THE
SOURCEBOOK
To Public Record Information

*The Comprehensive Guide to County, State, & Federal
Public Records Sources*

Sixth Edition

BRB Publications, Inc.
www.brbpub.com

Dedicated to the Searching & Understanding of Public Records

BRB
Publications

THE
SOURCEBOOK
TO PUBLIC RECORD INFORMATION - *Six Edition*

Edited by: Peter J. Weber and Michael Sankey

©2005 By BRB Publications, Inc.
206 West Julie Dr, Suite 2
Tempe, AZ 85283
800-929-3811   Fax 800-929-4981

www.brbpub.com

ISBN 1-879792-77-X

The sourcebook to public record information : the
comprehensive guide to county, state, & federal public
records sources / [edited by Peter J. Weber and Michael
Sankey]. -- 6th ed.
  p. cm.
    ISBN 1-879792-77-X

    1. Public records--United States--States--Information
services--Directories. 2. Courts--United States--States
--Directories. 3. Public records--United States--States
--Computer network resources.   I. Weber, Peter J.
(Peter Julius), 1952- II. Sankey, Michael L., 1949-

JK468.P76S693 2004   352.3'87'02573
                    QBI04-200388

Replaces *The Guide to Background Investigations*

Contents

Section II: Public Records Arranged by State   63

Each State Chapter is Organized as Follows:

1. State Agencies
2. State Licensing Boards
3. Federal Courts

4. County Courts
5. Recording Offices
6. County Locator and Map

Information about Canada, Guam, Puerto Rico and The Virgin Islands is located on pages 1917-1925

Introduction

Complex and Mysterious?

The access to and use of current public records is one of the fundamental pillars of our democratic society.

Yet, the words "Public Records" often convey a complex, almost mysterious source of information that is perceived as difficult to access, hard to decipher, and likely to be of interest only to private investigators and reporters.

This view could not be further from the truth!

Your Access to Over 20,000 Government Agencies

Herein, we will examine these paper trails that begin or are maintained at the federal, state, county, and in certain instances, the city and town level. This *Sourcebook* is especially useful for these applications:

Legal Research

Background Investigation

Pre-Employment and Tenant Screening

Locating People

Locating Assets

Skiptracing

Genealogy

This *Sourcebook* reveals where records are kept, outlines the access requirements, gives searching hints and tells which agencies are online. Over 20,000 government agencies are profiled so you can explore the depths of the public record industry.

Public records are meant to be used for the benefit of society. As a member of the public, you or someone in authority is entitled to review the public records held by government agencies. Whether you are a business owner, a reporter, an investigator, or even a father trying to check on your daughter's first date, you can access public records to meet your needs.

Equipped with the information contained in these pages, you can find the facts, gain access to the information you need, and even track your own "information trail!"

What Is New in the Sixth Edition

The Sixth Edition contains 96 additional pages compared to last year's book. Not only has the research for this year's edition led to an enormous amount of updated material, but we have also added many new phone numbers and online access sites. The majority of this additional information comes is found in—

- Statewide Court Record Systems

- Local Phone Numbers for Assessor, Treasurer, Vital Records, and Voter Registration Departments

- Over 500 Additional Online Accessible Sources for Searching Occupational Licenses

Also, included again this year are—

- State Maps

- Canadian Driving Records and Criminal Records

About The Guide to Background Investigations and Educational Records

In 2003, BRB Publications purchased the rights to a very successful publication known as *The Guide to Background Investigations*. Interestingly, the majority of the content found in the last three editions of *The Guide* was researched and provided by BRB Publications. Thus, rather than publish two very similar books, BRB Publications chose to print one book – *The Sourcebook* – and incorporate the best of both products into one.

Since there was no room to place the content from the Guide's Educational Records Section in *The Sourcebook*, a separate reference was published. *The National Directory to College and University Student Records* profiles more than 5,000 accredited, post secondary institutions from the U.S. and Canada. The good news for loyal Guide users is the cost of purchasing both *The Sourcebook* and the *National Guide* is still only half of the cost of purchasing *The Guide*.

Updated Information on the Internet

The Sixth Edition of *The Sourcebook to Public Record Information* represents thousands of hours of research right up to the day of printing. We have compiled what we feel is the most up-to-date and unique compendium of its kind. However, users should also remember that the information reported in *The Sourcebook* can, and does change. For those of you who need to know more or need to have this information constantly updated, we recommend an expanded version of this product. ***The Public Records Research System*** (PRRS) is available as a subscription service on the Internet. Updated weekly, PRRS contains all the information found in *The Sourcebook*, *The National Directory to College and University Student Records*, and *The County Locator*. For additional information, visit www.publicrecordsources.com.

Thank You from the Research and Editorial Staff at BRB Publications—

BRB Publications is 100% devoted to the understanding of public records. We hope you find the Sixth Edition of *The Sourcebook* to be a valuable asset.

Kiala Flanagan

Jill Von Rotz

Annette Talley

William Roberts

Robert Peterson

Peter J. Weber

Michael Sankey

How This Book Is Organized

General Layout

The Sourcebook is organized into two Sections--

1. Public Record Primer
2. 51 Individual State Chapters (with an Appendix of Canadian Provinces and U.S. Territories)

The Public Record Primer

The purpose of *The Public Record Primer* is to assist the reader in knowing *where categories of records can be found* and *how to search*. The Primer contains many searching hints and is an excellent overall source of information that will especially help those not familiar with searching government records.

An important discussion starting on page 7 examines privacy issues including public information vs. personal information and how records enter the public domain.

The **Searching Federal Court Records** chapter (page 25) contains an excellent article (on page 34) contributed by Alan Schlein, author of *Find it Online! The Complete Guide to Online Research* (Facts on Demand Press). Mr. Schlein presents a unique dissertation about the best federal government internet sites for finding usual information quickly and efficiently.

Another important chapter is **Using a Public Record Vendor** (page 56) that contains a wealth of information about using commercial public record vendors.

The State Chapters

The individual state chapters in *The Sourcebook* have been compiled into an easy to use format. Six sub-chapters or sections are presented in this order:

1. State Public Record Agencies
2. State Licensing and Regulatory Boards
3. Federal Courts (U.S. District and Bankruptcy)
4. County Courts
5. County Recorder Offices
6. County Locator
7. Canadian Provinces and U.S. Territories

Information Found in the Agency Profiles

The depth of knowledge presented about each government agency is what separates this *Sourcebook* from a typical address and phone listing reference book. The beginning of each state and/or county sub-chapter has an overall discussion of the public records policies, with important characteristics and searching hints.

The following details have been researched and presented (when applicable) within each profile:

- **Agency Facts**: office hours; time zone; websites.

- **Searching Facts**: methods of access; indexing; search requirements; if records are available online; when free public access terminals are at the counter; turnaround times, how far back (years) records are kept.

- **Privacy Facts**: restrictions the agencies impose on searchers or types of searchers; when signed releases or notarized statements are required.

- **Fees**: access fees, copy fees; certification fees; expedited fees, if credit cards accepted; what types of checks accepted; to whom to make the check payable.

- **Misc:** how to purchase databases or customized lists; if more than one agency must be visited in the county to get all records; if results will or will not be returned by fax, etc.

Using The County Locator

The County Locator portion of each state chapter is extremely useful when it is unclear in which county to perform a localized record search. This section contains two cross-reference indices. The City/County Cross Reference will indicate in what county(s) a "place" (city or town) is located. There are over 40,000 places referenced. The ZIP Code/City Cross Reference assists those people who have an address with ZIP Code, but are unsure in which county the ZIP in located.

Keep in mind that over 8,000 ZIP Codes cross county lines.

Note: Useful features added to *The Sourcebook* this year are the maps showing each state's county borders, county seats, and major cities.

Section I

Public Record Primer

Guidelines for Searching Public Records

Definition of Public Records

The strict **definition** of **public records** is—

> *"Those records maintained by government agencies*
> *that are open without restriction to public inspection,*
> *either by statute or by tradition."*

If access to a record that is held by a government agency is restricted in some way, then it is not a public record.

Accessibility Paradox

Adding to the mystique of government records is the accessibility paradox. For example, in some states a specific category of records is severely restricted, and therefore those records are not "public," while the very same category of records may be 100% open in other states. Among these categories are criminal histories, vehicle ownership records and workers' compensation records.

At times, you will see the following box printed on pages throughout the *Sourcebook*. We are not trying to fill up space. As your public record searching takes you from state-to-state, this is the one important adage to keep in mind.

> "Just because records are maintained in a certain way in
> your state or county, do not assume that any other county or
> state does things the same way you are used to."

Public vs. Private vs. Personal

Before reading further, let us define types of records held by government or by private industry. Of course, not all information about a company or individual is public. The boundaries between public and private information are not well understood, and continually undergo intense scrutiny. The following is an introduction to the subject from a viewpoint of a professional record searcher.

Public Record

Public records are records of **incidents** or **actions** filed or recorded with a government agency for the purpose of notifying others about the matter — the "public." The **deed** to your house recorded at the county recorder's office is a public record — it is a legal requirement that you record with the county recorder. Anyone requiring details about your property may review or copy the documents.

Public Information

Your **telephone listing** in the phone book is public information; that is, you freely furnished the information to ease the flow of commercial and private communications.

Personal Information

Any information about a person or business that the person or business might consider private and confidential in nature, such as your **Social Security Number**, is personal information. Such information will remain private to a limited extent unless it is disclosed to some outside entity that could make it public. **Personal information may be found in either public records or in public information.**

How Personal Information Enters the Public Domain

Many people confuse the three categories above, lump them into one and wonder how "big brother" accumulated so much information about them. Therefore, these distinctions are important. The reality is that **much of this information is given willingly**.

Actually, there are two ways that personal information can enter the public domain — statutory and voluntary. In a **voluntary** transaction, you **share** personal information of your own free will. In a **statutory** transaction, you **disclose** personal information because the law requires you to.

The confusion of terms used today feeds the increasing conflict between privacy advocates and commercial interests. This, in turn, is driving legislation towards more and more **restrictions** on the **dissemination of personal information** — the same personal information that, in fact, is willingly shared by most people and companies in order to participate in our market economy.

Where Public Records are Held

There are two places you can find public records—

1. at a government agency

2. within the database of a private company

Government agencies maintain records in a variety of ways. While many state agencies and highly populated county agencies are computerized, many others use microfiche, microfilm, and paper to store files and indexes. Agencies that have converted to computer will not necessarily place complete file records on their system; they are more apt to include only an index, pointer or summary data to the files.

Private enterprises develop their databases in one of two ways: they buy the records in bulk from government agencies; or they send personnel to the agencies and compile this information by using a copy machine or keying information into a laptop computer. The database is then available for internal use or for resale purposes. An example of such a company is *Superior Information* (800 848-0489). Superior maintains a very comprehensive database of civil judgments, tax liens, Uniform Commercial Code filings, and bankruptcy data gathered from the Mid-Atlantic States.

The Common Methods Used to Access Public Records

The following is a look at the various methods available to access public records.

Visit in Person

This is easy if you live close by. Many courthouses and recorders offices have free access terminals open to the public. Certain records, such as corporate or UCC records generally found at the Secretary of State, can be viewed or pulled for free, but will incur a fee for copies. A signed release is a common requirement for accessing motor vehicle and criminal records.

Mail, Fax, or Telephone

Although some agencies permit phone or fax requests, the majority of agencies prefer mail requests. Some agencies consider fax requesting to be an expedited service that incurs higher fees. Agencies that permit telephone requests may merely answer "Yes" or "No" to questions such as "Does John Doe have a civil court case in his name?" We have indicated when telephone and fax requesting is available, as well as the extent of the service.

Online

The Internet may serve as a free means to certain agency records or may be the conduit to a subscription or commercial site. Also, private dial systems (non-Internet) still exist for some subscription services. Subscription online access of public records is much more prevalent at the state level compared to the county level. Keep in mind many agencies, such as DMVs, only provide access to pre-approved, high volume, ongoing accounts. Typically, this access involves fees and a specified, minimum amount of usage.

However, there is a definite trend of certain agencies posting public record data on the Internet for free. Two examples are Secretary of State offices (whose records include corporation, UCC and tax liens) and county/city tax assessor offices (whose records reveal property ownership). Usually this information is limited to name indexes and summary data, rather than document images. In addition, a growing number of state licensing boards are posting their membership lists on the net (although addresses and phone numbers of the licensed individuals typically are not listed).

Also, the Internet is a good place to find *general* information about government agencies. Many websites enable one to download, read and/or print current forms, policies and regulations.

Hire Someone Else

As mentioned previously, one method to access public records is from a vendor. These companies must comply with state and federal laws, thus if the government agency will not release a record, chances are a vendor company will not either. There are a variety of companies that can be hired to perform record searches. An excellent, quick source to find the right vendor for a particular need is www.publicrecordsources.com or *Public Records Online* by Facts on Demand Press.

Bulk or Database Purchases

Many agencies offer programs to purchase all or parts of their database for statistical or commercial purposes. The restrictions vary widely from state to state, even within the same record type or category. Typically, records are available (to those who qualify) in the following media types; magnetic tapes, FTP, cartridges, paper printouts, labels, disks, CDs, microfiche and/or microfilm. Throughout the individual state chapters, we have indicated where these bulk purchases are available, to whom, and for what purposes as well as the costs involved.

Using the Freedom of Information Act and Other Acts

The Federal Freedom of Information Act has no bearing on state, county or local government agencies because these agencies are subject to that state's individual act. Further, the government agencies profiled in this book generally already have systems in place to release information and the act is not needed. However, if you are trying to obtain records from agencies beyond the scope of this book, there are many useful internet sites that will give you the information you need to complete such a request. We can recommend these sites:

> www.usdoj.gov/04foia/
>
> www.spj.org/foia.asp

Fees, Charges, and Usage

Public records are not necessarily free of charge, certainly not if they are maintained by private industry. Remember that **public records are records of incidents or transactions**. These incidents can be civil or criminal court actions, recordings, filings or occurrences such as speeding tickets or accidents. **It costs money** (time, salaries, supplies, etc.) **to record and track these events**. Common charges found at the government level include copy fees (to make copies of the document), search fees (for clerical personnel to search for the record), and certification fees (to certify a document as being accurate and coming from the particular agency). Fees can vary from $.10 per page for copies to a $52.00 search fee for government personnel to do the actual look-up. Some government agencies will allow you to walk in and view records at no charge. Fewer will release information over the phone for no fee.

If a private enterprise is in the business of maintaining a public records database, it generally does so to offer these records for resale. Typical clients include financial institutions, the legal industry, the insurance industry, and pre-employment screening firms among others. Usually, records are sold via online access or on a CD-ROM.

Also, there are a number of public record vendors (we call them search firms) companies that will do a name search — for a fee. These companies do not warehouse the records, but search on demand for a specific name.

Private companies usually offer different price levels based on volume of usage, while government agencies have one price per category, regardless of the amount of requests.

Using Identifiers

Every source will require certain identifiers to process a search request. For example, the agency (or vendor) may ask for the full name, Social Security Number, date of birth and last known address of the person to be checked. These "Identifiers" serve two different, though related purposes.

First, these identifiers ensure that the repository will be able to access its records to conduct a search. For example, the files may be indexed by name or Social Security Number. Thus, the office simply may not be able to process a record request if it does not have one or the other of these identifiers.

Second, the identifiers act as an important safeguard for both the requesting party and the subject of the search. There is always the chance that the "Harold Johnson" on whom a given repository has a record is not the same "Harold Johnson" on whom a check has been requested. However, the possibility of a misidentification can be decreased substantially if other identifiers can be matched on the individual.

In general, each record source listed in *The Sourcebook* will include the identifiers required to process a search (as well as some other information that the record-holder said would be "helpful"). This is the minimum data required for the office to proceed with your search.

As a general rule, information beyond the minimum should be provided whenever possible. Every available piece of information can aid their search. For example, maiden, alias or other previous names should always be included. Although no repository can be expected to give a 100% positive identification (without a fingerprint card), the more pointers matched, the smaller the chance of a mistake.

A Few Myths About Searching Public Records Online

The availability of online public records is not as widespread as one might think. According to our research:

- only 35% of public records can be found online;
- nearly every free government public record website contains no personal identifiers beyond the name.

The government agencies that offer online access on a fee or subscription basis generally do disclose at least partial personal identifiers. Very few give Social Security Numbers anymore, and those that do may cloak or mask the first 5 digits. Some even cloak the month and day of the DOB and only release the year of birth. This is a real problem for employers who are hiring and others that require a certain amount of due diligence. Adverse information may have to be checked by a hands on search.

Also, many government websites offering online record access include a warning or disclosure statement that the data can have errors and/or should be used for informational purposes only. For example, a criminal record check from such as source may not in and by itself comply with the Fair Credit Reporting Act regulations involving pre-employment screening.

The last section of this book examines over 200 private companies that offer online access to their proprietary databases (or gateways) of public record information. Keep in mind they hold many records that may not be otherwise found online via the government online sources.

Public Record & Public Information Categories

The following descriptions of the record categories fall into our definitions of either "public records" or "public information."

In considering these definitions, keep the following points in mind:

♦ Very little government record information is truly open to the public. Even presumably harmless information is subject to restrictions somewhere in the U.S.A. Likewise items that you believe should be highly confidential are probably considered "public information" in one or more states.

♦ Just because your state or county has certain rules, regulations and practices regarding the accessibility and content of public records does not mean that any other state or county follows the same rules.

Business Records

Corporation Records (found at the state level)

Checking to see if a company is incorporated is considered a "**status check**." The information that results from a status check typically includes the date of incorporation, status, type, registered agent and, sometimes, officers or directors. This is a good way to find the start of a paper trail and/or to find affiliates of the subject of your search. Some states permit status checks over the telephone.

If available, articles of incorporation (or amendments to them) as well as copies of annual reports may also provide useful information about a business or business owner. However, corporate records may *not* be a good source for a business address because most states allow corporations to use a registered agent as their address for service of process.

Partnership Records (found at the state level)

Some state statutes require registration of certain kinds of partnerships at the state level. Sometimes, these partner names and addresses may be available from the same office that handles corporation records. Some states have a department created specifically to administer limited partnerships and the records associated with them. These filings provide a wealth of information about other partners. Such information can be used to uncover other businesses that may be registered as well.

Limited Liability Companies (found at state level)

A newer form of business entity, similar to a corporation but has the favorable tax characteristics of a partnership, is known as the Limited Liability Company (LLC). An LLC is legal in most every state. An offspring of this, which many states now permit, is the Limited Liability Partnership (LLP).

Trademark and Trade Name (found at state or county levels)

"Trade names" and "trademarks" are relative terms. A trademark may be known as a "service mark." Trade names may be referred to as "fictitious names," "assumed names," or "DBAs." States (or counties) will not let two entities register and use the same (or close to the same) name or trademark

Typically, the agency that oversees corporation records usually maintains the files for trademarks and/or trade names. Most states will allow verbal status checks of names or worded marks. Some states will administer "fictitious names" at the state level while county agencies administer "trade names," or vice versa.

Sales Tax Registrations (found at state level)

Any individual or firm that sells applicable goods or services to an end-user, is required to register with the appropriate state agency. Such registration is necessary to collect applicable sales tax on the goods and services, and to ensure remittance of those taxes to the state.

45 states collect some sort of sales tax on a variety of goods and services. Of these, 38 will at the very least confirm that a tax permit exists. Each sales tax registrant is given a special state tax permit number, which may be called by various names, including tax ID number or seller's permit number. These numbers are not to be confused with the federal employer identification number.

SEC and Other Financial Data

The Federal Securities and Exchange Commission (SEC) is the public repository for information about publicly held companies. These companies are required to share their material facts with existing and prospective stockholders. See page 33 for information about the SEC database EDGAR.

Private companies, on the other hand, are not subject to public scrutiny. Their financial information is public information only to the extent that the company itself decides to disclose information.

Lien and Security Interest Records

Uniform Commercial Code (found at state and sometimes at county or city levels)

All 50 states and the District of Columbia have passed a version of the model Uniform Commercial Code (UCC). UCC filings are used to record liens in financing transactions such as equipment loans, leases, inventory loans, and accounts receivable financing. The Code allows potential lenders to be notified that certain assets of a debtor are already used to secure a loan or lease. *Therefore, examining UCC filings is an excellent way to find bank accounts, security interests, financiers, and assets.*

Revised Article 9 (see pages 48-50) of the Code made significant changes to the location of filings and records. Prior to July 2001, of the 7.5 million new UCC financing statements filed annually, 2.5 million were filed at the state level; 5 million were filed at the local level. Now, less than 3% of filings are done so at the local level. Although there are significant variations among state statutes, the state level is now the best starting place to uncover liens filed against an individual or business.

Tax Liens (found at state and sometimes at county or city levels)

The federal government and every state have some sort of taxes, such as those associated with sales, income, withholding, unemployment, and/or personal property. When these taxes go unpaid, the appropriate state agency can file a lien on the real or personal property of the subject. *Normally, the state agency that maintains UCC records also maintains tax liens.*

Individuals vs. Businesses

Tax liens filed against individuals are frequently maintained at separate locations from those liens filed against businesses. For example, a large number of states require liens filed against businesses to be filed at a central state location (i.e., Secretary of State's office) and liens against individuals to be filed at the county level (i.e., Recorder, Register of Deeds, Clerk of Court, etc.).

State vs. Federal Liens

Liens on a company may not all be filed in the same location. A federal tax lien will not necessarily be filed (recorded) at the same location/jurisdiction as a lien filed by the state. This holds true for both individual liens and as well as business liens filed against personal property. Typically, state tax liens on personal property will be found where UCCs are filed. *Tax liens on real property will be found where real property deeds are recorded*, with few exceptions. Unsatisfied state and federal tax liens may be renewed if prescribed by individual state statutes. However, once satisfied, the time the record will remain in the repository before removal varies by jurisdiction.

Real Estate and Tax Assessor (found at county and local levels)

Traditionally, real estate records are public so that everyone can know who owns what property. Liens on real estate must be public so a buyer knows all the facts. The county (or parish) recorder's office is the record source. However, many private companies purchase entire county record databases and create their own database for commercial purposes.

This category of public record is perhaps the fastest growing in regards to being freely accessible over the Internet. We have indicated all the recorder offices that offer web **name queries;** many more offer location searches (using maps and parcel numbers to locate an address).

Bankruptcies (found at federal court level)

This entails case information about people and businesses that have filed for protection under the bankruptcy laws of the United States. Only federal courts handle bankruptcy cases. Many types of financial records maintained by government agencies are considered public records; bankruptcy records, unlike some other court records, are in this class of fully open court records. There are several private companies that compile databases with names and dates of these records.

Important Individual Records

Criminal Records (found at state level, county courts, and federal courts)

Every state has a central repository of major misdemeanor, felony arrest records and convictions. States submit criminal record activity to the National Crime Information Center (which is not open to the public). *Not all states open their criminal records to the public.* Of those states that *will* release records to the public, many require fingerprints or signed release forms. The information that *could be* disclosed on the report includes the arrest record, criminal charges, fines, sentencing and incarceration information.

In states where records are not released, the best places to search for criminal record activity is at the city or county level with the county or district court clerk. Many of these searches can be done with a phone call. For further information regarding the use of criminal records, *The Criminal Records Manual* by Derek Hinton, Facts On Demand Press.

Litigation and Civil Judgments (found at county, local, and federal courts)

Actions under federal laws are found at U.S. District Courts. Actions under state laws are found within the state court system at the county level. Municipalities also have courts. Records of civil litigation case and records about judgments are often collected by commercial database vendors. For more information, please refer to the **County Court Records** chapter.

Motor Vehicle Records (found at state level, but, on occasion, accessible at county level)

The retrieval industry often refers to driving records as "MVRs." Typical information on an MVR might include full name, address, Social Security Number, physical description and date of birth along with the conviction and accident history. Also, the license type, restrictions and/or endorsements can provide background data on an individual.

In recent years there have been major changes regarding the release of motor vehicle data to the public. This is a direct result of the Driver's Privacy Protection Act (DPPA). States must differentiate between *permissible users* (14 are designated in DPPA) and *casual requesters* to determine who may receive a record and/or how much personal information is reported on the record. For example, if a state DMV chooses to sell a record to a "casual requester," the record can contain personal information (address, etc.) only with the consent of the subject.

Pay particular attention to the restriction requirements mentioned in this category throughout this publication. Refer to pages 54-56 for more about this subject. Also, for those interested in extensive, detailed information about either driver or vehicle records, refer to BRB Publications' *The MVR Book*.

Vehicle and Vessel Ownership, Registration, VINs, Titles, and Liens (found at state and, on occasion, at county level)

State repositories of vehicle/vessel registration and ownership records hold a wide range of information. Generally, record requesters submit a name to uncover vehicle(s) owned or submit vehicle information to obtain an owner name and address. However, this category of record information is also subject to the DPPA as described above.

The original language of DPPA required the states to offer an "opt out" option to drivers and vehicle owners, if they (the states) sold marketing lists or individual records to casual requesters (those requesters not specifically mentioned in DPPA). Public Law 106-69 reversed this. Effective June 1, 2000, states automatically opt out all individuals, unless the individual specifically asks to be included. While nearly all states have this "opt in" procedure in place, very few individuals request to be placed on marketing lists and such.

Passage of Public Law 106-69 was dramatic since it essentially did away with sales of:

- marketing lists;
- records (with addresses and other personal information) to "casual" requesters;
- record databases to information vendors and database compilers (except for vehicle recall purposes, etc.)

Accident Reports (found at state level or local level)

The State Police or Department of Public Safety usually maintains accident reports. For the purposes of this publication, "accident records" are designated as those prepared by the investigating officer. Copies of a *citizen's* accident report are not usually available to the public and are not reviewed herein. Typical information found on a state accident report includes drivers' addresses and license numbers as well as a description of the incident. Accidents investigated by local officials or minor accidents where the damage does not exceed a reporting limit (such as $1,000), are not available from state agencies. When state DMV's hold accident reports, they follow the DPPA guidelines with regards to record requests.

Occupational Licensing and Business Registration (found at state boards)

Occupational licenses and business registrations contain a plethora of information readily available from various state agencies. A common reason to call these agencies is to corroborate professional or industry credentials. Often, a telephone call to the agency may secure an address and phone number.

GED Records (found at state level)

By contacting the state offices that oversee GED Records, one can verify whether someone truly received a GED certificate for the high school education equivalency. These records are useful for pre-employment screening or background checking purposes. Most state agencies will verify over the phone the existence of a GED certificate. Many even offer copies of transcripts free-of-charge. When doing a record search, you must know the name of the student at the time of the test and a general idea of the year and test location. GED Records are *not* useful when trying to locate an individual.

Hunting and Fishing Licenses (found at state, county and local levels)

We have singled out one type of state license that merits a closer look. When trying to locate an individual, state hunting and fishing license information can be very informative. Currently 44 states maintain a central repository of fishing and/or hunting license records and 31 states permit access in some capacity by the public.

The trend is that many of these record repositories are becoming more computerized and are getting away from the days of storing in boxes in the basement. This movement began in 1992 when the U.S. Fish and Wildlife Service implemented a Migratory Bird Harvest Information Program that changed state hunting licensing procedures. Under this cooperative program, many states began to computerize their collection of licensees' names and addresses. The release of these records for investigative or search purposes may depend upon individual "state sunshine laws."

Workers' Compensation Records (found at state level)

Research at state workers' compensation boards is generally limited to determining if an employee has filed a claim and/or obtaining copies of the claim records themselves. With the passage of the Americans with Disabilities Act (ADA) in the early 1990s, using information from workers' compensation boards for pre-employment screening was virtually eliminated. However, *a review of workers' compensation histories may be conducted after a conditional job offer has been made* and when medical information is reviewed. The legality of performing this review is subject to individual state statutes, which vary widely.

Voter Registration (found at state and county levels)

Voting Registration Records are a good place to find addresses and voting history, and can generally be viewed at the local level.

Every state has a central election agency or commission, and most have a central repository of voter information collected from the county level agencies. The degree or level of accessibility to these records varies widely from state to state. Over half of the states will sell portions of the registered voter database, but only 10 states permit individual searching by name. Most states only allow access for political purposes such as "Get Out the Vote" campaigns or compilation of campaign contribution lists. Nearly every state and local agency blocks the release of Social Security Numbers and telephone numbers found on these records.

Vital Records: Birth, Death, Marriage, and Divorce Records (found at state and county levels)

Copies of vital record certificates are needed for a variety of reasons — social security, jobs, passports, family history, litigation, lost heir searching, proof of identity, etc. Most states understand the urgency of these requests, and many offer an expedited service. *A number of states will take requests over the phone if you use a credit card.* Searchers must also be aware that in many instances certain vital records are *not* kept at the state level. The searcher must then turn to city and county record repositories to find the information needed.

Most states offer expedited fax and online ordering through the services of an outside vendor known as VitalChek. This state endorsed vendor maintains individual fax order telephone lines at each state office they service. They require the use of a credit card and with that an extra fee in the range of

$5.50 to $10.05. Their website www.vitalchek.com is also a good place to order vital records online from many states; keep in mind that results are still mailed.

Older vital records are usually found in the state archives. There is an excellent website of extensive historical genealogy-related databases at http://ancestry.com/mainv.htm. Another source of historical vital record information is the Family History Library of the Church of Jesus Christ of Latter Day Saints (located at 35 North West Temple, Salt Lake City 84150). They have millions of microfilmed records from church and civil registers from all over the world.

Credit Information and Social Security Numbers

Social Security Numbers

The Social Security Number (SSN) is the subject of a persistent struggle between privacy rights groups and various business interests. The truth is that many individuals gave up the privacy of their number by writing it on a voter registration form, product registration form, or any of a myriad of other voluntary disclosures made over the years. It is probable that a good researcher can still legally find the SSN of anyone (along with at least an approximate birth date) with some ease. In the past, a major source of finding a SSN was in the "header" of a credit report. But not any more, see below.

Credit Information

Credit data is derived from financial transactions of people or businesses. **Private companies maintain this information; government only regulates access.** Certain credit information about individuals is restricted by law, such as the Fair Credit Reporting Act, at the federal level and by even more restrictive laws in many states. Credit information about businesses is not restricted by law and is fully open to anyone who requests (pays for) it.

A credit report essentially has two parts — the credit header and the credit history. A credit header is essentially the upper portion of a credit report containing the Social Security Number, age, phone number, last several addresses, and any AKAs. Recently, access to credit header information (see below) has been closed to most business entities.

Credit Header Ban Went Into Effect July 1st, 2001

July 1st, 2001 was an important date for skiptracers, fraud investigators, and other businesses that rely on "credit headers." This information has always been available without the consent of the individual subject. Per a federal court ruling, beginning July 1st 2001, access to credit header information was treated in the same manner as access to credit reports—there has to be permission granted by the individual.

The basis of this ban is traced to the Gramm-Leach-Bliley Act (GLB). Section 502 of this act prohibits a financial institution from disclosing nonpublic personal information about a consumer to non-affiliated third parties unless a consumer has elected not to opt out from disclosure. Trans Union and other members of the Individual References Services Group (IRSG), among others, filed suit in an effort to keep this information open for "appropriate commercial purposes." The ruling, dated April 30th, denied this argument. The sale of credit headers seemed to be on borrowed time anyway—originally, the ban was to begin November 2000. However, due to the lawsuits and action involving the FTC, a provision changed the start of the ban until July 1st, 2001.

Impact of Changes

The impact of the ruling (and an FTC opinion) was far ranging. The ruling restricted credit bureaus from selling the above-mentioned data to information vendors who compile their own proprietary databases. But there are some alternatives to those business entities that rely on this type of public record information. The data is grandfathered. Provider companies that purchased files from the credit bureaus can continue to sell the data to their customers. Although data will never be updated from the credit bureaus, the existing data can still be used without the restrictions imposed by the ruling.

The Gramm-Leach-Bliley Act did not deny access to public record sources or databases that may contain age, SSN, phone, prior addresses, and AKAs. The Act only forbade financial institutions from disclosing this data. Therefore, those businesses that were shut-off from credit headers had to investigate alternative sources of public records.

Additional Record Sources Worth Reviewing

Education and Employment

Information about an employee's or prospective employee's schooling, training, education, and jobs is important to any employer. Learning institutions maintain their own records of attendance, completion and degree/certification granted. Also, employers will confirm certain information about former employees. This is an example of private information that becomes public by voluntary disclosure. As part of your credit record, this information would be considered restricted. If, however, you disclose this information to Who's Who, or to a credit card company, it becomes public information.

Environment

Information about hazards to the environment is critical. There is little tradition and less law regarding how open or restricted information is at the state and local (recorder's office) levels. Most information on hazardous materials, soil composition, even OSHA inspection reports is public record. But many federal websites have removed information since 9-11-2001.

OSHA stands for Occupational Safety and Health Administration, which is part of the U.S. Department of Labor. Their website is www.osha.gov.

Another federal government source is the U.S. Environmental Protection Agency found at www.epa.gov/records. According to *Find it Online* author Alan Schlein, the EPA "...no longer allows direct access to the Envirofacts databases, which explain what toxic chemicals are found in water, hazardous waste, toxic waste, and Superfund sites, and is broken down by community. The EPA had originally created the database to provide the public with direct access to the wealth of information contained in its databases. The public is no longer able to access the information."

The same can be said for the U.S. Geological Survey (www.usgs.gov); this agency has removed a number of its reports on water resources.

Medical

Medical record Information about an individual's medical status and history are summarized in various repositories that are accessible only to authorized insurance and other private company employees. Medical information is neither public information nor a closed record. Like credit information, it is not meant to be shared with anyone unless you give authorization.

Military

Each branch maintains its own records. Much of this, such as years of service and rank, is open public record. However, some details in the file of an individual may be subject to restrictions on access — approval by the subject may be required.

For more information about military records, turn to page 33.

More About Searching State Agency Records

The previous chapter includes a wealth of knowledge about the various types of public records found at the state level. This chapter in the Primer explains how to use the State Agencies Sections found in each state chapter in the body of this *Sourcebook*.

Major State Offices

Each state chapter begins with a list of four important state offices that may be helpful to your record searching needs. This is followed by several helpful websites.

Governor's Office

The office of the Governor is a good place to start if you are looking for an obscure agency, phone number or address. We have found that typically the person who answers the phone will point you in the right direction if he or she cannot answer your question.

Attorney General's Office

This is another excellent starting point. For example, if you are looking for a non-profit organization, the Attorney General's Office may be able to help you out.

State Archives

The state archives contain an abundance of historical documents and records, especially useful to those interested in genealogy.

State Legislation

Most state legislative bodies offer free internet access to bill text and status, some even offer subject queries. Notwithstanding federal guidelines, the state legislatures and legislators control the policies and provisions for the release of state held information. Every year there is a multitude of bills introduced in state legislatures that would, if passed, create major changes in the access and retrieval of records and personal information.

State Court Administrator

The court administrator oversees the state court system, which is also known as the county court system. The state judicial website is a good place to find opinions from the state supreme court and for appeals court opinions. In some states, the state court administration office oversees a statewide online access system to court records. Some of these systems are commercial fee-based. Other systems offer free access, but are usually very limited in comparison. **This year we have added full profiles of each statewide system.**

How to Read and Use the State Agency Profiles

After the preceding four state offices mentioned, the various state agency profiles are presented, starting with the state criminal records agency. Each of these state agency profiles is broken into distinct segments that create a total picture of record searching, including access methods and privacy restrictions.

Indexing and Storage

This segment examines the following—

- How many years of records are accessible
- How long before new records are available
- How records are indexed and in what format are they maintained.

Searching

This segment looks in depth at the searching requirements and when privacy restrictions are in place. For example, here you learn what the agencies requirements are for doing a search, such as if a signed release is needed from the subject, or if a certain state form must be used.

Access Methods

The following access methods are both listed and described in a detailed paragraph—

- Mail
- Phone
- In person
- Fax
- Online

Here you will learn the turnaround time for mail requests, if there is free internet access, if the agency will release any information over the phone, fax, etc. In addition, there is a section describing expedited services or bulk database purchases, when applicable.

Fee and Payments

Fee coverage includes search fees, copy fees, certification fees, and expedite fees. Also covered: if credit cards are accepted, if personal checks (many agencies only accept business checks) are accepted, and whom to make the check payable.

Special Situations in State Records

We won't waste your time reading about agencies if the record data is truly unavailable. The following special situations are noted—

- When the state agency does not release any information period, except to government personnel.
- When the records are not maintained by a state level agency…and where to find these records if they are held at the local level.

Searching State Occupational Licensing Boards

The Privacy Question

While some agencies consider this information private and confidential, most agencies freely release at least some basic data over the phone or by mail.

Our research indicates that many agencies appear to make their own judgments regarding what specifically is private and confidential in their files. For example, approximately 45% of the agencies indicate that they will disclose adverse information about a registrant, and many others will only disclose selected portions of the information or merely verify a credential.

In any event, the basic rule to follow when you contact a licensing agency is to **ask for the specific kinds of information available.**

What Information May Be Available

An agency may be willing to release part or all of the following—

- Field of Certification
- Status of License/Certificate
- Date License/Certificate Issued
- Date License/Certificate Expires
- Current or Most Recent Employer
- Social Security Number
- Address of Subject
- Complaints, Violations or Disciplinary Actions

How to Use the State Licenses Section

Each *State Licenses* section is separated into three parts—

1. Licenses Searchable Online
2. Licensing Quick Finder
3. Licensing Agency Information

A "Key Number" ties the sections together.

The License Searchable Online List

This is a list of boards and their corresponding URLs that offer **free internet access** to their records. This means that you can do a name search or query from this website.

Using the Quick Finder

The place to start a verification search is in the **Licensing Quick Finder.** Here you will find, licenses, registrations or occupations listed in alphabetical order.

Although we reflect the official name used in a state for most items, names of some of the major license types have been standardized to make them easier to locate. For example, some states use the word "Physician" rather than "Medical Doctor." We have chosen to use the latter.

Agency Information

This section gives the address and telephone number of the agency or board where the records are maintained.

Use the "Key Number"

The **Key Number** is the *identifying number* for the agency that maintains information about this license. By matching the Key Number found in the Quick Finder to the profile in the Agency Information, you will have the address and other details about how this agency operates. The key number follows the "#" sign in the Quick Finder Section.

An Example of How to Use the Sections

Let us say the following appears in the *Quick Finder Section*:

Beautician #3   216-123-4536

As stated above, the Key Number, which follows the # sign, leads you to the Agency Information Section, where you will find the Agency or Board's address and phone number. For example, "#3" refers to the following:

3 Department of Health & Social Services, Division of Public Health, 123 Sesame Street, Mapletown, OH 44414, 216-123-4536

Search Fees

Several trends are observed when verifying search fees of the various licensing agencies. They are—

1. There is no charge to verify if a particular person is licensed; this can usually be done by phone.

2. The fee for copies or faxes ranges from $.25 to $2.00.

3. A fee of $5 to $20 usually applies to written requests. This is due to the fact that written certifications give more information than verbal inquiries, i.e. disciplinary action, exam scores, specific dates.

4. A fee that is $25 or more is typically for a list of licensed professionals. For example, a hospital might need a roster of registered nurses in a certain geographic area.

Searching Tip – Distinguish the Type of Agency

Within the agency category listings, it is important to note that there are five general types of agencies. When you are verifying credentials, you should be aware of what distinguishes each type, which in turn could alter the questions you ask.

Private Certification

Private Licensing and Certification — requires a proven level of minimum competence before a license is granted. These professional licenses separate the true "professions" from the third category below. In many of these professions, the certification body, such as the American Institute of Certified Public Accountants, is a private association whereas the licensing body, such as the New York State Education Department, is the licensing agency. Also, many professions may provide additional certifications in specialty areas.

State Certification

State Licensing and Certification — requires certification through an *examination* and/or other *requirements supervised* directly *by the state* rather than by a private association.

By Individual

Individual Registration — required if an individual intends to offer specified products or services in the designated area, but does not require certification that the person has met minimum requirements. An everyday example would be registering a handgun in a state that does not require passing a gun safety course.

By Business

Business Registration — required if a business intends to do business or offer specified products or services in a designated area, such as registering a liquor license. Some business license agencies require testing or a background check. Others merely charge a fee after a cursory review of the application.

Special Permits

Permits — give the grantee specific permission to do something, whether it is to sell hotdogs on the corner or to erect a three story high sign. Permits are usually granted at the local level rather than the state level of government.

Other Forms of Licensing and Registration

Although the state level is where much of the licensing and registration occurs, you should be aware of other places you may want to search.

Local Government Agencies

Local government agencies at both the **county** and **municipal levels** require a myriad of business registrations and permits in order to do business (construction, signage, etc.) within their borders. Even where you think a business or person, such as a remodeling contractor, should have local registrations you want to check out, it is still best to start at the state level.

County Recording Office and City Hall

If you decide to check on local registrations and permits, call the offices at both the county — try the **county recording office** — and municipal level — try **city hall** — to find out what type of registrations may be required for the person or business you are checking out.

Like the state level, you should expect that receiving basic information will only involve a phone call and that you will not be charged for obtaining a status summary.

Professional Associations

As mentioned above, many professional licenses are based on completion of the requirements of professional associations. In addition, there are *many professional designations* from such associations that *are not recognized as official licenses by government*. Other designations are basic certifications in fields that are so specialized that they are not of interest to the states, but rather only to the professionals within an industry. For example, if your company needs to hire an investigator to check out a potential fraud against you, you might want to hire a CFE — Certified Fraud Examiner — who has met the minimum requirements for that title from the Association of Certified Fraud Examiners.

Other Media Sources

Mail Lists and Databases

Many agencies make their lists available in reprinted or computer form, and a few maintain online access to their files. If you are interested in the availability of licensing agency information in bulk (e.g. mailing lists, magnetic tapes, disks) or online, call the agency and ask about formats that are available.

Vendor Databases

A number of private vendors also compile lists from these agencies and make them available online or on CD-ROM. We do not necessarily suggest these databases for credential searching because they may not be complete, may not be up-to-date and may not contain all the information you can obtain directly from the licensing agency. However, these databases are extremely valuable as a general source of background information on an individual or company that you wish to do business with.

Searching Federal Court Records

First published in May 1993, BRB Publication's The Sourcebook of Federal Courts *provided the first truly complete coverage of where and how to search for case records in the U.S. Federal Courts. Now, this information is fully revised and integrated into* The Sourcebook.

In addition to detailing how to obtain Federal Court information, another objective of this publication is to show searchers how the Federal Court system has evolved during the past few years. One problem searchers encounter is that older records may be in a different form or in a different location from newer records. For example, a searcher can go astray trying to find bankruptcy cases in Ohio unless he or she knows about changes in Dayton.

One development that continues to change the fundamental nature of Federal Courts case record access is, of course, computerization. Now, every Federal Court in the United States has converted to a computerized index.

Federal Court Structure

The Federal Court system includes three levels of courts, plus some special courts, described as follows—

Supreme Court of the United States

The Supreme Court of the United States is the court of last resort in the United States. It is located in Washington, DC, where it hears appeals from the United States Courts of Appeals and from the highest courts of each state.

United States Court of Appeals

The United States Court of Appeals consists of thirteen appellate courts that hear appeals of verdicts from the courts of general jurisdiction. They are designated as follows:

The Federal Circuit Court of Appeals hears appeals from the U.S. Claims Court and the U.S. Court of International Trade. It is located in Washington, DC.

The District of Columbia Circuit Court of Appeals hears appeals from the district courts in Washington, DC as well as from the Tax Court.

Eleven geographic **Courts of Appeals** — each of these appeal courts covers a designated number of states and territories. The chart on the pages 30-31 lists the circuit numbers (1 through 11) and location of the Court of Appeals for each state.

United States District Courts

The United States District Courts are the courts of general jurisdiction, or trial courts, and are subdivided into two categories—

The District Courts are courts of general jurisdiction, or trial courts, for federal matters, excluding bankruptcy. Essentially, this means they hear cases involving federal law and cases where there is diversity of citizenship. Both **civil** and **criminal** cases come before these courts.

The Bankruptcy Courts generally follow the same geographic boundaries as the U.S. District Courts. There is at least one bankruptcy court for each state; within a state there may be one or more judicial districts and within a judicial district there may be more than one location (division) where the courts hear cases. While civil lawsuits may be filed in either state or federal courts depending upon the applicable law, all bankruptcy actions are filed with the U.S. Bankruptcy Courts.

Special Courts/Separate Courts

The Special Courts/Separate Courts have been created to hear cases or appeals for certain areas of litigation demanding special expertise. Examples include the U.S. Tax Court, the Court of International Trade and the U.S. Claims Court.

How Federal Trial Courts are Organized

At the federal level, all cases involve federal or U.S. constitutional law or interstate commerce. The task of locating the right court is seemingly simplified by the nature of the federal system—

- All court locations are based upon the plaintiff's county of domicile.

- All civil and criminal cases go to the U.S. District Courts.

- All bankruptcy cases go to the U.S. Bankruptcy Courts.

However, a plaintiff or defendant may have cases in any of the 500 court locations, so it is really not all that simple to find them.

There is at least one District and one Bankruptcy Court in each state. In many states there is more than one court, often divided further into judicial districts — e.g., the State of New York consists of four judicial districts, the Northern, Southern, Eastern and Western. Further, many judicial districts contain more than one court location (usually called a division).

The Bankruptcy Courts generally use the same hearing locations as the District Courts. If court locations differ, the usual variance is to have fewer Bankruptcy Court locations.

Case Numbering

When a case is filed with a federal court, a case number is assigned. This is the primary indexing method. Therefore, in searching for case records, you will need to know or find the applicable case number. If you have the number in good form already, your search should be fast and reasonably inexpensive.

You should be aware that case numbering procedures are not consistent throughout the Federal Court system: one judicial district may assign numbers by district while another may assign numbers by location (division) within the judicial district or by judge. Remember that case numbers appearing in legal text citations may not be adequate for searching unless they appear in the proper form for the particular court.

All the basic civil case information that is entered onto docket sheets, and into computerized systems like PACER (see below), starts with standard form JS-44, the Civil Cover Sheet, or the equivalent.

Docket Sheet

As in the state court system, information from cover sheets, and from documents filed as a case goes forward, is recorded on the **docket sheet**, which then contains the case history from initial filing to its current status. While docket sheets differ somewhat in format, the basic information contained on a docket sheet is consistent from court to court. As noted earlier in the state court section, all docket sheets contain:

- Name of court, including location (division) and the judge assigned;

- Case number and case name;

- Names of all plaintiffs and defendants/debtors;

- Names and addresses of attorneys for the plaintiff or debtor;

- Nature and cause (e.g., U.S. civil statute) of action;

- Listing of documents filed in the case, including docket entry number, the date and a short description (e.g., 12-2-92, #1, Complaint).

Assignment of Cases and Computerization

Traditionally, cases were assigned within a district by county. Although this is still true in most states, the introduction of computer systems to track dockets has led to a more flexible approach to case assignment, as is the case in Minnesota and Connecticut. Rather than blindly assigning all cases from a county to one judge, their districts are using random numbers and other logical methods to balance caseloads among their judges.

This trend may appear to confuse the case search process. Actually, the only problem the searcher may face is to figure out where the case records themselves are located. Finding cases has become significantly easier with the wide availability of PACER from remote access and onsite terminals in each court location with the same district-wide information base.

Computerized Indexes are Available

Computerized courts generally index each case record by the names of some or all the parties to the case — the plaintiffs and defendants (debtors and creditors in Bankruptcy Court) as well as by case number. Therefore, when you search by name you will first receive a listing of all cases in which the name appears, both as plaintiff and defendant.

Electronic Access to Federal Courts

Numerous programs have been developed for electronic access to Federal Court records. In recent years the Administrative Office of the United States Courts in Washington, DC has developed three innovative public access programs: VCIS, PACER, and the Case Management/ Electronic Case Files (CM/ECF) project. The most useful program for online searching is PACER.

PACER

PACER, the acronym for **P**ublic **A**ccess to **E**lectronic **C**ourt **R**ecords, provides docket information online for open cases at **all U.S. Bankruptcy courts** and **most U.S. District courts**. Access is via either a commercial dial-up system (user fee of $.60 a minute) or through the Internet (user fee is $.07 per page). Cases for the U.S. Court of Federal Claims are also available.

Each court controls its own computer system and case information database; therefore, there are some variations among jurisdictions as to the information offered.

Sign-up and technical support is handled at the PACER Service Center in San Antonio, Texas (800) 676-6856. You can sign up for all or multiple districts at once. In many judicial districts, when you sign up for PACER access, you will receive a PACER Primer that has been customized for each district. The primer contains a summary of how to access PACER, how to select cases, how to read case numbers and docket sheets, some searching tips, who to call for problem resolution, and district specific program variations.

A continuing problem with PACER is that each court determines when records will be purged and how records will be indexed, leaving you to guess how a name is spelled or abbreviated and how much information about closed cases your search will uncover. A PACER search for anything but open cases **cannot** take the place of a full seven-year search of the federal court records available by written request from the court itself or through a local document retrieval company. Many districts report that they have closed records back a number of years, but at the same time indicate they purge docket items every six months.

Before Accessing PACER, Search the "National" U.S. Party/Case Index

It is no longer necessary to call each court in every state and district to determine where a debtor has filed bankruptcy, or if someone is a defendant in Federal litigation. National and regional searches of district and bankruptcy filings can be made with one call (via modem) to the U.S. Party/Case Index.

The **U.S. Party/Case Index** is a national index for U.S. district, bankruptcy, and appellate courts. This index allows searches to determine whether or not a party is involved in federal litigation almost anywhere in the nation.

The U.S. Party/Case Index provides the capability to perform national or regional searches on party name and Social Security Number in the bankruptcy index, party name and nature of suit in the civil index, and party name in the criminal and appellate indices.

The search will provide a list of case numbers, filing locations and filing dates for those cases matching the search criteria. If you need more information about the case, you must obtain it from the court directly or through that court's individual PACER system.

You may access the U.S. Party/Case Index by dialup connection or via the Internet. The internet site for the U.S. Party/Case Index is http://pacer.uspci.uscourts.gov. The toll-free dial-up number for the U.S. Party/Case Index is 800-974-8896. For more information, call the PACER service center at 800-676-6856.

In accordance with Judicial Conference policy, most courts charge a $.60 per minute access fee for the traditional dial-up service or $.07 per page for internet service.

RACER

RACER stands for Remote Access to Court Electronic Records. Accessed through the Internet, RACER offers access to the same records as PACER. At present, searching RACER is free in a few courts. Normally the fee structure is $.07 per page.

Miscellaneous Online Systems

Some courts have developed their own online systems. In addition to RACER, Idaho's Bankruptcy and District Courts have other searching options available on their website. Likewise, the Southern District Court of New York offers CourtWeb, which provides information to the public on selected recent rulings of those judges who have elected to make information available in electronic form.

Case Management/Electronic Case Files (CM/ECF)

Electronic Case Files (ECF) is a prototype system for the filing of cases electronically. This service, initially introduced in January 1996, enables participating attorneys and litigants to electronically submit pleadings and corresponding docket entries to the court via the Internet, thereby eliminating substantial paper handling and processing time. ECF permits any interested parties to instantaneously access the entire official case docket and documents on the Internet of selective civil and bankruptcy cases within these jurisdictions.

The federal judiciary's *Case management/Electronic Case Files (CM/ECF)* project is designed to replace the aging electronic docketing and case management systems in more than 200 bankruptcy, district and appellate courts by 2005. CM/ECF will provide the capability for courts to have case file documents in electronic format and to accept filings over the Internet. About two-thirds of all federal courts are currently operational as we go to press, and the remaining courts are in the process of implementing CM/ECF.

It is important to note that when you search ECF, you are ONLY searching cases that have been filed electronically. A case may not have been filed electronically through CM-ECF, so you must still conduct a search using PACER if you want to know if a case exists.

One important feature of this system is their *National Locator*, known as the *United States Party Index*. This is a name search, used to locate the specific court where records are available.

For further information about CM/ECF visit http://pacer.psc.uscourts.gov/cmecf/index.html.

VCIS

Another access system is **VCIS** (Voice Case Information System). At one time, nearly all of the U.S. Bankruptcy Court judicial districts provide **VCIS**, a means of accessing information regarding open bankruptcy cases by merely using a touch-tone telephone. **VCIS** is gradually being phased out, and now only a few dozen courts allow **VCIS** dialup. Still, there is no charge. Individual names are entered last name first with as much of the first name as you wish to include. For example, Carl R. Ernst could be entered as ERNSTC or ERNSTCARL. Do not enter the middle initial. Business names are entered as they are written, without blanks.

VCIS, like the RACER System, is being replaced by newer technology. **Each Bankruptcy Court that now offers VCIS access includes that court's VCIS phone number(s) in its profile.**

Federal Courts Searching Hints

- VCIS should *only* be used to locate information about open cases. Do not attempt to use VCIS as a substitute for a PACER search.

- Since this publication includes the counties of jurisdiction for each court, the list of counties in each Court profile is a good starting point for determining where case records may or may not be found.

- Before performing a general PACER search to determine whether cases exist under a particular plaintiff, debtor, or defendant name, first be certain to review that Court's profile, which may indicate the earliest dates of case records available on PACER. Also, searchers need to be sure that the Court's case index includes all cases, open and closed, for that particular period. Be aware that some courts purge older, closed cases after a period of time, making such a PACER search incomplete. Wherever known, this publication indicates within the court profiles the purge timeframe for PACER records. Times vary from court to court and state to state.

- Experience shows that court personnel are typically not aware of — nor concerned about — the types of searches performed by readers of this publication. Court personnel often focus on only open cases, whereas a searcher may want to know as much about closed cases as open ones. Thus, court personnel are sometimes fuzzy in answering questions about how far back case records go on PACER, and whether closed cases have been purged. If you are looking for cases older than a year or two, there is no substitute for a real, onsite search performed by the court itself or by a local search expert (if that court allows full access to its indexes).

- Some courts may be more willing than others to give out information by telephone. This is because most courts have converted from the old card index system to fully computerized indexes that are easily accessible while on the phone.

Federal Records Centers and the National Archives

After a federal case is closed, the documents are held by Federal Courts themselves for a number of years, then stored at a designated Federal Records Center (FRC). After 20 to 30 years, the records are then transferred from the FRC to the regional archives offices of the National Archives and Records Administration (NARA). The length of time between a case being closed and its being moved to an FRC varies widely by district. Each court has its own transfer cycle and determines access procedures to its case records, even after they have been sent to the FRC.

When case records are sent to an FRC, the boxes of records are assigned accession, location, and box numbers. These numbers, which are called case locator information, **must be obtained from the originating court in order to retrieve documents from the FRC.** Some courts will provide such information over the telephone, but others require a written request. This information is now available on PACER in certain judicial districts. The Federal Records Center for each state is listed as follows:

State	Circuit	Appeals Court	Federal Records Center
AK	9	San Francisco, CA	Anchorage (Some records are in temporary storage in Seattle)
AL	11	Atlanta, GA	Atlanta
AR	8	St. Louis, MO	Fort Worth
AZ	9	San Francisco, CA	Los Angeles
CA	9	San Francisco, CA	Los Angeles (Central & Southern CA) San Francisco (Eastern & Northern CA)
CO	10	Denver, CO	Denver
CT	2	New York, NY	Boston
DC		Washington, DC	Washington, DC
DE	3	Philadelphia, PA	Philadelphia
FL	11	Atlanta, GA	Atlanta
GA	11	Atlanta, GA	Atlanta
GU	9	San Francisco, CA	San Francisco
HI	9	San Francisco, CA	San Francisco
IA	8	St. Louis, MO	Kansas City, MO
ID	9	San Francisco, CA	Seattle
IL	7	Chicago, IL	Chicago
IN	7	Chicago, IL	Chicago
KS	10	Denver, CO	Kansas City, MO
KY	6	Cincinnati, OH	Atlanta
LA	5	New Orleans, LA	Fort Worth
MA	1	Boston, MA	Boston
MD	4	Richmond, VA	Philadelphia
ME	1	Boston, MA	Boston
MI	6	Cincinnati, OH	Chicago

State	Circuit	Appeals Court	Federal Records Center
MN	8	St. Louis, MO	Chicago
MO	8	St. Louis, MO	Kansas City, MO
MS	5	New Orleans, LA	Atlanta
MT	9	San Francisco, CA	Denver
NC	4	Richmond, VA	Atlanta
ND	8	St. Louis, MO	Denver
NE	8	St. Louis, MO	Kansas City, MO
NH	1	Boston, MA	Boston
NJ	3	Philadelphia, PA	New York
NM	10	Denver, CO	Denver
NV	9	San Francisco, CA	Los Angeles (Clark County, NV) San Francisco (Other NV counties)
NY	2	New York, NY	New York
OH	6	Cincinnati, OH	Chicago; Dayton has some bankruptcy
OK	10	Denver, CO	Fort Worth
OR	9	San Francisco, CA	Seattle
PA	3	Philadelphia, PA	Philadelphia
PR	1	Boston, MA	New York
RI	1	Boston, MA	Boston
SC	4	Richmond, VA	Atlanta
SD	8	St. Louis, MO	Denver
TN	6	Cincinnati, OH	Atlanta
TX	5	New Orleans, LA	Fort Worth
UT	10	Denver, CO	Denver
VA	4	Richmond, VA	Philadelphia
VI	3	Philadelphia, PA	New York
VT	2	New York, NY	Boston
WA	9	San Francisco, CA	Seattle
WI	7	Chicago, IL	Chicago
WV	4	Richmond, VA	Philadelphia
WY	10	Denver, CO	Denver

Notes to the Chart:

GU is Guam, PR is Puerto Rico, and VI is the Virgin Islands.

According to some odd logic, the following Federal Records Centers are not located in the city named above, but are actually somewhere else. Below are the exceptions:

Atlanta—in East Point, GA; Boston—in Waltham, MA; Los Angeles—in Laguna Niguel, CA; New York—in Bayonne, NJ; San Francisco—in San Bruno, CA

Searching Other Federal Records Online

EDGAR

EDGAR, the Electronic Data Gathering Analysis, and Retrieval system was established by the Securities and Exchange Commission (SEC) to allow companies to make required filing to the SEC by direct transmission. As of May 6, 1996, all public domestic companies are required to make their filings on EDGAR, except for filings made to the Commission's regional offices and those filings made on paper due to a hardship exemption.

EDGAR is an extensive repository of U.S. corporation information and it is available online.

What Information is Available on EDGAR?

Companies must file the following reports with the SEC:

- 10-K, an annual financial report, which includes audited year-end financial statements.

- 10-Q, a quarterly report, unaudited.

- 8K - a report detailing significant or unscheduled corporate changes or events.

- Securities offering and trading registrations and the final prospectus.

The list above is not conclusive. There are other miscellaneous reports filed, including those dealing with security holdings by institutions and insiders. Access to these documents provides a wealth of information.

How to Access EDGAR Online

EDGAR is searchable online at: http://www.sec.gov/info/edgar.shtml. A number of private vendors offer access to EDGAR records. LEXIS/NEXIS acts as the data wholesaler or distributor on behalf of the government. LEXIS/NEXIS sells data to information retailers, including its own NEXIS service.

Aviation Records

The Federal Aviation Association (FAA) is the U.S. government agency with the responsibility of all matters related to the safety of civil aviation. The FAA, among other functions, provides the system that registers aircraft, and documents showing title or interest in aircraft. Their website, at www.faa.gov, is the ultimate source of aviation records, airports and facilities, safety regulations, and civil research and engineering.

The Aircraft Owners and Pilots Association is the largest organization of its kind with 340,000+ members. Their website is www.aopa.org and is an excellent source of information regarding the aviation industry.

Another excellent source of aircraft information is *Jane's World Airlines* at www.janes.com.

Military Records

This topic is so broad that there can be a book written about it, and in fact there is! *The Armed Forces Locator Directory* from MIE Publishing (800-937-2133) is an excellent source. The book, now in its 8th edition, covers every conceivable topic regarding military records. Their website www.militaryusa.com offers free access to some useful databases.

The Privacy Act of 1974 (5 U.S.C. 552a) and the Department of Defense directives require a written request, signed and dated, to access military personnel records. For further details, visit the NPRC site listed below.

Military Internet Sources

There are a number of great internet sites that provide valuable information on obtaining military and military personnel records. The National Personnel Records Center (NPRC), maintained by the National Archives & Records Administration, is on the Internet at www.nara.gov/regional/mpr.html. This site is full of useful information and links. Other excellent sites include:

www.army.mil	The official site of the U.S. Army
www.af.mil	The official site of the U.S. Air Force
www.navy.mil	The official site of the U.S. Navy
www.usmc.mil	The official site of the U.S. Marine Corps
www.arng.army.mil	The official site of the Army National Guard
www.ang.af.mil	The official site of the Air National Guard
www.uscg.mil/USCG.shtm	The official site of the U.S. Coast Guard

Best U.S. Government Gateways

The remainder of this Chapter (pages 34-39) is written and contributed by online pioneer and award winning journalist Alan M. Schlein, author of Find It Online.

We sincerely thank Alan for permitting the use of his material in The Sourcebook. *Alan can be reached at* www.deadlineonline.com. *Check out his website— it is a great source with lots of useful links!*

In the U.S., almost every federal government agency is online. There is a nationwide network of depository libraries, including the enormous resources of the National Archives (www.nara.gov), the twelve presidential libraries, and four national libraries (the Library of Congress, the National Agricultural Library, the National Library of Education and the National Library of Medicine). There are almost 5000 government websites from more than forty-two U.S. departments and agencies.

Because there are so many government websites, you may need to turn to the hundreds of websites, called *government gateways*, that organize and link government sites, in order to find the starting point for your research. Some gateways are simply collections of links. Others provide access to bulletin boards of specific government agencies so that you find and contact employees with specific knowledge. Guides are becoming increasingly important in light of the growing number of reports and publications that are no longer printed but simply posted online.

Best Government Gateways (listed alphabetically)

Documents Center
www.lib.umich.edu/govdocs/index.html

> Documents Center is a clearinghouse for local, state, federal, foreign, and international government information. It is one of the more comprehensive online searching aids for all kinds of government information on the Internet. It is especially useful as a meta-site of meta-sites.

Federal Web Locators
www.infoctr.edu/fwl/

> This web locator is really two sites in one: a federal government website (www.infoctr.edu/fwl) and a separate site that tracks federal courts (www.infoctr.edu/fwl/fedweb.juris.htm), both of which are browsable by category or by keyword. Together they provide links to thousands of government agencies and departments.

FedLaw
www.thecre.com/fedlaw/default.htm

> FedLaw is an extremely broad resource for federal legal and regulatory research containing 1,600+ links to law-related information. It has very good topical and title indices that group web links into hundreds of subjects. It is operated by the General Services Administration (GSA).

Fedstats
www.fedstats.gov

A terrific collection of statistical sites from the federal government and a good central clearinghouse for other federal statistics sites.

FedWorld Information Network
www.fedworld.gov

FedWorld helps you search over thirty million U.S. government pages. It is a massive collection of 15,000 files and databases of government sites, including bulletin boards that can help you identify government employees with expertise in a broad range of subjects. A surprising number of these experts will take the time to discuss questions from the general public.

FirstGov
www.firstgov.gov

Responding to the need for a central clearinghouse of U.S. federal government sites, the U.S. government developed FirstGov and linked every federal agency to its site as well as every state government. It has an easy-to-use search tool, allowing you to specify if you want federal or state agencies and to easily locate business regulations and vital records. It also lets you look for federal government phone numbers and email addresses. This is an easy-to-use starting point, powered by the AlltheWeb search engine. Also, check out the FAQs of the U.S. government for questions and answers about the U.S. government (www.faq.gov).

Google's Uncle Sam
www.google.com/unclesam

Google's Uncle Sam site is a search engine geared to looking at U.S. government sites. It is an easy-to-use tool if you know what you are looking for.

Healthfinder
www.healthfinder.gov

This is a great starting point for health-related government information. See the Health and Medicine Information Tools sidebar in Chapter 5, Specialized Tools, for more health sites.

InfoMine: Scholarly Internet Resource Collections
http://infomine.ucr.edu

InfoMine provides collections of scholarly internet resources, best for academics. It is one of the best academic resources anywhere, from the librarians at the University of California Riverside. Its Government Information section is easily searchable by subject. It has detailed headings and its resource listings are very specific. Since it is run by a university, some of its references are limited to student use only.

SearchGov.com
www.searchgov.com

A private company that has an effective search for U.S. government sites.

Speech & Transcript Center
www.freepint.com/gary/speech.htm

This site links directly to websites containing transcripts of speeches. Pulled together by former George Washington University reference librarian and *Invisible Web* author Gary Price, it encompasses government resources, business leaders, and real audio. A large section is devoted to U.S. and international government speech transcripts – including Congressional hearings, testimony and transcripts.

U.S. Federal Government Agencies Directory
www.lib.lsu.edu/gov/fedgov.html

This directory of federal agencies is maintained by Louisiana State Univ. It links to hundreds of federal government internet sites. It is divided by branch and agency and is very thorough, but focus on your target because it is easy to lose your way or become overwhelmed en route.

U.S. Government Information
www.libraries.colorado.edu/ps/gov/us/federal.htm

This is a gem of a site from the University of Colorado and a good starting point. It is not as thorough as the LSU site above, but still very valuable.

Best U.S. Federal Government Websites

U.S. tax dollars are put to good and visible use here. A few of the government's web pages are rated as excellent. Some can be used in lieu of commercial tools but only if you have the time to invest.

A few of the top government sites – the Census and the Securities and Exchange Commission – are models of content and presentation. They are very deep, very thorough, and easy to use. If only the rest of the federal government would follow suit. Unfortunately, the best of the federal government is just that: the best. Not all agencies maintain such detailed and relevant resources.

Following are the crown jewels of the government's collection, in ranked order:

U.S. Census Bureau
www.census.gov

Without question, this is the U.S. government's top site. It is saturated with information and census publications – at times overwhelmingly so – but worth every minute of your time. A few hours spent here is a worthwhile investment for almost anyone seeking to background a community, learn about business, or find any kind of demographic information. You can search several ways: alphabetically by subject, by word, by location, and by geographic map. The only problem is the sheer volume of data.

One feature, the Thematic Mapping System, allows users to extract data from Census CD-ROMs and display them in maps by state or county. You can create maps on all kinds of subjects – for example, tracking violent crime to farm income. The site also features the Statistical Abstract of the U.S. with a searchable index at www.census.gov/statab/www/stateabs.html

The potential uses of census data are infinite. Marketers use it to find community information. Reporters search out trends by block, neighborhood or region. Educators conduct research. Businesses evaluate new business prospects. Genealogists trace family trees – though full census data is not available for seventy-two years from the date the census is taken. You can even use it to identify ideal communities in which to raise a family. Jennifer LaFleur, now at *The Dallas Morning News* did a story while at *The San Jose Mercury News* using the census site to find eligible bachelors in specific areas of San Jose.

Additional census resources include:

1990 U.S. Census LOOKUP
http://venus.census.gov/cdrom/lookup/

This site provides detailed census data down to the county level.

State and County QuickFacts
http://quickfacts.census.gov/qfd/

At all its levels, this site has very easy-to-use census information.

Census FactFinder
http://factfinder.census.gov

An easy way to find quickie facts from within the Census' huge website. This is an excellent and easy to use site. Start here when looking for Census documents, since it has a search capability.

Census Industry Statistics
www.census.gov/main/www/industries.html

Industry-by-industry statistics.

And one other census-related site that is superb is the University of Virginia's Fisher Library's historical census data browser, going all the way back to 1790. It can be found at http://fisher.lib.virginia.edu/collections/stats/histcensus/

U.S. Securities and Exchange Commission (SEC)
www.sec.gov

Only the Census site is better than the SEC site, which is a first-rate, must-stop place for information shopping on U.S. companies. Its EDGAR database search site (www.sec.gov/edaux/searches.htm) is easy to use and provides access to documents that companies and corporations are required to file under regulatory laws.

The SEC site is a great starting point for information about specific companies and industry trends. The SEC requires all publicly-held corporations and some large privately-held corporations to disclose detailed financial information about their activities, plans, holdings, executives' salaries and stakes, legal problems and so forth. For more details, see Chapter 9, Business Tools.

Library of Congress (LOC)
www.loc.gov

This site is an extraordinary collection of documents. Thomas, the Library's Congressional online center site (http://thomas.loc.gov/home) provides an exhaustive collection of congressional documents, including bill summaries, voting records and the full Congressional Record, which is the official record of Congressional action. This LOC site also links to many international, federal, state and local government sites. You can also access the library's more than five million records online, some versions in full-text and some in abstract form. Though the library's entire 121 million item collection is not yet available online, the amount online increases daily. In addition to books and papers, it includes an extensive images collection ranging from Frank Lloyd Wright's designs to the Dead Sea Scrolls to the world's largest online collection of baseball cards. The Library of Congress also has a terrific collection of international data on its website at www.loc.gov/rr/international/portals.html.

Superintendent of Documents Home Page (GPO)
www.access.gpo.gov/su_docs

The GPO is the federal government's primary information printer and distributor. All federally funded information from every agency is sent here, which makes the GPO's holdings priceless. Luckily, the GPO site is well-constructed and easy to use. For example, it has the full text of the *Federal Register*, which lists all federal regulations and proposals, and full-text access to the *Congressional Record*. The GPO also produces an online version of the *Congressional Directory*, providing details on every congressional district, profiles of members, staff profiles, maps of every district and historical documents about Congress. This site will expand exponentially over the next few years, as the number of materials go out of print and online. GPO Access also allows you to electronically retrieve much of the bureaucratic paper in Washington, electronically, from the Government Printing Office including searching more than seventy databases and indices. If you need some help finding things, use the topic-specific finder at this site.

National Technical Information Service (NTIS)
www.ntis.gov

The best place to find federal government reports related to technology and science. NTIS is the nation's clearinghouse for unclassified technical reports of government-sponsored research. NTIS collects, indexes, abstracts, and sells U.S. and foreign research – mostly in science, technology, behavioral, and social science data.

IGnet
www.ignet.gov

This is a truly marvelous collection of reports and information from the Inspector Generals of about sixty federal agency departments. They find waste and abuse within government agencies. It is well worth checking when starting research on government-related matters.

General Accounting Office GAO Reports
www.gao.gov/decisions/decision.htm

The Comptroller General Opinions from the last sixty days are posted on this GAO website. These reports and opinions are excellent references. For historical opinions back to 1996 go to www.access.gpo.gov/su_docs/aces/aces170.shtml.

White House
www.whitehouse.gov

This site would not make this list if not for its economic statistics page at www.whitehouse.gov/fsbr/es_br.html and the transcript of every official action the U.S. President takes at www.whitehouse.gov/news. Unfortunately, as with many government sites, its primary focus is in promoting itself.

DefenseLINK – U.S. Department of Defense (DOD)
www.defenselink.mil

This is the brand-name site for Pentagon-related information. There is a tremendous amount of data here – categorized by branch of service – including U.S. troop deployments worldwide. To the Pentagon's credit, they have made this a very easy site to use.

Defense Technical Information Center (DTIC)
www.dtic.mil

The DTIC site is loaded with links and defense information – everything from contractors to weapon systems. It even includes de-classified information about the Gulf War. It is the best place to start for defense information. You can even find a list of all military-related contracts, including beneficiary communities and the kinds of contracts awarded. The only problem with the site is there is no search engine to make it easy to find information.

Bureau of Transportation Statistics
www.bts.gov

The U.S. Department of Transportation's enormous collection of information about every facet of transportation. There is a lot of valuable material here including the Transportation Statistics Annual Report. It also holds financial data for airlines and searchable databases containing information about fatal accidents and on-time statistics for airlines, which can be narrowed to your local airport.

National Archives and Records Administration
www.nara.gov

A breathtaking collection of research online, for example the National Archives has descriptions of more than 170,000 documents related to the Kennedy assassination. It also contains a world-class database holding descriptions of more than 95,000 records held by the Still Picture and Motion Picture, Sound and Video Branches. This site also links to the twelve Presidential Archives with their records of every person ever mentioned in Executive Branch correspondence. You can view an image of the original document. The Archives Research Center Online has great collections of family history/genealogy research and veteran's service records.

FedWorld.gov
`www.fedworld.gov`

This thorough government clearinghouse site, run by the Commerce Department's National Technical Information Service, offers access to Firstgov, the U.S. Government's comprehensive site, but also allows you to search government publications, U.S. Supreme Court decisions and helps you find government jobs.

Federal Consumer Information Center National Contact Center
`www.info.gov`

While this is largely a telephone service that gets more than a million calls a year, this website tries to provide a way through the maze of federal agencies. It includes a clearinghouse of phone numbers for all federal agencies, state, and local government sites as well.

SciTechResources.gov
`www.scitechresources.gov`

This is a tremendous directory of about 700 science and technology resources on U.S. government sites from the U.S. Department of Commerce, National Technical Information Service.

Department of Homeland Security
`www.whitehouse.gov/homeland/`

While the U.S. Government has made the Department of Homeland Security a separate agency, it maintains the website under the White House's auspices. As a result, it has good information, but is, like the White House site, more about public relations for the current president and his staff, than it is about information. Nonetheless, you can find useful information about the current threat level and information about what U.S. state and local governments are doing on homeland security as well.

Bureau of National Affairs, The
`www.bna.com`

An expensive but useful group of topic-focused newsletters providing details on U.S. government action at different federal agencies like the Daily Labor Report, Bankruptcy Law Daily, and the Biotech Watch. This private company has hundreds of newsletters you will not find elsewhere.

Searching County Court Records

The County Court Records Sections

The purpose of the County Court Records Sections is to provide quick yet detailed access information on the more than 6,400 major courts that have jurisdiction over significant criminal and civil cases under state law.

Included in *The Sourcebook* are all state felony courts, larger claim civil courts, and probate courts in the United States. Since most courts have jurisdiction over a number of categories of cases, we also include many of the courts that hear misdemeanor, eviction, and small claims court cases. In addition, each County Court Records Section begins with an introduction that summarizes where other major categories of court cases — DUI, preliminary hearings, and juvenile cases — can be found.

The term "County Courts," as used in this publication, refers to those courts of original jurisdiction (trial courts) within each state's court system that handle...

- **Felonies**　　　　　-- Generally defined as crimes punishable by one year or more of jail time
- **Civil Actions**　　　-- For money damages (usually greater than $3,000)
- **Probate**　　　　　-- Estate matters
- **Misdemeanors**　　-- Generally defined as minor infractions with a fine or minimal jail time
- **Evictions**　　　　-- Landlord/tenant actions
- **Small Claims**　　　-- Actions for minor money damages (generally under $3,000)

Useful Applications

The County Court Record Sections are especially useful for four kinds of applications—

General litigation searching/background searching... Combined with the *Federal Court section*, you have complete coverage of all the important courts in the United States.

Employment background checking... Included is full coverage of local criminal courts at the felony level, and many misdemeanor courts as well.

Tenant background checking... Courts where landlord/tenant cases are filed are indicated in the state introduction charts, and most of the courts handling such cases are profiled.

Asset searching... The probate courts have records of wills and estate matters that can be used to determine assets, related parties, and useful addresses.

Reading the State Court Charts

On the first page of each County Court Records Section are three charts. Together, they present that state's court structure.

When searching for case records, keep in mind that many of the higher level courts also handle appeals from lower courts.

The First Chart

The chart at the top of the page summarizes the structure of the court system, listing the court of general jurisdiction, followed underneath by the courts of limited, municipal, and special jurisdiction. Court types with an asterisk (*) after their names are profiled in *The Sourcebook*.

The number of case record locations is indicated for each court. Where two classifications of courts are combined into one location and only one entry appears in the profiles, the number of combined courts is noted. The number of locations for courts not profiled in *The Sourcebook* are estimates.

Where useful, the number and type of organization of each of the classifications of court are indicated under the "How Organized" column.

The Civil and Criminal Charts

The other two charts consolidate information about what types of cases each court hears, i.e. the "jurisdiction" of the type of court.

Where more than one court has jurisdiction for a particular kind of civil case, the minimum and maximum claim fields clarify whether there is overlapping jurisdiction in the state. In most states, the lower and upper court civil claim limits dovetail nicely between the court levels, so you can readily tell which court has the type of civil case you are concerned about.

Although these charts oversimplify complex sets of state statutes, their purpose is to provide you with a practical starting point to help you decide where to search for case records.

Beyond the Charts

When you cannot make a determination to your satisfaction where to search, we suggest you contact that state's administrator of courts by telephone or visit their internet site.

The address, telephone number, and internet address of the administrative office in each state are listed under the heading "Administration."

Reading the Court Profiles

Basic Information

The 3,140 U.S. counties (and where applicable, parishes, boroughs, independent cities, etc.) are listed in alphabetical order, within each state. When a county has more than one court profiled, the courts appear in order beginning with the court of general jurisdiction, then proceeding down to more limited jurisdictions. Each profile specifically lists the types of cases handled by that court. If a level of court has divisions, civil courts are listed before criminal courts. Where more than one court of the same type is located in a county, they are listed in alphabetical order by the name of the city where they are located.

All city/ZIP Code combinations have been verified against our latest version of *The County Locator* database for accuracy. In addition to the address and telephone number, the time zone is indicated (see below for an explanation of the abbreviations used). Fax numbers are given for most courts.

Watch for Name Variations From State to State

Do not assume that the structure of the court system in another state is anything like your own. In one state, the Circuit Court may be the highest trial court whereas in another it is a limited jurisdiction court. Examples are: New York, where the Supreme Court is not very "supreme" and the downstate court structure varies from upstate; and Tennessee, where circuit courts are in districts.

Access and Searching Details

Each court profile indicates acceptable searching methods including phone, fax mail, in person, and online. The profiles also indicate all fees (including search, copy and certification) and acceptable payment methods. For example, some courts accept credit cards, some do not accept personal checks, and some may bill for copies.

Here are some searching hints to keep in mind:

- When a county has multiple courts of the same level, general information is provided to help determine which office to search in, depending upon the subject's address.

- In many instances two types of courts within a county (e.g., circuit and district) are combined. When phoning or writing these courts, we recommend that your request specifically state that you want both courts included in the search.

- Be aware that the number of courts that no longer conduct name searches has risen. For these courts, you must hire a local retriever, directly or through a search company, to search for you. It should be noted that usually these courts still take specific document copy requests by mail. Because of long mail turnaround times and court fees, local retrievers are frequently used even when the court will honor a request by mail. A court's entry indicates if it is one of the many to offer a **public access terminal** where in person searchers can freely view case documents or indexes.

Index and Record Systems

Most profiles of the civil courts indicate whether the plaintiffs as well as the defendants are indexed. A plaintiff search is useful, for example, to determine if someone is especially litigious.

During the past decade, thousands of courts have installed computerized indexing systems. The year when computer indexing started in each of these courts is indicated in the profile of most of the automated courts. Computerized systems are considerably faster and easier to search, allowing for more indexing capability than the microfilm and card indexes that preceded them.

Search Requirements

There is a strong tendency for courts to overstate their search requirements. For civil cases, the usual reasonable requirement is a defendant (or plaintiff) name — full name if it is a common name — and the time frame to search —e.g., 1993-2002. For criminal cases, the court may require more identification, such as date of birth (DOB), to ascertain the correct individual. Other information "required" by courts — such as Social Security Number (SSN) — is often just "helpful" to narrow the search on a common name. Further, we have indicated when certain pieces of information may be helpful but are not required.

Restricted Records

Most courts have a number of types of case records, such as juvenile and adoptions, which are not released without a court order. These restricted record types are indicated in each profile.

Fees and Other Requirements

As mentioned above, search, copy, and certification fees are given for most courts, as well as fax fees if known. Where specified, we indicate whether the court requires a self-addressed stamped envelope (SASE) to accompany a written search request. Even where it is not indicated, we recommend including a SASE to make sure the results are returned to you.

Some Court Basics

Before trudging into a courthouse and demanding to view a document, you should first be aware of some basic court procedures. Whether the case is filed in a state, municipal, or federal court, each case follows a similar process.

A **civil case** usually commences when a plaintiff files a complaint with a court against defendants. The defendants respond to the complaint with an answer. After this initial round, there may be literally hundreds of activities before the court issues a judgment. These activities can include revised complaints and their answers, motions of various kinds, discovery proceedings (including depositions) to establish the documentation and facts involved in the case. All of these activities are listed on a **docket sheet**, which may be a piece of paper or a computerized index.

Once the court issues a judgment, either party may appeal the ruling to an appellate division or court. In the case of a money judgment, the winning side can usually file it as a judgment lien with the county recorder. Appellate divisions usually deal only with legal issues and not the facts of the case.

In a **criminal case**, the plaintiff is a government jurisdiction. The Government brings the action against the defendant for violation of one or more of its statutes.

In a **bankruptcy case,** which can be heard only in federal courts, there is neither defendant nor plaintiff. Instead, the debtor files voluntarily for bankruptcy protection against creditors, or the creditors file against the debtor in order to force the debtor into involuntary bankruptcy.

State Court Structure

The secret to determining where a state court case is located is to understand how the court system is structured in that particular state. The general structure of all state court systems has four parts:

Appellate courts	**Limited jurisdiction trial courts**
Intermediate appellate courts	**General jurisdiction trial courts**

The two highest levels, appellate and intermediate appellate courts, only hear cases on appeal from the trial courts. Opinions of these appellate courts are of interest primarily to attorneys seeking legal precedents for new cases.

General jurisdiction trial courts usually handle a full range of civil and criminal litigation. These courts usually handle felonies and larger civil cases.

Limited jurisdiction trial courts come in two varieties. First, many limited jurisdiction courts handle smaller civil claims (usually $10,000 or less), misdemeanors, and pretrial hearing for felonies. Second, some of these courts, sometimes called special jurisdiction courts, are limited to one type of litigation, for example the Court of Claims in New York which only handles liability cases against the state.

Some states, for instance Iowa, have consolidated their general and limited jurisdiction court structure into one combined court system. In other states there may be a further distinction between state-supported courts and municipal courts. Notable is the state of New York where nearly 1,300 Justice Courts handle misdemeanors, local ordinance violations, and traffic violations including DWI.

Generalizations should not be made about where specific types of cases are handled in the various states. Misdemeanors, probate, landlord/tenant (eviction), domestic relations, and juvenile cases may be handled in either or both the general and limited jurisdiction courts. To help you locate the correct court to perform your search in, this *Sourcebook* specifically lists the types of cases handled by each court.

Types of Litigation in Trial Courts

Criminal

Criminal cases are categorized as *felonies* or *misdemeanors*. A general rule, a felony involves a jail term of one year or more, whereas a misdemeanor may only involve a monetary *fine*.

Civil

Civil cases are categorized as *tort*, *contract*, and *real property* rights. Torts can include *automobile accidents*, *medical malpractice*, and *product liability* cases. Actions for small money damages, typically under $3,000, are known as *small claims*.

Other

Other types of cases that frequently are handled by separate courts or specialized divisions of courts include *juvenile*, *probate* (wills and estates), and *domestic relations*.

How Courts Maintain Records

Case Numbering

When a case is filed, it is assigned a case number. This is the primary indexing method in every court. Therefore, in searching for case records, you will need to know — or find — the applicable case number. If you have the number in good form already, your search should be fast and reasonably inexpensive.

You should be aware that case numbering procedures are not consistent throughout a state court system. One district may assign numbers by district while another may assign numbers by location (division) within the district, or by judge. Remember: case numbers appearing in legal text citations may not be adequate for searching unless they appear in the proper form for the particular court in which you are searching.

All basic civil case information is entered onto docket sheets.

Docket Sheet

Information from cover sheets and from documents filed as a case goes forward is recorded on the docket sheet. The docket sheet then contains an outline of the case history from initial filing to its current status. While docket sheets differ somewhat in format, the basic information contained on a docket sheet is consistent from court to court. All docket sheets contain:

- Name of court, including location (division) and the judge assigned;
- Case number and case name;
- Names of all plaintiffs and defendants/debtors;
- Names and addresses of attorneys for the plaintiff or debtor;
- Nature and cause (e.g., statute) of action.

Computerization

Most courts are computerized, which means the docket sheet data is entered into a computer system. Within a state or judicial district, the courts *may* be linked together via a single computer system.

Docket sheets from cases closed before the advent of computerization may not be in the computer system. For pre-computer cases, most courts keep summary case information on microfilm, microfiche, or index cards.

Case documents are not generally available on computer because courts are still experimenting with and developing electronic filing and imaging of court documents. Generally, documents are only available to be copied by contacting the court where the case records are located.

Additional State Court Resources

The National Center for State Courts

www.ncsconline.org

NASCIO - Click on a State then the Judicial Link

https://www.nascio.org/aboutNascio/profiles/

Searching Recording Office Records

Combined, the Recording Offices section for each state section contains 4,266 local recording offices where Uniform Commercial Code and real estate records are maintained.

The Lowdown on Recorded Documents

Documents filed and recorded at local county, parish, city or town offices represent some of the best opportunities to gain access to open public records, moreso if they are available for searching online by name. In fact, recorded documents are one of the most available types of public records that can be viewed online and obtained over the Internet, either for free or at a reasonable fee. Even better, if you are lucky enough to live in close proximity, you can visit your local office and, for free, view complete records and acquire copies.

Real Estate

As mentioned previously, real estate records are public so that everyone can know who owns what property. Liens on real estate must be public so a buyer knows all the facts. The county (or parish or city) recorder's office is the source. Also, access is also available from many private companies that purchase entire county record databases and create their own database for commercial purposes.

Uniform Commercial Code (UCC)

UCC filings are to personal property what mortgages are to real estate property. UCCs are in the category of financial records that must be fully open to public scrutiny so that other potential lenders are on notice about which assets of the borrower have been pledged as collateral.

As with tax liens, UCC recordings are filed, according to state law, either at the state or local (county, town, parish) level. Until June 30, 2001, liens on certain types of companies required dual filing (must file at BOTH locations, thus records can be searched at BOTH locations). As of July 1, 2001, UCC filings other than those that go into real estate records are no longer filed at the local filing offices in most states, but older filings can still be located there until 2008. As with real estate records, there are a number of private companies who have created their own databases for commercial resale.

A Great Source of Information

Although recorded documents are a necessity to making an informed business-related decision, they are also a virtual treasure trove of data. UCC filing documents give you the names and addresses of creditors and debtors, describe the asset offered for collateral, the date of the filing, and whether or not the loan has been satisfied. This information contained on the statements can lead an experienced investigator to other avenues along the information trail. For example, if the collateral is a plane or a vessel, this will lead to registration records; if the debtor is a business, other names on the filing may lead to other traceable business partners or ventures.

How the Recording Offices Section is Organized

General Organization

The mailing address, telephone, time zone and fax number are listed for each office. If online access is available from the agencies, a detailed profile is provided. Included are other categories of information offered online from this or a related agency, such as tax assessor information and vital records, licenses, etc. Searching fees are listed. Other important phone numbers in the county are listed to the extent that we have researched and verified these numbers. Examples are telephone numbers for the assessor, treasurer, vital records, and elections offices.

An introduction to each state Recording Offices section contains a summary of the facts about where and how real estate records are maintained, as well as indicating information about Uniform Commercial Code and tax lien filings. It mentions any unusual conditions pertaining to real estate, tax lien and UCC searching in that state. A list of some of the other liens that are filed at the local level is also included.

Recording Office Searching Rules

The general rules for background searching of UCC records are as follows:

- *Except in local filing states, a search at the state level is adequate to locate all UCC records on a subject.*
- *Mortgage record searches will include any real estate related UCC filings.*

See the sections below for discussions of special collateral rules.

Due diligence searching, however, usually demands searching the local records in dual filing states as well, especially for older UCC records.

Special Categories of Collateral

Real Estate Related UCC Collateral

A specific purpose of lien statutes under both the UCC and real estate laws is to put a buyer or potential secured creditor on notice that someone has a prior security interest in real or personal property. UCC financing statements are to personal property what mortgages or deeds of trust are to real property.

One problem addressed by the UCC is that certain types of property have the characteristics of both real and personal property. In those instances, it is necessary to have a way to provide lien notice to two different categories of interested parties: those who deal with the real estate aspect of the property and those who deal with the "personal" aspect of the property.

In general, our definition of real estate related UCC collateral is any property that in one form is attached to land, but that in another form is not attached. For the sake of simplicity, we can define the characteristics of two broad types of property that meet this definition:

Property that is initially attached to real property, but then is separated.
Three specific types of collateral have this characteristic: *minerals* (including oil and gas), *timber*, and *crops*. These things are grown on or extracted from land. While they are on or in the ground they are thought of as real property, but once they are harvested or extracted they become personal property. Some states have a separate central filing system for crops.

*Property that is initially personal property, but then is attached to land, generally called **fixtures**.*
Equipment such as telephone systems or heavy industrial equipment permanently affixed to a building are examples of fixtures. It is important to realize that what is a fixture, like beauty, is in the eye of the beholder, since it is a vague concept at best.

UCC financing statements applicable to real estate related collateral must be filed where the real estate and mortgage records are kept, which is generally at the county level — except in Connecticut, Rhode Island and Vermont where the Town/City Clerk maintains these records. The chart gives the titles of the local official who maintains these records.

Consumer Goods

Among the state-to-state variations, some states required filing where real estate is filed for certain consumer goods. However, as of July 1, 2001 all non-realty related UCC filings in most states, including consumer goods, now go only to the central filing office in the state.

Equipment Used in Farming Operations

33 states required only local filing for equipment used in farming operations. However as of July 1, 2001, all non-realty-related UCC filing has been centralized.

Searching Note

If you are looking for information on subjects that might have these types of filings against them, a search of county records may still be revealing even if you would normally search only at the state level.

The Importance of Revised Article 9

Revised Article 9

On July 1, 2001, Revised Article 9 became law in 46 states and the District of Columbia, with 4 states adopting the law later; Alabama (January 1, 2002), Connecticut (October 1, 2001), Florida (January 1, 2002) and Mississippi (January 1, 2002). Under this new law, most UCC filings will go to the state where a business is organized, not where the collateral or chief executive offices are located. Thus, you will find new filings against IBM only in Delaware (IBM and many other public companies are Delaware corporations), and not in New York or in any other states where it has branch offices. Therefore, you will need to know where a company is organized in order to know where to find new UCC filings against it.

The place to file against individuals is the state where the person resides.

However, the new law does not apply to federal tax liens, which are still generally filed where the chief executive office is located. IBM's chief executive offices, for example, may still be in New York State.

As stated above, realty-related UCC filings continue to go to land recording offices where the property is located.

How to Search for Filings Under Old Article 9

Under old Article 9, Uniform Commercial Code financing statements and changes to them might be filed at two or three government agencies in each state, depending upon the type of collateral involved in the transaction. Each state's UCC statute contained variations on a nationally recommended Model Act. Each variation is explained below. The charts appear at the end of this chapter.

You will still need to know about where UCC filings are located under old Article 9 because the transition period to Revised Article 9 is five years long. UCC filings on record before July 1, 2001 remain effective until they lapse, which is generally five years from initial filing date.

A lot of UCC filings against IBM, for example, made before July 1, 2001 will still be on record in New York's central filing office, and may also be found in county filing offices since New York was a dual filing state, as explained below.

Under old Article 9, 33 states were central filing states. Central filing states are those where most types of personal property collateral require filing of a UCC financing statement only at a central filing location within that state.

Under old Article 9, five states had statewide UCC database systems. Some of these systems are still in effect under Revised Article 9. Minnesota and **Wisconsin** were central filing states with a difference: UCC financing statements filed at the county level are also entered into a statewide database. In **North Dakota** UCC financing statements may be filed at either the state or county level, and all filings are entered into a statewide database. In **Louisiana**, **Nebraska**, and **Georgia**, UCC financing statements may be filed with **any** county (parish). Under Revised Article 9, Minnesota has established a county/state system like North Dakota in all but six county offices, and Nebraska is now a central filing state. In each of these six states the records are entered into a central, statewide database that is available for searching in each county, as well as at the state agency (no state agency in Louisiana or Georgia).

Under old Article 9, eight states required dual filing of certain types of UCC financing statements. The usual definition of a dual filing state is one in which financing statements containing collateral such as inventory, equipment or receivables *must* be filed in *both* a central filing office, usually with the Secretary of State, and in a local (county) office where the collateral or business is located. The three states below were also dual filing states, with a difference. Under Revised Article 9, no dual filing is required within a state

Under old Article 9, the filing systems in three states, MA, NH, and PA, can be described as triple filing because the real estate portion of the filings goes to an office separate from the UCC filing offices. In Massachusetts and New Hampshire, UCC filings were submitted to the town/city while real estate filings go to the county. In Pennsylvania, county government was separated into the *Prothonotary* for UCC filings and the *Recorder* for real estate filings. The local filing offices for non-realty-related UCC filings no longer take filings under Revised Article 9, but they will continue to perform searches of the old records.

Some counties in other states do have separate addresses for real estate recording, but this is usually just a matter of local departmentalization.

Under old Article 9, Kentucky and Wyoming were the only *local filing only* states. In both of these states a few filings were also found at the state level because filings for out of state debtors went to the Secretary of State. And in Wyoming, filings for Wyoming debtor accounts receivable and farm products require dual filing. However, under Revised Article 9, all filings have been centralized.

The Old Article 9 UCC Locator Chart

This handy chart will tell you at a glance where UCC and real estate records are filed under old Article 9 on a state-by-state basis. Under Revised Article 9, effective July 1, 2001 except as noted later for Alabama, Connecticut, Florida and Mississippi, all new personal property filings go to the central filing office.

State	Most Personal Property		All Real Property
	Central Filing Office	Local Filing Office	Filing Office
AK	Department of Natural Resources		District Recorder
AL	Secretary of State		Judge of Probate
AR	Secretary of State	and Circuit Clerk	Circuit Clerk
AZ	Secretary of State		County Recorder
CA	Secretary of State		County Recorder
CO	Secretary of State	or any County Recorder (as of July 1, 1996)	County Clerk & Recorder
CT	Secretary of State		Town/City Clerk
DC	County Recorder		County Recorder
DE	Secretary of State		County Recorder
FL	Secretary of State		Clerk of Circuit Court
GA	None	Clerk Superior Court	Clerk of Superior Court
HI	Bureau of Conveyances		Bureau of Conveyances
IA	Secretary of State		County Recorder
ID	Secretary of State		County Recorder
IL	Secretary of State		County Recorder
IN	Secretary of State		County Recorder
KS	Secretary of State		Register
KY	Secretary of State (Out of state only)	County Clerk	County Clerk
LA	None	Clerk of Court	Clerk of Court
MA	Secretary of the Commonwealth	and Town/City Clerk	Register of Deeds
MD	Department of Assessments & Taxation	and Clerk of Circuit Court (until 7/1/95)	Clerk of Circuit Court
ME	Secretary of State		County Register
MI	Secretary of State		County Register
MN	Secretary of State or Recorder		County Recorder
MO	Secretary of State	and County Recorder	County Recorder
MS	Secretary of State	and Chancery Clerk	Chancery Clerk

| State | Most Personal Property | | All Real Property |
	Central Filing Office	Local Filing Office	Filing Office
MT	Secretary of State		Clerk & Recorder
NC	Secretary of State	and Register of Deeds	Register of Deeds
ND	Secretary of State or County Register		County Register
NE	Secretary of State (Out of state only)	County Clerk	County Register
NH	Secretary of State	and Town/City Clerk	County Register
NJ	Secretary of State		County Clerk/Register
NM	Secretary of State		County Clerk
NV	Secretary of State		County Recorder
NY	Secretary of State	and County Clerk (Register)	County Clerk (Register)
OH	Secretary of State	and County Recorder	County Recorder
OK	Oklahoma County Clerk		County Clerk
OR	Secretary of State		County Clerk
PA	Department of State	and Prothonotary	County Recorder
RI	Secretary of State		County Clerk & Recorder
SC	Secretary of State		County Register/Clerk
SD	Secretary of State		County Register
TN	Secretary of State		County Register
TX	Secretary of State		County Clerk
UT	Division of Corporations & Commercial Code		County Recorder
VA	Corporation Commission	and Clerk of Circuit Court	Clerk of Circuit Court
VT	Secretary of State	and Town/City Clerk (until 7/1/95)	Town/City Clerk
WA	Department of Licensing		County Auditor
WI	Dept. of Financial Institutions		County Register
WV	Secretary of State		County Clerk
WY	Secretary of State (Out of state and A/R only)	County Clerk	County Clerk

Using the County Locator Section

A list at the end of each state section cross references place names to counties. Comprised of every official U.S. Postal Service place name, the city/county cross references contain more that 40,000 entries. This information is summarized from the BRB publication The County Locator.

The cross references contain a special feature that identifies ZIP Codes that cross county lines.

Using ZIP Codes When Searching For Public Records

A place name (capitalized type) may be listed more than once in the city/county cross-references. For example,

> LOS GATOS (95030) Santa Clara (88), Santa Cruz (12)
> LOS GATOS Santa Clara

This duplicate listing indicates that the bulk of LOS GATOS addresses is in Santa Clara county, but those addresses with the ZIP Code 95030 may be in Santa Cruz county. Specifically, ZIP Code 95030 is approximately 88% in Santa Clara and 12% in Santa Cruz.

Note: county names are listed in upper and lower case type, and place names are always capitalized.

10,000 Problems Pointed Out

Multiple county ZIP Codes always appear, as in the above example, before the main entry for a place name. The percentages may not always add up to 100% because of rounding off. Counties that represent less than 1% of the addresses in a ZIP Code have also been eliminated. In all, there are almost 10,000 ZIP Codes shown in this *Sourcebook* that cross county lines.

Using Multiple County Information

The special multiple county entries put you on notice that addresses within a ZIP Code may not be in the county usually associated with that place name. This information can be crucial to finding public records, including court cases that are filed based on the location of property or residence. Remember, if you search in the wrong county, then you may get a false "no hit" response.

Non-Geographic Zip Codes

When trying to locate public records based upon place names and ZIP Codes, be aware that 10,000 ZIP Codes are useless in determining county of residence because they are assigned exclusively to post office boxes or rural routes. Anyone can have a post office box in any county. Never use an address containing one of these non-geographic ZIP Codes to determine where to search.

Maps

This year's edition of The Sourcebook contains 116 pages of useful state maps and tables. County outlines and major cities are shown.

For More Extensive Information

BRB Publications has several products that take a deeper look at counties, place names and ZIP Codes. The Public Record Research System on CD and on the Web each contain an additional 40,000 place names, as well as information about the characteristics of each ZIP Code. For example, these products indicate whether the ZIP Code only contains post office boxes, high rise building, or general delivery.

A resource recently added to the above products is the Adjoining County Lookup. This gives the user the ability to choose a subject county and find all adjoining counties with most recent Census population numbers.

For more information, visit www.publicrecordsources.com or www.brbpub.com

Motor Vehicle Records and The Driver's Privacy Protection Act

The Driver's Privacy Protection Act Title XXXI — Protection of Privacy of Information in State Motor Vehicle Records — was attached as an amendment to the Violent Crime Control Act of 1994 and was signed by President Clinton late in that summer. The intent of the DPPA is to protect the personal privacy of persons licensed to drive by prohibiting certain disclosures of information maintained by the states. This federal mandate declared that the federal government had the right to restrict or prohibit the release of personal information of persons licensed to drive or own motor vehicles. States were given three years to comply.

The profiles of the state motor vehicle departments throughout this book often refer to DPPA and permissible users. Therefore, we are printing a copy of the Act's permissible uses.

Personal Information and the Permissible Uses

The Act prohibits disclosure of personal information from the driver history, vehicle registration, title files held by state DMVs, except for 14 specific "permissible uses." The Act's definition of *Personal Information* is..

"..information that identifies an individual, including an individual's photograph, social security number, driver identification number, name, address (but not the 5-digit zip code), telephone number, and medical or disability information, but does not include information on vehicular accidents, driving violations, and driver's status."

The permissible uses do, in general, permit ongoing, legitimate businesses and individuals to obtain full record data, but with added compliance procedures. The following text, taken directly from the Act, details these 14 Permissible Uses—

§2721. Prohibition on release and use of certain personal information from State motor vehicle records

"(a) IN GENERAL.--Except as provided in subsection (b), a State department of motor vehicles, and any officer, employee, or contractor, thereof, shall not knowingly disclose or otherwise make available to any person or entity personal information about any individual obtained by the department in connection with a motor vehicle record.

"(b) PERMISSIBLE USES.--Personal information referred to in subsection (a) shall be disclosed for use in connection with matters of motor vehicle or driver safety and theft, motor vehicle emissions, motor vehicle product alterations, recalls, or advisories, performance monitoring of motor vehicles and dealers by motor vehicle manufacturers, and removal of non-owners records from the original owner records of motor vehicle manufacturers to carry out the purposes of the Automobile Information Disclosure Act, the Motor Vehicle Information and Cost Saving Act, the National Traffic and Motor Vehicle Safety Act of 1966, the Anti-Car Theft Act of 1992, and the Clean Air Act, and may be disclosed as follows:

"(1) For use by **any government agency**, including any court or law enforcement agency, in carrying out its functions, or any private person or entity acting on behalf of a Federal, State, or local agency in carrying out its functions.

"(2) For use in connection with matters of motor vehicle or **driver safety** and **theft**; motor vehicle emissions; motor vehicle product alterations, recalls, or advisories; performance monitoring of motor vehicles, motor vehicle parts and dealers; motor vehicle **market research** activities, including survey research; and removal of non-owner records from the original owner records of motor vehicle manufacturers.

"(3) For use in the normal course of business by a legitimate business or its agents, employees, or contractors, but only--

"(A) to **verify the accuracy of personal information submitted** by the individual to the business or its agents, employees, or contractors; and

"(B) if such information as so submitted is not correct or is no longer correct, to obtain the correct information, but only for the purposes of preventing fraud by, **pursuing legal remedies** against, or **recovering on a debt** or security interest against, the individual.

"(4) For use in connection with any civil, criminal, administrative, or arbitral proceeding in any Federal, State, or local court or agency or before any self-regulatory body, including the service of process, **investigation in anticipation of litigation**, and the execution or enforcement of judgments and orders, or pursuant to an order of a Federal, State, or local court.

"(5) For use in **research activities**, and for use in producing statistical reports, so long as the personal information is not published, redisclosed, or used to contact individuals.

"(6) For use by **any insurer or insurance support organization**, or by a self-insured entity, or its agents, employees, or contractors, in connection with claims investigation activities, antifraud activities, rating or underwriting.

"(7) For use in providing notice to the owners of towed or impounded vehicles.

"(8) For use by any **licensed private investigative agency** or licensed security service for any purpose permitted under this subsection.

"(9) For use by an employer or its agent or insurer to obtain or verify information relating to a holder of a commercial driver's license that is required under the Commercial Motor Vehicle Safety Act of 1986 (49 U.S.C. App. 2710 et seq.)

"(10) For use in connection with the operation of private toll transportation facilities.

"(11) For any other use in response to requests for individual motor vehicle records if the State has obtained the express consent of the person to whom such personal information pertains.

"(12) For bulk distribution for surveys, marketing or solicitations if if the State has obtained the express consent of the person to whom such personal information pertains.

"(13) For use by any requester, if the requester demonstrates it has obtained the written consent of the individual to whom the information pertains.

"(14) For any other use specifically authorized under the law of the State that holds the record, if such use is related to the operation of a motor vehicle or public safety.

"(c) RESALE OR REDISCLOSURE.--An authorized recipient of personal information (except a recipient under subsection (b)(11) or (12) may resell or redisclose the information only for a use permitted under subsection (b) (but not for uses under subsection (b) (11) or (12). An authorized recipient under subsection (b)(11) may resell or redisclose personal information for any purpose. An authorized recipient under subsection (b)(12) may resell or redisclose personal information pursuant to subsection (b)(12). Any authorized recipient (except a recipient under subsection (b)(11)) that resells or rediscloses personal information covered by this title must keep for a period of 5 years records identifying each person or entity that receives information and the permitted purpose for which the information will be used and must make such records available to the motor vehicle department upon request.

"(d) WAIVER PROCEDURES.--A State motor vehicle department may establish and carry out procedures under which the department or its agents, upon receiving a request for personal information that does not fall within one of the exceptions in subsection (b), may mail a copy of the request to the individual about whom the information was requested, informing such individual of the request, together with a statement to the effect that the information will not be released unless the individual waives such individual's right to privacy under this section.

Using a Public Record Vendor

Hiring Someone to Obtain the Record

There are five main categories of public record professionals: distributors and gateways; search firms; local document retrievers; investigative firms; and information brokers.

Distributors and Gateways (Proprietary Database Vendors)

Distributors are automated public record firms who combine public sources of bulk data and/or online access to develop their own database product(s). Primary Distributors include companies that collect or buy public record information from its original source and reformat the information in some useful way. They tend to focus on one or a limited number of types of information, although a few firms have branched into multiple information categories.

Gateways are companies that either compile data from or provide an automated gateway to Primary Distributors. Gateways thus provide "one-stop shopping" for multiple geographic areas and/or categories of information.

Companies can be *both* Primary Distributors and Gateways. For example, a number of online database companies are both primary distributors of corporate information and also gateways to real estate information from other Primary Distributors

Search Firms

Search firms are companies that furnish public record search and document retrieval services through outside online services and/or through a network of specialists, including their own employees or correspondents (see Retrievers below). There are three types of Search Firms.

Search Generalists offer a full range of search capabilities in many public record categories over a wide geographic region. They may rely on gateways, primary distributors and/or networks of retrievers. They combine online proficiency with document retrieval expertise.

Search Specialists focus either on one geographic region — like Ohio — or on one specific type of public record information — like driver/vehicle records.

Application Specialists focus on one or two types of services geared to specific needs. In this category are pre-employment screening firms and tenant screening firms. Like investigators, they search many of the public record categories in order to prepare an overall report about a person or business. An excellent source to find the nation's leading screening firms is www.napbs.com, the webpage for the newly formed National Association of Professional Background Screeners.

Local Document Retrievers

Local document retrievers use their own personnel to search specific requested categories of public records usually in order to obtain documentation for legal compliance (e.g., incorporations), for lending, and for litigation. They do not usually review or interpret the results or issue reports in the sense that investigators do, but rather return documents with the results of searches. They tend to be localized, but there are companies that offer a national network of retrievers and/or correspondents.

The retriever or his/her personnel goes directly to the agency to look up the information. A retriever may be relied upon for strong knowledge in a local area, whereas a search generalist has a breadth of knowledge and experience in a wider geographic range.

The 750+ members of the **Public Record Retriever Network (PRRN)** can be found, by state and counties served, at www.brbpub.com/PRRN. This organization has set industry standards for the retrieval of public record documents and operates under a Code of Professional Conduct. Using one of these record retrievers is an excellent way to access records in those jurisdictions that do not offer online access.

Private Investigation Firms

Investigators use public records as tools rather than as ends in themselves, in order to create an overall, comprehensive "picture" of an individual or company for a particular purpose. They interpret the information they have gathered in order to identify further investigation tracks. They summarize their results in a report compiled from all the sources used.

Many investigators also act as Search Firms, especially as tenant or pre-employment screeners, but this is a different role from the role of Investigator per se, and screening firms act very much like investigators in their approach to a project. In addition, an investigator may be licensed and may perform the types of services traditionally thought of as detective work, such as surveillance.

Information Brokers

There is one additional type of firm that occasionally utilizes public records. **Information Brokers** (IB) gather information that will help their clients make informed business decisions. Their work is usually done on a custom basis with each project being unique. IBs are extremely knowledgeable in online research of full text databases and most specialize in a particular subject area, such as patent searching or competitive intelligence. The Association of Independent Information Professionals (AIIP), at www.aiip.org, has over 700 experienced professional information specialist members from 21 countries.

Which Type of Vendor is Right for You?

With all the variations of vendors and the categories of information, the obvious question is; "How do I find the right vendor to go to for the public record information I need?" Before you start calling every interesting online vendor that catches your eye, you need to narrow your search to the **type** of vendor for your needs. To do this, ask yourself the following questions—

What is the Frequency of Usage?

If you have on-going, recurring requests for a particular type of information, it is probably best to choose a different vendor then if you have infrequent requests. Setting up an account with a primary distributor, such as LEXIS or Westlaw will give you an inexpensive per search fee, but the monthly minimum requirements will be prohibitive to the casual requester, who would be better off finding a vendor who accesses or is a gateway to one of these vendors..

What is the Complexity of the Search?

The importance of hiring a vendor who understands and can interpret the information in the final format increases with the complexity of the search. Pulling a corporation record in Maryland is not difficult, but doing an online criminal record search in Maryland, when only a portion of the felony records are online, is not so easy.

Thus, part of the answer to determining which vendor or type of vendor to use is to become conversant with what is (and is not) available from government agencies. Without knowing what is available (and what restrictions apply), you cannot guide the search process effectively. Once you are comfortable knowing the kinds of information available in the public record, you are in a position to find the best method to access needed information.

What are the Geographic Boundaries of the Search?

A search of local records close to you may require little assistance, but a search of records nationally or in a state 2,000 miles away will require seeking a vendor who covers the area you need to search. Many national primary distributors and gateways combine various local and state databases into one large comprehensive system available for searching. However, if your record searching is narrowed by a region or locality, then an online source that specializes in a specific geographic region (like Superior Information Services in NJ) may be an alternative to a national vendor. Keep in mind that many national firms allow you to order a search online, even though results cannot be delivered immediately and some hands-on local searching is required.

Of course, you may want to use the government agency online system, if available, for the kind of information you need.

10 Questions to Ask a Public Records Vendor

(Or a Vendor Who Uses Online Sources)

The following discussion focuses specifically on automated sources of information because many valuable types of public records have been entered into a computer and, therefore, require a computer search to obtain reliable results. The original version of the text to follow was written by **Mr. Leroy Cook.** Mr. Cook is the founder and Director of ION and The Investigators Anywhere Resource Line (800-338-3463, http://ioninc.com). Mr. Cook has graciously allowed us to edit the article and reprint it for our readers.

1. Where does he or she get the information?

You may feel awkward asking a vendor where he or she obtained the information you are purchasing. The fake Rolex watch is a reminder that even buying physical things based on looks alone — without knowing where they come from — is dangerous.

Reliable information vendors *will* provide verification material such as the name of the database or service accessed, when it was last updated, and how complete it is.

It is important that you know the gathering process in order to better judge the reliability of the information being purchased. There *are* certain investigative sources that a vendor will not be willing to disclose to you. However, that type of source should not be confused with the information that is being sold item by item. Information technology has changed so rapidly that some information vendors may still confuse "items of information" with "investigative reports." Items of information sold as units are *not* investigative reports. The professional reputation of an information vendor is a guarantee of sorts. Still, because information as a commodity is so new, there is little in the way of an implied warranty of fitness.

2. How long does it take for the new information or changes to get into the system?

Any answer *except* a clear, concise date and time or the vendor's personal knowledge of an ongoing system's methods of maintaining information currency is a reason to keep probing. In view of the preceding question, this one might seem repetitive, but it *really* is a different issue. Microfiche or a database of records may have been updated last week at a courthouse or a DMV, but the department's computer section may also be working with a three-month backlog. In this case, a critical incident occurring one month ago would *not* show up in the information updated last week. The importance of timeliness is a variable to be determined by you, but to be truly informed you need to know how "fresh" the information is. Ideally, the mechanism by which you purchase items of information *should* include an update or statement of accuracy — as a part of the reply — *without* having to ask.

3. What are the searchable fields? Which fields are mandatory?

If your knowledge of "fields" and "records" is limited to the places where cattle graze and those flat, round things that play music, you *could* have a problem telling a good database from a bad one. An MVR vendor, for example, should be able to tell you that a subject's middle initial is critical when pulling an Arizona driving record. You don't have to become a programmer to use a computer and you needn't know a database management language to benefit from databases, *but* it is very helpful to understand how databases are constructed and (*at the least*) what fields, records, and indexing procedures are used.

As a general rule, the computerized, public-record information world is not standardized from county to county or from state to state; in the same way, there is little standardization within or between information vendors. Look at the system documentation from the vendor. The manual should include this sort of information.

4. How much latitude is there for error (misspellings or inappropriate punctuation) in a data request?

If the vendor's requirements for search data appear to be concise and meticulous, then you're probably on the right track. Some computer systems will tell (or "flag") an operator when they make a mistake such as omitting important punctuation or using an unnecessary comma. Other systems allow you to make inquiries by whatever means or in whatever format you like — and then tell you the requested information has *not* been found. In this instance, the desired information may *actually* be there, but the computer didn't understand the question because of the way in which it was asked. It is easy to misinterpret "no record found" as "there is no record." Please take note that the meanings of these two phrases are quite different.

5. What method is used to place the information in the repository and what error control or edit process is used?

In some databases, information may be scanned in or may be entered by a single operator as it is received and, in others, information may be entered *twice* to allow the computer to catch input errors by searching for non-duplicate entries. You don't have to know *everything* about all the options, but the vendor selling information in quantity *should*.

6. How many different databases or sources does the vendor access *and* how often?

The chance of obtaining an accurate search of a database increases with the frequency of access and the vendor's/searcher's level of knowledge. If he or she only makes inquiries once a month — and the results are important — you may need to find someone who sells data at higher volume. The point here is that it is better to find someone who specializes in the type of information you are seeking than it is to utilize a vendor who *can* get the information, but actually specializes in another type of data.

7. Does the price include assistance in interpreting the data received?

A report that includes coding and ambiguous abbreviations may look impressive in your file, but may not be too meaningful. For all reports, except those you deal with regularly, interpretation assistance can be *very* important. Some information vendors offer searches for information they really don't know much about through sources that they only use occasionally. Professional pride sometimes prohibits them from disclosing their limitations — until *you* ask the right questions.

8. Do vendors "keep track" of requesters and the information they seek (usage records)?

This may not seem like a serious concern when you are requesting information you're legally entitled to; however, there *is* a possibility that your usage records could be made available to a competitor. Most probably, the information itself is *already* being (or will be) sold to someone else, but you may not necessarily want *everyone* to know what you are requesting and how often. If the vendor keeps records of who-asks-what, the confidentiality of that information should be addressed in your agreement with the vendor.

9. Will the subject of the inquiry be notified of the request?

If your inquiry is sub rosa or if the subject's discovery of the search could lead to embarrassment, double check! There are laws that mandate the notification of subjects when certain types of inquires are made into their files. If notification is required, the way it is accomplished could be critical.

10. Is the turnaround time and cost of the search made clear at the outset?

You should be crystal clear about what you expect and/or need; the vendor should be succinct when conveying exactly what will be provided and how much it will cost. Failure to address these issues can lead to disputes and hard feelings.

These are excellent questions and concepts to keep in mind when searching for the right public record vendor to meet your needs.

Section II

Public Records Arranged by State

Includes Appendix with Profiles of Certain Agencies in
the U.S. Territories and Canada

Alabama

General Help Numbers:

Governor's Office
600 Dexter Ave, #N-104
Montgomery, AL 36130
www.governor.state.al.us

334-242-7100
Fax 334-353-0004
8AM-5PM

Attorney General's Office
State House
11 S. Union Street, 3rd Fl
Montgomery, AL 36130
www.ago.state.al.us

334-242-7300
Fax 334-242-4891
8AM-5PM

Legislative Records
State House
11 S Union St
Montgomery, AL 36130-4600
www.legislature.state.al.us

334-242-7826 (Senate)
334-242-7637 (House)
Fax 334-242-0937
8:30AM-4:30PM

State Archives
Archives & History Department
Reference Room, PO Box 300100
Montgomery, AL 36130-0100
www.archives.state.al.us

334-242-4435
Fax 334-240-3433
8AM-5PM T-F,
9AM-5PM SA

State Specifics:

Capital:	Montgomery Montgomery County
Time Zone:	CST
Number of Counties:	67
Population:	4,500,752
Website:	www.alabama.gov

State Agencies

Criminal Records

Alabama Bureau of Investigation, Identification Unit - Record Checks, PO Box 1511, Montgomery, AL 36102-1511 (Courier: 301 S Ripley St, Montgomery, AL 36104); 334-353-4340, 8AM-5PM.

www.dps.state.al.us/public/abi/

Indexing & Storage: Records are available from 1942 on. It takes about 7 days before new records are available for inquiry.

Searching: The request must be on state form ABI-46. The form can be obtained from the webpage or call to have copy sent. Include the following in your request-notarized release from subject, date of birth, Social Security Number, full name, race, sex. Fingerprints optional. 100% of the record files have fingerprints. The following data is not released: juvenile records.

Access by: mail, in person.

Fee & Payment: The fee is $25.00 per name. For those entities entitled by statute to an FBI

fingerprint check, the fee is $49.00 per name. The FBI check is not available to the public or employers not entitled per statute. Fee payee: Alabama Bureau of Investigation. Cashier checks and money orders accepted. No personal checks accepted. No credit cards accepted.

Mail search: Turnaround time: 7 days. No SASE is required.

In person search: You may bring in the required release and request form.

Statewide Court Records

Director of Courts, 300 Dexter Ave, Montgomery, AL 36104-3741; 334-242-0300, 334-242-2099 (Fax), 8AM-5PM.

www.alacourt.gov/

Note: Except for certain online research capabilities, all court record access must be done at the local level.

Access by: online.

Online search: In the past, commercial remote access to the State Judicial Information System (SJIS) was offered, but this is no longer available. This agency reccommends searchers to contact a commercial vendor at www.alacourt.com. State Supreme Court and Appellette decisions are available at www.alalinc.net and at website above.

Sexual Offender Registry

Department of Public Safety, Sexual Offender Registry, PO Box 1511, Montgomery, AL 36102-1511 (Courier: 301 S Ripley, Montgomery, AL 36109); 334-353-1172, 334-353-2563 (Fax), 8AM-5PM.

www.dps.state.al.us

Note: Sections 15-20-21 to 37, Code of Alabama 1975, makes it a class C felony for any criminal sex offender to violate most provisions of the Alabama Community Notification Act.

Indexing & Storage: Records are available from 08/01/98. It takes about 7 days before new records are available for inquiry. Records are normally destroyed after the death of the offender.

Searching: Include the following in your request-name, DOB, and SSN. The following data is not released: information on the victim.

Access by: mail, phone, fax, in person, online.

Fee & Payment: None

Mail search: Turnaround time: 7 days. A SASE is required.

Phone search: Limited searching available.

Fax search: Requests may be faxed.

In person search: Time permitting.

Online search: Sex offender data and a felony fugitives list are available online at www.dps.state.al.us/public/abi/system. Search by name, ZIP Code or geographic area.

Incarceration Records

Alabama Department of Corrections, Central Records Office, PO Box 301501, Montgomery, AL 36130 334-240-9500, 8AM-5PM.

http://doc.state.al.us

Indexing & Storage: Records are available on current and former inmates by mail; current inmates only online. No information is available on youthful offenders. It takes about 7 days before new records are available for inquiry. Records are kept indefinitely.

Searching: Include the following in your request-full name; AIS number helpful, as is DOB and SSN.

Access by: mail, online. Questions regarding specifc inmates can be sent to pio@doc.state.al.us.

Fee & Payment: There is no fee.

Mail search: Turnaround time: 2-3 days. No SASE is required.

Online search: Only information on current inmates is available online at this time. Location, AIS number, physical identifiers, projected release date are released.

Corporation, Limited Partnership, Limited Liability Company, Limited Liability Partnerships, Trade Names, Trademarks, Servicemarks

Secretary of State, Corporations Division, PO Box 5616, Montgomery, AL 36103-5616 (Courier: 11 S Union St, Ste 207, Montgomery, AL 36104); 334-242-5324, 334-242-5325 (Trademarks), 334-240-3138 (Fax), 8AM-5PM.

www.sos.state.al.us

Note: The office for Trademarks, Trade Names, and Servicemarks is located in Room 200.

Indexing & Storage: Records are available for corporations, active or inactive. All information here on file is considered public information. It takes 1 month before new records are available for inquiry. Records are indexed on images and on inhouse computer.

Searching: Include the following in your request-full name of business. In addition to the articles of incorporation, corporation records include the following information: Officers, Prior (Merged) names, Inactive and Reserved names.

Access by: mail, phone, fax, in person, online.

Fee & Payment: There is no search fee, but copies are $1.00 per page. Fee payee: Secretary of State. Prepayment required. The agency will invoice members of the AL state bar. Personal checks & credit cards accepted.

Mail search: Turnaround time: 1 week. A SASE is requested.

Phone search: available.

Fax search: Search requests accepted by fax.

In person search: Call first for page amount before going to their office.

Online search: The website has free searches of corporate and UCC records. Search individual files for Active Names at http://arc-sos.state.al.us/CGI/SOSCRP01.MBR/INPUT.

Expedited service: Expedited service is available for mail and phone searches, call for fees. Turnaround time: 24 to 48 hours. Expedited service ends at Noon each day.

Uniform Commercial Code, Federal & State Tax Liens

UCC Division - SOS, UCC Records, PO Box 5616, Montgomery, AL 36103-5616 (Courier: 11 South Union St, Suite 200, Montgomery, AL 36104); 334-242-5231, 334-353-8269 (Fax), 8AM-5PM.

www.sos.state.al.us/

Indexing & Storage: It takes 72 hours before new records are available for inquiry. Records are indexed on inhouse computer. Records are normally destroyed after 1 year after lapse date.

Searching: Use search request form UCC-11. The search includes tax liens. Federal and state tax liens on individuals may also be filed at the county

level. All tax liens on businesses are filed here. Include the following in your request-debtor name or file number.

Access by: mail, in person, online.

Fee & Payment: In addition to the $20.00 search fee per debter name, the copy fee is $1.00 per page and certification is $5.00 per filing. Fee payee: Secretary of State. Prepayment required. Prepaid accounts available, minimum $500 deposit. Personal checks accepted. Credit cards accepted, convenience fee added.

Mail search: Turnaround time: 72 hours.

In person search: Turnaround time is 72 hours unless an expedited fee of $100 is paid for immediate service. However, if workload is light, they may do the search that day without the expedited fee.

Online search: The agency has UCC information available to search at the web address, there is no fee. Corporation data is also available. You can search by debtor's name or file number. Collateral information and /or image is not available to view online.

Other access: Bulk sale by CD for $1,500 plus $300 a week for updates.

Expedited service: This service is available for an additional $100.00, usually same day service.

Sales Tax Registrations
Access to Records is Restricted

Alabama Department of Revenue, Sales, Use and Business Tax Division, 4303 Gordon Persons Bldg, 50 N Ripley St, Montgomery, AL 36104; 334-353-7867, 334-242-8916 (Fax), 8AM-5PM.

www.ador.state.al.us

Note: According to state law 40-2A-10, Code of Alabama 1975, this agency is unable to release any information about tax registrations. Note, their website has motor vehicle dealer regulatory license information.

Birth Certificates

Center for Health Statistics, Record Services Division, PO Box 5625, Montgomery, AL 36103-5625 (Courier: RSA Tower Suite 1150, 201 Monroe St, Montgomery, AL 36104); 334-206-5418, 334-262-9563 (Fax), 8AM-5PM.

http://ph.state.al.us/chs/VitalRecords/VRECORDS.HTMl

Note: Certificates can, also, be delivered in any County Health Department for any vital record event occurring in AL. Delivery time is usually 15-30 minutes.

Indexing & Storage: Records are available from 1908 to present. New records are available for inquiry immediately. Records are indexed on microfiche, inhouse computer.

Searching: Birth certificates under 125 years old may be requested by an immediate family member or person with legal right to certificate. Include the following in your request-full name, names of father, full maiden name of mother, date of birth, county, reason for information request. Include a daytime phone number and a signature.

Access by: mail, phone, fax, in person, online.

Fee & Payment: Fee is $12.00, add $4.00 per name for each additional copy. Fee payee: State Board of Health Prepayment required. Credit cards accepted for phone, fax and expedited requests only. Personal checks accepted. Credit cards accepted: MasterCard, Visa, AmEx, Discover.

Mail search: Turnaround time: 5 to 10 days. No SASE is required.

Phone search: Telephone requests allowed using a credit card, see expedited service.

Fax search: Same criteria as phone searching.

In person search: Also, go to the nearest County Health Department.

Online search: Online ordering is available from a designated vendor - www.vitalchek.com.

Expedited service: Expedited service is available for phone, fax and online orders. Turnaround time: 1 day. Additional expedite fee is $10.00, use of credit card is $5.50, add overnight shipping fee if needed.

Death Records

Center for Health Statistics, Record Services Division, PO Box 5625, Montgomery, AL 36103-5625 (Courier: RSA Tower Suite 1150, 201 Monroe St, Montgomery, AL 36104); 334-206-5418, 334-262-9563 (Fax), 8AM-5PM.

http://ph.state.al.us/chs/VitalRecords/VRECORDS.HTMl

Note: Certificates can, also, be delivered in any County Health Department for any vital record event occurring in AL. Delivery time is usually 15-30 minutes.

Indexing & Storage: Records are available from 1908 on. New records are available for inquiry immediately. Records are indexed on microfiche, inhouse computer.

Searching: Must be immediate family for ordering death records less than 25 years old. Include the following in your request-full name, date of death, names of parents with mother's maiden name, county or city, reason for information request, and signature and daytime phone of requester.

Access by: mail, phone, fax, in person, online.

Fee & Payment: Fee is $12.00, add $4.00 per copy for each additional copy. Fee payee: State Board of Health Prepayment required. Personal checks accepted. Credit cards accepted: MasterCard, Visa, AmEx, Discover.

Mail search: Turnaround time: 5 to 10 days. No SASE is required.

Phone search: Telephone requests allowed using a credit card, see expedited service.

Fax search: Same criteria as phone searching.

In person search: Also, you can go to the nearest County Health Department.

Online search: Online ordering is available from a designated vendor - www.vitalchek.com.

Other access: Index to records are available on microfilm for $40.00 per roll. There are 6 rolls of records for 1908 through 1959.

Expedited service: Expedited service is available for phone, fax and online orders. Additional expedite fee is $10.00, use of credit card is $5.50, add overnight shipping fee if needed.

Marriage Certificates

Center for Health Statistics, Record Services Division, PO Box 5625, Montgomery, AL 36103-5625 (Courier: RSA Tower Suite 1150, 201 Monroe St, Montgomery, AL 36104); 334-206-5418, 334-262-9563 (Fax), 8AM-5PM.

http://ph.state.al.us/chs/VitalRecords/VRECORDS.HTMl

Note: Certificates can, also, be delivered in any County Health Department for any vital record event occurring in AL. Delivery time is usually 15-30 minutes.

Indexing & Storage: Records are available from 1936 to present. New records are available for inquiry immediately. Records are indexed on microfiche, inhouse computer.

Searching: Include the following in your request-names of husband and wife, date of marriage, county of license issue. Include a daytime phone number and signature of requester.

Access by: mail, phone, fax, in person, online.

Fee & Payment: Fee is $12.00, add $4.00 per copy for additional copies. Fee payee: State Board of Health Prepayment required. Personal checks accepted. Credit cards accepted: MasterCard, Visa, AmEx, Discover.

Mail search: Turnaround time: 5 to 10 days. No SASE is required.

Phone search: Telephone requests allowed using a credit card, see expedited service.

Fax search: Same criteria as phone searches.

In person search: Also, you can go to the nearest County Health Department.

Online search: Online ordering is available from a designated vendor - www.vitalchek.com.

Other access: Microfilm rolls are available for purchase at $40.00 each. There are 11 rolls available which includes index to records for 1936 to 1969.

Expedited service: Expedited service is available for phone, fax and online orders. Turnaround time: 1 to 2 days. Additional expedite fee is $10.00, use of credit card is $5.50, add overnight shipping fee if needed.

Divorce Records

Center for Health Statistics, Record Services Division, PO Box 5625, Montgomery, AL 36103-5625 (Courier: RSA Tower Suite 1150, 201 Monroe St, Montgomery, AL 36104); 334-206-5418, 334-206-2659 (Fax), 8AM-5PM.

http://ph.state.al.us/chs/VitalRecords/VRECORDS.HTMl

Note: Certificates can, also, be delivered in any County Health Department for any vital record event occurring in AL. Delivery time is usually 15-30 minutes.

Indexing & Storage: Records are available from 1950 to present. New records are available for inquiry immediately. Records are indexed on inhouse computer, microfiche.

Searching: Include the following in your request-names of husband and wife, date of divorce, county. Include a daytime phone number, all requests must have signature of the requester.

Access by: mail, phone, fax, in person, online.

Fee & Payment: Fee is $12.00, add $4.00 per copy for additional copies. Fee payee: State Board of Health Prepayment required. Personal checks accepted. Credit cards accepted: MasterCard, Visa, AmEx, Discover.

Mail search: Turnaround time: 5 to 10 days. No SASE is required.

Phone search: Telephone requests allowed using a credit card, see expedited service.

Fax search: Same criteria as phone searches.

In person search: Also, you can go to the nearest County Health Department.

Online search: Online ordering is available from a designated vendor - www.vitalchek.com.

Other access: There is one microfilm roll of index for records for 1950-59 available for $40.00.

Expedited service: Expedited service is available for phone, fax and online orders. Turnaround time: 1 to 2 days. Additional expedite fee is $10.00, use of credit card is $5.50, add overnight shipping fee if needed.

Workers' Compensation Records

Department of Industrial Relations, Disclosure Unit-Central Cashier, 649 Monroe Street, Rm. 2684, Montgomery, AL 36131; 334-242-8981, 334-242-2304 (Fax), 7AM-5PM.

http://dir.alabama.gov/wc/

Indexing & Storage: Records are available on computer in index form. Retention period is based on type of record. Actual file copies are placed on microfilm after 6 months. Older records (pre 1986) are on microfiche and must be searched by SSN. It takes 3 days before new records are available for inquiry. Records are normally destroyed after 12 years.

Searching: Must have a written, notarized release from claimant. Include the following in your request-claimant name, Social Security Number.

Access by: mail, fax, in person.

Fee & Payment: The fee is $8.00 per record. Fee payee: Department of Industrial Relations, Workers Compensation. Prepayment required. Personal checks accepted. No credit cards accepted.

Mail search: Turnaround time: 1 week. No SASE is required.

Fax search: Records can be returned (not ordered) by fax for an additional $1.00 per page.

In person search: A notarized release form is required.

Driver Records

Department of Public Safety, Driver Records-License Division, PO Box 1471, Montgomery, AL 36102-1471 (Courier: 301 S Ripley Street, Montgomery, AL 36104); 334-242-4400, 334-242-4639 (Fax), 8AM-5PM.

www.dps.state.al.us/

Note: Ticket information must be secured at the local level.

Indexing & Storage: Records are available for convictions in last three years for moving violations, and accidents. New records are available for inquiry immediately.

Searching: Some juvenile records are considered confidential and are not released. The driver's address and personal information is not included, even if the requester is a DPPA permissible user, for mail or in person requesters. The address is released online. Need full name, DOB and license number to obtain a record. Use Form MV-DPPA1 if you are a permissible user.

Access by: mail, in person, online.

Fee & Payment: The fee is $5.75 per record, online is higher. Fee payee: Alabama DPS, Drivers

License Division. Prepayment required. Personal checks not accepted. Credit cards accepted.

Mail search: Turnaround time: 3 to 5 days. Providing a self-addressed return envelope usually means quicker service.

In person search: Locations offering driving records and crash reports include Birmingham, Dothan, Foley, Huntsville, Jacksonville, Mobile, Montgomery, Opelika, Sheffield, and Tuscalossa.

Online search: Alabama Interactive has been designated the state's agent for online access of state driving records. A Subscriber Registration Agreement must be submitted and both Alabama Interactive and the Alabama DPS must approve all customers. There is a $75.00 annual administrative fee for new accounts and the search fee is $7.00 per record. The driver license number is needed to search. The system, open 24 hours daily, is Internet-based. Alabama Interactive can be reached at 2 N. Jackson St, #301, Montgomery AL, 36104, (866) 353-3468, www.alabamainteractive.org.

Vehicle Ownership, Vehicle Identification

Motor Vehicle Division, Records & Registration Unit, PO Box 327630, Montgomery, AL 36132-7630 (Courier: 50 North Ripley St, #1229, 1202 Gordon Persons Bldg, Montgomery, AL 36140); 334-242-9056 (Registration), 334-242-9102 (Title Inquiry), 334-353-8038 (Fax), 8AM-5PM.

www.ador.state.al.us/motorvehicle/index.html

Indexing & Storage: Records are available 24 years for title records and 10 years for registration records. It takes 4-6 weeks before new records are available for inquiry. Records are normally destroyed after 24 years.

Searching: The restrictions specified under the DPPA (Driver's Privacy Protection Act) apply. Access is restricted to permissible users who must use Form MV-DPPA1. Non-permissible users must have notarized release of subject. The address of the title or registration holder must be included as part of the request. The following data is not released: bulk information or lists for commercial purposes.

Access by: mail.

Fee & Payment: Fees are $3.00 per record per year for registration records and $15.00 per year for title searches (includes lien data). Fee payee: Alabama Department of Revenue. Prepayment required. Only certified funds are accepted. No credit cards accepted.

Mail search: Turnaround time: 1 to 2 weeks. No SASE is required.

Accident Reports

Alabama Department of Public Safety, Accident Records, PO Box 1471, Montgomery, AL 36102-1471 (Courier: 502 Washington Ave,

Montgomery, AL 36104); 334-242-4241, 8AM-5PM.

Indexing & Storage: Records are available for a minimum of 10 years. After 2 years, they put reports on microfiche. It takes 2 weeks before new records are available for inquiry.

Searching: Include the following in your request-date of accident, location of accident, county. Also, submit names of drivers.

Access by: mail, in person.

Fee & Payment: The fee is $15.00 and prepayment is required. Fee payee: Alabama DPS, Accident Reports. Only certified funds or cash is accepted. No credit cards accepted.

Mail search: Turnaround time: within 2 weeks. A SASE is requested.

In person search: Locations offering driving records and crash reports include Birmingham, Dothan, Foley, Huntsville, Jacksonville, Mobile, Montgomery, Opelika, Sheffield, and Tuscalossa. Turnaround time is while you wait.

Vessel Ownership, Vessel Registration

Dept of Conservation & Natural Resources, Marine Police Div. Boat Reg. Records, PO Box 301451, Montgomery, AL 36130 (Courier: 64 N Union St, Montgomery, AL 36104); 334-242-3673, 334-242-0336 (Fax), 8AM-5PM.

www.dcnr.state.al.us

Note: Records are not freely open to the public. Must give reason why record is requested.

Indexing & Storage: Records are available from 1985 to the present. Records are indexed on computer. All mechanically propelled, sail or rental boats must be registered. It takes 2 months before new records are available for inquiry. Records are normally destroyed after 7 years.

Searching: Vessels that have been commercially documented by the Coast Guard are not required to register with Alabama. Liens are not recorded here, but at the central state locations for UCC filings. Include the following in your request-one of the following is required; owner's name, hull id #, current decal #, or registration #. For purged records, the registration # is required to search.

Access by: mail, phone, fax, in person.

Fee & Payment: There is no search fee, except for bulk searches (see below) or lengthy lists ($1.00 per record). Fee payee: Department of Conservation. Prepayment required. No credit cards accepted.

Mail search: Turnaround time: 1 to 2 days. No SASE is required.

Phone search: Records are available by phone.

Fax search: Turnaround time is within 1 day.

In person search: Immediate records available, if list not lengthy. Request must be in writing.

Other access: This agency accepts e-mail requests for records at rthornell@dcnr.state.al.us. This agency will sell all or parts of its database. Fees start at $100.00 for the first 2,500 records.

Voter Registration

Access to Records is Unavailable from the Agency

Secretary of State-Elections Division, PO Box 5616, State Capitol E-210, Montgomery, AL 36103; 334-242-4337, 334-242-2940 (Fax), 8AM-5PM.

www.sos.state.al.us/election/index.cfm

Note: Individual name requests must be done at the county level, there are no restrictions.

GED Certificates

State Dept of Education, GED Testing Office, 401 Adams Ave #280, Montgomery, AL 36104; 334-353-4886, 334-353-4884 (Fax), 8AM-5PM.

www.acs.cc.al.us/ged/ged.aspx

Note: Release of your GED information is prohibited without written authorization

Searching: Requests should be writing. Include the following in your request-a signed release, name, year of test, date of birth, Social Security Number, and city of testing. All required for a verification or for copy of transcript.

Access by: mail, fax, in person.

Fee & Payment: There is no verification or search fee, but there is a $5.00 fee for either a copy of grades, transcript or diploma. Fee payee: GED Testing. Only cashier's checks and money orders are accepted. No credit cards accepted.

Mail search: Turnaround time: 1-2 days. No SASE is required.

Fax search: Turnaround time is same day. Results will be called or faxed.

In person search: Turnaround time is a few minutes.

Hunting and Fishing License Information

Access to Records is Unavailable from the Agency

Conservation & Natural Resources Department, Department of License Section, 64 N Union Street, Room 457, Montgomery, AL 36130-1456; 334-353-5239, 334-242-0771 (Fax), 8AM-5PM.

Note: They do not have a central computerized database. Records must be hand searched and are grouped by issuing agent. This makes searching very time consuming and thus it is discouraged. However, the agency will sell a list of lifetime license purchasers.

Alabama State Licensing Agencies
Licenses Searchable Online

Abortion/Reproductive Health Center #31 .... www.adph.org/providers/
Ambulatory Surgery Center #31 .... www.adph.org/providers/
Anesthesiologist Assistant #19 .... www.docboard.org/al/
Architect #8 .... www.boa.state.al.us/rostersearch/rostersearch.asp
Assisted Living Facility/Unit #31 .... www.adph.org/providers/
Auctioneer #9 .... www.auctioneer.state.al.us/roster/roster-search-form.asp
Birthing Center #31 .... www.adph.org/providers/
Cerebral Palsy Center #31 .... www.adph.org/providers/
Check Casher #5 .... www.bank.state.al.us/search_all_licensee.asp
Chiropractor #10 ... ...   www.alabamainteractive.org/asbce/VerificationEntryPoint.do;jsessionid=ap_JoQrUmjsg
Consumer Finance Company #5 .... www.bank.state.al.us/search_all_licenses.asp
Contractor, General #7 .... www.genconbd.state.al.us/DATABASE-LIVE/roster.asp
Electrical Contractor #14 .... www.aecb.state.al.us/Search/new_search.asp
Electrician, Journeyman #14 .... www.aecb.state.al.us/Search/new_search.asp
Engineer/Engineer in Training #27 .... www.bels.alabama.gov
Forester #26 .... www.alsbrf.org
Gas Fitter #46 .... http://pgfb.state.al.us/lookup.asp
Geologist #37 .... www.algeobd.state.al.us/geology%20roster.doc
Heating/Air Conditioning Contractor #38 .... www.hvacboard.state.al.us/Lic_Search/searchform.asp
Home Builder #53 .... www.hblb.state.al.us/Lic_Search/all-ind.asp
Home Health Agency #31 .... www.adph.org/providers/
Home Inspector #42 .... www.sos.state.al.us/sosinfo/inquiry.cfm
Hospice #31 .... www.adph.org/providers/
Hospital #31 .... www.adph.org/providers/
Insurance Adjuster #39 .... www.aldoi.org/LicenseeSearch/
Insurance Agent #39 .... www.aldoi.org/LicenseeSearch/
Insurance Broker/Producer #39 .... www.aldoi.org/LicenseeSearch/
Insurance Corp/Company/Partnership #39 .... www.aldoi.org/CompanySearch/
Landscape Architect #18 .... www.abela.state.al.us/architects.html
Lender/Loan Source #5 .... www.bank.state.al.us/search_all_licenses.asp
Marriage/Family Therapist #9 .... www.mft.state.al.us/Search/search.asp
Medical Doctor #19 .... www.docboard.org/al/
Medical Gas Piper #46 .... http://pgfb.state.al.us/lookup.asp
Mental Health Center #31 .... www.adph.org/providers/
Mortgage Broker #5 .... www.bank.state.al.us/search_all_licenses.asp
Notary Public #42 .... www.sos.state.al.us/sosinfo/inquiry.cfm?area=notaries%20public
Nursing Home #31 .... www.adph.org/providers/
Nursing Home Administrator #22 .... www.alboenha.state.al.us/logon.html
Optometrist #20 .... www.al-optometry.org
Osteopathic Physician #19 .... www.docboard.org/al/
Pawn Shop #5 .... www.bank.state.al.us/search_all_licenses.asp
Petroleum Product Seller #30 .... www.agi.state.al.us/Bonded.asp
Physical Therapist/Therapist Asst #24 .... www.pt.state.al.us/License/searchform.asp
Physician Assistant #19 .... www.docboard.org/al/
Physiological Lab, Independent Clinical #31 .... www.adph.org/providers/
Plumber #46 .... http://pgfb.state.al.us/lookup.asp
Podiatrist #4 .... www.alabamapodiatryboard.org/pages/licensee.html
Preneed Sales Agent #39 .... www.aldoi.org/LicenseeSearch/
Public Accountant-CPA-Non Licensee #25 .... www.asbpa.state.al.us/register/register.asp
Real Estate Agent/Sales #2 .... www.arec.state.al.us/search.asp
Real Estate Appraiser #43 .... http://reab.state.al.us/appraisers/searchform.asp
Real Estate Broker #2 .... www.arec.state.al.us/search.asp
Rehabilitation Center #31 .... www.adph.org/providers/
Reinsurance Intermediary #39 .... www.aldoi.org/LicenseeSearch/
Renal Disease (End Stage) Treatm't Ctr. #31 ..... www.adph.org/providers/
Rural Primary Care Hospital #31 .... www.adph.org/providers/

School Superintendent #49.................................www.alsde.edu/html/super_listing.asp?menu=none&footer=general
Sleep Disorder Center #31 .... www.adph.org/providers/
Social Worker #58.....................................www.abswe.state.al.us/Lic_Search/search.asp
Social Worker, Independent Practice #58 ....www.abswe.state.al.us/Lic_Search/searchpip.asp
Sports Agent #42 ....www.sos.state.al.us/cf/sportsagents/sasrch1.cfm
Surplus Line Broker #39 ....www.aldoi.org/LicenseeSearch/
Surveyor, Land #27.......................................www.bels.alabama.gov
Therapist, Marriage and Family #9 ....www.mft.state.al.us/Search/search.asp
U-Pick Location #30 ....www.agi.state.al.us/PDFs/UPick.PDF
X-ray (Portable) Supplier #31 ....www.adph.org/providers/

Alabama Licensing Quick Finder

Aband'd Mine Land Reclamation #32 ... 205-945-8671
Abortion/Reproductive Health Ctr #31.. 334-206-5175
Aircraft/Pilot-related Personnel #51......205-731-1557
Ambulatory Surgery Center #31............334-206-5175
Anesthesiologist Assistant #19.............334-242-4116
Architect #8.......................................334-242-4179
Assisted Living Facility/Unit #31...........334-206-5175
Attorney #3 334-269-1515
Auctioneer #9.........................334-269-9990 x14
Audiologist #28 334-269-1434
Bank #5...334-242-3452
Beauty Shop/Booth Rental #11 334-242-1918
Beauty Shop/Salon #11.......................334-242-1918
Bee, Queen & Package Shipper #30 .. 334-240-7239
Birthing Center #31.............................334-206-5175
Boxer/Wrestler - not regulated #52 334-242-1380
Broker/Dealer Agent #48 334-242-2984
Cerebral Palsy Center #31..................334-206-5175
Certified Regis. Nurse Practitioner #21.334-242-0767
Charitable Filing #48...........................334-242-2984
Check Casher #5 334-242-3452
Check Seller #48 334-242-2984
Chiropractor #10.................................205-755-8000
Clinical Nurse Specialist #21 334-242-0767
Consumer Finance Company #5...........334-242-3452
Contractor, General #7 334-272-5030
Cosmetic Studio #11 334-242-1918
Cosmetologist/Cosmetology Instruct. #11
....334-242-1918
Cosmetologist/Esthetician/Manicurist Mgr. #11
....334-242-1918
Cosmetologist/Esthetician/Manicurist Master #11
....334-242-1918
Cosmetology Mgr. Pending Exam #11..334-242-1918
Cosmetology School/Instructor/Pending Exam #11
....334-242-1918
Cosmetology Student/Apprentice #11..334-242-1918
Cosmetology, Restrict'd Managing #11.334-242-1918
Counselor, Professional #15 205-458-8716
Dental Hygienist #12...........................205-985-7267
Dentist #12..205-985-7267
Dietitian/Nutritionist #33.....................334-242-4505
Education Administrator #49 334-242-9977
Electrical Contractor #14....................334-269-9990
Electrician, Journeyman #14...............334-269-9990
Embalmer #17 334-242-4049
Emergency Medical Technician #50 334-206-5383
Engineer/Engineer in Training #27......334-242-5568
Esthetician School/Salon #11..............334-242-1918
Esthetician Student/Instr'r/School/Pending Exam #11
....334-242-1918
Esthetician/Esthetician Apprentice #11.334-242-1918
Firefighter #36....................................205-391-3743
Forester #26 334-353-3640
Funeral Director #17...........................334-242-4049
Gas Fitter #46....................................205-945-4857
Geologist #37.........................334-269-9990 x10
Ginseng Dealer #30............................334-240-7239

Hearing Instrument Dealer #35 334-242-1925
Heating/Air Conditioning Contract'r #38 334-242-5550
Home Builder #53................................334-242-2230
Home Health Agency #31 334-206-5175
Home Inspector #42............................334-242-7205
Hospice #31.......................................334-206-5175
Hospital #31.......................................334-206-5175
Industrial Revenue Bond #48 334-242-2984
Insurance Adjuster #39 334-241-4126
Insurance Agent #39...........................334-241-4126
Insurance Broker/Producer #39 334-241-4126
Insurance Corp/Company/Partner #39 . 334-241-4126
Interior Designer #54...........................205-879-6785
Investment Advisor #48.......................334-242-2984
Investment Advisor Rep. #48 334-242-2984
Landscape Architect #18.....................334-262-1351
Landscape Designer #55 334-240-7241
Landscape Planter #55 334-240-7241
Law Enforcement Personnel #44 334-242-4047
Lead Abatement Contractor #59 334-206-5373
Lead Abatement Professional #59 334-206-5373
Legal/Dental Svc Representative #39.. 334-241-4126
Lender/Loan Source #5.......................334-242-3452
Livestock Market Operator #30 334-240-7208
LPG-Liquif'd Petrol. Gas Broker #40....334-242-5649
Manicurist Salon/School/Student/Instructor #11
....334-242-1918
Manicurist/Manicurist Apprentice/Pending Exam #11
....334-242-1918
Marriage/Family Therapist #9........ 334-269-9990 x14
Massage Therapist #56.......................334-269-9990
Medical Doctor #19.............................334-242-4116
Medical Gas Piper #46 205-945-4857
Mental Health Center #31 334-206-5175
Midwife Nurse #21..............................334-242-0767
Mine Personnel #34............................205-254-1275
Mine Safety and Inspection #32...........205-254-1275
Mobile Home Manufacturer #41...........334-242-4036
Mobile Home Setup/Installer/Sales #41 334-242-4036
Mortgage Broker #5............................334-242-3452
Motor Club Representative #39 334-241-4126
Notary Public #42...............................334-242-7205
Nurse Anesthetist #21 334-242-0767
Nurse-LPN/RN #21.............................334-242-0767
Nursing Disciplinary Action #21 334-242-0767
Nursing Home #31..............................334-206-5175
Nursing Home Administrator #22..........334-271-6214
Occup. Therapist Assistant #57 334-353-4466
Occupational Therapist #57.................334-353-4466
Optometrist #20..................................205-481-9993
Osteopathic Physician #19..................334-242-4116
Pawn Shop #5....................................334-242-3452
Pest Control #30.................................334-240-7239
Pesticide Applicator/Dealer #30...........334-240-7239
Petroleum Product Seller #30 334-240-7127
Pharmacist #23..................................205-967-0130
Physical Therapist/Therapist Asst #24.334-242-4064
Physician Assistant #19 334-242-4116

Physiological Lab, Indep't Clinical #31. 334-206-5175
Pilot/Bar Pilot #45...............................251-432-2639
Plant & Quarantine Inspector #30........334-240-7239
Plumber #46 205-945-4857
Podiatrist #4 205-995-8537
Polygraph Examiner #47......................334-260-1182
Preneed Sales Agent #39 334-241-4126
Psychological Technician #16..............334-242-4127
Psychologist #16................................334-242-4127
Public Accountant-CPA-Non Licensee Owners #25
....334-242-5700
Real Estate Agent/Sales #2 334-242-5544
Real Estate Appraiser #43 334-242-8747
Real Estate Broker #2.........................334-242-5544
Rehabilitation Center #31 334-206-5175
Reinsurance Intermediary #39.............334-241-4126
Renal Disease End Stage Treatm't Ctr. #31
....334-206-5175
Rural Primary Care Hospital #31 334-206-5175
School Bus Driver #49.........................334-242-9730
School Counselor #49..........................334-242-9977
School Superintendent #49..................334-242-9977
Securities Broker/Dealer #48 334-242-2984
Securities Seller #48...........................334-242-2984
Shampoo Assistant #11 334-242-1918
Sleep Disorder Center #31...................334-206-5175
Social Worker #58 334-242-5860
Social Worker Private Indep't Prac. #58334-242-5860
Soil Classifier #1................................334-242-2620
Speech Pathologist/Audiologist #28 334-269-1434
Sports Agent #42................................334-242-7591
Subcontractor #7................................334-272-5030
Surface Mining (non-fuel) #32..............334-242-8265
Surplus Line Broker #39......................334-241-4126
Surveyor, Land #27.............................334-242-5568
Teacher #49 334-242-9977
Teacher, Elementary School #49..........334-242-9977
Therapist, Marriage & Family #9.... 334-269-9990 x14
Timeshare Real Estate Seller #43 334-242-8747
Timeshare Seller #2............................334-242-5544
Tree Surgeon #55 334-240-7241
U-Pick Location #30 334-240-7100
Veterinarian #29.................................256-353-3544
Veterinary Premise Permit #29.............256-353-3544
Veterinary Technician #29....................256-353-3544
Weights & Measures #30.....................334-240-7134
X-ray (Portable) Supplier #31 334-206-5175

Alabama Licensing Agency Information

1 Soil and Water Conservation Committee, 100 N Union St #334 (PO Box 304800 - 36130), Montgomery, AL 36104-3702; 334-242-2620, Fax: 334-242-0551.
www.swcc.state.al.us/
Email: vpayne@swcc.state.al.us

2 Real Estate Commission, 1201 Carmichael Way, Montgomery, AL 36106; 334-242-5544, Fax: 334-270-9118.
www.arec.state.al.us/   Email: arec@arec.state.al.us
Search Database at
www.arec.state.al.us/search.asp

3 Alabama State Bar Association, PO Box 671 (415 Dexter Ave), Montgomery, AL 36101; 334-269-1515, Fax: 334-261-6310.
www.alabar.org   Email: info@alabar.org

4 Board of Podiatry, 311 Saint Charles St, Homewood, AL 35209; 205-995-8537, Fax: 205-995-8537.
www.alabamapodiatryboard.org
Email: alpodboard@aol.com
Search Database at www.alabamapodiatryboard.org/pages/licensee.html

5 State Banking Department, Licensing and Registration, 401 Adams St, #680, Montgomery, AL 36130; 334-242-3452, Fax: 334-242-3500.
www.bank.state.al.us
Search Database at www.bank.state.al.us/search_all_licenses.asp Note: Bureau of Loans fax number is 334-353-5961.

7 License Board for General Contractors, 2525 Fairlane Drive, Montgomery, AL 36116; 334-272-5030, Fax: 334-395-5336.
www.genconbd.state.al.us
Search Database at www.genconbd.state.al.us/DATABASE-LIVE/roster.asp

8 Board for Registration of Architects, 770 Washington Ave, #150, Montgomery, AL 36130-4450; 334-242-4179, Fax: 334-242-4531.
www.boa.state.al.us/
Email: cgainey@boa.state.al.us
Search Database at
www.boa.state.al.us/rostersearch/rostersearch.asp

9 Board of Auctioneers, and, Board of Examiners in Marriage & Family Therapy, 610 S McDonough St, Montgomery, AL 36104-5612; 334-269-9990, Fax: 334-263-6115.
www.auctioneer.state.al.us
Email: ALAUCBD@aol.com
Search Database at
www.auctioneer.state.al.us/roster/roster-search-form.asp

10 Board of Chiropractic Examiners, 737 Logan Road, Clanton, AL 35045; 205-755-8000, Fax: 205-755-0081.
http://chiro.state.al.us
Email: sbolton@chiro.state.al.us
Search Database at
www.alabamainteractive.org/asbce/VerificationEntryPoint.do;jsessionid=ap_JoQrUmjsg Note: Verification is on-line.

11 Board of Cosmetology, RSA Union Bldg, 100 N Union St #320 (PO Box 301750), Montgomery, AL 36130; 334-242-1918, Fax: 334-242-1926.
www.aboc.state.al.us
Email: cosmetology@aboc.state.al.us

12 Board of Dental Examiners, 5346 Stadium Trace Pkwy #112, Hoover, AL 35244; 205-985-7267, Fax: 205-985-0674.
www.dentalboard.org   Email: BDEAAL@bellsouth.net

14 Board of Electrical Contractors, 660 Adams Ave #301, Montgomery, AL 36104; 334-269-9990, Fax: 334-263-6115.
www.aecb.state.al.us
Email: alelectricalbd@aol.com Search Database at
www.aecb.state.al.us/Search/new_search.asp

15 Board of Examiners in Counseling, 950 22nd St N. #670, Birmingham, AL 35203; 205-458-8716, Fax: 205-458-8718.
www.abec.state.al.us
Email: fhemphill@abec.state.al.us

16 Board of Examiners in Psychology, 660 Adams Ave, #360, Mongomery, AL 36104; 334-242-4127.
www.psychology.state.al.us
Email: albdpsychology@mindspring.com

17 Board of Funeral Service, Box 309522, Montgomery, AL 36130; 334-242-4049, Fax: 334-353-7988.

18 Board of Landscape Architects, 908 S Hull St, Montgomery, AL 36104; 334-262-1351, Fax: 334-262-1351.
www.abela.state.al.us/
Email: abela@bellsouth.net   Search Database at
www.abela.state.al.us/architects.html

19 Board of Medical Examiners, PO Box 887 (848 Washington Ave), Montgomery, AL 36101; 334-242-4116, Fax: 334-242-4155.
www.albme.org
Email: webmaster@albme.org
Search Database at www.docboard.org/al/
Note: Will sell lists at $.05 per record.

20 Board of Optometry, 1431 2nd Ave, N, Bessemer, AL 35020; 205-481-9993, Fax: 205-481-9959.   www.al-optometry.org
Email: fwallace@al-optometry.org
Search Database at www.al-optometry.org

21 Board of Nursing, 770 Washington Ave #250, Montgomery, AL 36104; 334-242-4060, Fax: 334-242-4360.   www.abn.state.al.us
Email: abn@abn.state.al.us Note: Individial verifications are $30.00 each. A group online license verification is available by subscription.

22 Board of Nursing Home Administrators, 4156 Carmichael Road, Montgomery, AL 36106; 334-271-6214, Fax: 334-244-6509.
www.alboenha.state.al.us
Search Database at
www.alboenha.state.al.us/logon.html

23 Board of Pharmacy, 1 Perimeter Park S, #425 South, Birmingham, AL 35243; 205-967-0130, Fax: 205-967-1009.
www.albop.com

24 Board of Physical Therapy, 100 N Union St, #627, Montgomery, AL 36130-5040; 334-242-4064, Fax: 334-240-3288.
www.pt.state.al.us
Email: kbrown@pt.state.al.us   Search Database at
www.pt.state.al.us/License/searchform.asp Note: Will sell directories of licensees for $50.00 each.

25 Board of Public Accountancy, PO Box 300375 (770 Washington Ave, #236), Montgomery, AL 36130-0375; 334-242-5700, Fax: 334-240-2711.
www.asbpa.state.al.us
Search Database at
www.asbpa.state.al.us/register/register.asp

26 Board of Registration for Foresters, 513 Madison Ave, Montgomery, AL 36130; 334-353-3640, Fax: 334-353-3641.
www.alsbrf.org
Email: psears@almore.rr.com
Search Database at www.alsbrf.org

27 Board of Licensure for Professional Engineers & Land Surveyors, PO Box 304451 (100 North Union St #382), Montgomery, AL 36130-4451; 334-242-5568, Fax: 334-242-5105.
www.bels.alabama.gov
Email: bonnie.kelly@bels.alabama.gov
Search Database at www.bels.alabama.gov

28 Board of Examiners for Speech-Language Pathology & Audiology, PO Box 304760 (400 S Union St #225), Montgomery, AL 36130-4760; 334-269-1434, Fax: 334-269-6379.
www.mindspring.com/~abespa/
Email: abespa@mindspring.com

29 Board of Veterinary Medical Examiners, 2128 6th Avenue SE, Bldg 5 Ste 501, Decatur, AL 35601; 256-353-3544, Fax: 256-350-5629.
http://asbvme.us
Email: asbvme@mindspring.com

30 Department of Agriculture & Industries, Executive Division - Licensing, PO Box 3336 (1445 Federal Dr), Montgomery, AL 36109; 334-240-7282, 800-642-7761.
www.agi.state.al.us Note: Fax number for the Pesticide Management Section is 334-240-7168. Weights & Measures fax is 334-240-7175. Admin Dept. fax is 334-240-7194.

31 Department of Health, Provider Services Division - Licensing, 434 Monroe St, Montgomery, AL 36130-3017; 334-206-5175, Fax: 334-206-5219.
www.adph.org
Search Database at www.adph.org/providers/
Note: Enter search area by clicking on "Facility Directory."

32 Department of Industrial Relations, State Programs Division, 649 Monroe St, Montgomery, AL 36131-5200; 334-242-8265, Fax: 334-242-8403.
www.dir.state.al.us/sp

33 Dietetic/Nutrition Examiners Board, 400 S Union St #445, Montgomery, AL 36104-0500; 334-242-4505, Fax: 334-834-6398. Note: Will sell mail list for $50.00. Verification by phone, mail no charge.

34 Examiners of Mine Personnel, Division of Safety and Inspection, PO Box 10444 (11 W Oxmoor), Birmingham, AL 35202; 205-254-1275, Fax: 205-945-8685.

35 Hearing Aid Dealers, Executive Secretary, 400 S Union St, #445, Montgomery, AL 36130-3010; 334-242-1925, Fax: 334-834-6398. Note: Mail lists are available for $25.00. Verifications made by phone and mail.

36 Fire College & Personnel Standards Commission, 2501 Phoenix Dr, Tuscaloosa, AL 35405; 205-391-3779, Fax: 205-391-3747. www.alabamafirecollege.org

37 Board of Licensure of Professional Geologists, 610 S McDonough St, Montgomery, AL 36104; 334-269-9990 x10, Fax: 334-263-6115. www.algeobd.state.al.us/ Email: ALGEOBD@aol.com

38 Heating & Air Conditioning Contractors Board, 100 N Union St, #630, Montgomery, AL 36130; 866-855-1912, 334-242-5550, Fax: 334-353-7050. www.hvacboard.state.al.us Search Database at www.hvacboard.state.al.us/ Lic_Search/searchform.asp

39 Department of Insurance, Agent Licensing Division, 201 Monroe St #1700, Mongomery, AL 36104; 334-269-3550, Fax: 334-240-3282. www.aldoi.gov Search Database at www.aldoi.org/LicenseeSearch/

40 Liquefied Petroleum Gas Board, 818 S Perry St, Montgomery, AL 36104; 334-242-5649, Fax: 334-240-3255. www.lpgb.state.al.us

41 Manufactured Housing Commission, 350 S Decatur St, Montgomery, AL 36104; 334-242-4036, Fax: 334-240-3178. www.amhc.state.al.us

42 Registrations for Sports Agents and Notaries, Office of the Secretary of State, PO Box 5616, Montgomery, AL 36103-5616; 334-242-7205, Fax: 334-353-8993. www.sos.state.al.us Email: wsullivan@sos.al.gov   Search Database at www.sos.state.al.us/sosinfo/inquiry.cfm

43 Office of the Secretary of State, Real Estate Appraisers Licensing, PO Box 304355 (100 North Union St #370), Montgomery, AL 36104; 334-242-8747, Fax: 334-242-8749. http://reab.state.al.us/ Email: lbrooks@reab.state.al.us

44 Peace Officers Standards & Training Commission, PO Box 300075 (100 Union St, RSA Union Bldg, #600), Montgomery, AL 36130-0075; 334-242-4045, Fax: 334-242-4633. www.apostc.state.al.us

45 Pilotage Commission, PO Box 273, Mobile, AL 36601; 251-432-2639, Fax: 251-432-9964.

46 Plumbers & Gas Fitters Examining Board, 11 W Oxmoor, #104, Birmingham, AL 35209; 205-945-4857, Fax: 205-945-9915. www.pgfb.state.al.us Email: staff@pgfb.state.al.us Search Database at http://pgfb.state.al.us/lookup.asp

47 Polygraph Examiners Board, PO Box 1511, Montgomery, AL 36102-1511; 344-260-1182.

48 Securities Commission, 770 Washington Ave, #570, Montgomery, AL 36130; 334-242-2984, Fax: 334-242-0240. www.asc.state.al.us Email: asc@asc.state.al.us

49 Department of Education, Teacher Education & Certification, PO Box 302101 (50 N Ripley St), Montgomery, AL 36104; 334-242-9977, Fax: 334-242-0498. www.alsde.edu Email: tcert@alsde.edu

50 Department of Health, Emergency Medical Services Division, PO Box 303017, Birmingham, AL 36130-3017; 334-206-5383, Fax: 334-206-5260. www.adph.org/ems/

51 Department of Transportation, Flight Standards District Office, 1500 Urban Center Dr #250, Vestavia Hills, AL 35242; 205-731-1557, Fax: 205-731-0939. www.faa.gov/fsdo/bhm/

52 Department of Revenue, Athletic Commission - Inactive, 50 N Ripley St Rm 4131, Montgomery, AL 36132; 334-242-1380.

53 Home Builders Licensure Board, 400 S Union St #195, Montgomery, AL 36130; 334-242-2230, Fax: 334-263-1397. www.hblb.state.al.us/ Search Database at www.hblb.state.al.us/Lic_Search/search.asp

54 Board of Registration for Interior Designers, PO Box 11026 (65 Bagby Dr #3B), Birmingham, AL 53202; 205-879-6785.

55 Department of Agriculture & Industries, Plant Protection & Pesticide Management Division, PO Box 3336 - Beard Building, Montgomery, AL 36109-0336; 334-240-7243, Fax: 334-240-7168. www.agi.state.al.us/ Email: commone@agi.state.al.us

56 Board of Massage Therapy, 610 S McDonough St, Montgomery, AL 36104; 334-269-9990, Fax: 334-263-6115. www.almtbd.state.al.us/ Email: almtbd@aol.com

57 Board of Occupational Therapy, PO Box 304510 (64 N Union St #734), Montgomery, AL 36130-4510; 334-353-4466, Fax: 334-353-4465. www.asbot.state.al.us/ Email: acosby@asbot.state.al.us

58 Board of Social Work Examiners, 100 N Union St. #736, Montgomery, AL 36130; 888-879-3672, 334-242-5860, Fax: 334-242-0280. www.abswe.state.al.us Search Database at www.abswe.state.al.us/Lic_Search/searchpip.asp

59 Department of Public Health, Indoor Air Quality/Lead Branch, Div. of Comm. Environmental Protection - Lead Contractors, P.O. Box 303017, (201 Monroe St, The RSA Tower, Suite 1250), Montgomery, AL 36130-3017; 800-819-7644, 334-206-5373. www.adph.org/lead/

Alabama Federal Courts

The following list indicates the district and division name for each county in the state. If the bankruptcy court location is different from the district court, then the location of the bankruptcy court appears in parentheses.

County/Court Cross Reference

Autauga	Middle	Montgomery	Henry	Middle	Dothan (Montgomery)
Baldwin	Southern	Mobile	Houston	Middle	Dothan (Montgomery)
Barbour	Middle	Montgomery	Jackson	Northern	Huntsville (Decatur)
Bibb	Northern	Birmingham (Tuscaloosa)	Jefferson	Northern	Birmingham
Blount	Northern	Birmingham	Lamar	Northern	Jasper (Tuscaloosa)
Bullock	Middle	Montgomery	Lauderdale	Northern	Florence (Decatur)
Butler	Middle	Montgomery	Lawrence	Northern	Huntsville (Decatur)
Calhoun	Northern	Birmingham (Anniston)	Lee	Middle	Opelika (Montgomery)
Chambers	Middle	Opelika (Montgomery)	Limestone	Northern	Huntsville (Decatur)
Cherokee	Northern	Gadsden (Anniston)	Lowndes	Middle	Montgomery
Chilton	Middle	Montgomery	Macon	Middle	Opelika (Montgomery)
Choctaw	Southern	Mobile	Madison	Northern	Huntsville (Decatur)
Clarke	Southern	Mobile	Marengo	Southern	Selma (Mobile)
Clay	Northern	Birmingham (Anniston)	Marion	Northern	Jasper (Tuscaloosa)
Cleburne	Northern	Birmingham (Anniston)	Marshall	Northern	Gadsden (Anniston)
Coffee	Middle	Dothan (Montgomery)	Mobile	Southern	Mobile
Colbert	Northern	Florence (Decatur)	Monroe	Southern	Mobile
Conecuh	Southern	Mobile	Montgomery	Middle	Montgomery
Coosa	Middle	Montgomery	Morgan	Northern	Huntsville (Decatur)
Covington	Middle	Montgomery	Perry	Southern	Selma (Mobile)
Crenshaw	Middle	Montgomery	Pickens	Northern	Birmingham (Tuscaloosa)
Cullman	Northern	Huntsville (Decatur)	Pike	Middle	Montgomery
Dale	Middle	Dothan (Montgomery)	Randolph	Middle	Opelika (Montgomery)
Dallas	Southern	Selma (Mobile)	Russell	Middle	Opelika (Montgomery)
De Kalb	Northern	Gadsden (Anniston)	Shelby	Northern	Birmingham
Elmore	Middle	Montgomery	St. Clair	Northern	Gadsden (Anniston)
Escambia	Southern	Mobile	Sumter	Northern	Birmingham (Tuscaloosa)
Etowah	Northern	Gadsden (Anniston)	Talladega	Northern	Birmingham (Anniston)
Fayette	Northern	Jasper (Tuscaloosa)	Tallapoosa	Middle	Opelika (Montgomery)
Franklin	Northern	Florence (Decatur)	Tuscaloosa	Northern	Birmingham (Tuscaloosa)
Geneva	Middle	Dothan (Montgomery)	Walker	Northern	Jasper (Tuscaloosa)
Greene	Northern	Birmingham (Tuscaloosa)	Washington	Southern	Mobile
Hale	Southern	Selma (Mobile)	Wilcox	Southern	Selma (Mobile)
			Winston	Northern	Jasper (Tuscaloosa)

Standards for Federal Courts: The search fee is $20.00 per item (one party name or case number). Certification fee is $7.00 per document. Copy fee is $.50 per page. All fees standard unless noted in profile. Mail Search: always enclose a stamped self addressed envelope unless otherwise noted. Most courts accept fax requests or will suggest a copying/search vendor. Before releasing records, all courts require prepayment unless noted in profile.

Open records are located at the court unless otherwise noted. District courts index by defendant and plaintiff as well as by case number. Bankruptcy courts usually index by debtor and case number. While most courts now have their indexes on computer, many still maintain index card files as well.

The universal PACER sign-up number is 800-676-6856. Find PACER and the Party/Case Index on the Web at http://pacer.psc.uscourts.gov. PACER dial-up access is $.60 per minute. Courts offering internet access via RACER, PACER, Web-PACER or the new CM-ECF charge $.07 per page fee unless noted as free.

US District Court

Middle District of Alabama

Dothan Division c/o Montgomery Division, PO Box 711, Montgomery, AL 36101 (courier address: 15 Lee St, Montgomery, AL 36104), 334-223-7308. www.almd.uscourts.gov

Counties: Coffee, Dale, Geneva, Henry, Houston.

Indexing & Storage: New cases available in the index immediately after filing date. Open records are located at the Montgomery Division.

Fee & Payment: Payment may be made by money order, cashier check. Business checks are not accepted. Personal checks are not accepted.

Phone Search: No searching by telephone.

In Person Search: Permitted.

PACER: PACER is available online at http://pacer.almd.uscourts.gov. Case records go back to 1994. New records are online after 1 day.

Electronic Filing: Currently in the process of implementing CM/ECF.

Montgomery Division Records Search, PO Box 711, Montgomery, AL 36101-0711 (courier address: 15 Lee St, Montgomery, AL 36104), 334-223-7308. www.almd.uscourts.gov

Counties: Autauga, Barbour, Bullock, Butler, Chilton, Coosa, Covington, Crenshaw, Elmore, Lowndes, Montgomery, Pike.

Indexing & Storage: New cases available in the index immediately after filing date. Records are also indexed on microfiche.

Fee & Payment: Payment may be made by money order, cashier check, business check. Personal checks are not accepted. Payee: Clerk, U.S. District Court.

Phone Search: No searching by telephone.

In Person Search: Fee charged if court conducts your in person search for you. Public allowed to search the microfiche index.

PACER: PACER is available online at http://pacer.almd.uscourts.gov. Case records go back to 1994. New records are online after 1 day.

Electronic Filing: Electronic filing information online at https://ecf.alsd.uscourts.gov

Opelika Division c/o Montgomery Division, PO Box 711, Montgomery, AL 36101 (courier address: 15 Lee St, Montgomery, AL 36104), 334-223-7308. www.almd.uscourts.gov

Counties: Chambers, Lee, Macon, Randolph, Russell, Tallapoosa.

Indexing & Storage: New cases available in the index immediately after filing date. Open records are located at the Montgomery Division.

Fee & Payment: Payment may be made by money order, cashier check. Business checks are not accepted. Personal checks are not accepted.

Phone Search: No searching by telephone.

Mail Search: A SASE not required.

In Person Search: Permitted.

PACER: PACER is available online at http://pacer.almd.uscourts.gov. Case records go back to 1994. New records are online after 1 day.

Electronic Filing: Currently in the process of implementing CM/ECF.

U.S. Bankruptcy Court

Middle District of Alabama

Montgomery Division PO Box 1248, Montgomery, AL 36102-1248 (courier address: 1 Church St, Montgomery, AL 36104), 334-954-3800, Fax: 334-954-3819. www.almb.uscourts.gov

Counties: Autauga, Barbour, Bullock, Butler, Chambers, Chilton, Coffee, Coosa, Covington, Crenshaw, Dale, Elmore, Geneva, Henry, Houston, Lee, Lowndes, Macon, Montgomery, Pike, Randolph, Russell, Tallapoosa.

Indexing & Storage: Cases indexed by debtor as well as by case number. New cases available in the index 3 days after filing date.

Fee & Payment: Payment may be made by money order, cashier check, business check. Personal checks are not accepted. Court may bill on request. Payee: Clerk of Court. Will fax back for $1.50 per page.

Phone Search: Docket information is available by phone. Automated voice case information service (VCIS) is available. Call VCIS at 334-954-3868. Will fax back for $1.50 per page.

In Person Search: Fee charged if court conducts your in person search for you.

PACER: WebPacer is at https://ecf.almb.uscourts.gov. Document images available. NIBS court. Case records go back to case 89-02000. Records purged every 6 months. New civil records are online after 2-3 days.

Electronic Filing: Electronic filing information online at https://ecf.almb.uscourts.gov

U.S. District Court

Northern District of Alabama

Birmingham Division Room 104, U.S. Courthouse, 1729 5th Ave N, Birmingham, AL 35203 (courier: Use mail address for courier delivery) 205-278-1700. www.alnd.uscourts.gov

Counties: Bibb, Blount, Calhoun, Clay, Cleburne, Greene, Jefferson, Pickens, Shelby, Sumter, Talladega, Tuscaloosa.

Indexing & Storage: New cases available in the index 2-3 days after filing date. Records are also indexed on microfiche.

Fee & Payment: Payment may be made by money order, cashier check, personal check. Payee: Clerk of Court.

Phone Search: All public information will be released over the phone.

In Person Search: Fee charged if court conducts your in person search for you.

PACER: PACER is available online at http://pacer.alnd.uscourts.gov. Document images available. Case records go back to 1994. Records purged every 18 months. New records are online after 1 day.

Florence Division PO Box 776, Florence, AL 35630 (courier address: 210 Court St, Florence, AL 35631), 205-760-5815, Fax: 205-760-5727. www.alnd.uscourts.gov

Counties: Colbert, Franklin, Lauderdale.

Indexing & Storage: New cases available in the index 2-3 days after filing date. Records are also indexed on microfiche. Some case files may be held in Birmingham if a Birmingham judge is assigned.

Fee & Payment: Payment may be made by money order, cashier check, personal check. Payee: U.S. District Court.

Phone Search: Only docket information available by phone.

Mail Search: A SASE not required.

In Person Search: Fee charged if court conducts your in person search for you.

PACER: PACER is available online at http://pacer.alnd.uscourts.gov. Document images available. Case records go back to 1994. Records purged every 18 months. New records are online after 1 day.

Gadsden Division c/o Birmingham Division, Room 140, U.S. Courthouse, 1729 5th Ave N, Birmingham, AL 35203 (courier address: Use mail address for courier delivery) 205-278-1700. www.alnd.uscourts.gov

Counties: Cherokee, De Kalb, Etowah, Marshall, St. Clair.

Indexing & Storage: New cases available in the index 2-3 days after filing date. Open records are located at the Birmingham Division.

Fee & Payment: Payment may be made by money order, cashier check. Business checks are not accepted. Personal checks are not accepted.

Phone Search: No searching by telephone.

In Person Search: Permitted.

PACER: PACER is available online at http://pacer.alnd.uscourts.gov. Document images available. Case records go back to 1994. Records

purged every 18 months. New records are online after 1 day.

Huntsville Division Clerk's Office, U.S. Post Office & Courthouse #302, 101 Holmes Ave NE, Huntsville, AL 35801 (courier address: Use mail address for courier delivery) 205-534-6495. www.alnd.uscourts.gov

Counties: Cullman, Jackson, Lawrence, Limestone, Madison, Morgan.

Indexing & Storage: New cases available in the index 2 days after filing date. Records are also indexed on microfiche.

Fee & Payment: Payment may be made by money order, cashier check, personal check. Payee: U.S. District Court Clerk.

Phone Search: All public information will be released over the phone.

Mail Search: All requests for criminal searches will be sent to Birmingham. Include SASE for return.

In Person Search: Fee charged if court conducts your in person search for you.

PACER: PACER is available online at http://pacer.alnd.uscourts.gov. Document images available. Case records go back to 1994. Records purged every 18 months. New records are online after 1 day.

Jasper Division c/o Birmingham Division, Room 140, U.S. Courthouse, 1729 5th Ave N, Birmingham, AL 35203 (courier address: Use mail address for courier delivery) 205-278-1700. www.alnd.uscourts.gov

Counties: Fayette, Lamar, Marion, Walker, Winston.

Indexing & Storage: New cases available in the index 2-3 days after filing date. Open records are located at the Birmingham Division. Some case records may be held in Florence, depending upon the judge assigned.

Fee & Payment: Payment may be made by money order, cashier check. Business checks are not accepted. Personal checks are not accepted.

Phone Search: No searching by telephone.

In Person Search: Permitted.

PACER: PACER is available online at http://pacer.alnd.uscourts.gov. Document images available. Case records go back to 1994. Records purged every 18 months. New records are online after 1 day.

U.S. Bankruptcy Court

Northern District of Alabama

Anniston Division PO Box 2008, Anniston, AL 36202-2008 (courier address: 914 Noble St, Anniston, AL36202), 256-741-1500, Fax: 256-741-1503. www.alnb.uscourts.gov

Counties: Calhoun, Cherokee, Clay, Cleburne, De Kalb, Etowah, Marshall, St. Clair, Talladega.

Indexing & Storage: Cases indexed by debtor as well as by case number. New cases available in the index immediately after filing date.

Fee & Payment: Payment may be made by money order, cashier check, personal check. Payee: Clerk, U.S. Bankruptcy Court, Northern District.

Phone Search: Automated voice case information service (VCIS) is available. Call VCIS at 877-466-8879.

In Person Search: Fee charged if court conducts your in person search for you.

PACER: PACER is available online at http://pacer.alnb.uscourts.gov. Records go back to October 31, 1976. New civil records are online after 1 day.

Electronic Filing: Electronic filing information online at https://ecf.alnb.uscourts.gov

Birmingham Division Room 120, 1800 5th Ave N, Birmingham, AL 35203 (courier address: Use mail address for courier delivery) 205-714-4000, Fax: 205-714-3913. www.alnb.uscourts.gov

Counties: Blount, Jefferson, Shelby.

Indexing & Storage: Cases indexed by debtor as well as by case number. New cases available in the index immediately after filing date. Along with the debtor's name and the case number, the searcher must provide the year the case was closed and the location where the case was filed.

Fee & Payment: Payment may be made by money order, cashier check, personal check. Payee: Clerk, U.S. Bankruptcy Court.

Phone Search: Only docket information available by phone. Automated voice case information service (VCIS) is available. Call VCIS at 877-466-0795 or 205-254-7337.

In Person Search: Fee charged if court conducts your in person search for you.

PACER: PACER is available online at http://pacer.alnb.uscourts.gov. Case records go back to 1994. Records purged every six months. New civil records are online after 1 day.

Electronic Filing: Electronic filing information online at https://ecf.alnb.uscourts.gov

Decatur Division PO Box 2748, Decatur, AL 35602 (courier address: Room 220, 400 Well St, Decatur, AL 35601), 256-584-7900, Fax: 256-584-7977. www.alnb.uscourts.gov

Counties: Colbert, Cullman, Franklin, Jackson, Lauderdale, Lawrence, Limestone, Madison, Morgan. The part of Winston County North of Double Springs is handled by this division.

Indexing & Storage: Cases indexed by debtor as well as by case number. New cases available in the index immediately after filing date. Along with the debtor's name and the case number, the searcher must provide the year the case was closed and the location where the case was filed.

Fee & Payment: Payment may be made by money order, cashier check, personal check. Payee: Clerk, U.S. Bankruptcy Court.

Phone Search: If a searcher calls, the court will indicate charges but not release information. Automated voice case information service (VCIS) is available. Call VCIS at 877-466-0796 or 256-353-2817.

In Person Search: Fee charged if court conducts your in person search for you.

PACER: PACER is available online at http://pacer.alnb.uscourts.gov. Case records go back to 1994. Records purged every six months. New civil records are online after 1 day.

Electronic Filing: Electronic filing information online at https://ecf.alnb.uscourts.gov

Tuscaloosa Division PO Box 3226, Tuscaloosa, AL 35403 (courier address: 1118 Greensboro Ave, Tuscaloosa, AL 35401), 205-752-0426, Fax: 205-752-6468. www.alnb.uscourts.gov

Counties: Bibb, Fayette, Greene, Lamar, Marion, Pickens, Sumter, Tuscaloosa, Walker, Winston. The part of Winston County North of Double Springs is handled by Decatur Division.

Indexing & Storage: Cases indexed by debtor as well as by case number. New cases available in the index 2 days after filing date. Card indexes are maintained on cases filed prior to October 1, 1979. Computer indexes only on cases filed commencing October 1, 1979.

Fee & Payment: Payment may be made by money order, cashier check, business check. Personal checks are not accepted. Payee: Clerk, U.S. Bankruptcy Court.

Phone Search: Automated voice case information service (VCIS) is available. Call VCIS at 877-466-9267 or 205-752-0426.

In Person Search: Fee charged if court conducts your in person search for you.

PACER: PACER is available online at http://pacer.alnb.uscourts.gov. Case records go back to 1994. Records never purged. New civil records are online after 1 day.

Electronic Filing: Electronic filing information online at https://ecf.alnb.uscourts.gov

U.S. District Court

Southern District of Alabama

Mobile Division Clerk, 113 St Joseph St, Mobile, AL 36602 (courier address: Use mail address for courier delivery) 251-690-2371, Fax: 251-694-4297. www.als.uscourts.gov

Counties: Baldwin, Choctaw, Clarke, Conecuh, Escambia, Mobile, Monroe, Washington.

Indexing & Storage: New cases available in the index immediately after filing date.

Fee & Payment: Payment may be made by money order, cashier check, personal check. Payee: Clerk, U.S. District Court.

Phone Search: Will only check docket information for a case number over the phone.

In Person Search: Fee charged if court conducts your in person search for you.

PACER: PACER is available online at http://pacer.alsd.uscourts.gov. Case records go back to 1994. New records are online after 1 day.

Electronic Filing: Electronic filing information online at https://ecf.almd.uscourts.gov

Selma Division c/o Mobile Division, 113 St Joseph St, Mobile, AL 36602 (courier address: Use mail address for courier delivery) 251-690-2371, Fax: 251-694-4297. www.als.uscourts.gov

Counties: Dallas, Hale, Marengo, Perry, Wilcox.

Indexing & Storage: New cases available in the index immediately after filing date. Open records are located at the Mobile Division.

Fee & Payment: Payment may be made by money order, cashier check. Business checks are not accepted. Personal checks are not accepted.

Phone Search: No searching by telephone.

In Person Search: Permitted.

PACER: PACER is available online at http://pacer.alsd.uscourts.gov. Case records go back to 1994. New records are online after 1 day.

Electronic Filing: Currently in the process of implementing CM/ECF.

U.S. Bankruptcy Court

Southern District of Alabama

Mobile Division Clerk, 201 St. Louis St, Mobile, AL 36602 (courier address: Use mail address for courier delivery) 251-441-5391, Fax: 251-441-6286. www.alsb.uscourts.gov

Counties: Baldwin, Choctaw, Clarke, Conecuh, Dallas, Escambia, Hale, Marengo, Mobile, Monroe, Perry, Washington, Wilcox.

Indexing & Storage: Cases indexed by debtor as well as by case number. New cases available in the index immediately after filing date. District wide computer searches are available for information from 1985 for this court.

Fee & Payment: Payment may be made by money order, cashier check, business check. Personal checks are not accepted. Payee: Clerk, U.S. Bankruptcy Court.

Phone Search: Only the name and case number is released over the phone. Automated voice case information service (VCIS) is available. Call VCIS at 251-441-5637.

Mail Search: A SASE not required.

In Person Search: Fee charged if court conducts your in person search for you.

PACER: Court uses new CM/ECF system for PACER. Case records go back to 1994. New civil records are online after 1 day.

Electronic Filing: Electronic filing information online at https://ecf.alsb.uscourts.gov

Alabama County Courts

Court	Jurisdiction	No. of Courts	How Organized
Circuit Courts*	General	17	40 Circuits
District Courts*	Limited	15	67 Districts
Combined Courts*		61	
Municipal Courts	Municipal	253	
Probate Courts*	Probate	68	

* Profiled in this Sourcebook.

Court	CIVIL								
	Tort	Contract	Real Estate	Min. Claim	Max. Claim	Small Claims	Estate	Eviction	Domestic Relations
Circuit Courts*	X	X	X	$3000	No Max				X
District Courts*	X	X	X	$3000	$10,000	$3000		X	
Municipal Courts									
Probate Courts*							X		

Court	CRIMINAL				
	Felony	Misdemeanor	DWI/DUI	Preliminary Hearing	Juvenile
Circuit Courts*	X				
District Courts*		X	X	X	X
Municipal Courts		X	X		
Probate Courts*					

ADMINISTRATION   Director of Courts, 300 Dexter Ave, Montgomery, AL, 36104; 334-242-0300, Fax: 334-242-2099. www.alacourt.gov

COURT STRUCTURE   Circuit Courts are the courts of general jurisdiction; District Courts have limited jurisdiction in civil matters. These courts are combined in all but eight larger counties. Barbour, Coffee, Jefferson, St. Clair, Talladega, and Tallapoosa Counties have two court locations within the county.

Jefferson County (Birmingham), Madison (Huntsville), Marshall, and Tuscaloosa Counties have separate criminal divisions for Circuit and/or District Courts. Misdemeanors committed with felonies are tried with the felony. The Circuit Courts are appeals courts for misdemeanors.

District Courts can receive guilty pleas in felony cases.

ONLINE ACCESS   The state has a remote access program called (SJIS), but it is only open to government agencies. They recommend new users to contact a designated private vendor. For more information, visit their web site at www.alacourt.com. Note that fees are involved.

State Supreme Court and Appellette decisions are available at www.alalinc.net.

ADDITIONAL INFORMATION   Although in most counties Circuit and District courts are combined, each index may be separate. Therefore, when you request a search of both courts, be sure to state that the search is to cover "both the Circuit and District Court records." Several offices do not perform searches. Some offices do not have public access computer terminals.

Autauga County

Circuit & District Court 134 N Court St, #114, Prattville, AL 36067-3049; Civil phone: 334-361-3736; Criminal phone: 334-361-3737. Hours: 8AM-5PM (CST). *Felony, Misdemeanor, Civil, Eviction, Small Claims.*

Civil Records: Access: Mail, online, in person. Both court and visitors may perform in person searches. No search fee. Required to search: name, years to search. Civil cases indexed by defendant, plaintiff. Civil records on computer since 1977 and in books from 1950. Online access at www.alacourt.com.

Criminal Records: Access: Mail, online, in person. Both court and visitors may perform in person searches. No search fee. Required to search: name, years to search; also helpful: DOB, SSN. Criminal records on computer since 1977 and in books from 1950. Online access via www.alacourt.com.

General Information: Public Access terminal is available. No sealed, adoptions, youthful offenders or juvenile records released. Copy fee: $.25 per page. Cert fee: $2.25. Payee: Circuit Court. Only cashiers checks and money orders accepted. Prepayment required. Mail turnaround time 1-2 weeks.

Probate Court 176 W 5th, Prattville, AL 36067; 334-361-3728/4842; Fax: 334-361-3740. Hours: 8:30AM-5PM (CST). *Probate.*

Baldwin County

Circuit & District Court 312 Courthouse Sq #10, Bay Minette, AL 36507; 251-937-0370; Civil phone: 251-937-0299; Criminal phone: 251-937-0280. Hours: 8AM-4:30PM (CST). *Felony, Misdemeanor, Civil, Eviction, Small Claims.*
Note: Court will not do name searches.

Civil Records: Access: Online, in person. Visitors must perform in person searches for themselves. Search fee: none. Required to search: name, years to search. Civil cases indexed by defendant, plaintiff. Civil records indexed on computer from 1977, index books by case # to early 1900s. Online access at www.alacourt.com.

Criminal Records: Access: Online, in person. Visitors must perform in person searches for themselves. Search fee: none. Required to search: name, years to search, DOB. Criminal records indexed on computer from 1977, index books by case # to early 1900s. Online access via www.alacourt.com.

General Information: Public Access terminal is available. No sealed, adoptions, youthful offenders or juvenile records released. Copy fee: $.25 per page. Cert fee: $1.25 per page. Payee: Circuit Court Clerk. Only cashiers checks and money orders accepted. Prepayment required.

Probate Court PO Box 459, Bay Minette, AL 36507; 251-937-9561; Fax: 251-937-0252. Hours: 8AM-4:30PM (CST). *Probate.*
Note: Online access to probate property records is at www.deltacomputersystems.com/al/al05/probatea.html.

Barbour County

Circuit & District Court - Clayton Division PO Box 219, Clayton, AL 36016; 334-775-8366; Probate phone: 334-775-8371; Fax: 334-775-1125. Hours: 8AM-4:30PM (CST). *Felony, Misdemeanor, Civil, Eviction, Small Claims, Probate.*
Note: Probate court is separate from this court, and can be contacted at the telephone number above.

Civil Records: Access: Phone, mail, online, in person. Both court and visitors may perform in person searches. Search fee: $5.00 per name. Fee is per

division. Required to search: name, years to search. Civil cases indexed by defendant. Civil records on computer back to 1993; books from 1977; archives back to 1920. Online access at www.alacourt.com.

Criminal Records: Access: Mail, online, in person. Both court and visitors may perform in person searches. Search fee: $5.00 per name. $5.00 per division. Required to search: name, years to search, DOB; also helpful: SSN. Criminal records on computer back to 1993, books from 1977; archives back to 1920. Online access via www.alacourt.com.

General Information: Public Access terminal is available. No sealed, adoptions, youthful offenders records released. Fee to fax results is $.50 per page. Copy fee: $.50 per page. Cert fee: $1.50. Payee: David S Nix. Business checks accepted. Mail requests: SASE required. Mail turnaround time 2-3 days.

Circuit & District Court - Eufaula Division 303 E Broad St, Rm 201, Eufaula, AL 36027; 334-687-1515/16; Probate phone: 334-687-1530; Fax: 334-687-1599. Hours: 8AM-4:30PM (CST). *Misdemeanor, Civil, Eviction, Small Claims, Probate.*
Probate court is separate from this court at Rm 101, and can be contacted at the telephone number above.

Civil Records: Access: Online, in person. Visitors must perform in person searches for themselves. No search fee. Required to search: name, years to search. Civil cases indexed by defendant, plaintiff. Civil records on computer from 1993. Index from 1977 to present, records are easily searched, prior to 1977 more difficult to search. Online access through SJIS. See state introduction or visit www.alacourt.com. If case number is known, will provide copies within 2 days.

Criminal Records: Access: Online, in person. Visitors must perform in person searches for themselves. No search fee. Required to search: name, years to search; also helpful: DOB, SSN. Criminal records on computer from 1993. Index from 1977 to present, records are easily searched, prior to 1977 more difficult to search. Online access through SJIS. See state introduction or visit www.alacourt.com. If case number is known, will provide copies within 2 days.

General Information: Public Access terminal is available. No sealed, adoptions, youthful offenders or juvenile records released. Copy fee: $.25 per page. Cert fee: $3.00. Payee: Clerk of Courts. Personal checks accepted. Prepayment required.

Bibb County

Circuit & District Court Bibb County Courthouse, PO Box 185, Centreville, AL 35042; 205-926-3103 Civil (Circuit); Civil phone: 205-926-3100 (Dist); Criminal phone: 205-926-3107; Probate phone: 205-926-3108; Fax: 205-926-3132. Hours: 8AM-4:30PM (CST). *Felony, Misdemeanor, Civil, Eviction, Small Claims, Probate.*
Note: Probate court is separate from this court, and can be contacted at the telephone number above.

Civil Records: Access: Mail, online, in person. Both court and visitors may perform in person searches. No search fee. Required to search: name, years to search. Civil cases indexed by defendant. Civil records on index book back to 1940s. Online access at www.alacourt.com.

Criminal Records: Access: Mail, online, in person. Both court and visitors may perform in person searches. No search fee. Required to search: name, years to search, DOB; also helpful: SSN. Criminal records on computer from 1988, on index books back to 1940s. Online access via www.alacourt.com.

General Information: Public Access terminal is available. No sealed, adoptions, youthful offenders or

juvenile records released. Copy fee: $.25 per page. Cert fee: $1.00 plus $.25 per page. Payee: John H Stacy, Clerk. Business checks accepted. Prepayment required. Mail requests: SASE required. Mail turnaround time 3-4 days.

Blount County

Circuit & District Court 220 2nd Ave East, #208, Oneonta, AL 35121; 205-625-4153. Hours: 8AM-5PM (CST). *Felony, Misdemeanor, Civil, Eviction, Small Claims.*

Civil Records: Access: Mail, online, in person. Both court and visitors may perform in person searches. No search fee. Required to search: name, years to search. Civil cases indexed by defendant, plaintiff. Civil records on computer from March 1994, on index books from 1977. Online access at www.alacourt.com.

Criminal Records: Access: Mail, online, in person. Both court and visitors may perform in person searches. No search fee. Required to search: name, years to search, DOB; also helpful: SSN. Criminal records on computer from March 1994, on index books from 1977. Online access via www.alacourt.com.

General Information: Public Access terminal is available. No sealed, adoptions, youthful offenders or juvenile records released. Copy fee: $.25 per page. Cert fee: $1.25. Payee: Mike Chriswell. No personal checks accepted. Prepayment required. Mail requests: SASE required. Mail turnaround time up to 1 month.

Probate Court 220 2nd Ave E, Oneonta, AL 35121; 205-625-4191/4180; Fax: 205-625-4206. Hours: 8AM-5PM (CST). *Probate.*

Bullock County

Circuit & District Court PO Box 230, Union Springs, AL 36089; 334-738-2280; Probate phone: 334-738-2250; Fax: 334-738-2282. Hours: 8AM-4:30PM (CST). *Felony, Misdemeanor, Civil, Eviction, Small Claims, Probate.*
Note: Probate court is separate from this court, and can be contacted at the telephone number above.

Civil Records: Access: Phone, fax, mail, online, in person. Both court and visitors may perform in person searches. No search fee. Required to search: name, years to search. Civil cases indexed by defendant, plaintiff. Civil records on index books back to 1930s; on computer back to 1995. Online access at www.alacourt.com.

Criminal Records: Access: Phone, fax, mail, online, in person. Only the court performs in person searches; visitors may not. No search fee. Required to search: name, years to search, DOB; also helpful: SSN, signed release. Criminal records on index books back to 1930s; on computer back to 1995. Online access via www.alacourt.com.

General Information: No sealed, adoptions, youthful offenders or juvenile records released. No fee to fax results. Prepayment required. Mail requests: SASE required. Mail turnaround time depends on clerk availability.

Butler County

Circuit & District Court PO Box 236, Greenville, AL 36037; 334-382-3521; Probate phone: 334-382-3512; Fax: 334-382-7488. Hours: 7:30AM-4:30PM (CST). *Felony, Misdemeanor, Civil, Eviction, Small Claims, Probate.*
Note: Probate court is separate from this court, and can be contacted at the telephone number above.

Civil Records: Access: Mail, online, in person. Both court and visitors may perform in person searches. Search fee: $5.00 per name. Fee is for first 2-3 years. Required to search: name, years to search. Civil cases indexed by defendant, plaintiff. Civil records on computer from 1992, books to 1979. Online access at www.alacourt.com.

Criminal Records: Access: Mail, online, in person. Both court and visitors may perform in person searches. Search fee: $5.00 per name. Fee for first 2-3 years. Required to search: name, years to search; also helpful: SSN, DOB. Criminal records on computer from 1992, books to 1979. Online access via www.alacourt.com.

General Information: Public Access terminal is available. No sealed, adoptions, youthful offenders or juvenile records released. Fee to fax results is $1.00 per page. Copy fee: $1.00 per page. Cert fee: $1.50 per page. Payee: Butler County District Court. Business checks accepted. Prepayment required. Mail requests: SASE requested. Turnaround time 1-2 weeks.

Calhoun County

Circuit Court 25 W 11th St, #300, Anniston, AL 36201; 256-231-1750; Fax: 256-231-1826. Hours: 8AM-4:30PM (CST). *Felony, Civil Actions Over $10,000.*

Civil Records: Access: Online, in person. Visitors must perform in person searches for themselves. No search fee. Required to search: name, years to search. Civil cases indexed by defendant, plaintiff. Civil records indexed on computer from 1970s, prior in books. Online access at www.alacourt.com.

Criminal Records: Access: Online, mail, in person. Visitors must perform in person searches for themselves. No search fee. Required to search: name, years to search, DOB; also helpful: SSN. Criminal records indexed on computer from 1970s, prior on books. Online access via www.alacourt.com. The County sex offender registry is online at www.calhouncountysheriff.org/html/Framsex.html. From Sept. 1999 forward only.

General Information: Public Access terminal is available. No sealed, adoptions, youthful offenders or juvenile records released. Copy fee: $.25 per page. Cert fee: $1.00. Personal checks accepted. Prepayment required. Mail turnaround time 2-4 days.

District Court 25 W 11th St, Box 9, Anniston, AL 36201; 256-231-1850; Fax: 256-231-1863. Hours: 8AM-4:30PM (CST). *Misdemeanor, Civil Actions Under $10,000, Eviction, Small Claims.*

Civil Records: Access: Online, in person. Visitors must perform in person searches for themselves. No search fee. Required to search: name, years to search. Civil cases indexed by defendant, plaintiff. Civil records on computer from 1989, books from 1977 to 1989. Online access at www.alacourt.com.

Criminal Records: Access: Online, in person. Visitors must perform in person searches for themselves. No search fee. Required to search: name, years to search; also helpful: SSN. Criminal records on computer from 1989, books from 1977 to 1989. Online access via www.alacourt.com.

General Information: Public Access terminal is available. No sealed, adoptions, youthful offenders or juvenile records released. Copy fee: $.25 per page. Cert fee: $1.25. Payee: District Court. Personal checks accepted. Prepayment required.

Probate Court 1702 Noble St, #102, Anniston, AL 36201; 256-241-2825. Hours: 8AM-4:30PM (CST). *Probate.*

Chambers County

Circuit & District Court Chambers County Courthouse - Clerks Office, Lafayette, AL 36862; 334-864-4348; Probate phone: 334-864-4372. Hours: 8AM-4:30PM (CST). *Felony, Misdemeanor, Civil, Eviction, Small Claims, Probate.*

Note: Probate court is separate from this court, and can be contacted at the telephone number above.

Civil Records: Access: Mail, online, in person. Both court and visitors may perform in person searches. No search fee. Required to search: name, years to search. Civil cases indexed by defendant, plaintiff. Civil records on computer from 4/93, on index books to early 1900s. Online access at www.alacourt.com.

Criminal Records: Access: Mail, online, in person. Only the court performs in person searches; visitors may not. No search fee. Required to search: name, years to search; also helpful: DOB, SSN. Criminal records are computerized since 1993. Online access via www.alacourt.com.

General Information: Public Access terminal is available. No sealed, adoptions, youthful offenders or juvenile records released. Copy fee: $.25 per page. Cert fee: $1.00. Business checks accepted. Mail requests: SASE required. Mail turnaround time 1 week.

Cherokee County

Circuit & District Court 100 Main St, Rm 203, Centre, AL 35960-1532; 256-927-3340. Hours: 8AM-4:30PM (CST). *Felony, Misdemeanor, Civil, Eviction, Small Claims.*

Civil Records: Access: Mail, online, in person. Visitors must perform in person searches for themselves. No search fee. Required to search: name, years to search. Civil cases indexed by defendant, plaintiff. Civil records on books from 1977. Online access at www.alacourt.com.

Criminal Records: Access: Mail, online, in person. Visitors must perform in person searches for themselves. No search fee. Required to search: name, years to search; also helpful: DOB, SSN. Criminal records on books from 1977. Online access via www.alacourt.com.

General Information: Public Access terminal is available. No sealed, adoptions, youthful offenders or juvenile records released. Copy fee: $.25 per page. Cert fee: $1.00. Payee: Circuit Clerk. Business checks accepted. Prepayment required. Mail turnaround time up to 2 weeks.

Probate Court 100 Main St, Rm 204, Centre, AL 35960; 256-927-3363; Fax: 256-927-6949. Hours: 8AM-4PM M-F, 8AM-Noon Sat (CST). *Probate.*

Chilton County

Circuit & District Court PO Box 1946, Clanton, AL 35046; 205-755-4275 Dist; 280-1844 Dist.; Probate phone: 205-755-1555. Hours: 8AM-5PM (CST). *Felony, Misdemeanor, Civil, Eviction, Small Claims, Probate.*

Note: Probate court is separate from this court, and can be contacted at the telephone number above.

Civil Records: Access: Online, in person. Visitors must perform in person searches for themselves. No search fee. Required to search: name, years to search. Civil cases indexed by defendant, plaintiff. Civil records on computer from 9/93, on books from 1950s. Online access at www.alacourt.com.

Criminal Records: Access: Online, in person. Visitors must perform in person searches for themselves. No search fee. Required to search: name, years to search; also helpful: DOB, SSN. Criminal records on computer since 1977. Online access via www.alacourt.com.

General Information: Public Access terminal is available. No sealed, adoptions, youthful offenders or juvenile records released. Copy fee: $.25 per page. Cert fee: $1.00. Payee: Clerk. Business checks accepted. Prepayment required.

Choctaw County

Circuit & District Court Choctaw County Courthouse, #10, PO Box 428, Butler, AL 36904; 205-459-2155; Probate phone: 205-459-2417. Hours: 8AM-4:30PM (CST). *Felony, Misdemeanor, Civil, Eviction, Small Claims, Probate.*

Note: Probate court is separate from this court, and can be contacted at the telephone number above.

Civil Records: Access: Online, in person. Both court and visitors may perform in person searches. No search fee. Required to search: name, years to search. Civil cases indexed by defendant, plaintiff. Civil records on index books from 1940. Putting records on computer starting September 1994. Online access at www.alacourt.com.

Criminal Records: Access: Online, in person. Visitors must perform in person searches themselves. No search fee. Required to search: name, years to search; also helpful: DOB, SSN. Criminal records on index books from 1940. Putting records on computer starting September 1994. Online access via www.alacourt.com.

General Information: Public Access terminal is available. No sealed, adoptions, youthful offenders or juvenile records released. Copy fee: $.25 per page. Cert fee: $1.00. Payee: Circuit Clerk. Business checks accepted. Prepayment required.

Clarke County

Circuit & District Court PO Box 921, Grove Hill, AL 36451; 251-275-3363; Probate phone: 251-275-3251. Hours: 8AM-5PM (CST). *Felony, Misdemeanor, Civil, Eviction, Small Claims, Probate.*

Note: Probate court is separate from this court, and can be contacted at the telephone number above.

Civil Records: Access: Mail, online, in person. Both court and visitors may perform in person searches. Search fee: $5.00 per name. Required to search: name, years to search. Civil cases indexed by defendant, plaintiff. Civil records on index cards from 1977. Online access at www.alacourt.com.

Criminal Records: Access: Mail, online, in person. Both court and visitors may perform in person searches. Search fee: $5.00 per name. Required to search: name, years to search; also helpful: DOB, SSN. Criminal records on index cards from 1977. Online access via www.alacourt.com.

General Information: Public Access terminal is available. No sealed, adoptions, youthful offenders or juvenile records released. Will not fax results. Copy fee: $.40 per page. Cert fee: $2.50. Payee: Circuit Clerk. Business checks accepted. Prepayment required. Mail turnaround time 1 week.

Clay County

Circuit & District Court PO Box 816, Ashland, AL 36251; 256-354-7926; Probate phone: 256-354-2198. Hours: 8AM-4:30PM (CST). *Felony, Misdemeanor, Civil, Eviction, Small Claims, Probate.*

Note: Probate court is separate from this court, and can be reached at the telephone number given above.

Civil Records: Access: Mail, online, in person. Visitors must perform in person searches for themselves. No search fee. Required to search: name, years to search. Civil cases indexed by defendant, plaintiff. Overall records go back to 1977; computerized records go back to 1994. Online access at www.alacourt.com.

Criminal Records: Access: Mail, online, in person. Visitors must perform in person searches for themselves. No search fee. Required to search: name, years to search; also helpful: SSN, DOB, signed release. Overall records go back to 1977;

computerized records go back to 1994. Online access via www.alacourt.com.

General Information: Public Access terminal is available. No sealed, adoptions, youthful offenders or juvenile records released. Fee to fax results is $1.00 per page. Copy fee: $.50 per page. Cert fee: $1.25. Payee: Circuit Clerk. Business checks accepted. Prepayment required. Mail turnaround time is 10-14 days.

Cleburne County

Circuit & District Court 120 Vickery St Rm 202, Heflin, AL 36264; 256-463-2651; Probate phone: 256-463-5655; Fax: 256-463-2257. Hours: 8AM-4:30PM (CST). *Felony, Misdemeanor, Civil, Eviction, Small Claims, Probate.*

Note: Probate court is separate from this court, and can be contacted at the telephone number above.

Civil Records: Access: Phone, mail, online, in person. Both court and visitors may perform in person searches. No search fee. Required to search: name, years to search. Civil cases indexed by defendant, plaintiff. Civil records on computer from 1993, on books and cards from 1900. Online access at www.alacourt.com.

Criminal Records: Access: Mail, online, in person. Only the court performs in person searches; visitors may not. No search fee. Required to search: name, years to search, DOB; also helpful: SSN. Criminal records on computer from 1993, on books and cards from 1900. Online access via www.alacourt.com.

General Information: No sealed, adoptions, youthful offenders or juvenile records released. Copy fee: $.25 per page. Cert fee: $1.00. Payee: Clerk. Only cashiers checks and money orders accepted. Prepayment required. Mail requests: SASE required. Mail turnaround time 1-2 days.

Coffee County

Circuit & District Court - Elba Division 230 M Court Ave, Elba, AL 36323; 334-897-2954. Hours: 8;30AM-noon, 1-4;30PM (CST). *Felony, Misdemeanor, Civil, Eviction, Small Claims, Probate.*

Civil Records: Access: Mail, online, in person. Both court and visitors may perform in person searches. No search fee. Required to search: name, years to search. Civil cases indexed by defendant. Civil records on computer back to 8/1993. Online access at www.alacourt.com.

Criminal Records: Access: Mail, online, in person. Only the court performs in person searches; visitors may not. No search fee. Required to search: name, years to search; also helpful: DOB. Criminal records on computer back to 8/1993. Online access via www.alacourt.com.

General Information: Public Access terminal is available. No sealed, adoptions, youthful offenders or juvenile records released. Copy fee: $.25 per page. Cert fee: $1.25. Payee: Circuit Clerk. Business checks accepted. Mail requests: SASE required. Mail turnaround time 3-4 days.

Circuit & District Court - Enterprise Division PO Box 311284, Enterprise, AL 36331; 334-347-2519. Hours: 8AM-5PM (CST). *Felony, Misdemeanor, Civil, Eviction, Small Claims.*

Civil Records: Access: Mail, fax, online, in person. Both court and visitors may perform in person searches. No search fee. Required to search: name, years to search. Civil cases indexed by defendant, plaintiff. Civil records on computer since 8/1993. Online access at www.alacourt.com.

Criminal Records: Access: Mail, online, in person. Both court and visitors may perform in person searches. No search fee. Required to search: name, years to search, DOB; also helpful: SSN. Criminal

records on computer since 8/1993. Online access via www.alacourt.com.

General Information: Public Access terminal is available. No sealed, adoptions, youthful offenders or juvenile records released. Copy fee: $.25 per page. Cert fee: $1.25. Payee: Clerk of Courts. Only cashiers checks and money orders accepted. Prepayment required. Mail turnaround time up to 1 week.

Probate Court - Enterprise Division PO Box 311247, Enterprise, AL 36331; 334-347-2688; Fax: 334-347-2095. Hours: 8AM-4:30PM (CST). *Probate.*

Colbert County

Circuit Court Colbert County Courthouse, 201 N Main St, Tuscumbia, AL 35674; 256-386-8512; Probate phone: 256-386-8542. Hours: 8AM-4:30PM (CST). *Felony, Civil Actions Over $10,000, Probate.*

Note: Probate court is separate from this court, and can be contacted at the telephone number above.

Civil Records: Access: Online, in person. Visitors must perform in person searches for themselves. No search fee. Required to search: name, years to search. Civil cases indexed by defendant, plaintiff. Civil records on computer from 1993, books from 1959. Online access at www.alacourt.com.

Criminal Records: Access: Online, in person. Visitors must perform in person searches for themselves. No search fee. Required to search: name, years to search; also helpful: DOB, SSN. Criminal records on computer from 1993, books prior. Online access at www.alacourt.com.

General Information: Public Access terminal is available. No sealed, youthful offenders or juvenile records released. Copy fee: $.25 per page. Cert fee: $1.00. Payee: Circuit Court Clerk. Business checks accepted. Prepayment required.

District Court Colbert County Courthouse, 201 N Main St, Tuscumbia, AL 35674; 256-386-8518. Hours: 8AM-Noon; 1PM-4:30PM (CST). *Misdemeanor, Civil Actions Under $10,000, Eviction, Small Claims.*

Civil Records: Access: Online, in person. Visitors must perform in person searches for themselves. No search fee. Required to search: name, years to search. Civil cases indexed by defendant, plaintiff. Civil records on computer from 1993, prior on books. Online access at www.alacourt.com.

Criminal Records: Access: Online, in person. Visitors must perform in person searches for themselves. No search fee. Required to search: name, years to search; also helpful: SSN. Criminal records on computer from 1993, prior on books. Online access via www.alacourt.com.

General Information: Public Access terminal is available. No sealed, adoptions, youthful offenders or juvenile records released. Copy fee: $.25 per page. Cert fee: $1.00. Payee: District Clerk. Only cashiers checks and money orders accepted. Prepayment required.

Conecuh County

Circuit & District Court PO Box 107, Evergreen, AL 36401; 251-578-2066; Probate phone: 251-578-1221. Hours: 8AM-4:30PM (CST). *Felony, Misdemeanor, Civil, Eviction, Small Claims, Probate.*

Note: Probate court is separate from this court, and can be contacted at the telephone number above.

Civil Records: Access: In person only. Both court and visitors may perform in person searches. No search fee. Required to search: name, years to search. Civil cases indexed by defendant, plaintiff. Civil records on index cards from 1977, on computer back to 12/1994. Online access at www.alacourt.com.

Criminal Records: Access: In person only. Both court and visitors may perform in person searches. No search fee. Required to search: name, years to search, DOB; also helpful: SSN. Criminal records on index cards from 1977, on computer back to 1994. Online access via www.alacourt.com.

General Information: Public Access terminal is available. No sealed, adoptions, youthful offenders or juvenile records released. Fee to fax results is $1.00 per page. Copy fee: $.50 per page. Cert fee: $2.50. Payee: Circuit Clerk, George Hendrix. Business checks accepted. Prepayment required.

Coosa County

Circuit & District Court PO Box 98, Rockford, AL 35136; 256-377-4988; Probate phone: 256-377-4919; Fax: 256-377-1599. Hours: 8AM-4:30PM (CST). *Felony, Misdemeanor, Civil, Eviction, Small Claims, Probate.*

Note: Probate court is separate from this court, and can be contacted at the telephone number above.

Civil Records: Access: Online, in person. Visitors must perform in person searches for themselves. No search fee. Required to search: name, years to search. Civil cases indexed by plaintiff. Civil records on books from the late 1800s, computerized records go back to July 1994. Online access at www.alacourt.com.

Criminal Records: Access: Online, in person, fax, mail. Visitors must perform in person searches for themselves. No search fee. Required to search: name, years to search; also helpful: DOB, SSN. Criminal records on books from the late 1800s, computerized records go back to July 1994. Online access via www.alacourt.com.

General Information: No sealed, adoptions, youthful offenders or juvenile records released. Copy fee: $.25 per page. Cert fee: $1.00. Payee: Clerk of Court. Business checks accepted. Prepayment required. Mail requests: SASE required. Mail turnaround time is 2-3 days.

Covington County

Circuit & District Court Covington County Courthouse, Andalusia, AL 36420; 334-428-2520; Probate phone: 334-428-2510. Hours: 8AM-5PM (CST). *Felony, Misdemeanor, Civil, Eviction, Small Claims, Probate.*

Note: Probate court is separate from this court, and can be contacted at the telephone number above.

Civil Records: Access: Online, in person. Both court and visitors may perform in person searches. Search fee: Copy fee only. Required to search: name, years to search. Civil cases indexed by defendant, plaintiff. Civil records on computer from 3/94; prior on books to 1920. Online access at www.alacourt.com. Also, online access to probate records is by subscription at www.recordsusa.com/Alabama/CovingtonCnAl.htm. Credit card-username-password required; choose monthly or per-use plan. Visit the website or call Lisa at 601-264-7701 for information.

Criminal Records: Access: Online, in person. Visitors must perform in person searches for themselves. Search fee: Copy fee only. Required to search: name, years to search, DOB; also helpful: SSN. Criminal records on computer from 3/94; prior on books to 1920. Online access via www.alacourt.com.

General Information: Public Access terminal is available. No sealed, adoptions, youthful offenders or juvenile records released. Copy fee: $.25 per page. Cert fee: $1.00. Payee: Circuit Clerk. Business checks accepted. Prepayment required.

Crenshaw County

Circuit & District Court PO Box 167, Luverne, AL 36049; 334-335-6575; Probate phone: 334-335-6568; Fax: 334-335-2076. Hours: 8AM-4:30PM (CST). *Felony, Misdemeanor, Civil, Eviction, Small Claims, Probate.*

Note: Probate court is separate from this court, and can be contacted at the telephone number above. Porbate Ct. address is PO Box 328, Luverne 36049.

Civil Records: Access: Mail, online, in person. Both court and visitors may perform in person searches. No search fee. Required to search: name, years to search. Civil cases indexed by defendant, plaintiff. Civil records on computer from 1993, on book from 1977. Online access at www.alacourt.com.

Criminal Records: Access: Mail, online, in person. Both court and visitors may perform in person searches. No search fee. Required to search: name, years to search, DOB; also helpful: SSN. Criminal records on computer from 1993, on book from 1977. Online access via www.alacourt.com.

General Information: Public Access terminal is available. No sealed, adoptions, youthful offenders or juvenile records released. Will fax results. Copy fee: $.50 per page. Cert fee: $1.00. Payee: Circuit Clerk. Only cashiers checks and money orders accepted. Mail requests: SASE requested. Turnaround time 2-3 days.

Cullman County

Circuit Court Cullman County Courthouse, Rm 303, 500 2nd Ave SW, Cullman, AL 35055; 256-775-4654; Probate phone: 256-775-4652. Hours: 8AM-4:30PM (CST). *Felony, Civil Actions Over $10,000, Probate.*

Civil Records: Access: Phone, mail, online, in person. Both court and visitors may perform in person searches. No search fee. Required to search: name, years to search. Civil cases indexed by defendant, plaintiff. Civil records on computer back to 1993, index back to 1977; books from 1900s. Online access at www.alacourt.com.

Criminal Records: Access: Mail, online, in person. Both court and visitors may perform in person searches. No search fee. Required to search: name, years to search, DOB; also helpful: SSN. Criminal records on computer back to 1993; index back to 1977; prior in books. Online access via www.alacourt.com.

General Information: Public Access terminal is available. No sealed, adoptions, youthful offenders or juvenile records released. Copy fee: $.25 per page. Add postage costs if by mail. Cert fee: $1.00 per document. Payee: Robert Bates, Circuit Clerk. Business checks accepted. Prepayment required. Mail requests: SASE not required. Mail turnaround time 10 days.

District Court 500 2nd Ave SW, Courthouse Rm 211, Cullman, AL 35055-4197; 256-775-4660. Hours: 8AM-4:30PM (CST). *Misdemeanor, Civil Actions Under $10,000, Eviction, Small Claims.*

Civil Records: Access: Mail, online, in person. Visitors must perform in person searches for themselves. No search fee. Required to search: name, years to search. Civil cases indexed by defendant. Civil records on computer from 11/92, on books 10 yrs back. Online access at www.alacourt.com.

Criminal Records: Access: Mail, online, in person. Visitors must perform in person searches for themselves. No search fee. Required to search: name, years to search, DOB; also helpful: SSN. Criminal records on computer from 11/92, on books 10 yrs back. Online access via www.alacourt.com.

General Information: Public Access terminal is available. No sealed, adoptions, youthful offenders or

juvenile records released. Copy fee: $.25 per page. Cert fee: $1.25. Payee: District Clerk. Only cashiers checks and money orders accepted. Prepayment required. Mail requests: SASE required. Mail turnaround time 1 week.

Dale County

Circuit & District Court PO Box 1350, Ozark, AL 36361; 334-774-5003; Probate phone: 334-774-2754. Hours: 8AM-4:30PM (CST). *Felony, Misdemeanor, Civil, Eviction, Small Claims, Probate.*

Note: Probate court is separate from this court, and can be contacted at the telephone number above.

Civil Records: Access: Online, in person. Visitors must perform in person searches for themselves. No search fee. Required to search: name, years to search. Civil cases indexed by defendant, plaintiff. Civil records on computer from 8/92, on books and index cards from the 1920s. Online access at www.alacourt.com.

Criminal Records: Access: Online, in person. Visitors must perform in person searches for themselves. No search fee. Required to search: name, years to search, DOB; also helpful: SSN. Criminal records on computer from 8/92, on books and index cards from the 1920s. Online access via www.alacourt.com.

General Information: Public Access terminal is available. No sealed, adoptions, youthful offenders or juvenile records released. Copy fee: $.25 per page. Cert fee: $1.00. Payee: Dale County Circuit Clerk. Only cashiers checks and money orders accepted. Prepayment required.

Dallas County

Circuit Court PO Box 1148, Selma, AL 36702; 334-874-2523. Hours: 8AM-5PM (CST). *Felony, Civil Actions Over $10,000, Probate.*

Note: Probate court is separate from this court, and can be contacted 334-876-4830.

Civil Records: Access: Mail, online, in person. Both court and visitors may perform in person searches. No search fee. Required to search: name, years to search. Civil cases indexed by defendant, plaintiff. Civil records on computer from 1980, on microfiche from the late 1800s, index books prior. Online access at www.alacourt.com.

Criminal Records: Access: Phone, mail, online, in person. Both court and visitors may perform in person searches. No search fee. Required to search: name, years to search, DOB; also helpful: SSN. Criminal records on computer from 1980, on microfiche from the late 1800s, index books prior. Online access via www.alacourt.com.

General Information: Public Access terminal is available. No sealed, adoptions, youthful offenders or juvenile records released. Copy fee: $.25 per page. Cert fee: $1.00. Payee: Dallas County Circuit Court. Personal checks accepted. Prepayment required. Mail requests: SASE required. Mail turnaround time less than 1 week for civil cases.

District Court PO Box 1148, Selma, AL 36702; 334-874-2523. Hours: 8AM-5PM (CST). *Misdemeanor, Civil Actions Under $10,000, Eviction, Small Claims.*

Note: Probate court is separate form this court, and can be reached at 334-876-4830.

Civil Records: Access: Phone, mail, online, in person. Visitors must perform in person searches for themselves. No search fee. Required to search: name, years to search. Civil cases indexed by defendant. Civil records on books from 1967, on computer since 1993. Online access at www.alacourt.com.

Criminal Records: Access: Mail, online, in person. Visitors must perform in person searches for themselves. No search fee. Required to search: name, years to search; also helpful: DOB, SSN. Criminal records on books from 1967, on computer since 1993. Online access via www.alacourt.com.

General Information: No sealed, adoptions, youthful offenders or juvenile records released. Copy fee: $.25 per page. Cert fee: $1.00. Payee: District Clerk. Personal checks accepted. Prepayment required.

De Kalb County

Circuit & District Court PO Box 681149, Fort Payne, AL 35968; 256-845-8525; Probate phone: 256-845-8510. Hours: 8AM-4PM (CST). *Felony, Misdemeanor, Civil, Eviction, Small Claims, Probate.*

Note: Probate court is separate from this court, and can be contacted at the telephone number above.

Civil Records: Access: Mail, online, in person. Both court and visitors may perform in person searches. No search fee. Required to search: name, years to search. Civil cases indexed by defendant. Civil records on computer from August 1991, on books from 1959. Online access at www.alacourt.com.

Criminal Records: Access: Mail, online, in person. Both court and visitors may perform in person searches. No search fee. Required to search: name, years to search; also helpful: DOB, SSN. Criminal records on computer from August 1991, on books from 1959. Online access via www.alacourt.com.

General Information: Public Access terminal is available. No sealed, adoptions, youthful offenders or juvenile records released. Copy fee: $.25 per page. Cert fee: $1.25. Business checks accepted. Turnaround time 1 week.

Elmore County

Circuit & District Court - Civil Division PO Box 310, Wetumpka, AL 36092; 334-567-1123; Probate phone: 334-567-1139; Fax: 334-567-5957. Hours: 8AM-4:30PM (CST). *Civil, Probate.*

Note: Probate court is separate from this court, but can be contacted at the telephone number above.

Civil Records: Access: Online, in person. Visitors must perform in person searches for themselves. No search fee. Required to search: name, years to search. Civil cases indexed by defendant, plaintiff. Civil records on computer from 1997, books from 1930. Online access at www.alacourt.com.

General Information: Public Access terminal is available. No sealed, adoptions, youthful offenders or juvenile records released. Copy fee: $.25 per page. Cert fee: $1.25. Payee: Circuit Court Clerk. Business checks accepted. Prepayment required.

Circuit Court - Criminal Division PO Box 310, 8935 US Hwy 23, Wetumpka, AL 36092; 334-567-1123; Fax: 334-567-5957. Hours: 8AM-4:30PM (CST). *Felony, Misdemeanor.*

Criminal Records: Access: Online, in person. Visitors must perform in person searches for themselves. No search fee. Required to search: name, years to search, DOB, SSN. Criminal records on computer from mid 1991, books from 1960-1992. Online access through SJIS. See state introduction.

General Information: Public Access terminal is available. No sealed, adoptions, youthful offenders or juvenile records released. Copy fee: $.25 per page. Cert fee: $1.00. Payee: Circuit Court Clerk. Only cashiers checks and money orders accepted. Prepayment required.

Escambia, County

Circuit & District Court PO Box 856, Brewton, AL 36427; 251-867-0305; Probate phone: 251-867-0201; Fax: 251-867-0365. Hours: 8AM-4:30PM (CST). *Felony, Misdemeanor, Civil, Eviction, Small Claims, Probate.*

Note: Probate court is separate from this court, and can be contacted at the telephone number above.

Civil Records: Access: Mail, fax, online, in person. Both court and visitors may perform in person searches. No search fee. Required to search: name, years to search. Civil cases indexed by defendant, plaintiff. Civil records on computer from 10/93, books and cards back to 1990. Online access at www.alacourt.com.

Criminal Records: Access: Mail, fax, online, in person. Both court and visitors may perform in person searches. No search fee. Required to search: name, years to search, DOB. Criminal records on computer from 10/93, books and cards back to 1950. Online access via www.alacourt.com.

General Information: Public Access terminal is available. No sealed, adoptions, youthful offenders or juvenile records released. Fee to fax results is $1.00 per document and $.25 per page. Copy fee: $.25 per page. Cert fee: $1.00. Payee: Escambia County Circuit Court. Business checks accepted. Prepayment required. Mail requests: SASE required. Mail turnaround time 2-3 days.

Etowah County

Circuit & District Court 801 Forrest Ave #202, Gadsden, AL 35901; 256-549-2150/5430; Probate phone: 256-549-5333. Hours: 8:30AM-4:30PM (CST). *Felony, Misdemeanor, Civil, Eviction, Small Claims.*

Note: Probate court is separate from this court.

Civil Records: Access: Mail, online, in person. Both court and visitors may perform in person searches. No search fee. Required to search: name, years to search. Civil cases indexed by defendant, plaintiff. Civil records on computer from 1984, index on computer since 1977, books prior to 1977. Online access at www.alacourt.com.

Criminal Records: Access: Mail, online, in person. Both court and visitors may perform in person searches. No search fee. Required to search: name, years to search; also helpful: DOB, SSN. Criminal records on computer from 1984, index on computer since 1977, books prior to 1977. Online access via www.alacourt.com.

General Information: Public Access terminal is available. No sealed, adoptions, youthful offenders or juvenile records released. Will not fax results. Copy fee: $.25 per page. Cert fee: $1.25. Payee: Clerk of Court. Only cashiers checks and money orders accepted. Prepayment required. Mail requests: SASE requested. Turnaround time 4-6 weeks.

Probate Court 801 Forest Ave, #202, Gadsden, AL 35901; 256-549-2150; Fax: 256-546-1149. *Probate.*

Fayette County

Circuit & District Court PO Box 906, Fayette, AL 35555; 205-932-4617; Probate phone: 205-932-4519. Hours: 8AM-4:30PM (CST). *Felony, Misdemeanor, Civil, Eviction, Small Claims, Probate.*

Note: Probate court is separate from this court, and can be contacted at the telephone number above.

Civil Records: Access: Online, mail, fax, in person. Visitors must perform in person searches for themselves. No search fee. Required to search: name, years to search. Civil cases indexed by defendant.

Civil records on computer from 3/94, on books and cards from 1977. Online access at www.alacourt.com.

Criminal Records: Access: Online, mail, fax, in person. Visitors must perform in person searches for themselves. No search fee. Required to search: name, years to search, DOB; also helpful: SSN. Criminal records on computer from 3/94, on books and cards from 1977. Online access via www.alacourt.com.

General Information: Public Access terminal is available. No sealed, adoptions, youthful offenders or juvenile records released. Copy fee: $.25 per page. Cert fee: $1.00. Payee: Circuit Clerk. Business checks accepted. Prepayment required.

Franklin County

Circuit & District Court PO Box 160, Russellville, AL 35653; 256-332-8861; Probate phone: 256-332-8802. Hours: 8AM-4:30PM (CST). *Felony, Misdemeanor, Civil, Eviction, Small Claims, Probate.*

Note: Probate court is separate from this court, and can be contacted at the telephone number above or PO Box 70.

Civil Records: Access: Mail, online, in person. Both court and visitors may perform in person searches. No search fee. Required to search: name, years to search; also helpful: address. Civil cases indexed by defendant, plaintiff. Civil records on computer from 1993, on index books prior. SSN and DOB helpful, but records are not indexed by SSN. Online access at www.alacourt.com.

Criminal Records: Access: Mail, online, in person. Both court and visitors may perform in person searches. No search fee. Required to search: name, years to search, DOB; also helpful: SSN. Criminal records on computer from 1993, on index books prior. SSN and DOB helpful, but records are not indexed by SSN. Online access via www.alacourt.com.

General Information: Public Access terminal is available. No sealed, youthful offenders or juvenile released. Copy fee: $.25 per page. Cert fee: $1.00. Payee: Circuit Court Clerk. Business checks accepted. Prepayment required. Mail requests: SASE required. Mail turnaround time 3-4 days.

Geneva County

Circuit & District Court PO Box 86, Geneva, AL 36340; 334-684-5620; Probate phone: 334-684-5640; Fax: 334-684-5605. Hours: 8AM-5PM (CST). *Felony, Misdemeanor, Civil, Eviction, Small Claims, Probate.*

Note: Probate court is separate from this court, and can be contacted at the telephone number above.

Civil Records: Access: Mail, online, in person. Visitors must perform in person searches for themselves. No search fee. Required to search: name, years to search; also helpful: address. Civil cases indexed by defendant, plaintiff. Civil records on computer from 1992, index cards from the 1950s. Online access at www.alacourt.com.

Criminal Records: Access: Mail, online, in person. Visitors must perform in person searches for themselves. No search fee. Required to search: name, years to search, DOB; also helpful: SSN. Criminal records on computer from 1992, index cards from the 1950s. Online access via www.alacourt.com.

General Information: Public Access terminal is available. No sealed, adoptions, youthful offenders or juvenile records released. Copy fee: $.25 per page. Cert fee: $1.50. Payee: Circuit Clerk, Valerie Thomley. Business checks accepted. Out of state personal checks not accepted. Prepayment required. Mail requests: SASE not required. Mail turnaround time 1 week.

Greene County

Circuit & District Court PO Box 307, Eutaw, AL 35462; 205-372-3598; Probate phone: 205-372-3340. Hours: 8AM-12;00-1-4;30PM (CST). *Felony, Misdemeanor, Civil, Eviction, Small Claims, Probate.*

Note: Probate court is separate from this court, and can be contacted at the telephone number above.

Civil Records: Access: Mail, online, in person. Both court and visitors may perform in person searches. No search fee. Required to search: name, years to search; also helpful: DOB, SSN and signed release. Civil cases indexed by defendant, plaintiff. Civil records on books from 1984. Online access at www.alacourt.com.

Criminal Records: Access: Mail, online, in person. Visitors must perform in person searches for themselves. No search fee. Required to search: name, years to search; also helpful: DOB, SSN and signed release. Criminal records on books from 1984. Online access via www.alacourt.com.

General Information: Public Access terminal is available. No sealed, adoptions, youthful offenders or juvenile records released. Copy fee: $.25 per page. Cert fee: $1.25. Payee: Circuit Clerk. Business checks accepted. Prepayment required. Mail requests: SASE required. Mail turnaround time 1 week.

Hale County

Circuit & District Court Hale County Courthouse, Rm 8, PO Drawer 99, Greensboro, AL 36744; 334-624-4334; Probate phone: 334-624-8740. Hours: 8AM-4;30PM (CST). *Felony, Misdemeanor, Civil, Eviction, Small Claims, Probate.*

Note: Probate court is separate from this court, and can be contacted at the telephone number above.

Civil Records: Access: Mail, online, in person. Both court and visitors may perform in person searches. No search fee. Required to search: name, years to search. Civil cases indexed by defendant, plaintiff. Civil records on books from 1985. Online access at www.alacourt.com.

Criminal Records: Access: Mail, online, in person. Both court and visitors may perform in person searches. No search fee. Required to search: name, years to search; also helpful: DOB, SSN. Criminal records on books from 1985. Online access via www.alacourt.com.

General Information: No sealed, adoptions, youthful offenders or juvenile records released. Will fax results to local and toll free lines. Copy fee: $.25 per page. Cert fee: $1.00. Payee: Clerk of the Court. Business checks accepted. No personal checks accepted. Prepayment required. Mail requests: SASE required. Mail turnaround time 1 week.

Henry County

Circuit & District Court 101 W Court St, #J, Abbeville, AL 36310-2135; 334-585-2753; Probate phone: 334-585-3257; Fax: 334-585-5006. Hours: 8AM-4:30PM (CST). *Felony, Misdemeanor, Civil, Eviction, Small Claims, Probate.*

Note: Probate court is separate from this court, and can be contacted at the telephone number above.

Civil Records: Access: Mail, online, in person. Both court and visitors may perform in person searches. Search fee: $3.00 per name. Required to search: name, years to search. Civil cases indexed by defendant. Civil records on computer from 1994, index cards 10 yrs back. Online access at www.alacourt.com.

Criminal Records: Access: Mail, online, in person. Both court and visitors may perform in person searches. Search fee: $3.00 per name. Required to search: name, years to search, DOB; also helpful:

SSN. Criminal records on computer from 5/93, index cards 10 yrs back. Online access via www.alacourt.com.

General Information: Public Access terminal is available. No sealed, adoptions, youthful offenders or juvenile records released. Copy fee: $.25 per page. Cert fee: $1.00. Payee: Circuit Clerk. Personal checks are not accepted. Prepayment required. Mail requests: SASE required. Mail turnaround time 2-3 days.

Houston County

Circuit & District Court PO Drawer 6406, Dothan, AL 36302; 334-677-4800/4872; Civil phone: Circ-334-677-4858; Dist-334-677-4868; Criminal phone: Circ-334-677-4863; Dist-334-677-4872; Probate phone: 334-677-4719. Hours: 7:30AM-4:30PM (CST). *Felony, Misdemeanor, Civil, Eviction, Small Claims, Probate.*

Note: Probate court is separate from this court, and can be contacted at the telephone number above.

Civil Records: Access: Mail, online, in person. Both court and visitors may perform in person searches. No search fee. Required to search: name, years to search. Civil cases indexed by defendant. Civil records on computer from 1977, index books from 1950s. Online access at www.alacourt.com.

Criminal Records: Access: Mail, online, in person. Both court and visitors may perform in person searches. No search fee. Required to search: name, years to search; also helpful: DOB, SSN. Criminal records on computer from 1977, index books from 1950s. Online access via www.alacourt.com.

General Information: Public Access terminal is available. No sealed, adoptions, youthful offenders or juvenile records released. Copy fee: $.25 per page. Cert fee: $1.00. Payee: Judy Byrd. Business checks accepted. Prepayment required. Mail turnaround time 1 week.

Jackson County

Circuit & District Court PO Box 397, Scottsboro, AL 35768; 256-574-9320; Civil phone: 256-574-9320; Criminal phone: 256-574-9320; Probate phone: 256-574-9290; Fax: 256-259-9981. Hours: 8AM-4:30PM (CST). *Felony, Misdemeanor, Civil, Eviction, Small Claims, Probate.*

Note: Probate court is at a separate office at the courthouse (PO Box 128) and can be contacted at the telephone number above or 256-574-9295.

Civil Records: Access: Mail, fax, online, in person. Both court and visitors may perform in person searches. No search fee. Required to search: name, years to search. Civil cases indexed by defendant. Civil records on computer from 5/1993, on cards from 1977. Online access at www.alacourt.com.

Criminal Records: Access: Mail, fax, online, in person. Both court and visitors may perform in person searches. No search fee. Required to search: name, years to search, DOB; also helpful: SSN. Criminal records on computer from 5/1993, on cards from 1977. Online access via www.alacourt.com.

General Information: Public Access terminal is available. No sealed, adoptions, youthful offenders or juvenile records released. Will fax results only if situation urgent enough to require quick return. Copy fee: $.25 per page. Cert fee: $2.00. Payee: Circuit Court Clerk. Only cashiers checks and money orders accepted. Prepayment required. Mail requests: SASE required. Mail turnaround time 1-2 weeks.

Jefferson County

Circuit Court - Bessemer Division Rm 606, Courthouse Annex, Bessemer, AL 35020; 205-481-4165. Hours: 8AM-5PM (CST). *Felony, Civil Actions Over $10,000.*

Civil Records: Access: Online, in person. Visitors must perform in person searches for themselves. No search fee. Required to search: name, years to search. Civil cases indexed by defendant, plaintiff. Civil records on computer from 1988, on index books from 1930s to 1977. Online access at www.alacourt.com.

Criminal Records: Access: Online, in person. Visitors must perform in person searches for themselves. No search fee. Required to search: name, years to search, DOB; also helpful: SSN. Criminal records on computer from 1988, on index books from 1930s to 1977. Online access via www.alacourt.com. Also, search imates (sheriff) at www.jeffcosheriff.org/sheriff/.

General Information: Public Access terminal is available. No sealed, adoptions, youthful offenders or juvenile records released. Copy fee: $.25 per page. Cert fee: $1.25. Payee: Clerk of Circuit Court. Only cashiers checks and money orders accepted. Prepayment required.

District Court - Bessemer Division Rm 506, Courthouse Annex, Bessemer, AL 35020; 205-481-4187. Hours: 8AM-5PM (CST). *Misdemeanor, Civil Actions Under $10,000, Eviction, Small Claims.*

Civil Records: Access: Online, in person. Visitors must perform in person searches for themselves. No search fee. Required to search: name, years to search. Civil cases indexed by defendant, plaintiff. Civil records on computer from 1986, on index cards from 1977, prior on docket books. Online access at www.alacourt.com.

Criminal Records: Access: Online, in person, mail. Visitors must perform in person searches for themselves. No search fee. Required to search: name, years to search, DOB; also helpful: SSN. Criminal records on computer from 1986, on index cards from 1977, prior on docket books. Online access via www.alacourt.com.

General Information: Public Access terminal is available. No sealed, adoptions, youthful offenders or juvenile records released. Copy fee: $.25 per page. Cert fee: $1.25. Payee: Bessemer District Court. Business checks accepted. Prepayment required. Mail requests: SASE required. Mail turnaround time is varies.

Circuit Court - Birmingham Civil Division 716 N 21st St, Rm 400, Birmingham, AL 35263; 205-325-5355. Hours: 8AM-5PM (CST). *Civil Actions Over $10,000 (Over $5,000 if jury trial).*

Civil Records: Access: Phone, mail, online, in person. Both court and visitors may perform in person searches. No search fee. Required to search: name, years to search. Civil cases indexed by defendant, plaintiff. Civil records on computer from 1976, on index books from 1976 to 1986, prior to 1976 archived. Online access at www.alacourt.com.

General Information: Public Access terminal is available. No sealed, adoptions, youthful offenders or juvenile records released. Copy fee: $.25 per page. Cert fee: $1.25. Payee: Clerk of Circuit Court. Business checks accepted. Prepayment required. Mail turnaround time 1-2 weeks.

Circuit Court - Birmingham Criminal Division 801 Richard Arrington Blvd, Rm 901, Birmingham, AL 35263; 205-325-5285. Hours: 8AM-4:55PM (CST). *Felony.*

Criminal Records: Access: Online, in person. Visitors must perform in person searches for themselves. No search fee. Required to search: name, years to search, DOB, signed release; also helpful: address, SSN. Criminal records on computer from 1960s, index books prior. Online access through SJIS. See state introduction.

General Information: Public Access terminal is available. No sealed, adoptions, youthful offenders, sex offender cases or juvenile records released. Copy fee: $.25 per page. Cert fee: $1.00. Payee: Clerk of Court. Only cashiers checks and money orders accepted. Prepayment required.

District Court - Birmingham Civil Division 716 Richard Arrington BLVD N, Birmingham, AL 35203; 205-325-5331. Hours: 8AM-5PM (CST). *Civil Actions Under $10,000, Eviction, Small Claims.*

Civil Records: Access: Phone, mail, online, in person. Both court and visitors may perform in person searches. No search fee. Required to search: name, years to search. Civil cases indexed by defendant, plaintiff. Civil records on computer from 1977, index books stored in warehouse. Online access at www.alacourt.com.

General Information: Public Access terminal is available. No sealed, adoptions, youthful offenders or juvenile records released. Copy fee: $.25 per page. Cert fee: $1.00. Payee: District Court. Only cashiers checks and money orders accepted. Prepayment required. Mail requests: SASE required. Mail turnaround time 1-2 days.

District Court - Birmingham Criminal Division 801 Richard Arrington Blvd N, Rm 207, Birmingham, AL 35203; 205-325-5309. Hours: 8AM-5PM (CST). *Misdemeanor.*

Criminal Records: Access: Mail, online, in person. Both court and visitors may perform in person searches. Search fee: $1.25. Required to search: name, DOB; also helpful: years to search, SSN, sex, date of arrest. Criminal records on computer from 1986. To search for records prior to 1987, require arrest date. Online access through SJIS. See state introduction.

General Information: Public Access terminal is available. No sealed, sexual abuse, adoptions, youthful offenders or juvenile records released. Copy fee: $.25 per page. Cert fee: $1.25. Payee: District Court. Only cashiers checks and money orders accepted. Prepayment required. Mail requests: SASE required. Mail turnaround time 5-10 days.

Probate Court 716 Richard Arrington Jr Blvd N., Birmingham, AL 35203; 205-325-5420/5411; Fax: 205-325-4885. Hours: 8AM-4:45PM (CST). *Probate.*

Lamar County

Circuit & District Court PO Box 434, Vernon, AL 35592; 205-695-7193; Probate phone: 205-695-9119; Fax: 205-695-1871. Hours: 8AM-4:30PM (CST). *Felony, Misdemeanor, Civil, Eviction, Small Claims, Probate.*

Note: Probate court is separate from this court, and can be contacted at the telephone number above.

Civil Records: Access: Mail, online, in person. Visitors must perform in person searches for themselves. No search fee. Required to search: name, years to search; also helpful: address. Civil cases indexed by defendant, plaintiff. Civil records on books from 1900; computerized records go back to 1995. Online access at www.alacourt.com.

Criminal Records: Access: Mail, fax, online, in person. Visitors must perform in person searches for themselves. No search fee. Required to search: name, years to search, DOB, signed release; also helpful: SSN. Criminal records on books from 1900; computerized records go back to 1995. Online access via www.alacourt.com.

General Information: Public Access terminal is available. No sealed, adoptions, youthful offenders or juvenile records released. Copy fee: $.25 per page. Cert fee: $2.25. Payee: Circuit Clerk. Only cashiers checks and money orders accepted. Prepayment required. Will bill copy fees. Mail requests: SASE required. Mail turnaround time 1-2 days.

Lauderdale County

Circuit Court PO Box 795, Florence, AL 35631; 256-760-5710; Criminal phone: 256-760-5713; Probate phone: 256-760-5800. Hours: 8AM-Noon, 1-5PM (CST). *Felony, Civil Actions Over $10,000, Probate.*

Note: Probate court is separate from this court, and can be contacted at the telephone number above.

Civil Records: Access: Online, in person. Visitors must perform in person searches for themselves. No search fee. Required to search: name, years to search. Civil cases indexed by defendant, plaintiff. Civil records on computer from 1977, index books from the 1930s. Online access at www.alacourt.com.

Criminal Records: Access: Online, in person. Visitors must perform in person searches for themselves. No search fee. Required to search: name, years to search, DOB; also helpful: SSN. Criminal records on computer from 1977, index books from the 1930s. Online access via www.alacourt.com.

General Information: Public Access terminal is available. No sealed, adoptions, youthful offenders or juvenile records released. Copy fee: $.25 per page. Cert fee: $1.00. Payee: Circuit Court Clerk. Personal checks accepted. Prepayment required.

District Court PO Box 776, Florence, AL 35631; 256-760-5726; Civil phone: 256-760-5722; Criminal phone: 256-760-5724; Fax: 256-760-5727. Hours: 8AM-Noon, 1-5PM (CST). *Misdemeanor, Civil Actions Under $10,000, Eviction, Small Claims.*

Civil Records: Access: Mail, fax, online, in person. Visitors must perform in person searches for themselves. No search fee. Required to search: name, years to search. Civil cases indexed by defendant, plaintiff. Civil records on computer from 1986, books from the 1930s. Online access at www.alacourt.com.

Criminal Records: Access: Mail, fax, online, in person. Visitors must perform in person searches for themselves. No search fee. Required to search: name, years to search, DOB; also helpful: SSN. Criminal records on computer from 1986, books from the 1930s. Online access via www.alacourt.com.

General Information: Public Access terminal is available. No sealed, adoptions, youthful offenders or juvenile records released. No fee to fax results. Copy fee: $.25 per page. Cert fee: $1.00. Payee: Circuit Clerk. Personal checks accepted. Prepayment required. Mail turnaround time 1 week.

Lawrence County

Circuit & District Court PO Box 249, Moulton, AL 35650; 256-974-2432; Civil phone: 256-974-2435; Criminal phone: 256-974-2436; Probate phone: 256-974-2439. Hours: 8AM-4PM (CST). *Felony, Misdemeanor, Civil, Eviction, Small Claims, Probate.*

Note: Probate court is separate from this court, and can be contacted at the telephone number above.

Civil Records: Access: Online, in person. Visitors must perform in person searches for themselves. No search fee. Required to search: name, years to search.

Civil cases indexed by defendant. Civil records on computer from mid-1994, on books and index cards from 1920s. Online access at www.alacourt.com.

Criminal Records: Access: Online, in person. Visitors must perform in person searches for themselves. No search fee. Required to search: name, years to search; also helpful: DOB, SSN. Criminal records on computer from mid-1994, on books and index cards from 1920s. Online access via www.alacourt.com.

General Information: Public Access terminal is available. No sealed, adoption, youthful offender, juvenile records released. Copy fee: $.25 per page. Cert fee: $1.00. Payee: Clerk. Prepayment required.

Lee County

Circuit & District Court 2311 Gateway Dr, Rm 104, Opelika, AL 36801; 334-749-7141; Fax: 334-737-3520. Hours: 8:30AM-4:30PM (CST). *Felony, Misdemeanor, Civil, Eviction, Small Claims.*

Note: Probate court is separate from this court, and can be contacted at 334-745-9761 or at Lee County Courthouse, 215 S 9 St, Opelika, AL 36801.

Civil Records: Access: Phone, mail, online, in person. Only the court performs in person searches; visitors may not. No search fee. Required to search: name, years to search. Civil cases indexed by defendant, plaintiff. Civil records on computer from 1980s, on index cards from 1988. Online access at www.alacourt.com.

Criminal Records: Access: Phone, mail, online, in person. Only the court performs in person searches; visitors may not. No search fee. Required to search: name, years to search; also helpful: DOB, SSN. Criminal records on computer from 1980s, on index cards from 1988. Online access via www.alacourt.com.

General Information: No sealed, adoptions, youthful offenders or juvenile records released. Copy fee: $.50 per page. Cert fee: $1.00. Payee: Clerk's Office. Only cashiers checks and money orders accepted. Mail requests: SASE required. Mail turnaround time 1 week.

Limestone County

Circuit & District Court 200 Washington St West, Athens, AL 35611; 256-233-6406; Probate phone: 256-233-6427. Hours: 8AM-4:30PM (CST). *Felony, Misdemeanor, Civil, Eviction, Small Claims, Probate.*

Note: Probate court is separate from this court, and can be contacted at the telephone number above.

Civil Records: Access: Mail, online, in person. Both court and visitors may perform in person searches. No search fee. Required to search: name, years to search. Civil cases indexed by defendant, plaintiff. Civil records on computer since 1992; prior in docket books. Online access at www.alacourt.com.

Criminal Records: Access: Mail, in person, online. Both court and visitors may perform in person searches. No search fee. Required to search: name, years to search, DOB; also helpful: SSN, sex. Criminal records on computer since 1992, prior in docket books. Online access via www.alacourt.com.

General Information: Public Access terminal is available. No juvenile, youthful offender records released. Copy fee: $.25 per page. Cert fee: $1.00. Payee: Clerk of Court. Personal checks accepted. Prepayment required. Mail requests: SASE required. Mail turnaround time 2 weeks.

Lowndes County

Circuit & District Court PO Box 876, Hayneville, AL 36040; 334-548-2252; Probate phone: 334-548-2365. Hours: 8AM-4:30PM (CST). *Felony, Misdemeanor, Civil, Eviction, Small Claims, Probate.*

Note: Probate court is separate from this court, and can be contacted at the telephone number above.

Civil Records: Access: Mail, online, in person. Both court and visitors may perform in person searches. Search fee: $10.00 per name. Required to search: name, years to search. Civil cases indexed by defendant, plaintiff. Civil records on index cards from 1977; computerized since 1996. Online access at www.alacourt.com.

Criminal Records: Access: Mail, online, in person. Both court and visitors may perform in person searches. Search fee: $10.00 per name. Required to search: name, years to search; also helpful: DOB, SSN. Criminal records on index cards from 1977; computerized since 1996. Online access via www.alacourt.com.

General Information: Public Access terminal is available. No sealed, adoptions, youthful offenders or juvenile records released. Will fax results to local or toll free line. Copy fee: $.25 per page. Cert fee: $1.00. Payee: District Court Clerk. Business checks accepted. Mail requests: SASE required. Mail turnaround time up to 1 week.

Macon County

Circuit & District Court PO Box 830723, Tuskegee, AL 36083; 334-724-2614; Probate phone: 334-724-2611. Hours: 8AM-12;00-1-4:30PM (CST). *Felony, Misdemeanor, Civil, Eviction, Small Claims, Probate.*

Note: Probate court is separate from this court, and can be contacted at the telephone number above.

Civil Records: Access: Mail, online, in person. Both court and visitors may perform in person searches. Search fee: $10.00 per name. Required to search: name, years to search. Civil cases indexed by defendant, plaintiff. Civil records on index books from 1977; on computer back to 1993. Online access at www.alacourt.com.

Criminal Records: Access: Mail, online, in person. Only the court performs in person searches; visitors may not. Search fee: $10.00 per name. Required to search: name, years to search; also helpful: DOB, SSN. Criminal records go back to 1977; on computer back to 1993. Online access via www.alacourt.com.

General Information: No sealed, adoption, youthful offender, juvenile records released. Will fax results to local or toll free line. Copy fee: $.25 per page. Cert fee: $2.50 per page. Payee: Office of Circuit Clerk. Business checks accepted. Prepayment required. Mail requests: SASE not required. Mail turnaround time 30 days.

Madison County

Circuit Court - Civil 100 N Side Square, Courthouse, Huntsville, AL 35801; 256-532-3381; Probate phone: 256-532-3330. Hours: 8AM-5PM (CST). *Civil Actions Over $10,000, Probate.*

Note: Probate court is separate from this court, and can be contacted at the telephone number above

Civil Records: Access: Online, in person. Visitors must perform in person searches for themselves. No search fee. Required to search: name, years to search; also helpful: address. Civil cases indexed by defendant, plaintiff. Civil records on computer from 1977, index books from 1937. Online access through SJIS. See state introduction.

General Information: Public Access terminal is available. No sealed, adoptions, youthful offenders or juvenile records released. Copy fee: $.25 per page. Cert fee: $1.00. Personal checks accepted. Prepayment required.

Circuit Court - Criminal
100 N Side Square, Courthouse, Huntsville, AL 35801-4820; 256-532-3386. Hours: 8:30AM-5PM (CST). *Felony.*

Criminal Records: Access: Online, in person. Visitors must perform in person searches for themselves. No search fee. Required to search: name, years to search; also helpful: DOB, SSN. Criminal records on computer from 1977, books from 1937. Online access through SJIS. See state introduction.

General Information: Public Access terminal is available. No sealed, adoptions, youthful offenders or juvenile records released. Copy fee: $.25 per page. Cert fee: $1.25. Payee: Circuit Court Clerk. Personal checks accepted. Prepayment required.

District Court
100 N Side Square, Rm 822 Courthouse, Huntsville, AL 35801; Civil phone: 256-532-3622; Criminal phone: 256-532-3373; Fax: 256-532-6972. Hours: 8:30AM-5PM (CST). *Misdemeanor, Civil Actions Under $10,000, Eviction, Small Claims.*

Civil Records: Access: Online, in person. Visitors must perform in person searches for themselves. No search fee. Required to search: name, years to search. Civil cases indexed by defendant, plaintiff. Civil records on computer from 1982, index books prior. Online access at www.alacourt.com.

Criminal Records: Access: Online, in person. Visitors must perform in person searches for themselves. No search fee. Required to search: name, years to search; also helpful: DOB, SSN. Criminal records on computer from 1982, index books prior since 1979. Online access via www.alacourt.com.

General Information: Public Access terminal is available. No sealed, adoptions, youthful offenders or juvenile records released. Copy fee: $.25 per page. Cert fee: $1.25. Payee: District Court. Only cashiers checks and money orders accepted. Prepayment required.

Marengo County

Circuit & District Court
PO Box 480566, Linden, AL 36748; 334-295-2220. Hours: 8AM-4:30PM (CST). *Felony, Misdemeanor, Civil, Eviction, Small Claims, Probate.*

Civil Records: Access: Mail, online, in person. Both court and visitors may perform in person searches. No search fee. Required to search: name, years to search. Civil cases indexed by defendant, plaintiff. Civil records on computer from 6/94, on books and index cards from 1965. Online access at www.alacourt.com.

Criminal Records: Access: Mail, online, in person. Both court and visitors may perform in person searches. No search fee. Required to search: name, years to search; also helpful: DOB, SSN. Criminal records on computer from 6/94, on books and index cards from 1965. Online access via www.alacourt.com.

General Information: Public Access terminal is available. No sealed, adoptions, youthful offenders or juvenile records released. Copy fee: $.25 per page. Cert fee: $1.00. Payee: Circuit Clerk. Business checks accepted. Prepayment required. Mail turnaround time 1 week.

Marion County

Circuit & District Court
PO Box 1595, Hamilton, AL 35570; 205-921-7451; Probate phone: 205-921-2471. Hours: 8AM-5PM (CST). *Felony, Misdemeanor, Civil, Eviction, Small Claims, Probate.*

Note: Probate court is separate from this court, and can be contacted at the telephone number above.

Civil Records: Access: Mail, online, in person. Both court and visitors may perform in person searches. No search fee. Required to search: name, years to search. Civil cases indexed by plaintiff. Civil cases indexed by defendant, plaintiff. Civil records on computer from 5/94, on books from 1950s. Online access at www.alacourt.com.

Criminal Records: Access: Mail, online, in person. Both court and visitors may perform in person searches. No search fee. Required to search: name, years to search; also helpful: DOB, SSN. Criminal records on computer from 5/94, on books from 1950s. Online access via www.alacourt.com.

General Information: Public Access terminal is available. No sealed, adoptions, youthful offenders or juvenile records released. Copy fee: $.50 per page. Cert fee: $1.50. Payee: Circuit Clerk. Only cashiers checks and money orders accepted. Mail requests: SASE required. Mail turnaround time 7-10 days.

Marshall County

Circuit & District Court - Albertville Division
133 S.Emmet St., Albertville, AL 35950; 256-878-4522/4521/4515. Hours: 8AM-4:30PM (CST). *Felony, Misdemeanor, Civil, Eviction, Small Claims.*

Civil Records: Access: Mail, online, in person. Both court and visitors may perform in person searches. No search fee. Required to search: name, years to search. Civil cases indexed by defendant. Civil records on computer from 8/92, on index books from 1974. Online access at www.alacourt.com.

Criminal Records: Access: In person only. Both court and visitors may perform in person searches. No search fee. Required to search: name, years to search, DOB; also helpful: SSN. Criminal records on computer from 8/92, on index books from 1974. Online access via www.alacourt.com.

General Information: Public Access terminal is available. No sealed, adoptions, youthful offenders or juvenile records released. Copy fee: $.25 per page. Cert fee: $1.25. Payee: Clerk of Courts. Business checks accepted. Prepayment required.

Circuit Court - Guntersville Civil Division
424 Blount Ave #201, Guntersville, AL 35976; 256-571-7788; Probate phone: 256-571-7764. Hours: 8AM-12;00-1-4:30PM (CST). *Civil Actions Over $10,000, Small Claims, Probate.*

Note: Probate court is separate from this court, and can be contacted at the telephone number above

Civil Records: Access: Online, in person. Visitors must perform in person searches for themselves. No search fee. Required to search: name, years to search. Civil cases indexed by defendant, plaintiff. Civil records on computer for past 3 years, on index books early 1900s. Online access through SJIS. See state introduction.

General Information: Public Access terminal is available. No sealed, adoptions, youthful offenders or juvenile records released. Copy fee: $.25 per page. Cert fee: $1.00. Payee: Circuit Clerk. Business checks accepted. Prepayment required. Mail requests: SASE required.

Circuit Court - Guntersville Criminal Division
424 Blount Ave #201, Guntersville, AL 35976; 256-571-7791. Hours: 8AM-12;00-1-4:30PM (CST). *Felony, Misdemeanor.*

Criminal Records: Access: Online, In person. Visitors must perform in person searches for themselves. No search fee. Required to search: name, years to search; also helpful: DOB, SSN. Criminal records on computer from 1992, on index books from 1984, prior back to 1930s. Online access through SJIS. See state introduction.

General Information: Public Access terminal is available. No sealed, adoptions, youthful offenders or

juvenile records released. Copy fee: $.25 per page. Cert fee: $1.00. Payee: Circuit Clerk. Business checks accepted. Prepayment required.

Mobile County

Circuit Court
205 Government St #C-913, Mobile, AL 36644-2913; 251-574-8786. Hours: 8AM-5PM (CST). *Felony, Civil Actions Over $10,000.*

Civil Records: Access: Online, in person. Visitors must perform in person searches for themselves. No search fee. Required to search: name, years to search. Civil cases indexed by defendant. Civil records on computer from 1977, microfiche from early 1900s. Online access at www.alacourt.com.

Criminal Records: Access: Online, in person. Visitors must perform in person searches for themselves. No search fee. Required to search: name, years to search; also helpful: DOB, SSN. Criminal records on computer from 1977, microfiche from early 1900s. Online access via www.alacourt.com.

General Information: Public Access terminal is available. No sealed, adoptions, youthful offenders or juvenile records released. Copy fee: $.25 per page. Cert fee: $1.25. Payee: Circuit Clerk. Only cashiers checks and money orders accepted. Prepayment required.

District Court
205 Government St, Mobile, AL 36644; 251-574-8520, 251-690-8525 (small claims); Civil phone: 251-574-8526; Criminal phone: 251-574-8511; Probate phone: 251-574-8502; Fax: 251-574-4840. Hours: 8AM-5PM (CST). *Misdemeanor, Civil Actions Under $10,000, Eviction, Small Claims, Probate.*

Note: Probate court is a separate court and can be reached at the telephone number given above.

Civil Records: Access: Phone, fax, mail, online, in person. Both court and visitors may perform in person searches. No search fee. Required to search: name, years to search. Civil cases indexed by defendant, plaintiff. Civil records on computer from 1977, index books from 1950s. Online access at www.alacourt.com. Access to the Probate court's recordings database is free at www.mobilecounty.org/probatecourt/recordssearch.htm. A second search is at www.mobilecounty.org/probatecourt/judicial.asp.

Criminal Records: Access: Phone, fax, mail, online, in person. Both court and visitors may perform in person searches. No search fee. Required to search: name, years to search, DOB; also helpful: SSN. Criminal records on computer from 1977, index books from 1950s. Online access via www.alacourt.com.

General Information: Public Access terminal is available. No sealed, youthful offenders, protected files or juvenile records released. Will not fax results. Copy fee: $.25 per page. Cert fee: $1.25. Payee: Clerk, District Court. Business checks accepted if pre-approved. Prepayment required. Mail requests: SASE required. Mail turnaround time 7 days.

Monroe County

Circuit & District Court
County Courthouse, 65 N Alabama Ave, Monroeville, AL 36460; 251-743-2283; Probate phone: 251-743-4107. Hours: 8AM-5PM (CST). *Felony, Misdemeanor, Civil, Eviction, Small Claims, Probate.*

Note: Probate court is separate from this court, and can be contacted at the telephone number above.

Civil Records: Access: Mail, online, in person. Both court and visitors may perform in person searches. No search fee. Required to search: name, years to search. Civil cases indexed by defendant. Civil records on index cards from 1977 and on computer since July 1994. Online access at www.alacourt.com.

Criminal Records: Access: Mail, online, in person. Both court and visitors may perform in person searches. No search fee. Required to search: name, years to search; also helpful: DOB, SSN. Criminal records on index cards from 1977 and on computer since July 1994. Online access via www.alacourt.com.

General Information: Public Access terminal is available. No sealed, adoptions, youthful offenders or juvenile records released. Copy fee: $.25 per page. Cert fee: $1.25 per page. Payee: John Sawyer, Circuit Clerk. Business checks accepted. Prepayment required. Mail requests: SASE required. Mail turnaround time 1 week.

Montgomery County

Circuit Court PO Box 1667, Montgomery, AL 36102-1667; 334-832-1260; Probate phone: 334-832-1237. Hours: 8AM-1100-11;30- 4PM (CST). *Felony, Civil Actions Over $10,000, Probate.*

Note: Probate court is separate from this court, and can be contacted at the telephone number above.

Civil Records: Access: Mail, online, in person. Both court and visitors may perform in person searches. No search fee. Required to search: name, years to search. Civil cases indexed by defendant, plaintiff. Civil records on computer from 1982, microfiche from 1976. Online access at www.alacourt.com.

Criminal Records: Access: Mail, online, in person. Both court and visitors may perform in person searches. No search fee. Required to search: name, years to search; also helpful: DOB, SSN. Criminal records on computer from 1982, microfiche from 1976. Online access via www.alacourt.com.

General Information: Public Access terminal is available. No sealed, youthful offenders or juvenile records released. Copy fee: $.25 per page. Cert fee: $1.25. Payee: Circuit Clerk. Business checks accepted. Prepayment required. Mail requests: SASE required. Mail turnaround time 3-4 days.

District Court PO Box 1667, Montgomery, AL 36102; 334-832-4950. Hours: 8AM-11:30AM, 12:30PM-4PM (CST). *Misdemeanor, Civil Actions Under $10,000, Eviction, Small Claims.*

Civil Records: Access: Mail, online, in person. Both court and visitors may perform in person searches. No search fee. Required to search: name, years to search. Civil cases indexed by defendant. Civil records on computer from the 1980s, index books from 1977. Online access at www.alacourt.com.

Criminal Records: Access: Mail, online, in person. Both court and visitors may perform in person searches. No search fee. Required to search: name, years to search; also helpful: DOB, SSN. Criminal records on computer from the 1980s, index books from 1977. Online access via www.alacourt.com.

General Information: Public Access terminal is available. No sealed, youthful offender, juvenile records released. Copy fee: $.25 per page. Cert fee: $1.00. Payee: District Court. Only cashiers checks and money orders accepted. Mail requests: SASE required. Mail turnaround time 3-4 days.

Morgan County

Circuit Court PO Box 668, Decatur, AL 35602; 256-351-4790; Probate phone: 256-351-4675. Hours: 8AM-4:30PM (CST). *Felony, Civil Actions Over $10,000, Probate.*

Note: Probate court is separate from this court, and can be contacted at the telephone number above.

Civil Records: Access: Online, in person. Visitors must perform in person searches for themselves. No search fee. Required to search: name, years to search. Civil cases indexed by defendant, plaintiff. Civil records on computer from 1994, on microfiche from

1950s, books from 1965. Online access at www.alacourt.com.

Criminal Records: Access: Online, in person. Visitors must perform in person searches for themselves. No search fee. Required to search: name, years to search; also helpful: DOB, SSN. Criminal records on computer from 1992. Online access via www.alacourt.com.

General Information: Public Access terminal is available. No sealed, adoption, youthful offender, juvenile records released. Copy fee: $.25 per page. Cert fee: $1.25 per page. Payee: John Pat Orr, Circuit Clerk. Only cashiers checks and money orders accepted. Prepayment required.

District Court PO Box 668, Decatur, AL 35602; 256-351-4649. Hours: 8:30AM-4:30PM (CST). *Misdemeanor, Civil Actions Under $10,000, Eviction, Small Claims.*

Civil Records: Access: Online, in person. Visitors must perform in person searches for themselves. No search fee. Required to search: name, years to search. Civil cases indexed by defendant. Civil records on computer from 1992, books from 1960. Online access at www.alacourt.com.

Criminal Records: Access: Online, in person, mail. Visitors must perform in person searches for themselves. No search fee. Required to search: name, years to search; also helpful: DOB, SSN. Criminal records on computer from 1992, books from 1960. Online access via www.alacourt.com.

General Information: Public Access terminal is available. No sealed, adoption, youthful offender, juvenile records released. Copy fee: $.25 per page. Cert fee: $1.00. Payee: District Court. Only cashiers checks and money orders accepted. Prepayment required. Mail requests: SASE required. Mail turnaround time is varies.

Perry County

Circuit & District Court PO Box 505, Marion, AL 36756; 334-683-6106; Probate phone: 334-683-2210. Hours: 8AM-4:30PM (CST). *Felony, Misdemeanor, Civil, Eviction, Small Claims, Probate.*

Note: Probate court is separate from this court, and can be contacted at the telephone number above.

Civil Records: Access: Mail, online, in person. Both court and visitors may perform in person searches. No search fee. Required to search: name, years to search. Civil cases indexed by defendant, plaintiff. Civil records on books from 1900s, on computer back to 1990. Online access at www.alacourt.com.

Criminal Records: Access: Mail, online, in person. Both court and visitors may perform in person searches. No search fee. Required to search: name, years to search; also helpful: DOB, SSN. Criminal records on index cards back to 1900, computerized back to 1990. Online access via www.alacourt.com.

General Information: Public Access terminal is available. No sealed, adoption, youthful offender, juvenile records released. Copy fee: $.25 per page. Cert fee: $1.25 per page. Payee: District Court Clerk. Business checks accepted. Prepayment required. Mail requests: SASE required. Mail turnaround time 2-3 days.

Pickens County

Circuit & District Court PO Box 418, Carrollton, AL 35447; 205-367-2050; Probate phone: 205-367-2010. Hours: 8AM-4:30PM (CST). *Felony, Misdemeanor, Civil, Eviction, Small Claims, Probate.*

Civil Records: Access: Mail, online, in person. Only the court performs in person searches; visitors may not. No search fee. Required to search: name, years to search. Civil cases indexed by defendant, plaintiff.

Civil records on computer from 10/93, on books and index cards from 1840s. Online access at www.alacourt.com.

Criminal Records: Access: Mail, online, in person. Only the court performs in person searches; visitors may not. No search fee. Required to search: name, years to search; also helpful: DOB, SSN. Criminal records on computer, on books and index cards from 1840s. Online access via www.alacourt.com.

General Information: No sealed, adoption, youthful offender, juvenile records released. Copy fee: $.25 per page. Cert fee: $1.00. Payee: District Court. Business checks accepted. Prepayment required. Mail requests: SASE required. Mail turnaround time 1-2 weeks.

Pike County

Circuit & District Court 120 W Church St, Troy, AL 36081; 334-566-4622; Probate phone: 334-566-1246. Hours: 8AM-5PM (CST). *Felony, Misdemeanor, Civil, Eviction, Small Claims, Probate.*

Note: Probate court is separate from this court, and can be contacted at the telephone number above.

Civil Records: Access: Mail, online, in person. Both court and visitors may perform in person searches. Search fee: $5.00 per name. Required to search: name, years to search. Civil cases indexed by defendant, plaintiff. Civil records on computer from 1977, on books from 1938. Online access at www.alacourt.com.

Criminal Records: Access: Mail, online, in person. Both court and visitors may perform in person searches. Search fee: $5.00 per name. Required to search: name, years to search, DOB, SSN. Criminal records on computer from 1977, on books from 1938. Online access via www.alacourt.com.

General Information: Public Access terminal is available. No sealed, adoption, youthful offender, juvenile records released. Will not fax results. Copy fee: $.25 per page. Cert fee: $1.00. Payee: Pike County Circuit/District Court. Only cashiers checks and money orders accepted. Prepayment required. Mail requests: SASE required. Mail turnaround time same day.

Randolph County

Circuit & District Court PO Box 328, Wedowee, AL 36278; 256-357-4551; Probate phone: 256-357-4933. Hours: 8AM-Noon, 1-5PM (CST). *Felony, Misdemeanor, Civil, Eviction, Small Claims, Probate.*

Note: Probate court is separate from this court, and can be contacted at the telephone number above.

Civil Records: Access: Online, in person. Visitors must perform in person searches for themselves. No search fee. Required to search: name, years to search. Civil cases indexed by defendant, plaintiff. Civil records on computer from 1994. Online access at www.alacourt.com.

Criminal Records: Access: Online, in person. Visitors must perform in person searches for themselves. No search fee. Required to search: name, years to search; also helpful: DOB, SSN. Criminal records on computer from 1977. Online access via www.alacourt.com.

General Information: Public Access terminal is available. No sealed, adoption, youthful offender, juvenile records released. Copy fee: $.25 per page. Cert fee: $1.50. Payee: Kim S Benefield. Business checks accepted. Prepayment required.

Russell County

Circuit & District Court PO Box 518, Phenix City, AL 36868; 334-298-0516; Probate phone: 334-298-7979; Fax: 334-297-6250. Hours: 8:30AM-4:PM (EST). *Felony, Misdemeanor, Civil, Eviction, Small Claims, Probate.*
Civil Records: Access: Mail, in person. Visitors must perform in person searches for themselves. No search fee. Required to search: name, years to search. Civil cases indexed by defendant, plaintiff. Civil records on computer from 1988, books from 1800s (prior to 1940 extremely difficult to find). Online access at www.alacourt.com.from 1988 to present.
Criminal Records: Access: Mail, in person. Visitors must perform in person searches for themselves. No search fee. Required to search: name, years to search; also helpful: DOB, SSN. Criminal records on computer from 1988, books from 1800s (prior to 1940 extremely difficult to find). Online access via www.alacourt.com.from 1988 to present.
General Information: Public Access terminal is available. No sealed, adoption, youthful offender, juvenile records released. Will not fax results. Copy fee: $.25 per page. Cert fee: $1.00. Payee: Clerk of Circuit Court. Business checks accepted. Prepayment required. Mail turnaround time 2 weeks.

Shelby County

Circuit & District Court PO Box 1810, Columbiana, AL 35051; 205-669-3760; Probate phone: 205-669-3711. Hours: 8AM-4:30PM (CST). *Felony, Misdemeanor, Civil, Eviction, Small Claims, Probate.*
Note: Probate court is separate from this court, and can be contacted at the telephone number above.
Civil Records: Access: Mail, fax, online, in person. Visitors must perform in person searches for themselves. No search fee. Required to search: name, years to search. Civil cases indexed by defendant, plaintiff. Civil records on computer from 1993, on index books from 1820s. Online access at www.alacourt.com.
Criminal Records: Access: Mail, fax, online, in person. Visitors must perform in person searches for themselves. No search fee. Required to search: name, years to search, DOB; also helpful: SSN. Criminal records on computer from 1993, on index books from 1820s. Online access via www.alacourt.com.
General Information: Public Access terminal is available. No sealed, adoption, youthful offender, juvenile records released. Copy fee: $.25 per page. Cert fee: $1.00. Payee: Mary Harris, Circuit Clerk. Only cashiers checks and money orders accepted. Prepayment required.

St. Clair County

Circuit & District Court - Ashville Division PO Box 1569, Ashville, AL 35953; 205-594-2184; Probate phone: 205-594-2120. Hours: 8AM-5PM (CST). *Felony, Misdemeanor, Civil, Eviction, Small Claims, Probate.* www.stclairco.com/
Note: Probate court is separate from this court, and can be contacted at the telephone number above.
Civil Records: Access: Mail, online, in person. Both court and visitors may perform in person searches. No search fee. Required to search: name, years to search. Civil cases indexed by defendant, plaintiff. Civil records on computer from 1/94, in books from 1800s, no index before 1940. Online access at www.alacourt.com. Also, online access to probate records is by subscription at www.recordsusa.com/Alabama/CovingtonCnAl.htm. Credit card-username-password required; choose

monthly or per-use plan. Visit the website or call Lisa at 601-264-7701 for information.
Criminal Records: Access: Mail, online, in person. Both court and visitors may perform in person searches. No search fee. Required to search: name, years to search, DOB; also helpful: SSN. Criminal records on computer from 1/94, in books from 1800s, no index before 1940. Online access via www.alacourt.com.
General Information: Public Access terminal is available. No sealed, adoption, youthful offender, juvenile records released. Copy fee: $.25 per page. Cert fee: $1.25. Payee: Jeff Wyatt Circuit Clerk. Business checks accepted. Prepayment required. Mail requests: SASE required. Mail turnaround time 10 days.

Circuit & District Court - Pell City Division 1815 Cogswell Ave, #217, Pell City, AL 35125; 205-338-2511; Circuit: 205-338-7224 District; Probate phone: 205-338-9449. Hours: 8AM-5PM (CST). *Felony, Misdemeanor, Civil, Eviction, Small Claims, Probate.*
Note: Probate court is separate from this court, and can be contacted at the telephone number above.
Civil Records: Access: Mail, online, in person. Both court and visitors may perform in person searches. No search fee. Required to search: name, years to search. Civil cases indexed by defendant, plaintiff. Civil records on computer from 11/93, on books from 1970s. Online access at www.alacourt.com. Also, online access to probate records is by subscription at www.recordsusa.com/Alabama/CovingtonCnAl.htm. Credit card-username-password required; choose monthly or per-use plan. Visit the website or call Lisa at 601-264-7701 for information.
Criminal Records: Access: Mail, online, in person. Both court and visitors may perform in person searches. No search fee. Required to search: name, years to search, DOB; also helpful: SSN, signed release. Criminal records on computer from 11/93, on books from 1950s. Online access via www.alacourt.com.
General Information: Public Access terminal is available. No sealed, adoption, youthful offender, juvenile records released. Copy fee: $.25 per page. Cert fee: $1.25. Payee: Clerk of Courts. Business checks accepted. Prepayment required. Mail requests: SASE required. Mail turnaround time 7-14 days.

Sumter County

Circuit & District Court PO Box 936, (115 Franklin St), Livingston, AL 35470; 205-652-2291; Probate phone: 205-652-7281. Hours: 8AM-4:30PM (CST). *Felony, Misdemeanor, Civil, Eviction, Small Claims.*
Civil Records: Access: Mail, online, in person. Both court and visitors may perform in person searches. No search fee. Required to search: name, years to search. Civil cases indexed by defendant, plaintiff. Civil records on computer from early 1995, on index books from 1962. Online access at www.alacourt.com.
Criminal Records: Access: Mail, online, in person. Both court and visitors may perform in person searches. No search fee. Required to search: name, years to search; also helpful: DOB, SSN. Criminal records on computer from early 1995, on index books from 1962. Online access via www.alacourt.com.
General Information: Public Access terminal is available. No sealed, adoption, youthful offender, juvenile records released. Will not fax results. Copy fee: $.50 per page. Cert fee: $1.50. Payee: Circuit Court Clerk. Business checks accepted. Prepayment required. Mail requests: SASE required. Mail turnaround time 2 weeks.

Probate Court PO Box 1040, Livingston, AL 35470; 205-652-7281; Fax: 205-652-2606. Hours: 8AM-4PM (CST). *Probate.*

Talladega County

Circuit & District Court - Northern Division PO 6137, 148 E. St N, Talladega, AL 35161; 256-761-2102. Hours: 8AM-5PM (CST). *Felony, Misdemeanor, Civil, Eviction, Small Claims, Probate.*
Civil Records: Access: Online, in person. Visitors must perform in person searches for themselves. No search fee. Required to search: name, years to search. Civil cases indexed by defendant, plaintiff. Civil records on computer from 1989, index books from 1970s. Online access at www.alacourt.com.
Criminal Records: Access: Online, in person. Visitors must perform in person searches for themselves. No search fee. Required to search: name, years to search; also helpful: DOB, SSN. Criminal records on computer from 1989, index books from 1970s. Online access via www.alacourt.com.
General Information: Public Access terminal is available. No sealed, adoption, youthful offender, juvenile records released. Copy fee: $.25 per page. Cert fee: $1.25. Payee: Circuit Court Clerk. Business checks accepted. Prepayment required.

District Court - Southern Division PO Box 183, Sylacauga, AL 35150; 256-245-4352. Hours: 7:30AM-4:30AM (CST). *Misdemeanor, Civil Actions Under $10,000, Eviction, Small Claims.*
Civil Records: Access: Mail, online, in person. Visitors must perform in person searches for themselves. No search fee. Required to search: name, years to search. Civil cases indexed by defendant. Civil records on computer from 1977, on index books and cards prior to 1982 at the Northern Division District Court. Online access at www.alacourt.com.
Criminal Records: Access: Mail, online, in person. Visitors must perform in person searches for themselves. No search fee. Required to search: name, years to search; also helpful: DOB, SSN. Criminal records on computer from 1977, on index books and cards prior to 1982 at the Northern Division District Court. Online access via www.alacourt.com.
General Information: Public Access terminal is available. No juvenile, youthful offender records released. Will fax results to local or toll free line. Copy fee: $.25 per page. Cert fee: $1.25. Payee: Clerk of District Court. Business checks accepted. Prepayment required. Mail requests: SASE required. Mail turnaround time up to 7-10 days.

Probate Court PO Box 737, Talladega, AL 35161; 256-362-4175; Probate phone: 256-761-2125; Fax: 256-761-2128. Hours: 8AM-5PM (CST). *Probate.*

Tallapoosa County

Circuit & District Court - Eastern Division Tallapoosa County Courthouse, Dadeville, AL 36853; 256-825-1098; Probate phone: 256-825-4266. Hours: 8AM-5PM (CST). *Felony, Misdemeanor, Civil, Eviction, Small Claims, Probate.*
Note: Probate court is separate from this court, and can be contacted at the telephone number above.
Civil Records: Access: Mail, online, in person. Only the court performs in person searches; visitors may not. Search fee: $3.00 per name. Required to search: name, years to search. Civil cases indexed by defendant, plaintiff. Civil records on computer from 1993, on index books from 1977. Online access at www.alacourt.com.
Criminal Records: Access: Mail, online, in person. Only the court performs in person searches; visitors

may not. Search fee: $3.00 per name. Required to search: name, years to search, DOB; also helpful: SSN. Criminal records on computer from 1993, on index books from 1977. Online access via www.alacourt.com.

General Information: No sealed, adoption, youthful offender, juvenile records released. Copy fee: $.50 per page. Cert fee: $1.00. Payee: Circuit Clerk. Business checks accepted. Prepayment required. Mail requests: SASE required. Mail turnaround time 1-2 weeks.

Circuit & District Court - Western Division

PO Box 189, Alexander City, AL 35011; 256-329-8123/234-4361. Hours: 8AM-5PM (CST). *Felony, Misdemeanor, Civil, Eviction, Small Claims.*

Civil Records: Access: Mail, online, in person. Both court and visitors may perform in person searches. Search fee: $3.00 per name. Required to search: name, years to search. Civil cases indexed by defendant, plaintiff. Civil records on index books from 1977, prior in docket books; on computer back to 1994. Online access via www.alacourt.com.

Criminal Records: Access: Mail, online, in person. Both court and visitors may perform in person searches. Search fee: $3.00 per name. Required to search: name, years to search, DOB; also helpful: SSN, signed release. Criminal records on index books from 1977, prior in docket books; on computer back to 1994. Online access via www.alacourt.com.

General Information: No sealed, adoption, youthful offender, juvenile records released. Will fax results to local or toll free line. Copy fee: $.50 per page. Cert fee: $1.00. Payee: Clerk of Courts. Business checks accepted. Prepayment required. Mail requests: SASE requested. Turnaround time up to 2 weeks.

Tuscaloosa County

Circuit Court - Civil

714 Greensboro Ave, Tuscaloosa, AL 35401; 205-349-3870; Civil phone: Circ-205-349-3870 X260; Dist: X357; Probate phone: 205-349-3870 X203. Hours: 8:30AM-5PM (CST). *Civil Actions over $10,000.*

Note: Probate court is separate from this court, and can be contacted at the telephone number above.

Civil Records: Access: Online, in person. Visitors must perform in person searches for themselves. No search fee. Required to search: name, years to search. Civil cases indexed by defendant, plaintiff. Civil records on computer from 1977, index books early 1900s. Online access at www.alacourt.com.

General Information: Public Access terminal is available. No sealed, adoption, youthful offender, juvenile records released. Copy fee: $.25 per page. Cert fee: $1.00. Payee: Circuit Clerk. Business checks accepted. Prepayment required.

District Courts - Civil

714 Greensboro Ave, Tuscaloosa, AL 35401; 205-349-3870; Civil phone: 205-349-3870 x355; Probate phone: 205-349-3870 x203. Hours: 8:30AM-5PM (CST). *Civil Actions Under $10,000, Probate.*

Note: Probate court is separate from this court and can be contacted at the telephone number above.

Civil Records: Access: Online, in person. Visitors must perform in person searches for themselves. No search fee. Required to search: name, years to search. Civil cases indexed by defendant, plaintiff. Civil records on computer from 1977, index books early 1900s. Online access at www.alacourt.com.

General Information: Public Access terminal is available. No sealed, adoption, youthful offender, juvenile records released. Copy fee: $.25 per page. Cert fee: $1.00. Payee: District Clerk. Business checks accepted. Prepayment required.

Circuit Court - Criminal

714 Greensboro Ave, 3rd Fl, Tuscaloosa, AL 35401; 205-349-3870 X326. Hours: 8AM-5PM (CST). *Felony.*

Criminal Records: Access: Mail, online, in person. Both court and visitors may perform in person searches. No search fee. Required to search: name, years to search, DOB; also helpful: SSN. Criminal records on computer and index books back to 1977. Online access through SJIS. See state introduction.

General Information: Public Access terminal is available. No sealed, adoption, youthful offender, juvenile records released. Will not fax results. Copy fee: $.25 per page. Cert fee: $1.00. Payee: Circuit Clerk. Business checks accepted. Prepayment required. Mail requests: SASE required. Mail turnaround time 1-2 days.

District Court - Criminal Division

PO Box 1687, Tuscaloosa, AL 35403; 205-349-3870 X357. Hours: 8:30AM-5PM (CST). *Misdemeanor.*

Criminal Records: Access: Phone, mail, online, in person. Both court and visitors may perform in person searches. No search fee. Required to search: name, years to search, signed release; also helpful: DOB, SSN. Criminal records on computer from 1985, books in storage from early 1965. Online access through SJIS. See state introduction.

General Information: Public Access terminal is available. No sealed, youthful offender records released. Will fax results to local or toll free line. Copy fee: $.25 per page. Cert fee: $1.25. Payee: District Court Clerk. Business checks accepted. Prepayment required. Mail requests: SASE preferred. Turnaround time 5 days.

Walker County

Circuit & District Court

PO Box 749, Jasper, AL 35502; 205-384-7268; Fax: 205-384-7271. Hours: 8AM-4:30PM (CST). *Felony, Misdemeanor, Civil, Eviction, Small Claims, Probate.*

Note: Probate court is separate from this court, and can be contacted at PO Box 502 or at 205-384-7281.

Civil Records: Access: Online, in person. Visitors must perform in person searches for themselves. No search fee. Required to search: name, years to search. Civil cases indexed by defendant, plaintiff. Civil records on computer from 3/93, on index books from 1920s. Online access at www.alacourt.com.

Criminal Records: Access: Online, in person. Visitors must perform in person searches for themselves. No search fee. Required to search: name, years to search. Criminal records on computer from 3/93, on index books from 1920s. Online access via www.alacourt.com.

General Information: Public Access terminal is available. No sealed, adoption, youthful offender, juvenile records released. Copy fee: $.25 per page. Cert fee: $1.00. Payee: Vinita Thomspon, Circuit Clerk. Only cashiers checks and money orders accepted. Prepayment required.

Washington County

Circuit & District Court

PO Box 548, Chatom, AL 36518; 251-847-2239. Hours: 8AM-4:30PM (CST). *Felony, Misdemeanor, Civil, Eviction, Small Claims, Probate.*

www.millry.net/~spgrimes

Civil Records: Access: Online, in person. Visitors must perform in person searches for themselves. No search fee. Required to search: name, years to search. Civil cases indexed by defendant. Civil records on computer since September 1994; prior 7 years on index cards. Online access at www.alacourt.com. Also, online access to probate records is by subscription at www.recordsusa.com/Alabama/CovingtonCnAl.htm. Credit card-username-password

required; choose monthly or per-use plan. Visit the website or call Lisa at 601-264-7701 for information.

Criminal Records: Access: Online, in person. Visitors must perform in person searches for themselves. No search fee. Required to search: name, years to search, DOB; also helpful: SSN. Criminal records on computer since September 1994; prior 7 years on index cards. Online access via www.alacourt.com.

General Information: Public Access terminal is available. No sealed, adoption, youthful offender, juvenile records released. Copy fee: $.25 per page. Cert fee: $1.00. Payee: Circuit Clerk. Only cashiers checks and money orders accepted. Prepayment required.

Wilcox County

Circuit & District Court

PO Box 608, Camden, AL 36726; 334-682-4126; Probate phone: 334-682-4883. Hours: 8AM-Noon, 1-5PM (CST). *Felony, Misdemeanor, Civil, Eviction, Small Claims, Probate.*

Note: Probate court is separate from this court, and can be contacted at the telephone number above.

Civil Records: Access: Mail, online, in person. Visitors must perform in person searches for themselves. No search fee. Required to search: name, years to search, address. Civil cases indexed by defendant, plaintiff. Civil records on computer since 1995; prior records on index books from 1970s, prior to 1970s in vault. Online access at www.alacourt.com.

Criminal Records: Access: Mail, online, in person. Visitors must perform in person searches for themselves. No search fee. Required to search: name, years to search; also helpful: DOB. Criminal records on computer since 1995; prior records on index books from 1970s, prior to 1970s in vault. Online access via www.alacourt.com.

General Information: No sealed, adoption, youthful offender, juvenile records released. Copy fee: $.25 per page. Cert fee: $1.50. Payee: Circuit Clerk. Business checks accepted. Prepayment required.

Winston County

Circuit & District Court

PO Box 309, Double Springs, AL 35553; 205-489-5533; Probate phone: 205-489-5219; Fax: 205-489-1225. Hours: 8AM-4:30PM (CST). *Felony, Misdemeanor, Civil, Eviction, Small Claims, Probate.*

Note: Probate court is separate from this court, and can be contacted at the telephone number above.

Civil Records: Access: Online, in person. Visitors must perform in person searches for themselves. No search fee. Required to search: name, years to search. Civil cases indexed by defendant, plaintiff. Civil records on index books from 1977, on computer since June 1994 including pending cases. Online access at www.alacourt.com.

Criminal Records: Access: Online, in person. Visitors must perform in person searches for themselves. No search fee. Required to search: name, years to search, DOB; also helpful: SSN. Criminal records on index books from 1977, on computer since June 1994 including pending cases. Online access via www.alacourt.com.

General Information: Public Access terminal is available. No sealed, adoption, youthful offender, juvenile records released. Copy fee: $.25 per page. Cert fee: $1.00. Payee: Circuit Clerk. Business checks accepted. Prepayment required.

Alabama Recording Offices

ORGANIZATION: 67 counties, 71 recording offices. The recording officer is Judge of Probate. Four counties have two recording offices-Barbour, Coffee, Jefferson, and St. Clair. See the notes under each county regarding how to determine which office is appropriate to search. The state is in the Central Time Zone (CST).

REAL ESTATE RECORDS: Most counties do not perform real estate searches. Copy fees vary. Certification fees vary. Tax records are located at the Assessor's Office.

UCC RECORDS: Alabama adopted Revised Article 9 effective 01/01/2002. Financing statements are filed at the state level; real estate related collateral with the County Judge of Probate. Prior to 01/01/2002, consumer goods and farm collateral were filed with the county Judge of Probate. Only one-third of counties will perform UCC searches. Use search request form UCC-11. Search fees vary from $2.00 to $12.00 per debtor. Copies usually cost $1.00 per page.

TAX LIEN RECORDS: Federal and state tax liens on personal property of businesses are filed with the Secretary of State. Other federal and state tax liens are filed with the County Judge of Probate. Counties do not perform separate tax lien searches although the liens are usually filed in the same index with UCC financing statements.

OTHER LIENS: Mechanics, judgment, lis pendens, hospital, vendor.

ONLINE ACCESS: There is no statewide system, but a limited number of counties offer free online access to recorded documents and tax assessor data.

Autauga County

County Judge of Probate, 176 W. 5th St., Prattville, AL 36067-3041. **Phone**-334-361-3731, R/E Recording- 334-361-3732, UCC Recording- 334-361-3732; fax-334-361-3740; hours 8:30AM-5PM
Will not search records. UCC copy- $1.00 per page. Cert fee: $3.00 per doc. Payee: Autauga County Judge of Probate. **Online Access to Property, Assessor, Map records:** Access to the GIS-property information database and Tax Office is free at www.emapsplus.com/ALAutauga/maps/. Click on search by name. **Other phones:** Assessor-334-361-3709; Treasurer-334-361-3701; Appraiser-334-361-3712; Elections-334-361-3728.

Baldwin County

County Judge of Probate, PO Box 459, Bay Minette, AL 36507. **Phone**-County Judge of Probate, R/E & UCC Recording- 251-937-0230; fax-251-580-2563; hours 8AM-4:30PM www.probate.co.baldwin.al.us
Will search UCC records. UCC search per debtor- $2.00 per name. UCC copy- $1.00 per page. Will not search real estate or tax lien records. Cert fee: $3.00 per doc. Payee: Baldwin County Judge of Probate. **Online Access to Property, Deed, Recording, UCC records:** Access to recordings, deeds, and UCCs is at the website, see the "Recording" box. Also, search property appraiser records at www.deltacomputersystems.com/AL/AL05/pappraisala.html. Also, Online access to probate's property information is free at www.deltacomputersystems.com/al/al05/probatea.html. Property tax information is at www.deltacomputersystems.com/AL/AL05/plinkquerya.html. **Other phones:** Assessor-251-937-0245; Treasurer-251-937-0282; Appraiser-251-937-0245; Elections-251-937-0399.

Barbour County (Clayton Division)

County Judge of Probate, PO Box 158, Clayton, AL 36016. **Phone**-334-775-8371; fax-334-775-1126; hours 8AM-5PM
File and search here for addresses in Clayton. File and search for Eufaula addresses there. For other addresses in the county, call for where to file. Will not search

records. Record copy- $.50 per page. Cert fee: $2.50 per doc. Payee: Barbour County Judge of Probate. **Other phones:** Assessor-334-775-1110; Treasurer-334-775-3203.

Barbour County (Eufaula Division)

County Judge of Probate, PO Box 758, Eufaula, AL 36072. **Phone**-334-687-1530; fax-334-687-0921; hours 8AM-5PM
File and search for Eufaula addresses here. File and search for Clayton addresses there. For other addresses in the county, call for where to file. Will not search records. UCC copy- $1.00 per page. RE record copy- $.50 per page. Cert fee: $3.00 per doc. Payee: Barbour County Judge of Probate. **Other phones:** Assessor-334-687-1575; Treasurer-334-775-3203.

Bibb County

County Judge of Probate, 8 Court Sq W, #A, Centerville, AL 35042. **Phone**-205-926-3104, R/E Recording- 205-926-3108; fax-205-926-3131; hours 8AM-4:30PM
May or may not search UCC records. Search per debtor- $6.00. UCC copy- $1.00 per page. Will not search real estate or tax lien records. RE record copy- $1.00 per page. Cert fee: $1.00 per doc. Payee: Bibb County Judge of Probate. **Phones:** Assessor-205-926-3105; Treasurer-205-926-3114.

Blount County

County Judge of Probate, 220 2nd Ave East, Oneonta, AL 35121. **Phone**-205-625-4180; fax-205-625-4206; hours 8AM-4PM
Will not search records. Record copy- $1.00 per page. Cert fee: $4.00 per doc. Payee: Blount County Judge of Probate. **Other phones:** Assessor-205-625-4117; Treasurer-205-625-4117.

Bullock County

County Judge of Probate, PO Box 71, Union Springs, AL 36089. **Phone**-County Judge of Probate, R/E & UCC Recording- 334-738-2250; fax-334-738-3839; hours 8AM-4:30PM. Will search UCC records. UCC copy- $1.00 per page. Will not search real estate or tax lien records. RE record copy- $1.50 per page,

or $3.10 per deed. Cert fee: $3.50 per doc. Payee: Bullock County Judge of Probate. **Other phones:** Assessor-334-738-2888; Elections-334-738-2250; Vital Records-334-738-2250.

Butler County

County Judge of Probate, PO Box 756, Greenville, AL 36037. **Phone**-County Judge of Probate, R/E & UCC Recording- 334-382-3512; fax-334-382-5489; hours 8AM-4PM M,T,Th,F; 8AM-Noon W
Will search UCC records. UCC copy- $1.00 per page. Will search tax liens. Will not search real estate records. RE record copy- $1.00 per page. Cert fee: $3.00 per doc. Payee: Butler County Judge of Probate. **Other phones:** Assessor-334-382-3221.

Calhoun County

County Judge of Probate, 1702 Noble St, #102, Anniston, AL 36201. **Phone**-256-241-2825; fax-256-231-1728; hours 8AM-4:30PM
Will not search UCC or tax lien records. Will help searchers find a specific property. Record copy- $1.00 per page. Cert fee: $3.00 per doc. Payee: Calhoun County Judge of Probate. **Other phones:** Assessor-256-241-2855; Tax Collector-256-241-2840.

Chambers County

County Judge of Probate, Courthouse, Lafayette, AL 36862. **Phone**-334-864-4384, R/E Recording- 334-864-4397, UCC Recording- 334-864-4393; fax-334-864-4394; hours 8AM-4:30PM
Will search UCC records. Search per debtor- $5.00. UCC copy- $1.00 per page. Will not search real estate or tax lien records. Cert fee: $3.00 per doc. Payee: County Judge of Probate. **Online Access to Real Estate, UCC records:** Access real estate and UCC information for a $49.95 monthly fee. For information, call 706-643-1010. Records are live and go back 5 years. **Other phones:** Assessor-334-864-4389; Appraiser-334-864-4379; Elections-334-864-4380; vital records-334-864-4393; Tax Collector-334-864-4386.

Cherokee County

County Judge of Probate, 100 Main St #204, Centre, AL 35960. **Phone-**256-927-3363; fax-256-927-6949; hours 8AM-4PM M-F; 8AM-Noon Sat
Will not search records. UCC copy- $1.00 per page. Cert fee: $3.00 per doc. Payee: County Judge of Probate. **Other phones:** Assessor-256-927-5527.

Chilton County

County Judge of Probate, PO Box 270, Clanton, AL 35046. **Phone-**County Judge of Probate, R/E & UCC Recording- 205-755-1555; fax-205-280-7204; hours 8AM-4PM. Will not search records. UCC copy- $1.00 per page. RE record copy- $.50 per page. Cert fee: $2.00 per doc. Payee: Chilton County Judge of Probate. **Other phones:** Assessor-205-755-0155; Appraiser-205-755-0160.

Choctaw County

County Judge of Probate, 117 S. Mulberry, Courthouse, Butler, AL 36904. **Phone-**205-459-2417; fax-205-459-4248; hours 8AM-4:30PM
Will search UCC records. Search per debtor- $10.00. UCC copy- $.50 per page. Will not search real estate or tax lien records. Cert fee: $3.00 per doc. Payee: County Judge of Probate. **Other phones:** Assessor-205-459-2412; Treasurer-205-459-2411.

Clarke County

County Judge of Probate, PO Box 10, Grove Hill, AL 36451. **Phone-**County Judge of Probate, R/E & UCC Recording- 251-275-3251; fax-251-275-8517; hours 8AM-5PM
Will search UCC records. Search per debtor- $20.00. Must submit UCC-11 form. UCC copy- $1.00 per page. Will not search real estate or tax lien records. Cert fee: $3.00; UCCs are $5.00 per file plus copy fee. Payee: Clarke County Judge of Probate. **Other phones:** Assessor-251-275-3376; Treasurer-251-275-3507; Appraiser-251-275-3010; Elections-251-275-3251; vital records-251-275-3251 (marriages); Circuit Clerk (divorce records)-251-275-3163.

Clay County

County Judge of Probate, PO Box 1120, Ashland, AL 36251. **Phone-**256-354-3006; fax-256-354-4778; hours 8AM-4:30PM. Will not search records. UCC copy- $1.00 per page. Cert fee: $4.00 per doc. Payee: County Judge of Probate. **Other phones:** Assessor-256-354-2454.

Cleburne County

County Judge of Probate, 120 Vickery St, Rm 101, Heflin, AL 36264. **Phone-**County Judge of Probate, R/E & UCC Recording- 256-463-5655; fax-256-463-1044; hours 8AM-5PM. Will search UCC records. Search per debtor- none. UCC copy- $.50 per page. Will not search real estate or tax lien records. RE record copy- $1.00 per page. Cert fee: $6.00 per doc. Payee: County Judge of Probate. **Other phones:** Assessor-256-463-5419; Treasurer-256-463-2873; Appraiser-256-463-2873; Elections-256-463-5299; Vital Records-256-463-2296.

Coffee County (Elba Division)

County Judge of Probate, 230-P N. Court Ave, Elba, AL 36323. **Phone-**334-897-2211, R/E Recording- 334-897-2211/12, UCC Recording- 334-897-2211/12; fax-334-897-2028; hours 8AM-4:30PM
Will not search records. UCC copy- $1.00 per page. Cert fee: $3.00. Payee: Coffee County Judge of Probate. **Other phones:** Elections-334-897-2211/12.

Coffee County (Enterprise Division)

County Judge of Probate, PO Box 311247, Enterprise, AL 36331. **Phone-**334-347-2688; fax-334-347-2095; hours 8AM-4:30PM
Will not search records. Record copy- $1.00 per page. Cert fee: $3.00 per doc. Payee: County Judge of Probate. **Other phones:** Assessor-334-347-8734.

Colbert County

County Judge of Probate, PO Box 47, Tuscumbia, AL 35674. **Phone-**256-386-8546; fax-256-386-8547; hours 8AM-4:30PM
Will not search records. UCC copy- $1.00 per page. Cert fee: $3.00 per doc. Payee: Colbert County Judge of Probate. **Other:** Assessor-256-386-8530.

Conecuh County

County Judge of Probate, PO Box 149, Evergreen, AL 36401. **Phone-**251-578-1221; fax-251-578-7034; hours 8AM-4:30PM
Will not search records. UCC copy- $1.00 per page. Cert fee: $3.00. Payee: Conecuh County Judge of Probate. **Other phones:** Assessor-251-578-7019.

Coosa County

County Judge of Probate, PO Box 218, Rockford, AL 35136. **Phone-**County Judge of Probate, R/E & UCC Recording- 256-377-4919; fax-256-377-1549; hours 8AM-4PM
Will not search UCC records or tax liens. Will look up specific real estate book and page number. Record copy- $1.00 per page. Cert fee: $3.00 for 1st page; $1.00 each add'l. Payee: Coosa County Judge of Probate. **Other phones:** Assessor-256-377-4919; Appraiser-256-377-4916.

Covington County

County Judge of Probate, PO Box 789, Andalusia, AL 36420-0789. **Phone-**334-428-2518/2519, R/E Recording- 334-428-2518, UCC Recording- 334-428-2519; fax-334-428-2563; hours 8AM-5PM
Will not search records. .RE record copy- $1.00 per page. Cert fee: $5.00 per doc. Payee: Probate Judge. **Online Access to Real Estate records:** Access to real estate recording records via a private company subscription service is at www.recordsusa.com/Alabama/CovingtonCnAl.htm. **Other phones:** Assessor-334-428-2540.

Crenshaw County

County Judge of Probate, PO Box 328, Luverne, AL 36049-0328. **Phone-**334-335-6568, R/E Recording-334-335-6568 x227, UCC Recording- 334-335-6568 x227; fax-334-335-4749; hours 8AM-4:30PM
Will not search records. Record copy- $1.00 per page. Cert fee: $3.00 per doc. Payee: Crenshaw County Judge of Probate. **Other phones:** Assessor-334-335-6568 x231; Treasurer-334-335-6568 x222; Appraiser-334-335-6568 x236; Elections-334-335-6568 x254; Vital Records-334-335-2471.

Cullman County

County Judge of Probate, PO Box 970, Cullman, AL 35055. **Phone-**County Judge of Probate, R/E & UCC Recording- 256-775-4807; fax-256-775-4813; hours 8AM-4:30PM. Will not search records. Record copy- $.30 per page. Cert fee: $2.00 per doc. Payee: County Judge of Probate. **Other phones:** Assessor-256-775-4844; Appraiser-256-775-4825; Elections-256-775-4815.

Dale County

County Judge of Probate, PO Box 580, Ozark, AL 36361-0580. **Phone-**County Judge of Probate, R/E & UCC Recording- 334-774-2754; fax-334-774-0468; hours 8AM-5PM

Will not search records. UCC copy- $1.00 per page. RE record copy- $.25 per page; $1.00 if they do. Cert fee: $4.00 per doc. Payee: Dale County Judge of Probate. **Other phones:** Assessor-334-774-2226; Appraiser-334-774-7208; Elections-334-774-9038; Vital Records-334-774-5146.

Dallas County

County Judge of Probate, PO Box 987, Selma, AL 36702-0987. **Phone-**334-874-2516; 8:30AM-4:30PM
Will search UCC records. Search per debtor- $25.00. UCC copy- $1.50 per page. UCC search includes tax liens if requested. Separate state/federal tax lien search fee- $5.00 per debtor. Will not search real estate records. Payee: Dallas County Judge of Probate. **Other phones:** Assessor-334-874-2520; Tax Collector-334-874-2519.

De Kalb County

County Judge of Probate, 300 Grand SW #100, Courthouse, Fort Payne, AL 35967. **Phone-**256-845-8510; fax-256-845-8514; hours 7:45AM-4:15PM
Will not search records. Record copy- $.25 per page. Cert fee: $3.00 per doc. Payee: De Kalb County Judge of Probate. **Online Access to Property, Assessor, Mapping records:** Access to property information on the GIS site is free at www.emapsplus.com/aldekalb/maps/. Click on Owner to search by name. **Other phones:** Assessor-256-845-8515; Treasurer-256-845-8520.

Elmore County

County Judge of Probate, PO Box 280, Wetumpka, AL 36092. **Phone-**County Judge of Probate, R/E & UCC Recording- 334-567-1143, UCC Recording- 334-567-1143 or 1145; fax-334-567-1144; hours 8AM-4:30PM
Will not search records. Record copy- $1.00 per page. Cert fee: $3.00 per doc. Payee: County Judge of Probate. **Other phones:** Assessor-334-567-1118; Treasurer-334-567-1156; Appraiser-334-567-1117; Elections-334-567-1140; Vital Records-334-567-1145.

Escambia County

County Judge of Probate, PO Box 557, Brewton, AL 36427. **Phone-**251-867-0206, R/E Recording- 251-867-0291, UCC Recording- 251-867-0291; fax-251-867-0284; hours 8AM-4PM www.clerk.co.escambia.fl.us
Will not search records. UCC copy- $1.00 per page. Cert fee: $1.00 per doc. Payee: Escambia County Judge of Probate. **Online Access to Property Appraiser records:** Access to county appraisal data is free at http://property.co.escambia.al.us/search.php?type=appraisal. **Other phones:** Assessor- 251-867-0214; Appraiser-251-867-9168.

Etowah County

County Judge of Probate, PO Box 187, Gadsden, AL 35902. **Phone-**256-549-5341; fax-256-546-1149; hours 8AM-5PM
Will not search records. UCC copy- $1.00 per page. Cert fee: $1.50 per doc. Payee: Etowah County Judge of Probate. **Online Access to Property Appraisal, Property Tax records:** Access to property data through a private company is free at www.deltacomputersystems.com/AL/AL31/pappraisala.html. Also, tax records are at www.deltacomputersystems.com/AL/AL31/plinkquerya.html.
Other phones: Assessor-256-549-5341 x121.

Fayette County

County Judge of Probate, PO Box 670, Fayette, AL 35555. **Phone-**205-932-4519; fax-205-932-7600; hours 8AM-4PM. Will not search records. UCC copy- $1.00 per page. RE record copy- $.50 per page. Cert fee: $1.00 per doc. Payee: Fayette County Judge of Probate. **Other phones:** Assessor-205-932-6081; Treasurer-205-932-4510; Appraiser-205-932-6081; Elections-205-932-5432.

Franklin County

County Judge of Probate, PO Box 70, Russellville, AL 35653. **Phone**-256-332-8801, R/E Recording- 256-332-8804, UCC Recording- 256-332-8804; fax-256-332-8423; hours 8AM-5PM; 8AM-Noon Sat
Will not search records. Record copy- $1.00 per page. Cert fee: $4.00 per doc. Payee: County Judge of Probate. **Other phones:** Assessor-256-332-8831; Treasurer-256-332-8850; Elections-256-332-8805.

Geneva County

County Judge of Probate, PO Box 430, Geneva, AL 36340-0430. **Phone**-County Judge of Probate, R/E & UCC Recording- 334-684-5647; fax-334-684-5602; hours 8AM-5PM
Will not search records. Record copy- $1.00 per page. Cert fee: $2.00 per doc. Payee: Geneva County Judge of Probate. **Other phones:** Assessor-334-684-3119; Appraiser-334-684-5713; Elections-334-684-5655; Main Number-334-684-5600.

Greene County

County Judge of Probate, PO Box 790, Eutaw, AL 35462-0790. **Phone**-205-372-3340, R/E Recording-205-372-3340 or 6945, UCC Recording- 205-372-3340 or 6945; fax-205-372-0499; hours 8AM-4PM
Will search UCC records. Search per debtor- $9.00. UCC copy- $1.00 per page. Will not search real estate or tax lien records. RE record copy-$1. ea. Cert fee: $3.00 per page. Payee: Greene County Judge of Probate. **Other phones:** Assessor-205-372-3202; Appraiser-205-372-3202; Elections-205-372-3340 or 6943; Vital Records-205-372-3340 or 6945.

Hale County

County Judge of Probate, 1001 Main St, Courthouse, Greensboro, AL 36744. **Phone**-County Judge of Probate, R/E & UCC Recording- 334-624-8740; fax-334-624-8725; hours 8AM-4PM
Will search UCC records. Search per debtor- $5.00. UCC copy- $2.00 per page. Tax liens not included in UCC search. Separate federal/state combined tax lien search- $5.00 per debtor. Will not search real estate records. RE record copy- $1.00 per page. Cert fee: $3.00 per doc. Payee: County Judge of Probate. **Other phones:** Assessor-334-624-3854; Treasurer-334-624-4257; Appraiser-334-624-0705.

Henry County

County Judge of Probate, 101 Court Sq, #A, Abbeville, AL 36310. **Phone**-County Judge of Probate, R/E & UCC Recording- 334-585-3257; fax-334-585-3610; hours 8AM-4:30PM. Will not search records. Record copy- $1.00 per page. Cert fee: $2.00 per doc. Payee: Henry County Judge of Probate. **Other phones:** Assessor-334-585-3043.

Houston County

County Judge of Probate, PO Drawer 6406, Dothan, AL 36302. **Phone**-County Judge of Probate, R/E & UCC Recording- 334-677-4723; fax-334-677-4733; hours 8AM-4:30PM. Will not search UCC records. UCC copy- $1.00 per page. Payee: Houston County Judge of Probate. **Other phones:** Assessor-334-677-4714.

Jackson County

County Judge of Probate, PO Box 128, Scottsboro, AL 35768. **Phone**-256-574-9292; fax-256-574-9318; hours 8AM-4:30PM
Will search UCC records. UCC search per debtor-$20.00. UCC copy- $1.00 per page. Will not search real estate or tax lien records. Cert fee: $5.00 per doc + $1.00 per page. Payee: Jackson County Judge of Probate. **Other phones:** Assessor-256-574-9270.

Jefferson County (Bessemer Division)

County Judge of Probate, 1801 3rd Ave., Bessemer, AL 35020. **Phone**-205-481-4100; hours 8AM-4:45PM
Will search UCC records. UCC search per debtor-$20.00. UCC copy- $1.00 per page. Will not search real estate or tax lien records. RE record copy- $1.00 per page. Cert fee: $2.00 per doc. Payee: Jefferson County Judge of Probate. **Other phones:** Assessor-205-481-4125.

Jefferson County (Birmingham Division)

County Judge of Probate, 716 N. 21st St, Courthouse, Birmingham, AL 35203. **Phone**-205-325-5112, R/E Recording- 205-325-5411, UCC Recording- 205-325-5411; fax-205-325-1437; hours 8AM-4:45PM
Will not search UCC records. UCC copy- $1.00 per page. Will search tax liens including federal tax liens- $20.00 per debtor. Will not search real estate records. Payee: Jefferson County Judge of Probate. **Online Access to Property Tax, Unclaimed Property, Inmate records:** Access to the property tax due database is free at http://tc.jeffcointouch.com/tax collection/HTML/index.asp. No name searching. Also, access to the unclaimed property list is free at www.jeffcointouch.com/unclaimed/alpha.asp?section=directory Also, access the sheriff's most wanted list at www.jeffcosheriff.net/mostwanted/pictures.asp. **Other phones:** Assessor-205-325-5505; Treasurer-205-325-5372; Vital Records-205-325-5182.

Lamar County

County Judge of Probate, PO Box 338, Vernon, AL 35592. **Phone**-205-695-9119; fax-205-695-9253; hours 8AM-5PM M,T,Th,F; 8AM-Noon W,Sat
Will not search records. UCC copy- $1.00 per page. RE record copy- $9.00 1st page, $3.00 each add'l. Payee: County Judge of Probate. **Other phones:** Assessor-205-695-9139; Treasurer-205-695-7151.

Lauderdale County

County Judge of Probate, PO Box 1059, Florence, AL 35631-1059. **Phone**-256-760-5800; fax-256-760-5807; hours 8AM-5PM
Will not search records. UCC copy- $1.00 per page. Cert fee: $1.00. Payee: Lauderdale County Judge of Probate. **Online Access to Real Estate, Appraisal, Property Tax records:** Access to property appraisal data is free at http://deltacomputersystems.com/AL/AL41/pappraisala.html. Also, property tax records are at http://deltacomputersystems.com/AL/AL41/plinkquerya.html. **Other phones:** Assessor-256-760-5785.

Lawrence County

County Judge of Probate, PO Box 310, Moulton, AL 35650. **Phone**-County Judge of Probate, R/E & UCC Recording- 256-974-2440; fax-256-974-3188; hours 8AM-4PM
Will not search records. UCC copy fee- $1.00 per page. RE record copy- $.25 per page. Cert fee: $3.00 per doc. Payee: Lawrence County Judge of Probate. **Other phones:** Assessor-256-974-2476; Treasurer-256-974-2441; Appraiser-256-974-2546; Elections-256-974-2440; Vital Records-256-974-2440.

Lee County

County Judge of Probate, PO Drawer 2266, Opelika, AL 36803. **Phone**-334-745-9761; fax-334-745-5082; hours 8:30AM-4:30PM
Will search UCC records. UCC search per debtor-$5.00. UCC copy- $1.00 per page. Will not search real estate or tax lien records. Cert fee: $3.00. Payee: Lee County Judge of Probate. **Online Access to Real Estate, Appraisal, Property Tax, Sex Offender records:** Assess to property appraisal records is at http://deltacomputersystems.com/AL/AL43/pappraisala.html. Also, search property tax records at http://deltacomputersystems.com/AL/AL41/plinkquerya.html. Also search the sheriff's sex offender list at www.leecountysheriff.org/offenders.html. **Other phones:** Assessor-334-745-9786.

Limestone County

County Judge of Probate, PO Box 1145, Athens, AL 35612. **Phone**-County Judge of Probate, R/E & UCC Recording- 256-233-6427; fax-256-233-6474; hours 8AM-4:30PM
Will not search records. Record copy- $1.00 per page. Cert fee: $3.00 per doc. Payee: County Judge of Probate. **Other phones:** Assessor-256-233-6435; Appraiser-256-233-6437; Elections-256-233-6427.

Lowndes County

County Judge of Probate, PO Box 5, Hayneville, AL 36040-0005. **Phone**-334-548-2365; fax-334-548-5398; hours 8AM-4:30PM
Will not search UCC records. UCC copy- $1.00 per page. Separate federal/state combined tax lien search- $5.00 per debtor. Real estate owner, mortgage, and property transfer searches available. RE record copy- $1.00 per page. Cert fee: $4.00 per doc. Payee: Lowndes County Judge of Probate. **Other phones:** Assessor-334-548-2271; Appraiser-334-548-5619.

Macon County

County Judge of Probate, 101 E. Northside St., #101, Tuskegee, AL 36083-1731. **Phone**-334-724-2611, R/E Recording- 334-724-2508, UCC Recording- 334-724-2508; fax-334-724-2512; hours 8:30AM-4:30PM
Will not search records. Record copy- $1.00 per page. Cert fee: $5.00 per doc. Payee: County Judge of Probate. **Other phones:** Assessor-334-724-2603; Treasurer-334-724-5120; Appraiser-334-724-2607; Elections-334-724-2617; Vital Records-334-724-2611.

Madison County

County Judge of Probate, 100 Northside Sq, Rm 101, Huntsville, AL 35801-4820. **Phone**-County Judge of Probate, R/E & UCC Recording- 256-532-3339; fax-256-532-3338; hours 8:30AM-5PM
Will not search records. Record copy- $1.00 per page. Cert fee: $2.00 per doc. Payee: Madison County Judge of Probate. **Other phones:** Assessor-256-532-3350; Treasurer-256-532-3370; Appraiser-256-532-3350; Elections-256-532-3332.

Marengo County

County Judge of Probate, PO Box 480668, Linden, AL 36748. **Phone**-334-295-2210, R/E Recording- 334-295-2212, UCC Recording- 334-295-2212; fax-334-295-2254; hours 8AM-4:30PM
Will search UCC records. UCC search fee-$5.00 per name. UCC copy- $3.00. Will not search tax liens. Will perform a limited real estate search; provide date, name, etc. RE record copy- $2.00 per page including certification. Cert fee: $2.00. Payee: Marengo County Judge of Probate. **Other phones:** Assessor-334-295-2215; Appraiser-334-295-2250; Elections-334-295-2210.

Marion County

County Judge of Probate, PO Box 1687, Hamilton, AL 35570. **Phone**-County Judge of Probate, R/E & UCC Recording- 205-921-2471; fax-205-921-5109; hours 8AM-Noon, 1-5PM
Will not search records. Record copy- $1.00 per copy. Cert fee: $1.00 per copy. Payee: Marion County Judge of Probate. **Online Access to Property Tax, Land, Mapping records:** Access the county GIS-mapping and property information data for free at www.marioncountymaps.com/FrameSet.htm. **Other phones:** Assessor-205-921-2606; Treasurer-

205-921-3561; Appraiser-205-921-2606; Elections-205-921-2471; Vital Records-205-921-2471.

Marshall County

County Judge of Probate, 425 Gunter Ave, Guntersville, AL 35976. **Phone**-256-571-7767, R/E Recording- 256-571-7764 x208, UCC Recording- 256-571-7764 x208; fax-256-571-7732; 8AM-4:30PM
Will not search records. UCC copy- $1.00 per page. Cert fee: $.50 per doc. Payee: Marshall County Judge of Probate. **Online Access to Property, GIS Mapping records:** Access to property data requires free registration and password at www.marshallgis.org. **Other phones:** Assessor-256-571-5733; Treasurer-256-571-7758; Elections-256-571-7764 x202.

Mobile County

County Judge of Probate, PO Box 7, Mobile, AL 36601. **Phone**-251-574-8497, R/E Recording- 251-690-8497, UCC Recording- 251-690-8497; fax-251-690-4939; 8AM-5PM www.mobile-county.net/probate/
Will not search records. Record copy- $1.00 per page. Cert fee: $2.00 per doc. Payee: Mobile County Judge of Probate. **Online Access to Deed, UCC, Property, Incs, Marriage, Estate Claim, Mortgage, Real/Personal Property, Voter Registration records:** Access to the Probate court's recordings database is free at www.mobilecounty.org/probatecourt/recordssearch.htm. Marriages and estate claims are in a separate index here. Also, search real and personal property at http://apps.siteonestudio.com/siteone/towns/mobilecoproptax/. Search registered voters at www.mobilecounty.org/probatecourt/voters/index.asp. Also, City of Mobile property ownership data is free at http://maps.cityofmobile.org/webmapping.htm. click on Property ownership data and choose to search by name. **Other phones:** Assessor-251-574-8530; Treasurer-251-690-8585; Appraiser-251-690-8531; Elections-251-574-8480; Vital Records-251-574-8490.

Monroe County

County Judge of Probate, PO Box 665, Monroeville, AL 36461-0665. **Phone**-251-743-4107, R/E Recording- 251-743-4107 x121, UCC Recording- 251-743-4107 x121; fax-251-575-4756; hours 8AM-5PM M,T,W,F; 8AM-Noon Th
Will search UCC records. UCC search per debtor- $20.00 per name. UCC copy- $1.00 per page. Will search tax liens. Will not search real estate records. RE record copy- $1.00 per page. Cert fee: $1.00. Payee: Monroe County Judge of Probate. **Other phones:** Assessor-251-743-4107 x124; Appraiser-251-743-4107 x124; Elections-251-743-4107 x120; Vital Records-251-743-4107 x121.

Montgomery County

County Judge of Probate, PO Box 223, Montgomery, AL 36195. **Phone**-334-832-1237, R/E Recording- 334-832-1236/1237; hours 8AM-5PM
Will not search records. Record copy- $1.00 per page. Cert fee: $2.00 per doc. Payee: Montgomery County Judge of Probate. **Online Access to Unclaimed Property records:** Access to Probate Court's unclaimed property list is free at www.mc-ala.org/probate/unclprop/default.asp. **Other phones:** Assessor-334-832-4950.

Morgan County

County Judge of Probate, PO Box 848, Decatur, AL 35602-0848. **Phone**-County Judge of Probate, R/E & UCC Recording- 256-351-4680; hours 8AM-4:30PM
Will not search records. UCC copy- $1.00 per page. Cert fee: $3.00 per doc. Payee: Morgan County Judge of Probate. **Online Access to Property, Appraisal, Assessor, Tax Payment records:** Access is free at www.deltacomputersystems.com/AL/AL52/INDEX.html. Also, search property assessor data at www.deltacomputersystems.com/AL/AL52/plinkqu

erya.html. There is a property tax payment search at https://secure.termnetinc.com/morgan/paymentType.jsp but no name searching. **Other phones:** Assessor-256-351-4690.

Perry County

County Judge of Probate, PO Box 478, Marion, AL 36756. **Phone**-County Judge of Probate, R/E & UCC Recording- 334-683-2210; fax-334-683-2211; hours 8AM-4:30PM
Will not search records. UCC copy- $1.00 per page. Cert fee: $3.00 per certification. Payee: Perry County Judge of Probate. **Other phones:** Assessor-334-683-2219; Appraiser-334-683-2221; Elections-334-683-2210; Collector-334-683-2220.

Pickens County

County Judge of Probate, PO Box 370, Carrollton, AL 35447. **Phone**-County Judge of Probate, R/E & UCC Recording- 205-367-2010; fax-205-367-2011; hours 8AM-4PM
Will not search records. Record copy- $1.00 per page. Cert fee: $3.00 per instrument. Payee: Pickens County Judge of Probate. **Other phones:** Assessor-205-367-2041; Elections-205-367-2010.

Pike County

County Judge of Probate, 120 W Church St, Troy, AL 36081. **Phone**-County Judge of Probate, R/E & UCC Recording- 334-566-1246; fax-334-566-8585; hours 8AM-5PM
Will not search records. UCC copy- $.50 per page. Cert fee: $2.50. Payee: Pike County Judge of Probate. **Other phones:** Assessor-334-566-0706; Treasurer-334-566-6374; Appraiser-334-566-0706; Elections-334-566-1246.

Randolph County

County Judge of Probate, PO Box 249, Wedowee, AL 36278. **Phone**-256-357-4933; fax-256-357-9053; hours 8AM-5PM
Will not search records. Record copy- $1.00 per record. Cert fee: $2.00. Payee: County Judge of Probate. **Other phones:** Assessor-256-357-4343.

Russell County

County Judge of Probate, PO Box 700, Phenix City, AL 36868-0700. **Phone**-County Judge of Probate, R/E & UCC Recording- 334-298-7979; fax-334-298-7979; hours 8:30AM-5PM
Will search UCC records. Search fee is $20.00. UCC copy- $1.00 per page. Will not search real estate or tax lien records. RE record copy- $1.00 per page. Cert fee: $3.00 per doc. Payee: County Judge of Probate. **Other phones:** Assessor-334-298-4441; Treasurer-334-298-6426; Appraiser-334-297-8996.

Shelby County

County Judge of Probate, PO Box 825, Columbiana, AL 35051. **Phone**-205-669-3720; fax-205-669-3714; hours 8AM-4:30PM www.shelbycountyalabama.com
Will not search records. UCC copy- $1.00 per page. Payee: Shelby County Judge of Probate. **Online Access to Recording, Land, Judgment, Deed, UCC, Notary, Fictitious Name, Marriage, Probate, Property Tax records:** Access to the probate court recording data is free at www.shelbycountyalabama.com/probate/. Search property tax records at www.shelbycountyalabama.com/taxc_search.asp. **Other phones:** Assessor-205-669-3902; Appraiser-205-669-3902.

St. Clair County
(Northern Congressional District)

County Judge of Probate, PO Box 220, Ashville, AL 35953. **Phone**-County Judge of Probate, R/E & UCC Recording- 205-594-2124; fax-205-594-2125; hours 8AM-5PM www.stclairco.com/index.php

Will not search records. Record copy- $1.00 per page. Cert fee: $3.00 per doc. Payee: Judge of Probate. **Online Access to Property, Appraisal, Assessor records:** property appraiser data is free at www.deltacomputersystems.com/AL/AL59/pappraisala.html. Also, access to county assessor data is free at www.deltacomputersystems.com/AL/AL59/plinkquerya.html. Access to real estate recording records via a private company subscription service is at www.recordsusa.com/Alabama/StClairCnAl.htm. **Other phones:** Assessor-205-594-2160; Appraiser-205-594-2168; Vital Records-334-206-5418.

St. Clair County
(Southern Congressional District)

County Judge of Probate, 1815 Cogswell Ave, #212, Pell City, AL 35125. **Phone**-County Judge of Probate, R/E & UCC Recording- 205-338-9449; fax-205-884-1182; hours 8AM-5PM
Will not search records. UCC copy- $1.00 per page. Cert fee: $3.00 per doc. Payee: St. Clair Judge of Probate. **Online Access to Property, Appraisal, Assessor records:** property appraiser data is free at www.deltacomputersystems.com/AL/AL59/pappraisala.html. Also, access to county assessor data is free at www.deltacomputersystems.com/AL/AL59/plinkquerya.html. Access to real estate recording records via a private company subscription service is at www.recordsusa.com/Alabama/StClairCnAl.htm. **Other phones:** Assessor-205-884-2395; Appraiser-205-884-2395.

Sumter County

County Judge of Probate, PO Box 1040, Livingston, AL 35470-1040. **Phone**-County Judge of Probate, R/E & UCC Recording- 205-652-7281; fax-205-652-6206; hours 8AM-4PM
Will not search records. Record copy- $1.00 per copy. Cert fee: $3.00 per doc. Payee: Sumter County Judge of Probate. **Other phones:** Assessor-205-652-2424; Treasurer-205-652-2731; Appraiser-205-652-2424; Elections-205-652-7281; Vital Records-205-652-7281.

Talladega County

County Judge of Probate, PO Box 737, Talladega, AL 35161. **Phone**-County Judge of Probate, R/E & UCC Recording- 256-362-4175; fax-256-761-2128; hours 8AM-5PM
Will not search records. Record copy- $1.00 per page. Cert fee: $4.00 per doc. Payee: Talladega County Judge of Probate. **Other phones:** Assessor-256-761-2123.

Tallapoosa County

County Judge of Probate, 125 N. Broadnax St., Courthouse, Rm 126, Dadeville, AL 36853. **Phone**-County Judge of Probate, R/E & UCC Recording- 256-825-1090; fax-256-825-1604; hours 8AM-5PM
Will not search records. UCC copy- $1.00 per page. Cert fee: $3.00 per instrument. Payee: County Judge of Probate. **Other phones:** Assessor-256-825-7831; Appraiser-256-825-7831.

Tuscaloosa County

County Judge of Probate, PO Box 20067, Tuscaloosa, AL 35402-0067. **Phone**-205-349-3870 x205/6; hours 8:30AM-5PM www.tuscco.com
Will not search UCC records or tax liens. Will search real estate names as time permits. Record copy- $1.00 per page. Cert fee: $2.00 per doc. Payee: Judge of Probate. **Online Access to Real Estate, Lien, UCC, Grantor/Grantee, Probate, Marriage, Mortgage, Incs, Property, Jail, Sex Offender, Most Wanted records:** Access to the records database is free at www.tuscco.com/OnlineServices.cfm. Included are searches for mortgages, incorporations, bonds, discharges, exemptions. Also, property and assessor

data is at www.emapsplus.com/ALTuscaloosa/maps/. Click on owner search. Also, a search is proposed for probate and judgment records at www.tuscco.com/RecordsRoom_Probate.cfm. Also, search for inmates, most wanted, sex offenders, and missing persons at www.tcsoal.org. **Other phones:** Assessor-205-349-3870 x370.

Walker County

County Judge of Probate, PO Box 502, Jasper, AL 35502-0502. **Phone-**205-384-7282, R/E Recording- 205-384-7281; fax-205-384-7005; hours 8AM-4PM
Will search UCC records. Search per debtor- $12.00 + $1.00 per record found. UCC copy- $1.00 per page. Will not search real estate or tax lien records. RE record copy- $1.00 per page. Cert fee: $3.00 per doc. Payee: County Judge of Probate. **Online Access to Sex Offender records:** Search the county sheriff's sex offender list at www.walkercount

y.com/sexoffenders.htm. **Other phones:** Assessor-205-384-7265; Treasurer-205-384-7276.

Washington County

County Judge of Probate, PO Box 549, Chatom, AL 36518. **Phone-** 251-847-2201; fax-251-847-3677; hours 8AM-4:30PM
Will not search records. Record copy- $1.00 per page for 1st 10, then $.50 per page. Cert fee: $3.00 per doc. Payee: Washington County Judge of Probate. **Online Access to Real Estate records:** Access to real estate recording records via a private company subscription service is at www.recordsusa.com/Alabama/WashingtonCnAl.htm. **Other phones:** Assessor-251-847-2780; Treasurer-251-847-2208; Elections-251-847-2201.

Wilcox County

County Judge of Probate, PO Box 668, Camden, AL 36726. **Phone-**County Judge of Probate, R/E & UCC

Recording- 334-682-4883; fax-334-682-9484; hours 8-11:30AM,Noon-4:30PM
Will search UCC records. UCC copy- $1.00 per page. Will not search real estate or tax lien records. RE record copy- $1.00 per page. Cert fee: $3.00 per cert; $1.00 per page. Payee: Wilcox County Judge of Probate. **Other phones:** Assessor-334-682-4625; Treasurer-334-682-9112.

Winston County

County Judge of Probate, PO Box 27, Double Springs, AL 35553. **Phone-**County Judge of Probate, R/E & UCC Recording- 205-489-5219; fax-205-489-5135; hours 8AM-4:30PM (8AM-Noon 1st Sat of month)
Will not search records. Record copy- $1.00 per page. Cert fee: $3.00 per doc. Payee: Winston County Judge of Probate. **Other phones:** Assessor-205-489-5166; Appraiser-205-489-5166; Vital Records-205-489-5219 (marriages).

Alabama County Locator

You will usually be able to find the city name in the City/County Cross Reference below. In that case, it is a simple matter to determine the county from the cross reference. However, only the official US Postal Service city names are included in this index. There are an additional 40,000 place names that people use in their addresses. Therefore, we have also included a ZIP/City Cross Reference immediately following the City/County Cross Reference.

If you know the ZIP Code but the city name does not appear in the City/County Cross Reference index, look up the ZIP Code in the ZIP/City Cross Reference, find the city name, then look up the city name in the City/County Cross Reference. For example, you want to know the county for an address of Menands, NY 12204. There is no "Menands" in the City/County Cross Reference. The ZIP/City Cross Reference shows that ZIP Codes 12201-12288 are for the city of Albany. Looking back in the City/County Cross Reference, Albany is in Albany County.

Alabama City/County Cross Reference

ABBEVILLE Henry
ABERNANT Tuscaloosa
ADAMSVILLE Jefferson
ADDISON (35540) Winston(95), Cullman(4)
ADGER (35006) Jefferson(91), Walker(6), Tuscaloosa(2)
AKRON Hale
ALABASTER Shelby
ALBERTA Wilcox
ALBERTVILLE (35951) Marshall(73), De Kalb(26)
ALBERTVILLE Marshall
ALEXANDER CITY (35010) Tallapoosa(95), Elmore(2), Coosa(1)
ALEXANDER CITY Tallapoosa
ALEXANDRIA Calhoun
ALICEVILLE (35442) Pickens(87), Sumter(11)
ALLEN Clarke
ALLGOOD Blount
ALMA Clarke
ALPINE Talladega
ALTON Jefferson
ALTOONA (35952) Etowah(57), Blount(41)
ANDALUSIA (36420) Covington(97), Escambia(2)
ANDALUSIA (36421) Covington(98), Conecuh(1)
ANDERSON (35610) Lauderdale(74), Limestone(25)
ANNEMANIE Wilcox
ANNISTON (36203) Calhoun(79), Talladega(20)
ANNISTON Calhoun
ARAB (35016) Marshall(82), Cullman(14), Blount(2)
ARDMORE (35739) Limestone(77), Madison(22)
ARITON (36311) Dale(66), Barbour(23), Coffee(10)
ARLEY Winston
ARLINGTON (36722) Wilcox(97), Marengo(2)
ASHFORD Houston
ASHLAND Clay
ASHVILLE St. Clair
ATHENS Limestone
ATMORE (36502) Escambia(93), Monroe(3), Baldwin(2)
ATMORE Escambia
ATTALLA Etowah
AUBURN (36830) Lee(90), Macon(9)
AUBURN Lee
AUBURN UNIVERSITY Lee
AUTAUGAVILLE Autauga
AXIS Mobile

BAILEYTON (35019) Cullman(73), Morgan(26)
BANKS (36005) Pike(67), Bullock(32)
BANKSTON Fayette
BAY MINETTE Baldwin
BAYOU LA BATRE Mobile
BEAR CREEK Marion
BEATRICE Monroe
BEAVERTON Lamar
BELK Fayette
BELLAMY Sumter
BELLE MINA Limestone
BELLWOOD Geneva
BERRY (35546) Fayette(65), Tuscaloosa(31), Walker(3)
BESSEMER (35022) Jefferson(95), Shelby(4)
BESSEMER Jefferson
BIGBEE Washington
BILLINGSLEY (36006) Autauga(59), Chilton(41)
BIRMINGHAM (35244) Jefferson(53), Shelby(46)
BIRMINGHAM (35242) Shelby(90), Jefferson(9)
BIRMINGHAM Jefferson
BLACK Geneva
BLOUNTSVILLE Blount
BOAZ (35957) Marshall(78), De Kalb(18), Blount(3)
BOAZ Etowah
BOLIGEE Greene
BOLINGER Choctaw
BON AIR Talladega
BON SECOUR Baldwin
BOOTH Autauga
BOYKIN Wilcox
BRANTLEY (36009) Crenshaw(94), Coffee(5)
BREMEN (35033) Cullman(90), Walker(9)
BRENT (35034) Bibb(98), Perry(1)
BREWTON (36426) Escambia(98), Conecuh(1)
BREWTON Escambia
BRIDGEPORT Jackson
BRIERFIELD (35035) Bibb(97), Shelby(2)
BRILLIANT Marion
BROOKLYN Conecuh
BROOKSIDE Jefferson
BROOKWOOD (35444) Tuscaloosa(97), Jefferson(2)
BROWNSBORO Madison
BRUNDIDGE (36010) Pike(77), Coffee(21)
BRYANT Jackson
BUCKS Mobile
BUHL Tuscaloosa

BURNT CORN Monroe
BURNWELL Walker
BUTLER Choctaw
BYNUM Calhoun
CALERA (35040) Shelby(86), Chilton(13)
CALVERT Washington
CAMDEN Wilcox
CAMP HILL (36850) Tallapoosa(76), Chambers(19), Lee(3)
CAMPBELL Clarke
CAPSHAW Limestone
CARBON HILL (35549) Walker(83), Fayette(16)
CARDIFF Jefferson
CARLTON Clarke
CARROLLTON Pickens
CASTLEBERRY (36432) Conecuh(67), Escambia(32)
CATHERINE Wilcox
CECIL (36013) Montgomery(94), Macon(5)
CEDAR BLUFF Cherokee
CENTRE Cherokee
CENTREVILLE Bibb
CHANCELLOR (36316) Geneva(53), Coffee(46)
CHAPMAN Butler
CHATOM Washington
CHELSEA Shelby
CHEROKEE Colbert
CHILDERSBURG Talladega
CHOCCOLOCCO Calhoun
CHUNCHULA Mobile
CITRONELLE (36522) Mobile(95), Washington(4)
CLANTON (35046) Chilton(97), Coosa(2)
CLANTON Chilton
CLAY Jefferson
CLAYTON Barbour
CLEVELAND Blount
CLINTON Greene
CLIO Barbour
CLOPTON (36317) Henry(88), Barbour(6), Dale(5)
CLOVERDALE Lauderdale
COALING Tuscaloosa
CODEN Mobile
COFFEE SPRINGS (36318) Geneva(70), Coffee(29)
COFFEEVILLE Clarke
COKER Tuscaloosa
COLLINSVILLE (35961) De Kalb(79), Etowah(10), Cherokee(10)
COLUMBIA (36319) Henry(51), Houston(48)
COLUMBIANA Shelby
COOK SPRINGS St. Clair

COOSADA Elmore
CORDOVA Walker
COTTONDALE Tuscaloosa
COTTONTON Russell
COTTONWOOD Houston
COURTLAND Lawrence
COWARTS Houston
COY Wilcox
CRAGFORD (36255) Clay(97), Tallapoosa(2)
CRANE HILL Cullman
CREOLA Mobile
CROMWELL Choctaw
CROPWELL St. Clair
CROSSVILLE (35962) De Kalb(93), Marshall(6)
CUBA Sumter
CULLMAN Cullman
CUSSETA (36852) Lee(74), Chambers(25)
DADEVILLE Tallapoosa
DALEVILLE (36322) Dale(95), Coffee(2), Geneva(2)
DANVILLE (35619) Lawrence(49), Morgan(49)
DAPHNE Baldwin
DAUPHIN ISLAND Mobile
DAVISTON (36256) Tallapoosa(96), Clay(3)
DAWSON De Kalb
DAYTON Marengo
DE ARMANVILLE Calhoun
DEATSVILLE (36022) Elmore(82), Autauga(17)
DECATUR (35603) Morgan(98), Lawrence(1)
DECATUR Morgan
DEER PARK Washington
DELMAR Winston
DELTA (36258) Clay(55), Cleburne(29), Randolph(15)
DEMOPOLIS Marengo
DETROIT (35552) Marion(56), Lamar(43)
DICKINSON Clarke
DIXONS MILLS Marengo
DOCENA Jefferson
DOLOMITE Jefferson
DORA (35062) Jefferson(52), Walker(47)
DOTHAN (36303) Houston(92), Dale(7)
DOTHAN Houston
DOUBLE SPRINGS Winston
DOUGLAS Marshall
DOZIER (36028) Covington(56), Crenshaw(43)
DUNCANVILLE (35456) Tuscaloosa(98), Bibb(1)
DUTTON Jackson

EAST TALLASSEE Tallapoosa
EASTABOGA (36260) Calhoun(64), Talladega(35)
ECHOLA Tuscaloosa
ECLECTIC Elmore
EDWARDSVILLE Cleburne
EIGHT MILE Mobile
ELBA Coffee
ELBERTA Baldwin
ELDRIDGE (35554) Fayette(64), Walker(29), Marion(5)
ELKMONT Limestone
ELMORE Elmore
ELROD Tuscaloosa
EMELLE Sumter
EMPIRE (35063) Walker(72), Blount(19), Jefferson(8)
ENTERPRISE (36330) Coffee(90), Dale(9)
ENTERPRISE Coffee
EPES Sumter
EQUALITY (36026) Elmore(61), Coosa(38)
ESTILLFORK Jackson
ETHELSVILLE Pickens
EUFAULA Autauga
EUFAULA Barbour
EUTAW Greene
EVA (35621) Morgan(91), Cullman(8)
EVERGREEN Conecuh
EXCEL Monroe
FACKLER Jackson
FAIRFIELD Jefferson
FAIRHOPE Baldwin
FALKVILLE (35622) Morgan(78), Cullman(21)
FAUNSDALE Marengo
FAYETTE (35555) Fayette(92), Tuscaloosa(5), Lamar(1)
FITZPATRICK (36029) Macon(49), Bullock(32), Montgomery(18)
FIVE POINTS Chambers
FLAT ROCK (35966) Jackson(64), De Kalb(35)
FLOMATON Escambia
FLORALA Covington
FLORENCE Lauderdale
FOLEY Baldwin
FOREST HOME (36030) Butler(96), Wilcox(3)
FORKLAND Greene
FORT DAVIS Macon
FORT DEPOSIT (36032) Lowndes(75), Butler(24)
FORT MITCHELL Russell
FORT PAYNE (35967) De Kalb(96), Cherokee(3)
FORT PAYNE De Kalb
FORT RUCKER Dale
FOSTERS Tuscaloosa
FRANKLIN Monroe
FRANKVILLE Washington
FRISCO CITY Monroe
FRUITDALE Washington
FRUITHURST Cleburne
FULTON Clarke
FULTONDALE Jefferson
FURMAN Wilcox
FYFFE De Kalb
GADSDEN (35907) Etowah(98), Calhoun(1)
GADSDEN Etowah
GAINESTOWN Clarke
GAINESVILLE (35464) Sumter(86), Greene(13)
GALLANT (35972) Etowah(75), St. Clair(24)

GALLION (36742) Marengo(95), Hale(4)
GANTT Covington
GARDEN CITY Cullman
GARDENDALE Jefferson
GAYLESVILLE Cherokee
GENEVA Geneva
GEORGIANA (36033) Butler(98), Conecuh(1)
GERALDINE De Kalb
GILBERTOWN Choctaw
GLEN ALLEN Fayette
GLENWOOD (36034) Crenshaw(70), Pike(29)
GOODSPRINGS Walker
GOODWATER (35072) Clay(47), Coosa(32), Tallapoosa(18)
GOODWAY Monroe
GORDO (35466) Pickens(93), Tuscaloosa(6)
GORDON Houston
GOSHEN (36035) Pike(76), Crenshaw(23)
GRADY (36036) Montgomery(75), Crenshaw(24)
GRAHAM Randolph
GRAND BAY Mobile
GRANT Marshall
GRAYSVILLE Jefferson
GREEN POND Bibb
GREENSBORO Hale
GREENVILLE Butler
GROVE HILL Clarke
GROVEOAK (35975) De Kalb(92), Marshall(7)
GUIN (35563) Marion(91), Fayette(4), Lamar(4)
GULF SHORES Baldwin
GUNTERSVILLE (35976) Marshall(97), Blount(2)
GURLEY (35748) Madison(94), Jackson(5)
HACKLEBURG Marion
HALEYVILLE (35565) Winston(66), Marion(28), Franklin(4)
HAMILTON Marion
HANCEVILLE Cullman
HARDAWAY Macon
HARPERSVILLE Shelby
HARTFORD Geneva
HARTSELLE Morgan
HARVEST (35749) Madison(74), Limestone(25)
HATCHECHUBBEE Russell
HAYDEN Blount
HAYNEVILLE Lowndes
HAZEL GREEN Madison
HEADLAND (36345) Henry(83), Houston(10), Dale(6)
HEFLIN (36264) Cleburne(92), Randolph(7)
HELENA Shelby
HENAGAR (35978) De Kalb(79), Jackson(20)
HIGDON (35979) De Kalb(66), Jackson(33)
HIGHLAND HOME (36041) Crenshaw(97), Montgomery(2)
HILLSBORO Lawrence
HODGES (35571) Franklin(69), Marion(30)
HOLLINS Clay
HOLLY POND Cullman
HOLLYTREE Jackson
HOLLYWOOD Jackson
HOLY TRINITY Russell
HONORAVILLE (36042) Crenshaw(54), Butler(45)

HOPE HULL (36043) Montgomery(65), Lowndes(34)
HORTON (35980) Marshall(66), Blount(33)
HOUSTON Winston
HUNTSVILLE Madison
HURTSBORO (36860) Russell(86), Bullock(8), Macon(4)
HUXFORD Escambia
IDER De Kalb
IRVINGTON Mobile
JACHIN Choctaw
JACK Coffee
JACKSON Clarke
JACKSONS GAP Tallapoosa
JACKSONVILLE Calhoun
JASPER (35503) Walker(92), Winston(7)
JASPER Walker
JEFFERSON Marengo
JEMISON Chilton
JONES (36749) Dallas(53), Autauga(46)
JOPPA (35087) Cullman(50), Morgan(37), Marshall(11)
KANSAS Walker
KELLERMAN Tuscaloosa
KELLYTON (35089) Tallapoosa(60), Coosa(39)
KENNEDY (35574) Lamar(55), Pickens(33), Fayette(11)
KENT Elmore
KILLEN Lauderdale
KIMBERLY Jefferson
KINSTON (36453) Coffee(53), Geneva(42), Covington(3)
KNOXVILLE (35469) Greene(52), Tuscaloosa(47)
LACEYS SPRING (35754) Morgan(98), Marshall(1)
LAFAYETTE Chambers
LAMISON Wilcox
LANETT Chambers
LANGSTON (35755) Marshall(58), Jackson(41)
LAPINE (36046) Crenshaw(51), Montgomery(48)
LAVACA Choctaw
LAWLEY (36793) Bibb(68), Chilton(24), Perry(7)
LEEDS (35094) Jefferson(76), Shelby(13), St. Clair(10)
LEESBURG (35983) Cherokee(98), De Kalb(1)
LEIGHTON Colbert
LENOX Conecuh
LEROY Washington
LESTER Limestone
LETOHATCHEE (36047) Lowndes(68), Montgomery(31)
LEXINGTON Lauderdale
LILLIAN Baldwin
LINCOLN (35096) Talladega(89), Calhoun(10)
LINDEN Marengo
LINEVILLE (36266) Clay(82), Randolph(17)
LISMAN Choctaw
LITTLE RIVER Baldwin
LIVINGSTON Sumter
LOACHAPOKA Lee
LOCKHART Covington
LOCUST FORK Blount
LOGAN (35098) Cullman(89), Winston(10)
LOUISVILLE Barbour
LOWER PEACH TREE (36751) Monroe(47), Wilcox(28), Clarke(23)
LOWNDESBORO Lowndes

LOXLEY Baldwin
LUVERNE Crenshaw
LYNN Winston
MADISON (35756) Limestone(81), Madison(18)
MADISON Madison
MAGNOLIA Marengo
MAGNOLIA SPRINGS Baldwin
MALCOLM Washington
MALVERN Geneva
MAPLESVILLE (36750) Chilton(94), Bibb(5)
MARBURY (36051) Autauga(43), Elmore(30), Chilton(26)
MARGARET St. Clair
MARION Perry
MARION JUNCTION (36759) Dallas(94), Perry(5)
MATHEWS (36052) Montgomery(93), Bullock(6)
MAYLENE Shelby
MC CALLA (35111) Tuscaloosa(62), Jefferson(35), Bibb(1)
MC INTOSH Washington
MC KENZIE (36456) Butler(74), Covington(12), Conecuh(12)
MC SHAN Pickens
MC WILLIAMS Wilcox
MEGARGEL Monroe
MELVIN Choctaw
MENTONE (35984) De Kalb(81), Cherokee(18)
MERIDIANVILLE Madison
MEXIA Monroe
MIDLAND CITY (36350) Dale(91), Houston(8)
MIDWAY (36053) Barbour(79), Bullock(20)
MILLBROOK Elmore
MILLERS FERRY Wilcox
MILLERVILLE Clay
MILLPORT (35576) Lamar(89), Pickens(10)
MILLRY (36558) Washington(84), Choctaw(15)
MINTER (36761) Dallas(59), Lowndes(39), Wilcox(1)
MOBILE Mobile
MONROEVILLE Monroe
MONTEVALLO (35115) Shelby(83), Chilton(15), Bibb(1)
MONTGOMERY Montgomery
MONTROSE Baldwin
MOODY St. Clair
MOORESVILLE Limestone
MORRIS Jefferson
MORVIN Clarke
MOULTON Lawrence
MOUNDVILLE (35474) Hale(87), Tuscaloosa(12)
MOUNT HOPE (35651) Lawrence(98), Franklin(1)
MOUNT MEIGS Montgomery
MOUNT OLIVE Jefferson
MOUNT VERNON Mobile
MULGA Jefferson
MUNFORD Talladega
MUSCADINE Cleburne
MUSCLE SHOALS Colbert
MYRTLEWOOD Marengo
NANAFALIA Marengo
NATURAL BRIDGE Winston
NAUVOO (35578) Walker(79), Winston(20)
NEEDHAM Choctaw
NEW BROCKTON Coffee
NEW CASTLE Jefferson

NEW HOPE (35760) Madison(88), Marshall(11)
NEW MARKET Madison
NEWBERN (36765) Hale(85), Perry(14)
NEWELL Randolph
NEWTON (36352) Houston(55), Dale(42), Geneva(1)
NEWVILLE (36353) Henry(72), Dale(27)
NORMAL Madison
NORTHPORT Tuscaloosa
NOTASULGA (36866) Macon(73), Tallapoosa(20), Lee(5)
OAK HILL Wilcox
OAKMAN (35579) Walker(98), Tuscaloosa(1)
ODENVILLE St. Clair
OHATCHEE Calhoun
ONEONTA Blount
OPELIKA (36801) Lee(98), Chambers(1)
OPELIKA (36804) Lee(97), Macon(1), Russell(1)
OPELIKA Lee
OPP (36467) Covington(95), Coffee(4)
ORANGE BEACH Baldwin
ORRVILLE Dallas
OWENS CROSS ROADS Madison
OZARK Dale
PAINT ROCK Jackson
PALMERDALE Jefferson
PANOLA Sumter
PANSEY Houston
PARRISH Walker
PAUL Conecuh
PELHAM Shelby
PELL CITY St. Clair
PENNINGTON Choctaw
PERDIDO (36562) Baldwin(90), Escambia(9)
PERDUE HILL Monroe
PEROTE Bullock
PETERMAN (36471) Monroe(96), Conecuh(3)
PETERSON Tuscaloosa
PETREY Crenshaw
PHENIX CITY (36870) Lee(72), Russell(27)
PHENIX CITY (36867) Russell(90), Lee(9)
PHENIX CITY Russell
PHIL CAMPBELL (35581) Franklin(87), Marion(12)
PIEDMONT (36272) Calhoun(61), Cherokee(26), Etowah(8), Cleburne(3)
PIKE ROAD Montgomery
PINCKARD Dale
PINE APPLE Wilcox
PINE HILL Wilcox
PINE LEVEL Montgomery
PINSON (35126) Jefferson(96), Blount(3)
PISGAH (35765) Jackson(92), De Kalb(7)
PITTSVIEW Russell
PLANTERSVILLE (36758) Dallas(90), Autauga(7), Chilton(1)

PLEASANT GROVE Jefferson
POINT CLEAR Baldwin
PRAIRIE Wilcox
PRATTVILLE Autauga
PRINCETON Jackson
QUINTON (35130) Walker(65), Jefferson(34)
RAGLAND St. Clair
RAINBOW CITY Etowah
RAINSVILLE De Kalb
RALPH (35480) Tuscaloosa(97), Greene(2)
RAMER Montgomery
RANBURNE Cleburne
RANDOLPH (36792) Bibb(72), Chilton(27)
RANGE Conecuh
RED BAY Franklin
RED LEVEL (36474) Covington(97), Conecuh(2)
REFORM Pickens
REMLAP (35133) Blount(93), St. Clair(6)
REPTON (36475) Conecuh(64), Monroe(35)
RIVER FALLS Covington
RIVERSIDE St. Clair
ROANOKE (36274) Randolph(93), Chambers(6)
ROBERTSDALE Baldwin
ROCKFORD Coosa
ROGERSVILLE (35652) Lauderdale(98), Limestone(1)
RUSSELLVILLE (35654) Franklin(80), Colbert(14), Lawrence(5)
RUTLEDGE (36071) Crenshaw(97), Butler(2)
RYLAND Madison
SAFFORD (36773) Dallas(89), Marengo(10)
SAGINAW Shelby
SAINT ELMO Mobile
SAINT STEPHENS Washington
SALEM (36874) Lee(95), Russell(4)
SALITPA Clarke
SAMANTHA Tuscaloosa
SAMSON (36477) Geneva(91), Coffee(8)
SARALAND Mobile
SARDIS (36775) Dallas(81), Lowndes(18)
SATSUMA Mobile
SAWYERVILLE Hale
SAYRE Jefferson
SCOTTSBORO (35769) Jackson(70), Marshall(29)
SCOTTSBORO Jackson
SEALE Russell
SECTION (35771) Jackson(96), De Kalb(3)
SELMA (36701) Dallas(98), Perry(1)
SELMA (36703) Dallas(97), Autauga(2)
SELMA Dallas
SEMINOLE Baldwin
SEMMES Mobile
SHANNON Jefferson

SHEFFIELD Colbert
SHELBY Shelby
SHORTER Macon
SHORTERVILLE Henry
SILAS Choctaw
SILURIA Shelby
SILVERHILL Baldwin
SIPSEY Walker
SKIPPERVILLE (36374) Dale(60), Barbour(39)
SLOCOMB (36375) Geneva(84), Houston(15)
SMITHS Lee
SMITHS STATION Lee
SNOW HILL Wilcox
SOMERVILLE Morgan
SPANISH FORT Baldwin
SPRING GARDEN Cherokee
SPRINGVILLE (35146) St. Clair(81), Blount(17), Jefferson(1)
SPROTT Perry
SPRUCE PINE Franklin
STANTON Chilton
STAPLETON Baldwin
STEELE St. Clair
STERRETT Shelby
STEVENSON Jackson
STOCKTON Baldwin
SULLIGENT Lamar
SUMITON Walker
SUMMERDALE Baldwin
SUNFLOWER Washington
SWEET WATER Marengo
SYCAMORE Talladega
SYLACAUGA Talladega
SYLVANIA De Kalb
TALLADEGA (35160) Talladega(96), Clay(3)
TALLADEGA Talladega
TALLASSEE (36078) Elmore(81), Tallapoosa(18)
TANNER Limestone
THEODORE Mobile
THOMASTON Marengo
THOMASVILLE (36784) Clarke(79), Marengo(16), Wilcox(3)
THORSBY Chilton
TIBBIE Washington
TITUS (36080) Elmore(98), Coosa(1)
TONEY (35773) Madison(72), Limestone(27)
TOWN CREEK (35672) Lawrence(97), Colbert(2)
TOWNLEY Walker
TOXEY Choctaw
TRAFFORD (35172) Blount(83), Jefferson(16)
TRENTON Jackson
TRINITY (35673) Lawrence(78), Morgan(21)
TROY (36079) Pike(93), Coffee(6)
TROY (36081) Pike(98), Bullock(1)
TROY Pike
TRUSSVILLE (35173) Jefferson(81), St. Clair(18)

TUSCALOOSA Tuscaloosa
TUSCUMBIA Colbert
TUSKEGEE Macon
TUSKEGEE INSTITUTE Macon
TYLER (36785) Lowndes(75), Dallas(25)
UNION GROVE (35175) Marshall(89), Morgan(10)
UNION SPRINGS Bullock
UNIONTOWN (36786) Perry(88), Hale(5), Marengo(5)
URIAH Monroe
VALHERMOSO SPRINGS Morgan
VALLEY (36854) Chambers(74), Lee(25)
VALLEY Lee
VALLEY HEAD De Kalb
VANCE Tuscaloosa
VANDIVER Shelby
VERBENA (36091) Chilton(95), Autauga(3)
VERNON Lamar
VINA (35593) Franklin(85), Marion(14)
VINCENT (35178) Shelby(70), St. Clair(29)
VINEGAR BEND Washington
VINEMONT Cullman
VREDENBURGH Monroe
WADLEY (36276) Randolph(68), Chambers(15), Clay(11), Tallapoosa(4)
WAGARVILLE Washington
WALKER SPRINGS Clarke
WALNUT GROVE Etowah
WARD (36922) Choctaw(91), Sumter(8)
WARRIOR (35180) Jefferson(55), Blount(44)
WATERLOO Lauderdale
WATSON Jefferson
WATTSVILLE St. Clair
WAVERLY (36879) Chambers(50), Lee(49)
WEAVER Calhoun
WEBB Houston
WEDOWEE Randolph
WELLINGTON Calhoun
WEOGUFKA Coosa
WEST BLOCTON (35184) Bibb(98), Tuscaloosa(1)
WEST GREENE Greene
WESTOVER Shelby
WETUMPKA Elmore
WHATLEY (36482) Clarke(97), Monroe(2)
WILMER Mobile
WILSONVILLE Shelby
WILTON Shelby
WINFIELD (35594) Fayette(56), Marion(43)
WING (36483) Covington(63), Escambia(36)
WOODLAND Randolph
WOODSTOCK (35188) Bibb(88), Tuscaloosa(11)
WOODVILLE (35776) Jackson(82), Marshall(15), Madison(1)
YORK Sumter

Alabama ZIP/City Cross Reference

ZIP Range	City	ZIP Range	City	ZIP Range	City	ZIP Range	City
35004-35004	MOODY	35143-35143	SHELBY	35563-35563	GUIN	35768-35769	SCOTTSBORO
35005-35005	ADAMSVILLE	35144-35144	SILURIA	35564-35564	HACKLEBURG	35771-35771	SECTION
35006-35006	ADGER	35146-35146	SPRINGVILLE	35565-35565	HALEYVILLE	35772-35772	STEVENSON
35007-35007	ALABASTER	35147-35147	STERRETT	35570-35570	HAMILTON	35773-35773	TONEY
35010-35011	ALEXANDER CITY	35148-35148	SUMITON	35571-35571	HODGES	35774-35774	TRENTON
35013-35013	ALLGOOD	35149-35149	SYCAMORE	35572-35572	HOUSTON	35775-35775	VALHERMOSO SPRINGS
35014-35014	ALPINE	35150-35151	SYLACAUGA	35573-35573	KANSAS	35776-35776	WOODVILLE
35015-35015	ALTON	35160-35161	TALLADEGA	35574-35574	KENNEDY	35800-35899	HUNTSVILLE
35016-35016	ARAB	35171-35171	THORSBY	35575-35575	LYNN	35901-35905	GADSDEN
35019-35019	BAILEYTON	35172-35172	TRAFFORD	35576-35576	MILLPORT	35906-35906	RAINBOW CITY
35020-35023	BESSEMER	35173-35173	TRUSSVILLE	35577-35577	NATURAL BRIDGE	35907-35907	GADSDEN
35031-35031	BLOUNTSVILLE	35175-35175	UNION GROVE	35578-35578	NAUVOO	35950-35951	ALBERTVILLE
35032-35032	BON AIR	35176-35176	VANDIVER	35579-35579	OAKMAN	35952-35952	ALTOONA
35033-35033	BREMEN	35178-35178	VINCENT	35580-35580	PARRISH	35953-35953	ASHVILLE
35034-35034	BRENT	35179-35179	VINEMONT	35581-35581	PHIL CAMPBELL	35954-35954	ATTALLA
35035-35035	BRIERFIELD	35180-35180	WARRIOR	35582-35582	RED BAY	35956-35957	BOAZ
35036-35036	BROOKSIDE	35181-35181	WATSON	35584-35584	SIPSEY	35958-35958	BRYANT
35038-35038	BURNWELL	35182-35182	WATTSVILLE	35585-35585	SPRUCE PINE	35959-35959	CEDAR BLUFF
35040-35040	CALERA	35183-35183	WEOGUFKA	35586-35586	SULLIGENT	35960-35960	CENTRE
35041-35041	CARDIFF	35184-35184	WEST BLOCTON	35587-35587	TOWNLEY	35961-35961	COLLINSVILLE
35042-35042	CENTREVILLE	35185-35185	WESTOVER	35592-35592	VERNON	35962-35962	CROSSVILLE
35043-35043	CHELSEA	35186-35186	WILSONVILLE	35593-35593	VINA	35963-35963	DAWSON
35044-35044	CHILDERSBURG	35187-35187	WILTON	35594-35594	WINFIELD	35964-35964	DOUGLAS
35045-35046	CLANTON	35188-35188	WOODSTOCK	35601-35609	DECATUR	35966-35966	FLAT ROCK
35048-35048	CLAY	35200-35299	BIRMINGHAM	35610-35610	ANDERSON	35967-35968	FORT PAYNE
35049-35049	CLEVELAND	35401-35407	TUSCALOOSA	35611-35614	ATHENS	35971-35971	FYFFE
35051-35051	COLUMBIANA	35440-35440	ABERNANT	35615-35615	BELLE MINA	35972-35972	GALLANT
35052-35052	COOK SPRINGS	35441-35441	AKRON	35616-35616	CHEROKEE	35973-35973	GAYLESVILLE
35053-35053	CRANE HILL	35442-35442	ALICEVILLE	35617-35617	CLOVERDALE	35974-35974	GERALDINE
35054-35054	CROPWELL	35443-35443	BOLIGEE	35618-35618	COURTLAND	35975-35975	GROVEOAK
35055-35058	CULLMAN	35444-35444	BROOKWOOD	35619-35619	DANVILLE	35976-35976	GUNTERSVILLE
35060-35060	DOCENA	35446-35446	BUHL	35620-35620	ELKMONT	35978-35978	HENAGAR
35061-35061	DOLOMITE	35447-35447	CARROLLTON	35621-35621	EVA	35979-35979	HIGDON
35062-35062	DORA	35448-35448	CLINTON	35622-35622	FALKVILLE	35980-35980	HORTON
35063-35063	EMPIRE	35449-35449	COALING	35630-35634	FLORENCE	35981-35981	IDER
35064-35064	FAIRFIELD	35452-35452	COKER	35640-35640	HARTSELLE	35983-35983	LEESBURG
35068-35068	FULTONDALE	35453-35453	COTTONDALE	35643-35643	HILLSBORO	35984-35984	MENTONE
35070-35070	GARDEN CITY	35456-35456	DUNCANVILLE	35645-35645	KILLEN	35986-35986	RAINSVILLE
35071-35071	GARDENDALE	35457-35457	ECHOLA	35646-35646	LEIGHTON	35987-35987	STEELE
35072-35072	GOODWATER	35458-35458	ELROD	35647-35647	LESTER	35988-35988	SYLVANIA
35073-35073	GRAYSVILLE	35459-35459	EMELLE	35648-35648	LEXINGTON	35989-35989	VALLEY HEAD
35074-35074	GREEN POND	35460-35460	EPES	35649-35649	MOORESVILLE	35990-35990	WALNUT GROVE
35077-35077	HANCEVILLE	35461-35461	ETHELSVILLE	35650-35650	MOULTON	35999-35999	GADSDEN
35078-35078	HARPERSVILLE	35462-35462	EUTAW	35651-35651	MOUNT HOPE	36003-36003	AUTAUGAVILLE
35079-35079	HAYDEN	35463-35463	FOSTERS	35652-35652	ROGERSVILLE	36004-36004	EUFAULA
35080-35080	HELENA	35464-35464	GAINESVILLE	35653-35654	RUSSELLVILLE	36005-36005	BANKS
35082-35082	HOLLINS	35466-35466	GORDO	35660-35660	SHEFFIELD	36006-36006	BILLINGSLEY
35083-35083	HOLLY POND	35468-35468	KELLERMAN	35661-35662	MUSCLE SHOALS	36008-36008	BOOTH
35085-35085	JEMISON	35469-35469	KNOXVILLE	35670-35670	SOMERVILLE	36009-36009	BRANTLEY
35087-35087	JOPPA	35470-35470	LIVINGSTON	35671-35671	TANNER	36010-36010	BRUNDIDGE
35089-35089	KELLYTON	35471-35471	MC SHAN	35672-35672	TOWN CREEK	36013-36013	CECIL
35091-35091	KIMBERLY	35473-35473	NORTHPORT	35673-35673	TRINITY	36015-36015	CHAPMAN
35094-35094	LEEDS	35474-35474	MOUNDVILLE	35674-35674	TUSCUMBIA	36016-36016	CLAYTON
35096-35096	LINCOLN	35475-35476	NORTHPORT	35677-35677	WATERLOO	36017-36017	CLIO
35097-35097	LOCUST FORK	35477-35477	PANOLA	35699-35699	DECATUR	36020-36020	COOSADA
35098-35098	LOGAN	35478-35478	PETERSON	35739-35739	ARDMORE	36022-36022	DEATSVILLE
35111-35111	MC CALLA	35480-35480	RALPH	35740-35740	BRIDGEPORT	36023-36023	EAST TALLASSEE
35112-35112	MARGARET	35481-35481	REFORM	35741-35741	BROWNSBORO	36024-36024	ECLECTIC
35114-35114	MAYLENE	35482-35482	SAMANTHA	35742-35742	CAPSHAW	36025-36025	ELMORE
35115-35115	MONTEVALLO	35485-35487	TUSCALOOSA	35744-35744	DUTTON	36026-36026	EQUALITY
35116-35116	MORRIS	35490-35490	VANCE	35745-35745	ESTILLFORK	36027-36027	EUFAULA
35117-35117	MOUNT OLIVE	35491-35491	WEST GREENE	35746-35746	FACKLER	36028-36028	DOZIER
35118-35118	MULGA	35501-35504	JASPER	35747-35747	GRANT	36029-36029	FITZPATRICK
35119-35119	NEW CASTLE	35540-35540	ADDISON	35748-35748	GURLEY	36030-36030	FOREST HOME
35120-35120	ODENVILLE	35541-35541	ARLEY	35749-35749	HARVEST	36031-36031	FORT DAVIS
35121-35121	ONEONTA	35542-35542	BANKSTON	35750-35750	HAZEL GREEN	36032-36032	FORT DEPOSIT
35123-35123	PALMERDALE	35543-35543	BEAR CREEK	35751-35751	HOLLYTREE	36033-36033	GEORGIANA
35124-35124	PELHAM	35544-35544	BEAVERTON	35752-35752	HOLLYWOOD	36034-36034	GLENWOOD
35125-35125	PELL CITY	35545-35545	BELK	35754-35754	LACEYS SPRING	36035-36035	GOSHEN
35126-35126	PINSON	35546-35546	BERRY	35755-35755	LANGSTON	36036-36036	GRADY
35127-35127	PLEASANT GROVE	35548-35548	BRILLIANT	35756-35758	MADISON	36037-36037	GREENVILLE
35128-35128	PELL CITY	35549-35549	CARBON HILL	35759-35759	MERIDIANVILLE	36038-36038	GANTT
35130-35130	QUINTON	35550-35550	CORDOVA	35760-35760	NEW HOPE	36039-36039	HARDAWAY
35131-35131	RAGLAND	35551-35551	DELMAR	35761-35761	NEW MARKET	36040-36040	HAYNEVILLE
35133-35133	REMLAP	35552-35552	DETROIT	35762-35762	NORMAL	36041-36041	HIGHLAND HOME
35135-35135	RIVERSIDE	35553-35553	DOUBLE SPRINGS	35763-35763	OWENS CROSS ROADS	36042-36042	HONORAVILLE
35136-35136	ROCKFORD	35554-35554	ELDRIDGE	35764-35764	PAINT ROCK	36043-36043	HOPE HULL
35137-35137	SAGINAW	35555-35555	FAYETTE	35765-35765	PISGAH	36045-36045	KENT
35139-35139	SAYRE	35559-35559	GLEN ALLEN	35766-35766	PRINCETON	36046-36046	LAPINE
35142-35142	SHANNON	35560-35560	GOODSPRINGS	35767-35767	RYLAND	36047-36047	LETOHATCHEE

36048-36048 LOUISVILLE	36370-36370 PANSEY	36556-36556 MALCOLM	36801-36804 OPELIKA
36049-36049 LUVERNE	36371-36371 PINCKARD	36558-36558 MILLRY	36830-36832 AUBURN
36051-36051 MARBURY	36373-36373 SHORTERVILLE	36559-36559 MONTROSE	36849-36849 AUBURN UNIVERSITY
36052-36052 MATHEWS	36374-36374 SKIPPERVILLE	36560-36560 MOUNT VERNON	36850-36850 CAMP HILL
36053-36053 MIDWAY	36375-36375 SLOCOMB	36561-36561 ORANGE BEACH	36851-36851 COTTONTON
36054-36054 MILLBROOK	36376-36376 WEBB	36562-36562 PERDIDO	36852-36852 CUSSETA
36057-36057 MOUNT MEIGS	36401-36401 EVERGREEN	36564-36564 POINT CLEAR	36853-36853 DADEVILLE
36061-36061 PEROTE	36419-36419 ALLEN	36567-36567 ROBERTSDALE	36854-36854 VALLEY
36062-36062 PETREY	36420-36421 ANDALUSIA	36568-36568 SAINT ELMO	36855-36855 FIVE POINTS
36064-36064 PIKE ROAD	36425-36425 BEATRICE	36569-36569 SAINT STEPHENS	36856-36856 FORT MITCHELL
36065-36065 PINE LEVEL	36426-36427 BREWTON	36570-36570 SALITPA	36858-36858 HATCHECHUBBEE
36066-36068 PRATTVILLE	36429-36429 BROOKLYN	36571-36571 SARALAND	36859-36859 HOLY TRINITY
36069-36069 RAMER	36431-36431 BURNT CORN	36572-36572 SATSUMA	36860-36860 HURTSBORO
36071-36071 RUTLEDGE	36432-36432 CASTLEBERRY	36574-36574 SEMINOLE	36861-36861 JACKSONS GAP
36072-36072 EUFAULA	36435-36435 COY	36575-36575 SEMMES	36862-36862 LAFAYETTE
36075-36075 SHORTER	36436-36436 DICKINSON	36576-36576 SILVERHILL	36863-36863 LANETT
36078-36078 TALLASSEE	36439-36439 EXCEL	36577-36577 SPANISH FORT	36865-36865 LOACHAPOKA
36079-36079 TROY	36441-36441 FLOMATON	36578-36578 STAPLETON	36866-36866 NOTASULGA
36080-36080 TITUS	36442-36442 FLORALA	36579-36579 STOCKTON	36867-36870 PHENIX CITY
36081-36082 TROY	36444-36444 FRANKLIN	36580-36580 SUMMERDALE	36871-36871 PITTSVIEW
36083-36083 TUSKEGEE	36445-36445 FRISCO CITY	36581-36581 SUNFLOWER	36872-36872 VALLEY
36087-36088 TUSKEGEE INSTITUTE	36446-36446 FULTON	36582-36582 THEODORE	36874-36874 SALEM
36089-36089 UNION SPRINGS	36449-36449 GOODWAY	36583-36583 TIBBIE	36875-36875 SEALE
36091-36091 VERBENA	36451-36451 GROVE HILL	36584-36584 VINEGAR BEND	36877-36877 SMITHS
36092-36093 WETUMPKA	36453-36453 KINSTON	36585-36585 WAGARVILLE	36877-36877 SMITHS STATION
36100-36199 MONTGOMERY	36454-36454 LENOX	36586-36586 WALKER SPRINGS	36879-36879 WAVERLY
36201-36207 ANNISTON	36455-36455 LOCKHART	36587-36587 WILMER	36901-36901 BELLAMY
36250-36250 ALEXANDRIA	36456-36456 MC KENZIE	36590-36590 THEODORE	36903-36903 BOLINGER
36251-36251 ASHLAND	36457-36457 MEGARGEL	36600-36612 MOBILE	36904-36904 BUTLER
36253-36253 BYNUM	36458-36458 MEXIA	36613-36613 EIGHT MILE	36906-36906 CROMWELL
36254-36254 CHOCCOLOCCO	36460-36462 MONROEVILLE	36614-36695 MOBILE	36907-36907 CUBA
36255-36255 CRAGFORD	36467-36467 OPP	36701-36703 SELMA	36908-36908 GILBERTOWN
36256-36256 DAVISTON	36469-36469 EVERGREEN	36720-36720 ALBERTA	36910-36910 JACHIN
36257-36257 DE ARMANVILLE	36469-36469 PAUL	36721-36721 ANNEMANIE	36911-36911 LAVACA
36258-36258 DELTA	36470-36470 PERDUE HILL	36722-36722 ARLINGTON	36912-36912 LISMAN
36260-36260 EASTABOGA	36471-36471 PETERMAN	36723-36723 BOYKIN	36913-36913 MELVIN
36261-36261 EDWARDSVILLE	36473-36473 RANGE	36726-36726 CAMDEN	36915-36915 NEEDHAM
36262-36262 FRUITHURST	36474-36474 RED LEVEL	36727-36727 CAMPBELL	36916-36916 PENNINGTON
36263-36263 GRAHAM	36475-36475 REPTON	36728-36728 CATHERINE	36919-36919 SILAS
36264-36264 HEFLIN	36476-36476 RIVER FALLS	36731-36731 DAYTON	36921-36921 TOXEY
36265-36265 JACKSONVILLE	36477-36477 SAMSON	36732-36732 DEMOPOLIS	36922-36922 WARD
36266-36266 LINEVILLE	36480-36480 URIAH	36736-36736 DIXONS MILLS	36925-36925 YORK
36267-36267 MILLERVILLE	36481-36481 VREDENBURGH	36738-36738 FAUNSDALE	
36268-36268 MUNFORD	36482-36482 WHATLEY	36740-36740 FORKLAND	
36269-36269 MUSCADINE	36483-36483 WING	36741-36741 FURMAN	
36270-36270 NEWELL	36501-36501 ALMA	36742-36742 GALLION	
36271-36271 OHATCHEE	36502-36504 ATMORE	36744-36744 GREENSBORO	
36272-36272 PIEDMONT	36505-36505 AXIS	36745-36745 JEFFERSON	
36273-36273 RANBURNE	36507-36507 BAY MINETTE	36747-36747 LAMISON	
36274-36274 ROANOKE	36509-36509 BAYOU LA BATRE	36748-36748 LINDEN	
36275-36275 SPRING GARDEN	36510-36510 BIGBEE	36749-36749 JONES	
36276-36276 WADLEY	36511-36511 BON SECOUR	36750-36750 MAPLESVILLE	
36277-36277 WEAVER	36512-36512 BUCKS	36751-36751 LOWER PEACH TREE	
36278-36278 WEDOWEE	36513-36513 CALVERT	36752-36752 LOWNDESBORO	
36279-36279 WELLINGTON	36515-36515 CARLTON	36753-36753 MC WILLIAMS	
36280-36280 WOODLAND	36518-36518 CHATOM	36754-36754 MAGNOLIA	
36301-36305 DOTHAN	36521-36521 CHUNCHULA	36756-36756 MARION	
36310-36310 ABBEVILLE	36522-36522 CITRONELLE	36758-36758 PLANTERSVILLE	
36311-36311 ARITON	36523-36523 CODEN	36759-36759 MARION JUNCTION	
36312-36312 ASHFORD	36524-36524 COFFEEVILLE	36760-36760 MILLERS FERRY	
36313-36313 BELLWOOD	36525-36525 CREOLA	36761-36761 MINTER	
36314-36314 BLACK	36526-36526 DAPHNE	36762-36762 MORVIN	
36316-36316 CHANCELLOR	36527-36527 SPANISH FORT	36763-36763 MYRTLEWOOD	
36317-36317 CLOPTON	36528-36528 DAUPHIN ISLAND	36764-36764 NANAFALIA	
36318-36318 COFFEE SPRINGS	36529-36529 DEER PARK	36765-36765 NEWBERN	
36319-36319 COLUMBIA	36530-36530 ELBERTA	36766-36766 OAK HILL	
36320-36320 COTTONWOOD	36532-36533 FAIRHOPE	36767-36767 ORRVILLE	
36321-36321 COWARTS	36535-36535 FOLEY	36768-36768 PINE APPLE	
36322-36322 DALEVILLE	36538-36538 FRANKVILLE	36769-36769 PINE HILL	
36323-36323 ELBA	36539-36539 FRUITDALE	36771-36771 PRAIRIE	
36330-36331 ENTERPRISE	36540-36540 GAINESTOWN	36773-36773 SAFFORD	
36340-36340 GENEVA	36541-36541 GRAND BAY	36775-36775 SARDIS	
36343-36343 GORDON	36542-36542 GULF SHORES	36776-36776 SAWYERVILLE	
36344-36344 HARTFORD	36543-36543 HUXFORD	36778-36778 SNOW HILL	
36345-36345 HEADLAND	36544-36544 IRVINGTON	36779-36779 SPROTT	
36346-36346 JACK	36545-36545 JACKSON	36782-36782 SWEET WATER	
36349-36349 MALVERN	36547-36547 GULF SHORES	36783-36783 THOMASTON	
36350-36350 MIDLAND CITY	36548-36548 LEROY	36784-36784 THOMASVILLE	
36351-36351 NEW BROCKTON	36549-36549 LILLIAN	36785-36785 TYLER	
36352-36352 NEWTON	36550-36550 LITTLE RIVER	36786-36786 UNIONTOWN	
36353-36353 NEWVILLE	36551-36551 LOXLEY	36790-36790 STANTON	
36360-36361 OZARK	36553-36553 MC INTOSH	36792-36792 RANDOLPH	
36362-36362 FORT RUCKER	36555-36555 MAGNOLIA SPRINGS	36793-36793 LAWLEY	

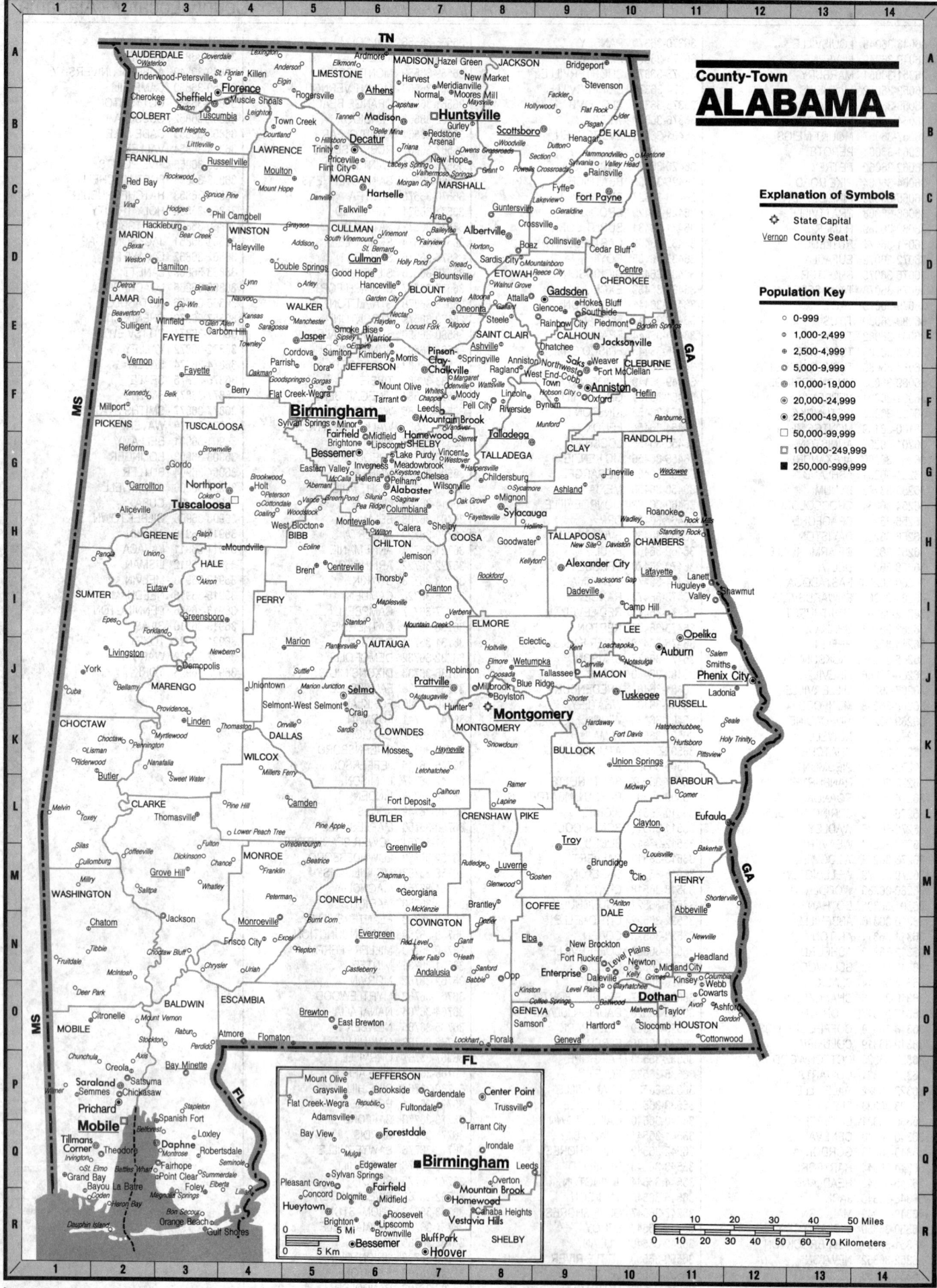

County-Town
ALABAMA

Explanation of Symbols

✧ State Capital
Vernon County Seat

Population Key

- ○ 0-999
- ⊙ 1,000-2,499
- ⊕ 2,500-4,999
- ◎ 5,000-9,999
- ◉ 10,000-19,000
- ⬤ 20,000-24,999
- ⬤ 25,000-49,999
- □ 50,000-99,999
- ▢ 100,000-249,999
- ■ 250,000-999,999

COUNTIES

(67 Counties)

CITIES AND TOWNS

Note: The first name is that of the city or town, second, that of the county in which it is located, then the population and location on the map.

Explanation of symbols: • – Census Designated Place (CDP)

Alaska

General Help Numbers:

Governor's Office
PO Box 110001
Juneau, AK 99811-0001
www.gov.state.ak.us

907-465-3500
Fax 907-465-3532
8AM-5PM

Attorney General's Office
Law Department
PO Box 110300
Juneau, AK 99811-0300
www.law.state.ak.us

907-465-3600
Fax 907-465-2075
8AM-4:30PM

Legislative Records
Alaska State Legislative Affairs Agency
Legislative Information Office
120 4th St #111-State Capitol
Juneau, AK 99801-1182
www.legis.state.ak.us

907-465-4648
Fax 907-465-2864
8AM-5PM

State Archives
Alaska State Archives
141 Willoughby Ave
Juneau, AK 99801-1720
www.archives.state.ak.us

907-465-2270
Fax 907-465-2465
9AM-5PM

State Specifics:

Capital:
Juneau
Juneau Borough

Time Zone:
AK (Alaska Standard Time)*
* Alaska's Aleutian Islands are HT (Hawaii Standard Time)

Number of Counties:
23

Population:
648,818

Web Site:
www.state.ak.us

State Agencies

Criminal Records

Department of Public Safety, Records and Identification, 5700 E Tudor Rd, Anchorage, AK 99507; 907-269-5765, 907-269-5091 (Fax), 8AM-4:30PM.

www.dps.state.ak.us

Note: The state has a "Request for Criminal Justice Information Form" (one for the subject and one for third parties) for "Any Person" reports, which can

be requested by email from tracey_brown@dps.state.ak.us.

Indexing & Storage: Records are available for 10 years from the unconditional discharge date of the incident.

Searching: To receive full record, requester must provide verification of status as "Interested Party" defined as person who employs, appoints or permits the subject to have supervisory power over others, primarily in the child care industry. Include

the following in your request-set of fingerprints, full name. "Any Person" reports are processed for those who are not "Interested Person" qualified and who have a release, proper letter of explanation, and fingerprints. Approximately 62% of records are fingerprint-supported. The following data is not released: sealed records.

Access by: mail, in person.

Fee & Payment: The fee is $35.00 per search. The subject may - in person - request a search for

$20.00, without fingerprints. This also applies to government agencies. If authorized, a requester may also request a national check by the FBI for an additional $24.00. Fee payee: State of Alaska. Prepayment required. No credit cards and no personal checks accepted.

Mail search: Results of search are also sent to the subject.

In person search: Results are usually returned by mail.

Other access: Name searching of limited trial court records and calendars are available free online at www.state.ak.us/courts/names.htm. See the Statewide Court Records profile.

Statewide Court Records

Office of the Administrative Director, Alaska Court System, 820 W 4th Ave, Anchorage, AK 99501; 907-264-8269, 907-264-8291 (Fax), 8AM-4:30PM.

www.state.ak.us/courts/

Indexing & Storage: Records are available online only. It takes up to 3 months before new records are available for inquiry.

Searching: Records are not destroyed.

Access by: online. No searching by mail.

Online search: The home web page gives access to Appellate opinions. You may do a name search of a nearly statewide Alaska Trial Courts database index at www.state.ak.us/courts/names.htm. Search results give case number, file date, disposition date, charge, and sentence. The index gives the name used on the first pleading only. The index is updated every 90 days. This search in and by itself is not FCRA-compliant for employment screening purposes. The civil/criminal name index is available to anyone who sends a blank CD-ROM each quarter to the Administrative Director.

Sexual Offender Registry

Department of Public Safety, Permits and Licensing-SOCR Unit, 5700 E Tudor Rd, Anchorage, AK 99507; 907-269-0396, 907-269-5091 (Fax), 8AM-4:30PM.

www.dps.state.ak.us/nSorcr/asp/

Note: AS 18.65.087 authorizes the Department of Public Safety to maintain a central registry of sex offenders required to register under AS 12.63.010 and to make information about the offender available to the public.

Indexing & Storage: Records are available since August 10, 1994. There are no levels or classes of sexual offenders in this state. All registration forms of offenders who register locally are forwarded to this address.

Searching: Only offenders convicted of the sex offenses specified under AS 12.63.100 are required to register. Persons who have been arrested or charged with a sex offense are not required to register unless the arrest or charge results in a conviction. The following information about those offenders available to the public: name, address, photograph, place of employment, date of birth, crime for which convicted, date of conviction and place and court of conviction. The following data is not released: sealed records.

Access by: mail, in person, online.

Mail search: Turnaround time: 2-4 days.

In person search: Results are usually returned by mail.

Online search: Name searching and geographic searching is available at the website.

Incarceration Records

Alaska Department of Corrections, DOC Classification Office, 4500 Diplomacy Drive, Suite 340, Anchorage, AK 99508-5918; 907-269-7426, 907-269-7439 (Fax), 8AM-4:30PM.

www.correct.state.ak.us

Indexing & Storage: Records are available on current and former inmates. It takes 1 to 2 days before new records are available for inquiry.

Searching: Location, physical identifiers, charges, bail data, conviction and sentencing data are released. Include the following in your request-full name; DOB and SSN helpful.

Access by: mail.

Fee & Payment: No fee for search.

Mail search: Turnaround time: 1-3 days.

Corporation, Trademarks, Servicemarks, Fictitious Name, Assumed Name, Limited Partnership, Limited Liability Company, Limited Liability Partnership

Corporation Section, Department of Community & Econ Dev, PO Box 110808, Juneau, AK 99811-0808 (Courier: 150 Third Street Rm 217, Juneau, AK 99801); 907-465-2530, 907-465-3257 (Fax), 8AM-5PM.

www.dced.state.ak.us/bsc/corps.htm

Indexing & Storage: Records are available from early 1900's on. Prior to 1960, the records are kept at the State Archives. You must go through this office in order to get records. New records are available for inquiry immediately. Records are indexed on microfiche, inhouse computer.

Searching: All information contained is considered public record. Include the following in your request-full name of business. In addition to the articles of incorporation, corporation records include the following information: Annual Reports, Officers, Directors, DBAs, Prior (Merged) names, Inactive and Reserved names.

Access by: mail, phone, fax, in person, online.

Fee & Payment: A copy of a document that is more than one page is $10.00. A copy of all documents pertaining to one file is $30.00 up to 50 pages and an additional $1.00 per page after 50 pages. A copy of a biennial report is $1.00. Fee payee: State of Alaska. Prepayment required. Personal checks accepted. Credit cards accepted: MasterCard, Visa.

Mail search: Turnaround time: 1 to 2 weeks.

Phone search: You can make a search request only if you are local and you plan to pick-up.

Fax search: Typical fax searches involve use of a credit card.

In person search: All results are mailed unless request is being processed using expedited service. The agency will call the requester when his/her request has been processed and is ready for pick-up, if it is a local call.

Online search: At the website, one can access status information on corps, LLCs, LLP, LP (all both foreign and domestic), registered and reserved names, as well as trademark information. Search by entity name, registered agent name, or by officer name. There is no fee. The trademark query is at www.dced.state.ak.us/bsc/TrdStart.cfm.

Other access: For bulk purchase, the requester must use a third party. Call 907-465-2530 for more information.

Expedited service: Expedited service is available for mail, phone and in person searches. Turnaround time: 48 hours. Add $50.00 per business name.

Uniform Commercial Code

UCC Central File Systems Office, State Recorder's Office, 550 West 7th Ave #1200A, Anchorage, AK 99501-3564; 907-269-8873, 907-269-8899, 907-269-8945 (Fax), 8AM-3:30PM.

www.dnr.state.ak.us/ssd/ucc/index.cfm

Note: The statewide recording system consists of 34 separate recording districts serviced by a total of 14 separate offices.

Indexing & Storage: Records are available from 1961 when the UCC system was established. Records are computerized since October 20, 1986 or earlier if with continuations. Records are kept on microfiche since 1981 or prior if continuations filed.

Searching: Use request form UCC-11. Search results include all filings up to one year after lapse. All tax liens are filed at the local District Recorder offices. Include the following in your request-debtor name. All requests must be in writing.

Access by: mail, fax, in person, online.

Fee & Payment: Fee to search by name is $15.00 per debtor name. For information and copies, fee is $25.00 per debtor name. Certification costs an additional $5.00. Single page copies are $2.00 each. Also, see In Person searching for those fees. Fee payee: Alaska Department of Revenue. Prepayment required. Personal checks accepted. Credit cards accepted: MasterCard, Visa.

Mail search: Turnaround time: 1 to 2 days. No SASE is required.

Fax search: Credt cards accepted.

In person search: A public access terminal is available. There is no fee to use the terminal, and a $2.00 per document (not page) when requesting copies in person.

Online search: One can search by granter-grantee name, date, document number or dcoument type at www.dnr.state.ak.us/ssd/ucc/search.cfm. There is no fee.

Other access: Bulkmedia of the entire UCC database can be purchased from the State Recorder's Office (907-269-8881).

Federal Tax Liens, State Tax Liens

Records not maintained by a state level agency.

Note: All tax liens are filed at local District Recorder Offices.

Sales Tax Registrations

State does not impose sales tax.

Birth Certificates

Department of Health & Social Services, Bureau of Vital Statistics, 5441 Commercial Blvd, Juneau, AK 99801; 907-465-3391, 907-465-3618 (Fax), 8AM-4:30PM.

www.hss.state.ak.us/dph/bvs/

Indexing & Storage: Records are available from 1913 to present. New records are available for inquiry immediately. Records are indexed on microfiche, inhouse computer.

Searching: Person requesting must be a parent or guardian or give a justifying reason for request. No adoption information will be given except according to statute. Records are public after 100 years. Include the following in your request-full name, names of parents, mother's maiden name, date of birth, place of birth, reason for information request, relationship to person of record. Also, include a day time phone number.

Access by: mail, phone, fax, in person.

Fee & Payment: The $20.00 search fee includes a 3 year search. Add $1.00 per year searched for each year over 3 years. Fee payee: Bureau of Vital Statistics. Prepayment required. Personal checks accepted. Credit cards accepted: MasterCard, Visa, AmEx, Discover.

Mail search: Turnaround time: 2 weeks. No SASE is required.

Phone search: See expedited services.

Fax search: See expedited services.

In person search: Turnaround time 10 minutes.

Expedited service: Expedited service is available for mail, phone and fax searches. Turnaround time: 2 days. Add $11.00 for using a credit card and $15.50 for Fed Ex or $11.75 for Express Mail.

Death Records

Department of Health & Social Services, Bureau of Vital Statistics, 5441 Commercial Blvd, Juneau, AK 99801; 907-465-3391, 907-465-3618 (Fax), 8AM-4:30PM.

www.hss.state.ak.us/dph/bvs/

Indexing & Storage: Records are available from 1913 to present. New records are available for inquiry immediately. Records are indexed on microfiche, inhouse computer.

Searching: You must be next of kin or have a notarized release statement from immediate family. Records are public after 50 years. Include the following in your request-full name, date of death, place of death, names of parents, reason for information request, relationship to person of record. Also, include a daytime phone number.

Access by: mail, phone, fax, in person.

Fee & Payment: The $20.00 search fee includes a 3 year search. Add $1.00 per year searched for each year over 3 years. Fee payee: Bureau of Vital Statistics. Prepayment required. Personal checks accepted. Credit cards accepted: MasterCard, Visa, AmEx, Discover.

Mail search: Turnaround time: 2 weeks.

Phone search: See expedited service.

Fax search: See expedited service.

In person search: Turnaround time 10 minutes.

Expedited service: Expedited service is available for mail, phone and fax searches. Turnaround time: 2 days. Add $11.00 for using a credit card and add $15.50 for Fed Ex or $11.75 for Express Mail.

Marriage Certificates

Department of Health & Social Services, Bureau of Vital Statistics, 5441 Commercial Blvd, Juneau, AK 99801; 907-465-3391, 907-465-3618 (Fax), 8AM-4:30PM.

www.hss.state.ak.us/dph/bvs/

Indexing & Storage: Records are available from 1913 to present. New records are available for inquiry immediately. Records are indexed on microfiche, inhouse computer.

Searching: Person requesting must be one of the registrants or an attorney representing a registrant. Records are public after 50 years. Include the following in your request-names of husband and wife, date of marriage, place or county of marriage. Include wife's maiden name and a daytime phone number.

Access by: mail, phone, fax, in person.

Fee & Payment: The $20.00 search fee includes a 3 year search. Add $1.00 per year searched for each year over 3 years. Fee payee: Bureau of Vital Statistics. Prepayment required. Personal checks accepted. Credit cards accepted: MasterCard, Visa.

Mail search: Turnaround time: 2 weeks.

Phone search: See expedited service.

Fax search: See expedited service.

In person search: Turnaround time 10 minutes.

Expedited service: Expedited service is available for mail, phone and fax searches. Turnaround time: 2 days. Add $11.00 for using a credit card and add $15.50 for Fed Ex or $11.75 for Express Mail.

Divorce Records

Department of Health & Social Services, Bureau of Vital Statistics, 5441 Commercial Blvd, Juneau, AK 99801; 907-465-3391, 907-465-3618 (Fax), 8AM-4:30PM.

www.hss.state.ak.us/dph/bvs/

Indexing & Storage: Records are available from 1950 to present. New records are available for inquiry immediately. Records are indexed on microfiche, inhouse computer.

Searching: Person requesting must be one of the registrants or an attorney representing a registrant. Records are public after 50 years. Include the following in your request-names of husband and wife, date of divorce, place of divorce. Also, include a daytime phone number.

Access by: mail, phone, fax, in person.

Fee & Payment: The $20.00 search fee includes a 3 year search. Add $1.00 per year searched for each year over 3 years. Fee payee: Bureau of Vital Statistics. Prepayment required. Personal checks accepted. Credit cards accepted: MasterCard, Visa, AmEx, Discover.

Mail search: Turnaround time: 2 weeks. No SASE is required.

Phone search: See expedited service.

Fax search: See expedited service.

In person search: Turnaround time 10 minutes.

Workers' Compensation Records

Workers' Compensation, PO Box 25512, Juneau, AK 99802 (Courier: 1111 W Eighth St, Room 307, Juneau, AK 99802); 907-465-2790, 907-465-2797 (Fax), 8AM-4:30PM.

www.labor.state.ak.us/wc/wc.htm

Indexing & Storage: Records are available from 1982 on the computer if active, and prior to 1982 the records are on microfilm and/or microfiche to the 1960s. It takes one week before new records are available for inquiry.

Searching: All requests must be in writing. To receive a copy of a file, a signed medical release from claimant is required. Include the following in your request-claimant name, Social Security Number, date of accident. All requests handled on a first come first serve basis.

Access by: mail, phone, fax, in person.

Fee & Payment: Copies cost $.35 per page for active files and $.75 per page for microfilmed files. A computer printout costs $.50 per screen. There is no search fee. Fee payee: State of Alaska. Large orders require prepayment. Personal checks accepted. No credit cards accepted.

Mail search: Turnaround time: 10 to 14 days. No SASE is required.

Phone search: The agency will let you know if a file exists.

Fax search: Fax searching available.

In person search: Records are still returned by mail.

Driver Records

Division of Motor Vehicles, Driver's Records, 2760 Sherwood Lane #B, Juneau, AK 99801; 907-465-4361 (Motor Vehicle Reports Desk), 907-465-4363 (Licensing), 907-465-5509 (Fax), 8AM-5PM.

www.state.ak.us/dmv

Note: Copies of tickets are only released, in writing, to the participant, legal representative, or insurance representative.

Indexing & Storage: Records are available for minor moving violations and suspensions for three years, major moving violations for five years. Convictions are automatically purged from public record by conviction date. Accidents are reported only if action is taken.

Searching: Records are considered confidential. Any private company or individual requester must have a signed release from the licensee or a subpoena. High volume requesters may maintain these forms rather than send in with requests. Include the following in your request-name, driver's license number, date of birth. Driver's residence and mailing address are included as part of the search report.

Access by: mail, in person, online.

Fee & Payment: Search costs $5.00 per record. Prepayment is required. Fee payee: State of Alaska. Personal checks accepted. Credit cards are accepted.

Mail search: Turnaround time: 3 to 4 working days. No SASE is required.

In person search: Turnaround time is while you wait.

Online search: Online access costs $5.00 per record. Inquiries may be made at any time, 24 hours a day. Batch inquiries may call back within thirty minutes for responses. Search by the first four letters of driver's name, license number and date of birth. At present, there is only one phone line available for users; you may experience a busy signal.

Vehicle Ownership, Vehicle Identification, Vessel Registration

Division of Motor Vehicles, Research, 1300 W Benson Blvd #200, Anchorage, AK 99503-3600; 907-269-5551, 8:30AM-4:30PM.

www.state.ak.us/dmv

Note: All powered boats, and all non-powered boats over 10 ft or with auxiliary power units used on any water of the state must be registered.

Indexing & Storage: Records are available for 7 years to present. However, until Jan. 1, 2001, all boat registrations were done through the US Coast Guard.

Searching: Record requests are honored for employment, insurance, court or impound purposes. Otherwise, a signed release is required, signed by requester, attesting to purpose of request. Use of Form 851-Request for Vehicle Record is recommended.

Access by: mail, in person.

Fee & Payment: The fee is $5.00 per record. There is no fee to do a vessel search. Fee payee: State of Alaska. Prepayment required. No credit cards accepted.

Mail search: Turnaround time: 2 to 3 weeks. No SASE is required.

In person search: Turnaround time depends on workload and complexity of request. Typically, requests are processed within 5 to 10 days, but can extend to 5 weeks or more.

Other access: The entire master tape file of registration information is available at a cost of approximately $50 per 1,000 records. Call the Director's Office (907-269-5551) for more information.

Accident Reports

Department of Public Safety, Driver Services, 2760 Sherwood Lane #B, Juneau, AK 99801; 907-465-4361, 907-463-5509 (Fax), 8AM-5PM.

www.state.ak.us/dmv

Indexing & Storage: Records are available from seven years. Records are normally destroyed after seven years.

Searching: Only legal representatives and insurance agents of the participants, or the participant him/herself may obtain copies. The lawyer or legal representative must have a notarized request, an insurance agent a signed request with reason. Items required for search include names, date of incident, city, physical location of the accident.

Access by: mail, phone, in person.

Fee & Payment: The fee is $5.00 per record. Fee payee: State of Alaska, Department of Public Safety. Prepayment required. Personal checks accepted. No credit cards accepted.

Mail search: Turnaround time: 1 to 2 weeks. No SASE is required.

Phone search: Phone requests are available for pre-approved accounts.

In person search: Turnaround time is while you wait.

Vessel Ownership

Records not maintained by a state level agency.

Note: Alaska is not a title state. Liens are filed with the Department of Natural Resources, Recorder's Section at 907-269-8882.

Voter Registration

Division of Elections, PO Box 110017, Juneau, AK 99811-0017 (Courier: Court Plaza Building, 4th Floor, 240 Main Street, Juneau, AK 99801); 907-465-4611, 907-465-3203 (Fax), 8AM-5PM.

www.elections.state.ak.us

Note: There are four regional Elections Offices, besides this office. Each has access to the election records database.

Indexing & Storage: Records are available from 1968. It takes 1 day before new records are available for inquiry. Records are normally destroyed after placed on microfilm and become permanent.

Searching: Searching by name is permitted. The following data is not released: Social Security Number, place or date of birth, phone number, and voter ID #.

Access by: mail, phone, fax, in person.

Fee & Payment: There is no fee. There is a copy fee of $.20 per copy if request exceeds 20 copies. Prepayment required. Personal cehcks accepted.

Mail search: Turnaround time: 1 day.

Phone search: Records search if search time not lengthy.

Fax search: Fax searching available.

In person search: Turnaround time is immediate unless extensive lists or requests for older records are presented.

Other access: The agency offers the complete record database on CD-ROM for $178. Individual districts (there are 40) can be purchased on disk for $20.00 per district.

GED Certificates

Department of Labor, Employment Security Division, PO Box 25509, Juneau, AK 99802-5509 (Courier: 1111 8th Street #210, Juneau, AK 99801); 907-465-4685, 907-465-8753 (Fax), 8AM-4:30PM.

www.ajcn.state.ak.us/abe/

Indexing & Storage: It takes 1 day before new records are available for inquiry.

Searching: Include the following in your request-full name, DOB, SSN, year of test and city of test. All requesters must include a signed release. E-mail requests accepted at ged@labor.state.ak.us.

Access by: mail, fax, in person.

Fee & Payment: There is no fee for a verification or a transcript copy. There is a $10.00 fee for a copy of a diploma.

Mail search: Turnaround time: 1 to 2 weeks. No SASE is required.

Fax search: A written release form is required.

In person search: Simple requests may be processed while you wait.

Hunting and Fishing License Information

Department of Fish & Game, Licensing Section, PO Box 25525, Juneau, AK 99802-5525 (Courier: 1255 W 8th St, Juneau, AK 99802); 907-465-2376, 907-465-2440 (Fax), 8AM-5PM.

www.adfg.state.ak.us/

Indexing & Storage: Records are available from 10 years to present. It takes 4 weeks before new records are available for inquiry.

Searching: Information used to search includes name, SSN, DOB, address, driver's license number, or year license issued. The following data is not released: Social Security Numbers or telephone numbers.

Access by: mail, phone, fax, in person.

Fee & Payment: No fee unless you request a large list. For certified copies the turnaround time is 6 weeks. Fee payee: State of Alaska. Prepayment required. Personal checks accepted. Credit cards accepted.

Mail search: Turnaround time: within 3 weeks. No SASE is required.

Phone search: Limited number of requests given over the phone.

Fax search: Same criteria as phone searches.

In person search: Large lists will not be processed immediately.

Other access: The vendor file is available for $25 on paper or disk. The entire license file is available for $350 on CD.

Alaska State Licensing Agencies
Licenses Searchable Online

Acupuncturist #20	www.dced.state.ak.us/occ/search3.htm
Anesthetist, Dental, General/Permit #20	www.dced.state.ak.us/occ/search3.htm
Architect #20	www.dced.state.ak.us/occ/search3.htm
Athletic Event Promoter #20	www.dced.state.ak.us/occ/search3.htm
Athletic Trainer #20	www.dced.state.ak.us/occ/search3.htm
Attorney #11	www.alaskabar.org/index.cfm?id=4954
Audiologist/Hearing Aid Dealer #20	www.dced.state.ak.us/occ/search3.htm
Bail Bondsman #13	www.dced.state.ak.us/ins/apps/InsLicStart.cfm
Bank #23	www.dced.state.ak.us/bsc/pub/2003_directory.pdf
Barber #20	www.dced.state.ak.us/occ/search3.htm
Barber Shop Owner/School/Instructor #20	www.dced.state.ak.us/occ/search3.htm
BIDCOS/CFAB #23	www.dced.state.ak.us/bsc/pub/2003_directory.pdf
Big Game Guide/Assistant/Transporter #20	www.dced.state.ak.us/occ/search3.htm
Boxer #20	www.dced.state.ak.us/occ/search3.htm
Boxing Physician #20	www.dced.state.ak.us/occ/search3.htm
Boxing/Wrestling Personnel #20	www.dced.state.ak.us/occ/search3.htm
Chiropractor #20	www.dced.state.ak.us/occ/search3.htm
Collection Agency/Operator #20	www.dced.state.ak.us/occ/search3.htm
Concert Promoter #20	www.dced.state.ak.us/occ/search3.htm
Construction Contractor #20	www.dced.state.ak.us/occ/search3.htm
Contractor, Civil/Elect./Mech./Mining/Petrol. #20	www.dced.state.ak.us/occ/search3.htm
Contractor, Residential #20	www.dced.state.ak.us/occ/search3.htm
Cosmetologist/Hairdresser #20	www.dced.state.ak.us/occ/search3.htm
Cosmetology Shop Owner/School/Instructor #20	www.dced.state.ak.us/occ/search3.htm
Counselor, Professional #20	www.dced.state.ak.us/occ/OccSearch/main.cfm
Credit Union #23	www.dced.state.ak.us/bsc/pub/2003_directory.pdf
Defibrillator Technician #17	http://chems.alaska.gov/emsdata/
Dental Hygienist #20	www.dced.state.ak.us/occ/search3.htm
Dentist/Dental Examiner #20	www.dced.state.ak.us/occ/search3.htm
Dietitian/Nutritionist #20	www.dced.state.ak.us/occ/OccSearch/main.cfm
Drug Distributor/Drug Room #20	www.dced.state.ak.us/occ/search3.htm
Electrical Administrator #20	www.dced.state.ak.us/occ/search3.htm
Emergency Medical Technician #17	http://chems.alaska.gov/emsdata/
Employment Agency Operator Permit #5	www.dced.state.ak.us/occ/search3.htm
Engineer #20	www.dced.state.ak.us/occ/search3.htm
Esthetician #20	www.dced.state.ak.us/occ/search3.htm
Funeral Director/Establishment #20	www.dced.state.ak.us/occ/search3.htm
Geologist #20	www.dced.state.ak.us/occ/search3.htm
Guide/Outfitter, Hunting #20	www.dced.state.ak.us/occ/search3.htm
Hairdresser/Esthetician #20	www.dced.state.ak.us/occ/search3.htm
Hearing Aid Dealer #20	www.dced.state.ak.us/occ/search3.htm
Independent Adjuster #13	www.dced.state.ak.us/ins/apps/InsLicStart.cfm
Insurance Agent, Managing General #13	www.dced.state.ak.us/ins/apps/InsLicStart.cfm
Insurance Occupation #13	www.dced.state.ak.us/ins/apps/InsLicStart.cfm
Insurance Producer #13	www.dced.state.ak.us/ins/apps/InsLicStart.cfm
Landscape Architect #20	www.dced.state.ak.us/occ/search3.htm
Lobbyist/Lobbyist Employer #9	www.state.ak.us/local/akpages/ADMIN/apoc/lobcov.htm
Marriage & Family Therapist #20	www.dced.state.ak.us/occ/OccSearch/main.cfm
Mechanical Administrator #20	www.dced.state.ak.us/occ/search3.htm
Medical Doctor/Surgeon #20	www.dced.state.ak.us/occ/search3.htm
Midwife #20	www.dced.state.ak.us/occ/OccSearch/main.cfm
Mortician/Embalmer #20	www.dced.state.ak.us/occ/search3.htm
Naturopathic Physician #20	www.dced.state.ak.us/occ/search3.htm
Nurse #20	www.dced.state.ak.us/occ/search3.htm
Nurse Anesthetist #20	www.dced.state.ak.us/occ/search3.htm
Nurse-RN/LPN #20	www.dced.state.ak.us/occ/search3.htm
Nurses' Aide #20	www.dced.state.ak.us/occ/search3.htm
Nursing Home Administrator #20	www.dced.state.ak.us/occ/search3.htm
Occupational Therapist/Assistant #20	www.dced.state.ak.us/occ/search3.htm
Optician, Dispensing #20	www.dced.state.ak.us/occ/search3.htm

Optometrist #20 ....www.dced.state.ak.us/occ/search3.htm
Osteopathic Physician #20 ....www.dced.state.ak.us/occ/search3.htm
Paramedic #20 ....www.dced.state.ak.us/occ/search3.htm
Parenteral Sedation (Dental) #20 ....www.dced.state.ak.us/occ/search3.htm
Pharmacist/Pharmacist Intern #20...........................www.dced.state.ak.us/occ/search3.htm
Pharmacy, Pharmacy Technician #20 ....www.dced.state.ak.us/occ/search3.htm
Physical Therapist/Assistant #20..............................www.dced.state.ak.us/occ/search3.htm
Physician Assistant #20 ....www.dced.state.ak.us/occ/search3.htm
Pilot, Marine #20 ....www.dced.state.ak.us/occ/search3.htm
Podiatrist #20 ....www.dced.state.ak.us/occ/search3.htm
Premium Finance Company #23 ....www.dced.state.ak.us/bsc/pub/2003_directory.pdf
Process Server #10 ....www.dps.state.ak.us/PermitsLicensing/images/CPSlist.pdf
Psychologist/Psychological Assistant #20.................www.dced.state.ak.us/occ/search3.htm
Public Accountant-CPA #20 ....www.dced.state.ak.us/occ/OccSearch/main.cfm
Real Estate Agent/Broker/Assoc. #20 ....www.dced.state.ak.us/occ/search3.htm
Real Estate Appraiser #20 ....www.dced.state.ak.us/occ/search3.htm
Referee #20 ....www.dced.state.ak.us/occ/OccSearch/main.cfm
Reinsurance Intermediary Broker/Mgr. #13...............www.dced.state.ak.us/ins/apps/InsLicStart.cfm
School Administrator #1..www.eed.state.ak.us/TeacherCertification/CertSearchForm.cfm
School Special Service #1 ....www.eed.state.ak.us/TeacherCertification/CertSearchForm.cfm
Small Loan Company #23 ....www.dced.state.ak.us/bsc/pub/2003_directory.pdf
Social Worker #20 ....www.dced.state.ak.us/occ/OccSearch/main.cfm
Social Worker, Clinical #20...www.dced.state.ak.us/occ/OccSearch/main.cfm
Speech/Language Pathologist #20.............................www.dced.state.ak.us/occ/search3.htm
Surplus Line Broker #13 ....www.dced.state.ak.us/ins/apps/InsLicStart.cfm
Surveyor, Land #20 ....www.dced.state.ak.us/occ/search3.htm
Tattoo Artist/Body Piercer #20...................................www.dced.state.ak.us/occ/search3.htm
Teacher #1..www.eed.state.ak.us/TeacherCertification/CertSearchForm.cfm
Thrift #23...www.dced.state.ak.us/bsc/pub/2003_directory.pdf
Transporter, Game #20 ....www.dced.state.ak.us/occ/search3.htm
Trust Company #23 ....www.dced.state.ak.us/bsc/pub/2003_directory.pdf
Underground Storage Tank Worker/Contractor #20.........www.dced.state.ak.us/occ/search3.htm
Vessel Agent #20..www.dced.state.ak.us/occ/search3.htm
Veterinarian/Veterinary Technician #20 ....www.dced.state.ak.us/occ/search3.htm
Viatical Settlement Broker #13 ....www.dced.state.ak.us/ins/apps/InsLicStart.cfm
Waste Water System Operator #3..............................www.dec.state.ak.us/fco/opcert/index.html
Wrestler #20 ....www.dced.state.ak.us/occ/OccSearch/main.cfm

Alaska Licensing Quick Finder

Acupuncturist #20 907-465-2695	Chiropractor #20 907-465-2589	Funeral Director/Establishment #20 607-465-2695
Aircraft-related Occupation #18 907-271-2158	Collection Agency/Operator #20 907-465-2695	Fur Dealer #4 907-465-2376
Alcohol Establishment #21 907-269-0350	Concealed Handgun Registrant #10 907-269-0392	Game Farm #4 907-465-2376
Alcohol Server #21 907-269-0350	Concert Promoter #20 907-465-2534	Geologist #20 907-465-2695
Amusement Ride #7 907-269-4963	Construction Contractor #20 907-465-2546	Guide, Sport Fishing #6 907-267-2369
Anesthetist, Dental, Gen'l/Permit #20 .. 907-465-2542	Contractor, Civil/Elect./Mech./Mining/Petrol. #20	Guide, Sport Fishing, Kenai Only #8.... 907-260-4882
Architect #20 907-465-2540	 907-465-2546	Guide/Outfitter, Hunting #20 907-465-2543
Art Exhibit (Cabaret) #21 907-269-0350	Contractor, Residential #20 907-465-2546	Hairdresser/Esthetician #20 907-465-2547
Asbestos Removal Worker #22 907-269-4960	Cosmetologist/Hairdresser #20 907-465-2547	Hearing Aid Dealer #20 907-465-2695
Asbestos Worker #227 907-269-4960	Cosmetology Shop Owner/School/Instructor #20	Hunting Guide #20 907-465-2543
Athletic Event Promoter #20 907-465-2695	 907-465-2547	Independent Adjuster #13 907-465-2515
Athletic Trainer #20 907-465-2695	Counselor, Professional #20 907-465-2551	Insurance Agent, Man'g General #13 .. 907-465-2515
Attorney #11 907-272-7469	Credit Union #23 907-465-2521	Insurance Occupation #13 907-465-2515
Audiologist/Hearing Aid Dealer #20 907-465-2695	Crewmember (Fishing Boat) #4 907-465-2376	Insurance Producer #13 907-465-2515
Bail Bondsman #13 907-465-2515	Defibrillator Technician #17 907-465-3029	Investment Advisor #12 907-465-2521
Bank #23 907-465-2521	Dental Hygienist #20 907-465-2542	Investment Broker/Dealer/Related Occupation #12
Barber #20 907-465-2547	Dentist/Dental Examiner #20 907-465-2542	 907-465-2521
Barber Shop Owner/School/Instr. #20... 907-465-2547	Dietitian/Nutritionist #20 907-465-2534	Landscape Architect #20 907-465-2540
BIDCOS/CFAB #23 907-465-2521	Drug Distributor/Drug Room #20 907-465-2589	Lobbyist/Lobbyist Employer #9 907-465-4864
Big Game Guide/Assistant/Transporter #20	Electrical Administrator #20 907-465-2589	Marriage & Family Therapist #20 907-465-2551
...... 907-465-2543	Electrician #7 907-269-4963	Mechanical Administrator #20 907-465-2589
Boiler Operator #7 907-269-4963	Elevator #7 907-269-4963	Medical Doctor/Surgeon #20 907-465-2541
Boxer #20 907-465-2695	Emergency Medical Technician #17 907-465-3029	Midwife #20 907-465-2580
Boxing Physician #20 907-465-2695	Employment Agency Operator #5...... 907-269-8160	Mobile Home Dealer #20 907-465-2547
Boxing/Wrestling Personnel #20 907-465-2695	Engineer #20 907-465-2540	Mortician/Embalmer #20 607-465-2695
Broker/Dealer #12 907-465-2521	Esthetician #20 907-465-2547	Naturopathic Physician #20 907-465-2695
Charter Boat, Sport Fishing #6 907-267-2369	Explosives Handler #22 907-269-4960	Notary Public #19 907-465-3509
Child Care Provider/Home/Center/Group Home #16	Fisher #4 907-465-2376	Nurse #20 907-465-2544
...... 907-465-4756	Fishing Operation, Kenai #8 907-260-4882	Nurse Anesthetist #20 907-465-2544

Nurse-RN/LPN #20 907-465-2544
Nurses' Aide #20 907-269-8169
Nursing Home Administrator #20 907-465-2695
Occupational Therapist/Assistant #20 .. 907-465-2580
Optician, Dispensing #20 907-465-5470
Optometrist #20 907-465-2580
Osteopathic Physician #20 907-465-2541
Painter #22 907-269-4960
Paramedic #20 907-465-2541
Parenteral Sedation (Dental) #20 907-465-2542
Pesticide Applicator #2 907-745-3236
Pharmacist/Pharmacist Intern #20 907-465-2589
Pharmacy #20 907-465-2589
Pharmacy Technician #20 907-465-2589
Physical Therapist/Assistant #20 907-465-2580
Physician Assistant #20...................... 907-269-8163
Pilot, Aircraft #18 907-271-2158
Pilot, Marine #20 907-465-2548

Plumber #7 907-269-4963
Podiatrist #20.................................... 907-465-2541
Premium Finance Company #23.......... 907-465-2521
Process Server #10 907-269-0393
Psychologist/Psychological Assist. #20 907-465-3811
Public Accountant-CPA #20 907-465-3817
Real Estate Agent/Broker/Assoc. #20.. 907-269-8162
Real Estate Appraiser #20 907-465-2542
Referee #20 907-465-2695
Reinsurance Intermediary Broker/Mgr. #13
.... 907-465-2515
School Administrator #1 907-465-2831
School Special Service #1................... 907-465-2831
Securities Agent #12 907-465-2521
Security Guard #10............................. 907-269-0393
Skilift #7 907-269-4963
Small Loan Company #23 907-465-2521
Social Worker #20 907-465-2551

Social Worker, Clinical #20 907-465-2551
Speech/Language Pathologist #20....... 907-465-2534
Surplus Line Broker #13...................... 907-465-2515
Surveyor, Land #20 907-465-2540
Tattoo Artist/Body Piercer #20 907-465-2547
Taxidermist #4 907-465-2376
Teacher #1 907-465-2831
Thrift #23 907-465-2521
Transporter, Game #20 907-465-2543
Trapper #4 907-465-2376
Trust Company #23............................. 907-465-2521
Underground Storage Tank Worker/Contractor #20
.... 907-465-5470
Vessel Agent #20 907-465-2548
Veterinarian/Veterinary Tech. #20 907-465-5470
Viatical Settlement Broker #13............. 907-465-2515
Waste Water System Operator #3........ 907-465-5140
Wrestler #20...................................... 907-465-2695

Alaska Licensing Agency Information

1 Department of Education & Early Development, Teacher Education & Certification, 801 W 10th St, #200, Juneau, AK 99801-1894; 907-465-2831, Fax: 907-465-2441.
www.eed.state.ak.us/TeacherCertification/
Email: tcwebmail@eed.state.ak.us
Search Database at
www.eed.state.ak.us/TeacherCertification/CertSearchForm.cfm

2 Department of Environmental Conservation, Division of Environmental Health, 500 S Alaska St, Palmer, AK 99645; 907-745-3236, Fax: 907-745-8125.
www.state.ak.us/dec/deh/pesticides/home.htm
Email: dick_barrett@dec.state.ak.us

3 Department of Environmental Conservation, Facility Construction & Operation, 410 Willoughby Ave, #303, Juneau, AK 99801-1795; 907-465-5140, Fax: 907-465-5177.
www.state.ak.us/local/akpages/ENV.CONSERV/
Search Database at
www.dec.state.ak.us/fco/opcert/index.html

4 Department of Fish & Game, Licensing Section, PO Box 25525, Juneau, AK 99802-5525; 907-465-2376, Fax: 907-265-6430.
www.state.ak.us/local/akpages/FISH.GAME/admin/license/crew.htm
Email: Kris_Wright@fishgame.state.ak.us

5 Department of Labor, Department of Commerce, Div of Occupational Licensing, 550 W 7th Ave #1500, Anchorage, AK 99501-3567; 907-269-8160, Fax: 907-261-8156.
www.dced.state.ak.us/occ Search Database at
www.dced.state.ak.us/occ/search3.htm

6 Department of Fish and Game, Division of Sport Fish - RTS, 333 Raspberry Rd, Anchorage, AK 99518-1599; 907-267-2369, Fax: 907-267-2422.
www.sf.adfg.state.ak.us/statewide/Guides/guide.cfm

7 Department of Labor, Labor & Safety Standards, Mechanical Inspection Section, 3301 Eagle St #302, Anchorage, AK 99503-4149; 907-269-4963, Fax: 907-269-4932.
www.labor.state.ak.us/lss/mihome.htm
Email: Anchorage_LSS-MI@labor.state.ak.us

8 Department of Natural Resources, Division of Parks & Outdoor Recreation - Kenai, 514 Funny River Rd, Soldotna, AK 99669; 907-260-4882, Fax: 907-260-5992.
www.dnr.state.ak.us/parks/

9 Public Offices Commission, PO Box 110222 (240 Main. St, Rm 201), Juneau, AK 99811-0222; 907-465-4864, Fax: 907-465-4832.
www.state.ak.us/local/akpages/ADMIN/apoc/lobcov.htm
Email: tammy_kempton@admin.stae.ak.us
Search Database at
www.state.ak.us/local/akpages/ADMIN/apoc/lobcov.htm Note: Download directories of licensed lobbyists at the website. The Anchorage phone is 907-276-4176.

10 Alaska State Troopers, Dept. of Public Safety/ Permits & Licensing Unit, 5700 E Tudor Rd, Anchorage, AK 99507-1225; 907-269-0391, Fax: 907-269-5609.
www.dps.state.ak.us/PermitsLicensing/index.asp
Email: maryellen_thomas@dps.state.ak.us

11 Alaska Bar Association, Board of Governors, PO Box 100279 (550 W 7th Ave #1900), Anchorage, AK 99510-0279; 907-272-7469, Fax: 907-272-2932.
www.alaskabar.org
Email: info@alaskabar.org Search Database at
www.alaskabar.org/index.cfm?id=4954 Note: Recent yearly bar exam name results are available at www.alaskabar.org/ada.cfm?id=5239.

12 Department of Community & Economic Development, Division of Banking; Securities Section, PO Box 110807, Juneau, AK 99811-0807; 907-465-2521, Fax: 907-465-1230.
www.dced.state.ak.us/bsc/secur.htm
Email: dbsc@dced.state.ak.us

13 Department of Community & Economic Development, Division of Insurance, PO Box 110805 (9th Floor State Office Bldg), Juneau, AK 99811-0805; 907-465-2515, Fax: 907-465-3422.
www.dced.state.ak.us/insurance/
Email: insurance@dced.state.ak.us Search Database at
www.dced.state.ak.us/ins/apps/InsLicStart.cfm

16 Department of Health & Social Services, Division of Public Asst - Child Care Licensing, SE, PO Box 110640 (SE Division Only), Juneau, AK 99811; 907-465-4756, Fax: 907-465-6982.
www.hss.state.ak.us/dpa
Search Database at
www.hss.state.ak.us/dpa/programs/ccare/
Note: There are 3 other divisions that handle facility licensing: Anchorage Area.: 907-343-4748; South Central Alaska (except Anchorage): 907-269-4600; Fairbanks: 907-451-3198.

17 Department of Health & Social Services, Division of Public Health/Section of Community Health and EMS, 410 Willoughby Rm 109 Box 110616, Juneau, AK 99811-0616; 907-465-3027, Fax: 907-465-4101.
www.chems.alaska.gov
Email: matt_anderson@health.state.ak.us
Search Database at
http://chems.alaska.gov/emsdata/

18 Federal Aviation Administration, FSDO, 4510 W International Airport Rd, Anchorage, AK 99502; 907-271-2158, Fax: 907-271-3877.

19 Notary Public Section, Office of Lieutenant Governor, PO Box 110015, State Capitol, Juneau, AK 99811-0015; 907-465-3509, Fax: 907-465-5400.
www.gov.state.ak.us/ltgov
Email: notary@gov.state.ak.us

20 Department of Community & Economic Development, Div of Occupational Licensing, PO Box 110806, Juneau, AK 99811-0806; 907-465-2534, Fax: 907-465-2974.
www.dced.state.ak.us/occ
Email: license@dced.state.ak.us
Search Database at
www.dced.state.ak.us/occ/search3.htm Note: You may download business license lists at
www.dced.state.ak.us/occ/buslic4.cfm.

21 Department of Revenue, Alcoholic Beverage Control Board, 5848 E. Tudor Rd, Anchorage, AK 99507-1286; 907-269-0350, Fax: 907-272-9412.
www.abc.revenue.state.ak.us

22 Department of Labor, Labor & Safety Standards, OSH, PO Box 107022, Anchorage, AK; 907-269-4960.
www.labor.state.ak.us/lss/oshhome.htm

23 Department of Community & Economic Development, Division of Banking; Banking Section, PO Box 110807, Juneau, AK 99811; 907-465-2521, Fax: 907-465-1231.
www.dced.state.ak.us/bsc/banking.htm
Search Database at
www.dced.state.ak.us/bsc/pub/2003_directory.pdf

Alaska Federal Courts

The following list indicates the district and division name for each county in the state. If the bankruptcy court location is different from the district court, then the location of the bankruptcy court appears in parentheses.

County/Court Cross Reference

Aleutian Islands, East	Anchorage
Aleutian Islands, West	Anchorage
Anchorage Borough Borough	Anchorage
Bethel	Fairbanks (Anchorage)
Bristol Bay Borough Borough	Anchorage
Fairbanks North Star Borough Borough	Fairbanks (Anchorage)
Haines. Borough Borough	Juneau (Anchorage)
Juneau Borough Borough	Juneau (Anchorage)
Kenai Peninsula Borough Borough	Anchorage
Ketchikan Gateway Borough Borough	Ketchikan (Anchorage)
Kodiak Island Borough Borough	Anchorage
Matanuska-Susitna Borough Borough	Anchorage
Nome	Nome (Anchorage)
North Slope Borough Borough	Fairbanks (Anchorage)
Northwest Arctic Borough	Fairbanks (Anchorage)
Prince of Wales-Outer Ketchikan	Juneau (Anchorage)
Sitka Borough Borough	Juneau (Anchorage)
Southeast Fairbanks	Fairbanks (Anchorage)
Valdez-Cordova	Anchorage
Wade Hampton	Fairbanks (Anchorage)
Wrangell-Petersburg	Juneau (Anchorage)
Yakutat	Juneau (Anchorage)
Yukon-Koyukuk	Fairbanks (Anchorage)

Standards for Federal Courts: The search fee is $20.00 per item (one party name or case number). Certification fee is $7.00 per document. Copy fee is $.50 per page. All fees standard unless noted in profile. Mail Search: always enclose a stamped self addressed envelope unless otherwise noted. Most courts accept fax requests or will suggest a copying/search vendor. Before releasing records, all courts require prepayment unless noted in profile.

Open records are located at the court unless otherwise noted. District courts index by defendant and plaintiff as well as by case number. Bankruptcy courts usually index by debtor and case number. While most courts now have their indexes on computer, many still maintain index card files as well.

The universal PACER sign-up number is 800-676-6856. Find PACER and the Party/Case Index on the Web at http://pacer.psc.uscourts.gov. PACER dial-up access is $.60 per minute. Also courts offering internet access via RACER, PACER, Web-PACER or the new CM-ECF charge $.07 per page fee unless noted as free.

US District Court
District of Alaska

Anchorage Division Room 229, 222 W 7th Ave, Anchorage, AK 99513-7564 (courier: Use mail address for courier delivery) 907-677-6100, 866-243-3814. www.akd.uscourts.gov

Counties: Aleutian Islands-East, Aleutian Islands-West, Anchorage Borough, Bristol Bay Borough, Dillingham, Kenai Peninsula Borough, Kodiak Island Borough, Lake and Peninsula, Matanuska-Susitna Borough, Valdez-Cordova.

Indexing & Storage: New cases available in the index immediately after filing date. An index card system was used to index files prior to May 1987. Records after May 1987 are on computer. If a case was tried, the file will be sent to the Anchorage Federal Records Center. If the case did not go to trial, the file will be sent to the Seattle Federal Records Center. Case records are sent to a Center after the case is closed.

Fee & Payment: Payment may be made by money order, cashier check, personal check. Payee: Clerk, U.S. District Court.

Phone Search: Only docket information available by phone.

In Person Search: Fee charged if court conducts your in person search for you.

PACER: Toll-free access: 888-271-6212. Local access: 907-677-6178. Records purged every 6 months. New records are online after 1 day.

Other Online Access: Court does not participate in the U.S. party case index.

Fairbanks Division Room 332, 101 12th Ave, Fairbanks, AK 99701 (courier address: Use mail address for courier delivery) 907-451-5791, 866-243-3813. www.akd.uscourts.gov

Counties: Bethel, Denali, Fairbanks North Star Borough, North Slope Borough, Northwest Arctic Borough, Southeast Fairbanks, Wade Hampton, Yukon-Koyukuk.

Indexing & Storage: New cases available in the index 1-2 days after filing date.

Fee & Payment: Payment may be made by money order, cashier check, personal check. Prepayment is required unless other arrangements have been made. Payee: U.S. District Court.

Phone Search: Only docket information available by phone.

In Person Search: Fee charged if court conducts your in person search for you.

PACER: Toll-free access: 888-271-6212. Local access: 907-677-6178. Records purged every 6 months. New records are online after 1 day.

Other Online Access: Court does not participate in the U.S. party case index.

Juneau Division PO Box 020349, 709 W. 9th Ave., Rm 979, Juneau, AK 99802-0349 (courier address: Room 979, Federal Bldg-U.S. Courthouse, 709 W 9th, Juneau, AK 99802), 907-586-7458, 866-243-3812. www.akd.uscourts.gov

Counties: Haines Borough, Juneau Borough, Prince of Wales-Outer Ketchikan, Sitka Borough, Skagway-Hoonah-Angoon, Wrangell-Petersburg.

Indexing & Storage: New cases available in the index immediately after filing date. Case files are indexed on computer and then stored in file cabinets. If the case was tried, the file will be sent to the divison where it was filed. If the case did not go to trial, it will be sent to the Seattle Federal Records Center some time after the case is closed.

Fee & Payment: Payment may be made by money order, cashier check, personal check. Payee: Clerk, U.S. District Court.

Phone Search: Only docket information available by phone.

In Person Search: Fee charged if court conducts your in person search for you. Public may view original case files.

PACER: Toll-free access: 888-271-6212. Local access: 907-677-6178. Records purged every 6 months. New records are online after 1 day.

Other Online Access: Court does not participate in the U.S. party case index.

Ketchikan Division 648 Mission St, Room 507, Ketchikan, AK 99901 (courier address: Use mail address for courier delivery) 907-247-7576. www.akd.uscourts.gov

Counties: Ketchikan Gateway Borough.

Indexing & Storage: New cases available in the index immediately after filing date. Case files are indexed on computer and then stored in file cabinets. If the case was tried, the file will be sent to the Anchorage Division. If the case did not go to trial, it will be sent to the Seattle Federal Records Center. Case records are sent to a Center after the case is closed.

Fee & Payment: Payment may be made by money order, cashier check, business check. Personal checks are not accepted. Payee: Clerk, U.S. District Court.

Phone Search: Only docket information available by phone.

In Person Search: Fee charged if court conducts your in person search for you.

PACER: Toll-free access: 888-271-6212. Local access: 907-677-6178. Records purged every 6 months. New records are online after 1 day.

Other Online Access: Court does not participate in the U.S. party case index.

Nome Division PO Box 130, Nome, AK 99762 (courier address: 2nd Floor, Federal Bldg, Front St, Nome, AK 99762), 907-443-5216, Fax: 907-443-2192. www.akd.uscourts.gov

Counties: Nome.

Indexing & Storage: New cases available in the index immediately after filing date. Records have been retained at this court since 1960. No records have been sent to the repository.

Fee & Payment: Payment may be made by money order, cashier check, personal check. Prepayment is not required, but is preferred. For copies, make checks payable to Alaska Court System. For searches and certified copies, make checks payable to U.S. District Court. Prefer not to fax results, but will in expedited cases at cost of fax, search and copies.

Phone Search: Only docket information available by phone. The court prefers that requests be submitted in writing. Prefer not to fax results, but will in expedited cases at cost of fax, search and copies.

Mail Search: A SASE not required.

In Person Search: Fee charged if court conducts your in person search for you.

PACER: Toll-free access: 888-271-6212. Local access: 907-677-6178. Records purged every 6 months. New records are online after 1 day.

Other Online Access: Court does not participate in the U.S. party case index.

U.S. Bankruptcy Court

District of Alaska

Anchorage Division Historic Courthouse, Suite 138, 605 W 4th Ave, Anchorage, AK 99501-2296 (Use mail address for courier delivery) 907-271-2655.

http://www2.akb.uscourts.gov/mainpage.htm

Counties: All boroughs and districts in Alaska.

Indexing & Storage: Cases indexed by debtor as well as by case number. New cases available in the index 1-2 days after filing date. To insure accuracy, the court advises including a social security number or tax ID number. If the case was tried, it will be sent to Anchorage Federal Records Center. If the case did not go to trial, it will be sent to Seattle Federal Records Center. Case records are sent to a Center 60 days after the case is closed.

Fee & Payment: Payment may be made by money order, cashier check, personal check. Payee: Clerk, U.S. Bankruptcy Court.

Phone Search: Accession numbers will be released over the phone if a case number is provided. If the case number is unknown, the information must be requested in writing with the $20.00 search fee. Automated voice case information service (VCIS) is available. Call VCIS at 888-878-3110 or 907-271-2658.

In Person Search: Fee charged if court conducts your in person search for you. The copy machine works on a debit card system. Cards may be purchased at the State Law Library.

PACER: PACER is available online at http://pacer.akb.uscourts.gov. Document images available. Records purged 6 months. New civil records are online after 2 days.

Electronic Filing: Electronic filing information online at https://ecf.akb.uscourts.gov

Other Online Access: The RACER system has been replaced by the ECF/PACER system. Access fee is $.07 per page.

Alaska Local Courts

Court	Jurisdiction	No. of Courts	How Organized
Superior Courts*	General		4 Districts
District Courts*	Limited	6	4 Districts
Combined Courts*		16	
Magistrate Courts*	Limited	40	4 Districts

* Profiled in this Sourcebook

CIVIL									
Court	Tort	Contract	Real Estate	Min. Claim	Max. Claim	Small Claims	Estate	Eviction	Domestic Relations
Superior Courts*	X	X	X	$0	No Max		X	X	X
District Courts*	X	X		$0	$50,000	$7500		X	X
Magistrate Courts*	X	X		$0	$7500	$7500			

CRIMINAL					
Court	Felony	Misdemeanor	DWI/DUI	Preliminary Hearing	Juvenile
Superior Courts*	X				X
District Courts*		X	X	X	X
Magistrate Courts*		X	X	X	

ADMINISTRATION   Office of the Administrative Director, 820 W 4th Ave, Anchorage, AK, 99501; 907-264-8269, Fax: 907-264-8291. www.state.ak.us/courts

COURT STRUCTURE   Alaska is not organized into counties, but rather into 15 boroughs (3 unified home rule municipalities that are combination borough and city, and 12 boroughs) and 12 home rule cities, which do not directly coincide with the 4 Judicial Districts into which the judicial system is divided. In other words, judicial boundaries cross borough boundaries. Alaska has a unified, centrally administered, and totally state-funded judicial system. Municipal governments do not maintain separate court systems.

The four levels of courts in the Alaska Court System are the supreme court, the court of appeals, the superior court and the district court. The supreme court and the court of appeals are appellate courts, while the superior and district courts are trial courts. Probate is handled by the superior courts.

The superior court is the trial court of general jurisdiction. There are 34 superior court judgeships located throughout the state. The district court is a trial court of limited jurisdiction. The district court currently has 17 judges in the state. The superior court serves as an appellate court for appeals from civil and criminal cases which have been tried in the district court.

We have listed the courts by their borough or home rule city in keeping with a convenient alphabetical format. You should search through the city court location names to determine the correct court for your search.

The First District encompasses all of S.E. Alaska. Magistrates act as judicial officers. This 1st District has five trial/Superior courts: Ketchikan, Wrangell, Petersburg, Sitka and Juneau. District Magistrate Courts are Haines, Skagway, Yakutat, Angoon, Kake, Hoona, Craig.

ONLINE ACCESS   You may do a name search of a nearly statewide Alaska Trial Courts database index at www.state.ak.us/courts/names.htm. Search results give case number, file date, disposition date, charge, and sentence. The index gives the name used on the first pleading only. The index is updated every 90 days. This search in and by itself is not FCRA-compliant for employment screening purposes. The civil/criminal name index is available to anyone who sends a blank CD-ROM each quarter to the Administrative Director. The home web page gives access to Appellate opinions.

ADDITIONAL INFORMATION   Documents may not be filed by fax in any Alaska court without prior authorization of a judge.

The fees established by court rules for Alaska courts are: search fee - $15.00 per hour or fraction thereof; certification fee - $5.00 per document and $2.00 per additional copy of the document. Copy fee is $.25 per page.

Magistrate Courts vary widely in how records are maintained and in the hours of operation (some are open only a few hours per week)

Aleutian Islands District

Unalaska District Court (3rd District) PO
Box 245, Unalaska, AK 99685-0245; 907-581-1266; Fax: 907-581-2809. Hours: 8AM-4:30PM (AK). *Felony, Misdemeanor, Civil.*
www.state.ak.us/courts

Civil Records: Access: In person, mail, online. Only the court performs in person searches; visitors may not. Search fee: $15.00 per name. Required to search: name, DOB. Civil records on computer back to 1992. Search names on the Alaska Trial Courts database at www.state.ak.us/courts/names.htm. Search gives basic info.

Criminal Records: Access: In person, mail, online. Only the court performs in person searches; visitors may not. Search fee: $15.00 per name. Required to search: name, years to search, DOB. Criminal records on computer back to 1992. Online access to criminal records is the same as civil.

General Information: Will fax results to local or toll free line. Copy fee: $.25 per page. Cert fee: $5.00. Payee: State of Alaska. Prepayment required. Mail turnaround time 1-2 weeks.

Sand Point Magistrate Court (3rd District) *Felony, Misdemeanor, Civil Actions Under $7,500, Small Claims.*
Note: Court closed; records at Cordova Court.

St Paul Island Magistrate Court (3rd District), *Misdemeanor, Civil Actions Under $7,500, Small Claims.*
Note: Court closed. See Seward Magistrate Court in Kenai penisula Borough.

Anchorage Borough

Superior & District Court (3rd District)
825 W 4th, Anchorage, AK 99501-2004; 907-264-0491; Probate phone: 907-264-0436; Fax: 907-264-0873. Hours: 8AM-4:30PM (AK). *Felony, Misdemeanor, Civil, Eviction, Small Claims, Probate.*
www.state.ak.us/courts

Civil Records: Access: Fax, mail, in person. Both court and visitors may perform in person searches. Search fee: $15.00 per hour. Required to search: name, years to search; also helpful: address. Civil cases indexed by defendant, plaintiff. Civil records on computer from 1990, on microfiche and archived from 1977 to 1989, on roll index from 1940s. Search names on the Alaska Trial Courts database at www.state.ak.us/courts/names.htm. Search gives case number only.

Criminal Records: Access: Fax, mail, in person. Both court and visitors may perform in person searches. Search fee: $15.00 per hour. Required to search: name, years to search; also helpful: address, DOB, SSN. Criminal records on computer from 1990, on microfiche and archived from 1977 to 1989, on roll index from 1940s. Online access to criminal records is the same as civil.

General Information: Public Access terminal is available. No adoption, juvenile, sealed or mental records released. No fee to fax results. Local faxing only. Copy fee: $.25 per page. Cert fee: $5.00. Payee: Alaska Court System. Personal checks accepted. Prepayment required. Mail requests: SASE required. Mail turnaround time 2-3 weeks.

Bethel District

Superior & District Court (4th District)
PO Box 130, Bethel, AK 99559-0130; 907-543-2298; Fax: 907-543-4419. Hours: 8AM-4:30PM,9-4;30 W (AK). *Felony, Misdemeanor, Civil, Eviction, Small Claims, Probate.*
www.state.ak.us/courts

Civil Records: Access: Fax, mail, in person, online. Visitors must perform in person searches for themselves. Search fee: $15.00 per name. Required to search: name, years to search. Civil cases indexed by defendant, plaintiff. Civil records on computer back to 1983, on microfiche, archived and on index from 1977. Search names on the Alaska Trial Courts database at www.state.ak.us/courts/names.htm. Search gives case number only.

Criminal Records: Access: Fax, mail, in person, online. Visitors must perform in person searches for themselves. Search fee: $15.00 per name. Required to search: name, years to search, DOB; also helpful- case number. Criminal records on computer back to 1983, on microfiche, archived and on index from 1977. Online access to criminal records is the same as civil.

General Information: Public Access terminal is available. No adoption, juvenile, guardianship or mental records released. Fee to fax results is $.25 per page. Copy fee: $.25 per page. Cert fee: $5.00 plus $2.00 per page after first. Payee: Clerk of Court. Personal checks accepted. Prepayment required. Mail requests: SASE required. Mail turnaround time 2 weeks.

Aniak District Court (4th District) PO Box
147, Aniak, AK 99557-0147; 907-675-4325; Fax: 907-675-4278. Hours: 8AM-4:30PM (AK). *Misdemeanor, Civil Actions Under $7,500, Small Claims.*

Civil Records: Access: Phone, mail, fax, in person. Both court and visitors may perform in person searches. Search fee: $15.00 per search. Required to search: name plus DOB, SSN, years to search. Civil records go back to 1960; on computer back to 1998.

Criminal Records: Access: Phone, mail, fax, in person. Both court and visitors may perform in person searches. Search fee: $15.00 per search. Required to search: name, years to search, DOB. Civil records go back to 1960; on computer back to 1998.

General Information: Will fax results. Copy fee: $.25 per page. Cert fee: $5.00 per document. Payee: Aniak District Court. Prepayment required. Mail turnaround time 1-2 weeks.

Quinhagak Magistrate Court (Bethel Area) c/o Bethel Clerk, PO Box 130, Bethel, AK 99559-0130; 907-543-1105. *Misdemeanor, Civil Actions Under $7,500, Small Claims.*
Note: Court closed; records at Bethel Clerk of Courts at address and phone here.

Bristol Bay Borough

Naknek Magistrate Court (3rd District)
PO Box 229, Naknek, AK 99633-0229; 907-246-6151; Fax: 907-246-7418. Hours: 8:30AM-4PM (AK). *Felony, Misdemeanor, Civil Actions Under $7,500, Small Claims.*
www.state.ak.us/courts
Note: Naknek is 3NA on the state court record numbers. Some Lake and Peninsula cases heard here.

Civil Records: Access: Mail, in person, online. Only the court performs in person searches; visitors may not. Search fee: $15.00 per hour. Records go back to 1970's; computerized from 1993. Search names on the Alaska Trial Courts database at www.state.ak.us/courts/names.htm. Search gives case number only.

Criminal Records: Access: Mail, in person, online. Only the court performs in person searches; visitors may not. Search fee: $15.00 per hour. Required to search: name, years to search. Records go back to 1970's; computerized from 1993. Online access to criminal records is the same as civil.

General Information: Cert fee: $10.00. Payee: Alaska Court System. Prepayment required. Mail turnaround time same day.

Denali Borough

Healy Magistrate Court (4th District) PO
Box 298, Healy, AK 99743-0298; 907-683-2213; Fax: 907-683-1383. Hours: 8AM-4:30PM (AK). *Misdemeanor, Civil Actions Under $7,500, Small Claims.*
www.state.ak.us/courts
Note: Felony cases are at Fairbanks Superior & District Court.

Civil Records: Access: Phone, mail, fax, in person, online. Both the court and visitors may perform in person searches. Search fee: $15.00 per hour. Required to search: name, years to search, DOB. Records on computer back to 1972. Search names on the Alaska Trial Courts database at www.state.ak.us/courts/names.htm. Search gives case number only.

Criminal Records: Access: Phone, mail, fax, in person, online. Both the court and visitors may perform in person searches. Search fee: $15.00 per name. Required to search: name, years to search, DOB. Records on computer back to 1972. Online access to criminal records is the same as civil.

General Information: Public Access terminal is available. Copy fee: $.25. Cert fee: $5.00. Payee: State of Alaska. Personal check accepted. No credit cards accepted. Prepayment required. Mail requests: SASE required. Mail turnaround time 2 weeks.

Dillingham District

Dillingham Superior Court (3rd District)
PO Box 909, Dillingham, AK 99576-0909; 907-842-5215; Fax: 907-842-5746. Hours: 8AM-4:30PM (AK). *Felony, Misdemeanor, Civil, Small Claims.*
www.state.ak.us/courts

Civil Records: Access: In person, mail, online. Only the court performs in person searches; visitors may not. Search fee: $15.00. Search names on the Alaska Trial Courts database at www.state.ak.us/courts/names.htm. Search gives case number only.

Criminal Records: Access: In person, mail, online. Only the court performs in person searches; visitors may not. Search fee: $15.00 per name. Required to search: name, years to search, DOB. Online access to criminal records is the same as civil.

General Information: Copy fee: $.25 per page. Cert fee: $5.00. Payee: State of Alaska. Cashiers checks, money orders, personal checks accepted. Prepayment required. Mail requests: SASE required. Mail turnaround time 1-2 weeks.

Fairbanks North Star Borough

Superior & District Court (4th District)
101 Lacey St, Fairbanks, AK 99701-4761; 907-452-9277; Civil phone: 907-452-9267; Criminal phone: 907-452-9289; Probate phone: 907-452-9256; Fax: 907-452-9330. Hours: 8AM-4:30PM (AK). *Felony, Misdemeanor, Civil, Eviction, Small Claims, Probate.*
www.state.ak.us/courts/courtdir.htm

Civil Records: Access: In person, online. Visitors must perform in person searches for themselves. No search fee. Required to search: name, years to search. Civil cases indexed by defendant, plaintiff. Civil records on computer from 1988, on microfiche, archived and on index from 1900s. Search names on the Alaska Trial Courts database at www.state.ak.us/courts/names.htm. Search gives case number only. Access to the previous 3 months of Fairbanks eviction, divorce and probate cases are at www.state.ak.us/courts/akct.htm. Click on Trial Court Reports. Access to closed civil cases goes back 6 months.

Criminal Records: Access: In person, online. Visitors must perform in person searches for themselves. No search fee. Required to search: name, years to search, DOB. Criminal records on computer from 1988, on microfiche, archived and on index from 1900s. Online access to criminal records is the same as civil.

General Information: Public Access terminal is available. No adoption, juvenile, guardianship or mental records released. Copy fee: $.25 per page. Cert fee: $5.00 plus $2.00 per copy after first. Payee: Clerk of Court. Personal checks accepted. In person only. Prepayment required.

Haines Borough

District Court (1st District) PO Box 169, Haines, AK 99827-0169; 907-766-2801; Fax: 907-766-3148. Hours: 8AM-N, 1-4:30PM (AK). *Misdemeanor, Civil Actions Under $50,000, Small Claims.*

www.state.ak.us/courts

Felony cases are at Juneau Superior & District Court.

Civil Records: Access: Phone, fax, mail, in person, online. Only the court performs in person searches; visitors may not. Search fee: $15.00 per hour if time consuming. Required to search: name, years to search; also helpful: address. Civil cases indexed by defendant, plaintiff. Civil records on computer since 1993, index from 1960s. Search names on the Alaska Trial Courts database at www.state.ak.us/courts/names.htm. Search gives case number only. Limited information is available by phone.

Criminal Records: Access: Phone, fax, mail, in person, online. Only the court performs in person searches; visitors may not. Search fee: $15.00 per hour if time consuming. Required to search: name, years to search; also helpful: address, DOB, SSN. Criminal records on computer since 1993, index from 1960s. Online access to criminal records is the same as civil.

General Information: No juvenile records released. Copy fee: $.25 per page. Cert fee: $5.00 plus $2.00 per each add'l document requested at same time. Payee: Alaska Court System. Personal checks accepted. Prepayment required. Mail requests: SASE required. Mail turnaround time 1-2 days.

Juneau Borough

Superior & District Court (1st District) Dimond Courthouse, PO Box 114100, Juneau, AK 99811-4100; 907-463-4700; Fax: 907-463-3788. Hours: 8AM-4:30PM,M-Th, 9AM-4;30 F (AK). *Felony, Misdemeanor, Civil, Eviction, Small Claims, Probate.*

www.state.ak.us/courts/courtdir.htm

Civil Records: Access: Fax, mail, in person, online. Both court and visitors may perform in person searches. Search fee: $15.00 per hour. Required to search: name, years to search. Civil cases indexed by defendant. Civil records on computer back to 1987, on microfiche from 1960 to 1986, on index from 1959 to 1987. Search names on the Alaska Trial Courts database at www.state.ak.us/courts/names.htm. Search gives case number only.

Criminal Records: Access: Fax, mail, in person, online. Both court and visitors may perform in person searches. Search fee: $15.00 per hour. Required to search: name, years to search. Criminal records on computer back to 1987, on microfiche from 1960 to 1986, on index from 1959 to 1987. Online access to criminal records is the same as civil.

General Information: Public Access terminal is available. No adoption, juvenile, guardianship or mental records released. Copy fee: $.25 per page. Cert fee: $5.00 plus $2.00 per page after first. Payee: Juneau Trial Court. Personal checks accepted.

Prepayment required. Mail requests: SASE required. Mail turnaround time 2-5 days.

Kenai Peninsula Borough

Superior & District Court (3rd District) 125 Trading Bay Dr, #100, Kenai, AK 99611; 907-283-3110; Fax: 907-283-8535. Hours: 8AM-4:30PM (AK). *Felony, Misdemeanor, Civil, Eviction, Small Claims, Probate.*

www.state.ak.us/courts

Civil Records: Access: Mail, in person, online. Both court and visitors may perform in person searches. Search fee: $15.00 per hour. Required to search: name, years to search. Civil cases indexed by defendant, plaintiff. Civil records on computer from 1983, on microfiche, archived and on index from 1959. Search names on the Alaska Trial Courts database at www.state.ak.us/courts/names.htm. Search gives case number only.

Criminal Records: Access: Mail, in person, online. Both court and visitors may perform in person searches. Search fee: $15.00 per hour. Required to search: name, years to search, DOB. Criminal records on computer from 1983, on microfiche, archived and on index from 1959. Online access to criminal records is the same as civil.

General Information: Public Access terminal is available. No adoption, guardianship, children's, conservatorship or coroner records released. Copy fee: $.25 per page. Cert fee: $5.00 plus $2.00 per page after first. Payee: Clerk of Court. Personal checks accepted. Prepayment required. Mail requests: SASE not required. Mail turnaround time 1 week.

District Court (3rd District) 3670 Lake St, #400, Homer, AK 99603-9647; 907-235-8171; Fax: 907-235-4257. Hours: 8AM-4:30PM (AK). *Misdemeanor, Civil Actions Under $50,000, Small Claims.*

www.state.ak.us/courts/courtdir.htm

Civil Records: Access: Phone, fax, mail, in person, online. Both court and visitors may perform in person searches. Search fee: $15.00 per hour. Required to search: name, years to search. Civil cases indexed by defendant, plaintiff. Civil records on computer back to 1984. Search names on the Alaska Trial Courts database at www.state.ak.us/courts/names.htm. Search gives case number only. Phone access limited to name searches.

Criminal Records: Access: Phone, fax, mail, in person, online. Both court and visitors may perform in person searches. Search fee: $15.00 per hour. Required to search: name, years to search. Criminal records on computer back to 1984. Online access to criminal records is the same as civil.

General Information: Public Access terminal is available. No confidential or sealed records released. Will fax results to local or toll free line. Copy fee: $.25 per page. Cert fee: $5.00. Payee: Alaska Court System. Personal checks accepted. Prepayment required. Mail requests: SASE required. Mail turnaround time 5 days.

Seward Magistrate Court (3rd District) PO Box 1929, 5th and Adams Sts, Seward, AK 99664-1929; 907-224-3075; Fax: 907-224-7192. Hours: 8AM-4:30PM (AK). *Misdemeanor, Civil Actions Under $7,500, Small Claims.*

www.state.ak.us/courts

Civil Records: Access: In person, mail, online. Both court and visitors may perform in person searches. Search fee: $15.00 per name; may do for free as time permits. Civil records on computer since 1983. Search names on the Alaska Trial Courts database at www.state.ak.us/courts/names.htm. Search gives case number only.

Criminal Records: Access: In person, mail, online. Only the court performs in person searches; visitors

may not. Search fee: $15.00 per name. Required to search: name, years to search, DOB. Criminal records on computer since 1983. Online access to criminal records is the same as civil.

General Information: Public Access terminal is available. Court recommends against faxing back results. Copy fee: $.25 per page. Cert fee: $5.00. Payee: State of Alaska. Prepayment required. Mail requests: SASE helpful. Turnaround time 1-2 weeks.

Ketchikan Gateway Borough

Superior & District Court (1st District) 415 Main, Rm 400, Ketchikan, AK 99901-6399; 907-225-3195; Fax: 907-225-7849. Hours: 8AM-4:30PM M-Th, 9AM-4:30PM Fridays (AK). *Felony, Misdemeanor, Civil, Eviction, Small Claims, Probate.*

www.state.ak.us/courts/names.htm

Civil Records: Access: Fax, mail, in person, online. Both court and visitors may perform in person searches. Search fee: $15.00 per hour. Required to search: name, years to search. Civil cases indexed by defendant, plaintiff. Civil records on computer from 1983, on microfiche from 1972 to 1989, index from 1972. Search names on the Alaska Trial Courts database at www.state.ak.us/courts/names.htm. Search gives case number only.

Criminal Records: Access: Fax, mail, in person, online. Both court and visitors may perform in person searches. Search fee: $15.00 per hour. Required to search: name, years to search, DOB. Criminal records on computer from 1983, on microfiche from 1972 to 1989, index from 1972. Online access to criminal records is the same as civil.

General Information: Public Access terminal is available. No confidential probate or children's records released. No fee to fax results. Copy fee: $.25 per page. Cert fee: $5.00. Payee: Alaska Court System. Personal checks accepted. Prepayment required. Mail requests: SASE required. Mail turnaround time 2 weeks.

Kodiak Island Borough

Superior & District Court (3rd District) 204 Mission Road, Rm 10, Kodiak, AK 99615-7312; 907-486-1600; Fax: 907-486-1660. Hours: 8AM-4:30PM M,T,Th,F; 9AM-4:30PM W (AK). *Felony, Misdemeanor, Civil, Eviction, Small Claims, Probate.*

www.state.ak.us/courts

Civil Records: Access: Mail, fax, in person, online. Both court and visitors may perform in person searches. Search fee: $15.00 per hour. Required to search: name, years to search; also helpful: address. Civil cases indexed by defendant, plaintiff. Civil records on computer from 1982, on microfiche, index and archived from 1959. Search names on the Alaska Trial Courts database at www.state.ak.us/courts/names.htm. Search gives case number only.

Criminal Records: Access: Mail, fax, in person, online. Both court and visitors may perform in person searches. Search fee: $15.00 per hour. Required to search: name, years to search; also helpful: address, DOB, SSN. Criminal records on computer from 1982, on microfiche, index and archived from 1959. Online access to criminal records is the same as civil.

General Information: Public Access terminal is available. No adoption, juvenile, guardianship or mental records released. Copy fee: $.25 per page. Cert fee: $5.00 plus $2.00 per add'l copy. Payee: Clerk of Court. Personal checks accepted. Prepayment required. Mail requests: SASE required. Mail turnaround time 1-3 weeks.

Matanuska-Susitna Borough

Superior & District Court (3rd District)
435 S Denali, Palmer, AK 99645-6437; Civil phone: 907-746-8108; Criminal phone: 907-746-8104; Fax: 907-746-4151. Hours: 8AM-4:30PM (AK). *Felony, Misdemeanor, Civil, Eviction, Small Claims, Probate.*
www.state.ak.us/courts
Civil Records: Access: Mail, in person, online. Both court and visitors may perform in person searches. Search fee: $15.00 per hour. Required to search: name, years to search; also helpful: address. Civil cases indexed by defendant, plaintiff. Civil records on computer from 1988, on microfiche, archived and index from 1974. Search names on the Alaska Trial Courts database at www.state.ak.us/courts/names.htm. Search gives case number only.
Criminal Records: Access: Mail, in person, online. Both court and visitors may perform in person searches. Search fee: $15.00 per hour. Required to search: name, years to search; also helpful: address, DOB, SSN. Criminal records on computer from 1988, on microfiche, archived and index from 1974. Online access to criminal records is the same as civil.
General Information: Public Access terminal is available. No adoption, juvenile, guardianship or mental records released. Copy fee: $.25 per page. Cert fee: $5.00. A second copy is $2.00 per document. Payee: State of Alaska. Personal checks accepted. Prepayment required. Mail requests: SASE required. Mail turnaround time 1-3 weeks.

Nome District

Superior & District Court (2nd District)
PO Box 1110, Nome, AK 99762-1110; 907-443-5216; Fax: 907-443-2192. Hours: 8AM-4:30PM (AK). *Felony, Misdemeanor, Civil, Eviction, Small Claims, Probate.*
www.state.ak.us/courts/courtdir.htm
Civil Records: Access: Fax, mail, in person, online. Both court and visitors may perform in person searches. Search fee: $15.00 per hour or fraction of. Required to search: name, years to search; also helpful: DOB. Civil cases indexed by defendant, plaintiff. Civil records on computer from 1983, on microfiche from 1960 to 1983, on index and archived from 1960. Search names on the Alaska Trial Courts database at www.state.ak.us/courts/names.htm. Search gives case number only.
Criminal Records: Access: Fax, mail, in person, online. Both court and visitors may perform in person searches. Search fee: $15.00 per hour or fraction of. Required to search: name, years to search; also helpful: DOB, SSN. Criminal records on computer from 1983, on microfiche from 1960 to 1983, on index and archived from 1960. Online access to criminal records is the same as civil.
General Information: Public Access terminal is available. No adoption, juvenile, guardianship or mental records released. Will fax results to toll-free number only. Copy fee: $.25 per page. Cert fee: $5.00 plus $2.00 per copy after first. Payee: Nome Trial Courts. Personal checks accepted. Prepayment required. Mail requests: SASE required. Mail turnaround time 5 days.

Gambell Magistrate Court (2nd District)
PO Box 1110, Nome, AK 99762-1110; 907-443-5216. *Misdemeanor, Civil Actions Under $7,500, Small Claims.*
Note: Court is vacant. Records at Superior Court in Nome at address and phone listed here.

Unalakleet Magistrate Court (2nd District)
PO Box 250, Unalakleet, AK 99684-0250; 907-624-3015; Fax: 907-624-3118. Hours: 8AM-4PM (AK). *Misdemeanor, Civil Actions Under $7,500, Small Claims.*
Note: This is a one-person court and very quiet.
Civil Records: Access: In person, mail, fax. Only the court performs in person searches; visitors may not. Search fee: $15.00 per hour. Required to search: name, years to search.
Criminal Records: Access: In person, mail, fax. Only the court performs in person searches; visitors may not. Search fee: $15.00 per hour. Required to search: name, years to search.
General Information: Will fax results for free. No copy fee. Payee: Magistrate Court. Prepayment required. Mail requests: SASE not required. Mail turnaround time 1-2 weeks.

North Slope Borough

Superior & District Court (2nd District)
PO Box 270, Barrow, AK 99723-0270; 907-852-4800 X80; Fax: 907-852-4804. Hours: 8AM-4:30PM (AK). *Felony, Misdemeanor, Civil, Eviction, Small Claims, Probate.*
www.state.ak.us/courts
Civil Records: Access: Fax, mail, in person, online. Both court and visitors may perform in person searches. Search fee: $15.00 per hour. Required to search: name, years to search; also helpful: address. Civil cases indexed by defendant, plaintiff. Civil records on computer from 1983, prior on microfiche. Search names on the Alaska Trial Courts database at www.state.ak.us/courts/names.htm. Search gives case number only.
Criminal Records: Access: Fax, mail, in person, online. Both the court and visitors may perform in person searches. Search fee: $15.00 per hour. Required to search: name, years to search; also helpful: address, DOB, SSN. Criminal records on computer from 1983, prior on microfiche. Online access to criminal records is the same as civil.
General Information: Public Access terminal is available. No confidential records released. No fee to fax results. Copy fee: $.25 per page. Cert fee: $5.00 plus $2.00 per page after first. Payee: Alaska Court System. Personal checks accepted. Prepayment required. Mail requests: SASE required. Mail turnaround time 3 weeks.

Northwest Arctic Borough

Superior & District Court (2nd District)
PO Box 317, 605 3rd Ave, Kotzebue, AK 99752-0317; 907-442-3208; Fax: 907-442-3974. Hours: 8AM-4:30PM (AK). *Felony, Misdemeanor, Civil, Eviction, Small Claims, Probate.*
www.state.ak.us/courts
Note: This court holds records for the closed Magistrate Court formerly in Ambler.
Civil Records: Access: Phone, fax, mail, in person, online. Both court and visitors may perform in person searches. Search fee: $15.00. Required to search: name, years to search. Civil cases indexed by defendant and plaintiff. Civil records on computer from 1983, prior records on microfiche, archived and index from 1966. Search names on the Alaska Trial Courts database at www.state.ak.us/courts/names.htm. Search gives case number only. Copy of check required for fax access.
Criminal Records: Access: Mail, fax, in person, online. Both court and visitors may perform in person searches. Search fee: $15.00. Required to search: name, years to search, DOB; also helpful: SSN. Criminal records on computer from 1983, prior records on microfilm, archived and index from 1966. Online access to criminal records is the same as civil.

General Information: Public Access terminal is available. No adoption, juvenile, guardianship or mental records released. Copy fee: $.25 per page. Cert fee: $5.00 plus $2.00 per page after first. Notary fee is $3.00. Payee: Alaska Court System. Personal checks accepted. Prepayment required. Mail turnaround time 2-3 days.

Kiana Magistrate Court (2nd District)
PO Box 317, Kotzebue, AK 99752-0317; 907-442-3208. Hours: 10AM-3PM M,W,F (AK). *Misdemeanor, Civil Actions Under $7,500, Small Claims.*
Note: Court is temporarily vacant; for records, contact Kotzebue Court at address and phone here.

Selawik Magistrate Court (2nd District)
PO Box 317, Kotzebue, AK 99752; 907-442-3208; Fax: 907-442-3974. Hours: variable (AK). *Misdemeanor, Civil Actions Under $7,500, Small Claims.*
Note: Contact the Kotzebue Court for record information; Kotzebue court address and phones given here.

Prince of Wales-Outer Ketchikan District

Craig Magistrate Court (1st District)
PO Box 646, Craig, AK 99921-0646; 907-826-3316/3306; Fax: 907-826-3904. Hours: 8AM-4:30PM (AK). *Misdemeanor, Civil Actions Under $7,500, Small Claims.*
www.state.ak.us/courts
Note: Felony cases are at Ketchican Superior & District Court.
Civil Records: Access: In person, phone, fax, mail, online. Only the court performs in person searches; visitors may not. Search fee: $15.00 per name. Required to search: name, years to search; also helpful: DOB. Search names on the Alaska Trial Courts database at www.state.ak.us/courts/names.htm. Search gives case number only.
Criminal Records: Access: In person, phone, fax, mail, online. Only the court performs in person searches; visitors may not. Search fee: $15.00 per name. Required to search: name, years to search; also helpful: DOB. Online access to criminal records is the same as civil.
General Information: Will fax results for free. Copy fee: $.25. Cert fee: $5.00. Payee: Alaska Court System. Prepayment required. Mail requests: SASE requested. Turnaround time 2 weeks.

Sitka Borough

Superior & District Court (1st District)
304 Lake St, Rm 203, Sitka, AK 99835-7759; 907-747-3291; Fax: 907-747-6690. Hours: 8AM-4:30PM (AK). *Felony, Misdemeanor, Civil, Eviction, Small Claims, Probate.*
www.state.ak.us/courts
Civil Records: Access: Phone, fax, mail, in person, online. Both court and visitors may perform in person searches. Search fee: $15.00 per hour. Required to search: name. Civil cases indexed by defendant, plaintiff. Civil records on computer from 1983, on microfilm and archived from 1970 to 1987, on index from 1960. Search names on the Alaska Trial Courts database at www.state.ak.us/courts/names.htm. Search gives case number only.
Criminal Records: Access: Phone, fax, mail, in person, online. Both court and visitors may perform in person searches. Search fee: $15.00 per hour. Required to search: name. Criminal records on computer from 1983, on microfilm and archived from 1970 to 1987, on index from 1960. Online access to criminal records is the same as civil.
General Information: Public Access terminal is available. No adoption, juvenile, guardianship or

mental records released. No fee to fax results to toll free number. Copy fee: $.25 per page. Cert fee: $5.00. Payee: Alaska Court System. Personal checks accepted. Prepayment required. Mail requests: SASE required. Mail turnaround time 1 week.

Skagway-Yakutat-Angoon District

Hoonah District Court (1st District) PO
Box 430, Hoonah, AK 99829-0430; 907-945-3668; Fax: 907-945-3637. Hours: 8AM-Noon, 1-4:30PM (AK). *Misdemeanor, Civil Actions Under $50,000, Small Claims.*
www.state.ak.us/courts
Note: Felony cases are at Juneau Superior & District Court.

Civil Records: Access: Mail, in person. Only the court performs in person searches; visitors may not. No search fee. Required to search: name, years to search. Civil cases indexed by defendant, plaintiff. Civil records on index from 1971 to present.
Criminal Records: Access: Mail, in person. Only the court performs in person searches; visitors may not. No search fee. Required to search: name, years to search; also helpful: DOB. Criminal records on index from 1971 to present.
General Information: No confidential, juvenile or sex related records released. Will fax results to toll-free number only. Copy fee: $.25 per page. Cert fee: $5.00 plus $2.00 per page after first. Payee: Alaska Court System. Personal checks accepted. Prepayment required. Mail requests: SASE not required. Mail turnaround time 2-3 days.

Angoon Magistrate Court (1st District)
PO Box 250, Angoon, AK 99820-0123; 907-788-3229; Fax: 907-788-3108. Hours: 1PM-4:30PM (AK). *Misdemeanor, Civil Actions Under $7,500, Small Claims.*
Note: Felony cases are at Sitka Superior & District Court.

Civil Records: Access: Phone, mail, fax, in person. Only the court performs in person searches; visitors may not. Search fee: $15.00 per hour. Required to search: name, years to search. Records go back to 1994.
Criminal Records: Access: Phone, mail, fax, in person. Only the court performs in person searches; visitors may not. Search fee: $15.00 per hour. Required to search: name, years to search, date of birth. Records go back to 1994.
General Information: Fee to fax results is $5.00 per page or $15.00 per document. Copy fee: $.25 per page. Cert fee: $5.00 per doc. Payee: Alaska Court System. Personal checks and money orders accepted. Prepayment required. Mail requests: SASE helpful. Turnaround time 1 week.

Pelican Magistrate Court (1st District)
304 Lake St #203, Sitka, AK 99835; 907-747-3291; Fax: 907-747-6690. *Misdemeanor, Civil Actions Under $7,500, Small Claims.*
Note: This Pelican court closed permanently on 12/31/99. All records are at the Sitka court, address and phone given here.

Skagway District Magistrate Court PO
Box 495, Skagway, AK 99840-0495; 907-983-2368; Fax: 907-983-3801. Hours: 8AM-N, 1-4PM M-T-W; 8AM-N, 1-3:30PM Thurs (AK). *Misdemeanor, Civil Actions Under $7,500, Small Claims.*
Note: Hours will vary from Summer to Winter. Felony cases are at Juneau Superior & District Court.

Civil Records: Access: Mail, fax, in person. Only the court performs in person searches; visitors may not. Search fee: $15.00 per hour. Civil records go back to 1970; on computer back to 1998.

Criminal Records: Access: In person, fax, mail. Only the court performs in person searches; visitors may not. Search fee: $15.00 per hour. Required to search: name, years to search, DOB. Criminal records go back to 1970; on computer back to 1998. No charge for a simple name search.
General Information: Will fax to toll-free numbers no charge. Copy fee: $.25 per page. Cert fee: $5.00 per doc. Payee: State of Alaska. Prepayment required. Mail turnaround time 1-2 weeks.

Yakutat Magistrate Court (1st District)
PO Box 426, Yakutat, AK 99689-0426; 907-784-3274; Fax: 907-784-3257. Hours: 9AM-4:30PM M-Th (AK). *Misdemeanor, Civil Actions Under $7,500, Small Claims.*
Note: Felony cases are at Juneau Superior & District Court. Telephone number subject to change.

Civil Records: Access: Phone, mail, fax, in person, email. Only the court performs in person searches; visitors may not. No search fee. Required to search: name. Civil records go back to 1998; on computer back to 1976.
Criminal Records: Access: Mail, fax, in person, email. Only the court performs in person searches; visitors may not. No search fee. Required to search: name, DOB. Criminal records go back to 1959; on computer back to 1998.
General Information: Copy fee: $.25 per page. Cert fee: $5.00. Payee: Alaska Court System. Prepayment required.

Southeast Fairbanks District

Delta Junction Magistrate Court (4th
District) PO Box 401, Delta Junction, AK 99737-0401; 907-895-4211; Fax: 907-895-4204. Hours: 8AM-Noon, 1-4:30PM (AK). *Misdemeanor, Civil Actions Under $7,500, Small Claims.*
www.state.ak.us/courts
Note: Felony cases are at Fairbanks Superior & District Court.

Civil Records: Access: In person, mail, online. Only the court performs in person searches; visitors may not. No search fee. Search names on the Alaska Trial Courts database at www.state.ak.us/courts/names.htm. Search gives case number only.
Criminal Records: Access: phone, mail, fax, in person, online. Only the court performs in person searches; visitors may not. Search fee: $15.00 per hour. Required to search: name, years to search. Criminal records computerized go back to 1980; prior records go back to mid-70's. Online access to criminal records is the same as civil.
General Information: Copy fee: $.25 per page. Cert fee: $5.00. Payee: District Court. Prepayment required. Mail turnaround time 1 week.

Tok Magistrate Court (4th District) PO
Box 187, Tok, AK 99780-0187; 907-883-5171; Fax: 907-883-4367. Hours: 8AM-Noon; 1PM-4:30PM (AK). *Misdemeanor, Civil Actions Under $7,500, Small Claims.*
www.state.ak.us/courts
Note: Felony cases are at Fairbanks Superior & District Court.

Civil Records: Access: In person, phone, mail, online. Visitors must perform in person searches for themselves. No search fee. Required to search: Name, DOB, SSN. Civil records computerized since 1994. Search names on the Alaska Trial Courts database at www.state.ak.us/courts/names.htm. Search gives case number only.
Criminal Records: Access: In person, phone, mail, online. Visitors must perform in person searches for themselves. No search fee. Required to search: name, years to search, DOB. Criminal records computerized

since 1994. Online access to criminal records is the same as civil.
General Information: Public Access terminal is available. Will fax results. Copy fee: $.25 per page. Cert fee: $5.00. Prepayment required. Mail turnaround time 5 days.

Valdez-Cordova District

Superior & District Court (3rd District)
PO Box 127, 213 Meals, Valdez, AK 99686-0127; 907-835-2266; Fax: 907-835-3764. Hours: 8AM-4:30PM (AK). *Felony, Misdemeanor, Civil, Eviction, Small Claims, Probate.*
www.state.ak.us/courts

Civil Records: Access: Fax, mail, in person, online. Only the court performs in person searches; visitors may not. No search fee. Required to search: name, years to search; also helpful: address. Civil cases indexed by defendant, plaintiff. Civil records on computer from 1984, on microfiche, archived and index from 1960. Search names on the Alaska Trial Courts database at www.state.ak.us/courts/names.htm. Search gives case number only.
Criminal Records: Access: Fax, mail, in person, online. Only the court performs in person searches; visitors may not. No search fee. Required to search: name, years to search; also helpful: address, DOB, SSN. Criminal records on computer from 1984, on microfiche, archived and index from 1960. Online access to criminal records is the same as civil.
General Information: No adoption, juvenile, guardianship or mental records released. Will fax results for $15.00 fee. Copy fee: $.25 per page. Cert fee: $5.00. Payee: Valdez Trial Court of Alaska. Personal checks accepted. Prepayment required. Mail requests: SASE required. Mail turnaround time 1-3 weeks.

Cordova Court (3rd District) PO Box 898,
Cordova, AK 99574-0898; 907-424-3378; Fax: 907-424-7581. Hours: 8AM-4:30PM (AK). *Felony, Misdemeanor, Civil, Small Claims, Probate.*
www.state.ak.us/courts

Civil Records: Access: Phone, mail, fax, in person, online. Both court and visitors may perform in person searches. No search fee. Required to search: DOB, years to search. Civil records on computer back to 1993; other records back to 1975. Search names on the Alaska Trial Courts database at www.state.ak.us/courts/names.htm. Search gives case number only. Access by phone if time allows.
Criminal Records: Access: Phone, mail, fax, in person, online. Both court and visitors may perform in person searches. Search fee: $15.00 per hour. Required to search: name, years to search, DOB. Criminal records on computer back to 1993; other records back to 1975. Online access to criminal records is the same as civil. Will take phone requests if time allows.
General Information: Public Access terminal is available. Will not fax results. Copy fee: $.25. Cert fee: $5.00. Payee: State of Alaska. Prepayment required. Mail turnaround time 1 week.

Glennallen District Court (3rd District)
PO Box 86, Glennallen, AK 99588-0086; 907-822-3405. Hours: 8AM-4:30PM (AK). *Misdemeanor, Civil, Small Claims.*
www.state.ak.us/courts

Civil Records: Access: Mail, in person, online. Only the court performs in person searches; visitors may not. Search fee: $15.00 per hour. Records go back to 1960; on computer back to 1992. Search names on the Alaska Trial Courts database at www.state.ak.us/courts/names.htm. Search gives case number only.
Criminal Records: Access: Mail, in person, online. Only the court performs in person searches; visitors

may not. Search fee: $15.00 per hour. Required to search: name, years to search, DOB. Records go back to 1960; on computer back to 1992. Online access to criminal records is the same as civil.

General Information: Copy fee: $.25 per page. Cert fee: $5.00 per document. Payee: Alaska Court System. Prepayment required. Mail turnaround time 1-2 weeks.

Whittier Magistrate Court (3rd District)

825 W 4th Ave, Anchorage, AK 99501-2004; 907-264-0479. *Misdemeanor, Civil Actions Under $7,500, Small Claims.*

Note: Court closed; records available at the address and phone above.

Wade Hampton District

Chevak Magistrate Court (Bethel Area)

PO Box 238, Chevak, AK 99563-0238; 907-858-7231; Fax: 907-858-7230. Hours: 8AM-4:30PM (AK). *Misdemeanor, Civil Actions Under $7,500, Small Claims.*

Note: Felony cases at Bethel Superior & District Court.

Civil Records: Access: Mail, fax, in person. Only the court performs in person searches; visitors may not. Search fee: $15.00. Required to search: name, years to search. Civil records go back to 1993; on computer back to 1997.

Criminal Records: Access: Mail, fax, in person. Both court and visitors may perform in person searches. Search fee: $15.00 per hour. Required to search: name, years to search, address, DOB, SSN, signed release. Criminal records go back to 1993; on computer back to 1997.

General Information: Will fax results. Copy fee: $.25 per page. Cert fee: $3.00. Payee: Magistrate Court. Prepayment required. Mail turnaround time 1-2 weeks.

Emmonak Magistrate Court (Bethel Area)

PO Box 176, Emmonak, AK 99581-0176; 907-949-1748; Fax: 907-949-1535. Hours: 8AM-4:30PM (AK). *Misdemeanor, Civil Actions Under $15,000, Small Claims.*

Note: Felony cases are at Bethel Superior & District Court.

Civil Records: Access: In person, mail. Only the court performs in person searches; visitors may not. Search fee: $15.00 per hour. Required to search: years to search, DOB, SSN, signed release. Overall records go back to 1995. Computerized records go back to 2000.

Criminal Records: Access: In person, mail. Only the court performs in person searches; visitors may not. Search fee: $15.00 per hour. Required to search: name, years to search, address, DOB, signed release; also helpful: SSN. Overall records go back to 1995. Computerized records go back to 2000.

General Information: Copy fee: $.25 per page. Cert fee: $5.00. Payee: Magistrate Court. Prepayment required. Mail turnaround time 1-2 weeks.

St Mary's Magistrate Court (Bethel Area)

PO Box 269, St Mary's, AK 99658-0183; 907-438-2912; Fax: 907-438-2819. Hours: 8AM-noon, 1-4:30PM (AK). *Misdemeanor, Civil Actions Under $10,000, Small Claims.*

Note: Felony cases are at Bethel Superior & District Court.

Civil Records: Access: In person, mail. Only the court performs in person searches; visitors may not. Search fee: $15.00 per hour. Civil records computerized go back to 1996.

Criminal Records: Access: In person, mail. Only the court performs in person searches; visitors may not. Search fee: $15.00 per hour. Required to search:

name, years to search; also helpful: DOB. Criminal records computerized go back to 1996.

General Information: Will fax back results. Copy fee: $.25 per page. Prepayment required. Mail turnaround time 3 weeks.

Wrangell-Petersburg District

Petersburg Superior & District Court (1st District)

PO Box 1009, Petersburg, AK 99833-1009; 907-772-3824; Fax: 907-772-3018. Hours: 8AM-4:30PM (AK). *Felony, Misdemeanor, Civil, Eviction, Small Claims, Probate.*

www.state.ak.us/courts

Civil Records: Access: Phone, fax, mail, in person, online. Only the court performs in person searches; visitors may not. Search fee: none unless on microfilm-$15.00 hr. Required to search: name, years to search; also helpful: address. Civil cases indexed by defendant, plaintiff. Civil records on computer from 1988, on microfiche and index from 1960s, archived from 1920s. Search names on the Alaska Trial Courts database at www.state.ak.us/courts/names.htm. Search gives case number only.

Criminal Records: Access: Phone, fax, mail, in person, online. Only the court performs in person searches; visitors may not. Search fee: None except a $15.00 per hour fee on archive cases. Required to search: name, years to search; also helpful: address, DOB. Criminal records on computer from 1988, on microfiche and index from 1960s, archived 1920s. Online access to criminal records is the same as civil.

General Information: No adoption, juvenile, guardianship or mental records released. Outgoing fax limited to 10 pages; call for fee. Copy fee: $.25 per page. Cert fee: $5.00. Payee: Alaska Court System. Personal checks accepted. Prepayment required. Mail requests: SASE required. Mail turnaround time 1 week.

Wrangell Superior & District Court (1st District)

PO Box 869, Wrangell, AK 99929-0869; 907-874-2311; Fax: 907-874-3509. Hours: 8AM-4:30PM (AK). *Felony, Misdemeanor, Civil, Eviction, Small Claims, Probate.*

www.state.ak.us/courts

Note: The TDD office can be reached at 907-874-2313.

Civil Records: Access: Phone, fax, mail, in person, online. Only the court performs in person searches; visitors may not. Search fee: $15.00 per hour. Search fee is charged for all written responses. Required to search: name, years to search. Civil cases indexed by defendant, plaintiff. Civil records on computer from 1988, on microfiche and card files from 1959, archived from 1900s. Search names on the Alaska Trial Courts database at www.state.ak.us/courts/names.htm. Search gives case number and court location only.

Criminal Records: Access: Phone, fax, mail, in person, online. Only the court performs in person searches; visitors may not. Search fee: $15.00 per hour. Required to search: name, years to search, DOB. Criminal records on computer from 1988, on microfiche and card files from 1959, archived from 1900s. Online access to criminal records is the same as civil.

General Information: No adoption, juvenile, guardianship or mental records released. Fee to fax results is $15.00 per document. Copy fee: $.25 per page. Cert fee: $5.00 plus $2.00 per copy after first. Payee: Alaska Court System or State of Alaska. Personal checks accepted. Prepayment required. Mail requests: SASE required. Mail turnaround time 3 days.

Kake Magistrate Court (1st District)

PO Box 100, Kake, AK 99830-0100; 907-785-3651; Fax: 907-785-3152. Hours: 8AM-Noon (AK). *Misdemeanor, Civil Actions Under $7,500, Small Claims.*

Civil Records: Access: In person, mail. Only the court performs in person searches; visitors may not. No search fee.

Criminal Records: Access: In person, mail. Only the court performs in person searches; visitors may not. No search fee. Required to search: name, years to search, DOB, SSN, signed release.

General Information: Payee: Alaska Court System. Prepayment required. Mail turnaround time 1-2 weeks.

Yukon-Koyukuk District

Fort Yukon Magistrate Court (4th District)

PO Box 211, Fort Yukon, AK 99740-0211; 907-662-2336; Fax: 907-662-2824. Hours: 9:30AM-3PM (AK). *Misdemeanor, Civil Actions Under $7,500, Small Claims.*

Note: Felony cases are at Fairbanks Superior & District Court.

Civil Records: Access: Fax, mail, in person. Only the court performs in person searches; visitors may not. No search fee. Required to search: name, DOB. Records go back to 1960s.

Criminal Records: Access: Fax, mail, in person. Only the court performs in person searches; visitors may not. Search fee: $15.00 per hour. Required to search: name, years to search, DOB. Records go back to 1960s.

General Information: Will fax results to local or toll free line. Payee: District Court. Prepayment required. Mail turnaround time 1-2 weeks.

Galena Magistrate Court (4th District)

PO Box 167, Galena, AK 99741-0167; 907-656-1322; Fax: 907-656-1546. Hours: 8AM-4:30PM (AK). *Misdemeanor, Civil Actions Under $7,500, Small Claims.*

Note: Felony cases are at Fairbanks Superior & District Court.

Civil Records: Access: In person, mail. Only the court performs in person searches; visitors may not. No search fee. Civil record computerized since 1995.

Criminal Records: Access: In person, mail. Only the court performs in person searches; visitors may not. Search fee: $15.00 per hour. Required to search: name, years to search. Criminal records computerized since 1995.

General Information: Payee: Magistrate Court. Prepayment required. Mail turnaround time 1-2 weeks.

McGrath Magistrate Court (4th District)

PO Box 167, Galena, AK 99741-0167; 907-656-1322; Fax: 907-656-1546. Hours: 8:30AM-4:30PM (AK). *Misdemeanor, Civil Actions Under $7,500, Small Claims.*

Note: McGrath Court is vacant. Court records at Galena Magistrate Court, address and phone here.

Nenana Magistrate Court (4th District)

PO Box 449, Nenana, AK 99760-0449; 907-832-5430; Fax: 907-832-5841. Hours: 8:30AM-4PM (AK). *Misdemeanor, Civil Actions Under $7,500, Small Claims.*

www.state.ak.us/courts/names.htm

Note: Felony cases are at Fairbanks Superior & District Court.

Civil Records: Access: In person, phone, online. Both the court and visitors may perform in person searches. No search fee. Required to search: name, years to search, DOB. Search names on the Alaska Trial Courts database at www.state.ak.us/courts/names.htm. Search gives case number only.

Criminal Records: Access: In person, phone, online. Both the court and visitors may perform in person searches. No search fee. Required to search: name, years to search, DOB. Criminal records on computer back to 1995. Online access to criminal records is the same as civil.

General Information: Public Access terminal is available. Copy fee: $.25 per page.

Tanana Magistrate Court (4th District)

PO Box 449, Nenana, AK 99777; 907-366-7243; Fax: 907-832-5841. Hours: Th-F 2nd full week each month (AK). *Misdemeanor, Civil Actions Under $7,500, Small Claims.*

www.state.ak.us/courts

Note: Magistrate may also be contacted by phone at 907-832-5430. Felony cases are at Fairbanks Superior & District Court.

Civil Records: Access: In person, phone, mail. Both the court and visitors may perform in person searches. No search fee.

Criminal Records: Access: In person, phone, mail. Both the court and visitors may perform in person searches. No search fee. Required to search: name, years to search, DOB, signed release.

General Information: Public Access terminal is available. Will not fax results. Copy fee: $.25 per page. Payee: Magistrate Court. Prepayment required. Mail turnaround time 1-2 weeks.

Alaska Recording Offices

ORGANIZATION: The 23 Alaskan counties are called boroughs. However, real estate recording is done under a system that was established at the time of the Gold Rush (whenever that was) of 34 Recording Districts. Some of the Districts are identical in geography to boroughs, such as the Aleutian Islands, but other boroughs and districts overlap. Therefore, you need to know which recording district any given town or city is located in. A helpful web site www.dnr.state.ak.us/recorders/findYourDistrict.htm

The entire state except the Aleutian Islands is in the Alaska Time Zone (AK).

REAL ESTATE RECORDS: Districts do not perform real estate searches. Certification fees are usually $5.00 per document. Copies usually cost $1.25 for the first page, $.25 per additional page.

UCC RECORDS: Financing statements are filed at the state level, except for real estate related collateral, which are filed with the District Recorder. However, prior to 07/2001, consumer goods and farm collateral were filed at the District Recorder and can be searched there. All districts will perform UCC searches now at $15.00 per debtor name for information and $25.00 with copies. Use search request form UCC-11. Copies ordered separately usually cost $2.00 per financing statement.

TAX LIEN RECORDS: All state and federal tax liens are filed with the District Recorder. Districts do not perform separate tax lien searches.

ONLINE ACCESS: Online access to the state recorder's office database from the Dept. of Natural Resources is available free at www.dnr.state.ak.us/recorders/search. This includes property information, liens, deeds, bankruptcies and more. Images go back to 6/2001; index to 2000. Also, a DNR "land records" database is searchable at www.dnr.state.ak.us/cgi-bin/lris/landrecords.

Aleutian Islands District

District Recorder, 550 W 7th Ave, #1200, #1140, Anchorage, AK 99501. **Phone**-907-269-8899, R/E Recording- 907-762-2444; hours 8AM-3:30PM
Will search UCC records. Information request only (per debtor)- $15.00. Information and copy request (per debtor)- $25.00. + $1.00. per page. UCC copy- $2.00 per financing statement. Will not search real estate or tax lien records. RE record copy- $1.25 1st page, $.25 each add'l. Cert fee: $5.00 per doc. Payee: Department of Revenue. **Online Access to Real Estate, UCC records:** Access is on the statewide DNR system at www.dnr.state.ak.us/ssd/recoff/search.cfm. **Other phones:** Assessor-907-343-6770.

Anchorage District

District Recorder, 550 W 7th Ave, #1200, #1140, Anchorage, AK 99501. **Phone**-907-269-8879, R/E Recording- 907-762-2443; hours 8AM-3:30PM
Will search UCC records. Information request only (per debtor)- $15.00. Information and copy request (per debtor)- $25.00 + $1.00. per page. UCC copy- $2.00 per financing statement. Will not search real estate or tax lien records. RE record copy- $1.25 1st page, $.25 each add'l. Cert fee: $5.00 per doc. Payee: Department of Revenue. **Online Access to Real Estate, UCC, Property Tax, Most Wanted, Stolen Vehicle records:** on the statewide DNR system at www.dnr.state.ak.us/ssd/recoff/search.cfm. UCC records can be accessed by phone at 907-269-8899. Also, access to Anchorage real estate property taxes are free at www.muni.org/services/departments/treasury/property/viewer.cfm Also, the sheriff's most wanted and stolen vehicle lists are at www.muni.org/apd1/apd911.cfm. Also, court list of divorces from 6/25/2003 to 10/22/2003 is at www.state.ak.us/courts/WEBDIV.3AN.
Other phones: Assessor-907-343-6770.

Barrow District

District Recorder, 1648 S Cushman St. #201, Fairbanks, AK 99701-6206. **Phone**-907-452-3521; fax-907-452-2951; hours 8:00AM-4PM
Will search UCC records. Information request only (per debtor)- $15.00. Information and copy request (per debtor)- $25.00. UCC copy- $2.00 per financing statement. Will not search real estate or tax lien records. RE record copy- $1.25 1st page, $.25 each add'l. Cert fee: $5.00 per doc. Payee: Department of Revenue. **Online Access to Real Estate, UCC records:** on the statewide DNR system at www.dnr.state.ak.us/ssd/recoff/search.cfm. **Other phones:** Assessor-907-459-1000.

Bethel District

District Recorder, PO Box 426, Bethel, AK 99559. **Phone**-907-543-3391; fax-907-543-7053; hours 9:15AM-Noon, 1-3:15PM
Will search UCC records. Information request only (per debtor)- $15.00. Information and copy request (per debtor)- $25.00. UCC copy- $2.00 per financing statement. Will not search real estate or tax lien records. RE record copy- $1.25 1st page, $.25 each add'l. Cert fee: $5.00 per doc. Payee: Department of Revenue. **Online Access to Real Estate, UCC records:** on the statewide DNR system at www.dnr.state.ak.us/ssd/recoff/search.cfm Or at akrecorder.info. **Other phones:** Assessor-907-543-2296; Treasurer-907-543-2298.

Bristol Bay District

District Recorder, 550 W 7th Ave, #1200, #1140, Anchorage, AK 99501. **Phone**-907-269-8879, R/E Recording- 907-762-2443; hours 8AM-3:30PM
Will search UCC records. Information request only (per debtor)- $15.00. Information and copy request (per debtor)- $25.00 + $1.00. per page. UCC copy- $2.00 per financing statement. Will not search real estate or tax lien records. RE record copy- $1.25 1st page, $.25 each add'l. Cert fee: $5.00 per doc. Payee: Department of Revenue. **Online Access to Real Estate, UCC records:** on the statewide DNR

system at www.dnr.state.ak.us/ssd/recoff/search.cfm. **Other phones:** Assessor-907-343-6770.

Cape Nome District

District Recorder, Box 431, Nome, AK 99762. **Phone**-907-443-5178; fax-907-452-2951; hours 8AM-12:30PM
Will search UCC records. Information request only (per debtor)- $15.00. Information and copy request (per debtor)- $25.00. UCC copy- $2.00 per financing statement. Will not search real estate or tax lien records. RE record copy- $1.25 1st page, $.25 each add'l. Cert fee: $5.00 per doc. Payee: Department of Revenue. **Online Access to Real Estate, UCC records:** on the statewide DNR system at www.dnr.state.ak.us/ssd/recoff/search.cfm.

Chitina District

District Recorder, Box 2023, Valdez, AK 99686. **Phone**-907-835-2266, R/E Recording- 907-745-9683, UCC Recording- 907-269-8899; hours 8:30AM-4PM
www.dnr.state.ak.us/recorders
The Chitna office records are now in Valdez, address and telephone given here. Will not search records. UCC copy- $2.00 per financing statement. RE record copy- $1.25 1st page, $.25 each add'l. Cert fee: $5.00 per doc. Payee: Department of Revenue. **Online Access to Real Estate, UCC, Deed records:** Access is on the statewide DNR system at www.dnr.state.ak.us/ssd/recoff/search.cfm. **Other phones:** Elections-907-451-2835; Vital Records-907-465-8606.

Cordova District

District Recorder, 550 W 7th Ave, #1200, #1140, Anchorage, AK 99501. **Phone**-907-269-8879, R/E Recording- 907-762-2443; hours 8AM-3:30PM
Will search UCC records. Information request only (per debtor)- $15.00. Information and copy request (per debtor)- $25.00. UCC copy- $2.00 per financing statement. Will not search real estate or tax lien records. RE record copy- $1.25 1st page, $.25 each add'l. Cert fee: $5.00 per doc. Payee: Department of Revenue. **Online Access to Real**

Estate, UCC records: on the statewide DNR system at www.dnr.state.ak.us/ssd/recoff/search.cfm. **Other phones:** Assessor-907-343-6770.

Fairbanks District

District Recorder, 1648 S Cushman St. #201, Fairbanks, AK 99701-6206. **Phone**-907-452-3521; fax-907-269-8912; hours 8:00AM-3:30pm www.co.fairbanks.ak.us Will search UCC records. Information request only (per debtor)- $15.00. Information and copy request (per debtor)- $25.00. UCC copy- $2.00 per financing statement. Will not search real estate or tax lien records. RE record copy- $1.25 1st page, $.25 each add'l. Cert fee: $5.00 per doc. Payee: Department of Revenue. **Online Access to Real Estate, UCC, Cemetery records:** Access to the Fairbanks North Star Borough property database is free at www.co.fairbanks.ak.us/PropertyDB/default.asp. Also, access is on the statewide DNR system at www.dnr.state.ak.us/ssd/recoff/search.cfm. Also, access to cemetery records for a fee is via a private company at www.ancestry.com/search/rectype/inddbs/4044.htm. **Other phones:** Assessor-907-459-1000.

Fort Gibbon District

District Recorder, 1648 S Cushman St. #201, Fairbanks, AK 99701-6206. **Phone**-907-452-3521; fax-907-452-2951; hours 8:30AM-4PM Will search UCC records. Information request only (per debtor)- $15.00. Information and copy request (per debtor)- $25.00. UCC copy- $2.00 per financing statement. Will not search real estate or tax lien records. RE record copy- $1.25 1st page, $.25 each add'l. Cert fee: $5.00 per doc. Payee: Department of Revenue. **Online Access to Real Estate, UCC records:** Access is on the statewide DNR system at www.dnr.state.ak.us/ssd/recoff/search.cfm. **Other phones:** Assessor-907-459-1000.

Haines District

District Recorder, 400 Willoughby, 3rd Fl, Juneau, AK 99801. **Phone**-907-465-3449; hours 8:30AM-4PM Will search UCC records. Information request only (per debtor)- $15.00. Information and copy request (per debtor)- $25.00. UCC copy- $2.00 per financing statement. Will not search real estate or tax lien records. RE record copy- $1.25 1st page, $.25 each add'l. Cert fee: $5.00 per doc. Payee: Department of Revenue. **Online Access to Real Estate, UCC records:** on the statewide DNR system at www.dnr.state.ak.us/ssd/recoff/search.cfm. **Other phones:** Assessor-907-586-5220.

Homer District

District Recorder, 195 E Bunnell Ave., #A, Homer, AK 99603. **Phone**-907-235-8136; hours 8:30AM-12;00, 1-4PM Will search UCC records. Information request only (per debtor)- $15.00. Information and copy request (per debtor)- $25.00. UCC copy- $2.00 per financing statement. Will not search real estate or tax lien records. RE record copy- $1.25 1st page, $.25 each add'l. Cert fee: $5.00 per doc. Payee: Department of Revenue. **Online Access to Real Estate, UCC, Assessor records:** Access is on the statewide DNR system at www.dnr.state.ak.us/ssd/recoff/search.cfm. Also, access the the borough tax assessor rolls is free at www.borough.kenai.ak.us/assessingdept/Parcel_QUERY/SEARCH.HTM.

Iliamna District

District Recorder, 550 W 7th Ave, #1200, #1140, Anchorage, AK 99501. **Phone**-907-269-8899, R/E Recording- 907-762-2443; hours 8AM-3:30PM Will search UCC records. Information request only (per debtor)- $15.00. Information and copy request (per debtor)- $25.00 + $1.00. per page. UCC copy-

$2.00 per financing statement. Will not search real estate or tax lien records. RE record copy- $1.25 1st page, $.25 each add'l. Cert fee: $5.00 per doc. Payee: Department of Revenue. **Online Access to Real Estate, UCC records:** on the statewide DNR system at www.dnr.state.ak.us/ssd/recoff/search.cfm. **Other phones:** Assessor-907-343-6770.

Juneau District

District Recorder, 400 Willoughby, 3rd Fl, Juneau, AK 99801. **Phone**-907-465-3449; hours 8:30AM-4PM www.juneau.org/cbj/index.php Will search UCC records. Information request only (per debtor)- $15.00. Information and copy request (per debtor)- $25.00. UCC copy- $2.00 per financing statement. Will not search real estate or tax lien records. RE record copy- $1.25 1st page, $.25 each add'l. Cert fee: $5.00 per doc. Payee: Department of Revenue. **Online Access to Real Estate, UCC, Assessor records:** Access to City of Juneau Property Records database is free online at www.juneau.org/assessordata/sqlassessor.php. Also includes link access to Juneau rentals data and the Records home page. Access is via the statewide DNR system at www.dnr.state.ak.us/ssd/recoff/search.cfm. **Other phones:** Assessor-907-586-5220.

Kenai District

District Recorder, 120 Trading Bay Rd #230, #230, Kenai, AK 99611. **Phone**-907-283-3118; R/E Recording- 907-225-3142; hours 8:30AM-4PM www.dnr.state.ak.us/ssd/recoff/default.htm Will search UCC records. Information request only (per debtor)- $15.00. Information and copy request (per debtor)- $25.00. UCC copy- $2.00 per financing statement. Will not search real estate or tax lien records. RE record copy- $1.25 1st page, $.25 each add'l. Cert fee: $5.00 per doc. Payee: Department of Revenue. **Online Access to Assessor, Real Estate, UCC records:** Kenai Peninsula Borough Assessing Dept. Public Information Search Page is at www.borough.kenai.ak.us/assessingdept/Parcel_QUERY/SEARCH.HTM. Also, access data on the statewide DNR system at www.dnr.state.ak.us/ssd/recoff/search.cfm. **Other phones:** Assessor-907-343-6770.

Ketchikan District

District Recorder, 415 Main St, Rm 310, Ketchikan, AK 99901. **Phone**-907-225-3142; fax-907-247-3142; hours 8:30AM-4PM; closed for lunch hour. Will search UCC records. Information request only (per debtor)- $15.00. Information and copy request (per debtor)- $25.00. UCC copy- $2.00 per financing statement. Will not search real estate or tax lien records. RE record copy- $1.25 1st page, $.25 each add'l. Cert fee: $5.00 per doc. Payee: Department of Revenue. **Online Access to Real Estate, UCC records:** on the statewide DNR system at www.dnr.state.ak.us/ssd/recoff/search.cfm. **Other phones:** Assessor-907-225-0277.

Kodiak District

District Recorder, 204 Mission Rd, Rm 110, Kodiak, AK 99615. **Phone**-907-486-9432; fax-907-486-9432; hours 8:00AM-Noon, 1-4PM Will not search records. UCC copy- $2.00 per financing statement. RE record copy- $1.25 1st page, $.25 each add'l. Cert fee: $5.00 per doc. Payee: Department of Revenue. **Online Access to Real Estate, UCC, Assessor records:** Access is on the statewide DNR system at www.dnr.state.ak.us/ssd/recoff/search.cfm. Also, search property assessor real property records free at www.kib.co.kodiak.ak.us. Click on "Real Property Records." **Other phones:** Assessor-907-486-9310.

Kotzebue District

District Recorder, 1648 S. Cushman St. #201, Fairbanks, AK 99701-6206. **Phone**-907-452-3521; fax-907-452-2951; hours 8:00AM-4PM Will search UCC records. Information request only (per debtor)- $15.00. Information and copy request (per debtor)- $25.00. UCC copy- $2.00 per financing statement. Will not search real estate or tax lien records. RE record copy- $1.25 1st page, $.25 each add'l. Cert fee: $5.00 per doc. Payee: Department of Revenue. **Online Access to Real Estate, UCC records:** on the statewide DNR system at www.dnr.state.ak.us/ssd/recoff/search.cfm. **Other phones:** Assessor-907-459-1000.

Kuskokwim District

District Recorder, PO Box 426, Bethel, AK 99559. **Phone**-907-543-3391; fax-907-543-7053; hours 9:15AM-Noon, 1-3:15PM Will search UCC records. Information request only (per debtor)- $15.00. Information and copy request (per debtor)- $25.00. UCC copy- $2.00 per financing statement. Will not search real estate or tax lien records. RE record copy- $1.25 1st page, $.25 each add'l. Cert fee: $5.00 per doc. Payee: Department of Revenue. **Online Access to Real Estate, UCC records:** on the statewide DNR system at www.dnr.state.ak.us/ssd/recoff/search.cfm.

Kvichak District

District Recorder, 550 W 7th Ave, #1200, #1140, Anchorage, AK 99501. **Phone**-907-269-8899, R/E Recording- 907-762-2443; hours 8AM-3:30PM Will search UCC records. Information request only (per debtor)- $15.00. Information and copy request (per debtor)- $25.00. UCC copy- $2.00 per financing statement. Will not search real estate or tax lien records. RE record copy- $1.25 1st page, $.25 each add'l. Cert fee: $5.00 per doc. Payee: Department of Revenue. **Online Access to Real Estate, UCC records:** on the statewide DNR system at www.dnr.state.ak.us/ssd/recoff/search.cfm. **Other phones:** Assessor-907-343-6770.

Manley Hot Springs District

District Recorder, 1648 S Cushman St. #201, Fairbanks, AK 99701-6206. **Phone**-907-452-3521; fax-907-452-2951; hours 8:30AM-4PM Will search UCC records. Information request only (per debtor)- $15.00. Information and copy request (per debtor)- $25.00. UCC copy- $2.00 per financing statement. Will not search real estate or tax lien records. RE record copy- $1.25 1st page, $.25 each add'l. Cert fee: $5.00 per doc. Payee: Department of Revenue. **Online Access to Real Estate, UCC records:** on the statewide DNR system at www.dnr.state.ak.us/ssd/recoff/search.cfm. **Other phones:** Assessor-907-459-1000.

Mount McKinley District

District Recorder, 1648 S Cushman St. #201, Fairbanks, AK 99701-6206. **Phone**-907-452-3521; fax-907-452-2951; hours 8:30AM-4PM Will search UCC records. Information request only (per debtor)- $15.00. Information and copy request (per debtor)- $25.00. UCC copy- $2.00 per financing statement. Will not search real estate or tax lien records. RE record copy- $1.25 1st page, $.25 each add'l. Cert fee: $5.00 per doc. Payee: Department of Revenue. **Online Access to Real Estate, UCC records:** on the statewide DNR system at www.dnr.state.ak.us/ssd/recoff/search.cfm. **Other phones:** Assessor-907459-1000.

Nenana District

District Recorder, 1648 S Cushman St. #201, Fairbanks, AK 99701-6206. **Phone**-907-452-3521; fax-907-452-2951; hours 8:30AM-4PM

Will search UCC records. Information request only (per debtor)- $15.00. Information and copy request (per debtor)- $25.00. UCC copy- $2.00 per financing statement. Will not search real estate or tax lien records. RE record copy- $1.25 1st page, $.25 each add'l. Cert fee: $5.00 per doc. Payee: Department of Revenue. **Online Access to Real Estate, UCC records:** on the statewide DNR system at www.dnr.state.ak.us/ssd/recoff/search.cfm. **Other phones:** Assessor-907-459-1000.

Nulato District

District Recorder, 1648 S Cushman St. #201, Fairbanks, AK 99701-6206. **Phone**-907-452-3521; fax-907-452-2951; hours 8:30AM-4PM

Will search UCC records. Information request only (per debtor)- $15.00. Information and copy request (per debtor)- $25.00. UCC copy- $2.00 per financing statement. Will not search real estate or tax lien records. RE record copy- $1.25 1st page, $.25 each add'l. Cert fee: $5.00 per doc. Payee: Department of Revenue. **Online Access to Real Estate, UCC records:** on the statewide DNR system at www.dnr.state.ak.us/ssd/recoff/search.cfm. **Other phones:** Assessor-907-459-1000.

Palmer District

District Recorder, 1800 Glenn Hwy #7, Palmer, AK 99645. **Phone**-907-745-3080; fax-907-745-0958; hours 8:30AM-4PM

Will search UCC records. Information request only (per debtor)- $15.00. Information and copy request (per debtor)- $25.00. UCC copy- $2.00 per financing statement. Will not search real estate or tax lien records. RE record copy- $1.25 1st page, $.25 each add'l. Cert fee: $5.00 per doc. Payee: Department of Revenue. **Online Access to Real Estate, UCC records:** on the statewide DNR system at www.dnr.state.ak.us/ssd/recoff/search.cfm.

Petersburg District

District Recorder, 415 Main St, Rm 310, Ketchikan, AK 99901. **Phone**-907-225-3142; fax-907-247-3142; hours 8:30AM-4PM; closed for lunch hour.

Will search UCC records. Information request only (per debtor)- $15.00. Information and copy request (per debtor)- $25.00. UCC copy- $2.00 per financing statement. Will not search real estate or tax lien records. RE record copy- $1.25 1st page, $.25 each add'l. Cert fee: $5.00 per doc. Payee: Department of Revenue. **Online Access to Real Estate, UCC records:** on the statewide DNR system at www.dnr.state.ak.us/ssd/recoff/search.cfm. **Other phones:** Assessor-907-225-0277.

Rampart District

District Recorder, 1648 S. Cushman St. #201, Fairbanks, AK 99701-6206. **Phone**-907-452-3521; fax-907-452-2951; hours 8AM-4PM

Will search UCC records. Information request only (per debtor)- $15.00. Information and copy request (per debtor)- $25.00. UCC copy- $2.00 per financing statement. Will not search real estate or tax lien records. RE record copy- $1.25 1st page, $.25 each add'l. Cert fee: $5.00 per doc. Payee: Department of Revenue. **Online Access to Real Estate, UCC records:** on the statewide DNR system at www.dnr.state.ak.us/ssd/recoff/search.cfm. **Other phones:** Assessor-907-459-1000.

Seldovia District

District Recorder, 195 E Bunnell Ave., #A, Homer, AK 99603. **Phone**-907-235-8136; hours 8:30-12.;00AM, 1-4PM

Will search UCC records. Information request only (per debtor)- $15.00. Information and copy request (per debtor)- $25.00. UCC copy- $2.00 per financing statement. Will not search real estate or tax lien records. RE record copy- $1.25 1st page, $.25 each add'l. Cert fee: $5.00 per doc. Payee: Department of Revenue. **Online Access to Real Estate, UCC, Assessor records:** on statewide DNR system at www.dnr.state.ak.us/ssd/recoff/search.cfm. Also, access the the borough tax assessor rolls is free at www.borough.kenai.ak.us/assessingdept/Parcel_QUERY/SEARCH.HTM.

Seward District

District Recorder, Box 246, Seward, AK 99664. **Phone**-907-224-3075, R/E Recording- 907-224-7032; fax- 907-224-7192; hours 8:30AM-4PM www.dnr.state.ak.us/recorders

Will search UCC records. Information request only (per debtor)- $15.00. Information and copy request (per debtor)- $25.00. UCC copy- $2.00 per financing statement. Will not search real estate or tax lien records. RE record copy- $1.25 1st page, $.25 each add'l. Cert fee: $5.00 per doc. Payee: Department of Revenue. **Online Access to Real Estate, UCC, Assessor records:** on statewide DNR system at www.dnr.state.ak.us/ssd/recoff/search.cfm. Also, access the the borough tax assessor rolls is free at www.borough.kenai.ak.us/assessingdept/Parcel_QUERY/SEARCH.HTM.

Sitka District

District Recorder, 210C Lake St, Sitka, AK 99835. 907-747-3275; hours 8:30AM-Noon, 1-4PM M-Th

Will search UCC records. Information request only (per debtor)- $15.00. Information and copy request (per debtor)- $25.00. UCC copy- $2.00 per financing statement. Will not search real estate or tax lien records. RE record copy- $1.25 1st page, $.25 each add'l. Cert fee: $5.00 per doc. Payee:

Department of Revenue. **Online Access to Real Estate, UCC records:** on the statewide DNR system at www.dnr.state.ak.us/ssd/recoff/search.cfm. **Other phones:** Assessor-907-343-6770.

Skagway District

District Recorder, 400 Willoughby, 3rd Fl, Juneau, AK 99801. **Phone**-907-465-3449; hours 8:30AM-4PM

Will not search records. UCC copy- $2.00 per financing statement. RE record copy- $1.25 1st page, $.25 each add'l. Cert fee: $5.00 per doc. Payee: Department of Revenue. **Online Access to Real Estate, UCC records:** on the statewide DNR system at www.dnr.state.ak.us/ssd/recoff/search.cfm.

Talkeetna District

District Recorder, 1800 Glenn Hwy #7, Palmer, AK 99645. **Phone**-907-745-3080; fax-907-745-0958; hours 8:30AM-4PM

Will search UCC records. Information request only (per debtor)- $15.00. Information and copy request (per debtor)- $25.00. UCC copy- $2.00 per financing statement. Will not search real estate or tax lien records. RE record copy- $1.25 1st page, $.25 each add'l. Cert fee: $5.00 per doc. Payee: Department of Revenue. **Online Access to Real Estate, UCC records:** on the statewide DNR system at www.dnr.state.ak.us/ssd/recoff/search.cfm.

Valdez District

District Recorder, Box 2023, Valdez, AK 99686. **Phone**-907-835-2266; hours 8:30AM-Noon, 1-4PM

Will search UCC records. Information request only (per debtor)- $15.00. Information and copy request (per debtor)- $25.00. UCC copy- $2.00 per financing statement. Will not search real estate or tax lien records. RE record copy- $1.25 1st page, $.25 each add'l. Cert fee: $5.00 per doc. Payee: Department of Revenue. **Online Access to Real Estate, UCC records:** on the statewide DNR system at www.dnr.state.ak.us/ssd/recoff/search.cfm.

Wrangell District

District Recorder, 415 Main St, Rm 310, Ketchikan, AK 99901. **Phone**-907-225-3142; fax-907-247-3142; hours 8:30AM-4PM; closed for lunch hour.

Will search UCC records. Information request only (per debtor)- $15.00. Information and copy request (per debtor)- $25.00. UCC copy- $2.00 per financing statement. Will not search real estate or tax lien records. RE record copy- $1.25 1st page, $.25 each add'l. Cert fee: $5.00 per doc. Payee: Department of Revenue. **Online Access to Real Estate, UCC records:** on the statewide DNR system at www.dnr.state.ak.us/ssd/recoff/search.cfm. **Other phones:** Assessor-907-225-0277.

Alaska County Locator

You will usually be able to find the city name in the City/County Cross Reference below. In that case, it is a simple matter to determine the county from the cross reference. However, only the official US Postal Service city names are included in this index. There are an additional 40,000 place names that people use in their addresses. Therefore, we have also included a ZIP/City Cross Reference immediately following the City/County Cross Reference.

If you know the ZIP Code but the city name does not appear in the City/County Cross Reference index, look up the ZIP Code in the ZIP/City Cross Reference, find the city name, then look up the city name in the City/County Cross Reference. For example, you want to know the county for an address of Menands, NY 12204. There is no "Menands" in the City/County Cross Reference. The ZIP/City Cross Reference shows that ZIP Codes 12201-12288 are for the city of Albany. Looking back in the City/County Cross Reference, Albany is in Albany County.

Alaska City/County Cross Reference

ADAK Aleutian Islands, West
AKIACHAK Bethel
AKIAK Bethel
AKUTAN Aleutian Islands, East
ALAKANUK Wade Hampton
ALEKNAGIK Dillingham
ALLAKAKET Yukon-Koyukuk
AMBLER Northwest Arctic
ANAKTUVUK PASS North Slope Borough
ANCHOR POINT Kenai Peninsula Borough
ANCHORAGE Anchorage Borough
ANDERSON Denali
ANGOON Yakutat
ANIAK Bethel
ANVIK Yukon-Koyukuk
ARCTIC VILLAGE Yukon-Koyukuk
ATKA Aleutian Islands, West
ATQASUK North Slope Borough
AUKE BAY Juneau Borough
BARROW North Slope Borough
BEAVER Yukon-Koyukuk
BETHEL Bethel
BETTLES FIELD Yukon-Koyukuk
BIG LAKE Matanuska-Susitna Borough
BREVIG MISSION Nome
BUCKLAND Northwest Arctic
CANTWELL Denali
CENTRAL Yukon-Koyukuk
CHALKYITSIK Yukon-Koyukuk
CHEFORNAK Bethel
CHEVAK Wade Hampton
CHICKEN Southeast Fairbanks
CHIGNIK Lake & Peninsula
CHIGNIK LAGOON Lake & Peninsula
CHIGNIK LAKE Lake & Peninsula
CHITINA Valdez-Cordova
CHUGIAK Anchorage Borough
CIRCLE Yukon-Koyukuk
CLAM GULCH Kenai Peninsula Borough
CLARKS POINT Dillingham
CLEAR Denali
COFFMAN COVE Prince of Wales-Outer
   Ketchikan
COLD BAY Aleutian Islands, East
COOPER LANDING Kenai Peninsula
   Borough
COPPER CENTER Valdez-Cordova
CORDOVA Valdez-Cordova
CRAIG Prince of Wales-Outer Ketchikan
CROOKED CREEK Bethel
DEERING Northwest Arctic
DELTA JUNCTION Southeast Fairbanks
DENALI NATIONAL PARK Denali
DILLINGHAM Dillingham
DOUGLAS Juneau Borough
DUTCH HARBOR Aleutian Islands, West
EAGLE Southeast Fairbanks
EAGLE RIVER Anchorage Borough
EEK Bethel
EGEGIK Lake & Peninsula
EIELSON AFB Fairbanks North Star
   Borough

EKWOK Dillingham
ELFIN COVE Yakutat
ELIM Nome
ELMENDORF AFB Anchorage Borough
EMMONAK Wade Hampton
ESTER Fairbanks North Star Borough
FAIRBANKS Fairbanks North Star Borough
FALSE PASS Aleutian Islands, East
FLAT Yukon-Koyukuk
FORT GREELY Southeast Fairbanks
FORT RICHARDSON Anchorage Borough
FORT WAINWRIGHT Fairbanks North Star
   Borough
FORT YUKON Yukon-Koyukuk
GAKONA Valdez-Cordova
GALENA Yukon-Koyukuk
GAMBELL Nome
GIRDWOOD Anchorage Borough
GLENNALLEN Valdez-Cordova
GOODNEWS BAY Bethel
GRAYLING Yukon-Koyukuk
GUSTAVUS Yakutat
HAINES Haines Borough
HEALY Denali
HOLY CROSS Yukon-Koyukuk
HOMER Kenai Peninsula Borough
HOONAH Yakutat
HOOPER BAY Wade Hampton
HOPE Kenai Peninsula Borough
HOUSTON Matanuska-Susitna Borough
HUGHES Yukon-Koyukuk
HUSLIA Yukon-Koyukuk
HYDABURG Prince of Wales-Outer
   Ketchikan
HYDER Prince of Wales-Outer Ketchikan
ILIAMNA Lake & Peninsula
INDIAN Anchorage Borough
JUNEAU Juneau Borough
KAKE Wrangell-Petersburg
KAKTOVIK North Slope Borough
KALSKAG Bethel
KALTAG Yukon-Koyukuk
KARLUK Kodiak Island Borough
KASIGLUK Bethel
KASILOF Kenai Peninsula Borough
KENAI Kenai Peninsula Borough
KETCHIKAN Ketchikan Gateway Borough
KIANA Northwest Arctic
KING COVE Aleutian Islands, East
KING SALMON (99613) Bristol Bay
   Borough(84), Lake & Peninsula(15)
KIPNUK Bethel
KIVALINA Northwest Arctic
KLAWOCK Prince of Wales-Outer
   Ketchikan
KOBUK Northwest Arctic
KODIAK Kodiak Island Borough
KOTLIK Wade Hampton
KOTZEBUE Northwest Arctic
KOYUK Nome
KOYUKUK Yukon-Koyukuk
KWETHLUK Bethel

KWIGILLINGOK Bethel
LAKE MINCHUMINA Yukon-Koyukuk
LARSEN BAY Kodiak Island Borough
LEVELOCK Lake & Peninsula
LOWER KALSKAG Bethel
MANLEY HOT SPRINGS Yukon-Koyukuk
MANOKOTAK Dillingham
MARSHALL Wade Hampton
MC GRATH Yukon-Koyukuk
MEKORYUK Bethel
METLAKATLA Prince of Wales-Outer
   Ketchikan
MEYERS CHUCK Prince of Wales-Outer
   Ketchikan
MINTO Yukon-Koyukuk
MOOSE PASS Kenai Peninsula Borough
MOUNTAIN VILLAGE Wade Hampton
NAKNEK Bristol Bay Borough
NAPAKIAK Bethel
NENANA Yukon-Koyukuk
NEW STUYAHOK Dillingham
NIGHTMUTE Bethel
NIKISKI Kenai Peninsula Borough
NIKOLAI Yukon-Koyukuk
NIKOLSKI Aleutian Islands, West
NINILCHIK Kenai Peninsula Borough
NOATAK Northwest Arctic
NOME Nome
NONDALTON Lake & Peninsula
NOORVIK Northwest Arctic
NORTH POLE Fairbanks North Star
   Borough
NORTHWAY Southeast Fairbanks
NUIQSUT North Slope Borough
NULATO Yukon-Koyukuk
NUNAM IQUA Wade Hampton
NUNAPITCHUK Bethel
OLD HARBOR Kodiak Island Borough
OUZINKIE Kodiak Island Borough
PALMER Matanuska-Susitna Borough
PEDRO BAY Lake & Peninsula
PELICAN Yakutat
PERRYVILLE Lake & Peninsula
PETERSBURG Wrangell-Petersburg
PILOT POINT Lake & Peninsula
PILOT STATION Wade Hampton
PLATINUM Bethel
POINT BAKER Prince of Wales-Outer
   Ketchikan
POINT HOPE North Slope Borough
POINT LAY North Slope Borough
PORT ALEXANDER Wrangell-Petersburg
PORT ALSWORTH Lake & Peninsula
PORT HEIDEN Lake & Peninsula
PORT LIONS Kodiak Island Borough
PRUDHOE BAY North Slope Borough
QUINHAGAK Bethel
RAMPART Yukon-Koyukuk
RED DEVIL Bethel
RUBY Yukon-Koyukuk
RUSSIAN MISSION Wade Hampton

SAINT GEORGE ISLAND Aleutian Islands,
   West
SAINT MARYS Wade Hampton
SAINT MICHAEL Nome
SAINT PAUL ISLAND Aleutian Islands,
   West
SALCHA Fairbanks North Star Borough
SAND POINT Aleutian Islands, East
SAVOONGA Nome
SCAMMON BAY Wade Hampton
SELAWIK Northwest Arctic
SELDOVIA Kenai Peninsula Borough
SEWARD Kenai Peninsula Borough
SHAGELUK Yukon-Koyukuk
SHAKTOOLIK Nome
SHELDON POINT Wade Hampton
SHISHMAREF Nome
SHUNGNAK Northwest Arctic
SITKA Sitka Borough
SKAGWAY Yakutat
SKWENTNA Matanuska-Susitna Borough
SLEETMUTE Bethel
SOLDOTNA Kenai Peninsula Borough
SOUTH NAKNEK Bristol Bay Borough
STEBBINS Nome
STERLING Kenai Peninsula Borough
STEVENS VILLAGE Yukon-Koyukuk
SUTTON Matanuska-Susitna Borough
TAKOTNA Yukon-Koyukuk
TALKEETNA Matanuska-Susitna Borough
TANACROSS Southeast Fairbanks
TANANA Yukon-Koyukuk
TATITLEK Valdez-Cordova
TELLER Nome
TENAKEE SPRINGS Yakutat
TETLIN Southeast Fairbanks
THORNE BAY Prince of Wales-Outer
   Ketchikan
TOGIAK Dillingham
TOK Southeast Fairbanks
TOKSOOK BAY Bethel
TRAPPER CREEK Matanuska-Susitna
   Borough
TULUKSAK Bethel
TUNTUTULIAK Bethel
TUNUNAK Bethel
TWO RIVERS Fairbanks North Star
   Borough
TYONEK Kenai Peninsula Borough
UNALAKLEET Nome
UNALASKA Aleutian Islands, West
VALDEZ Valdez-Cordova
VENETIE Yukon-Koyukuk
WAINWRIGHT North Slope Borough
WALES Nome
WARD COVE Ketchikan Gateway Borough
WASILLA Matanuska-Susitna Borough
WHITE MOUNTAIN Nome
WHITTIER Valdez-Cordova
WILLOW Matanuska-Susitna Borough
WRANGELL Wrangell-Petersburg
YAKUTAT Yakutat-Not Used

Alaska ZIP/City Cross Reference

ZIP	City		ZIP	City		ZIP	City		ZIP	City
99500-99504	ANCHORAGE		99637-99637	TOKSOOK BAY		99733-99733	CIRCLE		99922-99922	HYDABURG
99505-99505	FORT RICHARDSON		99638-99638	NIKOLSKI		99734-99734	PRUDHOE BAY		99923-99923	HYDER
99506-99506	ELMENDORF AFB		99639-99639	NINILCHIK		99736-99736	DEERING		99925-99925	KLAWOCK
99507-99530	ANCHORAGE		99640-99640	NONDALTON		99737-99737	DELTA JUNCTION		99926-99926	METLAKATLA
99540-99540	INDIAN		99641-99641	NUNAPITCHUK		99738-99738	EAGLE		99927-99927	POINT BAKER
99546-99546	ADAK		99643-99643	OLD HARBOR		99739-99739	ELIM		99928-99928	WARD COVE
99547-99547	ATKA		99644-99644	OUZINKIE		99740-99740	FORT YUKON		99929-99929	WRANGELL
99548-99548	CHIGNIK LAKE		99645-99645	PALMER		99741-99741	GALENA		99950-99950	KETCHIKAN
99549-99549	PORT HEIDEN		99647-99647	PEDRO BAY		99742-99742	GAMBELL			
99550-99550	PORT LIONS		99648-99648	PERRYVILLE		99743-99743	HEALY			
99551-99551	AKIACHAK		99649-99649	PILOT POINT		99744-99744	ANDERSON			
99552-99552	AKIAK		99650-99650	PILOT STATION		99745-99745	HUGHES			
99553-99553	AKUTAN		99651-99651	PLATINUM		99746-99746	HUSLIA			
99554-99554	ALAKANUK		99652-99652	BIG LAKE		99747-99747	KAKTOVIK			
99555-99555	ALEKNAGIK		99653-99653	PORT ALSWORTH		99748-99748	KALTAG			
99556-99556	ANCHOR POINT		99654-99654	WASILLA		99749-99749	KIANA			
99557-99557	ANIAK		99655-99655	QUINHAGAK		99750-99750	KIVALINA			
99558-99558	ANVIK		99656-99656	RED DEVIL		99751-99751	KOBUK			
99559-99559	BETHEL		99657-99657	RUSSIAN MISSION		99752-99752	KOTZEBUE			
99561-99561	CHEFORNAK		99658-99658	SAINT MARYS		99753-99753	KOYUK			
99563-99563	CHEVAK		99659-99659	SAINT MICHAEL		99754-99754	KOYUKUK			
99564-99564	CHIGNIK		99660-99660	SAINT PAUL ISLAND		99755-99755	DENALI NATIONAL PARK			
99565-99565	CHIGNIK LAGOON		99661-99661	SAND POINT		99756-99756	MANLEY HOT SPRINGS			
99566-99566	CHITINA		99662-99662	SCAMMON BAY		99757-99757	LAKE MINCHUMINA			
99567-99567	CHUGIAK		99663-99663	SELDOVIA		99758-99758	MINTO			
99568-99568	CLAM GULCH		99664-99664	SEWARD		99759-99759	POINT LAY			
99569-99569	CLARKS POINT		99665-99665	SHAGELUK		99760-99760	NENANA			
99571-99571	COLD BAY		99666-99666	SHELDON POINT		99761-99761	NOATAK			
99572-99572	COOPER LANDING		99666-99666	NUNAM IQUA		99762-99762	NOME			
99573-99573	COPPER CENTER		99667-99667	SKWENTNA		99763-99763	NOORVIK			
99574-99574	CORDOVA		99668-99668	SLEETMUTE		99764-99764	NORTHWAY			
99575-99575	CROOKED CREEK		99669-99669	SOLDOTNA		99765-99765	NULATO			
99576-99576	DILLINGHAM		99670-99670	SOUTH NAKNEK		99766-99766	POINT HOPE			
99577-99577	EAGLE RIVER		99671-99671	STEBBINS		99767-99767	RAMPART			
99578-99578	EEK		99672-99672	STERLING		99768-99768	RUBY			
99579-99579	EGEGIK		99674-99674	SUTTON		99769-99769	SAVOONGA			
99580-99580	EKWOK		99675-99675	TAKOTNA		99770-99770	SELAWIK			
99581-99581	EMMONAK		99676-99676	TALKEETNA		99771-99771	SHAKTOOLIK			
99583-99583	FALSE PASS		99677-99677	TATITLEK		99772-99772	SHISHMAREF			
99584-99584	FLAT		99678-99678	TOGIAK		99773-99773	SHUNGNAK			
99585-99585	MARSHALL		99679-99679	TULUKSAK		99774-99774	STEVENS VILLAGE			
99586-99586	GAKONA		99680-99680	TUNTUTULIAK		99775-99775	FAIRBANKS			
99587-99587	GIRDWOOD		99681-99681	TUNUNAK		99776-99776	TANACROSS			
99588-99588	GLENNALLEN		99682-99682	TYONEK		99777-99777	TANANA			
99589-99589	GOODNEWS BAY		99683-99683	TRAPPER CREEK		99778-99778	TELLER			
99590-99590	GRAYLING		99684-99684	UNALAKLEET		99779-99779	TETLIN			
99591-99591	SAINT GEORGE ISLAND		99685-99685	UNALASKA		99780-99780	TOK			
99599-99599	ANCHORAGE		99686-99686	VALDEZ		99781-99781	VENETIE			
99602-99602	HOLY CROSS		99687-99687	WASILLA		99782-99782	WAINWRIGHT			
99603-99603	HOMER		99688-99688	WILLOW		99783-99783	WALES			
99604-99604	HOOPER BAY		99689-99689	YAKUTAT		99784-99784	WHITE MOUNTAIN			
99605-99605	HOPE		99690-99690	NIGHTMUTE		99785-99785	BREVIG MISSION			
99606-99606	ILIAMNA		99691-99691	NIKOLAI		99786-99786	AMBLER			
99607-99607	KALSKAG		99692-99692	DUTCH HARBOR		99788-99788	CHALKYITSIK			
99608-99608	KARLUK		99693-99693	WHITTIER		99789-99789	NUIQSUT			
99609-99609	KASIGLUK		99694-99694	HOUSTON		99790-99790	FAIRBANKS			
99610-99610	KASILOF		99695-99695	ANCHORAGE		99791-99791	ATQASUK			
99611-99611	KENAI		99697-99697	KODIAK		99801-99811	JUNEAU			
99612-99612	KING COVE		99701-99701	FAIRBANKS		99820-99820	ANGOON			
99613-99613	KING SALMON		99702-99702	EIELSON AFB		99821-99821	AUKE BAY			
99614-99614	KIPNUK		99703-99703	FORT WAINWRIGHT		99824-99824	DOUGLAS			
99615-99619	KODIAK		99704-99704	CLEAR		99825-99825	ELFIN COVE			
99620-99620	KOTLIK		99705-99705	NORTH POLE		99826-99826	GUSTAVUS			
99621-99621	KWETHLUK		99706-99712	FAIRBANKS		99827-99827	HAINES			
99622-99622	KWIGILLINGOK		99714-99714	SALCHA		99829-99829	HOONAH			
99624-99624	LARSEN BAY		99716-99716	TWO RIVERS		99830-99830	KAKE			
99625-99625	LEVELOCK		99720-99720	ALLAKAKET		99832-99832	PELICAN			
99626-99626	LOWER KALSKAG		99721-99721	ANAKTUVUK PASS		99833-99833	PETERSBURG			
99627-99627	MC GRATH		99722-99722	ARCTIC VILLAGE		99835-99835	SITKA			
99628-99628	MANOKOTAK		99723-99723	BARROW		99836-99836	PORT ALEXANDER			
99629-99629	WASILLA		99724-99724	BEAVER		99840-99840	SKAGWAY			
99630-99630	MEKORYUK		99725-99725	ESTER		99841-99841	TENAKEE SPRINGS			
99631-99631	MOOSE PASS		99726-99726	BETTLES FIELD		99850-99850	JUNEAU			
99632-99632	MOUNTAIN VILLAGE		99727-99727	BUCKLAND		99901-99901	KETCHIKAN			
99633-99633	NAKNEK		99729-99729	CANTWELL		99903-99903	MEYERS CHUCK			
99634-99634	NAPAKIAK		99730-99730	CENTRAL		99918-99918	COFFMAN COVE			
99635-99635	NIKISKI		99731-99731	FORT GREELY		99919-99919	THORNE BAY			
99636-99636	NEW STUYAHOK		99732-99732	CHICKEN		99921-99921	CRAIG			

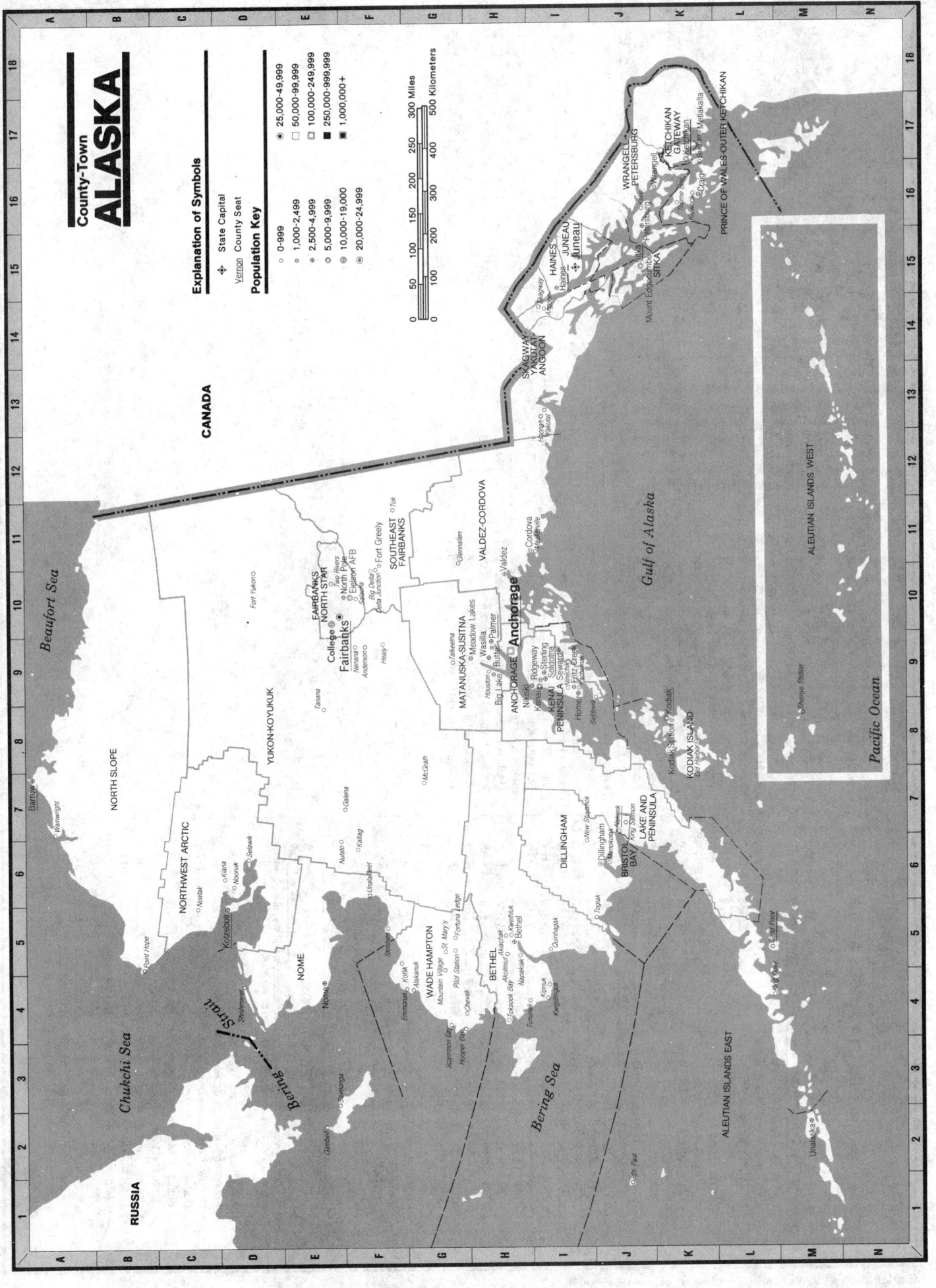

County-Town
ALASKA

Explanation of Symbols

State Capital

Vernon County Seat

Population Key

○ 0-999
⊙ 1,000-2,499
⊕ 2,500-4,999
◉ 5,000-9,999
⊚ 10,000-19,000
◎ 20,000-24,999

● 25,000-49,999
□ 50,000-99,999
▣ 100,000-249,999
■ 250,000-999,999
■ 1,000,000+

300 Miles
500 Kilometers

CANADA

RUSSIA

Beaufort Sea

Chukchi Sea

Bering Strait

Bering Sea

Gulf of Alaska

Pacific Ocean

NORTH SLOPE

NORTHWEST ARCTIC

NOME

YUKON-KOYUKUK

WADE HAMPTON

BETHEL

DILLINGHAM

BRISTOL BAY

LAKE AND PENINSULA

ALEUTIAN ISLANDS EAST

ALEUTIAN ISLANDS WEST

FAIRBANKS NORTH STAR

SOUTHEAST FAIRBANKS

MATANUSKA-SUSITNA

ANCHORAGE

KENAI PENINSULA

VALDEZ-CORDOVA

KODIAK ISLAND

SKAGWAY-YAKUTAT-ANGOON

HAINES

JUNEAU

SITKA

WRANGELL-PETERSBURG

KETCHIKAN GATEWAY

PRINCE OF WALES-OUTER KETCHIKAN

Barrow
Wainwright
Point Hope
Kivalina
Noatak
Kiana
Noorvik
Selawik
Kotzebue
Shishmaref
Shungnak
Gambell
Savoonga
Nome
Teller
Stebbins
Emmonak
Kotlik
Alakanuk
Scammon Bay
Hooper Bay
Mountain Village
St. Mary's
Pilot Station
Chevak
Toksook Bay
Nunapitchuk
Akiachak
Kwethluk
Bethel
Tununak
Kipnuk
Kasigluk
Napakiak
Quinhagak
Togiak
Manokotak
Dillingham
Aleknagik
New Stuyahok
Naknek
King Salmon
St. Paul
King Cove
Sand Point
Cold Bay
Unalaska
Fort Yukon
Galena
Nulato
Kaltag
Unalakleet
Tanana
McGrath
Fairbanks
College
North Pole
Eielson AFB
Salcha
Two Rivers
Big Delta
Delta Junction
Fort Greely
Nenana
Anderson
Healy
Tok
Northway
Tanacross
Talkeetna
Meadow Lakes
Wasilla
Houston
Big Lake
Butte
Palmer
Nikiski
Kenai
Ridgeway
Sterling
Soldotna
Seward
Homer
Fritz Creek
Anchor Point
Seldovia
Glennallen
Cordova
McCarthy
Valdez
Kodiak
Kodiak Station
Old Harbor
Skagway
Yakutat
Haines
Mount Edgecumbe
Sitka
Angoon
Hoonah
Wrangell
Petersburg
Thorne Bay
Craig
Klawock
Ketchikan
Saxman
Metlakatla
Shemya Station

Aleutian Islands West

BOROUGHS AND CENSUS AREAS

(25 Boroughs and Census Areas)

Name of Borough or Census Area	Population	Location on Map
ALEUTIANS EAST Borough	2,464	L-3
ALEUTIANS WEST Census Area	9,478	M-11
ANCHORAGE Borough	226,338	H-8
BETHEL Census Area	13,656	H-4
BRISTOL BAY Borough	1,410	J-6
DILLINGHAM Census Area	4,012	I-6
FAIRBANKS NORTH STAR Borough	77,720	E-10
HAINES Borough	2,117	I-15
JUNEAU Borough	26,751	I-15
KENAI PENINSULA Borough	40,802	I-8
KETCHIKAN GATEWAY Borough	13,828	K-17
KODIAK ISLAND Borough	13,309	K-7
LAKE AND PENINSULA Borough	1,668	J-7
MATANUSKA-SUSITNA Borough	39,683	G-8
NOME Census Area	8,288	E-4
NORTH SLOPE Borough	5,979	B-7
NORTHWEST ARCTIC Borough	6,113	C-6
PRINCE OF WALES-OUTER KETCHIKAN Census Area	6,278	L-15
SITKA Borough	8,588	K-15
SKAGWAY-YAKUTAT-ANGOON Census Area	4,385	H-13
SOUTHEAST FAIRBANKS Census Area	5,913	F-11
VALDEZ-CORDOVA Census Area	9,952	H-11
WADE HAMPTON Census Area	5,791	G-4
WRANGELL-PETERSBURG Census Area	7,042	J-16
YUKON-KOYUKUK Census Area	8,478	D-8
TOTAL	550,043	

CITIES AND TOWNS

Note: The first name is that of the city or town, second, that of the county in which it is located, then the population and location on the map.

- ● Adak Station, Aleutians West Census Area, 4,633 ... N-12
- Anchorage, Anchorage Borough, 226,338 ... H-9
- Barrow, North Slope Borough, 3,469 ... A-7
- Bethel, Bethel Census Area, 4,674 ... H-5
- ● Big Lake, Matanuska-Susitna Borough, 1,477 ... H-9
- ● Butte, Matanuska-Susitna Borough, 2,039 ... H-9
- ● College, Fairbanks North Star Borough, 11,249 ... E-10
- Cordova, Valdez-Cordova Census Area, 2,110 ... I-11
- Craig, Prince of Wales-Outer Ketchikan Census Area, 1,260 ... K-16
- Dillingham, Dillingham Census Area, 2,017 ... J-6
- ● Eielson AFB, Fairbanks North Star Borough, 5,251 ... F-10
- Fairbanks, Fairbanks North Star Borough, 30,843 ... E-10
- ● Fort Greely, Southeast Fairbanks Census Area, 1,147 ... F-11
- ● Fritz Creek, Kenai Peninsula Borough, 1,426 ... I-9
- Haines, Haines Borough, 1,238 ... I-14
- Homer, Kenai Peninsula Borough, 3,660 ... I-9
- Juneau, Juneau Borough, 26,751 ... I-15
- Kenai, Kenai Peninsula Borough, 6,327 ... I-9
- Ketchikan, Ketchikan Gateway Borough, 8,263 ... K-17
- Kodiak, Kodiak Island Borough, 6,365 ... K-8
- ● Kodiak Station, Kodiak Island Borough, 2,025 ... K-8
- Kotzebue, Northwest Arctic Borough, 2,751 ... D-5
- ● Meadow Lakes, Matanuska-Susitna Borough, 2,374 ... G-9
- ● Metlakatla, Prince of Wales-Outer Ketchikan Census Area, 1,407 ... K-17
- Mount Edgecumbe, Sitka ... J-15
- ● Nikiski, Kenai Peninsula Borough, 2,743 ... I-8
- Nome, Nome Census Area, 3,500 ... E-4
- North Pole, Fairbanks North Star Borough, 1,456 ... E-10
- Palmer, Matanuska-Susitna Borough, 2,866 ... H-9
- Petersburg, Wrangell-Petersburg Census Area, 3,207 ... J-16
- ● Ridgeway, Kenai Peninsula Borough, 2,018 ... I-9
- Seward, Kenai Peninsula Borough, 2,699 ... I-9
- Sitka, Sitka Borough, 8,588 ... J-16
- Soldotna, Kenai Peninsula Borough, 3,482 ... I-9
- ● Sterling, Kenai Peninsula Borough, 3,802 ... I-9
- Unalaska, Aleutians West Census Area, 3,089 ... M-3
- Valdez, Valdez-Cordova Census Area, 4,068 ... H-10
- Wasilla, Matanuska-Susitna Borough, 4,028 ... H-9
- Wrangell, Wrangell-Petersburg Census Area, 2,479 ... K-16

Explanation of symbols: ● – Census Designated Place (CDP)

Arizona

General Help Numbers:

Governor's Office
1700 W Washington   602-542-4331
Phoenix, AZ 85007   Fax 602-542-1381
www.governor.state.az.us   8AM-5PM

Attorney General's Office
1275 W Washington   602-542-5025
Phoenix, AZ 85007   Fax 602-542-4085
www.attorneygeneral.state.az.us   8AM-5PM

Legislative Records
Arizona Legislature   602-542-3559 Senate
1700 W Washington   602-542-4221 House
Phoenix, AZ 85007   Fax 602-542-4099
www.azleg.state.az.us   8AM-5PM

State Archives
1700 W Washington, Room 342   602-542-4159
Phoenix, AZ 85007   Fax 602-542-4402
www.dlapr.lib.az.us/archives   8AM-5PM

State Specifics:

Capital: Phoenix
          Maricopa County

Time Zone: MST
Note that Arizona does not go on daylight Savings Time

Number of Counties: 15

Population: 5,580,811

Web Site: www.az.gov/webapp/portal/

State Agencies

Criminal Records

Department of Public Safety, Applicant Team One, PO Box 18430//Mail Code 2250, Phoenix, AZ 85005-8430 (Courier: 2320 N 20th Ave, Phoenix, AZ 85005); 602-223-2223, 602-223-2972 (Fax), 8AM-5PM.

www.dps.state.az.us

Indexing & Storage: Records are available from 1988. It takes about 14 days before new records are available for inquiry. Records are indexed on computer back to 1983; non-automated records may go back as far as 1960's, depending on

charge. Records are normally destroyed after age 99 or 2 years after subject's death.

Searching: Record access is limited to agencies that have specific authorization by law including employers or pre-employment search firms located in AZ. Fingerprints are required for a search. Include the following in your request-full set of fingerprints plus demographic information on the applicant. Be sure to address requests to Applicant Team One.

Access by: mail.

Fee & Payment: The fee is $5.00 per name. Fee payee: Department of Public Safety. Only

cashier's checks and money orders accepted. No credit cards accepted.

Mail search: Turnaround time: 2 to 3 days. Arizona employers may call 602-223-2223 to request fingerprint cards and forms. No SASE is required.

Statewide Court Records

Administrative Offices of the Courts, Arizona Supreme Court Bldg, 1501 W Washington, Phoenix, AZ 85007-3231; 602-542-9301, 602-542-9484 (Fax), 8AM-5PM.

www.supreme.state.az.us/

Note: Except for certain online research capabilities, all court record access must be done at the local level.

Access by: online. No searching by mail.

Online search: The web offers Public Access to Court Case Information, a valuable online service providing a resource for information about court cases from 137 out of 180 courts in Arizona. Counties not covered include Maricopa, Pima, Yavapai, and Mohave. Access information includes: detailed case information, i.e., case type, charges, filing and disposition dates; the parties in the case, not including victims and witnesses; and the court mailing address & location. Go to www.supreme.state.az.us/publicaccess/default.htm Opinions from the AZ Supreme Court and Court of Appeals are available from the website.

Sexual Offender Registry

Department of Public Safety, Sex Offender Compliance, PO Box 6638//Mail Code 9999, Phoenix, AZ 85005-6638 (Courier: 2102 W Encanto, Phoenix, AZ 85009); 602-255-0611, 602-223-2915 (Fax), 8AM-5PM.

www.azsexoffender.com/

Note: The county sheriff is responsible for registering sex offenders living within their county. Arizona has approximately 12,000 registered sex offenders.

Indexing & Storage: Records are available on or after June 1,1996 with risk assessment scores of Level 2 (Intermediate) or Level 3 (High).

Access by: mail, online.

Mail search: Turnaround time: 2 to 3 days. No SASE is required.

Online search: Searching of Level 2 and Level 3 offender is available online at the website above. Search for an individual by name, or search by ZIP Code or address for known offenders. The site also lists, with pictures, absconders, who are individuals whose whereabouts are unknown.

Incarceration Records

Arizona Department of Corrections, Records Department, 1601 W. Jefferson St., Phoenix, AZ 85007; 602-542-5586, 602-542-1638 (Fax), 8AM-5PM.

www.adc.state.az.us

Indexing & Storage: Records are available on current and former inmates. It takes about 7 days before new records are available for inquiry. Records are normally destroyed after 25 years.

Searching: Include the following in your request-Full name, ADC number, and what you want. DOB, and SSN helpful.

Access by: fax, online.

Fee & Payment: Fee is $.25 for every copy. Fee payee: Arizona Department of Corrections. No searching by mail; mail is returned.

Fax search: Fax requires full name, the DOB and SSN are helpful.

Online search: For online search, you must provide last name, first initial or ADC number. Location, ADC number, physical Identifiers and sentencing information are released. Inmates admitted and released from 1972 to 1985 may not be searchable on the web. Also available is ADC

Fugitives - an alphabetical Inmate Datasearch listing of Absconders and Escapees from ADC.

Other access: A private company offers free web access at www.vinelink.com/index.jsp.

Corporation, Limited Liability Company Records

Corporation Commission, Corporation Records, 1300 W Washington, Room 101, Phoenix, AZ 85007; 602-542-3026 (Status), 602-542-3285 (Annual Reports), 602-542-3414 (Fax), 8AM-5PM.

www.cc.state.az.us/corp/index.htm

Note: Fictitious Name & Assumed Name records are found at the county level.

Indexing & Storage: Records are available from 1809 on. You must go through this office for records. If copies are needed for historical records, it can take as long as 4 to 6 weeks due to the filming process. It takes after 2-3 months before new records are available for inquiry. Records are indexed on microfiche, inhouse computer, microfilm.

Searching: Include the following in your request-full name of business, specific records that you need copies of. In addition to the articles of incorporation, corporation records include the following information: Annual Reports, Officers, Directors, Prior (Merged) Names, Inactive and Reserved Names.

Access by: mail, in person, online.

Fee & Payment: There is no charge for a search. Copies cost $.50 per page. An additional $5.00 is charged for each document for an LLC. The cost for the Good Standing is $10.00. Fee payee: Arizona Corporation Commission. Prepayment required. Personal checks accepted. No credit cards accepted.

Mail search: Turnaround time: 3 to 5 days. Enclose a check marked "Not to exceed $10.00." A SASE is requested.

In person search: Turnaround time is while you wait for up to 5 corporate names.

Online search: The website provides free access to all corporation information. Also, an online system called STARPAS functions 24 hours a day, 7 days a week. Go to http://starpas.cc.state.az.us/instruct.html.

Other access: To purchase the database, call 602-364-4433.

Expedited service: Expedited service is available for mail and in person searches. Turnaround time: 24 hours. Add $35.00 per request. The fee applies to large orders that must be completed within 24 hours. Generally, smaller orders or single document orders do not require this fee.

Fictitious Name, Assumed Name

Records not maintained by a state level agency.

Note: Records are found at the county level.

Trademarks/Servicemarks, Trade Names, Limited Partnership Records

Secretary of State, Trademarks/Tradenames/Limited Partnership Division, 1700 W Washington, 7th Floor, Phoenix, AZ 85007 (Courier: Customer Service, 14 N 18th Ave, Phoenix, AZ); 602-542-6187, 602-542-7386 (Fax), 8AM-5PM.

www.azsos.gov/business_services/trademarksandtradenames.htm

Indexing & Storage: Records are available from 1984 to present on computer. It takes 1 to 3 days before new records are available for inquiry.

Searching: Provide the entity name, owner name or file number to search.

Access by: mail, phone, in person, online.

Fee & Payment: There is no search fee, but certification is $3.00 plus the copy fee of $.10 per page. Fee payee: Secretary of State. Prepayment required. Personal checks accepted. No credit cards accepted.

Mail search: Turnaround time: 1 to 3 days. Trademarks may take longer. A SASE is requested.

Phone search: They will give general information at no charge over the phone for up to 3 searches, such as owner's name, date of application, mailing address & expiration date.

In person search: If there are more than 5 pages of copy, service is overnight. You may view microfiche at no charge.

Online search: The website links to three searchable databases. One searches for Registered Names, Trade Names, and Trademarks. Also available is the full Trade Name and Trademark index in data format. Anther lists the registerd names in alpha order and states the type of records available.

Other access: Bulk purchase is available on microfiche.

Expedited service: Expedited service is available for mail, phone and in person searches. Add $25.00 per filing.

Uniform Commercial Code, Federal Tax Liens, State Tax Liens

UCC Division, Secretary of State, 1700 W Washington, 7th Floor, Phoenix, AZ 85007 (Courier: Customer Service Center, 14 North 18th Ave, Phoenix, AZ 85007); 602-542-6187, 602-542-7386 (Fax), 8AM - 5PM.

www.sosaz.com/business_services/ucc.htm

Indexing & Storage: Records are available from 3/80 to present on microfiche and from 06/95 to present on the Internet.

Searching: Use search request form UCC-11. The search includes tax liens recorded here. Please note that tax liens recorded on individuals may be filed at the county level and not here. Include the following in your request-debtor name.

Access by: mail, phone, fax, in person, online.

Fee & Payment: The search fee is $6.00 per debtor name, except via the web which is no charge. Copies are $.10 each. Certification is an additional $3.00. Fee payee: Secretary of State.

Prepayment required. Personal checks accepted. No credit cards accepted.

Mail search: Turnaround time: 5 days.

Phone search: Records are available by phone.

Fax search: Records are available by fax.

In person search: They ususally do not charge expedited fees for same day service, if the counter is not busy. Be sure to visit the 18th Ave address.

Online search: UCC records can be searched for free over the website. Searching can be done by debtor, secured party name, or file number. From this site you can also pull down a weekly microfiche file of filings (about 10 megabytes). Note there are 2 searches - a pre 07/01/01 search of the old database, and a strict Revised Article 9 which is current up within 4 days of present.

Other access: E-mail requests are accepted. Microfilm of filings is available for purchase.

Expedited service: Expedited service is available for mail and phone searches. Turnaround time: same day if possible. Add $25.00 per package.

Sales Tax Registrations

Revenue Department, Transaction (Sales) Tax Licenses and Registration, 1600 W Monroe, Phoenix, AZ 85007; 602-542-4565, 602-542-4772 (Fax), 8AM-5PM.

www.revenue.state.az.us

Indexing & Storage: Records are available from 1980.

Searching: This agency will only confirm that a business is registered and whether it is active. It will provide no other information without a power of attorney. Include the following in your request-business name. The tax permit number is very helpful.

Access by: mail, phone, in person.

Mail search: A SASE is requested. No fee for mail request.

Phone search: They will confirm license on phone, if given permit #.

In person search: No fee for request.

Birth Certificates

Department of Health Services, Vital Records Section, PO Box 3887, Phoenix, AZ 85030 (Courier: 2727 W Glendale Ave, Phoenix, AZ 85051); 602-255-3260, 602-364-1300 (Recording), 602-249-3040 (Fax), 8AM-5PM.

www.hs.state.az.us/vitalrcd/index.htm

Note: A certificate of birth resulting in stillbirth is available as of 08/09/2001.

Indexing & Storage: Records are available from late 1800's to present. Records are computerized from 1950 to present. Records are indexed on file folders.

Searching: Must by 18 years of age or older to request a record and be the person named or that person's parent or legal guardian. Records 75 years or older available to the public for a $2.00 fee. Include the following in your request-full name, names of parents, mother's maiden name, date of birth, place of birth, relationship to person of record, reason for information request. Bring a government issued picture ID (or send a copy) with signature.

Access by: mail, fax, in person, online.

Fee & Payment: Certified copies of birth certificates for births occurring 1990 to present are $10.00 each. Prior certified records are $15.00 each. Fee payee: Vital Records Section. Prepayment required. Credit cards accepted: MasterCard, Visa, AmEx, Discover.

Mail search: Turnaround time: 2 weeks. No SASE is required.

Fax search: Include the following additional information on the request: copy of government ID with your signature, return address, phone #, credit card #, and expiration date. Fee is $5.50 plus copy cost. Turnaround time is 2 days.

In person search: Turnaround time is usually less than 1 hour.

Online search: Records may be ordered online via www.vitalchek.com, a state-endorsed vendor. Images of birth certificates from 1887 to 1929 are available free online at http://genealogy.az.gov. Death certificates 1878-1953 are also available.

Expedited service: Expedited service is available for fax and online ordering. Turnaround time: 1 day. There is an additional $27.00 fee to use a credit card have the results returned by courier.

Death Records

Department of Health Services, Vital Records Section, PO Box 3887, Phoenix, AZ 85030 (Courier: 2727 W Glendale Ave, Phoenix, AZ 85051); 602-255-3260, 602-364-1300 (Recording), 602-249-3040 (Fax), 8AM-5PM.

www.hs.state.az.us/vitalrcd/index.htm

Indexing & Storage: Records are available from late 1800's to present. New records are available for inquiry immediately. Records are indexed on file folders.

Searching: Must have notarized release from immediate family. Only immediate family, attorney or funeral director acting for immediate family can get records. Records 50 years or older are available to the public for a $2.00 fee. Include the following in your request-full name, date of death, place of death, relationship to person of record, reason for information request. Send a copy of your ID or your signature must be notarized.

Access by: mail, fax, in person, online.

Fee & Payment: The search fee is $4.00 for the first 10 years and $3.00 each add'l. A certified photocopy is $10.00. The fee for use of a credit card is $5.50. Fee payee: Vital Records Section. Prepayment required. Personal checks accepted. Credit cards accepted: MasterCard, Visa, AmEx, Discover.

Mail search: Turnaround time: 2 weeks. A SASE is requested.

Fax search: Include the following additional information on the request: copy of government ID with signature, return address, phone #, credit card #, and expiration date. Fee is $5.00 for processing/handling. Certification fee is $6.00.

In person search: Turnaround time is usually 30-50 minutes.

Online search: Death certificate images 1878-1953 are available free online at http://genealogy.az.gov. Also available are images of birth certificates from 1887 to 1928. Records may be ordered online via www.vitalchek.com, a state-endorsed vendor.

Expedited service: Expedited service is available for fax and online orders. There is an additional

$27.00 fee to use a credit card have the results returned by courier.

Marriage Certificates, Divorce Records

Records not maintained by a state level agency.

Note: These records are not available from the state; they must be requested from the county or court of issue.

Workers' Compensation Records

State Compensation Fund, Claims Information, 3030 N 3rd Street, Phoenix, AZ 85012; 602-631-2000 x4, 602-631-2869 (Copy Room), 8AM-5PM.

www.statefund.com

Indexing & Storage: Records are available from 1926 on. New records are available for inquiry immediately. Records are indexed on microfilm, inhouse computer.

Searching: Records that are closed or inactive are stored on microfilm. All active records are on the in-house computer. Claim and policy records are confidential, but you can get claim records with release from claimant. Most other records are public. Include the following in your request-claimant name, Social Security Number, claim number. Requester must have signed release from claimant or policyholder prior to obtaining confidential records. Copies of legal, claims, and policy working files are not released otherwise.

Access by: mail, in person.

Fee & Payment: Copies are $.25 per page. There is no search fee. Fee payee: State Compensation Fund. Requesters will be billed. Personal checks accepted. No credit cards accepted.

Mail search: Turnaround time: 1 to 2 weeks. No SASE is required.

In person search: Simple requests will receive immediate service.

Driver Records

Motor Vehicle Division, Correspondence Unit, PO Box 2100, Mail Drop 539M, Phoenix, AZ 85001-2100 (Courier: Customer Records Services, 1801 W Jefferson, Rm 111, Phoenix, AZ 85007); 602-712-8420, 8AM-5PM.

www.dot.state.az.us/MVD/mvd.htm

Note: Arizona will suspend the license for unpaid out-of-state tickets.

Indexing & Storage: Records are available for either a thirty-nine month record or for a five-year record. CDL records may be available for ten years. It takes 2 weeks before new records are available for inquiry.

Searching: Any person requesting a motor vehicle record shall identify himself and state the reason for the request. ID may be required. Certain requesters, identified by law, are labeled as "exempt" (generally, in line with DPPA requirements). Include the following in your request-full name, date of birth, driver's license number. Exempt requesters need only supply 2 out of the 3 items required to search. The driver's mailing address is provided as part of the record to exempt requesters.

Access by: mail, in person, online.

Fee & Payment: The fees are $3.00 for 39 month records ($2.00 if picked up overnight at counter) and $5.00 for certified 5 year records. Electronic access fees differ. Insurers may only receive the 39 month record. All non-exempt requests must be signed and notarized. Fee payee: Motor Vehicle Division, Record Services. Prepayment required. Personal checks accepted. No credit cards accepted.

Mail search: Turnaround time: 1 week to 10 days. If express mail is requested, then envelope must be pre-paid. If mail requester is not DPPA permissible, the requester's signature must be notarized. No SASE is required.

In person search: Records are available at any of the MVD field offices. There is a limit of 4 requests for immediate service. There is a $1.00 discount if requests are picked up next day.

Online search: Arizona's online system is interactive and open 24 hours daily. Fee is $3.25 per record. This system is primarily for those requesters who qualify per DPPA. For more information call 602-712-7235.

Other access: Overnight cartridge ordering is available. Fee is $2.00 for 39 month record, $3.00 for 5 year record. Call 602-712-7235 for details.

Vehicle Ownership, Vehicle Identification

Motor Vehicle Division - Director's Office, Record Services Section, PO Box 2100, Mail Drop 504M, Phoenix, AZ 85001-2100 (Courier: Customer Records Services, 1801 W Jefferson, Rm 111, Phoenix, AZ 85007); 602-712-8420, 8AM-5PM.

www.dot.state.az.us/MVD/mvd.htm

Indexing & Storage: Records are available for 5 years to present. It takes 2 weeks before new records are available for inquiry.

Searching: The record searcher must state the reason for the request and have his/her signature notarized. Records are not given by merely giving a plate license number or a name for ownership searches. The vehicle's owner, VIN, and plate number must be submitted to receive a vehicle history. If not a permissible use, need notarized release from subject.

Access by: mail, in person, online.

Fee & Payment: The fee is $3.00, $2.00 if walk-in is willing to pick up the next day, and $5.00 if the record is certified. Fee payee: Motor Vehicle Division. Prepayment required. Money orders and checks are accepted through the mail. Walk-ins may pay with cash. Personal checks accepted. No credit cards accepted.

Mail search: Turnaround time: 1 week to 10 days. A SASE is requested.

In person search: You may request information in person.

Online search: Online access is offered only to permissible users. Fee is $3.00 per record. The system is open 24 hours a day, seven days a week. For more information, call 602-712-7235.

Accident Reports

Department of Public Safety, Accident Reports, PO Box 6638, Mail Drop 1110, Phoenix, AZ 85005 (Courier: 2102 W Encanto, 1st Floor, Phoenix, AZ 85005-6638), 602-223-2230, 8AM-5PM.

Indexing & Storage: It takes 2 weeks before new records are available for inquiry. Records are indexed on inhouse computer. Records are normally destroyed after 25 years.

Searching: A written request is required and the requester must state his/her connection to the incident. Include the following in your request-relationship to person of record, date of accident, location of accident, full name, report number.

Access by: mail, in person, online.

Fee & Payment: The fee is $9.00 per record for up to first 9 pages, then $1.00 for each additional page. Fee payee: Department of Public Safety. Prepayment required; Business check or money order. Personal checks accepted in person with ID. No credit cards accepted.

Mail search: Turnaround time: 1 week to 14 days. A SASE is requested. No fee for mail request.

In person search: Turnaround time is while you wait, provided record is on file.

Online search: Reports are available for purchase through a third-party provider online at https://www.vectrareports.com/index.aspx. Registration required. Single reports are available, also commericial user accounts.

Vessel Ownership, Vessel Registration

Game & Fish Dept, Watercraft Department, 2221 W Greenway Rd, Phoenix, AZ 85023-4399; 602-942-3000, 602-789-3729 (Fax), 8AM-5PM M-F.

www.azgf.com

Note: Lien information is recorded at the county level. Maricopa County has some liens from other counties.

Indexing & Storage: Records are available from 1977 to present. Records are indexed on computer for the last 5 years. No titles are issued. All watercraft must be registered unless they are non-motorized. Records are normally destroyed after microfilmed.

Searching: To search, the following information is required: Arizona #, hull ID, owner's name, and a picture ID.

Access by: mail, phone, fax, in person.

Fee & Payment: There is no search fee.

Mail search: Turnaround time is within 30 days. No SASE is required.

Phone search: Only lawyers, private investigators, and government representatives can search by phone or fax.

Fax search: Same criteria as phone searching.

In person search: Turnaround time is normally immediate.

Other access: Commercial records are given as bulk lists, CDs or labels.

Voter Registration

Records not maintained by a state level agency.

Note: Records are only maintained at the county recorder offices. Their records are permitted to be sold in bulk only for political related purposes. Go to the county level to can confirm names on a single inquiry basis.

GED Certificates

Department of Education, GED Testing, 1535 W Jefferson, Phoenix, AZ 85007; 602-254-0265, 602-258-4977 (Fax), 8AM-5PM.

www.ade.az.gov/adult-ed/

Note: This agency will not do a verification only; a transcript must be purchased.

Indexing & Storage: Records are available from 1945 to present. It takes 3 to 4 weeks before new records are available for inquiry.

Searching: Request forms are available from the website. Include the following in your request-name at date of test, date of birth, Social Security Number, signed release, year of test and test site. All requests must be in writing, all require student signature.

Access by: mail, in person.

Fee & Payment: There is a $10.00 fee for a copy of transcript. This agency will not do a verification only; a transcript must be purchased. Fee payee: AZ Department of Education

Mail search: Turnaround time: 5 to 7 days. No SASE is required.

In person search: Counter serivce is available.

Hunting and Fishing License Information

Game & Fish Department, Information & Licensing Division, 2221 W Greenway Rd, Phoenix, AZ 85023-4399; 602-942-3000, 602-789-3924 (Fax), 8AM-5PM.

www.azgfd.com

Note: This agency will also release watercraft registration information within specific legal constraints.

Indexing & Storage: Records are available for past 3 years. It takes 30 days before new records are available for inquiry. Records are normally destroyed after placed on microfilm.

Searching: Records are not available to the public except as a mailing list. They will release certain data to attorneys for pending litigation.

Access by: mail.

Fee & Payment: Prepayment required. Fee payee: Arizona Game & Fish. Personal checks accepted. Credit cards accepted: MasterCard, Visa.

Mail search: Turnaround time: variable. Must complete a request form. No SASE is required.

Other access: There is a program to purchase the database or portions of. You can get 3 years of approximately 160,000 to 190,000 names for $.10 per name, which includes addresses. This is available for commercial purposes only. Lists are completed within 30 days.

Arizona State Licensing Agencies

Licenses Searchable Online

Acupuncturist Chiropractor #11 .... www.azchiroboard.com/ASPSearch.htm
Advance Fee Loan Broker #5 .... www.azbanking.com/Lists/Lists.htm
Aerial Applicator, Pesticide #33 .... www.kellysolutions.com/az/Pilots/index.asp
Agricultural Grower/Seller #33 .... www.kellysolutions.com/az/RUPBuyers/index.asp
Agricultural Pest Control Advisor #33 .... www.kellysolutions.com/az/PCA/index.asp
Ambulatory Surgical Center #43 .... www.hs.state.az.us/als/medical/index.htm
Applicator (Pesticide), Private/Commercial #33 .... www.kellysolutions.com/AZ/Applicators/index.asp
Architect #29 .... www.btr.state.az.us
Assayer #29 .... www.btr.state.az.us
Assisted Living Facility #49 .... www.hs.state.az.us/als/hcb/index.htm
Attorney #30 .... www.azbar.org/content.cfm?text=/LegalResources/findlawyer
Audiologist #49 .... www.hs.state.az.us/als/hcb/index.htm
Bank #5 .... www.azbanking.com/Lists/Lists.htm
Behavioral Health Emergency/Resi. Svcs #47 .... www.hs.state.az.us/als/databases/
Behavioral Outpatient Clinic/Rehab Center #47 .... www.hs.state.az.us/als/databases/
Charity #71 .... www.sosaz.com/scripts/Charity_Search.dll
Charter School #38 .... www.ade.state.az.us/CharterSchools/search/
Child Residential Home #37 .... www.hs.state.az.us/als/databases/providers_cc.pdf
Chiropractor #11 .... www.azchiroboard.com/ASPSearch.htm
Citrus Fruit Broker/Dealer/Packer/Shipper #35 .... www.kellysolutions.com/az
Clinic, Recovery Core/Rural Health #43 .... www.hs.state.az.us/als/medical/index.htm
Collection Agency #5 .... www.azbanking.com/Lists/Lists.htm
Consumer Lender #5 .... www.azbanking.com/Lists/Lists.htm
Contractor #70 .... www.rc.state.az.us/clsc/AZROCLicenseQuery
Court Reporter #63 .... www.supreme.state.az.us/cr/pdf/merged%20directory2wpd.pdf
Credit Union #5 .... www.azbanking.com/Lists/Lists.htm
Day Care Establishment #45 .... www.hs.state.az.us/als/childcare/index.htm
Debt Management #5 .... www.azbanking.com/Lists/Lists.htm
Deferred Presentment Company #5 .... www.azbanking.com/Lists/DPC_List.HTML
Degree Program, Vocational #6 .... http://azppse.state.az.us/directory.html
Detoxification Service #47 .... www.hs.state.az.us/als/databases/
Developmentally Disabled Group Home #49 .... www.hs.state.az.us/als/hcb/index.htm
Dispensing Naturopath #19 .... www.npbomex.az.gov/directories.html
Dry Well Registration #41 .... www.adeq.state.az.us/environ/water/permits/drywell.html
Embalmer #15 .... www.funeralbd.state.az.us/dir.htm
Engineer #29 .... www.btr.state.az.us
Escrow Agent #5 .... www.azbanking.com/Lists/Lists.htm
Family Day Care Home #37 .... www.hs.state.az.us/als/databases/providers_cc.pdf
Feed Dealer #33 .... www.kellysolutions.com/az/feeddealers/index.asp
Fertilizer Dealer #33 .... www.kellysolutions.com/az/fertdealers/index.asp
Fertilizer Product #33 .... www.kellysolutions.com/AZ/Fertilizer/fertilizerindex.asp
Food Packer/Grower/Shipper, Contract #35 .... www.kellysolutions.com/az
Foster Care Home #49 .... www.hs.state.az.us/als/hcb/index.htm
Fruit/Vegetable Broker/Dealer #35 .... www.kellysolutions.com/az
Funeral Director #15 .... www.funeralbd.state.az.us/dir.htm
Funeral Preneed Trust Company #5 .... www.azbanking.com/Lists/Lists.htm
Geologist #29 .... www.btr.state.az.us
Headstart Facility #45 .... www.hs.state.az.us/als/childcare/index.htm
Hearing Aid Dispenser #49 .... www.hs.state.az.us/als/hcb/index.htm
Home Health Agency #43 .... www.hs.state.az.us/als/medical/index.htm
Home Inspector #29 .... www.btr.state.az.us
Homeopathic Physician #16 .... http://home.mindspring.com/~bhme/
Hospice #43 .... www.hs.state.az.us/als/medical/index.htm
Hospital #43 .... www.hs.state.az.us/als/medical/index.htm
Infirmary #43 .... www.hs.state.az.us/als/medical/index.htm
Insurance Agent / Broker P&C #51 .... www.id.state.az.us/
Landscape Architect #29 .... www.btr.state.az.us
Liquor Producer/Whsle #52 .... www.azll.com/query.htm
Liquor Retail Co-Operative/Agent/Mgr. #52 .... www.azll.com/query.htm
Lobbyist #71 .... www.azsos.gov/scripts/Lobbyist_Search.dll

Long Term Care Facility #49	www.hs.state.az.us/als/hcb/index.htm
Massage Therapy School #19	http://massagetherapy.az.gov/approvedschools.htm
Medical Doctor, Intern/Resident #17	www.bomex.org/getlicense.asp
Medical Facility #49	www.hs.state.az.us/als/hcb/index.htm
Midwife, Lay #50	www.hs.state.az.us/als/midwife/
Money Transmitter #5	www.azbanking.com/Lists/Lists.htm
Mortgage Banker/Broker #5	www.azbanking.com/Lists/Lists.htm
Motor Vehicle Dealer/Sales Finance #5	www.azbanking.com/Lists/Lists.htm
Naturopathic Physician/Medical Assistant #19	www.npbomex.az.gov/directories.html
Naturopathic School #19	www.npbomex.az.gov/School%20Directory.html
Notary Public #71	www.sosaz.com/scripts/Notary_Search.dll
Optometrist #22	www.asbo.state.az.us
Osteopathic Physician #23	http://docfinder.state.az.us
Outpatient Physical Therapy #43	www.hs.state.az.us/als/medical/index.htm
Out-Patient Surgical Ctr./Treatment Clinic #43	www.hs.state.az.us/als/medical/index.htm
P&C Broker/P&C Mgr Agent, also Life/Disability #51	www.id.state.az.us/
Pesticide Company #72	www.sb.state.az.us/spccsearch.htm
Pesticide Custom Applicator #33	www.kellysolutions.com/az/CustomAppl/index.asp
Pesticide Registration #33	www.kellysolutions.com/az/pesticideindex.htm
Pesticide Seller #33	www.kellysolutions.com/az/Dealers/index.asp
Pharmacist #24	www.pharmacy.state.az.us/
Physical Therapist/Therapist Assistant #25	www.ptboard.state.az.us
Physician Assistant #17	www.bomex.org/getlicense.asp
Physiotherapist #11	www.azchiroboard.com/ASPSearch.htm
Political Action Committee #71	www.azsos.gov/scripts/superpac.cgi
Post-Secondary Educ. Institution #6	http://azppse.state.az.us/directory.html
Post-Secondary Voc. Program, Private #6	http://azppse.state.az.us/directory.html
Premium Finance Company #5	www.azbanking.com/Lists/Lists.htm
Preschool #45	www.hs.state.az.us/als/childcare/index.htm
Property Tax Agent #8	www.appraisal.state.az.us/Directory/taxaoat.txt
Psychologist #27	http://psychboard.az.gov/dir.html
Public Accountant-CPA #7	www.accountancy.state.az.us/scripts/BOAsearch.exe
Public Accounting Firm-CPA/PA #7	www.accountancy.state.az.us/scripts/BOAsearch.exe
Real Estate Agent/Broker/Sales #55	www.re.state.az.us/db.html
Real Estate Appraiser #8	www.appraisal.state.az.us/Directory/approut.txt
Real Estate Firm #55	www.re.state.az.us/db.html
Rehabilitation Agency #43	www.hs.state.az.us/als/medical/index.htm
Renal Disease Facility #43	www.hs.state.az.us/als/medical/index.htm
Sales Finance Company #5	www.azbanking.com/Lists/Lists.htm
School Bus Transportation Provider #1	www.dps.state.az.us/license/schoolbusdriver/default.asp
Seed Dealer #33	www.kellysolutions.com/az/SeedDealers/index.asp
Seed Labeler #33	www.kellysolutions.com/az/SeedLabelers/index.asp
Speech Pathology #43	www.hs.state.az.us/als/medical/index.htm
Speech-Language Pathologist #49	www.hs.state.az.us/als/hcb/index.htm
Surveyor, Land #29	www.btr.state.az.us
Telemarketing Firm #71	www.sosaz.com/scripts/TS_Search_engine.cgi
Trust Company #5	www.azbanking.com/Lists/Lists.htm
Trust Div. of Chartered Fin. Inst. #5	www.azbanking.com/Lists/Lists.htm
Well Drilling Firm #58	http://water.az.gov/adwr/content/drillers/default.asp
X-ray, Portable #43	www.hs.state.az.us/als/medical/index.htm

Arizona Licensing Quick Finder

Acupuncturist #25	602-542-3095	
Acupuncturist Chiropractor #11	602-864-5088	
Adult Care Home Manager #68	602-364-2273	
Advance Fee Loan Broker #5	602-255-4421	
Aerial Applicator, Pesticide #33	602-542-0904	
Aesthetician #12	480-784-4539	
Aesthetics Instructor #12	480-784-4539	
Agricultural Aircraft Pilot #33	602-542-0904	
Agricultural Grower Permit #33	602-542-0904	
Agricultural Grower/Seller #33	602-542-0904	
Agricultural Pest Control Advisor #33	602-542-0904	
Agricultural Seller Permit #33	602-542-0904	
Air Pollution Source #39	602-771-2338	
Air Quality Permit #65	602-506-6970	
Aircraft Dealer - Wreckers/Salvage #57	602-294-9144	
Aircraft Dealer/Retail #57	602-294-9144	
Aircraft Mfg/Importer/Dist./Transp'r #57	602-294-9144	
Aircraft Owner #57	602-294-9144	
Aircraft Pilot Trainer School/Instr. #57	602-294-9144	
Aircraft Use Fuel Dealer/Mfg #56	602-542-4565	
Ambulance Service #48	602-364-3184	
Ambulatory Surgical Center #43	602-364-3030	
Amusement Park #56	602-542-4565	
Amusement Printing/Advertising #56	602-542-4565	
Applicator, Pesticide, Private/Commercial #33	602-542-0904	
Appraiser, Real/Personal Property #56	602-542-4565	
Aquifer Protection Permit #41	602-771-4644	
Architect #29	602-364-4930	
Assayer #29	602-364-4930	
Assisted Living Facility #49	602-364-2536	
Attorney #30	602-252-4804	
Audiologist #49	602-364-2536	
Bank #5	602-255-4421	
Barber School/Instruction #9	602-542-4498	
Barber/Barber Shop #9	602-542-4498	
Bathing Place #65	602-506-6970	
Bedding/Furniture Manufacturer #65	602-506-6970	

Behavioral Health Emergency/Residential Svcs #47 602-343-2595
Behavioral Outpatient Clinic #47 602-343-2595
Behavioral Outpatient Rehab Ctr. #47 .602-343-2595
Bingo Operation #56 602-542-4565
Bondsman (Insurance) #51 602-912-8470
Bone Densitometer Operator #66 602-255-4845 x242
Bottled Water Processor #65 602-506-6970
Boxer #3 602-364-1721
Boxing Physician #3 602-364-1721
Boxing Professional #3 602-364-1721
Campground Membership Broker/Salesman #55 602-468-1414
Cannabis/Controlled Substance Dealer #56 602-542-4565
Cemetery Broker/Salesman #55 602-468-1414
Charity #71 602-542-6670
Charter School #38 602-542-5968
Child Adoption Agency #37 602-364-2536
Child Foster Home #37 602-364-2536
Child Placing Agency #37 602-364-2536
Child Residential Home #37 602-364-2539
Chiropractor #11 602-864-5088
Citrus Fruit Broker/Dealer/Packer/Shipper #35 602-542-0944
Clinic, Recovery Core #43 602-364-3030
Clinic, Rural Health #43 602-364-3030
Clinical Laboratory #44 602-542-1197
Collection Agency #5 602-255-4421
Commercial Leasing #56 602-542-4565
Concealed Weapon Permit #53 602-256-6280
Consumer Lender #5 602-255-4421
Contractor #70 602-542-1525
Cosmetologist #12 480-784-4539
Cosmetology Instructor #12 480-784-4539
Cosmetology or Nail Technology Salon/School #12 480-784-4539
Counselor, Professional #10 602-542-1864
Court Reporter #63 602-364-0878
Credit Union #5 602-255-4421
Cremationist #15 602-542-3095
Crematory #15 602-542-3095
Day Care Establishment #45 602-364-2536
Debt Management #5 602-255-4421
Deferred Presentment Company #5 602-255-4421
Degree Program, Vocational #6 602-542-5709
Dental Assistant #13 602-242-1492
Dental Hygienist #13 602-242-1492
Dentist #13 602-242-1492
Denturist #13 602-242-1492
Detoxification Service #47 602-343-2595
Develop'y Disabled Group Home #49 ...602-364-2536
Dispensing Naturopath #19 602-542-8242
Dog Racing Kennel #54 602-364-1700
Drug Mfg/Wholesaler #24 623-463-2727
Dry Well Registration #41 602-771-4385
DUI Education Agency #47 602-343-2595
DUI Screening/Treatment Agency #47...602-343-2595
Embalmer #15 602-542-3095
Embalmer Assistant #15 602-542-3095
Emergency Medical Tech. Instruct. #48 602-364-3150
Emergency Medical Technician #48 602-364-3186
Emergency Response Divis'n#66 602-255-4845 x239
Engineer #29 602-364-4930
Environmental Laboratory #44 602-542-1197
Escrow Agent #5 602-255-4421
Falconer #59 602-942-3000
Family Day Care Home #37 602-364-2539
Feed Dealer #33 602-542-0904
Feed Distribution, Commercial #34 602-542-0814
Feed, Wholesale #56 602-542-4565
Fertilizer Dealer #33 602-542-0904
Fertilizer Distribution, Commercial #34 .602-542-0814
Fertilizer Product #33 602-542-0904
Field Trial License #59 602-942-3000
Food Establishment #65 602-506-6970

Food Packer/Grower/Shipper, Contract #35 602-542-0944
Foster Care Home #49 602-364-2536
Fruit/Vegetable Broker/Dealer #35 602-542-0944
Funeral Director #15 602-542-3095
Funeral Establishment #15 602-542-3095
Funeral Preneed Trust Company #5 602-255-4421
Fur Dealer #59 602-942-3000
Game Farm, Private #59 602-942-3000
Game Resident Guide #59 602-942-3000
Geologist #29 602-364-4930
Groom #54 602-364-1700
Guidance Counselor #38 602-542-4367
Hazardous Waste Facility #40 602-771-4153
Headstart Facility #45 602-364-2536
Hearing Aid Dispenser #49 602-364-2536
Home Health Agency #43 602-364-3030
Home Inspector #29 602-364-4930
Homeopathic Physician #16 602-542-3095
Horse or Greyhound Racing #54 602-364-1700
Horse Owner/Trainer #54 602-364-1700
Hospice #43 602-364-3030
Hospital #43 602-364-3030
Hotel/Motel/Tourist Court #65 602-506-6970
Hunting & Fishing License Dealer #59 ..602-942-3000
Industrial Laser #66 ....602-255-4845 x237
Infirmary #43 602-364-3030
Insurance Agent #51 602-912-8470
Insurance Broker P&C only #51 602-912-8470
Intern #15 602-542-3095
Investment Advisor #32 602-542-0678
Investment Advisor Rep. #32 602-542-0678
Jockey #54 602-364-1700
Landscape Architect #29 602-364-4930
Laser Light Show #56 602-255-4845
Laser, Medical #66 ....602-255-4845 x237
Liquor Producer/Whsle #52 602-542-5141
Liquor Retail Co-Operative/Agent/Mgr. #52 602-542-5141
Lobbyist #71 602-542-8683
Long Term Care Facility #49 602-364-2536
Lottery Retailer #4 480-921-4400
LPG Service Agency/Rep #2 602-255-5211
Marriage & Family Therapist #10 602-542-1864
Massage Therapy School #19 602-542-8242
Medical Doctor, Intern/Resident #17....480-551-2700
Medical Facility #49 602-364-2536
Mental Health Screening/Evaluation/Treatment #47 602-343-2595
Midwife, Lay #50 602-364-2536
Mine Reclamation Plan #67 602-542-5971
Mining #56 602-542-4565
Mining Elevator/Diesel #67 602-542-5971
Mining Operator/Start-up #67 602-542-5971
Minnow Dealer #59 602-942-3000
Mobile Home Dealer/Broker/Seller #36.602-364-1063
Mobile Home Installer/Mfg. #36 602-364-1063
Money Transmitter #5 602-255-4421
Mortgage Banker, Commercial #5 602-255-4421
Mortgage Banker/Broker #5 602-255-4421
Motor Vehicle Dealer/Sales Finance #5 602-255-4421
MRI License #66 ....602-255-4845 x237
Nail Technician #12 480-784-4539
Nail Technology Instructor #12 480-784-4539
Naturopathic Medical Asst. #19 602-542-8242
Naturopathic Physician #19 602-542-8242
Naturopathic School #19 602-542-8242
Notary Public #71 602-542-4086
Nuclear Medicine Tech. #66 ....602-255-4845 x242
Nurse-LPN #20 602-331-8111
Nurse-RN #20 602-331-8111
Nurses' Aide #20 602-331-8111
Nursing Care Inst. Adminitrator #68 602-364-2273
Occupational Therapist/Assistant #21...602-589-8352
Oil & Gas Production #56 602-542-4565
Optical Establishment #14 602-542-3095

Optician #14 602-542-3095
Optometrist #22 602-542-3095
Osteopathic Physician #23 480-657-7703
Outpatient Physical Therapy #43 602-364-3030
Out-Patient Surgical Ctr./Treatment Clinic #43 602-364-3030
P&C Broker #51 602-912-8470
P&C Managing Agent, also Life/Disability #51 602-912-8470
Pesticide Appl./Supv./Advisor #72 602-255-3664
Pesticide Company #72 602-255-3664
Pesticide Custom Applicator #33 602-542-0904
Pesticide Distribution #34 602-542-0949
Pesticide Qualifying Party #72 602-255-3664
Pesticide Registration/Seller #33 602-542-0904
Pharmacist/Pharmacy Intern #24 623-463-2727
Physical Therapist/Therapy Assist #25. 602-542-3095
Physician Assistant #17 480-551-2700
Physiotherapist #11 602-864-5088
Pipeline #56 602-542-4565
Plant Operator #41 602-771-4644
Podiatrist #26 602-542-3095
Political Action Committee #71 602-542-8683
Pollutant Discharge Permit #41 602-771-4644
Post-Secondary Educ. Institution #6 602-542-5709
Post-Secondary Voc. Program, Private #6 602-542-5709
Premium Finance Company #5 602-255-4421
Pre-Need Endorsed Establish't #15 602-542-3095
Pre-Need Salesperson #15 602-542-3095
Preschool #45 602-364-2536
Private Car, Rail & Aircraft #56 602-542-4565
Private Investigator #53 602-223-2361
Property Broker #51 602-912-8470
Property Tax Agent #8 602-542-1539
Psychiatric Unit #47 602-343-2595
Psychologist #27 602-542-8162
Public Accountant-CPA #7 602-364-0804
Public Accounting Firm-CPA/PA #7 602-364-0804
Publishing #56 602-542-4565
Radiation Machine Possession Facility #66 ....602-255-4845 x231
Radiation Therapy Tech. #66 ....602-255-4845 x242
Radioactive Material #66 ....602-255-4845 x227
Radioactive Materials Lab #66 ....602-255-4845 x246
Radiologic Technologist #66 ....602-255-4845 x242
Radiology Practical Tech. #66 .....602-255-4845 x242
Radon Mitigation Specialist #66..602-255-4845 x244
Real Estate Agent/Broker/Sales #55 ...602-468-1414
Real Estate Appraiser #8 602-542-1539
Real Estate Division #62 602-542-1704
Real Estate Firm #55 602-468-1414
Real Estate School/Instr./Course #55..602-468-1414
Rehabilitation Agency #43 602-364-3030
Rehabilitation Unit #47 602-343-2595
Renal Disease Facility #43 602-364-3030
Rental of Personal Property #56 602-542-4565
Respiratory Therapist #28 602-542-5995
Restaurant/Bar #56 602-542-4565
Retail Sales Outlet #56 602-542-4565
Risk Management Company #51 602-912-8470
Sales Finance Company #5 602-255-4421
Sanitarian #46 602-230-5911
School Bus Driver/Driver Instructor #1. 602-223-2646
School Bus Transportation Provider #1 602-223-2646
School Librarian #38 602-542-4367
School Psychologist/Psychometrist #38 602-542-4367
School Superintendent #38 602-542-4367
School Supervisor #38 602-542-4367
Scientific Collector #59 602-942-3000
Securities Salesperson/Dealer #32 602-542-0678
Security Guard #53 602-223-2361
Seed Dealer #33 602-542-0904
Seed Labeler #33 602-542-0904
Self Insured Employer #60 602-542-1836
Sewage/Sludge Pumping Vehicle #40. 602-771-4153
Shooting Preserve License #59 602-942-3000

Social Worker #10 602-542-1864
Solid Waste Facility #40 602-771-4153
Speech Pathology #43 602-364-3030
Speech-Language Pathologist #49 602-364-2536
Spray Process Appli./Sterilizer/Renovator #65
.... 602-506-6970
Subdivision Public Report #55 602-468-1414
Substance Abuse Counselor #10 602-542-1864
Substance Abuse Treatment Svc #47..602-343-2595
Surety #51 602-912-8470
Surplus Line Broker #51 602-912-8470
Surveyor, Land #29 602-364-4930
Tanning Facility #66 .... 602-255-4845 x237
Taxidermist #59 602-942-3000
Teacher, Elementary/Special Edu. #38.602-542-4367
Telemarketing Firm #71....................... 602-542-6670
Timbering #56....................................... 602-542-4565
Timeshare Public Report #55 602-468-1414

Tobacco Product Distributor #56.......... 602-542-4565
Trailer Coach Park #65 602-506-6970
Transporting/Towing Company #56..... 602-542-4565
Travel Agent, Limited #51 602-912-8470
Trust Company #5 602-255-4421
Trust Div. of Chartered Fin. Inst. #5... 602-255-4421
Vehicle Emis. Fleet Insp. Station #42 ... 602-207-7007
Vehicle Emission Fleet Inspector #42.. 602-207-7007
Vendor/Concession on State Park Land #69
.... 602-542-2155
Veterinary Medicine/Surgery #73 602-364-1738
Veterinary Premise (Hospital) #73 602-364-1738
Veterinary Technician #73.................... 602-364-1738
Vocational Rehabilitation #61.............. 602-542-3294
Waste Water Collection/Treatment/Construction #41
.... 602-771-4644
Waste Water Facility Operator #41 602-771-4644
Waste Water Reuse #41 602-771-4644

Water Distribution System Operator #41602-771-4644
Water Quality Certification #41 602-771-4644
Water Rights Assignment #58.............. 602-417-2405
Water Transporter, out of state #58..... 602-417-2405
Watercraft Registration Agent #59 602-942-3000
Weighmaster, Public #2 602-255-5211
Weights/Measures Rep./Svc. Agency #2
.... 602-255-5211
Well Drilling Firm #58 .... 602-417-2470 x 7141
Well Registration/Construction #58...... 602-417-2405
White Amor Stocking License #59 602-942-3000
Wildlife Hobby License #59.................. 602-942-3000
Wildlife Holding Permit #59 602-942-3000
Wildlife Rehab/Service License #59 602-942-3000
X-ray Supplier #66...................... 602-255-4845 x231
X-ray, Portable #43 602-364-3030
Zoo #59 602-942-3000

Arizona Licensing Agency Information

1 Department of Public Safety, Student Transportation, PO Box 6638 - Mail Drop 1250, Phoenix, AZ 85005-6638; 602-223-2646, Fax: 602-223-2923. www.dps.state.az.us Search Database at www.dps.state.az.us/licen se/schoolbusdriver/default.asp

2 Department of Weights & Measures, 4425 W Olive Av #134, Glendale, AZ 85302-3844; 602-255-5211, Fax: 602-255-1950. www.weights.az.gov

3 Boxing Commission, 1110 W Washington, #260, Phoenix, AZ 85007; 602-364-1721, Fax: 602-364-1703.

4 Arizona State Lottery, PO Box2913, AZ 85063-2913., 4740 E University Dr, Phoenix, AZ 85034; 800-921-4400, Fax: 480-921-4512. www.arizonalottery.com Email: feedback@arizonalottery.com

5 Banking Department, 2910 N 44th St, #310, Phoenix, AZ 85018; 602-255-4421, Fax: 602-381-1225. www.azbanking.com Email: mailbox@azbanking.com Search Database at www.azbanking.com/Lists/Lists.htm Note: Online or phone verifications ONLY.

6 Board for Private Postsecondary Education, 1400 W Washington, Rm 260, Phoenix, AZ 85007; 602-542-5709, Fax: 602-542-1253. http://azppse.state.az.us Search Database at http://azppse.state.az.us/directory.html

7 Board of Accountancy, 100 N,.15th Ave #16, Phoenix, AZ 85007; 602-364-0804, Fax: 602-364-0903. www.accountancy.state.az.us Email: info@mail.accountancy.state.az.us Search Database at www.accountancy.state.az.us/scripts/BOAsearch.e xe Note: Lists of names and addresses are available for $1.00 per name.

8 Board of Appraisal, 1400 W Washington, #360, Phoenix, AZ 85007; 602-542-1539, Fax: 602-542-1598. www.appraisal.state.az.us Email: appraisal@appraisal.state.az.us Search Database at www.appraisal.state.az.us/Directory/directory.html

9 Board of Barbers, 1400 W Washington, Rm 220, Phoenix, AZ 85007; 602-542-4498.

10 Board of Behavioral Health Examiners, 1400 W Washington St #350, Phoenix, AZ 85007; 602-542-1882, Fax: 602-542-1830.

www.bbhe.state.az.us Email: azbbhe@bbhe.state.az.us Note: A public record request form is available at www.bbhe.state.az.us/Forms/pubinfo.pdf. Fee for verifications is $15.00; copies are $.25 each.

11 Board of Chiropractic Examiners, 5060 N 19th Ave #416, Phoenix, AZ 85015; 602-864-5088, Fax: 602-864-5099. www.azchiroboard.com Email: merriejoh@earthlink.net Search Database at www.azchiroboard.com Note: Acupuncture and physiotherapy are certifications under a Chiropractic license.

12 Information Services, Board of Cosmetology, 1721 E Broadway Rd, Tempe, AZ 85282; 480-784-4539, Fax: 480-255-3680. www.cosmetology.state.az.us/

13 Board of Dental Examiners, 5060 N 19th Ave, #406, Phoenix, AZ 85015; 602-242-1492, Fax: 602-242-1445. www.azdentalboard.org

14 Board of Dispensing Opticians, 1400 W Washington, Rm 230, Phoenix, AZ 85007; 602-542-3095, Fax: 602-542-3093. Email: director@asbdo.state.az.us

15 Board of Funeral Directors & Embalmers, 1400 W Washington, Room 230, Phoenix, AZ 85007; 602-542-3095, Fax: 602-542-3093. www.funeralbd.state.az.us

16 Board of Homeopathic Medical Examiners, 1400 W Washington, Rm 230, Phoenix, AZ 85007; 602-542-3095, Fax: 602-542-3093. www.az.gov/webapp/portal/displaycontent.jsp?id= 2244 Email: bhme@mindspring.com Note: A public records request must be completed.

17 Board of Medical Examiners, 9545 E Doubletree Ranch Dr, Scottsdale, AZ 85258-5539; 480-551-2700, Fax: 480-551-2704. www.bomex.org Email: questions@bomex.org Search Database at www.bomex.org/getlicense.asp

19 Board of Naturopathic Physicians Examiners, 1400 W Washington, Rm 230, Phoenix, AZ 85007; 602-542-8242, Fax: 602-542-3093. www.npbomex.az.gov Email: gail.anthony@npbomex.az.gov Search at www.npbomex.az.gov/directories.html Note: Licensing lookup may be under construction.

20 Board of Nursing, 1651 E Morton, #210, Phoenix, AZ 85020-7605; 602-331-8111, Fax: 602-906-9365. www.azboardofnursing.org Email: az@azbn.org Note: You may request verification via email only at www.azboardofnursing.org/verification.htm.

21 Board of Occupational Therapy Examiners, 5060 N 19th Av #209, Phoenix, AZ 85015; 602-589-8352, Fax: 602-589-8354. www.mindspring.com/~abote/ Email: azot@mindspring.com

22 Board of Optometry, 1400 W Washington, Rm 230, Phoenix, AZ 85007; 602-542-3095, Fax: 602-542-3093. www.asbo.state.az.us Email: margaret.whelan@webmail.state.az.us Search Database at www.asbo.state.az.us

23 Board of Osteopathic Medicine & Surgery Examiners, 9535 E Doubletree Ranch Rd, Scottsdale, AZ 85258-5539; 480-657-7703, Fax: 480-657-7715. www.azosteoboard.org Email: information@azostedboard.org Search Database at http://docfinder.state.az.us

24 Board of Pharmacy, 4425 W Olive #140, Glendale, AZ 85302-3844; 623-463-2727, Fax: 623-934-0583. www.pharmacy.state.az.us Email: info@azsbp.com

25 Board of Physical Therapy & Acupuncture, 1400 W Washington, Rm 230, Phoenix, AZ 85007; 602-542-3095, Fax: 602-542-3093. www.ptboard.state.az.us Email: info@ptboard.state.az.us Search Database at www.ptboard.state.az.us Note: Online searching will be available 1/1/2003.

26 Board of Podiatry Examiners, 1400 W Washington, Rm 230, Phoenix, AZ 85007; 602-542-3095, Fax: 602-542-3093. www.podiatry.state.az.us/ Search Database at www.podiatry.state.az.us/

27 Board of Psychologist Examiners, 1400 W Washington St, Rm 235, Phoenix, AZ 85007; 602-542-8162, Fax: 602-542-8279. http://psychboard.az.gov Email: info@psychboard.az.gov Search Database at http://psychboard.az.gov/dir.html Note: Will sell lists of licensees.

28 Board of Respiratory Care Examiners, 1400 W Washington, #200, Phoenix, AZ 85007; 602-542-5995, Fax: 602-542-5900. www.rb.state.az.us Email: recept@rb.state.az.us

29 Board of Technical Registration, 1110 W Washington #240, Phoenix, AZ 85007; 602-364-4930, Fax: 602-364-4931. www.btr.state.az.us Email: azbtrweb@yahoo.com Search Database at www.btr.state.az.us

30 State Bar of Arizona, 111 W Monroe, #1800, Phoenix, AZ 85003-1742; 602-252-4804, Fax: 602-271-4930. www.azbar.org
Email: azbar@azbar.org Search Database at www.azbar.org/content.cfm?text=/LegalResources/findlawyer

31 Community College Board of Directors, 1400 W. Washington #210, Phoenix, AZ 85007; 602-364-0613, Fax: 602-364-0615.
Email: collins@stbd.cc.az.us

32 Registration Department, Securities Division, Corporation Commission, 1300 W Washington, 3rd Fl, Phoenix, AZ 85007; 602-542-4242, Fax: 602-594-7470.
www.ccsd.cc.state.az.us/licensing_and_registration/index.asp Email: accsec@ccsd.cc.state.az.us

33 Department of Agriculture, Environmental Services Division, 1688 W Adams St, Phoenix, AZ 85007; 602-542-0904, Fax: 602-542-5420; 602-542-0466. www.agriculture.state.az.us
Email: adaweb@getnet.com
Search Database at www.kellysolutions.com/az/

34 Department of Agriculture, Environmental Services Division, 1688 W Adams St, 1st Fl, Phoenix, AZ 85007; 602-542-5578, Fax: 602-542-0466. www.kellysolutions.com/az/
Email: adaweb@getnet.com

35 Department of Agriculture, Plant Services, Citrus, Fruit & Vegetable Standardization, 1688 W Adams, Phoenix, AZ 85007; 602-542-0947, Fax: 602-542-0898. www.kellysolutions.com/az
Email: cfv@agriculture.state.az.us
Search Database at www.kellysolutions.com/az

36 Department of Building & Fire Safety, 1110 W. Washington #100, Phoenix, AZ 85007; 602-364-1063, Fax: 602-364-1052.

37 Dept of Health Services, Child Care Facility Licensing, 150 N 18th Ave, Phoenix, AZ 85007; 602-364-2539, Fax: 602-364-4768.
www.hs.state.az.us/als/childcare/index.htm

38 Department of Education, Teacher Certification Unit, PO Box 6490 (1535 W Jefferson St, Bin 34), Phoenix, AZ 85005; 602-542-4367, Fax: 602-542-1141.
www.ade.state.az.us Email: ade@ade.az.gov

39 Department of Environmental Quality, Office of Air Quality, 1110 W. Washington, Phoenix, AZ 85007; 602-771-2338, Fax: 602-771-2299.
www.adeq.state.az.us

40 Department of Environmental Quality, Office of Waste Programs, 1110 W. Washington, Phoenix, AZ 85007; 602-771-4208, Fax: 602-771-4208. www.adeq.state.az.us

41 Department of Environmental Quality, Office of Water Quality, 1110 W. Washington, Phoenix, AZ 85007; 602-771-4644, Fax: 602-771-4834.
www.adeq.state.az.us

42 Department of Environmental Quality, Vehicle Emissions Section, 600 N 40th St, Phoenix, AZ 85008; 602-207-7007, Fax: 602-207-7020.
www.adeq.state.az.us/environ/air/vei/index.html
Email: gibbons.john@ev.state.az.us

43 Department of Health Services, Facilities Licensing, 150 N 18th Ave #450, Phoenix, AZ 85007-3245; 602-364-3030, Fax: 602-364-4764.
www.hs.state.az.us/als/index.htm Search at www.hs.state.az.us/als/medical/index.htm

44 Department of Health Services, Bureau of State Lab Services/Licensure/Cert, 1520 W. Adams, Phoenix, AZ 85007; 602-542-1197, Fax: 602-542-0760. www.hs.state.az.us

45 Child Care Licensing, Division of Child Care, 150 N 18th Ave, 4th Fl, Phoenix, AZ 85007; 602-364-2536, Fax: 602-364-4806.
www.hs.state.az.us/als/childcare/index.htm Note: No license searches, only provider lists.

46 Department of Health Services, Food Protection & Institutional Sanitation Section, 3815 N Black Canyon Hwy, Phoenix, AZ 85015; 602-230-5912, Fax: 602-230-5817.
www.hs.state.az.us

47 Department of Health Services, Office of Behavioral Health Licensure, 150 N.18th Ave, Phoenix, AZ 85007; 602-343-2595, Fax: 602-364-4801. www.hs.state.az.us
Search Database at www.hs.state.az.us/als/databases/

48 Arizona Department of Health Services, Bureau of EMS, 150 N. 18th Ave #540, Phoenix, AZ 85007; 602-364-3150, Fax: 602-364-3568.
www.hs.state.az.us/bems/

49 Department of Health Services, The Division of Licensing Services, 150 N 18th Ave, Phoenix, AZ 85007; 602-364-2536, Fax: 602-364-4768.
www.hs.state.az.us Search Database at www.hs.state.az.us/als/hcb/index.htm

50 Department of Health Services, Office of Women & Children, 150 N 18th Ave, Phoenix, AZ 85017-5253; 602-364-2536, Fax: 602-364-4808.
www.hs.state.az.us Search Database at www.hs.state.az.us/als/midwife/

51 Department of Insurance, Licensing Section, 2910 N 44th St, #210, Phoenix, AZ 85018-7256; 602-912-8470, Fax: 602-912-8453.
www.id.state.az.us Email: licensing@id.state.az.us
Search Database at www.id.state.az.us/

52 Department of Liquor License & Control, 800 W Washington, 5th Fl, Phoenix, AZ 85007; 602-542-5141, Fax: 602-542-5707. www.azll.com
Search Database at www.azll.com/query.htm
Note: Search recently issued, expired, closed, suspended and inactive licenses at the website.

53 Department of Public Safety, Security Guard & Private Investigator Licensing, PO Box 6328 (2102 W Encanto Blvd, 85009), Phoenix, AZ 85005-6328; 602-223-2361, Fax: 602-223-2938.
www.dps.state.az.us/

54 Department of Racing, Licensing Division, 1110 W Washington #260, Phoenix, AZ 85007; 602-364-1700, Fax: 602-364-1703.
www.racing.state.az.us Email: ador@racing.state.az.us

55 Department of Real Estate, 2910 N 44th St #100, Phoenix, AZ 85018; 602-468-1414, Fax: 602-468-0562. www.re.state.az.us
Email: cdowns@adre.org
Search Database at www.re.state.az.us/db.html

56 Department of Revenue, License & Registration, PO Box 29002, Phoenix, AZ 85038-9069; 602-542-4565. www.revenue.state.az.us

57 Department of Transportation, Aeronautics Division, 255 E Osborn #101, Phoenix, AZ 85012; 602-294-9144, Fax: 602-294-9141.
www.dot.state.az.us/Aero/index.htm
Email: aeroinfo@dot.state.az.us

58 Department of Water Resources, PO Box 458 (500 N 3rd St, 85004), Phoenix, AZ 85001-0458; 602-417-2400, Fax: 602-417-2401.
http://water.az.gov/adwr/

59 Game & Fish Department, 2222 W Greenway Rd, Phoenix, AZ 85023; 602-942-3000, Fax: 602-789-3921. http://azgfd.com

60 Division of Administration, Industrial Commission of Arizona, 800 W Washington, 3rd Fl, Phoenix, AZ 85007; 602-542-4653, Fax: 602-542-3070. www.ica.state.az.us

61 Special Fund Division, Industrial Commission of Arizona, 800 W Washington, 4th Fl, Rm 401, Phoenix, AZ 85007; 602-542-3294, Fax: 602-542-3696. www.ica.state.az.us

63 Arizona Supreme Court, Court Reporter Program, 1501 W. Washington St, #104, Phoenix, AZ 85007-3231; 602-364-0878, Fax: 602-307-1210. www.supreme.state.az.us/cr/
Email: courtrep@supreme.sp.state.az.us

65 Maricopa Environmental Services, 1001 N Central, #550, Phoenix, AZ 85004; 602-506-6970, Fax: 602-506-6862.
www.maricopa.gov/envsvc/default.asp
Email: webmail@mail.maricopa.co

66 Medical Radiologic Technology Board of Examiners, 4814 S 40th St, Phoenix, AZ 85040-2940; 602-255-4845, Fax: 602-437-0705.
www.arra.state.az.us
Email: agodwin@arra.state.az.us

67 Mine Inspector, 1700 W Washington, #400, Phoenix, AZ 85007-2805; 602-542-5971, Fax: 602-542-5335. www.asmi.state.az.us
Email: admin@mi.state.az.us

68 Nursing Care Board, 1400 W Washington, #230, Phoenix, AZ 85007; 602-364-2273.
www.nciabd.state.az.us
Email: information@nciabd.state.az.us

69 Parks Board, 1300 W Washington, #221, Phoenix, AZ 85007; 602-542-2155, Fax: 602-542-4180. www.pr.state.az.us Email: info@pr.state.az.us

70 Registrar of Contractors, 800 W Washington, 6th Fl, Phoenix, AZ 85007; 602-542-1525, Fax: 602-542-1599. www.rc.state.az.us
Email: webmaster@roc1.rc.state.az.us
Search Database at
www.rc.state.az.us/clsc/AZROCLicenseQuery

71 Secretary of State, 1700 W Washington St, 7th Fl, Phoenix, AZ 85007-2888; 602-542-4285, Fax: 602-542-6172. www.sosaz.com
Email: lobbyist@azsos.gov
Search Database at www.sosaz.com Note: Search lobbyists using the public body's name, lobbyist's name or the lobbyist's employee's name.

72 Structural Pest Control Commission, 9535 E Doubletree Ranch Rd, Scottsdale, AZ 85258-5514; 602-255-3664, Fax: 602-255-1281.
www.sb.state.az.us

73 Veterinary Medical Examining Board, 1400 W Washington, #240, Phoenix, AZ 85007; 602-364-1738, Fax: 602-542-3093. www.vetbd.state.az.us

Arizona Federal Courts

The following list indicates the district and division name for each county in the state. If the bankruptcy court location is different from the district court, then the location of the bankruptcy court appears in parentheses.

County/Court Cross Reference

Apache	Prescott (Phoenix)	Mohave	Prescott (Yuma)
Cochise	Tucson	Navajo	Prescott (Phoenix)
Coconino	Prescott (Phoenix)	Pima	Tucson
Gila	Phoenix (Tucson)	Pinal	Phoenix (Tucson)
Graham	Tucson	Santa Cruz	Tucson
Greenlee	Tucson	Yavapai	Prescott (Phoenix)
La Paz	Phoenix (Yuma)	Yuma	Phoenix (Yuma)
Maricopa	Phoenix		

Standards for Federal Courts: The search fee is $20.00 per item (one party name or case number). Certification fee is $7.00 per document. Copy fee is $.50 per page. All fees standard unless noted in profile. Mail Search: always enclose a stamped self addressed envelope unless otherwise noted. Most courts accept fax requests or will suggest a copying/search vendor. Before releasing records, all courts require prepayment unless noted in profile.

Open records are located at the court unless otherwise noted. District courts index by defendant and plaintiff as well as by case number. Bankruptcy courts usually index by debtor and case number. While most courts now have their indexes on computer, many still maintain index card files as well.

The universal PACER sign-up number is 800-676-6856. Find PACER and the Party/Case Index on the Web at http://pacer.psc.uscourts.gov. PACER dial-up access is $.60 per minute. Also, courts offering internet access via RACER, PACER, Web-PACER or the new CM-ECF charge $.07 per page fee unless noted as free.

US District Court

District of Arizona

Phoenix Division Sandra Day O'Connor U.S. Courthouse, #130, 401 W. Washington Street, SPC 1, Phoenix, AZ 85025-2118 (courier address: Use mail address for courier delivery) 602-322-7200. www.azd.uscourts.gov

Counties: Gila, La Paz, Maricopa, Pinal, Yuma. Some Yuma cases handled by San Diego Division of the Southern District of California.

Indexing & Storage: New cases available in the index 2-3 weeks after filing date. Records are also indexed on microfiche.

Fee & Payment: Payment may be made by money order, cashier check, business check, Mastercard. In state personal checks are also accepted. Payee: Clerk, U.S. District Court.

Phone Search: No searching by telephone. If case number is known by the caller, basic information will be released over the phone.

Mail Search: All information is public unless the file is sealed. Include SASE for return.

In Person Search: Fee charged if court conducts your in person search for you.

PACER: PACER is available online at http://pacer.azd.uscourts.gov. Case records go back to 1994. Records purged every 12 months. New records are online after 1-3 days.

Prescott Division 101 W Goodwin St, U.S. Post Office Bldg, Prescott, AZ 86303 (courier address: Use mail address for courier delivery) 928-445-6598. www.azd.uscourts.gov

Counties: Apache, Coconino, Mohave, Navajo, Yavapai.

Indexing & Storage: Cases indexed by as well as by case number. New cases available in the index after filing date. Open records are located at the Phoenix Division.

Fee & Payment: Payment may be made by. Personal checks are not accepted.

Phone Search: No searching by telephone.

Mail Search: A SASE not required.

In Person Search: Permitted.

PACER: PACER is available online at http://pacer.azd.uscourts.gov. Case records go back to 1994. Records purged every 12 months. New records are online after 1-3 days.

Tucson Division U.S. Court House, 405 W. Congress Ste 1500, Tucson, AZ 85701-5010 (courier address: Use mail address for courier delivery) 520-205-4200, Fax: 520-205-4209. www.azd.uscourts.gov

Counties: Cochise, Graham, Greelee, Pima, Santa Cruz. The Globe Division was closed effective January 1994, and all case records for that division are now found here.

Indexing & Storage: New cases available in the index immediately after filing date.

Fee & Payment: Payment may be made by money order, cashier check, business check. In state personal checks are also accepted. A copy service may be used in lieu of court staff; the copy service has a one day turnaround. Payee: Clerk, U.S. District Court.

Phone Search: Only docket information available by phone.

Mail Search: A SASE not required.

In Person Search: Fee charged if court conducts your in person search for you.

PACER: PACER is available online at http://pacer.azd.uscourts.gov. Case records go back to 1994. Records purged every 12 months. New records are online after 1-3 days.

U.S. Bankruptcy Court

District of Arizona

Phoenix Division PO Box 34151, (2929 N Central, 9th Fl), Phoenix, AZ 85067-4151 (courier address: Use mail address for courier delivery) 602-640-5800. www.azb.uscourts.gov

Counties: Apache, Coconino, Maricopa, Navajo, Yavapai.

Indexing & Storage: Cases indexed by debtor as well as by case number. New cases available in the index immediately after filing date. Creditors are also indexed from case # 95-1668 forward. Case files are stored alphabetically. Individuals cannot request files from the Federal Records Center themselves.

Fee & Payment: Payment may be made by money order, cashier check, business check. Personal checks are not accepted. Payee: Clerk, U.S. Bankruptcy Court.

Phone Search: Only docket information available by phone. Automated voice case information service (VCIS) is available. Call VCIS at 602-640-5820 or 888-549-5336.

In Person Search: Fee charged if court conducts your in person search for you.

PACER: PACER is available online at http://pacer.azb.uscourts.gov. Records purged every six months. New civil records are online after 1 week.

Electronic Filing: Searching of electronically filed cases requires registration and password with the court. Electronic filing information online at https://ecf.azb.uscourts.gov

Tucson Division Suite 8112, 110 S Church Ave, Tucson, AZ 85701-1608 (courier address: Use mail address for courier delivery) 520-620-7500. www.azb.uscourts.gov

Counties: Cochise, Gila, Graham, Greenlee, Pima, Pinal, Santa Cruz.

Indexing & Storage: Cases indexed by debtor as well as by case number. New cases available in the index immediately after filing date. Records are also indexed by adversary case number if applicable. A master list of creditors is available for each case from 1995 on.

Fee & Payment: Payment may be made by money order, cashier check, business check. Personal checks are not accepted. Payee: Clerk, U.S. Bankruptcy Court.

Phone Search: Only docket and cover sheet information will be released over the phone. Automated voice case information service (VCIS) is available. Call VCIS at 888-299-6032.

In Person Search: Fee charged if court conducts your in person search for you. Copies obtained at the Office of the Bankruptcy Clerk or through an off-site copy service.

PACER: PACER is available online at http://pacer.azb.uscourts.gov. Case records go back to 1914. Records purged every six months. New civil records are online after 1 week.

Electronic Filing: Searching of electronically filed cases requires registration and password with

the court. Electronic filing information online at https://ecf.azb.uscourts.gov

Yuma Division PO Box 13011, (325 W 19th St), Yuma, AZ 853656 (courier address: Use mail address for courier delivery., 325 W 19th St, Yuma, AZ 853654), 928-783-2288. www.azb.uscourts.gov

Counties: La Paz, Mohave, Yuma.

Indexing & Storage: Cases indexed by debtor as well as by case number. New cases available in the index immediately after filing date.

Fee & Payment: Payment may be made by money order, cashier check, business check. Personal checks are not accepted. Payee: Clerk, U.S. Bankruptcy Court.

Phone Search: Docket information is available by phone. Call VCIS at 888-299-6032.

In Person Search: Fee charged if court conducts your in person search for you.

PACER: PACER is available online at http://pacer.azb.uscourts.gov. Case records go back to the mid 1980's. Records purged every six months. New civil records are online after 1 day.

Electronic Filing: Searching of electronically filed cases requires registration and password with the court. Electronic filing information online at https://ecf.azb.uscourts.gov

Arizona County Courts

Court	Jurisdiction	No. of Courts	How Organized
Superior Courts*	General	15	15 Counties
Justice of the Peace Courts*	Limited	79	79 Precincts
Municipal Courts	Municipal	85	

* Profiled in this Sourcebook.

CIVIL									
Court	Tort	Contract	Real Estate	Min. Claim	Max. Claim	Small Claims	Estate	Eviction	Domestic Relations
Superior Court*	X	X	X	$5000	No Max			X	
Justice of the Peace Courts*	X	X	X	$0	$10,000	$2500		X	X
Municipal Courts									X

CRIMINAL					
Court	Felony	Misdemeanor	DWI/DUI	Preliminary Hearing	Juvenile
Superior Court*	X	X			X
Justice of the Peace Courts*		X	X	X	
Municipal Courts		X	X		

ADMINISTRATION

Administrative Office of the Courts, Arizona Supreme Court Bldg, 1501 W Washington, Phoenix, AZ, 85007; 602-542-9301, Fax: 602-542-9484.

www.supreme.state.az.us

COURT STRUCTURE

The Superior is the court of general jurisdiction. Justice, and Municipal courts generally have separate jurisdiction over case types as indicated in the text. Most courts will search their records by plaintiff or defendant. Estate cases are handled by Superior Court. Fees are the same as for civil and criminal case searching.

ONLINE ACCESS

The Arizona Judicial Branch offers Public Access to Court Case Information, a valuable online service providing a resource for information about court cases from 137 out of 180 superior, justice, and municipal courts in Arizona. Access information includes: detailed case information, i.e., case type, charges, filing and disposition dates; the parties in the case, not including victims and witnesses; and the court mailing address and location. Go to www.supreme.state.az.us/publicaccess. Opinions from the AZ Supreme Court and Court of Appeals are available from the web site.

The Maricopa and Pima county courts maintain their own systems, but will also, under current planning, be part of ACAP. These two counties provide ever-increasing online access to the public.

ADDITIONAL INFORMATION

Public access to all Maricopa County court case indexes is available at a central location - 1 W Madison Ave in downtown Phoenix. Copies, however, must be obtained from the court where the case is heard.

As of Fall, 2001, Justice Courts accept civil actions up to $10.000; the increase is due to higher value claims in landlord/tenant cases. Civil cases between $5,000 and $10,000 may be filed at either Justice or Superior Courts.

Many offices do not perform searches due to personnel and/or budget constraints. As computerization of record offices increases across the state, more record offices are providing public access computer terminals.

Fees across all jurisdictions, as established by the Arizona Supreme Court and State Legislature, are as follows as of August 9, 2001: search - Superior Court: $18.00 per name; lower courts: $17.00 per name; certification - Superior Court: $18.00 per document; lower courts: $17.00 per document; copies - $.50 per page. Courts may choose to charge no fees.

Apache County

Superior Court PO Box 365, St Johns, AZ 85936; 928-337-7550; Fax: 928-337-2771. Hours: 8AM-5PM (MST). *Felony, Civil Actions Over $5,000, Probate.* www.co.apache.az.us/clerk
Civil Records: Access: Mail, in person, online. Both court and visitors may perform in person searches. Search fee: $18.00 per name. Required to search: name, years to search; also helpful: address. Civil cases indexed by defendant, plaintiff. Civil records on computer and docket books. Online access to records from 1995 forward is free at www.supreme.state.az.us/publicaccess/.
Criminal Records: Access: Mail, in person, online. Both court and visitors may perform in person searches. Search fee: $18.00 per name. Add $5.00 if no SASE or not a toll free fax. Required to search: name, years to search, DOB; also helpful: address, SSN. Criminal records on computer and docket books. Online access to records from 1995 forward is free at www.supreme.state.az.us/publicaccess/.
General Information: Public Access terminal is available. No juvenile dependencies, mental health, victims, sealed or adoption records released. Will fax results to local or toll free line. Copy fee: $.50 per page. Cert fee: $18.00. Payee: Clerk of the Court. Business checks accepted. Credit cards accepted. Prepayment required. Mail requests: SASE required. Mail turnaround time is 2 days.

Chinle Justice Court PO Box 888, Chinle, AZ 86503; 928-674-5922; Fax: 928-674-5926. Hours: 8AM-5PM (MST). *Misdemeanor, Civil Actions Under $10,000, Eviction, Small Claims.*
Civil Records: Access: Fax, mail, in person, online. Both court and visitors may perform in person searches. Search fee: $17.00 per name. Required to search: name, years to search; also helpful: address. Civil cases indexed by defendant. Civil records on docket books from 1977, computerized back to 2000. Online access to records is free at www.supreme.state.az.us/publicaccess/.
Criminal Records: Access: Fax, mail, in person, online. Both court and visitors may perform in person searches. Search fee: $17.00 per name. Required to search: name, years to search; also helpful: address, DOB, SSN. Criminal records on docket books from 1977, computerized back to 2000. Online access to records is at www.supreme.state.az.us/publicaccess/. Phone access is discouraged.
General Information: Public Access terminal is available. No juvenile, mental health, victims, sealed or adoption records released. Fee to fax results is $1.25 per page. Copy fee: $1.25 per page. Cert fee: $17.00. Payee: Chinle Justice Court. Business checks accepted. Prepayment required. Mail requests: SASE required. Mail turnaround time 1-2 days.

Puerco Justice Court PO Box 610, Sanders, AZ 86512; 928-688-2954; Fax: 928-688-2244. Hours: 8AM-Noon, 1-5PM (MST). *Misdemeanor, Civil Actions Under $10,000, Eviction, Small Claims.*
Civil Records: Access: Mail, in person, online. Only the court performs in person searches; visitors may not. Search fee: $17.00 per name. Required to search: name, years to search; also helpful: address. Civil cases indexed by defendant. Civil records on docket books. Online access to records is free at www.supreme.state.az.us/publicaccess/.
Criminal Records: Access: Mail, in person, online. Only the court performs in person searches; visitors may not. Search fee: $17.00 per name. Required to search: name, years to search, DOB; also helpful: address, SSN. Criminal records on docket books. Online access to records is free at www.supreme.state.az.us/publicaccess/.

General Information: No juvenile, mental health, victims, sealed or adoption records released. Copy fee: $.50 per page. Cert fee: $17.00. Payee: Sanders Justice Court. Only cashiers checks and money orders accepted. Prepayment required. Mail requests: SASE required. Mail turnaround time ASAP.

Round Valley Justice Court PO Box 1356, Springerville, AZ 85938; 928-333-4613; Fax: 928-333-4205. Hours: 8AM-Noon, 1-5PM (MST). *Misdemeanor, Civil Actions Under $10,000, Eviction, Small Claims.*
Civil Records: Access: Phone, fax, mail, in person, online. Both court and visitors may perform in person searches. Search fee: $17.00 per name. Required to search: name, years to search; also helpful: address. Civil cases indexed by defendant, plaintiff. Civil records on docket books from 1990, computerized since 02/96. Online access to records is free at www.supreme.state.az.us/publicaccess/.
Criminal Records: Access: Phone, fax, mail, in person, online. Both court and visitors may perform in person searches. Search fee: $17.00 per name. Required to search: name, years to search; also helpful: address, DOB, SSN. Criminal records on docket books from 1990, computerized since 02/96. Online access to records is free at www.supreme.state.az.us/publicaccess/.
General Information: Public Access terminal is available. No juvenile, mental health, victims, sealed or adoption records released. Copy fee: $.50 per page. Cert fee: $17.00. Payee: Round Valley Justice Court. Only cashiers checks and money orders accepted. Prepayment required. Mail requests: SASE required. Mail turnaround time 5 working days.

St Johns Justice Court PO Box 308, St Johns, AZ 85936; 928-337-7558; Fax: 928-337-2683. Hours: 8AM-5PM (MST). *Misdemeanor, Civil Actions Under $10,000, Eviction, Small Claims.*
Civil Records: Access: Mail, in person, online. Both court and visitors may perform in person searches. Search fee: $17.00 per name. Required to search: name, years to search; also helpful: address. Civil cases indexed by defendant. Civil records on docket books since 1972; on computer since 1996. Online access to records is free at www.supreme.state.az.us/publicaccess/.
Criminal Records: Access: Mail, in person, online. Both court and visitors may perform in person searches. Search fee: $17.00 per name. Required to search: name, years to search, DOB; also helpful: address, SSN. Criminal records on docket books since 1972; on computer since 1996. Online access to records is at www.supreme.state.az.us/publicaccess/.
General Information: No juvenile, mental health, victims, sealed or adoption records released. Copy fee: $.50 per page. Cert fee: $17.00. Payee: St John's Justice Court. Only cashiers checks and money orders accepted. Prepayment required. Mail requests: SASE required. Mail turnaround time 48 hours.

Cochise County

Superior Court PO Box CK, Bisbee, AZ 85603; 520-432-8604; Fax: 520-432-4850. 8AM-5PM (MST). *Felony, Civil Actions Over $5,000, Probate.* www.co.cochise.az.us/Court/Crtclerk.htm
Civil Records: Access: Fax, mail, in person, email, online. Both court and visitors may perform in person searches. Search fee: $18.00 per name per year. Required to search: name, years to search. Civil cases indexed by defendant, plaintiff. Civil records on computer since 1996 and on index books from 1881 to present. Online access to records is free at www.supreme.state.az.us/publicaccess/.
Criminal Records: Access: Fax, mail, in person, email, online. Both court and visitors may perform in person searches. Search fee: $18.00 per name. Per

every 5 years. Required to search: name, years to search; also helpful: DOB, SSN. Criminal records on computer since 1996; prior records on index books. Online access to records is free at www.supreme.state.az.us/publicaccess/.
General Information: Public Access terminal is available. (Records after 1/1/96 available.) No juvenile, mental health, victims, sealed or adoption records released. Fee to fax results is $.50 per page. Copy fee: $.50 per page. Cert fee: $18.00. Payee: Clerk of Superior Court. Only cashiers checks and money orders accepted. Prepayment required. Mail requests: SASE required. Mail turnaround: 7-14 days.

Benson Justice Court 126 W 5th St, #1, Benson, AZ 85602; 520-586-8100; Fax: 520-586-9647. Hours: 8AM-5PM (MST). *Misdemeanor, Civil Actions Under $10,000, Eviction, Small Claims.*
Civil Records: Access: Fax, mail, in person, online. Only the court performs in person searches; visitors may not. Search fee: $17.00 per name. Required to search: name, years to search; also helpful: address. Civil cases indexed by defendant. Online access to records is at www.supreme.state.az.us/publicaccess/.
Criminal Records: Access: Fax, mail, in person, online. Only the court performs in person searches; visitors may not. Search fee: $17.00 per name. Required to search: name, years to search; also helpful: address, DOB, SSN. Online access to records is free at www.supreme.state.az.us/publicaccess/.
General Information: No juvenile, mental health, victims, sealed records released. No fee to fax results. Copy fee: $.50 per page. Cert fee: $17.00. Payee: Benson Justice Court. Only cashiers checks and money orders accepted. Prepayment required. Mail requests: SASE required. Mail turnaround: 1-3 days.

Bisbee Justice Court 207 N Judd Dr, Bisbee, AZ 85603; 520-432-9542; Fax: 520-432-9594. Hours: 8AM-5PM (MST). *Misdemeanor, Civil Actions Under $10,000, Eviction, Small Claims.*
Civil Records: Access: Fax, mail, in person, online. Only the court performs in person searches; visitors may not. Search fee: $17.00 per name. Required to search: name, years to search; also helpful: address. Civil cases indexed by defendant, plaintiff. Civil records on computer from 1992. Some records on dockets. Online access to records is free at www.supreme.state.az.us/publicaccess/.
Criminal Records: Access: Fax, mail, in person, online. Only the court performs in person searches; visitors may not. Search fee: $17.00 per name. Required to search: name, years to search; also helpful: address, DOB, SSN. Criminal records on computer from 7/92. Some records on dockets; computerized records since 1992. Online access to records is at www.supreme.state.az.us/publicaccess/.
General Information: No juvenile, mental health, victims, sealed or adoption records released. No fee to fax results. Copy fee: $.50 per page. Cert fee: $17.00. Payee: Bisbee Justice Court #1. Personal checks accepted. Prepayment required. Mail requests: SASE required. Mail turnaround time 1-7 days.

Bowie Justice Court PO Box 317, Bowie, AZ 85605; 520-847-2303; Fax: 520-847-2242. Hours: 8AM-5PM (MST). *Misdemeanor, Civil Actions Under $10,000, Eviction, Small Claims.*
Civil Records: Access: Phone, fax, mail, in person, online. Only the court performs in person searches; visitors may not. Search fee: $17.00 per name. Required to search: name, years to search; also helpful: address. Civil cases indexed by defendant. Civil records on computer from 7/85, some from 1994. Files maintained for 5 years after closure. Online access to records is free at www.supreme.state.az.us/publicaccess/.

Criminal Records: Access: Phone, fax, mail, in person, online. Only the court performs in person searches; visitors may not. Search fee: $17.00 per name. Required to search: name, years to search, DOB; also helpful: address, SSN. Criminal records on computer from 1989. Files maintained for 5 years after closure. Online access to records is free at www.supreme.state.az.us/publicaccess/.

General Information: No juvenile, mental health, victims, sealed or adoption records released. Will fax results $2.00 per page. Copy fee: $.50 per page. Cert fee: $17.00. Payee: Bowie Justice Court. Only cashiers checks and money orders accepted. Visa, MC accepted. Prepayment required. Mail requests: SASE required. Mail turnaround time 1-3 days.

Douglas Justice Court 661 G Ave, Douglas, AZ 85607; 520-805-5640; Fax: 520-364-3684. Hours: 8AM-5PM (MST). *Misdemeanor, Civil Actions Under $10,000, Eviction, Small Claims.*

Civil Records: Access: Fax, mail, in person, online. Only the court performs in person searches; visitors may not. Search fee: $17.00 per name. Required to search: name, years to search; also helpful: address. Civil cases indexed by defendant, plaintiff. Civil records on computer from 1991. Some records on dockets. Online access to records is free at www.supreme.state.az.us/publicaccess/.

Criminal Records: Access: Fax, mail, in person, online. Only the court performs in person searches; visitors may not. Search fee: $17.00 per name. Required to search: name, years to search, DOB; also helpful: address, SSN. Criminal records on computer from 1990. Some records on dockets. Online access to records is at www.supreme.state.az.us/publicaccess/.

General Information: No juvenile, mental health, victims, sealed or adoption records released. Fee to fax certified search results is $.50 per page. Copy fee: $.50 per page. Cert fee: $17.00. Payee: Douglas Justice Court. Personal checks accepted. Prepayment required. Mail requests: SASE required. Mail turnaround time 1-7 days.

Sierra Vista Justice Court 4001 E Foothills Dr, Sierra Vista, AZ 85635; 520-803-3801; Fax: 520-439-9106. 8AM-5PM (MST). *Misdemeanor, Civil Actions Under $10,000, Eviction, Small Claims.*

Civil Records: Access: Fax, mail, in person, online. Only the court performs in person searches; visitors may not. Search fee: $17.00 per name. Required to search: name, years to search; also helpful: address. Civil cases indexed by plaintiff and defendant. Civil records on computer since 08/96. Online access to records is at www.supreme.state.az.us/publicaccess/. In person access requires a written request.

Criminal Records: Access: Fax, mail, in person, online. Only the court performs in person searches; visitors may not. Search fee: $17.00 per name. Required to search: name, years to search; also helpful: address, DOB, SSN. Criminal records by case number, on computer back to 8/1996. Online access to records is free at www.supreme.state.az.us/publicaccess/. In person access requires a written request.

General Information: No juvenile, mental health, victims, sealed, financial, or adoption records released. Will fax results to local or toll free line. Copy fee: $.50 per page. Cert fee: $17.00. Payee: Cochise County Treasurer. Personal checks accepted. Visa, MC accepted. Prepayment required. Mail requests: SASE required. Mail turnaround: 3-7 days.

Willcox Justice Court 450 S Haskell, Willcox, AZ 85643; 520-384-7000; Fax: 520-384-4305. Hours: 8AM-5PM (MST). *Misdemeanor, Civil Actions Under $10,000, Eviction, Small Claims.*

Civil Records: Access: Phone, fax, mail, in person, online. Only the court performs in person searches; visitors may not. Search fee: $17.00. Required to search: name; also helpful: years to search, address. Civil cases indexed by defendant, plaintiff. Civil records on computer from 1996. Some records on dockets. Online access to records is free at www.supreme.state.az.us/publicaccess/.

Criminal Records: Access: Phone, fax, mail, in person, online. Only the court performs in person searches; visitors may not. Search fee: $17.00. Required to search: name, DOB; also helpful: years to search, address, SSN. Criminal records on computer from 1996. Some records on dockets. Online access to records is at www.supreme.state.az.us/publicaccess/.

General Information: No juvenile, mental health, victims, sealed or adoption records released. No fee to fax results. Copy fee: $.50 per page. Cert fee: $17.00. Payee: Willcox Justice Court. Only cashiers checks and money orders accepted. Prepayment required. Mail requests: SASE required. Mail turnaround time usually 1-3 days.

Coconino County

Superior Court 200 N San Francisco St, Flagstaff, AZ 86001; 928-779-6535. 8AM-5PM (MST). *Felony, Civil Actions Over $5,000, Probate.*

Civil Records: Access: Mail, in person, online. Both court and visitors may perform in person searches. Search fee: $22.00 per name per year. Required to search: name, years to search; also helpful: address. Civil cases indexed by defendant. Civil records on handwritten ledger books from 1890. Some records on microfiche and dockets; computer from 1994. Online access to records is free at www.supreme.state.az.us/publicaccess/.

Criminal Records: Access: Mail, in person, online. Both court and visitors may perform in person searches. Search fee: $22.00 per name per year. Required to search: name, years to search, DOB; also helpful: address, SSN. Criminal records on handwritten ledger books from 1890. Some records on microfiche and dockets; computer from 1994. Online access to records is free at www.supreme.state.az.us/publicaccess/.

General Information: No mental health, victims, sealed or adoption records released. Copy fee: $.50 per page. Cert fee: $18.00. Payee: Clerk of Superior Court. Business checks accepted. Prepayment required. Mail requests: SASE required. Mail turnaround time 2 weeks.

Flagstaff Justice Court 200 N San Franciso St., Flagstaff, AZ 86001; 928-779-6806. Hours: 8AM-5PM (MST). *Misdemeanor, Civil Actions Under $10,000, Eviction, Small Claims.*

Civil Records: Access: Mail, in person, online. Only the court performs in person searches; visitors may not. Search fee: $17.00 per name. Required to search: name, years to search; also helpful: address. Civil records on docket books. Will only maintain records for 5 years. Online access to records is free at www.supreme.state.az.us/publicaccess/.

Criminal Records: Access: Mail, in person, online. Only the court performs in person searches; visitors may not. Search fee: $17.00 per name per year. Required to search: name, years to search, DOB; also helpful: address, SSN. Criminal records on computer since 1987. Will only maintain records for 5 years. Online access to records is free at www.supreme.state.az.us/publicaccess/.

General Information: No juvenile, mental health, victims, sealed or adoption records released. Copy fee: $.50 per page. Cert fee: $17.00. Payee: Flagstaff Justice Court. Only cashiers checks and money orders accepted. Prepayment required. Mail requests: SASE required. Mail turnaround time 14-20 days.

Fredonia Justice Court PO Box 559, 112 N Main, Fredonia, AZ 86022-0559; 928-643-7472; Fax: 928-643-7491. Hours: 8AM-5PM (MST). *Misdemeanor, Civil Actions Under $10,000, Eviction, Small Claims.*

Civil Records: Access: Mail, in person. Only the court performs in person searches; visitors may not. Search fee: $17.00 per name. Required to search: name, years to search; also helpful: address. Civil cases indexed by number. Civil records on docket books. Will only maintain records for 5 years. Online access to records is free at www.supreme.state.az.us/publicaccess/.

Criminal Records: Access: Mail, in person. Only the court performs in person searches; visitors may not. Search fee: $17.00 per name. Required to search: name, years to search, DOB; also helpful: address, SSN. Criminal records for misdemeanors on computer from 1992, all others on docket books. Online access to records is free at www.supreme.state.az.us/publicaccess/.

General Information: Public Access terminal is available. No juvenile, mental health, victims, sealed or adoption records released. Copy fee: $.50 per page. Cert fee: $17.00. Payee: Justice Court. Only cashiers checks and money orders accepted. Prepayment required. Mail requests: SASE required. Mail turnaround time 5 days from date request/received.

Page Justice Court PO Box 1565, Page, AZ 86040; 928-645-8871; Fax: 928-645-1869. Hours: 8AM-5PM (MST). *Misdemeanor, Civil Actions Under $10,000, Eviction, Small Claims.*

Civil Records: Access: Mail, in person, online. Only the court performs in person searches; visitors may not. Search fee: $17.00 per name. Required to search: name, years to search; also helpful: address. Civil cases indexed by defendant. Civil records on computer since 9/96; prior on docket books. Will only maintain records for 5 years. Online access to records is free at www.supreme.state.az.us/publicaccess/.

Criminal Records: Access: Mail, in person, online. Only the court performs in person searches; visitors may not. Search fee: $17.00 per name. Required to search: name, years to search, DOB; also helpful: address, SSN. Criminal records for misdemeanors on computer from 1987, felony since 1991, all others on docket books. Online access to records is free at www.supreme.state.az.us/publicaccess/.

General Information: No juvenile, mental health, victims, sealed or adoption records released. Copy fee: $.50 per page. Cert fee: $17.00. Payee: Page Justice Court. Only cashiers checks and money orders accepted. Visa, MC accepted. Prepayment required. Mail requests: SASE required. Mail turnaround time 5 days.

Williams Justice Court 700 W Rail Road Ave, Williams, AZ 86046; 928-635-2691. Hours: 8AM-N; 1-5PM (MST). *Misdemeanor, Civil Actions Under $10,000, Eviction, Small Claims.*

Civil Records: Access: Mail, in person, online. Both court and visitors may perform in person searches. Search fee: $17.00 per name. Required to search: name, years to search; also helpful: address. Civil cases indexed by defendant, plaintiff. Civil records on docket books. Will only maintain records for 5 years. Online access to records is free at www.supreme.state.az.us/publicaccess/.

Criminal Records: Access: Mail, in person, online. Both court and visitors may perform in person searches. Search fee: $17.00 per name. Required to search: name, years to search, DOB; also helpful: address, SSN. Criminal records on docket books. Online access to records is free at www.supreme.state.az.us/publicaccess/.

General Information: No juvenile, mental health, victims, sealed or adoption records released. Will not fax results. Copy fee: $1.25 per page. Cert fee: $17.00. Payee: Williams Justice Court. Only cashiers checks and money orders accepted. Prepayment required. Mail requests: SASE required. Mail turnaround time 2-3 weeks.

Gila County

Superior Court 1400 E Ash, Globe, AZ 85501; 928-425-3231 X8553. Hours: 8AM-5PM (MST). *Felony, Civil Actions Over $5,000, Probate.*
Civil Records: Access: Mail, in person, online. Both court and visitors may perform in person searches. Search fee: $18.00 per name per year. Required to search: name, years to search; also helpful: address. Civil cases indexed by defendant, plaintiff. Civil records indexed on computer from 1982. On microfiche from 1913 to 1982. Some records on docket books and index cards. Online access to records is at www.supreme.state.az.us/publicaccess/.
Criminal Records: Access: Mail, in person, online. Both court and visitors may perform in person searches. Search fee: $18.00 per name. Required to search: name, years to search, DOB; also helpful: address, SSN. Criminal records on computer from 1913. Online access to records is free at www.supreme.state.az.us/publicaccess/.
General Information: Public Access terminal is available. No juvenile prior to June 1996, mental health, victims, sealed or adoption records released. Will not fax results. Copy fee: $.50 per page. Cert fee: $18.00. Payee: Clerk of Superior Court. Personal checks accepted. Prepayment required. Mail requests: SASE required. Mail turnaround: 10 days to 2 weeks.

Globe Regional Justice Court Globe/Miami Magistrate Court, 1400 E Ash, Globe, AZ 85501; 928-425-3231 x8545; Fax: 928-425-4773. Hours: 8AM-5PM (MST). *Misdemeanor, Civil Actions Under $10,000, Eviction, Small Claims.*
Note: This courts holds the records for the justice courts formally located in Miami and Hayden/Winkelman.
Civil Records: Access: Mail, fax, in person, online. Only the court performs in person searches; visitors may not. Search fee: $17.00 per name. Required to search: name, years to search. Civil cases indexed by defendant, plaintiff. Civil records on computer from 1995. Some records on dockets. Will retain criminal and civil for 5 years. Online access to records is free at www.supreme.state.az.us/publicaccess/.
Criminal Records: Access: Mail, fax, in person, online. Only the court performs in person searches; visitors may not. Search fee: $17.00 per name. Required to search: name, years to search; also helpful: SSN, DOB, signed release. Criminal records on computer from 1995. Some records on dockets. Will retain criminal and civil for 5 years. Online access to records is free at www.supreme.state.az.us/publicaccess/.
General Information: No juvenile, mental health, victims, sealed or adoption records released. Will fax results to local or toll free line. Copy fee: $.50 per page. Cert fee: $17.00. Payee: Globe Justice Court. Business checks accepted. Prepayment required. Mail requests: SASE required. Mail turnaround: 2-4 days.

Payson Justice Court 714 S Beeline Hwy #103, Payson, AZ 85541; 928-474-5267; Fax: 928-474-6214. 8AM-5PM (MST). *Misdemeanor, Civil Actions Under $10,000, Eviction, Small Claims.*
Note: This court holds the records for the Pine Justice Court which is closed.
Civil Records: Access: Fax, mail, in person, online. Only the court performs in person searches; visitors may not. Search fee: $17.00 per name. Required to search: name, years to search; also helpful: address. Civil cases indexed by party names; defendant and

---

plaintiff. Civil records on computer since 1992. Records on dockets. Will retain criminal and civil for 5 years. Online access to records is free at www.supreme.state.az.us/publicaccess/.
Criminal Records: Access: Phone, fax, mail, in person, online. Only the court performs in person searches; visitors may not. Search fee: $17.00 per name. Required to search: name, years to search, DOB; also helpful: address, SSN. Criminal records on computer since 1992. Records on dockets. Will retain criminal and civil for 5 years. Online access to records is free at www.supreme.state.az.us/publicaccess/.
General Information: No juvenile, mental health, victims, sealed or adoption records released. Copy fee: $.50 per page. Cert fee: $17.00. Payee: Payson Justice Court. No personal checks accepted. Prepayment required. Mail requests: SASE required. Mail turnaround time 10 days.

Winkleman Justice Court 1400 E Ash St, c/o Globe Regional Justice Court, Globe, AZ 85501-1414. *Misdemeanor, Civil Actions Under $10,000, Eviction, Small Claims.*
Note: Now part of the Globe Regional Justice Court.

Graham County

Superior Court 800 Main St, Safford, AZ 85546-3803; 928-428-3100; Fax: 928-428-0061. Hours: 8AM-5PM (MST). *Felony, Civil Actions Over $5,000, Probate.*
Civil Records: Access: Fax, mail, in person, online. Both court and visitors may perform in person searches. Search fee: $18.00 per name. Required to search: name, years to search. Civil cases indexed by defendant, plaintiff. Civil records on dockets. Online access to records is free at www.supreme.state.az.us/publicaccess/.
Criminal Records: Access: Phone, fax, mail, in person, online. Both court and visitors may perform in person searches. Search fee: $18.00 per name per year. Required to search: name, years to search. Criminal records on dockets. Online access to records is free at www.supreme.state.az.us/publicaccess/.
General Information: Public Access terminal is available. No mental health, victims, sealed or adoption records released. Will fax results for $5.00. Copy fee: $.50 per page. Cert fee: $18.00. Payee: Clerk of Superior Court. Personal checks accepted. Prepayment required. Mail requests: SASE required. Mail turnaround time 3 days minimum.

Justice Court Precinct #1 800 W Main St, Safford, AZ 85546; 928-428-1210; Fax: 928-428-3523. Hours: 8AM-5PM (MST). *Misdemeanor, Civil Actions Under $10,000, Eviction.*
Civil Records: Access: Mail, in person, online. Both court and visitors may perform in person searches. Search fee: $17.00 per name. Required to search: name, years to search; also helpful: address. Civil cases indexed by case number. Civil records on computer from 1995, on dockets prior. Online access to records is free at www.supreme.state.az.us/publicaccess/.
Criminal Records: Access: Mail, in person, online. Both court and visitors may perform in person searches. Search fee: $17.00 per name. Required to search: name, years to search, DOB; also helpful: address, SSN. Criminal records on computer from 1995, on dockets prior. Online access to records is free at www.supreme.state.az.us/publicaccess/.
General Information: No juvenile, mental health, victims, sealed or adoption records released. Will fax results to local or toll free line. Copy fee: $.50 per page. Cert fee: $17.00. Payee: Safford Justice Court. Only cashiers checks and money orders accepted. Prepayment required. Mail requests: SASE required. Mail turnaround time 2 days.

Pima Justice Court Precinct #2 PO Box 1159, 136 W Center St, Pima, AZ 85543; 928-485-2771; Fax: 928-485-9961. Hours: 8AM-5PM (MST). *Misdemeanor, Civil Actions Under $10,000, Eviction, Small Claims.*
www.supreme.state.az.us
Civil Records: Access: Fax, mail, in person, online. Both court and visitors may perform in person searches. Search fee: $17.00 per name. Required to search: name, years to search; also helpful: address, docket number. Civil cases indexed by defendant. Civil records on dockets back to 1985; on computer back to 1995. Retained for 5 years. Online access to records is at www.supreme.state.az.us/publicaccess/.
Criminal Records: Access: Fax, mail, in person, online. Both court and visitors may perform in person searches. Search fee: $17.00 per name. Required to search: name, years to search, DOB; also helpful: address, SSN, docket number. Criminal records on dockets back to 1985; on computer back to 1995. Retained for 5 years. Online access to records is free at www.supreme.state.az.us/publicaccess/.
General Information: No juvenile, mental health, victims, sealed or adoption records released. Will fax results $17.00 per doc. Copy fee: $.50. Cert fee: $17.00. Payee: Graham Justice Court. Only cashiers checks and money orders accepted. Prepayment required. Mail requests: SASE required. Mail turnaround time 2 weeks.

Greenlee County

Superior Court PO Box 1027, Clifton, AZ 85533; 928-865-4242; Fax: 928-865-5358. Hours: 8AM-5PM (MST). *Felony, Civil Actions Over $5,000, Probate.*
Civil Records: Access: Mail, in person, online. Both court and visitors may perform in person searches. Search fee: $18.00 per name per year. Required to search: name, years to search. Civil cases indexed by defendant, plaintiff. Civil records in docket books from 1911; on computer from 12/97. Online access to records is at www.supreme.state.az.us/publicaccess/.
Criminal Records: Access: Mail, in person, online. Both court and visitors may perform in person searches. Search fee: $18.00 per name per year. Required to search: name, years to search. Criminal records on computer since 12/97; on books from 1911. Online access to records is free at www.supreme.state.az.us/publicaccess/.
General Information: No adoptions released. Will fax results to local or toll free line. Copy fee: $.50 per page. Cert fee: $18.00. Payee: Clerk of Superior Court. Personal checks accepted. Prepayment required. Mail requests: SASE required. Mail turnaround time 7 days.

Justice Court Precinct #1 PO Box 517, Clifton, AZ 85533; 928-865-4312; Fax: 928-865-5644. Hours: 9AM-5PM (MST). *Misdemeanor, Civil Actions Under $10,000, Eviction, Small Claims.*
Civil Records: Access: Mail, in person, online. Only the court performs in person searches; visitors may not. Search fee: $17.00 per name. Required to search: name, years to search. Civil cases indexed by defendant, plaintiff. Civil records in docket books. Online access to records is free at www.supreme.state.az.us/publicaccess/.
Criminal Records: Access: Mail, in person, online. Only the court performs in person searches; visitors may not. Search fee: $17.00 per name. Required to search: name, years to search; also helpful: DOB, SSN. Criminal records in docket books. Online access to records is free at www.supreme.state.az.us/publicaccess/.
General Information: No juvenile, sealed, victims, mental health or adoption records released. No copy fee. Cert fee: $17.00. Payee: Justice of the Peace.

Only cashiers checks and money orders accepted. Prepayment required. Mail requests: SASE not required. Mail turnaround time 1 week.

Justice Court Precinct #2 PO Box 208, Duncan, AZ 85534; 928-359-2536; Fax: 928-359-1936. Hours: 9AM-5PM (MST). *Misdemeanor, Civil Actions Under $10,000, Eviction, Small Claims.*
Civil Records: Access: Mail, in person, online. Both court and visitors may perform in person searches. Search fee: $17.00 per name. Required to search: name, years to search. Civil cases indexed by defendant, plaintiff. Civil records on computer since 1996. Documents retained for 5 years. Online access to records is free at www.supreme.state.az.us/publicaccess/.
Criminal Records: Access: Mail, in person, online. Both court and visitors may perform in person searches. Search fee: $17.00 per name. Required to search: name, years to search. Criminal Records computerized since 1996. Online access to records is free at www.supreme.state.az.us/publicaccess/.
General Information: Public Access terminal is available. No juvenile, victims, sealed, mental health or adoption records released. Will fax results for no fee. Copy fee: $.50 per page. Cert fee: $17.00. Payee: Justice Court. Personal checks not accepted. Prepayment required. Mail turnaround time 2 days.

La Paz County

Superior Court 1316 Kofa Ave, #607, Parker, AZ 85344; 928-669-6131; Fax: 928-669-2186. Hours: 8AM-5PM (MST). *Felony, Civil Actions Over $5,000, Probate.*
www.co.la-paz.az.us/courts.htm
Civil Records: Access: Mail, in person, online. Both court and visitors may perform in person searches. Search fee: $18.00 per name per year. Required to search: name, years to search; also helpful: address. Civil cases indexed by defendant, plaintiff. Civil records computerized since 1996, to 1983 on docket books. For records prior to 1983, check with Yuma County Superior Court. Online access to records is free at www.supreme.state.az.us/publicaccess/.
Criminal Records: Access: Mail, in person, online. Both court and visitors may perform in person searches. Search fee: $18.00 per name per year. Required to search: name, years to search; also helpful: address, DOB, SSN. Criminal records computerized since 1993, to 1983 on docket books. For records prior to 1983, check with Yuma County Superior Court. Online access to records is free at www.supreme.state.az.us/publicaccess/.
General Information: No dependency or adoption records released. Copy fee: $.50 per page. Cert fee: $18.00. Payee: Clerk of Superior Court. Business checks accepted. Prepayment required. Mail requests: SASE required. Mail turnaround time 2-3 days.

Parker Justice Court 1105 Arizona Ave, Parker, AZ 85344; 928-669-2504; Fax: 928-669-2915. Hours: 8AM-5PM (MST). *Misdemeanor, Civil Actions Under $10,000, Eviction, Small Claims.*
Civil Records: Access: Mail, in person, online. Only the court performs in person searches; visitors may not. Search fee: $17.00. Required to search: name, years to search; also helpful: address. Civil cases indexed by defendant. Civil records on dockets back to 1800s, computerized since 1996. Online access to records is at www.supreme.state.az.us/publicaccess/.
Criminal Records: Access: Mail, in person, online. Only the court performs in person searches; visitors may not. Search fee: $17.00. Required to search: name, years to search, DOB; also helpful: address, SSN. Criminal records on dockets back to 1800s, computerized since 1996. Online access to records is free at www.supreme.state.az.us/publicaccess/.

General Information: No juvenile, mental health, victims or sealed records released. Copy fee: $.50 per page. Cert fee: $17.00. Payee: Clerk of Justice Court. Only cashiers checks and money orders accepted. Prepayment required. Mail requests: SASE required. Mail turnaround time 2-3 weeks.

Quartzsite Justice Court PO Box 580, Quartzsite, AZ 85346; 928-927-6313; Fax: 928-927-4842. Hours: 8AM-5PM (MST). *Misdemeanor, Civil Actions Under $10,000, Eviction, Small Claims.*
Civil Records: Access: Fax, mail, in person, online. Both court and visitors may perform in person searches. Search fee: $17.00 per name/year. Required to search: name, years to search. Civil cases indexed by defendant, plaintiff. Civil records computerized since 07/96. Files retained for 5 yrs after final disposition. Online access to records is free at www.supreme.state.az.us/publicaccess/.
Criminal Records: Access: Fax, mail, in person, online. Both court and visitors may perform in person searches. Search fee: $17.00 per name. Required to search: name, years to search, date of offense; also helpful: DOB, SSN, offense. Criminal records computerized since 07/96. Files retained for 5 yrs after final disposition. Online access to records is free at www.supreme.state.az.us/publicaccess/.
General Information: No juvenile, mental health, victims, sealed or adoption records released. Copy fee: $.50 per page. Cert fee: $17.00. Payee: Quartsite Justice Court. Only cashiers checks and money orders accepted. Prepayment required. Mail requests: SASE required. Mail turnaround time within 3 weeks.

Salome Justice Court PO Box 661, Salome, AZ 85348; 928-859-3871; Fax: 928-859-3709. Hours: 8AM-5PM (MST). *Misdemeanor, Civil Actions Under $10,000, Eviction, Small Claims.*
Civil Records: Access: Mail, in person, online. Only the court performs in person searches; visitors may not. Search fee: $17.00. Required to search: name, years to search; also helpful: address. Civil cases indexed by defendant. Civil records on dockets from mid-1960s. Records destroyed after 5 years. Computerized back to 1996. Online access to records is free at www.supreme.state.az.us/publicaccess/.
Criminal Records: Access: Mail, in person, online. Only the court performs in person searches; visitors may not. Search fee: $17.00. Required to search: name, years to search, DOB; also helpful: address, SSN. Criminal records on dockets from mid-1960s. Records destroyed after 5 years. Computerized back to 1996. Online access to records is free at www.supreme.state.az.us/publicaccess/.
General Information: No juvenile, mental health, victims, sealed or adoption records released. Copy fee: $.50 per page. Cert fee: $17.00. Payee: Salome Justice Court. Only cashiers checks and money orders accepted. Prepayment required. Mail requests: SASE not required. Mail turnaround time 2-3 days.

Maricopa County

Superior Court 601 W. Jackson St., Phoenix, AZ 85003; 602-506-3360; Fax: 602-506-7619. Hours: 8AM-5PM (MST). *Felony, Civil Actions Over $5,000, Probate.*
www.superiorcourt.maricopa.gov
Civil Records: Access: Fax, mail, online, in person. Both court and visitors may perform in person searches. Search fee: $18.00 per name. Required to search: name, years to search. Civil cases indexed by defendant, plaintiff. Civil records on computer from 7/87, on microfiche from 1969 to present. Some records on docket books. Access to civil case dockets at www.superiorcourt.maricopa.gov/docket/index.asp. Case file can be printed. Also, access to probate court dockets is at www.superiorcourt.maricopa.gov/docket/probate/inde

x.asp. Family court filings are at www.superiorcourt.maricopa.gov/docket/family/index.asp.
Criminal Records: Access: Fax, mail, online, in person. Both court and visitors may perform in person searches. Search fee: $18.00 per name. Required to search: name, years to search; also helpful: DOB. Criminal records on computer from 7/87, on microfiche from 1969 to present. Some records on docket books. Access to criminal case dockets is at www.superiorcourt.maricopa.gov/docket/criminal/index.asp.
General Information: Public Access terminal is available. No mental health, victims, sealed or adoption records released. Will fax results $18.50 1st page, $.50 each add'l. Copy fee: $.50 per page. Cert fee: $18.00. Payee: Clerk of Superior Court. Personal checks accepted. Prepayment required. Mail requests: SASE not required. Mail turnaround time 2 weeks.

Buckeye Justice Court 100 N Apache Rd, Buckeye, AZ 85326; 623-386-4289; Fax: 623-386-5796. Hours: 8AM-5PM (MST). *Misdemeanor, Civil Actions Under $10,000, Eviction, Small Claims.*
www.superiorcourt.maricopa.gov/justiceCourts
Civil Records: Access: Mail, in person. Only the court performs in person searches; visitors may not. Search fee: $17.00 per name. Required to search: name, years to search. Civil cases indexed by defendant, plaintiff. Civil records on dockets by number, computerized since 1990.
Criminal Records: Access: Mail, in person. Only the court performs in person searches; visitors may not. Search fee: $17.00 per name. Required to search: name, years to search, DOB. Criminal records on dockets by number, computerized since 1990.
General Information: No juvenile, mental health, victims, sealed or adoption records released. Will fax results to local or toll free line. Copy fee: $.50 per page. Cert fee: $17.00. Payee: Buckeye Justice Court. Personal checks accepted. Visa, MC accepted. Prepayment required. Mail requests: SASE required. Mail turnaround time 1-2 weeks.

Central Phoenix Justice Court 1 W Madison St, Phoenix, AZ 85003; 602-254-1488; Fax: 602-254-1496. Hours: 8AM-5PM (MST). *Misdemeanor, Civil Actions Under $10,000, Eviction, Small Claims.*
www.superiorcourt.maricopa.gov/justiceCourts
Civil Records: Access: Phone, fax, mail, in person. Visitors must perform in person searches for themselves. Search fee: $17.00 per name. Required to search: name, years to search. Civil cases indexed by defendant, plaintiff. Civil records on computer since 1985.
Criminal Records: Access: Mail, fax, in person. Visitors must perform in person searches for themselves. Search fee: $17.00 per name. Required to search: name, years to search, DOB, SSN. Criminal records on computer since 1985.
General Information: Public Access terminal is available. (Allows public access to electronic Justice Courts countywide.) No sealed records released. Will fax results to local or toll-free number if 3 pages or less. Copy fee: $.50 per page. Cert fee: $17.00. Payee: Central Phoenix Justice Court. Personal checks accepted with DL. Visa, MC accepted. Visa, MC. Prepayment required. Mail requests: SASE required. Mail turnaround time 1-2 weeks.

Chandler Justice Court 2051 W Warner Rd, #20, Chandler, AZ 85224; 480-963-6691. Hours: 8AM-5PM (MST). *Misdemeanor, Civil Actions Under $10,000, Eviction, Small Claims.*
www.superiorcourt.maricopa.gov/justiceCourts
Civil Records: Access: Mail, in person. Only the court performs in person searches; visitors may not.

Search fee: $17.00 per name. Required to search: name, years to search; also helpful: address. Civil records on dockets by number; records go back 5 years; on computer back to 1991.

Criminal Records: Access: Mail, in person. Only the court performs in person searches; visitors may not. Search fee: $17.00 per name. Required to search: name, years to search, DOB; also helpful: address, SSN. Criminal records on dockets by number; records on computer go back to 1991.

General Information: No juvenile, mental health, victims, sealed or adoption records released. Copy fee: $.50 per page. Cert fee: $17.00. Payee: Clerk of Justice Court. Personal checks accepted. Visa, MC accepted. Prepayment required. Mail requests: SASE required. Mail turnaround time 1-2 weeks.

East Mesa Justice Court 4811 E Julep #128, Mesa, AZ 85205; 480-985-0188; Fax: 480-396-6327. Hours: 8AM-5PM (MST). *Misdemeanor, Civil Actions Under $10,000, Eviction, Small Claims.* www.superiorcourt.maricopa.gov/justiceCourts
Civil Records: Access: Mail, in person. Only the court performs in person searches; visitors may not. Search fee: $17.00 per name. Required to search: name, years to search; also helpful: address. Civil cases indexed by defendant, plaintiff. Civil records on computer since 1990. Prior records in docket books by number.

Criminal Records: Access: Mail, in person. Only the court performs in person searches; visitors may not. Search fee: $17.00 per name. Required to search: name, years to search, DOB; also helpful: address, SSN. Criminal records on computer since 1990. Prior records in docket books by number.

General Information: No juvenile, mental health, victims, sealed or adoption records released. Copy fee: $.50 per page. Cert fee: $17.00. Payee: East Mesa Justice Court. Personal checks accepted. Visa, MC accepted. Prepayment required. Mail requests: SASE required. Mail turnaround time 1-2 weeks.

East Phoenix Justice Court #1 1 W Madison St #1, Phoenix, AZ 85003; 602-254-1599; Fax: 602-254-1603. Hours: 8AM-5PM (MST). *Misdemeanor, Civil Actions Under $10,000, Eviction, Small Claims.* www.superiorcourt.maricopa.gov/justiceCourts
Civil Records: Access: Phone, mail, in person. Visitors must perform in person searches for themselves. No search fee. Required to search: name, years to search. Civil cases indexed by defendant, plaintiff. Civil records on dockets by number; computerized records since 1990's.

Criminal Records: Access: Phone, mail, in person. Visitors must perform in person searches for themselves. No search fee. Required to search: name, years to search, DOB. Criminal records on dockets by number; computerized records since 1990's.

General Information: Public Access terminal is available. (Allows public access to electronic Justice Courts countywide.) No mental health, victims or sealed records released. Copy fee: $.50 per page. Cert fee: $17.00. Payee: East Phoenix #1 Justice Court. Personal checks accepted. Visa, MC accepted. Credit cards only if paid in person. Prepayment required. Mail requests: SASE required. Mail turnaround time 1-2 weeks.

East Phoenix Justice Court #2 4109 N 12th St, Phoenix, AZ 85014; 602-266-3741; Fax: 602-277-9442. Hours: 8AM-5PM (MST). *Misdemeanor, Civil Actions Under $10,000, Eviction, Small Claims.* www.superiorcourt.maricopa.gov/justiceCourts
Civil Records: Access: Mail, in person. Both court and visitors may perform in person searches. Search fee: $17.00 per name. Required to search: name, years

to search. Civil cases indexed by defendant, plaintiff. Civil records on computer since 1981.
Criminal Records: Access: Mail, in person. Both court and visitors may perform in person searches. Search fee: $17.00 per name. Required to search: name, years to search, DOB. Criminal records computerized since 1991.
General Information: No juvenile, mental health, victims, sealed or adoption records released. Copy fee: $.50 per page. Cert fee: $17.00. Payee: East Phoenix #2 Justice Court. Personal checks accepted. Visa, MC accepted. Prepayment required. Mail requests: SASE required. Mail turnaround time immediate.

East Tempe Justice Court 1845 E Broadway #8, Tempe, AZ 85282; 480-967-8856; Fax: 480-921-7413. Hours: 8AM-5PM (MST). *Misdemeanor, Civil Actions Under $10,000, Eviction, Small Claims.* www.superiorcourt.maricopa.gov/justiceCourts
Civil Records: Access: Mail, in person. Only the court performs in person searches; visitors may not. No search fee. Required to search: name, years to search. Civil cases indexed by defendant, plaintiff. Civil records on computer by case number. This court charges no search fee, but for bulk name searches this court refers you to the central Office of Administration.
Criminal Records: Access: Mail, in person. Only the court performs in person searches; visitors may not. No search fee. Required to search: name, years to search, DOB. Criminal records on computer by case number. This court charges no search fee, but for bulk name searches this court refers you to the central Office of Administration.
General Information: No juvenile, mental health, victims, sealed records released. Copy fee: $.50 per page. Cert fee: $17.00. Payee: Tempe Justice Court. Personal checks accepted. Visa, MC accepted. Prepayment required. Mail requests: SASE required.

Gila Bend Justice Court PO Box 648 (209 E. Pima St), Gila Bend, AZ 85337; 928-683-2651; Fax: 928-683-6412. Hours: 8AM-5PM (MST). *Misdemeanor, Civil Actions Under $10,000, Eviction, Small Claims.* www.superiorcourt.maricopa.gov/justiceCourts
Civil Records: Access: Mail, in person. Only the court performs in person searches; visitors may not. Search fee: $17.00 per name. Required to search: name, years to search. Civil cases indexed by defendant, plaintiff. Civil records on computer since 1987. Public access terminal only in main Phoenix court.
Criminal Records: Access: Mail, in person. Only the court performs in person searches; visitors may not. Search fee: $17.00 per name. Required to search: name, years to search; also helpful: DOB. Criminal records on computer since 1987. Public access terminal only in main Phoenix court.
General Information: No juvenile, mental health, victims, sealed or adoption records released. Copy fee: $.50 per page. Certification fee is included in search fee. Payee: Gila Bend Justice Court. Personal checks accepted. Visa, MC accepted. Prepayment required. Mail requests: SASE required. Mail turnaround time 1-2 weeks.

Glendale Justice Court 5222 W Glendale, Glendale, AZ 85301; 623-939-9477; Fax: 623-842-2260. Hours: 8AM-5PM (MST). *Misdemeanor, Civil Actions Under $10,000, Eviction, Small Claims.* www.superiorcourt.maricopa.gov/justiceCourts
Civil Records: Access: Mail, in person. Only the court performs in person searches; visitors may not. Search fee: $17.00 per name. Required to search: name, years to search. Civil records on dockets by case number, computerized since 1993. Public access

for all searches at Justice Court Admin, 1 W Madison St, Phoenix in person only.
Criminal Records: Access: Mail, in person. Only the court performs in person searches; visitors may not. Search fee: $17.00 per name. Required to search: name, years to search, DOB; also helpful: SSN. Criminal records on dockets by case number, computerized since 1992. Public access for all searches at Justice Court Admin, 1 W Madison, Phoenix in person only.
General Information: No juvenile, mental health, victims, sealed or adoption records released. Copy fee: $.50 per page. Cert fee: $17.00. Payee: Glendale Justice Court. Personal checks accepted. Visa, MC accepted. Prepayment required. Mail requests: SASE required. Mail turnaround time 1-2 weeks.

Maryvale Justice Court 4622 W Indian School Rd Bldg D, Phoenix, AZ 85031; 623-245-0432; Fax: 623-245-1216. Hours: 8AM-5PM (MST). *Misdemeanor, Civil Actions Under $10,000, Eviction, Small Claims.* www.superiorcourt.maricopa.gov/justiceCourts
Civil Records: Access: Mail, in person. Only the court performs in person searches; visitors may not. Search fee: $17.00 per name. Required to search: name, years to search, address. Civil records on dockets by number.
Criminal Records: Access: Mail, in person. Only the court performs in person searches; visitors may not. Search fee: $17.00 per name. Required to search: name, years to search, address, DOB; also helpful: SSN, aliases. Criminal records on dockets by number.
General Information: No juvenile, mental health, victims, sealed or adoption records released. Copy fee: $.50 per page. Cert fee: $17.00. Payee: Maryvale Justice Court. Personal checks accepted. Visa, MC accepted. Prepayment required. Mail requests: SASE required. Mail turnaround time 2-4 weeks.

North Mesa Justice Court 1837 S Mesa Dr #A-201, Mesa, AZ 85210; 480-926-9731; Fax: 480-926-7763. Hours: 8AM-5PM (MST). *Misdemeanor, Civil Actions Under $10,000, Eviction, Small Claims.* www.superiorcourt.maricopa.gov/justiceCourts
Civil Records: Access: Fax, mail, in person. Only the court performs in person searches; visitors may not. Search fee: $17.00 per name, limit 3 names. Required to search: name, years to search. Civil cases indexed by defendant, plaintiff. Civil records on computer by case number. Public access terminal only in main Phoenix court.
Criminal Records: Access: Fax, mail, in person. Only the court performs in person searches; visitors may not. Search fee: $17.00 per name, limit 3 names. Required to search: name, years to search, offense; also helpful: DOB. Criminal records on computer by case number. Public access terminal only in main Phoenix court.
General Information: No juvenile, mental health, victims or sealed records released. No fee to fax results. Copy fee: $.50 per page. Cert fee: $17.00. Payee: North Mesa Justice Court. Personal checks accepted. Visa, MC accepted. Prepayment required. Mail requests: SASE required. Mail turnaround time 1-2 weeks.

North Valley Justice Court 5222 W Glendale, Glendale, AZ 85301; 623-915-2877; Fax: 623-463-0670. Hours: 8AM-5PM (MST). *Misdemeanor, Civil Actions Under $10,000, Eviction, Small Claims.* www.superiorcourt.maricopa.gov/justiceCourts
Civil Records: Access: Mail, in person. Only the court performs in person searches; visitors may not. Search fee: $17.00 per name. Required to search: name, years to search. Civil records on dockets by

case number; on computer back to 1999. Public access for all searches at Justice Court Admin, 1 W Madison St, Phoenix in person only.

Criminal Records: Access: Mail, in person. Only the court performs in person searches; visitors may not. Search fee: $17.00 per name. Required to search: name, years to search, DOB; also helpful: SSN. Criminal records on dockets by case number; on computer back to 1999. Public access for all searches at Justice Court Admin, 1 W Madison, Phoenix in person only.

General Information: No juvenile, mental health, victims, sealed or adoption records released. Copy fee: $.50 per page. Cert fee: $17.00. Payee: North Valley Justice Court. Personal checks accepted. Visa, MC accepted. Prepayment required. Mail requests: SASE required. Mail turnaround time 1-2 weeks.

Northeast Phoenix Justice Court 10255 N
32nd St, Phoenix, AZ 85028; 602-494-0620; Fax: 602-953-2315. Hours: 8AM-5PM (MST). *Misdemeanor, Civil Actions Under $10,000, Eviction, Small Claims.*
www.superiorcourt.maricopa.gov/justiceCourts

Civil Records: Access: Mail, in person. Only the court performs in person searches; visitors may not. Search fee: $17.00 per name; no fee if records are on-site. Required to search: name, years to search; also helpful: address. Civil cases indexed by defendant, plaintiff. Civil records on computer since 1993. Records on dockets by name and case number.

Criminal Records: Access: Phone, mail, in person. Only the court performs in person searches; visitors may not. Search fee: $17.00 per name; no fee if records are on-site. Required to search: name, years to search, DOB; also helpful: address, SSN. Criminal records on dockets by name and case number.

General Information: No juvenile, mental health, victims, sealed or adoption records released. Copy fee: $.50 per page. Cert fee: $17.00. Payee: Clerk of Justice Court-Northeast. Visa, MC accepted. Personal checks accepted for civil filings; for traffic-cashier's check or MO only. Prepayment required. Mail requests: SASE required. Mail turnaround time 1-2 weeks.

Northwest Phoenix Justice Court 8230 E
Butherus Drive, Scottsdale, AZ 85260; 602-395-0293; Fax: 602-678-4508. Hours: 8AM-5PM (MST). *Misdemeanor, Civil Actions Under $10,000, Eviction, Small Claims.*
www.superiorcourt.maricopa.gov/justiceCourts/
Note: This court is co-located with the Scottsdale Justice Court.

Civil Records: Access: Mail, in person. Only the court performs in person searches; visitors may not. Search fee: $17.00 per name. Required to search: name, years to search. Civil cases indexed by defendant, plaintiff. Civil records on dockets. Will retain criminal and civil for 5 years; computerized records since 1987.

Criminal Records: Access: Mail, in person. Only the court performs in person searches; visitors may not. Search fee: $17.00 per name. Required to search: name, years to search. Criminal records on dockets. Will retain criminal and civil for 5 years; computerized records since 1987.

General Information: Copy fee: $.50 per page. Cert fee: $17.00. Payee: Northwest Phoenix Justice Court. Personal checks accepted. Visa, MC accepted. Prepayment required. Mail requests: SASE required. Mail turnaround time 1 week.

Peoria Justice Court 11601 N 19th Ave,
Phoenix, AZ 85029; 602-395-0294. Hours: 8AM-5PM (MST). *Misdemeanor, Civil Actions Under $10,000, Eviction, Small Claims.*
www.superiorcourt.maricopa.gov/justiceCourts

Civil Records: Access: Phone, fax, mail, in person. Only the court performs in person searches; visitors may not. Search fee: $17.00 per name. Required to search: name, years to search. Civil cases indexed by defendant, plaintiff. Civil records on computer by case number.

Criminal Records: Access: Phone, fax, mail, in person. Only the court performs in person searches; visitors may not. Search fee: $17.00 per name. Required to search: name, years to search; also helpful: DOB. Criminal records on computer by case number.

General Information: No juvenile, mental health, victims, sealed or adoption records released. Will fax results for $1.25 per page, but only to local area codes. Copy fee: $.50 per page. Cert fee: $17.00. Payee: Peoria Justice Court. Personal checks accepted. Visa, MC accepted. Prepayment required. Mail requests: SASE required. Mail turnaround time 1-2 weeks.

Scottsdale Justice Court 8230 E Butherus
Dr, Scottsdale, AZ 85260; 480-443-6600; Fax: 480-443-5981. 8AM-5PM (MST). *Misdemeanor, Civil Actions Under $10,000, Eviction, Small Claims.*
www.superiorcourt.maricopa.gov/justiceCourts

Civil Records: Access: Phone, mail, in person. Only the court performs in person searches; visitors may not. Search fee: $17.00 per name. Required to search: name, years to search. Civil cases indexed by defendant, plaintiff. Civil records on computer since 1985. Records kept for 5 years on closed cases.

Criminal Records: Access: Phone, mail, in person. Only the court performs in person searches; visitors may not. Search fee: $17.00 per name. Required to search: name, years to search. Criminal records on computer since 1985. Records kept for 5 years on closed cases.

General Information: No juvenile, mental health, victims, sealed or adoption records released. Copy fee: $.50 per page. Cert fee: $17.00. Payee: Scottsdale Justice Court. Personal checks accepted. Visa, MC accepted. Prepayment required. Mail requests: SASE required. Mail turnaround time 2-3 weeks.

South Mesa/Gilbert Justice Court 55 E
Civic Center Dr #102, Gilbert, AZ 85296-3468; 480-926-3051; Fax: 480-545-1638. Hours: 8AM-5PM (MST). *Misdemeanor, Civil Actions Under $10,000, Eviction, Small Claims.*
www.superiorcourt.maricopa.gov/justiceCourts

Civil Records: Access: Mail, in person. Only the court performs in person searches; visitors may not. Search fee: $17.00 per name. Required to search: name, years to search, DOB, SSN, signed release. Civil cases indexed by defendant, plaintiff. Civil records on computer by case number back to 1994. Public access terminal at Justice Court Admin 1 W Madison St, Phoenix, AZ.

Criminal Records: Access: Mail, in person. Only the court performs in person searches; visitors may not. Search fee: $17.00 per name. Required to search: name, years to search, DOB, SSN, signed release. Criminal records on computer by case number; computerized back to 1994. Public access terminal at Justice Court Admin 1 West Madison, Phoenix, AZ.

General Information: No juvenile, mental health, victims, sealed or adoption records released. Copy fee: $.50 per page. Cert fee: $17.00. Payee: South Mesa/Gilbert Justice Court. Only cashiers checks and money orders accepted. Prepayment required. Mail requests: SASE required. Mail turnaround time 1-2 weeks.

South Phoenix Justice Court 217 E
Olympic Dr, Phoenix, AZ 85040; 602-243-0318; Fax: 602-243-6389. Hours: 8AM-5PM (MST). *Misdemeanor, Civil Actions Under $10,000, Eviction, Small Claims.*
www.superiorcourt.maricopa.gov/justiceCourts

Civil Records: Access: In person only. Visitors must perform in person searches for themselves. No search fee. Required to search: name, years to search; also helpful: address. Civil cases indexed by defendant, plaintiff. Civil records on computer since 1990, on dockets by number.

Criminal Records: Access: In person only. Visitors must perform in person searches for themselves. No search fee. Required to search: name, years to search; also helpful: DOB. Criminal records on dockets by number.

General Information: Public Access terminal is available. No juvenile, mental health, victims, sealed or adoption records released. Copy fee: $.50 per page. Cert fee: $17.00. Payee: South Phoenix Justice Court. Personal checks accepted. Visa, MC accepted. Prepayment required.

Tolleson Justice Court 9550 W Van Buren
#6, Tolleson, AZ 85353; 623-936-1449; Fax: 623-936-4859. 8AM-5PM (MST). *Misdemeanor, Civil Actions Under $10,000, Eviction, Small Claims.*
www.superiorcourt.maricopa.gov/justiceCourts

Civil Records: Access: Mail, in person. Only the court performs in person searches; visitors may not. Search fee: $17.00 per name. Required to search: name, years to search; also helpful: address. Civil cases indexed by defendant, plaintiff. Civil records on computer since 1993.

Criminal Records: Access: Mail, in person. Only the court performs in person searches; visitors may not. Search fee: $17.00 per name. Required to search: name, years to search, DOB; also helpful: address, SSN. Criminal records on computer since 1993.

General Information: No juvenile, mental health, victims, sealed or adoption records released. Copy fee: $.50 per page. Cert fee: $17.00. Payee: Tolleson Justice Court. Personal checks accepted. Visa, MC accepted. Prepayment required. Mail requests: SASE required. Mail turnaround time 1-2 weeks.

West Mesa Justice Court 2050 W University
Dr, Mesa, AZ 85201; 480-964-2958; Fax: 480-969-1098. Hours: 8AM-5PM (MST). *Misdemeanor, Civil Actions Under $10,000, Eviction, Small Claims.*
www.superiorcourt.maricopa.gov/justiceCourts

Civil Records: Access: In person, mail. Only the court performs in person searches; visitors may not. Search fee: $17.00 per name. Required to search: name, years to search. Civil cases indexed by defendant, plaintiff. Civil records on computer since 1990 by case number.

Criminal Records: Access: In person, mail. Only the court performs in person searches; visitors may not. Search fee: $17.00 per name. Required to search: name, years to search, DOB; also helpful: SSN. Criminal records on computer since 1990 by case number.

General Information: No juvenile, mental health, victims, sealed or adoption records released. Copy fee: $.50 per page. Cert fee: $17.00. Payee: West Mesa Justice Court. Personal checks accepted. Visa, MC accepted. Prepayment required.

West Phoenix Justice Court 1 W Madison
St, Phoenix, AZ 85003; 602-256-0292; Fax: 602-256-7959. Hours: 8AM-5PM (MST). *Misdemeanor, Civil Actions Under $10,000, Eviction, Small Claims.*
www.superiorcourt.maricopa.gov/justiceCourts

Civil Records: Access: Mail, in person. Both court and visitors may perform in person searches. Search fee: $17.00 per name. Required to search: name, years

to search. Civil cases indexed by defendant, plaintiff. Civil records on computer since 1993.

Criminal Records: Access: In person. Both court and visitors may perform in person searches. Search fee: $17.00 per name. Required to search: name, years to search, DOB. Criminal records on computer by case number.

General Information: Public Access terminal is available. No juvenile, mental health, victims, sealed or adoption records released. Copy fee: $.50 per page. Cert fee: $17.00. Payee: West Phoenix Justice Court. Personal checks accepted. Visa, MC accepted. Prepayment required. Mail requests: SASE required. Mail turnaround time is 1-2 days.

West Tempe Justice Court 8240 S Kyrene Rd # 113, Building A, Tempe, AZ 85284; 480-705-7349; Fax: 480-785-4577. Hours: 8AM-5PM (MST). *Misdemeanor, Civil Actions Under $10,000, Eviction, Small Claims.*
www.superiorcourt.maricopa.gov/justiceCourts

Civil Records: Access: Mail, in person. Only the court performs in person searches; visitors may not. No search fee. Required to search: name, years to search. Civil cases indexed by defendant, plaintiff. Civil records on computer by case number.

Criminal Records: Access: Mail, in person. Only the court performs in person searches; visitors may not. No search fee. Required to search: name, years to search, DOB. Criminal records on computer by case number.

General Information: No juvenile, mental health, victims, sealed records released. Copy fee: $.50 per page. Cert fee: $17.00. Payee: Tempe Justice Court. Personal checks accepted. Visa, MC accepted. Prepayment required. Mail requests: SASE required.

Wickenburg Justice Court 155 N Tegner, #D, Wickenburg, AZ 85390; 602-506-1554; Fax: 928-684-9639. Hours: 8AM-5PM (MST). *Misdemeanor, Civil Actions Under $10,000, Eviction, Small Claims.*
www.superiorcourt.maricopa.gov/justiceCourts/
Town Court telephone number is 928-684-5451.

Civil Records: Access: Mail, in person. Only the court performs in person searches; visitors may not. Search fee: $17.00 per name. Required to search: name, years to search; also helpful: address. Civil cases indexed by defendant, plaintiff. Civil records on computer since 1994.

Criminal Records: Access: Mail, in person. Only the court performs in person searches; visitors may not. Search fee: $17.00 per name. Required to search: name, years to search, DOB; also helpful: SSN. Criminal records on computer by name and case number.

General Information: No juvenile, mental health, victims, sealed records released. Copy fee: $.50 per page. Cert fee: $17.00. Payee: Wickenburg Justice Court. Personal checks accepted. Visa, MC accepted. Prepayment required. Mail requests: SASE required. Mail turnaround time 1-2 weeks.

Mohave County

Superior Court PO Box 7000, Kingman, AZ 86402-7000; 928-753-0713; Fax: 928-753-0781. Hours: 8AM-5PM (MST). *Felony, Civil Actions Over $5,000, Probate.*
www.mohavecourts.com

Civil Records: Access: Phone, fax, mail, in person. Both court and visitors may perform in person searches. Search fee: $18.00 per name. Fee is per source. Required to search: name, years to search. Civil cases indexed by defendant, plaintiff. Civil records on computer since 11/95; prior records on microfiche and index books.

Criminal Records: Access: Phone, fax, mail, in person. Both court and visitors may perform in person searches. Search fee: $18.00 per name per yr. Required to search: name, years to search; also helpful: DOB, SSN. Criminal records on computer since 11/95; prior records on microfiche and index books.

General Information: Public Access terminal is available. No juvenile, mental health, victims, sealed or adoption records released. Will fax results for $18.00. Copy fee: $.50 per page. Cert fee: $18.00. Payee: Clerk of Superior Court. Business checks accepted. Prepayment required. Mail requests: SASE required. Mail turnaround time 3 days.

Bullhead City Justice Court 2225 Trane Rd, Bullhead City, AZ 86442; 928-758-0709 x2015; Fax: 928-753-7840. Hours: 8AM-5PM (MST). *Misdemeanor, Civil Actions Under $10,000, Eviction, Small Claims.*
www.mohavecourts.com

Civil Records: Access: Phone, mail, in person. Only the court performs in person searches; visitors may not. No search fee. Required to search: name, years to search. Civil cases indexed by defendant, plaintiff. Civil records on computer from 1988. Some records on docket books. Records retained for 5 years. Will only search back to 1988 unless w/docket number.

Criminal Records: Access: Mail, in person. Only the court performs in person searches; visitors may not. Search fee: $17.00 per name. Required to search: name, years to search; also helpful: DOB, SSN. Criminal records on computer from 1988. Some records on docket books. Records retained for 5 years. Will only search back to 1988 unless w/docket number.

General Information: No juvenile, mental health, victims, sealed or adoption records released. Copy fee: $.50 per page. Cert fee: $17.00. Payee: Bullhead City Justice Court. Personal checks accepted. Prepayment required. Mail requests: SASE requested. Turnaround time 2-3 days.

Kingman/Cerbat Justice Court 524 W Beale St, PO Box 29, Kingman, AZ 86401-0029; 928-753-0710; Fax: 928-753-7840. Hours: 8AM-5PM (MST). *Misdemeanor, Civil Actions Under $10,000, Eviction, Small Claims.*

Civil Records: Access: Phone, fax, mail, in person. Only the court performs in person searches; visitors may not. Search fee: $17.00 per name. Required to search: name, years to search. Civil cases indexed by defendant, plaintiff. Civil records on computer from 1988. Some records on docket books. Records retained for 5 years.

Criminal Records: Access: Phone, fax, mail, in person. Only the court performs in person searches; visitors may not. Search fee: $17.00 per name. Required to search: name, years to search; also helpful: DOB, SSN. Criminal records on computer from 1988. Some records on docket books. Records retained for 5 years.

General Information: No juvenile, mental health, victims, sealed or adoption records released. Will fax results $.50 per page. Copy fee: $.50 per page. Cert fee: $17.00. Payee: Kingman/Cerbat Justice Court. Personal checks accepted. Visa, MC accepted. Prepayment required. Mail requests: SASE required. Mail turnaround time 2-3 days.

Lake Havasu Consolidated Court 2001 College Dr #148, Lake Havasu City, AZ 86403; 928-453-0705; Fax: 928-680-0193. Hours: 8AM-5PM (MST). *Misdemeanor, Civil Actions Under $10,000, Eviction, Small Claims.*

Civil Records: Access: Mail, fax, in person. Only the court performs in person searches; visitors may not. Search fee: $17.00 per name. Required to search:

name, years to search. Civil cases indexed by defendant, plaintiff. Civil records on computer from 1988. Some records on docket books. Records retained for 5 years after closed/satisfied.

Criminal Records: Access: Fax, mail, in person. Only the court performs in person searches; visitors may not. Search fee: $17.00 per name. Required to search: name, years to search; also helpful: DOB. Criminal records on computer from 1988. Some records on docket books. Records retained for 5 years after closed/satisfied.

General Information: No juvenile or victims records released. Will fax non-certified results. Copy fee: $.50 per page. Cert fee: $17.00. Payee: Lake Havasu Consoldiated Court. Personal checks accepted. Prepayment required. Mail requests: SASE required. Mail turnaround time 2-3 days.

Moccasin Justice Court HC-65 PO Box 90, Moccasin, AZ 86022; 928-643-7104; Fax: 928-643-6206. Hours: 8AM-5PM (MST). *Misdemeanor, Civil Actions Under $10,000, Eviction, Small Claims.*
Note: This court is also the Magistrate Court for Colorado City.

Civil Records: Access: Mail, in person. Only the court performs in person searches; visitors may not. Search fee: $17.00 per name. Required to search: name, years to search. Civil cases indexed by defendant, plaintiff. Civil records on docket books. Records retained for 5 years.

Criminal Records: Access: Mail, in person. Only the court performs in person searches; visitors may not. Search fee: $17.00 per name. Required to search: name, years to search. Criminal records on docket books. Records retained for 5 years.

General Information: No juvenile, mental health, victims, sealed or adoption records released. Copy fee: $.50 per page. Cert fee: $17.00. Payee: Moccasin Justice Court. Personal checks accepted. Prepayment required. Mail requests: SASE required. Mail turnaround time 7-14 days.

Navajo County

Superior Court PO Box 668, Holbrook, AZ 86025; 928-524-4188; Fax: 928-524-4261. Hours: 8AM-5PM (MST). *Felony, Civil Actions Over $5,000, Probate.*

Civil Records: Access: Phone, fax, mail, in person, online. Both court and visitors may perform in person searches. Search fee: $18.00 per document. Required to search: name, years to search. Civil cases indexed by defendant, plaintiff. Civil records on docket books, index cards and microfiche back to 1890; computerized back to 1994. Online access to records is free at www.supreme.state.az.us/publicaccess/.

Criminal Records: Access: Phone, fax, mail, in person, online. Both court and visitors may perform in person searches. Search fee: $18.00 per document. Required to search: name, years to search; also helpful: DOB, SSN. Criminal records on docket books, index cards and microfiche back to 1890; computerized back to 1994. Online access to records is free at www.supreme.state.az.us/publicaccess/.

General Information: Public Access terminal is available. No juvenile, mental health, victims, sealed or adoption records released. Fee to fax results is $18.00. Copy fee: $.50 per page. Cert fee: $18.00. Payee: Clerk of Superior Court. Only cashiers checks and money orders accepted. Prepayment required. Mail requests: SASE required. Mail turnaround time 3 days.

Holbrook Justice Court PO Box 366, Holbrook, AZ 86025; 928-524-4720; Fax: 928-524-4725. Hours: 8AM-5PM (MST). *Misdemeanor, Civil Actions Under $10,000, Eviction, Small Claims.*
www.supreme.state.az.us

Civil Records: Access: Mail, in person, online. Both the court and visitors may perform in person searches. Search fee: $19.00 per name. Required to search: name, years to search. Civil cases indexed by defendant, plaintiff. Civil records on computer since 1994. Records on dockets and index cards back for 5 years. Online access to records is free at www.supreme.state.az.us/publicaccess/.

Criminal Records: Access: Mail, in person, online. Both the court and visitors may perform in person searches. Search fee: $19.00 per name. Required to search: name, years to search. Criminal records on computer since 1992. Records on dockets and stat books back for 5 years. Online access to records is free at www.supreme.state.az.us/publicaccess/.

General Information: Public Access terminal is available. No victim names or sealed records released. Copy fee: $.50 per page. Cert fee: $19.00. Payee: Holbrook Justice Court. Business checks accepted. Prepayment required. Mail requests: SASE required. Mail turnaround time 1 week.

Kayenta Justice Court PO Box 38, Kayenta, AZ 86033; 928-697-3522; Fax: 928-697-3528. Hours: 8AM-Noon,1-5PM (MST). *Misdemeanor, Civil Actions Under $10,000, Eviction, Small Claims.*
Note: If planning to make an in-person search, call to make an appointment.

Civil Records: Access: Mail, in person, online. Only the court performs in person searches; visitors may not. Search fee: $17.00 per name. Required to search: name, years to search, address. Civil cases indexed by defendant, plaintiff. Civil records on docket books and index cards; on computer back to 1994. Online access to records is free at www.supreme.state.az.us/publicaccess/.

Criminal Records: Access: Mail, in person, online. Only the court performs in person searches; visitors may not. Search fee: $17.00 per name. Required to search: name, years to search, address, DOB, SSN, signed release. Criminal records on docket books and index cards; on computer back to 1994. Online access to records is free at www.supreme.state.az.us/publicaccess/.

General Information: Public Access terminal is available. No victim's names released. Copy fee: $.50 per page. Cert fee: $17.00. Payee: Kayenta Justice Court. Only cashiers checks and money orders accepted. Prepayment required. Mail requests: SASE required. Mail turnaround time 1 week.

Pinetop-Lakeside Justice Court PO Box 2020, (1360 Neils Hansen Dr), Lakeside, AZ 85929; 928-368-6200; Fax: 928-368-8674. Hours: 8AM-5PM (MST). *Misdemeanor, Civil Actions Under $10,000, Eviction, Small Claims.*

Civil Records: Access: Fax, mail, in person, online. Only the court performs in person searches; visitors may not. Search fee: $17.00 per name. Required to search: name, years to search. Civil cases indexed by case number. Civil records on electronic dockets by case number and case files by numeric. Online access to records is free at www.supreme.state.az.us/publicaccess/.

Criminal Records: Access: Fax, mail, in person, online. Only the court performs in person searches; visitors may not. Search fee: $17.00 per name. Required to search: name, years to search. Criminal records on electronic dockets by case number and case files by alpha back to 1970. Computerized back to 1996. Online access to records is free at www.supreme.state.az.us/publicaccess/.

General Information: No victim's names released. No fee to fax results. Copy fee: $.50 per page. Cert fee: $17.00. Payee: Pinetop-Lakeside Justice Court. Personal checks accepted. Prepayment required. Mail requests: SASE requested. Turnaround time 7-10 days.

Show Low Justice Court PO Box 3085, (561 E Duece of Clubs), Show Low, AZ 85902-3085; 928-532-6030; Fax: 928-532-6035. Hours: 8AM-5PM (MST). *Misdemeanor, Civil Actions Under $10,000, Eviction, Small Claims.*

Civil Records: Access: Fax, mail, in person, online. Only the court performs in person searches; visitors may not. Search fee: $17.00 per name. Required to search: name, years to search. Civil cases indexed by defendant, plaintiff. Civil records on computer. Online access to records is free at www.supreme.state.az.us/publicaccess/. In person access requires a written request.

Criminal Records: Access: Fax, mail, in person, online. Only the court performs in person searches; visitors may not. Search fee: $17.00 per name per year. Required to search: name, years to search; also helpful: DOB, SSN. Criminal records on computer for five years. Online access to records is free at www.supreme.state.az.us/publicaccess/. In person access requires a written request.

General Information: No victim's names released. Copy fee: $.50 per page. Cert fee: $17.00. Payee: Show Low Justice Court. Personal checks accepted. Prepayment required. Mail requests: SASE required. Mail turnaround time 1 week.

Snowflake Justice Court 145 S Main St #D, Snowflake, AZ 85937; 928-536-4141; Fax: 928-536-3511. Hours: 8AM-5PM (MST). *Misdemeanor, Civil Actions Under $10,000, Eviction, Small Claims.*

Civil Records: Access: Phone, fax, mail, in person, online. Only the court performs in person searches; visitors may not. Search fee: $17.00 per name. Required to search: name, years to search. Civil cases indexed by defendant, plaintiff. Civil records on computer back to 6/96, prior on docket books and index cards. Misdemeanors, DUI's and traffic records kept for 3 years, others held for 5 years. Online access to records is free at www.supreme.state.az.us/publicaccess/.

Criminal Records: Access: Fax, mail, in person, online. Only the court performs in person searches; visitors may not. Search fee: $17.00 per name. Required to search: name, years to search; also helpful: DOB, SSN. Criminal records on computer back to 6/96, prior on docket books and index cards. Misdemeanors, DUI's and traffic records kept for 3 years, others held for 5 years. Online access to records is free at www.supreme.state.az.us/publicaccess/.

General Information: No victim's names or search warrants released, no juvenile records released. Copy fee: $1.25 per page. Cert fee: $17.00. Payee: Snowflake Justice Court. Only cashiers checks and money orders accepted. Prepayment required. Mail requests: SASE required. Mail turnaround time 2 weeks.

Winslow Justice Court Box 808, Winslow, AZ 86047; 928-289-6840; Fax: 928-289-6847. Hours: 8AM-5PM (MST). *Misdemeanor, Civil Actions Under $10,000, Eviction, Small Claims.*

Civil Records: Access: Fax, mail, in person, online. Only the court performs in person searches; visitors may not. Search fee: $20.00. Required to search: name, years to search. Civil cases indexed by defendant, plaintiff. Civil records on docket books; on computer since 1994. Online access to records is free at www.supreme.state.az.us/publicaccess/.

Criminal Records: Access: Fax, mail, in person, online. Only the court performs in person searches; visitors may not. Search fee: $20.00. Required to search: name, years to search; also helpful: DOB, SSN. Criminal records on docket books; on computer since 1995. Online access to records is free at www.supreme.state.az.us/publicaccess/.

General Information: No victim's names released. Will fax results to local or toll free line. Copy fee:

$.50 per page. Cert fee: $20.00. Payee: Winslow Justice Court. Personal checks accepted. Prepayment required. Mail requests: SASE required. Mail turnaround time 1 week.

Pima County

Superior Court 110 W Congress, Tucson, AZ 85701; 520-740-3240; Fax: 520-798-3531. Hours: 8AM-5PM (MST). *Felony, Civil Actions Over $5,000, Probate.*
www.cosc.co.pima.az.us
Note: Address correspondence to attention of civil or criminal section.

Civil Records: Access: Phone, mail, in person, online. Both court and visitors may perform in person searches. Search fee: $18.00 per name. Required to search: name, years to search, DOB. Civil cases indexed by defendant, plaintiff. Civil records on computer since 1980s, on microfilm since late 1800s. Online access to superior court records is free at www.cosc.co.pima.az.us/record_search/.

Criminal Records: Access: Mail, in person, online. Both court and visitors may perform in person searches. Search fee: $18.00 per name. Add $5.00 for postage and handling. Required to search: name, years to search, DOB. Criminal records on computer since 1980s, on microfilm since late 1800s. Online access to superior court records is free at www.cosc.co.pima.az.us/record_search/. Cases without dispositions are not included online.

General Information: Public Access terminal is available. No juvenile, mental health, adoption, victims or sealed records released. Fee to fax results is $5.00 plus $.50 per page. Copy fee: $.50 per page. Cert fee: $18.00. Payee: Clerk of Superior Court. Only cashiers checks and money orders accepted. Visa, MC accepted. In person only. Prepayment required. Mail requests: SASE not required. Mail turnaround time 14 days; include $5.00 mailing fee.

Ajo Justice Court 111 La Mina, Ajo, AZ 85321; 520-387-7684. Hours: 8AM-5PM (MST). *Misdemeanor, Civil Actions Under $10,000, Eviction, Small Claims.*

Civil Records: Access: Mail, in person, online. Only the court performs in person searches; visitors may not. No search fee. Required to search: name, years to search. Civil cases indexed by defendant, plaintiff. Civil records on computer since 1987, prior in docket books. Online access to records is free at www.supreme.state.az.us/publicaccess/.

Criminal Records: Access: Mail, in person, online, fax. Only the court performs in person searches; visitors may not. Search fee: $17.00 per name. Required to search: name, years to search. Criminal records on computer since 1987, prior in docket books. Online access to records is free at www.supreme.state.az.us/publicaccess/.

General Information: No juvenile, sealed, victim records released. Copy fee: $.50 per page. Cert fee: $17.00. Payee: Ajo Justice Court. Personal checks accepted. Prepayment required. Mail requests: SASE not required. Mail turnaround time 2 weeks.

Green Valley Justice Court 601 N LaCanada, Green Valley, AZ 85614; 520-648-0658; Fax: 520-648-2235. Hours: 8AM-5PM (MST). *Misdemeanor, Civil Actions Under $10,000, Eviction, Small Claims.*

Civil Records: Access: Mail, in person, online. Only the court performs in person searches; visitors may not. Search fee: $17.00 per name. Required to search: name, years to search. Civil cases indexed by defendant, plaintiff. Civil records on computer back to 1996; card files prior. Online access to records is free at www.supreme.state.az.us/publicaccess/. Clerk will only search computerized records.

Criminal Records: Access: Mail, in person, online. Only the court performs in person searches; visitors may not. Search fee: $17.00 per name. Required to search: name, years to search, DOB. Criminal records on computer back to 1996; card files prior. Online access to records is free at www.supreme.state.az.us/publicaccess/. Clerk will only search computerized records.

General Information: No juvenile, mental health, victims, sealed or adoption records released. Copy fee: $.50 per page. Cert fee: $17.00. Payee: Green Valley Justice Court. Personal checks accepted. Prepayment required. Mail requests: SASE required. Mail turnaround time 14 days.

Pima County Consolidated Justice Court

115 N Church Ave, Tucson, AZ 85701; 520-740-3171; Fax: 520-884-0346. Hours: 8AM-4;30PM, M-F, 7;30-12;00 Sat. (MST). *Misdemeanor, Civil Actions Under $10,000, Eviction, Small Claims.*

http://jp.co.pima.az.us

Civil Records: Access: Fax, mail, online, in person. Both court and visitors may perform in person searches. Search fee: $10.00 per name. Required to search: name, years to search. Civil cases indexed by defendant, plaintiff. Civil records on computer since 1988, on docket books prior. Online access is free http://geronimo.jp.co.pima.az.us/casesearch/. You can search docket information for civil, criminal or traffic cases by name, docket or citation number.

Criminal Records: Access: Fax, mail, online, in person. Both court and visitors may perform in person searches. Search fee: $17.00 per name. Required to search: name, years to search, DOB, SSN. Criminal records on computer since 1988, on docket books prior. Online access to criminal records is the same as civil.

General Information: Public Access terminal is available. No information about set-aside judgments, unserved search warrants or felony warrants released. Copy fee: $1.25 per page. Cert fee: $17.00 per page. Payee: Pima County Justice Court. Personal checks accepted. Visa, MC accepted. Visa, MC. Prepayment required. Mail requests: SASE required. Mail turnaround time 10 days.

Pinal County

Superior Court

PO Box 2730, Florence, AZ 85232-2730; 520-866-5300; Fax: 520-866-5320, Hours: 8AM-5PM (MST). *Felony, Civil Actions Over $5,000, Probate.*

www.co.pinal.az.us/clerksc

Civil Records: Access: Phone, mail, in person, online. Both court and visitors may perform in person searches. Search fee: $18.00 per name. Required to search: name, years to search. Civil cases indexed by defendant, plaintiff. Civil records on computer from 1987. Some records on docket books back to 1775. Online access to records is free at www.supreme.state.az.us/publicaccess/.

Criminal Records: Access: Phone, mail, in person, online. Both court and visitors may perform in person searches. Search fee: $18.00 per name. Required to search: name, years to search. Criminal records on computer from 1987. Some records on docket books back to 1775. Online access to records is free at www.supreme.state.az.us/publicaccess/.

General Information: Public Access terminal is available. No victim names, adoption records released. Fee to fax results is $.50 per page. Copy fee: $.50 per page. Cert fee: $18.00. Payee: Clerk of Superior Court. Business checks accepted. Prepayment required. Mail requests: SASE required. Mail turnaround time 2 days.

Apache Junction Justice Court

575 N Idaho, #200, Apache Junction, AZ 85219; 480-982-2921; Fax: 520-866-6153. Hours: 8AM-5PM (MST). *Misdemeanor, Civil Actions Under $10,000, Eviction, Small Claims.*

http://co.pinal.az.us/JusticeCourts/

Note: Yes, the area code for the fax number is different than the voice number.

Civil Records: Access: Fax, mail, in person, online. Both court and visitors may perform in person searches. Search fee: $17.00. Required to search: name, years to search. Civil cases indexed by defendant, plaintiff. Civil records on computer since 1999. Records retained for 5 years. Online access to records is at www.supreme.state.az.us/publicaccess/.

Criminal Records: Access: Fax, mail, in person, online. Only the court performs in person searches; visitors may not. Search fee: $17.00. Required to search: name, years to search. Criminal records on computer since 1993. Records retained for 5 years. Online access to records is free at www.supreme.state.az.us/publicaccess/.

General Information: Will fax results $1.25 per page. Copy fee: $.50 per page. Cert fee: $17.00. Payee: Apache Junction Justice Court. Personal checks accepted. Prepayment required. Mail turnaround time varies.

Casa Grande Justice Court

820 E Cottonwood Lane, Bldg B, Casa Grande, AZ 85222; 520-836-5471; Fax: 520-866-7404. Hours: 8AM-5PM (MST). *Misdemeanor, Civil Actions Under $10,000, Eviction, Small Claims.*

http://co.pinal.az.us/JusticeCourts

Civil Records: Access: Mail, in person, online. Only the court performs in person searches; visitors may not. Search fee: $17.00 per name. Required to search: name, years to search. Civil cases indexed by defendant, plaintiff. Civil records on computer since 1999, index back to 1995. Online access to records is free at www.supreme.state.az.us/publicaccess/.

Criminal Records: Access: Mail, in person, online. Only the court performs in person searches; visitors may not. Search fee: $17.00 per name. Required to search: name, years to search, DOB; also helpful: SSN. Criminal records on computer since 1999, index back to 1995. Online access to records is free at www.supreme.state.az.us/publicaccess/.

General Information: No juvenile, mental health, victims, sealed or adoption records released. Copy fee: $.50. Cert fee: $17.00. Payee: Casa Grande Justice Court. Business checks must be pre-approved. Visa, MC accepted. Prepayment required. Mail requests: SASE required. Mail turnaround time 1 day.

Eloy Justice Court

PO Box 586, Eloy, AZ 85231; 520-466-9221; Fax: 520-466-4473. Hours: 8AM-Noon, 1-5PM (MST). *Misdemeanor, Civil Actions Under $10,000, Eviction, Small Claims.*

http://co.pinal.az.us/JusticeCourts

Civil Records: Access: Mail, in person, online. Only the court performs in person searches; visitors may not. No search fee. Required to search: name, years to search. Civil cases indexed by defendant, plaintiff. Civil records on computer since 8/92. On docket books and index cards from 1981. Online access to records is at www.supreme.state.az.us/publicaccess/.

Criminal Records: Access: Mail, in person, online. Only the court performs in person searches; visitors may not. No search fee. Required to search: name, years to search, DOB. Criminal records on computer since 8/92. On docket books and index cards from 1981. Online access to records is free at www.supreme.state.az.us/publicaccess/.

General Information: No juvenile, mental health, victims, sealed or adoption records released. Copy fee: $.50 per page. Cert fee: $17.00. Payee: Eloy

Justice Court. No personal checks accepted. Prepayment required. Mail requests: SASE required. Mail turnaround time 1-2 weeks.

Florence Justice Court

PO Box 1818, Florence, AZ 85232; 520-866-7194; Fax: 520-866-7190. Hours: 8AM-5PM (MST). *Misdemeanor, Civil Actions Under $10,000, Eviction, Small Claims.*

http://co.pinal.az.us/JusticeCourts

Civil Records: Access: Mail, in person, online. Only the court performs in person searches; visitors may not. Search fee: $17.00 per name. Required to search: name, years to search. Civil cases indexed by defendant, plaintiff. Civil records are on computer since January 1999. Online access to records is free at www.supreme.state.az.us/publicaccess/.

Criminal Records: Access: Mail, in person, online. Only the court performs in person searches; visitors may not. Search fee: $17.00 per name. Required to search: name, years to search. Criminal records are on computer since January 1999. Online access to records is free at www.supreme.state.az.us/publicaccess/.

General Information: No juvenile, mental health, victims, sealed or adoption records released. Copy fee: $.50 per page. Cert fee: $17.00. Payee: Florence Justice Court. Only cashiers checks and money orders accepted. Prepayment required. Mail requests: SASE required. Mail turnaround time 1 week.

Mammoth Justice Court

PO Box 777, Mammoth, AZ 85618; 520-487-2262; Fax: 520-866-7839. Hours: 8AM-5PM (MST). *Misdemeanor, Civil Actions Under $10,000, Eviction, Small Claims.*

http://co.pinal.az.us/JusticeCourts

Civil Records: Access: Mail, fax, in person, online. Both court and visitors may perform in person searches. Search fee: $17.00 per name. Required to search: name, years to search. Civil cases indexed by defendant, plaintiff. Civil records on docket books. Misdemeanor and civil records retained for 7 years; on computer back 5 years. Online access to records is free at www.supreme.state.az.us/publicaccess/.

Criminal Records: Access: Mail, in person, online. Both court and visitors may perform in person searches. Search fee: $17.00 per name. Required to search: name, years to search, DOB. Criminal records on docket books. Misdemeanor and civil records retained for 7 years; on computer back 5 years. Online access to records is free at www.supreme.state.az.us/publicaccess/.

General Information: Public Access terminal is available. No juvenile, mental health, victims, sealed or adoption records released. Will fax results to local or toll free line. Copy fee: $.50 per page. Cert fee: $7.00. Payee: Mammoth Justice Court. Personal checks accepted. Prepayment required. Mail requests: SASE required. Mail turnaround time 2 days.

Maricopa Justice Court

44625 W Garvey Rd, Maricopa, AZ 85239; 520-568-2451; Fax: 520-568-2924. Hours: 8AM-5PM (MST). *Misdemeanor, Civil Actions Under $10,000, Eviction, Small Claims.*

http://co.pinal.az.us/JusticeCourts

Civil Records: Access: Fax, mail, in person, online. Only the court performs in person searches; visitors may not. Search fee: $17.00 per name. Required to search: name, years to search. Civil cases indexed by defendant. Civil records on computer since 1999; on dockets to 1993. Online access to records is free at www.supreme.state.az.us/publicaccess/.

Criminal Records: Access: Fax, mail, in person, online. Only the court performs in person searches; visitors may not. Search fee: $17.00 per name. Required to search: name, years to search. Criminal records on computer since 1999; on dockets to 1993. Online access to records is free at www.supreme.state.az.us/publicaccess/.

General Information: No juvenile, mental health, victims, sealed or adoption records released. Copy fee: $.50 per page. Cert fee: $17.00. Payee: Maricopa Justice Court. Personal checks accepted. Prepayment required. Mail requests: SASE required. Mail turnaround time 7 days.

Oracle Justice Court PO Box 3924, Oracle, AZ 85623; 520-896-9250; Fax: 520-868-7812. Hours: 8AM-5PM (MST). *Misdemeanor, Civil Actions Under $10,000, Eviction, Small Claims.* http://co.pinal.az.us/JusticeCourts

Civil Records: Access: Mail, in person, online. Both court and visitors may perform in person searches. Search fee: $17.00 per name. Required to search: name, years to search; also helpful: address. Civil cases indexed by defendant. Civil records on docket books and computer back to 1991. Online access to records is at www.supreme.state.az.us/publicaccess/.

Criminal Records: Access: Mail, in person, online. Both court and visitors may perform in person searches. Search fee: $17.00 per name. Required to search: name, years to search, DOB; also helpful: address, SSN. Criminal records on docket books and computer back to 1991. Online access to records is free at www.supreme.state.az.us/publicaccess/.

General Information: Public Access terminal is available. No juvenile, mental health, victims, sealed, adoption records released. Fee to fax results is $1.00 per page. Copy fee: $1.50 per page. Cert fee: $17.00. Payee: Oracle Justice Court. Personal checks not accepted; money orders, cashier's checks or cash only. Prepayment required. Mail requests: SASE required. Mail turnaround time is 1 day.

Superior/Kearny Justice Court 60 E Main St, Superior, AZ 85273; 520-689-5871; Fax: 520-689-2369. Hours: 8AM-Noon, 1-5PM (MST). *Misdemeanor, Civil Actions Under $10,000, Eviction, Small Claims.* http://co.pinal.az.us/JusticeCourts

Civil Records: Access: Fax, mail, in person. Only the court performs in person searches; visitors may not. Search fee: $17.00 per name. Required to search: name, years to search. Civil cases indexed by defendant, plaintiff. Civil records go back 5 years; computerized records go back 5 years. Online access to records is free at www.supreme.state.az.us/publicaccess/.

Criminal Records: Access: Fax, mail, in person, online. Only the court performs in person searches; visitors may not. Search fee: $17.00 per name. Required to search: name, years to search, DOB; also helpful: SSN. Criminal records go back 5 years; computerized records go back 5 years. Online access to records is free at www.supreme.state.az.us/publicaccess/.

General Information: No juvenile, mental health, victims, sealed or adoption records released. No fee to fax results. Copy fee: $1.50 per page. Cert fee: $17.00. Payee: Superior/Kearny Justice Court. Personal checks accepted. Prepayment required. Mail requests: SASE required. Mail turnaround time 3 days.

Santa Cruz County

Superior Court PO Box 1265, Nogales, AZ 85628; 520-375-7700; Fax: 520-761-7857. Hours: 8AM-5PM (MST). *Felony, Civil Actions Over $5,000, Probate.* http://sccazcourts.org

Civil Records: Access: Mail, fax, in person, online. Both court and visitors may perform in person searches. Search fee: $18.00 per year/source. Required to search: name, years to search. Civil cases indexed by defendant, plaintiff. Civil records on microfiche from 1898 to 1950. Records on docket books from 1950 to 1996; on computer after 1996.

Online access to records is free at www.supreme.state.az.us/publicaccess/.

Criminal Records: Access: Mail, fax, in person, online. Both court and visitors may perform in person searches. Search fee: $18.00 per year/source. Required to search: name, years to search, DOB; also helpful: SSN. Criminal records archived on microfiche from 1898 to 1989. Records on docket books from 1977 to 1996; on computer after 1996. Online access to records is free at www.supreme.state.az.us/publicaccess/.

General Information: Public Access terminal is available. No mental health, victims, sealed or adoption records released. Fee to fax results is $.50 per page. Copy fee: $.50 per page. Cert fee: $18.00. Payee: Clerk of Superior Court. Personal checks accepted. Prepayment required. Mail requests: SASE required. Mail turnaround time 1 1/2 weeks.

East Santa Cruz County Justice Court - Precinct #2 PO Box 100, Patagonia, AZ 85624; 520-455-5796; Fax: 520-455-5513 (Attn: Justice Court). Hours: 8:30AM-5PM (MST). *Misdemeanor, Civil Actions Under $10,000, Eviction, Small Claims.*

Civil Records: Access: Mail, in person, online. Only the court performs in person searches; visitors may not. Search fee: $17.00 per name. Required to search: name, years to search; also helpful: address. Civil cases indexed by plaintiff. Civil records on docket books. Online access to records is free at www.supreme.state.az.us/publicaccess/.

Criminal Records: Access: Mail, in person, online. Only the court performs in person searches; visitors may not. Search fee: $17.00 per name. Required to search: name, years to search, DOB, SSN, signed release; also helpful: address. Criminal records on docket books. Online access to records is free at www.supreme.state.az.us/publicaccess/.

General Information: No juvenile, mental health, victims, sealed or adoption records released. Will fax results to local or toll free line. Copy fee: $.50 per page. Cert fee: $17.00. Payee: East Santa Cruz County Justice Court. Personal checks accepted. Prepayment required. Mail requests: SASE not required. Mail turnaround time 3-5 days.

Santa Cruz Justice Court PO Box 1150, Nogales, AZ 85628; 520-761-7853; Fax: 520-761-7929. Hours: 8AM-5PM (MST). *Misdemeanor, Civil Actions Under $10,000, Eviction, Small Claims.* www.sccazcourts.org

Civil Records: Access: Fax, mail, in person, online. Both court and visitors may perform in person searches. Search fee: $17.00 per name. Required to search: name, years to search; also helpful: address. Civil cases indexed by defendant, plaintiff. Civil records go back to 1975; on computer back to 2/96. Online access to records is free at www.supreme.state.az.us/publicaccess/. Also, weekly court calendars are at www.sccazcourts.org/court_calendars.htm.

Criminal Records: Access: Fax, mail, in person, online. Both court and visitors may perform in person searches. Search fee: $17.00 per name. Required to search: name, years to search, DOB; also helpful: address, SSN. Criminal records go back to 1975; on computer back to 2/96. Online access to records is free at www.supreme.state.az.us/publicaccess/. Also, weekly court calendars are at www.sccazcourts.org/court_calendars.htm.

General Information: Public Access terminal is available. No juvenile, mental health, victims, sealed or adoption records released. Will fax results. Copy fee: $.50 per page. Cert fee: $17.00. Payee: Santa Cruz Justice Court. Personal checks accepted. Prepayment required. Mail requests: SASE required. Mail turnaround time 1-3 weeks.

Yavapai County

Superior Court Yavapai County Courthouse, Prescott, AZ 86301; 928-771-3312; Fax: 928-771-3111. Hours: 8AM-5PM (MST). *Felony, Civil Actions Over $1,000, Probate.*

Civil Records: Access: Fax, mail, in person, online. Both court and visitors may perform in person searches. Search fee: $18.00 per name. Required to search: name, years to search. Civil cases indexed by defendant, plaintiff. Civil records archived from 1900s. Some records on handwritten index book. Access to Superior Court records is free at www.supreme.state.az.us/publicaccess/.

Criminal Records: Access: Fax, mail, in person, online. Both court and visitors may perform in person searches. Search fee: $18.00 per name per year. Required to search: name, years to search, offense. Criminal records archived from 1900s. Some records on handwritten index book. Free access to Court records at www.supreme.state.az.us/publicaccess/.

General Information: Public Access terminal is available. No juvenile, mental health, victims, sealed or adoption records released. Will fax results $.50 per page. Copy fee: $.50 per page. Cert fee: $18.00. Payee: Clerk of Superior Court. Personal checks accepted. Prepayment required. Mail requests: SASE required. Mail turnaround time 10 days.

Bagdad Justice Court PO Box 243, Bagdad, AZ 86321; 928-633-2141; Fax: 928-633-4451. Hours: 8AM-5PM M; 8:00AM-4:00PM T-Th (MST). (MST). *Misdemeanor, Civil Actions Under $10,000, Eviction, Small Claims.*

Civil Records: Access: Mail, in person, online. Only the court performs in person searches; visitors may not. Search fee: $17.00 per name. Required to search: name, years to search; also helpful: address. Civil records on computer since 3/94. Records on docket books and index cards. Records purged after 10 years. Online access to records is free at www.supreme.state.az.us/publicaccess/.

Criminal Records: Access: Mail, in person, online. Only the court performs in person searches; visitors may not. Search fee: $17.00 per name. Required to search: name, years to search, DOB; also helpful: address, SSN. Criminal records on computer since 3/94. Records on docket books and index cards. Records purged after 5 years. Online access to records is free at www.supreme.state.az.us/publicaccess/.

General Information: No juvenile, mental health, victims, sealed or adoption records released. Will not fax results. Copy fee: $.50 per page. Cert fee: $17.00. Payee: Bagdad Justice Court. Only cashiers checks and money orders accepted. Prepayment required. Mail requests: SASE required. Mail turnaround time 2 days.

Mayer Justice Court PO Box 245, Mayer, AZ 86333; 928-771-3355. Hours: 8AM-5PM (MST). *Misdemeanor, Civil Actions Under $10,000, Eviction, Small Claims.*

Civil Records: Access: Mail, in person, online. Only the court performs in person searches; visitors may not. Search fee: $17.00 per name. Required to search: name, years to search. Civil cases indexed by defendant, plaintiff. Civil records on computer back to 1989. Records purged after 5 years. Online access to records is at www.supreme.state.az.us/publicaccess/.

Criminal Records: Access: Mail, in person, online. Only the court performs in person searches; visitors may not. Search fee: $17.00 per name. Required to search: name, years to search; also helpful: DOB. Criminal records on computer back to 1989. Records purged after 5 years. Online access to records is free at www.supreme.state.az.us/publicaccess/.

General Information: No juvenile, mental health, victims, sealed or adoption records released. Copy fee: $.50 per page. Cert fee: $17.00. Payee: Mayer Justice Court. Only cashiers checks and money orders accepted. Prepayment required. Mail requests: SASE required. Mail turnaround time 4 days.

Prescott Justice Court
Yavapai County Courthouse, 120 S. Cortez, Rm 103, Prescott, AZ 86301; 928-771-3300; Fax: 928-771-3302. Hours: 8AM-5PM (MST). *Misdemeanor, Civil Actions Under $10,000, Eviction, Small Claims.* www.co.yavarai.az.us

Civil Records: Access: Fax, mail, in person. Both court and visitors may perform in person searches. Search fee: $17.00. Required to search: name, years to search; also helpful: address. Civil cases indexed by defendant, plaintiff. Civil records are indexed on computer then purged after 5 years. Searches only for past 5 years.

Criminal Records: Access: Fax, mail, in person. Both court and visitors may perform in person searches. Search fee: $17.00. Required to search: name, years to search, DOB; also helpful: address, SSN. Criminal records are indexed on computer then purged after 5 years. Searches only available for past 5 years.

General Information: Public Access terminal is available. No juvenile, victims or sealed records released. Will fax results $17.00 per doc. Copy fee: $.50 per page. Cert fee: $17.00 per document. Payee: City of Prescott. No two party checks accepted. Visa, MC, AmEX accepted. Prepayment required. Mail requests: SASE required. Mail turnaround: 2 days.

Seligman Justice Court
PO Box 56, Seligman, AZ 86337-0056; 928-422-3281; Fax: 928-422-3282. Hours: 8AM-5PM (MST). *Misdemeanor, Civil Actions Under $10,000, Eviction, Small Claims.*

Civil Records: Access: Phone, fax, mail, in person, online. Both court and visitors may perform in person searches. No search fee. Required to search: name, years to search; also helpful: address. Civil cases indexed by defendant, plaintiff. Civil records on computer. Records purged after 5 years. Online access to records is free at www.supreme.state.az.us/publicaccess/.

Criminal Records: Access: Phone, fax, mail, in person, online. Both court and visitors may perform in person searches. No search fee. Required to search: name, years to search, DOB; also helpful: address, SSN. Criminal records on computer. Records purged after 5 years. Online access to records is free at www.supreme.state.az.us/publicaccess/.

General Information: No juvenile or victims records released. No fee to fax results. Copy fee: $1.25 per page. Cert fee: $17.00. Payee: Seligman Justice Court. Business checks accepted. Prepayment required. Mail requests: SASE required. Mail turnaround time 2 days.

Verde Valley Justice Court
10 S 6th St, Cottonwood, AZ 86326; 928-639-5820; Fax: 928-639-5828. Hours: 8AM-5PM (MST). *Misdemeanor, Civil Actions Under $10,000, Eviction, Small Claims.*

Civil Records: Access: Mail, in person, online. Both court and visitors may perform in person searches. Search fee: $17.00. Required to search: name, years to search; also helpful: address. Civil cases indexed by defendant, plaintiff. Civil records on computer from 6/99. Records purged after 5 years. Online access to records is at www.supreme.state.az.us/publicaccess/.

Criminal Records: Access: Mail, in person, online. Both court and visitors may perform in person searches. Search fee: $17.00. Required to search: name, years to search, DOB; also helpful: address, SSN. Criminal records computerized since 6/99.

Records purged after 5 years. Online access to records is free at www.supreme.state.az.us/publicaccess/.

General Information: No juvenile, mental health, victims, sealed or adoption records released. Copy fee: $.50 per page. Cert fee: $17.00. Payee: Verde Valley Justice Court. Prepayment required. Mail requests: SASE required. Mail turnaround time 2 days.

Yarnell Justice Court
PO Box 65, Justice Court Bldg, Yarnell, AZ 85362; 928-427-3318; Fax: 928-771-3362. Hours: 8AM-5PM (MST). *Misdemeanor, Civil Actions Under $10,000, Eviction, Small Claims.*

Civil Records: Access: Mail, in person, online. Only the court performs in person searches; visitors may not. Search fee: $17.00 per name. Required to search: name, years to search. Civil cases indexed by defendant, plaintiff. Civil records on computer from 1989. Prior records on docket books. Records purged after 10 years. Online access to records is free at www.supreme.state.az.us/publicaccess/.

Criminal Records: Access: Mail, in person, online. Only the court performs in person searches; visitors may not. Search fee: $17.00 per name. Required to search: name, years to search. Criminal records on computer from 1989. prior on docket books. Records purged after 5 years. Online access to records is free at www.supreme.state.az.us/publicaccess/.

General Information: No juvenile, mental health, victims, sealed or adoption records released. Copy fee: $.50 per page. Cert fee: $17.00. Payee: Yarnell Justice Court. Only cashiers checks and money orders accepted. Prepayment required. Mail requests: SASE required. Mail turnaround time 5 days.

Yuma County

Superior Court
168 S 2nd Ave, Yuma, AZ 85364; 928-329-2164; Civil phone: 928-329-2164; Criminal phone: 928-329-2167; Probate phone: 928-329-2163; Fax: 928-329-2007. Hours: 8AM-5PM (MST). *Felony, Civil Actions Over $5,000, Probate.*

Civil Records: Access: Fax, mail, in person, online. Both court and visitors may perform in person searches. Search fee: $18.00 per name. Required to search: name, years to search. Civil cases indexed by defendant or plantiff. Civil records on docket books from 1900s, new and pending cases from November 1994 on computer. Online access to records is free at www.supreme.state.az.us/publicaccess/.

Criminal Records: Access: Fax, mail, in person, online. Both court and visitors may perform in person searches. Search fee: $18.00 per name. Required to search: name, years to search. Criminal records on docket books from 1900s, new and pending cases from November 1994 on computer. Online access to records is at www.supreme.state.az.us/publicaccess/.

General Information: Public Access terminal is available. No adoption, mental health records released. Will fax results $18.00 per doc. Copy fee: $.50 per page. Cert fee: $18.00. Payee: Clerk of Superior Court. Business checks accepted. Visa, MC accepted. Prepayment required. Mail requests: SASE required. Mail turnaround time 1 week.

Somerton Justice Court
PO Box 458, 350 W Main St, Somerton, AZ 85350; 928-627-2722; Fax: 928-627-1076. Hours: 8AM-5PM (MST). *Misdemeanor, Civil Actions Under $10,000, Eviction, Small Claims.* www.somertoncourts.com

Civil Records: Access: Phone, fax, mail, in person, online. Both court and visitors may perform in person searches. No search fee. Required to search: name, years to search. Civil cases indexed by defendant. Civil records on computer. Online access to records is free the website above as well as at www.supreme.state.az.us/publicaccess/.

Criminal Records: Access: Phone, fax, mail, in person, online. Only the court performs in person searches; visitors may not. No search fee. Required to search: name, years to search, DOB, SSN, offense, date of offense. Criminal records on computer. Online access to records is free at the website above as well at www.supreme.state.az.us/publicaccess/.

General Information: No set aside judgment records released. Will fax results $1.25 per page. Copy fee: $1.25 per page. Cert fee: $17.00. Payee: Somerton Justice Court. Business checks accepted. Prepayment required. Mail requests: SASE required. Mail turnaround time 2-4 days.

Wellton Justice Court
PO Box 384, Wellton, AZ 85356; 928-785-3321; Fax: 928-785-4933. Hours: 8AM-5PM (MST). *Misdemeanor, Civil Actions Under $10,000, Eviction, Small Claims.*

Civil Records: Access: Phone, fax, mail, in person, online. Only the court performs in person searches; visitors may not. No search fee. Required to search: name, years to search. Civil cases indexed by defendant, plaintiff. Civil records on computer to 1992. Online access to records is free at www.supreme.state.az.us/publicaccess/.

Criminal Records: Access: Phone, fax, mail, in person, online. Only the court performs in person searches; visitors may not. No search fee. Required to search: name, years to search, offense, date of offense. Criminal records on computer to 1992. Online access to records is free at www.supreme.state.az.us/publicaccess/.

General Information: No set aside judgment records released. Will fax results to local or toll free line. Copy fee: $.50 per page. No cert fee. Payee: Wellton Justice Court. Personal checks accepted. Credit cards accepted: Visa, MC, Discover, AmEx. Prepayment required. Mail requests: SASE not required. Mail turnaround time same day.

Yuma Justice Court
168 S 2nd Ave, Yuma, AZ 85364; 928-329-2180; Fax: 928-329-2005. Hours: 8AM-5PM (MST). *Misdemeanor, Civil Actions Under $10,000, Eviction, Small Claims.*

Civil Records: Access: Mail, in person, online. Both court and visitors may perform in person searches. Search fee: $17.00 per name. Required to search: name, years to search. Civil cases indexed by defendant. Civil records on computer. Purged after 5 years. Info available only for cases after 09/01/97; computerized records since 1997. Online access to records is at www.supreme.state.az.us/publicaccess/.

Criminal Records: Access: Mail, in person, online. Only the court performs in person searches; visitors may not. Search fee: $17.00 per name. Required to search: name, years to search. Criminal records on computer. Purged after 5 years. Info available only for cases after 09/01/97; computerized records since 1997. Online access to records is free at www.supreme.state.az.us/publicaccess/.

General Information: Will not release victim's names. Copy fee: $.50 per page. Cert fee: $17.00. Payee: Justice Court #1. Personal checks accepted. Visa, MC accepted. Prepayment required. Mail requests: SASE required. Mail turnaround time 2-4 days.

Arizona Recording Offices

ORGANIZATION: 15 counties, 16 recording offices. The Navajo Nation is profiled here. The recording officer is County Recorder. Recordings are usually placed in a Grantor/Grantee index. The entire state is in the Mountain Time Zone (MST), and does not change to daylight savings time. Note that no less than four new telephone area codes have added in recent years: 480 and 623 for east and west Phoenix Metro area respectively, 520 for south and southeastern state, 924 for west and north of state.

REAL ESTATE RECORDS: Counties do not perform real estate searches. Copy fees are usually $1.00 per page. Certification fees are usually $3.00 per document.

UCC RECORDS: Financing statements are filed at the state level, except for real estate related collateral, which are filed with the County Recorder. However, prior to 07/2001, consumer goods and farm collateral were filed at the County Recorder and these older records can be searched there. All counties will perform UCC searches. Use search request form UCC-3. Search fees are generally $10.00 per debtor name. Copies usually cost $1.00 per page.

TAX LIEN RECORDS: Federal and state tax liens on personal property of businesses are filed with the Secretary of State. Other federal and state tax liens are filed with the County Recorder. Several counties will do a separate tax lien search.

OTHER LIENS: Executions, judgments, labor.

ONLINE ACCESS: A number of county assessor offices offer online access:. The Secretary of State offers online access to UCC records at www.sosaz.com/scripts/UCC_Search.dll

Apache County

County Recorder, PO Box 425, St. Johns, AZ 85936. **Phone-**County Recorder, R/E & UCC Recording- 928-337-7515; fax-928-337-7676; hours 8AM-5PM www.co.apache.az.us/Recorder/
Will search UCC records. Search per debtor- $10.00. UCC copy- $1.00 per page. UCC search does not include tax liens. Separate federal & state combined tax lien search- $10.00 per debtor. Will not search real estate records. RE record copy- $1.00 per page. Cert fee: $3.00 per doc. Payee: Apache County Recorder. **Online Access to Real Estate, Recording, Deed, Judgment, Lien, records:** Access to the Apache County Recorder is free at www.thecountyrecorder.com/Search.aspx?CountyKey =5. Index goes back to 1985. Also, search the assessor property tax records for free at www.co.mohave.az.us/apache/assessor/assessdatalink.a sp. **Other phones:** Assessor-928-337-7521; Treasurer-928-337-7513; Elections-928-337-7537.

Cochise County

County Recorder, PO Box 184, Bisbee, AZ 85603. **Phone-**County Recorder, R/E & UCC Recording- 520-432-8350; fax-520-432-8368; hours 8AM-5PM www.co.cochise.az.us
Will search UCC records. Search per debtor- $10.00. UCC copy- $1.00 per page. Will not search real estate or tax lien records. RE record copy- $1.00 per page. Cert fee: $3.00 per cert. Payee: Cochise County Recorder. **Online Access to Treasurer Back Tax, Restaurant Inspection records:** Access to the treasurer's back tax list is free at http://209.180.126.252/treasurer/backtax.htm. Also, search the restaurant inspections results at www.co.cochise.az.us/ccwebsite/SelectDistrict.asp.
Other phones: Assessor-520-432-8650; Treasurer-520-432-8400; Elections-520-432-8970; Voter Registration-520-432-8354.

Coconino County

County Recorder, 110 E. Cherry Ave, Flagstaff, AZ 86001. **Phone-**County Recorder, R/E & UCC Recording- 928-779-6585; fax-928-779-6739; hours 8AM-5PM http://co.coconino.az.us/recorder/
Will search UCC records. Search per debtor- $10.00. UCC copy- $1.00 per page. Tax liens included in UCC search if requested with extra $2.00 fee. Also charge $1.00 per finding. Separate federal/state combined tax lien search- $10.00 per debtor. Real estate record owner searches available. $1.00 per page. Cert fee: $3.00 per doc. Payee: Coconino County Recorder. **Online Access to Recording, Grantor/Grantee, Real Estate records:** Access to county iCRIS system is free at http://coco-criswf.infomagic.net/icris/splash.jsp. Registration required. Documents: $1.00 to print; signup and request documents at 800-793-6181. Online records go back to 1983; images back to 3/1999. **Other phones:** Assessor-928-779-6502; Treasurer-928-779-6615; Appraiser/Auditor-928-779-6502; Elections-928-779-6589; Vital Records-602-364-1300.

Gila County

County Recorder, 1400 E. Ash St, Globe, AZ 85501. **Phone-**928-425-3231, R/E Recording- 928-425-3231 x8738, UCC Recording- 928-425-3231 x8738; fax-928-425-9270; 8AM-5PM http://recorder.co.gila.az.us
Will search UCC records. Search per debtor- $18.00. UCC copy- $1.00 per page. Will do a tax lien search. Tax lien search fee- $10.00 per hour. Will search real estate records. RE record copy- $1.00 per page. Cert fee: $3.00 per doc. Payee: Gila County Recorder. **Online Access to Recording, Deed, Lien, Grantor/Grantee records:** Access to the recorder's index are free at http://63.241.138.77/icris/splash.jsp. Search for free, but copies are $1.00 per page. Records go back to 1985, images back to 1998. **Other phones:** Assessor-928-425-3231 x8720; Treasurer-928-425-3231 x8701; Elections-928-425-3231 x8740.

Graham County

County Recorder, 921 Thatcher Blvd., Safford, AZ 85546. **Phone-**County Recorder, R/E & UCC Recording- 928-428-3560; fax-928-348-8625; hours 8AM-5PM www.graham.az.gov
Will search UCC records. Search per debtor- $10.00. UCC copy- $1.00 per finding. Will not search real estate or tax lien records. RE record copy- $1.00 per page. Cert fee: $3.00 per instrument. Payee: Graham County Recorder. **Online Access to Assessor, Property, Most Wanted, Recording, Deed, Divorce, Judgment, Lien records:** Access the assessor database of property and assessments is free at www.co.mohave.az.us/graham/assessor/assessdatalink. asp. Search the most wanted list at www.eaznet.com/~gcso/wanted.htm Also access to recorder records is at www.thecountyrecorder.co m/Search.aspx?CountyKey=1.Index goes back to 1984. **Other phones:** Assessor-928-428-2828; Treasurer-928-428-3440; Elections-928-428-3930.

Greenlee County

County Recorder, PO Box 1625, Clifton, AZ 85533-1625. **Phone-**928-865-2632, UCC Recording- 928-865-2632 or 928-865-1717; fax-928-865-4417; hours 8AM-5PM www.thecountyrecorder.com
Will search UCC records. Search per debtor- $10.00. UCC copy- $1.00 per page. Will not search real estate or tax lien records. Cert fee: $3.00 per doc. Payee: Greenlee County Recorder. **Online Access to Real Estate, Deed, Lien, Judgment, Vital Statistic, Recording records:** Access to County recorder records is free at www.thecountyrecorder.com/Se arch.aspx?CountyKey=2. Index back to 1973. **Other phones:** Assessor-928-865-5302; Treasurer-928-865-3422; Elections-928-865-1717.

La Paz County

County Recorder, 1112 Joshua Ave, #201, Parker, AZ 85344. **Phone-**County Recorder, R/E & UCC Recording- 928-669-6136; fax-928-669-5638; hours 8AM-5PM

Will search UCC records. Search per debtor- $10.00 + per $1.00 per doc. UCC copy- $1.00 per page. Will not search real estate or tax lien records. RE record copy- $1.00 per page. Cert fee: $3.00 per doc. Payee: La Paz County Recorder. **Online Access to Recorder, Deed, Judgment, Lien records:** Access to the county recorder document index only is free at www.thecountyrecorder.com. **Other phones:** Assessor-928-669-6165; Treasurer-928-669-6145; Elections-928-669-6115; Vital Records-928-669-6131 (marriages only).

Maricopa County

County Recorder, 111 S. 3rd Ave #103, Phoenix, AZ 85003. **Phone**-602-506-3535; fax-602-506-3273; hours 8AM-5PM http://recorder.maricopa.gov
Will search UCC records. Search per debtor- $9.00. UCC copy- $1.00 per page. Will search federal tax liens. Tax lien search fee- $10.00. Will not search real estate records. Cert fee: $3.00 per doc. Payee: Maricopa County Recorder. **Online Access to Real Estate, Lien, Property, Assessor records:** Access by direct dial-up or the Internet. Dial-up access requires one-time set-up fee of $300 + $.06 per minute. Dial-up hours are 8am-10pm M-F, 8-5 S-S. Records date back to 1983. For add'l info, contact Linda Kinchloe, 602-506-3637. Also, access to Recorder's database is at http://recorder.maricopa.gov/recdocdata. Records go back to 1983. Also search data back to 2002 for free at the clerk's office. Also search most wanted list at www.mcso.org/submenu.asp?file=mostwanted. The Assessor database is at www.maricopa.gov/assessor. Residential data available. Also, perform tax appeal lookups at SBOE site at www.sboe.state.az.us/cgi-bin/name_lookup.pl. Search inmates at www.mcso.org/submenu.asp?file=MugIndex. **Other phones:** Assessor-602-506-3406.

Mohave County

County Recorder, PO Box 70, Kingman, AZ 86402-0070. **Phone**-County Recorder, R/E & UCC Recording- 928-753-0701; fax-928-753-0727; hours 8AM-5PM www.co.mohave.az.us
Will search UCC records. Search per debtor- $10.00. UCC copy- $1.00 per page. Will not search real estate or tax lien records. RE record copy- $1.00 per page. Cert fee: $3.00 per doc. Payee: Mohave County Recorder. **Online Access to Real Estate, Grantor/Grantee, Lien, Assessor, Most Wanted, Sex Offender records:** the Recorder's System is free at http://icris.co.mohave.az.us/splash.jsp. Registration and password is required. Sheriff's most wanted list is at www.co.mohave.az.us/mcso/wanted.htm. Also, access the Assessor's property database free (no registration) at www.co.mohave.az.us/1moweb/depts_files/assessor.htm. A sales history database is also here. Sex offender list is at www.ctaz.com/~mcso/page19.html. Also, the treasurer's tax sale parcel search is at www.co.mohave.az.us/1moweb/depts_files/treasure_files/taxsale.asp. Also, health inspection ratings for food establishments are at www.co.mohave.az.us/webapts/aptsnew.htm. **Other phones:** Assessor-928-753-0703; Treasurer-928-753-0737; Appraiser/ Auditor-928-753-0703; Elections-928-753-0733; Vital Records-602-364-1300 (Phoenix).

Navajo County

County Recorder, PO Box 668, Holbrook, AZ 86025-0668. **Phone**-928-524-4194; fax-928-524-4308; hours 8AM-5PM www.co.navajo.az.us
Will search UCC records. Search per debtor- $10.00. UCC copy- $1.00 per page. UCC search includes tax liens if requested. Separate federal/state combined tax lien search- $10.00 per debtor. Will not search real estate records. Cert fee: $3.00 per seal.

Payee: Navajo County Recorder. **Online Access to Property, Assessor, Grantor/Grantee, Recording, UCC, Tax Lien, Death, Tax Sale records:** Access to the recorder's database of land information, UCCs, Liens, and Grantor/Grantee indices is free at www.thecountyrecorder.com/Introduction.aspx?CountyKey=4. Documents go back to 1989; images to 1995. Also, access to the property assessor database is free at http://co.navajo.az.us/theCountyRecorder/DataSearch/WebForm1.aspx. Also, search a list of tax sales property at the county website. **Other phones:** Assessor-928-524-4086; Treasurer-928-524-4172.

Navajo Nation

County Recorder, State Rd 264 West, Window Rock, AZ 86515. **Phone**-928-871-7365; fax-928-871-7381; hours 8AM-Noon, 1-5PM www.co.navajo.az.us
Recording is handled by Navajo County. While assessing is performed by Navajo Nation, the Assessor is county assessor located at Navajo County. Will search UCC records. Search per debtor- $.50. UCC copy- $1.00 per page. Will not search real estate or tax lien records. Cert fee: $3.00 per page. Payee: Navajo Nation Business Regulatory Dept. **Online Access to Property, Assessor, Grantor/Grantee, Recording, UCC, Tax Lien, Death, Tax Sale records:** Access to the recorder's database of land information, UCCs, Liens, and Grantor/Grantee indices is free at www.thecountyrecorder.com/Introduction.aspx?CountyKey=4. Documents go back to 1989; images to 1995. Also, access to the property assessor database is free at http://co.navajo.az.us/theCountyRecorder/DataSearch/WebForm1.aspx. Also, a list of tax sales property is via the Navajo County website. **Other phones:** Assessor-928-524-4086; Treasurer-928-524-4172.

Pima County

County Recorder, 115 N. Church Ave, Tucson, AZ 85701. **Phone**-520-740-4350; fax-520-623-1785; hours 8AM-5PM www.recorder.co.pima.az.us
Will search UCC records. Search per debtor- $10.00. UCC copy- $1.00 per page. Tax liens not included in UCC search. Tax lien search fee- $10.00 per debtor. Will not search real estate records. RE record copy- $1.00 per page. Cert fee: $3.00 per doc. Payee: Pima County Recorder. **Online Access to Assessor, Real Estate, Lien, Recording, Deed, Most Wanted, Sex Offender records:** Access to the recorder's Research Records database is free at www.recorder.co.pima.az.us/research.html. Click "Enter Here" and use the word "public" for user name and password. Records go back to 1987. Also, records on the Pima County Tax Assessor database are free at www.asr.co.pima.az.us/apiq/index.html. Also, a name/parcel/property tax lookup may be performed free on the SBOE site at www.sboe.state.az.us/cgi-bin/name_lookup.pl. Also, search the property tax inquiry database at www.to.co.pima.az.us/inquiry.html. Sex offender list- www.pimasheriff.org/sexnot.html. Inmates at- www.pimasheriff.net/inmate/index.html. **Other phones:** Assessor-520-740-8630.

Pinal County

County Recorder, PO Box 848, Florence, AZ 85232-0848. **Phone**-County Recorder, R/E & UCC Recording- 520-866-7100, UCC Recording- 520-866-6179; fax-520-866-7170; hours 8AM-5PM http://co.pinal.az.us
Will search UCC records. Search per debtor- $10.00. UCC copy- $1.00 per page. Will search state tax liens. Tax lien search fee- $10.00 per debtor. Will not search real estate records. Cert fee: $3.00 per doc. Payee: Pinal County Recorder. **Online Access to Grantor/Grantee, Tax Bill, Tax Lien, Tax Sale,**

Assessor records: the county recorder's index is free at http://apps.co.pinal.az.us/Recorder/Search/. Also, access to the county treasurer's database of tax liens, tax bills, and tax sales is available free at http://co.pinal.az.us/treasurer. Click on appropriate "Tax Searches" button. Search the assessor's property tax database at http://apps.co.pinal.az.us/Assessor/Search/. **Other phones:** Assessor-520-866-6361; Treasurer-520-866-6425; Appraiser/ Auditor-520-866-6361; Elections-520-866-6236.

Santa Cruz County

County Recorder, 2150 N. Congress, County Complex, Nogales, AZ 85621. **Phone-**County Recorder, R/E & UCC Recording- 520-375-7990; fax-520-761-7938; hours 8AM-5PM
Will search UCC records. Search per debtor- $10.00. UCC copy- $1.00 per page. Will not search real estate or tax lien records. RE record copy- $1.00 per page. Cert fee: $3.00 per doc + $1.00 per page copy. Payee: Santa Cruz County Recorder. **Online Access to Assessor, Property records:** Access to the County Assessor data is free at www.co.mohave.az.us/santacruz/assessor/assessdatalink.asp. **Other phones:** Assessor-520-375-8030; Treasurer-520-375-7980; Appraiser/ Auditor-520-375-8030; Elections-520-375-7990; Courthouse Main-520-375-7800.

Yavapai County

County Recorder, 1015 Fair St, Rm 228, Prescott, AZ 86305. **Phone**-928-771-3244; fax-928-771-3258; hours 8AM-5PM www.co.yavapai.az.us
A second office is located at 10 S 6th St, Cottonwood AZ 86326, phone 928-639-5807, fax: 928-639-5812. Will search UCC records. Search per debtor- $10.00. UCC copy- $1.00 per page. Separate federal/state combined tax lien search- $10.00 per debtor. Will not perform open-ended real estate records searches. Cert fee: $3.00 per seal. Payee: Yavapai County Recorder. **Online Access to Assessor, Real Estate, Recording, Inmate/Offender records:** Access to the recording office iCRIS database is free at http://icris.co.yavapai.az.us/icris/splash.jsp. Records from 1976 to present; images from 1986 to present. Also, assessor and land records on the County Geographic Information Systems (GIS) database are free at http://mapserver.co.yavapai.az.us/gis/yavgis/. Information also at http://mapserver.co.yavapai.az.us/parcelinfo/map.asp. Also, the board of supervisors tax sale list is at www.co.yavapai.az.us/events/TaxSales/BOS/taxsalelist.htm. Search the county offender/inmate list for free at www.vinelink.com/offender/searchNew.jsp?siteID=3007. **Other phones:** Assessor-520-771-3220; Treasurer-928-771-3233; Elections-928-771-3250; Voter Registration-928-771-3248.

Yuma County

County Recorder, 410 S Maiden Lane, Yuma, AZ 85364-2311. **Phone**-928-373-6020, R/E Recording-928-373-6029, UCC Recording- 928-373-6028; fax-928-373-6024; hours 8AM-5PM
Will search UCC records. Search per debtor- $10.00. UCC copy- $1.00 per page. Will not search real estate or tax lien records. Cert fee: $3.00 per doc. Payee: Yuma County Recorder. **Online Access to Property, Assessor records:** Access county property data at http://itax.co.yuma.az.us:8080/itax/taxSplash.jsp; free registration is required. **Other phones:** Assessor-928-373-6040; Treasurer-928-539-7781; Elections-928-373-1014; Vital Records-928-317-4530.

Arizona County Locator

You will usually be able to find the city name in the City/County Cross Reference below. In that case, it is a simple matter to determine the county from the cross reference. However, only the official US Postal Service city names are included in this index. There are an additional 40,000 place names people use in their addresses. We have included a ZIP/City Cross Reference following the City/County Cross Reference.

If you know the ZIP Code but the city name does not appear in the City/County Cross Reference index, look up the ZIP Code in the ZIP/City Cross Reference, find the city name, then look up the city name in the City/County Cross Reference.

Arizona City/County Cross Reference

AGUILA Maricopa
AJO Pima
ALPINE Apache
AMADO (85645) Pima(90), Santa Cruz(9)
ANTHEM Maricopa
APACHE JUNCTION (85220) Pinal(85), Maricopa(14)
APACHE JUNCTION Pinal
ARIVACA Pima
ARIZONA CITY Pinal
ARLINGTON Maricopa
ASH FORK Yavapai
AVONDALE Maricopa
BAGDAD Yavapai
BAPCHULE Pinal
BELLEMONT Coconino
BENSON (85602) Cochise(93), Pima(6)
BISBEE Cochise
BLACK CANYON CITY Yavapai
BLUE Greenlee
BLUE GAP Navajo
BOUSE La Paz
BOWIE Cochise
BUCKEYE Maricopa
BULLHEAD CITY Mohave
BYLAS Graham
CAMERON Coconino
CAMP VERDE Yavapai
CAREFREE Maricopa
CASA GRANDE Pinal
CASHION Maricopa
CATALINA Pima
CAVE CREEK Maricopa
CENTRAL Graham
CHAMBERS Apache
CHANDLER Maricopa
CHANDLER HEIGHTS Maricopa
CHINLE Apache
CHINO VALLEY Yavapai
CHLORIDE Mohave
CIBICUE Navajo
CIBOLA La Paz
CLARKDALE Yavapai
CLAY SPRINGS Navajo
CLAYPOOL Gila
CLIFTON Greenlee
COCHISE Cochise
COLORADO CITY Mohave
CONCHO Apache
CONGRESS Yavapai
COOLIDGE Pinal
CORNVILLE Yavapai
CORTARO Pima
COTTONWOOD Yavapai
CROWN KING Yavapai
DATELAND Yuma
DENNEHOTSO Apache
DEWEY Yavapai
DOLAN SPRINGS Mohave
DOUGLAS Cochise
DRAGOON Cochise
DUNCAN Greenlee
EAGAR Apache
EDEN Graham
EHRENBERG La Paz
EL MIRAGE Maricopa
ELFRIDA Cochise
ELGIN Santa Cruz
ELOY Pinal

FLAGSTAFF Coconino
FLORENCE Pinal
FOREST LAKES Coconino
FORT APACHE Navajo
FORT DEFIANCE Apache
FORT HUACHUCA Cochise
FORT MCDOWELL Maricopa
FORT MOHAVE Mohave
FORT THOMAS Graham
FOUNTAIN HILLS Maricopa
FREDONIA Coconino
GADSDEN Yuma
GANADO Apache
GILA BEND Maricopa
GILBERT Maricopa
GLENDALE Maricopa
GLOBE Gila
GOLDEN VALLEY Mohave
GOODYEAR Maricopa
GRAND CANYON Coconino
GRAY MOUNTAIN Coconino
GREEN VALLEY Pima
GREER Apache
HACKBERRY Mohave
HAPPY JACK Coconino
HAYDEN Gila
HEBER Navajo
HEREFORD Cochise
HIGLEY Maricopa
HOLBROOK Navajo
HOTEVILLA Navajo
HOUCK Apache
HUACHUCA CITY Cochise
HUALAPAI Mohave
HUMBOLDT Yavapai
INDIAN WELLS Navajo
IRON SPRINGS Yavapai
JEROME Yavapai
JOSEPH CITY Navajo
KAIBITO Coconino
KAYENTA Navajo
KEAMS CANYON Navajo
KEARNY Pinal
KINGMAN Mohave
KIRKLAND Yavapai
KYKOTSMOVI VILLAGE Navajo
LAKE HAVASU CITY Mohave
LAKE MONTEZUMA Yavapai
LAKESIDE Navajo
LAVEEN Maricopa
LEUPP Coconino
LITCHFIELD PARK Maricopa
LITTLEFIELD Mohave
LUKACHUKAI Apache
LUKE AFB Maricopa
LUKEVILLE Pima
LUPTON Apache
MAMMOTH Pinal
MANY FARMS Apache
MARANA (85653) Pima(84), Pinal(15)
MARBLE CANYON Coconino
MARICOPA Pinal
MAYER Yavapai
MC NARY Apache
MC NEAL Cochise
MEADVIEW Mohave
MESA (85212) Maricopa(92), Pinal(7)
MESA Maricopa
MIAMI Gila

MOHAVE VALLEY Mohave
MORENCI Greenlee
MORMON LAKE Coconino
MORRISTOWN Maricopa
MOUNT LEMMON Pima
MUNDS PARK Coconino
NACO Cochise
NAZLINI Apache
NEW RIVER Maricopa
NOGALES Santa Cruz
NORTH RIM Coconino
NUTRIOSO Apache
OATMAN Mohave
ORACLE Pinal
OVERGAARD Navajo
PAGE Coconino
PALO VERDE Maricopa
PARADISE VALLEY Maricopa
PARKER La Paz
PARKS Coconino
PATAGONIA Santa Cruz
PAULDEN Yavapai
PAYSON Gila
PEACH SPRINGS Mohave
PEARCE Cochise
PEORIA Maricopa
PERIDOT Gila
PETRIFIED FOREST NATL PK Apache
PHOENIX Maricopa
PICACHO Pinal
PIMA Graham
PINE Gila
PINEDALE Navajo
PINETOP Navajo
PINON Navajo
PIRTLEVILLE Cochise
POLACCA Navajo
POMERENE Cochise
POSTON La Paz
PRESCOTT Yavapai
PRESCOTT VALLEY Yavapai
QUARTZSITE La Paz
QUEEN CREEK (85242) Maricopa(61), Pinal(38)
RED ROCK Pinal
RED VALLEY Apache
RILLITO Pima
RIMROCK Yavapai
RIO RICO Santa Cruz
RIO VERDE Maricopa
ROCK POINT Apache
ROLL Yuma
ROOSEVELT Gila
ROUND ROCK Apache
SACATON Pinal
SAFFORD Graham
SAHUARITA Pima
SAINT DAVID Cochise
SAINT JOHNS Apache
SAINT MICHAELS Apache
SALOME La Paz
SAN CARLOS Gila
SAN LUIS Yuma
SAN MANUEL Pinal
SAN SIMON Cochise
SANDERS Apache
SASABE Pima
SAWMILL Apache
SCOTTSDALE Maricopa

SECOND MESA Navajo
SEDONA (86336) Yavapai(67), Coconino(32)
SEDONA Coconino
SEDONA Yavapai
SELIGMAN Yavapai
SELLS Pima
SHONTO Navajo
SHOW LOW Navajo
SIERRA VISTA Cochise
SKULL VALLEY Yavapai
SNOWFLAKE Navajo
SOLOMON Graham
SOMERTON Yuma
SONOITA (85637) Santa Cruz(82), Pima(17)
SPRINGERVILLE Apache
STANFIELD Pinal
SUN CITY Maricopa
SUN CITY WEST Maricopa
SUN VALLEY Navajo
SUPAI Coconino
SUPERIOR Pinal
SURPRISE Maricopa
TACNA Yuma
TAYLOR Navajo
TEEC NOS POS Apache
TEMPE Maricopa
TEMPLE BAR MARINA Mohave
THATCHER Graham
TOLLESON Maricopa
TOMBSTONE Cochise
TONALEA Coconino
TONOPAH Maricopa
TONTO BASIN Gila
TOPAWA Pima
TOPOCK Mohave
TORTILLA FLAT Maricopa
TSAILE Apache
TUBA CITY Coconino
TUBAC Santa Cruz
TUCSON (85739) Pima(57), Pinal(42)
TUCSON Pima
TUMACACORI Santa Cruz
VAIL Pima
VALENTINE Mohave
VALLEY FARMS Pinal
VERNON Apache
WADDELL Maricopa
WELLTON Yuma
WENDEN La Paz
WHITE MOUNTAIN LAKE Navajo
WHITERIVER Navajo
WICKENBURG Maricopa
WIKIEUP Mohave
WILLCOX (85643) Cochise(98), Graham(1)
WILLCOX Cochise
WILLIAMS Coconino
WILLOW BEACH Mohave
WINDOW ROCK Apache
WINKELMAN (85292) Pinal(54), Gila(45)
WINSLOW Navajo
WITTMANN Maricopa
WOODRUFF Navajo
YARNELL Yavapai
YOUNG Gila
YOUNGTOWN Maricopa
YUCCA Mohave
YUMA Yuma

Arizona ZIP/City Cross Reference

85000-85086 PHOENIX	85352-85352 TACNA	85640-85640 TUMACACORI	86321-86321 BAGDAD
85086-85086 ANTHEM	85353-85353 TOLLESON	85641-85641 VAIL	86322-86322 CAMP VERDE
85087-85087 NEW RIVER	85354-85354 TONOPAH	85643-85644 WILLCOX	86323-86323 CHINO VALLEY
85098-85099 PHOENIX	85355-85355 WADDELL	85645-85645 AMADO	86324-86324 CLARKDALE
85201-85216 MESA	85356-85356 WELLTON	85646-85646 TUBAC	86325-86325 CORNVILLE
85217-85220 APACHE JUNCTION	85357-85357 WENDEN	85648-85648 RIO RICO	86326-86326 COTTONWOOD
85221-85221 BAPCHULE	85358-85358 WICKENBURG	85650-85650 SIERRA VISTA	86327-86327 DEWEY
85222-85222 CASA GRANDE	85359-85359 QUARTZSITE	85652-85652 CORTARO	86329-86329 HUMBOLDT
85223-85223 ARIZONA CITY	85360-85360 WIKIEUP	85653-85653 MARANA	86330-86330 IRON SPRINGS
85224-85226 CHANDLER	85361-85361 WITTMANN	85654-85654 RILLITO	86331-86331 JEROME
85227-85227 CHANDLER HEIGHTS	85362-85362 YARNELL	85655-85655 DOUGLAS	86332-86332 KIRKLAND
85228-85228 COOLIDGE	85363-85363 YOUNGTOWN	85662-85662 NOGALES	86333-86333 MAYER
85230-85230 CASA GRANDE	85364-85369 YUMA	85670-85670 FORT HUACHUCA	86334-86334 PAULDEN
85231-85231 ELOY	85371-85371 POSTON	85671-85671 SIERRA VISTA	86335-86335 RIMROCK
85232-85232 FLORENCE	85372-85373 SUN CITY	85700-85737 TUCSON	86336-86336 SEDONA
85233-85234 GILBERT	85374-85374 SURPRISE	85738-85738 CATALINA	86337-86337 SELIGMAN
85235-85235 HAYDEN	85375-85376 SUN CITY WEST	85739-85777 TUCSON	86338-86338 SKULL VALLEY
85236-85236 HIGLEY	85377-85377 CAREFREE	85901-85902 SHOW LOW	86339-86341 SEDONA
85237-85237 KEARNY	85378-85379 SURPRISE	85911-85911 CIBICUE	86342-86342 LAKE MONTEZUMA
85239-85239 MARICOPA	85380-85385 PEORIA	85912-85912 WHITE MOUNTAIN LAKE	86343-86343 CROWN KING
85240-85240 MESA	85387-85387 SURPRISE	85920-85920 ALPINE	86351-86351 SEDONA
85241-85241 PICACHO	85390-85390 WICKENBURG	85922-85922 BLUE	86401-86402 KINGMAN
85242-85242 QUEEN CREEK	85501-85502 GLOBE	85923-85923 CLAY SPRINGS	86403-86406 LAKE HAVASU CITY
85244-85244 CHANDLER	85530-85530 BYLAS	85924-85924 CONCHO	86411-86411 HACKBERRY
85245-85245 RED ROCK	85531-85531 CENTRAL	85925-85925 EAGAR	86412-86412 HUALAPAI
85246-85246 CHANDLER	85532-85532 CLAYPOOL	85926-85926 FORT APACHE	86413-86413 GOLDEN VALLEY
85247-85247 SACATON	85533-85533 CLIFTON	85927-85927 GREER	86426-86427 FORT MOHAVE
85248-85249 CHANDLER	85534-85534 DUNCAN	85928-85928 HEBER	86429-86430 BULLHEAD CITY
85250-85252 SCOTTSDALE	85535-85535 EDEN	85929-85929 LAKESIDE	86431-86431 CHLORIDE
85253-85253 PARADISE VALLEY	85536-85536 FORT THOMAS	85930-85930 MC NARY	86432-86432 LITTLEFIELD
85254-85262 SCOTTSDALE	85539-85539 MIAMI	85931-85931 FOREST LAKES	86433-86433 OATMAN
85263-85263 RIO VERDE	85540-85540 MORENCI	85932-85932 NUTRIOSO	86434-86434 PEACH SPRINGS
85264-85264 FORT MCDOWELL	85541-85541 PAYSON	85933-85933 OVERGAARD	86435-86435 SUPAI
85266-85267 SCOTTSDALE	85542-85542 PERIDOT	85934-85934 PINEDALE	86436-86436 TOPOCK
85268-85269 FOUNTAIN HILLS	85543-85543 PIMA	85935-85935 PINETOP	86437-86437 VALENTINE
85271-85271 SCOTTSDALE	85544-85544 PINE	85936-85936 SAINT JOHNS	86438-86438 YUCCA
85272-85272 STANFIELD	85545-85545 ROOSEVELT	85937-85937 SNOWFLAKE	86439-86439 BULLHEAD CITY
85273-85273 SUPERIOR	85546-85546 SAFFORD	85938-85938 SPRINGERVILLE	86440-86440 MOHAVE VALLEY
85274-85277 MESA	85547-85547 PAYSON	85939-85939 TAYLOR	86441-86441 DOLAN SPRINGS
85278-85278 APACHE JUNCTION	85548-85548 SAFFORD	85940-85940 VERNON	86442-86442 BULLHEAD CITY
85279-85279 FLORENCE	85550-85550 SAN CARLOS	85941-85941 WHITERIVER	86443-86443 TEMPLE BAR MARINA
85280-85289 TEMPE	85551-85551 SOLOMON	85942-85942 WOODRUFF	86444-86444 MEADVIEW
85290-85290 TORTILLA FLAT	85552-85552 THATCHER	86001-86011 FLAGSTAFF	86445-86445 WILLOW BEACH
85291-85291 VALLEY FARMS	85553-85553 TONTO BASIN	86015-86015 BELLEMONT	86446-86446 MOHAVE VALLEY
85292-85292 WINKELMAN	85554-85554 YOUNG	86016-86016 GRAY MOUNTAIN	86502-86502 CHAMBERS
85296-85299 GILBERT	85601-85601 ARIVACA	86017-86017 MUNDS PARK	86503-86503 CHINLE
85301-85308 GLENDALE	85602-85602 BENSON	86018-86018 PARKS	86504-86504 FORT DEFIANCE
85309-85309 LUKE AFB	85603-85603 BISBEE	86020-86020 CAMERON	86505-86505 GANADO
85310-85318 GLENDALE	85605-85605 BOWIE	86021-86021 COLORADO CITY	86506-86506 HOUCK
85320-85320 AGUILA	85606-85606 COCHISE	86022-86022 FREDONIA	86507-86507 LUKACHUKAI
85321-85321 AJO	85607-85608 DOUGLAS	86023-86023 GRAND CANYON	86508-86508 LUPTON
85322-85322 ARLINGTON	85609-85609 DRAGOON	86024-86024 HAPPY JACK	86509-86509 CHAMBERS
85323-85323 AVONDALE	85610-85610 ELFRIDA	86025-86025 HOLBROOK	86510-86510 PINON
85324-85324 BLACK CANYON CITY	85611-85611 ELGIN	86028-86028 PETRIFIED FOREST NATL PK	86511-86511 SAINT MICHAELS
85325-85325 BOUSE	85613-85613 FORT HUACHUCA		86512-86512 SANDERS
85326-85326 BUCKEYE	85614-85614 GREEN VALLEY	86029-86029 SUN VALLEY	86514-86514 TEEC NOS POS
85327-85327 CAVE CREEK	85615-85615 HEREFORD	86030-86030 HOTEVILLA	86515-86515 WINDOW ROCK
85328-85328 CIBOLA	85616-85616 HUACHUCA CITY	86031-86031 INDIAN WELLS	86520-86520 BLUE GAP
85329-85329 CASHION	85617-85617 MC NEAL	86032-86032 JOSEPH CITY	86535-86535 DENNEHOTSO
85331-85331 CAVE CREEK	85618-85618 MAMMOTH	86033-86033 KAYENTA	86538-86538 MANY FARMS
85332-85332 CONGRESS	85619-85619 MOUNT LEMMON	86034-86034 KEAMS CANYON	86540-86540 NAZLINI
85333-85333 DATELAND	85620-85620 NACO	86035-86035 LEUPP	86544-86544 RED VALLEY
85334-85334 EHRENBERG	85621-85621 NOGALES	86036-86036 MARBLE CANYON	86545-86545 ROCK POINT
85335-85335 EL MIRAGE	85622-85622 GREEN VALLEY	86038-86038 MORMON LAKE	86547-86547 ROUND ROCK
85336-85336 GADSDEN	85623-85623 ORACLE	86039-86039 KYKOTSMOVI VILLAGE	86549-86549 SAWMILL
85337-85337 GILA BEND	85624-85624 PATAGONIA	86040-86040 PAGE	86556-86556 TSAILE
85338-85338 GOODYEAR	85625-85625 PEARCE	86042-86042 POLACCA	
85339-85339 LAVEEN	85626-85626 PIRTLEVILLE	86043-86043 SECOND MESA	
85340-85340 LITCHFIELD PARK	85627-85627 POMERENE	86044-86044 TONALEA	
85341-85341 LUKEVILLE	85628-85628 NOGALES	86045-86045 TUBA CITY	
85342-85342 MORRISTOWN	85629-85629 SAHUARITA	86046-86046 WILLIAMS	
85343-85343 PALO VERDE	85630-85630 SAINT DAVID	86047-86047 WINSLOW	
85344-85344 PARKER	85631-85631 SAN MANUEL	86052-86052 NORTH RIM	
85345-85345 PEORIA	85632-85632 SAN SIMON	86053-86053 KAIBITO	
85346-85346 QUARTZSITE	85633-85633 SASABE	86054-86054 SHONTO	
85347-85347 ROLL	85634-85634 SELLS	86301-86305 PRESCOTT	
85348-85348 SALOME	85635-85636 SIERRA VISTA	86312-86312 PRESCOTT VALLEY	
85349-85349 SAN LUIS	85637-85637 SONOITA	86313-86313 PRESCOTT	
85350-85350 SOMERTON	85638-85638 TOMBSTONE	86314-86314 PRESCOTT VALLEY	
85351-85351 SUN CITY	85639-85639 TOPAWA	86320-86320 ASH FORK	

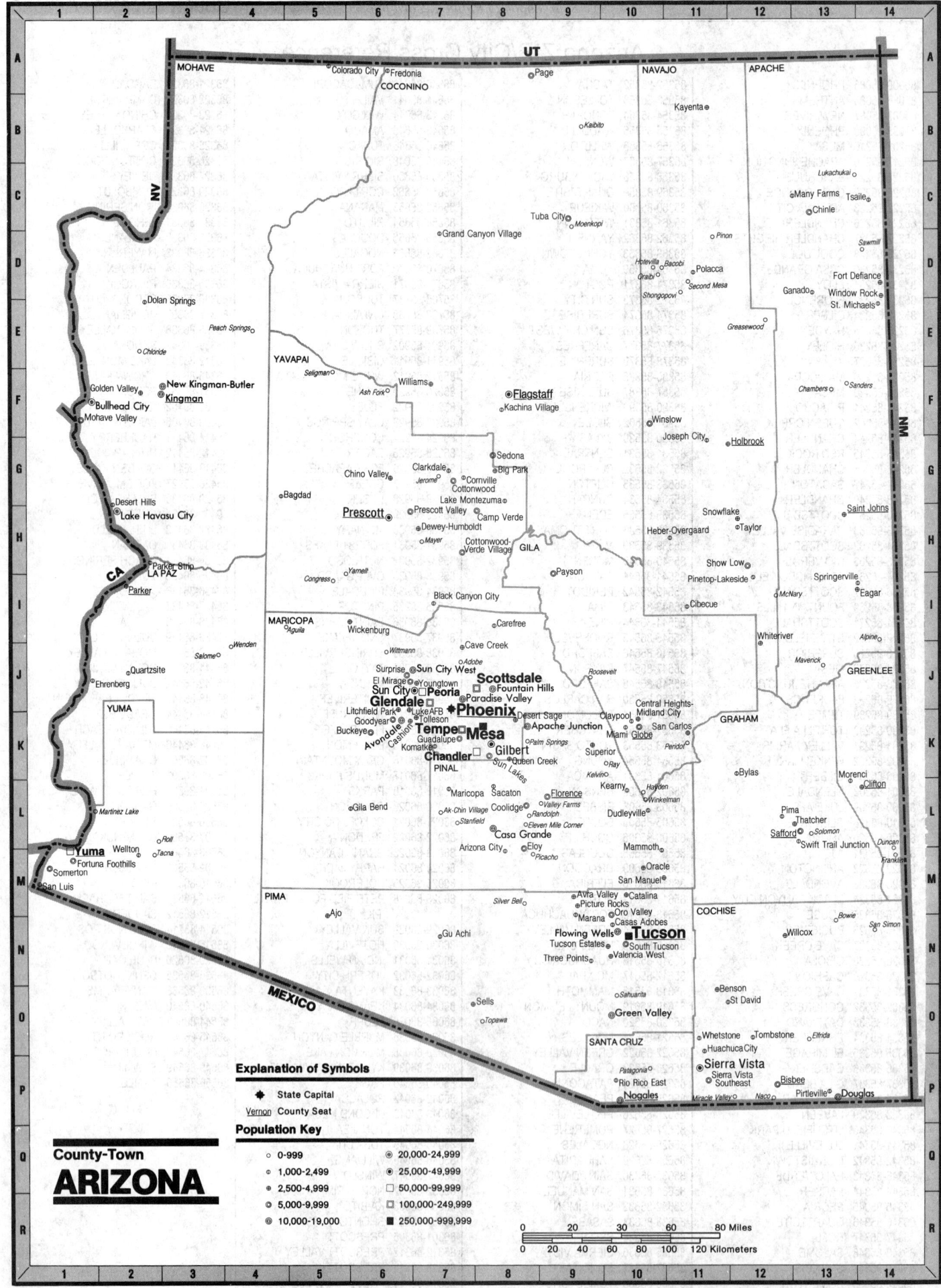

County-Town

ARIZONA

Explanation of Symbols

✦ State Capital
Vernon County Seat

Population Key

○ 0-999	◉ 20,000-24,999
○ 1,000-2,499	◉ 25,000-49,999
◦ 2,500-4,999	☐ 50,000-99,999
◎ 5,000-9,999	☐ 100,000-249,999
◉ 10,000-19,000	■ 250,000-999,999

Explanation of symbols: ● — Census Designated Place (CDP)

Arkansas

General Help Numbers:

Governor's Office
State Capitol, #250
Little Rock, AR 72201
www.accessarkansas.org/governor

501-682-2345
Fax 501-682-3597
8AM-5PM

Attorney General's Office
323 Center St #200
Little Rock, AR 72201
www.ag.state.ar.us

501-682-2007
Fax 501-682-8084
8AM-5PM

Legislative Records
Elections Department
State Capitol, Room 026
Little Rock, AR 72201
www.arkleg.state.ar.us

501-682-5070
Fax 501-682-3408
8AM-5PM

State Archives
State Archives
One Capitol Mall
Little Rock, AR 72201
www.ark-ives.com/

501-682-6900

8AM-4:30PM M-SA

State Specifics:

Capital:	Little Rock Pulaski County
Time Zone:	CST
Number of Counties:	75
Population:	2,725,714
Web Site:	www.state.ar.us

State Agencies

Criminal Records

Arkansas State Police, Identification Bureau, #1 State Police Plaza Dr, Little Rock, AR 72209; 501-618-8500, 501-618-8404 (Fax), 7:30AM-4:30PM.

www.asp.state.ar.us

Note: Under Act 63 of the 1st Ext Sess of 2003, employers and professional licensing boards are permitted access to felony arrests not yet resulting in disposition. Generally if such arrest is more than three years old, state personnel will research record.

Indexing & Storage: Records are available for the past 25 years. Older records are located in the off-site State Archives. It takes 2-3 weeks before new records are available for inquiry. Records are indexed on computer by name, and on fingerprint cards. Records are normally destroyed after it is determined the subject will probably not commit a crime again (i.e.death).

Searching: You must use the Bureau's request form. Include the following in your request-notarized release from subject, name, date of birth, sex, Social Security Number, driver's license number. Fingerprints are not required, but may be included. 100% of the arrest records are fingerprint supported. The following data is not released: pardons and juvenile reocrds.

Access by: mail, in person, online.

Fee & Payment: The fee is $20.00 per record. Fee payee: Arkansas State Police. Prepayment required. Personal checks accepted, credit or debit cards are not.

Mail search: Turnaround time: 5 to 7 days. A SASE is required.

In person search: Bring in signed, notarized release. Results of less than 10 request can usually be done as you wait.

Online search: Online access is, but only to employers and professional licensing boards. Registration is required. Agents or 3rd party vendors representing employers are blocked from access, per the state legislators. There is an additional $2.00 to the standard $20.00 search fee. Searches are conducted by name. Search results includes registered sex offenders. Accounts must maintain the signed release documents in-house for three years.

Statewide Court Records

Administrative Office of Courts, 625 Marshall Street, 1100 Justice Bldg, Little Rock, AR 72201-1078; 501-682-9400, 501-682-9410 (Fax), 8AM-5PM.

www.courts.state.ar.us

Note: There is no statewide access to county court records. Except for certain online research capabilities, all court record access must be done at the local level.

Access by: online. No searching by mail.

Online search: The home web page gives online access to Supreme and Appellate opinions.

Sexual Offender Registry

Access to Records is Restricted

Arkansas Crime Information Center, Sexual Offender Registry, One Capitol Mall, Little Rock, AR 72201; 501-682-2222, 501-682-2269 (Fax).

www.acic.org/Registration/index.htm

Note: Based on information obtained from the risk assessment process, offenders are assigned the following levels: Level 1: Low Risk; Level 2: Moderate Risk; Level 3: High Risk; Level 4: Sexually Violent Predator. ACIC provides information on registered sex offenders to all law enforcement agencies in the county where the offender resides. Local law enforcement agencies release names of those determined most likely to re-offend.

Incarceration Records

Arkansas Department of Corrections, Records Supervisor, 7500 Corrections Circle, Pine Bluff, AR 71603; 870-267-6424, 8AM-4:30PM.

www.accessarkansas.org/doc/inmate_info/

Indexing & Storage: Records are available on current and former inmates; however, the online access is limited to current inmates. It takes 2-3 weeks before new records are available for inquiry.

Searching: Include the following in your request-first and last name or ADC number. The location, ADC number, physical Identifiers and sentencing information, release dates are released.

Access by: mail, online.

Fee & Payment: There is no fee.

Mail search: Turnaround time: 5 to 7 days. A mail search can also be directed through the Attorney General's office (phone 510-682-2007).

Online search: The online access at the website has many search criteria capabilites. Also, a private company offers free web access at www.vinelink.com/index.jsp, including state, DOC, and many county jail systems.

Corporation, Fictitious Name, Limited Liability

Company, Limited Partnership

Secretary of State, Business Services Div, State Capitol Bldg, Little Rock, AR 72201 (Courier: Commercial Service Division, Victory Bldg - 1401 W Capitol Ave, Little Rock, AR 72201); 501-682-3409, 888-233-0325, 501-682-3437 (Fax), 8AM-5PM (4:30 on F).

www.sos.arkansas.gov/corps/

Indexing & Storage: Records are available from late 1800's on. Corporation records are on computer from 1987 on. Prior records, such as dissolved corporations, may be in paper files. New records are available for inquiry immediately. Records are indexed on inhouse computer, file folders.

Searching: Franchise tax information is not released except for names and addressees of parties involved and certain information about the shares of stock. Include the following in your request-full name of business. In addition to the articles of incorporation, corporation records include the following information: Prior (Merged) names, Reserved names, Good standing. Officers listed on franchise tax form is now public information.

Access by: mail, phone, in person, online.

Fee & Payment: There are no search fees. Copies are $.50 a page. Certification of records is an additional $5.00. Fee payee: Secretary of State. Prepayment required. Personal checks accepted. No credit cards accepted.

Mail search: Turnaround time: same day if possible. Call first for copy fees. Records prior to 1988 will take longer to search. No SASE is required. Copies cost $.50 per page, minimum $2.50 by mail.

Phone search: They will give incorporation dates, history, agent name, and status over the phone.

In person search: Copies cost $.50 per page.

Online search: The Internet site permits free searching of corporation records. You can search by name, registered agent, or filing number.

Other access: Bulk release of records is available for $.50 per page. Contact Julia 501-682-3409 or visit website for details.

Trademarks/Servicemarks

Secretary of State, Trademarks Section, State Capitol Bldg, Little Rock, AR 72201 (Courier: Business & Commercial Services Div, Victory Bldg - 1401 W Capitol Ave, Little Rock, AR 72201); 501-682-3409, 888-233-0325, 501-682-3437 (Fax), 8AM-5PM (4:30PM on F).

www.sos.arkansas.gov/corps/trademk/

Indexing & Storage: Records are available from the 1950s. It takes 24-48 hours before new records are available for inquiry. Records are indexed on inhouse computer.

Searching: Include the following in your request-name.

Access by: mail, phone, in person, online, email.

Fee & Payment: There is no search fee, copy fees are $.50 per copy. Fee payee: Secretary of State. Prepayment required. Personal checks accepted. No credit cards accepted.

Mail search: Turnaround time: 3 to 4 working days. Minimum fee for copies by mail is $2.50. No SASE is required.

Phone search: They will give information over the phone.

In person search: Turnaround time is within a few minutes.

Online search: Searching is available at no fee over the Internet site. Search by name, owner, city, or filing number. You can also requests via email at corprequest@sosmail.state.ar.us.

Other access: Records can be provided in bulk for $.50 per page. Call 501-682-3409 or visit website for details.

Uniform Commercial Code, Federal Tax Liens

UCC Division - Commercial Srvs, Secretary of State, State Capitol Bldg, Little Rock, AR 72201 (Courier: Commercial Service Division, Victory Bldg - 1401 W Capitol Ave, Little Rock, AR 72201); 501-682-5078, 501-682-3500 (Fax), 8AM-5PM.

www.sos.arkansas.gov

Indexing & Storage: Records are available from 1962. Records are indexed on cards. You can make requests by fax, but they will be returned by mail. Records are not searched by phone, but they will inform if there is anything on file. It takes 24 hours before new records are available for inquiry.

Searching: Use search request form UCC-11. A search includes federal tax liens on businesses, via a lien search certificate. Federal tax liens on individuals and all state tax liens (AKA municipal judgments before 1978) are filed at the county. Include the following in your request-debtor name.

Access by: mail, fax, online.

Fee & Payment: A lien search certificate is $6.00. Photostat copies of financing statements are $6.00 for the first page, $.50 each additional, maximum $100.00. The fee for certification of a copy of a filed financing statement is $.50 Fee payee: Secretary of State. Personal checks accepted. No credit cards accepted.

Mail search: Turnaround time: 1 to 2 days. No SASE is required.

Fax search: There is an additional fee of $5.00 to return by fax.

Online search: Subscribers of INA (Information Netwrok of Arkansas) can search by file number or charter number; subscription fees and search fees involved. Check website for details. UCC Download is available via the Interent, but only to subscribers. Fee is $2,000.00 per month for weekly, bi-weekly or monthly downloads. Watch notifications are available for a $35.00 monthly fee.

State Tax Liens

Records not maintained by a state level agency.

Note: Records are at the county level.

Sales Tax Registrations

Finance & Administration Department, Sales & Use Tax Office - Reg. Dept, PO Box 1272, Little Rock, AR 72203; 501-682-1895, 501-682-7900 (Fax), 8AM-4:30PM.

www.state.ar.us/dfa/taxes/salestax/

Indexing & Storage: Records are available from the 1940s.

Searching: This agency will only confirm that a business is registered. They will provide no other information. All searches are based upon tax permit number

Access by: mail, phone, fax, in person.

Mail search: Turnaround time: 3 to 5 days. A SASE is requested. No fee for mail request.

Phone search: No fee for telephone request. This is the recommended search request method.

Fax search: Fax searching available.

In person search: No fee for request.

Birth Certificates

Arkansas Department of Health, Division of Vital Records, 4815 W Markham St, Slot 44, Little Rock, AR 72205; 501-661-2174, 501-661-2336 (Message Number), 506-661-2726 (Credit Card Line), 800-637-9314 (Toll Free), 501-663-2832 (Fax), 8AM-4:30PM.

www.healthyarkansas.com

Note: Three types of records are available; certification copy, actual copy, and wallet size copy.

Indexing & Storage: Records are available from 1914 on. New records are available for inquiry immediately. Records are indexed on microfiche, inhouse computer.

Searching: Must have a signed release from person of record if requester is not a member of parents, grandparents or spouse. Include your name, address and signature on the request. Include the following in your request-full name, names of parents, mother's maiden name, date of birth, place of birth, relationship to person of record, reason for information request. Also include your phone number.

Access by: mail, phone, fax, in person, online.

Fee & Payment: The fee is $12.00 for the first copy and $10.00 for each add'l of same record. Fee payee: Division of Vital Records. Prepayment required. Personal checks accepted. Credit cards accepted: MasterCard, Visa, AmEx, Discover.

Mail search: Turnaround time: 4 weeks. No SASE is required.

Phone search: See expedited service. You must use a credit card. Turnaround time is 1 week.

Fax search: See expedited service.

In person search: Turnaround time: While you wait.

Online search: Records may requested from www.vitalchek.com, a state-endorsed vendor. Expedited service fees apply.

Other access: Research projects require the approval of the director.

Expedited service: Expedited service is available for phone, online, and fax requests. Turnaround time: 1-5 days. Add $10.95 for use of credit card and additional funds for the delivery method desired.

Death Records

Arkansas Department of Health, Division of Vital Records, 4815 W Markham St, Slot 44, Little Rock, AR 72205; 501-661-2174, 501-661-2336 (Message number), 501-661-2726 (Credit Card Line), 501-663-2832 (Fax), 8AM-4:30PM.

www.healthyarkansas.com

Note: This agency does not hold the actual records, but does have an index of all deaths since 1914 and some death index records for Fort Smith and Little Rock prior to 1914.

Indexing & Storage: Records are available from 1914 on. New records are available for inquiry immediately. Records are indexed on microfiche, inhouse computer.

Searching: Must have a signed release from immediate family member if requester is not a member of family. Include the following in your request-full name, date of death, place of death, relationship to person of record, reason for information request, wife's maiden name. Include requester's signature and phone number.

Access by: mail, phone, fax, in person, online.

Fee & Payment: The fee is $10.00 for the first copy and $8.00 for each add'l of same record. Add $6.00 if you use a credit card. Fee payee: Division of Vital Records. Prepayment required. Personal checks accepted. Credit cards accepted: MasterCard, Visa, AmEx, Discover.

Mail search: Turnaround time: 4 weeks. Turnaround time with a credit card is 1 week. No SASE is required.

Phone search: You must use a credit card.

Fax search: You must use a credit card or prepay before record is sent.

In person search: Turnaround time is usually 1 to 2 hours.

Online search: Records may requested from www.vitalchek.com, a state-endorsed vendor. Expedited service fees apply.

Expedited service: Expedited service is available for online, phone and fax searches. Turnaround time: 1-5 days. Add $10.95 for use of credit card and additional funds for the delivery method desired.

Marriage Certificates

Arkansas Department of Health, Division of Vital Records, 4815 W Markham St, Slot 44, Little Rock, AR 72205; 501-661-2174, 501-661-2336 (Message Number), 501-661-2726 (Credit Card Line), 501-663-2832 (Fax), 8AM-4:30PM.

www.healthyarkansas.com

Indexing & Storage: Records are available from 1917 on. New records are available for inquiry immediately. Records are indexed on microfiche, inhouse computer.

Searching: Must have a signed release from person of record if requester is not a member of immediate family. Include the following in your request-full names of husband and wife, registration number, date of marriage, place or county of marriage, wife's maiden name. Requester must sign request and provide phone number.

Access by: mail, phone, fax, in person, online.

Fee & Payment: The fee is $10.00, add $6.00 if you use a credit card. Fee payee: Division of Vital Records. Prepayment required. Personal checks accepted. Credit cards accepted: MasterCard, Visa, AmEx, Discover.

Mail search: Turnaround time: 4 weeks. Turnaround time with a credit card is 1 week. No SASE is required.

Phone search: You may call in your request, but you must use a credit card. Turnaround time is 1 week.

Fax search: A credit card is required or must prepay before records sent.

In person search: Turnaround time is 30 minutes to an hour.

Online search: Records may requested from www.vitalchek.com, a state-endorsed vendor. Expedited service fees apply.

Expedited service: Expedited service is available for online, phone and fax searches. Turnaround time: 1-5 days. Add $10.95 for use of credit card and additional funds for the delivery method desired.

Divorce Records

Arkansas Department of Health, Department of Vital Records, 4815 W Markham St, Slot 44, Little Rock, AR 72205; 501-661-2174, 501-661-2336 (Message Number), 866-209-9482 (Credit Card Line), 800-637-9314, 501-663-2832 (Fax), 8AM-4:30PM.

www.healthyarkansas.com

Indexing & Storage: Records are available from 1923 to present. It takes 30 days before new records are available for inquiry. Records are indexed on mainframe computer and microfiche.

Searching: Must have a signed release from person of record if requester is not a member of the immediate family. Include the following in your request-names of husband and wife, date of divorce, place of divorce. Signature of requester required.

Access by: mail, phone, fax, in person, online.

Fee & Payment: The fee is $10.00. Fee payee: Division of Public Records. Prepayment required. Personal checks accepted. Credit cards accepted: MasterCard, Visa, AmEx, Discover.

Mail search: Turnaround time: 4 weeks. Turnaround time with a credit card is 1 week. No SASE is required.

Phone search: See expedited service. You must use a credit card. Turnaround time is 1 week.

Fax search: See expedited service.

In person search: Turnaround time is within 1 hour.

Online search: Records may requested from www.vitalchek.com, a state-endorsed vendor. See expedited service.

Expedited service: Expedited service is available for online, phone and fax searches. Turnaround time: 1-5 days. Add $10.95 for use of credit card and additional funds for the delivery method desired.

Workers' Compensation Records

Workers Compensation Department, Operations/Compliance, 324 Spring Street, PO Box 950, Little Rock, AR 72203-0950; 501-682-3930, 800-622-4472, 501-682-6761 (Fax), 8AM-4:30PM M-F.

www.awcc.state.ar.us

Indexing & Storage: Records are available from 1940's on. New records are available for inquiry immediately. Records are indexed on microfilm, index cards, inhouse computer.

Searching: Only written requests are accepted. You may fax a request, but it is returned by mail. Include the following in your request-claimant name, Social Security Number, place of employment at time of accident, file number (if known). The following data is not released: Social Security Numbers or medical information.

Access by: mail, phone, fax, in person, online.

Fee & Payment: The fee is $5.00 per name searched and $.50 per page for copies. Fee payee: Workers' Compensation Commission. An invoice is mailed with the results of the request. Personal checks accepted. No credit cards accepted.

Mail search: Turnaround time: 10 days. No SASE is required.

Phone search: Records are available by phone.

Fax search: Same criteria as mail searching.

In person search: You may make copies at $.50 per page. You are allowed to look through the files without charge.

Online search: To perform an online claim search, one must be a subscriber to the Information Network of Arkansas (INA). Records are from May 1, 1997 forward. There is an annual $50 subscriber fee to INA. Each record request is $3.50; if more than 20 are ordered in one month, the fee is $2.50 each request over 20. For more information, visit www.awcc.state.ar.us/electron.html

Driver Records

Department of Driver Services, Driving Records Division, PO Box 1272, Room 1130, Little Rock, AR 72203-1272 (Courier: 1900 W 7th, #1130, Little Rock, AR 72201); 501-682-7207, 501-682-7908, 501-682-2075 (Fax), 8AM-4:30PM.

www.accessarkansas.org/dfa/driverservices/

Note: Copies of tickets must be requested from the local jurisdiction where the ticket was issued.

Indexing & Storage: Records are available for 3 years for moving violations, 3 years for employment or insurance purposes and are retained indefinitely for departmental purposes. DWI and suspensions show until all requirements are met. It takes less than 1 day before new records are available for inquiry. Records are indexed on inhouse computer.

Searching: Arkansas requires signed authorization by the driver to obtain a driving record. Volume requesters must have these authorizations on file. Violations on an interstate highway not exceeding 75 mph won't show on records requested for insurance purposes. Include the following in your request-full name, driver's license number, date of birth. Driver's address is included as part of the search report for permissible requesters.

Access by: mail, in person, online.

Fee & Payment: Fees are $7.00 for insurance record and $10.00 for CDLs. There is a full charge for a "no record found." Fee payee: State of Arkansas, Driver Services. Prepayment required. Personal checks accepted. No credit cards accepted.

Mail search: Turnaround time: 24 hours. Requester must enclose written release, full name, DOB, driver's license number, and proper fees. No SASE is required.

In person search: The state will process up to 5 requests while you wait.

Online search: Access is available through the Information Network of Arkansas (INA). The system offers both batch and interactive service. The system is only available to INA subscribers

who have statutory rights to the data. The record fee is $8.00, or $11.00 for commercial drivers. Visit www.state.ar.us/ina.html.

Other access: High volume requesters use magnetic tape-to-tape for overnight access.

Vehicle Ownership, Vehicle Identification

Office of Motor Vehicles, MV Title Records, PO Box 1272, Room 1100, Little Rock, AR 72203 (Courier: 7th & Battery Sts, Ragland Bldg, Room 1100, Little Rock, AR 72201); 501-682-4692, 800-662-8247, 8AM-4:30PM.

www.accessarkansas.org/dfa/

Indexing & Storage: Records are available from 1950 for titles; license plate records from 1968 on microfilm; plate number and name from 1981 on microfiche. It takes 4 to 6 weeks before new records are available for inquiry.

Searching: Vehicle registration information cannot be sold or used for solicitation purposes. Requesters that do not have DPPA approved purpose, cannot receive records with personal information, unless consent of subject is given. Include the following in your request-vehicle make and VIV. Approved account holders may request via e-mail. The following data is not released: Social Security Numbers or date of birth.

Access by: mail, phone, fax, in person.

Fee & Payment: The fee for vehicle and/or ownership searches is $1.00 per copy and $1.00 per search. Fee payee: Department of Finance and Administration. Prepayment required. If mailing a check to open a new account, place "Attn: Search Account" on the request. If mailing an information request, place "Attn: Correspondence Desk" on the request. Personal checks accepted. No credit cards accepted.

Mail search: Turnaround time: 24 hours. No SASE is required.

Phone search: Searching by phone is available for established accounts. A $25.00 deposit is required.

Fax search: For approved account holders only.

In person search: Turnaround time: while you wait.

Other access: The bulk purchase of records, except for recall or statistical purposes, is prohibited.

Accident Reports

Arkansas State Police, Crash Records Section, 1 State Police Plaza Drive, Little Rock, AR 72209; 501-618-8130, 501-618-8131 (Fax), 8AM-5PM.

www.asp.state.ar.us/cr/cr.html

Indexing & Storage: Records are available from 1995 to present. It takes 10 days before new records are available for inquiry.

Searching: Include the following in your request-date of accident, location, name of at least on driver.

Access by: mail, phone, in person.

Fee & Payment: The fee is $10.00 per record. There is no charge for a "no record found." Payment will be refunded. Fee payee: Arkansas State Police, Accident Records. Prepayment required. Personal checks accepted. No credit cards accepted.

Mail search: Turnaround time: 3 to 4 weeks. A SASE is requested.

Phone search: Limited information is available.

In person search: Turnaround time is while you wait, if staffing available.

Vessel Ownership, Vessel Registration

Office of Motor Vehicles, Boat Registration, PO Box 1272, Little Rock, AR 72203; 501-682-4692, 501-682-1116 (Fax), 8AM-4:30PM.

www.arkansas.gov/dfa/motorvehicle/index.html

Note: Lien information may be filed at the Secretary of State.

Indexing & Storage: Records are available from 1980. All boats propelled by sail or machinery must be registered. Vessels are not titled in this state. New records are available for inquiry immediately.

Searching: Motor vehicle title, registration and lien information is available for users that qualify under DPPA. Onging requesters should become account holders. Include the following in your request-name and address of requester and account number if applicable. Search by name or registration number or hull number.

Access by: mail, phone, fax, in person.

Fee & Payment: The search fee is $1.00 per search and $1.00 per copy of a record. Fee payee: Office of Motor Vehicles. Prepayment required. Personal checks accepted. No credit cards accepted.

Mail search: Turnaround time: 2 weeks. No SASE is required.

Phone search: Requests only accepted for account holders.

Fax search: Requests only accepted for account holders.

In person search: Records are usually obtained at once, unless they require extensive research.

Other access: Bulk access to approved users is available via FTP.

Voter Registration

Access to Records is Restricted

Secretary of State, Voter Services, State Capitol, Room 026, Little Rock, AR 72201; 501-682-3526, 501-682-3548 (Fax), 8AM-5PM.

www.sosweb.state.ar.us/elections.html

Note: The state will sell the voter database for voting or election purposes. All individual search requests must be at the local County Clerk's office. The SSN will not be released. Requests for bulk release of records must be in writing and state "pursuant to the Freedom of Information Act." Information released on a CD includes name, address, and DOB, as well as district data.

GED Certificates

GED Testing, Dept of Workforce Education, #3 Capitol Mall, Room 305D, Little Rock, AR 72201; 501-682-1978 (Main Number), 501-682-1982 (Fax), 8AM-4:30PM.

http://dwe.arkansas.gov/ged.htm

Indexing & Storage: Records are available from 1980 forward. It takes on month before new records are available for inquiry.

Searching: For verification or for a copy of a transcript, all of the following is required: a signed release, name, year of test, date of birth, and SSN.

Access by: mail, fax, in person.

Fee & Payment: There is no fee.

Mail search: Turnaround time is within a week. No SASE is required.

Fax search: Turnaround time is next day, but results returned by mail.

In person search: Records can be accessed immediately.

Expedited service: Will provide expedited service if needed for immediate hiring or enrollment in college. Turnaround time: 1 day or less.

Hunting and Fishing License Information

Game & Fish Commission, Attn: Records, Two Natural Resources Dr, Little Rock, AR 72205; 501-223-6300, 800-364-4263, 501-223-6425 (Fax), 8AM-4:30PM.

www.agfc.com

Note: Lists maintained here include fish farmers, put & take pay lakes, shell buyers, commercial game breeders, commercial shooting resorts, fur dealers, and bull frog permits.

Indexing & Storage: Records are available for 2 to 3 years then purged. It takes 4 days before new records are available for inquiry. Records are indexed on inhouse computer.

Searching: Must mention request is under the Freedom of Information Act. Include the following in your request-full name. Addresses are given and telephone numbers, if available.

Access by: mail, fax, in person.

Fee & Payment: The search and copy fee is $2.00. Fee payee: Game & Fish Commission. Personal checks accepted. No credit cards accepted.

Mail search: Turnaround time: 1 to 2 days. No SASE is required.

Fax search: Records are available by fax.

In person search: Some searches require 1 to 2 days to process.

Arkansas State Licensing Agencies

Licenses Searchable Online

Aesthetician #49	www.arkansas.gov/cos/
Agriculture Education #32	www.as-is.org/directory/search_lic.html
Architect #6	www.state.ar.us/arch/search.html
Asbestos Abatement Inspector/Planner/Trainer #28	www.adeq.state.ar.us/compsvs/webmaster/databases.htm
Asbestos Removal Worker #28	www.adeq.state.ar.us/compsvs/webmaster/databases.htm
Athletic Trainer #24	www.aratb.org/search.php
Attorney #43	http://courts.state.ar.us/attylist/new/
Bank #38	www.sos.arkansas.gov/corps/search_all.php
Business Education Teacher #32	www.as-is.org/directory/search_lic.html
Career Education Coordinator #32	www.as-is.org/directory/search_lic.html
Career Orientation Teacher #32	www.as-is.org/directory/search_lic.html
Cemetery, Perpetual Care #39	www.ark.org/arsec/database/dbsearch.cgi?dbname=7&LIMIT=20&LISTALL=ON
Child Care Provider #26	www.state.ar.us/childcare/search.html
Chiropractor #9	www.accessarkansas.org/asbce/search.html
Contractor #23	www.state.ar.us/clb/search.html
Cosmetologist/Cosmetology Instructor #49	www.arkansas.gov/cos/
Counselor, Professional #51	www.state.ar.us/abec/search.php
Dental Hygienist #11	www.asbde.org
Dentist #11	www.asbde.org
Electrologist/Electrolysis Instructor #49	www.arkansas.gov/cos/
Embalmer/Embalmer Apprentice #12	www.accessarkansas.org/fdemb/
Engineer/Engineer in Training #19	www.accessarkansas.org/pels/search.php
Fire Equipment/Sprinkler Inspector/Repairer #56	www.arfireprotection.org/roster/index.html
Funeral Director/Apprentice #12	www.accessarkansas.org/fdemb/
Funeral Home/Crematory #12	www.accessarkansas.org/fdemb/
Insurance Agency #38	www.sos.arkansas.gov/corps/search_all.php
Insurance Sales Agent #2	www.accessarkansas.org/insurance/license/search.php
Investment Advisor #39	www.ark.org/arsec/database/search.html
Landscape Architect #6	www.state.ar.us/arch/search.html
Lobbyist #38	www.sosweb.state.ar.us/elections_ethics.html
Manicurist #49	www.arkansas.gov/cos/
Marriage & Family Therapist #51	www.state.ar.us/abec/search.php
Medical Corporation #31	https://www.armedicalboard.org/licenseverf/
Medical Doctor/Surgeon #31	https://www.armedicalboard.org/licenseverf/
Midwife Nurse #15	www.accessarkansas.org/nurse/registry/index.html
Mortgage Loan Broker/Company #39	www.ark.org/arsec/database/search.html
Motor Vehicle Dealer/Distributor #55	www.armvc.com/licensee_search/index.html
Motor Vehicle Mfg/Rep, New #55	www.armvc.com/licensee_search/index.html
Notary Public #38	www.sos.arkansas.gov/corps/notary/
Nurse #15	www.accessarkansas.org/nurse/registry/index.html
Nurse Anesthetist #15	www.accessarkansas.org/nurse/registry/index.html
Nurse-LPN #15	www.accessarkansas.org/nurse/registry/index.html
Occupational Therapist/Assistant #31	https://www.armedicalboard.org/licenseverf/
Optician #50	www.ark.org/directory/detail2.cgi?ID-1050
Optometrist #16	www.arbo.org/odfinder/LicSearch.asp
Osteopathic Physician #31	https://www.armedicalboard.org/licenseverf/
Physical Therapist #3	www.arptb.org/ptroster/search.php
Physician Assistant #31	https://www.armedicalboard.org/licenseverf/
Political Action Committee #38	www.sosweb.state.ar.us/elections_ethics.html
Public Accountant-CPA #18	www.arkansas.gov/asbpa/
Real Estate Agent/Broker/Sales #37	www.accessarkansas.org/arec/db/
Real Estate Appraiser #37	www.arkansas.gov
Respiratory Care Practitioner #31	https://www.armedicalboard.org/licenseverf/
School Counselor #32	www.as-is.org/directory/search_lic.html

School Principal/Admin/Super #32 .... www.as-is.org/directory/search_lic.html
Securities Agent #39.. www.ark.org/arsec/database/search.html
Securities Broker/Dealer #39 .... www.ark.org/arsec/database/search.html
Social Worker #40 .... www.state.ar.us/swlb/search/index.html
Solid Waste Facility Operator #28 .... www.adeq.state.ar.us/compsvs/webmaster/databases.htm
Surveyor, Land #19 .... www.accessarkansas.org/pels/search.php
Surveyor-in-Training #19 .... www.accessarkansas.org/pels/search.php
Teacher #32.. www.as-is.org/directory/search_lic.html
Waste Water Treatment Plant Operator #28 .... www.adeq.state.ar.us/compsvs/webmaster/databases.htm

Arkansas Licensing Quick Finder

Abstractor #48 870-942-8064
Acupuncturist #46 501-228-0644
Aesthetician #49 501-682-2168
Agricultural Consultant #33 501-225-1598
Agriculture Education #32 501-682-4695
Alcohol/Drug Abuse Treatm't Program #25
.... 501-280-4500
Anesthetician #15 501-682-2200
Announcer, Athletic Event (Ring) #4 501-666-5544
Architect #6 501-682-3171
Armored Car Guard #42 501-618-8600
Asbestos Abatement Inspector/Planner #28
.... 501-682-0718
Asbestos Abatement Training Provider #28
.... 501-682-0718
Asbestos Removal Worker #28 501-682-0718
Athletic Manager #4 501-666-5544
Athletic Promoter/Matchmaker #4 501-666-5544
Athletic Trainer #24 501-683-4076
Attorney #43 501-682-6849
Auctioneer #5 501-682-1156
Audiologist #41 501-320-4319
Bail Bondsman #2 501-682-9050
Bank #38 501-682-3409
Barber Instructor #7 501-682-4035
Barber/Barber Technician #7 501-682-4035
Birthing Center #25 501-661-2518
Boiler Inspector/Installer/Repairer #27 .. 501-682-4513
Boiler Operator #27 501-682-4513
Boxer #4 501-666-5544
Boxing/Wrestling Referee #4 501-666-5544
Burglar Alarm System Agent/Mgr. #42 .. 501-618-8600
Business Education Teacher #32 501-682-4695
Career Education Coordinator #32 501-682-4695
Career Orientation Teacher #32 501-682-4695
Cemetery, Perpetual Care #39 501-324-9260
Check Casher #10 501-376-1438
Chemicals, List 1 Whlse Distributor #17 501-682-0190
Child Care Provider #26 501-682-9699
Chiropractor #9 501-682-9015
Claims Adjuster #2 501-371-2750
Clinics, Health #25 501-661-2518
Collection Agency #10 501-376-1438
Collection Agency Collector/Mgr. #10 .. 501-376-1438
Contractor #23 501-372-4661
Cosmetologist/Cosmetology Instr. #49.. 501-682-2168
Counselor, Professional #51 870-901-7055
Court Reporter #8 501-682-6850
Dental Assistant #11 501-682-2085
Dental Hygienist #11 501-682-2085
Dentist #11 501-682-2085
Dietitian #29 .... 501-221-0566, 580-9294
Drugs, Legend, Wholesale Distrib. #17. 501-682-0190
Egg Grader #53 501-907-2400
Electrical Contractor #27 501-682-4549
Electrician Journeyman/ Master #27 501-682-4549
Electrologist/Electrolysis Instructor #49. 501-682-2168
Elevator/Lifting Device Inspector #27 ... 501-682-4531

Embalmer/Embalmer Apprentice #12 .. 501-682-0574
Emergency Medical Technician #25 501-661-2284
Emergency Medical Tech.-Paramedic #25
.... 501-661-2284
Employment Agency Manager #27 501-682-4505
Employment Agent/Counselor #27 501-682-4505
Engineer/Engineer in Training #19 501-682-2824
Exterminator #33 501-225-1598
Fire Equipment Inspect'/Repairer #56... 501-661-7903
Fire Extinguisher Sprinkler Inspect. #56 501-661-7903
Forester #20 501-296-1998
Funeral Director/Apprentice #12 501-682-0574
Funeral Home/Crematory #12 501-682-0574
Gas Fitter/Trainee #25 501-661-2242
Geologist #21 501-683-0150
Grain Warehouseman #33 501-225-1598
Greyhound Racing #36 501-682-1467
Handgun, Concealed #42 501-618-8600
Health Facility #25 501-661-2201
Hearing Instrument Dispenser #14 501-663-5869
HMO #25 501-661-2518
Home Health Agency #25 501-661-2518
Home Inspector #38 501-682-3409
Homebuilders #23 501-372-4661
Horse Racing #36 501-682-1467
Hospice Facility #25 501-661-2518
Hospital Maintenance Plumber #25 501-661-2698
Industrial Maintenance Electrician #27 . 501-682-4549
Insurance Agency #38 501-682-3409
Insurance Sales Agent #2 501-371-2750
Investment Advisor #39 501-324-9260
Laboratory #25 501-661-2191
Landscape Architect #6 501-682-3393
Liquor Distributor #1 501-682-1105
Livestock Brand #53 501-907-2400
Livestock Dealer #53 501-907-2400
Lobbyist #38 501-682-1010
LPG Safety Supervisor #30 501-683-4100
Manicurist #49 501-682-2168
Manufactured Home Dealer/Mfg #54 ... 501-324-9032
Manufactured Home Installer #54 501-324-9032
Manufactured Home Salesperson #54.. 501-324-9032
Marriage & Family Therapist #51 870-901-7055
Martial Arts #4 501-666-5544
Massage Therapy Tech. (Masseur/Masseuse) #22
.... 501-623-0444
Medical Corporation #31 501-296-1802
Medical Doctor/Surgeon #31 501-296-1802
Medicare Certified Facility #25 501-661-2201
Midwife Nurse #15 501-682-2200
Mortgage Loan Broker/Company #39 .. 501-324-9260
Motor Vehicle Dealer/Distributor #55 ... 501-682-1428
Motor Vehicle Dealer/Seller, Used #42. 501-618-8600
Motor Vehicle Mfg/Rep, New #55 501-682-1428
Notary Public #38 501-682-3409
Nurse #15 501-682-2200
Nurse Anesthetist #15 501-682-2200
Nurse-LPN #15 501-682-2200

Nurseryman #33 501-225-1598
Nursing Home Administrator #52 501-682-1873
Occupational Therapist/Assistant #31 . 501-296-1802
Optician #50 870-572-2847
Optometrist #16 501-268-4351
Osteopathic Physician #31 501-296-1802
Permanent Cosmetic/Tattoo Artist #25 . 501-661-2171
Pesticide Applicator #33 501-225-1598
Petroleum Dealer #30 501-683-4100
Pharmacist #17 501-682-0190
Pharmacist Intern #17 501-682-0190
Pharmacy Technician #17 501-682-0190
Pharmacy, Hospital #17 501-682-0190
Pharmacy, Institutional #17 501-682-0190
Pharmacy, Specialty #17 501-682-0190
Pharmacy-In-State, Retail #17 501-682-0190
Pharmacy-Out-of-State, Retail #17 501-682-0190
Physical Therapist #3 501-228-7100
Physician Assistant #31 501-296-1802
Podiatrist #34 501-664-3668
Political Action Committee #38 501-682-1010
Polygraph Examiner #42 501-618-8600
Precious Metals Dealer #42 501-618-8600
Private Investigator #42 501-618-8600
Psychological Examiner #13 501-682-6167
Psychologist #13 501-682-6167
Public Accountant-CPA #18 501-682-1520
Pump Installer #45 501-682-1025
Radiologic Technician #25 501-661-2306
Real Estate Agent/Broker/Sales #37 ... 501-683-8010
Real Estate Appraiser #37 501-683-8010
Residential Journeyman #27 501-682-4549
Respiratory Care Practitioner #31 501-296-1802
School Counselor #32 501-682-4344
School Principal/Admin/Super #32 501-682-4344
Securities Agent #39 501-324-9260
Securities Broker/Dealer #39 501-324-9260
Security Guard #42 501-618-8600
Seed Dealer #33 501-225-1598
Septic Tank Cleaner #25 501-661-2171
Social Worker #40 501-372-5071
Solid Waste Facility Operator #28 501-682-0585
Speech Pathologist #41 501-320-4319
State Trooper #42 501-618-8282
Supplier of Med. Equipment, Legend Device, Medical
Gas #17 501-682-0190
Surveyor, Land #19 501-682-2824
Surveyor-in-Training #19 501-682-2824
Teacher #32 501-682-4695
Veterinarian #44 501-224-2836
Veterinary Technician #44 501-224-2836
Waste Water Treatment Plant Operator #28
.... 501-682-0998
Water Supply Operator #25 501-661-2623
Water Well Driller #45 501-682-1025
Wrestler #4 501-666-5544

Arkansas Licensing Agency Information

1 Alcoholic Beverage Control Division, 1515 W 7th St #503, Little Rock, AR 72201; 501-682-1105, Fax: 501-682-2221.

2 Department of Insurance, Licensing Division, 1200 W 3rd St, Little Rock, AR 72201; 800-282-9134, Fax: 501-371-2618.
www.accessarkansas.org/insurance/index.html
Email: Insurance.License@mail.state.ar.us
Search Database at www.accessarkansas.org/insurance/license/search.php

3 Board of Physical Therapy, 9 Shackelford Plaza, #3, Little Rock, AR 72211; 501-228-7100, Fax: 501-228-0294.
www.arptb.org
Email: axptb@sbcglobal.net
Search Database at www.arptb.org/ptroster/search.php

4 Athletic Commission, 809 N Palm St, Little Rock, AR 72205-1946; 501-666-5544, Fax: 501-666-5546.

5 Auctioneers Licensing Board, 101 E Capital, #112B, Little Rock, AR 72201; 501-682-1156, Fax: 501-682-1158.
www.state.ar.us/directory/detail2.cgi?ID=962
Email: betty.king@mail.state.ar.us

6 Board of Architecture, 101 E Capitol, #208, Little Rock, AR 72201; 501-682-3171, Fax: 501-682-3172.
www.accessarkansas.org/arch
Email: arch@mac.state.ar.us
Search Database at
www.state.ar.us/arch/search.html

7 Board of Barber Examiners, 103 E 7th St Rm 212, Little Rock, AR 72201-4512; 501-682-4035, Fax: 501-682-2806.
www.state.ar.us/directory/detail2.cgi?ID=1044
Email: charles.kirkpatrick@mail.state.ar.us

8 Board of Certified Court Reporter Examiners, 625 Marshall St, Justice Bldg, Little Rock, AR 72201; 501-682-6850, Fax: 501-682-6877 c/o Renee.   Email: renee.herndon@mail.state.ar.us

9 Board of Chiropractic Examiners, 101 E Capital, #209, Little Rock, AR 72201; 501-682-9015, Fax: 501-682-9016.
www.accessarkansas.org/asbce/
Email: ann.gates@mail.state.ar.us
Search Database at
www.accessarkansas.org/asbce/search.html

10 Board of Collection Agencies, 523 S Louisiana St, #460, Little Rock, AR 72201; 501-376-1438, Fax: 501-372-5383.
www.asbca.org/

11 Board of Dental Examiners, 101 E Capitol Ave, #111, Little Rock, AR 72201; 501-682-2085, Fax: 501-682-3543.
www.asbde.org
Email: asbde@arkansas.gov
Search Database at www.asbde.org

12 Board of Embalmers & Funeral Directors, 101 E Capitol Ave, #113, Little Rock, AR 72201; 501-682-0574, Fax: 501-682-0575.
www.accessarkansas.org/fdemb
Search Database at
www.accessarkansas.org/fdemb

13 Board of Examiners in Psychology, 101 E Capitol Ave, #415, Little Rock, AR 72201; 501-682-6167, Fax: 501-682-6165.
www.accessarkansas.org/abep/
Email: rebecca.wright@arkansas.gov Note: They do accept verifications by phone or fax. They require a written request only plus a $10.00 per per verification. A form may be downloaded from their website to fill out and return. They do not have web access for verification.

14 Board of Hearing Instrument Dispensers, 305 N Monroe, Little Rock, AR 72205; 501-663-5869, Fax: 501-663-6359.

15 Board of Nursing, 1123 S University, University Tower Bldg, #800, Little Rock, AR 72204-1619; 501-686-2700, Fax: 501-686-2714.
www.accessarkansas.org/nurse
Search Database at
www.accessarkansas.org/nurse/registry/index.html

16 Board of Optometry, 407 N. Elm St., Searcy, AR 72143; 501-268-4351, Fax: 501-268-5631.
www.aroptometry.org/
Email: hflippin@cswnet.com
Search Database at
www.arbo.org/odfinder/LicSearch.asp

17 Board of Pharmacy, 101 E Capitol, #218, Little Rock, AR 72201; 501-682-0190, Fax: 501-682-0195.   www.arkansas.gov/asbp
Email: margaret.lincourt@arkansas.gov

18 Board of Public Accountancy, 101 E Capitol, #450, Little Rock, AR 72201; 501-682-1520, Fax: 501-682-5538.
www.arkansas.gov/asbpa/
Search Database at www.arkansas.gov/asbpa/

19 Board of Registration for Engineers/Land Surveyors, PO Box 3750, Little Rock, AR 72203; 501-682-2824, Fax: 501-682-2827.
www.state.ar.us/pels/
Email: joseph.clement@mail.state.ar.us
Search Database at
www.accessarkansas.org/pels/search.php

20 Board of Registration for Foresters, PO Box 7424, Little Rock, AR 72217; 501-296-1998, Fax: 501-296-1949.
http://members.aol.com/JOSTNIX/rf.htm
Email: robert.mcfarland@arkansas.org

21 Board of Registration for Professional Geologists, 3815 W Roosevelt Rd, Little Rock, AR 72204; 501-683-0150, Fax: 501-663-7360.
www.state.ar.us/agc/BOR.htm
Email: connie.raper@arkansas.gov

22 Board of Massage Therapy, PO Box 20739, Hot Springs, AR 71903-0739; 501-623-0444, Fax: 501-623-4130.
www.arkansasmassagetherapy.com/
Email: info@arkansasmassagetherapy.com

23 Contractors Licensing Board, 4100 Richards Road, North Little Rock, AR 72117; 501-372-4661, Fax: 501-372-2247.
www.accessarkansas.org/clb/
Search Database at
www.state.ar.us/clb/search.html

24 State Board of Athletic Training, 9 Shackleford Plaza #3, Littlle Rock, AR 72211; 501-683-4076, Fax: 501-228-0294.
www.aratb.org   Email: aratb@sbcglobal.net
Search Database at www.aratb.org/search.php

25 Department of Health, Bureau of Health Resources; Administration/Licencing, 4815 West Markham, Little Rock, AR 72205-3867; 501-661-2000, Fax: 501-280-4901.
www.healthyarkansas.com/index.html

26 Department of Human Services, Division of Child Care & Early Childhood Education, PO Box 1437 Slot S140, Little Rock, AR 72203; 501-682-4891, Fax: 501-682-4897.
www.accessarkansas.org/childcare/
Email: Jennifer.Spriggs@mail.state.ar.us
Search Database at
www.state.ar.us/childcare/search.html

27 Department of Labor, 10421 W Markham, Little Rock, AR 72205; 501-682-4500, Fax: 501-682-4535.
www.arkansas.gov/labor/
Email: sharon.adams@arkansas.gov Note: Online rosters available.

28 Department of Environmental Quality, 8001 National Dr, Little Rock, AR 72209; 501-682-0680, Fax: 501-682-0707.
www.adeq.state.ar.us
Email: rogersk@adeq.state.ar.us
Search Database at
www.adeq.state.ar.us/compsvs/webmaster/databases.htm

29 Dietetics Licensing Board, PO Box 1016, Little Rock, AR 72115; 501-221-0566, Fax: 501-843-0878.

30 Liquefied Petroleum Gas Board, 3800 Richards Rd, North Little Rock, AR 72117; 501-683-4100.

31 Medical Board, 2100 Riverside Dr., Little Rock, AR 72202-1435; 501-296-1802, Fax: 501-296-1805.
www.armedicalboard.org
Email: asmb@mail.state.ar.us
Search Database at
https://www.armedicalboard.org/licenseverf/
Note: They also offer online verification system that includes additional professional information.

32 Department of Education, Office of Teacher Education & Licensure, State Education Bldg, Rm 106, Capitol Mall #4, Little Rock, AR 72201; 501-682-4695, Fax: 501-682-4898.
http://arkedu.state.ar.us/teachers/
Email: gmorris@arkedu.k12.ar.us
Search Database at www.as-is.org/directory/search_lic.html

33 Plant Board, PO Box 1069 (One Natural Resources Dr), Little Rock, AR 72203; 501-225-1598, Fax: 501-225-3590.
www.plantboard.org
Email: info@aspb.state.ar.us

34 Arkansas Board of Podiatric Medicine, 2001 Georgia Ave, Little Rock, AR 72207-5014; 501-664-3668, Fax: 501-666-3338. Note: Verifications in writing are free if a toll free fax number is provided, and/or a self addressed stamped envelope is provided with request.

36 Racing Commission, 1515 W. 7th St #505, Little Rock, AR 72203; 501-682-1467, Fax: 501-682-5273.
www.arkansas.gov/dfa/racing/
Email: bob.cohen@dfa.state.ar.us

37 Real Estate Commission, 612 Summit St, Little Rock, AR 72201; 501-683-8010, Fax: 501-682-8020.
www.arkansas.gov/arec/
Search Database at www.arkansas.gov/arec/

38 Secretary of State, 256 State Capitol, Little Rock, AR 72201; 501-682-3409, Fax: 501-682-3437.   www.sosweb.state.ar.us/corps/
Search Database at www.sosweb.state.ar.us/corps/

39 Securities Department, 201 W Markham, Heritage West Bldg, 3rd Fl, Little Rock, AR 72201; 501-324-9260, Fax: 501-324-9268.
www.accessarkansas.org/arsec/
Search Database at www.accessarkansas.org/asbce/search.html

40 Social Work Licensing Board, 2020 W 3rd St #503, POB 250381, Little Rock, AR 72225; 501-372-5071, Fax: 501-372-6301.
www.accessarkansas.org/swlb/
Email: swlb@mail.state.ar.us
Search Database at
www.state.ar.us/swlb/search/index.html

41 Speech Pathology & Audiology, Arkansas Children's Hospital, 800 Marshall St., Little Rock, AR 72202; 501-364-4319, Fax: 501-364-6881.
www.archildrens.org

42 Regulartory Service Section, State Police Admin. Svcs. Section, #1 State Police Plaza Drive, Little Rock, AR 72209; 501-618-8600, Fax: 501-618-8621.
www.asp.state.ar.us
Email: info@asp.state.ar.us

43 Supreme Court, 625 Marshall, Justice Bldg, Little Rock, AR 72201; 501-682-6849, Fax: 501-682-6877.
http://courts.state.ar.us
Email: arsclib@mail.state.ar.us
Search Database at
http://courts.state.ar.us/attylist/new/

44 Veterinary Medical Examining Board, PO Box 8505, Little Rock, AR 72215; 501-224-2836, Fax: 501-224-1100.
Email: sherry.glover@aspb.ar.gov Note: Veterinary/Tech Roster (hard copy printed) each year- $25.00.

45 Water Well Construction Commission, 101 E Capitol #350, Little Rock, AR 72201; 501-682-1025, Fax: 501-682-3991.
www.accessarkansas.org/awwcc

46 Board of Acupuncture & Related Techniques, 5110 Kavanaugh Blvd, Little Rock, AR 72207; 501-228-0644.
www.state.ar.us/directory/detail2.cgi?ID=1254

48 Abstractor's Board of Examiners, #5 Pinecrest Circle, Sheridan, AR 72150; 870-942-8064, Fax: 870-942-3101.
www.ark.org

49 Board of Cosmetology, 101 E Capitol #108, Little Rock, AR 72201; 501-682-2168, Fax: 501-682-5640.
www.arkansas.gov/cos/
Search Database at www.arkansas.gov/cos/

50 Board of Dispensing Opticians, Box 627, Helena, AR 72342; 870-572-2847, Fax: 870-572-2847.   www.ark.org
Search Database at
www.ark.org/directory/detail2.cgi?ID-1050

51 Board of Examiners for Counselors & Marriage/Family Therapists, 124 South Jackson #312 (PO Box 70, AR 71754), Magnolia, AR 71754-0070; 870-901-7055, Fax: 870-234-1842.
www.accessarkansas.org/abec/
Email: arboec@global.net
Search Database at
www.state.ar.us/abec/search.php Note: They provide lists in e-mail, fax, land line and written requests.

52 Department of Human Services, Office of Long Term Care, 7th & Main Streets, Little Rock, AR 72203; 501-682-1001.
www.medicaid.state.ar.us/general/units/OLTC/index.htm

53 Livestock & Poultry Commission, 1 Natural Resources Dr, PO Box 8505, Little Rock, AR 72215; 501-907-2400, Fax: 501-907-2425.
www.arlpc.org
Email: info@arlpc.org

54 Manufactured Home Commission, 523 S Louisiana #500, Little Rock, AR 72201; 501-324-9032, Fax: 501-324-9032.

55 Motor Vehicle Commission, 101 E Capitol #212, Little Rock, AR 72201; 501-682-1428, Fax: 501-682-5573.
www.armvc.com
Email: amvc@mail.state.ar.us
Search Database at
www.armvc.com/licensee_search/index.html

56 Fire Protection Licensing Board, 7509 Cantrell Rd #103-A, Little Rock, AR 72207; 501-661-7903, Fax: 501-603-3540.
www.arfireprotection.org
Email: afplb@aristotle.net
Search Database at
www.arfireprotection.org/roster/index.html

Arkansas Federal Courts

The following list indicates the district and division name for each county in the state. If the bankruptcy court location is different from the district court, then the location of the bankruptcy court appears in parentheses.

County/Court Cross Reference

County	District	Division
Arkansas	Eastern	Pine Bluff (Little Rock)
Ashley	Western (Eastern)	El Dorado (Little Rock)
Baxter	Western	Harrison (Fayetteville)
Benton	Western	Fayetteville
Boone	Western	Harrison (Fayetteville)
Bradley	Western (Eastern)	El Dorado (Little Rock)
Calhoun	Western (Eastern)	El Dorado (Little Rock)
Carroll	Western	Harrison (Fayetteville)
Chicot	Eastern	Pine Bluff (Little Rock)
Clark	Western (Eastern)	Hot Springs (Little Rock)
Clay	Eastern	Jonesboro (Little Rock)
Cleburne	Eastern	Batesville (Little Rock)
Cleveland	Eastern	Pine Bluff (Little Rock)
Columbia	Western (Eastern)	El Dorado (Little Rock)
Conway	Eastern	Little Rock
Craighead	Eastern	Jonesboro (Little Rock)
Crawford	Western	Fort Smith (Fayetteville)
Crittenden	Eastern	Jonesboro (Little Rock)
Cross	Eastern	Helena (Little Rock)
Dallas	Eastern	Pine Bluff (Little Rock)
Desha	Eastern	Pine Bluff (Little Rock)
Drew	Eastern	Pine Bluff (Little Rock)
Faulkner	Eastern	Little Rock
Franklin	Western	Fort Smith (Fayetteville)
Fulton	Eastern	Batesville (Little Rock)
Garland	Western (Eastern)	Hot Springs (Little Rock)
Grant	Eastern	Pine Bluff (Little Rock)
Greene	Eastern	Jonesboro (Little Rock)
Hempstead	Western (Eastern)	Texarkana (Little Rock)
Hot Spring	Western (Eastern)	Hot Springs (Little Rock)
Howard	Western (Eastern)	Texarkana (Little Rock)
Independence	Eastern	Batesville (Little Rock)
Izard	Eastern	Batesville (Little Rock)
Jackson	Eastern	Batesville (Little Rock)
Jefferson	Eastern	Pine Bluff (Little Rock)
Johnson	Western	Fort Smith (Fayetteville)
Lafayette	Western (Eastern)	Texarkana (Little Rock)
Lawrence	Eastern	Jonesboro (Little Rock)
Lee	Eastern	Helena (Little Rock)
Lincoln	Eastern	Pine Bluff (Little Rock)
Little River	Western (Eastern)	Texarkana (Little Rock)
Logan	Western	Fort Smith (Fayetteville)
Lonoke	Eastern	Little Rock
Madison	Western	Fayetteville
Marion	Western	Harrison (Fayetteville)
Miller	Western (Eastern)	Texarkana (Little Rock)
Mississippi	Eastern	Jonesboro (Little Rock)
Monroe	Eastern	Helena (Little Rock)
Montgomery	Western (Eastern)	Hot Springs (Little Rock)
Nevada	Western (Eastern)	Texarkana (Little Rock)
Newton	Western	Harrison (Fayetteville)
Ouachita	Western (Eastern)	El Dorado (Little Rock)
Perry	Eastern	Little Rock
Phillips	Eastern	Helena (Little Rock)
Pike	Western (Eastern)	Hot Springs (Little Rock)
Poinsett	Eastern	Jonesboro (Little Rock)
Polk	Western	Fort Smith (Fayetteville)
Pope	Eastern	Little Rock
Prairie	Eastern	Little Rock
Pulaski	Eastern	Little Rock
Randolph	Eastern	Jonesboro (Little Rock)
Saline	Eastern	Little Rock
Scott	Western	Fort Smith (Fayetteville)
Searcy	Western	Harrison (Fayetteville)
Sebastian	Western	Fort Smith (Fayetteville)
Sevier	Western (Eastern)	Texarkana (Little Rock)
Sharp	Eastern	Batesville (Little Rock)
St. Francis	Eastern	Helena (Little Rock)
Stone	Eastern	Batesville (Little Rock)
Union	Western (Eastern)	El Dorado (Little Rock)
Van Buren	Eastern	Little Rock
Washington	Western	Fayetteville
White	Eastern	Little Rock
Woodruff	Eastern	Helena (Little Rock)
Yell	Eastern	Little Rock

Standards for Federal Courts: The search fee is $20.00 per item (one party name or case number). Certification fee is $7.00 per document. Copy fee is $.50 per page. All fees standard unless noted in profile. Mail Search: always enclose a stamped self addressed envelope unless otherwise noted. Most courts accept fax requests or will suggest a copying/search vendor. Before releasing records, all courts require prepayment unless noted in profile.

Open records are located at the court unless otherwise noted. District courts index by defendant and plaintiff as well as by case number. Bankruptcy courts usually index by debtor and case number. While most courts now have their indexes on computer, many maintain card indices.

The universal PACER sign-up number is 800-676-6856. Find PACER and the Party/Case Index on the Web at http://pacer.psc.uscourts.gov. PACER dial-up access is $.60 per minute. Also, courts offering internet access via RACER, PACER, Web-PACER or the new CM-ECF charge $.07 per page fee unless noted as free.

US District Court

Eastern District of Arkansas

Batesville Division c/o Little Rock Division, PO Box 869, Little Rock, AR 72201-3325 (courier address: 600 W Capital, Room 402, Little Rock, AR 72201), 501-604-5351. www.are.uscourts.gov

Counties: Cleburne, Fulton, Independence, Izard, Jackson, Sharp, Stone.

Indexing & Storage: Cases indexed by as well as by case number. New cases available in the index after filing date. Open records are located at the Little Rock Division.

Fee & Payment: Payment may be made by money order, cashier check. Business checks are not accepted. Personal checks are not accepted.

Phone Search: Will search name.

In Person Search: Permitted.

PACER: There is no PACER access to this court.

Other Online Access: Search records on the Internet using RACER at www.are.uscourts.gov/perl/bkplog.html. Access fee is $.07 per page.

Helena Division c/o Little Rock Division, 600 W Capital Rm 402, Little Rock, AR 72201-3325 (courier: 600 W Capital, Room 402, Little Rock, AR 72201), 501-604-5351. www.are.uscourts.gov

Counties: Cross, Lee, Monroe, Phillips, St. Francis, Woodruff.

Indexing & Storage: Cases indexed by as well as by case number. New cases available in the index after filing date. Open records are located at the Little Rock Division.

Fee & Payment: Payment may be made by money order, cashier check. Business checks are not accepted. Personal checks are not accepted.

Phone Search: Will search name.

In Person Search: Permitted.

PACER: Search records online using RACER at www.are.uscourts.gov/perl/bkplog.html. Access fee is $.07 per page. Document images available. Records purged every five years. New records online after 1 day.

Jonesboro Division PO Box 7080, Jonesboro, AR 72403 (courier address: Federal Office Bldg, Room 312, 615 S Main St, Jonesboro, AR 72401), 870-972-4610, Fax: 870-972-4612. www.are.uscourts.gov

Counties: Clay, Craighead, Crittenden, Greene, Lawrence, Mississippi, Poinsett, Randolph.

Indexing & Storage: New cases available in the index immediately after filing date.

Fee & Payment: Payment may be made by money order, cashier check, personal check. Payee: Clerk, U.S. District Court.

Phone Search: Docket information available.

Mail Search: A SASE not required.

In Person Search: Fee charged if court conducts your in person search for you.

PACER: There is no PACER access to this court.

Other Online Access: Search records on the Internet using RACER at www.are.uscourts.gov/perl/bkplog.html. Access fee is $.07 per page. Document images available.

Little Rock Division Room 402, 600 W Capitol, Little Rock, AR 72201 (courier address: Use mail address for courier delivery) 501-604-5351. www.are.uscourts.gov

Counties: Conway, Faulkner, Lonoke, Perry, Pope, Prairie, Pulaski, Saline, Van Buren, White, Yell.

Indexing & Storage: New cases available in the index immediately after filing date. Records are also indexed on microfiche.

Fee & Payment: Payment may be made by money order, cashier check, personal check, Visa, Mastercard. Payee: Clerk, U.S. District Court.

Phone Search: Docket information available by phone.

In Person Search: Fee charged if court conducts your in person search for you.

PACER: There is no PACER access to this court.

Other Online Access: Search records on the Internet using RACER at www.are.uscourts.gov/perl/bkplog.html. Access fee is $.07 per page. Document images available.

Pine Bluff Division PO Box 8307, Pine Bluff, AR 71611-8307 (courier address: U.S. Post Office & Courthouse, 100 E 8th St, Room 3103, Pine Bluff, AR 71601), 870-536-1190, Fax: 870-536-6330. www.are.uscourts.gov

Counties: Arkansas, Chicot, Cleveland, Dallas, Desha, Drew, Grant, Jefferson, Lincoln.

Indexing & Storage: New cases available in the index immediately after filing date. Records are on the computer from 1989. Records are also indexed on microfiche.

Fee & Payment: Payment may be made by money order, cashier check, personal check. Prepayment is required for copies and certification. Payee: U.S. District Clerk.

Phone Search: Phone searching is not available.

In Person Search: Fee charged if court conducts your in person search for you.

PACER: There is no PACER access to this court.

Other Online Access: Search records on the Internet using RACER at www.are.uscourts.gov/perl/bkplog.html. Access fee is $.07 per page. Document images available.

U.S. Bankruptcy Court

Eastern District of Arkansas

Little Rock Division PO Drawer 3777, Little Rock, AR 72203 (courier address: Room 101, 600 W Capitol, Little Rock, AR 72201), 501-918-5500, Fax: 501-918-5520. www.areb.uscourts.gov

Counties: Same counties as included in Eastern District of Arkansas, plus the counties included in the Western District divisions of El Dorado, Hot Springs and Texarkana. All bankruptcy cases in Arkansas prior to mid-1993 were heard here.

Indexing & Storage: Cases indexed by debtor and creditors as well as by case number. New cases available in the index immediately after filing date. Records are also indexed on microfiche.

Fee & Payment: Payment may be made by money order, cashier check, personal check, Visa or Mastercard. Debtor's checks are not accepted. Payee: Clerk, U.S. Bankruptcy Court. Will fax results if copy fee is paid.

Phone Search: Only the basic information not provided on the VCIS will be released over the phone. This includes the case number, chapter, judge, attorney, trustee, date if case closed, etc. Automated voice case information service (VCIS) is available. Call VCIS at 800-891-6741 or 501-918-5555. Will fax results if copy fee is paid.

In Person Search: Permitted.

PACER: Court uses new CM/ECF system for PACER. Records purged every six months. New civil records are online after 1 day.

Electronic Filing: Electronic filing information online at https://ecf.areb.uscourts.gov

U.S. District Court

Western District of Arkansas

El Dorado Division PO Box 1566, El Dorado, AR 71731 (courier address: Room 205, 101 S Jackson, El Dorado, AR 71730), 870-862-1202. www.arwd.uscourts.gov

Counties: Ashley, Bradley, Calhoun, Columbia, Ouachita, Union.

Indexing & Storage: New cases available in the index immediately after filing date. Files are maintained numerically by year.

Fee & Payment: Payment may be made by money order, cashier check, personal check, Visa, Mastercard. Prepayment is required for out of state searchers. Payee: Clerk, U.S. District Court.

Phone Search: Only docket information available.

In Person Search: Fee charged if court conducts your in person search for you.

PACER: PACER is available online at http://pacer.arwd.uscourts.gov. Records purged every five years. New records online after 1 day.

Other Online Access: Only "Pending Cases" information is available online at www.arwd.uscourts.gov/caseinfo.cfm. This court now participates in PACER. Court does not participate in the U.S. party case index.

Fayetteville Division PO Box 6420, Fayetteville, AR 72702 (courier: Room 510, 35 E Mountain, Fayetteville, AR 72702), 479-521-6980, Fax: 479-575-0774. www.arwd.uscourts.gov

Counties: Benton, Madison, Washington.

Indexing & Storage: New cases available in the index immediately after filing date. Files are maintained numerically by year.

Fee & Payment: Payment may be made by money order, cashier check, personal check, Visa, Mastercard. Prepayment is required for out of state searchers. Payee: Clerk, Western District of Arkansas.

Phone Search: Only docket information available.

Mail Search: A SASE not required.

In Person Search: Fee charged if court conducts your in person search for you. Searches can be done in person for free if no written record is furnished.

PACER: PACER is available online at http://pacer.arwd.uscourts.gov. Records purged every five years. New records online after 1 day.

Other Online Access: Only "Pending Cases" information is available online at www.arwd.uscourts.gov/caseinfo.cfm. This court now participates in PACER. Court does not participate in the U.S. party case index.

Fort Smith Division

Fort Smith Division PO Box 1547, Fort Smith, AR 72902 (courier address: Judge Isaac C. Parker Federal Bldg #1038, 6th & Rogers Ave, Fort Smith, AR 72901), 479-783-6833, Fax: 479-783-6308. www.arwd.uscourts.gov

Counties: Crawford, Franklin, Johnson, Logan, Polk, Scott, Sebastian.

Indexing & Storage: New cases available in the index immediately after filing date. Files are maintained numerically by year.

Fee & Payment: Payment may be made by money order, cashier check, personal check, Visa, Mastercard. Prepayment is required for out of state searchers. Payee: Clerk of Court.

Phone Search: Only docket information available.

Mail Search: A SASE not required.

In Person Search: Fee charged if court conducts your in person search for you.

PACER: PACER is available online at http://pacer.arwd.uscourts.gov. Records purged every five years. New records online after 1 day.

Other Online Access: Only "Pending Cases" information is available online at www.arwd.uscourts.gov/caseinfo.cfm. This court now participates in PACER. Court does not participate in the U.S. party case index.

Hot Springs Division

Hot Springs Division PO Drawer 6486, Hot Springs, AR 71902 (courier address: Federal Bldg Room 347, 100 Reserve, Hot Springs, AR 71901), 501-623-6411. www.arwd.uscourts.gov

Counties: Clark, Garland, Hot Springs, Montgomery, Pike.

Indexing & Storage: New cases available in the index immediately after filing date. Files are maintained numerically by year.

Fee & Payment: Payment may be made by money order, cashier check, personal check, Visa, MC.

Prepayment is required for out of state searchers. Payee: Clerk, Western District of Arkansas.

Phone Search: Searching inot available by phone.

In Person Search: Fee charged if court conducts your in person search for you.

PACER: PACER is available online at http://pacer.arwd.uscourts.gov. Records purged every five years. New records online after 1 day.

Other Online Access: Only "Pending Cases" information is available online at www.arwd.uscourts.gov/caseinfo.cfm. This court now participates in PACER. Court does not participate in the U.S. party case index.

Texarkana Division

Texarkana Division PO Box 2746, Texarkana, AR 75504-2746 (courier address: 500 State Line Ave, Room 302, Texarkana, AR 71854), 870-773-3381. www.arwd.uscourts.gov

Counties: Hempstead, Howard, Lafayette, Little River, Miller, Nevada, Sevier.

Indexing & Storage: New cases available in the index immediately after filing date. Files are maintained numerically by year. Records are also indexed by microfiche.

Fee & Payment: Payment may be made by money order, cashier check, personal check, Visa, Mastercard. Prepayment is required for out of state searchers. Payee: Clerk of the Court.

Phone Search: Case numbers are released by phone. Anything else will depend on workload of deputy clerk.

Mail Search: A SASE not required.

In Person Search: Fee charged if court conducts your in person search for you.

PACER: PACER is available online at http://pacer.arwd.uscourts.gov. Records purged every five years. New records online after 1 day.

Other Online Access: Only "Pending Cases" information is available online at www.arwd.uscourts.gov/caseinfo.cfm. This court now participates in PACER. Court does not participate in the U.S. party case index.

U.S. Bankruptcy Court
Western District of Arkansas

Fayetteville Division

Fayetteville Division PO Box 3097, Fayetteville, AR 72702-3097 (courier address: 35 E Mountain, Room 316, Fayetteville, AR 72701), 479-582-9800, Fax: 479-582-9825. www.arb.uscourts.gov

Counties: Same counties as included in the U.S. District District Court - Western District of Arkansas except that counties included in the divisions of El Dorado and Texarkana are heard in Little Rock.

Indexing & Storage: Cases indexed by debtor and creditors as well as by case number. New cases available in the index immediately after filing date.

Fee & Payment: Payment may be made by money order, cashier check, personal check, Visa. Personal checks are not accepted from debtors. Licensed attorneys may be invoiced for copywork. Payee: Clerk, U.S. Bankruptcy Court.

Phone Search: Only the basic information not provided on the VCIS will be released over the phone. This includes the case number, chapter, judge, attorney, and trustee. Automated voice case information service (VCIS) is available. Call VCIS at 800-891-6741 or 501-918-5555.

In Person Search: Fee charged if court conducts your in person search for you.

PACER: Court uses new CM/ECF system for PACER. Records purged every six months. New civil records are online after 1 day.

Electronic Filing: Electronic filing information online at https://ecf.arwb.uscourts.gov

Arkansas County Courts

Court	Jurisdiction	No. of Courts	How Organized
Circuit Courts*	General	38	28 Circuits
District Courts*	Limited	126	
City Courts	Limited	1084	
Court of Common Pleas	Limited	4	
Justice of the Peace Courts	Limited	55	
Police Courts	Limited	5	

* Profiled in this Sourcebook.

Court	CIVIL								
	Tort	Contract	Real Estate	Min. Claim	Max. Claim	Small Claims	Estate	Eviction	Domestic Relations
Circuit Courts*	X	X	X	$5000	No Max		X		X
District Courts*		X	X	$0	$5000	$5000		X	
City Courts		X	X	$0	$300				
Court of Common Pleas		X		$500	$1000				
Justice of the Peace Courts						$300			
Police Courts		X	X	$0	$300				

Court	CRIMINAL				
	Felony	Misdemeanor	DWI/DUI	Preliminary Hearing	Juvenile
Circuit Courts*	X				
District Courts*		X	X	X	
City Courts		X	X	X	
Court of Common Pleas					
Justice of the Peace Courts		X			
Police Courts		X	X		

ADMINISTRATION

Administrative Office of Courts, 625 Marshall St, 1100 Justice Bldg, Little Rock, AR, 72201; 501-682-9400, Fax: 501-682-9410. www.courts.state.ar.us/

COURT STRUCTURE

Circuit Courts are the courts of general jurisdiction and are arranged in 28 circuits. Circuit courts consist of five subject matter divisions: criminal, civil, probate, domestic relations, and juvenile. The Circuit Clerk handles the records and recordings; however, some counties have a County Clerk that handles probate. District courts, formerly known as municipal courts before passage of Amendment 80 to the Arkansas Constitution, exercise county-wide jurisdiction over misdemeanor cases, preliminary felony cases, and civil cases in matters of less than $5,000, including small claims. The City Courts operate in smaller communities where District Courts do not exist and exercise city-wide jurisdiction.

ONLINE ACCESS

There is a very limited internal online computer system at the Administrative Office of Courts. The home web page gives online access to Supreme and Appellate opinions.

ADDITIONAL INFORMATION

Many courts that allow written search requests require an SASE. Fees vary widely across jurisdictions as do prepayment requirements.

Arkansas County

Circuit Court - Northern District 302 S
College St, Stuttgart, AR 72160; 870-673-2056; Probate phone: 870-673-7311; Fax: 870-673-3869. Hours: 8AM-4;30PM (CST). *Felony, Civil Actions, Probate.*

Note: The court is not bonded to search Civil or Chancery records. Probate has a different Clerk.

Civil Records: Access: In person only. Visitors must perform in person searches for themselves. No search fee. Required to search: name, years to search. Civil cases indexed by defendant, plaintiff. Civil records in files from 1913, prior to 1913 records located in DeWitt (946-4219).

Criminal Records: Access: In person only. Visitors must perform in person searches for themselves. No search fee. Required to search: name, years to search, DOB. Criminal records in files from 1913, prior to 1913 records located in DeWitt (946-4219).

General Information: No juvenile records released. Copy fee: $.50 per page. Cert fee: $4.00. Personal checks accepted. Prepayment required.

Circuit Court - Southern District 101
Courthouse Sq, De Witt, AR 72042; 870-946-4219; Fax: 870-946-1394. Hours: 8AM-4:30PM (closed btw12 & 12:30) (CST). *Felony, Civil Actions Over $5,000.*

Civil Records: Access: Fax, mail, in person. Both court and visitors may perform in person searches. Search fee: $6.00 per name. Required to search: name, years to search. Civil cases indexed by defendant, plaintiff. Civil records in files from 1923, computerized since 1995, prior records (the two other courts in this county also) located at this court.

Criminal Records: Access: Fax, mail, in person. Both court and visitors may perform in person searches. Search fee: $6.00 per name. Required to search: name, DOB; also helpful: SSN. Criminal records in files from 1923, computerized since 1995, prior records (the two other courts in this county also) located at this court. Search request must be in writing.

General Information: Public Access terminal is available. No juvenile, expunged records released. Will fax results for $1.00 per copy. Copy fee: $.50 per page. Cert fee: $4.00. Payee: Arkansas County Circuit Clerk. Personal checks accepted. Prepayment required. Mail requests: SASE requested. Turnaround time 1-2 days.

Stuttgart District Court PO Box 848, 514 S.
Main, Stuttgart, AR 72160; 870-673-7951; Fax: 870-673-6522. Hours: 8AM-4:30PM (CST). *Misdemeanor, Civil Actions Under $5,000, Eviction, Small Claims.*

Civil Records: Access: Phone, mail, fax, in person. Both court and visitors may perform in person searches. No search fee. Required to search: name plus SSN. Records go back to 1990; on computer back to 1991.

Criminal Records: Access: Phone, mail, fax, in person. Both court and visitors may perform in person searches. No search fee. Required to search: name, years to search, SSN; also helpful: DOB. Records go back to 1990; on computer back to 1991.

General Information: Will fax results. Copy fee: $0.25. No cert fee. Mail requests: SASE required. Mail turnaround time 3 days.

Ashley County

Circuit Court Ashley County Courthouse, 205 E
Jefferson, Hamburg, AR 71646; 870-853-2030; Fax: 870-853-2034. Hours: 8AM-4:30PM (CST). *Felony, Civil Actions Over $5,000, Probate.*

Civil Records: Access: Mail, in person. Visitors must perform in person searches for themselves. No search fee. Required to search: name, years to search. Civil cases indexed by defendant, plaintiff. Civil records on files and index cards from 1950s.

Criminal Records: Access: Mail, in person. Visitors must perform in person searches for themselves. No search fee. Required to search: name, years to search; also helpful: DOB, SSN. Criminal records on files and index cards from 1950s. No name searches by mail, must have case numbers. Mail requests must have case numbers.

General Information: No juvenile records released. Fee to fax results is $1.00 per page. Copy fee: $.50 per page. Cert fee: $2.50. Payee: Circuit Clerk's Office. Personal checks accepted. Prepayment required. Mail requests: SASE required.

Hamburg District Court PO Box 72,
Hamburg, AR 71646; 870-853-8326; Fax: 870-853-8600. Hours: 8AM-4:30PM (CST). *Misdemeanor, Civil Actions Under $5,000, Eviction, Small Claims.*

Civil Records: Access: Mail, in person. Both court and visitors may perform in person searches. Search fee: $5.00. Civil records go back 10 years; on computer back to 1989.

Criminal Records: Access: Mail, in person. Both court and visitors may perform in person searches. Search fee: $5.00. Required to search: name, years to search, DOB. Criminal records go back to 1976; on computer back to 1989.

General Information: Public Access terminal is available. Will not fax results. Cert fee: $10.00. Payee: District Court. Prepayment required. Mail turnaround time 1-2 days.

Baxter County

Circuit Court 1 E 7th St Courthouse Sq, Mountain
Home, AR 72653; 870-425-3475; Fax: 870-424-5105. Hours: 8AM-4:30PM (CST). *Felony, Civil Actions Over $5,000, Probate.*

Civil Records: Access: Fax, mail, in person. Both court and visitors may perform in person searches. Search fee: $6.00 per name. Required to search: name, years to search. Civil cases indexed by defendant, plaintiff. Civil records on computer from 1982, on criminal fee book from early 1900s.

Criminal Records: Access: Mail, in person. Both court and visitors may perform in person searches. Search fee: $6.00 per name. Required to search: name, years to search, SSN. Criminal records on computer from 1982, on criminal fee book from early 1900s.

General Information: Public Access terminal is available. No adoption or juvenile records released. Will fax results $5.00 per page. Copy fee: $.25 per page. Cert fee: $5.00. Payee: Baxter County Clerk. Personal checks accepted. Prepayment required. Mail requests: SASE required. Mail turnaround time 1-2 days.

District Court 720 S Hickory, Mountain Home,
AR 72653; 870-425-3140; Civil phone: 870-425-8910; Fax: 870-425-8470. Hours: 8AM-4:30PM (CST). *Misdemeanor, Civil Actions Under $5,000, Eviction, Small Claims.*

Civil Records: Access: In person, mail. Only the court performs in person searches; visitors may not. No search fee. Civil records go back to 1980's; computerized records since 1995.

Criminal Records: Access: In person, mail. Only the court performs in person searches; visitors may not.

No search fee. Required to search: name, years to search, DOB, SSN. Criminal records go back to 1980's; computerized since 1995.

General Information: Copy fee: $.25 per page. Cert fee: $5.00. Turnaround time 1-2 days.

Benton County

Circuit Court 102 NE "A" St, Bentonville, AR
72712; 479-271-1015; Probate phone: 479-271-5727; Fax: 479-271-5719. Hours: 8AM-4:30PM (CST). *Felony, Civil Actions Over $5,000, Probate.*
www.co.benton.ar.us

Civil Records: Access: Phone, mail, online, in person. Visitors must perform in person searches for themselves. No search fee. Required to search: name, years to search. Civil cases indexed by defendant, plaintiff. Civil records on computer from 1991, on dockets from 1880s. Civil court docket information is free online at http://64.217.42.130:5061. Use "option" 21.

Criminal Records: Access: Phone, mail, online, in person. Visitors must perform in person searches for themselves. No search fee. Required to search: name, years to search. Criminal records on computer from 1991, on dockets from 1880s. Online access to criminal records is the same as civil.

General Information: Public Access terminal is available. No juvenile records released. Will fax results to lcoal or toll free line. Copy fee: $.10 per page. Cert fee: $2.00. Payee: Benton County Circuit Clerk. Personal checks accepted. Prepayment required. Mail turnaround time in 24 hours.

District Court 117 W Central, Bentonville, AR
72712; 479-271-3120; Fax: 479-271-3134. Hours: 8AM-4:30PM (CST). *Misdemeanor, Civil Actions Under $5,000,Small Claims.*

Civil Records: Access: In person, mail. Only the court performs in person searches; visitors may not. No search fee. Civil records on computer back to 1996; other records go back to 1985.

Criminal Records: Access: In person, mail. Only the court performs in person searches; visitors may not. No search fee. Required to search: name, years to search, DOB. Criminal records on computer back to 1992; other records go back to 1982.

General Information: Will fax results to local or toll free line. Copy fee: $.25 per page. Cert fee: $5.00. Payee: Bentonville District Court. Prepayment required. Mail turnaround time 5 days.

Boone County

Circuit Court 100 N Main St #200, Harrison, AR
72601; 870-741-5560; Fax: 870-741-4335. Hours: 8AM-4:30PM (CST). *Felony, Civil Actions Over $5,000.*

Note: Probate records are in the County Clerk's office, 870-741-8428.

Civil Records: Access: Mail, in person. Both court and visitors may perform in person searches. Search fee: $5.00. Required to search: name, years to search. Civil cases indexed by defendant, plaintiff. Civil records archived from 1940, index from 1977, computerized from 1990.

Criminal Records: Access: Mail, in person. Both court and visitors may perform in person searches. Search fee: $5.00. Required to search: name, years to search. Criminal records archived from 1940, index from 1977, computerized from 1990.

General Information: Public Access terminal is available. No indictments or juvenile records released. Fee to fax results is $5.00 per document. Copy fee: $.25 per page. Cert fee: $5.00. Payee: Circuit Clerk. Personal checks accepted. Prepayment required. Mail requests: SASE required. Mail turnaround time 1 day.

District Court PO Box 968, Harrison, AR 72602; 870-741-2788; Fax: 870-741-4329. Hours: 8AM-4:30PM (CST). *Misdemeanor, Civil Actions Under $5,000, Eviction, Small Claims.*
Civil Records: Access: In person, mail. Both court and visitors may perform in person searches. Search fee: None. Required to search: name and years to search. Records indexed since 1996.
Criminal Records: Access: In person, mail. Both court and visitors may perform in person searches. No search fee. Required to search: name, years to search; also helpful: DOB. Records indexed since 1990.
General Information: Will fax results for $1.00 per page. Copy fee: $.25 per copy. Cert fee: $5.00. Payee: Boone County District Court. Prepayment required. Mail turnaround time 2 weeks.

Bradley County

Circuit Court Bradley County Courthouse - Records, 101 E Cedar, Warren, AR 71671; 870-226-2272; Probate phone: 870-226-3464; Fax: 870-226-8401. Hours: 8AM-4:30PM (CST). *Felony, Civil Actions Over $5,000, Probate.*
Civil Records: Access: In person only. Visitors must perform in person searches for themselves. No search fee. Required to search: name, years to search. Civil cases indexed by defendant, plaintiff. Civil records (active cases) on dockets, retired cases on indexes from 1880, no computerization.
Criminal Records: Access: Mail, in person. Both court and visitors may perform in person searches. Search fee: $6.00. Required to search: name, years to search; also helpful: DOB, SSN. Criminal records (active cases) on dockets, retired cases on indexes from 1880, no computerization.
General Information: No juvenile released. Copy fee: $.50 per page. Cert fee: $3.00. Payee: Circuit Court. Personal checks accepted. Prepayment required. Mail requests: SASE required. Mail turnaround time 1 week.

District Court PO Box 352, Warren, AR 71671; 870-226-2567; Fax: 870-226-2567. Hours: 8AM-4:30PM (CST). *Misdemeanor, Civil Actions Under $5,000, Eviction, Small Claims.*
Civil Records: Access: In person, mail. Only the court performs in person searches; visitors may not. Search fee: $6.00 per name. Computerized records since 1993.
Criminal Records: Access: In person, mail. Only the court performs in person searches; visitors may not. Search fee: $6.00 per name. Required to search: name, years to search, SSN. Computerized records since 1993.
General Information: Will fax results to local or toll free line. No copy fee. Cert fee: $5.00. Payee: District Court. Prepayment required. Mail requests: SASE required. Mail turnaround time 1 week.

Calhoun County

Circuit Court PO Box 1175, Hampton, AR 71744; 870-798-2517. Hours: 8AM-4:30PM (CST). *Felony, Civil Actions Over $5,000, Probate.*
Civil Records: Access: Mail, in person. Both court and visitors may perform in person searches. Search fee: $6.00. Required to search: name, years to search. Civil cases indexed by defendant, plaintiff. Civil records on dockets from 1851.
Criminal Records: Access: Mail, in person. Visitors must perform in person searches for themselves. Search fee: $6.00. Required to search: name, years to search, DOB; also helpful: SSN. Criminal records on dockets from 1851.
General Information: Public Access terminal is available. No juvenile or adoption released. Copy fee: $.25 per page. Cert fee: $5.00. Payee: Calhoun County Clerk. Personal checks accepted. Prepayment

required. Mail requests: SASE required. Mail turnaround time 1-3 days.

District Court PO Box 783, Hampton, AR 71744; 870-798-2753; Civil phone: 870-798-2165; Fax: 870-798-3665. Hours: 8AM-4:30PM (CST). *Misdemeanor, Civil Actions Under $5,000, Eviction, Small Claims.*
Note: Municipal Clerk at the city is 870-798-3201.
Civil Records: Access: In person, mail. Both court and visitors may perform in person searches. No search fee.
Criminal Records: Access: In person, mail. Both court and visitors may perform in person searches. No search fee. Required to search: name, years to search, SSN.
General Information: Will fax results. Cert fee: $5.00 per doc. Turnaround time 2 days.

Carroll County

Berryville Circuit Court - Eastern District Carroll County Circuit Court, PO Box 71, Berryville, AR 72616; 870-423-2422; Probate phone: 870-423-2022; Fax: 870-423-4796. Hours: 8:30AM-4:30PM (CST). *Felony, Civil Actions Over $5,000, Eviction, Probate.*
Civil Records: Access: Mail, in person. Both court and visitors may perform in person searches. Search fee: $6.00 per name. Required to search: name, years to search. Civil cases indexed by defendant, plaintiff. Civil records on computer from 1997, on index books since 1869.
Criminal Records: Access: Fax, mail, in person. Both court and visitors may perform in person searches. Search fee: $6.00 per name. Required to search: name, years to search, DOB, SSN. Criminal records on computer back to 1997, on index books since 1869.
General Information: Public Access terminal is available. No juvenile records released. Fee to fax results is $1.00 per page. Copy fee: $.25 per page; $.50 per page if mailed. Cert fee: $2.00 per document. Payee: Circuit Clerk of Carroll County. Personal checks accepted. Prepayment required. Mail requests: SASE required. Mail turnaround time 1-2 days.

Eureka Springs Circuit Court - Western District 44 S Main, PO Box 109, Eureka Springs, AR 72632; 479-253-8646. Hours: 8:30AM-4:30PM (CST). *Felony, Civil Actions Over $5,000, Eviction, Probate.*
Civil Records: Access: In person only. Visitors must perform in person searches for themselves. No search fee. Required to search: name, years to search. Civil cases indexed by defendant, plaintiff. Civil records on indexes from 1883.
Criminal Records: Access: Phone, mail, in person. Both court and visitors may perform in person searches. Search fee: $6.00 per name. Required to search: name, years to search; also helpful: DOB. Criminal records on indexes from 1883, computerized since 02/21/02.
General Information: Public Access terminal is available. (Only for recent criminal cases.) No expunged criminal records released. Fee to fax results is $1.00 per page. Copy fee: $.50 by mail or $.25 in person. Cert fee: $2.00; $5.00 for Probate records. Payee: Circuit Clerk of Carroll County or County Clerk. Personal checks accepted. Prepayment required. Mail requests: SASE required. Mail turnaround time varies.

Berryville District Court 103 S Springs, Berryville, AR 72616; 870-423-6247; Fax: 870-423-7069. Hours: 8AM-4:30PM (CST). *Misdemeanor, Civil Actions Under $5,000, Small Claims.*
Civil Records: Access: Mail, fax, in person. Both court and visitors may perform in person searches. No

search fee. Required to search: name, DOB. Records computerized since 1987.
Criminal Records: Access: In person, mail. Both court and visitors may perform in person searches. No search fee. Required to search: name, years to search; also helpful: DOB. Records computerized since 1987.
General Information: Copy fee: $.25 per page. Prepayment required. Mail turnaround time 1-2 days.

Eureka Springs District Court Courthouse, 44 S Main, Eureka Springs, AR 72632; 479-253-8574; Fax: 479-253-6887. Hours: 8AM-5PM (CST). *Misdemeanor, Civil Actions Under $5,000, Small Claims.*
www.cityofeurekasprings.org/muncourt.html
Civil Records: Access: Phone, mail, in person. Both court and visitors may perform in person searches. No search fee. Records on computer back to 1990.
Criminal Records: Access: Phone, mail, in person. Both court and visitors may perform in person searches. No search fee. Required to search: name, years to search. Criminal records on computer back to 1990.
General Information: Mail requests: SASE required. Mail turnaround time 1 week.

Chicot County

Circuit Court 108 Main St, County Courthouse, Lake Village, AR 71653; 870-265-8010; Probate phone: 870-265-8000; Fax: 870-265-8012. Hours: 8AM-4:30PM (CST). *Felony, Civil Actions Over $5,000, Probate.*
Note: Probate court is located here at the same address, in a separate office.
Civil Records: Access: Mail, in person. Both court and visitors may perform in person searches. Search fee: $6.00 per name. Required to search: name, years to search. Civil cases indexed by defendant, plaintiff. Civil records on dockets and files from 1900s; computerized since 1999.
Criminal Records: Access: Mail, in person. Both court and visitors may perform in person searches. Search fee: $6.00 per name. Required to search: name, years to search. Criminal records on dockets and files from 1900s; computerized records since 1999.
General Information: No juvenile records released. Copy fee: $.50 per page. Cert fee: $2.00 per doc plus copy fee. Payee: Circuit Clerk. Personal checks accepted. Prepayment required. Mail requests: SASE required. Mail turnaround time 1-2 days.

Lake Village District Court PO Box 832, Lake Village, AR 71653; 870-265-3283. Hours: 9AM-5PM (CST). *Misdemeanor, Civil Actions Under $5,000, Eviction, Small Claims.*
Civil Records: Access: Phone, mail, fax, in person. Both court and visitors may perform in person searches. Search fee: $5.00 per name. Civil records on computer go back to 10/02; other records go back to 1977.
Criminal Records: Access: Mail, in person. Both court and visitors may perform in person searches. Search fee: $5.00 per name. Required to search: name, years to search; also helpful: DOB, SSN. Criminal records on computer go back to 8/2000; other records go back to 1977.
General Information: Payee: Lake Village District Court. Prepayment required. Mail requests: SASE required. Mail turnaround time ASAP.

Clark County

Circuit Court PO Box 576, Arkadelphia, AR 71923; 870-246-4281. Hours: 8:30AM-4:30PM (CST). *Felony, Civil Actions Over $5,000, Probate.*
Civil Records: Access: Mail, in person. Both court and visitors may perform in person searches. Search

fee: $5.00 per name. Required to search: name, years to search. Civil cases indexed by defendant, plaintiff. Civil records on computer since 1985.

Criminal Records: Access: Mail, in person. Both court and visitors may perform in person searches. Search fee: $5.00 per name. Required to search: name, years to search. Criminal records on computer since 1985.

General Information: Public Access terminal is available. No juvenile records released. Will fax results for $1.00 per page. Copy fee: $.50 per page. Cert fee: $5.00. Payee: Penny R Ross Circuit Clerk. Personal checks accepted. Prepayment required. Mail requests: SASE required. Mail turnaround time 1-2 days.

District Court PO Box 449, Arkadelphia, AR 71923; 870-246-9552. Hours: 8:30AM-4:30PM (CST). *Misdemeanor, Civil Actions Under $5,000, Eviction, Small Claims.*

Civil Records: Access: Phone, mail, fax, in person. Both court and visitors may perform in person searches. No search fee. Records go back to 1980; on computer since 1990.

Criminal Records: Access: Phone, mail, fax, in person. Both court and visitors may perform in person searches. No search fee. Required to search: name, years to search; also helpful: DOB. Records go back to 1980; on computer since 1990.

General Information: Mail requests: SASE required. Mail turnaround time 3 days.

Clay County

Corning Circuit Court 800 SW @nd St, Corning, AR 72422-2715; 870-857-3271; Fax: 870-857-9201. Hours: 8AM-4:30PM (CST). *Felony, Civil Actions Over $5,000, Probate.*

Civil Records: Access: Mail, in person. Both court and visitors may perform in person searches. Search fee: $6.00 per name. Required to search: name, years to search. Civil cases indexed by defendant, plaintiff. Civil records on books from 1893.

Criminal Records: Access: In person. Both court and visitors may perform in person searches. No search fee. Required to search: name, years to search; also helpful: DOB, SSN. Criminal records on books from 1893. Court personnel will not do a name search, but will pull specific case data if docket number given.

General Information: No juvenile records released. Copy fee: $1.00 per page if mailed, $.25 if in person. Cert fee: $5.00. Payee: Circuit Clerk. Personal checks accepted. Prepayment required. Mail turnaround time 1-2 days.

Piggott Circuit Court 151 S 2nd, Piggott, AR 72454; 870-598-2524; Probate phone: 870-598-2813; Fax: 870-598-2524. Hours: 8AM-4:30PM (CST). *Felony, Civil Actions Over $5,000.*

Civil Records: Access: In person only. Visitors must perform in person searches. No search fee. Required to search: name, years to search. Civil cases indexed by defendant, plaintiff. Civil records on books from 1893.

Criminal Records: Access: In person only. Visitors must perform in person searches. No search fee. Required to search: name, years to search, DOB, SSN. Criminal records on books from 1893.

General Information: No expunged criminal records released. Will fax results $5.00 per doc. Copy fee: $.25 per page. Cert fee: $5.00 per page. Payee: Circuit Clerk. Personal checks accepted. Prepayment required.

District Court 151 S 2nd Ave, Piggott, AR 72454; 870-598-2265. Hours: 8AM-4:30PM (CST). *Misdemeanor, Civil Actions Under $5,000, Eviction, Small Claims.*

Note: Office is open 20 hours per week only. For eviction information the court says to contact Clay County Sheriff, 151 S 2nd St, Piggott, AR 72454, 870-598-2266.

Civil Records: Access: Mail, in person. Only the court performs in person searches; visitors may not. Search fee: $8.00. Records on computer back to 1998.

Criminal Records: Access: Mail, in person. Only the court performs in person searches; visitors may not. Search fee: $8.00. Required to search: name, years to search, SSN; also helpful: DOB. Records on computer back to 1998.

General Information: Will fax results to local or toll free line. Payee: District Court. Prepayment required. Mail requests: SASE required. Mail turnaround time 3-4 days.

Cleburne County

Circuit Court PO Box 543, Heber Springs, AR 72543; 501-362-8149; Fax: 501-362-4650. Hours: 8:30AM-4:30PM (CST). *Felony, Civil Actions Over $5,000, Probate.*

Civil Records: Access: Fax, mail, in person. Both court and visitors may perform in person searches. Search fee: $6.00 per name. Required to search: name, years to search. Civil cases indexed by defendant, plaintiff. Civil records on dockets from 1883.

Criminal Records: Access: Phone, mail, in person. Both court and visitors may perform in person searches. Search fee: $6.00 per name. Required to search: name, years to search. Criminal records on dockets from 1883.

General Information: No juvenile records released. Will fax results for $4.00 1st page; $1.00 each add'l page. Copy fee: $.25 per page. Cert fee: $1.00 per document. Payee: Circuit Clerk. Personal checks accepted. Prepayment required. Mail requests: SASE required. Mail turnaround time 1-2 days.

District Court 102 E Main, Heber Springs, AR 72543; 501-362-6585; Fax: 501-362-4661. Hours: 8:30AM-4:30PM (CST). *Misdemeanor, Civil Actions Under $5,000, Small Claims, Eviction.*

Civil Records: Access: Phone, mail, fax, in person. Both court and visitors may perform in person searches. No search fee. Civil records on computer back to 1989.

Criminal Records: Access: Phone, mail, fax, in person. Both court and visitors may perform in person searches. No search fee. Required to search: name, years to search, offense, DOB. Criminal records on computer back to 1989.

General Information: Public Access terminal is available. Turnaround time 10 working days.

Cleveland County

Circuit Court PO Box 368, Rison, AR 71665; 870-325-6521; Fax: 870-325-6144. Hours: 8AM-4:30PM (CST). *Felony, Civil Actions Over $5,000, Probate.*

Civil Records: Access: Mail, in person. Visitors must perform in person searches for themselves. No search fee. Required to search: name, years to search. Civil cases indexed by defendant, plaintiff. Civil records from 1980.

Criminal Records: Access: Mail, in person. Both court and visitors may perform in person searches. No search fee. Required to search: name, years to search, DOB. Criminal records from 1980.

General Information: Public Access terminal is available. No juvenile or adoption records released. Fee to fax results is $1.00 per page. Copy fee: $.25 per

page. Cert fee: $5.00. Payee: Clerk of Circuit Court. Personal checks accepted. Prepayment required. Mail turnaround time is same day, if possible.

District Court PO Box 405, City Hall, Rison, AR 71665; 870-325-7382; Fax: 870-325-6152. Hours: 8AM-4PM (CST). *Misdemeanor, Civil Actions Under $5,000, Eviction, Small Claims.*

Civil Records: Access: In person only. Both court and visitors may perform in person searches. No search fee. Computerized records go back 3 years.

Criminal Records: Access: In person only. Both court and visitors may perform in person searches. No search fee. Required to search: name, years to search, SSN. Computerized records go back 3 years.

Columbia County

Circuit Court 1 Court Sq #3, Magnolia, AR 71753-3595; 870-235-3700; Fax: 870-235-3786. Hours: 8AM-4:30PM (CST). *Felony, Civil Actions Over $5,000, Probate.*

Civil Records: Access: Mail, in person. Both court and visitors may perform in person searches. Search fee: $10.00 per name. Required to search: name, years to search. Civil cases indexed by defendant, plaintiff. Civil records on dockets and index cards; computerized records since 8/97.

Criminal Records: Access: Mail, in person. Both court and visitors may perform in person searches. Search fee: $10.00 per name. Required to search: name, years to search, DOB, SSN. Criminal records on dockets and index cards; computerized records since 8/97.

General Information: No juvenile or adoption. Copy fee: $.50 self serve $1.00 per page by court. Cert fee: $3.00. Payee: Circuit Clerk. Personal checks accepted. Prepayment required. Mail requests: SASE required. Mail turnaround time 2-4 days.

Magnolia District Court 121 S Jefferson, Magnolia, AR 71753; 870-234-7312. Hours: 8AM-5PM (CST). *Misdemeanor, Civil Actions Under $5,000, Eviction, Small Claims.*

Civil Records: Access: Mail, in person. Both court and visitors may perform in person searches. No search fee. Search request should include DOB and SSN. Civil records available since 1993.

Criminal Records: Access: Mail, in person. Only the court performs in person searches; visitors may not. Search fee: $1.00 per name. Search request should include name, DOB and SSN, years to search; also helpful: address. Criminal records available sine 1987.

General Information: Copy fee: $1.00 per page. Cert fee: $5.00. Payee: District Court Clerk. Prepayment required. Mail requests: SASE required. Mail turnaround time 3 days.

Conway County

Circuit Court Conway County Courthouse, Rm 206, Morrilton, AR 72110; 501-354-9617; Probate phone: 501-354-9621; Fax: 501-354-9612. Hours: 8AM-5PM (CST). *Felony, Civil Actions Over $5,000, Probate.*

Civil Records: Access: Phone, fax, mail, in person. Both court and visitors may perform in person searches. Search fee: $8.00 per name. Required to search: name, years to search. Civil cases indexed by defendant, plaintiff. Civil records (child support) on computer. All others on dockets from 1900s.

Criminal Records: Access: Phone, mail, in person. Both court and visitors may perform in person searches. Search fee: $8.00 per name. Required to search: name, years to search, DOB; also helpful: sex, SSN. Criminal records indexed in books back to 1900s.

General Information: No juvenile records released. Fee to fax results is $1.00 per page. Copy fee: $1.00 per page. Cert fee: $5.00. Payee: Circuit Clerk.

Personal checks accepted. Prepayment required. Mail requests: SASE required. Mail turnaround time 1-2 days.

District Court Conway County Courthouse, PO Box 127, Morrilton, AR 72110; 501-354-9615; Fax: 501-354-9633. Hours: 8AM-4:30PM (CST). *Misdemeanor, Civil Actions Under $5,000, Eviction, Small Claims.*

Civil Records: Access: In person, mail. Both court and visitors may perform in person searches. No search fee. Computerized records since 1994.

Criminal Records: Access: In person, mail. Only the court performs in person searches; visitors may not. No search fee. Required to search: name, years to search; also helpful: DOB. Computerized records since 1994.

General Information: Public Access terminal is available. Copy fee: $1.00. Cert fee: $5.00. Payee: District Court Clerk. Prepayment required. Mail turnaround time 1-2 days.

Craighead County

Jonesboro Circuit Court PO Box 120, Jonesboro, AR 72403; 870-933-4530; Fax: 870-933-4534. Hours: 8AM-5PM (CST). *Felony, Civil Actions Over $5,000, Probate.*

Civil Records: Access: Fax, mail, in person. Both court and visitors may perform in person searches. Search fee: $6.00 per name. Required to search: name, years to search. Civil cases indexed by defendant, plaintiff. Civil records on computer from 1972, on microfiche from 1800s.

Criminal Records: Access: Fax, mail, in person. Both court and visitors may perform in person searches. Search fee: $6.00 per name. Required to search: name, years to search, DOB; also helpful: address, SSN. Criminal records on computer from 1972, on microfiche from 1800s.

General Information: Public Access terminal is available. No juvenile records released. Will fax results $1.00 per page. Copy fee: $.50 per page. Cert fee: $3.00. Payee: Circuit Clerk. Personal checks accepted. Prepayment required. Mail requests: SASE required. Mail turnaround time 1-2 days.

Lake City Circuit Court PO Box 537, Lake City, AR 72437; 870-237-4342; Fax: 870-237-8174. Hours: 8AM-5PM (CST). *Felony, Civil Actions Over $5,000, Probate.*

Civil Records: Access: Mail, fax, in person. Both court and visitors may perform in person searches. Search fee: $6.00 per name. Required to search: name, years to search, address. Civil cases indexed by defendant, plaintiff. Civil records on computer from 1976.

Criminal Records: Access: Mail, fax, in person. Both court and visitors may perform in person searches. Search fee: $6.00 per name. Required to search: name, years to search, address, DOB; also helpful: SSN. Criminal records on computer from 1976.

General Information: Public Access terminal is available. No adoption records released. Will fax results to local or toll free line. Copy fee: $.25 per page. Cert fee: $3.00. Payee: Circuit Clerk. Business checks accepted. Prepayment required. Mail requests: SASE required. Mail turnaround time 1-2 days.

District Court 410 W Washington, Jonesboro, AR 72401; 870-933-4508; Fax: 870-933-4582. Hours: 8AM-5PM (CST). *Misdemeanor, Civil Actions Under $5,000, Eviction, Small Claims.*

Civil Records: Access: In person, mail. Only the court may perform in person searches. Search fee: $4.00 per name. Required to search: name, DOB. Computerized records go back 10 years.

Criminal Records: Access: In person, mail. Only the court performs in person searches; visitors may not. Search fee: $4.00 per name. Required to search: name, years to search, SSN. Computerized records go back 10 years.

General Information: Will fax results. Copy fee: $.20 per page. Cert fee: $2.00 each. Payee: District Court. Prepayment required. Mail turnaround time 1-2 days.

Crawford County

Circuit Court County Courthouse, 300 Main St, Rm 22, Van Buren, AR 72956; 479-474-1821; Probate phone: 479-474-1312; Fax: 479-471-0622. Hours: 8AM-5PM (CST). *Felony, Civil Actions Over $5,000, Probate.*
www.crawford-county.org/circuit_court.htm
Note: Probate same add.

Civil Records: Access: Mail, in person. Both court and visitors may perform in person searches. Search fee: $6.00 per name. Required to search: name, years to search. Civil cases indexed by defendant, plaintiff. Civil records on computer from 1992, on dockets from 1877.

Criminal Records: Access: Mail, in person. Both court and visitors may perform in person searches. Search fee: $6.00 per name. Required to search: name, years to search. Criminal records on computer from 1992, on dockets from 1877.

General Information: Public Access terminal is available. No juvenile records released. Will fax results to local or toll free line. Copy fee: $1.00 per page (mail) self serve $.50. Cert fee: $2.00. Payee: Circuit Clerk. Personal checks accepted. Prepayment required. Mail requests: SASE required. Mail turnaround time 1-2 days.

District Court 1003 Broadway, Van Buren, AR 72956; 479-474-1671; Fax: 479-471-5010. Hours: 8AM-5PM, (CST). *Misdemeanor, Civil Actions Under $5,000, Eviction, Small Claims.*

Civil Records: Access: In person, mail. Both court and visitors may perform in person searches. No search fee. Records available from 1975, computerized from 2000.

Criminal Records: Access: In person, mail. Both court and visitors may perform in person searches. No search fee. Required to search: name, years to search; also helpful: DOB, SSN. Specific court cases prior to 2000 need the conviction date. Records available from 1975, computerized from 2000.

General Information: Public Access terminal is available. (Terminal is only available on Fridays.) Copy fee: $.50. Cert fee: $10.00 per document. Payee: Van Buren District Court. Prepayment required. Mail requests: SASE required. Mail turnaround time 2-3 days.

Crittenden County

Circuit Court 100 Court St, Marion, AR 72364; 870-739-3248; Fax: 870-739-3287. Hours: 8AM-4:30PM (CST). *Felony, Civil Actions Over $5,000, Probate.*

Civil Records: Access: Mail, in person. Both court and visitors may perform in person searches. Search fee: $6.00 per name. Required to search: name, years to search. Civil cases indexed by plaintiff only. Civil records on dockets from 1930s.

Criminal Records: Access: In person only. Visitors must perform in person searches for themselves. No search fee. Required to search: name, case number. Criminal records on dockets or microfiche from 1930s. Case number required for mail search. The court suggests to send criminal record inquires to Ark. State Police, 501-681-8100.

General Information: No juvenile records released. Fee to fax results is $4.50 per document. Copy fee:

$.25 per page. Cert fee: $3.00. Payee: Circuit Court. Personal checks accepted. Prepayment required. Mail requests: SASE required. Mail turnaround time 1-2 days.

District Court PO Box 766, West Memphis, AR 72303; 870-732-7560; Civil phone: 870-732-7563; Fax: 870-732-7538/7566. Hours: 8AM-5PM (CST). *Misdemeanor, Civil Actions Under $5,000, Eviction, Small Claims.*

Civil Records: Access: Phone, fax, mail, in person. Both court and visitors may perform in person searches. No search fee. Required to search: name, years to search, DOB or SSN. Civil records on computer back to 1989; other records go back to 1945.

Criminal Records: Access: Phone, mail, in person. Both court and visitors may perform in person searches. No search fee. Required to search: name, years to search; also helpful: SSN, race, sex, DOB. Criminal records on computer back to 1989; other records go back to 1945.

General Information: Public Access terminal is available. No fee to fax results. Copy fee: $.25 per page. No cert fee. Payee: District Court. Prepayment required. Mail turnaround time 2-3 days.

Cross County

Circuit Court County Courthouse, 705 E Union, Rm 9, Wynne, AR 72396; 870-238-5720; Probate phone: 870-238-5735. Hours: 8AM-4PM (CST). *Felony, Civil Actions Over $5,000, Probate.*

Civil Records: Access: In person only. No search fee. Required to search: name, years to search. Civil cases indexed by defendant. Civil records (child support) on computer. All on dockets from 1800s.

Criminal Records: Access: In person only. Visitors must perform in person searches for themselves No search fee. Required to search: name, years to search; also helpful: SSN. Criminal records (child support) on computer. All on dockets from 1800s.

General Information: No juvenile records released. Copy fee: $.25 per page. Cert fee: $3.00. Payee: Cross County Circuit Court. Personal checks accepted. Prepayment required.

District Court 205 Mississippi St, Wynne, AR 72396; 870-238-9171; Fax: 870-238-3930. Hours: 8AM-4PM (CST). *Misdemeanor, Civil Actions Under $5,000, Eviction, Small Claims.*

Civil Records: Access: Mail, in person. Both court and visitors may perform in person searches. Search fee: $5.00. Required to search: name, years to search. Records on computer back to 1986.

Criminal Records: Access: Mail, in person. Both court and visitors may perform in person searches. Search fee: $5.00. Required to search: name, years to search, signed release; also helpful: SSN. Records on computer back to 1986.

General Information: Fee to fax results is $2.00 per document. Copy fee: $.50 per page. Cert fee: $5.00. Payee: Cross County Court. Prepayment required. Mail turnaround time 1-2 days.

Dallas County

Circuit Court Dallas County Courthouse, Fordyce, AR 71742; 870-352-2307; Fax: 870-352-7179. Hours: 8:30AM-4:30PM (CST). *Felony, Civil Actions Over $5,000, Probate.*

Civil Records: Access: Phone, fax, mail, in person. Both court and visitors may perform in person searches. Search fee: $6.00. Required to search: name, years to search. Civil cases indexed by defendant, plaintiff. Civil records go back to 1863; on computer back to 8/1997.

Criminal Records: Access: In person only. Visitors must perform in person searches for themselves. No search fee. Required to search: name, years to search,

DOB; also helpful: SSN. Criminal records go back to 1863; on computer back to 8/1997.

General Information: Public Access terminal is available. No juvenile records released. Will fax results $2.00 plus $.25 per page. Copy fee: $.25 per page. Cert fee: $5.00. Payee: Circuit Clerk. Business checks accepted. Law firm accounts, money orders and cashier checks allowed. Prepayment required. Mail requests: SASE required. Mail turnaround time 1-2 days.

District Court 202 W 3rd St, Fordyce, AR 71742; 870-352-2332; Fax: 870-352-3414. Hours: 8AM-4:30PM (CST). *Misdemeanor, Civil Actions Under $5,000, Eviction, Small Claims.*

Civil Records: Access: In person, mail. Only the court performs in person searches; visitors may not. No search fee. Required to search: None. Computerized records since 1997.

Criminal Records: Access: In person only. Only the court performs in person searches; visitors may not. No search fee. Required to search: name, years to search, SSN; also helpful: DOB. Computerized records since 1997.

General Information: Public Access terminal is available. Copy fee: $.25. No cert fee. Payee: Dallas County District Court. Checks or cash accepted. Turnaround time 1-2 days.

Desha County

Circuit Court PO Box 309, Arkansas City, AR 71630; 870-877-2411; Probate phone: 870-877-2323; Fax: 870-877-3407. Hours: 8AM-4PM (CST). *Felony, Civil Actions Over $5,000, Probate.*

Civil Records: Access: Fax, mail, in person. Both court and visitors may perform in person searches. Search fee: $5.00 per name. Required to search: name, years to search. Civil cases indexed by defendant, plaintiff. Civil records on dockets from 1920s; on computer back to 1997.

Criminal Records: Access: Fax, mail, in person. Both court and visitors may perform in person searches. Search fee: $5.00 per name. Required to search: name, years to search, SSN. Criminal records on dockets from 1920s, on computer back to 1997.

General Information: Public Access terminal is available. No juvenile records released. No fee to fax results. Copy fee: $.50 per page. Cert fee: $3.50. Payee: Skippy Leek, Circuit Court Clerk. Personal checks accepted. Prepayment required. Mail requests: SASE required. Mail turnaround time 1-2 days.

District Court PO Box 157, Dumas, AR 71639-2226; 870-382-6972; Fax: 870-382-1106. Hours: 8AM-4:30PM (CST). *Misdemeanor, Civil Actions Under $5,000, Eviction, Small Claims.*

Civil Records: Access: In person, mail. Only the court performs in person searches; visitors may not. Search fee: $5.00 per name. Required to search: name, years to search, signed release; also helpful: address. Civil records go back to 1988.

Criminal Records: Access: In person, mail. Only the court performs in person searches; visitors may not. Search fee: $5.00 per name. Required to search: name, years to search, signed release; also helpful: address. Criminal records go back to 1988.

General Information: Copy fee: $5.00 per doc. Cert fee: $5.00. Payee: Dumas District Court. Prepayment required. Mail turnaround time 1-2 days.

Drew County

Circuit Court 210 S Main, Monticello, AR 71655; 870-460-6250; Fax: 870-460-6246. Hours: 8AM-4:30PM (CST). *Felony, Civil Actions Over $5,000, Probate.*

Civil Records: Access: Phone, fax, mail, in person. Both court and visitors may perform in person searches. No search fee. Required to search: name, years to search. Civil cases indexed by defendant, plaintiff. Civil records on dockets from 1846; on computer back to 1996 approx.

Criminal Records: Access: In person only. Visitors must perform in person searches for themselves. No search fee. Required to search: name, years to search. Criminal records on dockets from 1846; on computer back to 1997 approx.

General Information: Public Access terminal is available. No juvenile or expunged records released. Will fax results $1.25 1st page, $1.00 each add'l. Copy fee: $.50 per page. Cert fee: $.50 per page + $2.00 per document. Payee: Drew County Circuit Clerk. Personal checks accepted. Prepayment required. Mail requests: SASE required. Mail turnaround time 1-2 days.

District Court PO Box 505, Monticello, AR 71655; 870-367-4420; Fax: 870-460-9056. Hours: 8AM-4:30PM (CST). *Misdemeanor, Civil Actions Under $5,000, Eviction, Small Claims.*

Civil Records: Access: Mail, fax, in person. Only the court performs in person searches; visitors may not. Search fee: none. Required to search: name, years to search, DOB, SSN, signed release. Records overall since 1980, on computer since 1987.

Criminal Records: Access: Mail, fax, in person. Only the court performs in person searches; visitors may not. No search fee. Required to search: name, years to search, DOB; also helpful: sex, signed release. Records overall since 1980, on computer since 1987.

General Information: Will fax results to local or toll free line. Turnaround time 1-2 days.

Faulkner County

Circuit Court PO Box 9, Conway, AR 72033; 501-450-4911; Fax: 501-450-4948. Hours: 8AM-4:30PM (CST). *Felony, Civil Actions Over $5,000, Probate.*

Civil Records: Access: Fax, mail, in person. Both court and visitors may perform in person searches. Search fee: $6.00 per name. Required to search: name, years to search. Civil cases indexed by defendant, plaintiff. Civil records on computer back to 1987; on docket from 1800s.

Criminal Records: Access: Fax, mail, in person. Both court and visitors may perform in person searches. Search fee: $6.00 per name. Required to search: name, years to search. Criminal records on computer back to 1987; on docket from 1800s.

General Information: Public Access terminal is available. No juvenile records released. Will fax results $1.00 if local, $3.50 plus $.25 per page if long distance. Copy fee: $.25 per page. Cert fee: $3.00. Payee: Faulkner County Circuit Clerk. Personal checks accepted. Prepayment required. Mail requests: SASE required. Mail turnaround time 1-2 days.

District Court 810 Parkway, Conway, AR 72032; 501-450-6112; Fax: 501-450-6184. Hours: 8AM-4:30PM (CST). *Misdemeanor, Civil Actions Under $5,000, Small Claims.*

Civil Records: Access: Mail, fax, in person. Both court and visitors may perform in person searches. No search fee. Required to search: name, years to search, DOB, signed release; also helpful: address, SSN. Computerized records go back to 1993.

Criminal Records: Access: Mail, fax, in person. Both court and visitors may perform in person searches. No search fee. Required to search: name, years to search, DOB, signed release; also helpful: address, SSN. Computerized records go back to 1993.

General Information: Public Access terminal is available. Will fax results to local or toll free number. Cert fee: $5.00. Payee: Conway District Court. Prepayment required. Mail turnaround time 2 days.

Franklin County

Charleston Circuit Court 607 E main, Charleston, AR 72933; 479-965-7332; Probate phone: 479-965-2129. Hours: 8AM-4:30PM (CST). *Felony, Civil Actions Over $5,000, Probate.*

Civil Records: Access: Mail, in person. Both court and visitors may perform in person searches. Search fee: $6.00 per name. Required to search: name, years to search, DOB. Civil cases indexed by defendant, plaintiff. Civil records on dockets from 1900s.

Criminal Records: Access: Mail, in person. Both court and visitors may perform in person searches. Search fee: $6.00 per name. Required to search: name, years to search, DOB. Criminal records on dockets from 1900s.

General Information: No juvenile records released. Will fax results $1.00 per page. Copy fee: $.25 per page. Cert fee: $5.00. Payee: Franklin County. Personal checks accepted. Prepayment required. Mail requests: SASE required. Mail turnaround time 1-2 days.

Ozark Circuit Court PO Box 1112, 211 W Commercial, Ozark, AR 72949; 479-667-3818; Probate phone: 479-667-3607; Fax: 479-667-5174. Hours: 8AM-4:30PM (CST). *Felony, Civil Actions Over $5,000, Probate.*

Note: Probate is maintained at the County Clerk's Office.

Civil Records: Access: Fax, mail, in person. Both court and visitors may perform in person searches. Search fee: $6.00 per name. Required to search: name, years to search. Civil cases indexed by plaintiff. Civil records on dockets from 1900s.

Criminal Records: Access: Fax, mail, in person. Both court and visitors may perform in person searches. Search fee: $6.00 per name. Required to search: name, years to search. Criminal records on dockets from 1900s.

General Information: No juvenile records released. Will fax results $1.00 per page. Copy fee: $.25 per page. Cert fee: $2.00. Payee: Circuit Clerk. Personal checks accepted. Prepayment required. Mail requests: SASE required. Mail turnaround time 1-2 days.

District Court PO Box 426, Charleston, AR 72933; 479-965-7455; Fax: 479-965-9980. Hours: 8AM-5PM (CST). *Misdemeanor, Civil Actions Under $5,000, Small Claims.*

Civil Records: Access: Mail, fax, in person. Both court and visitors may perform in person searches. No search fee. Civil records on computer.

Criminal Records: Access: Mail, fax, in person. Both court and visitors may perform in person searches. No search fee. Required to search: name, years to search, DOB; also helpful-SSN, signed release. Criminal records on computer back to 1/2000.

General Information: Will fax back results. No copy fee. No cert fee. Turnaround time 1-2 days.

Fulton County

Circuit Court PO Box 485, Salem, AR 72576; 870-895-3310; Fax: 870-895-3383. Hours: 8AM-4:30PM (CST). *Felony, Civil Actions Over $5,000, Probate.*

Civil Records: Access: Mail, in person. Both court and visitors may perform in person searches. Search fee: $6.00 per name. Required to search: name, years to search. Civil cases indexed by defendant, plaintiff. Civil records on dockets from 1900s; on computer back to 2000.

Criminal Records: Access: Mail, in person. Both court and visitors may perform in person searches. Search fee: $6.00 per name. Required to search: name, years to search. Criminal records on dockets from 1900s; on computer back to 2000.

General Information: Public Access terminal is available. (Public terminal includes years 2000 and forward only.) No juvenile records released. Will fax results. Copy fee: $.20 per page. No cert fee. Payee: Fulton County Clerks. Personal checks accepted. Prepayment required. Mail requests: SASE required. Mail turnaround time 1-2 days.

District Court PO Box 928, Salem, AR 72576; 870-895-4136; Fax: 870-895-4114. Hours: 8AM-4:30PM (CST). *Misdemeanor, Civil Actions Under $5,000, Eviction, Small Claims.*
Civil Records: Access: In person, mail. Only the court may perform in person searches. No search fee. Computerized records since 1995.
Criminal Records: Access: In person, mail, phone. Both court and visitors may perform in person searches. No search fee. Required to search: name, years to search, DOB. Computerized records since 1995.
General Information: Mail requests: SASE required. Mail turnaround time 1 week.

Garland County

Circuit Court Garland County Courthouse, 501 Ouachita Ave, Rm 207, Hot Springs, AR 71901; Civil phone: 501-622-3630; Criminal phone: 501-622-3640; Probate phone: 501-622-3610; Fax: 501-609-9043. Hours: 8AM-5PM (CST). *Felony, Civil Actions Over $5,000, Probate.*
Note: Probate records are handled by the County Clerk, phone number above.
Civil Records: Access: In person only. Visitors must perform in person searches for themselves. No search fee. Required to search: name; also helpful: years to search. Civil cases indexed by defendant, plaintiff. Civil records on microfiche and docket from 1900s; on computer back to 1989.
Criminal Records: Access: Fax, mail, in person. Both court and visitors may perform in person searches. No search fee. Required to search: name, years to search; also helpful: DOB, SSN, maiden name, race, aliases, sex. Criminal records on microfiche and docket from 1900s; on computer back to 1989.
General Information: Public Access terminal is available. No expunged, sealed records released. Fee to fax results is $2.00 plus $.25 per page. Copy fee: $.25 per page. Cert fee: $.50. Payee: Garland County Circuit Clerk. Personal checks accepted. Prepayment required. Mail requests: SASE required. Mail turnaround time 1-2 days.

District Court 607 Ouachita, Hot Springs, AR 71901; 501-321-6765; Fax: 501-321-6764. Hours: 8AM-4:30PM (CST). *Misdemeanor, Civil Actions Under $5,000, Eviction, Small Claims.*
Civil Records: Access: In person, mail. Both court and visitors may perform in person searches. No search fee. Required to search: name, DOB, SSN, years to search. Civil record on computer back to 2000.
Criminal Records: Access: In person, mail. Both court and visitors may perform in person searches. No search fee. Required to search: name, years to search, offense. Criminal records on computer back to 1990.
General Information: Will fax results. Copy fee: $.25 per page. Cert fee: $5.00 per document. Payee: HSDC. Prepayment required. Mail turnaround time 1-2 days.

Grant County

Circuit Court Grant County Courthouse, 101 W Center, Rm 106, Sheridan, AR 72150; 870-942-2631; Fax: 870-942-3564. Hours: 8AM-4:30PM (CST). *Felony, Civil Actions Over $5,000, Probate.*
Civil Records: Access: In person only. Visitors must perform in person searches for themselves. No search fee. Required to search: name, years to search. Civil cases indexed by defendant, plaintiff. Civil records on dockets and index from 1877.
Criminal Records: Access: In person only. Visitors must perform in person searches for themselves. No search fee. Required to search: name, years to search. Criminal records on dockets and index from 1982.
General Information: No juvenile, probate or adoption records released. Will fax specific case file documents $ 3.00 per fax. Copy fee: $.25 per page. Cert fee: $5.00. Payee: Circuit Clerk. Personal checks accepted. Prepayment required.

District Court PO Box 603, Sheridan, AR 72150; 870-942-3464; Fax: 870-942-8885. Hours: 8AM-4:15PM (CST). *Misdemeanor, Civil Actions Under $5,000, Eviction, Small Claims.*
Civil Records: Access: In person, mail. Both court and visitors may perform in person searches. No search fee. Computerized records since 1992.
Criminal Records: Access: In person, mail. Both court and visitors may perform in person searches. No search fee. Required to search: name, years to search. Computerized records since 1992.
General Information: Copy fee: $.25. Cert fee: $5.00. Payee: Grant County District Court. Personal checks accepted. Mail requests: SASE required. Mail turnaround time 3 days.

Greene County

Circuit Court 320 W Court #124, Paragould, AR 72450; 870-239-6330; Fax: 870-239-3550. Hours: 8AM-4:30PM (CST). *Felony, Civil Actions Over $5,000, Probate.*
Civil Records: Access: Fax, mail, in person. Both court and visitors may perform in person searches. Search fee: $6.00 per name. Required to search: name, years to search. Civil cases indexed by plaintiff. Civil records on computer from 1980, on index from 1830.
Criminal Records: Access: Fax, mail, in person. Both court and visitors may perform in person searches. Search fee: $6.00 per name. Required to search: name, years to search; also helpful: DOB, SSN. Criminal records computerized since 1986, archived to 1876.
General Information: Public Access terminal is available. No juvenile records released. For fax back, $1.00 for first 3 pages then $.25 per page. Copy fee: $.20 per page. Cert fee: $3.00. Payee: Greene County Circuit Clerk. Personal checks accepted. Prepayment required. Mail requests: SASE required. Mail turnaround time 1-2 days.

District Court 320 W Court, Rm 227, Paragould, AR 72450; 870-239-7507; Fax: 870-239-7506. Hours: 8AM-4:30PM (CST). *Misdemeanor, Civil Actions Under $5,000, Eviction, Small Claims.*
www.gccourt.com
Civil Records: Access: In person, mail. Only the court performs in person searches; visitors may not. No search fee. Required to search: name, years to search, DOB or SSN. Records on computer back to 1989.
Criminal Records: Access: In person, mail. Only the court performs in person searches; visitors may not. Search fee: $5.00 per name. Required to search: name, years to search, DOB or SSN. Records on computer back to 1989.

General Information: Copy fee: $.50 per page. Cert fee: $5.00. Payee: District Clerk. Only cashiers checks and money orders accepted. Prepayment required. Mail requests: SASE required. Mail turnaround time 2 days.

Hempstead County

Circuit Court PO Box 1420, Hope, AR 71802; 870-777-2384; Probate phone: 870-777-2241; Fax: 870-777-7827. Hours: 8AM-4PM (CST). *Felony, Civil Actions Over $5,000, Probate.*
Note: Probate is handled by the County Clerk at same address.
Civil Records: Access: Phone, fax, mail, in person. Both court and visitors may perform in person searches. Search fee: $6.00 per name. Required to search: name, years to search. Civil cases indexed by defendant, plaintiff. Civil records on dockets from 1910.
Criminal Records: Access: Phone, fax, mail, in person. Both court and visitors may perform in person searches. Search fee: $6.00 per name. Required to search: name, years to search, DOB, SSN. Criminal records on dockets from 1910; computerized since 198.
General Information: No juvenile records released. kathyt@nezperce.org. Copy fee: $.50 per page. Cert fee: $5.00. Payee: Circuit Clerk. Personal checks accepted. Prepayment required. Mail requests: SASE required. Mail turnaround time 1-2 days.

District Court PO Box 1420, Hope, AR 71802-1420; 870-777-2525; Fax: 870-777-7830. Hours: 8AM-4PM (CST). *Misdemeanor, Civil Actions Under $5,000, Eviction, Small Claims.*
Civil Records: Access: Mail, in person. Both court and visitors may perform in person searches. Search fee: $5.00 per name. Required to search: name, years to search. Civil records not computerized.
Criminal Records: Access: Mail, in person. Both court and visitors may perform in person searches. Search fee: $5.00 per name. Required to search: name, years to search, SSN, DOB. Criminal records on computer back to 1987.
General Information: Will not fax results. Copy fee: $1.00 per page. Cert fee: $5.00. Payee: District Court. Prepayment required. Mail turnaround time less than 1 week.

Hot Spring County

Circuit Court 210 Locust St, PO Box 1200, Malvern, AR 72104; 501-332-2281; Probate phone: 501-332-2291. Hours: 8:00AM-4:30PM (CST). *Felony, Civil Actions Over $5,000.*
Civil Records: Access: Mail, in person. Both court and visitors may perform in person searches. Search fee: $5.00 per name. Required to search: name, years to search. Civil cases indexed by plaintiff. Civil records on dockets from 1800s.
Criminal Records: Access: Mail, in person. Both court and visitors may perform in person searches. Search fee: $5.00 per name. Required to search: name, years to search, DOB or SSN. Criminal records on dockets from 1800s.
General Information: No juvenile records released. Copy fee: $.50 per page. Cert fee: $5.00. Payee: Circuit Clerk. Personal checks accepted. Prepayment required. Mail requests: SASE required. Mail turnaround time 1-2 days.

Malvern District Court 305 Locust St, Rm 201, Malvern, AR 72104; 501-332-7604; Fax: 501-332-3144. Hours: 8AM-4:30PM (CST). *Misdemeanor, Civil Actions Under $5,000, Eviction, Small Claims.*
Note: Formerly known as Malvern Muni. Court before 7/1/01.

Civil Records: Access: Mail, fax, in person. Visitors must perform in person searches for themselves. No search fee. Required to search: name, years to search and DOB or SSN. Records computerized back to 1994.

Criminal Records: Access: Mail, fax, in person. Visitors must perform in person searches for themselves. No search fee. Required to search: name, years to search, DOB; also helpful: address, SSN. Records computerized back to 1994.

General Information: Will fax results for $.25 per page. Copy fee: $.25. Prepayment required. Mail requests: SASE required. Mail turnaround time 3 days.

Howard County

Circuit Court 421 N Main, Rm 7, Nashville, AR 71852; 870-845-7506; Probate phone: 870-845-7503. Hours: 8AM-4:30PM (CST). *Felony, Civil Actions Over $5,000, Probate.*

Note: Probate is handled by the County Clerk at this address.

Civil Records: Access: Phone, mail, in person. Both court and visitors may perform in person searches. Search fee: $6.00. Required to search: name, years to search. Civil cases indexed by defendant, plaintiff. Civil records on dockets from 1873.

Criminal Records: Access: In person only. Visitors must perform in person searches for themselves. No search fee. Required to search: name, years to search, DOB. Criminal records on dockets from 1873.

General Information: Public Access terminal is available. No juvenile or sealed records released. Will fax results for $.50 per page. Copy fee: $.25 per page. Cert fee: $2.00. Payee: Circuit Clerk. Personal checks accepted. Prepayment required. Mail requests: SASE required. Mail turnaround time 1 week.

District Court 426 N Main, ##7, Nashville, AR 71852-2009; 870-845-7522; Fax: 870-845-3705. Hours: 8AM-4:30PM (CST). *Misdemeanor, Civil Actions Under $5,000, Eviction, Small Claims.*

Civil Records: Access: In person, mail. Visitors must perform in person searches for themselves. No search fee. Civl records viewable since 1989.

Criminal Records: Access: In person, mail. Both court and visitors may perform in person searches. No search fee. Required to search: name, years to search, DOB; also helpful: address, SSN. Criminal records viewable past 7 years.

General Information: Will fax results to local or toll free line. No copy fee. Cert fee: $5.00. Prepayment required. Mail turnaround time 1-3 days.

Independence County

Circuit Court PO Box 2155, (192 E.Main and Broad St), Batesville, AR 72503; 870-793-8833; Fax: 870-793-8888. Hours: 8AM-4:30PM (CST). *Felony, Civil Actions Over $5,000.*

Civil Records: Access: In person only. Visitors must perform in person searches for themselves. No search fee. Required to search: name, years to search; also helpful: address. Civil cases indexed by defendant, plaintiff. Civil judgments on computer from 1980, all others on index books from 1970s.

Criminal Records: Access: In person, mail. Both court and visitors may perform in person searches. Search fee: $6.00 per name. Required to search: name, years to search, DOB; also helpful: address. Criminal records on index books from 1970s.

General Information: No juvenile records released. Copy fee: $.25 per page. No cert fee. Payee: Circuit Clerk. Personal checks accepted. Prepayment required. Mail requests: SASE required. Mail turnaround time varies, but usually same day.

District Court 368 E Main, Rm 205, Batesville, AR 72501; 870-793-8817; Fax: 870-793-8875. Hours: 8AM-4:30PM (CST). *Misdemeanor, Civil Actions Under $5,000, Eviction, Small Claims.*

Civil Records: Access: In person, mail. Both court and visitors may perform in person searches. No search fee. Civil reocrds go back to 1975.

Criminal Records: Access: In person, mail. Both court and visitors may perform in person searches. No search fee. Required to search: name, years to search. Criminal records go back to 1975.

General Information: Will fax results. No copy fee. No cert fee. Payee: District Court. Only cashiers checks and money orders accepted. Prepayment required. Mail requests: SASE required. Mail turnaround time 1-2 days.

Izard County

Circuit Court PO Box 95, Melbourne, AR 72556; 870-368-4316; Fax: 870-368-4748. Hours: 8:30AM-4:30PM (CST). *Felony, Civil Actions Over $5,000, Probate.*

Civil Records: Access: Fax, mail, in person. Visitors must perform in person searches for themselves. Search fee: $6.00 per name. Required to search: name, years to search, address. Civil cases indexed by plaintiff. Civil records on judgment books from 1889.

Criminal Records: Access: Fax, mail, in person. Both court and visitors may perform in person searches. Search fee: $6.00 per name. Required to search: name, years to search, DOB; also helpful: address. Criminal records on judgment books from 1889.

General Information: No juvenile records released. No fee to fax results locally; is $1.00 per page if long distance. Copy fee: $.20 per page. Cert fee: $5.00. Payee: Izard County and Circuit Clerk. Personal checks accepted. Prepayment required. Mail requests: SASE required. Mail turnaround time 2 weeks.

District Court PO Box 337, Melbourne, AR 72556; 870-368-4390; Fax: 870-368-2267. Hours: 8:30AM-4:30PM (CST). *Misdemeanor, Civil Actions Under $5,000, Small Claims.*

Civil Records: Access: Mail, fax, in person. Both court and visitors may perform in person searches. Search fee: $6.00. Required to search: name, years to search, DOB. Civil records go back to 1977; on computer back to 1993.

Criminal Records: Access: Mail, fax, in person. Both court and visitors may perform in person searches. Search fee: $6.00. Required to search: name, years to search, DOB. Criminal records go back to 1977; on computer back to 1993.

General Information: Will fax results for $1.00 per page. Copy fee: $.20 per page. Cert fee: $5.00. Payee: District Court. Prepayment required. Mail turnaround time varies.

Jackson County

Circuit Court Jackson County Courthouse, 208 Main St, Newport, AR 72112; 870-523-7423; Fax: 870-523-3682. Hours: 8AM-4:30PM (CST). *Felony, Civil Actions Over $5,000, Probate.*

Civil Records: Access: In person only. Visitors must perform in person searches for themselves. No search fee. Required to search: name, years to search. Civil cases indexed by defendant, plaintiff. Civil records on dockets from 1800s.

Criminal Records: Access: In person, mail. Visitors must perform in person searches for themselves. No search fee. Required to search: name, years to search. Criminal records on dockets from 1800s, computized back to 1997.

General Information: Public Access terminal is available. No juvenile records released. Copy fee: $.25 per page. Cert fee: $3.00. Payee: Circuit Clerk.

Personal checks accepted. Prepayment required. Mail requests: SASE required. Mail turnaround time is 1-2 days.

District Court 615 3rd St, Newport, AR 72112; 870-523-9555; Civil phone: Ext 118; Criminal phone: Ext 119; Probate phone: Ext 120; Fax: 870-523-4365. Hours: 8AM-4:30PM (CST). *Misdemeanor, Civil Actions Under $5,000, Eviction, Small Claims.*

Civil Records: Access: Phone, mail, fax, in person. Both court and visitors may perform in person searches. No search fee. Civil records go back to 1987.

Criminal Records: Access: Mail, fax, in person. Both court and visitors may perform in person searches. No search fee. Required to search: name, years to search, DOB. Criminal records go back to 1993 on computer, searchable to 1950.

General Information: Public Access terminal is available. Will fax results to local or toll free line. Cert fee: $3.00. Payee: Newport District Court. Prepayment required. Mail requests: SASE required. Mail turnaround time 5-7 days.

Jefferson County

Circuit Court PO Box 7433, Pine Bluff, AR 71611; Civil phone: 870-541-5307; Criminal phone: 870-541-5306. Hours: 8:30PM-5PM (CST). *Felony, Civil Actions Over $5,000, Probate.*

Civil Records: Access: In person only. Visitors must perform in person searches for themselves. No search fee. Required to search: name, years to search. Civil cases indexed by defendant, plaintiff. Civil records on dockets from 1950.

Criminal Records: Access: In person only. Visitors must perform in person searches for themselves. No search fee. Required to search: name, years to search, DOB. Criminal records on dockets from 1950.

General Information: Public Access terminal is available. No juvenile records released. Copy fee: $.50 per page. Cert fee: $.50. Payee: Circuit Clerk. Only cashiers checks and money orders accepted. Prepayment required.

District Court 200 E 8th Ave, Pine Bluff, AR 71601; 870-543-1860 Div.I; 850-7584 Div. II; Fax: 870-543-1889. Hours: 8AM-5PM (CST). *Misdemeanor, Civil Actions Under $5,000, Eviction, Small Claims.*

Civil Records: Access: In person, mail. Both court and visitors may perform in person searches. Search fee: $5.00.

Criminal Records: Access: In person, mail. Both court and visitors may perform in person searches. Search fee: $5.00. Required to search: name, years to search; also helpful: DOB, SSN. Criminal records go back to 1989; computerized records since 1997.

General Information: No copy fee. No cert fee. Payee: District Court. Only cashiers checks and money orders accepted. Mail requests: SASE required. Mail turnaround time 1-2 days.

Johnson County

Circuit Court PO Box 189, Clarksville, AR 72830-0189; 479-754-2977; Probate phone: 479-754-3967; Fax: 479-754-4235. Hours: 8AM-4:30PM (CST). *Felony, Civil Actions Over $5,000, Probate.*

Note: Probate is handled by County Clerk, PO Box 57.

Civil Records: Access: Fax, mail, in person. Both court and visitors may perform in person searches. No search fee. Required to search: name, years to search. Civil cases indexed by defendant, plaintiff. Civil records on index from 1900s. Fax access limited to 800#'s.

Criminal Records: Access: Mail, in person. Both court and visitors may perform in person searches. No search fee. Required to search: name, years to search, DOB; also helpful: SSN. Criminal records on index from 1900s. Fax access limited to 800#'s.

General Information: No juvenile records released. No fee to fax results. Will fax to 800 numbers only. Copy fee: $.50 per page. Cert fee: $1.00. Personal checks accepted. Mail requests: SASE required. Mail turnaround time 1-2 days.

District Court PO Box 581, Clarksville, AR 72830; 479-754-8533; Fax: 479-754-6014. Hours: 8AM-4PM (CST). *Misdemeanor, Civil Actions Under $5,000, Eviction, Small Claims.*
Civil Records: Access: In person, mail. Both court and visitors may perform in person searches. No search fee. Required to search: name. Civil records go back 10 years.
Criminal Records: Access: In person, mail. Both court and visitors may perform in person searches. No search fee. Required to search: name, years to search; also helpful: DOB, SSN.
General Information: Turnaround time 1-2 days.

Lafayette County

Circuit Court #3 Courthouse Sq, Lewisville, AR 71845; 870-921-4878; Probate phone: 870-921-4633; Fax: 870-921-4879 (Crim). Hours: 8AM-4:30PM (CST). *Felony, Civil Actions Over $5,000, Probate.*
Note: Civil fax is 870-921-4879. Probate is located at #2 Courthouse Sq.
Civil Records: Access: Phone, mail, in person. Both court and visitors may perform in person searches. Search fee: $6.00 per name. Required to search: name, years to search. Civil cases indexed by defendant, plaintiff. Civil records on dockets from 1950s.
Criminal Records: Access: Mail, in person. Visitors must perform in person searches for themselves. No search fee. Required to search: name, years to search. Criminal records on dockets from 1950s.
General Information: No juvenile records released without written order form the judge. Copy fee: $.50 per page. Cert fee: $3.00. Payee: Circuit Clerk. Personal checks accepted. Prepayment required. Mail requests: SASE required. Mail turnaround time 2 days.

District Court 110 E Fourth, #1, Lewisville, AR 71845; 870-921-5555; Fax: 870-921-4256. Hours: 8AM-4:30PM (CST). *Misdemeanor, Civil Actions Under $5,000, Eviction, Small Claims.*
Civil Records: Access: In person only. Both court and visitors may perform in person searches. No search fee.
Criminal Records: Access: In person only. Both court and visitors may perform in person searches. No search fee. Required to search: name, years to search, DOB, SSN.

Lawrence County

Circuit Court PO Box 581, 315 W. Main St., Rm 7, Walnut Ridge, AR 72476; 870-886-1112; Probate phone: 870-886-1111; Fax: 870-886-1128. Hours: 8AM-4:30PM (CST). *Felony, Civil Actions Over $5,000, Probate.*
Note: They also oversee domestic relations and juvenile cases.
Civil Records: Access: Mail, in person. Visitors must perform in person searches for themselves. Search fee: $6.00. Required to search: name, years to search. Civil cases indexed by defendant, plaintiff. Civil records on index from 1981, on docket sheets from 1960s.
Criminal Records: Access: Mail, in person. Visitors must perform in person searches for themselves. Search fee: $6.00. Required to search: name, years to

search. Criminal records on index from 1981, on docket sheets from 1960s.
General Information: Public Access terminal is available. No juvenile records released. Will fax results for $1.00 per page. Copy fee: $.50 per page. Cert fee: $3.00 per document. Payee: Circuit Clerk. Personal checks accepted. Prepayment required. Mail requests: SASE required. Mail turnaround time 1 day.

Walnut Ridge District Court 201 SW 2nd St, Walnut Ridge, AR 72476; 870-886-3905. Hours: 8AM-4:30PM (CST). *Misdemeanor, Civil Actions Under $5,000, Eviction, Small Claims.*
Civil Records: Access: In person, mail. Both court and visitors may perform in person searches. No search fee. Computerized records since 1992.
Criminal Records: Access: In person, mail. Both court and visitors may perform in person searches. No search fee. Required to search: name, years to search, offense. Computerized records since 1992.
General Information: Will fax results to local or toll free line. Turnaround time 2-3 days.

Lee County

Circuit Court 15 E Chestnut, Marianna, AR 72360; 870-295-7710; Fax: 870-295-7766. Hours: 8:30AM-4:30PM (CST). *Felony, Civil Actions Over $5,000, Probate.*
Civil Records: Access: In person only. Visitors must perform in person searches for themselves. No search fee. Required to search: name, years to search. Civil cases indexed by defendant, plaintiff. Civil records on index books from 1873; computerized records since 1/2002.
Criminal Records: Access: In person only. Only the court performs in person searches; visitors may not. No search fee. Required to search: name, years to search, DOB. Criminal records on index books from 1873; computerized records since 1/2002.
General Information: No juvenile records released. Copy fee: $.25 per page. Cert fee: $2.50. Payee: Circuit Court. Personal checks accepted. Prepayment required.

District Court 45 W Mississippi, Marianna, AR 72360; 870-295-3813; Fax: 870-295-5726. Hours: 8AM-Noon; 1-5PM (CST). *Misdemeanor, Civil Actions Under $5,000, Eviction, Small Claims.*
Civil Records: Access: In person, mail. Only the court performs in person searches; visitors may not. No search fee. Computerized records since 1994.
Criminal Records: Access: In person, mail. Only the court performs in person searches; visitors may not. No search fee. Required to search: name, years to search. Computerized records since 1994.
General Information: Copy fee: $.10 per page. Cert fee: $2.00 per document. Payee: City of Marianna. Personal checks accepted. Mail requests: SASE requested. Turnaround time 5 days.

Lincoln County

Circuit Court Courthouse, 300 S Drew, Star City, AR 71667; 870-628-3154; Probate phone: 870-628-5114; Fax: 870-628-5546. Hours: 8AM-4:30PM (CST). *Felony, Civil Actions Over $5,000, Probate.*
Civil Records: Access: In person only. Both court and visitors may perform in person searches. No search fee. Required to search: name, years to search. Civil cases indexed by defendant, plaintiff. Civil records on index from 1920, archived from 1920.
Criminal Records: Access: In person only. Visitors must perform in person searches for themselves. No search fee. Criminal records on index from 1920, archived from 1920.
General Information: No sealed records released. Copy fee: $.50 per page. Cert fee: $3.00. Payee:

Lincoln County Circuit Court. Personal checks accepted. Prepayment required.

Lincoln County District Court 300 S Drew St, Star City, AR 71667; 870-628-4904; Civil phone: 870-628-4166. Hours: 8AM-4:30PM (CST). *Misdemeanor, Civil Actions Under $5,000, Eviction, Small Claims.*
Civil Records: Access: Mail, in person. Both court and visitors may perform in person searches. Search fee: $6.00 per name. Required to search: name, years to search, DOB. Civil records go back to 1980.
Criminal Records: Access: Mail, in person. Both court and visitors may perform in person searches. Search fee: $6.00 per name. Required to search: name, years to search, DOB, signed release; also helpful: address, SSN, DL#. Criminal records go back to 1980; on computer back to 1991.
General Information: No fee to fax 5 pages or less; if 6 or more, $.50 per page. Copy fee: $.50 per page. Cert fee: $25.00. Payee: District Court of Star City. Prepayment required. Mail turnaround time 3-5 days.

Little River County

Circuit Court PO Box 575, Ashdown, AR 71822; 870-898-7211; Probate phone: 870-898-7210; Fax: 870-898-5783. Hours: 8AM-4:30PM (CST). *Felony, Civil Actions Over $5,000, Probate.*
Civil Records: Access: Phone, mail, in person. Both court and visitors may perform in person searches. Search fee: $6.00 per name. Required to search: name, years to search. Civil cases indexed by plaintiff. Civil records docket books from early 1900s.
Criminal Records: Access: In person only. Both court and visitors may perform in person searches. No search fee. Required to search: name, years to search, DOB. Criminal records on docket books back to 1868. Direct criminal records searches to AR state plolice; 870-777-4641.
General Information: No juvenile records released. Will fax results to local or toll free line. Copy fee: $.50 per page. Cert fee: $5.00. Payee: Circuit Clerk. Personal checks accepted. Prepayment required.

District Court 351 N 2nd St, #8, Ashdown, AR 71822; 870-898-7230; Fax: 870-898-7262. Hours: 8:30AM-4:30PM (CST). *Misdemeanor, Civil Actions Under $5,000, Eviction, Small Claims.*
Civil Records: Access: In person, mail. Both court and visitors may perform in person searches. No search fee. Civil records on computer since 1987.
Criminal Records: Access: In person, mail. Both court and visitors may perform in person searches. No search fee. Required to search: name, years to search; also helpful: DOB, SSN. Criminal records on computer since 1987.
General Information: Public Access terminal is available. Copy fee: $.50 per page. Cert fee: $5.00 per document. Payee: District Court. Only cashiers checks and money orders accepted. Mail requests: SASE required. Mail turnaround time 1 week.

Logan County

Circuit Court Courthouse, 25 W Walnut, Paris, AR 72855; 479-963-2164; Probate phone: 479-963-2618; Fax: 479-963-3304. Hours: 8AM-4:30PM (CST). *Felony, Civil Actions Over $5,000, Probate.*
Civil Records: Access: Fax, mail, in person. Visitors must perform in person searches for themselves. Search fee: $6.00 per name. Required to search: name, years to search. Civil cases indexed by defendant, plaintiff. Civil records on criminal index from 1901.
Criminal Records: Access: In person only. Visitors must perform in person searches for themselves. No search fee. Required to search: name, years to search. Criminal records on criminal index from 1901.

General Information: Will fax results $2.00 per page. Copy fee: $.50 per page. Cert fee: $5.00. Payee: Circuit Clerk. Personal checks accepted. Prepayment required.

Paris District Court Paris Courthouse, Paris, AR 72855; 479-963-3792; Fax: 479-963-2762. Hours: 8:30AM-4:30PM (CST). *Misdemeanor, Civil Actions Under $5,000, Eviction, Small Claims.*
Civil Records: Access: In person, mail. Both court and visitors may perform in person searches. No search fee. Civil records go back to the 1970's; computerized records since 1994.
Criminal Records: Access: In person, mail. Both court and visitors may perform in person searches. No search fee. Required to search: name, years to search; also helpful: DOB. Criminal records go back to 1970's; computerized records since 1994.
General Information: Public Access terminal is available. Will fax results to local or toll free line. No copy fee. No cert fee. Mail requests: SASE required. Mail turnaround time 1-2 days.

Lonoke County

Circuit Court PO Box 218 Attn: Circuit Clerk, Lonoke, AR 72086; 501-676-2316; Probate phone: 501-676-2368. Hours: 8AM-4:30PM (CST). *Felony, Civil Actions Over $5,000, Probate.*
Civil Records: Access: In person only. Visitors must perform in person searches for themselves. No search fee. Required to search: name, years to search. Civil cases indexed by defendant. Civil records on computer from 1989, on dockets from 1918's.
Criminal Records: Access: Mail, in person. Both court and visitors may perform in person searches. Search fee: $6.00 per name. Required to search: name, years to search, SSN. Criminal records on computer from 1989, on dockets from 1918's (not for public use).
General Information: Public Access terminal is available. No juvenile records released. Copy fee: $.25 per page. Cert fee: $6.00. Payee: Circuit Clerk. Personal checks accepted. Prepayment required. Mail requests: SASE required. Mail turnaround time 1-2 days.

Lonoke District Court 107 W 2nd St, Lonoke, AR 72086-2701; 501-676-3585; Fax: 501-676-2500. Hours: 8AM-4:30PM (CST). *Misdemeanor, Civil Actions Under $5,000, Eviction, Small Claims.*
Civil Records: Access: Mail, in person. Both court and visitors may perform in person searches. Search fee: $5.00. Computerized records since 1999.
Criminal Records: Access: Mail, in person. Both court and visitors may perform in person searches. No search fee. Required to search: name, years to search. Computerized records since 1999.
General Information: No copy fee. No cert fee. Payee: District Court. Prepayment required. Mail requests: SASE required. Mail turnaround time is 1-2 days.

Madison County

Circuit Court PO Box 416 (Courthouse), Huntsville, AR 72740; 479-738-2215; Probate phone: 479-738-2747; Fax: 479-738-2735. Hours: 8AM-4:30PM (CST). *Felony, Civil Actions Over $5,000, Probate.*
Note: Probate is in the County Clerk's office, PO Box 37.479-738-1544
Civil Records: Access: In person only. Both court and visitors may perform in person searches. Search fee: $10.00. Required to search: name, years to search; also helpful: address. Civil cases indexed by defendant, plaintiff. Civil records on dockets back to 1892.

Criminal Records: Access: In person only. Both court and visitors may perform in person searches. Search fee: $10.00. Required to search: name, years to search; also helpful: address, DOB, SSN. Criminal records on dockets back to 1906.
General Information: No juvenile records released. Will fax specific document for $5.00 per fax; if over 20 pages, add $.25 each add'l page. Copy fee: $.25 per page. Cert fee: $2.00. Payee: Circuit Clerk. Personal checks accepted. Prepayment required.

District Court PO Box 549, Huntsville, AR 72740; 479-738-2911; Fax: 479-738-6846. Hours: 8AM-4:30PM (CST). *Misdemeanor, Civil Actions Under $5,000, Eviction, Small Claims.*
Civil Records: Access: Mail. fax, in person. Both court and visitors may perform in person searches, but court will search only if time permits. No search fee. Records go back to 1991; computerized records since 1999.
Criminal Records: Access: In person, mail, fax. Both court and visitors may perform in person searches, but court will search only if time permits. No search fee. Required to search: name, years to search, DOB, SSN. Criminal records go back to 1991; on computer back to 1999.
General Information: No copy fee. Cert fee: $5.00. Payee: City of Huntsville. Personal checks accepted. Mail requests: SASE required. Mail turnaround time 1 week.

Marion County

Circuit Court PO Box 385, Yellville, AR 72687; 870-449-6226; Fax: 870-449-4979. Hours: 8AM-4:30PM (CST). *Felony, Civil Actions Over $5,000, Probate.*
Civil Records: Access: In person only. Visitors must perform in person searches for themselves. No search fee. Required to search: name, years to search. Civil cases indexed by plaintiff. Civil records on dockets from 1956, records are not computerized.
Criminal Records: Access: Mail, in person. Both court and visitors may perform in person searches. Search fee: $6.00 per name. Required to search: name, years to search. Criminal records on dockets from 1956, records are not computerized.
General Information: No juvenile or adoption records released. Will fax results for $1.00 per page (for specific case information). Copy fee: $.25 per page. Cert fee: $5.00. Payee: Marion County Circuit Clerk. Personal checks accepted. Prepayment required. Mail requests: SASE required. Mail turnaround time 1 day.

District Court PO Box 301, Yellville, AR 72687; 870-449-6030. Hours: 8AM-4:30PM (CST). *Misdemeanor, Civil Actions Under $5,000, Small Claims.*
Civil Records: Access: Mail, in person. Both court and visitors may perform in person searches. No search fee. Civil records go back to 1985.
Criminal Records: Access: Mail, in person. Both court and visitors may perform in person searches. No search fee. Required to search: name, years to search, DOB. Criminal records go back to 1985; on computer back to 1996.
General Information: Will fax results to local or toll free line. Copy fee: $.25 per page. Cert fee: $5.00. Prepayment required. Mail turnaround time 1-2 days.

Miller County

Circuit Court 412 Laurel St Rm 109, Texarkana, AR 71854; 870-774-4501; Fax: 870-772-5293. Hours: 8AM-4:30PM (CST). *Felony, Civil Actions Over $5,000, Probate.*
Note: Probate is at the County Clerk's office.

Civil Records: Access: Phone, mail, in person, online. Both court and visitors may perform in person searches. Search fee: $6.00 per name. Required to search: name, years to search. Civil cases indexed by defendant, plaintiff. Civil records from index from 1850s. Access to court dockets is by subscription at www.recordsusa.com/Arkansas/MillerCnAr.htm. Base fee is $49.95 per month and also includes land imaging and unlimited instrument access.
Criminal Records: Access: Mail, in person, online. Both court and visitors may perform in person searches. Search fee: $6.00 per name. Required to search: name, years to search. Criminal records on index from 1850s; computerized records since 2000. Online access to criminal records is the same as civil.
General Information: Public Access terminal is available. No expunged records released. Will fax results to local or toll free line. Copy fee: $1.00 per page. Cert fee: $3.50. Payee: Miller County Circuit Clerk. Personal checks accepted. Prepayment required. Mail requests: SASE required. Mail turnaround time 1-2 days.

District Court 2300 East St, Texarkana, AR 71854; 870-772-2780; Fax: 870-773-3595. Hours: 8AM-4:30PM (CST). *Misdemeanor, Eviction.*
Civil Records: Access: Mail, in person. Both court and visitors may perform in person searches. Search fee: $25.00 per search. Civil records on computer back to 1997.
Criminal Records: Access: In person, mail. Only the court may perform in person searches. Search fee: $25.00 per search. Required to search: name, years to search, DOB. Criminal records on computer back to 1997.
General Information: Will fax results to local or toll free line. Copy fee: $1.00. Cert fee: $25.00. Payee: Miller County Court. Only cashiers checks and money orders accepted. Prepayment required. Mail requests: SASE required. Mail turnaround time 2 days.

Mississippi County

Blytheville Circuit Court PO Box 1498, Blytheville, AR 72316; 870-762-2332; Fax: 870-763-8148. Hours: 9AM-4:30PM (CST). *Felony, Civil Actions Over $5,000, Probate.*
Civil Records: Access: In person only. Visitors must perform in person searches for themselves. No search fee. Required to search: name, years to search. Civil cases indexed by plaintiff. Civil records prior on index from 1940.
Criminal Records: Access: In person only. Both court and visitors may perform in person searches. No search fee. Required to search: name, years to search, DOB, SSN. Criminal records prior on index from 1940. Court will search 7 years only.
General Information: No juvenile records released. Will fax results $5.00 per doc. Copy fee: $.25 per page. Cert fee: $3.00. Payee: Circuit Clerk. Personal checks accepted. Prepayment required.

Osceola Circuit Court County Courthouse, PO Box 466 (200 W Hale), Osceola, AR 72370; 870-563-6471. Hours: 9AM-4:30PM (CST). *Felony, Civil Actions Over $5,000, Probate.*
Civil Records: Access: Mail, in person. Visitors must perform in person searches for themselves. No search fee. Required to search: name, years to search. Civil cases indexed by defendant, plaintiff. Civil records computerized since 1992, on index from 1940.
Criminal Records: Access: In person only. Visitors must perform in person searches for themselves. No search fee. Required to search: name, years to search, DOB, SSN. Criminal records on computer (not for public use) since 1992.
General Information: Public Access terminal is available. No juvenile records released. Copy fee:

$.25 per page. Cert fee: $3.00. Payee: Circuit Clerk. Personal checks accepted. Prepayment required.

Blytheville District Court 121 N 2nd St, #104, Blytheville, AR 72315; 870-763-7513; Fax: 870-762-0433. Hours: 8AM-5PM (CST). *Misdemeanor, Civil Actions Under $5,000, Small Claims.*
Civil Records: Access: Mail, fax, in person. Both court and visitors may perform in person searches. Search fee: $4.00 per name. Civil records go back to 1960; on computer back to 1987.
Criminal Records: Access: Mail, fax, in person. Both court and visitors may perform in person searches. Search fee: $4.00 per name. Required to search: name, years to search; also helpful: DOB, SSN. Criminal records go back to 1960; on computer back to 1987.
General Information: Will fax results to local or toll free line. Copy fee: $.50 per page. Cert fee: $5.00. Payee: City of Blytheville. Prepayment required. Mail turnaround time 1-2 days.

Osceola District Court 397 W Keiser, Osceola, AR 72370; 870-563-1303; Fax: 870-563-8439. Hours: 8AM-4PM (CST). *Misdemeanor, Civil Actions Under $5,000, Small Claims.*
Civil Records: Access: Mail, in person, fax. Only the court may perform in person searches. Search fee: $5.00. Required to search: name, DOB and SSN. Records computerized for at least 7 years.
Criminal Records: Access: Mail, in person. Only the court may perform in person searches. Search fee: $5.00. Required to search: name, years to search; also helpful: address, DOB, SSN. Records computerized for at least 7 years.
General Information: Will fax results to local or toll free line. Copy fee: $.50 per page. Cert fee: $1.00 per page. Payee: Osceola District Court. Prepayment required. Mail turnaround time 1-2 days.

Monroe County

Circuit Court 123 Madison St, Courthouse, Clarendon, AR 72029; 870-747-3615; Fax: 870-747-3710. Hours: 8AM-4:30PM (CST). *Felony, Civil Actions Over $5,000, Probate.*
Civil Records: Access: Fax, mail, in person. Both court and visitors may perform in person searches. No search fee. Required to search: name, years to search. Civil cases indexed by defendant, plaintiff. Civil records on index books from 1931.
Criminal Records: Access: In person only. Visitors must perform in person searches for themselves. No search fee. Required to search: name, years to search. Criminal records on index books from 1933.
General Information: No juvenile records released. Will fax results $2.50 per page and $2.50 per doc. Add $.50 per page if more than 10. Copy fee: $.50 per page. Cert fee: $2.50. Payee: Monroe County Circuit Clerk. Personal checks accepted. Prepayment required. Mail requests: SASE required. Mail turnaround time 1-2 days.

District Court City Hall, 270 Madison St, Clarendon, AR 72029; 870-747-5200; Fax: 870-747-9969. Hours: 8AM-5PM (CST). *Misdemeanor, Civil Actions Under $5,000, Small Claims.*
Civil Records: Access: Mail, in person. Both court and visitors may perform in person searches. No search fee. Required to search: name, years to search, DOB. Records go back to 1988, on computer since 1994.
Criminal Records: Access: Mail, in person. Both court and visitors may perform in person searches. No search fee. Required to search: name, years to search, DOB, SSN. Records go back to 1988, on computer since 1994.
General Information: Will fax results to local or toll free line. Copy fee: $.25. Cert fee: $5.00. Payee:

Clarendon District Court. Prepayment required. Mail turnaround time is 1-2 days.

Montgomery County

Circuit Court PO Box 369, Courthouse, Mount Ida, AR 71957; 870-867-3521; Fax: 870-867-2177. Hours: 8AM-4:30PM (CST). *Felony, Civil Actions Over $5,000, Probate.*
Civil Records: Access: Phone, fax, mail, in person. Both court and visitors may perform in person searches. No search fee. Required to search: name, years to search; also helpful: address. Civil cases indexed by defendant, plaintiff. Civil records on card files from 1960s.
Criminal Records: Access: In person only. Visitors must perform in person searches for themselves. No search fee. Required to search: name, years to search; also helpful: address, DOB, SSN. Criminal records on card files from 1960s.
General Information: No juvenile or adoption records released. Copy fee: $.50 per page. Cert fee: $5.00. Payee: Circuit Clerk. Personal checks accepted. Prepayment required. Mail requests: SASE required. Mail turnaround time 1 day.

District Court PO Box 548, Mount Ida, AR 71957; 870-867-2221. Hours: 8AM-4:30PM M-Th, other days hours may vary (CST). *Misdemeanor, Civil Actions Under $5,000, Eviction, Small Claims.*
Civil Records: Access: In person, mail. Both court and visitors may perform in person searches. No search fee. Required to search: name, years to search, DOB, SSN. Records go back to 1973; computerized records go back to 1993.
Criminal Records: Access: In person, mail. Both court and visitors may perform in person searches. No search fee. Required to search: name, years to search, DOB, SSN. Records go back to 1973; computerized records go back to 1993.
General Information: No fee to fax results. No copy fee. No cert fee. Turnaround time 1-2 days.

Nevada County

Circuit Court PO Box 204, Prescott, AR 71857; 870-887-2511; Fax: 870-887-1911. Hours: 8AM-5PM (CST). *Felony, Civil Actions Over $5,000, Probate.*
Civil Records: Access: Phone, fax, mail, in person. Both court and visitors may perform in person searches. Search fee: $6.00 per name. Required to search: name, years to search. Civil cases indexed by defendant, plaintiff. Civil records on index since 1850.
Criminal Records: Access: In person, mail. Both court and visitors may perform in person searches. Search fee: $6.00 per name. Required to search: name, years to search, DOB. Criminal records on index since 1850.
General Information: No juvenile records released. Will fax results $.25 per page. Copy fee: $.25 per page. Cert fee: $2.00 plus $.25 per page. Payee: Nevada County Circuit Clerk. Personal checks accepted. Prepayment required. Mail requests: SASE required. Mail turnaround time 1-2 days.

District Court PO Box 22, Prescott, AR 71857; 870-887-6016; Fax: 870-887-3244. Hours: 8AM-5PM (CST). *Misdemeanor, Civil Actions Under $5,000, Small Claims.*
Civil Records: Access: Phone, mail, fax, in person. Both court and visitors may perform in person searches. Search fee: $6.00. Records on computer go back to 1994.
Criminal Records: Access: Phone, mail, fax, in person. Both court and visitors may perform in person searches. Search fee: $6.00. Required to search: name, years to search, DOB, SSN. Records on computer go back to 1994.

General Information: Will fax results to local or toll free line. Cert fee: $2.00. Prepayment required. Mail turnaround time 2-5 days.

Newton County

Circuit Court PO Box 410, Jasper, AR 72641; 870-446-5125; Fax: 870-446-5155. Hours: 8AM-4:30PM (CST). *Felony, Civil Actions Over $5,000, Probate.*
Civil Records: Access: Fax, mail, in person. Both court and visitors may perform in person searches. Search fee: $6.00 per name. Required to search: name, years to search. Civil cases indexed by defendant, plaintiff. Civil records on dockets from 1800s.
Criminal Records: Access: Fax, mail, in person. Both court and visitors may perform in person searches. Search fee: $6.00 per name. Required to search: name, years to search, DOB. Criminal records on dockets from 1800s.
General Information: No juvenile records released. Will fax results $2.50 1st page, $.50 each add'l. Copy fee: $.25 per page. Cert fee: $5.00. Payee: Circuit Clerk. Personal checks accepted. Prepayment required. Mail requests: SASE required. Mail turnaround time varies.

District Court PO Box 550, Jasper, AR 72641; 870-446-5335; Fax: 870-446-2234. Hours: 8AM-4:30PM (CST). *Misdemeanor, Civil Actions Under $5,000, Eviction, Small Claims.*
Civil Records: Access: Phone, mail, fax, in person. Only the court performs in person searches; visitors may not. No search fee. Required to search: name plus years to search, and DOB or SSN. Records go back to 1984, civil records not computerized.
Criminal Records: Access: Phone, mail, fax, in person. Only the court performs in person searches; visitors may not. No search fee. Required to search: name plus years to search, and DOB or SSN. Records go back to 1972, on computer back to 1993.
General Information: Will fax results to local or toll free line. Copy fee: $.25 per page. Cert fee: $10.00. Payee: District Court. Prepayment required. Mail turnaround time is 24 hours.

Ouachita County

Circuit Court PO Box 667, Camden, AR 71701; 870-837-2230 (Circuit); Probate phone: 870-837-2220; Fax: 870-837-2252. Hours: 8AM-4:30PM (CST). *Felony, Civil Actions Over $5,000, Probate.*
Civil Records: Access: In person only. Visitors must perform in person searches for themselves. No search fee. Required to search: name, years to search. Civil cases indexed by defendant, plaintiff. Civil records archived from 1950s; on computer back to 3/1999.
Criminal Records: Access: In person only. Visitors must perform in person searches for themselves. No search fee. Required to search: name, years to search; also helpful: DOB, SSN. Criminal records archived from 1950s; on computer back to 3/1999.
General Information: Public Access terminal is available. No juvenile records released. Will fax results for $3.00 per fax plus copy fee. Copy fee: $1.00 per page. Cert fee: $2.50. Payee: Circuit Clerk of Ouachita County. Personal checks accepted. Prepayment required.

District Court 213 Madison St, Camden, AR 71701; 870-836-0331; Fax: 870-837-5530. Hours: 8AM-4:30PM (CST). *Misdemeanor, Civil Actions Under $5,000, Eviction, Small Claims.*
Civil Records: Access: Mail, fax, in person. Both court and visitors may perform in person searches. Search fee: $5.00 per name. Required to search: name, years to search. Records go back to 1950; computerized since 1987.

Criminal Records: Access: Mail, fax, in person. Both court and visitors may perform in person searches. Search fee: $5.00 per name. Required to search: name, years to search, DOB; also helpful: SSN. Records go back to 1950; computerized since 1987.

General Information: Will fax results to local or toll free line. Copy fee: $.25. Cert fee: $5.00. Payee: District Court. Prepayment required. Mail turnaround time 1-2 days.

Perry County

Circuit Court PO Box 358, Perryville, AR 72126; 501-889-5126; Fax: 501-889-5759. Hours: 8AM-4:30PM (CST). *Felony, Civil Actions Over $5,000, Probate.*

Civil Records: Access: In person only. Visitors must perform in person searches for themselves. No search fee. Required to search: name, years to search. Civil cases indexed by defendant, plaintiff. Civil records on computer from 1997, on dockets from 1974.

Criminal Records: Access: In person only. Visitors must perform in person searches for themselves. No search fee. Required to search: name, years to search, DOB. Criminal records on computer from 1997, on dockets from 1974.

General Information: Public Access terminal is available. No juvenile or adoption records released. Copy fee: $.50 for first page, $.25 each add'l. Cert fee: $5.00. Payee: Circuit Clerk. Personal checks accepted. Prepayment required.

District Court PO Box 186, Perryville, AR 72126; 501-889-5296; Fax: 501-889-5835. Hours: 8AM-4:30PM (CST). *Misdemeanor, Civil Actions Under $5,000, Eviction, Small Claims, Traffic.*

Civil Records: Access: Mail, fax, in person. Only the court performs in person searches; visitors may not Search fee: $2.00. Records back to 1993.

Criminal Records: Access: In person, mail. Only the court performs in person searches; visitors may not Search fee: $2.00. Required to search: name, years to search, DOB, SSN. Computerized records back to 1997, prior on hard copy back to 1993.

General Information: Will fax results. Payee: District Court. Prepayment required. Mail turnaround time 3-5 days.

Phillips County

Circuit Court Courthouse, 620 Cherry St #206, Helena, AR 72342; 870-338-5515; Probate phone: 870-338-5505; Fax: 870-338-5513. Hours: 8AM-4:30PM (CST). *Felony, Civil Actions Over $5,000, Probate.*

Civil Records: Access: Mail, in person. Visitors must perform in person searches for themselves. Search fee: $6.00 per name. Required to search: name, years to search, DOB. Civil cases indexed by plaintiff. Civil records on fee books from 1970; on computer back to 1998.

Criminal Records: Access: Mail, in person. Visitors must perform in person searches for themselves. Search fee: $6.00 per name. Required to search: name, years to search; also helpful-DOB, SSN. Criminal records on fee books from 1970; on computer back to 1998.

General Information: Public Access terminal is available. No juvenile records released. Fee to fax results is $1.00 per document. Copy fee: $.25 per page. Cert fee: $3.00. Payee: Circuit Clerk Wanda McIntosh. Personal checks accepted. Prepayment required. Mail requests: SASE required. Mail turnaround time is 1-3 days.

District Court 226 Perry ST, City Hall, Helena, AR 72342; 870-338-8825; Fax: 870-338-8676. Hours: 8AM-4:30PM (CST). *Misdemeanor, Civil Actions Under $5,000, Eviction, Small Claims.*

Civil Records: Access: In person, mail. Both court and visitors may perform in person searches. Search fee: $9.00. Computerized from 1993-2000.

Criminal Records: Access: In person, mail. Both court and visitors may perform in person searches. Search fee: $5.00 per name. Required to search: name, years to search, address, DOB, SSN. Computerized back to 1993.

General Information: Copy fee: $.25 per page. Cert fee: $2.50 per page. Payee: City of Helena District Court. Prepayment required. Mail turnaround time 3 days.

Pike County

Circuit Court PO Box 219, Murfreesboro, AR 71958; 870-285-2231; Fax: 870-285-3281. Hours: 8AM-4:30PM (CST). *Felony, Civil Actions Over $5,000, Probate.*

Civil Records: Access: Fax, mail, in person. Both court and visitors may perform in person searches. Search fee: $6.00 per name. Required to search: name, years to search. Civil cases indexed by defendant. Civil records archived from 1895. Some records on dockets books, computerized since 1989.

Criminal Records: Access: Fax, mail, in person. Both court and visitors may perform in person searches. Search fee: $6.00 per name. Required to search: name, years to search, DOB. Criminal records archived from 1895. Some records on dockets, fee books. Computerized records from 1992.

General Information: No juvenile or adoption records released. Will fax results for $1.50 1st 3 pages, $.50 each add'l. Copy fee: $.50 per page. Cert fee: $5.00. Payee: Pike County Clerk. Prepayment required. Mail turnaround time 1 week.

District Court PO Box 197, Murfreesboro, AR 71958; 870-285-3865; Fax: 870-285-3865. Hours: 8:30AM-4:30PM (CST). *Misdemeanor, Civil Actions Under $5,000, Eviction, Small Claims.*

Civil Records: Access: In person, mail. Both court and visitors may perform in person searches. No search fee.

Criminal Records: Access: In person, mail. Both court and visitors may perform in person searches. Search fee: $6.00 per name. Required to search: name, years to search, offense.

General Information: Will fax results. Payee: Pike County District Court. Prepayment required. Mail turnaround time 2-3 days.

Poinsett County

Circuit Court PO Box 46, Harrisburg, AR 72432; 870-578-4420; Fax: 870-578-4427. Hours: 8:30AM-4:30PM (CST). *Felony, Civil Actions Over $5,000, Probate.*

Civil Records: Access: Mail, in person. Both court and visitors may perform in person searches. Search fee: $6.00 per name. Required to search: name, years to search. Civil cases indexed by defendant, plaintiff. Civil records on computer from 1985. Some records on dockets. All requests must be in writing.

Criminal Records: Access: Mail, in person. Both court and visitors may perform in person searches. Search fee: $6.00 per name. Required to search: name, years to search, DOB. Criminal records on computer from 1985. Some records on dockets. All requests must be in writing.

General Information: No juvenile records released. Copy fee: $.25 per page. Cert fee: $2.00. Payee: Circuit Clerk. Personal checks accepted. Prepayment required. Mail requests: SASE required. Mail turnaround time 1-2 days.

Harrisburg District Court 202 N East St, Harrisburg, AR 72432; 870-578-4110; Fax: 870-578-4123. Hours: 8:30AM-4:30PM (CST). *Misdemeanor, Civil Actions Under $5,000, Eviction, Small Claims.*

Civil Records: Access: Mail, in person. Both court and visitors may perform in person searches. Search fee: $2.00. Required to search: name, DOB, SSN, signed release. Civil records go back to 1978.

Criminal Records: Access: Mail, in person. Both court and visitors may perform in person searches. Search fee: $2.00. Required to search: name, years to search; also helpful: DOB, SSN, signed release. Criminal records on computer back to 1987. Court does not allow public access to computer index.

General Information: Copy fee: $.25 per page. Cert fee: $5.00. Payee: Harrisburg District Court. Prepayment required. Mail turnaround time is 1 day.

Lepanto District Court PO Box 610, Lepanto, AR 72354; 870-475-2415; Fax: 870-475-3161. Hours: 8:30AM-4:30PM (CST). *Misdemeanor, Civil Actions Under $5,000, Eviction, Small Claims.*

Civil Records: Access: Mail, in person. Both court and visitors may perform in person searches. Search fee: $2.00. Required to search: name, DOB, SSN, signed release. Civil records go back to 1978.

Criminal Records: Access: Mail, in person. Both court and visitors may perform in person searches. Search fee: $2.00. Required to search: name, years to search; also helpful: DOB, SSN, signed release. Criminal records on computer back to 1987. All requests must be in writing. Court does not allow public access to computer index.

General Information: Copy fee: $.25 per page. Cert fee: $5.00. Payee: District Court. Prepayment required. Mail turnaround time is 1-2 days.

Marked Tree District Court #1 Elm St, Marked Tree, AR 72365; 870-358-2024; Fax: 870-358-7867. Hours: 8:30AM-4:30PM (CST). *Misdemeanor, Civil Actions Under $5,000, Eviction, Small Claims.*

Civil Records: Access: Mail, in person. Both court and visitors may perform in person searches. Search fee: $2.00. Required to search: name, DOB, SSN, signed release. Civil records go back to 1978.

Criminal Records: Access: Mail, in person. Both court and visitors may perform in person searches. Search fee: $2.00. Required to search: name, years to search; also helpful: DOB, SSN, signed release. Criminal records on computer back to 1987. Court does not allow public access to computer index.

General Information: Copy fee: $.25 per page. Cert fee: $5.00. Payee: District Court. Prepayment required. Mail turnaround time is 1-2 days.

Trumann District Court PO Box 120, Trumann, AR 72472; 870-483-7771; Fax: 870-483-2620. Hours: 8:30AM-4:30PM (CST). *Misdemeanor, Civil Actions Under $5,000, Eviction, Small Claims.*

Civil Records: Access: Mail, in person. Both court and visitors may perform in person searches. No search fee. Required to search: name, DOB, SSN, signed release. Civil records go back to 1978.

Criminal Records: Access: Mial, in person. Both court and visitors may perform in person searches. No search fee. Required to search: name, years to search; also helpful: DOB, SSN, signed release. Criminal records on computer back to 1987. Court does not allow public access to computer index.

General Information: Copy fee: $.25 per page. Cert fee: $5.00. Payee: District Court. Prepayment required. Mail turnaround time is 1-2 days.

Tyronza District Court PO Box 275, Tyronza, AR 72386; 870-487-2168; Fax: 870-487-2729. Hours: 8AM-4:30PM (CST). *Misdemeanor, Civil Actions Under $5,000, Eviction, Small Claims.*

Civil Records: Access: Mail, In person. Both court and visitors may perform in person searches. Search fee: $2.00. Required to search: name, DOB, SSN, signed release. Civil records go back to 1978.

Criminal Records: Access: Mail, in person. Both court and visitors may perform in person searches. Search fee: $2.00. Required to search: name, years to search; also helpful: DOB, SSN, signed release. Criminal records on computer back to 1987. All requests must be in writing. Court does not allow public access to computer index.

General Information: Copy fee: $.25 per page. Cert fee: $5.00. Payee: District Court. Prepayment required.

Polk County

Circuit Court 507 Church St, Mena, AR 71953; 479-394-8100; Probate phone: 479-394-8123. Hours: 8AM-4:30PM (CST). *Felony, Civil Actions Over $5,000, Probate.*

Note: Probate is handled separately from the court.

Civil Records: Access: Mail, in person. Both court and visitors may perform in person searches. Search fee: $6.00 per name. Required to search: name, years to search. Civil cases indexed by defendant, plaintiff. Civil records on dockets and index from late 1800s.

Criminal Records: Access: Mail, in person. Both court and visitors may perform in person searches. Search fee: $6.00 per name. Required to search: name, years to search, DOB. Criminal records on dockets and index from late 1800s.

General Information: Public Access terminal is available. No juvenile records released. Will fax results to local or toll free line. Copy fee: $.25 per page. $.50 for legal size copies. Cert fee: $2.00. Payee: Circuit Clerk. Personal checks accepted. Prepayment required. Mail turnaround time 1-2 days.

District Court Courthouse, 507 Church St, Mena, AR 71953; 479-394-8140; Fax: 479-394-6199. Hours: 8AM-4:30PM (CST). *Misdemeanor, Civil Actions Under $5,000, Eviction, Small Claims.*

Civil Records: Access: In person only. Visitors must perform in person searches for themselves. No search fee. Civil records go back 10 years; computerized records go back 10 years.

Criminal Records: Access: In person only. Visitors must perform in person searches for themselves. No search fee. Required to search: name, years to search, DOB; also helpful: SSN. Criminal records go back 10 years; computerized records go back 10 years.

Pope County

Circuit Court 100 W Main, Russellville, AR 72801; 479-968-7499; Probate phone: 479-968-6064. Hours: 8AM-5PM (CST). *Felony, Civil Actions Over $5,000.*

Civil Records: Access: In person only. Visitors must perform in person searches for themselves. No search fee. Required to search: name, years to search. Civil cases indexed by defendant, plaintiff. Civil records on dockets from early 1900s; on computer back to 1998.

Criminal Records: Access: In person only. Visitors must perform in person searches for themselves. No search fee. Required to search: name, years to search, DOB; also helpful: SSN. Criminal records on dockets from early 1900s; on computer back to 1998.

General Information: Public Access terminal is available. No juvenile records released. Copy fee: If the court makes the copy, the fee is $1.00 per page, otherwise $.15. Cert fee: $3.00. Payee: Pope County. Personal checks accepted. Prepayment required.

District Court 205 W Second, Russellville, AR 72801; 479-968-1393; Fax: 479-968-4166. Hours: 8AM-5PM (CST). *Misdemeanor, Civil Actions Under $5,000, Small Claims.*

Civil Records: Access: Phone, fax, mail, in person. Both court and visitors may perform in person searches. No search fee. Required to search: name, DOB, years to search. Civil records go back to 1970s; on computer back to 1991.

Criminal Records: Access: Phone, fax, mail, in person. Both court and visitors may perform in person searches. No search fee. Required to search: name, years to search; also helpful: DOB. Criminal records go back to 1970s; on computer back to 1991.

General Information: Will fax results to local or toll free line. Copy fee: $.25 per page. Cert fee: $5.00. Payee: District Court. Prepayment required. Mail turnaround time 2-3 days.

Prairie County

Circuit Court - Southern District PO Box 283, De Valls Bluff, AR 72041; 870-998-2314; Fax: 870-998-2314. Hours: 8AM-4:30PM (CST). *Felony, Civil Actions Over $5,000, Probate.*

Civil Records: Access: Phone, fax, mail, in person. Both court and visitors may perform in person searches. Search fee: $6.00. Required to search: name, years to search. Civil cases indexed by defendant, plaintiff. Civil records on dockets from 1800s.

Criminal Records: Access: Phone, fax, mail, in person. Both court and visitors may perform in person searches. Search fee: $6.00. Required to search: name, years to search, DOB, SSN. Criminal records on dockets from 1800s.

General Information: No juvenile or adoption records released. Will fax results $1.00 per page. Copy fee: $.25 per page. Cert fee: $6.00. Payee: Circuit Clerk. Personal checks accepted. Prepayment required. Mail requests: SASE required. Mail turnaround time 1 day.

Circuit Court - Northern District PO Box 1011, Des Arc, AR 72040; 870-256-4434; Fax: 870-256-4434. Hours: 8AM-4:30PM (CST). *Felony, Civil Actions Over $5,000, Probate.*

Civil Records: Access: Mail, in person. Both court and visitors may perform in person searches. Search fee: $6.00 per name. Required to search: name, years to search. Civil cases indexed by defendant, plaintiff. Civil records on dockets from 1800s; limited records on computer.

Criminal Records: Access: Mail, in person. Both court and visitors may perform in person searches. Search fee: $6.00 per name. Required to search: name, years to search. Criminal records on dockets from 1800s; limited records on computer.

General Information: No juvenile, adoption records released. Fee to fax results is $1.005 per page. Copy fee: $.25 per page. Cert fee: $6.00. Payee: Circuit Clerk. Personal checks accepted. Prepayment required. Mail requests: SASE required. Mail turnaround time 1 day.

Des Arc District Court PO Box 389, Des Arc, AR 72040; 870-256-3011; Fax: 870-256-4612. Hours: 8AM-4:30PM (CST). *Misdemeanor, Civil Actions Under $5,000, Eviction, Small Claims.*

Civil Records: Access: In person, mail. Both court and visitors may perform in person searches. No search fee. Civil records available since 1988.

Criminal Records: Access: In person, mail. Both court and visitors may perform in person searches. No search fee. Required to search: name, years to search. Criminal records available since 1988.

General Information: Copy fee: $.50. Turnaround time 1-2 days.

Pulaski County

District Court 3001 W Roosevelt, Little Rock, AR 72204; 501-340-6824; Fax: 501-340-6899. Hours: 8AM-4:30PM (CST). *Misdemeanor, Civil Actions Under $5,000, Eviction, Small Claims.*

Civil Records: Access: Phone, mail, in person. Both court and visitors may perform in person searches. No search fee. Required to search: DOB, SNS, case number. Overall records and computerized records go to 1988.

Criminal Records: Access: Phone, mail, in person. Both court and visitors may perform in person searches. No search fee. Required to search: name, years to search; also helpful: SSN.

General Information: Copy fee: $.50 per page. Turnaround time 2-3 days.

Circuit Court Courthouse, Rm 102, 401 W Markham St, #102, Little Rock, AR 72201; 501-340-8431; Probate phone: 501-340-8411; Fax: 501-340-8420. Hours: 8:30AM-4:30PM (CST). *Felony, Civil Actions Over $5,000, Probate.*

Note: Probate is handled by the Chancery Court #120 until July 1, 2001.

Civil Records: Access: In person only. Visitors must perform in person searches for themselves. No search fee. Required to search: name, years to search. Civil cases indexed by defendant, plaintiff. Civil records on computer from 1982, on microfiche from 1974 to 1982, archived from 1900.

Criminal Records: Access: In person only. Visitors must perform in person searches for themselves. No search fee. Required to search: name, years to search, DOB, SSN. Criminal records on computer from 1982, on microfiche from 1974 to 1982, archived from 1900.

General Information: Public Access terminal is available. No expunged records released. Copy fee: $.25 per page. Cert fee: $2.50. Payee: Circuit Clerk. Personal checks accepted. Prepayment required.

Randolph County

Circuit Court 107 W Broadway, Pocahontas, AR 72455; 870-892-5522; Probate phone: 870-892-5822; Fax: 870-892-8794. Hours: 8AM-4:30PM (CST). *Felony, Civil Actions Over $5,000, Probate.*

Note: Probate records are located at the same address, right down the hall.

Civil Records: Access: Mail, in person. Both court and visitors may perform in person searches. Search fee: $6.00 per name. Required to search: name, years to search. Civil cases indexed by defendant, plaintiff. Civil records on criminal index from 1836.

Criminal Records: Access: Mail, in person. Both court and visitors may perform in person searches. Search fee: $6.00 per name. Required to search: name, years to search, DOB. Criminal records on criminal index from 1836.

General Information: Public Access terminal is available. (DuDs only are available.) No juvenile records released. Will fax results for $1.00 per page prepaid. Copy fee: $.25 per page. Cert fee: $2.00. Payee: Circuit Clerk. Personal checks accepted. Prepayment required. Mail requests: SASE required. Mail turnaround time same day.

District Court 1510 Pace Rd, Pocahontas, AR 72455; 870-892-4033; Fax: 870-892-4392. Hours: 8:00AM-4:30PM (CST). *Misdemeanor, Civil Actions Under $5,000, Eviction, Small Claims.*

Civil Records: Access: In person, mail. Both court and visitors may perform in person searches. Search fee: $6.00. Required to search: name, years to search, DOB, SSN. Records maintained since 1980s.

Criminal Records: Access: In person, mail. Both court and visitors may perform in person searches.

Search fee: $6.00. Required to search: name, years to search, DOB, SSN. Records maintained since 1970s.
General Information: Will fax results to local or toll free line. Copy fee: $.25. Cert fee: $5.00. Payee: District Court. Prepayment required. Mail turnaround time 1 day.

Saline County

Circuit Court 200 N Main St, Benton, AR 72015; 501-303-5615; Probate phone: 501-303-5630; Fax: 501-303-5675. Hours: 8AM-4:30PM (CST). *Felony, Civil Actions Over $5,000, Probate.*
www.salinecounty.org
Note: Probate add;215 N Main,Benton,Ar. 72015
Civil Records: Access: In person only. Visitors must perform in person searches for themselves. No search fee. Required to search: name, years to search. Civil cases indexed by defendant, plaintiff. Civil records on computer since 1992, prior on docket books.
Criminal Records: Access: In person only. Visitors must perform in person searches for themselves. No search fee. Required to search: name, years to search. Criminal records on computer since 1992, prior on docket books.
General Information: Public Access terminal is available. No juvenile records released. Will fax results for $1.00 per page. Copy fee: $.25 per page. Cert fee: $3.00. Payee: Circuit Court. Personal checks accepted. Prepayment required.

Benton District Court 1605 Edison Ave #19, Benton, AR 72015; 501-303-5670/1 & 5975; Fax: 501-776-5696. Hours: 8AM-4:30PM (CST). *Misdemeanor, Civil Actions Under $5,000, Eviction, Small Claims.*
Civil Records: Access: In person, mail. Both court and visitors may perform in person searches. Search fee: $5.00 per name. Required to search: name. Civil records go back to 1982.
Criminal Records: Access: In person, mail. Both court and visitors may perform in person searches. Search fee: $5.00 per name. Required to search: name, years to search; also helpful: DOB, SSN. Criminal records go back to 1994 on computer.
General Information: Will fax results. Copy fee: $5.00. Turnaround time 72 hours.

Scott County

Circuit Court PO Box 2165, 190 W First St Box 10, Waldron, AR 72958; 479-637-2642. Hours: 8AM-4:30PM (CST). *Felony, Civil Actions Over $5,000, Probate.*
Civil Records: Access: Phone, mail, fax, in person. Both court and visitors may perform in person searches. No search fee. Required to search: name, years to search. Civil cases indexed by defendant, plaintiff. Civil records on index books from 1882.
Criminal Records: Access: Phone, mail, fax, in person. Both court and visitors may perform in person searches. No search fee. Required to search: name, years to search, DOB, SSN. Criminal records on index books from 1882.
General Information: No juvenile or adoption records released. Will fax results for no fee. Copy fee: $.25 per page. Cert fee: $5.00. Payee: Scott County. Personal checks accepted. Prepayment required. Mail requests: SASE required. Mail turnaround time 1 week.

District Court 100 W 1st St, Box 15, Waldron, AR 72958; 479-637-4694; Fax: 479-637-4712. Hours: 8AM-4:30PM (CST). *Misdemeanor, Civil Actions Under $5,000, Eviction, Small Claims.*
Civil Records: Access: In person, mail. Both court and visitors may perform in person searches. No search fee. Records on computer go back to 1998.

Criminal Records: Access: In person, mail. Both court and visitors may perform in person searches. No search fee. Required to search: name, years to search. Records go back to 1998; on computer back to 10/1998.
General Information: No cert fee. Turnaround time 1-2 days.

Searcy County

Circuit Court PO Box 998, Marshall, AR 72650; 870-448-3807. Hours: 8AM-4:30PM (CST). *Felony, Civil Actions Over $5,000, Probate.*
Civil Records: Access: Mail, in person. Visitors must perform in person searches for themselves. No search fee. Required to search: name, years to search. Civil cases indexed by defendant, plaintiff. Civil records archived from 1881. Some records on dockets.
Criminal Records: Access: In person only. Visitors must perform in person searches for themselves. No search fee. Required to search: name, years to search, offense; also helpful: DOB, SSN. Criminal records archived from 1881. Some records on dockets.
General Information: No juvenile or adoption records released. Copy fee: $.25 per page. Fee is for civil division only. Cert fee: $3.00 per doc. Payee: Searcy County Clerk. Personal checks accepted. Prepayment required. Mail requests: SASE required. Mail turnaround time 1-2 days.

District Court PO Box 885, Marshall, AR 72650; 870-448-5411; Fax: 870-448-5927. Hours: 9AM-5PM (CST). *Misdemeanor, Civil Actions Under $5,000, Eviction, Small Claims.*
Civil Records: Access: In person, mail. Both court and visitors may perform in person searches. No search fee.
Criminal Records: Access: In person, mail. Both court and visitors may perform in person searches. No search fee. Required to search: name, years to search, DOB, SSN.
General Information: Cert fee: $5.00 per document. Turnaround time 1 week.

Sebastian County

Circuit Court - Greenwood Division PO Box 310, County Courthouse, Greenwood, AR 72936; 479-996-4175; Fax: 479-996-6885. Hours: 8AM-5PM (CST). *Felony, Civil Actions Over $5,000, Probate.*
www.sebastiancountyonline.com
Note: Records from both Circuit Courts-Fort Smith and Greenwood Division-are on the same computer system, but copies of case files must be pulled from the individual courts.
Civil Records: Access: Mail, in person. Both court and visitors may perform in person searches. Search fee: $6.00 per name. Required to search: name, years to search. Civil cases indexed by defendant, plaintiff. Civil records on computer from 10/87, on dockets from 1900.
Criminal Records: Access: Mail, in person. Both court and visitors may perform in person searches. Search fee: $6.00 per name. Required to search: name, years to search; also helpful: SSN. Criminal records on computer from 10/87, on dockets from 1900.
General Information: Public Access terminal is available. No juvenile records released. Will fax results $1.00 per page. Copy fee: $1.00 per page. Cert fee: $2.50. Payee: Circuit Clerk. Personal checks accepted. Prepayment required. Mail requests: SASE required. Mail turnaround time 1-2 weeks.

Circuit Court - Fort Smith 35 S 6th St,Rm 203, PO Box 1179, Fort Smith, AR 72902; 479-782-1046. Hours: 8AM-5PM (CST). *Felony, Civil Actions Over $5,000, Probate.*
www.sebastiancountyonline.com
Note: Records from both Circuit Courts-Fort Smith and Greenwood Division-are on the same computer system, but copies of case files must be pulled from the individual courts. Closed files in this Circuit are maintained at 40 S 4th St in Fort Smith.
Civil Records: Access: Fax, mail, in person. Both court and visitors may perform in person searches. Search fee: $6.00 per name. Required to search: name, years to search; also helpful: address. Civil cases indexed by defendant, plaintiff. Civil records computerized from 1988, on dockets from 1900.
Criminal Records: Access: Fax, mail, in person. Both court and visitors may perform in person searches. Search fee: $6.00 per name. Required to search: name, years to search; also helpful: address, DOB, SSN. Criminal records computerized from 1988, on dockets from 1900. Court will only perform searches for criminal justice purposes.
General Information: Public Access terminal is available. (Records go back to 1988 on computer.) No juvenile records released. Will fax results $1.00 per page. Copy fee: $1.00 per page. The fee is $.50 if in person, $1.00 for mail requesters. Cert fee: $2.50. Payee: Circuit Clerk. Personal checks accepted. Prepayment required. Mail requests: SASE required. Mail turnaround time 1-2 weeks.

Fort Smith District Court Courthouse, 35 S 6th St, Fort Smith, AR 72901; 479-784-2420; Fax: 479-784-2438. Hours: 8:30AM-5PM (CST). *Misdemeanor, Civil Actions Under $5,000, Traffic, Small Claims.*
Civil Records: Access: Phone, fax, mail, in person. Both court and visitors may perform in person searches. No search fee. Record stored from 1984. If copies are reuqired, then your request must be in writing.
Criminal Records: Access: Phone, fax, mail, in person. Both court and visitors may perform in person searches. No search fee. Required to search: name, years to search, DOB; also helpful: SSN. Records are computerized since 1986. If copies are reuqired, then your request must be in writing.
General Information: Public Access terminal is available. Fee to fax results is $.50 per page. Copy fee: $.50 per page. Cert fee: $5.00. Payee: Fort Smith District Court. Prepayment required. Mail turnaround time 1-2 days.

Sevier County

Circuit Court 115 N 3rd, Courthouse, De Queen, AR 71832; 870-584-3055; Probate phone: 870-642-2852; Fax: 870-642-3119. Hours: 8AM-4:30PM (CST). *Felony, Civil Actions Over $5,000, Probate.*
Note: Probate court is located in the same building at County Clerk; probate phone is above.
Civil Records: Access: Phone, mail, fax, in person. Visitors must perform in person searches for themselves. Search fee: none. Required to search: name, years to search. Civil cases indexed by defendant, plaintiff. Civil records archived from 1900.
Criminal Records: Access: In person only. Visitors must perform in person searches for themselves. Search fee: none. Required to search: name, years to search, DOB. Criminal records index goes back to 1961, prior back to 1912.
General Information: Public Access terminal is available. No juvenile records released. Fee to fax results is $5.00 per document; free if to a toll-free number. Copy fee: $.50 per page. Cert fee: $5.00 per document. Payee: Circuit Clerk. Personal checks

accepted. Prepayment required. Mail requests: SASE required. Mail turnaround time 3 days.

District Court 115 N 3rd St, Rm 215, De Queen, AR 71832; 870-584-7311; Fax: 870-642-6651. Hours: 8AM-4:30PM (CST). *Misdemeanor, Civil Actions Under $5,000, Eviction, Small Claims.*
Civil Records: Access: In person, mail. Both court and visitors may perform in person searches. No search fee. Records available since 1991.
Criminal Records: Access: In person, mail. Both court and visitors may perform in person searches. No search fee. Required to search: name, years to search, DOB. Records available since 1991.
General Information: Turnaround time 1-2 weeks.

Sharp County

Circuit Court PO Box 307, Ash Flat, AR 72513; 870-994-7361; Fax: 870-994-7712. Hours: 8AM-4PM (CST). *Felony, Civil Actions Over $5,000, Probate.*
Civil Records: Access: Fax, mail, in person, online. Both court and visitors may perform in person searches. Search fee: $6.00 per name. Required to search: name, years to search. Civil cases indexed by defendant, plaintiff. Civil records on card files from 1970s. Some records on dockets, computerized since 1986. The court has outsourced online access to civil, probate, criminal, and all recordings to www.ecourtstor.com. Fees are involved.
Criminal Records: Access: In person, online. Visitors must perform in person searches for themselves. No search fee. Required to search: name, years to search; also helpful: DOB, SSN. Criminal records on card files from 1970s. Some records on dockets, computerized since 1986. The court has outsourced online access to civil, probate, criminal, and all recordings to www.ecourtstor.com. Fees are involved.
General Information: Public Access terminal is available. No juvenile or expunged records released. No fee to fax results. Will fax to toll free numbers only. Copy fee: $.25 per page. Cert fee: $5.00. Payee: Sharp County Clerk. Personal checks accepted. Prepayment required. Mail requests: SASE required. Mail turnaround time 1 day.

District Court PO Box 2, Ash Flat, AR 72513; 870-994-2745; Fax: 870-994-7901. Hours: 8AM-4PM (CST). *Misdemeanor, Civil Actions Under $5,000, Eviction, Small Claims.*
Civil Records: Access: In person, mail. Both court and visitors may perform in person searches. No search fee.
Criminal Records: Access: In person, mail. Both court and visitors may perform in person searches. No search fee. Required to search: name, years to search; also helpful: DOB, SSN.
General Information: Public Access terminal is available. Turnaround time 1 day.

St. Francis County

Circuit Court PO Box 1775, Forrest City, AR 72336; 870-261-1715; Fax: 870-261-1723. Hours: 8AM-4:30PM (CST). *Felony, Civil Actions Over $5,000, Probate.*
Civil Records: Access: Fax, mail, in person. Both court and visitors may perform in person searches. Search fee: $5.00 per name. Required to search: name, years to search. Civil cases indexed by defendant, plaintiff. Civil records on index from 1982, archived from 1920s.
Criminal Records: Access: Fax, mail, in person. Both court and visitors may perform in person searches. Search fee: $5.00 per name. Required to search: name, years to search, DOB, SSN. Criminal records on index from 1982, archived from 1920s.

General Information: No juvenile records released. No fee to fax results. Local or toll free calls only. Copy fee: $.25 per page. Cert fee: $3.00. Payee: Circuit Clerk. Personal checks accepted. Prepayment required. Mail requests: SASE required. Mail turnaround time 2-3 days.

District Court 615 East Cross, Forrest City, AR 72335; 870-261-1410; Fax: 870-261-1411. Hours: 8AM-4:30PM (CST). *Misdemeanor, Civil Actions Under $5,000, Eviction, Small Claims.*
Civil Records: Access: In person, mail. Only the court performs in person searches; visitors may not. Search fee: $5.00 per name. Civil records on computer since 1994.
Criminal Records: Access: In person, mail. Only the court performs in person searches; visitors may not. Search fee: $5.00 per name. Required to search: name, years to search. Criminal records on computer since 1990.
General Information: Will fax results. Copy fee: $.25 per page. Cert fee: $5.00 per page. Payee: District Court. Prepayment required. Mail turnaround time 5 days.

Stone County

Circuit Court 107 W Mail #D, Mountain View, AR 72560; 870-269-3271; Fax: 870-269-2303. Hours: 8AM-4:30PM (CST). *Felony, Civil Actions Over $5,000, Probate.*
www.16thdistrictark.org
Civil Records: Access: In person only. Visitors must perform in person searches for themselves. No search fee. Required to search: name, years to search. Civil cases indexed by defendant, plaintiff. Civil records on dockets from 1960s; computerized records since 1992. Mountain View Abstract Corp does searches by mail. Call 870-269-3470.
Criminal Records: Access: In person only. Visitors must perform in person searches for themselves. No search fee. Required to search: name, years to search, DOB; also helpful: SSN. Criminal records on dockets from 1960s; computerized records since 1992.
General Information: Public Access terminal is available. No juvenile or adoption records released. Copy fee: $.25 per page. Cert fee: $5.00. Payee: Stone County Clerk. Personal checks accepted. Prepayment required.

District Court 107 W Main, #H, Mountain View, AR 72560; 870-269-3465. Hours: 8AM-4:30PM (CST). *Misdemeanor, Civil Actions Under $5,000, Eviction, Small Claims.*
Civil Records: Access: Phone, fax, mail, in person. Both court and visitors may perform in person searches. No search fee. Required to search: names, years to search. Records available since 1984, not computerized.
Criminal Records: Access: Phone, fax, mail, in person. Both court and visitors may perform in person searches. No search fee. Required to search: name, years to search; also helpful: DOB, SSN. Records on computer since 1990.
General Information: Cert fee: $3.00. Payee: District Court. Prepayment required. Mail turnaround time varies.

Union County

Circuit Court PO Box 1626, El Dorado, AR 71730; 870-864-1940. Hours: 8:30AM-5PM (CST). *Felony, Civil Actions Over $5,000, Probate.*
Civil Records: Access: In person, online. Visitors must perform in person searches themselves. No search fee. Required to search: name, years to search. Civil cases indexed by defendant, plaintiff. Civil records on computer back to 1996 on dockets from 1800s. Online access to circuit court dockets by subscription through RecordsUSA.com. Credit card,

username and password is required; choose either monthly or per-use plan. Visit the website for sign-up or call Lisa at 601-264-7701 for information.
Criminal Records: Access: In person, online. Visitors must perform in person searches themselves No search fee. Required to search: name, years to search, DOB; also helpful: SSN. Criminal records on computer back to 1996 on dockets from 1800s. Online access to criminal dockets is the same as civil.
General Information: Public Access terminal is available. No juvenile records released. Fee to fax results is $1.00 per page. Copy fee: $.50 per page. Cert fee: $3.00. Payee: Circuit Clerk. Personal checks accepted. Prepayment required.

District Court 250 American #A, El Dorado, AR 71730; 870-864-1950; Fax: 870-864-1955. Hours: 8:30AM-5PM (CST). *Misdemeanor, Civil Actions Under $5,000, Eviction, Small Claims.*
Civil Records: Access: In person, fax, mail. Both court and visitors may perform in person searches. No search fee. Computerized records since 1987.
Criminal Records: Access: In person, fax, mail. Both court and visitors may perform in person searches. No search fee. Required to search: name, years to search, DOB; also helpful: SSN. Computerized records since 1987.
General Information: Turnaround time 1-2 days.

Van Buren County

Circuit Court 451 Main St, Clinton, AR 72031; 501-745-4140. Hours: 8AM-5PM (CST). *Felony, Civil Actions Over $5,000, Probate.*
Civil Records: Access: Mail, in person. Visitors must perform in person searches for themselves. Search fee: $1.00. Required to search: name, years to search; also helpful: address. Civil cases indexed by defendant, plaintiff. Civil records on computer from 1987, archived from 1900s.
Criminal Records: Access: Mail, in person. Both court and visitors may perform in person searches. Search fee: $1.00 per name. Required to search: name, years to search; also helpful: address, DOB, SSN. Criminal records on computer from 1987, archived from 1900s.
General Information: Public Access terminal is available. No juvenile or adoption records released. Will fax results to local or toll free line. Copy fee: $1.00 per page. $.50 for microfilm copies. Cert fee: $5.00. Payee: Van Buren County Clerk's Office. Personal checks accepted. Prepayment required. Mail requests: SASE required. Mail turnaround time 7-10 days.

District Court PO Box 181, Clinton, AR 72031; 501-745-8894; Fax: 501-745-5810. Hours: 8AM-5PM (CST). *Misdemeanor, Civil Actions Under $5,000, Small Claims.*
Civil Records: Access: Phone, mail, fax, in person. Visitors must perform in person searches for themselves. No search fee. Civil records on computer back to 1992; in books back to 1992.
Criminal Records: Access: Phone, mail, fax, in person. Both court and visitors may perform in person searches. Search fee: $5.00 per name. Required to search: name, years to search, DOB, SSN; also helpful-docket or ticket number. Criminal records on computer back to 1992; in books back to 1992; computerized sincee 1992.
General Information: Cert fee: $5.00. Payee: Clinton District Court. Prepayment required.

Washington County

Circuit Court 280 N College, #302, Fayetteville, AR 72701; 479-444-1538; Probate phone: 479-444-1711; Fax: 479-444-1537. Hours: 8AM-4:30PM (CST). *Felony, Civil Actions Over $5,000, Probate.*
www.co.washington.ar.us/

Note: Probate is at same address.

Civil Records: Access: Fax, mail, in person, online. Both court and visitors may perform in person searches. No search fee. Required to search: name, years to search. Civil cases indexed by defendant, plaintiff. Civil records on computer from 1992, on index from 1950. Online case index at www.co.washington.ar.us/resolution/. Civil cases indexed from 1992 forward. This is a commercial system, $50.00 per month prepaid.

Criminal Records: Access: Fax, mail, in person, online. Both court and visitors may perform in person searches. No search fee. Required to search: name, years to search; also helpful: address, DOB, SSN. Criminal records on computer from 1992, on index from 1950. Online case index at www.co.washington.ar.us/resolution/. Civil cases indexed from 1992 forward. This is a commercial system, $50.00 per month prepaid.

General Information: Public Access terminal is available. No juvenile records released. Will fax results $5.00 per doc. Copy fee: $.15 per page. Cert fee: $2.00. Payee: Circuit Clerk. Personal checks accepted. Prepayment required. Mail turnaround time 1-2 days.

Fayetteville District Court 100 B West Rock, Fayetteville, AR 72701; 479-587-3596; Fax: 479-444-3480. Hours: 8AM-5PM (CST). *Misdemeanor, Civil Actions Under $5,000, Small Claims.*
www.co.washington.ar.us

Civil Records: Access: Phone, mail, fax, in person. Both court and visitors may perform in person searches. Search fee: $5.00 per name. Required to search: name, years to search. Civil records on computer go back to 1984.

Criminal Records: Access: In person, mail. Only the court may perform in person searches. Search fee: $5.00 per name. Required to search: name, years to search, DOB, SSN, signed release; also helpful: address. Criminal records on computer go back to 1984.

General Information: Will fax results. Copy fee: $5.00 per document. Payee: City of Fayetteville. Prepayment required. Mail turnaround time 1 week.

White County

Circuit Court 301 W Arch, Searcy, AR 72143; 501-279-6223; Probate phone: 501-279-6204; Fax: 501-279-6218. Hours: 8AM-4:30PM (CST). *Felony, Civil Actions Over $5,000, Probate.*

Civil Records: Access: Mail, in person. Both court and visitors may perform in person searches. Search fee: $6.00 per name. Required to search: name, years to search; also helpful: address. Civil cases indexed by plaintiff.

Criminal Records: Access: Mail, in person. Both court and visitors may perform in person searches. Search fee: $6.00 per name. Required to search: name, years to search, DOB, SSN; also helpful: address. Criminal records on dockets from 1982.

General Information: No juvenile records released. Will fax results $1.00 per page. Copy fee: $.50 per

page. Cert fee: $2.50. Payee: Circuit Clerk. Personal checks accepted. Prepayment required. Mail requests: SASE required. Mail turnaround time 1 day.

Searcy District Court 311 N Gum, Searcy, AR 72143; 501-268-7622/279-1040; Fax: 501-207-5712. Hours: 8:00AM-4:30PM (CST). *Misdemeanor, Civil Actions Under $5,000, Small Claims.*

Civil Records: Access: Mail, fax, phone, in person. Only the court performs in person searches; visitors may not. Search fee: $6.00. Required to search: name plus SSN, years to search. Records go back to 1998; on computer since 6/1995.

Criminal Records: Access: In person, phone, fax, mail. Only the court performs in person searches; visitors may not. Search fee: $6.00 if after 6/1995; $10.00 if before and $15.00 is record found. Required to search: name, years to search, DOB, SSN. Records go back since 1993; on computer since 6/1995.

General Information: Will fax results. Copy fee: $.50 per page. Cert fee: $10.00. Payee: Searcy District Court. Prepayment required. Mail turnaround time 5 days.

Woodruff County

Circuit Court PO Box 492, Augusta, AR 72006; 870-347-8703; Probate phone: 870-347-2871; Fax: 870-347-2915. Hours: 8AM-4PM (CST). *Felony, Civil Actions Over $5,000.*
Note: Probate is handled by the County Clerk.

Civil Records: Access: Phone, mail, in person, fax. Both court and visitors may perform in person searches. No search fee. Required to search: name, years to search. Civil cases indexed by defendant, plaintiff. Civil records on dockets from 1982.

Criminal Records: Access: Phone, mail, in person. Both court and visitors may perform in person searches. No search fee. Required to search: name, years to search, DOB. Criminal records on dockets from 1980.

General Information: No juvenile records released. Copy fee: $.50 per page. Cert fee: $5.00. Payee: Circuit Clerk. Personal checks accepted. Prepayment required. Mail requests: SASE required. Mail turnaround time 1-2 days.

District Court PO Box 381, Augusta, AR 72006; 870-347-2790; Fax: 870-347-2436. Hours: 8:30AM-5PM (CST). *Misdemeanor, Civil Actions Under $5,000, Eviction, Small Claims.*

Civil Records: Access: In person, mail. Only the court may perform in person searches. Search fee: $5.00 per name. Computerized records go back to 1995.

Criminal Records: Access: In person, mail. Only the court may perform in person searches. Search fee: $5.00 per name. Required to search: name, years to search, DOB, signed release. Computerized records go back to 1995.

General Information: No fee to fax results. Cert fee: $.25. Payee: Augusta District Court. Prepayment required. Mail turnaround time 10 days.

Yell County

Danville Circuit Court PO Box 219, Danville, AR 72833; 479-495-4850; Fax: 479-495-4875. Hours: 8AM-4PM (CST). *Felony, Civil Actions Over $5,000, Probate.*

Civil Records: Access: Mail, fax, in person. Both court and visitors may perform in person searches. Search fee: $6.00 per name. Required to search: name, years to search; also helpful: address. Civil cases indexed by defendant. Civil records on dockets from 1900s.

Criminal Records: Access: Mail, fax, in person. Both court and visitors may perform in person searches. Search fee: $6.00 per name. Required to search: name, years to search, DOB; also helpful: address. Criminal records on dockets from 1900s.

General Information: No juvenile or adoption records released. Will fax results for $3.00 if lengthy. Copy fee: $.25 per page. Cert fee: $5.00. Payee: Circuit Clerk of Yell County. Personal checks accepted. Prepayment required. Mail requests: SASE required. Mail turnaround time 1 day.

Dardanelle Circuit Court County Courthouse, PO Box 457, Dardanelle, AR 72834; 501-229-4404. Hours: 8AM-4PM (CST). *Felony, Civil Actions Over $5,000, Probate.*

Civil Records: Access: Mail, in person. Both court and visitors may perform in person searches. Search fee: $6.00 per name. Required to search: name, years to search. Civil cases indexed by defendant. Civil records on dockets from 1800s.

Criminal Records: Access: Mail, in person. Both court and visitors may perform in person searches. Search fee: $6.00 per name. Required to search: name, years to search; also helpful: DOB. Criminal records on dockets from 1800s.

General Information: No adoption or juvenile records released. Will fax results for a fee of $3.00 per document. Copy fee: $.25 per page. Cert fee: $5.00. Payee: Circuit Clerk of Yell County. Personal checks accepted. Prepayment required. Mail requests: SASE required. Mail turnaround time 1 day.

District Court County Courthouse, Dardanelle, AR 72834; 501-229-1389. Hours: 8AM-4PM (CST). *Misdemeanor, Civil Actions Under $5,000, Eviction, Small Claims.*

Civil Records: Access: In person, mail. Both court and visitors may perform in person searches. Search fee: $3.00 per name. Civil records go back to 1982.

Criminal Records: Access: In person, mail. Both court and visitors may perform in person searches. Search fee: $3.00 per name. Required to search: name, years to search, signed release; also helpful: address, DOB, SSN. Criminal records go back to 1982, on computer back to 1994.

General Information: Will fax results to local or toll free line. Copy fee: $.25 per copy. No cert fee. Payee: District Court. Prepayment required. Mail turnaround time 2-4 days.

Arkansas Recording Offices

ORGANIZATION: 75 counties, 85 recording offices. The recording officer is the Clerk of Circuit Court, who is Ex Officio Recorder. Ten counties have two recording offices - Arkansas, Carroll, Clay, Craighead, Franklin, Logan, Mississippi, Prairie, Sebastian, and Yell. See the notes under each county for how to determine which office is appropriate to search. The entire state is in the Central Time Zone (CST).

REAL ESTATE RECORDS: Most counties do not perform real estate searches. Copy fees and certification fees vary.

UCC RECORDS: Prior to 07/01 this was a dual filing state. Financing statements were filed at the state level and with the Circuit Clerk, except for consumer goods, farm and real estate related collateral, which were filed only with the Circuit Clerk. Now all financing statements are filed at the state level, except for real estate related collateral, which is still filed with the Circuit Clerk. Most counties will perform UCC searches. Use search request form UCC-11. Search fees are usually $10.00 per debtor name. Copy fees vary.

TAX LIEN RECORDS: Federal tax liens on personal property of businesses are filed with the Secretary of State. Other federal and all state tax liens are filed with the Circuit Clerk. Many counties will perform separate tax lien searches. Search fees are usually $6.00 per name.

OTHER LIENS: Mechanics, lis pendens, judgments, hospital, child support, materialman.

ONLINE ACCESS: There is no statewide access. Benton county offers records via their web site. Also, there is a commercial system available for a limited number of participating counties. Registration and logon is required, the signup fee is $200 minimum plus $.10 per minute usage. For signup or information call 479-631-8054 or visit www.arcountydata.com

Arkansas County (Northern District)

County Circuit Clerk, 302 S. College St., Stuttgart, AR 72160. **Phone-**County Circuit Clerk, R/E & UCC Recording- 870-673-2056; fax-870-673-3869; hours 8AM-4;30PM
Will search UCC records. Search per debtor- $6.00. UCC copy- $1.00 per page. Will not search real estate or tax lien records. Cert fee: $4.00 per doc. Payee: Arkansas County Circuit Clerk. **Online Access to Assessor, Property records:** Registration and logon is required to search all participating counties' assessor records at www.arcountydata.com. Signup fee is $200 min. + $.10 per minute usage. For signup or information call 479-631-8054 or visit the website. **Other phones:** Assessor-870-673-6586.

Arkansas County (Southern District)

County Circuit Clerk, 101 Court Sq, De Witt, AR 72042. **Phone-**County Circuit Clerk, R/E & UCC Recording- 870-946-4219; fax-870-946-1394; hours 8AM-Noon,12:30-4:30PM
Will search UCC records. Search per debtor- $6.00. UCC copy- $.50 per copy. $1.00 for fax copy. Will not search real estate or tax lien records. RE record copy- $.50 per page. Cert fee: $4.00 per doc. Payee: County Circuit Clerk. **Other phones:** Assessor-870-946-1795; Treasurer-870-946-4210; Elections-870-846-4347; Tax Collector-870-946-2911.

Ashley County

County Circuit Clerk, 205 E. Jefferson St, Courthouse, Hamburg, AR 71646. **Phone-**County Circuit Clerk, R/E & UCC Recording- 870-853-2030; fax-870-853-2034; hours 8AM-4:30PM
Will search UCC records. Search per debtor- $6.00. UCC copy fee- $.50 per page. Will not search real estate or tax lien records. Cert fee: $2.50 per doc. Payee: Ashley County Circuit Clerk. **Other phones:** Assessor-870-853-2060; Treasurer-870-853-2010; Elections-870-853-2020; Tax Collector-870-853-2050.

Baxter County

County Circuit Clerk, 1 E. 7th St #103, Courthouse Sq, Mountain Home, AR 72653. **Phone-**870-425-3475; fax-870-424-5105; hours 8AM-4:30PM
Records are now filed at the office of the Secretary of State. Will search UCC records. Search per debtor- $6.00. UCC copy- $6.00 1st page; $1.00 each add'l. UCC search includes tax liens. Separate federal/state combined tax lien search- $6.00 per debtor. Property transfer searches available. RE record copy- $6.00 1st page; $1.00 each add'l. Cert fee: $5.00 per doc. Payee: Baxter County Circuit Clerk. **Online Access to Assessor, Property, Real Estate Recording records:** Registration and logon is required to search all participating counties' assessor records at www.arcountydata.com. Signup fee is $200 min. + $.10 per minute usage. For signup or information call 479-631-8054 or visit the website. **Other phones:** Assessor-870-425-3453; Tax Collector-870-425-3444.

Benton County

County Circuit Clerk, 215 E. Central St, #6, Bentonville, AR 72712. **Phone-**County Circuit Clerk, R/E & UCC Recording- 479-271-1017; fax-479-271-5719; hours 8AM-4:30PM www.co.benton.ar.us
Will not search records. Record copy- $.10 per page. Cert fee: $2.00 per page. Payee: Benton County Circuit Clerk. **Online Access to Real Estate, Deed, Circuit Court, Lien, Plats, Property Tax, Judgment, Medical Lien, Inmate, Personal Property records:** County Assessor, tax collector, medical liens, plats and circuit court information is free online at http://64.217.42.130:5061. Land records are at https://www.etitlesearch.com/services.asp. Call 870-856-3055 for subscription info. Also, registration and logon required to search assessor records at www.arcountydata.com. Signup fee is $200 min. + $.10 per minute usage. For info, call 479-631-8054Access to county land court records is also by subscription; visit www.recordsusa.com/Arkansas/bentonCnAr.htm or phone 800-932-5029. $49.95/$79.90 monthly. Also, search property data free at www.countyservice.net/bentax.html. Inmate records are at www.co.benton.ar.us/Sheriff/Inmate.htm. **other phones:** Assessor-479-271-1037; Treasurer-479-271-1018; Elections-479-271-1013; Tax Collector-479-271-1040.

Boone County

County Circuit Clerk, 100 N Main, Courthouse, #200, Harrison, AR 72601. **Phone-**County Circuit Clerk, R/E & UCC Recording- 870-741-5560; fax-870-741-4335; hours 8AM-4:30PM
Will not search records. Record copy- $.25 per page. Cert fee: $5.00 per doc. Payee: Boone County Circuit Clerk. **Online Access to Real Estate Recording, Assessor, Property records:** Land records at https://www.etitlesearch.com/services.asp. You can do a name search; choose from $45.00 monthly subscription or per click account. Also, registration and logon is required to search all participating counties' assessor records at www.arcountydata.com. Signup fee is $200 min. + $.10 per minute usage. For signup or more information call 479-631-8054 or visit www.arcountydata.com. Also www.eCourtStor.com or 888-485-8462. **Other phones:** Assessor-870-741-3783; Elections-870-741-8428; Tax Collector-870-741-6646; Marriages-870-741-8428.

Bradley County

County Circuit Clerk, 101 E. Cedar St, Courthouse, Warren, AR 71671. **Phone-**County Circuit Clerk, R/E & UCC Recording- 870-226-2272; fax-870-226-8401; hours 8AM-4:30PM
Will not search records. UCC copy- $1.00 per page. RE record copy- $.50 per page. Cert fee: $3.00 per doc. Payee: Bradley County Circuit Clerk. **Other phones:** Assessor-870-226-2211; Treasurer-870-226-8402; Elections-870-226-3464.

Calhoun County

County Circuit Clerk, PO Box 1175, Hampton, AR 71744. **Phone-**County Circuit Clerk, R/E & UCC Recording- 870-798-2517; fax-870-798-2428; hours 8AM-4:30. Will search UCC records. Search per debtor- $6.00. UCC copy- $1.00 per page. Will not search real estate or tax lien records. RE record copy- $.25 per copy. Cert fee: $4.00 per doc. Payee: Calhoun County Circuit Clerk. **Other phones:** Assessor-870-798-2740; Treasurer-870-798-2827; Tax Collector-870-798-2357.

Carroll County (Eastern District)

County Circuit Clerk, PO Box 71, Berryville, AR 72616. **Phone-**County Circuit Clerk, R/E & UCC Recording- 870-423-2422; fax-870-423-4796; hours 8:30AM-4:30PM

Will search UCC records. Search per debtor- $6.00. UCC copy fee- $.25 per page. UCC search includes tax liens if requested. Separate federal/state combined tax lien search- $6.00 per debtor. Will not search real estate records. Cert fee: $2.00 per doc. Payee: Carroll County Circuit Clerk. **Online Access to Assessor, Property, Jail records:** Registration and logon is required to search all participating counties' assessor records at www.arcountydata.com. Signup fee is $200 min. + $.10 per minute usage. For signup or information call 479-631-8054 or visit the website. Also, access to the weekly county jail roster is free at www.carrollcounty.org/sheriff/jail.phtm. **Other phones:** Assessor-870-423-2388; Treasurer-870-423-3189; Appraiser-870-423-2388; Elections-870-423-2022; Vital Records-870-423-2022; Tax Collector-870-423-2867.

Carroll County (Western District)

County Circuit Clerk, PO Box 109, Eureka Springs, AR 72632. **Phone-**479-253-8646, R/E Recording- 870-423-2422, UCC Recording- 870-423-2422; fax-479-253-6013; hours 8:30AM-4:30PM

Will search UCC records. Search per debtor- $6.00. Copy fee is $.25 per page. UCC search includes tax liens if requested. Separate federal/state combined tax lien search- $6.00 per debtor. Will not search real estate records. RE record copy- $.25 per page. Cert fee: $2.00. Payee: Carroll County Circuit Clerk. **Online Access to Assessor, Property, Jail records:** Registration and logon is required to search all participating counties' assessor records at www.arcountydata.com. Signup fee is $200 min. + $.10 per minute usage. For signup or information call 479-631-8054 or visit the website. Also, access to the weekly county jail roster is free at www.carrollcounty.org/sheriff/jail.phtm. **Other phones:** Assessor-870-423-2388; Treasurer-870-423-3189; Appraiser-870-423-2388; Elections-870-423-2022; Vital Records-870-423-2022 (marriage); Tax Collector-870-423-2867.

Chicot County

County Circuit Clerk, 108 Main St, Courthouse, Lake Village, AR 71653. **Phone-**870-265-8010, R/E Recording- 870-265-236; fax-870-265-8012; hours 8AM-4:30PM

Will search UCC records. Search per debtor- $6.00. UCC copy- $.50 per page. Tax liens not included in UCC search. Will not search real estate records. RE record copy- $.50 per page. Cert fee: $2.00 per cert. Payee: County Circuit Clerk. **Other phones:** Assessor-870-265-8025; Tax Collector-870-265-8040.

Clark County

County Circuit Clerk, PO Box 576, Arkadelphia, AR 71923. **Phone-**County Circuit Clerk, R/E & UCC Recording- 870-246-4281; fax-870-846-1416; hours 8:30AM-4:30PM

Will search UCC records. Search per debtor- $5.00. UCC copy fee- $1.00 per page. $.25 if you make your own. Will not search real estate or tax lien records. RE record copy- $1.00 per page. $.25 if you make you own. Cert fee: $5.00 per doc. Payee: Clark County Circuit Clerk. **Online Access to Real Estate Recording records:** Land records are at https://www.etitlesearch.com/services.asp. You can do a name search, fees involved. **Other phones:** Assessor-870-246-4431; Treasurer-870-246-4361; Tax Collector-870-246-2211.

Clay County (Eastern District)

County Circuit Clerk, 151 S Second St, Piggott, AR 72454. **Phone-**County Circuit Clerk, R/E & UCC Recording- 870-598-2524; fax-870-598-1107; hours 8AM-Noon,1-4:30PM

Will search UCC records. Search per debtor- $10.00. UCC copy- $.25 per page. UCC search includes tax liens. Separate federal/state combined tax lien search- $8.00 per debtor. Will not search real estate records. RE record copy- $.25 per page. Cert fee: $5.00 per cert. Payee: Clay County Circuit Clerk. **Other phones:** Assessor-870-598-3870; Treasurer-870-598-3879; Elections-870-598-2813; Vital Records-870-598-2813.

Clay County (Western District)

County Circuit Clerk, 800 W. Second St., Corning, AR 72422. **Phone-**870-857-3271; fax-870-857-9201; hours 8AM-Noon, 1PM-4:30PM

Will search UCC records. Search per debtor- $6.00. UCC copy fee- $1.00 per page. UCC search includes tax liens. Separate federal/state combined tax lien search- $6.00 per debtor. Will not search real estate records. Cert fee: $5.00 per cert. Payee: Clay County Circuit Clerk. **Other phones:** Assessor-870-857-3133; Tax Collector-870-855-3011.

Cleburne County

County Circuit Clerk, PO Box 543, Heber Springs, AR 72543. **Phone-**County Circuit Clerk, R/E & UCC Recording- 501-362-8149; fax-501-362-4650; hours 8:30AM-4:30PM

Will search UCC records. Search per debtor- $6.00. UCC copy fee- $6.00 1st page, $2.00 add'l. UCC search includes tax liens if requested. Separate federal/state combined tax lien search- $6.00 per debtor. Will not search real estate records. Cert fee: $1.00 per cert. Payee: Cleburne County Circuit Clerk. **Other phones:** Assessor-501-362-8147; Tax Collector-501-362-8124.

Cleveland County

County Circuit Clerk, PO Box 368, Rison, AR 71665. **Phone-**County Circuit Clerk, R/E & UCC Recording- 870-325-6521; fax-870-325-6144; 8AM-4:30PM

Will search UCC records under the FOIA. UCC copy fee- $.25 per page. Will not search real estate or tax lien records. RE record copy- $.25 per page. Cert fee: $8.00 1st pg, $3.00 each add'l. Payee: Cleveland County Circuit Clerk. **Other phones:** Assessor-870-325-6695; Treasurer-870-325-6681; Elections-870-325-6521; Tax Collector-870-325-6681.

Columbia County

County Circuit Clerk, PO Box 327, Magnolia, AR 71753. **Phone-**County Circuit Clerk, R/E & UCC Recording- 870-235-3700; fax-870-235-3786; hours 8AM-4:30PM. Will not search UCC records. UCC copy fee- $.50 per page. Will not search tax liens. Will search real estate records. Cert fee: $3.00. Payee: County Circuit Clerk. **Other phones:** Assessor-870-235-4380; Appraiser-870-235-4380; Elections-870-235-3774; Tax Collector-870-235-3704.

Conway County

County Circuit Clerk, 115 S. Moose St, County Courthouse, Rm 206, Morrilton, AR 72110. **Phone-**County Circuit Clerk, R/E & UCC Recording- 501-354-9617; fax-501-354-9612; hours 8AM-5PM

Will search UCC records. UCC search per debtor- $8.00. UCC copy- $.50 per page. Will not search real estate or tax lien records. RE record copy- $.50 per page. Cert fee: $5.00 per doc. Payee: Conway County Circuit Clerk. **Other phones:** Assessor-501-354-9622; Treasurer-501-354-9623; Elections-501-354-9621; Tax Collector-501-354-9600.

Craighead County (East District)

County Circuit Clerk, PO Box 537, Lake City, AR 72437. **Phone-**County Circuit Clerk, R/E & UCC Recording- 870-237-4342; fax-870-237-8174; hours 8AM-5PM. Will search UCC records. Search per debtor- $6.00. UCC copy fee- $5.00 per page. Will not search real estate or tax lien records. Cert fee: $3.00 per doc. Payee: County Circuit Clerk.

Craighead County (West District)

County Circuit Clerk, PO Box 120, Jonesboro, AR 72401. **Phone-**870-933-4530; fax-870-933-4534; hours 8AM-5PM. Will search UCC records. Search per debtor- $6.00. Copy fee is $.50 per page. Will not search tax liens. Will search real estate records. Copy fee-$.25 per page. Cert fee: $3.00 per doc. Payee: Craighead County Circuit Clerk. **Online Access to Assessor, Property, Personal Property, Assessor, Real Estate records:** Registration and logon is required to search all participating counties' assessor records at www.arcountydata.com. Signup fee is $200 min. + $.10 per minute usage. For signup or information call 479-631-8054 or visit the website. Also, land records are at https://www.etitlesearch.com/servi ces.asp. Name searching; choose from $100.00 monthly subscription or per click account. Also, search personal property, real estate, and assessor records free at www.cratax.countyservice.net. **Other phones:** Assessor-870-933-4570; Tax Collector-870-933-4540.

Crawford County

County Circuit Clerk, 300 Main, Courthouse - Rm 22, Van Buren, AR 72956-5799. **Phone-**County Circuit Clerk, R/E & UCC Recording- 479-474-1821; hours 8AM-5PM Will search UCC records. Search per debtor- $6.00. UCC copy fee- $1.00 per page. Will not search real estate or tax lien records. Cert fee: $2.00 per doc. Payee: County Circuit Clerk. **Online Access to Real Estate Recording records:** Land records are at https://www.etitlesearch.com/serv ices.asp. Name searching; choose from $30.00 monthly subscription or per click account. **Other phones:** Assessor-479-471-1751; Tax Collector-479-474-6641.

Crittenden County

County Circuit Clerk, 100 Court St., Marion, AR 72364. **Phone-**County Circuit Clerk, R/E & UCC Recording- 870-739-3248; fax-870-739-3072; hours 8AM-4:30PM. Will search UCC records. Search per debtor- $6.00. UCC copy- $.25 per page. Separate federal/state combined tax lien search- $6.00 per debtor. Will not search real estate records. RE record copy- $.25 per page. Cert fee: $3.00 per doc. Payee: Crittenden County Circuit Clerk. **Online Access to Assessor, Property records:** Registration and logon is required to search all participating counties' assessor records at www.arcountydata.com. Signup fee is $200 min. + $.10 per minute usage. For signup or information call 479-631-8054 or visit the website. **Other phones:** Assessor-870-739-3606; Treasurer-870-739-4112; Appraiser-870-739-3606; Elections-870-739-4434.

Cross County

County Circuit Clerk, 705 E Union, Rm 9, Wynne, AR 72396. **Phone-**County Circuit Clerk, R/E & UCC Recording- 870-238-5720; fax-870-238-5739; hours 8AM-4PM. Will search UCC records. Search per debtor- $6.00. Copy fee is $1.00 per page. UCC search includes tax liens if requested. Separate federal/state combined tax lien search- $6.00 per debtor. Will not search real estate records. RE record copy- $.25 per page. Cert fee: $3.00 per doc. Payee: Cross County Circuit Clerk. **Other phones:** Assessor and Appraiser- 870-238-5715; Treasurer-870-238-5725; Elections-870-238-5735; Vital Records-870-238-5735; Tax Collector-870-238-5710.

Dallas County

County Circuit Clerk, 206 W 3rd St, Courthouse, Fordyce, AR 71742-3299. **Phone**-County Circuit Clerk, R/E & UCC Recording- 870-352-2307; fax-870-352-7179; hours 8:30AM-4:30PM
Will search UCC records. Search per debtor- $6.00. UCC copy fee- $.50 per page. UCC search includes tax liens. Separate federal/state combined tax lien search- $6.00 per debtor. Will not search real estate records. RE record copy- $.50 per page. Cert fee: $3.00 per doc. Payee: Dallas County Circuit Clerk. **Other phones:** Assessor-870-352-7983; Treasurer-870-352-2333; Appraiser-870-352-3342; Elections-870-352-3965; Vital Records-870-352-7688; Tax Collector-870-352-5181.

Desha County

County Circuit Clerk, PO Box 309, Arkansas City, AR 71630. **Phone**-870-877-2411; fax-870-877-3407; hours 8AM-4PM
Will search UCC records. Search per debtor- $6.00. UCC copy- $.50 per page. Will not search real estate or tax lien records. Cert fee: $3.00 per doc. Payee: Circuit Clerk of Desha County. **Online Access to Real Estate, Recording records:** Access to county recorder records is by subscription at www.recordsusa.com. Credit card, username and password is required; Visit the website or call Lisa at 601-264-7701 for information. **Other phones:** Assessor-870-877-2431; Tax Collector-870-877-2353.

Drew County

County Circuit Clerk, 210 S. Main, Monticello, AR 71655. **Phone**-County Circuit Clerk, R/E & UCC Recording- 870-460-6250; fax-870-460-6246; hours 8AM-4:30PM
Will search UCC records. Search per debtor- $6.00. UCC copy- $.50 per page. Will search tax liens. Tax lien search fee- $6.00 per debtor. Real estate owner, mortgage, and property transfer searches available. RE record copy- $.50 per page. Cert fee: $2.00 per doc. Payee: Drew County Circuit Clerk. **Online Access to Real Estate, Deed, Circuit Court, Lien, Judgment records:** Access to county land and court records is by subscription; visit www.recordsusa.com/Arkansas/drewCnAr.htm or phone 800-932-5029 or 888-85-IMAGE. Monthly packages are $49.95 or $79.90. **Other phones:** Assessor-870-460-6240; Tax Collector-870-460-6225.

Faulkner County

Faulkner County Circuit Clerk, PO Box 9, Conway, AR 72033. **Phone**-Faulkner County Circuit Clerk, R/E & UCC Recording- 501-450-4911; fax-501-450-4948; hours 8AM-4:30PM
Will search UCC records. Search per debtor- $10.00. UCC copy fee- $6.00 per name + $2.00 each add'l page to maximum of $100.00. Will not search real estate or tax lien records. RE record copy- $.25 per copy. Cert fee: $3.00 per doc. Payee: Faulkner County Circuit Clerk. **Online Access to Assessor, Property records:** Registration and logon is required to search all participating counties' assessor records at www.arcountydata.com. Signup fee is $200 min. + $.10 per minute usage. For signup or information call 479-631-8054 or visit the website. **Other phones:** Assessor-501-450-4905; Treasurer-501-450-4902; Elections-501-450-4909; Tax Collector-501-450-4902.

Franklin County (Charleston Dist.)

County Circuit Clerk, 607 E Main St, Charleston, AR 72933. **Phone**-County Circuit Clerk, R/E & UCC Recording- 479-965-7332; fax-479-965-9322; hours 8AM-Noon, 12:30-4:30PM. Will not search records. Record copy fee- $.25 per page. Cert fee: $2.00 per doc. Payee: Franklin County Circuit Clerk. **Other phones:** Assessor-479-965-7797.

Franklin County (Ozark District)

County Circuit Clerk, PO Box 1112, Ozark, AR 72949. 479-667-3818; fax-479-667-5174; 8AM-4:30PM
Will not search records. Record copy- $.25 per page. Cert fee: $2.00 per instrument. Payee: Franklin County Circuit Clerk. **Other phones:** Assessor-479-667-2415.

Fulton County

County Circuit Clerk, PO Box 485, Salem, AR 72576-0485. **Phone**-870-895-3310; fax-870-895-3383; hours 8AM-4:30PM. Will search UCC records. Search per debtor- $6.00. UCC copy fee- $.20 per copy. UCC search includes tax liens. Separate federal/state combined tax lien search- $6.00 per debtor. Will not search real estate records. RE record copy- $.20 per page. Cert fee: No charge. Payee: Fulton County Circuit Clerk. **Online Access to Assessor, Property records:** Registration and logon is required to search all participating counties' assessor records at www.arcountydata.com. Signup fee is $200 min. + $.10 per minute usage. For signup or information call 479-631-8054 or visit the website. **Other phones:** Assessor-870-895-3592; Treasurer-870-895-3522; Vital Records-501-661-2336; Tax Collector-870-895-2547.

Garland County

County Circuit Clerk, Courthouse - Rm207, Quachita & Hawthorn Sts, Hot Springs, AR 71901. **Phone**-County Circuit Clerk, R/E & UCC Recording- 501-622-3630; fax-501-609-9043; hours 8AM-5PM
Will not search records. Record copy- $.25 per page. Cert fee: $.50 per cert. Payee: Garland County Circuit Clerk. **Online Access to Sex Offender records:** Access to the sheriff's sex offender list is free at www.hsnp.com/megan/garland_index.cgi. No recording records available through Garland County; reportedly available via a private provider County Professional Solicitations, PO Box 55, Brenton, AR 72015. **Other phones:** Assessor-501-622-3730; Treasurer-501-622-3650; Elections-501-622-3610; Tax Collector-501-622-3710.

Grant County

County Circuit Clerk, 101 W. Center, Rm 106, Courthouse, Sheridan, AR 72150. **Phone**-County Circuit Clerk, R/E & UCC Recording- 870-942-2631; fax-870-942-3564; hours 8AM-4:30PM
Will search UCC records. Search per debtor- $10.00. UCC copy- $.25 per page. UCC search includes tax liens if requested. Separate federal/state combined tax lien search- $6.00 per debtor. Real estate owner, mortgage, and property transfer searches available. RE record copy- $.25 per page. Cert fee: $5.00 per doc. Payee: Grant County Circuit Clerk. **Other phones:** Assessor-870-942-3711; Treasurer-870-942-2031; Elections-870-942-4363; Tax Collector-870-942-4315.

Greene County

County Circuit Clerk, 320 W. Court St, Rm 124, Paragould, AR 72450. **Phone**-County Circuit Clerk, R/E & UCC Recording- 870-239-6330; fax-870-239-3550; hours 8AM-4:30PM
Will search UCC records. Search per debtor- $6.00. UCC copy- $6.00 +$.50. Tax liens not included in UCC search. Federal/state combined tax lien search- $6.00 per debtor. Will not search real estate records. Cert fee: $3.00 per doc. Payee: Greene County Circuit Clerk. **Online Access to Assessor, Property records:** Registration and logon is required to search all participating counties' assessor records at www.arcountydata.com. Signup fee is $200 min. + $.10 per minute usage. For signup or information call 479-631-8054 or visit the website. **Other phones:** Assessor-870-239-6303; Treasurer-870-239-6304; Elections-870-239-6311.

Hempstead County

County Circuit Clerk, PO Box 1420, Hope, AR 71802. **Phone**-County Circuit Clerk, R/E & UCC Recording- 870-777-2384; fax-870-777-7827; hours 8AM-4PM
Will search UCC records. Search per debtor- $10.00. UCC copy- $1.00 per page. Will not search real estate or tax lien records. Cert fee: $5.00 per doc. Payee: County Circuit Clerk. **Other phones:** Assessor and Appraiser- 870-777-6190; Treasurer-870-777-3141; Elections-870-777-2241; Vital Records-501-661-2000; Tax Collector-870-777-4103.

Hot Spring County

Circuit Clerk, PO Box 1220, Malvern, AR 72104. **Phone**-501-332-2281; hours 8AM-4:30PM
Will search UCC records. Search per debtor- $10.00. UCC copy fee- $.50 per page. Will not search real estate or tax lien records. RE record copy- $.50 per page. Cert fee: $5.00 per doc. Payee: Hot Spring County Circuit Clerk. **Other phones:** Assessor-501-332-2461; Treasurer-501-337-7411; Elections-501-332-2291; Tax Collector-501-332-7211.

Howard County

County Circuit Clerk, 421 N. Main St, Rm 7, Nashville, AR 71852. **Phone**-County Circuit Clerk, R/E & UCC Recording- 870-845-7506; hours 8AM-4:30PM
Will search UCC records. Search per debtor- $6.00. UCC copy- $2.00 per page. Will search tax liens. Tax lien search fee- $6.00 per debtor. Will not search real estate records. RE record copy- $.50 per page. Cert fee: $2.00 + $.50 per page. Payee: Howard County Circuit Clerk. **Other phones:** Assessor-870-845-7511; Treasurer-870-845-7504; Elections-870-845-7503.

Independence County

County Circuit Clerk, PO Box 2155, Batesville, AR 72503. **Phone**-870-793-8865, R/E Recording- 870-793-8833; fax-870-793-8888; hours 8AM-4:30PM
Will search UCC records. Search per debtor- $6.00. UCC copy- $.25 per page. Will not search real estate or tax lien records. Payee: Independence County Circuit Clerk. **Online Access to Real Estate Recording records:** Land records are at https://www.etitlesearch.com/services.asp. You can do a name search; choose from $200.00 monthly subscription or per click account. **Other phones:** Assessor-870-793-8842.

Izard County

County Circuit Clerk, PO Box 95, Melbourne, AR 72556. **Phone**-County Circuit Clerk, R/E & UCC Recording- 870-368-4316; fax-870-368-4748; hours 8:30AM-4:30PM. Will search UCC records. Search per debtor- $6.00. UCC copy- $.25 per page. Will not search tax liens or real estate records. RE record copy- $.25 per page. Cert fee: $5.00 per cert. Payee: Izard County Circuit Clerk. **Online Access to Assessor, Property records:** Registration and logon is required to search all participating counties' assessor records at www.arcountydata.com. Signup fee is $200 min. + $.10 per minute usage. For signup or info call 479-631-8054 or visit the website. **Other phones:** Assessor-870-368-7810; Elections-870-368-4316; Tax Collector-870-368-4394.

Jackson County

County Circuit Clerk, 208 Main St, Courthouse, Newport, AR 72112. **Phone**-870-523-7423, R/E Recording- 870-523-3826; fax-870-523-3682; hours 8AM-4:30PM. Will not search records. UCC copy- $.25 per page. Cert fee: $3.00 per doc. Payee: Jackson County Circuit Clerk. **Other phones:** Assessor-870-523-7410; Tax Collector-870-523-7401.

Jefferson County

County Circuit Clerk, PO Box 7433, Pine Bluff, AR 71611. **Phone**-870-541-5309, R/E Recording- 870-541-5360, UCC Recording- 870-541-5304; fax-none; hours 8:30AM-5PM. Will search UCC records. Search per debtor- $6.00. UCC copy- $.50 per page. Will not search real estate or tax lien records. RE record copy- $2.00 1st 2 pages, $3.00 next 3, then $.25 per page. Cert fee: $.50 per doc. Payee: Jefferson County Circuit Clerk. **Other phones:** Assessor-870-541-5338; Tax Collector-870-541-5302.

Johnson County

County Circuit Clerk, PO Box 189, Clarksville, AR 72830-0189. **Phone**-County Circuit Clerk, R/E & UCC Recording- 479-754-2977; fax-479-754-4235; hours 8AM-4:30PM. Will not search records. UCC copy fee- $.50 per page. RE record copy- $1.00 per page. Cert fee: $1.00 per page. Payee: Johnson County Circuit Clerk. **Online Access to Assessor, Property records:** May be online. Registration and logon is required to search participating counties at www.arcountydata.com. Signup fee is $200 min. + $.10 per minute usage. For signup or information call 479-631-8054 or visit www.arcountydata.com. **Other phones:** Assessor-479-754-8839; Appraiser-479-754-8839; Tax Collector-479-754-3056.

Lafayette County

County Circuit Clerk, 3 Courthouse Sq, Third & Spruce, Lewisville, AR 71845. **Phone**-County Circuit Clerk, R/E & UCC Recording- 870-921-4878; fax-870-421-4879; hours 8AM-4:30PM
Will search UCC records. Search per debtor- $6.00. Copy fee is $.50 per page. Will not search tax liens. Will search real estate records. Cert fee: $3.00 + $.50 per page. Payee: Lafayette County Circuit Clerk. **Other phones:** Assessor-870-921-4808; Treasurer-870-921-4755; Tax Collector-870-921-4755.

Lawrence County

County Circuit Clerk, PO Box 581, Walnut Ridge, AR 72476. **Phone**-County Circuit Clerk, R/E & UCC Recording- 870-886-1112; fax-870-886-1128; hours 8AM-4:30PM. Will search UCC records. Search per debtor- $6.00. UCC copy- $.50 per page. Will not search tax liens. Will search for deed with a date or book and page. RE record copy- $.50 per page. Cert fee: $3.00 per doc. Payee: Lawrence County Circuit Clerk. **Other phones:** Assessor-870-886-1135; Treasurer-870-886-1116; Elections-870-866-1111; Tax Collector-870-886-1114.

Lee County

County Circuit Clerk, 15 E. Chestnut St, Courthouse, Marianna, AR 72360. **Phone**-County Circuit Clerk, R/E & UCC Recording- 870-295-7710; fax-870-295-7712; hours 8:30AM-4:30PM
Will search UCC records. Search per debtor- $6.00.Will not search real estate or tax lien records. RE record copy- $.25 per page. Cert fee: $2.50 per doc. Payee: Lee County Circuit Clerk. **Other phones:** Assessor-870-295-7750; Tax Collector-870-295-5296.

Lincoln County

County Circuit Clerk, 300 S. Drew St, Star City, AR 71667. **Phone**-County Circuit Clerk, R/E & UCC Recording- 870-628-3154; fax-870-628-5546; hours 8AM-5PM
Will search UCC records. Search per debtor- $6.00. UCC copy- $.50 per page. Will not search tax liens or real estate records. Cert fee: $3.00 per doc. Payee: Lincoln County Circuit Clerk. **Other phones:** Assessor-870-628-4401; Tax Collector-870-628-4816.

Little River County

County Circuit Clerk, PO Box 575, Ashdown, AR 71822-0575. **Phone**-870-898-7211; fax-870-898-7207; hours 8:30AM-4:30PM
Will search UCC records. Search per debtor- $6.00. UCC copy- $.50 per page. Separate federal/state combined tax lien search- $6.00 per debtor. Will not search real estate records. Cert fee: $5.00 per doc. Payee: Little River County Circuit Clerk. **Other phones:** Assessor-870-898-7204.

Logan County (Northern District)

County Circuit Clerk, 25 W. WALNUT Courthouse, Paris, AR 72855. **Phone**-479-963-2164, R/E Recording- 479-963-2618; fax-479-963-3304; hours 8AM-4:30PM
Will search UCC records. Search per debtor- $6.00. UCC copy- $.25 per page. Will not search real estate or tax lien records. Cert fee: $5.00 per doc. Payee: Logan County Circuit Clerk. **Other phones:** Assessor-479-963-2716; Tax Collector-479-963-2038.

Logan County (Southern District)

County Circuit Clerk, 366 N Broadway #2, Courthouse, Booneville, AR 72927. **Phone**-479-675-2894; fax-479-675-0577; hours 8AM-Noon, 1-4:30PM
Will search UCC records. Search per debtor- $6.00.Will not search real estate or tax lien records. RE record copy- $.25 per page. Cert fee: $5.00 per doc. Payee: Logan County Circuit Clerk. **Other phones:** Assessor-479-675-3942; Tax Collector-479-675-5131.

Lonoke County

County Circuit Clerk, PO Box 219, Lonoke, AR 72086-0219. **Phone**-County Circuit Clerk, R/E & UCC Recording-501-676-2316; hours 8AM-4:30PM
Will search UCC records; mail requests must include a SASE for return of results. Search per debtor- $10.00.Will not search real estate or tax lien records. Cert fee: $6.00 per doc. Payee: Lonoke County Circuit Clerk. **Online Access to Assessor, Property records:** Registration and logon is required to search all participating counties' assessor records at www.arcountydata.com. Signup fee is $200 min. + $.10 per minute usage. For signup or information call 479-631-8054 or visit the website. **Other phones:** Assessor-501-676-6938.

Madison County

County Circuit Clerk, PO Box 416, Huntsville, AR 72740. **Phone**-County Circuit Clerk, R/E & UCC Recording- 479-738-2215; fax-479-738-1544; hours 8AM-4:30PM
Will search UCC records. Search per debtor- $10.00. UCC copy fee- $.25 per page. Will not search tax liens. Will search UCC real estate records. RE record copy- $.25 per page. Cert fee: $2.00 per doc. Payee: County Circuit Clerk. **Other phones:** Assessor-479-738-2325; Treasurer-479-738-6514; Elections-479-738-2747; Tax Collector-479-738-6673.

Marion County

County Circuit Clerk, PO Box 385, Yellville, AR 72687. **Phone**-County Circuit Clerk, R/E & UCC Recording- 870-449-6226; fax-870-449-4979; hours 8AM-4:30PM
Will search UCC records. Search per debtor- $6.00. UCC copy fee- $.25 per page. Will not search real estate or tax lien records. RE record copy- $.25 per page. Cert fee: $5.00 + $.25 per page. Payee: Marion County Circuit Clerk. **Other phones:** Assessor-870-449-4113; Treasurer-870-449-6331; Tax Collector-870-449-6253.

Miller County

County Circuit Clerk, 412 Laurel St., County Courthouse, #109, Texarkana, AR 71854. **Phone**-870-774-4501; fax-870-772-5293; hours 8AM-4:30PM
Will search UCC records. Search per debtor- $6.00. UCC copy- $1.00 per page. Tax liens not included in UCC search. Separate federal/state combined tax lien search- $6.00 per debtor. Mortgage searches available. RE record copy- $1.00 per copy. Cert fee: $3.50 per doc. Payee: Miller County Circuit Clerk. **Online Access to Land, Deed records:** Access to recorder land records and images are via a private company at www.recordsusa.com/Arkansas/MillerCnAr.htm. Subscription required; basic monthly package including court dockets is $49.95. Call 888-85-IMAGE or visit the website. **Other phones:** Assessor-870-772-1502; Tax Collector-870-772-0003.

Mississippi County (Chickasawba District)

County Circuit Clerk, PO Box 1498, Blytheville, AR 72316-1498. **Phone**-870-762-2332; fax-870-762-8148; 9AM-4:30PM. Will search UCC records. Search per debtor- $6.00. UCC copy fee- $.25 per page. Will not search real estate or tax lien records. Copy fee- $.25 per page. Cert fee: $3.00 per doc. Payee: Mississippi County Circuit Clerk. **Other phones:** Assessor-870-763-6860; Tax Collector-870-762-2152.

Mississippi County (Osceola Dist.)

County Circuit Clerk, PO Box 466, Osceola, AR 72370. **Phone**-870-563-6471; fax-870-563-5063; hours 9AM-4:30PM. Will search UCC records. Search per debtor- $6.00. UCC copy fee- $.25 per page. Separate federal/state combined tax lien search- $6.00 per debtor. Will not search real estate records. Cert fee: $3.00 per doc. Payee: Mississippi County Circuit Clerk. **Other phones:** Assessor-870-563-2682; Tax Collector-870-762-2152.

Monroe County

County Circuit Clerk, 123 Madison St, Clarendon, AR 72029. **Phone**-870-747-3615; fax-870-747-3710; hours 8AM-4:30PM. Will search UCC records. Search per debtor- $6.00. UCC copy- $.25 per page. Will not search real estate or tax lien records. RE record copy- $.25 per page. Cert fee: $2.50 per doc. Payee: Monroe County Circuit Clerk. **Other phones:** Assessor-870-747-3847; Treasurer-870-747-3722; Tax Collector-870-747-3722.

Montgomery County

County Circuit Clerk, PO Box 369, Mount Ida, AR 71957-0369. **Phone**-870-867-3521; fax-870-867-2177; hours 8AM-4:30PM
Will search UCC records. Search per debtor- $6.00. UCC copy- $.50 per page. Will not search real estate or tax lien records. RE record copy- $1.00 if from vault; $.50 otherwise. Cert fee: $5.00 per doc. Payee: Montgomery County Circuit Clerk. **Other phones:** Assessor-870-867-3271; Treasurer-870-867-3411; Tax Collector-870-867-3155.

Nevada County

County Circuit Clerk, PO Box 204, Prescott, AR 71857. **Phone**-870-887-2511; fax-870-887-1911; 8AM-5PM
Will search UCC records. Search per debtor- $6.00. UCC copy- $.25 per page. UCC search includes tax liens if requested. Separate federal/state combined tax lien search- $6.00 per debtor. Real estate record owner and mortgage searches available. RE record copy- $.25 per page. Cert fee: $2.00 per doc. Payee: Nevada County Circuit Clerk. **Other phones:** Assessor-870-887-3410; Tax Collector-870-887-2811.

Newton County

County Circuit Clerk, PO Box 410, Jasper, AR 72641. **Phone**-870-446-5125; fax-870-446-5755; hours 8AM-4:30PM. Will not search records. Record copy- $.25 per page. Cert fee: $5.00 per doc. Payee: Newton County Circuit Clerk. **Other phones:** Assessor-870-446-2937; Treasurer-870-446-2936; Tax Collector-870-446-2936.

Ouachita County

County Circuit Clerk, PO Box 667, Camden, AR 71701. **Phone**-County Circuit Clerk, R/E & UCC Recording- 870-837-2230; fax-870-837-2252; hours 8AM-4:30PM. Will search UCC records. Search per debtor- $10.00. Will not search real estate or tax lien records. RE record copy- $.50 per page. Cert fee: $2.50 per doc. Payee: Ouachita County Circuit Clerk. **Other phones:** Assessor-870-837-2240; Treasurer-870-837-2250; Appraiser-870-837-2240; Elections-870-837-2220; Vital Records-501-661-2336.

Perry County

County Circuit Clerk, PO Box 358, Perryville, AR 72126. **Phone**-501-889-5126; fax-501-889-5759; hours 8AM-4:30PM. Will not search records. RE record copy- $1.00 per copy. Cert fee: $5.00 per doc. Payee: Perry County Circuit Clerk. **Other phones:** Assessor-501-889-2865; Treasurer-501-889-5285; Tax Collector-501-889-2710.

Phillips County

County Circuit Clerk, 620 Cherry St., Courthouse, #206, Helena, AR 72342. **Phone**-County Circuit Clerk, R/E & UCC Recording- 870-338-5515; fax-870-338-5513; hours 8AM-4:30PM

Will search UCC records. Search per debtor- $6.00. UCC copy fee- $.25 per page. Will not search real estate or tax lien records. RE record copy- $.25 per page. Cert fee: $3.00 per page. Payee: Phillips County Circuit Clerk. **Online Access to Real Estate Recording records:** Land records are at https://www.etitlesearch.com/services.asp. You can do a name search; choose from $25.00 monthly subscription or per-click account. **Other phones:** Assessor-870-338-5535; Treasurer-870-338-5510; Tax Collector-870-338-5580.

Pike County

County Circuit Clerk, PO Box 219, Murfreesboro, AR 71958. **Phone**-County Circuit Clerk, R/E & UCC Recording- 870-285-2231; fax-870-285-3281; hours 8AM-4:30PM

Will search UCC records. Search per debtor- $6.00. UCC copy- $.50 per page. Separate federal/state combined tax lien search- $6.00 per debtor. Will not search real estate records. RE record copy- $.50 per page. Cert fee: $5.00 per doc. Payee: Pike County Circuit Clerk. **Online Access to Assessor, Property records:** Registration and logon is required to search all participating counties' assessor records at www.arcountydata.com. Signup fee is $200 min. + $.10 per minute usage. For signup or information call 479-631-8054 or visit the website. **Other phones:** Assessor-870-285-3316; Treasurer-870-285-2422; Tax Collector-870-285-2422.

Poinsett County

County Circuit Clerk, PO Box 46, Harrisburg, AR 72432-0046. **Phone**-870-578-4420; fax-870-578-4427; hours 8:30AM-4:30PM

Will search UCC records. Search per debtor- $6.00. Copy fee is $.50 per page. Will not search real estate or tax lien records. Cert fee: $2.00 per doc. Payee: Poinsett County Circuit Clerk. **Online Access to Assessor, Property records:** Registration and logon is required to search all participating counties' assessor records at www.arcountydata.com.

Signup fee is $200 min. + $.10 per minute usage. For signup or information call 479-631-8054 or visit the website. **Other phones:** Assessor-870-578-4430; Treasurer-870-578-4405; Tax Collector-870-578-4405.

Polk County

County Circuit Clerk, 507 Church, Courthouse, Mena, AR 71953. **Phone**-County Circuit Clerk, R/E & UCC Recording- 479-394-8100; fax-479-394-8170; hours 8AM-4:30PM

Will search UCC records. Search per debtor- $6.00. UCC copy- $5.00 per UCC. Federal tax liens not included in UCC search. Separate federal/state tax lien search-$6.00 per debtor. Will not search real estate records. RE record copy- $.50 per page. Cert fee: $2.00 per doc. Payee: Polk County Circuit Clerk. **Online Access to Real Estate, Deed, Circuit Court, Lien, Judgment records:** Access to county land and court records is by subscription; visit www.recordsusa.com/Arkansas/PolkCnAr.htm or phone 800-932-5029 or 888-85-IMAGE. Monthly packages are $49.95 or $79.90 per month. **Other phones:** Assessor-479-394-8121; Treasurer-479-394-8150; Appraiser-479-394-8121; Elections-479-394-8123; Tax Collector-479-394-8150.

Pope County

County Circuit Clerk, 100 W. Main, 3rd Fl, County Courthouse, Russellville, AR 72801. **Phone**-County Circuit Clerk, R/E & UCC Recording- 479-968-7499, UCC Recording- 479-968-6989; fax-none; 8AM-5PM Will search UCC records. UCC search per debtor- $6.00. UCC copy fee- $.50 per page. Will not search real estate or tax lien records. RE record copy- $.50 per page. Cert fee: $3.00 per doc. Payee: Pope County Circuit Clerk. **Online Access to Assessor, Property records:** Registration and logon is required to search all participating counties' assessor records at www.arcountydata.com. Signup fee is $200 min. + $.10 per minute usage. For signup or information call 479-631-8054 or visit the website. Also, free access to assessor data is at www.county service.net/poptax.html. Last name and zip code are required. **Other phones:** Assessor-479-968-7418; Treasurer-479-968-7016; Tax Collector-479-968-7016.

Prairie County (Northern District)

County Circuit Clerk, PO Box 1011, Des Arc, AR 72040. **Phone**-870-256-4434; fax-870-256-4434; hours 8AM-4:30PM

Will search UCC records. Search per debtor- $6.00. UCC copy- $1.00 per page. Will not search real estate or tax lien records. Cert fee: $3.00 per doc. Payee: Prairie County Circuit Clerk. **Other phones:** Assessor-870-256-4692; Treasurer-870-256-4137; Tax Collector-870-256-4137.

Prairie County (Southern District)

County Circuit Clerk, PO Box 283, De Valls Bluff, AR 72041-0283. **Phone**-County Circuit Clerk, R/E & UCC Recording- 870-998-2314; fax-870-998-2314; hours 8AM-Noon, 1-4:30PM

Will search UCC records. Search per debtor- $6.00. UCC copy fee- $.25 per page. Will not search real estate or tax lien records. Cert fee: $6.00 per doc. Payee: Prairie County Circuit Clerk. **Other phones:** Assessor-870-256-4692; Treasurer-870-256-4786; Tax Collector-870-256-4764.

Pulaski County

County Circuit Clerk, 401 W. Markham St, Rm S216, Little Rock, AR 72201. **Phone**-501-340-8433; fax-501-340-8889; hours 8:30AM-4:30PM

Will not search records. UCC copy- $1.00 per page. Cert fee: $2.50 per doc. Payee: Pulaski County Circuit Clerk. **Online Access to Assessor, Property, Personal Property records:** Registration and logon is required to search all participating counties' assessor

records at www.arcountydata.com. Signup fee is $200 min. + $.10 per minute usage. For signup or information call 479-631-8054 or visit the website. Also, search the personal property and real estate database for free at www.pultax.countyservice.net. For personal property, click on "Access Vehicles." Name and zip code required. **Other phones:** Assessor-501-340-6170; Treasurer-501-340-8345; Elections-340-8683 (Vote); Tax Collector-501-340-8345.

Randolph County

County Circuit Clerk, 107 W. Broadway, Pocahontas, AR 72455. **Phone**-County Circuit Clerk, R/E & UCC Recording- 870-892-5522; fax-870-892-8794; hours 8AM-4:30PM

Will search UCC records. Search per debtor- $6.00. UCC copy- $.25 per page. Tax liens not included in UCC search. Separate federal tax lien search-$6.00 per debtor. Will not search real estate records. RE record copy- $.50 per page. Cert fee: $2.00 per cert. Payee: County Circuit Clerk. **Other phones:** Assessor-870-892-3200; Treasurer-870-892-5238; Elections-870-892-5822; Tax Collector-870-892-5491.

Saline County

County Circuit Clerk, 200 N. Main St. #113, Benton, AR 72018. **Phone**-501-303-5615; fax-501-303-5675; hours 8AM-4:30PM

Will search UCC records. Search per debtor- $6.00. UCC copy- $.25 per page. Will not search real estate or tax lien records. RE record copy- $.25 per page. Cert fee: $3.00 per doc. Payee: Saline County Circuit Clerk. **Online Access to Assessor, Property, Real Estate Recording records:** Registration and logon is required to search all participating counties' assessor records at www.arcountydata.com. Signup fee is $200 min. + $.10 per minute usage. For signup or information call 479-631-8054 or visit the website. Also, land records are at https://www.etitlesearch.com/services.asp. You can do a name search; choose from $25.00 monthly subscription or per-click account. Also, search assessor real estate and personal property records free at www.countyservice.net/saltax.html. **Other phones:** Assessor-501-776-5622; Treasurer-501-776-5633; Tax Collector-501-776-5633.

Scott County

County Circuit Clerk, PO Box 2165, Waldron, AR 72958. **Phone**-County Circuit Clerk, R/E & UCC Recording- 479-637-2642; fax-479-637-0124; hours 8AM-4:30PM. Will search UCC records. Search per debtor- $6.00. Will not search tax liens or real estate records. RE record copy- $.25 per page. Cert fee: $5.00 per doc. Payee: Scott County Circuit Clerk. **Other phones:** Assessor-479-637-2666; Treasurer-479-637-2780; Tax Collector-479-637-4156.

Searcy County

County Circuit Clerk, PO Box 998, Marshall, AR 72650. **Phone**-870-448-3807; fax-870-448-5005; hours 8AM-4:30PM. Will search UCC records. Search per debtor- $8.00. Copy fee is $.50 per copy. Tax lien search fee- $6.00 per search. Will not search real estate records. Cert fee: $5.00 per doc. Payee: Searcy County Circuit Clerk. **Other phones:** Assessor-870-448-2464; Treasurer-870-448-3828; Appraiser-870-448-2464; Tax Collector-870-448-5050.

Sebastian County (Fort Smith District)

County Clerk and Recorder, PO Box 1089, Fort Smith, AR 72902-1089. **Phone**-County Clerk and Recorder, R/E & UCC Recording- 479-782-5065; fax-479-784-1567; 8AM-5PM www.sebastiancountyonline.com Will search UCC records. Search per debtor- $6.00. UCC copy- $6.00 1st page; $.50 add'l. Tax lien search fee- $6.00. Will not search real estate records. Cert fee: $2.50 per doc. Payee: Sebastian County Clerk and Recorder. **Online Access to Assessor, Property records:** Registration and logon is required to search all participating counties' assessor records at www.arcountydata.com. Signup fee is $200 min. + $.10 per minute usage. For signup or information call 479-631-8054 or visit the website. **Other phones:** Assessor-479-783-8948; Elections-479-782-5065.

Sebastian County (Southern District)

County Clerk, PO Box 428, Greenwood, AR 72936. **Phone-**County Clerk, R/E & UCC Recording- 479-996-4195; fax-479-996-4165; hours 8AM-5PM
Will search UCC records. Search per debtor- $6.00. UCC copy- $5.00 per doc + $2.00 per attachment. Will not search real estate or tax lien records. RE record copy- $.50 per page. Cert fee: $3.00 per doc. Payee: Sebastian County Clerk-Doris Tate. **Online Access to Assessor, Property records:** Registration and logon is required to search all participating counties' assessor records at www.arcountydata.com. Signup fee is $200 min. + $.10 per minute usage. For signup or information call 479-631-8054 or visit the website. **Other phones:** Assessor-479-996-6591; Elections-479-996-4195; Vital Records-479-996-4195 (marriages).

Sevier County

County Circuit Clerk, 115 N. 3rd St, De Queen, AR 71832. **Phone-**County Circuit Clerk, R/E & UCC Recording- 870-584-3055; fax-870-642-3119; hours 8AM-4:30PM. Will not search records. Record copy-$.25 per page. Cert fee: $5.00 per cert. Payee: Sevier County Circuit Clerk. **Other phones:** Assessor-870-584-3182; Treasurer-870-642-2358; Tax Collector-870-642-2358.

Sharp County

County Circuit Clerk, PO Box 307, Ash Flat, AR 72513. **Phone-**County Circuit Clerk, R/E & UCC Recording- 870-994-7361; fax-870-994-7712; hours 8AM-4PM
Will search UCC records. Search per debtor- $6.00. UCC copy- $.25 per page. Will not search real estate or tax lien records. RE record copy- $.25 per page. Cert fee: $5.00 per doc. Payee: Sharp County Circuit Clerk. **Online Access to Assessor, Property, Real Estate records:** Registration and logon is required to search all participating counties' assessor records at www.arcountydata.com. Signup fee is $200 min. + $.10 per minute usage. For signup or information call 479-631-8054 or visit the website. Also, land records are available at https://www.etitlesearch.com/services.asp. You can do a name search; choose from $25.00 monthly subscription or per-click account. **Other phones:** Assessor-870-994-7328; Treasurer-870-994-7347; Elections-870-994-7361; Tax Collector-870-994-7347.

St. Francis County

County Circuit Clerk, PO Box 1775, Forrest City, AR 72336-1775. **Phone-**County Circuit Clerk, R/E & UCC Recording- 870-261-1715, UCC Recording- 870-261-1721; fax-870-261-1723; hours 8AM-4:30PM
Will search UCC records. Search per debtor- $6.00. Separate federal/state combined tax lien search- $6.00 per debtor. Will not search real estate records. RE record copy- $.25 per page. Cert fee: $3.00 per page. Payee: St. Francis County Circuit Clerk. **Online Access to Assessor, Property records:** Registration and logon is required to search all participating counties' assessor records at www.arcountydata.com. Signup fee is $200 min. + $.10

per minute usage. For signup or information call 479-631-8054 or visit the website. **Other phones:** Assessor-870-261-1710; Treasurer-870-261-1705; Tax Collector-870-261-1792.

Stone County

County Circuit Clerk, 107 W Main #D, Mountain View, AR 72560. **Phone-**County Circuit Clerk, R/E & UCC Recording- 870-269-3271; fax-870-269-2303; hours 8AM-4:30PM
Will search UCC records. Search per debtor- $6.00. UCC copy fee- $5.00 1st 3 pages, $1.00 each add'l. Will not search real estate or tax lien records. RE record copy- $.25 per page. Cert fee: $5.00 per doc. Payee: Stone County Circuit Clerk. **Online Access to Assessor, Property records:** Registration and logon is required to search all participating counties' assessor records at www.arcountydata.com. Signup fee is $200 min. + $.10 per minute usage. For signup or information call 479-631-8054 or visit the website. **Other phones:** Assessor-870-269-3524; Treasurer-870-269-8426; Elections-870-269-5550; Tax Collector-870-269-8426.

Union County

County Circuit Clerk, PO Box 1626, El Dorado, AR 71731-1626. **Phone-**870-864-1940; fax-870-864-1994; hours 8:30AM-5PM
Will search UCC records. Search per debtor- $6.00. UCC copy- $5.00 1st 3 pages; $1.00 each add'l. UCC search includes tax liens if requested. Separate federal/state combined tax lien search- $12.00 per debtor. Will not search real estate records. RE record copy- $.50 per page. Cert fee: $1.00 per page. Payee: Union County Circuit Clerk. **Online Access to Real Estate, Deed, Circuit Court, Lien, Judgment records:** Access to county land and court records is by subscription; visit www.recordsusa.com/Arkansas/UnionCnAr.htm or phone 800-932-5029 or 888-85-IMAGE. Monthly packages are $49.95 or $79.90 per month. **Other phones:** Assessor-870-864-1920; Treasurer-870-864-1928; Tax Collector-870-864-1928.

Van Buren County

County Circuit Clerk, 451 Main St. #2, Clinton, AR 72031-9806. **Phone-**County Circuit Clerk, R/E & UCC Recording- 501-745-4140; fax-501-745-7400; hours 8AM-5PM
Will not search UCC records. UCC copy fee- $.50 per page. Will not search tax liens. Real estate owner, mortgage, and property transfer searches available. Cert fee: $5.00 per doc. Payee: Van Buren County Circuit Clerk. **Online Access to Real Estate Recording records:** Land records are at https://www.etitlesearch.com/services.asp. You can do a name search; call 870-856-3055 for subscription information. **Other phones:** Assessor-501-745-2464; Treasurer-501-745-2400; Appraiser-501-745-2474; Elections-501-745-4140.

Washington County

County Circuit Clerk, 280 N. College, #302, Courthouse, Fayetteville, AR 72701. **Phone-**479-444-1538; fax-479-444-1537; hours 8AM-4:30PM
www.co.washington.ar.us
Will search UCC records. Search per debtor- $6.00. UCC copy- $.15 per page. Tax liens not included in UCC search. Separate federal/state combined tax lien search- $0.00. Will not search real estate records. RE record copy- $.15 per page. Cert fee: $2.00 per doc. Payee: Washington County Circuit Clerk. **Online Access to Real Estate, Lien, UCC, Recording, Court, Inmate, Vital Statistic records:** Search Clerk's index of real estate (back to '97), liens,

and UCCs (to '92) free at www.co.washington.ar.us/resolution/. Username and password required. Also, search property records free at www.co.washington.ar.us/PropertySearch/MapSearch.asp. Also, search court record archives at www.co.washington.ar.us/ArchiveSearch/CourtRecordSearch.asp. Land records are also at https://www.etitlesearch.com/services.asp. You can do a name search, fees involved, call 870-856-3055 for info. **Other phones:** Assessor-479-444-1520; Treasurer-479-444-1526; Tax Collector-479-444-1526.

White County

County Circuit Clerk, White County Courthouse, 300 N. Spruce, Searcy, AR 72143. **Phone-**501-279-6203; fax-501-279-6233; hours 8AM-4:30PM
Will search UCC records. Search per debtor- $10.00. UCC copy fee- $.50 per page. Separate federal/state combined tax lien search- $9.00 per debtor. Will not search real estate records. RE record copy- $.50 per page. Cert fee: $2.50 per doc. Payee: White County Circuit Clerk. **Online Access to Assessor, Property records:** Registration and logon is required to search all participating counties' assessor records at www.arcountydata.com. Signup fee is $200 min. + $.10 per minute usage. For signup or information call 479-631-8054 or visit the website. **Other phones:** Assessor-501-279-6205; Treasurer-501-279-6206; Tax Collector-501-279-6206.

Woodruff County

County Circuit Clerk, PO Box 492, Augusta, AR 72006. **Phone-**County Circuit Clerk, R/E & UCC Recording- 870-347-2391; fax-870-347-8703; hours 8AM-4PM. Will search UCC records. Search per debtor- $10.00. UCC copy- $.50 per page. Tax liens not included in UCC search. Separate federal/state combined tax lien search- $6.00 per debtor. Will not search real estate records. Cert fee: $5.00 per doc. Payee: Woodruff County Circuit Clerk. **Online Access to Real Estate Recording records:** Land records are available at https://www.etitlesearch.com/services.asp. You can do a name search; choose from $25.00 monthly subscription or per-click account. **Other phones:** Assessor-870-347-5151; Treasurer-870-347-5416; Tax Collector-870-347-5151.

Yell County (Danville District)

County Circuit Clerk, PO Box 219, Danville, AR 72833. **Phone-**County Circuit Clerk, R/E & UCC Recording- 479-495-4850; fax-479-495-4875; hours 8AM-4PM
Will search UCC records. Search per debtor- $6.00. UCC copy fee- $.25 per sheet. Tax liens not included in UCC search. Tax lien search fee- $6.00 per debtor. Will not search real estate records. Cert fee: $5.00 per doc. Payee: Yell County Circuit Clerk. **Other phones:** Assessor-479-495-2940; Treasurer-479-495-2933; Elections-479-495-4850; Vital Records-479-495-4850.

Yell County (Dardanelle District)

County Circuit Clerk, PO Box 457, Dardanelle, AR 72834. **Phone-**479-229-4404; fax-479-229-5634; hours 8AM-4PM
Will search UCC records. Search per debtor- $6.00. UCC copy- $.50 per page. Tax liens not included in UCC search. Tax lien search $6.00 per debtor. Will not search real estate records. Cert fee: $5.00 per doc. Payee: Yell County Circuit Clerk. **Other phones:** Assessor-479-229-2693.

Arkansas County Locator

You will usually be able to find the city name in the City/County Cross Reference below. In that case, it is a simple matter to determine the county from the cross reference. However, only the official US Postal Service city names are included in this index. There are an additional 40,000 place names that people use in their addresses. Therefore, we have also included a ZIP/City Cross Reference immediately following the City/County Cross Reference.

If you know the ZIP Code but the city name does not appear in the City/County Cross Reference index, look up the ZIP Code in the ZIP/City Cross Reference, find the city name, then look up the city name in the City/County Cross Reference. For example, you want to know the county for an address of Menands, NY 12204. There is no "Menands" in the City/County Cross Reference. The ZIP/City Cross Reference shows that ZIP Codes 12201-12288 are for the city of Albany. Looking back in the City/County Cross Reference, Albany is in Albany County.

Arkansas City/County Cross Reference

ADONA (72001) Perry(53), Conway(46)
ALCO (72610) Stone(95), Searcy(4)
ALEXANDER (72002) Saline(93), Pulaski(6)
ALICIA Lawrence
ALIX Franklin
ALLEENE Little River
ALMA Crawford
ALMYRA Arkansas
ALPENA (72611) Boone(50), Carroll(49)
ALPINE Clark
ALTHEIMER Jefferson
ALTUS (72821) Franklin(75), Johnson(24)
AMAGON Jackson
AMITY (71921) Clark(54), Pike(29), Hot Spring(16)
ANTOINE Pike
ARKADELPHIA (71923) Clark(96), Hot Spring(3)
ARKADELPHIA Clark
ARKANSAS CITY Desha
ARMOREL Mississippi
ASH FLAT (72513) Fulton(48), Sharp(45), Izard(6)
ASHDOWN Little River
ATKINS (72823) Pope(97), Conway(2)
ATKINS Pope
AUBREY Lee
AUGUSTA Woodruff
AUSTIN Lonoke
AVOCA Benton
BALCH Jackson
BALD KNOB White
BANKS Bradley
BARLING Sebastian
BARTON Phillips
BASS Newton
BASSETT Mississippi
BATES Scott
BATESVILLE Independence
BAUXITE Saline
BAY Craighead
BEARDEN (71720) Ouachita(85), Dallas(11), Calhoun(3)
BEAVER Carroll
BEE BRANCH (72013) Van Buren(96), Conway(3)
BEEBE White
BEECH GROVE Greene
BEEDEVILLE Jackson
BEIRNE Clark
BELLA VISTA Benton
BELLEVILLE Yell
BEN LOMOND Sevier
BENTON (72015) Saline(98), Grant(1)
BENTON Saline
BENTONVILLE Benton
BERGMAN Boone
BERRYVILLE Carroll
BEXAR Fulton
BIG FLAT (72617) Baxter(75), Searcy(18), Stone(6)

BIGELOW (72016) Perry(52), Pulaski(47)
BIGGERS (72413) Randolph(92), Clay(7)
BIRDEYE Cross
BISCOE Prairie
BISMARCK Hot Spring
BLACK OAK Craighead
BLACK ROCK Lawrence
BLAKELY Garland
BLEVINS Hempstead
BLUE MOUNTAIN Logan
BLUFF CITY Nevada
BLUFFTON (72827) Yell(89), Scott(10)
BLYTHEVILLE Mississippi
BOARD CAMP Polk
BOLES Scott
BONNERDALE (71933) Hot Spring(46), Garland(35), Montgomery(17)
BONO (72416) Craighead(77), Greene(22)
BOONEVILLE (72927) Logan(85), Scott(8), Sebastian(5)
BOSWELL Izard
BRADFORD (72020) Jackson(48), White(37), Independence(13)
BRADLEY Lafayette
BRANCH Franklin
BRICKEYS Lee
BRIGGSVILLE Yell
BRINKLEY (72021) Monroe(98), Woodruff(1)
BROCKWELL Izard
BROOKLAND Craighead
BRUNO Marion
BRYANT (72022) Saline(96), Pulaski(3)
BRYANT Saline
BUCKNER (71827) Lafayette(78), Nevada(21)
BULL SHOALS Marion
BURDETTE Mississippi
CABOT (72023) Lonoke(75), Pulaski(23)
CADDO GAP Montgomery
CALDWELL St. Francis
CALE Nevada
CALICO ROCK (72519) Baxter(66), Stone(18), Izard(14)
CALION Union
CAMDEN (71701) Ouachita(97), Calhoun(2)
CAMDEN Ouachita
CAMP Fulton
CANEHILL Washington
CARAWAY (72419) Craighead(94), Poinsett(5)
CARLISLE (72024) Lonoke(96), Prairie(3)
CARTHAGE (71725) Dallas(92), Cleveland(7)
CASA (72025) Perry(80), Conway(18), Yell(2)
CASH (72421) Craighead(77), Poinsett(19), Jackson(2)
CASSCOE Arkansas
CAVE CITY (72521) Sharp(69), Independence(30)

CAVE SPRINGS Benton
CECIL (72930) Franklin(80), Sebastian(19)
CEDARVILLE Crawford
CENTER RIDGE (72027) Conway(97), Faulkner(1)
CENTERTON Benton
CENTERVILLE Yell
CHARLESTON (72933) Franklin(83), Sebastian(16)
CHARLOTTE Independence
CHATFIELD Crittenden
CHEROKEE VILLAGE (72529) Sharp(77), Fulton(22)
CHEROKEE VILLAGE Sharp
CHERRY VALLEY (72324) Cross(90), Poinsett(9)
CHESTER Crawford
CHIDESTER Ouachita
CHOCTAW Van Buren
CLARENDON Monroe
CLARKEDALE Crittenden
CLARKRIDGE Baxter
CLARKSVILLE Johnson
CLEVELAND (72030) Conway(52), Van Buren(47)
CLINTON (72031) Van Buren(95), Stone(2), Conway(1)
COAL HILL Johnson
COLLEGE STATION Pulaski
COLLINS Drew
COLT (72326) St. Francis(87), Cross(12)
COLUMBUS (71831) Hempstead(60), Howard(40)
COMBS Madison
COMPTON (72624) Newton(83), Carroll(16)
CONCORD (72523) Cleburne(87), Independence(12)
CONWAY Faulkner
CORD Independence
CORNING Clay
COTTER Baxter
COTTON PLANT (72036) Woodruff(88), Monroe(11)
COVE Polk
COY Lonoke
CRAWFORDSVILLE Crittenden
CROCKETTS BLUFF Arkansas
CROSSETT Ashley
CRUMROD Phillips
CURTIS Clark
CUSHMAN Independence
DAMASCUS (72039) Van Buren(71), Faulkner(28)
DANVILLE Yell
DARDANELLE (72834) Yell(98), Logan(1)
DATTO Clay
DE QUEEN Sevier
DE VALLS BLUFF Prairie
DE WITT Arkansas
DECATUR Benton
DEER Newton

DELAPLAINE Greene
DELAWARE Logan
DELIGHT Pike
DELL Mississippi
DENNARD Van Buren
DERMOTT (71638) Chicot(84), Drew(12), Desha(3)
DES ARC Prairie
DESHA Independence
DIAMOND CITY Boone
DIAZ Jackson
DIERKS (71833) Howard(94), Sevier(5)
DODDRIDGE Miller
DOLPH Izard
DONALDSON Hot Spring
DOVER Pope
DRASCO (72530) Cleburne(94), Stone(5)
DRIVER Mississippi
DUMAS (71639) Desha(97), Lincoln(2)
DYER Crawford
DYESS Mississippi
EARLE (72331) Crittenden(95), Cross(4)
EDGEMONT (72044) Cleburne(80), Stone(19)
EDMONDSON Crittenden
EGYPT Craighead
EL DORADO Union
EL PASO (72045) White(98), Faulkner(1)
ELAINE Phillips
ELIZABETH (72531) Baxter(53), Fulton(46)
ELKINS (72727) Madison(50), Washington(49)
ELM SPRINGS Washington
EMERSON Columbia
EMMET (71835) Nevada(78), Hempstead(21)
ENGLAND (72046) Lonoke(81), Pulaski(10), Jefferson(7)
ENOLA Faulkner
ETHEL Arkansas
ETOWAH Mississippi
EUDORA Chicot
EUREKA SPRINGS Carroll
EVANSVILLE Washington
EVENING SHADE Sharp
EVERTON (72633) Boone(59), Marion(37), Searcy(3)
FAIRFIELD BAY (72088) Van Buren(91), Cleburne(8)
FARMINGTON Washington
FAYETTEVILLE Washington
FERNDALE Pulaski
FIFTY SIX Stone
FISHER (72429) Poinsett(97), Cross(3)
FLIPPIN Marion
FLORAL (72534) Independence(86), Cleburne(13)
FORDYCE (71742) Dallas(96), Calhoun(3)
FOREMAN Little River
FORREST CITY St. Francis
FORT SMITH Sebastian
FOUKE Miller

FOUNTAIN HILL (71642) Ashley(82), Drew(17)
FOX Stone
FRANKLIN Izard
FRENCHMANS BAYOU Mississippi
FRIENDSHIP Hot Spring
FULTON Hempstead
GAMALIEL Baxter
GARFIELD Benton
GARLAND CITY (71839) Miller(96), Lafayette(4)
GARNER White
GASSVILLE Baxter
GATEWAY Benton
GENOA Miller
GENTRY Benton
GEPP (72538) Fulton(94), Baxter(5)
GILBERT Searcy
GILLETT (72055) Arkansas(89), Jefferson(10)
GILLHAM (71841) Sevier(89), Polk(10)
GILMORE Crittenden
GLENCOE Fulton
GLENWOOD (71943) Pike(56), Montgomery(39), Hot Spring(4)
GOODWIN St. Francis
GOSHEN Washington
GOSNELL Mississippi
GOULD (71643) Lincoln(88), Desha(11)
GRADY (71644) Jefferson(64), Lincoln(35)
GRANNIS Polk
GRAPEVINE Grant
GRAVELLY (72838) Yell(93), Scott(6)
GRAVETTE Benton
GREEN FOREST Carroll
GREENBRIER Faulkner
GREENLAND Washington
GREENWAY Clay
GREENWOOD Sebastian
GREGORY Woodruff
GRIFFITHVILLE (72060) White(70), Prairie(29)
GRUBBS Jackson
GUION Izard
GURDON Clark
GUY Faulkner
HACKETT Sebastian
HAGARVILLE (72839) Johnson(97), Pope(2)
HAMBURG Ashley
HAMPTON Calhoun
HARDY (72542) Sharp(86), Fulton(13)
HARRELL Calhoun
HARRIET (72639) Searcy(95), Marion(4)
HARRISBURG Poinsett
HARRISON Boone
HARTFORD Sebastian
HARTMAN Johnson
HARVEY (72841) Scott(81), Yell(18)
HASTY Newton
HATFIELD Polk
HATTIEVILLE (72063) Conway(94), Pope(5)
HATTON Polk
HAVANA (72842) Yell(98), Logan(1)
HAYNES Lee
HAZEN Prairie
HEBER SPRINGS Cleburne
HECTOR Pope
HELENA Phillips
HENDERSON Baxter
HENSLEY (72065) Saline(84), Pulaski(11), Grant(4)
HERMITAGE Bradley
HETH (72346) St. Francis(94), Cross(4), Crittenden(1)
HICKORY PLAINS Prairie
HICKORY RIDGE (72347) Cross(80), Jackson(18)
HIGDEN (72067) Cleburne(89), Van Buren(10)
HIGGINSON White

HINDSVILLE (72738) Madison(80), Washington(12), Benton(6)
HIWASSE Benton
HOLLY GROVE (72069) Monroe(91), Phillips(8)
HOPE Hempstead
HORATIO Sevier
HORSESHOE BEND Izard
HOT SPRINGS NATIONAL PARK Garland
HOT SPRINGS VILLAGE (71909) Garland(74), Saline(25)
HOT SPRINGS VILLAGE Garland
HOUSTON Perry
HOWELL Woodruff
HOXIE Lawrence
HUGHES (72348) St. Francis(48), Crittenden(45), Lee(5)
HUMNOKE (72072) Lonoke(90), Jefferson(9)
HUMPHREY (72073) Arkansas(77), Jefferson(22)
HUNT Johnson
HUNTER Woodruff
HUNTINGTON Sebastian
HUTTIG Union
IDA Cleburne
IMBODEN (72434) Randolph(71), Lawrence(28)
IVAN Dallas
JACKSONPORT Jackson
JACKSONVILLE (72076) Pulaski(95), Lonoke(4)
JACKSONVILLE Pulaski
JASPER Newton
JEFFERSON (72079) Jefferson(85), Grant(14)
JENNIE Chicot
JEROME Drew
JERSEY Bradley
JERUSALEM (72080) Van Buren(48), Conway(41), Pope(10)
JESSIEVILLE Garland
JOHNSON Washington
JOINER Mississippi
JONES MILLS Hot Spring
JONESBORO (72401) Craighead(98), Greene(1)
JONESBORO Craighead
JUDSONIA White
JUNCTION CITY Union
KEISER Mississippi
KENSETT White
KEO Lonoke
KINGSLAND Cleveland
KINGSTON (72742) Madison(91), Newton(8)
KIRBY Pike
KNOBEL (72435) Clay(93), Greene(6)
KNOXVILLE Johnson
LA GRANGE Lee
LAFE (72436) Greene(84), Clay(15)
LAKE CITY Craighead
LAKE VILLAGE Chicot
LAKEVIEW Baxter
LAMAR (72846) Johnson(97), Pope(2)
LAMBROOK Phillips
LANEBURG Nevada
LANGLEY Pike
LAVACA Sebastian
LAWSON Union
LEACHVILLE (72438) Mississippi(87), Craighead(12)
LEAD HILL (72644) Boone(89), Marion(10)
LEOLA (72084) Grant(54), Hot Spring(27), Dallas(18)
LEPANTO (72354) Poinsett(78), Mississippi(21)
LESLIE (72645) Van Buren(42), Searcy(34), Stone(22)
LETONA White
LEWISVILLE Lafayette
LEXA (72355) Phillips(88), Lee(11)
LIGHT Greene

LINCOLN Washington
LITTLE ROCK (72210) Pulaski(92), Saline(7)
LITTLE ROCK Pulaski
LITTLE ROCK AIR FORCE BASE Pulaski
LOCKESBURG Sevier
LOCUST GROVE (72550) Independence(56), Cleburne(28), Stone(14)
LONDON (72847) Pope(62), Johnson(37)
LONOKE Lonoke
LONSDALE (72087) Saline(57), Garland(42)
LOUANN Ouachita
LOWELL Benton
LUXORA Mississippi
LYNN Lawrence
MABELVALE (72103) Saline(79), Pulaski(20)
MADISON St. Francis
MAGAZINE Logan
MAGNESS Independence
MAGNOLIA (71753) Columbia(98), Union(1)
MAGNOLIA Columbia
MALVERN (72104) Hot Spring(98), Saline(1)
MAMMOTH SPRING (72554) Fulton(68), Sharp(31)
MANILA Mississippi
MANSFIELD (72944) Sebastian(59), Scott(40)
MARBLE FALLS Newton
MARCELLA Stone
MARIANNA Lee
MARION Crittenden
MARKED TREE Poinsett
MARMADUKE Greene
MARSHALL (72650) Searcy(90), Stone(9)
MARVELL (72366) Phillips(96), Monroe(1), Lee(1)
MAUMELLE Pulaski
MAYFLOWER Faulkner
MAYNARD Randolph
MAYSVILLE Benton
MC CASKILL Hempstead
MC CRORY (72101) Woodruff(89), Jackson(8), Cross(2)
MC CRORY Cross
MC CRORY Woodruff
MC DOUGAL Clay
MC GEHEE Desha
MC NEIL Columbia
MC RAE White
MELBOURNE Izard
MELLWOOD Phillips
MENA Polk
MENIFEE Conway
MIDLAND Sebastian
MIDWAY Baxter
MINERAL SPRINGS Howard
MINTURN Lawrence
MOKO Fulton
MONETTE Craighead
MONROE Monroe
MONTICELLO Drew
MONTROSE Ashley
MORO (72368) Lee(90), Monroe(9)
MORRILTON Conway
MORROW Washington
MOSCOW Jefferson
MOUNT HOLLY Union
MOUNT IDA Montgomery
MOUNT JUDEA Newton
MOUNT PLEASANT Izard
MOUNT VERNON (72111) Faulkner(64), White(35)
MOUNTAIN HOME (72653) Baxter(98), Marion(1)
MOUNTAIN HOME Baxter
MOUNTAIN PINE Garland
MOUNTAIN VIEW (72560) Stone(98), Izard(1)

MOUNTAINBURG Crawford
MULBERRY (72947) Crawford(61), Franklin(38)
MURFREESBORO Pike
NASHVILLE (71852) Howard(87), Hempstead(6), Pike(6)
NATURAL DAM (72948) Crawford(95), Washington(4)
NEW BLAINE Logan
NEW EDINBURG (71660) Cleveland(96), Bradley(3)
NEWARK Independence
NEWHOPE (71959) Pike(60), Howard(39)
NEWPORT Jackson
NORFORK Baxter
NORMAN Montgomery
NORPHLET Union
NORTH LITTLE ROCK Pulaski
O KEAN Randolph
OAK GROVE Carroll
OAKLAND Marion
OARK (72852) Johnson(90), Newton(5), Madison(4)
ODEN Montgomery
OGDEN Little River
OIL TROUGH Independence
OKOLONA Clark
OLA (72853) Perry(64), Yell(35)
OMAHA (72662) Boone(98), Carroll(1)
ONEIDA Phillips
ONIA Stone
OSCEOLA Mississippi
OXFORD Izard
OZAN Hempstead
OZARK (72949) Franklin(97), Johnson(1), Logan(1)
OZONE (72854) Johnson(94), Newton(5)
PALESTINE (72372) St. Francis(85), Lee(14)
PANGBURN (72121) White(69), Cleburne(30)
PARAGOULD Greene
PARIS Logan
PARKDALE (71661) Ashley(88), Chicot(11)
PARKIN Cross
PARKS Scott
PARON (72122) Saline(69), Pulaski(30)
PARTHENON Newton
PATTERSON Woodruff
PEA RIDGE Benton
PEACH ORCHARD (72453) Greene(89), Clay(10)
PEARCY (71964) Garland(90), Hot Spring(9)
PEEL Marion
PELSOR (72856) Pope(52), Newton(47)
PENCIL BLUFF Montgomery
PERRY (72125) Perry(71), Conway(28)
PERRYVILLE (72126) Perry(96), Pulaski(3)
PETTIGREW (72752) Madison(84), Johnson(14)
PICKENS (71662) Lincoln(53), Desha(46)
PIGGOTT Clay
PINDALL Searcy
PINE BLUFF (71602) Jefferson(98), Grant(1)
PINE BLUFF Jefferson
PINEVILLE Izard
PLAINVIEW (72857) Yell(70), Perry(29)
PLEASANT GROVE Stone
PLEASANT PLAINS (72568) Independence(92), White(7)
PLUMERVILLE Conway
POCAHONTAS Randolph
POLLARD Clay
PONCA Newton
POPLAR GROVE (72374) Phillips(98), Lee(1)
PORTIA Lawrence
PORTLAND (71663) Ashley(65), Chicot(34)
POTTSVILLE Pope
POUGHKEEPSIE Sharp
POWHATAN Lawrence

POYEN (72128) Grant(98), Hot Spring(1)
PRAIRIE GROVE Washington
PRATTSVILLE Grant
PRESCOTT (71857) Nevada(96), Hempstead(3)
PRIM Cleburne
PROCTOR (72376) Crittenden(98), St. Francis(1)
PYATT Marion
QUITMAN (72131) Cleburne(82), Faulkner(9), Van Buren(7)
RATCLIFF (72951) Logan(58), Franklin(41)
RAVENDEN (72459) Lawrence(50), Randolph(35), Sharp(13)
RAVENDEN SPRINGS Randolph
RECTOR (72461) Clay(91), Greene(8)
REDFIELD (72132) Jefferson(84), Grant(15)
REYDELL Jefferson
REYNO Randolph
RISON (71665) Cleveland(98), Jefferson(1)
RIVERVALE Poinsett
ROE (72134) Monroe(82), Arkansas(13), Prairie(3)
ROGERS Benton
ROLAND Pulaski
ROMANCE White
ROSE BUD (72137) White(58), Cleburne(41)
ROSIE Independence
ROSSTON Nevada
ROUND POND St. Francis
ROVER Yell
ROYAL Garland
RUDY Crawford
RUSSELL White
RUSSELLVILLE Pope
SAFFELL (72572) Lawrence(66), Independence(33)
SAGE Izard
SAINT CHARLES Arkansas
SAINT FRANCIS Clay
SAINT JOE (72675) Marion(60), Searcy(39)
SAINT PAUL Madison
SALADO Independence
SALEM Fulton
SARATOGA (71859) Hempstead(60), Howard(40)
SCOTLAND Van Buren

SCOTT (72142) Pulaski(62), Lonoke(37)
SCRANTON Logan
SEARCY White
SEDGWICK Lawrence
SHERIDAN (72150) Grant(98), Jefferson(1)
SHERRILL Jefferson
SHERWOOD (72120) Pulaski(96), Faulkner(3)
SHIRLEY (72153) Van Buren(93), Stone(6)
SIDNEY (72577) Sharp(73), Izard(26)
SILOAM SPRINGS Benton
SIMS Montgomery
SMACKOVER (71762) Union(96), Ouachita(3)
SMITHVILLE (72466) Lawrence(63), Sharp(36)
SNOW LAKE Desha
SOLGOHACHIA Conway
SPARKMAN (71763) Dallas(92), Ouachita(4), Clark(2)
SPRINGDALE (72764) Washington(97), Benton(2)
SPRINGDALE Washington
SPRINGFIELD Conway
SPRINGTOWN Benton
STAMPS (71860) Lafayette(94), Columbia(5)
STAR CITY (71667) Lincoln(97), Cleveland(1)
STATE UNIVERSITY Craighead
STEPHENS (71764) Ouachita(57), Columbia(35), Nevada(5), Union(1)
STEPROCK White
STORY Montgomery
STRAWBERRY (72469) Lawrence(80), Sharp(19)
STRONG Union
STURKIE Fulton
STUTTGART (72160) Arkansas(96), Prairie(1), Jefferson(1)
SUBIACO Logan
SUCCESS Clay
SULPHUR ROCK (72579) Independence(94), Sharp(5)
SULPHUR SPRINGS Benton
SUMMERS Washington
SUMMIT Marion
SWEET HOME Pulaski
SWIFTON Jackson

TAYLOR (71861) Columbia(63), Lafayette(36)
TEXARKANA Miller
THIDA Independence
THORNTON (71766) Calhoun(97), Ouachita(2)
TICHNOR Arkansas
TILLAR (71670) Desha(81), Drew(18)
TILLY (72679) Pope(61), Van Buren(25), Searcy(12)
TIMBO Stone
TOMATO Mississippi
TONTITOWN Washington
TRASKWOOD (72167) Saline(80), Hot Spring(14), Grant(4)
TRUMANN Poinsett
TUCKER Jefferson
TUCKERMAN Jackson
TUMBLING SHOALS Cleburne
TUPELO Jackson
TURNER Phillips
TURRELL Crittenden
TWIST Cross
TYRONZA (72386) Poinsett(63), Mississippi(18), Crittenden(17)
ULM Prairie
UMPIRE (71971) Howard(78), Pike(21)
UNIONTOWN Crawford
URBANA Union
VALLEY SPRINGS (72682) Marion(83), Boone(16)
VAN BUREN Crawford
VANDERVOORT Polk
VANNDALE Cross
VENDOR Newton
VILLAGE Columbia
VILONIA Faulkner
VIOLA Fulton
VIOLET HILL Izard
WABASH Phillips
WABBASEKA (72175) Jefferson(98), Arkansas(1)
WALCOTT Greene
WALDENBURG Poinsett
WALDO (71770) Columbia(88), Nevada(11)
WALDRON Scott
WALNUT RIDGE (72476) Lawrence(91), Randolph(3), Craighead(2), Greene(2)
WARD (72176) Lonoke(98), Prairie(1)

WARM SPRINGS Randolph
WARREN (71671) Bradley(97), Cleveland(2)
WASHINGTON Hempstead
WATSON Desha
WAVELAND Yell
WEINER (72479) Poinsett(85), Jackson(9), Craighead(4)
WESLEY (72773) Madison(98), Washington(1)
WEST FORK Washington
WEST HELENA Phillips
WEST MEMPHIS Crittenden
WEST POINT White
WEST RIDGE Mississippi
WESTERN GROVE (72685) Newton(92), Searcy(4), Boone(2)
WHEATLEY (72392) St. Francis(78), Monroe(14), Woodruff(5), Lee(1)
WHEELER Washington
WHELEN SPRINGS Clark
WHITE HALL Jefferson
WICKES (71973) Polk(93), Howard(6)
WIDEMAN Izard
WIDENER St. Francis
WILBURN Cleburne
WILLIFORD Sharp
WILLISVILLE Nevada
WILMAR (71675) Drew(92), Bradley(7)
WILMOT (71676) Ashley(94), Chicot(5)
WILSON Mississippi
WILTON Little River
WINCHESTER Drew
WINSLOW (72959) Washington(87), Crawford(12)
WINTHROP Little River
WISEMAN (72587) Izard(94), Fulton(5)
WITTER Madison
WITTS SPRINGS (72686) Searcy(90), Pope(9)
WOODSON Pulaski
WOOSTER Faulkner
WRIGHT Jefferson
WRIGHTSVILLE Pulaski
WYNNE Cross
YELLVILLE Marion
YORKTOWN Lincoln

Arkansas ZIP/City Cross Reference

71601-71612	PINE BLUFF	71663-71663	PORTLAND	71749-71749	JUNCTION CITY	71833-71833	DIERKS
71612-71612	WHITE HALL	71665-71665	RISON	71750-71750	LAWSON	71834-71834	DODDRIDGE
71613-71613	PINE BLUFF	71666-71666	MC GEHEE	71751-71751	LOUANN	71835-71835	EMMET
71630-71630	ARKANSAS CITY	71667-71667	STAR CITY	71752-71752	MC NEIL	71836-71836	FOREMAN
71631-71631	BANKS	71670-71670	TILLAR	71753-71754	MAGNOLIA	71837-71837	FOUKE
71634-71634	COLLINS	71671-71671	WARREN	71758-71758	MOUNT HOLLY	71838-71838	FULTON
71635-71635	CROSSETT	71674-71674	WATSON	71759-71759	NORPHLET	71839-71839	GARLAND CITY
71638-71638	DERMOTT	71675-71675	WILMAR	71762-71762	SMACKOVER	71840-71840	GENOA
71639-71639	DUMAS	71676-71676	WILMOT	71763-71763	SPARKMAN	71841-71841	GILLHAM
71640-71640	EUDORA	71677-71677	WINCHESTER	71764-71764	STEPHENS	71842-71842	HORATIO
71642-71642	FOUNTAIN HILL	71678-71678	YORKTOWN	71765-71765	STRONG	71844-71844	LANEBURG
71643-71643	GOULD	71701-71711	CAMDEN	71766-71766	THORNTON	71845-71845	LEWISVILLE
71644-71644	GRADY	71720-71720	BEARDEN	71767-71767	HAMPTON	71846-71846	LOCKESBURG
71646-71646	HAMBURG	71721-71721	BEIRNE	71768-71768	URBANA	71847-71847	MC CASKILL
71647-71647	HERMITAGE	71722-71722	BLUFF CITY	71769-71769	VILLAGE	71851-71851	MINERAL SPRINGS
71649-71649	JENNIE	71724-71724	CALION	71770-71770	WALDO	71852-71852	NASHVILLE
71650-71650	JEROME	71725-71725	CARTHAGE	71772-71772	WHELEN SPRINGS	71853-71853	OGDEN
71651-71651	JERSEY	71726-71726	CHIDESTER	71801-71802	HOPE	71854-71854	TEXARKANA
71652-71652	KINGSLAND	71728-71728	CURTIS	71820-71820	ALLEENE	71855-71855	OZAN
71653-71653	LAKE VILLAGE	71730-71731	EL DORADO	71822-71822	ASHDOWN	71857-71857	PRESCOTT
71654-71654	MC GEHEE	71740-71740	EMERSON	71823-71823	BEN LOMOND	71858-71858	ROSSTON
71655-71657	MONTICELLO	71742-71742	FORDYCE	71825-71825	BLEVINS	71859-71859	SARATOGA
71658-71658	MONTROSE	71743-71743	GURDON	71826-71826	BRADLEY	71860-71860	STAMPS
71659-71659	MOSCOW	71744-71744	HAMPTON	71827-71827	BUCKNER	71861-71861	TAYLOR
71660-71660	NEW EDINBURG	71745-71745	HARRELL	71828-71828	CALE	71862-71862	WASHINGTON
71661-71661	PARKDALE	71747-71747	HUTTIG	71831-71831	COLUMBUS	71864-71864	WILLISVILLE
71662-71662	PICKENS	71748-71748	IVAN	71832-71832	DE QUEEN	71865-71865	WILTON

Range	City
71866-71866	WINTHROP
71901-71903	HOT SPRINGS NATIONAL PARK
71909-71910	HOT SPRINGS VILLAGE
71913-71914	HOT SPRINGS NATIONAL PARK
71920-71920	ALPINE
71921-71921	AMITY
71922-71922	ANTOINE
71923-71923	ARKADELPHIA
71929-71929	BISMARCK
71931-71931	BLAKELY
71932-71932	BOARD CAMP
71933-71933	BONNERDALE
71935-71935	CADDO GAP
71937-71937	COVE
71940-71940	DELIGHT
71941-71941	DONALDSON
71942-71942	FRIENDSHIP
71943-71943	GLENWOOD
71944-71944	GRANNIS
71945-71945	HATFIELD
71946-71946	HATTON
71949-71949	JESSIEVILLE
71950-71950	KIRBY
71951-71951	HOT SPRINGS NATIONAL PARK
71952-71952	LANGLEY
71953-71953	MENA
71956-71956	MOUNTAIN PINE
71957-71957	MOUNT IDA
71958-71958	MURFREESBORO
71959-71959	NEWHOPE
71960-71960	NORMAN
71961-71961	ODEN
71962-71962	OKOLONA
71964-71964	PEARCY
71965-71965	PENCIL BLUFF
71966-71966	ODEN
71968-71968	ROYAL
71969-71969	SIMS
71970-71970	STORY
71971-71971	UMPIRE
71972-71972	VANDERVOORT
71973-71973	WICKES
71998-71999	ARKADELPHIA
72001-72001	ADONA
72002-72002	ALEXANDER
72003-72003	ALMYRA
72004-72004	ALTHEIMER
72005-72005	AMAGON
72006-72006	AUGUSTA
72007-72007	AUSTIN
72009-72009	BALCH
72010-72010	BALD KNOB
72011-72011	BAUXITE
72012-72012	BEEBE
72013-72013	BEE BRANCH
72014-72014	BEEDEVILLE
72015-72015	BENTON
72016-72016	BIGELOW
72017-72017	BISCOE
72018-72018	BENTON
72020-72020	BRADFORD
72021-72021	BRINKLEY
72022-72022	BRYANT
72023-72023	CABOT
72024-72024	CARLISLE
72025-72025	CASA
72026-72026	CASSCOE
72027-72027	CENTER RIDGE
72028-72028	CHOCTAW
72029-72029	CLARENDON
72030-72030	CLEVELAND
72031-72031	CLINTON
72032-72035	CONWAY
72036-72036	COTTON PLANT
72037-72037	COY
72038-72038	CROCKETTS BLUFF
72039-72039	DAMASCUS
72040-72040	DES ARC
72041-72041	DE VALLS BLUFF
72042-72042	DE WITT
72043-72043	DIAZ
72044-72044	EDGEMONT
72045-72045	EL PASO
72046-72046	ENGLAND
72047-72047	ENOLA
72048-72048	ETHEL
72051-72051	FOX
72052-72052	GARNER
72053-72053	COLLEGE STATION
72055-72055	GILLETT
72057-72057	GRAPEVINE
72058-72058	GREENBRIER
72059-72059	GREGORY
72060-72060	GRIFFITHVILLE
72061-72061	GUY
72063-72063	HATTIEVILLE
72064-72064	HAZEN
72065-72065	HENSLEY
72066-72066	HICKORY PLAINS
72067-72067	HIGDEN
72068-72068	HIGGINSON
72069-72069	HOLLY GROVE
72070-72070	HOUSTON
72071-72071	HOWELL
72072-72072	HUMNOKE
72073-72073	HUMPHREY
72074-72074	HUNTER
72075-72075	JACKSONPORT
72076-72078	JACKSONVILLE
72079-72079	JEFFERSON
72080-72080	JERUSALEM
72081-72081	JUDSONIA
72082-72082	KENSETT
72083-72083	KEO
72084-72084	LEOLA
72085-72085	LETONA
72086-72086	LONOKE
72087-72087	LONSDALE
72088-72088	FAIRFIELD BAY
72089-72089	BRYANT
72099-72099	LITTLE ROCK AIR FORCE BASE
72100-72100	NORTH LITTLE ROCK
72101-72101	MC CRORY
72102-72102	MC RAE
72103-72103	MABELVALE
72104-72104	MALVERN
72105-72105	JONES MILLS
72106-72106	MAYFLOWER
72107-72107	MENIFEE
72108-72108	MONROE
72110-72110	MORRILTON
72111-72111	MOUNT VERNON
72112-72112	NEWPORT
72113-72113	MAUMELLE
72114-72119	NORTH LITTLE ROCK
72120-72120	SHERWOOD
72121-72121	PANGBURN
72122-72122	PARON
72123-72123	PATTERSON
72124-72124	NORTH LITTLE ROCK
72125-72125	PERRY
72126-72126	PERRYVILLE
72127-72127	PLUMERVILLE
72128-72128	POYEN
72129-72129	PRATTSVILLE
72130-72130	PRIM
72131-72131	QUITMAN
72132-72132	REDFIELD
72133-72133	REYDELL
72134-72134	ROE
72135-72135	ROLAND
72136-72136	ROMANCE
72137-72137	ROSE BUD
72139-72139	RUSSELL
72140-72140	SAINT CHARLES
72141-72141	SCOTLAND
72142-72142	SCOTT
72143-72149	SEARCY
72150-72150	SHERIDAN
72152-72152	SHERRILL
72153-72153	SHIRLEY
72156-72156	SOLGOHACHIA
72157-72157	SPRINGFIELD
72158-72158	BENTON
72159-72159	STEPROCK
72160-72160	STUTTGART
72164-72164	SWEET HOME
72165-72165	THIDA
72166-72166	TICHNOR
72167-72167	TRASKWOOD
72168-72168	TUCKER
72169-72169	TUPELO
72170-72170	ULM
72173-72173	VILONIA
72175-72175	WABBASEKA
72176-72176	WARD
72178-72178	WEST POINT
72179-72179	WILBURN
72180-72180	WOODSON
72181-72181	WOOSTER
72182-72182	WRIGHT
72183-72183	WRIGHTSVILLE
72189-72189	MC CRORY
72190-72199	NORTH LITTLE ROCK
72200-72207	LITTLE ROCK
72208-72208	FERNDALE
72209-72297	LITTLE ROCK
72301-72303	WEST MEMPHIS
72310-72310	ARMOREL
72311-72311	AUBREY
72312-72312	BARTON
72313-72313	BASSETT
72314-72314	BIRDEYE
72315-72317	BLYTHEVILLE
72319-72319	GOSNELL
72320-72320	BRICKEYS
72321-72321	BURDETTE
72322-72322	CALDWELL
72323-72323	CHATFIELD
72324-72324	CHERRY VALLEY
72325-72325	CLARKEDALE
72326-72326	COLT
72327-72327	CRAWFORDSVILLE
72328-72328	CRUMROD
72329-72329	DRIVER
72330-72330	DYESS
72331-72331	EARLE
72332-72332	EDMONDSON
72333-72333	ELAINE
72335-72336	FORREST CITY
72338-72338	FRENCHMANS BAYOU
72339-72339	GILMORE
72340-72340	GOODWIN
72341-72341	HAYNES
72342-72342	HELENA
72346-72346	HETH
72347-72347	HICKORY RIDGE
72348-72348	HUGHES
72350-72350	JOINER
72351-72351	KEISER
72352-72352	LA GRANGE
72353-72353	LAMBROOK
72354-72354	LEPANTO
72355-72355	LEXA
72358-72358	LUXORA
72359-72359	MADISON
72360-72360	MARIANNA
72364-72364	MARION
72365-72365	MARKED TREE
72366-72366	MARVELL
72367-72367	MELLWOOD
72368-72368	MORO
72369-72369	ONEIDA
72370-72370	OSCEOLA
72372-72372	PALESTINE
72373-72373	PARKIN
72374-72374	POPLAR GROVE
72376-72376	PROCTOR
72377-72377	RIVERVALE
72378-72378	ROUND POND
72379-72379	SNOW LAKE
72381-72381	TOMATO
72383-72383	TURNER
72384-72384	TURRELL
72385-72385	TWIST
72386-72386	TYRONZA
72387-72387	VANNDALE
72389-72389	WABASH
72390-72390	WEST HELENA
72391-72391	WEST RIDGE
72392-72392	WHEATLEY
72394-72394	WIDENER
72395-72395	WILSON
72396-72397	WYNNE
72397-72397	MC CRORY
72401-72404	JONESBORO
72410-72410	ALICIA
72411-72411	BAY
72412-72412	BEECH GROVE
72413-72413	BIGGERS
72414-72414	BLACK OAK
72415-72415	BLACK ROCK
72416-72416	BONO
72417-72417	BROOKLAND
72419-72419	CARAWAY
72421-72421	CASH
72422-72422	CORNING
72424-72424	DATTO
72425-72425	DELAPLAINE
72426-72426	DELL
72427-72427	EGYPT
72428-72428	ETOWAH
72429-72429	FISHER
72430-72430	GREENWAY
72431-72431	GRUBBS
72432-72432	HARRISBURG
72433-72433	HOXIE
72434-72434	IMBODEN
72435-72435	KNOBEL
72436-72436	LAFE
72437-72437	LAKE CITY
72438-72438	LEACHVILLE
72439-72439	LIGHT
72440-72440	LYNN
72441-72441	MC DOUGAL
72442-72442	MANILA
72443-72443	MARMADUKE
72444-72444	MAYNARD
72445-72445	MINTURN
72447-72447	MONETTE
72449-72449	O KEAN
72450-72451	PARAGOULD
72453-72453	PEACH ORCHARD
72454-72454	PIGGOTT
72455-72455	POCAHONTAS
72456-72456	POLLARD
72457-72457	PORTIA
72458-72458	POWHATAN
72459-72459	RAVENDEN
72460-72460	RAVENDEN SPRINGS
72461-72461	RECTOR
72462-72462	REYNO
72464-72464	SAINT FRANCIS
72465-72465	SEDGWICK
72466-72466	SMITHVILLE
72467-72467	STATE UNIVERSITY
72469-72469	STRAWBERRY
72470-72470	SUCCESS
72471-72471	SWIFTON
72472-72472	TRUMANN
72473-72473	TUCKERMAN
72474-72474	WALCOTT
72475-72475	WALDENBURG
72476-72476	WALNUT RIDGE
72478-72478	WARM SPRINGS
72479-72479	WEINER
72482-72482	WILLIFORD
72501-72503	BATESVILLE
72512-72512	HORSESHOE BEND
72513-72513	ASH FLAT
72515-72515	BEXAR
72516-72516	BOSWELL
72517-72517	BROCKWELL
72519-72519	CALICO ROCK
72520-72520	CAMP
72521-72521	CAVE CITY
72522-72522	CHARLOTTE
72523-72523	CONCORD

72524-72524 CORD	72658-72659 NORFORK	72843-72843 HECTOR
72525-72525 CHEROKEE VILLAGE	72660-72660 OAK GROVE	72844-72844 HUNT
72526-72526 CUSHMAN	72661-72661 OAKLAND	72845-72845 KNOXVILLE
72527-72527 DESHA	72662-72662 OMAHA	72846-72846 LAMAR
72528-72528 DOLPH	72663-72663 ONIA	72847-72847 LONDON
72529-72529 CHEROKEE VILLAGE	72666-72666 PARTHENON	72851-72851 NEW BLAINE
72530-72530 DRASCO	72668-72668 PEEL	72852-72852 OARK
72531-72531 ELIZABETH	72669-72669 PINDALL	72853-72853 OLA
72532-72532 EVENING SHADE	72670-72670 PONCA	72854-72854 OZONE
72533-72533 FIFTY SIX	72672-72672 PYATT	72855-72855 PARIS
72534-72534 FLORAL	72675-72675 SAINT JOE	72856-72856 PELSOR
72536-72536 FRANKLIN	72677-72677 SUMMIT	72857-72857 PLAINVIEW
72537-72537 GAMALIEL	72679-72679 TILLY	72858-72858 POTTSVILLE
72538-72538 GEPP	72680-72680 TIMBO	72860-72860 ROVER
72539-72539 GLENCOE	72682-72682 VALLEY SPRINGS	72863-72863 SCRANTON
72540-72540 GUION	72683-72683 VENDOR	72865-72865 SUBIACO
72542-72542 HARDY	72685-72685 WESTERN GROVE	72867-72867 WAVELAND
72543-72543 HEBER SPRINGS	72686-72686 WITTS SPRINGS	72901-72919 FORT SMITH
72544-72544 HENDERSON	72687-72687 YELLVILLE	72921-72921 ALMA
72545-72545 HEBER SPRINGS	72701-72704 FAYETTEVILLE	72923-72923 BARLING
72546-72546 IDA	72711-72711 AVOCA	72924-72924 BATES
72550-72550 LOCUST GROVE	72712-72712 BENTONVILLE	72926-72926 BOLES
72553-72553 MAGNESS	72714-72715 BELLA VISTA	72927-72927 BOONEVILLE
72554-72554 MAMMOTH SPRING	72716-72716 BENTONVILLE	72928-72928 BRANCH
72555-72555 MARCELLA	72717-72717 CANEHILL	72930-72930 CECIL
72556-72556 MELBOURNE	72718-72718 CAVE SPRINGS	72932-72932 CEDARVILLE
72557-72557 MOKO	72719-72719 CENTERTON	72933-72933 CHARLESTON
72560-72560 MOUNTAIN VIEW	72721-72721 COMBS	72934-72934 CHESTER
72561-72561 MOUNT PLEASANT	72722-72722 DECATUR	72935-72935 DYER
72562-72562 NEWARK	72727-72727 ELKINS	72936-72936 GREENWOOD
72564-72564 OIL TROUGH	72728-72728 ELM SPRINGS	72937-72937 HACKETT
72565-72565 OXFORD	72729-72729 EVANSVILLE	72938-72938 HARTFORD
72566-72566 PINEVILLE	72730-72730 FARMINGTON	72940-72940 HUNTINGTON
72567-72567 PLEASANT GROVE	72732-72732 GARFIELD	72941-72941 LAVACA
72568-72568 PLEASANT PLAINS	72733-72733 GATEWAY	72943-72943 MAGAZINE
72569-72569 POUGHKEEPSIE	72734-72734 GENTRY	72944-72944 MANSFIELD
72571-72571 ROSIE	72735-72735 GOSHEN	72945-72945 MIDLAND
72572-72572 SAFFELL	72736-72736 GRAVETTE	72946-72946 MOUNTAINBURG
72573-72573 SAGE	72737-72737 GREENLAND	72947-72947 MULBERRY
72575-72575 SALADO	72738-72738 HINDSVILLE	72948-72948 NATURAL DAM
72576-72576 SALEM	72739-72739 HIWASSE	72949-72949 OZARK
72577-72577 SIDNEY	72740-72740 HUNTSVILLE	72950-72950 PARKS
72578-72578 STURKIE	72741-72741 JOHNSON	72951-72951 RATCLIFF
72579-72579 SULPHUR ROCK	72742-72742 KINGSTON	72952-72952 RUDY
72581-72581 TUMBLING SHOALS	72744-72744 LINCOLN	72955-72955 UNIONTOWN
72583-72583 VIOLA	72745-72745 LOWELL	72956-72957 VAN BUREN
72584-72584 VIOLET HILL	72747-72747 MAYSVILLE	72958-72958 WALDRON
72585-72585 WIDEMAN	72749-72749 MORROW	72959-72959 WINSLOW
72587-72587 WISEMAN	72751-72751 PEA RIDGE	
72601-72602 HARRISON	72752-72752 PETTIGREW	
72610-72610 ALCO	72753-72753 PRAIRIE GROVE	
72611-72611 ALPENA	72756-72758 ROGERS	
72612-72612 BASS	72760-72760 SAINT PAUL	
72613-72613 BEAVER	72761-72761 SILOAM SPRINGS	
72615-72615 BERGMAN	72762-72766 SPRINGDALE	
72616-72616 BERRYVILLE	72767-72767 SPRINGTOWN	
72617-72617 BIG FLAT	72768-72768 SULPHUR SPRINGS	
72618-72618 BRUNO	72769-72769 SUMMERS	
72619-72619 BULL SHOALS	72770-72770 TONTITOWN	
72623-72623 CLARKRIDGE	72773-72773 WESLEY	
72624-72624 COMPTON	72774-72774 WEST FORK	
72626-72626 COTTER	72775-72775 WHEELER	
72628-72628 DEER	72776-72776 WITTER	
72629-72629 DENNARD	72801-72812 RUSSELLVILLE	
72630-72630 DIAMOND CITY	72820-72820 ALIX	
72631-72632 EUREKA SPRINGS	72821-72821 ALTUS	
72633-72633 EVERTON	72822-72823 ATKINS	
72634-72634 FLIPPIN	72824-72824 BELLEVILLE	
72635-72635 GASSVILLE	72826-72826 BLUE MOUNTAIN	
72636-72636 GILBERT	72827-72827 BLUFFTON	
72638-72638 GREEN FOREST	72828-72828 BRIGGSVILLE	
72639-72639 HARRIET	72829-72829 CENTERVILLE	
72640-72640 HASTY	72830-72830 CLARKSVILLE	
72641-72641 JASPER	72832-72832 COAL HILL	
72642-72642 LAKEVIEW	72833-72833 DANVILLE	
72644-72644 LEAD HILL	72834-72834 DARDANELLE	
72645-72645 LESLIE	72835-72835 DELAWARE	
72648-72648 MARBLE FALLS	72837-72837 DOVER	
72650-72650 MARSHALL	72838-72838 GRAVELLY	
72651-72651 MIDWAY	72839-72839 HAGARVILLE	
72653-72654 MOUNTAIN HOME	72840-72840 HARTMAN	
72655-72655 MOUNT JUDEA	72841-72841 HARVEY	
72657-72657 TIMBO	72842-72842 HAVANA	

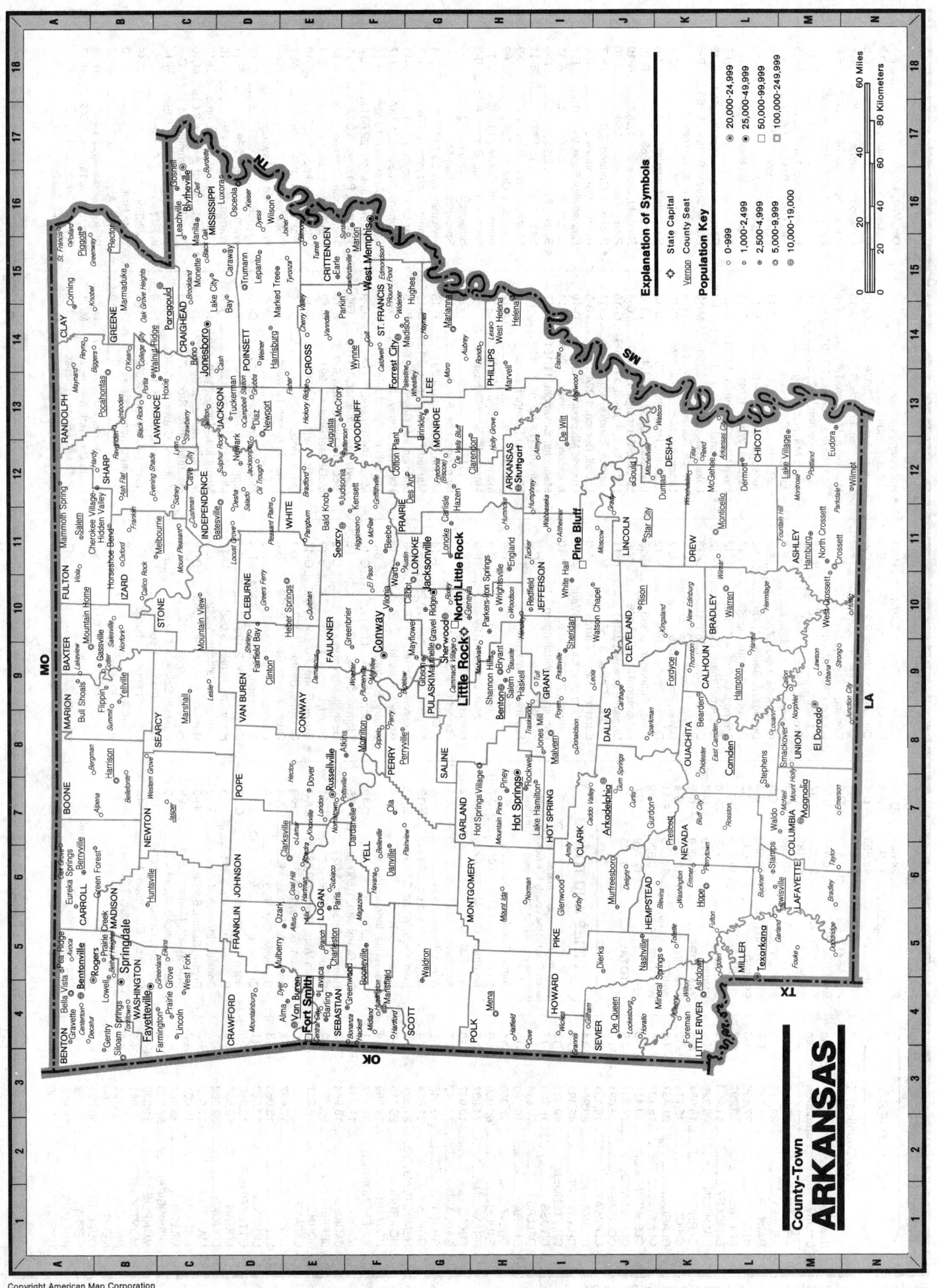

County-Town
ARKANSAS

Copyright American Map Corporation

COUNTIES

(75 Counties)

Name of County	Population	Location on Map
ARKANSAS	21,653	H-12
ASHLEY	24,319	M-11
BAXTER	31,186	A-9
BENTON	97,499	A-3
BOONE	28,297	A-7
BRADLEY	11,793	K-10
CALHOUN	5,826	K-9
CARROLL	18,654	A-5
CHICOT	15,713	L-12
CLARK	21,437	I-6
CLAY	18,107	A-14
CLEBURNE	19,411	D-10
CLEVELAND	7,781	J-9
COLUMBIA	25,691	M-6
CONWAY	19,151	E-8
CRAIGHEAD	68,956	C-14
CRAWFORD	42,493	D-4
CRITTENDEN	49,939	E-15
CROSS	19,225	E-13
DALLAS	9,614	J-8
DESHA	16,798	K-12
DREW	17,369	K-11
FAULKNER	60,006	E-9
FRANKLIN	14,897	D-5
FULTON	10,037	A-10
GARLAND	73,397	G-7
GRANT	13,948	I-9
GREENE	31,804	B-14
HEMPSTEAD	21,621	J-5
HOT SPRING	26,115	I-7
HOWARD	13,569	I-4
INDEPENDENCE	31,192	C-11
IZARD	11,364	B-10
JACKSON	18,944	D-13
JEFFERSON	85,487	I-10
JOHNSON	18,221	D-6
LAFAYETTE	9,643	M-6
LAWRENCE	17,457	C-12
LEE	13,053	G-13
LINCOLN	13,690	J-11
LITTLE RIVER	13,966	K-3
LOGAN	20,557	E-5
LONOKE	39,268	G-11
MADISON	11,618	B-5
MARION	12,001	A-8
MILLER	38,467	L-5
MISSISSIPPI	57,525	C-16
MONROE	11,333	G-12
MONTGOMERY	7,841	H-5
NEVADA	10,101	K-6
NEWTON	7,666	B-7
OUACHITA	30,574	K-8
PERRY	7,969	F-8
PHILLIPS	28,838	H-13
PIKE	10,086	I-5
POINSETT	24,664	D-14
POLK	17,347	H-4
POPE	45,883	D-7
PRAIRIE	9,518	F-11
PULASKI	349,660	G-8
RANDOLPH	16,558	A-12
SAINT FRANCIS	28,497	F-14
SALINE	64,183	G-7
SCOTT	10,205	G-4
SEARCY	7,841	C-8
SEBASTIAN	99,590	E-4
SEVIER	13,637	J-3
SHARP	14,109	B-12
STONE	9,775	C-10
UNION	46,719	M-8
VAN BUREN	14,008	D-8
WASHINGTON	113,409	B-4
WHITE	54,676	E-11
WOODRUFF	9,520	F-12
YELL	17,759	F-6
TOTAL	**2,350,725**	

CITIES AND TOWNS

Note: The first name is that of the city or town, second, that of the county in which it is located, then the population and location on the map.

Alma, Crawford, 2,959 ..... E-4
Arkadelphia, Clark, 10,014 ..... J-7
Arkansas City, Desha, 523 ..... L-13
Ash Flat, Sharp, 667 ..... B-12
Ashdown, Little River, 5,150 ..... K-4
Atkins, Pope, 2,834 ..... F-8
Augusta, Woodruff, 2,759 ..... E-12
Bald Knob, White, 2,653 ..... E-12
Barling, Sebastian, 4,078 ..... E-4
Batesville, Independence, 9,187 ..... D-12
Bay, Craighead, 1,660 ..... D-15
Bearden, Ouachita, 1,021 ..... K-9
Beebe, White, 4,455 ..... F-11
• Bella Vista, Benton, 9,083 ..... A-4
Benton, Saline, 18,177 ..... H-9
Bentonville, Benton, 11,257 ..... A-4
Berryville, Carroll, 3,212 ..... A-6
Blytheville, Mississippi, 22,906 ..... C-17
Bono, Craighead, 1,220 ..... C-14
Booneville, Logan, 3,804 ..... F-5
Brinkley, Monroe, 4,234 ..... G-13
Bryant, Saline, 5,269 ..... H-9
Bull Shoals, Marion, 1,534 ..... A-9
Cabot, Lonoke, 8,319 ..... G-10
Camden, Ouachita, 14,380 ..... L-8
Caraway, Craighead, 1,178 ..... D-15
Carlisle, Lonoke, 2,253 ..... G-11
Cave City, Independence/Sharp, 1,503 ..... C-12
Charleston, Franklin, 2,128 ..... E-5
• Cherokee Village-Hidden Valley, Fulton/Sharp, 4,416 ..... B-12

Clarendon, Monroe, 2,072 ..... H-13
Clarksville, Johnson, 5,833 ..... E-6
Clinton, Van Buren, 2,213 ..... D-9
Conway, Faulkner, 26,481 ..... F-9
Corning, Clay, 3,323 ..... A-14
Cotton Plant, Woodruff, 1,150 ..... F-13
Crossett, Ashley, 6,282 ..... M-11
Danville, Yell, 1,585 ..... F-6
Dardanelle, Yell, 3,722 ..... F-7
De Queen, Sevier, 4,633 ..... J-4
De Witt, Arkansas, 3,553 ..... I-12
Dermott, Chicot, 4,715 ..... L-12
Des Arc, Prairie, 2,001 ..... G-12
Diaz, Jackson, 1,363 ..... D-13
Dierks, Howard, 1,263 ..... J-5
Dover, Pope, 1,055 ..... E-7
Dumas, Desha, 5,520 ..... K-12
Earle, Crittenden, 3,393 ..... E-15
El Dorado, Union, 23,146 ..... M-9
England, Lonoke, 3,351 ..... H-11
Eudora, Chicot, 3,155 ..... M-13
Eureka Springs, Carroll, 1,900 ..... A-6
• Fairfield Bay, Cleburne/Van Buren, 2,332 ..... D-10
Farmington, Washington, 1,322 ..... C-4
Fayetteville, Washington, 42,099 ..... B-4
Flippin, Marion, 1,006 ..... B-9
Fordyce, Dallas, 4,729 ..... K-9
Foreman, Little River, 1,267 ..... K-4
Forrest City, St. Francis, 13,364 ..... F-14
Fort Smith, Sebastian, 72,798 ..... E-4
Gassville, Baxter, 1,167 ..... A-9
Gentry, Benton, 1,726 ..... B-3
Gibson, Pulaski, 4,288 ..... G-10
Glenwood, Pike, 1,354 ..... I-6
Gosnell, Mississippi, 3,783 ..... C-16
Gould, Lincoln, 1,470 ..... J-12
Gravel Ridge, Pulaski, 3,846 ..... G-10
Gravette, Benton, 1,412 ..... A-4
Green Forest, Carroll, 2,050 ..... B-6
Greenbrier, Faulkner, 2,130 ..... F-9
Greenwood, Sebastian, 3,984 ..... F-4
Gurdon, Clark, 2,199 ..... J-7
Hamburg, Ashley, 3,098 ..... M-11
Hampton, Calhoun, 1,562 ..... L-9
Harrisburg, Poinsett, 1,943 ..... D-14
Harrison, Boone, 9,922 ..... B-7
Haskell, Saline, 1,342 ..... H-9
Hazen, Prairie, 1,668 ..... G-12
Heber Springs, Cleburne, 5,628 ..... E-10
Helena, Phillips, 7,491 ..... H-15
Hope, Hempstead, 9,643 ..... K-6
Horseshoe Bend, Fulton/Izard/Sharp, 2,239 ..... B-11
Hot Springs, Garland, 32,462 ..... H-8

• Hot Springs Village, Garland/Saline, 6,361 ..... H-8
Hoxie, Lawrence, 2,676 ..... C-13
Hughes, St. Francis, 1,810 ..... G-15
Huntsville, Madison, 1,605 ..... B-6
Jacksonville, Pulaski, 29,101 ..... G-10
Jasper, Newton, 332 ..... C-7
Jones Mill, Hot Spring 3,611 ..... I-8
Jonesboro, Craighead, 46,535 ..... C-14
Judsonia, White, 1,915 ..... E-12
Kensett, White, 1,741 ..... F-11
Lake City, Craighead, 1,833 ..... C-15
Lake Hamilton, Garland, 1,331 ..... I-7
Lake Village, Chicot, 2,791 ..... M-13
Lavaca, Sebastian, 1,253 ..... E-4
Leachville, Mississippi, 1,743 ..... C-15
Lepanto, Poinsett, 2,033 ..... D-15
Lewisville, Lafayette, 1,424 ..... L-6
Lincoln, Washington, 1,460 ..... C-4
Little Rock, Pulaski, 175,795 ..... G-11
Lonoke, Lonoke, 4,022 ..... G-11
Lowell, Benton, 1,224 ..... B-5
Luxora, Mississippi, 1,338 ..... D-16
Madison, St. Francis, 1,263 ..... F-14
Magnolia, Columbia, 11,151 ..... M-7
Malvern, Hot Spring, 9,256 ..... I-8
Mammoth Spring, Fulton, 1,097 ..... A-12
Manila, Mississippi, 2,635 ..... C-16
Mansfield, Scott/Sebastian, 1,018 ..... F-4
Marianna, Lee, 5,910 ..... G-14
Marion, Crittenden, 4,391 ..... F-16
Marked Tree, Poinsett, 3,100 ..... D-15
Marmaduke, Greene, 1,164 ..... B-15
Marshall, Searcy, 1,318 ..... C-9
Marvell, Phillips, 1,545 ..... H-14
Maumelle, Pulaski, 6,714 ..... G-9
Mayflower, Faulkner, 1,415 ..... G-9
McCrory, Woodruff, 1,971 ..... E-13
McGehee, Desha, 4,997 ..... K-12
Melbourne, Izard, 1,562 ..... C-11
Mena, Polk, 5,475 ..... H-4
Mineral Springs, Howard, 1,004 ..... K-5
Monette, Craighead, 1,115 ..... C-15
Monticello, Drew, 8,116 ..... L-11
Morrilton, Conway, 6,551 ..... F-8
Mount Ida, Montgomery, 775 ..... H-6
Mountain Home, Baxter, 9,027 ..... A-9
Mountain View, Stone, 2,439 ..... C-10
Murfreesboro, Pike, 1,542 ..... J-6
Nashville, Howard, 4,639 ..... J-5
Newark, Independence, 1,159 ..... D-12
Newport, Jackson, 7,459 ..... D-13
• North Crossett, Ashley, 3,358 ..... M-11
North Little Rock, Pulaski, 61,741 ..... G-10

Ola, Yell, 1,090 ..... F-7
Osceola, Mississippi, 8,930 ..... D-16
Ozark, Franklin, 3,330 ..... E-5
Paragould, Greene, 18,540 ..... C-15
Paris, Logan, 3,674 ..... E-6
• Parkers-Iron Springs, Pulaski, 3,611 ..... H-10
Parkin, Cross, 1,847 ..... E-15
Pea Ridge, Benton, 1,620 ..... A-5
Perryville, Perry, 1,141 ..... F-8
Piggott, Clay, 3,777 ..... A-16
Pine Bluff, Jefferson, 57,140 ..... I-11
Piney, Garland, 2,500 ..... H-7
Pocahontas, Randolph, 6,151 ..... B-13
• Prairie Creek, Benton, 1,268 ..... B-5
• Prairie Grove, Washington, 1,761 ..... C-4
Prescott, Nevada, 3,673 ..... K-6
Rector, Clay, 2,268 ..... B-15
Redfield, Jefferson, 1,082 ..... H-10
Rison, Cleveland, 1,258 ..... J-10
Rockwell, Garland, 2,514 ..... H-7
Rogers, Benton, 24,692 ..... B-5
Russellville, Pope, 21,260 ..... E-7
Salem, Fulton, 1,474 ..... A-11
Salem, Saline, 2,950 ..... H-9
Searcy, White, 15,180 ..... E-11
Shannon Hills, Saline, 1,755 ..... H-9
Sheridan, Grant, 3,098 ..... I-9
Sherwood, Pulaski, 18,893 ..... G-10
Siloam Springs, Benton, 8,151 ..... B-3
Smackover, Union, 2,232 ..... M-8
Springdale, Benton, 29,941 ..... B-4
Stamps, Lafayette, 2,478 ..... L-6
Star City, Lincoln, 2,138 ..... J-11
Stephens, Ouachita, 1,137 ..... L-7
Stuttgart, Arkansas, 10,420 ..... H-12
Texarkana, Miller, 22,631 ..... L-4
Trumann, Poinsett, 6,304 ..... D-15
Tuckerman, Jackson, 2,020 ..... D-13
Van Buren, Crawford, 14,979 ..... E-4
Vilonia, Faulkner, 1,133 ..... F-10
Waldo, Columbia, 1,495 ..... M-7
Waldron, Scott, 3,024 ..... G-4
Walnut Ridge, Lawrence, 4,388 ..... C-13
Ward, Lonoke, 1,269 ..... F-11
Warren, Bradley, 6,455 ..... L-10
Watson Chapel, Jefferson, 2,019 ..... I-10
• West Crossett, Ashley, 2,019 ..... M-10
West Fork, Washington, 1,607 ..... C-4
West Helena, Phillips, 9,695 ..... H-14
West Memphis, Crittenden, 28,259 ..... F-16
White Hall, Jefferson, 3,849 ..... I-10
Wilmot, Ashley, 1,047 ..... N-12
Wilson, Mississippi, 1,068 ..... D-16
Wrightsville, Pulaski, 1,062 ..... H-10
Wynne, Cross, 8,187 ..... F-14
Yellville, Marion, 1,181 ..... B-9

Explanation of symbols: • – Census Designated Place (CDP)

California

General Help Numbers:

Governor's Office
State Capitol, 1st Floor
Sacramento, CA 95814
www.governor.ca.gov/state
/govsite/gov_homepage.jsp

916-445-2841
Fax 916-445-4633
8:30AM-5PM

Attorney General's Office
Justice Department
PO Box 944255
Sacramento, CA 94244-2550
http://caag.state.ca.us

916-445-9555
Fax 916-324-5205
8AM-5PM

Legislative Records
State Capitol, Room B-32
Sacramento, CA 95814
www.leginfo.ca.gov

916-445-2323

8AM-5PM

State Archives
1020 "O" St
Sacramento, CA 95814
www.ss.ca.gov/archives/
archives.htm

916-653-7715/2246
Fax 916-653-7363
9:30AM-4PM

State Specifics:

Capital:	Sacramento
	Sacramento County
Time Zone:	PST
Number of Counties:	58
Population:	35,484,453

Web Site:
www.state.ca.us/state/portal/myca_homepage.jsp

State Agencies

Criminal Records

Access to Records is Restricted

Department of Justice, Records Search Section, PO Box 903417, Sacramento, CA 94203-4170 (Courier: 4949 Broadway, Sacramento, CA 95820); 916-227-3460 (Dept of Justice), 916-227-3849 (General Information), 916-227-3812 (Sealing & Dismissal), 8AM-5PM.

www.caag.state.ca.us

Note: SEVERE LIMITATIONS! Penal Code Sec. 11105.3 limits access to searches involving child care, education, the handicaped and mentally impaired. The subject can obtain their own copy.

Statewide Court Records

Administration Office of Courts, Office of Cummunications, 455 Golden Gate Ave, San Francisco, CA 94102-3660; 415-865-4200, 415-865-4205 (Fax), 8AM-5PM.

www.courtinfo.ca.gov

Note: Except for certain online research capabilities, all court record access must be done at the local level.

Access by: limited online.

Online search: There is no statewide online computer access available for county court records. The website offers access to all opinions from the Supreme and Appeals courts from 1850 to present. Opinions not certified for publications are available for last 60 days.

Sexual Offender Registry

Department of Justice, Sexual Offender Program, PO Box 903387, Sacramento, CA 94203-3870 (Courier: 4949 Broadway, Rm H216, Sacramento, CA 95820); 900-448-3000 (Fee Search), 916-227-4199 (Tracking), 916-227-4345 (Fax), 8AM-5PM.

www.caag.state.ca.us

Note: There are over 99,715 registered sexual offenders in CA.

Searching: Offender informatiion can be accessed 3 ways: 1) in person at DOJ offices, sheriff offices, and police departments in cities with population exceeding 200,000; 2) fee-based phone system from DOJ; 3) mail requests to DOJ. Include the following in your request-full name; also helpful DOB and SSN.

Access by: mail, phone.

Mail search: Turnaround time: 3 to 5 business days. Names searches are $4.00 per name and the request must contain 6 names or more. Mail requests are available to businesses and organizations.

Phone search: The public may call the CA Sexual Offender 900 service at 900-448-3000. There is a fee of $10.00 per call for checks on up to two names.

Incarceration Records

California Department of Corrections, Communications Office, PO Box 942883, Sacramento, CA 94283-0001; 916-557-5933, 916-445-6713 (24 Hour Inmate Locator), 916-445-7682 (Dept. of Corrections Main), 916-327-1988 (Fax), 8AM-5PM.

www.corr.ca.gov

Note: The state provides no online searching, however a private company offers free web access to state/DOC records at www.vinelink.com/index.jsp.

Indexing & Storage: Records are available on current and former inmates. It takes about 70 days before new records are available for inquiry.

Searching: Please note that for new or transferring inmates it can take up to seven business days to update location information. Include the following in your request-full name, DOB, your fax and phone numbers; also helpful: inmate number. Location, conviction and sentencing information, and county of conviction are released. Agency prefers to return results via fax. The following data is not released: case specifics, which should be acquired from the courts.

Access by: mail, phone, fax.

Fee & Payment: There is no fee.

Mail search: Turnaround time: 4-6 days.

Phone search: The Inmate Locator help line at 916-445-6713 is open 24 hours daily. Provides an inmate's location, mailing addresses and relevant phone numbers.

Fax search: Records are available by fax.

Corporation, Limited Liability Company, Limited Partnerships, Limited Liability Partnerships,

Secretary of State, Information Retrieval/Certification Unit, 1500 11th Street, 3rd Fl, Sacramento, CA 95814; 916-657-5448 x1, 8AM-4:30PM.

www.ss.ca.gov

Indexing & Storage: New records are available for inquiry immediately. Records are indexed on microfiche, inhouse computer.

Searching: Include the following in your request-full name of business. In addition to the articles of incorporation, corporation records include the following information: Statement of Officers (up to 2), Prior (merged) or amended names, Inactive and Reserved names. Reserved names are not available on the online search.

Access by: mail, phone, fax, in person, online.

Fee & Payment: Statement of Officers or articles of incorporation and amendments is $1.00 first page, $.50 each add'l. A status report with officers is $4.00. Add $5.00 for certification for any document. Fee payee: Secretary of State. Prepayment required. Personal checks accepted. No credit cards accepted.

Mail search: Turnaround time: 3 to 5 weeks. A SASE is requested.

Phone search: Only pre-paid accounts have telephone access to corporate status and name availability/reservation. Fee is $4.00 per name searched.

Fax search: Return of documents and/or status information is an additional $5.00 per document.

In person search: Turnaround time is while you wait for computer printouts of status reports, or if expediate fee paid.

Online search: The website at http://kepler.ss.ca.gov/list.html offers access to more than 2 million records including corporation, LLC, LP and LLP. Information available includes status, file number, date of filing and agent for service of process. Please note the file is updated weekly (not daily).

Expedited service: Over-the counter requests for immediate service, other than for compuer printouts of status reports, entails an additional $10.00 fee.

Trademarks/Servicemarks, Limited Partnership Records

Secretary of State, Trademark Unit, PO Box 944225, Sacramento, CA 94244-2250 (Courier: 1500 11th Street, Rm 345, Sacramento, CA 95814); 916-653-4984 (Trademark/Servicemarks), 916-653-3365 (Partnership Information), 8AM-5PM.

www.ss.ca.gov

Indexing & Storage: Records are available for active and expired records. It takes 2 to 3 weeks before new records are available for inquiry. Records are indexed on index cards.

Searching: Include the following in your request-trademark/servicemark name. Information returned includes name of trademark, name of owner and address, and date of filing.

Access by: mail, phone, in person.

Fee & Payment: Copies are $1.00 per page and $.50 each add'l. Certification is $5.00 per document. A Certificate of Status is $5.00. Fee payee: Secretary of State. Prepayment required. Personal checks accepted. No credit cards accepted.

Mail search: Turnaround time: 2 to 3 weeks. A SASE is requested. No fee for mail request.

Phone search: No fee for telephone request of a name search. There is a limit of 2 searches per call.

In person search: You can wait for results. If lists are presented, then the results are returned by mail.

Assumed Name, Fictitious Name

Records not maintained by a state level agency.

Note: Records are found at the county level.

Uniform Commercial Code, Federal Tax Liens, State Tax Liens

UCC Division, Secretary of State, PO Box 942835, Sacramento, CA 94235. (Courier: 1500 11th St, Room 255, Sacramento, CA 95814); 916-653-3516 x2, 8AM-5PM.

www.ss.ca.gov/business/ucc/ucc.htm

Note: This office does not currently offer fax service, but may make it available in the near future.

Indexing & Storage: Records are available for current records and expired records up to 1 year after lapse. There is an index on computer dating back to 1965. Records are indexed on inhouse computer.

Searching: Use search request form UCC-11; one form per debtor name. The search includes federal and some state tax liens on businesses. Federal tax liens on individuals are filed at the county level, state tax liens are filed at either location. Include the following in your request-debtor name. Item 3b-3d on the UCC11 provide fields for narrowing the search by a specific address, by a date range or by a Social Security or federal tax number

Access by: mail, in person, online.

Fee & Payment: The search fee is $10.00 per debtor name. The copy fee is $1.00 for the first page of the document and $.50 each additional page. There is a certification fee of $5.00 if the state seal is needed. Fee payee: Secretary of State. Prepayment required. Credit cards are only for over-the-counter services. Those conducting business frequently with this office may utilize a prepaid account option. Personal checks accepted. Credit cards accepted: MasterCard, Visa.

Mail search: Records are available by mail.

In person search: There is an additional $6.00 special handling fee for each document received over the counter.

Online search: Direct Access provides dial-up searching via PC and modem. This provides limited search capabilities, it's primarily used to verify filings. The data available contains names and file dates, but not colateral. Fees range from $1-3 dollars, depending on type of search. Each page scroll is $.25. Requesters operate from a prepaid account.

Sales Tax Registrations

Board of Equalization, Sales and Use Tax Department, PO Box 942879, Sacramento, CA 94279-0001; 916-445-6362, 800-400-7115 (In California Only), 916-324-4433 (Fax), 8AM-5PM.

www.boe.ca.gov

Note: A list of the field offices is available at www.boe.ca.gov/info/phone.htm.

Searching: This Board will provide owners' name, firm name, business address, account number, starting date, whether account is active or closed and, if closed, the closing date. The responsibility of assisting taxpayers in verifying the validity of resale certificates is primarily at the District level, but this office will provide search services. Requesters must provide the name of the business, its location, and the permit #.

Access by: mail, phone, fax, online.

Fee & Payment: No charge is required for verification of resale certificates and permits. However, a fee for other requests, such as those received from attorneys and collection agencies, is $3.00 per name searched. Fee payee: Board of Equalization. Prepayment required. Monthly billing is available for ongoing requesters. Personal checks accepted. No credit cards accepted.

Mail search: Turnaround time: 2 weeks. A SASE is requested.

Phone search: No fee for telephone request. The 24 hour phone service is offered to verify a seller's permit is valid. Calls are not limited to number of requests.

Fax search: Generally, turnaround time is 2 weeks.

Online search: The Internet site provides a permit verification service. Permit number is needed. System is open 5AM to midnight.

Other access: Lists, available for a fee, are sorted in a number of ways including CA Industry Code. For further information and fees, call the Technical Services Division at 916-445-5848

Birth Certificates

State Department of Health Svcs, Office of Vital Records - MS 5103, PO Box 997410, Sacramento, CA 95899-7410 (Courier: 1501 Capitol Ave, Rm 71-1110, Sacramento, CA 95814); 916-445-2684 (Recording), 916-445-1719 (Attendant), 8AM-4:30PM.

www.dhs.ca.gov/chs/default.htm

Indexing & Storage: Records are available from July 1905 on. It takes 1 to 3 months before new records are available for inquiry. Records are indexed on microfiche, inhouse computer. Records are normally destroyed after (records kept indefinitely).

Searching: Certified records are not open to the public. Requester must be related to the subject or attorney representing subject or subject's family. However, persons who are not eligible to receive a Certified Copy can receive a Certified Informational Copy. Include the following in your request-full name, mother's full maiden name, date of birth, place of birth, father's full name is optional. Certifed copy must included notarized signature of requester. If you do not use their form, the search may be delayed 2-3 weeks.

Access by: mail.

Fee & Payment: The fee for a certified copy is $15.00, if the birth date is not known, a fee of $15.00 is charged for each decade searched. Fee payee: Office of Vital Records. Prepayment required. Personal checks and money orders accepted. No credit cards accepted.

Mail search: Turnaround time: may exceed 1 month. Always include your daytime phone number. No SASE is required. Download and use the request form at the website.

Expedited service: Expedited service is available for mail searches. Turnaround time: 1-2 days. Add $7.00 per event for express mail delivery service. You may send request by special mail (express, registered, etc.) and mark "Urgent."

Death Records

State Department of Health Svcs, Office of Vital Records - MS 5103, PO Box 997410, Sacramento, CA 95899-7410 (Courier: 1501 Capitol Ave, Rm 71-1110, Sacramento, CA 95814); 916-445-2684, 916-445-1719 (Attendant), 8AM-4:30PM.

www.dhs.ca.gov/chs/default.htm

Indexing & Storage: Records are available from July 1905 to present. It takes 1 to 3 months before new records are available for inquiry. Records are indexed on microfiche, inhouse computer. Records are normally destroyed after (records kept indefinitely).

Searching: Certified records are not open to the public. Requester must be related to the subject or attorney representing subject or subject's family. However, persons who are not eligible to receive a Certified Copy can receive a Certified Informational Copy. Include the following in your request-full name, date of death, date of birth, place of death, Social Security Number. Certifed copy must included notarized signature of requester. There will be a 2-3 week delay if you do not use their form.

Access by: mail, online.

Fee & Payment: Search fee is $13.00 per name for each decade searched. Fee payee: Office of Vital Records. Prepayment required. Personal checks accepted. Will not accept credit cards.

Mail search: Turnaround time: 1 month or more. Download and use the request form at the website.

Online search: No online searching of this agency directly. Death records from 1940-1997 can be accessed   at http://userdb.rootsweb.com/ca/death/search.cgi. The site is maintained by a private entity, but the data is provided but this agency.

Expedited service: Expedited service is available for mail searches Turnaround time: 1-2 days. Add $7.00 per event for express delivery service. Send request by special mail (express, registered, etc.) and mark "Urgent."

Marriage Certificates

State Department of Health Svcs, Office of Vital Records - MS 5103, PO Box 997410, Sacramento, CA 95899-7410 (Courier: 1501 Capitol Ave, Rm 71-1110, Sacramento, CA 95814); 916-445-2684, 916-445-1719 (Attendant), 8AM-4:30PM.

www.dhs.ca.gov/chs/default.htm

Note: Records between 1986 to 1997 and 2000 to present must be searched at the county level; state does not have access to these records.

Indexing & Storage: Records are available from July 1905 to March 1986 and 1998 to 2000. Records are indexed on microfiche and some on inhouse computer.

Searching: Include the following in your request-names of husband and wife, date of marriage, place or county of marriage.

Access by: mail.

Fee & Payment: Search fee is $13.00 per name for each decade searched. Fee payee: Office of Vital Records. Prepayment required. Personal checks & money orders accepted.

Mail search: Turnaround time: 1 month or more. No SASE is required. Download and use the request form at the website.

Expedited service: Expedited service is available for mail searches. Turnaround time: 1-2 days. Add $7.00 per event for express delivery service. Send request by special mail (express, registered, etc.) and mark "Urgent."

Divorce Records

State Department of Health Svcs, Office of Vital Records - MS 5103, PO Box 997410, Sacramento, CA 95899-7410 (Courier: 1501 Capitol Ave, Rm 71-1110, Sacramento, CA 95814); 916-445-2684, 916-445-1719 (Attendant), 8AM-4:30PM.

www.dhs.ca.gov/chs/default.htm

Indexing & Storage: Records are available from 1962 to 1984 for certificate of record only. All divorce records are found at the county court issuing the decree. Records are indexed on microfiche.

Searching: Include the following in your request-names of husband and wife, place of divorce, date of divorce.

Access by: mail.

Fee & Payment: Search fee is $13.00 per name for decade searched. Fee payee: Office of Vital Records. Prepayment required. Personal checks accepted.

Mail search: Turnaround time: 1 month or more. No SASE is required. Download and use the request form at the website.

Expedited service: Expedited service is available for mail searches. Turnaround time: 1-2 days. Add $7.00 per event for express delivery service. Send request by special mail (express, registered, etc.) and mark "Urgent."

Workers' Compensation Records

Division of Workers' Compensation, Headquarters, 455 Golden Gate Ave, 9th Fl, San Francisco, CA 94102; 415-703-4600, 415-703-4717 (Fax), 8AM-5PM.

www.dir.ca.gov/dwc/dwc_home_page.htm

Note: Per law, no addresses of any injured workers are given out. There are 3 claims offices as follows - San Francisco (415-703-4955); Los Angeles (213-576-7300; and Sacramento (916-263-2774).

Indexing & Storage: Records are available for varying periods depending on injury.

Searching: Using the proper forms, one can either view a file or ask if records exist. This authorization process does not require the signature or approval of the claimant. Forms may be faxed. All forms must be obtained from this agency and require approval before a searcher can present a request at the district office.

Access by: mail, fax, in person.

Fee & Payment: There is no search fee.

Mail search: Turnaround time: variable. You must use "Request for WCAB Case # Search Form" and the agency will let you know if there is a record. The state suggests that out-of-state requesters use a local CA retriever who already has the necessary authorization to search. No SASE is required.

Fax search: Turnaround is usually 1 week.

In person search: Requester must be authorized first (by this office) with either the "Request to View a WCAB Case File" or "Request for DWC Authorization # for Access to Index Cards." Then, with a case number, requester can visit any of the 25 district offices.

Driver Records

Department of Motor Vehicles, Information Services Branch, PO Box 944247, Mail Station G199, Sacramento, CA 94244-2470 (Courier: 2415 First Ave, Sacramento, CA 95818); 916-657-8098, 916-657-5564 (Requester Accounts), 8AM-5PM.

www.dmv.ca.gov

Note: The public counter is closed for record access by walk-in requesters. Copies of tickets are not available at the state level.

Indexing & Storage: Records are available for 3 years from accidents and minor moving violations dates and 7 years for major violations. A Failure to Appear is reported for 5 years, and 10 years if for a DUI offense. It takes 10 days or more before new records are available for inquiry. Records are normally destroyed after the Director determines they are no longer necessary to retain.

Searching: Commercial requesters/users who meet certain criteria must maintain a Commercial Requester Account, which may require a $50,000 bond if confidential address information is released. For more information about a Requester Account call (916) 657-5564. Include the following in your request-driver's license number, full name, date of birth. Non-commercial requesters are known as "casual requesters." These requests may be held for 10 days and the state notifies the licensee of each release. If released, address is shielded unless a permissible use shown. The following data is not released: mental health records, medical records, pending records, and Social Security Numbers.

Access by: mail, phone, online.

Fee & Payment: Manual searches are $5.00; electronic MCRS are $2.00; full name and DOB-$4.00; guarantor's signature-$20.00; license status only $1.00 via an approved vendor. Fee payee: California Department of Motor Vehicles. Prepayment required. Personal checks accepted. No credit cards accepted.

Mail search: Turnaround time: 1 to 2 weeks. Individuals mailing any request forms may be subject to a 10 day delay and a notice to subject(s) of the record request.

Phone search: Available, however, records are only released to the subject. Call 916-657-6525.

Online search: The department offers online access, but a $10,000 one-time setup fee is required. The fee is $2.00 per record. The system is available 24 hours, 7 days a week. For more information call 916-657-5582.

Other access: Employers may monitor their drivers in the Pull Notice Program. The DMV informs the organization when there is activity on enrolled drivers. Call 916-657-6346 for details.

Vehicle Ownership and Identification, Vessel Ownership and Registration

Department of Motor Vehicle, Office of Information Services, PO Box 944247, MS-G199, Sacramento, CA 94244-2470 (Courier: 2415 First Ave, Sacramento, CA 95818); 916-657-8098, 916-657-5564 (Commercial Accounts), 916-657-6893 (Vessel Registration), 8AM-5PM.

www.dmv.ca.gov

Note: All watercraft must be registered if over 8 ft (except rowboats).

Indexing & Storage: Records are available for thirtteen years when microfilmed.

Searching: It is suggested to use departmental forms, which can be obtained from the Public Contact Unit at the address above or fax request to 916-657-7243. There are two types of requesters: "casual requesters" and "requester account holders." For those businesses and entities who need to access on a regular basis, call 916-657-5564. A bond may be required.

Access by: mail, online.

Fee & Payment: Current record by license, VIN or CF#, by registration owner name and address-$5.00; magnetic tape inquiry-$2.00; owner as of data by license, VIN or CF#-$5.00; current automated history data-$5.00; photocopies-$20.00 per year. Fee payee: California Department of Motor Vehicles. Prepayment required. Personal checks accepted. No credit cards accepted.

Mail search: Turnaround time: 1 to 2 weeks. A SASE is requested.

Online search: 24 hour online access is limited to certain Authorized Vendors. Requesters are may not use the data for direct marketing, solicitation, nor resell for those purposes. A bond is required and very high fees are involved. For more information, call the Electronic Access Administration Section at 916-657-5582.

Other access: California offers delivery of registration information on magnetic tape, disk or paper within special parameters. Release of information is denied for commercial marketing purposes.

Accident Reports

Department of Motor Vehicles, Accident Reports, PO Box 942884, Sacramento, CA 94284, 916-675-5651 (Fax), 8AM-5PM (open at 9AM of F).

www.dmv.ca.gov

Note: Most accident reports are held by the California Highway Patrol or local law enforcement agency that filed the report. There are

115 area offices of the California Highway Patrol. Fees vary. Limited reports are held by this office.

Indexing & Storage: It takes 30 to 60 days before new records are available for inquiry. Records are normally destroyed after 4 years.

Searching: Reports are made if there was property damage of more than $750 ($500 for accidents prior to January 1, 2003). Include the following in your request-name and DOB of driver, location, date, and name of requester. Copies of SR-1 accident reports are provided to limited requesters by the Department of Motor Vehicles.

Access by: mail.

Fee & Payment: The fee is $20.00.

Mail search: SR-1 accident reports are available by mail from this office.

Voter Registration
Access to Records is Restricted

Secretary of State, Elections Division, 1500 11th Street, Sacramento, CA 95814; 916-657-2166, 916-653-3214 (Fax), 8AM-5PM.

Note: Records are not open and cannot be viewed at this agency. Individual verification must be done at the local level. The state will sell CDs with all or portions of the statewide database for political or pre-approved purposes. Call for details.

GED Certificates

Dept of Education, State GED Office, 1430 N st Suite 5408, Sacramento, CA 94244-0273; 916-445-8049, 800-331-6316, 8AM-5PM.

www.cde.ca.gov/ta/tg/gd/

Indexing & Storage: Records are available from July 1990, prior are archived. It takes 2 months before new records are available for inquiry.

Searching: To verify or to obtain a copy of a transcript, all of the following is required: a signed release, name, date of birth, date/year of test, SSN, and city of test.

Access by: mail.

Fee & Payment: There is no fee for verifications. Score reports are provided without charge; there is a $12 fee (money order only) for duplicate certificates. Fee payee: Ca Dept of Ed Prepayment required. Personal checks not accepted.

Mail search: Turnaround time is 7-10 working days or 2-3 weeks if the information is older than 1990. No SASE is required.

Hunting and Fishing License Information
Access to Records is Restricted

Department of Fish & Game, License & Revenue Branch, 3211 "S" St, Sacramento, CA 95816; 916-227-2245, 916-227-2261 (Fax), 9AM-5PM.

www.dfg.ca.gov

Note: Records are not available to the public.

California State Licensing Agencies
Licenses Searchable Online

Acupuncturist #1 .... www.acupuncture.ca.gov
Administrative Services #26 .... www.ctc.ca.gov/credentialinfo/credinfo.html
Adoption Agency #50 .... www.ccld.ca.gov/docs/ccld_search/ccld_search.aspx
Air Conditioning Contractor #28 .... http://www2.cslb.ca.gov/CSLB_LIBRARY/Name+Request.asp
Alarm Company/Employee/Mgr. #22 .... www.dca.ca.gov/bsis/lookup.htm
Apprentice Program #53 .... www.dir.ca.gov/databases/das/aigstart.asp
Architect #7 .... www.cab.ca.gov/querylic.htm
Asbestos Consultant/Surveillance #52 .... www.dir.ca.gov/databases/doshcaccsst/caccsst_query_1.html
Asbestos Contractor #52 .... www.dir.ca.gov/databases/doshacru/acrusearch.html
Asbestos Trainer #52 .... www.dir.ca.gov/databases/doshcaccsst/aheratp.asp
Asbestos Worker/Trainee #52 .... www.dir.ca.gov/DOSH/ACRU/TP_AsbestosTrainingCertificates.html
Athletic Event Mgr/Promoter/Matchmaker #3 .... www.dca.ca.gov/csac/directories.htm
Attorney #23 .... http://members.calbar.ca.gov/search/member.aspx
Audiologist #42 .... www.slpab.ca.gov/
Automobile Dealer/Repair #19 .... www.smogcheck.ca.gov/stdPage.asp?Body=/Consumer/verify_a_license.htm
Bank #11 .... www.dfi.ca.gov/directry/tl.asp
Bar Association #23 .... www.calsb.org/rm/brelsch.htm
Barber Instructor/School #4 .... www.barbercosmo.ca.gov/license.htm
Barber Shop/Barber/Barber Apprentice #4 .... www.barbercosmo.ca.gov/license.htm
Baton Training Facility/Instructor #22 .... www.dca.ca.gov/bsis/lookup.htm
Boxer #3 .... www.dca.ca.gov/csac/directories.htm
Brake & Lamp Adjuster #19 .... www.smogcheck.ca.gov/stdPage.asp?Body=/Consumer/verify_a_license.htm
Brake Station #19 .... www.smogcheck.ca.gov/stdPage.asp?Body=/Consumer/verify_a_license.htm
Building Contractor, General-Class B #28 .... http://www2.cslb.ca.gov/CSLB_LIBRARY/Name+Request.asp
Business/Industrial Dev. Company #11 .... www.dfi.ca.gov/directry/bidco.asp
Cabinet/Millwork Contractor #28 .... http://www2.cslb.ca.gov/CSLB_LIBRARY/Name+Request.asp
Care Facility for Children, Transitional #50 .... www.ccld.ca.gov/docs/ccld_search/ccld_search.aspx
Care Facility for Chronically Ill #50 .... www.ccld.ca.gov/docs/ccld_search/ccld_search.aspx
Cemetery, Cemetery Broker/Sales Agent #25 .... www.cfb.ca.gov/lookup.htm
Child Care Center #50 .... www.ccld.ca.gov/docs/ccld_search/ccld_search.aspx
Chiropractic Business #46 .... www.chiro.ca.gov/licsearch/
Chiropractor #46 .... www.chiro.ca.gov/licsearch/
Clinic Pharmaceutical Permit #13 .... www.pharmacy.ca.gov/license_lookup.htm
Community Treatment Facility #50 .... www.ccld.ca.gov/docs/ccld_search/ccld_search.aspx
Concrete Contractor/Company #28 .... http://www2.cslb.ca.gov/CSLB_LIBRARY/Name+Request.asp
Conscious Sedation Permit #9 .... www.dbc.ca.gov/license_verification.html
Continuing Education Provider #8 .... www.bbs.ca.gov/weblokup.htm
Contractor, Busi./Individual #28 .... www.cslb.ca.gov
Cosmetician/Cosmetologist #4 .... www.barbercosmo.ca.gov/license.htm
Cosmetology School #4 .... www.dca.ca.gov/barber/schools_list.pdf
Cosmetology/Electrology Business/Instructor #4 .... www.barbercosmo.ca.gov/license.htm
Court Reporter (Shorthand Reporter) #29 .... www.courtreportersboard.ca.gov
CPA/CPA Firm #6 .... www.dca.ca.gov/cba/lookup.htm
Crane Operator #52 .... www.dir.ca.gov/databases/crane/cranesearch.html
Credit Union #11 .... www.dfi.ca.gov/directry/cu.asp
Cremated Remains Disposer #25 .... www.cfb.ca.gov/lookup.htm
Crematory #25 .... www.cfb.ca.gov/lookup.htm
Day Care, Adult/Child #50 .... www.ccld.ca.gov/docs/ccld_search/ccld_search.aspx
Dental Anesthesia Permit #9 .... www.dbc.ca.gov/license_verification.html
Dental Assistant #27 .... www.comda.ca.gov/licensestatus.html
Dental Assistant, Extended Function #27 .... www.comda.ca.gov/licensestatus.html
Dental Hygienist #27 .... www.comda.ca.gov/licensestatus.html
Dental Registered Provider #9 .... www.dbc.ca.gov/license_verification.html
Dentist #9 .... www.dbc.ca.gov/license_verification.html
Dentist Fictitious Name #9 .... www.dbc.ca.gov/license_verification.html
Development Corporation #11 .... www.dfi.ca.gov/directry/directry.asp
Driving School #49 .... http://eg.dmv.ca.gov/olinq/Welcome.jsp
Drug Wholesaler/Drug Room #13 .... www.pharmacy.ca.gov/license_lookup.htm
Drywall Contractor #28 .... http://www2.cslb.ca.gov/CSLB_LIBRARY/Name+Request.asp

Earthwork/Paving Contractor #28 ....http://www2.cslb.ca.gov/CSLB_LIBRARY/Name+Request.asp
Electrical (General) & Electric Sign Contr. #28...........http://www2.cslb.ca.gov/CSLB_LIBRARY/Name+Request.asp
Electrologist #4 ....www.barbercosmo.ca.gov/license.htm
Electrology School #4 ....www.dca.ca.gov/barber/schools_list.pdf
Electronics & Appliance Repair #20 ....www.bear.ca.gov/look-up.htm
Elevator Installation Contractor #28.........................http://www2.cslb.ca.gov/CSLB_LIBRARY/Name+Request.asp
Embalmer/Embalmer Apprentice #25.......................www.cfb.ca.gov/lookup.htm
Engineer (various disciplines) #10............................www.dca.ca.gov/pels/l_lookup.htm
Esthetician #4 ....www.barbercosmo.ca.gov/license.htm
Family Child Care Home #50 ....www.ccld.ca.gov/docs/ccld_search/ccld_search.aspx
Farm Labor Contractor #53 ....www.dir.ca.gov/databases/dlselr/Farmlic.html
Fencing Contractor #28 ....http://www2.cslb.ca.gov/CSLB_LIBRARY/Name+Request.asp
Firearm Permit #22 ....www.dca.ca.gov/bsis/lookup.htm
Firearm Training Facility/Instructor #22 ....www.dca.ca.gov/bsis/lookup.htm
Flooring/Floor Covering Contractor #28 ....http://www2.cslb.ca.gov/CSLB_LIBRARY/Name+Request.asp
Foster Family Agency #50 ....www.ccld.ca.gov/docs/ccld_search/ccld_search.aspx
Fumigation #44 ....www.cdpr.ca.gov/docs/license/currlic.htm
Funeral Director/Establishment #25 ....www.cfb.ca.gov/lookup.htm
Funerary Training Establishment/Apprentice #25 ......www.cfb.ca.gov/lookup.htm
Garment Mfg #53..www.dir.ca.gov/databases/dlselr/Garmreg.html
Geologist #18...www.dca.ca.gov/geology/
Geologist, Engineering #18 ....www.dca.ca.gov/geology/
Geophysicist #18..www.dca.ca.gov/geology/
Glazier #28 ....http://www2.cslb.ca.gov/CSLB_LIBRARY/Name+Request.asp
Group Home #50 ....www.ccld.ca.gov/docs/ccld_search/ccld_search.aspx
Healing Art Supervisor #31 ....www.dhs.ca.gov/applications/search/search.asp
Hearing Aid Dispenser #34 ....www.dca.ca.gov/hearingaid/
Heating & Warm-Air Vent. Contractor #28 ....http://www2.cslb.ca.gov/CSLB_LIBRARY/Name+Request.asp
Home Furnishings #21 ... ... http://www2.dca.ca.gov/pls/wllpub/wllqryna$lcev2.startup?p_qte_code=LIC&p_qte_pgm_code=5710
Horse Racing Entity #24 ....www.chrb.ca.gov/license_search.htm
Horse Racing Occupation #24...................................www.chrb.ca.gov/license_search.htm
Hospital Pharmaceutical Exemptee #13....................www.pharmacy.ca.gov/license_lookup.htm
Hydrogeologist #18...www.dca.ca.gov/geology/
Hypodermic Needle & Syringe Dist. #13 ....www.pharmacy.ca.gov/license_lookup.htm
Industrial Loan Company, Premium #11 ....www.dfi.ca.gov/directry/tl.asp
Infant Center #50..www.ccld.ca.gov/docs/ccld_search/ccld_search.aspx
Insulation/Accoustical Contractor #28 ....http://www2.cslb.ca.gov/CSLB_LIBRARY/Name+Request.asp
Insurance Adjuster #32..www.insurance.ca.gov/docs/FS-Licensestatus.htm
Insurance Agent/Broker #32.....................................www.insurance.ca.gov/docs/FS-Licensestatus.htm
Insurance Company #32...www.insurance.ca.gov/docs/insurer.htm
Lamp Station #19..www.smogcheck.ca.gov/stdPage.asp?Body=/Consumer/verify_a_license.htm
Landscape Architect #35 ....www.latc.dca.ca.gov/licenseeinfo/search.htm
Landscaping Contractor #28.....................................http://www2.cslb.ca.gov/CSLB_LIBRARY/Name+Request.asp
Legal Specialist #23..www.calsb.org/ls/lscounty.htm
Legal Specialization Provider #23 ....http://members.calbar.ca.gov/search/cert.aspx
Lobbyist #47 ....http://cal-access.ss.ca.gov/Lobbying/
Locksmith/Locksmith Company #22 ....www.dca.ca.gov/bsis/lookup.htm
Mammographic Facility #31......................................www.dhs.ca.gov/applications/search/search.asp
Manicurist #4 ....www.barbercosmo.ca.gov/license.htm
Marriage & Family Therapist #8................................www.bbs.ca.gov/weblokup.htm
Masonry Contractor #28 ....http://www2.cslb.ca.gov/CSLB_LIBRARY/Name+Request.asp
Medical Doctor/Surgeon #36 ... ... http://www2.dca.ca.gov/pls/wllpub/wllqryna$lcev2.startup?p_qte_code=MDX&p_qte_pgm_code=6301
Medical Evaluator #52...www.dir.ca.gov/databases/imc/imcstartnew.asp
Midwife #36 ... ... http://www2.dca.ca.gov/pls/wllpub/wllqryna$lcev2.startup?p_qte_code=LM&p_qte_pgm_code=6200
Money Orders Issuer #11...www.dfi.ca.gov/directry/pi.asp
Nuclear Medicine Technologist #31...........................www.dhs.ca.gov/applications/search/search.asp
Nurse #16 ....www.rn.ca.gov/online/online.htm
Nursing Continuing Edu. Provider #16 ....www.rn.ca.gov/online/online.htm
Occupational Therapist/Thera. Asst. #51 ... ...
http://www2.dca.ca.gov/pls/wllpub/wllqryna$lcev2.startup?p_qte_code=OT&p_qte_pgm_code=1475
Optometrist #12..www.optometry.ca.gov/search.asp
Optometry Practice/Branch Office #12 ....www.optometry.ca.gov/search.asp
Ornamental Metal Contractor #28 ....http://www2.cslb.ca.gov/CSLB_LIBRARY/Name+Request.asp
Osteopath #36 ....www.docboard.org/cx/
Painting/Decorating Contractor #28..........................http://www2.cslb.ca.gov/CSLB_LIBRARY/Name+Request.asp

Parking/Highway Improvement Contr. #28 ....http://www2.cslb.ca.gov/CSLB_LIBRARY/Name+Request.asp
Patrol Operator, Private #22 ....www.dca.ca.gov/bsis/lookup.htm
Payment Instrument Issuer #11 ....www.dfi.ca.gov/directry/directry.asp
Pest Control Field Rep./Operator #44 ....www.cdpr.ca.gov/docs/license/currlic.htm
Pesticide Applicator #44 ....www.cdpr.ca.gov/docs/license/currlic.htm
Pharmaceutical Dist., Out-of-State #13 ....www.pharmacy.ca.gov/license_lookup.htm
Pharmaceutical Whlse./Exemptee #13.......................www.pharmacy.ca.gov/license_lookup.htm
Pharmacist/Pharmacist Intern #13 ....www.pharmacy.ca.gov/license_lookup.htm
Pharmacy #13...www.pharmacy.ca.gov/license_lookup.htm
Pharmacy Technician #13 ....www.pharmacy.ca.gov/license_lookup.htm
Pharmacy, Non-resident #13 ....www.pharmacy.ca.gov/license_lookup.htm
Physical Therapist/Assistant #38 ... http://www2.dca.ca.gov/pls/wllpub/wllqryna$lcev2.startup?p_qte_code=PT&p_qte_pgm_code=6800
Physician Assistant #39 ... ... http://www2.dca.ca.gov/pls/wllpub/wllqryna$lcev2.startup?p_qte_code=PA&p_qte_pgm_code=7000
Plastering Contractor #28 ....http://www2.cslb.ca.gov/CSLB_LIBRARY/Name+Request.asp
Plumber #28 ....http://www2.cslb.ca.gov/CSLB_LIBRARY/Name+Request.asp
Podiatrist #14..www.bpm.ca.gov
Polygraph Examiner #48 ....www.californiapolygraph.com/members/roster.htm
Polygraph Examiner of Sex Offenders #48 ....www.californiapolygraph.com/members/roster.htm
Premium Finance Company #11 ....www.dfi.ca.gov/directry/pf.asp
Private Investigator #22 ....www.dca.ca.gov/bsis/lookup.htm
Psychiatric Technician #17 ....www.bvnpt.ca.gov/licverif.htm
Psychological Assistant #15 ....www.psychboard.ca.gov
Psychologist #15..www.psychboard.ca.gov
Psychologist, Educational #8....................................www.bbs.ca.gov/weblokup.htm
Psychologist, Registered #15 ....www.psychboard.ca.gov/
Public Accountant-CPA #6 ....www.dca.ca.gov/cba/lookup.htm
Public Works Trainer #53 ....www.dir.ca.gov/databases/das/pwaddrstart.asp
Radioactive Material Licensee #31...........................www.dhs.ca.gov/applications/search/search.asp
Radiologic Technologist #31......................................www.dhs.ca.gov/applications/search/search.asp
Real Estate Agent/Sales #33....................................www.dre.ca.gov/licstats.htm
Real Estate Broker/Corporation #33.........................www.dre.ca.gov/licstats.htm
Refrigeration Contractor #28 ....http://www2.cslb.ca.gov/CSLB_LIBRARY/Name+Request.asp
Registered Veterinary Technicians #40.....................www.vmb.ca.gov/lic1list.htm
Repossessor Agency/Mgr./Employee #22 ....www.dca.ca.gov/bsis/lookup.htm
Residential Care for Elderly #50 ....www.ccld.ca.gov/docs/ccld_search/ccld_search.aspx
Residential Facility, Adult #50 ....www.ccld.ca.gov/docs/ccld_search/ccld_search.aspx
Respiratory Care Practitioner #41 ....www.rcb.ca.gov/license_verification_forms_instructions.htm
Roofing Contractor #28 ....http://www2.cslb.ca.gov/CSLB_LIBRARY/Name+Request.asp
Sanitation System Contractor #28.............................http://www2.cslb.ca.gov/CSLB_LIBRARY/Name+Request.asp
Security Guard #22 ....www.dca.ca.gov/bsis/lookup.htm
Service Contract Seller (Appliance) #20...................www.bear.ca.gov/look-up.htm
Sheet Metal Contractor #28.......................................http://www2.cslb.ca.gov/CSLB_LIBRARY/Name+Request.asp
Shelter, Temporary #50 ....www.ccld.ca.gov/docs/ccld_search/ccld_search.aspx
Smog Check Station/Technician #19.........................www.smogcheck.ca.gov/stdPage.asp?Body=/Consumer/verify_a_license.htm
Social Rehabilitation Facility #50 ....www.ccld.ca.gov/docs/ccld_search/ccld_search.aspx
Social Worker, Clinical #8...www.bbs.ca.gov/weblokup.htm
Social Worker, Clinical Associate #8 ....www.bbs.ca.gov/weblokup.htm
Solar Energy Contractor #28 ....http://www2.cslb.ca.gov/CSLB_LIBRARY/Name+Request.asp
Specialty Contractor-Class C #28.............................http://www2.cslb.ca.gov/CSLB_LIBRARY/Name+Request.asp
Speech Pathologist/Audiologist Aide #42..................www.slpab.ca.gov
Speech Pathology Assistant #42...............................www.slpab.ca.gov
Speech-Language Pathologist #42............................www.slpab.ca.gov
Steel Contractor, Reinforcing/Structural #28 ....http://www2.cslb.ca.gov/CSLB_LIBRARY/Name+Request.asp
Studio Teacher #53 ....www.dir.ca.gov/databases/dlselr/StudTch.html
Support Center, Adult #50 ....www.ccld.ca.gov/docs/ccld_search/ccld_search.aspx
Surgical Clinic Pharm., Nonprofit #13.......................www.pharmacy.ca.gov/license_lookup.htm
Surveyor, Land #10 ....www.dca.ca.gov/pels/l_lookup.htm
Swimming Pool Contractor #28 ....http://www2.cslb.ca.gov/CSLB_LIBRARY/Name+Request.asp
Talent Agency #53..www.dir.ca.gov/databases/dlselr/Talag.html
Tax Education Provider #45 ....www.ctec.org/internal.asp?pid=8
Tax Preparer #45...www.ctec.org/verify.asp
Termite Control #44 ....www.cdpr.ca.gov/docs/license/currlic.htm
Thrift & Loan Company #11..www.dfi.ca.gov/directry/directry.asp
Tile Contractor, Ceramic/Mosaic #28 ....http://www2.cslb.ca.gov/CSLB_LIBRARY/Name+Request.asp
Trainer, Public Works #53 ....www.dir.ca.gov/databases/das/pwaddrstart.asp

Travelers Checks Issuer #11 ....www.dfi.ca.gov/directry/tc.asp
Trust Company #11 ....www.dfi.ca.gov/directry/trust.asp
Veterinarian #40 ....www.vmb.ca.gov/lic1list.htm
Veterinary Food/Animal Drug Retailer #13 ....www.pharmacy.ca.gov/license_lookup.htm
Veterinary Premises #40 ....www.vmb.ca.gov/lic1list.htm
Vocational Nurse #17 ....www.bvnpt.ca.gov/licverif.htm
Water Well Driller #28 ....http://www2.cslb.ca.gov/CSLB_LIBRARY/Name+Request.asp
X-ray Machine Registration #31 ....www.dhs.ca.gov/applications/search/search.asp
X-ray Technician #31 ....www.dhs.ca.gov/applications/search/search.asp

California Licensing Quick Finder

Acupuncturist #1 916-263-2680
Administrative Services #26 916-445-7254
Adoption Agency #50 916-274-6200
Agricultural Engineer #10 916-263-2222
Air Conditioning Contractor #28 916-255-3985
Alarm Company/Employee/Mgr. #22 ...800-952-5210
Announcer, Athletic Event (Ring) #3 916-263-2195
Apprentice Program #53........................415-703-5100
Arbitrator, Consumer (Lemon Law)
Auto Mfg. Arbitration Program #2.........916-323-3406
Architect #7...916-445-3394
Asbestos Consultant/Surveillance #52..415-703-5100
Asbestos Contractor #52 415-703-5100
Asbestos Trainer #52 415-703-5100
Asbestos Worker/Trainee #52.............415-703-5100
Athletic Event Box Office Employee/Ticket Seller #3
....916-263-2195
Athletic Event Mgr/Promoter/Matchmaker #3
....916-263-2195
Athletic Event-related Occupation #3...916-263-2195
Athletic Gym #3 916-263-2195
Athletic Trainer/Second #3 916-263-2195
Attorney #23 415-538-2577
Audiologist #42 916-263-2666
Automobile Dealer/Repair #19 916-322-4010
Bank #11...800-622-0620
Bar Association #23.............................415-538-2577
Barber Instructor/School #4 916-445-7061
Barber Shop/Barber/Barber Appren. #4 916-445-7061
Baton Training Facility/Instructor #22...800-952-5210
Bedding Mfg./Renovator/Retailer/Whlse. #21
....800-952-5210
Boiler, Hot Water & Steam Fitting #28 .916-255-3985
Boxer #3..916-263-2195
Boxing Second #3................................916-263-2195
Brake & Lamp Adjuster #19..................916-322-4010
Brake Station #19 916-322-4010
Building Contr., General-Class B #28 ..916-255-3985
Building Moving/Demolition #28 916-255-3985
Business/Industrial Dev. Company #11800-622-0620,
916-323-0189
Cabinet/Millwork Contractor #28 916-255-3985
Care Facility for Children, Transitional #50
....916-274-6200
Care Facility for Chronically Ill #50.......916-274-6200
Cemetery, Cemetery Broker/Sales Agent #25
....916-322-7737
Child Care Center #50..........................916-274-6200
Chiropractic Business #46....................916-263-5355
Chiropractor #46.................................916-263-5355
Clinic Pharmaceutical Permit #13 916-445-5014
Clinical Nurse Specialist #16
...................................800-838-6828 L, 916-322-3350
Community Treatment Facility #50........916-274-6200
Concrete Contractor/Company #28.......916-255-3985
Conscious Sedation Permit #9 916-263-2300
Continuing Education Provider #8.........916-445-4933
Contractor, Busi./Individual #28 800-321-2752
Cosmetician/Cosmetologist #4 916-445-7061
Cosmetology School #4........................916-445-7061
Cosmetology/Electrology Business/Instructor #4
....916-445-7061

Court Reporter (Shorthand Reporter) #29
....916-263-3660
CPA/CPA Firm #6..................................916-263-3680
Crane Operator #52 415-703-5100
Credit Union #11...................................800-622-0620
Cremated Remains Disposer #25 916-322-7737
Crematory #25......................................916-322-7737
Day Care, Adult/Child #50....................916-274-6200
Dental Anesthesia Permit #9................916-263-2300
Dental Assistant #27 916-263-2595
Dental Assistant, Exten'd Function #27 916-263-2595
Dental Hygienist #27 916-263-2595
Dental Registered Provider #9 916-263-2300
Dentist #9 916-263-2300
Dentist Fictitious Name #9 916-263-2300
Development Corporation #11
..................................800-622-0620, 916-323-0189
Driving School #49 916-657-6077
Drug Wholesaler/Drug Room #13 916-445-5014
Dry Cleaning Plant #21 916-574-0280
Drywall Contractor #28.........................916-255-3985
Earthwork/Paving Contractor #28 916-255-3985
Electrical (General) & Electric Sign Contr. #28
....916-255-3985
Electrologist #4 916-445-7061
Electrology School #4...........................916-445-7061
Electroneuromyographer #38.................916-263-2550
Electronics & Appliance Repair #20.....916-574-2069
Elementary School Teacher #26...........916-445-7254
Elevator Installation Contr. #28 916-255-3985
Embalmer/Embalmer Apprentice #25 ..916-322-7737
Engineer (various disciplines) #10 916-263-2222
Esthetician #4 916-445-7061
Family Child Care Home #50 916-274-6200
Farm Labor Contractor #53..................415-703-4854
Fencing Contractor #28........................916-255-3985
Fire Protection #28 916-255-3985
Firearm Permit #22...............................800-952-5210
Firearm Training Facility/Instr. #22......800-952-5210
Flooring/Floor Covering Contr. #28.......916-255-3985
Foster Family Agency #50....................916-274-6200
Fumigation #44....................................916-263-2540
Fundraiser to Establish Training School #43
....916-324-9328
Funeral Director/Establishment #25.....916-322-7737
Funerary Training Establishment/Apprentice #25
....916-322-7737
Furniture & Bedding Retailer #21.........916-574-0280
Furniture Mfg./Retailer/Whlse. #21 916-574-0280
Garment Mfg #53.................................415-703-4848
Geologist #18 916-263-2113
Geologist, Engineering #18..................916-263-2113
Geophysicist #18..................................916-263-2113
Glazier #28 916-255-3985
Group Home #50 916-274-6200
Healing Art Supervisor #31 916-445-6430
Hearing Aid Dispenser #34 916-263-2288
Heating & Warm-Air Vent. Contr. #28 ..916-255-3985
Home Furnishings #21..........................916-574-0280
Home Improvement Salesperson #28..800-321-2752
Horse Racing Entity #24......................916-263-6000
Horse Racing Occupation #24 916-263-6000
Hospital Pharmaceutical Exemptee #13916-445-5014

Hydrogeologist #18 916-263-2113
Hypodermic Needle & Syringe Dist. #13916-445-5014
Industrial Loan Company, Premium #11
...................................800-622-0620, 916-323-0189
Infant Center #50.................................916-274-6200
Insulation/Accoustical Contr. #28.........916-255-3985
Insurance Adjuster #32 916-322-3555
Insurance Agent/Broker #32 916-322-3555
Insurance Company #32.......................916-322-3555
Investment Advisors #30......................916-445-3062
Kickboxer, Amateur #3.........................916-263-2195
Kickboxer/Full Contact Karate #3 916-263-2195
Kinesiological Electromyographer #38..916-263-2550
Lamp Station #19 916-322-4010
Landscape Architect #35......................916-445-4954
Landscaping Contractor #28 916-255-3985
Lathing Contractor #28.........................916-255-3985
Legal Specialist #23............................415-538-2577
Legal Specialization Provider #23........415-538-2577
Lobbyist #47..916-653-6224
Locksmith/Locksmith Company #22 800-952-5210
Mammographic Facility #31 916-323-2772
Manicurist #4 916-445-7061
Manufactured Housing Contractor #28. 916-255-3985
Marriage & Family Therapist #8...........916-445-4933
Masonry Contractor #28.......................916-255-3985
Medical Doctor/Surgeon #36................916-263-2635
Medical Evaluator #52..........................415-703-5100
Midwife #36 916-263-2393
Midwife Nurse #16.....800-838-6828 L, 916-322-3350
Money Orders Issuer #11
...................................800-622-0620, 916-323-0189
Notary Public #37................................916-653-3595
Nuclear Medicine Technologist #31.....916-445-8820
Nurse #16.............800-838-6828 L, 916-322-3350
Nurse Anesthetist #16800-838-6828 L, 916-322-3350
Nursing Continuing Edu. Provider #16
...................................800-838-6828 L, 916-322-3350
Nursing Home Administrator #5...916-916-552-8780
Occupational Therapist #51 916-322-3394
Occupational Therapist Assistant #51 .916-322-3394
Optician, Dispensing #36 916-263-2634
Optometric Corporation #12.................916-323-8720
Optometrist #12...................................916-323-8720
Optometrist Diagnostic/Pharmaceutical #12
....916-323-8720
Optometry Practice/Branch Office #12 . 916-323-8720
Ornamental Metal Contractor #28........916-255-3985
Osteopath #36.....................................916-263-3100
Painting/Decorating Contractor #28.....916-255-3985
Parking/Highway Improvement Contr. #28
....916-255-3985
Patrol Operator, Private #22 800-952-5210
Payment Instrument Issuer #11
...................................800-622-0620, 916-323-0189
Pest Control Field Rep./Operator #44.. 916-263-2540
Pesticide Applicator #44.......................916-263-2540
Pharmaceutical Dist., Out-of-State #13 916-445-5014
Pharmaceutical Whlse./Exemptee #13. 916-445-5014
Pharmacist/Pharmacist Intern #13.......916-445-5014
Pharmacy #13 916-445-5014
Pharmacy Technician #13.....................916-445-5014
Pharmacy, Non-resident #13 916-445-5014

Photogrammetrist #10 916-263-2222
Physical Therapist/Assistant #38 916-263-2550
Physician Assistant #39 916-263-2670
Pipeline Contractor #28 916-255-3985
Plastering Contractor #28 916-255-3985
Plumber #28 916-255-3985
Podiatrist #14 916-263-2382
Polygraph Examiner #48 800-593-8598
Polygraph Examiner of Sex Offenders #48
.... 800-593-8598
Premium Finance Company #11
.... 800-622-0620, 916-323-0189
Private Investigator #22 800-952-5210
Psychiatric Mental Health Nurse #16
.... 800-838-6828 L, 916-322-3350
Psychiatric Technician #17 916-263-7800
Psychoanalyst, Research #36 916-263-2370
Psychological Assistant #15 916-263-2699
Psychologist #15 916-263-2699
Psychologist, Educational #8 916-445-4933
Psychologist, Registered #15 916-263-2699
Public Accountant-CPA #6 916-263-3680
Public Health Nurse #16
.... 800-838-6828 L, 916-322-3350
Public Works Trainer #53 415-703-5100
Radioactive Material Licensee #31 916-445-0931
Radiologic Technologist #31 916-445-8820
Real Estate Agent/Sales #33 916-227-0931
Real Estate Broker/Corporation #33 916-227-0931

Refrigeration Contractor #28 916-255-3985
Registered Veterinary Tech. #40 916-263-2613
Repossessor Agency/Mgr./Employee #22
.... 800-952-5210
Residential Care for Elderly #50 916-274-6200
Residential Facility, Adult #50 916-274-6200
Respiratory Care Practitioner #41 916-323-9983
Roofing Contractor #28 916-255-3985
Sanitation System Contractor #28 916-255-3985
Sanitizer of Home Furnishings #21 916-574-0280
Savings & Loan Association #11
.... 800-622-0620, 916-323-0189
Secondary School Teacher #26 916-445-7254
Securities Broker/Dealer #30 916-445-3062
Security Guard #22 800-952-5210
Service Contract Seller, Appliance #20. 916-574-2069
Sheet Metal Contractor #28 916-255-3985
Shelter, Temporary #50 916-274-6200
Smog Check Station/Technician #19 ... 916-322-4010
Social Rehabilitation Facility #50 916-274-6200
Social Worker, Clinical #8 916-445-4933
Social Worker, Clinical Associate #8.... 916-445-4933
Solar Energy Contractor #28 916-255-3985
Sparring Permit #3 916-263-2195
Specialty Contractor-Class C #28 916-255-3985
Specialty Sublicenses, Limited #28 916-255-3985
Speech Pathologist/Audiologist Aide #42
.... 916-263-2666
Speech Pathology Assistant #42 916-263-2666

Speech-Language Pathologist #42 916-263-2666
Steel Contractor #28 916-255-3985
Studio Teacher #53 415-703-4854
Support Center, Adult #50 916-274-6200
Surgical Clinic Pharm., Nonprofit #13.. 916-445-5014
Surveyor, Land #10 916-263-2222
Surveyor-in-Training #10 916-263-2222
Swimming Pool Contractor #28 916-255-3985
Talent Agency #53 415-703-4846
Tax Education Provider #45 916-492-0457
Tax Interviewer #45 916-492-0457
Tax Preparer #45 916-492-0457
Termite Control #44 916-263-2540
Thermal Insulation Manufacturer #21 .. 916-574-0280
Thrift & Loan #11 .... 800-622-0620, 916-323-0189
Tile Contractor, Ceramic/Mosaic #28... 916-255-3985
Trainer, Public Works #53 415-703-5100
Travelers Checks Issuer #11
.... 800-622-0620, 916-323-0189
Trust Company #11 ...... 800-622-0620, 916-323-0189
Upholsterer, Custom #21 800-952-5210
Veterinarian #40 916-263-2610
Veterinary Food/Animal Drug Retailer #13
.... 916-445-5014
Veterinary Premises #40 916-263-2610
Vocational Nurse #17 916-263-7800
Water Well Driller #28 916-255-3985
X-ray Machine Registration #31 916-445-0931
X-ray Technician #31 916-323-2775

California Licensing Agency Information

1 Acupuncture Board, 444 N. 3rd Street, #260, Sacramento, CA 95825-3233; 916-445-3021, Fax: 916-263-3015. www.acupuncture.ca.gov Search Database at www.acupuncture.ca.gov

2 Arbitration Certification Program, 401 S St #201, Sacramento, CA 95814; 916-323-3406, Fax: 916-323-3968. www.dca.ca.gov/acp/arbprocess.htm Email: acp@dca.ca.gov

3 Athletic Commission, 1424 Howe Ave, #33, Sacramento, CA 95825; 916-263-2195, Fax: 916-263-2197. www.dca.ca.gov/csac/ Search Database at www.dca.ca.gov/csac/directories.htm

4 Board of Barbering & Cosmetology, 400 R St, #5100 (PO Box 944226), Sacramento, CA 95814-6200; 916-445-1254, Fax: 916-323-5037. www.barbercosmo.ca.gov Email: barbercosmo@dca.ca.gov Search Database at www.barbercosmo.ca.gov/license.htm Note: 800-952-5210 is number when calling in-state.

5 Nursing Home Administrator Program, PO Box 942732 (1800 3rd St #162), Sacramento, CA 95234-7320; 916-552-8780, Fax: 916-552-8777. www.dhs.ca.gov Email: nhap@dhs.ca.gov

6 Board of Accountancy, 2000 Evergreen St, #250, Sacramento, CA 95815-3832; 916-263-3680, Fax: 916-263-3673. www.dca.ca.gov/cba/ Email: enforcementinfo@cba.ca.gov Search Database at www.dca.ca.gov/cba/lookup.htm Note: Search either individual or company names.

7 Architects Board, 400 R St, #4000, Sacramento, CA 95814-6238; 916-445-3393, Fax: 916-445-8524. www.cab.ca.gov Email: cab@dca.ca.gov Search Database at www.cab.ca.gov/querylic.htm

8 Board of Behavioral Sciences, 400 R St, #3150, Sacramento, CA 95814-6200; 916-445-4933, Fax: 916-323-0707. www.bbs.ca.gov

Email: BBSWebMaster@bbs.ca.gov Search Database at www.bbs.ca.gov/weblokup.htm

9 Dental Board, 1432 Howe Ave, #85-B, Sacramento, CA 95825-3241; 916-263-2300, Fax: 916-263-2140. www.dca.ca.gov Email: DentalBoard@dca.ca.gov Search Database at www.dbc.ca.gov/license_verification.html

10 Board of Professional Engineers & Land Surveyors, 2535 Capitol Oaks Dr #300, Sacramento, CA 95833-2944; 916-263-2222, Fax: 916-263-2246. www.dca.ca.gov/pels Email: bpels-license-verifications@dca.ca.gov Search Database at www.dca.ca.gov/pels/l_lookup.htm Note: Member lists may be downloaded. Engineers include: civil, fire protection, electrical, mechanical, geotechnical, structural, traffic, oil, nuclear, control system, chemical, industrial, manufacturing, metallurgical, petroleum, corrosion, quality, safety.

11 Department of Financial Institutions, Consumer Affairs, 1801 13th Street #2124, Sacramento, CA 95814; 916-322-5966. www.dfi.ca.gov/consumer/ Search Database at www.dfi.ca.gov/directry/directry.asp

12 Board of Optometry, 400 R St, #4090, Sacramento, CA 95814-6200; 916-323-8720, 800-547-4576, Fax: 916-445-8711. www.optometry.ca.gov Email: boardemail@dea.ca.gov Search Database at www.optometry.ca.gov/search.asp

13 Board of Pharmacy, 400 R St, #4070, Sacramento, CA 95814-6200; 916-445-5014, Fax: 916-327-6308. www.pharmacy.ca.gov Search Database at www.pharmacy.ca.gov/license_lookup.htm

14 Board of Podiatric Medicine, 1420 Howe Ave, #8, Sacramento, CA 95825-3229; 916-263-2647, Fax: 916-263-2651. www.bpm.ca.gov Email: bpm@dca.ca.gov Search Database at www.bpm.ca.gov

15 Board of Psychology, 1422 Howe Ave, #22, Sacramento, CA 95825-3200; 916-263-2699, Fax: 916-263-2697. www.psychboard.ca.gov Email: bopmail@dca.ca.gov Search Database at www.psychboard.ca.gov

16 Board of Registered Nursing, 400 R St, #4030, Sacramento, CA 95814-6200; 916-322-3350, Fax: 916-327-4402. www.rn.ca.gov Email: brnappdesk@dca.ca.gov Search Database at www.rn.ca.gov/online/online.htm Note: The toll-free number is available 24 hours a day. Also, a license verification request form is available online at www.ncsbn.org/public/regulation/res/verific ation.pdf.

17 Board of Vocational Nursing & Psychiatric Technicians, 2535 Capitol Oaks Dr, #205, Sacramento, CA 95833; 916-263-7800, Fax: 916-263-7855. www.bvnpt.ca.gov Email: webmaster@bvnpt.ca.gov Search Database at www.bvnpt.ca.gov/licverif.htm

18 Board for Geologists & Geophysicists, 2535 Capitol Oaks Dr, #300A, Sacramento, CA 95833; 916-263-2113, Fax: 916-263-2099. www.dca.ca.gov/geology Email: geology@dca.ca.gov Search Database at www.dca.ca.gov/geology/ Note: To search directories, click on "Directory of Licenses."

19 Bureau of Automotive Repair, PO Box 989001, West Sacramento, CA 95798-9001; 916-322-4000, Fax: 916-322-4274. www.smogcheck.ca.gov/stdhome.asp Search Database at www.smogcheck.ca.gov/st dPage.asp?Body=/Consumer/verify_a_license.htm

20 Department of Consumer Affairs, Bureau of Electronic & Appliance Repair, 3485 Orange Grove Ave., North Highlands, CA 95660; 916-574-2069, Fax: 916-574-2120. www.bear.ca.gov Email: beartalk@dca.ca.gov Search Database at www.bear.ca.gov/look-up.htm

21 Department of Consumer Affairs, Bureau of Home Furnishings & Thermal Insulation, 3485 Orange Grove Ave, North Highlands, CA 95660; 916-574-0280, Fax: 916-574-2449. www.dca.ca.gov/bhfti/

22 Bureau of Security & Investigative Services, 401 S St #101, Sacramento, CA 95814; 916-322-4000, Fax: 916-445-1694. www.dca.ca.gov/bsis Email: bsis@dca.ca.gov Search Database at www.dca.ca.gov/bsis/lookup.htm

23 State Bar of California, California Committee of Bar Examiners, 180 Howard St, San Francisco, CA 94105; 415-538-2577, Fax: 415-538-2361. www.calbar.ca.gov/state/calbar/calbar_home.jsp Email: memrec@calbar.ca.gov Search Database at www.calbar.ca.gov/state/calbar/calbar_home.jsp Note: The member records online database does not include judges or deceased former members.

24 Horse Racing Board, 1010 Hurley Way, #300, Sacramento, CA 95825; 916-263-6000, Fax: 916-263-6042. www.chrb.ca.gov Search Database at www.chrb.ca.gov/license_search.htm

25 Cemetery and Funeral Bureau, 400 R St, #3080, Sacramento, CA 95814; 916-327-3219. www.cfb.ca.gov Search Database at www.dca.ca.gov/cemetery/lookup.htm

26 Commission on Teacher Credentialing, 1900 Capitol Ave (95814-4213), Sacramento, CA 95814-7000; 916-445-7254, Fax: 916-445-7255. www.ctc.ca.gov Email: credentials@ctc.ca.gov Search Database at www.ctc.ca.gov/credentialinfo/credinfo.html

27 Committee on Dental Auxiliaries, 1428 Howe Ave, #58, Sacramento, CA 95825; 916-263-2595, Fax: 916-263-2709. www.comda.ca.gov Search Database at www.comda.ca.gov/licensestatus.html

28 Contractors License Board, PO Box 26000 (9821 Business Park Dr), Sacramento, CA 95826; 916-255-3900, 800-321-2752, Fax: 916-361-7497. www.cslb.ca.gov Email: licensing@dca.cslb.ca.gov Search Database at http://www2.cslb.ca.gov/CSLB_LIBRARY/Name+Request.asp

29 Court Reporters Board of California, 2535 Capitol Oaks Dr, #230, Sacramento, CA 95833; 916-263-3660, Fax: 916-263-3664. www.courtreportersboard.ca.gov Search Database at www.courtreportersboard.ca.gov Note: To search, click on "License Verification."

30 Department of Corporations, 1515 K St #200, Sacramento, CA 95814; 916-445-7205. www.corp.ca.gov Email: Webmaster@corp.ca.gov

31 Department of Health Services, Radiological Health Branch, PO Box 942732, Sacramento, CA 94234-7320; 916-445-0931, Fax: 916-324-3610. www.dhs.ca.gov/rhb/ Search Database at www.dhs.ca.gov/applications/search/search.asp

32 Department of Insurance, Producer Licensing Bureau, 320 Capitol Mall, Sacramento, CA 95814; 916-322-3555, Fax: 916-327-6907. www.insurance.ca.gov

Email: license.bureau@insurance.ca.gov Search Database at www.insurance.ca.gov/docs/FS-Licensestatus.htm

33 Department of Real Estate, 2201 Broadway, Sacramento, CA 95818-2500; 916-227-0931, Fax: 916-227-0925. www.dre.ca.gov Search Database at www.dre.ca.gov/licstats.htm

34 Hearing Aid Dispensers Examining Committee, PO Box 980490, West Sacramento, CA 95798-0490; 916-327-3433, Fax: 916-445-1696. www.dca.ca.gov/hearingaid/ Email: hearingaid@dca.ca.gov Search Database at www.dca.ca.gov/hearingaid/

35 Landscape Architects Technical Committee, 400 R St, #4000, Sacramento, CA 95814-6200; 916-445-4954, Fax: 916-324-2333. www.latc.dca.ca.gov Email: latc@dca.ca.gov Search Database at www.latc.dca.ca.gov/licenseeinfo/search.htm

36 Medical Board of California, 1426 Howe Ave, #54, Sacramento, CA 95825-3236; 916-263-2382, Fax: 916-263-2567. www.medbd.ca.gov Note: Facilities and professionals may search at www.docboard.org/ca/df/casearch.htm; logon and password required.

37 Office of the Secretary of State, 1500 11th St, 2nd Fl, Sacramento, CA 95814; 916-653-3595, Fax: 916-653-9580. www.ss.ca.gov/business/notary/notary.htm Email: notaries@ss.ca.gov

38 Physical Therapy Examining Committee, 1418 Howe Ave #16, Sacramento, CA 95825-3204; 916-561-8200, Fax: 916-263-2560. www.ptb.ca.gov

39 Department of Consumer Affairs, Physician Assistant Committee, 1424 Howe Ave, #35, Sacramento, CA 95825-3237; 916-263-2670, Fax: 916-263-2671. www.physicianassistant.ca.gov/index.html

40 Veterinary Medical Board, 1420 Howe Ave, #6, Sacramento, CA 95825-3228; 916-263-2610, Fax: 916-263-2621. www.vmb.ca.gov Email: vmb@dca.ca.gov Search Database at www.vmb.ca.gov/lic1list.htm

41 Respiratory Care Board of California, 444 N 3rd St #270, Sacramento, CA 95814; 916-323-9983, Fax: 916-323-9999. www.rcb.ca.gov Email: rcbinfo@dca.ca.gov Search Database at www.rcb.ca.gov/license_verification_forms_instructions.htm Note: Click on "License Verification On-Line"

42 Speech Language Pathology & Audiology Board, 1422 Howe Ave, #3, Sacramento, CA 95825; 916-263-2666, Fax: 916-263-2668. www.slpab.ca.gov Email: slpab@dca.ca.gov

43 Board of Guide Dogs for the Blind, 400 R St #5100-A, Sacramento, CA 95814; 916-324-9328, Fax: 916-324-9340. www.dca.ca.gov/guidedogboard Email: guidedogboard@dca.ca.gov

44 Structural Pest Control Board, 1418 Howe Ave #18, Sacramento, CA 95825-3280; 916-263-8700, Fax: 916-263-2469.

www.cdpr.ca.gov Search Database at www.cdpr.ca.gov/docs/license/currlic.htm

45 Tax Preparer Program, CA Tax Education Council, PO Box 2890, Sacramento, CA 95812-2840; 877-850-2832. www.ctec.org Email: info@ctec.org Search Database at www.ctec.org/verify.asp

46 California Board of Chiropractic Examiners, 2525 Natromas Park Dr #260, Sacramento, CA 95833-2931; 916-263-5355, Fax: 916-263-5369. www.chiro.ca.gov/default.asp Search Database at www.chiro.ca.gov/licsearch/

47 Secretary of State, Political Reform Division, 1500 11th Street, Room 495, Sacramento, CA 95814; 916-653-6224, Fax: 916-653-5045. http://cal-access.ss.ca.gov Email: PoliticalReform@ss.ca.gov Search Database at http://cal-access.ss.ca.gov/Lobbying/

48 Association of Polygraph Examiners, 969-G Edgewater Blvd #330, Foster City, CA 94404; 800-593-8598. www.californiapolygraph.com Email: bod@californiapolygraph.com Search Database at www.californiapolygraph.com/members/roster.htm

49 Driving School Complaint Unit, Occupational Licensing, PO Box 932342 L228, Sacramento, CA 94232-3420; 916-657-6077, 916-657-8921. www.dmv.ca.gov/vehindustry/ol/drschool_faq.htm Search Database at http://eg.dmv.ca.gov/olinq/Welcome.jsp

50 Department of Social Services, Community Care Licensing Division, 744 P St, Sacramento, CA 95814; 916-274-6200, Fax: 916-274-6206. http://ccld.ca.gov Email: cclwebmaster@dss.ca.gov Search Database at www.ccld.ca.gov/docs/ccld_search/ccld_search.aspx

51 Board of Occupational Therapy, 444 N 3rd St, #410, Sacramento, CA 95814; 916-322-3394, Fax: 916-445-6167. www.bot.ca.gov Email: cbot@dca.ca.gov Search Database at http://www2.dca.ca.gov/pls/wllpub/wllqryna$lcev2.startup?p_qte_code=OT&p_qte_pgm_code=1475 Note: Will provide certification/ letter of good standing.

52 Department of Industrial Relations, Division of Occupational Health, 455 Golden Gate Ave, 10th Fl, San Francisco, CA 94102; 415-703-5100, Fax: 415-703-5135. www.dir.ca.gov Search Database at www.dir.ca.gov/dirdatabases.html

53 Division of Labor Standards Enforcement, Licensing and Registration Unit, PO Box 420603, San Francisco, CA 94142; 415-703-5100, Fax: 415-703-4808. www.dir.ca.gov Email: DLSE.licensing@dir.ca.gov Search Database at www.dir.ca.gov/dirdatabases.html

California Federal Courts

The following list indicates the district and division name for each county in the state. If the district or division name of the bankruptcy court is different from the civil/criminal court, it appears in parentheses.

For California counties of Alameda, Contra Costa, Del Norte, Humboldt, Lake, Marin, Mendocino, Napa, San Francisco, San Mateo, and Sonoma in the Northern District of California District Court, cases may be filed at either the San Francisco Division or Oakland Division. From there a case may be assigned to either division. Records are available electronically or on public access terminals at either Division, and at the San Jose Division. To find the actual locations of records, first search by name to find case numbers; the first number of the case number indicates the file location: 3~=San Francisco, 4~=Oakland., 5~=San Jose.

County/Court Cross Reference

Alameda	Northern	Oakland/SF (Oakland)
Alpine	Eastern	Sacramento
Amador	Eastern	Sacramento
Butte	Eastern	Sacramento
Calaveras	Eastern	Sacramento (Modesto)
Colusa	Eastern	Sacramento
Contra Costa	Northern	Oakland/SF (Oakland)
Del Norte	Northern	San Francisco/Oakland (Santa Rosa)
El Dorado	Eastern	Sacramento
Fresno	Eastern	Fresno
Glenn	Eastern	Sacramento
Humboldt	Northern	San Francisco/Oakland (Santa Rosa)
Imperial	Southern	San Diego
Inyo	Eastern	Fresno
Kern	Eastern	Fresno
Kings	Eastern	Fresno
Lake	Northern	San Francisco/Oakland (Santa Rosa)
Lassen	Eastern	Sacramento
Los Angeles	Central	Los Angeles (Western)
Madera	Eastern	Fresno
Marin	Northern	San Francisco/Oakland (Santa Rosa)
Mariposa	Eastern	Fresno
Mendocino	Northern	San Francisco/Oakland (Santa Rosa)
Merced	Eastern	Fresno
Modoc	Eastern	Sacramento
Mono	Eastern	Sacramento
Monterey	Northern	San Jose
Napa	Northern	San Francisco/Oakland (Santa Rosa)
Nevada	Eastern	Sacramento
Orange	Central	Santa Ana (Southern)
Placer	Eastern	Sacramento
Plumas	Eastern	Sacramento
Riverside	Central	Riverside (Eastern)
Sacramento	Eastern	Sacramento
San Benito	Northern	San Jose
San Bernardino	Central	Riverside (Eastern)
San Diego	Southern	San Diego
San Francisco	Northern	San Francisco/Oakland (San Francisco)
San Joaquin	Eastern	Sacramento (Modesto)
San Luis Obispo	Central	Los Angeles (Western)
San Mateo	Northern	San Francisco/Oakland (San Francisco)
Santa Barbara	Central	Los Angeles (Western)
Santa Clara	Northern	San Jose
Santa Cruz	Northern	San Jose
Shasta	Eastern	Sacramento
Sierra	Eastern	Sacramento
Siskiyou	Eastern	Sacramento
Solano	Eastern	Sacramento
Sonoma	Northern	San Francisco/Oakland (Santa Rosa)
Stanislaus	Eastern	Fresno (Modesto)
Sutter	Eastern	Sacramento
Tehama	Eastern	Sacramento
Trinity	Eastern	Sacramento
Tulare	Eastern	Fresno
Tuolumne	Eastern	Fresno (Modesto)
Ventura	Central	Los Angeles (Western)
Yolo	Eastern	Sacramento
Yuba	Eastern	Sacramento

Standards for Federal Courts: The search fee is $20.00 per item (one party name or case number). Certification fee is $7.00 per document. Copy fee is $.50 per page. All fees standard unless noted in profile. Mail Search: always enclose a stamped self addressed envelope unless otherwise noted. Most courts accept fax requests or will suggest a copying/search vendor. Before releasing records, all courts require prepayment unless noted in profile. Open records are located at the court unless otherwise noted. District courts index by defendant and plaintiff as well as by case number. Bankruptcy courts usually index by debtor and case number. While most courts now have their indexes on computer, many still maintain index card files as well.

The universal PACER sign-up number is 800-676-6856. Find PACER and the Party/Case Index on the Web at http://pacer.psc.uscourts.gov. PACER

dial-up access is $.60 per minute. Also, courts offering internet access via RACER, PACER, Web-PACER or the new CM-ECF charge $.07 per page fee unless noted as free.

U.S. District Court

Central District of California

Los Angeles (Western) Division U.S. Courthouse, Attn: Correspondence, 312 N Spring St, Room G-8, Los Angeles, CA 90012 (courier address: Use mail address for courier delivery) 213-894-5261. www.cacd.uscourts.gov
Counties: Los Angeles, San Luis Obispo, Santa Barbara, Ventura.

Indexing & Storage: New cases available in the index 3 days after filing date. In general, criminal case records from 1989 back and civil from 1994 back have been sent to the Federal Records Center.
Fee & Payment: Payment may be made by money order, cashier check, business check. Personal checks are not accepted. Payee: Clerk, U.S. District Court.
Phone Search: No searching by telephone.
In Person Search: Fee charged if court conducts your in person search for you. Persons with a valid ID may search microfiche.
PACER: PACER is available online at http://pacer.cacd.uscourts.gov. Document images available. New records are online after 2 days.
Electronic Filing: Electronic filing information online at https://ecf.cacd.uscourts.gov
Opinions Online: Court opinions are online at www.cacd.uscourts.gov

Riverside (Eastern) Division U.S. District Court, PO Box 13000, Riverside, CA 92502-3000 (courier address: 3470 12th St., Riverside, CA 92501), 951-328-4450. www.cacd.uscourts.gov
Counties: Riverside, San Bernardino.
Indexing & Storage: New cases available in the index 3 days after filing date.
Fee & Payment: Payment may be made by money order, cashier check, business check. Personal checks are not accepted. Payee: Clerk, U.S. District Court.
Phone Search: No searching by telephone.
In Person Search: Fee charged if court conducts your in person search for you.
PACER: PACER is available online at http://pacer.cacd.uscourts.gov. Document images available. New records are online after 2 days.
Electronic Filing: Electronic filing information online at https://ecf.cacd.uscourts.gov
Opinions Online: at www.cacd.uscourts.gov

Santa Ana (Southern) Division 411 W 4th St Rm 1053, Santa Ana, CA 92701-4516 (courier address: Use mail address for courier delivery) 714-338-4750. www.cacd.uscourts.gov
Counties: Orange.
Indexing & Storage: New cases available in the index 3 days after filing date.
Fee & Payment: Payment may be made by money order, cashier check, business check. Personal checks are not accepted. Prepayment is required unless a deposit account is set up with the court. Payee: Clerk, U.S. District Court.
Phone Search: Only docket information available.
In Person Search: Fee charged if court conducts your in person search for you.
PACER: PACER is available online at http://pacer.cacd.uscourts.gov. Document images available. New records are online after 2 days.
Electronic Filing: Electronic filing information online at https://ecf.cacd.uscourts.gov
Opinions Online: at www.cacd.uscourts.gov

U.S. Bankruptcy Court

Central District of California

Los Angeles Division 255 E Temple St, Roybal Bldg, #945, Los Angeles, CA 90012 (courier address: Use mail address for courier delivery) 213-894-3118, Fax: 213-894-1261. www.cacb.uscourts.gov
Counties: Los Angeles (cases filed in certain northern Los Angeles County ZIP Codes may be shared with the San Fernando Valley Division.).
Indexing & Storage: Cases indexed by debtor as well as by case number. New cases available in the index immediately after filing date. Records are indexed on microfiche.
Fee & Payment: Payment may be made by money order, cashier check. Business checks are not accepted. Personal checks are not accepted. Payee: Clerk, U.S. Bankruptcy Court.
Phone Search: Automated voice case information service (VCIS) is available. VCIS: 213-894-4111.
In Person Search: Fee charged if court conducts your in person search for you.
PACER: PACER is available online at https://pacer.login.uscourts.gov/cgi-bin/login.pl?court_id=CACBLA. Document images available. Records purged once a year. New civil records are online after 1 day.
Electronic Filing: Currently in the process of implementing CM/ECF.

Riverside (East) Division 3420 12th St #125, Riverside, CA 92501-3819 (courier address: Use mail address for courier delivery) 951-774-1000. www.cacb.uscourts.gov
Counties: Riverside, San Bernardino.
Indexing & Storage: Cases indexed by debtor as well as by case number. New cases available in the index immediately after filing date. Files are stored in numerical sequence. The time that records are kept at the Riverside court is varied. There is no set time limit before they are sent to the Los Angeles Federal Records Center.
Fee & Payment: Payment may be made by money order, cashier check. Business checks are not accepted, Visa or Mastercard. Personal checks are not accepted. Payee: U.S. Bankruptcy Court.
Phone Search: Only docket information available by phone. Automated voice case information service (VCIS) available. VCIS at 951-774-1150.
Mail Search: Include the case number, document title, document number (if available), your phone number, and any applicable fees. Include SASE for return.
In Person Search: Fee charged if court conducts your in person search for you. Records are available for public inspection. Copies available from West Coast Copy Svc, 909-788-4371.
PACER: PACER is available online at https://pacer.login.uscourts.gov/cgi-bin/login.pl?court_id=CACBLA. Document images available. Records purged once a year. New civil records are online after 1 day.
Electronic Filing: Currently in the process of implementing CM/ECF.

San Fernando Valley Division 21041 Burbank Blvd, Woodland Hills, CA 91367 (courier address: Use mail address for courier delivery) 818-587-2900. www.cacb.uscourts.gov
Counties: Los Angeles, Ventura (cases filed in certain northern Los Angeles County ZIP Codes are shared with the Los Angeles Division, and cases filed in certain eastern Ventura County ZIP Codes are shared with the Ventura Division).
Indexing & Storage: Cases indexed by debtor as well as by case number. New cases available in the index immediately after filing date.
Fee & Payment: Payment may be made by money order, cashier check. Business checks are not accepted. Personal checks are not accepted. Payee: Clerk, U.S. Bankruptcy Court.
Phone Search: Automated voice case data service (VCIS) is available. Call VCIS at 818-587-2936.
In Person Search: Fee charged if court conducts your in person search for you.
PACER: PACER is available online at https://pacer.login.uscourts.gov/cgi-bin/login.pl?court_id=CACBLA. Document images available. Records purged once a year. New civil records are online after 1 day.
Electronic Filing: Currently in the process of implementing CM/ECF.
Other Online Access: Currently in the process of implementing CM/ECF.

Santa Ana Division Ronald Reagan Federal Bldg & U.S. Courthouse, 411 W 4th St #2030, Santa Ana, CA 92701-4593 (courier address: Use mail address for courier delivery) 714-836-5300. www.cacb.uscourts.gov
Counties: Orange.
Indexing & Storage: Cases indexed by debtor and creditors as well as by case number. New cases available in the index 24-48 hours after filing date.

Fee & Payment: Payment may be made by money order, cashier check, business check. Personal checks are not accepted. Prepayment is required unless prior arrangements have been made. Payee: U.S. Bankruptcy Court.
Phone Search: Docket information available by phone. Automated voice case information service (VCIS) is available. Call VCIS at 714-338-5401.
In Person Search: Fee charged if court conducts your in person search for you.
PACER: PACER is available online at https://pacer.login.uscourts.gov/cgi-bin/login.pl?court_id=CACBLA. Document images available. Case records go back to June 3, 1991. New civil records are online after 1 day.
Electronic Filing: Currently in the process of implementing CM/ECF.

Santa Barbara (Northern) Division 1415 State St, Santa Barbara, CA 93101 (courier address: Use mail address for courier delivery) 805-884-4800. www.cacb.uscourts.gov
Counties: San Luis Obispo, Santa Barbara, Ventura. Certain Ventura County ZIP Codes are assigned to the new office in San Fernando Valley.
Indexing & Storage: Cases indexed by debtor as well as by case number. New cases available in the index immediately after filing date. There is no set time for sending records to the repository.
Fee & Payment: Payment may be made by money order, cashier check. Business checks are not accepted. Personal checks are not accepted. Payee: U.S. Bankruptcy Court.
Phone Search: Automated voice case information service (VCIS) is available. VCIS: 805-884-4805.
Mail Search: Include case number, document title, document number (if available), your phone number and applicable fees. Include SASE.
In Person Search: Fee charged if court conducts your in person search for you.
PACER: PACER is available online at https://pacer.login.uscourts.gov/cgi-bin/login.pl?court_id=CACBLA. Document images available. New civil records are online after 1 day.
Electronic Filing: Currently in the process of implementing CM/ECF.

U.S. District Court

Eastern District of California

Fresno Division U.S. Courthouse, Room 5000, 1130 "O" St, Fresno, CA 93721-2201 (courier address: Use mail address for courier delivery) 559-498-7483. www.caed.uscourts.gov
Counties: Fresno, Inyo, Kern, Kings, Madera, Mariposa, Merced, Stanislaus, Tulare, Tuolumne.
Indexing & Storage: New cases available in the index 24 hours after filing date. Records are stored by case type and case number.
Fee & Payment: Payment may be made by money order, cashier check, personal check. Payee: Clerk, U.S. District Court.
Phone Search: Only docket information available by phone.
Mail Search: A SASE not required.
In Person Search: Fee charged if court conducts your in person search for you. Court will copy a maximum of 20 pages, otherwise searchers must contact an outside copy service. Iin person only between 8:30AM and 4:30PM.
PACER: PACER is available online at http://pacer.caed.uscourts.gov. Local access: 916-498-6567. Case records go back to 1994 (some

earlier). Records purged at varying intervals. New records are online after 1 day.

Opinions Online: Court opinions are online at www.caed.uscourts.gov

Other Online Access: Search records using RACER at https://racer.caed.uscourts.gov/. Access fee is $.07 per page. Document images available.

Sacramento Division 501 I St, Sacramento, CA 95814 (courier address: Use mail address for courier delivery) 916-930-4000, Fax: 916-930-4015. www.caed.uscourts.gov

Counties: Alpine, Amador, Butte, Calaveras, Colusa, El Dorado, Glenn, Lassen, Modoc, Mono, Nevada, Placer, Plumas, Sacramento, San Joaquin, Shasta, Sierra, Siskiyou, Solano, Sutter, Tehama, Trinity, Yolo, Yuba.

Indexing & Storage: New cases available in the index immediately after filing date. Archived records are stored by case number. A case number can be researched by the plaintiff's or defendant's name. Archived case records indexed on microfiche.

Fee & Payment: Payment may be made by money order, cashier check, business check. Personal checks are not accepted. Payee: Clerk, U.S. District Court.

Phone Search: Only docket information available.

In Person Search: Fee charged if court conducts your in person search for you. For copy service, call 916-448-8875. A 24-hour drop box is located on the premises.

PACER: PACER is available online at http://pacer.caed.uscourts.gov. Local access: 916-498-6567. Case records go back to 1994 (some earlier). Records purged at varying intervals. New records are online after 1 day.

Opinions Online: Court opinions are online at www.caed.uscourts.gov

Other Online Access: Search records on the Internet using RACER at https://racer.caed.uscourts.gov/. Access fee is $.07 per page. Document images available.

U.S. Bankruptcy Court

Eastern District of California

Fresno Division Room 2656, 1130 O Street, Fresno, CA 93721 (courier address: Use mail address for courier delivery) 559-498-7217. www.caeb.uscourts.gov

Counties: Fresno, Inyo, Kern, Kings, Madera, Mariposa, Merced, Tulare. Three Kern ZIP Codes, 93243 and 93523-24, are handled by San Fernando Valley in the Central District.

Indexing & Storage: Cases indexed by debtor as well as by case number. New cases available in the index immediately after filing date.

Fee & Payment: Payment may be made by money order, cashier check, business check. Personal checks are not accepted. Payee: Clerk, U.S. Bankruptcy Court.

Phone Search: Only docket information available by phone. Automated voice case information service (VCIS) is available. Call VCIS at 916-498-5583 or 916-498-5584.

In Person Search: Fee charged if court conducts your in person search for you.

PACER: PACER is available online at http://pacer.caeb.uscourts.gov/pacerhome.html. Document images available. Records purged every six months. New civil records are online after 1 day.

Modesto Division PO Box 5276, Modesto, CA 95352 (courier address: Suite C, 1130 12th St, Modesto, CA 95354), 209-521-5160. www.caeb.uscourts.gov

Counties: Calaveras, San Joaquin, Stanislaus, Tuolumne. The following ZIP Codes in San Joaquin County are handled by the Sacramento Division: 95220, 95227, 95234, 95237, 95240-95242, 95253, 95258, and 95686.Mariposa and Merced counties were transferred to the Fresno Division as of January 1, 1995.

Indexing & Storage: Cases indexed by debtor as well as by case number. New cases available in the index 1 day after filing date. Case numbers can be researched by using the debtor's name.

Fee & Payment: Payment may be made by money order, cashier check, personal check. Payee: Clerk, U.S. Bankruptcy Court.

Phone Search: Only docket information available by phone. Automated voice case information service (VCIS) is available. Call VCIS at 916-498-5583 or 916-498-5584.

Mail Search: A SASE not required.

In Person Search: Fee charged if court conducts your in person search for you.

PACER: PACER is available online at http://pacer.caeb.uscourts.gov/pacerhome.html. Document images available. Records purged every six months. New civil records are online after 1 day.

Sacramento Division U.S. Courthouse, 501 I St, Rm 3-200, Sacramento, CA 95814 (courier address: Use mail address for courier delivery) 916-930-4400. www.caeb.uscourts.gov

Counties: Alpine, Amador, Butte, Colusa, El Dorado, Glenn, Lassen, Modoc, Mono, Nevada, Placer, Plumas, Sacramento, Shasta, Sierra, Siskiyou, Solano, Sutter, Tehama, Trinity, Yolo, Yuba. This court also handles the following ZIP Codes in San Joaquin County: 95220, 95227, 95234, 95237, 95240-95242, 95253, 95258, and 95686.

Indexing & Storage: Cases indexed by debtor as well as by case number. New cases available in the index immediately after filing date.

Fee & Payment: Payment may be made by money order, cashier check, business check. Personal checks are not accepted. Payee: Clerk, U.S. Bankruptcy Court.

Phone Search: Only docket information available by phone. Automated voice case information service (VCIS) is available. Call VCIS at 916-498-5583 or 916-498-5584.

In Person Search: Fee charged if court conducts your in person search for you. You must make an appointment in order to conduct a search yourself.

PACER: PACER is available online at http://pacer.caeb.uscourts.gov/pacerhome.html. Document images available. Records purged every six months. New civil records are online after 1 day.

U.S. District Court

Northern District of California

Oakland Division 1301 Clay St, Ste 400S, Oakland, CA 94612-5212 (courier address: Use mail address for courier delivery) 510-637-3530. www.cand.uscourts.gov

Counties: Alameda, Contra Costa(Note: Cases may be filed here or at San Francisco Div.; records available electronically at either; the 1st number of

the case number indicates the file location: 3=SF, 4=Oak., 5=SJ.

Indexing & Storage: New cases available in the index immediately after filing date. Records are stored by case number, however, a case number can be researched by using the plaintiff's or defendant's name. Records on computer since 1994. Records are also indexed on microfiche.

Fee & Payment: Payment may be made by money order, cashier check, personal check. Payee: Clerk, U.S. District Court.

Phone Search: Only docket information available.

In Person Search: Fee charged if court conducts your in person search for you. Use public pay copier for copies.

PACER: PACER is available online at http://pacer.cand.uscourts.gov. Records purged every six months. New records online after 1 day.

Electronic Filing: ECF cases data back to 4/2001. Electronic filing information online at https://ecf.cand.uscourts.gov

San Francisco Division 450 Golden Gate Ave, 16th Fl, San Francisco, CA 94102 (courier address: Use mail address for courier delivery) 415-522-2000. www.cand.uscourts.gov

Counties: Del Norte, Humboldt, Lake, Marin, Mendocino, Napa, San Francisco, San Mateo, Sonoma(Note: Cases may be filed here or at Oakland Div; records available electronically at either; the 1st number of the case number indicates the file location: 3=SF, 4=Oak., 5=SJ.

Indexing & Storage: New cases available in the index immediately after filing date. Records are stored by case number, however, a case number can be researched by using the plaintiff's or defendant's name. Records on computer since 1994. Records are also indexed on microfiche.

Fee & Payment: Payment may be made by money order, cashier check, personal check. Payee: Clerk, U.S. District Court.

Phone Search: Only docket information available by phone.

In Person Search: Fee charged if court conducts your in person search for you. Use public pay copier for copies.

PACER: PACER is available online at http://pacer.cand.uscourts.gov. Records purged every six months. New records are online after 1 day.

Electronic Filing: ECF cases data back to 4/2001. Electronic filing information online at https://ecf.cand.uscourts.gov

San Jose Division Room 2112, 280 S 1st St, San Jose, CA 95113 (courier address: Use mail address for courier delivery) 408-535-5364. www.cand.uscourts.gov

Counties: Monterey, San Benito, Santa Clara, Santa Cruz.

Indexing & Storage: New cases available in the index immediately after filing date. Records are stored by case number, however, a case number can be researched by using the plaintiff's or defendant's name. Records are also indexed on microfiche.

Fee & Payment: Payment may be made by money order, cashier check, personal check. Payee: Clerk, U.S. District Court.

Phone Search: Only docket information available by phone.

In Person Search: Fee charged if court conducts your in person search for you. Use public pay copier for copies.

PACER: PACER is available online at http://pacer.cand.uscourts.gov. Records purged every six months. New records are online after 1 day.
Electronic Filing: ECF includes civil cases filed after 4/1/2001 and criminal and miscellaneous cases after 1/1/2004. Electronic filing information online at https://ecf.cand.uscourts.gov

U.S. Bankruptcy Court
Northern District of California

Oakland Division PO Box 2070, Oakland, CA 94604 (courier address: 1300 Clay St, Room 300, Oakland, CA 94612), 510-879-3600. www.canb.uscourts.gov
Counties: Alameda, Contra Costa.
Indexing & Storage: Cases indexed by debtor as well as by case number. New cases available in the index 2 days after filing date.
Fee & Payment: Payment may be made by money order, cashier check, business check. Personal checks are not accepted. Payee: Clerk, U.S. Bankruptcy Court.
Phone Search: Automated voice case information service (VCIS) is available. Call VCIS at 888-457-0604 or 415-705-3160.
In Person Search: Fee charged if court conducts your in person search for you.
PACER: PACER is available online at http://pacer.canb.uscourts.gov. Records purged every six months to one year. New civil records are online after 1 day.
Electronic Filing: Electronic filing information online at https://ecf.canb.uscourts.gov

San Francisco Division PO Box 7341, San Francisco, CA 94120-7341 (courier address: 235 Pine St, 19th Fl, San Francisco, CA 94104), 415-268-2300. www.canb.uscourts.gov
Counties: San Francisco, San Mateo.
Indexing & Storage: Cases indexed by debtor as well as by case number. New cases available in the index 3-4 working days after filing date. All searches are conducted by a copy service. To reach them, call 415-781-4910. Records are also indexed on microfiche.
Fee & Payment: Payment may be made by money order, cashier check, business check. Personal checks are not accepted. Payee: Clerk of the Court.
Phone Search: Only information available from dockets of open cases is released over the phone. Automated voice case information service (VCIS) is available. Call VCIS at 888-457-0604 or 415-705-3160.
Mail Search: A SASE not required.
In Person Search: Fee charged if court conducts your in person search for you.
PACER: PACER is available online at http://pacer.canb.uscourts.gov. Records purged

every six months to one year. New civil records are online after 1 day.
Electronic Filing: Electronic filing information online at https://ecf.canb.uscourts.gov

San Jose Division Room 3035, 3rd Fl, 280 S 1st St, San Jose, CA 95113-3099 (courier address: Use mail address for courier delivery) 408-535-5118. www.canb.uscourts.gov
Counties: Monterey, San Benito, Santa Clara, Santa Cruz.
Indexing & Storage: Cases indexed by debtor as well as by case number. New cases available in the index 1-2 days after filing date.
Fee & Payment: Payment may be made by money order, cashier check, business check. Personal checks are not accepted. Payee: Clerk, U.S. Bankruptcy Court.
Phone Search: Only basic information, such as date of filing is released over the phone. Automated voice case information service (VCIS) is available. Call VCIS at 888-457-0604 or 415-705-3160.
In Person Search: Fee charged if court conducts your in person search for you. Copying from BK Copy Center is available.
PACER: PACER is available online at http://pacer.canb.uscourts.gov. Records purged every six months to one year. New civil records are online after 1 day.
Electronic Filing: Electronic filing information online at https://ecf.canb.uscourts.gov

Santa Rosa Division 99 South E St, Santa Rosa, CA 95404 (courier address: Use mail address for courier delivery) 369-525-8539, Fax: 369-579-0374. www.canb.uscourts.gov
Counties: Del Norte, Humboldt, Lake, Marin, Mendocino, Napa, Sonoma.
Indexing & Storage: Cases indexed by debtor as well as by case number. New cases available in the index immediately after filing date.
Fee & Payment: Payment may be made by money order, cashier check, business check. Personal checks are not accepted. This court will not bill. Payee: Clerk - U.S. Bankruptcy Court.
Phone Search: Names and accession numbers will be released over the phone. Automated voice case information service (VCIS) is available. Call VCIS at 888-457-0604 or 415-705-3160.
In Person Search: Fee charged if court conducts your in person search for you. This court urges use of their contracted copy service, Attorney's Diversified (707-545-5455).
PACER: PACER is available online at http://pacer.canb.uscourts.gov. Records purged every six months to one year. New civil records are online after 1 day.
Electronic Filing: Electronic filing information online at https://ecf.canb.uscourts.gov

U.S. District Court
Southern District of California

San Diego Division Clerk of Court, Room 4290, 880 Front St, San Diego, CA 92101-8900 (courier address: Use mail address for courier delivery) 619-557-5600, Fax: 619-557-6684. www.casd.uscourts.gov
Counties: Imperial, San Diego. Court also handles some cases from Yuma County, AZ.
Indexing & Storage: New cases available in the index 24 hours after filing date.
Fee & Payment: Payment may be made by money order, cashier check, personal check. A contract copying services is available. Payee: U.S. District Court.
Phone Search: No searching by telephone.
Mail Search: A SASE not required.
In Person Search: Fee charged if court conducts your in person search for you. There is a contract copy service.
PACER: PACER is available online at http://pacer.casd.uscourts.gov. Document images available. New records are online after 1 day.
Other Online Access: A computer bulletin board is accessible at 619-557-6779.

U.S. Bankruptcy Court
Southern District of California

San Diego Division Office of the Clerk, U.S. Courthouse, 325 West "F" St., San Diego, CA 92101 (Use mail address for courier delivery) 619-557-5620. www.casb.uscourts.gov
Counties: Imperial, San Diego.
Indexing & Storage: Cases indexed by debtor as well as by case number. New cases available in the index 3 days after filing date.
Fee & Payment: Payment may be made by money order, cashier check, personal check. Payee: Clerk, U.S. Bankruptcy Court.
Phone Search: Only docket information available by phone. Automated voice case information service (VCIS) available. Call VCIS 619-557-6521
Mail Search: A SASE not required.
In Person Search: Fee charged if court conducts your in person search for you.
PACER: PACER is available online at http://pacer.casb.uscourts.gov. Document images available. Records purged every six months. New civil records are online after 3 days.

Electronic Filing: Electronic filing information online at http://ecf.casb.uscourts.gov

California County Courts

Court	Jurisdiction	No. of Courts	How Organized
Superior Courts*	General	29	
Limited Superior Courts*	Limited	122	
Combined Superior Courts*	Limited & General	58	

* Profiled in this Sourcebook.

Court	CIVIL								
	Tort	Contract	Real Estate	Min. Claim	Max. Claim	Small Claims	Estate	Eviction	Domestic Relations
General Jurisdiction*	X	X	X	$25,000	No Max		X		X
Limited Jurisdiction*	X	X	X	$0	$25,000	$5000		X	

Court	CRIMINAL				
	Felony	Misdemeanor	DWI/DUI	Preliminary Hearing	Juvenile
General Jurisdiction*	X	X	X		X
Limited Jurisdiction*		X	X	X	

ADMINISTRATION   Administrative Office of Courts, 455 Golden Gate Ave, San Francisco, CA, 94102; 415-865-4200, Fax: 415-865-4205. www.courtinfo.ca.gov

COURT STRUCTURE   In July, 1998, the judges in individual counties were given the opportunity to vote on unification of superior and municipal courts within their respective counties. By late 2000, all counties had voted to unify these courts. Courts that were formally Municipal Courts are now known as Limited Jurisdiction Superior Courts. In some counties, superior and municipal courts were combined into one superior court. Civil under $25,000 is a Limited Civil Court, over $25,000 is an Unlimited Civil Court, and if both are over and under, then the court is a Combined Civil Court.

It is important to note that Limited Courts may try minor felonies not included under our felony definition.

Due to its large number of courts, the Los Angeles County section is arranged uniquely in this book. Each Branch or Division of the Los Angeles Superior Court is given by name, which usually indicates a court's general jurisdictional and geographic boundary (the actual jurisdiction area is noted in the text). The court name is followed by the District it is located in - South Central, West, Northeast, Central, etc. Also, a court name may mention whether its jurisdiction is "Civil" only or "Criminal" only.

ONLINE ACCESS   There is no statewide online computer access available. However, a number of counties have developed their own online access sytems and provide Internet access at no fee. The site at www.courtinfo.ca.gov offers access to all opinions from the Supreme and Appeals courts from 1850 to present. Opinions not certified for publications are available for last 60 days. This site also contains very useful information about the state court system, inlcuding opinions form the Supreme and Appeals courts.

Los Angeles County - As of 2003, all felony and misdemeanor defendant records in Los Angeles County are available online for a fee at www.lasuperiorcourt.org/onlineservices/criminalindex/. Search fee is $4 to $5. Historical Superior Court felony indices go back to 1973; misdemeanor cases vary - some go back to 1982, others only until 1991. Case disposition information also varies; generally, if the entire criminal case was automated at the time of sentencing, then an accurate case disposition should be included, but if it was not automated or the electronic data was somehow compromised, then the case disposition will not be available online. Keep in mind this is a new system that is still being tested.

ADDITIONAL INFORMATION   If there is more than one court of a type within a county, where the case is tried and where the record is held depends on how a citation is written, where the infraction occurred, or where the filer chose to file the case.

Some courts now require signed releases from the subject in order to perform criminal searches and will no longer allow the public to conduct such searches.

Personal checks are acceptable by state law.

Although fees are set by statute, courts interpret them differently. For example, the search fee is supposed to be $6.00 per name per year searched, but many courts charge only $5.00 per name. Generally, certification is $6.60 per document and copies are usually $.75 per page, but can range from $.50 to $1.10, and in Los Angeles County copies are $.57 each.

A convenient Los Angeles County Court Locator web page is available free at www.lasuperiorcourt.org/locations/

Alameda County

Superior Court - Criminal 1225 Fallon St Rm 107, Oakland, CA 94612; 510-272-6777; Fax: 510-835-4850. Hours: 8:30AM-4PM (PST). *Felony.* www.co.alameda.ca.us/courts/index.shtml
Note: Located at the Rene C Davidson Alameda County Courthouse.

Criminal Records: Access: Mail, in person. Both court and visitors may perform in person searches. Search fee: $5.00 per name. There is no fee if you do the search. Required to search: name, years to search, signed release; also helpful: DOB, SSN. Criminal records on computer back 10 years; on microfiche from 1940, archived and indexed from 1880. At the website, search "Find Your Court Date" to determine if a name has an upcoming court date.
General Information: Public Access terminal is available. No probation, medical, adoption, juvenile or sealed records released. Will fax results. Copy fee: $.75 per page. Cert fee: $6.60. Payee: Clerk of Superior Court. Personal checks accepted. Prepayment required. Mail requests: SASE required. Mail turnaround time 1 week.

Superior Court - Civil 1225 Fallon St, Rm 109, Oakland, CA 94612; 510-272-6503. Hours: 8:30AM-4:30PM (PST). *Civil Actions Over $25,000, Probate.* www.co.alameda.ca.us/courts/index.shtml
Note: Located at the Rene C Davidson Courthouse.

Civil Records: Access: Mail, in person, online. Both court and visitors may perform in person searches. Search fee: $5.00 per name per year. Additional $5.00 fee for years prior to 1974. Required to search: name, years to search. Civil cases indexed by defendant, plaintiff. Civil records on computer from 1974, on microfiche and archived from 1900s. Online access to calendars, limited civil case summaries and complex litigations are free from Register of Actions/Domain Web at the website. Search limited cases by number; litigations by case name or number. At the website, search "Find Your Court Date" to determine if a name has an upcoming court date.
General Information: Public Access terminal is available. No sealed records nor adoption records released unless court ordered. Copy fee: $.75 per page. Cert fee: $6.60. Payee: Superior Court. Personal checks accepted. Prepayment required. Mail requests: SASE required. Mail turnaround time 2 weeks.

Superior Court South Branch/Hayward - Civil 24405 Amador St Rm 108, Hayward, CA 94544; 510-670-5060. Hours: 8:30AM-5PM (PST). *Civil, Probate.* www.co.alameda.ca.us/courts/index.shtml
Note: Located at the Hayward Hall of Justice.

Civil Records: Access: Mail, in person, online. Visitors must perform in person searches for themselves. Search fee: $5.00 per name. Required to search: name, years to search. Civil cases indexed by defendant, plaintiff. Civil records on computer from 1974, on microfiche and archived from 1900s. Online

access to calendars, limited civil case summaries and complex litigations are free from Register of Actions/Domain Web at the website. Search limited cases by number; litigations by case name or number. At the website, search "Find Your Court Date" to determine if a name has an upcoming court date.
General Information: Public Access terminal is available. No sealed files, paternity or adoption records released. Copy fee: $.75 per page. Cert fee: $6.60 per document. Payee: Clerk of Superior Court. Personal checks accepted. Prepayment required. Mail requests: SASE required. Mail turnaround time 2-3 weeks.

Alameda Branch Superior Court 2233 Shoreline Dr, Alameda, CA 94501; 510-268-4209; Civil phone: 510-268-4219; Criminal phone: 510-268-7494; Fax: 510-268-4273. Hours: 8:30AM-5:00PM (PST). *Felony, Misdemeanor, Civil Actions Under $25,000, Eviction, Small Claims.* www.co.alameda.ca.us/courts/index.shtml
Note: Co-extensive with the city limits of Alameda only. Located at the George E McDonald Hall of Justice.

Civil Records: Access: Mail, in person, online. Both court and visitors may perform in person searches. Search fee: $5.00 per name. Required to search: name, years to search. Civil cases indexed by defendant, plaintiff. Civil records on computer since 1987. Online access to calendars, limited civil case summaries and complex litigations are free from Register of Actions/Domain Web at the website. Search limited cases by number; litigations by case number.
Criminal Records: Access: Mail, in person. Both court and visitors may perform in person searches. Search fee: $5.00 per name. Required to search: name, years to search, DOB, signed release; also helpful: SSN. Criminal records on computer 7 years back. At the website, search "Find Your Court Date" to determine if a name has an upcoming court date. Only seven year search available.
General Information: Public Access terminal is available. No confidential records released. Will fax results to local or toll free line. Copy fee: $.75 per page. Cert fee: $6.60 per document. Payee: Alameda Superior Court. Personal checks accepted. Credit cards accepted. Accepted in person only. Prepayment required. Mail requests: SASE required. Mail turnaround time 1 week.

Berkeley/Albany Superior Court - Civil 2000 Center St, Rm 202, Berkeley, CA 94704; 510-644-6423. Hours: 8:30AM-4:00PM (PST). *Civil Actions Under $25,000, Eviction, Small Claims.* www.co.alameda.ca.us/courts/index.shtml
Note: Co-extensive with the city limits of Berkeley and Albany.

Civil Records: Access: Mail, in person, online. Both court and visitors may perform in person searches. Search fee: $5.00 per name. Required to search: name, years to search. Civil cases indexed by

defendant, plaintiff. Civil records on computer from 1986. Online access to calendars, limited civil case summaries and complex litigations are free from Register of Actions/Domain Web at the website. Search limited cases by number; litigations by case name or number. At the website, search "Find Your Court Date" to determine if a name has an upcoming court date.
General Information: Public Access terminal is available. No sealed, judge's notes or confidential records released. Copy fee: $.75 per page. Cert fee: $6.60. Payee: Berkeley Superior Court. Personal checks accepted. Prepayment required. Mail requests: SASE required. Mail turnaround time 1 week.

Fremont Superior Court 39439 Paseo Padre Pky, Fremont, CA 94538; Civil phone: 510-795-2360; Criminal phone: 510-795-2300; Fax: 510-795-2349. 8:30AM-5PM (PST). *Misdemeanor, Civil Actions Under $25,000, Eviction, Small Claims.* www.co.alameda.ca.us/courts/index.shtml
Note: Jurisdiction includes Fremont, Newark and Union City. Located at the Fremont Hall of Justice.

Civil Records: Access: Fax, mail, in person, online. Both court and visitors may perform in person searches. Search fee: $5.00 per name. Required to search: name, years to search. Civil cases indexed by defendant, plaintiff. Civil records on computer from 1990. Online access to calendars, limited civil case summaries and complex litigations are free at the DomainWeb section at the website. Search limited cases by number; litigations by case name or number.
Criminal Records: Access: Fax, mail, in person. Both court and visitors may perform in person searches. Search fee: $5.00 per name. Required to search: name, years to search, DOB, signed release. Criminal records on computer only go back 7 years. At the website, search "Find Your Court Date" to determine if a name has an upcoming court date.
General Information: Public Access terminal is available. (Public terminal for civil only.) No sealed or confidential records released. Will fax civil results only, $1.00 per page. Copy fee: $.75 per page. Cert fee: $6.75. Payee: Fremont Superior Court. Personal checks accepted. Prepayment required. Mail requests: SASE required. Mail turnaround time 1 week.

Hayward Superior Court 24405 Amador St, Hayward, CA 94544; Civil phone: 510-670-5059; Criminal phone: 510-670-6434; Fax: 510-670-5953. Hours: 8:30AM-4PM (PST). *Misdemeanor, Civil Actions Under $25,000, Eviction, Small Claims.* www.co.alameda.ca.us/courts/index.shtml
Note: Formerly San Leandro/Hayward Superior Ct. Includes the cities of San Leandro, Hayward and adjoining unincorporated areas of Castro Valley and San Lorenzo. Located at the Hayward Hall of Justice.

Civil Records: Access: Fax, mail, in person, online. Both court and visitors may perform in person searches. Search fee: $5.00 per name. Required to search: name, years to search. Civil cases indexed by defendant, plaintiff. Civil records on computer back

20 years; also on paper index. Online access to calendars, limited civil case summaries and complex litigations are free from Register of Actions/Domain Web at the website. Search limited cases by number; litigations by case name or number.

Criminal Records: Access: Mail, in person. Both court and visitors may perform in person searches. Search fee: $5.00 per name. Fee is per case. Required to search: name, years to search, DOB, signed release; also helpful: SSN. Criminal records on computer back 20 years; also on paper index. At the website, search "Find Your Court Date" to determine if a name has an upcoming court date.

General Information: Public Access terminal is available. No sealed or confidential records released. No fee to fax results. Copy fee: $.75 per page. Cert fee: $6.60. Payee: Clerk of the Court. Personal checks accepted. Visa, MC accepted. ATM card accepted. Prepayment required. Mail requests: SASE required. Mail turnaround time 2 weeks.

Oakland/Piedmont/Emeryville Superior Court - Civil
600 Washington St, 4th Fl, #4020, Oakland, CA 94607; 510-268-4222; Fax: 510-268-7807. Hours: 8:30AM-4PM (PST). *Civil Actions Under $25,000, Eviction, Small Claims.*
www.co.alameda.ca.us/courts/index.shtml
Note: Comprises the cities of Oakland, Piedmont and Emeryville. Located at the Allen E Broussard Justice Center.

Civil Records: Access: Mail, in person, online. Both court and visitors may perform in person searches. Search fee: $5.00 per name. Required to search: name, years to search. Civil cases indexed by defendant, plaintiff. Civil records on computer from 1990. Online access to calendars, limited civil case summaries and complex litigations are free from Register of Actions/Domain Web at the website. Search limited cases by number; litigations by case name or number. At the website, search "Find Your Court Date" to determine if a name has an upcoming court date.

General Information: Public Access terminal is available. No sealed or confidential records released. Copy fee: $.75 per page. Cert fee: $6.60. Payee: Oakland Superior Court. Personal checks accepted. Prepayment required. Mail requests: SASE required. Mail turnaround time 2-3 weeks.

Oakland/Piedmont/Emeryville Superior Court - Criminal
661 Washington St, 2nd Fl, Oakland, CA 94607; 510-268-7700; Fax: 510-268-7705. 8:30AM-5PM (PST). *Misdemeanor, Felony.*
www.co.alameda.ca.us/courts/index.shtml
Note: Comprises the cities of Oakland, Piedmont and Emeryville, Albany and Berkeley. Located at the Wiley W Manuel Courthouse.

Criminal Records: Access: Mail, in person. Both court and visitors may perform in person searches. Search fee: $5.00 per name. Required to search: name, years to search. Criminal records on computer from 1994, maintained since 1972. At the website, search "Find Your Court Date" to determine if a name has an upcoming court date.

General Information: Public Access terminal is available. No sealed or confidential records released. Copy fee: $.75 per page. Cert fee: $6.60 per document. Payee: Oakland Superior Court. Personal checks accepted. Prepayment required. Mail requests: SASE required. Mail turnaround time 1 week.

Pleasanton Superior Court
5672 Stoneridge Dr, Hall of Justice, Pleasanton, CA 94588; 925-803-7123; Civil phone: 925-551-6886; Criminal phone: 925-803-7995; Probate phone: 925-551-6886; Fax: 925-803-7979 (civ) 925-551-6862 (crim). Hours: 8:30AM-4PM (PST). *Misdemeanor, Civil Actions over $25,000, Eviction, Small Claims, Probate.*
www.co.alameda.ca.us/courts/index.shtml
Note: Includes the cities of Livermore, Dublin, Sunol and Pleasanton and all areas east to San Joaquin County line, north of Highway 580 to Contra Costa line. Located at the Gale/Schenone Hall of Justice.

Civil Records: Access: Mail, in person, online. Both court and visitors may perform in person searches. Search fee: $5.00 per name. Required to search: name, years to search. Civil cases indexed by defendant, plaintiff. Civil records on computer from 1990. Online access to calendars, civil case summaries, probate, family law, and and complex litigations are free from Register of Actions/Domain Web at the website. Search all cases by case number.

Criminal Records: Access: Mail, in person. Both court and visitors may perform in person searches. Search fee: $5.00 per name. Required to search: name, years to search; also helpful: address, DOB. Criminal records on computer from 1990. At the website, search "Find Your Court Date" to determine if a name has an upcoming court date within five days.

General Information: Public Access terminal is available. No records older than 10 years are released. Copy fee: $.75 per page. Cert fee: $6.60 per document. Payee: Alameda County Superior Court. Personal checks accepted. Visa, MC accepted. Prepayment required. Mail requests: SASE required. Mail turnaround time 4-6 weeks.

Berkeley/Albany Superior Court - Traffic
2000 Center St, Berkeley, CA 94704; 510-644-6888; Fax: 510-849-2813. Hours: 8:30AM-4:PM (PST). *Traffic.*
www.co.alameda.ca.us/courts/index.shtml
Note: This court no longer handles Misdemeanor cases; records are at the Oakland/Piedmont/Emeryville Superior Ct Criminal Div. at 661 Washington St, Oakland. Co-extensive with the city limits of Berkeley and Albany. Located at the Berkeley Courthouse.

Alpine County

Superior Court
PO Box 518, Markleeville, CA 96120; 530-694-2113; Fax: 530-694-2119. Hours: 8AM-Noon, 1-5PM (PST). *Felony, Misdemeanor, Civil, Eviction, Small Claims, Probate.*
www.alpine.courts.ca.gov
Civil Records: Access: Mail, in person. Both court and visitors may perform in person searches. Search fee: $5.00 per name per year. Required to search: name, years to search. Civil cases indexed by defendant, plaintiff. Civil records on index file from 1981, archived from 1800s. Computer records go back 10 years.

Criminal Records: Access: Mail, in person. Both court and visitors may perform in person searches. Search fee: $5.00 per name per year. Required to search: name, years to search; also helpful-SSN. Criminal records on index file from 1981, archived from 1800s. Computer records go back 10 years.

General Information: No juvenile, paternity, adoption or sealed released. Fee to fax results is $1.00 per page. Copy fee: $.50 per page. Cert fee: $6.60 per page. Payee: Alpine County Superior Court. Personal checks accepted. Prepayment required. Mail requests: SASE required. Mail turnaround time 1 week.

Amador County

Superior Court
108 Court St, Jackson, CA 95642; Civil phone: 209-223-6463; Criminal phone: 209-223-6320. Hours: 9.:3AM-4PM (PST). *Felony, Misdemeanor, Civil, Eviction, Small Claims, Probate.*
www.amadorcourt.org
Civil Records: Access: Mail, in person. Both court and visitors may perform in person searches. Search fee: $5.00 per name; clerk will search for specific information only. Required to search: name, years to search. Civil cases indexed by defendant, plaintiff. Civil records on computer from 1989, archived and indexed from 1800s. Court calendars are by date up to 10 days ahead at www.amadorcourt.org/courtcal/courtcal.html. Tentative rulings including previous year are free at www.amadorcourt.org/rulings/rulings.html.

Criminal Records: Access: Mail, in person. Only the court performs in person searches; visitors may not. Search fee: $5.00 per name. $5.00 for search by case number. Required to search: name, years to search. Criminal records on computer from 1989, archived and indexed from 1800s. Court calendars are by date up to 10 days ahead at www.amadorcourt.org/courtcal/courtcal.html. Tentative rulings including previous year are free at www.amadorcourt.org/rulings/rulings.html. Phone & fax access limited to agency searches.

General Information: No adoption, juvenile or paternity records released. Will fax results to 800 numbers only. Copy fee: $1.00 for first page, $.20 each add'l. Cert fee: $6.60. Payee: Superior Court Clerk. Personal checks accepted. Prepayment required. Mail requests: SASE required. Mail turnaround time 7-14 days.

Butte County

Superior Court
One Court St, Oroville, CA 95965; 530-532-7002; Civil phone: 530-532-7009; Criminal phone: 530-532-7012; Probate phone: 530-532-7017; Fax: 530-892-8516. Hours: 8:30AM-4PM *Felony, Misdemeanor, Small Claims, Eviction.*
www.courtinfo.ca.gov/courts/trial/butte
Note: This courthouse physically holds most criminal court files for the county; however, one can search the countywide computer index at any court. Civil cases were transferred to the Chico court in 2003.

Civil Records: Access: Fax, mail, in person, online. Both court and visitors may perform in person searches. Search fee: $5.00 per name. Required to search: name, years to search; also helpful: address. Civil cases indexed by defendant, plaintiff. Civil records on computer from 1988, on microfiche from 1983 thru 1988. Limited case index searching by name is free online at www.buttecourt.ca.gov/online_index/cmssearch.cfm. There is also a calendar lookup at www.buttecourt.ca.gov/calendarlookup/cmscalendarlookup.cfm.

Criminal Records: Access: Mail, in person, online. Both court and visitors may perform in person searches. Search fee: $5.00 per name. Required to search: name, years to search; also helpful: DOB. Criminal records on computer from 1988, on microfiche from 1983 thru 1988. Limited case index searching by name is free online at www.buttecourt.ca.gov/online_index/cmssearch.cfm. There is also a calendar lookup, see above.

General Information: Public Access terminal is available. No juvenile, paternity or adoption records released. Will fax results $5.00 1st page, $1.00 each add'l. Copy fee: $.50 per page. $1.00 minimum. Cert fee: $6.60 per document. Payee: Butte County Superior Court. Personal checks accepted. Visa, MC accepted. Prepayment required. Mail requests: SASE helpful. Turnaround time 2-5 days.

Chico Branch - Superior Court 655
Oleander Ave, Chico, CA 95926; 530-892-9407 (Traffic); Civil phone: 530-892-0849; Criminal phone: 530-532-7011. Hours: 8:30AM-4PM (PST). *Misdemeanor, Civil Actions, Eviction, Small Claims, Probate.*

Note: Active county Probate case records are located here; closed cases are archived in the basement at the main Superior Court in Oroville. This court handles civil cases previously handled by Oroville court.

Civil Records: Access: Mail, in person, online. Only the court performs in person searches; visitors may not. Search fee: $5.00 per name. Required to search: name, years to search. Civil cases indexed by defendant, plaintiff. Civil records in index files. Records destroyed after 10 years. Limited case index searching by name is free online at www.buttecourt.ca.gov/online_index/cmssearch.cfm. There is also a calendar lookup at www.buttecourt.ca.gov/calendarlookup/cmscalendarlookup.cfm.

Criminal Records: Access: Mail, in person, online. Only the court performs in person searches; visitors may not. Search fee: $5.00 per name. Required to search: name, years to search; also helpful: DOB. Criminal records in index files. Records destroyed after 10 years. Limited case index searching by name is free online at www.buttecourt.ca.gov/online_index/cmssearch.cfm. There is also a calendar lookup, see civil.

General Information: Public Access terminal is available. No sealed records released. Copy fee: $1.00 for first page, $.50 each add'l. Cert fee: $6.60. Payee: Superior Court. Personal checks accepted. Prepayment required. Mail requests: SASE required. Mail turnaround time 4 weeks.

Gridley Branch - Superior Court 239
Sycamore, Gridley, CA 95948; 530-846-5701 or 538-7551. Hours: 8AM-1PM 1st & 3rd Tuesday of month (PST). *Misdemeanor-Traffic, Eviction, Small Claims.*

Note: Only open cases are found at this location. Closed cases must be searched at either Chico or Oroville. When court is closed (all but 2 days a month) calls are routed to the Oroville court.

Civil Records: Access: Mail, online. Only the court performs in person searches; visitors may not. Search fee: $5.00 per name. Limited case index searching by name is free online at www.buttecourt.ca.gov/online_index/cmssearch.cfm. There is also a calendar lookup at www.buttecourt.ca.gov/calendarlookup/cmscalendarlookup.cfm.

Criminal Records: Access: Mail, online. Only the court performs in person searches; visitors may not. Search fee: $5.00 per name. Required to search: name, years to search. Limited case index searching by name is free online at www.buttecourt.ca.gov/online_index/cmssearch.cfm. There is also a calendar lookup, see above.

General Information: Copy fee: $.50 per page with $1.00 minimum. Cert fee: $6.60. Payee: Butte County Superior Court. Prepayment required. Mail turnaround time 2-15 days.

Paradise Branch - Superior Court 747
Elliott Rd, Paradise, CA 95969; 530-532-7018. Hours: 8:30AM-4PM (PST). *Misdemeanor-Traffic, Eviction, Small Claims.*
Civil Records: Civil records are located in the Chico Superior Court.
Criminal Records: Criminal records are located in the Oroville Superior Court.

Calaveras County

Superior Court 891 Mt Ranch Rd, San Andreas, CA 95249; 209-754-6311 info; Civil phone: 209-754-6310; Criminal phone: 209-754-6338; Probate phone: 209-754-6310; Fax: 209-754-6689. Hours: 8AM-4PM (PST). *Misdemeanor, Civil, Small Claims, Probate.*
www.co.calaveras.courts.ca.gov

Civil Records: Access: Phone, mail, in person. Both court and visitors may perform in person searches. Search fee: $5.00 per name. Fee is for each 15 year period. Required to search: name, years to search. Civil cases indexed by defendant, plaintiff. Civil records on computer since 6/96; in index books and microfiche from 1975.

Criminal Records: Access: Mail, in person. Both court and visitors may perform in person searches. Search fee: $5.00 per name. Fee is for each 15 year period. Required to search: name, years to search, DOB; also helpful: aliases. Criminal records on computer since 6/96; in index books and microfiche from 1975.

General Information: No juvenile or confidential records released. Will not fax results. Copy fee: $.50 per page. Cert fee: $6.60. Payee: Calaveras Superior Court. Personal checks accepted. Prepayment required. Mail requests: SASE required. Mail turnaround time 2-3 weeks.

Colusa County

Superior Court 532 Oak St, Colusa, CA 95932; 530-458-5149; Fax: 530-458-2230. Hours: 8:30AM-5PM (PST). *Felony, Civil Actions Over $25,000, Probate.*
Note: Since 1995, the records have been combined for both courts in this county; prior records must be searched at the individual courts. Dept. 1's courtroom is at 547 Market St.

Civil Records: Access: Mail, in person. Both court and visitors may perform in person searches. Search fee: $5.00 per name. Required to search: name, years to search. Civil cases indexed by defendant, plaintiff. Civil records on computer from 1986, in index files from 1800s.

Criminal Records: Access: Mail, in person. Both court and visitors may perform in person searches. Search fee: $5.00 per name. Required to search: name, years to search. Criminal records on computer from 1986, in index files from 1800s.

General Information: Public Access terminal is available. No juvenile, paternity (except Judgment) or adoption records released. Copy fee: $.50 per page. Cert fee: $6.60. Payee: Colusa County Superior Court. Personal checks accepted. Prepayment required. Mail requests: SASE required. Mail turnaround: 7 days.

Colusa Superior Court 532 Oak St, Colusa, CA 95932; 530-458-5149; Fax: 530-458-2230. Hours: 8:30AM-5PM (PST). *Felony, Misdemeanor, Civil, Eviction, Small Claims.*
www.colusa.courts.ca.gov
Note: Since 1995, records from both courts in this county have been combined; prior records must be searched at the individual courts.
Civil Records: Access: Mail, in person. Both court and visitors may perform in person searches. Search fee: $5.00 per name per year. Required to search: name, years to search. Civil cases indexed by defendant, plaintiff. Civil records on computer from 1994, index books prior.
Criminal Records: Access: Mail, in person. Both court and visitors may perform in person searches. Search fee: $5.00 per name per year. Required to search: name, years to search, DOB. Criminal records on computer from 1994, index books prior.

General Information: Public Access terminal is available. No sealed records released. Copy fee: $.50 per page. Cert fee: $6.60. Payee: Colusa Superior Court. Personal checks accepted. Prepayment required. Mail requests: SASE required. Mail turnaround time 1-2 days.

Contra Costa County

Superior Court 725 Court St, Martinez, CA 94553; 925-646-2950; Civil phone: 925-646-2951; Criminal phone: 925-646-2440. Hours: 8AM-3PM (PST). *Felony, Civil Actions Over $25,000, Probate.*
www.cc-courts.org/
Note: The Family Law Center can be reached at 925-957-7866.

Civil Records: Access: Mail, online, in person. Both court and visitors may perform in person searches. Search fee: $5.00 per name. Required to search: name, years to search. Civil cases indexed by defendant, plaintiff. Civil records on computer from 1987, on microfiche from 1900s. Civil case, Probate, Family and Small Claims information is free at www.cc-courts.org/civilcms.htm. Visitors can view microfiche.

Criminal Records: Access: Mail, in person. Both court and visitors may perform in person searches. Search fee: $5.00 per name. Required to search: name, DOB. Criminal records on computer from 1987, on microfiche from 1900s. Send written requests to Rm 127. Visitors can view microfiche.

General Information: No adoption, juvenile or sealed records released. Copy fee: $1.00 per page. Cert fee: $6.60 per document. Payee: Clerk of the Superior Court. Business checks accepted. Prepayment required. Mail requests: SASE required. Mail turnaround time 1 week.

Walnut Creek Branch - Superior Court
640 Ygnacio Valley Rd, Walnut Creek, CA 94596-3820; Civil phone: 925-646-6579; Criminal phone: 925-646-6572. Hours: 8AM-3PM (PST). *Felony, Misdemeanor, Civil Actions Under $25,000, Eviction, Small Claims.*
www.co.contra-costa.ca.us
Note: Includes Alamo, Canyon, Danville, Lafayette, Moraga, Orinda, Rheem, San Ramon, St Mary's College, Walnut Creek and Ygnacio Valley. Effective 01/01/99, this court has all civil records formerly at the municipal court in Concord.

Civil Records: Access: Phone, mail, online, in person. Both court and visitors may perform in person searches. Search fee: $5.00 per name. Add $5.00 archive retrieval fee for older cases. In person searching of microfiche is free. Required to search: name; also helpful: years to search. Civil cases indexed by defendant, plaintiff. Civil records on computer from 1991. Records are destroyed after 10 years. Civil case, Probate, Family and Small Claims data is free at www.cc-courts.org/civilcms.htm.

Criminal Records: Access: Mail, in person. Both court and visitors may perform in person searches. Search fee: $5.00 per name. Add $5.00 archive retrieval fee for older cases. In person searching of microfiche is free. Required to search: name, years to search, DOB. Criminal records go back 10 years.

General Information: No probation reports or sealed case records released. Copy fee: $1.00 per page. Cert fee: $6.60. Payee: Walnut Creek Superior Court. Personal checks accepted. Prepayment required. Mail requests: SASE required. Mail turnaround time: 4 days.

Pittsburg Branch - Superior Court 45

Civic Ave, Pittsburg, CA 94565-0431; Civil phone: 925-427-8159; Criminal phone: 925-427-8173. Hours: 8AM-3PM; (PST). *Felony, Misdemeanor, Civil Actions $25,000 and under, Eviction, Small Claims.*

www.co.contra-costa.ca.us

Note: Includes Antioch, Bay Pt., Bradford Island, Brentwood, Byron, Discovery Bay, Knightsen, Oakley, Pittsburg.

Civil Records: Access: Mail, online, in person. Both court and visitors may perform in person searches. Search fee: $5.00 per name. Required to search: name, years to search. Civil cases indexed by defendant, plaintiff. Civil records on computer from 1991. Records are destroyed after 10 years. Civil case, Probate, Family and Small Claims information is free at www.cc-courts.org/index.htm.

Criminal Records: Access: Mail, in person. Both court and visitors may perform in person searches. Search fee: $5.00 per name. Required to search: name, years to search, DOB. Criminal records on computer from 1991, index files for 10 years. Records are destroyed after 10 years. Visitor may search microfiche only.

General Information: No probation reports released. Copy fee: $1.00 per page. Cert fee: $6.60. Payee: Superior Court. Personal checks accepted. Prepayment required. Mail requests: SASE required. Mail turnaround time 2 days.

Richmond Superior Court 100 37th St Rm

185, Richmond, CA 94805; Civil phone: 510-374-3137; Criminal phone: 510-374-3158. Hours: 8AM-3PM (PST). *Misdemeanor, Civil Actions Under $25,000, Eviction, Small Claims.*

www.co.contra-costa.ca.us

Note: Includes Crockett, El Cerrito, El Sobrante, Hercules, Kensington, North Richmond, Pinole, Point Richmond, Port Costa, Richmond, Rodeo, Rollingwood and San Pablo.

Civil Records: Access: Mail, in person, online. Both court and visitors may perform in person searches. Search fee: $5.00 per name. Required to search: name. Civil cases indexed by defendant, plaintiff. Civil records on computer from 1991. Records are destroyed after 10 years. Civil case, Probate, Family and Small Claims information is free at www.cc-courts.org/civilcms.htm.

Criminal Records: Access: Mail, in person. Only the court performs in person searches; visitors may not. Search fee: $5.00 per name. There is an additional fee for retrieval of archive files. Required to search: name, years to search; also helpful: address, DOB, SSN. Criminal records on computer from 1991, index files from 1983. Records are destroyed after 10 years.

General Information: No probation reports released. Copy fee: $1.00 per page. Cert fee: $6.60. Payee: Richmond Superior Court. Personal checks accepted. Prepayment required. Mail requests: SASE required. Mail turnaround time 5 days.

Del Norte County

Superior Court 450 "H" St, Rm 209, Crescent City, CA 95531; 707-464-8115; Fax: 707-465-4005. Hours: 8AM-5PM (PST). *Felony, Misdemeanor, Civil, Eviction, Small Claims, Probate.*

Civil Records: Access: Fax, mail, in person. Only the court performs in person searches; visitors may not. Search fee: $5.00 per name per year. Required to search: name, years to search. Civil cases indexed by defendant, plaintiff. Civil records archived and in index files.

Criminal Records: Access: Mail, fax, in person. Only the court performs in person searches; visitors may not. Search fee: $5.00 per name per year. Required to search: name, years to search, DOB,

middle name; also helpful-SSN. Criminal records archived and in index files.

General Information: No adoption, juvenile, probate, LPS conservatorship released. Copy fee: $.50 per page. Cert fee: $7.00. Plus $.50 per page. Payee: Superior Court. Personal checks accepted. Prepayment required. Mail requests: SASE required. Mail turnaround time 1-2 days.

El Dorado County

Placerville Branch - Superior Court 495

Main St, Placerville, CA 95667; 530-621-6426; Criminal phone: 530-622-6427; Fax: 530-622-9774. Hours: 8AM-2PM (PST). *Felony.*

http://eldocourtweb.eldoradocourt.org/

Note: Also handles Juvenile and Family Law.

Civil Records: Access: Mail, in person. Both court and visitors may perform in person searches. Search fee: $5.00 per name. Required to search: name, years to search. Civil cases indexed by defendant, plaintiff. Civil records on computer from 2000, in hardbound books from 1979 to 1999, prior archived in Placerville.

Criminal Records: Access: Mail, fax, in person. Both court and visitors may perform in person searches. Search fee: $5.00 per name. Required to search: name, years to search. Criminal records on computer from 2000, in hardbound books from 1979 to 1999, prior archived in Placerville.

General Information: No adoption, juvenile, mental or confidential released. Will not fax results. Copy fee: $.50 per page. Cert fee: $6.60. Payee: Superior Court. Personal checks accepted. Prepayment required. Mail requests: SASE required. Mail turnaround time 2 weeks.

South Lake Tahoe Branch - Superior Court - Civil 1354 Johnson Blvd #2, South Lake

Tahoe, CA 96150; 530-573-3075; Fax: 530-544-6532. 8AM-2PM (PST). *Civil, Eviction, Probate.*

http://eldocourtweb.eldoradocourt.org

Civil Records: Access: Mail, in person. Both court and visitors may perform in person searches. Search fee: $5.00 per name. Required to search: name, years to search; also helpful-case number. Civil cases indexed by defendant, plaintiff. Civil records on computer from 1989, in hardbound books from 1979 to 1989, prior archived in Placerville. Judge's weekly tentative rulings may be free online at the website.

General Information: No adoption, juvenile, mental or confidential released. Copy fee: $.50 per page. Cert fee: $6.60. Payee: Superior Court. Personal checks accepted. Prepayment required. Mail requests: SASE required. Mail turnaround time 2 weeks.

South Lake Tahoe Branch - Superior Court - Criminal 1354 Johnson Blvd #1, South

Lake Tahoe, CA 96150; 530-573-3044; Fax: 530-542-9102. Hours: 8AM-2PM (PST). *Felony, Misdemeanor.*

http://eldocourtweb.eldoradocourt.org

Criminal Records: Access: Mail, in person. Both court and visitors may perform in person searches. Search fee: $5.00 per name. Required to search: name, years to search; also helpful: DOB, SSN. Criminal records on computer from 1991, index files from 1983. Records are destroyed after 10 years. Judge's weekly tentative rulings may be free online at the website. Faxed record requests must be prepaid.

General Information: No probation reports released. Copy fee: $.50 per page. Cert fee: $6.60. Payee: El Dorado Superior Court. Personal checks accepted. Credit cards not accepted. Prepayment required. Mail requests: SASE required. Mail turnaround time 2 weeks.

Cameron Park Branch - Superior Court

3321 Cameron Park Dr, Cameron Park, CA 95682; 530-621-5867; Fax: 530-672-2413. Hours: 8AM-3PM (PST). *Civil, Probate.*

http://eldocourtweb.eldoradocourt.org/

Note: This is a Trial and Law & Motion court. Only records after 2000 are housed here. Records from 1999 and prior are available at the Placerville Branch Superior Court.

Civil Records: Access: Mail, in person. Both court and visitors may perform in person searches. Search fee: $5.00 per name. Required to search: name, years to search. Civil records on computer from 2000, index cards prior. Records are destroyed after 10 years.

General Information: Will not fax results. Copy fee: $.50 per page. Cert fee: $6.60 per document. Payee: Superior Court. Personal checks accepted. Prepayment required. Mail requests: SASE required. Mail turnaround time 1 week.

Westen Slope Branch Superior Court

2850 Fairlane Ct, Bldg C, Placerville, CA 95667; Civil phone: 530-621-7470; Criminal phone: 530-621-7464. Hours: 8AM-3PM M-F (PST). *Misdemeanor, Small Claims, Evictions, Traffic.*

http://eldocourtweb.eldoradocourt.org/

Note: Also known as the Fairlane Branch. Also hears felony arraignments.

Civil Records: Access: Mail, in person. Both court and visitors may perform in person searches. Search fee: $5.00 per name per year. Required to search: name, years to search. Civil cases indexed by defendant, plaintiff. Civil records on computer from 2000. Judge's weekly tentative rulings may be free online at the website. Send search requests to Dept. 8.

Criminal Records: Access: Mail, in person. Both court and visitors may perform in person searches. Search fee: $5.00 per name. Required to search: name, years to search; also helpful: DOB. Criminal records on computer from 2000, prior on index books, index files from 1983. Records are destroyed after 10 years. Address search requests to Dept 7.

General Information: No probation reports released. Copy fee: $.50 per page. Cert fee: $6.60. Payee: El Dorado County Superior Courts. Personal checks accepted. Prepayment required. Mail requests: SASE required. Mail turnaround time 2 weeks.

Fresno County

Superior Court 1100 Van Ness Ave, #401, Fresno, CA 93724; Civil phone: 559-488-3453; Criminal phone: 559-488-3142 misd.; 559-488-3388 felony; Probate phone: 559-488-3618; Fax: 559-488-1976 civ; 559-488-6799 felony fax; 488-1654 misd. Fax. Hours: 8AM-3PM; clerk open to researcher 9AM-3PM (PST). *Felony, Misdemeanor, Civil, Small Claims, Probate.*

www.co.fresno.ca.us/2810/

Note: Felony address is B-102; Misdemeanor address is Rm 402; Civil unlimited is RM 401.

Civil Records: Access: Phone, fax, mail, in person, online. Both court and visitors may perform in person searches. Search fee: $5.00 per name. Required to search: name, years to search. Civil cases indexed by defendant, plaintiff. Civil records on computer back to 1976, on microfiche, index files and archived from 1800s. Online access to civil, probate, family, small claims cases is free at http://banweb.co.fresno.ca.us/plsql/ck_public_qry_main.cp_main_idx.

Criminal Records: Access: Phone, fax, mail, in person. Both court and visitors may perform in person searches. Search fee: $5.00 per name. Required to search: name, years to search. Criminal records on computer back to 1976, microfiche, index files and archived from 1800s.

General Information: Public Access terminal is available. No confidential, adoption or juvenile records released. Copy fee: $.50 per page. Cert fee: $6.60. Payee: Superior Court Clerk's Office. Personal checks accepted. Prepayment required. Mail requests: SASE required. Mail turnaround time 3-5 days.

Clovis Division - Superior Court 1011 5th

St, Clovis, CA 93612; 559-299-4964; Fax: 559-299-2595. Hours: 8AM-3PM (PST). *Traffic, Misdemeanor, Civil Actions Under $25,000, Eviction, Small Claims.*
www.fresno.ca.gov/2810/default.htm
Note: Includes Alder Springs, Auberry, Big Creek, Burroughs Valley, Clovis, Friant, Huntington Lake, Millerton Lake, Pine Ridge, Prather, Shaver, Tollhouse, and Watts. Does felony welfare fraud cases only.

Civil Records: Access: Mail, in person, online. Only the court performs in person searches; visitors may not. Search fee: $5.00. Required to search: name, years to search. Civil cases indexed by defendant, plaintiff. Civil records on computer and index files from 1983. Records destroyed after 10 years. Online access to civil, probate, family, small claims cases is free at http://banweb.co.fresno.ca.us/plsql/ck_publ ic_qry_main.cp_main_idx.
Criminal Records: Access: Mail, in person. Only the court performs in person searches; visitors may not. Search fee: $5.00. Required to search: name, years to search, DOB. Criminal records on computer and index files from 1983. Records destroyed after 10 years.
General Information: No probation reports released. Will not fax results. Copy fee: $.50 per page. Cert fee: $6.60. Payee: Clovis Superior Court. Personal checks accepted. Prepayment required. Mail requests: SASE required. Mail turnaround time 1 week.

Coalinga Division - Superior Court 160 W

Elm St, Coalinga, CA 93210; 559-935-2017/2018; Fax: 559-935-5324. Hours: 8AM-3PM (PST). *Misdemeanor, Civil Actions Under $25,000, Eviction, Small Claims.*
www.fresno.ca.gov/2810/default.htm
Note: Includes Coalinga and Huron.

Civil Records: Access: Mail, in person, online. Only the court performs in person searches; visitors may not. No search fee. Required to search: name, years to search; also helpful: address. Civil cases indexed by defendant, plaintiff. Civil records on index cards and are computerized since 1990. Will only search back 10 years. Free access to civil, probate, family, small claims at http://banweb.co.fresno.ca.us/plsql/ck_pu blic_qry_main.cp_main_idx.
Criminal Records: Access: Mail, in person. Only the court performs in person searches; visitors may not. No search fee. Required to search: name, years to search, DOB; also helpful: address. Criminal records on computer from 1990, on index cards prior. Will only search back 10 years, Traffic 10 years.
General Information: No confidential records or cases not finished released. Copy fee: $.50 per page. Cert fee: $6.60. Payee: Superior Court. Personal checks accepted. Prepayment required. Mail requests: SASE required. Mail turnaround time 1 week.

Firebaugh Division - Superior Court 1325

"O" St, Firebaugh, CA 93622; 559-659-2011/2012; Fax: 559-659-6228. Hours: 8AM-3PM (PST). *Misdemeanor, Civil Actions Under $25,000, Eviction, Small Claims.*
www.fresno.ca.gov/2810/default.htm
Note: Includes Firebaugh and Mendota.

Civil Records: Access: Phone, fax, mail, in person, online. Only the court performs in person searches; visitors may not. Search fee: $5.00 per name. Required to search: name, years to search. Civil cases

indexed by defendant, plaintiff. Civil records on computer from 1990, index cards prior. Will only search back 7 years. Free access to civil, probate, family, small claims cases at http://banweb.co.f resno.ca.us/plsql/ck_public_qry_main.cp_main_idx.
Criminal Records: Access: Phone, fax, mail, in person. Only the court performs in person searches; visitors may not. Search fee: $5.00 per name. Required to search: name, years to search, DOB. Criminal records on computer from 1990. Will only search back 7 years.
General Information: No confidential records released. Will not fax results. Copy fee: $.50 per page. Cert fee: $6.60. Payee: Firebaugh Superior Court. Personal checks accepted. Prepayment required. Mail requests: SASE required. Mail turnaround time 1 week.

Fowler Division - Superior Court PO Box

400, Fowler, CA 93625; 559-834-3215; Fax: 559-834-1645. 8AM-3PM (PST). *Misdemeanor, Civil Actions Under $25,000, Eviction, Small Claims.*
www.fresno.ca.gov/2810/default.htm
Note: This court holds the records for the closed courts in Caruthers, Parlier, and Selma (no criminal) as well as cases from the cities of Bowles, Del Rey, Fowler, Kinopburg, Monmouth, and Raisin City (no criminal).

Civil Records: Access: Mail, in person, online. Only the court performs in person searches; visitors may not. Search fee: $5.00 per name. Required to search: name, years to search. Civil cases indexed by defendant, plaintiff. Civil records on index cards. Will only search back 7 years. Online access to civil, probate, family, small claims cases is free at http://banweb.co.fresno.ca.us/plsql/ck_public_qry_ma in.cp_main_idx.
Criminal Records: Access: Mail, in person. Only the court performs in person searches; visitors may not. Search fee: $5.00 per name. Required to search: name, years to search; also helpful: DOB, SSN. Criminal records on computer from 1990, index cards prior. Will only search back 7 years.
General Information: No confidential records released. Copy fee: $.50 per page. Cert fee: $6.60. Payee: Fowler Superior Court. Personal checks accepted. Prepayment required. Mail requests: SASE required. Mail turnaround time 1 week.

Kerman Division - Superior Court 719 S

Madera Ave, Kerman, CA 93630; 559-846-7371/7372; Fax: 559-846-5751. Hours: 8AM-3PM M-F (PST). *Misdemeanor, Civil Actions Under $25,000, Eviction, Small Claims.*
www.fresno.ca.gov/2810/default.htm
Note: The court holds preliminary hearings for felonies. Includes Biola, Biola Junction, Cantua, Five Points, Helm, Kerman, Rolinda, San Joaquin, and Tranquility.

Civil Records: Access: Phone, mail, in person, online. Both court and visitors may perform in person searches. No search fee. Required to search: name, years to search. Civil cases indexed by defendant, plaintiff. Civil records on index cards, computerized since 1994. Court will only search back 7 years. Online access to civil, probate, family, small claims cases is free at http://banweb.co.fresno.ca.us/pl sql/ck_public_qry_main.cp_main_idx.
Criminal Records: Access: Phone, mail, in person. Only the court performs in person searches; visitors may not. No search fee. Required to search: name, years to search. Criminal records on computer from 1994 index cards prior. Court will only search back 7 years. May have terminals available at archives location; 1963 E St, Kerman, CA, call 559-233-2800.
General Information: No confidential records released. Copy fee: $.50 per page. Cert fee: $7.00.

Payee: Superior Court. Personal checks accepted. Prepayment required. Mail requests: SASE required. Mail turnaround time 1 week.

Kingsburg Division - Superior Court 1600

California St, Kingsburg, CA 93631; 559-897-2241; Fax: 559-897-1419. Hours: 8AM-3PM (PST). *Felony, Misdemeanor.*
www.fresno.ca.gov/2810/default.htm
Note: This court includes records from the branch court closed in Riverdale, Selma/Parlick/Fowler (criminal only), and cases from the cities of Burrel, Camden, Kingsburg, Lanare, Laton, and Riverdale.

Civil Records: Access: Mail, in person, online. Only the court performs in person searches; visitors may not. Search fee: $5.00 per name. Required to search: name, years to search. Online access to civil, probate, family, small claims cases is free at http://banweb.co.fresno.ca.us/plsql/ck_public_qry_ma in.cp_main_idx.
Criminal Records: Access: Mail, in person. Only the court performs in person searches; visitors may not. Search fee: $5.00 per name. Required to search: name, years to search, DOB. Criminal records on computer from April, 1994, index cards prior.
General Information: No confidential records released. Will not fax results. Copy fee: $.50 per page. Cert fee: $7.00. Payee: Superior Court. Personal checks accepted. Prepayment required. Mail requests: SASE required. Mail turnaround time 1 week.

Reedley Division - Superior Court 815

"G" St, Reedley, CA 93654; 559-638-3114; Fax: 559-637-1534. Hours: 8AM-3PM (PST). *Misdemeanor, Civil Actions Under $25,000, Eviction, Small Claims.*
www.fresno.ca.gov/2810/default.htm
Note: Includes Badger, Cedarbrook, Cedar Pines, Centerville, Dunlap, Hume, Kings River Canyon, Navalencia, Minkler, Miramonte, Orange Cove, Piedra, Reedley, Sanger, Squaw Valley, Trimmer Springs and Wahtoke.

Civil Records: Access: Mail, in person, online. Both court and visitors may perform in person searches. Search fee: $5.00 per name. Required to search: name, years to search. Civil cases indexed by defendant, plaintiff. Civil records on computer back 10 years, index cards prior. Will only search back 7 years. Online access to civil, probate, family, small claims cases is free at http://banweb.co.fresno.ca.u s/plsql/ck_public_qry_main.cp_main_idx.
Criminal Records: Access: Mail, in person. Both court and visitors may perform in person searches. Search fee: $5.00 per name. Required to search: name, years to search, DOB. Criminal records on computer back 10 years, index cards prior. Will only search back 7 years.
General Information: No confidential records released. Copy fee: $.50 per page. Cert fee: $6.60. Payee: Reedley Superior Court. Personal checks accepted. Prepayment required. Mail requests: SASE required. Mail turnaround time 1 week.

Sanger Division - Superior Court c/o

Reedley Division Superior Court, 815 "G" St, Reedley, CA 93654; 559-638-3114; Fax: 559-637-1534. Hours: 8AM-Noon, 1-4PM (1-4 for phone calls) (PST). *Misdemeanor, Civil Actions Under $25,000, Eviction, Small Claims.*
www.fresno.ca.gov/2810/default.htm
Note: This court closed as of 07/03. Case files went to the Court in Reedley. The Sanger court had jurisdiction over Centerville, Minkler, Piedra, Sanger, and Trimmer Springs.

Selma Division - Superior Court 127 E Mercer St, Fowler, CA 93626. *Misdemeanor, Civil Actions Under $25,000, Eviction, Small Claims.*
Note: This court closed as of 06/03. Criminal case files went to the Court in Kingsburg. Civil and small claims to court in Fowler.

Glenn County

Superior Court 526 W Sycamore, Willows, CA 95988; 530-934-6446; Fax: 530-934-6728. Hours: 8AM-5PM (PST). *Felony, Misdemeanor, Civil, Small Claims, Probate.*
Note: Records from the municipal court were combined with this court when the courts were consolidated.Records-530-934-6461
Civil Records: Access: Mail, in person. Both court and visitors may perform in person searches. Search fee: $5.00 per name. Required to search: name, years to search. Civil cases indexed by defendant, plaintiff. Civil records on computer back to 1996, on microfiche, archived and in index file from 1894.
Criminal Records: Access: Mail, in person. Both court and visitors may perform in person searches. Search fee: $5.00 per search. Required to search: name, years to search; also helpful: DOB. Criminal records on computer back to 1996, on microfiche, archived and in index file from 1894.
General Information: Public Access terminal is available. No adoption, juvenile or paternity released. Copy fee: $.50 per page. Cert fee: $7.00. Payee: Superior Court. Personal checks accepted. Prepayment required. Mail requests: SASE required. Mail turnaround time 1 day.

Humboldt County

Superior Court 825 5th St, 421 I St., Eureka, CA 95501; 707-445-7256. Hours: 10AM-4PM (PST). *Felony, Civil, Probate.*
Note: Countywide searching can be done from this court, records computerized for 10 years. The former Eureka, Eel River, and North Humboldt Muni. Court Divisions have been combined with this court. Physical address is at 421 I St.
Civil Records: Access: Mail, in person. Both court and visitors may perform in person searches. Search fee: $5.00 per name. Required to search: name, years to search. Civil cases indexed by defendant, plaintiff. Civil records on computer back to 1993; on microfiche and archived from 1964.
Criminal Records: Access: Mail, in person. Both court and visitors may perform in person searches. Search fee: $5.00 per name. Required to search: name, years to search; also helpful: DOB. Criminal records on computer back to 1985; on microfiche and archived from 1964.
General Information: No probation, medical, adoption, juvenile or sealed records released. Copy fee: $.50 per page. Cert fee: $6.60. Payee: Humboldt Superior Court. Personal checks accepted. Prepayment required. Mail requests: SASE required. Mail turnaround time 3 weeks.

Garberville Branch - Superior Court C/O Eureka Superior Court, 825 5th St, Eureka, CA 95501; 707-445-7256. Hours: 9AM-3PM Fri only (PST). *Misdemeanor, Eviction, Small Claims.*
Note: Court is open one day a week no longer opens new civil cases. All mail inquires or research are directed to the Superior Court in Eureka.

Klamath/Trinity Branch - Superior Court, Eureka, CA 95501. *Misdemeanor, Civil Actions Under $25,000, Eviction, Small Claims.*
Note: Records for this branch are housed at the main court in Eureka.

Imperial County

Imperial Branch - Superior Court 939 W Main St, El Centro, CA 92243; Civil phone: 760-482-4217; Criminal phone: 760-482-4256; Fax: 760-482-4219/Cri760-482-4918. Hours: 8AM-4PM (PST). *Felony, Misdemeanor, Civil, Eviction, Small Claims, Probate.*
Note: All record searching for Imperial county must be done at each location.
Civil Records: Access: Mail, in person. Both court and visitors may perform in person searches. Search fee: $5.00 per name. Required to search: name, years to search. Civil cases indexed by defendant, plaintiff. Civil records on microfiche from 1972, in index file from 1917.
Criminal Records: Access: Mail, in person. Both court and visitors may perform in person searches. Search fee: $5.00 per name. Required to search: name, years to search. Criminal records on microfiche from 1972, index file from 1917.
General Information: No adoptions, juvenile, medical, probation or sealed records released. Will fax results for $1.00. Copy fee: $1.00 for first page, $.50 each add'l. Cert fee: $7.00. Payee: Imperial County Superior Court. Personal checks accepted. Prepayment required. Mail requests: SASE required. Mail turnaround time 2 weeks.

Brawley Branch - Superior Court 220 Main St., Brawley, CA 92227; 760-351-2840; Fax: 760-351-7703. Hours: 8AM-4PM (PST). *Misdemeanor, Civil Actions Under $25,000, Eviction, Small Claims.*
Note: There is no countywide database in this county.
Civil Records: Access: Phone, fax, mail, in person. Both court and visitors may perform in person searches. Search fee: $5.00 per name. Required to search: name, years to search. Civil cases indexed by defendant, plaintiff. Civil records on computer back 2 years (traffic from 1991), in index files from 1983. Records destroyed after 10 years.
Criminal Records: Access: Phone, fax, mail, in person. Only the court performs in person searches; visitors may not. Search fee: $5.00 per name. Required to search: name, years to search, DOB. Criminal records on computer back 2 years (traffic only from 1991), in index files from 1983. Records destroyed after 10 years.
General Information: No probation reports released. Copy fee: $1.00 for first page, $.50 each add'l. Cert fee: $6.60. Payee: Brawley Superior Court. Personal checks accepted. Prepayment required. Mail requests: SASE required. Mail turnaround time 1 week.

Calexico Branch - Superior Court 415 4th St, Calexico, CA 92231; 760-357-3726; Fax: 760-357-6571. Hours: 8AM-4PM (PST). *Misdemeanor, Civil Actions Under $25,000, Eviction, Small Claims.*
Note: There is no countywide database in this county.
Civil Records: Access: Fax, mail, in person. Both court and visitors may perform in person searches. Search fee: $5.00 per name. Required to search: name, years to search. Civil cases indexed by defendant, plaintiff. Civil records on computer from 1991, index files from 1983. Records destroyed after 10 years.
Criminal Records: Access: Fax, mail, in person. Only the court performs in person searches; visitors may not. Search fee: $5.00 per name. Required to search: name, years to search. Criminal records on computer from 1991, index files from 1983. Records destroyed after 10 years.
General Information: No probation reports released. Copy fee: $1.00 per page,$.50 Add'l. Cert fee: $7.00. Payee: Superior Court. Personal checks accepted.

Write case number on check. Prepayment required. Mail requests: SASE required. Mail turnaround time within 2 weeks.

Winterhaven Branch - Superior Court PO Box 1087 (2124 Winterhaven Dr), Winterhaven, CA 92283-1087; 760-572-0354; Fax: 760-572-2683. 8AM-Noon, 1-4PM (PST). *Eviction, Small Claims.*
Note: Misdemeanor and civil records have been moved to the Calexico Branch. Only small claims and traffic records remain here.

Inyo County

Superior Court PO Drawer U, 168 N Edwards St, Independence, CA 93526; 760-878-0218. Hours: 8AM- 4PM (PST). *Felony, Civil Actions Over $25,000, Probate.*
Note: There is no countywide database; branch court must be searched separately.
Civil Records: Access: Mail, in person. Both court and visitors may perform in person searches. Search fee: $6.00 per name. Required to search: name, years to search. Civil cases indexed by defendant, plaintiff. Civil records on computer to mid-1999, on microfiche and in index files from 1800s.
Criminal Records: Access: Mail, in person. Both court and visitors may perform in person searches. Search fee: $6.00 per name. Required to search: name, years to search. Criminal records on computer back to 1993, on microfiche and in index files from 1800s.
General Information: No adoptions, juvenile, medical, probation or sealed records released. Will fax to 800 number, no fee; otherwise $1.00 per page. Copy fee: $1.00 per page. Cert fee: $7.00 plus $1.00 per page after the first. Payee: Inyo Superior Court. Personal checks or credit cards accepted. Prepayment required. Mail requests: SASE required. Mail turnaround time 2-3 business days.

Bishop Branch - Superior Court 301 W Line St, Bishop, CA 93514; 760-872-4971. Hours: 8AM-4PM (open 12-1) (PST). *Misdemeanor, Civil Actions Under $25,000, Eviction, Small Claims.*
Note: There is no countywide database, each branch court must be searched.
Civil Records: Access: Mail, in person. Only the court performs in person searches; visitors may not. Search fee: $6.00 per name. Required to search: name, years to search. Civil cases indexed by defendant, plaintiff. Civil records on index cards. Will only search back 7 years.
Criminal Records: Access: Mail, in person. Only the court performs in person searches; visitors may not. Search fee: $6.00 per name. Required to search: name, years to search. Criminal records on computer from 1993, index cards prior. Will only search back 7 years.
General Information: No confidential records released. Will fax to 800 number, no fee; otherwise $1.00 per page. Copy fee: $1.00 per page. Cert fee: $8.00 plus $1.00 per page after the first. Payee: Superior Court. Personal checks or credit cards accepted. Prepayment required. Mail requests: SASE required. Mail turnaround time 1 week.

Independence Limited Branch - Superior Court PO Drawer 518, 168 N Edwards St, Independence, CA 93526; 760-878-0319; Fax: 760-878-0334. Hours: 9AM-5PM (PST). *Misdemeanor, Civil Actions Under $25,000, Eviction, Small Claims.*
Note: There is no countywide database, each branch court must be searched.
Civil Records: Access: Mail, in person. Both court and visitors may perform in person searches. Search fee: $6.00 per name. Required to search: name, years

to search. Civil cases indexed by defendant, plaintiff. Civil records on computer back to 1999, in index books and index cards. Will only search back 7 years.

Criminal Records: Access: Mail, in person. Both court and visitors may perform in person searches. Search fee: $6.00 per name. Required to search: name, years to search, DOB. Criminal records on computer from 2/1993, index books and index cards prior. Will only search back 7 years.

General Information: No confidential records released. Copy fee: $1.00 per page. Cert fee: $7.00 plus $1.00 per page after the first. Payee: Inyo County Court. Personal checks or credit cards accepted. Prepayment required. Mail requests: SASE required. Mail turnaround time 1 week.

Kern County

Superior Court 1415 Truxtun Ave, Bakersfield, CA 93301; 661-868-5393; Criminal phone: 661-868-4888; Fax: 800-487-4567 (civ only). 8AM-5PM (PST). *Felony, Civil Actions, Eviction, Small Claims.* www.co.kern.ca.us/courts

Civil Records: Access: Mail, fax, in person. Both court and visitors may perform in person searches. Search fee: $5.00 per name per year. Required to search: name, years to search. Civil cases indexed by defendant, plaintiff. Civil records on microfiche from 1964, archived and in index file from 1800s.

Criminal Records: Access: Mail, in person. Both court and visitors may perform in person searches. Visitors may search counter index which excludes identifiers; court searches electronically with identifiers. Search fee: $5.00 per name per year. A $5.00 court surcharge added Aug 1, 2003. Required to search: name, years to search, DOB. Criminal records on computer from 1989, on microfiche, archived, and in index files. Current court calendars are free at www.co.kern.ca.us/courts/crimcal/courtcalendar.asp.

General Information: Public Access terminal is available. (Civil records on microfiche only, which you can search yourself; civil records soon to be computerized.) No adoptions, juvenile, medical, probation or sealed records released. Copy fee: $.75 per page. Cert fee: $6.60. Payee: Kern County Superior Court. Personal checks accepted. Prepayment required. Mail requests: SASE required. Mail turnaround time 1 day to 1 week.

Delano/McFarland Branch Superior Court - North Division 1122 Jefferson St, Delano, CA 93215; 661-720-5800; Criminal phone: x3; Fax: 661-721-1237. Hours: 8AM-5PM (PST). *Misdemeanor, Civil Actions Under $25,000, Eviction, Small Claims.* www.co.kern.ca.us/courts

Civil Records: Access: Fax, mail, in person. Both court and visitors may perform in person searches. Search fee: $5.00 per name per year. Required to search: name, years to search. Civil cases indexed by defendant, plaintiff. Civil records in index files from 1983. Records destroyed after 10 years.

Criminal Records: Access: Mail, in person. Both court and visitors may perform in person searches. Visitors may search counter index which excludes identifiers; court searches electronically with identifiers. Search fee: $5.00 per name per year. Required to search: name, years to search; also helpful: DOB. Criminal records on computer from 1988, in index files from 1983. Records destroyed after 10 years. Current court calendars are free at www.co.kern.ca.us/courts/crimcal/courtcalendar.asp.

General Information: Public Access terminal is available. (Criminal records only.) No probation reports released. Copy fee: $.75 per page. Cert fee: $6.60. Payee: Superior Court Kern County-Delano/McFarland Branch. Personal checks accepted.

Prepayment required. Mail requests: SASE required. Mail turnaround time 2 days.

Kern River Branch Superior Court - East Division 7046 Lake Isabella Blvd, Lake Isabella, CA 93240; 760-549-2000; Fax: 760-549-2120. Hours: 8AM-4PM M-Th 8AM-5PM F (PST). *Misdemeanor, Civil Actions Under $25,000, Eviction, Small Claims.* www.co.kern.ca.us/courts/ Note: Includes the communities of Lake Isabella, Kern River, Weldon, Onxy, and Mt Mesa.

Civil Records: Access: Phone, fax, mail, in person. Only the court performs in person searches; visitors may not. Search fee: $5.00. Required to search: name, DOB, years to search. Civil cases indexed by defendant, plaintiff. Civil records on computer from 1991, in index files from 1983. Records destroyed after 10 years.

Criminal Records: Access: Phone, mail, in person. Both the court and visitors may perform in person searches. Search fee: $5.00. Required to search: name, years to search. Criminal records on computer from 1991, in index files from 1983. Records destroyed after 10 years. Current court calendars are free at www.co.kern.ca.us/courts/crimcal/courtcalendar.asp.

General Information: Public Access terminal is available. No probation reports released. Copy fee: $1.10 per page. Cert fee: $6.60 per document. Payee: East Kern Superior Court. Personal checks accepted. Visa, AmEx accepted. Prepayment required. Mail requests: SASE required. Mail turnaround: 2 days.

Lamont/Arvin Branch Superior Court - South Division 12022 Main St, Lamont, CA 93241; 661-868-5800; Fax: 661-845-9142. Hours: 8AM-5PM (PST). *Misdemeanor, Civil Actions Under $25,000, Eviction, Small Claims.* www.co.kern.ca.us/courts

Civil Records: Access: Mail, in person. Only the court performs in person searches; visitors may not. Search fee: $5.00 per name. Required to search: name, years to search. Civil cases indexed by defendant, plaintiff. Civil records on computer from 1989. Records destroyed after 10 years.

Criminal Records: Access: Fax, mail, in person. Both court and visitors may perform in person searches. Visitors may search counter index which excludes identifiers; court searches electronically with identifiers. Search fee: $5.00 per name. Required to search: name, years to search, DOB; also helpful CA DL#, SSN, signed release. Criminal records on computer from 1989. Records destroyed after 10 years. Current court calendars are free online at www.co.kern.ca.us/courts/crimcal/courtcalendar.asp.

General Information: Public Access terminal is available. (Criminal only.) No probation reports released. No fee to fax results. Copy fee: $.75 per page. Cert fee: $6.60. Payee: Superior Court Lamont Branch. Personal checks accepted. Visa, AmEx accepted. Prepayment required. Mail requests: SASE required. Mail turnaround time 2 days.

Mojave Branch Superior Court - East Division 1773 Hwy 58, Mojave, CA 93501; 661-824-7100; Fax: 661824-7089. Hours: 8AM-5PM (PST). *Misdemeanor, Civil Actions Under $25,000, Eviction, Small Claims.* www.co.kern.ca.us/courts/ Note: Includes California City, Edwards AFB, Mojave, Boron, Rosemond, Cantil, and Tehachapi.

Civil Records: Access: Mail, fax, in person. Only the court performs in person searches; visitors may not. Search fee: $5.00 per name. Required to search: name, years to search. Civil cases indexed by defendant, plaintiff. Civil records on computer from 1991, in index files from 1983. Records destroyed after 10 years.

Criminal Records: Access: Mail, fax, in person. Only the court performs in person searches; visitors may not. Search fee: $5.00. Required to search: name, years to search, DOB. Criminal records on computer from 1991, in index files from 1983. Current court calendars are free online at www.co.kern.ca.us/courts/crimcal/courtcalendar.asp.

General Information: Public Access terminal is available. No probation reports released. Will not fax results. Copy fee: $.75 per page. Cert fee: $6.60 per page. Payee: East Kern Superior Court. Personal checks accepted. Visa, AmEx accepted; there is a $7.50 credit card charge. Additional fee charged for use of credit card. Prepayment required. Mail requests: SASE required. Mail turnaround time up to 1 week.

Ridgecrest Branch Superior Court - East Division 132 E Coso St, Ridgecrest, CA 93555; 760-384-5900; Civil phone: 760-384-5986; Fax: 760-384-5899. Hours: 8AM-5PM (PST). *Misdemeanor, Civil Actions Under $25,000, Eviction, Small Claims.* www.co.kern.ca.us/courts/ Note: Includes the communities of Ridgecrest, Inyokern, China lake, Johanesburg, and Randsburg.

Civil Records: Access: Mail, in person. Both court and visitors may perform in person searches. Search fee: $5.00 per name. Required to search: name, years to search. Civil cases indexed by defendant, plaintiff. Civil records on computer from 1990, in index files from 1983. Records destroyed after 10 years.

Criminal Records: Access: Mail, in person,phone, fax. Only the court performs in person searches; visitors may not. Search fee: $5.00 per name. Required to search: name, years to search; also helpful: DOB, SSN. Criminal records on computer from 1990, in index files from 1983. Records destroyed after 5 years. Current court calendars are free online at www.co.kern.ca.us/courts/crimcal/courtcalendar.asp.

General Information: Public Access terminal is available. No probation reports released. Will not fax results. Copy fee: $.75 per page. Cert fee: $6.60. Payee: Kern County Superior Court. Personal checks accepted. Visa, AmEx accepted. Prepayment required. Mail requests: SASE required. Mail turnaround time 2 days.

Shafter/Wasco Branch Superior Court - North Division 325 Central Valley Hwy, Shafter, CA 93263; 661-746-7500; Fax: 661-746-0545. Hours: 8AM-5PM (PST). *Misdemeanor, Civil Actions Under $25,000, Eviction, Small Claims.* www.co.kern.ca.us/courts

Civil Records: Access: Phone, fax, mail, in person. Both court and visitors may perform in person searches. Visitors may search counter index that excludes identifiers; court searches electronically with identifiers. Search fee: $5.00 per name per year. Required to search: name, years to search; also helpful: address. Civil cases indexed by defendant, plaintiff. Civil records go back to 1994.

Criminal Records: Access: Mail, in person. Both court and visitors may perform in person searches. Visitors may search counter index which excludes identifiers; court searches electronically with identifiers. Search fee: $5.00 per name. Required to search: name, years to search, DOB; also helpful: address, SSN. Criminal records on computer since 1988, traffic since 1991. Current court calendars are free online at www.co.kern.ca.us/courts/crimcal/courtcalendar.asp. Phone searches limited to a few names only.

General Information: Public Access terminal is available. (Terminal has criminal only.) No probation reports released. No fee to fax results. Copy fee: $.75

per page. Cert fee: $6.60 or $10.00 if a dissolution. Payee: Superior Court North Division. Personal checks accepted. Prepayment required. Mail requests: SASE required. Mail turnaround time 2 days.

Superior Court Metropolitan Division

1215 Truxtun Ave, Bakersfield, CA 93301; 661-868-2482; Fax: 661-868-2695. Hours: 8AM-5PM (PST). *Misdemeanor, Traffic.*
www.co.kern.ca.us/courts
Note: Formerly Bakersfield Muni. Court. Includes Bakersfield, Oildale, Edison, Glenville, Woody.

Criminal Records: Access: Mail, in person. Both court and visitors may perform in person searches. Visitors may search counter index which excludes identifiers; court searches electronically with identifiers. Search fee: $5.00 per name per year. Required to search: name, years to search. Criminal records on computer since 1988, microfilm since 1952. Current court calendars are free online at www.co.kern.ca.us/courts/crimcal/courtcalendar.asp.
General Information: Public Access terminal is available. No probation reports, rap sheets, medical or financial released. No fee to fax results. Will only fax one or two pages due to time constraints. Copy fee: $.75 per page. Cert fee: $6.60. Payee: Superior Court of California. Personal checks accepted. Prepayment required. Mail requests: SASE helpful. Turnaround time is 1 week.

Taft Branch Superior Court - South

Division 311 N Lincoln St, Taft, CA 93268; 661-763-8531; Fax: 661-763-2439. Hours: 8AM-Noon,1-5PM (PST). *Misdemeanor, Civil Actions Under $25,000, Eviction, Small Claims.*
www.co.kern.ca.us/courts
Civil Records: Access: Phone, mail, in person. Both court and visitors may perform in person searches. Search fee: $5.00 per name. Required to search: name, years to search; also helpful: address. Civil cases indexed by defendant, plaintiff. Civil records on computer from 1988, in index files from 1983. Records destroyed after 10 years.
Criminal Records: Access: Phone, mail, in person. Both court and visitors may perform in person searches. Search fee: $5.00 per name. Purchase of complaint and docket required. Required to search: name, years to search, DOB; also helpful: address, SSN. Criminal records on computer from 1988, in index files from 1983. Records destroyed after 10 years. Current court calendars are free online at www.co.kern.ca.us/courts/crimcal/courtcalendar.asp.
General Information: Public Access terminal is available. No probation reports released. Copy fee: $.75 per page. Cert fee: $6.60. Payee: South Taft Court. Personal checks accepted. Visa, MC, AmEx accepted. Prepayment required. Mail requests: SASE required. Mail turnaround time 2 days.

Kings County

Superior Court - Criminal

1426 South Dr, Hanford, CA 93230; 559-582-3211 X4838; Fax: 559-584-7054. 8AM-5PM (PST). *Felony, Misdemeanor.*
Criminal Records: Access: Mail, in person. Both court and visitors may perform in person searches. Search fee: $5.00 per name. Required to search: name, years to search, DOB. Criminal records on computer from 1991, in index files from 1983. Records destroyed after 10 years.
General Information: Public Access terminal is available. No probation or police reports released. Will not fax results. Copy fee: $.50 per page. Cert fee: $6.60. Payee: Kings County Superior Court. Personal checks accepted. Credit cards not accepted. Prepayment required. Mail requests: SASE required. Mail turnaround time 1 week.

Superior Court - Civil

1426 South Dr, Hanford, CA 93230; 559-582-3211 X2430; Fax: 559-584-0319. Hours: 8AM-5PM (PST). *Civil Actions, Eviction, Small Claims, Probate.*
Civil Records: Access: Mail, in person. Both court and visitors may perform in person searches. Search fee: $5.00 per name. Required to search: name, years to search. Civil cases indexed by defendant, plaintiff. Civil records on computer from 1989, on microfiche and archived from 1970s, in index file from 1914.
General Information: Public Access terminal is available. No adoptions, juvenile, medical, probation or sealed records released. Copy fee: $.50 per page. Cert fee: $6.60. Payee: Superior Court of the State of California. Business checks accepted. Checks accepted with proper identification. Prepayment required. Mail requests: SASE required. Mail turnaround time 1 week.

Avenal Division Superior Court

501 E Kings St, Avenal, CA 93204; 559-386-5225; Fax: 559-386-9452. Hours: 8AM-5PM (PST). *Misdemeanor, Civil Actions Under $25,000, Eviction, Small Claims.*
Civil Records: Access: Phone, fax, mail, in person. Both court and visitors may perform in person searches. Search fee: $5.00 per name. Required to search: name, years to search. Civil records on index cards, computerized.
Criminal Records: Access: Fax, mail, in person. Both court and visitors may perform in person searches. Search fee: $5.00 per name. Required to search: name, years to search, DOB. Criminal records on computer from 1991, index cards prior.
General Information: Public Access terminal is available. (Civil only.) No juvenile or adoption records released. Copy fee: $.50 per page. Cert fee: $6.60. Payee: Avenal Superior Court. Personal checks accepted. Prepayment required. Mail requests: SASE required. Mail turnaround time 1 week.

Corcoran Division Superior Court

1000 Chittenden Ave, Corcoran, CA 93212; 559-992-5193/5194; Fax: 559-992-5933. Hours: 8AM-5PM (PST). *Misdemeanor, Civil Actions Under $25,000, Eviction, Small Claims.*
Civil Records: Access:
Mail, in person. Only the court performs in person searches; visitors may not. Search fee: $5.00 per name. Required to search: name, years to search; also helpful: address. Civil cases indexed by defendant, plaintiff. Civil records on computer from 1990, index cards to 1974. Will only search back 7 years.
Criminal Records: Access: Mail, in person. Only the court performs in person searches; visitors may not. Search fee: $5.00 per name. Required to search: name, years to search, DOB; also helpful: address, aka's. Criminal records on computer from 1990, index cards to 1974. Will only search back 7 years.
General Information: No juvenile or adoption records released. Will not fax results. Copy fee: $.50 per page. Cert fee: $6.60. Payee: Kings County Superior Court. Personal checks accepted. Prepayment required. Mail requests: SASE required. Mail turnaround time 1 week.

Lemoore Division Superior Court

449 "C" St, Lemoore, CA 93245; 559-924-7757; Fax: 559-925-0319. 8AM-5PM (PST). *Misdemeanor, Civil Actions Under $25,000, Eviction, Small Claims.*
Note: Court says to search records at Hanford court;1426 S. Dr.,Hanford,Ca.93230,Ph-559-582-3211x4838 Criminal

Civil Records: Access: Mail, in person. Both court and visitors may perform in person searches. Search fee: $5.00 per name. Required to search: name, years to search. Civil cases indexed by defendant, plaintiff. Civil records computerized since 1990, on index cards

back to 1977. In person access limited. Fax requests are accepted, though the court will recommend a fax processing service. There is an add'l charge for fax requests.
Criminal Records: Access: Mail, in person. Both court and visitors may perform in person searches. Search fee: $5.00 per name. Required to search: name, years to search, date of birth. Criminal records on computer since 1990, index cards back to 1977. Fax requests are accepted, though the court will recommend a fax processing service. There is an add'l charge for fax requests.
General Information: Copy fee: $.50 per page. Cert fee: $6.60. Payee: Clerk of Courts. Personal checks accepted. Prepayment required. Mail requests: SASE required. Mail turnaround time 10 days.

Lake County

Superior Court

255 N Forbes St, Lakeport, CA 95453; 707-263-2374; Fax: 707-262-1327. Hours: 8AM-1PM (PST). *Felony, Misdemeanor, Civil, Eviction, Small Claims, Probate.*
www.courtinfo.ca.gov/courts/trial/lake/lakeport.htm
Note: This court holds the records for the former Northlake Muni. Court. Please note that there are also felony records at the South Lake Branch, and both courts should be checked when doing a criminal record search.

Civil Records: Access: Mail, in person. Only the court performs in person searches; visitors may not. Search fee: $5.00 per name. Required to search: name, years to search. Civil cases indexed by defendant, plaintiff. Civil records on computer from 1991, on microfiche, archived, and in index files from 1800s.
Criminal Records: Access: Mail, in person. Only the court performs in person searches; visitors may not. Search fee: $5.00 per name. Required to search: name, years to search, DOB. Criminal records on computer from 1991, on microfiche, archived, and in index files from 1800s.
General Information: No adoptions, juvenile, medical, probation or sealed records released. Copy fee: $.25 per page. Cert fee: $6.60. Payee: Lake County Superior Court. Personal checks accepted. Prepayment required. Mail requests: SASE required. Mail turnaround time 1-3 weeks.

South Lake Division - Superior Court

7000 S Center Dr, Clearlake, CA 95422; 707-994-4859; Civil phone: 707-994-8262; Criminal phone: 707-994-6598; Fax: 707-994-1625. Hours: 8AM-1PM; Phone hours 8:30AM-12:30PM (PST). *Felony, Misdemeanor, Civil Actions Under $25,000, Eviction, Small Claims.*
www.co.lake.ca.us
Note: There are some felony cases here that will not be on the computer index at the Superior Court in Lakeport. The court recommends searching both courts when doing criminal record searches.

Civil Records: Access: Mail, in person. Visitors must perform in person searches for themselves. Search fee: $5.00 per name. Required to search: name, years to search. Civil cases indexed by defendant, plaintiff. Civil records on index books.
Criminal Records: Access: Mail, in person. Only the court performs in person searches; visitors may not. Search fee: $5.00 per name. Required to search: name, years to search, DOB. Criminal records on computer from 1990, index books prior.
General Information: No police reports or sealed records released. Copy fee: $.25 per page. Cert fee: $6.60. Payee: Lake County Superior Court. Personal checks accepted. Prepayment required. Mail requests: SASE required. Mail turnaround time 1 week for civil or 30 days for criminal.

Lassen County

Superior Court 220 S Lassen St, #2, Susanville, CA 96130; 530-251-8189 (dept 1), 251-8205 (dept 2). 7:30AM-5:30PM (PST). *Felony, Misdemeanor, Civil, Eviction, Small Claims, Probate.*
www.lassencourt.org
Civil Records: Access: Phone, mail, in person. Both court and visitors may perform in person searches. Search fee: $5.00 per name. Required to search: name, years to search. Civil cases indexed by defendant, plaintiff. Civil records on computer from 11/89, archived and in index files from 1900s.
Criminal Records: Access: Phone, mail, in person. Both court and visitors may perform in person searches. Search fee: $5.00 per name. Required to search: name, years to search. Criminal records on computer from 11/89, archived and in index files from 1900s.
General Information: No adoptions, juvenile, medical, probation or sealed records released. Copy fee: $1.50 for first page, $.50 each add'l. Cert fee: $6.60. Payee: Lassen County Superior Court. Business checks accepted. Prepayment required. Mail requests: SASE required. Mail turnaround: 1-5 days.

Los Angeles County

Los Angeles Superior Court - Central District - Civil
110 N Grand Ave, Rm 426, Los Angeles, CA 90012; 213-974-6135 (974-5171 if over $25,000); Fax: 213-621-2701. Hours: 8:30AM-4:30PM *Civil Actions, Eviction, Small Claims.*
www.lasuperiorcourt.org
Note: Any civil cases here under $25,000 are co-extensive with the city limits of Los Angeles and includes the City of San Fernando and sections designated as San Pedro, West Los Angeles, Van Nuys, Venice and the unincorporated county area known as Florence.
Civil Records: Access: Phone, mail, online, in person. Both court and visitors may perform in person searches. Search fee: $5.00 per name. Required to search: name, years to search. Civil cases indexed by defendant, plaintiff. Civil records on computer from 1991, index files from 1983. Records destroyed after 10 years. Online access is free at www.lasuperiorcourt.org. Court location, case number required to search. Includes civil, small claims, probate and unlawful detainer records. Three other Courts in Los Angeles County handle civil cases over $25,000; they are Norwalk, Palmdale, and Van Nuys.
General Information: Public Access terminal is available. No probation reports released. Copy fee: $.57 per page. Cert fee: $6.60. Payee: Los Angeles Superior Court. Personal checks accepted. Visa, MC accepted. Prepayment required. Mail requests: SASE required. Mail turnaround time 24 hours, more if busy.

Los Angeles Superior Court - Central District - Felony
210 W Temple St, Rm M-6, Los Angeles, CA 90012; 213-974-5259; Criminal phone: 213-974-6535 Felony; 974-6141 Misd.; Fax: 213-617-1224 (for agencies only). Hours: 8:30AM-4:30PM (PST). *Felony, Misdemeanor.*
www.lasuperiorcourt.org
Note: This court now handles felonies and misdemeanors; they can do misdemeanor searches for the Central District area of downtown LA, East LA, and Hollywood.
Criminal Records: Access: Mail, in person, online. Only the court performs in person searches; visitors

may not. Search fee: $5.00 per name. Required to search: name, years to search, DOB, sex. Criminal records on microfiche and index files since 1956, computerized misdemeanors since 1988; felonies since 1996. Felony and misdemeanor defendant records are online for a fee at www.lasuperiorcourt.org/OnlineServices/criminalindex/. Search fee is $4 to $4.75. In requests, court suggests to include full spelling of middle name.
General Information: No adoptions, juvenile, medical, probation or sealed records released. Copy fee: $.57 per page. Cert fee: $6.60. Payee: Los Angeles Superior Court. Personal checks accepted. Prepayment required. Mail requests: SASE required. Mail turnaround time 24 hours; up to 3 weeks if busy.

Los Angeles Superior Court - Probate Department
111 N Hill St, Rm 258, Los Angeles, CA 90012; 213-974-5471. Hours: 8AM-4PM (PST). *Probate.* www.lasuperiorcourt.org/probate
Note: Case summaries (notes) available free at web site; search by case number. Also, probate for current cases in Central Dist., Burbank, Compton, Glendale, Lancaster, Long Beach, Pasadena, Pomona, San Fernando, Santa Monica, Torrance District Courts.

Airport Superior Court - West District
11701 S La Cienega Blvd, Los Angeles, CA 90045; 310-727-6020; Criminal phone: 310-727-6100. 8:30AM-4:30PM (PST). *Felony, Misdemeanor.*
www.lasuperiorcourt.org/Locations/LAX.htm
Note: New Court in 2000, includes the areas of Palms, Mar Vista, Rancho Park, Marina del Rey, Venice, Playa del Rey and Sawtelle. Holds records for the former West LA Court covering Culver, El Segundo, Hawthorne.

Criminal Records: Access: In person, online. Only the court performs in person searches; visitors may not. Search fee: $5.00 per name. Required to search: name, years to search; also helpful: DOB, address. Criminal records index goes back to. Felony and misdemeanor defendant records are online for a fee at www.lasuperiorcourt.org/OnlineServices/criminalindex/. Search fee is $4 to $4.75. Will do search if you have a case number.
General Information: No probation reports released. Will not fax results. Copy fee: $.57 per page. Cert fee: $6.60. Payee: Los Angeles Superior Court. Personal checks accepted. Prepayment required.

Alhambra Superior Court - Northeast District
150 W Commonwealth Ave, Alhambra, CA 91801; Civil phone: 626-308-5521; Criminal phone: 626-308-5525. Hours: 8AM-4:30PM (PST). *Misdemeanor, Civil Actions Under $25,000, Eviction, Small Claims.*
www.lasuperiorcourt.org
Note: Includes cities of Alhambra, Monterey Park, San Gabriel, Temple City and the unincorporated County area known as South San Gabriel. Address the specific division (criminal, civil, small claims) in correspondence.
Civil Records: Access: Mail, online, in person. Only the court performs in person searches; visitors may not. Search fee: $5.00 per name. Required to search: name, years to search. Civil cases indexed by defendant, plaintiff. Civil records on computer back to 1991, index files from 1983. Records destroyed after 10 years. Online access is free at www.lasuperiorcourt.org. Court location, case number required to search. Includes civil, small claims, and unlawful detainer records.
Criminal Records: Access: Mail, in person, online. Only the court performs in person searches; visitors may not. Search fee: $5.00 per name. Required to search: name, years to search, DOB; also helpful: CDL. Criminal records on computer from 1996, index

files from 1991. Records destroyed after 10 years. Felony and misdemeanor defendant records are online for a fee at www.lasuperiorcourt.org/OnlineServices/criminalindex/. Search fee is $4 to $4.75.
General Information: No probation records released. Copy fee: $.57 per page. Cert fee: $6.60. Payee: Los Angeles Superior Court. Personal checks accepted. Prepayment required. Mail requests: SASE required. Mail turnaround time 2 days.

Bellflower Superior Court - Southeast District
10025 E Flower St, Bellflower, CA 90706; 562-804-8025; Civil phone: 562-804-8011; Criminal phone: 562-804-8018. Hours: 8AM-4:30PM (PST). *Misdemeanor, Civil Actions Under $25,000, Eviction, Small Claims.*
www.lasuperiorcourt.org/Locations/LosCerritos.htm
Note: Includes Artesia, Bellflower, Hawaiian Gardens, Lakewood and Cerritos. Specify civil or criminal search request. Small claims phone is 562-804-8011.

Civil Records: Access: Mail, online, in person. Both court and visitors may perform in person searches. Search fee: $5.00 per name. Required to search: name, years to search. Civil cases indexed by defendant, plaintiff. Civil records on computer from 1991, index files from 1983. Records destroyed after 10 years. Online access is free at www.lasuperiorcourt.org. Court location, case number required to search. Includes civil, small claims, probate and unlawful detainer records. Always specify that it is a "civil records" search request.
Criminal Records: Access: Mail, in person, online. Only the court performs in person searches; visitors may not. Search fee: $5.00 per name. Required to search: name, years to search, DOB; also helpful: SSN, sex. Criminal records on computer from 1991, index files from 1983. Records destroyed after 10 years. Criminal defendant records are online for fee at www.lasuperiorcourt.org/OnlineServices/criminalindex/. Search fee is $4 to $4.75. Always specify that it is a "criminal records" search request.
General Information: Public Access terminal is available. (Terminal contains civil index only.) No probation reports released. Copy fee: $.57 per page. Cert fee: $6.60 per document. Payee: Los Angeles Superior Court. Personal checks accepted. Visa, MC, Discover accepted. Prepayment required. Mail requests: SASE required. Mail turnaround: 2-3 days.

Beverly Hills Superior Court - West District
9355 Burton Way, Beverly Hills, CA 90210; 310-860-0070. Hours: 8;30AM-4:30PM (PST). *Misdemeanor, Civil Actions Under $25,000, Eviction, Small Claims.*
www.lasuperiorcourt.org
Includes cities of Beverly Hills and West Hollywood.

Civil Records: Access: Phone, mail, online, in person. Both court and visitors may perform in person searches. Search fee: $5.00 per name. Fee is per data bank per year. Required to search: name, years to search; also helpful: address. Civil cases indexed by defendant, plaintiff. Civil records on computer from 1991, index files from 1983. Records destroyed after 10 years. Online access is free at www.lasuperiorcourt.org. Court location, case number required to search. Includes civil, small claims and unlawful detainer records.
Criminal Records: Access: Phone, mail, in person, online. Only the court performs in person searches; visitors may not. Search fee: $5.00 per name. Fee is per data bank per year. Required to search: name, years to search, DOB; also helpful: address, SSN, sex, signed release. Criminal records on computer from 1991, index files from 1983. Records destroyed after 10 years. Felony and misdemeanor defendant records are online for a fee at

www.lasuperiorcourt.org/OnlineServices/criminalindex/. Search fee is $4 to $4.75.

General Information: No probation, arrest records released. Copy fee: $.57 per page. Cert fee: $6.60. Court location, case number, and last name are all required to search. Available for civil, small claims, and unlawful detainer records. Payee: Los Angeles Superior Court. Personal checks accepted. Visa, MC, Discover accepted. Use Visa or Discover; plus user fees. Prepayment required. Mail requests: SASE required. Mail turnaround time 3 days.

Burbank Superior Court - North Central

District 300 E Olive Ave, Burbank, CA 91502-1215; Civil phone: 818-557-3482 Civ; 818-557-3461 Sm Claims; Criminal phone: 818-557-3466; Fax: 818-953-9455 Civil. Hours: 8:15AM-4:30PM (PST). *Felony, Misdemeanor, Civil Actions, Eviction, Small Claims.* www.lasuperiorcourt.org

Civil Records: Access: Mail, online, in person. Both court and visitors may perform in person searches. Search fee: $5.00 per name. Required to search: name, years to search. Civil cases indexed by defendant, plaintiff. Civil records on computer from 1991, index files from 1983. Limited civil records destroyed ten years after judgment. Online access is free at www.lasuperiorcourt.org. Court location, case number required to search. Includes civil, small claims, probate and unlawful detainer records.

Criminal Records: Access: Mail, in person, online. Only the court performs in person searches; visitors may not. Search fee: $5.00 per name. Required to search: name, years to search, DOB. Criminal records on computer from 1991, index files from 1983. Records destroyed after ten years. Felony and misdemeanor defendant records are online for a fee at www.lasuperiorcourt.org/OnlineServices/criminalindex/. Search fee is $4 to $4.75.

General Information: No probation reports released. They may charge a $3.37 fee for faxing back results. Copy fee: $.57 per page. Cert fee: $6.60. Domestic judgments are certified for $11.00. Payee: Los Angeles Superior Court. Personal checks accepted. Prepayment required. Mail requests: SASE required. Mail turnaround time 3-5 days.

Compton Superior Court - South

Central District 200 W Compton Blvd, Compton, CA 90220; Civil phone: 310-603-7812; Criminal phone: 310-603-7112; Fax: 310-223-5941. Hours: 8:30AM-4:30PM (PST). *Felony, Misdemeanor, Civil Actions, Eviction, Small Claims.* www.lasuperiorcourt.org

Note: Includes cities of Carson, Compton, Lynwood and Paramount and the unincorporated portions of county that surround them.

Civil Records: Access: Mail, online, in person. Both court and visitors may perform in person searches. Search fee: $5.00 per name. Fee is per year prior to 1991. Required to search: name, years to search. Civil cases indexed by defendant, plaintiff. Civil records on computer from 1991, index files from 1983. Records destroyed after 10 years. Online access is free at www.lasuperiorcourt.org. Court location, case number required to search. Includes civil, small claims, probate and unlawful detainer records.

Criminal Records: Access: Mail, in person, online. Both court and visitors may perform in person searches. Search fee: $5.00 per name. Required to search: name, years to search, DOB. Criminal records maintained per G.C. 68152(E). Felony and misdemeanor defendant records are online for a fee at www.lasuperiorcourt.org/OnlineServices/criminalindex/. Search fee is $4 to $4.75.

General Information: Public Access terminal is available. No complaint records released. Copy fee: $.57 per page. Cert fee: $6.60 per document. Payee:

Los Angeles Superior Court-Compton. Personal checks accepted. Visa, MC, Discover accepted. Prepayment required. Mail requests: SASE required. Mail turnaround time 7 days.

Culver City Superior Court - West

District 4130 Overland Ave, Culver City, CA 90230; 310-202-3181; Civil phone: 310-202-3160; Fax: 310-836-8345. 8:30AM-4:30PM (PST). *Civil Actions Under $25,000, Eviction, Small Claims.* www.lasuperiorcourt.org

Note: Includes Culver City and surrounding unincorporated areas including Angelus Vista, portions of Marina del Rey, View Park and Windsor Hills, all surrounded by the City of Los Angeles, on south bounded by Inglewood. No longer handles misdemeanors as of 2000

Civil Records: Access: Mail, online, in person. Only the court performs in person searches; visitors may not. Search fee: $5.00 per name. Required to search: name, years to search. Civil cases indexed by defendant, plaintiff. Civil records on computer from 1987, index files from 1983. Records destroyed after 10 years. Online access is free at www.lasuperiorcourt.org. Court location, case number required to search. Includes civil, small claims, probate and unlawful detainer records.

General Information: No probation reports released. Copy fee: $.57 per page. Cert fee: $6.60. Payee: Los Angeles Superior Court. Personal checks accepted. Prepayment required. Mail requests: SASE required. Mail turnaround time 2 days.

Downey Superior Court - Southeast

District 7500 E Imperial Hwy, Downey, CA 90242; Civil phone: 562-803-7052; Criminal phone: 562-803-7049. Hours: 8:30AM-4:30PM T-F; 8:30AM-6PM M (PST). *Misdemeanor, Civil Actions Under $25,000, Eviction, Small Claims.* www.lasuperiorcourt.org

Note: Comprises the cities of Downey, Norwalk and La Mirada.

Civil Records: Access: Mail, online, in person. Both court and visitors may perform in person searches. Search fee: $5.00 per name. Required to search: name, years to search. Civil cases indexed by defendant, plaintiff. Civil records on microfiche from 1964, archived and index file from 1800s. Online access is free at www.lasuperiorcourt.org. Court location, case number required to search. Includes civil, small claims, and unlawful detainer records.

Criminal Records: Access: Mail, in person, online. Only the court performs in person searches; visitors may not. Search fee: $5.00 per name. Required to search: name, years to search; also helpful: DOB. Criminal records on computer from 1989, on microfiche, archived, and index files. Felony and misdemeanor defendant records are online for a fee at www.lasuperiorcourt.org/OnlineServices/criminalindex/. Search fee is $4 to $4.75. Mail or in person - court may choose not to run lists of names.

General Information: No adoptions, juvenile, medical, probation or sealed records released. Copy fee: $.57 per page. Cert fee: $6.60. Payee: Los Angeles Superior Court. Personal checks accepted. Credit cards accepted. Prepayment required. Mail requests: SASE required. Mail turnaround time 5 days.

East Los Angeles Superior Court -

Central District 214 S Fetterly Ave, Los Angeles, CA 90022; Civil phone: 323-780-2017; Criminal phone: 323-780-2025. Hours: 8AM-4:30PM (PST). *Misdemeanor, Civil Actions Under $25,000, Eviction, Small Claims.* www.lasuperiorcourt.org

Includes cities of Montebello and Commerce and adjacent unincorporated territory bordering Monterey Park on the north and Los Angeles on the west.

Civil Records: Access: Mail, online, in person. Only the court performs in person searches; visitors may not. Search fee: $5.00 per name. Required to search: name, years to search. Civil cases indexed by defendant, plaintiff. Civil records on computer from 1991, index files from 1983. Records destroyed after 10 years. Online access is free at www.lasuperiorcourt.org. Court location, case number required to search. Includes civil, small claims, probate and unlawful detainer records.

Criminal Records: Access: Mail, in person, online. Only the court performs in person searches; visitors may not. Search fee: $5.00 per name. Required to search: name, years to search, DOB; also helpful: SSN. Criminal records on computer from 1991, index files from 1983. Records destroyed after 10 years. Felony and misdemeanor defendant records are online for a fee at www.lasuperiorcourt.org/OnlineServices/criminalindex/. Search fee is $4 to $4.75.

General Information: No probation reports released. Copy fee: $.57 per page. Cert fee: $6.60. Payee: Superior Court of East Los Angeles. Personal checks accepted. Credit cards accepted: Discover. Prepayment required. Mail requests: SASE required. Mail turnaround time 2 days.

El Monte Superior Court - East District

11234 E Valley Blvd, El Monte, CA 91731; Civil phone: 626-575-4117; Criminal phone: 626-575-4121; Fax: 626-444-9029. Hours: 8AM-4:30PM (PST). *Misdemeanor, Civil Actions Under $25,000, Eviction, Small Claims.* www.lasuperiorcourt.org

Note: Includes cities of El Monte, South El Monte, La Puente, Rosemead and adjacent unincorporated county area.

Civil Records: Access: Mail, online, in person. Only the court performs in person searches; visitors may not. No search fee. Required to search: name, years to search. Civil cases indexed by defendant, plaintiff. Civil records on computer since 1989, microfiche since 1980. Records destroyed after 10 years. Online access is free at www.lasuperiorcourt.org. Court location, case number required to search. Includes civil, small claims, and unlawful detainer records.

Criminal Records: Access: Phone, mail, in person, online. Only the court performs in person searches; visitors may not. Search fee: $5.00 per name. Required to search: name, years to search; also helpful: DOB. Criminal records on computer since 1985, microfiche since 1980. Felony and misdemeanor defendant records are online for a fee at www.lasuperiorcourt.org/OnlineServices/criminalindex/. Search fee is $5.

General Information: Will not release unlawful detainer for 60 days. No probation reports, medical records, search warrants, rap sheet, and any sealed cases per CCP Sec 1161.2(e), CLETS report, transcripts or sealed records released. Copy fee: $.57 per page. Cert fee: $6.60. Payee: Los Angeles Superior Court. Two-party checks not accepted. Write "not to exceed $x.xx" on check. Prepayment required. Mail requests: SASE required. Mail turnaround time 5 days.

Glendale Superior Court - NorthCentral

District Los Angeles Superior Court, 600 E Broadway, Glendale, CA 91206; Civil phone: 818-500-3551; Criminal phone: 818-500-3530; Fax: 818-548-0486 Civ; 548-0236 Crim. Hours: 8:15AM-4:30PM (PST). *Misdemeanor, Civil Actions Under $25,000, Eviction, Small Claims.* www.lasuperiorcourt.org

Note: Includes cities of Glendale, LaCanada-Flintridge and unincorporated county are known as

Montrose, La Crescenta, Verdugo City, Highway Highlands, and Kogel Canyon.

Civil Records: Access: Mail, online, in person. Only the court performs in person searches; visitors may not. Search fee: $5.00 per name. Required to search: name, years to search. Civil cases indexed by defendant, plaintiff. Civil records on computer from 1990, small claims from 07/92, index files from 1983. Records destroyed after 10 years. Online access is free at www.lasuperiorcourt.org. Court location, case number required to search. Includes civil, small claims, probate and unlawful detainer records.

Criminal Records: Access: Mail, in person, online. Only the court performs in person searches; visitors may not. Search fee: $5.00 per name. Required to search: name, years to search. Criminal records on computer from 1990, microfilm past 10 years. Felony and misdemeanor defendant records are online for a fee at www.lasuperiorcourt.org/OnlineServices/criminalindex/. Search fee is $4 to $4.75.

General Information: No probation reports, police reports, CII records released. Copy fee: $.57 per page. Cert fee: $6.60. Payee: Los Angeles Superior Court. Personal checks accepted. Visa, MC accepted. Prepayment required. Mail requests: SASE required. Mail turnaround time 2 weeks.

Hollywood Superior Court - Central District
5925 Hollywood Blvd, Los Angeles, CA 90028; 323-856-5747. Hours: 8:30AM-4:30PM (PST). *Misdemeanor.*
www.lasuperiorcourt.org
Note: High-grade and low-grade Misdemeanors for the Hollywood area.

Criminal Records: Access: Mail, in person, online. Only the court performs in person searches; visitors may not. Search fee: $5.00 per name. Required to search: name, years to search, DOB. Criminal records on computer go back 10 years, prior on microfiche. Felony and misdemeanor defendant records are online for a fee at www.lasuperiorcourt.org/OnlineServices/criminalindex/. Search fee is $4 to $4.75. Mail or in person request will be expedited if a SASE provided.

General Information: No probation, driver's license, medical, arrest report or confidential reports released. Copy fee: $.57 per page. Cert fee: $6.60 per document. Payee: Los Angeles Superior Court. Personal checks accepted. Credit cards accepted (except AMEX). Prepayment required. Mail requests: SASE required. Mail turnaround time 2-3 days.

Huntington Park Superior Court - Southeast District
6548 Miles Ave, Huntington Park, CA 90255; Civil phone: 323-586-6365; Criminal phone: 323-586-6362; Fax: 323-589-6769. Hours: 8AM-4:30PM (PST). *Misdemeanor, Civil Actions Under $25,000, Eviction, Small Claims.*
www.lasuperiorcourt.org
Note: Includes cities of Bell, Bell Gardens, Cudahy, Huntington Park, Maywood and Vernon. Also includes South Gate, Hollydale and unincorporated area of Walnut Park from closed court at South Gate.

Civil Records: Access: Mail, online, in person. Only the court performs in person searches; visitors may not. Search fee: $5.00 per name. Required to search: name, years to search. Civil cases indexed by defendant, plaintiff. Civil records on computer from 1991, index files from 1983. Records destroyed after 10 years. Online access is free at www.lasuperiorcourt.org. Court location, case number required to search. Includes civil, small claims, probate and unlawful detainer records.

Criminal Records: Access: Phone, mail, in person, online. Only the court performs in person searches; visitors may not. Search fee: $5.00 per name. Required to search: name, years to search; also helpful: DOB. Criminal records on computer from 1991, index files from 1983. Records destroyed after 10 years. Felony and misdemeanor defendant records are online for a fee at www.lasuperiorcourt.org/OnlineServices/criminalindex/. Search fee is $4 to $4.75.

General Information: No probation reports released. Copy fee: $.57 per page. Cert fee: $6.60 per document. Payee: Los Angeles Superior Court. Personal checks accepted. Visa, MC, Discover accepted. Prepayment required. Mail requests: SASE required. Mail turnaround time 2 days.

Inglewood Superior Court - Southwest District
1 Regent St, Inglewood, CA 90301; 310-419-5132; Civil phone: 310-419-5132; Criminal phone: 310-419-5128; Fax: 310-674-4862 (680-7055 Civ. Fax). Hours: 8AM-4:30PM (PST). *Misdemeanor, Civil Actions Under $25,000, Eviction, Small Claims.*
www.lasuperiorcourt.org
Note: Includes cities of Inglewood, Hawthorne, El Segundo, Lennox and adjoining unincorporated area.

Civil Records: Access: Mail, online, in person. Only the court performs in person searches; visitors may not. Search fee: $5.00 per name. Required to search: name, years to search. Civil cases indexed by defendant, plaintiff. Civil records on computer from 1991, index files from 1983. Records destroyed after 10 years. Online access is free at www.lasuperiorcourt.org. Court location, case number required to search. Includes civil, small claims, probate and unlawful detainer records.

Criminal Records: Access: Mail, in person. Only the court performs in person searches; visitors may not. Search fee: $5.00 per name. Required to search: name, years to search; also helpful: DOB. Criminal records on computer from 1991, index files from 1983. Records destroyed after 10 years. Felony and misdemeanor defendant records are online for a fee at www.lasuperiorcourt.org/OnlineServices/criminalindex/. Search fee is $4 to $4.75.

General Information: No probation reports released. Copy fee: $.57 per page. Cert fee: $6.60. Payee: Los Angeles Superior Court. Personal checks accepted. Credit cards accepted: Visa, MC, Discover, AmEx. Visa, Discover. Prepayment required. Mail requests: SASE required. Mail turnaround time 2 days.

Lancaster Superior Court - North District
42011 4th St, Lancaster, CA 93534; 661-974-7200. Hours: 8AM-4:30PM (PST). *Felony, Misdemeanor, Civil, Small Claims, Probate.*
www.lasuperiorcourt.org
Note: Formerly Antelope; includes Lancaster, City of Palmdale, and unincorporated County territory including Acton, Agua Dulce, Fairmont, Lake Hughes, Llano, Leona Valley, Littlerock, Pearblossom, Quartz Hill, Roosevelt, Green Valley Big Pines, Lake Elizabeth

Civil Records: Access: Phone, mail, online, in person. Only the court performs in person searches; visitors may not. Search fee: $5.00 per name. Required to search: name, years to search. Civil cases indexed by defendant, plaintiff. Civil records on computer since 1989, index books since 1983. Records destroyed after 10 years. Online access is free at www.lasuperiorcourt.org. Court location, case number required to search. Includes civil, small claims, probate and unlawful detainer records.

Criminal Records: Access: Mail, in person, online. Only the court performs in person searches; visitors may not. Search fee: $5.00 per name. Required to search: name, years to search; also helpful: case number. Criminal records on computer since 1989, index books since 1983. Records destroyed after 10 years. Felony and misdemeanor defendant records are for a fee at www.lasuperiorcourt.org/OnlineServices/criminalindex/. Search fee is $4 to $4.75. Mail or in person - court may choose not to run lists of names.

General Information: No probation reports released. Copy fee: $.57 per page. Cert fee: $6.60. Payee: Los Angeles Superior Court. Personal checks accepted; must be pre-imprinted. Prepayment required. Mail requests: SASE required. Mail turnaround: 2 days.

Long Beach Superior Court - South District
415 W Ocean Blvd, Long Beach, CA 90802; 562-491-6201; Civil phone: 562-491-6234 Civ; 562-491-6235 Sm Claims; Criminal phone: 562-491-6226/6227; Probate phone: 562-491-5928; Fax: 562-437-0147 (Criminal). Hours: 8:30AM-4:30PM (PST). *Misdemeanor, Civil Actions Under $25,000, Eviction, Small Claims.*
www.lasuperiorcourt.org
Note: Includes cities of Long Beach and Signal Hill and adjoining unincorporated area. Address requests to civil or criminal division.

Civil Records: Access: Mail, online, in person. Both court and visitors may perform in person searches. Search fee: $5.00 per name. Required to search: name, years to search. Civil cases indexed by defendant, plaintiff. Civil records on computer from 1991, index files from 1983. Records destroyed after 10 years. Online access is free at www.lasuperiorcourt.org. Court location, case number required to search. Includes civil, small claims, probate and unlawful detainer records.

Criminal Records: Access: Mail, in person, online. Both court and visitors may perform in person searches. Search fee: $5.00 per name. Required to search: name, years to search, DOB. Criminal records on computer from 1991, index files from 1983. Records destroyed after 10 years. Felony and misdemeanor defendant records are online for a fee at www.lasuperiorcourt.org/OnlineServices/criminalindex/. Search fee is $4 to $4.75.

General Information: No probation reports released. Copy fee: $.57 per page. Cert fee: $6.60. Payee: Los Angeles Superior Court. Personal checks accepted. Credit cards accepted: Discover. Accepted in person only. Prepayment required. Mail requests: SASE required. Mail turnaround time 2 days.

Malibu Superior Court - West District
23525 W Civic Center Way, Malibu, CA 90265; 310-317-1335; Fax: 310-456-0194. Hours: 8AM-4:30PM (PST). *Misdemeanor, Civil Actions Under $25,000, Eviction, Small Claims.*
www.lasuperiorcourt.org
Note: Includes Malibu, Agoura Hills, Calabasas, Westlake Village, Hidden Hills and unincorporated areas known as Topanga and Chatsworth Lake, bounded by Ventura County on the west and north, Pacific Ocean on the south and City of Los Angeles on the east.

Civil Records: Access: Mail, online, in person. Only the court performs in person searches; visitors may not. Search fee: $5.00 per name. Required to search: name, years to search. Civil cases indexed by defendant, plaintiff. Civil records on computer from 1991, index files from 1983. Records destroyed after 10 years. Online access is free at www.lasuperiorcourt.org. Court location, case number required to search. Includes civil, small claims, probate and unlawful detainer records.

Criminal Records: Access: Mail, in person, online. Only the court performs in person searches; visitors may not. Search fee: $5.00 per name. Required to search: name, years to search; also helpful: DOB. Criminal records on computer from 1991, index files from 1983. Records destroyed after 10 years. Felony and misdemeanor defendant records are online for a fee at www.lasuperiorcourt.org/OnlineServices/ criminalindex/. Search fee is $4 to $4.75.

General Information: No probation reports released. Copy fee: $.57 per page. Cert fee: $6.60. Court location, case number, and last name are all required to search. Available for civil, small claims, and unlawful detainer records. Payee: Los Angeles Superior Court. Personal checks accepted. Prepayment required. Mail requests: SASE required. Mail turnaround time 1-5 days.

Metropolitan Branch Superior Court - Central District
1945 S Hill St Rm 200, Los Angeles, CA 90007; 213-744-4023; Fax: 213-744-1879. Hours: 8AM-4:30PM (PST). *Misdemeanor.* www.lasuperiorcourt.org

Note: Vehicle Code misdemeanor and traffic citations for the incorporated City of Los Angeles excluding the areas known as San Pedro, West Los Angeles and communities of San Fernando Valley and the unincorporated County area more commonly known as Florence

Criminal Records: Access: Mail, in person, online. Only the court performs in person searches; visitors may not. Search fee: $5.00 per name. Required to search: name, years to search, DOB. Criminal records on computer from 1991, index files from 1983. Records destroyed after 10 years. Felony and misdemeanor defendant records are online for a fee at www.lasuperiorcourt.org/OnlineServices/criminalinde x/. Search fee is $4 to $4.75.

General Information: No probation, driver's license, medical, arrest report or confidential reports released. Copy fee: $.57 per page. Cert fee: $6.60. Payee: Los Angeles Superior Court. Personal checks accepted. Credit cards accepted. Prepayment required. Mail requests: SASE requested. Turnaround time 2-3 days.

Norwalk Superior Court - Southeast District
12720 Norwalk Blvd, Norwalk, CA 90650; 562-807-7340. Hours: 8:30AM-4:30PM (PST). *Felony, Civil Actions Over $25,000, Probate.* www.lasuperiorcourt.org

Civil Records: Access: Mail, online, in person. Both court and visitors may perform in person searches. Search fee: $5.00 per name. Required to search: name, years to search. Civil cases indexed by defendant, plaintiff. Civil records on computer from 1991, index files from 1983. Online access is free at www.lasuperiorcourt.org. Court location, case number required to search. Includes civil, small claims, probate and unlawful detainer records.

Criminal Records: Access: Mail, in person, online. Both court and visitors may perform in person searches. Search fee: $5.00 per name. Required to search: name, years to search, DOB; also helpful: SSN, sex. Criminal records on computer from 1991, index files from 1983. Felony and misdemeanor defendant records are online for a fee at www.lasuperiorcourt.org/OnlineServices/criminalinde x/. Search fee is $4 to $4.75.

General Information: Public Access terminal is available. (Public terminal to find case number only.) No probation reports released. Copy fee: $.57 per page. Cert fee: $6.60. Payee: Los Angeles Superior Court. Personal checks accepted. Credit cards accepted. Prepayment required. Mail requests: SASE required. Mail turnaround time 2-10 days.

Pasadena Superior Court - Northeast District
300 E Walnut, Pasadena, CA 91101; Civil phone: 626-356-5695; Criminal phone: 626-356-5254; Fax: 626-568-3903. Hours: 8:30AM-4:30PM (PST). *Misdemeanor, Civil Actions Under $25,000, Eviction, Small Claims.* www.lasuperiorcourt.org

Note: Includes cities of Pasadena, South Pasadena, San Marino, Sierra Madre and the area of Altadena and East Pasadena.

Civil Records: Access: Mail, online, in person. Both court and visitors may perform in person searches. Search fee: $5.00 per name. Required to search: name, years to search. Civil cases indexed by defendant, plaintiff. Civil records on computer from 1991, index files from 1983. Records destroyed after 10 years. Online access is free at www.lasuperiorcourt.org. Court location, case number required to search. Includes civil, small claims, probate and unlawful detainer records.

Criminal Records: Access: Mail, in person, online. Only the court performs in person searches; visitors may not. Search fee: $5.00 per name. Required to search: name, years to search. Criminal records on computer from 1991, index files from 1983. Records destroyed after 10 years. Felony and misdemeanor defendant records are online for a fee at www.lasuperiorcourt.org/OnlineServices/criminalinde x/. Search fee is $4 to $4.75.

General Information: No probation reports released. Copy fee: $.57 per page. Cert fee: $6.60. Payee: Los Angeles Superior Court. Personal checks accepted. Prepayment required. Mail requests: SASE required. Mail turnaround time 2 days.

Pomona Superior Court - East District
350 W Mission Blvd, Pomona, CA 91766; 909-802-9944; Fax: 909-865-6767. Hours: 8AM-4:30PM; Phone Hours: 8AM-Noon, 2-4PM (PST). *Misdemeanor, Civil Actions Under $25,000, Eviction, Small Claims.* www.lasuperiorcourt.org

Note: Includes cities of Pomona, Claremont, La Verne, Walnut, San Dimas and unincorporated area including Diamond Bar. Also, 909-802-9944 is good phone number.

Civil Records: Access: Fax, mail, online, in person. Both court and visitors may perform in person searches. Search fee: $5.00 per name. Required to search: name, years to search. Civil cases indexed by defendant, plaintiff. Civil records on computer from 1990, index files from 1983. Records destroyed after 10 years. Online access is free at www.lasuperiorcourt.org. Court location, case number required to search. Includes civil, small claims, probate and unlawful detainer records.

Criminal Records: Access: Mail, in person, online. Only the court performs in person searches; visitors may not. Search fee: $5.00 per name. Required to search: name, years to search, DOB. Criminal records on computer from 1990, index files from 1983. Records destroyed after 10 years. Felony and misdemeanor defendant records are online for a fee at www.lasuperiorcourt.org/OnlineServices/criminalinde x/. Search fee is $4 to $4.75. Drop box available.

General Information: No probation, mental health or police reports released. Copy fee: $.57 per page. Cert fee: $6.60 per document. Court location, case number, and last name are all required to search. Available for civil, small claims, and unlawful detainer records. Payee: Los Angeles Superior Court. Personal checks accepted. Prepayment required. Mail requests: SASE required. Mail turnaround time 2-4 days.

Redondo Beach Superior Court - Southwest District
117 W Torrance Blvd, Redondo Beach, CA 90277-3638; 310-798-6875; Fax: 310-376-4051. Hours: 8:15AM-4:30PM (PST). *Civil Actions over $25,000.* www.lasuperiorcourt.org

Note: Also known as the Southwest District South Bay Court - Beach Cities Branch

Civil Records: Access: Mail, online, in person. Only the court performs in person searches; visitors may not. Search fee: $5.00 per name. Required to search: name, years to search. Civil cases indexed by defendant, plaintiff. Civil records on computer from 1991, index files from 1983. Records destroyed after 10 years. Online access is free at www.lasuperiorcourt.org. Court location, case number required to search. Includes civil, small claims, probate and unlawful detainer records.

General Information: Unlawful detainers held for 60 days. Copy fee: $.57 for first page, $.20 each add'l. Cert fee: $6.60. Payee: Los Angeles Superior Court. Personal checks accepted. Prepayment required. Mail requests: SASE required. Mail turnaround: 3-4 days.

San Fernando Superior Court - North Valley District
900 3rd St, #1137, San Fernando, CA 91340; 818-898-2401; Criminal phone: 818-898-2655 Felony, 818-898-2407 Misc. Hours: 8:30AM-4:30PM (PST). *Felony, Misdemeanor, Small Claims.* www.lasuperiorcourt.org

Includes Granada Hills, Northridge, Chatsworth, Sunland, Tujunga, Pacoima, Mission Hills, Sylmar, Arleta, Lake View Terrace, Sun Valley and City of San Fernando. They merged with the Newhall Court to become the North Valley District Court

Criminal Records: Access: Mail, online, in person. Only the court performs in person searches; visitors may not. Search fee: $5.00 per name. Required to search: name, years to search; also helpful: DOB. Criminal records on computer from 1988. Records destroyed after 10 years. Felony and misdemeanor defendant records are online for a fee at www.lasuperiorcourt.org/OnlineServices/criminalinde x/. Search fee is $4 to $4.75. The Misdemeanor clerk's office is Rm 1137.

General Information: No probation reports or arrest reports released. Copy fee: $.57 per page. Cert fee: $6.60. Payee: Los Angeles Superior Court. Personal checks accepted. No 3rd party checks. Credit cards accepted. Prepayment required. Mail requests: SASE required. Mail turnaround time 2 days.

San Pedro Superior Court - South District
505 S Centre St, Rm 202, San Pedro, CA 90731; 310-519-6014; 519-6016 Traffic; Civil phone: 310-519-6015. Hours: 8:30AM-4:30PM (civ, sm claims & criminal); 8AM-4:30PM (traffic) (PST). *Civil Actions, Eviction, Small Claims, Traffic.* www.lasuperiorcourt.org

Note: Includes San Pedro, Wilmington and a county strip in Torrance extending up to Western Ave.

Civil Records: Access: Mail, online, in person. Only the court performs in person searches; visitors may not. Search fee: $5.00 per name. Required to search: name, years to search. Civil cases indexed by defendant, plaintiff. Civil records on computer go back 10 years; on index files from 1984. Records destroyed after 10 years. Online access is free at www.lasuperiorcourt.org. Court location, case number required to search. Includes civil, small claims, probate and unlawful detainer records. Also, search for open traffic citations at www.lasuperiorcourt.org/traffic/index.asp?RT=CI.

General Information: No probation, arrest, records released. Will fax results for $3.37 per page. Copy fee: $.57 per page. Cert fee: $6.60. Payee: Los Angeles Superior Court. Personal checks accepted.

Credit cards accepted: Visa. Additional 6% fee charged. Prepayment required. Mail requests: SASE required. Mail turnaround time 2 days.

Santa Clarita Superior Court - North Valley District
23747 W Valencia Blvd, Santa Clarita, CA 91355; 661-253-7316; Civil phone: 661-253-7313; Criminal phone: 661-253-7384; Fax: 661-254-4107. 8AM-4:30PM (PST). *Misdemeanor, Civil Actions Under $25,000, Eviction, Small Claims.* www.lasuperiorcourt.org
Note: Formerly known as Newhall Sup. Court, it includes Saugus, Valencia, Santa Clarita and unincorporated area bound by Ventura County line (west), Kern County line (north), Agua Dulce on the east, and Glendale and Los Angeles city limits (south).
Civil Records: Access: Mail, online, in person. Only the court performs in person searches; visitors may not. Search fee: $5.00 per name. There is no fee to view records on microfiche or for first 3 records searched in person. Required to search: name, years to search. Civil cases indexed by defendant, plaintiff. Civil records on computer from 1991, index files from 1983. Records destroyed after 10 years, many records on microfiche. Online access is free at www.lasuperiorcourt.org. Court location, case number required to search. Includes civil, small claims, probate and unlawful detainer records. Call first for permission to fax request.
Criminal Records: Access: Mail, in person, online. Only the court performs in person searches; visitors may not. Search fee: $5.00 per name,5 name limit. Required to search: name, years to search; also helpful: DOB, SSN. Criminal records on computer from 1991, index files from 1983. Records destroyed after 10 years, many records on microfiche. Felony and misdemeanor defendant records online for a fee at www.lasuperiorcourt.org/OnlineServices/criminalindex/. Search fee is $4 to $4.75.
General Information: No probation, or police reports w/out court approval released. Copy fee: $.57 per page. Cert fee: $6.60. Payee: Los Angeles Superior Court. Personal checks accepted. Prepayment required. Mail requests: SASE required. Mail turnaround time 7-10 days.

Santa Monica Superior Court - West District
1725 Main St, Rm 224, Santa Monica, CA 90401; 310-260-3522; Civil phone: 310-587-2442 Limited/Sm Claims; 310-587-2442 Unlim.; Criminal phone: 310-587-2442; Probate phone: 310-260-3771; Fax: 310-576-1399. Hours: 8:30AM-4:30PM (PST). *Misdemeanor, Civil Actions Under $25,000, Eviction, Small Claims.* www.lasuperiorcourt.org
Note: Includes City of Santa Monica and the unincorporated territory of the Veteran's Admin. facilities located at West Los Angeles.
Civil Records: Access: Mail, online, in person. Both court and visitors may perform in person searches. Search fee: $5.00 per name. Required to search: name, years to search. Civil cases indexed by defendant, plaintiff. Civil records on computer from 1991, index files from 1983. Records destroyed after 10 years. Online access is free at www.lasuperiorcourt.org. Court location, case number required to search. Includes civil, small claims, probate and unlawful detainer records.

Criminal Records: Access: Mail, in person, online. Only the court performs in person searches; visitors may not. Search fee: $5.00 per name. Required to search: name, years to search. Criminal records on computer from 1991, index files from 1983. Records destroyed after 10 years. Felony and misdemeanor defendant records are online for a fee at www.lasuperiorcourt.org/OnlineServices/criminalindex/. Search fee is $4 to $4.75.
General Information: No probation reports or unlawful detainer records released. Copy fee: $.57 per page. Cert fee: $6.60. Payee: Los Angeles Superior Court. Personal checks accepted. Prepayment required. Mail requests: SASE required. Mail turnaround time 1-2 days.

South Gate Superior Court - Southeast District
Civil Actions Under $25,000, Eviction, Small Claims, Traffic.
Note: This court is closed, all records are at Huntington park Superior Court.

Torrance Superior Court - Southwest District
825 Maple Ave, Torrance, CA 90503-5058; 310-222-6505, 222-6501 Admin.; Civil phone: 310-222-8809 Civ, 222-6400 Sm Claims; Criminal phone: 310-222-6506; Probate phone: 310-222-8803; Fax: 310-783-5108 Crim; 310-782-7326 Civil fax. Hours: 8:30AM-4:30PM (PST). *Misdemeanor, Civil, Traffic, Eviction, Small Claims.* www.lasuperiorcourt.org
Note: Includes cities of Torrance, Gardena, Rolling Hills, Rolling Hills Estates, Manhattan Beach, Lomita, Redondo Beach, Hermosa Beach, Palos Verdes Estates, Rancho Palos Verdes, and Lawndale.
Civil Records: Access: Mail, online, in person. Only the court performs in person searches; visitors may not. Search fee: $5.00 per name. Required to search: name, years to search. Civil cases indexed by defendant, plaintiff. Civil records on computer from 1991, index files from 1983. Records destroyed after 10 years. Online access is free at www.lasuperiorcourt.org. Court location, case number required to search. Includes civil, small claims, probate and unlawful detainer records. Also, search for open traffic citations at www.lasuperiorcourt.org/traffic/index.asp?RT=CI.
Criminal Records: Access: Mail, in person, online. Only the court performs in person searches; visitors may not. Search fee: $5.00 per name. Required to search: name, years to search, DOB. Criminal records on computer from 1991, index files from 1983. Records destroyed after 10 years. Criminal defendant records are online for a fee at www.lasuperiorcourt.org/OnlineServices/criminalindex/. Search fee is $4 to $4.75.
General Information: No probation reports, medical or psychiatric reports, criminal history rap sheets released. Copy fee: $.57 per page. Cert fee: $6.60. Payee: LA Superior Court. Personal checks accepted. Prepayment required. Mail requests: SASE required. Mail turnaround time 5 days.

Van Nuys Superior Court - Northwest District - Civil
6230 Sylmar St, Van Nuys, CA 91401; 818-374-2208. Hours: 8:30AM-4:30PM (PST). *Civil Actions, Eviction, Small Claims, Family Law, Probate.* www.lasuperiorcourt.org
Note: Small Claims for Sherman Oaks, Van Nuys, Reseda, North Hollywood, Woodland Hills, Canoga Park, Tarzana, Porter Ranch, Winnetka and Panorama City. Civil jurisdiction depends on whether limited or general.
Civil Records: Access: Mail, online, in person. Both court and visitors may perform in person searches. Search fee: $5.00 per name. Required to search: name, years to search. Civil cases indexed by

defendant, plaintiff. Civil records on computer from 1991, index files from 1983. Records destroyed after 10 years. Online access is free at www.lasuperiorcourt.org. Court location, case number required to search. Includes civil, small claims, probate and unlawful detainer records.
General Information: Public Access terminal is available. No probation reports or arrest reports released. Will not fax results. Copy fee: $.57 per page. Cert fee: $6.60. Payee: Los Angeles Superior Court or LASC. Personal checks and credit cards accepted. Prepayment required. Mail requests: SASE required. Mail turnaround time 2-3 days.

Van Nuys Superior Court - Northwest District - Criminal
14400 Erwin St Mall, 2nd Fl, Van Nuys, CA 91401; 818-374-2903. Hours: 8:30AM-4:30PM (PST). *Felony, Misdemeanor.* www.lasuperiorcourt.org
Note: Misdemeanors for that part of city known as Sherman Oaks, Van Nuys, Reseda, North Hollywood, Woodland Hills, Canoga Park, Tarzana, Proter Ranch, Winnetka and Panorama City
Criminal Records: Access: Phone, mail, in person, online. Only the court performs in person searches; visitors may not. Search fee: $5.00 per name. Required to search: name, years to search, sex; also helpful: DOB. Criminal records on computer from 1991, index files from 1983. Felony and misdemeanor defendant records are online for a fee at www.lasuperiorcourt.org/OnlineServices/criminalindex/. Search fee is $4 to $4.75.
General Information: No probation reports or arrest reports released. Will not fax results. Copy fee: $.57 per page. Cert fee: $6.60. Payee: Los Angeles Superior Court. Personal checks accepted. Prepayment required. Mail requests: SASE required. Mail turnaround time 2-3 days.

West Covina Superior Court - East District
1427 W Covina Pky, West Covina, CA 91790; Civil phone: 626-813-3236 Civ, 626-813-3226 Sm Claims; Criminal phone: 626-813-3239; Fax: 626-338-7364. Hours: 8AM-4:30PM (PST). *Misdemeanor, Civil Actions Under $25,000, Eviction, Small Claims.* www.lasuperiorcourt.org
Note: Formerly known as Citrus Court, this includes cities of Azusa, Baldwin Park, Covina, Glendora, Industry, Irwindale, Valinda, West Covina and surrounding unincorporated County area.
Civil Records: Access: Mail, online, in person. Both court and visitors may perform in person searches. Search fee: $5.00 per name. Required to search: name, years to search. Civil cases indexed by defendant, plaintiff. Civil records on computer from 1991, index files from 1983. Records destroyed after 10 years. Online access is free at www.lasuperiorcourt.org. Court location, case number required to search. Includes civil, small claims, probate and unlawful detainer records.
Criminal Records: Access: In person, online. Both court and visitors may perform in person searches. Search fee: $5.00 per name. Required to search: name, years to search. Criminal records on computer from 1991, index files from 1983. Records destroyed after 10 years. Felony and misdemeanor defendant records are online for a fee at www.lasuperiorcourt.org/OnlineServices/criminalindex/. Search fee is $4 to $4.75. Direct criminal records searches to; LA County Court,Felony- 213-974-6145, add; 210 W.Temple St.,LA CA. 90012.
General Information: Public Access terminal is available. No probation reports released. Copy fee: $.57 per page. Cert fee: $6.60. Payee: Los Angeles Superior Court. Personal checks accepted.

Prepayment required. Mail requests: SASE required. Mail turnaround time 1 week.

West Los Angeles Superior Court - West District
1633 Purdue Ave, Los Angeles, CA 90025; 310-914-7477; Fax: 310-312-2902. Hours: 8:30AM-4:30PM (PST). *Civil Actions Under $25,000, Eviction, Small Claims.* www.lasuperiorcourt.org

Note: Includes the areas of Palms, Mar Vista, Rancho Park, Marina del Rey, Venice, Playa del Rey and Sawtelle. Holds records for the former Robertson branch. Criminal felony and misdemeanors are at the new Airport Court.

Civil Records: Access: Phone, mail, online, in person. Both court and visitors may perform in person searches. Search fee: $5.00 per name. Required to search: name, years to search. Civil cases indexed by defendant, plaintiff. Online access is free at www.lasuperiorcourt.org. Court location, case number required to search. Includes civil, small claims, probate and unlawful detainer records.

Criminal Records: Access: Mail, in person, online. Both court and visitors may perform in person searches. Search fee: $5.00 per name. Required to search: name, years to search; also helpful: DOB. Felony and misdemeanor defendant records are online for a fee at www.lasuperiorcourt.org/OnlineServices/criminalindex/. Search fee is $4 to $4.75. Felony and misdemeanor records have been moved to the Airport Court.

General Information: Public Access terminal is available. Copy fee: $.57 per page. Cert fee: $6.60. Payee: Los Angeles Superior Court. Personal checks accepted. Prepayment required. Mail requests: SASE required. Mail turnaround time 1-5 days.

Whittier Superior Court - Southeast District
7339 S Painter Ave, Whittier, CA 90602; Civil phone: 562-907-3127; Criminal phone: 562-907-3113. 8AM-4:30PM (PST). *Misdemeanor, Civil Actions Under $25,000, Eviction, Small Claims.* www.lasuperiorcourt.org

Note: Includes cities of Whittier, Santa Fe Springs, Pico Rivera, La Habra Heights plus unincorporated territory in the Whittier area including areas designated as Los Nietos and South Whittier.

Civil Records: Access: Mail, online, in person. Both court and visitors may perform in person searches. No search fee. Required to search: name, years to search. Civil cases indexed by defendant, plaintiff. Civil records on computer from 1991, index files from 1983. Records destroyed after 10 years. Online access is free at www.lasuperiorcourt.org. Court location, case number required to search. Includes civil, small claims, probate and unlawful detainer records.

Criminal Records: Access: Mail, in person, online. Only the court performs in person searches; visitors may not. Search fee: $5.00 per name. Required to search: name, years to search; also helpful: DOB. Criminal records computerized since 1987. Felony and misdemeanor defendant records online for a fee at www.lasuperiorcourt.org/OnlineServices/criminalindex/. Search fee is $4 to $4.75.

General Information: No probation reports released. Copy fee: $.57 per page. Cert fee: $6.60 per document. Payee: Los Angeles Superior Court. Personal checks accepted. Visa, MC, Discover accepted. Prepayment required. Mail requests: SASE required. Mail turnaround time 2 days.

Santa Anita Superior Court - Northeast District
300 W Maple Ave, Monrovia, CA 91016; 626-301-4056; Civil phone: 626-301-4050; Criminal phone: 626-301-4051; Fax: 626-357-7825. Hours: 8AM-4:30PM (PST). *Civil Actions Under $25,000, Eviction, Small Claims.* www.lasuperiorcourt.org

Note: Includes cities of Monrovia, Arcadia, Duarte, Bradbury and unincorporated county territory in surrounding area. This court no longer handles misdemeanor records, cases refered to Alhambra court.

Civil Records: Access: Mail, online, in person. Only the court performs in person searches; visitors may not. Search fee: $5.00 per name. Required to search: name, years to search. Civil cases indexed by defendant, plaintiff. Civil records on computer from 1991, ion microfiche from 1983. Records destroyed after 10 years. Online access is free at www.lasuperiorcourt.org. Court location, case number required to search. Includes civil, small claims, probate and unlawful detainer records.

General Information: Will not release unlawful detainers less than 60 days old. No sealed, criminal history information, arrest reports or any documents containing witness information records released. Copy fee: $.57 per page. Cert fee: $6.60. Payee: Los Angeles Superior Court. Personal checks accepted. Visa, MC, Discover accepted. Prepayment required. Mail requests: SASE required. Mail turnaround time 2 days.

Madera County

Superior Court 209 W Yosemite Ave, Madera, CA 93637; 559-675-7944; Civil phone: 559-675-7996; Criminal phone: 559-675-7734; Fax: 559-675-0701. Hours: 8AM-4PM (PST). *Felony, Civil, Probate, Eviction, Small Claims.*

Note: The Superior and Muni. courts located in the City of Madera have combined into a consolidated court. There is no countywide database of records; each court must be searched.

Civil Records: Access: Mail, fax, in person. Both court and visitors may perform in person searches. Search fee: $5.00 per name. There is no fee if searcher comes to court and does search. Required to search: name, years to search. Civil cases indexed by defendant, plaintiff. Civil records on microfiche, archived and index file from 1893.

Criminal Records: Access: Mail, fax, in person. Both court and visitors may perform in person searches. Search fee: $5.00 per name. There is no fee if searcher comes to court and does search. Required to search: name, years to search; also helpful: DOB, signed release. Criminal records on microfiche, archived and index file from 1893.

General Information: Public Access terminal is available. No adoptions, juvenile, medical, probation or sealed records released. Copy fee: $.50 per page. Cert fee: $6.60. Payee: Madera Superior Court. Personal checks accepted. Prepayment required. Mail requests: SASE required. Mail turnaround time 2-3 weeks.

Sierra Division - Superior Court
40601 Road 274, Bass Lake, CA 93604; 559-642-3235; Fax: 559-642-3445. Hours: 8;30AM-4;30PM (PST). *Felony, Misdemeanor, Civil Actions Under $25,000, Eviction, Small Claims, Probate.*

Note: There is no countywide database of records. Each court must be searched.

Civil Records: Access: Mail, in person. Only the court performs in person searches; visitors may not. Search fee: $5.00 per name. Required to search: name, years to search. Civil cases indexed by defendant, plaintiff. Civil records on index cards. Will only search back 7 years.

Criminal Records: Access: Mail, in person. Only the court performs in person searches; visitors may not. Search fee: $5.00 per name. Required to search: name, years to search; also helpful: DOB. Criminal records on computer (traffic only), index cards for criminal.

General Information: No adoptions, juvenile, medical, probation or sealed records released. Copy fee: $.50 per page. Cert fee: $6.60. Payee: Madera Superior Court. Personal checks accepted. Prepayment required. Mail requests: SASE required. Mail turnaround time 1-2 weeks.

Marin County

Superior Court PO Box 4988, San Rafael, CA 94913-4988; Civil phone: 415-473-6407; Criminal phone: 415-473-6225. Hours: 8:30AM-4PM (PST). *Felony, Misdemeanor, Civil, Eviction, Small Claims, Probate.* www.co.marin.ca.us/courts

Civil Records: Access: Phone, mail, in person, online. Both court and visitors may perform in person searches. Search fee: $5.00 per name per year. Required to search: name, years to search. Civil cases indexed by defendant, plaintiff. Civil records on computer from 1986, on microfiche from 1973 to 1985, archived from 1900 to 1972, on reel from 1900. Online access to the current court calendar is free at www.co.marin.ca.us/depts/MC/main/courtcal/name.cfm. Phone requests are limited to one name.

Criminal Records: Access: Mail, in person, online. Both court and visitors may perform in person searches. Search fee: $5.00 per name per year. Required to search: name, years to search. Criminal records on computer from 1986, on microfiche from 1973 to 1985, archived from 1900 to 1972, on reel from 1900. Online Access to the active criminal calendar is the same as civil. Phone requests are limited to one name.

General Information: Public Access terminal is available. No adoptions, paternity, sole custody, juvenile, medical, probation or sealed records released. Will not fax results. Copy fee: $1.00 per page. Cert fee: $7.00 abstract,$ 6.00. Payee: Marin County Superior Court. Personal checks accepted. Out-of-state checks not accepted. Write "not to exceed $x.xx" on check. Call first. Prepayment required. Mail requests: SASE required. Mail turnaround time 3 weeks.

Mariposa County

Superior Court 5088 Bullion St (PO Box 28), Mariposa, CA 95338; 209-966-2005; Civil phone: 209-966-6599; Criminal phone: 209-966-2005; Probate phone: 209-966-6599; Fax: 209-742-6860. Hours: 8:30AM-4PM (PST). *Felony, Misdemeanor, Civil, Small Claims, Eviction, Probate.* www.mariposacourts.org

Note: This former municipal court is now known as Department 2.

Civil Records: Access: Phone, fax, mail, in person. Both court and visitors may perform in person searches. Search fee: $5.00 per name. Fee applies to years prior to 1990. No fee for computer records search. Required to search: name, years to search. Civil records on computer from 1989, on microfiche and index files from 1800s. Phone access limited to short searches.

Criminal Records: Access: Phone, fax, mail, in person. Both court and visitors may perform in person searches. Search fee: $5.00 per name per year. Required to search: name, years to search. Criminal records on computer from 1989, on microfiche and index files from 1800s.

General Information: Public Access terminal is available. No adoptions, juvenile, medical, probation or sealed records released. Copy fee: $.50 per page. Cert fee: $6.60 per document. Payee: Mariposa Superior Court. Personal checks accepted. Prepayment required. Mail requests: SASE required. Mail turnaround time 2-3 days.

Mendocino County

Superior Court 100 N State & Perkins Sts (PO Box 996 Civ; PO Box 337 Crim), Ukiah, CA 95482; Civil phone: 707-463-4481; Criminal phone: 707-463-4486; Fax: 707-463-4655. Hours: 8AM-2;30 PM (noon on F) (PST). *Felony, Civil Actions Over $25,000, Probate.*
www.mendocino.courts.ca.gov
Civil Records: Access: Mail, in person, online. Both court and visitors may perform in person searches. Search fee: $5.00 per name. Fee for mail search only. Required to search: name, years to search. Civil cases indexed by defendant, plaintiff. Civil records on computer from 1990s, on microfilm from 1800 to 1940. Search index at www.mendocino.courts.ca.gov/caseindex.html.
Criminal Records: Access: Mail, in person, online. Both court and visitors may perform in person searches. Search fee: $5.00 per case. Required to search: name, years to search. Criminal records on computer from 1990s, on microfilm from 1800 to 1940. Search index at www.mendocino.courts.ca.gov/caseindex.html.
General Information: Public Access terminal is available. No adoptions, juvenile, medical, probation or sealed records released. Copy fee: $1.00 for first page, $.50 each add'l. Cert fee: $6.60. Payee: Mendocino Superior Court. Personal checks accepted. Prepayment required. Mail requests: SASE required. Mail turnaround time 2 weeks.

Ten Mile Branch - Superior Court 700 S Franklin St, Fort Bragg, CA 95437; 707-964-3192; Fax: 707-961-2611. Hours: 8AM-2:30PM (noon on F) (PST). *Felony, Misdemeanor, Civil Actions, Eviction, Small Claims.*
www.mendocino.courts.ca.gov/fortbragg.html
Civil Records: Access: Mail, in person, online. Only the court may perform in person searches. Search fee: $5.00 per name. Required to search: name, years to search. Civil cases indexed by defendant, plaintiff. Will only search back 7 years. Search index at www.mendocino.courts.ca.gov/caseindex.html.
Criminal Records: Access: Mail, in person, online. Only the court may perform in person searches. Search fee: $5.00 per name. Required to search: name, years to search, DOB. Criminal records go back to 1990; on computer back 1995; will only search back 7 years. Search index at www.mendocino.courts.ca.gov/caseindex.html.
General Information: No juvenile or probation records released. Will not fax results. Copy fee: $1.00 for first page, $.50 each add'l. Cert fee: $6.60. Payee: Superior Court. Personal checks accepted. Prepayment required. Mail requests: SASE required. Mail turnaround time 2 weeks.

Willits Branch - Superior Court 125 E Commercial St, Rm 100, Willits, CA 95490; 707-459-7800; Fax: 707-459-7818. Hours: 8AM-2;30PM (noon on F) (PST). *Felony, Misdemeanor, Civil Actions Under $25,000, Eviction, Small Claims.*
www.mendocino.courts.ca.gov
Civil Records: Access: Mail, in person, online. Only the court performs in person searches; visitors may not Search fee: $5.00 per name. Required to search: name, years to search. Civil cases indexed by defendant, plaintiff. Civil records on computer since 1992, index files prior. Search index at www.mendocino.courts.ca.gov/caseindex.html.
Criminal Records: Access: Mail, in person, online. Both court and visitors may perform in person

searches. Search fee: $5.00 per name. Required to search: name, years to search, DOB. Criminal records on computer since 1992, index files prior. Search index at www.mendocino.courts.ca.gov/caseindex.html.
General Information: No probation reports released. Copy fee: $1.00 for 1st page & $.50 per additional page. Cert fee: $6.60. Payee: MCSC. Personal checks accepted. Prepayment required. Mail requests: SASE required. Mail turnaround time 1 week.

Anderson Branch in Boonville - Superior Court, CA; Fax: 707-895-2349. *Misdemeanor, Civil Actions Under $25,000, Eviction, Small Claims.*
Note: This court was closed. Records were transferred to Ukiah. Everything east of Mile post marker 13.6 on Highway 128 is now in Ukiah; everything west is in Ft Bragg.

Round Valley Branch - Superior Court, *Misdemeanor, Civil Actions Under $25,000, Eviction, Small Claims.*
Note: This court has been merged with the Willits Division.

Arena Branch - Superior Court
www.mendocino.courts.ca.gov/ptarena.html
Note: Effective June 30, 2003, operations for the Arena Branch of the Superior Court have been merged with the Ten Mile Court in Fort Bragg.

Merced County

Superior Court 627 W 21st St, Merced, CA 95340; 209-385-7531; Fax: 209-725-9223. Hours: 8AM-4PM (PST). *Felony, Civil Actions Over $25,000, Probate.*

Civil Records: Access: Mail, in person. Both court and visitors may perform in person searches. Search fee: $5.00 per name. Required to search: name, years to search. Civil cases indexed by defendant, plaintiff. Civil records in index files from 1900s, computer from 1979, on microfiche from 1900s.
Criminal Records: Access: Mail, in person. Both court and visitors may perform in person searches. Search fee: $5.00 per name. Required to search: name, years to search. Criminal records in index files from 1900s, computer from 1979, on microfiche from 1900s.
General Information: Public Access terminal is available. No juvenile nor adoption records released. Copy fee: $.50 per page. Cert fee: $6.60. Payee: Merced County Superior Court. Business checks accepted. Prepayment required. Mail requests: SASE required. Mail turnaround time 1 week.

4, 5, 7 & 8 Divisions - Merced Limited Superior Court 670 W 22nd St, Merced, CA 95340; 209-725-4113; Civil phone: 209-385-7337; Criminal phone: 209-385-7335; Fax: 209-725-4114. Hours: 8AM-4PM M-F (civil); Noon-4PM M-F (civ only) (PST). *Misdemeanor, Civil Actions Under $25,000, Eviction, Small Claims.*
Civil Records: Access: Mail, in person. Search fee: $5.00 per name. Required to search: name, years to search. Civil cases indexed by defendant, plaintiff. Civil records on computer from 1992, index cards prior. Will only search back 7 years.
Criminal Records: Access: Mail, in person. Both court and visitors may perform in person searches. Search fee: $5.00 per name. Required to search: name, years to search. Criminal records on computer from 1992; prior on microfiche. Will only search back 7 years.
General Information: Public Access terminal is available. No juvenile or probation records released.

Copy fee: $.50 per page. Cert fee: $6.60. Payee: Merced County Superior Court. Only cashiers checks and money orders accepted. Prepayment required. Mail requests: SASE required. Mail turnaround time 2-5 days.

Los Banos Branch - Superior Court 445 "I" St, Los Banos, CA 93635; 209-725-4124; Fax: 209-725-4125. Hours: 8AM-4PM (PST). *Misdemeanor, Civil Actions Under $25,000, Eviction, Small Claims.*
Note: This court was combined with the old Dos Palos and Gustine Muni. Courts.
Civil Records: Access: Mail, in person. Only the court may perform in person searches. Search fee: $5.00 per name. Required to search: name, years to search. Civil cases indexed by defendant, plaintiff. Civil records on microfiche.
Criminal Records: Access: Mail, in person. Only the court may perform in person searches. Search fee: $5.00 per name. Required to search: name, years to search; also helpful: DOB. Criminal records on microfiche.
General Information: No juvenile or probation records released. Will fax results to local or toll free line. Copy fee: $.50 per page. Cert fee: $6.60 per document. Payee: Merced Superior Court. Personal checks accepted. Prepayment required. Mail requests: SASE required. Mail turnaround time 2-3 days.

Modoc County

Superior Court 205 S East St, Alturas, CA 96101; 530-233-6515/6; Fax: 530-233-6500. Hours: 8:30AM-5PM (PST). *Felony, Misdemeanor, Civil, Small Claims, Eviction, Probate.*
Civil Records: Access: Mail, in person. Only the court performs in person searches; visitors may not. Search fee: $5.00 per name. Required to search: name, years to search. Civil cases indexed by plaintiff. Civil records in index file from 1874, computerized since 07/25/95.
Criminal Records: Access: Fax, mail, in person. Only the court performs in person searches; visitors may not. Search fee: $5.00 per name. Required to search: name, years to search; also helpful: DOB. Criminal records computerized since 1991.
General Information: No adoptions, juvenile, medical, probation or sealed records released. Copy fee: $.50 per page. Cert fee: $6.60. Payee: Modoc County Superior Courts. Personal checks accepted. Prepayment required. Mail requests: SASE required. Mail turnaround time 1-2 weeks.

Mono County

Superior Court - Bridgeport Branch PO Box 537, Bridgeport, CA 93517; 760-932-5239. Hours: 8:30AM-5PM (PST). *Felony, Civil, Probate.*
Civil Records: Access: Mail, in person. Only the court performs in person searches; visitors may not. Search fee: $5.00 per name. Required to search: name, years to search. Civil cases indexed by defendant, plaintiff. Civil records in index files from 1873.
Criminal Records: Access: Mail, in person. Only the court performs in person searches; visitors may not. Search fee: $5.00 per name. Required to search: name, years to search. Criminal records in index files from 1873.
General Information: No adoptions, juvenile, medical, probation or sealed records released. Copy fee: $.50 per page. Cert fee: $6.60 first page and $1.10 each additional. Payee: Mono County Superior Court. Personal checks accepted. Prepayment required. Mail requests: SASE required. Mail turnaround time 1-3 weeks.

Mammoth Lakes Division - Superior Court

PO Box 1037, Mammoth Lakes, CA 93546; 760-924-5444; Fax: 760-924-5419. Hours: 9AM-5PM (PST). *Felony, Misdemeanor, Civil, Eviction, Small Claims.*
www.monosuperiorcourt.ca.gov

Civil Records: Access: Mail, in person. Only the court performs in person searches; visitors may not. Search fee: $5.00 per name. Required to search: name, years to search. Civil cases indexed by defendant, plaintiff. Civil records on index cards. Will only search back 10 years.

Criminal Records: Access: Mail, in person. Only the court performs in person searches; visitors may not. Search fee: $5.00 per name. Required to search: name, years to search. Criminal records on computer from 1989, index cards prior. Will only search back 7 years.

General Information: No juvenile or probation records released. Copy fee: $1.10 per page. Cert fee: $6.60 plus copy fee. Payee: Mono Superior Court. Personal checks accepted. Prepayment required. Mail requests: SASE required. Mail turnaround time 1 week.

Monterey County

Superior Court - Monterey Branch

1200 Aguajito Rd, 1st Fl, Monterey, CA 93940; 831-647-5800. Hours: 9:30AM-4PM (PST). *Civil, Probate.*
http://65.119.109.232/
Note: This court holds the civil records from the city of Salinas. Criminal records for Monterey are held in Salinas.

Civil Records: Access: Mail, in person. Both court and visitors may perform in person searches. Search fee: $5.00 per name per year. Required to search: name, years to search. Civil cases indexed by defendant, plaintiff. Some cCivil records computerized since 07/03, on microfiche from 1973, index books prior. Although historical records are not online, access to calendars and current cases is free at the web page.

General Information: No juvenile or probation records released. Copy fee: $.75 per page. Cert fee: $7.00 general; $10.00 if for final re dissolution. Payee: Superior Court. Personal checks accepted. Prepayment required. Mail requests: SASE required. Mail turnaround time 1 week.

Superior Court - Salinas Division

240 Church St, Rm 318 PO Box 1819, Salinas, CA 93902; 831-755-5400. Hours: 8AM-4PM (PST). *Felony, Misdemeanor.*
www.co.monterey.ca.us/court
Note: All criminal records are filed at the Salinas courthouse. All civil, probate, and family law cases are files at the Monterey courthouse.

Criminal Records: Access: Mail, in person, online. Both court and visitors may perform in person searches. Search fee: $5.00 per name. Required to search: name, years to search; also helpful: DOB. Felony records computerized since 1998, on microfiche to 1940s. Misdemeanor records computerized since 1992, on microfiche since 1986. Online access to calendars and current cases is free at www.co.monterey.ca.us/court/calendar.asp.

General Information: No adoptions, juvenile, medical, probation or sealed records released. Copy fee: $.75 per page. Cert fee: $6.60. Payee: Clerk of Court. Personal checks accepted. Prepayment required. Mail requests: SASE required. Mail turnaround time 1 week.

King City Division - Consolidated Trial Court

250 Franciscan Way (PO Box 647), King City, CA 93930; 831-386-5200. Hours: 8AM-5PM; Public Hours: 9:30AM-4PM (PST). *Felony, Misdemeanor, Civil Actions Under $25,000, Eviction, Small Claims.*
www.co.monterey.ca.us/court
Note: Encompasses the cities of King City, Greenfield, Soledad, areas south of King City to the San Luis Obispo County line.

Civil Records: Access: Mail, in person, online. Both court and visitors may perform in person searches. Search fee: $5.00 per name. Required to search: name, years to search. Civil cases indexed by defendant, plaintiff. Civil records on computer from 1992, index files from 1983. Records destroyed after 10 years. Online access to calendars and current cases is free online at www.co.monterey.ca.us/court/calendar.asp.

Criminal Records: Access: Mail, in person, online. Both court and visitors may perform in person searches. Search fee: $5.00 per name. Required to search: name, years to search; also helpful: DOB. Criminal records on computer from 1992, index files from 1983. Records destroyed after 10 years. Online access to criminal records is the same as civil.

General Information: No probation reports released. Copy fee: $.75 per page. Cert fee: $7.00. Payee: Monterey County Courts. Personal checks accepted. Visa, AmEx accepted. Additional fee charged. Prepayment required. Mail requests: SASE requested. Turnaround time 2-4 week.

Superior Court - Marina Division

3180 Del Monte Blvd, Marina, CA 93933; 831-883-5300; Fax: 831-884-0106. Hours: 8AM-4PM M-W, 8AM-2PM Fri; Closed Thursdays (PST). *Small Claims, Traffic.*
www.co.monterey.ca.us/court

Napa County

Superior Court - Civil Division

825 Brown St, Napa, CA 94559; 707-299-1130; Criminal phone: 702-299-1180; Fax: 707-253-4229. Hours: 8AM-5PM (PST). *Civil, Eviction, Small Claims, Probate.*
www.napa.courts.ca.gov

Civil Records: Access: Mail, in person. Both court and visitors may perform in person searches. Search fee: $5.00 per name per year. Required to search: name, years to search. Civil cases indexed by defendant, plaintiff. Civil records on computer since 1989; prior records on index books or microfilm back to 1800s. Access to Tentative Rulings is online free at www.napa.courts.ca.gov/Civil/civil_tentative.asp.
These only go back about 1 week.

General Information: Public Access terminal is available. No adoptions, juvenile, medical, probation or sealed records released. Copy fee: $1.00 per page. Cert fee: $6.60 per document. Payee: Napa Superior Court. Personal checks accepted. Prepayment required. Mail requests: SASE required. Mail turnaround time 2 weeks.

Superior Court - Criminal Division

1111 3rd St, Napa, CA 94559; 707-299-1180; Fax: 707-253-4673. Hours: 8AM-5PM (PST). *Felony, Misdemeanor.*
www.napa.courts.ca.gov

Criminal Records: Access: Mail, in person, fax, online. Both court and visitors may perform in person searches. Search fee: $5.00 per name per year. Required to search: name, years to search, DOB; also helpful: address, SSN. Misdemeanor records on computer back to 1986 and felonies back to 1989. Online access is at www.napa.courts.ca.gov/. There is no fee to search by case number; but fees are incurred if records are ordered or to search by name.

General Information: Public Access terminal is available. No adoptions, juvenile, medical, probation or sealed records released. Copy fee: $1.00 per page. Cert fee: $6.60. Payee: Napa Superior Court. Personal checks accepted. Prepayment required. Mail requests: SASE required. Mail turnaround time 2 weeks.

Nevada County

Superior Court - Civil Division

201 Church St, #5, Nevada City, CA 95959; Civil phone: 530-265-1294; Criminal phone: 530-265-1311; Probate phone: 530-265-1293. Hours: 8AM-5PM (PST). *Civil, Eviction, Small Claims.*
www.court.co.nevada.ca.us
Note: The phone number for Family Law, Probate and Juvenile is 530-265-1293. The phone number for Evictions and Small Claims is 530-265-1294.

Civil Records: Access: Phone, mail, in person, online. Both court and visitors may perform in person searches. Search fee: $5.00 per name. Required to search: name, years to search. Civil cases indexed by defendant, plaintiff. Civil records on computer back to 1983. Cases with previous disposition are available on microfilm in most cases. Some of the Limited Civil, Small Claims and Unlawful Detainer cases have been destroyed. Access to case calendar is free at www.court.co.nevada.ca.us/cgi/dba/casecal/db.cgi.

General Information: Public Access terminal is available. No probation reports released. Copy fee: $.50 per page. Cert fee: $6.60. plus copy fees. Payee: Superior Court. Personal checks accepted. Prepayment required. Mail requests: SASE required. Mail turnaround time 2 days.

Superior Court - Criminal

201 Church St #7, Nevada City, CA 95959; 530-265-1311; Fax: 530-478-1938. Hours: 8AM-5PM (PST). *Felony, Misdemeanor.*
www.courts.co.nevada.ca.us

Criminal Records: Access: Phone, mail, in person, online. Only the court performs in person searches; visitors may not. Search fee: No fee unless extensive research required. Required to search: name, years to search; also helpful: DOB. Criminal records on computer from 1987, prior in books back to 1800s. Access to case calendar is free at www.court.co.nevada.ca.us/cgi/dba/casecal/db.cgi.

General Information: No adoptions, paternit, juvenile, medical, probation or sealed records released. Will fax results to local or toll free line. Copy fee: $.50 per page. Cert fee: $6.60 per document. Payee: Nevada County Superior Courts. Personal checks accepted. Prepayment required. Mail requests: SASE required. Mail turnaround time 2 weeks.

Truckee Branch - Superior Court

10075 Levon Ave, #301, Truckee, CA 96161; Civil phone: 530-582-7837; Criminal phone: 530-582-7835; Fax: 530-582-7875. Hours: 8AM-5PM (PST). *Misdemeanor, Civil, Eviction, Small Claims.*
http://court.co.nevada.ca.us

Civil Records: Access: Mail, in person, online. Both court and visitors may perform in person searches. Search fee: $5.00 per name. Required to search: name, years to search. Civil cases indexed by defendant, plaintiff. Civil records on computer from 1991, index files from 1983. Records destroyed after 10 years. Access to case calendar is free at www.court.co.nevada.ca.us/cgi/dba/casecal/db.cgi.

Criminal Records: Access: Mail, in person, online. Both court and visitors may perform in person searches. Search fee: $5.00 per name. Required to search: name, years to search. Criminal records on computer from 1991, index files from 1983. Records destroyed after 10 years. Access to case calendar is free at www.court.co.nevada.ca.us/cgi/dba/casecal/db.cgi. **General Information:** Public Access terminal is available. No probation reports released. Copy fee: $.50 per page. Cert fee: $6.60. Payee: Superior Court. Personal checks accepted. Prepayment required. Mail requests: SASE required. Mail turnaround time 1 week.

Orange County

Superior Court - Civil 700 Civic Center Dr W, Santa Ana, CA 92701; 714-834-2200. Hours: 8AM-4PM (PST). *Civil Actions, Small Claims.*
www.occourts.org
Note: This court handles civil actions over $25,000 countywide, but the limited civil and small claims cases are for this central jurisdiction venue (Santa Ana area) only.

Civil Records: Access: Mail, in person. Both court and visitors may perform in person searches. Search fee: $5.00 per name per index. Required to search: name, years to search. Civil cases indexed by defendant, plaintiff. Civil records on computer from mid 1980s, partial prior to 1986, microfiche and index file from 1900s. Civil cases index involving $25,000+ for the county can be purchased on CD; however, index only goes back to 12/31/01. Civil and family court calendars are online at www.occourts.org/calendars/.
General Information: Public Access terminal is available. No adoptions, juvenile, medical, probation or sealed records released. Will not fax results. Copy fee: $.80 per page. Cert fee: $6.60 per document. Payee: Clerk of the Court. Personal checks accepted. Prepayment required. Mail requests: SASE required. Mail turnaround time 1-2 weeks.

Superior Court - Criminal Operations 700 Civic Center Dr W, Santa Ana, CA 92701; 714-834-2200; Criminal phone: 714-834-2266. Hours: 8AM-4PM (PST). *Felony, Misdemeanor.*
www.occourts.org
Criminal Records: Access: Mail, in person. Both court and visitors may perform in person searches. Search fee: $5.00 per name per year. Required to search: name, years to search, DOB. Criminal records on computer from 1988, on microfiche and archived from 1966, index files from 1918. Felony name index for the county can be purchased on CD; however, index only goes back to 12/31/01.
General Information: No adoptions, juvenile, medical, probation or sealed records released. Copy fee: $.80 per page. Cert fee: $6.60 per document. Payee: Clerk of the Court. Personal checks accepted. Prepayment required. Mail requests: SASE required. Mail turnaround time 1-2 weeks.

Central Orange County Superior Court - Limited Jurisdiction 700 Civic Ctr Dr W (PO Box 1138, 92702), Santa Ana, CA 92701; Civil phone: 714-834-3580; Criminal phone: 714-834-3575; Fax: 714-953-9032. Hours: 8AM-4PM (PST). *Misdemeanor, Civil Actions Under $25,000, Eviction, Small Claims.*
www.occourts.org/
Note: Includes cities of Santa Ana, Orange, Tustin and surrounding unincorporated territories including Cowan Heights, El Modena, Tustin Marine Air Base, Lemon Heights, Modjeska, Orange Park Acres, Silverado Canyon and Villa Park.
Civil Records: Access: Mail, in person. Both the court and visitors may perform in person searches. Search fee: $5.00 per name per year. Required to search: name, years to search. Civil cases indexed by defendant, plaintiff. Civil records on index files and microfiche from 1985. Records destroyed after 10

years. Civil and family court calendars are online at www.occourts.org/calendars/.
Criminal Records: Access: Mail, in person. Both the court and visitors may perform in person searches. Search fee: $5.00 per name per year. Required to search: name, years to search, DOB. Criminal records on index files and microfiche from 1986; on computer since 1995. Records destroyed after 7 years, no physical file available then.
General Information: Public Access terminal is available. (Terminal is in Rm K107.) No probation reports released. Copy fee: $.80 per page. Cert fee: $6.60. Payee: Clerk of Court. Personal checks accepted. Visa, MC accepted. Prepayment required. Mail requests: SASE required. Mail turnaround time 2-4 days.

Harbor - Laguna Hills Superior Court - Civil Division 23141 Moulton Pkwy, Laguna Hills, CA 92653; 949-472-6964. Hours: 8AM-4PM (PST). *Civil Actions Under $25,000, Eviction, Small Claims.*
www.occourts.org/
Note: Formerly known as South Orange, this includes Aliso Viejo, Capistrano Bch, Coto De Caza, Dana Pt, Laguna (various), Lake Forest, Mission Viejo, Rancho St. Margarita, San Clemente, San Juan Capistrano, Trabuco Canyon.
Civil Records: Access: Mail, in person. Both court and visitors may perform in person searches. Search fee: $5.00 per name per year. Fee only applies if court does search and case number is required. Required to search: name, years to search. Civil cases indexed by defendant, plaintiff. Civil records in index files and on microfiche back to 1987; on computer back to 2000. Civil and family court calendars are online at www.occourts.org/calendars/.
General Information: Public Access terminal is available. No unlawful detainer records released for 60 days. Copy fee: $.80 per page. Cert fee: $6.60. Payee: Clerk of Court. Personal checks accepted. Visa, MC, Discover accepted. Prepayment required. Mail requests: SASE required. Mail turnaround time 2-3 days.

Harbor - Laguna Niguel Superior Court - Criminal Division 30143 Crown Valley Parkway, Justice Center, Laguna Niguel, CA 92677; 949-249-5000. Hours: 8AM-4PM (PST). *Misdemeanor.*
www.occourts.org/
Note: Also known as South Orange County Superior Court. Includes Capistrano Bch, Coto De Caza, Dana Pt, Laguna Hills, Laguna Niguel, Mission Viejo, Rancho St. Margarita, San Clemente, San Juan Capistrano, Trabuco Canyon.
Criminal Records: Access: Mail, in person. Both court and visitors may perform in person searches. Search fee: $5.00 per name per year. Required to search: name, years to search, DOB; also helpful: SSN. Criminal records on computer since 1987; prior records on books.
General Information: No probation report, unlawful detainer records released. Copy fee: $.80 per page. Cert fee: $6.60. Payee: Clerk of Court. Personal checks accepted. Visa, MC, Discover accepted. Prepayment required. Mail requests: SASE required. Mail turnaround time 2-3 days.

Harbor - Newport Beach Superior Court 4601 Jamboree Rd #104, Newport Beach, CA 92660-2595; 949-476-4699. Hours: 8AM-4PM (PST). *Misdemeanor, Civil Actions Under $25,000, Eviction, Small Claims.*
www.occourts.org
Note: Includes Balboa Island, Corona Del Mar, Costa Mesa, Newport Beach, Irvine, Santa Ana Heights,

John Wayne/Orange Co Airport, Lido Isle and surrounding unincorporated areas.

Civil Records: Access: Mail, in person. Both court and visitors may perform in person searches. Search fee: $5.00 per name. Required to search: name, years to search. Civil cases indexed by defendant, plaintiff. Civil records go back 10 years; computerized records go back 3 years. Civil and family court calendars are online at www.occourts.org/calendars/.
Criminal Records: Access: Mail, in person. Only the court performs in person searches; visitors may not. Search fee: $5.00 per name. Required to search: name, years to search; also helpful: DOB. Criminal records on computer go back 10 years; on microfiche -- felonies kept 75 years, misdemeanors 5 years.
General Information: No probation reports nor police reports released. Copy fee: $.80. Cert fee: $6.60 per document. Payee: Clerk of Court. Personal checks accepted. Checks must be in-state and be imprinted with name and address. Visa, MC, Discover accepted. Prepayment required. Mail requests: SASE required. Mail turnaround time 5-10 days.

North Orange County Superior Court 1275 N Berkeley Ave, PO Box 5000, Fullerton, CA 92838-0500; 714-773-4555; 773-4667 (Small Claims); Civil phone: 714-773-4664; Criminal phone: 714-773-4668. Hours: 7:30AM-4PM (PST). *Felony, Misdemeanor, Civil Actions Under $25,000, Eviction, Small Claims.*
www.occourts.org/
Note: Includes the cities of Anaheim, Brea, Buena Park, Fullerton, La Habra, La Palma, Placentia, Yorba Linda and surrounding unincorporated area including Anaheim Hills.

Traffic phone: 714-773-4615.
Civil Records: Access: Mail, in person. Both court and visitors may perform in person searches. Search fee: $5.00 per name, per year, per index. Fee also applies to requests by case number. Required to search: name, years to search. Civil cases indexed by defendant, plaintiff. Civil records on computer from 1991, index files from 1983. Records destroyed after 10 years. Family court calendars are online at www.occourts.org/calendars/.
Criminal Records: Access: Mail, in person. Only the court performs in person searches; visitors may not. Search fee: $5.00 per name per index. Required to search: name, years to search. All Criminal records are on computer. Records destroyed after 5-7 years from date of conviction. Felony name index for the county can be purchased on CD; however, index only goes back to 12/31/01.
General Information: No probation reports or UD's for 60 days released. Copy fee: $.80 per page. Cert fee: $6.60 per document. Payee: Clerk of Court. Personal checks accepted with proper ID. Visa, MC, Discover accepted. Prepayment required. Mail requests: SASE required. Mail turnaround time 5 days.

West Orange County Superior Court 8141 13th St, Westminster, CA 92683; 714-896-7181; Civil phone: 714-896-7191; Criminal phone: 714-896-7351; Fax: 714-896-7404 (civ); 896-7219 (criminal). Hours: 8AM-4PM (PST). *Misdemeanor, Civil Actions Under $25,000, Eviction, Small Claims.*
www.occourts.org
Note: Includes the cities of Cypress, Fountain Valley, Garden Grove, Huntington Beach, Los Alamitos, Rossmore, Seal Beach, Stanton, Sunset Beach, Surfside, Westminster and adjoining and unincorporated territory.
Civil Records: Access: Mail, in person. Both court and visitors may perform in person searches. Search fee: $5.00 per name per year per index. Required to

search: name, years to search. Civil cases indexed by defendant, plaintiff. Civil records on computer back to 1992, microfiche from 1983. Records destroyed after 10 years. Civil and family court calendars are online at www.occourts.org/calendars/.

Criminal Records: Access: Mail, in person. Both court and visitors may perform in person searches. Search fee: $5.00 per name per year per index. Required to search: name, years to search, DOB. Criminal records on computer back to 1996, microfiche from 1983. Misdemeanor records destroyed after 10 years.

General Information: No probation reports, unlawful detainer (under 60 days old) records released. Will not fax results. Copy fee: $.80 per page. Cert fee: $6.60 per document. Payee: Clerk of Court. Personal checks accepted. Visa, MC, Discover accepted. Prepayment required. Mail requests: SASE required. Mail turnaround time 2 days.

Orange County Probate Court 341 The City Dr, Orange, CA 92868; 714-935-8043. Hours: 8AM-5PM (PST). *Probate.*
www.occourts.org
Note: Jurisdiction includes juvenile, family law, and mental health filings. Search court calendars free at www.occourts.org/calendars/calendarsprob.asp.

Placer County

Superior Court 101 Maple St, Auburn, CA 95603; Civil phone: 530-889-6550; Criminal phone: 530-886-1200. Hours: 8AM-3PM (PST). *Felony, Civil, Eviction, Probate.*
www.placercourts.org
Civil Records: Access: Phone, mail, in person. Both court and visitors may perform in person searches. Search fee: $5.00 per year for records prior to 1974; 1975 and forward are $5.00 per name. Required to search: name, years to search. Civil cases indexed by defendant, plaintiff. Civil records on computer from 1992, on microfiche from 1974, archived and index file from 1800s.
Criminal Records: Access: Phone, mail, in person. Both court and visitors may perform in person searches. Search fees: Same fees as civil. Required to search: name, years to search. Criminal records on computer from 1992, on microfiche from 1974, archived and index file from 1800s.
General Information: Public Access terminal is available. No adoptions, juvenile, medical, paternity, probation or sealed records released. Copy fee: $1.00 for first page, $.50 each add'l. Cert fee: $6.60. Payee: Clerk of the Court. Personal checks accepted. Prepayment required. Mail requests: SASE required. Mail turnaround time 2 weeks.

Auburn Branch - Superior Court 11532 "B" Ave, Auburn, CA 95603; 530-886-1200; Fax: 530-886-1209. Hours: 8AM-3PM Office (8AM-3PM phone hours) (PST). *Felony, Misdemeanor.*
www.placercourts.org
Note: Includes Auburn, Penryn, Newcastle, Bowman, Colfax, Weimar, Alta, Dutch Flat, Loomis. Also includes criminal for Roseville, Rocklin, Lincoln criminal as of 12/8/97.
Criminal Records: Access: Mail, in person. Both court and visitors may perform in person searches. Search fee: $5.00 per name per year. Required to search: name, years to search, DOB. Criminal Records indexed on computer back to 1992; felonies back to 1999; records go back 10 years.
General Information: Public Access terminal is available. No probation reports or copies of warrants released. Will not fax results. Copy fee: $1.00 per page. Cert fee: $6.60. Payee: Clerk of the Court. Personal checks accepted. Prepayment required. Mail

requests: SASE required. Mail turnaround time 2 weeks.

Tahoe Division - Superior Court PO Box 5669, Tahoe City, CA 96145; 530-581-6336; Fax: 530-581-6344. Hours: 8AM-3PM (PST). *Misdemeanor, Civil, Eviction, Small Claims.*
www.placercourts.org
Note: This court does all areas of law with the exception of Adoptions and Probate.
Civil Records: Access: Mail, in person. Only the court may perform in person searches. Search fee: $5.00 per name. Required to search: name, years to search. Civil cases indexed by defendant, plaintiff. Civil records computerized since 1999, previous on index cards.
Criminal Records: Access: Mail, in person. Only the court may perform in person searches. Search fee: $5.00 per name. Required to search: name, years to search. Criminal records on index cards. Will only search back 7 years; computerized records since 1999.
General Information: No probation reports released. Copy fee: $1.00 per page. Cert fee: $6.60. Payee: Clerk of Court. Personal checks accepted. Write "not to exceed $x.xx" on check. Prepayment required. Mail requests: SASE required. Mail turnaround time 1 week.

Lincoln Division - Superior Court
www.placercourts.org
Note: This Lincoln Division is now fully consolidated with the Roseville Court. All traffic cases have been transferred to Roseville custody; all small claims cases have been transferred to Historic Courthouse at 101 Maple St, Auburn, CA 95603, 530-889-6550.

Roseville Division - Superior Court 300 Taylor St, Roseville, CA 95678; 916-783-1600; Fax: 916-783-1690. Hours: 8AM-3PM (PST). *Traffic.*
www.placercourts.org
Note: This court holds the records for the Foresthill Division Court which has closed; and Lincoln Court Traffic only.

Plumas County

Superior Court - Civil Division 520 Main St, Rm 104, Quincy, CA 95971; 530-283-6305; Criminal phone: 530-283-6232; Fax: 530-283-6415. Hours: 8AM-5PM (PST). *Civil, Small Claims, Probate.*
www.plumascourt.ca.gov
Civil Records: Access: Phone, fax, mail, in person. Both court and visitors may perform in person searches. Search fee: $5.00 per name per year. Required to search: name, years to search. Civil cases indexed by defendant, plaintiff. Civil records on computer from 1993, archived from 1980, index file from 1850.
General Information: No adoptions, juvenile, confidential, medical, probation or sealed records released. Will fax results $5.00 per doc. Copy fee: $1.00 per page. Cert fee: $7.00. Payee: Plumas County Courts. Personal checks accepted. Prepayment required. Mail requests: SASE required. Mail turnaround time 1 week.

Superior Court - Criminal Division 520 Main St, Rm 104, Quincy, CA 95971; 530-283-6232; Fax: 530-283-6415. Hours: 8AM-5PM (PST). *Felony, Misdemeanor.*
www.plumascourt.ca.gov
Criminal Records: Access: Mail, in person. Only the court performs in person searches; visitors may not. Search fee: $5.00 per name. Required to search: name, years to search, DOB; also, signed release if juvenile. Criminal records indexed on computer back to 1989.
General Information: No probation reports, financial statements or juvenile released. Will fax

results. Copy fee: $1.00 per page. Cert fee: $7.00. Payee: Superior Court. Personal checks accepted. Prepayment required. Mail requests: SASE required. Mail turnaround time 1-2 days.

Chester Branch - Superior Court 1st & Willow Way (PO Box 722), Chester, CA 96020; 530-258-2646; Fax: 530-258-2652. Hours: 8AM-4PM (PST). *Civil Actions Under $25,000, Eviction, Small Claims.*
www.psln.com/pccourt
Civil Records: Access: Phone, mail, in person. Only the court performs in person searches; visitors may not. Search fee: $5.00 per name per year. Required to search: name, years to search. Civil cases indexed by defendant, plaintiff. Traffic on computer, index cards for civil records. Will only search back 7 years. Records on computer go back 13 years.
General Information: No probation reports released. Fee to fax results is $5.00 per document. Copy fee: $1.00 per page. Cert fee: $6.60 to $10.00. Payee: Superior Court. Personal checks accepted. Prepayment required. Mail requests: SASE required. Mail turnaround time 1-2 days.

Portola Branch - Superior Court 161 Nevada St (PO Box 1054), Portola, CA 96122; 530-832-4286; Fax: 530-832-5838. Hours: 8AM-3:30PM (PST). *Civil Actions Under $25,000, Eviction, Small Claims, Traffic.*
Civil Records: Access: Phone, fax, mail, in person. Only the court performs in person searches; visitors may not. Search fee: $5.00 per name. Required to search: name, years to search. Civil cases indexed by defendant, plaintiff. Traffic on computer, computer for civil records. Court will only search back 10 years.
Criminal Records: Access: Phone, mail, in person. Only the court performs in person searches; visitors may not. Search fee: $5.00 per name. Required to search: name, years to search. Traffic on computer, computer for criminal records. Court will only search back 10 years.
General Information: No probation reports released. Will not fax results. Copy fee: $1.00 per page. Cert fee: $6.60. Payee: Superior Court. Personal checks accepted. Prepayment required. Mail requests: SASE required. Mail turnaround time ASAP.

Greenville Branch - Superior Court PO Box 706 (115 Hwy 89), Greenville, CA 95947; 530-284-7213; Fax: 530-284-0857. Hours: 8AM-4PM (PST). *Small Claims.*

Riverside County

Superior Court - Civil Division 4050 Main St, Riverside, CA 92501; 951-955-1960; Probate phone: 951-955-1970; Fax: 909-955-1751. Hours: 8AM-4PM (PST). *Civil Actions, Small Claims, Probate.*
www.courts.co.riverside.ca.us/
Note: All Superior Court Files and Limited Jurisdiction files except for those cases filed within the Mt. San Jacinto Judicial District and Three Lakes Judicial District.
Civil Records: Access: Phone, fax, mail, online, in person. Both court and visitors may perform in person searches. No search fee. Required to search: name, years to search. Civil cases indexed by defendant, plaintiff. Civil records on computer and microfiche from 1970, index file from 1956, archived from 1900s. Access to civil records is free at the web page. Online records date back to 1991 for Riverside, 1994 for Corona, and 1996 forward for most of the remaining limited court cases. Also, civil indexes are on CD-Rom including DOBs. CD-Rom fee is $25.00 per month per department. Overall index goes back to 10/91 and complete name index history is $300 per

department. For info, contact S Griffin at 909-955-1431.

General Information: Public Access terminal is available. No adoptions, juvenile, medical, probation, unlawful detainers for 60 days or sealed records released. Will fax results $1.00 per page. Copy fee: $.50 per page. Cert fee: $7.00. Payee: Riverside County Superior Court. Personal checks accepted. Visa, MC, Discover accepted. Prepayment required. Mail requests: SASE required. Mail turnaround time 3 days.

Superior Court - Criminal Division 4100
Main St, Riverside, CA 92501; 951-955-2300; Fax: 951-955-4007. Hours: 7:30AM-4PM (PST). *Felony, Misdemeanor.*
www.courts.co.riverside.ca.us
Criminal Records: Access: Phone, fax, mail, online, in person. Both court and visitors may perform in person searches. No search fee. Required to search: name, years to search, DOB; also helpful: SSN. Criminal Records on microfiche and computer since 1970, index file from 1956. For free Internet access to records visit the web page. Includes Desert and Riverside felony, misdemeanor, & traffic; and misdemeanor from Corona, Palm Springs, Indio and Blythe. Also, criminal indexes are on CD-Rom including DOBs. CD-Rom fee is $25.00 per month per department. Overall index goes back to 6/90 and complete name index history is $300.00 per department. For info, contact S Griffin at 909-955-1431.
General Information: Public Access terminal is available. No adoptions, juvenile, medical, probation, unlawful detainers for 60 days or sealed records released. Will fax results $1.00 for 1st page, $.50 each add'l. Must pay fax fee by credit card. Copy fee: $.50 per page. Cert fee: $7.00. Payee: Clerk of the Court. Personal checks accepted. Visa, MC, Discover accepted. Prepayment required. Mail requests: SASE required. Mail turnaround time 1 day to 1 week.

Blythe Division - Superior Court 265 N
Broadway, Blythe, CA 92225; Civil phone: 760-921-7981; Criminal phone: 760-921-7828 (incl: traffic); Fax: 760-921-7941 civ.; 921-7942 crim. Hours: 7:30AM-4PM (PST). *Felony, Misdemeanor, Civil Actions, Eviction, Small Claims.*
www.courts.co.riverside.ca.us/
Note: Includes Blythe, Ripley. Phone for Family Law is 760-921-7982.
Civil Records: Access: Phone, fax, mail, online, in person. Both court and visitors may perform in person searches. Search fee: none. Required to search: name, years to search. Civil cases indexed by defendant, plaintiff. Civil records on computer from 1991, index files from 1983. Records destroyed after 10 years. See Riverside Division for online information. Also, see Riverside Civil Division for information on name indexes back to 3/89 on CD-rom.
Criminal Records: Access: Phone, fax, mail, online, in person. Both court and visitors may perform in person searches. Search fee: none. Required to search: name, years to search; also helpful: DOB, sex. Criminal records on computer from 1991, index files from 1983. Records destroyed after 10 years. See Riverside Division for online information. Also, see Riverside Criminal Division for information on name indexes back to 11/89 on CD-rom. See Riverside Division for information on name indexes on CD-rom.
General Information: Public Access terminal is available. No probation reports released. Will charge $1.00 per page to fax in or fax results out. Copy fee: $.50 per page. Cert fee: $7.00. Payee: Clerk of the Court. Personal checks accepted. Visa, MC, Discover accepted. Prepayment required. Mail requests: SASE required. Mail turnaround time 2 days.

Corona Branch - Superior Court, CA; 909-272-5620. *Felony, Misdemeanor, Civil Actions Under $25,000, Eviction, Small Claims.*
www.courts.co.riverside.ca.us
Note: This court closed as of 7/03.

Banning Division - Superior Court 155 E
Hays St, Banning, CA 92220; Civil phone: 909-922-7155; Criminal phone: 909-922-7145; Fax: 909-922-7160 civ; 909-922-7150 crim. Hours: 7:30AM-4PM (PST). *Felony, Misdemeanor, Civil Actions Under $25,000, Eviction, Small Claims.*
www.courts.co.riverside.ca.us
Note: Includes Banning, Cabazon, Highland Springs, Poppet Flatt, Silent Valley, Beaumont, Calimesa, Cherry Valley and Whitewater.
Civil Records: Access: Phone, fax, mail, online, in person. Both the court and visitors may perform in person searches. No search fee. Required to search: name, years to search; also helpful-case number. Civil cases indexed by defendant, plaintiff. Civil records on computer from 1991, index files from 1983. Records destroyed after 10 years. See Riverside Division location for online information. Also, see Riverside Civil Division for information on name indexes back to 3/89 on CD-rom. Phone and fax access limited to short searches.
Criminal Records: Access: Phone, fax, mail, online, in person. Only the court performs in person searches; visitors may not. No search fee. Required to search: name, years to search; also helpful-case number. Criminal records on computer back to 1992, index files from 1983. Records destroyed after 10 years. See Riverside Division for online information. Also, see Riverside Criminal Division for information on name indexes back to 11/89 on CD-rom. Will perform phone searches for one or two names only.
General Information: Public Access terminal is available. (Public terminal for civil in person searches only.) No probation reports released. Fee to fax results is $1.00 per page. Copy fee: $.50 per page. Cert fee: $6.60. Payee: Clerk of the Court. Personal checks accepted. Visa, MC, Discover accepted. Prepayment required. Mail requests: SASE required. Mail turnaround time 2 days.

Hemet Division - Superior Court 880 N
State St, Hemet, CA 92543; 951-766-2322; Fax: 951-766-2317. Hours: 7:30AM-4PM (PST). *Civil Actions Under $25,000, Eviction, Small Claims.*
www.courts.co.riverside.ca.us/
Note: Includes Aguanga, Anza, Gilman Hot Springs, Hemet, Idylwild, Mountain Center, Pine Cove, Redec, Sage, San Jacinto, Sobba Hot Spring, Valle Vista and Winchester.
Civil Records: Access: Mail, online, in person. Both court and visitors may perform in person searches. No search fee. Required to search: name, years to search. Civil cases indexed by defendant, plaintiff. Civil records on computer from 1996, index files from 1983. Records destroyed after 10 years. See Riverside Division location for online information. Also, see Riverside Civil Division for information on name indexes back to 3/89 on CD-rom.
General Information: Copy fee: $.50 per page. Cert fee: $6.60. Payee: Clerk of the Court. Personal checks accepted. Visa, MC, Discover accepted. Prepayment required. Mail requests: SASE required.

Indio Division - Superior Court 46-200
Oasis St, Indio, CA 92201; 760-863-8426; Civil phone: 760-863-8208; Criminal phone: 760-863-8206; Probate phone: 760-863-8207; Fax: 760-863-8707. Hours: 7:30AM-4PM (PST). *Misdemeanor, Civil Actions Under $25,000, Eviction, Small Claims, Probate.*
www.courts.co.riverside.ca.us/

Note: Includes Desert Center, Eagle Mountain, Indio, La Quinta, Coachella, Bermuda Dunes, Mecca, North Shore, Pinyon Pines, Palm Springs, Salton Sea, Oasis, Thermal. Most Palm Springs records are here.
Civil Records: Access: Phone, fax, mail, online, in person. Visitors must perform in person searches for themselves. No search fee. Required to search: name, years to search. Civil cases indexed by defendant, plaintiff. Civil records on computer from 1993, index files from 1983. Records destroyed after 10 years. See Riverside Division for online information. Also, see Riverside Civil Division for information on name indexes back to 3/89 on CD-rom. Phone & fax access limited to short searches.
Criminal Records: Access: Phone, fax, mail, online, in person. Visitors must perform in person searches for themselves. No search fee. Required to search: name, years to search, signed release. Criminal records on computer from 1993, index files from 1983. Records destroyed after 10 years. See Riverside Division for online information. Also, see Riverside Criminal Division for information on name indexes back to 11/89 on CD-rom.
General Information: Public Access terminal is available. No probation reports released. Will fax results $1.00 per page. Copy fee: $.50 per page. Cert fee: $7.00. Payee: Clerk of the Court. Personal checks accepted. Visa, MC, Discover accepted. Prepayment required. Mail requests: SASE required. Mail turnaround time 2 days.

Palm Springs Division - Superior Court
Misdemeanor, Evictions, Traffic.
Note: This Court closed as of 07/03. Records sent to court in Indio.

Southwest Justice Center - Superior Court 30755 "D" Auld Rd, #1226, Murrieta, CA
92563; 951-304-5000; Fax: 951-304-5250. Hours: 7:30AM-4PM (PST). *Felony, Misdemeanor, Family Law.*
www.courts.co.riverside.ca.us/
Note: This is a new court (01/01/03) that took in the criminal court cases from the closed Superior Courts in Lake Elsinore and Perris.
Criminal Records: Access: Fax, mail, online, in person. Both court and visitors may perform in person searches. No search fee. Required to search: name, years to search. Criminal records on computer since 1992; prior records on fiche. See Riverside Division for online information. See Riverside Criminal Division for information on name indexes back to 11/89 on CD-Rom. Phone & fax access limited to short searches.
General Information: Public Access terminal is available. No adoptions, juvenile, medical, probation or sealed records released. Will fax results for $1.00 per page. Copy fee: $.50 per page. Cert fee: $6.60 per document. Payee: Clerk of the Court. Personal checks accepted. Visa, MC, Discover accepted. Prepayment required. Mail requests: SASE required. Mail turnaround time 1 week.

Temecula Branch - Superior Court 41002
County Center Dr, Temecula, CA 92591; 951-600-6400; Fax: 951-600-6423. Hours: 7:30AM-4PM (PST). *Civil Actions Under $25,000, Eviction, Small Claims.*
www.courts.co.riverside.ca.us/
Note: Civil records for the former Lake Elsinore and Perris Branches are stored here. Includes Perris, Sun City, Romoland, Homeland, Lakeview, Glenn Valley, Mead Valley, Quail Valley, Nuevo.
Civil Records: Access: Phone, mail, online, in person. Both court and visitors may perform in person searches. Visitors may search on computer only. No search fee. Required to search: name, years to search,

DOB. Civil cases indexed by defendant, plaintiff. Civil records on computer go back 10-12 years; records held for 10 years. See Riverside Division location for online information. Also, see Riverside Civil Division for information on name indexes back to 3/89 on CD-rom.

General Information: Public Access terminal is available. No confidential, adoption or sealed records released. Unlawful detainers not released for 60 days. Will not fax results. Copy fee: $.50 per page. Cert fee: $7.00 per document. Payee: Clerk of the Court. Personal checks accepted. Visa, MC, Discover accepted. Prepayment required. Mail requests: SASE required. Mail turnaround time 7 days.

Lake Elsinore Division - Superior Court
Note: This court closed 01/01/03. Refer to the Riverside Superior Court for case files.

Perris Branch - Superior Court
Note: This court closed 01/01/03. Refer to the Riverside Superior Court for case files.

Sacramento County

Superior Court 720 9th St Rm 102, Sacramento, CA 95814; 916-874-5522; Civil phone: 916-874-6868; Criminal phone: 916-874-5744; Fax: 916-874-5620. Hours: 8:30AM-4:30PM (PST). *Felony, Misdemeanor, Civil.*
www.saccourt.com
Note: Probate is located at 3341 Power Inn Rd, Sacramento 95826 (916-875-3400). The Galt, Elk Grove, and Walnut Grove branches closed. This court now holds their records.

Civil Records: Access: Phone, fax, mail, online, in person. Both court and visitors may perform in person searches. Search fee: $5.00 per name per year. Also charge $9.00 per hour for court. Required to search: name, years to search; also helpful: address. Civil cases indexed by defendant, plaintiff. Civil records on microfiche and archived from 1937, index books from 1800s. All court records for the county are free on the Internet at www.saccourt.com.

Criminal Records: Access: Phone, mail, online, in person. Both court and visitors may perform in person searches. Search fee: $5.00 per name. Required to search: name, years to search; also helpful: address, DOB, SSN. Criminal records on computer since 1993 (Superior), on microfiche and archived from 1962. All court records back to 1993 are free on the Internet at www.saccourt.com.

General Information: No adoptions, juvenile, medical, probation or sealed records released. Copy fee: $.50 per page. Cert fee: $6.60. Payee: Superior Court. Personal checks accepted. Prepayment required. Mail requests: SASE required. Mail turnaround time 1-3 weeks.

Carol Miller Justice Center 301 Bicentennial Circle, Sacramento, CA 95826; 916-875-7800/7354. Hours: 8:30AM-4:30PM (PST). *Small Claims, Evictions, Traffic, Juvenile.*
www.saccourt.com/geninfo/location/cmjc.asp

Galt Division - Superior Court
Misdemeanor, Small Claims.
Note: This court is closed as of 03/03. Misdemenaor records and files are now housed at the Sacramento Superior Court. Traffic records were sent to the Carol Miller Justice Center (916-875-7354/875-7800).

South Sacramento Superior Court - Elk Grove Branch *Misdemeanor, Civil Actions Under $25,000, Eviction, Small Claims.*
www.saccourt.com
Note: This court has been closed. All records are located at the Superior Court in Sacramento.

Walnut Grove Branch - Superior Court
Note: This court was closed, records are now at the Superior Court in Sacramento.

San Benito County

Superior Court Courthouse, 440 5th St-Rm 205, Hollister, CA 95023; 831-636-4057; Fax: 831-636-2046. Hours: 8AM-4PM (PST). *Felony, Misdemeanor, Civil, Small Claims, Eviction, Probate.*
www.sanbenito.courts.ca.gov/
Note: As of 11/2000, Small Claims, Family Law, and Eviction records are located at the Limited Jurisdiction Court, 390 5th St, Hollister. Phone: 831-630-5115. Fax: 831-636-4117. Same search requirements as stated below.

Civil Records: Access: Mail, in person. Both court and visitors may perform in person searches. Search fee: $5.00 per name. Required to search: name, years to search. Civil cases indexed by defendant, plaintiff. Civil records on computer since 1990, index books and archived from 1873.

Criminal Records: Access: Mail, in person. Both court and visitors may perform in person searches. Search fee: $5.00 per name. Required to search: name, years to search. Criminal records on computer since 1989, index books and archived from 1900.

General Information: Public Access terminal is available. No adoptions, juvenile, medical, probation or sealed records released. Will not fax results. Copy fee: $.50 per page. Cert fee: $7.00. Payee: Superior Court. Personal checks accepted. Prepayment required. Mail requests: SASE required. Mail turnaround time 1-2 weeks.

San Bernardino County

Barstow District - Superior Court 235 E Mountain View, Barstow, CA 92311; 760-256-4814; Civil phone: 760-256-4907; Criminal phone: 760-256-4785. Hours: 8AM-4PM (PST). *Felony, Misdemeanor, Civil, Eviction, Small Claims.*
www.sbcounty.gov/courts/
Note: Includes the City of Barstow and the unincorporated areas of Yermo, Lenwood, Daggett, Hinkley and Baker.

Civil Records: Access: Mail, in person, online. Both court and visitors may perform in person searches. Search fee: $5.00 per name per year. Required to search: name, years to search. Civil cases indexed by defendant, plaintiff. Civil records on computer from 1991, index books and microfilm. Microfilm is 3 to 4 weeks current. Records destroyed after 10 years. Online access to civil cases is free at www.sbcounty.gov/courts/genInfo/openaccess.htm. Daily calendars are at the main website.

Criminal Records: Access: Mail, in person, online. Both court and visitors may perform in person searches. Search fee: $5.00 per name per year. Required to search: name, years to search. Criminal records on computer from 1999, index books and microfilm. Microfilm is 3 to 4 weeks current. Records destroyed after 10 years. Online access to criminal cases is free at www.sbcounty.gov/courts/genInfo/openaccess.htm. Also, the daily criminal docket is free at the court main website.

General Information: No probation or confidential reports released. Will not fax results. Copy fee: $.50 per page. Cert fee: $6.60. Payee: Clerk of the Court. Only cashiers checks and money orders accepted. Visa, MC, Discover, AmEx accepted. Accepted for filings only. Prepayment required. Mail requests: SASE required. Mail turnaround time 2-5 days.

Central District - Superior Court 351 N Arrowhead Ave, San Bernardino, CA 92415; Civil phone: 909-387-3922; Criminal phone: 909-384-1888; Fax: 909-387-4428 (387-4993 criminal). Hours: 8AM-4PM (PST). *Felony, Misdemeanor, Civil, Eviction, Small Claims, Probate.*
www.sbcounty.gov/courts

Civil Records: Access: Mail, fax, in person, online. Both court and visitors may perform in person searches. Search fee: $5.00 per name per year. Required to search: name, years to search. Civil cases indexed by defendant, plaintiff. Civil records on computer from 1992, microfiche from 1972, archived and index file from 1856. Online access to civil cases is free at www.sbcounty.gov/courts/genInfo/openaccess.htm. Online access to "Probate Notes" is free at www.co.san-bernardino.ca.us/courts/ Click on Probate. Daily calendars are at the website. Address mail search access requests to Research Dept.

Criminal Records: Access: Mail, in person, online. Both court and visitors may perform in person searches. Search fee: $5.00 per name per year. Required to search: name, years to search, DOB, SSN. Criminal records on computer from 1996, microfiche from 1972, archived and index file from 1856. Online access to criminal cases is free at www.sbcounty.gov/courts/genInfo/openaccess.htm. Also, the daily criminal docket is free at the court main website.

General Information: Public Access terminal is available. No adoptions, juvenile, medical, probation or sealed records released. Will not fax results. Copy fee: $.50 per page. Cert fee: $6.60. Payee: Superior Court. Business checks accepted. Prepayment required. Mail requests: SASE required. Mail turnaround time 1-2 weeks.

Joshua Tree District - Superior Court
6527 White Feather Rd (PO Box 6602), Joshua Tree, CA 92252; 760-366-5770; Civil phone: 760-366-5770; Criminal phone: 760-366-5775; Fax: 760-366-4156. Hours: 8AM-4PM (PST). *Felony, Misdemeanor, Civil, Eviction, Small Claims.*
www.sbcounty.gov/courts/
Note: Includes the incorporated area of City of Twenty-Nine Palms, Town of Yucca Valley and unicorporated areas of Morongo Valley, Pioneertown, Landers, Johnson Valley and Wonder Valley.

Civil Records: Access: Mail, in person, online. Both court and visitors may perform in person searches. Search fee: $5.00 per name per year. Required to search: name, years to search. Civil cases indexed by defendant, plaintiff. Civil records on computer from 1991, index books from 1983. Records destroyed after 10 years. Online access to civil cases is free at www.sbcounty.gov/courts/genInfo/openaccess.htm. Daily calendars are at the main website.

Criminal Records: Access: Mail, in person, online. Both court and visitors may perform in person searches. Search fee: $5.00 per name per year. Required to search: name, years to search, DOB. Criminal records on computer from 1991, index books from 1983. Records destroyed after 10 years. Online access to criminal cases is free at www.sbcounty.gov/courts/genInfo/openaccess.htm. Also, the daily criminal docket is free at the court main website.

General Information: Public Access terminal is available. No probation reports, confidential records released. Will not fax results. Copy fee: $.50 per page. Cert fee: $6.60. Payee: Joshua Tree Superior Court. Personal checks accepted. Prepayment required. Mail requests: SASE required. Mail turnaround time 1 week.

Rancho Cucamonga District - Superior Court

8303 N Haven Ave, Rancho Cucamonga, CA 91730; 909-945-4131 info.; Civil phone: 909-945-4131; Criminal phone: 909-350-9764; Fax: 909-945-4154. Hours: 8AM-4PM (PST). *Felony, Misdemeanor, Civil, Eviction, Small Claims, Probate.*

www.co.san-bernardino.ca.us/courts/

Note: Formerly West District Superior Ct. Includes cities of Montclair, Ontario, Upland, Rancho Cucamonga, Alta Loma, Etiwanda, Guasti and surrounding unincorporated area of Mt Baldy.

Civil Records: Access: Phone, fax, mail, in person, online. Both court and visitors may perform in person searches. Search fee: $5.00 per name. Required to search: name, years to search. Civil cases indexed by defendant, plaintiff. Civil records on computer since April 1994, index cards prior. Records destroyed after 10 years. Online access to civil cases is free at www.sbcounty.gov/courts/genInfo/openaccess.htm. Online access to "Probate Notes" is free at www.co.san-bernardino.ca.us/courts/ Click on Probate. Daily calendars are at the main website.

Criminal Records: Access: Phone, fax, mail, in person, online. Both court and visitors may perform in person searches. Search fee: $5.00 per name. Required to search: name, years to search; also helpful: DOB. Criminal records computerized since 1994, also on index cards and microfiche. Online access to criminal cases is free at www.sbcounty.gov/courts/genInfo/openaccess.htm. Also, the daily criminal docket is free at the court main website.

General Information: Public Access terminal is available. No probation reports released. Will not fax results. Copy fee: $.50 per page. Cert fee: $6.60. Payee: Superior Court. Personal checks accepted. Only checks over $10.00 accepted. Visa, AmEx accepted for civil records. Prepayment required. Mail requests: SASE required. Mail turnaround time 2-4 days.

Victorville District - Superior Court

14455 Civic Dr, Victorville, CA 92392; Civil phone: 760-245-6215; Criminal phone: 760-245-6215; Fax: 760-243-8790 (civil); 8794 (criminal). Hours: 8AM-4PM (PST). *Felony, Misdemeanor, Civil, Eviction, Small Claims, Probate.*

www.sbcounty.gov/courts/

Note: Includes the Cities of Victorville, Adelanto Hesperia and the areas of Apple Valley, El Mirage, Helendale, Lucerne Valley, Oro Grande, Phelan, Pinon Hill and Wrightwood.

Civil Records: Access: Mail, in person, online. Both court and visitors may perform in person searches. Search fee: $5.00 per name. Required to search: name, years to search. Civil cases indexed by defendant, plaintiff. Civil records on microfiche from 1982 to July 1999, on computer from 1989 to present, index books prior. Records destroyed after 10 years. Online access to civil cases is free at www.sbcounty.gov/courts/genInfo/openaccess.htm. Also, daily calendars are at the main website.

Criminal Records: Access: Mail, in person, online. Only the court performs in person searches; visitors may not. Search fee: $5.00 per name. Required to search: name, years to search; also helpful: DOB, date of offense. Criminal index books by defendant 1986 - present. Online access to criminal cases is free at www.sbcounty.gov/courts/genInfo/openaccess.htm. Also, the daily criminal docket is free at the court main website. Only court allowed to search computer index.

General Information: Public Access terminal is available. No probation reports released. Will not fax results. Copy fee: $.50 per page. Cert fee: $6.60. Payee: Superior Court. Personal checks accepted.

$5.00 minimum. Prepayment required. Mail requests: SASE required. Mail turnaround time within 1 week.

Big Bear Lake District - Superior Court

PO Box 2806 (477 Summit Blvd.), Big Bear Lake, CA 92315; 909-866-0150; Fax: 909-866-0160. Hours: 8AM-4PM (PST). *Misdemeanor, Civil Actions Under $25,000, Eviction, Small Claims.*

www.sbcounty.gov/courts

Civil Records: Access: Mail, in person, online. Both court and visitors may perform in person searches. Search fee: $5.00 per name per year. Required to search: name, years to search. Civil cases indexed by defendant, plaintiff. Civil records on computer since 9/1/96; prior on index books. Will only search back 7 years. Online access to civil cases is free at www.sbcounty.gov/courts/genInfo/openaccess.htm. Daily calendars are at the main website.

Criminal Records: Access: Mail, in person, online. Both court and visitors may perform in person searches. Search fee: $5.00 per name per year. Required to search: name, years to search, DOB; also helpful: SSN. Criminal records on index books. Will only search back 7 years. Online access to criminal cases is free at www.sbcounty.gov/courts/genInfo/openaccess.htm. Also, the daily criminal docket is free at the court main website.

General Information: No probation reports released. Copy fee: $.50 per page. Cert fee: $6.60. Payee: Superior Court. Personal checks accepted. Prepayment required. Mail requests: SASE required. Mail turnaround time 1 week.

Central Division Branch - Superior Court

351 N Arrowhead, San Bernardino, CA 92415-0220; Civil phone: 909-885-0139; Criminal phone: 909-384-1888; Probate phone: 909-387-3952; Fax: 909-387-4428. Hours: 8AM-4PM (PST). *Misdemeanor, Civil Actions, Eviction, Small Claims, Probate.*

www.sbcounty.gov/courts/

Note: Includes the City of Bernardino, cities of Grand Terrace, Loma Linda, Colton and Highland and the unincorporated area of Del Rosa, Devore, Muscoy, Patton, Verdemont. Specify which city you are searching in.

Civil Records: Access: Phone, mail, fax, in person, online. Both court and visitors may perform in person searches. Search fee: $5.00 per name. Required to search: name, years to search. Civil cases indexed by defendant, plaintiff. Civil records on computer from 1991, index files from 1983, microfiche from 1972. Online access to civil cases is free at www.sbcounty.gov/courts/genInfo/openaccess.htm. Online access to "Probate Notes" is free at www.co.san-bernardino.ca.us/courts/ Click on Probate. Daily calendars are at the main website.

Criminal Records: Access: Mail, in person, online. Both court and visitors may perform in person searches. Search fee: $5.00 per name. Required to search: name, years to search; also helpful: DOB. Criminal records on computer from 1991, index files from 1983, microfiche from 1972. Online access to criminal cases is free at www.sbcounty.gov/courts/genInfo/openaccess.htm. Also, the daily criminal docket is free at the court main website.

General Information: No probation reports released. Fee to fax results is $1.00 per page. Copy fee: $.50 per page. Cert fee: $6.60 per document. Payee: San Bernardino Superior Court. Personal checks accepted. Prepayment required. Mail requests: SASE required. Mail turnaround time 7-10 days.

Chino Division - Superior Court

13260 Central Ave, Chino, CA 91710; 909-356-5337; Criminal phone: 909-465-5260; Fax: 909-465-5221. Hours: 8AM-4PM (PST). *Felonies, Misdemeanor, Eviction, Small Claims.*

www.sbcounty.gov/courts/

Note: Includes City of Chino and surrounding unincorporated area. Rancho Cucamonga Courts handles all civil cases since 01/01/99.

Civil Records: Access: Fax, mail, in person. Only the court performs in person searches; visitors may not. Search fee: $5.00 per name. Required to search: name, years to search; also helpful: address. Civil cases indexed by defendant, plaintiff. Civil records on computer from 1991, index books from 1983. Records destroyed after 10 years. Daily calendars are at the main website.

Criminal Records: Access: Mail, in person, online. Only the court performs in person searches; visitors may not. Search fee: $5.00 per name. Required to search: name, years to search, DOB; also helpful: address. Criminal records on computer from 1991, index books from 1983. Records destroyed after 10 years. Online access to criminal cases is free at www.sbcounty.gov/courts/genInfo/openaccess.htm. Also, the daily criminal docket is free at the court main website.

General Information: No probation reports released. Copy fee: $.50 per page. Cert fee: $6.60. Payee: Chino Superior Court. Personal checks accepted. Prepayment required. Mail requests: SASE required. Mail turnaround time 2 days.

Fontana Division - Superior Court

17780 Arrow Hwy, Fontana, CA 92335; 909-350-9322. Hours: 8AM-4PM (PST). *Felony, Misdemeanor, Civil Actions Under $25,000, Traffic.*

www.sbcounty.gov/courts/

Note: Includes the Cities of Fontana, Rialto, Crestmore and the unincorporated areas of Lytle Creek Canyon and Bloomington.

Civil Records: Access: Mail, in person, online. Only the court performs in person searches; visitors may not. Search fee: $5.00 per name. Required to search: name, years to search; also helpful: address. Civil cases indexed by defendant, plaintiff. Civil records on computer from 1987, microfilm prior. Records destroyed after 10 years. Online access to civil cases is free at www.sbcounty.gov/courts/genInfo/openaccess.htm. Daily calendars are at the main website.

Criminal Records: Access: Mail, in person, online. Both court and visitors may perform in person searches. Search fee: $5.00 per name. Required to search: name, years to search; also helpful: DOB. Criminal records on computer from 1987, microfilm prior. Records destroyed after 10 years. Online access to criminal cases is free at www.sbcounty.gov/courts/genInfo/openaccess.htm. Also, the daily criminal docket is free at the court main website.

General Information: No probation reports or police records released. Copy fee: $.50 per page. Cert fee: $6.60. Payee: Fontana Courts. Personal checks accepted. Prepayment required. Mail requests: SASE required. Mail turnaround time 2-5 days.

Needles District - Superior Court

1111 Bailey Ave, Needles, CA 92363; 760-326-9245; Fax: 760-326-9254. Hours: 8AM-4PM (PST). *Felony, Misdemeanor, Civil Actions Under $25,000, Eviction, Small Claims.*

www.sbcounty.gov/courts

Civil Records: Access: Mail, in person, online. Only the court performs in person searches; visitors may not. Search fee: $5.00 per name. Required to search: name, years to search. Civil cases indexed by plaintiff.

Civil records in index books. Will only search back 7 years. Online access to civil cases is free at www.sbcounty.gov/courts/genInfo/openaccess.htm. Daily calendars are at the main website.

Criminal Records: Access: Mail, in person, online. Only the court performs in person searches; visitors may not. Search fee: $5.00 per name. Required to search: name, years to search. Criminal records on computer from 1990, index books prior. Will only search back 7 years. Online access to criminal cases is free at www.sbcounty.gov/courts/genInfo/openaccess.htm. Also, the daily criminal docket is free at the court main website.

General Information: No probation reports released. Copy fee: $.50 per page. Cert fee: $6.60. Payee: Superior Court. Personal checks accepted. Prepayment required. Mail requests: SASE required. Mail turnaround time 1-2 weeks.

Redlands District - Superior Court
216 Brookside Ave, Redlands, CA 92373; Civil phone: 909-885-4260; Criminal phone: 909-885-1269; Fax: 909-798-8588. Hours: 8AM-4PM (PST). *Traffic Misdemeanor, Eviction, Small Claims.*
www.sbcounty.gov/courts/
Note: All felonies and non-traffic misdemeanors are filed at Central Dist. Court. This Court's district includes Redlands, Yucaipa and the unincorporated areas of Angeles Oaks, Barton Flats, Colton, Forest Home, Grand Terrace, Highland, Loma Linda and Mentone.

Civil Records: Access: Mail, in person. Visitors must perform in person searches for themselves. Search fee: $5.00 per name. Required to search: name, years to search. Civil cases indexed by defendant, plaintiff. Civil records on computer from 1991, index books prior. Records destroyed after 10 years. Daily calendars are at the main website.

Criminal Records: Access: Mail, in person, online. Visitors must perform in person searches for themselves. Search fee: $5.00 per name. Required to search: name, years to search, DOB. Criminal records on computer from 1998, index books prior. Records destroyed after 10 years. Online access to criminal cases is free at www.sbcounty.gov/courts/genInfo/openaccess.htm. Also, the daily criminal docket is free at the court main website.

General Information: Public Access terminal is available. No probation reports released. Will not fax results. Copy fee: $.50 per page. Exemplified copy $20.00. Cert fee: $6.60. Payee: Superior Court. Prepayment required. Mail requests: SASE required. Mail turnaround time 2 days.

Twin Peaks District - Superior Court
26010 State Hwy 189 (PO Box 394), Twin Peaks, CA 92391; 909-336-0620; Fax: 909-336-0683. Hours: 8AM-4:30PM Monday only (PST). *Traffic Misdemeanor, Civil under $25,000, Eviction, Small Claims.*
www.sbcounty.gov/courts/
Note: Felony and misdemeanors are now heard at the San Bernardino District Courthouse. For information on Twin Peaks cases Tuesdays to Fridays, call the San Bernardino District Courthouse.

Civil Records: Access: Mail, in person, online. Both the court and visitors may perform in person searches. Search fee: $5.00 per name per year. Required to search: name, years to search. Civil cases indexed by defendant, plaintiff. Civil records on index cards. Will only search back 7 years. Online access to civil cases is free at www.sbcounty.gov/courts/genInfo/openaccess.htm. Daily calendars are at the main website.

Criminal Records: Access: Mail, in person, online. Both the court and visitors may perform in person searches. Search fee: $5.00 per name per year. Required to search: name, years to search, DOB. Criminal records on computer from 1990, index cards prior. Will only search back 7 years. Online access to criminal cases is free at www.sbcounty.gov/courts/genInfo/openaccess.htm. Also, the daily criminal docket is free at the court main website.

General Information: Public Access terminal is available. No probation or arrest reports released. Will not fax results. Copy fee: $.50 per page. Cert fee: $6.60. Payee: Superior Court. No personal checks accepted. Mail requests: SASE required. Mail turnaround time 1 week.

San Diego County

Superior Court - Civil
Hall of Justice, PO Box 120128 (330 W Broadway), San Diego, CA 92112-0128; Civil phone: 619-531-3141; Probate phone: 619-236-3781. Hours: 8:30AM-4:30PM (PST). *Civil, Probate, Eviction, Small Claims, Probate.*
www.sandiego.courts.ca.gov/superior
Note: Now has Central Division Limited Jurisdiction civil cases. For any San Diego County requests, always specify which division - Central, East, North or South. Probate is located at the Madge Bradley Bldg, 1409 4th Ave, 92101.

Civil Records: Access: Mail, in person, online. Both court and visitors may perform in person searches. Search fee: $5.00 per name. Required to search: name, years to search. Civil cases indexed by defendant, plaintiff. Civil records index on computer from 06/74. The court sells a county-wide CD-ROM of civil, domestic, mental health, and probate indices, generally from 1974 to 1999. Also, the court's five day calendar is free at www.sandiego.courts.ca.gov/superior/online/searchcal.html. New case searching is at www.sandiego.courts.ca.gov/superior/online/newfiles/newfile.html. Also, there is a free party name case search at www.sandiego.courts.ca.gov:8080/CISPublic/enter.

General Information: Public Access terminal is available. No probation reports released. Will not fax results. Copy fee: $.50 per page. Cert fee: $6.60 per document. Payee: Clerk of Superior Court. Personal checks accepted. Prepayment required. Mail requests: SASE required. Mail turnaround time 1 day.

Superior Court - Criminal
PO Box 120128 (220 W Broadway), San Diego, CA 92112-0128; 619-531-3040 Misdemeanor. Hours: 8:30AM-4:30PM (PST). *Felony, Misdemeanor.*
www.sandiego.courts.ca.gov/superior/
Note: Both General and Limited Criminal records are located here.

Criminal Records: Access: Mail, in person. Both court and visitors may perform in person searches. Search fee: $5.00 per name. Fee is per index. Required to search: name, years to search, DOB. Criminal records on computer from 1974 to present, paper ledgers from 1860s. The county system sells a CD-ROM of criminal records; felonies from 6/1974 to 1999; misdemeanors back 10 years. Also, the court's five day calendar is free at www.sandiego.courts.ca.gov/superior/online/searchcal.html. New case searching is at www.sandiego.courts.ca.gov/superior/online/newfiles/newfile.html. Also, there is a free party name case search at www.sandiego.courts.ca.gov:8080/CISPublic/enter.

General Information: Public Access terminal is available. No adoptions, juvenile, medical, probation or sealed records released. Will not fax results. Copy fee: $.50 per page. Cert fee: $6.60. Payee: San Diego Superior Court. No out of state personal checks. Prepayment required. Mail requests: SASE required. Mail turnaround time 1 week.

East County Division - Superior Court
250 E Main St, El Cajon, CA 92020; 619-441-4100; Civil phone: 619-441-4461; Criminal phone: 619-441-4342; Probate phone: 619-441-6770 (family law). Hours: 8AM-4:30PM (PST). *Felony, Misdemeanor, Civil, Small Claims, Eviction.*
www.sandiego.courts.ca.gov
Note: Court now houses the former municipal court records. Includes El Cajon, La Mesa, Lemon Grove, Santee and unincorporated towns of Alpine, Boulevard, Campo, Dulzura, Grossmont, Jacumba, Jamul, Julian, Lakeside, Mesa Grande, Ramona, Spring Valley, Tecate.

Civil Records: Access: Mail, in person, online. Both court and visitors may perform in person searches. Search fee: $5.00 per name. Required to search: name, years to search. Civil cases indexed by defendant, plaintiff. Civil records on computer since 1974; microfilm prior. Online searching of 5-day calendars is free at www.sandiego.courts.ca.gov/superior/online/searchcal.html. New case searching is at www.sandiego.courts.ca.gov/superior/online/newfiles/newfile.html. Also, there is a free party name case search at www.sandiego.courts.ca.gov:8080/CISPublic/enter.

Criminal Records: Access: Mail, in person, online. Both court and visitors may perform in person searches. Search fee: $5.00 per name. Required to search: name, years to search; also helpful: DOB. Criminal records on computer since 1974; microfilm prior. The county system sells a CD-ROM of criminal records; felonies from 6/1974 to 1999; misdemeanors back 10 years. Also, the court's five day calendar is free at www.sandiego.courts.ca.gov/superior/online/searchcal.html. New case searching is at www.sandiego.courts.ca.gov/superior/online/newfiles/newfile.html. Also, there is a free party name case search at www.sandiego.courts.ca.gov:8080/CISPublic/enter.

General Information: Public Access terminal is available. Copy fee: $.50 per page. Cert fee: $6.60. Payee: Clerk of Superior Court. Personal checks accepted. Law firm and Calif. checks with preprinted name and address only. Prepayment required. Mail requests: SASE required. Mail turnaround time 3-5 days.

North County Branch - Superior Court
325 S Melrose Dr, Vista, CA 92081; 760-726-9595; Probate phone: 760-806-6150. Hours: 8:30AM-4:30PM (PST). *Felony, Misdemeanor, Civil Actions, Eviction, Small Claims, Probate.*
www.sandiego.courts.ca.gov
Note: Includes Cities of Oceanside, Del Mar, Carlsbad, Solana Beach, Encinitas, Escondido, San Marcos, Vista and unincorporated towns of Del Dios, Olivehain, San Luis Rey, San Pasqual, Rancho Santa Fe, Valley Ctr., Bonsall, Palomar Mt., Borrego Spr., Pala, etc.

Civil Records: Access: Mail, in person, online. Both court and visitors may perform in person searches. Search fee: $5.00 per name. Required to search: name, years to search. Civil cases indexed by defendant, plaintiff. Civil records on computer back to 1993; prior on microfiche and index books. Online searching of 5-day calendars is free at www.sandiego.courts.ca.gov/superior/online/searchcal.html. New case searching is at www.sandiego.courts.ca.gov/superior/online/newfiles/newfile.html. Also, there is a free party name case search at www.sandiego.courts.ca.gov:8080/CISPublic/enter.

Criminal Records: Access: Mail, in person, online. Both court and visitors may perform in person searches. Search fee: $5.00 per name. Required to search: name, years to search. Criminal records on computer back to 1993; prior on microfiche and index books. The county system sells a CD-ROM of criminal records; felonies from 6/1974 to 1999; misdemeanors back 10 years. Also, the court's five day calendar is free at www.sandiego.courts.ca.gov/superior/online/searchca l.html. New case searching is at www.sandiego.courts.ca.gov/superior/online/newfiles /newfile.html. Also, there is a free party name case search at www.sandiego.courts.ca.gov:8080/CISPublic/enter.

General Information: Public Access terminal is available. No sealed or confidential documents released. Copy fee: $.50 per page. Cert fee: $6.60. Payee: Clerk of the Superior Court. Personal checks accepted. Out of state checks not accepted. Prepayment required. Mail requests: SASE required. Mail turnaround time 2-3 days.

South County Branch - Superior Court

500-C 3rd Ave, Chula Vista, CA 91910; Civil phone: 619-691-4439; Criminal phone: 619-691-4726; Fax: 619-691-4969 (Civil) 4864 is Criminal. Hours: 8:30AM-4:30PM (PST). *Felony, Misdemeanor, Civil Actions, Probate, Eviction, Small Claims.*
www.sandiego.courts.ca.gov
Note: Includes National City, Chula Vista, Coronado, Imperial Beach and that portion of the City of San Diego lying south of the City of Chula Vista and contiguous unincorporated areas. Family phone is 619-691-4875

Civil Records: Access: Fax, mail, in person, online. Both court and visitors may perform in person searches. Search fee: $5.00 per name per year. Required to search: name, years to search. Civil cases indexed by defendant, plaintiff. Civil records on computer; for case files prior to 1991, contact Superior Court's Main Records Division, Downtown. Online searching of 5-day calendars is free at www.sandiego.courts.ca.gov/superior/online/searchca l.html. New case searching is at www.sandiego.courts.ca.gov/superior/online/newfiles /newfile.html. Also, there is a free party name case search at www.sandiego.courts.ca.gov:8080/CISPublic/enter.

Criminal Records: Access: Phone, fax, mail, in person, online. Both court and visitors may perform in person searches. Search fee: $5.00 per name. Required to search: name, years to search, DOB. Criminal records on computer, cases files in or before 1986 on microfiche. The county system sells a CD-ROM of criminal records; felonies from 6/1974 to 1999; misdemeanors back 10 years. Also, the court's five day calendar is free at www.sandiego.courts.ca.gov/superior/online/searchca l.html. New case searching is at www.sandiego.courts.ca.gov/superior/online/newfiles /newfile.html. Also, there is a free party name case search at www.sandiego.courts.ca.gov:8080/CISPublic/enter.

General Information: Public Access terminal is available. Copy fee: $.60 per page. Cert fee: $6.60. Payee: Superior Court (Civil)-Clerk of the Court (Criminal). Personal checks accepted. Prepayment required. Mail requests: SASE required. Mail turnaround time up to 1 week (civil) or depends on availability of clerk (criminal).

Kearny Mesa Branch - Central Division

8950 Clairemont Mesa Blvd, San Diego, CA 92123; 858-694-2066 Small Claims; Fax: 858-694-2252. Hours: 8AM-4PM (PST). *Small Claims, Traffic, Infractions.*
www.sandiego.courts.ca.gov/superior/index.html
Note: Traffic phone is 858-565-1006. Some minor infractions are heard at this court.

Ramona Branch - East Division

1428 Montecito Rd, Ramona, CA 92065; 760-738-2435. Hours: 8AM-4:30PM (PST). *Misdemeanor, Civil Actions Under $25,000, Eviction, Small Claims.*
www.sandiego.courts.ca.gov
Note: Jurisdiction over the northeast area of the county. Closed noon to 1PM T, W, TH.

Civil Records: Access: Mail, in person, online. Only the court performs in person searches; visitors may not. Search fee: $5.00 per name. Required to search: name, years to search. Civil cases indexed by defendant, plaintiff. Civil records on computer from 1991, index files since 1983. Files destroyed after 10 years. Online searching of 5-day calendars is free at www.sandiego.courts.ca.gov/superior/online/searchca l.html. New case searching is at www.sandiego.courts.ca.gov/superior/online/newfiles /newfile.html. Also, there is a free party name case search at www.sandiego.courts.ca.gov:8080/CISPublic/enter.

Criminal Records: Access: Mail, in person, online Mail, in person. Only the court performs in person searches; visitors may not. Search fee: $5.00 per name. Required to search: name, years to search, SSN; also helpful: DOB. Criminal records on computer from 1991, index files since 1983. Files destroyed after 10 years. The county system sells a CD-ROM of criminal records; felonies from 6/1974 to 1999; misdemeanors back 10 years. Also, the court's five day calendar is free at www.sandiego.courts.ca.gov/superior/online/searchca l.html. New case searching is at www.sandiego.courts.ca.gov/superior/online/newfiles /newfile.html. Also, there is a free party name case search at www.sandiego.courts.ca.gov:8080/CISPublic/enter.

General Information: No probation reports or DMV records released. Will not fax results. Copy fee: $.50 per page. Cert fee: $6.60. Payee: Clerk of the Court. Personal checks accepted. Visa, MC accepted. Prepayment required. Mail requests: SASE required. Mail turnaround time 2-3 days.

San Marcos Branch - North Divison

Misdemeanor, Traffic.
Note: On July 14th 2003, they moved into the Superior Court at 325 S Melrose Dr #350, Annex Bldg, Vista CA 92081.

San Francisco County

Superior Court - Criminal Division

850 Bryant St, #101 & 102, San Francisco, CA 94107/94103; 415-553-1159/9394. Hours: 8AM-4:30PM (PST). *Felony.*
http://sfgov.org/site/courts_page.asp?id=3664
Note: Telephone number for misdemeanor records department 415-553-1665. Court manager telephone is 415-553-1897.

Criminal Records: Access: Mail, in person. Both court and visitors may perform in person searches. Search fee: $5.00 per name per year. Add warehouse retrieval fee of $5.00 for archived records. Required to search: name, years to search, DOB. If searching by mail, direct your request to "Prior Convictions.".

General Information: No medical, probation or sealed records released. No fee to fax results, as long as prepaid. Copy fee: $1.00 per page. Cert fee: $6.60. Payee: Clerk of the Superior Court. Personal checks

accepted with ID. Cashier checks and money orders accepted. Prepayment required. Mail requests: SASE required. Mail turnaround time 1 week.

Superior Court - Civil Division

400 McAllister St, Rm 103, San Francisco, CA 94102; 415-551-4000 (general info); Civil phone: 415-551-3888; Probate phone: 415-551-3892. Hours: 8AM-4PM daily, except Wed. 10AM-Noon (PST). *Civil, Small Claims, Eviction, Probate.*
http://sfgov.org/site/courts_index.asp

Civil Records: Access: Mail, in person, online. Both court and visitors may perform in person searches. Search fee: $5.00 per name per year. Required to search: name, years to search. Civil cases indexed by defendant, plaintiff. Civil records on computer since 1987 for unlimited jurisdiction; 1992 for Limited jurisdiction; prior records on microfilm and microfiche. For pre-1987 records, contact: Research at 415-551-3813. Access to the case management system including probate is free at www.sfgov.org.

General Information: Public Access terminal is available. No medical, probation or sealed records released without court order. Will not fax results. Copy fee: $1.00 per page. Cert fee: $6.60 plus $1.00 per page copy fee. Payee: San Francisco Superior Court. Personal checks accepted. Visa, MC accepted. Prepayment required. Mail requests: SASE required. Mail turnaround time 2-3 weeks; in person turnaround is 5 days.

Limited Superior - Civil Division

400 McAllister St, Rm 103, San Francisco, CA 94107; 415-551-3802(Records Section); Civil phone: 415-551-4000; Fax: 415-551-3801. Hours: 8AM-4:30PM, Wed 8Am-3PM (PST). *Civil Actions Under $25,000, Eviction, Small Claims.*
www.sfgov/courts
Note: Includes all of San Francisco County, including former municipal court on Folsom St.

Civil Records: Access: Mail, in person, online. Both court and visitors may perform in person searches. Search fee: $5.00 per name per year. No charge if easily pulled from computer. Required to search: name, years to search. Civil cases indexed by defendant, plaintiff. Civil records on computer from 1991, index files from 1983. Records destroyed after 10 years. Online access to the case management system is free at www.sftc.org.

General Information: Public Access terminal is available. No sealed records released. Will not fax results. Copy fee: $1.00 per page. Cert fee: $6.60 plus $1.00 per page & copy fee. Payee: Superior Court. Personal checks accepted. Prepayment required. Mail requests: SASE required. Mail turnaround time 2 days.

Superior Court - Misdemeanor Division

850 Bryant St, Rm 101, San Francisco, CA 94103; 415-553-1665 (Records Dept); Criminal phone: 415-553-9395. Hours: 8AM-4:30PM (PST). *Misdemeanor.*
www.ci.sf.ca.us/courts
Note: Includes all of San Francisco County

Criminal Records: Access: Mail, in person, online. Both court and visitors may perform in person searches. Search fee: $5.00 per name per year. Required to search: name, years to search; also helpful: DOB. Criminal records (pending) on computer from 1991, index files from 1983. Records are destroyed after 10 years. Online access to the case management system is free at www.sftc.org.

General Information: No probation reports released. Copy fee: $1.00 per page. Microfilm copies $1.50 per page. Cert fee: $1.75. Payee: Superior Court. Personal checks accepted. Prepayment required. Mail requests: SASE required. Mail turnaround time 3-4 weeks.

San Joaquin County

Superior Court - Civil 222 E Weber Ave, Rm 303, Stockton, CA 95202-2709; 209-468-2355; Civil phone: 209-468-2933; Probate phone: 209-468-2843; Fax: 209-468-0539. Hours: 7:30AM-4PM (office); 8AM-5PM M-F (phones) (PST). *Civil Actions, Eviction, Small Claims, Probate.*
www.stocktoncourt.org/courts/
Note: Includes City of Stockton and suburban areas Farmington and Linden, Delta area and surrounding unincorporated areas

Civil Records: Access: Mail, in person, online. Both court and visitors may perform in person searches. Search fee: $5.00 per name. No fee if search is done by customer. Required to search: name, years to search. Civil cases indexed by defendant, plaintiff. Civil records on computer from 1996; indices/books from 1850-1973; Microfiche 1973-1996. Records destroyed after 10 years. Free access to case summaries, with name searching, at www.stocktoncourt.org/courts/caseinfo.htm. Free access to court calendars at www.stocktoncourt.org/stkcrtwwwV5web/SCCalDay Index.html.
General Information: Public Access terminal is available. No probation, confidential records released. Will not fax results. Copy fee: $.50 per page. Cert fee: $6.60. Payee: Superior Court. Personal checks accepted. Prepayment required. Mail requests: SASE required. Mail turnaround time 5-7 days.

Superior Court - Criminal Division 222 E Weber Ave, Rm 101, Stockton, CA 95202; 209-468-2935; Criminal phone: 209-468-2935. Hours: 7:30AM-5PM (PST). *Felony, Misdemeanor.*
www.stocktoncourt.org/courts
Criminal Records: Access: Mail, in person, online. Both court and visitors may perform in person searches. Search fee: $5.00 per name. Required to search: name, years to search; also helpful: DOB, SSN. Criminal Records on computer since 1991, on microfiche since 1972, older records archived to 1800s. Online access to court calendars is free at www.stocktoncourt.org/stkcrtwwwV5web/SCCalDay Index.html. Includes Register of Actions and case summaries by case number. Mail access only for authorized agencies.
General Information: Public Access terminal is available. No juvenile, medical, probation, sealed records released. Copy fee: $.50 per page. Cert fee: $6.60 per document. Payee: San Joaquin Superior Court. Personal checks accepted. Prepayment required. Mail requests: SASE required. Mail turnaround time 1-2 weeks.

Lodi Division - Superior Court 315 W Elm St (Civil), 230 W Elm St (Criminal), Lodi, CA 95240; 209-331-2104; Civil phone: 209-331-2101; Criminal phone: 209-331-2121; Fax: 209-331-2135. Hours: 8AM-4PM (PST). *Misdemeanor (Traffic), Civil Actions Under $25,000, Eviction, Small Claims.*
www.stocktoncourt.org/courts/
Note: Includes City of Lodi, eight mile road to Sacramento County line, towns of Acampo, Clements, Lockeford, Terminous, Thornton, Woodbridge.
Civil Records: Access: Phone, mail, fax, in person, online. Both court and visitors may perform in person searches. Search fee: $5.00 per name. Required to search: name, years to search. Civil cases indexed by defendant, plaintiff. Civil records on computer from 1994, index files from 1989. Records destroyed after 10 years. Online access to court calendars is free at www.stocktoncourt.org/stkcrtwwwV5web/SCCalDay Index.html. Also, Register of Actions and case summaries are by case number.

Criminal Records: Access: Phone, mail, fax, in person, online. Both court and visitors may perform in person searches. Search fee: $5.00 per name. Required to search: name, years to search, DOB; also helpful: address, SSN, sex. Criminal records on computer from 1991, index files from 1983. Records destroyed after 10 years. Online access to court calendars is free at www.stocktoncourt.org/stkcrtwwwV5web/SCCalDay Index.html. Includes Register of Actions and case summaries by case number.
General Information: Public Access terminal is available. (Criminal records only.) No probation reports released. Will not fax results. Copy fee: $.50 per page. Cert fee: $6.60. Payee: Superior Court. Personal checks accepted. Prepayment required. Mail requests: SASE required. Mail turnaround time 5 days.

Manteca Branch - Superior Court 315 E Center St, Manteca, CA 95336; Civil phone: 209-239-9188; Criminal phone: 209-239-1316. Hours: 8AM-4PM (PST). *Felony, Misdemeanor, Civil Actions Under $25,000, Eviction, Small Claims.*
www.stocktoncourt.org/courts/
Note: Includes Cities of Manteca, Ripon, Escalon, French Camp, Lathrop and surrounding unincorporated areas.

Civil Records: Access: Mail, in person, online. Only the court performs in person searches; visitors may not. Search fee: $5.00 per name. Required to search: name, years to search. Civil cases indexed by defendant, plaintiff.
Microfiche since 1986, index files from 1983. Records destroyed after 10 years. Online access to court calendars is free at www.stocktoncourt.org/stkcrtwwwV5web/SCCalDay Index.html. Also, Register of Actions and case summaries are by case number.
Criminal Records: Access: Mail, in person, online. Only the court performs in person searches; visitors may not. Search fee: $5.00 per name. Required to search: name, years to search; also helpful: DOB. Criminal records on computer since 1990, microfiche since 1986, index files from 1983. Records destroyed after 10 years. Online access to court calendars is free at www.stocktoncourt.org/stkcrtwwwV5web/SCCalDay Index.html. Includes Register of Actions and case summaries by case number. Special request form required to view files in person.
General Information: No judge's notes, probation or police reports released. Copy fee: $.50 per page. Cert fee: $6.60. Payee: Superior Court. Personal checks accepted. Prepayment required. Mail requests: SASE required. Mail turnaround time 1-2 days.

Tracy Branch - Superior Court 475 E 10th St, Tracy, CA 95376; Civil phone: 209-831-5902; Criminal phone: 209-831-5900; Fax: 209-831-5919. Hours: 8AM-4PM (PST). *Felony, Misdemeanor, Civil Actions Under $25,000, Eviction, Small Claims.*
www.stocktoncourt.org/courts/
Note: Includes Cities of Tracy, Banta, portion of Vernalis and surrounding unincorporated area.
Civil Records: Access: Phone, mail, in person, online. Only the court performs in person searches; visitors may not. Search fee: $5.00 per name. If on computer, no charge. Required to search: name, years to search. Civil cases indexed by defendant, plaintiff. Civil records on computer since 03/95; on index files from 1983. Records destroyed after 10 years. Online access to court calendars is free at www.stocktoncourt.org/stkcrtwwwV5web/SCCalDay Index.html. Also, Register of Actions and case summaries are by case number.

Criminal Records: Access: Mail, in person, online. Only the court performs in person searches; visitors may not. Search fee: $5.00 per name. Required to search: name, years to search, DOB. Criminal records on computer from 1991; on index files from 1983. Records destroyed after 10 years. Online access to court calendars is free at www.stocktoncourt.org/stkcrtwwwV5web/SCCalDay Index.html. Includes Register of Actions and case summaries by case number.
General Information: No probation reports, DMV history and criminal history records released. Will not fax results. Copy fee: $.50 per page. Cert fee: $6.60. Payee: Tracy Superior Court. Personal checks accepted. Prepayment required. Mail requests: SASE required. Mail turnaround time 5-10 days.

San Luis Obispo County

Superior Court - Civil Division 1035 Palm St, Rm 385, Government Center, San Luis Obispo, CA 93408; 805-781-5677; Probate phone: 805-781-5242. Hours: 8:30AM-4PM (PST). *Civil Actions, Small Claims, Eviction, Probate.*
www.slocourts.net
Note: This Court has jurisdiction over all of San Luis Obispo County for Civil actions over $25,000, and also the current and former "limited jurisdiction" (under $25,000) civil cases in the immediate area.

Civil Records: Access: Mail, in person. Both court and visitors may perform in person searches. Search fee: $5.00 per name. Required to search: name, years to search. Civil cases indexed by defendant, plaintiff. Civil records on computer from 1975, index files from 1865. Records destroyed after 10 years.
General Information: Public Access terminal is available. No probation reports released. Will not fax results. Copy fee: $1.00 per page. Cert fee: $6.60. Payee: Superior Court. Personal checks accepted. Prepayment required. Mail requests: SASE required. Mail turnaround time 2-5 days.

Superior Court - Criminal Division Government Center, Rm 220, 1050 Monterey St., San Luis Obispo, CA 93408; 805-781-5670. Hours: 8:30AM-4PM (PST). *Felony, Misdemeanor.*
www.slocourts.net
Note: Due to re-organization of the courts in this city, this court handles misdemeanor cases which were formerly handled by the limited jurisdiction court. The civil cases are located at the Superior Court - Civil Division.
Criminal Records: Access: Mail, in person. Both court and visitors may perform in person searches. Search fee: $5.00 per name. Required to search: name, years to search. Criminal records on computer and microfiche from 1975, archived and index file from late 1800s.
General Information: Public Access terminal is available. No adoptions, juvenile, medical, probation or sealed records released. Will not fax results. Copy fee: $.50 per page. Cert fee: $6.60. Payee: Superior Court Criminal Court Operations. Personal checks accepted. Prepayment required. Mail requests: SASE required. Mail turnaround time 2-5 days.

Grover Beach Branch - Superior Court 214 S 16th St, Grover Beach, CA 93433-2299; Civil phone: 805-473-7077; Criminal phone: 805-473-7072. Hours: 8:30AM-4PM (PST). *Misdemeanor, Civil Actions Under $25,000, Eviction, Small Claims.*
www.slocourts.net
Note: Includes Nipomo, Grover Beach, Arroyo Grande, Pismo Beach, Oceano, South Coast unincorporated areas.
Civil Records: Access: Phone, mail, in person. Both court and visitors may perform in person searches.

Search fee: First name is free, then $5.00 per name. Required to search: name, years to search. Civil cases indexed by defendant, plaintiff. Civil records on index cards to 1976; on computer back to 1986. Records destroyed after 10 years.

Criminal Records: Access: Phone, mail, in person. Both court and visitors may perform in person searches. Search fee: First name is free, then $5.00 per name. Required to search: name, years to search. Criminal records on index cards to 1976; on computer back to 1986. Records destroyed after 10 years.

General Information: Public Access terminal is available. No probation reports released. Will not fax results. Copy fee: $1.00 per page. Cert fee: $6.60. Payee: Superior Court. Personal checks accepted. Prepayment required. Mail requests: SASE required. Mail turnaround time 2-3 weeks if civil; 1 week if criminal.

Paso Robles Branch - Superior Court

549 10th St, Paso Robles, CA 93446-2593; Civil phone: 805-237-3079; Criminal phone: 805-237-3080. Hours: 8:30AM-4PM (PST). *Misdemeanor, Civil Actions Under $25,000, Eviction, Small Claims.*

www.slocourts.net/

Note: Includes Atascadero, Templeton, Paso Robles, San Miguel, Shandon, Cholame, areas north and east of the Cuesta Grade.

Civil Records: Access: Phone, mail, in person. Both the court and visitors may perform in person searches. Search fee: $5.00 per name. Search is free if only one name. Required to search: name, years to search. Civil cases indexed by defendant, plaintiff. Civil records on computer from 1975, index files from 1983. Records destroyed after 10 years. Mail requests limited to 5 at a time.

Criminal Records: Access: Phone, mail, in person. Both the court and visitors may perform in person searches. Search fee: $5.00. Search is free for only one name. Required to search: name, years to search; also helpful: DOB. Criminal records on computer from 1975, index files from 1983. Records destroyed after 10 years. Mail requests limited to 5 at a time.

General Information: Public Access terminal is available. No driving histories, rap sheets, sealed or probation reports released. Copy fee: $1.00 per page. Cert fee: $6.60 per document. Payee: Superior Court. Personal checks accepted. Prepayment required. Mail requests: SASE required. Mail turnaround time 1-2 days.

San Mateo County

Superior Court 400 County Center, Redwood City, CA 94063; Civil phone: 650-363-4711; Criminal phone: 650-363-4302; Fax: 650-363-4914. Hours: 8AM-4PM (PST). *Felony, Civil Actions Over $25,000, Probate.*

www.sanmateocourt.org

Note: Southern Area Limited Criminal, lower-value civil actions, evictions and small claims are also located here.

Civil Records: Access: Mail, in person, online. Both court and visitors may perform in person searches. Search fee: $5.00 per name. Required to search: name, years to search. Civil cases indexed by defendant, plaintiff. Civil records and Family Law on computer from 1978; index books prior. Online access to civil, probate, family and small claims records is free at www.sanmateocourt.org. Click on Open Access.

Criminal Records: Access: Mail, in person. Both court and visitors may perform in person searches. Search fee: $5.00 per name. Required to search: name, years to search; also helpful: address, DOB, SSN. Criminal records on computer since 1964; prior on books. Criminal matters only filed by Belmont,

Foster City, Half Moon Bay, San Carlos, Menlo Pk, East Palo Alto and unicorporated areas are heard at the Southern Branch.

General Information: Public Access terminal is available. No confidential jackets on conservatorships & guardianships, adoptions, juvenile, medical, probation or sealed records released. Copy fee: $.75 per page per side. Cert fee: $6.60 per document. Payee: Superior Court. Personal checks accepted. Prepayment required. Mail requests: SASE required. Mail turnaround time 1 week.

Northern Branch - Superior Court 1050

Mission Rd, South San Francisco, CA 94080; 650-877-5773. Hours: 8AM-4PM (PST). *Misdemeanor, Small Claims, Traffic.*

www.sanmateocourt.org

Note: Includes Brisbane, Daly City (including Westlake), Pacifica, San Bruno, South San Francisco, the northern coastal towns and all unincorporated areas in the north end of the county including Colma, Bart and Broadmoor. Small Claims phone is 650-877-5778.

Civil Records: Access: Mail, in person, online. Both court and visitors may perform in person searches. Search fee: $5.00 per name. Required to search: name, years to search. Civil cases indexed by defendant, plaintiff. Online access to civil, probate, family and small claims records is free at www.sanmateocourt.org. Click on Open Access.

Criminal Records: Access: Mail, in person. Both court and visitors may perform in person searches. Search fee: $5.00 per name. Required to search: name, years to search; also helpful: DOB. Criminal records on computer back to 1991, index files from 1983. Records destroyed after 10 years.

General Information: Public Access terminal is available. No probation reports or confidential information records released. Will fax results to local or toll free line. Copy fee: $.75 per page. Cert fee: $6.60 per document. Payee: Superior Court. Personal checks accepted. Prepayment required. Mail requests: SASE required. Mail turnaround time 2 days to 2 weeks.

San Mateo Central Branch 800 N Humboldt

St, San Mateo, CA 94401; 650-573-3936 Main; 650-573-2616 Traf.; Fax: 650-342-5438. Hours: 8AM-4PM (PST). *Small Claims, Traffic, Infractions.*

www.co.sanmateo.ca.us/sanmateocourts/

Note: Small claims phone is 650-573-2628. Includes small claims for Belmont, Burlingame, El Granada, Foster City, Half Moon Bay, Hillsborough, Millbrae, Miramar, Montara, Moss Beach, SF Int. Airport, San Mateo and adjoing unincorporated areas.

Superior Court - Southern Branch 400

County Center, Redwood City, CA 94063; Civil phone: 650-363-4576; Criminal phone: 650-363-4203. Hours: 8AM-4PM (PST). *Misdemeanor, Civil, Eviction, Small Claims.*

www.sanmateocourt.org

Note: Limited Criminal - Includes Atherton, Belmont, Foster City, Half Moon Bay, Menlo Park, Portola Valley, Redwood City, San Carlos, Woodside, East Palo Alto and unicorporated areas including La Honda, Pescadera, and San Gregorio.

Civil Records: Access: Mail, in person, online. Both court and visitors may perform in person searches. Search fee: $5.00 per name. Required to search: name, years to search. Civil cases indexed by defendant, plaintiff. Civil Records on computer since 1978. Online access to civil and small claims records is free at www.sanmateocourt.org. Click on Open Access.

Criminal Records: Access: Mail, in person. Both court and visitors may perform in person searches. Search fee: $5.00 per name. Required to search:

name, years to search. Limited Criminal records on computer from 1991, index files from 1983. Records destroyed after 10 years. Only limited criminal cases for the Southern District can be found at this location.

General Information: Public Access terminal is available. No probation reports or confidential information records released. Copy fee: $.75 per page. Cert fee: $6.60 per document. Payee: Superior Court. Personal checks accepted. Write "not to exceed $x.xx" on check. Visa/MC accepted. Credit card accepted in person only. Prepayment required. Mail requests: SASE required. Mail turnaround time 2 weeks.

Santa Barbara County

Superior Court - Civil - Anacapa Division

Box 21107 (1100 Anacapa St), Santa Barbara, CA 93121; 805-568-2220; Civil phone: 805-568-2238; Criminal phone: 805-568-2753; Fax: 805-568-2219. Hours: 8AM-4PM; closed on mandatory furlough days; call for dates. (PST). *Civil Actions, Eviction, Small Claims, Probate.*

www.sbcourts.org/index.htm

Note: Also known as the Anacapa Division. Includes the City of Santa Barbara, Goleta, and adjacent unicorporated areas, Carpenteria and Montecito.

Civil Records: Access: Phone, fax, mail, in person. Both court and visitors may perform in person searches. Search fee: $5.00 per name. Required to search: name, years to search. Civil cases indexed by defendant, plaintiff. Civil records on computer and microfiche from 1975, archived and index file from 1920. A CD-rom of monthy court indices from all divisions is for $40.00.

General Information: Public Access terminal is available. No adoptions, juvenile, medical, probation or sealed records released. Copy fee: $.75 per page. Cert fee: $6.60; if marriage dissolution, is $10.00. Payee: Superior Court. Personal checks accepted. Visa, MC accepted. Prepayment required. Mail requests: SASE required. Mail turnaround time 1 week.

Superior Court - Criminal - Figueroa Division

118 E Figueroa St, Santa Barbara, CA 93101; 805-568-2735; Civil phone: 805-568-2238; Criminal phone: 805-568-2752/2753; Fax: 805-568-3208. Hours: 7:45AM-4PM; closed on mandatory furlough days; call for dates. (PST). *Felony, Misdemeanor.*

www.sbcourts.org/index.htm

Note: Includes the City of Santa Barbara, Goleta and adjacent unincorporated areas, Carpenteria, Montecito. For civil cases call Anacapa Division at 805-568-2220.

Criminal Records: Access: Mail, in person. Both court and visitors may perform in person searches. Search fee: $5.00 per name. Required to search: name, years to search; also helpful: DOB. Criminal records on computer from 1991, index files from 1983, microfiche from 1975. Records destroyed after 10 years. A CD-rom of monthy court indices from all divisions is $40.00. Will accept fax requests from gov't agencies only.

General Information: Public Access terminal is available. No probation reports released. Copy fee: $.75 per page. Cert fee: $6.60 per document. Payee: Clerk of the Court. Personal checks accepted. Prepayment required. Mail requests: SASE required. Mail turnaround time 3-5 days.

Santa Maria Cook Division - Superior Court

312-C E Cook St (PO Box 5369), Santa Maria, CA 93454-5369; 805-346-7414; Civil phone: 805-346-7405; Fax: 805-346-7616. Hours: 7:30AM-4PM; closed on mandatory furlough days; call for dates. (PST). *Civil Actions Under $25,000, Probate, Eviction, Small Claims.*

www.sbcourts.org/general_info/index.htm

Note: This Cook Division handles Civil; its sister court (Miller Division) handles Criminal. Includes Betteravia, Casmalia, Cuyama, Guadalupe, Gary, Los Alamos, New Cuyama, Orcutt, Santa Maria, Sisquoc, Tepusquet and sections of the Vandenburg Air Force Base

Civil Records: Access: Mail, in person. Both court and visitors may perform in person searches. Search fee: $5.00 per name. Required to search: name, years to search. Civil cases indexed by defendant, plaintiff. Civil records in index files from 1983. Records destroyed after 10 years.

General Information: Public Access terminal is available. No probation reports, financial, judges notes, confidential or sealed records released. Will fax results. Copy fee: $.75 per page. Cert fee: $6.60. Payee: Clerk of Court. Personal checks accepted. Visa, MC accepted. Prepayment required. Mail requests: SASE required. Mail turnaround: 5 days.

Santa Maria Miller Division - Superior Court

312-M E Cook St, Bldg E, Santa Maria, CA 93454-5165; 805-346-7590; Criminal phone: 805-346-7565; Fax: 805-346-7591. Hours: 8AM-3PM; closed on mandatory furlough days; call for dates. (PST). *Felony, Misdemeanor, Traffic.*

Note: Miller Division is in the same building complex as the Cook Division, which handles civil, small claims, family cases. Miller includes the same jurisdictional area as Cook Division.

Criminal Records: Access: Mail, fax, in person. Both court and visitors may perform in person searches. Search fee: $5.00 per name. Required to search: complete name and alias, years to search, DOB. Criminal records in index files from 7/1963. A CD-rom of monthly court indices from all divisions is $40.00.

General Information: Public Access terminal is available. No probation reports, financial, judges notes, confidential or sealed records released. Will fax results for $1.00 per page. Copy fee: $.75 per page. Cert fee: $6.60. Payee: Clerk of Court. Personal checks accepted. Visa, MC accepted. Prepayment required. Mail requests: SASE required. Mail turnaround time 7 days.

Lompoc Division - Superior Court

115 Civic Center Plz, Lompoc, CA 93436; Civil phone: 805-737-7796; Criminal phone: 805-737-7790; Fax: 805-737-7786. Hours: 8:30AM-4PM; closed on mandatory furlough days; call for dates. (PST). *Felony. Misdemeanor, Civil Actions Under $25,000, Eviction, Small Claims.*

www.sbcourts.org/index.htm

Includes Lompoc and adjacent unincorporated areas including sections of Vandenburg Air Force Base.

Civil Records: Access: Mail, in person. Both court and visitors may perform in person searches. Search fee: $5.00. Required to search: name, years to search. Civil cases indexed by defendant, plaintiff. Civil records on computer from 1991, index files from 1983. Records destroyed after 10 years.

Criminal Records: Access: Mail, in person. Both court and visitors may perform in person searches. Search fee: $5.00. Required to search: name, DOB; also helpful: address. Criminal records on computer from 1991, index files from 1983. Records destroyed after 10 years. Includes Solvang

jurisdiction filings from 1997 to present. A CD-Rom of weekly court indices from all divisions is $48.00.

General Information: Public Access terminal is available. No probation reports released. Will fax results for $1.00 per page. Copy fee: $.75 per side. Cert fee: $6.60 per document. Payee: Clerk of the Superior Court. Personal checks accepted. Prepayment required. Mail requests: SASE required. Mail turnaround time 5 days.

Solvang Division - Superior Court

1745 Mission Dr, #C, Solvang, CA 93463; 805-686-5040; Fax: 805-686-5079. Hours: 8AM-3PM; closed on mandatory furlough days; call for dates. (PST). *Misdemeanor, Small Claims, Traffic.*

www.sbcourts.org/

Note: Includes the City of Solvang, Buelton, and adjacent unincorporated areas, Los Olivos and Santa Ynez.

Civil Records: Access: Phone, mail, in person. Both court and visitors may perform in person searches. Search fee: $5.00. Required to search: name, years to search. Civil cases indexed by defendant, plaintiff. Civil records on computer from 1997 to present, index lists prior.

Criminal Records: Access: Mail, in person. Both court and visitors may perform in person searches. No search fee. Required to search: name, years to search, DOB. Criminal records on computer from 1988 to 1997. There are no criminal filings at this court since 01/97.

General Information: Public Access terminal is available. No sealed or confidential records released. Copy fee: $.75 per page. Cert fee: $6.75. Payee: Superior Court. Personal checks accepted. Visa, MC accepted. Credit cards are only accepted at the counter, and by phone. Prepayment required. Mail requests: SASE required. Mail turnaround: 1 week.

Santa Clara County

Superior Court - Civil

191 N 1st St, San Jose, CA 95113; 408-882-2100. Hours: 8:30AM-4PM (PST). *Civil, Eviction, Probate.*

www.sccsuperiorcourt.org

Note: Handles cases for San Jose, Milpitas, Santa Clara, Los Gatos and Campbell areas.

Civil Records: Access: Mail, in person, online. Both court and visitors may perform in person searches. Search fee: $5.00 per name per year. Required to search: name, years to search. Civil records on computer 1993 to present; prior on books to 1800s. Civil, Family, Probate, and Small Claims case records and court calendars are free online at www.sccaseinfo.org.

General Information: Public Access terminal is available. No probation reports or confidential records released. Copy fee: $1.00 per page. Cert fee: $6.60 per document. Payee: Superior Court. Personal checks accepted. Prepayment required. Mail requests: SASE required. Mail turnaround time 2 weeks.

Superior Court - Criminal

191 N 1st St, San Jose, CA 95113-1001; 408-808-6600; Criminal phone: 408-808-6600. Hours: 8:30AM-4PM (PST). *Felony, Misdemeanor.*

www.sccsuperiorcourt.org

Note: Includes the Cities of Alviso, Campbell, Los Gatos, Milpitas, Monte Sereno, San Jose, Santa Clara, and Saratoga.

Criminal Records: Access: Mail, in person. Both court and visitors may perform in person searches. Search fee: $5.00 per name per year. Required to search: name, years to search, DOB. Criminal indexes on microfiche from 1975-present. Old files are kept in archives or on microfilm.

General Information: No probation, confidential or sealed records released. Will not fax results. Copy fee:

$1.00 per page. Postage also charged based on number of pages copied. Cert fee: $6.60 per document. Payee: Santa Clara Superior Court. Personal checks accepted. Prepayment required. Mail requests: SASE required. Mail turnaround time 3-7 days.

South County Facility - Superior Court

12425 Monterey Rd, San Martin, CA 95046-9590; 408-695-5000; Civil phone: 408-695-5012; Criminal phone: 408-695-5014. Hours: 8:30AM-4PM (PST). *Felony, Misdemeanor, Civil Actions Under $25,000, Eviction, Small Claims.*

http://sccsuperiorcourt.org

Note: Jurisdiction includes the Cities of Gilroy, Morgan Hill, San Martin and surrounding unincorporated areas. Traffic case phone number is 408-695-5011.

Civil Records: Access: Mail, in person, onliine. Both court and visitors may perform in person searches. Search fee: $5.00 per name per year. Required to search: name, years to search. Civil records on microfiche. Civil, Family, Probate, and Small Claims case records and court calendars are free online at www.sccaseinfo.org.

Criminal Records: Access: Mail, in person. Both court and visitors may perform in person searches. Search fee: $5.00 per name per year. Required to search: name, years to search; also helpful: DOB. Same record keeping as civil.

General Information: No adoptions, juvenile, medical, probation or sealed records released. Copy fee: $1.00 per page. Cert fee: $6.60 per document. Payee: Superior Court. Personal checks accepted. Prepayment required. Mail requests: SASE required. Mail turnaround time 1 week.

Palo Alto Facility - Superior Court

270 Grant Ave, Palo Alto, CA 94306; 650-462-3800. Hours: 8:30AM-4PM (PST). *Felony, Misdemeanor, Small Claims.* www.sccsuperiorcourt.org

Note: Includes Palo Alto, Mountain View, Los Altos, Los Altos Hills, Stanford University, Sunnyvale and the surrounding unincorporated areas.

Civil Records: Access: Mail, in person, online. Both court and visitors may perform in person searches. Search fee: $5.00 per name per year. Required to search: name, years to search. Civil, Family, Probate, and Small Claims case records and court calendars are free online at www.sccaseinfo.org.

Criminal Records: Access: Mail, in person. Both court and visitors may perform in person searches. Search fee: $5.00 per name per year. Required to search: name, years to search; also helpful: DOB. Criminal Records on microfiche.

General Information: No probation, doctor report, pretrial report records released. Copy fee: $1.00 per page. Cert fee: $6.60 per document. Payee: Superior Court. Personal checks accepted. Prepayment required. Mail requests: SASE required. Mail turnaround time 1 week.

Sunnyvale Facility - Superior Court

270 Grant Ave, #204, Palo Alto, CA 94306; 408-462-3800. 8:30AM-3PM (PST). *Felony, Misdemeanor.*

www.sccsuperiorcourt.org

Note: Court closed; records now at Palo Alto Court facility; address and phone given here. Also, traffic and small claims are filed at the Palo Alto Facility.

Los Gatos Facility - Superior Court

14205 Capri Dr, Los Gatos, CA 95032; 408-370-4440. Hours: 8:30AM-4PM (PST). *Small Claims.*

http://sccsuperiorcourt.org

Note: Includes the towns of Los Gatos and Monte Sereno and the cities of Campbell, Saratoga, and surrounding unincorporated areas as well as San Jose,

Milpitas and Santa Clara. Mailing address is Superior Court in San Jose at 191 N 1st St, 95113.

Civil Records: Access: Phone, mail, in person, online. Both court and visitors may perform in person searches. Search fee: $5.00 per name per year. Required to search: name, years to search. Civil cases indexed by defendant, plaintiff. Civil record index on microfiche. Civil, Family, Probate, and Small Claims case records and court calendars are free online at www.sccaseinfo.org. Mail Requests must be sent to 191 N. First St, San Jose CA 95113.

General Information: Copy fee: $1.10 per page. Cert fee: $6.60 per document. Payee: Superior Court. Personal checks accepted. Prepayment required.

Santa Cruz County

Superior Court - Civil 701 Ocean St, Rm 110, Santa Cruz, CA 95060; 831-454-2020. Hours: 8AM-4PM (PST). *Civil, Probate.* www.santacruzcourt.org/ Note: This court also handles Family Law.

Civil Records: Access: Phone, mail, in person, online. Both court and visitors may perform in person searches. Search fee: $5.00 per name. Required to search: name, years to search. Civil cases indexed by defendant, plaintiff. Civil records on computer back to 6/1985; microfiche, archived and index books from 1880. Search the index free at http://sccounty01.co.santa-cruz.ca.us/supct/calendar/IndexMenu.htm. Includes probate also.

General Information: Public Access terminal is available. No adoptions, juvenile, medical, probation or sealed records released. Copy fee: $.50 per page. Cert fee: $6.60 plus $1.10 per page. Payee: Superior Court. Personal checks accepted. Prepayment required. Mail requests: SASE required. Mail turnaround time 10-15 days.

Superior Court - Criminal 701 Ocean St, Rm 120, Santa Cruz, CA 95060; 831-454-2230; Fax: 831-454-2215. Hours: 8AM-4PM (PST). *Felony, Misdemeanor.* www.santacruzcourt.org

Criminal Records: Access: Fax, mail, in person. Both court and visitors may perform in person searches. Search fee: $5.00 per name. Required to search: name; also helpful: years to search, DOB. Criminal records on computer since 1985; also on microfiche index by party name back; other records go back to 1880's.

General Information: Public Access terminal is available. No juvenile, probation or sealed records released. Will fax results to local or toll free line. Copy fee: $.50 per page. Cert fee: $6.60 plus $1.10 per page. Payee: Clerk of Court. Personal checks accepted. Prepayment required. Mail requests: SASE required. Mail turnaround time 2-4 weeks.

Watsonville Division - Superior Court 1430 Freedom Blvd, Watsonville, CA 95076; 831-763-8060. 8AM-4PM (PST). *Misdemeanor, Civil Actions Under $25,000, Eviction, Small Claims.* www.santacruzcourt.org/ Note: Includes all of Santa Cruz County.

Civil Records: Access: Mail, in person, online. Search fee: $5.00 per name. Required to search: name, years to search. Civil cases indexed by defendant, plaintiff. Civil records on computer from 1992, index books prior. Records destroyed after 10 years. Searc the index at http://sccounty01.co.santa-cruz.ca.us/supct/calendar/IndexMenu.htm. Includes small claims.

Criminal Records: Access: Mail, in person. Both court and visitors may perform in person searches. Search fee: $5.00 per name. Required to search: name, years to search; also helpful: DOB. Criminal records on computer from 1992, index books prior. Records destroyed after 10 years.

General Information: No probation or juvenile records released. Copy fee: $.50 per page. Cert fee: $6.60 plus $1.10 per page. Payee: Superior Court. Personal checks accepted. Prepayment required. Mail requests: SASE required. Mail turnaround time 2-5 days.

Shasta County

Superior Court 1500 Court St, Redding, CA 96001; 530-245-6789; Fax: 530-225-5564 Civil; 245-6483 Criminal. Hours: 8:30AM-4:30PM (PST). *Felony, Misdemeanor, Civil, Small Claims, Eviction, Probate.* www.shastacourts.com Note: Address Rm 319 for civil division and Rm 219 for criminal division.

Civil Records: Access: Phone, mail, in person, online. Both court and visitors may perform in person searches. Search fee: $5.00 per name per year. Required to search: name, years to search. Civil cases indexed by defendant, plaintiff. Civil records on computer from 1992, index books prior. Access to the civil division index is at www.shastacourts.com/indexes.php.

Criminal Records: Access: Mail, in person, online. Both court and visitors may perform in person searches. Search fee: $5.00 per name per year. Required to search: name, years to search. Criminal records on computer from 1992, index books prior. Online access to the criminal division index is free at www.shastacourts.com/indexes.php. Also, the Integrated Justice System Access at www.shastacourts.com/access.shtml is limited to attorneys involved on county cases.

General Information: Public Access terminal is available. No probation or confidential records released. Will fax results to local or toll free line. Copy fee: $.50 per page. Cert fee: $6.60 per document. Payee: Superior Court. Personal checks accepted. Prepayment required. Mail requests: SASE required. Mail turnaround time 2-7 days.

Burney Branch - Superior Court 20509 Shasta St, Burney, CA 96013; 530-335-3571; Fax: 530-225-5684. Hours: 8AM-Noon, 1-4:30PM (PST). *Misdemeanor, Civil, Eviction, Small Claims.* www.shastacourts.com/page.php?page=burney Note: Civil actions handled by Redding Branch since 1992. Prior civil limited jurisdiction records maintained here.

Civil Records: Access: Mail, in person. Only the court performs in person searches; visitors may not. Search fee: $5.00 per name per year. Required to search: name, years to search. Civil cases indexed by defendant, plaintiff. Civil records on computer from 1993, index books prior.

Criminal Records: Access: Mail, in person, online. Only the court performs in person searches; visitors may not. Search fee: $5.00 per name per year. Required to search: name, years to search, DOB. Criminal records on computer from 1993, index books prior. Online access to the criminal division index is free at www.shastacourts.com/indexes.php. Also, the Integrated Justice System Access at www.shastacourts.com/access.shtml is limited to attorneys involved on county cases.

General Information: No probation, juvenile, or DMV reports released. Copy fee: $1.00 1st page; $.50 each add'l. Cert fee: $6.60 per document. Payee: Superior Court. Personal checks accepted. Prepayment required. Mail requests: SASE required. Mail turnaround time 2-14 days.

Sierra County

Superior Court PO Box 476, Courthouse Sq, Downieville, CA 95936; 530-289-3698; Fax: 530-289-0205. Hours: 8AM-Noon, 1-5PM (PST). *Felony, Misdemeanor, Civil, Eviction, Small Claims, Probate.* www.sierracourt.org

Civil Records: Access: Phone, fax, mail, in person. Only the court performs in person searches; visitors may not. Search fee: $5.00 per name per year. Required to search: name, years to search. Civil cases indexed by defendant, plaintiff. Civil records on computer from 1985, index books from 1852.

Criminal Records: Access: Phone, fax, mail, in person. Both court and visitors may perform in person searches. Search fee: $5.00 per name per year. Required to search: name, years to search. Criminal records on computer from 1985, index books from 1852.

General Information: No adoptions, juvenile, medical, probation or sealed records released. Will fax results $1.00 per page. Copy fee: $1.00 per page. Cert fee: $7.00 per document. Payee: Superior Court. Personal checks accepted. Prepayment required. Mail requests: SASE required. Mail turnaround time 2-4 days.

Siskiyou County

Superior Court 311 4th St PO Box 1026, Yreka, CA 96097; Civil phone: 530-842-8196; Criminal phone: 530-842-8195; Fax: 530-842-0164(Civ); 530-842-8178(Crim). Hours: 8AM-5PM; 8AM-3PM (phone hours) (PST). *Felony, Misdemeanor, Civil, Probate.* www.siskiyou.courts.ca.gov

Civil Records: Access: Phone, mail, in person, online. Both court and visitors may perform in person searches. Search fee: $5.00 per name. Fee is per 10 years searched. Required to search: name, years to search. Civil cases indexed by defendant, plaintiff. Civil records on computer since 1991, archived and index book from 1900. Access superior court records free at www.siskiyou.courts.ca.gov/CaseHistory.asp. Includes traffic but not juvenile.

Criminal Records: Access: Mail, in person, online. Both court and visitors may perform in person searches. Search fee: $5.00 per name. Fee is per 10 years searched. Required to search: name, years to search. Criminal records on computer since 1991, archived and index book from 1900. Online access to criminal records is available; see civil.

General Information: Public Access terminal is available. No adoptions, juvenile, medical, probation or sealed records released. Will fax results to local or toll free line. Copy fee: $.50 per page. Cert fee: $6.60. Payee: Siskiyou Superior Court. Personal checks accepted. Prepayment required. Mail requests: SASE required. Mail turnaround time 1 week.

Weed Branch - Superior Court 550 Main St, Weed, CA 96094; 530-938-2483; Civil phone: 530-842-0107; Fax: 530-842-0109. Hours: 8AM-4PM (PST). *Misdemeanor, Small Claims.* www.siskiyou.courts.ca.gov

Civil Records: Access: Mail, fax, in person, online. Both court and visitors may perform in person searches. Search fee: $5.00 per name per 10 years. Required to search: full name, years to search. Civil cases indexed by defendant, plaintiff. Civil records go back to 1980; on computer since 1995. Access to county superior court records is free at www.siskiyou.courts.ca.gov/CaseHistory.asp. Includes traffic but not juvenile.

Criminal Records: Access: Mail, fax, in person, online. Both court and visitors may perform in person searches. Search fee: $5.00 per name per 10 years.

Required to search: full name, years to search, DOB, SSN. Criminal records go back to 1994; computerized records back 7 years. Online access to criminal records is available; see civil.

General Information: Public Access terminal is available. Fee to fax results is $1.00 per page. Copy fee: $.50 per page. Cert fee: $6.60 per document. Payee: Siskiyou Superior Court. Personal checks accepted only from party to the case. Prepayment required. Mail requests: SASE required. Mail turnaround time 10 days.

Dorris Branch - Superior Court PO Box 828, 324 N. Pine St, Dorris, CA 96023; 530-397-3161; Fax: 530-397-3169. Hours: 8AM-Noon, 1-4PM (PST). *Civil Actions Under $25,000, Eviction, Small Claims.*
www.siskiyou.courts.ca.gov
Note: All new misdemeanor cases are referred to Weed, CA Branch. This court only maintains a few criminal records for a year

Civil Records: Access: Mail, in person, online. Only the court performs in person searches; visitors may not. Search fee: $5.00 per name. Required to search: name, years to search. Civil records on computer back to 1998; prior on books back to 1992. Access to county superior court records is free at www.siskiyou.courts.ca.gov/CaseHistory.asp. Includes traffic but not juvenile.

General Information: Public Access terminal is available. (Available at the Yreka Main court only.) No probation reports released. Copy fee: $.50 per page. Cert fee: $6.60. Payee: Siskiyou Superior Court. Personal checks accepted. Prepayment required. Mail requests: SASE required. Mail turnaround: 10 days.

Solano County

Superior Court - Civil 600 Union Ave, Fairfield, CA 94533; 707-421-6053; Probate phone: 707-421-6471; Fax: 707-435-2950. Hours: 8AM-3PM (PST). *Civil, Eviction, Probate.*
www.solanocourts.com/
Note: Northern Solano Muni. Ct. has been combined with this Court. Probate is a separate office at the same address. Probate fax-707-421-6961. Small claims phone-707-421-7435. Includes Fairfield, Suisun, Vacaville, Dixon, Rio Vista, and surrounding area.

Civil Records: Access: Phone, mail, online, in person. Both court and visitors may perform in person searches. Search fee: $5.00 per name. Required to search: name, years to search. Civil cases indexed by defendant, plaintiff. Civil records on computer since 1992, microfiche since 1971, archived and index files since 1800s. Online access to civil records is free at http://courtconnect.solanocourts.com/pls/bprod_cc/ck_public_qry_main.cp_main_idx. Also, civil tentative rulings and probate notes are free at www.solanocourts.com/civil_tent.htm. Phone access limited to short searches.

General Information: Public Access terminal is available. No sealed records released. Copy fee: $1.00 per page. Cert fee: $6.60. Payee: Solano County Courts. Personal checks accepted. Prepayment required. Mail requests: SASE required. Mail turnaround time 2-3 days.

Superior Court - Criminal 530 Union Ave, #200, Fairfield, CA 94533; 707-421-7440; 421-7834 Sup Court Records; Fax: 707-421-7439. Hours: 8AM-3PM (PST). *Felony, Misdemeanor.*
www.solanocourts.com
Note: The Northern Solano Muni. Court has been combined with the Superior Court. This court includes Fairfield, Suisun, Vacaville, Dixon, Rio Vista and the adjacent unicorported areas.

Criminal Records: Access: Mail, in person, online. Visitors must perform in person searches themselves. Search fee: $5.00 per name. Required to search: name, years to search; also helpful: DOB, SSN. Superior Court records on computer since 1992, microfiche since 1971; Muni. Court records on computer for past 10 years. Online access to criminal records is free at http://courtconnect.solanocourts.com/pls/bprod_cc/ck_public_qry_main.cp_main_idx. Phone questions can only be answered between 10AM and 3PM. Records from this court are found only at this court, not at other divisions.

General Information: No probation reports released. Copy fee: $1.00 for first page. Cert fee: $6.60. Payee: Solano Superior Court. Personal checks accepted. Prepayment required. Mail requests: SASE required. Mail turnaround time 1-3 weeks.

Vallejo Branch - Superior Court 321 Tuolumne St, Vallejo, CA 94590; Civil phone: 707-553-5346; Criminal phone: 707-553-5341; Fax: 707-553-5661. Hours: 8AM-3PM (PST). *Misdemeanor, Civil, Eviction, Small Claims, Felony, Probate.*
www.solanocourts.com/
Note: Includes Cities of Vallejo and Benicia and the adjacent unincorporated areas.

Civil Records: Access: Mail, in person, online. Both court and visitors may perform in person searches. Search fee: $5.00 per name. Required to search: name, years to search. Civil cases indexed by defendant, plaintiff. Civil records on computer from 1991, index files from 1983. Records destroyed after 10 years. Online access to civil records is free at the website; click on "Court Connect.". Also, civil tentative rulings and probate notes are free at www.solanocourts.com/civil_tent.htm.

Criminal Records: Access: Mail, in person, online. Only the court performs in person searches; visitors may not. Search fee: $5.00 per name. Required to search: name, years to search. Criminal records on computer from 1991, index files from 1983. Records destroyed after 10 years. Online access to criminal records is free at http://courtconnect.solanocourts.com/pls/bprod_cc/ck_public_qry_main.cp_main_idx.

General Information: Public Access terminal is available. (Civil access only.) No probation reports released. Will not fax results. Copy fee: $1.00 per page. Cert fee: $6.60. Payee: Superior Court. Personal checks accepted. Visa, AmEx accepted. Prepayment required. Mail requests: SASE required. Mail turnaround time 2 days.

Sonoma County

Superior Court - Criminal 600 Administration Dr, Rm 105J, Santa Rosa, CA 95403-0281; 707-565-1100. Hours: 8AM-3PM, M,W,F; 8-6PM Th (PST). *Felony, Misdemeanor, Probate.*
www.sonomasuperiorcourt.com
Civil Records: Access: Phone, mail, in person. Both court and visitors may perform in person searches. Search fee: $15.00 per hour. Required to search: name, years to search. Civil cases indexed by defendant, plaintiff. Civil records on computer from 1985, microfiche and index books from 1850 to 1984. Phone access limited to 2 names or cases per call.

Criminal Records: Access: Phone, mail, in person. Both court and visitors may perform in person searches. Search fee: $15.00 per hour. Required to search: name, years to search, DOB. Criminal Records on computer back to 1985, microfiche and index books 1850 to 1984. Misdemeanor records can be destroyed after 10 years.

General Information: Public Access terminal is available. No adoptions, juvenile, medical, probation or sealed records released. Copy fee: $1.00 per page. 10 page limit. If more than 10 pages must wait 3-5 days. Cert fee: $6.60 plus $1.00 per page. Payee:

Superior Court. No out of state personal checks accepted. Prepayment required. Mail requests: SASE required. Mail turnaround time 2-3 weeks.

Superior Court - Civil Division 600 Administration Dr, Rm 107J, Santa Rosa, CA 95403; 707-565-1100. Hours: 8AM-3PM M,T,W,F; till 6PM TH (PST). *Civil, Eviction, Small Claims.*
www.sonomasuperiorcourt.com
Civil Records: Access: Mail, in person. Both court and visitors may perform in person searches. Search fee: $15.00 per hour; minimum is $5.00. Required to search: name, years to search. Civil cases indexed by defendant, plaintiff. Civil records on computer to 10/84, index files prior. Judgment records destroyed after 10 years, dismissals after 1. Computer index include criminal from 10/1984.

General Information: Public Access terminal is available. No probation reports or sealed records released. Copy fee: $1.00 per page. Cert fee: $6.60. Payee: Superior Court. Personal checks accepted. Prepayment required. Mail requests: SASE required. Mail turnaround time 3 days to 2 weeks.

Stanislaus County

Superior Court - Criminal 800 11 St, Rm 140, PO Box 1098, Modesto, CA 95353; 209-558-6000. 8AM-Noon, 1-4PM (PST). *Felony, Misdemeanor.*
www.stanct.org/courts/index.html
Note: Physical address Zip Code is 95354

Criminal Records: Access: Mail, in person. Both court and visitors may perform in person searches. Search fee: $5.00 per name per year. Required to search: name, years to search. Criminal Records on microfiche since 1974, archived back to 1800s.

General Information: No adoptions, juvenile, medical, probation or sealed records released. Copy fee: $.50 per page. Cert fee: $6.60. Payee: Superior Court Clerk. Personal checks accepted. Prepayment required. Mail requests: SASE required. Mail turnaround time 1-2 weeks.

Superior Court - Civil 1100 "I" St, PO Box 828, Modesto, CA 95353; 209-558-6000; Fax: 209-525-4348 (civil). Hours: 8AM-3PM (PST). *Civil, Eviction, Small Claims, Probate.*
www.stanct.org/courts/criminal/index.html
Note: Ceres Branch has been closed and records transferred here.

Civil Records: Access: Mail, fax, in person, online. Both court and visitors may perform in person searches. Search fee: $5.00 per name. Required to search: name, years to search. Civil cases indexed by defendant, plaintiff. Civil records on computer from 1991, in index files from 1983. Records destroyed after 10 years. The case index is searchable by name and year at www.stanct.org/case_index/.

General Information: Public Access terminal is available. No probation or juvenile records released. Copy fee: $.50 per page. Cert fee: $6.60. Payee: Superior Court. Personal checks accepted. Prepayment required. Mail requests: SASE required. Mail turnaround time 2-5 days.

Turlock Division - Superior Court 300 Starr Ave, Turlock, CA 95380; 209-558-6000; Fax: 209-664-8009. Hours: 8AM-Noon, 12:30-4PM (PST). *Small Claims.* www.co.stanislaus.ca.us/courts

Sutter County

Superior Court - Civil Division 463 2nd St, Rm 211, Courthouse East, 2nd Fl, Yuba City, CA 95991; 530-822-7352; Fax: 530-822-7192. Hours: 8AM-5PM (PST). *Civil, Eviction, Small Claims, Probate.* www.suttercourts.com
Civil Records: Access: Mail, in person. Both court and visitors may perform in person searches. Search fee: $5.00 per name. Required to search: name, years

to search. Civil cases indexed by defendant, plaintiff. Civil records in index books and archived from 1800s, on computer back to 1/95.

General Information: Public Access terminal is available. No adoptions, juvenile, medical, probation or sealed records released. Copy fee: $.50 per page. Cert fee: $6.60. Payee: Superior Court. Personal checks accepted. Prepayment required. Mail requests: SASE required. Mail turnaround time 2 days if records on site.

Superior Court - Criminal Division 446
2nd St, Yuba City, CA 95991; 530-822-7360; Fax: 530-822-7159. Hours: 8AM-5PM (PST). *Felony, Misdemeanor.* www.suttercourts.com

Criminal Records: Access: Fax, mail, in person. Both court and visitors may perform in person searches. Search fee: $5.00 per name. Required to search: name, years to search. Criminal records in index books and archived from 1800s, computerized since 1995.

General Information: Public Access terminal is available. No police reports or probation records released. Will fax results to local or toll free line. Copy fee: $.50 per page. Cert fee: $6.60. Payee: Sutter County Superior Court. Personal checks accepted. Prepayment required. Mail turnaround time 1 week.

Tehama County

Superior Court - Civil Division PO Box 310,
Red Bluff, CA 96080; 530-527-6441. Hours: 8AM-5PM (PST). *Civil, Small Claims, Eviction, Probate, Family Law.*

Civil Records: Access: Mail, in person. Only the court may perform in person searches. Search fee: $2.50 per name. Fee is $5.00 if years before 1991 are requested. Required to search: name, years to search. Civil cases indexed by defendant, plaintiff. Civil records on computer back to 1992, archived and index books from 1900s.

General Information: No adoptions, juvenile, mental, probation or sealed records released. Will not fax results. Copy fee: $.50 per page. Cert fee: $6.60 per document. Payee: Tehama County Superior Court Clerk. Personal checks accepted. Prepayment required. Mail requests: SASE required. Mail turnaround time same day.

Superior Court - Criminal Division 445
Pine St, PO Box 1170, Red Bluff, CA 96080; 530-527-3563; Criminal phone: 530-527-7314; Fax: 530-527-0956. Hours: 8AM-5PM (PST). *Felony, Misdemeanor.*

Criminal Records: Access: Mail, in person. Both court and visitors may perform in person searches. Search fee: $5.00 per name. Required to search: name, years to search; also helpful: DOB. Criminal records on computer from 1991, index cards prior. Will only search back 7 years.

General Information: No probation reports released. Copy fee: $.50 per page. Cert fee: $7.10. Payee: Superior Court. Personal checks accepted. Prepayment required. Mail requests: SASE required. Mail turnaround time within 1 week.

Corning Branch - Superior Court 720
Hoag St, Corning, CA 96021; 530-824-4601; Fax: 530-824-6457. Hours: 8AM-5PM (PST). *Misdemeanor, Civil Actions Under $25,000, Eviction, Small Claims.*

Civil Records: Access: Mail, in person. Both court and visitors may perform in person searches. Search fee: $5.00 per name. Required to search: name, years to search. Civil cases indexed by defendant, plaintiff. Civil records on index cards. Will only search back 7 years; records on computer since 1990. Requests must be in writing.

Criminal Records: Access: Mail, in person. Only the court may perform in person searches. Search fee: $2.50. Required to search: name, years to search; also helpful: DOB. Criminal records on computer from 1990, index cards prior. Will only search back 7 years. Requests must be in writing.

General Information: No probation reports released. Will fax results to local or toll free line, if paid in advance. Copy fee: $.50 per page. Cert fee: $6.60. Payee: Tehama Superior Court. Personal checks accepted. Prepayment required. Mail requests: SASE required. Mail turnaround time 1 week.

Trinity County

Superior Court 101 Court St (PO Box 1258),
Weaverville, CA 96093; 530-623-1208; Fax: 530-623-3762. 9AM-4PM (PST). *Felony, Misdemeanor, Civil, Eviction, Small Claims, Probate.*

Civil Records: Access: Mail, in person. Both court and visitors may perform in person searches. Search fee: $5.00 per name per year. Required to search: name, years to search. Civil cases indexed by defendant, plaintiff. Civil records on microfiche, archived and index files from 1900s.

Criminal Records: Access: Mail, in person. Both court and visitors may perform in person searches. Search fee: $5.00 per name per year. Required to search: name, years to search. Criminal records on microfiche, archived and index files from 1900s.

General Information: No adoptions, juvenile, medical, probation or sealed records released. Copy fee: $.50 per page. Cert fee: $6.60 per document. Payee: Superior Court. Personal checks accepted. Prepayment required. Mail requests: SASE required. Mail turnaround time 2-3 weeks.

Tulare County

Superior Court Courthouse, 221 S Mooney,
Visalia, CA 93291; Civil phone: 559-733-6454; Criminal phone: 559-733-6830; Fax: 559-737-4547. Hours: 8AM-4PM (PST). *Felony, Civil, Eviction, Small Claims, Probate.*
www.tularesuperiorcourt.ca.gov
Note: This court has records from Exeter, Woodlake, Farmersville, Goshen and Three Rivers. Address criminal record requests to Rm 124 and civil to Rm 201.

Civil Records: Access: Mail, in person. Both court and visitors may perform in person searches. Search fee: $5.00 per name. Required to search: name, years to search. Civil cases indexed by defendant, plaintiff. Civil records on computer back to 2/1986; microfiche and index books from 1800s. Daily calendar and civil and probate recommendations at www.tularesuperiorcourt.ca.gov.

Criminal Records: Access: Mail, in person. Both court and visitors may perform in person searches. Search fee: $5.00 per name. Required to search: name, years to search, DOB or SSN. Criminal records on computer back to 2/1986; microfiche and index books from 1800s. Daily calendar and civil and probate recommendations are at www.tularesuperiorcourt.ca.gov.

General Information: Public Access terminal is available. No adoptions, juvenile, mental, probation reports or sealed records released. Copy fee: $.50 per page. Cert fee: $6.60. Payee: Tulare County Superior Court. Personal checks accepted. Prepayment required. Mail requests: SASE required. Mail turnaround time 1 week.

Dinuba Division - Superior Court 640 S
Alta Dinuba, Dinuba, CA 93618; 559-591-5815. 8AM-4PM (PST). *Felony, Misdemeanor, Civil Actions Under $25,000, Eviction, Small Claims.*
http:/www.tularesuperiorcourt.ca.gov

Note: Includes Dinuba, Cutler, Orosi, Seville, Traver, London, Delf, Orange Cove.

Civil Records: Access: Mail, in person. Both court and visitors may perform in person searches. Search fee: $5.00 per name. Required to search: name, years to search. Civil cases indexed by defendant, plaintiff. Civil records on computer from 1993, index files from 1983. Records destroyed after 10 years.

Criminal Records: Access: Mail, in person. Both court and visitors may perform in person searches. Search fee: $5.00 per name. Required to search: name, years to search, DOB. Criminal records on computer from 1993, index files from 1983. Records destroyed after 10 years.

General Information: Public Access terminal is available. No probation reports released. Will not fax results. Copy fee: $.50 per page. Cert fee: $6.60. Payee: Dinuba Superior Court. In state checks accepted. Prepayment required. Mail requests: SASE required. Mail turnaround time 2-3 days.

Porterville Division - Superior Court 87 E
Morton Ave, Porterville, CA 93257; 559-782-4710; Fax: 559-782-4805. Hours: 8AM-4PM (PST). *Misdemeanor, Civil Actions Under $25,000, Eviction, Small Claims.*
Note: Includes Porterville, Springville, Camp Nelson, Johnsondale, Terra Bella, Ducor, Richgrove, Poplar, Strathmore and surrounding areas.

Civil Records: Access: Mail, in person. Both court and visitors may perform in person searches. Search fee: $5.00 per name. also is per case. Required to search: name, years to search, DOB, SSN, case #. Civil cases indexed by defendant, plaintiff. Civil records on computer from February, 1992, index book prior. Records destroyed after 10 years.

Criminal Records: Access: Mail, in person. Both court and visitors may perform in person searches. Search fee: $5.00 per name. Also is per case. Required to search: name, years to search; also helpful: DOB, SSN, case #. Criminal records on computer from February, 1992, index book prior. Records destroyed after 10 years.

General Information: Public Access terminal is available. No probation reports released. Copy fee: $.50 per page. Cert fee: $6.60 per document. Payee: Porterville Superior Court. Personal checks accepted. Prepayment required. Mail requests: SASE required. Mail turnaround time 3-5 days.

Tulare/Pixley Division - Superior Court
425 E Kern St (PO Box 1136), Tulare, CA 93275; 559-685-2556; Fax: 559-685-2663. Hours: 8AM-4PM (PST). *Misdemeanor, Civil Actions Under $25,000, Eviction, Small Claims.*
Note: Includes Tulare, Pixley, Tipton, Earlimart, Alpaugh, Allensworth, Woodville, Waukena and surrounding areas.

Civil Records: Access: Mail, fax, in person. Both court and visitors may perform in person searches. Search fee: $5.00 per name. Required to search: name, years to search. Civil cases indexed by defendant, plaintiff. Civil records in index books. Records destroyed after 10 years; on computer back to 1992.

Criminal Records: Access: Mail, fax, in person. Both court and visitors may perform in person searches. Search fee: $5.00 per name. Required to search: name, years to search, DOB; also helpful: address, SSN. Criminal records in index books. Records destroyed after 10 years; on computer back to 1992.

General Information: Public Access terminal is available. No probation reports released. Copy fee: $.50 per page. Cert fee: $6.60. Payee: Superior Court. Personal checks accepted. Prepayment required. Mail requests: SASE required. Mail turnaround: 2 days.

Tuolumne County

Superior Court - Civil 41 W Yaney, Sonora, CA 95370; 209-533-5555; Fax: 209-533-6944. Hours: 8AM-5PM (PST). *Civil, Eviction, Small Claims, Probate.*

www.courtinfo.ca.gov/courts/trial/tuolumne

Note: Departments 1, 2, and 5. The small claims court can be reach at 209-533-6509.

Civil Records: Access: Mail, in person. Both court and visitors may perform in person searches. Search fee: $5.00 per name. Fee is per record. Required to search: name, years to search. Civil cases indexed by defendant, plaintiff. Civil records on computer back to 1994, microfiche and archived from 1900s, index files from 1800s.

General Information: Public Access terminal is available. No adoptions, juvenile, medical, probation or sealed records released. Copy fee: $.50 per page. Cert fee: $6.60. Payee: Superior Court. Personal checks accepted. Out of state checks not accepted. Prepayment required. Mail requests: SASE required. Mail turnaround time 1 week.

Superior Court - Criminal 60 N Washington St, Sonora, CA 95370; 209-533-5563; Fax: 209-533-5581. Hours: 8AM-4PM (PST). *Felony, Misdemeanor, Traffic.*

www.courtinfo.ca.gov/courts/trial/tuolumne

Note: Departments 3 and 4. Traffic court can be reach at 209-533-5671.

Criminal Records: Access: Mail, in person. Both court and visitors may perform in person searches. Search fee: $5.00 per name. Required to search: name, years to search, DOB. Felony records on computer from 1993; misdemeanors from 1999; index files prior. Will only search back 7 years.

General Information: Public Access terminal is available. No sealed records released. Most records are public. Will only fax to public agencies. Copy fee: $.50 per page. Cert fee: $6.60. Payee: Tuolomne County Superior Court. Personal checks accepted. Prepayment required. Mail requests: SASE required. Mail turnaround time 1 week to 10 days.

Ventura County

Ventura Superior Court 800 S Victoria Ave (PO Box 6489), Ventura, CA 93006-6489; Civil phone: 805-654-2609; Criminal phone: 805-654-2611; Probate phone: 805-654-2264; Fax: 805-650-4032. 8AM-5PM (PST). *Felony, Misdemeanor, Civil, Eviction, Small Claims, Probate.*

http://courts.countyofventura.org

Civil Records: Access: Phone, mail, online, in person. Both court and visitors may perform in person searches. Search fee: $5.00 per name. Required to search: name, years to search. Civil cases indexed by defendant, plaintiff. Civil records prior to 10/93 are on microfiche, after are on computer. Access to case information, calendars and dockets is free at https://public.courts.ventura.org/casehome.htm. Also, access to civil court records 10/93-present is free at http://courts.countyofventura.org/civcase/case_home.asp. Search by defendant or plaintiff name, case number, or date. Search probate at www.cagenweb.com/ventura/Probate.html.

Criminal Records: Access: Phone, mail, online, in person. Both court and visitors may perform in person searches. Search fee: $5.00 per name. Required to search: name, years to search, DOB. Criminal records go back to 1893; criminal records on computer back to 1989. Access to case information, calendars and dockets is free at https://public.courts.ventura.org/casehome.htm.

General Information: Public Access terminal is available. No adoptions, mental health, paternity actions, juvenile, medical, probation or sealed records

released. Copy fee: $.50 per page. Cert fee: $7.00 per document. Payee: Superior Court. Personal checks accepted. Visa, MC, AmEx, Discover cards accepted. Additional fee charged. Prepayment required. Mail requests: SASE required. Mail turnaround: 5-10 days.

East County Superior Court PO Box 1200 (3855F Alamo St), Simi Valley, CA 93062-1200; Civil phone: 805-582-8086; Criminal phone: 805-582-8080. Hours: 8AM-11:30AM; 1:30PM-5PM (PST). *Misdemeanor, Civil, Eviction, Small Claims, Family Law.*

http://courts.countyofventura.org

Note: Other phones are: Eviction 582-8086; Small Claims 582-8078; Family Law 582-8086.

Civil Records: Access: Phone, mail, online, in person. Both court and visitors may perform in person searches. Search fee: $5.00 per name. Fee is per court. Required to search: name, years to search. Civil records go back to 4/92. Access to civil court records 10/93-present is free online at the website. Search by defendant or plaintiff name, case number, or date. Access to case information, calendars and dockets is free at https://public.courts.ventura.org/casehome.htm.

Criminal Records: Access: Phone, mail, in person, online. Both court and visitors may perform in person searches. Search fee: $5.00 per name. Fee is per court. Required to search: name, years to search, DOB. Same record keeping as civil. Access to case information, calendars and dockets is free at https://public.courts.ventura.org/casehome.htm.

General Information: Public Access terminal is available. No adoptions, mental health, paternity actions, juvenile, medical, probation or sealed records released. Will not fax results. Copy fee: $.50 per page. Cert fee: $7.00. Payee: Ventura County Superior Courts. Personal checks accepted. Credit cards accepted: Visa, MC, Discover, AmEx. Additional fee charged. Prepayment required. Mail turnaround time 5 days.

Yolo County

Superior Court 725 Court St, Rm 308, Woodland, CA 95695; 800-944-0990, 530-666-8598; Civil phone: 530-666-8170; Criminal phone: 530-666-8050; Fax: 530-666-8576. Hours: 8AM-3PM (PST). *Felony, Misdemeanor, Civil, Eviction, Small Claims, Probate.*

www.yolocourts.com

Note: Phone numbers will change in Fall, 2004; see www.yolocourts.com for new numbers. Address civil requests to Rm 103 and criminal to Rm 111. Small claims phone is 530-666-8060.

Civil Records: Access: Phone, mail, in person. Both court and visitors may perform in person searches. Search fee: $5.00 per name. Required to search: name, years to search. Civil cases indexed by defendant, plaintiff. Civil records on computer from 1995, microfiche, archived and index files from 1800s. Calendars are online free at www.yolocourts.com/calendar_daily.html. Search Probate Notes at www.yolocourts.com/probate_notes.html.

Criminal Records: Access: Phone, mail, in person. Both court and visitors may perform in person searches. Search fee: $5.00 per name. Required to search: name, years to search; also helpful: DOB. Criminal records on computer from 1995, microfiche, archived and index files from 1800s. Calendars are free at www.yolocourts.com/calendar_daily.html.

General Information: No adoptions, juvenile, medical, probation or sealed records released. Copy fee: $1.00 per page. Cert fee: $6.60. Payee: Yolo Superior Court. Personal checks accepted. Prepayment required. Mail requests: SASE required. Mail turnaround time 2 weeks.

Yuba County

Superior Court 215 5th St, #200, Marysville, CA 95901; 530-749-7600; Fax: 530-749-7351. Hours: 8:30AM-4:30PM (PST). *Felony, Misdemeanor, Civil, Small Claims, Probate.*

Civil Records: Access: Mail, in person. Both court and visitors may perform in person searches. Search fee: $5.00 per name. Required to search: name, years to search. Civil cases indexed by defendant, plaintiff. Civil records on computer from 1992, index books through 1962, archives and index files from 1854.

Criminal Records: Access: Mail, in person. Both court and visitors may perform in person searches. Search fee: $5.00 per name. Required to search: name, years to search. Criminal records on computer from 1992, index books through 1962, archives and index files from 1854.

General Information: Public Access terminal is available. No adoptions, paternity, juvenile, medical, probation or sealed records released. Copy fee: $1.00 per page. Cert fee: $6.60 per document. Payee: Yuba County Superior Court. Personal checks accepted. Prepayment required. Mail requests: SASE required. Mail turnaround time 1-4 weeks.

Marysville Civil Limited Superior Court 215 5th St #200, Marysville, CA 95901; 530-749-7600; Fax: 530-749-7354. Hours: 8:30AM-4:30PM (PST). *Civil Actions Under $25,000, Eviction, Small Claims.*

Civil Records: Access: Mail, in person. Both court and visitors may perform in person searches. Search fee: $5.00 per name. Required to search: name, years to search, DOB. Civil cases indexed by defendant, plaintiff. Civil records on computer through 1993, index books prior back to 1850's.

General Information: Public Access terminal is available. No labor commissioner judgment, juvenile, or judge's records released. Will fax results $20.00 per doc and $1.00 per page. Copy fee: $1.00 per page. Cert fee: $6.60. Payee: Yuba County Superior Court. Personal checks accepted. Prepayment required. Mail requests: SASE required. Mail turnaround time 2 days.

California Recording Offices

ORGANIZATION: 58 counties, 58 recording offices. The recording officer is County Recorder. Recordings are usually located in a Grantor/Grantee or General index. The entire state is in the Pacific Time Zone (PST).

REAL ESTATE RECORDS: Most counties do not perform real estate name searches. Copy fees and certification fees vary.

UCC RECORDS: Financing statements are filed at the state level, except for real estate related collateral, which are filed with the County Recorder. However, prior to 07/2001, consumer goods and farm collateral were also filed at the County Recorder and these older records can be searched there. All counties will perform UCC searches. Use search request form UCC-11. Search fees are usually $15.00 per debtor name. Copy costs vary.

TAX LIEN RECORDS: Federal and state tax liens on personal property of businesses are filed with the Secretary of State. Other federal and state tax liens are filed with the County Recorder. Some counties will perform separate tax lien searches. Fees vary for this type of search.

OTHER LIENS: Judgment (note - many judgments are also filed at the Sec. of State), child support, mechanic.

ONLINE ACCESS: A number of counties offer online access to assessor and real estate information. The system in Los Angeles is a commercial subscription system.

Alameda County

County Recorder, 1106 Madison St, 1st Fl, Oakland, CA 94607. **Phone**-510-272-6362; fax-510-272-6382; hours 8:30AM-4:30PM www.co.alameda.ca.us Will search UCC records. Search per debtor- $15.00. Copy fee is $2.00 per page. Tax liens not included in UCC search. Separate federal tax lien search- $15.00 per debtor. Will not search real estate records. RE record copy- $.50 per page. Cert fee: $.50 per doc. Payee: Alameda County Recorder. **Online Access to Assessor, Recording, Deed, Mortgage, Lien, Fictitious Business Name, Property Tax records:** The clerk-recorder's official public records and fictitious name databases are free at http://rechart1.co.alameda.ca.us/localization/menu.asp. Also, access to the Property Assessment database is free at www.co.alameda.ca.us/assessor/property_info/; property tax info is now available at www.co.alameda.ca.us/treasurer/tax_info/. No name searching at either site. **Other phones:** Assessor-510-272-3755; Treasurer-510-272-6800.

Alpine County

County Recorder, PO Box 217, Markleeville, CA 96120. **Phone**-County Recorder, R/E & UCC Recording- 530-694-2286; fax-530-694-2491; hours 9AM-Noon,1-4PM. Will search UCC records. Search per debtor- $5.00. UCC copy fee- $1.00 1st page; $.50 each add'l. Will not search real estate or tax lien records. Cert fee: $1.75 per cert. Payee: Alpine County Recorder. **Other phones:** Assessor-530-694-2283; Treasurer-530-694-2286.

Amador County

County Recorder, 500 Argonaut Lane, Jackson, CA 95642. **Phone**-County Recorder, R/E & UCC Recording- 209-223-6468; fax-209-223-6204; 8AM-5PM www.co.amador.ca.us/depts/recorder/index.htm Will not search records. Copy fees are $2.00 for 1st page, $1 each add'l. Cert fee: $4.00 per cert. Payee: Amador County Recorder. **Online Access to Recording, Deed, Lien, Judgment, Fictitious name, Tax Sale records:** Access to the county clerk database is free at www.co.amador.ca.us/depts/recorder/criis.htm or www.criis.com/amador/recorded.htm Also, tax sale data is at www.co.amador.ca.us/depts/treasurer/index.htm; earch by year. **Other phones:** Assessor-209-223-6351; Treasurer-209-223-6364; Appraiser-209-223-6351; Elections-209-223-6465; Vital Records-209-223-6468.

Butte County

County Recorder, 25 County Ctr Dr, Oroville, CA 95965-3375. **Phone**-County Recorder, R/E & UCC Recording- 530-538-7691; fax-530-538-7975; hours 9AM-5PM; Recording hours: 9AM-4PM http://clerk-recorder.buttecounty.net Will not search records. Record copy- $2.00 per page. Cert fee: $2.00 per cert. Payee: Butte County Recorder. **Online Access to Real Estate, Recording, Fictitious Business Name, Inmate records:** Access to the County Recorder's database of official documents is free at http://clerk-recorder.buttecounty.net/Riimsweb/Asp/ORInquiry.asp. Records go back to 1988. Marriages, births and deaths are no longer available. Search fictitious business names free at http://clerk-recorder.buttecounty.net/RiimsWeb/ASP/FBNInquiry.asp. Also, search the inmate list free at www.vinelink.com/offender/searchNew.jsp?siteID=5099. **Other phones:** Assessor-530-538-7721; Treasurer-530-538-7576; Appraiser/ Auditor-530-538-7721; Elections-530-538-7761; Vital Records-530-538-7690.

Calaveras County

County Recorder, 891 Mountain Ranch Rd, Government Ctr, San Andreas, CA 95249. **Phone**-209-754-6372; fax-209-754-6733; hours 8AM-4PM Will not search records. Record copy- $1.00 1st page, $.50 each add'l. Cert fee: $1.00 per cert. Payee: Calaveras County Recorder. **Online Access to Property Tax, Assessor records:** Access to the GIS Project of property information is free at www.co.calaveras.ca.us/departments/gisproj.html. Click on "Parcel Information System" or, search at www.co.calaveras.ca.us/propertysearch/parcelhome.asp . No name searching at either site. **Other phones:** Assessor-209-754-6356; Treasurer-209-754-6350; Appraiser/ Auditor-209-754-6356; Elections-209-754-6376; Vital Records-209-754-6372.

Colusa County

County Recorder, 546 Jay St, Colusa, CA 95932. **Phone**-County Recorder, R/E & UCC Recording- 530-458-0500; fax-530-458-0512; hours 8:30AM-5PM www.colusacountyclerk.com Will not search records. Record copy- $1.00 per page. Cert fee: $1.00 per doc. Payee: Colusa County Recorder. **Other phones:** Assessor-530-458-0450; Treasurer-530-458-0440; Appraiser/ Auditor-530-458-0450; Elections-530-458-0500; Vital Records-530-458-0500.

Contra Costa County

County Recorder, PO Box 350, Martinez, CA 94553. **Phone**-925-646-2360; fax-925-646-2135; 8AM-4PM www.co.contra-costa.ca.us/depart/elect/Rindex.html The County Clerk is located at 822 Main St, Martinez, CA 94553, 925-646-2955. Will not search records. Record copy- $1.00 per page. Cert fee: $2.50 per cert. Payee: Contra Costa County Recorder. **Online Access to Recording, Fictitious Business Name, Deed, Lien, Judgment, Real Estate, Most Wanted records:** Recorder office records back to 1992 are free at www.criis.com/contra/srecord.shtml. By order of governor, vital statistic records have been removed from the internet. Fictitious Business names are at www.criis.com/contracosta/sfictitious.shtml. Marriage records are no longer online. Search the sheriff's most wanted list at www.cocosheriff.org/wanted/wanted.htm. **Other phones:** Assessor-925-313-7400 (resi); 313-7500 (busi).

Del Norte County

County Recorder, 981 H St #160, Crescent City, CA 95531. **Phone**-County Recorder, R/E & UCC Recording- 707-464-7216; fax-707-464-0321; hours 8AM-Noon,1-5PM. Will not search records. Record copy- $2.00 1st page, $1.00 each add'l. Cert fee: $2.00 per seal. Payee: Del Norte County Recorder. **Online Access to Tax Sale records:** Access to tax sales lists is free through a private company at www.bid4assets.com. **Other phones:** Assessor-707-464-7200; Treasurer-707-464-7283; Elections-707-465-0383; Vital Records-707-464-7216.

El Dorado County

County Recorder, 360 Fair Lane, Placerville, CA 95667-4197. **Phone**-County Recorder, R/E & UCC Recording- 530-621-5490; fax-530-621-2147; hours 8AM-5PM (No recordings after 4PM) Will not search records. Record copy- $1.00 1st page, $.50 each add'l. Cert fee: $1.00 per cert. Payee: El Dorado County Recorder. **Online Access to Real Estate, Personal Property, Vital Statistic, Fictitious Name records:** Access to the Recorder's index is available free at http://main.co.el-dorado.ca.us/CGI/WWB012/WWM501/R. Records go back to 1949. Search business licenses at http://main.co.el-dorado.ca.us/CGI/WWB012/WWM200/T?S=A Official records on the recorder database are free at http://main.co.el-dorado.ca.us/CGI/WWB012/WWM501/C. Search by date range, name or document number.

Search inmates at www.vinelink.com/offender/searchNew.jsp?siteID=5099 County non-confidential marriages and fictitious names are free at http://main.co.el-dorado.ca.us/CGI/WWB012/WWM500/C. Births and deaths have been removed. **Other phones:** Assessor-530-621-5719; Treasurer-530-621-5800; Vital Records-530-621-5490.

Fresno County

County Recorder, PO Box 766, Fresno, CA 93712. **Phone-**County Recorder, R/E & UCC Recording- 559-488-3471; fax-559-488-6774; hours 9AM-4PM www.co.fresno.ca.us/0420/recorders_web/index.htm Husband and wife count as one search, if so indicated. Will not search records. Copy fee-$1.50 1st page; $.50 each add'l. Cert fee: $1.00 per cert. Payee: Fresno County Recorder. **Online Access to Recorder, Property, Birth, Death, Marriage, Lien, Deed, Mortgage, Inmate records:** Access to the county recorder database is free at www.criis.com/fresno/srecord.shtml. Marriage records are at www.criis.com/fresno/smarriage.shtml. County Birth Records and death records have been removed from the internet. Also, search inmate info on private company website at www.vinelink.com/index.jsp. **Other phones:** Assessor-559-488-3514; Treasurer-559-488-3486; Vital Records-559-488-3476.

Glenn County

County Recorder, 526 W. Sycamore St, Willows, CA 95988. **Phone-**County Recorder, R/E & UCC Recording- 530-934-6412; fax-530-934-6305; hours 8AM-5PM. Will not search records. Record copy-$1.50 per page. Cert fee: $2.00 per cert. Payee: Glenn County Recorder. **Other phones:** Assessor-530-934-6402; Treasurer-530-934-6410; Appraiser/Auditor-530-934-6402; Elections-530-934-6414; Vital Records-530-934-6412.

Humboldt County

County Recorder, 825 Fifth St, 5th Fl, Eureka, CA 95501. **Phone-**County Recorder, R/E & UCC Recording- 707-445-7593; fax-707-445-7324; hours 8:30AM-5PM www.co.humboldt.ca.us/recorder/ Will not search records. Copy fee-$2.00 1st page; $1.00 each add'l. Cert fee: $2.00 per cert. Payee: Humboldt County Recorder. **Online Access to Inmate, Offender records:** Access to the county correction facility inmate lists is free at www.vinelink.com/offender/searchNew.jsp?siteID=5099. **Other phones:** Assessor-707-445-7663; Treasurer-707-445-7331; Elections-707-445-7481; Vital Records-707-445-7382.

Imperial County

County Recorder, 940 Main St, Rm 202, El Centro, CA 92243-2865. **Phone-**760-482-4272, R/E Recording-760-482-4275, UCC Recording- 760-482-4275; hours 9AM-4:30PM Will not search UCC records. UCC copy fee- $1.00 per page add'l $.50. Separate federal/state combined tax lien search- $15.00 per debtor. Will not search real estate records. Cert fee: $2.00 per cert. Payee: Imperial County Clerk/Recorder. **Online Access to Inmate, Offender, Most Wanted records:** Search the county inmate list for free at www.vinelink.com/offender/searchNew.jsp?siteID=5011. View the sheriff office most wanted list at www.icso.org/most_wanted.htm. **Other phones:** Assessor-760-482-4244; Treasurer-760-482-6281; Vital Records-760-482-4272.

Inyo County

County Recorder, PO Box F, Independence, CA 93526. **Phone-**County Recorder, R/E & UCC Recording- 760-878-0222; fax-760-878-1805; hours 9-Noon,1-5PM Will search UCC records. Search per debtor- $15.00. Copy fee is $1.00 per page. Will search tax liens.

Will not search real estate records. RE record copy-$1.00 per page. Cert fee: $3.00 for 1st page; $1.00 each add'l. Payee: Inyo County Recorder. **Online Access to Recording, Fictitious Business Name records:** Access to the county clerk recording database is free at www.criis.com/inyo/official.shtml. Fictitious names are also available. Vital statistics are not available. **Other phones:** Assessor-760-878-0302; Treasurer-760-878-0333; Appraiser-760-878-0302; Elections-760-878-0223; Vital Records-760-878-0410.

Kern County

County Recorder, 1655 Chester Ave, Hall of Records, Bakersfield, CA 93301. **Phone-**661-868-6400, R/E Recording- 661-868-6448, UCC Recording- 661-868-6448; fax-661-868-6401; hours 8AM-5PM; Recording 8AM-2PM; Copy Service 8AM-5PM www.co.kern.ca.us/recorder Will not search records. UCC copy fee- $3.00 1st page, $.50 each add'l. RE record copy- $.50 per page. Payee: Kern County Recorder. **Online Access to Assessor, Property Tax, Fictitious Business Name, Vital Statistic, Recording, Real Estate, Tax Collector, Unclaimed Property records:** Assessor database records are available free at http://assessor.co.kern.ca.us/kips/property_search.asp. Search marriages at http://recorderonline.co.kern.ca.us/cgi-bin/msearch.mbr/input. Purchase Birth, Death records from Vitalchek at www.vitalchek.com. Also, search county clerk's fictitious business name database free at www.co.kern.ca.us/ctyclerk/dba/default.asp. The recorders database of deeds is free at http://recorder.co.kern.ca.us/kips/property_search.asp. Fictitious business names and property tax assessment data at http://kerndata.com. Tax collector data at www.kcttc.co.kern.ca.us/payment/mainsearch.aspx. Unclaimed property at www.kcttc.co.kern.ca.us/searches/unclaimed_monies.cfm. **Other phones:** Assessor-661-868-3485; Treasurer-661-868-3490; Appraiser/Auditor-661-868-3485; Elections-661-868-3590; Vital Records-661-868-6449.

Kings County

County Recorder, 1400 W. Lacey Blvd., Hanford, CA 93230. **Phone-**County Recorder, R/E & UCC Recording- 559-582-3211 x2470; fax-559-582-6639; hours 8AM-3PM www.countyofkings.com Will not search records. You may search records in person with office assistance. Copy fee is $1.00 per page. Cert fee: $2.00 per cert. Payee: Kings County Clerk Recorder. **Online Access to Inmate records:** Search inmate info on private company website at www.vinelink.com/index.jsp. **Other phones:** Assessor-559-582-3211 x2486; Treasurer-559-582-3211 x2477; Elections-559-582-3211 x2439; Vital Records-559-582-3211 x2470.

Lake County

County Recorder, 255 N. Forbes, Rm 223, Lakeport, CA 95453. **Phone-**County Recorder, R/E & UCC Recording- 707-263-2293; fax-707-263-3703; hours 9AM-5PM. Will search UCC records. Search per debtor- $15.00. Copy fee is $1.00 for 1st page and $.50 each add'l. Will not search real estate or tax lien records. RE record copy- $1.00 for 1st pg., $.50 each add'l pg. Cert fee: $1.00 per cert. Payee: Lake County Recorder. **Other phones:** Assessor-707-263-2302; Treasurer-707-263-2236; Elections-707-263-2372; Vital Records-707-263-2293.

Lassen County

County Recorder, 220 S. Lassen St, #5, Susanville, CA 96130. **Phone-**County Recorder, R/E & UCC Recording- 530-251-8234; fax-530-257-3480; hours Public hours- 10AM-Noon, 1-3PM; Phone hours-8AM-N http://clerk.lassencounty.org Will not search records. Record copy-$1.50 per page. Cert fee: $1.75 1st page. Payee: Lassen

County Recorder. **Online Access to Real Estate, Recording, Tax Sale records:** Access to the county recorder database is available free at http://icris.lassencounty.org/icris/splash.jsp. Registration is required. Recorded documents go back to 7/1985. Access to tax sales lists is free via a private company at www.bid4assets.com. **Other phones:** Assessor-530-251-8241; 251-8242; Treasurer-530-251-8220; Elections-530-251-8217; Vital Records-530-251-8234.

Los Angeles County

County Recorder, PO Box 53195, Real Estate Records Section, Los Angeles, CA 90053-0115. **Phone-**562-462-2125, 800-815-2666; fax-562-864-1250 for record requests; hours 8AM-5PM http://regrec.co.la.ca.us The county sells a variety of data; view lists/details at http://assessor.co.la.ca.us/extranet/Outsidesales/catalog.aspx. There is an application for real estate record form at http://regrec.co.la.ca.us/recorder/apprealstaterec.htm. Will search UCC records. Search per debtor- $.50 per year with $1.00 min. See certification fee. Will not search tax liens. Will not name search real estate records. Search fee with document number is $.50 per name per year. To request a credit card order by telephone, please contact the Real estate Records Section at 562-462-2133. Cert fee: $6.00 for 1st page; $3.00 each add'l. Payee: Los Angeles County Recorder; no out of state checks. Credit card orders-add $6.00. All major card accepted. **Online Access to Assessor, Fictitious Business Name, Inmate, Property Tax, Sex Offender, Most Wanted records:** For assessments use the PDB Inquiry System dial-up svc.; $100 monthly + $1.00 per inquiry, also $75 sign-up fee for 3-year dial-up with usage fee of $6.50 per hr or $.11 per minute. PDB registration data is at: http://assessor.co.la.ca.us/extranet/outsidesales/online.aspx. Tax info line: 213-974-3838. County most wanted list- www.lapdonline.org/get_involved/most_wanted/most_wanted_main.htm. Search county inmates at http://app1.lasd.org/iic/ajis_search.cfm. Property assessor data (no name searching) is free at http://assessormap.co.la.ca.us/mapping/viewer.asp. Fictitious Names- http://regrec.co.la.ca.us/fbn/FBN.cfm. Sex offenders- http://gismap.co.la.ca.us/sols/viewer.asp. **Other phones:** Assessor-562-974-3211; Treasurer-562-974-2101.

Madera County

County Recorder, 209 W. Yosemite, Madera, CA 93637. **Phone-**County Recorder, R/E & UCC Recording- 559-675-7724; fax-559-675-7870; hours 8AM-3:30PM www.madera-county.com Will not search records. Copy fee is $1.00 for 1st page, $.50 each add'l. Cert fee: $1.75 per cert. Payee: Madera County Recorder. **Other phones:** Assessor-559-675-7710; Treasurer-559-675-7713; Elections-559-675-7720; Vital Records-559-675-7724.

Marin County

County Recorder, PO Box C, San Rafael, CA 94913. **Phone-**County Recorder, R/E & UCC Recording- 415-499-6092; fax-415-499-7893; hours 9AM-4PM research and copies; 9AM-3PM Recording www.co.marin.ca.us/depts/AR/main/index.cfm Will not search records. Copy fee is $2.00 per page. Cert fee: $3.00 per cert. Payee: Marin County Recorder. **Online Access to Real Estate, Property Tax, Grantor/Grantee, Recording, Vital Statistic, Business Name, Booking Log records:** Search the county Grantor/Grantee index free at www.co.marin.ca.us/depts/AR/RiiMs/index.asp. Also, search the property tax database at www.co.marin.ca.us/depts/AR/COMPASS/index.asp but there is no name searching. Also, search the real estate sales lists by month and year by selecting the year. Search vital records for document index number at www.co.marin.ca.us/depts/AR/VitalStatistics/index.asp.

Birth records go back to 1967; deaths to 1979. Marriage records go back to 1948. Search business names at http://marinfo.marin.org/Bizmo/index.cfm. Sheriff's booking log is at www.co.marin.ca.us/depts/SO/bklog/XMLProj/index.asp. **Other phones:** Assessor-415-499-7215; Treasurer-415-499-6145; Vital Records-415-499-6094.

Mariposa County

County Recorder, PO Box 35, Mariposa, CA 95338. **Phone**-209-966-5719; hours 8AM-5PM (Recording hours 8AM-3:30PM)
Will not search records. Record copy- $1.00 per page. Cert fee: $1.00 per doc. Payee: Mariposa County Recorder. **Other phones:** Assessor-209-966-2332; Treasurer-209-966-2621.

Mendocino County

County Recorder, 501 Low Gap Rd, Rm 1020, Ukiah, CA 95482. **Phone**-County Recorder, R/E & UCC Recording- 707-463-4376; fax-707-463-4257; hours 8AM-5PM www.co.mendocino.ca.us
Will not search UCC records or tax liens. Will search real estate records. Record copy- $2.50 + $.50. Cert fee: $1.00 per cert. Payee: Mendocino County Recorder. **Online Access to Inmate, Offender records:** Access to the county inmate list is free at www.vinelink.com/offender/searchNew.jsp?siteID=5009. **Other phones:** Assessor-707-463-4311; Treasurer-707-463-4388; Appraiser/ Auditor-707-463-4311; Elections-707-463-4374; Vital Records-707-463-4371.

Merced County

County Recorder, 2222 M St, Merced, CA 95340. **Phone**-209-385-7627; fax-209-385-7626; hours 8AM-4:30PM http://web.co.merced.ca.us/recorder/
Will not search records. Copy fee is $3.00 for 1st page; $1 each add'l. Cert fee: $2.00 per cert. Payee: Merced County Recorder. **Online Access to Recorder, Grantor/Grantee, Deed, Real Estate, Most Wanted, Missing Person, Sex Offender records:** Access to the recorder official records index PARIS system is free at http://139.151.191.2/cgi-bin/odsmnu1.html/input. Search the county most wanted and missing person sites for free at www.co.merced.ca.us/sheriff/. Short list of high risk sex offenders is at www.co.merced.ca.us/da/so_high_risk.htm. **Other phones:** Assessor-209-385-7631; Treasurer-209-385-7307.

Modoc County

County Recorder, 204 Court St, Alturas, CA 96101. **Phone**-County Recorder, R/E & UCC Recording- 530-233-6205; fax-530-233-6666; hours 8:30AM-Noon, 1-5PM
Will search UCC records. Search per debtor- $10.00. Copy fee is $1.00 for 1st page; $.50 each add'l. Will not search real estate or tax lien records. RE record copy- $1.00 per page. Cert fee: $1.00 per cert. Payee: Modoc County Recorder. **Online Access to Recording, Fictitious Business Name, Tax Sale records:** Access to the county clerk recording database soon to be available free at www.criis.com/modoc/official.shtml. Fictitious names may also be found. Also, access to tax sales lists is free through a private company at www.bid4assets.com. **Other phones:** Assessor-530-233-6217; 233-6218; Treasurer-530-233-6223; Appraiser/ Auditor-530-233-6221; Elections-530-233-6201; Vital Records-530-233-6205.

Mono County

County Recorder, PO Box 237, Bridgeport, CA 93517. **Phone**-County Recorder, R/E & UCC Recording- 760-932-5530; fax-760-932-5531; hours 9AM-5PM
Will search UCC records. Search per debtor- $15.00 per name per 5 years. UCC copy- $.05 per page. UCC search does not include tax liens. Tax lien

search fee- $2.00 per year per debtor. Real estate record owner searches available. RE record copy- $.05 per page. Cert fee: $1.75 per cert. Payee: Mono County Recorder. **Other phones:** Assessor-760-932-5510; Treasurer-760-932-5480; Elections-760-932-5537; Vital Records-760-932-5535.

Monterey County

County Recorder, PO Box 29, Salinas, CA 93902. **Phone**-County Recorder, R/E & UCC Recording- 831-755-5041; fax-831-755-5064; hours 8AM-5PM www.co.monterey.ca.us/recorder/
Will not search records. Copy fee is $1.00 per page. Cert fee: $2.00 per cert. Payee: Monterey County Recorder. **Online Access to Inmate, Offender, Most Wanted, Tax Sale records:** Access to the county jail inmates list is avaialble free at www.vinelink.com/offender/searchNew.jsp?siteID=5099. The county tax defaulted property list is at www.co.monterey.ca.us/taxcollector/Auction.htm. Search assessor data (no name searching) atwww.co.monterey.ca.us/assessor/intro2asmt-query.htm. **Other phones:** Assessor-831-755-5035; Treasurer-831-755-5015; Vital Records-813-755-5041.

Napa County

County Recorder, PO Box 298, Napa, CA 94559-0298. **Phone**-County Recorder, R/E & UCC Recording- 707-253-4246; fax-707-259-8149; hours 8AM-5PM www.mynapa.info/Gov/Departments/DeptDefault.asp?DID=28000
Will not search UCC records. Tax lien search fee- $5.00 per debtor per year. Real estate record owner searches available. Record copy- $2.00 per page. Cert fee: $3.00 per cert. Payee: Napa County Recorder. **Online Access to Property Tax, Tax Sale, Property, Recording, Deed, Judgment, Lien, Inmate records:** Access to recorder data is by subscription; tentative fee is $3600 per year. Index goes back to May, 1996; images go back to March, 1999. For information and sign-up, call Dawnette Martindale at 707-253-4327. Search property free by street address at www.co.napa.ca.us/MyProperty/. Also, search limited property data at the GIS site at http://gis.napa.ca.gov/mapdisclaimer.asp. No name searching. Also, recording data avaialble on CD-rom for $25.00 per week. Also, access the Treasurer's property tax data on a subscription online service; username/password is required. For info call 707-253-4311 x0. Access the county Dept of Corrections inmate list at www.vinelink.com/offender/searchNew.jsp?siteID=5099. **Other phones:** Assessor-707-253-4466; Treasurer-707-253-4311; Elections-707-253-4321; Vital Records-707-253-4246.

Nevada County

County Recorder, 950 Maidu Ave, Nevada City, CA 95959. **Phone**-530-265-1221; fax-530-265-1497; hours 9AM-4PM http://recorder.co.nevada.ca.us
Will not search records. Copy fee is $3.00 for 1st page; $.50 each add'l. Cert fee: $1.00 per cert. Payee: Nevada County Recorder. **Online Access to Recording, Fictitious Name, Property Tax, GIS, Real Estate records:** Access to the county clerk database of recordings and assumed names is free at www.criis.com/nevada/official.shtml. Also, search property tax payment records at http://treas-tax.co.nevada.ca.us/searchtax.php; no name searching. Also, subscription access to Recorders full database is $200 per month fee. Also, daily/weekly/monthly CD-Roms are available. Also, search the GIS mapping site by adddress for property info for free at http://63.205.214.10:1711. Will fax results for add'l $2.00 per page. **Other phones:** Assessor-530-265-1232; Treasurer-530-265-1285; Elections-530-265-1298.

Orange County

County Recorder, PO Box 238, Santa Ana, CA 92702-0238. **Phone**-714-834-2887 (questions), R/E Records-714-834-2500 (recorded info only); fax-714-834-2675; hours 8AM-4:30PM www.oc.ca.gov/recorder
For questions about requesting documents, call 714-834-2461. Fax requests not accepted. Will search UCC records. Search per debtor- $15.00 per five years. Record copy- $1.00 per page. Cert fee: $1.00 per cert. Payee: Orange County Clerk-Recorder. **Online Access to Grantor/Grantee, Deed, Lien, Judgment, Fictitious Business Name, Property Tax, Wanted, Missing Person, Inmate, Arrest records:** Orange County Grantor/Grantee index is free online at http://cr.ocgov.com/grantorgrantee/index.asp. Fictitious business names at http://cr.ocgov.com/fbn/index.asp. Also, search property tax records at http://tax.ocgov.com/tcweb/search_page.asp; no name searching. Search sheriff's wanted, missing persons and blotter lists at www.ocsd.org; click on "Crime Bulletins." For inmates, arrests (search by date only), arrest warrants, click on "e-services." Also, search inmate/offender lists at www.vinelink.com/offender/searchNew.jsp?siteID=5004. **Other phones:** Assessor-714-834-2727; Treasurer-714-834-2682; Vital Records-714-834-2568.

Placer County

County Recorder, 2954 Richardson Dr., Auburn, CA 95603. **Phone**-County Recorder, R/E & UCC Recording- 530-886-5600; fax-530-886-5687; hours 8AM-5PM (Recording hours 9AM-4PM)
www.placer.ca.gov/clerk/clerk.htm
Will search UCC records. Search per debtor- $10.00. Copy fee is $2.00 per page. Will not search real estate or tax lien records. RE record copy- $2.00 for 1st page. Cert fee: $2.00 per doc. Payee: Placer County Recorder. **Online Access to Recording, Fictitious Name, Marriage, Most Wanted, Missing Person, Jail, Assessor, Property Tax records:** Recorder office records are free at the website. County Birth and death records have been removed from the web. Marriage records at www.criis.com/placer/smarriage.shtml. Search county Fictitious Business Names at www.criis.com/placer/sfictitious.shtml. Search sheriff's most wanted, missing person, and sex offender map at www.placer.ca.gov/sheriff/aware/. County in-custody roster is at www.placer.ca.gov/sheriff/jail/icr.htm. The assessor's property assessment data is free at www.placer.ca.gov/assessor/assessment-inquiry.htm, no name searching. **Other phones:** Assessor-530-889-4300; Elections-530-886-5650; Vital Records-530-886-5600.

Plumas County

County Recorder, 520 Main St, Rm 102, Quincy, CA 95971. **Phone**-530-283-6218; fax-530-283-6155; hours 8AM-5PM. Will search UCC records. Search per debtor- $10.00. UCC copy fee- $1.00 per page. UCC search includes tax liens if requested. Separate federal/state combined tax lien search- $10.00 per debtor. Will not search real estate records. Cert fee: $1.00 per cert. Payee: Plumas County Recorder. **Other phones:** Assessor-530-283-6380; Treasurer-530-283-6260; Elections-530-283-6256.

Riverside County

County Recorder, PO Box 751, Attn: County Recorder/Clerk, Riverside, CA 92502-0751. **Phone**-County Recorder, R/E & UCC Recording- 951-486-7000; fax-951-486-7007; 8AM-4:30PM (recording hours 8AM-2PM) http://riverside.asrclkrec.com
Will not search UCC records. Copy fee is $2.00 for 1st page; $1.00 each add'l page (certified). Separate federal/state combined tax lien search is available. Will search real estate records. RE record copy- $2.00 1st page, $1.00 each add'l. Cert fee:

$1.00 per cert. Payee: Riverside County Recorder. **Online Access to Assessor, Property Tax, Fictitious Name, Grantor/Grantee, Wanted, Missing Person records:** Property tax information from the County Treasurer database is free from EZproperty.com at https://riverside.ca.ezgov.com/ezproperty/review_searc h.jsp. Also, access to county fictitious name database is at http://riverside.asrclkrec.com/OS.asp. The FBN search is free; a fee is charged for documents from Grantor/Grantee index and assessor data at www.enetwizard.com/shop/affiliates/11467_01/. Also, access sheriff's most wanted, missing person, sex offender map at www.co.riverside.ca.us/sheriff/crime/. **Other phones:** Assessor-951-955-6250; Treasurer-951-955-3900; Vital Records-951-486-7000.

Sacramento County

County Recorder, PO Box 839, Sacramento, CA 95812-0839. **Phone-**916-874-6334; 800-313-7133, R/E Recording- 916-874-6334, UCC Recording- 916-874-6334; hours 8AM-5PM (recording 8AM-3PM) www.saccounty.net
Assessor office is at 3701 Power Inn Rd. Will search UCC records; mail requests accepted. Search per debtor- $10.00 per name. Copy fee is $10.50 for 1st page; $1.00 each add'l. Will not search real estate or tax lien records. RE record copy- $10.50 per doc. Cert fee: $.50 per cert. Payee: Sacramento County Clerk and Recorder. **Online Access to Assessor, Grantor/Grantee, Deed, Business License, Wanted Suspect, Inmate records:** Access to the Dept. of Finance Clerk-recorder Grantor/Grantee index is free at www.erosi.saccounty.net/Inputs.asp. Online records go back to 1965. Search restaurant inspections at www.emd.saccounty.net/eh/emdfoodprotect.htm. Also, recorder data may (was not at press time) be at www.criis.com/sacramento/official.shtml and may include Birth, Death, Marriages. Also search property tax and parcels at www.eproptax.saccounty.net; no name searching. Search fictitious names at www.efbn.saccounty.net. Also, search City of West Sacramento business licenses at www.ci.west-sacramento.ca.us/cityhall/departments/finance/buslic/blf ind.cfm. Search the county wanted suspect list at www.crimealert.org/wanted.cfm. Inmates list is at www.vinelink.com/index.jsp. **Other phones:** Assessor-916-875-0700; Treasurer-916-874-6725; Appraiser/ Auditor-916-875-0700; Elections-916-874-6451; Vital Records-916-874-7850.

San Benito County

County Recorder, 440 Fifth St, Rm 206, Hollister, CA 95023. **Phone-**County Recorder, R/E & UCC Recording- 831-636-4046; fax-831-636-2939; hours 8AM-5PM (Recording hours 9AM-4PM)
Will not search records. Record copy- $2.00 1st page, $1.00 per add'l. Cert fee: $3.00 per doc. Payee: San Benito County Clerk/Recorder. **Online Access to Most Wanted records:** Access the sheriff's most wanted list at www.sbcsheriff.org/wanted.html. **Other phones:** Assessor-831-636-4043; Elections-831-636-4016; Vital Records-831-636-4029.

San Bernardino County

County Recorder, 222 W. Hospitality Ln., 1st Fl, San Bernardino, CA 92415-0022. **Phone-**County Recorder, R/E & UCC Recording- 909-387-8306; fax-909-386-9050; 8AM-4:30PM www.co.san-bernardino.ca.us
Will not search UCC records. UCC copy- $1.25 per page. Will not do federal tax lien search. Will not search real estate records. Cert fee: $3.25 per page. Payee: San Bernardino County Recorder. **Online Access to Recorder, Assessor, Fictitious Name, Grantor/Grantee, Inmate, Property Tax records:** Records on the County Assessor database are free at www.co.san-bernardino.ca.us/tax/trsearch.asp. No name searching. Also, for automated call distribution,

call 909-387-8306; for fictitious names information, call 909-386-8970. Search fictitious business names at www.co.san-bernardino.ca.us/ACR/FBNSearch.asp. Also, Auditor/Controller Grantor/Grantee recording index back to 1980 is free at http://acrparis.co.san-bernardino.ca.us/cgi-bin/odsmnu1.html/input. Property can also be searched on PIMS system, registration required, https://nppublic.co.san-bernardino.ca.us/newp ims/. Also, search the inmates/offender list at www.vinelink.com/offender/searchNew.jsp?siteID=50 06. **Other phones:** Assessor-909-387-6730; Treasurer-909-387-8308; Appraiser/ Auditor-909-387-6730; Elections-909-387-8300; Vital Records-909-387-8314; Admin.-909-387-8924.

San Diego County

County Recorder, PO Box 121750, San Diego, CA 92112. **Phone-**County Recorder, R/E & UCC Recording- 619-238-8158; fax-619-557-4155; hours 8AM-5PM www.sdarcc.com
Will search UCC records. Search per debtor- $15.00. UCC copy- $2.00 per page. Tax liens not included in UCC search. Tax lien search- $10.00 per debtor. Real estate owner, mortgage, and property transfer searches available. RE record copy- $2.00 per page. Cert fee: $1.00 per cert. Payee: San Diego Recorder/Clerk. **Online Access to Assessor, Fictitious Name, Real Estate, Grantor/Grantee, Inmates, Most Wanted, Warrant, Sex Offender, Pets, Missing Children, Tax Sale records:** Records on the County Assessor/Recorder/County Clerk Online Services site are free at www.sdcounty.ca.gov/arc c/arcc_home.html including fictitious business names, indexes, maps, property information. Grantee/grantor index search by name for individual record data at http://arcc.san-diego.ca.us/services/grantorgrantee. Search inmates at www.sdsheriff.net/wij/wij.aspx. Search property characteristics data at http://arcc.co.san-diego.ca.us/services/propchar/. Search property data at www.sdcounty.ca.gov/arcc/services/propsales_search.ht ml; no name searching. **Other phones:** Assessor-619-236-3771; Treasurer-619-236-3121; Vital Records-619-237-0502.

San Francisco County

County Recorder, 1 Dr. Carlton E. Goodlet Pl., City Hall, Rm 190, San Francisco, CA 94102. **Phone-**415-554-4176; fax-415-554-4179; hours 8AM-4PM www.sfgov.org
Will not search records. Record copy- $3.00 per page; $.50 after 3rd page. Cert fee: $1.00 per doc. Payee: San Francisco County Assessor-Recorder. **Online Access to Assessor, Property, Fictitious Business Name, Birth, Death records:** access the City Property Tax database for free at https://services.sfgov.org/ptx/intro.asp. Click on "begin." No name searching; address or block/lot number is required. Also search parcel addresses on the GIS site at http://gispub.sfgov.org/website/sfparc el/index.htm. Fictitious business names are also searchable at http://services.sfgov.org/bns/start.asp. Limited vital statistic information is searchable at www.sfgenealogy.com/sf/, a privately operated site. **Other phones:** Assessor-415-554-5516.

San Joaquin County

County Recorder, PO Box 1968, Stockton, CA 95201. **Phone-**209-468-3939; fax-209-468-8040; hours 8AM-5PM www.co.san-joaquin.ca.us
Will not search records. Record copy- $1.00 per page. Cert fee: $1.00 per page. Payee: San Joaquin County Recorder. **Online Access to Property, Most Wanted, Missing Person records:** Search county property information for free at www.co.san-joaquin.ca.us/commdev/cgi-bin/cdd.exe. No name searching. Sheriff most wanted and missing person pages at http://207.104.50.55/wanted/information.jsp.

Other phones: Assessor-209-468-2630; Treasurer-209-468-2133; Vital Records-803-245-8075.

San Luis Obispo County

County Recorder, 1144 Monterey St, #C, San Luis Obispo, CA 93408. **Phone-**County Recorder, R/E & UCC Recording- 805-781-5080; fax-805-781-1111; hours 8AM-5PM www.sloclerkrecorder.org
There is also a North County office at 5955 Capistrano, #B, Atascadero CA 93422, 805-461-6041. Will search UCC records; mail requests only. Use their UCC-3 form for search requests. Search per debtor- $10.00. UCC copy- $1.00 per page. Will not search real estate or tax lien records. RE record copy- $1.00 per page. Cert fee: $1.00 per cert. Payee: San Luis Obispo County Recorder. **Online Access to Grantor/Grantee, Deed, Judgment, Lien, Real Estate, Mortgage, Divorce, Fictitious Business Name, Missing Person, Most Wanted, Bad Check records:** Search the county recorder database for free at www.sloclerkrecorder.org/recorder/searchform.cfm. Search fictitious names are available at www.sloclerkrecorder.org/countyclerk/fbnstartpage.ht m. Also, search the assessor property tax rolls for free at www.slocoassr.net/#; no name searching. There is also an "unsecured roll" search. Also, search the sheriff's alerts page for missing persons and most wanted at http://slosheriff.org/alerts.php. Check bad check writers at www.sloda.com/page10.html. **Other phones:** Assessor-805-781-5643; Treasurer-805-781-5842; Elections-805-781-5228; Vital Records-805-781-5080.

San Mateo County

County Recorder, 555 County Ctr, 1st Fl, Redwood City, CA 94063. **Phone-**County Recorder, R/E & UCC Recording- 650-363-4713; fax-650-363-4843; hours 8AM-5PM www.care.co.sanmateo.ca.us
Will not search records. Record copy- $2.00 1st page, $1.00 each add'l. Cert fee: $1.00 per cert. Payee: San Mateo County Recorder. **Online Access to Property Tax, Fictitious Name records:** Records on the county property tax data is free online at http://smctweb1.co.sanmateo.ca.us/index.html. Search by address or parcel ID#. There is also a secured property search, but no name searching. Also, search fictitious business names for free at www.care.co.sanmateo.ca.us/business/fictitious/default. asp. **Other phones:** Assessor-650-363-4500; Treasurer-650-363-4840; Appraiser/ Auditor-650-363-4500; Elections-650-312-5222; Vital Records-650-363-4500.

Santa Barbara County

County Recorder, PO Box 159, Santa Barbara, CA 93102-0159. **Phone-**County Recorder, R/E & UCC Recording- 805-568-2250; fax-805-568-2266; hours 8AM-4:30PM www.sb-democracy.com
County also has a branch office in Santa Maria at 511 E Lakeside Pkwy, #115, 93455, 805-346-8370; but that office does not handle recordings. Will not search records. Copy fee is $1.00 per page. Cert fee: $2.00 per cert. Payee: Santa Barbara County Recorder. **Online Access to Assessor, Recorder, Real Estate, Lien, Deed, Vital Statistic, Judgment, Property Tax, Most Wanted records:** Access to assessor online property info system (OPIS) in free at the website with parcel number. Records go back 10 years. Database is free to view but only subscribers will be able to download. Full access requires registration. Contact Larry Herrera for an account. herrera@co.santa-barbara.ca.us. Also, search the records database for free at www.sb-democracy.com/opis/logon.htf. Logon as "public" password "access." Also search property tax bills at http://taxes.co.santa-barbara.ca.us/property tax.asp; click on View/Search Secured Property Tax Bills. No name searching. Search the Sheriff's most wanted list at www.sbsheriff.org/mw/index.html. **Other phones:** Assessor-805-568-2550; Treasurer-805-568-

2490; Appraiser/ Auditor-805-568-2550; Elections-805-568-2200; Vital Records-805-568-2257.

Santa Clara County

County Clerk/Recorder, 70 W. Hedding St, 1st Fl, East Wing, County Gov't Ctr, San Jose, CA 95110. **Phone**-408-299-2481, R/E Recording- 408-299-5667; fax-408-280-1768; hours 8AM-4:30PM www.clerkrecordersearch.org

Will not search UCC records. Tax lien search fee-$15.00 per debtor. Will search by real estate document type in index. RE record copy- $5.00 for the 1st page, $1.00 each add'l. Cert fee: $2.00 per cert. Payee: Santa Clara County Recorder. **Online Access to Recording, Grantor/Grantee, Fictitious Business Name, Assessor, Tax Collector records:** Access to the County Clerk-Recorder database is free at www.clerkrecordersearch.org/cgi-bin/odsmnu1.html/input. Also, search fictitious business names for free at www.clerkrecordersearch.org/cgi-bin/FBNSearch.html/input. Also search the assessment roll free at www.scc-assessor.org/ari/home. No name searching. Also, search the tax collector database at http://payments.scctax.org/payment/jsp/startup.jsp. No name searching. Also, search for county sex offenders at www.sjpd.org/SexOffenders.cfm. **Other phones:** Assessor-408-299-5500; Vital Records-408-299-5669; Official Record Copies-408-299-5670.

Santa Cruz County

County Recorder, 701 Ocean St, Rm 230, Rm 230, Santa Cruz, CA 95060. **Phone**-831-454-2800; fax-831-454-3169; 8AM-4PM www.co.santa-cruz.ca.us/rcd/
Will search UCC records. Search per debtor- $15.00. Copy fee is $1.75 per page. Will not search real estate or tax lien records. Cert fee: $2.50 per cert. Payee: Santa Cruz County Recorder. **Online Access to Assessor, Property Tax, Fictitious Business Name, Recording, Deed, Judgment, Vital Statistic, Inmate records:** Access to the assessor's parcel information data is free at http://sccounty01.co.santa-cruz.ca.us/ASR/. No name searching. Also, search for property information using the GIS map at http://gis.co.santa-cruz.ca.us. Search fictitious business names at http://sccounty01.co.santa-cruz.ca.us/clerkrecorder/Asp/FBNInquiry.asp. Search city business licenses at www.ci.santa-cruz.ca.us/bldb/index.html. Search inmate list at www.vinelink.com/offender/searchNew.jsp?siteID=5099. Also, access to the recorder's official records is free at http://sccounty01.co.santa-cruz.ca.us/clerkrecorder/Asp/ORInquiry.asp. Online indexes go back to 1978. Births, Deaths, and Marriages are also searchable back to 1984. **Other phones:** Assessor-831-454-2002; Elections-831-454-2060.

Shasta County

County Recorder, 1500 Court St, Rm 102, Redding, CA 96001. **Phone**-530-225-5671; fax-530-225-5152; hours 8AM-5PM www.co.shasta.ca.us
Will not search records. Record copy- $1.00 1st page; $.50 each add'l. Cert fee: $1.00 per doc. Payee: Shasta County Recorder. **Online Access to Assessor, Recorder, Real Estate, Vital Statistic records:** Search assessor and recorded documents at www.co.shasta.ca.us/Departments/AssessorRecorder/PubInqDisclaimer.shtml Also, a private site lists various birth, death, and marriage records of the county at http://myclouds.tripod.com/shasta/shastaco.html. Records on the City of Redding Parcel Search By Parcel Number Server are free at http://cor400.ci.redding.ca.us/nd/gow3lkap.ndm/input. CA state law has now removed owner names. **Other phones:** Assessor-530-225-3600.

Sierra County

County Recorder, PO Drawer D, Downieville, CA 95936. **Phone**-County Recorder, R/E & UCC Recording- 530-289-3295; hours 9AM-Noon,1-4PM www.sierracounty.ws
Will search UCC records. Search per debtor- $5.00. Copy fee is $1.00 per page. Will not search tax liens. Real estate record owner searches available. RE record copy- $1.00 per page. Cert fee: $1.75 per cert. Payee: Sierra County Recorder. **Online Access to Tax Sale records:** Access to tax sales lists is free through a private company at www.bid4assets.com. **Other phones:** Assessor-530-289-3283; Treasurer-530-289-3286; Appraiser/ Auditor-530-289-3283; Elections-530-289-3295; Vital Records-530-289-3295.

Siskiyou County

County Recorder, PO Box 8, Yreka, CA 96097. **Phone**-530-842-8065; fax-530-842-8077; hours 8AM-4PM
Will not search records. Cert fee: $1.00 per doc. Payee: Siskiyou County Recorder. **Online Access to Recording, Deed, Lien, Land, Fictitious Business Name, Tax Sale records:** Access to the Recorder records database is available free at www.criis.com/siskiyou/srecord_current.shtml. Also, access to the fictitious names database is at www.criis.com/siskiyou/sfictitious.shtml. Also, access to tax sales lists is free through a private company at www.bid4assets.com. **Other phones:** Assessor-530-842-8036; Vital Records-530-842-8065.

Solano County

County Recorder, 701 Texas St, Fairfield, CA 94533. **Phone**-County Recorder, R/E & UCC Recording- 707-421-6290; fax-707-421-6911; hours 8AM-4PM; 8AM-3:30PM recording hours; copies 8AM-3P www.solanocounty.com
Will not search UCC or tax line records. Copy fee is $4.00 for 1st page; $2.00 each add'l. Real estate owner, mortgage, and property transfer searches available. Searches only performed to 1974 and only if searcher is purchasing copies. Cert fee: $4.00 per cert. Payee: Solano County Recorders Office. **Online Access to Property Tax, Recording, Grantor/Grantee, Deed, Judgment, Lien, Death, Inmate records:** recorder's and assessor's indexes are free at www.solanocounty.com/assessrecord/. Also, search the treasurer/tax collector/county clerk property tax database free at www.solanocounty.com/resources/scips/tax/situssearch.asp?navid=531. No name searching. Also, search the county jail inmate list at www.vinelink.com/offender/searchNew.jsp?siteID=5099. **Other phones:** Assessor-707-421-6200; Treasurer-707-421-7485; Appraiser/ Auditor-707-421-6210; Elections-707-421-7485; Vital Records-707-421-6294.

Sonoma County

County Recorder, PO Box 1709, Santa Rosa, CA 95406-1709. **Phone**-707-565-2651; fax-707-565-3905; hours 8AM-4:30PM www.sonoma-county.org/
Will not search UCC records or tax liens. Separate federal/state combined tax lien search- $15.00 per debtor. Will not search real estate records. Record copy- $1.75 per page. Cert fee: $2.00 per doc. Payee: Sonoma County Recorder. **Other phones:** Assessor-707-565-1888.

Stanislaus County

County Recorder, PO Box 1008, Modesto, CA 95353. **Phone**-County Recorder, R/E & UCC Recording- 209-525-5260; fax-209-525-5207; hours 8AM-Noon,1-4PM www.co.stanislaus.ca.us
Assessor is located at 1010 10th St. #2400. Will search UCC records. Search per debtor- $8.00. Copy fee is $3.00 1st page, $2.00 each add'l. Will not search real estate or tax lien records. RE copy- $3.00 per page. Cert fee: $2.00 per doc. Payee: Stanislaus

County Recorder. **Online Access to Recording, Fictitious Name, Deed, Lien, Land, Most Wanted, Missing Person records:** Recorder office records index of recent records are free at www.criis.com/stanislaus/srecord_current.shtml. Birth, death and marriage records have been removed from the internet. County Fictitious Business Name records are at www.criis.com/stanislaus/sfictitious.shtml. Also, search sheriff's missing persons and most wanted lists at www.stanislaussheriff.com/crimebulletin/. **Other phones:** Assessor-209-525-6461; Elections-209-525-5200; Vital Records-209-525-5291.

Sutter County

County Recorder, PO Box 1555, Yuba City, CA 95992-1555. **Phone**-County Recorder, R/E & UCC Recording- 530-822-7134; fax-530-822-7214; hours 8AM-5PM www.suttercounty.org
Will not search records. Record copy- $1.25 per page. Cert fee: $2.25 per doc. Payee: Sutter County Recorder. **Online Access to Recorder, Grantor/Grantee, Real Estate, Fictitious Name records:** Access to the recorder's database is free at www.suttercounty.org/apps/RecordsQuery/. Records go back to 12/29/1994. **Other phones:** Assessor-530-822-7160; Treasurer-530-822-7117; Appraiser/ Auditor-530-822-7160; Elections-530-822-7120; Vital Records-530-822-7134.

Tehama County

County Recorder, PO Box 250, Red Bluff, CA 96080. **Phone**-County Recorder, R/E & UCC Recording- 530-527-3350; fax-530-527-1745; hours 8AM-5PM www.tehamacountyadmin.org
Will not search records. Copy fee is $1.50 per page. Cert fee: $1.50 per cert. Payee: Tehama County Recorder. **Online Access to Inmate records:** Access to the county sheriff inmate list is at www.tehamaso.org/inmates/ICURRENT.HTM. **Other phones:** Assessor-530-527-5931; Treasurer-530-527-4535; Appraiser/ Auditor-530-527-5931; Elections-530-527-8190; Vital Records-530-527-3350.

Trinity County

County Recorder, PO Box 1215, Weaverville, CA 96093-1258. **Phone**-530-623-1215; fax-530-623-8398; 8AM-5PM www.trinitycounty.org/Departments/assessor-clerk-elect/clerkrecorder.htm
Will not search records. Copy fee is $1.25 per page. Cert fee: $2.00 per cert. Payee: Trinity County Recorder. **Online Access to Fictitious Business Name records:** Access to the Recorder's fictitous business names database is available free at http://halfile.trinitycounty.org. For user name, enter "fbn"; leave password field empty. **Other phones:** Assessor-530-623-1257; Treasurer-530-623-1251; Elections-530-623-1220; Vital Records-530-623-1215.

Tulare County

County Recorder, 221 S. Mooney Blvd., County Civic Ctr, Rm 103, Visalia, CA 93291-4593. **Phone**-559-733-6377; fax-559-740-4329; hours 8AM-5PM; (recording hours 8AM-3PM) www.co.tulare.ca.us
Will search UCC records. Search per debtor- $15.00. Will not search real estate or tax lien records. Payee: Tulare County Recorder. **Online Access to Recording, Deed, Judgment, Lien, Vital Statistic, Fictitious Name records:** Search the recorders database including births, marriages, deaths for free at http://209.78.90.65/riimsweb/orinquiry.asp. **Other phones:** Assessor-559-733-6361; Elections-559-733-6377.

Tuolumne County

County Recorder, 2 S. Green St, County Admin. Ctr, Sonora, CA 95370. **Phone**-209-533-5531; fax-209-533-6543; hours 8AM-5PM

Will search UCC records. Copy fee is $3.00 per page. Will not search real estate or tax lien records. RE record copy- $2.00 1st page, $1.00 per add'l. Cert fee: $1.00 per doc. Payee: Tuolumne County Recorder. **Other phones:** Assessor-209-533-5535; Treasurer-209-533-5544; Appraiser/ Auditor-209-533-5535; Elections-209-533-5570; Vital Records-209-533-5531.

Ventura County

County Recorder, 800 S. Victoria Ave, Government Ctr, Ventura, CA 93009. **Phone**-805-654-2292, R/E Recording- 805-654-3665, UCC Recording- 805-654-3665; fax- 805-654-2392; hours 8AM-4PM www.countyofventura.org
Will not search UCC records; copy fee is $3.00 per page. Will not search real estate or tax lien records. RE record copy- $2.00 1st page, $1.00 each add'l. Cert fee: $3.00 for 1st page; $1.00 each add'l. Payee: Ventura County Recorder. **Online Access to Recording, Fictitious Name, Birth, Death, Marriage,**

Most Wanted, Property Tax records: Access to the county clerks database is free. Also, search property tax data for free at http://prop-tax.countyofventura.org/pisearch.asp; no name searching. Also, the county most wanted list is at www.vcsd.org/wanted_main.htm.
Other phones: Assessor-805-654-2181; Treasurer-805-654-3735; Vital Records-805-654-3666.

Yolo County

County Recorder, PO Box 1130, Woodland, CA 95776-1130. **Phone**-530-666-8130; fax-530-666-8109; hours 8AM-4PM www.yolocounty.org/org/Recorder
Will not search records. Copy fee is $3.50 for 1st page; $.50 each add'l. Cert fee: $2.00 per cert. Payee: Yolo County Recorder. **Online Access to Assessor, Birth, Death, Marriage, Fictitious Business Name, Davis Cemetery records:**
Access to recordings on the county clerk database are free at www.criis.com/yolo/srecord_current.shtml. Marriage records at www.criis.com/yolo/smarriage.shtml. County Fictitious Business Name records are

at www.criis.com/yolo/sfictitious.shtml. County Birth records Death records have been removed from the Internet. Also, City of Davis business licenses are free at www.city.davis.ca.us/ed/business/. Davis Cemetery District search is free at http://www2.dcn.org/orgs/cemetery. **Other phones:** Assessor-530-666-8135; Treasurer-530-666-8625.

Yuba County

County Recorder, 915 8th St #107, Marysville, CA 95901. **Phone**-530-741-6547, R/E Recording- 530-749-7850; fax-530-749-7854; hours 8AM-5PM
Will search UCC records. Search per debtor- $10.00. Copy fee is $2.00 for 1st page; $.50 each add'l. Will not search real estate or tax lien records. RE record copy- $2.00 1st page; $.50 each add'l. Cert fee: $1.50 per cert. Payee: Yuba County Recorder. **Other phones:** Assessor-530-749-7820; Treasurer-530-749-7840; Elections-530-749-7855; Vital Records-530-749-7850; Clerk-530-749-7851.

California County Locator

You will usually be able to find the city name in the City/County Cross Reference below. In that case, it is a simple matter to determine the county from the cross reference. However, only the official US Postal Service city names are included in this index. There are an additional 40,000 place names that people use in their addresses. Therefore, we have also included a ZIP/City Cross Reference immediately following the City/County Cross Reference.

If you know the ZIP Code but the city name does not appear in the City/County Cross Reference index, look up the ZIP Code in the ZIP/City Cross Reference, find the city name, then look up the city name in the City/County Cross Reference. For example, you want to know the county for an address of Menands, NY 12204. There is no "Menands" in the City/County Cross Reference. The ZIP/City Cross Reference shows that ZIP Codes 12201-12288 are for the city of Albany. Looking back in the City/County Cross Reference, Albany is in Albany County.

California City/County Cross Reference

ACAMPO San Joaquin
ACTON Los Angeles
ADELANTO San Bernardino
ADIN (96006) Modoc(66), Lassen(33)
AGOURA HILLS Los Angeles
AGUANGA Riverside
AHWAHNEE (93601) Madera(96), Mariposa(3)
ALAMEDA Alameda
ALAMO Contra Costa
ALBANY Alameda
ALBION Mendocino
ALDERPOINT Humboldt
ALHAMBRA Los Angeles
ALISO VIEJO Orange
ALLEGHANY Sierra
ALPAUGH Tulare
ALPINE San Diego
ALTA Placer
ALTA LOMA San Bernardino
ALTADENA Los Angeles
ALTAVILLE Calaveras
ALTURAS Modoc
ALVISO Santa Clara
AMADOR CITY Amador
AMBOY San Bernardino
AMERICAN CANYON Napa
ANAHEIM Orange
ANDERSON Shasta
ANGELS CAMP Calaveras
ANGELUS OAKS San Bernardino
ANGWIN Napa
ANNAPOLIS Sonoma
ANTELOPE Sacramento
ANTIOCH Contra Costa
ANZA Riverside
APPLE VALLEY San Bernardino
APPLEGATE Placer
APTOS Santa Cruz
ARBUCKLE (95912) Colusa(98), Yolo(1)
ARCADIA Los Angeles
ARCATA Humboldt
ARMONA Kings
ARNOLD Calaveras
AROMAS (95004) Monterey(53), San Benito(46)
ARROYO GRANDE San Luis Obispo
ARTESIA Los Angeles
ARTOIS Glenn
ARVIN Kern
ATASCADERO San Luis Obispo
ATHERTON San Mateo
ATWATER Merced
ATWOOD Orange
AUBERRY Fresno
AUBURN (95602) Placer(73), Nevada(26)
AUBURN Placer
AVALON Los Angeles
AVENAL Kings
AVERY Calaveras
AVILA BEACH San Luis Obispo
AZUSA Los Angeles
BADGER Tulare
BAKER San Bernardino

BAKERSFIELD Kern
BALDWIN PARK Los Angeles
BALLICO Merced
BANGOR (95914) Butte(90), Yuba(10)
BANNING Riverside
BANTA San Joaquin
BARD Imperial
BARSTOW San Bernardino
BASS LAKE Madera
BAYSIDE Humboldt
BEALE AFB Yuba
BEAUMONT Riverside
BECKWOURTH Plumas
BELDEN Plumas
BELL Los Angeles
BELL GARDENS Los Angeles
BELLA VISTA Shasta
BELLFLOWER Los Angeles
BELMONT San Mateo
BELVEDERE TIBURON Marin
BEN LOMOND Santa Cruz
BENICIA Solano
BENTON Mono
BERKELEY (94708) Alameda(83), Contra Costa(16)
BERKELEY Alameda
BERRY CREEK Butte
BETHEL ISLAND Contra Costa
BEVERLY HILLS Los Angeles
BIEBER Lassen
BIG BAR Trinity
BIG BEAR CITY San Bernardino
BIG BEAR LAKE San Bernardino
BIG BEND Shasta
BIG CREEK Fresno
BIG OAK FLAT Tuolumne
BIG PINE Inyo
BIG SUR Monterey
BIGGS Butte
BIOLA Fresno
BIRDS LANDING Solano
BISHOP (93514) Inyo(93), Mono(6)
BISHOP Inyo
BLAIRSDEN-GRAEAGLE Plumas
BLOCKSBURG Humboldt
BLOOMINGTON San Bernardino
BLUE JAY San Bernardino
BLUE LAKE Humboldt
BLYTHE Riverside
BODEGA Sonoma
BODEGA BAY Sonoma
BODFISH Kern
BOLINAS Marin
BONITA San Diego
BONSALL San Diego
BOONVILLE Mendocino
BORON (93516) Kern(93), San Bernardino(6)
BORON Kern
BORREGO SPRINGS (92004) San Diego(94), Imperial(5)
BOULDER CREEK Santa Cruz
BOULEVARD San Diego
BOYES HOT SPRINGS Sonoma

BRADLEY (93426) Monterey(69), San Luis Obispo(30)
BRANDEIS Ventura
BRANSCOMB Mendocino
BRAWLEY Imperial
BREA Orange
BRENTWOOD Contra Costa
BRIDGEPORT Mono
BRIDGEVILLE (95526) Humboldt(90), Trinity(10)
BRISBANE San Mateo
BROOKDALE Santa Cruz
BROOKS Yolo
BROWNS VALLEY Yuba
BROWNSVILLE Yuba
BRYN MAWR San Bernardino
BUELLTON Santa Barbara
BUENA PARK Orange
BURBANK Los Angeles
BURLINGAME San Mateo
BURNEY Shasta
BURNT RANCH Trinity
BURREL Fresno
BURSON Calaveras
BUTTE CITY Glenn
BUTTONWILLOW Kern
BYRON (94514) Contra Costa(89), Alameda(9), San Joaquin(1)
CABAZON Riverside
CADIZ San Bernardino
CALABASAS Los Angeles
CALEXICO Imperial
CALIENTE Kern
CALIFORNIA CITY Kern
CALIFORNIA HOT SPRINGS Tulare
CALIMESA Riverside
CALIPATRIA Imperial
CALISTOGA (94515) Napa(88), Sonoma(11)
CALLAHAN Siskiyou
CALPELLA Mendocino
CALPINE Sierra
CAMARILLO Ventura
CAMBRIA San Luis Obispo
CAMINO El Dorado
CAMP MEEKER Sonoma
CAMP NELSON Tulare
CAMP PENDLETON San Diego
CAMPBELL Santa Clara
CAMPO San Diego
CAMPO SECO Calaveras
CAMPTONVILLE (95922) Yuba(85), Sierra(14)
CANBY Modoc
CANOGA PARK Los Angeles
CANTIL Kern
CANTUA CREEK Fresno
CANYON Contra Costa
CANYON COUNTRY Los Angeles
CANYONDAM Plumas
CAPAY Yolo
CAPISTRANO BEACH Orange
CAPITOLA Santa Cruz
CARDIFF BY THE SEA San Diego

CARLOTTA Humboldt
CARLSBAD San Diego
CARMEL Monterey
CARMEL VALLEY Monterey
CARMICHAEL Sacramento
CARNELIAN BAY Placer
CARPINTERIA Santa Barbara
CARSON Los Angeles
CARUTHERS Fresno
CASMALIA Santa Barbara
CASPAR Mendocino
CASSEL Shasta
CASTAIC Los Angeles
CASTELLA Shasta
CASTRO VALLEY Alameda
CASTROVILLE Monterey
CATHEDRAL CITY Riverside
CATHEYS VALLEY Mariposa
CAYUCOS San Luis Obispo
CAZADERO Sonoma
CEDAR GLEN San Bernardino
CEDAR RIDGE Nevada
CEDARPINES PARK San Bernardino
CEDARVILLE Modoc
CERES Stanislaus
CERRITOS Los Angeles
CHALLENGE (95925) Butte(56), Yuba(43)
CHATSWORTH (91311) Los Angeles(98), Ventura(1)
CHATSWORTH Los Angeles
CHESTER Plumas
CHICAGO PARK Nevada
CHICO Butte
CHILCOOT Plumas
CHINESE CAMP Tuolumne
CHINO San Bernardino
CHINO HILLS San Bernardino
CHOLAME San Luis Obispo
CHOWCHILLA (93610) Madera(97), Merced(2)
CHUALAR Monterey
CHULA VISTA San Diego
CIMA San Bernardino
CITRUS HEIGHTS Sacramento
CITY OF INDUSTRY Los Angeles
CLAREMONT Los Angeles
CLARKSBURG Yolo
CLAYTON Contra Costa
CLEARLAKE Lake
CLEARLAKE OAKS Lake
CLEARLAKE PARK Lake
CLEMENTS San Joaquin
CLIO Plumas
CLIPPER MILLS Butte
CLOVERDALE (95425) Sonoma(98), Mendocino(1)
CLOVIS Fresno
COACHELLA Riverside
COALINGA Fresno
COARSEGOLD Madera
COBB Lake
COLEVILLE Mono
COLFAX Placer
COLLEGE CITY Colusa

COLOMA El Dorado
COLTON (92324) San Bernardino(96), Riverside(3)
COLUMBIA Tuolumne
COLUSA Colusa
COMPTCHE Mendocino
COMPTON Los Angeles
CONCORD Contra Costa
COOL El Dorado
COPPEROPOLIS Calaveras
CORCORAN (93212) Kings(97), Tulare(2)
CORNING Tehama
CORONA (92880) Riverside(98), San Bernardino(1)
CORONA Riverside
CORONA DEL MAR Orange
CORONADO San Diego
CORTE MADERA Marin
COSTA MESA Orange
COTATI Sonoma
COTTONWOOD (96022) Tehama(51), Shasta(48)
COULTERVILLE (95311) Mariposa(92), Tuolumne(7)
COURTLAND Sacramento
COVELO Mendocino
COVINA Los Angeles
COYOTE Santa Clara
CRESCENT CITY Del Norte
CRESCENT MILLS Plumas
CRESSEY Merced
CREST PARK San Bernardino
CRESTLINE San Bernardino
CRESTON San Luis Obispo
CROCKER NAT BANK San Francisco
CROCKETT Contra Costa
CROWS LANDING Stanislaus
CULVER CITY Los Angeles
CUPERTINO Santa Clara
CUTLER Tulare
CUTTEN Humboldt
CUYAMA Santa Barbara
CYPRESS Orange
DAGGETT San Bernardino
DALY CITY San Mateo
DANA POINT Orange
DANVILLE Contra Costa
DARDANELLE Tuolumne
DARWIN Inyo
DAVENPORT Santa Cruz
DAVIS Yolo
DAVIS CREEK Modoc
DEATH VALLEY Inyo
DEER PARK Napa
DEL MAR San Diego
DEL REY Fresno
DELANO (93215) Kern(92), Tulare(7)
DELANO Kern
DELHI Merced
DENAIR Stanislaus
DESCANSO San Diego
DESERT CENTER Riverside
DESERT HOT SPRINGS Riverside
DI GIORGIO Kern
DIABLO Contra Costa
DIAMOND BAR Los Angeles
DIAMOND SPRINGS El Dorado
DILLON BEACH Marin
DINUBA (93618) Tulare(98), Fresno(1)
DIXON Solano
DOBBINS Yuba
DORRIS Siskiyou
DOS PALOS (93620) Merced(85), Fresno(14)
DOS RIOS Mendocino
DOUGLAS CITY Trinity
DOUGLAS FLAT Calaveras
DOWNEY Los Angeles
DOWNIEVILLE Sierra
DOYLE Lassen
DRYTOWN Amador
DUARTE Los Angeles
DUBLIN Alameda

DUCOR Tulare
DULZURA San Diego
DUNCANS MILLS Sonoma
DUNLAP Fresno
DUNNIGAN Yolo
DUNSMUIR (96025) Siskiyou(93), Shasta(6)
DURHAM Butte
DUTCH FLAT Placer
EAGLEVILLE Modoc
EARLIMART Tulare
EARP San Bernardino
EAST IRVINE Orange
ECHO LAKE El Dorado
EDISON Kern
EDWARDS Kern
EL CAJON San Diego
EL CENTRO Imperial
EL CERRITO Contra Costa
EL DORADO El Dorado
EL DORADO HILLS El Dorado
EL GRANADA San Mateo
EL MACERO Yolo
EL MONTE Los Angeles
EL NIDO Merced
EL PORTAL Mariposa
EL SEGUNDO Los Angeles
EL SOBRANTE Contra Costa
EL TORO Orange
EL VERANO Sonoma
ELDRIDGE Sonoma
ELK Mendocino
ELK CREEK (95939) Glenn(94), Colusa(5)
ELK GROVE Sacramento
ELMIRA Solano
ELVERTA (95626) Sacramento(84), Placer(12), Sutter(2)
EMERYVILLE Alameda
EMIGRANT GAP Placer
EMPIRE Stanislaus
ENCINITAS San Diego
ENCINO Los Angeles
ESCALON San Joaquin
ESCONDIDO San Diego
ESPARTO Yolo
ESSEX San Bernardino
ETNA Siskiyou
EUREKA Humboldt
EXETER Tulare
FAIR OAKS Sacramento
FAIRFAX Marin
FAIRFIELD Solano
FALL RIVER MILLS Shasta
FALLBROOK San Diego
FARMERSVILLE Tulare
FARMINGTON (95230) Stanislaus(34), San Joaquin(33), Calaveras(28), Tuolumne(2)
FAWNSKIN San Bernardino
FEATHER FALLS Butte
FELLOWS Kern
FELTON Santa Cruz
FERNDALE Humboldt
FIDDLETOWN (95629) El Dorado(75), Amador(24)
FIELDS LANDING Humboldt
FILLMORE Ventura
FINLEY Lake
FIREBAUGH (93622) Fresno(89), Madera(8), Merced(2)
FISH CAMP (93623) Mariposa(81), Madera(18)
FIVE POINTS Fresno
FLORISTON Nevada
FLOURNOY Tehama
FOLSOM Sacramento
FONTANA San Bernardino
FOOTHILL RANCH Orange
FORBESTOWN (95941) Butte(84), Yuba(15)
FOREST FALLS San Bernardino
FOREST KNOLLS Marin
FOREST RANCH Butte

FORESTHILL Placer
FORESTVILLE Sonoma
FORKS OF SALMON Siskiyou
FORT BIDWELL Modoc
FORT BRAGG Mendocino
FORT DICK Del Norte
FORT IRWIN San Bernardino
FORT JONES Siskiyou
FORT ORD Monterey
FORTUNA Humboldt
FOUNTAIN VALLEY Orange
FOWLER Fresno
FRAZIER PARK Kern
FREEDOM Santa Cruz
FREMONT Alameda
FRENCH CAMP San Joaquin
FRENCH GULCH Shasta
FRESNO Fresno
FRIANT (93626) Fresno(58), Madera(41)
FT ORD Monterey
FULLERTON Orange
FULTON Sonoma
GALT (95632) Sacramento(95), San Joaquin(4)
GARBERVILLE Humboldt
GARDEN GROVE Orange
GARDEN VALLEY El Dorado
GARDENA Los Angeles
GASQUET (95543) Del Norte(98), Trinity(2)
GAZELLE Siskiyou
GEORGETOWN El Dorado
GERBER Tehama
GEYSERVILLE Sonoma
GILROY Santa Clara
GLEN ELLEN Sonoma
GLENCOE Calaveras
GLENDALE Los Angeles
GLENDORA Los Angeles
GLENHAVEN Lake
GLENN Glenn
GLENNVILLE Kern
GOLD RUN Placer
GOLETA Santa Barbara
GONZALES Monterey
GOODYEARS BAR Sierra
GOSHEN Tulare
GRANADA HILLS Los Angeles
GRAND TERRACE San Bernardino
GRANITE BAY Placer
GRASS VALLEY Nevada
GRATON Sonoma
GREEN VALLEY LAKE San Bernardino
GREENBRAE Marin
GREENFIELD Monterey
GREENVIEW Siskiyou
GREENVILLE Plumas
GREENWOOD El Dorado
GRENADA Siskiyou
GRIDLEY Butte
GRIMES Colusa
GRIZZLY FLATS El Dorado
GROVELAND (95321) Tuolumne(97), Mariposa(2)
GROVER BEACH San Luis Obispo
GUADALUPE Santa Barbara
GUALALA Mendocino
GUASTI San Bernardino
GUATAY San Diego
GUERNEVILLE Sonoma
GUINDA Yolo
GUSTINE Merced
HACIENDA HEIGHTS Los Angeles
HALF MOON BAY San Mateo
HAMILTON CITY Glenn
HANFORD Kings
HAPPY CAMP Siskiyou
HARBOR CITY Los Angeles
HARMONY San Luis Obispo
HAT CREEK Shasta
HATHAWAY PINES Calaveras
HAWAIIAN GARDENS Los Angeles
HAWTHORNE Los Angeles
HAYFORK Trinity

HAYWARD Alameda
HEALDSBURG Sonoma
HEBER Imperial
HELENDALE San Bernardino
HELM Fresno
HEMET Riverside
HERALD Sacramento
HERCULES Contra Costa
HERLONG Lassen
HERMOSA BEACH Los Angeles
HESPERIA San Bernardino
HICKMAN Stanislaus
HIDDEN VALLEY LAKE Lake
HIGHLAND San Bernardino
HILMAR Merced
HINKLEY San Bernardino
HOLLISTER San Benito
HOLT San Joaquin
HOLTVILLE Imperial
HOLY CITY Santa Clara
HOMELAND Riverside
HOMEWOOD Placer
HONEYDEW Humboldt
HOOD Sacramento
HOOPA Humboldt
HOPLAND Mendocino
HORNBROOK Siskiyou
HORNITOS Mariposa
HORSE CREEK Siskiyou
HUGHSON Stanislaus
HUME Fresno
HUNTINGTON BEACH Orange
HUNTINGTON LAKE Fresno
HUNTINGTON PARK Los Angeles
HURON Fresno
HYAMPOM Trinity
HYDESVILLE Humboldt
IDYLLWILD Riverside
IGO Shasta
IMPERIAL Imperial
IMPERIAL BEACH San Diego
INDEPENDENCE Inyo
INDIAN WELLS Riverside
INDIO Riverside
INGLEWOOD Los Angeles
INVERNESS Marin
INYOKERN (93527) Kern(93), Inyo(3), Tulare(2)
IONE Amador
IRVINE Orange
ISLETON Sacramento
IVANHOE Tulare
JACKSON Amador
JACUMBA San Diego
JAMESTOWN Tuolumne
JAMUL San Diego
JANESVILLE Lassen
JENNER Sonoma
JOHANNESBURG Kern
JOLON Monterey
JOSHUA TREE San Bernardino
JULIAN San Diego
JUNCTION CITY Trinity
JUNE LAKE Mono
KAWEAH Tulare
KEELER Inyo
KEENE Kern
KELSEYVILLE Lake
KENTFIELD Marin
KENWOOD Sonoma
KERMAN Fresno
KERNVILLE (93238) Kern(89), Tulare(10)
KETTLEMAN CITY Kings
KEYES Stanislaus
KING CITY Monterey
KINGS BEACH Placer
KINGS CANYON NATIONAL PK Tulare
KINGSBURG (93631) Fresno(83), Tulare(11), Kings(4)
KIRKWOOD Alpine
KIT CARSON Amador
KLAMATH Del Norte
KLAMATH RIVER Siskiyou

KNEELAND Humboldt
KNIGHTS LANDING (95645) Sutter(84), Yolo(15)
KNIGHTSEN Contra Costa
KORBEL Humboldt
KYBURZ El Dorado
LA CANADA FLINTRIDGE Los Angeles
LA COUNTY TAX COLLECTOR Los Angeles
LA CRESCENTA Los Angeles
LA GRANGE (95329) Tuolumne(57), Mariposa(34), Stanislaus(8)
LA HABRA (90631) Orange(87), Los Angeles(12)
LA HABRA Orange
LA HONDA San Mateo
LA JOLLA San Diego
LA MESA San Diego
LA MIRADA (90638) Los Angeles(98), Orange(1)
LA MIRADA Los Angeles
LA PALMA Orange
LA PUENTE Los Angeles
LA QUINTA Riverside
LA VERNE Los Angeles
LADERA RANCH Orange
LAFAYETTE Contra Costa
LAGUNA BEACH Orange
LAGUNA HILLS Orange
LAGUNA NIGUEL Orange
LAGUNITAS Marin
LAKE ARROWHEAD San Bernardino
LAKE CITY Modoc
LAKE ELSINORE Riverside
LAKE FOREST Orange
LAKE HUGHES Los Angeles
LAKE ISABELLA Kern
LAKEHEAD Shasta
LAKEPORT Lake
LAKESHORE Fresno
LAKESIDE San Diego
LAKEVIEW Riverside
LAKEWOOD Los Angeles
LAMONT Kern
LANCASTER Los Angeles
LANDERS San Bernardino
LARKSPUR Marin
LATHROP San Joaquin
LATON (93242) Fresno(84), Kings(15)
LAWNDALE Los Angeles
LAYTONVILLE Mendocino
LE GRAND Merced
LEBEC (93243) Kern(73), Los Angeles(26)
LEE VINING Mono
LEGGETT Mendocino
LEMON COVE Tulare
LEMON GROVE San Diego
LEMOORE Kings
LEWISTON Trinity
LIKELY Modoc
LINCOLN Placer
LINCOLN ACRES San Diego
LINDEN (95236) San Joaquin(95), Calaveras(4)
LINDSAY Tulare
LITCHFIELD Lassen
LITTLE LAKE Inyo
LITTLERIVER Mendocino
LITTLEROCK Los Angeles
LIVE OAK Sutter
LIVERMORE (94551) Alameda(97), Contra Costa(2)
LIVERMORE Alameda
LIVINGSTON Merced
LLANO Los Angeles
LOCKEFORD San Joaquin
LOCKWOOD Monterey
LODI San Joaquin
LOLETA Humboldt
LOMA LINDA San Bernardino
LOMA MAR San Mateo
LOMITA Los Angeles
LOMPOC Santa Barbara

LONE PINE Inyo
LONG BARN Tuolumne
LONG BEACH Los Angeles
LOOKOUT Modoc
LOOMIS Placer
LOS ALAMITOS Orange
LOS ALAMOS Santa Barbara
LOS ALTOS Santa Clara
LOS ANGELES Los Angeles
LOS BANOS Merced
LOS GATOS (95033) Santa Cruz(66), Santa Clara(33)
LOS GATOS Santa Clara
LOS MOLINOS Tehama
LOS OLIVOS Santa Barbara
LOS OSOS San Luis Obispo
LOST HILLS Kern
LOTUS El Dorado
LOWER LAKE Lake
LOYALTON Sierra
LUCERNE Lake
LUCERNE VALLEY San Bernardino
LUDLOW San Bernardino
LYNWOOD Los Angeles
LYOTH San Joaquin
LYTLE CREEK San Bernardino
MACDOEL Siskiyou
MAD RIVER Trinity
MADELINE Lassen
MADERA Madera
MADISON Yolo
MAGALIA Butte
MALIBU (90265) Los Angeles(94), Ventura(5)
MALIBU Los Angeles
MAMMOTH LAKES Mono
MANCHESTER Mendocino
MANHATTAN BEACH Los Angeles
MANTECA San Joaquin
MANTON (96059) Tehama(67), Shasta(32)
MARCH AIR FORCE BASE Riverside
MARICOPA (93252) Kern(60), Santa Barbara(24), Ventura(12), San Luis Obispo(2)
MARINA Monterey
MARINA DEL REY Los Angeles
MARIPOSA Mariposa
MARKLEEVILLE Alpine
MARSHALL Marin
MARTELL Amador
MARTINEZ Contra Costa
MARYSVILLE Yuba
MATHER Sacramento
MAXWELL Colusa
MAYWOOD Los Angeles
MC FARLAND Kern
MC KITTRICK Kern
MCARTHUR (96056) Lassen(54), Shasta(31), Modoc(14)
MCARTHUR Lassen
MCCLELLAN Sacramento
MCCLELLAN AFB Sacramento
MCCLOUD Siskiyou
MCKINLEYVILLE Humboldt
MEADOW VALLEY Plumas
MEADOW VISTA Placer
MECCA Riverside
MENDOCINO Mendocino
MENDOTA Fresno
MENIFEE Riverside
MENLO PARK San Mateo
MENTONE San Bernardino
MERCED Merced
MERIDIAN (95957) Sutter(97), Colusa(2)
MI WUK VILLAGE Tuolumne
MIDDLETOWN Lake
MIDPINES Mariposa
MIDWAY CITY Orange
MILFORD Lassen
MILL CREEK Tehama
MILL VALLEY Marin
MILLBRAE San Mateo
MILLVILLE Shasta

MILPITAS Santa Clara
MINERAL Tehama
MIRA LOMA Riverside
MIRAMONTE (93641) Fresno(90), Tulare(10)
MIRANDA Humboldt
MISSION HILLS Los Angeles
MISSION VIEJO Orange
MOBIL OIL CREDIT CORPORATION Contra Costa
MOCCASIN Tuolumne
MODESTO Stanislaus
MOJAVE Kern
MOKELUMNE HILL Calaveras
MONO HOT SPRINGS Fresno
MONROVIA Los Angeles
MONTAGUE Siskiyou
MONTARA San Mateo
MONTCLAIR San Bernardino
MONTE RIO Sonoma
MONTEBELLO Los Angeles
MONTEREY Monterey
MONTEREY PARK Los Angeles
MONTGOMERY CREEK Shasta
MONTGOMERY WARD Contra Costa
MONTROSE Los Angeles
MOORPARK Ventura
MORAGA Contra Costa
MORENO VALLEY Riverside
MORGAN HILL Santa Clara
MORONGO VALLEY San Bernardino
MORRO BAY San Luis Obispo
MOSS BEACH San Mateo
MOSS LANDING Monterey
MOUNT AUKUM El Dorado
MOUNT HAMILTON Santa Clara
MOUNT HERMON Santa Cruz
MOUNT LAGUNA San Diego
MOUNT SHASTA Siskiyou
MOUNT WILSON Los Angeles
MOUNTAIN CENTER Riverside
MOUNTAIN PASS San Bernardino
MOUNTAIN RANCH Calaveras
MOUNTAIN VIEW Santa Clara
MT BALDY Los Angeles
MURPHYS Calaveras
MURRIETA Riverside
MYERS FLAT Humboldt
NAPA Napa
NATIONAL CITY San Diego
NAVARRO Mendocino
NEEDLES San Bernardino
NELSON Butte
NESTOR San Diego
NEVADA CITY Nevada
NEW ALMADEN Santa Clara
NEW CUYAMA Santa Barbara
NEWARK Alameda
NEWBERRY SPRINGS San Bernardino
NEWBURY PARK Ventura
NEWCASTLE Placer
NEWHALL Los Angeles
NEWMAN Stanislaus
NEWPORT BEACH Orange
NEWPORT COAST Orange
NICASIO Marin
NICE Lake
NICOLAUS Sutter
NILAND Imperial
NIPOMO San Luis Obispo
NIPTON San Bernardino
NORCO Riverside
NORDEN Nevada
NORTH FORK Madera
NORTH HIGHLANDS Sacramento
NORTH HILLS Los Angeles
NORTH HOLLYWOOD Los Angeles
NORTH PALM SPRINGS Riverside
NORTH SAN JUAN (95960) Nevada(61), Sierra(31), Yuba(6)
NORTHRIDGE Los Angeles
NORWALK Los Angeles
NOVATO Marin

NUBIEBER Lassen
NUEVO Riverside
O NEALS Madera
OAK PARK Ventura
OAK RUN Shasta
OAK VIEW Ventura
OAKDALE Stanislaus
OAKHURST Madera
OAKLAND Alameda
OAKLEY Contra Costa
OAKVILLE Napa
OBRIEN Shasta
OCCIDENTAL Sonoma
OCEANO San Luis Obispo
OCEANSIDE San Diego
OCOTILLO Imperial
OJAI Ventura
OLANCHA Inyo
OLD STATION Shasta
OLEMA Marin
OLIVEHURST Yuba
OLYMPIC VALLEY Placer
ONTARIO San Bernardino
ONYX Kern
ORANGE Orange
ORANGE COVE (93646) Fresno(90), Tulare(10)
ORANGEVALE Sacramento
OREGON HOUSE Yuba
ORICK Humboldt
ORINDA Contra Costa
ORLAND Glenn
ORLEANS Humboldt
ORO GRANDE San Bernardino
OROSI Tulare
OROVILLE Butte
OXNARD Ventura
PACIFIC GROVE Monterey
PACIFIC PALISADES Los Angeles
PACIFICA San Mateo
PACOIMA Los Angeles
PAICINES San Benito
PALA San Diego
PALERMO Butte
PALM DESERT Riverside
PALM SPRINGS Riverside
PALMDALE Los Angeles
PALO ALTO (94303) Santa Clara(51), San Mateo(48)
PALO ALTO San Mateo
PALO ALTO Santa Clara
PALO CEDRO Shasta
PALO VERDE Imperial
PALOMAR MOUNTAIN San Diego
PALOS VERDES PENINSULA Los Angeles
PANORAMA CITY Los Angeles
PARADISE Butte
PARAMOUNT Los Angeles
PARKER DAM San Bernardino
PARLIER Fresno
PASADENA Los Angeles
PASKENTA Tehama
PASO ROBLES San Luis Obispo
PATTERSON Stanislaus
PATTON San Bernardino
PAUMA VALLEY San Diego
PAYNES CREEK Tehama
PEARBLOSSOM Los Angeles
PEBBLE BEACH Monterey
PENN VALLEY Nevada
PENNGROVE Sonoma
PENRYN Placer
PERRIS Riverside
PESCADERO San Mateo
PETALUMA Sonoma
PETROLIA Humboldt
PHELAN San Bernardino
PHILLIPSVILLE Humboldt
PHILO Mendocino
PICO RIVERA Los Angeles
PIEDMONT Alameda
PIEDRA Fresno

PIERCY Mendocino
PILOT HILL El Dorado
PINE GROVE Amador
PINE VALLEY San Diego
PINECREST Tuolumne
PINOLE Contra Costa
PINON HILLS San Bernardino
PIONEER Amador
PIONEERTOWN San Bernardino
PIRU Ventura
PISMO BEACH San Luis Obispo
PITTSBURG Contra Costa
PIXLEY Tulare
PLACENTIA Orange
PLACERVILLE El Dorado
PLANADA Merced
PLATINA (96076) Tehama(46), Trinity(27), Shasta(25)
PLAYA DEL REY Los Angeles
PLEASANT GROVE (95668) Sutter(72), Placer(27)
PLEASANT HILL Contra Costa
PLEASANTON Alameda
PLEASANTON Contra Costa
PLYMOUTH Amador
POINT ARENA Mendocino
POINT MUGU NAWC Ventura
POINT REYES STATION Marin
POLLOCK PINES El Dorado
POMONA (91766) Los Angeles(95), San Bernardino(4)
POMONA Los Angeles
POPE VALLEY Napa
PORT COSTA Contra Costa
PORT HUENEME Ventura
PORT HUENEME CBC BASE Ventura
PORTERVILLE Tulare
PORTOLA Plumas
PORTOLA VALLEY San Mateo
POSEY Tulare
POTRERO San Diego
POTTER VALLEY Mendocino
POWAY San Diego
PRATHER Fresno
PRINCETON (95970) Glenn(79), Colusa(20)
PROBERTA Tehama
QUINCY Plumas
RACKERBY Yuba
RAIL ROAD FLAT Calaveras
RAISIN Fresno
RAMONA San Diego
RANCHITA San Diego
RANCHO CORDOVA Sacramento
RANCHO CUCAMONGA San Bernardino
RANCHO MIRAGE Riverside
RANCHO PALOS VERDES Los Angeles
RANCHO SANTA FE San Diego
RANCHO SANTA MARGARITA Orange
RANDSBURG Kern
RAVENDALE Lassen
RAYMOND (93653) Madera(79), Mariposa(20)
RED BLUFF Tehama
RED MOUNTAIN Kern
REDCREST Humboldt
REDDING Shasta
REDLANDS (92373) San Bernardino(96), Riverside(3)
REDLANDS San Bernardino
REDONDO BEACH Los Angeles
REDWAY Humboldt
REDWOOD CITY San Mateo
REDWOOD ESTATES Santa Clara
REDWOOD VALLEY Mendocino
REEDLEY (93654) Fresno(97), Tulare(2)
REPRESA Sacramento
RESCUE El Dorado
RESEDA Los Angeles
RIALTO San Bernardino
RICHGROVE Tulare
RICHMOND Contra Costa
RICHVALE Butte

RIDGECREST (93555) Kern(98), San Bernardino(1)
RIDGECREST Kern
RIMFOREST San Bernardino
RIO DELL Humboldt
RIO LINDA Sacramento
RIO NIDO Sonoma
RIO OSO Sutter
RIO VISTA (94571) Solano(94), Sacramento(5)
RIPLEY (92272) Riverside(98), San Diego(1)
RIPON San Joaquin
RIVER PINES Amador
RIVERBANK Stanislaus
RIVERDALE (93656) Fresno(88), Kings(11)
RIVERSIDE Riverside
ROBBINS Sutter
ROCKLIN Placer
RODEO Contra Costa
ROHNERT PARK Sonoma
ROSAMOND (93560) Kern(98), Los Angeles(1)
ROSEMEAD Los Angeles
ROSEVILLE Placer
ROSS Marin
ROUGH AND READY Nevada
ROUND MOUNTAIN Shasta
ROWLAND HEIGHTS Los Angeles
RUMSEY Yolo
RUNNING SPRINGS San Bernardino
RUTHERFORD Napa
RYDE Sacramento
SACRAMENTO (95837) Sacramento(70), Sutter(29)
SACRAMENTO Sacramento
SAINT HELENA Napa
SALIDA Stanislaus
SALINAS Monterey
SALTON CITY Imperial
SALYER Trinity
SAMOA Humboldt
SAN ANDREAS Calaveras
SAN ANSELMO Marin
SAN ARDO Monterey
SAN BERNARDINO San Bernardino
SAN BRUNO San Mateo
SAN CARLOS San Mateo
SAN CLEMENTE Orange
SAN DIEGO San Diego
SAN DIMAS Los Angeles
SAN FERNANDO Los Angeles
SAN FRANCISCO San Francisco
SAN FRANCISCO San Mateo
SAN GABRIEL Los Angeles
SAN GERONIMO Marin
SAN GREGORIO San Mateo
SAN JACINTO Riverside
SAN JOAQUIN Fresno
SAN JOSE Santa Clara
SAN JUAN BAUTISTA San Benito
SAN JUAN CAPISTRANO Orange
SAN LEANDRO Alameda
SAN LORENZO Alameda
SAN LUCAS Monterey
SAN LUIS OBISPO San Luis Obispo
SAN LUIS REY San Diego
SAN MARCOS San Diego
SAN MARINO Los Angeles
SAN MARTIN Santa Clara
SAN MATEO San Mateo
SAN MIGUEL (93451) San Luis Obispo(58), Monterey(41)
SAN PABLO Contra Costa
SAN PEDRO Los Angeles
SAN QUENTIN Marin
SAN RAFAEL Marin
SAN RAMON Contra Costa
SAN SIMEON San Luis Obispo
SAN YSIDRO San Diego
SANGER Fresno
SANTA ANA Orange
SANTA BARBARA Santa Barbara

SANTA CLARA Santa Clara
SANTA CLARITA Los Angeles
SANTA CRUZ Santa Cruz
SANTA FE SPRINGS Los Angeles
SANTA MARGARITA San Luis Obispo
SANTA MARIA (93454) Santa Barbara(98), San Luis Obispo(1)
SANTA MARIA Santa Barbara
SANTA MONICA Los Angeles
SANTA PAULA Ventura
SANTA RITA PARK Merced
SANTA ROSA Sonoma
SANTA YNEZ Santa Barbara
SANTA YSABEL San Diego
SANTEE San Diego
SARATOGA Santa Clara
SAUSALITO Marin
SCOTIA Humboldt
SCOTT BAR Siskiyou
SCOTTS VALLEY Santa Cruz
SEAL BEACH Orange
SEASIDE Monterey
SEBASTOPOL Sonoma
SEELEY Imperial
SEIAD VALLEY Siskiyou
SELMA Fresno
SEQUOIA NATIONAL PARK Tulare
SHAFTER Kern
SHANDON San Luis Obispo
SHASTA Shasta
SHASTA LAKE Shasta
SHAVER LAKE Fresno
SHEEP RANCH Calaveras
SHERIDAN Placer
SHERMAN OAKS Los Angeles
SHINGLE SPRINGS El Dorado
SHINGLETOWN Shasta
SHOSHONE Inyo
SIERRA CITY Sierra
SIERRA MADRE Los Angeles
SIERRAVILLE Sierra
SIGNAL HILL Los Angeles
SILVERADO Orange
SIMI VALLEY Ventura
SKYFOREST San Bernardino
SLOUGHHOUSE Sacramento
SMARTVILLE (95977) Nevada(62), Yuba(37)
SMITH RIVER Del Norte
SNELLING Merced
SODA SPRINGS Nevada
SOLANA BEACH San Diego
SOLEDAD Monterey
SOLVANG Santa Barbara
SOMERSET El Dorado
SOMES BAR Siskiyou
SOMIS Ventura
SONOMA Sonoma
SONORA Tuolumne
SOQUEL Santa Cruz
SOULSBYVILLE Tuolumne
SOUTH DOS PALOS Merced
SOUTH EL MONTE Los Angeles
SOUTH GATE Los Angeles
SOUTH LAKE TAHOE El Dorado
SOUTH PASADENA Los Angeles
SOUTH SAN FRANCISCO San Mateo
SPRECKELS Monterey
SPRING VALLEY San Diego
SPRINGVILLE Tulare
SQUAW VALLEY Fresno
STANDARD Tuolumne
STANDISH Lassen
STANTON Orange
STEVENSON RANCH Los Angeles
STEVINSON Merced
STEWARTS POINT Sonoma
STINSON BEACH Marin
STIRLING CITY Butte
STOCKTON San Joaquin
STONYFORD Colusa
STORRIE Plumas
STRATFORD Kings

STRATHMORE Tulare
STRAWBERRY Tuolumne
STRAWBERRY VALLEY (95981) Yuba(66), Plumas(33)
STUDIO CITY Los Angeles
SUGARLOAF San Bernardino
SUISUN CITY Solano
SULTANA Tulare
SUMMERLAND Santa Barbara
SUN CITY Riverside
SUN VALLEY Los Angeles
SUNLAND Los Angeles
SUNNYVALE Santa Clara
SUNOL Alameda
SUNSET BEACH Orange
SURFSIDE Orange
SUSANVILLE Lassen
SUTTER Sutter
SUTTER CREEK Amador
SYLMAR Los Angeles
TAFT Kern
TAHOE CITY Placer
TAHOE VISTA Placer
TAHOMA El Dorado
TALMAGE Mendocino
TARZANA Los Angeles
TAYLORSVILLE Plumas
TECATE San Diego
TECOPA Inyo
TEHACHAPI Kern
TEHAMA Tehama
TEMECULA Riverside
TEMPLE CITY Los Angeles
TEMPLETON San Luis Obispo
TERMO Lassen
TERRA BELLA Tulare
THE SEA RANCH Sonoma
THERMAL (92274) Riverside(65), Imperial(34)
THORNTON San Joaquin
THOUSAND OAKS (91362) Ventura(83), Los Angeles(16)
THOUSAND OAKS Ventura
THOUSAND PALMS Riverside
THREE RIVERS Tulare
TIPTON Tulare
TOLLHOUSE Fresno
TOLUCA LAKE Los Angeles
TOMALES Marin
TOPANGA Los Angeles
TOPAZ Mono
TORRANCE Los Angeles
TRABUCO CANYON Orange
TRACY (95391) San Joaquin(88), Alameda(11)
TRACY San Joaquin
TRANQUILLITY Fresno
TRAVER Tulare
TRAVIS AFB Solano
TRES PINOS San Benito
TRINIDAD Humboldt
TRINITY CENTER (96091) Trinity(56), Siskiyou(43)
TRONA San Bernardino
TRUCKEE (96161) Nevada(89), Placer(10)
TRUCKEE Nevada
TUJUNGA Los Angeles
TULARE Tulare
TULELAKE (96134) Modoc(71), Siskiyou(28)
TUOLUMNE Tuolumne
TUPMAN Kern
TURLOCK Stanislaus
TUSTIN Orange
TWAIN Plumas
TWAIN HARTE Tuolumne
TWENTYNINE PALMS San Bernardino
TWIN BRIDGES El Dorado
TWIN PEAKS San Bernardino
UKIAH Mendocino
UNION CITY Alameda
UNIVERSAL CITY Los Angeles
UPLAND San Bernardino

UPPER LAKE Lake
VACAVILLE Solano
VALENCIA Los Angeles
VALLECITO Calaveras
VALLEJO Solano
VALLEY CENTER San Diego
VALLEY FORD Sonoma
VALLEY HOME Stanislaus
VALLEY SPRINGS Calaveras
VALLEY VILLAGE Los Angeles
VALYERMO Los Angeles
VAN NUYS Los Angeles
VENICE Los Angeles
VENTURA Ventura
VERDUGO CITY Los Angeles
VERNALIS (95385) Stanislaus(76), San Joaquin(23)
VICTOR San Joaquin
VICTORVILLE San Bernardino
VIDAL San Bernardino
VILLA GRANDE Sonoma
VILLA PARK Orange
VINA Tehama
VINEBURG Sonoma
VINTON Plumas
VISALIA Tulare
VISTA San Diego
VOLCANO Amador

WALLACE Calaveras
WALNUT Los Angeles
WALNUT CREEK Contra Costa
WALNUT GROVE (95690) Sacramento(73), Solano(17), San Joaquin(8)
WARNER SPRINGS San Diego
WASCO Kern
WASHINGTON Nevada
WATERFORD Stanislaus
WATSONVILLE (95076) Santa Cruz(86), Monterey(13)
WATSONVILLE Santa Cruz
WAUKENA Tulare
WEAVERVILLE Trinity
WEED Siskiyou
WEIMAR Placer
WELDON Kern
WENDEL Lassen
WEOTT Humboldt
WEST COVINA Los Angeles
WEST HILLS (91307) Los Angeles(94), Ventura(5)
WEST HILLS Los Angeles
WEST HOLLYWOOD Los Angeles
WEST POINT Calaveras
WEST SACRAMENTO Yolo

WESTLAKE VILLAGE (91361) Ventura(74), Los Angeles(25)
WESTLAKE VILLAGE Los Angeles
WESTLAKE VILLAGE Ventura
WESTLEY Stanislaus
WESTMINSTER Orange
WESTMORLAND Imperial
WESTPORT Mendocino
WESTWOOD (96137) Plumas(70), Lassen(29)
WHEATLAND Yuba
WHISKEYTOWN Shasta
WHITE WATER Riverside
WHITETHORN (95589) Humboldt(95), Mendocino(4)
WHITMORE Shasta
WHITTIER Los Angeles
WILDOMAR Riverside
WILLIAMS Colusa
WILLITS Mendocino
WILLOW CREEK Humboldt
WILLOWS Glenn
WILMINGTON Los Angeles
WILSEYVILLE Calaveras
WILTON Sacramento
WINCHESTER Riverside
WINDSOR Sonoma
WINNETKA Los Angeles

WINTERHAVEN Imperial
WINTERS (95694) Yolo(85), Solano(14)
WINTON Merced
WISHON Madera
WITTER SPRINGS Lake
WOFFORD HEIGHTS Kern
WOODACRE Marin
WOODBRIDGE San Joaquin
WOODLAKE Tulare
WOODLAND Yolo
WOODLAND HILLS Los Angeles
WOODY Kern
WRIGHTWOOD San Bernardino
YERMO San Bernardino
YETTEM Tulare
YOLO Yolo
YORBA LINDA Orange
YORKVILLE Mendocino
YOSEMITE NATIONAL PARK Mariposa
YOUNTVILLE Napa
YREKA Siskiyou
YUBA CITY Sutter
YUCAIPA (92399) San Bernardino(98), Riverside(1)
YUCCA VALLEY San Bernardino
ZAMORA Yolo
ZENIA Trinity

California ZIP/City Cross Reference

90000-90068	LOS ANGELES
90069-90069	WEST HOLLYWOOD
90070-90189	LOS ANGELES
90201-90201	BELL
90202-90202	BELL GARDENS
90209-90213	BEVERLY HILLS
90220-90224	COMPTON
90230-90233	CULVER CITY
90239-90242	DOWNEY
90245-90245	EL SEGUNDO
90247-90249	GARDENA
90250-90251	HAWTHORNE
90254-90254	HERMOSA BEACH
90255-90255	HUNTINGTON PARK
90260-90261	LAWNDALE
90262-90262	LYNWOOD
90263-90265	MALIBU
90266-90267	MANHATTAN BEACH
90270-90270	MAYWOOD
90272-90272	PACIFIC PALISADES
90274-90274	PALOS VERDES PENINSULA
90275-90275	RANCHO PALOS VERDES
90277-90278	REDONDO BEACH
90280-90280	SOUTH GATE
90290-90290	TOPANGA
90291-90291	VENICE
90292-90292	MARINA DEL REY
90293-90293	PLAYA DEL REY
90294-90294	VENICE
90295-90295	MARINA DEL REY
90296-90296	PLAYA DEL REY
90300-90398	INGLEWOOD
90400-90411	SANTA MONICA
90500-90510	TORRANCE
90601-90612	WHITTIER
90620-90622	BUENA PARK
90623-90623	LA PALMA
90624-90624	BUENA PARK
90630-90630	CYPRESS
90631-90633	LA HABRA
90637-90639	LA MIRADA
90640-90640	MONTEBELLO
90650-90659	NORWALK
90660-90665	PICO RIVERA
90670-90671	SANTA FE SPRINGS
90680-90680	STANTON
90701-90702	ARTESIA
90703-90703	CERRITOS
90704-90704	AVALON
90706-90707	BELLFLOWER
90710-90710	HARBOR CITY
90711-90715	LAKEWOOD
90716-90716	HAWAIIAN GARDENS
90717-90717	LOMITA
90720-90721	LOS ALAMITOS
90723-90723	PARAMOUNT
90731-90734	SAN PEDRO
90740-90740	SEAL BEACH
90742-90742	SUNSET BEACH
90743-90743	SURFSIDE
90744-90744	WILMINGTON
90745-90747	CARSON
90748-90748	WILMINGTON
90749-90749	CARSON
90755-90755	SIGNAL HILL
90800-90899	LONG BEACH
91001-91003	ALTADENA
91006-91007	ARCADIA
91009-91010	DUARTE
91011-91012	LA CANADA FLINTRIDGE
91016-91017	MONROVIA
91020-91021	MONTROSE
91023-91023	MOUNT WILSON
91024-91025	SIERRA MADRE
91030-91031	SOUTH PASADENA
91040-91041	SUNLAND
91042-91043	TUJUNGA
91046-91046	VERDUGO CITY
91050-91051	PASADENA
91052-91052	LA COUNTY TAX COLLECTOR
91066-91077	ARCADIA
91100-91107	PASADENA
91108-91108	SAN MARINO
91109-91117	PASADENA
91118-91118	SAN MARINO
91121-91191	PASADENA
91200-91210	GLENDALE
91214-91214	LA CRESCENTA
91221-91222	GLENDALE
91224-91224	LA CRESCENTA
91225-91226	GLENDALE
91301-91301	AGOURA HILLS
91302-91302	CALABASAS
91303-91305	CANOGA PARK
91306-91306	WINNETKA
91307-91308	WEST HILLS
91309-91309	CANOGA PARK
91310-91310	CASTAIC
91311-91313	CHATSWORTH
91316-91316	ENCINO
91319-91320	NEWBURY PARK
91321-91322	NEWHALL
91324-91330	NORTHRIDGE
91331-91334	PACOIMA
91335-91337	RESEDA
91340-91341	SAN FERNANDO
91342-91342	SYLMAR
91343-91343	NORTH HILLS
91344-91344	GRANADA HILLS
91345-91346	MISSION HILLS
91350-91350	SANTA CLARITA
91351-91351	CANYON COUNTRY
91352-91353	SUN VALLEY
91354-91355	VALENCIA
91356-91357	TARZANA
91358-91358	THOUSAND OAKS
91359-91359	WESTLAKE VILLAGE
91360-91360	THOUSAND OAKS
91361-91361	WESTLAKE VILLAGE
91362-91362	THOUSAND OAKS
91363-91363	WESTLAKE VILLAGE
91364-91371	WOODLAND HILLS
91372-91372	CALABASAS
91375-91376	AGOURA HILLS
91377-91377	OAK PARK
91380-91380	SANTA CLARITA
91381-91381	STEVENSON RANCH
91382-91383	SANTA CLARITA
91384-91384	CASTAIC
91385-91385	VALENCIA
91386-91387	CANYON COUNTRY
91388-91388	VAN NUYS
91390-91390	SANTA CLARITA
91392-91392	SYLMAR
91393-91393	NORTH HILLS
91394-91394	GRANADA HILLS
91395-91395	MISSION HILLS
91396-91396	WINNETKA
91399-91399	WOODLAND HILLS
91400-91401	VAN NUYS
91402-91402	PANORAMA CITY
91403-91403	SHERMAN OAKS
91404-91411	VAN NUYS
91412-91412	PANORAMA CITY
91413-91413	SHERMAN OAKS
91416-91416	ENCINO
91423-91423	SHERMAN OAKS
91426-91436	ENCINO
91461-91494	VAN NUYS
91495-91495	SHERMAN OAKS
91496-91499	VAN NUYS
91500-91526	BURBANK
91600-91603	NORTH HOLLYWOOD
91604-91604	STUDIO CITY
91605-91606	NORTH HOLLYWOOD
91607-91607	VALLEY VILLAGE
91608-91608	UNIVERSAL CITY
91609-91609	NORTH HOLLYWOOD
91610-91610	TOLUCA LAKE
91611-91612	NORTH HOLLYWOOD
91614-91614	STUDIO CITY
91615-91616	NORTH HOLLYWOOD
91617-91617	VALLEY VILLAGE
91618-91618	UNIVERSAL CITY
91618-91618	NORTH HOLLYWOOD
91701-91701	ALTA LOMA
91702-91702	AZUSA
91706-91706	BALDWIN PARK
91708-91708	CHINO
91709-91709	CHINO HILLS
91710-91710	CHINO
91711-91711	CLAREMONT
91714-91716	CITY OF INDUSTRY
91718-91720	CORONA
91722-91724	COVINA
91729-91730	RANCHO CUCAMONGA
91731-91732	EL MONTE
91733-91733	SOUTH EL MONTE
91734-91735	EL MONTE
91737-91737	ALTA LOMA
91739-91739	RANCHO CUCAMONGA
91740-91741	GLENDORA
91743-91743	GUASTI
91744-91744	LA PUENTE
91745-91745	HACIENDA HEIGHTS
91746-91747	LA PUENTE
91748-91748	ROWLAND HEIGHTS
91749-91749	LA PUENTE
91750-91750	LA VERNE
91752-91752	MIRA LOMA
91754-91756	MONTEREY PARK
91758-91758	ONTARIO
91759-91759	MT BALDY
91760-91760	NORCO
91761-91762	ONTARIO
91763-91763	MONTCLAIR
91764-91764	ONTARIO
91765-91765	DIAMOND BAR
91766-91769	POMONA
91770-91772	ROSEMEAD
91773-91773	SAN DIMAS
91775-91778	SAN GABRIEL

91780-91780	TEMPLE CITY	92173-92173	SAN YSIDRO	92341-92341	GREEN VALLEY LAKE
91784-91786	UPLAND	92174-92177	SAN DIEGO	92342-92342	HELENDALE
91788-91789	WALNUT	92178-92178	CORONADO	92345-92345	HESPERIA
91790-91793	WEST COVINA	92179-92199	SAN DIEGO	92346-92346	HIGHLAND
91795-91795	WALNUT	92201-92203	INDIO	92347-92347	HINKLEY
91797-91797	BALDWIN PARK	92210-92210	INDIAN WELLS	92350-92350	LOMA LINDA
91797-91797	POMONA	92211-92211	PALM DESERT	92351-92351	BAKER
91798-91798	ONTARIO	92220-92220	BANNING	92352-92352	LAKE ARROWHEAD
91799-91799	POMONA	92222-92222	BARD	92353-92353	LAKEVIEW
91800-91899	ALHAMBRA	92223-92223	BEAUMONT	92354-92354	LOMA LINDA
91901-91901	ALPINE	92225-92226	BLYTHE	92356-92356	LUCERNE VALLEY
91902-91902	BONITA	92227-92227	BRAWLEY	92357-92357	LOMA LINDA
91903-91903	ALPINE	92230-92230	CABAZON	92358-92358	LYTLE CREEK
91905-91905	BOULEVARD	92231-92232	CALEXICO	92359-92359	MENTONE
91906-91906	CAMPO	92233-92233	CALIPATRIA	92363-92363	NEEDLES
91908-91908	BONITA	92234-92235	CATHEDRAL CITY	92364-92364	NIPTON
91909-91915	CHULA VISTA	92236-92236	COACHELLA	92365-92365	NEWBERRY SPRINGS
91916-91916	DESCANSO	92239-92239	DESERT CENTER	92366-92366	MOUNTAIN PASS
91917-91917	DULZURA	92240-92241	DESERT HOT SPRINGS	92368-92368	ORO GRANDE
91921-91921	CHULA VISTA	92242-92242	EARP	92369-92369	PATTON
91931-91931	GUATAY	92243-92244	EL CENTRO	92371-92371	PHELAN
91932-91933	IMPERIAL BEACH	92247-92248	LA QUINTA	92372-92372	PINON HILLS
91934-91934	JACUMBA	92249-92249	HEBER	92373-92375	REDLANDS
91935-91935	JAMUL	92250-92250	HOLTVILLE	92376-92377	RIALTO
91941-91944	LA MESA	92251-92251	IMPERIAL	92378-92378	RIMFOREST
91945-91946	LEMON GROVE	92252-92252	JOSHUA TREE	92382-92382	RUNNING SPRINGS
91947-91947	LINCOLN ACRES	92253-92253	LA QUINTA	92384-92384	SHOSHONE
91948-91948	MOUNT LAGUNA	92254-92254	MECCA	92385-92385	SKYFOREST
91950-91951	NATIONAL CITY	92255-92255	PALM DESERT	92386-92386	SUGARLOAF
91962-91962	PINE VALLEY	92256-92256	MORONGO VALLEY	92389-92389	TECOPA
91963-91963	POTRERO	92257-92257	NILAND	92391-92391	TWIN PEAKS
91976-91979	SPRING VALLEY	92258-92258	NORTH PALM SPRINGS	92392-92395	VICTORVILLE
91980-91987	TECATE	92259-92259	OCOTILLO	92397-92397	WRIGHTWOOD
91990-91995	POTRERO	92260-92261	PALM DESERT	92398-92398	YERMO
92003-92003	BONSALL	92262-92264	PALM SPRINGS	92399-92399	YUCAIPA
92004-92004	BORREGO SPRINGS	92266-92266	PALO VERDE	92400-92427	SAN BERNARDINO
92007-92007	CARDIFF BY THE SEA	92267-92267	PARKER DAM	92500-92517	RIVERSIDE
92008-92013	CARLSBAD	92268-92268	PIONEERTOWN	92518-92518	MARCH AIR FORCE BASE
92014-92014	DEL MAR	92270-92270	RANCHO MIRAGE	92519-92522	RIVERSIDE
92018-92018	CARLSBAD	92272-92272	RIPLEY	92530-92532	LAKE ELSINORE
92019-92022	EL CAJON	92273-92273	SEELEY	92536-92536	AGUANGA
92023-92024	ENCINITAS	92274-92274	THERMAL	92539-92539	ANZA
92025-92027	ESCONDIDO	92275-92275	SALTON CITY	92543-92546	HEMET
92028-92028	FALLBROOK	92276-92276	THOUSAND PALMS	92548-92548	HOMELAND
92029-92033	ESCONDIDO	92277-92278	TWENTYNINE PALMS	92549-92549	IDYLLWILD
92036-92036	JULIAN	92280-92280	VIDAL	92551-92557	MORENO VALLEY
92037-92039	LA JOLLA	92281-92281	WESTMORLAND	92561-92561	MOUNTAIN CENTER
92040-92040	LAKESIDE	92282-92282	WHITE WATER	92562-92564	MURRIETA
92046-92046	ESCONDIDO	92283-92283	WINTERHAVEN	92567-92567	NUEVO
92049-92052	OCEANSIDE	92284-92284	YUCCA VALLEY	92570-92572	PERRIS
92053-92053	NESTOR	92285-92285	LANDERS	92581-92583	SAN JACINTO
92054-92054	OCEANSIDE	92286-92286	YUCCA VALLEY	92584-92584	MENIFEE
92055-92055	CAMP PENDLETON	92292-92292	PALM SPRINGS	92585-92587	SUN CITY
92056-92058	OCEANSIDE	92301-92301	ADELANTO	92589-92593	TEMECULA
92059-92059	PALA	92304-92304	AMBOY	92595-92595	WILDOMAR
92060-92060	PALOMAR MOUNTAIN	92305-92305	ANGELUS OAKS	92596-92596	WINCHESTER
92061-92061	PAUMA VALLEY	92307-92308	APPLE VALLEY	92599-92599	PERRIS
92064-92064	POWAY	92309-92309	BAKER	92601-92601	ATWOOD
92065-92065	RAMONA	92310-92310	FORT IRWIN	92602-92604	IRVINE
92066-92066	RANCHITA	92311-92312	BARSTOW	92605-92605	HUNTINGTON BEACH
92067-92067	RANCHO SANTA FE	92313-92313	GRAND TERRACE	92606-92606	IRVINE
92068-92068	SAN LUIS REY	92314-92314	BIG BEAR CITY	92607-92607	LAGUNA NIGUEL
92069-92069	SAN MARCOS	92315-92315	BIG BEAR LAKE	92609-92609	EL TORO
92070-92070	SANTA YSABEL	92316-92316	BLOOMINGTON	92610-92610	FOOTHILL RANCH
92071-92072	SANTEE	92317-92317	BLUE JAY	92612-92612	IRVINE
92073-92073	SAN DIEGO	92318-92318	BRYN MAWR	92613-92613	ORANGE
92074-92074	POWAY	92319-92319	CADIZ	92614-92614	IRVINE
92075-92075	SOLANA BEACH	92320-92320	CALIMESA	92615-92615	HUNTINGTON BEACH
92078-92079	SAN MARCOS	92321-92321	CEDAR GLEN	92616-92620	IRVINE
92081-92081	VISTA	92322-92322	CEDARPINES PARK	92621-92622	BREA
92082-92082	VALLEY CENTER	92323-92323	CIMA	92623-92623	IRVINE
92083-92085	VISTA	92324-92324	COLTON	92624-92624	CAPISTRANO BEACH
92086-92086	WARNER SPRINGS	92325-92325	CRESTLINE	92625-92625	CORONA DEL MAR
92088-92088	FALLBROOK	92326-92326	CREST PARK	92626-92628	COSTA MESA
92090-92090	EL CAJON	92327-92327	DAGGETT	92629-92629	DANA POINT
92091-92091	RANCHO SANTA FE	92328-92328	DEATH VALLEY	92630-92630	LAKE FOREST
92092-92093	LA JOLLA	92329-92329	PHELAN	92631-92631	BREA
92096-92096	SAN MARCOS	92332-92332	ESSEX	92632-92635	FULLERTON
92100-92117	SAN DIEGO	92333-92333	FAWNSKIN	92637-92637	LAGUNA HILLS
92118-92118	CORONADO	92334-92337	FONTANA	92640-92640	FULLERTON
92119-92142	SAN DIEGO	92338-92338	LUDLOW	92641-92645	GARDEN GROVE
92143-92143	SAN YSIDRO	92339-92339	FOREST FALLS	92646-92649	HUNTINGTON BEACH
92145-92172	SAN DIEGO	92340-92340	HESPERIA	92650-92650	EAST IRVINE
92651-92652	LAGUNA BEACH				
92653-92654	LAGUNA HILLS				
92655-92655	MIDWAY CITY				
92656-92656	ALISO VIEJO				
92657-92657	NEWPORT COAST				
92658-92663	NEWPORT BEACH				
92664-92669	ORANGE				
92670-92670	PLACENTIA				
92672-92674	SAN CLEMENTE				
92675-92675	SAN JUAN CAPISTRANO				
92676-92676	SILVERADO				
92677-92677	LAGUNA NIGUEL				
92678-92679	TRABUCO CANYON				
92680-92681	TUSTIN				
92683-92685	WESTMINSTER				
92686-92687	YORBA LINDA				
92688-92688	RANCHO SANTA MARGARITA				
92690-92692	MISSION VIEJO				
92693-92693	SAN JUAN CAPISTRANO				
92694-92694	MISSION VIEJO				
92694-92694	LADERA RANCH				
92697-92698	IRVINE				
92698-92698	ALISO VIEJO				
92701-92707	SANTA ANA				
92708-92708	FOUNTAIN VALLEY				
92709-92710	IRVINE				
92711-92712	SANTA ANA				
92713-92720	IRVINE				
92725-92725	SANTA ANA				
92728-92728	FOUNTAIN VALLEY				
92730-92730	IRVINE				
92735-92735	SANTA ANA				
92780-92782	TUSTIN				
92799-92799	SANTA ANA				
92800-92809	ANAHEIM				
92811-92811	ATWOOD				
92812-92817	ANAHEIM				
92821-92823	BREA				
92825-92825	ANAHEIM				
92831-92838	FULLERTON				
92840-92846	GARDEN GROVE				
92850-92850	ANAHEIM				
92856-92859	ORANGE				
92860-92860	NORCO				
92861-92861	VILLA PARK				
92862-92869	ORANGE				
92870-92871	PLACENTIA				
92877-92883	CORONA				
92885-92887	YORBA LINDA				
92899-92899	ANAHEIM				
93001-93009	VENTURA				
93010-93012	CAMARILLO				
93013-93014	CARPINTERIA				
93015-93016	FILLMORE				
93020-93021	MOORPARK				
93022-93022	OAK VIEW				
93023-93024	OJAI				
93030-93036	OXNARD				
93040-93040	PIRU				
93041-93041	PORT HUENEME				
93042-93042	POINT MUGU NAWC				
93043-93043	PORT HUENEME CBC BASE				
93044-93044	PORT HUENEME				
93060-93061	SANTA PAULA				
93062-93063	SIMI VALLEY				
93064-93064	BRANDEIS				
93065-93065	SIMI VALLEY				
93066-93066	SOMIS				
93067-93067	SUMMERLAND				
93093-93099	SIMI VALLEY				
93101-93111	SANTA BARBARA				
93116-93118	GOLETA				
93120-93190	SANTA BARBARA				
93199-93199	GOLETA				
93201-93201	ALPAUGH				
93202-93202	ARMONA				
93203-93203	ARVIN				
93204-93204	AVENAL				
93205-93205	BODFISH				
93206-93206	BUTTONWILLOW				
93207-93207	CALIFORNIA HOT SPRINGS				
93208-93208	CAMP NELSON				

93210-93210 COALINGA	93450-93450 SAN ARDO	93633-93633 KINGS CANYON NATIONAL PK	94096-94098 SAN BRUNO
93212-93212 CORCORAN	93451-93451 SAN MIGUEL		94099-94099 SOUTH SAN FRANCISCO
93214-93214 CUYAMA	93452-93452 SAN SIMEON	93634-93634 LAKESHORE	94100-94199 SAN FRANCISCO
93215-93216 DELANO	93453-93453 SANTA MARGARITA	93635-93635 LOS BANOS	94203-94299 SACRAMENTO
93217-93217 DI GIORGIO	93454-93458 SANTA MARIA	93637-93639 MADERA	94300-94310 PALO ALTO
93218-93218 DUCOR	93460-93460 SANTA YNEZ	93640-93640 MENDOTA	94400-94497 SAN MATEO
93219-93219 EARLIMART	93461-93461 SHANDON	93641-93641 MIRAMONTE	94501-94502 ALAMEDA
93220-93220 EDISON	93463-93464 SOLVANG	93642-93642 MONO HOT SPRINGS	94503-94503 AMERICAN CANYON
93221-93221 EXETER	93465-93465 TEMPLETON	93643-93643 NORTH FORK	94504-94504 MOBIL OIL CREDIT
93222-93222 FRAZIER PARK	93475-93475 OCEANO	93644-93644 OAKHURST	CORPORATION
93223-93223 FARMERSVILLE	93483-93483 GROVER BEACH	93645-93645 O NEALS	94506-94506 DANVILLE
93224-93224 FELLOWS	93501-93502 MOJAVE	93646-93646 ORANGE COVE	94507-94507 ALAMO
93225-93225 FRAZIER PARK	93504-93505 CALIFORNIA CITY	93647-93647 OROSI	94508-94508 ANGWIN
93226-93226 GLENNVILLE	93510-93510 ACTON	93648-93648 PARLIER	94509-94509 ANTIOCH
93227-93227 GOSHEN	93512-93512 BENTON	93649-93649 PIEDRA	94510-94510 BENICIA
93230-93232 HANFORD	93513-93513 BIG PINE	93650-93650 FRESNO	94511-94511 BETHEL ISLAND
93234-93234 HURON	93514-93515 BISHOP	93651-93651 PRATHER	94512-94512 BIRDS LANDING
93235-93235 IVANHOE	93516-93516 BORON	93652-93652 RAISIN	94513-94513 BRENTWOOD
93237-93237 KAWEAH	93517-93517 BRIDGEPORT	93653-93653 RAYMOND	94514-94514 BYRON
93238-93238 KERNVILLE	93518-93518 CALIENTE	93654-93654 REEDLEY	94515-94515 CALISTOGA
93239-93239 KETTLEMAN CITY	93519-93519 CANTIL	93656-93656 RIVERDALE	94516-94516 CANYON
93240-93240 LAKE ISABELLA	93522-93522 DARWIN	93657-93657 SANGER	94517-94517 CLAYTON
93241-93241 LAMONT	93523-93524 EDWARDS	93660-93660 SAN JOAQUIN	94518-94522 CONCORD
93242-93242 LATON	93526-93526 INDEPENDENCE	93661-93661 SANTA RITA PARK	94523-94523 PLEASANT HILL
93243-93243 LEBEC	93527-93527 INYOKERN	93662-93662 SELMA	94524-94524 CONCORD
93244-93244 LEMON COVE	93528-93528 JOHANNESBURG	93664-93664 SHAVER LAKE	94525-94525 CROCKETT
93245-93246 LEMOORE	93529-93529 JUNE LAKE	93665-93665 SOUTH DOS PALOS	94526-94526 DANVILLE
93247-93247 LINDSAY	93530-93530 KEELER	93666-93666 SULTANA	94527-94527 CONCORD
93249-93249 LOST HILLS	93531-93531 KEENE	93667-93667 TOLLHOUSE	94528-94528 DIABLO
93250-93250 MC FARLAND	93532-93532 LAKE HUGHES	93668-93668 TRANQUILLITY	94529-94529 CONCORD
93251-93251 MC KITTRICK	93534-93539 LANCASTER	93669-93669 WISHON	94530-94530 EL CERRITO
93252-93252 MARICOPA	93541-93541 LEE VINING	93670-93670 YETTEM	94531-94531 ANTIOCH
93254-93254 NEW CUYAMA	93542-93542 LITTLE LAKE	93673-93673 TRAVER	94533-94534 FAIRFIELD
93255-93255 ONYX	93543-93543 LITTLEROCK	93675-93675 SQUAW VALLEY	94535-94535 TRAVIS AFB
93256-93256 PIXLEY	93544-93544 LLANO	93700-93888 FRESNO	94536-94539 FREMONT
93257-93258 PORTERVILLE	93545-93545 LONE PINE	93901-93915 SALINAS	94540-94545 HAYWARD
93260-93260 POSEY	93546-93546 MAMMOTH LAKES	93920-93920 BIG SUR	94546-94546 CASTRO VALLEY
93261-93261 RICHGROVE	93549-93549 OLANCHA	93921-93923 CARMEL	94547-94547 HERCULES
93262-93262 SEQUOIA NATIONAL PARK	93550-93552 PALMDALE	93924-93924 CARMEL VALLEY	94548-94548 KNIGHTSEN
93263-93263 SHAFTER	93553-93553 PEARBLOSSOM	93925-93925 CHUALAR	94549-94549 LAFAYETTE
93265-93265 SPRINGVILLE	93554-93554 RANDSBURG	93926-93926 GONZALES	94550-94551 LIVERMORE
93266-93266 STRATFORD	93555-93556 RIDGECREST	93927-93927 GREENFIELD	94552-94552 CASTRO VALLEY
93267-93267 STRATHMORE	93558-93558 RED MOUNTAIN	93928-93928 JOLON	94553-94553 MARTINEZ
93268-93268 TAFT	93560-93560 ROSAMOND	93930-93930 KING CITY	94555-94555 FREMONT
93270-93270 TERRA BELLA	93561-93561 TEHACHAPI	93932-93932 LOCKWOOD	94556-94556 MORAGA
93271-93271 THREE RIVERS	93562-93562 TRONA	93933-93933 MARINA	94557-94557 HAYWARD
93272-93272 TIPTON	93563-93563 VALYERMO	93940-93940 MONTEREY	94558-94559 NAPA
93274-93275 TULARE	93570-93570 KEENE	93941-93941 FT ORD	94560-94560 NEWARK
93276-93276 TUPMAN	93581-93582 TEHACHAPI	93941-93941 FORT ORD	94561-94561 OAKLEY
93277-93277 VISALIA	93584-93586 LANCASTER	93941-93944 MONTEREY	94562-94562 OAKVILLE
93280-93280 WASCO	93590-93591 PALMDALE	93950-93950 PACIFIC GROVE	94563-94563 ORINDA
93282-93282 WAUKENA	93592-93592 TRONA	93953-93953 PEBBLE BEACH	94564-94564 PINOLE
93283-93283 WELDON	93596-93596 BORON	93954-93954 SAN LUCAS	94565-94565 PITTSBURG
93285-93285 WOFFORD HEIGHTS	93599-93599 PALMDALE	93955-93955 SEASIDE	94566-94566 PLEASANTON
93286-93286 WOODLAKE	93601-93601 AHWAHNEE	93960-93960 SOLEDAD	94567-94567 POPE VALLEY
93287-93287 WOODY	93602-93602 AUBERRY	93962-93962 SPRECKELS	94568-94568 DUBLIN
93290-93292 VISALIA	93603-93603 BADGER	94002-94003 BELMONT	94569-94569 PORT COSTA
93300-93399 BAKERSFIELD	93604-93604 BASS LAKE	94005-94005 BRISBANE	94570-94570 MORAGA
93401-93401 SAN LUIS OBISPO	93605-93605 BIG CREEK	94010-94012 BURLINGAME	94571-94571 RIO VISTA
93402-93402 LOS OSOS	93606-93606 BIOLA	94013-94017 DALY CITY	94572-94572 RODEO
93403-93410 SAN LUIS OBISPO	93607-93607 BURREL	94018-94018 EL GRANADA	94573-94573 RUTHERFORD
93412-93412 LOS OSOS	93608-93608 CANTUA CREEK	94019-94019 HALF MOON BAY	94574-94574 SAINT HELENA
93420-93421 ARROYO GRANDE	93609-93609 CARUTHERS	94020-94020 LA HONDA	94575-94575 MORAGA
93422-93423 ATASCADERO	93610-93610 CHOWCHILLA	94021-94021 LOMA MAR	94576-94576 DEER PARK
93424-93424 AVILA BEACH	93611-93613 CLOVIS	94022-94024 LOS ALTOS	94577-94579 SAN LEANDRO
93426-93426 BRADLEY	93614-93614 COARSEGOLD	94025-94026 MENLO PARK	94580-94580 SAN LORENZO
93427-93427 BUELLTON	93615-93615 CUTLER	94027-94027 ATHERTON	94581-94581 NAPA
93428-93428 CAMBRIA	93616-93616 DEL REY	94028-94028 PORTOLA VALLEY	94582-94582 PLEASANTON
93429-93429 CASMALIA	93618-93618 DINUBA	94029-94029 MENLO PARK	94582-94583 SAN RAMON
93430-93430 CAYUCOS	93619-93619 CLOVIS	94030-94031 MILLBRAE	94585-94585 SUISUN CITY
93431-93431 CHOLAME	93620-93620 DOS PALOS	94035-94035 MOUNTAIN VIEW	94586-94586 SUNOL
93432-93432 CRESTON	93621-93621 DUNLAP	94037-94037 MONTARA	94587-94587 UNION CITY
93433-93433 GROVER BEACH	93622-93622 FIREBAUGH	94038-94038 MOSS BEACH	94588-94588 PLEASANTON
93434-93434 GUADALUPE	93623-93623 FISH CAMP	94039-94043 MOUNTAIN VIEW	94589-94592 VALLEJO
93435-93435 HARMONY	93624-93624 FIVE POINTS	94044-94045 PACIFICA	94593-94593 CROCKER NAT BANK
93436-93438 LOMPOC	93625-93625 FOWLER	94059-94059 REDWOOD CITY	94594-94594 MONTGOMERY WARD
93440-93440 LOS ALAMOS	93626-93626 FRIANT	94060-94060 PESCADERO	94595-94598 WALNUT CREEK
93441-93441 LOS OLIVOS	93627-93627 HELM	94061-94065 REDWOOD CITY	94599-94599 YOUNTVILLE
93442-93443 MORRO BAY	93628-93628 HUME	94066-94067 SAN BRUNO	94601-94607 OAKLAND
93444-93444 NIPOMO	93629-93629 HUNTINGTON LAKE	94070-94071 SAN CARLOS	94608-94608 EMERYVILLE
93445-93445 OCEANO	93630-93630 KERMAN	94074-94074 SAN GREGORIO	94609-94619 OAKLAND
93446-93447 PASO ROBLES	93631-93631 KINGSBURG	94080-94083 SOUTH SAN FRANCISCO	94620-94620 PIEDMONT
93448-93449 PISMO BEACH		94085-94091 SUNNYVALE	94621-94661 OAKLAND

94662-94662 EMERYVILLE	95044-95044 REDWOOD ESTATES	95343-95344 MERCED	95467-95467 HIDDEN VALLEY LAKE
94666-94666 OAKLAND	95045-95045 SAN JUAN BAUTISTA	95345-95345 MIDPINES	95468-95468 POINT ARENA
94701-94705 BERKELEY	95046-95046 SAN MARTIN	95346-95346 MI WUK VILLAGE	95469-95469 POTTER VALLEY
94706-94706 ALBANY	95050-95056 SANTA CLARA	95347-95347 MOCCASIN	95470-95470 REDWOOD VALLEY
94707-94720 BERKELEY	95060-95065 SANTA CRUZ	95348-95348 MERCED	95471-95471 RIO NIDO
94801-94802 RICHMOND	95066-95067 SCOTTS VALLEY	95350-95358 MODESTO	95472-95473 SEBASTOPOL
94803-94803 EL SOBRANTE	95070-95071 SARATOGA	95360-95360 NEWMAN	95476-95476 SONOMA
94804-94805 RICHMOND	95073-95073 SOQUEL	95361-95361 OAKDALE	95480-95480 STEWARTS POINT
94806-94806 SAN PABLO	95075-95075 TRES PINOS	95363-95363 PATTERSON	95481-95481 TALMAGE
94807-94808 RICHMOND	95076-95077 WATSONVILLE	95364-95364 PINECREST	95482-95482 UKIAH
94820-94820 EL SOBRANTE	95100-95139 SAN JOSE	95365-95365 PLANADA	95485-95485 UPPER LAKE
94850-94875 RICHMOND	95140-95140 MOUNT HAMILTON	95366-95366 RIPON	95486-95486 VILLA GRANDE
94901-94903 SAN RAFAEL	95141-95196 SAN JOSE	95367-95367 RIVERBANK	95487-95487 VINEBURG
94904-94904 GREENBRAE	95201-95219 STOCKTON	95368-95368 SALIDA	95488-95488 WESTPORT
94911-94913 SAN RAFAEL	95220-95220 ACAMPO	95369-95369 SNELLING	95490-95490 WILLITS
94914-94914 KENTFIELD	95221-95221 ALTAVILLE	95370-95370 SONORA	95492-95492 WINDSOR
94915-94915 SAN RAFAEL	95222-95222 ANGELS CAMP	95372-95372 SOULSBYVILLE	95493-95493 WITTER SPRINGS
94920-94920 BELVEDERE TIBURON	95223-95223 ARNOLD	95373-95373 STANDARD	95494-95494 YORKVILLE
94922-94922 BODEGA	95224-95224 AVERY	95374-95374 STEVINSON	95497-95497 THE SEA RANCH
94923-94923 BODEGA BAY	95225-95225 BURSON	95375-95375 STRAWBERRY	95501-95503 EUREKA
94924-94924 BOLINAS	95226-95226 CAMPO SECO	95376-95378 TRACY	95511-95511 ALDERPOINT
94925-94925 CORTE MADERA	95227-95227 CLEMENTS	95379-95379 TUOLUMNE	95514-95514 BLOCKSBURG
94926-94926 COTATI	95228-95228 COPPEROPOLIS	95380-95382 TURLOCK	95518-95518 ARCATA
94927-94928 ROHNERT PARK	95229-95229 DOUGLAS FLAT	95383-95383 TWAIN HARTE	95519-95519 MCKINLEYVILLE
94929-94929 DILLON BEACH	95230-95230 FARMINGTON	95384-95384 VALLEY HOME	95521-95521 ARCATA
94930-94930 FAIRFAX	95231-95231 FRENCH CAMP	95385-95385 VERNALIS	95524-95524 BAYSIDE
94931-94931 COTATI	95232-95232 GLENCOE	95386-95386 WATERFORD	95525-95525 BLUE LAKE
94933-94933 FOREST KNOLLS	95233-95233 HATHAWAY PINES	95387-95387 WESTLEY	95526-95526 BRIDGEVILLE
94937-94937 INVERNESS	95234-95234 HOLT	95388-95388 WINTON	95527-95527 BURNT RANCH
94938-94938 LAGUNITAS	95236-95236 LINDEN	95389-95389 YOSEMITE NATIONAL PARK	95528-95528 CARLOTTA
94939-94939 LARKSPUR	95237-95237 LOCKEFORD	95390-95390 RIVERBANK	95531-95532 CRESCENT CITY
94940-94940 MARSHALL	95240-95242 LODI	95391-95391 TRACY	95534-95534 CUTTEN
94941-94942 MILL VALLEY	95245-95245 MOKELUMNE HILL	95397-95397 MODESTO	95536-95536 FERNDALE
94945-94945 NOVATO	95246-95246 MOUNTAIN RANCH	95401-95409 SANTA ROSA	95537-95537 FIELDS LANDING
94946-94946 NICASIO	95247-95247 MURPHYS	95410-95410 ALBION	95538-95538 FORT DICK
94947-94949 NOVATO	95248-95248 RAIL ROAD FLAT	95412-95412 ANNAPOLIS	95540-95540 FORTUNA
94950-94950 OLEMA	95249-95249 SAN ANDREAS	95415-95415 BOONVILLE	95542-95542 GARBERVILLE
94951-94951 PENNGROVE	95250-95250 SHEEP RANCH	95416-95416 BOYES HOT SPRINGS	95543-95543 GASQUET
94952-94955 PETALUMA	95251-95251 VALLECITO	95417-95417 BRANSCOMB	95545-95545 HONEYDEW
94956-94956 POINT REYES STATION	95252-95252 VALLEY SPRINGS	95418-95418 CALPELLA	95546-95546 HOOPA
94957-94957 ROSS	95253-95253 VICTOR	95419-95419 CAMP MEEKER	95547-95547 HYDESVILLE
94960-94960 SAN ANSELMO	95254-95254 WALLACE	95420-95420 CASPAR	95548-95548 KLAMATH
94963-94963 SAN GERONIMO	95255-95255 WEST POINT	95421-95421 CAZADERO	95549-95549 KNEELAND
94964-94964 SAN QUENTIN	95257-95257 WILSEYVILLE	95422-95422 CLEARLAKE	95550-95550 KORBEL
94965-94966 SAUSALITO	95258-95258 WOODBRIDGE	95423-95423 CLEARLAKE OAKS	95551-95551 LOLETA
94970-94970 STINSON BEACH	95267-95296 STOCKTON	95424-95424 CLEARLAKE PARK	95552-95552 MAD RIVER
94971-94971 TOMALES	95296-95296 LYOTH	95425-95425 CLOVERDALE	95553-95553 MIRANDA
94972-94972 VALLEY FORD	95297-95298 STOCKTON	95426-95426 COBB	95554-95554 MYERS FLAT
94973-94973 WOODACRE	95301-95301 ATWATER	95427-95427 COMPTCHE	95555-95555 ORICK
94974-94974 SAN QUENTIN	95303-95303 BALLICO	95428-95428 COVELO	95556-95556 ORLEANS
94975-94975 PETALUMA	95304-95304 BANTA	95429-95429 DOS RIOS	95558-95558 PETROLIA
94976-94976 CORTE MADERA	95305-95305 BIG OAK FLAT	95430-95430 DUNCANS MILLS	95559-95559 PHILLIPSVILLE
94977-94977 LARKSPUR	95306-95306 CATHEYS VALLEY	95431-95431 ELDRIDGE	95560-95560 REDWAY
94978-94978 FAIRFAX	95307-95307 CERES	95432-95432 ELK	95562-95562 RIO DELL
94979-94979 SAN ANSELMO	95309-95309 CHINESE CAMP	95433-95433 EL VERANO	95563-95563 SALYER
94998-94998 NOVATO	95310-95310 COLUMBIA	95435-95435 FINLEY	95564-95564 SAMOA
94999-94999 PETALUMA	95311-95311 COULTERVILLE	95436-95436 FORESTVILLE	95565-95565 SCOTIA
95001-95001 APTOS	95312-95312 CRESSEY	95437-95437 FORT BRAGG	95567-95567 SMITH RIVER
95002-95002 ALVISO	95313-95313 CROWS LANDING	95439-95439 FULTON	95568-95568 SOMES BAR
95003-95003 APTOS	95314-95314 DARDANELLE	95441-95441 GEYSERVILLE	95569-95569 REDCREST
95004-95004 AROMAS	95315-95315 DELHI	95442-95442 GLEN ELLEN	95570-95570 TRINIDAD
95005-95005 BEN LOMOND	95316-95316 DENAIR	95443-95443 GLENHAVEN	95571-95571 WEOTT
95006-95006 BOULDER CREEK	95317-95317 EL NIDO	95444-95444 GRATON	95573-95573 WILLOW CREEK
95007-95007 BROOKDALE	95318-95318 EL PORTAL	95445-95445 GUALALA	95585-95585 LEGGETT
95008-95009 CAMPBELL	95319-95319 EMPIRE	95446-95446 GUERNEVILLE	95587-95587 PIERCY
95010-95010 CAPITOLA	95320-95320 ESCALON	95448-95448 HEALDSBURG	95589-95589 WHITETHORN
95011-95011 CAMPBELL	95321-95321 GROVELAND	95449-95449 HOPLAND	95595-95595 ZENIA
95012-95012 CASTROVILLE	95322-95322 GUSTINE	95450-95450 JENNER	95601-95601 AMADOR CITY
95013-95013 COYOTE	95323-95323 HICKMAN	95451-95451 KELSEYVILLE	95602-95604 AUBURN
95014-95016 CUPERTINO	95324-95324 HILMAR	95452-95452 KENWOOD	95605-95605 WEST SACRAMENTO
95017-95017 DAVENPORT	95325-95325 HORNITOS	95453-95453 LAKEPORT	95606-95606 BROOKS
95018-95018 FELTON	95326-95326 HUGHSON	95454-95454 LAYTONVILLE	95607-95607 CAPAY
95019-95019 FREEDOM	95327-95327 JAMESTOWN	95456-95456 LITTLERIVER	95608-95609 CARMICHAEL
95020-95021 GILROY	95328-95328 KEYES	95457-95457 LOWER LAKE	95610-95611 CITRUS HEIGHTS
95023-95024 HOLLISTER	95329-95329 LA GRANGE	95458-95458 LUCERNE	95612-95612 CLARKSBURG
95026-95026 HOLY CITY	95330-95330 LATHROP	95459-95459 MANCHESTER	95613-95613 COLOMA
95030-95033 LOS GATOS	95333-95333 LE GRAND	95460-95460 MENDOCINO	95614-95614 COOL
95035-95036 MILPITAS	95334-95334 LIVINGSTON	95461-95461 MIDDLETOWN	95615-95615 COURTLAND
95037-95038 MORGAN HILL	95335-95335 LONG BARN	95462-95462 MONTE RIO	95616-95617 DAVIS
95039-95039 MOSS LANDING	95336-95337 MANTECA	95463-95463 NAVARRO	95618-95618 EL MACERO
95041-95041 MOUNT HERMON	95338-95338 MARIPOSA	95464-95464 NICE	95619-95619 DIAMOND SPRINGS
95042-95042 NEW ALMADEN	95340-95341 MERCED	95465-95465 OCCIDENTAL	95620-95620 DIXON
95043-95043 PAICINES	95342-95342 ATWATER	95466-95466 PHILO	95621-95621 CITRUS HEIGHTS

95622-95622 NICOLAUS	95709-95709 CAMINO	95968-95968 PALERMO	96070-96070 OBRIEN
95623-95623 EL DORADO	95712-95712 CHICAGO PARK	95969-95969 PARADISE	96071-96071 OLD STATION
95624-95624 ELK GROVE	95713-95713 COLFAX	95970-95970 PRINCETON	96073-96073 PALO CEDRO
95625-95625 ELMIRA	95714-95714 DUTCH FLAT	95971-95971 QUINCY	96074-96074 PASKENTA
95626-95626 ELVERTA	95715-95715 EMIGRANT GAP	95972-95972 RACKERBY	96075-96075 PAYNES CREEK
95627-95627 ESPARTO	95717-95717 GOLD RUN	95973-95973 CHICO	96076-96076 PLATINA
95628-95628 FAIR OAKS	95720-95720 KYBURZ	95974-95974 RICHVALE	96078-96078 PROBERTA
95629-95629 FIDDLETOWN	95721-95721 ECHO LAKE	95975-95975 ROUGH AND READY	96079-96079 SHASTA LAKE
95630-95630 FOLSOM	95722-95722 MEADOW VISTA	95976-95976 CHICO	96080-96080 RED BLUFF
95631-95631 FORESTHILL	95724-95724 NORDEN	95977-95977 SMARTVILLE	96084-96084 ROUND MOUNTAIN
95632-95632 GALT	95726-95726 POLLOCK PINES	95978-95978 STIRLING CITY	96085-96085 SCOTT BAR
95633-95633 GARDEN VALLEY	95728-95728 SODA SPRINGS	95979-95979 STONYFORD	96086-96086 SEIAD VALLEY
95634-95634 GEORGETOWN	95735-95735 TWIN BRIDGES	95980-95980 STORRIE	96087-96087 SHASTA
95635-95635 GREENWOOD	95736-95736 WEIMAR	95981-95981 STRAWBERRY VALLEY	96088-96088 SHINGLETOWN
95636-95636 GRIZZLY FLATS	95741-95743 RANCHO CORDOVA	95982-95982 SUTTER	96089-96089 SHASTA LAKE
95637-95637 GUINDA	95746-95746 GRANITE BAY	95983-95983 TAYLORSVILLE	96090-96090 TEHAMA
95638-95638 HERALD	95747-95747 ROSEVILLE	95984-95984 TWAIN	96091-96091 TRINITY CENTER
95639-95639 HOOD	95757-95759 ELK GROVE	95986-95986 WASHINGTON	96092-96092 VINA
95640-95640 IONE	95762-95762 EL DORADO HILLS	95987-95987 WILLIAMS	96093-96093 WEAVERVILLE
95641-95641 ISLETON	95763-95763 FOLSOM	95988-95988 WILLOWS	96094-96094 WEED
95642-95642 JACKSON	95765-95765 ROCKLIN	95991-95993 YUBA CITY	96095-96095 WHISKEYTOWN
95643-95643 PLACERVILLE	95776-95776 WOODLAND	96001-96003 REDDING	96096-96096 WHITMORE
95644-95644 KIT CARSON	95798-95799 WEST SACRAMENTO	96006-96006 ADIN	96097-96097 YREKA
95645-95645 KNIGHTS LANDING	95800-95842 SACRAMENTO	96007-96007 ANDERSON	96099-96099 REDDING
95646-95646 KIRKWOOD	95843-95843 ANTELOPE	96008-96008 BELLA VISTA	96101-96101 ALTURAS
95648-95648 LINCOLN	95851-95899 SACRAMENTO	96009-96009 BIEBER	96103-96103 BLAIRSDEN-GRAEAGLE
95650-95650 LOOMIS	95901-95901 MARYSVILLE	96010-96010 BIG BAR	96104-96104 CEDARVILLE
95651-95651 LOTUS	95903-95903 BEALE AFB	96011-96011 BIG BEND	96105-96105 CHILCOOT
95652-95652 MCCLELLAN AFB	95910-95910 ALLEGHANY	96013-96013 BURNEY	96106-96106 CLIO
95652-95652 MCCLELLAN	95912-95912 ARBUCKLE	96014-96014 CALLAHAN	96107-96107 COLEVILLE
95653-95653 MADISON	95913-95913 ARTOIS	96015-96015 CANBY	96108-96108 DAVIS CREEK
95654-95654 MARTELL	95914-95914 BANGOR	96016-96016 CASSEL	96109-96109 DOYLE
95655-95655 MATHER	95915-95915 BELDEN	96017-96017 CASTELLA	96110-96110 EAGLEVILLE
95656-95656 MOUNT AUKUM	95916-95916 BERRY CREEK	96019-96019 SHASTA LAKE	96111-96111 FLORISTON
95658-95658 NEWCASTLE	95917-95917 BIGGS	96020-96020 CHESTER	96112-96112 FORT BIDWELL
95659-95659 NICOLAUS	95918-95918 BROWNS VALLEY	96021-96021 CORNING	96113-96113 HERLONG
95660-95660 NORTH HIGHLANDS	95919-95919 BROWNSVILLE	96022-96022 COTTONWOOD	96114-96114 JANESVILLE
95661-95661 ROSEVILLE	95920-95920 BUTTE CITY	96023-96023 DORRIS	96115-96115 LAKE CITY
95662-95662 ORANGEVALE	95922-95922 CAMPTONVILLE	96024-96024 DOUGLAS CITY	96116-96116 LIKELY
95663-95663 PENRYN	95923-95923 CANYONDAM	96025-96025 DUNSMUIR	96117-96117 LITCHFIELD
95664-95664 PILOT HILL	95924-95924 CEDAR RIDGE	96027-96027 ETNA	96118-96118 LOYALTON
95665-95665 PINE GROVE	95925-95925 CHALLENGE	96028-96028 FALL RIVER MILLS	96119-96119 MADELINE
95666-95666 PIONEER	95926-95929 CHICO	96029-96029 FLOURNOY	96120-96120 MARKLEEVILLE
95667-95667 PLACERVILLE	95930-95930 CLIPPER MILLS	96031-96031 FORKS OF SALMON	96121-96121 MILFORD
95668-95668 PLEASANT GROVE	95931-95931 COLLEGE CITY	96032-96032 FORT JONES	96122-96122 PORTOLA
95669-95669 PLYMOUTH	95932-95932 COLUSA	96033-96033 FRENCH GULCH	96123-96123 RAVENDALE
95670-95670 RANCHO CORDOVA	95934-95934 CRESCENT MILLS	96034-96034 GAZELLE	96124-96124 CALPINE
95671-95671 REPRESA	95935-95935 DOBBINS	96035-96035 GERBER	96125-96125 SIERRA CITY
95672-95672 RESCUE	95936-95936 DOWNIEVILLE	96037-96037 GREENVIEW	96126-96126 SIERRAVILLE
95673-95673 RIO LINDA	95937-95937 DUNNIGAN	96038-96038 GRENADA	96127-96127 SUSANVILLE
95674-95674 RIO OSO	95938-95938 DURHAM	96039-96039 HAPPY CAMP	96128-96128 STANDISH
95675-95675 RIVER PINES	95939-95939 ELK CREEK	96040-96040 HAT CREEK	96129-96129 BECKWOURTH
95676-95676 ROBBINS	95940-95940 FEATHER FALLS	96041-96041 HAYFORK	96130-96130 SUSANVILLE
95677-95677 ROCKLIN	95941-95941 FORBESTOWN	96044-96044 HORNBROOK	96132-96132 TERMO
95678-95678 ROSEVILLE	95942-95942 FOREST RANCH	96045-96045 HORSE CREEK	96133-96133 TOPAZ
95679-95679 RUMSEY	95943-95943 GLENN	96046-96046 HYAMPOM	96134-96134 TULELAKE
95680-95680 RYDE	95944-95944 GOODYEARS BAR	96047-96047 IGO	96135-96135 VINTON
95681-95681 SHERIDAN	95945-95945 GRASS VALLEY	96048-96048 JUNCTION CITY	96136-96136 WENDEL
95682-95682 SHINGLE SPRINGS	95946-95946 PENN VALLEY	96049-96049 REDDING	96137-96137 WESTWOOD
95683-95683 SLOUGHHOUSE	95947-95947 GREENVILLE	96050-96050 KLAMATH RIVER	96140-96140 CARNELIAN BAY
95684-95684 SOMERSET	95948-95948 GRIDLEY	96051-96051 LAKEHEAD	96141-96141 HOMEWOOD
95685-95685 SUTTER CREEK	95949-95949 GRASS VALLEY	96052-96052 LEWISTON	96142-96142 TAHOMA
95686-95686 THORNTON	95950-95950 GRIMES	96053-96053 MCARTHUR	96143-96143 KINGS BEACH
95687-95687 VACAVILLE	95951-95951 HAMILTON CITY	96054-96054 LOOKOUT	96145-96145 TAHOE CITY
95689-95689 VOLCANO	95953-95953 LIVE OAK	96055-96055 LOS MOLINOS	96146-96146 OLYMPIC VALLEY
95690-95690 WALNUT GROVE	95954-95954 MAGALIA	96056-96056 MCARTHUR	96148-96148 TAHOE VISTA
95691-95691 WEST SACRAMENTO	95955-95955 MAXWELL	96057-96057 MCCLOUD	96150-96158 SOUTH LAKE TAHOE
95692-95692 WHEATLAND	95956-95956 MEADOW VALLEY	96058-96058 MACDOEL	96160-96162 TRUCKEE
95693-95693 WILTON	95957-95957 MERIDIAN	96059-96059 MANTON	96635-96688 FPO
95694-95694 WINTERS	95958-95958 NELSON	96061-96061 MILL CREEK	
95695-95695 WOODLAND	95959-95959 NEVADA CITY	96062-96062 MILLVILLE	
95696-95696 VACAVILLE	95960-95960 NORTH SAN JUAN	96063-96063 MINERAL	
95697-95697 YOLO	95961-95961 OLIVEHURST	96064-96064 MONTAGUE	
95698-95698 ZAMORA	95962-95962 OREGON HOUSE	96065-96065 MONTGOMERY CREEK	
95699-95699 DRYTOWN	95963-95963 ORLAND	96067-96067 MOUNT SHASTA	
95701-95701 ALTA	95965-95966 OROVILLE	96068-96068 NUBIEBER	
95703-95703 APPLEGATE	95967-95967 PARADISE	96069-96069 OAK RUN	

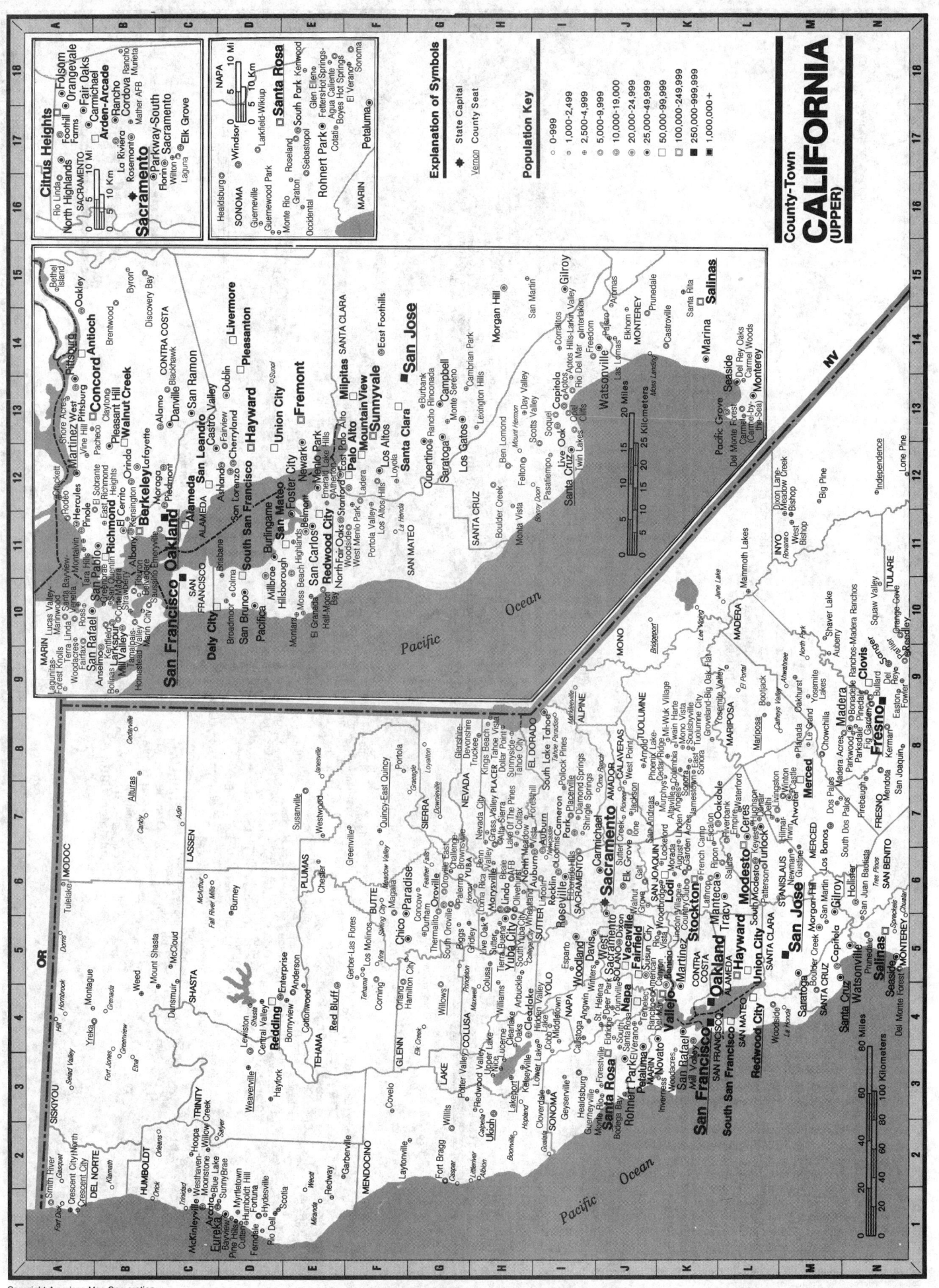

CALIFORNIA

County-Town

(UPPER)

Explanation of Symbols

⊕ State Capital

Vernon County Seat

Population Key

- ○ 0-999
- ⊙ 1,000-2,499
- ◉ 2,500-4,999
- ● 5,000-9,999
- ⊡ 10,000-19,000
- ▣ 20,000-24,999
- ▢ 25,000-49,999
- □ 50,000-99,999
- ■ 100,000-249,999
- ■ 250,000-999,999
- ■ 1,000,000+

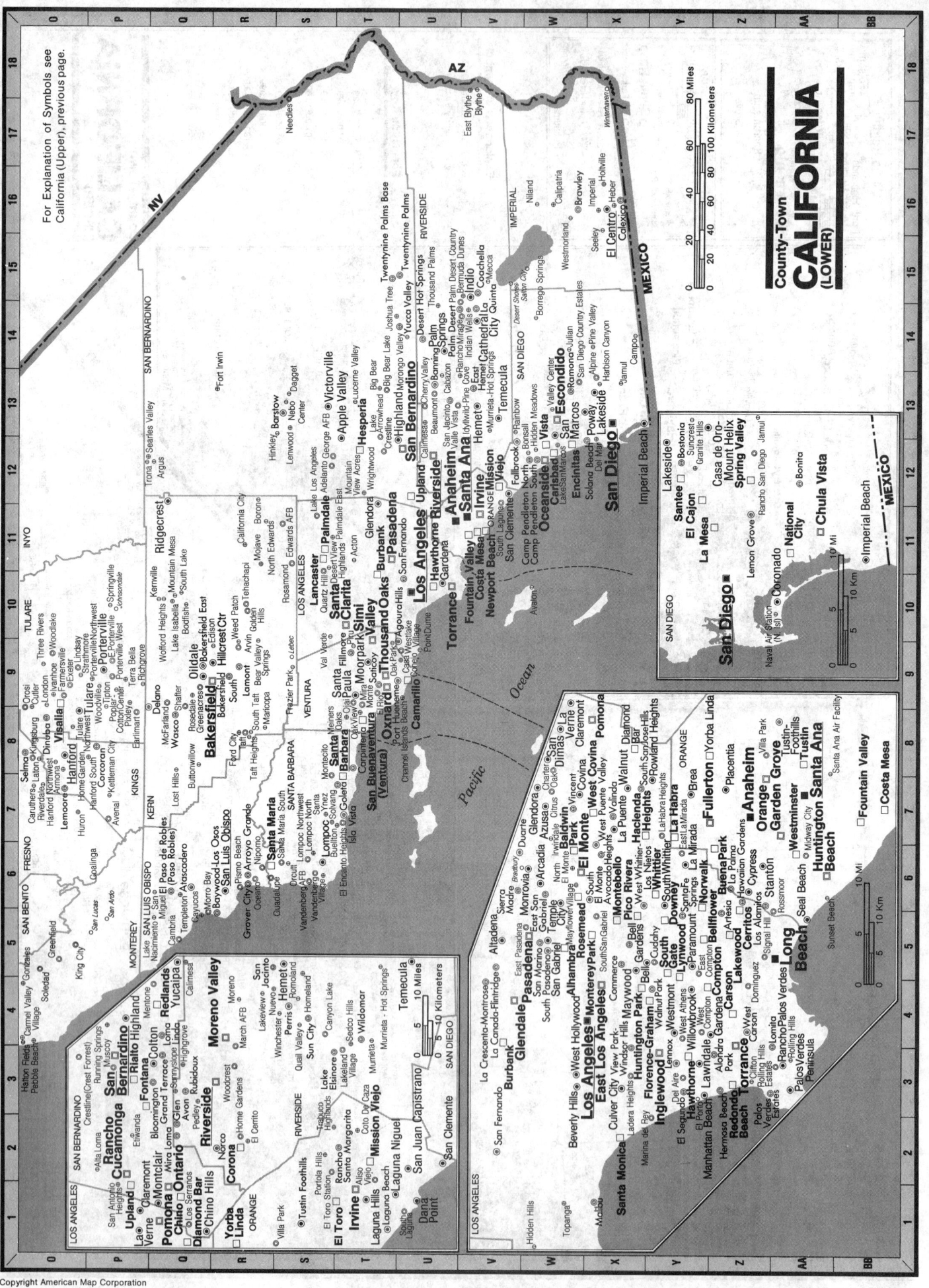

For Explanation of Symbols see
California (Upper), previous page.

County-Town
CALIFORNIA
(LOWER)

Copyright American Map Corporation

COUNTIES

(58 Counties)

Name of County	Population	Location on Map
ALAMEDA	1,279,182	L-4
ALPINE	1,113	I-8
AMADOR	30,039	J-7
BUTTE	182,120	F-6
CALAVERAS	31,998	J-8
COLUSA	16,275	G-4
CONTRA COSTA	803,732	K-5
DEL NORTE	23,460	B-1
EL DORADO	125,995	I-8
FRESNO	667,490	N-7
GLENN	24,798	F-3
HUMBOLDT	119,118	B-2
IMPERIAL	109,303	V-15
INYO	18,281	L-11
KERN	543,477	Q-7
KINGS	101,469	P-7
LAKE	50,631	G-3
LASSEN	27,598	C-6
LOS ANGELES	8,863,164	S-10
MADERA	88,090	L-10
MARIN	230,096	J-3
MARIPOSA	14,302	L-8
MENDOCINO	80,345	F-1
MERCED	178,403	M-6
MODOC	9,678	A-6
MONO	9,956	J-9
MONTEREY	355,660	N-5
NAPA	110,765	I-4
NEVADA	78,510	G-7
ORANGE	2,410,556	V-11
PLACER	172,796	H-7
PLUMAS	19,739	E-6
RIVERSIDE	1,170,413	U-16
SACRAMENTO	1,041,219	I-6
SAN BENITO	36,697	N-6
SAN BERNARDINO	1,418,380	Q-14
SAN DIEGO	2,498,016	V-13
SAN FRANCISCO	723,959	K-3
SAN JOAQUIN	480,628	J-6
SAN LUIS OBISPO	217,162	P-5
SAN MATEO	649,623	L-4
SANTA BARBARA	369,608	S-7
SANTA CLARA	1,497,577	L-5
SANTA CRUZ	229,734	M-4
SHASTA	147,036	C-4
SIERRA	3,318	G-7
SISKIYOU	43,531	A-3
SOLANO	340,421	J-5
SONOMA	388,222	I-2
STANISLAUS	370,522	M-6
SUTTER	64,415	I-5
TEHAMA	49,625	E-3
TRINITY	13,063	C-3
TULARE	311,921	O-10
TUOLUMNE	48,456	J-8
VENTURA	669,016	S-8
YOLO	141,092	I-4
YUBA	58,228	G-6
TOTAL	29,760,021	

CITIES AND TOWNS

Note: The first name is that of the city or town, second, that of the county in which it is located, then the population and location on the map.

•Acton, Los Angeles, 1,471 ... T-11
Adelanto, San Bernardino, 8,517 ... S-12
Agoura Hills, Los Angeles, 20,390 ... V-9
Alameda, Alameda, 76,459 ... C-11
•Alamo, Contra Costa, 12,277 ... C-13
Albany, Alameda, 16,327 ... B-11
Alhambra, Los Angeles, 82,106 ... W-5
•Aliso Viejo, Orange, 7,612 ... T-1
•Alondra Park, Los Angeles, 12,215 ... Z-3
•Alpine, San Diego, 9,695 ... X-13
Alta Loma, San Bernardino ... P-12
•Alta Sierra, Nevada, 5,709 ... H-7
•Altadena, Los Angeles, 42,658 ... V-5
Altaville, Calaveras ... K-7
Alturas, Modoc, 3,231 ... B-8
•American Canyon, Napa, 7,706 ... J-4
Anaheim, Orange, 266,406 ... U-11
Anderson, Shasta, 8,299 ... E-4
Angels, Calaveras, 2,409 ... K-7
•Angwin, Napa, 3,503 ... I-4
Antioch, Contra Costa, 62,195 ... A-14
Apple Valley, San Bernardino, 46,079 ... T-12
•Aptos, Santa Cruz, 9,061 ... I-13
•Aptos Hills-Larkin Valley, Santa Cruz, 2,205 ... I-14
•Arbuckle, Colusa, 1,912 ... H-5
Arcadia, Los Angeles, 48,290 ... W-6
Arcata, Humboldt, 15,197 ... C-1
•Arden-Arcade, Sacramento, 92,040 ... B-17
Argus, San Bernardino ... Q-12
•Armona, Kings, 3,122 ... O-8
•Arnold, Calaveras, 3,788 ... J-8
•Aromas, Monterey/San Benito, 2,275 ... J-14
Arroyo Grande, San Luis Obispo, 14,378 ... R-6
Artesia, Los Angeles, 15,464 ... Z-5
Arvin, Kern, 9,286 ... R-9
•Ashland, Alameda, 16,590 ... D-12
Atascadero, San Luis Obispo, 23,138 ... Q-6
Atherton, San Mateo, 7,163 ... E-12
Atwater, Merced, 22,282 ... M-7
•Auberry, Fresno, 1,866 ... M-9
Auburn, Placer, 10,592 ... I-6
•August, San Joaquin, 6,376 ... K-6
Avalon, Los Angeles, 2,918 ... W-10
Avenal, Kings, 9,770 ... P-7
•Avocado Heights, Los Angeles, 14,232 ... X-6
Azusa, Los Angeles, 41,333 ... W-7
Bakersfield, Kern, 174,820 ... R-9
Bakersfield East, Kern ... Q-9
Bakersfield South, Kern ... R-9
Baldwin Park, Los Angeles, 69,330 ... W-6
Banning, Riverside, 20,570 ... U-12
Barstow, San Bernardino, 21,472 ... S-13
•Bayview, Humboldt, 1,318 ... C-1
•Bayview-Montalvin, Contra Costa, 3,988 ... A-11
•Baywood-Los Osos, San Luis Obispo, 14,377 ... R-5
•Beale AFB, Yuba, 6,912 ... H-6
•Bear Valley Springs, Kern, 1,593 ... R-10
Beaumont, Riverside, 9,685 ... U-12
Bell, Los Angeles, 34,365 ... X-5
Bell Gardens, Los Angeles, 42,355 ... X-5
Bellflower, Los Angeles, 61,815 ... Y-5
Belmont, San Mateo, 24,127 ... E-11
Belvedere, Marin, 2,147 ... B-10
•Ben Lomond, Santa Cruz, 7,884 ... H-13
Benicia, Solano, 24,437 ... K-5
Berkeley, Alameda, 102,724 ... B-11
•Bermuda Dunes, Riverside, 4,571 ... H-15
•Bethel Island, Contra Costa, 2,115 ... A-15
Beverly Hills, Los Angeles, 31,971 ... W-3
•Big Bear City, San Bernardino, 4,920 ... T-13
Big Bear Lake, San Bernardino, 5,351 ... T-13
•Big Pine, Inyo, 1,158 ... M-12
Biggs, Butte, 1,581 ... G-5
Bishop, Inyo, 3,475 ... M-11
•Blackhawk, Contra Costa, 6,199 ... C-13
•Bloomington, San Bernardino, 15,116 ... Q-3
Blue Lake, Humboldt, 1,235 ... C-1
Blythe, Riverside, 8,428 ... V-18
•Bodega Bay, Sonoma, 1,127 ... J-3
•Bodfish, Kern, 1,283 ... Q-10
•Bolinas, Marin, 1,098 ... B-9
•Bonadelle Ranchos-Madera Ranchos, Madera, 5,705 ... N-8
•Bonita, San Diego, 12,542 ... AA-12
Bonnyview, Shasta ... E-4
•Bonsall, San Diego, 1,881 ... W-12
•Bootjack, Mariposa, 1,295 ... L-9
•Boron, Kern, 2,101 ... R-12
•Borrego Springs, San Diego, 2,244 ... W-14
•Bostonia, San Diego, 13,670 ... Y-12
•Boulder Creek, Santa Cruz, 6,725 ... M-4
•Boyes Hot Springs, Sonoma, 5,973 ... E-18
Brawley, Imperial, 18,923 ... W-16
Brea, Orange, 32,873 ... Y-7
Brentwood, Contra Costa, 7,563 ... B-15
Bridgeport, Mono ... J-10
Brisbane, San Mateo, 2,952 ... D-11
•Broadmoor, San Mateo, 3,739 ... D-10
•Buellton, Santa Barbara, 3,506 ... T-7
Buena Park, Orange, 68,784 ... Z-6
Bullard, Fresno ... N-9
Burbank, Los Angeles, 93,643 ... T-10
•Burbank, Santa Clara, 4,902 ... G-13
Burlingame, San Mateo, 26,801 ... D-11
•Burney, Shasta, 3,423 ... D-6
•Buttonwillow, Kern, 1,301 ... Q-8
Byron, Contra Costa ... B-15
•Cabazon, Riverside, 1,588 ... H-13
Calexico, Imperial, 18,633 ... X-16
California City, Kern, 5,955 ... R-11
Calimesa, Riverside, 4,647 ... U-13
Calipatria, Imperial, 2,690 ... W-16
Calistoga, Napa, 4,468 ... I-4
Camarillo, Ventura, 52,303 ... U-9
•Cambria, San Luis Obispo, 5,382 ... Q-5
•Cambrian Park, Santa Clara, 2,998 ... G-13
•Cameron Park, El Dorado, 11,897 ... I-7
•Camp Pendleton North, San Diego, 10,373 ... W-12
•Camp Pendleton South, San Diego, 11,299 ... W-12
Campbell, Santa Clara, 36,048 ... G-13
Campo, San Diego ... X-14
•Canyon Lake, Riverside, 7,938 ... S-4
Capitola, Santa Cruz, 10,171 ... M-5
Carlsbad, San Diego, 63,126 ... W-12
•Carmel Valley Village, Monterey, 4,407 ... O-4
Carmel Woods, Monterey ... L-13
Carmel-by-the-Sea, Monterey, 4,239 ... L-13
•Carmichael, Sacramento, 48,702 ... A-17
Carpinteria, Santa Barbara, 13,747 ... T-8
Carson, Los Angeles, 83,995 ... Z-4
•Caruthers, Fresno, 1,603 ... O-7
•Casa Conejo, Ventura, 3,286 ... V-9
•Casa de Oro-Mount Helix, San Diego, 30,727 ... Z-12
Castle, Merced ... M-7
•Castro Valley, Alameda, 48,619 ... C-12
•Castroville, Monterey, 5,272 ... K-14
Cathedral City, Riverside, 30,085 ... V-14
•Cayucos, San Luis Obispo, 2,960 ... Q-5
•Central Valley, Shasta, 4,340 ... D-4
Ceres, Stanislaus, 26,314 ... L-7
Cerritos, Los Angeles, 53,240 ... Z-5
•Challenge-Brownsville, Yuba, 1,096 ... G-6
•Channel Islands Beach, Ventura, 3,317 ... U-9
•Charter Oak, Los Angeles, 8,858 ... W-8
•Cherry Valley, Riverside, 5,945 ... U-13
•Cherryland, Alameda, 11,088 ... D-12
•Chester, Plumas, 2,082 ... E-6
Chico, Butte, 40,079 ... G-5
Chino, San Bernardino, 59,682 ... Q-1
•Chino Hills, San Bernardino, 27,608 ... Q-1
Chowchilla, Madera, 5,930 ... M-8
Chula Vista, San Diego, 135,163 ... AA-11
•Citrus, Los Angeles, 9,481 ... W-7
•Citrus Heights, Sacramento, 107,439 ... A-17
Claremont, Los Angeles, 32,503 ... W-9
Clayton, Contra Costa, 7,317 ... B-13
Clearlake, Lake, 11,804 ... H-4
•Clearlake Oaks, Lake, 2,419 ... H-4
Clifton, Los Angeles ... Z-3
Cloverdale, Sonoma, 4,924 ... I-3
Clovis, Fresno, 50,323 ... N-9
Coachella, Riverside, 16,896 ... V-15
Coalinga, Fresno, 8,212 ... P-6
•Cobb, Lake, 1,477 ... I-4
Colfax, Placer, 1,306 ... H-6
Colma, San Mateo, 1,103 ... D-10
Colton, San Bernardino, 40,213 ... Q-3
•Columbia, Tuolumne, 1,799 ... K-8
Colusa, Colusa, 4,934 ... H-5
Commerce, Los Angeles, 12,135 ... X-5
Compton, Los Angeles, 90,454 ... Z-4
Concord, Contra Costa, 111,348 ... B-13
•Concow, Butte, 1,392 ... G-6
Corcoran, Kings, 13,364 ... P-8
Corning, Tehama, 5,870 ... F-5
Corona, Riverside, 76,095 ... R-2
Coronado, San Diego, 26,540 ... AA-10
•Corralitos, Santa Cruz, 2,513 ... I-14
Corte Madera, Marin, 8,272 ... B-10
Costa Mesa, Orange, 96,357 ... V-11
Cotati, Sonoma, 5,714 ... E-17
•Coto De Caza, Orange, 2,853 ... T-2
•Cottonwood, Shasta, 1,747 ... E-4
•Country Club, San Joaquin, 9,325 ... K-6
•Covelo, Mendocino, 1,057 ... F-3
Covina, Los Angeles, 43,207 ... W-7
Crescent City, Del Norte, 4,380 ... A-1
•Crescent City North, Del Norte, 3,853 ... A-1
•Crestline, San Bernardino, 8,594 ... T-12
•Crockett, Contra Costa, 3,228 ... A-12
Cudahy, Los Angeles, 22,817 ... Y-5
Culver City, Los Angeles, 38,793 ... X-3
Cupertino, Santa Clara, 40,263 ... G-13
•Cutler, Tulare, 4,450 ... O-9
•Cutten, Humboldt, 1,516 ... D-1
Cypress, Orange, 42,655 ... Z-4
Dagget, San Bernardino ... S-13
Daly City, San Mateo, 92,311 ... C-10
Dana Point, Orange, 31,896 ... U-1
Danville, Contra Costa, 31,306 ... C-13
Davis, Yolo, 46,209 ... I-5
•Day Valley, Santa Cruz, 2,842 ... I-13
•Deer Park, Napa, 1,825 ... J-4
•Del Aire, Los Angeles, 8,040 ... Y-3
Del Mar, San Diego, 4,860 ... X-12
•Del Monte Forest, Monterey, 5,069 ... L-13
•Del Rey, Fresno, 1,150 ... N-9
Del Rey Oaks, Monterey, 1,661 ... L-13
Delano, Kern, 22,762 ... Q-8
•Delhi, Merced, 3,280 ... L-7
•Denair, Stanislaus, 3,693 ... L-7
Desert Hot Springs, Riverside, 11,668 ... U-14
•Desert View Highlands, Los Angeles, 2,154 ... S-11
Diamond Bar, Los Angeles, 53,672 ... X-8
•Diamond Springs, El Dorado, 2,872 ... I-7
Dinuba, Tulare, 12,743 ... O-8
•Discovery Bay, Contra Costa, 5,351 ... B-15
Dixon, Solano, 10,401 ... J-5
•Dixon Lane-Meadow Creek, Inyo, 2,561 ... L-11
•Dollar Point, Placer, 1,449 ... H-8
Dominguez, Los Angeles ... Z-4
Dos Palos, Merced, 4,196 ... M-7
Downey, Los Angeles, 91,444 ... Y-5
Downieville, Sierra ... G-7
Duarte, Los Angeles, 20,688 ... V-6
Dublin, Alameda, 23,229 ... D-13
Dunsmuir, Siskiyou, 2,129 ... C-5
•Durham, Butte, 4,784 ... G-5
•Earlimart, Tulare, 5,881 ... P-8
•East Blythe, Riverside, 1,511 ... V-18
•East Compton, Los Angeles, 7,967 ... Y-5
•East Foothills, Santa Clara, 14,898 ... F-14
•East Hemet, Riverside, 17,611 ... U-12
•East La Mirada, Los Angeles, 9,367 ... Y-6
•East Los Angeles, Los Angeles, 126,379 ... X-4
•East Palo Alto, San Mateo, 23,451 ... E-12
•East Pasadena, Los Angeles, 5,910 ... W-5
•East Porterville, Tulare, 5,790 ... P-9
•East Richmond Heights, Contra Costa, 3,266 ... B-11
•East San Gabriel, Los Angeles, 12,736 ... W-6
•East Sonora, Tuolumne, 1,675 ... K-8
•Easton, Fresno, 1,877 ... N-9
Edison, Kern ... R-9
•Edwards AFB, Kern, 7,423 ... S-11
El Cajon, San Diego, 88,693 ... Y-12
El Centro, Imperial, 31,384 ... X-16
El Cerrito, Contra Costa, 22,869 ... B-11
•El Cerrito, Riverside, 4,490 ... D-2
•El Dorado Hills, El Dorado, 6,395 ... I-6
El Encanto Heights, Santa Barbara ... T-7
•El Granada, San Mateo, 4,426 ... E-19
El Monte, Los Angeles, 106,209 ... W-6
El Paso de Robles (Paso Robles), San Luis Obispo, 18,583 ... Q-6
El Porto, Los Angeles ... Y-3
•El Rio, Ventura, 6,419 ... T-9
El Segundo, Los Angeles, 15,223 ... Y-3
•El Sobrante, Contra Costa, 9,852 ... B-12
•El Toro, Orange, 62,685 ... T-1
•El Toro Station, Orange, 6,869 ... T-1
•El Verano, Sonoma, 3,498 ... J-4
•Eldridge, Sonoma, 1,144 ... J-4
•Elk Grove, Sacramento, 17,483 ... J-6
•Elkhorn, Monterey, 1,458 ... J-14
•Emerald Lake Hills, San Mateo, 3,328 ... E-11
Emeryville, Alameda, 5,740 ... C-11
Empire, Stanislaus ... L-7
Encinitas, San Diego, 55,386 ... W-12
Enterprise, Shasta ... D-4
Escalon, San Joaquin, 4,437 ... K-7
Escondido, San Diego, 108,635 ... W-13
•Esparto, Yolo, 1,487 ... I-5
Etiwanda, San Bernardino ... P-2
Eureka, Humboldt, 27,025 ... D-1
Exeter, Tulare, 7,276 ... O-9
•Fair Oaks, Sacramento, 26,867 ... A-17
Fairfax, Marin, 6,931 ... A-10
Fairfield, Solano, 77,211 ... J-5
•Fairview, Alameda, 9,045 ... D-12
•Fallbrook, San Diego, 22,095 ... V-12
Farmersville, Tulare, 6,235 ... O-9
•Felton, Santa Cruz, 5,350 ... H-12
Ferndale, Humboldt, 1,331 ... D-1
•Fetters Hot Springs-Agua Caliente, Sonoma, 2,024 ... E-18
Fig Garden, Fresno ... N-9
Fillmore, Ventura, 11,992 ... T-9
Firebaugh, Fresno, 4,429 ... N-8
•Florence-Graham, Los Angeles, 57,147 ... Y-4
•Florin, Sacramento, 24,330 ... C-17
Folsom, Sacramento, 29,802 ... A-18
Fontana, San Bernardino, 87,535 ... P-3
•Foothill Farms, Sacramento, 17,135 ... A-17
•Ford City, Kern, 3,781 ... R-8
•Foresthill, Placer, 1,409 ... H-7
•Forestville, Sonoma, 2,443 ... J-3
Fort Bragg, Mendocino, 6,078 ... G-2
Fort Irwin, San Bernardino ... R-13
Fortuna, Humboldt, 8,788 ... B-1
Foster City, San Mateo, 28,176 ... E-11
Fountain Valley, Orange, 53,691 ... V-11
Fowler, Fresno, 3,208 ... N-9
•Frazier Park, Kern, 2,201 ... S-9
•Freedom, Santa Cruz, 8,361 ... I-14
Fremont, Alameda, 173,339 ... E-13
•French Camp, San Joaquin, 3,018 ... K-6
Fresno, Fresno, 354,202 ... N-9
Fullerton, Orange, 114,144 ... Z-7
Galt, Sacramento, 8,889 ... J-6
Garberville, Humboldt ... F-2
•Garden Acres, San Joaquin, 8,547 ... K-6
Garden Grove, Orange, 143,050 ... AA-7
Gardena, Los Angeles, 49,847 ... U-10
•George AFB, San Bernardino, 5,085 ... S-12
•Gerber-Las Flores, Tehama, 1,143 ... F-5
Geyserville, Sonoma ... I-3
Gilroy, Santa Clara, 31,487 ... M-6
•Glen Avon, Riverside, 12,663 ... Q-2
•Glen Ellen, Sonoma, 1,191 ... E-18
Glendale, Los Angeles, 180,038 ... V-4
Glendora, Los Angeles, 47,828 ... T-11
•Glenshire-Devonshire, Nevada, 2,133 ... G-8
•Golden Hills, Kern, 5,423 ... R-10
Goleta, Santa Barbara ... T-7
Gonzales, Monterey, 4,660 ... O-4
Grand Terrace, San Bernardino, 10,946 ... Q-3
•Granite Hills, San Diego, 3,157 ... Y-12
Grass Valley, Nevada, 9,048 ... H-7
•Graton, Sonoma, 1,409 ... E-16
•Greenacres, Kern, 7,379 ... Q-9
Greenbrae, Marin ... B-10
Greenfield, Monterey, 7,464 ... O-5
•Greenville, Plumas, 1,396 ... F-7
Gridley, Butte, 4,631 ... H-5
•Groveland-Big Oak Flat, Tuolumne, 2,753 ... K-8
Grover City, San Luis Obispo, 11,656 ... R-6
Guadalupe, Santa Barbara, 5,479 ... R-6
•Guerneville, Sonoma, 1,966 ... J-3
Guernewood Park, Sonoma ... D-16
Gustine, Merced, 3,931 ... M-7
•Hacienda Heights, Los Angeles, 52,354 ... X-7
Half Moon Bay, San Mateo, 8,886 ... E-10
•Hamilton City, Glenn, 1,811 ... G-5
Hanford, Kings, 30,897 ... O-8
Hanford Northwest, Kings ... O-8
Hanford South, Kings ... P-8
•Harbison Canyon, San Diego, 2,122 ... X-13
Hatton Fields, Monterey ... O-4
Hawaiian Gardens, Los Angeles, 13,639 ... Z-6
Hawthorne, Los Angeles, 71,349 ... U-10
•Hayfork, Trinity, 2,605 ... D-3
Hayward, Alameda, 111,498 ... L-5
Healdsburg, Sonoma, 9,469 ... I-3
•Heber, Imperial, 2,566 ... X-16
Hemet, Riverside, 36,094 ... V-13
Hercules, Contra Costa, 16,829 ... A-11
Hermosa Beach, Los Angeles, 18,219 ... Z-3
Hesperia, San Bernardino, 50,418 ... T-12
Hidden Hills, Los Angeles, 1,729 ... W-1
•Hidden Meadows, San Diego, 2,371 ... W-12
•Hidden Valley Lake, Lake, 1,961 ... I-4
•Highgrove, Riverside, 3,175 ... Q-3
Highland, San Bernardino, 34,439 ... U-12
•Highlands, San Mateo, 2,644 ... E-11
Hillcrest Center, Kern ... R-9
Hillsborough, San Mateo, 10,667 ... E-11
•Hilmar-Irwin, Merced, 3,392 ... L-7
Hinkley, San Bernardino ... S-12
Hollister, San Benito, 19,212 ... N-6
Holtville, Imperial, 4,820 ... X-16
•Home Garden, Kings, 1,549 ... O-8
•Home Gardens, Riverside, 7,780 ... R-2
•Homeland, Riverside, 3,312 ... S-5
Hoopa, Humboldt ... C-2
Hughson, Stanislaus, 3,259 ... L-7
•Humboldt Hill, Humboldt, 2,865 ... D-1
Huntington Beach, Orange, 181,519 ... AA-6
Huntington Park, Los Angeles, 56,065 ... X-4
Huron, Fresno, 4,766 ... O-7
•Hydesville, Humboldt, 1,131 ... D-1
•Idyllwild-Pine Cove, Riverside, 2,853 ... U-13
Imperial, Imperial, 4,113 ... X-16
Imperial Beach, San Diego, 26,512 ... BB-11
Independence, Inyo ... N-12
Indian Wells, Riverside, 2,647 ... V-14
Indio, Riverside, 36,793 ... V-15
Inglewood, Los Angeles, 109,602 ... Y-3
•Interlaken, Santa Cruz, 6,404 ... I-14
•Inverness, Marin, 1,422 ... K-3
Ione, Amador, 6,516 ... J-7
Irvine, Orange, 110,330 ... V-11
Irwindale, Los Angeles, 1,050 ... W-7
•Isla Vista, Santa Barbara, 20,395 ... T-7
•Ivanhoe, Tulare, 3,293 ... O-9
Jackson, Amador, 3,545 ... J-7
Jamestown, Tuolumne, 2,178 ... K-8
•Jamul, San Diego, 2,258 ... X-13
•Joshua Tree, San Bernardino, 3,898 ... T-14
•Julian, San Diego, 1,284 ... W-14
•Kelseyville, Lake, 2,861 ... H-3
•Kensington, Contra Costa, 4,974 ... B-11
•Kentfield, Marin, 6,030 ... B-10
Kenwood, Sonoma ... E-18
Kerman, Fresno, 5,448 ... N-8
•Kernville, Kern, 1,656 ... Q-10
•Kettleman City, Kings, 1,411 ... P-7
•Keyes, Stanislaus, 2,878 ... L-7
King City, Monterey, 7,634 ... O-5
•Kings Beach, Placer, 2,796 ... H-8
Kingsburg, Fresno, 7,205 ... O-8
La Canada Flintridge, Los Angeles, 19,378 ... V-5
•La Crescenta-Montrose, Los Angeles, 16,968 ... V-4
La Habra, Orange, 51,266 ... Y-7
La Habra Heights, Los Angeles, 6,226 ... Y-7
La Mesa, San Diego, 52,931 ... Z-11
La Mirada, Los Angeles, 40,452 ... Y-6
La Palma, Orange, 15,392 ... Z-6
La Puente, Los Angeles, 36,955 ... X-7
La Quinta, Riverside, 11,215 ... V-14
•La Riviera, Sacramento, 10,986 ... B-17
La Verne, Los Angeles, 30,897 ... W-8
Ladera, San Mateo ... F-12
•Ladera Heights, Los Angeles, 6,316 ... X-3
Lafayette, Contra Costa, 23,501 ... B-12
•Laguna, Sacramento, 9,828 ... C-17
Laguna Beach, Orange, 23,170 ... T-1
•Laguna Hills, Orange, 46,731 ... T-1
Laguna Niguel, Orange, 44,400 ... T-1
•Lagunitas-Forest Knolls, Marin, 1,821 ... A-9
•Lake Arrowhead, San Bernardino, 6,539 ... T-12
Lake Elsinore, Riverside, 18,285 ... S-3
•Lake Isabella, Kern, 3,323 ... Q-10
•Lake Los Angeles, Los Angeles, 7,977 ... S-11
•Lake Nacimiento, San Luis Obispo, 1,556 ... Q-5
•Lake of the Pines, Nevada, 3,890 ... H-6
•Lake San Marcos, San Diego, 3,802 ... W-12
•Lakeland Village, Riverside, 5,159 ... T-3

Explanation of symbols: •– Census Designated Place (CDP)

Colorado

General Help Numbers:

Governor's Office

136 State Capitol Bldg
Denver, CO 80203-1792

303-866-2471
Fax 303-866-2003
8AM-5PM

www.colorado.gov/governor/l

Attorney General's Office

Department of Law
1525 Sherman St, 5th Floor
Denver, CO 80203
www.ago.state.co.us

303-866-4500
Fax 303-866-5691
8AM-5PM

Legislative Records

State Capitol, 200 E Colfax Ave
Devcer, CO 80203-1776
www.leg.state.co.us/

303-866-3055
303-866-4011
8AM-5PM

State Archives

Archives & Public Records
1313 Sherman St, Room 1B-20
Denver, CO 80203
http://statearchives.us/colorado.htm

303-866-2055
Fax 303-866-2257
8AM-4:30PM

State Specifics:

Capital:

Denver
Denver County

Time Zone:

MST

Number of Counties:

64

Population:

4,550,688

Web Site:

www.state.co.us

State Agencies

Criminal Records

Bureau of Investigation, State Repository, Identification Unit, 690 Kipling St, Suite 3000, Denver, CO 80215; 303-239-4208, 303-239-5858 (Fax), 8AM-4:30PM.

http://cbi.state.co.us

Indexing & Storage: Records are available from 1967 on. Records prior to 1967 are in on-site computer archives. It takes less than 72 hours before new records are available for inquiry. Records are indexed on inhouse computer, fingerprint cards. Records are not destroyed or removed.

Searching: The requester must sign a disclaimer stating "This record shall not be used for the direct

solicitation of business for pecuniary gain." Include the following in your request-full name, date of birth, and disclaimer. The SSN, race, and gender are optional. Fingerprints are optional unless statutorily-required. Records are 100% fingerprint supported. If charged after fingerprinted, the practice of notifying the state is becoming more common, though this not yet statewide. The following data is not released:

sealed records, juvenile records and pending mental comps.

Access by: mail, in person, online.

Fee & Payment: Name check-$13.00 per name; fingerprint search-$16.50 per fingerprint. A state mandated fingerprint search plus notification of subsequent arrest in CO-$19.50; or nationwide fingerprint search-$22.00. Internet searches are $6.85 each. Fee payee: Colorado Bureau of Investigations (CBI). Prepayment required. No personal checks accepted. Credit cards accepted: MasterCard, Visa.

Mail search: Turnaround time: 3 days. No SASE is required.

In person search: You may request information in person.

Online search: There is an Internet access at www.cbirecordscheck.com. Requesters must use a credit card, an account does not need to be established. However, account holders may set up a batch system. The fee is $6.85 per record.

Statewide Court Records

State Court Administrator, 1301 Pennsylvania St, Suite 300, Denver, CO 80203-2416; 303-861-1111, 800-888-0001, 303-837-2340 (Fax), 8AM-5PM.

www.courts.state.co.us

Note: Except for certain online research capabilities, all court record access must be done at the local level.

Access by: online. No searching by mail.

Online search: Search opinions at the website. As a result of an initiative of the Colorado Judicial Branch, all district court and all county court records are available at www.cocourts.com. This is not an official state site and fees are involved.

Sexual Offender Registry

Colorado Bureau of Investigation, SOR Unit, 690 Kipling St, Suite 4000, Denver, CO 80215; 303-239-4222, 303-233-8336 (Fax), 8AM-4:30PM.

http://sor.state.co.us

Note: Each police or sheriff's agency is required to maintain a list of convicted sex offenders in their jurisdiction and is required to release that information to any citizen of the jurisdiction who requests it.

Searching: Requesters are screened for purpose, they must be at least 18 years of age. Include the following in your request-name, address.

Access by: mail, in person, online.

Fee & Payment: The CBI may assess reasonable fees for the search, retrieval, and copying of information requested. Fee payee: CBI

Mail search: Turnaround time: 5 days. Lists of names can be ordered by city or by ZIP Code.

In person search: Lists of names can be ordered by city or by ZIP Code.

Online search: The website gives access to only certain high-risk registered sex offenders in the following categories: Sexually Violent Predator (SVP), Multiple Offenses, and Failed to Register.

Incarceration Records

Colorado Department of Corrections, Offender Records Customer Support, 2862 South Circle Dr.

#418, Colorado Springs, CO 80906-4195; 719-226-4884, 719-226-4880 (Locator Service), 719-226-4899 (Fax), 8AM-5PM.

www.doc.state.co.us/index.html

Indexing & Storage: Records are available on current and former inmates. This office can release: sentence information (crime/sentencing court/docket #); location of incarceration; parole eligibility date/approved parole date; and mandatory release date. It takes 4 weeks before new records are available for inquiry. Records are normally destroyed after 10 years.

Searching: Include the following in your request-full name, date of birth, signed release (for full information).

Access by: mail, phone, fax.

Fee & Payment: Fee is $1.00 per page. Prepayment required. No credit cards or personal checks accepted.

Mail search: Turnaround time: 2-4 weeks. No SASE is required.

Phone search: The Locator Service phone line is open from 8:00 AM to 5:00 PM. Only very basic information is available.

Fax search: Fax requesting is available.

Corporation, Trademarks, Servicemarks, Fictitious Name, Limited Liability Company, Assumed Name, Trade Name

Secretary of State, Business Division, 1560 Broadway, Suite 200, Denver, CO 80202; 303-894-2200 x2 (Business Entities), 303-869-4864 (Fax), 7:30AM-5PM.

www.sos.state.co.us

Indexing & Storage: Records are available for all active companies. Inactive company records are archived. New records are available for inquiry immediately. Records are indexed on microfilm, inhouse computer. Records are normally destroyed after once scanned & available on web.

Searching: Include the following in your request-full name of business.

Access by: mail, phone, fax, in person, online.

Fee & Payment: There is no fee for searching active companies online. There is a $5.00 per business name searched via paper request, $100.00 fee for archived records. The copy fee is $.50 per page. Certifcation is $2.00. Fee payee: Secretary of State. Personal checks accepted. No credit cards accepted.

Mail search: Turnaround time: 2 to 3 days.

Phone search: Limit of 3 names.

Fax search: Orders requested by fax are processed the same as other searches.

In person search: A public access terminal offers free searching.

Online search: The Sec. of State's Business Record Search page offers free searching of corporate names and associate information at www.sos.state.co.us/pubs/business/main.htm. Effective 07/04, some e-filing documents are available. Click on Business Center. Also, search for charitable nonprofit members of CANPO - Colorado Association of Nonprofit Organizations - at www.canpo.org/directory_members_search.cfm.

Search trade names at www.businesstax.state.co.us/tradenames/.

Other access: Various informaion is available as a one time order or via subscription. Transmittal can be through CDs, tapes or FTP.

Expedited service: Expedited service is available for mail, in person and fax searches. Turnaround time: 1 day. Add $50.00 per business name.

Uniform Commercial Code, Federal Tax Liens, State Tax Liens

Secretary of State, UCC Division, 1560 Broadway, Suite 200, Denver, CO 80202; 303-894-2200 x2, 303-869-4864 (Fax), 7:30AM-5PM.

www.sos.state.co.us

Note: State tax liens are handled by the Department of Revenue. These liens can be filed at any one of the state's county recording offices, and so should be searched as such.

Indexing & Storage: Records are available from 1966. Records are indexed on computer from 1979, and on microfiche from 1987 to 1997. It takes 5 days before new records are available for inquiry. Records are normally destroyed after scanning and placed online.

Searching: Use search request form UCC-11. The search includes all tax liens recorded at the state level. This includes all IRS liens. Include the following in your request-debtor name.

Access by: mail, phone, fax, in person, online.

Fee & Payment: The search fee is $13.00 per name searched. Copies are $1.25 per page. Fee payee: Secretary of State. Personal checks accepted. No credit cards accepted.

Mail search: Turnaround time: 10 days. A SASE is requested.

Phone search: The latest 4 liens are available by telephone, press 2 when connected using number listed above.

Fax search: Fax searching available.

In person search: Simple requests may be processed while you wait.

Online search: There is free record searching at this agency's website. More extensive data is also available via supscription for ongoing business requesters.

Other access: Various informaion is available as a one time order or via subscription. Transmittal can be through CDs, tapes or FTP.

Expedited service: Expedited service is available for mail, phone and in person searches. Turnaround time: 1 day. There is a $50.00 fee per debtor name.

Sales Tax Registrations

Revenue Department, Taxpayers Services Office, 1375 Sherman St, Denver, CO 80261 (Courier: 1625 Broadway, Ste 805, Denver, CO 80261); 303-238-7378, 303-866-3211 (Fax), 8AM-4:30PM.

www.revenue.state.co.us

Indexing & Storage: Records are available from 1988 and are computerized. It takes 2 weeks before new records are available for inquiry. Records are indexed on computer. Records are normally destroyed after 10 years.

Searching: This agency will confirm that a business is registered. Include the following in your request-business name. They will also search by tax permit number.

Access by: phone, in person, online.

Fee & Payment: There is no search fee. The agency will not honor mail requests.

Phone search: No fee for telephone request. They will only search by trade name.

In person search: They will release the owner's name if petitioned in writing.

Online search: You can verfiy a sales tax license or exemption number at www.taxview.state.co.us.

Birth Certificates

Department of Public Health & Environment, Vital Records Section HSVR-A1, 4300 Cherry Creek Dr S, Denver, CO 80246-1530; 303-756-4464 (Recorded Message), 303-692-2224 (Credit Card Ordering), 303-692-2234 (General Information), 800-423-1108 (Fax), 8:30AM-4:30PM.

www.cdphe.state.co.us/hs/certs.asp

Note: Certified copies for birth years 1910 to present can also be ordered at most county health departments.

Indexing & Storage: Records are available from 1910 to present. New records are available for inquiry immediately. Records are indexed on microfiche, inhouse computer.

Searching: The person named on the record, members of the immediate family, legal representatives of those named above, and others demonstrating a direct and tangible interest in the record may request a copy. Include the following in your request-full name, names of parents, mother's maiden name, date of birth, place of birth, relationship to person of record, reason for information request. Birth Certificates are filed under person of record's last name.

Access by: mail, phone, fax, in person, online.

Fee & Payment: Search fee is $15.00 per name. Add $6.00 if you use a credit card. Add $6.00 per name requested for additional copies. You can order by fax using a credit card. Also include copy of requester's ID (government issued). Fee payee: Vital Records. Prepayment required. Personal checks accepted. Credit cards accepted: MasterCard, Visa, AmEx, Discover.

Mail search: Turnaround time: 2 weeks. Include a daytime telephone number. No SASE is required.

Phone search: You must use a credit card for an additional $6.00 fee. Turnaround time is 5 working days.

Fax search: Turnaround time 5 days, credit card required.

In person search: Turnaround time is 30-45 minutes.

Online search: Records can be ordered online from a state designated vendor - VitalChek. Go to www.vitalchek.com/default.asp

Expedited service: Expedited service is available for online searches. Turnaround time: next day. Add credit card fee ($6.00) and express delivery fee.

Death Records

Department of Public Health & Environment, Vital Records Section HSVR-A1, 4300 Cherry Creek Dr S, Denver, CO 80246-1530; 303-756-4464 (Recorded Message), 303-692-2224 (Credit Card Ordering), 303-692-2234, 800-423-1108 (Fax), 8:30AM-4:30PM.

www.cdphe.state.co.us/hs/certs.asp

Indexing & Storage: Records are available from 1900 to present. It takes within 4 weeks before new records are available for inquiry. Records are indexed on microfiche, inhouse computer.

Searching: Certified copies may be issued to: parents; grandparents; stepparents; siblings; spouse; adult children, stepchildren or grandchildren of the deceased; legal representatives of above; genealogists, probate reseachers or those with a tangible interest. Include the following in your request-full name, date of death, place of death, names of parents, relationship to person of record, reason for information request. Death certificates are indexed by decedent's last name and the year of death. Include date of birth or age at death.

Access by: mail, phone, fax, in person, online.

Fee & Payment: Search fee is $15.00 per name. Add $6.00 if you use a credit card. Add $6.00 per name requested for an additional copy. Also include copy of requester's ID (government issued). Fee payee: Vital Records. Prepayment required. Personal checks accepted. Credit cards accepted: MasterCard, Visa, AmEx, Discover.

Mail search: Turnaround time: 2 weeks. Also include a day time phone number.

Phone search: You must use a credit card. Turnaround time is 5 working days.

Fax search: Same criteria as phone searching.

In person search: You may request records in person for same day service. Turnaround time 30-45 minutes.

Online search: Records can be ordered online from a state designated vendor - VitalChek. Go to www.vitalchek.com/default.asp

Expedited service: Expedited service is available for fax searches. Turnaround time: next day. Add use of credit card fee ($6.00) and express delivery fee.

Marriage Certificates

Department of Public Health & Environment, Vital Records Section, 4300 Cherry Creek Dr S, Denver, CO 80246-1530; 303-756-4464 (Recorded Message), 303-692-2224 (Credit Card Ordering), 303-692-2234, 800-423-1108 (Fax), 8:30AM-4:30PM.

www.cdphe.state.co.us/hs/certs.asp

Note: Records available include 1900 to 1939, and 1975 to present. Verifications for the years 1940 to 1974 are not available from this office and must be obtained from the county where the license was obtained.

Indexing & Storage: It takes 6 months before new records are available for inquiry.

Searching: Records are open to the public. This agency refers to the records as "verifications." Include the following in your request-date of marriage, county of license issue. Also include copy of requester's ID (government issued). The index for records from 1900 to 1939 is by groom only.

Access by: mail, phone, fax, in person, online.

Fee & Payment: The state fee for a marriage verification is $15.00. If the year is not known and the entire index is searched, there is an additional

$5.00. Fee payee: Vital Records. Prepayment required. Credit card use is only for fax, phone, and Internet searches. Personal checks accepted. Credit cards accepted: MasterCard, Visa, AmEx, Discover.

Mail search: Turnaround time: 2 weeks.

Phone search: Turnaround time is 5 days. There is an additional $6.00 fee for use of a credit card.

Fax search: Use of credit card (extra $6.00) required, turnaround time 1 day.

In person search: Turnaround time is 30 to 45 minutes. These indexes can also be searched, for no fee, at many public libraries throughout the state and at State Archives.

Online search: Search marriages from 1975 to present in the state of Colorado at www.sctc.state.co.us/marriages/default.aspx. There is no fee. Also, records can be ordered online from a state designated vendor - VitalChek. Go to www.vitalchek.com/default.asp

Expedited service: Expedited service is available. Use of credit card is required (extra $6.00 fee). Total fee depends on delivery service requested.

Divorce Records

Department of Public Health & Environment, Vital Records Section, 4300 Cherry Creek Dr S, Denver, CO 80246-1530; 303-756-4464 (Recorded Message), 303-692-2224 (Credit Card Ordering), 303-692-2234, 800-423-1108 (Fax), 8:30AM-4:30PM.

www.cdphe.state.co.us/hs/certs.asp

Note: This office holds records from 1900 to 1939, and 1968 to present. Searches must be performed at the county level for all other years.

Indexing & Storage: Records are available 1968 to current within this office. Records are available 1900-1939 at State Office. It takes 6 months before new records are available for inquiry.

Searching: Records are open to the public. Include the following in your request-date of action, county. Alos include copy of requester's ID (government issued). The agency only has an INDEX of the records and will provide a certified verification. Actual copies of the dissolution must be obtained from the county where the event was finalized.

Access by: mail, phone, fax, in person, online.

Fee & Payment: The state fee for a divorce verification is $15.00. If the year is not known and the entire index is searched, there is an additional $5.00. Fee payee: Vital Records. Prepayment required. Personal checks accepted. Credit cards accepted: MasterCard, Visa, AmEx, Discover.

Mail search: Turnaround time: 2 weeks.

Phone search: A credit card is required with an additional fee of $6.00. Turnaround time is 5 business days.

Fax search: Same criteria as phone searching, but turnaround time is 5 business days.

In person search: Records can be obtained across the counter within 30 to 45 minutes.

Online search: Search all divorces/dissolutions from 1851 to 1939 and 1968 to present at www.sctc.state.co.us/marriages/divorces.aspx. There is no fee.

Expedited service: Expedited service is available for online searches. Turnaround time: 1 day. Use of credit card is required (extra $6.00 fee). Total fee depends on delivery service requested.

Workers' Compensation Records

Division of Workers' Compensation, Customer Service, 1515 Arapahoe St, Tower 2, Ste 500, Denver, CO 80202-2117; 303-318-8700, 303-318-8710 (Fax), 8AM-5PM.

www.coworkforce.com/DWC/

Indexing & Storage: Records are available as far back 1979, many records have been scanned and are stored electonically. If the physical records have been destroyed, the wage information is still on computer. New records are available for inquiry immediately. Records are indexed on inhouse computer.

Searching: If you are not a party to the claim, you must have a notarized release from claimant not older than 90 days. Judges notes, transcripts and depositions are not released. Older purged files will get a screen print only. Include the following in your request-claimant name, Social Security Number, DOB. There is a search form that is suggested. The form is not yet available from the web page.

Access by: mail, phone, fax, in person.

Fee & Payment: There is no search fee, copies are $.25 per page, rush copies are $.50 per page, the fee to return via fax is $1.00 per page. Certification is $2.00. Fee payee: Division of Workers' Compensation. Prepayment required. Approved accounts are billed monthly. Personal checks not accepted. No credit cards accepted.

Mail search: Turnaround time: 1 to 2 days. A SASE is requested.

Phone search: Limited information is given over the phone only if caller is a party to the case.

Fax search: Turnaround time is 1-2 days, unless otherwise requested.

In person search: You should call first so that they can locate records. Bring ID and notarized statement.

Other access: Lists and/or labels of carriers, adjusting companies, and attorneys are available upon request. Fees range from $3.00 to $7.00 (for list, not per name) plus postage.

Driver Records

Motor Vehicle Business Group, Driver Control, Denver, CO 80261-0016 (Courier: 1881 Pierce Street, Lakewood, CO 80214); 303-205-5613, 303-205-5990 (Fax), 8AM-5PM.

www.mv.state.co.us

Note: Copies of tickets may be obtained this address for a fee of $2.20 per record. All requests must be submitted in writing and include the driver's name, DOB, and the specific ticket number.

Indexing & Storage: Records are available for up to 7 years. It takes 3 to 12 days before new records are available for inquiry.

Searching: Address and personal data is given to certain pre-approved, permissible requesters. Otherwise the "Requester Release and Information Request/Notice of Intended Use" form must be signed by requester. Include the following in your request-name, date of birth, driver's license number. The middle initial and DL are optional, but suggested.

Access by: mail, in person, online.

Fee & Payment: The fee for manually processed records is $2.20 per record, $2.70 if certified. Online access has been privatized, there is no state fee. Fee payee: Department of Revenue. Prepayment required. Personal checks accepted. No credit cards accepted.

Mail search: Turnaround time: 24 hours. No SASE is required.

In person search: Turnaround time is immediate. Up to 50 records will be processed while you wait.

Online search: Online access is available via a state-designated vendor. The vendors receive nightly updates from the state of the entire DMV record history file, then charge a processing fee per record to users and customers. These vendors provide access online to end users. Call Mary Tuttle at 303-205-5762 for a list of the vendors.

Other access: Colorado offers FTP retrieval for high volume users, call 303-205-5762.

Vehicle Ownership, Vehicle Identification

Motor Vehicle Business Group, Title, Registration and Emissions, Denver, CO 80261-0016 (Courier: 1881 Pierce Street, Lakewood, CO 80214); 303-205-5607 (Titles), 303-205-5765 (Registration), 303-205-5990 (Fax), 8AM-5PM.

www.mv.state.co.us/mv.html

Indexing & Storage: Records are available 10 years back plus the current year. It takes (varies - depend on when county submits record) before new records are available for inquiry. Records are normally destroyed after being microfilmed.

Searching: Handicap and disabled vet plate data are not released. Include the following in your request-Vehicle Identification Number. To obtain vehicle or ownership information, or for title and lien records, the requester's driver license number, and the Requestor Release and Information Request Form (DR 2539) and Affidavit of Intended Use (DR2489) are required.

Access by: mail, in person.

Fee & Payment: The fee for searches is $2.20 per record. Fee payee: Department of Revenue. Prepayment required. Personal checks accepted. No credit cards accepted.

Mail search: Turnaround time: 24 hours.

In person search: Turnaround time is while you wait.

Other access: Bulk requests of vehicle information on magnetic tape, computer paper, and on microfiche are available. Direct inquires to the Data Services Section, Motor Vehicle Extractions, MVBG, Driver Control, Denver, CO 80261-0016.

Expedited service: Will expedite if a prepaid FedEx envelope is provided with request.

Accident Reports

Motor Vehicle Business Group, Driver Control, Denver, CO 80261-0016 (Courier: 1881 Pierce Street, Lakewood, CO 80261); 303-205-5613, 8AM-5PM.

www.mv.state.co.us

Indexing & Storage: Records are available for 6 years plus current year from date of the accident. It takes 30 to 60 days before new records are available for inquiry.

Searching: Use of "Requestor Release and Information Request" Form DR 2559 is required. If requester is not involved in accident, permission must be given by one of involved drivers. Include the following in your request-full name, date of accident, location of accident, and requester's mailing address.

Access by: mail, in person.

Fee & Payment: The fee is $2.20 per record for walk-in or mail-in searches. Fee payee: Department of Revenue. Prepayment required. Personal checks accepted. No credit cards accepted.

Mail search: Turnaround time: variable. No SASE is required.

In person search: Turnaround time depends on availability of report.

Vessel Ownership, Vessel Registration

Colorado State Parks, Registration, 13787 S Highway 85, Littleton, CO 80125; 303-791-1920, 303-470-0782 (Fax), 8AM-5PM.

http://parks.state.co.us/boating/

Note: Liens must be searched at the Secretary of State.

Indexing & Storage: Records are available since 1994. Older records are available on microfiche. All sail and motorized vessels must be registered.

Searching: To search, a Release of Registration Records Form must be completed and signed. The following data is not released: residence addresses.

Access by: mail, fax, in person.

Fee & Payment: There is a $2.00 search fee plus a $1.00 charge per page for copies. Fee payee: Colorado State Parks. Prepayment required. Personal checks accepted. No credit cards accepted.

Mail search: Turnaround time: 1-3 weeks. No SASE is required.

Fax search: Turnaround time varies. Results are faxed or mailed back.

In person search: Availability depends on how extensive search is.

Voter Registration

Department of State, Elections Department, 1560 Broadway #200, Denver, CO 80202; 303-894-2200 x6307, 303-894-7732 (Fax), 8:30AM-5PM.

www.sos.state.co.us/pubs/elections/main.htm

Indexing & Storage: Records are available for the current year only. It takes 1-2 days before new records are available for inquiry.

Searching: Voters may request not to have their information released. Include the following in your request-a signed statement requesting confidentiality. Provide name and address or DOB to search. The following data is not released: Social Security Numbers.

Access by: mail, fax, in person.

Fee & Payment: The fee is $.50 per name. Fee payee: Department of State. Prepayment required. No credit cards accepted.

Mail search: Turnaround time: 2 to 3 days. A SASE is requested.

Fax search: Same criteria as mail searching.

In person search: Availability depends on how extensive search is.

Other access: The entire database is available on tape or CD-ROM. The cost is $500. No customization is available.

GED Certificates

Colorado Dept of Education, GED Testing, 201 E Colfax Ave Rm 100, Denver, CO 80203; 303-866-6613, 8AM-4:55PM.

www.cde.state.co.us/index_adult.htm

Searching: All written requests must have a yes or no answer to the following question in the upper right hand corner of the request: Did the person who received the GED ever attend a Colorado public school (as in elementary or high school)? All of the following are required to search: a signed release, name, date/year of test, date of birth, SSN, and location of testing.

Access by: mail, in person.

Fee & Payment: The search fee $22.00 per transcript. Fee payee: GED Testing. Prepayment required. Money orders & personal checks accepted. No credit cards accepted.

Mail search: Turnaround time: 14 working days. The agency requests use of their request form, which can be downloaded from the web site. No SASE is required.

In person search: Turnaround time is 24 hours, you must come back next day.

Hunting and Fishing License Information

Access to Records is Restricted

Department of Natural Resources, Division of Wildlife, 6060 Broadway, Denver, CO 80216; 303-297-1192, 303-294-0874 (Fax), 8AM-5PM.

www.wildlife.state.co.us

Note: The state attorney general has decided that no information on holders of individual hunting and fishing licenses can be given to the public. It is only available to law enforcement officials or to the licensed individual.

Colorado State Licensing Agencies
Licenses Searchable Online

Acupuncturist #14..www.dora.state.co.us/pls/real/ARMS_Search.Set_Up
Architect/Architectural Firm #15 ....www.dora.state.co.us/pls/real/ARMS_Search.Set_Up
Asbestos Inspector/Mgmt. Planner/Worker/Supv./Designer #5 www.cdphe.state.co.us/ap/asbeshom.asp
Attorney #4 ....www.coloradosupremecourt.com/Search/AttSearch.asp
Audiologist #14 ....www.dora.state.co.us/pls/real/ARMS_Search.Set_Up
Barber #16...www.dora.state.co.us/pls/real/ARMS_Search.Disclaimer_Page
Bus, Charter/Scenic/Childrens #30 ....www.dora.state.co.us/pls/real/puc_permit.search_form
Charitable Organization #37......................................www.sos.state.co.us/cgi-forte/fortecgi?serviceName=ccsaprodaccess&template
                Name=/sessauto/mainMenu_outer_form.forte&hasr=T&hast=T
Chiropractor #17...www.dora.state.co.us/pls/real/ARMS_Search.Disclaimer_Page
Common Carrier/Contract Carrier #30 ....www.dora.state.co.us/pls/real/puc_permit.search_form
Contractor Registration #41 ....www.dora.state.co.us/pls/real/ARMS_Search.Disclaimer_Page
Cosmetologist #16..www.dora.state.co.us/pls/real/ARMS_Search.Disclaimer_Page
Counselor, Professional #20 ....www.dora.state.co.us/pls/real/ARMS_Search.Disclaimer_Page
Credit Union #9 ....www.dora.state.co.us/financial-services/homeregu.html
Dental Hygienist #18...www.dora.state.co.us/pls/real/ARMS_Search.Disclaimer_Page
Dentist #18 ....www.dora.state.co.us/pls/real/ARMS_Search.Disclaimer_Page
Electrical Contractor #41 ....www.dora.state.co.us/pls/real/ARMS_Search.Disclaimer_Page
Electrician Journeyman/Master #41 ....www.dora.state.co.us/pls/real/ARMS_Search.Disclaimer_Page
Engineer/Engineer in Training #19 ....www.dora.state.co.us/pls/real/ARMS_Search.Disclaimer_Page
Family Therapist #20...www.dora.state.co.us/pls/real/ARMS_Search.Disclaimer_Page
Fundraising Consultant #37 ....www.sos.state.co.us/cgi-forte/fortecgi?serviceName=ccsaprodaccess&template
                Name=/sessauto/mainMenu_outer_form.forte&hasr=T&hast=T
HazMat Carrier #30 ....www.dora.state.co.us/pls/real/puc_permit.search_form
Hearing Aid Dealer #14 ....www.dora.state.co.us/pls/real/ARMS_Search.Set_Up
Household Goods/Property Carrier #30 ....www.dora.state.co.us/pls/real/puc_permit.search_form
Insurance Agency/Company #10 ....www.dora.state.co.us/pls/real/INS_Agent.Search_Form
Insurance Producer #10...www.dora.state.co.us/pls/real/INS_Agent.Search_Form
Land Surveyor/Land Surveyor Intern #19 ....www.dora.state.co.us/pls/real/ARMS_Search.Disclaimer_Page
Lead Abatement Firm #5..www.cdphe.state.co.us/ap/asbeshom.asp
Lead Abatement Inspector/Risk Assessor/ Worker/Supv. #5 ..www.cdphe.state.co.us/ap/asbeshom.asp
Life Care Institution #9 ....www.dora.state.co.us/financial-services/homeregu.html
Limousine #30..www.dora.state.co.us/pls/real/puc_permit.search_form
Lobbyist #37 ....www.sos.state.co.us/cgi-forte/fortecgi?serviceName=lobbyprodaccess&template
                Name=/sessauto/inquiryHome_outer_form.forte&hasr=T&hast=T
Lobbyist Employer #37...www.sos.state.co.us/pubs/elections/employer_clientdir.pdf
Lobbyist Volunteer #37..www.state.co.us/gov_dir/leg_dir/vollob03.pdf
Manicurist #16..www.dora.state.co.us/pls/real/ARMS_Search.Disclaimer_Page
Manufactured Housing Dealer #22.............................www.dola.state.co.us/doh/Documents/dealers.htm
Manufactured Housing Mfg. #22 ....www.dola.state.co.us/doh/Documents/parkt.htm
Marriage Therapist #20..www.dora.state.co.us/pls/real/ARMS_Search.Disclaimer_Page
Medical Doctor #21...www.dora.state.co.us/pls/real/ARMS_Search.Disclaimer_Page
Midwife #28 ....www.dora.state.co.us/pls/real/ARMS_Search.Disclaimer_Page
Nurse / Nurses' Aide #1...www.dora.state.co.us/pls/real/ARMS_Search.Disclaimer_Page
Nursing Care Facility #23 ....www.dora.state.co.us/pls/real/ARMS_Search.Set_Up
Nursing Home Administrator #23 ....www.dora.state.co.us/pls/real/ARMS_Search.Set_Up
Off-Road Charter #30..www.dora.state.co.us/pls/real/puc_permit.search_form
Optometrist #33..www.dora.state.co.us/pls/real/ARMS_Search.Disclaimer_Page
Outfitter #24...www.dora.state.co.us/pls/real/ARMS_Search.Disclaimer_Page
Pharmacist/Pharmacist Intern/Pharmacy #26 ....www.dora.state.co.us/pls/real/ARMS_Search.Disclaimer_Page
Physical Therapist #32..www.dora.state.co.us/pls/real/ARMS_Search.Disclaimer_Page
Physician Assistant #21 ....www.dora.state.co.us/pls/real/ARMS_Search.Disclaimer_Page
Plumber Journeyman/Master/Residential #35 ....www.dora.state.co.us/pls/real/ARMS_Search.Disclaimer_Page
Podiatrist #27 ....www.dora.state.co.us/pls/real/ARMS_Search.Disclaimer_Page
Psychologist #20 ....www.dora.state.co.us/pls/real/ARMS_Search.Disclaimer_Page
Public Accountant-CPA #13 ....www.dora.state.co.us/pls/real/ARMS_Search.Disclaimer_Page
Real Estate Agent/Broker/Sales #12.........................www.dora.putate.co.us/pls/real/re_estate_home
Real Estate Appraiser #12 ....www.dora.state.co.us/pls/real/re_estate_home
Respiratory Therapist #16..www.dora.state.co.us/pls/real/ARMS_Search.Disclaimer_Page

River Outfitter #38	www.dora.state.co.us/pls/real/ARMS_Search.Disclaimer_Page
Savings & Loan Association #9	www.dora.state.co.us/financial-services/homeregu.html
Securities Broker/Dealer #34	http://pdpi.nasdr.com/pdpi/disclaimer_frame.htm
Social Worker #20	www.dora.state.co.us/pls/real/ARMS_Search.Disclaimer_Page
Solicitor, Paid #37	www.sos.state.co.us/cgi-forte/fortecgi?serviceName=ccsaprodaccess&template
	Name=/sessauto/mainMenu_outer_form.forte&hasr=T&hast=T
Stock Broker #34	http://pdpi.nasdr.com/pdpi/disclaimer_frame.htm
Towing Carrier #30	www.dora.state.co.us/pls/real/puc_permit.search_form
Veterinarian/Veterinary Student #31	www.dora.state.co.us/pls/real/ARMS_Search.Disclaimer_Page
Wireman, Residential #41	www.dora.state.co.us/pls/real/ARMS_Search.Disclaimer_Page

Colorado Licensing Quick Finder

Acupuncturist #14	303-894-2464	
Architect/Architectural Firm #15	303-894-7441	
Artificial Inseminator #31	303-894-7755	
Asbestos Building Inspector #5	303-692-3158	
Asbestos Inspector/Mgmt. Planner #5	303-692-3158	
Asbestos Project Designer #5	303-692-3158	
Asbestos Worker/Supervisor #5	303-692-3158	
Attorney #4	303-893-8096	
Audiologist #14	303-894-2464	
Bail Bond Agent #10	303-894-7583	
Bank, Commercial/Industrial #8	303-894-7575	
Barber #16	303-894-7772	
Bulk Milk Hauler #6	303-692-3643	
Bus, Charter/Scenic/Childrens #30	303-894-2867	
Charitable Organization #37	303-894-2200	
Child Care Facility #29	800-799-5876	
Chiropractor #17	303-894-7762	
Collection Agency #3	303-866-5706	
Commercial Driving School #7	303-205-5841	
Common Carrier/Contract Carrier #30	303-894-2870	
Contractor Registration #41	303-894-2300	
Cosmetologist #16	303-894-7772	
Counselor, Professional #20	303-894-7766	
Court Reporter #36	303-837-3695	
Credit Union #9	303-894-2336	
Dairy Farm #6	303-692-3643	
Dairy Plant #6	303-692-3643	
Debt Management Company #8	303-894-7575	
Dental Hygienist #18	303-894-7758	
Dentist #18	303-894-7758	
Egg Seller #2	303-239-4140	
Electrical Contractor #41	303-894-2300	
Electrician Journeyman/Master #41	303-894-2300	
Engineer/Engineer in Training #19	303-894-7788	
Family Care Home #29	303-866-5958	
Family Therapist #20	303-894-7766	
Food Plant Operator #2	303-239-4140	
Fundraising Consultant #37	303-894-2200	
Greyhound Racing #11	303-205-2990	
HazMat Carrier #30	303-894-2868	
Hearing Aid Dealer #14	303-894-2464	
Horse Racing #11	303-205-2990	
Household Goods/Property Carrier #30	303-894-2868	
Insurance Agency/Company #10	303-894-2419	
Insurance Producer #10	303-894-2419	
Investment Advisor #34	303-894-2320	
Kennel #2	303-239-4166	
Land Surveyor/Surveyor Intern #19	303-894-7788	
Lead Abatement Firm #5	303-692-3158	
Lead Abatement Inspector/Risk Assessor #5	303-692-3158	
Lead Abatement Worker/Supvr #5	303-692-3158	
Life Care Institution #9	303-894-2336	
Limousine #30	303-894-2867	
Liquor Control #39	303-205-2300	
Lobbyist #37	303-894-2200	
Lobbyist Employer #37	303-894-2200	
Lobbyist Volunteer #37	303-894-2200	
Manicurist #16	303-894-7772	
Manufactured Housing Dealer #22	303-866-4616	
Manufactured Housing Mfg./Instal #22	303-866-4616	
Marriage Therapist #20	303-894-7766	
Medical Doctor #21	303-894-7690	
Midwife #28	303-894-2464	
Milk/Cream Sampler/Tester #6	303-692-3643	
Money Order Company #8	303-894-7575	
Motor Vehicle Buyer/Wholesaler #42	303-205-5604	
Motor Vehicle Dealer/Salesperson#42	303-205-5604	
Motor Vehicle Manufacturer Rep. #42	303-205-5604	
Notary Public #37	303-894-2680	
Nurse #1	303-894-2430	
Nursery #2	303-239-4140	
Nurses' Aide #1	303-894-2816	
Nursing Care Facility #23	303-894-7800	
Nursing Home Administrator #23	303-894-7760	
Off-Road Charter #30	303-894-2867	
Optometrist #33	303-894-7750	
Outfitter #24	303-894-7778	
Pesticide Applicator #2	303-239-4140	
Pet Animal/Bird Dealer #2	303-239-4166	
Pharmacist/Pharmacist Intern #26	303-894-7750	
Pharmacy #26	303-894-7750	
Physical Therapist #32	303-894-2440	
Physician Assistant #21	303-894-7690	
Physiotherapist #32	303-894-2440	
Plumber Journeyman/Master/Residential #35	303-894-2300 x110	
Podiatrist #27	303-894-2464	
Psychiatric Technician #1	303-894-2430	
Psychologist #20	303-894-7766	
Public Accountant-CPA #13	303-894-7441	
Public Adjuster #10	303-894-7499	
Real Estate Agent/Broker/Sales #12	303-894-2166	
Real Estate Appraiser #12	303-894-2166	
Respiratory Therapist #16	303-894-7851, 303-894-2440	
River Outfitter #38	303-894-7772	
Savings & Loan Association #9	303-894-2336	
School Administrator/Principal #40	303-866-6628	
School Special Svc Associate #40	303-866-6628	
Securities Broker/Dealer /Sales #34	303-894-2320	
Ski Lift #25	303-894-7785	
Small Business Development Credit Corp. #9	303-894-2336	
Social Worker #20	303-894-7766	
Solicitor, Paid #37	303-894-2200	
Solicitor/Telemarketer #3	303-866-5079	
Stock Broker #34	303-894-2320	
Substitute Teacher #40	303-866-6968	
Teacher #40	303-866-6628	
Towing Carrier #30	303-894-2846	
Tramway #25	303-894-7785	
Trust Company #8	303-894-7575	
Veterinarian #31	303-894-7755	
Veterinary Student #31	303-894-7755	
Vocational Education Teacher #40	303-866-6628	
Wireman, Residential #41	303-894-2300	

Colorado Licensing Agency Information

1 Board of Nursing, 1560 Broadway, #880, Denver, CO 80202; 303-894-2430, Fax: 303-894-2821. www.dora.state.co.us/nursing Search Database at www.dora.state.co.us/real/ARMS_Search.Disclaimer_Page

2 Agriculture Department, 700 Kipling St, #4000, Lakewood, CO 80215-8000; 303-239-4100, Fax: 303-239-4125. www.ag.state.co.us Email: jim.thurman@ag.state.co.us

3 Attorney General's Office, 1525 Sherman St, 5th Fl, Denver, CO 80203; 303-866-4500, Fax: 303-866-5691. www.ago.state.co.us Email: attorney.general@state.co.us

4 Colorado Supreme Court, Board of Law Examiners, 600 17th St, Dominion Plaza Bldg, #910S, Denver, CO 80202; 303-893-8096, Fax: 303-534-3643. www.coloradosupremecour

t.com/Regulation/Contacts.htm Email: kuenhold@amigo.net Search database at www.coloradosupremecourt.com/Search/AttSearch.asp

5 Department of Public Health & Environment, Air Pollution Control Division, 4300 Cherry Creek Dr S, Denver, CO 80246; 303-692-3150, Fax: 303-782-0278. Email: larry.dover@state.co.us www.cdphe.state.co.us/ap/asbeshom.asp

6 Consumer Protection Division, Department of Public Health and Environment, 4300 Cherry Creek, Denver, CO 80246-1530; 303-692-3620, Fax: 303-753-6809. www.cdphe.state.co.us/cp/Dairy/dairy.asp

7 Department of Revenue, 1375 Sherman St, Denver, CO 80261; 303-866-3091, Fax: 303-205-5634. www.taxcolorado.com

8 Division of Banking, 1560 Broadway, #1175, Denver, CO 80202; 303-894-7575, Fax: 303-894-7570. www.dora.state.co.us/Banking Email: Banking@dora.state.co.us

9 Division of Financial Services, 1560 Broadway, #1520, Denver, CO 80202; 303-894-2336, Fax: 303-894-7886. www.dora.state.co.us/financial-services Search Database at www.dora.state.co.us/financial-services/homeregu.html

10 Division of Insurance, 1560 Broadway, #850, Denver, CO 80202; 303-894-7499, Fax: 303-894-7455. www.dora.state.co.us/Insurance Email: nancy.ryan@dora.state.co.us Search database at www.dora.state.co.us/pls/real/INS_Search.Disclaimer_Page

11 Division of Racing Events, 1881 Pierce St, #108, Lakewood, CO 80214; 303-205-2990, Fax: 303-205-2950.
www.revenue.state.co.us/racing_dir/coracing.html
Email: Racing@spike.dor.state.co.us

12 Division of Real Estate, 1900 Grant St, #600, Denver, CO 80203; 303-894-2166, Fax: 303-894-2683.
www.dora.state.co.us/real-estate/index.html
Search Database at www.dora.state.co.us/pls/real/re_estate_home

13 Division of Registrations, Board of Accountancy, 1560 Broadway, #1340, Denver, CO 80202; 303-894-7800, Fax: 303-894-7802.
www.dora.state.co.us/Accountants
Email: robert.longway@state.co.us   Search Database at www.dora.state.co.us/pls/real/ARMS_Search.Disclaimer_Page

14 Division of Registrations, Audiology Registration Ofc / Acupuncture Licensing, 1560 Broadway, #1550, Denver, CO 80202; 303-894-2464, Fax: 303-894-7802. www.dora.state.co.us
Email: acupuncture@dora.state.co.us
Search Database at www.dora.state.co.us/pls/real/ARMS_Search.Set_Up

15 Division of Registrations, Board of Examiners of Architects, 1560 Broadway, #1340, Denver, CO 80202; 303-894-7801, Fax: 303-894-7802.
www.dora.state.co.us/Architects/
Email: robert.longway@dora.state.co.us   Search database at www.dora.state.co.us/pls/real/ARMS_Search.Disclaimer_Page

16 Division of Registrations, Office of Barber & Cosmetologist Licensing, 1560 Broadway, #1340, Denver, CO 80202; 303-894-7772, Fax: 303-894-7802.
www.dora.state.co.us/Barbers_Cosmetologists
Email: barber-cosmetology@dora.state.co.us
Search Database at www.dora.state.co.us/pls/real/ARMS_Search.Disclaimer_Page

17 Division of Registrations, Board of Chiropractors, 1560 Broadway, #1310, Denver, CO 80202; 303-894-7762, Fax: 303-894-7764.
www.dora.state.co.us/chiropratic
Search Database at www.dora.state.co.us/pls/real/ARMS_Search.Disclaimer_Page

18 Division of Registrations, Board of Dental Examiners, 1560 Broadway, #1310, Denver, CO 80202; 303-894-7758, Fax: 303-894-7764.
www.dora.state.co.us/dental
Email: Dental@dora.state.co.us
Search Database at www.dora.state.co.us/pls/real/ARMS_Search.Disclaimer_Page

19 Division of Registrations, Board of Reg for Prof Engineers and Land Surveyors, 1560 Broadway, #1370, Denver, CO 80202; 303-894-7788, Fax: 303-894-7790.
www.dora.state.co.us/Engineers_Surveyors/
Search Database at www.dora.state.co.us/pls/real/ARMS_Search.Disclaimer_Page

20 Division of Registrations, Mental Health Licening Section, 1560 Broadway, #1370, Denver, CO 80202; 303-894-7766, Fax: 303-894-7747.
www.dora.state.co.us/Mental-Health
Email: MentalHealth@dora.state.co.us
Search Database at www.dora.state.co.us/pls/real/ARMS_Search.Disclaimer_Page

21 Div of Registrations, Dept of Regulatory Agencies, Board of Medical Examiners, 1560 Broadway, #1300, Denver, CO 80202-5140; 303-894-7690, Fax: 303-894-7692.
www.dora.state.co.us/medical/
Email: medical@dora.state.co.us
Search Database at www.dora.state.co.us/pls/real/ARMS_Search.Disclaimer_Page

22 Division of Housing, 1313 Sherman St Rm 518, Denver, CO 80203; 303-866-2033, Fax: 303-866-4077. www.dola.state.co.us/doh/Index.htm
Email: dola.helpdesk@state.co.us

23 Division of Registrations, Board of Examiners of Nursing Home Adminstrators, 1560 Broadway, #1300, Denver, CO 80202; 303-894-7690, Fax: 303-894-7694. www.dora.state.co.us/registrations
Search Database at www.dora.state.co.us/real/ARMS_Search.Set_Up

24 Division of Registrations, Office of Outfitters Registration, 1560 Broadway, #1340, Denver, CO 80202; 303-894-7778, Fax: 303-894-7802.
www.dora.state.co.us/Outfitters
Email: Outfitters@dora.state.co.us
Search Database at www.dora.state.co.us/pls/real/ARMS_Search.Disclaimer_Page

25 Division of Registrations, Colorado Tramway Passenger Safety Board, 1560 Broadway, #1300, Denver, CO 80202; 303-894-7785, Fax: 303-894-7790. www.dora.state.co.us/Tramway
Email: webmaster@dora.state.co.us

26 Division of Registrations, Board of Pharmacy, 1560 Broadway, #1310, Denver, CO 80202-5146; 303-894-7750, Fax: 303-894-7764.
www.dora.state.co.us/Pharmacy
Email: pharmacy@dora.state.co.us
Search Database at www.dora.state.co.us/pls/real/ARMS_Search.Disclaimer_Page

27 Division of Registrations, Podiatry Board, 1560 Broadway, #1545, Denver, CO 80202; 303-894-2464, Fax: 303-894-7885.
www.dora.state.co.us/Podiatrists
Email: podiatrists@dora.state.co.us
Search Database at www.dora.state.co.us/pls/real/ARMS_Search.Disclaimer_Page

28 Division of Registrations, Midwives Registration, 1560 Broadway, #1545, Denver, CO 80202; 303-894-2464, Fax: 303-894-7885.
www.dora.state.co.us/Midwives
Email: midwives@dora.state.co.us
Search Database at www.dora.state.co.us/pls/real/ARMS_Search.Disclaimer_Page

29 Department of Human Services, Division of Child Care, 1575 Sherman St, Denver, CO 80202; 800-799-5958, Fax: 303-866-4453.
www.cdhs.state.co.us/childcare/home.html

30 Public Utilities Commission, Department of Regulatory Agencies, 1580 Logan St, DL 2, Denver, CO 80203; 800-456-0858, 303-894-2070.
www.dora.state.co.us/puc/index.htm
Email: terry.willert@dora.state.co.us
Search Database at www.dora.state.co.us/real/puc_permit.search_form

31 Division of Registrations, Board of Veterinary Medicine, 1560 Broadway, #1310, Denver, CO 80202-5146; 303-894-7755, Fax: 303-894-7764.
www.dora.state.co.us/Veterinarians
Search Database at www.dora.state.co.us/pls/real/ARMS_Search.Disclaimer_Page

32 Division of Registrations, Physical Therapy Registration, 1560 Broadway, #1545, Denver, CO 80202; 303-894-2440, Fax: 303-894-7885.
www.dora.state.co.us/Physical-Therapy

Email: pt@dora.state.co.us
Search Database at www.dora.state.co.us/pls/real/ARMS_Search.Disclaimer_Page

33 Division of Registrations, Board of Optometry Examiners, 1560 Broadway, #1310, Denver, CO 80202-5146; 303-894-7751, Fax: 303-894-7764.
www.dora.state.co.us/Optometry
Email: optometry@dora.state.co.us
Search Database at www.dora.state.co.us/pls/real/ARMS_Search.Disclaimer_Page

34 Department of Regulatory Agencies, Division of Securities, 1580 Lincoln, #420, Denver, CO 80203-1506; 303-894-2320, Fax: 303-861-2126.
www.dora.state.co.us/Securities/brokers.htm
Email: Securities@DORA.state.co.us
Search Database at http://pdpi.nasdr.com/pdpi/disclaimer_frame.htm

35 Examining Board of Plumbers, 1580 Logan St, #550, Denver, CO 80203-1941; 303-894-2300, Fax: 303-894-2310.
www.dora.state.co.us/Plumbing
Email: Plumbing@dora.state.co.us   Search Database at www.dora.state.co.us/pls/real/ARMS_Search.Disclaimer_Page

36 Judicial Department, Human Resources Office, 1301 Pennsylvania St, #300, Denver, CO 80203; 303-837-3695, Fax: 303-837-2340.
www.courts.state.co.us

37 Licensing Division, Office of Secretary of State, 1560 Broadway, #200, Denver, CO 80202; 303-894-2200, Fax: 303-869-4864.
www.sos.state.co.us/pubs/business/main.htm
Email: licensing@sos.state.co.us
Search Database at www.sos.state.co.us/pubs/bingo_raffles/main.htm
Note: The Colorado Assoc. of NonProfit Organizations member list is avaialble free at www.canpo.org/directory_members_search.cfm.

38 Division of Registrations, Outfitters Registration, 1560 Broadway, #1340, Denver, CO 80202; 303-894-7778, Fax: 303-470-0782.
www.dora.state.co.us/Outfitters
Email: outfitters@dora.state.co.us
Search Database at www.dora.state.co.us/real/ARMS_Search.Disclaimer_Page   Note: For a list of all registered outfitters, please send a check or money order in the amount of $11.00 to: Office of Outfitters Reg. 1560 Broadway #1340, Denver, CO 80202.

39 Revenue Department, Alcohol Control Division, 1881 Pierce, #108A, Lakewood, CO 80214; 303-205-2300, Fax: 303-205-2341.
www.revenue.state.co.us/liquor_dir/licenses.htm
Email: nhamby@spike.dor.state.co.us

40 Department of Education, 201 E Colifax, Denver, CO 80203; 303-866-6600, Fax: 303-830-0793. www.cde.state.co.us/index_license.htm
Email: webmaster@cde.state.co.us

41 Electrical Board, 1580 Logan St, #550, Denver, CO 80203-1939; 303-894-2300, Fax: 303-894-2310. www.dora.state.co.us/Electrical
Email: roberta.aceves@dora.state.co.us
Search Database at www.dora.state.co.us/real/ARMS_Search.Disclaimer_Page

42 Motor Vehicle Dealer Board, 1881 Pierce St Rm 142, Lakewood, CO 80215; 303-205-5604, Fax: 303-205-5977. www.mv.state.co.us
Email: dealers@spike.dor.state.co.us.

Colorado Federal Courts

The following list indicates the district and division name for each county in the state.

County/Court Cross Reference

Adams	Denver	Fremont	Denver	Montrose	Denver
Alamosa	Denver	Garfield	Denver	Morgan	Denver
Arapahoe	Denver	Gilpin	Denver	Otero	Denver
Archuleta	Denver	Grand	Denver	Ouray	Denver
Baca	Denver	Gunnison	Denver	Park	Denver
Bent	Denver	Hinsdale	Denver	Phillips	Denver
Boulder	Denver	Huerfano	Denver	Pitkin	Denver
Chaffee	Denver	Jackson	Denver	Prowers	Denver
Cheyenne	Denver	Jefferson	Denver	Pueblo	Denver
Clear Creek	Denver	Kiowa	Denver	Rio Blanco	Denver
Conejos	Denver	Kit Carson	Denver	Rio Grande	Denver
Costilla	Denver	La Plata	Denver	Routt	Denver
Crowley	Denver	Lake	Denver	Saguache	Denver
Custer	Denver	Larimer	Denver	San Juan	Denver
Delta	Denver	Las Animas	Denver	San Miguel	Denver
Denver	Denver	Lincoln	Denver	Sedgwick	Denver
Dolores	Denver	Logan	Denver	Summit	Denver
Douglas	Denver	Mesa	Denver	Teller	Denver
Eagle	Denver	Mineral	Denver	Washington	Denver
El Paso	Denver	Moffat	Denver	Weld	Denver
Elbert	Denver	Montezuma	Denver	Yuma	Denver

US District Court

District of Colorado

Denver Division U.S. Courthouse, 901 19th Street, Denver, CO 80294-3589 (courier address: Use mail address for courier delivery) 303-844-3433. www.co.uscourts.gov

Counties: All counties in Colorado.

Indexing & Storage: New cases available in the index immediately after filing date.

Fee & Payment: Payment may be made by money order, cashier check, personal check, Visa, Mastercard. No prepayment required for copies unless the bill is over $100.00. Payee: Clerk, U.S. District Court.

Phone Search: Over the phone, the court will release anything of public record, although they will not read long excerpts over the phone.

In Person Search: Fee charged if court conducts your in person search for you.

PACER: PACER is available online at http://pacer.cod.uscourts.gov. Case records go back to 1994. Records purged on a varying schedule. New records are online after 1 day.

U.S. Bankruptcy Court

District of Colorado

Denver Division U.S. Custom House, Room 114, 721 19th St, Denver, CO 80202-2508 (courier address: Use mail address for courier delivery) 303-844-4045. www.cob.uscourts.gov/bindex.htm

Counties: All counties in Colorado.

Indexing & Storage: Cases indexed by debtor as well as by case number. New cases available in the index 24-48 hours after filing date. Records are also on microfilm of all cases prior to June 1990.

Fee & Payment: Payment may be made by money order, cashier check, personal check. Personal checks are not accepted from debtors. Payee: Clerk, U.S. Bankruptcy Court.

Phone Search: Automated voice case information service (VCIS) is available. Call VCIS at 303-844-0267.

Mail Search: A SASE not required.

In Person Search: Fee charged if court conducts your in person search for you. View records from 8:00AM-4:45PM in Room 114.

PACER: PACER is available online at http://pacer.cob.uscourts.gov. Case records go back to July 1981. New civil records are online after 1 day.

Electronic Filing: Electronic filing information online at https://ecf.cob.uscourts.gov

Standards for Federal Courts: The search fee is $20.00 per item (one party name or case number). Certification fee is $7.00 per document. Copy fee is $.50 per page. All fees standard unless noted in profile. Mail Search: always enclose a stamped self addressed envelope unless otherwise noted. Most courts accept fax requests or will suggest a copying/search vendor. Before releasing records, all courts require prepayment unless noted in profile.

Open records are located at the court unless otherwise noted. District courts index by defendant and plaintiff as well as by case number. Bankruptcy courts usually index by debtor and case number. While most courts now have their indexes on computer, many still maintain index card files as well.

The universal PACER sign-up number is 800-676-6856. Find PACER and the Party/Case Index on the Web at http://pacer.psc.uscourts.gov. PACER dial-up access is $.60 per minute. Also, courts offering internet access via RACER, PACER, Web-PACER or the new CM-ECF charge $.07 per page fee unless noted as free.

Colorado County Courts

Court	Jurisdiction	No. of Courts	How Organized
District Courts*	General	14	22 Districts
County Courts*	Limited	17	63 Counties
Combined Courts*		49	
Denver Probate Courts*	Probate	1	
Municipal Courts	Municipal	206	
Denver Juvenile Courts	Special	1	
Water Courts	Special	7	7 Districts

* Profiled in this Sourcebook.

Court	CIVIL								
	Tort	Contract	Real Estate	Min. Claim	Max. Claim	Small Claims	Estate	Eviction	Domestic Relations
District Courts*	X	X	X	$0	No Max		X		X
County Courts*	X	X	X	$0	$15,000	$7500		X	
Denver Probate Courts*							X		
Denver Juvenile Courts									
Water Courts			X	$0	No Max				

Court	CRIMINAL				
	Felony	Misdemeanor	DWI/DUI	Preliminary Hearing	Juvenile
District Courts*	X				X
County Courts*		X	X	X	
Denver Probate Courts*					
Denver Juvenile Courts					X
Water Courts					

ADMINISTRATION   State Court Administrator, 1301 Pennsylvania St, Suite 300, Denver, CO, 80203; 303-861-1111, Fax: 303-837-2340. www.courts.state.co.us

COURT STRUCTURE   As of 9/1/2001, the maximum civil claim in County Courts was increased to $15,000. The District and County Courts have overlapping jurisdiction over civil cases involving less than $15,000 ($10,000 prior to 9/1/2001). Fortunately, District and County Courts are combined in most counties. Combined courts usually search both civil or criminal indexes for a single fee, except as indicated in the profiles.

Municipal courts only have jurisdiction over traffic, parking, and ordinance violations.

ONLINE ACCESS   There is no official government system, but as result of an initiative of the Colorado Judicial Branch, all district courts and all county courts are available on the Internet at www.cocourts.com. Real-time records include civil, civil water, small claims, domestic, felony, misdemeanor, and traffic cases and can be accessed by name or case number. Court records go as far back as 1995. There is a fee for this subscription Internet access, generally $6.00 per search and there are discounts for volume users. Contact Jeff Mueller, Major Accounts, by telephone at 866-COCOURT, or by email at Jeffm@cocourts.com.

Opinions from the Court of Appeals are available from the web site.

ADDITIONAL INFORMATION

November 15, 2001, Broomfield City & County came into existence, derived from the counties of Adams, Boulder, Jefferson and Weld. A District and County Court (presumed to be 17th Judicial District) was established.

All state agencies require a self-addressed, stamped envelope (SASE) for return of information.

Co-located with seven district courts are divisions known as Water Courts. The Water Courts are located in Weld, Pueblo, Alamosa, Montrose, Garfield, Routt, and La Platta counties; see the District Court discussion for those counties to determine the jurisdictional area for the Water Court. Water Court records are maintained by the Water Clerk and fees are similar to those for other court records. To retrieve a Water Court record, one must furnish the Case Number or the Legal Description (section, township, and range) or the Full Name of the respondent (note that the case number or legal description are preferred).

PROBATE COURTS

Denver is the only county where Probate Court is separate from the District Court.

Adams County

17th District Court 1100 Judicial Center Dr, Brighton, CO 80601; 303-659-1161; Civil phone: 303-654-3237; Criminal phone: 303-654-3314; Probate phone: 303-654-3237; Fax: 303-654-3216. Hours: 8AM-5PM; closed from Noon-1pm (MST). *Felony, Civil Actions Over $10,000, Probate.*
www.17thjudicialdistrict.com
Note: The District and County courts have combined, but records are searched separately unless requester asks to search both courts (at no extra fee).

Civil Records: Access: Mail, in person, online. Both court and visitors may perform in person searches. Search fee: $5.00 per name. Fee is $10.00 for cases before 1976. There is no fee if search done by party of case. Required to search: name, years to search. Civil cases indexed by defendant, plaintiff. Civil records on computer from Jan 1976, index books back to early 1900s. Civil records online access at www.cocourts.com.

Criminal Records: Access: Mail, in person, online. Both court and visitors may perform in person searches. Search fee: $5.00 per name. Fee is $10.00 for cases before 1976. Required to search: name, years to search, DOB. Criminal records on computer from Jan 1976, index books back to early 1900s. Online access to criminal records is at www.cocourts.com.

General Information: No adoptions, sealed, juvenile, mental health or expunged cases released. Copy fee: $.75 per page. Cert fee: $10.00. Payee: Clerk of the District Court. Personal checks accepted. Credit cards accepted. Accepted in person only. Prepayment required. Mail requests: SASE required. Mail turnaround time 2 days.

County Court 1100 Judicial Center Dr, Brighton, CO 80601; 303-659-1161; Civil phone: 303-654-3335; Criminal phone: 303-654-3314. 8AM-5PM; closed from Noon-1PM (MST). *Misdemeanor, Civil Actions Under $15,000, Eviction, Small Claims.*
www.17thjudicialdistrict.com/
Note: The District and County courts have combined, but records are searched separately unless specifically asked to search both courts for no additional fee.

Civil Records: Access: Mail, in person, online. Both court and visitors may perform in person searches. Search fee: $5.00 per name. $10.00 per name for pre-computer records. Required to search: name, years to search. Civil cases indexed by defendant, plaintiff. Civil records on computer from Jan 1990, index books back to 1965. Civil records online access at www.cocourts.com.

Criminal Records: Access: Mail, in person, online. Both court and visitors may perform in person searches. Search fee: $5.00 per name. $10.00 per name for pre-computer records. Required to search:

name, years to search, DOB. Criminal records on computer from Jan 1990, index books back to 1965. Online access to criminal records is at www.cocourts.com.

General Information: No adoptions, sealed, juvenile, mental health or expunged cases released. Copy fee: $.75 per page. Cert fee: $10.00. Payee: Adams County Combined Court. Personal checks accepted. Visa, MC accepted. Prepayment required. Mail requests: SASE required. Mail turnaround time 2 working days.

Alamosa County

Alamosa Combined Court 702 4th St, Alamosa, CO 81101; 719-589-4996; Fax: 719-589-4998. Hours: 8AM-noon, 1-4PM (MST). *Felony, Misdemeanor, Civil, Eviction, Small Claims, Probate, Traffic.*
Civil Records: Access: Mail, in person, online. Only the court performs in person searches; visitors may not. Search fee: $5.00 per name. Required to search: name, years to search. Civil cases indexed by defendant, plaintiff. Civil records on computer from May 1978, index books back to 1913. Civil records online access at www.cocourts.com.
Criminal Records: Access: Mail, in person, online. Only the court performs in person searches; visitors may not. Search fee: $5.00 per name. Required to search: name, years to search, DOB. Criminal records on computer from May 1978, index books back to 1913. Online access to criminal records is at www.cocourts.com.
General Information: No adoptions, juvenile, mental health, sealed or expunged cases released. Fee to fax results is $10.00 minimum plus $1.00 per page after 1st 10. Copy fee: $.75 per page. Cert fee: $10.00. Payee: Clerk, Combined Court. Personal checks accepted. Prepayment required. Mail requests: SASE required. Mail turnaround time 10 days.

Arapahoe County

18th District Court 7325 S Potomac St, Centennial, CO 80112; 303-649-6355. Hours: 8AM-noon, 1:15-4PM (MST). *Felony, Civil Actions Over $15,000, Probate.*
www.courts.state.co.us/district/18th/18dist.htm
Civil Records: Access: Phone, mail, in person, online. Both court and visitors may perform in person searches. Search fee: $5.00 per name. Required to search: name, years to search. Civil cases indexed by defendant, plaintiff. Civil records on computer from 1985, microfiche back to 1903. Civil records online access at www.cocourts.com.
Criminal Records: Access: Phone, mail, in person, online. Both court and visitors may perform in person searches. Search fee: $5.00 per name. Required to search: name, years to search, DOB. Criminal records on computer from 1985, microfiche back to 1903.

Online access to criminal records is at www.cocourts.com.
General Information: No adoptions, sealed, juvenile, mental health or expunged cases released. Will not fax results. Copy fee: $.75 per page. Cert fee: $10.00. Payee: Clerk of District Court. Personal checks accepted. Prepayment required. Mail requests: SASE required. Mail turnaround time 7-10 days.

Arapahoe County Court Division A 1790 W Littleton Blvd, Littleton, CO 80120-2060; 303-798-4591. Hours: 8AM-Noon-1;30-4PM (MST). *Misdemeanor, Civil Actions Under $15,000, Eviction, Small Claims.*
www.courts.state.co.us/district/18th/18dist.htm
Civil Records: Access: Mail, in person, online. Both court and visitors may perform in person searches. Search fee: $5.00 per name. Required to search: name, years to search. Civil cases indexed by defendant, plaintiff. Civil records on computer from 1986, index cards from 1965, microfiche from 1861 in District Court. Civil records online access at www.cocourts.com. Registration required; transaction fee. Only court performs searches prior to March 1986.
Criminal Records: Access: Mail, in person, online. Both court and visitors may perform in person searches. Search fee: $5.00 per name. Required to search: name, years to search, DOB. Criminal records on computer from 1986, index cards from 1965, microfiche from 1861 in District Court. Online access to criminal records is at www.cocourts.com. Only court performs searches prior to March 1986.
General Information: No adoptions, sealed, juvenile, mental health or expunged cases released. Copy fee: $.75 per page. Cert fee: $10.00. Payee: Clerk of County Court. Personal checks accepted. Visa, MC, Discover accepted. Prepayment required. Mail requests: SASE required. Mail turnaround time 2 weeks.

Arapahoe County Court Division B 15400 E 14th Pl, Aurora, CO 80011; 303-363-8004; Fax: 303-363-7155. Hours: 8AM-N, 1:15-4PM (MST). *Misdemeanor, Civil Actions Under $15,000, Eviction, Small Claims.*
www.courts.state.co.us/district/18th/18dist.htm
Civil Records: Access: Phone, mail, in person, online. Only the court performs in person searches; visitors may not. Search fee: $5.00 per name or $25.00 per hour. Required to search: name, years to search. Civil cases indexed by defendant, plaintiff. Civil records on computer from April 1986, microfiche from 1980-1983, index cards from 1980. Civil records online access at www.cocourts.com.
Criminal Records: Access: Phone, mail, in person, online. Only the court performs in person searches; visitors may not. Search fee: $5.00 per name pr $25.00 per hour. Required to search: name, years to

search, DOB. Criminal records on computer from April 1986, microfiche from 1980-1983, index cards from 1980. Online access to criminal records is at www.cocourts.com.
General Information: No adoptions, sealed, juvenile, mental health or expunged cases released. Will fax results. Copy fee: $.75 per page. Cert fee: $10.00. Payee: Clerk of County Court. Personal checks accepted. Visa, MC accepted. Prepayment required. Mail requests: SASE required. Mail turnaround time 5-10 days.

Archuleta County

Archuleta Combined Courts PO Box 148, Pagosa Springs, CO 81147; 970-264-2400; Fax: 970-264-2407. 8AM-4PM (MST). *Felony, Misdemeanor, Civil, Eviction, Small Claims, Probate.*
Civil Records: Access: Mail, in person, online. Only the court performs in person searches; visitors may not. Search fee: $5.00 per name. Specific case information is $2.00 per file. Required to search: name, years to search. Civil cases indexed by defendant, plaintiff. Civil records on index cards from 1976, index books back to 1885, on computer since 08/95. Civil records online access at www.cocourts.com.
Criminal Records: Access: Mail, in person, online. Only the court performs in person searches; visitors may not. Search fee: $5.00 per name. Specific case information $2.00 per file. Required to search: name, years to search, DOB. Criminal records on index cards from 1976, index books back to 1885, on computer since 08/95. Online access to criminal records is at www.cocourts.com.
General Information: No adoptions, sealed, juvenile, mental health or expunged cases released. Will fax results to local or toll free line, otherwise $1.00 per page. Copy fee: $.75 per page. Cert fee: $10.00. Payee: Archuleta Combined Court. Personal checks accepted. Prepayment required. Mail requests: SASE required. Mail turnaround time 5 days.

Baca County

Baca County District & County Courts 741 Main St, Springfield, CO 81073; 719-523-4555. Hours: 8AM-5PM (MST). *Felony, Misdemeanor, Civil, Eviction, Small Claims, Probate.*
www.courts.state.co.us/district/15th/15dist.htm
Civil Records: Access: Mail, in person, online. Only the court performs in person searches; visitors may not. Search fee: $5.00 per name. Required to search: name, years to search. Civil cases indexed by defendant, plaintiff. Civil records on index cards from 1945, index books back to 1910, computerized since 1995. Civil records online access at www.cocourts.com.
Criminal Records: Access: Mail, in person, online. Only the court performs in person searches; visitors may not. Search fee: $5.00 per name. Required to search: name, years to search, DOB. Criminal records on index cards from 1945, index books back to 1910, computerized since 1995. Online access to criminal records is at www.cocourts.com.
General Information: No adoptions, sealed, juvenile, mental health or expunged cases released. Will fax results for $1.00 per page. If only two pages-nothing lengthy. Copy fee: $.75 per page. Cert fee: $10.00. Payee: Baca County Courts. Personal checks accepted. Prepayment required. Mail requests: SASE required. Mail turnaround time 1-2 days.

Bent County

16th District Court Bent County Courthouse, 725 Bent, Las Animas, CO 81054; 719-456-1353; Fax: 719-456-0040. Hours: 8AM-12, 1-5PM (MST). *Felony, Misdemeanor, Civil, Eviction, Small Claims, Probate.*
www.courts.state.co.us/district/16th/16dist.htm
Civil Records: Access: Mail, in person, online. Only the court performs in person searches; visitors may not. Search fee: $5.00 per name. Required to search: name, years to search. Civil cases indexed by defendant, plaintiff. Civil records on index cards from 1975, prior to 1975 some on microfilm, on computer from 11/95 forward- all indexes available at this office. Civil records online access at www.cocourts.com.
Criminal Records: Access: Mail, in person, online. Only the court performs in person searches; visitors may not. Search fee: $5.00 per name. Required to search: name, years to search, DOB. Criminal records on index cards from 1975, prior to 1975 some on microfilm, on computer from 11/95 forward- all indexes available at this office. Online access to criminal records is at www.cocourts.com.
General Information: No adoptions, sealed, juvenile, mental health or expunged cases released. Will fax results to local or toll free line. Copy fee: $.75 per page. Cert fee: $10.00. Payee: Clerk of Combined Court. Personal checks accepted. Prepayment required. Mail requests: SASE required. Mail turnaround time 4-5 days.

Boulder County

20th District & County Courts 6th & Canyon, 1777 6th St, Boulder, CO 80306; 303-441-3750. 8AM-4PM (MST). *Felony, Misdemeanor, Civil, Eviction, Small Claims, Probate.*
Civil Records: Access: Mail, in person, online. Only the court performs in person searches; visitors may not. Search fee: $5.00 per name. Required to search: name, years to search. Civil cases indexed by defendant, plaintiff. Civil records on computer from 1983, microfiche prior from 1977, all prior records in books. Civil records online access at www.cocourts.com.
Criminal Records: Access: Mail, in person, online. Only the court performs in person searches; visitors may not. Search fee: $5.00 per name. Required to search: name, years to search, DOB, signed release. Criminal records on computer from 1983, microfiche prior from 1977, all prior records in books. Online access to criminal records is at www.cocourts.com.
General Information: No adoptions, sealed, juvenile, mental health or expunged cases released. Currently will not fax results. Copy fee: $.75 per page. Cert fee: $10.00. Payee: 20th Judicial District. Business checks accepted. Attorney checks accepted. Visa, MC accepted. Prepayment required. Mail turnaround: 5 days.

Broomfield County

Broomfield Municipal Court (District & County) 17 DesCombes Dr, Broomfield, CO 80020; 720-887-2100; Fax: 720-887-2122. Hours: 8AM-5PM (MST). *Felony, Misdemeanor, Civil, Eviction, Small Claims, Probate.*
www.co.broomfield.co.us
Note: This is a new county created in late 2001, record keeping is limited. Older records should be searched in Adams, Boulder, Jefferson or Weld counties. This court holds Municipal court records prior to county organization.
Civil Records: Access: Mail, in person, online. Court performs searches. No search fee. Civil cases indexed by defendant, plaintiff. Civil records on computer since 11/01. Online access is at www.cocourts.com.

Criminal Records: Access: Mail, in person, online. Court performs searches. Search fee: $5.00 per name. Required to search: name, also helpful: address, DOB. Online access is at www.cocourts.com.
General Information: No Juvenile or protective custody records released. Copy fee: $.75. Cert fee: $10.00. Payee: Broomfield County Courts. Will accept credit cards and checks. Prepayment required. Mail requests: SASE required. Mail turnaround time 2-3 days.

Chaffee County

11th District & County Courts PO Box 279, Salida, CO 81201; 719-539-2561/6031; Fax: 719-539-6281. Hours: 8AM-5PM (MST). *Felony, Misdemeanor, Civil, Eviction, Small Claims, Probate.*
www.courts.state.co.us/district/11th/dist11.htm
Note: This court combined in 2002; formerly two courts: one county court, one district court.

Civil Records: Access: Phone, mail, in person, online. Only the court performs in person searches; visitors may not. Search fee: $5.00 per name. Fee applies if 3 or more files involved. Required to search: name, years to search. Civil cases indexed by defendant, plaintiff. Civil records on computer back to 1995; index cards from April 1976, index books back to late 1800s. Civil records online access at www.cocourts.com.
Criminal Records: Access: Phone, mail, in person, online. Only the court performs in person searches; visitors may not. Search fee: $5.00 per name. Fee applies if 3 or more files involved. Required to search: name, years to search, DOB. Criminal records on computer back to 1995; index cards back to April 1976, index books back to late 1800s. Online access to criminal records is at www.cocourts.com.
General Information: No adoptions, sealed, juvenile, mental health or expunged cases released. Fee to fax results is $.50 per page. Copy fee: $.75 per page. Cert fee: $10.00. Payee: Clerk of District Court. Personal checks accepted. Prepayment required. Mail requests: SASE required. Mail turnaround: 2-3 days.

Cheyenne County

District & County Courts PO Box 696, Cheyenne Wells, CO 80810; 719-767-5649. Hours: 8AM-4PM, till noon on Fri (MST). *Felony, Misdemeanor, Civil, Eviction, Small Claims, Probate.*
www.courts.state.co.us/district/15th/15dist.htm
Civil Records: Access: Mail, in person, online. Only the court performs in person searches; visitors may not. Search fee: $5.00 per name. Required to search: name, years to search. Civil cases indexed by defendant, plaintiff. Civil records on computer since 11/1/95, index cards from 1960, index books back to early 1900s. Civil records online access at www.cocourts.com.
Criminal Records: Access: Mail, in person, online. Only the court performs in person searches; visitors may not. Search fee: $5.00 per name. Required to search: name, years to search, DOB, notorized signed release. Criminal records on computer since 11/1/95, index cards from 1960, index books back to early 1900s. Online access to criminal records is at www.cocourts.com.
General Information: No adoptions, sealed, juvenile, mental health or expunged cases released. Will fax results for $1.00 per page. Copy fee: $.75 per page. Cert fee: $10.00 per document. Payee: Cheyenne County Combined Court. Business checks accepted. Prepayment required. Will bill attorneys only. Mail requests: SASE required. Mail turnaround time 5-7 days.

Clear Creek County

Clear Creek Combined Courts PO Box 367, Georgetown, CO 80444; 303-569-3273; Fax: 303-569-3274. 8AM-4PM (MST). *Felony, Misdemeanor, Civil, Eviction, Small Claims, Probate.*
Civil Records: Access: Mail, in person, online. Both court and visitors may perform in person searches. Search fee: $5.00 per name. Required to search: name, years to search. Civil cases indexed by defendant, plaintiff. Civil records on index cards from 1976, ledger books back to late 1800. Civil records online access at www.cocourts.com. No searches done on records prior to 1976.
Criminal Records: Access: Mail, in person, online. Both court and visitors may perform in person searches. Search fee: $5.00 per name. Required to search: name, years to search, DOB. Criminal records on index cards from 1976, ledger books back to late 1800, computerized since 9/95. Online access to criminal records is at www.cocourts.com.
General Information: No adoptions, sealed, juvenile, mental health or expunged cases released. Copy fee: $.75 per page. Cert fee: $10.00. Payee: Clerk of Combined Court. Personal checks accepted. Prepayment required. Mail requests: SASE required. Mail turnaround time 1 week.

Conejos County

12th District & County Courts 6683 County Road 13, Conejos, CO 81129; 719-376-5466; Fax: 719-376-5939. Hours: 8AM-4PM (MST). *Felony, Misdemeanor, Civil, Eviction, Small Claims, Probate.*
Civil Records: Access: Mail, in person, online. Only the court performs in person searches; visitors may not. Search fee: $5.00 per name. Required to search: name, years to search. Civil cases indexed by defendant, plaintiff. Civil records on computer since 6/94, on index cards from 1980. Civil records online access at www.cocourts.com.
Criminal Records: Access: Mail, in person, online. Only the court performs in person searches; visitors may not. Search fee: $5.00 per name. Required to search: name, years to search, DOB. Criminal records on computer since 6/94, on index cards from 1980. Online access to criminal records is at www.cocourts.com.
General Information: No adoptions, sealed, juvenile, mental health or expunged cases released. Will not fax results. Copy fee: $.75 per page. Cert fee: $10.00. Payee: Conejos Combined Court. Personal checks accepted. Prepayment required. Mail requests: SASE required. Mail turnaround time 2 weeks.

Costilla County

12th District & County Courts PO Box 301, San Luis, CO 81152; 719-672-3681; Fax: 719-672-4493. Hours: 8AM-Noon, 1-4PM (MST). *Felony, Misdemeanor, Civil, Eviction, Small Claims, Probate.*
www.courts.state.co.us/district/12th/12dist.htm
Civil Records: Access: Mail, in person, online. Both court and visitors may perform in person searches. Search fee: $5.00 per name. Records prior to 1994 are $25.00 per hour. Required to search: name, years to search; also helpful: address. Civil cases indexed by defendant, plaintiff. Civil records on index cards from 1970, index books back to 1865, indexed on computer since 1994. In CO state archives prior to 1970. Civil records online access at www.cocourts.com.
Criminal Records: Access: Fax, mail, in person, online. Only the court performs in person searches; visitors may not. Search fee: $5.00 per name, records prior to 1994 are $25.00 per hour. Required to search: name, years to search, DOB; also helpful: address, SSN. Criminal records on index cards from 1970,

index books back to 1865, indexed on computer since 1994. In CO state archived prior to 1970. Online access to criminal records is at www.cocourts.com.
General Information: No adoptions, sealed, juvenile, mental health, certain criminal cases or expunged cases released. Fee to fax results is $10.00 per document. Copy fee: $.75 per page. Cert fee: $10.00 per document. Payee: Costilla Combined Courts. Personal checks accepted. Prepayment required. Mail requests: SASE required. Mail turnaround time 1-2 weeks.

Crowley County

16th District & County Courts 110 E 6th St, #303, Ordway, CO 81063; 719-267-4468; Fax: 719-267-3753. 8AM-5PM (MST). *Felony, Misdemeanor, Civil, Eviction, Small Claims, Probate.*
www.courts.state.co.us/district/16th/16dist.htm
Civil Records: Access: Phone, mail, fax, in person, online. Only the court performs in person searches; visitors may not. Search fee: $5.00 per name. Required to search: name, years to search. Civil cases indexed by defendant, plaintiff. Civil records on computer back to 1993, fiche since 1980s, index books back to 1925. Civil records online access at www.cocourts.com.
Criminal Records: Access: Mail, fax, in person, online. Only the court performs in person searches; visitors may not. Search fee: $5.00 per name. Required to search: name, years to search, DOB, SSN. Criminal records on computer back to 1993, fiche since 1980s, index books back to 1925. Online access to criminal records is at www.cocourts.com.
General Information: No adoptions, sealed, juvenile, mental health or expunged cases released. Fee to fax results is $1.00 per page. Copy fee: $.75 per page. Cert fee: $10.00. Payee: Crowley Combined Court. Personal checks accepted. Prepayment required. Mail requests: SASE required. Mail turnaround time 3-5 days.

Custer County

11th District & County Courts PO Box 60, Westcliffe, CO 81252; 719-783-2274; Fax: 719-783-2995. 8AM-2PM (MST). *Felony, Misdemeanor, Civil, Eviction, Small Claims, Probate.*
www.courts.state.co.us/district/11th/dist11.htm
Civil Records: Access: Mail, in person, online. Only the court may perform in person searches. Search fee: $5.00 per name. Required to search: name, years to search. Civil cases indexed by defendant, plaintiff. Civil records on index cards from 1973, ledger books back to 1965, on computer since 1993, archived from 1879-1972. Civil records online access at www.cocourts.com.
Criminal Records: Access: Mail, in person, online. Only the court may perform in person searches. Search fee: $5.00 per name. Required to search: name, years to search, DOB. Criminal records on index cards from 1973, ledger books back to 1965, on computer since 1993, archived from 1879-1972. Online access to criminal records is at www.cocourts.com.
General Information: No adoptions, sealed, juvenile, mental health or expunged cases released. Will fax results for $1.00 per page. Copy fee: $.75 per page. Cert fee: $10.00. Payee: Custer Combined Court. Personal checks accepted. Prepayment required. Mail requests: SASE required. Mail turnaround time 1-2 weeks.

Delta County

District & County Courts 501 Palmer St, Rm 338, Delta, CO 81416; 970-874-6280. Hours: 9AM-4PM (MST). *Felony, Misdemeanor, Civil, Eviction, Small Claims, Probate.*
www.7thjudicialdistrictco.org/delta.html

Civil Records: Access: Mail, in person, online. Only the court performs in person searches; visitors may not. Search fee: $5.00 per name. Required to search: name, years to search. Civil cases indexed by defendant, plaintiff. Civil records on computer back to 10/1994, index cards from 1972, index books back to 1900. Civil records online access at www.cocourts.com. Also, weekly dockets for the 7th district courts are at www.7thjudicialdistrictco.org/docket.html.
Criminal Records: Access: Mail, in person, online. Only the court performs in person searches; visitors may not. Search fee: $5.00 per name. Required to search: name, years to search, DOB, signed release. Criminal records on computer back to 10/1994, index cards from 1972, index books back to 1900. Online access to criminal records is at www.cocourts.com. Also, weekly dockets are available, see civil, above.
General Information: No adoptions, sealed, juvenile, mental health or expunged cases released. Will fax results for $1.00 per page prepaid. Copy fee: $.75 per page. Cert fee: $10.00. Payee: Clerk of Court. Only cashiers checks and money orders accepted. Prepayment required. Mail requests: SASE required. Mail turnaround time 10 days.

Denver County

2nd District Court 1437 Bannock, Office of the Court Clerk, Denver, CO 80202; 720-865-8301. Hours: 8AM-4PM (MST). *Felony, Civil Actions Over $10,000.*
www.courts.state.co.us/district/02nd/02dist.htm
Civil Records: Access: Mail, in person, online. Both court and visitors may perform in person searches. No search fee. Required to search: name, years to search. Civil cases indexed by defendant, plaintiff. Civil records on computer from 1974, index books back to the late 1800s if convicted of criminal charges. Online access to civil records is at www.denvergov.org/court/civilcourts.asp, and also at www.cocourts.com.
Criminal Records: Access: Mail, in person, online. Both court and visitors may perform in person searches. No search fee. Required to search: name, years to search, DOB. Criminal records on computer from 1974, index books back to the late 1800s if convicted of criminal charges. Online access to criminal records is at www.cocourts.com and at www.denvergov.org/court/courtselect.asp.
General Information: No adoptions, sealed, juvenile, mental health or expunged cases released. Copy fee: $.75 per page. Cert fee: $10.00. Payee: Denver District Court. Personal checks accepted. Prepayment required. Mail requests: SASE required. Mail turnaround time 1 week.

County Court - Civil Division 1515 Cleveland Pl, 4th Fl, Denver, CO 80202; 303-640-5161; Fax: 303-640-4730. Hours: 8AM-5PM (MST). *Civil Actions Under $15,000, Eviction, Small Claims.*
www.courts.state.co.us/district/counties.htm
Civil Records: Access: Mail, in person, online. Only the court may perform in person searches. No search fee. Required to search: name, years to search. Civil cases indexed by defendant, plaintiff. Civil records on computer from 1987, microfiche since 1965. Online searching of Denver County Civil Division court cases is at www.denvergov.org/court/civilcourts.asp. Search by name, business name, or case number. You can also search at www.cocourts.com.
General Information: No adoptions, sealed, juvenile, mental health or expunged cases released. Will not fax results. Copy fee: $1.00 per page. Cert fee: $10.00. Payee: Denver County Court. Personal checks accepted. Prepayment required. Mail requests: SASE required. Mail turnaround time 1 week.

County Court - Criminal Division 1437 Bannock St Rm 111A, Denver, CO 80202; 720-865-7820. Hours: 8AM-5PM (MST). *Misdemeanor.* www.courts.state.co.us/district/02nd/02dist.htm

Criminal Records: Access: Mail, in person, online. Only the court may perform in person searches. No search fee. Required to search: name, years to search, DOB; also helpful: address. Criminal records computerized since 1978. Online access to criminal records at www.denvergov.org/court/courtselect.asp

General Information: No adoptions, sealed, juvenile, mental health or expunged cases released. Will fax results for $5.00 per name plus $.75 per page. Copy fee: $.75 per page. Cert fee: $10.00. Payee: Denver County Court. Personal checks accepted. Prepayment required. Mail requests: SASE required. Mail turnaround time 1 week.

Probate Court 1437 Bannock, Rm 230, Denver, CO 80202; 720-865-8310; Fax: 720-865-8576. Hours: 8:30AM-4PM (MST). *Probate.* www.courts.state.co.us/district/02nd/02dist.htm

Dolores County

22nd District & County Courts PO Box 511, Dove Creek, CO 81324; 970-677-2258. Hours: 8AM-5PM M, T, TH; 8AM-Noon F (MST). *Felony, Misdemeanor, Civil, Eviction, Small Claims, Probate.*

Note: Office is closed on Wednesday.

Civil Records: Access: Phone, mail, in person. Only the court performs in person searches; visitors may not. No search fee. Required to search: name, years to search. Civil cases indexed by defendant, plaintiff. Civil records on index cards from 1972, index books back to 1895, on computer from 06/95 to present. Civil records online access at www.cocourts.com.

Criminal Records: Access: Phone, mail, in person, online. Only the court performs in person searches; visitors may not. No search fee. Required to search: name, years to search, DOB. Criminal records on index cards from 1972, index books back to 1895, on computer from 06/95 to present. Online access to criminal records is at www.cocourts.com.

General Information: No adoptions, sealed, juvenile, mental health or expunged cases released. Will not fax results. Copy fee: $.75 per page. Cert fee: $10.00. Payee: Dolores County Combined. Only cashiers checks and money orders accepted. Prepayment required. Mail requests: SASE required. Mail turnaround time 1 week.

Douglas County

Douglas County Combined Court 4000 Justice Way, #2009, Castle Rock, CO 80104; 303-663-7200. Hours: 8:30AM-Noon; 1:15PM-4PM (MST). *Felony, Misdemeanor, Civil, Eviction, Small Claims, Probate.* www.courts.state.co.us/district/18th/18dist.htm

Civil Records: Access: Mail, in person, online. Both court and visitors may perform in person searches. Search fee: $5.00 per name. $20.00 per hour for extensive search. Required to search: name, years to search. Civil cases indexed by defendant, plaintiff. Civil records on computer back to 1/1988, index cards from 1975, index books to 1880s. Civil records online access at www.cocourts.com.

Criminal Records: Access: Mail, in person, online. Both court and visitors may perform in person searches. Search fee: $5.00 per name. $20.00 per hour for extensive search. Required to search: name, years to search. Criminal records on computer back to 1/1988, index cards from 1975, index books to 1880s. Online access to criminal records is at www.cocourts.com.

General Information: No adoptions, sealed, juvenile, mental health or expunged cases released.

Copy fee: $.75 per page. Cert fee: $10.00. Payee: Clerk of Court. Only cashiers checks and money orders accepted. Prepayment required. Mail requests: SASE required. Mail turnaround time 1-2 weeks.

Eagle County

Eagle Combined Court PO Box 597, Eagle, CO 81631; 970-328-6373; Fax: 970-328-6328. 8AM-12;00-1-4PM (MST). *Felony, Misdemeanor, Civil, Eviction, Small Claims, Probate.*

Civil Records: Access: Fax, mail, in person, online. Visitors must perform in person searches for themselves. Search fee: $5.00 per name. Required to search: name, years to search. Civil cases indexed by defendant, plaintiff. Civil records on computer since 09/95; prior on fiche to 1970, books to 1930. Civil records online access at www.cocourts.com.

Criminal Records: Access: Fax, mail, in person, online. Visitors must perform in person searches for themselves. Search fee: $5.00 per name. Required to search: name, years to search, DOB. Criminal records on computer since 09/95; prior on fiche to 1970, books to 1930. Online access to criminal records is at www.cocourts.com.

General Information: No adoptions, sealed, juvenile, mental health or expunged cases released. Will fax results $1.00 per page. Fax fee must be paid with credit card. Copy fee: $.75 per page. Cert fee: $10.00. Payee: Eagle Combined Courts. Personal checks accepted. Visa, MC accepted. Prepayment required. Mail requests: SASE required. Mail turnaround time 5-7 days.

El Paso County

El Paso Combined Court PO Box 2980, Colorado Springs, CO 80901-2980; 719-448-7599; Fax: 719-448-7685. Hours: 8AM-5PM (closed at noon 1 hr) (MST). *Felony, Misdemeanor, Civil Actions, Probate.* www.gofourth.org

Note: Records for the County and District Courts are combined.

Civil Records: Access: Fax, mail, in person, online. Both court and visitors may perform in person searches. Search fee: $5.00 per name. Required to search: name, years to search. Civil cases indexed by defendant, plaintiff. Civil records on computer from Jan, 1975, index cards to 1975, index books to 1861. Civil records online access at www.cocourts.com.

Criminal Records: Access: Fax, mail, in person, online. Both court and visitors may perform in person searches. Search fee: $5.00 per name; if pre-1975, fee is $20.00 per hour. Required to search: name, years to search, DOB; also helpful: SSN. Criminal records on computer from Jan, 1975, index cards to 1975, index books to 1861. Online access to criminal records is at www.cocourts.com.

General Information: No adoptions, sealed, juvenile, mental health, expunged cases or other access restricted cases released. Fee is fax results is $.75 per page plus $1.50 if long distance. Copy fee: $.75 per page. Cert fee: $10.00. Payee: Clerk of District Court. Personal checks accepted. Visa, MC, Discover accepted. Prepayment required. Mail requests: SASE required. Mail turnaround time 5-7 days.

Elbert County

Elbert District & County Courts PO Box 232, Kiowa, CO 80117; 303-621-2131. Hours: 8AM-4PM (MST). *Felony, Misdemeanor, Civil, Eviction, Small Claims, Probate.* www.courts.state.co.us/district/18th/18dist.htm

Civil Records: Access: Mail, in person, online. Only the court performs in person searches; visitors may not. Search fee: $5.00 per name. Required to search:

full name, years to search. Civil cases indexed by defendant, plaintiff. Civil records on computer back to 1995, index cards from 1978-1994, index books from 1920s, archived prior to 1920. Civil records online access at www.cocourts.com.

Criminal Records: Access: Mail, in person, online. Only the court performs in person searches; visitors may not. Search fee: $5.00 per name. Required to search: full name, years to search, DOB, signed release. Criminal records on computer back to 1995, index cards from 1978, index books from 1920s. Online access to criminal records is at www.cocourts.com.

General Information: No adoptions, sealed, juvenile, mental health or expunged cases released. Copy fee: $.75 per page. Cert fee: $10.00. Payee: Elbert Combined Courts. Business checks accepted. Prepayment required. Mail requests: SASE required. Mail turnaround time 1-2 weeks.

Fremont County

District & County Courts 136 Justice Center Rd, Rm 103, Canon City, CO 81212; 719-269-0100; Fax: 719-269-0134. Hours: 8AM-5PM (MST). *Felony, Misdemeanor, Civil, Eviction, Small Claims, Probate, Tarffic.* www.courts.state.co.us/district/11th/dist11.htm

Civil Records: Access: Mail, fax, in person, online. Only the court performs in person searches; visitors may not. Search fee: $5.00 per name. Required to search: name, years to search; also helpful: address. Civil cases indexed by defendant, plaintiff. Civil records computerized since 1995, on index cards from 1978, index books in Denver back to 1861. Civil records online access at www.cocourts.com.

Criminal Records: Access: Mail, fax, in person, online. Only the court performs in person searches; visitors may not. Search fee: $5.00 per name. Required to search: name, years to search; also helpful: address, DOB. Criminal records computerized since 1995, on index cards from 1978. Online access to criminal records is at www.cocourts.com.

General Information: No adoptions, sealed, juvenile, mental health or expunged cases released. Copy fee: $.75 per page. Cert fee: $10.00. Payee: Clerk of the Combined Courts. Personal checks accepted. Prepayment required. Mail requests: SASE required. Mail turnaround time up to 14 working days.

Garfield County

9th District & County Courts 109 8th St #104, Glenwood Springs, CO 81601; 970-945-5075; Fax: 970-945-8756. Hours: 8AM-5PM (MST). *Felony, Misdemeanor, Civil, Eviction, Small Claims, Probate.* www.courts.state.co.us/district/09th/dist09.htm

Note: This court handles cases in the county for the area east of New Castle.

Civil Records: Access: Mail, in person, online. Only the court performs in person searches; visitors may not. Search fee: $5.00 per name. Required to search: name, years to search. Civil cases indexed by defendant, plaintiff. Civil records on computer from 1992, on fiche from 1970, index books back to late 1800s. Civil records online access at www.cocourts.com.

Criminal Records: Access: Mail, in person, online. Only the court performs in person searches; visitors may not. Search fee: $5.00 per name. Required to search: name, years to search. Criminal records on computer from 1992, on fiche from 1970, index books back to late 1800s. Online access to criminal records is at www.cocourts.com.

General Information: No adoptions, sealed, juvenile, mental health or expunged cases released.

Will fax results for $1.00 per page. Copy fee: $.75 per page. Cert fee: $10.00. Payee: Garfield Combined Courts. Personal checks accepted. Visa, MC accepted. Prepayment required. Mail requests: SASE required. Mail turnaround time 1-2 weeks.

County Court - Rifle 110 E 18th St, Rifle, CO 81650; 970-625-5100; Fax: 970-625-1125. Hours: 8AM-5PM (MST). *Misdemeanor, Civil Actions Under $15,000, Eviction, Small Claims.*
www.courts.state.co.us/district/09th/dist09.htm
Note: This court handles cases in the county for the area from New Castle to the west.

Civil Records: Access: Phone, fax, mail, in person, online. Only the court performs in person searches; visitors may not. No search fee. Required to search: name, years to search. Civil cases indexed by defendant, plaintiff. Civil records on index cards from 1965, computerized since 1994. Civil records online access at www.cocourts.com.
Criminal Records: Access: Phone, fax, mail, in person, online. Only the court performs in person searches; visitors may not. No search fee. Required to search: name, years to search, DOB. Criminal records on index cards from 1965, computerized since 1994. Online access to criminal records is at www.cocourts.com.
General Information: No adoptions, sealed, juvenile, mental health or expunged cases released. Will fax results $1.00 per page to send or receive. Copy fee: $.75 per page. Cert fee: $10.00 per page. Payee: Associate County Court. Personal checks accepted. Visa, MC accepted. Prepayment required. Mail requests: SASE required. Mail turnaround time 1 week.

Gilpin County

1st District & County Courts 2960 Dory Hill Rd #200, Golden, CO 80403-8768; 303-582-5323; Fax: 303-582-3112. Hours: 8AM-5PM (MST). *Felony, Misdemeanor, Civil, Eviction, Small Claims, Probate.*

Civil Records: Access: Mail, in person, online. Only the court performs in person searches; visitors may not. Search fee: $5.00 per name. Fee is for past 7 years. Required to search: name, years to search. Civil cases indexed by defendant, plaintiff. Civil records on computer (County-1993, District-1994), on index cards from 1970s, index books from 1950s. Civil records online access at www.cocourts.com.
Criminal Records: Access: Mail, in person, online. Only the court performs in person searches; visitors may not. Search fee: $10.00 per name. Fee is for past 7 years. Required to search: name, years to search, DOB. Criminal records on computer (County-1993, District-1994), on index cards from 1970s, index books from 1950s. Online access to criminal records is at www.cocourts.com.
General Information: No adoptions, sealed, juvenile, mental health or expunged cases released. Will fax results to local or toll free line. Copy fee: $.75 per page. Cert fee: $10.00. Payee: Clerk of the Combined Courts. Personal checks accepted. Prepayment required. Mail requests: SASE required. Mail turnaround time 5 days.

Grand County

14th District & County Courts PO Box 192, Hot Sulphur Springs, CO 80451; 970-725-3357. Hours: 8AM-4PM (MST). *Felony, Misdemeanor, Civil, Eviction, Small Claims, Probate.*

Civil Records: Access: Phone, mail, in person, online. Only the court performs in person searches; visitors may not. Search fee: $5.00 per name if 1976-1991. $20.00 if pre-1976. No fee 1992-present. Required to search: name, years to search. Civil cases indexed by defendant, plaintiff. Civil records on

computer from July, 1991, fiche from 1970, index books from 1900. Civil records online access at www.cocourts.com. Phone requests accepted only if no fees involved.
Criminal Records: Access: Phone, mail, in person, online. Only the court performs in person searches; visitors may not. Search fee: $5.00 per name if 1976-1991. $20.00 if pre-1976. No fee 1992-present. Required to search: name, years to search, DOB. Criminal records on computer from July, 1991, fiche from 1970, index books from 1900. Online access to criminal records is at www.cocourts.com. Phone requests accepted only if no fees involved.
General Information: No adoptions, sealed, juvenile, mental health or expunged cases released. Copy fee: $.75 per page. Cert fee: $10.00. Payee: Grand County Combined Court. Personal checks accepted. Prepayment required. Mail requests: SASE required. Mail turnaround time 1 week.

Gunnison County

7th District & County Courts 200 E Virginia Ave, Gunnison, CO 81230; 970-641-3500; Fax: 970-641-6876. Hours: 8:30AM-4:30PM M-Th; 8:30AM-3PM F (MST). *Felony, Misdemeanor, Civil, Eviction, Small Claims, Probate.*
www.courts.state.co.us/district/07th/dist07.htm
Civil Records: Access: Mail, in person, online. Only the court performs in person searches; visitors may not. Search fee: $5.00 per name. Required to search: name, years to search. Civil cases indexed by defendant. Civil records on computer from 1994, index cards from 1977, index books back to 1877. Civil records online access at www.cocourts.com.
Criminal Records: Access: Mail, in person, online. Only the court performs in person searches; visitors may not. Search fee: $5.00 per name. Required to search: name, years to search, DOB. Criminal records on computer from 1994, index cards from 1977, index books back to 1877. Online access to criminal records is at www.cocourts.com.
General Information: No adoptions, sealed, juvenile, mental health or expunged cases released. Will fax results. Copy fee: $.75 per page. Cert fee: $10.00. Payee: Gunnison Combined Courts. Personal checks accepted. Prepayment required. Mail requests: SASE required. Mail turnaround time 1-2 days.

Hinsdale County

7th District & County Courts PO Box 245, Lake City, CO 81235; 970-944-2227; Fax: 970-944-2289. Hours: 8:30-Noon MWF (Jun-Aug) 8:30-12:00 TF (Sept-May) (MST). *Felony, Misdemeanor, Civil, Eviction, Small Claims, Probate.*
www.courts.state.co.us/district/07th/dist07.htm
Civil Records: Access: Phone, fax, mail, in person, online. Only the court performs in person searches; visitors may not. No search fee. Required to search: name, years to search. Civil cases indexed by defendant, plaintiff. Civil records on index cards from 1975, index books back to 1900. Civil records online access at www.cocourts.com.
Criminal Records: Access: Phone, fax, mail, in person, online. Only the court performs in person searches; visitors may not. Search fee: Fee depends on time required for search. Required to search: name, years to search, DOB. Criminal records on index cards from 1975, index books back to 1900. Online access to criminal records is at www.cocourts.com.
General Information: No adoptions, sealed, juvenile, mental health or expunged cases released. Will fax results $.75 per page. 1-10 pgs $2.00, 11-20 pgs $5.00, 21-30 pgs $10.00. Copy fee: $.75 per page. Cert fee: $10.00. Payee: Clerk of the Combined Courts. Personal checks accepted. Prepayment required. Mail requests: SASE required. Mail turnaround time 2-4 weeks.

Huerfano County

3rd District & County Courts 401 Main St, #304, Walsenburg, CO 81089; 719-738-1040; Fax: 719-738-1267. Hours: 8AM-4PM (MST). *Felony, Misdemeanor, Civil, Eviction, Small Claims, Probate.*
www.courts.state.co.us/district/03rd/03dist.htm
Civil Records: Access: Mail, in person, online. Only the court performs in person searches; visitors may not. Search fee: $5.00 per name. Required to search: name, years to search. Civil cases indexed by defendant, plaintiff. Civil records on computer from 1995 (county court only), index cards from 1978, index books from 1861. Civil records online access at www.cocourts.com.
Criminal Records: Access: Mail, in person, online. Only the court performs in person searches; visitors may not. Search fee: $5.00 per name. Required to search: name, years to search, DOB. Criminal records on computer from 1995 (county court only), index cards from 1978, index books from 1861. Online access to criminal records is at www.cocourts.com.
General Information: No adoptions, sealed, juvenile, mental health or expunged cases released. Fee to fax results is $2.00 per page. Copy fee: $.75 per page. Cert fee: $10.00. Payee: Huerfano County Combined Courts. Personal checks accepted. Prepayment required. Mail requests: SASE required. Mail turnaround time 2 weeks.

Jackson County

8th District & County Courts PO Box 308, Walden, CO 80480; 970-723-4363. Hours: 9AM-1PM (MST). *Felony, Misdemeanor, Civil, Eviction, Small Claims, Probate.*
www.courts.state.co.us/district/08th/08dist.htm
Civil Records: Access: Mail, in person, online. Both court and visitors may perform in person searches. No search fee. Required to search: name, years to search. Civil cases indexed by defendant, plaintiff. Civil records on computer since 1994; prior on index cards from 1974, index books from the 1900s. Civil records online access at www.cocourts.com.
Criminal Records: Access: Mail, in person, online. Both court and visitors may perform in person searches. No search fee. Required to search: name, years to search, DOB. Criminal records on computer since 1994; prior on index cards from 1974, index books from the 1900s. Online access to criminal records is at www.cocourts.com.
General Information: No adoptions, sealed, juvenile, mental health or expunged cases released. Will fax results to a local or toll free line. Copy fee: $.75 per page. Will bill in excess of 10 pages. Cert fee: $10.00. Payee: Clerk of the Combined Courts. Personal checks accepted. Prepayment required. If a file has been pulled and exceeds 10 pages, will bill the requesting party. Mail requests: SASE required. Mail turnaround time 2 weeks.

Jefferson County

1st District & County Courts 100 Jefferson County Parkway, Golden, CO 80401-6002; 303-271-6267; Fax: 303-271-6188. Hours: 8AM-4PM (MST). *Felony, Misdemeanor, Civil, Eviction, Small Claims, Probate, Traffic.*
Civil Records: Access: Mail, in person, online. Both court and visitors may perform in person searches. Search fee: $5.00 per name. Fee is per case. Add $5.00 if search includes microfilm records. Required to search: name, years to search; also helpful: address. Civil cases indexed by defendant, plaintiff. Civil records on computer from 1985, microfiche from 1975, index books from 1963-1974, archived prior to 1963. Civil records online access at www.cocourts.com.

Criminal Records: Access: Mail, in person, online. Both court and visitors may perform in person searches. Search fee: $5.00 per name. Fee varies depending on number of years searched. Add $5.00 if search includes microfilm records. Required to search: name, years to search, DOB; also helpful: address. Criminal records on computer from 1985, microfiche from 1975, index books from 1963-1974, archived prior to 1963. Online access to criminal records is at www.cocourts.com.

General Information: No adoptions, sealed, juvenile, mental health or expunged cases released. Will not fax results. Copy fee: $.75 per page. Cert fee: $10.00. Payee: Clerk of Combined Courts. Personal checks accepted. Prepayment required. Mail requests: SASE required. Mail turnaround time 1 week.

Kiowa County

15th District & County Courts PO Box 353, Eads, CO 81036; 719-438-5558; Fax: 719-438-5300. Hours: 9AM-4PM (MST). *Felony, Misdemeanor, Civil, Eviction, Small Claims, Probate.*

www.courts.state.co.us/district/15th/15dist.html

Civil Records: Access: Phone, fax, mail, in person, online. Only the court performs in person searches; visitors may not. Search fee: $5.00 per name. Required to search: name, years to search. Civil cases indexed by defendant, plaintiff. Civil records on index cards from the 1960s, index books from 1889. Recent records are computerized. Civil records online access at www.cocourts.com.

Criminal Records: Access: Phone, fax, mail, in person, online. Only the court performs in person searches; visitors may not. Search fee: $5.00 per name. Required to search: name, years to search, DOB. Criminal records on index cards from the 1960s, index books from 1889. Recent records are computerized. Online access to criminal records is at www.cocourts.com.

General Information: No adoptions, sealed, juvenile, mental health or expunged cases released. Will fax results $1.00 per doc. Copy fee: $.75 per page. Cert fee: $10.00. Payee: Kiowa County Court. Business checks accepted. Prepayment required. Mail requests: SASE required. Mail turnaround: 1 week.

Kit Carson County

Kit Carson Combined Court 251 16th St, #301, Burlington, CO 80807; 719-346-5524. Hours: 8AM-4PM (MST). *Felony, Misdemeanor, Civil, Eviction, Small Claims, Probate.*

www.courts.state.co.us/district/13th/13dist.htm

Civil Records: Access: Mail, in person, online. Only the court performs in person searches; visitors may not. Search fee: $5.00 per name. Required to search: name, years to search. Civil cases indexed by defendant, plaintiff. Civil records on index cards from 1910, index books from 1889. Civil records online access at www.cocourts.com.

Criminal Records: Access: Mail, in person, online. Only the court performs in person searches; visitors may not. No search fee. Required to search: name, years to search, DOB. Criminal records on index cards from 1910, index books from 1889. Online access to criminal records is at www.cocourts.com.

General Information: No adoptions, sealed, juvenile, mental health or expunged cases released. Will fax results $5.00 per doc. Copy fee: $.75 per page. Cert fee: $10.00. Payee: Combined Courts. No personal checks accepted. Prepayment required. Mail requests: SASE required. Mail turnaround: 1 week.

La Plata County

La Plata Combined Courts 1060 E 2nd Ave, Durango, CO 81301; 970-247-2304; Fax: 970-247-4348 Cri; 259-0258 Civ. Hours: 8AM-4PM (MST). *Felony, Misdemeanor, Civil, Small Claims, Probate.* Note: Fax for civil section is 970-259-0258.

Civil Records: Access: Mail, in person, online. Only the court performs in person searches; visitors may not. Search fee: $5.00 per name. Fee is per case and can be as much as $20.00. Required to search: name, years to search. Civil cases indexed by defendant, plaintiff. Civil records on computer from 1990, index cards from 1976, index books from 1874. Civil records online access at www.cocourts.com.

Criminal Records: Access: Mail, in person, online. Only the court performs in person searches; visitors may not. Search fee: $5.00 per name. Fee is per case and can be as much as $20.00. Required to search: name, years to search, DOB. Criminal records on computer from 1990, index cards from 1976, index books from 1874. Online access to criminal records is at www.cocourts.com.

General Information: No adoptions, sealed, juvenile, mental health or expunged cases released. Fee to fax results is $3.00 per document. Copy fee: $.75 per page. Cert fee: $15.00. Payee: Clerk of the Combined Courts. Personal checks accepted. Prepayment required. Mail requests: SASE required. Mail turnaround time 3-7 days.

Lake County

Lake County Combined Courts PO Box 55, Leadville, CO 80461; 719-486-0535. Hours: 8AM-Noon, 1-4PM (MST). *Felony, Misdemeanor, Civil, Eviction, Small Claims, Probate.*

Civil Records: Access: Mail, in person, online. Only the court performs in person searches; visitors may not. Search fee: $20.00 per name. Required to search: name, years to search. Civil cases indexed by defendant, plaintiff. Civil records on index cards from 1988 (District), 1970 (County), index books from 1865. Civil records online access at www.cocourts.com.

Criminal Records: Access: Mail, in person, online. Only the court performs in person searches; visitors may not. Search fee: $20.00 per name. Required to search: name, years to search, DOB. Criminal records on index cards from 1988 (District), 1970 (County), index books from 1865. Online access to criminal records is at www.cocourts.com.

General Information: No adoptions, sealed, juvenile, mental health or expunged cases released. Copy fee: $.75 per page. Cert fee: $10.00. Payee: Lake County Court. Business checks accepted. Prepayment required. Mail requests: SASE required. Mail turnaround time 7 days.

Larimer County

8th District Court 201 La Porte Ave, #100, Ft Collins, CO 80521; 970-498-6100; Fax: 970-498-6110. Hours: 8AM-4PM (MST). *Felony, Civil Actions Over $10,000, Probate.*

www.courts.state.co.us/district/08th/08dist.htm

Civil Records: Access: Phone, mail, in person, online. Both court and visitors may perform in person searches. Search fee: $5.00 per name. Required to search: name; also helpful: years to search. Civil cases indexed by defendant, plaintiff. Civil records on computer from 1976, index books back to 1861. Civil records online access at www.cocourts.com.

Criminal Records: Access: Mail, in person, online. Only the court performs in person searches; visitors may not. Search fee: $5.00 per name. Required to search: name; also helpful: years to search, DOB, SSN. Criminal records on computer from 1976, index

books back to 1861. Online access to criminal records is at www.cocourts.com.

General Information: No adoptions, sealed, juvenile, mental health or expunged cases released. Copy fee: $.75 per page. Cert fee: $10.00. Payee: Clerk of District Court. Personal checks accepted. Prepayment required. Mail requests: SASE required. Mail turnaround time 7-10 days.

County Court 201 La Porte Ave, #100, Ft Collins, CO 80521; 970-498-6100; Fax: 970-498-6110. Hours: 8AM-4PM (MST). *Misdemeanor, Civil Actions Under $15,000, Eviction, Small Claims.*

www.courts.state.co.us/district/08th/08dist.htm

Civil Records: Access: Mail, in person, online. Both the court and visitors may perform in person searches. Search fee: $5.00 per name. Required to search: name, years to search; also helpful: address. Civil cases indexed by defendant, plaintiff. Some records on computer from 1986, index cards from 1965. Civil records online access at www.cocourts.com.

Criminal Records: Access: Mail, in person, online. Both the court and visitors may perform in person searches. Search fee: $5.00 per name. Required to search: name, years to search, DOB, signed release, offense; also helpful: address. Some records on computer from 1986, index cards from 1965. Online access to criminal records is at www.cocourts.com.

General Information: No sealed cases released. Copy fee: $.75 per page. Cert fee: $10.00. Payee: Larimer County Combined Court. Personal checks accepted. Prepayment required. Mail requests: SASE required. Mail turnaround time 3-5 days.

Las Animas County

3rd District Court 200 E 1st St, Rm 304, Trinidad, CO 81082; 719-846-3316/2221; Fax: 719-846-9367. Hours: 8AM-5PM (MST). *Felony, Misdemeanor, Civil, Eviction, Small Claims, Probate.*

www.courts.state.co.us/district/03rd/03dist.htm

Civil Records: Access: Mail, in person, online. Both court and visitors may perform in person searches. Search fee: $5.00 per name. Required to search: name, years to search. Civil cases indexed by defendant, plaintiff. Civil records on index cards from 1976, index books to 1950. Civil records online access at www.cocourts.com.

Criminal Records: Access: Mail, in person, online. Both court and visitors may perform in person searches. Search fee: $5.00 per name. Required to search: name, years to search, DOB; also helpful: SSN. Criminal records on index cards from 1976, index books to 1950. Online access to criminal records is at www.cocourts.com.

General Information: No adoptions, sealed, juvenile, mental health or expunged cases released. Fee to fax results is $2.00 per page. Copy fee: $.75 per page. Cert fee: $10.00. Payee: Combined courts. Only cashiers checks and money orders accepted. Prepayment required. Mail requests: SASE required. Mail turnaround time 1 week.

Lincoln County

18th District & County Courts PO Box 128, Hugo, CO 80821; 719-743-2455. Hours: 8AM-5PM (MST). *Felony, Misdemeanor, Civil, Eviction, Small Claims, Probate.*

www.courts.state.co.us/district/18th/18dist.htm

Civil Records: Access: Phone, mail, in person, online. Only the court performs in person searches; visitors may not. Search fee: $5.00. Required to search: name, years to search. Civil cases indexed by defendant, plaintiff. Civil records on computer since 12/94, index cards from 1977, index books back to 1889, archived 10 years back. Civil records online access at www.cocourts.com.

Criminal Records: Access: Phone, mail, in person, online. Only the court performs in person searches; visitors may not. Search fee: $5.00. Required to search: name, years to search, DOB. Criminal records on computer since 12/94, index cards from 1977, index books back to 1889, archived 10 years back. Online access to criminal records is at www.cocourts.com.

General Information: No adoptions, sealed, juvenile, mental health or expunged cases released. Copy fee: $.75 per page. Cert fee: $10.00. Payee: Lincoln County Combined Courts. Personal checks accepted. Prepayment required. Mail requests: SASE required. Mail turnaround time within 10 days.

Logan County

13th District Court 110 N.Riverview Rd. Rm 205, Sterling, CO 80751; 970-522-6565; Fax: 970-522-6566. Hours: 8AM-4PM (MST). *Felony, Civil Actions Over $10,000, Probate.*
www.courts.state.co.us/district/13th/13dist.htm
Civil Records: Access: Mail, in person, online. Only the court performs in person searches; visitors may not. Search fee: $5.00 per name. Required to search: name, years to search. Civil cases indexed by defendant, plaintiff. Civil records computerized since 08/95, on index cards from 1973, index books back to 1887. Civil records online access at www.cocourts.com.
Criminal Records: Access: Mail, in person, online. Only the court performs in person searches; visitors may not. Search fee: $5.00 per name. Required to search: name, years to search, DOB. Criminal records computerized since 08/95, on index cards from 1973, index books back to 1887. Online access to criminal records is at www.cocourts.com.
General Information: No adoptions, sealed, juvenile, mental health or expunged cases released. Fee to fax results is $1.00 per page local; $2.00 per page long distance. Copy fee: $.75 per page. Cert fee: $10.00. Payee: Logan District Court. Personal checks accepted. Prepayment required. Mail requests: SASE required. Mail turnaround time 1 week.

County Court 110 N Riverview Rd, Rm 210, Sterling, CO 80751; 970-522-1572; Fax: 970-526-5359. Hours: 8AM-4PM (MST). *Misdemeanor, Civil Actions Under $15,000, Eviction, Small Claims.*
www.courts.state.co.us/district/counties.htm
Note: Fax number will change in late 2003.
Civil Records: Access: Phone, mail, in person, online. Both court and visitors may perform in person searches. Search fee: $5.00 per name. Required to search: name, years to search. Civil cases indexed by defendant, plaintiff. Civil records on computer since 08/95; prior on index cards from 1972 and index books from 1965. Civil records online access at www.cocourts.com.
Criminal Records: Access: In person, online. Both court and visitors may perform in person searches. Search fee: $5.00 per name. Required to search: name, years to search, DOB. Criminal records on computer since 08/95; prior on index cards from 1972 and index books from 1965. Online access to criminal records is at www.cocourts.com.
General Information: No adoptions, sealed, juvenile, mental health or expunged cases released. Will fax results for $2.00 per document. Copy fee: $.75 per page. Cert fee: $10.00. Payee: Logan County Court. Business checks accepted. Prepayment required.

Mesa County

Mesa County Combined Court Mesa County District Court, PO Box 20000-5030, Grand Junction, CO 81502; 970-257-3625. 8AM-4PM (MST). *Felony, Civil Actions Over $10,000, Probate.*
Civil Records: Access: Phone, mail, in person, online. Both court and visitors may perform in person searches. Search fee: $5.00 per name. Required to search: name, years to search. Civil cases indexed by defendant, plaintiff. Civil records on computer since 1994, on microfiche to 1985, books from late 1800s. Civil records online access at www.cocourts.com.
Criminal Records: Access: Mail, in person, online. Only the court performs in person searches; visitors may not. Search fee: $5.00 per name. Required to search: name, years to search, DOB. Criminal records on computer since 1994, on microfiche to 1985, books from late 1800s. Online access to criminal records is at www.cocourts.com.
General Information: No adoptions, sealed, juvenile, mental health or expunged cases released. Will not fax results. Copy fee: $.75 per page. Cert fee: $10.00. Payee: Mesa County Combined Court. Business checks accepted. Visa, MC accepted. Prepayment required. Mail requests: SASE required. Mail turnaround time 5-7 days.

Mineral County

12th District & County Courts PO Box 427, Creede, CO 81130; 719-658-2575. Hours: 8AM-12;00-1-3PM (MST). *Felony, Misdemeanor, Civil, Eviction, Small Claims, Probate.*
Note: Mineral County, PO Box 337, Creede,CO.81130
Civil Records: Access: Mail, in person, online. Only the court performs in person searches; visitors may not. Search fee: $5.00 per name. Required to search: name, years to search. Civil cases indexed by defendant, plaintiff. Civil records on computer since July 1993, on index cards from 1977, index books back to 1893. Civil records online access at www.cocourts.com.
Criminal Records: Access: Mail, in person, online. Only the court performs in person searches; visitors may not. Search fee: $5.00 per name. Required to search: name, years to search, DOB. Criminal records on computer since July 1993, on index cards from 1977, index books back to 1893. Online access to criminal records is at www.cocourts.com.
General Information: No adoptions, sealed, juvenile, mental health or expunged cases released. Copy fee: $.75 per page. Cert fee: $10.00. Payee: Mineral Combined Courts. Personal checks accepted. Prepayment required. Mail requests: SASE required. Mail turnaround time 2-3 days.

Moffat County

Moffat County Combined Court 221 W Victory Wy, #300, Craig, CO 81625; 970-824-8254. Hours: 8AM-4PM (MST). *Felony, Misdemeanor, Civil, Eviction, Small Claims, Probate.*
Civil Records: Access: Phone, mail, in person, online. Only the court performs in person searches; visitors may not. Search fee: $5.00 for records 1976-91; $20.00 prior to 1976. Required to search: name, years to search. Civil cases indexed by defendant, plaintiff. Civil records on computer from 1992, index cards from 1976, either microfilmed or archived back to 1911. Civil records online access at www.cocourts.com.
Criminal Records: Access: Mail, in person, online. Only the court performs in person searches; visitors may not. Search fee: $5.00 1976-1991; $20.00 prior to 1976. Required to search: name, years to search, DOB. Criminal records on computer from 1992, index cards from 1976, either microfilmed or archived

back to 1911. Online access to criminal records is at www.cocourts.com.
General Information: No adoptions, sealed, juvenile, mental health or expunged cases released. Copy fee: $.75 per page. Cert fee: $10.00. Payee: Moffat County Combined Courts. Personal checks accepted. Prepayment required. Mail requests: SASE required. Mail turnaround time 1-2 weeks.

Montezuma County

22nd District Court 109 W Main St, #210, Cortez, CO 81321; 970-565-1111. Hours: 8AM-4PM (MST). *Felony, Civil Actions Over $15,000, Probate.*
www.courts.state.co.us/district/22nd/22distindex.htm
Civil Records: Access: Phone, mail, in person, online. Only the court performs in person searches; visitors may not. Search fee: $5.00 per name or case number, or $20.00 per hour to search. Required to search: name, years to search. Civil cases indexed by defendant, plaintiff. Civil records on computer back to 6/95, microfiche up to 1988, index cards from 1975, index books back to late 1890s. Civil records online access at www.cocourts.com.
Criminal Records: Access: Mail, in person, online. Only the court performs in person searches; visitors may not. Search fee: $5.00 per name or case number, or $20.00 per hour to search. Required to search: name, years to search, DOB. Criminal records on computer back to 6/95, microfiche up to 1988, index cards from 1975, index books back to late 1890s. Online access to criminal records is at www.cocourts.com.
General Information: No adoptions, sealed, juvenile, mental health or expunged cases released. Will not fax results. Copy fee: $.75 per page. Cert fee: $10.00. Payee: Montezuma District Court. Personal checks accepted. Prepayment required. Will bill mailing and copy costs. Mail requests: SASE required. Mail turnaround time 1-2 weeks.

County Court 601 N Mildred Rd, Cortez, CO 81321; 970-565-7580. Hours: 8AM-4PM (MST). *Misdemeanor, Civil Actions Under $15,000, Eviction, Small Claims.*
www.courts.state.co.us/district/22nd/22distindex.htm
Civil Records: Access: Mail, in person, online. Only the court performs in person searches; visitors may not. Search fee: $5.00. Required to search: name, years to search. Civil cases indexed by defendant, plaintiff. Civil records on computer since 1993. Civil records online access at www.cocourts.com.
Criminal Records: Access: Mail, in person, online. Only the court performs in person searches; visitors may not. Search fee: $5.00. Required to search: name, years to search, DOB. Criminal records on index cards from 1975, index books prior. Online access to criminal records is at www.cocourts.com.
General Information: No adoptions, sealed, juvenile, mental health or expunged cases released. Will not fax results. Copy fee: $.75 per page. Cert fee: $10.00. Payee: Montezuma County Court. Personal checks accepted. Prepayment required. Mail requests: SASE required. Mail turnaround time 5-7 days.

Montrose County

7th District & County Courts 1200 N Grand Ave, #A, Montrose, CO 81401-3164; 970-252-4300; 242-4309; Fax: 970-252-4309. Hours: 9AM-4PM (MST). *Felony, Misdemeanor, Civil, Eviction, Small Claims, Probate.* www.courts.state.co.us
Civil Records: Access: Mail, in person, online. Search fee: $5.00 per name. Required to search: name, years to search. Civil cases indexed by defendant, plaintiff. Civil records on index cards from 1975, index books back to 1890. Civil records online access at www.cocourts.com. Also, weekly dockets

for the 7th district county courts only are at www.7thjudicialdistrictco.org/docket.html.

Criminal Records: Access: Mail, in person, online, fax. Only the court performs in person searches; visitors may not. Search fee: $5.00 per name. Required to search: name, years to search, DOB. Criminal records on index cards from 1975, index books back to 1890. Online access to criminal records is at www.cocourts.com. Also, County Court weekly dockets are available, see civil, above.

General Information: No adoptions, sealed, juvenile, mental health or expunged cases released. Copy fee: $.75 per page. Cert fee: $10.00. Payee: Montrose Combined Courts. Personal checks accepted. Prepayment required. Mail requests: SASE required. Mail turnaround time 10 days.

Morgan County

13th District Court PO Box 130, Ft Morgan, CO 80701; 970-542-3435; Fax: 970-542-3436. Hours: 8AM-4PM (MST). *Felony, Civil Actions Over $10,000, Probate.*

www.courts.state.co.us/district/13th/13dist.htm

Civil Records: Access: Fax, mail, in person, online. Only the court performs in person searches; visitors may not. Search fee: $5.00. Required to search: name, years to search. Civil cases indexed by defendant, plaintiff. Civil records on index cards from 1967, index books back to 1906; computerized since 08/95. Civil records online access at www.cocourts.com.

Criminal Records: Access: Fax, mail, in person, online. Only the court performs in person searches; visitors may not. Search fee: None$5.00. Required to search: name, years to search, DOB, SSN; also helpful: signed release. Criminal records on index cards from 1967, index books back to 1906, computerized since 08/95. Online access to criminal records is at www.cocourts.com.

General Information: No adoptions, sealed, juvenile, mental health or expunged cases released. Will fax results if less than 5 pages. Copy fee: $.75 per page. Cert fee: $10.00. Payee: Morgan District Court. Personal checks accepted. Prepayment required. Mail requests: Written and SASE required. Mail turnaround time is 1 week.

County Court PO Box 695, Ft Morgan, CO 80701; 970-542-3414; Fax: 970-542-3416. Hours: 8AM-3PM (MST). *Misdemeanor, Civil Actions Under $15,000, Eviction, Small Claims.*

www.courts.state.co.us/district/13th/13dist.htm

Civil Records: Access: Mail, in person, online. Only the court performs in person searches; visitors may not. Search fee: $5.00 per name. Required to search: name, years to search. Civil cases indexed by defendant, plaintiff. Civil records on computer since 08/95; prior on index cards from 1980. Civil records online access at www.cocourts.com.

Criminal Records: Access: Mail, in person, online. Only the court performs in person searches; visitors may not. Search fee: $5.00 per name. Required to search: name, years to search, DOB. Criminal records on computer since 08/95; prior on index cards from 1980. Online access to criminal records is at www.cocourts.com.

General Information: Copy fee: $.75 per page. Cert fee: $10.00. Payee: Morgan County Court. Personal checks accepted. Prepayment required. Mail turnaround time is 7 days.

Otero County

Otero County Combined Courts Courthouse Rm 207, 13 W 3rd St, La Junta, CO 81050; 719-384-4951; Fax: 719-384-4991. Hours: 8AM-5PM (MST). *Felony, Civil, Probate.*

www.courts.state.co.us/district/16th/16dist.htm

Note: While this court has been "combined" with the County Court, there are separate offices and record databases.

Civil Records: Access: Mail, in person, online. Only the court performs in person searches; visitors may not. Search fee: $5.00 per name. Required to search: name, years to search. Civil cases indexed by defendant, plaintiff. Civil records on index cards from 1978, 'index books back to 1889, microfiche from 1889-1992. Civil records online access at www.cocourts.com.

Criminal Records: Access: Mail, in person, online. Only the court performs in person searches; visitors may not. Search fee: $5.00 per name. Required to search: name, years to search, DOB. Criminal records on index cards from 1978, index books back to 1889, microfiche from 1889-1992. Online access to criminal records is at www.cocourts.com.

General Information: No adoptions, sealed, juvenile, mental health or expunged cases released. Will fax results for $1.00 per page. Copy fee: $.75 per page. Cert fee: $10.00. Payee: Otero County Combined Courts. Personal checks accepted. Prepayment required. Mail requests: SASE required. Mail turnaround time 10 days.

Ouray County

7th District & County Courts PO Box 643, Ouray, CO 81427; 970-325-4405; Fax: 970-325-7364. Hours: 8:30AM-Noon, 1-4PM M-TH; Closed Fri (MST). *Felony, Misdemeanor, Civil, Eviction, Small Claims, Probate.*

www.courts.state.co.us/district/07th/dist07.htm

Civil Records: Access: Mail, in person, online. Only the court performs in person searches; visitors may not. Search fee: $5.00 per name. Required to search: name, years to search. Civil cases indexed by defendant, plaintiff. Civil records on computer since 1994, index cards from 1976, index books back to 1886, archived prior to 1925. Civil records online access at www.cocourts.com.

Criminal Records: Access: Mail, in person, online. Only the court performs in person searches; visitors may not. Search fee: $5.00 per name. Required to search: name, years to search, DOB. Criminal records on computer since 1994, index cards from 1976, index books back to 1886, archived prior to 1925. Online access to criminal records is at www.cocourts.com.

General Information: No adoptions, sealed, juvenile, financial, drug/alcohol evaluations, mental health or expunged cases released. Fee to fax results is $10.00 per 5 five pages returned. Copy fee: $.75 per page. Cert fee: $10.00. Payee: Ouray Combined Courts. Personal checks accepted. Prepayment required. Mail requests: SASE requested. Turnaround time 1 week.

Park County

Park County Combined Courts PO Box 190, Fairplay, CO 80440; 719-836-2940; Fax: 719-836-2892. Hours: 8AM-5PM (MST). *Felony, Misdemeanor, Civil, Eviction, Small Claims, Probate.*

www.courts.state.co.us/district/11th/dist11.htm

Civil Records: Access: Mail, in person, online. Only the court performs in person searches; visitors may not. Search fee: $5.00 per name. Required to search: name, years to search. Civil cases indexed by defendant, plaintiff. Civil records computerized since 1995, on index cards from 1978, index books back to 1950, archived prior to 1950. Civil records online access at www.cocourts.com.

Criminal Records: Access: Mail, in person, online. Only the court performs in person searches; visitors may not. Search fee: $5.00 per name. Required to

search: name, years to search, DOB, signed release. Criminal records computerized since 1995, on index cards from 1978, index books back to 1950, archived prior to 1950. Online access to criminal records is at www.cocourts.com.

General Information: No adoptions, sealed, juvenile, mental health or expunged cases released. Fee to fax results is $1.00 per page. Copy fee: $.75 per page. Cert fee: $10.00. Payee: Park County Combined Court. Personal checks accepted. Prepayment required. Mail requests: SASE required. Mail turnaround time within 1 week.

Phillips County

13th District & County Courts 221 S Interocean, Holyoke, CO 80734; 970-854-3279; Fax: 970-854-3179. Hours: 8AM-1PM (MST). *Felony, Misdemeanor, Civil, Eviction, Small Claims, Probate.*

www.courts.state.co.us/district/13th/13dist.htm

Civil Records: Access: Phone, fax, mail, in person. Only the court performs in person searches; visitors may not. No search fee. Required to search: name, years to search. Civil cases indexed by defendant, plaintiff. Civil records on computer since 1995; records go back to 1880. Civil records online access at www.cocourts.com.

Criminal Records: Access: Phone, fax, mail, in person. Only the court performs in person searches; visitors may not. No search fee. Required to search: name, years to search, DOB. Criminal records on computer since 1995; records go back to 1880. Online access to criminal records is at www.cocourts.com.

General Information: No adoptions, sealed, juvenile, mental health or expunged cases released. Copy fee: $.75 per page. Cert fee: $10.00. Payee: Phillips County Combined Court. Personal checks accepted. Prepayment required. Mail requests: SASE required. Mail turnaround time 1-3 days.

Pitkin County

9th District & County Courts 506 E Main St, #300, Aspen, CO 81611; 970-925-7635; Fax: 970-925-6349. Hours: 8AM-Noon, 1-5PM (MST). *Felony, Misdemeanor, Civil, Eviction, Small Claims, Probate.*

www.courts.state.co.us/district/09th/dist09.htm

Civil Records: Access: Phone, mail, fax, in person, online, email. Both court and visitors may perform in person searches. Search fee: No fee for computer search. Required to search: name, years to search. Civil cases indexed by defendant. Civil records on computer back to 1990, microfiche from 1940-1970, index cards from 1975. Civil records online access at www.cocourts.com. Search probate 1881-1953 at www.colorado.gov/dpa/doit/archives/probate/pitkin_probate.htm.

Criminal Records: Access: Mail, fax, in person, online. Both court and visitors may perform in person searches. Search fee: There is no fee for searching computer, otherwise rate determined by time and volume. Required to search: name, years to search, DOB, SSN. Criminal records on computer back to 1990, microfiche from 1940-1970, index cards from 1975. Online access to criminal records is at www.cocourts.com.

General Information: No adoptions, sealed, juvenile, mental health or expunged cases released. Fee to fax results is $1.00 per page. Copy fee: $.75 per page. Cert fee: $10.00. Payee: Pitkin County Combined Court. Only cashiers checks and money orders accepted. Visa, MC accepted. Prepayment required. Mail turnaround time 1 week.

Prowers County

15th District Court 301 S Main St, #300, Lamar, CO 81052-2834; 719-336-7424; Fax: 719-336-9757. Hours: 8AM-5PM (MST). *Felony, Civil Actions Over $10,000, Probate.*
www.courts.state.co.us/district/15th/15dist.htm
Civil Records: Access: Fax, mail, in person, online. Only the court performs in person searches; visitors may not. Search fee: $5.00. Required to search: name, years to search. Civil cases indexed by defendant, plaintiff. Civil records computerized since 1995, on microfiche from 1920, index books from the late 1800s. Civil records online access at www.cocourts.com.
Criminal Records: Access: Fax, mail, in person, online. Only the court performs in person searches; visitors may not. Search fee: $5.00. Required to search: name, years to search, DOB. Criminal records computerized since 1995, on microfiche from 1920, index books from the late 1800s. Online access to criminal records is at www.cocourts.com.
General Information: No adoptions, sealed, juvenile, mental health or expunged cases released. Will fax results $1.00 per page. Copy fee: $.75 per page. Cert fee: $10.00. Payee: Clerk of District Court. Only cashiers checks and money orders accepted. Prepayment required. Mail requests: SASE required. Mail turnaround time 1 week.

County Court 301 S Main St #100, Lamar, CO 81052-2634; 719-336-7416; Fax: 719-336-4145. 8AM-12;00-1-5PM (MST). *Misdemeanor, Civil Actions Under $15,000, Eviction, Small Claims.*
www.courts.state.co.us/district/15th/15dist.htm
Civil Records: Access: Mail, phone, in person, online. Only the court performs in person searches; visitors may not. No search fee. Required to search: name, years to search. Civil cases indexed by defendant, plaintiff. Civil records on computer since 10/95, prior on books to 1965. Civil records online access at www.cocourts.com.
Criminal Records: Access: Mail, in person, online, fax. Only the court performs in person searches; visitors may not. Search fee: $5.00 per name-1st. 5 names. Required to search: name, years to search; also helpful: DOB. Criminal records on computer since 10/95, prior on books to 1965. Online access to criminal records is at www.cocourts.com.
General Information: No adoptions, sealed, juvenile, mental health or expunged cases released. Copy fee: $.75 per page. Cert fee: $10.00. Payee: Prowers County Court. Only cashiers checks and money orders accepted. Prepayment required. Mail requests: SASE required. Mail turnaround: 7-14 days.

Pueblo County

Combined Courts 320 W 10th St, Pueblo, CO 81003; 719-583-7000; Civil phone: 719-583-7026; Probate phone: 719-583-7030; Fax: 719-583-7126. Hours: 8AM-5PM (MST). *Felony, Misdemeanor, Civil, Eviction, Small Claims, Probate.*
Civil Records: Access: Mail, in person, online. Only the court performs in person searches; visitors may not. Search fee: $5.00 per name. Required to search: name, years to search; also helpful: address. Civil cases indexed by defendant, plaintiff. Civil records on computer from 1976, index books back to the 1890s. Civil records online access at www.cocourts.com.
Criminal Records: Access: Mail, in person, online. Only the court performs in person searches; visitors may not. Search fee: $5.00 per name. Required to search: name, years to search, DOB; also helpful: address. Criminal records on computer from 1976, index books back to the 1890s. Online access to criminal records is at www.cocourts.com.

General Information: No adoptions, sealed, juvenile, mental health or expunged cases released. Will fax results for $1.00 per page. Copy fee: $.75 per page. Cert fee: $10.00. Payee: Clerk of Court. Personal checks accepted. Prepayment required. Mail requests: SASE required. Mail turnaround: 3-5 days.

Rio Blanco County

9th District & County Courts 555 Main St, Rm 303, PO Box 1150, Meeker, CO 81641; 970-878-5622. Hours: 8AM-Noon, 1-5PM (MST). *Felony, Misdemeanor, Civil, Eviction, Small Claims, Probate.*
www.courts.state.co.us/district/09th/dist09.htm
Civil Records: Access: Phone, mail, in person. Only the court performs in person searches; visitors may not. Search fee: $5.00 per name. May charge for lengthy in-person search request. Required to search: name; also helpful: years to search. Civil cases indexed by defendant, plaintiff. Civil records on computer since 8/1994, on index cards from April 1976, index books back to 1889. Civil records online access at www.cocourts.com.
Criminal Records: Access: Phone, mail, in person, online. Only the court performs in person searches; visitors may not. Search fee: $5.00 per name. May charge for lengthy in-person search request. Required to search: name, years to search; also helpful: DOB. Criminal records on computer since 8/1994, on index cards from April 1976, index books back to 1889. Online access to criminal records is at www.cocourts.com.
General Information: No adoptions, sealed, juvenile, mental health or expunged cases released. Fee to fax results is $1.00 per page. Copy fee: $.75 per page. Cert fee: $10.00. Payee: Clerk of the Combined Courts. Business checks accepted. Prepayment required. Mail requests: SASE required. Mail turnaround time 2 days.

Rio Grande County

12th District & County Courts 6th & Cherry, PO Box 427, Del Norte, CO 81132; 719-657-3394. 8AM-Noon, 1-4PM (MST). *Felony, Misdemeanor, Civil, Eviction, Small Claims, Probate.*
Civil Records: Access: Mail, in person, online. Only the court performs in person searches; visitors may not. Search fee: $5.00 per name, additional $25.00 to search archived records. Required to search: name, years to search. Civil cases indexed by defendant, plaintiff. Civil records on computer from 5/95, County on index cards from 1950s, District from 1977. All on index books from the 1800s. Online access to civil records 1995 to present is at www.cocourts.com.
Criminal Records: Access: Mail, in person, online. Only the court performs in person searches; visitors may not. Search fee: $5.00 per name, additional $25.00 to search archived records. Required to search: name, DOB; also helpful: years to search. Criminal records on computer from 5/95, County on index cards from 1950s, District from 1977. All on index books from the 1800s. Online access to criminal records is at www.cocourts.com.
General Information: No adoptions, sealed, juvenile, mental health or expunged cases released. Will fax results for $1.00 per page. Copy fee: $.75 per page. Cert fee: $10.00. Payee: Rio Grande Combined Court. Personal and business checks accepted. Prepayment required. Mail requests: SASE required. Mail turnaround time 2-4 days.

Routt County

Routt Combined Courts PO Box 773117, Steamboat Springs, CO 80477; 970-879-5020; Fax: 970-879-3531. Hours: 8AM12;00-1-4PM (MST). *Felony, Misdemeanor, Civil, Eviction, Small Claims, Probate.*
Civil Records: Access: Mail, in person, online. Both court and visitors may perform in person searches. Search fee: $5.00 for 1976-1991; prior to 1976 $20.00. There is no fee to search computer records. Required to search: name, years to search. Civil cases indexed by defendant. Civil records on computer back to 1994, on index cards from 1977, microfiche from 1/1977 to 12/1990, archived from 1877. Civil records online access at www.cocourts.com.
Criminal Records: Access: Mail, in person, online. Both court and visitors may perform in person searches. Search fee: Same fees as civil. Required to search: name, years to search, DOB, maiden name, aliases. Criminal records on computer back to 1994, on index cards from 1977, microfiche from 1/1977 to 12/1990, archived from 1877. Online access to criminal records is at www.cocourts.com.
General Information: No adoptions, sealed, juvenile, mental health or expunged cases released. Copy fee: $.75 per page. Cert fee: $10.00 per document. Payee: Routt Combined Court. Personal checks accepted. Visa/MC accepted. Prepayment required. Mail requests: SASE required. Mail turnaround time 7-10 days.

Saguache County

12th District & County Courts PO Box 164, Saguache, CO 81149; 719-655-2522; Fax: 719-655-2522. Hours: 8AM-Noon, 1-5PM (MST). *Felony, Misdemeanor, Civil, Eviction, Small Claims, Probate.*
Civil Records: Access: Mail, in person, online. Only the court performs in person searches; visitors may not. No search fee. Required to search: name, years to search. Civil cases indexed by defendant, plaintiff. Civil records on computer since 06/94, on index cards from 1980s, index books back to 1866. Civil records online access at www.cocourts.com.
Criminal Records: Access: Mail, in person, online. Only the court performs in person searches; visitors may not. No search fee. Required to search: name, years to search, DOB. Criminal records on computer since 06/94, on index cards from 1980s, index books back to 1866. Online access to criminal records is at www.cocourts.com.
General Information: No adoptions, sealed, juvenile, mental health or expunged cases released. Copy fee: $.75 per page. Cert fee: $10.00. Payee: Saguache Combined Courts. Personal checks accepted. Prepayment required. Mail requests: SASE required. Mail turnaround time 10-12 days.

San Juan County

6th District & County Courts PO Box 900, Silverton, CO 81433; 970-387-5790. Hours: 8AM-4PM T & TH, 8AM-Noon W (MST). *Felony, Misdemeanor, Civil, Eviction, Small Claims, Probate.*
Civil Records: Access: Phone, mail, in person, online. Only the court may perform in person searches. Search fee: $20.00 per hour. Fee is for lengthy search. Required to search: name, years to search. Civil cases indexed by defendant, plaintiff. Civil records on computer since 1995; prior on index cards from 1975, index books back to 1876. Civil records online access at www.cocourts.com.
Criminal Records: Access: Mail, in person, online. Only the court may perform in person searches. Search fee: $8.00 per name. Required to search: name, years to search, DOB, signed release. Criminal

records on computer since 1995; prior on index cards from 1975, index books back to 1876. Online access to criminal records is at www.cocourts.com.

General Information: No adoptions, sealed, juvenile, mental health, open domestic, probate or expunged cases released. Will fax results to local or toll free line. Copy fee: $.75 per page. Cert fee: $10.00. Payee: San Juan County Court. Business checks accepted. Prepayment required. Mail requests: SASE required. Mail turnaround time 1 week.

San Miguel County

7th District & County Courts PO Box 919, Telluride, CO 81435; 970-728-3891; Fax: 970-728-6216. Hours: 9AM-Noon, 1-4PM (MST). *Felony, Misdemeanor, Civil, Eviction, Small Claims, Probate.*

www.7thjudicialdistrictco.org

Civil Records: Access: Phone, mail, in person, online. Only the court performs in person searches; visitors may not. Search fee: $5.00 per name if after 1994. Required to search: name, years to search. Civil cases indexed by defendant, plaintiff. Civil records on index cards from 1970, index books back to 1861, archived back to 1880; on computer back to 1994. Civil records online access at www.cocourts.com. Will do very limited phone searches back to 1994.

Criminal Records: Access: Phone, mail, in person, online. Only the court performs in person searches; visitors may not. Search fee: $5.00 per name if after 1994. Required to search: name, years to search, DOB. Criminal records on index cards from 1970, index books back to 1861, archived back to 1880; on computer back to 1994. Online access to criminal records is at www.cocourts.com. Will do very limited phone searches back to 1994.

General Information: No adoptions, sealed, juvenile, mental health or expunged cases released. Will fax results if prepaid. Copy fee: $.75 per page. Cert fee: $10.00. Payee: Combined Courts. Personal checks accepted. Prepayment required. Mail requests: SASE required. Mail turnaround time 30 days.

Sedgwick County

13th District & County Courts Third & Pine, Julesburg, CO 80737; 970-474-3627; Fax: 970-474-2026. 8AM-1PM (MST). *Felony, Misdemeanor, Civil, Eviction, Small Claims, Probate.*

www.courts.state.co.us/district/13th/13dist.htm

Civil Records: Access: Fax, mail, in person, online. Both court and visitors may perform in person searches. Search fee: The court reserves the right to charge if an extensive search is required. Required to search: name; also helpful: years to search. Civil cases indexed by defendant, plaintiff. Civil records on index cards from early 1970s, index books back to 1889; on computer back to 8/1995. Civil records online access at www.cocourts.com.

Criminal Records: Access: Fax, mail, in person, online. Both court and visitors may perform in person searches. Search fee: The court reserves the right to charge if an extensive search is required. Required to search: name, DOB; also helpful: years to search. Criminal records on index cards from early 1970s, index books back to 1889; on computer back to 8/1995. Online access to criminal records is at www.cocourts.com.

General Information: No adoptions, sealed, juvenile, mental health or expunged cases released. Fee to fax results is $5.00 per document. Copy fee: $.75 per page. Cert fee: $10.00. Payee: Sedgwick County Combined Court. Personal checks accepted. Prepayment required. Mail requests: SASE required. Mail turnaround time 1-2 days.

Summit County

Summit Combined Courts PO Box 185, Breckenridge, CO 80424; 970-453-2241 District; 970-453-2272 County. Hours: 8AM-Noon, 1-4PM (MST). *Felony, Misdemeanor, Civil, Eviction, Small Claims, Probate.* www.courts.state.co.us

Note: District Court uses PO Box 269.

Civil Records: Access: In person, online. Visitors must perform in person searches for themselves. No search fee. Required to search: name. Civil cases indexed by defendant, plaintiff. Civil records on computer back to 1995, index cards from the early 1970s, index books back to 1861, archived from 1980 and prior. Civil records online access at www.cocourts.com.

Criminal Records: Access: In person, online. Visitors must perform in person searches for themselves. No search fee. Required to search: name, DOB, signed release. Criminal records name index on computer as of 09/95. Online access to criminal records is at www.cocourts.com.

General Information: No adoptions, sealed, juvenile, mental health or expunged cases released. Copy fee: $.75 per page. Cert fee: $10.00. Only cashiers checks and money orders accepted. Cash accepted in person. Prepayment required.

Teller County

Teller Combined Courts PO Box 997, Cripple Creek, CO 80813; 719-689-2574. Hours: 9AM-Noon; 1PM-4PM (MST). *Felony, Misdemeanor, Civil, Eviction, Small Claims, Probate.*

www.tellercountycourts.com

Civil Records: Access: Mail, in person, online. Only the court performs in person searches; visitors may not. Search fee: $5.00 per name. If not on computer, fee is $20.00 per hour. Required to search: name, years to search. Civil cases indexed by defendant, plaintiff. Civil records computerized back to 1988, on index cards from 1960, index books back to 1899. Civil records online access at www.cocourts.com. Also, a record request form is to download at https://33.securedata.net/gofourth/pub_data_req_form.htm.

Criminal Records: Access: Mail, in person, online. Only the court performs in person searches; visitors may not. Search fee: $5.00 per name. If records not on computer, fee is $20.00 per hour. Required to search: name, years to search, DOB; also helpful: address, SSN. Criminal records computerized back to 1988, on index cards from 1960, index books back to 1899. Online access to criminal records is at www.cocourts.com.

General Information: No adoptions, sealed, juvenile, mental health or expunged cases released. Will fax results for $1.00 per page. Copy fee: $.75 per page. Cert fee: $10.00. Payee: Teller County Combined Courts. Any form of payment is acceptable, including Visa/MC. Prepayment required. Mail requests: SASE required. Mail turnaround time 5-7 days; 4-6 weeks if not computerized.

Washington County

Washington County Combined Court PO Box 455 (26861 Hwy 34), Akron, CO 80720; 970-345-2756; Fax: 970-345-2829. Hours: 8AM-Noon, 1-5PM (MST). *Felony, Misdemeanor, Civil, Eviction, Small Claims, Probate.*

www.courts.state.co.us/district/13th/13dist.htm

Civil Records: Access: Phone, mail, in person, online. Only the court may perform in person searches. No search fee. Required to search: name, years to search. Civil cases indexed by defendant. Civil records on index cards from 1970, index books

back to 1887; computerized since 1995. Civil records online access at www.cocourts.com.

Criminal Records: Access: Phone, mail, in person, online. Only the court performs in person searches; visitors may not. No search fee. Required to search: name, years to search, DOB. Criminal records on index cards from 1970, index books back to 1887; computerized since 1995. Online access to criminal records is at www.cocourts.com.

General Information: No adoptions, sealed, juvenile, mental health or expunged cases released. Will fax results. Copy fee: $.75 per page. Cert fee: $10.00. Payee: Washington County Combined Court. Personal checks accepted. Prepayment required. Mail requests: SASE required. Mail turnaround: 2-3 days.

Weld County

19th District & County Courts PO Box 2038, Greeley, CO 80632; 970-351-7300; Fax: 970-336-7245. Hours: 8AM-4PM closed at noon for 1 hour (MST). *Felony, Misdemeanor, Civil, Eviction, Small Claims, Probate.*

Note: Probate/ water offices can be faxed at 970-3469136

Civil Records: Access: Mail, in person, online. Only the court performs in person searches; visitors may not. Search fee: $10.00 per name. Required to search: name, years to search. Civil cases indexed by defendant, plaintiff. Civil records on computer from 1975 (District), 1990 (County), index cards from 1958, index books back to 1876. Civil records online access at www.cocourts.com. Fees involved.

Criminal Records: Access: Mail, in person, online. Only the court performs in person searches; visitors may not. Search fee: $10.00 per name. Required to search: name, years to search; also helpful: DOB. Criminal records on computer from 1975 (District), 1990 (County), index cards from 1958, index books back to 1876. Online access to criminal records is at www.cocourts.com. Fees involved.

General Information: No adoptions, sealed, juvenile, mental health or expunged cases released. Copy fee: $.75 per page. Cert fee: $20.00. Payee: Clerk of Combined Court. Personal checks accepted. Prepayment required. Mail requests: SASE required. Mail turnaround time 3 days.

Yuma County

13th District & County Courts PO Box 347, Wray, CO 80758; 970-332-4118; Fax: 970-332-4119. Hours: 8AM-4PM (MST). *Felony, Misdemeanor, Civil, Eviction, Small Claims, Probate.*

www.courts.state.co.us/district/13th/13dist.htm

Civil Records: Access: Mail, in person, online. Only the court performs in person searches; visitors may not. Search fee: $5.00 per name. Required to search: name, years to search. Civil cases indexed by defendant. Civil records on index cards from 1982, index books back to 1889. Civil records online access at www.cocourts.com.

Criminal Records: Access: Mail, in person, online. Only the court performs in person searches; visitors may not. Search fee: $5.00 per name. Required to search: name. Criminal records on index cards from 1982, index books back to 1889. Online access to criminal records is at www.cocourts.com.

General Information: No adoptions, sealed, juvenile, mental health or expunged cases released. Will fax results to local or toll free line. Copy fee: $.75 per page. Cert fee: $10.00. Payee: Yuma County Combined Court. Personal checks accepted. Prepayment required. Mail requests: SASE required. Mail turnaround time 2-5 days.

Colorado Recording Offices

ORGANIZATION: 63 counties, 63 recording offices. The recording officer is County Clerk and Recorder. The entire state is in the Mountain Time Zone (MST).

November 15, 2001, Broomfield City and County comes into existence, derived from portions of Adams, Boulder, Jefferson and Weld counties. County offices are located at 1 Descombes Dr, Broomfield, CO 80020; 303-469-3301; hours 8AM-5PM. To determine if an address is in Broomfield, parcel search by address at www.co.broomfield.co.us/centralrecords/assessor.shtml

REAL ESTATE RECORDS: Counties do not perform real estate searches. Copy fees are usually $1.25 per page and certification fees are usually $1.00 per document. Tax records are located in the Assessor's Office.

UCC RECORDS: Financing statements are filed at the state level, except for real estate related collateral, which are filed with the County Clerk & Recorder. However, prior to 07/2001, consumer goods and farm collateral were also filed at the County Clerk & Recorder and these older records can be searched there. Nearly all counties perform UCC searches. Use search request form UCC-11. Search fees are usually $5.00 per debtor name for the first year and $2.00 for each additional year searched (or $13.00 for a five year search). Copies usually cost $1.25 per page.

TAX LIEN RECORDS: Federal and some state tax liens on personal property are filed with the Secretary of State. Other federal and state tax liens are filed with the County Clerk and Recorder. Many counties will perform tax lien searches, usually at the same fees as UCC searches. Copies usually cost $1.25 per page.

OTHER LIENS: Judgments, motor vehicle, mechanics.

ONLINE ACCESS: To date, over 20 Colorado Counties offer free access to property assessor records. Also, the state archives provides limited inheritance tax records for 14 Colorado counties at www.colorado.gov/dpa/doit/archives/inh_tax/index.html; generally records extend forward only to the 1940s.

At the state level, the Secretary of State offers web access to UCCs, and the Department of Revenue offers trade name searches. See the State Agencies section for details.

Adams County

County Clerk & Recorder, 450 S. 4th Ave, Admin. Bldg., Brighton, CO 80601-3197. **Phone**-County Clerk & Recorder, R/E & UCC Recording- 303-654-6020; fax-303-654-6009;   hours-8AM-4:30PM www.co.adams.co.us
Will search UCC records. Search per debtor- $5.00. UCC copy- $1.25 per page. UCC search includes tax liens. Will not search real estate records. RE record copy- $1.25 per page. Cert fee: $1.00 per cert. Payee: Adams County Clerk and Recorder. **Online Access to Assessor, Property records:** Adams County Assessor database records are free at www.co.adams.co.us/gis/html/QuickSearchFSIE.htm. Also, search property information on the GIS mapping page for free at www.co.adams.co.us/gis/. **Other phones:** Assessor-303-654-6038; Treasurer-303-654-6160; Elections-303-920-7800.

Alamosa County

County Clerk & Recorder, PO Box 630, Alamosa, CO 81101. **Phone**-719-589-6681; fax-719-589-6118; hours 8AM-4:30PM. Will search UCC records. Search per debtor-. UCC copy- $1.25 per page. Tax liens not included in UCC search. Separate tax lien search available. Tax lien search fee- $5.00 per debtor for 1st year, $2.00 each add'l year. Will not search real estate records. Payee: Alamosa County Clerk and Recorder. **Other phones:** Assessor-719-589-6365; Treasurer-719-589-3626;   Elections-719-589-6681; Vital Records-719-589-6681.

Arapahoe County

County Clerk & Recorder, 5334 S. Prince St, Adminstration Bldg, Littleton, CO 80166-0060. **Phone**-County Clerk & Recorder, R/E & UCC Recording- 303-795-4200, UCC Recording- 303-795-4520; fax-303-794-4625;   hours-7AM-4:30PM www.co.arapahoe.co.us
Will not search UCC records. UCC copy- $1.25 per page. Tax lien search fee- $5.00 1st year; $2.00 each add'l year. Will not search real estate records. Cert fee: $1.00 per doc. Payee: Arapahoe County Clerk and Recorder. **Online Access to Assessor, Property Tax, Real Estate, Deed, Judgment, Lien, Recording, Personal Property records:** Access to the recorders database is available free at www.co.arapahoe.co.us/Apps/LegalDocuments/default.aspx. Also, tax and personal property records on the Arapahoe County Assessor database are free at www.co.arapahoe.co.us/AS/index.asp. Click on "online tools" to choose database to search. Also search parcels by address from this site. **Other phones:** Assessor-303-795-4600;   Treasurer-303-795-4550;   Appraiser/ Auditor-303-795-4611; Elections-303-795-4511; Vital Records-303-756-4464.

Archuleta County

County Clerk & Recorder, PO Box 2589, Pagosa Springs, CO 81147-2589. **Phone**-County Clerk & Recorder, R/E & UCC Recording- 970-264-8350; fax-970-264-8357; hours 8AM-4PM
Will not search UCC or real estate records. Will do a federal tax lien search, but not state tax liens. Record copy- $1.25 per page. Cert fee: $1.00 per cert. Payee: Archuleta County Clerk and Recorder. **Other phones:** Assessor-970-264-8310; Treasurer-970-264-8325; Elections-970-264-8350.

Baca County

County Clerk & Recorder, 741 Main St, Courthouse, Springfield, CO 81073. **Phone**-County Clerk & Recorder, R/E & UCC Recording- 719-523-4372; fax-719-523-4881;   hours-8:30AM-4:30PM www.bacacounty.net
Will not search UCC records. Will search tax liens. Will not search real estate records. Record copy-$1.25 per page. Cert fee: $.50 per cert. Payee: Baca County Clerk and Recorder. **Other phones:** Assessor-719-523-4332;   Treasurer-719-523-4262; Appraiser/ Auditor-719-523-4332; Elections-719-523-4372; Vital Records-719-523-6665.

Bent County

County Clerk & Recorder, PO Box 350, Las Animas, CO 81054. **Phone**-County Clerk & Recorder, R/E & UCC Recording- 719-456-2009; fax-719-456-0375; hours 8:30AM-4:30PM
Will search UCC records. Search per debtor- $5.00. UCC copy- $1.25 per page. Will not search real estate or tax lien records. RE record copy- $1.25 per page. Cert fee: $1.00 per cert. Payee: Bent County Clerk and Recorder. **Other phones:** Assessor-719-456-2010; Treasurer-719-456-2211; Elections-719-456-2009; Vital Records-719-456-6042.

Boulder County

County Clerk & Recorder, 1750 33rd St #201, Boulder, CO 80301. **Phone**-303-413-7770; hours 8AM-5PM www.co.boulder.co.us/clerk
Will search UCC records. Search per debtor-$5.00 for 5 years. UCC copy- $1.25 per page. UCC search includes tax liens. Will not search real estate records. RE record copy- $1.25 per page. Cert fee: $1.00 per cert. Payee: Boulder County Clerk and

Recorder. **Online Access to Assessor, Property Tax, Voter Registration, Recording, Grantor/Grantee, Deed, Judgment, Lien, Most Wanted records:** Search the assessor's property database for free at www.co.boulder.co.us/assessor/disclaimer.htm. No name searching. Also, recorder data is on the iCris system at http://icris.co.boulder.co.us/splash.jsp. To search free, login as public, password public. Also, search property tax records at www.co.boulder.co.us/treas/disclaim.htm. No name searching. Also, the county treasurer offers data electronically and on microfiche. Alpha index by owner name is $25.00 per set. Also, search voter registration at www.co.boulder.co.us. Click on "Check your Voter Registration." Name and DOB required. Search the county sheriff's most wanted at www.co.boulder.co.us/Sheriff/most_wanted/wanted.htm. **Other phones:** Assessor-303-441-3530; Treasurer-303-441-3520; Elections-303-413-7740.

Broomfield County

County/City Clerk & Recorder, One DesCombes Dr, Broomfield, CO 80020. **Phone-**303-469-3301; fax-303-438-6252; hours 8AM-5PM www.co.broomfield.co.us Became a county in 2001; further information is at website. Includes Zip Codes 80005, 80020, 80021, 80038, 80234. Will not search records. UCC copy- $1.25 per page. RE record copy- $.50 per page. Cert fee: $1.00 per doc. Payee: City and County of Broomfield. **Online Access to Real Estate, Assessor, Voter Registration records:** Access assessor property records for free at http://ims.ci.broomfield.co.us/website/htmlviewer/Parcelsearch/. Search by address or parcel ID only. Also, search property and tax assessment data for free at http://info.ci.broomfield.co.us/Tax/. No name searching. Also search voter registration records at www.ci.broomfield.co.us/election/voter_inquiry/.
Other phones: Central Records, all departments-303-464-5819.

Chaffee County

County Clerk & Recorder, PO Box 699, Salida, CO 81201. **Phone-**719-539-6913, R/E Recording- 719-539-4004; fax-719-539-8588; hours 8AM-4PM Recording; 8AM-5PM for researching.
This agency will not search records. UCC copy- $1.25 per page. Cert fee: $1.00 per cert. Payee: Chaffee County Clerk and Recorder. **Other phones:** Assessor-719-539-4016; Treasurer-719-539-6808; Elections-719-539-6913.

Cheyenne County

County Clerk & Recorder, PO Box 567, Cheyenne Wells, CO 80810. **Phone-**County Clerk & Recorder, R/E & UCC Recording- 719-767-5685; fax-719-767-5540; hours 8AM-4PM
Will not search records. UCC copy- $1.25 per page. Cert fee: $1.00 per cert. Payee: Cheyenne County Clerk and Recorder. **Other phones:** Assessor-719-767-5664; Treasurer-719-767-5657; Elections-719-767-5685; Vital Records-719-767-5661.

Clear Creek County

County Clerk & Recorder, PO Box 2000, Georgetown, CO 80444-2000. **Phone-**County Clerk & Recorder, R/E & UCC Recording- 303-679-2339; fax-303-679-2416; hours 8:30AM-4:30PM www.co.clearcreek.co.us/depts/clerk.htm
Will not search records. Record copy- $1.25 per page. Cert fee: $1.00 per cert. Payee: Clear Creek County Clerk and Recorder. **Other phones:** Assessor-303-679-2322; Treasurer-303-679-2353; Appraiser/ Auditor-303-679-2322; Elections-303-679-2339; Vital Records-303-679-2357.

Conejos County

County Clerk & Recorder, PO Box 127, Conejos, CO 81129-0127. **Phone-**County Clerk & Recorder, R/E & UCC Recording- 719-376-5422; fax-719-376-5661; hours 8AM-4:30PM
Will search UCC records. UCC search per debtor- $5.00 per year + $2.00 each year after. UCC copy- $1.25 per page. Will search tax liens including federal tax liens. Tax lien search fee- $5.00 1st year; $2.00 each add'l. Will not search real estate records. RE record copy- $1.25 per page. Cert fee: $1.00 per cert. Payee: Conejos County Clerk and Recorder. **Other phones:** Assessor-719-376-5585; Treasurer-719-376-5919; Elections-719-376-5422; Vital Records-719-376-5787.

Costilla County

County Clerk & Recorder, PO Box 308, San Luis, CO 81152. **Phone-**County Clerk & Recorder, R/E & UCC Recording- 719-672-3301; fax-719-672-3962; hours 8AM-Noon, 1-5PM
Will not search records. Record copy- $1.25 per page. Cert fee: $1.00 per page. Payee: Costilla County Clerk and Recorder. **Other phones:** Assessor-719-672-3642; Treasurer-719-672-3642; Elections-719-672-3301; Vital Records-719-672-3301.

Crowley County

County Clerk & Recorder, 631 Main #104, Ordway, CO 81063-1092. **Phone-**719-267-4643, R/E Recording- 719-267-5555 x3, UCC Recording- 719-267-5555 x3; fax-719-267-4608; hours 8AM-4PM
Will not search records. UCC and tax lien copy fee is $1.25 per page off computer; $.50 if paper copy. RE record copy- $1.25 per page. Cert fee: $1.00 per cert. Payee: County Clerk and Recorder. **Other phones:** Assessor-719-267-4421 x5; Treasurer-719-267-4624 x4; Elections-719-267-5555 x3.

Custer County

County Clerk & Recorder, PO Box 150, Westcliffe, CO 81252. **Phone-**County Clerk & Recorder, R/E & UCC Recording- 719-783-2441; fax-719-783-2885; hours 8AM-4PM
Will search UCC records. Search per debtor- $15.00 for 1st yr; $5.00 each add'l yr. UCC copy- $1.25 per page. UCC search includes tax liens if requested. Will not search real estate records. RE record copy- $1.25 per page. Cert fee: $1.00 per cert. Payee: Custer County Clerk and Recorder. **Other phones:** Assessor-719-783-2218; Treasurer-719-783-2341; Appraiser/ Auditor-719-783-2218; Elections-719-783-2441; Vital Records-719-783-2441.

Delta County

County Clerk & Recorder, 501 Palmer St, #211, Delta, CO 81416. **Phone-**County Clerk & Recorder, R/E & UCC Recording- 970-874-2150; fax-970-874-2161; hours 8:30AM-4:30PM
Will not search records. Record copy- $1.25 per page. Cert fee: $1.00 per cert. Payee: Delta County Clerk and Recorder. **Other phones:** Assessor-970-874-2120; Treasurer-970-874-2135; Appraiser/ Auditor-970-874-2120; Elections-970-874-2150; Vital Records-970-874-2150.

Denver County

County Clerk & Recorder, 201 W Colfax Ave Dept 101, Denver, CO 80202. **Phone-**720-865-8400; fax-720-865-8580; hours 9AM-4PM www.denvergov.org
Will search UCC records. Search per debtor-$5.00 per name, 1st year, $2.00 add'l 1 year. UCC copy- $1.00 per page. Tax liens not included in UCC search. Separate tax lien searches performed at same cost as UCC searches Will not search real estate records. RE record copy- $1.25 per page. Cert fee: $1.00 per cert. Payee- Denver County Clerk

and Recorder. **Online Access to Assessor, Real Estate, Property Tax, Personal Property, Contract, Inmates, Solicitation Arrest, Restaurant records:** Search the Denver City and Denver County Assessor database free at www.denvergov.org/realproperty.asp. Search business personal property at www.denvergov.org/PersProperty.asp. Also, search real estate property tax data for free at www.denvergov.org/treasurypt/PropertyTax.asp. Address or parcel number required to search. Search restaurant inspections-www.denvergov.org/eh/search.asp. Ssearch county contracts at www.denvergov.org/contracts/contrak.asp. Search county inmates list at www.vinelink.com/offender/searchNew.jsp?siteID=6001; Prostitution solicitation arrests are at www.denvergov.org/johnstv/. **Other phones:** Assessor-720-913-4162; Treasurer-720-865-7070; Appraiser/ Auditor-720-913-4032; Elections-720-913-8683; Vital Records-303-436-7350.

Dolores County

County Clerk & Recorder, PO Box 58, Dove Creek, CO 81324-0058. **Phone-**County Clerk & Recorder, R/E & UCC Recording- 970-677-2381; fax-970-677-2815; hours 8:30AM-4:30PM
Will search UCC records they have onhand. UCC search per debtor- $5.00 for 1st year; $2.00 each add'l year. UCC copy- $1.25 per page. Will search tax liens. Tax lien search fee- $5.00 1st year, $2.00 each add'l. Will search real estate records. RE record copy- $1.25 per page. Cert fee: $1.00 per cert. Payee: Dolores County Clerk and Recorder. **Other phones:** Assessor-970-677-2385; Treasurer-970-677-2386; Appraiser/ Auditor-970-677-2385; Elections-970-677-2381; Vital Records-970-677-2381.

Douglas County

County Clerk & Recorder, PO Box 1360, Castle Rock, CO 80104. **Phone-**County Clerk & Recorder, R/E & UCC Recording- 303-660-7446; fax-303-814-2776; hours 8AM-4:30PM www.douglas.co.us/recording
Will search UCC records. Search per debtor-$5.00 per year; $2.00 each add'l year. UCC copy- $1.25 per page. Will not search real estate or tax lien records. RE record copy- $1.25 per page. Cert fee: $1.00 per cert. Payee: Douglas County Clerk and Recorder. **Online Access to Deed, Grantor/Grantee, Judgment, Lien, Mortgage, UCC, Vital Statistic, Assessor, Property records:** Access recorders data for free at https://secure.douglas.co.us/nasapp/pubdocaccess/simplesearch.jsp. Click on "Advance Search" to search by name. Also, county assessor records are free at www.douglas.co.us/assessor_search/default/htm.
Other phones: Assessor-303-660-7450; Treasurer-303-660-7455; Appraiser-303-660-7450; Elections-303-660-7444.

Eagle County

County Clerk & Recorder, PO Box 537, Eagle, CO 81631. **Phone-**970-328-8710, R/E Recording- 970-328-8723, UCC Recording- 970-328-8723; fax-970-328-8716; hours 8AM-5PM www.eagle-county.com
Will search UCC records. Search per debtor- $5.00 1st year; $2.00 per name ea add'l year. UCC copy- $1.00 per page. UCC search includes tax liens. Will not search real estate records. Cert fee: $1.00 per cert. Payee: Eagle County Clerk and Recorder. **Online Access to Assessor, Property, Grantor/Grantee, Property Sale, Most Wanted records:** County Assessor-Treasurer database records are free at www.eagle-county.com/Goodturns/assessor/search.asp?. Also, view sheriff's most wanted list www.eaglesheriff.com/Website/extraextra/mostwanted.asp. **Other phones:** Assessor-970-328-8640; Treasurer-970-328-8860; Elections-970-328-8715.

El Paso County

County Clerk & Recorder, PO Box 2007, Colorado Springs, CO 80901-2007. 719-520-6200; fax-719-520-6230; hours 8AM-5PM www.car.elpasoco.com
Will not search records. Copy fee-$1.25 per page. Cert fee: $1.00 per cert. Payee: El Paso County Clerk and Recorder. **Online Access to Assessor, Public Trustee Sale, Inmate, Contractor, Granter-Grantee records:** county Assessor database records are free at http://land.elpasoco.com/default.htm. Also, the public trust weekly sale list is at http://put.elpasoco.com/ptweeklysale.aspx. Search the county contractor list www.pprbd.org/contrnames.html. Search the recorder's Grantor/Grantee index at www.car.elpasoco.com/rcdquery.asp. **Other phones:** Assessor-719-520-6600; Treasurer-719-520-6666; Elections-719-520-8683; Vital Records-719-520-7475.

Elbert County

County Clerk & Recorder, PO Box 37, Kiowa, CO 80117. **Phone-**303-621-3129, 303-621-3116, R/E Recording-303-621-3128, UCC Recording- 303-621-3128; fax-303-621-3168; hours 8AM-4:30PM
Will search UCC records. Search per debtor- $5.00 per 5 years. UCC copy- $1.00 per page. Will not search real estate or tax lien records. RE record copy- $1.25 per page. Cert fee: $1.00 per cert. Payee: Elbert County Clerk and Recorder. **Online Access to Will records:** Access to county will records from 1887 to 1966 is available free at www.colorado.gov/dpa/doit/archives/wills/1elbert.html. **Other phones:** Assessor-303-621-3101; Treasurer-303-621-3117; Elections-303-621-3127.

Fremont County

County Clerk & Recorder, 615 Macon Ave, Rm 102, Canon City, CO 81212-3311. **Phone-**719-276-7336; fax-719-275-1594; hours 8:30AM-4:30PM
Will search UCC records. Search per debtor-. UCC copy- $1.25 per page. Will not search real estate or tax lien records. Cert fee: $1.00 per cert. Payee: Fremont County Clerk and Recorder. **Online Access to Assessor, Property, Property Sale records:** Access to the assessors database is free at www.qpublic.net/fremont/search1.html. **Other phones:** Assessor-719-276-7310; Treasurer-719-276-7380; Elections-719-276-7332.

Garfield County

County Clerk & Recorder, 109 8th St, #200, Glenwood Springs, CO 81601. **Phone-**970-945-2377, R/E Recording- 970-945-2377 x1845; fax-970-947-1078; hours 8:30AM-5PM
Will search UCC records. Search per debtor- $5.00 1 year, $2.00 @ additional year. UCC copy- $1.25 per page. Tax liens not included in UCC search. Tax lien search- $5.00 per debtor. Will not search real estate records. RE record copy- $1.25 per page. Cert fee: $1.00 per cert. Payee: Garfield County Clerk and Recorder. **Online Access to Assessor, Treasurer records:** Search the assessor and treasurer at www.mitchandco.com/realEstate/garfield/index.cfm. **Other phones:** Assessor-970-945-9134; Elections-970-945-2377 x1770; Vital Records-970-945-2377 x1950.

Gilpin County

County Clerk & Recorder, PO Box 429, Central City, CO 80427. **Phone-**303-582-5321; fax-303-582-3086; hours 8AM-5PM. Will not search records. Record copy- $1.25 per page. Cert fee: $1.00 per cert. Payee: Gilpin County Clerk and Recorder. **Online Access to Marriage records:** Access to county marriage records from 1864 to 1944 is available free at www.colorado.gov/dpa/doit/archives/marriage/gilpin_index.htm. **Other phones:** Assessor-303-582-5451; Treasurer-303-582-5222; Appraiser/ Auditor-303-582-5451; Elections-303-582-5321.

Grand County

County Clerk & Recorder, PO Box 120, Hot Sulphur Springs, CO 80451. **Phone-**970-725-3347 x273; fax-970-725-0100; hours-8:30AM-5PM www.gcgovernment.com
Will not search records. UCC copy- $.25 per page. Cert fee: $1.00 per cert. Payee: Grand County Clerk and Recorder. **Online Access to Property, Assessor, Grantor/Grantee, Recording records:** Access to the Clerk&Recorder database is free at http://co.grand.co.us/Clerk/lookup/. Also, the assessor database is searchable for free at http://co.grand.co.us/Assessor/PropertySearch/. Also, property ownership information is free at www.co.grand.co.us/Assessor/Download_Page.html. **Other phones:** Assessor-970-725-3347 x219; Treasurer-970-725-3347 x269; Elections-970-725-3347 x224; Vital Records-970-725-3347 x213.

Gunnison County

County Clerk & Recorder, 221 N Wisconsin #C, Courthouse, Gunnison, CO 81230. **Phone-**970-641-1516, R/E Recording- 970-641-2038; fax-970-641-7690; hours 8AM-5PM www.co.gunnison.co.us
Will not search records. Record copy- $1.25 per page. Cert fee: $1.00 per cert. Payee: Gunnison County Clerk and Recorder. **Other phones:** Assessor-970-641-1085; Treasurer-970-641-2231; Elections-970-641-7927.

Hinsdale County

County Clerk & Recorder, PO Box 9, Lake City, CO 81235. **Phone-**970-944-2228; fax-970-944-2202; hours 7AM-5:30PM
Will not search UCC or real estate records. UCC copy- $1.00 per page. Tax lien search fee- $5.00 per 1st year. RE record copy- $1.25 per page. Cert fee: $1.00 per cert. Payee: Hinsdale County Clerk and Recorder. **Other phones:** Assessor-970-944-2224; Treasurer-970-944-2223; Elections-970-944-2228.

Huerfano County

County Clerk & Recorder, 410 Main St., Courthouse, #204, Walsenburg, CO 81089. **Phone-**719-738-2380; fax-719-738-2364; hours 8AM-4PM
Will not search UCC records. UCC copy- $1.25 per page. Separate tax lien search is available. Treasurer performs tax lien searches. Will not search real estate records. Cert fee: $1.00 per cert. Payee: County Clerk and Recorder. **Other phones:** Assessor-719-738-1280; Treasurer-719-782-1191.

Jackson County

County Clerk & Recorder, PO Box 337, Walden, CO 80480-0337. **Phone-**970-723-4334; fax-970-723-3214; hours 8AM-5PM
Will search UCC records. Search per debtor-$5.00 1st year; $2.00 each add'l year. UCC copy- $1.25 per page. UCC search includes tax liens. Separate tax lien search costs same as UCC search. Will not search real estate records. RE record copy- $1.25 per page. Cert fee: $1.00 per cert. Payee: Jackson County Clerk and Recorder. **Other phones:** Assessor-970-723-4751; Treasurer-970-723-4220; Elections-970-723-4334; Vital Records-970-723-4334.

Jefferson County

County Clerk & Recorder, 100 Jefferson County Parkway, #2530, Golden, CO 80419-2530. **Phone-**303-271-8121; fax-303-271-8180; hours 8:30AM-4:30PM http://co.jefferson.co.us/ext/dpt/officials/clkrec/index.htm
Will search UCC records. Search per debtor- $5.00 per 1st year. UCC copy- $1.25 per page. Will not search tax liens. Real estate record owner and mortgage searches available. RE record copy- $1.25 per page. Cert fee: $1.00 per cert. Payee: Jefferson County Clerk and Recorder. **Online Access to**

Assessor, Property, Grantor/Grantee, Deed, Judgment, Recording records: records on the county Assessor database are available free at http://ww14.co.jefferson.co.us/ats/splash.do. No name searching. Also, search the recorder's Grantor/Grantee index for free at http://ww14.co.jefferson.co.us/crint/disclaimer.htm. **Other phones:** Assessor-303-271-8666; Treasurer-303-271-8330; Elections-303-271-8111; Vital Records-303-271-6450.

Kiowa County

County Clerk & Recorder, PO Box 37, Eads, CO 81036-0037. **Phone-**County Clerk & Recorder, R/E & UCC Recording- 719-438-5421; fax-719-438-5327; hours 8AM-4:30PM. Will not search records. UCC copy- $1.25 per page. Cert fee: $.50 per cert. Payee: County Clerk and Recorder. **Other phones:** Assessor-719-438-5521; Treasurer-719-438-5831; Elections-719-438-5421; Vital Records-719-438-5590.

Kit Carson County

County Clerk & Recorder, PO Box 249, Burlington, CO 80807-0249. **Phone-**719-346-8638; fax-719-346-7242; hours 8AM-4PM
Will not search real estate or UCC records. UCC copy- $1.00 per page. Tax lien search fee- $13.00 per debtor for 5 years, $2.00 each add'l year. RE record copy- $1.25 per page. Cert fee: $1.00 per cert. Payee: Kit Carson County Clerk and Recorder. **Other phones:** Assessor-719-346-8946; Treasurer-719-346-8434; Elections-719-346-8638; Vital Records-719-346-8133.

La Plata County

County Clerk & Recorder, PO Box 519, Durango, CO 81302-0519. **Phone-**970-382-6294, R/E Recording-970-382-6280/6281; fax-970-382-6299; hours 8AM-5PM http://co.laplata.co.us
Will not search records. UCC copy- $1.25 per page. Cert fee: $1.25 per cert. Payee: La Plata County Clerk and Recorder. **Online Access to Real Estate, Sale, Property records:** Records on the county Real Estate Search Page are free at www.laplatainfo.com/search2.html. This is basic property data; for sales and tax data, there is a subscription service for $20.00 per month, credit cards accepted. **Other phones:** Assessor-970-382-6221; Treasurer-970-382-6245.

Lake County

County Clerk & Recorder, PO Box 917, Leadville, CO 80461. **Phone-**County Clerk & Recorder, R/E & UCC Recording- 719-486-4131, UCC Recording- 719-894-2200; fax-719-486-3972; hours 9AM-5PM
Will not search records. Record copy- $1.25 per page. Cert fee: $1.00 per cert. Payee: Lake County Clerk and Recorder. **Other phones:** Assessor-719-486-0413; Treasurer-719-486-0530; Elections-719-486-1410; Vital Records-719-486-0708.

Larimer County

County Clerk & Recorder, PO Box 1280, Fort Collins, CO 80522-1280. **Phone-**County Clerk & Recorder, R/E & UCC Recording- 970-498-7860; fax-970-498-7830; hours 7:30AM-4:30PM www.larimer.org
Will search UCC records. Search per debtor- $5.00 per name. UCC copy- $1.00 per page. UCC search includes tax liens. Separate tax lien search costs the same as UCC search. Will not search real estate records. Cert fee: $1.00 per cert. Payee: Larimer County Clerk and Recorder. **Online Access to Property Tax, Assessor, Treasurer, UCC, Lien, Deed, Judgment, Recording, Voter Registration, Most Wanted records:** Search the county Public Record Databases for free at www.larimer.org/databases/index.htm. Also, search the county sheriff most wanted list for free at www.co.larimer.co.us/Sheriff/MostWanted/Wanted0.ht

m. **Other phones:** Assessor-970-498-7050; Treasurer-970-498-7020; Elections-970-498-7820; Vital Records-970-498-5710.

Las Animas County

County Clerk & Recorder, PO Box 115, Trinidad, CO 81082. **Phone-**719-846-3314; fax-719-845-2573; hours 8AM-4PM
Will not search records. UCC copy- $1.25 per page. Cert fee: $2.25 per cert. Payee: Las Animas County Clerk and Recorder. **Other phones:** Assessor-719-846-2295; Treasurer-719-846-2295.

Lincoln County

County Clerk & Recorder, PO Box 67, Hugo, CO 80821-0067. **Phone-**719-743-2444; fax-719-743-2524; hours 8AM-4:30PM
Will not search records. UCC copy- $1.00 per page. RE record copy- $1.25 per page. Cert fee: $1.00 per cert. Payee: Lincoln County Clerk and Recorder. **Other phones:** Assessor-719-743-2358; Treasurer-719-743-2633; Elections-719-743-2444; Vital Records-719-743-2796.

Logan County

County Clerk & Recorder, 315 Main St #3, Logan County Courthouse, Sterling, CO 80751. **Phone-**County Clerk & Recorder, R/E & UCC Recording-970-522-1544; fax-970-522-2063; hours 8AM-5PM www.loganco.gov/departments.htm
Will search UCC records prior to 1/2001. Search per debtor- $5.00 per name per year; $2.00 each add'l year. UCC copy- $1.25 per page. Will not search real estate or tax lien records. RE record copy- $1.25 per page. Cert fee: $1.00 per cert. Payee: Logan County Clerk and Recorder. **Online Access to Assessor, Real Estate records:** Access to the assessor's Property Search database is free at www.loganco-assessor.org/search.asp?. **Other phones:** Assessor-970-522-2797; Treasurer-970-522-2462; Elections-970-522-1544; Vital Records-970-522-1544 (marriage); Birth & Death Certificates-970-522-3741.

Mesa County

County Clerk & Recorder, PO Box 20000-5007, Grand Junction, CO 81502-5007. **Phone-**County Clerk & Recorder, R/E & UCC Recording- 970-244-1679; fax-970-256-1588;   hours-8:30AM-4:30PM www.co.mesa.co.us
an interactive Voice Response System lets callers access real property data at 970-256-1563. Fax back service available. Will search UCC records. Search per debtor-. UCC copy- $1.25 per page. UCC search includes federal tax liens only. Separate federal/state combined tax lien search- $5.00 per debtor per year or $13.00 forr 5-year search. Will not search real estate records. RE record copy- $1.25 per page. Cert fee: $1.00 per cert. Payee: Mesa County Clerk and Recorder. **Online Access to Grantor/Grantee, Judgment, Lien, Real Estate, Assessor, Real Estate, Property Tax, Voter Registration records:** Records on the county Assessor database are free at www.co.mesa.co.us. Click on "Assessor Lookup" and search by address or parcel number. Search on the GIS-mapping/property page at www.gjcity.org/CityDeptWebPages/PublicWorksAnd Utilities/TechnicalServices/GIS.htm. Also, search the Grantor/Grantee index, liens, judgments, mortgages, etc. at www.co.mesa.co.us/sireweb/sireweb.asp. **Other phones:** Assessor-970-244-1610; Treasurer-970-244-1824; Elections-970-244-1662; Vital Records-970-248-6900 (birth/death); Marriage Records-970-244-1679.

Mineral County

County Clerk & Recorder, PO Box 70, Creede, CO 81130. **Phone-**County Clerk & Recorder, R/E & UCC Recording- 719-658-2440; fax-719-658-2931; hours 8AM-4PM

Will not search records. UCC copy- $1.25 per page. Cert fee: $1.00 per page. Payee: Mineral County Clerk and Recorder. **Other phones:** Assessor-719-658-2669; Treasurer-719-658-2325; Elections-719-658-2440; Vital Records-719-658-2497.

Moffat County

County Clerk & Recorder, 221 W. Victory Way, Craig, CO 81625-2716. **Phone-**County Clerk & Recorder, R/E & UCC Recording- 970-824-9104; fax-970-824-4975; hours 8AM-4PM. Will not search records. UCC copy- $1.00 per page. RE record copy- $1.25 per page. Payee: Moffat County Clerk and Recorder. **Online Access to Most Wanted records:** Access the sheriff's most wanted list at www.moffatcountysher iff.com/mostwanted.htm. **Other phones:** Assessor-970-824-9102; Treasurer-970-824-9111; Elections-970-824-9104; Vital Records-970-824-8233.

Montezuma County

County Clerk & Recorder, 109 W. Main St, Rm #108, Cortez, CO 81321. **Phone-**970-565-3728, R/E Recording- 970-565-3728 x3, UCC Recording- 303-894-2200; fax-970-564-0215; hours 8:30AM-4:30PM www.co.montezuma.co.us
Will not search records. Record copy- $1.25 per page. Cert fee: $1.00 per cert. Payee: Montezuma County Clerk and Recorder. **Online Access to Property Tax, Property Sale records:** Access to county property information is free at http://itax.co.montezuma.co.us/itax/taxSplash.jsp and registration is required. **Other phones:** Assessor-970-565-3428; Treasurer-970-565-7550; Elections-970-565-3728 x4; Vital Records-970-565-3728 x3.

Montrose County

County Clerk & Recorder, PO Box 1289, Montrose, CO 81402. **Phone-**970-249-3362, R/E Recording- 970-249-3362 x2; fax-970-249-0757; 8:30AM-4:30PM
Will not search records. RE record copy- $1.25 per page. Cert fee: $1.00 per cert. Payee: Montrose County Clerk and Recorder. **Online Access to Property, Assessor records:** Access to Property Information Search System is free at http://itax.co.montrose.co.us/itax/taxSplash.jsp. Free registration is required. **Other phones:** Assessor-970-249-3753; Treasurer-970-249-3565; Elections-970-249-3362 x3; Vital Records-970-249-3362 x0.

Morgan County

County Clerk & Recorder, PO Box 1399, Fort Morgan, CO 80701. **Phone-**County Clerk & Recorder, R/E & UCC Recording- 970-542-3521; fax-970-542-3520; hours 8AM-4PM
Will not search records. Record copy- $1.25 per page. Cert fee: No extra fee. Payee: Morgan County Clerk and Recorder. **Online Access to Assessor records:** Search the assessor database at morgancounty.coloproperty.com/search/search.cfm.
Other phones: Assessor-970-542-3512; Treasurer-970-542-3518; Appraiser/ Auditor-970-542-3512; Elections-970-542-3521; Vital Records-970-867-4918.

Otero County

County Clerk & Recorder, PO Box 511, La Junta, CO 81050-0511. **Phone-**719-383-3020, R/E Recording- 719-383-3023; fax-719-383-3026; hours 8AM-5PM
Will not search records. Record copy- $1.25 per page. Cert fee: $1.00 per cert. Payee: Otero County Clerk and Recorder. **Online Access to Assessor records:** For property information go to www.oterocountyassessor.net. **Other phones:** Assessor-719-383-3010; Treasurer-719-383-3030; Elections-719-383-3024; Vital Records-719-383-3040.

Ouray County

County Clerk & Recorder, PO Bin C, Ouray, CO 81427. **Phone-**County Clerk & Recorder, R/E & UCC

Recording- 970-325-4961, UCC Recording- 970-894-2200; fax-970-325-0452; hours 9AM-5PM http://co.ouray.co.us
Will search UCC records. Search per debtor-. UCC copy- $1.25 per page. Will not search real estate or tax lien records. RE record copy- $1.25 per page. Payee: Ouray County Clerk and Recorder. **Other phones:** Assessor-970-325-4371; Treasurer-970-325-4487; Elections-970-325-4961; Vital Records-970-325-4487.

Park County

County Clerk & Recorder, PO Box 220, Fairplay, CO 80440. **Phone-**719-836-4222, R/E Recording- 719-836-4222 or 4224, UCC Recording- 719-836-4222 or 4224; fax-719-836-4348; hours 7AM-5PM www.parkco.org
Will not search r records. Record copy- $1.25 per page. Cert fee: $1.00 per cert. Payee: Park County Clerk and Recorder. **Online Access to Assessor, Property Tax, Divorce records:** Records on the county Assessor database are free at www.parkco.org/Search2.asp? including tax information, owner, address, building characteristics, legal and deed information. Also, county divorce records from 1957 to 1974 are free at www.colorado.gov/dpa/doit/archives/divorce/1park.htm . **Other phones:** Assessor-719-836-2771 x186; Treasurer-719-836-2771 x242; Elections-719-836-4223; Vital Records-719-836-4227.

Phillips County

County Clerk & Recorder, 221 S. Interocean, Holyoke, CO 80734. **Phone-**County Clerk & Recorder, R/E & UCC Recording- 970-854-3131; fax-970-854-4745; hours 8AM-4:30PM
Will not search records. Record copy- $1.25 per page. Cert fee: $1.00 per cert. Payee: Phillips County Clerk and Recorder. **Other phones:** Assessor-970-854-3151; Treasurer-970-852-2822; Appraiser/ Auditor-970-854-3151; Elections-970-854-3131; Vital Records-970-854-3350.

Pitkin County

County Clerk & Recorder, 530 E. Main St., #101, Aspen, CO 81611. **Phone-**County Clerk & Recorder, R/E & UCC Recording- 970-920-5180; fax-970-920-5196; hours 8:30AM-4:30PM www.aspenpitkin.com
Will search UCC records. UCC search per debtor- $13.00 per 5 year search. UCC copy- $1.25 per page. Will not search real estate or tax lien records. RE record copy- $1.25 per page. Cert fee: $1.00 per cert. Payee: Pitkin County Clerk and Recorder. **Online Access to Assessor, Inmates, Divorce, Probate, Grantor/Grantee records:** Records on the county Assessor database are free at www.mitchandco.com/realestate/pitkin/index.cfm. Search recorded documents at www.pitkinassessor.org/Clerk/search.asp. Also, the sheriff's current inmate list is free at www.aspenpitkin.com/depts/28/inmates.cfm. Divorce records 1931 to 1964 are at www.colorado.gov/dpa/doit/archives/divorce/1pitkin.ht m. Also, probate records from 1881 to 1953 are at www.colorado.gov/dpa/doit/archives/probate/pitkin_pr obate.htm. Grantor/Grantee index at www.pitkinassessor.org/clerk. **Other phones:** Assessor-970-920-5160; Treasurer-970-920-5170; Elections-970-920-5180.

Prowers County

County Clerk & Recorder, 301 S. Main St #210, Lamar, CO 81052. **Phone-**County Clerk & Recorder, R/E & UCC Recording- 719-336-8011; fax-719-336-5306; hours 8:30AM-4:30PM
Will search UCC records. Search per debtor- $5.00 for 1st year; $2.00 each add'l year. UCC copy- $1.00 per page. Will not search real estate or tax lien records. RE record copy- $1.25 per page. Cert

fee: $1.00 per cert. Payee: Prowers County Clerk and Recorder. **Other phones:** Assessor-719-336-8000; Treasurer-719-336-8081; Appraiser/ Auditor-719-336-8000; Elections-719-336-8011; Vital Records-719-336-2606.

Pueblo County

County Clerk & Recorder, PO Box 878, Pueblo, CO 81002-0878. **Phone**-719-583-6625, R/E Recording-719-583-6629; fax-719-583-4625; hours 8AM-4:30PM www.co.pueblo.co.us/clerk/
Will search UCC records but not real estate-related UCC filings. UCC search per debtor- $5.00 per name for 1st year, $2.00 each add'l year. UCC copy- $1.25 per page. Will search tax liens. Federal/state combined tax lien search- $5.00 per debtor for 1st year; $2.00 each add'l year. Will not search real estate records. RE record copy- $1.25 per page. Cert fee: $1.00 per doc. Payee: Pueblo County Clerk and Recorder. **Online Access to Assessor, Real Estate, Property Sale, Registered Voter records:** Access to the county assessor database is free at http://assessor.co.pueblo.co.us. Also, access to voter registration data is free at www.co.pueblo.co.us; click on "Registered Voters". **Other phones:** Assessor-719-583-6564; Treasurer-719-583-6015; Appraiser/ Auditor-719-583-6596; Elections-719-583-6620; Vital Records-719-583-4555; Main switchboard-719-583-6000.

Rio Blanco County

County Clerk & Recorder, PO Box 1067, Meeker, CO 81641. **Phone**-970-878-5068; hours 8AM-5PM
Will not search real estate or UCC records. UCC copy- $1.25 per page. Tax lien records filed with real property records. Cert fee: $1.00 per cert. Payee: Rio Blanco County Clerk and Recorder. **Other phones:** Assessor-970-878-5686; Treasurer-970-878-3614; Elections-970-878-5068; Vital Records-970-878-5068.

Rio Grande County

County Clerk & Recorder, PO Box 160, Del Norte, CO 81132. **Phone**-County Clerk & Recorder, R/E & UCC Recording- 719-657-3334, UCC Recording- 719-657-3334 real estate only; fax-719-657-2621; hours 8AM-4PM www.qpublic.net/riogrande/
Will not search records. Record copy- $1.25. Cert fee: $1.00 per doc. Payee: Rio Grande County Clerk and Recorder. **Online Access to Property Tax, Assessor, Sale records:** Access to the proeprty assessor's data is available free at www.qpublic.net/riogrande/search1.html. A property sale search is also at the assessor website. **Other phones:** Assessor-719-657-3326; Treasurer-719-657-2747; Appraiser/ Auditor-719-657-3326; Elections-719-657-3334; Vital Records-719-657-3334.

Routt County

County Clerk & Recorder, PO Box 773598, Steamboat Springs, CO 80477. **Phone**-County Clerk & Recorder, R/E & UCC Recording- 970-870-5556; fax-970-870-1329; hours 8AM-4:30PM; Recording hours- 8AM-4PM www.co.routt.co.us
Will search UCC records. UCC copy- $1.25 per page. UCC search includes tax liens. Will not search real estate records. Cert fee: $1.00 per doc. Payee: Routt County Clerk and Recorder. **Online Access to Real Estate, Assessor, Treasurer, Deed, Judgment, Property Sale records:** Records on the county Assessor/Treasurer Property Search database are free at www.co.routt.co.us/assessor.html. Also, records on the Routt County Clerk and Recorder Reception Search database are free at www.co.routt.co.us/clerk.html. **Other phones:** Assessor-970-879-2756; Treasurer-970-870-5555; Appraiser/ Auditor-970-870-5554; Elections-970-870-5556; Vital Records-970-879-1632.

Saguache County

County Clerk & Recorder, PO Box 176, Saguache, CO 81149-0176. **Phone**-719-655-2512; fax-719-655-2730; hours 8AM-4PM
Will not search records. UCC copy- $1.25 per page. Cert fee: $1.00 per cert. Payee: Saguache County Clerk and Recorder. **Online Access to Recording, Real estate, Deed, Lien, Death, Marriage records:** Access to the Recorder data base is free at www.thecountyrecorder.com/Search.aspx?CountyKey =6. Index goes back to 1984; images back to 1986. Also, search the Assessor propert database at www.qpublic.net/co/saguache/. **Other phones:** Assessor-719-655-2521; Treasurer-719-655-2656.

San Juan County

County Clerk & Recorder, PO Box 466, Silverton, CO 81433-0466. **Phone**-County Clerk & Recorder, R/E & UCC Recording- 970-387-5671; fax-970-387-5671; hours 9AM-5PM
Will search UCC records. Search per debtor- $13.00. UCC copy- $1.25 per page. Will not search real estate or tax lien records. Cert fee: $.75 per page. Payee: San Juan County Clerk and Recorder. **Other phones:** Assessor-970-387-5632; Treasurer-970-389-5488; Elections-970-387-5671; Vital Records-970-387-5488.

San Miguel County

County Clerk & Recorder, PO Box 548, Telluride, CO 81435-0548. **Phone**-County Clerk & Recorder, R/E & UCC Recording- 970-728-3954; fax-970-728-4808; hours 9AM-5PM
Will not search records. Record copy- $1.25 per copy. Cert fee: $1.00 per cert. Payee: San Miguel County Clerk and Recorder. **Online Access to Most Wanted records:** Access the sheriff's most wanted list at www.sanmiguelsheriff.com/rewards.html. **Other phones:** Assessor-970-728-3174; Treasurer-970-728-4451; Appraiser/ Auditor-970-728-3174; Elections-970-728-3954; Vital Records-970-728-4451.

Sedgwick County

County Clerk & Recorder, PO Box 50, Julesburg, CO 80737. **Phone**-County Clerk & Recorder, R/E & UCC Recording- 970-474-3346; fax-970-474-0954; hours 8AM-4PM
Will not search or retrieve UCC records unless provided the book and page number. UCC copy- $1.25 per page. Will not search real estate or tax lien records. RE record copy- $1.25 per page. Cert fee: $1.00 per cert. Payee: Sedgwick County Clerk and Recorder. **Other phones:** Assessor-970-474-2531; Treasurer-970-474-3473; Elections-970-474-3346; Vital Records-970-474-3473.

Summit County

County Clerk & Recorder, PO Box 1538, Breckenridge, CO 80424. **Phone**-County Clerk & Recorder, R/E & UCC Recording- 970-453-3475; fax-970-453-3540; hours-8AM-5PM www.co.summit.co.us
Will search UCC records. Search per debtor-. UCC copy- $1.25 per page. UCC search includes tax liens. Will not search real estate records. RE record copy- $1.25 per page. Cert fee: $1.00 per cert. Payee: Summit County Clerk and Recorder. **Online Access to Property, GIS-mapping records:** Access to the GIS-mapping site property data is free at www.co.summit.co.us/scripts/esrimap.dll. **Other phones:** Assessor-970-453-3480; Treasurer-970-453-3440; Appraiser/ Auditor-970-453-3480; Elections-970-453-3479; Vital Records-970-453-3472.

Teller County

County Clerk & Recorder, PO Box 1010, Cripple Creek, CO 80813-1010. **Phone**-719-689-2951, R/E Recording- 719-689-2951 x4; fax-719-689-3524; hours 8AM-4:30PM www.co.teller.co.us
Will search UCC records. Search per debtor-. UCC copy- $1.00 per page. Separate tax lien search costs same as UCC search. Will not search real estate records. Cert fee: $1.00 per cert. Payee: Teller County Clerk and Recorder. **Online Access to Real Estate, Grantor/Grantee, Assessor, Property Tax records:** Access the county clerk real estate database free at http://data.co.teller.co.us/AsrData/wc.dll?D oc~GrantSearch. Records go back to 1978; fee for documents is $1.25 per page. Also, search the assessor database free at http://data.co.teller.co.us/AsrData/wc.d ll?AsrDataProc~OwnerNameSearch. **Other phones:** Assessor-719-689-2941; Treasurer-719-689-2985; Elections-719-689-2951 x5 or x6; Vital Records-719-689-2951 x4.

Washington County

County Clerk & Recorder, PO Box L, Akron, CO 80720-0380. **Phone**-County Clerk & Recorder, R/E & UCC Recording- 970-345-6565, UCC Recording- 303-894-2200; fax-970-345-6607; hours 8AM-4:30PM
Will not search real estate or UCC records. UCC copy- $1.00 per page. RE record copy- $1.25 per page. Cert fee: $1.00 per cert. Payee: Washington County Clerk. **Other phones:** Assessor-970-345-6662; Treasurer-970-345-6601; Appraiser/ Auditor-970-345-6662; Elections-970-345-6565; Vital Records-970-345-6627.

Weld County

County Clerk & Recorder, PO Box 459, Greeley, CO 80632-0459. **Phone**-970-304-6530, R/E Recording-970-304-6530 x3065, UCC Recording- 970-304-6530 x3065; fax-970-353-1964; hours 8AM-5PM www.co.weld.co.us
Will not search real estate or UCC records. UCC copy- $1.25 per page. Tax lien search fee- $5.00 1st year, $2.00 each add'l year. Cert fee: $1.00 per cert. Payee: Weld County Clerk and Recorder. **Online Access to Real Estate, Assessor, Treasurer, Property Tax, Most Wanted, Sex Offender records:** Search property information on the map server database at http://maps.merrick.com/website/weld/ or click on the "Property Information" button then search assessor data by name. Also, search the treasurer's property database for free at www.co.weld.co.us/departments/treas urer/tax/index1.cfm. Also, access the sheriff's most wanted and sex offender pages at www.co.weld.co.us/Sheriff/. **Other phones:** Assessor-970-304-3845 x3650; Treasurer-970-304-3845 x3260; Elections-970-304-6525 x3070.

Yuma County

County Clerk & Recorder, 310 Ash St, #F, Wray, CO 80758. **Phone**-County Clerk & Recorder, R/E & UCC Recording- 970-332-5809; fax-970-332-5919; hours 8:30AM-4:30PM
Will search UCC records only thru 12-31-99. Search per debtor-$5.00 1st year, $2.00 each additional year. UCC copy- $1.25 per page. Will not search real estate or tax lien records. RE record copy- $1.25 per page. Cert fee: $1.00 per cert. Payee: Yuma County Clerk and Recorder. **Other phones:** Assessor-970-332-5032; Treasurer-970-332-4965; Appraiser/ Auditor-970-332-5032; Elections-970-332-5809; Vital Records-970-332-5809; Birth/Death Records-970-332-4431/970- 848-3878.

Colorado County Locator

You will usually be able to find the city name in the City/County Cross Reference below. In that case, it is a simple matter to determine the county from the cross reference. However, only the official US Postal Service city names are included in this index. There are an additional 40,000 place names that people use in their addresses. Therefore, we have also included a ZIP/City Cross Reference immediately following the City/County Cross Reference.

If you know the ZIP Code but the city name does not appear in the City/County Cross Reference index, look up the ZIP Code in the ZIP/City Cross Reference, find the city name, then look up the city name in the City/County Cross Reference. For example, you want to know the county for an address of Menands, NY 12204. There is no "Menands" in the City/County Cross Reference. The ZIP/City Cross Reference shows that ZIP Codes 12201-12288 are for the city of Albany. Looking back in the City/County Cross Reference, Albany is in Albany County.

Colorado City/County Cross Reference

AGATE Elbert
AGUILAR Las Animas
AKRON Washington
ALAMOSA (81101) Alamosa(98), Conejos(1)
ALAMOSA Alamosa
ALLENSPARK (80510) Boulder(95), Larimer(4)
ALMA Park
ALMONT Gunnison
AMHERST Phillips
ANTON Washington
ANTONITO Conejos
ARAPAHOE Cheyenne
ARBOLES Archuleta
ARLINGTON (81021) Kiowa(80), Lincoln(19)
ARRIBA Lincoln
ARVADA (80003) Jefferson(86), Adams(13)
ARVADA Jefferson
ASPEN Pitkin
ATWOOD Logan
AULT Weld
AURORA (80010) Adams(52), Arapahoe(47)
AURORA (80011) Arapahoe(61), Adams(38)
AURORA (80014) Arapahoe(91), Denver(8)
AURORA Adams
AURORA Arapahoe
AUSTIN Delta
AVON Eagle
AVONDALE Pueblo
BAILEY Park
BASALT (81621) Eagle(68), Pitkin(31)
BATTLEMENT MESA Garfield
BAYFIELD La Plata
BEDROCK Montrose
BELLVUE Larimer
BENNETT (80102) Adams(51), Arapahoe(44), Elbert(3)
BERTHOUD (80513) Larimer(90), Weld(9)
BETHUNE Kit Carson
BEULAH Pueblo
BLACK HAWK Gilpin
BLANCA Costilla
BONCARBO Las Animas
BOND Eagle
BOONE Pueblo
BOULDER Boulder
BOYERO Lincoln
BRANSON Las Animas
BRECKENRIDGE Summit
BRIGGSDALE Weld
BRIGHTON (80603) Weld(54), Adams(45)
BRIGHTON Adams
BRISTOL Prowers
BROOMFIELD (80020) Broomfield(77), Jefferson(11), Adams(8), Boulder(2)
BROOMFIELD (80021) Jefferson(84), Broomfield(15)
BROOMFIELD Boulder

BRUSH (80723) Morgan(98), Washington(1)
BUENA VISTA Chaffee
BUFFALO CREEK Jefferson
BURLINGTON Kit Carson
BURNS Eagle
BYERS (80103) Arapahoe(87), Adams(12)
CAHONE Dolores
CALHAN (80808) El Paso(97), Elbert(2)
CAMPO Baca
CANON CITY Fremont
CAPULIN Conejos
CARBONDALE (81623) Garfield(62), Eagle(15), Pitkin(11), Gunnison(9)
CARR (80612) Weld(95), Larimer(4)
CASCADE El Paso
CASTLE ROCK Douglas
CEDAREDGE Delta
CENTER (81125) Saguache(67), Rio Grande(31), Alamosa(1)
CENTRAL CITY Gilpin
CHAMA Costilla
CHERAW Otero
CHEYENNE WELLS Cheyenne
CHIMNEY ROCK Archuleta
CHROMO Archuleta
CIMARRON (81220) Gunnison(81), Montrose(18)
CLARK Routt
CLIFTON Mesa
CLIMAX Lake
COAL CREEK Fremont
COALDALE Fremont
COALMONT Jackson
COKEDALE Las Animas
COLLBRAN Mesa
COLORADO CITY Pueblo
COLORADO SPRINGS (80926) El Paso(98), Fremont(1)
COLORADO SPRINGS El Paso
COMMERCE CITY Adams
COMO Park
CONEJOS Conejos
CONIFER Jefferson
COPE Washington
CORTEZ Montezuma
CORY Delta
COTOPAXI Fremont
COWDREY Jackson
CRAIG Moffat
CRAWFORD (81415) Delta(80), Montrose(19)
CREEDE Mineral
CRESTED BUTTE Gunnison
CRESTONE Saguache
CRIPPLE CREEK Teller
CROOK Logan
CROWLEY Crowley
DACONO Weld
DE BEQUE (81630) Mesa(63), Garfield(36)
DEER TRAIL (80105) Arapahoe(63), Elbert(26), Adams(9)

DEL NORTE (81132) Rio Grande(88), Saguache(11)
DELTA (81416) Delta(96), Montrose(3)
DENVER (80221) Adams(87), Denver(12)
DENVER (80234) Adams(97), Broomfield(2)
DENVER (80212) Denver(77), Jefferson(18), Adams(3)
DENVER (80216) Denver(60), Adams(39)
DENVER (80222) Denver(94), Arapahoe(5)
DENVER (80230) Denver(98), Adams(1)
DENVER (80247) Denver(69), Arapahoe(27), Adams(3)
DENVER (80249) Denver(96), Adams(3)
DENVER (80235) Jefferson(61), Denver(38)
DENVER Adams
DENVER Denver
DENVER Jefferson
DILLON Summit
DINOSAUR Moffat
DIVIDE Teller
DOLORES Montezuma
DOVE CREEK (81324) Dolores(98), San Miguel(1)
DRAKE Larimer
DUMONT Clear Creek
DUPONT Adams
DURANGO La Plata
EADS Kiowa
EAGLE Eagle
EASTLAKE Adams
EATON Weld
ECKERT Delta
ECKLEY Yuma
EDWARDS Eagle
EGNAR (81325) Dolores(85), San Miguel(14)
EL JEBEL Eagle
ELBERT (80106) El Paso(60), Elbert(37), Douglas(2)
ELDORADO SPRINGS Boulder
ELIZABETH Elbert
EMPIRE Clear Creek
ENGLEWOOD (80110) Arapahoe(98), Denver(1)
ENGLEWOOD (80112) Arapahoe(90), Douglas(5), Denver(4)
ENGLEWOOD Arapahoe
ERIE (80516) Weld(59), Boulder(40)
ESTES PARK Larimer
EVANS Weld
EVERGREEN (80439) Jefferson(88), Clear Creek(11)
EVERGREEN Jefferson
FAIRPLAY Park
FIRESTONE Weld
FLAGLER (80815) Kit Carson(86), Washington(13)
FLEMING Logan
FLORENCE Fremont
FLORISSANT (80816) Teller(78), Park(21)
FORT COLLINS Larimer

FORT GARLAND Costilla
FORT LUPTON Weld
FORT LYON Bent
FORT MORGAN Morgan
FOUNTAIN El Paso
FOWLER (81039) Otero(91), Pueblo(6), Crowley(1)
FOXTON Jefferson
FRANKTOWN Douglas
FRASER Grand
FREDERICK Weld
FRISCO Summit
FRUITA Mesa
GALETON Weld
GARCIA Costilla
GARDNER Huerfano
GATEWAY Mesa
GENOA (80818) Lincoln(83), Washington(16)
GEORGETOWN Clear Creek
GILCREST Weld
GILL Weld
GLADE PARK Mesa
GLEN HAVEN Larimer
GLENWOOD SPRINGS Garfield
GOLDEN (80403) Jefferson(74), Gilpin(21), Boulder(4)
GOLDEN Jefferson
GRANADA (81041) Prowers(92), Baca(7)
GRANBY Grand
GRAND JUNCTION Mesa
GRAND LAKE Grand
GRANITE (81228) Lake(62), Chaffee(37)
GRANT Park
GREELEY Weld
GREEN MOUNTAIN FALLS El Paso
GROVER Weld
GUFFEY Park
GULNARE Las Animas
GUNNISON Gunnison
GYPSUM (81637) Eagle(91), Garfield(8)
HAMILTON (81638) Moffat(59), Routt(30), Rio Blanco(9)
HARTMAN Prowers
HARTSEL Park
HASTY Bent
HASWELL (81045) Kiowa(63), Lincoln(20), Cheyenne(16)
HAXTUN (80731) Phillips(55), Logan(23), Yuma(21)
HAYDEN Routt
HENDERSON Adams
HEREFORD Weld
HESPERUS La Plata
HILLROSE Morgan
HILLSIDE Fremont
HOEHNE Las Animas
HOLLY (81047) Prowers(92), Kiowa(4), Baca(2)
HOLYOKE (80734) Phillips(95), Yuma(4)
HOMELAKE Rio Grande
HOOPER (81136) Alamosa(94), Saguache(5)

HOT SULPHUR SPRINGS Grand
HOTCHKISS Delta
HOWARD Fremont
HUDSON (80642) Weld(67), Adams(32)
HUGO Lincoln
HYGIENE Boulder
IDAHO SPRINGS Clear Creek
IDALIA Yuma
IDLEDALE Jefferson
IGNACIO La Plata
ILIFF Logan
INDIAN HILLS Jefferson
JAMESTOWN Boulder
JAROSO Costilla
JEFFERSON Park
JOES Yuma
JOHNSTOWN Weld
JULESBURG Sedgwick
KARVAL Lincoln
KEENESBURG (80643) Weld(88),
    Adams(11)
KERSEY Weld
KIM Las Animas
KIOWA Elbert
KIRK Yuma
KIT CARSON Cheyenne
KITTREDGE Jefferson
KREMMLING (80459) Grand(98),
    Summit(1)
LA JARA Conejos
LA JUNTA Otero
LA SALLE Weld
LA VETA Huerfano
LAFAYETTE Boulder
LAKE CITY Hinsdale
LAKE GEORGE (80827) Teller(71),
    Park(28)
LAKEWOOD (80226) Jefferson(98),
    Denver(1)
LAKEWOOD Jefferson
LAMAR (81052) Prowers(98), Bent(1)
LAPORTE Larimer
LARKSPUR Douglas
LAS ANIMAS Bent
LAZEAR Delta
LEADVILLE Lake
LEWIS Montezuma
LIMON (80828) Lincoln(70), Elbert(29)
LIMON Lincoln
LINDON Washington
LITTLETON (80128) Jefferson(94),
    Arapahoe(5)
LITTLETON Arapahoe
LITTLETON Douglas
LITTLETON Jefferson
LIVERMORE Larimer
LOG LANE VILLAGE Morgan
LOMA Mesa
LONGMONT (80504) Weld(75),
    Boulder(22), Larimer(1)
LONGMONT Boulder
LOUISVILLE Boulder
LOUVIERS Douglas
LOVELAND (80537) Larimer(98), Weld(1)
LOVELAND Larimer
LUCERNE Weld
LYONS (80540) Larimer(53), Boulder(46)

MACK Mesa
MAHER Delta
MANASSA Conejos
MANCOS (81328) Montezuma(96), La
    Plata(3)
MANITOU SPRINGS El Paso
MANZANOLA (81058) Otero(78),
    Crowley(21)
MARVEL La Plata
MASONVILLE Larimer
MATHESON Elbert
MAYBELL Moffat
MC CLAVE Bent
MC COY (80463) Eagle(80), Routt(20)
MEAD Weld
MEEKER (81641) Rio Blanco(93),
    Moffat(4), Garfield(1)
MEREDITH Pitkin
MERINO (80741) Logan(90),
    Washington(7), Morgan(1)
MESA Mesa
MESA VERDE NATIONAL PARK
    Montezuma
MILLIKEN Weld
MINTURN Eagle
MODEL (81059) Las Animas(77), Otero(22)
MOFFAT Saguache
MOLINA Mesa
MONARCH Chaffee
MONTE VISTA (81144) Rio Grande(96),
    Alamosa(3)
MONTROSE (81401) Montrose(96),
    Ouray(3)
MONTROSE Montrose
MONUMENT El Paso
MORRISON Jefferson
MOSCA Alamosa
NATHROP Chaffee
NATURITA Montrose
NEDERLAND Boulder
NEW CASTLE Garfield
NEW RAYMER (80742) Weld(66),
    Morgan(33)
NIWOT Boulder
NORWOOD San Miguel
NUCLA Montrose
NUNN Weld
OAK CREEK Routt
OHIO CITY Gunnison
OLATHE Montrose
OLNEY SPRINGS (81062) Crowley(94),
    Pueblo(5)
OPHIR San Miguel
ORCHARD (80649) Morgan(55), Weld(44)
ORDWAY (81063) Crowley(95), Lincoln(4)
OTIS (80743) Washington(97), Logan(2)
OURAY Ouray
OVID Sedgwick
PADRONI Logan
PAGOSA SPRINGS Archuleta
PALISADE Mesa
PALMER LAKE El Paso
PAOLI Phillips
PAONIA Delta
PARACHUTE Garfield
PARADOX Montrose
PARKER Douglas

PARLIN Gunnison
PARSHALL Grand
PEETZ Logan
PENROSE Fremont
PEYTON El Paso
PHIPPSBURG Routt
PIERCE Weld
PINE (80470) Jefferson(69), Park(30)
PINECLIFFE Boulder
PITKIN Gunnison
PLACERVILLE San Miguel
PLATTEVILLE Weld
PLEASANT VIEW Montezuma
PONCHA SPRINGS Chaffee
POWDERHORN Gunnison
PRITCHETT (81064) Baca(77), Las
    Animas(22)
PRYOR Huerfano
PUEBLO (81008) Pueblo(84), El Paso(15)
PUEBLO Pueblo
RAMAH (80832) Elbert(48), El Paso(46),
    Lincoln(5)
RAND Jackson
RANGELY Rio Blanco
RED CLIFF Eagle
RED FEATHER LAKES Larimer
RED WING Huerfano
REDVALE Montrose
RICO Dolores
RIDGWAY Ouray
RIFLE (81650) Garfield(96), Rio Blanco(3)
ROCKVALE Fremont
ROCKY FORD Otero
ROGGEN Weld
ROLLINSVILLE Gilpin
ROMEO Conejos
RUSH (80833) El Paso(49), Lincoln(40),
    Elbert(10)
RYE Pueblo
SAGUACHE Saguache
SALIDA Chaffee
SAN ACACIO Costilla
SAN LUIS Costilla
SAN PABLO Costilla
SANFORD (81151) Conejos(77),
    Costilla(21), Rio Grande(1)
SARGENTS Saguache
SEDALIA Douglas
SEDGWICK Sedgwick
SEGUNDO Las Animas
SEIBERT (80834) Kit Carson(90),
    Washington(9)
SEVERANCE Weld
SHAWNEE Park
SHERIDAN LAKE Kiowa
SILT Garfield
SILVER CLIFF Custer
SILVER PLUME Clear Creek
SILVERTHORNE Summit
SILVERTON San Juan
SIMLA (80835) Elbert(89), El Paso(10)
SLATER Moffat
SLICK ROCK San Miguel
SNOWMASS Pitkin
SNOWMASS VILLAGE Pitkin
SNYDER Morgan

SOMERSET (81434) Gunnison(90),
    Delta(9)
SOUTH FORK Rio Grande
SPRINGFIELD Baca
STARKVILLE Las Animas
STEAMBOAT SPRINGS Routt
STERLING Logan
STONEHAM Weld
STONINGTON Baca
STRASBURG (80136) Adams(66),
    Arapahoe(33)
STRATTON Kit Carson
SUGAR CITY (81076) Crowley(94),
    Lincoln(3), Kiowa(1)
SWINK Otero
TABERNASH Grand
TELLURIDE San Miguel
TIMNATH Larimer
TOPONAS Routt
TOWAOC Montezuma
TRINCHERA Las Animas
TRINIDAD Las Animas
TWIN LAKES Lake
TWIN LAKES CPO Lake
TWO BUTTES (81084) Baca(89),
    Prowers(10)
U S A F ACADEMY El Paso
VAIL Eagle
VERNON Yuma
VICTOR Teller
VILAS Baca
VILLA GROVE Saguache
VIRGINIA DALE Larimer
VONA Kit Carson
WALDEN Jackson
WALSENBURG Huerfano
WALSH Baca
WARD Boulder
WATKINS (80137) Arapahoe(59),
    Adams(40)
WELDONA Morgan
WELLINGTON (80549) Larimer(95),
    Weld(4)
WESTCLIFFE Custer
WESTMINSTER (80031) Adams(93),
    Jefferson(6)
WESTMINSTER Adams
WESTON Las Animas
WETMORE (81253) Custer(69),
    Fremont(26), Pueblo(4)
WHEAT RIDGE Jefferson
WHITEWATER Mesa
WIGGINS (80654) Morgan(92), Weld(4),
    Adams(2)
WILD HORSE Cheyenne
WILEY (81092) Prowers(60), Bent(36),
    Kiowa(3)
WINDSOR (80550) Weld(94), Larimer(5)
WINDSOR Weld
WINTER PARK Grand
WOLCOTT Eagle
WOODLAND PARK Teller
WOODROW Washington
WOODY CREEK Pitkin
WRAY Yuma
YAMPA Routt
YELLOW JACKET Montezuma
YODER El Paso

Colorado ZIP/City Cross Reference

ZIP Range	City	ZIP Range	City	ZIP Range	City	ZIP Range	City
80001-80007	ARVADA	80454-80454	INDIAN HILLS	80651-80651	PLATTEVILLE	81001-81015	PUEBLO
80010-80019	AURORA	80455-80455	JAMESTOWN	80652-80652	ROGGEN	81019-81019	COLORADO CITY
80020-80021	BROOMFIELD	80456-80456	JEFFERSON	80653-80653	WELDONA	81020-81020	AGUILAR
80022-80022	COMMERCE CITY	80457-80457	KITTREDGE	80654-80654	WIGGINS	81021-81021	ARLINGTON
80024-80024	DUPONT	80459-80459	KREMMLING	80701-80701	FORT MORGAN	81022-81022	AVONDALE
80025-80025	ELDORADO SPRINGS	80461-80461	LEADVILLE	80705-80705	LOG LANE VILLAGE	81023-81023	BEULAH
80026-80026	LAFAYETTE	80463-80463	MC COY	80720-80720	AKRON	81024-81024	BONCARBO
80027-80028	LOUISVILLE	80465-80465	MORRISON	80721-80721	AMHERST	81025-81025	BOONE
80030-80031	WESTMINSTER	80466-80466	NEDERLAND	80722-80722	ATWOOD	81026-81026	EADS
80033-80034	WHEAT RIDGE	80467-80467	OAK CREEK	80723-80723	BRUSH	81027-81027	BRANSON
80035-80036	WESTMINSTER	80468-80468	PARSHALL	80726-80726	CROOK	81028-81028	BRISTOL
80037-80037	COMMERCE CITY	80469-80469	PHIPPSBURG	80727-80727	ECKLEY	81029-81029	CAMPO
80038-80038	BROOMFIELD	80470-80470	PINE	80728-80728	FLEMING	81030-81030	CHERAW
80040-80047	AURORA	80471-80471	PINECLIFFE	80729-80729	GROVER	81032-81032	COKEDALE
80101-80101	AGATE	80473-80473	RAND	80731-80731	HAXTUN	81033-81034	CROWLEY
80102-80102	BENNETT	80474-80474	ROLLINSVILLE	80732-80732	HEREFORD	81036-81036	EADS
80103-80103	BYERS	80475-80475	SHAWNEE	80733-80733	HILLROSE	81038-81038	FORT LYON
80104-80104	CASTLE ROCK	80476-80476	SILVER PLUME	80734-80734	HOLYOKE	81039-81039	FOWLER
80105-80105	DEER TRAIL	80477-80477	STEAMBOAT SPRINGS	80735-80735	IDALIA	81040-81040	GARDNER
80106-80106	ELBERT	80478-80478	TABERNASH	80736-80736	ILIFF	81041-81041	GRANADA
80107-80107	ELIZABETH	80479-80479	TOPONAS	80737-80737	JULESBURG	81042-81042	GULNARE
80108-80109	CASTLE ROCK	80480-80480	WALDEN	80740-80740	LINDON	81043-81043	HARTMAN
80110-80113	ENGLEWOOD	80481-80481	WARD	80741-80741	MERINO	81044-81044	HASTY
80116-80116	FRANKTOWN	80482-80482	WINTER PARK	80742-80742	NEW RAYMER	81045-81045	HASWELL
80117-80117	KIOWA	80483-80483	YAMPA	80743-80743	OTIS	81046-81046	HOEHNE
80118-80118	LARKSPUR	80487-80488	STEAMBOAT SPRINGS	80744-80744	OVID	81047-81047	HOLLY
80120-80130	LITTLETON	80497-80498	SILVERTHORNE	80745-80745	PADRONI	81049-81049	KIM
80131-80131	LOUVIERS	80501-80504	LONGMONT	80746-80746	PAOLI	81050-81050	LA JUNTA
80132-80132	MONUMENT	80510-80510	ALLENSPARK	80747-80747	PEETZ	81052-81052	LAMAR
80133-80133	PALMER LAKE	80511-80511	ESTES PARK	80749-80749	SEDGWICK	81054-81054	LAS ANIMAS
80134-80134	PARKER	80512-80512	BELLVUE	80750-80750	SNYDER	81055-81055	LA VETA
80135-80135	SEDALIA	80513-80513	BERTHOUD	80751-80751	STERLING	81057-81057	MC CLAVE
80136-80136	STRASBURG	80514-80514	DACONO	80754-80754	STONEHAM	81058-81058	MANZANOLA
80137-80137	WATKINS	80515-80515	DRAKE	80755-80755	VERNON	81059-81059	MODEL
80138-80138	PARKER	80516-80516	ERIE	80757-80757	WOODROW	81062-81062	OLNEY SPRINGS
80150-80155	ENGLEWOOD	80517-80517	ESTES PARK	80758-80758	WRAY	81063-81063	ORDWAY
80160-80166	LITTLETON	80520-80520	FIRESTONE	80759-80759	YUMA	81064-81064	PRITCHETT
80201-80214	DENVER	80521-80528	FORT COLLINS	80801-80801	ANTON	81065-81065	PRYOR
80215-80215	LAKEWOOD	80530-80530	FREDERICK	80802-80802	ARAPAHOE	81066-81066	RED WING
80216-80225	DENVER	80532-80532	GLEN HAVEN	80804-80804	ARRIBA	81067-81067	ROCKY FORD
80226-80226	LAKEWOOD	80533-80533	HYGIENE	80805-80805	BETHUNE	81069-81069	RYE
80227-80227	DENVER	80534-80534	JOHNSTOWN	80806-80806	BOYERO	81070-81070	SEGUNDO
80228-80228	LAKEWOOD	80535-80535	LAPORTE	80807-80807	BURLINGTON	81071-81071	SHERIDAN LAKE
80229-80231	DENVER	80536-80536	LIVERMORE	80808-80808	CALHAN	81073-81073	SPRINGFIELD
80232-80232	LAKEWOOD	80537-80539	LOVELAND	80809-80809	CASCADE	81074-81074	STARKVILLE
80233-80299	DENVER	80540-80540	LYONS	80810-80810	CHEYENNE WELLS	81075-81075	STONINGTON
80301-80329	BOULDER	80541-80541	MASONVILLE	80812-80812	COPE	81076-81076	SUGAR CITY
80401-80419	GOLDEN	80542-80542	MEAD	80813-80813	CRIPPLE CREEK	81077-81077	SWINK
80420-80420	ALMA	80543-80543	MILLIKEN	80814-80814	DIVIDE	81081-81081	TRINCHERA
80421-80421	BAILEY	80544-80544	NIWOT	80815-80815	FLAGLER	81082-81082	TRINIDAD
80422-80422	BLACK HAWK	80545-80545	RED FEATHER LAKES	80816-80816	FLORISSANT	81084-81084	TWO BUTTES
80423-80423	BOND	80546-80546	SEVERANCE	80817-80817	FOUNTAIN	81087-81087	VILAS
80424-80424	BRECKENRIDGE	80547-80547	TIMNATH	80818-80818	GENOA	81089-81089	WALSENBURG
80425-80425	BUFFALO CREEK	80548-80548	LAPORTE	80819-80819	GREEN MOUNTAIN FALLS	81090-81090	WALSH
80426-80426	BURNS	80548-80548	VIRGINIA DALE	80820-80820	GUFFEY	81091-81091	WESTON
80427-80427	CENTRAL CITY	80549-80549	WELLINGTON	80821-80821	HUGO	81092-81092	WILEY
80428-80428	CLARK	80550-80551	WINDSOR	80822-80822	JOES	81101-81102	ALAMOSA
80429-80429	CLIMAX	80553-80553	FORT COLLINS	80823-80823	KARVAL	81120-81120	ANTONITO
80430-80430	COALMONT	80601-80603	BRIGHTON	80824-80824	KIRK	81121-81121	ARBOLES
80432-80432	COMO	80610-80610	AULT	80825-80825	KIT CARSON	81122-81122	BAYFIELD
80433-80433	CONIFER	80611-80611	BRIGGSDALE	80826-80826	LIMON	81123-81123	BLANCA
80434-80434	COWDREY	80612-80612	CARR	80827-80827	LAKE GEORGE	81124-81124	CAPULIN
80435-80435	DILLON	80614-80614	EASTLAKE	80828-80828	LIMON	81125-81125	CENTER
80436-80436	DUMONT	80615-80615	EATON	80829-80829	MANITOU SPRINGS	81126-81126	CHAMA
80437-80437	EVERGREEN	80620-80620	EVANS	80830-80830	MATHESON	81127-81127	CHIMNEY ROCK
80438-80438	EMPIRE	80621-80621	FORT LUPTON	80831-80831	PEYTON	81128-81128	CHROMO
80439-80439	EVERGREEN	80622-80622	GALETON	80832-80832	RAMAH	81129-81129	CONEJOS
80440-80440	FAIRPLAY	80623-80623	GILCREST	80833-80833	RUSH	81130-81130	CREEDE
80441-80441	FOXTON	80624-80624	GILL	80834-80834	SEIBERT	81131-81131	CRESTONE
80442-80442	FRASER	80631-80639	GREELEY	80835-80835	SIMLA	81132-81132	DEL NORTE
80443-80443	FRISCO	80640-80640	HENDERSON	80836-80836	STRATTON	81133-81133	FORT GARLAND
80444-80444	GEORGETOWN	80642-80642	HUDSON	80840-80841	U S A F ACADEMY	81134-81134	GARCIA
80446-80446	GRANBY	80643-80643	KEENESBURG	80860-80860	VICTOR	81135-81135	HOMELAKE
80447-80447	GRAND LAKE	80644-80644	KERSEY	80861-80861	VONA	81136-81136	HOOPER
80448-80448	GRANT	80645-80645	LA SALLE	80862-80862	WILD HORSE	81137-81137	IGNACIO
80449-80449	HARTSEL	80646-80646	LUCERNE	80863-80863	WOODLAND PARK	81138-81138	JAROSO
80451-80451	HOT SULPHUR SPRINGS	80648-80648	NUNN	80864-80864	YODER	81140-81140	LA JARA
80452-80452	IDAHO SPRINGS	80649-80649	ORCHARD	80866-80866	WOODLAND PARK	81141-81141	MANASSA
80453-80453	IDLEDALE	80650-80650	PIERCE	80900-80997	COLORADO SPRINGS	81143-81143	MOFFAT

81144-81144 MONTE VISTA	81221-81221 COAL CREEK	81243-81243 POWDERHORN	81325-81325 EGNAR
81146-81146 MOSCA	81222-81222 COALDALE	81244-81244 ROCKVALE	81326-81326 HESPERUS
81147-81147 PAGOSA SPRINGS	81223-81223 COTOPAXI	81246-81246 CANON CITY	81327-81327 LEWIS
81148-81148 ROMEO	81224-81225 CRESTED BUTTE	81247-81247 GUNNISON	81328-81328 MANCOS
81149-81149 SAGUACHE	81226-81226 FLORENCE	81248-81248 SARGENTS	81329-81329 MARVEL
81150-81150 SAN ACACIO	81227-81227 MONARCH	81249-81249 SILVER CLIFF	81330-81330 MESA VERDE NATIONAL
81151-81151 SANFORD	81228-81228 GRANITE	81250-81250 COTOPAXI	PARK
81152-81152 SAN LUIS	81230-81231 GUNNISON	81251-81251 TWIN LAKES	81331-81331 PLEASANT VIEW
81153-81153 SAN PABLO	81232-81232 HILLSIDE	81251-81251 TWIN LAKES CPO	81332-81332 RICO
81154-81154 SOUTH FORK	81233-81233 HOWARD	81252-81252 WESTCLIFFE	81333-81333 SLICK ROCK
81155-81155 VILLA GROVE	81235-81235 LAKE CITY	81253-81253 WETMORE	81334-81334 TOWAOC
81157-81157 PAGOSA SPRINGS	81236-81236 NATHROP	81290-81290 FLORENCE	81335-81335 YELLOW JACKET
81201-81201 SALIDA	81237-81237 OHIO CITY	81301-81303 DURANGO	81401-81402 MONTROSE
81210-81210 ALMONT	81239-81239 PARLIN	81320-81320 CAHONE	81410-81410 AUSTIN
81211-81211 BUENA VISTA	81240-81240 PENROSE	81321-81321 CORTEZ	81411-81411 BEDROCK
81212-81215 CANON CITY	81241-81241 PITKIN	81323-81323 DOLORES	81413-81413 CEDAREDGE
81220-81220 CIMARRON	81242-81242 PONCHA SPRINGS	81324-81324 DOVE CREEK	81414-81414 CORY
81415-81415 CRAWFORD	81432-81432 RIDGWAY	81615-81615 SNOWMASS VILLAGE	81640-81640 MAYBELL
81416-81416 DELTA	81433-81433 SILVERTON	81620-81620 AVON	81641-81641 MEEKER
81418-81418 ECKERT	81434-81434 SOMERSET	81621-81621 BASALT	81642-81642 MEREDITH
81419-81419 HOTCHKISS	81435-81435 TELLURIDE	81623-81623 CARBONDALE	81643-81643 MESA
81420-81420 LAZEAR	81501-81506 GRAND JUNCTION	81624-81624 COLLBRAN	81645-81645 MINTURN
81421-81421 MAHER	81520-81520 CLIFTON	81625-81626 CRAIG	81646-81646 MOLINA
81422-81422 NATURITA	81521-81521 FRUITA	81628-81628 EL JEBEL	81647-81647 NEW CASTLE
81423-81423 NORWOOD	81522-81522 GATEWAY	81630-81630 DE BEQUE	81648-81648 RANGELY
81424-81424 NUCLA	81523-81523 GLADE PARK	81631-81631 EAGLE	81649-81649 RED CLIFF
81425-81425 OLATHE	81524-81524 LOMA	81632-81632 EDWARDS	81650-81650 RIFLE
81426-81426 OPHIR	81525-81525 MACK	81633-81633 DINOSAUR	81652-81652 SILT
81427-81427 OURAY	81526-81526 PALISADE	81635-81635 PARACHUTE	81653-81653 SLATER
81428-81428 PAONIA	81527-81527 WHITEWATER	81636-81636 BATTLEMENT MESA	81654-81654 SNOWMASS
81429-81429 PARADOX	81601-81602 GLENWOOD SPRINGS	81637-81637 GYPSUM	81655-81655 WOLCOTT
81430-81430 PLACERVILLE	81610-81610 DINOSAUR	81638-81638 HAMILTON	81656-81656 WOODY CREEK
81431-81431 REDVALE	81611-81612 ASPEN	81639-81639 HAYDEN	81657-81658 VAIL

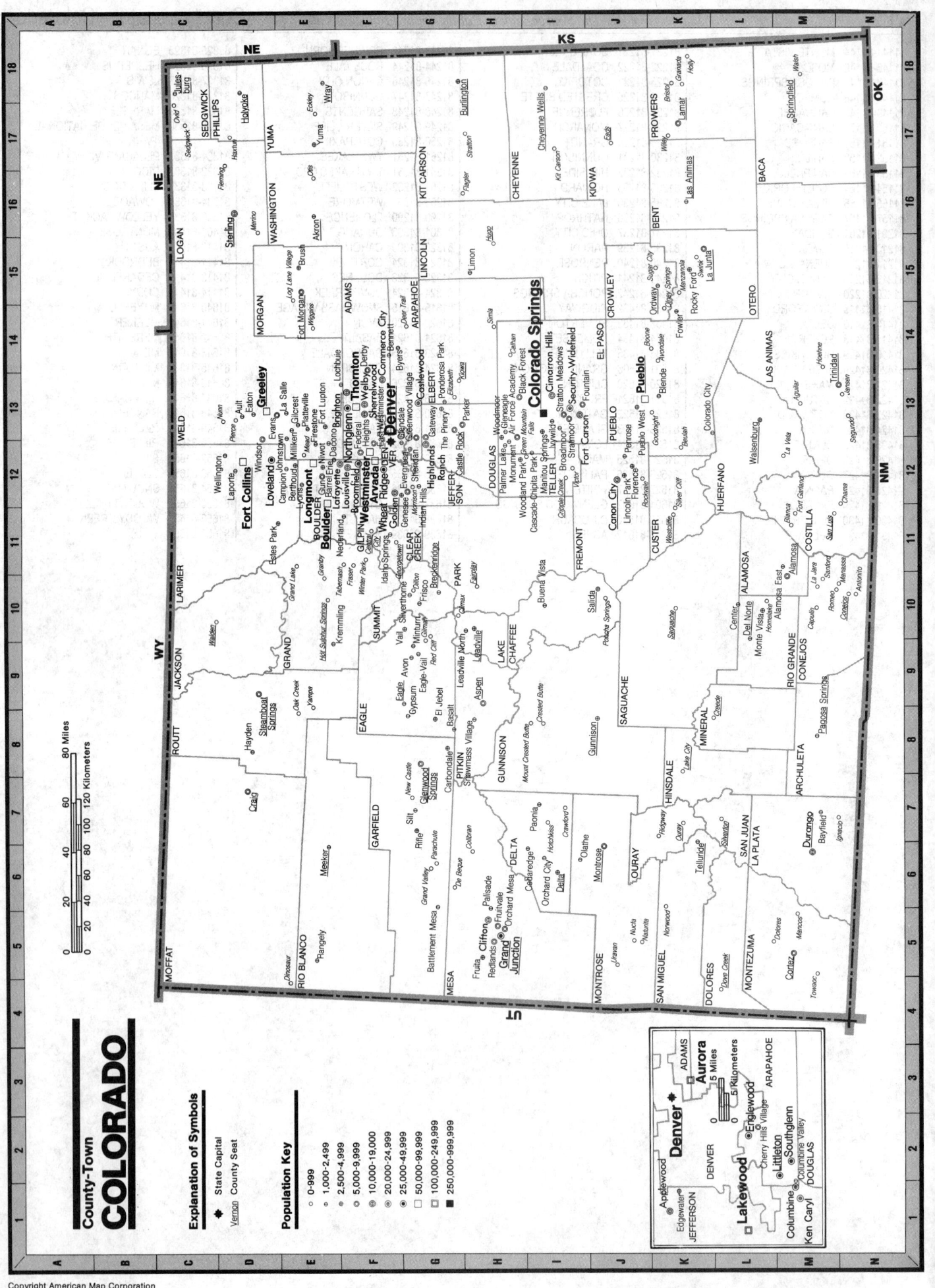

COLORADO
County-Town

Explanation of Symbols

✦ State Capital

Vernon ◉ County Seat

Population Key

○ 0-999
⊙ 1,000-2,499
⊕ 2,500-4,999
◉ 5,000-9,999
◎ 10,000-19,999
◉ 20,000-24,999
◉ 25,000-49,999
◉ 50,000-99,999
☐ 100,000-249,999
■ 250,000-999,999

COUNTIES

(63 Counties)

Name of County	Population	Location on Map
ADAMS	265,038	F-14
ALAMOSA	13,617	L-10
ARAPAHOE	391,511	G-14
ARCHULETA	5,345	M-7
BACA	4,556	L-16
BENT	5,048	K-16
BOULDER	225,339	E-11
CHAFFEE	12,684	H-9
CHEYENNE	2,397	H-16
CLEAR CREEK	7,619	G-11
CONEJOS	7,453	M-9
COSTILLA	3,190	M-11
CROWLEY	3,946	J-14
CUSTER	1,926	K-11
DELTA	20,980	H-6
DENVER	467,610	F-12
DOLORES	1,504	K-4
DOUGLAS	60,391	H-12
EAGLE	21,928	F-8
EL PASO	397,014	J-14
ELBERT	9,646	G-13
FREMONT	32,273	I-11
GARFIELD	29,974	F-7
GILPIN	3,070	F-11
GRAND	7,966	E-9
GUNNISON	10,273	H-7
HINSDALE	467	K-7
HUERFANO	6,009	L-11
JACKSON	1,605	C-9
JEFFERSON	438,430	G-12
KIOWA	1,688	J-16
KIT CARSON	7,140	G-16
LA PLATA	32,284	L-6
LAKE	6,007	H-9
LARIMER	186,136	C-10
LAS ANIMAS	13,765	L-13
LINCOLN	4,529	G-15
LOGAN	17,567	C-15
MESA	93,145	G-4
MINERAL	558	K-8
MOFFAT	11,357	C-5
MONTEZUMA	18,672	L-4
MONTROSE	24,423	J-4
MORGAN	21,939	D-14
OTERO	20,185	L-14
OURAY	2,295	J-6
PARK	7,174	G-10
PHILLIPS	4,189	D-17
PITKIN	12,661	G-8
PROWERS	13,347	K-17
PUEBLO	123,051	J-13
RIO BLANCO	5,972	E-4
RIO GRANDE	10,770	M-9
ROUTT	14,088	C-8
SAGUACHE	4,619	J-8
SAN JUAN	745	L-6
SAN MIGUEL	3,653	K-4
SEDGWICK	2,690	C-17
SUMMIT	12,881	F-10
TELLER	12,468	H-12
WASHINGTON	4,812	D-15
WELD	131,821	C-13
YUMA	8,954	D-17
TOTAL	**3,294,394**	

CITIES AND TOWNS

Note: The first name is that of the city or town, second, that of the county in which it is located, then the population and location on the map.

● Air Force Academy, El Paso, 9,062		H-13
Akron, Washington, 1,599		E-16
Alamosa, Alamosa, 7,579		M-10
● Alamosa East, Alamosa, 1,389		M-11
● Applewood, Jefferson, 11,069		
Arvada, Adams/Jefferson, 89,235		F-12
Aspen, Pitkin, 5,049		H-9
Ault, Weld, 1,107		D-13
Aurora, Adams/Arapahoe/ Douglas, 222,103		K-3
Avon, Eagle, 1,798		F-9
Basalt, Eagle/Pitkin, 1,128		G-8
● Battlement Mesa, Garfield, 1,477		G-6
Bayfield, La Plata, 1,090		M-7
Bennett, Adams, 1,757		F-14
Berthoud, Larimer, 2,990		E-12
● Black Forest, El Paso, 8,143		H-13
Blende, Pueblo		K-13
Boulder, Boulder, 83,312		E-11
Breckenridge, Summit, 1,285		G-10
Brighton, Adams/Weld, 14,203		F-13
Broomfield, Adams/Boulder/ Jefferson/Weld, 24,638		E-15
Brush, Morgan, 4,165		D-15
Buena Vista, Chaffee, 1,752		I-10
Burlington, Kit Carson, 2,941		G-18
● Byers, Arapahoe, 1,065		F-14
● Campion, Larimer, 1,692		E-12
Canon City, Fremont, 12,687		J-12
Carbondale, Garfield, 3,004		G-8
● Cascade-Chipita Park, El Paso, 1,479		H-13
Castle Rock, Douglas, 8,708		G-13
Castlewood, Arapahoe, 24,392		G-13
Cedaredge, Delta, 1,380		I-6
Center, Rio Grande/Saguache, 1,963		L-10
Central City, Gilpin, 335		F-11
● Cherry Hills Village, Arapahoe, 5,245		L-2
Cheyenne Wells, Cheyenne, 1,128		I-18
● Cimarron Hills, El Paso, 11,160		I-13
Clifton, Mesa, 12,671		H-5
● Colorado City, Pueblo, 1,149		K-13
Colorado Springs, El Paso, 281,140		I-13
● Columbine, Arapahoe/Jefferson, 23,969		M-1
● Columbine Valley, Arapahoe, 1,071		M-2
Commerce City, Adams, 16,466		F-13
● Conejos, Conejos		N-10
Cortez, Montezuma, 7,284		M-5
Craig, Moffat, 8,091		D-7
Creede, Mineral, 362		L-8
Cripple Creek, Teller, 584		I-12
Dacono, Weld, 2,228		E-12
Del Norte, Rio Grande, 1,674		L-10
Delta, Delta, 3,789		I-6
Denver, Denver, 467,610		F-12
Derby, Adams, 6,043		F-14
Dove Creek, Dolores, 643		L-4
Durango, La Plata, 12,430		M-6
Eads, Kiowa, 780		J-17
Eagle, Eagle, 1,580		F-9
Eagle-Vail, Eagle, 1,922		G-9
Eaton, Weld, 1,959		D-13
Edgewater, Jefferson, 4,613		K-1
El Jebel, Eagle, 2,605		G-8
Englewood, Arapahoe, 29,387		L-2
Erie, Boulder/Weld, 1,258		E-12
Estes Park, Larimer, 3,184		D-11
Evans, Weld, 5,877		D-13
Evergreen, Jefferson, 7,582		H-10
Fairplay, Park, 387		H-10
Federal Heights, Adams, 9,342		F-12
Firestone, Weld, 1,358		E-12
Florence, Fremont, 2,990		J-12
Fort Carson, El Paso, 11,309		I-13
Fort Collins, Larimer, 87,758		D-12
Fort Lupton, Weld, 5,159		E-13
Fort Morgan, Morgan, 9,068		E-15
Fountain, El Paso, 9,984		I-13
Fowler, Otero, 1,154		K-14
Frisco, Summit, 1,601		G-10
Fruita, Mesa, 4,045		H-5
● Fruitvale, Mesa, 5,222		H-5
● Gateway, Douglas, 7,510		G-12
Genesee, Jefferson, 2,737		F-12
Georgetown, Clear Creek, 891		F-11
Gilcrest, Weld, 1,084		E-13
Glendale, Arapahoe, 2,453		G-12
● Gleneagle, El Paso, 1,661		H-13
Glenwood Springs, Garfield, 6,561		G-8
Golden, Jefferson, 13,116		F-12
Grand Junction, Mesa, 29,034		H-5
Greeley, Weld, 60,536		D-13
● Greenwood Village, Arapahoe, 7,589		G-13
● Gunbarrel, Boulder, 9,388		E-12
Gunnison, Gunnison, 4,636		J-8
Gypsum, Eagle, 1,750		F-8
● Hayden, Routt, 1,444		D-8
● Highlands Ranch, Douglas, 10,181		G-12
Holyoke, Phillips, 1,931		D-18
Hot Sulphur Springs, Grand, 347		E-10
Hugo, Lincoln, 660		H-15
● Idaho Springs, Clear Creek, 1,834		F-11
● Indian Hills, Jefferson		G-12
Ivywild, El Paso		I-13
Johnstown, Weld, 1,579		E-12
Julesburg, Sedgwick, 1,295		C-18
● Ken Caryl, Jefferson, 24,391		M-1
Kiowa, Elbert, 275		G-13
Kremmling, Grand, 1,166		E-9
La Junta, Otero, 7,637		K-15
La Salle, Weld, 1,783		E-13
Lafayette, Boulder, 14,548		F-12
Lake City, Hinsdale, 223		K-8
Lakewood, Jefferson, 126,481		L-1
Lamar, Prowers, 8,343		K-17
Laporte, Larimer		D-12
Las Animas, Bent, 2,481		K-16
Leadville, Lake, 2,629		H-10
● Leadville North, Lake, 1,757		H-10
Limon, Lincoln, 1,831		H-15
● Lincoln Park, Fremont, 3,728		J-12
Littleton, Arapahoe/Douglas, 33,685		M-2
Lochbuie, Weld, 1,168		E-13
Longmont, Boulder, 51,555		E-12
Louisville, Boulder, 12,361		F-12
Loveland, Larimer, 37,352		D-12
Lyons, Boulder, 1,227		E-12
● Manitou Springs, El Paso, 4,535		I-13
Meeker, Rio Blanco, 2,098		E-6
Milliken, Weld, 1,605		E-13
Minturn, Eagle, 1,066		G-9
Monte Vista, Rio Grande, 4,324		L-10
Montrose, Montrose, 8,854		J-6
Monument, El Paso, 1,020		H-13
Nederland, Boulder, 1,099		F-11
● Niwot, Boulder, 2,666		E-12
Northglenn, Adams/Weld, 27,195		F-13
Olathe, Montrose, 1,263		I-6
Orchard City, Delta, 2,218		I-6
Orchard Mesa, Mesa, 5,977		H-5
Ordway, Crowley, 1,025		K-15
Ouray, Ouray, 644		K-7
● Pagosa Springs, Archuleta, 1,207		
Palisade, Mesa, 1,871		H-6
Palmer Lake, El Paso, 1,480		H-12
Paonia, Delta, 1,403		I-7
Parker, Douglas, 5,450		G-13
Penrose, Fremont, 2,235		J-12
Platteville, Weld, 1,515		E-13
● Ponderosa Park, Elbert, 1,640		J-13
Pueblo, Pueblo, 98,640		J-13
● Pueblo West, Pueblo, 4,386		J-13
Rangely, Rio Blanco, 2,278		E-5
● Redlands, Mesa, 9,355		H-5
Rifle, Garfield, 4,636		G-7
Rocky Ford, Otero, 4,162		K-15
Saguache, Saguache, 584		K-10
Salida, Chaffee, 4,737		J-10
San Luis, Costilla, 800		M-11
● Security-Widefield, El Paso, 23,822		
Sheridan, Arapahoe, 4,976		G-12
Sherrelwood, Adams, 16,636		F-13
Silt, Garfield, 1,095		G-7
Silverthorne, Summit, 1,768		F-10
Silverton, San Juan, 716		L-7
Snowmass Village, Pitkin, 1,449		H-8
Southglenn, Arapahoe, 43,087		M-2
Springfield, Baca, 1,475		M-17
● Steamboat Springs, Routt, 6,695		D-9
Sterling, Logan, 10,362		D-16
● Stratmoor, El Paso, 5,854		I-13
Stratton Meadows, El Paso		I-13
Telluride, San Miguel, 1,309		K-6
● The Pinery, Douglas, 4,885		G-13
Thornton, Adams, 55,031		F-13
Trinidad, Las Animas, 8,580		N-13
Vail, Eagle, 3,659		G-10
Walden, Jackson, 890		C-10
Walsenburg, Huerfano, 3,300		L-13
● Welby, Adams, 10,218		F-13
Wellington, Larimer, 1,340		D-12
Westcliffe, Custer, 312		K-11
● Westminster, Adams/Jefferson, 74,625		F-12
● Westminster East, Adams, 5,197		F-12
Wheat Ridge, Jefferson, 29,419		F-12
Windsor, Weld, 5,062		D-12
Woodland Park, Teller, 4,610		H-12
● Woodmoor, El Paso, 3,858		H-13
Wray, Yuma, 1,998		E-18
Yuma, Yuma, 2,719		E-17

Connecticut

General Help Numbers:

Governor's Office

State Capitol, 210 Capitol Ave   860-566-4840
Hartford, CT 06106   Fax 860-566-4677
www.state.ct.us/governor   8AM-5PM

Attorney General's Office

PO Box 120   860-808-5318
Hartford, CT 06141-0120   Fax 860-808-5387
www.cslib.org/attygenl   8:30AM-4:30PM

Legislative Records

State Library, Bill Room 231   860-757-6550
Hartford, CT 06106   Fax 860-757-6594
www. cga.state.ct.us/default.asp   9AM-5PM

State Archives

History & Genealogy Unit   860-757-6580
231 Capitol Ave   Fax 860-757-7767
Hartford, CT 06106   9AM-5PM M-F
www.cslib.org/archives.htm

State Specifics:

Capital: Hartford
    Hartford County

Time Zone: EST

Number of Counties: 8

Population: 3,483,372

Web Site: www.state.ct.us

State Agencies

Criminal Records

Department of Public Safety, Bureau of Identification, PO Box 2794, Middletown, CT 06757-9294 (Courier: 1111 Country Club Rd, Middleton, CT 06457); 860-685-8480, 860-685-8361 (Fax), 8:30AM-4:30PM.

www.state.ct.us/dps/spbi.htm

Note: DPS-846-C Form "State Police Bureau of Identification Request" can be downloaded from the website.

Indexing & Storage: Records are available from the 1950's on. Records were first computerized in 1983. It takes about 30 days before new records are available for inquiry. Records are normally destroyed after subject reaches 100th birthdate.

Searching: Records are open to the public using a name search. Fingerprint searches are not available to the public. Pending case information is available. Include the following in your request-date of birth. Request forms may be downloaded from the website. Approximately 90% of the records on file are fingerprint supported. The

following data is not released: dismissals or juvenile records.

Access by: mail, in person.

Fee & Payment: The fee is $25.00 per request. Fee payee: Commissioner of Public Safety. Prepayment required. Personal checks accepted. No credit cards accepted.

Mail search: Turnaround time: 7 to 10 days. Records must be in writing.

In person search: Request must be on agency form; results are mailed only. If you come in-person, the results are still mailed.

Statewide Court Records

Chief Court Administrator, 231 Capitol Ave, Hartford, CT 06106; 860-757-2100, 860-757-2270 (External Affairs), 860-757-2215 (Fax), 8AM-5PM.

www.jud.state.ct.us

Note: Specific requests for case information should be obtained from the court itself.

Indexing & Storage: Records are available for all data entry completed by close of business the previous day. Records are normally destroyed (actually unavailable, not destroyed) after being termed "erased" or sealed.

Access by: online. No searching by mail.

Online search: Online access allows for civil, housing and family cases only at the party name inquiry page at www.jud2.state.ct.us/Civil_Inquiry/GetParty.asp. Assignment lists and calendars are also available free at www.jud2.state.ct.us. Opinions from the Supreme and Appellete courts are available from the general website.

Sexual Offender Registry

Department of Public Safety, Sex Offender Registry Unit, PO Box 2794, Middletown, CT 06757-9294 (Courier: 1111 Country Club Rd, Middleton, CT 06457); 860-685-8060, 860-685-8349 (Fax), 8:30AM-4:30PM.

www.state.ct.us/dps/Sex_Offender_Registry.htm

Note: It is suggested to visit local law enforcement if you cannot search online.

Indexing & Storage: Records are available from October 1, 1988. It takes 1 day before new records are available for inquiry. Records are normally destroyed after registry term expires.

Searching: Include the following in your request-date of birth. The following data is not released: names of victims and treatment information.

Access by: online.

Fee & Payment: There is no fee. The agency will not honor written requests.

Online search: The website has two searches: those convicted of a CT law, and those offenders who violated a law in a different state but are living in CT. Search by name or location, ZIP Code, or entire list.

Incarceration Records

Connecticut Department of Corrections, Public Information Office, 24 Wolcott Hill Rd, Wethersfield, CT 06109, 860-692-7780 (Locater), 860-692-7783 (Fax), 8:30AM-4:30PM.

www.ct.gov/doc/site/default.asp

Indexing & Storage: Records are available on current and former inmates, except for the website which is current only. Computerized records go back to 1970. It takes about 30 days before new records are available for inquiry.

Searching: Records are open to the public using a name search. Location, conviction and sentencing information, bond, and release dates are released. Include the following in your request-name; DOB and SSN are helpful.

Access by: mail, phone, online.

Fee & Payment: There is no fee.

Mail search: Turnaround time: 7 to 10 days.

Phone search: For phone search, use the "Locater" number listed above.

Online search: Current inmates may be searched at www.ctinmateinfo.state.ct.us/searchop.asp.

Corporation, Limited Partnership, Trademarks, Servicemarks, Limited Liability Company, Limited Liability Partnership, Statutory Trust Records

Secretary of State, Commercial Recording Division, 30 Trinity St, Hartford, CT 06106; 860-509-6003, 860-509-6069 (Fax), 8:30AM-4PM.

www.sots.state.ct.us

Note: Assumed names are found at the town level.

Indexing & Storage: New records are available for inquiry immediately. Records are indexed on microfilm, inhouse computer.

Searching: Include the following in your request-full name of business, specific records that you need copies of. In addition to the articles of incorporation, corporation records include the following information: Annual Reports, Officers, Directors, Prior (merged) names, Inactive and Reserved names.

Access by: mail, phone, fax, in person, online.

Fee & Payment: The search fee is $20.00 per business name for copies of documents on record. Add $5.00 for certification. Fee payee: Secretary of State. Prepayment required. Personal checks accepted. Credit cards accepted: MasterCard, Visa.

Mail search: Turnaround time: 2 to 3 days. No SASE is required.

Phone search: Only limited, basic information is available by phone.

Fax search: Requests accepted by fax.

In person search: Certain, limited information is available at no charge.

Online search: Click on the CONCORD option at the website for free access to corporation and UCC records. The system is open from 7AM to 11PM. You can search by business name only.

Expedited service: Expedited service is available on limited filings for an add'l $25.00 per business name. Turnaround time: 24 hours. The fee is per transaction requested; review is one transaction, copy is another, etc.

Uniform Commercial Code, Federal Tax Liens, State Tax Liens

UCC Division, Secretary of State, PO Box 150470, Hartford, CT 06115-0470 (Courier: 30 Trinity St, Hartford, CT 06106); 860-509-6002, 860-509-6069 (Fax), 8:30AM-4PM.

www.sots.state.ct.us

Indexing & Storage: Records are available from 8/94 on computer, earlier records are on microfilm from 10/80. It takes one month or less before new records are available for inquiry.

Searching: Use search request form UCC-11. The search includes tax liens. Include the following in your request-debtor name or original.

Access by: mail, fax, in person, online.

Fee & Payment: UCC searches include tax liens and are free if requested in person, $25.00 per name by mail. Copies are $20.00 for a plain copy or $25.00 for a certified copy. Fee payee: Secretary of State. Prepayment required. Credit cards are accepted for in-person searching only. Personal checks accepted. Credit cards accepted: MasterCard, Visa.

Mail search: Turnaround time: 3 to 5 days.

Fax search: Use of credit card required.

In person search: Walk-in service available, excepted for prepared documents.

Online search: Records may be accessed at no charge on the Internet. Click on the CONCORD ON-LINE option (lower right corner). The system is open 7AM to 11PM.

Other access: Bulk lists and CDs are available for purchase. Call the Financial Area at 860-509-6165.

Sales Tax Registrations

Dept of Revenue - Taxpayer Services Division, Sales Tax Registrations, 25 Sigourney St, Hartford, CT 06106; 860-297-4885, 860-297-5714 (Fax), 8AM-5PM.

www.ct.gov/drs/site/default.asp

Indexing & Storage: It takes up to 3 weeks before new records are available for inquiry. Records are normally destroyed after 5 years after date of abatement for abated taxpayer files and 5 years after "out-of-business notice" for out-of-business taxpayer files.

Searching: This agency will only confirm that the business is registered and active. They will provide no other information. Include the following in your request-business name. They will also search by tax permit number. Authorized business representatives may request copies of their records only by mail, fax, or in person.

Access by: mail, phone, fax, in person.

Fee & Payment: There is no search fee

Mail search: Turnaround time: 1 day.

Phone search: Records available by phone only to verify a permit was issued.

Fax search: Same criteria as mail searches.

In person search: If the question is more than "has a permit been issued," the requester must have documents completed and have legal authority to make request.

Birth Certificates, Death Records, Marriage Certificates

Access to Records is Restricted

Department of Public Health, Vital Records Section MS# 11VRS, PO Box 340308, Hartford, CT 06134-0308 (Courier: 410 Capitol Ave, Hartford, CT 06134); 860-509-7897, 860-509-7964 (Fax), 8:30AM-4:30PM M-F.

www.dph.state.ct.us/OPPE/hpvital.htm

Note: The state is in the process of microfilming birth, death and marriage records. You must contact the town/city clerk of occurrence to obtain copies of records. The website has a list of towns and phone numbers. Records are $5.00 each at the town level.

Divorce Records

Records not maintained by a state level agency.

Note: The state does not maintain divorce records; records are available from the Chief Clerks of the 15 Judicial District Courts; See the County Courts Section. The State Vital Records Section (860-509-7897) will also provide contact info for the 15 courts.

Workers' Compensation Records

Workers Compensation Commission, 21 Oak Street, Hartford, CT 06106; 860-493-1500, 860-247-1361 (Fax), 7:45AM-4:30PM.

http://wcc.state.ct.us

Note: All files are kept at one of the eight district offices. This agency will forward the request to the proper district office, or you can order direct from the D. Office. Requesters with authorization may e-mail requests to peter.miecznikowski@state.ct.us.

Indexing & Storage: Records are available on microfilm from 1914 thru 1985 and computerized from 1985 forward, for insurance coverage files. The case files since 1995 are indexed on computer. Records are not destroyed. It takes 1 month before new records are available for inquiry.

Searching: Claims information is not released without a signed release from the employee, for employment checks. Include the following in your request-claimant name, Social Security Number (if available), date of injury, name and address of employer. Include as much information as possible. The following data is not released: medical records, commissioner's notes.

Access by: mail, phone, fax, in person.

Fee & Payment: Fees vary depending upon the nature of the request and are determined at that time. Fee payee: Workers Compensation Commission. Personal checks accepted. No credit cards accepted.

Mail search: Turnaround time: variable. A SASE is requested.

Phone search: You may call for information.

Fax search: A mail request must follow.

In person search: You may request information in person.

Other access: The agency will sell self-insured lists for $5.00.

Driver Records

Department of Motor Vehicles, Copy Records Unit, 60 State St., Wethersfield, CT 06161-0503; 860-263-5154, 8:30AM-4:30PM T-F.

www.ct.gov/dmv/site/default.asp

Note: Copies of tickets may be obtained from the Superior Court Records Center, 860-741-3714 for a fee of $3.00, or $5.00 for certified copy.

Indexing & Storage: Records are available for 3/5/10 years to present, dependent upon the type of violation. It takes 5 to 7 days before new records

are available for inquiry. Records are normally destroyed after 5 years at the discretion of the commissioner. The state does not report accidents on the driving record.

Searching: Mail and in person requesters must complete Form J-23 and state permissible use. Casual requests must include evidence of the individual's consent. The form can be ordered from the web at http://dmvct.org/formsrec.htm or by calling 860-263-5700. Include the following in your request-two forms of ID (one with photo), signed Form J-23. The driver's license number, name and address are needed when searching, the DOB is optional. A DWI first offense violation will not appear if the offender attends an "Accelerated Alcohol Class."

Access by: mail, in person, online.

Fee & Payment: The fee for walk-in or mail-in driving records is $20.00 per record (the highest fee for a driving record in the US). The fee for ordering online is $15.00. The fee for a license status check is $20.00. Fee payee: Department of Motor Vehicles. Prepayment required. Personal checks accepted. No credit cards accepted.

Mail search: Turnaround time: 2 weeks. A SASE is requested.

In person search: The state will process up to 3 requests (at one time) for walk-in requesters who have a permissible use as stipulated in C.G.S.#14-10. Please note the office is closed on Mondays.

Online search: Online access is provided to approved businesses that enter into written contract. The contract requires a prepayment with minimum hits annually and a surety bond. Fee is $15.00 per record. The address is part of the record. For more information, call 203-805-6093. The program is open 24/7.

Other access: Batch requests are available for approved users, call 203-805-6093 for details.

Vehicle Ownership, Vehicle Identification

Department of Motor Vehicles, Copy Record Unit, 60 State St, Wethersfield, CT 06161-1896; 860-263-5154, 8:AM-4:30PM T- F.

www.ct.gov/dmv/site/default.asp

Note: Section 14-10 of the Connecticut General Statutes regulates the release of record information in accordance with federal DPPA guidelines.

Indexing & Storage: Records are available for 3 years to present. Any records prior to this period may be destroyed at the discretion of the commissioner. It takes six weeks before new records are available for inquiry.

Searching: Permissible users of the information are listed on back of Form J-23. Otherwise, requester must include evidence of subject's written consent. Form J-23 can be downloaded from the website or obtained calling 860-263-5700. Include the following in your request-two forms of ID and one must contain a photo of the person signing the Form. Name searches and license plate searches are available to J-23 approved requesters. Businesses requesting for permissible purposes may only confirm the accuracy of personal information submitted by an individual to them.

Access by: mail, in person, online.

Fee & Payment: Title searches-$17.50 per search; most other records are $20.00 each, including current owner searches. Certification is an

additional $20.00. A copy of an original title or registration application is $7.00. A full charge is for a "no record found." Fee payee: Department of Motor Vehicles. Prepayment required. Personal checks accepted. No credit cards accepted.

Mail search: Turnaround time: 3 to 4 working days. The agency requests that you use their Form J-23. A SASE is requested.

In person search: The state will process up to 3 requests (file information only) for walk-in customers. Drop off requests accepted. Please note the office is closed on Mondays.

Online search: Vehicle record information is available on a volume basis to approved businesses that enter into a written agreement. The contract requires an annual fee and a surety bond. For more information, call 860-805-6093.

Accident Reports

Department of Public Safety, Reports and Records Unit, PO Box 2794, Middletown, CT 06457-9294; 860-685-8250, 8:30AM-4:30PM.

Indexing & Storage: Records are available from 10 years to present. Searching by name only goes back 5 years.

Searching: The request should include data and location of incident, names of operators, and the 8 digit case number (if known). The following data is not released: pending cases or sealed records.

Access by: mail, phone.

Fee & Payment: Prepayment of the $8.00 search fee per record is required. Fee payee: Commissioner of Public Safety. Personal checks accepted. No credit cards accepted.

Mail search: Turnaround time: 2 to 4 weeks. A SASE is requested.

Phone search: Confirmation of records are available by phone.

Vessel Ownership, Vessel Registration

Department of Motor Vehicles, Marine Vessel Section, 60 State Street, Wethersfield, CT 06161-3032; 860-263-5151, 860-263-5555 (Fax), 8AM-5PM T-F; til 12:30 PM Sat.

www.ct.gov/dmv/cwp/view.asp?A=818&Q=245044

Note: Lien information is found at the Secretary of State.

Indexing & Storage: Records are available from 1981, records are maintained on computer for 4 years then placed on microfiche. All motorized boats any length, and all vessels over 19.5 ft without motor must be registered. Records are normally destroyed after 5 years.

Searching: All requests must be in writing. Requests follow requirements of DPPA. Use Form J-23B. Include the following in your request-photo ID and money. Either the name, CT registration number or hull number is needed to do a search.

Access by: mail, in person.

Fee & Payment: The fee is $20.00 for a current owner search or for a copy of the registration and $17.50 for a complete boat history. Certification is an additional $20.00. Fee payee: Department of Motor Vehicles. Prepayment required. Personal checks accepted. No credit cards accepted.

Mail search: Turnaround time: 1 to 2 weeks. No SASE is required.

In person search: Results are returned by mail. The agency is closed to the public on Mondays.

Other access: Bulk list information is available by contract. The fee depends on data requested. Call 860-263-5241 for ordering procedures.

Voter Registration
Records not maintained by a state level agency.
Note: Records are open at the town level. There are 169 towns.

GED Certificates
Department of Education, GED Records, 25 Industrial Park Rd, Middletown, CT 06457; 860-807-2110, 860-807-2112 (Fax), 8AM-5PM.

www.state.ct.us/sde/

Searching: Include the following in your request-signed release, Social Security Number, date of birth. The year of the test is helpful. For records prior to 1982, the location of the test is needed.

Access by: mail, fax, in person.

Fee & Payment: There is no search fee.

Mail search: Turnaround time: 2 to 3 days. No SASE is required.

Fax search: There is no fee to fax back to a local phone number.

In person search: Photo ID is required.

Hunting and Fishing License Information
Department of Environmental Protection, License Division, 79 Elm St, Hartford, CT 06106; 860-424-3105, 860-424-4072 (Fax), 9AM-4PM.

www.dep.state.ct.us

Indexing & Storage: Records are available from 1995 to present. It takes 1 day before new records are available for inquiry. Records are indexed on inhouse computer. Records are normally destroyed after 10 years.

Searching: Only deer tag information is released. Include the following in your request-full name, address. All requests must be in writing.

Access by: mail, in person.

Fee & Payment: There is no search fee. Copies are $.50 per page. Fee payee: Department of Environmental Protection. Prepayment required. Personal checks accepted. No credit cards accepted.

Mail search: Turnaround time: 1 to 3 days. No SASE is required.

In person search: Must have the request in writing.

Other access: CDs are available, usually $5.00 per disk.

Connecticut State Licensing Agencies

Licenses Searchable Online

Acupuncturist #11 .... www.dph.state.ct.us/scripts/hlthprof.asp
Alcohol/Drug Counselor #11 .... www.dph.state.ct.us/scripts/hlthprof.asp
Antenna Service Dealer/Technician #5 .... www.dcpaccess.state.ct.us/DCPPublic/LicenseLookup.asp
Appraiser, MVPD/MVR #2 .... www.ct-clic.com
Architect #3 .... www.dcpaccess.state.ct.us/DCPPublic/LicenseLookup.asp
Architectural Firm #3 .... www.dcpaccess.state.ct.us/DCPPublic/LicenseLookup.asp
Asbestos Abatement Worker/Supr. #31 .... www.state.ct.us/dph/scripts/hlthprof.asp
Asbestos Consultant/Contractor #31 .... www.state.ct.us/dph/scripts/hlthprof.asp
Athletic Promoter #7 .... www.dcpaccess.state.ct.us/DCPPublic/LicenseLookup.asp
Attorney/Attorney Firm #1 .... www.jud2.state.ct.us/Civil_Inquiry/GetAtty.asp
Audiologist #11 .... www.dph.state.ct.us/scripts/hlthprof.asp
Auto Insurance Adjuster #2 .... www.ct-clic.com
Bail Bond Agent #2 .... www.ct-clic.com
Bail Enforcement Agent #13 .... www.state.ct.us/dps/SLFU/BailEnforcementLicensed.htm
Bail Enforcement Firearm Instructor #13 .... www.state.ct.us/dps/SLFU/BailEnforcementFirearmsPermit.htm
Bailbondsman #13 .... www.state.ct.us/dps/SLFU/BailBondsmanLicensed.htm
Bakery #8 .... www.dcpaccess.state.ct.us/DCPPublic/LicenseLookup.asp
Bank #6 .... www.state.ct.us/dob/pages/banklist.htm
Bank & Trust Company #6 .... www.state.ct.us/dob/pages/bcharter.htm
Bank Branch #6 .... www.state.ct.us/dob/pages/branch1.htm
Barber #11 .... www.dph.state.ct.us/scripts/hlthprof.asp
Bazaar/Raffle Permit #12 .... www.ct-clic.com/
Bedding Mfg/Renovation #4 .... www.dcpaccess.state.ct.us/DCPPublic/LicenseLookup.asp
Bedding Supply/Sterilizer #4 .... www.dcpaccess.state.ct.us/DCPPublic/LicenseLookup.asp
Beekeeper #14 .... www.caes.state.ct.us/InspectandRegandGeneral/inspecti.htm
Beverage/Water Bottler #4 .... www.dcpaccess.state.ct.us/DCPPublic/LicenseLookup.asp
Bingo Registration #12 .... www.ct-clic.com/
Boxer/Boxing Professional #7 .... www.dcpaccess.state.ct.us/DCPPublic/LicenseLookup.asp
Building Contractor #7 .... www.dcpaccess.state.ct.us/DCPPublic/LicenseLookup.asp
Casino #12 .... www.ct-clic.com/
Casino Occupation #12 .... www.ct-clic.com/
Casualty Adjuster #2 .... www.ct-clic.com
Check Cashing Service #6 .... www.state.ct.us/dob/pages/chckcash.htm
Child Caring Agency/Facility #37 .... www.state.ct.us/dcf/Licensed_Facilities/listing_CCF.asp
Child Placing Agency #37 .... www.state.ct.us/dcf/Licensed_Facilities/listing_CPA.asp
Child Psychiatric Clinic #37 .... www.state.ct.us/dcf/Licensed_Facilities/listing_OPCC.asp
Chiropractor #11 .... www.dph.state.ct.us/scripts/hlthprof.asp
Coach, High/Grade School #9 .... www.state.ct.us/sde/
Collection Agency #6 .... www.state.ct.us/dob/pages/collect.htm
Collection Agency, Consumer #6 .... www.state.ct.us/dob/pages/collect.htm
College/University #29 .... www.ctdhe.org/database/default.htm
Contractor, Mechanical #4 .... www.dcpaccess.state.ct.us/DCPPublic/LicenseLookup.asp
Cosmetologist #11 .... www.dph.state.ct.us/scripts/hlthprof.asp
Counselor, Professional #11 .... www.dph.state.ct.us/scripts/hlthprof.asp
Credit Union #6 .... www.state.ct.us/dob/pages/culist.htm
Day Treatment Facility, Extended #37 .... www.state.ct.us/dcf/Licensed_Facilities/listing_EDT.asp
Debt Adjuster #6 .... www.state.ct.us/dob/pages/debtadj.htm
Dental Anes/Conscious Sedation Permittee #11 .... www.dph.state.ct.us/scripts/hlthprof.asp
Dentist/Dental Hygienist #11 .... www.dph.state.ct.us/scripts/hlthprof.asp
Dessert Mfg, Frozen #8 .... www.dcpaccess.state.ct.us/DCPPublic/LicenseLookup.asp
Dietician/Nutritionist #11 .... www.dph.state.ct.us/scripts/hlthprof.asp
Dog Racing Owner/Trainer #12 .... www.ct-clic.com/
Druggist Liquor Permittee #15 .... www.dcpaccess.state.ct.us/DCPPublic/LicenseLookup.asp
Electrical Contractor/Inspector #7 .... www.dcpaccess.state.ct.us/DCPPublic/LicenseLookup.asp
Electrical Journeyman/Apprentice #4 .... www.dcpaccess.state.ct.us/DCPPublic/LicenseLookup.asp
Electrical Sign Installer #7 .... www.dcpaccess.state.ct.us/DCPPublic/LicenseLookup.asp

Electrician #7	www.dcpaccess.state.ct.us/DCPPublic/LicenseLookup.asp
Electrologist/Hypertricologist #11	www.dph.state.ct.us/scripts/hlthprof.asp
Electronics Service Dealer/Technician #5	www.dcpaccess.state.ct.us/DCPPublic/LicenseLookup.asp
Elevator Inspector/Mechanic #4	www.dcpaccess.state.ct.us/DCPPublic/LicenseLookup.asp
Embalmer #11	www.dph.state.ct.us/scripts/hlthprof.asp
Emergency Medical Svc Professional #11	www.dph.state.ct.us/scripts/hlthprof.asp
Engineer #4	www.dcpaccess.state.ct.us/DCPPublic/LicenseLookup.asp
Family Residence, Permanent #37	www.state.ct.us/dcf/Licensed_Facilities/listing_PFR.asp
Farm Winery #15	www.dcpaccess.state.ct.us/DCPPublic/LicenseLookup.asp
Fire Investigator, PI #13	www.state.ct.us/dps/SLFU/PrivateDetectivesLicensed.htm
Fire Protection Inspector/Contractor #4	www.dcpaccess.state.ct.us/DCPPublic/LicenseLookup.asp
Funeral Director/Home #11	www.dph.state.ct.us/scripts/hlthprof.asp
Glazier #4	www.dcpaccess.state.ct.us/DCPPublic/LicenseLookup.asp
Hairdresser #11	www.dph.state.ct.us/scripts/hlthprof.asp
Health Care Ctr. Insurer #2	www.ct-clic.com
Health Club #4	www.dcpaccess.state.ct.us/DCPPublic/LicenseLookup.asp
Hearing Instrument Specialist #11	www.dph.state.ct.us/scripts/hlthprof.asp
Heating, Piping, Cooling Cont./Journeyman #4	www.dcpaccess.state.ct.us/DCPPublic/LicenseLookup.asp
Homeopathic Physician #11	www.dph.state.ct.us/scripts/hlthprof.asp
Honey Bee Registration #14	www.caes.state.ct.us/InspectandRegandGeneral/inspecti.htm
Hypertrichologist #11	www.dph.state.ct.us/scripts/hlthprof.asp
Insurance Adjuster/Public Adjuster #2	www.ct-clic.com
Insurance Agent, Fraternal #2	www.ct-clic.com
Insurance Appraiser #2	www.ct-clic.com
Insurance Company/Producer/Consultant #2	www.ct-clic.com
Interior Designer #4	www.dcpaccess.state.ct.us/DCPPublic/LicenseLookup.asp
Juice Producer #8	www.dcpaccess.state.ct.us/DCPPublic/LicenseLookup.asp
Land Surveyor Firm #3	www.dcpaccess.state.ct.us/DCPPublic/LicenseLookup.asp
Landscape Architect #3	www.dcpaccess.state.ct.us/DCPPublic/LicenseLookup.asp
Lead Abatement Professional #11	www.dph.state.ct.us/scripts/hlthprof.asp
Lead Planner/Project Designer #11	www.dph.state.ct.us/scripts/hlthprof.asp
Legalized Gaming Occupation #12	www.ct-clic.com/
Liquor License #15	www.dcpaccess.state.ct.us/DCPPublic/LicenseLookup.asp
Liquor Mfg/Dist/Whlse #15	www.dcpaccess.state.ct.us/DCPPublic/LicenseLookup.asp
Liquor Store/Broker/Shipper #15	www.dcpaccess.state.ct.us/DCPPublic/LicenseLookup.asp
Loan Company, Small #6	www.state.ct.us/dob/pages/smalloan.htm
Lobbyist #18	www.ethics.state.ct.us/publicinfo.htm
Lottery #12	www.ct-clic.com/
Lottery Sales Agent #12	www.ct-clic.com/
Marriage & Family Therapist #11	www.dph.state.ct.us/scripts/hlthprof.asp
Marshall, State #34	www.jud.state.ct.us/faq/marshals.htm
Martial Arts Facility #4	www.dcpaccess.state.ct.us/DCPPublic/LicenseLookup.asp
Massage Therapist #11	www.dph.state.ct.us/scripts/hlthprof.asp
Mausoleum #11	www.dph.state.ct.us/scripts/hlthprof.asp
Medical Doctor #11	www.dph.state.ct.us/scripts/hlthprof.asp
Medical Response Technician #11	www.dph.state.ct.us/scripts/hlthprof.asp
Midwife #11	www.dph.state.ct.us/scripts/hlthprof.asp
Mobile Home Park/Seller #17	www.dcpaccess.state.ct.us/DCPPublic/LicenseLookup.asp
Money Forwarder #6	www.state.ct.us/dob/pages/$forward.htm
Mortgage (1st) Broker/Lender #6	www.state.ct.us/dob/pages/1stmtg.htm
Mortgage (2nd) Broker/Lender #6	www.state.ct.us/dob/pages/2ndmtg.htm
Naturopathic Physician #11	www.dph.state.ct.us/scripts/hlthprof.asp
New Home Construction Contractor #4	www.dcpaccess.state.ct.us/DCPPublic/LicenseLookup.asp
Nurse #11	www.dph.state.ct.us/scripts/hlthprof.asp
Nurse, Advance Registered Practice #11	www.dph.state.ct.us/scripts/hlthprof.asp
Nurse-LPN #11	www.dph.state.ct.us/scripts/hlthprof.asp
Nursery Plant Dealer #14	www.caes.state.ct.us/InspectandRegandGeneral/inspecti.htm
Nursery, Plant #14	www.caes.state.ct.us/InspectandRegandGeneral/inspecti.htm
Nursing Home Administrator #11	www.dph.state.ct.us/scripts/hlthprof.asp
Occupational Therapist/Assistant #11	www.dph.state.ct.us/scripts/hlthprof.asp
Off-Track Betting #12	www.ct-clic.com/
Optical Shop #11	www.dph.state.ct.us/scripts/hlthprof.asp

Optician #11	www.dph.state.ct.us/scripts/hlthprof.asp
Optometrist #11	www.dph.state.ct.us/scripts/hlthprof.asp
Osteopathic Physician #11	www.dph.state.ct.us/scripts/hlthprof.asp
Paramedic #11	www.dph.state.ct.us/scripts/hlthprof.asp
Pesticide Applicator #26	www.kellysolutions.com/CT/Applicators/index.htm
Pesticide-related Business #26	www.kellysolutions.com/CT/Business/index.htm
Pharmacist/Pharmacist Intern #4	www.dcpaccess.state.ct.us/DCPPublic/LicenseLookup.asp
Pharmacy #4	www.dcpaccess.state.ct.us/DCPPublic/LicenseLookup.asp
Pharmacy Technician #4	www.dcpaccess.state.ct.us/DCPPublic/LicenseLookup.asp
Physical Therapist/Assistant #11	www.dph.state.ct.us/scripts/hlthprof.asp
Physician #11	www.dph.state.ct.us/scripts/hlthprof.asp
Physician Assistant #11	www.dph.state.ct.us/scripts/hlthprof.asp
Pipefitter #7	www.dcpaccess.state.ct.us/DCPPublic/LicenseLookup.asp
Plumber #4	www.dcpaccess.state.ct.us/DCPPublic/LicenseLookup.asp
Podiatrist #11	www.dph.state.ct.us/scripts/hlthprof.asp
Premium Finance Company #2	www.ct-clic.com
Private Detective Company #13	www.state.ct.us/dps/SLFU/PrivateDetectivesLicensed.htm
Private Investigator #13	www.state.ct.us/dps/SLFU/PrivateDetectivesLicensed.htm
Private Occupational School #29	www.ctdhe.org/database/default.htm
Psychologist #11	www.dph.state.ct.us/scripts/hlthprof.asp
Public Service Technician #4	www.dcpaccess.state.ct.us/DCPPublic/LicenseLookup.asp
Radiographer #11	www.dph.state.ct.us/scripts/hlthprof.asp
Real Estate Agent/Broker/Sales #17	www.dcpaccess.state.ct.us/DCPPublic/LicenseLookup.asp
Real Estate Appraiser #17	www.dcpaccess.state.ct.us/DCPPublic/LicenseLookup.asp
Reinsurance Intermediary #2	www.ct-clic.com
Rental Car Company #2	www.ct-clic.com
Respiratory Care Practitioner #11	www.dph.state.ct.us/scripts/hlthprof.asp
Risk Purchasing/Retention Group #2	www.ct-clic.com
Sales Finance Company #6	www.state.ct.us/dob/pages/salefinc.htm
Sanitarian #11	www.dph.state.ct.us/scripts/hlthprof.asp
Savings & Loan Association Bank #6	www.state.ct.us/dob/pages/bcharter.htm
Savings Bank #6	www.state.ct.us/dob/pages/bcharter.htm
School Administrator/Supervisor #9	www.state.ct.us/sde/
School Guidance Counselor #9	www.state.ct.us/sde/
School Library Media Associate #9	www.state.ct.us/sde/
School Principal/Superintendent #9	www.state.ct.us/sde/
School Psychologist /Social Worker #9	www.state.ct.us/sde/
Security Company, Private #13	www.state.ct.us/dps/SLFU/PrivateSecurityLicensed.htm
Security Service #13	www.state.ct.us/dps/SLFU/PrivateDetectivesLicensed.htm
Sheet Metal Cont./Journeyman #4	www.dcpaccess.state.ct.us/DCPPublic/LicenseLookup.asp
Shorthand Court Reporter #4	www.dcpaccess.state.ct.us/DCPPublic/LicenseLookup.asp
Social Worker #11	www.dph.state.ct.us/scripts/hlthprof.asp
Solar Energy Contractor/Journeyman #4	www.dcpaccess.state.ct.us/DCPPublic/LicenseLookup.asp
Speech Pathologist #11	www.dph.state.ct.us/scripts/hlthprof.asp
Speech/Language Pathologist #9	www.state.ct.us/sde/
Sprinkler Layout Technician #4	www.dcpaccess.state.ct.us/DCPPublic/LicenseLookup.asp
Student Athlete Agent #4	www.dcpaccess.state.ct.us/DCPPublic/LicenseLookup.asp
Subsurface Sewage Cleaner/Installer #11	www.dph.state.ct.us/scripts/hlthprof.asp
Surplus Line Broker #2	www.ct-clic.com
Surveyor, Land #3	www.dcpaccess.state.ct.us/DCPPublic/LicenseLookup.asp
Teacher #9	www.state.ct.us/sde/
Utilization Review Company #2	www.ct-clic.com
Vending Machine Operator #8	www.dcpaccess.state.ct.us/DCPPublic/LicenseLookup.asp
Vendor, Itinerent #4	www.dcpaccess.state.ct.us/DCPPublic/LicenseLookup.asp
Veterinarian #11	www.dph.state.ct.us/scripts/hlthprof.asp
Viatical Settlement Broker/Provider #2	www.ct-clic.com
Weigher #8	www.dcpaccess.state.ct.us/DCPPublic/LicenseLookup.asp
Weights/Measures Dealer/Repairer/Regulator #8	www.dcpaccess.state.ct.us/DCPPublic/LicenseLookup.asp
Well Driller #7	www.dcpaccess.state.ct.us/DCPPublic/LicenseLookup.asp
Wrestler/Wrestling Manager #7	www.dcpaccess.state.ct.us/DCPPublic/LicenseLookup.asp
Youth Camp #11	www.dph.state.ct.us/BRS/Youth_camps/youthcamps.htm

Connecticut Licensing Quick Finder

Acupuncturist #11 860-509-7603
Air Emission Permittee #30 860-424-4152
Airport/Heliport #43 860-594-2544
Alcohol/Drug Counselor #11 860-509-7603
Ambulance #11 860-509-7552
Amusement Park #25 860-685-8470
Antenna Svcs Dealer/Technician #5 860-566-3275
Appraiser, MVPD/MVR #2 860-297-3954
Aquaculture Operation #20 203-874-0696
Arborist #26 860-424-3369
Architect #3 860-713-6145
Architectural Firm #3 860-713-6145
Asbestos Abatement Worker/Supr. #31 860-509-7559
Asbestos Consultant/Contractor #31 860-509-7559
Assisted Living Service #11 860-509-7400
Athletic Promoter #7 860-566-6980
Attorney/Attorney Firm #1 860-568-5157
Audiologist #11 860-509-7603
Auto Auction #44 203-805-6307
Auto Insurance Adjuster #2 860-297-3954
Auto Parts Manufacturer #27 860-263-5057
Auto Racing Permit #27 860-263-5057
Auto Renter/Leasor #27 860-263-5057
Backflow Tester #11 860-509-7333
Bail Bond Agent #2 860-297-3954
Bail Enforcement Agent #13 860-685-8046
Bail Enforcement Firearm Instructor #13860-685-8160
Bailbondsman #13 860-685-8046
Bait Seller (Live Bait) #10 860-424-3474
Bakery #8 860-713-6160
Bank #6 860-240-8299
Bank & Trust Company #6 860-240-8299
Bank Branch #6 860-240-8299
Banking Office, Non-depository #6 860-240-8299
Barber #11 860-509-7603
Bazaar/Raffle Permit #12 860-594-5480
Bedding Mfg/Renovation #4 860-713-6000
Bedding Supply/Sterilizer #4 860-713-6000
Beekeeper #14 203-974-8479
Beverage/Water Bottler #4 860-713-6000
Bingo Registration #12 860-594-5480
Bird/Poultry Permit/Buyer #22 860-713-2512
Boxer/Boxing Professional #7 860-713-6155
Broker/Dealer Agent #6 860-240-8299
Building Contractor #7 860-566-2825
Building Inspector #33 860-685-8330
Building Official #25 860-685-8330
Bus Driver #23 860-263-5720
Business Opportunity Offering #6 860-240-8299
Car Dealer #27 860-263-5056
Carnival/Circus Operator #25 860-685-8470
Casino #12 860-594-0643
Casino Occupation #12 860-594-0643
Casualty Adjuster #2 860-297-3954
Cattle/Swine Dealer #22 860-713-2512
Charitable Solicitor #36 860-808-5030
Charter Fishing Vessel #42 860-434-6043
Chauffeur/Livery Company #24 860-594-2865
Check Cashing Service #6 860-240-8299
Cheese Dealer #22 860-713-2512
Child Caring Agency/Facility #37 860-550-6445
Child Clinic (Well Child) #11 860-509-7444
Child Placing Agency #37 860-550-6445
Child Psychiatric Clinic #37 860-550-6445
Chiropractor #11 860-509-7603
Cigarette Seller/Dist. #21 860-297-5962
Coach, High/Grade School #9 860-713-6969
Coastal/Tidal/Navigatable Waters Permit #32 860-424-3034
Collection Agency #6 860-240-8299
Collection Agency, Consumer #6 860-240-8299
College/University #29 860-947-1822
Community Assoc. Manager #7 860-713-6150
Community Living arrangement for Mentally Retarded #38 860-418-6081
Conch/Depuration/Oyster License #20 . 203-874-0696
Construction Inspector #25 860-685-8310
Contractor, Mechanical #4 860-713-6135
Controlled Substance License #7 860-713-6065
Convalescent Hursing Home #11 860-509-7400
Cosmetologist #11 860-509-7603
Counselor, Professional #11 860-509-7603
Crane Operator #25 860-685-8470
Cranes/Hoisting Equipment #25 860-685-8470
Credit Union #6 860-240-8299
Crematorium #11 860-509-7296
Cross-Connection Survey Insp. #11 860-509-7333
Dairy Laboratory Analyst #22 860-713-2512
Dairy Sample Collector #22 860-713-2512
Dairy Transporter #22 860-713-2512
Day Care Provider #11 860-509-8000
Day Treatment Facility, Extended #37 . 860-550-6445
Debt Adjuster #6 860-240-8299
Demolition Operator #25 860-685-8470
Dental Anes/Conscious Sedation Permittee #11 860-509-7603
Dentist/Dental Hygienist #11 860-509-7603
Dessert Mfg, Frozen #8 860-713-6160
Diesel Fuel Distributor #21 860-297-5962
Dietician/Nutritionist #11 860-509-7603
Digger of Shellfish #20 203-874-0696
Dog Racing Owner/Trainer #12 860-594-0643
Dog Training Facility #22 860-713-2512
Driver Education Instr/School #27 860-263-5057
Driving Instructor #23 .... 860-263-5720/5442
Driving School #23 860-263-5442
Druggist Liquor Permittee #15 860-713-6200
Egg Grader #22 860-713-2513
Electrical Contr./Inspector #7 860-566-2825
Electrical Journeyman/Apprentice #4 ... 860-713-6000
Electrical Sign Installer #7 860-566-2825
Electrician #7 860-566-2825
Electrologist/Hypertricologist #11 860-509-7603
Electronics Service Dealer/Tech. #5 860-566-3275
Elevator Inspector/Mechanic #4 860-713-6000
Embalmer #11 860-509-7603
Emergency Medical Svc Prof'l #11 860-509-7603
Emissions Technician #35 203-805-6244
Employment Agency #39 860-263-6790
EMS First Responder #11 860-509-7552
EMS Instructor #11 860-509-7975
Engineer #4 860-713-6000
Enviromental Professional #40 860-424-3705
Environmental Lab Director #11 860-509-7389
Explosive Handler #25 860-685-8470
Explosive Hauler #25 860-685-8470
Family Planning Clinic #11 860-509-8000
Family Residence, Permanent #37 860-550-6445
Farm Winery #15 860-713-6200
Fire Investigator, PI #13 860-685-8046
Fire Officer/Driver/Instructor #41 . 860-627-6363 x225
Fire Protection Inspector/Contr. #4 860-713-6000
Fire/Life Safety Educator #41 .... 860-627-6363 x225
Firearms Dealer #13 860-685-8046
Firearms Registration #19 860-685-8290
Firefighter #41 .... 860-627-6363 x225
Fireworks Display Operator #25 860-685-8470
Fireworks Occupation/Permit #25 860-685-8470
Fisher #10 860-424-3105
Fishery #10 860-424-3474
Food Service Inspector #11 860-509-7297
Food Tester #11 860-509-7297
Forest Products Harvestor/Practitioner #10 860-424-3630
Fruit Storage #22 860-713-2548
Fund Raiser, Paid #36 860-808-5030
Funeral Director/Home #11 860-509-7603
Fur Breeder #22 860-713-2512
Fur Buyer #10 860-424-3011
Game Breeder #10 860-424-3011
Gasoline Dealer #8 860-713-6160
Glazier #4 860-713-6000
Gun Dealer #19 860-685-8290
Hairdresser #11 860-509-7603
Hatchery #20 203-874-0696
Hazardous Material Tech. #41 .... 860-627-6363 x225
Hazardous Waste Disposer #40 860-424-3372
Hazardous Waste Transporter #40 860-424-3372
Health Care Ctr. Insurer #2 860-297-3814
Health Club #4 860-713-6000
Hearing Instrument Specialist #11 860-509-7603
Heating, Piping, Cooling Contractor/Journeyman #4 860-713-6000
Home Health Aide Agency #11 860-509-7400
Home Health Aide Homemaker #11 860-509-7400
Home Heating Oil Seller #8 860-713-6160
Home Improvement Contr./Seller #4 ... 860-713-6110
Home Inspector #4 860-713-6145
Homeopathic Physician #11 860-509-7603
Honey Bee Registration #14 203-974-8479
Hospice #11 860-509-7400
Hospital #11 860-509-7400
Hypertrichologist #11 860-509-7603
Industrial Truck #24 860-594-2874
Insurance Adjuster/Public Adjuster #2 . 860-297-3954
Insurance Agent, Fraternal #2 860-297-3954
Insurance Appraiser #2 860-297-3954
Insurance Company/Producer #2 860-297-3845
Insurance Consultant #2 860-297-3954
Interior Designer #4 860-566-2825
Investment Advisor/Agent #6 860-240-8299
Issuer Agent (Financial) #6 860-240-8299
Juice Producer #8 860-713-6160
Junkyard Operator #27 860-263-5057
Kennel #22 860-713-2512
Laboratory, Animal #11 860-509-7400
Laboratory, Clinical #11 860-509-7400
Land Surveyor Firm #3 860-713-6145
Landscape Architect #3 860-713-6145
Lead Abatement Professional #11 860-509-7603
Lead Abatement Worker/Supv'r #31 860-509-7559
Lead Abatement/Consultant Contractor #31 860-509-7559
Lead Consultant #31 860-509-7559
Lead Planner/Project Designer #11 860-509-7603
Legalized Gaming Occupation #12 860-594-0643
Lender #6 860-240-8200
Lender, Correspondent #6 860-240-8299
Liquor License #15 860-713-6200
Liquor Mfg/Dist/Whlse #15 860-713-6200
Liquor Permittee #15 860-713-6200
Liquor Store/Broker/Shipper #15 860-713-6200
Livestock Dealer #22 860-713-2512
Loan Broker/Originator #6 860-240-8299
Loan Company, Small #6 860-240-8299
Lobbyist #18 860-566-4472
Lobster Seller #10 860-424-6043
Lottery #12 860-594-0643
Lottery Sales Agent #12 860-594-0643
Marine Fishing License #42 860-434-6043
Marriage & Family Therapist #11 860-609-7603
Marshall, State #34 860-566-7109
Martial Arts Facility #4 860-713-6000
Massage Therapist #11 860-509-7603
Materialman #21 860-297-5962
Maternity Home #11 860-509-7400
Mausoleum #11 860-509-7603
Medical Doctor #11 860-509-7603
Medical Gas/Vacuum System #4 860-713-6135
Medical Response Technician #11 860-509-7603
Medication Administration for Mentally Retarded #38 860-418-6081
Mental Health Facility/Clinic #11 860-509-7400
Midwife #11 860-509-7603
Mikdwife Nurse #11 .... 860-509-7603/7570

Milk Dealer/Producer #22 860-713-2512	Plumber #4 860-713-6000	Shorthand Court Reporter #4 860-713-6000
Milk/Cream Weigher #22 860-713-2512	Plumbing Inspector #25 860-685-8310	Social Worker #11 860-509-7603
Mobile Home Park/Seller #17 860-713-6150	Podiatrist #11 860-509-7603	Solar Energy Contr./Journeyman #4... 860-713-6000
Money Forwarder #6 860-240-8299	Police Officer #45 203-238-6694	Solid Waste Facility Operator #40 860-424-4051
Money Order/Traveler Check Issuer #6 860-240-8299	Poultry Buyer #22 860-713-2512	Special Effects Permit #25 860-685-8470
Mooring Space #43 860-594-2544	Premium Finance Company #2 860-297-3916	Speech Pathologist #11 860-509-7603
Mooring/Swim Float #32 860-424-3034	Private Detective Company #13 860-685-8046	Speech/Language Pathologist #9 860-713-6969
Mortgage (1st) Broker/Lender #6 860-240-8299	Private Investigator #13 860-685-8046	Sprinkler Layout Technician #4 860-713-6000
Mortgage (2nd) Broker/Lender #6 860-240-8299	Private Occupational School #29 860-947-1822	Student Athlete Agent #4 860-713-6000
Motion Picture Theater #25 860-685-8470	Psychologist #11 860-509-7603	Substance Abuse Clinic #11 860-509-7400
Motion Picture Theater Mgr #25 860-685-8470	Public Accountant-CPA #16 860-509-6179	Subsurface Sewage Cleaner/Instal. #11 860-509-7603
Motor Bus Company #24 860-594-2865	Public Service Technician #4 860-713-6000	Subsurface Sewage Installer/Cleaner #31
Motor Vehicle Recycler #27 860-263-5056	Radiation Permittee #30 860-424-3029	 860-509-7559
Mover, Household Goods #24 860-594-2863	Radiographer #11 860-509-7603	Surplus Line Broker #2 860-297-3868
Naturopathic Physician #11 860-509-7603	Real Estate Agent/Broker/Sales #17... 860-713-6150	Surveyor, Land #3 860-713-6145
New Home Construction Contr. #4... 860-713-6000	Real Estate Appraiser #17 860-713-6150	Tattoo Artist #11 860-509-8000
Notary Public #16 860-509-6200	Recycler #40 860-424-3365	Taxable Entity #21 860-297-4874
Nurse #11 .... 860-509-7603/7570	Reinsurance Intermediary #2 860-297-3954	Taxi Company #24 860-594-2865
Nurse, Advance Registered Practice #11	Rental Car Company #2 860-297-3953	Taxidermist #10 860-424-3105
.... 860-509-7603/7570	Residence for Mentally Retarded #38.. 860-418-6081	Teacher #9 860-713-6969
Nurse-LPN #11 860-509-7603	Residential Care Home #11 860-509-7400	Theatre Manager #25 860-685-8470
Nursery Plant Dealer #14 203-974-8481	Respiratory Care Practitioner #11 860-509-7603	Tobacco Products Permit #21 860-297-5962
Nursery, Plant #14 203-974-8481	Rest Home #11 860-509-7400	Towing Operator #27 860-263-5056
Nurses' Aide #11 860-509-7603	Risk Purchasing/Retention Group #2... 860-297-3880	Training Home for Mentally Retarded #38
Nursing Home #11 860-509-7400	Safety Officer #41 .... 860-627-6363 x225	 860-418-6081
Nursing Home Administrator #11 860-509-7603	Sales Finance Company #6 860-240-8299	Trapper #10 860-424-3105
Occupational Therapist/Assistant #11.. 860-509-7603	Sanitarian #11 860-509-7603	Tree Surgeon #7 860-566-2825
Off-Track Betting #12 860-594-0643	Sanitarian, Registered #31 860-509-7559	Truck Driver #23 860-263-5720
Optical Shop #11 860-509-7603	Savings & Loan Association Bank #6 .. 860-240-8299	Underground Storage Tank #40 860-424-3374
Optician #11 860-509-7603	Savings Bank #6 860-240-8299	Utilization Review Company #2 860-297-3862
Optometrist #11 860-509-7603	School Administrator/Supervisor #9... 860-713-6969	Vehicle Dealer #27 860-263-5056
Osteopathic Physician #11 860-509-7603	School Bus Driver #23 860-263-5720	Vehicle Repairer #27 860-263-5057
Outpatient Clinic #11 860-509-7400	School Guidance Counselor #9 860-713-6969	Vending Machine Operator #8 860-713-6160
Parachute Jump Area #43 860-594-2544	School Library Media Associate #9... 860-713-6969	Vendor, Itinerent #4 860-713-6000
Paramedic #11 860-509-7603	School Principal/Superintendent #9... 860-713-6969	Veterinarian #11 860-509-7603
Pawnbroker #21 860-297-4874	School Psychologist #9 860-713-6969	Viatical Settlement Broker/Provider #2 . 860-297-3882
Pesticide Applicator #26 860-424-3369	School Social Worker #9 860-713-6969	Waste Disposal Permittee #40 860-424-3360
Pesticide-related Business #26 860-424-3369	Scientific Collector #10 860-424-3589	Water Distribnt'n System Operator #11 860-509-8000
Pet Groomer #22 860-713-2512	SCOR #6 860-240-8299	Water Treatment Plant Operator #11... 860-509-8000
Pet Store Operator #22 860-713-2512	Seafood Dealer #42 860-434-6043	Weigher #8 860-713-6000
Pharmacist/Pharmacist Intern #4 860-713-6000	Securities Agent #6 860-240-8299	Weights/Measures Dealer/Repairer/Regulator #8
Pharmacy #4 860-713-6000	Securities Broker/Dealer #6 860-240-8299	 860-713-6000
Pharmacy Technician #4 860-713-6000	Security Company, Private #13 860-685-8046	Well Driller #7 860-566-2825
Physical Therapist/Assistant #11 860-509-7603	Security Guard #13 860-685-8046	Wildlife Control Operator/Rehabil. #10 . 860-424-3011
Physician #11 860-509-7603	Security Service #13 860-685-8046	Winery, Small #21 860-297-5962
Physician Assistant #11 860-509-7603	Septic Tank Cleaner #11 860-509-8000	Wrestler/Wrestling Manager #7 860-566-2825
Pilot, Marine #43 860-443-3856	Sewage Disposal System Instal'r #11.. 860-509-8000	Youth Camp #11 .... 860-509-8045, 800-282-6063
Pipefitter #7 860-566-2825	Sheet Metal Cont./Journeyman #4... 860-713-6000	
Plan Review Technician #25 860-685-8310	Shellfish Professional #20 203-874-0696	

Connecticut Licensing Agency Information

1 Attorney Registration, Statewide Grievance Committee, 287 Main St, East Hartford, CT 06118; 860-568-5157. Search Database at www.jud2.state.ct.us/Civil_Inquiry/GetAtty.asp

2 Department of Insurance, Licensing Division, PO Box 816 (153 Market St), Hartford, CT 06142-0816; 860-297-3845, Fax: 860-297-3978. www.ct.gov/cid
Email: ctinsdept.licensing@po.state.ct.us
Search Database at www.ct-clic.com Note: Fees for pre-programed lists: printed report-$7.88 + $.25 per page, labels-$7.88 + $.25 per 100 labels, Diskette-$7.88 + $.17 per diskette, CD-ROM-$7.88 + $.57 per CD, E-mail-$7.88.

3 Department of Consumer Protection, Board of Architects, 165 Capitol Ave, #110, Hartford, CT 06106; 860-713-6135, Fax: 860-713-7239. Search Database at www.dcpaccess.state.ct.us/DCPPublic/LicenseLookup.asp Note: Lists can be downloaded at www.dcpaccess.state.ct.us/DCPRosterDownload/pRosterDownload.asp.

4 Department of Consumer Protection, Board of Trades Division, 165 Capitol Ave, Hartford, CT 06106; 860-713-6000, Fax: 860-713-7239. www.dcp.state.ct.us
Email: License.services@po.state.ct.us Search Database at www.dcpaccess.state.ct.us/verify.htm Note: Lists can be downloaded at www.dcpaccess.state.ct.us/DCPRosterDownload/pRosterDownload.asp.

5 Department of Consumer Protection/Occupational Licensing, Board of Television & Radio Service Examiners, 165 Capitol Ave, Hartford, CT 06106; 860-713-6135, Fax: 860-713-7239. www.state.ct.us/dcp/ Search Database at www.dcpaccess.state.ct.us/verify.htm

6 Department of Banking, 260 Constitution Plaza, Hartford, CT 06103-1800; 860-240-8299, Fax: 860-240-8178. www.state.ct.us/dob
Email: john.burke@po.state.ct.us
Search Sourcebase at www.state.ct.us/dob

7 Department of Consumer Protection, Occupational Licensing Division, 165 Capitol

Ave, Hartford, CT 06106; 860-713-6300, Fax: 860-713-7239. www.dcpaccess.state.ct.us
Email: license.services@po.state.ct.us Search Database at www.dcpaccess.state.ct.us/verify.htm Note: Lists can be downloaded at www.dcpaccess.state.ct.us/DCPRosterDownload/pRosterDownload.asp.

8 Department of Consumer Protection, Food Standards Division, 165 Capitol Ave, State Office Bldg, Hartford, CT 06106-1630; 860-713-6160, Fax: 860-713-7229. www.dcp.state.ct.us/licensing/food.htm
Email: license.services@po.state.ct.us
Search Database at www.dcpaccess.state.ct.us/DCPPublic/LicenseLookup.asp Note: Lists can be downloaded at www.dcpaccess.state.ct.us/DCPRosterDownload/pRosterDownload.asp.

9 Department of Education, Bureau of Certification & Professional Development, PO Box 150471, Rm 243, Hartford, CT 06115-0471; 860-713-6969, Fax: 860-713-7017. www.state.ct.us/sde/

Email: teacher.cert@po.state.ct.us   Note: License verification available through "Freedom of Information" (FOI). Request must be submitted in writing.

10 Department of Environmental Protection, Bureau of Natural Resources, 79 Elm St, Hartford, CT 06106; 860-424-3010, Fax: 860-424-4078. www.dep.state.ct.us/burnatr/index.htm

11 Department of Public Health, Health Care or Environmental Health Licensing, PO Box 340308 (410 Capital Ave, MS 12MQA), Hartford, CT 06134-0308; 860-509-7603, Fax: 860-509-7607. www.dph.state.ct.us
Search Database at www.dph.state.ct.us/scripts/hlthprof.asp

12 Division of Special Revenue, Licensing Section, PO Box 11424 (555 Russell Rd), Newington, CT 06111; 860-594-0643, Fax: 860-594-0696. www.dosr.state.ct.us/ Email: dosr@po.state.ct.us
Search Database at www.ct-clic.com/

13 Division of State Police, Special Licensing & Firearms Division, 1111 Country Club Rd, Middletown, CT 06457; 860-685-8046, Fax: 860-685-8496. www.state.ct.us/dps/SLFU/ Email: DPS.Spec.Licensing@po.state.ct.us
Search Database at www.state.ct.us/dps/SLFU/

14 Office of the State Entomologist, Connecticut Agricultural Experiment Station, PO Box 1106 (125 Huntington St), New Haven, CT 06504; 203-974-8466.
www.caes.state.ct.us/InspectandRegandGeneral/inspecti.htm

15 Department of Consumer Protection, Liquor Control Divison, 165 Capitol Ave, Hartford, CT 06106; 860-713-6200, Fax: 860-713-7235. Email: dosr@po.state.ct.us   Search Database at www.dcpaccess.state.ct.us/DCPPublic/LicenseLookup.asp   Note: Lists can be downloaded at www.dcpaccess.state.ct.us/DCPRosterDownload/pRosterDownload.asp.

16 Office of the Secretary of the State, Records Division, PO Box 150470 (30 Trinity St), Hartford, CT 06115; 860-509-6200, Fax: 860-509-6230. www.sots.state.ct.us
Email: rls@po.state.ct.us

17 Department of Consumer Protection, Real Estate Division, 165 Capitol Ave, Rm 110, Hartford, CT 06106; 860-713-6150, Fax: 860-713-7230. www.dcp.state.ct.us/licensing/realestate.htm
Email: license.services@po.state.ct.us
Search Database at www.dcpaccess.state.ct.us/verify.htm
Note: Lists can be downloaded at www.dcpaccess.state.ct.us/DCPRosterDownload/pRosterDownload.asp.

18 Ethics Commission, 18 Trinity St, Hartford, CT 06106; 860-566-4472, Fax: 860-566-3806. www.ethics.state.ct.us   Search Database at www.ethics.state.ct.us/publicinfo.htm   Note: May not have full lobbyist rosters. Also search reports and enforcement actions.

19 Department of Public Safety, Division of State Police, Licensing/Registration, 1111 Country Club Rd, Middletown, CT 06457-9294; 860-685-8290.

20 Department of Agriculture, Bureau of Aquaculture, PO Box 97 (190 Rogers Ave), Milford, CT 06460; 203-874-0696. www.state.ct.us/doag/

21 Department of Revenue Svcs, Audit Unit (Licensing), PO Box 2937 (25 Sigourney St, 06106), Hartford, CT 06104; 860-297-5962, Fax: 860-297-4797. www.drs.state.ct.us

22 Department of Agriculture, Bureau of Regulation & Inspection, 165 Capitol Avenue, Hartford, CT 06106; 860-713-2500, Fax: 860-713-2514. www.state.ct.us/doag
Email: ctdeptag@po.state.ct.us

23 Department of Motor Vehicles, Specialized Licenses & Permits, 60 State St, Wethersfield, CT 06109; 860-263-5720. www.ct.gov/dmv/site/default.asp

24 Department of Transportation, Motor Transport Svcs, PO Box 317546 (2800 Berlin Turnpike,), Newington, CT 06131-7546; 860-594-2865, Fax: 860-594-2859.

25 Department of Public Safety, Division of Fire, Emergency & Building Svcs, PO Box 2794 (1111 Country Club Rd), Middletown, CT 06457-9294; 860-685-8470. www.state.ct.us/dps/DFEBS/index.html

26 Department of Environmental Protection, Pesticide Division, Bureau of Waste Management, 79 Elm St, Hartford, CT 06106; 860-424-3369, Fax: 860-509-8457. www.dep.state.ct.us/wst/pesticides/index.htm
Search Database at www.kellysolutions.com/CT/

27 Department of Motor Vehicles, Dealer and Repairer Division, 60 State St, Wethersfield, CT 06109; 860-263-5057, Fax: 860-263-5554. www.ct.gov/dmv/site/default.asp   Note: Licenses cannot be verified by phone; must use form J23 available at all DMV offices.

29 CT Department of Higher Education, Academic Affairs, 61 Woodland St, Hartford, CT 06105-2326; 860-947-1801, Fax: 860-947-1310. www.ctdhe.org   Email: info@ctdhe.org

30 Department of Environmental Protection, Bureau of Air Mgmt; Compliance & Filed Ops Div., 79 Elm St, Hartford, CT 06106; 860-424-4152.

31 Department of Public Health, Asbestos Licensure, PO Box 340308 (410 Capitol Ave, MS 12 APP), Hartford, CT 06134; 860-509-7559. www.dph.state.ct.us   Search Database at www.state.ct.us/dph/scripts/hlthprof.asp

32 Department of Environmental Protection, Office of Long Island Sound Programs, 79 Elm St, Hartford, CT 06106; 860-424-3034. www.dep.state.ct.us

33 Department of Public Safety, Office of Education & Data Management, PO Box 2794 (1111 County Club Rd), Middletown, CT 06457-9294; 860-685-8330, Fax: 860-685-8611. www.state.ct.us/dps/dfebs/oedm/oedmbcol.htm

34 State Marshall Commission, State of Connecticut Judicial Branch, 765 Asylum Ave, Hartford, CT 06105; 860-566-7109. www.jud.state.ct.us   Email: rob.rudewicz@po.state.ct.us Search Database at www.jud.state.ct.us/faq/marshals.htm

35 Department of Motor Vehicles, Emissions Divison, 55 West Main St, Rowland State Gov. Ctr, Waterbury, CT 06072; 800-842-8222, 203-805-6244. www.ct.gov/dmv/cwp/view.asp?a=800&Q=244982

36 Department of Consumer Protection, Public Charities Unit - Ofc. of the Attorney General, 55 Elm St, Hartford, CT 06106; 860-808-5030.

37 DCF Licensing, Department of Children & Families, 505 Hudson St, Hartford, CT 06106; 860-550-6445. www.state.ct.us/dcf/

38 Department of Mental Retardation, 460 Capitol Ave, Hartford, CT 06106; 860-418-6000. www.dmr.state.ct.us/

39 Department of Labor, Wage and Workplace Standards, 200 Folly Brook Blvd, Wethersfield, CT 06109; 860-263-6790. www.ctdol.state.ct.us/wgwkstnd/wgemenu.htm

40 Department of Environmental Protection, Bureau of Waste Management, 79 Elm St, 2nd Fl, Hartford, CT 06106; 860-424-3705. www.dep.state.ct.us/wst/prgactiv.htm

41 Commission on Fire Prevention & Control, Director of Certification, 34 Perimeter Rd, Windsor Locks, CT 06096; 860-623-6363 x225, Fax: 860-654-1889. www.ct.gov/cfpc/taxonomy/ct_taxonomy.asp
Email: denice.fortin@po.state.ct.us

42 Department of Environmental Protection, Marine Fisheries Division, PO Box 719 (333 Ferry Rd), Old Lyme, CT 06371; 860-434-6043, Fax: 860-434-6150. www.dep.state.ct.us/burnatr/fishing/fdhome.htm

43 Department of Transportation, Bureau of Aviation and Ports, State Pier, New London, CT 06320; 860-443-3856. www.dot.state.ct.us/permits/ap_mplv.htm
Email: Kevin.Lynch@po.state.ct.us

44 Department of Motor Vehicles, Fiscal Services Divison, 55 W Main St, Waterbury, CT 06702; 203-805-6307, Fax: 203-805-6161.

45 Police Officers Standards & Training Council, Certification, Assessment & Audit Unit, 285 Preston Ave, Meriden, CT 06450; 203-238-6694, Fax: 203-238-6643. www.post.state.ct.us
Email: gary.pfeifer@po.state.ct.us

Connecticut Federal Courts

The following list indicates the district and division name for each county in the state. If the bankruptcy court location is different from the district court, then the location of the bankruptcy court appears in parentheses.

County/Court Cross Reference

Fairfield	Bridgeport	New Haven	New Haven
Hartford	Hartford	New London	New Haven
Litchfield	New Haven (Hartford)	Tolland	Hartford
Middlesex	New Haven (Hartford)	Windham	Hartford

Standards for Federal Courts: The search fee is $20.00 per item (one party name or case number). Certification fee is $7.00 per document. Copy fee is $.50 per page. All fees standard unless noted in profile. Mail Search: always enclose a stamped self addressed envelope unless otherwise noted. Most courts accept fax requests or will suggest a copying/search vendor. Before releasing records, all courts require prepayment unless noted in profile. Open records are located at the court unless otherwise noted. District courts index by defendant and plaintiff as well as by case number. Bankruptcy courts usually index by debtor and case number. While most courts now have their indexes on computer, many still maintain index card files as well.

The universal PACER sign-up number is 800-676-6856. Find PACER and the Party/Case Index on the Web at http://pacer.psc.uscourts.gov. PACER dial-up access is $.60 per minute. Also, courts offering internet access via RACER, PACER, Web-PACER or the new CM-ECF charge $.07 per page fee unless noted as free.

US District Court

Bridgeport Division Office of the clerk, Room 400, 915 Lafayette Blvd, Bridgeport, CT 06604 (Use mail address for courier delivery) 203-579-5861. www.ctd.uscourts.gov
Counties: Fairfield (prior to 1993). Since January 1993, cases from any county may be assigned to any of the divisions in the district.
Indexing & Storage: New cases available in the index immediately after filing date. Records are stored by docket number, accession number and box number.
Fee & Payment: Payment may be made by money order, cashier check. Business and personl checks are not accepted. Payee: Clerk, U.S. District Court.
Phone Search: Only docket information available.
Mail Search: A SASE not required.
In Person Search: Fee charged if court conducts your in person search for you.
PACER: PACER online at http://pacer.ctd.uscourts.gov. New records are online after 1 day.
Electronic Filing: Electronic filing information online at https://ecf.ctd.uscourts.gov

Hartford Division 450 Main St, Hartford, CT 06103 (Use mail address for courier delivery) 860-240-3200. www.ctd.uscourts.gov
Counties: Hartford, Tolland, Windham (prior to 1993). Since 1993, cases from any county may be assigned to any of the divisions in the district.

Indexing & Storage: New cases available in the index immediately after filing date. Records are kept where the assigned judge sits, and are stored by the federal record number system.
Fee & Payment: Payment may be made by money order, cashier check, personal check. Payee: Clerk, U.S. District Court.
Phone Search: Only docket information available.
In Person Search: Fee charged if court conducts your in person search for you.
PACER: PACER online at http://pacer.ctd.uscourts.gov. New records are online after 1 day.
Electronic Filing: https://ecf.ctd.uscourts.gov

New Haven Division 141 Church St, New Haven, CT 06510 (courier address: Use mail address for courier delivery) 203-773-2140. www.ctd.uscourts.gov
Counties: Litchfield, Middlesex, New Haven, New London (prior to 1993). Since 1993, cases from any county may be assigned to any of the divisions in the district.
Indexing & Storage: New cases available in the index immediately after filing date. Older records are indexed on microfiche. District wide searches are available for information from 1982 to the present from this court.
Fee & Payment: Payment may be made by money order, cashier check, business check. Personal checks are not accepted. $20.00 search fee charged for each add'l name searched. Payee: District Court Clerk.
Phone Search: Only docket information available by phone.
In Person Search: Fee charged if court conducts your in person search for you.
PACER: PACER online at http://pacer.ctd.uscourts.gov. New records are online after 1 day.
Electronic Filing: Electronic filing information online at https://ecf.ctd.uscourts.gov

U.S. Bankruptcy Court

Bridgeport Division 915 Lafayette Blvd, Bridgeport, CT 06604 (courier address: same) 203-579-5808. www.ctb.uscourts.gov
Counties: Fairfield.
Indexing & Storage: Cases indexed by debtor as well as by case number. New cases available in the index immediately after filing date. District wide searches are available from this division.
Fee & Payment: Payment may be made by money order, cashier check, business check. Personal checks are not accepted. Payee: Clerk, U.S. Bankruptcy Court.

Phone Search: Automated voice case information service (VCIS) is available. Call VCIS at 800-800-5113 or 860-240-3345.
In Person Search: Fee charged if court conducts your in person search for you.
PACER: PACER online at http://pacer.ctb.uscourts.gov. Document images available. Records purged every 6 months. New civil records are online after 1 day.
Electronic Filing: https://ecf.ctb.uscourts.gov/

Hartford Division 450 Main St, Hartford, CT 06103 (Use mail address for courier delivery) 860-240-3675. www.ctb.uscourts.gov
Counties: Hartford, Litchfield, Middlesex, Tolland, Windham.
Indexing & Storage: Cases indexed by debtor as well as by case number. New cases available in the index 1 week after filing date.
Fee & Payment: Payment may be made by money order, cashier check, personal check. Payee: Clerk, U.S. Bankruptcy Court.
Phone Search: Only docket information available by phone. Automated voice case information service (VCIS) is available. Call VCIS at 800-800-5113 or 860-240-3345.
In Person Search: Fee charged if court conducts your in person search for you.
PACER: PACER online at http://pacer.ctb.uscourts.gov. Document images available. Records purged every 6 months. New civil records are online after 1 day.
Electronic Filing: Electronic filing information online at https://ecf.ctb.uscourts.gov/

New Haven Division The Connecticut Financial Center, 157 Church St, 18th Floor, New Haven, CT 06510 (courier address: Use mail address for courier delivery) 203-773-2009. www.ctb.uscourts.gov
Counties: New Haven, New London.
Indexing & Storage: Cases indexed by debtor as well as by case number. New cases available in the index 1 week after filing date.
Fee & Payment: Payment may be made by money order, cashier check, personal check. Payee: Clerk, U.S. Bankruptcy Court.
Phone Search: Only docket information available by phone. Automated voice case information service (VCIS) is available. Call VCIS at 800-800-5113 or 860-240-3345.
In Person Search: Fee charged if court conducts your in person search for you.
PACER: PACER online at http://pacer.ctb.uscourts.gov. Document images available. Records purged every 6 months. New civil records are online after 1 day.
Electronic Filing: https://ecf.ctb.uscourts.gov/

Connecticut County Courts

Court	Jurisdiction	No. of Courts	How Organized
Judicial District Courts*	General	15	15 Geographic Areas
Geographic Area Courts*	Limited	20	20 Geographic Areas
Probate Courts*	Probate	129	

* Profiled in this Sourcebook.

CIVIL									
Court	Tort	Contract	Real Estate	Min. Claim	Max. Claim	Small Claims	Estate	Eviction	Domestic Relations
Judicial District Courts*	X	X	X	No Min	No Max				X
Geographic Area Courts*						$3500		X	
Probate Courts*							X		

CRIMINAL					
Court	Felony	Misdemeanor	DWI/DUI	Preliminary Hearing	Juvenile
Judicial District Courts*	X				X
Geographic Area Courts*		X	X	X	
Probate Courts*					

ADMINISTRATION   Chief Court Administrator, 231 Capitol Av, Hartford, CT, 06106; 860-757-2100, Fax: 860-757-2130. www.jud.state.ct.us

COURT STRUCTURE   The Superior Court is the sole court of original jurisdiction for all causes of action, except for matters over which the probate courts have jurisdiction as provided by statute. The state is divided into 15 Judicial Districts, 20 Geographic Area Courts, and 14 Juvenile Districts. The Superior Court - comprised primarily of the Judicial District Courts and the Geographical Area Courts - has five divisions: Criminal, Civil, Family, Juvenile, and Administrative Appeals. When not combined, the Judicial District Courts handle felony and civil cases while the Geographic Area Courts handle misdemeanors, and most handle small claims.

Divorce records are maintained by the Chief Clerk of the Judicial District Courts.

ONLINE ACCESS   The Judicial Branch provides access to civil, small claims and/or family court records via the Internet, located online at www.jud2.state.ct.us. Click on "Party Name Inquiry." The site contains party name search, assignment lists and calendars. Also, questions about the fuller commercial system available through Judicial Information Systems should be directed to the CT JIS Office at 860-282-6500. There is currently no online access to criminal records; however, criminal and motor vehicle data is available for purchase in database format. Opinions from the Supreme and Appellete courts are available from the general web site.

PROBATE   Probate is handled by city Probate Courts, which we have listed, and are not part of the state court system. Information request requirements are consistent across the state; requesters must provide full name of decedent, year and place of death, and SASE. There is no search fee; the certification fee is $5.00 for 1st 2 pages and $2.00 for each additional page; and, the copy fee is $1.00 per page.

Fairfield County

Bridgeport Judicial District Court 1061 Main St, Attn: criminal or civil, Bridgeport, CT 06604; 203-579-6527. Hours: 9AM-5PM (EST). *Felony, Civil Actions, Divorce.*
Civil Records: Access: Mail, online, in person. Only the court performs in person searches; visitors may not. No search fee. Required to search: name, years to search. Civil cases indexed by defendant, plaintiff. Civil records on computer from 1990, on microfiche from 1975 to 1990, prior on index cards. After 5 years sent to Records Center at Enfield, CT. Access to civil, family, and small claims case records is free online at www.jud.state.ct.us.
Criminal Records: Access: Mail, in person. Only the court performs in person searches; visitors may not. No search fee. Required to search: name, years to search, DOB. Criminal records on computer since 1997, on microfiche from 1975 to 1996.
General Information: No sealed, adoption records released. Copy fee: $1.00 per page. Cert fee: $2.00. Payee: Chief Clerk Superior Court. Personal checks accepted. Prepayment required. Mail requests: SASE required. Mail turnaround time 2-3 weeks for civil, 4 weeks for criminal.

Danbury Judicial District Court 146 White St, Danbury, CT 06810; 203-207-8600. Hours: 9AM-5PM (EST). *Felony, Civil Actions, Divorce, Eviction, Small Claims.*
Civil Records: Access: Mail, online, in person. Only the court performs in person searches; visitors may not. No search fee. Required to search: name, years to search. Civil cases indexed by plaintiff and defendant. Civil records on microfilm from 11-87, prior on index cards. Access to civil and family case records is free online at www.jud.state.ct.us.
Criminal Records: Access: Mail, in person. Only the court performs in person searches; visitors may not. No search fee. Required to search: name, years to search, DOB. Criminal records on microfilm from 11-87, prior on index cards but only list docket number and disposal date.
General Information: No sealed records released. Copy fee: $1.00 per page. Cert fee: $2.00 and copy fees. Payee: Clerk of Superior Court. ID required with personal check. Prepayment required. Mail turnaround time 2-4 days for civil and family, 3-4 days for motor vehicle and criminal.

Stamford-Norwalk Judicial District Court 123 Hoyt St, Stamford, CT 06905; Civil phone: 203-965-5307; Criminal phone: 203-965-5208. Hours: 9AM-5PM (EST). *Felony, Misdemeanors, Civil Actions, Divorce.*
Civil Records: Access: Mail, online, in person. Both court and visitors may perform in person searches. No search fee. Required to search: name, years to search. Civil cases indexed by defendant, plaintiff. Only pending civil cases on computer, on microfiche from 1970s, on index cards from 1958. Access to current civil case records is free online at www.jud.state.ct.us.
Criminal Records: Access: Mail, in person. Both court and visitors may perform in person searches. No search fee. Required to search: name, years to search. Only pending cases on computer, on microfiche from 1970s, on index cards from 1962.
General Information: Public Access terminal is available. No sealed records released. Will not fax results. Copy fee: $1.00 per page. Cert fee: $2.00. Payee: Clerk of Superior Court. Personal checks accepted. Prepayment required.

Geographical Area Court #2 172 Golden Hill St, Bridgeport, CT 06604; Civil phone: 203-579-6527; Criminal phone: 203-579-6560. Hours: 9AM-4PM (EST). *Misdemeanor, Eviction, Small Claims.*
Note: Serving the towns of Bridgeport, Easton, Fairfield, Monroe, Stratford and Trumbull.
Civil Records: Access: Phone, mail, online, in person. Both court and visitors may perform in person searches. No search fee. Required to search: name, years to search. Civil cases indexed by defendant. Civil records pending and from 1990 on computer, on microfiche from 1982 to 1990, prior on index cards. After microfilmed and entered on index cards, sent to Records Center at Enfield, CT. Access to civil, family, and small claims case records is free online at www.jud.state.ct.us.
Criminal Records: Access: In person only. Visitors must perform in person searches for themselves. No search fee. Required to search: name, years to search. Criminal records pending and from 1990 on computer, on microfiche from 1982. Refer mail requests to the state criminal records agency, PO Box 2794, Middletown CT 06457, www.state.ct.us/dps/SPBI.htm.
General Information: No sealed records released. Copy fee: $1.00 per page. Cert fee: $3.00. Payee: Clerk of Superior Court. Personal checks accepted. Prepayment required. Mail turnaround time up to 4 weeks.

Geographical Area Court #20 17 Belden Ave, Norwalk, CT 06850; 203-846-3237; Civil phone: 203-846-4206; Criminal phone: 203-846-3237. Hours: 9AM-5PM (EST). *Misdemeanor, Eviction, Small Claims.*
Note: Serving the towns of New Canaan, Norwalk, Weston, Westport and Wilton.
Civil Records: Access: Online, in person. Visitors must perform in person searches for themselves. No search fee. Required to search: name, years to search. Civil cases indexed by defendant, plaintiff. Civil records on computer from 1986. Access to small claims case records is free online at www.jud.state.ct.us.
Criminal Records: Access: In person only. Visitors must perform in person searches for themselves. No search fee. Required to search: name, years to search; also helpful: DOB. Criminal records on computer from 1986, prior records on index cards.
General Information: Copy fee: $1.00 per page. Cert fee: $2.00. Payee: Superior Court GA #20. Only cashiers checks and money orders accepted. Prepayment required.

Geographical Area Court #3 146 White St, Danbury, CT 06810; 203-207-8600. Hours: 9AM-5PM (EST). *Misdemeanor, Eviction, Small Claims.*
Note: Serving the towns of Bethel, Brookfield, Danbury, New Fairfield, Newtown, Redding, Ridgefield and Sherman.
Civil Records: Access: Mail, online, in person. Only the court performs in person searches; visitors may not. No search fee. Required to search: name, years to search. Civil cases indexed by defendant. Civil records on microfilm from 11-87, prior on index cards, but only list docket number and disposal date, then referred to Records Center at Enfield, CT. Access to civil, family, and small claims case records is free online at www.jud.state.ct.us. In person searches are returned by mail.
Criminal Records: Access: In person only. Visitors must perform in person searches for themselves. No search fee. Required to search: name, years to search; also helpful: DOB. Criminal records on computer from 11/9/87. The court refers all requests to one of the 2 statewide agencies.

General Information: No youthful offender or dispositions by dismissal after 20 days from date of judgment records released. Copy fee: $1.00 per page. Cert fee: $2.00. Payee: Clerk of Superior Court. Personal checks accepted. Prepayment required. Mail requests: SASE required.

Bethel Probate Court 1 School St, PO Box 144, Bethel, CT 06801; 203-794-8508; Fax: 203-794-8587. Hours: 9AM-1:00PM (EST). *Probate.*

Bridgeport Probate District 202 State St, McLevy Hall, 3rd Fl, Bridgeport, CT 06604; 203-576-3945; Fax: 203-576-7898. Hours: 8;30AM-5PM M-Th; 8;30AM-4PM F (EST). *Probate.*

Brookfield Probate Court 100 Pocono Rd, PO Box 5192, Brookfield, CT 06804; 203-775-3700; Fax: 203-775-5316. 9AM-4:30PM (EST). *Probate.*

Danbury Probate Court 155 Deer Hill Ave, Danbury, CT 06810; 203-797-4521; Fax: 203-796-1563. Hours: 8:30AM-4:30PM (EST). *Probate.*

Darien Probate Court Town Hall, 2 Renshaw Rd, Darien, CT 06820; 203-656-7342; Fax: 203-656-0774. Hours: 8:30AM-12:30PM, 1:30-4:30PM; 9AM-12:30PM Fri July-Labor Day (EST). *Probate.*

Fairfield Probate Court Independence Hall, 725 Old Post Rd, Fairfield, CT 06824; 203-256-3041; Fax: 203-256-3044. Hours: 9AM-5PM, 9AM-4:30PM (Jun-Aug) (EST). *Probate.*

Greenwich Probate Court 101 Field Point Rd, PO Box 2540, Greenwich, CT 06836; 203-622-3766; Fax: 203-622-6451. Hours: 8AM-4PM, 8AM-Noon Fri July-Aug (EST). *Probate.*

New Canaan Probate Court 77 Main St, New Canaan, CT 06840; 203-594-3050; Fax: 203-594-3128. Hours: 8:30AM-4:30PM; (8:30AM-1PM Fri July-Aug) (EST). *Probate.*

New Fairfield Probate Court 4 Brush Hill Rd, New Fairfield, CT 06812; 203-312-5627; Fax: 203-312-5627. Hours: 9AM-Noon T-Th (and by app't) (EST). *Probate.*

Newtown Probate Court Edmond Town Hall, 45 Main St, Newtown, CT 06470; 203-270-4280; Fax: 203-270-4283. Hours: 8:30AM-Noon,1-4:30PM (EST). *Probate.*

Norwalk Probate Court 125 East Ave, PO Box 2009, Norwalk, CT 06852-2009; 203-854-7737; Fax: 203-854-7825. Hours: 9AM-4:30PM (EST). *Probate.*
Note: District includes Town of Wilton

Redding Probate Court Town Hall, Lonetown Rd, PO Box 1125, Redding, CT 06875-1125; 203-938-2326; Fax: 203-938-8816. Hours: 9AM-1PM (EST). *Probate.*

Ridgefield Probate Court Town Hall, 400 Main St, Ridgefield, CT 06877; 203-431-2776; Fax: 203-431-2772. Hours: 8:30AM-4:30PM (EST). *Probate.*

Shelton Probate Court 40 White St, PO Box 127, Shelton, CT 06484; 203-924-8462; Fax: 203-924-8943. Hours: 9AM-5PM; 9AM-6:30PM 1st & 3rd Tues. of month (EST). *Probate.*

Sherman Probate Court Mallory Town Hall, Rt. 39 Center, PO Box 39, Sherman, CT 06784; 860-355-1821; Fax: 860-350-5041. Hours: 9AM-Noon Tu (and by app't) (EST). *Probate.*

Stamford Probate Court 888 Washington Blvd, 8th Fl, PO Box 10152, Stamford, CT 06904-2152; 203-323-2149; Fax: 203-964-1830. Hours: 9AM-4PM (EST). *Probate.*

Stratford Probate Court 468 Birdseye St, 2nd Fl, Stratford, CT 06615; 203-385-4023; Fax: 203-375-6253. Hours: 9:30AM-4:30PM (EST). *Probate.*

Trumbull Probate Court Town Hall, 5866 Main St, Trumbull, CT 06611-5416; 203-452-5068; Fax: 203-452-5092. 9AM-4:30PM (EST). *Probate.*
Note: District includes Town of Easton,and Monroe.

Westport Probate Court Town Hall, 110 Myrtle Ave, Westport, CT 06880; 203-341-1100; Fax: 203-341-1102. 9AM-4:30PM (EST). *Probate.*
Note: District includes Town of Weston

Hartford County

Hartford Judicial District Court - Civil 95 Washington St, Hartford, CT 06106; 860-548-2700; Fax: 860-548-2711. Hours: 9AM-5PM (EST). *Civil Actions, Divorce.* www.jud.state.ct.us
Civil Records: Access: Mail, online, in person. Both court and visitors may perform in person searches. No search fee. Required to search: name, years to search. Civil cases indexed by defendant, plaintiff. Civil records on computer if active, otherwise on microfiche, older records at Enfield Records Center. Access to civil case records is free online at www.jud.state.ct.us.
General Information: Public Access terminal is available. Copy fee: $1.00 per page. Cert fee: $2.00. Payee: Clerk of Superior Court. Personal checks accepted. Visa, MC accepted. Accepted in person only. $10.00 minimum. Prepayment required. Mail requests: SASE required. Mail turnaround: 7-10 days.

Hartford Judicial District Court - Criminal 101 LaFayette St, Hartford, CT 06106; 860-566-1630. Hours: 9AM-5PM (EST). *Felony.*
Note: Hartford Judicial shares ph line and add with Geoghraphical Court.
Criminal Records: Access: Mail, in person. Only the court performs in person searches; visitors may not. No search fee. Required to search: name, years to search; also helpful: DOB. Criminal records on computer from 1989.
General Information: No youthful offender records or dismissals released. Copy fee: $1.00 per page. Cert fee: $3.00. Payee: Clerk of Superior Court. Personal checks accepted. Prepayment required. Mail requests: SASE required. Mail turnaround time 7-10 days.

New Britain Judicial District Court 20 Franklin Sq, New Britain, CT 06051; Civil phone: 860-515-5180; Criminal phone: 860-515-5080. Hours: 9AM-5PM (EST). *Felony, Civil Actions, Small Claims, Divorce.*
Civil Records: Access: Phone, mail, online, in person. Both court and visitors may perform in person searches. No search fee. Required to search: name, years to search. Civil cases indexed by plaintiff. Civil records on computer up to one year after closing, index cards back to 1989, prior in Hartford. Access to civil, family, and small claims case records is free online at www.jud.state.ct.us.
Criminal Records: Access: Phone, mail, in person. Both court and visitors may perform in person searches. No search fee. Required to search: name, years to search. Criminal records on computer for 2 years, then purged when cases sent to State Record Center.
General Information: Public Access terminal is available. Certain paternity, family case studies and sealed records not released. Copy fee: $1.00 per page. Cert fee: $2.00. Payee: Clerk of Superior Court. Prepayment required. Mail requests: SASE required. Mail turnaround time 3 days.

Geographic Area Court #15 20 Franklin Sq, New Britain, CT 06051; Civil phone: 860-515-5180; Criminal phone: 860-515-5080. Hours: 9AM-5PM (EST). *Misdemeanor, Eviction, Small Claims.*
Note: Serving the towns of Berlin, New Britain, Newington, Rocky Hill and Wethersfield.
Civil Records: Access: Mail, online, in person. Only the court performs in person searches; visitors may not. No search fee. Required to search: name, years to search. Civil cases indexed by defendant, plaintiff. Civil records on computer for 3 years, then on microfiche. All info in archives at Record Center at Enfield, CT. Access to civil, family, and small claims case records is free online at www.jud.state.ct.us.
Criminal Records: Access: Mail, in person. Only the court performs in person searches; visitors may not. No search fee. Required to search: name, years to search, DOB. Criminal records on computer from 1985, then on microfiche. All info in archives at Record Center @ Enfield, CT. Data is purged every two years.
General Information: Public Access terminal is available. No sealed records released. Copy fee: $1.00 per page. Cert fee: $2.00. Certification fee is for criminal division. Civil fee varies. Payee: Clerk of Superior Court. No out-of-state checks accepted. Prepayment required. Mail requests: SASE required. Mail turnaround time 1 month.

Geographical Area Court #12 410 Center St, Manchester, CT 06040; 860-647-1091. Hours: 9AM-5PM; Phone Hours: 9AM-4PM (EST). *Misdemeanor, Eviction, Small Claims.*
Note: Evictions are handled by a special Housing Court, 18 Trinity, Hartford, CT, 860-566-8550. Serving the towns of East Hartford, Glastonbury, Manchester, Marlborough and South Windsor.
Civil Records: Access: Mail, online, in person. Both court and visitors may perform in person searches. No search fee. Required to search: name, years to search. Civil cases indexed by defendant. Civil records on computer for 3 years. Access to family and small claims case records is free online at www.jud.state.ct.us.
Criminal Records: Access: Mail, in person. Only the court performs in person searches; visitors may not. No search fee. Required to search: name, years to search, DOB. Criminal records on computer since 1999, available since 1979. In person search results returned by mail only.
General Information: No non disclosable records released. Copy fee: $1.00 per page. Cert fee: $3.00. Payee: Clerk of Superior Court. Prepayment required. Mail requests: SASE required. Mail turnaround time 1-2 weeks.

Geographical Area Court #13 111 Phoenix, Enfield, CT 06082; 860-741-3727. Hours: 9AM-5PM (EST). *Misdemeanor.*
Note: Eviction cases are handled by Hartford Housing, 860-756-7920. Serving the towns of East Granby, East Windsor, Enfield, Granby, Simsbury, Suffield, Windsor and Windsor Locks.
Civil Records: Access: In person only. Visitors must perform in person searches for themselves. No search fee. Required to search: name, years to search. Civil cases indexed by defendant. Civil records on computer for 1 year, microfiche by year, archived at Record Center at Enfield, CT.
Criminal Records: Access: In person, mail. Visitors must perform in person searches for themselves. No search fee. Required to search: name, years to search, DOB. Criminal records on computer for 3 years, microfiche by year, archived at Record Center at Enfield, CT.
General Information: Copy fee: $1.00 per page. Cert fee: $3.00 per 1st page. Payee: Clerk of Superior

Court. Will take personal check with ID. Prepayment required.

Geographical Area Court #17 131 N Main St, Bristol, CT 06010; 860-582-8111. Hours: 9AM-5PM (EST). *Misdemeanor, Eviction, Small Claims.* www.jud2.state.ct.us
Note: Serving the towns of Bristol, Burlington, Plainville, Plymouth and Southington.
Civil Records: Access: Phone, mail, in person. No search fee. Required to search: name, years to search. Civil cases indexed by defendant. Civil records on computer from 1997, on microfiche from 1982, prior on index cards from 1979-1992, microfiche 1988-1992 and docket books.
Criminal Records: Access: In person, mail. Only the court performs in person searches; visitors may not. No search fee. Required to search: name, years to search, DOB. Criminal records on computer from 1986, on microfiche from 1982, prior on index cards from 1979-1992, microfiche 1988-1996 and docket books; records on computer for 5 years, then put on microfiche.
General Information: No dismissals, not guilty, youthful offender or NOLLE records released. Copy fee: $1.00 per page. No cert fee. Payee: Clerk of Superior Court. Personal checks accepted. Prepayment required. Mail requests: SASE required. Mail turnaround time 1-2 days.

Geographical Area Court #14 101 LaFayette St, Hartford, CT 06106; 860-566-1630. Hours: 9-5PM (EST). *Misdemeanor.*
Note: Serving the towns of Avon, Bloomfield, Canton, Farmington, Hartford and West Hartford.
Criminal Records: Access: Mail, in person. Only the court performs in person searches; visitors may not. No search fee. Required to search: name, years to search, DOB. Computerized records for past 3 years.
General Information: Copy fee: $1.00 per page. Cert fee: $2.00. Payee: Clerk of Superior Court. Only cashiers checks and money orders accepted. Prepayment required. Mail requests: SASE required. Mail turnaround time 1 week.

Avon Probate Court 60 W Main St, Avon, CT 06001-0578; 860-409-4348; Fax: 860-409-4368. 9am-2;30M,T,Th;9-12;00-W,Fri (EST). *Probate.*

Berlin Probate Court 1 Liberty Sq, PO Box 400, New Britain, CT 06050-0400; 860-826-2696; Fax: 860-826-2695. 9AM-4PM (EST). *Probate.*
Note: District includes Town of New Britain, Kennsington, East Berlin

Bloomfield Probate Court Town Hall, 800 Bloomfield Ave, Bloomfield, CT 06002; 860-769-3548; Fax: 860-242-1167. Hours: 9AM-1PM, 2AM-4:30PM (EST). *Probate.*

Bristol Probate Court 111 N Main St, City Hall, 3rd Fl, Bristol, CT 06010; 860-584-6230; Fax: 860-584-3818. Hours: 9AM-5PM (EST). *Probate.*

Burlington Probate Court 200 Spielman Highway, Burlington, CT 06013; 860-673-2108; Fax: 860-673-8607. Hours: 1PM-6PM M-Th (and by app't) (EST). *Probate.*

Canton Probate Court Canton Town Hall, 3rd Fl, 4 Market St, PO Box 175, Collinsville, CT 06022-0175; 860-693-7851; Fax: 860-693-7889. Hours: 9AM-12PM M; 8:30AM-2PM Tu; 8:30AM-4PM W; 8:30AM-2PM Th; 9AM-12PM F (passports and other times by app't) (EST). *Probate.*

East Granby Probate Court PO Box 542, 9 Center St, East Granby, CT 06026-0542; 860-653-3434; Fax: 860-653-7085. Hours: 9AM-Noon T, W-Th (and by app't) (EST). *Probate.*

East Hartford Probate Court Town Hall, 740 Main St, East Hartford, CT 06108; 860-291-7278; Fax: 860-291-7211. 9AM-4PM (EST). *Probate.*

East Windsor Probate Court Town Hall, 1540 Sullivan Ave, South Windsor, CT 06074; 860-644-2511 X271; Fax: 860-648-5047. Hours: 8AM-2PM (EST). *Probate.*
Note: District includes Town of South Windsor

Enfield Probate Court 820 Enfield St, Enfield, CT 06082; 860-253-6305; Fax: 860-253-6388. Hours: 9AM-4:30PM (EST). *Probate.*

Farmington Probate Court One Monteith Dr, Farmington, CT 06032; 860-675-2360; Fax: 860-673-8262. Hours: 9AM-4PM (EST). *Probate.*

Glastonbury Probate Court PO Box 6523, 2155 Main St, Glastonbury, CT 06033-6523; 860-652-7629; Fax: 860-368-2520. Hours: 9:30AM-4:30PM (EST). *Probate.*

Granby Probate Court 15 N Granby Rd, Town Hall, PO Box 240, Granby, CT 06035-0240; 860-844-5314; Fax: 860-653-4769. Hours: 9AM-12:30 M, T,W (EST). *Probate.*

Hartford Probate Court 250 Constitution Plaza, 3rd Fl, Hartford, CT 06103; 860-757-9150; Fax: 860-724-1503. Hours: 9AM-4PM M-F; (4-6:30PM Mon. by app't) (EST). *Probate.*

Manchester Probate Court 66 Center St, Manchester, CT 06040; 860-647-3227; Fax: 860-647-3236. 8:30AM-Noon, 1-4:30PM (EST). *Probate.*

Marlborough Probate Court 26 N Main St, PO Box 29, Marlborough, CT 06447; 860-295-6239; Fax: 860-295-0317. 10:30-12;00 M; 10;30-N,1-4PM T,W;9am-12pm TH-and by app't) (EST). *Probate.*

New Hartford Probate Court 530 Main, New Hartford, CT 06057; 860-379-3254. 8;30-3pm-M,T,Th,; 8am-6pm-W;8-12;00-Fri (EST). *Probate.*
Note: Also serving;Barkhamsted,and Hartland

Newington Probate Court 66 Cedar St, Rear, Newington, CT 06111; 860-665-1285; Fax: 860-665-1331. Hours: 9AM-4PM M-W, F; 9AM-6PM Th (EST). *Probate.* Note: District includes towns of Rocky Hill, Wethersfield, Newington

Plainville Probate Court 1 Central Sq, Plainville, CT 06062; 860-793-0221 x250; Fax: 860-793-2424. Hours: 9AM-3PM M-Th; 9AM-1PM F (EST). *Probate.*

Simsbury Probate Court 933 Hopmeadow St, PO Box 495, Simsbury, CT 06070; 860-658-3277; Fax: 860-658-3206. 8:30-1, 2-4:30 M-F *Probate.*

Southington Probate Court Town Hall, 75 Main St, PO Box 165, Southington, CT 06489; 860-276-6253; Fax: 860-276-6255. Hours: 8:30AM-4:30PM M-W, F; 8:30AM-7PM Th (EST). *Probate.*

Suffield Probate Court 83 Mountain Rd, Town Hall, Suffield, CT 06078; 860-668-3835; Fax: 860-668-3029. 9AM-1PM (and by app't) (EST). *Probate.*

West Hartford Probate Court 50 S Main St, West Hartford, CT 06107; 860-523-3174; Fax: 860-236-8352. Hours: 8:30AM-4:30PM (EST). *Probate.*

Windsor Locks Probate Court Town Office Bldg, 50 Church St, Windsor Locks, CT 06096; 860-627-1450; Fax: 860-627-1451. Hours: 9AM-2PM M-Th (EST). *Probate.*

Windsor Probate Court 275 Broad St, PO Box 342, Windsor, CT 06095; 860-285-1976; Fax: 860-285-1909. Hours: 8:30AM-4:30PM M-Th; 8:30AM-Noon Fri (EST). *Probate.*

Litchfield County

Litchfield Judicial District Court PO Box 247, Litchfield, CT 06759; 860-567-0885; Fax: 860-567-4779. Hours: 9AM-5PM (EST). *Felony, Civil Actions, Divorce.*
Civil Records: Access: Fax, mail, online, in person. Only the court performs in person searches; visitors may not. No search fee. Required to search: name, years to search. Civil cases indexed by defendant, plaintiff. Pending cases only on computer, on index cards from 1972. Access to civil case records is free online at www.jud.state.ct.us.
Criminal Records: Access: Fax, mail, in person. Only the court performs in person searches; visitors may not. No search fee. Required to search: name, years to search; also helpful: DOB. Pending cases only on computer, on index cards from 1972.
General Information: No sealed files released. No fee to fax results. Copy fee: $1.00 per page. Cert fee: $2.00. Payee: Clerk of Superior Court. Personal checks accepted. Prepayment required. Mail requests: SASE required. Mail turnaround time 3-4 weeks.

Geographical Area Court #18 80 Doyle Rd (PO Box 667), Bantam, CT 06750; 860-567-3942. Hours: 9AM-5PM (EST). *Misdemeanor, Eviction, Small Claims.*
Note: Serving Barkhamsted, Bethlehem, Bridgewater, Canaan, Colebrook, Cornwall, Goshen, Hartland, Harwinton, Kent, Litchfield, Morris, New Hartford, New Milford, Norfolk, North Canaan, Roxbury, Salisbury, Sharon, Thomaston, Torrington, Warren, Wash & Winchester
Civil Records: Access: Mail, online, in person. Both court and visitors may perform in person searches. No search fee. Required to search: name, years to search. Civil cases indexed by defendant. Civil records on computer for 2 years, on microfiche from 1986. Access to small claims case records is free online at www.jud.state.ct.us.
Criminal Records: Access: Mail, in person. Only the court performs in person searches; visitors may not. No search fee. Required to search: name, years to search, DOB; also helpful: address. Criminal records on computer for 1 year, microfiche from 1986, on index cards for 40 years. Archived at Records Center at Enfield, CT.
General Information: No youthful offender or non-discloseable records released. Copy fee: $1.00 per page. Cert fee: $3.00. Payee: Clerk of Superior Court. Personal checks accepted. Prepayment required. Mail requests: SASE required. Mail turnaround: 1 week.

Barkhamsted Probate Court *Probate.*
Note: Merged w/ New Hartford-860-379-3254

Canaan Probate Court Town Hall, 100 Pease St, PO Box 905, Canaan, CT 06018-0905; 860-824-7114; Fax: 860-824-3139. Hours: 9AM-1PM (and by app't) (EST). *Probate.*

Cornwall Probate Court PO Box 157, Town Office Bldg, Cornwall, CT 06753-0157; 860-672-2677; Fax: 860-672-2677. Hours: 9AM-12PM T & Th (EST). *Probate.*

Harwinton Probate Court Town Hall, 100 Bentley Dr, Harwinton, CT 06791; 860-485-1403; Fax: 860-485-0051. Hours: 1-6PM Tu-W (and by app't) (EST). *Probate.*

Kent Probate Court Town Hall, 41 Kent Green Blvd, PO Box 185, Kent, CT 06757-0185; 860-927-3729; Fax: 860-927-1313. Hours: 9AM-Noon Tu & Th (and by app't) (EST). *Probate.*

Litchfield Probate Court 74 West St, PO Box 505, Litchfield, CT 06759; 860-567-8065; Fax: 860-567-2538. 9AM-1PM (and by app't) (EST). *Probate.*

Note: District includes towns of Morris, Warren, and Litchfield

New Hartford Probate Court Town Hall, 530 Main St, PO Box 308, New Hartford, CT 06057; 860-379-3254; Fax: 860-379-0940. Hours: 8AM-3PM (till 12 on F) Wed. 9-6 PM (EST). *Probate.*
Note: We serve the towns of New Hartford, Barkhamsted, and Hartkand

New Milford Probate Court 10 Main St, New Milford, CT 06776; 860-355-6029; Fax: 860-355-6002. Hours: 9AM-Noon, 1-4PM M-Th, closed Friday (EST). *Probate.*
Note: District includes Town of Bridgewater. Also open by appt and mon.open till 5pm

Norfolk Probate Court 19 Maple Ave, PO Box 648, Norfolk, CT 06058; 860-542-5134; Fax: 860-542-5876. Hours: 9AM-Noon T & TH (and by app't) (EST). *Probate.*

Plymouth Probate Court 80 Main St, Terryville, CT 06786; 860-585-4014; Fax: 860-585-4098. Hours: 9AM-2PM Tu & Th (and by app't) (EST). *Probate.*

Roxbury Probate Court Town Hall, 29 North St, PO Box 203, Roxbury, CT 06783; 860-354-1184; Fax: 860-355-3091. Hours: 9AM-3PM Tu-Th (and by app't) (EST). *Probate.*

Salisbury Probate Court Town Hall, 27 Main St, PO Box 525, Salisbury, CT 06068; 860-435-5183; Fax: 860-435-5172. Hours: 9AM-Noon (and by app't) (EST). *Probate.*

Sharon Probate Court 63 Main St, PO Box 1177, Sharon, CT 06069; 860-364-5514; Fax: 860-364-5789. Hours: 2-4PM M-W & F (and by app't) (EST). *Probate.*

Thomaston Probate Court 158 Main St, Town Hall Bldg, PO Box 136, Thomaston, CT 06787; 860-283-4874; Fax: 860-283-1013 (police dept). Hours: 3-6PM M-Th (and by app't) (EST). *Probate.*

Torrington Probate Court Municipal Bldg, 140 Main St, Torrington, CT 06790; 860-489-2215; Fax: 860-496-5910. Hours: 8:30AM-4:30PM, M-W; 8:30AM-6:30PM, Tu; 8:30AM-12:30PM, F (EST). *Probate.* Note: District includes Town of Goshen

Washington Probate Court Town Hall, 2 Bryan Mem. Plaza, PO Box 295, Washington Depot, CT 06794; 860-868-7974; Fax: 860-868-0512. Hours: 9AM-Noon, 1-3PM M,W,F (and by app't) (EST). *Probate.* www.washingtonct.org/probate.html

Watertown Probate Court PO Box 84, Woodbury, CT 06798; 203-263-2417; Fax: 203-263-2748. Hours: 9AM-Noon, 1-3PM (EST). *Probate.*
Note: Waterbury probate Court merged with Woodbury Probate Court on 01/08/03.

Winchester Probate Court 338 Main St, PO Box 625, Winsted, CT 06098; 860-379-5576; Fax: 860-738-7053. Hours: 9AM-12,1-4PM M-W, 9Am-2PM, 3-7PM Th, til noon Fri (EST). *Probate.*
Note: District includes towns of Colebrook, Winsted

Woodbury Probate Court 281 Main St, South, PO Box 843, Woodbury, CT 06798; 203-263-2417; Fax: 203-263-2748. Hours: 9AM-Noon, 1PM-4PM M-Th (EST). *Probate.*
Note: District includes Town of Bethlehem, Watertown and Oakville

Middlesex County

Middlesex District Court - Criminal & GA Court #9 1 Court St, 1st Fl, Middletown, CT 06457-3348; 860-343-6445. Hours: 9AM-5PM (EST). *Felony, Misdemeanor.*
Note: Serving the towns of Chester, Clinton, Cromwell, Deep River, Durham, East Haddam, East Hampton, Essex, Haddam, Killingworth, Middlefield, Middletown, Old Saybrook, Portland and Westbrook.
Criminal Records: Access: Mail, in person. Only the court performs in person searches; visitors may not. No search fee. Required to search: name, years to search, DOB, signed release; also helpful: address, SSN. Criminal records on computer for 1 year from disposition or sentence, on microfiche prior to 1984, prior on index cards to 1961.
General Information: No youthful offender records or dismissals released. Copy fee: $1.00 per page. Cert fee: $2.50. Payee: Clerk, Superior Court. Personal checks accepted. Prepayment required. Mail requests: SASE required. Mail turnaround time 3-4 days.

Middlesex Judicial District Court - Civil 1 Court St, 2nd Fl, Middletown, CT 06457-3374; 860-343-6400; Fax: 860-343-6423. Hours: 9AM-5PM *Civil Actions, Divorce, Eviction, Small Claims.*
Civil Records: Access: Mail, online, in person. Only the court performs in person searches; visitors may not. Search fee: None. Required to search: name, years to search; also helpful: type of case, docket number. Civil cases indexed by defendant, plaintiff. Civil records on computer 1 year post-judgment; on index card back 15 years, prior on docket books, microfiche. Access to civil and family case records is free online at www.jud.state.ct.us.
General Information: No sealed records released. Will not fax results. Copy fee: $1.00 per page. Cert fee: $2.00; judgment file copy-$15.00 ($25 if certified); judgment in foreclosure action-$20.00; Exemplification copies-$20.00. Payee: Clerk, Superior Court. Personal checks accepted. Name and address must be on pre-printed check. Prepayment required. Mail requests: SASE required. Mail turnaround time 1 week.

Clinton Probate Court 50 E Main St, PO Box 130, Clinton, CT 06413-0130; 860-669-6447; Fax: 860-669-6447 (call first). Hours: 10AM-3PM M-Th (Fri. by app't) (EST). *Probate.*

Deep River Probate Court Town Hall, 174 Main St, PO Box 391, Deep River, CT 06417; 860-526-6026; Fax: 860-526-6094 (call first). Hours: 9AM-Noon M,F;9am-5pmT,Th;9-12;00 and 2:30-5PM on W (EST). *Probate.*

East Haddam Probate Court PO Box 217, 7 Main St, East Haddam, CT 06423; 860-873-5028; Fax: 860-873-5025. Hours: 10AM-2PM (and by app't) (EST). *Probate.*

East Hampton Probate Court 20 E High St, Annex, East Hampton, CT 06424; 860-267-9262; Fax: 860-267-6453. Hours: 9AM-2PM M-Th (EST). *Probate.*

Essex Probate Court Town Hall, 29 West Ave, Essex, CT 06426; 860-767-4340 X125; Fax: 860-767-2538. Hours: 9AM-1PM (and by app't) (EST). *Probate.* www.essexprobate.com

Haddam Probate Court 30 Field Park Dr, Haddam, CT 06438; 860-345-8531; Probate phone: 860-345-8531 x210; Fax: 860-345-3730. Hours: 10AM-2PM T-Th (and by app't) (EST). *Probate.*

Killingworth Probate Court 323 Route 81, Killingworth, CT 06419; 860-663-2304; Fax: 860-663-3305. Hours: 9AM-Noon M,W,F (and by app't) (EST). *Probate.*

Middletown Probate Court 94 Court St, Middletown, CT 06457; 860-347-7424; Fax: 860-346-1520. Hours: 8:30AM-4:30PM (EST). *Probate.*
Note: District includes towns of Cornwall, Durham, Middlefield

Old Saybrook Probate Court 251 Main St, Old Saybrook, CT 06475; 860-395-3128; Fax: 860-395-3125. Hours: 9AM-1PM M,T,TH,F (Wed. eves by app't) (EST). *Probate.*
Note: Court is open on Wed. evenings, also

Portland Probate Court 33 E Main St, PO Box 71, Portland, CT 06480; 860-342-6739; Fax: 860-342-6775. Hours: 9AM-2PM (EST). *Probate.*

Saybrook Probate Court 203 Middlesex Ave (no Mail), PO Box 628, Chester, CT 06412; 860-526-0013 X221; Fax: 860-526-0004. Hours: 9:30AM-12:30PM Tue, Wed, Thur (and by app't) (EST). *Probate.* Note: District includes Town of Chester

Westbrook Probate Court 866 Boston Post Rd, Westbrook, CT 06498; 860-399-5661; Fax: 860-399-3092. Hours: 1-4:30PM (EST). *Probate.*

New Haven County

Ansonia-Milford Judicial District Court 14 W River St (PO Box 210), Milford, CT 06460; 203-877-4293. Hours: 9AM-4PM (EST). *Felony, Civil Actions, Divorce.*
Civil Records: Access: Mail, fax, online, in person. Only the court performs in person searches; visitors may not. No search fee. Required to search: name, years to search. Civil cases indexed by defendant, plaintiff. Civil records on computer back to 1993, on index cards from 1978. Purged computer records are on microfilm. Maintain 75 years at Records Center at Enfield, CT. Access to civil, family, and small claims case records is free online at www.jud.state.ct.us.
Criminal Records: Access: Mail, in person. Only the court performs in person searches; visitors may not. No search fee. Required to search: name, years to search, DOB; also helpful-SSN. Criminal records on computer back to 1993, on index cards from 1978. Purged computer records are on microfilm. Maintain 75 years at Records Center at Enfield, CT.
General Information: Will fax results only to toll-free or local numbers. Copy fee: $1.00 per page. Payee: Clerk of Superior Court. Personal checks accepted. Prepayment required. Mail requests: SASE required. Mail turnaround time 1-2 weeks.

Meriden Judicial District Court 54 W Main St, Rm 128, Meriden, CT 06451; 203-238-6666. Hours: 9AM-4PM (EST). *Civil Actions, Divorce, Eviction, Housing Small Claims.*
Civil Records: Access: Mail, online, in person. Only the court performs in person searches; visitors may not. No search fee. Required to search: name, years to search. Civil cases indexed by defendant, plaintiff. Pending and 1 yr after disposed cases on computer, on microfiche from 1984, prior on index cards. Access to civil, family, and small claims case records is free online at www.jud.state.ct.us.
General Information: No acknowledgments of paternity, agreements to support prior to 10/01/95 records released. Copy fee: $1.00 per page. Cert fee: $2.00. Payee: Clerk of Superior Court. In state personal checks accepted. Prepayment required. Mail requests: SASE required. Mail turnaround: 1-2 days.

New Haven Judicial District Court 235 Church St, New Haven, CT 06510; 203-503-6800; Fax: 203-789-6424. 9AM-5PM (EST). *Felony, Civil Actions, Family, Divorce, Small Claims.*
www.jud.state.ct.us/directory/directory/location/newhaven.htm
Civil Records: Access: Phone, mail, online, in person. Both the court (all cases) and visitors (live cases only) may perform in person searches. No search fee. Required to search: name, years to search. Civil cases indexed by defendant, plaintiff. Pending cases on computer, disposed cases deleted after 1 year, on microfiche from 1972, prior on index cards. Access to civil and family case records is free online at www.jud.state.ct.us.
Criminal Records: Access: Mail, in person. Only the court performs in person searches; visitors may not. No search fee. Required to search: name, years to search, DOB. Pending criminal cases on computer, disposed deleted after 1 year, prior on index cards.
General Information: Public Access terminal is available. (Live civil cases only.) No sealed records released. Copy fee: $1.00 per page. Cert fee: $2.00. Payee: Clerk of Superior Court. CT personal checks accepted if address on check matches address on drivers license. Prepayment required. Mail requests: SASE required. Mail turnaround time 2-5 weeks.

Waterbury Judicial District Court 300 Grand St, Waterbury, CT 06702; 203-591-3300; Civil phone: Small claims: 203-591-3320; Criminal phone: 203-236-8100; Fax: 203-591-3325. Hours: 9AM-5PM (EST). *Civil Actions, Small Claims, Divorce.*
Note: Address mail requests for Misdemeanor criminal searches to 400 Grand St. (Geographical Area Court #4)
Civil Records: Access: Fax, mail, online, in person. Only the court performs in person searches; visitors may not. No search fee. Required to search: name, years to search. Civil cases indexed by defendant. Civil records on computer back to 1990; none-computer records go back to 1900. Access to civil, family, and small claims case records is free online at www.jud.state.ct.us. Phone access limited to one search.
General Information: Copy fee: $1.00 per page. Cert fee: $5.00. Payee: Clerk of Superior Court. Personal checks accepted. Prepayment required. Mail requests: SASE required. Mail turnaround: 1-2 weeks.

Geographical Area Court #22 14 W River St, Milford, CT 06460; 203-874-0674 (Small Claims); Civil phone: 203-877-4293; Criminal phone: 203-874-1116. Hours: 1-2:30PM, 4-5PM (EST). *Misdemeanor, Eviction, Housing Small Claims.*
Note: Serving the towns of Milford and West Haven.
Civil Records: Access: Mail, online, in person. Only the court performs in person searches; visitors may not. No search fee. Required to search: name, years to search. Civil cases indexed by defendant, plaintiff. Civil records on computer for 6 months, after disposal, on microfiche from 1986, prior on index cards and docket books. Access to civil, family, and small claims case records is free online at www.jud.state.ct.us.
Criminal Records: Access: Mail, in person. Only the court performs in person searches; visitors may not. No search fee. Required to search: name, years to search; also helpful: DOB. Criminal records on computer for 6 months, after disposal, on microfiche from 1986, prior on index cards and docket books.
General Information: Copy fee: $1.00 per page. Cert fee: $2.00. Payee: Clerk of Superior Court. Personal checks accepted. Prepayment required. Mail requests: SASE required. Mail turnaround time 1 week.

Geographical Area Court #23 121 Elm St, New Haven, CT 06510; 203-789-7461; Civil phone: 203-503-6800; Fax: 203-789-7492. Hours: 9AM-5PM (EST). *Misdemeanor, Eviction.*
Note: Small claims is located at 235 Church St, Clerk's Office, New Haven, CT 06510, 203-503-6800. Serving the towns of Bethany, Branford, East Haven, Guilford, Madison, New Haven, North Branford and Woodbridge.
Civil Records: Access: Mail, online, in person. Only the court performs in person searches; visitors may not. No search fee. Required to search: name, years to search. Civil records on log book for small claims. Records go back to 1800s. Access to civil, family, and small claims case records is free online at www.jud.state.ct.us.
Criminal Records: Access: Mail, in person. Only the court performs in person searches; visitors may not. No search fee. Required to search: name, years to search, DOB. Criminal records on computer back 13 months, microfiche from 1986, prior archived for criminal and motor vehicle. In person search results mailed back.
General Information: No dismissals, juvenile records released. Copy fee: $1.00 per page. Cert fee: $2.00. Payee: Superior Court. Personal checks accepted. Prepayment required. Mail requests: SASE required. Mail turnaround time 2-3 weeks.

Geographical Area Court #4 400 Grand St, Waterbury, CT 06702; 203-236-8100; Fax: 203-236-8099. Hours: 9AM-5PM (EST). *Felony, Misdemeanor, Traffic.* www.jud.state.ct.us
Note: Serving the towns of Middlebury, Naugatuck, Prospect, Southbury, Waterbury, Watertown, Wolcott and Woodbury.
Criminal Records: Access: Phone, mail, in person. Only the court performs in person searches; visitors may not. No search fee. Required to search: name, years to search; also helpful: DOB. Criminal records on computer since 1985. No certification of records available.
General Information: No youthful offenders records or dismissals released. Copy fee: $1.00 per page. Payee: Clerk of Superior Court. Personal checks accepted. Prepayment required. Mail requests: SASE required. Mail turnaround time 1-2 weeks.

Geographical Area Court #5 106 Elizabeth St, Derby, CT 06418; 203-735-7438; Civil phone: 203-735-9654; Criminal phone: 203-735-7438. Hours: 9AM-5PM (EST). *Misdemeanor, Eviction, Small Claims.*
Note: Serving the towns of Ansonia, Beacon Falls, Derby, Orange, Oxford, Seymour and Shelton.
Civil Records: Access: Mail, in person. Only the court performs in person searches; visitors may not. No search fee. Required to search: name, years to search. Civil cases indexed by defendant, plaintiff. Pending and records for 1 yr after disposal on computer, prior on index cards. They only hold small claims civil records in this office. Access to small claims case records is free online at www.jud.state.ct.us. In person search results are mailed back.
Criminal Records: Access: Mail, in person. Only the court performs in person searches; visitors may not. No search fee. Required to search: name, years to search, DOB. Pending and records for 1 yr after disposal on computer, on microfiche from 1986, prior on index cards. In person search results returned by mail only.
General Information: No sealed records released. Copy fee: $1.00 per page. Cert fee: $2.00. Payee: Clerk of Superior Court. Personal checks accepted. Prepayment required. Mail requests: SASE not required. Mail turnaround time 1-2 weeks.

Geographical Area Court #7 54 W Main St, Meriden, CT 06451; Criminal phone: 203-238-6130; Fax: 203-238-6016. Hours: 9AM-5PM (EST). *Misdemeanor, Small Claims.*
Note: Serving the towns of Cheshire, Hamden, Meriden, North Haven and Wallingford.
Civil Records: Access: Mail, online, in person. Only the court performs in person searches; visitors may not. No search fee. Required to search: name, years to search. Civil cases indexed by defendant, plaintiff. Pending and 1 yr after disposed cases on computer, on microfiche from 1985, prior on index cards. All manual records by docket number. Access to civil, family, and small claims case records is free online at www.jud.state.ct.us.
Criminal Records: Access: Phone, mail, in person. Only the court performs in person searches; visitors may not. No search fee. Required to search: name, years to search, DOB. Criminal records on computer since 1986, purged every 6 months and maintained in Enfield, CT.
General Information: No sealed records released. Copy fee: $1.00 per page. Cert fee: $10.00. Payee: Clerk of Superior Court. Personal checks accepted. Prepayment required. Mail requests: SASE required. Mail turnaround time 1-2 days.

Bethany Probate Court Town Hall, 40 Peck Rd, Bethany, CT 06524; 203-393-3744; Fax: 203-393-0821. 9AM-Noon, by appt (EST). *Probate.*

Branford Probate Court PO Box 638, 1019 Main St, Branford, CT 06405-0638; 203-488-0318; Fax: 203-315-4715. Hours: 9AM-Noon, 1-4:30PM (till Noon, Fridays in Summer) (EST). *Probate.*

Cheshire Probate Court 84 S Main St, Cheshire, CT 06410; 203-271-6608; Fax: 203-271-6628. Hours: 8:30AM-1PM, 1:30PM-4PM M-Th (EST). *Probate.* Note: District includes town of Prospect. Courts cosed on Fridays.

Derby Probate Court 253 Main St, 2nd Fl, Ansonia, CT 06401; 203-734-1277; Fax: 203-736-1434. 8:30AM-5PM M-Th; 8;30-4 F (EST). *Probate.* Note: District includes towns of Ansonia, Seymour

East Haven Probate Court 250 Main St, Town Hall, East Haven, CT 06512; 203-468-3895; Fax: 203-468-5155. Hours: 9:30AM-4:30PM, M; 9:30AM-3:30PM, Tu; 8:30AM-3:30PM, W; 8:30AM-4:30PM, Th; 9AM-1PM, F; (EST). *Probate.*

Guilford Probate Court Town Hall, 31 Park St, Guilford, CT 06437; 203-453-8006; Fax: 203-453-8132. Hours: 9AM-Noon,1-4PM M,T,Th,F; 9AM-Noon W (EST). *Probate.*

Hamden Probate Court Govt. Center, 2750 Dixwell Ave, Hamden, CT 06518; 203-287-7082; Fax: 203-287-7087. 8:30AM-4:30PM *Probate.*

Madison Probate Court 8 Campus Dr, Madison, CT 06443; 203-245-5661; Fax: 203-245-5653. 9AM-3PM (and by app't) (EST). *Probate.*

Meriden Probate Court City Hall ,142 E Main St, Rm 113, Meriden, CT 06450; 203-630-4150; Fax: 203-630-4043. Hours: 8:30AM-7PM M; 8:30-4:30 T-F (EST). *Probate.*

Milford Probate Court Parsons Government Office Complex, 70 W River St, PO Box 414, Milford, CT 06460; 203-783-3205; Fax: 203-783-3364. Hours: 9AM-5PM (EST). *Probate.*

Naugatuck Probate Court Town Hall, 229 Church St, Naugatuck, CT 06770; 203-720-7046; Fax: 203-720-5476. Hours: 8:45AM-4PM M-Th ;8:45AM-2PM F (EST). *Probate.* Note: District includes Town of Beacon Falls

New Haven Probate Court 200 Orange St, 1st Fl, PO Box 905, New Haven, CT 06504; 203-946-4880; Fax: 203-946-5962. Hours: 9AM-4PM (EST). *Probate.*

North Branford Probate Court 909 Foxon Rd, PO Box 214, North Branford, CT 06471; 203-484-6007; Fax: 203-484-6017. Hours: 8:45AM-12:45PM (EST). *Probate.*

North Haven Probate Court 18 Church St, PO Box 175, North Haven, CT 06473-0175; 203-239-5321 X775; Fax: 203-239-1874. Hours: 8:30AM-4:30PM M-Th (and by app't) (EST). *Probate.*

Orange Probate Court 525 Orange Center Rd, Orange, CT 06477; 203-891-2160; Fax: 203-891-2161. Hours: 8:30AM-Noon (EST). *Probate.*

Oxford Probate Court Town Hall, Rt. 67, Oxford, CT 06478; 203-888-2543 x3014; Fax: 203-888-2136. Hours: 7-9PM Mon, 7-9PM Tu-W, 1-5PM, 9AM-5PM, 7-9PM Th (EST). *Probate.*

Southbury Probate Court Townhall Annex, 421 Main St South, PO Box 674, Southbury, CT 06488; 203-262-0641; Fax: 203-264-9310. Hours: 9AM-4:30PM (and by app't) (EST). *Probate.*

Wallingford Probate Court Town Hall, 45 S Main St, Rm 114, Wallingford, CT 06492; 203-294-2100; Fax: 203-294-2109. Hours: 9AM-5PM (EST). *Probate.*

Waterbury Probate Court 236 Grand St, Waterbury, CT 06702; 203-755-1127; Fax: 203-597-0824. Hours: 9AM-4:45PM MTWF; 9AM-6PM Th; 9AM-Noon Sat (EST). *Probate.*
Note: District includes towns of Middlebury, Wolcott

West Haven Probate Court 355 Main St, PO Box 127, West Haven, CT 06516; 203-937-3552/3/4/5; Fax: 203-937-3556. Hours: 9AM-4PM (EST). *Probate.*

Woodbridge Probate Court Town Hall, 11 Meetinghouse Ln, Woodbridge, CT 06525; 203-389-3410; Fax: 203-387-5878. Hours: 9AM-1PM M, 9AM-2PM W (EST). *Probate.*

New London County

New London Judicial District Court 70 Huntington St, New London, CT 06320; 860-443-5363. Hours: 9AM-5PM (EST). *Felony, Civil Actions, Divorce.*
Civil Records: Access: Mail, online, in person. No search fee. Required to search: exact name, years to search. Civil cases indexed by defendant, plaintiff. Civil records pending and 1 yr after disposed on computer, on microfiche from mid-70s. Access to civil and family case records is free online at www.jud.state.ct.us. In person access limited to five names.
Criminal Records: Access: Mail, in person. Only the court performs in person searches; visitors may not. No search fee. Required to search: name, years to search; also helpful: DOB. Criminal records on computer from 1991, prior on index cards.
General Information: Public Access terminal is available. (Civil records only on terminal.) No sealed or youthful offender records released. Copy fee: $1.00 per page. Cert fee: $2.00. Payee: Clerk of Superior Court. Personal checks accepted. Prepayment required. Mail requests: SASE required. Mail turnaround time 2 weeks.

Norwich Judicial District Court 1

Courthouse Sq, Norwich, CT 06360; 860-887-3515; Fax: 860-887-8643. Hours: 9AM-5PM (EST). *Civil Actions, Divorce.*

www.jud.state.ct.us

Civil Records: Access: Phone, mail, fax, online, in person. Both court and visitors may perform in person searches. No search fee. Required to search: name, years to search. Civil cases indexed by defendant, plaintiff. Pending and disposed cases on computer from 1992, on microfiche from 1975, prior on index cards. Access to civil case records is free online at www.jud.state.ct.us.

General Information: Public Access terminal is available. No criminal search warrant, acknowledgment of paternity prior to 1995, sealed records released. Copy fee: $1.00 per page. Judgment copies $15.00. Cert fee: $2.00. Certified copy of Judgment $25.00. Payee: Clerk of Superior Court. Personal checks accepted. Checks must have imprinted name and address and match valid CT driver license. Prepayment required. Mail requests: SASE required. Mail turnaround time up to 2 months.

Geographical Area Court #10 112 Broad St,

New London, CT 06320; 860-443-8343; Civil phone: 860-443-8346. Hours: 9AM-5PM (EST). *Misdemeanor, Eviction, Small Claims.*

www.jud.state.ct.us

Note: Serving the towns of East Lyme, Groton, Ledyard, Lyme, New London, North Stonington, Old Lyme, Stonington and Waterford.

Civil Records: Access: Mail, online, in person. Both court and visitors may perform in person searches. No search fee. Required to search: name, years to search. Civil cases indexed by defendant. Civil records on index cards and docket books. Access to civil, family, and small claims case records is free online at www.jud.state.ct.us.

Criminal Records: Access: Mail, in person. Only the court performs in person searches; visitors may not. No search fee. Required to search: name, years to search, DOB. Criminal records on computer for 2 years; on microfiche back to 1962.

General Information: No sealed, dismissed, youth or program records released. Copy fee: $1.00 per page. No cert fee. Certification available from State Record Center. Payee: Clerk, Superior Court. Personal checks accepted. Prepayment required. Mail requests: SASE required. Mail turnaround time up to 2 months.

Geographical Area Court #21 1 Courthouse

Sq, Norwich, CT 06360; Civil phone: 860-887-3515; Criminal phone: 860-889-7338. Hours: 1-2:30PM, 4-5PM (EST). *Misdemeanor, Eviction, Small Claims.*

www.jud.state.ct.us

Note: Serving the towns of Bozrah, Colchester, Franklin, Griswold, Lebanon, Lisbon, Montville, Norwich, Preston, Salem, Sprague and Voluntown.

Civil Records: Access: Mail, online, in person. No search fee. Required to search: name, years to search. Civil cases indexed by defendant. Pending and 2-4 years history of disposed on computer, on microfiche from 1986, prior on index cards and docket books. Small claims, evictions not on computer. Access to civil case records is free online at www.jud.state.ct.us.

Criminal Records: Access: In person only. Visitors must perform in person searches for themselves. No search fee. Required to search: name, years to search, DOB. Pending and 2-4 years history of disposed on computer, on microfiche from 1986, prior on index cards and docket books. Small claims, evictions not on computer. Mail requests are referred to the Judicial Records Center in Enfield.

General Information: Public Access terminal is available. No youthful offender or dismissed/erased records released. Copy fee: $1.00 per page. Cert fee:

$2.00. Certified copy of Judgment $15.00. Payee: Superior Court GA #21. Personal checks accepted. Prepayment required. Mail requests: SASE required. Mail turnaround time 1-2 weeks.

Bozrah Probate Court Town Hall, 2nd Fl, One

River Rd, Bozrah, CT 06334; 860-889-2958; Fax: 860-887-7571. Hours: 10AM-1PM M,W (and by app't) (EST). *Probate.*

Colchester Probate Court Town Hall, 127

Norwich Ave, Colchester, CT 06415; 860-537-7290; Fax: 860-537-7298. Hours: 12:30PM-4:30PM M,F; 9AM-4:30PM T,W,TH (EST). *Probate.*

Note: The court also holds records for former probate court in Lebanon fro Jan '03 to date.

East Lyme Probate Court PO Box 519, 108

Pennsylvania Ave, Niantic, CT 06357; 860-739-6931; Fax: 860-739-6930. Hours: 8:30AM-4:30PM (EST). *Probate.*

Griswold Probate Court Town Hall, 32

School St, PO Box 369, Jewett City, CT 06351; 860-376-7060 x213; Fax: 860-376-0216. Hours: 5PM-8PM M; 1PM-5PM T-F (EST). *Probate.*

Lebanon Probate Court *Probate.*

Note: Court records now located at Colchester Probate Court at 860-537-7290.

Ledyard Probate Court 741 Colonel Ledyard

Hwy, Rte 17, Ledyard, CT 06339; 860-464-3219; Probate phone: 860-464-3218; Fax: 860-464-8531. Hours: 8:30AM-12:30PM Mon; 8:30AM-4:30PM Wed; 8:30AM-3:30PM W; closed Fri (app't only) (EST). *Probate.*

Lyme Probate Court Town Hall, 480 Hamburg

Rd, Lyme, CT 06371; 860-434-7733; Fax: 860-434-2989. Hours: 2-4PM T-Th (and by app't) (EST). *Probate.*

Montville Probate Court 310 Norwich-New

London Turnpike, Uncasville, CT 06382; 860-848-3030 X319; Fax: 860-848-2116. Hours: 9AM-1PM M,T,Th,F; 9AM-4PM W (EST). *Probate.*

New London Probate Court 181 State St,

Municipal Bldg, PO Box 148, New London, CT 06320; 860-443-7121; Fax: 860-437-8155. Hours: 9AM-4PM (EST). *Probate.*

Note: District includes Town of Waterford

North Stonington Probate Court 391

Norwich Westerly Rd, Route #2, PO Box 204, North Stonington, CT 06359; 860-535-8441; Fax: 860-535-8441 (call first). Hours: 9AM-Noon M & W; 1-4PM T,1-4:30PM Th (EST). *Probate.*

Norwich Probate Court PO Box 38, 100

Broadway, Rm 122, Norwich, CT 06360; 860-887-2160; Fax: 860-887-2401. Hours: 9AM-4:30PM (EST). *Probate.*

Note: District includes Towns of Franklin, Lisbon, Preston, Sprague, Voluntown

Old Lyme Probate Court 52 Lyme St,

Memorial Town Hall, Old Lyme, CT 06371; 860-434-1605 X222; Fax: 860-434-9283. Hours: 9AM-Noon, 1-4PM (EST). *Probate.*

Salem Probate Court 270 Hartford Rd, Salem,

CT 06420; 860-859-3873, 203-859-3036 (After hours); Fax: 860-537-0547. Hours: 10:00-Noon Fridays and app't (EST). *Probate.*

Stonington Probate Court 152 Elm St, PO

Box 312, Stonington, CT 06378; 860-535-5090; Fax: 860-535-0520. Hours: 9AM-Noon, 1-4PM (EST). *Probate.* Note: District includes Town of Mystic

Tolland County

Tolland Judicial District Court - Civil 69

Brooklyn St, Rockville, CT 06066; 860-896-4920. Hours: 9AM-5PM (EST). *Civil Actions, Divorce.*

Civil Records: Access: Mail, online, in person. Only the court performs in person searches; visitors may not. No search fee. Required to search: name, years to search. Civil cases indexed by defendant, plaintiff. Civil records on computer from 2001, on microfiche from 1980, all prior on index cards. Access to civil and family case records is free online at www.jud.state.ct.us.

General Information: No youthful offender, dismissed or not guilty verdict records released. Copy fee: $1.00 per page. Cert fee: $2.00. Payee: Clerk of Superior Court. Personal checks accepted. Prepayment required. Mail requests: SASE required. Mail turnaround time 1-2 weeks.

Tolland Judicial District Court - Criminal

20 Park St, Vernon, CT 06066; 860-870-3200. Hours: 9AM-5PM (EST). *Felony.*

Note: The address can use either Rockville or Vernon, but the US Postal Service will sometimes return mail addressed to Rockville.

Criminal Records: Access: In person only. Only the court performs in person searches; visitors may not. No search fee. Required to search: name, years to search; also helpful: DOB. Criminal records are for active cases only. Completed cases must be searched State Police. Mail requests should be sent to the State Police Bureau in Middletown, CT.

General Information: No youthful offender, dismissed or not guilty verdict records released. Copy fee: $1.00 per page. Cert fee: $2.00. Payee: Clerk of Superior Court. Personal checks accepted. Prepayment required. Mail requests: SASE required. Mail turnaround time 1 week.

Geographical Area Court #19 20 Park St,

PO Box 980, Rockville, CT 06066-0980; 860-870-3200. Hours: 9AM-4PM (EST). *Misdemeanor.*

www.jud2.state.ct.us

Note: Serving the towns of Andover, Bolton, Columbia, Coventry, Ellington, Hebron, Mansfield, Somers, Stafford, Tolland, Union, Vernon and Willington.

Criminal Records: Access: Mail, in person. Only the court performs in person searches; visitors may not. No search fee. Required to search: name, years to search, DOB. Criminal records on computer approx. 2 yrs from disposition, on microfiche from 1985, prior on index cards.

General Information: No youthful offender records released. Will not fax results. Copy fee: $1.00 per page. Cert fee: $2.00. Payee: Clerk of Superior Court. Personal checks accepted. Prepayment required. Mail requests: SASE required. Mail turnaround time 7-14 days.

Hebron Probate Court 15 Gilead St, Hebron,

CT 06248; 860-228-5971; Fax: 860-228-4859. Hours: 8AM-Noon Tu Wed; 8A-10AM Fri (and by app't) (EST). *Probate.*

Andover Probate Court 222 Bolton Center

Rd, Bolton, CT 06043; 860-647-7979; Fax: 860-649-8674. Hours: 8:30-4:30PM M,T-Th; 8:30-4PM TH; 8:30-1PM Fri (EST). *Probate.*

Note: District includes towns of Andover, Bolton and Columbia

Ellington Probate Court PO Box 268, 14 Park

Pl, Rockville, CT 06066; 860-872-0519; Fax: 860-870-5140. Hours: M-closed,T,W-9am-4pm,Th-9am-7pm,Fri-9am-1pm (EST). *Probate.*

Note: District includes Towns of Vernon, Ellington.

Mansfield Probate Court 4 S Eagleville Rd, Storrs, CT 06268; 860-429-3313; Fax: 860-429-4088. Hours: 9AM-12PM, 2PM-5PM, Tu; 2-5PM W; 2-6:0PM, Th; 9AM-12pm, F (EST). *Probate.*

Stafford Probate Court Town Hall, 1 Main St, PO Box 63, Stafford Springs, CT 06076; 860-684-1783; Fax: 860-684-7173. Hours: 9AM-Noon, 1-4:30PM M; 9AM-Noon Tu-F (and by app't) (EST). *Probate.*

Note: District includes towns of Union, Stafford and Somers. Somers Probate Court was merged in with this court in Jan. 1999.

Tolland Probate Court 21 Tolland Green, Tolland, CT 06084; 860-871-3640; Fax: 860-871-3641. Hours: 9AM-1:30 M-W; 4:30-7:30PM Th (and by app't) (EST). *Probate.*

Note: District includes Town of Willington

Windham County

Windham Judicial District Court 155 Church St, Putnam, CT 06260; 860-928-7749; Fax: 860-928-7076. Hours: 9AM-5PM (EST). *Civil Actions, Divorce.*

Civil Records: Access: Phone, mail, online, in person. Only the court performs in person searches; visitors may not. No search fee. Required to search: name, years to search. Civil cases indexed by defendant, plaintiff. Civil records on computer for 1 year, prior on index cards, prior to 1970s archived. Access to civil and family case records is free online at www.jud.state.ct.us.

General Information: No sealed, dismissed criminal, not guilty verdict records released. Copy fee: $1.00 per page. Cert fee: $2.00. Payee: Clerk of Superior Court. Personal checks accepted. Prepayment required. Mail requests: SASE required. Mail turnaround time 1-2 days.

Geographical Area Court #11 120 School St, #110, Danielson, CT 06239-3024; 860-779-8480; Fax: 860-779-8488. Hours: 9AM-5PM (EST). *Felony, Misdemeanor, Eviction, Small Claims.*

Note: Serving the towns of Ashford, Brooklyn, Canterbury, Chaplin, Eastford, Hampton, Killingly, Plainfield, Pomfret, Putnam, Scotland, Sterling, Thompson, Windham and Woodstock.

Civil Records: Access: Phone, mail, online, in person. Both the court and visitors may perform in person searches. No search fee. Required to search: name, years to search. Civil cases indexed by defendant. Small claims records on computer since 08/96; all other records on index cards. Access to small claims case records is free online at www.jud.state.ct.us.

Criminal Records: Access: Phone, mail, in person. Only the court performs in person searches; visitors may not. No search fee. Required to search: name, years to search, DOB. Pending criminal and 1 year after disposed on computer, on microfiche from 1986, prior on index cards.

General Information: Public Access terminal is available. (Civil only is available.) No sealed records released. Will not fax results. Copy fee: $1.00 per page. Cert fee: $2.00. Payee: Clerk of Superior Court. Personal checks accepted. Prepayment required. Mail requests: SASE required. Mail turnaround time 1-2 weeks.

Ashford Probate Court 20 Pompey Hollow Rd, PO Box 61, Ashford, CT 06278; 860-429-4986; Fax: 860-429-1114. Hours: 1PM-3:30PM TH (and by app't) (EST). *Probate.*

Brooklyn Probate Court Town Hall, 4 Wolf Den Rd, PO Box 356, Brooklyn, CT 06234-0356; 860-774-5973; Fax: 860-779-3744. Hours: 11AM-4:30PM T (and by app't) (EST). *Probate.*

Canterbury Probate Court, CT. *Probate.*

Note: Closed. See Plainfield Probate District.

Chaplin Probate Court c/o Eastford Probate District, PO Box 61, Ashford, CT 06278-0061; 860-974-1885; Fax: 860-974-0624. *Probate.*

Eastford Probate Court PO Box 207, 16 Westford Rd, Eastford, CT 06242-0207; 860-974-3024; Fax: 860-974-0624. Hours: 2-4PM T (and by app't) (EST). *Probate.*

Hampton Probate Court Town Hall, 164 Main St, PO Box 143, Hampton, CT 06247; 860-455-9132 x8; Fax: 860-455-0517. Hours: 1-4PM T, Th (EST). *Probate.*

Killingly Probate Court 172 Main St, Danielson, CT 06239; 860-779-5319; Fax: 860-779-5394. Hours: 8:30AM-Noon, 1-4:30PM M-F (EST). *Probate.*

Plainfield Probate Court Town Hall, 8 Community Ave, Plainfield, CT 06374; 860-230-3031; Fax: 860-230-3033. Hours: 8:30-3:30PM M-Th; 8:30AM-Noon F (EST). *Probate.*

Note: The Probate Court merged into this court in Jan. 2003.

Pomfret Probate Court 5 Haven Rd, Rt. 44, Pomfret Center, CT 06259; 860-974-0186; Fax: 860-974-3950. Hours: 10AM-4PM T-TH (and by app't) (EST). *Probate.*

Putnam Probate Court PO Box 548, Putnam, CT 06260; 860-963-6868; Fax: 860-963-6814. Hours: 8:30AM-4:30PM M-F. (EST). *Probate.*

Sterling Probate Court, CT. *Probate.*

Note: This court merged into the Plainfield Probate Court.

Thompson Probate Court 815 Riverside Dr, Town Hall, PO Box 74, North Grosvenordale, CT 06255; 860-923-2203; Fax: 860-923-3836. Hours: 8;30-11;00 -M,T,W,F;Th-3-6pm;S-9-12;00(and by app't) (EST). *Probate.*

Windham Probate Court 979 Main St, PO Box 34, Willimantic, CT 06226; 860-465-3049; Fax: 860-465-3012. Hours: 9AM-1PM M-Th; 9AM-Noon F (EST). *Probate.*

Note: District includes Willimanitc, Scottland and Windham.

Woodstock Probate Court 415 Route 169, Woodstock, CT 06281; 860-928-2223; Fax: 860-963-7557. Hours: 3PM-6PM, W, 1:30PM-4:30PM, Th (and by app't) (EST). *Probate.*

Connecticut Recording Offices

ORGANIZATION: 8 counties and 170 towns/cities. There is no county recording in this state. The recording officer is Town/City Clerk. Be careful not to confuse searching in the following towns/cities as equivalent to a county-wide search: Fairfield, Hartford, Litchfield, New Haven, New London, Tolland, and Windham. The entire state is in the Eastern Time Zone (EST).

REAL ESTATE RECORDS: Many towns do not perform real estate searches. Copy fees are usually $1.00 per page. Certification fees are usually $1.00 per document or per page.

UCC RECORDS: Connecticut adopted Revised Article 9 on October 1, 2001. Financing statements are filed at the state level, except for real estate related collateral, which are filed only with the Town/City Clerk. Some towns will perform UCC searches. Copies usually cost $1.00 per page.

TAX LIEN RECORDS: All federal and state tax liens on personal property are filed with the Secretary of State. Federal and state tax liens on real property are filed with the Town/City Clerk. Towns will not perform tax lien searches.

OTHER LIENS: Mechanics, judgments, lis pendens, municipal, welfare, carpenter, sewer & water, city/town.

ONLINE ACCESS: A number of towns offer free access to assessor information. The State's Municipal Public Access Initiative has produced a website of Town and Municipality general information at http://www.munic.state.ct.us/. Also, a private vendor has placed assessor records from a number of towns on the Internet. Visit http://data.visionappraisal.com

Andover Town

Town Clerk, 17 School Rd., Andover, CT 06232-0328. **Phone**-Town Clerk, R/E & UCC Recording- 860-742-0188; fax-860-742-7535; hours M 8:3AM-7PM; Tues-Th 8:30AM-3PM; F 8:30AM-12PM. Will not search records. Record copy- $1.00 per page. Cert fee: $1.00 per cert. Payee: Andover Town Clerk. **Other phones:** Assessor-860-742-7305; Treasurer-860-742-4035; Elections-860-742-7305; Vital Records-860-742-0188; Tax Collector-860-742-4035.

Ansonia City

City Clerk, 253 Main St, City Hall, Ansonia, CT 06401. **Phone**-203-736-5980; hours 8AM-5:30PM, M, T, W, F; 8AM-6:30PM, TH. Will not search records. UCC copy- $1.00 per page. They will make copies; you must provide volume, book and page numbers. Cert fee: $1.00 per cert. Payee: Ansonia City Clerk. **Other phones:** Assessor-203-734-5950; Treasurer-203-734-5920; Elections-203-736-5970; Vital Records-203-736-5980.

Ashford Town

Town Clerk, 25 Pompey Hollow Rd, Ashford, CT 06278. **Phone**-860-429-7044; fax-860-487-2025; hours 8:30AM-3PM M-W & F; 7-9PM Wed Will not search records. UCC copy- $1.00 per page. Cert fee: $2.00 per page. Payee: Town of Ashford. **Other phones:** Assessor-860-429-8583.

Avon Town

Town Clerk, 60 W. Main St, Avon, CT 06001. **Phone**-860-409-4310; fax-860-677-8428; hours 8:30AM-4:30PM (Summer hours: 8AM-4:45PM M-Th) Will not search records. UCC copy- $1.00 per page. Cert fee: $1.00 per cert. Payee: Avon Town Clerk. **Online Access to Property Assessor records:** property data is available free at www.avonassessor.com/index.shtml. **Other phones:** Assessor-860-409-4335; Elections-860-409-4350; Vital Records-860-409-4310.

Barkhamsted Town

Town Clerk, 67 Ripley Hill Rd., Pleasant Valley, CT 06063. **Phone**-Town Clerk, R/E & UCC Recording- 860-379-8665; fax-860-379-9284; hours 9AM-4PM (F open until 1PM) Will not search records. Record copy- $1.00 per page. Cert fee: $1.00 per doc. Payee: Town of Barkhamsted. **Other phones:** Assessor-860-379-3600; Treasurer-860-379-8285; Elections-860-738-4695; Vital Records-860-379-8665.

Beacon Falls Town

Town Clerk, 10 Maple Ave, Beacon Falls, CT 06403. **Phone**-Town Clerk, R/E & UCC Recording- 203-729-8254; fax-203-720-1078; hours 9AM-Noon, 1-4PM Will not search records. Record copy- $1.00 per page. Cert fee: $1.00 per cert. Payee: Beacon Falls Town Clerk. **Other phones:** Assessor-203-723-5253; Vital Records-203-729-8254.

Berlin Town

Town Clerk, 240 Kensington Rd, Kensington, CT 06037. **Phone**-860-828-7075, R/E Recording- 860-828-7035, UCC Recording- 860-828-7035; fax-860-828-8628; hours M-W, 8:30AM-4:30PM; Th 8:30AM-7PM; F 8:30AM-1PM www.town.berlin.ct.us Will not search records. UCC copy- $1.00 per page. Payee: Berlin Town Clerk. **Online Access to Real Estate, Marriage, Recorder, Assessor records:** Access recorders index for free at www.town.berlin.ct.us/resolution/. The assessor database is searchable at http://data.visionappraisal.com/BerlinCT/. **Other phones:** Assessor-860-828-7039; Treasurer-860-828-7023; Elections-860-828-7035; Vital Records-860-828-7035.

Bethany Town

Town Clerk, 40 Peck Rd, Bethany, CT 06524-3338. **Phone**-203-393-2100 x104, x105, R/E Recording- 203-393-2100 x104,x105,x106; fax-203-393-0821; hours 9:00AM-4:30PM (no copying or recording after 4PM). Will not search records. Record copy- $1.00 per page. Cert fee: $1.00 per cert. Payee: Bethany Town Clerk. **Other phones:** Assessor-203-393-2100 x112; Treasurer-203-393-2100 x100; Vital Records-203-393-2100 x104, x105, x106.

Bethel Town

Town Clerk, 1 School St., Bethel, CT 06801. **Phone**-Town Clerk, R/E & UCC Recording- 203-794-8505; fax-203-794-8588; hours 9AM-5PM M-F Will not search records. Record copy- $1.00 per page. Cert fee: $1.00 per cert. Payee: Bethel Town Clerk. **Other phones:** Assessor-203-794-8507; Vital Records-203-794-8505.

Bethlehem Town

Town Clerk, PO Box 160, Bethlehem, CT 06751. **Phone**-Town Clerk, R/E & UCC Recording- 203-266-7510; fax-203-266-7670; hours 9AM-Noon T,W,Th,F,Sat www.ci.bethlehem.ct.us Will not search records. Record copy- $1.00 per page. Cert fee: $1.00 per page. Payee: Bethlehem Town Clerk. **Other phones:** Assessor-203-266-5479; Treasurer-203-266-7677; Elections-203-266-7961; Vital Records-203-266-7510.

Bloomfield Town

Town Clerk, PO Box 337, Bloomfield, CT 06002. **Phone**-860-769-3506, R/E Recording- 860-769-3507; fax-860-769-3597; hours 9AM-5PM Will not search records. UCC copy- $1.00 per page. Cert fee: $1.00 per cert. Payee: Town of Bloomfield. **Other phones:** Assessor-860-769-3530; Elections-860-769-3507; Vital Records-860-769-3507.

Bolton Town

Town Clerk, 222 Bolton Ctr Rd, Bolton, CT 06043-7698. **Phone**-860-649-8066, R/E Recording- 860-649-8066 x106, UCC Recording- 860-649-8066 x107; fax-860-643-0021; hours 9AM-4PM M,W,Th; 9AM-5PM, 6-8PM T; 9AM-3PM F Will not search records. Record copy- $1.00 per page. Cert fee: $1.00 per cert. Payee: Bolton Town Clerk. **Other phones:** Assessor-860-649-8066 x100; Treasurer-860-649-7780; Elections-860-649-8066 x116; Vital Records-860-649-8066 x106.

Bozrah Town

Town Clerk, I River Rd, Bozrah, CT 06334. **Phone**-860-889-2689; fax-860-887-5449; hours 9AM-4PM T,W; 9AM-4PM Th; 9AM-Noon Fri

Will not search records. UCC copy- $1.00 per page. Payee: Bozrah Town Clerk. **Other phones:** Assessor-860-889-2689.

Branford Town

Town Clerk, PO Box 150, Branford, CT 06405. **Phone-**203-488-6305; fax-203-481-5561; hours 9AM-4:30PM (9AM-4PM Recording hours)
Will not search records. UCC copy- $1.00 per page. Cert fee: $1.00 per cert. Payee: Branford Town Clerk. **Online Access to Assessor records:** Search the town assessor database at http://data.visionappraisal.com/BranfordCT/. Free registration for full data. **Other phones:** Assessor-203-488-2039 x144.

Bridgeport Town

Town Clerk, 45 Lyon Terrace, City Hall, Rm 124, Bridgeport, CT 06604. **Phone-**203-576-7207; hours 9AM-4:30PM; Recording until 4PM
Will not search records. Record copy- $1.00 per page. Cert fee: $1.00 per page. Payee: Bridgeport Town Clerk. **Other phones:** Assessor-203-576-7077; Treasurer-203-576-7286; Appraiser/ Auditor-203-576-7241; Elections-203-576-7281; Vital Records-203-576-7445; City Hall Information-203-576-7200.

Bridgewater Town

Town Clerk, PO Box 216, Bridgewater, CT 06752-0216. **Phone-**Town Clerk, R/E & UCC Recording-860-354-5102; fax-860-350-5944; hours 8AM-Noon M,W,F; 8AM-5PM T. Will not search records. UCC copy- $1.00 per page. Cert fee: $1.00 per cert. Payee: Bridgewater Town Clerk. **Other phones:** Assessor-860-355-9379; Treasurer-860-354-2683; Elections-860-354-5102; Vital Records-860-354-5102.

Bristol City

City Clerk, PO Box 114, Bristol, CT 06011-0114. **Phone-**860-584-7600, R/E Recording- 860-584-6200, UCC Recording- 860-584-6200; hours 8:30AM-5PM
Will not search records. Record copy- $1.00 per page. Cert fee: $1.00 per cert. Payee: Bristol City Clerk. **Other phones:** Assessor-860-584-6240; Treasurer-860-584-6285; Elections-860-584-6200; Vital Records-860-584-6200.

Brookfield Town

Town Clerk, PO Box 5106, Brookfield, CT 06804-5106. **Phone-**203-775-7314, R/E Recording- 203-775-7313; fax-203-775-5231; hours 8:30AM-4:30PM; Most Th to 7PM-Call. www.brookfield.org
Will not search records. UCC copy- $1.00 per page. Cert fee: $1.00 per cert. Payee: Brookfield Town Clerk. **Online Access to Assessor records:** Search the town assessor field cards online at http://data.visionappraisal.com/BrookfieldCT/. Free registration for full data. **Other phones:** Assessor-203-775-7302; Treasurer-203-775-7308; Elections-203-775-7343; Vital Records-203-775-7313.

Brooklyn Town

Town Clerk, PO Box 356, Brooklyn, CT 06234. **Phone-**Town Clerk, R/E & UCC Recording- 860-774-9543; fax-860-779-3744; hours M-W 9AM-4:30PM; Th 9AM-6PM; F 9AM-1PM www.brooklynct.org
Will not search records. Record copy- $1.00 per page. Cert fee: $1.00 per page. Payee: Town of Brooklyn. **Other phones:** Assessor-860-774-5611; Treasurer-860-779-3411; Elections-860-779-3411; Vital Records-860-774-9543.

Burlington Town

Town Clerk, 200 Spielman Highway, Burlington, CT 06013. **Phone-**860-673-2108; fax-860-675-9312; hours 8:30AM-4PM
Will not search records. Record copy- $1.00 per page. Cert fee: $1.00 per cert. Payee: Burlington Town Clerk. **Other phones:** Assessor-860-673-3901.

Canaan Town

Town Clerk, PO Box 47, Falls Village, CT 06031. **Phone-**860-824-0707; fax-860-824-4506; hours 9AM-3PM. Will not search records. Record copy- $1.00 per page. Cert fee: $5.00 per cert. Payee: Town of Canaan. **Other phones:** Assessor-860-824-0707; Treasurer-860-824-0707; Appraiser/ Auditor-860-824-0707; Elections-860-824-0707; Vital Records-860-824-0707.

Canterbury Town

Town Clerk, PO Box 27, Canterbury, CT 06331-0027. **Phone-**Town Clerk, R/E & UCC Recording- 860-546-9377; fax-860-546-9295; hours 9AM-4PM M-W; 9AM-6:30PM TH; 9AM-1:30PM F
Will not search records. Record copy- $1.00 per page. Cert fee: $1.00 per cert. Payee: Canterbury Town Clerk. **Other phones:** Assessor-860-546-6035; Treasurer-860-546-2089; Elections-860-546-9377; Vital Records-860-546-9377.

Canton Town

Town Clerk, PO Box 168, Collinsville, CT 06022. **Phone-**Town Clerk, R/E & UCC Recording- 860-693-7870; fax-860-693-7840; hours 8:30AM-4:30PM
Will not search records. Record copy- $1.00 per page. Cert fee: $1.00 per cert. Payee: Town of Canton. **Other phones:** Assessor-860-693-7842; Treasurer-860-693-7852; Elections-860-693-7870; Vital Records-860-693-7870.

Chaplin Town

Town Clerk, PO Box 286, Chaplin, CT 06235. **Phone-**Town Clerk, R/E & UCC Recording- 860-455-9455; fax-860-455-0027; hours 9am-3pm M, W, Th; 1pm-7pm Tues
Will not search records. Record copy- $1.00 per page. Cert fee: $1.00 per cert. Payee: Town of Chaplin. **Other phones:** Assessor-860-455-9333; Treasurer-860-455-2170; Appraiser/ Auditor-860-455-9333; Elections-860-455-9455; Vital Records-860-455-9455.

Cheshire Town

Town Clerk, 84 S. Main St, Town Hall, Cheshire, CT 06410. **Phone-**Town Clerk, R/E & UCC Recording-203-271-6601; hours 8:30AM-4PM (Recording until 3:30PM) www.cheshirect.org
Will not search records. Record copy- $1.00 per page. Cert fee: $1.00 per cert. Payee: Cheshire Town Clerk. **Other phones:** Assessor-203-271-6620; Vital Records-203-271-6601.

Chester Town

Town Clerk, PO Box 218, Chester, CT 06412-0218. **Phone-**860-526-0013 x511, R/E Recording- 860-526-0013, UCC Recording- 860-526-0013; fax-860-526-0004; hours 9AM-N, 1-4PM M,W,Th; 9AM-N, 1-7PM T; 9AM-Noon Fri. www.chesterct.com
Will not search records. Record copy fee- $1.00 per page. Cert fee: $1.00 per cert. Payee: Chester Town Clerk. **Online Access to Assessor records:** Search the Assessor's Taxpayer Information System database at http://data.visionappraisal.com/ChesterCT. Free registration for full data. **Other phones:** Assessor-860-526-0013 x512; Treasurer-860-526-0013; Elections-860-526-0013 x211; Vital Records-860-526-0013.

City of New London

City Clerk, 181 State St, New London, CT 06320. **Phone-**City Clerk, R/E & UCC Recording- 860-447-5205; fax-860-447-1644; hours 8:30AM-3:50PM www.ci.new-london.ct.us
File here only for the city of New London, not for the county. There is no county filing in Connecticut. Will not search records. Record copy- $1.00 per page. Cert fee: $1.00 per cert. Payee: New London City

Clerk. **Online Access to Assessor records:** Search the city assessor's database at http://data.visionappraisal.com//NewLondonCT. Free registration required for full access. **Other phones:** Assessor-860-447-5216; Treasurer-860-447-5209; Appraiser/ Auditor-860-447-5216; Elections-860-447-5206; Vital Records-860-447-5205; Tax Collector-860-447-5208.

Clinton Town

Town Clerk, 54 E. Main St, Clinton, CT 06413. **Phone-**Town Clerk, R/E & UCC Recording- 860-669-9101; hours 9AM-4PM
Will not search records. UCC copy fee- $13.00 per 1st page and $5.00 per page each document. RE record copy- $1.00 per page. Cert fee: $1.00 per cert. Payee: Clinton Town Clerk. **Online Access to Assessor records:** Search Assessor records at http://data.visionappraisal.com/ClintonCT/. **Other phones:** Assessor-860-669-9269; Treasurer-860-669-9465; Elections-860-669-6436; Vital Records-860-669-9101.

Colchester Town

Town Clerk, 127 Norwich Ave, Colchester, CT 06415. **Phone-**Town Clerk, R/E & UCC Recording- 860-537-7215; fax-860-537-0547; hours 8:30AM-4:30PM M-W & F; 8:30-7PM Th www.colchesterct.net
Will not search records. Record copy- $1.00 per page. Cert fee: $1.00 per doc. Payee: Town of Colchester. **Online Access to Assessor records:** Search the town assessor database at http://data.visionappraisal.com/ColchesterCT/. Free registration for full data. **Other phones:** Assessor-860-537-7205; Treasurer-860-537-7225; Elections-860-537-7204; Vital Records-860-537-7215.

Colebrook Town

Town Clerk, PO Box 5, Colebrook, CT 06021. **Phone-**860-379-3359 ext 213, R/E Recording- 203-379-3359; fax-860-379-7215; hours 9AM-12;00-1-4:30PM
Will not search records. UCC copy- $1.00 per page. Cert fee: $1.00 per cert. Payee: Colebrook Town Clerk. **Online Access to Assessor records:** Assessor records are at http://data.visionappraisal.com/ColebrookCT/. **Other phones:** Assessor-203-379-3738.

Columbia Town

Town Clerk, 323 Jonathan Trumbull Hwy, Columbia, CT 06237. **Phone-**860-228-3284; fax-860-228-2335; hours 8:30AM-3PM M-W; 9AM-7PM Th; 8AM-Noon Fri
Will not search records. Record copy- $1.00 per page. Cert fee: $1.00 per cert. Payee: Columbia Town Clerk. **Other phones:** Assessor-860-228-9555.

Cornwall Town

Town Clerk, PO Box 97, Cornwall, CT 06753-0097. **Phone-**Town Clerk, R/E & UCC Recording- 860-672-2709; hours 9AM-4PM M-Th
Will not search records. Record copy- $1.00 per page. Cert fee: $1.00 per cert. Payee: Cornwall Town Clerk. **Other phones:** Assessor-860-672-2703; Treasurer-860-672-2707; Vital Records-860-672-2709.

Coventry Town

Town Clerk, 1712 Main St, Coventry, CT 06238. **Phone-**Town Clerk, R/E & UCC Recording- 860-742-7966; fax-860-742-8911; hours 8:30AM-4:30PM M-W; 8:30AM-6:30PM Th; 8:30AM-1:30PM
Will not search records. Record copy- $1.00 per page. Cert fee: $1.00 per cert. Payee: Town of Coventry. **Other phones:** Assessor-860-742-4067; Treasurer-860-742-3528; Elections-860-742-4061; Vital Records-860-742-7966.

Cromwell Town

Town Clerk, 41 West St, Cromwell, CT 06416-2100. **Phone**-860-632-3440; fax-860-632-3425; hours 8:30AM-4PM www.cromwellct.com
Will not search records. Record copy- $1.00 per page. Cert fee: $1.00 per cert. Payee: Town of Cromwell. **Other phones:** Assessor-860-632-3442; Treasurer-860-632-3440; Elections-860-632-3418; Vital Records-860-632-3440.

Danbury City

Town Clerk, 155 Deer Hill Ave, City Hall, Danbury, CT 06810. **Phone**-203-797-4531; hours 8:30AM-4:30PM www.ci.danbury.ct.us
Will not search records. UCC copy- $1.00 per page. Cert fee: $1.00 per cert. Payee: City of Danbury. **Online Access to Assessor, Land, Permits, Water Information records:** Search the city assessor database at http://data.visionappraisal.com/DanburyCT/. Free registration for full data. Also, search land, permits, and other records on the city public access at www.ci.danbury.ct.us/Public_Documents/DanburyCT_WebDocs/publicaccess. Follow prompts and use "public" for username and password. Site may be temporarily down. **Other phones:** Assessor-203-797-4556; Treasurer-203-797-4650.

Darien Town

Town Clerk, 2 Renshaw Rd, Darien, CT 06820-5397. **Phone**-203-656-7307; hours 8:30AM-4:30PM
Will not search records. Record copy- $1.00 per page. Cert fee: $1.00 per cert. Payee: Town of Darien. **Other phones:** Assessor-203-656-7310; Treasurer-203-656-7334.

Deep River Town

Town Clerk, 174 Main St, Town Hall, Deep River, CT 06417. **Phone**-Town Clerk, R/E & UCC Recording- 860-526-6024; fax-860-526-6023; hours 9AM-Noon,1-4PM
Will not search UCC records by name. UCC copy- $1.00 per page. Will not search real estate or tax lien records. RE record copy- $1.00 per page. Cert fee: $1.00 per cert. Payee: Deep River Town Clerk. **Other phones:** Assessor-860-526-6029; Elections-860-526-6024; Vital Records-860-526-6024.

Derby City

Town Clerk, 35 Fifth St, Derby, CT 06418-1897. **Phone**-Town Clerk, R/E & UCC Recording- 203-736-1462; fax-203-736-1458; hours 9AM-5PM
Will not search records. UCC copy- $1.00 per page. Cert fee: $1.00 per cert. Payee: Derby Town Clerk. **Other phones:** Assessor-203-736-1455; Treasurer-203-736-1452; Appraiser/ Auditor-203-736-1452; Elections-203-736-1462; Vital Records-203-736-1462.

Durham Town

Town Clerk, PO Box 428, Durham, CT 06422. **Phone**-860-349-3452, R/E Recording- 860-349-3453, UCC Recording- 860-349-3453; fax-860-349-0547; hours 9AM-4:30PM M-F, 10AM-N Sat except holiday weekends http://townofdurhamct.org
Will not search records. Record copy- $1.00 per page. Cert fee: $1.00 per cert. Payee: Durham Town Clerk. **Other phones:** Assessor-860-349-3452; Treasurer-860-349-3625; Elections-860-349-3452; Vital Records-860-349-3453.

East Granby Town

Town Clerk, PO Box TC, East Granby, CT 06026-0459. **Phone**-Town Clerk, R/E & UCC Recording- 860-653-6528; fax-860-653-4017; hours 8:30AM-Noon, 1-4PM M-Th; 8:30am-1PM F
Will not search records. UCC copy- $1.00 per page. Cert fee: $1.00 per doc. Payee: Town of East Granby. **Other phones:** Assessor-860-653-2852;

Treasurer-860-653-0096; Elections-860-653-0097; Vital Records-860-653-6528; Selectmen-860-653-2576.

East Haddam Town

Town Clerk, PO Box K, Town Office Bldg, East Haddam, CT 06423. **Phone**-860-873-5027; hours 9AM-4PM M,W,Th; 9AM-Noon F (T open until 7PM) http://easthaddam.org
Will not search records. Record copy- $1.00 per page. Cert fee: $1.00 per page. Payee: East Haddam Town Clerk. **Other phones:** Assessor-860-873-5026; Treasurer-860-873-5022; Elections-860-873-5027; Vital Records-860-873-5027.

East Hampton Town

Town Clerk, 20 E. High St, Town Hall, East Hampton, CT 06424. **Phone**-860-267-2519, R/E Recording- 203-267-2519; fax-860-267-1027; hours 8AM-4PM M,W,Th; 8AM-7:30PM T; 8AM-12:30PM F
Will not search records. UCC copy- $1.00 per page. Cert fee: $2.00 per page. Payee: East Hampton Town Clerk. **Other phones:** Assessor-203-267-2510.

East Hartford Town

Town Clerk, 740 Main St, East Hartford, CT 06108-3126. **Phone**-860-291-7230; fax-860-289-0831; hours 8:30AM-4:30PM www.ci.east-hartford.ct.us
Will search UCC records. UCC copy- $1.00 per page. Will not search real estate or tax lien records. Cert fee: $1.00 per cert. Payee: Town Clerk, East Hartford. **Other phones:** Assessor-860-291-7260 x268; Vital Records-860-291-7230.

East Haven Town

Town Clerk, 250 Main St, East Haven, CT 06512-3034. **Phone**-203-468-3201; fax-203-468-3372; hours 8:30AM-4:15PM
Will not search records. Record copy- $1.00 per page. Cert fee: $1.00 per cert. Payee: East Haven Town Clerk. **Other phones:** Assessor-203-468-3233; Vital Records-203-468-3201.

East Lyme Town

Town Clerk, PO Box 519, Niantic, CT 06357. **Phone**-Town Clerk, R/E & UCC Recording- 860-739-6931; fax-860-739-6930; hours 8:30AM-4:30PM
Will not search records. Record copy- $1.00 per page. Cert fee: $1.00 per cert. Payee: East Lyme Town Clerk. **Online Access to Assessor records:** Search the town assessor database at http://data.visionappraisal.com/EastLymeCT/. Free registration for full data. **Other phones:** Assessor-860-739-6931; Treasurer-860-739-6931; Vital Records-860-739-6931.

East Windsor Town

Town Clerk, PO Box 213, Broad Brook, CT 06016-0213. **Phone**-860-623-9467, R/E Recording- 860-292-8255, UCC Recording- 860-292-8255; fax-860-623-4798; hours 8:30-4:30PM M,T,W; 8:30AM-7:30PM Th; 8:30AM-12:30P
Will not search records. Record copy- $1.00 per page. Cert fee: $1.00 per cert. Payee: Town of East Windsor. **Other phones:** Assessor-860-623-8878; Treasurer-860-292-5909; Elections-860-292-5915; Vital records-860-292-8255; Selectmen-860-623-8122.

Eastford

Town Clerk, PO Box 273, Eastford, CT 06242. **Phone**-860-974-1885; fax-860-974-0624; hours 10AM-Noon, 1-4PM T,W
Will not search records. UCC copy- $1.00 per page. Cert fee: $1.00 per copy/document. Payee: Eastford Town Clerk. **Other phones:** Assessor-860-974-1291; Treasurer-860-974-0133; Elections-860-974-1885; Vital Records-860-974-1885.

Easton Town

Town Clerk, PO Box 61, Easton, CT 06612. **Phone**-203-268-6291; fax-203-261-6080; hours 9AM-2PM
Will not search records. Record copy- $1.00 per page + $20.00. Cert fee: $1.00 per cert. Payee: Town of Easton. **Other phones:** Assessor-203-268-6291; Treasurer-203-268-6291; Appraiserr-203-268-6291; Elections-203-268-6291; Vital Records-203-268-6291.

Ellington Town

Town Clerk, PO Box 187, Ellington, CT 06029-0187. **Phone**-Town Clerk, R/E & UCC Recording- 860-870-3105; hours 9AM-7PM M; 9AM-4:30PM T-F
Will not search records. Record copy- $1.00 per page. Cert fee: $1.00 per cert. Payee: Ellington Town Clerk. **Other phones:** Assessor-860-870-3109; Treasurer-860-870-3115; elections-860-870-3107; Vital Records-860-870-3105; Tax Collector-860-870-3113.

Enfield Town

Town Clerk, 820 Enfield St, Enfield, CT 06082-2997. **Phone**-860-253-6440, R/E Recording- 860-253-6435, UCC Recording- 860-253-6435; hours 9AM-5PM www.enfield.org
Will not search records. Record copy- $1.00 per page. Cert fee: $1.00 per doc. Payee: Town of Enfield. **Online Access to Tax Sale records:** Search the town's tax sale list free at www.enfield.org/Link_Tax.HTM. Use Control+F and search for name. **Other phones:** Assessor-860-253-6339; Treasurer-860-253-6330; Elections-860-253-6320; Vital Records-860-253-6440.

Essex Town

Town Clerk, PO Box 98, Essex, CT 06426. **Phone**-Town Clerk, R/E & UCC Recording- 860-767-4344 x129; fax-860-767-4560; hours 9AM-4PM
Will not search records. Record copy- $1.00 per copy. Cert fee: $1.00 per page. Payee: Essex Town Clerk. **Online Access to Property, Assessor records:** Access to property data is at http://data.visionappraisal.com/EssexCT/. **Other phones:** Assessor-860-767-4340 x124; Treasurer-860-767-4340 x127; Elections-860-767-4344 x129; Vital records-860-767-4344 x129.

Fairfield Town

Town Clerk, 611 Old Post Rd, Fairfield, CT 06430-6690. **Phone**-Town Clerk, R/E & UCC Recording-203-256-3090; hours (8:30AM-5PM 4:30PM Memorial Day-Labor Day)
Will not search records. Record copy- $1.00 per page. Cert fee: $1.00 per page. Payee: Fairfield Town Clerk. **Online Access to Assessor records:** Search the town assessor database at http://data.visionappraisal.com/FairfieldCT/. Free registration for full data. **Other phones:** Assessor-203-256-3110; Elections-203-256-3090; Vital Records-203-256-3090.

Farmington Town

Town Clerk, 1 Monteith Drive, Farmington, CT 06032-1053. **Phone**-860-673-8247, R/E Recording- 860-673-2380; fax-860-675-7140; hours 8:30AM-4:30PM
Will not search records. UCC copy- $1.00 per page. Cert fee: $1.00 per cert. Payee: Farmington Town Clerk. **Online Access to Assessor, Property records:** Access to the property assessor data is free at www.farmington-ct.org/As2002/index.php. **Other phones:** Assessor-860-673-2370.

Franklin Town

Town Clerk, 7 Meeting House Hill Rd, Town Hall, Franklin, CT 06254. **Phone**-860-642-7352; fax-860-642-6606; hours 8:30AM-3PM M-Th; 6PM-8PM T
Will not search records. UCC copy- $1.00 per page. Cert fee: $1.00 per cert. Payee: Franklin Town Clerk. **Other phones:** Assessor-860-642-6475; Treasurer-860-642-6055.

Glastonbury Town

Town Clerk, 2155 Main St, Glastonbury, CT 06033. **Phone**-Town Clerk, R/E & UCC Recording- 860-652-7616; fax-860-652-7639; hours 8AM-4:30PM www.glasct.org

Will not search records. Record copy- $1.00 per page. Cert fee: $1.00 per page. Payee: Glastonbury Town Clerk. **Online Access to Property, Assessor records:** Search town property information free on the GIS Interactive Mapping site at http://gis.glasct.org. Click on the binoculars for "Parcels" page where you can name search. Also, search town assessor data at http://data.visionappraisal.com/GlastonburyCT/. Free registration for full data. Land record indexes access is free at http://town.glasct.org/wb_or1 or www.glasct.org - click on General Information, important links or town dept and then town clerk. **Other phones:** Assessor-860-652-7600; Treasurer-860-652-7586; Elections-860-652-7616; Vital Records-860-652-7616.

Goshen Town

Town Clerk, PO Box 54, Goshen, CT 06756-0054. **Phone**-Town Clerk, R/E & UCC Recording- 860-491-3647; 9AM-Noon,1-4PM M-Th; 9AM-1PM F

Will not search records. Record copy- $1.00 per page. Cert fee: $1.00 per doc. Payee: Town Clerk. **Online Access to Assessor records:** Search the town assessor database at http://data.visionappraisal.com/goshenCT/. Free registration for full data. **Other phones:** Assessor-860-491-2115; Treasurer-860-491-2308; Elections-860-491-2308 x236; Vital Records-860-491-3647; Tax Office-860-491-3275 X226.

Granby Town

Town Clerk, 15 N. Granby Rd, Granby, CT 06035. **Phone**-860-844-5308; hours 9AM-Noon,1-4PM

Will not search records. UCC copy- $1.00 per page. Cert fee: $1.00 per cert. Payee: Town of Granby. **Online Access to Assessor records:** Search the town assessor's database at http://data.visionappraisal.com /GranbyCT. Free registration for full data. **Other phones:** Assessor-203-844-5311.

Greenwich Town

Town Clerk, PO Box 2540, Greenwich, CT 06836. **Phone**-203-622-7897; hours 8AM-4PM

Will not search records. Record copy- $1.00 per page. Cert fee: $1.00 per cert. Payee: Town of Greenwich. **Other phones:** Assessor-203-622-7885.

Griswold Town

Town Clerk, PO Box 369, Jewett City, CT 06351. **Phone**-860-376-7060 x100, R/E Recording- 860-376-7060 x101, UCC Recording- 860-376-7060 x101; fax-860-376-7070; hours 8:30AM-4PM M,T,Th,F; 8:30AM-Noon W www.griswold-ct.org

Will not search records. Record copy- $1.00 per page. Cert fee: $1.00 per page. Payee: Town of Griswold. **Other phones:** Assessor-860-376-7060 x105; Treasurer-860-376-7060 x205; Appraiser/Auditor-860-376-7060 x105; Elections-860-376-7060 x208; Vital Records-860-376-7060 x101.

Groton Town

Town Clerk, 45 Fort Hill Rd, Groton, CT 06340. **Phone**-Town Clerk, R/E & UCC Recording- 860-441-6642; hours 8:30AM-4:30PM M-W & F; 9AM-4:30PM Th. Will not search records. UCC copy- $1.00 per page. Cert fee: $1.00 per cert. Payee: Groton Town Clerk. **Other phones:** Assessor-860-441-6660; Treasurer-860-441-6609; Elections-860-441-6640; Vital Records-860-441-6640.

Guilford Town

Town Clerk, 31 Park St, Town Hall, Guilford, CT 06437. **Phone**-203-453-8001; hours 8:30AM-4:30PM www.ci.guilford.ct.us   Will not search records. UCC

copy- $1.00 per page. Cert fee: $1.00 per cert. Payee: Guilford Town Clerk. **Other phones:** Assessor-203-453-8010; Treasurer-203-453-8022.

Haddam Town

Town Clerk, PO Box 87, Haddam, CT 06438. **Phone**-860-345-8531; fax-860-345-3730; hours 9AM-4PM M,T,W, 9AM-7PM Th; 9AM-Noon F

Will not search records. UCC copy- $1.00 per page. Cert fee: $1.00 per cert. Payee: Town of Haddam. **Other phones:** Assessor-860-345-8531 x213.

Hamden Town

Town Clerk, 2372 Whitney Ave, Memorial Town Hall, Hamden, CT 06518. **Phone**-203-287-2510, R/E Recording- 203-287-2500; fax-203-287-2518; hours 9AM-4PM. Will not search records. Record copy- $1.00 per page. Cert fee: $1.00 per cert. Payee: Hamden Town Clerk. **Online Access to Assessor records:** Search the town assessor's database at http://data.visionappraisal.com/hamdenct. Free registration required for full access. **Other phones:** Assessor-203-287-2529; Treasurer-203-387-2530; Appraiser/ Auditor-203-287-2520; Elections-203-287-2609; Vital Records-203-287-2510.

Hampton Town

Town Clerk, PO Box 143, Hampton, CT 06247-0143. **Phone**-860-455-9132, R/E Recording- 860-455-9132 x1, UCC Recording- 860-455-9132 x1; fax-860-455-0517; hours 9AM-4PM T,Th; 6-8PM Th

Will not search records. Record copy- $1.00 per page. Cert fee: $1.00 per cert. Payee: Hampton Town Clerk. **Other phones:** Assessor-860-455-9132 x5; Treasurer-860-455-9132 x7; Elections-860-455-9132 x1; Vital Records-860-455-9132 x1.

Hartford City

City Clerk, 550 Main St, Hartford, CT 06103-2992. **Phone**-860-543-8580, R/E Recording- 860-722-8040; fax-860-772-8041; hours 8:30AM-4:30 PM

Will not search records. UCC copy- $1.00 per page. Cert fee: $1.00 per cert. Payee: Hartford City Clerk. **Other phones:** Assessor-860-543-8540; Treasurer-860-543-8530.

Hartland Town

Town Clerk, PO Box 297, East Hartland, CT 06027. **Phone**-860-653-0285; fax-860-653-0452; hours 10AM-N, 1-4PM M,T,W

www.munic.state.ct.us/hartland/hartland.htm

Will not search records. Record copy- $1.00 per page. Cert fee: $1.00 per cert. Payee: Hartland Town Clerk. **Other phones:** Assessor-860-653-0609 X106; Vital Records-860-653-0285; Selectmen-860-653-6800; Tax Collector-860-653-0609 x105.

Harwinton Town

Town Clerk, 100 Bentley Drive, Town Hall, Harwinton, CT 06791. **Phone**-Town Clerk, R/E & UCC Recording- 860-485-9613; fax-860-485-0051; hours 8:30AM-4PM. Will not search records. Copy fee is $1.00 per page. Cert fee: $1.00 per cert. Payee: Harwinton Town Clerk. **Other phones:** Assessor-860-485-0898; Treasurer-860-485-9051; Elections-860-485-9613; Vital Records-860-485-9613.

Hebron Town

Town Clerk, PO Box 156, Hebron, CT 06248. **Phone**-860-228-5971 x124, R/E Recording- 860-228-5971, UCC Recording- 860-228-5971; fax-860-228-4859; hours 8AM-4PM M-W; 8AM-6PM Th; 8AM-1:00PM F www.hebronct.com

Will not search records. Record copy- $1.00 per page. Cert fee: $1.00 per cert. Payee: Hebron Town Clerk. **Other phones:** Assessor-860-228-5971; Treasurer-860-228-5971; Appraiser/ Auditor-860-228-

5971; Elections-860-228-5971; Vital Records-860-228-5971.

Kent Town

Town Clerk, PO Box 678, Kent, CT 06757-0678. **Phone**-860-927-3433; fax-860-927-4541; hours 9AM-4PM. Will not search records. UCC copy- $1.00 per page. Cert fee: $1.00 per page. Payee: Kent Town Clerk. **Online Access to Assessor, Property records:** Access to property assessor data is at http://data.visionappraisal.com/KentCT/. Free registration required. **Other phones:** Assessor-860-927-3160.

Killingly Town

Town Clerk, PO Box 6000, Danielson, CT 06239. **Phone**-860-779-5307, R/E Recording- 860-774-8601; fax-860-779-5394; hours 8:30AM-4:30PM

Will not search records. UCC copy- $1.00 per page. Cert fee: $1.00 per page. Payee: Killingly Town Clerk. **Other phones:** Assessor-860-779-5323; Treasurer-860-779-5337; Elections-203-779-5302; Vital Records-860-779-5307.

Killingworth Town

Town Clerk, 323 Route 81, Killingworth, CT 06419-1298. **Phone**-860-663-1616, R/E Recording- 860-663-1765; fax-860-663-3305; hours 9AM-Noon,1-4PM

Will not search records. Record copy- $1.00 per page. Cert fee: $1.00 per cert. Payee: Town of Killingworth. **Other phones:** Assessor-203-663-2002; Vital Records-860-663-1616.

Lebanon Town

Town Clerk, 579 Exeter Rd, Town Hall, Lebanon, CT 06249. **Phone**-860-642-7319; hours 9AM-4PM M,T,F; 9AM-7PM Th

Will not search records. Record copy- $1.00 per page. Cert fee: $1.00 per cert. Payee: Town of Lebanon. **Online Access to Assessor, Property records:** property data is at http://data.visionappraisal.com/LebanonCT/. Free registration required. **Other phones:** Assessor-860-642-6141; Vital Records-860-642-7319.

Ledyard Town

Town Clerk, 741 Col. Ledyard Highway, Ledyard, CT 06339. **Phone**-860-464-3259; fax-860-464-1126; hours 8:30AM-4:30PM Mon-Fri www.town.ledyard.ct.us

Will not search records. Record copy- $1.00 per page. Cert fee: $1.00 per cert. Payee: Town of Ledyard. **Other phones:** Assessor-860-464-3237; Treasurer-860-464-3228; Vital Records-860-464-3259.

Lisbon Town

Town Clerk, 1 Newent Rd, RD 2 Town Hall, Lisbon, CT 06351-9802. **Phone**-860-376-2708; fax-860-376-6545; hours 9AM-4PM M-Th; 6PM-8PM W; 9AM-2PM F; 9AM-Noon Sat. Will not search records. UCC copy- $1.00 per page. Cert fee: $1.00 per cert. Payee: Lisbon Town Clerk. **Other phones:** Assessor-860-376-5115; Treasurer-860-376-3400.

Litchfield Town

Town Clerk, PO Box 488, Litchfield, CT 06759-0488. **Phone**-Town Clerk, R/E & UCC Recording- 860-567-7561; hours 9AM-4:30PM. Will not search records. Record copy- $1.00 per page. Cert fee: $1.00 per cert. Payee: Litchfield Town Clerk. **Other phones:** Assessor-860-567-7559; Treasurer-860-567-7554; Vital Records-860-567-7561; Registrar-860-567-7558.

Lyme Town

Town Clerk, 480 Hamburg Rd., Town Hall, Lyme, CT 06371. **Phone**-Town Clerk, R/E & UCC Recording-860-434-7733; fax-860-434-2989; hours 9AM-4PM

Will not search records. Record copy- $1.00 per page. Cert fee: $1.00 per cert. Payee: Lyme Town Clerk. **Online Access to Assessor, Property records:** property data is at http://data.visionappraisal.com/L

ymeCT/. Free registration required. **Other phones:** Assessor-860-434-8094; Treasurer-860-434-7733; Appraiser/ Auditor-860-434-8094; Elections-860-434-7733; Vital Records-860-434-7733.

Madison Town

Town Clerk, 8 Campus Dr., Madison, CT 06443-2538. **Phone-**Town Clerk, R/E & UCC Recording- 203-245-5672; fax-203-245-5613; hours 8:30AM-4PM www.madisonct.org
Will search UCC records. UCC copy- $1.00 per page. Will not search real estate or tax lien records. RE record copy- $1.00 per page. Cert fee: $1.00 per cert. Payee: Madison Town Clerk. **Online Access to Assessor, Property records:** Search the town assessor database at http://data.visionappraisal.com/MadisonCT/. Free Registration required for full access. **Other phones:** Assessor-203-245-5652; Elections-203-245-5671; Vital Records-203-245-5672.

Manchester Town

Town Clerk, PO Box 191, Manchester, CT 06045-0191. **Phone-**Town Clerk, R/E & UCC Recording-860-647-3037; fax-860-647-3029; hours 8:30AM-5PM www.ci.manchester.ct.us/Town_Clerk/index.htm
Will not search real estate UCC records. Record copy- $1.00 per page. Will search tax liens. Cert fee: $1.00 per cert. Payee: Manchester Town Clerk. **Online Access to Assessor records:** Search the town assessor database at http://data.visionappraisal.com/ManchesterCT/. Free registration required for full access. **Other phones:** Assessor-860-647-3016; Treasurer-860-647-3023; Appraiser-860-647-3017; Elections-860-647-3037; Vital Records-860-647-3037.

Mansfield Town

Town Clerk, 4 S. Eagleville Rd, Mansfield, CT 06268. **Phone-**860-429-3302; hours 8:15AM-4:30PM M-W; 8:15AM-6:30PM Th; 8AM-Noon F www.mansfieldct.org
Will not search records. Record copy- $1.00 per page. Cert fee: $1.00 per page. Payee: Town of Mansfield. **Other phones:** Assessor-860-429-3327; Elections-860-429-3369.

Marlborough Town

Town Clerk, PO Box 29, Marlborough, CT 06447. **Phone-**Town Clerk, R/E & UCC Recording- 860-295-6206, UCC Recording- 860-298-6206; fax-860-295-0317; hours 8AM-4:30PM M-Th; 8AM-7PM T; 8AM-Noon F
Will not search records. Record copy- $1.00 per page. Cert fee: $1.00 per doc. Payee: Marlborough Town Clerk. **Other phones:** Assessor-860-295-6201; Treasurer-860-295-6165.

Meriden City

City Clerk, 142 E. Main St, Meriden, CT 06450-8022. **Phone-**City Clerk, R/E & UCC Recording- 203-630-4030; fax-203-630-4059; hours 9AM-7PM M; 9AM-5PM T-F www.cityofmeriden.org/government/
Will not search records. Record copy- $1.00 per page. Cert fee: $1.00 per page. Payee: Meriden City Clerk. **Other phones:** Assessor-203-630-4071; Elections-203-630-4075; Vital Records-203-630-4030.

Middlebury Town

Town Clerk, PO Box 392, Middlebury, CT 06762-0392. **Phone-**Town Clerk, R/E & UCC Recording-203-758-2557; fax-203-758-2915; hours 9AM-Noon,1-5PM www.middlebury-ct.org
Will not search records. Record copy- $1.00 per page. Cert fee: $1.00 per cert. Payee: Middlebury Town Clerk. **Other phones:** Assessor-203-758-1447; Treasurer-203-758-1770; Elections-203-758-2557; Vital Records-203-758-2557.

Middlefield Town

Town Clerk, PO Box 179, Middlefield, CT 06455. **Phone-**Town Clerk, R/E & UCC Recording- 860-349-7116; fax-860-349-7115; hours 9AM-5PM M; 9AM-4PM T-Th; 9AM-3PM F www.munic.state.ct.us/MIDDLEFIELD/contents.htm
Will not search records. UCC copy- $1.00 per page. Cert fee: $1.00 per cert. Payee: Middlefield Town Clerk. **Online Access to Assessor records:** Search the town assessor database at http://data.visionappraisal.com/MiddlefieldCT/. Free registration required for full data. **Other phones:** Assessor-860-349-7111; Treasurer-860-349-7114; Elections-860-349-7119; Vital Records-860-349-7116.

Middletown City

City Clerk, PO Box 1300, Middletown, CT 06457. **Phone-**City Clerk, R/E & UCC Recording- 860-344-3459; fax-860-344-3591; hours 8:30AM-4:30PM www.cityofmiddletown.com/Departments.htm
Will not search records. Record copy- $1.00 per page. Cert fee: $1.00 per cert. Payee: Middletown Town Clerk. **Other phones:** Assessor-860-344-3454; Treasurer-860-344-3438; Elections-860-344-3459; Vital Records-860-344-3474.

Milford City

City Clerk, 70 W River St, Milford, CT 06460-3364. **Phone-**City Clerk, R/E & UCC Recording- 203-783-3210; hours 8:30AM-5PM www.ci.milford.ct.us
Will search UCC records. UCC copy- $1.00 per page. Will not search real estate or tax lien records. RE record copy- $1.00 per page. Cert fee: $1.00 per cert. Payee: Milford City Clerk. **Online Access to Assessor records:** Search the city assessor's database at http://data.visionappraisal.com/milfordct/. Free registration required for full data. **Other phones:** Assessor-203-783-3215; Treasurer-203-783-3257; Appraiser/ Auditor-203-783-3215; Elections-203-783-3339 (DEM); 203-783-3242 (REP); Vital Records-203-783-3210.

Monroe Town

Town Clerk, 7 Fan Hill Rd, Monroe, CT 06468-1800. **Phone-**203-452-5417, R/E Recording- 203-452-5427, UCC Recording- 203-452-5427; fax-203-261-6197; hours 9AM-5PM
Will not search records. Record copy- $1.00 per page. Cert fee: $1.00 per cert. Payee: Town of Monroe. **Other phones:** Assessor-203-452-5469; Treasurer-203-452-5433; Appraiser/ Auditor-203-452-5469; Elections-203-452-5414; Vital Records-203-452-5427.

Montville Town

Town Clerk, 310 Norwich-New London Tpke., Town Hall, Uncasville, CT 06382. **Phone-**860-848-1349; fax-860-848-1521; hours 9AM-5PM
Will not search records. UCC copy- $1.00 per page. Cert fee: $1.00 per cert. Payee: Montville Town Clerk. **Other phones:** Assessor-860-848-8221 #5; Treasurer-860-848-0139.

Morris Town

Town Clerk, PO Box 66, Morris, CT 06763-0066. **Phone-**Town Clerk, R/E & UCC Recording- 860-567-7433; fax-860-567-7432; hours 9AM-Noon, 1-4PM
Will not search records. Record copy- $1.00 per page. Cert fee: $1.00 per cert. Payee: Morris Town Clerk. **Other phones:** Assessor-860-567-7435; Treasurer-860-567-7435; Elections-860-567-7433; Vital Records-860-567-7433.

Naugatuck Town

Town Clerk, 229 Church St, Town Hall, Naugatuck, CT 06770. **Phone-**203-720-7000, R/E Recording- 203-720-7055; fax-203-720-7099; hours 8:30AM-4PM

Will not search records. Record copy- $1.00 per page. Cert fee: $1.00 per cert. Payee: Naugatuck Town Clerk. **Online Access to Assessor records:** Search the town assessor database at http://data.visionappraisal.com/NaugatuckCT/. Free registration required for full data. **Other phones:** Assessor-203-720-7016; Treasurer-203-720-7021; Elections-203-720-7047; Vital Records-203-720-7055.

New Britain Town

Town Clerk, 27 W. Main St, New Britain, CT 06051. **Phone-**860-826-3344; fax-860-826-3348; hours 8:15AM-3:45PM M-W & F; 8:15AM-6:45PM Th
Will not search records. UCC copy- $1.00 per page. Cert fee: $1.00 per cert. Payee: New Britain Town Clerk. **Online Access to Assessor records:** Search the city assessor database at http://data.visionappraisal.com/NewbritainCT/. Free registration for full data. **Other phones:** Assessor-860-826-3323.

New Canaan Town

Town Clerk, 77 Main St, Town Hall, New Canaan, CT 06840. **Phone-**203-594-3070; fax-203-594-3130; hours 8:30AM-4:30PM www.newcanaan.info
Will not search records. UCC copy- $1.00 per page. RE record copy- $.25 per page. Cert fee: $1.00 per cert. Payee: New Canaan Town Clerk. **Online Access to Assessor, Property records:** Access to property data is at http://data.visionappraisal.com/NewCanaanCT/. Free registration required. **Other phones:** Assessor-203-594-3005; Treasurer-203-594-3024; Elections-203-594-3060; Vital Records-203-594-3070.

New Fairfield Town

Town Clerk, 4 Brushhill Rd, New Fairfield, CT 06812. **Phone-**203-312-5616, R/E Recording- 203-746-8110; hours 8:30AM-5PM T-F; 8:30AM-Noon Sat
Will not search records. Record copy- $1.00 per page. Cert fee: $2.00 per cert. Payee: New Fairfield Town Clerk. **Other phones:** Assessor-203-312-5624.

New Hartford Town

Town Clerk, PO Box 426, New Hartford, CT 06057. **Phone-**Town Clerk, R/E & UCC Recording- 860-379-5037; fax-860-379-1367; hours 9AM-Noon, 12:40-4PM M,T,Th; 9AM-Noon, 1PM-6PM W; www.town.new-hartford.ct.us/home.html
Will not search records. Record copy- $1.00 per page. Cert fee: $1.00 per cert. Payee: New Hartford. **Online Access to Assessor, Property records:** Access to property data is at http://data.visionappraisal.com/NewhartfordCT/. Free registration required. **Other phones:** Assessor-860-379-5235; Treasurer-860-379-3389; Elections-860-738-9721; Vital Records-860-379-5037.

New Haven City

City Clerk, 200 Orange St, Rm 202, New Haven, CT 06510. **Phone-**203-946-8339, R/E Recording- 203-946-8344, UCC Recording- 203-946-8344; fax-203-946-6974; hours 9AM-5PM. Will not search records. UCC copy- $1.00 per page. Cert fee: $1.00 per page. Payee: New Haven City Clerk. **Online Access to Assessor records:** Search the city assessor database at http://data.visionappraisal.com/NewhavenCT/. Free registration required for full data. **Other phones:** Assessor-203-787-8066; Treasurer-203-946-8300; Elections-203-946-8346; Vital Records-203-946-8084.

New Milford Town

Town Clerk, 10 Main St, New Milford, CT 06776. **Phone-**860-355-6020; fax-860-355-6002; hours 9AM-5PM www.newmilford.org/agencies/home.htm
Will not search records. Record copy- $1.00 per page. Cert fee: $1.00 per cert. Payee: New Milford Town Clerk. **Online Access to Assessor records:** Search

the town assessor database at http://data.visionappraisal.com/NewMilfordCT/. Free registration required for full access. **Other phones:** Assessor-860-355-6070; Vital Records-860-355-6020.

Newington Town

Town Clerk, 131 Cedar St, Newington, CT 06111-2696. **Phone**-Town Clerk, R/E & UCC Recording-860-665-8545;   hours-8:30AM-4:30PM www.ci.newington.ct.us
Will not search records. Record copy- $1.00 per page. Cert fee: $1.00 per page. Payee: Newington Town Clerk. **Other phones:** Assessor-860-665-8530; Elections-860-665-8516; Vital Records-860-665-8545.

Newtown Town

Town Clerk, 45 Main St, Newtown, CT 06470. **Phone**-203-270-4210; hours 8AM-4:30PM. Will not search records. Record copy- $1.00 per page. Cert fee: $1.00 per cert. Payee: Town of Newtown. **Other phones:** Assessor-203-270-4240;   Treasurer-203-270-4221; Elections-203-270-4250; Vital Records-203-270-4210.

Norfolk Town

Town Clerk, PO Box 552, Norfolk, CT 06058-0552. **Phone**-860-542-5679; hours 8:30AM-N, 1-4PM M-Th, 8:30AM-N F. Will not search records. All land records copy fee- $1.00 per page. Cert fee: $1.00 per doc. Payee: Town of Norfolk. **Other phones:** Assessor-860-542-5287;   Treasurer-860-542-5679; Elections-860-542-5679; Vital Records-860-542-5679.

North Branford Town

Town Clerk, PO Box 287, North Branford, CT 06471-0287. **Phone**-203-484-6015; hours 8:30AM-4:30PM Will not search records. Record copy- $1.00 per page. Cert fee: $1.00 per cert. Payee: North Branford Town Clerk. **Other phones:** Assessor-203-484-6013; Treasurer-203-484-6002; Vital Records-203-484-6015.

North Canaan Town

Town Clerk, PO Box 338, North Canaan, CT 06018. **Phone**-860-824-3138;   fax-860-824-3139;   hours 9:30AM-Noon, 1-4PM; Fri till 1PM
Will search UCC records. UCC copy- $1.00 per page. Will not search real estate or tax lien records. RE record copy- $1.00 per page. Cert fee: $1.00 per cert. Payee: North Canaan Town Clerk. **Other phones:** Assessor-860-824-3137.

North Haven Town

Town Clerk, 18 Church St, Town Hall, North Haven, CT 06473. **Phone**-203-239-5321 x541; hours 8:30AM-4:30PM
Will not search records. Record copy- $1.00 per page. Cert fee: $1.00 per cert. Payee: North Haven Town Clerk. **Other phones:** Assessor-203-239-5321 x700; Elections-203-239-5321 x755; Vital Records-203-239-5321 x541.

North Stonington Town

Town Clerk, 40 Main St, North Stonington, CT 06359. **Phone**-Town Clerk, R/E & UCC Recording- 860-535-2877 x21; fax-860-535-4554; hours 9AM-4PM www.munic.state.ct.us/N_Stonington/
Will not search records. Record copy- $1.00 per page. Cert fee: $1.00 per cert. Payee: North Stonington Town Clerk. **Other phones:** Assessor-860-535-2877 x23; Treasurer-860-535-2877 x10; Elections-860-535-2877 x28; Vital Records-860-535-2877 x21.

Norwalk City

Town Clerk, PO Box 5125, Norwalk, CT 06856-5125. **Phone**-203-854-7746;   fax-203-854-7817;   hours 8:30AM-4:30PM M T W F; 8:30 AM-7PM Th www.norwalkct.org
Will not search records. Record copy- $1.00 per page. Cert fee: $1.00 per cert. Payee: Town Clerk of Norwalk. **Online Access to Property, Assessor records:** Access to Norwalk property records is free at www.norwalkct.org/norwalk/pckls.asp. Site may be temporarily down. **Other phones:** Assessor-203-854-7887; Elections-203-854-7746; Vital Records-203-854-7746.

Norwich City

City Clerk, 100 Broadway, City Hall, Rm 215, Norwich, CT 06360. **Phone**-860-823-3732; fax-860-823-3790; 8:30AM-4:30PM www.norwichct.org
Will not search records. UCC copy- $1.00 per page. Cert fee: $1.00 per cert. Payee: Norwich City Clerk. **Online Access to Assessor, Real Estate records:** Search the city assessor's database at http://data.visionappraisal.com/NorwichCT. Free registration required for full data. Also, access to the clerk's town land records is online by subscription. Index goes back to 1928 and images to 1997. Fee is $350.00   per   year;   sign-up   online   at www.norwichct.org/clerk.htm or call 860-823-3732. **Other phones:** Assessor-860-823-3732.

Old Lyme Town

Town Clerk, 52 Lyme St, Old Lyme, CT 06371. **Phone**-Town Clerk, R/E & UCC Recording- 860-434-1605 x221; fax-860-434-9283; hours 9AM-Noon,1-4PM. Will not search records. Record copy- $1.00 per page. Cert fee: $1.00 per cert. Payee: Old Lyme Town Clerk. **Online Access to Assessor records:** Search the town Assessor's database at http://data.visionappraisal.com/OLDLYMECT. Free registration required for full access. **Other phones:** Assessor-860-434-1605 x218; Treasurer-860-434-1605 x232;   Appraiser/   Auditor-860-434-1605   x218; Elections-860-434-1605 x230; Vital Records-860-434-1605 x221.

Old Saybrook Town

Town Clerk, 302 Main St, Old Saybrook, CT 06475. **Phone**-Town Clerk, R/E & UCC Recording- 860-395-3135; fax-860-395-5014; hours 8:30AM-4:30PM www.oldsaybrookct.com
Will not search records. Record copy- $1.00 per page. Cert fee: $1.00 per cert. Payee: Old Saybrook Town Clerk. **Online Access to Real Estate records:** Real Estate Sales records on the Assessor's database are free at http://oldsaybrookct.com/assessor/. No name searching. **Other phones:** Assessor-860-395-3137; Treasurer-860-395-3073;   Elections-860-395-3135; Vital Records-860-395-3135.

Orange Town

Town Clerk, 617 Orange Center Rd., Town Hall, Orange, CT 06477. **Phone**-203-891-2122, R/E Recording- 203-795-0751; fax-203-891-2185; hours 8:30AM-4:30PM
Will not search records. UCC copy- $1.00 per page. Cert fee: $1.00 per cert. Payee: Orange Town Clerk. **Other phones:** Assessor-203-891-2122 x722.

Oxford Town

Town Clerk, 486 Oxford Rd, Oxford, CT 06478. **Phone**-203-888-2543; fax-203-888-2136; hours 9AM-5PM M-Th; 7-9PM Mon & Th
Will not search records. Record copy- $1.00 per page. Cert fee: $1.00 per cert. Payee: Oxford Town Clerk. **Other phones:** Assessor-203-888-2543; Treasurer-203-888-2543;   Elections-203-888-2543; Vital Records-203-888-2543.

Plainfield Town

Town Clerk, 8 Community Ave, Town Hall, Plainfield, CT 06374. **Phone**-860-564-4075, R/E Recording- 860-230-3009, UCC Recording- 860-230-3009; hours 8:30AM-4:30PM M,T,W; 8:30AM-6:30PM Th; 8:30AM-1PM

Closed for lunch, 1-2PM. Will not search records. Record copy- $1.00 per page. Cert fee: $1.00 per cert. Payee: Town of Plainfield. **Other phones:** Assessor-860-230-3006;   Treasurer-860-230-3003; Elections-860-230-3024; Vital Records-860-230-3009.

Plainville Town

Town Clerk, 1 Central Sq, Municipal Ctr, Plainville, CT 06062. **Phone**-860-793-0221; hours 8:30AM-4:30PM Will not search records. UCC copy- $1.00 per page. Cert fee: $1.00 per page. Payee: Town of Plainville. **Other phones:** Assessor-860-793-0221 x242.

Plymouth Town

Town Clerk, 80 Main St, Town Hall, Terryville, CT 06786. **Phone**-Town Clerk, R/E & UCC Recording- 860-585-4039; fax-860-585-4015; hours 8:30-4:30PM Will not search records. Record copy- $1.00 per page. Cert fee: $1.00 per page. Payee: Plymouth Town Clerk. **Other phones:** Assessor-860-585-4006; Treasurer-860-585-4009;   Elections-860-585-4033; Vital Records-860-585-4039.

Pomfret Town

Town Clerk, 5 Haven Rd, Pomfret Center, CT 06259. **Phone**-Town Clerk, R/E & UCC Recording- 860-974-0343; fax-860-974-3950; hours 9AM-4PM
Will not search records. Record copy- $1.00 per page. Cert fee: $1.00 per doc. Payee: Town of Pomfret. **Online Access to Assessor records:. Other phones:** Assessor-860-974-1674; Vital Records-860-974-0343.

Portland Town

Town Clerk, PO Box 71, Portland, CT 06480. **Phone**-Town Clerk, R/E & UCC Recording- 860-342-6743; fax-860-342-0001; hours 9AM-4:30PM
Will not search records. Record copy- $1.00 per page. Cert fee: $1.00 per cert. Payee: Portland Town Clerk. **Other phones:** Assessor-860-342-6744; Treasurer-860-342-6726;   Elections-860-342-6743; Vital Records-860-342-6743.

Preston Town

Town Clerk, 389 Route 2, Town Hall, Preston, CT 06365-8830. **Phone**-860-887-9821; fax-860-885-1905; hours 9AM-4:30PM T-F; Th until 6:30
Will not search records. Record copy- $1.00 per page. Cert fee: $1.00 per cert. Payee: Preston Town Clerk. **Online Access to Assessor records:** Search the town assessor database at http://data.visiona ppraisal.com/PrestonCT/. Free registration for full data. **Other phones:** Assessor-860-889-2529.

Prospect Town

Town Clerk, 36 Center St, Prospect, CT 06712-1699. **Phone**-203-758-4461;   fax-203-758-4466;   hours 8:30AM-4PM. Will not search records. Record copy- $1.00 per page. Cert fee: $1.00 per page. Payee: Prospect Town Clerk. **Other phones:** Assessor-203-758-4461; Vital Records-203-758-4461.

Putnam Town

Town Clerk, 126 Church St, Putnam, CT 06260. **Phone**-Town Clerk, R/E & UCC Recording- 860-963-6807;   fax-860-963-2001;   hours 8:30AM-Noon,1-4:30PM www.putnamct.us Will not search records. Record copy- $1.00 per page. Cert fee: $1.00 per cert. Payee: Town of Putnam. **Online Access to Assessor, Property records:** Access to property data is at http://data.visionappraisal.com/PutnamCT/. Free registration. **Other phones:** Assessor-860-963-6802; Treasurer-860-963-6809.

Redding Town

Town Clerk, PO Box 1028, Redding, CT 06875-1028. **Phone**-Town Clerk, R/E & UCC Recording- 203-938-2377; fax-203-938-8816; hours 9AM-4:30PM. Will not search records. Record copy- $1.00 per page. Cert fee: $1.00 per cert. Payee: Redding Town Clerk. **Other phones:** Assessor-203-938-2626; Treasurer-203-938-3616; Appraiser/ Auditor-203-938-2626; Elections-203-938-5012; Vital Records-203-938-2377.

Ridgefield Town

Town Clerk, 400 Main St, Ridgefield, CT 06877. **Phone**-203-431-2783; fax-203-431-2722; hours 8:30AM-4:30PM www.ridgefieldct.org/government/townclerk/townclerk.htm Will not search records. Record copy- $1.00 per page. Cert fee: $1.00 per instrument. Payee: Ridgefield Town Clerk. **Other phones:** Assessor-203-431-2706; Treasurer- 203-431-2763; Elections- 203-431-2771/2772; Vital Records-203-431-2783.

Rocky Hill Town

Town Clerk, 761 Old Main St., Rocky Hill, CT 06067. **Phone**-860-258-2705; hours 8:30AM-4:30PM Will not search records. UCC copy- $1.00 per page. Cert fee: $1.00 per cert. Payee: Rocky Hill Town Clerk. **Online Access to Land, Marriage, Death, Trade Name, Recording records:** Access to the Town Clerk's Index Search is free at www.ci.rocky-hill.ct.us/resolution/. Land records go back to 1973; Marriages/Deaths to 1990; trade names to 1987; maps to 1982. **Other phones:** Assessor-860-258-2772; Elections-860-258-2715.

Roxbury Town

Town Clerk, 29 North St., Roxbury, CT 06783-1405. **Phone**-Town Clerk, R/E & UCC Recording- 860-354-3328; fax-860-354-0560; hours 9AM-Noon, 1-4PM T & Th; 9AM-Noon F Will not search records. Record copy- $1.00 per page. Cert fee: $1.00 per page. Payee: Roxbury Town Clerk. **Online Access to Assessor, Property records:** Access to property data is at www.visionappraisal.com/databases/ct/index.htm. Free registration required. **Other phones:** Assessor-860-354-2634; Treasurer-860-354-9938; Vital Records-860-354-3328.

Salem Town

Town Clerk, 270 Hartford Rd, Town Office Bldg., Salem, CT 06420. **Phone**-Town Clerk, R/E & UCC Recording- 860-859-3873 x170; fax-860-859-1184; hours 8AM-4PM M-W; 8AM-5PM Th; 8AM-N Fri. www.salemct.gov Will not search records. Record copy- $1.00 per page. Cert fee: $1.00 per page. Payee: Town of Salem. **Other phones:** Assessor-860-859-3873 x130; Treasurer-860-859-3873 x125; Elections-860-859-3873 x230; Vital Records-860-859-3873 x170; Tax Collector-860-859-3873 x150.

Salisbury Town

Town Clerk, PO Box 548, Salisbury, CT 06068. **Phone**-860-435-5182; fax-860-435-5172; 9AM-4PM Will not search records. Record copy- $1.00 per page. Cert fee: $1.00 per cert. Payee: Salisbury Town Clerk. **Other phones:** Assessor-860-435-5176; Treasurer-860-435-5174; Vital Records-860-435-5182.

Scotland Town

Town Clerk, PO Box 122, Scotland, CT 06264. **Phone**-Town Clerk, R/E & UCC Recording- 860-423-9634; fax-860-423-3666; hours 9AM-3PM M,T,Th- Noon-8PM W; Closed Friday Will not search records. UCC copy- $1.00 per page. Cert fee: $1.00 per cert. Payee: Scotland Town Clerk. **Other phones:** Assessor-860-423-9634; Treasurer-860-423-9634.

Seymour Town

Town Clerk, 1 1st St, Town Hall, Seymour, CT 06483-2817. **Phone**-203-888-0519; hours 9AM-5PM (No Recording after 4:15PM) Will not search records.

UCC copy- $1.00 per page. Cert fee: $1.00 per cert. Payee: Seymour Town Clerk. **Other phones:** Assessor-203-881-5013; Treasurer-203-888-0581.

Sharon Town

Town Clerk, PO Box 224, Sharon, CT 06069. **Phone**-860-364-5224; fax-860-364-5224; hours M- Th 8:30AM-Noon, 1-4PM ; Fri 8:30AM-Noon Will not search records. Record copy- $1.00 per page. Cert fee: $1.00 per cert. Payee: Sharon Town Clerk. **Online Access to Assessor records:** Access assessor data at http://data.visionappraisal.com/SharonCT/. **Other phones:** Assessor-860-364-0205; Treasurer-860-364-5789; Vital Records-860-364-5224.

Shelton City

City Clerk, PO Box 364, Shelton, CT 06484-0364. **Phone**-203-924-1555, R/E Recording- 203-924-1555 x377; fax-203-924-1721; hours 8AM-5:30PM www.cityofshelton.org Will not search records. UCC copy- $1.00 per page. Cert fee: $1.00 per cert. Payee: Shelton City Clerk. **Other phones:** Assessor-203-924-1555 x335; Treasurer-203-924-1555 x318; Elections-203-924-1555 x337; Vital Records-203-924-1555 x321.

Sherman Town

Town Clerk, PO Box 39, Sherman, CT 06784-0039. **Phone**-Town Clerk, R/E & UCC Recording- 860-354-5281; fax-860-350-5041; hours 9AM-Noon, 1-4PM T,W,Th,F; 9AM-Noon Sat Will not search records. UCC copy- $1.00 per page. Cert fee: $1.00 per cert. Payee: Town of Sherman. **Other phones:** Assessor-860-355-0376; Treasurer-860-355-1139; Vital Records-860-354-5281.

Simsbury Town

Town Clerk, PO Box 495, Simsbury, CT 06070. **Phone**-860-658-3243; fax-860-658-3206; hours 8:30AM-4:30PM. Will not search records. UCC copy- $1.00 per page. Cert fee: $1.00 per cert. Payee: Town of Simsbury. **Other phones:** Assessor-860-658-3251.

Somers Town

Town Clerk, PO Box 308, Somers, CT 06071. **Phone**-860-763-8206; fax-860-763-8228; 8:30AM-4:30PM M-W,F; 8:30AM-7PM Th www.somersnow.com Will not search records. UCC copy- $1.00 per page. RE record copy- $.50 per page. Cert fee: $1.00 per doc. Payee: Somers Town Clerk. **Other phones:** Assessor-860-763-8203; Treasurer-860-763-8204; Elections-860-763-8211; Vital Records-860-763-8206.

South Windsor Town

Town Clerk, 1540 Sullivan Ave, South Windsor, CT 06074. **Phone**-860-644-2511 x225, R/E Recording-860-644-2511 x225/226/227; fax-860-644-3781; hours 8AM-4:30PM www.southwindsor.org Will not search records. Record copy fee- $1.00 per page. Cert fee: $1.00 per cert. Payee: Town of South Windsor. **Online Access to Property Transfer records:** Access to town clerk's lists of property transfers by year are free at www.southwindsor.org/TownHall/Property%20Transfer/property.htm. Search back to 1999. **Other phones:** Assessor-860-644-2511 x213; Treasurer-860-644-2511 x261; Elections-860-644-2511 x275; Vital Records-860-644-2511 x225/226/227; Tax collector-860-644-2511 X220.

Southbury Town

Town Clerk, 501 Main St South, Southbury, CT 06488-2295. **Phone**-Town Clerk, R/E & UCC Recording-203-262-0657; fax-203-264-9762; 8:30AM-4:30PM Will not search records. Record copy- $1.00 per page. Cert fee: $1.00 per cert. Payee: Southbury Town Clerk. **Other phones:** Assessor-203-262-0674;

Treasurer-203-262-0663; Elections-203-262-0657; Vital Records-203-262-0657.

Southington Town

Town Clerk, PO Box 152, Southington, CT 06489. **Phone**-860-276-6211; fax-860-276-6229; hours 8:30AM-4PM M, T, W, F; 8:30AM-7PM TH www.southington.org Will not search records. UCC copy- $1.00 per page. Cert fee: $1.00 per cert. Payee: Southington Town Clerk. **Online Access to Most Wanted records:** Access to the Town's most wanted list is at www.southingtonpolice.org/warrant.htm. Assessor-860-276-6205; Treasurer-860-276-6228; Elections-860-276-6268; Vital Records-860-276-6211.

Sprague Town

Town Clerk, PO Box 162, Baltic, CT 06330. **Phone**-860-822-3001; fax-860-822-3013; hours 8:00AM-4:30PM M-T (W Open Until 5:30PM) Will not search records. UCC copy- $1.00 per page. RE record copy- $1.50 per page. Cert fee: $1.00 per cert. Payee: Town of Sprague. **Other phones:** Assessor-860-822-3002; Treasurer-860-822-3004.

Stafford Town

Town Clerk, PO Box 11, Stafford Springs, CT 06076. **Phone**-Town Clerk, R/E & UCC Recording- 860-684-1765; fax-860-684-1765; hours 8:15AM-4PM M-W; 8:15AM-6:30PM Th; 8AM-Noon F Will not search records. UCC copy- $1.00 per page. Payee: Stafford Town Clerk. **Other phones:** Assessor-860-684-1788; Treasurer-860-684-1772; Elections-860-684-1765; Vital Records-860-684-1765.

Stamford City

City Clerk, PO Box 10152, Stamford, CT 06904. **Phone**-City Clerk, R/E & UCC Recording- 203-977-4054, UCC Recording- 203-977-4707; fax-203-977-4943; hours 8:00AM-3:45PM www.cityofstamford.org/Welcome.htm Will not search records. UCC copy- $1.00 per page. RE record copy- $.50 per page. Cert fee: $1.00 per cert. Payee: City of Stamford. **Online Access to Assessor, Real Estate, Personal Property, City Businesses records:** Access to the city tax assessor database is free online at www.cityofstamford.org/Tax/main.htm. Also, search the city registry of trade names for free at www.cityofstamford.org/TradeNames/default.htm. Also, access assessor at http://data.visionappraisal.com/StamfordCT/. **Other phones:** Assessor-203-977-4019; Treasurer-203-977-4185; Elections-203-977-4011; Vital Records-203-977-4055.

Sterling Town

Town Clerk, PO Box 157, Oneco, CT 06373-0157. **Phone**-Town Clerk, R/E & UCC Recording- 860-564-2657; fax-860-564-1660; hours 8:30AM-3:30PM-M,T,TH; 8AM-6PM-W; 8AM-NOON-F Will not search records. Record copy- $1.00 per page. Cert fee: $1.00 per cert. Payee: Sterling Town Clerk. **Other phones:** Assessor-860-564-3030; Treasurer-860-564-2904; Elections-860-564-2657; Vital Records-860-564-2657.

Stonington Town

Town Clerk, PO Box 352, Stonington, CT 06378. **Phone**-Town Clerk, R/E & UCC Recording- 860-535-5060; fax-860-535-5062; hours 8:30AM-4PM www.townofstonington.com Will not search records. Record copy- $1.00 per page. Cert fee: $1.00 per cert. Payee: Stonington Town Clerk. **Other phones:** Assessor-860-535-5098; Elections-860-535-5047; Vital Records-860-535-5060; Finance Phone:-860-535-5070.

Stratford Town

Town Clerk, 2725 Main St, Rm 101, Stratford, CT 06615. **Phone**-203-385-4020; fax-203-385-4005; hours 8AM-4:30PM www.townofstratford.com
Will not search records. Record copy- $1.00 per page. Cert fee: $1.00 per page; $2.00 per certification. Payee: Town of Stratford. **Other phones:** Assessor-203-385-4025; Elections-203-385-4048; Vital Records-203-385-4020.

Suffield Town

Town Clerk, 83 Mountain Rd, Town Hall, Suffield, CT 06078. **Phone**-860-668-3880; fax-860-668-3898; hours 8:30AM-4:30PM; Summer: 8AM-4:30PM M-Th; 8AM-1PM F www.suffieldtownhall.com
Will not search records. Record copy- $1.00 per page. Cert fee: $1.00 per page. Payee: Town of Suffield. **Online Access to Assessor records:** Search the town assessor's database at http://data.visionappraisal.com/SuffieldCT. Free registration required for full access. **Other phones:** Assessor-860-668-3866; Treasurer-860-668-3851; Appraiser/ Auditor-860-668-3850; Elections-860-668-3880; Vital Records-860-668-3880.

Thomaston Town

Town Clerk, 158 Main St, Thomaston, CT 06787. **Phone**-Town Clerk, R/E & UCC Recording- 860-283-4141; fax-860-283-1013; hours 9AM-4:30PM
Will not search records. Record copy- $1.00 per page. Cert fee: $1.00 per cert. Payee: Thomaston Town Clerk. **Other phones:** Assessor-860-283-0305; Treasurer-860-283-9678.

Thompson Town

Town Clerk, PO Box 899, No. Grosvenor Dale, CT 06255. **Phone**-860-923-9900; fax-860-923-3836; hours 9AM-5PM. Will not search records. Record copy-$1.00 per page. Cert fee: $1.00 per cert. Payee: Town of Thompson. **Online Access to Assessor records:** Search the town assessor database at http://data.visionappraisal.com/ThompsonCT/. Free registration for full data. **Other phones:** Assessor-860-923-2259; Treasurer-860-923-3593; Elections-860-923-9900.

Tolland Town

Town Clerk, 21 Tolland Green, Hicks Memorial Muni. Ctr, Tolland, CT 06084. **Phone**-Town Clerk, R/E & UCC Recording- 860-871-3630; fax-860-871-3663; hours 8:30AM-4PM MTW; 8:30AM-7:30PM TH; 8:30 AM-Noon F
Do not confuse this town with the County of Tolland. Only Town of Tolland filings go here. Will not search records. Record copy- $1.00 per page. Cert fee: $1.00 per doc. Payee: Town Clerk. **Other phones:** Assessor-860-871-3650; Treasurer-860-871-3658; Elections-860-871-3634; Vital Records-860-871-3630.

Torrington City

Town Clerk, 140 Main St, City Hall, Torrington, CT 06790. **Phone**-860-489-2236, R/E Recording- 860-489-2238, UCC Recording- 860-489-2237; fax-860-489-2548; hours 8AM-4:30PM www.torrington-ct.org
Will search UCC records. UCC copy- $1.00 per page. Will not search real estate or tax lien records. Cert fee: $1.00 per cert. Payee: Town of Torrington. **Online Access to Assessor, Property records:** Access to property data is at http://data.visionappraisal.com/TorringtonCT/. Free registration required. **Other phones:** Assessor-860-489-2222; Treasurer-860-489-2334; Elections-860-489-2239; Vital Records-860-489-2236.

Trumbull Town

Town Clerk, 5866 Main St, Trumbull, CT 06611. **Phone**-203-452-5035; fax-203-452-5094; hours 9AM-5PM. Will not search records. Record copy- $1.00 per page. Cert fee: $1.00 per cert. Payee: Trumbull Town Clerk. **Other phones:** Assessor-203-452-5016; Treasurer-203-452-5014; Elections-203-452-5058; Vital Records-203-452-5035.

Union Town

Town Clerk, 1043 Buckley Highway, Route 171, Union, CT 06076-9520. **Phone**-Town Clerk, R/E & UCC Recording- 860-684-3770; fax-860-684-8830; hours 9AM-Noon T,Th; 9AM-Noon, 1-3PM W
Will not search records. Record copy- $1.00 per page. Cert fee: $1.00 per cert. Payee: Union Town Clerk. **Other phones:** Assessor-860-684-5705; Treasurer-860-684-8831; Elections-860-684-3770; Vital Records-860-684-3770; Tax Collector-860-684-8834.

Vernon Town

Town Clerk, 14 Park Pl, Rockville, CT 06066. **Phone**-Town Clerk, R/E & UCC Recording- 860-870-3662; fax-860-870-3683; hours 8:30AM-4:30PM M-W; 8:30AM-7PM Thurs.; 8:30AM-1PM Friday www.munic.state.ct.us/VERNON/
Will not search records. UCC copy- $1.00 per page. Cert fee: $1.00 per cert. Payee: Town of Vernon. **Other phones:** Assessor-860-870-3625; Treasurer-860-870-3660 (Tax Collector); Elections-860-870-3685 (Reg of Voters); Vital Records-860-870-3662.

Voluntown Town

Town Clerk, PO Box 96, Voluntown, CT 06384-0096. **Phone**-Town Clerk, R/E & UCC Recording- 860-376-4089; fax-860-376-3295; hours 9AM-2PM; 6-8PM T Evening www.voluntown.gov
Will not search records. UCC copy- $1.00 per page. Copy fee-$1.00 per page. Cert fee: $1.00 per cert. Payee: Town of Voluntown. **Other phones:** Assessor-860-376-3927; Treasurer-860-376-3927.

Wallingford Town

Town Clerk, Omit PO Box, Wallingford, CT 06492. **Phone**-Town Clerk, R/E & UCC Recording- 203-294-2145; fax-203-294-2150; hours 9AM-5PM
Will not search records. Record copy- $1.00 per page. Cert fee: $1.00 per cert. Payee: Town Clerk. **Other phones:** Assessor-203-294-2001; Treasurer-203-294-2042; Appraiser/ Auditor-203-294-2001; Elections-203-294-2125; Vital Records-203-294-2145.

Warren Town

Town Clerk, 7 Sackett Hill Rd, Town Hall, Warren, CT 06754. **Phone**-860-868-0090; fax-860-868-7746; hours 10AM-4PM W,Th; 10AM-Noon M,F
Will not search records. UCC copy- $1.00 per page. Cert fee: $1.00 per cert. Payee: Warren Town Clerk. **Other phones:** Assessor-860-868-7881.

Washington Town

Town Clerk, PO Box 383, Washington Depot, CT 06794. **Phone**-860-868-2786; fax-860-868-3103; hours 9AM-Noon, 1-4:45PM
Will not search records. Record copy- $1.00 per page. Cert fee: $1.00 per page. Payee: Town of Washington. **Other phones:** Assessor-860-868-0398; Vital Records-860-868-2786.

Waterbury City

Town Clerk, 235 Grand St, City Hall, Waterbury, CT 06702. **Phone**-Town Clerk, R/E & UCC Recording-203-574-6806; fax-203-574-6887; hours 8:30AM-4:30PM
Will not search records. UCC copy- $1.00 per page. Cert fee: $1.00 per page. Payee: Waterbury Town Clerk. **Online Access to Assessor, Property, Real**

Estate Sale records: Access to the assessor property data is free at www.waterburyrealestate.org/Waterbury208/LandRover.asp and also at http://data.visionappraisal.com/watertownct/. **Other phones:** Assessor-203-574-6821; Elections-203-574-6751; Vital Records-203-574-6801.

Waterford Town

Town Clerk, 15 Rope Ferry Rd, Waterford, CT 06385. **Phone**-Town Clerk, R/E & UCC Recording- 860-444-5831; fax-860-437-0352; hours 8AM-4PM
Will not search records. UCC copy- $1.00 per page. Cert fee: $1.00 per cert. Payee: Waterford Town Clerk. **Other phones:** Assessor-860-444-5820; Vital Records-860-444-5831.

Watertown Town

Town Clerk, 37 DeForest St, Watertown, CT 06795. **Phone**-Town Clerk, R/E & UCC Recording- 860-945-5230; fax-860-945-2706; hours 9AM-5PM www.watertownct.org
Will not search records. **Other phones:** Assessor-860-945-5235; Treasurer-860-945-5261; Elections-860-945-5230; Vital Records-860-945-5230.

West Hartford Town

Town Clerk, 50 S. Main St, Rm 313 Town Hall Common, West Hartford, CT 06107-2431. **Phone**-860-523-3148; fax-860-523-3522; hours 8:30AM-4:30PM
Will not search records. UCC copy- $1.00 per page. Cert fee: $1.00 per cert. Payee: Town of West Hartford. **Online Access to Assessor, Property records:** Access to the assessor property records requires a $50 annual subscription for one user; $200 for 5 users. Details and sign-up are at www.westhartford.org/whprs/. **Other phones:** Assessor-860-523-3119; Treasurer-860-523-3188; Appraiser/ Auditor-860-523-3119; Elections-860-523-3181; Vital Records-860-523-3151.

West Haven City

City Clerk, PO Box 526, West Haven, CT 06516. **Phone**-203-937-3534, R/E Recording- 203-937-3535; fax-203-937-3706; hours 9AM-5PM
Will not search records. Record copy- $1.00 per page. Cert fee: $1.00 per cert. Payee: West Haven City Clerk. **Online Access to Assessor records:** Search the town assessor's database at http://data.visionappraisal.com/Westhavenct/. Free registration required for full access. **Other phones:** Assessor-203-937-3517.

Westbrook Town

Town Clerk, 866 Boston Post Rd, Westbrook, CT 06498-1881. **Phone**-860-399-3044; fax-860-399-3092; hours 9AM-4PM M-W & F; 9AM-7PM Th; 9AM-Noon Friday
Will not search records. Record copy- $1.00 per page. Cert fee: $1.00 per cert. Payee: Westbrook Town Clerk. **Other phones:** Assessor-860-399-3045.

Weston Town

Town Clerk, PO Box 1007, Weston, CT 06883. **Phone**-203-222-2616, R/E Recording- 203-222-2617; fax-203-222-8871; hours 9AM-4:30PM www.weston-ct.com
Will not search records. UCC copy fee- $1.00 per page. RE record copy- $.50 per page. Cert fee: $1.00 per cert. Payee: Weston Town Clerk. **Online Access to Land, Marriage, Death, Trade Name, Grantor/Grantee records:** Access the Town Clerk's index records free online at www.weston-ct.com/resolution/. For username and password use cott, cott. Maps and surveys are also available. Search page access at www.weston-ct.com/resolution. **Other phones:** Assessor-203-222-2606; Elections-203-222-2616; Vital Records-203-222-2616; General Information-203-222-2500.

Westport Town

Town Clerk, PO Box 549, Westport, CT 06881. **Phone-**Town Clerk, R/E & UCC Recording- 203-341-1110; fax-203-341-1112; hours 8:30AM-4:30PM www.ci.westport.ct.us/govt/services
Will not search records. Record copy- $1.00 per page. Cert fee: $1.00 per cert. Payee: Westport Town Clerk. **Online Access to Assessor records:** Access to the assessments database at www.ci.westport.ct.us/govt/services/finance/assessor/default.asp. **Other phones:** Assessor-203-341-1070; Elections-203-341-1115; Vital Records-203-341-1110; Main number-203-341-1000.

Wethersfield Town

Town Clerk, 505 Silas Deane Highway, Wethersfield, CT 06109. **Phone-**Town Clerk, R/E & UCC Recording- 860-721-2880; fax-860-721-2994; hours 8AM-4:30PM www.wethersfieldct.com/govt.htm
Will not search records. Record copy- $1.00 per page. Cert fee: $1.00 per cert. Payee: Wethersfield Town. **Online Access to Assessor, Property records:** Access to property data is at http://data.visionappraisal.com/WethersfieldCT/. Free registration required. **Other phones:** Assessor-860-721-2810; Treasurer-860-721-2861; Elections-860-721-2819; Vital Records-860-721-2880.

Willington Town

Town Clerk, 40 Old Farms Rd, Willington, CT 06279. **Phone-**Town Clerk, R/E & UCC Recording- 860-487-3121; fax-860-487-3103; hours 9AM-2PM (M open 6-8PM) www.willingtonct.org
Will not search records. Record copy- $1.00 per page. Cert fee: $1.00 per cert. Payee: Willington Town Clerk. **Other phones:** Assessor-860-487-3122; Treasurer-860-487-3133; Elections-860-487-3120; Vital Records-860-487-3121.

Wilton Town

Town Clerk, 238 Danbury Rd, Wilton, CT 06897. **Phone-**Town Clerk, R/E & UCC Recording- 203-563-0106; fax-203-563-0130; hours 8:30AM-4:30PM www.munic.state.ct.us/WILTON/wilton.htm
Will not search records. Record copy- $1.00 per page. Cert fee: $1.00 per page + $1.00. Payee: Town of Wilton. **Online Access to Assessor records:** Search the town assessor database at http://data.visionappraisal.com/WiltonCT/. Free registration for full data. **Other phones:** Assessor-203-563-0121; Treasurer-203-563-0114; Elections-203-563-0112; Vital Records-203-563-0106.

Winchester Town

Town Clerk, 338 Main St, Town Hall, Winsted, CT 06098-1697. **Phone-**Town Clerk, R/E & UCC Recording- 860-738-6963; fax-860-738-6595; hours 8AM-4PM M-W, 8AM-7PM Th, 8AM-noon F www.townofwinchester.org
Will search UCC records. UCC copy- $1.00 per page. Will not search real estate or tax lien records. RE record copy- $1.00 per page. Cert fee: $1.00 per cert. Payee: Town of Winchester. **Online Access to Property, Assessor records:** Access town property tax data after free registration at http://data.visionappraisal.com/WinchesterCT/. **Other phones:** Assessor-860-379-5461; Treasurer-860-738-6961; Appraiser/ Auditor-860-379-5461; Elections-860-379-2713 x355; Vital Records-860-738-6963.

Windham Town

Town Clerk, PO Box 94, Willimantic, CT 06226. **Phone-**860-465-3013; fax-860-465-3012; hours 8AM-5PM M-W; 8AM-7:30PM Th; 8AM-Noon F www.windhamct.com
Will not search records. Record copy- $1.00 per page. Cert fee: $1.00 per cert. Payee: Windham Town Clerk. **Other phones:** Assessor-860-465-3025; Treasurer-860-465-3013.

Windsor Locks Town

Town Clerk, 50 Church St, Town Office Bldg., Windsor Locks, CT 06096. **Phone-**Town Clerk, R/E & UCC Recording- 860-627-1441; hours 8AM-4PM M-W; 8AM-6PM Th; 8AM-1PM F
Will not search records. Record copy- $1.00 per page. Cert fee: $1.00 per cert. Payee: Town of Windsor Locks. **Online Access to Assessor records:** Search the town assessor database at http://data.visionappraisal.com/WINDSORLOCKSCT/. Free registration for full data. **Other phones:** Assessor-860-627-1448; Treasurer-860-627-1449; Elections-860-654-1619; Vital Records-860-627-1441.

Windsor Town

Town Clerk, PO Box 472, Windsor, CT 06095-0472. **Phone-**Town Clerk, R/E & UCC Recording- 860-285-1902; fax-860-285-1909; hours 8AM-5PM M,W-F; 8AM-6PM T www.townofwindsorct.com
Will not search records. Record copy- $1.00 per page or $1.37 without a stamped envelope. Cert fee: $1.00 per cert. Payee: Town of Windsor. **Online Access to Assessor, Real Estate records:** Search the town clerk's land records index for free at www.townofwindsorct.com/records.htm. Index goes

back to 1970. Also, search the town assessor's Taxpayer Information System database at http://data.visionappraisal.com/WINDSORCT/. Free registration required for full access. Searce page: www.townofwindsorct.com (town services-index only). **Other phones:** Assessor-860-285-1817; Treasurer-860-285-1890; Elections-860-285-1902; Vital Records-860-285-1902.

Wolcott Town

Town Clerk, 10 Kenea Ave, Town Hall, Wolcott, CT 06716. **Phone-**Town Clerk, R/E & UCC Recording-203-879-8100; fax-203-879-8105; hours 8:30AM-4:30PM (Recording until 4PM)
Will not search records. Record copy- $1.00 per page. Cert fee: $1.00 per cert. Payee: Wolcott Town Clerk. **Other phones:** Assessor-203-879-8100; Treasurer-203-879-8100; Elections-203-879-8100; Vital Records-203-879-8100.

Woodbridge Town

Town Clerk, 11 Meetinghouse Lane, Woodbridge, CT 06525. **Phone-**Town Clerk, R/E & UCC Recording-203-389-3422; fax-203-389-3473; hours 8AM-4PM www.munic.state.ct.us/woodbridge/townclerk.html
Will not search records. Record copy- $1.00 per page. Cert fee: $1.00 per cert. Payee: Woodbridge Town Clerk. **Online Access to Assessor records:** Search the town assessor's database at http://data.visionappraisal.com/woodbridgeCT. Free registration required for full data. **Other phones:** Assessor-203-389-3416; Treasurer-203-389-3414; Appraiser/ Auditor-203-389-3414; Elections-203-389-3408; Vital Records-203-389-3424.

Woodbury Town

Town Clerk, PO Box 369, Woodbury, CT 06798-3407. **Phone-**203-263-2144; fax-203-263-4755; hours 8:30AM-4:30PM (Summer Hours 8AM-4PM)
Will not search records. Record copy- $1.00 per page. Cert fee: $1.00 per cert. Payee: Woodbury Town Clerk. **Other phones:** Assessor-203-263-2435; Treasurer-203-263-2449; Elections-203-263-4750; Vital Records-203-263-2144.

Woodstock Town

Town Clerk, 415 Route 169, Town Hall, Woodstock, CT 06281. **Phone-**860-928-6595; fax-860-963-7557; hours 8:30AM-4:30PM M,T,Th; 8:30AM-6PM W; 8:30AM-3PM F
Will not search records. UCC copy- $1.00 per page. Cert fee: $1.00 per cert. Payee: Town of Woodstock. **Other phones:** Assessor-860-928-6929.

Connecticut County Locator

You will usually be able to find the city name in the City/County Cross Reference below. In that case, it is a simple matter to determine the county from the cross-reference. However, only the official US Postal Service city names are included in this index. Included is a ZIP/City Cross Reference following the City/County Cross Reference. If you know the ZIP Code but the city name does not appear in the City/County Cross list, look up the ZIP Code in the ZIP/City Cross Reference, find the city name, then look up the city in the City/County Cross Reference.

Connecticut City/County Cross Reference

ABINGTON Windham
AMSTON Tolland
ANDOVER Tolland
ANSONIA New Haven
ASHFORD Windham
AVON Hartford
BALLOUVILLE Windham
BALTIC (06330) New London(92), Windham(7)
BANTAM Litchfield
BARKHAMSTED Litchfield
BEACON FALLS New Haven
BETHANY New Haven
BETHEL Fairfield
BETHLEHEM Litchfield
BLOOMFIELD Hartford
BOLTON Tolland
BOTSFORD Fairfield
BOZRAH New London
BRANFORD New Haven
BRIDGEPORT Fairfield
BRIDGEWATER Litchfield
BRISTOL Hartford
BROAD BROOK Hartford
BROOKFIELD Fairfield
BROOKLYN Windham
BURLINGTON Hartford
CANAAN Litchfield
CANTERBURY Windham
CANTON Hartford
CANTON CENTER Hartford
CENTERBROOK Middlesex
CENTRAL VILLAGE Windham
CHAPLIN Windham
CHESHIRE New Haven
CHESTER Middlesex
CLINTON Middlesex
COBALT Middlesex
COLCHESTER (06415) New London(90), Middlesex(9)
COLEBROOK Litchfield
COLLINSVILLE Hartford
COLUMBIA Tolland
CORNWALL Litchfield
CORNWALL BRIDGE Litchfield
COS COB Fairfield
COVENTRY Tolland
CROMWELL Middlesex
DANBURY Fairfield
DANIELSON Windham
DARIEN Fairfield
DAYVILLE Windham
DEEP RIVER Middlesex
DERBY New Haven
DURHAM Middlesex
EAST BERLIN Hartford
EAST CANAAN Litchfield
EAST GLASTONBURY Hartford
EAST GRANBY Hartford
EAST HADDAM Middlesex
EAST HAMPTON Middlesex
EAST HARTFORD Hartford
EAST HARTLAND Hartford
EAST HAVEN New Haven
EAST KILLINGLY Windham
EAST LYME New London
EAST WINDSOR Hartford
EAST WINDSOR HILL Hartford
EAST WOODSTOCK Windham
EASTFORD (06242) Windham(96), Tolland(3)

EASTON Fairfield
ELLINGTON Tolland
ENFIELD Hartford
ESSEX Middlesex
FABYAN Windham
FAIRFIELD Fairfield
FALLS VILLAGE Litchfield
FARMINGTON Hartford
GALES FERRY New London
GAYLORDSVILLE Litchfield
GEORGETOWN Fairfield
GILMAN New London
GLASGO New London
GLASTONBURY Hartford
GOSHEN Litchfield
GRANBY Hartford
GREENS FARMS Fairfield
GREENWICH Fairfield
GROSVENOR DALE Windham
GROTON New London
GUILFORD New Haven
HADDAM Middlesex
HADLYME New London
HAMDEN New Haven
HAMPTON Windham
HANOVER New London
HARTFORD Hartford
HARWINTON Litchfield
HAWLEYVILLE Fairfield
HEBRON Tolland
HIGGANUM Middlesex
IVORYTON Middlesex
JEWETT CITY New London
KENSINGTON Hartford
KENT Litchfield
KILLINGWORTH Middlesex
LAKESIDE Litchfield
LAKEVILLE Litchfield
LEBANON New London
LEDYARD New London
LITCHFIELD Litchfield
MADISON New Haven
MANCHESTER (06040) Hartford(98), Tolland(1)
MANCHESTER Hartford
MANSFIELD CENTER (06250) Tolland(97), Windham(2)
MANSFIELD DEPOT Tolland
MARION Hartford
MARLBOROUGH Hartford
MASHANTUCKET New London
MELROSE Hartford
MERIDEN New Haven
MIDDLE HADDAM Middlesex
MIDDLEBURY New Haven
MIDDLEFIELD Middlesex
MIDDLETOWN Middlesex
MILFORD New Haven
MILLDALE Hartford
MONROE Fairfield
MONTVILLE New London
MOODUS Middlesex
MOOSUP Windham
MORRIS Litchfield
MYSTIC New London
NAUGATUCK New Haven
NEW BRITAIN Hartford
NEW CANAAN Fairfield
NEW FAIRFIELD Fairfield
NEW HARTFORD Litchfield
NEW HAVEN New Haven

NEW LONDON New London
NEW MILFORD Litchfield
NEW PRESTON MARBLE DALE Litchfield
NEWINGTON Hartford
NEWTOWN Fairfield
NIANTIC New London
NORFOLK Litchfield
NORTH BRANFORD New Haven
NORTH CANTON Hartford
NORTH FRANKLIN New London
NORTH GRANBY Hartford
NORTH GROSVENORDALE Windham
NORTH HAVEN New Haven
NORTH STONINGTON New London
NORTH WESTCHESTER New London
NORTH WINDHAM Windham
NORTHFIELD Litchfield
NORTHFORD New Haven
NORWALK Fairfield
NORWICH New London
OAKDALE New London
OAKVILLE Litchfield
OLD GREENWICH Fairfield
OLD LYME New London
OLD MYSTIC New London
OLD SAYBROOK Middlesex
ONECO Windham
ORANGE New Haven
OXFORD New Haven
PAWCATUCK New London
PEQUABUCK Litchfield
PINE MEADOW Litchfield
PLAINFIELD Windham
PLAINVILLE Hartford
PLANTSVILLE Hartford
PLEASANT VALLEY Litchfield
PLYMOUTH Litchfield
POMFRET Windham
POMFRET CENTER Windham
POQUONOCK Hartford
PORTLAND Middlesex
PRESTON New London
PROSPECT New Haven
PUTNAM Windham
QUAKER HILL New London
QUINEBAUG Windham
REDDING Fairfield
REDDING CENTER Fairfield
REDDING RIDGE Fairfield
RIDGEFIELD Fairfield
RIVERSIDE Fairfield
RIVERTON Litchfield
ROCKFALL Middlesex
ROCKY HILL Hartford
ROGERS Windham
ROXBURY Litchfield
SALEM New London
SALISBURY Litchfield
SANDY HOOK Fairfield
SCOTLAND Windham
SEYMOUR New Haven
SHARON Litchfield
SHELTON Fairfield
SHERMAN (06784) Fairfield(98), Litchfield(1)
SIMSBURY Hartford
SOMERS Tolland
SOMERSVILLE Tolland
SOUTH BRITAIN New Haven
SOUTH GLASTONBURY Hartford
SOUTH KENT Litchfield

SOUTH LYME New London
SOUTH WILLINGTON Tolland
SOUTH WINDHAM Windham
SOUTH WINDSOR Hartford
SOUTH WOODSTOCK Windham
SOUTHBURY New Haven
SOUTHINGTON Hartford
SOUTHPORT Fairfield
STAFFORD Tolland
STAFFORD SPRINGS (06076) Tolland(93), Windham(6)
STAFFORDVILLE Tolland
STAMFORD Fairfield
STERLING Windham
STEVENSON Fairfield
STONINGTON New London
STORRS MANSFIELD Tolland
STRATFORD Fairfield
SUFFIELD Hartford
TACONIC Litchfield
TAFTVILLE New London
TARIFFVILLE Hartford
TERRYVILLE Litchfield
THOMASTON Litchfield
THOMPSON Windham
TOLLAND Tolland
TORRINGTON Litchfield
TRUMBULL Fairfield
UNCASVILLE New London
UNIONVILLE Hartford
VERNON ROCKVILLE Tolland
VERSAILLES New London
VOLUNTOWN (06384) New London(97), Windham(2)
W HARTFORD Hartford
WALLINGFORD New Haven
WASHINGTON DEPOT Litchfield
WATERBURY New Haven
WATERFORD New London
WATERTOWN Litchfield
WAUREGAN Windham
WEATOGUE Hartford
WEST CORNWALL Litchfield
WEST GRANBY Hartford
WEST HARTFORD Hartford
WEST HARTLAND Hartford
WEST HAVEN New Haven
WEST MYSTIC New London
WEST SIMSBURY Hartford
WEST SUFFIELD Hartford
WESTBROOK Middlesex
WESTON Fairfield
WESTPORT Fairfield
WETHERSFIELD Hartford
WILLIMANTIC Windham
WILLINGTON Tolland
WILTON Fairfield
WINCHESTER CENTER Litchfield
WINDHAM Windham
WINDSOR Hartford
WINDSOR LOCKS Hartford
WINSTED Litchfield
WOLCOTT New Haven
WOODBRIDGE New Haven
WOODBURY Litchfield
WOODSTOCK Windham
WOODSTOCK VALLEY Windham
YANTIC New London

Connecticut ZIP/City Cross Reference

06001-06001 AVON	06117-06117 WEST HARTFORD	06371-06371 OLD LYME	06500-06511 NEW HAVEN
06002-06002 BLOOMFIELD	06118-06118 EAST HARTFORD	06372-06372 OLD MYSTIC	06512-06512 EAST HAVEN
06006-06006 WINDSOR	06119-06119 W HARTFORD	06373-06373 ONECO	06513-06513 NEW HAVEN
06010-06011 BRISTOL	06119-06119 WEST HARTFORD	06374-06374 PLAINFIELD	06514-06514 HAMDEN
06013-06013 BURLINGTON	06120-06126 HARTFORD	06375-06375 QUAKER HILL	06515-06515 NEW HAVEN
06016-06016 BROAD BROOK	06127-06127 W HARTFORD	06376-06376 SOUTH LYME	06516-06516 WEST HAVEN
06018-06018 CANAAN	06127-06127 WEST HARTFORD	06377-06377 STERLING	06517-06518 HAMDEN
06019-06019 CANTON	06128-06128 EAST HARTFORD	06378-06378 STONINGTON	06519-06521 NEW HAVEN
06020-06020 CANTON CENTER	06129-06129 WETHERSFIELD	06379-06379 PAWCATUCK	06524-06524 BETHANY
06021-06021 COLEBROOK	06131-06131 NEWINGTON	06380-06380 TAFTVILLE	06525-06525 WOODBRIDGE
06022-06022 COLLINSVILLE	06132-06132 HARTFORD	06382-06382 UNCASVILLE	06530-06540 NEW HAVEN
06023-06023 EAST BERLIN	06133-06133 W HARTFORD	06383-06383 VERSAILLES	06600-06610 BRIDGEPORT
06024-06024 EAST CANAAN	06133-06133 WEST HARTFORD	06384-06384 VOLUNTOWN	06611-06611 TRUMBULL
06025-06025 EAST GLASTONBURY	06134-06134 HARTFORD	06385-06386 WATERFORD	06612-06612 EASTON
06026-06026 EAST GRANBY	06137-06137 W HARTFORD	06387-06387 WAUREGAN	06614-06615 STRATFORD
06027-06027 EAST HARTLAND	06137-06137 WEST HARTFORD	06388-06388 WEST MYSTIC	06650-06699 BRIDGEPORT
06028-06028 EAST WINDSOR HILL	06138-06138 EAST HARTFORD	06389-06389 YANTIC	06701-06710 WATERBURY
06029-06029 ELLINGTON	06140-06199 HARTFORD	06401-06401 ANSONIA	06712-06712 PROSPECT
06030-06030 FARMINGTON	06226-06226 WILLIMANTIC	06403-06403 BEACON FALLS	06716-06716 WOLCOTT
06031-06031 FALLS VILLAGE	06230-06230 ABINGTON	06404-06404 BOTSFORD	06720-06749 WATERBURY
06032-06032 FARMINGTON	06231-06231 AMSTON	06405-06405 BRANFORD	06750-06750 BANTAM
06033-06033 GLASTONBURY	06232-06232 ANDOVER	06408-06408 CHESHIRE	06751-06751 BETHLEHEM
06034-06034 FARMINGTON	06233-06233 BALLOUVILLE	06409-06409 CENTERBROOK	06752-06752 BRIDGEWATER
06035-06035 GRANBY	06234-06234 BROOKLYN	06410-06411 CHESHIRE	06753-06753 CORNWALL
06037-06037 KENSINGTON	06235-06235 CHAPLIN	06412-06412 CHESTER	06754-06754 CORNWALL BRIDGE
06039-06039 LAKEVILLE	06237-06237 COLUMBIA	06413-06413 CLINTON	06755-06755 GAYLORDSVILLE
06040-06041 MANCHESTER	06238-06238 COVENTRY	06414-06414 COBALT	06756-06756 GOSHEN
06043-06043 BOLTON	06239-06239 DANIELSON	06415-06415 COLCHESTER	06757-06757 KENT
06045-06045 MANCHESTER	06241-06241 DAYVILLE	06416-06416 CROMWELL	06758-06758 LAKESIDE
06049-06049 MELROSE	06242-06242 EASTFORD	06417-06417 DEEP RIVER	06759-06759 LITCHFIELD
06050-06053 NEW BRITAIN	06243-06243 EAST KILLINGLY	06418-06418 DERBY	06762-06762 MIDDLEBURY
06057-06057 NEW HARTFORD	06244-06244 EAST WOODSTOCK	06419-06419 KILLINGWORTH	06763-06763 MORRIS
06058-06058 NORFOLK	06245-06245 FABYAN	06420-06420 SALEM	06770-06770 NAUGATUCK
06059-06059 NORTH CANTON	06246-06246 GROSVENOR DALE	06422-06422 DURHAM	06776-06776 NEW MILFORD
06060-06060 NORTH GRANBY	06247-06247 HAMPTON	06423-06423 EAST HADDAM	06777-06777 NEW PRESTON MARBLE
06061-06061 PINE MEADOW	06248-06248 HEBRON	06424-06424 EAST HAMPTON	DALE
06062-06062 PLAINVILLE	06249-06249 LEBANON	06426-06426 ESSEX	06778-06778 NORTHFIELD
06063-06063 PLEASANT VALLEY	06250-06250 MANSFIELD CENTER	06430-06432 FAIRFIELD	06779-06779 OAKVILLE
06063-06063 BARKHAMSTED	06251-06251 MANSFIELD DEPOT	06436-06436 GREENS FARMS	06781-06781 PEQUABUCK
06064-06064 POQUONOCK	06254-06254 NORTH FRANKLIN	06437-06437 GUILFORD	06782-06782 PLYMOUTH
06065-06065 RIVERTON	06255-06255 NORTH GROSVENORDALE	06438-06438 HADDAM	06783-06783 ROXBURY
06066-06066 VERNON ROCKVILLE	06256-06256 NORTH WINDHAM	06439-06439 HADLYME	06784-06784 SHERMAN
06067-06067 ROCKY HILL	06258-06258 POMFRET	06440-06440 HAWLEYVILLE	06785-06785 SOUTH KENT
06068-06068 SALISBURY	06259-06259 POMFRET CENTER	06441-06441 HIGGANUM	06786-06786 TERRYVILLE
06069-06069 SHARON	06260-06260 PUTNAM	06442-06442 IVORYTON	06787-06787 THOMASTON
06070-06070 SIMSBURY	06262-06262 QUINEBAUG	06443-06443 MADISON	06790-06790 TORRINGTON
06071-06071 SOMERS	06263-06263 ROGERS	06444-06444 MARION	06791-06791 HARWINTON
06072-06072 SOMERSVILLE	06264-06264 SCOTLAND	06447-06447 MARLBOROUGH	06793-06794 WASHINGTON DEPOT
06073-06073 SOUTH GLASTONBURY	06265-06265 SOUTH WILLINGTON	06450-06454 MERIDEN	06795-06795 WATERTOWN
06074-06074 SOUTH WINDSOR	06266-06266 SOUTH WINDHAM	06455-06455 MIDDLEFIELD	06796-06796 WEST CORNWALL
06075-06075 STAFFORD	06267-06267 SOUTH WOODSTOCK	06456-06456 MIDDLE HADDAM	06798-06798 WOODBURY
06076-06076 STAFFORD SPRINGS	06268-06269 STORRS MANSFIELD	06457-06459 MIDDLETOWN	06801-06801 BETHEL
06077-06077 STAFFORDVILLE	06277-06277 THOMPSON	06460-06460 MILFORD	06804-06804 BROOKFIELD
06078-06078 SUFFIELD	06278-06278 ASHFORD	06461-06461 BRIDGEPORT	06807-06807 COS COB
06079-06079 TACONIC	06279-06279 WILLINGTON	06466-06466 MILFORD	06810-06811 DANBURY
06080-06080 SUFFIELD	06280-06280 WINDHAM	06467-06467 MILLDALE	06812-06812 NEW FAIRFIELD
06081-06081 TARIFFVILLE	06281-06281 WOODSTOCK	06468-06468 MONROE	06813-06817 DANBURY
06082-06083 ENFIELD	06282-06282 WOODSTOCK VALLEY	06469-06469 MOODUS	06820-06820 DARIEN
06084-06084 TOLLAND	06320-06320 NEW LONDON	06470-06470 NEWTOWN	06824-06828 FAIRFIELD
06085-06087 UNIONVILLE	06330-06330 BALTIC	06471-06471 NORTH BRANFORD	06829-06829 GEORGETOWN
06088-06088 EAST WINDSOR	06331-06331 CANTERBURY	06472-06472 NORTHFORD	06830-06836 GREENWICH
06089-06089 WEATOGUE	06332-06332 CENTRAL VILLAGE	06473-06473 NORTH HAVEN	06838-06838 GREENS FARMS
06090-06090 WEST GRANBY	06333-06333 EAST LYME	06474-06474 NORTH WESTCHESTER	06840-06842 NEW CANAAN
06091-06091 WEST HARTLAND	06334-06334 BOZRAH	06475-06475 OLD SAYBROOK	06850-06860 NORWALK
06092-06092 WEST SIMSBURY	06335-06335 GALES FERRY	06477-06477 ORANGE	06870-06870 OLD GREENWICH
06093-06093 WEST SUFFIELD	06336-06336 GILMAN	06478-06478 OXFORD	06875-06875 REDDING CENTER
06094-06094 WINCHESTER CENTER	06337-06337 GLASGO	06479-06479 PLANTSVILLE	06876-06876 REDDING RIDGE
06095-06095 WINDSOR	06338-06338 MASHANTUCKET	06480-06480 PORTLAND	06877-06877 RIDGEFIELD
06096-06096 WINDSOR LOCKS	06339-06339 LEDYARD	06481-06481 ROCKFALL	06878-06878 RIVERSIDE
06098-06098 WINSTED	06340-06340 GROTON	06482-06482 SANDY HOOK	06879-06879 RIDGEFIELD
06100-06106 HARTFORD	06350-06350 HANOVER	06483-06483 SEYMOUR	06880-06881 WESTPORT
06107-06107 W HARTFORD	06351-06351 JEWETT CITY	06484-06484 SHELTON	06883-06883 WESTON
06107-06107 WEST HARTFORD	06353-06353 MONTVILLE	06487-06487 SOUTH BRITAIN	06888-06889 WESTPORT
06108-06108 EAST HARTFORD	06354-06354 MOOSUP	06488-06488 SOUTHBURY	06890-06890 SOUTHPORT
06109-06109 WETHERSFIELD	06355-06355 MYSTIC	06489-06489 SOUTHINGTON	06896-06896 REDDING
06110-06110 W HARTFORD	06357-06357 NIANTIC	06490-06490 SOUTHPORT	06897-06897 WILTON
06110-06110 WEST HARTFORD	06359-06359 NORTH STONINGTON	06491-06491 STEVENSON	06900-06928 STAMFORD
06111-06111 NEWINGTON	06360-06360 NORWICH	06492-06495 WALLINGFORD	
06112-06115 HARTFORD	06365-06365 PRESTON	06497-06497 STRATFORD	
06117-06117 W HARTFORD	06370-06370 OAKDALE	06498-06498 WESTBROOK	

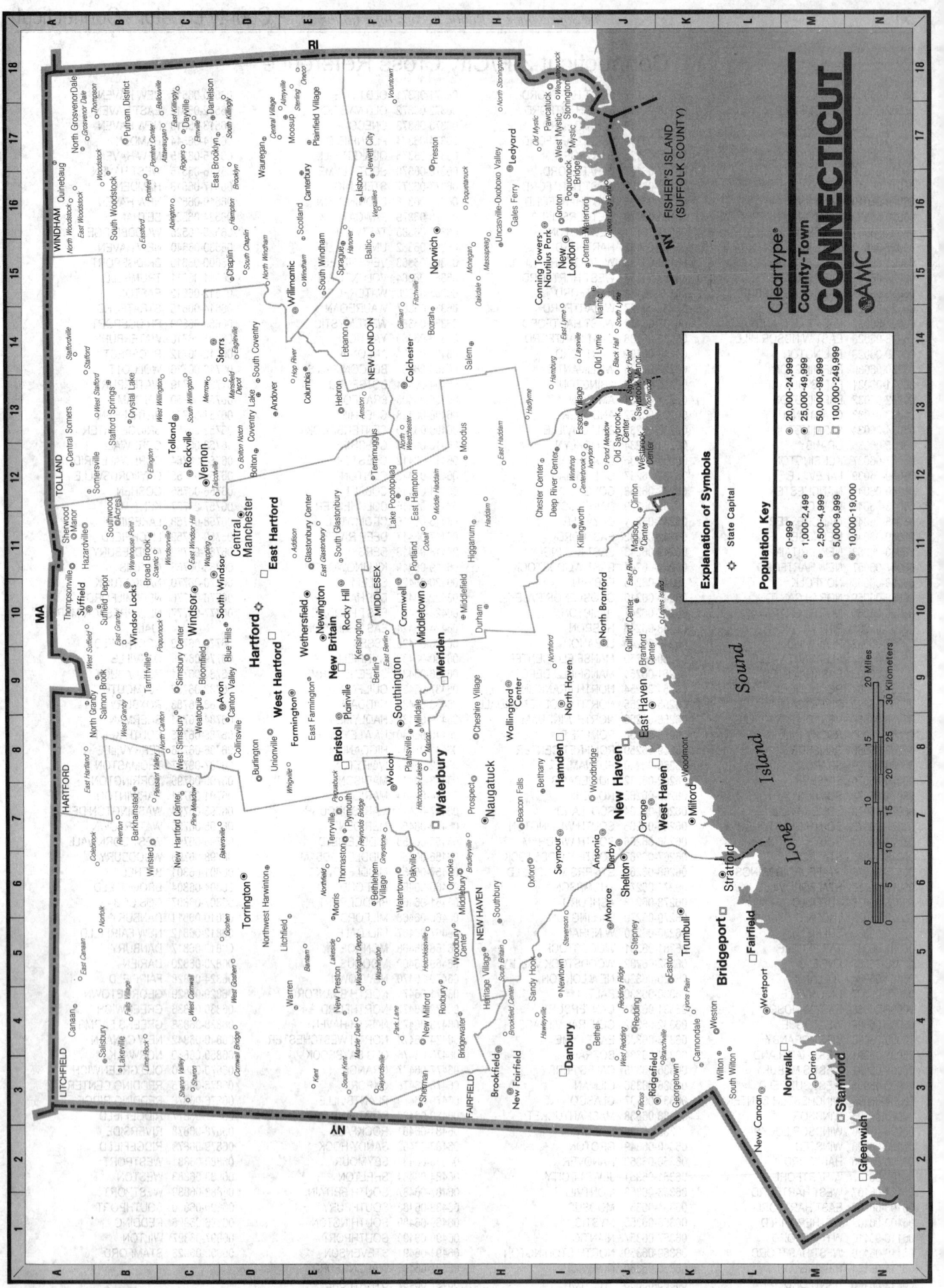

CONNECTICUT

Cleartype®
County-Town

AMC

Explanation of Symbols

State Capital

Population Key

⊚ 0-999
⊙ 1,000-2,499
⊛ 2,500-4,999
⊙ 5,000-9,999
⊛ 10,000-19,000
⊚ 20,000-24,999
⊛ 25,000-49,999
□ 50,000-99,999
▢ 100,000-249,999

Explanation of symbols:

●– Census Designated Place (CDP)

▲ *italics* – Township (shown on the map)

● *italics* – Township shown which is also a CDP

italics – Township (not shown on the map)

Delaware

General Help Numbers:

Governor's Office

820 N. French St
Wilmington, DE 19801
www.state.de.us/governor/index.shtm

302-577-3210
Fax 302-577-3118
8AM-5:30PM

Attorney General's Office

Carvel State Office Bldg
820 N French St
Wilmington, DE 19801
www.state.de.us/attgen

302-577-8400
Fax 302-577-6630
8:30AM-5PM

Legislative Records

Division of Research
PO Box 1401
Wilmington, DE 19903
www.legis.state.de.us/Legislature.nsf?Open

302-744-4114
800-282-8545 (In-state)
8AM-4:30PM

State Archives

121 Duke of York St
Dover, DE 19901
www.archives.lib.de.us

302-744-5000
Fax 302-739-6710
8:30AM-4:15PM M-F
(till 8PM on E & TH)

State Specifics:

Capital:	Dover
	Kent County
Time Zone:	EST
Number of Counties:	3
Population:	817,491
Web Site:	http://delaware.gov

State Agencies

Criminal Records

Delaware State Police, State Bureau of Identification, PO Box 430, Dover, DE 19903-0430 (Courier: 1407 N Dupont Highway, Dover, DE 19930); 302-739-5880, 302-739-4794 (Fingerprinting/Crim. Background), 302-739-5888 (Fax), 8AM-4PM.

www.state.de.us/dsp/

Indexing & Storage: Records are available from 1935. It takes up to 3 days before new records are available for inquiry. Records are normally destroyed after expunged, otherwise kept indefinitely.

Searching: Must have a signed release from the subject for the fingerprint search and release of information. Will not expedite requests; their policy is first come first served. You do not need to use the state's forms. Include the following in your request-fingerprints, full name, signed release. The following data is not released: traffic ticket information.

Access by: mail, in person.

Fee & Payment: The search fee is $35.00 per request. Fee payee: Delaware State Police. Prepayment required. Funds must be certified or money order. Credit cards accepted for in person searches only

Mail search: Turnaround time: 14 days. Must have a signed release and full set of fingerprints. A SASE is requested.

In person search: It can take up to 14 days before records are ready for pickup.

Statewide Court Records

Administrative Office of the Courts, Supreme Court of Delaware, 820 N French, 11th Fl, Wilmington, DE 19801; 302-255-0090, 302-255-2217 (Fax), 8:30AM-5PM.

http://courts.state.de.us

Note: Except for certain online research capabilities, all court record access must be done at the local level.

Access by: online. No searching by mail.

Online search: Supreme Court Final Orders and Opinions are available at http://courts.state.de.us/supreme/opinions.htm. There is no statewide access to trial court data.

Sexual Offender Registry

Delaware State Police, Sex Offender Central Registry, PO Box 430, Dover, DE 19903-0430 (Courier: 1407 N Dupont Highway, Dover, DE 19901); 302-739-5882, 302-739-5888 (Fax), 8AM-4PM.

www.state.de.us/dsp/sexoff/

Note: There are three Tiers or Levels of offenders in the state. The public is only made aware of Tiers 2 and 3 via the Internet through public notification programs by local law enforcement. Door-to-door is used for Tier 3 notification.

Indexing & Storage: Records are available from 06/24/94. It takes up to 3 days before new records are available for inquiry.

Searching: Name searching is not available in the state except through the web page.

Access by: online.

Online search: Statewide registry can be searched at the web site. The site gives the ability to search by Last Name, Development, and city or Zip Code. Any combination of these fields may be used; however, a search cannot be performed if both a city and Zip Code are entered.

Incarceration Records

Delaware Department of Corrections, Central Records, 511 Maple Parkway, Dover, DE 19901; 302-739-5387 (Locator), 302-739-7486 (Fax), 8AM-4PM.

www.state.de.us/correct/index.htm

Note: The Department of Correction does not offer the public access to an automated database of offender information.

Indexing & Storage: Records are available on current and former inmates. It takes up to 5 days before new records are available for inquiry. Records are normally destroyed after three years.

Searching: However, the public may receive basic information about an offender, including whether the individual is incarcerated in Delaware, where the individual is incarcerated and, how to contact an offender, by calling the number above. Include the following in your request-name and DOB.

Access by: phone. No searching by mail.

Phone search: Call the Department's Office of Community Relations at 302-739-5601 Ext. 246.

Other access: An escapees list is available at www.state.de.us/correct/Data/Escapees.htm. Most wanted: www.state.de.us/dsp/wanted/wanted.htm.

Corporation, General Partnerships, Limited Partnerships Trademarks, Servicemarks, Limited Liability Company, Limited Liability Partnerships

Secretary of State, Corporation Records, PO Box 898, Dover, DE 19903 (Courier: 401 Federal Street #4, Dover, DE 19901); 302-739-3073, 302-739-3812 (Fax), 8AM-4:30PM.

www.state.de.us/corp

Note: There is no online access to the public; however, there is a system available to only registered agents.

Indexing & Storage: Records are available from the formation of the Division. Indexes are maintained on imaging system and in-house computer. Delaware Registered Agents have online access. New records are available for inquiry immediately.

Searching: Include the following in your request-full name of business. In addition to the articles of incorporation, corporation records include the following information: Annual Reports, Officers, Directors, Prior (merged) names, Inactive and Reserved names.

Access by: mail, phone, fax, in person, online.

Fee & Payment: Record search is $30.00. Certification is $30.00 plus $2.00 per page. Plain copies are $10.00 first page and $2.00 each additional. Fee payee: Delaware Secretary of State. Prepayment required. Personal checks accepted. Credit cards accepted: MasterCard, Visa, Discover.

Mail search: Turnaround time: 3 - 5 days. No SASE is required.

Phone search: There is no fee for general information given over the phone.

Fax search: Fax requests can be received by fax, but are not returned by fax.

In person search: Requests are returned by regular mail unless expedite fee is paid.

Online search: Information is available at https://sos-res.state.de.us/tin/GINameSearch.jsp. The entity information provided on this website, free of charge, consists of the entity name, file number, incorporation/formation date, registered agent name, address, phone number and residency. Additional, detailed information can be obtained for a fee of $20.00.

Expedited service: Expedited services available for mail, fax, phone, and in person. Add $2.00 for 24 hour service for plain copies. Otherwise, fees will basically double if 24 hours. If same day, then 133% higher. $1,000 for one hour service. $500 for 2 hour service. Ouch.

Uniform Commercial Code, Federal Tax Liens

UCC Division, Secretary of State, PO Box 793, Dover, DE 19903 (Courier: Townsend Bldg, 401 Federal Street #4, Dover, DE 19901); 302-739-3077, 302-739-3813 (Fax), 8:30AM-4:30PM.

www.state.de.us/corp/ucc.shtml

Note: Effective December 1, 2001, all non "Search to Reflect" UCC Searches are referred to a Delaware Authorized Searcher, who performs the search. The website maintains a list of these private vendors.

Indexing & Storage: Records are available from 1967. Records are computerized since 1992. Records are indexed on inhouse computer.

Searching: Use search request form UCC-11, downloadable from web. The search includes federal tax liens on businesses since 1976. Federal tax liens on individuals may show here, also. All state tax liens are filed at the county level. Include the following in your request-debtor name.

Access by: mail, fax, in person.

Fee & Payment: Copies are $2.00 a page, $10.00 minimum. Add $25.00 for certification. Fee payee: Secretary of State. Prepayment required. Volume users may establish an account. Personal checks accepted. Credit cards accepted: MasterCard, Visa, Discover.

Mail search: Turnaround time: 5 to 7 business days. You may request information by mail. No SASE is required.

Fax search: Same criteria as searching by mail.

In person search: Results are mailed or you must come back in 7 business days.

Other access: Bulk purchase of paper copies is $2.00 per page.

Expedited service: Expedited service is available for mail and phone searches. Three levels of expedited service are available at extra fees as follows: 24 hrs-$25.00; same day-$50.00; 2 hrs-$75.00.

State Tax Liens

Records not maintained by a state level agency.

Note: Records are at the county level.

Sales Tax Registrations

Finance Department - Div. Rev., Groos Receipt Tax Registration, PO Box 8750, Wilmington, DE 19899-8750 (Courier: Carvel State Office Bldg, 820 N French St, 9th Fl, Wilmington, DE 19801); 302-577-8238, 302-577-8203 (Fax), 8AM-4:30PM.

www.state.de.us/revenue/obt/lic_gr.htm

Note: This state has a gross receipts tax, not a sales tax per se. They will release the information found on the face of the business licensee issued to the business.

Indexing & Storage: Records are available for the past 3 years.

Searching: This agency will do an alpha search for a business name and will provide the business name, address and business license number, type of business, and amount of license fee paid. They will not release business owner or officer names. Include the following in your request-business name. The federal tax ID can also be used.

Access by: mail, phone, fax, in person.

Mail search: Turnaround time: 1 week. A SASE is requested. No fee for mail request.

Phone search: No fee for telephone request. There is a limit of 3 searches per phone call.

Fax search: There is no fee for fax searches. Turnaround time is 2 days.

In person search: No fee for request.

Birth Certificates

Department of Health, Office of Vital Statistics, PO Box 637, Dover, DE 19903 (Courier: William Penn & Federal Sts, Jesse Cooper Bldg, Dover, DE 19901); 302-744-4549, 302-736-1862 (Fax), 8AM-4:30PM (Counter closes at 4:15 PM).

www.state.de.us/dhss/dph/ss/vitalstats.html

Indexing & Storage: Records are available from 72 years. Prior records are at the State Archives. It takes 1 month before new records are available for inquiry. Records are indexed on microfilm, microfiche, and index cards.

Searching: Must have a signed release from person of record or immediate family member. Others may only obtain records if they demonstrate the record is needed for the determination or protection of their personal property rights or for genealogical uses. Include the following in your request-full name, names of parents, mother's maiden name, date of birth, place of birth, reason for information request, relationship to person of record, photo ID.

Access by: mail, fax, in person, online.

Fee & Payment: Search fee is $10.00 per name for every 5 years searched. Add $6.00 if you use a credit card via vitalchek.com. Fee payee: Office of Vital Statistics. Prepayment required. Personal checks accepted. Credit cards accepted by vitalchek.

Mail search: Turnaround time: 1 day to 1 week. No SASE is required.

Fax search: Available from VitalChek. Use of credit card and photo ID required.

In person search: Turnaround time is generally 10 minutes or less.

Online search: Access available at vitalchek.com, a state designated vendor.

Death Records

Department of Health, Office of Vital Statistics, PO Box 637, Dover, DE 19903 (Courier: William Penn & Federal Sts, Jesse Cooper Bldg, Dover, DE 19901); 302-744-4549, 302-736-1862 (Fax), 8AM-4:30PM.

www.state.de.us/dhss/dph/ss/vitalstats.html

Indexing & Storage: Records are available for the past 40 years. Prior records are at the State Archives. It takes 3 days before new records are available for inquiry. Records are indexed on microfilm, microfiche, and index cards.

Searching: Must have a signed release from immediate family member. Include the following in your request-full name, date of death, place of death, names of parents, reason for information request, relationship to person of record, photo ID.

Access by: mail, fax, in person, online.

Fee & Payment: The search fee is $10.00 per name for every 5 years searched. Add $6.00 if you use a credit card via vitalchek.com. Fee payee: Office of Vital Statistics. Prepayment required. Personal checks accepted. Credit cards accepted by vitalcheck.com

Mail search: Turnaround time: 1 day. No SASE is required.

Fax search: Records are available from VitalChek. Use of credit card and photo ID required.

In person search: Turnaround time is 10 to 15 minutes.

Online search: Access available at vitalchek.com, a state designated vendor.

Marriage Certificates

Department of Health, Office of Vital Statistics, PO Box 637, Dover, DE 19903 (Courier: William Penn & Federal Sts, Jesse Cooper Bldg, Dover, DE 19901); 302-739-4549, 302-739-1862 (Fax), 8AM-4:30PM.

Indexing & Storage: Records are available for 40 years. Prior records are in the State Public Archives. It takes 1 month before new records are available for inquiry. Records are indexed on microfilm, microfiche, and index cards.

Searching: Must have a signed release from person or persons of record or immediate family member. Include the following in your request-names of husband and wife, date of marriage, place or county of marriage, relationship to person of record, reason for information request, wife's maiden name, photo ID.

Access by: mail, fax, in person, online.

Fee & Payment: The search fee is $10.00 per name for every 5 years searched. Add $6.00 if you use a credit card via vitalchek.com. Fee payee: Office of Vital Statistics. Prepayment required. Personal checks accepted. Credit cards accepted: MasterCard, Visa, AmEx, Discover.

Mail search: Turnaround time: 1 day. No SASE is required.

Fax search: This is available through VitalChek. Credit card and photo ID are required.

In person search: Turnaround time is 10 to 15 minutes.

Online search: Access is available via VitalChek.com, a state designated vendor.

Divorce Records

Records not maintained by a state level agency.

Note: This agency will verify whether a divorce occurred after 1935, but will issue no copies of the record. For records 1976 to present, go to the Family Court at the county; prior to 1976, go to the Prothonotary at the county level.

Workers' Compensation Records

Labor Department, Industrial Accident Board, 4425 N Market Street, 3rd Fl, Wilmington, DE 19802; 302-761-8200 x2, 302-761-6601 (Fax), 8AM-4:30PM.

www.delawareworks.com/industrialaffairs/services/workerscomp.shtml

Note: Case records must have been adjudicated to be considered public. First reports of injury only (non-adjudicated) are not covered under FOIA.

Indexing & Storage: Records are available from 1985. New records are available for inquiry immediately.

Searching: Must have signed authorization from injured party in letter form or a court subpoena.

They will not honor out-of-state requests. Information required includes claimant name, SSN, and date of accident.

Access by: mail.

Fee & Payment: There is no fee. Copies are $.25 each. Fee payee: DOL/IA. Prepayment required. Payment is for copies only. Personal checks accepted. No credit cards accepted.

Mail search: Turnaround time: 2 to 5 days. A SASE is requested.

Driver Records

Division of Motor Vehicles, Driver Services, PO Box 698, Dover, DE 19903 (Courier: 303 Transportation Circle, Dover, DE 19901); 302-744-2506, 302-739-2602 (Fax), 8AM-4:30PM M-T-TH-F; 12:00PM-8PM W.

www.dmv.de.gov/

Note: For tickets: Delaware does not keep copies of tickets in a central repository for request purposes and suggests you go to the appropriate local jurisdiction.

Indexing & Storage: Records are available for 3 years to present for public record purposes. It takes 2 to 3 weeks before new records are available for inquiry.

Searching: Records cannot be sold from one vendor to another. Vendors can only sell to the end users. Casual requesters can obtain records only with MV703 Form requiring notarized signature of requester. Include the following in your request-full name, driver's license number, date of birth. Authorized account holders must have an application and contract on file. The following data is not released: Social Security Numbers or medical information.

Access by: mail, in person, online.

Fee & Payment: The fee for all search modes is $15.00 per request. Fee payee: Division of Motor Vehicles. Prepayment required. Personal checks accepted. No credit cards accepted.

Mail search: Turnaround time: 3 to 5 days. A SASE is requested.

In person search: Three requests will be processed while you wait, additional requests are processed overnight. Walk-in requesters may obtain records from centers in Wilmington, New Castle, Dover, and Georgetown.

Online search: Online searching is single inquiry only, no batch request mode is offered. Searching is done by driver's license number or name and DOB. A signed contract application and valid "business license" is required. Access is provided 24 hours daily through a 900 number at a fee of $1.50 per minute, plus the $15.00 per record fee. For more information, call 302-744-2606.

Other access: Tape-to-tape is offered for high volume, batch requesters. The $1.50 per minute line charge also applies. Also, this agency will release data from the driver license file on tapes or cartridges, but this cannot be resold.

Vehicle Ownership, Vehicle Identification

Division of Motor Vehicles, Correspondence Section, PO Box 698, Dover, DE 19903 (Courier: 303 Transportation Circle, Dover, DE 19901); 302-744-2511, 302-744-2538, 302-739-2042 (Fax), 8AM-4:30PM M-T-TH-F; 12-8PM W.

www.dmv.de.gov/Vehicle_Services/ve_main.html

Indexing & Storage: Records are available for 3 years to present. It takes 2 to 3 weeks before new records are available for inquiry.

Searching: Those routinely seeking information must complete an Application and Contract for Direct Access to become an account holder. Casual requesters must use Form MV703 which requires notarized signature of subject.

Access by: mail, in person, online.

Fee & Payment: The fee for ownership, plate, and registration searches is $15.00 per record, $20.00 if certified. Fee payee: Division of Motor Vehicles. Prepayment required. Personal checks accepted. No credit cards accepted.

Mail search: Turnaround time: 3 to 5 days. A SASE is requested.

In person search: Turnaround time is while you wait.

Online search: There is an additional $1.00 per minute fee for using the online "900 number" system. Records are $4.00 each. The system is single inquiry mode and open from 8 AM to 4:30 PM, except on Wed. from noon to 8PM. For more information, call 302-744-2606. This program is strictly monitored and not available for non-permissible uses.

Other access: Bulk information can be obtained on a customized basis in tape, cartridge or paper format. However, the purpose of the request is carefully screened and information cannot be resold.

Accident Reports

Delaware State Police, Traffic Records, PO Box 430, Dover, DE 19903 (Courier: 1441 N Dupont Hwy, Dover, DE 19901); 302-739-5931, 302-739-5982 (Fax), 8AM-4PM.

Indexing & Storage: It takes 2 to 3 weeks before new records are available for inquiry.

Searching: Include the following in your request- full name, date of accident, location of accident.

Access by: mail, phone.

Fee & Payment: The fee is $25.00 per report, $60.00 if fatal accident report. Fee payee: Delaware State Police. Prepayment required. Personal checks accepted. No credit cards accepted.

Mail search: Turnaround time: 5 to 10 days. A SASE is requested.

Phone search: You can only verify if a report exists.

Vessel Ownership, Vessel Registration

Dept of Natural Resources & Environmental Control, Delaware Boat Registration Office, 89 Kings Highway, Dover, DE 19901; 302-739-3498, 302-739-6157 (Fax), 8AM-4:30PM.

www.dnrec.state.de.us/dnrec2000/Boating.asp

Note: Liens are filed with UCC filings, not at this location. Records are confidential and not released to general public per DPPA.

Indexing & Storage: Records are available from 1978 to present. Records are registration only, no titles, and are indexed on microfiche from 1978 to 1989. Records are computer indexed from 1990 to the present. All motorized craft are registered. It takes one month or less before new records are available for inquiry. Records are normally destroyed after original paperwork scanned.

Searching: No searching of records is allowed. However, they will verify information over the phone using "yes" and "no" only. Liens are not filed here, they are filed with UCCs. Either the owner's name, hull ID# or registration number must be submitted for a verification.

Access by: mail, phone, fax, in person.

Fee & Payment: There is no fee.

Mail search: Turnaround time: 3 days. Records are available by mail.

Phone search: They will verify information over the phone using "yes" and "no" only.

Fax search: If DPPA approved.

In person search: Verification only.

Voter Registration

Commissioner of Elections, Voter Registration Records, 111 S West St #10, Dover, DE 19904; 302-739-4277, 8AM-4:30PM.

www.state.de.us/election

Indexing & Storage: Records are available for both active and inactive records.

Searching: There is no individual record searching permitted, except in person. The following data is not released: Social Security Numbers or telephone numbers.

Access by: mail, in person.

Fee & Payment: There is no search fee, the copy fee is $.25 per copy. Fee payee: State of Delaware. Prepayment required. Personal checks accepted No credit cards accepted.

Mail search: Turnaround time: 7 to 10 days. Records are available by mail.

In person search: available.

Other access: The entire state database is available on tape for $250. Individual districts (432) are available on disk for $2.00 per district or $.025 per name on labels. Also, there are several different types of printed lists available.

GED Certificates

Department of Education, Adult Education - GED Testing, PO Box 1402, Dover, DE 19903; 302-739-3743, 302-739-1318 (Fax), 8AM-4:30PM.

www.doe.state.de.us

Searching: Consent of subject is needed for all third-party searches. Include the following in your request-signed release, name, date of birth, Social Security Number, location of test center. The year of the test is very helpful.

Access by: mail, fax, in person.

Fee & Payment: There is no fee for a verification. A duplicate certificate is available for $4.00. Fee payee: Department of Education Suggest using a money order. Personal checks not accpeted.

Mail search: Turnaround time: 2 to 3 weeks. No SASE is required.

Fax search: Same criteria as mail searching.

In person search: Requester must present a photo ID.

Hunting and Fishing License Information

Access to Records is Restricted

Division of Fish & Wildlife, License Records, 89 Kings Hwy, Dover, DE 19901; 302-739-5296, 302-739-6157 (Fax), 8AM-4:30PM.

www.dnrec.state.de.us/fw/index.htm

Note: Records are not on a computerized database, but kept on paper and filed alphabetically. They will release name, address, driver license number, and physical characteristics.

Delaware State Licensing Agencies

Licenses Searchable Online

Engineer #12 .... www.dape.org
Engineering Firm #12 .... www.dape.org
Insurance Broker/Dealer #8 .... www.state.de.us/inscom/berg/authorizedcompanies.htm
Optometrist #11 .... www.arbo.org/odfinder/LicSearch.asp
Real Estate Appraiser #11 .... www.asc.gov/content/category1/appr_by_state.asp
Teacher/Educator #4 .... http://deeds.doe.state.de.us/public/deeds_pc_findeducator.aspx

Delaware Licensing Quick Finder

Adult Entertainment #11 302-744-4506
Aesthetician #11 302-744-4518
Alarm Company/Employee #3 302-739-5991
Alcoholic Beverage Establishment #1 . 302-577-5222
Amateur Boxing-related #11 320-744-4533
Ambulance Attendant #18 302-739-4773
Architect #11 302-744-4505
Armored Car Agency/Employee #3 302-739-5991
Asbestos Abatement Worker #15 302-739-4611
Athletic Agent #11 302-744-4511
Athletic Trainer #11 302-744-4506
Attorney #2 302-739-4155
Audiologist #11 302-744-4533
Bail Enforcement Agent #3 302-739-5991
Barber #11 302-744-4518
Bodyworker #11 302-744-4506
Boiler Inspector #14 302-744-2735
Boxer/Boxing Professional #11 302-787-5720
Charitable Gaming Permittee #11 302-744-4530
Chiropractor #11 302-744-4509
Constable #3 302-739-5991
Contractor Class A #15 302-739-4611
Contractor, General #5 302-577-8778
Cosmetologist #11 302-744-4518
Counselor, Professional #11 302-744-4534
Deadly Weapons Dealer #11 302-744-4506
Dentist/Dental Hygienist #11 302-744-4518
Dental Radiographer #16 302-744-4546
Dietician/Nutritionist #11 302-744-4512
Electrical Inspector #11 302-744-4505
Electrician #11 302-744-4504

Electrologist #11 302-744-4518
Emergency Med'l Tech/Paramedic #11 302-739-6637
EMT-B #18 302-739-4773
Engineer /Engineering Firm #12 302-577-6500
Fire Company #18 302-739-4773
Funeral Director #11 302-744-4505
Gaming Control #11 302-744-4530
Geologist #11 302-744-4533
Harness Racing #6 302-698-4500
Hearing Aid Dealer/Fitter #11 302-744-4533
Horse Racing (Thorobred) #6 302-698-4500
Human Relations Specialist (Edu.)#13 . 888-759-9133
Insurance Adjuster/Advisor #8 302-739-4254
Insurance Agent/ Broker/Dealer #8 302-739-4254
Landscape Architect #11 302-744-4504
Library Media Specialist #13 888-759-9133
Lobbyist #9 302-739-2397
Massage #11 302-744-4506
Medical Doctor/Surgeon #11 302-744-4530
Medical Practice #11 302-744-4530
Mental Health Counselor #11 302-744-4507
Midwife Nurse #11 302-744-4517
Nail Technician #11 302-744-4518
Notary Public #9 302-739-3073
Nuclear Medicine Technologist #16 302-744-4546
Nurse #11 302-744-4517
Nursing Home Administrator #11 302-744-4505
Nutritionist #11 302-744-4512
Occupational Therapist/Assistant #11 .. 302-744-4511
Optometrist #11 302-744-4512
Osteopathic Physician #11 302-744-4529

Pesticide Applicator #10 302-698-4570
Pharmacist #11 302-744-4547
Pharmacy or related Business #11 320-744-4547
Physical Therapist/Assistant #11 302-744-4506
Physician Assistant #11 302-744-4507
Pilot, River #11 302-744-4504
Plumber #11 302-744-4504
Podiatrist #11 302-744-4530
Private Inv. Agency/Employee #3 302-739-5991
Private Security Agency/Employee #3 .. 302-739-5991
Professional Svc. Firm #15 302-739-4611
Project Monitor (Const.) #15 302-739-4611
Psychologist /Psychological Assist. #11 302-744-4534
Public Accountant-CPA #11 302-744-4505
Radiation Therapist #16 302-744-4546
Real Estate Agent/Broker #11 302-744-4519
Real Estate Appraiser #11 302-744-4505
Rental Car Insurer #8 302-739-4254
Respiratory Care Practioner #11 302-744-4507
School Admin. Supervisor/Asst. #4 302-739-4601
School Principal/Super/Counselor #4 .. 302-739-4601
Securities Agent #8 302-739-4254
Social Worker #11 302-744-4534
Speech Pathologist/Audiologist #11 302-744-4533
Surplus Lines Broker #8 302-739-4254
Surveyor, Land #11 302-744-4518
Teacher #4 302-739-4601
Veterinarian #11 302-744-4506
Waste Water Operator #17 302-739-5731
Water Supply Operator #7 302-739-5410
X-ray Technician #7 302-744-4546

Delaware Licensing Agency Information

1 Alcoholic Beverage Control Division, 820 N French St, Carvel State Office Bldg, Wilmington, DE 19801; 302-577-5222, Fax: 302-577-3204.

2 Board of Bar Examiners, 820 N French St 11th Fl., Wilmington, DE 19801-3545; 302-577-7038, Fax: 302-577-7037.   http://courts.state.de.us/bbe

3 State Police, State Bureau of Identification, Detective Licensing, PO Box 430, Dover, DE 19903; 302-739-5991, Fax: 302-739-5888. www.state.de.us/dsp/sbi.htm
Email: panderson@state.de.us

4 Department of Education, PO Box 1402 (401 Federal St), Dover, DE 19903; 302-739-4601, Fax: 302-739-3092. www.doe.state.de.us
Search Database at http://deeds.doe.state.de.us/public/deeds_pc_findeducator.aspx

5 Division of Revenue, 820 N French St, Carvel State Office Bldg, Wilmington, DE 19801; 302-577-8200, Fax: 302-577-8202.
www.state.de.us/revenue/index.htm
Email: wremington@state.de.us

6 Harness Racing Commission, 2320 S DuPont Hwy, Dover, DE 19901; 302-698-4500, Fax: 302-697-4748. www.state.de.us/deptagri
Email: johnwayne@dda.state.de.us

7 Health & Social Services Dept., Division of Public Health, PO Box 637 (Federal & Water Sts), Dover, DE 19903; 302-744-4701.
www.state.de.us/dhss/dph/index.htm
Email: dhssinfo@state.de.us

8 Insurance Department, Producer Licencing, 841 Silver Lake Blvd, Dover, DE 19904; 302-739-4254, Fax: 302-739-5280. www.state.de.us/inscom
Email: licensing@deins.state.de.us

9 Notary Division, Office of Sec of State, PO Box 898, Dover, DE 19903; 302-739-4114, Fax: 302-739-3812.   www.state.de.us/sos/nphome.shtml

10 Department of Agriculture, Pesticide Section, 2320 S DuPont Hwy, Dover, DE 19901; 302-698-4570, Fax: 302-697-6287.
www.state.de.us/deptagri/pesticides/index.htm
Email: grier.stayton@state.de.us

11 Division of Professional Regulations, Dept. of Admin. Svcs., 861 Silver Lake Blvd, Cannon Bldg #203, Dover, DE 19904; 302-739-4522, Fax: 302-739-2711. www.professionallicensing.state.de.us

12 Assoc. of Prof. Engineers, Engineering Licensing Board, 56 W Main St #208, Plaza 273, Christiana, DE 19702-1500; 302-368-6708, Fax: 302-368-6710.   www.dape.org

Email: office@dape.org Note: Searchable rosters link is on left hand margin of web page.

13 Department of Public Instruction, Office of Certification, PO Box 1402, Townsend Bldg, Dover, DE 19903; 888-759-9133, Fax: 302-739-5894. www.doe.state.de.us

14 Department of Public Safety, Division of Boiler Safety, PO Box 674, Dover, DE 19903-0674; 302-744-2735, Fax: 302-739-2526. www.delawareboilersafety.com

15 Division of Facilities Mgmt, 149 Transportation Circle, Dover, DE 19901; 302-739-3930, Fax: 302-739-3127.

16 Division of Public Health, Office of Radiation Control, PO Box 637, Dover, DE 19903; 302-744-4546, Fax: 302-739-3839.

17 Department of Natural Resources & Environmental Control, Division of Water Resources, 89 Kings Hwy, Dover, DE 19901; 302-739-4860, Fax: 302-739-8369.

18 Fire Prevention Comm., 1463 Chestnut Grove Rd, Dover, DE 19904; 302-739-3160, Fax: 302-739-4436. www.delawarestatefirecommission.com
Email: firecommission@state.de.us

Delaware Federal Courts

The following list indicates the district and division name for each county in the state.

County/Court Cross Reference

Kent ....Wilmington
New Castle ....Wilmington
Sussex ....Wilmington

US District Court

District of Delaware

Wilmington Division U.S. Courthouse, Lock Box 18, 844 N King St, Wilmington, DE 19801 (courier address: U.S. Courthouse, 844 N King St, Clerk's Office, 4th Floor, Room 4209, Wilmington, DE 19801), 302-573-6170. www.ded.uscourts.gov

Counties: All counties in Delaware.

Indexing & Storage: New cases available in the index 1 day after filing date.

Fee & Payment: Payment may be made by money order, cashier check, personal check. A copy vendor is used for civil court documents. Parcels Inc, 800-343-1742 -- orders may be placed with them directly. Payee: Clerk, U.S. District Court.

Phone Search: They will search civil and criminal cases from 1982 to the present over the phone. The only information released over the phone is whether a case was found and, if so, its case number.

Mail Search: Search can include all computer, microfiche and judgment indexes. A SASE not required.

In Person Search: Fee charged if court conducts your in person search for you.

PACER: PACER online at http://pacer.ded.usc ourts.gov. Records purged every few years. New records are online after 2 days.

Opinions Online: Court opinions are online at www.lawlib.widener.edu/pages/deopind.htm

U.S. Bankruptcy Court

District of Delaware

Wilmington Division 824 North Market St, 3rd Floor, Marine Midland Plaza, Wilmington, DE 19801 (Use mail address for courier delivery) 888-667-5530. www.deb.uscourts.gov

Counties: All counties in Delaware.

Indexing & Storage: Cases indexed by debtor as well as by case number. New cases available in the index 1 day after filing date.

Fee & Payment: Payment may be made by money order, cashier check, personal check. Payee: Clerk, U.S. Bankruptcy Court.

Phone Search: The only information that is released over the telephone is whether the search is positive or negative. If positive they will release the case number. Also, an automated voice case information service (VCIS) is still available. Call VCIS at 302-252-2560.

In Person Search: Fee charged if court conducts your in person search for you. There is an in-house private copy service that you must use.

PACER: Court uses new CM/ECF system for PACER. Records purged every four years. New civil records are online after 1 day.

Electronic Filing: https://ecf.deb.uscourts.gov

Other Online Access: Online access to WebPacer is available is available at www.deb.uscourts.gov and click on "Case Information." Chapter 11 filing lists are available free at www.deb.uscourts.gov /Chapter11/chapter11_filings.htm.

Standards for Federal Courts: The search fee is $20.00 per item (one party name or case number). Certification fee is $7.00 per document. Copy fee is $.50 per page. All fees standard unless noted in profile. Mail Search: always enclose a stamped self addressed envelope unless otherwise noted. Most courts accept fax requests or will suggest a copying/search vendor. Before releasing records, all courts require prepayment unless noted in profile.

Open records are located at the court unless otherwise noted. District courts index by defendant and plaintiff as well as by case number. Bankruptcy courts usually index by debtor and case number. While most courts now have their indexes on computer, many still maintain index card files as well.

The universal PACER sign-up number is 800-676-6856. Find PACER and the Party/Case Index on the Web at http://pacer.psc.uscourts.gov. PACER dial-up access is $.60 per minute. Also, courts offering internet access via RACER, PACER, Web-PACER or the new CM-ECF charge $.07 per page fee unless noted as free.

Delaware County Courts

Court	Jurisdiction	No. of Courts	How Organized
Superior Courts*	General	3	
Chancery Courts*	General	3	
Court of Common Pleas*	Limited	3	
Justice of the Peace Courts*	Municipal	19	
Alderman's Courts	Municipal	9	
Family Courts	Special	3	

* Profiled in this Sourcebook.

Court	CIVIL								
	Tort	Contract	Real Estate	Min. Claim	Max. Claim	Small Claims	Estate	Eviction	Domestic Relations
Superior Courts*	X	X	X	$50000	No Max				
Chancery Courts*	X	X	X	$0	No Max		X		
Court of Common Pleas*	X	X	X	$0	$50000				
Justice of the Peace Courts*			X	$0	$15000	$5000		X	
Alderman's Courts						$2500			
Family Courts									X

Court	CRIMINAL				
	Felony	Misdemeanor	DWI/DUI	Preliminary Hearing	Juvenile
Superior Courts*	X	X			
Chancery Courts*					
Court of Common Pleas*		X		X	
Justice of the Peace Courts*		X	X		
Alderman's Courts		X	X		
Family Courts		X			X

ADMINISTRATION

Administrative Office of the Courts, Supreme Court of Delaware, 820 N French, 11th Fl, Wilmington, DE, 19801; 302-255-0090, Fax: 302-255-2217. 8:30AM-5PM. http://courts.state.de.us/

COURT STRUCTURE

The Superior Court, the State's court of general jurisdiction, has original jurisdiction over criminal and civil cases except equity cases. The Court has exclusive jurisdiction over felonies and almost all drug offenses. The Court of Common Pleas has jurisdiction in civil cases where the amount in controversy, exclusive of interest, does not exceed $50,000. In criminal cases, the Court of Common Pleas handles all misdemeanors occurring in the State except certain drug-related offenses and traffic offenses. The Court of Chancery has jurisdiction to hear all matters relating to equity. The litigation in this tribunal deals largely with corporate issues, trusts, estates, other fiduciary matters, disputes involving the purchase of land and questions of title to real estate as well as commercial and contractual matters. The Justice of the Peace Court, the initial entry level into the court system for most citizens, has jurisdiction over civil cases in which the disputed amount is less than $15,000. In criminal cases, the Justice of the Peace Court hears certain misdemeanors and most motor vehicle cases (excluding felonies) and the Justices of the Peace may act as committing magistrates for all crimes.

ONLINE ACCESS

Chancery, Superior, Common Pleas and Supreme Court opinions and orders are available free online at http://courts.state.de.us/opinions. Supreme, Superior and Common Pleas Court calendars are available free at http://courts.state.de.us/calendars.

Chancery and Supreme Court filings are available at www.virtualdocket.com. Registration and fees required.

Kent County

Superior Court Office of Prothonotary, 38 The Green, Dover, DE 19901; 302-739-3184; Fax: 302-739-6717. Hours: 8AM-4:30PM (EST). *Felony, Misdemeanor, Civil Actions Over $50,000.*
http://courts.state.de.us/superior
Note: Court refers records request to State Agency-302-739-5961

Civil Records: Access: Mail, in person. Visitors must perform in person searches for themselves. No search fee. Required to search: name, years to search. Civil cases indexed by defendant, plaintiff. Judgments on computer from 1996, on microfiche from 1918.
Criminal Records: Access: In person only. No search fee. Required to search: name, years to search, DOB; also helpful: race. Judgments on computer from 1996, on microfiche from 1918. Contact Dept of Records for search assistance.
General Information: Public Access terminal is available. No sealed or psychological evaluation records released. Copy fee: $1.00 per page. Cert fee: $6.00 fee for 3 pages and $1.00 each add'l page. Payee: Prothonotary. Personal checks accepted. Prepayment required. Mail requests: SASE required.

Chancery Court 38 The Green, Dover, DE 19901; 302-736-2242; Probate phone: 302-744-2330; Fax: 302-736-2240. Hours: 8:30AM-4:30PM (EST). *Civil, Probate.* http://courts.state.de.us/chancery
Civil Records: Access: In person only. Visitors must perform in person searches for themselves. No search fee. Required to search: name, years to search. Civil cases indexed by defendant, plaintiff. Civil records on index books. The Court of Chancery oversees corporate and equity matters and guardianship. The Register of Wills oversees estate, and probate matters.
General Information: Public Access terminal is available. No juvenile, sealed or mental health records released. Fee to fax results is $10.00 1st page, $2.00 each add'l. Copy fee: $1.50 per page. Cert fee: $25.00 plus $1.50 per page. Payee: Register in Chancery (Register of Wills for Probate). Personal checks accepted. Prepayment required. May bill law firms and businesses. Turnaround time 24 hrs.

Court of Common Pleas 38 The Green, Dover, DE 19901; 302-739-4618; Fax: 302-739-4501. Hours: 8AM-4:30PM (EST). *Misdemeanor, Civil Actions Under $50,000.*
http://courts.state.de.us/commonpleas
Civil Records: Access: Mail, in person. Both court and visitors may perform in person searches. No search fee. Required to search: name, years to search. Civil cases indexed by defendant, plaintiff. Civil records on computer from 1992, on microfiche from 10/85, archived prior.
Criminal Records: Access: Mail, in person. Visitors must perform in person searches for themselves. No search fee. Required to search: name, years to search, DOB, offense, date of offense. Criminal records on computer from 1/94, on microfiche from 10/85, archived prior.
General Information: Public Access terminal is available. No sealed records released. Will fax results to local or toll free line. Copy fee: $1.00 per page. Cert fee: $10.00. Payee: Court of Common Pleas. Personal checks accepted. Prepayment required. Mail requests: SASE required. Mail turnaround:1-3 days.

Dover Justice of the Peace #16 480 Bank Ln, Dover, DE 19904; 302-739-4316; Fax: 302-739-6797. Hours: 8AM-4PM (EST). *Civil Actions Under $15,000, Eviction, Small Claims.*
http://courts.state.de.us/jpcourt
Civil Records: Access: Mail, in person. Both court and visitors may perform in person searches. No search fee. Required to search: name, years to search.

Civil cases indexed by defendant, plaintiff. Civil records computerized since 10/98.
General Information: Copy fee: $.25 per page. Cert fee: $10.00. Payee: JCP Court 16. Personal checks accepted. Prepayment required.

Dover Justice of the Peace #7 480 Bank Ln, Dover, DE 19903; 302-739-4554; Fax: 302-739-6797. Hours: Open 24 hours (EST). *Misdemeanor.*
http://courts.state.de.us/jpcourt
Criminal Records: Only the court performs in person searches; visitors may not. Search fee: $7.00 per name. Fee includes copy certification. Required to search: name, years to search, DOB, signed release; also helpful: address, offense, date of offense.
General Information: Payee: State of Delaware. Prepayment required.

Harrington Justice of the Peace #6 35 Cams Fortune Way, Harrington, DE 19952; 302-422-5922; Fax: 302-422-1527. Hours: 8AM-4PM (EST). *Misdemeanor.* http://courts.state.de.us/jpcourt
Criminal Records: Access: In person, mail. Only the court performs in person searches; visitors may not. No search fee. Required to search: name, years to search, DOB. Court form required for all searches.
General Information: Turnaround time 2-3 days.

Smyrna Justice of the Peace #8 100 Monrovia Ave, Smyrna, DE 19977; 302-653-7083; Fax: 302-653-2888. 8AM-4PM *Misdemeanor.*
http://courts.state.de.us/jpcourt
Criminal Records: Only the court performs in person searches; visitors may not. No search fee. Required to search: name, years to search; also helpful: DOB.

New Castle County

Superior Court Office of the Prothonotary, 500 N King St #500, Wilmington, DE 19801; 302-255-0800; Fax: 302-255-2264/66. Hours: 8:30AM-5PM (EST). *Felony, Misdemeanor, Civil Actions Over $50,000.*
http://courts.state.de.us/superior
Civil Records: Access: In person only. Visitors must perform in person searches for themselves. No search fee. Required to search: name, years to search. Civil cases indexed by defendant, plaintiff. Civil records on computer from 4/80, prior on microfiche.
Criminal Records: Access: In person only. Visitors must perform in person searches for themselves. No search fee. Required to search: name, DOB; also helpful: years to search. Criminal records on computer from 4/80, prior on microfiche.
General Information: Public Access terminal is available. No psychological evaluation, sealed records released. Copy fee: $1.50 per page. Cert fee: $6.00. Payee: Prothonotary's Office. Personal checks accepted. Prepayment required.

Chancery Court 500 N King St, #1551, Wilmington, DE 19801; 302-255-0544; Probate phone: 302-571-7545; Fax: 302-255-2213. Hours: 8:30AM-5PM (EST). *Civil, Probate.*
http://courts.state.de.us/chancery
Civil Records: Access: Phone, fax, mail, in person. Both court and visitors may perform in person searches. No search fee. Required to search: name; also helpful: years to search. Civil cases indexed by defendant, plaintiff. Civil records indexed on computer since 1963, in books prior to 1963. The civil records for the Court of Chancery deal with corporate and equity matters, there is no money jurisdiction. The Register of Wills oversees estates, guardianships and probate.
General Information: Public Access terminal is available. No guardianship records released. Will fax results $5.00 1st page, $2.00 each add'l. Copy fee:

$.50 per page. $2.00 if from microfilm. Cert fee: $10.00. Payee: Register in Chancery (Register of Wills for Probate). Personal checks accepted. Prepayment required. Will bill fax requests. Mail requests: SASE requested. Turnaround time 2 days.

Court of Common Pleas 500 N King St, Wilmington, DE 19801-3704; 302-255-0900; Fax: 302-255-2243. Hours: 8:30AM-4:30PM (EST). *Misdemeanor, Civil Actions Under $50,000.*
http://courts.state.de.us/commonpleas
Note: Fax for civil is 302-255-2245.
Civil Records: Access: Phone, fax, mail, in person. Both court and visitors may perform in person searches. No search fee. Required to search: name, years to search. Civil cases indexed by defendant, plaintiff. Civil records on computer from 1993; prior records on docket books.
Criminal Records: Access: Phone, fax, mail, in person. Both court and visitors may perform in person searches. No search fee. Required to search: name, years to search; also helpful: DOB. Criminal records on computer from 1993; prior records on docket books.
General Information: No closed records released. Will fax results $1.00 per page. Copy fee: $1.00 per page. Cert fee: $10.00. Payee: Court of Common Pleas. Personal checks accepted. Prepayment required. Mail requests: SASE required. Mail turnaround time up to 1 week.

Middletown Justice of the Peace #9 757 N Broad St, Middletown, DE 19709; 302-378-5221; Fax: 302-378-5220. Hours: 8AM-4PM M,T,; Noon-8PM Th F, (EST). *Civil Under$15,000, Misdemeanor, Eviction, Small Claims.*
http://courts.state.de.us/jpcourt
Note: Due to a court fire, criminal cases 7/24/2000 to 5/1/2001 are heard at New Castle JP Court 11, 323-4450. Civil cases were heard at Prices Corner JP Court 12, 995-8646. Now, all new cases are back at here at Middletown.
Civil Records: Access: In person only. Both court and visitors may perform in person searches. No search fee. Required to search: name, years to search. Civil cases indexed by defendant. Due to fire, records on computer only back to mid-1990s. The court will not do name searches, but will search if a civil action # is presented.
Criminal Records: Access: In person only. Visitors must perform in person searches for themselves. No search fee. Required to search: name, years to search, DOB. Due to fire, records on computer only back to mid-1990s.
General Information: Copy fee: $.25 per page. Cert fee: Civil record certification is $7.00, criminal is $10.00. Only cashiers checks and money orders accepted.

Prices Corner Justice of the Peace #12 212 Greenbank Rd, Wilmington, DE 19808; 302-995-8646; Fax: 302-995-8642. 8AM-4PM (EST). *Civil Actions Under $15,000, Eviction, Small Claims.*
http://courts.state.de.us/jpcourt
Civil Records: Access: Mail, in person. Visitors must perform in person searches for themselves. No search fee. Required to search: name, years to search.
General Information: No sealed, juvenile, adoption or mental health records released. Will fax results to lcoal or toll free line. Copy fee: $.25. Cert fee: $10.00. Payee: Justice of the Peace Court 12. Personal checks accepted. Prepayment required.

Wilmington Justice of the Peace #13 1010 Concord Ave, Concord Professional Center, Wilmington, DE 19802; 302-577-2550; Fax: 302-577-2526. Hours: 8AM-4PM (EST). *Civil Actions Under $15,000, Eviction, Small Claims.*

http://courts.state.de.us/jpcourt
Civil Records: Access: In person only. Visitors must perform in person searches for themselves. No search fee. Required to search: name, years to search. Civil cases indexed by defendant, plaintiff. Civil records are computerized since 09/01/99. The court will pull specific case data if CA# given, if and when time permitting.
General Information: No sealed, juvenile, adoption or mental health records released. Copy fee: $.25 per page. Cert fee: $10.00. Payee: Justice of the Peace Court #13. Personal checks accepted. Prepayment required.

New Castle Justice of the Peace #11 61
Christiana Rd, New Castle, DE 19720; 302-323-4450; Fax: 302-323-4452. Hours: Open 24 hours (EST). *Misdemeanor.* http://courts.state.de.us/jpcourt
Criminal Records: Access: In person, mail. Visitors must perform in person searches for themselves. Search fee: $7.00 per search. Required to search: name, years to search.
General Information: Copy fee: $7.00. Cert fee: $7.00. Payee: State of Delaware. Only cashiers checks and money orders accepted. Mail requests: SASE required. Mail turnaround time 2-3 weeks.

Prices Corner Justice of the Peace #10
210 Greenbank Rd, Wilmington, DE 19808; 302-995-8640; Fax: 302-995-8642. Hours: 8AM-11PM (EST). *Misdemeanor.* http://courts.state.de.us/jpcourt
Criminal Records: Access: In person, mail. Only the court performs in person searches; visitors may not. Search fee: $7.00 per name. Required to search: name, years to search, DOB.
General Information: Copy fee: $7.00. Cert fee: $7.00 included in search fee. Payee: Justice of the Peace Court 10. Only cashiers checks and money orders accepted. Prepayment required. Mail requests: SASE required. Mail turnaround time 2 weeks.

Wilmington Justice of the Peace #15 130
Hickman Rd, #13, Claymont, DE 19703; 302-798-5327; Fax: 302-798-4508. Hours: 8AM-4PM (EST). *Misdemeanor.* http://courts.state.de.us/jpcourt
Note: Effective 06/01/99, the court assumed DUI cases. This court was formally located at 716 Philadelphia Pike in Wilmington
Criminal Records: Access: In person, mail. Only the court performs in person searches; visitors may not. Search fee: $7.00 per name. Fee is per case & includes certification & copy fees. Required to search: name, years to search, DOB; also helpful: offense.
General Information: Copy fee: $.25 per page. Payee: State of Delaware. Prepayment required. Mail turnaround time 2-4 weeks.

Wilmington Justice of the Peace #20
Public Safety Bldg, 300 N Walnut St, Wilmington, DE 19801; 302-577-7234; Fax: 302-577-7237. Hours: 8AM-midnight (EST). *Misdemeanor.*
http://courts.state.de.us/jpcourt
Note: This court now also maintains the case records from the former JP Court #18.
Criminal Records: Access: In person only. Visitors must perform in person searches for themselves. Search fee: $7.00 only disposition available. Required to search: name, years to search.
General Information: Copy fee: $7.00-disposition (1copy only.). Cert fee: $7.00. Payee: Justice of the Peace Court #13. Only cashiers checks and money orders accepted.

Sussex County

Superior Court
PO Box 756 (The Circle), Georgetown, DE 19947; Civil phone: 302-856-5742; Criminal phone: 302-856-5741; Fax: 302-856-5739. Hours: 8AM-4:30PM (EST). *Felony, Misdemeanor, Civil Actions.* http://courts.state.de.us/superior
Civil Records: Access: In person only. Visitors must perform in person searches for themselves. No search fee. Required to search: name, years to search. Civil cases indexed by defendant, plaintiff. Civil records on computer from 6/91 or as far back as 1980 if case was pending in 1991; microfiche prior.
Criminal Records: Access: In person only. Visitors must perform in person searches for themselves. No search fee. Required to search: name, years to search, DOB. Criminal records on manual index; computerized records since 1983.
General Information: Public Access terminal is available. No divorce, victim info, sealed records, expungments, or CCDW permit records released. Copy fee: $.25 per page. Cert fee: $6.00 plus $1.00 per page after the 1st three. Payee: Prothonotary. Personal checks accepted. Prepayment required.

Chancery Court
34 The Circle, PO Box 424, Georgetown, DE 19947; 302-856-5775; Probate phone: 302-855-7875. 8:30AM-4:30PM (EST). *Civil, Probate.* http://courts.state.de.us/chancery
Civil Records: Access: Phone, mail, in person. Both court and visitors may perform in person searches. No search fee. Required to search: name, years to search. Civil cases indexed by defendant, plaintiff. Civil records on index books.
General Information: All records public. Will fax results for $10.00 plus $2.00 per each add'l page. Copy fee: $1.50 per page. Cert fee: $.25 plus copy fee. Fees charged by Register of Wills for Probate are separate. Payee: Register in Chancery (or Register of Wills for Probate). Personal checks accepted. Prepayment required. Mail turnaround time 1-3 days.

Court of Common Pleas
PO Box 426, Georgetown, DE 19947; 302-856-5333; Fax: 302-856-5056. Hours: 8:30AM-4:30PM (EST). *Misdemeanor, Civil Actions Under $50,000.* http://courts.state.de.us/commonpleas
Civil Records: Access: Phone, fax, mail, in person. Both the court and visitors may perform in person searches. Search fee: $10.00 per name. Required to search: name, years to search. Civil cases indexed by defendant. Civil records on computer from 1993, on microfiche from 09/53, archived prior.
Criminal Records: Access: Phone, fax, mail, in person. Both the court and visitors may perform in person searches. Search fee: $10.00 per name. Required to search: name, years to search, DOB, offense, date of offense. Criminal records on computer from 1994, on microfiche from 10/65, archived prior.
General Information: Public Access terminal is available. No closed case records released. No fee to fax results. Copy fee: $1.00 per page. Cert fee: $5.00. Payee: Court of Common Pleas. Personal checks accepted. Prepayment required. Mail requests: SASE required. Mail turnaround time 1-2 weeks.

Georgetown Justice of the Peace #17
23730 Shortly Rd, Georgetown, DE 19947; 302-856-1447; Fax: 302-856-4654. 8AM-4PM (EST). *Civil Actions Under $15,000, Eviction, Small Claims.* http://courts.state.de.us/jpcourt
Civil Records: Access: Mail, in person. Only the court performs in person searches; visitors may not. No search fee. Required to search: name, years to search. Civil cases indexed by defendant, plaintiff. Civil records on index books from 1966 to present.

General Information: Will not fax results. Copy fee: $.25 per page. Cert fee: $10.00. Payee: State of Delaware. Personal checks accepted. Prepayment required. Mail requests: SASE requested. Turnaround time 1-2 days.

Seaford Justice of the Peace #19 408 Stein
Hwy, Seaford, DE 19973; 302-629-5433; Fax: 302-628-6517. Hours: 8AM-4PM (EST). *Civil Actions Under $15,000, Eviction, Small Claims.* http://courts.state.de.us/jpcourt
Civil Records: Access: In person, mail. Visitors must perform in person searches for themselves. No search fee. Required to search: name, years to search. Civil cases indexed by defendant, plaintiff. Civil records in docket books since 1985; computerized records since 9/98. In person access requires identification.
General Information: Will not fax results. Copy fee: $1.00 per page. Cert fee: $10.00. Payee: State of Delaware. Personal checks accepted. Prepayment required. Mail turnaround time 5 days.

Justice of the Peace #6 35 Cams Fortune
Way, Harrington, DE 19952-1790; 302-422-5922; Fax: 302-422-1527. Hours: 8AM-4PM (EST). *Misdemeanor.* http://courts.state.de.us/jpcourt
Note: Some old civil cases also located here.
Criminal Records: Access: Mail, in person. Visitors must perform in person searches for themselves. No search fee. Required to search: name, years to search, DOB. Court refers written requests to State Bureau of Investigation in Dover at 302-739-5882.
General Information: No juvenile records released. Copy fee: $1.00 per page. Cert fee: $7.00. Payee: State of Delaware. Personal checks accepted. Visa, MC, Discover accepted. Prepayment required.

Georgetown Justice of the Peace #3 17
Shortly Rd, Georgetown, DE 19947; 302-856-1445; Fax: 302-856-5844. Hours: 24 hours daily (EST). *Misdemeanor.* http://courts.state.de.us/jpcourt
Criminal Records: Only the court performs in person searches; visitors may not. Search fee: $7.00 per name. Search fee includes certification. Also must be recent case. Required to search: name, years to search, DOB; also helpful: SSN. **General Information:** Payee: State. Prepayment required.

Millsboro Justice of the Peace #1 553 E
DuPont Hwy, Millsboro, DE 19966; 302-934-7268; Fax: 302-934-1414. Hours: 8AM-4PM (EST). *Misdemeanor.* http://courts.state.de.us/jpcourt
Criminal Records: Access: In person, mail. Only the court performs in person searches; visitors may not. No search fee. Required to search: name, years to search, DOB. Records available from 1983, computerized since 1990.
General Information: Copy fee: $.25 per page. Prepayment required. Mail turnaround time same day.

Rehoboth Beach Justice of the Peace #2 31 Rte 24, Rehoboth Beach, DE 19971-9738; 302-645-6163; Fax: 302-645-8842. Hours: 8AM-Midnight (EST). *Misdemeanor.*
http://courts.state.de.us/jpcourt
Criminal Records: Both court and visitors may perform in person searches. No search fee. Required to search: name, years to search, DOB. Records available since 1990, computerized since 1992.
General Information: Copy fee: $1.00 per page. Cert fee: $7.00. Payee: State. Prepayment required.

Seaford Justice of the Peace #4 408 Stein
Hwy, Seaford, DE 19973; 302-628-2036; Fax: 302-528-2049. Hours: 8:00 am - Midnight (EST). *Misdemeanor.* http://courts.state.de.us/jpcourt
Criminal Records: Visitors must perform in person searches for themselves. No search fee. Required to search: name, years to search.

Delaware Recording Offices

ORGANIZATION: Delaware has 3 counties and 3 recording offices. The recording officer is County Recorder in both jurisdictions. Delaware is in the Eastern Time Zone (EST).

REAL ESTATE RECORDS: Counties do not perform real estate searches, but will provide copies.

UCC RECORDS: Financing statements are filed at the state level, except for real estate related collateral, which are filed only with the County Recorder. All counties perform UCC searches. Copy and certification fees vary.

TAX LIEN RECORDS: Federal tax liens on personal property of businesses are filed with the Secretary of State. Other federal and all state tax liens on personal property are filed with the County Recorder. Copy and certification fees vary.

ONLINE ACCESS: There is no statewide online system for county recorded documents.

Kent County

County Recorder of Deeds, 414 Federal St., County Admin. Bldg, Rm 218, Dover, DE 19901. **Phone-**302-744-2314; fax-302-736-2035; hours 8:30AM-4:30PM Will not search records. Record copy- $1.00 per page. Cert fee: $5.00 per page. Payee: Kent County Recorder of Deeds. **Online Access to Sheriff Sale, Most Wanted records:** Access to sheriff sales lists is at www.co.kent.de.us/sheriff_na.htm. Also, City of Dover most wanted list is at www.doverpolice.org/wanted.htm. **Other phones:** Assessor-302-744-2401; Treasurer-302-744-2341; Prothonotary-302-739-5328.

New Castle County

County Recorder of Deeds, 800 French St, 4th Fl, Wilmington, DE 19801. **Phone-**County Recorder of Deeds, R/E & UCC Recording- 302-395-7700; fax-302-395-7732; hours 9AM-5PM www.ncc-deeds.com Will search UCC records. Search per debtor- $16.00. UCC copy- $1.00 per page. Will not search real estate or tax lien records. RE record copy- $.25 per page. Cert fee: $2.00 per page; $5.00 if pages supplied by Recorder office. Payee: New Castle County Recorder of Deeds. **Online Access to Real Estate, Property Assessor, Recorder, Deed, Marriage, Incs, Sex Offenders, Most Wanted records:** Records on the City of New Castle Geographic Information System database are free at www.2isystems.com/newcastle/Search2.CFM.

Property information can also be found at www.co.new-castle.de.us/LandUse/LandUse1.htm. No name searching. Also, access to the Recorder of Deeds database is free at www.ncc-deeds.com. Also, the sheriff's Most Wanted, sex offender and missing persons lists are at www.nccpd.com Also, City of New Castle provides an acreage search for free at www.2isystems.com/newcastle/Search2.CFM. **Other phones:** Assessor-302-395-5400; Treasurer-302-395-5177; Appraiser/ Auditor-302-395-5400; Elections-302-577-3464; Prothonotary-302-255-0800.

Sussex County

County Recorder of Deeds, PO Box 827, Georgetown, DE 19947-0827. **Phone-**302-855-7785; fax-302-855-7787; hours 8:30AM-4:30PM Will search UCC records. Search per debtor- $10.00. UCC copy- $2.00 per page. Will not search real estate or tax lien records. RE record copy- $5.00 1st page; $.50 each add'l pg. Cert fee: $5.00 per cert. Payee: Sussex County Recorder of Deeds. **Online Access to Real Estate, Property Tax, Sheriff Sale records:** Access to the tax information website is free at www.sussexcounty.net/proptax/index.cfm. Also, search the GIS-mapping page for free at www.smartmap.com/sussex/. At the map page, click on "search by" and choose "tax parcel (Name)". Also access to sheriff sales data is at www.sussexsheriff.com/SalesCont.htm. **Other phones:** Assessor-302-855-7824; Treasurer-302-855-7763; Prothontary-302-856-5740.

Delaware County Locator

You will usually be able to find the city name in the City/County Cross Reference below. In that case, it is a simple matter to determine the county from the cross reference. However, only the official US Postal Service city names are included in this index. There are an additional 40,000 place names that people use in their addresses. Therefore, we have also included a ZIP/City Cross Reference immediately following the City/County Cross Reference.

If you know the ZIP Code but the city name does not appear in the City/County Cross Reference index, look up the ZIP Code in the ZIP/City Cross Reference, find the city name, then look up the city name in the City/County Cross Reference. For example, you want to know the county for an address of Menands, NY 12204. There is no "Menands" in the City/County Cross Reference. The ZIP/City Cross Reference shows that ZIP Codes 12201-12288 are for the city of Albany. Looking back in the City/County Cross Reference, Albany is in Albany County.

Delaware City/County Cross Reference

BEAR New Castle
BETHANY BEACH Sussex
BETHEL Sussex
BRIDGEVILLE Sussex
CAMDEN WYOMING Kent
CHESWOLD Kent
CLAYMONT New Castle
CLAYTON (19938) Kent(89), New Castle(10)
DAGSBORO Sussex
DELAWARE CITY New Castle
DELMAR Sussex
DOVER Kent
DOVER AFB Kent
ELLENDALE Sussex
FARMINGTON Kent

FELTON Kent
FENWICK ISLAND Sussex
FRANKFORD Sussex
FREDERICA Kent
GEORGETOWN Sussex
GREENWOOD (19950) Sussex(65), Kent(34)
HARBESON Sussex
HARRINGTON Kent
HARTLY Kent
HOCKESSIN New Castle
HOUSTON Kent
KENTON Kent
KIRKWOOD New Castle
LAUREL Sussex
LEWES Sussex

LINCOLN Sussex
LITTLE CREEK Kent
MAGNOLIA Kent
MARYDEL Kent
MIDDLETOWN New Castle
MILFORD (19963) Sussex(61), Kent(38)
MILLSBORO Sussex
MILLVILLE Sussex
MILTON Sussex
MONTCHANIN New Castle
NASSAU Sussex
NEW CASTLE New Castle
NEWARK New Castle
OCEAN VIEW Sussex
ODESSA New Castle
PORT PENN New Castle

REHOBOTH BEACH Sussex
ROCKLAND New Castle
SAINT GEORGES New Castle
SEAFORD Sussex
SELBYVILLE Sussex
SMYRNA (19977) Kent(89), New Castle(10)
TOWNSEND New Castle
VIOLA Kent
WILMINGTON New Castle
WINTERTHUR New Castle
WOODSIDE Kent
YORKLYN New Castle

Delaware ZIP/City Cross Reference

BEAR New Castle
BETHANY BEACH Sussex
BETHEL Sussex
BRIDGEVILLE Sussex
CAMDEN WYOMING Kent
CHESWOLD Kent
CLAYMONT New Castle
CLAYTON (19938) Kent(89), New Castle(10)
DAGSBORO Sussex
DELAWARE CITY New Castle
DELMAR Sussex
DOVER Kent
DOVER AFB Kent
ELLENDALE Sussex
FARMINGTON Kent

FELTON Kent
FENWICK ISLAND Sussex
FRANKFORD Sussex
FREDERICA Kent
GEORGETOWN Sussex
GREENWOOD (19950) Sussex(65), Kent(34)
HARBESON Sussex
HARRINGTON Kent
HARTLY Kent
HOCKESSIN New Castle
HOUSTON Kent
KENTON Kent
KIRKWOOD New Castle
LAUREL Sussex
LEWES Sussex

LINCOLN Sussex
LITTLE CREEK Kent
MAGNOLIA Kent
MARYDEL Kent
MIDDLETOWN New Castle
MILFORD (19963) Sussex(61), Kent(38)
MILLSBORO Sussex
MILLVILLE Sussex
MILTON Sussex
MONTCHANIN New Castle
NASSAU Sussex
NEW CASTLE New Castle
NEWARK New Castle
OCEAN VIEW Sussex
ODESSA New Castle
PORT PENN New Castle

REHOBOTH BEACH Sussex
ROCKLAND New Castle
SAINT GEORGES New Castle
SEAFORD Sussex
SELBYVILLE Sussex
SMYRNA (19977) Kent(89), New Castle(10)
TOWNSEND New Castle
VIOLA Kent
WILMINGTON New Castle
WINTERTHUR New Castle
WOODSIDE Kent
YORKLYN New Castle

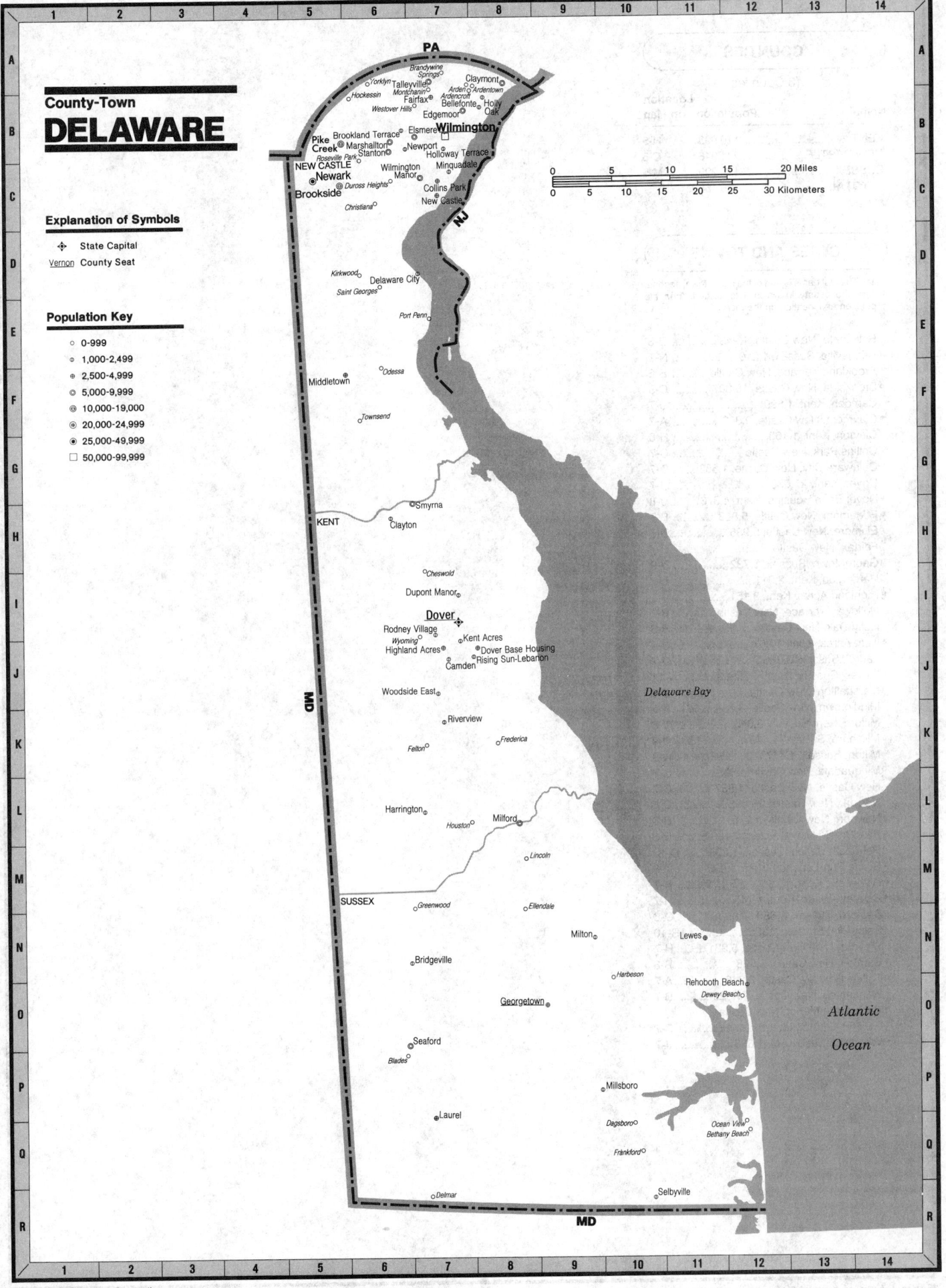

County-Town
DELAWARE

Explanation of Symbols

✛ State Capital

Vernon County Seat

Population Key

○ 0-999
◔ 1,000-2,499
⊕ 2,500-4,999
◎ 5,000-9,999
◉ 10,000-19,000
◉ 20,000-24,999
⬤ 25,000-49,999
□ 50,000-99,999

PA

Brandywine Springs
Claymont
Yorklyn
Talleyville
Hockessin
Montchanin
Arden Ardentown
Fairfax
Ardencroft
Bellefonte Holly
Westover Hills
Edgemoor
Oak

Pike Creek
Brookland Terrace
Elsmere
Wilmington
Brookside
Marshallton
Newport
Roseville Park
Stanton
Holloway Terrace
NEW CASTLE
Wilmington
Minquadale
Newark
Manor
Duross Heights
Collins Park
Brookside
New Castle
Christiana

NJ

Kirkwood
Delaware City
Saint Georges

Port Penn

Middletown
Odessa

Townsend

20 Miles

0   5   10   15   20 Miles
0   5   10   15   20   25   30 Kilometers

KENT
Smyrna
Clayton

Cheswold

Dupont Manor

Dover
Rodney Village
Kent Acres
Wyoming
Highland Acres
Dover Base Housing
Camden
Rising Sun-Lebanon

Woodside East

Riverview

Felton
Frederica

Delaware Bay

Harrington
Milford
Houston
Lincoln

SUSSEX
Greenwood
Ellendale

Milton
Lewes

Bridgeville

Harbeson
Rehoboth Beach
Dewey Beach

Georgetown

Atlantic
Ocean

Seaford
Blades

Millsboro

Laurel
Dagsboro
Ocean View
Bethany Beach
Frankford

Delmar
Selbyville

MD

COUNTIES

(3 Counties)

Name	Population	Location on Map
KENT	110,993	H-5
NEW CASTLE	441,946	C-5
SUSSEX	113,229	M-5
TOTAL	666,168	

CITIES AND TOWNS

Note: The first name is that of the city or town, second, that of the county in which it is located, then the population and location on the map.

Bellefonte, New Castle, 1,243 .... B-8
Bridgeville, Sussex, 1,210 .... N-7
Brookland Terrace, New Castle B-6
• Brookside, New Castle, 15,307 .... C-5
Camden, Kent, 1,899 .... J-7
• Claymont, New Castle, 9,800 .... A-7
Clayton, Kent, 1,163 .... H-6
Collins Park, New Castle C-7
Delaware City, New Castle, 1,682 .... D-7
Dover, Kent, 27,630 .... I-7
• Dover Base Housing, Kent, 4,376 .... J-8
• Edgemoor, New Castle, 5,853 .... B-7
Elsmere, New Castle, 5,935 .... B-7
Fairfax, New Castle B-7
Georgetown, Sussex, 3,732 .... O-9
Harrington, Kent, 2,311 .... L-7
• Highland Acres, Kent, 3,151 .... J-7
Holloway Terrace, New Castle B-7
Holly Oak, New Castle B-8
• Kent Acres, Kent, 1,807 .... J-7
Laurel, Sussex, 3,226 .... Q-7
Lewes, Sussex, 2,295 .... N-11
Marshallton, New Castle B-6
Middletown, New Castle, 3,834 .... F-5
Milford, Kent/Sussex, 6,040 .... L-8
Millsboro, Sussex, 1,643 .... P-9
Milton, Sussex, 1,417 .... N-9
Minquadale, New Castle C-7
New Castle, New Castle, 4,837 .... C-7
Newark, New Castle, 25,098 .... C-5
Newport, New Castle, 1,240 .... B-6
• Pike Creek, New Castle, 10,163 .... B-5
Rehoboth Beach, Sussex, 1,234 .... O-12
• Rising Sun-Lebanon, Kent, 2,177 .... J-8
• Riverview, Kent, 1,138 .... K-7
• Rodney Village, Kent, 1,745 .... I-7
Seaford, Sussex, 5,689 .... O-6
Selbyville, Sussex, 1,335 .... R-10
Smyrna, Kent/New Castle, 5,231 .... H-7
• Stanton, New Castle, 5,028 .... B-6
• Talleyville, New Castle, 6,346 .... A-7
Wilmington, New Castle, 71,529 .... B-7
• Wilmington Manor, New Castle,
   8,568 .... C-7
• Woodside East, Kent, 1,655 .... J-7

Explanation of symbols: ● – Census Designated Place (CDP)

District of Columbia

General Help Numbers:

Mayor's Office

1350 Pennsylvania Ave NW
Washington, DC 20004
http://dc.gov/mayor/index.shtm

202-727-2980
Fax 202-727-0505
8:30AM-5:30PM

Legislative Records

Council of the District of Columbia
441 4th Street, Rm 714
Washington, DC 20004
www.dccouncil.washington.dc.us

202-724-8050
Fax 202-347-3070
9AM-5:30PM

District Archives

Office of Archives/Public Records
1300 Naylor Ct NW
Washington, DC 20001-4225

202-671-1105
Fax 202-727-6076
9AM-3:30PM research hours

District Specifics:

Time Zone: EST

Population: 563,384

Web Site: www.washingtondc.gov

District Agencies

Criminal Records

Metropolitan Police Department, Identification and Records Section, 300 Indiana Ave NW, Rm 3055, Washington, DC 20001; 202-727-4245 (Police), 202-879-1373 (Superior Court), 202-638-5352 (Fax), 8AM-5PM.

www.mpdc.dc.gov/main.shtm

Note: Records are also available with less restrictions from the Superior Court, Criminal Div. at 500 Indiana NW, Rm 4001, phone 202-879-1373. The court record mail/fax search fee is $10.00; a signed release not required there.

Indexing & Storage: Records are available for 10 years. Records at Superior Court are indexed in microfilm from 1974 on, index cards from 1970 on, in house computer from 1978 on and Dist.

Archives from 1962 on. Police Dept. keeps felony records back to '92, misdemeanors to '97. It takes 1 day before new records are available for inquiry.

Searching: Include the following in your request-signed, notorized release from subject, full name (middle initial), date and place of birth, year. The SSN, race, curent address and case number, if known, are helpful. Fingerprints searches are not available. The following data is not released: pending cases.

Access by: mail, in person.

Fee & Payment: The fee is $7.00 per name from the Police Dept.; Search fee at Superior Court is $10.00. Fee payee: Superior Court, Criminal Division Out of state personal checks accepted. No credit cards accepted.

Mail search: Turnaround time: 2 to 4 weeks. A SASE is required.

In person search: Searching permitted at this address. Also, you may search in person for at the Superior Court, Criminal Div., 500 Indiana NW, Rm 4001.

Sexual Offender Registry

Metropolitan Police Department, Sex Offender Registry Unit, 300 Indiana Ave NW, Rm 3009, Washington, DC 20001; 202-727-4407, 202-727-9292 (Fax), 8AM-5PM.

www.mpdc.dc.gov/serv/sor/sor.shtm

Note: In general, an offense requiring registration is a felony sexual assault (regardless of the age of the victim); an offense involving sexual abuse or exploitation of minors; or sexual abuse of wards, patients, or clients.

Indexing & Storage: It takes 1 day before new records are available for inquiry.

Searching: Searchers can visit any police station and inspect a public registry that will contain current information on all registered sex offenders in the District of Columbia. The following data is not released: pending cases.

Access by: fax, in person, online.

Fax search: Records may be requested by fax.

In person search: Records for all classes may be searched at this office and all local police stations in DC.

Online search: A list of Class A & B registered sex offenders is provided on the website.

Incarceration Records

District of Columbia Department of Corrections, DC Detention Facility, Office of Records, 1901 D. Street, S.E., Washington, DC 20003; 202-673-8136, 202-673-8136 option 2 (VINE Inmate Information Line), 202-673-8257 (Administration), 8AM-5PM.

www.mpdc.dc.gov/main.shtm

Indexing & Storage: Records are available on current and former inmates. It takes 1 day before new records are available for inquiry. Records are normally destroyed after never; records are archived.

Searching: For full information, a subpeona or signed release is required. The reason for the search must be stated in your request. For general "public" information, this agency prefers that you access the VINE telephone locator system. Include the following in your request-first and last name, DOB. SSN and PVID number helpful and requested. Type of data released varies depending on request.

Access by: mail.

Mail search: Turnaround time: 2 to 4 weeks minimum. For a search, you must provide first and last name, DOB; SSN and/or PVID number helpful.

Corporation, Limited Partnership, Limited Liability Company Records

Department of Consumer & Regulatory Affairs, Corporations Division, 941 N Capitol St NE, Washington, DC 20002, 202-442-4432, 202-442-4523 (Fax), 8:30AM-4PM.

http://dcra.dc.gov/dcra/site/default.asp

Indexing & Storage: Records are available from the 1850s. There is no trademark or servicemark statute. Records are indexed on inhouse computer.

Searching: Include the following in your request-full name of business. The website provides download capability of forms.

Access by: mail, phone, in person.

Fee & Payment: The fee is $35.00 per certifed legal document, plain copies are not available. A Good Standing is $15.00, $18.00 for partnerships, and $30.00 if a not-for-profit. Fee payee: DC Treasury. Prepayment required. Personal checks accepted. Credit cards accepted for in person searches only.

Mail search: Turnaround time: 5 to 10 days.

Phone search: They will release agent's name and address, date of incorporation, and status over the phone at no fee. Names and addresses of Officers and Directors will not be released over the phone, unless time permits.

In person search: You may request information in person. There is no fee unless copies of documents are needed. You may use a credit card.

Other access: For information concerning lists and bulk file purchases, contact the Office of Information Services.

Uniform Commercial Code, Federal Tax Liens, State Tax Liens

UCC Recorder, District of Columbia Recorder of Deeds, 515 D Street NW, Washington, DC 20001; 202-727-0400, 202-727-5374, 8:30AM-4:30PM.

www.washington.dc.us.landata.com/

Note: Records from 1983 forward are located in Room 101, prior records are in Room 304. This agency will not perform name searches (you must do yourself or hire someone).

Indexing & Storage: Records are available from the 1900's. Records are indexed on microfiche.

Searching: Local tax liens are called district tax liens. Include the following in your request-debtor name. Searches from 1973 forward are not performed by state personnel. Use the inhouse terminal or the website. Searches prior to 1973 need a book and page number.

Access by: mail, in person, online.

Fee & Payment: Copies cost $2.25 per page. Fee payee: DC Treasurer. Prepayment required. Personal checks accepted. Credit cards accepted for online service only.

Mail search: Turnaround time: 2 weeks. No name searches.

In person search: There is a public access terminal available to look up names to find instrument numbers.

Online search: Search the index by name or document number at the website. Registration is required. There are two commercial plans to purchase images. Note this for all recorded documents, not just UCC. A Subscriber pays $175 per month for unlimited views of images and $2.00 per document image downloaded. Accounts are also available for larger firms with multiple users. A registered "non-subscriber" pays no fee to view documents and $4.00 per document mage downloaded.

Sales Tax Registrations

Office of Tax and Revenue, Sales Tax Certificates, 941 N. Capitol Street NE, Washington, DC 20002; 202-727-4829, 202-442-6550 (Fax), 8:15AM-4:30PM.

http://brc.dc.gov/tax/tax.asp

Indexing & Storage: Records are available from the 1980's. Records are computerized since 1990, otherwise are hard copies.

Searching: This agency will only confirm that a tax certificate number is registered. If a request is made to search by company name, requester should talk to the agency's legal department. They will provide no other information. Include the

following in your request-business name, tax certification number, federal employer identification number, address.

Access by: mail, phone, fax, in person.

Mail search: Turnaround time: 3 to 5 days. A SASE is requested. No fee for mail request.

Phone search: No fee for telephone request.

Fax search: Same criteria as mail searches.

In person search: Immediate turnaround time.

Birth Certificates

Department of Health, Vital Records Division, 825 North Capitol St NE, 1st Fl, Washington, DC 20002; 202-442-9009, 202-442-4848 (Fax), 8:30AM-3:30PM.

http://dchealth.dc.gov/index.asp

Indexing & Storage: Records are available from 1874 to present. New records are available for inquiry immediately. Records are indexed on microfiche, inhouse computer. Records are normally destroyed after (records not destroyed).

Searching: Records less than 100 years old are only released to person of record or immediate family members or to legal representative of family. Requester should include a copy of photo ID and daytime phone number. Include the following in your request-full name, date of birth, place of birth, names of parents, name of the hospital.

Access by: mail, phone, fax, in person, online.

Fee & Payment: The $18.00 fee is for the short form of birth certificate for every consecutive 3 years searched. The archival long form costs $23.00. All copies are certified. Fee payee: DC Treasurer. Prepayment required. Credit cards are only accepted for expedited services. Personal checks accepted. Credit cards accepted: MasterCard, Visa, AmEx, Discover.

Mail search: Turnaround time: 2 weeks. All genealogical searches must be done by mail and cannot be expedited. No SASE is required.

Phone search: Phone requests are considered expedited and extra fees are involved.

Fax search: See expedited services.

In person search: Simple requests may be processed while you wait.

Online search: Orders may be placed online via a state designated vendor at www.vitalchek.com.

Expedited service: Expedited service is available for fax and online orders. Expedited service is available from VitalChek 800-255-2414 and requires a credit card and additional $9.95 service fee and $12.95 for 7-10 day delivery or $29.95 for 3-5 day service.

Death Records

Department of Health, Vital Records Division, 825 North Capitol St NE, 1st Fl, Washington, DC 20002; 202-442-9009, 800-255-2414 (Vital Chek), 8:30AM-3:30PM.

http://dchealth.dc.gov/index.asp

Note: Request forms are available from the website.

Indexing & Storage: Records are available from August 1874 on. New records are available for inquiry immediately. Records are indexed on microfiche, inhouse computer.

Searching: Records up to 50 years old are only released to immediate family members of person of record or to legal representative of family. Requester should include copy of a photo ID and daytime phone number. Include the following in your request-full name, date of death, Social Security Number.

Access by: mail, phone, fax, in person, online.

Fee & Payment: The fee is $18.00 per record. All copies are certified. Fee payee: DC Treasurer. Prepayment required. Credit cards are only accepted for expedited services. Personal checks accepted. Credit cards accepted: MasterCard, Visa, AmEx, Discover.

Mail search: Turnaround time: 2 weeks. Genealogical searches must be in writing and cannot be expedited. No SASE is required.

Phone search: See expedited services.

Fax search: See expedited services.

In person search: Turnaround time is 1/2 hour unless extensive search required.

Online search: Orders may be placed online via a state designated vendor at www.vitalchek.com.

Expedited service: Expedited service is available for fax and online orders. Expedited service is available from VitalChek 800-255-2414 and requires a credit card and additional $9.95 service fee and $10.00 for 3-5 day delivery or $17.00 for 2-3 day delivery, or $23.95 for overnight delivery.

Marriage Certificates

Superior Court House, Marriage Bureau, 500 Indiana Ave, NW, Room 4485, Washington, DC 20001; 202-879-4840, 202-879-1280 (Fax), 9AM-4PM.

Indexing & Storage: Records are available from 1811 on. New records are available for inquiry immediately. Records are indexed on microfilm, books (volumes).

Searching: Include the following in your request-both names, wife's maiden name, date of marriage.

Access by: mail, in person.

Fee & Payment: Search fee is $10.00. Extra copies are $.50 per page. To search prior to 1921 there is an additional $10.00 per year charge to search. Fee payee: Clerk of the Superior Court. Prepayment required. Only money orders are accepted unless requester is an attorney or a minister/priest/rabbi. No personal checks accepted. No credit cards accepted.

Mail search: Turnaround time: 2 weeks. A SASE is requested.

In person search: Turnaround time is within the same day.

Divorce Records

Superior Court House, Divorce Records, 500 Indiana Ave, NW, Room 4230, Washington, DC 20001; 202-879-1261, 202-879-1572 (Fax), 8:30AM-5PM.

Indexing & Storage: Records are available from 1956 on. Records prior to 1956 are located at the US District Court at 202-273-0520. New records are available for inquiry immediately. Records are indexed on microfilm, books (volumes).

Searching: Include the following in your request-names of husband and wife, date of divorce, year divorce case began, case number (if known). The following data is not released: sealed records.

Access by: mail, fax, in person.

Fee & Payment: Search fee is $10.00. Certification is $6.50. Copy fee is $.50 per page. Fee payee: Clerk of the Superior Court. Prepayment required. Use either a money order or a cashier's check if ordering by mail. No credit cards accepted.

Mail search: Turnaround time: 3-6 weeks. Written requests must include requester's phone number so the court can call back with the charge. A SASE is requested.

Fax search: Requesters must prepay before records are returned.

In person search: Turnaround time is same day for record after 1993. Prior records are kept off site and will take longer to retrieve.

Workers' Compensation Records

Office of Workers' Compensation, PO Box 56098 2nd Floor, Washington, DC 20011 (Courier: 77 P St, NE 2nd Fl, Washington, DC 20011); 202-671-1000, 202-671-1929 (Fax), 8:30AM-5PM.

www.does.dc.gov/main.shtm

Indexing & Storage: Records are available from June 1982 on. Records are archived after a year and will take longer to locate. Records are only from private employers. New records are available for inquiry immediately. Records are indexed on inhouse computer.

Searching: Only claimant or parties to claim can access records. All others must have signed release from claimant. Include the following in your request-claimant name, Social Security Number, date of accident, employer.

Access by: mail, fax, in person.

Fee & Payment: There is no search fee, copies are $.25 per page. Fee payee: DC Treasurer. Prepayment required. Personal checks accepted. No credit cards accepted.

Mail search: Turnaround time: 2 to 3 days. A SASE is requested.

Fax search: Limit 2 pages, turnaround time is 2-3 days.

In person search: Limited to interested parties or with signed release from claimant.

Driver Records

Department of Motor Vehicles, Driver Records Division, 65 K Street NE, Rm 200A, Washington, DC 20002; 202-727-1530, 202-727-5000 (General), 8:15AM-4PM.

www.dmv.dc.gov

Note: Copies of tickets are available from the Bureau of Traffic Adjudication, same address. The fee is $1.00 per ticket.

Indexing & Storage: Records are available for 3 years for moving violations, suspensions/revocations for 5 years, and DWIs for an indefinite period. Accidents are listed on the record if there is a conviction, but fault is not indicated.

Searching: The agency's policy is stricter than DPPA. Personal information is suppressed unless authority is granted by subject. Mail requesters must submit name and DL number; DOB is optional. Online requesters must submit DL, name and DOB; the sex and middle initial is optional.

The following data is not released: SSN, height, and weight

Access by: mail, in person, online.

Fee & Payment: The cost for a driving record is $7.00 for a three or five year record and $10.00 for a ten year record. Fee payee: DC Treasurer. Prepayment required. Personal checks accepted. Credit cards accepted for in person requests.

Mail search: Turnaround time: 3 days. No SASE is required.

In person search: Walk-in requesters may obtain up to 5 records at once. Additional records are available the next day.

Online search: Online requests are taken throughout the day and are available in batch the next morning after 8:15 am. There is no minimum order requirement. Fee is $7.00 per record. Billing is a "bank" system which draws from pre-paid account. Requesters are restricted to high volume, ongoing users. Each requester must be approved and sign a contract. For more information, call 202-727-5692.

Vehicle Ownership, Vehicle Identification

Department of Motor Vehicles, Vehicle Control Division, 301 "C" St, NW, Room 1063, Washington, DC 20001; 202-727-5000, 8:15AM-4PM M-T-TH-F.

www.dmv.dc.gov

Searching: Records are classified as either "Authorized" or "General." Authorized is for law enforcement. General records (DPPA permissible use purposes) suppress the SSN but show personal information. Casual requesters must have permission of the subject. The following data is not released: Social Security Numbers or financial information.

Access by: mail, in person.

Fee & Payment: The current fee is $7.00 per request for VIN, registration or lien information. Fee payee: DC Treasurer. Prepayment required. Cash is accepted for in person transactions. Personal checks accepted. No credit cards accepted.

Mail search: Turnaround time: 10 days. No SASE is required.

In person search: You may request information in person.

Other access: Bulk requests can be obtained for commercial purposes upon approval by the Director, Department of Motor Vehicles if it is determined that the requested use "is for the public interest." Commercial purposes are not permitted.

Accident Reports

Metro. Police Dept., Accident Report Section, 300 Indiana Ave NW, Room 3075, Washington, DC 20001; 202-727-4357, 7AM-4PM (8PM on Wed).

www.dmv.washingtondc.gov

Note: This office holds the officer investigated accident reports known as PD-10s. "Citizen reports" are no longer required (effective 12/12/03), but older reports may be secured for $2.00 each at the Insurance Operations Branch at 202-727-4601.

Searching: Include the following in your request-date of accident, location of accident, full name. The six-digit report number is extremely helpful if known. The agency will not perform a name search.

Access by: mail, in person.

Fee & Payment: The fee is $3.00 per report for walk-in or mail-in requests. Fee payee: DC Treasurer. Prepayment required. Personal checks accepted. No credit cards accepted.

Mail search: Turnaround time: 3 days. A SASE is requested.

In person search: You may request information in person.

Vessel Ownership, Vessel Registration

Access to Records is Restricted

Metropolitan Police Dept, Harbor Patrol, 550 Water St SW, Washington, DC 20024; 202-727-4582, 202-727-3663 (Fax), 7AM-3PM.

http://mpdc.dc.gov/main.shtm

Note: All vessels regardless of size must be titled and registered. Information is not open to the public. Any emergency requests must be in writing and the agency will use some discretion in release of data for lawful purposes.

Voter Registration

DC Board of Elections and Ethics, Voter Registration Records, 441 4th St NW, #250 North, Washington, DC 20001; 202-727-2525, 8:30AM-4:45PM.

www.dcboee.org

Indexing & Storage: Records are available for active records. The database is updated every four months.

Searching: Records are open to the public. The following data is not released: Social Security Numbers or date of birth.

Access by: mail, phone, fax, in person.

Fee & Payment: There is no fee for a search, but there is a $.25 copy fee. Fee payee: DC Treasurer. Prepayment required. If purchasing the database, certified funds are required. No credit cards accepted.

Mail search: Turnaround time: 7 to 10 days.

Phone search: For verification purposes only.

Fax search: Fax searching available.

In person search: Information is available immediately.

Other access: Records can be purchased on CD, tape, and printed lists. A variety of data is available from party registration to voter history. Minimum fee is $50 plus $10 for a CD. Call at 202-727-2525 for details.

GED Certificates

GED Testing Center, State Education Agency, 4200 Connecticut Ave NW, MB1005, Washington, DC 20008; 202-274-7173, 202-274-6507 (Fax), 9AM-1PM.

www.dcadultliteracy.org/

Searching: An examinee must request in writing that an official score report or verification be sent to a specific institution, employer, or other organization. Include the following in your request-a signed release, name at time of test,

DOB, date/year test, SSN, and city of test. Test records for 1997 to present are maintained under SSN. Records prior to 1997 are filed by year.

Access by: mail, in person.

Fee & Payment: There is no fee for verification. Copies of transcripts are $5.00 per copy. Fee payee: UDC - GED Testing Center Money orders are accepted. No credit cards accepted.

Mail search: Turnaround time: 7-10 business days.

In person search: Results are still mailed within two weeks.

Fishing & Hunting License Information

Access to Records is Restricted

Environmental Health Regulation, Fisheries & Wildlife Division, 51 N Street NE - 5th Fl, Washington, DC 20002-3323; 202-535-2266, 202-535-1359 (Fax), 8AM-5PM.

http://dchealth.dc.gov/about/index_environmental.shtm

Note: Hunting of any kind is prohibited within the District of Columbia. Fishing records are not available to the public, they are only released as a Freedom of Information Act request. Certain data may be released to attorneys for pending litigation or statistical use with a written request.

District of Columbia Licensing Agencies
Licenses Searchable Online

Acupuncturist #2 .... http://dchealth.dc.gov/prof_license/services/search_licensing.asp
Addiction Counselor #2.. http://dchealth.dc.gov/prof_license/services/search_licensing.asp
Alcohol Mfg./Vendor/Dist. #1 .... http://app.abra.dc.gov/services/license_holders.asp
Alcohol Servers/Sellers #1.. http://app.abra.dc.gov/services/license_holders.asp
Alcohol Suspended/Revoked Licenses #1 .... http://app.abra.dc.gov/services/suspended_licenses.asp
Appraiser, Real Estate #5... www.asc.gov/content/category1/appr_by_state.asp
Attorney #3 .... www.dcbar.org/find_a_member/index.cfm
Attorney Discipline Case #3....................................... www.dcbar.org/for_the_public/complaints/discipline01.cfm
Bank #10.. http://dbfi.dc.gov/dbfi/cwp/view,a,3,q,585840,dbfiNav,|31299|.asp
Check Casher #10 .... http://app.dbfi.dc.gov/ifs/default.asp
Chiropractor #2 .... http://dchealth.dc.gov/prof_license/services/search_licensing.asp
Counselor, Professional #2... http://dchealth.dc.gov/prof_license/services/search_licensing.asp
Dance Therapist #2 .... http://dchealth.dc.gov/prof_license/services/search_licensing.asp
Dental Hygienist #2... http://dchealth.dc.gov/prof_license/services/search_licensing.asp
Dentist #2... http://dchealth.dc.gov/prof_license/services/search_licensing.asp
Dietitian/Nutritionist #2.. http://dchealth.dc.gov/prof_license/services/search_licensing.asp
Educational Institution, Higher #8 ... http://dcra.dc.gov/dcra/cwp/view,a,1342,q,600631,dcraNav_GID,1697,dcraNav,|33466|.asp
Insurance Company #12... http://disb.dc.gov/disr/cwp/view,a,1300,q,581346,disrnav_gid,1644.asp
Investment Advisor #7 .... www.nasdbrokercheck.com
Investment Advisor Rep. #7... www.nasdbrokercheck.com
Lobbyist #9 .... http://ocf.dc.gov/rep/repocf4.shtm
Massage Therapist #2 .... http://dchealth.dc.gov/prof_license/services/search_licensing.asp
Medical Doctor #2... http://dchealth.dc.gov/prof_license/services/search_licensing.asp
Midwife Nurse #2 .... http://dchealth.dc.gov/prof_license/services/search_licensing.asp
Money Lender #10... http://app.dbfi.dc.gov/ifs/default.asp
Money Transmitter #10.. http://app.dbfi.dc.gov/ifs/default.asp
Mortgage Broker/Lender #10....................................... http://app.dbfi.dc.gov/ifs/default.asp
Naturopath #2 .... http://dchealth.dc.gov/prof_license/services/search_licensing.asp
Nurse Anesthetist #2 .... http://dchealth.dc.gov/prof_license/services/search_licensing.asp
Nurse, Clinical #2.. http://dchealth.dc.gov/prof_license/services/search_licensing.asp
Nurse-LPN #2... http://dchealth.dc.gov/prof_license/services/search_licensing.asp
Nurse-RN #2... http://dchealth.dc.gov/prof_license/services/search_licensing.asp
Nursing Home Administrator #2.................................... http://dchealth.dc.gov/prof_license/services/search_licensing.asp
Occupational Therapist #2.. http://dchealth.dc.gov/prof_license/services/search_licensing.asp
Optometrist #2 .... www.arbo.org/odfinder/LicSearch.asp
Osteopath #2.. http://dchealth.dc.gov/prof_license/services/search_licensing.asp
Pharmacist/Pharmacy #2... http://dchealth.dc.gov/prof_license/services/search_licensing.asp
Physical Therapist #2 .... http://dchealth.dc.gov/prof_license/services/search_licensing.asp
Physician Assistant #2.. http://dchealth.dc.gov/prof_license/services/search_licensing.asp
Podiatrist #2... http://dchealth.dc.gov/prof_license/services/search_licensing.asp
Political Campaign Contributor #9 .... http://ocf.dc.gov/dsearch/dsearch.asp
Psychologist #2... http://dchealth.dc.gov/prof_license/services/search_licensing.asp
Real Estate Appraiser #5.. www.asc.gov/content/category1/appr_by_state.asp
Real Estate School #5 ... . http://dcra.dc.gov/dcra/cwp/view,a,1342,q,600757,dcraNav_GID,1697,dcraNav,|33466|.asp
Recreational Therapist #2.. http://dchealth.dc.gov/prof_license/services/search_licensing.asp
Respiratory Care #2... http://dchealth.dc.gov/prof_license/services/search_licensing.asp
Sales Finance Company #10....................................... http://app.dbfi.dc.gov/ifs/default.asp
Securities Agent #7... www.nasdbrokercheck.com
Securities Broker/Dealer #7 .... www.nasdbrokercheck.com
Social Worker #2... http://dchealth.dc.gov/prof_license/services/search_licensing.asp
Taxi Dispatch #16.. www.dctaxi.dc.gov/dctaxi/cwp/view.asp?a=1187&q=487917
Taxi Fleet/Company #16.. www.dctaxi.dc.gov/dctaxi/cwp/view.asp?a=1187&q=487910
Taxi Insurer #16.. www.dctaxi.dc.gov/dctaxi/cwp/view.asp?a=1187&q=487938

District of Columbia Licensing Quick Finder

Acupuncturist #2 202-442-9200
Addiction Counselor #2 202-442-9200
Air Conditioning/Refrigeration #5 202-442-4459
Alcohol Mfg./Vendor/Dist. #1 202-442-4423
Alcohol Servers/Sellers/Permit #1 202-442-4423
Alcohol Suspended/Revoked Licenses #1
....202-442-4423
Appraiser, Real Estate #5....................202-442-4472
Architect #5...202-442-4461
Asbestos Abatement Worker/Contr. #5.202-442-4459
Attorney #3 202-626-3475
Attorney Discipline Case #3 202-638-1501
Auctioneer #5..202-442-9200
Automobile Repossessor #5.................202-442-9200
Bank #10..202-727-1563
Barber #5 202-442-4459
Bingo Operation #13.............................202-645-8041
Boxing Event/Professional #5 202-442-4472
Check Casher #10.................................202-727-1563
Chiropractor #2 202-442-9200
Contractor, Mechnaical/Residential #5..202-442-4459
Cosmetologist #5 202-442-4459
Counselor, Professional #2 202-442-9200
Credit Union #10...................................202-727-1563
Dance Therapist #2 202-442-9200
Dental Hygienist #2..............................202-442-9200
Dentist #2..202-442-9200
Dietitian/Nutritionist #2.........................202-442-9200
Educational Institution, Higher #8.........202-442-5377
Electrician #5 202-442-4459
Emergency Medical Technician #11 202-442-9111
Engineer #5...202-442-4459
Engineer, Steam #5..............................202-442-4459
Fair Housing Provider #5......................202-442-4400
Firearms Instructor #14 410-799-0191
Firearms Permit #14.............................410-799-0191
Funeral Director #5...............................202-442-4461
Gas Fitter #5 202-442-4459

Hearing Aid Dispenser #2 202-442-9200
Insurance Broker/Agent #12................202-727-7425
Insurance Company #12 202-727-7425
Interior Designer #5..............................202-442-4461
Investment Advisor #7..........................202-442-4934
Investment Advisor Rep. #7.................202-442-4934
K-9 Units #14...410-799-0191
Lobbyist #9..202-671-0550
Lottery Retailer #13 202-645-8042
Massage Therapist #2..........................202-442-9200
Mechanic, Master #5.............................202-442-9200
Medical Doctor #2.................................202-442-9200
Midwife Nurse #2 202-442-9200
Money Lender #10.................................202-727-1563
Money Transmitter #10 202-727-1563
Mortgage Broker/Lender #10 202-727-1563
Motor Vehicle Dealer/Salesperson #5..202-442-9200
Naturopath #2 202-442-9200
Notary Public #15..................................202-727-3117
Nurse Anesthetist #2 202-442-9200
Nurse, Clinical #2 202-442-9200
Nurse-LPN #2..202-442-9200
Nurse-RN #2..202-442-9200
Nursing Home Administrator #2 202-442-9200
Occupational Therapist #2 202-442-9200
Optometrist #2 202-442-9200
Osteopath #2 202-442-9200
Parking Lot Attendant #5 202-442-9200
Pesticide Applicator #4.........................202-535-2299
Pesticide Dealer #4 202-535-2299
Pesticide Employee/Operator #4 202-535-2299
Pharmacist/Pharmacy #2 202-442-9200
Physical Therapist #2 202-442-9200
Physician Assistant #2 202-442-9200
Plumber #5 202-727-7170
Podiatrist #2..202-442-9200
Political Campaign Contributor #9........202-671-0550
Private Investigator #14........................410-799-0191

Property Manager #5 202-442-9200
Psychologist #2 202-442-9200
Psychometrist/School Psychologist #8 202-442-5377
Public Accountant #5............................202-442-4461
Real Estate Agent/Broker/Sales #5 202-442-4400
Real Estate Appraiser #5 202-442-4472
Real Estate School #5..........................202-442-4400
Recreational Therapist #2 202-442-9200
Respiratory Care #2 202-442-9200
Sales Finance Company #10...............202-727-1563
Savings & Loan Company #10 202-727-1563
School Athletic Trainer/Coach #8 202-442-5377
School Attendance Officer/Worker #8..202-442-5377
School Counselor #8.............................202-442-5377
School Librarian/Media Specialist #8...202-442-5377
School Social Worker #8.......................202-442-5377
School, Degree/Non-Degree Granting #5
....202-442-4314 or 4465
Securities Agent #7..............................202-442-4934
Securities Broker/Dealer #7 202-442-4934
Security Agency #14 410-799-0191
Security Alarm Dealer/Agent #5..........202-442-9200
Security Guard #14 410-799-0191
Social Worker #2 202-442-9200
Solicitor #5..202-442-9200
Solid Waste Collector #5......................202-442-9200
Speech Language Pathologist/Audiologist #8
....202-442-5377
Steam Fitter #5.....................................202-442-4459
Surveyor, Land #5 202-442-4459
Taxi Dispatch/Taxi Fleet/Company #16 202-645-6018
Taxi Insurer #16 202-645-6018
Teacher/Teacher Trainer #8 202-442-5377
Tour Guide #5 202-442-9200
Trust Company #10...............................202-727-1563
Veterinarian #5 202-442-9200
Wrestling Event/Professional #5 202-442-4472

Licensing Agency Information

1 Department of Consumer Regulatory Affairs, Alcohol & Beverage Control Division, 941 N Capitol St NE #7200, Washington, DC 20002-4259; 202-442-4423, Fax: 202-727-9685. www.abra.dc.gov Search Database at http://app.abra.dc.gov/services/license_holders.asp

2 Department of Consumer & Regulatory Affairs, Health Professional Licensing, 825 N Capitol St NE, 2nd Fl, Washington, DC 20002-4210; 202-442-9200, Fax: 202-442-9431. http://dchealth.dc.gov/prof_license/services/main.asp Search Database at http://dchealth.dc.gov/prof_license/services/search_licensing.asp

3 District of Columbia Bar Association, 1250 H St NW, 6th Fl, Washington, DC 20005; 202-737-4700, Fax: 202-626-3471. www.dcbar.org Search Database at www.dcbar.org/find_a_member/index.cfm

4 Department of Health, Bureau of Hazardous & Toxic Substances, 51 N St NE, 3rd Fl, #3032, Washington, DC 20002; 202-535-2299, Fax: 202-535-2483. http://doh.dc.gov/services/administration_offices/environmental/services2/tsd/index.shtm Email: gholmes@dchealth.com Note: Also, check licensees through the Dept. of Consumer Affairs at 202-442-4400.

5 Department of Consumer & Regulatory Affairs, License & Certification Division - Central Verifications, 941 N Capitol St NE, Washington, DC 20002-4259; 202-442-9200. http://dcra.dc.gov/about/index_bandc.shtm

7 Department of Insurance & Securities Regulation, Securities Bureau, 810 1st St NE #602, Washington, DC 20002-4227; 202-727-8000, Fax: 202-442-0661. www.disr.dc.gov Email: Maurice.goff@dc.gov

8 District of Columbia Public Schools, Licensure & Credentials, 825 N Capitol St NE, 6th Floor, Washington, DC 20002; 202-442-5377, Fax: 202-442-5311. www.k12.dc.us/dcps/home.html

9 Director of Campaign Finance, Office of Campaign Finance, 2000 14th St NW, #420, Washington, DC 20009; 202-671-0550, Fax: 202-671-0658. http://ocf.dc.gov/index.shtm

10 Economic Development, Banking & Financial Institutions Office, 1400 L St NW #400, Washington, DC 20005; 202-727-1563, Fax: 202-727-1290. http://dbfi.dc.gov/dbfi Search Database at http://app.dbfi.dc.gov/ifs/default.asp

11 Emergency, Health & Medical Svcs. Office, 64 New York Ave NE #5000, Washington, DC 20002; 202-671-4222, Fax: 202-671-0707. http://doh.dc.gov/services/administration_offices/ehms/services.shtm Email: sadams@dchealth.com

12 Department of Insurance & Securities Regulation, Insurance Licensing Division, 810 1st St NE #701, Washington, DC 20002; 202-727-8000. www.disr.washingtondc.gov Email: disr@dcgov.org

13 Lottery & Charitable Games Control Board, 2101 Martin Luther King Jr Ave SE, Washington, DC 20020; 202-645-8041, Fax: 202-645-0006.

14 Metropolitian Police Department, Licensing Division, 7751 Washington Blvd, Jessup, MD 20794; 410-799-0191, Fax: 410-799-5934.

15 Notary Commissions & Authentications Section, Office of the Secretary, 441 4th St NW #810A South, Washington, DC 20001; 202-727-3117, Fax: 202-727-8457.

16 DC Taxicab Commission, 2041 Martin Luther King Junior Ave, SE, #204, Washaington, DC 20020-7024; 202-645-6018, Fax: 202-889-3604. www.dctaxi.dc.gov/dctaxi/site/default.asp Email: dctc@dc.gov Search Database at www.dctaxi.dc.gov/dctaxi/site/default.asp

District of Columbia Federal Courts

US District Court

District of Columbia

Washington DC Division U.S. Courthouse, Clerk's Office, Room 1225, 333 Constitution Ave NW, Washington, DC 20001 (courier address: Use mail address for courier delivery) 202-727-2947, Fax: 202-354-3524. www.dcd.uscourts.gov

Counties: Entire District of Columbia.

Indexing & Storage: New cases available in the index 48 hours after filing date. Civil records are indexed on computer since 1987 with an archive program available of some older cases, microfiche from 1932 to mid-1991. Criminal records are indexed on computer since mid-1991, microfiche from 1932 to mid-1991. District wide searches are available from this court. Archived records are not available over the phone; the court must be contacted in writing and will be made available through a copy service. Turnaround time: 3-5 days.

Fee & Payment: Payment may be made by. Payee: Clerk, U.S. District Court.

Phone Search: Searchers calling locally will not be given information over the phone. Out of state calls will be given the 3 most current docket entries only.

In Person Search: Fee charged if court conducts your in person search for you. Local inquiries must be made in person. Copying available from I.T.S., 202-857-3800.

PACER: PACER is available online at http://pacer.dcd.uscourts.gov.

Electronic Filing: Electronic filing information online at https://ecf.dcd.uscourts.gov

Opinions Online: Court opinions are online at www.dcd.uscourts.gov/court-opinions.html

U.S. Bankruptcy Court

District of Columbia

Washington DC Division E Barrett Prettyman Courthouse, Room 4400, 333 Constitution Ave NW, Washington, DC 20001 (courier address: Use mail address for courier delivery) 202-565-2500. www.dcb.uscourts.gov

Counties: District of Columbia.

Indexing & Storage: Cases indexed by debtor and creditors as well as by case number. New cases available in the index 24 hours after filing date. Records are indexed on computer from 1990 to present. For records prior to 1990,

Fee & Payment: Payment may be made by money order, cashier check, business check. Personal checks are not accepted. Cash accepted in person. Payee: Clerk, U.S. Bankruptcy Court.

Phone Search: Automated voice case information service (VCIS) is available. Call VCIS at 202-208-1365.

In Person Search: Permitted. Outside copy service available for more than 10 copies; call I.T.S., 202-857-3837.

PACER: PACER is available online at http://pacer.dcb.uscourts.gov. Case records go back to 1994. Records purged every six months. New civil records are online after 2 days.

Electronic Filing: Electronic filing information online at https://ecf.dcb.uscourts.gov/

Standards for Federal Courts: The search fee is $20.00 per item (one party name or case number). Certification fee is $7.00 per document. Copy fee is $.50 per page. All fees standard unless noted in profile. Mail Search: always enclose a stamped self addressed envelope unless otherwise noted. The courts accept fax requests or will suggest a copying/search vendor. Before releasing records, all courts require prepayment unless noted in profile.

Open records are located at the court unless otherwise noted. District courts index by defendant and plaintiff as well as by case number. Bankruptcy courts usually index by debtor and case number. While most courts now have their indexes on computer, many still maintain index card files as well.

The universal PACER sign-up number is 800-676-6856. Find PACER and the Party/Case Index on the Web at http://pacer.psc.uscourts.gov. PACER dial-up access is $.60 per minute. Also, courts offering internet access via RACER, PACER, Web-PACER or the new CM-ECF charge $.07 per page fee unless noted as free.

District of Columbia Courts

Court	Jurisdiction	No. of Courts	How Organized
Superior Courts*	General	3	
Probate/Tax Court*	Special	1	

* Profiled in this Sourcebook.

Court	CIVIL								
	Tort	Contract	Real Estate	Min. Claim	Max. Claim	Small Claims	Estate	Eviction	Domestic Relations
Superior Courts*	X	X	X	$5000	No Max	$5000		X	X
Probate/Tax Courts*							X		

Court	CRIMINAL				
	Felony	Misdemeanor	DWI/DUI	Preliminary Hearing	Juvenile
Superior Courts*	X	X	X	X	X
Probate/Tax Courts*					

ADMINISTRATION Executive Office, 500 Indiana Av NW, Room 1500, Washington, DC, 20001; 202-879-1700, Fax: 202-879-4829. www.dcsc.gov

COURT STRUCTURE The Superior Court in DC is divided into 17 divisions, 4 of which are shown in this book: Criminal, Civil, Family, and Tax-Probate. The Tax-Probate Division of the Superior Court handles probate. Eviction is part of the court's Landlord and Tenant Branch (202-879-4879).

ONLINE ACCESS The Superior Court and Court of Appeals offer access to opinions at www.dcbar.org

Superior Court - Criminal Division 500 Indiana Ave NW, Rm 4001, Washington, DC 20001; 202-879-1373; Fax: 202-879-0146. Hours: 8:30AM-5PM (EST). *Felony, Misdemeanor.*
www.dcsc.gov
Criminal Records: Access: Mail, fax, in person. Visitors must perform in person searches for themselves. Search fee: $10.00 (name search). Required to search: name, years to search, DOB. Criminal records on computer from 1978, on microfiche from 1974, on index from 1970, archived from 1962. This court recommends that you contact the Metro DC Police to perform a "police clearance" record check for $7.00. ID and signed release is required. Metro Police is at 202-727-4245, ID & Records Sec., Mail Correspondence Sec., 300 Indiana Av NW, DC 2001. See the State section under District of Columbia "Criminal Records.".
General Information: Public Access terminal is available. (Three public access terminals available.) No sealed records released. Will not fax results. No copy fee. No cert fee. Turnaround time depends on case involved.

Superior Court - Civil Division 500 Indiana Ave NW JM 170, Washington, DC 20001; 202-879-1133; Criminal phone: 202-879-1373; Fax: 202-879-8335. Hours: 8:30AM-5PM M-F; 9AM-Noon S (EST). *Civil Actions, Small Claims.*
www.dcbar.org/dcsc/
Note: Small Claims is a separate branch that handles claims of $5,000 or less.
Civil Records: Access: Phone, mail, in person, online. Both court and visitors may perform in person searches. Search fee: $10.00 per name. Required to search: name. Civil cases indexed by defendant, plaintiff. Civil records on computer from 1983, on microfiche, archived and on index from 1976. Limited cases are free via the e-Filing Project. Attorneys and legal professionals participating in the project must register for the CourtLink eFile service either by logging onto www.courtlink.com or calling 1-888-529-7587. Only out-of-District inquires are taken by phone.
General Information: Public Access terminal is available. No sealed records released. Copy fee: $.25 per page. Cert fee: $5.00. Payee: Clerk-Superior Court of DC. Only cashiers checks and money orders accepted. Prepayment required. Mail requests: SASE

required. Mail turnaround time depends on case involved.

Superior Court - Landlord & Tenant Branch 500 Indiana Ave NW Rm JM 255, Washington, DC 20001; 202-879-4879. Hours: 8:30AM-5PM M-F; 9AM-Noon S; 6:30pm-8pm Wed evenings (EST). *Eviction.*
www.dcsc.gov
Note: This information applies to the Landlord & Tenant Branch only.
Civil Records: Access: In person, mail. Both court and visitors may perform in person searches. Search fee: $10.00. Required to search: name, years to search; also helpful-case number. Civil records go back to 1994; computerized records go back 5 years. Only out-of-District inquires are taken by phone.
General Information: Public Access terminal is available. Copy fee: $.50 each. Cert fee: $5.00. Payee: Clerk-Superior Court of DC. Prepayment required. Mail turnaround time depends on case involved.

Superior Court - Probate Division 500 Indiana Ave NW, Washington, DC 20001; 202-879-1499; Fax: 202-393-5849/879-1452(auditing). Hours: 9AM-4PM (EST). *Probate.*

District of Columbia Recording Offices

ORGANIZATION:

District of Columbia is in the Eastern Time Zone (EST).

REAL ESTATE RECORDS:

The District does not perform real estate searches.

UCC RECORDS:

Financing statements are filed with the Recorder, including real estate related collateral. UCC searches performed for $30.00 per debtor name. Copies cost $2.25 per page.

TAX LIEN RECORDS:

Federal tax liens on personal property of businesses are filed with the Secretary of State. Other federal and all state tax liens on personal property are filed with the Recorder.

ONLINE ACCESS:

Search the recorders database at http://www.washington.dc.us.landata.com/. Registration is required; images are available for free, temporarily. Also, search the real property tax database for free at http://cfo.washingtondc.gov/services/tax/property/database.shtm

District of Columbia

Recorder of Deeds, 515 D St NW, Rm 203, Washington, DC 20001. **Phone**-202-727-5374, 202-727-7110; hours 8:30AM-4:30PM

Will not search real estate records. Record copy fee is $2.25 per page. A $6.60 surcharge is added to each Land Document or General Document processed. Cert fee: $2.25 per page. Payee: D.C. Treasurer.

Online Access to Real Estate, Assessor, Recording, Deed, Judgment, Lien, UCC, Legislation, Most Wanted, Missing records: Search the recorders database at www.washington.dc.us.landata.com. Registration is required; search index for free; $4.00 fee to view and copy. Subscribe for $175.00 per month or per use, and get docs for $2.00 per page. Records go back to 1973. Search Unclaimed property at http://cfo.washingtondc.gov/services/financial/unclaimed_property/search/index.shtm.

Search the DC legislation record at www.dccouncil.washington.dc.us/lims/SearchForm.asp. Search most wanted and missing persons at http://mpdc.dc.gov/serv/solvers/solvers.shtm. **Other phones:** Assessor-202-727-0421; Treasurer-202-727-6055.

District of Columbia County Locator

You will usually be able to find the city name in the City/County Cross Reference below. In that case, it is a simple matter to determine the county from the cross reference. However, only the official US Postal Service city names are included in this index. There are an additional 40,000 place names that people use in their addresses. Therefore, we have also included a ZIP/City Cross Reference immediately following the City/County Cross Reference.

If you know the ZIP Code but the city name does not appear in the City/County Cross Reference index, look up the ZIP Code in the ZIP/City Cross Reference, find the city name, then look up the city name in the City/County Cross Reference. For example, you want to know the county for an address of Menands, NY 12204. There is no "Menands" in the City/County Cross Reference. The ZIP/City Cross Reference shows that ZIP Codes 12201-12288 are for the city of Albany. Looking back in the City/County Cross Reference, Albany is in Albany County.

District of Columbia
City/County Cross Reference

ANACOSTIA ANNEX District of Columbia
NAVAL ANACOST ANNEX District of Columbia
WASHINGTON District of Columbia
WASHINGTON NAVY YARD District of Columbia

District of Columbia
ZIP/City Cross Reference

20000-20099	WASHINGTON
20201-20330	WASHINGTON
20332-20373	WASHINGTON
20373-20373	ANACOSTIA ANNEX
20373-20373	NAVAL ANACOST ANNEX
20374-20374	WASHINGTON
20374-20374	WASHINGTON NAVY YARD
20375-20376	WASHINGTON
20376-20376	WASHINGTON NAVY YARD
20380-20388	WASHINGTON
20388-20388	WASHINGTON NAVY YARD
20389-20391	WASHINGTON
20391-20391	WASHINGTON NAVY YARD
20392-20398	WASHINGTON
20398-20398	WASHINGTON NAVY YARD
20401-20599	WASHINGTON
56901-56920	WASHINGTON

Florida

General Help Numbers:

Governor's Office
The Capitol – 400 S Monroe St   850-488-4441
Tallahassee, FL 32399-0001   Fax 850-487-0801
www.myflorida.com/b_eog/owa/b_eog_www.html.main_p
age   8AM-5PM

Attorney General's Office
Legal Affairs Department   850-414-3300
The Capitol, PL-01   Fax 850-410-1630
Tallahassee, FL 32399-1050   8AM-5PM
http://myfloridalegal.com/

Legislative Records
Legislative Information Services Division 850-488-4371
111 W Madison St, Rm 704   Fax 850-921-5334
Tallahassee, FL 32399-1400   8AM-5PM
www.leg.state.fl.us/Welcome/index.cfm

State Archives
Archives & Records   850-245-6700
R A Gray Bldg, 500 S Bronough   Fax 850-488-4894
Tallahassee, FL 32399-1400   8AM-5PM
http://dlis.dos.state.fl.us/barm/

State Specifics:

Capital: Tallahassee
                                 Leon County

Time Zone: EST*

* Florida's ten western-most counties are CST:
They are: Bay, Calhoun, Escambia, Gulf, Holmes,
Jackson, Okaloosa, Santa Rosa, Walton, Washington.

Number of Counties: 67

Population: 16,396,515

Web Site: www.myflorida.com/

State Agencies

Criminal Records

Florida Department of Law Enforcement, User Services Bureau, PO Box 1489, Tallahassee, FL 32302 (Courier: 2331 Phillip Rd, Tallahassee, FL 32308); 850-410-8109, 850-410-8107, 850-410-8201 (Fax), 8AM-5PM.

www.fdle.state.fl.us

Indexing & Storage: Records are available from the early 1930's. It takes 1 day before new records are available for inquiry. Records are indexed on microfilm, NIST Archive inhouse computer.

Searching: The SSN is suppressed except for the last 4 digits. Include the following in your request-date of birth, race, sex, name. You can submit fingerprints, for the same fee, but it is not required. 100% of the arrest records are fingerprint-

supported. The following data is not released: sealed or expunged records, juvenile records prior to 10/94.

Access by: mail, in person, online.

Fee & Payment: The fee is $23.00 per individual. Pre-paid accounts receive turnaround time of two to five working days. Fee payee: Department of Law Enforcement. Prepayment required. Personal checks accepted. Credit cards accepted only for online requests.

Mail search: Turnaround time: 5 working days. No SASE is required.

In person search: In person requests are treated the same as mail requests; processing takes 5 working days.

Online search: Criminal history information from 1967 forward may be ordered over the Department Program Internet site at www2.fdle.state.fl.us. The $23.00 fee applies. Juvenile records from 10/1994 forward are also available. Credit card ordering will return records to your screen or via email. Search state's most wanted list at www3.fdle.state.fl.us/fdle/wpersons_search.asp.

Expedited service: Expedited service is available for mail and phone searches. Turnaround time: overnight delivery.

Statewide Court Records

Office of the State Courts Administrator, Supreme Court Bldg, 500 S Duval, Tallahassee, FL 32399-1900; 850-922-5081, 850-488-0156 (Fax), 8AM-5PM.

www.flcourts.org

Note: Except for certain online research capabilities, all court record access must be done at the local level.

Searching: The Clerk of the Circuit Court cannot place an image or copy of the following documents on a publicly available Internet website for general public display.

Access by: online.

Online search: 53 Clerk of Courts/Recorders give access to index data at www.myflorida.com, a government sponsored website. Supreme Court dockets are available at website listed above.

Sexual Offender Registry

Florida Department of Law Enforcement, Sexual Offender/Predator Unit, PO Box 1489, Tallahassee, FL 32302 (Courier: 2331 Phillips Rd, Tallahassee, FL 32308); 888-357-7332, 850-410-8572, 850-410-8599 (Fax), 8AM-5PM.

http://www3.fdle.state.fl.us/sexual_predators/index.asp

Note: Chapter 97-299, Laws of Florida, requires certain sex offenders to directly register with law enforcement or to have information compiled by the Department of Corrections, with the information to be provided to FDLE.

Indexing & Storage: Records are available from 07/01/96. It takes 1 day before new records are available for inquiry.

Searching: Under Chapter 119, Florida Statutes, the Public Records Law, any of the public records of the Department of Law Enforcement are available for review upon request, subject to statutorily-authorized editing of exempt or confidential information. Include the following in your request-name or address.

Access by: mail, phone, fax, in person, online.

Fee & Payment: If documents need printing or are substandard forms, then fees may be involved.

Mail search: Turnaround time: 5 working days. No SASE required.

Phone search: The toll free number is manned from 8AM until 7PM.

Fax search: Search criteria is the same phone search.

In person search: In person requests are treated the same as mail requests; processing takes 5 working days.

Online search: Search the registry from the web page. Searching can be done by name or by geographic area.

Incarceration Records

Florida Department of Corrections, Central Records Office, 2601 Blair Stone Rd, Tallahassee, FL 32399-2500; 850-488-2533, 850-488-1503 (Records), 850-922-0000 (Parole Commission), 850-413-8302 (Fax), 8AM-5PM.

www.dc.state.fl.us

Note: Full records are housed at the individual institutions, though inmate information available through this agency and the website should sufficiently fullfill most searches.

Indexing & Storage: Records are available on current and former inmates. It takes 1 day before new records are available for inquiry. Records are indexed on paper, then scanned and stored in database. Image database goes back to 1997. Records are normally destroyed after imaging the paper records.

Searching: Location, DOC number, physical identifiers, conviction information, and release dates are released. Include the following in your request-first and last name and DOB. The SSN and DOC number are helpful.

Access by: mail, phone, fax, in person, online.

Fee & Payment: Fee is $.15 per copy. There is $12.00 per hour search fee (minimum is $12.00). Fee payee: Florida Department of Corrections

Mail search: Turnaround time: 14-30 working days. No SASE is required.

Phone search: Searching limited to general "public" information is available by phone.

Fax search: Fax requesting available.

In person search: In person requesters must call for appointment for a Public File Review; please call two weeks in advance.

Online search: Extensive search capabilities are offered from the website. Click on Inmate Population Information Search. Also, a private company offers free web access at www.vinelink.com/index.jsp. Includes state, DOC, and 44 county jail systems.

Other access: The monthly-updated inmate database is available for $83.00.

Corporation, Limited Partnership, Limited Liability Company, Trademarks, Servicemarks, Fictitious Names, Federal Tax Liens

Division of Corporations, Department of State, PO Box 6327, Tallahassee, FL 32314 (Courier: 409 E Gaines St, Tallahassee, FL 32399); 800-755-5111 (Telephone Inquiries), 850-245-6053 (Copy Requests), 850-245-6056 (Annual Reports), 8AM-5PM.

www.sunbiz.org

Note: This agency recommends accessing the Internet site. Send requests for Judgment Lien Filings to PO Box 6250.

Indexing & Storage: Records are available from the late 1800's. New records are available for inquiry immediately. Records are indexed on inhouse computer, on-line.

Searching: Other fees note - LLC status is $5.00, LLC certified copy of record is $30.00. Include the following in your request-full name of business. In addition to the articles of incorporation, corporation records include the following information: Annual Reports (date of filing and updates), Officers, Directors, Prior (merged) names, Inactive names, and US Tax ID number. The following data is not released: addresses of judges and police.

Access by: mail, phone, fax, in person, online.

Fee & Payment: In person copies are $1.00 per page, certified copies are $8.75 for the first 8 pages and $1.00 for each additional page, not to exceed $52.50. By mail, a flat fee of $8.75 for certification and $10.00 for copies. Fee payee: Secretary of State. Prepayment required. Personal checks accepted. Accepts credit cards for online filing of annuals, only.

Mail search: Turnaround time: 2 to 3 days.

Phone search: The agency will release information for $4.00 per entity via the 800 number. Add $1.00 to have the information retruned by fax.

Fax search: Results returned by fax for $1.00 per page.

In person search: available.

Online search: The state's excellent Internet site gives detailed information on all corporate, trademark, limited liability company and limited partnerships (from 01/96): fictitious names (from 01/97); and lien records (from 01/97).

Other access: This agency offers record purchases on microfiche sets and on CD disks.

Uniform Commercial Code

UCC Filings, FLORIDAUCC, Inc, 2670 Executive Center Circle West, #100, Tallahassee, FL 32301; 850-222-8526, 8AM-5PM.

www.floridaucc.com

Note: The Secretary of State privatized the filing and searching of UCC. The vendor, FLORIDAUCC, is responsible for all filings, photocopy and certification requests, forms, and database availability for searches.

Indexing & Storage: Records are available from 1966, if active, 1997 forward on the web. Records are on computer and microfiche. Records filed by electronic process are available in image format. New records are available for inquiry immediately. Records are normally destroyed after 1997, if lapsed.

Searching: Information on Tax Liens is maintained at the Department of State, Division of Corporations. Tax liens are not filed here, unlerss filed as a UCC. It is suggested to search tax liens at the county level. Include the following in your request-debtor name. The agency will not do a search. You must hire an outside firm, the web page, or use the state designated vendor.

Access by: mail, in person, online.

Fee & Payment: Fees are $1.00 per page for mail searching. Fee payee: Secretary of State.

Prepayment required. Personal checks accepted. No credit cards accepted.

Mail search: Turnaround time: 3 to 5 days. No SASE is required.

In person search: Simple requests may be processed while you wait.

Online search: The state Internet site allows access for no charge. Search by name or document number, for records 1997 to present. Tax Liens are not included with UCC filing information.

Other access: Microfilm reels and CD's of images are available for bulk purchase requesters. Call for more information.

State Tax Liens

Records not maintained by a state level agency.

Note: These records are filed and found at the county level.

Sales Tax Registrations

Florida Department of Revenue, Sales Tax Registration Records, 168 Blountstown Highway #C, Tallahassee, FL 32304-3702; 850-488-9925, 850-922-5936 (Fax), 8AM-5PM.

www.state.fl.us/dor

Indexing & Storage: Records are available for 5 years, then they are purged.

Searching: This agency will confirm that a business is registered and has filed returns with the department. The following are required to search; business name, tax ID number, and business location. Federal ID is helpful. They can also search by the owner's name.

Access by: mail, fax, in person.

Fee & Payment: There is no fee.

Mail search: The turnaround time is 7-10 days.

Fax search: Same criteria as mail searching.

In person search: Records are still returned by mail.

Birth Certificates

Department of Health, Office of Vital Statistics, PO Box 210, Jacksonville, FL 32231-0042 (Courier: 1217 Pearl St, Jacksonville, FL 32202); 904-359-6900 x9000, 877-550-7330 (Order Line), 877-550-7428 (Fax Order Line), 904-359-6993 (Fax), 8AM-5PM.

www.doh.state.fl.us

Note: The website includes general information and ordering instructions. The vendor www.vitalchek.com also can process orders via online or by fax.

Indexing & Storage: Records are available from 1865 to present, however few records were filed prior to 1917. It takes 4 weeks after birth before new records are available for inquiry. Records are indexed on microfiche, inhouse computer.

Searching: Certified copies released only to individual named, if of legal age, or to parents or legal guardians. All letters or applications must include a copy of a picture id of the applicant and the signature and relationship must be notarized. Include the following in your request-full name, names of parents including mother's maiden name, date of birth, county. Include relationsip of requester to subject and ID.

Access by: mail, phone, fax, in person.

Fee & Payment: Fee is $9.00 for a computer print or $14.00 for a certifed photocopy. Extra fees involved for expedited services. $4.00 per copy when ordering additional same name at the same time. Fee payee: Office of Vital Statistics. Prepayment required. Personal checks accepted. All major credit cards accepted.

Mail search: Turnaround time: 10 to 15 days. No SASE is required.

Phone search: See expedited services. This is an automated phone service open 24 hours daily.

Fax search: See expedited services.

In person search: Turnaround time is same day.

Other access: Commemorative birth certificates in large size, signed by the governor, and suitable for framing are available. The fee is $34.00 or $25.00 when ordered in conjunction with other certified copies of the same record. Allow 4 to 6 weeks for delivery.

Expedited service: Expedited service is available for mail, phone and fax searches. Fax phone is 877-550-7428. Add $10.00 for "2 to 3 day rush service" or $23.00 for overnight service. Add $5.00 for use of credit card (required for phone or fax service).

Death Records

Department of Health, Office of Vital Statistics, PO Box 210, Jacksonville, FL 32231-0042 (Courier: 1217 Pearl St, Jacksonville, FL 32202); 904-359-6900, 877-550-7330 (Order Line), 877-550-7428 (Fax Order Line), 904-359-6993 (Fax), 8AM-5PM.

www.doh.state.fl.us

Note: The website contains general information, ordering instructions, and forms. The vendor www.vitalchek.com also can process orders via online or by fax.

Indexing & Storage: Records are available from 1877 to present. It takes 4 weeks after death before new records are available for inquiry. Records are indexed on microfiche, inhouse computer.

Searching: The death certificate minus cause of death is public information. Cause is released 50 years after death to public. Otherwise, requester must be family member or demonstrate legal interest in the estate. Include the following in your request-full name, sex, date of death, county. The following data is not released: cause of death.

Access by: mail, phone, fax, in person.

Fee & Payment: Fee is $5.00 for the first year searched. If the specific year is not known, additional years may be searched for $2.00 per year with a maximum fee of $55.00. Add $4.00 per copy when ordering additional copies at the same time. Fee payee: Office of Vital Statistics. Prepayment required. Personal checks accepted. Credit cards accepted: MasterCard, Visa, AmEx, Discover.

Mail search: Turnaround time: 10 to 15 days. No SASE is required.

Phone search: See expedited service. Order line is open 24 hours daily.

Fax search: See expedited service.

In person search: Turnaround time is same day.

Expedited service: Expedited service is available for mail, phone and fax searches. Fax phone is 877-550-7428. Add $10.00 for "2 to 3 day rush service" or $23.00 for overnight service. Add $5.00 for use of credit card (required for phone or fax service).

Marriage Certificates

Department of Health, Office of Vital Statistics, PO Box 210, Jacksonville, FL 32231-0042 (Courier: 1217 Pearl St, Jacksonville, FL 32202); 904-359-6900 x9000, 877-550-7330, 904-359-6993 (Fax), 8AM-5PM.

www.doh.state.fl.us

Note: The website contains general information, ordering instructions and order forms to download. The vendor www.vitalchek.com also can process orders via online or by fax.

Indexing & Storage: Records are available from 1927 to present on microfiche, from 1970 to present on computer.

Searching: Records are indexed by husband's name and/or by wife's maiden name. Include date of marriage and county of marriage in request. The following data is not released: Social Security Numbers.

Access by: mail, phone, fax, in person.

Fee & Payment: The fee is $5.00 per name for the first year searched. Additional years may be searched for $2.00 per year with a maximum fee of $55.00. Add $4.00 per copy when ordering additional copies at the same time. Credit card fee is $5.00 Fee payee: Office of Vital Statistics. Prepayment required. Personal checks accepted. Credit cards accepted: MasterCard, Visa, AmEx, Discover.

Mail search: Turnaround time: 15 to 20 days. No SASE is required.

Phone search: See expedited service.

Fax search: See expedited service.

In person search: Turnaround time is same day.

Other access: A large size, commemorative marriage certificate signed by the governor is available for $30.00 or $25.00 when ordered in conjunction with other certified copies of the same record. Allow 4 to 6 weeks for delivery.

Expedited service: Expedited service is available for mail, phone and fax searches. Use 904-359-6633 for the fax number. Add $10.00 for "2 to 3 day rush service" or $23.00 for overnight service. Add $5.00 for use of credit card (required for phone or fax service).

Divorce Records

Department of Health, Office of Vital Statistics, PO Box 210, Jacksonville, FL 32231-0042 (Courier: 1217 Pearl St, Jacksonville, FL 32202); 904-359-6900 x9000, 877-550-7330, 904-359-6993 (Fax), 8AM-5PM.

www.doh.state.fl.us

Note: The website provides general information and ordering instructions. The vendor www.vitalchek.com also can process orders via online or by fax.

Indexing & Storage: Records are available from 1927 to present. It takes 6-8 weeks after divorce before new records are available for inquiry.

Searching: Records are indexed by husband's name only. Include county of divorce in request. In each of the last 5 years in Florida, there have been 140,000 marriages and 80,000 divorces per year. (This is over 1025 per court day.)

Access by: mail, phone, fax, in person.

Fee & Payment: Fees are $5.00 per request for the first year and $2.00 per year for each additional search year, with a maximum search fee of $55.00. Add $4.00 per copy per name when ordering additional copies at the same time. Fee payee: Office of Vital Statistics. Prepayment required. Personal checks accepted. Credit cards accepted: MasterCard, Visa, AmEx, Discover.

Mail search: Turnaround time: 15 to 20 days. No SASE is required.

Phone search: See expedited service.

Fax search: See expedited service.

In person search: The fee is nonrefundable. Turnaround time is same day.

Expedited service: Expedited service is available for mail, phone and fax searches. Use 904-359-6633 for the fax number. Turnaround time: 2 days. Add $10.00 for "2 to 3 day rush service" or $23.00 for overnight service. Add $5.00 for use of credit card (required for phone or fax service).

Workers' Compensation Records

Workers Compensation Division, Information Management Unit, 200 E Gaines St, Tallahassee, FL 32399-4226; 850-488-3030, 850-414-7341 (Fax), 7:30AM-5PM.

www.fldfs.com/wc/

Note: All information that would identify an ill or injured worker contained on the first notice of injury (DWC-1) is confidential and may not be disclosed to the public.

Indexing & Storage: Records are available from 1985 on microfilm. Indexes are also on microfiche (older) and on an image process (recent). It takes 3 days (imaged) before new records are available for inquiry. Records are indexed on microfilm, microfiche.

Searching: To get medical records you must have a signed release of subject, except for legal representatives or an involved insurance company. Include the following in your request-claimant name, Social Security Number, date of accident.

Access by: mail, fax, in person.

Fee & Payment: There is no search fee, but copies are $.15 per page after 14 pages. Fee payee: Workers Compensation Trust Fund. Prepayment required. Personal checks accepted. No credit cards accepted.

Mail search: Turnaround time: 2 weeks. They will send an invoice, and will send you the copies after they receive the check. No SASE is required.

Fax search: Same criteria as mail searching.

In person search: Requests are still returned by mail, unless you have a subpoena.

Driver Records

Division of Drivers Licenses, Bureau of Records, PO Box 5775, Tallahassee, FL 32314-5775 (Courier: 2900 Apalachee Pky, MS90, Neil Kirkman Bldg, Tallahassee, FL 32399); 850-488-0250, 850-922-9000, 850-487-7080 (Fax), 8AM-5PM.

www.hsmv.state.fl.us

Note: Copies of tickets may be obtained from the same address listed above. The search fee is $2.00 plus $.50 copy fee or $1.00 for certified copies.

Indexing & Storage: Records are available for a 3 year record or for a 7 year record. Accidents will appear only if convicted of a violation.

Searching: Florida did not adopt the amendment to DPPA. Casual requesters can obtain personal information without consent if the subject has not opted out. Either the driver license number or the name, DOB and sex are required for ordering.

Access by: mail, in person, online.

Fee & Payment: The fee is $3.10 for a certified three or seven year record. Uncertified or online is $2.10. There is a full charge for a "no record found." Fee payee: Division of Drivers Licenses. Prepayment required. Personal checks accepted. No credit cards accepted.

Mail search: Turnaround time: 10 days. No SASE is required.

In person search: Normally, up to 50 requests can be processed for walk-in requests, while you wait. Some Clerks of Courts will also process driving records.

Online search: Online requests an sold on an interactive basis. The state differentiates between high and low volume users. Requesters with 5,000 or more records per month are considered Network Providers. Call 850-488-6264 to become a Provider. Requesters with less than 5,000 requests per month (called Individual Users) are directed to a Provider. A list of providers is found at the website. Check the status of any Florida Driver License free at https://www4.hsmv.state.fl.us/dlstatus.html. Simply enter the driver license number.

Other access: This agency will process magnetic tape requests. Also, they will provide customized database searches of the license information. Call 850-487-4467 for more details.

Vehicle Ownership, Vehicle Identification

Division of Motor Vehicles, Information Research Unit, Neil Kirkman Bldg, A-126, Tallahassee, FL 32399; 850-488-5665, 850-921-6122, 850-488-8983 (Fax), 8AM-4:30PM.

www.hsmv.state.fl.us

Note: The state has not converted from an opt-out to an opt-in policy, but otherwise is in compliiance with the DPPA.

Indexing & Storage: Records are available for 12 years.

Searching: Casual requesters cannot obtain personal information without consent of subject. Please submit the city (residence) and DOB if doing a name search.

Access by: mail, in person, online.

Fee & Payment: The fee for a computer printout of information is $.50, $1.00 per page copy fee, add $3.00 if certification is needed. The current license plate registration or copy of title is $2.00. A complete microfilm title history can be $15.00 or more. Fee payee: Division of Motor Vehicles. Prepayment required. Personal checks accepted. No credit cards accepted.

Mail search: Turnaround time: 2 to 3 weeks. If records are on microfiche, the wait may be as long as 4 weeks. No SASE is required.

In person search: In cases when the information is not readily available the wait is 2 to 3 days.

Online search: Florida has contracted to release vehicle information through approved Network Providers. Accounts must first be approved by the state. For each record accessed, the charge is $.50 plus a transactional fee, and the subscriber fee. Users must work from an estimated 2 1/2 month pre-paid bank. New subscribers must complete an application with the Department 850-488-6710.

Other access: A user may obtain ownership information by county or statewide vehicle class code basis. For more information, call the Motor Vehicle Data Listing Information Services at 850-488-6710 or fax 850-922-1276.

Accident Reports

DHSMV- MS-28, Crash Records-Room A-325, 2900 Apalachee Prky, Tallahassee, FL 32399-0537; 850-488-5017, 850-488-1009 (Older Homicide Records (5 yrs)), 850-922-0488 (Fax), 8AM-4:45PM.

www.hsmv.state.fl.us

Note: They will not provide homicide reports, which must come from the investigating agency.

Indexing & Storage: Records are available from 1942 to the present. Records are stored on microfilm from 1983 forward. It takes 12 weeks before new records are available for inquiry. Records are indexed on microfilm and computer.

Searching: Records sealed by court order and juvenile information cannot be accessed. Homicide reports less than 5 years old should be requested from the local law enforcement agency that wrote the report, if over 5 years call 850-188-1009. Include the following in your request-the full name of driver, exact date of crash (after 1983), county and city, local agency that investigated. For reports prior to 1983 the exact date, county, location and if crash involved a fatality must be supplied with request.

Access by: mail, in person.

Fee & Payment: The cost is $2.00 per report, $25.00 if homicide. You cannot search by phone; however, you can call to determine if report is available. Fee payee: Department of Highway Safety and Motor Vehicles. Prepayment required. Personal checks accepted. No credit cards accepted.

Mail search: Turnaround time: 2 to 4 weeks. A SASE is requested.

In person search: You may request information in person at the customer service counter on 1st floor (Room B-133).

Other access: List or bulk purchase is available by special request.

Vessel Ownership, Vessel Registration

Dept of Highway Safety, Vessel Records, Bureau of Titles & Registrations, 2900 Apalachee Parkway, MS 68, Tallahassee, FL 32399; 850-922-9000, 850-921-1935 (Fax), 8AM-5PM.

www.hsmv.state.fl.us

Note: The state does not offer online access, but has outsourced some online access to vendors. Check the web page for details.

Indexing & Storage: Records are available for 10 yrs to present. Records indexed on computer. Motorized vessels must be titled and registered. Registration of non-powered vessels is not required, but non-powered vessels 16 ft and over must be titled. Liens show on records. It takes 6 weeks before new records are available for inquiry. Records are normally destroyed after 10 years.

Searching: A written request is required for all searches. To search one of the following is required: Florida registration #, title #, hull id #, or the exact name. If doing name search, submit DOB and city.

Access by: mail, in person.

Fee & Payment: $.50 per page for computer print-out. $1.00 per photocopy of record. Additional $3.00 for each item to be certified. Fee payee: Dept of Highway Safety. Personal checks accepted. No credit cards accepted.

Mail search: Turnaround time: 1-2 weeks. No SASE is required.

In person search: Simple requests may be processed while you wait.

Other access: A bulk purchase program is available for magnetic tape, labels or printed list. There is a $50.00 deposit required and a fee of $.01 per record.

Voter Registration

Access to Records is Restricted

Dept of State - Division of Elections, 500 South Bronough St, RA Gray Building, Room 316, Tallahassee, FL 32399-0250; 850-245-6200, 850-245-6217 (Fax), 8AM-5PM.

http://election.dos.state.fl.us

Note: All individual searching must be done at the county level. However, the state maintains a central voter file for data and statistical purposes.

GED Certificates

GED Transcripts/Certificates, 325 W Gaines St Rm 634, Tallahassee, FL 32399; 850-245-0449, 850-245-0990 (Fax), 8AM-5PM.

www.firn.edu/doe/workforce/ged_dipl.htm

Indexing & Storage: It takes 24 hours or less before new records are available for inquiry. Records are normally destroyed after never.

Searching: To verify, the following is required: name, date of birth, year of test, SSN, and county/city of test. If known, the GED Diploma number is helpful. A signed release is needed to get a copy of a transcript or diploma.

Access by: mail, phone, fax, in person.

Fee & Payment: The fee is $4.00 per copy of transcript or diploma. There is no fee for verification. Fee payee: FDOE. Pre-payment required. Money orders and cashiers' checks are required. Personal checks and credit cards are not accepted.

Mail search: Turnaround time 7-10 working days. A SASE is required

Phone search: Depending on workload, personnel may be able to verify over the telephone.

Fax search: Requests are accepted via fax.

In person search: Suggest to call first.

Hunting and Fishing License Information

Fish & Wildlife Cons. Comm, Licensing & Permit Board, 2590 Executive Center Circle, #200, Tallahassee, FL 32301; 850-488-3641, 850-414-8212 (Fax), 8AM-5PM.

www.floridaconservation.org

Indexing & Storage: Records are available from 2/97 forward.

Searching: Requests must be in writing. The agency will release address, telephone number, and type of license. Include the following in your request-name, date of birth.

Access by: mail, in person.

Fee & Payment: There is no search fee.

Mail search: Turnaround time: 2 to 4 days.

In person search: Turnaround time while you wait.

Other access: Will sell entire database of records.

Florida State Licensing Agencies
Licenses Searchable Online

Acupuncturist #1 .... http://ww2.doh.state.fl.us/irm00praes/praslist.asp
Air Ambulance #20 .... www.doh.state.fl.us/ems/emslookup.html
Air Conditioning Contractor #16 .... https://www.myfloridalicense.com/licensing/wl11.jsp?SID=
Alcoholic Beverage Permit #6 .... https://www.myfloridalicense.com/licensing/wl11.jsp?SID=
Ambulance Service #20 .... www.doh.state.fl.us/ems/emslookup.html
Architectural Business/Individual #30 .... https://www.myfloridalicense.com/licensing/wl11.jsp?SID=
Asbestos Remover/Contractor #16 .... https://www.myfloridalicense.com/licensing/wl11.jsp?SID=
Asbestos Surveyor Consultant #16 .... https://www.myfloridalicense.com/licensing/wl11.jsp?SID=
Assisted Living Facility #26 .... www.floridahealthstat.com/qs/owa/facilitylocator.facllocator
Athletic Agent #6 .... https://www.myfloridalicense.com/licensing/wl11.jsp?SID=
Athletic Trainer #1 .... http://ww2.doh.state.fl.us/irm00praes/praslist.asp
Attorney #23 .... www.flabar.org/newflabar/findlawyer.html
Auctioneer/Auction Company #22 .... https://www.myfloridalicense.com/licensing/wl11.jsp?SID=
Audiologist #1 .... http://ww2.doh.state.fl.us/irm00praes/praslist.asp
Automobile Repossessor #18 .... http://licgweb.doacs.state.fl.us/access/individual.html
Bank #5 .... www.dbf.state.fl.us/cf/dogi/Inst_search.cfm
Barber/Barber Assistant/Barber Shop #6 .... https://www.myfloridalicense.com/licensing/wl11.jsp?SID=
Boxer #6 .... https://www.myfloridalicense.com/licensing/wl11.jsp?SID=
Building Code Administrator #6 .... https://www.myfloridalicense.com/licensing/wl11.jsp?SID=
Building Contractor #16 .... https://www.myfloridalicense.com/licensing/wl11.jsp?SID=
Building Inspector #6 .... https://www.myfloridalicense.com/licensing/wl11.jsp?SID=
Chiropractic-related Occupation #1 .... http://ww2.doh.state.fl.us/irm00praes/praslist.asp
Chiropractor #1 .... http://ww2.doh.state.fl.us/irm00praes/praslist.asp
Clinical Lab Personnel #1 .... http://ww2.doh.state.fl.us/irm00praes/praslist.asp
Collection Agency #5 .... https://ssl.dbf.state.fl.us/cf/lic/pubinqry/pub2/index.cfm
Community Association Manager #6 .... https://www.myfloridalicense.com/licensing/wl11.jsp?SID=
Company in Receivership #14 .... www.fldfs.com/Receiver/receivership_list.asp
Construction Business #16 .... https://www.myfloridalicense.com/licensing/wl11.jsp?SID=
Continuing Edu. Provider, Medical #1 .... http://ww2.doh.state.fl.us/irm00praes/praslist.asp
Contractor, General #16 .... https://www.myfloridalicense.com/licensing/wl11.jsp?SID=
Cosmetologist, Hair Braider, Nails/Salon #6 .... https://www.myfloridalicense.com/licensing/wl11.jsp?SID=
Credit Union #5 .... www.dbf.state.fl.us/cf/dogi/Inst_search.cfm
Crematory #6 .... https://www.myfloridalicense.com/licensing/wl11.jsp?SID=
Dentist/Dental Assistant #1 .... http://ww2.doh.state.fl.us/irm00praes/praslist.asp
Dietician/Nutritionist #1 .... http://ww2.doh.state.fl.us/irm00praes/praslist.asp
Doctor, Limited License #1 .... http://ww2.doh.state.fl.us/irm00praes/praslist.asp
Electrical Contractor #16 .... https://www.myfloridalicense.com/licensing/wl11.jsp?SID=
Electrologist/Electrologist Facility #1 .... http://ww2.doh.state.fl.us/irm00praes/praslist.asp
Elevator Certificates of Operation #6 .... https://www.myfloridalicense.com/licensing/wl11.jsp?SID=
Embalmer #6 .... https://www.myfloridalicense.com/licensing/wl11.jsp?SID=
Emergency Medical Technician #20 .... www.doh.state.fl.us/ems/emslookup.html
Employee Leasing Company #16 .... https://www.myfloridalicense.com/licensing/wl11.jsp?SID=
Engineer #33 .... www.fbpe.org/search/
Engineering Firm #33 .... www.fbpe.org/search/
Finance Company, Consumer #5 .... https://ssl.dbf.state.fl.us/cf/lic/pubinqry/pub3/index.cfm
Financial Institution #5 .... www.dbf.state.fl.us/cf/dogi/Inst_search.cfm
Firearms Instructor #18 .... http://licgweb.doacs.state.fl.us/access/individual.html
Firearms License, Statewide #18 .... http://licgweb.doacs.state.fl.us/access/individual.html
Food Services Establishment #6 .... https://www.myfloridalicense.com/licensing/wl11.jsp?SID=
Funeral Director/Funeral Home #6 .... https://www.myfloridalicense.com/licensing/wl11.jsp?SID=
Geologist/Geology Firm #6 .... https://www.myfloridalicense.com/licensing/wl11.jsp?SID=
Health Facility #26 .... www.floridahealthstat.com/qs/owa/facilitylocator.facllocator
Hearing Aid Specialist #1 .... http://ww2.doh.state.fl.us/irm00praes/praslist.asp
Home Health Care Agency #26 .... www.floridahealthstat.com/qs/owa/facilitylocator.facllocator
Hospital #26 .... www.floridahealthstat.com/qs/owa/facilitylocator.facllocator
Hotel/Restaurant #6 .... https://www.myfloridalicense.com/licensing/wl11.jsp?SID=
Insect Sting Treatment Specialist #20 .... www.doh.state.fl.us/ems/emslookup.html
Installment Seller, Retail #5 .... www.dbf.state.fl.us/licensing/
Insurance Adjuster/Agent/Title Agent #14 .... www.fldfs.com/data/aar_alis1/
Insurance-related Company #14 .... www.fldfs.com/Data/CompanySearch/index.asp

Interior Design Business/Individual #30 .... https://www.myfloridalicense.com/licensing/wl11.jsp?SID=
International Bank Office #5 .... www.dbf.state.fl.us/cf/dogi/Inst_search.cfm
Kickboxer #6 .... https://www.myfloridalicense.com/licensing/wl11.jsp?SID=
Lab License #26 .... www.floridahealthstat.com/qs/owa/facilitylocator.facllocator
Landscape Architecture Business/Individual #30 .. https://www.myfloridalicense.com/licensing/wl11.jsp?SID=
Liquor Store #6 .... https://www.myfloridalicense.com/licensing/wl11.jsp?SID=
Lobbyist/Principal #28   ...   www.flsenate.gov/lobbyist/index.cfm?requesttimeout=500&mode=list&submenu=2&tab=lobbyist
Lodging Establishment #6 .... https://www.myfloridalicense.com/licensing/wl11.jsp?SID=
Marriage & Family Therapist #1............................ http://ww2.doh.state.fl.us/irm00praes/praslist.asp
Massage Therapist/School/Facility #1 .... http://ww2.doh.state.fl.us/irm00praes/praslist.asp
Mechanical Contractor #16.................................... https://www.myfloridalicense.com/licensing/wl11.jsp?SID=
Medical Doctor #1.. http://ww2.doh.state.fl.us/irm00praes/praslist.asp
Medical Faculty Certificate #1............................... http://ww2.doh.state.fl.us/irm00praes/praslist.asp
Mental Health Counselor #1.................................. http://ww2.doh.state.fl.us/irm00praes/praslist.asp
Midwife #1.. http://ww2.doh.state.fl.us/irm00praes/praslist.asp
Mortgage Broker School #5 .... https://ssl.dbf.state.fl.us/cf/lic/mbschools/index.cfm
Mortgage Broker/Firm #5...................................... https://ssl.dbf.state.fl.us/cf/lic/pubinqry/pub1/index.cfm
Motel/Restaurant #6 .... https://www.myfloridalicense.com/licensing/wl11.jsp?SID=
Nail Specialist #6 .... https://www.myfloridalicense.com/licensing/wl11.jsp?SID=
Naturopath #1 .... http://ww2.doh.state.fl.us/irm00praes/praslist.asp
Naturopathic Physician #1 .... http://ww2.doh.state.fl.us/irm00praes/praslist.asp
Notary Public #19 .... http://notaries.dos.state.fl.us/not001.html
Nuclear Radiology Physicist #1 .... http://ww2.doh.state.fl.us/irm00praes/praslist.asp
Nurse #1 .... http://ww2.doh.state.fl.us/irm00praes/praslist.asp
Nurse, Practical #1 .... http://ww2.doh.state.fl.us/irm00praes/praslist.asp
Nursing Assistant #1.. http://ww2.doh.state.fl.us/irm00praes/praslist.asp
Nursing Home Administrator #1............................. http://ww2.doh.state.fl.us/irm00praes/praslist.asp
Nutrition Counselor #1 .... http://ww2.doh.state.fl.us/irm00praes/praslist.asp
Occupational Therapist #1 .... http://ww2.doh.state.fl.us/irm00praes/praslist.asp
Optician/Optician Apprentice #1 .... http://ww2.doh.state.fl.us/irm00praes/praslist.asp
Optometrist #1 .... http://ww2.doh.state.fl.us/irm00praes/praslist.asp
Orthotist/Prosthetist #1 .... http://ww2.doh.state.fl.us/irm00praes/praslist.asp
Osteopathic Physician #1 .... http://ww2.doh.state.fl.us/irm00praes/praslist.asp
Paramedic #20... www.doh.state.fl.us/ems/emslookup.html
Pari-Mutuel Wagering #6....................................... https://www.myfloridalicense.com/licensing/wl11.jsp?SID=
Pedorthist #1.. http://ww2.doh.state.fl.us/irm00praes/praslist.asp
Pest Control Operator #4....................................... www.safepesticideuse.com/search/PersonSearch.asp
Pesticide Applicator #4 .... www.safepesticideuse.com/search/PersonSearch.asp
Pesticide Applicator, Comm./Private/Public #32 ... www.safepesticideuse.com/search/PersonSearch.asp
Pesticide Dealer #32... www.safepesticideuse.com/search/DealerSearch.asp
Pharmacist, Consulting #1 .... http://ww2.doh.state.fl.us/irm00praes/praslist.asp
Pharmacist/Pharmacist Intern #1.......................... http://ww2.doh.state.fl.us/irm00praes/praslist.asp
Physical Therapist/Assistant #1 .... http://ww2.doh.state.fl.us/irm00praes/praslist.asp
Physician Assistant #1 .... http://ww2.doh.state.fl.us/irm00praes/praslist.asp
Physicist, Medical #1 .... http://ww2.doh.state.fl.us/irm00praes/praslist.asp
Pilot, State/Deputy #6.. https://www.myfloridalicense.com/licensing/wl11.jsp?SID=
Plumbing Contractor #16 .... https://www.myfloridalicense.com/licensing/wl11.jsp?SID=
Polygraph Assn Member #34 .... www.floridapolygraph.org/directory/
Polygraph Examiner #34 .... www.floridapolygraph.org/directory/
Private Investigator/Agency #18 .... http://licgweb.doacs.state.fl.us/access/individual.html
Psychologist/Limited License Psychologist #1 ...... http://ww2.doh.state.fl.us/irm00praes/praslist.asp
Public Accountant-CPA #21 .... https://www.myfloridalicense.com/licensing/wl11.jsp?SID=
Racing, Dog/Horse #6 .... https://www.myfloridalicense.com/licensing/wl11.jsp?SID=
Radiologic Physician, Diagnostic/Therapeutic #1.. http://ww2.doh.state.fl.us/irm00praes/praslist.asp
Radioogist #1... http://ww2.doh.state.fl.us/irm00praes/praslist.asp
Real Estate Agent/Broker/Sales #24 .... https://www.myfloridalicense.com/licensing/wl11.jsp?sid=
Real Estate Appraiser #24..................................... https://www.myfloridalicense.com/licensing/wl11.jsp?sid=
Recovery Agent School/Instructor/Mgr. #18.......... http://licgweb.doacs.state.fl.us/access/agency.html
Recovery Agent/Agency/Intern #18....................... http://licgweb.doacs.state.fl.us/access/agency.html
Respiratory Care Therapist/Provider #1 .... http://ww2.doh.state.fl.us/irm00praes/praslist.asp
Roofing Contractor #16.. https://www.myfloridalicense.com/licensing/wl11.jsp?SID=
Sales Finance Company #5.................................... www.dbf.state.fl.us/licensing/
Savings & Loan Association, Charter #5 .... www.dbf.state.fl.us/cf/dogi/Inst_search.cfm
School Psychologist #1.. http://ww2.doh.state.fl.us/irm00praes/praslist.asp
Security Officer School #18 .... http://licgweb.doacs.state.fl.us/access/agency.html

Security Officer/Instructor #18 .... http://licgweb.doacs.state.fl.us/access/individual.html
Social Worker, Clinical/Master #1 .... http://ww2.doh.state.fl.us/irm00praes/praslist.asp
Solar Energy Contractor #16 .... https://www.myfloridalicense.com/licensing/wl11.jsp?SID=
Speech-Language Pathologist/Audiologist #1 .... http://ww2.doh.state.fl.us/irm00praes/praslist.asp
Surveyor, Mapping #6.. https://www.myfloridalicense.com/licensing/wl11.jsp?SID=
Swimming Pool/Spa Contractor #16 .... https://www.myfloridalicense.com/licensing/wl11.jsp?SID=
Talent Agency #6... https://www.myfloridalicense.com/licensing/wl11.jsp?SID=
Therapeutic Radiologic Physician #1..................... http://ww2.doh.state.fl.us/irm00praes/praslist.asp
Tobacco Wholesale #6 .... https://www.myfloridalicense.com/licensing/wl11.jsp?SID=
Trust Company #5 .... www.dbf.state.fl.us/cf/dogi/Inst_search.cfm
Underground Utility Contractor #16 .... https://www.myfloridalicense.com/licensing/wl11.jsp?SID=
Veterinarian/Veterinary Establishment #6 .... https://www.myfloridalicense.com/licensing/wl11.jsp?SID=
Visiting Mental Health Faculty #1 .... http://ww2.doh.state.fl.us/irm00praes/praslist.asp
X-ray, Pod, Assistant #1 .... http://ww2.doh.state.fl.us/irm00praes/praslist.asp
Yacht & Ship Broker/Salesman #6 .... https://www.myfloridalicense.com/licensing/wl11.jsp?SID=

Florida Licensing Quick Finder

Acupuncturist #1 850-488-0595
Adoption Service #9 850-921-2594
Adult & Foster Care #9 850-921-2594
Air Ambulance #20 850-245-4440
Air Conditioning Contractor #16 850-487-1395
Alcoholic Beverage Permit #6 850-487-6793
Ambulance Service #20......................850-245-4440
Animal Registration (Livestock Marks/Brands) #3
....850-922-0187
Architectural Business/Individual #30...850-487-1395
Asbestos Remover/Contractor #16 850-487-1395
Asbestos Surveyor Consultant #16 850-487-1395
Assisted Living Facility #26 850-487-2515
Athletic Agent #6..............................850-488-8500
Athletic Trainer #1............................850-488-0595
Attorney #23 850-487-1292
Auctioneer/Auction Company #22.......850-488-5189
Audiologist #1 850-488-0595
Automobile Dealer/Sales #13 850-488-4958
Automobile Repossessor #18 850-488-5381
Bail Bondsman #14 850-413-3137
Bank #5...850-410-9111
Barber/Barber Assist./Barber Shop #6.850-488-6888
Boxer #6..850-488-8500
Broker Dealer/Branch Office #5 850-410-9805
Broker/Dealer/Associated Person #5...850-410-9805
Building Code Administrator #6............850-487-1395
Building Contractor #16 850-487-1395
Building Inspector #6 850-487-1395
Cemetery Lot Salesperson #5.............850-410-9898
Child Care Center #10.......................850-487-3166
Child Care/Child Placing Facility #9 850-921-2594
Chiropractic-realted Occupation #1......850-488-0595
Chiropractor #1................................850-488-0595
Clinical Lab Personnel #1 850-488-0595
Clinical Laboratory #26......................850-487-3109
Collection Agency #5.........................850-410-9805
Community Association Manager #6.....850-487-1395
Company in Receivership #14 800-882-3054
Concealed Weapon License #18 850-488-5381
Construction Business #16.................850-487-1395
Continuing Edu. Provider, Medical #1..850-488-0595
Contractor, General #16.....................850-487-1395
Cosmetologist, Hair Braider, Nails/Salon #6
....850-488-5702
Credit Union #5................................850-410-9111
Crematory #6 850-488-8690
Day Care Center/Child Care Center/Nursery School
#10...850-487-3166
Dentist/Dental Assistant #1 850-488-0595
Dietician/Nutritionist #1.....................850-488-0595
Doctor, Limited License #1 850-488-0595
Electrical Contractor #16 850-488-3109
Electrologist/Electrologist Facility #1...850-488-0595
Elevator Certificates of Operation #6 ...904-488-9097
Embalmer #6...................................850-488-8690

Emergency Medical Technician #20 850-245-4440
Employee Leasing Company #16 850-487-1395
Engineer #33 850-521-0500
Engineering Firm #33........................ 850-521-0500
Feed Distributor #32......................... 850-488-7626
Fertilizer Distributor #32................... 850-487-2085
Finance Company, Consumer #5 850-410-9805
Financial Institution #5...................... 850-410-9111
Firearms Instructor #18 850-488-5381
Firearms License, Statewide #18........ 850-488-5381
Fishing, Commercial Fresh Water #25.. 904-488-4066
Food Services Establishment #6.......... 850-487-1395
Foster Family Home #9 850-921-2594
Fumigation Performance Special ID #4 850-921-4177
Funeral Director/Funeral Home #6....... 850-488-8690
Geologist/Geology Firm #6................. 850-488-1105
Guidance Counselor #2...................... 850-488-2317
Health Facility #26........................... 850-922-5455
Hearing Aid Specialist #1 850-488-0595
Home Health Care Agency #26 850-414-6010
Hospital #26.................................... 850-487-2717
Hotel/Restaurant #6 850-488-7891
In Home Family Day Care Center #10.. 850-487-3166
Insect Sting Treatment Specialist #20.. 850-245-4440
Installment Seller, Retail #5............... 850-410-9805
Insurance Adjuster/Agent/Title Agent #14
....850-413-3137
Insurance-related Company #14.......... 850-413-3137
Interior Design Business/Individual #30 850-487-1395
International Bank Office #5................. 850-410-9111
Investment Advisor #5....................... 850-410-9805
Investment Advisor (Credit Unions) #5 850-410-9805
Kickboxer #6.................................... 850-488-8500
Lab License #26 850-487-3109
Labor Org Business Agent #29 850-488-3131
Labor Organization #29...................... 850-488-3131
Landscape Architecture Business/Individual #30
....850-487-1395
Landscape Maint. & Pest Control Mgmt Co #4
....850-921-4177
Liquor Store #6 850-488-8288
Livestock Hauler #3.......................... 850-922-0187
Lobbyist/Principal #28....................... 850-922-4990
Lodging Establishment #6 850-487-1395
LPG-Liquefied Petroleum Gas Licensing #32
....850-921-8001
Marriage & Family Therapist #1 850-488-0595
Massage Therapist/School/Facility #1. 850-488-0595
Mechanical Contractor #16................. 850-487-1395
Medical Doctor #1............................. 850-488-0595
Medical Faculty Certificate #1 850-488-0595
Mental Health Counselor #1................ 850-488-0595
Midwife #1 850-488-0595
Milk Hauler/Tester #31...................... 850-487-1450
Mobile Home Dealer/Broker/Mfg #13.. 850-488-4958
Money Transmitter #5 850-410-9805

Mortgage Broker School #5 850-410-9805
Mortgage Broker/Firm #5 850-410-9805
Motel/Restaurant #6 904-488-1133
Nail Specialist #6............................... 850-487-1395
Naturopath #1 850-488-0595
Naturopathic Physician #1 850-488-0595
Notary Public #19 850-245-6975
Nuclear Radiology Physicist #1 850-488-0595
Nurse/Nurse, Practical #1 850-488-0595
Nursing Assistant #1 850-488-0595
Nursing Home Administrator #1........... 850-488-0595
Nutrition Counselor #1 850-488-0595
Occupational Therapist #1 850-488-0595
Optician/Optician Apprentice #1 850-488-0595
Optometrist #1 850-488-0595
Orphanage #9 850-921-2594
Orthotist/Prosthetist #1..................... 850-488-0595
Osteopathic Physician #1.................... 850-488-0595
Paramedic #20 850-245-4440
Pari-Mutuel Wagering #6 850-488-9161
Pedorthist #1 850-488-0595
Pest Control Operator #4 850-921-4177
Pest Control, Structural #4.................. 850-921-4177
Pesticide Applicator #4....................... 850-921-4177
Pesticide Applicator, Comm./Private/Public #32
....850-488-3314
Pesticide Dealer #32.......................... 850-488-3314
Pet Shop #25.................................... 904-488-6253
Pharmacist, Consulting #1 850-488-0595
Pharmacist/Pharmacist Intern #1......... 850-488-0595
PHPC Public Health Pest Control #4 ... 850-921-4177
Physical Therapist/Assistant #1 850-488-0595
Physician Assistant #1 850-488-0595
Physicist, Medical #1......................... 850-488-0595
Pilot, State/Deputy #6 850-488-0698
Plumbing Contractor #16 850-487-1395
Polygraph Assn Member #34.............. 954-321-4264
Polygraph Examiner #34...................... 954-321-4264
Private Investigator/Agency #18 850-488-5381
Psychologist/Limited License Psychologist #1
....850-488-0595
Public Accountant-CPA #21................. 850-487-1395
Racing, Dog/Horse #6......................... 850-488-9130
Radiologic Physician, Diagnostic/Therapeutic #1 850-
488-0595
Radiologist #1 850-488-0595
Real Estate Agent/Broker/Sales #24 ... 407-245-0800
Real Estate Appraiser #24 407-245-0800
Recovery Agent School/Instructor./Mgr. #18
....850-488-5381
Recovery Agent/Agency/Intern #18 850-488-5381
Recreational Vehicle Dealer #13 850-488-4958
Respiratory Care Therapist/Provider #1 850-488-0595
Roofing Contractor #16....................... 850-487-1395
Sales Finance Company #5.................. 850-410-9805
Savings & Loan Assoc., Charter #5..... 850-410-9111

School Admin./Superv'r, Principal #2 ... 850-488-2317	Solid Waste Facility Operator #8 850-922-6104	Timeshare Agent #5 850-410-9805
School Educ. Media Specialist #2 850-487-4822	Speech-Language Pathologist/Audiologist #1	Tobacco Wholesale #6 850-487-6793
School Psychologist #1 850-488-0595	 850-488-0595	Trust Company #5 850-410-9111
Securities Agent/Dealer #5 850-410-9805	Surveyor, Mapping #6 850-487-1395	Underground Utility Contractor #16 850-487-1395
Securities Registration #5 850-410-9805	Sweepstakes Operator, Game Promotions #18	Veterinarian/Veterinary Establishm't #6 850-487-1820
Security Officer School #18 850-488-5381	 850-488-5381	Visiting Mental Health Faculty #1 850-488-0595
Security Officer/Instructor #18 850-488-5381	Swimming Pool/Spa Contr. #16 850-487-1395	X-ray, Pod, Assistant #1 850-488-0595
Seed Dealer #32 850-487-3863	Talent Agency #6 850-487-1395	Yacht & Ship Broker/Salesman #6 850-488-1636
Social Worker, Clinical/Master #1 850-488-0595	Teacher #2 850-487-4822	Zoo #25 904-488-6253
Solar Energy Contractor #16 850-487-1395	Therapeutic Radiologic Physician #1 ... 850-488-0595	

Florida Licensing Agency Information

1 Department of Health, Division of Medical Quality Assurance, 4052 Bald Cypress Way, Tallahassee, FL 32399; 850-245-4111, Fax: 850-414-8209. www.doh.state.fl.us/mqa Search Database at http://ww2.doh.state.fl.us/irm00praes/praslist.asp

2 Education Center, Bureau of Teacher Certification, 325 W Gaines, #1514, Tallahassee, FL 32399; 850-488-2317, Fax: 850-245-9667. www.fldoe.org

3 Department of Agriculture & Consumer Services, Division of Animal Industry, 407 S Calhoun, Mayo Bldg, Rm 335, Tallahassee, FL 32399-0800; 850-410-0900, Fax: 850-487-3641. http://doacs.state.fl.us/ai/ai.html Email: brown@doacs.state.fl.us

4 Department of Agriculture & Consumer Services, Bureau of Entomology & Pest Control, 1203 Governors Square Blvd #300, Tallahassee, FL 32301; 850-921-4177, Fax: 850-410-0724. www.floridatermitehelp.org/ Email: galet@doacs.state.fl.us Search Database at www.safepesticideuse.com/search/PersonSearch.asp

5 Department of Financial Services, Banking & Finance Division, 200 E Gaines St, Larsen Bldg, Tallahassee, FL 32399; 850-410-9805, Fax: 850-410-9914. www.dbf.state.fl.us Search Database at www.dbf.state.fl.us/cf/dogi/Inst_search.cfm Note: Formerly the Dept of Banking and Finance.

6 Department of Business & Professional Regulation, DBPR Licensing, 1940 N Monroe St #300, Tallahassee, FL 32399; 850-487-1395, Fax: 850-488-1514. www.state.fl.us/dbpr Search Database at https://www.myfloridalicense.com/licensing/wl11.jsp?SID=

8 Department of Environmental Regulation, Division of Waste Management, 2600 Blair Stone Rd, Tallahassee, FL 32399-2400; 850-922-6104. www.dep.state.fl.us

9 Department of Children & Families, Interstate Corporate Office, 1317 Winewood Blvd, Bldg 7, #202, Tallahassee, FL 32399-0700; 850-487-2383, Fax: 850-488-0751. www.state.fl.us/cf_web/ Email: dcf-osc@dcf.state.state.us Note: This agency provides an informative searchable online list of children available for adoption through them.

10 Department of Health, Day Care Facilities Licensing, 3401 W Tharp, Tallahassee, FL 32303; 850-487-3166, Fax: 850-487-3168.

13 Department of Highway Safety & Motor Vehicles, Bureau of Field Operations, 2900 Apalachee Pkwy MS65, Tallahassee, FL 32399-0500; 850-488-4958, Fax: 850-922-9840. www.hsmv.state.fl.us

Email: Reynolds.Ron@hsmv.state.fl.us Note: List are available $25.00 each. Request must be in writing.

14 Department of Financial Services, Office of Insurance Regulation; Agents & Agency Licensing, 200 E Gaines St, Larsen Bldg, Tallahassee, FL 32399; 850-413-3137. www.fldfs.com Search Database at www.fldfs.com/data/aar_alis1/ Note: Formerly the Department of Insurance.

16 Department of Professional Regulation, Construction Industry Licensing Board, 1940 N Monroe St, Tallahassee, FL 32399; 850-487-1395, Fax: 850-487-9529. www.state.fl.us/dbpr Email: cathleen.o'dowd@mail.dbpr.state.fl.us Search Database at https://www.myfloridalicense.com/licensing/wl11.jsp?SID=

18 Division of Licensing, Bureau of License Issuance, Post Office Box 6687, Tallahassee, FL 32314-6687; 850-488-5381, Fax: 850-487-7950. http://licgweb.dos.state.fl.us Email: eshores@mail.dos.state.fl.us Search Database at http://licgweb.doacs.state.fl.us

19 Department of State, Division of Corporations, Division of Corporation, Notary Section, PO Box 6327, Tallahassee, FL 32314; 850-245-6975, Fax: 850-245-6966. http://notaries.dos.state.fl.us Email: gkoonce@mail.state.fl.us Search Database at http://notaries.dos.state.fl.us/not001.html

20 Emergency Medical Services, 4025 Esplanade Way Bin C-18, Tallahassee, FL 32399; 850-245-4440, Fax: 850-487-2911. www.doh.state.fl.us/ems Email: lisa_vanderwerf-hourigan@doh.state.fl.us Search Database at www.doh.state.fl.us/ems/emslookup.html

21 Board of Accountancy, Dept. of Business & Professional Regulation, 240 NW 76th Dr, Ste. A, Gainesville, FL 32607; 850-487-1395, Fax: 352-333-2508. www.state.fl.us/dbpr/cpa/index.shtml Email: CallCenter@dbpr.state.fl.us Search Database at https://www.myfloridalicense.com/licensing/wl11.jsp?SID=

22 Department of Business & Professional Regulation, Board of Auctioneers, 1940 N Monroe St, Tallahassee, FL 32399; 850-488-5189, Fax: 850-922-6959. www.state.fl.us/dbpr/pro/auct/auc_index.shtml Email: Julie.Baker@dbpr.state.fl.us Search Database at https://www.myfloridalicense.com/licensing/wl11.jsp?SID=

23 Board of Bar Examiners, 1891 Eider Ct, Tallahassee, FL 32399-1750; 850-487-1292, Fax: 850-414-6822. www.barexam.org/florida Search Database at www.flabar.org/newflabar/findlawyer.html

24 Department of Business & Professional Regulation, Real Estate Commission, 1940 N Monroe St, Talahassee, FL 32399; 407-245-0800. www.state.fl.us/dbpr/re/frec_welcome.shtml Search Database at https://www.myfloridalicense.com/licensing/wl11.jsp?sid=

25 Florida Fish & Wildlife Conservation Commision, 2590 Executive Center Cir, Tallahassee, FL 32301; 850-488-3641, Fax: 850-488-1961. www.marinefisheries.org

26 Facilities Licensing, Agency for Health Care Administration (AHCA), 2727 Mahan Dr, Tallahassee, FL 32308-5401; 850-414-9796, Fax: 850-487-6240. www.floridahealthstat.com Search Database at www.floridahealthstat.com/qs/owa/facilitylocator.facllocator

28 Lobbyist Registration, 111 W Madison St Rm G-68, Tallahassee, FL 32399-1425; 850-922-4990. www.leg.state.fl.us/lobbyist/index.cfm Search Database at www.flsenate.gov/lobbyist/index.cfm?requesttimeout=500&mode=list&submenu=2&tab=lobbyist

29 Department of Business and Professional Regulation, Farm and Child Labor Program, Post Office Box 1698, Tallahassee, FL 32302-1698; 850-488-3131. Email: Rebecca.Gregory@dbpr.state.fl.us

30 Department of Professional Regulation, Bureau of Architects, Interior Desigers & Landscape Architects, 1940 N Monroe St, Tallahassee, FL 32399-1027; 850-487-1395, Fax: 850-922-4191. www.state.fl.us/dbpr/pro/arch/arc_index.shtml Search Database at https://www.myfloridalicense.com/licensing/wl11.jsp?SID=

31 Department of Agriculture & Consumer Services, Division of Dairy Industry, 3125 Conner Blvd, Mail Stop C-27, Tallahassee, FL 32399-1650; 850-487-1450, Fax: 850-922-9444. http://doacs.state.fl.us/~dairy/index.html

32 Agricultural and Environmental Division, Bureau of Compliance Monitoring, 3125 Conner Blvd, Bldg 8, Tallahassee, FL 32399-1650; 850-488-8731. http://doacs.state.fl.us/onestop/index.html

33 Board of Professional Engineers, 2507 Calloway Rd. #200, Tallahassee, FL 32303-5267; 850-521-0500, Fax: 850-521-0521. www.fbpe.org Search Database at www.fbpe.org/search/

34 Florida Polygraph Association, Lt. Scott A. Gooding, BCSO, 2601 West Broward Boulevard, Ft. Lauderdale, FL 33311; 954-321-4264, Fax: 954-321-4566. www.floridapolygraph.org Search Database at www.floridapolygraph.org

Florida Federal Courts

The following list indicates the district and division name for each county in the state. If the bankruptcy court location is different from the district court, then the location of the bankruptcy court appears in parentheses.

County/Court Cross Reference

County	District	Division
Alachua	Northern	Gainesville (Tallahassee)
Baker	Middle	Jacksonville
Bay	Northern	Panama City (Tallahassee)
Bradford	Middle	Jacksonville
Brevard	Middle	Orlando
Broward	Southern	Fort Lauderdale (Miami)
Calhoun	Northern	Panama City (Tallahassee)
Charlotte	Middle	Fort Myers (Tampa)
Citrus	Middle	Ocala (Jacksonville)
Clay	Middle	Jacksonville
Collier	Middle	Fort Myers (Tampa)
Columbia	Middle	Jacksonville
Dade	Southern	Miami
De Soto	Middle	Fort Myers (Tampa)
Dixie	Northern	Gainesville (Tallahassee)
Duval	Middle	Jacksonville
Escambia	Northern	Pensacola
Flagler	Middle	Jacksonville
Franklin	Northern	Tallahassee
Gadsden	Northern	Tallahassee
Gilchrist	Northern	Gainesville (Tallahassee)
Glades	Middle	Fort Myers (Tampa)
Gulf	Northern	Panama City (Tallahassee)
Hamilton	Middle	Jacksonville
Hardee	Middle	Tampa
Hendry	Middle	Fort Myers (Tampa)
Hernando	Middle	Tampa
Highlands	Southern	Fort Pierce (Miami)
Hillsborough	Middle	Tampa
Holmes	Northern	Panama City (Tallahassee)
Indian River	Southern	Fort Pierce (Miami)
Jackson	Northern	Panama City (Tallahassee)
Jefferson	Northern	Tallahassee
Lafayette	Northern	Gainesville (Tallahassee)
Lake	Middle	Ocala (Orlando)
Lee	Middle	Fort Myers (Tampa)
Leon	Northern	Tallahassee
Levy	Northern	Gainesville (Tallahassee)
Liberty	Northern	Tallahassee
Madison	Northern	Tallahassee
Manatee	Middle	Tampa
Marion	Middle	Ocala (Jacksonville)
Martin	Southern	Fort Pierce (Miami)
Monroe	Southern	Key West (Miami)
Nassau	Middle	Jacksonville
Okaloosa	Northern	Pensacola
Okeechobee	Southern	Fort Pierce (Miami)
Orange	Middle	Orlando
Osceola	Middle	Orlando
Palm Beach	Southern	W. Palm Beach (Miami)
Pasco	Middle	Tampa
Pinellas	Middle	Tampa
Polk	Middle	Tampa
Putnam	Middle	Jacksonville
Santa Rosa	Northern	Pensacola
Sarasota	Middle	Tampa
Seminole	Middle	Orlando
St. Johns	Middle	Jacksonville
St. Lucie	Southern	Fort Pierce (Miami)
Sumter	Middle	Ocala (Jacksonville)
Suwannee	Middle	Jacksonville
Taylor	Northern	Tallahassee
Union	Middle	Jacksonville
Volusia	Middle	Orlando (Jacksonville)
Wakulla	Northern	Tallahassee
Walton	Northern	Pensacola
Washington	Northern	Panama City (Tallahassee)

Standards for Federal Courts: The search fee is $20.00 per item (one party name or case number). Certification fee is $7.00 per document. Copy fee is $.50 per page. All fees standard unless noted in profile. Mail Search: always enclose a stamped self addressed envelope unless otherwise noted. Most courts accept fax requests or will suggest a copying/search vendor. Before releasing records, all courts require prepayment unless noted in profile. Open records are located at the court unless otherwise noted. District courts index by defendant and plaintiff as well as by case number. Bankruptcy courts usually index by debtor and case number. While most courts now have their indexes on computer, many still maintain index card files as well.

The universal PACER sign-up number is 800-676-6856. Find PACER and the Party/Case Index on the Web at http://pacer.psc.uscourts.gov. PACER dial-up access is $.60 per minute. Also, courts offering internet access via RACER, PACER, Web-PACER or the new CM-ECF charge $.07 per page fee unless noted as free.

US District Court

Middle District of Florida

Fort Myers Division 2110 First St, Room 2-194, Fort Myers, FL 33901 (courier address: Use mail address for courier delivery) 239-461-2000. www.flmd.uscourts.gov

Counties: Charlotte, Collier, De Soto, Glades, Hendry, Lee.

Indexing & Storage: New cases available in the index immediately after filing date. The civil case index is computerized, but the criminal index is not. Records are also indexed on microfiche.

Fee & Payment: Payment may be made by money order, cashier check, personal check. Payee: Clerk, U.S. District Court.

Phone Search: Docket information is available by phone.

In Person Search: Fee charged if court conducts your in person search for you.

PACER: PACER is available online at http://pacer.flmd.uscourts.gov. Document images available. Records purged three years after case closed. New records are online after 1 day.

Electronic Filing: Electronic filing information online at https://ecf.flmd.uscourts.gov

Jacksonville Division PO Box 53558, Jacksonville, FL 32201 (courier address: Suite 9-150, 300 North Hogan St., Jacksonville, FL 32202), 904-549-1900. www.flmd.uscourts.gov

Counties: Baker, Bradford, Clay, Columbia, Duval, Flagler, Hamilton, Nassau, Putnam, St. Johns, Suwannee, Union.

Indexing & Storage: New cases available in the index 1 day after filing date.

Fee & Payment: Payment may be made by money order, cashier check, personal check. Payee: Clerk, U.S. District Court.

Phone Search: No searching by telephone.

In Person Search: Fee charged if court conducts your in person search for you.

PACER: PACER is available online at http://pacer.flmd.uscourts.gov. Document images available. Records purged three years after case closed. New records are online after 1 day.

Electronic Filing: Electronic filing information online at https://ecf.flmd.uscourts.gov

Ocala Division U.S. Court House, 207 NW Second St., Ocala, FL 34475 (courier address: U.S. Court House, 207 NW Second St., Ocala, FL 34475), 352-369-4860. www.flmd.uscourts.gov

Counties: Citrus, Lake, Marion, Sumter.

Indexing & Storage: Cases indexed by as well as by case number. New cases available in the index after filing date. Open records are located at the Jacksonville Division.

Fee & Payment: Payment may be made by money order, cashier check. Business checks are not accepted. Personal checks are not accepted.

Phone Search: No searching by telephone.

In Person Search: Permitted.

PACER: PACER is available online at http://pacer.flmd.uscourts.gov. Document images available. Records purged three years after case closed. New records are online after 1 day.

Orlando Division Room 218, 80 North Hughey Ave, Orlando, FL 32801 (courier address: Use mail address for courier delivery) 407-835-4200. www.flmd.uscourts.gov

Counties: Brevard, Orange, Osceola, Seminole, Volusia.

Indexing & Storage: New cases available in the index immediately after filing date. Records are stored by case number according to year closed.

Fee & Payment: Payment may be made by money order, cashier check, personal check. All checks, except foreign, are accepted. Payee: Clerk, U.S. District Court.

Phone Search: Docket information is available.

In Person Search: Fee charged if court conducts your in person search for you.

PACER: PACER is available online at http://pacer.flmd.uscourts.gov. Document images available. Records purged three years after case closed. New records are online after 1 day.

Electronic Filing: Electronic filing information online at https://ecf.flmd.uscourts.gov

Tampa Division Office of the clerk, 801 N Florida Ave #223, Tampa, FL 33602-4500 (courier address: Use mail address for courier delivery) 813-301-5400. www.flmd.uscourts.gov

Counties: Hardee, Hernando, Hillsborough, Manatee, Pasco, Pinellas, Polk, Sarasota.

Indexing & Storage: New cases available in the index 1 day after filing date.

Fee & Payment: Payment may be made by money order, cashier check, personal check. Payee: Clerk, U.S. District Court.

Phone Search: Only docket information available.

In Person Search: Fee charged if court conducts your in person search for you.

PACER: PACER is available online at http://pacer.flmd.uscourts.gov. Document images available. Records purged three years after case closed. New records are online after 1 day.

Electronic Filing: Electronic filing information online at https://ecf.flmd.uscourts.gov

U.S. Bankruptcy Court

Middle District of Florida

Jacksonville Division PO Box 559, Jacksonville, FL 32201 (courier address: Room 206, 311 W Monroe, Jacksonville, FL 32202), 904-301-6490. www.flmb.uscourts.gov

Counties: Baker, Bradford, Citrus, Clay, Columbia, Duval, Flagler, Hamilton, Marion, Nassau, Putnam, St. Johns, Sumter, Suwannee, Union, Volusia.

Indexing & Storage: Cases indexed by debtor as well as by case number. New cases available in the index immediately after filing date. This court has no specific time that they send closed records to the Atlanta Federal Records Center.

Fee & Payment: Payment may be made by money order, cashier check, business check. Personal checks are not accepted. Pacific Photo, 904-355-1062, is the contracted search and copy center for this district;. Payee: Clerk, U.S. Bankruptcy Court.

Phone Search: Automated voice case information service (VCIS) is available. Call VCIS at 866-879-1286 or 904-301-6490.

Mail Search: A SASE not required.

In Person Search: Permitted. Court uses a contracted search and copy service: Pacific Photo, 904-355-1062.

PACER: PACER is available online at http://pacer.flmb.uscourts.gov. Records purged every year. New civil records online after 1 week.

Electronic Filing: Electronic filing information online at https://ecf.flmb.uscourts.gov

Other Online Access: Court now participates in the U.S. party case index.

Orlando Division Suite 950, 135 W Central Blvd, Orlando, FL 32801 (courier address: Use mail address for courier delivery) 407-648-6365. www.flmb.uscourts.gov

Counties: Brevard, Lake, Orange, Osceola, Seminole.

Indexing & Storage: Cases indexed by debtor and creditors as well as by case number. New cases available in the index 1-2 days after filing date. This court has no specific time that they send closed records to the Atlanta Federal Records Center.

Fee & Payment: Payment may be made by money order, cashier check, business check. Personal checks are not accepted. Pacific Photo is the contracted search and copy center for this district; 904-355-1062. Payee: Clerk, U.S. Bankruptcy Court.

Phone Search: Automated voice case information service (VCIS) is available. VCIS: 866-879-1286.

In Person Search: Permitted. Public access terminals available. Court uses a contracted search and copy service, Pacific Photo; 407-425-7234. There is a 5 page photocopy limit at court; higher quanitities referred to Pacific Photo copy service.

PACER: PACER is available online at http://pacer.flmb.uscourts.gov. Case records go back to 1986. Records never purged. New civil records are online after 1 day.

Electronic Filing: Electronic filing information online at https://ecf.flmb.uscourts.gov

Other Online Access: Court now participates in the U.S. party case index.

Tampa Division 801 N Florida Ave #727, Tampa, FL 33602 (courier address: Use mail address for courier delivery) 813-301-5065. www.flmb.uscourts.gov

Counties: Charlotte, Collier, De Soto, Glades, Hardee, Hendry, Hernando, Hillsborough, Lee, Manatee, Pasco, Pinellas, Polk, Sarasota.

Indexing & Storage: Cases indexed by debtor as well as by case number. New cases available in the index immediately after filing date. This court has no specific time that they send closed records to the Atlanta Federal Records Center.

Fee & Payment: Payment may be made by money order, cashier check, business check. Personal checks are not accepted. Pacific Photo, 904-355-1062, is the contracted search and copy center for this district. Payee: Clerk, U.S. Bankruptcy Court.

Phone Search: Automated voice case information service (VCIS) is available. VCIS: 813-301-5210.

In Person Search: Permitted. Court uses a contracted search and copy service: Pacific Photo, 904-355-1062.

PACER: PACER is available online at http://pacer.flmb.uscourts.gov. Records purged every six months. New civil records are online after 1 day.

Electronic Filing: Electronic filing information online at https://ecf.flmb.uscourts.gov

Other Online Access: Court now participates in the U.S. party case index.

U.S. District Court

Northern District of Florida

Gainesville Division 401 SE First Ave, Room 243, Gainesville, FL 32601 (Use mail address for courier delivery) 352-380-2400, Fax: 352-380-2424. www.flnd.uscourts.gov

Counties: Alachua, Dixie, Gilchrist, Lafayette, Levy. Records for cases prior to July 1996 are maintained at the Tallahassee Division.

Indexing & Storage: New cases available in the index 3 days after filing date.

Fee & Payment: Payment may be made by money order, cashier check, personal check. Payee: Clerk, U.S. District Court.

Phone Search: Only 1-3 names may be searched over the phone, and only docket information will be released.

In Person Search: Fee charged if court conducts your in person search for you.

PACER: PACER is available online at http://pacer.flnd.uscourts.gov. Records purged three years after case closed. New records are online after 2 days.

Electronic Filing: Electronic filing information online at https://ecf.flnd.uscourts.gov

Panama City Division 30 W. Government St., Panama City, FL 32401 (courier address: Use mail address for courier delivery) 850-769-4556, Fax: 850-769-7528. www.flnd.uscourts.gov

Counties: Bay, Calhoun, Gulf, Holmes, Jackson, Washington.

Indexing & Storage: Cases indexed by as well as by case number. New cases available in the index after filing date.

Fee & Payment: Payment may be made by money order, cashier check. Business checks are not accepted. Personal checks are not accepted.

Phone Search: No searching by telephone.

In Person Search: Permitted.

PACER: PACER is available online at http://pacer.flnd.uscourts.gov. Records purged three years after case closed. New records are online after 2 days.

Electronic Filing: Currently in the process of implementing CM/ECF.

Pensacola Division U.S. Courthouse, 1 N Palafox St, #226, Pensacola, FL 32502 (courier address: Use mail address for courier delivery) 850-435-8440, Fax: 850-433-5972. www.flnd.uscourts.gov

Counties: Escambia, Okaloosa, Santa Rosa, Walton.

Indexing & Storage: New cases available in the index 2-3 days after filing date. Records are indexed on computer as of August 1992. District wide searches are available for information from August 1992 from this division. This division maintains records for the Panama City office.

Fee & Payment: Payment may be made by money order, cashier check, personal check. Payee: Clerk, U.S. District Court.

Phone Search: Only basic information is released over the phone. They will not release all docket information over the phone.

In Person Search: Fee charged if court conducts your in person search for you.

PACER: PACER is available online at http://pacer.flnd.uscourts.gov. Records purged three years after case closed. New records are online after 2 days.

Electronic Filing: Electronic filing information online at https://ecf.flnd.uscourts.gov

Tallahassee Division Suite 122, 111 North Adams St., Tallahassee, FL 32301 (courier address: Use mail address for courier delivery) 850-521-3501, Fax: 850-521-3656. www.flnd.uscourts.gov

Counties: Franklin, Gadsden, Jefferson, Leon, Liberty, Madison, Taylor, Wakulla.

Indexing & Storage: New cases available in the index immediately after filing date. Records are also indexed by year closed.

Fee & Payment: Payment may be made by money order, cashier check, personal check. Payee: Clerk, U.S. District Court.

Phone Search: Basic information about a case requested by name (case number) or by case number (names of parties or their attorneys, date of complaint, or general status) is available by telephone at no charge.

Mail Search: A SASE not required.

In Person Search: Fee charged if court conducts your in person search for you.

PACER: PACER is available online at http://pacer.flnd.uscourts.gov. Records purged three years after case closed. New records are online after 2 days.

Electronic Filing: Electronic filing information online at https://ecf.flnd.uscourts.gov

U.S. Bankruptcy Court
Northern District of Florida

Pensacola Division Suite 700, 220 W Garden St, Pensacola, FL 32502 (courier address: Use mail address for courier delivery) 850-435-8475. www.flnb.uscourts.gov/

Counties: Escambia, Okaloosa, Santa Rosa, Walton.

Indexing & Storage: Cases indexed by debtor as well as by case number. New cases available in the index 5-7 days after filing date.

Fee & Payment: Payment may be made by money order, cashier check, business check. Personal checks are not accepted. Payee: Clerk, U.S. Bankruptcy Court.

Phone Search: Automated voice case information service (VCIS) is available. Call VCIS at 850-942-8358.

Mail Search: A SASE not required.

In Person Search: Fee charged if court conducts your in person search for you.

PACER: PACER is available online at http://pacer.flnb.uscourts.gov. Case records go back to September 1985. Records purged when cases are closed. New civil records are online after 2 days.

Electronic Filing: Electronic filing information online at https://ecf.flnb.uscourts.gov/

Tallahassee Division Room 3120, 227 N Bronough St, Tallahassee, FL 32301-1378 (courier address: Use mail address for courier delivery) 850-942-8933. www.flnb.uscourts.gov/

Counties: Alachua, Bay, Calhoun, Dixie, Franklin, Gadsden, Gilchrist, Gulf, Holmes, Jackson, Jefferson, Lafayette, Leon, Levy, Liberty, Madison, Taylor, Wakulla, Washington.

Indexing & Storage: Cases indexed by debtor as well as by case number. New cases available in the index 2-3 days after filing date.

Fee & Payment: Payment may be made by money order, cashier check, business check. Personal checks are not accepted. Payee: Clerk, U.S. Bankruptcy Court.

Phone Search: Only docket information available by phone. Automated voice case information service (VCIS) is available. Call VCIS at 850-942-8358.

In Person Search: Fee charged if court conducts your in person search for you.

PACER: PACER is available online at http://pacer.flnb.uscourts.gov. Case records go back to 9/23/1985. Records purged every six months. New civil records are online after 1 day.

Electronic Filing: Electronic filing information online at https://ecf.flnb.uscourts.gov/

U.S. District Court
Southern District of Florida

Fort Lauderdale Division 299 E Broward Blvd, Fort Lauderdale, FL 33301 (courier address: Use mail address for courier delivery) 954-769-5400. www.flsd.uscourts.gov

Counties: Broward.

Indexing & Storage: New cases available in the index immediately after filing date. The full name of any party of the case, case number or case type is required to search for records. Civil cases are in the computer from August 1990 to present. Criminal cases are in the computer from January 1992. Cases from 1983 are on microfiche. Cases prior to 1983 are on microfilm. Records that are more than 5 years old are, at the discretion of the clerk, sent to the Atlanta Federal Records Center. Call records department to get location of records.

Fee & Payment: Payment may be made by money order, cashier check, business check, Visa, Mastercard. Personal checks are not accepted. Payee: U.S. Courts.

Phone Search: No searching by telephone. Only docket information available by phone.

In Person Search: Fee charged if court conducts your in person search for you. The copy service (954-832-0111) will pull records and make copies. Copy machines also available in lobby.

PACER: PACER is available online at http://pacer.flsd.uscourts.gov. Document images available. Records purged three years after case closed. New records are online after 1 day.

Fort Pierce Division U S Court House, 300 South Sixth Street, Miami, FL 33128 (courier address: Use mail address for courier delivery) 772-595-9691. www.flsd.uscourts.gov

Counties: Highlands, Indian River, Martin, Okeechobee, St. Lucie.

Indexing & Storage: New cases available in the index immediately after filing date. Open records are located at the Miami Division. Records are transferred to the Federal Records Center any time after 5 years at the discretion of the clerk.

Fee & Payment: Payment may be made by money order, cashier check, personal check. Payee: U.S. Court.

Phone Search: Docket information is available by phone.

In Person Search: Fee charged if court conducts your in person search for you.

PACER: PACER is available online at http://pacer.flsd.uscourts.gov. Document images available. Records purged three years after case closed. New records are online after 1 day.

Key West Division 301 Simonton St., Key West, FL 33040 (Use mail address for courier delivery) 305-295-8100. www.flsd.uscourts.gov

Counties: Monroe.

Indexing & Storage: New cases available in the index immediately after filing date. The full name of either party in the case, case number or case type is required to search for records. Open records are located at the Division. Records that are more than 5 years old are, at the discretion of the clerk, are sent to the Atlanta Federal Records Center. Call records department to get location of records.

Fee & Payment: Payment may be made by money order, cashier check, personal check. Payee: U.S. Courts.

Phone Search: No searching by telephone.

In Person Search: Fee charged if court conducts your in person search for you. The copy service will pull records and make copies for a fee. Copy machines also available in lobby.

PACER: PACER is available online at http://pacer.flsd.uscourts.gov. Document images available. Records purged three years after case closed. New records are online after 1 day.

Miami Division Room 150, 301 N Miami Ave, Miami, FL 33128-7788 (courier address: Use mail address for courier delivery) 305-523-5100. www.flsd.uscourts.gov

Counties: Dade, Miami-Dade.

Indexing & Storage: New cases available in the index 1 day after filing date. The full name of either party in the case, case number or case type is required to search for records. Records that are more than 5 years old are, at the discretion of the clerk, sent to the Atlanta Federal Records Center. Call records department to get location of records.

Fee & Payment: Payment may be made by money order, cashier check, personal check, Visa, Mastercard. Payee: U.S. Courts.

Phone Search: Only docket information available.

In Person Search: Fee charged if court conducts your in person search for you. Copy machines are available in the lobby area of the Records and Docketing Section. An onsite copy service can also pull records and make copies; call for more information.

PACER: PACER is available online at http://pacer.flsd.uscourts.gov. Document images available. Records purged three years after case closed. New records are online after 1 day.

West Palm Beach Division Room 402, 701 Clematis St, West Palm Beach, FL 33401 (courier address: Use mail address for courier delivery) 561-803-3400. www.flsd.uscourts.gov

Counties: Palm Beach.

Indexing & Storage: New cases available in the index immediately after filing date. The full name of either party in the case, case number or case type is required to search for records.

Fee & Payment: Payment may be made by money order, cashier check, business check, Visa, Mastercard. Personal checks are not accepted. Payee: U.S. Courts.

Phone Search: Docket information is available by phone.

In Person Search: Fee charged if court conducts your in person search for you. A copy service is available to pull records and copy. Self serve copiers also in the lobby.

PACER: PACER is available online at http://pacer.flsd.uscourts.gov. Document images available. Records purged three years after case closed. New records are online after 1 day.

U.S. Bankruptcy Court
Southern District of Florida

Miami Division Room 1517, 51 SW 1st Ave, Miami, FL 33130 (courier address: Use mail address for courier delivery) 305-536-5216. www.flsb.uscourts.gov

Counties: Broward, Dade, Highlands, Indian River, Martin, Miami-Dade, Monroe, Okeechobee, Palm Beach, St. Lucie. Cases may also be assigned to Fort Lauderdale or to West Palm Beach.

Indexing & Storage: Cases indexed by debtor and creditors as well as by case number. New cases available in the index 48 hours after filing date. Open case records may be held in the Fort Lauderdale or West Palm Beach office, depending on the judge assigned.

Fee & Payment: Payment may be made by money order, cashier check. Business checks are not accepted. Personal checks are not accepted. Checks from law firms are accepted. Payee: U.S. Courts.

Phone Search: Automated voice case information service (VCIS) is available. Call VCIS at 800-473-0226 or 305-536-5979.

In Person Search: Fee charged if court conducts your in person search for you.

PACER: PACER is available online at http://pacer.flsb.uscourts.gov. Records purged every six months. New civil records are online after 1 day.

Electronic Filing: Currently in the process of implementing CM/ECF.

Florida County Courts

Court	Jurisdiction	No. of Courts	How Organized
Circuit Courts*	General	10	20 Circuits
County Courts*	Limited	13	
Combined Courts*		81	

* Profiled in this Sourcebook.

Court	CIVIL								
	Tort	Contract	Real Estate	Min. Claim	Max. Claim	Small Claims	Estate	Eviction	Domestic Relations
Circuit Courts*	X	X	X	$15,000	No Max		X		X
County Courts*	X	X	X	$0	$15,000	$2500		X	

Court	CRIMINAL				
	Felony	Misdemeanor	DWI/DUI	Preliminary Hearing	Juvenile
Circuit Courts*	X				X
County Courts*		X	X	X	

ADMINISTRATION

Office of State Courts Administrator, Supreme Court Bldg, 500 S Duval, Tallahassee, FL, 32399-1900; 850-922-5082, Fax: 850-488-0156. www.flcourts.org

COURT STRUCTURE

All counties have combined Circuit and County Courts. The Circuit Court is the court of general jurisdiction.

ONLINE ACCESS

53 Clerk of Courts/Recorders give access to index data at www.myflorida.com, a government sponsored web site. Supreme Court dockets are available online at http://jweb.f lcourts.org/pls/docket/ds_docket_search. The Supreme Court dockets are available online at web site listed above. A large number of the courts do offer online access to the public, usually, through the Clerk of the Circuit Court. The Florida Legislature mandated that court documents must be imaged and available for inspection over a publicly available web site. In response to concerns of identity theft and fraud, the Florida Legislature recently passed new laws concerning privacy of public documents on public web sites. These laws now make it possible for certain of these documents viewed on the Clerk web sites to be either redacted of sensitive information or in some cases removed completely. The Clerk of the Circuit Court cannot place an image or copy of the following documents on a publicly available Internet web site for general public display: Military discharges; Death certificates; Court files, records or papers relating to Family Law, Juvenile Law or Probate Law cases.

ADDITIONAL INFORMATION

All courts have one address and switchboard; however, the divisions within a court are completely separate. Requesters should specify which court and which division, e.g., Circuit Civil, County Civil, etc., the request is directed to, even though some counties will automatically check both with one request.

Fees are set by statute and are as follows as of July 1, 2004: Search Fee - $1.50 per name per year; Certification Fee - $1.50 per document plus copy fee; Copy Fee - $1.00 per page; some county copy fees may vary.

Most courts have very lengthy phone recording systems.

Alachua County

Circuit & County Courts PO Box 600, 201 E University Ave, Gainesville, FL 32602; 352-374-3636; Civil phone: 352-374-3636; Criminal phone: 352-374-3681 (felony); Fax: 352-381-0144-felony, 338-3207-civil. Hours: 8:15AM-5PM (EST). *Felony, Misdemeanor, Civil, Eviction, Small Claims, Probate.* www.alachuaclerk.org
Note: Misdeamenor records phone number-352-337-6250. Fax number for ancient (older) records is 352-337-6158.
Civil Records: Access: Phone, fax, mail, in person. Both court and visitors may perform in person

searches. Search fee: $1.50 per name per year. Required to search: name, years to search; also helpful: address. Civil cases indexed by defendant, plaintiff. Civil records on computer from 1979, some records on docket books. Civil records can be searched www.clerk-alachua-fl.org/clerk/pubrec.html. Also, access an index of judgments & recorded documents at www.myfloridacounty.com. Fees involved to order copies; save $1.50 per record by becoming a subscriber. Also, search probate and other ancient records free at www.clerk-alachua-fl.org/archive/default.cfm.
Criminal Records: Access: Fax, mail, in person. Both court and visitors may perform in person

searches. Search fee: $1.50 per name per year. Required to search: name, years to search, DOB; also helpful-address, SSN, race, sex. Criminal records on computer since 1974.
General Information: No juvenile, child abuse or sexual battery records released. Will fax results for $1.50 per page. Copy fee: $1.50 per page. Cert fee: $1.50. Payee: Clerk of Circuit Court. No Personal checks accepted. Visa, MC, Discover accepted. Prepayment required. Mail requests: SASE not required.

Baker County

Circuit & County Courts - Civil 339 E Macclenny Ave, Macclenny, FL 32063; 904-259-0202, 904-259-0209 (Circuit civ); Civil phone: 904-259-0208 (Cty); Probate phone: 904-259-0209; Fax: 904-259-4176. Hours: 8:30AM-5PM (EST). *Civil, Eviction, Small Claims, Probate.*
http://bakercountyfl.org/clerk
Civil Records: Access: Mail, in person, online. Both the court and visitors may perform in person searches. Search fee: $1.50 per name per year. Required to search: name, years to search; also helpful: address. Civil cases indexed by defendant, plaintiff. Civil records on computer back to 1996; prior on index cards and docket books. Access an index of judgments, liens, recorded documents at www.myfloridacounty.com. Fees involved to order copies; save $1.50 per record by becoming a subscriber.
General Information: Public Access terminal is available. No juvenile, child abuse or sexual battery records released. Copy fee: $1.00 per page. Cert fee: $1.50. Payee: Clerk of Circuit Court. Business checks accepted. Prepayment required. Mail requests: SASE preferred. Turnaround time 2 days.

Circuit & County Courts - Criminal 339 E Macclenny Ave, Macclenny, FL 32063; 904-259-0206; Fax: 904-259-4176. Hours: 8:30AM-5PM (EST). *Felony, Misdemeanor.*
http://bakercountyfl.org/clerk/
Note: County Court Misdemeanor phone nubmer is 904-259-0204.
Criminal Records: Access: Mail, in person, online. Only the court performs in person searches; visitors may not. Search fee: $1.50 per name per year. Required to search: name, years to search, DOB. Criminal records on computer since 1989. Some records on docket books. Access the circuit-wide criminal quick lookup at http://circuit8.org/golem/gencrim.html. Account and password is required; restricted usage. Call the court for details.
General Information: No juvenile or guardianship records released. Copy fee: $1.00 per page. Cert fee: $1.50. Payee: Clerk of Circuit Court. Business checks accepted. Prepayment required. Mail requests: SASE required. Mail turnaround time 1-2 days.

Bay County

Circuit Court - Civil PO Box 2269, Panama City, FL 32402; Civil phone: 850-747-5715; Criminal phone: 850-747-5123; Probate phone: 850-747-5118; Fax: 850-747-5188. Hours: 8AM-4:30PM (CST). *Civil Actions Over $15,000, Probate.*
www.baycoclerk.com
Civil Records: Access: Phone, fax, mail, in person, online. Both court and visitors may perform in person searches. Search fee: $1.50 per name per year. Required to search: name, years to search. Civil cases indexed by defendant, plaintiff. Civil records on computer from 1984, on microfiche from 1950 to 1980, archived from 1913 to 1979. Some records on dockets. Access an index of judgments, liens, recorded documents at www.myfloridacounty.com. Fees involved to order copies; save $1.50 per record by becoming a subscriber. Also, search the clerk's case search database for free at www.clerk.co.bay.fl.us/ovationweb/search.aspx.
General Information: Public Access terminal is available. No juvenile, adoption, child abuse or sexual battery records released. Will fax results $2.00 per page. Copy fee: $1.00 per page. Cert fee: $1.50. Payee: Clerk of Circuit Court. Personal checks not accepted. Prepayment required. Mail turnaround time 2 days.

Circuit Court - Criminal PO Box 2269, Panama City, FL 32402; 850-747-5125; Fax: 850-747-5188. Hours: 8AM-4:30PM (CST). *Felony.*
www.baycoclerk.com
Criminal Records: Access: Fax, mail, in person, online. Both court and visitors may perform in person searches. Search fee: $1.50 per name per year. Required to search: name, years to search, DOB; also helpful: SSN, signed release. Criminal records on computer back to 1986, on microfilm from 1938 to 1982, prior archived. Search the clerk's case search database for free at www.clerk.co.bay.fl.us/ovationweb/search.aspx.
General Information: No sealed, juvenile or expunged records released. Will fax results $2.00 per doc. Copy fee: $1.00 per page. Cert fee: $1.50 per page. Payee: Clerk of Circuit Court. Personal checks accepted. Prepayment required. Mail requests: SASE requested. Turnaround time 3-5 days.

County Court - Civil PO Box 2269, Panama City, FL 32402; 850-747-5114; Fax: 850-747-5188. Hours: 8AM-4:30PM (CST). *Civil Actions Under $15,000, Eviction, Small Claims.*
www.baycoclerk.com
Civil Records: Access: Phone, fax, mail, in person, online. Both court and visitors may perform in person searches. Search fee: $1.50 per name per year. Required to search: name, years to search. Civil cases indexed by defendant, plaintiff. Civil records on computer from 1986, on microfiche from 1950 to 1980, archived from 1913 to 1979. Some records on docket books. Access an index of judgments, liens, recorded documents at www.myfloridacounty.com. Fees involved to order copies; save $1.50 per record by becoming a subscriber. Also, search the clerk's case search database for free at www.clerk.co.bay.fl.us/ovationweb/search.aspx.
General Information: Public Access terminal is available. No juvenile, child abuse or sexual battery records released. Will fax results $2.00 per page. Copy fee: $1.00 per page. Cert fee: $1.50 per page. Payee: Clerk of Circuit Court. Personal checks accepted. Prepayment required. Mail requests: SASE requested. Turnaround time 2 days.

County Court - Misdemeanor PO Box 2269, Panama City, FL 32402; 850-747-5146; Fax: 850-747-5188. Hours: 8AM-4:30PM (CST). *Misdemeanor.* www.baycoclerk.com
Criminal Records: Access: Phone, fax, mail, in person, online. Both court and visitors may perform in person searches. Search fee: $1.50 per name per year. Required to search: name, years to search; also helpful: DOB, SSN. Criminal records on computer from 1984, felonies on microfilm from 1950 to 1987, archived from 1913. Misdemeanors from 1996-present; pending cases back to 1980. Search the clerk's case search database for free at www.clerk.co.bay.fl.us/ovationweb/search.aspx.
General Information: Public Access terminal is available. No sealed or expunged records released. Will fax results $2.00 per doc. Copy fee: $1.00 per page. Cert fee: $1.50. Payee: Clerk of Circuit Court. Personal checks accepted. Prepayment required. Mail requests: SASE requested. Turnaround time 7-10 days.

Bradford County

Circuit Court PO Drawer B, Starke, FL 32091; 904-964-6280; Fax: 904-964-4454. Hours: 8AM-5PM (EST). *Felony, Civil Actions Over $15,000, Probate.*
http://circuit8.org
Civil Records: Access: Phone, mail, in person, online. Both court and visitors may perform in person searches. Search fee: $1.50 per name per year. Required to search: name, years to search. Civil cases

indexed by defendant, plaintiff. Civil records on computer since late 1987, others on index books. Access an index of judgments, liens, recorded documents at www.myfloridacounty.com. Fees involved to order copies; save $1.50 per record by becoming a subscriber.
Criminal Records: Access: Phone, mail, in person, online. Both court and visitors may perform in person searches. Search fee: $1.50 per name per year. Required to search: name, years to search, DOB, SSN. Criminal records on computer since 1989, others on index books. Access to the circuit-wide criminal quick lookup is at http://circuit8.org/golem/gencrim.html. Account and password is required; restricted usage.
General Information: Public Access terminal is available. No juvenile, child abuse or sexual battery records released. Copy fee: $1.00 per page. Cert fee: $1.50 per document. Payee: Clerk at Circuit Court. Business checks accepted. Prepayment required. Mail requests: SASE required. Mail turnaround time 1 week.

County Court PO Drawer B, Starke, FL 32091; 904-964-6280; Fax: 904-964-4454. Hours: 8AM-5PM (EST). *Misdemeanor, Civil Actions Under $15,000, Eviction, Small Claims.*
www.bradford-co-fla.org
Civil Records: Access: Mail, fax, in person, online. Only the court performs in person searches; visitors may not. Search fee: $1.50 per name per year. Required to search: name, years to search. Civil cases indexed by defendant, plaintiff. Civil records on computer back to 1989. Some records on docket books, some microfilm. Access an index of judgments, liens, recorded documents at www.myfloridacounty.com. Fees involved to order copies; save $1.50 per record by becoming a subscriber.
Criminal Records: Access: Mail, fax, in person. Only the court performs in person searches; visitors may not. Search fee: $1.50 per name per year. Required to search: name, years to search, DOB, SSN. Criminal records on computer back to 1988. Records back to 1970's on docket books.
General Information: No juvenile records released. Copy fee: $1.00 per page. Cert fee: $1.50 per document. Payee: Clerk of Court. Business checks accepted. Prepayment required. Mail requests: SASE required. Mail turnaround time 2 days.

Brevard County

Circuit Court - Civil PO Box 2767, Offical Records Copy Desk, Titusville, FL 32781-2767; 321-264-5245; Fax: 321-264-5246. Hours: 8AM-5PM (EST). *Civil, Eviction, Small Claims, Probate.*
www.brevardclerk.us
Civil Records: Access: Phone, fax, mail, online, in person. Both court and visitors may perform in person searches. Search fee: $1.50 per name per year. Required to search: name, years to search. Civil cases indexed by defendant, plaintiff. Civil records on computer since 1987, on microfiche since early 1900s. Some records on docket books. Access County Court records free from FACTSweb at http://factscfweb1.brevardclerk.us/facts/facts_main_page.cfm. Online records back to 1988 can be searched by name, case number or citation number.
General Information: Public Access terminal is available. No juvenile, child abuse or sexual battery victim records released. If local, no add'l chargel. Fax fee for long distance $3.00 1st page, $1.00 each add'l page. Copy fee: $1.00 per page. Cert fee: $1.50. Payee: Circuit Clerk. Personal checks accepted. Check by fax or phone accepted. Visa, MC, Discover accepted. Prepayment required. Mail requests: SASE not required. Mail turnaround time 1 week.

Circuit Court - Felony PO Box H, 700 S Park Ave, Titusville, FL 32781-0239; 321-264-5245; Fax: 321-264-5345. Hours: 8AM-5PM (EST). *Felony.* www.brevardclerk.us

Criminal Records: Access: Phone, fax, mail, online, in person. Both court and visitors may perform in person searches. Search fee: $1.50 per name per year. Required to search: name, DOB, SSN. Criminal records on computer since 1988, on microfiche from early 1900s. Some records on docket books. Online access to county criminal court records is free through FACTSweb at http://factscfweb1.clerk.co.brevard.fl.us/facts/facts_main_page.cfm. Search by name, case number or citation number.

General Information: Public Access terminal is available. No juvenile, child abuse, sexual battery or adoption records released. Will fax results $1.00 per page. Fax fee for long distance $2.00. Copy fee: $1.00 per page. Cert fee: $1.50. Payee: Circuit Clerk. Personal checks accepted. Visa, MC accepted. Prepayment required. Mail requests: SASE not required. Mail turnaround time 1 week; phone turnaround is same day.

County Court - Misdemeanor PO Box 2767, 700 S Park Ave, Bldg B, Titusville, FL 32781; 321-637-5445; Fax: 321-264-5246. Hours: 8AM-4:30PM (EST). *Misdemeanor.* www.brevardclerk.us

Criminal Records: Access: Phone, fax, mail, online, in person. Both court and visitors may perform in person searches. Search fee: $1.50 per name per year. Required to search: name, years to search, DOB; also helpful: SSN, race, sex, signed release. Criminal records on computer since 1990, on microfiche from early 1900s. Some records on docket books and index cards. Access to county criminal records is free from http://factscfweb1.brevardclerk.us/facts/facts_main_page.cfm. Online records back to 1988 can be searched by name, case number or citation number.

General Information: Public Access terminal is available. No juvenile, child abuse, sexual battery or adoption records released. Will fax results $1.00 per page. Fax fee for long distance $2.00 for 1st page. Copy fee: $1.00 per page. Cert fee: $1.50. Payee: Circuit Clerk. Personal checks accepted. Visa, MC, AmEx, Discover. Prepayment required. Mail requests: SASE not required. Mail turnaround time 1 week; phone turnaround is 2 days.

Broward County

Circuit & County Courts 201 SE 6th St, Ft Lauderdale, FL 33301; 954-712-7899; Civil phone: 954-831-5740; Criminal phone: 954-831-5680; Probate phone: 954-831-7154; Fax: 954-831-7166. Hours: 9AM-4PM (EST). *Felony, Misdemeanor, Civil, Eviction, Small Claims, Probate.* www.browardclerk.org

Civil Records: Access: Phone, fax, mail, online, in person, email. Both court and visitors may perform in person searches. Search fee: $1.50 per name per year. Add $4.00 for written response (affidavit). Required to search: name, years to search. Civil cases indexed by defendant, plaintiff. Civil records on computer from 1986. Some records on dockets. Will search back 10 years. The county clerk online fee system is being replaced by a web system. Basic information is free at www.browardclerk.org/bccoc2/default.asp. Search by name or case number or case type.

Criminal Records: Access: Phone, fax, mail, online, in person, email. Both court and visitors may perform in person searches. Search fee: $1.50 per name per year. Add $4.00 for written response (affidavit). Required to search: name, years to search, DOB; also helpful: SSN. Criminal records on computer since 1980. The county clerk online fee system is being replaced by a web system. The web allows basic info

free at www.browardclerk.org/bccoc2/default.asp Search by name or case number or case type. The "Premium Access" for detailed case information requires a fee, registration and password. Call 954-831-5654 for information or visit the website.

General Information: Public Access terminal is available. Copy fee: $1.00 per page. Cert fee: $1.50. Payee: Clerk of the Court. Only cashiers checks and money orders accepted. Prepayment required. Mail turnaround time 1-14 days.

Calhoun County

Circuit & County Court 20859 E Central Ave, #130 (425 E Central), Blountstown, FL 32424; 850-674-4545; Criminal phone: 850-674-8764; Fax: 850-674-5553. Hours: 8AM-4PM (CST). *Felony, Misdemeanor, Civil, Eviction, Small Claims, Probate.* www.calhounclerk.com

Civil Records: Access: Phone, mail, in person, online. Both court and visitors may perform in person searches. Search fee: $7.00 per name. Required to search: name, years to search. Civil cases indexed by defendant, plaintiff. Civil records on computer back to 1986, books from 1970s. Access an index of judgments, liens, recorded documents at www.myfloridacounty.com. Fees involved to order copies; save $1.50 per record by becoming a subscriber.

Criminal Records: Access: Phone, mail, in person. Both court and visitors may perform in person searches. Search fee: $7.00 per name. Required to search: name, years to search. Criminal records on computer back to 1986, on docket books from 1970s.

General Information: Public Access terminal is available. No juvenile, child abuse or sexual battery records released. Copy fee: $1.00 per page. Cert fee: $1.50. Payee: Clerk of Court. Personal checks accepted. Prepayment required. Mail requests: SASE required. Mail turnaround time 2 days.

Charlotte County

Circuit & County Courts - Civil Division PO Box 511687, Punta Gorda, FL 33951-1687; 941-637-2279; Fax: 941-637-2116. Hours: 8AM-5PM (EST). *Civil, Eviction, Small Claims, Probate.* http://co.charlotte.fl.us/clrkinfo/clerk_default.htm

Civil Records: Access: Mail, in person, online. Both court and visitors may perform in person searches. Search fee: $1.50 per name per year. Required to search: name, years to search. Civil cases indexed by defendant, plaintiff. Civil records on computer back to 1982, on microfiche since 1987. Online access to civil and probate records is by subscription, see the website. Original payment is $186.00 ($150 refundable) plus a usage fee based on number of transactions. Allows printing of copies. For more information, call 941-637-4848. Access an index of judgments, liens, recorded documents at www.myfloridacounty.com. Fees involved to order copies; save $1.50 per record by becoming a subscriber.

General Information: Public Access terminal is available. No juvenile, child abuse, sexual battery, adoption records released. Fee to fax results is $2.00 per page. Copy fee: $1.00 per page. Cert fee: $1.50 per document. Payee: Clerk of Circuit Court. Personal checks accepted. Prepayment required. Mail requests: SASE requested. Turnaround time 1-2 days.

Circuit & County Courts - Criminal Division PO Box 511687, Punta Gorda, FL 33951-1687; 941-637-2269; Fax: 941-637-2159. Hours: 8AM-5PM (EST). *Felony, Misdemeanor.* http://co.charlotte.fl.us/clrkinfo/clerk_default.htm

Criminal Records: Access: Phone, mail, in person, online. Both court and visitors may perform in person searches. Search fee: $1.50 per name per year.

Required to search: name, years to search, DOB; also helpful: address, SSN, race, sex. Criminal records on computer since 1985, misdemeanors on index cards, felonies on judgment books, imaging on disc from 1993. Online commercial access to criminal records by subscription from the website. For more information, call 941-637-2199. The free access at https://www.co.charlotte.fl.us/scripts/mgrqispi.dll?appname=MPI%20Criminal&prgname=PUBSEARCHF requires that you provide a name and birthdate.

General Information: Public Access terminal is available. No juvenile, child abuse or sexual battery records released. Fee to fax results is $2.00 per page. Copy fee: $1.00 per page. Cert fee: $1.50. Payee: Clerk of Circuit Court. Personal checks accepted. Prepayment required. Mail requests: SASE requested. Turnaround time 1 week.

Citrus County

Circuit Court 110 N Apopka, Rm 101, Inverness, FL 34450-4299; 352-341-6400; Fax: 352-341-6413. Hours: 8AM-5PM (EST). *Felony, Civil Actions Over $15,000, Probate.* www.clerk.citrus.fl.us

Marriage license data is found online at the web site.

Civil Records: Access: Phone, fax, mail, in person, online. Both court and visitors may perform in person searches. Search fee: $1.50 per name per year. Required to search: name, years to search; also helpful: address. Indicate on search request the type(s) of cases to search. Civil cases indexed by defendant, plaintiff. Civil records on computer from 1989, archived from 1940 to 1991. Some records on docket books. By phone only back to 1989. The web page has a subscription service to view court record index, fees are involved. Images are not on this system. Alsom there is an index of judgments, liens, recorded documents at www.myfloridacounty.com. Fees involved to order copies; save $1.50 per record by becoming a subscriber.

Criminal Records: Access: Phone, fax, mail, in person, online. Both court and visitors may perform in person searches. Search fee: $1.50 per name per year. Required to search: name, years to search, DOB; also helpful: address, SSN, race, sex. Criminal records on computer from 1989, on microfiche from 1948 to 1987, archived from 1940-1991. The web page has a subscription service to view court record index, fees are involved. Images are not on this system. By phone only back to 1989.

General Information: Public Access terminal is available. No juvenile, adoption, child abuse or sexual battery records released. Will fax results $1.00 per page if local; $2.00 per page long distance. Copy fee: $1.00 per page. Cert fee: $1.50. Payee: Clerk of Circuit Court. Personal checks accepted. Prepayment required. Mail requests: SASE required. Mail turnaround time 1-2 days.

County Court 110 N Apopka, Rm 101, Inverness, FL 34450; 352-341-6400; Fax: 352-341-6413. Hours: 8AM-5PM (EST). *Misdemeanor, Civil Actions Under $15,000, Eviction, Small Claims.* www.clerk.citrus.fl.us

Civil Records: Access: Phone, fax, mail, in person, online. Both court and visitors may perform in person searches. Search fee: $1.50 per name per year. Required to search: name, years to search; also helpful: address. Civil cases indexed by defendant, plaintiff. Civil records on computer from 1990, prior records on docket books. The web page has a subscription service to view court record index, fees are involved. Images are not on this system. Also, access an index of judgments, liens, recorded documents at www.myfloridacounty.com. Fees involved to order copies; save $1.50 per record by becoming a subscriber.

Criminal Records: Access: Phone, fax, mail, in person, online. Both court and visitors may perform in person searches. Search fee: $1.50 per name per year. Required to search: name, years to search, DOB; also helpful: address, SSN, race, sex. Criminal records on computer from 1990, prior records on docket books. The web page has a subscription service to view court record index, fees are involved. Images are not on this system.

General Information: Public Access terminal is available. (Criminal only.) No juvenile, child abuse or sexual battery records released. Will fax results $1.00 per page. Fax fee for long distance $2.00 per page. Copy fee: $1.00 per page. Cert fee: $1.50. Payee: Clerk of Circuit Court. Personal checks accepted. Prepayment required. Mail requests: SASE required. Mail turnaround time 1-3 days.

Clay County

Circuit Court PO Box 698, Green Cove Springs, FL 32043; 904-284-6302; Fax: 904-284-6390. Hours: 8:30AM-4:30PM (EST). *Felony, Civil Actions Over $15,000, Probate.*
http://clerk.co.clay.fl.us
Civil Records: Access: Mail, online, in person. Both court and visitors may perform in person searches. Search fee: $1.50 per name per year. Required to search: name, years to search; also helpful: address. Civil cases indexed by defendant, plaintiff. Civil records on computer from 1985, prior records on docket books. Clerk provides free access to records at http://clerk.co.clay.fl.us/asp/pub_pi_queryname.asp. Access an index of judgments, liens, recorded documents at www.myfloridacounty.com. Fees involved to order copies; save $1.50 per record by becoming a subscriber.
Criminal Records: Access: Mail, in person. Both court and visitors may perform in person searches. Search fee: $1.50 per name per year. Required to search: name, years to search, DOB; also helpful: address, SSN, race, sex. Criminal records (Felony) on computer from 1967, prior records on docket books. Access to criminal records is free at http://clerk.co.clay.fl.us/asp/cr_pi_queryname.asp.
General Information: Public Access terminal is available. No juvenile, child abuse or sexual battery records released. Copy fee: $1.00 per page. Cert fee: $1.50. Payee: Clerk of Circuit Court. Only cashiers checks and money orders accepted. Prepayment required. Mail turnaround time 1-3 days.

County Court PO Box 698, Green Cove Springs, FL 32043; 904-284-6316; Fax: 904-284-6390. Hours: 8:30AM-4:30PM (EST). *Misdemeanor, Civil Actions Under $15,000, Eviction, Small Claims.*
http://clerk.co.clay.fl.us
Civil Records: Access: Mail, online, in person. Both court and visitors may perform in person searches. Search fee: $1.50 per name per year. Required to search: name, years to search; also helpful: address. Civil cases indexed by defendant, plaintiff. Civil records on computer back to 1992, prior records on docket books. Online access to records is free at http://clerk.co.clay.fl.us/asp/pub_pi_queryname.asp. Online records go back to 1992.
Criminal Records: Access: Mail, in person, online. Both court and visitors may perform in person searches. Search fee: $1.50 per name per year. Required to search: name, years to search, DOB, SSN; also helpful: address, race, sex. Criminal records on computer back to 1992, prior records on docket books. Access to criminal records is free at http://clerk.co.clay.fl.us/asp/cr_pi_queryname.asp.
General Information: Public Access terminal is available. No juvenile, child abuse or sexual battery records released. Fee to fax results is $2.00 1st page; $1.00 each add'l. Copy fee: $1.00 per page. Cert fee:

$1.50. Payee: Clerk of Circuit Court. Personal checks accepted. Prepayment required. Mail turnaround time 1-2 days.

Collier County

Circuit Court PO Box 413044, Naples, FL 34101-3044; 239-732-2646; Criminal phone: 239-732-2648. Hours: 8AM-5PM (EST). *Felony, Civil Actions Over $15,000, Probate.*
www.clerk.collier.fl.us
Civil Records: Access: Mail, online, in person. Both court and visitors may perform in person searches. Search fee: $1.50 per name per year. Required to search: name, years to search. Civil cases indexed by defendant, plaintiff. Civil records on computer from 1990, on microfiche from 1922 to 1997, archived from 1922. Online access is free at www.clerk.collier.fl.us/clerkspublicac/Default.htm. Records include probate, traffic and domestic. Access an index of judgments, liens, recorded documents at www.myfloridacounty.com. Fees involved to order copies; save $1.50 per record by becoming a subscriber.
Criminal Records: Access: Mail, online, in person. Both court and visitors may perform in person searches. Search fee: $1.50 per name per year. Required to search: name, years to search, DOB; also helpful: SSN, add'l your phone number. Criminal records on computer from 1990, on microfiche from 1922 to 1994, archived from 1922. Criminal records access is free at www.clerk.collier.fl.us/clerkspublicac/Default.htm.
General Information: No sealed by court or statute records released. Copy fee: $1.50 per page. Cert fee: $1.50. Payee: Clerk of Circuit Court. Personal checks accepted. Prepayment required. Mail requests: SASE required. Mail turnaround time within 1 week.

County Court PO Box 413044, Naples, FL 34101-3044; Civil phone: 239-732-2646; Criminal phone: 239-732-2648; Fax: 239-774-8020. Hours: 8AM-5PM (EST). *Misdemeanor, Civil Actions Under $15,000, Eviction, Small Claims.*
www.clerk.collier.fl.us
Civil Records: Access: Mail, online, in person. Both court and visitors may perform in person searches. Search fee: $1.50 per name per year. Required to search: name, years to search; also helpful: address. Civil cases indexed by defendant, plaintiff. Civil records on computer from 1990, on microfiche from 1922 to 1995. Online access is free at www.clerk.collier.fl.us/clerkspublicac/Default.htm. Records include probate, traffic and domestic.
Criminal Records: Access: Mail, online, in person. Both court and visitors may perform in person searches. Search fee: $1.50 per name per year. Required to search: name, years to search, DOB; also helpful: address, SSN, race, sex. Criminal records on computer from 1990, on microfiche from 1922 to 1995. Criminal records access is free at www.clerk.collier.fl.us/clerkspublicac/Default.htm.
General Information: Public Access terminal is available. No juvenile, child abuse or sexual battery records released. Copy fee: $1.50 per page. Cert fee: $1.50. Payee: Clerk of County Court. Personal checks accepted. Prepayment required. Mail requests: SASE required. Mail turnaround time 1 week.

Columbia County

Circuit & County Courts PO Drawer 2069, Lake City, FL 32056; 386-758-1342; Civil phone: 386-758-1036; Criminal phone: 386-758-1164. Hours: 8AM-5PM (EST). *Felony, Misdemeanor, Circuit/County, Civil, Eviction, Small Claims, Probate.* www.columbiaclerk.com
Civil Records: Access: Mail, in person, online. Both court and visitors may perform in person searches.

Search fee: $1.50 per name per year. Fee is per department. Required to search: name, years to search. Civil cases indexed by defendant, plaintiff. Civil records on computer from 1987, archived from 1800s. DOB and SSN also helpful for searching. Access an index of judgments, liens, recorded documents at www.myfloridacounty.com. Fees involved to order copies; save $1.50 per record by becoming a subscriber.
Criminal Records: Access: In person only. Both court and visitors may perform in person searches. Search fee: $1.50 per name per year. Fee is per department. Required to search: name, years to search, DOB; also helpful: SSN. Criminal records on computer from 1987, archived from 1800s.
General Information: Public Access terminal is available. No names of victims of sex related offenses, juveniles, incompetence or mental health records released. Fee to fax results is $3.00 per page. Copy fee: $1.00 per page. Cert fee: $1.50. Payee: Clerk of Circuit Court. Cashier's check or money orders only. Prepayment required. Mail requests: SASE required. Mail turnaround time 1 day.

Dade County

Circuit & County Courts - Civil 73 W Flagler St, #242, Miami, FL 33130; 305-275-1155; Fax: 305-349-7410 Civil. Hours: 9AM-4PM (EST). *Civil, Eviction, Small Claims, Probate.*
www.miami-dadeclerk.com/dadecoc
Note: Better known as Miami-Dade County. The County Court hears civil actions up to $15,000.

Civil Records: Access: Phone, fax, mail, online, in person. Both court and visitors may perform in person searches. Search fee: $1.50 per name per year. Required to search: name, years to search. Civil and domestic relations cases indexed by plaintiff/petitioner, defendant/respondent. Civil and domestic relations records on computer back to 1973; archives from 1836; microfilm in county recorder office. Access a wealth of information through the Clerk of Court's online services website. Choose between Standard (free of charge) and Premier (fee-based) online services. By subscribing to the Premier service, you may access 3 advanced options: Civil/Family/Probate, Public Records, and Traffic. Fees are based on number of units purchased; minimum $5.00, paid in advance. Also, though limited, you may search felony, misdemeanor, civil and county ordinance violations free at. www.miami-dadeclerk.com/cjis/search1.asp. Also, search Civil/Family/Probate free at www.miami-dadeclerk.com/default.asp and choose Standard Case Search. Also, now search traffic cases free at www.miami-dadeclerk.com/spirit/publicsearch/defnamesearch.asp.
General Information: Public Access terminal is available. No juvenile, adoption, mental health records releases. Will not fax results. Copy fee: $1.00 per page. Cert fee: $1.50. Payee: Clerk of Circuit & County Courts. Personal checks and money orders accepted; will accept Visa/MC. Prepayment required. Mail requests: SASE requested. Turnaround time 10 days.

Circuit & County Courts - Criminal 1351 NW 12th St, #9000, Miami, FL 33125; 305-275-1155; Criminal phone: 305-548-5527; Fax: 305-548-5526. 9AM-4PM (EST). *Felony, Misdemeanor.*
www.miami-dadeclerk.com/dadecoc/
Note: Better known as Miami-Dade County. Although located in the same building, the records of the felony and the misdemeanor courts are not co-mingled. Search the Circuit Court for felony and the County Court for misdememanor records.

Criminal Records: Access: Phone, fax, mail, online, in person. Both court and visitors may perform in person searches. Search fee: $1.50 per year. Required to search: name, years to search, DOB; also helpful: address, SSN, race, sex. Criminal records on computer back to 1971, on microfiche from 1975, archived from 1836. The website offers free and Premier (Fee Based) Online Services. Though limited, you may search felony, misdemeanor, civil and county ordinance violations free at www.miami-dadeclerk.com/cjis/search1.asp. By subscribing to the Clerk's Premier Services, you will be able to access advanced options in three of the Clerk's internet-based systems: Civil/Family/Probate, Public Records, and Traffic. Fees are $.25 per search, paid in advance. Search traffic cases free at www.miami-dadeclerk.com/spirit/publicsearch/defnamesearch.asp.

General Information: Public Access terminal is available. No juvenile, child abuse or sexual battery records released. Copy fee: $1.00 per page. Cert fee: $1.50. Payee: Clerk of Circuit and County Court. Personal checks accepted. Visa, MC accepted. Credit cards accepted in person only. Prepayment required. Mail requests: SASE required. Mail turnaround time 10-15 days.

De Soto County

Circuit & County Courts 115 E Oak St, Arcadia, FL 34266; 863-993-4876; Civil phone: 863-993-4880; Probate phone: 863-993-4880; Fax: 863-993-4669. Hours: 8AM-5PM (EST). *Felony, Misdemeanor, Civil, Eviction, Small Claims, Probate.* http://12circuit.state.fl.us

Note: County Court & Evictions 863-993-4880.

Civil Records: Access: Phone, fax, mail, in person, online. Both court and visitors may perform in person searches. Search fee: $1.50 per name per year. Required to search: name, years to search. Civil cases indexed by defendant, plaintiff. Civil records on computer from 1986, on microfiche from 1974, archived from 1887. Access an index of judgments, liens, recorded documents at www.myfloridacounty.com. Fees involved to order copies; save $1.50 per record by becoming a subscriber.

Criminal Records: Access: Phone, fax, mail, in person. Both court and visitors may perform in person searches. Search fee: $1.50 per name per year. Required to search: name, years to search, DOB; also helpful: SSN, aliases. Criminal records on computer since 1986, archived since 1887.

General Information: Public Access terminal is available. No juvenile or sex related records released. Will fax results $1.00 per page. Copy fee: $1.00 per page. Cert fee: $1.50. Payee: Clerk of the Court. Personal checks accepted. Prepayment required. Mail requests: SASE requested. Turnaround time 2 days.

Dixie County

Circuit & County Courts PO Drawer 1206, Cross City, FL 32628-1206; 352-498-1200; Fax: 352-498-1201. Hours: 9AM-5PM (EST). *Felony, Misdemeanor, Civil, Eviction, Small Claims, Probate.*

Civil Records: Access: Mail, in person, online. Both the court and visitors may perform in person searches. Search fee: $1.50 per name per year. Required to search: name, years to search; also helpful: address. Civil cases indexed by defendant, plaintiff. Civil records on computer since 1987, archived to 1920's. Access an index of judgments, liens, recorded documents at www.myfloridacounty.com. Fees involved to order copies; save $1.50 per record by becoming a subscriber.

Criminal Records: Access: Mail, in person. Both the court and visitors may perform in person searches. Search fee: $1.50 per name per year. Required to search: name, years to search, DOB; also helpful: address, SSN, race, sex. Criminal records on computer since 1989, archived to 1920's.

General Information: No juvenile, child abuse or sexual battery records released. Fee to fax results is $1.00 per page. Copy fee: $1.00 per page. Cert fee: $1.50 per page. Payee: Clerk of Circuit Court. Personal checks accepted. Prepayment required. Mail requests: SASE required. Mail turnaround: 1 week.

Duval County

Circuit & County Courts - Civil Division
330 E Bay St, Jacksonville, FL 32202; 904-630-2038; Fax: 904-630-7506. Hours: 8:30AM-4:30PM (EST). *Civil, Eviction, Small Claims, Probate.* www.duval.fl.us.landata.com

Civil Records: Access: Fax, mail, online, in person. Both court and visitors may perform in person searches. Search fee: $1.50 per name per year. Required to search: name, years to search; also helpful: address. Civil cases indexed by defendant, plaintiff. Civil records (Circuit) on computer from 1968, county from 1984. County civil on index books from 1975 to 1986, prior on docket books. Circuit civil on index books from 1950s to 1968. Two sources are available. First, online access requires $100.00 setup fee, but no access charges. For more information, call 904-630-1212 x5115. Access an index of judgments, liens, recorded documents at www.myfloridacounty.com. Fees involved to order copies; save $1.50 per record by becoming a subscriber.

General Information: Public Access terminal is available. No juvenile, child abuse or sexual battery records released. Fee to fax results is $1.00 per page. Copy fee: $1.00 per page. Cert fee: $1.50. Payee: Clerk of Circuit Court. Business checks accepted. Prepayment required. Mail turnaround time for county records 5-7 days, circuit 2-4 days.

Circuit & County Courts - Criminal Division
330 E Bay St, Rm M101, Jacksonville, FL 32202; 904-630-2065; Fax: 904-630-7505. Hours: 8AM-5PM (EST). *Felony, Misdemeanor.* www.duval.fl.us.landata.com

Criminal Records: Access: Mail, fax, online, in person. Visitors must perform in person searches for themselves. No search fee. Required to search: name, years to search, DOB; also helpful: address, SSN, race, sex. Criminal records (Circuit) on computer from 1968, county from 1986. County civil on index books from 1975 to 1986, prior on docket books. Circuit civil on index books from 1900s to 1968. Online access to criminal records requires $100.00 setup fee, but no access charges. Records go back to 1992. For more information, call Leslie Peterson at 904-630-1212 x5115. Also, recorded documents are free at the Clerk of Circuit Court search site at www.duval.fl.us.landata.com/SearchDisclaimer.asp.

General Information: Public Access terminal is available. No juvenile, child abuse or sexual battery records released. Copy fee: $1.00 per page. Cert fee: $1.50. Payee: Clerk of the Court. Business checks accepted. Prepayment required. Mail requests: SASE helpful. Turnaround time 2-3 days.

Escambia County

Circuit & County Courts - Civil Division
190 Governmental Center, Pensacola, FL 32501; 850-595-4170; Civil phone: 850-595-4130 (Circ Ct. Civil); Probate phone: 850-595-4300. Hours: 8AM-5PM (CST). *Civil, Eviction, Small Claims, Probate.* www.clerk.co.escambia.fl.us

Note: Mail address is PO Box 333, Pensacola FL 32591-0333.

Civil Records: Access: Phone, fax, mail, in person, online. Both court and visitors may perform in person searches. Search fee: $1.00 per year per name. Required to search: name, years to search; also helpful: address. Civil cases indexed by defendant,

plaintiff. Couny civil records on computer from mid 1986, Circuit Court civil on computer from mid 1987. Prior on index books. Judgments and small claims on microfiche from 1952, evictions from 1973. Online access to county clerk records is free at www.clerk.co.escambia.fl.us/public_records.html. Search by name, citation, or case number. Small claims, traffic, and marriage data also available. Access an index of judgments, liens, recorded documents at www.myfloridacounty.com. Fees involved to order copies; save $1.50 per record by becoming a subscriber.

General Information: Public Access terminal is available. No juvenile, child abuse, adoption, mental health or sexual battery records released. Will fax results; $1.00 for call and $6.00 for cover letter per response. Copy fee: $1.00 per page. Cert fee: $1.50. Payee: Clerk of Circuit Court. Personal checks accepted. Prepayment required. Mail requests: SASE requested. Turnaround time 1-5 days.

Circuit & County Courts - Criminal Division
190 Governmental Center, Pensacola, FL 32501; 850-595-4150; Criminal phone: 850-595-4185 County; Fax: 850-595-4198. Hours: 8AM-5PM (CST). *Felony, Misdemeanor.* www.clerk.co.escambia.fl.us

Note: Misdemeanor records phone is 850-595-4185.

Criminal Records: Access: Fax, mail, in person, online. Both the court and visitors may perform in person searches. Search fee: $1.50 per name per year. Required to search: name, years to search, DOB; also helpful: address, SSN, race, sex. Criminal records on computer and microfiche from 1973, archived from 1940 to 1972. Online access to criminal records is free at www.clerk.co.escambia.fl.us/public_records.html. Search by name, citation, or case number.

General Information: Public Access terminal is available. No juvenile, child abuse, mental health, adoption or sexual battery records released. Will fax results $1.00 per page. Over 5 pages $2.00, each add'l group of 5 pages charge increases by $1.00, plus phone charge. Copy fee: $1.00 per page. Cert fee: $1.50. Payee: Clerk of Circuit Court. Personal checks accepted. Prepayment required. Mail requests: SASE requested. Turnaround time within 1 week.

Flagler County

Circuit & County Courts PO Box 787, Bunnell, FL 32110; Civil phone: 386-437-7430; Criminal phone: 386-437-7419; Fax: 386-437-7454 crim; 586-2116 civil. Hours: 8:30AM-4:30PM (EST). *Felony, Misdemeanor, Civil, Eviction, Small Claims, Probate.* http://clerk.co.flagler.fl.us

Civil Records: Access: Phone, fax, mail, in person, email, online. Both court and visitors may perform in person searches. Search fee: $1.50 per name per year. Required to search: name, years to search; also helpful: address. Civil cases indexed by defendant, plaintiff. Civil records on computer from 1990. All archived from 1917, some on index books. Access an index of judgments, liens, recorded documents at www.myfloridacounty.com. Fees involved to order copies; save $1.50 per record by becoming a subscriber.

Criminal Records: Access: Phone, fax, mail, in person, email. Both court and visitors may perform in person searches. Search fee: $1.50 per name per year. Required to search: name, years to search, DOB; also helpful: address, SSN, race, sex. Felony records on computer back to 1999; misdemeanors back to 1988. All archived from 1917, some on index books.

General Information: Public Access terminal is available. No juvenile, adoption, child abuse or sexual battery records released. Will fax results $1.00 per page. Copy fee: $1.00 per page. Cert fee: $1.50. Payee: Clerk of Circuit Court. Local business checks, money orders, or cashiers checks accepted. Prepayment required. Mail turnaround time 5-7 days.

Franklin County

Circuit & County Courts 33 Market St, #203, Apalachicola, FL 32320; 850-653-8862; Fax: 850-653-2261. Hours: 8:30AM-4:30PM (EST). *Felony, Misdemeanor, Civil, Eviction, Small Claims, Probate.* www.franklinclerk.com

Civil Records: Access: Mail, in person, online. Both court and visitors may perform in person searches. Search fee: $1.50 per name per year. Required to search: name, years to search; also helpful: address. Civil cases indexed by defendant, plaintiff. Civil records on computer from 3/92. Access an index of judgments, liens, recorded documents at www.myfloridacounty.com. Fees involved to order copies; save $1.50 per record by becoming a subscriber.

Criminal Records: Access: Mail, in person, online. Both court and visitors may perform in person searches. Search fee: $1.50 per name per year. Required to search: name, years to search, DOB; also helpful: address, SSN, race, sex. Criminal records on computer since 1989. Public records may be obtained at https://www.myfloridacounty.com/subscription/. Fees are involved.

General Information: Public Access terminal is available. No juvenile, child abuse or sexual battery records released. Will fax results if prepaid. Copy fee: $1.00 per page. Cert fee: $1.50. Payee: Clerk of Circuit Court. In county personal checks accepted. Prepayment required. Mail requests: SASE requested. Turnaround time 2-5 days.

Gadsden County

Circuit & County Courts - Criminal Division 24 N Adams, Quincy, FL 32351; 850-875-8610; Probate phone: 850-875-8622; Fax: 850-875-7265. Hours: 8:30AM-5PM (EST). *Felony, Misdemeanor.* www.co.leon.fl.us/court/court.htm Requests may be sent to PO Box 1649, ZIP is 32353

Criminal Records: Access: Fax, mail, in person. Only the court performs in person searches; visitors may not. Search fee: $1.50 per name per year. Required to search: name, years to search, DOB; also helpful: SSN. Criminal records on computer from 1984, some on index books and cards.

General Information: No juvenile or sex offender records released. Will fax results for $1.00 per page. Copy fee: $.25 per page. Cert fee: $1.15 per page. Payee: Clerk of Circuit Court. Personal checks accepted. Prepayment required. Mail requests: SASE not required. Mail turnaround time 3-5 days.

Circuit & County Courts - Civil Division PO Box 1649, Quincy, FL 32353; 850-875-8621; Fax: 850-875-8612. Hours: 8:30AM-5PM (EST). *Civil, Eviction, Small Claims, Probate.* www.clerk.co.gadsden.fl.us

Civil Records: Access: Phone, fax, mail, online, email, in person. Both court and visitors may perform in person searches. Search fee: $1.50 per name, per yr. Required to search: name, years to search. Civil cases indexed by defendant, plaintiff. Civil records on computer since 1984. Access to the index of civil court judgments, etc. are free from the County Clerk at www.clerk.co.gadsden.fl.us. Also, access an index of judgments, liens, recorded documents at www.myfloridacounty.com. Fees involved to order copies; save $1.50 per record by becoming a subscriber.

General Information: Public Access terminal is available. No juvenile, child abuse or sexual battery records released. Will fax results $1.00 per page. Copy fee: $.25 per page. Cert fee: $1.75. Payee: Clerk of Circuit Court. Only cashiers checks and money orders accepted. Prepayment required. Mail requests: SASE required. Mail turnaround time 1 week.

Gilchrist County

Circuit & County Courts PO Box 37, Trenton, FL 32693; 352-463-3170; Fax: 352-463-3166. Hours: 8;30AM-5PM (EST). *Felony, Misdemeanor, Civil, Eviction, Small Claims, Probate.* www.co.gilchrist.fl.us/cophone

Civil Records: Access: Mail, in person, online. Only the court performs in person searches; visitors may not. Search fee: $1.50 per name per year. Add $4.00 for written response (affidavit). Required to search: name, years to search; also helpful: address. Civil cases indexed by defendant, plaintiff. Civil records on computer from 1987, prior on index books. Search judgements and liens online at the website.

Criminal Records: Access: Mail, in person. Only the court performs in person searches; visitors may not. Search fee: $1.50 per name per year. Add $4.00 for written response (affidavit). Required to search: name, years to search, DOB; also helpful: address, SSN, race, sex. Criminal records on computer since 1989, prior on index books.

General Information: No juvenile, child abuse or sexual battery records released. Will fax results $1.00 per page; available for civil only. Copy fee: $1.00 per page. Cert fee: $1.50. Payee: Clerk of Circuit Court. Personal checks accepted. Prepayment required. Mail requests: SASE required. Mail turnaround: 2-3 days.

Glades County

Circuit & County Courts PO Box 10, Moore Haven, FL 33471; 863-946-6011; Fax: 863-946-0560. Hours: 8AM-5PM (EST). *Felony, Misdemeanor, Civil, Eviction, Small Claims, Probate.*

Civil Records: Access: Mail, in person, online. Only the court performs in person searches; visitors may not. Search fee: $1.50 per name per year. Add $4.00 for written response (affidavit). Required to search: name, years to search; also helpful: address. Civil cases indexed by defendant, plaintiff. Civil records on computer from 1991. Access an index of judgments, liens, recorded documents at www.myfloridacounty.com. Fees involved to order copies; save $1.50 per record by becoming a subscriber.

Criminal Records: Access: Mail, fax, in person. Only the court performs in person searches; visitors may not. Search fee: $1.50 per name per year. Add $4.00 for written response (affidavit). Required to search: name, years to search, DOB; also helpful: address, SSN, race, sex. Criminal records on computer from 1991.

General Information: No juvenile, child abuse or sexual battery records released. Will fax results for $3.00 per page. Copy fee: $1.00 per page. Cert fee: $1.50. Payee: Clerk of Circuit Court. Personal checks accepted. Prepayment required. Mail requests: SASE not required. Mail turnaround time 2-3 days.

Gulf County

Circuit & County Courts 1000 Cecil Costin Blvd, Port St Joe, FL 32456; 850-229-6112; Fax: 850-229-6174. Hours: 9AM-5PM (EST). *Felony, Misdemeanor, Civil, Eviction, Small Claims, Probate.* www.gulfclerk.com

Civil Records: Access: Fax, mail, in person, online. Only the court performs in person searches; visitors may not. Search fee: $1.50 per name per year. Required to search: name, years to search. Civil cases indexed by defendant, plaintiff. Civil records on computer from 1990; archived to 1925. Access an index of judgments, liens, recorded documents at www.myfloridacounty.com. Fees involved to order copies; save $1.50 per record by becoming a subscriber.

Criminal Records: Access: Fax, mail, in person. Only the court performs in person searches; visitors may not. Search fee: $1.50 per name per year. Required to search: name, years to search, DOB; also helpful: SSN. Criminal records on computer from 1990; archived to 1925.

General Information: No juvenile, adoption, child abuse or sexual battery records released. Will fax results $1.50 per page. Copy fee: $.15 per page. Cert fee: $1.50. Payee: Clerk of Circuit Court. Personal checks accepted. Prepayment required. Mail requests: SASE required. Mail turnaround time 1-3 days.

Hamilton County

Circuit & County Courts 207 NE 1st St, #106, Jasper, FL 32052; 386-792-1288; Fax: 386-792-3524. 8:30AM-4:30PM (EST). *Felony, Misdemeanor, Civil, Eviction, Small Claims, Probate.*

Civil Records: Access: Mail, in person, online. Both court and visitors may perform in person searches. Search fee: $1.50 per name per year. Required to search: name, years to search; also helpful: address. Civil records on computer from 1/91, county civil from 3/91. Access an index of judgments, liens, recorded documents at www.myfloridacounty.com. Fees involved to order copies; save $1.50 per record by becoming a subscriber.

Criminal Records: Access: Mail, in person. Both court and visitors may perform in person searches. Search fee: $1.50 per name per year. Required to search: name, years to search, DOB; also helpful: address, SSN, race, sex. Criminal records on computer since 1/89.

General Information: Public Access terminal is available. No juvenile, child abuse or sexual battery records released. Will fax results for $2.00 per page. Copy fee: $1.00 per page. Cert fee: $1.50. Payee: Clerk of Circuit Court. Personal checks accepted. Prepayment required. Mail requests: SASE requested. Turnaround time 2-3 days.

Hardee County

Circuit & County Courts PO Drawer 1749, Wauchula, FL 33873-1749; 863-773-4174; Fax: 863-773-4422. Hours: 8AM-5PM (EST). *Felony, Misdemeanor, Civil, Eviction, Small Claims, Probate.* www.jud10.org

Civil Records: Access: Mail, in person, online. Both court and visitors may perform in person searches. Search fee: $1.50 per name per year. Required to search: name, years to search; also helpful: address. Civil records on computer from 1984. Access an index of judgments, liens, recorded documents at www.myfloridacounty.com. Fees involved to order copies; save $1.50 per record by becoming a subscriber.

Criminal Records: Access: Mail, in person. Both court and visitors may perform in person searches. Search fee: $1.50 per name per year. Required to search: name, years to search, DOB; also helpful: address, race, sex. Criminal records on computer from 1984.

General Information: Public Access terminal is available. No juvenile, child abuse or sexual battery records released. Fee to fax results is $1.00 per page. Copy fee: $1.00 per page. Cert fee: $3.00 per document. Payee: Clerk of Circuit Court. Business checks accepted. Prepayment required. Mail requests: SASE requested. Turnaround time 3 days.

Hendry County

Circuit & County Courts PO Box 1760, LaBelle, FL 33975-1760; 863-675-5369; Criminal phone: 863-675-5214; Fax: 863-612-4748. Hours: 8:30AM-5PM (EST). *Felony, Misdemeanor, Civil, Eviction, Small Claims, Probate.*

Civil Records: Access: Mail, in person, online. Both court and visitors may perform in person searches. Search fee: $1.50 per name per year. Required to search: name, years to search; also helpful: address. Civil cases indexed by defendant, plaintiff. Civil records on computer since 5/92, archived from 1923, on microfiche prior to 1989 if filed. Access an index of judgments, liens, recorded documents at www.myfloridacounty.com. Fees involved to order copies; save $1.50 per record by becoming a subscriber.

Criminal Records: Access: Mail, in person. Both court and visitors may perform in person searches. Search fee: $1.50 per name per year plus $6.00. Required to search: name, years to search, DOB; also helpful: address, SSN, race, sex. Criminal records on computer since 1989, prior on microfiche, archived since 1923.

General Information: No juvenile, child abuse or sexual battery records released. Copy fee: $1.00 per page. Cert fee: $1.50. Payee: Clerk of Circuit Court. Only cashiers checks and money orders accepted. Prepayment required. Mail requests: SASE requested. Turnaround time varies.

Hernando County

Circuit & County Courts 20 N Main St, Brooksville, FL 34601; 352-540-6377; Civil phone: 352-540-6377; Criminal phone: 352-540-6444; Probate phone: 352-540-6366; Fax: 352-754-4247. Hours: 8AM-5PM (EST). *Felony, Misdemeanor, Civil, Eviction, Small Claims, Probate.* www.clerk.co.hernando.fl.us

Civil Records: Access: Mail, online, in person. Both court and visitors may perform in person searches. Search fee: $1.50 per name per year. Required to search: name, years to search. Civil cases indexed by defendant, plaintiff. Civil records on computer from 1982, archived from late 1800s. Online access to court records is now free at www.clerk.co.hernando.fl.us/SearchType.asp. Online records may go as far back as 1/1983. Your browser must be Javascript enables (MS Explorer 4.0 or above). Access an index of judgments, liens, recorded documents at www.myfloridacounty.com. Fees involved to order copies; save $1.50 per record by becoming a subscriber.

Criminal Records: Access: Mail, online, in person. Both court and visitors may perform in person searches. Search fee: $1.50 per name per year. Required to search: name, years to search, DOB; also helpful: SSN. Criminal records on computer from 1982, archived from late 1800s. Index and docket information is available for felony and misdemeanor records. Online access to criminal records is the same as civil.

General Information: Public Access terminal is available. No juvenile, child abuse or sexual battery records released. Copy fee: $1.00 per page. Cert fee: $1.50. Payee: Clerk of Circuit Court. Personal checks accepted. Prepayment required. Mail turnaround time approx. 5 days.

Highlands County

Circuit & County Courts 590 S Commerce Ave, Sebring, FL 33870-3867; Civil phone: 863-402-6591; Criminal phone: 863-402-6597; Fax: 863-402-6575. 8AM-5PM (EST). *Felony, Misdemeanor, Civil, Eviction, Small Claims, Probate.* www.clerk.co.highlands.fl.us

Civil Records: Access: Mail, in person, online. Both court and visitors may perform in person searches. Search fee: $1.50 per name per year. Required to search: name, years to search. Civil cases indexed by defendant, plaintiff. Civil cases indexed by defendant since 1992, prior on microfiche and film. Access to county clerk civil and probate records is free at www.clerk.co.highlands.fl.us/civil/search.masn, from 1991. Also includes small claims, probate, and tax deeds. Access an index of judgments, liens, recorded documents at www.myfloridacounty.com. Fees involved to order copies; save $1.50 per record by becoming a subscriber.

Criminal Records: Access: Mail, in person. Both court and visitors may perform in person searches. Search fee: $1.50 per name per year. Required to search: name, years to search; also helpful: SSN. Criminal records on computer since 1991, prior on microfiche and film.

General Information: Public Access terminal is available. No juvenile, child abuse or sexual battery records released. Copy fee: $1.00 per page. Cert fee: $2.00. Payee: Clerk of Courts. Personal checks accepted. Prepayment required. Mail turnaround time 1 week.

HillsBorough

Circuit & County Courts 419 Pierce St, Tampa, FL 33602; 813-276-8100; Civil phone: x7803; Criminal phone: x7802; Fax: 813-272-7707. Hours: 8AM-5PM (EST). *Felony, Misdemeanor, Civil, Eviction, Small Claims, Probate.* www.hillsclerk.com

Civil Records: Access: Fax, mail, online, in person. Both court and visitors may perform in person searches. Search fee: $1.50 per name per year. Required to search: name, years to search; also helpful: address. Civil cases indexed by defendant, plaintiff. Civil records on computer since 5/85, prior on microfiche. Online access to the Court Progress Dockets Search is free at http://publicrecord.hillsclerk.com. The old dialup Service has been discontinued. Also, access an index of judgments, liens, recorded documents at www.myfloridacounty.com. Fees involved to order copies; save $1.50 per record by becoming a subscriber.

Criminal Records: Access: Fax, mail, online, in person. Both court and visitors may perform in person searches. Search fee: $1.50 per name per year. Required to search: name, years to search, DOB; also helpful: address, SSN, race, sex. Criminal records on computer since 1989, prior on microfiche to 1975, archived 1953 to 1974. Online access to the Court Progress Dockets Search is free at http://207.156.115.81/pls/oridev/criminal_pack.ins.

General Information: Public Access terminal is available. No juvenile, child abuse or sexual battery records released. No fee to fax results. Fax account required. Copy fee: $1.00 per page. Cert fee: $1.50. Payee: Clerk of Circuit Court. Local personal checks accepted. Prepayment required. Mail turnaround time 1-2 days.

Holmes County

Circuit & County Courts PO Box 397, Bonifay, FL 32425; 850-547-1100; Fax: 850-547-6630. Hours: 8AM-4PM (CST). *Felony, Misdemeanor, Civil, Eviction, Small Claims, Probate.*

Civil Records: Access: Mail, in person, online. Both court and visitors may perform in person searches. Search fee: $1.50 per name per year. Required to search: name, years to search; also helpful: address. Civil cases indexed by defendant, plaintiff. Civil records on computer from 10/91, archived from early 1900s. Access an index of judgments, liens, recorded documents at www.myfloridacounty.com. Fees involved to order copies; save $1.50 per record by becoming a subscriber.

Criminal Records: Access: Mail, in person. Both court and visitors may perform in person searches. Search fee: $1.50 per name per year. Required to search: name, years to search, DOB; also helpful: address, SSN, race, sex. Criminal records on computer since 1989, prior archived since early 1900s.

General Information: Public Access terminal is available. No juvenile, child abuse or sexual battery records released. Copy fee: $1.00 per page. Cert fee: $1.50. Payee: Holmes County Clerk of Court. Personal checks accepted. Prepayment required. Mail requests: SASE required. Mail turnaround: 1 week.

Indian River County

Circuit & County Courts PO Box 1028, Vero Beach, FL 32961; 772-770-5185; Fax: 772-770-5008. Hours: 8:30AM-5PM (EST). *Felony, Misdemeanor, Civil, Eviction, Small Claims, Probate.* www.clerk.indian-river.org

Civil Records: Access: Mail, in person, online. Both court and visitors may perform in person searches. Search fee: $1.50 per name per year. Required to search: name, years to search; also helpful: address. Civil cases indexed by defendant, plaintiff. Civil records on computer since 1984, prior on microfiche. Online access to county recordings index is free at www.clerk.indian-river.org/recordssearch/ori.asp. Records go back to 1983. Full access to court records is via the clerk's subscription service. Fee is $200.00 per month. For information about free and fee access, call Gary at 772-567-8000 x216.

Criminal Records: Access: Mail, in person, online. Both court and visitors may perform in person searches. Search fee: $1.50 per name per year. Required to search: name, years to search, DOB; also helpful: address, SSN, race, sex. Criminal records on computer (Felony since 1986, Misdemeanor since 1983), both archived since 1925. Online access to criminal records is the same as civil.

General Information: Public Access terminal is available. No juvenile, child abuse or sexual battery records released. Will not fax results. Copy fee: $1.00 per page. Cert fee: $1.50. Payee: Clerk of Circuit Court. Only cashiers checks and money orders accepted. Prepayment required. Mail requests: SASE helpful. Turnaround time 2 days.

Jackson County

Circuit & County Courts PO Box 510, Marianna, FL 32447; 850-482-9552; Fax: 850-482-7849. Hours: 8AM-4:30PM (CST). *Felony, Misdemeanor, Civil, Eviction, Small Claims, Probate.* www.jacksonclerk.com

Civil Records: Access: Fax, mail, in person, online. Both court and visitors may perform in person searches. Search fee: $1.50 per name per year. Required to search: name, years to search; also helpful: address. Civil cases indexed by defendant, plaintiff. Civil records go back to 1900; computerized records go back to 1989. Access an index of judgments, liens, recorded documents at www.jacksonclerk.com or www.myfloridacounty.com. Fees involved to order copies; save $1.50 per record by becoming a subscriber.

Criminal Records: Access: Fax, mail, in person. Both court and visitors may perform in person searches. Search fee: $1.50 per name per year. Required to search: name, years to search, DOB; also helpful: address, SSN, race, sex. Criminal records go back to 1900; computerized records since 1989.

General Information: Public Access terminal is available. No juvenile, child abuse or sexual battery records released. Will fax results $3.00 1st page,

$1.00 each add'l. Copy fee: $1.00 per page. Cert fee: $1.50. Payee: Clerk of Circuit Court. Personal checks accepted. Visa, MC, AmEx accepted. Prepayment required. Mail requests: SASE helpful. Turnaround time 1-5 days.

Jefferson County

Circuit & County Courts Jefferson County Courthouse, Rm 10, Monticello, FL 32344; 850-342-0218; Fax: 850-342-0222. Hours: 8AM-5PM (EST). *Felony, Misdemeanor, Civil, Eviction, Small Claims, Probate.* www.myjeffersoncounty.com

Civil Records: Access: Mail, in person, online. Only the court may perform in person searches. Search fee: $1.50 per name per year. Required to search: name, years to search; also helpful: address. Civil cases indexed by defendant, plaintiff. Civil records on computer since 7/90, prior on dockets. Access an index of judgments, liens, recorded documents at www.myfloridacounty.com, for 01/1/73 to current. Fees involved to order copies; save $1.50 per record by becoming a subscriber.

Criminal Records: Access: Fax, mail, in person. Only the court performs in person searches; visitors may not. Search fee: $1.50 per name per year. Required to search: name, years to search, DOB; also helpful: address, SSN, race, sex. Criminal records on computer since 1989, prior on microfiche from 1969 to 1980, archived since 1950s, prior to 1950 on dockets.

General Information: No juvenile, child abuse or sexual battery records released. Fee to fax results is $2.00 per page. Copy fee: $1.00 per page. Cert fee: $1.50. Payee: Clerk of Circuit Court. Personal checks accepted. Prepayment required. Mail turnaround time 1 week.

Lafayette County

Circuit & County Courts PO Box 88, Mayo, FL 32066; 386-294-1600; Fax: 386-294-4231. Hours: 8AM-5PM (EST). *Felony, Misdemeanor, Civil, Eviction, Small Claims, Probate.*

Civil Records: Access: Phone, mail, fax, in person, online. Both court and visitors may perform in person searches. No search fee. Required to search: name, years to search; also helpful: address. Civil cases indexed by defendant, plaintiff. Civil records on computer since 1997, on books back to early 1900s. Access an index of judgments, liens, recorded documents at www.myfloridacounty.com. Fees involved to order copies; save $1.50 per record by becoming a subscriber.

Criminal Records: Access: Phone, mail, fax, in person. Both court and visitors may perform in person searches. Search fee: $1.50 per name per yr. Required to search: name, years to search, DOB; also helpful: address, SSN, race, sex. Criminal records computerized since 1989.

General Information: Public Access terminal is available. No juvenile, child abuse or sexual battery records released. Copy fee: $1.00 per page. Cert fee: $1.50. Payee: Clerk of Circuit Court. Personal checks accepted. Prepayment required. Mail requests: SASE required. Mail turnaround time 5-7 days.

Lake County

Circuit & County Courts 550 W Main St or PO Box 7800, Tavares, FL 32778; 352-742-4100; Civil phone: 352-742-4145; Criminal phone: 352-742-4126(Felony) 352-742-4128(Misdemeanor); Probate phone: 352-742-4122; Fax: 352-742-4166. Hours: 8:30AM-5PM (EST). *Felony, Misdemeanor, Civil, Eviction, Small Claims, Probate.* www.lakecountyclerk.org/default1.asp

Civil Records: Access: Fax, mail, in person, online. Both court and visitors may perform in person searches. Search fee: $1.50 per name per year, raises

to $1.50 on 07/04. Required to search: name, years to search. Civil cases indexed by defendant, plaintiff. Civil records on computer since 1984, county civil on index books since 11/51, circuit civil since 1888. Online access to Clerk of Court records is free at www.lakecountyclerk.org/services.asp?subject=Online_Court_Records. County civil records go back to 1985; Circuit records go back to 9/1984.

Criminal Records: Access: Fax, mail, in person. Both court and visitors may perform in person searches. Search fee: $1.50 per name per year, effective 07/04 will be $1.50. Required to search: name, years to search, DOB; also helpful: SSN, sex. Criminal records on computer since 1989, on microfiche since 1970s, archived since 1920s. Some on index books.

General Information: Public Access terminal is available. Expunged & sealed records will not be released. No juvenile, child abuse or sexual battery records released. Will fax results for $1.00 per page. Copy fee: $1.00 per page. Cert fee: $1.50, will be $1.50 effective 07/04. Payee: Clerk of Circuit Court. Personal checks accepted. Prepayment required. Mail requests: SASE helpful. Turnaround time 7-10 days.

Lee County

Circuit & County Courts PO Box 2469, Ft Myers, FL 33902; 239-335-2283. Hours: 7:45AM-5PM (EST). *Felony, Misdemeanor, Civil, Eviction, Small Claims, Probate, Traffic.* www.leeclerk.org

Civil Records: Access: Mail, online, in person. Both court and visitors may perform in person searches. Search fee: $1.50 per name per year. Required to search: name, years to search. Civil cases indexed by defendant, plaintiff. Civil records on computer since 1988, prior on microfilm and dockets. Access records at www.leeclerk.org/court_inquiry_disclaimer.htm. Online records go back to 1988. Includes traffic, felony, misdemeanor, civil, small claims and probate. Access an index of judgments, liens, recorded documents at www.leeclerk.org or www.myfloridacounty.com. Search free but fees involved to order certified copies; save the per-record copy fee by becoming a subscriber; sub fee is $25.00 per month.

Criminal Records: Access: Mail, online, in person. Both court and visitors may perform in person searches. Search fee: $1.50 per name per year. Required to search: name, years to search, DOB; also helpful: address, SSN, race, sex. Criminal records on computer-(Felony since 1978, Misdemeanor since 1986), prior on microfilm. Online access to criminal records is the same as civil.

General Information: Public Access terminal is available. No juvenile, child abuse or sexual offense records released. Will not fax results. Copy fee: $1.00 per page. Cert fee: $1.50 per document. Payee: Clerk of Circuit Court. Personal checks accepted. Prepayment required. Mail requests: SASE required. Mail turnaround time 5 days.

Leon County

Circuit & County Courts PO Box 726, Tallahassee, FL 32302; 850-577-4000; Civil phone: 850-577-4170; Criminal phone: 850-577-4070; Probate phone: 850-577-4180. Hours: 8:30AM-5PM (EST). *Felony, Misdemeanor, Civil, Eviction, Small Claims, Probate.* www.clerk.leon.fl.us

Civil Records: Access: Mail, online, in person. Both court and visitors may perform in person searches. Search fee: $1.50 per name per year. Required to search: name, years to search; also helpful: address. Civil cases indexed by defendant, plaintiff. Civil records on computer since 8/86, prior on docket books. Also, you may search cases and "High Profile Cases" (re: Election 2000) at www.clerk.leon.fl.us

under "Search Court Databases." Registration required. Access an index of judgments, liens, recorded documents at www.myfloridacounty.com. Fees involved to order copies; save $1.50 per record by becoming a subscriber.

Criminal Records: Access: Mail, online, in person. Both court and visitors may perform in person searches. Search fee: $1.50 per name per year. Required to search: name, years to search, DOB; also helpful: address, SSN, race, sex. Criminal records on computer since 1976, on microfiche since 1937, archived since late 1800s/early 1900s. Online access to criminal records is the same as civil.

General Information: Public Access terminal is available. No juvenile, child abuse or sexual battery records released. Copy fee: $1.00 per page. Cert fee: $1.50. Payee: Clerk of Circuit Court. Personal checks accepted. Prepayment required. Mail requests: SASE helpful. Turnaround time 1-5 days.

Levy County

Circuit & County Courts PO Box 610, Bronson, FL 32621; 352-486-5100; Civil phone: 352-486-5277; Criminal phone: 352-486-5272; Probate phone: 352-486-5459. Hours: 8AM-5PM (EST). *Felony, Misdemeanor, Civil, Eviction, Small Claims, Probate.* www.levyclerk.com

Civil Records: Access: Mail, in person, online. Both court and visitors may perform in person searches. Search fee: $1.50 per name per year. Required to search: name, years to search; also helpful: address. Civil cases indexed by defendant, plaintiff. Civil records on computer since 1986, microfiche since 1981 (in process), prior on docket books. Access an index of judgments, liens, recorded documents is at www.myfloridacounty.com. Fees involved to order copies; save $1.50 per record by becoming a subscriber. Also, access to the week's civil calendars is free at http://circuit8.org/civilcal.pdf.

Criminal Records: Access: Mail, in person. Both court and visitors may perform in person searches. Search fee: $1.50 per name per year. Required to search: name, years to search, DOB, signed release; also helpful: address, SSN, race, sex. Criminal records on computer from 1986 to present, prior on docket books. Access to the week's criminal calendars is free at http://circuit8.org/crimcal.pdf.

General Information: Public Access terminal is available. (Civil cases only.) No juvenile, child abuse or sexual battery records released. Copy fee: $1.00 per page. Cert fee: $1.50. Payee: Clerk of Circuit Court. Business checks accepted. Prepayment required. Mail requests: SASE required. Mail turnaround time 2-3 days.

Liberty County

Circuit & County Courts PO Box 399, Bristol, FL 32321; 850-643-2215; Fax: 850-643-2866. Hours: 8AM-5PM (EST). *Felony, Misdemeanor, Civil, Eviction, Small Claims, Probate.* www.libertyclerk.com

Civil Records: Access: Mail, in person. Both court and visitors may perform in person searches. Search fee: $1.50 per name per year. Required to search: name, years to search; also helpful: address. Civil cases indexed by defendant, plaintiff. Civil records on docket books. Access an index of judgments, liens, recorded documents at www.myfloridacounty.com. Fees involved to order copies; save $1.50 per record by becoming a subscriber.

Criminal Records: Access: Mail, in person. Both court and visitors may perform in person searches. Search fee: $1.50 per name per year. Required to search: name, years to search, DOB; also helpful: address, SSN, race, sex. Criminal records on docket books.

General Information: No juvenile, child abuse or sexual battery records released. Copy fee: $1.00 per page. Cert fee: $1.50. Payee: Clerk of Circuit Court. Business checks accepted. Prepayment required. Mail requests: SASE required. Mail turnaround: 1 week.

Madison County

Circuit & County Courts PO Box 237, Madison, FL 32341; 850-973-1500; Fax: 850-973-2059. Hours: 8AM-5PM (EST). *Felony, Misdemeanor, Civil, Eviction, Small Claims, Probate.*

Civil Records: Access: Phone, mail, in person, online. Both court and visitors may perform in person searches. Search fee: $1.50 per name per year. Required to search: name, years to search; also helpful: address. Civil cases indexed by defendant, plaintiff. Civil records on computer since 1988, prior on docket books. Access an index of judgments, liens, recorded documents at www.myfloridacounty.com. Fees involved to order copies; save $1.50 per record by becoming a subscriber.

Criminal Records: Access: Phone, mail, in person. Both court and visitors may perform in person searches. Search fee: $1.50 per name per year. Required to search: name, years to search, DOB; also helpful: address, SSN, race, sex. Criminal records on computer since 1988, prior on docket books.

General Information: No juvenile, child abuse or sexual battery records released. Copy fee: $1.00 per page. Cert fee: $1.50. Payee: Clerk of Circuit Court. Personal checks accepted. Prepayment required. Mail requests: SASE requested. Turnaround time 1-3 days.

Manatee County

Circuit & County Courts PO Box 25400, Bradenton, FL 34206; 941-749-1800; Fax: 941-741-4082. 8:30AM-5PM (EST). *Felony, Misdemeanor, Civil, Eviction, Small Claims, Probate.*
www.manateeclerk.com

Civil Records: Access: Phone, fax, mail, online, in person, email. Both court and visitors may perform in person searches. Search fee: $1.50 per name per year. Required to search: name, years to search; also helpful: address. Civil cases indexed by defendant, plaintiff. Civil records on computer since 9/80, prior on microfilm back to 1972. A subscription online service is $50 plus $60 per user fee advance; for sign-up information visit the website. Also, court records at Circuit clerk's office are free at www.manateeclerk.com/mpa/cvweb.asp. Access an index of judgments, liens, recorded documents at www.myfloridacounty.com. Fees involved to order copies; save $1.50 per record by becoming a subscriber.

Criminal Records: Access: Phone, fax, mail, online, in person, email. Both court and visitors may perform in person searches. Search fee: $1.50 per name per year. Required to search: name, years to search, DOB; also helpful: address, charge, race, sex. Criminal records on computer since 1981, prior on docket books back to 1972. Online access to criminal records is the same as civil.

General Information: Public Access terminal is available. No juvenile, adoption, child abuse or sexual battery victim records released. Will fax results for $1.00 per page. Copy fee: $1.00 per page. Cert fee: $1.50. Payee: Clerk of Circuit Court. Personal checks accepted. Visa, MC accepted. Prepayment required. Mail requests: SASE helpful. Turnaround time 2 days.

Marion County

Circuit & County Courts PO Box 1030, Ocala, FL 34478; 352-620-3892 (cty civ); Civil phone: 352-620-3891 (Circ); Criminal phone: 352-620-3861; Probate phone: 352-620-3874; Fax: 352-620-3300 (civ); 840-5668 (crim). Hours: 8AM-5PM (EST). *Felony, Misdemeanor, Civil, Eviction, Small Claims, Probate.*
www.marioncountyclerk.org

Civil Records: Access: Fax, mail, in person, online. Both court and visitors may perform in person searches. Search fee: $1.50 per name per year. Required to search: name, years to search; also helpful: address. Civil cases indexed by defendant, plaintiff. Civil records on computer since 1983, on microfiche since 1958. Online access to county clerk civil records is free online at www.marioncountyclerk.org/. Click on Case Search found on left side under Courts. Access an index of judgments, liens, recorded documents at www.myfloridacounty.com. Fees involved to order copies; save $1.50 per record by becoming a subscriber.

Criminal Records: Access: Fax, mail, in person. Both court and visitors may perform in person searches. Search fee: $1.50 per name per year. Required to search: name, years to search, DOB; also helpful: address, SSN, race, sex. Criminal records on computer. Felonies since 1984, on microfiche from 1950 to 1979, prior on index cards. Misdemeanors since 1983, on microfiche from 1900 to 1982, archived since 1900s, prior on index cards.

General Information: Public Access terminal is available. No juvenile records released. Will fax results to local or toll free line, otherwise fee involved. Copy fee: $1.00 per page. Cert fee: $1.50. Payee: Clerk of Court. Personal checks accepted. Prepayment required. Mail requests: SASE requested. Turnaround time 1-2 weeks.

Martin County

Circuit & County Courts PO Box 9016, Stuart, FL 34995; 772-288-5576; Fax: 772-288-5724; 288-5991 (civil). Hours: 8AM-5PM (EST). *Felony, Misdemeanor, Civil, Eviction, Small Claims, Probate.*
http://clerk-web.martin.fl.us/ClerkWeb

Civil Records: Access: Phone, fax, mail, online, in person. Both court and visitors may perform in person searches. Search fee: $1.50 per name per year. Required to search: name, years to search; also helpful: address. Civil cases indexed by defendant, plaintiff. Civil records on computer since 10/86, prior on microfiche, microfilm and archived. Online access to civil case information on the records division database is free at http://clerk-web.martin.fl.us/wb_or1. Also includes small claims, recordings, other document types.

Criminal Records: Access: Phone, fax, mail, online, in person. Both court and visitors may perform in person searches. Search fee: $1.50 per name per year prior to 1990. Required to search: name, years to search, DOB; also helpful: address, SSN. Criminal records on computer. Felonies since 1986, on microfiche since 1956, prior on index cards and docket books. Misdemeanors since 1985, on microfiche since 1973, prior on index cards and docket books. Online access to criminal records is the same as civil. Records indexed form 01/01/86, and images from 11/01/93.

General Information: Public Access terminal is available. No juvenile, child abuse or sexual battery records released. Will fax results $1.25 per page. Copy fee: $1.00 per page. Cert fee: $1.50. Payee: Clerk of Circuit Court. Personal checks accepted. Prepayment required. Mail turnaround time 1 week.

Monroe County

Circuit & County Courts 500 Whitehead St, Key West, FL 33040; 305-294-4641; Civil phone: 305-292-3310; Criminal phone: 305-292-3390; Fax: 305-295-3623. Hours: 8:30AM-5PM (EST). *Felony, Misdemeanor, Civil, Eviction, Small Claims, Probate.*
www.co.monroe.fl.us

Civil Records: Access: Mail, fax, in person, online. Both court and visitors may perform in person searches. Search fee: $1.50 per name per year. Required to search: name, years to search; also helpful: address. Civil cases indexed by defendant, plaintiff. Civil records on computer since 1983, on microfiche since 1972, prior on docket books. Some records purged after 2 years. Probate from 1972. Online access to civil cases is free at www.clerk-of-the-court.com/searchCivilCases.asp. Subscription is required for viewing full document library.

Criminal Records: Access: Mail, fax, in person, online. Both court and visitors may perform in person searches. Search fee: $1.50 per name per year. Required to search: name, years to search, DOB; also helpful: address, SSN, race, sex. Criminal records (pending felony and misdemeanors) on computer, others since 1992, non-pending on microfiche since 1945. Online access to criminal records is free at www.clerk-of-the-court.com/searchCriminalCases.asp. Includes traffic cases online. Subscription is required for viewing full document library.

General Information: Public Access terminal is available. No juvenile, child abuse or sexual battery records released. Fee to fax results is $1.00 per page. Copy fee: $1.00 per page. Cert fee: $1.50. Payee: Clerk of Circuit Court. Personal checks accepted. Prepayment required. Mail requests: SASE helpful. Turnaround time 1-2 weeks.

Nassau County

Circuit & County Courts PO Box 456, (76347 Veterans Way), Fernandina Beach, FL 32035; Civil phone: 904-548-4600; Criminal phone: 904-548-4607; Probate phone: 904-548-4600; Fax: 904-321-5723 civ; 491-3649 crim. Hours: 8:30AM-5PM (EST). *Felony, Misdemeanor, Civil, Eviction, Small Claims, Probate.*
www.nassauclerk.com

Civil Records: Access: Phone, fax, mail, in person, online. Only the court performs in person searches; visitors may not. Search fee: $1.50 per name per year. Required to search: name, years to search; also helpful: address. Civil cases indexed by defendant, plaintiff. Civil records on computer since 1993, on microfiche since 1982, prior on docket books. Access an index of judgments, liens, recorded documents at www.myfloridacounty.com. Fees involved to order copies; save $1.50 per record by becoming a subscriber.

Criminal Records: Access: Phone, fax, mail, in person. Only the court performs in person searches; visitors may not. Search fee: $1.50 per name per year. Required to search: name, years to search, DOB; also helpful: address, SSN, race, sex. Criminal records on computer since 1985, on microfiche since 1982, prior on docket books. Past 5 years only can be done on the phone.

General Information: No juvenile, child abuse or sexual battery records released. Will fax results for $1.00 per page. Copy fee: $1.00 per page. Cert fee: $1.50. Payee: Clerk of Circuit Court. Personal checks accepted. Prepayment required. Mail requests: SASE required. Mail turnaround time 1 week.

Okaloosa County

Circuit & County Courts 1250 N Eglin Pkwy, Shalimar, FL 32579; 850-651-7200; Fax: 850-651-7230. Hours: 8AM-5PM (CST). *Felony, Misdemeanor, Civil, Eviction, Small Claims, Probate.*
www.clerkofcourts.cc

Civil Records: Access: Mail, online, in person. Both court and visitors may perform in person searches. Search fee: $1.00 per year per name. Required to search: name, years to search; also helpful: address. Civil cases indexed by defendant, plaintiff. Civil records on computer from 6/86; archives from 1915; prior on index cards. 3 options available. Access to the full online system (civil, probate, traffic) requires monthly fee of $100.00. For more information, call 850-689-5821. Also, civil records are free at www.clerkofcourts.cc/orsearch/contract.htm. Records go back to 1/86. Search civil index by defendant or plaintiff, date, or file type. Access an index of judgments, liens, recorded documents at www.myfloridacounty.com. Fees involved to order copies; sve $1.50 per record by becoming a subscriber.

Criminal Records: Access: Mail, online, in person. Both court and visitors may perform in person searches. Search fee: $6.00 per name. Add $1.50 for each year searched prior to 6/1989. Required to search: name, years to search, DOB; also helpful: address, SSN, race, sex. Criminal records on computer from 6/86; archives from 1915; prior on index cards. Access to the full online system (civil, probate, traffic) requires monthly fee of $100.00. For more information, call 850-689-5821. Both felony and misdemeanor indexes can be searched. Also, the county clerk has placed traffic misdemeanor records free on the Internet at www.clerkofcourts.cc/orsearch/contract.htm.

General Information: Public Access terminal is available. No juvenile, child abuse or sexual battery records released. Copy fee: $1.00 per page. Cert fee: $2.00. Payee: Clerk of Circuit Court. Personal checks accepted. Prepayment required. Mail requests: SASE required. Mail turnaround time 1 week.

Okeechobee County

Circuit & County Courts 304 NW 2nd St, Rm 101, Okeechobee, FL 34972; 863-763-2131. Hours: 8:30AM-5PM (EST). *Felony, Misdemeanor, Civil, Eviction, Small Claims, Probate.*

Civil Records: Access: Mail, in person. Both court and visitors may perform in person searches. Search fee: $1.50 per name per year. Required to search: name, years to search; also helpful: address. Civil cases indexed by defendant, plaintiff. Civil records on computer since 1990, on index cards from 1983 to 1988.

Criminal Records: Access: Mail, in person. Both court and visitors may perform in person searches. Search fee: $1.50 per name per year. Required to search: name, years to search, DOB; also helpful: address, SSN, race, sex. Criminal records on computer since 1989, on index cards from 1932 to 1988.

General Information: No juvenile, child abuse or sexual battery records released. Copy fee: $1.00 per page. Cert fee: $1.50. Payee: Clerk of Circuit Court. Personal checks accepted. Prepayment required. Mail requests: SASE required. Mail turnaround time for criminal: 2 weeks; civil 1-2 weeks.

Orange County

Circuit & County Courts PO Box 4994, (425 N Orange Ave), Orlando, FL 32801-1544; 407-836-2060. 8AM-5PM (EST). *Felony, Misdemeanor, Civil, Eviction, Small Claims, Probate.*
http://orangeclerk.ocfl.net

Note: Mail requests should use room numbers; civil circuit-310; civil county-350; crim circuit-210; crim county-250.

Civil Records: Access: Mail, online, in person, email. Both court and visitors may perform in person searches. Search fee: $1.50 per name per year. Required to search: name, years to search. Civil cases indexed by defendant, plaintiff. Civil records are on computer as follows: Circuit civil-1992; Domestic civil-1992; Probate-1993; Traffic-1980. The Teleclerk countywide remote online system has been replaced by the free iclerk system at http://orangeclerk1.onetgov.net/restricted/iclerk/index.htm. Set your borwser "privacy" to "low." Use "public" as username and password. For more information, call 407-836-2060. This court also accepts email requests.

Criminal Records: Access: Mail, online, in person, email. Both court and visitors may perform in person searches. Search fee: $1.50 per name per year. Required to search: name, years to search, DOB. Criminal records on computer go back to 1990; prior records go back to 1987. The Teleclerk countywide remote online system has been replaced by the free iclerk system at http://orangeclerk1.onetgov.net/restricted/iclerk/index.htm. Though arrests only, the county posts postitution solicitation arrests at www.ocso.com/categories/arresting/developments.html. This court also accepts email requests.

General Information: Public Access terminal is available. (Available in Records Management Division.) No sex-related or adoption records released. Copy fee: $1.00 per page. For more information, call 407-836-2064 Cert fee: $1.50. Payee: Orange County Clerk of Courts. Personal checks accepted from Orange County only. Prepayment required. Mail requests: SASE helpful. Turnaround time 2 days.

County Court - Apopka Branch 1111 N Rock Springs Rd, Apopka, FL 32712; 407-654-1030. Hours: 7:30AM-5:30PM (EST). *Misdemeanor, Civil Actions Under $15,000, Eviction, Small Claims.*
http://orangeclerk.ocfl.net

Note: Records maintained at Orlando office.

Civil Records: Access: Mail, online, in person. Both court and visitors may perform in person searches. Search fee: $1.50 per name per year. Required to search: name, years to search. Civil cases indexed by defendant, plaintiff. Civil records (Pending) on computer. All dockets on microfilm or microfiche. Some records on index cards. The Teleclerk countywide remote online system has been replaced by the free Iclerk system at http://orangeclerk1.onetgov.net/restricted/iclerk/index.htm. Set your browser "privacy" to low. Use "public" as username and password. Probate records available.

Criminal Records: Access: Mail, online, in person. Both court and visitors may perform in person searches. Search fee: $1.50 per name. Required to search: name, years to search, DOB; also helpful: SSN. Criminal records (Pending) on computer. All dockets on microfilm or microfiche. Some records on index cards. Online access to criminal records is the same as civil. Though arrests only, the county posts postitution solicitation arrests at www.ocso.com/categories/arresting/developments.html.

General Information: Public Access terminal is available. No sex related or adoption records released.

Copy fee: $1.00 per page. Cert fee: $2.00. Payee: Clerk of County Court. Personal checks accepted. Prepayment required. Mail requests: SASE helpful. Turnaround time 2 days.

County Court - NE Orange Division 450 N Lakemont Ave, Winter Park, FL 32792; 407-671-1116. Hours: 7:30AM-5:30PM (EST). *Misdemeanor, Civil Actions Under $15,000, Eviction, Small Claims.*
http://orangeclerk.ocfl.net

Civil Records: Access: Phone, mail, online, in person. Only the court performs in person searches; visitors may not. Search fee: $1.50 per name per year. Required to search: name, years to search. Civil cases indexed by defendant, plaintiff. Civil records (Pending) on computer. All dockets on microfilm or microfiche. The Teleclerk countywide remote online system has been replaced by the free Iclerk system at http://orangeclerk1.onetgov.net/restricted/iclerk/index.htm. Set your browser "privacy" to "low." Use "public" as username and password.

Criminal Records: Access: Phone, mail, online, in person. Only the court performs in person searches; visitors may not. Search fee: $1.50 per name per year. Required to search: name, years to search, DOB; also helpful: SSN. Criminal records (Pending) on computer. All dockets on microfilm or microfiche. Online access to criminal records is the same as civil. Though arrests only, the county posts postitution solicitation arrests at www.ocso.com/categories/arresting/developments.html.

General Information: No sex related or adoption records released. Copy fee: $1.00 per page. Cert fee: $1.50. Payee: Clerk of County Court. Only cashiers checks and money orders accepted. Prepayment required. Mail requests: SASE helpful. Turnaround time 2 days.

County Court #3 Clerk of Courts, 475 W Story Rd, Ocoee, FL 34761; 407-667-6240. Hours: 8AM-5PM (EST). *Misdemeanor, Civil Actions Under $15,000, Eviction, Small Claims.*
http://orangeclerk.ocfl.net

Civil Records: Access: Mail, online, in person. Both court and visitors may perform in person searches. Search fee: $5.00 per name. Required to search: name, years to search. Civil cases indexed by defendant, plaintiff. Civil records go back to 1890; on computer back to 1990. All dockets on microfilm or microfiche. The Teleclerk countywide remote online system has been replaced by the free iclerk system at http://orangeclerk1.onetgov.net/restricted/iclerk/index.htm. Set your browser "privacy" to "low. Use "public" as username and password. For more information, call 407-836-2060.

Criminal Records: Access: Mail, online, in person. Both court and visitors may perform in person searches. Search fee: $5.00 per name. Required to search: name, years to search, DOB; also helpful: SSN. Criminal records go back to 1890; on computer back to 1990. All dockets are on microfilm or microfiche. Online access to criminal records is the same as civil. Though arrests only, the county posts postitution solicitation arrests at www.ocso.com/categories/arresting/developments.html.

General Information: Public Access terminal is available. No sex related or adoption records released. Copy fee: $1.00 per page. Cert fee: $2.00 per page. Payee: Clerk of County Court. Personal checks accepted. Visa, MC accepted. Accepted for civil payments only. Prepayment required. Mail requests: SASE helpful. Turnaround time 2 days depending on file.

Osceola County

Circuit Court - Civil 2 Courthouse Sq, Kissimmee, FL 34741; 407-343-3500; Probate phone: 407-343-3506. Hours: 8:30AM-5PM (EST). *Civil Actions Over $5,000, Probate.*
www.ninja9.org
Civil Records: Access: Mail, in person, online. Both court and visitors may perform in person searches. Search fee: $1.50 per name per year per division. Required to search: name, years to search. Civil cases indexed by defendant, plaintiff. Civil records on computer from 1990, on docket books from 1800s to 1990. Online access to court records on the Clerk of Circuit Court database are free at www.osceolaclerk.org. Also, access an index of judgments, liens, recorded documents at www.myfloridacounty.com. Fees involved to order copies; save $1.50 per record by becoming a subscriber.
General Information: Public Access terminal is available. (Only civil available.) No appeal records released. Will fax results if prepaid. Copy fee: $1.00 per page. Cert fee: $1.50. Payee: Clerk of Court. Business checks accepted. Prepayment required. Mail requests: SASE required. Mail turnaround time 1-2 days.

Circuit & County Courts - Criminal Division 2 Courthouse Sq, Kissimmee, FL 34741; 407-343-3543/3555. Hours: 8:30AM-5PM (EST). *Felony, Misdemeanor.*
www.osceolaclerk.com
Criminal Records: Access: Mail, in person, online. Both the court and visitors may perform in person searches as long as the case occurred 1990 or after. Search fee: $1.50 per name per year. Required to search: name, years to search, DOB, SSN. Criminal records on computer back to 1990, on index since 1978, prior on docket books from 1800s to 1978. Online access to criminal records is free at www.osceolaclerkcourt.org/search.htm. Includes party index and case summary searching. Serarch inmates at www.osceola.org/index.cfm?lsFuses=inmates.
General Information: Public Access terminal is available. No juvenile or sealed records released. Will fax results to local or toll free line. Copy fee: $1.00 per page. Cert fee: $1.50. Payee: Money orders payable to Clerk of the Court. Business checks accepted. Credit cards accepted; a surcharge is added. Prepayment required. Mail requests: SASE requested. Turnaround time 1 week.

County Court - Civil 2 Courthouse Sq, #2000, Kissimmee, FL 34741; 407-343-3500. Hours: 8:30AM-5PM (EST). *Eviction, Small Claims.*
www.osceolaclerk.com
Civil Records: Access: Mail, in person, online. Both court and visitors may perform in person searches. Search fee: $1.50 per name per year per division. Required to search: name, years to search. Civil cases indexed by defendant, plaintiff. Civil records on computer from 1991, on index cards from 1972 to 1991, on docket books from 1800s to 1972. Online access to court records on the Clerk of Circuit Court database are free at www.osceolaclerkcourt.org.
General Information: Public Access terminal is available. (Only civil available.) No juvenile records released. Will fax results if prepaid. Copy fee: $1.00 per page. Cert fee: $1.50. Payee: Clerk of Court. Business checks accepted. Prepayment required. Mail requests: SASE helpful. Turnaround time 1 week.

Palm Beach County

Circuit Court - Civil Division PO Box 4667, West Palm Beach, FL 33402; 561-355-2986; Fax: 561-355-4643. Hours: 8AM-5PM (EST). *Civil.*
www.pbcountyclerk.com
Civil Records: Access: Phone, mail, online, in person. Both court and visitors may perform in person searches. Search fee: $1.50 per name per year. Required to search: name, years to search; also helpful: address. Civil cases indexed by defendant, plaintiff. Civil records (Circuit) on computer from 1982, prior records on microfiche and dockets. County on computer from 1987, prior on microfilm. Access to the countywide is free. Civil index goes back to '88. Records also include probate, traffic and domestic. Contact Rowtera Simmons at 561-355-4277 for information. Also, access 15th judicial circuit records at http://web3172.co.palm-beach.fl.us. Registration and password is required. Service may be discontinued. Also, civil records only are free at http://courtcon.co.palm-beach.fl.us/pls/jiwp/ck_publ ic_qry_main.cp_main_idx.
General Information: Public Access terminal is available. No juvenile, child abuse or sexual battery records released. Copy fee: $1.00 per page. Cert fee: $1.50. Payee: Clerk of Circuit Court. Personal checks accepted. Prepayment required. Mail requests: SASE required. Mail turnaround time 1 week.

Circuit & County Courts - Criminal Division 205 N Dixie Hwy, West Palm Beach, FL 33401; 561-355-2519; Fax: 561-355-3802. Hours: 8AM-5PM (EST). *Felony, Misdemeanor.*
www.pbcountyclerk.com
Note: Faxes can only be received by state agencies.

Criminal Records: Access: Phone, fax, mail, online, in person. Both court and visitors may perform in person searches. Search fee: $1.50 per name per year. Required to search: name, years to search, DOB, aliases. Criminal records on computer & microfiche (some files) from 1970s, archived from 1920s. Access to the countywide criminal online system requires $145 setup and $65 per month fee. Records also include probate, traffic and domestic. Contact Mr. McArthur for information. Also, access to 15th judicial circuit records is at http://web3172.co.palm-beach.fl.us. Registration and password is required.
General Information: Public Access terminal is available. No juvenile, child abuse or sexual battery records released. Copy fee: $1.00 per page. Cert fee: $1.50. Payee: Clerk of Circuit Court. Personal checks accepted. Prepayment required. Mail requests: SASE not required. Mail turnaround time 1 day.

County Court - Civil Division 205 N Dixie HWY, West Palm Beach, FL 33402; 561-355-2500; Fax: 561-355-4643. Hours: 8AM-5PM (EST). *Eviction, Small Claims.*
www.pbcountyclerk.com
Civil Records: Access: Phone, mail, online, in person. Both court and visitors may perform in person searches. Search fee: $1.50 per name per year. Required to search: name, years to search; also helpful: address. Civil cases indexed by defendant, plaintiff. Civil records (Circuit) on computer from 1982, prior records on microfiche and dockets. County on computer from 1987, prior on microfilm. Access to the countywide remote online system requires $145 setup and $65 per month fees. Civil index goes back to '88. Records also include probate, traffic and domestic. Contact M. McArthur at 561-355-6846 for information.
General Information: Public Access terminal is available. No juvenile, child abuse or sexual battery records released. Copy fee: $1.00 per page. Cert fee: $1.50. Payee: Clerk of Circuit Court. Personal checks

accepted. Prepayment required. Mail requests: SASE required. Mail turnaround time 1 week.

Circuit Court - Probate Division PO Box 4238, West Palm Beach, FL 33402; 561-355-2900. Hours: 8AM-5PM (EST). *Probate.*
www.pbcountyclerk.com
Note: Online access to 15th judicial circuit records is available at http://web3172.co.palm-beach.fl.us. Registration and password is required.

Pasco County

Circuit & County Courts - Civil Division 38053 Live Oak Ave, Dade City, FL 33523; 352-521-4482. Hours: 8:30AM-5PM (EST). *Civil, Eviction, Small Claims, Probate.*
www.pascoclerk.com
Civil Records: Access: Mail, online, in person. Both court and visitors may perform in person searches. Search fee: $1.50 per name per year. Required to search: name, years to search. Civil cases indexed by defendant, plaintiff. Civil records on computer from 1985, on docket cards and docket books from 1900s. Online access to Clerk of Court records via the Internet is a subscription service. Monthly fees are involved. Probate records also available. Call 352-521-4274, ext 4767 for more information. Access an index of judgments, liens, recorded documents at www.myfloridacounty.com. Fees involved to order copies; save $1.50 per record by becoming a subscriber.
General Information: Public Access terminal is available. No adoption records released. Copy fee: $1.00 per page. Cert fee: $1.50. Payee: Clerk of Court. Personal checks accepted. Prepayment required. Mail turnaround time 2-4 days.

Circuit & County Courts - Criminal Division 38053 Live Oak Ave, Dade City, FL 33523-3894; 352-521-4504. Hours: 8:30AM-5PM (EST). *Felony, Misdemeanor.*
www.jud6.org
Criminal Records: Access: Mail, online, in person. Both court and visitors may perform in person searches. Search fee: $1.50 per name per year. Required to search: name, years to search, address, DOB; also helpful: SSN. Criminal records on computer since 1978. Access to the countywide criminal online system requires $100 deposit, $50 annual fee and $10 monthly minimum. There is a $.10 per screen charge. The system is open 24 hours daily. Search by name or case number. Call 352-521-4201 for more information.
General Information: Public Access terminal is available. No confidential, sealed or juvenile records released. Copy fee: $1.00 per page. Cert fee: $1.50. Payee: Clerk of Courts. Personal checks accepted. Out of state personal checks not accepted. Prepayment required. Mail turnaround time 2-4 days.

Pinellas County

Circuit & County Courts - Civil Division 315 Court St Rm 170, Clearwater, FL 33756; 727-464-3267; Fax: 727-464-4070. Hours: 8AM-5PM (EST). *Civil, Eviction, Small Claims, Probate.*
www.jud6.org
Civil Records: Access: Fax, mail, online, in person. Both court and visitors may perform in person searches. Search fee: $1.50 per name per year. Required to search: name, years to search. Civil cases indexed by defendant, plaintiff. Civil records on computer from 1980, on microfiche from 1900s to 1982, older data in warehouse. Access to the countywide civil online system requires $60 fee plus $5.00 a month and $.05 per screen over 100. Index goes back to 1972. Contact Sue Maskeny at 727-464-3779 for information. Includes probate and traffic

records. Also, you can access the clerk's criminal and other data as a free non-subscriber at https://pubtitles.co.pinellas.fl.us/login/loginx.jsp. However, you are on the clock and may be booted if you overuse the system. Also, access an index of judgments, liens, recorded documents at www.myfloridacounty.com. Fees involved to order copies; save $1.50 per record by becoming a subscriber.

General Information: Public Access terminal is available. No adoption or juvenile records released. Will fax results $1.00 per page. Copy fee: $1.00 per page. Cert fee: $1.50. Payee: Clerk of the Court. Personal checks accepted. Prepayment required. Mail requests: SASE helpful. Turnaround time 1 week.

Criminal Justice Center Circuit Criminal
Court Records, 14250 49th St N, Clearwater, FL 34622; 727-464-6793; Fax: 727-464-6233. Hours: 8AM-5PM (EST). *Felony.*
www.jud6.org
Criminal Records: Access: Fax, mail, online, in person. Both court and visitors may perform in person searches. Search fee: $1.50 per name per year. Required to search: name, years to search, DOB. Criminal records on computer from 1977, on microfilm from 1912 to 1976, on docket books from 1912. Access to the countywide criminal online system requires $60 fee plus $5.00 a month and $.05 per screen over 100. Criminal index goes back to 1972. Contact Sue Maskeny at 727-464-3779 for information. Also, you can access the clerk's criminal and other data as a free non-subscriber at https://pubtitles.co.pinellas.fl.us/login/loginx.jsp. However, you are on the clock and may be booted if you overuse the system.

General Information: Public Access terminal is available. Will fax results $1.00 per page. Copy fee: $1.00 per page. Cert fee: $1.50. Payee: Clerk of Circuit Court. Personal checks accepted. Prepayment required. Mail turnaround time 1 week.

County Court - Criminal Division 14250
49th St N, Clearwater, FL 34622-2831; 727-464-7000; Fax: 727-464-7040. Hours: 8AM-5PM (EST). *Misdemeanor.*
www.jud6.org
Criminal Records: Access: Mail, online, in person. Both court and visitors may perform in person searches. Search fee: $1.50 per name per year. Required to search: name, years to search; also helpful: address, DOB, SSN. Criminal records on computer since 10/77, prior on index books. Prior to 1993 on microfilm. Access to the countywide criminal online system requires $60 fee plus $5.00 a month and $.05 per screen over 100. Criminal index goes back to 1972. Contact Sue Maskeny at 727-464-3779 for information. Also, you can access the clerk's criminal and other data as a free non-subscriber at https://pubtitles.co.pinellas.fl.us/login/loginx.jsp. However, you are on the clock and may be booted if you overuse the system.

General Information: Public Access terminal is available. No sealed or non-arrested case records released. Copy fee: $1.00 per page. Cert fee: $1.50. Payee: Clerk of Courts. Personal checks accepted. Prepayment required. Mail turnaround time 3-5 days.

Polk County

Circuit Court - Civil Division PO Box 9000,
Drawer CC2, Bartow, FL 33831-9000; 863-534-4488; Probate phone: 863-534-4478; Fax: 863-534-7707. Hours: 8AM-5PM (EST). *Civil Actions Over $15,000, Probate.*
www.polk-county.net/clerk/clerk.html
Civil Records: Access: Phone, mail, online, in person. Both court and visitors may perform in person searches. Search fee: $1.50 per name per year.

Required to search: name. Civil cases indexed by defendant, plaintiff. Civil Records on computer since 1978; on microfiche from 1800s to 1978. Free internet access to limited records is at www.polkcountyclerk.net/public_records/public_index.html. Complete access to the database requires $150 setup fee, but there is no monthly fees. Call 863-534-7575 for more information.

General Information: Public Access terminal is available. No sex related cases, adoption, confidential, victims or child abuse records released. Will fax results to local or toll free line. Copy fee: $1.00 per page. Cert fee: $1.50. Payee: Clerk of Court. Personal checks accepted. Prepayment required. Mail requests: SASE required. Mail turnaround time 2-3 days.

Circuit & County Courts - Felony
Division PO Box 9000 Drawer CC9, Bartow, FL 33830; 863-534-4000; Fax: 863-534-4137. Hours: 8AM-5PM (EST). *Felony.*
www.polk-county.net/clerk/clerk.html
Criminal Records: Access: Phone, mail, in person. Both court and visitors may perform in person searches. Search fee: $4.00 per name. Required to search: name, years to search, DOB; also helpful: SSN. Criminal records on computer-felonies since 1977, misdemeanors purged periodically. Both on microfiche and archived since 1800s.

General Information: Public Access terminal is available. No sex related cases, victims or child abuse released. Copy fee: $1.00 per page. Cert fee: $1.50 per page. Payee: Clerk of Circuit Court. Personal checks accepted. Prepayment required. Mail turnaround time varies. Indicate on request when record is needed.

Circuit & County Courts - Misdemeanor
Division PO Box 9000, Drawer CC10, Bartow, FL 33831-9000; 863-534-4446; Fax: 863-534-4137. Hours: 8AM-5PM (EST). *Misdemeanor, Traffic.*
www.polk-county.net/clerk/clerk.html
Criminal Records: Access: Mail, in person. Both court and visitors may perform in person searches. Search fee: 3 year search: $4.10; lifetime: $5.10. Required to search: name, years to search, DOB; also helpful: SSN. Criminal records on computer; felonies since 1977, misdemeanors purged periodically. Both on microfiche and archived since 1800s.

General Information: Public Access terminal is available. No sex related cases, victims or child abuse released. Copy fee: $1.00 per page. Cert fee: $1.50. Payee: Clerk of Circuit Court. Personal checks accepted. Prepayment required. Mail turnaround time varies. Indicate on request when record is needed.

County Court - Civil Division PO Box 9000,
Drawer CC12, Bartow, FL 33830-9000; 863-534-4556 (County Court); Fax: 863-534-4045 (County Court). Hours: 8AM-5PM (EST). *Civil Actions Under $15,000, Eviction, Small Claims.*
www.polkcountyclerk.net
Civil Records: Access: Phone, mail, online, in person. Both court and visitors may perform in person searches. No search fee. Required to search: name, years to search. Civil cases indexed by defendant, plaintiff. Civil records on computer from 1983, on microfiche from 1961 to 1995. Case index information back to 1983 is free from the County Clerk's website at www.polkcountyclerk.net.

General Information: Public Access terminal is available. Copy fee: $1.00 per page. Cert fee: $1.50. Payee: Clerk of Court. Checks, cash, cashiers checks and money orders accepted. Prepayment required. Mail requests: SASE required. Mail turnaround time 1-5 days.

Putnam County

Circuit & County Courts - Civil Division
PO Box 758, Palatka, FL 32178; 386-329-0361; Fax: 386-329-0888. Hours: 8:30AM-5PM (EST). *Civil, Eviction, Small Claims, Probate.*
Civil Records: Access: Both court and visitors may perform in person searches. Search fee: $1.50 per name per year. Required to search: name, years to search. Civil cases indexed by defendant, plaintiff. Civil records on computer from 1984, on microfiche from 1973 to 1984, on index cards and docket books from 1900s to 1973. Access to the countywide remote online system requires $400 setup fee and $40. monthly charge plus $.05 per minute over 20 hours. Civil records go back to 1984. System includes criminal and real property records. Contact Ryel Christiansen to register. Access an index of judgments, liens, recorded documents at www.myfloridacounty.com. Fees involved to order copies; save $1.50 per record by becoming a subscriber.

General Information: Public Access terminal is available. No juvenile or incompetency records released. Fee to fax results is $2.25 per page. Copy fee: $1.00 per page. Cert fee: $1.50. Payee: Clerk of Court. Personal checks accepted. Prepayment required. Mail requests: SASE requested. Turnaround time 2-3 days.

Circuit & County Courts - Criminal
Division PO Box 758, Palatka, FL 32178; 386-329-0257; Fax: 386-329-0888. Hours: 8:30AM-5PM (EST). *Felony, Misdemeanor.*
Criminal Records: Access: Mail, fax, in person, email. Both court and visitors may perform in person searches. Search fee: $1.50 per name per year. Required to search: name, years to search; also helpful: DOB. Criminal records on computer from 1988, in files from 1930s to 1988. Access to the countywide criminal online system requires $400 setup fee and $40. monthly charge plus $.05 per minute over 20 hours. Criminal records go back to 1972. System includes civil and real property records. Contact Ryel Christiansen to register.

General Information: Public Access terminal is available. No juvenile records released. Fee to fax results is $2.25 per page. Copy fee: $1.00 per page. Cert fee: $1.50. Payee: Clerk of Circuit Court. Personal checks accepted. Prepayment required. Mail turnaround time 2-3 days.

Santa Rosa County

Circuit & County Courts - Civil Division
PO Box 472, Milton, FL 32572; 850-623-0135. Hours: 8AM-4:30PM (CST). *Civil, Eviction, Small Claims, Probate.*
www.santarosaclerk.com
Civil Records: Access: Fax, mail, in person, online. Both court and visitors may perform in person searches. Search fee: $1.50 per name per year. Required to search: name, years to search. Civil cases indexed by defendant, plaintiff. Civil records (Circuit) on computer from 1990, archived and on docket books from 1900s. County on computer from 1989, on microfiche from 1900s, on docket books from early 1900s. Access an index of judgments, liens, and court records free at http://oncoreweb.srccol.com/srccol/party5.asp or search at www.myfloridacounty.com where fees involved to order copies; save $1.50 per record by becoming a subscriber.

General Information: Public Access terminal is available. No adoption records released. Will fax results $2.00 per page. Copy fee: $1.00 per page. Cert fee: $1.50. Payee: Clerk of Courts. Personal checks accepted. Prepayment required. Mail requests: SASE required. Mail turnaround time ASAP.

Circuit & County Courts - Criminal Division
PO Box 472, Milton, FL 32572; 850-623-0135; Criminal phone: 850-983-1011; Fax: 850-626-5705. Hours: 8AM-4:30PM (CST). *Felony, Misdemeanor.*
www.co.santa-rosa.fl.us/santa_rosa/clerk/index.html
Note: Misdemeanor phone number is 850-623-0135 x1007 or x2140; fax 850-626-7849.

Criminal Records: Access: Mail, in person, online. Both court and visitors may perform in person searches. Search fee: $1.50 per name per year. Required to search: name, years to search, DOB; also helpful: SSN. Criminal records on computer back to 1989; felonies on index cards from 1925, misdemeanors on docket books from 1900s. Access an index of judgments, liens, and court records free at http://oncoreweb.srccol.com/srccol/party5.asp.

General Information: Public Access terminal is available. No records released before sentencing. Fee to fax results is $2.00 per page. Copy fee: $1.00 per page. Cert fee: $1.50 per page. Payee: Clerk's Office (include Division/Department name). Personal checks accepted. Prepayment required. Mail requests: SASE required. Mail turnaround time 1-5 days.

Sarasota County

Circuit & County Courts - Civil
PO Box 3079, Sarasota, FL 34230; 941-861-7400. Hours: 8:30AM-5PM (EST). *Civil, Eviction, Small Claims, Probate.*
www.sarasotaclerk.com
Civil Records: Access: Mail, online, in person. Both court and visitors may perform in person searches. Search fee: $1.50 per name per year. Required to search: name, years to search. Civil cases indexed by defendant, plaintiff. Civil records on computer from 1983, circuit & county on docket books from 1900s to 1983. Civil and DV case records from the Clerk of Circuit Court database are free online at www.clerk.co.sarasota.fl.us/srqapp/civilinq.asp.
Probate court records are at www.clerk.co.sarasota.fl.us/srqapp/probinq.asp.
Access an index of judgments, liens, recorded documents at www.myfloridacounty.com. Fees involved to order copies; save $1.50 per record by becoming a subscriber.
General Information: Public Access terminal is available. No adoption, mental health, or sealed records released. Copy fee: $1.00 per page. Cert fee: $1.50. Payee: Clerk of Circuit Court. Personal checks accepted. Credit cards will be accepted as of 07/97. Prepayment required. Mail requests: SASE helpful. Turnaround time 1 week.

Circuit & County Courts - Criminal
PO Box 3079, Sarasota, FL 34230; 941-861-7400. Hours: 8:30AM-5PM (EST). *Felony, Misdemeanor.*
www.sarasotaclerk.com
Criminal Records: Access: Mail, online, in person. Both court and visitors may perform in person searches. Search fee: $1.50 per name per year. Required to search: name, years to search, DOB, SSN. Criminal records on computer since 1983, (circuit) on docket books from 1900s to 1983, (county) on docket books from 1960s to 1983. Criminal and traffic case records from the Clerk of the Circuit Court database are free online at http://clerk.co.sarasota.fl.us/cvdisclaim.htm. Civil, probate and domestic records are also available.
General Information: Public Access terminal is available. No juvenile records released. Copy fee: $1.00 per page. Cert fee: $1.50. Payee: Clerk of Circuit Court. Personal checks accepted. Prepayment

required. Mail requests: SASE helpful. Turnaround time 1 week.

Seminole County

Circuit & County Courts - Civil Division
PO Box 8099, Sanford, FL 32772; 407-665-4330; Civil phone: 407-665-4366; Probate phone: 407-665-4374; Fax: 407-330-7193. Hours: 8AM-4:30PM (EST). *Civil, Eviction, Small Claims, Probate.*
www.18thcircuit.state.fl.us
Note: The felony court can be reached at 407-665-4380, and the misdemeanor court at 407-665-4342.
Civil Records: Access: Mail, in person, online. Both court and visitors may perform in person searches. Search fee: $1.50 per name per year. Required to search: name, years to search. Civil cases indexed by defendant, plaintiff. Civil records on computer since 1986, on microfiche since 1913. Access to the County Clerk's online records is free at www.seminoleclerk.org/OfficialRecords. Search by name, clerk's file number, or book & page.
General Information: Public Access terminal is available. No confidential files pursuant to law or sealed records released. Copy fee: $1.00 per page. Cert fee: $1.50 per document. Payee: Clerk of the Circuit Court. Personal checks accepted. Prepayment required. Mail requests: SASE required. Mail turnaround time 1 week.

Circuit & County Courts - Criminal Division
301 N Park Ave, Sanford, FL 32771; 407-665-4356 (Felony) 4377 (Misd); Fax: 407-330-7193. Hours: 8AM-4:30PM (EST). *Felony, Misdemeanor.*
www.seminoleclerk.org
Criminal Records: Access: Mail, in person. Both court and visitors may perform in person searches. Search fee: $1.50 per name per year. Required to search: name, years to search, DOB; also helpful: race, sex. Criminal records on computer from 1986; prior on microfiche.
General Information: Public Access terminal is available. No records of investigations which have not resulted in an arrest released. Local faxes $1.00 per page; out of state faxes $2.00 per page. Copy fee: $1.00 per page. Cert fee: $6.00. Payee: Clerk of Courts. Local personal and company checks allowed. Prepayment required. Mail requests: SASE not required. Mail turnaround time 2-4 days for felonies, no set time for misdemeanors.

St. Johns County

Circuit & County Courts - Civil Division
PO Drawer 300, St Augustine, FL 32085-0300; 904-819-3600; Fax: 904-819-3661. Hours: 8AM-5PM (EST). *Civil, Eviction, Small Claims, Probate.*
www.co.st-johns.fl.us
Civil Records: Access: Fax, mail, online, in person. Both court and visitors may perform in person searches. Search fee: $1.50 per name per year. Required to search: name, years to search. Civil cases indexed by defendant, plaintiff. Civil records on computer from 1984, on microfiche from 1976 to 1986, on docket books from 1820 to 1983. County on computer from 1991, microfiche from 1983 to 1991, docket books from 1820 to 1983. Access to the countywide remote online system requires $200 setup fee plus a monthly fee of $50. Searching is by name or case number. Call Mark Dearing at 904-819-3610 for more information. Also, access the county Clerk of Circuit Court recording database free at www.co.st-johns.fl.us/Const-Officers/Clerk-of-Court/doris/searchdocs.asp. Includes civil records. Access an index of judgments, liens, recorded documents at www.myfloridacounty.com. Fees involved to order copies; save $1.50 per record by becoming a subscriber at $25.00 per month.

General Information: Public Access terminal is available. No confidential or sealed records released. Fee to fax results: $2.00 for 1st page, $1.00 each add'l. Copy fee: $1.00 per page. Cert fee: $1.50. Payee: Clerk of Circuit Court. Personal checks accepted. Visa, MC accepted. Prepayment required. Mail requests: SASE required. Mail turnaround time 4-5 days.

Circuit & County Courts - Criminal Division
PO Drawer 300, St Augustine, FL 32085-0300; 904-819-3600; Civil phone: 904-819-3651; Criminal phone: 904-819-3615; Probate phone: 904-819-3654; Fax: 904-819-3666. Hours: 8AM-5PM (EST). *Felony, Misdemeanor.*
www.co.st-johns.fl.us
Criminal Records: Access: Fax, mail, online, in person. Both court and visitors may perform in person searches. Search fee: $1.50 per name per year. Required to search: name, years to search, DOB; also helpful: address, SSN. Criminal Records on computer. Felony since 1986, Misdemeanor since 1984. Felony on log books from 1950 to 1984. Access to the countywide criminal online system requires $200 setup fee plus a monthly fee of $50. Searching is by name or case number. Call Mark Dearing at 904-823-2333 x361 for more information.
General Information: Public Access terminal is available. No juvenile or sexual offense records released. Fee to fax results is $1.00 per page. Copy fee: $1.00 per page. Cert fee: $1.50. Payee: Clerk of Circuit Court. Personal checks accepted. Visa, MC accepted. Prepayment required. Escrow/billing accounts available to government agencies. Mail requests: SASE required. Mail turnaround time 4-5 days.

St. Lucie County

Circuit & County Courts - Civil Division
PO Drawer 700, Ft Pierce, FL 34954; 772-462-2758 (Circuit); Civil phone: 772-785-5880 (County); Fax: 772-462-1998 (Circ.); 772-785-5884 (Cty). Hours: 8AM-5PM (EST). *Civil, Eviction, Small Claims, Probate.*
www.slclerkofcourt.com
Note: Small claims phone is 772-785-5880; Small Claims and County Civil files and microfiche are located at the Courthouse Annex, 250 NW County Club Dr, Pt St. Lucie, FL 34986.
Civil Records: Access: Mail, in person, online. Both court and visitors may perform in person searches. Search fee: $1.50 per name per year. Required to search: name, years to search. Civil cases indexed by defendant, plaintiff. Circuit records on computer back to 1992. Circuit on microfiche from 1981 to 1992, County from 1981 to 1992. Circuit on docket books from 1900s to 1981, County from 1900s to 1981. Online access to civil records at http://public.slclerkofcourt.com. Case tracking and bond record tracking are available. Access an index of judgments, liens, recorded documents at www.myfloridacounty.com. Fees involved to order copies; save $1.50 per record by becoming a subscriber.
General Information: Public Access terminal is available. No sealed cases or adoption records released. Will fax results to local or toll free line. Copy fee: $1.00 per page. Cert fee: $1.50 per document. Payee: Clerk of Court. Personal checks accepted; drivers license & photo ID required. Prepayment required. Mail turnaround time 1 day.

Circuit & County Courts - Criminal Division
PO Drawer 700, Ft Pierce, FL 34954; 772-462-6900; Fax: 772-462-2833. Hours: 8AM-5PM (EST). *Felony, Misdemeanor.*
www.martin.fl.us/GOVT/co/schack

Criminal Records: Access: Fax, mail, in person, online. Both court and visitors may perform in person searches. Search fee: $1.50 per name per year. Required to search: name, years to search, DOB, signed release; also helpful: address, SSN, race, sex. Criminal records on computer back to 1982, on microfiche to 1960, on books prior to 1900s. Online access to bonds, traffic and misdemeanor records is free at http://public.slcclerkofcourt.com. Online records go back to 7/6/1992. Felony records only available to government agencies.

General Information: Public Access terminal is available. No sealed or expunged records released. Fee to fax results is $2.00 per page. Copy fee: $1.00 per page. Cert fee: $1.50. Payee: Clerk of Court. Only cashiers checks and money orders accepted. Prepayment required. Mail turnaround time 1-2 weeks; fax turnaround time 1-5 days.

Sumter County

Circuit & County Courts - Civil Division
209 N Florida St, Bushnell, FL 33513; 352-793-0211; Fax: 352-568-6608. Hours: 8:30AM-5PM (EST). *Civil, Eviction, Small Claims, Probate.*
Civil Records: Access: Fax, mail, in person, online. Both court and visitors may perform in person searches. Search fee: $1.50 per name per year. Required to search: name, years to search. Civil cases indexed by defendant, plaintiff. Civil records go back to 1800s; on computer go back to 12/1999; in docket books from 1986 to 11/30/99 (circuit only). Access an index of judgments, liens, recorded documents at www.myfloridacounty.com. Fees involved to order copies; save $1.50 per record by becoming a subscriber.

General Information: No juvenile or adoption records released. Will fax results $1.00 per page. Copy fee: $1.00 per page. Cert fee: $1.50 per document. Payee: Clerk of Circuit Court. Personal checks accepted. Prepayment required. Mail requests: SASE requested. Turnaround time 1 week; phone turnaround is 30 min. to 1 hour.

Circuit & County Courts - Criminal Division 209 N Florida St, Bushnell, FL 33513; 352-793-0211; Fax: 352-568-6608. Hours: 8:30AM-5PM (EST). *Felony, Misdemeanor.*
Criminal Records: Access: Mail, in person. Only the court performs in person searches; visitors may not. Search fee: $1.50 per name per year. Required to search: name, years to search, DOB. Criminal records (circuit) on computer since 2000, on index books from 1965 to 1999, prior in vaults. County on computer since 1982, on microfiche from 1960 to 1982, on docket books since early 1900s.

General Information: No juvenile records released. Fee to fax results is $1.00 per page. Copy fee: $1.00 per page. Cert fee: $1.50. Payee: Clerk of Court. Only cashiers checks and money orders accepted. Prepayment required. Mail requests: SASE requested. Turnaround time 1 week.

Suwannee County

Circuit & County Courts 200 S Ohio Ave, Live Oak, FL 32060; 386-362-0500; Fax: 386-362-0567. 8:30AM-5PM (EST). *Felony, Misdemeanor, Civil, Eviction, Small Claims, Probate.*
www.suwclerk.org/index2.html
Civil Records: Access: Mail, in person, online. Both court and visitors may perform in person searches. Search fee: $1.50 per name per year. Fee is per index. Required to search: name, years to search; also helpful: address. Civil cases indexed by defendant, plaintiff. Civil records on computer from 1983, archived from 1859 to 1983. Access to County Clerk of Circuit Court records is at

www.suwclerk.org/public.html. Written requests require prepayment.
Criminal Records: Access: Mail, in person, online. Both court and visitors may perform in person searches. Search fee: $1.50 per name per year. Fee is per index. Required to search: name, years to search, DOB, signed release; also helpful: address. Criminal records on computer from 1983, archived from 1859 to 1983. Access to County Clerk of Circuit Court records is at www.suwclerk.org/public.html. Criminal records may be temporarily unavailable. Written requests require prepayment.

General Information: Public Access terminal is available. No juvenile or adoption records released. Will fax results for $3.00 1st page plus $.50 each add'l. Copy fee: $1.00 per page. Cert fee: $1.50. Payee: Suwannee Court Clerk. Personal checks accepted. Prepayment required. Mail requests: SASE required. Mail turnaround time 1 week.

Taylor County

Circuit & County Courts PO Box 620, Perry, FL 32348; 850-838-3506; Fax: 850-838-3549. Hours: 8AM-5PM (EST). *Felony, Misdemeanor, Civil, Eviction, Small Claims, Probate.*
Civil Records: Access: Mail, in person, online. Only the court performs in person searches; visitors may not. Search fee: $1.50 per name per year. Required to search: name, years to search. Civil cases indexed by defendant, plaintiff. Civil records on computer back to 1982; on index from 1973 to 1991, prior on index books to 1856. Access an index of judgments, liens, recorded documents at www.myfloridacounty.com. Fees involved to order copies; save $1.50 per record by becoming a subscriber.
Criminal Records: Access: Mail, in person. Only the court performs in person searches; visitors may not. Search fee: $1.50 per name per year. Required to search: name, years to search, DOB; also helpful: SSN, race, sex. Criminal records on computer back to 1982; on index from 1973 to 1991, prior on index books to 1950.

General Information: Public Access terminal is available. No juvenile records released. Will fax results for $1.00 per fax plus copy cost. Copy fee: $1.00 per page. Cert fee: $1.50. Payee: Taylor County Clerk of Court. Business checks accepted. Prepayment required. Mail requests: SASE helpful. Turnaround time 1 week.

Union County

Circuit & County Courts Courthouse, Rm 103, Lake Butler, FL 32054; 386-496-3711; Fax: 386-496-1718. Hours: 8AM-5PM (EST). *Felony, Misdemeanor, Civil, Eviction, Small Claims, Probate.*
http://circuit8.org
Civil Records: Access: Fax, mail, in person, online. Only the court may perform in person searches; visitors may not. Search fee: $1.50 per name per year. Required to search: name, years to search. Civil cases indexed by defendant, plaintiff. Civil records on docket books from 1921. Access an index of judgments, liens, recorded documents at www.myfloridacounty.com. Fees involved to order copies; save $1.50 per record by becoming a subscriber.
Criminal Records: Access: Fax, mail, in person, online. Only the court performs in person searches; visitors may not. Search fee: $1.50 per name per year. Required to search: name, years to search, DOB; also helpful: SSN. Criminal records on docket books from 1921. Access the circuit-wide criminal quick lookup at http://circuit8.org/golem/gencrim.html. Account and password is required; restricted usage.

General Information: No juvenile records released. Will fax results $1.00 per page. Copy fee: $1.00 per

page. Cert fee: $1.50. Payee: Clerk of Court. Personal checks accepted. Prepayment required. Mail requests: SASE preferred. Turnaround time 2-3 days.

Volusia County

Circuit & County Courts - Civil Division
PO Box 6043, De Land, FL 32721; 386-736-5915; Fax: 386-822-5711. Hours: 8AM-4:30PM (EST). *Civil, Eviction, Small Claims, Probate.*
www.clerk.org
Civil Records: Access: Fax, mail, online, in person. Both court and visitors may perform in person searches. Search fee: $1.50 per name per year. Required to search: name, years to search. Civil cases indexed by defendant, plaintiff. Civil records on computer from 1986, on docket books from 1863 to 1986. Access to the countywide remote online system requires $125 setup fee plus a $25 monthly fee. Windows required. Search by name or case number. Call Thom White 386-736-5915 for more information. Criminal, probate and traffic records are also available. Access an index of judgments, liens, recorded documents at www.myfloridacounty.com. Fees involved to order copies; save $1.50 per record by becoming a subscriber.

General Information: Public Access terminal is available. No sealed records released. Fee to fax results is $1.00 per page. Copy fee: $1.00 per page. Cert fee: $1.50. Payee: Clerk of Circuit Court. Personal checks accepted. Prepayment required. Mail requests: SASE requested. Turnaround time 1-2 weeks.

Circuit & County Courts - Criminal Division PO Box 6043, De Land, FL 32721-6043; 386-736-5915; Fax: 386-740-5175. Hours: 8AM-4:30PM (EST). *Felony, Misdemeanor.*
www.clerk.org
Criminal Records: Access: Mail, online, in person. Both court and visitors may perform in person searches. Search fee: $1.50 per name per year. Required to search: name, years to search, DOB; also helpful: SSN, race, sex. Criminal records 1982 to present on computer, on microfiche from 1856 to 1988, on docket books prior to 1983. Two access methods are available. Access to the Clerk of Circuit Courts database of Citation Violations and 24-hour Arrest Reports is free at www.clerk.org/publicrecords/or.tshtml. Access to the countywide criminal online system requires $125 setup fee plus a $25 monthly fee. Windows required. Search by name or case number back to 1988. Call 904-822-5710 for more information. Civil, probate and traffic records are also available.

General Information: Public Access terminal is available. No confidential, sexual battery and juvenile records released. Will fax results $1.50 per page. Copy fee: $1.00 per page. Cert fee: $1.50. Payee: Clerk of Court. Personal and out of state checks accepted with proper ID. Prepayment required. Mail requests: SASE required. Mail turnaround time up to 1 week.

Wakulla County

Circuit & County Courts 3056 Crawfordville Hwy, Crawfordville, FL 32327; 850-926-0905; Civil phone: 850-926-0323; Criminal phone: 850-926-0359; Fax: 850-926-0938 (Civil); 926-0936 (Crim). Hours: 8AM-5PM (EST). *Felony, Misdemeanor, Civil, Eviction, Small Claims, Probate.*
www.wakullaclerk.com/
Note: Felony/Misdemeanor court can be reached at 850-926-0324.

Civil Records: Access: Phone, fax, mail, in person, online. Both court and visitors may perform in person searches. Search fee: $1.50 per name per year. Required to search: name, years to search. Civil cases indexed by defendant, plaintiff. Civil records on computer since 1990, on docket books from 1800s. Access an index of judgments, liens, recorded documents at www.myfloridacounty.com. Fees involved to order copies; save $1.50 per record by becoming a subscriber.

Criminal Records: Access: Fax, mail, in person. Both court and visitors may perform in person searches. Search fee: $1.50 per name per year. Required to search: name, years to search, DOB; also helpful: SSN. Criminal records on computer since 1990, on docket books from 1800s. Visitors may review docket books, only court performs name searches.

General Information: No juvenile, adoption records released. Fee to fax results is $1.00 per page. Copy fee: $1.00 per page. Cert fee: $1.50. Payee: Clerk of Court. Personal checks accepted. Prepayment required. Mail requests: SASE helpful. Turnaround time 3-4 days.

Walton County

Circuit & County Courts PO Box 1260, De Funiak Springs, FL 32435; 850-892-8115; Fax: 850-892-7551. Hours: 8AM-4:30PM (CST). *Felony, Misdemeanor, Civil, Eviction, Small Claims, Probate.*

www.co.walton.fl.us/clerk

Civil Records: Access: Fax, mail, online, in person. Only the court may perform in person searches;

visitors may not. Search fee: $1.50 per name per year. Required to search: name, years to search. Civil cases indexed by defendant, plaintiff. Civil records on computer from 1988, on dockets from 1900s. The website offers access to civil record indices.

Criminal Records: Access: Fax, mail, online, in person. Only the court may perform in person searches; visitors may not. Search fee: $1.50 per name per year. Required to search: name, years to search, DOB. Criminal records on computer from 1988, on dockets from 1900s. The websites offers access to felony judgments of guilt.

General Information: Public Access terminal is available. No sealed, expunged, or pre-sentence investigation records released. Will fax results $1.00 per page. Copy fee: $1.00 per page. Cert fee: $1.50. Payee: Clerk of Courts. Personal checks accepted. Prepayment required. Mail requests: SASE helpful. Turnaround time 24 hours.

Washington County

Circuit & County Courts PO Box 647, Chipley, FL 32428-0647; 850-638-6285; Fax: 850-638-6297. Hours: 8AM-4PM (CST). *Felony, Misdemeanor, Civil, Eviction, Small Claims, Probate.*

Civil Records: Access: Phone, fax, mail, in person, online. Both court and visitors may perform in person searches. Search fee: $1.50 per name per year. Required to search: name, years to search. Civil cases

indexed by defendant, plaintiff. Civil records on computer from 1985; on docket books from 1940. Access an index of judgments, liens, recorded documents at www.myfloridacounty.com. Fees involved to order copies; save $1.50 per record by becoming a subscriber.

Criminal Records: Access: Phone, fax, mail, in person. Only the court performs in person searches; visitors may not. Search fee: $1.50 per name per year. Required to search: name, years to search. Criminal records on computer back to 1981, on docket books from 1900.

General Information: Public Access terminal is available. (Only civil available.) No adoption or juvenile records released. Will fax results to local or toll free line. Copy fee: $1.00 per page. Cert fee: $1.50. Payee: Clerk of Court. Business checks accepted. Local personal checks accepted. Prepayment required. Mail requests: SASE requested. Turnaround time 1 day.

Florida Recording Offices

ORGANIZATION: 67 counties, 67 recording offices. The recording officer is Clerk of the Circuit Court. All transactions are recorded in the "Official Record," a grantor/grantee index. Some counties will search by type of transaction while others will return everything on the index. 57 counties are in the Eastern Time Zone (EST) and 10 are in the Central Time Zone (CST).

REAL ESTATE RECORDS: Any name searched in the "Official Records" will usually include all types of liens and property transfers for that name. Most counties will perform searches. In addition to the usual $1.00 per page copy fee, certification of documents usually cost $1.50 per document. Tax records are located at the Property Appraiser Office.

Note that a number of counties make their real estate records available online.

UCC RECORDS: Financing statements are filed at the state level, and real estate related collateral at the Clerk of the Circuit Court. Until 1/2002, farm related financing was also filed at the clerk's office. All but a few counties will perform UCC searches. Use search request form UCC-11. Search fees are usually $1.50 per debtor name per year searched and include all lien and real estate transactions on record. Copies usually cost $1.00 per page.

TAX LIEN RECORDS: Federal tax liens on personal property of businesses are filed with the Secretary of State. All other federal and state tax liens on personal property are filed with the county Clerk of Circuit Court. Usually tax liens on personal property are filed in the same index with UCC financing statements and real estate transactions. Most counties will perform a tax lien as part of a UCC search. Copies usually cost $1.00 per page.

OTHER LIENS: Judgments, hospital, mechanics, sewer, ambulance.

ONLINE ACCESS: There are numerous county agencies that provide online access to records, but the statewide system MyFlorida.com predominates. My Florida offers free access to the over 51 counties Circuit Clerks of Court recorded document indexes including real estate records liens, judgments, marriages, and deaths at www.myfloridacounty.com/services/officialrecords_intro.shtml. Fees involved to order copies; save $1.50 per record by becoming a subscriber. Subscription fee is $120.00 per year, plus monthly transaction fees for copies.

On or after October 1, 2002, any person preparing or filing a document for recording in the Official Record may not include a Social Security Number in such document unless required by law. The Clerk of the Circuit Court cannot place an image or copy of the following documents on a publicly available Internet website for general public display: Military discharges; Death certificates; Court files, records or papers relating to Family Law, Juvenile Law or Probate Law cases.

Any person has the right to request the Clerk/County Recorder to redact/remove his Social Security Number from an image or copy of an Official Record that has been placed on such Clerk/County Recorder's publicly available Internet website.

Alachua County

County Clerk of the Circuit Court, PO Box 600, Gainesville, FL 32602. **Phone**-352-374-3625; fax-352-491-4649; 8:30AM-5PM www.clerk-alachua-fl.org Will search UCC records. Search per debtor- $1.50 per name per year. UCC copy- $1.00 per page. Tax liens not included in UCC search. Separate federal/state combined tax lien search- $1.50 per year. Real estate owner, mortgage, and property transfer searches available. RE record copy- $1.00 per page. Cert fee: $1.50 per doc. Payee: Alachua County Clerk of the Circuit Court. **Online Access to Property Appraiser, Real Estate, Lien, Vital Statistic, Recording, Traffic Citation records:** Access to the Clerk of Courts recording database is free at www.alachuaclerk.org. Index goes back to 1971. Records go back to 1990. Also, search the County Appraiser's Property Search page free online at www.acpafl.org. Sales search and GIS search also here. Also search ancient records - pre-1940 plats, pre-1970 marriages, deeds, transcriptions and more - free at www.clerk-alachua-fl.org/archive/default.cfm. Search traffic citations at www.co.alachua.fl.us/traffic/. Access the clerk's recorded document index at www.myfloridacounty.com. See section intro for MyFlorida.com access details. Also, search tax roll data free at www.actcfl.org/collectmax/collect30.asp. **Other phones:** Treasurer-352-374-3605; Appraiser-352-374-5230; Finance Director-352-374-3605.

Baker County

County Clerk of the Circuit Court, 339 E. MacClenny Ave, MacClenny, FL 32063. **Phone**-904-259-0208; fax-904-259-4176; hours 8:30AM-5PM

Will search UCC records. Search per debtor- $1.50 per name per year. UCC copy- $1.00 per page. Will not search real estate or tax lien records. RE record copy- $1.00 per page. Cert fee: $1.50 per doc. Payee: Baker County Clerk of the Circuit Court. **Online Access to Real Estate, Lien, Recording, Property records:** Access the recorded document index at www.myfloridacounty.com. See section intro for MyFlorida.com access details. Also, search for free property data at www.emapsplus.com/FLBaker/maps/. Choose to search by owner. **Other phones:** Treasurer-904-259-6880; Appraiser-904-259-3191; Elections-904-259-6339.

Bay County

County Clerk of the Circuit Court, PO Box 2269, Panama City, FL 32402. **Phone**-850-747-5104; fax-850-747-5199; 8AM-4:30PM www.baycoclerk.com Will not search UCC or tax lien records. UCC copy- $1.00 per page. Real estate record owner searches available 1987 to present. Cert fee: $1.50 per doc. Payee: Bay County Clerk of the Circuit Court. **Online Access to Property Tax, Real Estate, Tax Lien, Recording, Appraiser, Property Sale records:** Access to the Clerk of the Circuit Court Recordings database is free at www.clerk.co.bay.fl.us/oncoreV2/. Records go back to 1/1987. Also, search the property appraiser database free at http://bcpa.elementaldata.com/search.asp or at www.qpublic.net/bay/search1.html; search the tax collector database for free at http://bctc.elementaldata.com/disclaimer.asp. Assessor database is free at http://bcpa.co.bay.fl.us/database.htm. Also, Access the recorded document index at www.myfloridacounty.com. See section intro for

MyFlorida.com access details. **Other phones:** Assessor-850-784-4095; Appraiser-850-784-4095.

Bradford County

County Clerk of the Circuit Court, PO Drawer B, Starke, FL 32091. **Phone**-County Clerk of the Circuit Court, R/E & UCC Recording- 904-966-6283; fax-904-964-4454; 8AM-5PM www.myfloridacounty.com Will not search records. Record copy- $1.00 per page. Cert fee: $1.50 per doc. Payee: Bradford County Clerk of the Circuit Court. **Online Access to Real Estate, Appraisal, Deed, Judgment, Marriage, Lien, Court records:** Access to the recorders database is free at www.mybradfordcounty.com. Click on "Official Records." Also, search the property appraiser database at www.bradfordappraiser.com/Search_F.asp. Access the clerk's recorded document index atwww.myfloridacounty.com. See section intro for MyFlorida.com access details. **Other phones:** Assessor-904-966-6217; Treasurer-904-966-6246; Appraiser-904-964-6280; Elections-904-966-6236; Vital Records-904-966-7383.

Brevard County

County Clerk of the Circuit Court, PO Box 2767, Titusville, FL 32781. **Phone**-321-264-5244, 264-5350; fax-321-264-5246; hours-8AM-5PM www.clerk.co.brevard.fl.us Will not search records. Record copy- $1.00 per page. Cert fee: $1.50 per doc. Payee: Brevard County Clerk of the Circuit Court. **Online Access to Real Estate, Lien, Marriage, Recording, Tax Sale, Property Appraiser, Personal Property records:** Access to the clerk's tax lien (1981-95), land records (1995 to present) and indexed records from 1981 to

9/30/1995 are at www.clerk.co.brevard.fl.us/pages/pubrec9.htm. Registration and a password is now required; application fee is $5.00. Marriage records also available; access is free. Search most wanted and arrests at www.sheriff.co.brevard.fl.us under "Departments." Property tax, sales and personal property records are at http://brevardpropertyappraiser.com/asp/disclaimer.asp. Also, tax deed sales are listed free at www.clerk.co.brevard.fl.us/taxdeed/taxdeed.HTM. For "public use" the clerk offers a public system at http://webfyi.clerk.co.brevard.fl.us/netfyi/instruct.html includes plats, traffic, courts and more. **Other phones:** Assessor-321-264-6700; Appraiser-321-264-6700.

Broward County

Director of County Records, 115 S Andrews Ave, Rm 114, Records Division, Fort Lauderdale, FL 33301. **Phone**-Director of County Records, R/E & UCC Recording- 954-357-7281; fax-954-357-7267; hours 7:30AM-5PM www.broward.org/records
Will search UCC records. Search per debtor- $1.50 per name per year. UCC copy- $1.00 per page. Tax liens not included in UCC search. Separate federal/state combined tax lien search- $1.00 per year. Real estate record owner and property searches available. Cert fee: $1.50 per doc. Payee: Broward County Board of County Commissioners. **Online Access to Property, Appraiser, Real Estate, Lien, Recording, Occupational License, Most Wanted, Arrest, Missing, Sex Offender records:** Access to the county records Public Search database 1978-present is free at http://205.166.161.12/oncoreV2/. At www.broward.org/cri03300.htm professional users may register and receive a password for add'l access options. Also, search the occupational license database at http://lsta.broward.org/olsearch/olsearch.asp. Search the sheriff's multiple databases at www.sheriff.org. Also, search property tax data for free at http://bcegov.co.broward.fl.us/revenue/nameform.htm. Search appraiser records for free online at www.bcpa.net/index.cfm?page=search. **Other phones:** Assessor-954-357-6904; Treasurer-954-357-7235; Appraiser-954-357-6908; Elections-954-357-7050; Vital Records-Birth 954-467-4413/Death 467-4424.

Calhoun County

County Clerk of the Circuit Court, 20859 SE Central Ave, Rm 130, Blountstown, FL 32424. **Phone**-County Clerk of the Circuit Court, R/E & UCC Recording-850-674-4545; fax-850-674-5553; hours 8AM-4PM www.calhounclerk.com
Will not search records. Record copy- $1.00 per page. Cert fee: $1.50 per doc. Payee: Calhoun County Clerk of the Circuit Court. **Online Access to Real Estate, Lien, Deed, Judgment, Recording records:** Access the recorded document index at www.myfloridacounty.com. See section intro for MyFlorida.com access details. **Other phones:** Assessor-850-674-8242; Appraiser-850-674-8242.

Charlotte County

County Clerk of the Circuit Court, PO Box 510156, Punta Gorda, FL 33951-0156. **Phone**-941-637-2245; fax-941-637-2172; 8AM-5PM www.co.charlotte.fl.us
Will search UCC records. Search per debtor- $1.50 per name per year. UCC copy- $1.00 per page per year, $1.00 to certify. Tax liens not included in UCC search. Separate federal/state combined tax lien search- $1.00 per year. Real estate record owner and mortgage searches available. RE record copy- $1.00 per page. Cert fee: $1.50 per doc. Payee: Clerk of the Circuit Court. **Online Access to Property Appraiser, Real Estate, Lien, Recording, Property Sale, Arrest, Most Wanted, Sex Offender records:** Property records are free at www.ccappraiser.com/record.asp. Sales records are also here and at the tax collector database, free at

www.cctaxcol.com/record.asp?. Search sheriff data at www.ccso.org/localcrime/crimedatabase.cfm. Also, recordings from the county clerk database are free at http://208.47.160.70. Search by book/page or grantor/grantee. A subscription service (CASWEB) is also available, which includes images, court records, recordings, etc. Bulk database record purchases, by year, are also available. Access the recorded document index at www.myfloridacounty.com. See section intro for MyFlorida.com access details. **Other phones:** Appraiser-941-743-1488.

Citrus County

County Clerk of the Circuit Court, 110 N. Apopka Ave. Rm101, Inverness, FL 34450-4299. **Phone**-352-341-6468; fax-352-341-6477; hours 8AM-5PM www.clerk.citrus.fl.us
Will search UCC records. Search per debtor- $1.50 per name per year. UCC copy- $1.00 per page. UCC search includes tax liens if requested. Separate federal/state combined tax lien search- $1.00 per year. Will search for any real estate records in the official records index. Cert fee: $1.50 per doc. Payee: Citrus County Clerk of the Circuit Court. **Online Access to Property Appraiser, Real Estate, Lien, Deed, Recording, Marriage, Property Tax, Sex Offender records:** Access to the Clerk records is free at www.clerk.citrus.fl.us/hart_wwwroot/. Search property tax records for free at http://citrustaxcollector.governmax.com. Search marriage license records free online at www.clerk.citrus.fl.us/marrsearch.asp. Search by first and last name. Also, Property records are free at www.pa.citrus.fl.us/ccpaask.html. Access the recorded document index at www.myfloridacounty.com. See section intro for MyFlorida.com access details. Also, search the sheriff sex offender list at www.sheriffcitrus.org/SexOffenders/SexOffPred.htm. **Other phones:** Appraiser-352-637-9820.

Clay County

County Clerk of the Circuit Court, PO Box 698, Green Cove Springs, FL 32043-0698. **Phone**-904-284-6317, R/E Recording- 904-284-6362, UCC Recording- 904-284-6362; fax-904-284-6390; hours 8:30AM-4:30PM http://clerk.co.clay.fl.us
Will search UCC records. Search per debtor- $1.50 per name per year. UCC copy- $1.00 per page. UCC search includes tax liens if requested. Separate federal/state combined tax lien search- $1.00 per year per debtor. Will search for any real estate records in official records, except title searches. RE record copy- $1.00 per page. Cert fee: $1.50 per doc. Payee: Clay County Clerk of the Circuit Court. **Online Access to Appraiser, Real Estate, Lien, Recording, Tangible Personal Property, Property Tax, Most Wanted, Sex Offender records:** The county clerk of circuit court allows free online access to recording records at http://clerk.co.clay.fl.us/ASP/or_queryname.asp. This replaces the commercial system. Records go back to 1990. Also, Property Appraiser's office records are free at www.ccpao.com/ccpao/ccpao.asp?page=Disclaimer. Also, search real estate and tangible personal property at www.claycountytax.com/Tax_Searchr/porr.html. Also, access the clerk's recorded document index atwww.myfloridacounty.com. See section intro for MyFlorida.com access details. Also, search sex offenders and most wanted at http://claysheriff.com. **Other phones:** Appraiser-904-284-6320.

Collier County

County Clerk of the Circuit Court, PO Box 413044, Naples, FL 34101-3044. **Phone**-239-732-2646, R/E Recording- 239-732-2606, UCC Recording- 239-732-2606; fax-239-774-8003; hours 8AM-5PM (No recording after 4:30PM) www.clerk.collier.fl.us

Will search UCC records. Search per debtor- $1.50 per name per year. UCC copy- $1.00 per page. UCC search includes tax liens if requested. Separate federal/state combined tax lien search- $1.00 per year. Real estate owner, mortgage, and property transfer searches available. RE record copy- $1.00 per page. Cert fee: $1.50 per doc. Payee: Collier County Clerk of the Circuit Court. **Online Access to Property Appraiser, Real Estate, Lien, UCC, Vital Statistic, Recording, Tax Sale, Wanted, Missing Person, Property Tax records:** Access to records on the Property Appraiser database are free at www.collierappraiser.com/Disclaimer.asp. The sheriff's wanted and missing persons lists are at www.colliersheriff.org. Access to clerk of courts court records, lien, real estate, UCCs and vital records is free at www.clerk.collier.fl.us/clerkspublicac/Default.htm. Lending agency data is available. Also search property tax rolls at www.colliertax.com/Search.asp. Tax deeds sales data is at www.clerk.collier.fl.us/OfficialRecords/Tax_Deeds/Tax%20Deeds.htm. Also, access the clerk's recorded document index at www.myfloridacounty.com. See section intro for MyFlorida.com access details. **Other phones:** Assessor-239-732-8141; Treasurer-239-732-6179; Appraiser-239-774-8175; Elections-239-732-8450; Vital Records-239-732-8205.

Columbia County

County Clerk of the Circuit Court, PO Box 2069, Lake City, FL 32056-2069. **Phone**-386-758-1342, R/E Recording- 386-758-1053, UCC Recording- 386-758-1053; fax-386-758-1337; hours 8AM-5PM www.columbiaclerk.com
Will search UCC records. UCC search per debtor- $1.50 per name per year. UCC copy- $1.00 per page. UCC search includes tax liens if requested. Separate federal/state combined tax lien search- $1.00 per year. Real estate owner, mortgage, and property transfer searches available. Cert fee: $1.50 per doc. Payee: Columbia County Clerk of the Circuit Court. **Online Access to Real Estate, Lien, Recording, Probate, Property Tax, Appraiser, GIS, Occupational License records:** Access to the Clerk of Circuit Courts recording database index is free at www.columbiaclerk.com. Click on Order Official Records. Search by name, book/page, file number of document type. A www.myfloridacounty.com website; fees are involved to order copies; see section intro for details. Search property appraiser records free at http://columbia.floridapa.com/GIS/Search_F.asp. Also, search the tax rolls and occupational licenses free at www.columbiataxcollector.com/collectmax/collect30.asp. **Other phones:** Assessor-386-758-1077; Treasurer-386-758-1042; Appraiser-386-758-1087; Elections-386-758-1028; Vital Records-386-758-1150.

Dade County

County Clerk of the Circuit Court, 22 N.W. 1st St, Miami, FL 33128. **Phone**-305-275-1155; fax-305-372-7775; hours 9AM-4PM www.metro-dade.com/clerk
Will search UCC records. Search per debtor- $1.50 per name per year. UCC copy- $1.00 per page. UCC search includes tax liens if requested. Separate federal/state combined tax lien search- $1.50 per year. Real estate owner, mortgage, and property transfer searches available. RE record copy- $1.00 per page. Cert fee: $1.50 per doc. Payee: Dade County Clerk of the Circuit Court. **Online Access to Real Estate, Recording, Judgment, Lien, Marriage, Tax Deed Sale, Property Appraiser, Property Tax records:** 3 sources available. Record access to 11 databases requires $125 initial setup fee and minimum $52 monthly fee for 208 minutes, $.25 ea. add'l minute. Records date back to 1975. Contact 305-596-8148 for info. 2nd service county recorder only. Fee is $50 per month, at www.miami-

dadeclerk.com/dadecoc/Premier_Services.asp. Third, recorder records are free at www.miami-dadeclerk.com/public-records/pubsearch.asp. Property search GIS site at www.emapsplus.com/FLDade/maps/. Tax Collector records, free at www.co.miami-dade.fl.us/proptax/. Search property at http://gisims2.co.miami-dade.fl.us/MyHome/propmap.asp. Tax deed sales: www.miami-dadeclerk.com/tax-deeds/home.asp. Also, www.miamidade.gov/public-records records search site. **Other phones:** Assessor-305-375-4099; Appraiser-305-375-5447.

De Soto County

County Clerk of the Circuit Court, 115 E. Oak St, Arcadia, FL 34266. **Phone-**County Clerk of the Circuit Court, R/E & UCC Recording- 863-993-4876; fax-863-993-4669; hours 8AM-5PM
Will search UCC records. Search per debtor- $1.50 per name per year. UCC copy- $1.00 per page. UCC search includes tax liens if requested. Separate federal/state combined tax lien search- $1.00 per year. Will not search real estate records. RE record copy- $1.00 per copy. Cert fee: $1.50 per doc. Payee: De Soto County Clerk of the Circuit Court. **Online Access to Real Estate, Lien, Recording, Property Tax, Inmate, Wanted records:** Access the recorded document index at www.myfloridacounty.com. See section intro for MyFlorida.com access details. Also, access property appraiser data at http://qpublic.net/desoto/search.html. Also, access to the tax collector data is free at www.qpublic.net/dctc/search.html. Search the sheriff's inmate list at http://65.40.25.25/Sheriff.htm - the most wanted list at www.desotosheriff.com/mostwanted.htm. **Other phones:** Assessor-863-993-4866; Appraiser-863-993-4866.

Dixie County

County Clerk of the Circuit Court, PO Box 1206, Cross City, FL 32628. **Phone-**County Clerk of the Circuit Court, R/E & UCC Recording- 352-498-1200; fax-352-498-1201; hours 9AM-Noon,1-5PM
Will not search records. Record copy- $1.00 per page. Cert fee: $1.50 per doc. Payee: Dixie County Clerk of the Circuit Court. **Online Access to Real Estate, Lien, Recording records:** Access the recorded document index at www.myfloridacounty.com. See section intro for MyFlorida.com access details. **Other phones:** Assessor-352-498-1212; Appraiser-352-498-1212; Elections-352-498-1216.

Duval County

County Clerk of the Circuit Court, 330 E. Bay St #103, Courthouse, Jacksonville, FL 32202. **Phone-**904-630-2043; fax-904-630-2959; hours 8:30AM-4:30PM
www.coj.net
Will search UCC records. Search per debtor- $1.50 per name per year. UCC copy- $1.00 per page. Will search tax liens. Tax lien search fee- $1.00 per debtor. Real estate record owner and mortgage searches available. Cert fee: $1.50 per doc. Payee: Duval County Clerk of the Circuit Court. **Online Access to Property Appraiser, Real Estate, Lien, Recording, Grantor/Grantee, Vital Statistic, Occupational License records:** Access to the Clerk of Circuit Court and City of Jacksonville Official Records (a grantor/grantee index) is free at www.duval.fl.us.landata.com/SearchDisclaimer.asp. Search the tax collector real estate data at http://tc.coj.net/realestate/. Also, search County Property Appraiser records for Duval County and City of Jacksonville at http://apps2.coj.net/pao. Search occupational licenses at http://tc.coj.net/occlicense/; Tangible property at http://tc.coj.net/tpproperty/ Access the clerk's recorded document index at www.myfloridacounty.com. See section intro for

MyFlorida.com access details. **Other phones:** Treasurer-904-630-2068; Appraiser-904-630-2020.

Escambia County

Clerk of the Circuit Court, 223 Palafox Pl, Old Courthouse, Pensacola, FL 32501. **Phone-**Clerk of the Circuit Court, R/E & UCC Recording- 850-595-3930; fax-850-595-4827; hours-8AM-5PM
www.clerk.co.escambia.fl.us
Will search UCC records. Search per debtor- $1.50 per name per year. UCC copy- $1.00 per page. UCC search includes tax liens if requested. Separate federal/state combined tax lien search- $1.00 per year. RE record copy- $1.00 per page. Cert fee: $1.50 per doc. Payee: Escambia Clerk of Circuit Court. **Online Access to Property Appraiser, Real Estate, Grantor/Grantee, Lien, Recording, Vital Statistic, Property Tax, Tax Sale records:** Access to the Clerk of Court database is free at www.clerk.co.escambia.fl.us/public_records.html. This includes grantor/grantee index and marriage, traffic, court records, tax sales. Also, access to the tax collector's Property Tax Inquiry database is free at http://ectc.co.escambia.fl.us/ectc/index2.html. Click on ECTC Online then on "Cyber-Tax." Tax sale info also available. Also, search the property appraiser real estate records at www.escpa.org/Search/. Access the recorded document index at www.myfloridacounty.com. See section intro for MyFlorida.com access details. Also, Sexual offenders, etc are at www.escambiaso.com/investigations.htm. **Other phones:** Assessor-850-434-2735; Treasurer-850-436-5200; Appraiser-850-434-2735.

Flagler County

County Clerk of the Circuit Court, PO Box 787, Recording Division, Bunnell, FL 32110. **Phone-**386-437-7433; fax-386-437-7406; hours 8AM-5PM
http://clerk.co.flagler.fl.us
Will search UCC records. Search per debtor- $1.50 per name per year. UCC copy- $1.00 per page. Will search tax liens. Tax lien search fee- $1.00 per debtor + $1.00 per year. Will search for any real estate records in general index. RE record copy- $1.00 per page. Cert fee: $1.50 per doc. Payee: Flagler County Clerk of the Circuit Court. **Online Access to Property Appraiser, Recording, Real Estate, Lien, Most Wanted, Sex Offender, Property Sale records:** The clerk's recording index is now on CD-ROM for $31.52. For information, contact Vickie Hunter at 386-437-7396. Also, property information from the tax appraiser is free at www.qpublic.net/flagler/search.html. Check sales at www.qpublic.net/flagler/flaglersearch.html. Also, access to the state recorders' meta-search site is free at www.myflaglercounty.com. Click on Official Records. Also, sheriff's most wanted and sex offender lists are at www.myfcso.com/fcso/. Access the recorded document index at www.myfloridacounty.com. See section intro for MyFlorida.com access details. **Other phones:** Assessor-386-437-7450; Treasurer-386-437-7414; Appraiser-386-437-7450; Elections-386-437-7447.

Franklin County

County Clerk of the Circuit Court, 33 Market St #203, Apalachicola, FL 32320. **Phone-**850-653-8861 x108 or x109; fax-850-653-2261; hours 8:30AM-4:30PM
www.franklinclerk.com
Toll-free phone is 850-697-2112. There is also an office at Carrabelle Annex, 203 5th St #5, Carrabelle, FL 32322; 850-697- 3263. Will search UCC records. Search per debtor- $1.50 per name per year. UCC copy- $1.00 per page. Will not search real estate or tax lien records. Cert fee: $1.50 per doc. Payee: Franklin County Clerk of the Circuit Court. **Online Access to Real Estate, Lien, Recording records:** Access the recorded document index at www.myfloridacounty.com. See section intro for

MyFlorida.com access details. **Other phones:** Treasurer-850-653-8861; Appraiser-850-653-9236.

Gadsden County

County Clerk of the Circuit Court, PO Box 1649, Quincy, FL 32353-1649. **Phone-**850-875-8601; fax-850-875-8612; hours-8:30AM-5PM
www.clerk.co.gadsden.fl.us
Will search UCC records. Search per debtor- $1.50 per name per year. UCC copy- $1.00 per page. UCC search includes tax liens. Separate federal/state combined tax lien search- $1.00 per year. Will search real estate records. Cert fee: $1.50 per doc. Payee: Gadsden County Clerk of the Circuit Court. **Online Access to Real Estate, Recording, Judgment, Deed, Lien, Vital Statistic, Property Appraiser records:** Access to records index is free at www.clerk.co.gadsden.fl.us/OfficialRecords/. Index records go back to 1985. Provides index numbers only. Also, access to the property appraiser database is free at www.qpublic.net/gadsden/search.html. Search tax collector records at www.gadsdentaxcollector.com/collectmax/collect30.asp. Search property sales at www.qpublic.net/gadsden/gadsensearch.html. No name searching. **Other phones:** Assessor-850-627-7168; Appraiser-850-627-7168.

Gilchrist County

County Clerk of the Circuit Court, PO Box 37, Trenton, FL 32693. **Phone-**County Clerk of the Circuit Court, R/E & UCC Recording- 352-463-3170; fax-352-463-3166; 8:30AM-5PM www.co.gilchrist.fl.us/cophone
Will not search records. UCC copy- $1.00 per page. Cert fee: $1.50 per doc. Payee: Gilchrist County Clerk of the Circuit Court. **Online Access to Real Estate, Property Appraiser, Lien, Recording, Deed, Judgment, Marriage, Death records:** Access to the property appraiser database is free at www.qpublic.net/gilchrist/search.html. Also, sales searches are at www.gcpaonline.net; click on Search. Access the recorded document index at http://mygilchristcounty.com or www.myfloridacounty.com. See section intro for MyFlorida.com access details. **Other phones:** Assessor-352-463-3190; Appraiser-352-463-3190; Elections-352-463-3194.

Glades County

County Clerk of the Circuit Court, PO Box 10, Moore Haven, FL 33471. **Phone-**County Clerk of the Circuit Court, R/E & UCC Recording- 863-946-6010; fax-863-946-0560; hours 8AM-5PM http://gladesclerk.com/
Will search UCC records. Search per debtor-$1.00 $1.50 per name per year. UCC copy- $1.00 per page. Tax lien search fee- $1.00 per debtor & $1.00 per year. Will search for any real estate records on general index. RE record copy- $1.00 per page. Cert fee: $1.50 per doc. Payee: Glades County Clerk of the Circuit Court. **Online Access to Real Estate, Lien, Recording records:** Access recorded document index at www.myfloridacounty.com. See section intro for MyFlorida.com access details. **Other phones:** Appraiser-863-946-6025.

Gulf County

County Clerk of the Circuit Court, 1000 Cecil G. Costin, Sr. Blvd. Rm. 148, Port St. Joe, FL 32456. **Phone-**850-229-6112, R/E Recording- 850-229-6113, UCC Recording- 850-229-6113; fax-850-229-6174; hours 9AM-5PM www.gulfclerk.com
Will not search UCC records or tax liens. Will search for any real estate records in general index. Record copy- $1.00 per page. Cert fee: $1.50 per doc. Payee: Gulf County Clerk of the Circuit Court. **Online Access to Real Estate, Lien, Deed, Judgment, Marriage, Death, Recording records:** Access the the clerk's recorded document index at www.myfloridacounty.com. See section intro for MyFlorida.com access details. **Other phones:**

Assessor-850-229-6115; Treasurer-850-229-6116; Appraiser-850-229-6115; Elections-850-229-6117; Vital Records-850-227-1276.

Hamilton County

County Clerk of the Circuit Court, 207 NE 1st St, Rm 106, Jasper, FL 32052. **Phone**-County Clerk of the Circuit Court, R/E & UCC Recording- 386-792-1288; fax-386-792-3524; hours 8:30AM-4:30PM Will search UCC records. Search per debtor- $1.50 per name per year. UCC copy- $1.00 per page. UCC search includes tax liens if requested. Separate federal/state combined tax lien search- $1.00 per debtor per year. Will search for any real estate records in general index. RE record copy- $1.00 per page. Cert fee: $1.50 per doc. Payee: Hamilton County Clerk of the Circuit Court. **Online Access to Real Estate, Lien, Recording records:** Access the recorded document index at www.myfloridacounty.com. See section intro for MyFlorida.com access details. **Other phones:** Assessor-386-792-2791; Treasurer-386-792-1288; Appraiser-386-792-1284; Elections-386-792-1426; Vital Records-386-792-1288.

Hardee County

County Clerk of the Circuit Court, PO Drawer 1749, Wauchula, FL 33873. **Phone**-863-773-4174; fax-863-773-3295; hours 8AM-5PM; 8AM-4PM Recording hours www.hardeeclerk.com Will search UCC records. Search per debtor- $1.50 per name per year. UCC copy- $1.00 per page. Will search tax liens. Will not search real estate records. RE record copy- $1.00 per page. Cert fee: $1.50 per doc. Payee: Hardee County Clerk of the Circuit Court. **Online Access to Real Estate, Recording, Lien, Property Appraiser, Most Wanted, Arrest, Inmate, Warrant records:** Access the recorded document index at www.myfloridacounty.com. See section intro for MyFlorida.com access details. Also, online assess to property appraiser data is free at www.hardeecounty.net/cfaps/appraiser/propform.cfm. Search the sheriff's most wanted, inmate, arrest, warrant and missing person lists at www.hardeeso.com. **Other phones:** Assessor-863-773-2196; Appraiser-863-773-2196.

Hendry County

County Clerk of the Circuit Court, PO Box 1760, La Belle, FL 33975-1760. **Phone**-County Clerk of the Circuit Court, R/E & UCC Recording- 863-675-5217, UCC Recording- 863-675-5202; fax-863-675-5238; hours 8:30AM-5PM www.hendryclerk.org Will search UCC records. Search per debtor- $1.50 per name per year. UCC copy- $1.00 per page. Will search tax liens. Separate federal/state combined tax lien search- $1.00 per year. Real estate owner, mortgage, and property transfer searches available. RE record copy- $1.00 per page. Cert fee: $1.50 per doc. Payee: Hendry County Clerk of the Circuit Court. **Online Access to Real Estate, Lien, Recording records:** Access the recorded document index at www.myfloridacounty.com. See section intro for MyFlorida.com access details. Also, access the property appraiser database at www.hendryprop.com/GIS/Search_F.asp. Official Records Database is found at http://64.45.229.253/offrec/ormain.htm Has images from April 12, 1990 -- Book 450 Page 1 to latest available. Web records are updated once a week. **Other phones:** Assessor-863-675-5270; Treasurer-863-675-5280; Appraiser-863-675-5270; Elections-863-675-5231; Vital Records-863-675-5217.

Hernando County

County Clerk of the Circuit Court, 20 N. Main, Rm 215, Brooksville, FL 34601. **Phone**-352-540-6768; fax-352-754-4243; hours-8AM-5PM www.clerk.co.hernando.fl.us

Will search UCC records. Search per debtor- $1.50 per name per year. UCC copy- $1.00 per page. Tax liens not included in UCC search. Separate federal/state combined tax lien search- $1.00 per debtor, per year. Real estate record owner and property searches available. RE record copy- $1.00 per page. Cert fee: $1.50 per doc. Payee: Hernando County Clerk of the Circuit Court. **Online Access to Property Appraiser, Real Estate, Lien, Marriage, Recording, Most Wanted, Arrest records:** Access to the clerk's Official Records database is now free at www.clerk.co.hernando.fl.us/disclaimer.asp. Your browser must be Javascript enabled. Includes recordings, marriages, and court records. Also, the county now offers 2 levels of the Public Inquiry System Property Appraiser Real Estate database - Easy Search and Real Time Search - free at www.co.hernando.fl.us/pa/propsearch.htm. Search by owner, address, or parcel key. Also, access the recorded document index at www.myfloridacounty.com. See section intro for MyFlorida.com access details. Search sheriff's most wanted and arrests (back to 1995) lists at www.hcso.hernando.fl.us. **Other phones:** Treasurer-352-754-4190; Appraiser-352-754-4190.

Highlands County

County Clerk of the Circuit Court, 590 S. Commerce Ave, Sebring, FL 33870. **Phone**-County Clerk of the Circuit Court, R/E & UCC Recording- 863-402-6590, UCC Recording- 800-822-5436; hours 8AM-5PM www.clerk.co.highlands.fl.us Will not search records. UCC copy- $1.00 per page. Cert fee: $1.50 per doc. Payee: Clerk of Court. **Online Access to Property Appraiser, Personal Property, Real Estate, Lien, Recording records:** Property appraiser records are free at www.appraiser.co.highlands.fl.us/search.html; tangible personal property records are available. Access the recorded document index at www.myfloridacounty.com. See section intro for MyFlorida.com access details. Also, online access to deeds, mortgages, judgments from the county recording database are free at www.clerk.co.highlands.fl.us/official/search.html. Records go back to 1983. Also, county tax collector database for personal property and real estate is free at www.collector.co.highlands.fl.us/search/index.html. **Other phones:** Assessor-863-402-6659; Treasurer-863-402-6685; Appraiser-863-402-6661; Elections-863-402-6654; Vital Records-863-402-6040.

Hillsborough County

County Clerk of the Circuit Court, PO Box 3249, Tampa, FL 33601-1110. **Phone**-813-276-8100 x4367, R/E Recording- 813-276-8100, UCC Recording- 813-276-8100; fax-813-276-2114; hours 8AM-5PM www.hillsclerk.com Will search UCC records. Search per debtor- $1.50 per name per year. UCC copy- $1.00 per page. UCC search includes tax liens. Separate federal/state combined tax lien search- $1.00 per year. Real estate owner, mortgage, and property transfer searches available. Copy fee-$1.00 per page. Cert fee: $1.50 per doc. Payee: Hillsborough County Clerk of the Circuit Court. **Online Access to Property Appraiser, Personal Property, Real Estate, Lien, Deed, Recording, Warrant, Inmate, Repo/Impound records:** Property appraiser records are free at www.hcpafl.org/disclaimer.html. Receive owner data, legal, sales, value summaries. The clerk's recordings index can be searched free at http://publicrecord.hillsclerk.com. Also, access recorded document index at www.myfloridacounty.com; See section intro for MyFlorida.com access details. Search sheriff's warrants, inmates, repo data free at www.hcso.tampa.fl.us/Page_Headers/online.htm. Images of official records from 1990 to current are at www.hillsclerk.com. **Other phones:** Appraiser-813-272-6100.

Holmes County

County Clerk of the Circuit Court, PO Box 397, Bonifay, FL 32425. **Phone**-850-547-1102, R/E Recording- 850-547-1100, UCC Recording- 850-547-1100; fax-850-547-6630; hours 8AM-4PM www.holmesclerk.com Will search UCC records. Search per debtor- $1.50 per name per year. UCC copy- $1.00 per page. Will not search real estate or tax lien records. RE record copy- $1.00 per page. Cert fee: $1.50 per doc. Payee: Holmes County Clerk of the Circuit Court. **Online Access to Real Estate, Lien, Recording records;** Access the recorded document index at www.myfloridacounty.com. See section intro for MyFlorida.com access details. **Other phones:** Assessor-850-547-1100; Treasurer-850-547-1115; Appraiser-850-547-1113; Elections-850-547-1107.

Indian River County

County Clerk of the Circuit Court, PO Box 1028, Vero Beach, FL 32961-1028. **Phone**-772-770-5185 x184; hours 8:30AM-5PM http://indian-river.fl.us Will search UCC records. Search per debtor- $1.50 per name per year. UCC copy- $1.00 per page. Tax liens not included in UCC search. Separate federal/state combined tax lien search- $1.00 per year per debtor. Will not search real estate records. RE record copy- $1.00 per page. Cert fee: $1.50 per doc. Payee: Indian River County Clerk of the Circuit Court. **Online Access to Property Appraiser, Real Estate, Lien, Vital Statistic, Inmate, Criminal History records:** Appraiser information is free, but only some of the recording office data is. Appraiser records are free at http://ircpa.irene.net/search.html. Also, access to Clerk's recording indices are free at www.clerk.indian-river.org/recordssearch/ori.asp. Records go back to 1983. Sheriff's data on inmates and criminal histories at www.ircsheriff.org/programs.cfm. Full real estate, lien and court and vital records from the Clerk is at their fee site; subscriptions start $100 per month, increasing with amount of access. For info about free and fee access, call 772-567-8000 x216. **Other phones:** Appraiser-772-567-8188.

Jackson County

County Clerk of the Circuit Court, PO Drawer 510, Marianna, FL 32447. **Phone**-County Clerk of the Circuit Court, R/E & UCC Recording- 850-482-9552; fax-850-482-7849; hours-8AM-4:30PM www.jacksonclerk.com Will search UCC records. UCC copy- $1.00 per page. Will not search real estate or tax lien records. RE record copy- $1.00 per page. Cert fee: $1.50 per doc. Payee: Jackson County Clerk of the Circuit Court. **Online Access to Real Estate, Lien, Recording, Marriage, Death, Probate, Property Tax records:** Access to the Clerk of Circuit Court Official Records database is free at www.jacksonclerk.com. Images will go back to 5/1996. Also, search property tax data for free at www.jacksoncountytaxcollector.com/SearchSelect.aspx Access the recorded document index at www.myfloridacounty.com. See section intro for MyFlorida.com access details. **Other phones:** Assessor-850-482-9646; Treasurer-850-482-9653; Appraiser-850-482-9646; Elections-850-482-9652; Vital Records-850-482-9552 (marriage only).

Jefferson County

County Clerk of the Circuit Court, Courthouse, Rm 10, Monticello, FL 32344. **Phone**-850-342-0218 x27, R/E Recording- 850-342-0218 x 227, UCC Recording- 850-342-0218 x 227; fax-850-342-0222; hours 8AM-5PM http://co.jefferson.fl.us Will search UCC records. Search per debtor- $1.50 per name per year. UCC copy- $1.00 per page. Will search tax liens. Separate federal tax lien search- $1.00 per debtor per year; state lien- $2.00

per debtor. Will search real estate records. RE copy-$1.00 per page. Cert fee: $1.50 per doc. Payee: Jefferson County Clerk of the Circuit Court. **Online Access to Property, Real Estate, Lien, Recording records:** Access Property Appraiser data free at http://qpublic.net/jefferson/search.html. Sales searches are also available. Also, online access to the Clerk of Circuit Court recordings database is free at www.myjeffersoncounty.com. Also, tax collector database is free at www.jeffersoncountytaxcollector.com/SearchSelect.aspx. Access the recorded document index at www.myfloridacounty.com. See section intro for MyFlorida.com access details. **Other phones:** Assessor-850-997-3356; Treasurer-850-342-0218 x 232; Appraiser-850-997-3356; Elections-850-997-3348.

Lafayette County

County Clerk of the Circuit Court, PO Box 88, Mayo, FL 32066. **Phone**-386-294-1600; fax-386-294-4231; hours 8AM-5PM www.lafayetteclerk.com
Will not search records. UCC copy- $1.00 per page. Cert fee: $1.50 per doc. Payee: Lafayette County Clerk of the Circuit Court. **Online Access to Real Estate, Lien, Recording records:** Access recorded document index at www.myfloridacounty.com. See section intro for MyFlorida.com access details. **Other phones:** Assessor-386-294-1991; Treasurer-386-294-1961; Appraiser-386-294-1991.

Lake County

County Clerk of the Circuit Court, PO Box 7800, Tavares, FL 32778-7800. **Phone**-County Clerk of the Circuit Court, R/E & UCC Recording- 352-253-2600; fax-352-253-2616; hours 8:30AM-5PM (Recording hours: 8:30AM-4:30PM) www.lakecountyclerk.org
Will search UCC records. Search per debtor- $1.50 per name per year. UCC copy- $1.00 per page. UCC search includes tax liens. Separate federal & state combined tax lien search- $1.00 per year. Will search real estate records. RE record copy- $1.50 per page. Cert fee: $1.50 per doc. Payee: Clerk of the Circuit Court. **Online Access to Property Appraiser, Recording, Real Estate, Lien, Marriage, Death records:** County clerk official records database is free at www.lakecountyclerk.org/services.asp?subject=Online_Official_Records. Records go as far back as 1974. Includes court records. Also, records on Property Assessor database are free at www.lakecopropappr.com/search.asp. Also, marriage records back to 11/2000 www.lakecountyclerk.org/departments.asp?subject=Marriage_Licenses. Also, access to the state recorders' meta-search site is free at www.myfloridacounty.com. Click on Official records. **Other phones:** Assessor-352-343-9748; Treasurer-352-742-9808; Appraiser-352-343-9748; Elections-352-343-9734; Vital Records-352-589-6424; Tax Collector-352-343-9622.

Lee County

County Clerk of the Circuit Court, PO Box 2278, Fort Myers, FL 33902-2278. **Phone**-239-335-2283; hours 7:45AM-5PM http://leeclerk.org/index.asp
There is also a Cape Coral Branch Office - Lee County Government Center, 1039 SE 9th Place, Cape Coral, FL 33990. Will search UCC records. Search per debtor-$1.50 per name per year. UCC copy- $1.00 per page. UCC search includes tax liens if requested. Separate federal/state combined tax lien search-$1.00 per year. Real estate owner, mortgage, and property transfer searches available. Cert fee: $1.50 per doc. Payee: Lee County Clerk of the Circuit Court. **Online Access to Property Appraiser, Real Estate, Occupational License, Lien, Recording, Business Tangible Property records:** Access to the appraiser database is free at www.leepa.org/Queries/SearchCriteria.htm, or the tax roll database at www.leetc.com/search_taxroll_real.asp or tax certificates at www.leetc.com/search_taxcert.asp.

Also, access to county "license" database is at www.leetc.com/search_occlic.asp. Tangible property: www.leetc.com/search_taxroll_tangible.asp. Search the clerk's data back to 1988 at www.leeclerk.org/wb_or1/disclaim.asp. Search bussiness tangible property at www.leepa.org/Tangible/Business%20Search.htm. Also a subscription service ($50 set-up/$25 per month) allows full access to clerk's records. Also, access the recorded document index at www.myfloridacounty.com. Fees involved. **Other phones:** Assessor-239-339-6100; Appraiser-239-335-2283.

Leon County

County Clerk of the Circuit Court, PO Box 726, Tallahassee, FL 32302. **Phone**-850-577-4030, R/E Recording- 850-577-4050; fax-850-921-1310; hours 8:30AM-5PM www.clerk.leon.fl.us
Online records at www.clerk.leon.fl.us MAY have ID information removed; some records MAY have been removed from this online service, though this is rare. Will search UCC records. Search per debtor- $1.50 per name per year. UCC copy- $1.00 per page. Tax liens not included in UCC search. Separate federal/state combined tax lien search- $1.00 per year. Will search for any real estate records in general index. Cert fee: $1.50 per doc. Payee: Leon County Clerk of the Circuit Court. **Online Access to Property Appraiser, Real Estate, Lien, Marriage, Recording, Permit, Foreclosure, Contractor, Most Wanted records:** Real Estate, lien, and foreclosure records from the County Clerk are free at www.clerk.leon.fl.us. Lending agency information is also available. Also, access to full document images requires user name and password, + $100 per month. Property Appraiser database records are free at www.co.leon.fl.us/propappr/search.cfm. Also, access recorded documents at www.myfloridacounty.com. Fees involved to order copies. Search contractors lists at www.leonpermits.org/contractors/. Also search tax collector rolls at http://dta.co.leon.fl.us/tax/default.asp. Search county data at www.tlcgis.org/tallahassee. Marriages are at http://cvweb.clerk.leon.fl.us/index_marriage.html. **Other phones:** Assessor-850-488-6102; Appraiser-850-488-6102.

Levy County

County Clerk of the Circuit Court, PO Drawer 610, Bronson, FL 32621. **Phone**-County Clerk of the Circuit Court, R/E & UCC Recording- 352-486-5229; fax-352-486-5166; hours 8AM-5PM www.levyclerk.com
Will not search UCC records or tax liens. Real estate owner, mortgage, and property transfer records available if you provide book and page number. Record copy- $1.00 per page. Cert fee: $1.50 per doc. Payee: Levy County Clerk of the Circuit Court. **Online Access to Real Estate, Lien, Recording, Property Tax, Property Appraiser, Warrant records:** Access the Clerk's recording data free at http://levyclerk.com/scripts/LevyClerk.exe?K. Search by name, book/page, file number or document type. Access the recorded document index at www.myfloridacounty.com. See section intro for MyFlorida.com access details. Also, search county warrants list at www.levyso.com/warrantlist.html. Also, access to the property appraiser data is free at www.qpublic.net/levy/search.html. Search tax collector data at www.levytaxcollector.com/collectmax/collect30.asp. **Other phones:** Appraiser-352-486-5222; Elections-352-486-5163; Vital Records-352-486-5274.

Liberty County

County Clerk of the Circuit Court, PO Box 399, Bristol, FL 32321. **Phone**-850-643-2215; fax-850-643-2866; hours 8AM-5PM www.libertyclerk.com
Will not search UCC records or tax liens. Will search real estate records. Record copy- $1.00 per page. Cert fee: $1.50 per doc. Payee: Liberty County

Clerk of the Circuit Court. **Online Access to Real Estate, Lien, Recording records:** Access recorded document index at www.myfloridacounty.com. See section intro for MyFlorida.com access details. **Other phones:** Assessor-850-643-2279; Treasurer-850-643-2442; Appraiser-850-643-2279.

Madison County

County Clerk of the Circuit Court, PO Box 237, Madison, FL 32341-0237. **Phone**-850-973-1500, R/E Recording- 850-973-1500 x27, UCC Recording- 850-973-1500 x27; fax-850-973-2059; hours 8AM-5PM www.madisonclerk.com
Will not search UCC records. Separate federal/state combined tax lien search- $1.00 per year. Real estate owner, mortgage, and property transfer searches available. Record copy- $1.00 per page. Cert fee: $1.50 per doc. Payee: Madison County Clerk of the Circuit Court. **Online Access to Real Estate, Lien, Recording, Property, Appraiser, Sale records:** Access the recorded document index at www.myfloridacounty.com. See section intro for MyFlorida.com access details. Official Records indexes are for past 10 years. Access the property appraiser's property cards and sale databases free at www.madisonpa.com/GIS/Search_F.asp. **Other phones:** Assessor-850-973-6133; Treasurer-850-973-1500; Appraiser-850-973-6133; Elections-850-973-6507.

Manatee County

County Clerk of the Circuit Court, PO Box 25400, Bradenton, FL 34206. **Phone**-941-741-4041, R/E Recording- 941-741-4040 or 4041; fax-941-741-4082; hours 8:30AM-5PM www.manateeclerk.com
Will search UCC records. Search per debtor- $1.50 per name per year. UCC copy- $1.00 per page. UCC search includes tax liens. Separate federal/state combined tax lien search- $1.00 per debtor per year. Real estate owner, mortgage, and property transfer searches available. RE record copy-$1.00 per page. Cert fee: $1.50 per doc. Payee: Manatee County Clerk of the Circuit Court. **Online Access to Property Appraiser, Real Estate, Lien, Recording, Deed, Judgment, Death, Marriage, Condominium, Foreclosure Sale, Tax Deed Sale, Most Wanted records:** Several sources exist. Search and view real estate and recordings records free from the Clerk of Circuit Court and Comptroller's database at www.clerkofcourts.com/PubRec/RecordedDocs/ormain.htm. Also, Access the recorded document index at www.myfloridacounty.com. Fees involved to order copies. Also, Property Appraiser records are free at www.manateepao.com. Tax deed sales are free at www.clerkofcourts.com/Sales/TaxDeeds/taxdeed.pdf. Also, property tax records are at www.taxcollector.com/dataaccess/design/1owner.asp. Search foreclosure sat www.clerkofcourts.com/Sales/Foreclosures/fore.htm. Most wanted list is at http://legal.firn.edu/sheriff/manatee/. **Other phones:** Assessor-941-748-8208; Treasurer-941-748-4800; Appraiser-941-748-8208; Elections-941-741-3823; Vital Records-941-748-0747.

Marion County

County Clerk of the Circuit Court, PO Box 1030, Ocala, FL 34478-1030. **Phone**-County Clerk of the Circuit Court, R/E & UCC Recording- 352-620-3925; fax-352-620-3930; hours-8AM-5PM www.marioncountyclerk.org
Will search UCC records. Search per debtor- $1.50 per name per year. UCC copy- $1.00 per page. Tax liens not included in UCC search. Separate federal/state combined tax lien search- $1.00 per year. Real estate owner, mortgage, and property transfer searches available. Cert fee: $1.50 per doc. Payee: Marion County Clerk of the Circuit Court. **Online Access to Property Appraiser, Real Estate, Recording, Tax Collector, Tax Deed Sale, Inmate,**

Sex Offender records: Property Appraiser records are free at www.propappr.marion.fl.us. Tax collector data at http://mariontaxcollector.governmax.com/collectmax/collect30.asp. Access the recorded document index at www.myfloridacounty.com. See section intro for MyFlorida.com access details. Also, search the jail inmate data at www.marionso.com:8000/search.asp. **Other phones:** Appraiser-352-368-8300.

Martin County

County Clerk of the Circuit Court, PO Box 9016, Stuart, FL 34995. **Phone-**County Clerk of the Circuit Court, R/E & UCC Recording- 772-288-5554; fax-772-223-7920; hours 8AM-5PM www.martin.fl.us/GOVT 772-288-552 is the direct telephone number for search requests. Will search UCC records. Search per debtor- $1.50 per name per year. UCC copy- $1.00 per page. Tax liens not included in UCC search. Separate tax lien search fee- $1.00 per debtor per year. Real estate record owner and mortgage searches available. RE record copy- $1.00 per page. Cert fee: $1.50 per doc. Payee: Clerk of the Circuit Court. **Online Access to Property Appraiser, Real Estate, Lien, Recording, Personal Property records:** Access to the clerk of the circuit court recordings database are free at http://clerk-web.martin.fl.us/wb_or1. Also, records on the county property appraiser database are free at http://paoweb.martin.fl.us. Choose from "Online Property Searches." Personal property searches are also available. The county tax collector data files are free at http://taxcol.martin.fl.us/advsrch_home.asp. Also, online access to the state recorders' meta-search site is free at www.myfloridacounty.com. **Other phones:** Assessor-772-288-5608; Treasurer-772-288-5595; Appraiser-772-288-5608; Elections-772-288-5637.

Monroe County

County Clerk of the Circuit Court, PO Box 1980, Key West, FL 33041-1980. **Phone-**305-292-3540, R/E Recording- 305-292-3507; fax-305-295-3623; hours 8:30AM-4:45PM www.co.monroe.fl.us Will search UCC records. Search per debtor- $1.50 per name per year. UCC copy- $1.00 per page. UCC search includes tax liens. Separate federal/state combined tax lien search- $1.00 per year. Real estate owner, mortgage, and property transfer searches available. RE record copy- $1.00 per page. Cert fee: $1.50 per doc. Payee: Monroe County Clerk of the Circuit Court. **Online Access to Real Estate, Recording, Deed, Lien, Property Tax, Occupational License, Arrest, Inmate, Warrant records:** Access to the clerk of circuit courts database is at www.clerk-of-the-court.com/searchOfficialRecords.asp. Also, access to property appraiser data is free at www.mcpafl.org/datacenter/mapdisc.asp? Also, search property tax and occupational licenses at www.monroetaxcollector.com/collectmax/collect30.asp . Also, search the sheriff database of arrests and inmates at http://www2.keysso.net. Search warrant lists at http://www2.keysso.net/WebWarrants/WebWarrantsA.htm. **Other phones:** Treasurer-305-292-3420; Vital Records-305-292-3507; Tax Collector-305-245-5000.

Nassau County

County Clerk of the Circuit Court, PO Box 456, Fernandina, FL 32035. **Phone-**904-548-4600; fax-904-548-4508; hours 9AM-5PM (Recording hours-9AM-4PM) www.nassauclerk.com Will search UCC records. Search per debtor- $1.50 per name per year. UCC copy- $1.00 per page. UCC search includes tax liens if requested. Separate federal/state combined tax lien search- $1.00 per year. Will not search real estate records. Cert fee: $1.50 per doc. Payee: Nassau County Clerk of the Circuit Court. **Online Access to Real Estate, Lien, Recording records:** recorded document

index at www.myfloridacounty.com. See section intro for MyFlorida.com access details. Also, the recorders database is at www.nassauclerk.org/OfficialRecords/. **Other phones:** Assessor-904-491-7300; Appraiser-904-491-7300.

Okaloosa County

County Clerk of the Circuit Court, PO Drawer 1359, Crestview, FL 32536. **Phone-**850-689-5847, R/E Recording- 850-689-5041, UCC Recording- 850-689-5041; fax-850-689-5886; hours 8AM-5PM www.clerkofcourts.cc Will search UCC records. Search per debtor- $1.50 per name per year. UCC copy- $1.00 per page. Tax liens not included in UCC search. Separate federal/state combined tax lien search- $1.00 per year. Real estate owner, mortgage, and property transfer searches available. Copy fee-$1.00 per page. Cert fee: $1.50 per doc. Payee: Okaloosa County Clerk of the Circuit Court. **Online Access to Property Appraiser, Real Estate, Lien, Recording, Vital Statistic, Property Tax, Occupational License records:** Several databases are available. Access to County online system requires a monthly usage fee of $100. No addresses listed. Lending agency, traffic and domestic records are. For info, call 850-689-5821. Access the clerk's land and official records for free at www.clerkofcourts.cc/orsearch/disclaimer.htm includes access to marriage, civil court, traffic records. Access tax collector data at http://okaloosa.governmax.com/collectmax/search_collect.asp?. Property Appraiser records are online at http://qpublic.net/okaloosa/search1.html; sales & sales lists are at www.okaloosapa.com. Also, Access recorded document index at www.myfloridacounty.com. See section intro for MyFlorida.com access details. **Other phones:** Treasurer-850-689-5801; Appraiser-850-689-5900; Elections-850-651-7272.

Okeechobee County

County Clerk of the Circuit Court, 304 N.W. 2nd St, Rm 101, Okeechobee, FL 34972. **Phone-**863-763-2131, R/E Recording- 863-763-0239, UCC Recording- 863-763-0239; hours-8:30AM-5PM www.clerk.co.okeechobee.fl.us Will search UCC records. Search per debtor- $1.50 per name per year. UCC copy- $1.00 per page. Will not search tax liens. Will search real estate records. Cert fee: $1.50 per doc. Payee: Okeechobee County Clerk of the Circuit Court. **Online Access to Property, Recording, Appraiser, GIS, Personal Property, Property Sale records:** Search the statewide recording database via www.myfloridacounty.com. There is a fee to order. Also, access to the property appraiser database is free at www.okeechobeepa.com/GIS/Search_F.asp. Property search on GIS site www.emapsplus.com/FLOkeechobee/maps/. **Other phones:** Assessor-863-763-4422; Treasurer-863-763-3421; Appraiser-863-763-4422; Elections-863-763-4014; Vital Records-863-462-5819.

Orange County

County Comptroller, PO Box 38, Official Records Dept., Orlando, FL 32802-0038. **Phone-**County Comptroller, R/E & UCC Recording- 407-836-5115; fax-407-836-5120; hours-7:30AM-4:30PM www.occompt.com Will search UCC records. Search per debtor- $1.50 per year per name. UCC copy- $1.00 per page. Tax liens not included in UCC search. Separate federal/state combined tax lien search- $1.50 per debtor per year. Real estate record owner and mortgage searches available. RE record copy- $1.00 per page. Cert fee: $1.50 per doc. Payee: Orange County Comptroller. **Online Access to Property Appraiser, Recording, Real Estate, Lien, Vital Statistic, Land Sale, Personal Property, Property Tax, Contractor records:** Real Estate, Lien, and

Marriage records on the county Comptroller database are free at www.occompt.com/2002/records.html. Lending Agency information is available. Also, property records on the Property Appraiser database are free at www.ocpafl.org/docs/disclaimer.html. At this main site, click on "Record Searches." Also search Tangible Personal Property records and residential sales. Search property tax data at www.octaxcol.com/dev/NameSearch.asp. Search contractor licenses: www.orangecountyfl.net/ebuildingContractorSearch/ContractorSearch.asp. Search inmates list for free at www.orangecountyfl.net/cms/Bailbond/default.htm. **Other phones:** Assessor-407-836-5044; Treasurer-407-836-5715; Appraiser-407-836-5000; Elections-407-836-2070; Vital Records-407-623-1182.

Osceola County

County Clerk of the Circuit Court, 2 Courthouse Sq, #2000, Kissimmee, FL 34741-5491. **Phone-**407-343-3500 x3517, R/E Recording- 407-343-3517, UCC Recording- 407-343-3517; fax-407-343-3534; hours 8:30AM-5PM; 8:30AM-4PM Recording hours www.osceolaclerk.com Access the recorded document index at www.myfloridacounty.com. See section intro for MyFlorida.com access details. Will search UCC records. Search per debtor- $1.50 per name per year. UCC copy- $1.00 per page. UCC search includes tax liens if requested. Separate federal/state combined tax lien search- $1.00 per year. Real estate owner, mortgage, and property transfer searches available. RE record copy- $1.00 per page. Cert fee: $1.50 per doc. Payee: Osceola County Clerk of the Circuit Court. **Online Access to Real Estate, Property Tax, Appraiser, Occupational License, Inmate records:** Access to the county Clerk of Circuit Court database features court records only at this time; see www.osceolaclerkcourt.org. Search occupation licenses and tax collector data at www.osceolataxcollector.com/collectmax/collect30.asp? Property appraiser records are free at http://ira.property-appraiser.org/ira/PASE/presentation/Osceola/search.asp or may you may also purchase property data; call 407-343-3700. Data comes as 8mm data cartridges, CD-ROM, or 3.5 inch diskettes. Fees vary; tax roll data is $75.00. Also, recording/land records are online at http://osceolarecorder.governmax.com/recordmax/record40.asp. Search inmate list at www.osceola.org/index.cfm?lsFuses=inmates. **Other phones:** Appraiser-407-343-3700; Elections-407-343-3900.

Palm Beach County

County Clerk of the Circuit Court, PO Box 4177, West Palm Beach, FL 33402. **Phone-**County Clerk of the Circuit Court, R/E & UCC Recording- 561-355-2991; fax-561-355-2633; hours-8AM-5PM www.pbcountyclerk.com A subscription full-index online records system and CD-Roms of indexes are planned. Will search UCC records. Search per debtor- $1.50 per name per year. UCC copy- $1.00 per page. Tax liens not included in UCC search. Separate federal/state combined tax lien search- $1.00 per year. Real Estate search includes all records on general index. RE record copy- $1.00 per page. Cert fee: $1.50 per doc. Payee: Palm Beach County Clerk of Circuit Court. **Online Access to Property Appraiser, Real Estate, Deed, Lien, Judgment, Recording, Vital Statistic, Property Tax, Personal Property, Occ License, Warrant, Sexual Predator, Sheriff Booking records:** Access to the clerk's recording database is free at www.pbcountyclerk.com/records_home.html. Records go back to 1968; includes marriage records 1979 to present. Images go back to 1990. Also, search real estate, property tax, personal property data at www.co.palm-beach.fl.us/tc_pubaccess/default.asp. Search sheriff bookings at www.pbso.org/blotter/criter

ia.cfm. Search warrants & sex predators at www.pbso.org/index.cfm?fa=crimestoppers. Property appraiser records are at www.co.palm-beach.fl.us/papa. Tax deeds at www.pbcountyclerk.com/dt_web2/or_sch_l.asp. Search occupational licenses at www.co.palm-beach.fl.us/tc_pubaccess/occ/occ_search.asp. **Other phones:** Assessor-561-355-2866; Appraiser-561-355-2866; Elections-561-355-2650; Vital Records-561-653-2350.

Pasco County

County Clerk of the Circuit Court, 38053 Live Oak Ave, Rm 205, Dade City, FL 33523-3894. **Phone-**352-521-4469 or 4408, R/E Recording- 352-521-4469; hours 8:30AM-5PM www.pascoclerk.com
Will search UCC records. Search per debtor- $1.50 per name per year. UCC copy- $1.00 per page. Separate federal/state combined tax lien search- $1.00 per year. Real estate owner, mortgage, and property transfer searches available. Cert fee: $1.50 per doc. Payee: Pasco County Clerk of the Circuit Court. **Online Access to Property Appraiser, Real Estate, Lien, Vital Statistic, Recording, Occ License, Personal Property, Wanted, Sexual Predator, Contractor/Permit records:** Several sources available. Access to real estate, liens, marriage records requires $25 annual fee plus a $50 deposit. Billing rate is $.05 per minute, $.03 evenings. For information, call 352-521-4529. Also, free access to indexes at www.pascoclerk.com. Click on "records." Also, access the document index at www.myfloridacounty.com. Fees involved to order copies. Search sheriff's wanted and sex predators at http://pascosheriff.com. Also, property appraiser data is at http://appraiser.pascogov.com w/ sales data & maps. Search tax records and occ. licenses at http://taxcollector.pascogov.com/search/prclsearch.asp. Contractors/permit at http://opal.pascocountyfl.net/. **Other phones:** Assessor-352-521-4433; Appraiser-352-521-4433.

Pinellas County

County Clerk of the Circuit Court, 315 Court St, Rm 150, Clearwater, FL 33756. **Phone-**727-464-4876; fax-727-464-4383; 8AM-5PM http://clerk.co.pinellas.fl.us
Will not name search UCC records; will retreive records if given book/page numbers. UCC copy- $1.00 per page. Tax liens not included in UCC search. Separate federal and/orstate combined tax lien search- $1.00 per year. Limited real estate owner, mortgage, and property transfer searches available; book and page number number must be provided. Cert fee: $1.50 per doc. Payee: Pinellas County Clerk of the Circuit Court. **Online Access to Property Appraiser, Real Estate, Lien, Judgment, Recording, Traffic/Boating Fine, Tax Collector, Personal Property, Tax Deed Sale, Accident Report records:** Assessor/property records are free at www.pao.co.pinellas.fl.us/search2.html. Also, search tax collector data free at www.autotech.com/search/default.cfm. Also, recording records are no longer at http://clerk.co.pinellas.fl.us. Tax deed sales lists are at http://pubtitlet.co.pinellas.fl.us/servlet/taxdeed.saledates.DM79. Search most wanted at www.co.pinellas.fl.us/sheriff/csprofiles.htm. Also, recorded document index is at www.myfloridacounty.com. Fees involved to order copies. Also, search tax collector data at www.visualgov.com/pinellascounty/. Search accident reports http://stockton.pcsonet.com/Crash%20Reports/policy.htm. **Other phones:** Assessor-727-464-3207; Appraiser-727-464-3207.

Polk County

County Clerk of the Circuit Court, PO Box 9000 Drawer CC-8, Bartow, FL 33831-9000. **Phone-**County Clerk of the Circuit Court, R/E & UCC Recording- 863-534-4516; fax-863-534-4008; hours 8AM-4:30PM www.polkcountyclerk.net

Will search UCC records. Search per debtor- $1.50 per year. UCC copy- $1.00 per page. UCC search includes tax liens. Separate federal/state combined tax lien search- $1.50 per year. Real Estate search includes all records on general index. RE record copy-$1.00 per page. Cert fee: $1.50 per doc. Payee: Clerk of the Circuit Court. **Online Access to Property Appraiser, Real Estate, Lien, Vital Statistic, Recording, Personal Property, Occ License Account, Tax Collector, Tax Deed Sale, Warrant, Most Wanted records:** Search the clerk database at www.polkcountyclerk.net/public_records/public_index.html for free court records, deeds, mortgages, plats, marriages, resolutions. For copies of documents, call 863-534-4524. Fee is $1.00 per page. Also, appraiser property and personal property records are free at www.polkpa.org. Also, search occupational license accounts at http://198.31.196.18/occupational_search/. Search tax collector data at www.autotech.com/search/default.cfm. Search tax deed sales at www.polkcountyclerk.net/Taxdeed/Taxdeed_Sale.html. Search the sheriff's warrant and most wanted lists at www.polksheriff.org/wanted/. **Other phones:** Assessor-863-534-4777; Appraiser-863-534-4777.

Putnam County

County Clerk of the Circuit Court, PO Box 758, Palatka, FL 32178-0758. **Phone-**386-329-0361, R/E Recording- 386-329-0256, UCC Recording- 386-329-0256; fax-386-329-0888; hours 8:30AM-5PM www.putnam-fl.com/clk/
Will search UCC records. Search per debtor- $1.50 per name per year. UCC copy- $1.00 per page. Separate federal/state combined tax lien search- $1.00 per year. Real estate owner, mortgage, and property transfer searches available. Cert fee: $1.50 per doc. Payee: Putnam County Clerk of the Circuit Court. **Online Access to Real Estate, Lien, Recording, Tax Appraiser, Property, GIS, Occ License, Warrant, Jail Log, Most Wanted records:** Access to the county clerk database requires a $400 setup fee and monthly charge of $40 + $.05 per minute over 20 hours. Includes civil court records and real property records back to 10/1983. For info, call 904-329-0353. Also, Access the recorded document index at www.myfloridacounty.com. Fees involved to order copies. The sheriff's warrants, jail, most wanted lists are at www.pcso.us. Also, search property data on the GIS site at www.emapsplus.com/FLPutnam/maps/. Also, search the online tax rolls at www.putnam-fl.com/app/disclaimer.htm. No name searching. Also, search the treasurer's tax rolls and occupational licensing at www.putnam-fl.com/txc/onlineinquiry.htm. **Other phones:** Appraiser-386-329-0286; Elections-386-329-0455; Vital Records-386-329-0420.

Santa Rosa County

County Clerk of the Circuit Court, PO Box 472, Milton, FL 32572. **Phone-**Clerk, R/E & UCC Recording- 850-983-1966; fax-850-983-1991; 8AM-4:30PM www.co.santa-rosa.fl.us/santa_rosa/clerk/
Will search UCC records. Search per debtor- $1.50 per year, 5 year maximum. UCC copy- $1.00 per page. UCC search includes tax liens if requested. Separate federal or state or combined tax lien search- $1.00 per year, 5 year maximum. Will not search real estate records. RE record copy- $1.00 per page. Cert fee: $1.50 per doc. Payee: Santa Rosa County Clerk of the Circuit Court. **Online Access to Property Appraiser, Real Estate, Lien, Deed, Recording, Marriage, Death, Judgment, Tax Collector, Fugitive records:** Access to the Clerk's index of recorded documents is at http://oncoreweb.srccol.com/oncoreweb/. Or, go to www.myflorida.com where you may search the index free; fees involved to order copies or view images. Also, access to the appraiser property records is free at

www.srcpa.org/property.html or at the main Property Appraiser page at www.srcpa.org click on "Record Search." Search for fugitives at www.santarosasheriff.org/fugitives.shtml. Also, search the real estate tax collector data for free at http://santarosataxcollector.governmax.com/collectmax/collect30.asp; occupational licenses at http://santarosataxcollector.governmax.com/collectmax/search_collect.asp?l_nm=occlic_bus_name&sid. **Other phones:** Assessor-850-983-1880; Treasurer-850-983-1950; Appraiser-850-983-1880; Elections-850-983-1900; Clerk of Courts-Research Dept-850-983-1970.

Sarasota County

County Clerk of the Circuit Court, PO Box 3079, Sarasota, FL 34230. **Phone-**Clerk, R/E & UCC Recording- 941-861-7400; hours 8:30AM-5PM www.sarasotaclerk.com
Will search UCC records. Search per debtor- $1.50 per name per year. UCC copy- $1.00 per page. UCC search includes tax liens if requested. Separate federal/state combined tax lien search-$1.00 per year. Real estate record owner and mortgage searches available. Offical RE record copy- $1.00 per page. Cert fee: $1.50 per doc. Payee: Sarasota County Clerk of the Circuit Court. **Online Access to Real Estate, Lien, Vital Statistic, Recording, Property Appraiser, Personal Property, records:** Access to the Clerk of Circuit Court recordings database are free at www.sarasotaclerk.com. Includes civil, criminal, and traffic court indexes. Also search indexes at www.sarasotaclerk.com. Marriage licenses may be searched; probate also available. Access the recorded document index at www.myfloridacounty.com. Fees involved to order copies. Also, search tax collector at http://sarasotataxcollector.governmax.com/collectmax/collect30.asp. Also, the Property Appraiser database is at www.sarasotaproperty.net/scpa_record_search.asp; includes subdivision/condominium sales. Search sheriff arrests back 30 days at www.sarasotasheriff.org/arrests.asp. **Other phones:** Appraiser-941-861-8200; Elections-941-861-8600; Vital Records-941-316-1043.

Seminole County

Clerk of the Circuit Court, PO Box 8099-Attn Recording Dept, Sanford, FL 32772-8099. **Phone-**407-665-4336, R/E Recording- 407-665-4409, UCC Recording- 407-665-4409; hours 8AM-4:30PM www.seminoleclerk.org
Will not search records. Record copy- $1.00 per page. Cert fee: $1.50 per doc. Payee: Seminole County Clerk of the Circuit Court. **Online Access to Property Appraiser, Real Estate, Lien, Recording records:** county clerk's recordings database is free at http://officialrecords.seminoleclerk.org/NV_Records/. Also, property appraisal records are free at www.scpafl.org/pls/web/web.seminole_county_disclaimer. There is also a map search. Also, search the tax collector personal property and real estate records for free at www.seminoletax.org/TaxSearch.htm. Also, sheriff's felon, offender, and sex offender lists are at www.seminolesheriff.org. **Other phones:** Appraiser-407-665-7502; Elections-407-65-7709.

St. Johns County

County Clerk of the Circuit Court, PO Drawer 300, St. Augustine, FL 32085-0300. **Phone-**904-819-3600, R/E Recording- 904-819-3632, UCC Recording- 904-819-3632; fax-904-819-3661; hours 8AM-5PM (No Recording after 4:15PM) www.co.st-johns.fl.us
Will search UCC records. Search per debtor- $1.50 per name per year. UCC copy- $1.00 per page. Tax liens included in UCC search if requested. Separate federal/state combined tax lien search-$1.00 per year. Real estate record owner and property searches available. RE record copy- $1.00 per page. Cert fee: $1.50 per doc. Payee: St. Johns County

Clerk of the Circuit Court. **Online Access to Property Appraiser, Real Estate, Lien, Recording, Civil, Probate, UCC, Property Tax, Occ. License, Most Wanted, Sex Offender records:** clerk's recording database is free at www.co.st-johns.fl. us/Const-Officers/Clerk-of-Court/doris/searchdocs.asp. Search by name, parcel ID, instrument type. Includes civil and probate records, UCCs. Access the recorded document index at www.myfloridacounty.com. See section intro for MyFlorida.com access details. Also, sheriff sex offender and wanted lists are at www.co.st-johns.fl.us/Const-Officers/Sheriff/index.html. Also, access to the county property appraiser database is at www.sjcpa.us/Disclaimer%20for%20as400.htm. Also, search property tax and occ. licenses at http://stjoh nstaxcollector.governmax.com. **Other phones:** Appraiser-904-823-2200; Elections-904-823-2238.

St. Lucie County

County Clerk of the Circuit Court, PO Box 700, Fort Pierce, FL 34954. **Phone**-County Clerk of the Circuit Court, R/E & UCC Recording- 772-462-6928, UCC Recording- 772-462-6927; fax-772-462-1283; hours 8AM-5PM www.stlucieco.gov
Will search UCC records. Search per debtor- $1.50 per name per year. UCC copy- $1.00 per page. Tax liens not included in UCC search. Federal/state combined tax lien search- $1.50 per year. Will search real estate records. RE copy- $1.50 per page. Cert fee: $1.50 per doc. Payee: St. Lucie County Clerk of the Circuit Court. **Online Access to Property Appraiser, Real Estate, Lien, Recording, Marriage, Fictitious Name, Personal Property, GIS, Sex Offender records:** Access to the clerk of circuit courts database of recordings, deeds, liens, mortgages, marriages, fictitious names is free at http://public.slcclerkofcourt.com. Business searching is also available for a small fee. Access the recorded document index at www.myfloridacounty.com. Fees involved to order copies. Also search property data free at www.emapsplus.com/FLStLucie/maps/. Also, sex offender list is at www.stluciesheriff.com/ex-offenders/index.asp. Also, property appraiser records are free online at www.paslc.org. Click on "Real estate" or "Personal property" to get search options. Search property tax rolls at http://216.77.1.194/tc/taxes/qui ck_tax.asp. **Other phones:** Assessor-772-462-1650; Treasurer-772-462-1476; Appraiser-772-462-1000; Vital Records-772-462-3800.

Sumter County

County Clerk of the Circuit Court, 209 N. Florida St, Rm 106, Bushnell, FL 33513. **Phone**-352-793-0215; fax-352-793-0218; hours 8:30AM-5PM
Will search UCC records. Search per debtor- $1.50 per name per year. UCC copy- $1.00 per page. UCC search includes tax liens if requested. Separate federal/state combined tax lien search- $1.00 per year. Real estate record owner and mortgage searches available. Cert fee: $1.50 per doc. Payee: Sumter County Clerk of the Circuit Court. **Online Access to Real Estate, Lien, Recording, Property Tax, Occ License records:** Access the recorded document index at www.myfloridacounty.com. See section intro for MyFlorida.com access details. Also, search tax collector and occupational licenses for free at http://sumtertaxcollector.governmax.com/collectmax/co llect30.asp. **Other phones:** Appraiser-352-793-0210.

Suwannee County

County Clerk of the Circuit Court, 200 S. Ohio Ave, Live Oak, FL 32060. **Phone**-Clerk of the Circuit Court, R/E & UCC Recording- 386-362-0554; fax-386-362-0548; 8:30AM-4:45PM www.suwclerk.org

Will search UCC records. Search per debtor- $1.50 per name per year. UCC copy- $1.00 per page. Tax liens not included in UCC search. Separate federal/state combined tax lien search- $1.00 per year. Will not search real estate records. RE record copy- $1.00 per year. Cert fee: $1.50 per doc. Payee: Suwannee County Clerk of the Circuit Court. **Online Access to Real Estate, Lien, Deed, Recording, Property Tax, Marriage, GIS, Inmate, Most Wanted records:** clerk's database index is free at www.suwclerk.org/public.html. This directs you to the statewide database; search index free; subscription required for documents. Also, search tax collector data free at www.suwanneecountytax.com/collectmax/co llect30.asp. Also, search property data on th4e GIS site at www.emapsplus.com/FLSuwannee/maps/. Also, search sheriff's most wanted and inmate lists at www.suwanneesheriff.com. **Other phones:** Treasurer-386-364-3414; Appraiser-386-362-1385; Elections-386-362-2616; Vital Records-386-362-0554.

Taylor County

County Clerk of the Circuit Court, PO Box 620, Perry, FL 32348. **Phone**-County Clerk of the Circuit Court, R/E & UCC Recording- 850-838-3506; fax-850-838-3549; hours 8AM-5PM www.taylorclerk.com
Will not search UCC records. Record copy- $1.00 per page. Cert fee: $1.50 per doc. Payee: Taylor County Clerk of the Circuit Court. **Online Access to Recording, Deed, Lien, Judgment, County Commissioner records:** Access the recorded document index at www.myfloridacounty.com. See section intro for MyFlorida.com access details. Also, access to county commission records is free at http://taco.perryfl.com/search.htm. Online records go back to 1988. **Other phones:** Assessor-850-838-3517; Treasurer-850-838-3517; Appraiser-850-838-3511; Elections-850-838-3515; Vital Records-850-838-3506.

Union County

County Clerk of the Circuit Court, State Rd 100, Courthouse Rm 103, Lake Butler, FL 32054. **Phone**-386-496-3711; fax-386-496-1718; hours 8AM-5PM
Will search UCC records. Search per debtor- $1.50 per name per year. UCC copy- $1.00 per page. UCC search includes tax liens. Separate federal/state combined tax lien search- $1.00 per debtor per year. Real estate owner, mortgage, and property transfer searches available. Cert fee: $1.50 per doc. Payee: Union County Clerk of the Circuit Court. **Online Access to Real Estate, Lien, Recording, Property, GIS records:** Access recorded document index at www.myfloridacounty.com. See section intro for MyFlorida.com access details. Also, search the GIS-mapping site for property data for free at www.emapsplus.com/FLUnion/maps/. **Other phones:** Treasurer-386-496-1026; Appraiser-386-496-3431; Elections-386-496-2236.

Volusia County

County Clerk of the Circuit Court, PO Box 6043, Deland, FL 32721. **Phone**-County Clerk of the Circuit Court, R/E & UCC Recording- 386-736-5912; fax-386-740-5104; hours 8AM-4:30PM www.clerk.org
Will search UCC records. Search per debtor- $1.50 per name per year. UCC copy- $1.50 per page. Tax liens not included in UCC search. Separate federal/state combined tax lien search- $1.50 per year. Real estate record owner searches available. Copy fee-$1.50 per page. Cert fee: $1.50 per doc. Payee: Volusia County Clerk of the Circuit Court. **Online Access to Property Appraiser, Real Estate, Lien, Vital Statistic, Recording, Citation Violation, Arrest, Property Sale, GIS, Inmate, Tax Deed Sale, Court, Personal Property records:** Recording data is

free at www.clerk.org/index.html. Click on Public Records. Recorder indices go back to 3/1996; soon back to 1990. County also offers full real Estate, lien, court and vital records on a commercial site. Initial set up is $100 with $25 monthly. For info, contact clerk. Also, search arrest ledger, tax deed sales and citations at this site. Inmate list is at http://volusia.org/correctio ns/search_page.htm. Access index of recorded documents at www.myfloridacounty.com. Fees involved to order copies. Also, search property appraiser data free at http://webserver.vcgov.org/vc_se arch.html. Also, search property free at www.emapsplus.com/FLVolusia/maps/. **Other phones:** Appraiser-386-736-5902.

Wakulla County

County Clerk of the Circuit Court, 3056 Crawfordville Hwy, Wakulla County Court House, Crawfordville, FL 32327. **Phone**-850-926-0905, R/E Recording- 850-926-0326, UCC Recording- 850-926-0326; fax-850-926-0938; hours 8AM-4PM
Will not search UCC or real estate records. Separate federal/state combined tax lien search- $1.00 per year. Record copy- $1.00 per page. Cert fee: $1.50 per doc. Payee: Wakulla County Clerk of the Circuit Court. **Online Access to Real Estate, Lien, Recording, Property Appraiser records:** recorded document index at www.myfloridacounty.com. See section intro for MyFlorida.com access details. Search property appraiser data at http://wakulla.acsgrm.co m/Property_Search.php. **Other phones:** Treasurer-850-926-3371; Appraiser-850-926-3271.

Walton County

County Clerk of the Circuit Court, PO Box 1260, De Funiak Springs, FL 32433. **Phone**-850-892-8115; fax-850-892-7551; 8AM-4PM www.co.walton.fl.us/clerk
Will search UCC records. Search per debtor- $1.50 per name per year. UCC copy- $1.00 per page. UCC search includes tax liens if requested. Separate federal/state combined tax lien search- $1.00 per year. Real estate owner, mortgage, and property transfer searches available. RE record copy- $1.00 per page. Cert fee: $1.50 per doc. Payee: Walton County Clerk of the Circuit Court. **Online Access to Real Estate, Lien, Vital Statistic, Grantor/Grantee, Property Tax records:** Records back to 1/1976 on the County Clerk database are free at www.co.walton.fl.us/clerk/orsearch/Default.aspx. This replaces of the commercial system. Also, property appraiser records are at http://propertyappraiser.co.w alton.fl.us/. Also, search tax collector data free at http://fl-walton-taxcollector.governmaxa.com/collectma x/collect30.asp. **Other phones:** Treasurer-850-892-8121; Appraiser-850-892-8123.

Washington County

County Clerk of the Circuit Court, PO Box 647, Chipley, FL 32428. **Phone**-County Clerk of the Circuit Court, R/E & UCC Recording- 850-638-6285; fax-850-638-6297; hours 8AM-4PM
Will not search records. Record copy- $1.00 per page. Cert fee: $1.50 per doc. Payee: Washington County Clerk of the Circuit Court. **Online Access to Recording, Deed, Judgment, Lien, Appraiser, Property Tax, Property Sale records:** recorded document index at www.mywashingtoncounty.com. See section intro for MyFlorida.com access details. Also, search the property appraiser sales and tax records for free at www.qpublic.net/washington/index-pa-search.html. Also, search the tax collector records for free at www.qpublic.net/wctc/index-tc-search.html. **Other phones:** Assessor-850-638-6275; Treasurer-850-638-6205; Appraiser-850-638-6205; Elections-850-638-6230; Vital Records-850-638-6230.

Florida County Locator

You will usually be able to find the city name in the City/County Cross Reference below. In that case, it is a simple matter to determine the county from the cross reference. However, only the official US Postal Service city names are included in this index. There are an additional 40,000 place names that people use in their addresses. Therefore, we have also included a ZIP/City Cross Reference immediately following the City/County Cross Reference.

If you know the ZIP Code but the city name does not appear in the City/County Cross Reference index, look up the ZIP Code in the ZIP/City Cross Reference, find the city name, then look up the city name in the City/County Cross Reference. For example, you want to know the county for an address of Menands, NY 12204. There is no "Menands" in the City/County Cross Reference. The ZIP/City Cross Reference shows that ZIP Codes 12201-12288 are for the city of Albany. Looking back in the City/County Cross Reference, Albany is in Albany County.

Florida City/County Cross Reference

ABMPS Dade
ALACHUA Alachua
ALFORD (32420) Jackson(95), Washington(4)
ALTAMONTE SPRINGS Seminole
ALTHA Calhoun
ALTOONA (32702) Lake(83), Marion(16)
ALTURAS Polk
ALVA (33920) Lee(85), Hendry(14)
ANNA MARIA Manatee
ANTHONY Marion
APALACHICOLA Franklin
APOLLO BEACH Hillsborough
APOPKA (32703) Orange(79), Seminole(20)
APOPKA Orange
ARCADIA De Soto
ARCHER (32618) Alachua(73), Levy(26)
ARGYLE Walton
ARIPEKA Pasco
ASTATULA Lake
ASTOR (32102) Lake(83), Volusia(16)
ATLANTIC BEACH Duval
AUBURNDALE Polk
AVON PARK (33825) Highlands(98), Polk(1)
AVON PARK Highlands
BABSON PARK Polk
BAGDAD Santa Rosa
BAKER (32531) Okaloosa(97), Santa Rosa(2)
BALM Hillsborough
BARBERVILLE Volusia
BARTOW Polk
BASCOM Jackson
BAY PINES Pinellas
BELL Gilchrist
BELLE GLADE Palm Beach
BELLEAIR BEACH Pinellas
BELLEAIR SHORES Pinellas
BELLEVIEW Marion
BEVERLY HILLS Citrus
BIG PINE KEY Monroe
BLOUNTSTOWN Calhoun
BOCA GRANDE Lee
BOCA RATON Palm Beach
BOKEELIA Lee
BONIFAY (32425) Holmes(90), Washington(9)
BONITA SPRINGS (34134) Lee(89), Collier(10)
BONITA SPRINGS Lee
BOSTWICK Putnam
BOWLING GREEN (33834) Hardee(75), Manatee(18), Polk(6)
BOYNTON BEACH Palm Beach
BRADENTON Manatee
BRADENTON BEACH Manatee
BRADLEY Polk
BRANDON Hillsborough
BRANFORD (32008) Suwannee(66), Gilchrist(25), Lafayette(6), Dixie(1)
BRISTOL Liberty
BRONSON Levy

BROOKER (32622) Bradford(82), Alachua(17)
BROOKSVILLE Hernando
BROOKSVILLE Pasco
BRYANT Palm Beach
BRYCEVILLE Nassau
BUNNELL Flagler
BUSHNELL Sumter
CALLAHAN Nassau
CAMPBELLTON Jackson
CANAL POINT (33438) Palm Beach(62), Martin(37)
CANAL POINT Palm Beach
CANDLER Marion
CANTONMENT Escambia
CAPE CANAVERAL Brevard
CAPE CORAL Lee
CAPTIVA Lee
CARRABELLE Franklin
CARYVILLE (32427) Washington(93), Holmes(6)
CASSADAGA Volusia
CASSELBERRY Seminole
CEDAR KEY Levy
CENTER HILL Sumter
CENTURY Escambia
CHATTAHOOCHEE Gadsden
CHIEFLAND Levy
CHIPLEY Washington
CHOKOLOSKEE Collier
CHRISTMAS Orange
CITRA Marion
CLARCONA Orange
CLARKSVILLE Calhoun
CLEARWATER Pinellas
CLEARWATER BEACH Pinellas
CLERMONT (34714) Lake(95), Polk(4)
CLERMONT Lake
CLEWISTON (33440) Hendry(98), Palm Beach(1)
COCOA Brevard
COCOA BEACH Brevard
COLEMAN Sumter
COPELAND Collier
CORTEZ Manatee
COTTONDALE (32431) Jackson(79), Washington(20)
CRAWFORDVILLE Wakulla
CRESCENT CITY Putnam
CRESTVIEW (32539) Okaloosa(89), Walton(10)
CRESTVIEW Okaloosa
CROSS CITY Dixie
CRYSTAL BEACH Pinellas
CRYSTAL RIVER Citrus
CRYSTAL SPRINGS Pasco
CYPRESS Jackson
DADE CITY (33523) Pasco(83), Hernando(16)
DADE CITY Pasco
DANIA Broward
DAVENPORT (33896) Polk(89), Osceola(10)
DAVENPORT Polk
DAY Lafayette

DAYTONA BEACH Volusia
DE LEON SPRINGS Volusia
DEBARY Volusia
DEERFIELD BEACH Broward
DEFUNIAK SPRINGS Walton
DELAND (32720) Volusia(86), Lake(13)
DELAND Volusia
DELRAY BEACH Palm Beach
DELTONA Volusia
DESTIN Okaloosa
DOCTORS INLET Clay
DOVER Hillsborough
DUNDEE Polk
DUNEDIN Pinellas
DUNNELLON (34431) Marion(81), Levy(18)
DUNNELLON Citrus
DUNNELLON Marion
DURANT Hillsborough
EAGLE LAKE Polk
EARLETON Alachua
EAST PALATKA Putnam
EASTLAKE WEIR Marion
EASTPOINT Franklin
EATON PARK Polk
EBRO (32437) Washington(88), Bay(11)
EDGEWATER Volusia
EGLIN AFB Okaloosa
ELFERS Pasco
ELKTON St. Johns
ELLENTON Manatee
ENGLEWOOD (34223) Sarasota(75), Charlotte(24)
ENGLEWOOD Charlotte
ENGLEWOOD Sarasota
ESTERO Lee
EUSTIS Lake
EVERGLADES CITY Collier
EVINSTON Alachua
FAIRFIELD Marion
FEDHAVEN Polk
FELDA Hendry
FELLSMERE Indian River
FERNANDINA BEACH Nassau
FERNDALE Lake
FLAGLER BEACH Flagler
FLEMING ISLAND Clay
FLORAHOME Putnam
FLORAL CITY Citrus
FORT LAUDERDALE Broward
FORT MC COY Marion
FORT MEADE Polk
FORT MYERS (33917) Lee(98), Charlotte(1)
FORT MYERS Lee
FORT MYERS BEACH Lee
FORT OGDEN De Soto
FORT PIERCE St. Lucie
FORT WALTON BEACH Okaloosa
FORT WHITE Columbia
FOUNTAIN Bay
FREEPORT Walton
FROSTPROOF Polk
FRUITLAND PARK Lake
GAINESVILLE Alachua

GENEVA Seminole
GEORGETOWN Putnam
GIBSONTON Hillsborough
GLEN SAINT MARY Baker
GLENWOOD Volusia
GOLDENROD Seminole
GONZALEZ Escambia
GOODLAND Collier
GOTHA Orange
GRACEVILLE (32440) Jackson(86), Holmes(13)
GRAHAM Bradford
GRAND ISLAND Lake
GRAND RIDGE (32442) Jackson(90), Calhoun(9)
GRANDIN Putnam
GRANT Brevard
GREEN COVE SPRINGS (32043) Clay(98), Putnam(1)
GREENSBORO Gadsden
GREENVILLE (32331) Madison(58), Jefferson(22), Taylor(19)
GREENWOOD Jackson
GRETNA Gadsden
GROVELAND Lake
GULF BREEZE (32561) Santa Rosa(54), Escambia(45)
GULF BREEZE Santa Rosa
GULF HAMMOCK Levy
HAINES CITY Polk
HALLANDALE Broward
HAMPTON (32044) Bradford(93), Alachua(6)
HAROLD Santa Rosa
HASTINGS St. Johns
HAVANA Gadsden
HAWTHORNE (32640) Alachua(58), Putnam(41)
HERNANDO Citrus
HIALEAH Dade
HIGH SPRINGS (32643) Alachua(61), Gilchrist(27), Columbia(10)
HIGH SPRINGS Alachua
HIGHLAND CITY Polk
HILLIARD Nassau
HOBE SOUND Martin
HOLDER Citrus
HOLIDAY Pasco
HOLLISTER Putnam
HOLLYWOOD Broward
HOLMES BEACH Manatee
HOLT (32564) Santa Rosa(87), Okaloosa(12)
HOMELAND Polk
HOMESTEAD Dade
HOMOSASSA Citrus
HOMOSASSA SPRINGS Citrus
HORSESHOE BEACH Dixie
HOSFORD Liberty
HOWEY IN THE HILLS Lake
HUDSON Pasco
HURLBURT FIELD Okaloosa
IMMOKALEE (34142) Collier(96), Lee(1), Hendry(1)
IMMOKALEE Collier

INDIALANTIC Brevard
INDIAN LAKE ESTATES Polk
INDIAN ROCKS BEACH Pinellas
INDIANTOWN Martin
INGLIS (34449) Levy(92), Citrus(7)
INTERCESSION CITY Osceola
INTERLACHEN Putnam
INVERNESS Citrus
ISLAMORADA Monroe
ISLAND GROVE Alachua
ISTACHATTA Hernando
JACKSONVILLE (32234) Duval(72),
    Clay(23), Nassau(3)
JACKSONVILLE Duval
JACKSONVILLE St. Johns
JACKSONVILLE BEACH Duval
JASPER Hamilton
JAY Santa Rosa
JENNINGS Hamilton
JENSEN BEACH Martin
JUPITER (33478) Palm Beach(93),
    Martin(6)
JUPITER Palm Beach
KATHLEEN (33849) Polk(93), Pasco(6)
KENANSVILLE Osceola
KEY BISCAYNE Dade
KEY COLONY BEACH Monroe
KEY LARGO Monroe
KEY WEST Monroe
KEYSTONE HEIGHTS (32656) Clay(83),
    Bradford(16)
KILLARNEY Orange
KINARD Calhoun
KISSIMMEE (34747) Osceola(98),
    Orange(1)
KISSIMMEE (34759) Polk(81), Osceola(18)
KISSIMMEE Osceola
LA CROSSE Alachua
LABELLE (33935) Hendry(82), Glades(17)
LABELLE Hendry
LACOOCHEE Pasco
LADY LAKE (32159) Lake(73), Sumter(26)
LADY LAKE (32162) Sumter(66),
    Marion(33)
LADY LAKE Lake
LAKE ALFRED Polk
LAKE BUTLER (32054) Union(88),
    Bradford(11)
LAKE CITY (32055) Columbia(97),
    Suwannee(2)
LAKE CITY Columbia
LAKE COMO Putnam
LAKE GENEVA Clay
LAKE HAMILTON Polk
LAKE HARBOR Palm Beach
LAKE HELEN Volusia
LAKE MARY Seminole
LAKE MONROE Seminole
LAKE PANASOFFKEE Sumter
LAKE PLACID Highlands
LAKE WALES Polk
LAKE WORTH Palm Beach
LAKELAND (33810) Polk(98),
    Hillsborough(1)
LAKELAND Polk
LAMONT (32336) Jefferson(65),
    Madison(19), Taylor(15)
LANARK VILLAGE Franklin
LAND O LAKES Pasco
LARGO Pinellas
LAUREL Sarasota
LAUREL HILL (32567) Walton(66),
    Okaloosa(33)
LAWTEY (32058) Bradford(96), Union(3)
LECANTO Citrus
LEE Madison
LEESBURG Lake
LEHIGH ACRES Lee
LITHIA (33547) Hillsborough(97), Polk(2)
LIVE OAK Suwannee
LLOYD Jefferson
LOCHLOOSA Alachua
LONG KEY Monroe

LONGBOAT KEY (34228) Sarasota(62),
    Manatee(37)
LONGWOOD Seminole
LORIDA Highlands
LOUGHMAN Polk
LOWELL Marion
LOXAHATCHEE Palm Beach
LULU Columbia
LUTZ (33559) Hillsborough(57), Pasco(42)
LYNN HAVEN Bay
MACCLENNY Baker
MAITLAND (32751) Orange(78),
    Seminole(21)
MAITLAND Orange
MALABAR Brevard
MALONE Jackson
MANASOTA Manatee
MANGO Hillsborough
MARATHON Monroe
MARATHON SHORES Monroe
MARCO ISLAND Collier
MARIANNA Jackson
MARY ESTHER Okaloosa
MASCOTTE Lake
MAYO Lafayette
MC ALPIN Suwannee
MC DAVID Escambia
MC INTOSH Marion
MELBOURNE Brevard
MELBOURNE BEACH Brevard
MELROSE (32666) Putnam(52),
    Alachua(18), Bradford(16), Clay(12)
MERRITT ISLAND Brevard
MEXICO BEACH Bay
MIAMI Dade
MIAMI BEACH Dade
MICANOPY (32667) Alachua(65),
    Marion(34)
MICCOSUKEE CPO Leon
MID FLORIDA Seminole
MIDDLEBURG Clay
MIDWAY Gadsden
MILLIGAN Okaloosa
MILTON Santa Rosa
MIMS (32754) Brevard(91), Volusia(8)
MINNEOLA Lake
MIRAMAR BEACH Walton
MOLINO Escambia
MONTICELLO (32344) Jefferson(98),
    Leon(1)
MONTICELLO Jefferson
MONTVERDE Lake
MOORE HAVEN Glades
MORRISTON (32668) Levy(81), Marion(18)
MOSSY HEAD Walton
MOUNT DORA (32757) Lake(93),
    Orange(6)
MOUNT DORA Lake
MOUNT DORA Seminole
MOUNT PLEASANT Gadsden
MULBERRY Polk
MURDOCK Charlotte
MYAKKA CITY Manatee
NALCREST Polk
NAPLES (34119) Collier(98), Lee(1)
NAPLES Collier
NEPTUNE BEACH Duval
NEW PORT RICHEY Pasco
NEW SMYRNA BEACH Volusia
NEWBERRY (32669) Alachua(79),
    Gilchrist(18), Levy(2)
NICEVILLE (32578) Okaloosa(92),
    Walton(7)
NICEVILLE Okaloosa
NICHOLS Polk
NOBLETON Hernando
NOCATEE De Soto
NOKOMIS Sarasota
NOMA Holmes
NORTH FORT MYERS (33917) Lee(98),
    Charlotte(1)
NORTH FORT MYERS Lee
NORTH PALM BEACH Palm Beach

NORTH PORT Sarasota
O BRIEN Suwannee
OAK HILL Volusia
OAKLAND Orange
OCALA Marion
OCHOPEE (34141) Collier(65), Dade(28),
    Monroe(5)
OCKLAWAHA Marion
OCOEE Orange
ODESSA (33556) Hillsborough(74),
    Pasco(25)
OKAHUMPKA Lake
OKEECHOBEE (34972) Okeechobee(98),
    Osceola(1)
OKEECHOBEE (34974) Okeechobee(89),
    Martin(3), Glades(3), Highlands(3)
OKEECHOBEE Okeechobee
OLD TOWN Dixie
OLDSMAR Pinellas
OLUSTEE Baker
ONA (33865) Hardee(97), De Soto(2)
ONECO Manatee
OPA LOCKA Dade
ORANGE CITY Volusia
ORANGE LAKE Marion
ORANGE PARK (32073) Clay(98),
    Duval(1)
ORANGE PARK Clay
ORANGE SPRINGS Marion
ORLANDO Brevard
ORLANDO Orange
ORMOND BEACH (32174) Volusia(98),
    Flagler(1)
ORMOND BEACH Volusia
OSPREY Sarasota
OSTEEN Volusia
OTTER CREEK Levy
OVERSTREET Gulf
OVIEDO Seminole
OXFORD (34484) Sumter(98), Marion(1)
OZONA Pinellas
PAHOKEE Palm Beach
PAISLEY Lake
PALATKA Putnam
PALM BAY Brevard
PALM BEACH Palm Beach
PALM BEACH GARDENS Palm Beach
PALM CITY (34990) Martin(95), St.
    Lucie(4)
PALM CITY Martin
PALM COAST Flagler
PALM HARBOR Pinellas
PALMDALE Glades
PALMETTO Manatee
PANACEA (32346) Wakulla(87),
    Franklin(12)
PANAMA CITY (32413) Bay(88),
    Walton(11)
PANAMA CITY Bay
PANAMA CITY BEACH (32413) Bay(88),
    Walton(11)
PANAMA CITY BEACH Bay
PARRISH Manatee
PATRICK A F B Brevard
PAXTON Walton
PENNEY FARMS Clay
PENSACOLA Escambia
PERRY Taylor
PIERSON Volusia
PINELAND Lee
PINELLAS PARK Pinellas
PINETTA Madison
PLACIDA Charlotte
PLANT CITY Hillsborough
PLYMOUTH Orange
POINT WASHINGTON Walton
POLK CITY Polk
POMONA PARK Putnam
POMPANO BEACH Broward
PONCE DE LEON (32455) Holmes(83),
    Walton(16)
PONTE VEDRA BEACH St. Johns
PORT CHARLOTTE Charlotte

PORT ORANGE Volusia
PORT RICHEY Pasco
PORT SAINT JOE (32456) Gulf(88),
    Bay(11)
PORT SAINT JOE Gulf
PORT SAINT LUCIE St. Lucie
PORT SALERNO Martin
PUNTA GORDA (33955) Charlotte(82),
    Lee(17)
PUNTA GORDA Charlotte
PUTNAM HALL Putnam
QUINCY Gadsden
RAIFORD (32083) Union(77), Bradford(22)
RAIFORD Union
REDDICK Marion
RIVER RANCH Polk
RIVERVIEW Hillsborough
ROCKLEDGE Brevard
ROSELAND Indian River
ROSEMARY BEACH (32461) Bay(50),
    Walton(50)
ROTONDA WEST Charlotte
RUSKIN Hillsborough
SAFETY HARBOR Pinellas
SAINT AUGUSTINE St. Johns
SAINT CLOUD Osceola
SAINT JAMES CITY Lee
SAINT LEO Pasco
SAINT MARKS Wakulla
SAINT PETERSBURG Pinellas
SALEM Taylor
SAN ANTONIO Pasco
SAN MATEO Putnam
SANDERSON Baker
SANFORD Seminole
SANIBEL Lee
SANTA ROSA BEACH Walton
SARASOTA (34243) Manatee(85),
    Sarasota(14)
SARASOTA Sarasota
SATELLITE BEACH Brevard
SATSUMA Putnam
SCOTTSMOOR Brevard
SEBASTIAN Brevard
SEBASTIAN Indian River
SEBRING Highlands
SEFFNER Hillsborough
SEMINOLE Pinellas
SEVILLE Volusia
SHADY GROVE Taylor
SHALIMAR Okaloosa
SHARPES Brevard
SILVER SPRINGS Marion
SNEADS Jackson
SOPCHOPPY Wakulla
SORRENTO Lake
SOUTH BAY Palm Beach
SOUTH FLORIDA Broward
SPARR Marion
SPRING HILL Hernando
STARKE (32091) Bradford(89), Clay(10)
STEINHATCHEE (32359) Dixie(62),
    Taylor(37)
STUART Martin
SUGARLOAF SHORES Monroe
SUMATRA Liberty
SUMMERFIELD Marion
SUMMERLAND KEY Monroe
SUMTERVILLE Sumter
SUN CITY Hillsborough
SUN CITY CENTER Hillsborough
SUNNYSIDE (32461) Bay(50), Walton(50)
SUWANNEE Dixie
SYDNEY Hillsborough
TALLAHASSEE Leon
TALLEVAST Manatee
TAMPA Hillsborough
TANGERINE Orange
TARPON SPRINGS Pinellas
TAVARES Lake
TAVERNIER Monroe
TELOGIA Liberty
TERRA CEIA Manatee

THONOTOSASSA Hillsborough
TITUSVILLE Brevard
TRENTON (32693) Gilchrist(64), Levy(35)
TRILBY Pasco
UMATILLA (32784) Lake(68), Marion(31)
VALPARAISO Okaloosa
VALRICO Hillsborough
VENICE Sarasota
VENUS (33960) Highlands(86), Glades(13)
VERNON (32462) Washington(71),
  Bay(17), Walton(10)
VERO BEACH Indian River
WABASSO Indian River
WACISSA Jefferson
WAKULLA SPRINGS Leon

WALDO (32694) Alachua(96), Bradford(3)
WAUCHULA Hardee
WAUSAU Washington
WAVERLY Polk
WEBSTER (33597) Sumter(84),
  Hernando(15)
WEIRSDALE (32195) Marion(83), Lake(16)
WELAKA Putnam
WELLBORN (32094) Suwannee(94),
  Columbia(5)
WEST PALM BEACH Palm Beach
WESTON Broward
WESTVILLE (32464) Holmes(63),
  Walton(36)
WEWAHITCHKA Calhoun

WEWAHITCHKA Gulf
WHITE SPRINGS (32096) Hamilton(52),
  Columbia(41), Suwannee(6)
WILDWOOD Sumter
WILLISTON (32696) Levy(91), Marion(8)
WIMAUMA (33598) Hillsborough(96),
  Manatee(3)
WINDERMERE Orange
WINTER BEACH Indian River
WINTER GARDEN (34787) Orange(96),
  Lake(3)
WINTER GARDEN Orange
WINTER HAVEN Polk
WINTER PARK (32792) Orange(68),
  Seminole(31)

WINTER PARK Orange
WINTER SPRINGS Seminole
WOODVILLE Leon
WORTHINGTON SPRINGS Union
YALAHA Lake
YANKEETOWN Levy
YOUNGSTOWN (32466) Bay(95),
  Washington(3), Calhoun(1)
YULEE Nassau
ZELLWOOD Orange
ZEPHYRHILLS (33540) Pasco(98),
  Hillsborough(1)
ZEPHYRHILLS Pasco
ZOLFO SPRINGS Hardee

Florida ZIP/City Cross Reference

32003-32003	ORANGE PARK	
32004-32004	PONTE VEDRA BEACH	
32006-32006	FLEMING ISLAND	
32007-32007	BOSTWICK	
32008-32008	BRANFORD	
32009-32009	BRYCEVILLE	
32011-32011	CALLAHAN	
32013-32013	DAY	
32024-32025	LAKE CITY	
32026-32026	RAIFORD	
32030-32030	DOCTORS INLET	
32033-32033	ELKTON	
32034-32035	FERNANDINA BEACH	
32038-32038	FORT WHITE	
32040-32040	GLEN SAINT MARY	
32041-32041	YULEE	
32042-32042	GRAHAM	
32043-32043	GREEN COVE SPRINGS	
32044-32044	HAMPTON	
32046-32046	HILLIARD	
32050-32050	MIDDLEBURG	
32052-32052	JASPER	
32053-32053	JENNINGS	
32054-32054	LAKE BUTLER	
32055-32056	LAKE CITY	
32058-32058	LAWTEY	
32059-32059	LEE	
32060-32060	LIVE OAK	
32061-32061	LULU	
32062-32062	MC ALPIN	
32063-32063	MACCLENNY	
32064-32064	LIVE OAK	
32065-32065	ORANGE PARK	
32066-32066	MAYO	
32067-32067	ORANGE PARK	
32068-32068	MIDDLEBURG	
32071-32071	O BRIEN	
32072-32072	OLUSTEE	
32073-32073	ORANGE PARK	
32079-32079	PENNEY FARMS	
32080-32080	SAINT AUGUSTINE	
32082-32082	PONTE VEDRA BEACH	
32083-32083	RAIFORD	
32084-32086	SAINT AUGUSTINE	
32087-32087	SANDERSON	
32091-32091	STARKE	
32092-32092	SAINT AUGUSTINE	
32094-32094	WELLBORN	
32095-32095	SAINT AUGUSTINE	
32096-32096	WHITE SPRINGS	
32097-32097	YULEE	
32099-32099	JACKSONVILLE	
32100-32100	DAYTONA BEACH	
32102-32102	ASTOR	
32105-32105	BARBERVILLE	
32110-32110	BUNNELL	
32111-32111	CANDLER	
32112-32112	CRESCENT CITY	
32113-32113	CITRA	
32114-32123	DAYTONA BEACH	
32123-32123	PORT ORANGE	
32124-32127	DAYTONA BEACH	
32127-32127	PORT ORANGE	
32128-32128	DAYTONA BEACH	
32129-32129	PORT ORANGE	
32130-32130	DE LEON SPRINGS	
32131-32131	EAST PALATKA	
32132-32132	EDGEWATER	
32133-32133	EASTLAKE WEIR	
32134-32134	FORT MC COY	
32135-32135	PALM COAST	
32136-32136	FLAGLER BEACH	
32137-32137	PALM COAST	
32138-32138	GRANDIN	
32139-32139	GEORGETOWN	
32140-32140	FLORAHOME	
32141-32141	EDGEWATER	
32142-32142	PALM COAST	
32145-32145	HASTINGS	
32147-32147	HOLLISTER	
32148-32149	INTERLACHEN	
32151-32151	FLAGLER BEACH	
32157-32157	LAKE COMO	
32158-32159	LADY LAKE	
32160-32160	LAKE GENEVA	
32162-32162	LADY LAKE	
32164-32164	PALM COAST	
32168-32170	NEW SMYRNA BEACH	
32173-32176	ORMOND BEACH	
32177-32178	PALATKA	
32179-32179	OCKLAWAHA	
32180-32180	PIERSON	
32181-32181	POMONA PARK	
32182-32182	ORANGE SPRINGS	
32183-32183	OCKLAWAHA	
32185-32185	PUTNAM HALL	
32187-32187	SAN MATEO	
32189-32189	SATSUMA	
32190-32190	SEVILLE	
32192-32192	SPARR	
32193-32193	WELAKA	
32195-32195	WEIRSDALE	
32198-32198	DAYTONA BEACH	
32200-32232	JACKSONVILLE	
32233-32233	ATLANTIC BEACH	
32234-32239	JACKSONVILLE	
32240-32240	JACKSONVILLE BEACH	
32241-32247	JACKSONVILLE	
32250-32250	JACKSONVILLE BEACH	
32254-32260	JACKSONVILLE	
32266-32266	NEPTUNE BEACH	
32267-32297	JACKSONVILLE	
32301-32304	TALLAHASSEE	
32305-32305	WAKULLA SPRINGS	
32305-32308	TALLAHASSEE	
32309-32309	MICCOSUKEE CPO	
32309-32318	TALLAHASSEE	
32320-32320	APALACHICOLA	
32321-32321	BRISTOL	
32322-32322	CARRABELLE	
32323-32323	LANARK VILLAGE	
32324-32324	CHATTAHOOCHEE	
32326-32327	CRAWFORDVILLE	
32328-32328	EASTPOINT	
32329-32329	APALACHICOLA	
32330-32330	GREENSBORO	
32331-32331	GREENVILLE	
32332-32332	GRETNA	
32333-32333	HAVANA	
32334-32334	HOSFORD	
32335-32335	SUMATRA	
32336-32336	LAMONT	
32337-32337	LLOYD	
32340-32341	MADISON	
32343-32343	MIDWAY	
32344-32345	MONTICELLO	
32346-32346	PANACEA	
32347-32348	PERRY	
32350-32350	PINETTA	
32351-32351	QUINCY	
32352-32352	MOUNT PLEASANT	
32352-32353	QUINCY	
32355-32355	SAINT MARKS	
32356-32356	SALEM	
32357-32357	SHADY GROVE	
32358-32358	SOPCHOPPY	
32359-32359	STEINHATCHEE	
32360-32360	TELOGIA	
32361-32361	WACISSA	
32362-32362	WOODVILLE	
32395-32399	TALLAHASSEE	
32400-32406	PANAMA CITY	
32407-32407	PANAMA CITY BEACH	
32408-32409	PANAMA CITY	
32410-32410	MEXICO BEACH	
32411-32413	PANAMA CITY	
32413-32413	PANAMA CITY BEACH	
32417-32417	PANAMA CITY	
32420-32420	ALFORD	
32421-32421	ALTHA	
32422-32422	ARGYLE	
32423-32423	BASCOM	
32424-32424	BLOUNTSTOWN	
32425-32425	BONIFAY	
32426-32426	CAMPBELLTON	
32427-32427	CARYVILLE	
32428-32428	CHIPLEY	
32430-32430	CLARKSVILLE	
32431-32431	COTTONDALE	
32432-32432	CYPRESS	
32433-32433	DEFUNIAK SPRINGS	
32434-32434	MOSSY HEAD	
32435-32435	DEFUNIAK SPRINGS	
32437-32437	EBRO	
32438-32438	FOUNTAIN	
32439-32439	FREEPORT	
32440-32440	GRACEVILLE	
32442-32442	GRAND RIDGE	
32443-32443	GREENWOOD	
32444-32444	LYNN HAVEN	
32445-32445	MALONE	
32446-32448	MARIANNA	
32449-32449	KINARD	
32449-32449	WEWAHITCHKA	
32452-32452	NOMA	
32453-32453	OVERSTREET	
32454-32454	POINT WASHINGTON	
32455-32455	PONCE DE LEON	
32456-32457	PORT SAINT JOE	
32459-32459	SANTA ROSA BEACH	
32460-32460	SNEADS	
32461-32461	SUNNYSIDE	
32461-32461	ROSEMARY BEACH	
32462-32462	VERNON	
32463-32463	WAUSAU	
32464-32464	WESTVILLE	
32465-32465	WEWAHITCHKA	
32466-32466	YOUNGSTOWN	
32500-32526	PENSACOLA	
32530-32530	BAGDAD	
32531-32531	BAKER	
32533-32533	CANTONMENT	
32534-32534	PENSACOLA	
32535-32535	CENTURY	
32536-32536	CRESTVIEW	
32537-32537	MILLIGAN	
32538-32538	PAXTON	
32539-32539	CRESTVIEW	
32540-32541	DESTIN	
32542-32542	EGLIN AFB	
32544-32544	HURLBURT FIELD	
32547-32549	FORT WALTON BEACH	
32550-32550	MIRAMAR BEACH	
32559-32559	PENSACOLA	
32560-32560	GONZALEZ	
32561-32562	GULF BREEZE	
32563-32563	HAROLD	
32563-32563	GULF BREEZE	
32564-32564	HOLT	
32565-32565	JAY	
32566-32566	GULF BREEZE	
32567-32567	LAUREL HILL	
32568-32568	MC DAVID	
32569-32569	MARY ESTHER	
32570-32572	MILTON	
32573-32576	PENSACOLA	
32577-32577	MOLINO	
32578-32578	NICEVILLE	
32579-32579	SHALIMAR	
32580-32580	VALPARAISO	
32581-32582	PENSACOLA	
32583-32583	MILTON	
32588-32588	NICEVILLE	
32589-32598	PENSACOLA	
32600-32614	GAINESVILLE	
32615-32616	ALACHUA	
32617-32617	ANTHONY	
32618-32618	ARCHER	
32619-32619	BELL	
32621-32621	BRONSON	
32622-32622	BROOKER	
32625-32625	CEDAR KEY	
32626-32626	CHIEFLAND	
32627-32627	GAINESVILLE	
32628-32628	CROSS CITY	
32631-32631	EARLETON	
32633-32633	EVINSTON	
32634-32634	FAIRFIELD	
32635-32635	GAINESVILLE	
32639-32639	GULF HAMMOCK	
32640-32640	HAWTHORNE	
32641-32641	GAINESVILLE	

32643-32643 HIGH SPRINGS	32799-32799 MID FLORIDA	33455-33455 HOBE SOUND	33834-33834 BOWLING GREEN
32644-32644 CHIEFLAND	32800-32899 ORLANDO	33458-33458 JUPITER	33835-33835 BRADLEY
32648-32648 HORSESHOE BEACH	32901-32902 MELBOURNE	33459-33459 LAKE HARBOR	33836-33837 DAVENPORT
32653-32653 GAINESVILLE	32903-32903 INDIALANTIC	33460-33464 LAKE WORTH	33838-33838 DUNDEE
32654-32654 ISLAND GROVE	32904-32904 MELBOURNE	33464-33464 BOCA RATON	33839-33839 EAGLE LAKE
32655-32655 HIGH SPRINGS	32905-32911 PALM BAY	33465-33467 LAKE WORTH	33840-33840 EATON PARK
32656-32656 KEYSTONE HEIGHTS	32912-32919 MELBOURNE	33468-33469 JUPITER	33841-33841 FORT MEADE
32658-32658 LA CROSSE	32920-32920 CAPE CANAVERAL	33470-33470 LOXAHATCHEE	33842-33842 FORT OGDEN
32662-32662 LOCHLOOSA	32922-32924 COCOA	33471-33471 MOORE HAVEN	33843-33843 FROSTPROOF
32663-32663 LOWELL	32925-32925 PATRICK A F B	33474-33474 BOYNTON BEACH	33844-33845 HAINES CITY
32664-32664 MC INTOSH	32926-32927 COCOA	33475-33475 HOBE SOUND	33846-33846 HIGHLAND CITY
32666-32666 MELROSE	32931-32932 COCOA BEACH	33476-33476 PAHOKEE	33847-33847 HOMELAND
32667-32667 MICANOPY	32934-32936 MELBOURNE	33477-33478 JUPITER	33848-33848 INTERCESSION CITY
32668-32668 MORRISTON	32937-32937 SATELLITE BEACH	33480-33480 PALM BEACH	33849-33849 KATHLEEN
32669-32669 NEWBERRY	32940-32941 MELBOURNE	33481-33481 BOCA RATON	33850-33850 LAKE ALFRED
32680-32680 OLD TOWN	32948-32948 FELLSMERE	33482-33484 DELRAY BEACH	33851-33851 LAKE HAMILTON
32681-32681 ORANGE LAKE	32949-32949 GRANT	33486-33488 BOCA RATON	33852-33852 LAKE PLACID
32683-32683 OTTER CREEK	32950-32950 MALABAR	33491-33491 CANAL POINT	33853-33853 LAKE WALES
32686-32686 REDDICK	32951-32951 MELBOURNE BEACH	33493-33493 SOUTH BAY	33854-33854 FEDHAVEN
32692-32692 SUWANNEE	32952-32954 MERRITT ISLAND	33496-33499 BOCA RATON	33855-33855 INDIAN LAKE ESTATES
32693-32693 TRENTON	32955-32956 ROCKLEDGE	33503-33503 BALM	33856-33856 NALCREST
32694-32694 WALDO	32957-32957 ROSELAND	33504-33504 BAY PINES	33857-33857 LORIDA
32696-32696 WILLISTON	32958-32958 SEBASTIAN	33508-33511 BRANDON	33858-33858 LOUGHMAN
32697-32697 WORTHINGTON SPRINGS	32959-32959 SHARPES	33513-33513 BUSHNELL	33859-33859 LAKE WALES
32701-32701 ALTAMONTE SPRINGS	32960-32969 VERO BEACH	33514-33514 CENTER HILL	33860-33860 MULBERRY
32702-32702 ALTOONA	32970-32970 WABASSO	33521-33521 COLEMAN	33862-33862 LAKE PLACID
32703-32704 APOPKA	32971-32971 WINTER BEACH	33523-33523 DADE CITY	33863-33863 NICHOLS
32706-32706 CASSADAGA	32976-32978 SEBASTIAN	33524-33524 CRYSTAL SPRINGS	33864-33864 NOCATEE
32707-32707 CASSELBERRY	33001-33001 LONG KEY	33525-33526 DADE CITY	33865-33865 ONA
32708-32708 WINTER SPRINGS	33002-33002 HIALEAH	33527-33527 DOVER	33867-33867 RIVER RANCH
32709-32709 CHRISTMAS	33004-33004 DANIA	33530-33530 DURANT	33868-33868 POLK CITY
32710-32710 CLARCONA	33008-33009 HALLANDALE	33534-33534 GIBSONTON	33870-33872 SEBRING
32712-32712 APOPKA	33010-33018 HIALEAH	33537-33537 LACOOCHEE	33873-33873 WAUCHULA
32713-32713 DEBARY	33019-33029 HOLLYWOOD	33538-33538 LAKE PANASOFFKEE	33875-33876 SEBRING
32714-32717 ALTAMONTE SPRINGS	33030-33035 HOMESTEAD	33539-33544 ZEPHYRHILLS	33877-33877 WAVERLY
32718-32718 CASSELBERRY	33036-33036 ISLAMORADA	33547-33547 LITHIA	33880-33888 WINTER HAVEN
32719-32719 WINTER SPRINGS	33037-33037 KEY LARGO	33548-33549 LUTZ	33890-33890 ZOLFO SPRINGS
32720-32721 DELAND	33039-33039 HOMESTEAD	33550-33550 MANGO	33896-33897 DAVENPORT
32722-32722 GLENWOOD	33040-33041 KEY WEST	33556-33556 ODESSA	33898-33898 LAKE WALES
32723-32724 DELAND	33042-33042 SUMMERLAND KEY	33558-33559 LUTZ	33900-33903 FORT MYERS
32725-32725 DELTONA	33043-33043 BIG PINE KEY	33563-33567 PLANT CITY	33903-33903 NORTH FORT MYERS
32726-32727 EUSTIS	33044-33044 SUGARLOAF SHORES	33568-33569 RIVERVIEW	33904-33904 CAPE CORAL
32728-32728 DELTONA	33045-33045 KEY WEST	33570-33570 RUSKIN	33905-33908 FORT MYERS
32730-32730 CASSELBERRY	33050-33050 MARATHON	33571-33571 SUN CITY CENTER	33909-33910 CAPE CORAL
32732-32732 GENEVA	33051-33051 KEY COLONY BEACH	33572-33572 APOLLO BEACH	33911-33913 FORT MYERS
32733-32733 GOLDENROD	33052-33052 MARATHON SHORES	33573-33573 SUN CITY CENTER	33914-33915 CAPE CORAL
32735-32735 GRAND ISLAND	33054-33056 OPA LOCKA	33574-33574 SAINT LEO	33916-33917 FORT MYERS
32736-32736 EUSTIS	33060-33069 POMPANO BEACH	33575-33575 RUSKIN	33917-33917 NORTH FORT MYERS
32738-32739 DELTONA	33070-33070 TAVERNIER	33576-33576 SAN ANTONIO	33918-33918 FORT MYERS
32744-32744 LAKE HELEN	33071-33077 POMPANO BEACH	33583-33584 SEFFNER	33918-33918 NORTH FORT MYERS
32745-32745 MOUNT DORA	33081-33081 HOLLYWOOD	33585-33585 SUMTERVILLE	33919-33919 FORT MYERS
32745-32745 MID FLORIDA	33082-33082 SOUTH FLORIDA	33586-33586 SUN CITY	33920-33920 ALVA
32746-32746 LAKE MARY	33083-33084 HOLLYWOOD	33587-33587 SYDNEY	33921-33921 BOCA GRANDE
32747-32747 LAKE MONROE	33090-33092 HOMESTEAD	33592-33592 THONOTOSASSA	33922-33922 BOKEELIA
32750-32750 LONGWOOD	33093-33097 POMPANO BEACH	33593-33593 TRILBY	33923-33923 BONITA SPRINGS
32751-32751 MAITLAND	33100-33102 MIAMI	33594-33595 VALRICO	33924-33924 CAPTIVA
32752-32752 LONGWOOD	33103-33104 ABMPS	33597-33597 WEBSTER	33925-33925 CHOKOLOSKEE
32753-32753 DEBARY	33107-33148 MIAMI	33598-33598 WIMAUMA	33926-33926 COPELAND
32754-32754 MIMS	33149-33149 KEY BISCAYNE	33600-33697 TAMPA	33927-33927 PUNTA GORDA
32756-32757 MOUNT DORA	33150-33154 MIAMI	33700-33743 SAINT PETERSBURG	33928-33928 ESTERO
32759-32759 OAK HILL	33154-33154 MIAMI BEACH	33744-33744 BAY PINES	33929-33929 EVERGLADES CITY
32762-32762 OVIEDO	33155-33239 MIAMI	33747-33747 SAINT PETERSBURG	33930-33930 FELDA
32763-32763 ORANGE CITY	33239-33239 MIAMI BEACH	33755-33767 CLEARWATER	33931-33932 FORT MYERS BEACH
32764-32764 OSTEEN	33242-33299 MIAMI	33767-33767 CLEARWATER BEACH	33933-33933 GOODLAND
32765-32766 OVIEDO	33300-33326 FORT LAUDERDALE	33769-33769 CLEARWATER	33934-33934 IMMOKALEE
32767-32767 PAISLEY	33327-33327 WESTON	33770-33771 LARGO	33935-33935 LABELLE
32768-32768 PLYMOUTH	33327-33394 FORT LAUDERDALE	33772-33772 SEMINOLE	33936-33936 LEHIGH ACRES
32771-32773 SANFORD	33401-33407 WEST PALM BEACH	33773-33774 LARGO	33937-33937 MARCO ISLAND
32774-32774 ORANGE CITY	33408-33408 NORTH PALM BEACH	33775-33776 SEMINOLE	33938-33938 MURDOCK
32775-32775 SCOTTSMOOR	33409-33410 WEST PALM BEACH	33777-33777 LARGO	33939-33942 NAPLES
32776-32776 SORRENTO	33410-33410 PALM BEACH GARDENS	33777-33777 SEMINOLE	33943-33943 OCHOPEE
32777-32777 TANGERINE	33411-33422 WEST PALM BEACH	33778-33779 LARGO	33944-33944 PALMDALE
32778-32778 TAVARES	33424-33426 BOYNTON BEACH	33780-33782 PINELLAS PARK	33945-33945 PINELAND
32779-32779 LONGWOOD	33427-33429 BOCA RATON	33784-33784 SAINT PETERSBURG	33946-33946 PLACIDA
32780-32783 TITUSVILLE	33430-33430 BELLE GLADE	33785-33785 INDIAN ROCKS BEACH	33947-33947 ROTONDA WEST
32784-32784 UMATILLA	33431-33434 BOCA RATON	33786-33786 BELLEAIR BEACH	33948-33949 PORT CHARLOTTE
32789-32790 WINTER PARK	33435-33437 BOYNTON BEACH	33801-33815 LAKELAND	33950-33951 PUNTA GORDA
32791-32791 LONGWOOD	33438-33438 CANAL POINT	33820-33820 ALTURAS	33952-33954 PORT CHARLOTTE
32792-32793 WINTER PARK	33439-33439 BRYANT	33821-33821 ARCADIA	33955-33955 PUNTA GORDA
32794-32794 MAITLAND	33440-33440 CLEWISTON	33823-33823 AUBURNDALE	33956-33956 SAINT JAMES CITY
32795-32795 LAKE MARY	33441-33443 DEERFIELD BEACH	33825-33826 AVON PARK	33957-33957 SANIBEL
32796-32796 TITUSVILLE	33444-33448 DELRAY BEACH	33827-33827 BABSON PARK	33959-33959 BONITA SPRINGS
32798-32798 ZELLWOOD	33454-33454 LAKE WORTH	33830-33831 BARTOW	33960-33960 VENUS

33961-33964	NAPLES
33965-33965	FORT MYERS
33969-33969	MARCO ISLAND
33970-33972	LEHIGH ACRES
33975-33975	LABELLE
33980-33981	PORT CHARLOTTE
33982-33983	PUNTA GORDA
33990-33993	CAPE CORAL
33994-33994	FORT MYERS
33999-34120	NAPLES
34133-34136	BONITA SPRINGS
34137-34137	COPELAND
34138-34138	CHOKOLOSKEE
34139-34139	EVERGLADES CITY
34140-34140	GOODLAND
34141-34141	OCHOPEE
34142-34143	IMMOKALEE
34145-34146	MARCO ISLAND
34201-34212	BRADENTON
34215-34215	CORTEZ
34216-34216	ANNA MARIA
34217-34217	BRADENTON BEACH
34218-34218	HOLMES BEACH
34219-34219	PARRISH
34220-34221	PALMETTO
34222-34222	ELLENTON
34223-34224	ENGLEWOOD
34228-34228	LONGBOAT KEY
34229-34229	OSPREY
34230-34243	SARASOTA
34250-34250	TERRA CEIA
34251-34251	MYAKKA CITY
34260-34260	MANASOTA
34264-34264	ONECO
34265-34266	ARCADIA
34267-34267	FORT OGDEN
34268-34268	NOCATEE
34269-34269	ARCADIA
34270-34270	TALLEVAST
34272-34272	LAUREL
34274-34275	NOKOMIS
34276-34278	SARASOTA
34280-34282	BRADENTON
34284-34285	VENICE
34286-34289	NORTH PORT
34292-34293	VENICE
34295-34295	ENGLEWOOD
34420-34421	BELLEVIEW
34423-34429	CRYSTAL RIVER
34430-34434	DUNNELLON
34436-34436	FLORAL CITY
34442-34442	HERNANDO
34445-34445	HOLDER
34446-34446	HOMOSASSA
34447-34447	HOMOSASSA SPRINGS
34448-34448	HOMOSASSA
34449-34449	INGLIS
34450-34453	INVERNESS
34460-34461	LECANTO
34464-34465	BEVERLY HILLS
34470-34483	OCALA
34484-34484	OXFORD
34487-34487	HOMOSASSA
34488-34489	SILVER SPRINGS
34491-34492	SUMMERFIELD
34498-34498	YANKEETOWN
34601-34605	BROOKSVILLE
34606-34608	SPRING HILL
34609-34610	BROOKSVILLE
34611-34611	SPRING HILL
34613-34614	BROOKSVILLE
34615-34630	CLEARWATER
34634-34635	BELLEAIR SHORES
34635-34635	INDIAN ROCKS BEACH
34636-34636	ISTACHATTA
34637-34639	LAND O LAKES
34640-34649	LARGO
34652-34656	NEW PORT RICHEY
34660-34660	OZONA
34661-34661	NOBLETON
34664-34666	PINELLAS PARK
34667-34667	HUDSON
34668-34668	PORT RICHEY

34669-34669	HUDSON
34673-34673	PORT RICHEY
34674-34674	HUDSON
34677-34677	OLDSMAR
34679-34679	ARIPEKA
34680-34680	ELFERS
34681-34681	CRYSTAL BEACH
34682-34685	PALM HARBOR
34688-34689	TARPON SPRINGS
34690-34691	HOLIDAY
34695-34695	SAFETY HARBOR
34697-34698	DUNEDIN
34705-34705	ASTATULA
34711-34715	CLERMONT
34729-34729	FERNDALE
34731-34731	FRUITLAND PARK
34734-34734	GOTHA
34736-34736	GROVELAND
34737-34737	HOWEY IN THE HILLS
34739-34739	KENANSVILLE
34740-34740	KILLARNEY
34741-34747	KISSIMMEE
34748-34749	LEESBURG
34753-34753	MASCOTTE
34755-34755	MINNEOLA
34756-34756	MONTVERDE
34758-34759	KISSIMMEE
34760-34760	OAKLAND
34761-34761	OCOEE
34762-34762	OKAHUMPKA
34769-34773	SAINT CLOUD
34777-34778	WINTER GARDEN
34785-34785	WILDWOOD
34786-34786	WINDERMERE
34787-34787	WINTER GARDEN
34788-34789	LEESBURG
34797-34797	YALAHA
34945-34951	FORT PIERCE
34952-34953	PORT SAINT LUCIE
34954-34954	FORT PIERCE
34956-34956	INDIANTOWN
34957-34958	JENSEN BEACH
34972-34974	OKEECHOBEE
34979-34982	FORT PIERCE
34983-34988	PORT SAINT LUCIE
34990-34991	PALM CITY
34992-34992	PORT SALERNO
34994-34997	STUART

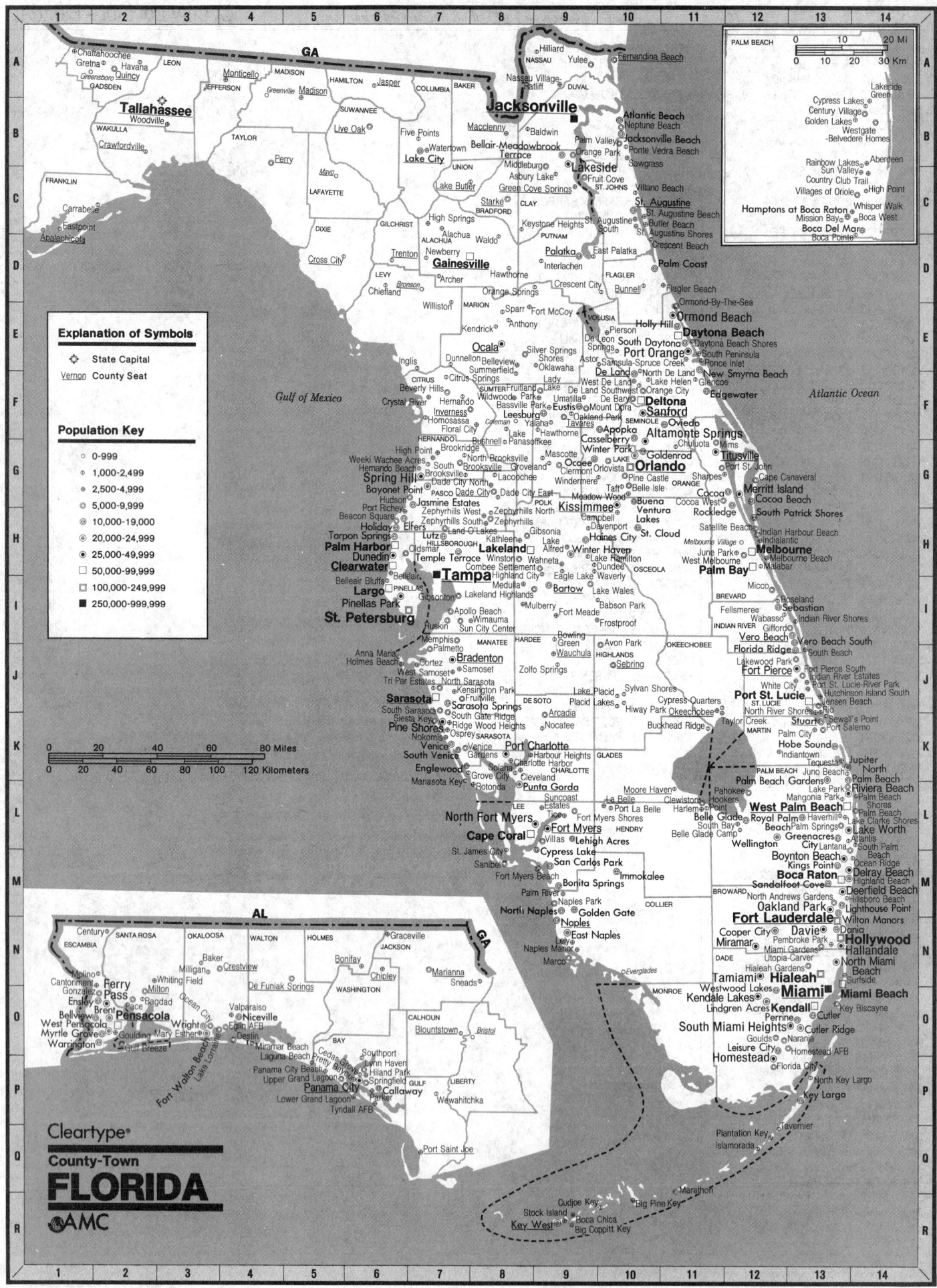

Cleartype®

County-Town

FLORIDA

AMC

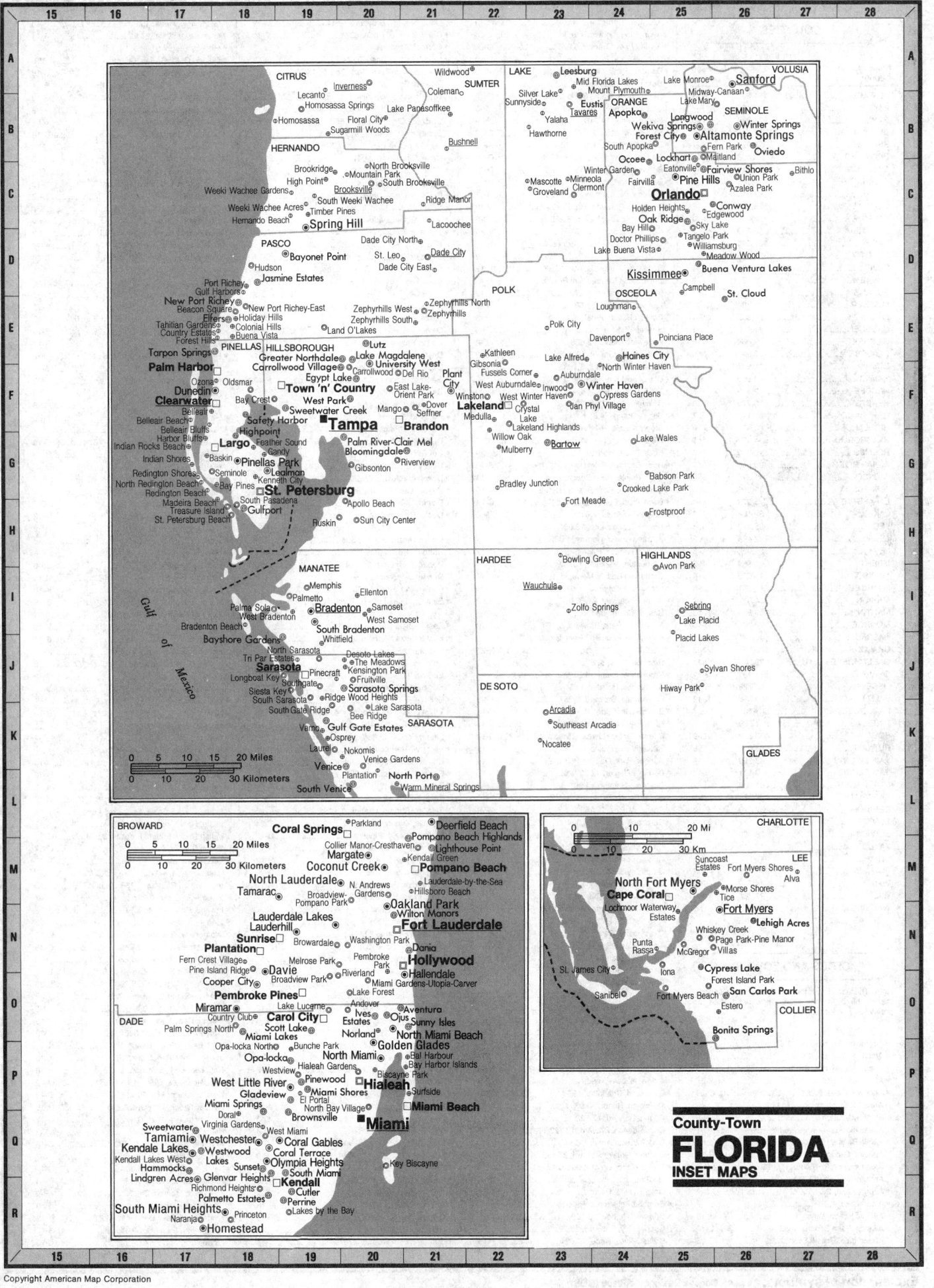

County-Town
FLORIDA
INSET MAPS

COUNTIES

(67 Counties)

Name of County	Population	Location on Map
ALACHUA	181,596	D-7
BAKER	18,486	A-7
BAY	126,994	O-5
BRADFORD	22,515	C-8
BREVARD	398,978	I-11
BROWARD	1,255,488	M-11
CALHOUN	11,011	O-7
CHARLOTTE	110,975	L-8
CITRUS	93,515	F-7
CLAY	105,986	C-8
COLLIER	152,099	M-10
COLUMBIA	42,613	A-7
DADE	1,937,094	N-11
DESOTO	23,865	J-8
DIXIE	10,585	C-5
DUVAL	672,971	A-9
ESCAMBIA	262,798	N-1
FLAGLER	28,701	D-10
FRANKLIN	8,967	C-1
GADSDEN	41,105	A-1
GILCHRIST	9,667	C-6
GLADES	7,591	K-10
GULF	11,504	P-7
HAMILTON	10,930	A-5
HARDEE	19,499	I-8
HENDRY	25,773	L-10
HERNANDO	101,115	G-7
HIGHLANDS	68,432	J-10
HILLSBOROUGH	834,054	H-7
HOLMES	15,778	N-5
INDIAN RIVER	90,208	I-11
JACKSON	41,375	N-6
JEFFERSON	11,296	A-3
LAFAYETTE	5,578	C-5
LAKE	152,104	E-9
LEE	335,113	L-8
LEON	192,493	A-3
LEVY	25,923	D-6
LIBERTY	5,569	P-7
MADISON	16,569	A-4
MANATEE	211,707	I-8
MARION	194,833	E-7
MARTIN	100,900	K-12
MONROE	78,024	O-10
NASSAU	43,941	A-8
OKALOOSA	143,776	N-3
OKEECHOBEE	29,627	I-11
ORANGE	677,491	G-11
OSCEOLA	107,728	H-10
PALM BEACH	863,518	K-12
PASCO	281,131	G-7
PINELLAS	851,659	I-6
POLK	405,382	G-9
PUTNAM	65,070	D-9
SAINT JOHNS	83,829	C-9
SAINT LUCIE	150,171	J-12
SANTA ROSA	81,608	N-2
SARASOTA	277,776	K-8
SEMINOLE	287,529	F-10
SUMTER	31,577	F-8
SUWANNEE	26,780	B-5
TAYLOR	17,111	B-4
UNION	10,252	B-7
VOLUSIA	370,712	E-9
WAKULLA	14,202	B-2
WALTON	27,760	N-4
WASHINGTON	16,919	O-5
TOTAL	12,937,926	

CITIES AND TOWNS

Note: The first name is that of the city or town, second, that of the county in which it is located, then the population and location on the map.

• Aberdeen, Palm Beach, 2,572 ... B-14
Alachua, Alachua, 4,529 ... C-7
Altamonte Springs, Seminole, 34,879 ... B-25
• Alva, Lee, 1,036 ... M-27
• Andover, Dade, 6,251 ... O-20
Anna Maria, Manatee, 1,744 ... J-6
Anthony, Marion ... E-8
Apalachicola, Franklin, 2,602 ... C-1
• Apollo Beach, Hillsborough, 6,025 ... I-7
Apopka, Orange, 13,512 ... G-10
Arcadia, DeSoto, 6,488 ... K-9
Archer, Alachua, 1,372 ... D-7
• Asbury Lake, Clay, 2,072 ... C-9
• Astor, Lake, 1,273 ... E-9
Atlantic Beach, Duval, 11,636 ... B-10
Atlantis, Palm Beach, 1,653 ... L-13
Auburndale, Polk, 8,858 ... F-23
• Aventura, Dade, 14,914 ... O-19
Avon Park, Highlands, 8,042 ... J-10
• Azalea Park, Orange, 8,926 ... C-26
• Babson Park, Polk, 1,125 ... I-9
• Bagdad, Santa Rosa, 1,457 ... O-2
Baker, Okaloosa ... N-3
Bal Harbour, Dade, 3,045 ... O-19
Baldwin, Duval, 1,450 ... B-9
Bartow, Polk, 14,716 ... I-9
• Baskin, Pinellas, 3,834 ... G-17
• Bassville Park, Lake, 2,752 ... F-9
Bay Harbor Islands, Dade, 4,703 ... O-19
• Bay Hill, Orange, 5,346 ... D-10
• Bay Pines, Pinellas, 4,171 ... C-18
• Bayonet Point, Pasco, 21,860 ... G-7
• Bayshore Gardens, Manatee, 17,062 ... J-19
• Beacon Square, Pasco, 6,265 ... G-6
• Bee Ridge, Sarasota, 6,406 ... K-20
• Bellair-Meadowbrook Terrace, Clay, 15,606 ... B-9
Belle Glade, Palm Beach, 16,177 ... L-12
• Belle Glade Camp, Palm Beach, 1,616 ... L-12
Belle Isle, Orange, 5,272 ... G-10
Belleair, Pinellas, 3,968 ... H-6
Belleair Beach, Pinellas, 2,070 ... F-3
Belleair Bluffs, Pinellas, 2,128 ... I-6
Belleview, Marion, 2,666 ... E-8
• Bellview, Escambia, 19,386 ... O-2
• Beverly Hills, Citrus, 6,163 ... F-7
• Big Coppitt Key, Monroe, 2,388 ... R-9
• Big Pine Key, Monroe, 4,206 ... R-10
Biscayne Park, Dade, 3,068 ... P-19
• Bithlo, Orange, 4,834 ... C-27
• Bloomingdale, Hillsborough, 13,912 ... G-21
Blountstown, Calhoun, 2,404 ... O-7
Boca Chica, Monroe ... R-9
• Boca Del Mar, Palm Beach, 17,754 ... C-13
• Boca Pointe, Palm Beach, 2,147 ... C-14
Boca Raton, Palm Beach, 61,492 ... M-13
• Boca West, Palm Beach, 2,847 ... C-14
Bonifay, Holmes, 2,612 ... N-6
• Bonita Springs, Lee, 13,600 ... M-9
Bowling Green, Hardee, 1,836 ... I-9
Boynton Beach, Palm Beach, 46,194 ... M-13
Bradenton, Manatee, 43,779 ... J-7
Bradenton Beach, Manatee, 1,657 ... I-18
• Brandon, Hillsborough, 57,985 ... F-21
• Brent, Escambia, 21,624 ... O-2
Bristol, Liberty, 937 ... O-8
• Broadview Park, Broward, 6,109 ... O-18
• Broadview-Pompano Park, Broward, 5,230 ... N-23
Bronson, Levy, 875 ... D-7
• Brookridge, Hernando, 2,805 ... G-7
Brooksville, Hernando, 7,440 ... G-7
• Browardale, Broward, 6,257 ... P-23
• Brownsville, Dade, 15,607 ... P-18
• Buckhead Ridge, Glades, 1,279 ... K-11
• Buena Ventura Lakes, Osceola, 14,148 ... G-10
Buena Vista, Pasco ... E-18
• Bunche Park, Dade, 4,388 ... O-18
Bunnell, Flagler, 1,873 ... D-10
Bushnell, Sumter, 1,998 ... F-8
• Butler Beach, St. Johns, 3,377 ... D-10
Callaway, Bay, 12,253 ... P-6
• Campbell, Osceola, 3,884 ... H-10
Cantonment, Escambia ... N-2
Cape Canaveral, Brevard, 8,014 ... G-12
Cape Coral, Lee, 74,991 ... L-8
• Carol City, Dade, 53,331 ... O-18
Carrabelle, Franklin, 1,200 ... C-2
• Carrollwood, Hillsborough, 7,195 ... E-20
• Carrollwood Village, Hillsborough, 15,051 ... E-19
Casselberry, Seminole, 18,911 ... F-10
Cedar Grove, Bay, 1,479 ... P-6
Century, Escambia, 1,989 ... N-2
• Century Village, Palm Beach, 8,363 ... B-14
• Charlotte Harbor, Charlotte, 3,327 ... K-8
• Charlotte Park, Charlotte, 2,225 ... K-8
Chattahoochee, Gadsden, 4,382 ... A-1
Chiefland, Levy, 1,917 ... D-6
Chipley, Washington, 3,866 ... O-6
• Chuluota, Seminole, 1,441 ... G-11
• Citrus Springs, Citrus, 2,213 ... F-7
Clearwater, Pinellas, 98,784 ... H-6
Clermont, Lake, 6,910 ... G-9
• Cleveland, Charlotte, 2,896 ... K-8
Clewiston, Hendry, 6,085 ... L-11
Cocoa, Brevard, 17,722 ... G-11
Cocoa Beach, Brevard, 12,123 ... G-12
• Cocoa West, Brevard, 6,160 ... G-11
Coconut Creek, Broward, 27,485 ... M-20
• Collier Manor-Cresthaven, Broward, 7,322 ... N-19
Colonial Hills, Pasco ... E-18
• Combee Settlement, Polk, 5,463 ... H-9
• Conway, Orange, 13,159 ... C-26
Cooper City, Broward, 20,791 ... N-12
Coral Gables, Dade, 40,091 ... P-18
Coral Springs, Broward, 79,443 ... M-19
• Coral Terrace, Dade, 23,255 ... P-18
• Cortez, Manatee, 4,509 ... J-7
• Country Club, Dade, 3,408 ... O-18
• Country Club Trail, Palm Beach, 4,599 ... C-14
Country Estates, Pasco ... E-18
Crawfordville, Wakulla ... B-2
• Crescent Beach, St. Johns, 1,081 ... D-10
Crescent City, Putnam, 1,859 ... D-10
Crestview, Okaloosa, 9,886 ... N-3
• Crooked Lake Park, Polk, 1,575 ... G-24
Cross City, Dixie, 2,041 ... D-5
• Crystal Lake, Polk, 5,300 ... F-23
Crystal River, Citrus, 4,044 ... F-7
• Cudjoe Key, Monroe, 1,714 ... R-10
• Cutler, Dade, 16,201 ... O-13
• Cutler Ridge, Dade, 21,268 ... O-13
• Cypress Gardens, Polk, 9,188 ... F-24
• Cypress Lake, Lee, 10,491 ... M-9
• Cypress Lakes, Palm Beach, 1,260 ... B-14
• Cypress Quarters, Okeechobee, 1,343 ... J-11
Dade City, Pasco, 5,633 ... G-8
Dade City East, Pasco ... G-8
• Dade City North, Pasco, 3,058 ... G-8
Dania, Broward, 13,024 ... N-13
Davenport, Polk, 1,529 ... H-9
Davie, Broward, 47,217 ... N-13
Daytona Beach, Volusia, 61,921 ... E-11
Daytona Beach Shores, Volusia, 2,335 ... E-11
• De Bary, Volusia, 7,176 ... F-10
De Funiak Springs, Walton, 5,120 ... N-5
De Land, Volusia, 16,491 ... F-11
• De Land Southwest, Volusia, 1,249 ... F-9
• De Leon Springs, Volusia, 1,481 ... E-10
Deerfield Beach, Broward, 46,325 ... M-13
• Del Rio, Hillsborough, 8,248 ... F-20
Delray Beach, Palm Beach, 47,181 ... M-13
• Deltona, Volusia, 50,828 ... F-10
• Desoto Lakes, Sarasota, 2,807 ... J-20
Destin, Okaloosa, 8,080 ... O-4
• Doctor Phillips, Orange, 7,963 ... D-11
• Doral, Dade, 3,126 ... Q-18
• Dover, Hillsborough, 2,606 ... F-21
Dundee, Polk, 2,335 ... H-9
Dunedin, Pinellas, 34,012 ... H-6
Dunnellon, Marion, 1,624 ... E-7
Eagle Lake, Polk, 1,758 ... H-9
• East Lake-Orient Park, Hillsborough, 6,171 ... F-20
• East Naples, Collier, 22,951 ... C-9
• East Palatka, Putnam, 1,989 ... D-9
• Eastpoint, Franklin, 1,577 ... C-1
Eatonville, Orange, 2,170 ... C-25
Edgewater, Volusia, 15,337 ... F-11
Edgewood, Orange, 1,062 ... C-25
• Eglin AFB, Okaloosa, 8,347 ... O-4
• Egypt Lake, Hillsborough, 14,580 ... F-19
El Portal, Dade, 2,457 ... P-18
• Elfers, Pasco, 12,356 ... G-6
• Ellenton, Manatee, 2,573 ... I-20
• Englewood, Charlotte/Sarasota, 15,025 ... K-7
• Ensley, Escambia, 16,362 ... O-2
• Estero, Lee, 3,177 ... O-26
Eustis, Lake, 12,967 ... F-6
• Fairview Shores, Orange, 13,192 ... C-25
Fairvilla, Orange ... C-24
• Feather Sound, Pinellas, 2,690 ... G-18
Fellsmere, Indian River, 2,179 ... I-12
Fern Crest Village, Broward ... N-17
• Fern Park, Seminole, 8,294 ... B-25
Fernandina Beach, Nassau, 8,765 ... A-10
• Ferry Pass, Escambia, 26,301 ... O-2
• Five Points, Columbia, 1,136 ... B-7
Flagler Beach, Flagler, 3,820 ... D-11
• Floral City, Citrus, 2,609 ... F-8
Florida City, Dade, 5,806 ... P-12
• Florida Ridge, Indian River, 12,218 ... I-12
• Forest City, Seminole, 10,638 ... B-25
Forest Hills, Pasco ... E-18
• Forest Island Park, Lee, 5,988 ... O-25
Fort Lauderdale, Broward, 149,377 ... N-13
Fort McCoy, Marion ... E-8
Fort Meade, Polk, 4,976 ... H-9
Fort Myers, Lee, 45,206 ... L-9
• Fort Myers Beach, Lee, 9,284 ... M-9
• Fort Myers Shores, Lee, 5,460 ... L-9
Fort Pierce, St. Lucie, 36,830 ... J-12
• Fort Pierce North, St. Lucie, 5,833 ... J-13
• Fort Pierce South, St. Lucie, 5,320 ... J-13
Fort Walton Beach, Okaloosa, 21,471 ... O-3
Frostproof, Polk, 2,808 ... I-9
• Fruit Cove, St. Johns, 5,904 ... C-9
Fruitland Park, Lake, 2,754 ... F-9
• Fruitville, Sarasota, 9,808 ... J-7
• Fussels Corner, Polk, 3,840 ... F-23
Gainesville, Alachua, 84,770 ... D-7
• Gandy, Pinellas, 3,164 ... G-18
• Gibsonia, Polk, 5,168 ... H-9
• Gibsonton, Hillsborough, 7,706 ... I-7
• Gifford, Indian River, 6,278 ... I-13
• Gladeview, Dade, 15,637 ... P-18
• Glencoe, Volusia, 2,282 ... F-11
• Glenvar Heights, Dade, 14,823 ... Q-18
• Golden Gate, Collier, 14,148 ... M-9
• Golden Glades, Dade, 25,474 ... O-19
• Golden Lakes, Palm Beach, 3,867 ... B-14
• Goldenrod, Orange/Seminole, 12,362 ... G-10
• Gonzalez, Escambia, 7,669 ... O-2
• Goulding, Escambia, 4,159 ... O-2
• Goulds, Dade, 7,284 ... O-12
Graceville, Jackson, 2,675 ... N-6
• Greater Northdale, Hillsborough, 16,318 ... E-6
Green Cove Springs, Clay, 4,497 ... C-9
Greenacres City, Palm Beach, 18,683 ... L-13
Gretna, Gadsden, 1,981 ... A-2
• Grove City, Charlotte, 2,374 ... K-7
Groveland, Lake, 2,300 ... G-9
Gulf Breeze, Santa Rosa, 5,530 ... O-2
• Gulf Gate Estates, Sarasota, 11,622 ... K-19
Gulf Harbors, Pasco ... D-18
Gulfport, Pinellas, 11,727 ... H-18
Haines City, Polk, 11,683 ... H-9
Hallandale, Broward, 30,996 ... N-13
• Hammocks, Dade, 10,897 ... Q-17
• Hamptons at Boca Raton, Palm Beach, 11,686 ... C-14
• Harbor Bluffs, Pinellas, 2,659 ... G-17
• Harbour Heights, Charlotte, 2,523 ... K-8
• Harlem, Hendry, 2,826 ... L-11
Havana, Gadsden, 1,654 ... A-2
Haverhill, Palm Beach, 1,058 ... L-13
Hawthorne, Alachua, 1,305 ... D-8
• Hawthorne, Lake, 1,804 ... F-9
• Hernando, Citrus, 2,103 ... F-7
• Hernando Beach, Hernando, 1,767 ... C-19
Hialeah, Dade, 188,004 ... M-13
Hialeah Gardens, Dade, 7,713 ... M-13
• High Point, Hernando, 2,814 ... G-7
• High Point, Palm Beach, 2,288 ... C-14
High Springs, Alachua, 3,144 ... C-7
Highland Beach, Palm Beach, 3,209 ... M-13
• Highland City, Polk, 1,919 ... H-9
• Highpoint, Pinellas, 13,818 ... G-18
• Hiland Park, Bay, 3,865 ... P-6
Hilliard, Nassau, 1,751 ... A-8
Hillsboro Beach, Broward, 1,748 ... M-13
• Hobe Sound, Martin, 11,507 ... K-13
• Holden Heights, Orange, 4,387 ... C-25
• Holiday, Pasco, 19,360 ... H-6
Holiday Hills, Pasco ... E-18
Holly Hill, Volusia, 11,141 ... E-11
Hollywood, Broward, 121,697 ... N-13
Holmes Beach, Manatee, 4,810 ... J-6
Homestead, Dade, 26,866 ... O-12
• Homestead AFB, Dade, 5,153 ... O-13
• Homosassa, Citrus, 2,113 ... F-7
• Homosassa Springs, Citrus, 6,271 ... B-19
Hookers Point, Hendry ... L-11
• Hudson, Pasco, 7,344 ... G-7
• Hutchinson Island South, St. Lucie, 3,893 ... J-13
• Immokalee, Collier, 14,120 ... M-10
Indialantic, Brevard, 2,844 ... H-12
Indian Harbour Beach, Brevard, 6,933 ... H-12
• Indian River Estates, St. Lucie, 4,858 ... J-13
Indian River Shores, Indian River, 2,278 ... I-13
Indian Rocks Beach, Pinellas, 3,963 ... G-17
Indian Shores, Pinellas, 1,405 ... G-17
• Indiantown, Martin, 4,794 ... K-12
Inglis, Levy, 1,241 ... E-7
Interlachen, Putnam, 1,160 ... D-9
Inverness, Citrus, 5,797 ... F-7
• Inwood, Polk, 6,824 ... F-23
• Iona, Lee, 9,565 ... N-25
• Islamorada, Monroe, 1,220 ... Q-12
• Ives Estates, Dade, 13,531 ... O-19
Jacksonville, Duval, 635,230 ... B-9
Jacksonville Beach, Duval, 17,839 ... B-10
• Jan Phyl Village, Polk, 5,308 ... F-23
• Jasmine Estates, Pasco, 17,136 ... G-7
Jasper, Hamilton, 2,099 ... A-6
• Jensen Beach, Martin, 9,884 ... J-13
• June Park, Brevard, 4,080 ... H-12
Juno Beach, Palm Beach, 2,121 ... K-13
Jupiter, Palm Beach, 24,986 ... K-13
• Kathleen, Polk, 2,743 ... H-8
• Kendale Lakes, Dade, 48,524 ... O-12
• Kendall, Dade, 87,271 ... O-13
• Kendall Green, Broward, 3,815 ... M-19
• Kendall Lakes West, Dade, 6,038 ... Q-17
Kendrick, Marion ... E-8
Kenneth City, Pinellas, 4,462 ... G-18
• Kensington Park, Sarasota, 3,026 ... J-7
• Key Biscayne, Dade, 8,854 ... O-13
• Key Largo, Monroe, 11,336 ... P-13
Key West, Monroe, 24,832 ... R-9
Keystone Heights, Clay, 1,315 ... C-8
• Kings Point, Palm Beach, 12,422 ... M-13
Kissimmee, Osceola, 30,050 ... G-10
La Belle, Hendry, 2,703 ... L-10

Explanation of symbols: •– Census Designated Place (CDP)

• Lacoochee, Pasco, 2,072 ... G-8
Lady Lake, Lake, 8,071 ... F-9
• Laguna Beach, Bay, 1,876 ... P-5
Lake Alfred, Polk, 3,622 ... H-9
Lake Buena Vista, Orange, 1,776 ... D-11
Lake Butler, Union, 2,116 ... C-7
Lake City, Columbia, 10,005 ... B-7
Lake Clarke Shores, Palm Beach, 3,364 ... L-13
Lake Forest, Broward ... O-19
Lake Hamilton, Polk, 1,128 ... H-9
Lake Helen, Volusia, 2,344 ... F-10
• Lake Lorraine, Okaloosa, 6,779 ... O-3
• Lake Lucerne, Dade, 9,478 ... O-18
• Lake Magdalene, Hillsborough, 15,973 ... E-19
Lake Mary, Seminole, 5,929 ... B-26
Lake Monroe, Seminole ... A-26
• Lake Panasoffkee, Sumter, 2,705 ... F-8
Lake Park, Palm Beach, 6,704 ... L-13
Lake Placid, Highlands, 1,158 ... J-10
• Lake Sarasota, Sarasota, 4,117 ... K-20
Lake Wales, Polk, 9,670 ... I-9
Lake Worth, Palm Beach, 28,564 ... L-13
Lakeland, Polk, 70,576 ... I-8
• Lakeland Highlands, Polk, 9,972 ... G-22
• Lakes by the Bay, Dade, 5,615 ... R-19
• Lakeside, Clay, 29,137 ... B-9
• Lakeside Green, Palm Beach, 2,994 ... B-14
• Lakewood Park, St. Lucie, 7,211 ... J-13
• Land O'Lakes, Pasco, 7,892 ... H-7
Lantana, Palm Beach, 8,392 ... L-13
Largo, Pinellas, 65,674 ... I-6
Lauderdale Lakes, Broward, 27,341 ... N-18
Lauderdale-by-the-Sea, Broward, 2,990 ... N-19
Lauderhill, Broward, 49,708 ... N-18
• Laurel, Sarasota, 8,245 ... K-20
• Lealman, Pinellas, 21,748 ... G-18
• Lecanto, Citrus, 1,243 ... B-19
Leesburg, Lake, 14,903 ... F-9
• Lehigh Acres, Lee, 13,611 ... L-9
• Leisure City, Dade, 19,379 ... O-12
• Lely, Collier, 3,014 ... N-9
Lighthouse Point, Broward, 10,378 ... M-13
• Lindgren Acres, Dade, 22,290 ... O-12
Live Oak, Suwannee, 6,332 ... B-6
• Lochmoor Waterway Estates, Lee, 4,091 ... N-25
• Lockhart, Orange, 11,636 ... B-25
Longboat Key, Manatee/Sarasota, 5,937 ... J-19
Longwood, Seminole, 13,316 ... B-25
• Loughman, Polk, 1,214 ... E-24
• Lower Grand Lagoon, Bay, 3,329 ... P-6
• Lutz, Hillsborough, 10,552 ... H-7
Lynn Haven, Bay, 9,298 ... P-6
Macclenny, Baker, 3,966 ... B-8
Madeira Beach, Pinellas, 4,225 ... G-18
Madison, Madison, 3,345 ... A-5
Maitland, Orange, 9,110 ... B-25
Malabar, Brevard, 1,977 ... H-12
• Manasota Key, Charlotte, 1,395 ... K-7
• Mango, Hillsborough, 8,700 ... F-21
Mangonia Park, Palm Beach, 1,453 ... L-13
• Marathon, Monroe, 8,857 ... Q-11
• Marco, Collier, 9,493 ... N-9
Margate, Broward, 42,985 ... M-19
Marianna, Jackson, 6,292 ... N-7
Mary Esther, Okaloosa, 4,139 ... O-3
Mascotte, Lake, 1,761 ... G-9
Mayo, Lafayette, 917 ... C-5
• McGregor, Lee, 6,504 ... N-25
• Meadow Wood, Orange, 4,876 ... D-11
• Medulla, Polk, 3,977 ... I-8
Melbourne, Brevard, 59,646 ... H-12
Melbourne Beach, Brevard, 3,021 ... H-12
• Melrose Park, Broward, 6,477 ... N-18
• Memphis, Manatee, 6,760 ... I-7
• Merritt Island, Brevard, 32,886 ... G-12
Miami, Dade, 358,548 ... O-13
Miami Beach, Dade, 92,639 ... N-13
• Miami Gardens-Utopia-Carver, Broward, 7,448 ... N-13
• Miami Lakes, Dade, 12,750 ... O-17
Miami Shores, Dade, 10,084 ... P-18
Miami Springs, Dade, 13,268 ... P-18
• Micco, Brevard, 8,757 ... I-12
• Mid Florida Lakes, Lake, 2,776 ... A-23
• Middleburg, Clay, 6,223 ... C-9
Midway-Canaan, Seminole ... A-26
Milligan, Okaloosa ... N-3
Milton, Santa Rosa, 7,216 ... O-2
• Mims, Brevard, 9,412 ... F-11
Minneola, Lake, 1,515 ... C-23
Miramar, Broward, 40,663 ... N-12
• Miramar Beach, Walton, 1,644 ... O-4
• Mission Bay, Palm Beach, 1,227 ... C-13
• Molino, Escambia, 1,207 ... N-2
Monticello, Jefferson, 2,573 ... A-4
Moore Haven, Glades, 1,432 ... L-11
• Morse Shores, Lee, 3,771 ... M-26
Mount Dora, Lake, 7,196 ... F-9
• Mount Plymouth, Lake, 1,752 ... B-24

Mulberry, Polk, 2,988 ... I-8
• Myrtle Grove, Escambia, 17,402 ... O-2
Naples, Collier, 19,505 ... N-9
• Naples Manor, Collier, 4,574 ... N-9
• Naples Park, Collier, 8,002 ... M-9
• Naranja, Dade, 5,790 ... R-17
• Nassau Village-Ratliff, Nassau, 4,047 ... A-9
Neptune Beach, Duval, 6,816 ... B-10
New Port Richey, Pasco, 14,044 ... E-18
• New Port Richey East, Pasco, 9,683 ... E-18
New Smyrna Beach, Volusia, 16,543 ... E-11
Newberry, Alachua, 1,644 ... D-7
Niceville, Okaloosa, 10,507 ... O-4
Nocatee, DeSoto ... K-9
• Nokomis, Sarasota, 3,448 ... K-7
• Norland, Dade, 22,109 ... O-19
• North Andrews Gardens, Broward, 9,002 ... M-12
North Bay Village, Dade, 5,383 ... P-19
• North Brooksville, Hernando, 1,459 ... G-7
• North De Land, Volusia, 1,493 ... E-10
• North Fort Myers, Lee, 30,027 ... L-9
• North Key Largo, Monroe, 1,490 ... P-13
North Lauderdale, Broward, 26,506 ... N-18
North Miami, Dade, 49,998 ... N-13
North Miami Beach, Dade, 35,359 ... N-13
• North Naples, Collier, 13,422 ... M-9
North Palm Beach, Palm Beach, 11,343 ... K-13
North Port, Sarasota, 11,973 ... L-21
North Redington Beach, Pinellas, 1,135 ... G-17
• North River Shores, Martin, 3,250 ... J-13
• North Sarasota, Sarasota, 6,702 ... J-7
North Winter Haven, Polk ... F-24
• Oak Ridge, Orange, 15,388 ... C-25
Oakland Park, Broward, 26,326 ... M-13
• Oakland Park, Lake, 1,743 ... F-9
Ocala, Marion, 42,045 ... E-8
• Ocean City, Okaloosa, 5,422 ... O-3
Ocean Ridge, Palm Beach, 1,570 ... M-14
Ocoee, Orange, 12,778 ... G-9
• Ojus, Dade, 15,519 ... O-19
Okeechobee, Okeechobee, 4,943 ... J-11
Oklawaha, Marion ... E-9
Oldsmar, Pinellas, 8,361 ... H-7
• Olympia Heights, Dade, 37,792 ... P-18
Opa-locka, Dade, 15,283 ... P-18
• Opa-locka North, Dade, 6,568 ... O-18
Orange City, Volusia, 5,347 ... F-10
Orange Park, Clay, 9,488 ... B-9
Orange Springs, Marion ... D-8
Orlando, Orange, 164,693 ... G-10
• Orlovista, Orange, 5,990 ... G-10
Ormond Beach, Volusia, 29,721 ... E-10
• Ormond-By-The-Sea, Volusia, 8,157 ... D-11
• Osprey, Sarasota, 2,597 ... K-7
Oviedo, Seminole, 11,114 ... F-11
Ozona, Pinellas ... F-18
• Pace, Santa Rosa, 6,277 ... O-2
• Page Park-Pine Manor, Lee, 5,116 ... N-26
Pahokee, Palm Beach, 6,822 ... L-12
Palatka, Putnam, 10,201 ... D-9
Palm Bay, Brevard, 62,632 ... H-12
Palm Beach, Palm Beach, 9,814 ... L-14
Palm Beach Gardens, Palm Beach, 22,965 ... K-13
Palm Beach Shores, Palm Beach, 1,040 ... L-14
• Palm City, Martin, 3,925 ... K-13
• Palm Coast, Flagler, 14,287 ... D-10
• Palm Harbor, Pinellas, 50,256 ... H-6
• Palm River, Collier, 3,507 ... M-9
• Palm River-Clair Mel, Hillsborough, 13,691 ... G-20
Palm Springs, Palm Beach, 9,763 ... L-13
• Palm Springs North, Dade, 5,300 ... O-17
• Palm Valley, St. Johns, 9,960 ... B-10
Palmetto, Manatee, 9,268 ... J-7
• Palmetto Estates, Dade, 12,293 ... Q-18
Panama City, Bay, 34,378 ... P-6
Panama City Beach, Bay, 4,051 ... P-5
Parker, Bay, 4,598 ... P-6
Parkland, Broward, 3,558 ... L-6
Pembroke Park, Broward, 4,933 ... O-18
Pembroke Pines, Broward, 65,452 ... O-18
Pensacola, Escambia, 58,165 ... O-2
• Perrine, Dade, 15,576 ... O-12
Perry, Taylor, 7,151 ... B-4
Pierson, Volusia, 2,988 ... E-10
• Pine Castle, Orange, 8,276 ... G-10
• Pine Hills, Orange, 35,322 ... C-25
• Pine Island Ridge, Broward, 5,244 ... N-4
Pinellas Park, Pinellas, 43,426 ... H-6
• Pinewood, Dade, 15,518 ... P-19
• Placid Lakes, Highlands, 2,045 ... K-10
Plant City, Hillsborough, 22,754 ... F-21
Plantation, Broward, 66,692 ... N-18
• Plantation, Sarasota, 1,885 ... L-20
• Plantation Key, Monroe, 4,405 ... Q-12
• Poinciana Place, Osceola, 3,618 ... E-10
Polk City, Polk, 1,439 ... E-22

Pompano Beach, Broward, 72,411 ... N-19
• Pompano Beach Highlands, Broward, 17,915 ... M-19
Ponce Inlet, Volusia, 1,704 ... E-11
Ponte Vedra Beach, St. Johns ... B-10
• Port Charlotte, Charlotte, 41,535 ... K-8
• Port La Belle, Hendry, 1,512 ... L-9
Port Orange, Volusia, 35,317 ... E-11
Port Richey, Pasco, 2,523 ... H-6
Port Saint Joe, Gulf ... Q-7
• Port Salerno, Martin, 7,786 ... K-13
• Port St. John, Brevard, 8,933 ... G-11
Port St. Lucie, St. Lucie, 55,866 ... J-13
• Port St. Lucie-River Park, St. Lucie, 4,874 ... J-12
• Pretty Bayou, Bay, 3,839 ... P-5
• Princeton, Dade, 7,073 ... R-18
Punta Gorda, Charlotte, 10,747 ... K-8
• Punta Rassa, Lee, 1,493 ... N-26
Quincy, Gadsden, 7,444 ... A-2
• Rainbow Lakes, Palm Beach, 1,496 ... C-14
Redington Beach, Pinellas, 1,626 ... G-17
Redington Shores, Pinellas, 2,366 ... G-17
• Richmond Heights, Dade, 8,583 ... Q-18
• Ridge Manor, Hernando, 1,947 ... C-21
• Ridge Wood Heights, Sarasota, 4,851 ... K-7
• Rio, Martin, 1,054 ... J-13
• Riverland, Broward, 5,376 ... O-18
• Riverview, Hillsborough, 6,478 ... G-20
Riviera Beach, Palm Beach, 27,639 ... L-13
Rockledge, Brevard, 16,023 ... G-12
• Roseland, Indian River, 1,379 ... I-12
• Rotonda, Charlotte, 3,576 ... L-8
Royal Palm Beach, Palm Beach, 14,589 ... L-13
• Ruskin, Hillsborough, 6,046 ... I-7
Safety Harbor, Pinellas, 15,124 ... F-18
Saint Augustine, St. Johns, 11,692 ... C-10
Saint Augustine Beach, St. Johns, 3,657 ... C-10
• Saint Augustine Shores, St. Johns, 4,411 ... C-10
• Saint Augustine South, St. Johns, 4,218 ... C-10
Saint Cloud, Osceola, 12,453 ... H-10
• Saint James City, Lee, 1,904 ... L-8
Saint Leo, Pasco, 1,009 ... D-20
Saint Petersburg, Pinellas, 238,629 ... I-7
Saint Petersburg Beach, Pinellas, 9,200 ... H-18
• Samoset, Manatee, 3,119 ... J-7
• Samsula-Spruce Creek, Volusia, 3,404 ... E-11
• San Carlos Park, Lee, 11,785 ... M-9
• Sandalfoot Cove, Palm Beach, 14,214 ... M-13
Sanford, Seminole, 32,387 ... F-10
Sanibel, Lee, 5,468 ... M-8
Sarasota, Sarasota, 50,961 ... J-7
• Sarasota Springs, Sarasota, 16,088 ... J-7
Satellite Beach, Brevard, 9,889 ... H-12
• Sawgrass, St. Johns, 2,999 ... C-10
• Scott Lake, Dade, 14,588 ... O-18
Sebastian, Indian River, 10,205 ... I-12
Sebring, Highlands, 8,900 ... J-10
• Seffner, Hillsborough, 5,371 ... F-20
Seminole, Pinellas, 9,251 ... G-17
Sewall's Point, Martin, 1,588 ... K-13
• Sharpes, Brevard, 3,348 ... G-11
• Siesta Key, Sarasota, 7,772 ... K-7
• Silver Lake, Lake, 1,573 ... B-23
• Silver Springs Shores, Marion, 6,421 ... E-8
• Sky Lake, Orange, 6,202 ... C-25
Sneads, Jackson, 1,746 ... N-8
• Solana, Charlotte, 1,128 ... K-8
• South Apopka, Orange, 6,360 ... B-25
South Bay, Palm Beach, 3,558 ... L-12
• South Beach, Indian River, 2,754 ... J-13
• South Bradenton, Manatee, 20,398 ... I-9
• South Brooksville, Hernando, 1,586 ... G-7
South Daytona, Volusia, 12,482 ... E-11
• South Gate Ridge, Sarasota, 5,924 ... K-7
South Miami, Dade, 10,404 ... Q-18
• South Miami Heights, Dade, 30,030 ... O-13
South Palm Beach, Palm Beach, 1,480 ... L-14
South Pasadena, Pinellas, 5,644 ... G-18
• South Patrick Shores, Brevard, 10,249 ... H-12
South Peninsula, Volusia ... E-11
• South Sarasota, Sarasota, 5,298 ... J-7
• South Venice, Sarasota, 11,951 ... K-7
• Southeast Arcadia, DeSoto, 4,145 ... K-23
• Southgate, Sarasota, 7,324 ... J-20
Southport, Bay ... P-6
Sparr, Marion ... E-8
• Spring Hill, Hernando, 31,117 ... G-7
Springfield, Bay, 8,715 ... P-6
Starke, Bradford, 5,226 ... C-8
• Stock Island, Monroe, 3,613 ... R-9
Stuart, Martin, 11,936 ... K-13
• Sugarmill Woods, Citrus, 4,073 ... B-19
Summerfield, Marion ... F-8
• Sun City Center, Hillsborough, 8,326 ... I-7
• Sun Valley, Palm Beach, 2,735 ... C-14
• Suncoast Estates, Lee, 4,483 ... L-9
• Sunny Isles, Dade, 11,772 ... O-19
• Sunnyside, Lake, 1,008 ... B-23

Sunrise, Broward, 64,407 ... N-19
• Sunset, Dade, 15,810 ... P-17
Surfside, Dade, 4,108 ... N-13
Sweetwater, Dade, 13,909 ... Q-17
Sweetwater Creek, Hillsborough ... F-19
• Sylvan Shores, Highlands, 2,155 ... J-10
Taft, Orange ... G-10
Tahitian Gardens, Pasco ... E-18
Tallahassee, Leon, 124,773 ... B-3
Tamarac, Broward, 44,822 ... N-18
• Tamiami, Dade, 33,845 ... N-12
Tampa, Hillsborough, 280,015 ... H-7
• Tangelo Park, Orange, 2,663 ... D-11
Tarpon Springs, Pinellas, 17,906 ... H-6
Tavares, Lake, 7,383 ... F-9
• Tavernier, Monroe, 2,433 ... P-12
• Taylor Creek, Okeechobee, 4,081 ... K-11
Temple Terrace, Hillsborough, 16,444 ... H-7
Tequesta, Palm Beach, 4,499 ... K-13
• The Meadows, Sarasota, 3,437 ... J-20
• Tice, Lee, 3,971 ... L-9
• Timber Pines, Hernando, 3,182 ... C-19
Titusville, Brevard, 39,394 ... G-11
• Town 'n' Country, Hillsborough, 60,946 ... F-19
Treasure Island, Pinellas, 7,266 ... H-18
Trenton, Gilchrist, 1,287 ... D-6
Tri Par Estates, Sarasota ... J-7
• Tyndall AFB, Bay, 4,318 ... P-6
Umatilla, Lake, 2,350 ... F-9
• Union Park, Orange, 6,890 ... C-26
• University West, Hillsborough, 23,760 ... F-20
• Upper Grand Lagoon, Bay, 7,855 ... P-5
Valparaiso, Okaloosa, 4,672 ... O-4
• Vamo, Sarasota, 3,325 ... K-19
Venice, Sarasota, 16,922 ... K-7
• Venice Gardens, Sarasota, 7,701 ... K-7
Vero Beach, Indian River, 17,350 ... I-13
• Vero Beach South, Indian River, 16,973 ... I-13
• Villages of Oriole, Palm Beach, 5,698 ... C-14
• Villano Beach, St. Johns, 1,867 ... C-10
• Villas, Lee, 9,898 ... L-9
Virginia Gardens, Dade, 2,212 ... P-18
• Wabasso, Indian River, 1,145 ... I-12
• Wahneta, Polk, 4,024 ... H-9
Waldo, Alachua, 1,017 ... D-8
• Warm Mineral Springs, Sarasota, 4,041 ... L-20
• Warrington, Escambia, 16,040 ... O-2
• Washington Park, Broward, 6,930 ... N-19
Watertown, Columbia, 3,340 ... B-7
Wauchula, Hardee, 3,253 ... J-9
• Waverly, Polk, 2,071 ... H-9
• Weeki Wachee Acres, Hernando, 1,394 ... G-7
• Weeki Wachee Gardens, Hernando, 1,170 ... C-19
• Wekiva Springs, Seminole, 23,026 ... B-25
• Wellington, Palm Beach, 20,670 ... L-12
West Auburndale, Polk ... F-23
• West Bradenton, Manatee, 4,528 ... I-19
• West De Land, Volusia, 3,389 ... F-10
• West Little River, Dade, 33,575 ... P-18
West Melbourne, Brevard, 8,399 ... H-12
West Miami, Dade, 5,727 ... P-18
West Palm Beach, Palm Beach, 67,643 ... L-13
• West Park, Hillsborough, 10,347 ... F-20
• West Pensacola, Escambia, 22,107 ... O-2
• West Samoset, Manatee, 3,819 ... J-7
West Winter Haven, Polk ... F-23
• Westchester, Dade, 29,883 ... P-18
• Westgate-Belvedere Homes, Palm Beach, 6,880 ... B-14
• Westview, Dade, 9,668 ... P-18
• Westwood Lakes, Dade, 11,522 ... P-18
Wewahitchka, Gulf, 1,779 ... P-7
• Whiskey Creek, Lee, 5,061 ... N-25
• Whisper Walk, Palm Beach, 3,037 ... C-14
• White City, St. Lucie, 4,645 ... J-13
• Whitfield, Manatee, 3,152 ... J-19
Whiting Field, Santa Rosa ... N-2
Wildwood, Sumter, 3,421 ... F-8
• Williamsburg, Orange, 3,093 ... D-11
Williston, Levy, 2,179 ... D-7
• Willow Oak, Polk, 4,017 ... F-22
Wilton Manors, Broward, 11,804 ... N-13
• Wimauma, Hillsborough, 2,932 ... I-7
Windermere, Orange, 1,371 ... G-10
• Winston, Polk, 9,118 ... H-8
Winter Garden, Orange, 9,745 ... C-24
Winter Haven, Polk, 24,725 ... H-9
Winter Park, Orange, 22,242 ... G-10
Winter Springs, Seminole, 22,151 ... B-26
• Woodville, Leon, 2,760 ... B-3
• Wright, Okaloosa, 18,945 ... O-3
• Yalaha, Lake, 1,168 ... B-23
• Yulee, Nassau, 6,915 ... A-9
Zephyrhills, Pasco, 8,220 ... H-8
• Zephyrhills North, Pasco, 2,320 ... H-8
• Zephyrhills South, Pasco, 2,514 ... H-8
• Zephyrhills West, Pasco, 4,249 ... H-8
Zolfo Springs, Hardee, 1,219 ... J-9

Explanation of symbols: •– Census Designated Place (CDP)

Georgia

General Help Numbers:

Governor's Office

203 State Capitol
Atlanta, GA 30334
www.ganet.org/governor/
index_flash.html

404-656-1776
Fax 404-657-7332
8AM-4:30PM

Attorney General's Office

40 Capitol Square SW
Atlanta, GA 30334-1300
www.law.state.ga.us

404-656-3300
Fax 404-651-9148
8AM-5PM

Legislative Records

State Capitol
General Assembly of Georgia
Atlanta, GA 30334
www.legis.state.ga.us

404-656-2370
Fax 404-656-5043
8:30AM-4:30PM

State Archives

Archives & History Department
330 Capitol Ave SE
Atlanta, GA 30260
www.sos.state.ga.us/archives/

404-656-2393
Fax 404-657-8427
8 AM - 4:45 PM

State Specifics:

Capital: Atlanta
Fulton County

Time Zone: EST

Number of Counties: 159

Population: 8,684,715

Web Site: www.georgia.com/home.asp

State Agencies

Criminal Records

Georgia Bureau of Investigation, Attn: GCIC, PO Box 370748, Decatur, GA 30037-0748 (Courier: 3121 Panthersville Rd, Decatur, GA 30034); 404-244-2639, 404-244-2878 (Fax), 8AM-4PM.

www.ganet.org/gbi

Note: GCIC is the central criminal records repository for the State. (Note: anyone with a signed release may make a record request at any local law enforcement office and the statewide record will be provided. Fees for this may vary; the maximum fee is $20.00.)

Indexing & Storage: Records are available from 1972 forward. It takes 1-3 days before new records are available for inquiry. Records are normally destroyed after court order.

Searching: Records are available here to employers, government agencies including licensing agencies, and adoption and foster care providers. Include the following in your request-name, set of fingerprints, date of birth, sex, race, Social Security Number. Certain law enforcement agencies, who are online, and local agencies may access and retrieve records for investigative/background purposes. These agencies

have the option of requesting a signed release from subject or including a set of fingerprints. The following data is not released: juvenile records, traffic ticket information or out-of-state or federal charges.

Access by: mail, in person, online.

Fee & Payment: Fee is $15.00 per name. If statutues require a FBI check, both state and FBI require one set of fingerprint cards, a total search fee of $24.00 per name is required plus the fingerprints. Agencies may establish an account. Fee payee: Georgia Bureau of Investigations.

Prepayment required. Money orders are accepted. No credit cards accepted.

Mail search: Turnaround time: 7 to 10 days. No SASE is required.

In person search: In-person requests are returned by mail in about 14 days.

Online search: There are three searchable databases found at www.cscj.org/crimjustinfo. They are for parolees, sexual offenders, and inmates. There is no online access to the criminal records database.

Statewide Court Records

Administrative Office of the Courts, 244 Washington St SW, #300, Atlanta, GA 30334-5900; 404-656-5171, 404-651-6449 (Fax), 8:30AM-5PM.

www.georgiacourts.org

Note: Except for certain online research capabilities, all court record access must be done at the local level.

Access by: online.

Online search: Supreme Court docket information and opinions are available from the web, but there is no online access available statewide for trial courts, although statewide access is being planned. A certified copy of a Supreme Court Opinion can be purchased online for $5.00 at www2.state.ga.us/Courts/Supreme/main_pp.html.

Sexual Offender Registry

Georgia Bureau of Investigations, GCIC - Sexual Offender Registry, PO Box 370748, Decatur, GA 30037-0748 (Courier: 3121 Panthersville Rd, Decatur, GA 30034); 404-244-2835, 404-212-3028 (Fax), 8AM-4PM.

www.ganet.org/gbi/disclaim.html

Note: The website outlines which offenders are in the searchable database at the website.

Indexing & Storage: Records are available from 07/01/96. It takes 1-3 days before new records are available for inquiry. Records are normally destroyed after 10 years unless more than one prior or who have been convicted of an aggravated offense such as aggravated child molestation, will remain on the registry for life.

Searching: As of July 1, 1999, sexual offenders who have more than one prior conviction for an offense listed in O.C.G.A. § 42-1-12, or who have been convicted of an aggravated offense such as aggravated child molestation, will remain on the registry for life.

Access by: mail, in person, online.

Fee & Payment: There is no fee.

Mail search: Turnaround time: 7 to 10 days.

In person search: In person requests are returned by mail in about 14 days if lists are involved.

Online search: Records may be searched at www.ganet.org/gbi/sorsch.cgi. Earliest records go back to 07/01/96. Searches may be conducted for sex offenders, absconders, and predators.

Incarceration Records

Georiga Department of Corrections, Inmate Records Office, Eastern Tower, 2 Martin Luther King, Jr. Drive, S.E., Atlanta, GA 30334-4900;

404-656-4593, 404-463-6232 (Fax), 8AM-4:30PM.

www.dcor.state.ga.us

Indexing & Storage: Records are available on current and former inmates. It takes 1-3 days before new records are available for inquiry. Records are normally destroyed after 15 years.

Searching: Include the following in your request-name; DOB, Inmate number or SSN are helpful. Location, physical identifiers, conviction information, release dates, and inmate number are released.

Access by: mail, phone, fax, in person, online.

Mail search: Turnaround time: 7 to 10 days. Requests in writing must be on letterhead. No SASE is required.

Phone search: Only general "public" information is released over the phone.

Fax search: Records are available by fax.

In person search: You may make your record request in person; use the agency form. Results are available in two days.

Online search: The website has an extensive array of search capabilities. Also, a private company offers free web access to DOC records at www.vinelink.com/index.jsp.

Corporation, Limited Partnership, Limited Liability Partnerships, Limited Liability Company Records

Sec of State - Corporation Division, Record Searches, 315 W Tower, #2 ML King Drive, Atlanta, GA 30334-1530; 404-656-2817, 8AM-5PM.

www.sos.state.ga.us/corporations

Note: Trade Names, Fictitious Names, Assumed Names and DBAs are found at the county level.

Indexing & Storage: Records are available from the 1960s, and earlier if the filer has moved records from the county level to the state level. Indexes are maintained on microfilm and document imaging systems. New records are available for inquiry immediately.

Searching: Date of incorporation, current status and registered name and address available at website or by phone. Officer names available at website only. Copies and/or certificates can be ordered by mail or from the web.

Access by: mail, phone, in person, online.

Fee & Payment: There is no fee for a website search; there is a $10.00 fee for a Certificate of Existence (good standing) or certified copies. Fee payee: Secretary of State. Prepayment required. Web requests must be paid by credit card. Personal checks accepted. Credit cards accepted: MasterCard, Visa, AmEx.

Mail search: Turnaround time: 1 week. No SASE is required.

Phone search: Limited verification information is available over the phone.

In person search: Immediate records only if expedited service fees paid.

Online search: Records are available from the corporation database on the Internet site above. The corporate database can be searched by entity

name or registered agent for no fee. Document image and certificates are available for a $10.00 fee at www.ganet.org/services/corp/corpsearch.shtml. Other services include name reservation, filing procedures, downloading of forms/applications.

Expedited service: Expedited service is available for mail and in person searches. Turnaround time: 24 hours. Add $50.00 per business name.

Trademarks/Servicemarks

Secretary of State, Trademark Division, 2 Martin Luther King, Room 315, W Tower, Atlanta, GA 30334; 404-656-2861, 404-657-6380 (Fax), 8AM-5PM.

www.sos.state.ga.us/corporations/trademarks.htm

Note: Applications and filing instructions can be obtained at the website.

Indexing & Storage: Records are available from the beginning of the Division and are maintained on computer. It takes 24 hours before new records are available for inquiry. Records are permanently retained.

Searching: Include the following in your request-registration number. Search by mark name or description or by owner name or by goods and services. Will not expedite requests.

Access by: mail, in person, online.

Fee & Payment: $10.00 per record. Fee payee: Secretary of State Prepayment required. Personal checks accepted. No credit cards accepted.

Mail search: Turnaround time: 2 to 3 days. No SASE is required.

In person search: They will take your request in person, but they will mail back the records.

Online search: A record database is searchable from the web site.

Uniform Commercial Code

Superior Court Clerks' Cooperative Authority, 1875 Century Blvd, #100, Atlanta, GA 30345; 404-327-9058, 404-327-7877 (Fax), 8:30AM-5PM.

www.gsccca.org/

Note: High volume, ongoing requesters can open a "search account" and receive expedited service.

Indexing & Storage: Records are available from 1-1-95, indexed on computer. It takes 3-4 days before new records are available for inquiry.

Searching: All uniform commercial code filings are filed at the county level. As of January 1, 1995, new UCC filings are indexed statewide (older filings are only available at the county). Submit a UCC-11 to the address above to search new filings. Include the following in your request-debtor name, Social Security or federal employer number. All tax liens are filed at the county level only.

Access by: mail, fax, in person, online.

Fee & Payment: Uncertified copies made by searcher are $.25 each. Certified copies are also available at the county level for $2.50 for first page. Fee payee: GSCCCA. Prepayment required. Personal checks accepted. Credit cards accepted.

Mail search: Turnaround time: 1 day. No SASE is required.

Fax search: However, this is only available to established accounts.

In person search: Simple requests may be processed while you wait.

Online search: Online name searching is available free at the website. Also search by secured party, tax payer ID, date, or file number. For certified searches, there is a monthly charge of $9.95 and a $.25 fee per image. Billing is monthly. The system is open 24 hours daily. The website also includes real estate indexes and images, lien index, and notary index.

Other access: The entire UCC Central Index System can be purchased on a daily, weekly, biweekly basis. For more information, contact the Director's office.

Expedited service: Expedited service is available online. Add $25.00 per search.

Federal Tax Liens, State Tax Liens

Records not maintained by a state level agency.

Note: All tax liens are filed at the county level.

Sales Tax Registrations

Sales & Use Tax Division, Registration Information, PO 49512, Atlanta, GA 30359-1512; 404-417-4490 (Registration), 404-417-6601 (General Info), 404-651-9490 (Fax), 8AM-4:30PM.

http://www2.state.ga.us/departments/dor

Indexing & Storage: Records are available for all active accounts, which are kept on computer. Inactive accounts are on microfilm.

Searching: This agency will confirm that a business is registered and active, but will not provide further information. Include the following in your request-tax permit number or business name.

Access by: mail, phone, in person.

Fee & Payment: No fee is involved.

Mail search: Turnaround time: 2 weeks. Please give reason for request. Requests in writing will be honored if over two.

Phone search: No fee for telephone request.

In person search: No fee for request. Generally, the information is returned by mail in two weeks.

Birth Certificates

Department of Human Resources, Vital Records Unit, 2600 Skyland Dr NE, Atlanta, GA 30319; 404-679-4701, 877-572-6343 (Credit Card Line), 404-679-4730 (Fax), 8AM-4PM.

http://health.state.ga.us/programs/vitalrecords/index.asp

Indexing & Storage: Records are available from 1919 to present. It takes 1 month before new records are available for inquiry. Records are indexed on inhouse computer.

Searching: For investigative purposes or distant relatives, a notarized, signed release from person of record is required. Include the following in your request-full name, names of parents, mother's maiden name, date of birth, place of birth.

Access by: mail, phone, fax, in person.

Fee & Payment: The fee is $10.00 per record. Add $5.00 per name requested for second copies.

Multi year searches are $10.00 per ten years or portions thereof. Credit card fee is $10.95 Fee payee: Georgia Department of Human Resources. Prepayment required. Credit cards accepted: MasterCard, Visa, AmEx, Discover.

Mail search: Turnaround time: 4 to 6 weeks. No SASE is required.

Phone search: See expedited services.

Fax search: Same criteria as phone searching.

In person search: Turnaround time is usually 30 minutes.

Expedited service: Expedited service is available for mail, phone and fax searches. Turnaround time: overnight delivery. Add $17.50 for overnight service plus use of credit card fee required.

Death Records

Department of Human Resources, Vital Records Unit, 2600 Skyland Dr NE, Atlanta, GA 30319; 404-679-4701, 877-572-6343 (Credit Card Line), 404-679-4730 (Fax), 8AM-4PM.

http://health.state.ga.us/programs/vitalrecords/index.asp

Indexing & Storage: Records are available from 1919 to present. It takes 1 month before new records are available for inquiry. Records are indexed on inhouse computer.

Searching: Death certificates are available to the general public. Cause of death is released to next of kin only. Include the following in your request-full name, date of death, place of death. Age at death, sex and race are helpful.

Access by: mail, phone, fax, in person.

Fee & Payment: The fee is $10.00 per name. Add $5.00 per name for second copies. Multi year searches are $10.00 per 10 years or portions thereof. Credit card fee is $10.95 Fee payee: Georgia Department of Human Resources. Prepayment required. Credit cards accepted: MasterCard, Visa, AmEx, Discover.

Mail search: Turnaround time: 3 to 4 weeks. No SASE is required.

Phone search: See expedited services.

Fax search: Same criteria as phone searching.

In person search: Turnaround time 30 minutes.

Other access: The death index is available for the years 1919-1998 on microfiche for $50.00.

Expedited service: Expedited service is available for mail, phone and fax searches. Turnaround time: overnight delivery. Add $17.50 for overnight delivery, plus include credit card fee.

Marriage Certificates

Department of Human Resources, Vital Records Unit, 2600 Skyland Dr NE, Atlanta, GA 30319; 404-679-4701, 877-572-6343 (Credit Card Line), 404-679-4730 (Fax), 8AM-4PM.

http://health.state.ga.us/programs/vitalrecords/index.asp

Indexing & Storage: Records are available from 1952 on. Prior to 1952, records must be obtained from the county probate office. It takes 1 month. before new records are available for inquiry. Records are indexed on inhouse computer.

Searching: Certified copies of marriage licenses are available to the general public; but copies of the marriage application are only issued to bride and groom. Records may not be ordered via e-

mail. Include the following in your request-full names of husband and wife, date of marriage, place or county of marriage.

Access by: mail, phone, fax, in person.

Fee & Payment: The search fee is $10.00 per name. Add $5.00 per name requested for second copies. Multi-year search are $10.00 per ten years or portions thereof. Credit card fee is $10.50 Fee payee: Georgia Department of Human Resources. Prepayment required. Credit cards accepted: MasterCard, Visa, AmEx, Discover.

Mail search: Turnaround time: 3 to 4 weeks. No SASE is required.

Phone search: See expedited services.

Fax search: Same criteria as phone searches.

In person search: Turnaround time 30 minutes.

Other access: The marriage index is available on microfiche for $50.00, the set includes the years 1964-1998.

Expedited service: Expedited service is available for mail, phone and fax searches. Turnaround time: overnight delivery. Add $17.50 for express delivery plus the credit card surcharge.

Divorce Records

Department of Human Resources, Vital Records Unit, 2600 Skyland Dr NE, Atlanta, GA 30319; 404-679-4701, 877-572-6343 (Credit Card Line), 404-679-4730 (Fax), 8AM-4PM.

http://health.state.ga.us/programs/vitalrecords/index.asp

Note: Divorce records are found at the county of issue. However, this agency will do search to identify the county of record, but cannot issue a record. Certified copies are only available at the county level.

Indexing & Storage: Records are available from the counties.

Access by: mail, phone, fax, in person.

Fee & Payment: The fee is $10.00, $5.00 for a second copy. Credit card fee is $10.95 Fee payee: GA Department of Human Resources. Personal checks accepted. Credit cards accepted: MasterCard, Visa, AmEx, Discover.

Mail search: Records are available by mail.

Phone search: See expedited services.

Fax search: Same criteria as phone searches.

In person search: Search of index availablity immediately.

Other access: Divorce microfiche indexes are available to the public, sold in complete set for the years 1919-1998 for $50.00.

Expedited service: Expedited service is available for fax and phone searches. Add $17.50 for express delivery plus the credit card use fee.

Workers' Compensation Records

State Board of Workers Compensation, 270 Peachtree St, NW, Atlanta, GA 30303-1299; 404-656-3875, 8AM-4:30PM.

www.sbwc.georgia.gov/

Indexing & Storage: Records are available from 1994. Records are maintained for 10 years. Records are indexed on inhouse computer.

Searching: Must have a court order signed by a judge to obtain records from this agency unless you are a party to the case. Include the following in your request-claimant name, Social Security Number.

Access by: mail.

Fee & Payment: The agency will bill for required fees. Fee payee: State Board of Workers Compensation. Personal checks accepted. No credit cards accepted.

Mail search: Turnaround time: 2 to 3 weeks. The fee is $7.00 for the first 10 pages plus $.50 per page for over 10 pages. Certification for a document is $7.00. No SASE is required. No fee for mail request.

Driver Records

Department of Motor Vehicle Safety, Driver's Services Section, MVR Unit, PO Box 80447, Conyers, GA 30013 (Courier: 2206 East View Parkway, Conyers, GA 30013); 678-413-8441, 8AM-3:30PM.

www.dmvs.ga.gov

Note: Copies of tickets are not available from a central depository. It is recommended you go directly to the issuing court.

Indexing & Storage: Records are available for either a 3 year record or a 7 year record. Accident involvement is shown if the driver was cited. The driver's address is part of the record. It takes ten days or more before new records are available for inquiry.

Searching: Georgia has strict rules concerning driver record access. If an individual requests a driving record on another, the driver's notarized signature is needed (except for court subpoena). Large requesters must have "bulk-user certificates" on file. The driver's full name, DOB and license number are required.

Access by: mail, in person, online.

Fee & Payment: $5.00 for a 3 year period; $7.00 for a 7 year period. Fee payee: Department of Motor Vehicle Safety. Prepayment required. No personal checks accepted. No credit cards accepted.

Mail search: Turnaround time: 2 weeks. No SASE is required.

In person search: Walk-in requesters may receive up to three records while waiting, additional requests are processed overnight. Walk-in requests are also available at most driver's license offices.

Online search: Through the coordinated efforts of the GA Department of Motor Vehicle Safety and the Georgia Technology Authority, driving records are now available via the Internet for "certified users, including insurance, employers, and car rental companies. Requesters must complete several applications and user agreement forms.The fees are $5.00 for a three-year record and $7.00 for a seven-year record. For further information, visit: https://online.dmvs.ga.gov/mvr/cert.asp.

Other access: Georgia no long offers magnetic tape processing for high volume users.

Expedited service: Has no regular policy for expediting requests.

Vehicle Ownership, Vehicle Identification

Department of Motor Vehicle Safety, Motor Vehicle Services - Research, PO Box 740381, Atlanta, GA 30374-0381; 404-362-6500, 404-362-2729 (Fax), 8AM-4:30PM.

www.dmvs.ga.gov

Indexing & Storage: Records are available from 1999 forward. New records are available for inquiry immediately. Records are normally destroyed after 5 years.

Searching: Records are not open to the general public and are restricted to authorized (notarized) agents or individuals, judgment creditor, tax collector, law enforcement officials, license dealers, etc. There is an online access mode for only GA licensed dealers. Include the following in your request-statement of reason for requests, fee; must be on letterhead. Records are only released to casual requesters with notarized consent of the subject

Access by: mail, in person, online.

Fee & Payment: Fees: $5.00 per record for VIN and title histories; $.50 for a title or tag search computer print-out. Certified tag or title record is $10.00. Lien information is considered part of the title history. There is a full charge for a "no record found." Fee payee: Department of Motor Vehicle Safety. Prepayment required. Personal checks accepted. No credit cards accepted.

Mail search: Turnaround time: 2 weeks. A SASE is requested.

In person search: Turnaround time is while you wait.

Online search: Online access available to Georgia dealers only; registration is required.

Expedited service: Will expedite if you provide a court date that indicates that the request must be received in a timely manner.

Accident Reports

Department of Motor Vehicle Safety, Accident Reporting Section, PO Box 80447, Conyers, GA 30013; 678-413-8647, 678-413-8584 (Fax), 8AM-4:30PM.

Indexing & Storage: Records are available for 10 years to present. It takes 30 days before new records are available for inquiry. Records are normally destroyed after 10 years.

Searching: Only persons involved in the accident or their legal representative may obtain a copy, unless the subject has given written permission. Include the following in your request-full name, date of accident, location of accident.

Access by: mail, phone, in person.

Fee & Payment: The fee for a report is $5.00. There is no charge for a "no record found." Fee payee: Department of Motor Vehicle Safety. Prepayment required. Cash, money orders, certified checks, and cashier's checks are all accepted. No personal checks accepted. No credit cards accepted.

Mail search: Turnaround time: 1 week to 10 days. No SASE is required.

Phone search: Record requests are accepted by telephone.

In person search: Request must be in writing. Turnaround time is within the hour.

Vessel Ownership, Vessel Registration

Georgia Dept of Natural Resources, Boat Registration Office, PO Box 105310, Atlanta, Georgia 30348-5310; 770-414-3337, 770-414-3344 (Fax), 8AM-4:30PM.

www.gadnr.org/

Note: Liens are at the county level and will not show on records at this location.

Indexing & Storage: Records are available from 1986 to present. Records are indexed on microfiche from 1986 to 1993 and on computer from 1994 to present. All motorized boats must be registered. All sailboats 12 ft or longer must be registered.

Searching: Either the name, registration # or hull # must be submitted.

Access by: mail, phone, fax, in person.

Fee & Payment: There is no search fee.

Mail search: Turnaround time: 1 to 2 weeks. No SASE is required.

Phone search: Verification only.

Fax search: Same criteria as mail searching.

In person search: Simple requests may be processed while you wait.

Voter Registration

Secretary of State, Elections Division, 2 Martin Luther King Dr SE, Suite 1104, Atlanta, GA 30334; 404-656-2871, 404-651-9531 (Fax), 8AM-5PM.

www.sos.state.ga.us/elections

Note: Data entry to the database is done at the county level.

Indexing & Storage: Records are available from 1995, on computer. Data is keyed in by county personnel onto the state computer.

Searching: Records may be ordered as a flat file in ASCII format directly from the website. Include the following in your request-full name, Social Security Number if available, date of birth, phone numer of requester. All requests must be in writing. Records may be requested at county level, also. The following data is not released: Social Security Numbers or bulk information or lists for commercial purposes.

Access by: mail, fax, online.

Fee & Payment: There is no fee for individual requests. Copies are $.25 per page. There are fees to purchase the database, and these fees can be found at the website. Prepayment required. Personal checks accpeted.

Mail search: Turnaround time: 2 to 3 days. No SASE is required.

Fax search: Fax searching of statutus is available.

Online search: Name and DOB needed to search registration information at the website. Go to "Poll Locator." The results will provide address and district-precinct information, no SSNs released.

Other access: CDs, Internet files, disks, and paper lists are available for purchase for non-commercial purposes. Look at the website for pricing.

GED Certificates

GED Testing Service, 1800 Century Pl #555, Atlanta, GA 30345; 404-679-1644, 8:30AM-4:30PM M-F.

www.dtae.org

Searching: Include the following in your request-a signed release, name, year and location of test, date of birth, and Social Security Number.

Access by: mail, in person.

Fee & Payment: The fee for a verification or for a copy of a transcript is $5.00 per record. A duplicate diploma is $8.00. Fee payee: GED Testing Services. Prepayment required. Money orders are accepted. No credit cards accepted.

Mail search: Turnaround time: 2 weeks. No SASE is required.

In person search: Records may only be picked up between 12 noon to 4PM Tues. through Fri.

Hunting and Fishing License Information

Access to Records is Restricted

Department of Natural Resources, Hunting & Fishing Licenses, 2189 Northlake Pkwy, Bldg 10, #108, Tucker, GA 30084; 770-918-6400, 770-414-3344 (Fax), 8AM-4:30PM.

www.georgiawildlife.com

Note: The request must be in writing and cite that under the Georgia Open Records Act you request that a search be done. The database may not be current for non-resident licenses and license purchases made via the website.

Georgia State Licensing Agencies

Licenses Searchable Online

Acupuncturist #41	www.medicalboard.state.ga.us/bdsearch/index.html
Air Conditioning Contractor #9	https://secure.sos.state.ga.us/myverification/
Architect #15	https://secure.sos.state.ga.us/myverification/
Athletic Agent #12	https://secure.sos.state.ga.us/myverification/
Athletic Trainer #16	https://secure.sos.state.ga.us/myverification/
Auctioneer/Auction Dealer #12	https://secure.sos.state.ga.us/myverification/
Audiologist #16	https://secure.sos.state.ga.us/myverification/
Bank #17	www.ganet.org/dbf/other_institutions.html
Barber/Barber Shop #19	https://secure.sos.state.ga.us/myverification/
Charity #45	www.sos.state.ga.us/securities/charitysearch.htm
Check Casher/Seller #17	www.ganet.org/dbf/other_institutions.html
Chiropractor #18	https://secure.sos.state.ga.us/myverification/
Cosmetologist/Cosmetology Shop #19	https://secure.sos.state.ga.us/myverification/
Counselor #10	https://secure.sos.state.ga.us/myverification/
Credit Union #17	www.ganet.org/dbf/other_institutions.html
Dental Hygienist #20	https://secure.sos.state.ga.us/myverification/
Dentist #20	https://secure.sos.state.ga.us/myverification/
Detox Specialist #41	www.medicalboard.state.ga.us/bdsearch/index.html
Dietitian #2	https://secure.sos.state.ga.us/myverification/
Drug Whlse/Retail/Mfg (Hospital) #31	https://secure.sos.state.ga.us/myverification/
EDP - Electronic Data Processor #17	www.ganet.org/dbf/other_institutions.html
Electrical Contractor #9	https://secure.sos.state.ga.us/myverification/
Embalmer #12	https://secure.sos.state.ga.us/myverification/
Engineer #11	https://secure.sos.state.ga.us/myverification/
Esthetician #19	https://secure.sos.state.ga.us/myverification/
Family Therapist #10	https://secure.sos.state.ga.us/myverification/
Forester #36	https://secure.sos.state.ga.us/myverification/
Funeral Director/Apprentice #12	https://secure.sos.state.ga.us/myverification/
Funeral Establishment #12	https://secure.sos.state.ga.us/myverification/
Geologist #44	https://secure.sos.state.ga.us/myverification/
Hearing Aid Dealer/Dispenser #21	https://secure.sos.state.ga.us/myverification/
Holding Company/Representative Office #17	www.ganet.org/dbf/other_institutions.html
Insurance Adjuster #8	www.inscomm.state.ga.us/AGENTS/agentstatus.asp
Insurance Agent / Counselor #8	www.inscomm.state.ga.us/AGENTS/agentstatus.asp
Interior Designer #15	https://secure.sos.state.ga.us/myverification/
Landscape Architect #27	https://secure.sos.state.ga.us/myverification/
Lobbyist #22	www.ethics.state.ga.us
Lobbyist Organization #22	www.ethics.state.ga.us
Low Voltage Contractor #9	https://secure.sos.state.ga.us/myverification/
Manicurist #19	https://secure.sos.state.ga.us/myverification/
Marriage Counselor #10	https://secure.sos.state.ga.us/myverification/
Medical Doctor #41	www.medicalboard.state.ga.us/bdsearch/index.html
Mortgage Institution #17	www.ganet.org/dbf/mortgage.html
Nail Care #19	https://secure.sos.state.ga.us/myverification/
Notary Public #3	www.gsccca.org/search/notary/search.asp
Nuclear Pharmacist #31	https://secure.sos.state.ga.us/myverification/
Nurse-LPN #2	https://secure.sos.state.ga.us/myverification/
Nurse-RN #28	https://secure.sos.state.ga.us/myverification/
Nursing Home Administrator #16	https://secure.sos.state.ga.us/myverification/
Occupational Therapist/Assistant #2	https://secure.sos.state.ga.us/myverification/
Optician, Dispensing #21	https://secure.sos.state.ga.us/myverification/
Optometrist #21	https://secure.sos.state.ga.us/myverification/
Osteopathic Physician #41	www.medicalboard.state.ga.us/bdsearch/index.html
Perfusionist #41	www.medicalboard.state.ga.us/bdsearch/index.html
Pesticide Applicator #4	www.kellysolutions.com/ga/Applicators/index.htm
Pesticide Contractor/Employee #4	www.kellysolutions.com/ga/Applicators/index.htm
Pharmacist #31	https://secure.sos.state.ga.us/myverification/
Pharmacy School, Clinic Researcher #31	https://secure.sos.state.ga.us/myverification/
Physical Therapist/Therapist Asst #2	https://secure.sos.state.ga.us/myverification/

Physician Assistant #41 .... www.medicalboard.state.ga.us/bdsearch/index.html
Plumber Journeyman/Contractor #9 .... https://secure.sos.state.ga.us/myverification/
Podiatrist #33 .... https://secure.sos.state.ga.us/myverification/
Poison Pharmacist #31 .... https://secure.sos.state.ga.us/myverification/
Private Detective #12 .... https://secure.sos.state.ga.us/myverification/
Psychologist #16 .... https://secure.sos.state.ga.us/myverification/
Public Accountant-CPA #14 .... https://secure.sos.state.ga.us/myverification/
Public Adjuster #8 .... www.inscomm.state.ga.us/AGENTS/agentstatus.asp
Real Estate Agent/Sales/Broker #46 .... www.arello.com
Real Estate Appraiser #46 .... www.asc.gov/content/category1/appr_by_state.asp
Real Estate Community Assn. Mgr. #46 .... www.arello.com
Rebuilder (Motor Vehicle) #12 .... https://secure.sos.state.ga.us/myverification/
Respiratory Care Practitioner #41 .... www.medicalboard.state.ga.us/bdsearch/index.html
Salvage Pool Operator/ Salvage Yard Dealer #12 .... https://secure.sos.state.ga.us/myverification/
School Librarian #40 .... https://secure.sos.state.ga.us/myverification/
Security Guard/Agency #12 .... https://secure.sos.state.ga.us/myverification/
Social Worker #10 .... https://secure.sos.state.ga.us/myverification/
Speech-Language Pathologist #16 .... https://secure.sos.state.ga.us/myverification/
Surplus Line Broker #8 .... www.inscomm.state.ga.us/AGENTS/agentstatus.asp
Surveyor, Land #11 .... https://secure.sos.state.ga.us/myverification/
Teacher #7 .... https://www.gapsc.com/Certificationchannel/newcertificationchannel.asp
Used Car Dealer/Parts Dist. #12 .... https://secure.sos.state.ga.us/myverification/
Utility Contractor #9 .... https://secure.sos.state.ga.us/myverification/
Veterinarian/Veterinary Technician #39 .... https://secure.sos.state.ga.us/myverification/
Waste Water Collection System Operator #43 .... https://secure.sos.state.ga.us/myverification/
Waste Water Laboratory Analyst #43 .... https://secure.sos.state.ga.us/myverification/
Waste Water Operator 1-4/ Water System Operator #43 . https://secure.sos.state.ga.us/myverification/
Water Laboratory Operator/Water Operator Cl. 1-4 #43 .. https://secure.sos.state.ga.us/myverification/

Georgia Licensing Quick Finder

Acupuncturist #41	404-657-6490
Air Conditioning Contr. #9	478-207-1416
Amusement Ride Inspector #48	404-679-0687
Animal Technician #39	478-207-1686
Architect #15	478-207-1401
Athletic Agent #12	478-207-1460
Athletic Trainer #16	478-207-1670
Attorney #47	404-527-8700
Auctioneer/Auction Dealer #12	478-207-1460
Audiologist #16	478-207-1670
Bank #17	770-986-1633
Barber/Barber Shop #19	478-207-1430
Cemetery #45	404-656-3920
Charity #45	404-656-3920
Check Casher/Seller #17	770-986-1633
Chiropractor #18	478-207-1686
Coin-operated Machine #6	404-417-4490
Cosmetologist/Cosmetology Shop #19	478-207-1430
Counselor #10	478-207-1670
Court Reporter #1	404-656-6422
Credit Union #17	770-986-1637
Dental Hygienist #20	478-207-1686
Dentist #20	478-207-1686
Detox Specialist #41	404-656-3913
Dietitian #2	478-207-1620
Drug Whlse/Retail/Mfg (Hospital) #31	478-207-1686
EDP - Electronic Data Processor #17	770-986-1633
Electrical Contractor #9	478-207-1416
Embalmer #12	478-207-1460
Emergency Medical Technician #49	404-679-0547
Engineer #11	478-207-1450
Esthetician #19	478-207-1430
Family Therapist #10	478-207-1670
Forester #36	478-207-1401
Funeral Director/Apprentice #12	478-207-1460
Funeral Establishment #12	478-207-1460
Geologist #44	478-207-1401
Hearing Aid Dealer/Dispenser #21	478-207-1686
Holding Company/Rep. Office #17	770-986-1633

Insurance Adjuster #8	404-656-2101
Insurance Agent #8	404-656-2101
Insurance Counselor #8	404-656-2101
Interior Designer #15	478-207-1401
Investment Advisor (Firm) #45	404-656-3920
Landfill Inspector/Operator #5	404-362-2696
Landscape Architect #27	478-207-1401
Liquor Control #6	404-417-4490
Lobbyist #22	404-463-1980
Lobbyist Organization #22	404-463-1980
Low Voltage Contractor #9	478-207-1416
Manicurist #19	478-207-1430
Marriage Counselor #10	478-207-1670
Medical Doctor #41	404-657-6489
Mortgage Institution #17	770-986-1269
Nail Care #19	478-207-1430
Notary Public #3	404-327-6023
Nuclear Pharmacist #31	478-207-1686
Nurse-LPN #2	478-207-1620
Nurse-RN #28	478-207-1640
Nursing Home Administrator #16	478-207-1670
Occupational Therapist/Assistant #2	478-207-1620
Optician, Dispensing #21	478-207-1686
Optometrist #21	478-207-1686
Osteopathic Physician #41	404-657-6489
Perfusionist #41	404-463-2292
Pesticide Applicator #4	404-656-4958
Pesticide Contr./Employee #4	404-656-4958
Pharmacist #31	478-207-1686
Pharmacy School, Clinic Researcher #31	478-207-1686
Physical Therapist/Therapist Asst #2	478-207-1620
Physician Assistant #41	404-657-4688
Plumber Journeyman/Contr. #9	478-207-1416
Podiatrist #33	478-207-1686
Poison Pharmacist #31	478-207-1686
Private Detective #12	478-207-1460
Psychologist #16	478-207-1670
Public Accountant-CPA #14	478-207-1401

Public Adjuster #8	404-656-2101
Real Estate Agent/Sales/Broker #46	404-656-3916
Real Estate Appraiser #46	404-656-3916
Real Estate Community Assn. Mgr. #46	404-656-3916
Rebuilder (Motor Vehicle) #12	478-207-1460
Respiratory Care Practitioner #41	404-656-3914
Salvage Pool Operator/Yard Dealer #12	478-207-1460
School Administrator/Supervisor #7	404-657-9000
School Bus Driver #51	678-413-8458
School Counselor / Media Specialist #7	404-657-9000
School Librarian #40	478-207-1401
School Social Worker #7	404-657-9000
Securities Salesperson/Dealer #45	404-656-3920
Security Guard/Agency #12	478-207-1460
Shorthand Court Reporter/Stenomask #1	404-656-6422
Social Worker #10	478-207-1670
Speech-Language Pathologist #16	478-207-1670
Surplus Line Broker #8	404-656-2101
Surveyor, Land #11	478-207-1450
Teacher #7	404-657-9000
Timber Dealer/Processor #4	404-656-4958
Tobacco Seller #6	404-417-4490
Truck Driver #51	678-413-8458
Used Car Dealer /Distributor #12	478-207-1460
Utility Contractor #9	478-207-1416
Veterinarian/Veterinary Technician #39	478-207-1686
Veterinary Faculty #39	478-207-1686
Waste Water Collection System Operator #43	912-207-1460
Waste Water Industrial Operator #43	912-207-1460
Waste Water Laboratory Analyst #43	912-207-1460
Waste Water Operator 1-4 #43	912-207-1460
Water Distribution System Operator #43	912-207-1460
Water Laboratory Operator #43	912-207-1460
Water Operator Class 1-4 #43	912-207-1460

Georgia Licensing Agency Information

1 Clerk of the Board, Board of Court Reporting, 244 Washington St SW, #300, Atlanta, GA 30334; 404-656-6422, Fax: 404-651-6449. www.georgiacourts.org/agencies/bcr Email: reisss@gaaoc.us

2 Examining Boards Division, Board of Examiners of Licensed Practical Nurses, 237 Coliseum Dr, Macon, GA 31217; 478-207-1620, Fax: 478-207-1633. www.sos.state.ga.us/plb/lpn Search Database at https://secure.sos.state.ga.us/myverification/

3 Clerks Authority, Notary Public Division, 1875 Century Blvd #100, Atlanta, GA 30345; 404-327-6023, Fax: 404-327-7887. www.gsccca.org/Projects/aboutnp.asp Email: mike.smith@gsccca.org Search Database at www.gsccca.org/search/notary/search.asp

4 Department of Agriculture, Pesticide Division, Capitol Sq, Rm 550, Atlanta, GA 30334; 404-656-4958, Fax: 404-657-8378. www.agr.state.ga.us Search Database at www.kellysolutions.com/ga/Applicators/index.htm

5 Department of Natural Resources, Environmental Protection Division, 4244 International Pky, #104, Atlanta, GA 30354; 404-362-2696, Fax: 404-362-2693. www.state.ga.us/dnr/environ/

6 Dept. of Revenue, Centralized Taxpayer Registration, 1800 Century Center RL NE, PO Box 49512, Atlanta, GA 30359-1512; 404-417-4490. http://www2.state.ga.us/Departments/DOR

7 Georgia Professional Standards Commission, Teacher Certification, 1452 Twin Towers East, Atlanta, GA 30334; 404-657-9000. www.gapsc.com/teachercertification.asp Note: To check teacher status, the SSN is required.

8 Licensing Division, Insurance Commissioner's Office, 2 Martin Luther King Jr Dr, West Tower, #908, Atlanta, GA 30334; 404-656-2101, Fax: 404-656-0874. www.gainsurance.org Search Database at www.inscomm.state.ga.us/AGENTS/agentstatus.asp

9 State Construction Industry Licensing Board, 237 Coliseum Dr, Macon, GA 31217; 478-207-1416, Fax: 478-207-1425. www.sos.state.ga.us/plb/construct Email: ckhouser@sos.state.ga.us Search Database at https://secure.sos.state.ga.us/myverification/ Note: They sell rosters for $25.00.

10 Examining Boards Division, Board of Prof. Counselors, Social Workers, & Marriage/Family Therapists, 237 Coliseum Dr, Macon, GA 31217; 478-207-1670, Fax: 478-207-1676. www.sos.state.ga.us/plb/counselors Search at https://secure.sos.state.ga.us/myverification/

11 Examining Boards Division, Professional Engineers & Land Surveyors Board, 237 Coliseum Dr, Macon, GA 31217-3858; 478-207-1450, Fax: 478-207-1456. www.sos.state.ga.us/plb/pels/ Email: pels@sos.state.ga.us Search Database at https://secure.sos.state.ga.us/myverification/ Note: They sell rosters for $25.00.

12 Professional Licensing, Licensing Boards, 237 Coliseum Dr, Macon, GA 31217; 478-207-1460, Fax: 478-207-1468. www.sos.state.ga.us/plb Search Database at https://secure.sos.state.ga.us/myverification/

14 Examining Boards Division, Board of Accountancy, 237 Coliseum Dr, Macon, GA 31217-3858; 478-207-1401, Fax: 478-207-1410. www.sos.state.ga.us/plb/accountancy Search at https://secure.sos.state.ga.us/myverification/

15 Examining Boards Division, Board of Architects and Interior Designers, 237 Coliseum Dr, Macon, GA 31217; 478-207-1401, Fax: 478-207-1410. www.sos.state.ga.us/plb/architects Search Database at https://secure.sos.state.ga.us/myverification/

16 Examining Boards Division, State Examining Board-Medical, 237 Coliseum Dr, Macon, GA 31217; 478-207-1670, Fax: 478-207-1676. www.sos.state.ga.us/plb/ Search Database at https://secure.sos.state.ga.us/myverification/

17 Department of Banking & Finance, Regulated Institutions, 2990 Brandywine Rd #200, Atlanta, GA 30341; 770-986-1633, Fax: 770-986-1654. www.ganet.org/dbf/dbf.html Search Database at www.ganet.org/dbf/regulated_institutions.html

18 Examining Boards Division, Board of Chiropractic Examiners, 237 Coliseum Dr, Macon, GA 31217; 478-207-1686, Fax: 478-207-1699. www.sos.state.ga.us/plb/chiro Search Database at https://secure.sos.state.ga.us/myverification/

19 Examining Boards Division, Board of Cosmetology, 237 Coliseum Drive, Macon, GA 31217; 478-207-1430, Fax: 478-207-1442. www.sos.state.ga.us/plb/barber_cosmet Search at https://secure.sos.state.ga.us/myverification/

20 Examining Boards Division, Board of Dentistry, 237 Coliseum Drive, Macon, GA 31217-3858; 478-207-1686, Fax: 478-207-1699. www.sos.state.ga.us/plb/dentistry Search at https://secure.sos.state.ga.us/myverification/

21 Examining Boards Division, Board of Hearing Aid Disp., Board of Dispensing Opticians, Examiners in Optometry, 237 Coliseum Dr, Macon, GA 31217; 478-207-1686, Fax: 478-207-1699. www.sos.state.ga.us/plb/opticians Search at https://secure.sos.state.ga.us/myverification/

22 State Ethics Commission, 205 Jesse Hill Jr Dr, #478 East Tower, Atlanta, GA 30334; 404-463-1980, Fax: 404-463-1988. www.ethics.state.ga.us Email: mailto:ethics@ethics.state.ga.us Search at www.ethics.state.ga.us Note: At the website, you may choose the type of Lobbyist lists to examine.

27 Examining Boards Division, Board of Landscape Architects, 237 Coliseum Dr, Macon, GA 31217-3858; 478-207-1401, Fax: 478-207-1410. www.sos.state.ga.us/plb/landscape Search Database at https://secure.sos.state.ga.us/myverification/

28 Examining Boards Division, Board of Nursing, 237 Coliseum Dr, Macon, GA 30217-3858; 478-207-1640, Fax: 478-207-1660. www.sos.state.ga.us/plb/rn Search Database at https://secure.sos.state.ga.us/myverification/

31 Examining Boards Division, Board of Pharmacy, 237 Coliseum Dr, Macon, GA 31217; 478-207-1686, Fax: 478-207-1699. www.sos.state.ga.us/plb/pharmacy Search at https://secure.sos.state.ga.us/myverification/

33 Examining Boards Division, Board of Podiatry Examiners, 237 Coliseum Dr, Macon, GA 31217; 478-207-1686, Fax: 478-207-1699.

www.sos.state.ga.us/plb/podiatry Search Database at https://secure.sos.state.ga.us/myverification/

36 Examining Boards Division, Board of Registration for Foresters, 237 Coliseum Dr, Macon, GA 31217; 478-207-1401, Fax: 478-207-1410. www.sos.state.ga.us/plb/foresters Search at https://secure.sos.state.ga.us/myverification/

39 Examining Boards Division, Board of Veterinary Medicine, 237 Coliseum Dr, Macon, GA 31217; 478-207-1686, Fax: 478-207-1699. www.sos.state.ga.us/plb/veterinary Search at https://secure.sos.state.ga.us/myverification/

40 Examining Boards Division, Board for the Certification of Librarians, 237 Coliseum Dr, Macon, GA 31217-3858; 478-207-1401, Fax: 478-207-1410. www.sos.state.ga.us/plb/librarians Search Database at https://secure.sos.state.ga.us/myverification/

41 Examining Boards Division, Composite Board of Medical Examiners, 2 Peachtree St, 10th Fl, Atlanta, GA 30303; 404-656-3913, Fax: 404-656-9723. www.medicalboard.state.ga.us Search Database at www.medicalboard.state.ga.us/bdsearch/index.html

43 Examining Boards Division, Water & Wastewater Treatment Plant Operators & Laboratory Analysts, 237 Coliseum Dr, Macon, GA 31217; 404-207-1460, Fax: 404-207-1468. www.sos.state.ga.us/plb/water Email: cmroehm@sos.state.ga.us Search Database at https://secure.sos.state.ga.us/myverification/ Note: Verification Letter from Board $25.00 fee, https://www.sos.state.ga.us/plb/water/download-forms.htm. For Excel format "Roster Request Form".

44 Examining Boards Division, Board of Registration for Professional Geologists, 237 Coliseum Dr, Macon, GA 31217-3858; 478-207-1401, Fax: 478-207-1410. www.sos.state.ga.us/plb/geologists/ Search at https://secure.sos.state.ga.us/myverification/

45 Securities & Business Regulation, Office of Sec of State, 2 MLK Jr Dr, West Tower, #802, Atlanta, GA 30334-1530; 404-656-3920, Fax: 404-657-8410. www.sos.state.ga.us/securities Email: securities@sos.state.ga.us Search Database at www.sos.state.ga.us/securities

46 Real Estate Commission/Appraiser Board, 229 Peachtree St NE, International Tower, #1000, Atlanta, GA 30303-1605; 404-656-3916, Fax: 404-656-6650. www.grec.state.ga.us Email: grecmail@grec.state.ga.us

47 State Bar of Georgia, 104 Marietta St NW #100, Atlanta, GA 30303; 404-527-8700, Fax: 404-527-8717. www.gabar.org

48 Department of Labor, Safety Engineering Division, 1700 Century Circle NE, Atlanta, GA 30345; 404-679-0687, Fax: 404-679-5818.

49 Emergency Medical Svcs, 2600 Skyland Dr, Atlanta, GA 30319; 404-679-0547, Fax: 404-679-0526. www.ph.dhr.state.ga.us/programs/ems/index.shtml

51 Department of Public Safety, Commercial Driver's License Unit, PO Box 1456, Atlanta, GA 30371-1456; 678-413-8458. www.state.ga.us/gsp/

Georgia Federal Courts

The following list indicates the district and division name for each county in the state. If the bankruptcy court location is different from the district court, then the location of the bankruptcy court appears in parentheses.

County/Court Cross Reference

County	District	Division
Appling	Southern	Brunswick (Savannah)
Atkinson	Southern	Waycross (Savannah)
Bacon	Southern	Waycross (Savannah)
Baker	Middle	Albany/Americus (Macon)
Baldwin	Middle	Macon
Banks	Northern	Gainesville
Barrow	Northern	Gainesville
Bartow	Northern	Rome
Ben Hill	Middle	Albany/Americus (Macon)
Berrien	Middle	Valdosta (Columbus)
Bibb	Middle	Macon
Bleckley	Middle	Macon
Brantley	Southern	Waycross (Savannah)
Brooks	Middle	Thomasville (Columbus)
Bryan	Southern	Savannah
Bulloch	Southern	Statesboro (Augusta)
Burke	Southern	Augusta
Butts	Middle	Macon
Calhoun	Middle	Albany/Americus (Macon)
Camden	Southern	Brunswick (Savannah)
Candler	Southern	Statesboro (Augusta)
Carroll	Northern	Newnan
Catoosa	Northern	Rome
Charlton	Southern	Waycross (Savannah)
Chatham	Southern	Savannah
Chattahoochee	Middle	Columbus
Chattooga	Northern	Rome
Cherokee	Northern	Atlanta
Clarke	Middle	Athens (Macon)
Clay	Middle	Columbus
Clayton	Northern	Atlanta
Clinch	Middle	Valdosta (Columbus)
Cobb	Northern	Atlanta
Coffee	Southern	Waycross (Savannah)
Colquitt	Middle	Thomasville (Columbus)
Columbia	Southern	Augusta
Cook	Middle	Valdosta (Columbus)
Coweta	Northern	Newnan
Crawford	Middle	Macon
Crisp	Middle	Albany/Americus (Macon)
Dade	Northern	Rome
Dawson	Northern	Gainesville
De Kalb	Northern	Atlanta
Decatur	Middle	Thomasville (Columbus)
Dodge	Southern	Dublin (Augusta)
Dooly	Middle	Macon
Dougherty	Middle	Albany/Americus (Macon)
Douglas	Northern	Atlanta
Early	Middle	Albany/Americus (Macon)
Echols	Middle	Valdosta (Columbus)
Effingham	Southern	Savannah
Elbert	Middle	Athens (Macon)
Emanuel	Southern	Statesboro (Augusta)
Evans	Southern	Statesboro (Augusta)
Fannin	Northern	Gainesville
Fayette	Northern	Newnan
Floyd	Northern	Rome
Forsyth	Northern	Gainesville
Franklin	Middle	Athens (Macon)
Fulton	Northern	Atlanta
Gilmer	Northern	Gainesville
Glascock	Southern	Augusta
Glynn	Southern	Brunswick (Savannah)
Gordon	Northern	Rome
Grady	Middle	Thomasville (Columbus)
Greene	Middle	Athens (Macon)
Gwinnett	Northern	Atlanta
Habersham	Northern	Gainesville
Hall	Northern	Gainesville
Hancock	Middle	Macon
Haralson	Northern	Newnan
Harris	Middle	Columbus
Hart	Middle	Athens (Macon)
Heard	Northern	Newnan
Henry	Northern	Atlanta
Houston	Middle	Macon
Irwin	Middle	Valdosta (Columbus)
Jackson	Northern	Gainesville
Jasper	Middle	Macon
Jeff Davis	Southern	Brunswick (Savannah)
Jefferson	Southern	Augusta
Jenkins	Southern	Statesboro (Augusta)
Johnson	Southern	Dublin (Augusta)
Jones	Middle	Macon
Lamar	Middle	Macon
Lanier	Middle	Valdosta (Columbus)
Laurens	Southern	Dublin (Augusta)
Lee	Middle	Albany/Americus (Macon)
Liberty	Southern	Savannah
Lincoln	Southern	Augusta
Long	Southern	Brunswick (Savannah)
Lowndes	Middle	Valdosta (Columbus)
Lumpkin	Northern	Gainesville
Macon	Middle	Macon
Madison	Middle	Athens (Macon)
Marion	Middle	Columbus
McDuffie	Southern	Augusta
McIntosh	Southern	Brunswick (Savannah)
Meriwether	Northern	Newnan
Miller	Middle	Albany/Americus (Macon)
Mitchell	Middle	Albany/Americus (Macon)
Monroe	Middle	Macon
Montgomery	Southern	Dublin (Augusta)
Morgan	Middle	Athens (Macon)
Murray	Northern	Rome
Muscogee	Middle	Columbus
Newton	Northern	Atlanta
Oconee	Middle	Athens (Macon)
Oglethorpe	Middle	Athens (Macon)
Paulding	Northern	Rome
Peach	Middle	Macon
Pickens	Northern	Gainesville

Pierce	Southern	Waycross (Savannah)
Pike	Northern	Newnan
Polk	Northern	Rome
Pulaski	Middle	Macon
Putnam	Middle	Macon
Quitman	Middle	Columbus
Rabun	Northern	Gainesville
Randolph	Middle	Columbus
Richmond	Southern	Augusta
Rockdale	Northern	Atlanta
Schley	Middle	Albany/Americus (Macon)
Screven	Southern	Statesboro (Augusta)
Seminole	Middle	Thomasville (Columbus)
Spalding	Northern	Newnan
Stephens	Northern	Gainesville
Stewart	Middle	Columbus
Sumter	Middle	Albany/Americus (Macon)
Talbot	Middle	Columbus
Taliaferro	Southern	Augusta
Tattnall	Southern	Statesboro (Augusta)
Taylor	Middle	Columbus
Telfair	Southern	Dublin (Augusta)
Terrell	Middle	Albany/Americus (Macon)
Thomas	Middle	Thomasville (Columbus)

Tift	Middle	Valdosta (Columbus)
Toombs	Southern	Statesboro (Augusta)
Towns	Northern	Gainesville
Treutlen	Southern	Dublin (Augusta)
Troup	Northern	Newnan
Turner	Middle	Albany/Americus (Macon)
Twiggs	Middle	Macon
Union	Northern	Gainesville
Upson	Middle	Macon
Walker	Northern	Rome
Walton	Middle	Athens (Macon)
Ware	Southern	Waycross (Savannah)
Warren	Southern	Augusta
Washington	Middle	Macon
Wayne	Southern	Brunswick (Savannah)
Webster	Middle	Albany/Americus (Macon)
Wheeler	Southern	Dublin (Augusta)
White	Northern	Gainesville
Whitfield	Northern	Rome
Wilcox	Middle	Macon
Wilkes	Southern	Augusta
Wilkinson	Middle	Macon
Worth	Middle	Albany/Americus (Macon)

Standards for Federal Courts: The search fee is $20.00 per item (one party name or case number). Certification fee is $7.00 per document. Copy fee is $.50 per page. All fees standard unless noted in profile. Mail Search: always enclose a stamped self addressed envelope unless otherwise noted. Most courts accept fax requests or will suggest a copying/search vendor. Before releasing records, all courts require prepayment unless noted in profile.

Open records are located at the court unless otherwise noted. District courts index by defendant and plaintiff as well as by case number. Bankruptcy courts usually index by debtor and case number. While most courts now have their indexes on computer, many still maintain index card files as well.

The universal PACER sign-up number is 800-676-6856. Find PACER and the Party/Case Index on the Web at http://pacer.psc.uscourts.gov. PACER dial-up access is $.60 per minute. Also, courts offering internet access via RACER, PACER, Web-PACER or the new CM-ECF charge $.07 per page fee unless noted as free.

US District Court

Middle District of Georgia

Albany/Americus Division PO Box 1906, Albany, GA 31702 (courier address: Room 106, 345 Broad Ave, Albany, 31701), 229-430-8432, Fax: 229-430-8538. www.gamd.uscourts.gov

Counties: Baker, Ben Hill, Calhoun, Crisp, Dougherty, Early, Lee, Miller, Mitchell, Schley, Sumter, Terrell, Turner, Webster, Worth. Ben Hill and Crisp were transfered from the Macon Division as of October 1, 1997.

Indexing & Storage: New cases available in the index immediately after filing date. Records are on the computer from 1991. Prior records are indexed on index cards. District wide searches are available from any division in district for files after 1/91.

Fee & Payment: Payment may be made by money order, cashier check, in-state business check. Personal checks not accepted. Payee: Clerk USDC.

Phone Search: Only docket information available.

In Person Search: Fee charged if court conducts your in person search for you.

PACER: PACER is available online at http://pacer.gamd.uscourts.gov. Case records go back to January 1991. Records never purged. New records are online after 1-2 days.

Athens Division PO Box 1106, Athens, GA 30603 (courier address: 115 E Hancock Ave, Athens, GA 30601), 706-227-1094, Fax: 706-546-2190. www.gamd.uscourts.gov

Counties: Clarke, Elbert, Franklin, Greene, Hart, Madison, Morgan, Oconee, Oglethorpe, Walton. Closed cases before April 1997 are located in the Macon Division.

Indexing & Storage: New cases available in the index 2 days after filing date.

Fee & Payment: Payment may be made by money order, cashier check, business check. Personal checks not accepted. Payee: U.S. District Court.

Phone Search: No searching by telephone.

In Person Search: Fee charged if court conducts your in person search for you. Public access terminal available.

PACER: PACER is available online at http://pacer.gamd.uscourts.gov. Case records go back to January 1991. Records never purged. New records are online after 1-2 days.

Columbus Division PO Box 124, Columbus, GA 31902 (courier address: Room 216, 120 12th St, Columbus, GA 31901), 706-649-7816. www.gamd.uscourts.gov

Counties: Chattahoochee, Clay, Harris, Marion, Muscogee, Quitman, Randolph, Stewart, Talbot, Taylor.

Indexing & Storage: New cases available in the index immediately after filing date.

Fee & Payment: Payment may be made by money order, cashier check, business check. Personal checks are not accepted. Payee: Clerk U.S. Courts.

Phone Search: No searching by telephone. Only docket information available by phone.

In Person Search: Fee charged if court conducts your in person search for you.

PACER: PACER is available online at http://pacer.gamd.uscourts.gov. Case records go back to January 1991. Records never purged. New records are online after 1-2 days.

Macon Division PO Box 128, Macon, GA 31202-0128 (courier address: 475 Mulberry, Suite 216, Macon, GA 31201), 912-752-3497, Fax: 912-752-3496. www.gamd.uscourts.gov

Counties: Baldwin, Ben Hill, Bibb, Bleckley, Butts, Crawford, Crisp, Dooly, Hancock, Houston, Jasper, Jones, Lamar, Macon, Monroe, Peach, Pulaski, Putnam, Twiggs, Upson, Washington,

Wilcox, Wilkinson.Athens Division cases closed before April 1997 are also located here.

Indexing & Storage: New cases available in the index immediately after filing date. Records after 1/91 can be searched at any court in this district.

Fee & Payment: Payment may be made by money order, cashier check, business check. Personal checks are not accepted. Payee: U.S. Courts. Will fax results for $3.00 per page.

Phone Search: Only docket information available by phone. Will fax results for $3.00 per page.

In Person Search: Fee charged if court conducts your in person search for you.

PACER: PACER is available online at http://pacer.gamd.uscourts.gov. Case records go back to January 1991. Records never purged. New records are online after 1-2 days.

Thomasville Division c/o Valdosta Division, PO Box 68, Valdosta, GA 31601 (courier address: Room 212, 401 N Patterson, Valdosta, GA 31603), 912-226-3651. www.gamd.uscourts.gov

Counties: Brooks, Colquitt, Decatur, Grady, Seminole, Thomas.

Indexing & Storage: Cases indexed by as well as by case number. New cases available in the index after filing date. Open records are located at the Valdosta Division.

Fee & Payment: Payment may be made by money order, cashier check. Business checks are not accepted. Personal checks are not accepted.

Phone Search: No searching by telephone.

In Person Search: Permitted.

PACER: PACER is available online at http://pacer.gamd.uscourts.gov. Case records go back to January 1991. Records never purged. New records are online after 1-2 days.

Valdosta Division PO Box 68, Valdosta, GA 31603 (courier address: Room 212, 401 N Patterson, Valdosta, GA 31601), 912-242-3616, Fax: 912-244-9547. www.gamd.uscourts.gov

Counties: Berrien, Clinch, Cook, Echols, Irwin, Lanier, Lowndes, Tift.

Indexing & Storage: New cases available in the index immediately after filing date.

Fee & Payment: Payment may be made by money order, cashier check, business check. Personal checks are not accepted. Payee: U.S. Courts.

Phone Search: Docket information is available.

Mail Search: A SASE not required.

In Person Search: Fee charged if court conducts your in person search for you.

PACER: PACER is available online at http://pacer.gamd.uscourts.gov. Case records go back to January 1991. Records never purged. New records are online after 1-2 days.

U.S. Bankruptcy Court

Middle District of Georgia

Columbus Division PO Box 2147, Columbus, GA 31902 (courier: 901 Front Ave, 1 Arsenal Pl, Columbus, GA 31902), 706-649-7837, Fax: 706-649-7845. www.gamb.uscourts.gov

Counties: Berrien, Brooks, Chattahoochee, Clay, Clinch, Colquitt, Cook, Decatur, Echols, Grady, Harris, Irwin, Lanier, Lowndes, Marion, Muscogee, Quitman, Randolph, Seminole, Stewart,Talbot, Taylor, Thomas, TiftThis court has records for the Thomasville and Valdosta branches, also Chapter 11 & 12 records for the Albany branch.

Indexing & Storage: Cases indexed by debtor as well as by case number. New cases available in the index immediately after filing date. An alias name of the debtor may be required to search for records.

Fee & Payment: Payment may be made by money order, cashier check, business check. Personal checks are not accepted. Payee: Clerk, U.S. Bankruptcy Court.

Phone Search: Docket information is available by phone. Automated voice case information service (VCIS) is available. Call VCIS at 800-211-3015 or 912-752-8183.

In Person Search: Fee charged if court conducts your in person search for you.

PACER: PACER is available online at http://pacer.gamb.uscourts.gov. Case records go back to March 1990 (some back to 1985). Records purged except last 12 months. New civil records are online after 1 day.

Electronic Filing: Currently in the process of implementing CM/ECF.

Macon Division PO Box 1957, Macon, GA 31201 (courier address: 433 Cherry St, Macon, GA 31202), 478-752-3506, Fax: 478-752-8157. www.gamb.uscourts.gov

Counties: Baldwin, Baker, Ben Hill, Bibb, Bleckley, Butts, Calhoun, Clarke, Crawford, Crisp, Dooly, Dougherty, Early, Elbert, Franklin, Greene, Hancock, Hart, Houston, Jasper, Jones, Lamar, Lee, Macon, Madison, Miller, Mitchell, Monroe, Morgan, Oconee, Oglethorpe,Peach, Pulaski, Putnam, Schley, Sumter, Terrell, Turner, Twiggs, Upson, Walton, Washington, Webster, Wilcox, Wilkinson, WorthThis court has records for the Athens branch as well as Chapter 7 & 13 records from the Albany branch.

Indexing & Storage: Cases indexed by debtor and creditors as well as by case number. New cases available in the index 1-2 days after filing date. Any alias name of the debtor may be required to search for records.

Fee & Payment: Payment may be made by money order, cashier check, business check. Personal checks are not accepted. Payee: Clerk, U.S. Bankruptcy Court.

Phone Search: This court will only search for basic information by phone and limits the number of searches to 3 per phone call. Automated voice case information service (VCIS) is available. Call VCIS at 800-211-3015 or 478-752-8183.

In Person Search: Fee charged if court conducts your in person search for you.

PACER: PACER is available online at http://pacer.gamb.uscourts.gov. Case records go back to March 1990 (some back to 1985). Records purged except last 12 months. New civil records are online after 1 day.

Electronic Filing: Currently in the process of implementing CM/ECF.

U.S. District Court

Northern District of Georgia

Atlanta Division 2211 U.S. Courthouse, 75 Spring St SW, Atlanta, GA 30303-3361 (courier address: Use mail address for courier delivery) 404-215-1660. www.gand.uscourts.gov

Counties: Cherokee, Clayton, Cobb, De Kalb, Douglas, Fulton, Gwinnett, Henry, Newton, Rockdale.

Indexing & Storage: New cases available in the index 1 day after filing date.

Fee & Payment: Payment may be made by money order, cashier check. Business checks are not accepted. Personal checks are not accepted. Payee: Clerk, U.S. District Court.

Phone Search: Only docket information available by phone.

Mail Search: A SASE not required.

In Person Search: Fee charged if court conducts your in person search for you.

PACER: PACER is available online at http://pacer.gand.uscourts.gov. Document images available. Records purged on a varied schedule. New records are online after 1 day.

Electronic Filing: Electronic filing information online at https://ecf.gand.uscourts.gov

Gainesville Division Federal Bldg, Room 201, 121 Spring St SE, Gainesville, GA 30501 (courier address: Use mail address for courier delivery) 678-450-2760. www.gand.uscourts.gov

Counties: Banks, Barrow, Dawson, Fannin, Forsyth, Gilmer, Habersham, Hall, Jackson, Lumpkin, Pickens, Rabun, Stephens, Towns, Union, White.

Indexing & Storage: New cases available in the index 24 hours after filing date.

Fee & Payment: Payment may be made by money order. Business checks are not accepted. Personal checks are not accepted. The court will only accept U.S. Postal money orders, law firm checks and cashier's checks. Payee: Clerk, U.S. District Court.

Phone Search: No searching by telephone.

In Person Search: Fee charged if court conducts your in person search for you.

PACER: PACER is available online at http://pacer.gand.uscourts.gov. Document images available. Records purged on a varied schedule. New records are online after 1 day.

Electronic Filing: Electronic filing information online at https://ecf.gand.uscourts.gov

Newnan Division PO Box 939, Newnan, GA 30264 (courier: 18 Greenville St, #352, Newnan, 30263), 678-423-3060. www.gand.uscourts.gov

Counties: Carroll, Coweta, Fayette, Haralson, Heard, Meriwether, Pike, Spalding, Troup.

Indexing & Storage: New cases available in the index immediately after filing date.

Fee & Payment: Payment may be made by money order, cashier check. Business checks are not accepted. Personal checks are not accepted. Only attorney firm checks will be accepted. Payee: Clerk, U.S. District Court.

Phone Search: Only docket information available.

Mail Search: A SASE not required.

In Person Search: Fee charged if court conducts your in person search for you.

PACER: PACER is available online at http://pacer.gand.uscourts.gov. Document images available. Records purged on a varied schedule. New records are online after 1 day.

Electronic Filing: Electronic filing information online at https://ecf.gand.uscourts.gov

Rome Division PO Box 1186, Rome, GA 30162-1186 (courier address: 600 E 1st St, Room 304, Rome, GA 30161), 706-291-5629. www.gand.uscourts.gov

Counties: Bartow, Catoosa, Chattooga, Dade, Floyd, Gordon, Murray, Paulding, Polk, Walker, Whitfield.

Indexing & Storage: New cases available in the index immediately after filing date. Records are also indexed on microfiche. Only records prior to 1978 are on index cards.

Fee & Payment: Payment may be made by money order, cashier check. Business checks are not accepted. Personal checks are not accepted. Attorney checks also accepted. Payee: Clerk, U.S. District Court.

Phone Search: Only docket information showing if a suit has been filed, date of filing, and if case is pending or closed will be released over the phone.

In Person Search: Fee charged if court conducts your in person search for you.

PACER: PACER is available online at http://pacer.gand.uscourts.gov. Document images availableRecords purged on a varied schedule. New records are online after 1 day.

Electronic Filing: Electronic filing information online at https://ecf.gand.uscourts.gov

U.S. Bankruptcy Court

Northern District of Georgia

Atlanta Division 1340 U.S. Courthouse, 75 Spring St SW, Atlanta, GA 30303-3361 (courier address: Use mail address for courier delivery) 404-215-1000. www.ganb.uscourts.gov

Counties: Cherokee, Clayton, Cobb, DeKalb, Douglas, Fulton, Gwinnett, Henry, Newton, Rockdale.

Indexing & Storage: Cases indexed by debtor as well as by case number. New cases available in the index 1-2 days after filing date. Records are also indexed on microfiche.

Fee & Payment: Payment may be made by money order, cashier check, business check. Personal checks are not accepted. Debtor's checks are not accepted. Payee: Clerk, U.S. Bankruptcy Court.

Phone Search: Docket information is available by phone. Automated voice case information service (VCIS) is available. Call VCIS at 800-510-8284 or 404-730-2866.

In Person Search: Permitted.

PACER: Court uses new CM/ECF system for PACER. Case records go back to August 1986. Records never purged. New civil records are online after 2 days.

Electronic Filing: Electronic filing information online at http://ecf.ganb.uscourts.gov

Gainesville Division 121 Spring St SE, Room 120, Gainesville, GA 30501 (courier address: Use mail address for courier delivery) 678-450-2700. www.ganb.uscourts.gov

Counties: Banks, Barrow, Dawson, Fannin, Forsyth, Gilmer, Habersham, Hall, Jackson, Lumpkin, Pickens, Rabun, Stephens, Towns, Union, White.

Indexing & Storage: Cases indexed by debtor as well as by case number. New cases available in the index 1-2 days after filing date. This court maintains index cards on older cases.

Fee & Payment: Payment may be made by money order, cashier check, personal check. Debtors checks not accepted. Payee: Clerk, U.S. Bankruptcy Court.

Phone Search: Docket information available by phone. Automated voice case information service (VCIS) is available. Call VCIS at 800-510-8284 or 404-730-2866.

In Person Search: Permitted.

PACER: Court uses new CM/ECF system for PACER. Case records go back to August 1986. Records never purged. New civil records are online after 2 days.

Electronic Filing: Electronic filing information online at http://ecf.ganb.uscourts.gov

Newnan Division Clerk, PO Box 2328, Newnan, GA 30264 (courier address: Room 220, 18 Greenville St, Newnan, GA 30263), 678-423-3000. www.ganb.uscourts.gov

Counties: Carroll, Coweta, Fayette, Haralson, Heard, Meriwether, Pike, Spalding, Troup.

Indexing & Storage: Cases indexed by debtor as well as by case number. New cases available in the index 1 day after filing date. Records are also indexed on microfiche.

Fee & Payment: Payment may be made by money order, cashier check, personal check. Debtor's checks are not accepted. Payee: Clerk, U.S. Bankruptcy Court.

Phone Search: Only docket information available by phone. The debtor's address and social security number will not be released. There is no charge if a case number is provided. Automated voice case information service (VCIS) is available. Call VCIS at 800-510-8284 or 404-730-2866.

Mail Search: A SASE not required.

In Person Search: Permitted.

PACER: Court uses new CM/ECF system for PACER. Case records go back to August 1986. Records never purged. New civil records are online after 2 days.

Electronic Filing: Electronic filing information online at http://ecf.ganb.uscourts.gov

Rome Division Clerk, 600 E 1st St, Room 339, Rome, GA 30161-3187 (courier address: Use mail address for courier delivery) 706-291-5639. www.ganb.uscourts.gov

Counties: Bartow, Catoosa, Chattooga, Dade, Floyd, Gordon, Murray, Paulding, Polk, Walker, Whitfield.

Indexing & Storage: Cases indexed by debtor as well as by case number. New cases available in the index 24 hours after filing date.

Fee & Payment: Payment may be made by money order, cashier check, personal check. Payee: Clerk, U.S. Bankruptcy Court.

Phone Search: Docket information is available by phone. Automated voice case information service (VCIS) is available. Call VCIS at 800-510-8284 or 404-730-2866.

In Person Search: Fee charged if court conducts your in person search for you.

PACER: Court uses new CM/ECF system for PACER. Case records go back to August 1986. Records never purged. New civil records are online after 2 days.

Electronic Filing: Electronic filing information online at http://ecf.ganb.uscourts.gov

U.S. District Court

Southern District of Georgia

Augusta Division PO Box 1130, Augusta, GA 30903 (courier address: Use mail address for courier delivery., 500 E Ford St, First Floor,), 706-849-4400. www.gasd.uscourts.gov

Counties: Burke, Columbia, Dodge, Glascock, Jefferson, Johnson, Laurens, Lincoln, McDuffie, Montgomery, Richmond, Taliaferro, Telfair, Treutlen, Warren, Wheeler, Wilkes.

Indexing & Storage: New cases available in the index immediately after filing date. Records are alphabetically indexed and stored by chronological case number order. Holds records for the unstaffed Dublin Divison.

Payment: Payment may be made by money order, cashier check, personal check. Payee: U.S. Courts.

Phone Search: Docket information available.

In Person Search: Fee charged if court conducts your in person search for you.

PACER: PACER is available online at http://pacer.gasd.uscourts.gov. Document images available. New records are online after 1 day.

Brunswick Division PO Box 1636, Brunswick, GA 31521 (courier address: Room 220, 801 Glouchester St, Brunswick, GA 31520), 912-280-1330. www.gasd.uscourts.gov

Counties: Appling, Camden, Glynn, Jeff Davis, Long, McIntosh, Wayne.

Indexing & Storage: New cases available in the index immediately after filing date. The records from the last 1 1/2 years are indexed on computer. Prior records are indexed on microfiche.

Fee & Payment: Payment may be made by money order, cashier check, personal check. Payee: Clerk, U.S. District Court.

Phone Search: Only docket information available.

In Person Search: Fee charged if court conducts your in person search for you.

PACER: PACER is available online at http://pacer.gasd.uscourts.gov. Document images available. New records are online after 1 day.

Savannah Division PO Box 8286, Savannah, GA 31412 (courier address: Room 306, 125 Bull St, Savannah, GA 31401), 912-650-4020, Fax: 912-650-4030. www.gasd.uscourts.gov

Counties: Atkinson, Bacon, Bulloch, Brantley, Bryan, Candler, Charlton, Chatham, Coffee, Effingham, Emanuel, Evans, Jenkins, Liberty, Pierce, Screven, Tattnall, Toombs, Ware.

Indexing & Storage: New cases available in the index immediately after filing date. Holds records for unstaffed Statesboro and Waycross Divisons. Records have been indexed on computer from 1992. Prior records are indexed on microfiche.

Fee & Payment: Payment may be made by money order, cashier check, personal check. Payee: Clerk, U.S. District Court.

Phone Search: No searching by telephone. Only docket information available by phone.

Mail Search: A SASE not required.

In Person Search: Fee charged if court conducts your in person search for you.

PACER: PACER is available online at http://pacer.gasd.uscourts.gov. Document images available. New records are online after 1 day.

U.S. Bankruptcy Court
Southern District of Georgia

Augusta Division PO Box 1487, Augusta, GA 30903 (courier address: 933 Broad St - 3rd Floor, Augusta, GA 30901), 706-724-2421. www.gas.uscourts.gov

Counties: Bulloch, Burke, Candler, Columbia, Dodge, Emanuel, Evans, Glascock, Jefferson, Jenkins, Johnson, Laurens, Lincoln, McDuffie, Montgomery, Richmond, Screven, Taliaferro, Tattnall, Telfair, Toombs, Treutlen, Warren, Wheeler, Wilkes.

Indexing & Storage: Cases indexed by debtor as well as by case number. New cases available in the index 24 hours after filing date. District wide searches are available for information from August 1986 from this court. This court handles files for the Statesboro and Dublin divisions as well as the Augusta files.

Fee & Payment: Payment may be made by money order, cashier check, business check. Personal checks are not accepted. Payee: Clerk, U.S. Bankruptcy Court.

Phone Search: If case number is provided over the phone, all docket information will be released.

In Person Search: Fee charged if court conducts your in person search for you.

PACER: PACER is available online at http://pacer.gasb.uscourts.gov. This appears to be a homogenization of RACER and PACER; the fee is $.07 per page. Document images available. Records purged annually.

Other Online Access: Court now participates in the U.S. party case index.

Savannah Division PO Box 8347, Savannah, GA 31412 (courier address: Room 213, 125 Bull St, Savannah, GA 31412), 912-650-4100. www.gas.uscourts.gov

Counties: Appling, Atkinson, Bacon, Brantley, Bryan, Camden, Charlton, Chatham, Coffee, Effingham, Glynn, Jeff Davis, Liberty, Long, McIntosh, Pierce, Ware, Wayne.

Indexing & Storage: Cases indexed by debtor as well as by case number. New cases available in the index immediately after filing date. Cases are also indexed by Social Security number. District wide searches are available for information from August 1, 1985 at this court. This court handles files for the Waycross and Brunswick divisions as well as the Savannah files.

Fee & Payment: Payment may be made by money order, cashier check, business check. Personal checks are not accepted. Payee: Clerk, U.S. Bankruptcy Court.

Phone Search: Phone search is limited to information on computer.

Mail Search: A SASE not required.

In Person Search: Fee charged if court conducts your in person search for you.

PACER: PACER is available online at http://pacer.gasb.uscourts.gov. This appears to be a homogenization of RACER and PACER; the fee is $.07 per page. Document images available. Records purged every six months. New civil records are online after 1 day.

Other Online Access: Court now participates in the U.S. party case index.

Georgia County Courts

Court	Jurisdiction	No. of Courts	How Organized
Superior Courts*	General	100	49 Circuits
State Courts*	Limited	69	69 Counties
Combined Courts*		43	
Magistrate Courts*	Limited	159	By County
Combined Superior/ Magistrate Court*		17	
Civil Courts*	Limited	2	Bibb, Richmond
County Recorder's Courts	Limited	4	Chatham, DeKalb, Gwinnett, Muscogee
Municipal Courts	Municipal	474	Includes City Court of Atlanta
Probate Courts*	Probate	159	By County
Juvenile Courts	Special	159	By County

* Profiled in this Sourcebook.

Court	CIVIL								
	Tort	Contract	Real Estate	Min. Claim	Max. Claim	Small Claims	Estate	Eviction	Domestic Relations
Superior Courts*	X	X	X	$0	No Max	X		X	X
State Courts*	X	X		$0	No Max	X		X	
Combined Courts*	X	X		$0	No Max	$0		X	
Magistrate Courts*	X	X		$0	$15,000	$15,000		X	
Combined Superior/ Magistrate Court*									
Civil Courts*	X	X		$0	$7500	$7500			
Recorder's Courts									
Municipal Courts									
Probate Courts*							X		
Juvenile Courts									

Court	CRIMINAL				
	Felony	Misdemeanor	DWI/DUI	Preliminary Hearing	Juvenile
Superior Courts*	X	X	X	X	
State Courts*		X	X	X	
Combined Courts*				X	
Magistrate Courts*		X		X	
Combined Superior/ Magistrate Court*			X	X	
Civil Courts*				X	
Recorder's Courts		X	X	X	
Municipal Courts		X	X	X	
Probate Courts*		X	X	X	
Juvenile Courts					X

ADMINISTRATION   Court Administrator, 244 Washington St SW, Suite 550, Atlanta, GA, 30334; 404-656-5171, Fax:

404-651-6449. www.georgiacourts.org/aoc/index.html

COURT STRUCTURE

Georgia's Superior Courts are arranged in 49 circuits of general jurisdiction, and these assume the role of a State Court if the county does not have one. The 69 State Courts, like Superior Courts, can conduct jury trials, but are limited jurisidiction. Each county has a Probate, a Juvenile, and a Magistrate Court; the latter has jurisdiction over civil actions under $15,000, also one type of misdemeanor related to passing bad checks.

Magistrate Courts also issue arrest warrants and set bond on all felonies. Magistrate Courts also have jurisdiction for bad checks, arrest warrants, preliminary hearings, and county ordinance violations.

Probate courts can, in certain cases, issue search and arrest warrants, and hear miscellaneous misdemeanors.

ONLINE ACCESS

Supreme Court docket information and opinions are available from the web. A certified copy of a Supreme Court Opinion can be purchased online for $5.00 at www2.state.ga.us/Courts/Supreme/main_pp.html. A limited number of courts offer Internet access to court records, but there is no online access available statewide, although statewide access is being planned.

ADDITIONAL INFORMATION

In many Georgia counties the courts will not perform criminal record searches, and, in many cases, will not do civil record searches. An in person search or the use of a record retriever is advised.

The Georgia Crime Information Center is the felony criminal history state repository.

Magistrate Courts also have jurisdiction for bad checks, arrest warrants, preliminary hearings, and county ordinance violations.

Appling County

Superior & State Court PO Box 269, 38 S. Main St., Baxley, GA 31513; 912-367-8126; Fax: 912-367-8180. Hours: 8AM-5PM (EST). *Felony, Misdemeanor, Civil.*

Civil Records: Access: In person only. Visitors must perform in person searches for themselves. No search fee. Required to search: name, years to search. Civil cases indexed by defendant, plaintiff. Civil records on docket books back to 1800s.

Criminal Records: Access: In person only. Visitors must perform in person searches for themselves. No search fee. Required to search: name, years to search, DOB; also helpful: SSN, race, sex. Criminal records on docket books back to 1800s.

General Information: No juvenile, adoption, sealed, sexual, mental health or expunged records released. Copy fee: $.25 for first page, $.10 each add'l. Cert fee: $2.50 plus $.50 per page after first. Payee: Court Clerk. Personal checks accepted.

Magistrate Court Box 366, Baxley, GA 31515; 912-367-8116; 367-8117; Fax: 912-367-8182. Hours: 8:30AM-5PM (EST). *Civil Actions Under $15,000, Eviction, Small Claims.* **Probate Court** 36 S Main St, #B, Appling County Courthouse, Baxley, GA 31513; 912-367-8114; Fax: 912-367-8166. Hours: 8:30AM-5PM (EST). *Probate.*

Atkinson County

Superior Court PO Box 6, South Main, Courthouse Sq, Pearson, GA 31642; 912-422-3343; Fax: 912-422-7025. Hours: 8AM-5PM (EST). *Felony, Misdemeanor, Civil.*

Civil Records: Access: In person only. Visitors must perform in person searches for themselves. No search fee. Required to search: name, years to search. Civil cases indexed by defendant. Civil records in docket books back to 1919.

Criminal Records: Access: In person only. Visitors must perform in person searches for themselves. No search fee. Required to search: name, years to search. Criminal records in docket books back to 1919.

General Information: Public Access terminal is available. No juvenile, adoption, sealed, sexual, mental health or expunged records released. Copy fee: $.25 per page. Cert fee: $2.50 plus $.50 per page after

first. Payee: Clerk of Superior Court. Personal checks accepted. Prepayment required.

Magistrate Court PO Box 674, Pearson, GA 31642; 912-422-7158; Fax: 912-422-7989. Hours: 8AM-5PM (EST). *Civil Actions Under $15,000, Eviction, Small Claims.*

Probate Court PO Box 855, Pearson, GA 31642; 912-422-3552; Fax: 912-422-7842. Hours: 8AM-5PM (EST). *Probate.*

Bacon County

Superior Court PO Box 376, Alma, GA 31510; 912-632-4915; Probate phone: 91-632-7661. Hours: 9AM-5PM (EST). *Felony, Misdemeanor, Civil.*

Civil Records: Access: Mail, in person. Both court and visitors may perform in person searches. No search fee. Required to search: name, years to search. Civil cases indexed by defendant, plaintiff. Civil records on index from 1970, archived to 1918, computerized since 2000.

Criminal Records: Access: Mail, in person. Both court and visitors may perform in person searches. No search fee. Required to search: name, years to search, DOB; also helpful: SSN, race, sex. Criminal records on index from 1970, archived to 1918, computerized since 2000.

General Information: Public Access terminal is available. No juvenile, adoption, sealed, sexual, mental health, expunged or first offender records released. Will fax results. Copy fee: $.25 per page. Cert fee: $2.50 plus $.50 per page after first. Payee: Clerk of Superior Court. Personal checks accepted. Prepayment required. Mail requests: SASE required. Mail turnaround time 1 week.

Magistrate Court Box 389, Alma, GA 31510; 912-632-5961; Fax: 912-632-7662. Hours: 9AM-5PM (EST). *Civil Actions Under $15,000, Eviction, Small Claims, Probate.*

Probate Court PO Box 389, Alma, GA 31510; 912-632-7661; Fax: 912-632-7662. Hours: 9AM-5PM (EST). *Probate.*

Baker County

Superior Court PO Box 10, Governmental Bldg, Newton, GA 39870; 229-734-3004; Fax: 229-734-7770. Hours: 9AM-5PM (EST). *Felony, Misdemeanor, Civil.*

Civil Records: Access: In person only. Visitors must perform in person searches for themselves. No search fee. Required to search: name, years to search. Civil cases indexed by defendant. Civil records on index from 1850.

Criminal Records: Access: In person only. Visitors must perform in person searches for themselves. No search fee. Required to search: name, years to search, DOB; also helpful: SSN, race, sex. Criminal records on index from 1850.

General Information: No juvenile, adoption, sealed, sexual or expunged records released. Copy fee: $.25 per page. Cert fee: $2.50 plus $.50 per page after first. Payee: Court Clerk. Personal checks accepted. Prepayment required.

Magistrate Court Box 548, Newton, GA 39870; 229-734-3009; Fax: 229-734-8822. Hours: 9AM-5PM (EST). *Civil Actions Under $15,000, Eviction, Small Claims.*

Probate Court PO Box 548, Newton, GA 39870; 229-734-3007; Fax: 229-734-8822. Hours: 9AM-5PM M-W & F; 9AM-Noon Th (EST). *Probate.* https://www.gaprobate.org/counties/baker/index.html

Baldwin County

Superior & State Court PO Drawer 987, Milledgeville, GA 31059-0987; 478-445-4007; Fax: 478-445-1404. Hours: 8:30AM-5PM (EST). *Felony, Misdemeanor, Civil.*

Civil Records: Access: In person only. Visitors must perform in person searches for themselves. No search fee. Required to search: name, years to search. Civil cases indexed by defendant, plaintiff. Civil records on docket from 1861; on computer back to 1996.

Criminal Records: Access: In person only. Visitors must perform in person searches for themselves. No search fee. Required to search: name, years to search. Criminal records on docket from 1861; on computer back to 1996.

General Information: Public Access terminal is available. No juvenile, adoption, sealed, sexual, mental health or expunged records released. Copy fee: $.25 per page. Cert fee: $2.50 plus $.50 per page after first. Personal checks accepted. Prepayment required.

Magistrate Court 121 N Wilkenson, #107, Milledgeville, GA 31061; 478-445-4446; Fax: 478-445-5918. Hours: 8:30AM-5PM (EST). *Civil Actions Under $15,000, Eviction, Small Claims.*

Probate Court 121 N Wilkinson St, #109, Milledgeville, GA 31061; 478-445-4807; Fax: 478-445-5178. Hours: 8:30AM-5PM (EST). *Probate.* https://www.gaprobate.org/counties/baldwin/index.html

Banks County

Superior Court PO Box 337, 144 Yorah Homer Road, Homer, GA 30547; 706-677-6240; Fax: 706-677-6294. Hours: 8:00AM-5PM (EST). *Felony, Misdemeanor, Civil.*
Civil Records: Access: In person only. Visitors must perform in person searches for themselves. No search fee. Required to search: name, years to search. Civil cases indexed by defendant, plaintiff. Civil records on docket from 1960.
Criminal Records: Access: In person only. Visitors must perform in person searches for themselves. No search fee. Required to search: name, years to search, DOB, signed release; also helpful: SSN, race, sex. Criminal records on docket from 1960.
General Information: Public Access terminal is available. No juvenile, adoption, sealed, sexual, mental health or expunged records released. Copy fee: $.25 per page. Cert fee: $3.75. Payee: Clerk of Superior Court. Personal checks accepted. Prepayment required.

Magistrate Court 144 Yonah Homer Rd 310, Homer, GA 30547-2614; 706-677-6270; Fax: 706-677-6215. Hours: 8:30AM-5PM (EST). *Civil Actions Under $15,000, Eviction, Small Claims.*

Probate Court 144 Yonah;Homer Rd., Homer, GA 30547; 706-677-6250; Fax: 706-677-2337. Hours: 8AM-5PM (EST). *Probate.* https://www.gaprobate.org/counties/banks/index.html

Barrow County

Superior Court PO Box 1280, Winder, GA 30680; 770-307-3035; Fax: 770-867-4800. Hours: 8AM-5PM (EST). *Felony, Misdemeanor, Civil.*
Civil Records: Access: In person only. Visitors must perform in person searches for themselves. No search fee. Required to search: name, years to search. Civil cases indexed by defendant, plaintiff. Civil records on computer from 1990, docket from 1915.
Criminal Records: Access: In person only. Visitors must perform in person searches for themselves. No search fee. Required to search: name, years to search, DOB; also helpful: SSN, race, sex. Criminal records on computer from 1990, docket from 1915.
General Information: Public Access terminal is available. No juvenile, adoption, sealed, sexual, mental health or expunged records released. Copy fee: $.25 per page. Cert fee: $2.50 plus $.50 per page after first. Payee: Clerk of Superior Court. Business checks accepted. Prepayment required.

Magistrate Court 30 N Broad St, #227, Winder, GA 30680; 770-307-3050; Fax: 770-868-1440. Hours: 8AM-5PM (EST). *Civil Actions Under $15,000, Eviction, Small Claims.*

Probate Court Barrow County Courthouse, 30 N Broad St, Winder, GA 30680; 770-307-3045; Fax: 770-307-4470. Hours: 8AM-5PM (EST). *Probate.* https://www.gaprobate.org/counties/barrow/index.html

Bartow County

Superior Court 135 W Cherokee, #233, Cartersville, GA 30120; 770-387-5025; Fax: 770-387-5611. Hours: 8AM-5PM (EST). *Felony, Misdemeanor, Civil.*
Civil Records: Access: In person only. Visitors must perform in person searches for themselves. No search fee. Required to search: name, years to search. Civil cases indexed by defendant, plaintiff. Civil records on computer from 9/92, on books from 1900s.
Criminal Records: Access: In person only. Visitors must perform in person searches for themselves. No search fee. Required to search: name, years to search, address, DOB, SSN, signed release. Criminal records on computer for 10 years, prior on books.
General Information: No juvenile, adoptions or sealed records released. Copy fee: $.25 per page. Cert fee: $2.50 plus $.25 each add'l page. Payee: Clerk of Superior Court. Personal checks accepted. Prepayment required.

Magistrate Court 135 W Cherokee Ave, #225, Cartersville, GA 30120; 770-387-5070; Fax: 770-387-5073. Hours: 7AM-5:30PM (EST). *Civil Actions Under $15,000, Eviction, Small Claims, Misdemeanors.*

Probate Court 135 W Cherokee, #243A, Cartersville, GA 30120; 770-387-5075; Fax: 770-387-5074. Hours: 8AM-5PM (EST). *Probate.* https://www.gaprobate.org/counties/bartow/index.html

Ben Hill County

Superior Court PO Box 1104, 115 S Sheridan, Fitzgerald, GA 31750; 229-426-5135; Fax: 229-426-5487. Hours: 8:30AM-4:30PM (EST). *Felony, Misdemeanor, Civil.*
Civil Records: Access: In person only. Visitors must perform in person searches for themselves. No search fee. Required to search: name, years to search. Civil cases indexed by defendant. Civil records on computer from 1994, archived from 1907, docket 1907.
Criminal Records: Access: In person only. Visitors must perform in person searches for themselves. No search fee. Required to search: name, years to search, signed release; also helpful: DOB, SSN. Criminal records on computer from 1994, archived from 1907, docket 1907.
General Information: Public Access terminal is available. No juvenile, adoption, sealed, sexual, mental health or expunged records released. Copy fee: $.25 per page; $1.00 per page if mailed. Cert fee: $2.00 plus $.50 per page. Payee: Clerk. Personal checks accepted. Prepayment required.

Magistrate Court Box 1163, Fitzgerald, GA 31750; 229-426-5140; Fax: 229-426-5123. Hours: 8:30AM-4:30PM (EST). *Civil Actions Under $15,000, Eviction, Small Claims.*

Probate Court 111 S Sheridan St, Fitzgerald, GA 31750; 229-426-5137; Fax: 229-426-5486. Hours: 8:30AM-4:30PM (EST). *Probate.*

Berrien County

Superior Court 101 E Marion Ave, # 3, Nashville, GA 31639; 229-686-5506. Hours: 8AM-4:30PM (EST). *Felony, Misdemeanor, Civil.*
Civil Records: Access: Mail, in person. Both court and visitors may perform in person searches. No search fee. Required to search: name, years to search. Civil cases indexed by defendant, plaintiff. Civil records on docket back to 1800.
Criminal Records: Access: Mail, in person. Both court and visitors may perform in person searches. No search fee. Required to search: name, years to search,

DOB; also helpful: SSN, race, sex. Criminal records on docket back to 1800.
General Information: No juvenile, adoption, sealed, sexual, mental health or expunged records released. Copy fee: $.25 per page. Cert fee: $2.50 plus $.50 per page after first. Payee: Court Clerk. Personal checks accepted. Prepayment required. Mail requests: SASE required. Mail turnaround time same day.

Magistrate Court PO Box 267, Nashville, GA 31639; 229-686-7019; Fax: 229-686-6328. Hours: 8:30AM-4:30PM (EST). *Civil Actions Under $15,000, Eviction, Small Claims.*

Probate Court 101 E Marion Ave, # 2, Nashville, GA 31639; 229-686-5213; Fax: 229-686-9495. Hours: 8AM-4;30-M-FRI (EST). *Probate.* https://www.gaprobate.org/counties/berrien/index.html
Note: The Superior Court is in #3.

Bibb County

Superior Court PO Box 1015, 601 Mulberry S, Rm 216, Macon, GA 31202; 478-621-6527. Hours: 8:30AM-5PM (EST). *Felony, Civil.*
Civil Records: Access: Mail, in person. Both court and visitors may perform in person searches. Search fee: $10.00 per name. Required to search: name, years to search. Civil cases indexed by defendant, plaintiff. Civil records on computer from 1993, on books from 1823.
Criminal Records: Access: Mail, in person. Both court and visitors may perform in person searches. Search fee: $10.00 per name. Required to search: name, years to search, DOB, signed release; also helpful: SSN. Criminal records on computer since 1989. Superior court calenders at www.co.bibb.ga.us/CalendarDirectory/CalendarDirectory.asp.
General Information: No adoption or sealed records released. Copy fee: $.25 per page. Fee is $1.00 if court makes copy. Cert fee: $2.50 plus $.50 per page after first. Payee: Superior Court Clerk. Only cashiers checks and money orders accepted. Prepayment required. Mail turnaround time same day.

State Court PO Box 5086, Macon, GA 31213-7199; 478-621-6676; Fax: 478-621-6326. Hours: 8AM-5PM (EST). *Misdemeanor, Civil.* www.co.bibb.ga.us/
Note: The court calendar can be found online. The website will have access to court record indexes in the near future.
Civil Records: Access: Mail, in person. Both court and visitors may perform in person searches. Search fee: $10.00 per name. Required to search: name, years to search. Civil cases indexed by defendant, plaintiff. Civil records on computer from 1989, docket from 1952. Civil court calendars are searchable online at www.co.bibb.ga.us/StateCourtClerk/Civil/Default.htm.
Criminal Records: Access: Mail, in person. Both court and visitors may perform in person searches. Search fee: $10.00 per name. Required to search: name, years to search, DOB; also helpful: SSN, race, sex. Criminal records on computer from 1989, docket from 1945.
General Information: Public Access terminal is available. No juvenile, adoption, sealed, sexual, mental health or expunged records released. Will fax to toll-free line if 5 pages or less, otherwise results mailed. Copy fee: $.50 per page. Cert fee: $2.50 plus $.50 per page. Exemplification is an add'l $5.00. Payee: Court Clerk. Business checks accepted. Prepayment required. Mail requests: SASE required. Mail turnaround time 1 day.

Civil & Magistrate Court 601 Mulberry #110, Bibb County Courthouse, Macon, GA 31201; 478-621-6495; Civil phone: 478-621-6495; Criminal

phone: 478-621-6505; Fax: 478-621-5861. Hours: 8AM-5PM (EST). *Civil Actions Under $25,000, Eviction, Small Claims.*
www.bibbcourt.com

Probate Court 207 Bibb County Courthouse, PO Box 6518, Macon, GA 31208-6518; 478-621-6494; Fax: 478-621-6686. Hours: 8AM-5PM (EST). *Probate.*
www.co.bibb.ga.us/probate

Bleckley County

Superior Court 306 SE 2nd St, Cochran, GA 31014; 478-934-6671; Fax: 478-934-3205. Hours: 8:30AM-5PM (EST). *Felony, Misdemeanor, Civil.*
Civil Records: Access: In person only. Visitors must perform in person searches for themselves. No search fee. Required to search: name, years to search. Civil cases indexed by defendant, plaintiff. Civil records archived from 1913, docket from 1913.
Criminal Records: Access: In person only. Visitors must perform in person searches for themselves. No search fee. Required to search: name, years to search, DOB; also helpful: SSN, race, sex. Criminal records archived from 1913, docket from 1913.
General Information: No juvenile, adoption, sealed, sexual, mental health or expunged records released. Copy fee: $.25 per page. Cert fee: $2.50 plus $.50 per page after first. Payee: Clerk of the Superior Court. Personal checks not accepted. Prepayment required.

Magistrate Court 306 2nd St SE, Cochran, GA 31014; 478-934-3202; Fax: 478-934-7826. Hours: 8:30AM-5PM (EST). *Civil Actions Under $15,000, Eviction, Small Claims.*

Probate Court 306 SE 2nd St, Cochran, GA 31014; 478-934-3204; Fax: 478-934-3205. Hours: 8:30AM-5PM (EST). *Probate.*
https://www.gaprobate.org/counties/bleckley/index.html

Brantley County

Superior Court PO Box 1067, 117 Brantley St, Nahunta, GA 31553; 912-462-5635; Fax: 912-462-6247. Hours: 8AM-5PM (EST). *Felony, Misdemeanor, Civil.*
Civil Records: Access: In person only. Visitors must perform in person searches for themselves. No search fee. Required to search: name, years to search. Civil cases indexed by defendant, plaintiff. Civil records on dockets from 1920; computerized records go back 1998.
Criminal Records: Access: In person only. Visitors must perform in person searches for themselves. No search fee. Required to search: name, years to search, DOB, SSN, signed release; also helpful: race, sex. Criminal records on dockets from 1920.
General Information: No juvenile, adoption, sealed, 1st offenders, expunged or confidential records released. Copy fee: $.25 per page. Cert fee: $2.50 plus $.50 per page after first. Payee: Superior Court Clerk. Personal checks accepted. Prepayment required.

Magistrate Court PO Box 998, Nahunta, GA 31553; 912-462-6780; Fax: 912-462-6897. Hours: 8AM-4:30PM (EST). *Civil Actions Under $15,000, Eviction, Small Claims.*

Probate Court PO Box 207, Nahunta, GA 31553; 912-462-5192; Fax: 912-462-8360. Hours: 8AM-5PM (EST). *Probate.*

Brooks County

Superior Court PO Box 630, Quitman, GA 31643; 229-263-4747/5150; Fax: 229-263-5050. 8AM-5PM (EST). *Felony, Misdemeanor, Civil.*
http://www2.state.ga.us/courts/superior/dca/dca2sohp.htm
Civil Records: Access: In person, phone if specific date is known. Visitors must perform in person

searches for themselves. No search fee. Required to search: name, years to search. Civil cases indexed by defendant, plaintiff. Civil records in books back to 1857.
Criminal Records: Access: In person only. Visitors must perform in person searches for themselves. No search fee. Required to search: name, years to search, DOB; also helpful: SSN, race, sex. Criminal records in books back to 1857.
General Information: Public Access terminal is available. No juvenile, adoption, sealed, sexual, mental health or expunged records released. Will fax results to local or toll free line. Copy fee: $.25 per page. Cert fee: $2.50 plus $.50 per page after first. Payee: Clerk Superior Court. Business checks accepted. Prepayment required.

Magistrate Court PO Box 387, Quitman, GA 31643; 229-263-9989; Fax: 229-263-7847. Hours: 8AM-5PM (EST). *Civil Actions Under $15,000, Eviction, Small Claims.*

Probate Court PO Box 665, Quitman, GA 31643; 229-263-5567; Fax: 229-263-5058. Hours: 8AM-5PM (EST). *Probate.*

Bryan County

Superior & State Court PO Box 670, Pembroke, GA 31321; 912-653-3872; Fax: 912-653-3870. Hours: 8AM-5PM (EST). *Felony, Misdemeanor, Civil.*
Civil Records: Access: Mail, in person. Visitors must perform in person searches for themselves. No search fee. Required to search: name, years to search. Civil cases indexed by defendant, plaintiff. Civil records on dockets from 1960, recent records are computerized since 9/93.
Criminal Records: Access: Mail, in person. Visitors must perform in person searches for themselves. No search fee. Required to search: name, years to search, DOB; also helpful: SSN, race, sex. Criminal records on dockets from 1960, recent records are computerized since 9/93.
General Information: Public Access terminal is available. No juvenile, adoption, sealed, sexual, mental health or expunged records released. Will fax results for $2.00 1st page, $1.00 each add'l, must be pre-paid. Copy fee: $.25 per page. Cert fee: $2.50 plus $.25 per page after first. Payee: Clerk of Superior & State Court. Personal checks accepted. Prepayment required. Mail requests: SASE requested. Turnaround time 1-2 days.

Magistrate Court Box 670, Pembroke, GA 31321; 912-653-3860; Fax: 912-653-5254. Hours: 8AM-5PM (EST). *Civil Actions Under $15,000, Eviction, Small Claims.*

Probate Court PO Box 418, Pembroke, GA 31321; 912-653-3856; Fax: 912-653-3845. Hours: 8:30AM-12, 1-5PM (EST). *Probate.*
www.georgiacourts.org/probate/bryan

Bulloch County

Superior & State Court Judicial Annex Bldg, 20 Siebald St, Statesboro, GA 30458; 912-764-9009; Fax: 912-764-5953. Hours: 8:00AM-5PM (EST). *Felony, Misdemeanor, Civil.*
Civil Records: Access: In person only,fax,mail. Both court or visitors may perform searches. No search fee. Required to search: name, years to search. Civil cases indexed by defendant. Civil records on computer from 1991, dockets back to 1796.
Criminal Records: Access: In person only,fax,mail. Both court or visitors may perform searches. No search fee. Required to search: name, years to search. Criminal records on computer from 1991, dockets back to 1796.

General Information: Public Access terminal is available. No juvenile, adoption, sexual, mental health or expunged records released. Copy fee: $.25 per page. Cert fee: $2.50 plus $.50 per page after first. Payee: Court Clerk. Personal checks accepted. Prepayment required. Mail requests: SASE required. Mail turnaround time is 7 days.

Magistrate Court Box 1004, Statesboro, GA 30459-1004; 912-764-6458, 912-764-5050; Fax: 912-489-6731. Hours: 8AM-5PM (EST). *Civil Actions Under $15,000, Eviction, Small Claims.*

Probate Court PO Box 1005, Statesboro, GA 30459; 912-489-8749; Fax: 912-764-8740. Hours: 8:00AM-5PM (EST). *Probate.*
https://www.gaprobate.org/counties/bulloch/index.html

Burke County

Superior & State Court PO Box 803, 111 E 6th St, Rm 107, Waynesboro, GA 30830; 706-554-2279; Fax: 706-554-7887. Hours: 9AM-5PM (EST). *Felony, Misdemeanor, Civil.*
Civil Records: Access: In person only. Visitors must perform in person searches for themselves. No search fee. Required to search: name, years to search. Civil cases indexed by defendant. Civil records on minute books back to 1856, indexed on computer since 1996.
Criminal Records: Access: In person only. Visitors must perform in person searches for themselves. No search fee. Required to search: name, years to search, DOB; also helpful: SSN, race, sex. Criminal records on minute books back to 1856, indexed on computer since 1996.
General Information: No juvenile, adoption, sexual, mental health or expunged records released. Copy fee: $.25 per page. Cert fee: $2.50 plus $.50 per page after first. Payee: Clerk of Superior Court. Personal checks accepted. Prepayment required.

Magistrate Court Box 401, Waynesboro, GA 30830; 706-554-4281; Fax: 706-554-8772. Hours: 8AM-5PM (EST). *Civil Actions Under $15,000, Eviction, Small Claims.*

Probate Court PO Box 322, Waynesboro, GA 30830; 706-554-3000; Fax: 706-554-6693. Hours: 9AM-5PM (EST). *Probate.*
https://www.gaprobate.org/counties/burke/index.html

Butts County

Superior Court PO Box 320, 26 3rd St, Jackson, GA 30233; 770-775-8215. Hours: 8AM-5PM (EST). *Felony, Misdemeanor, Civil.*
Civil Records: Access: In person, fax, mail. Visitors must perform in person searches for themselves. No search fee. Required to search: name, years to search. Civil cases indexed by defendant, plaintiff. Civil records on dockets from 1966, computerized since 1998.
Criminal Records: Access: In person, fax, mail. Visitors must perform in person searches for themselves. Search fee: None. Required to search: name, years to search, signed release; also helpful: DOB, SSN, race, sex. Criminal records on dockets from 1966, computerized since 1998.
General Information: Public Access terminal is available. No juvenile, adoption, sexual, mental health or expunged records released. Copy fee: $.25 per page. Cert fee: $2.50 plus $.50 per page. Payee: Clerk of Superior Court. Personal checks accepted. Prepayment required. Mail requests: SASE required. Mail turnaround time is 3-4 days.

Magistrate Court Box 457, Jackson, GA 30233; 770-775-8220; Fax: 770-775-1954. Hours: 8AM-5PM (EST). *Civil Actions Under $15,000, Eviction, Small Claims.*

Probate Court 25 3rd St, #7, Jackson, GA 30233; 770-775-8204; Fax: 770-775-8004. Hours: 8AM-5PM (EST). *Probate, Traffic.*
https://www.gaprobate.org/counties/butts/index.html

Calhoun County

Superior Court PO Box 69, Morgan, GA 39866; 229-849-2715; Fax: 229-849-0072. Hours: 8AM-5PM (EST). *Felony, Misdemeanor, Civil.*
Civil Records: Access: Mail, in person. Both court and visitors may perform in person searches. Search fee: $2.00. Required to search: name, years to search. Civil cases indexed by defendant, plaintiff. Civil records on dockets back to 1854.
Criminal Records: Access: In person only. Visitors must perform in person searches for themselves. No search fee. Required to search: name, years to search, DOB. Criminal records on dockets back to 1854.
General Information: No juvenile, adoption, sexual, mental health or expunged records released. Will fax results $1.50; no charge to toll-free numbers. Copy fee: $.25 per page. Cert fee: $3.00. Payee: Superior Court Clerk. Personal checks accepted. Prepayment required.

Magistrate & Probate Court PO Box 87, Morgan, GA 39866; 229-849-2115, 849-2116; Fax: 229-849-2117. 8AM-5PM (EST). *Civil Actions Under $15,000, Eviction, Small Claims, Probate.*

Camden County

Superior Court PO Box 550, 210 E 4th St, Woodbine, GA 31569; 912-576-5624. Hours: 9AM-5PM (EST). *Felony, Misdemeanor, Civil.*
Civil Records: Access: In person only. Visitors must perform in person searches for themselves. No search fee. Required to search: name, years to search. Civil cases indexed by defendant, plaintiff. Civil records on computer from 1989, on dockets from 1776.
Criminal Records: Access: In person only. Visitors must perform in person searches for themselves. No search fee. Required to search: name, years to search, signed release; also helpful: DOB, SSN. Criminal records on computer from 1989, on dockets from 1776.
General Information: Public Access terminal is available. No juvenile, adoption, sexual or expunged records released. Will not fax results. Copy fee: $.25 per page. Cert fee: $2.00 plus $.50 per page. Payee: Clerk of Superior Court. Personal checks accepted. Prepayment required.

Magistrate Court Box 386, Woodbine, GA 31569; 912-576-5658. Hours: 9AM-5PM (EST). *Civil Actions Under $15,000, Eviction, Small Claims.*

Probate Court PO Box 818, Woodbine, GA 31569; 912-576-3785; Fax: 912-576-5484. Hours: 9AM-5PM (EST). *Probate, Misdemeanor Drug.*

Candler County

Superior & State Court PO Drawer 830, Metter, GA 30439; 912-685-5257; Probate phone: 912-685-2357; Fax: 912-685-2946. Hours: 8:30AM-5PM (EST). *Felony, Misdemeanor, Civil.*
Civil Records: Access: Mail, in person. Visitors must perform in person searches for themselves. No search fee. Required to search: name, years to search. Civil cases indexed by defendant, plaintiff. Civil records on dockets from 1914.
Criminal Records: Access: Mail, in person. Visitors must perform in person searches for themselves. No search fee. Required to search: name, years to search. Criminal records on dockets from 1914.
General Information: Public Access terminal is available. No juvenile, adoption, mental health, expunged or sealed records released. Will fax results to local or toll free line. Copy fee: $.25 per page. Cert

fee: $2.00 plus $.50 per page. Payee: Clerk of Superior & State Court. Personal checks accepted. Prepayment required. Mail turnaround time 2 days.

Magistrate Court 1 Courthouse Sq, Metter, GA 30439; 912-685-2888; Fax: 912-685-6426. Hours: 8:30AM-5PM (EST). *Civil Actions Under $15,000, Eviction, Small Claims.*

Probate Court Courthouse Sq, Metter, GA 30439; 912-685-2357; Fax: 912-685-5130. Hours: 8:30AM-5PM (EST). *Probate.*
https://www.gaprobate.org/counties/candler/index.html

Carroll County

Superior & State Court PO Box 1620, Carrollton, GA 30117; 770-214-3125; Civil phone: 770-830-5835 Ext 2245&2246; Criminal phone: 770-830-5835 Ext 2247&2239; Probate phone: 770-830-5840; Fax: 770-830-5988. Hours: 8AM-5PM (EST). *Felony, Misdemeanor, Civil.*
Civil Records: Access: Mail, in person. Both court and visitors may perform in person searches. Search fee: $5.00 per name. Required to search: name, years to search. Civil cases indexed by defendant, plaintiff. Civil records on computer from 1986, docket.
Criminal Records: Access: Mail, in person. Both court and visitors may perform in person searches. Search fee: $5.00 per name. Required to search: name, years to search, DOB; also helpful: SSN, race, sex. Criminal records on computer from 1986 for State Court, but Superior Court records are not computerized.
General Information: No juvenile, adoption, sexual, mental health or expunged records released. Copy fee: $1.00 per page. Cert fee: $2.50 plus $.50 per page after first. Payee: Clerk of Superior & State Court. Personal checks accepted. Prepayment required. Mail requests: SASE required. Mail turnaround time 1 week.

Magistrate Court 108 Courtyard Sq, Carrollton, GA 30117; 770-830-5874; Fax: 770-830-5851. Hours: 9AM-5PM (EST). *Civil Actions Under $15,000, Eviction, Small Claims.*

Probate Court Carroll County Courthouse, 311 Newnan St, Rm 204, Carrollton, GA 30117; 770-830-5840; Fax: 770-830-5995. 8AM-5PM *Probate.*
https://www.gaprobate.org/counties/carroll/index.html

Catoosa County

Superior Court 875 Lafayette St, Ringgold, GA 30736; 706-935-4231. Hours: 8:30AM-5PM (EST). *Felony, Misdemeanor, Civil.*
Civil Records: Access: In person only. Visitors must perform in person searches for themselves. No search fee. Required to search: name, years to search. Civil cases indexed by defendant, plaintiff. Civil records on dockets from 1800.
Criminal Records: Access: In person only. Visitors must perform in person searches for themselves. No search fee. Required to search: name, years to search, DOB; also helpful: SSN, race, sex. Criminal records on dockets from 1800.
General Information: No juvenile, adoption, sexual, mental health or expunged records released. Copy fee: $1.00 per page. Cert fee: $2.50 plus $.50 per page after first. Payee: Superior Court - Court Clerk. Personal checks accepted. Prepayment required.

Magistrate Court 798 Lafayette St, Ringgold, GA 30736; 706-935-3114. Hours: 8:30AM-5PM (EST). *Civil Actions Under $15,00, Eviction, Small Claims.*

Probate Court 875 LaFayette St, Justice Bldg, Ringgold, GA 30736; 706-935-3511; Fax: 706-935-3519. Hours: 9AM-5PM (EST). *Probate.*

Note: This court will not perform mail searches.

Charlton County

Superior Court Courthouse, PO Box 760, Folkston, GA 31537; 912-496-2354. Hours: 8:30AM-5PM (EST). *Felony, Misdemeanor, Civil.*
Civil Records: Access: In person. Visitors must perform in person searches for themselves. No search fee. Required to search: name, years to search. Civil cases indexed by defendant. Civil records on index from 1954.
Criminal Records: Access: In person. Visitors must perform in person searches for themselves. No search fee. Required to search: name, years to search, DOB, SSN. Criminal records on index from 1954.
General Information: Public Access terminal is available. No juvenile, adoption, sexual, mental health or expunged records released. Will not fax results. Copy fee: $.25 per page. Cert fee: $2.50 plus $.50 per page after first. Payee: Court Clerk. Personal checks accepted.

Magistrate Court 100 B County St, Folkston, GA 31537; 912-496-2617; Fax: 912-496-2560. Hours: 9AM-4:30PM (EST). *Civil Actions Under $15,000, Eviction, Small Claims.*

Probate Court 100 S 3rd St, Folkston, GA 31537; 912-496-2230; Fax: 912-496-1156. Hours: 8AM-5PM (EST). *Probate.*
https://www.gaprobate.org/counties/charlton/index.html

Chatham County

Superior Court PO Box 10227, Savannah, GA 31412-0427; 912-652-7197; Civil phone: 912-652-7200; Criminal phone: 912-652-7209; Fax: 912-652-7380. Hours: 8AM-5PM (EST). *Felony, Civil.*
www.chathamcourts.org
Civil Records: Access: Mail, in person. Both court and visitors may perform in person searches. No search fee. Required to search: name, years to search. Civil cases indexed by defendant, plaintiff. Civil records on computer from 1984, archived back to 1900, dockets back to 1900s.
Criminal Records: Access: Mail, in person. Both court and visitors may perform in person searches. No search fee. Required to search: name, years to search, signed release; also helpful: DOB, SSN. Criminal records on computer from 1984, archived back to 1900, dockets back to 1900s.
General Information: Public Access terminal is available. No adoption records released. Will not fax results. Copy fee: $.25 per page. Cert fee: $2.00 plus $.50 per page. Payee: Court Clerk. Personal checks accepted. Prepayment required. Mail requests: SASE requested. Turnaround time 1 week.

State Court County Courthouse 133 Montgomery St, Savannah, GA 31401; 912-652-7224; Fax: 912-652-7229. 8AM-5PM (EST). *Misdemeanor, Civil.*
www.statecourt.org
Civil Records: Access: Mail, fax, in person. Both court and visitors may perform in person searches. No search fee. Required to search: name, years to search, address. Civil cases indexed by defendant, plaintiff. Civil records on computer from 1983, prior on books. Current state court cases only is free online at www.chathamcourts.org. Search by name or case number.
Criminal Records: Access: Mail, fax, in person. Both court and visitors may perform in person searches. No search fee. Required to search: name, years to search. Criminal records on computer from 1983, prior on books.
General Information: Public Access terminal is available. No first time criminal offender or sealed civil records released. Will fax results for $.50 per page. Copy fee: $1.00 per page. Cert fee: $2.50 plus

$.50 per page. Payee: Clerk of State Court. Only cashiers checks and money orders accepted. Prepayment required. Mail requests: SASE required. Mail turnaround time 2 days.

Magistrate Court 133 Montgomery St Rm 303 3rd Fl, Savannah, GA 31401; 912-652-7181; Fax: 912-652-7550. Hours: 8AM-5PM (EST). *Civil Actions Under $15,000, Eviction, Small Claims.* www.chathamcourts.org

Probate Court 133 Montgomery St, Rm 509, Savannah, GA 31401; 912-652-7264; Fax: 912-652-7262. Hours: 8AM-5PM (EST). *Probate.* www.chathamcourts.org

Chattahoochee County

Superior & Magistrate Court PO Box 120, Cusseta, GA 31805; 706-989-3424; Fax: 706-989-0396. Hours: 8AM-5PM (EST). *Felony, Misdemeanor, Civil, Eviction, Small Claims.* Note: Magistrate Court is 706-989-3643.

Civil Records: Access: In person only. Visitors must perform in person searches for themselves. No search fee. Required to search: name, years to search. Civil cases indexed by defendant, plaintiff. Civil records on dockets from 1854.
Criminal Records: Access: In person only. Visitors must perform in person searches for themselves. No search fee. Required to search: name, years to search, DOB; also helpful: SSN, race, sex. Criminal records on dockets from 1854.
General Information: Public Access terminal is available. No juvenile, adoption, sexual, mental health or expunged records released. Copy fee: $.25 per page. Cert fee: $2.50 plus $.50 per page after first. Payee: Court Clerk. Business checks accepted. Prepayment required.

Probate Court PO Box 119, Cusseta, GA 31805; 706-989-3603; Fax: 706-989-2015. Hours: 8AM-Noon, 1-5PM (EST). *Probate.*

Chattooga County

Superior & State Court PO Box 159, Summerville, GA 30747; 706-857-0706. Hours: 8:30AM-5PM (EST). *Felony, Misdemeanor, Civil, Eviction, Small Claims.*
Civil Records: Access: In person only. Visitors must perform in person searches for themselves. No search fee. Required to search: name, years to search. Civil cases indexed by defendant, plaintiff. Civil records on dockets from 1960.
Criminal Records: Access: In person only. Visitors must perform in person searches for themselves. No search fee. Required to search: name, years to search, DOB; also helpful: SSN, race, sex. Criminal records on dockets from 1960.
General Information: Public Access terminal is available. No juvenile, adoption, sexual, mental health or expunged records released. Copy fee: $.25 per page. Cert fee: $2.50 plus $.50 per page after first. Payee: Clerk of Court. Personal checks accepted. Prepayment required.

Magistrate Court 10017 Commerce St, Summerville, GA 30747; 706-857-0711; Fax: 706-857-0675. Hours: 9AM-5PM (EST). *Civil Actions Under $15,000, Eviction, Small Claims.*

Probate Court PO Box 467, 10035 Commerce St, Summerville, GA 30747; 706-857-0709; Fax: 706-857-0877. 8:30AM-Noon, 1-5PM *Probate.* https://www.gaprobate.org/counties/chattooga/index.html

Cherokee County

Superior & State Court 90 North St, # G170, Canton, GA 30114; 678-493-6501. Hours: 8AM-5PM (EST). *Felony, Misdemeanor, Civil.* Note: This court location also handles juvenile records.

Civil Records: Access: In person only. Visitors must perform in person searches for themselves. No search fee. Required to search: name. Civil cases indexed by defendant, plaintiff. Civil records on computer from 1990, archived 1900-1991, on dockets back to 1900.
Criminal Records: Access: In person only. Visitors must perform in person searches for themselves. No search fee. Required to search: name, years to search, DOB; also helpful: SSN, race, sex. Criminal records on computer from 1990, archived 1900-1990, on dockets back to 1900.
General Information: Public Access terminal is available. No juvenile, adoption, sexual, mental health, expunged or confidential records released. Copy fee: $.25 per page. Cert fee: $2.00 plus $.50 per add'l page. Payee: Clerk of Court. Only cashiers checks and money orders accepted. Prepayment required.

Magistrate Court 90 North St, #150, Canton, GA 30114; 678-493-6390. Hours: 8:30AM-5PM (EST). *Civil Actions Under $15,000, Eviction, Small Claims.* www.cccourt.com
Note: Search the magistrate court database online at www.cccourt.com. Court also has jurisdiction for bad checks, arrest warrants, preliminary hearings, and county ordinance violations.

Probate Court 90 North St, Rm 340, Canton, GA 30114; 678-493-6160; Fax: 678-493-6170. Hours: 8AM-5PM (EST). *Probate.* https://www.gaprobate.org/counties/cherokee/index.html

Clarke County

Superior & State Court PO Box 1805, Athens, GA 30603; 706-613-3190. Hours: 8AM-5PM (EST). *Felony, Misdemeanor, Civil.* http://athensclarke.allclerks.us
Note: Located at 325 E Washington, Rm 450, 30601. This court will perform no searches for the public.

Civil Records: Access: In person only. Visitors must perform in person searches for themselves. No search fee. Required to search: name, years to search. Civil cases indexed by defendant, plaintiff. Civil records on computer from 1993, docket books from 1801.
Criminal Records: Access: In person only. Visitors must perform in person searches for themselves. No search fee. Required to search: name, years to search, DOB. Criminal records on computer from 1993, docket books from 1801.
General Information: Public Access terminal is available. No juvenile, adoptions, sealed, sexual, mental health or expunged records released. Copy fee: In-house copies are $.25 each; by mail is $1.00 per page. Cert fee: $2.50 plus $.50 per page after first. Payee: County Clerk. Personal checks accepted. Prepayment required.

Magistrate Court PO Box 1868, 325 E Washington St, Athens, GA 30601; 706-613-3310; Fax: 706-613-3314. Hours: 8AM-5PM (EST). *Civil Actions Under $15,000, Eviction, Small Claims.*

Probate Court 325 E Washington St, #215, Athens, GA 30601; 706-613-3320; Fax: 706-613-3323. Hours: 8AM-5PM (EST). *Probate.*

Clay County

Superior Court PO Box 550, Ft Gaines, GA 39851; 229-768-2631; Fax: 229-768-3047. Hours: 8AM-4:30PM (EST). *Felony, Misdemeanor, Civil, Eviction.*
Civil Records: Access: In person only. Visitors must perform in person searches for themselves. No search fee. Required to search: name, years to search. Civil cases indexed by defendant, plaintiff. Civil records on computer from 1990, on dockets from 1854.
Criminal Records: Access: In person only. Visitors must perform in person searches for themselves. No search fee. Required to search: name, years to search. Criminal records on computer from 1990, on dockets from 1854.
General Information: Public Access terminal is available. No juvenile, adoption, sexual, mental health or expunged records released. Copy fee: $1.00 per page. Cert fee: $3.00. Payee: Superior Court Clerk. Personal checks accepted. Prepayment required.

Magistrate Court PO Box 73, Ft Gaines, GA 39851; 229-768-2841; Fax: 229-768-3047. Hours: 8AM-4:30PM (EST). *Civil Actions Under $15,000, Eviction, Small Claims.*

Probate Court PO Box 448, 210 S Washington, Ft Gaines, GA 39851; 229-768-2445; Fax: 229-768-2710. Hours: 8AM-4:30PM (EST). *Probate.*

Clayton County

Superior Court 9151 Tara Blvd, # ICL19, Jonesboro, GA 30236-4912; 770-477-3405. Hours: 8AM-5PM (EST). *Felony, Civil.* www.co.clayton.ga.us/superior_court/clerk_of_courts
Civil Records: Access: Mail, in person. Visitors must perform in person searches for themselves. No search fee. Required to search: name, years to search. Civil cases indexed by defendant. Civil records on docket books for all records, on computer from 1996, on microfilm from 1990, archived from 1858-1982, dockets to 1858. Court calendars are online at www.co.clayton.ga.us/courtcalendars/index.htm.
Criminal Records: Access: Mail, in person. Visitors must perform in person searches for themselves. No search fee. Required to search: name, years to search, DOB; also helpful: SSN, race, sex. Criminal record keeping same as civil. Court calendars online at www.co.clayton.ga.us/courtcalendars/index.htm.
General Information: Public Access terminal is available. (Civil records only.) No adoption, sexual, mental health or expunged records released. Copy fee: $1.00 per page. Cert fee: $2.50 plus $1.00 per page after first. Payee: Clerk of Superior Court. Only cashiers checks, money orders and attorney checks accepted. Prepayment required. Mail turnaround time is 1 week.

State Court 9151 Tara Blvd, #1CL181, Jonesboro, GA 30236; 770-477-3388. Hours: 8AM-5PM (EST). *Misdemeanor.* www.co.clayton.ga.us/state_court/clerk_of_courts
Criminal Records: Access: In person only. Visitors must perform in person searches for themselves. No search fee. Required to search: name, years to search. Criminal records on computer from 1985.
General Information: Public Access terminal is available. No juvenile, adoption, sexual, mental health or expunged records released. Copy fee: $.25 per page. Cert fee: $2.50 plus $.50 per page after first. Payee: Court Clerk. Business checks accepted. Prepayment required.

Magistrate Court 9151 Tara Blvd, #2TC08, Jonesboro, GA 30236-4912; 770-477-3444; Fax: 770-473-5750. Hours: 8AM-5PM (EST). *Civil Actions Under $15,000, Eviction, Small Claims.* www.co.clayton.ga.us/courts.htm

Probate Court 121 S McDonough St, Annex 3, Jonesboro, GA 30236-3694; 770-477-3299; Fax: 770-477-3306. Hours: 8AM-4;30PM (EST). *Probate.* www.co.clayton.ga.us/probate_court

Clinch County

Superior & State Court PO Box 433, Homerville, GA 31634; 912-487-5854; Fax: 912-489-3083. 8AM-5PM *Felony, Misdemeanor, Civil.*
Civil Records: Access: Mail, in person. Both court and visitors may perform in person searches. No search fee. Required to search: name, years to search. Civil cases indexed by defendant, plaintiff. Civil records on dockets from 1900.
Criminal Records: Access: Mail, in person. Both court and visitors may perform in person searches. No search fee. Required to search: name, years to search, DOB; also helpful: SSN, race, sex. Criminal records on dockets from 1900.
General Information: Public Access terminal is available. No juvenile, adoption, sexual, mental health or expunged records released. Will fax results for $3.00 per page. Copy fee: $.25 per page. Cert fee: $3.00. Payee: Court Clerk. Personal checks accepted. Prepayment required. Mail requests: SASE requested. Turnaround time 1-2 days.

Magistrate Court 100 Court Sq, Homerville, GA 31634; 912-487-2514; Fax: 912-487-3658. Hours: 9AM-12;00-1-5PM (EST). *Civil Actions Under $15,000, Eviction, Small Claims.*

Probate Court PO Box 364, Homerville, GA 31634; 912-487-5523; Fax: 912-487-3083. Hours: 9AM-12;00,1-5PM (EST). *Probate.*

Cobb County

Superior Court PO Box 3370, Marietta, GA 30061; 770-528-1300; Fax: 770-528-1382. Hours: 8AM-5PM (EST). *Felony, Misdemeanor, Civil.* www.cobbgasupctclk.com/index.htm
Civil Records: Access: Online, in person. Visitors must perform in person searches for themselves. No search fee. Required to search: name, years to search. Civil cases indexed by defendant, plaintiff. Civil records on computer from 1982, records on dockets from 1958. Civil or criminal indexes of Clerk of Superior Court are free at the website. Search by name, type or case number. Data is updated every Fri.
Criminal Records: Access: Mail, online, in person. Visitors must perform in person searches for themselves. No search fee. Required to search: name, years to search. Criminal records on computer from 1982, Records on dockets from 1958. Online access to criminal records is the same as civil.
General Information: Public Access terminal is available. No juvenile, adoption, sexual, mental health or expunged records released. Copy fee: $.25 per page. Cert fee: $2.00 plus $.50 per page. Payee: Clerk of Superior Court. Personal checks accepted. Prepayment required. Mail turnaround time 1-3 days.

State Court - Civil & Criminal Divisions
12 E Park Sq, Marietta, GA 30090-9630; Civil phone: 770-528-1203; Criminal phone: 770-528-1262. Hours: 8AM-5PM (EST). *Misdemeanor, Civil, Eviction.* www.cobbstatecourtclerk.com
Civil Records: Access: In person only. Visitors must perform in person searches for themselves. No search fee unless offsite (pre-1996), then $7.00. Required to search: name, years to search. Civil cases indexed by defendant, plaintiff. Civil records on computer since 03/10/97, docket books from 1965.
Criminal Records: Access: In person only. Both court and visitors may perform in person searches. Search fee: None unless offsite (pre-1996), then $7.00. Required to search: name, years to search,

offense; also helpful: DOB. Criminal records on computer since 1981, docket books from 1965.
General Information: Public Access terminal is available. No sealed records released. Copy fee: $.25 per page. Cert fee: $3.00. Payee: State Court Clerk. Prepayment required.

Magistrate Court 32 Waddell St, 3rd Fl, Marietta, GA 30090-9656; 770-528-8900; Fax: 770-528-8929. Hours: 8AM-5PM (EST). *Civil Actions Under $15,000, Small Claims.* www.cobbcounty.org/judicial/magistrate/index.htm

Probate Court 32 Waddell St, Marietta, GA 30060; 770-528-1990; Fax: 770-528-1996. Hours: 8AM-4:30PM (EST). *Probate.* https://www.gaprobate.org/counties/cobb/index.html

Coffee County

Superior & State Court 101 S Peterson Ave, Douglas, GA 31533; 912-384-2865. Hours: 8:30AM-5PM (EST). *Felony, Misdemeanor, Civil.*
Civil Records: Access: In person only. Visitors must perform in person searches for themselves. No search fee. Required to search: name. Civil cases indexed by defendant, plaintiff. Civil records on dockets.
Criminal Records: Access: In person only. Visitors must perform in person searches for themselves. No search fee. Required to search: name, years to search. Criminal records on dockets.
General Information: No juvenile, adoption, sexual, mental health or expunged records released. Copy fee: $.25 per page. Cert fee: $3.00. Payee: Clerk Superior Court. Business checks accepted.

Magistrate Court 101 S Peterson Ave, Douglas, GA 31533; 912-384-2983; Fax: 912-383-0800. Hours: 8:30AM-5PM (EST). *Civil Actions Under $15,000, Eviction, Small Claims.*

Probate Court 101 S Peterson Ave, Douglas, GA 31533; 912-384-5213; Fax: 912-384-0291. Hours: 8:30AM-5PM (EST). *Probate, Civil.* https://www.gaprobate.org/counties/coffee/index.html

Colquitt County

Superior & State Court PO Box 2827, Moultrie, GA 31776; 229-616-7420; Civil phone: 229-616-7066 Sup; 616-7420 state; Criminal phone: 229-616-7423 Sup; 616-7064 state. Hours: 8AM-5PM (EST). *Felony, Misdemeanor, Civil.* http://www2.state.ga.us/courts/superior/dca/dca2sohp.htm
Civil Records: Access: In person only. Visitors must perform in person searches for themselves. No search fee. Required to search: name, years to search. Civil cases indexed by defendant, plaintiff. Civil records go back to 1800s, civil records on dockets books, computerized records go back to 1999.
Criminal Records: Access: In person only. Visitors must perform in person searches for themselves. No search fee. Required to search: name, years to search. Criminal records on dockets books; computerized records go back to 1999.
General Information: Public Access terminal is available. No juvenile, adoption, sexual, mental health or expunged records released. Copy fee: $.25 per page w/out assistance, $1.00 per page w/assistance. Cert fee: $2.50. Payee: Court Clerk. Personal checks accepted. Prepayment required.

Magistrate Court PO Box 70, Moultrie, GA 31776; 229-616-7450; Fax: 229-616-7494. Hours: 8AM-5PM (EST). *Civil Actions Under $15,000, Eviction, Small Claims.*

Probate Court PO Box 264, Rm 108 Colquitt County Govt Bldg, Moultrie, GA 31776-0264; 229-616-7415; Fax: 229-616-7489. Hours: 8AM-5PM (EST). *Probate.*

Columbia County

Superior Court PO Box 2930, Evans, GA 30809; 706-312-7139; Fax: 706-312-7152. Hours: 8AM-5PM (EST). *Felony, Misdemeanor, Civil.*
Note: This court is located at 640 Ronald Reagan Dr in Evans, GA 30809.
Civil Records: Access: In person only. Visitors must perform in person searches for themselves. No search fee. Required to search: name, years to search. Civil cases indexed by plaintiff. Civil records on computer from 1987, prior on docket books.
Criminal Records: Access: In person only. Visitors must perform in person searches for themselves. No search fee. Required to search: name, years to search, DOB; also helpful: SSN, race, sex. Criminal records on computer from 1987, prior on docket books.
General Information: Public Access terminal is available. No juvenile, adoption, sexual, mental health or expunged records released. Copy fee: $.25 per page. Cert fee: $2.00 plus $.50 per page. Payee: Clerk of Superior Court. Personal checks not accepted. Prepayment required.

Magistrate Court PO Box 777, Evans, GA 30809; 706-868-3316; Fax: 706-868-3314. Hours: 8AM-5PM (EST). *Civil Actions Under $15,000, Eviction, Small Claims.*

Probate Court PO Box 525, Appling, GA 30802; 706-541-1254; Fax: 706-541-4001. Hours: 8AM-4;30PM (EST). *Probate.*

Cook County

Superior Court 212 N Hutchinson Ave, Adel, GA 31620; 229-896-7717. Hours: 8:30AM-4:30PM (EST). *Felony, Misdemeanor, Civil.*
Civil Records: Access: Phone, mail, in person. Both court and visitors may perform in person searches. Search fee: $10.00 per name, per 7 year period. Required to search: name, years to search. Civil cases indexed by defendant. Civil records on dockets books, microfilm.
Criminal Records: Access: Mail, in person. Both court and visitors may perform in person searches. Search fee: $10.00 per name per 7 year period. Required to search: name, years to search, DOB, signed release; also helpful: SSN, race, sex. Criminal records on dockets books, microfilm.
General Information: No juvenile, adoption, sexual, 1st offenders, mental health or expunged records released. Copy fee: $1.00 per page. Cert fee: $2.50 plus $.50 per page after first. Payee: Court Clerk. Business checks accepted. Prepayment required. Mail requests: SASE not required. Mail turnaround time same day.

Magistrate Court PO Box 772, Adel, GA 31620-0772; 229-896-3151; Fax: 229-896-5186. Hours: 8AM-4:30PM (EST). *Civil Actions Under $15,000, Eviction, Small Claims.*

Probate Court 212 N Hutchinson Ave, Adel, GA 31620; 229-896-3941; Fax: 229-896-6083. Hours: 8:30AM-5PM (EST). *Probate, Misdemeanor Traffic.*

Coweta County

Superior Court PO Box 943, 200 Court Sq, Newnan, GA 30264; 770-254-2693/2695; Fax: 770-254-3700. Hours: 8AM-5PM (EST). *Felony, Civil.*
Civil Records: Access: Mail, in person. Visitors must perform in person searches for themselves. No search fee. Required to search: name, years to search. Civil cases indexed by defendant, plaintiff. Civil records on computer from 1990, dockets books to 1970.
Criminal Records: Access: In person only. Both court and visitors may perform in person searches. No search fee. Required to search: name, years to search,

DOB; also helpful: SSN, race, sex. Criminal records on docket books back to 1919. Can only conduct felony searches from 1990 to present.

General Information: Public Access terminal is available. No juvenile, adoption, sexual, mental health or expunged records released. Copy fee: $.25 per page. Cert fee: $2.50 plus $.50 per page after first. Payee: Clerk of Superior & State Court. Business checks accepted. Prepayment required.

State Court 9A E Broad St, Newnan, GA 30263; 770-254-2699. 8AM-5PM *Misdemeanor, Civil.*
www.coweta.ga.us/Resources/stateclk.html
This is a new court in new location as of 5/2001.

Civil Records: Access: Phone, in person. Both court and visitors may perform in person searches. Search fee: None, unless records are off-site (pre-1990), fee is $5.00. Required to search: name, years to search. Civil cases indexed by defendant, plaintiff. Civil records on computer from 1990, dockets books to 1970. No real estate; this court handles general civil.

Criminal Records: Access: In person, mail. Both court and visitors may perform in person searches. Search fee: None, but if records are off-site (pre-1990), fee is $5.00. Required to search: name, years to search, DOB. Criminal records on docket books back to 1919; on computer from 1990. Can only conduct felony searches from 1990 to present.

General Information: Public Access terminal is available. No juvenile, adoption, sexual, mental health or expunged records released. Copy fee: $.25 per page. Cert fee: $2.50 plus $.50 per page after first. Payee: Clerk of Superior & State Court. Only cashiers checks and money orders accepted. Prepayment required. Mail requests: SASE required. Mail turnaround time is 2-3 days.

Magistrate Court 22-34 E Broad St, Newnan, GA 30263; 770-254-2610; Fax: 770-254-2614. Hours: 8AM-5PM (EST). *Civil Actions Under $15,000, Eviction, Small Claims.*

Probate Court 22 E Broad St, Newnan, GA 30263; 770-254-2640; Fax: 770-254-2648. Hours: 8AM-5PM (EST). *Probate.*
https://www.gaprobate.org/counties/coweta/index.html

Crawford County

Superior Court PO Box 1037, Roberta, GA 31058; 478-836-3328; Probate phone: 478-836-3313. 9AM-5PM (EST). *Felony, Misdemeanor, Civil.*
Civil Records: Access: In person, mail. Visitors must perform in person searches for themselves. Search fee: Copy fees apply. Required to search: name, years to search. Civil cases indexed by defendant, plaintiff. Civil records on dockets books to 1830, records computerized since 1998.

Criminal Records: Access: In person, mail. Visitors must perform in person searches for themselves. Search fee: Copy fees apply. Required to search: name, years to search, DOB; also helpful: SSN, race, sex. Criminal records on dockets books to 1830, records computerized since 1998.

General Information: Public Access terminal is available. No juvenile, adoption, sexual, mental health or expunged records released. Will fax results for $2.50 per page, prepaid. Copy fee: $.25 per page, $1.00 if done by clerk. Cert fee: $2.50 plus $.50 per page after first. Payee: Clerk of Superior Court. Personal checks not accepted. Prepayment required. Mail turnaround time is 2 days.

Magistrate Court PO Box 568, Roberta, GA 31078; 478-836-4439; Fax: 478-836-4340. Hours: 9AM-5PM (EST). *Civil Actions Under $15,000, Eviction, Small Claims.*

Probate Court PO Box 1028, Roberta, GA 31078; 478-836-3313; Fax: 478-836-4111. Hours: 9AM-5PM (EST). *Probate.*
https://www.gaprobate.org/counties/crawford/index.html
Note: The record search fee is $5.00. Traffic records here also.

Crisp County

Superior & Juvenile Court PO Box 747, Cordele, GA 31010-0747; 229-276-2616. Hours: 8:30AM-5PM (EST). *Felony, Misdemeanor, Civil Actions Over $15,000.*
Civil Records: Access: Mail, in person. Visitors must perform in person searches for themselves. No search fee. Required to search: name, years to search. Civil cases indexed by defendant. Civil records on docket books to 1905, computerized since 1994.

Criminal Records: Access: Mail, in person. Visitors must perform in person searches for themselves. No search fee. Required to search: name, years to search; also helpful: SSN. Criminal records on docket books to 1905, computerized since 1994.

General Information: Public Access terminal is available. No juvenile, adoption, sexual, mental health or expunged records released. Fee to fax results is $2.50 1st page, $1.00 each add'l. Copy fee: $.25 per page. Cert fee: $2.00 plus $.50 per page. Payee: Clerk of Superior Court. Personal checks accepted. Prepayment required. Mail requests: SASE required. Mail turnaround time 1-2 days.

Magistrate Court 210 S 7th St, Rm 102, Cordese, GA 31015; 229-276-2618; Fax: 229-276-2634. Hours: 8:30AM-5PM (EST). *Civil Actions Under $15,000, Eviction, Small Claims.*

Probate Court 210 S 7th St, Rm 103, Cordele, GA 31015; 229-276-2621; Fax: 229-273-9184. Hours: 9AM-5PM (EST). *Probate.*
https://www.gaprobate.org/counties/crisp/index.html

Dade County

Superior Court PO Box 417, Trenton, GA 30752; 706-657-4778; Sm Claims 706-657-4113; Probate phone: 706-657-4414. Hours: 8:30AM-5PM (EST). *Felony, Misdemeanor, Civil, Eviction, Small Claims.* www.gsccca.org/clerks
Civil Records: Access: Phone, fax, mail, in person. Both court and visitors may perform in person searches. No search fee. Required to search: name, years to search. Civil cases indexed by defendant, plaintiff. Civil records on computer back to 1/1999; prior on docket books.

Criminal Records: Access: Mail, fax, in person. Both court and visitors may perform in person searches. Search fee: $5.00 per name. Required to search: name, years to search, DOB, signed release. Criminal records on computer back to 1/1999; prior on docket books to 1900s.

General Information: Public Access terminal is available. No juvenile, adoption, sexual, mental health or expunged records released. Fee to fax results is $1.00 per page. Copy fee: $1.50 per page. Cert fee: $2.00 plus $.50 per page after first. Payee: Superior Court. Personal checks accepted. Prepayment required. Mail requests: SASE requested. Turnaround time 1 day.

Magistrate Court PO Box 1263, Trenton, GA 30752; 706-657-4113; Fax: 706-657-8618. Hours: 8AM-5PM (EST). *Civil Actions Under $15,000, Eviction, Small Claims.*

Probate Court PO Box 605, Trenton, GA 30752; 706-657-4414; Fax: 706-657-4305. Hours: 8:30AM-12;00,1-5PM (EST). *Probate.*
https://www.gaprobate.org/counties/dade/index.html

Dawson County

Superior Court 25 Tucker Ave, #106, Dawsonville, GA 30534; 706-344-3510; Fax: 706-344-3511. Hours: 8AM-5PM (EST). *Felony, Misdemeanor, Civil.*
Civil Records: Access: Phone, mail, fax, in person. Visitors must perform in person searches for themselves. No search fee. Required to search: name, years to search. Civil cases indexed by plaintiff. Civil records on computer back to 1994, prior in dockets books.

Criminal Records: Access: mail, fax, in person. Visitors must perform in person searches for themselves. No search fee. Required to search: name, years to search, DOB; also helpful: SSN, race, sex. Criminal records on computer back to 1994, prior in dockets books.

General Information: Public Access terminal is available. No juvenile, adoption, sexual, mental health or expunged records released. Copy fee: $.25 per page. Cert fee: $2.50. Payee: Superior Court. Prepayment required. Mail turnaround time is 1 week.

Magistrate Court PO Box 254, Dawsonville, GA 30534; 706-344-3730; Fax: 706-265-8480. Hours: 10AM-8PM (EST). *Civil Actions Under $15,000, Eviction, Small Claims.*

Probate Court 25 Tucker Ave, #102, Dawsonville, GA 30534; 706-344-3580; Fax: 706-265-6155. Hours: 8AM-5PM, closed for noon hour (EST). *Probate.*
https://www.gaprobate.org/counties/dawson/index.html

De Kalb County

Superior Court 556 N McDonough St, Decatur, GA 30030; 404-371-2836; Fax: 404-371-2635. 7:30AM-6PM (EST). *Felony, Misdemeanor, Civil.*
www.co.dekalb.ga.us/superior/index.htm
Civil Records: Access: In person, online. Visitors must perform in person searches for themselves. No search fee. Required to search: name, years to search. Civil cases indexed by defendant, plaintiff. Civil records on computer from 1988, prior archived. Online access is free at www.ojs.dekalbga.org.

Criminal Records: Access: In person, online. Visitors must perform in person searches for themselves. No search fee. Required to search: name, years to search, DOB; also helpful: SSN, race, sex. Criminal records on computer from 1988, on microfilm from 1947. Online access is free at www.ojs.dekalbga.org. Jail and inmate records are also available.

General Information: Public Access terminal is available. No juvenile, adoption, sexual, mental health or expunged records released. Copy fee: Copies made by the court are $1.00 per page, do it yourself is $.25 per page. Cert fee: $2.50 plus $.50 per page after first. Payee: Clerk of Superior Court. Personal checks accepted. Prepayment required. Mail turnaround time is 2-3 days if exact case number given.

State Court 556 N McDonough St, Decatur, GA 30030; 404-371-2261; Fax: 404-371-3064. Hours: 8:30AM-5PM (EST). *Misdemeanor, Civil.*
www.dekalbstatecourt.net
Civil Records: Access: Mail, in person, online. Visitors must perform in person searches for themselves. No search fee. Required to search: name, years to search. Civil cases indexed by defendant, plaintiff. Civil records on docket books. Online access is free at www.ojs.dekalbga.org. The court will perform limited searches.

Criminal Records: Access: In person, online,mail. Both court and visitors may perform in person searches. No search fee. Required to search: name. Criminal records on docket books. Online access is free at www.ojs.dekalbga.org. Jail and inmate records are also available.

General Information: Public Access terminal is available. Copy fee: $.50 per page. Cert fee: $5.00. Payee: Court Clerk. Only cashiers checks and money orders accepted. Prepayment required. Mail requests: SASE requested. Turnaround time 7 days.

Magistrate Court 120 W. Trinity Pl., Rm 210, Decatur, GA 30030; 404-371-4766. Hours: 8:30AM-5PM (EST). *Civil Actions Under $15,000, Eviction, Small Claims.* http://dekalbstatecourt.net
Note: Online access is available free at www.ojs.dekalbga.org. Court also has jurisdiction for bad checks, arrest warrants, preliminary hearings, and county ordinance violations.

Probate Court 103 County Courthouse, 556 N McDonough St, Rm 1100, Decatur, GA 30030; 404-371-2718; Fax: 404-371-7055. Hours: 8:30AM-4:00PM (EST). *Probate.*
www.co.dekalb.ga.us/probate

Decatur County

Superior & State Court PO Box 336, Bainbridge, GA 39818; 229-248-3025. Hours: 8AM-5PM (EST). *Felony, Misdemeanor, Civil.*
Civil Records: Access: In person only. Visitors must perform in person searches for themselves. No search fee. Required to search: name, years to search. Civil cases indexed by defendant, plaintiff. Civil records on docket books from 1823; computerized from 1996.
Criminal Records: Access: In person only. Visitors must perform in person searches for themselves. No search fee. Required to search: name, years to search, DOB; also helpful: SSN, race, sex. Criminal records on docket books from 1823; computerized from 1996.
General Information: Public Access terminal is available. No juvenile, adoption, sexual, mental health or expunged records released. Copy fee: $.25 per page. Cert fee: $2.00 plus $.50 per page. Payee: Court Clerk. No personal checks accepted. Prepayment required.

Magistrate Court 912 Spring Creek Rd, Box #3, Bainbridge, GA 39817; 229-248-3014; Fax: 229-248-3863. Hours: 9AM-5PM (EST). *Civil Actions Under $15,000, Eviction, Small Claims.*

Probate Court PO Box 234, Bainbridge, GA 39818; 229-248-3016; Fax: 229-248-3858. Hours: 9AM-5PM (EST). *Probate.*
https://www.gaprobate.org/counties/decatur/index.html
Note: The ZIP Code changed 7/1/2002.

Dodge County

Superior Court PO Drawer 4276, 5401 Anson Ave, Eastman, GA 31023; 478-374-2871. Hours: 9AM-5PM (EST). *Felony, Misdemeanor, Civil.*
Civil Records: Access: In person only. Visitors must perform in person searches for themselves. No search fee. Required to search: name, years to search. Civil cases indexed by defendant. Civil records on docket books.
Criminal Records: Access: In person only. Visitors must perform in person searches for themselves. No search fee. Required to search: name, years to search, DOB, signed release; also helpful: SSN, race, sex. Criminal records on docket books and computer.
General Information: No juvenile, adoption, sexual, mental health or expunged records released. Copy fee: $.25 per page. Cert fee: $2.00 plus $.50 per page after first. Payee: Court Clerk. Personal checks accepted. Prepayment required.

Magistrate Court 5018 Courthouse Circle, #202, Eastman, GA 31023; 478-374-7243/8144; Fax: 478-374-5716. Hours: 8:30AM-Noon; 1PM-4:30PM

(EST). *Civil Actions Under $15,000, Eviction, Small Claims.*

Probate Court PO Box 514, Eastman, GA 31023; 478-374-3775; Fax: 478-374-9197. Hours: 9AM-Noon, 1-5PM (EST). *Probate.*

Dooly County

Superior Court PO Box 326, Vienna, GA 31092-0326; 229-268-4234; Fax: 229-268-1427. Hours: 8:30AM-5PM (EST). *Felony, Misdemeanor, Civil.*
Civil Records: Access: Fax, mail, in person. Visitors must perform in person searches for themselves. No search fee. Required to search: name, years to search. Civil cases indexed by defendant, plaintiff. Civil records on computer since 1995. Prefer to have public perform searches.
Criminal Records: Access: In person. Visitors must perform in person searches for themselves. No search fee. Required to search: name, years to search, DOB, signed release; also helpful: SSN, race, sex. Criminal records on computer since 1995, docket books prior to 1857. Prefer to have public to perform searches.
General Information: No juvenile, adoption, sexual, mental health or expunged records released. Copy fee: $1.00 per page, self serve $.25. Cert fee: $2.50. Payee: Dooly County Superior Court Clerk. Personal checks accepted. Prepayment required.

Magistrate Court PO Box 336, Vienna, GA 31092; 229-268-4324; Fax: 229-268-3585. Hours: 8AM-Noon, 1-5PM (EST). *Civil Actions Under $15,000, Eviction, Small Claims.*

Probate Court PO Box 304, Vienna, GA 31092; 229-268-4217; Fax: 229-268-6142. Hours: 8AM-5PM M,T,Th,F; 8:30AM-Noon W & Sat or by appointment (EST). *Probate.*

Dougherty County

Superior & State Court PO Box 1827, Albany, GA 31702; 229-431-2198. Hours: 8:30AM-5PM (EST). *Felony, Misdemeanor, Civil.*
www.albany.ga.us/doco/court_system.htm
Civil Records: Access: Online, in person. Visitors must perform in person searches for themselves. No search fee. Required to search: name, years to search. Civil cases indexed by defendant, plaintiff. Civil records on computer from 1992, overall records go back to 1854. Access to pre-2003 civil and criminal court docket data is free at www.albany.ga.us/doco/clerk_court_rec.htm. The same system permits access to probate, tax, deeds, death certificate records, and older civil/criminal records.
Criminal Records: Access: Online, in person. Visitors must perform in person searches for themselves. No search fee. Required to search: name, years to search SSN. Criminal records on computer from 1992, overall records go back to 1854. Online access to criminal records is the same as civil.
General Information: Public Access terminal is available. No juvenile, adoption, sexual, mental health or expunged records released. Copy fee: If court makes copy then $1.00, if yourself then $.25. Cert fee: $3.00 for 1st page; $1.00 each add'l page. Payee: Court Clerk. Personal checks accepted. Prepayment required.

Magistrate Court 225 Pine Ave, Rm 308, Albany, GA 31701; 229-431-3216; Fax: 229-434-2692. Hours: 8:30AM-5PM (EST). *Civil Actions Under $15,000, Eviction, Small Claims.*
Note: Online access to court records is available through the county clerk's system at www.dougherty.ga.us.

Probate Court PO Box 1827, 225 Pine Ave, #123, Albany, GA 31702; 229-431-2102; Fax: 229-434-2694. Hours: 8:30AM-5PM (EST). *Probate.*
https://www.gaprobate.org/counties/dougherty/index.html
Note: Search the probate court index at www.dougherty.ga.us.

Douglas County

Superior Court Douglas County Courthouse, 8700 Hospital Dr, Douglasville, GA 30134; 770-920-7252. Hours: 8AM-5PM (EST). *Felony, Misdemeanor, Civil.*
Civil Records: Access: In person only. Visitors must perform in person searches for themselves. No search fee. Required to search: name, years to search. Civil cases indexed by defendant, plaintiff. Civil records on computer from 1994, prior on docket books to 1871.
Criminal Records: Access: In person only. Visitors must perform in person searches for themselves. No search fee. Required to search: name, years to search, DOB, signed release; also helpful: address, SSN. Criminal records on computer from 1994, prior on docket books to 1871.
General Information: Public Access terminal is available. No juvenile, adoption, sexual, mental health or expunged records released. Copy fee: $.25 per page. Cert fee: $2.50 plus $.50 per page. Payee: Clerk of Superior Court. Personal checks accepted. Prepayment required.

Magistrate Court 8700 Hospital Dr, Douglasville, GA 30134; 770-920-7215. Hours: 8AM-5PM (EST). *Civil Actions Under $15,000, Eviction, Small Claims.*

Probate Court 8700 Hospital Dr, Douglasville, GA 30134; 770-920-7249; Fax: 770-920-7381. Hours: 8AM-5PM (EST). *Probate.*

Early County

Superior & State Court PO Box 849, Blakely, GA 39823; 229-723-3033; Fax: 229-723-4411. 8AM-5PM (EST). *Felony, Misdemeanor, Civil.*
Civil Records: Access: In person only. Visitors must perform in person searches for themselves. No search fee. Required to search: name, years to search. Civil cases indexed by defendant, plaintiff. Civil records on dockets.
Criminal Records: Access: In person only. Visitors must perform in person searches for themselves. No search fee. Required to search: name, years to search, DOB; also helpful: SSN, race, sex. Criminal records on dockets.
General Information: No juvenile, adoption, sexual, mental health or expunged records released. Copy fee: $1.00 per page. Cert fee: $2.50 plus $.50 per page after first. Payee: Court Clerk. Personal checks accepted. Prepayment required.

Magistrate Court Early County Courthouse, Rm D, 111 Court Sq, Blakely, GA 39823; 229-723-3454 and 229-723-5492; Fax: 229-723-5246. Hours: 8AM-5PM (EST). *Civil Actions Under $15,000, Eviction, Small Claims, Probate.*

Echols County

Superior Court PO Box 213, Statenville, GA 31648; 229-559-5642; Fax: 229-559-5792. Hours: 8AM-Noon, 1-4:30PM (EST). *Felony, Misdemeanor, Civil.*
http://www2.state.ga.us/courts/superior/dca/dca2sohp.htm
Civil Records: Access: In person only. Visitors must perform in person searches for themselves. No search fee. Required to search: name, years to search. Civil cases indexed by defendant, plaintiff. Civil records on dockets books, computerized since 1995.
Criminal Records: Access: In person only. Visitors must perform in person searches for themselves. No

search fee. Required to search: name, years to search. Criminal records on dockets books, computerized since 1995.

General Information: No juvenile, adoption, sexual, mental health or expunged records released. Copy fee: $1.00 per page. Cert fee: $2.00 1st page, $.50 each additional page. Payee: Court Clerk. Personal checks accepted. Prepayment required.

Magistrate & Probate Court PO Box 118, Statenville, GA 31648; 229-559-7526; Fax: 229-559-8128. Hours: 8:00AM-4:30PM (EST). *Civil Actions Under $15,000, Eviction, Small Claims, Probate.*

Effingham County

Superior Court PO Box 387, Springfield, GA 31329; 912-754-2146. Hours: 8:30AM-5PM (EST). *Felony, Misdemeanor, Civil.*
Civil Records: Access: Mail, in person. Both court and visitors may perform in person searches. Search fee: $20.00 per name. Required to search: name, years to search. Civil cases indexed by defendant, plaintiff. Civil records on computer from 1991, dockets books.
Criminal Records: Access: Mail, in person. Both court and visitors may perform in person searches. Search fee: $20.00 per name. Required to search: name, years to search, DOB; also helpful: SSN, race, sex. Criminal records on computer from 1991, dockets books.
General Information: Public Access terminal is available. No juvenile, adoption, sexual, mental health or expunged records released. Copy fee: $.25 per page. Cert fee: $2.50 plus $.50 per add'l page. Payee: Court Clerk. Business checks accepted. Prepayment required. Mail requests: SASE required. Mail turnaround time 3-5 days.

Magistrate Court PO Box 819, Springfield, GA 31329; 912-754-2124/29/50; Fax: 912-754-4893. Hours: 8AM-5PM (EST). *Civil Actions Under $15,000, Eviction, Small Claims.*
www.georgiacourts.org/magistrate/effingham

Probate Court 901 Pine St, PO Box 387, Springfield, GA 31329; 912-754-2112; Fax: 912-754-3894. Hours: 8:30AM-5PM (EST). *Probate.*
https://www.gaprobate.org/counties/effingham/index.html

Elbert County

Superior & State Court PO Box 619, Elberton, GA 30635; 706-283-2005; Fax: 706-213-7286. Hours: 8AM-5PM (EST). *Felony, Misdemeanor, Civil.*
Civil Records: Access: Mail, in person. Visitors must perform in person searches for themselves. No search fee. Required to search: name, years to search. Civil cases indexed by defendant, plaintiff. Civil records on computer from 1986 (excluding felonies), dockets books prior.
Criminal Records: Access: Mail, in person. Visitors must perform in person searches for themselves. No search fee. Required to search: name, years to search. Criminal records on computer from 1986 (excluding felonies), dockets books prior.
General Information: Public Access terminal is available. No juvenile, adoption, sexual, mental health or expunged records released. Will fax results for $2.50 1st page and $1.00 each add'l. Copy fee: $.25 per page. Cert fee: $2.00 plus $.50 per page. Payee: Clerk of Court. Personal checks accepted. Prepayment required. Mail turnaround time 1 week.

Magistrate Court PO Box 763, Elberton, GA 30635; 706-283-2027; Fax: 706-283-2004. Hours: 8AM-5PM (EST). *Civil Actions Under $15,000, Eviction, Small Claims.*

Probate Court Elbert County Courthouse, Elberton, GA 30635; 706-283-2016; Fax: 706-283-9668. Hours: 8AM-5PM (EST). *Probate.*

Emanuel County

Superior & State Court PO Box 627, Swainsboro, GA 30401; 478-237-8911; Fax: 478-237-3570. Hours: 8AM-5PM (EST). *Felony, Misdemeanor, Civil.*
Civil Records: Access: In person only. Visitors must perform in person searches for themselves. No search fee. Required to search: name, years to search. Civil cases indexed by defendant, plaintiff. Civil records computerized since 1999, earlier on dockets books.
Criminal Records: Access: In person only. Visitors must perform in person searches for themselves. No search fee. Required to search: name, years to search, DOB; also helpful: SSN, race, sex. Criminal records computerized since 1999, earlier on dockets books.
General Information: No juvenile, adoption, sexual, mental health or expunged records released. Copy fee: $.25 per page. Cert fee: $2.50 plus $.50 per page. Payee: Court Clerk. Personal checks accepted. Prepayment required.

Magistrate Court 107 N Main St, Swainsboro, GA 30401; 478-237-7278; Fax: 478-237-2593. Hours: 8AM-5PM Fri-7;30-4;30 (EST). *Civil Actions Under $15,000, Eviction, Small Claims.*

Probate Court PO Box 70, Swainsboro, GA 30401; 478-237-7091; Fax: 478-237-2633. Hours: 8AM-5PM (EST). *Probate.*

Evans County

Superior & State Court PO Box 845, Claxton, GA 30417; 912-739-3868; Fax: 912-739-2504. Hours: 8AM-5PM (EST). *Felony, Misdemeanor, Civil.*
Civil Records: Access: In person only. Visitors must perform in person searches for themselves. No search fee. Required to search: name, years to search. Civil cases indexed by defendant, plaintiff. Civil records on computer from 1989, dockets bookstore 1915.
Criminal Records: Access: In person only. Visitors must perform in person searches for themselves. No search fee. Required to search: name, years to search, DOB; also helpful: SSN, race, sex. Criminal records on computer from 1989, dockets books to 1915.
General Information: Public Access terminal is available. No juvenile, adoption, sexual, mental health or expunged records released. Copy fee: $1.00 per page. Cert fee: $2.50 plus $.50 per page after first. Payee: Court Clerk. Personal checks accepted. Prepayment required.

Magistrate Court Courthouse Annex, 7 Freeman St, Claxton, GA 30417; 912-739-3745; Fax: 912-739-8856. Hours: 8AM-5PM (EST). *Civil Actions Under $15,000, Eviction, Small Claims.*

Probate Court 123 W Main St, PO Box 852, Claxton, GA 30417; 912-739-4080; Fax: 912-739-4077. Hours: 8AM-5PM (EST). *Probate.*
https://www.gaprobate.org/counties/effingham/index.html

Fannin County

Superior Court PO Box 1300, 420 W Main St, Blue Ridge, GA 30513; 706-632-2039; Probate phone: 706-632-3011. Hours: 9AM-5PM (EST). *Felony, Misdemeanor, Civil.*
http://9thjudicialdistrict-ga.org/dca9apphp.shtml
Civil Records: Access: In person only. Visitors must perform in person searches for themselves. No search fee. Required to search: name, years to search. Civil cases indexed by defendant, plaintiff. Civil records on docket books back to the early 1900s.

Criminal Records: Access: In person only. Visitors must perform in person searches for themselves. No search fee. Required to search: name, years to search, DOB, signed release; also helpful: SSN, race, sex. Criminal records on docket books back to the early 1900s.
General Information: No juvenile, adoption, or DD214 records released. Copy fee: $.25 per page. $1.00 per page if the court make copies. Cert fee: $2.50 plus $.50 per page after first. Payee: Fannin County Court Clerk. Personal checks accepted. Prepayment required.

Magistrate Court 420 W Main St, #7, Blue Ridge, GA 30513; 706-632-5558; Fax: 706-632-8236. Hours: 9AM-5PM (EST). *Civil Actions Under $15,000, Eviction, Small Claims, Misdemeanor.*

Probate Court 420 W Main St #2, Blue Ridge, GA 30513; 706-632-3011; Fax: 706-632-7167. Hours: 8AM-5PM (EST). *Probate.*

Fayette County

Superior Court PO Box 130, Fayetteville, GA 30214; 770-716-4290; Civil phone: 770-716-4294; Criminal phone: 770-716-4293. Hours: 8AM-5PM (EST). *Felony, Misdemeanor, Civil.*
www.admin.co.fayette.ga.us
Note: The court will copy and mail specific documents for $1.00 per page.

Civil Records: Access: In person only. Visitors must perform in person searches for themselves. No search fee. Required to search: name, years to search. Civil cases indexed by defendant, plaintiff. Civil records on computer since 1989; prior records on dockets books.
Criminal Records: Access: In person only. Visitors must perform in person searches for themselves. No search fee. Required to search: name, years to search, DOB; also helpful: SSN, race, sex. Criminal records on computer since 1989; prior records on dockets books.
General Information: Public Access terminal is available. No juvenile, adoption, sexual, mental health or expunged records released. Copy fee: $.25 per page. Cert fee: $2.00 plus $.50 per page after first. Payee: Court Clerk. Only cashiers checks and money orders accepted. Prepayment required.

Magistrate Court 1 Center Dr, Fayetteville, GA 30214-8401; 770-716-4230. 8AM-5PM (EST). *Civil Actions Under $15,000, Eviction, Small Claims.*

Probate Court 1 Center Dr., Fayetteville, GA 30214; 770-716-4220; Fax: 770-716-4854. Hours: 8AM-5PM (EST). *Probate.*
https://www.gaprobate.org/counties/fayette/index.html

Floyd County

Superior Court PO Box 1110, #3 Government Plaza, #101, Rome, GA 30163; 706-291-5190; Probate phone: 706-291-5131; Fax: 706-233-0035. 8AM-5PM (EST). *Felony, Misdemeanor, Civil.*
www.floydsuperiorcourt.org
Civil Records: Access: Phone, in person. Visitors must perform in person searches for themselves. No search fee. Required to search: name, years to search. Civil cases indexed by defendant, plaintiff. Civil records on computer since 11/95; prior on docket books to 1833. The court will only do a name search to determine if a case exists, then provides a case number.
Criminal Records: Access: In person only. Visitors must perform in person searches for themselves. No search fee. Required to search: name, years to search, signed release. Criminal records on computer since 11/95; prior on docket books back to 1833. The court will only do a name search to determine if a case exists, then provides a case number.

General Information: Public Access terminal is available. No juvenile, adoption, sexual, mental health or expunged records released. Will fax results $.50 per page. Copy fee: $.50 per page. Cert fee: $2.00 plus copy fee. Payee: Court Clerk. Personal checks accepted. Prepayment required. Mail turnaround time is 1 day.

Magistrate Court 3 Government Plaza, Rm 227, Rome, GA 30161; 706-291-5250; Fax: 706-291-5269. Hours: 8:45AM-4:45PM (EST). *Civil Actions Under $15,000, Eviction, Small Claims.*
Note: Copy and certification fees are $.50 a page, will fax results for an additional $.50 pe rpage. Court also has jurisdiction for bad checks, arrest warrants, preliminary hearings, and county ordinance violations.

Probate Court 3 Government Plaza, #201, County Admin. Offices, Rome, GA 30162; 706-291-5136/8; Fax: 706-291-5189. Hours: 8AM-5:00PM (EST). *Probate.*

Forsyth County

Superior & State Court 100 Courthouse Sq, Rm 010, Cumming, GA 30040; 770-781-2120; Fax: 770-886-2858. Hours: 8:30AM-5PM (EST). *Felony, Misdemeanor, Civil, Eviction, Small Claims.*
www.forsythco.com
Civil Records: Access: In person only. Visitors must perform in person searches for themselves. No search fee. Required to search: name, years to search. Civil cases indexed by defendant. Civil records on computer since 1996; prior records on docket books back to 1832.
Criminal Records: Access: In person only. Visitors must perform in person searches for themselves. No search fee. Required to search: name, years to search; also helpful: SSN. Criminal records on computer since late 1989.
General Information: Public Access terminal is available. No juvenile, adoption, sexual, mental health or expunged records released. Copy fee: $.25 per page. Cert fee: $2.50 plus $.50 per page after first. Payee: Court Clerk. Personal checks accepted. Prepayment required.

Magistrate Court 121 Dahlonega St, Cumming, GA 30040; 770-781-2211; Fax: 770-844-7581. Hours: 8AM-4:30PM (EST). *Civil Actions Under $15,000, Eviction, Small Claims, Probate.*

Probate Court County Courthouse Annex, Rm 101, 112 W Maple St, Cumming, GA 30130; 770-781-2140; Fax: 770-886-2839. Hours: 8:30AM-5PM (EST). *Probate.*

Franklin County

Superior Court PO Box 70, Carnesville, GA 30521; 706-384-2514. Hours: 8AM-5PM (EST). *Felony, Misdemeanor, Civil.*
Civil Records: Access: In person only. Visitors must perform in person searches for themselves. No search fee. Required to search: name, years to search. Civil cases indexed by defendant, plaintiff. Civil records on computer since 1995; prior records on docket books.
Criminal Records: Access: In person only. Visitors must perform in person searches for themselves. No search fee. Required to search: name, years to search, DOB; also helpful: SSN, race, sex. Criminal records on computer since 1995; prior records on docket books.
General Information: Public Access terminal is available. No juvenile, adoption, sexual, mental health or expunged records released. Copy fee: $.25 per page. Cert fee: $2.50 for 1st page, $.50 each add'l. Payee: Court Clerk. Personal checks accepted. Prepayment required.

Magistrate Court PO Box 467, Carnesville, GA 30521; 706-384-7473; Fax: 706-384-4346. Hours: 8AM-5PM (EST). *Civil Actions Under $15,000, Eviction, Small Claims.*

Probate Court PO Box 207, 9592 Lavonia Rd, Carnesville, GA 30521; 706-384-2403; Fax: 706-384-2636. Hours: 8AM-5PM (EST). *Probate.*
https://www.gaprobate.org/counties/franklin/index.html

Fulton County

Superior Court 136 Pryor St SW, Rm C-155, Superior Court Clerk, Atlanta, GA 30303; Civil phone: 404-730-5344; Fax: 404-302-8416. Hours: 8:30AM-5PM (EST). *Civil.*
www.fcclk.org
Civil Records: Access: In person, online. Both court and visitors may perform in person searches. Search fee: varies. Required to search: name, years to search. Civil cases indexed by defendant, plaintiff. Civil records on computer since 1972. Search civil cases free at www.fcclk.org/JudicialSearch/CivilSearch/civfrmdFC.htm.
General Information: Public Access terminal is available. No juvenile, adoption, sexual, mental health, sealed or expunged records released. Copy fee: $.25 per page. Cert fee: $2.50 for 1st page; $.50 each add'l. Payee: Clerk of Fulton Superior Court. Personal checks accepted. Prepayment required.

Superior Court 136 Pryor St SW, Rm C-515, Atlanta, GA 30303; 404-730-5770; Criminal phone: 404-730-5248; Fax: 404-893-2773. Hours: 8:30AM-5PM (EST). *Felony, Misdemeanor, Eviction.*
www.fcclk.org
Criminal Records: Access: In person only. Visitors must perform in person searches for themselves. No search fee. Required to search: name, years to search, DOB, signed release; also helpful: SSN, race, sex. Criminal records on computer from 1973.
General Information: Public Access terminal is available. No juvenile, adoption, sexual, mental health, sealed or expunged records released. Will not fax results. Copy fee: $.25 per page. Cert fee: $2.50 for 1st page; $.50 each add'l. Payee: Clerk of Superior Court. Personal checks accepted. Prepayment required.

State Court TG100 Justice Center Tower, 185 Central Ave SW, Atlanta, GA 30303; 404-730-5000; Fax: 404-730-8141 Civil; 335-3521 Criminal. Hours: 8:30AM-5PM (EST). *Misdemeanor, Civil.*
www.fultonstatecourt.com
Civil Records: Access: In person only. Both court and visitors may perform in person searches. Search fee: $15.00 if court performs search. Required to search: name, years to search. Civil cases indexed by defendant, plaintiff. Civil records on computer from 1984, books back to 1982.
Criminal Records: Access: In person only. Both court and visitors may perform in person searches. Search fee: $15.00 if court performs search. Required to search: name, years to search, DOB, signed release; also helpful: SSN, race, aliases, date of offense, sex, approximate arrest date. Criminal records on computer from 1984, books back to 1982.
General Information: Public Access terminal is available. No juvenile, adoption, sexual, mental health or expunged records released. Copy fee: $.25 per page. Cert fee: $2.50 per page. Payee: Court Clerk. Business checks accepted. Prepayment required.

Magistrate Court 185 Central Ave SW, TG-700, Justice Center Tower, Atlanta, GA 30303; 404-730-5045; Fax: 404-730-5027. 8:30AM-5PM (EST). *Civil Actions Under $15,000, Eviction, Small Claims.*

Probate Court 136 Pryor St., # 230, Atlanta, GA 30303; 404-730-4640; Fax: 404-730-8283. Hours: 8:30AM-5PM (EST). *Probate.*
https://www.gaprobate.org/counties/fulton/index.html

Gilmer County

Superior Court #1 Westside Sq, Ellijay, GA 30540; 706-635-4462; Fax: 706-635-1462. Hours: 8:30AM-5PM (EST). *Felony, Misdemeanor, Civil.*
http://9thjudicialdistrict-ga.org/dca9apphp.shtml
Civil Records: Access: In person only. Visitors must perform in person searches for themselves. No search fee. Required to search: name, years to search. Civil cases indexed by defendant, plaintiff. Civil records on docket books computerized records since 1994.
Criminal Records: Access: In person only. Visitors must perform in person searches for themselves. No search fee. Required to search: name, years to search, signed release; also helpful: DOB, SSN. Criminal records on docket books; computerized since 1994.
General Information: Public Access terminal is available. No juvenile, adoption, sealed, sexual, mental health, expunged or sealed records released. Copy fee: $.25 per page. Cert fee: $2.50 plus $.50 per page after first. Payee: Superior Court Clerk. Personal checks accepted. Prepayment required.

Magistrate Court 53 Sand St., Ellijay, GA 30540; 706-635-2515; Fax: 706-635-7756. Hours: 8:30AM-5PM (EST). *Civil Actions Under $15,000, Eviction, Small Claims.*

Probate Court 51 Sand St., Ellijay, GA 30540; 706-635-4763; Fax: 706-635-4761. Hours: 8:30AM-5PM (EST). *Probate.*
https://www.gaprobate.org/counties/gilmer/index.html

Glascock County

Superior Court PO Box 231, 62 E Main St, Gibson, GA 30810; 706-598-2084; Fax: 706-598-2577. Hours: Mon, tue, Thu, Fri 8am-5pm; Wed 8am-12pm (EST). *Felony, Misdemeanor, Civil.*
Civil Records: Access: In person only. Visitors must perform in person searches for themselves. No search fee. Required to search: name, years to search. Civil cases indexed by defendant, plaintiff. Civil records on computer from 1991, records go back to 1990.
Criminal Records: Access: In person only. Visitors must perform in person searches for themselves. No search fee. Required to search: name, years to search, DOB; also helpful: SSN, race, sex. Criminal records on computer from 1991 records go back to 1990.
General Information: Public Access terminal is available. (Public access in county cases only.) No juvenile, adoption, sexual, mental health or expunged records released. Copy fee: $.25 per page. Legal size copies $1.00 per page. Cert fee: $2.50 plus $.50 per page after first. Payee: Court Clerk. Personal checks accepted. Prepayment required.

Magistrate Court PO Box 201, Gibson, GA 30810; 706-598-2013; Fax: 706-598-3577. Hours: 8AM-5PM T, 8AM-8PM TH (EST). *Civil Actions Under $15,000, Eviction, Small Claims.*

Probate Court PO Box 277, Gibson, GA 30810; 706-598-3241; Fax: 706-598-2471. 8AM-Noon, 1-5PM-M.T,Th,Fri; 8am-12;00-W (EST). *Probate.*

Glynn County

Superior Court PO Box 1355, Brunswick, GA 31521; 912-554-7272; Fax: 912-267-5625. Hours: 8AM-5PM (EST). *Felony, Civil.*
Civil Records: Access: Phone, fax, mail, in person. Both court and visitors may perform in person searches. No search fee. Required to search: name, years to search. Civil cases indexed by defendant,

plaintiff. Civil records on computer back to 1987, archived and in docket books from 1800s.

Criminal Records: Access: Phone, fax, mail, in person. Both court and visitors may perform in person searches. No search fee. Required to search: name, years to search, DOB, signed release; also helpful: SSN, race, sex. Criminal records on computer back to 1987, index back to 1800s.

General Information: Public Access terminal is available. No juvenile, adoption, sexual, mental health or expunged records released. Fee to fax results is $5.00 per document. Copy fee: $.25 per page. If court does copy, fee is $.25 per page. Cert fee: $2.50 plus $.50 per page after first. Payee: Court Clerk. Personal checks accepted. Prepayment required. Will bill copy and cert fees. Mail requests: SASE requested. Turnaround time 1-3 days.

State Court 701 "H" St,. #104, Brunswick, GA 31520; 912-554-7325; Fax: 912-261-3849. Hours: 9AM-5PM (EST). *Misdemeanor, Civil.*

Civil Records: Access: In person only. Visitors must perform in person searches for themselves. No search fee. Required to search: name, years to search. Civil cases indexed by defendant. Civil records on dockets books to 1980; on computer back to 1994.

Criminal Records: Access: In person only. Visitors must perform in person searches for themselves. No search fee. Required to search: name, years to search. Criminal records on dockets books to 1979; on computer back to 1994.

General Information: Public Access terminal is available. No juvenile, adoption, sexual, mental health or expunged records released. Copy fee: $.25 per page. Cert fee: $2.00 plus $.50 per page. Payee: Clerk of State Court. Only cashiers checks and money orders accepted. Prepayment required.

Magistrate Court PO Box 1355, Brunswick, GA 31521; 912-554-7250; Fax: 912-267-5677. Hours: 8:00AM-5PM (EST). *Civil Actions Under $15,000, Eviction, Small Claims.*

Probate Court 701 H St, Box 302, Brunswick, GA 31520; 912-554-7231; Fax: 912-466-8001. 8:30AM-5PM *Probate, Civil, Small Claims.*
https://www.gaprobate.org/counties/glynn/index.html

Gordon County

Superior Court 100 Wall St, #102, Calhoun, GA 30701; 706-629-9533; Fax: 706-629-2139. Hours: 8:30AM-5PM (EST). *Felony, Misdemeanor, Civil.*

Civil Records: Access: Mail, in person. Both court and visitors may perform in person searches. No search fee. Required to search: name, years to search. Civil cases indexed by defendant, plaintiff. Civil records on computer since 03/97; prior records on docket books.

Criminal Records: Access: Mail, in person. Both court and visitors may perform in person searches. No search fee. Required to search: name, years to search. Criminal records on computer since 03/97; prior records on docket books.

General Information: Public Access terminal is available. (Public access records from 1997 to present.) No sealed records released. Will not fax results. Copy fee: $.25 per page. Cert fee: $2.50 plus $.25 per page. Payee: Superior Court Clerk. Personal checks accepted. Prepayment required. Mail requests: SASE required. Mail turnaround time 1-2 days.

Magistrate Court PO Box 1025, 100 Wall St, Calhoun, GA 30703; 706-629-6818 X121/122/143/144; Fax: 706-602-1751. Hours: 8:30AM-5PM (EST). *Civil Actions Under $15,000, Eviction, Small Claims.*

Probate Court PO Box 669, Calhoun, GA 30703; 706-629-7314; Fax: 706-629-4698. Hours: 8:30AM-5PM (EST). *Probate.*
https://www.gaprobate.org/counties/gordon/index.html

Grady County

Superior Court 250 N Broad St, Box 8, Cairo, GA 39828; 229-377-2912. Hours: 8AM-5PM (EST). *Felony, Misdemeanor, Civil.*

Civil Records: Access: In person only. Court will assist visitors with searches. No search fee. Required to search: name, years to search. Civil cases indexed by defendant, plaintiff. Civil records on computer since 1993; prior records on docket books from 1903.

Criminal Records: Access: In person only. Court will assist visitors with searches. No search fee. Required to search: name, years to search. Criminal records on computer since 1993; prior records on docket books from 1903.

General Information: Public Access terminal is available. No juvenile or adoption records released. Copy fee: $.25 per page. Cert fee: $2.00 plus $.50 per page. Payee: Superior Court Clerk. Personal checks accepted. Prepayment required. Mail turnaround time 3 days for case file copies.

Magistrate Court 250 N Broad St, Box 2, Cairo, GA 39828; 229-377-4132; Fax: 229-377-4127. Hours: 8AM-5PM (EST). *Civil Actions Under $15,000, Eviction, Small Claims.*

Probate Court Courthouse, 250 N Broad St #1, Box 1, Cairo, GA 39828; 229-377-4621; Fax: 229-378-8052. Hours: 8AM-5PM (EST). *Probate.*

Greene County

Superior & Juvenile Court 113 N Main St, #109, Greensboro, GA 30642; 706-453-3340; Fax: 706-453-9179. Hours: 8AM-5PM (EST). *Felony, Misdemeanor, Civil, Eviction, Small Claims.*

Civil Records: Access: In person only. Visitors must perform in person searches for themselves. No search fee. Required to search: name, years to search. Civil cases indexed by defendant, plaintiff. Overall records go back to 1700. Computerized records go back to 2000.

Criminal Records: Access: In person only. Visitors must perform in person searches for themselves. No search fee. Required to search: name, years to search; also helpful: SSN. Overall records go back to 1700. Computerized records go back to 2000.

General Information: No juvenile or adoption records released. Copy fee: $.25 per page. Cert fee: Fee is $2.50 plus $.25 per page. Payee: Superior Court Clerk. Personal checks accepted. Prepayment required.

Magistrate & Probate Court 113 N Main St, #113, Greensboro, GA 30642; 706-453-3346; Fax: 706-453-7649. 8AM-5PM (EST). *Civil Actions Under $15,000, Eviction, Small Claims, Probate.*
https://www.gaprobate.org/counties/greene/index.html

Gwinnett County

Superior & State Court PO Box 880 (75 Langley Dr.), Lawrenceville, GA 30046; 770-822-8100. Hours: 8AM-5PM (EST). *Felony, Misdemeanor, Civil, Eviction, Small Claims.*
www.gwinnettcourts.com/courts/Supcourt.htm

Civil Records: Access: Online, in person. Visitors must perform in person searches for themselves. No search fee. Required to search: name, years to search. Civil cases indexed by defendant, plaintiff. Civil records on computer from 1990, prior records on card index. Online access to court case party index is free online at www.gwinnettcourts.com/misc/casendx.htm. Search by name or case number.

Criminal Records: Access: Online, in person. Visitors must perform in person searches for themselves. No search fee. Required to search: name, years to search. Criminal records on computer from 1990, prior records on card index. Online access to criminal records is the same as civil.

General Information: Public Access terminal is available. No sealed records released. Copy fee: $.25 per page. Cert fee: $2.50 plus $.50 per page. Payee: Superior Court Clerk. Personal checks accepted. Prepayment required.

Magistrate Court 75 Langley Dr, Justice & Admin. Ctr, Lawrenceville, GA 30045-6900; 770-822-8080; Fax: 770-822-8075. Hours: 8AM-5PM (EST). *Civil Actions Under $15,000, Eviction, Small Claims.*
www.gwinnettcourts.com/courts/Magcourt.htm

Probate Court 75 Langley Dr, Justice & Admin. Ctr, Lawrenceville, GA 30045; 770-822-8250; Fax: 770-822-8274. 8:AM-4:30PM (EST). *Probate.*
www.gwinnettcourts.com/courts/Procourt.htm
Note: Search records by name for free at the web site; click on "Data Search."

Habersham County

Superior & State Court 555 Monroe St, Unit 35, Clarkesville, GA 30523; 706-754-2923; Probate phone: 706-754-2013. Hours: 8AM-5PM (EST). *Felony, Misdemeanor, Civil.*
www.co.habersham.ga.us

Civil Records: Access: Mail, in person. Visitors must perform in person searches for themselves. No search fee. Required to search: name, years to search. Civil cases indexed by defendant, plaintiff. Civil records on index books from 1819.

Criminal Records: Access: Mail, in person. Visitors must perform in person searches for themselves. No search fee. Required to search: name, years to search. Criminal records on index books from 1819.

General Information: Public Access terminal is available. No juvenile, adoption, sexual, mental health or expunged records released. Will fax results to local or toll free line. Copy fee: $.25 per page. Cert fee: $3.00 per document. Payee: Court Clerk. Personal checks accepted. Prepayment required. Mail turnaround time 1-2 days.

Magistrate Court PO Box 580, Clarkesville, GA 30523; 706-754-4871; Civil phone: 706-754-4871; Criminal phone: 706-754-0126; Fax: 706-839-7093. Hours: 8AM-5PM (EST). *Civil Actions Under $15,000, Eviction, Small Claims.*
www.co.habersham.ga.us

Probate Court Habersham County Courthouse, PO Box 625, Clarkesville, GA 30523; 706-754-2013; Fax: 706-754-5093. 8AM-5PM (EST). *Probate.*

Hall County

Superior & State Court PO Box 1336, Gainesville, GA 30503; 770-531-7025; Fax: 770-531-7070; 536-0702 real estate. Hours: 8AM-5PM (EST). *Felony, Misdemeanor, Civil.*

Civil Records: Access: In person only. Visitors must perform in person searches for themselves. No search fee. Required to search: name, years to search. Civil cases indexed by defendant, plaintiff. Civil records on computer back to 1989, dockets books from early 1900s in storage.

Criminal Records: Access: In person only. Visitors must perform in person searches for themselves. No search fee. Required to search: name, years to search. Criminal records on computer back to 1989, dockets books from early 1900s in storage.

General Information: No juvenile, adoption, sexual, mental health or expunged records released. Copy fee:

$1.00 per page. Cert fee: $2.00 plus $.50 per page. Payee: Court Clerk. Personal checks accepted. Prepayment required.

Magistrate Court PO Box 1435, Gainesville, GA 30503; 770-531-6912; Fax: 770-531-6917. Hours: 8AM-5PM (EST). *Civil Actions Under $15,000, Eviction, Small Claims, Misdemeanors.* www.hallcounty.org/clerk.asp

Probate Court Hall County Courthouse, Rm 123, 225 Green St, Gainesville, GA 30501; 770-531-6923; Fax: 770-531-4946. Hours: 8AM-4:30PM (EST). *Probate.* www.hallcounty.org/clerk.asp Note: The search fee is $4.00 per record

Hancock County

Superior Court PO Box 451, Courthouse Sq, Sparta, GA 31087; 706-444-6644; Fax: 706-444-6221. Hours: 9AM-5PM (EST). *Felony, Misdemeanor, Civil.*
Civil Records: Access: Mail, in person. Visitors must perform in person searches for themselves. Search fee: $5.00 per name. Required to search: name, years to search. Civil cases indexed by defendant, plaintiff. Civil records on docket books from 1991.
Criminal Records: Access: Mail, in person. Visitors must perform in person searches for themselves. Search fee: $5.00 per name. Required to search: name, years to search, DOB, signed release; also helpful: SSN, race, sex. Criminal records on books since 1991.
General Information: Public Access terminal is available. No juvenile, adoptions, sealed, sexual, mental health or expunged records released. Copy fee: $.25 per page. Cert fee: First page is $2.50, each add'l is $.50. Payee: Clerk of Superior Court. Personal checks accepted. Prepayment required. Mail requests: SASE required. Mail turnaround time 1 week.

Magistrate Court 603 Courthouse Sq, Sparta, GA 31087; 706-444-6234; Fax: 706-444-6178. Hours: 9AM-5PM (EST). *Civil Actions Under $15,000, Eviction, Small Claims.*

Probate Court 601 Courthouse Sq, Sparta, GA 31087; 706-444-5343; Fax: 706-444-8024. Hours: 8AM-5PM (EST). *Probate.* https://www.gaprobate.org/counties/hancock/index.html

Haralson County

Superior Court Drawer 849, 4485 Georgia Hwy 120, Buchanan, GA 30113; 770-646-2005; Probate phone: 770-646-2008; Fax: 770-646-2035. Hours: 8:30AM-5PM (EST). *Felony, Misdemeanor, Civil.*
Civil Records: Access: Mail, in person. Both court and visitors may perform in person searches. No search fee. Required to search: name, years to search. Civil cases indexed by defendant, plaintiff. Civil records on dockets books from the 1864.
Criminal Records: Access: Mail, in person. Both court and visitors may perform in person searches. No search fee. Required to search: name, years to search, signed release. Criminal records on dockets books from the 1864.
General Information: No juvenile, adoption, sexual, mental health or expunged records released. Copy fee: $.25 per page. Cert fee: $2.50 plus $.50 per page after first. Payee: Clerk of Superior Court. Personal checks accepted. Prepayment required. Mail requests: SASE required. Mail turnaround time 1 week.

Magistrate Court PO Box 1040, Buchanan, GA 30113; 770-646-2015; Fax: 770-646-12017. Hours: 8:30AM-5PM (EST). *Civil Actions Under $15,000, Eviction, Small Claims.*

Probate Court PO Box 620, Buchanan, GA 30113; 770-646-2008; Fax: 770-646-3419. Hours: 8:30AM-5PM (EST). *Probate.* https://www.gaprobate.org/counties/haralson/index.html

Harris County

Superior Court PO Box 528, Hamilton, GA 31811; 706-628-4944; Fax: 706-628-7039. Hours: 8AM-5PM (EST). *Felony, Misdemeanor, Civil.*
Civil Records: Access: In person only. Visitors must perform in person searches for themselves. No search fee. Required to search: name, years to search. Civil cases indexed by defendant, plaintiff. Civil records on dockets books from 1900; on computer back to 1999.
Criminal Records: Access: In person only. Visitors must perform in person searches for themselves. No search fee. Required to search: name, years to search, DOB; also helpful: race, sex. Criminal records on dockets books from 1900; on computer back to 1999.
General Information: Public Access terminal is available. Juvenile, adoption, sexual, mental health or expunged records are only released with a signed release. Copy fee: $.25 per page. Cert fee: $2.50 plus $.50 per page after first. Payee: Court Clerk. No personal checks accepted. Prepayment required.

Magistrate Court PO Box 347, Hamilton, GA 31811; 706-628-4977; Fax: 706-628-5416. Hours: 8AM-5PM (EST). *Civil Actions Under $15,000, Eviction, Small Claims.*

Probate Court PO Box 569, Hamilton, GA 31811; 706-628-5038; Fax: 706-628-7322. Hours: 8AM-5PM (No longer close at noon) (EST). *Probate.*

Hart County

Superior Court PO Box 386, Hartwell, GA 30643; 706-376-7189; Fax: 706-376-1277. Hours: 8:30AM-5PM (EST). *Felony, Misdemeanor, Civil.*
Civil Records: Access: In person only. Visitors must perform in person searches for themselves. No search fee. Required to search: name, years to search. Civil cases indexed by defendant, plaintiff. Civil records on computer back to 1991, dockets books from 1853.
Criminal Records: Access: In person only. Visitors must perform in person searches for themselves. No search fee. Required to search: name, years to search, DOB; also helpful: SSN, race, sex. Criminal records on computer back to 1991, dockets books from 1853.
General Information: Public Access terminal is available. No juvenile, adoption, sexual, mental health or expunged records released. Copy fee: $.25 per page. Cert fee: $2.50 plus $.50 per page after first. Payee: Clerk of Court. Personal checks accepted. Prepayment required.

Magistrate Court PO Box 698, Hartwell, GA 30643; 706-376-6817; Fax: 706-376-6821. Hours: 8:30AM-5PM (EST). *Civil Actions Under $15,000, Eviction, Small Claims.* www.hartmagcourt.com

Probate Court PO Box 1159, Hartwell, GA 30643; 706-376-2565; Fax: 706-376-9032. Hours: 8:30AM-5PM M-F (EST). *Probate.* https://www.gaprobate.org/counties/hart/index.html

Heard County

Superior Court PO Box 249, Franklin, GA 30217; 706-675-3301. Hours: 8:30AM-5PM (EST). *Felony, Misdemeanor, Civil.*
Civil Records: Access: In person only. Visitors must perform in person searches for themselves. No search fee. Required to search: name, years to search. Civil cases indexed by defendant, plaintiff. Civil records on docket books from 1800s.
Criminal Records: Access: In person only. Visitors must perform in person searches for themselves. No

search fee. Required to search: name, years to search, DOB, signed release; also helpful: SSN, race, sex. Criminal records on docket books from 1800s.
General Information: No juvenile, adoptions, sealed, sexual, mental health or expunged records released. Will fax results for $1.00 per page. Copy fee: $.25 per page. Cert fee: $2.50 plus $.50 per page after first. Payee: Court Clerk. Personal checks accepted. Prepayment required.

Magistrate Court PO Box 395, Franklin, GA 30217; 706-675-3002; Fax: 706-675-0819. Hours: 8:30AM-5PM (EST). *Civil Actions Under $15,000, Eviction, Small Claims.*

Probate Court PO Box 478, Franklin, GA 30217; 706-675-3353; Fax: 706-675-0819. Hours: 8:30AM-5PM (EST). *Probate.* https://www.gaprobate.org/counties/heard/index.html

Henry County

Superior Court One Courthouse Sq, McDonough, GA 30253; 770-954-2121. Hours: 8AM-5PM (EST). *Felony, Misdemeanor, Civil.*
Civil Records: Access: Phone, mail, in person. Visitors must perform in person searches for themselves. No search fee. Required to search: name, years to search. Civil cases indexed by defendant, plaintiff. Civil records on dockets books from 1800s.
Criminal Records: Access: In person only. Visitors must perform in person searches for themselves. No search fee. Required to search: name, years to search, DOB, signed release; also helpful: SSN, race, sex. Criminal records on dockets books from 1800s.
General Information: No juvenile, adoption, sexual, mental health or expunged records released. No fee to fax results. Copy fee: $.25 per page. Cert fee: $2.50 plus $.50 per add'l page. Payee: Clerk of Superior Court. Personal checks accepted. Prepayment required.

Magistrate Court 30 Atlanta St, McDonough, GA 30253; 770-954-2111; Fax: 770-954-2144. Hours: 8AM-5PM (EST). *Civil Actions Under $15,000, Eviction, Small Claims.*

Probate Court 99 Sims St., McDonough, GA 30253; 770-954-2303; Fax: 770-954-2308. Hours: 8AM-4:45PM (EST). *Probate.* https://www.gaprobate.org/counties/henry/index.html

Houston County

Superior Court 201 Perry Pkwy, Perry, GA 31069; 478-218-4720; Civil phone: 478-218-4740; Criminal phone: 478-218-4730; Fax: 478-218-4745. Hours: 8:30AM-5PM (EST). *Felony, Misdemeanor, Civil.*
www.houstoncountyga.org
Civil Records: Access: Phone, fax, mail, in person. Both court and visitors may perform in person searches. No search fee. Required to search: name, years to search. Civil cases indexed by defendant, plaintiff. Civil records on computer from 1984, dockets books back to 1823.
Criminal Records: Access: Fax, mail, in person. Both court and visitors may perform in person searches. No search fee. Required to search: name, years to search, DOB; also helpful: SSN, race, sex. Criminal records on computer from 1984, dockets books back to 1823.
General Information: Public Access terminal is available. No juvenile, adoption, mental health or expunged records released. Will fax results. Copy fee: $.25 per page. Cert fee: $2.50 plus $.50 per page after first. Payee: Court Clerk. No personal checks accepted. Prepayment required. Mail turnaround time 1-2 days.

State Court 202 Carl Vinson Pkwy, Warner Robins, GA 31088; 478-542-2105; Fax: 478-542-2077. Hours: 8AM-5PM (EST). *Misdemeanor, Civil.* www.houstoncountyga.com/
Note: The county recorder's office offers free online access to liens from the web site listed above.

Civil Records: Access: Mail, fax, in person. Visitors must perform in person searches for themselves. No search fee. Required to search: name, years to search. Civil cases indexed by defendant. Civil records on computer from 1987, dockets books from 1965.
Criminal Records: Access: In person only. Visitors must perform in person searches for themselves. No search fee. Required to search: name, years to search, DOB; also helpful: SSN, race, sex. Criminal records on computer from 1987, dockets books from 1965.
General Information: Public Access terminal is available. No juvenile, adoption, sexual, mental health or expunged records released. Copy fee: $.25 per page. Cert fee: $2.50 plus $.50 per page after first. Payee: Court Clerk. Only cashiers checks and money orders accepted. Prepayment required.

Magistrate Court 89 Cohen Walker Dr, Warner Robins, GA 31088; 478-987-4695; Fax: 478-987-5249. Hours: 8AM-5PM (EST). *Civil Actions Under $15,000, Eviction, Small Claims.*
http://georgiacourts.org/courts/magistrate/houston/

Probate Court PO Box 1801, 201 N. Perry Pkwy, Perry, GA 31069; 478-218-4710; Fax: 478-218-4715. Hours: 8AM-4PM (EST). *Probate.*
www.houstoncountyga.org/probate_court.htm

Irwin County

Superior Court 113 N Irwin Ave, Ocilla, GA 31774; 229-468-5356. Hours: 8AM-5PM (EST). *Felony, Misdemeanor, Civil.*
Civil Records: Access: Phone, mail, in person. Visitors must perform in person searches for themselves. No search fee. Required to search: name, years to search. Civil cases indexed by defendant, plaintiff. Civil records on dockets books from 1870s, records are not computerized. Court will not do general record searches, the specific case file must be given.
Criminal Records: Access: Phone, mail, in person. Visitors must perform in person searches themselves. No search fee. Required to search: name, years to search, DOB, signed release; also helpful: SSN, race, sex. Criminal records on dockets books from 1900, records are not computerized. Court will not do general record searches, the specific case file must be given.
General Information: Public Access terminal is available. No juvenile, adoption, sexual, mental health or expunged records released. Will fax results for $2.50 1st page, $1.00 each add'l page. Copy fee: $1.00 for first page, $.25 each add'l. Cert fee: $2.50 plus $.50 per page after first. Payee: Court Clerk. Personal checks accepted. Prepayment required. Mail turnaround time 2 days.

Magistrate Court 207 S Irwin Ave, # 3, Ocilla, GA 31774; 229-468-7671; Fax: 229-468-9672. Hours: 8AM-5PM (EST). *Civil Actions Under $15,000, Eviction, Small Claims.*

Probate Court 202 S Irwin Ave., Ocilla, GA 31774; 229-468-5138; Fax: 229-468-5702. Hours: 8:00-12:00 - 1:00-5:00 (EST). *Probate.*
https://www.gaprobate.org/counties/irwin/index.html

Jackson County

Superior & State Court PO Box 7, Jefferson, GA 30549; 706-367-6360; Criminal phone: 707-367-6369; Fax: 706-367-2468. Hours: 8AM-5PM (EST). *Felony, Misdemeanor, Civil.*
Civil Records: Access: In person only. Visitors must perform in person searches for themselves. No search fee. Required to search: name, years to search. Civil cases indexed by defendant, plaintiff. Civil records on computer from 1992, on dockets books from 1800s.
Criminal Records: Access: In person only. Visitors must perform in person searches for themselves. No search fee. Required to search: name, years to search, DOB; also helpful: SSN, race, sex. Criminal records on computer from 1992, on dockets books from 1800s.
General Information: Public Access terminal is available. No juvenile, adoption, sexual, mental health or expunged records released. Copy fee: $.25 per page. Cert fee: $2.50 plus $.50 per page after first. Payee: Court Clerk. Personal checks accepted. Prepayment required.

Magistrate Court PO Box 751, Commerce, GA 30529; 706-335-6545; Fax: 706-335-5221. Hours: 8AM-5PM (EST). *Civil Actions Under $15,000, Eviction, Small Claims.*

Probate Court 500 Jackson Pky, Jefferson, GA 30549; 706-367-6366; Fax: 706-367-7211. Hours: 8:AM-5PM (EST). *Probate.*
https://www.gaprobate.org/counties/jackson/index.html
Note: Jackson County Probate does not handle civil and criminal records.

Jasper County

Superior Court 126 W Green St, #110, Monticello, GA 31064; 706-468-4901; Fax: 706-468-4946. Hours: 8AM-5PM (EST). *Felony, Misdemeanor, Civil.*
Civil Records: Access: In person only. Visitors must perform in person searches for themselves. No search fee. Required to search: name, years to search. Civil cases indexed by defendant, plaintiff. Civil records on computer from 1990, dockets books from 1807.
Criminal Records: Access: In person only. Visitors must perform in person searches for themselves. No search fee. Required to search: name, years to search, DOB; also helpful: SSN, race, sex. Criminal records on computer from 1990, dockets books from 1807.
General Information: Public Access terminal is available. No juvenile, adoption, sexual, mental health or expunged records released. Will fax specific document for $2.50 per page. Copy fee: $.25 per page. Cert fee: $2.50 plus $.50 per page after first. Payee: Court Clerk. Personal checks accepted. Prepayment required.

Magistrate Court 126 W Green St #110, Monticello, GA 31064; 706-468-4909; Fax: 706-468-4946. Hours: 8:30AM-4:30PM (EST). *Civil Actions Under $15,000, Eviction, Small Claims.*
Note: Access records online via the state system at www.gsccca.org. Court also has jurisdiction for bad checks, arrest warrants, preliminary hearings, and county ordinance violations.

Probate Court Jasper County Courthouse, 126 W Green St, #111, Monticello, GA 31064; 706-468-4903; Fax: 706-468-4926. Hours: 8AM-4:30PM (EST). *Probate.*
https://www.gaprobate.org/counties/jasper/index.html

Jeff Davis County

Superior & State Court PO Box 429, Hazlehurst, GA 31539; 912-375-6615; Fax: 912-375-6637. Hours: 8AM-5PM (EST). *Felony, Misdemeanor, Civil.*
Civil Records: Access: Fax, mail, in person. Both court and visitors may perform in person searches. No search fee. Required to search: name, years to search. Civil cases indexed by defendant, plaintiff. Civil records on dockets books, limited records on computer back 3 years.
Criminal Records: Access: Fax, mail, in person. Both court and visitors may perform in person searches. Search fee: $3.00 per name. Required to search: name, years to search. Criminal records on dockets books.
General Information: No juvenile, confidential, adoption or sealed records released. Fee to fax results is $2.00 1st page, $1.00 each add'l. Copy fee: $.25 per page. Cert fee: $2.50 plus $.50 per page after first. Payee: Court Clerk. Personal checks accepted. Prepayment required. Mail requests: SASE requested. Turnaround time 1 week; fax is immediate on finding results.

Magistrate Court PO Box 568, Hazlehurst, GA 31539; 912-375-6630; Fax: 912-375-6629. Hours: 8AM-5PM (EST). *Civil Actions Under $15,000, Eviction, Small Claims.*
www.jeffdaviscourt.com

Probate Court PO Box 446, Hazlehurst, GA 31539; 912-375-6626; Fax: 912-375-6629. Hours: 9AM-5PM (EST). *Probate.*

Jefferson County

Superior & State Court PO Box 151, Louisville, GA 30434; 478-625-7922; Fax: 478-625-4037. Hours: 8AM-5PM (EST). *Felony, Misdemeanor, Civil.*
Civil Records: Access: Mail, in person. Both court and visitors may perform in person searches. No search fee. Required to search: name, years to search. Civil cases indexed by defendant, plaintiff. Civil records on dockets books from 1865; on computer back to 1995.
Criminal Records: Access: In person only. Both court and visitors may perform in person searches. No search fee. Required to search: name, years to search, DOB or SSN. Criminal records on dockets books from 1865; on computer back to 1995.
General Information: Public Access terminal is available. No juvenile, adoption, sexual, mental health or expunged records released. Will fax results. Copy fee: $.25 per page. Cert fee: $2.50 plus $1.00 per add'l page. Payee: Court Clerk. Personal checks accepted. Prepayment required.

Magistrate Court PO Box 749, Louisville, GA 30434; 478-625-8834; Fax: 478-625-4039. Hours: 8AM-5PM (EST). *Civil Actions Under $15,000, Eviction, Small Claims.*
www.jeffersoncourt.com

Probate Court PO Box 307, Louisville, GA 30434; 478-625-3258; Fax: 478-625-0245. Hours: 8AM-5PM (EST). *Probate.*
https://www.gaprobate.org/counties/jefferson/index.html

Jenkins County

Superior & State Court PO Box 659, Millen, GA 30442; 478-982-4683; Fax: 478-982-1274. Hours: 8:30AM-5PM (EST). *Felony, Misdemeanor, Civil.*
Civil Records: Access: In person only. Visitors must perform in person searches for themselves. No search fee. Required to search: name, years to search. Civil

cases indexed by defendant. Civil records on dockets books.

Criminal Records: Access: In person only. Visitors must perform in person searches for themselves. No search fee. Required to search: name, years to search, DOB; also helpful: SSN, race, sex. Criminal records on dockets books.

General Information: Public Access terminal is available. No juvenile, adoption, sexual, mental health or expunged records released. Copy fee: $.25 per page. Cert fee: $2.50 plus $.25 per page after first. Payee: Clerk of Court. Personal checks accepted. Prepayment required.

Magistrate Court PO Box 892, Millen, GA 30442; 478-982-5580; Fax: 478-982-4911. Hours: 8:30AM-5PM (EST). *Civil Actions Under $15,000, Eviction, Small Claims.*

Probate Court PO Box 904, 611 E Winthrope Ave, Millen, GA 30442; 478-982-5581; Fax: 478-982-2829. Hours: 8:30AM-5PM (EST). *Probate.*
https://www.gaprobate.org/counties/jenkins/index.html

Johnson County

Superior & Magistrate Court PO Box 321, Wrightsville, GA 31096; 478-864-3484; Fax: 478-864-1343. Hours: 9AM-5PM (EST). *Felony, Misdemeanor, Civil, Eviction, Small Claims.*

Civil Records: Access: In person only. Visitors must perform in person searches for themselves. No search fee. Required to search: name, years to search. Civil cases indexed by defendant, plaintiff. Civil records on computer from 1991, dockets books from 1859.

Criminal Records: Access: In person only. Visitors must perform in person searches for themselves. No search fee. Required to search: name, years to search, DOB; also helpful: SSN, race, sex. Criminal records on computer from 1991, dockets books from 1859.

General Information: No juvenile, adoption, sexual, mental health or expunged records released. Copy fee: $.25 per page. Cert fee: $3.00. Payee: Court Clerk. Personal checks accepted. Prepayment required.

Probate Court PO Box 264, Wrightsville, GA 31096; 478-864-3316; Fax: 478-864-0528. Hours: 9AM-5PM (EST). *Probate.*

Jones County

Superior Court PO Box 39, 110 S Jefferson St, Gray, GA 31032; 478-986-6671/6674. 8:30AM-4:30PM (EST). *Felony, Misdemeanor, Civil.*

Civil Records: Access: In person only. Visitors must perform in person searches for themselves. No search fee. Required to search: name, years to search. Civil cases indexed by defendant, plaintiff. Civil records on computer since 1989, dockets books from 1800s. The court will fax records not requiring a search, $5.00 minimum.

Criminal Records: Access: In person only. Visitors must perform in person searches for themselves. No search fee. Required to search: name, years to search, signed release. Criminal records on docket books, computerized since 1995.

General Information: Public Access terminal is available. No juvenile, adoption, sexual, mental health or expunged records released. Copy fee: $.50 per page. Cert fee: $2.50 plus $.50 per page after first. Payee: Superior Court. Personal checks accepted. Prepayment required.

Probate Court PO Box 1359, Gray, GA 31032; 478-986-6668; Fax: 478-986-1715. Hours: 8:30AM-4:30PM (EST). *Civil Actions Under $15,000, Eviction, Small Claims, Probate.*

Lamar County

Superior Court 326 Thomaston St, Box 7, Barnesville, GA 30204; 770-358-5145; Fax: 770-358-5814. Hours: 8AM-5PM (EST). *Felony, Misdemeanor, Civil.*

Civil Records: Access: In person only. Visitors must perform in person searches for themselves. No search fee. Required to search: name, years to search. Civil cases indexed by defendant. Civil records on dockets books from 1921; on computer back to 9/2000.

Criminal Records: Access: In person only. Visitors must perform in person searches for themselves. No search fee. Required to search: name, years to search, DOB, offense, date of offense; also helpful: SSN, race, sex. Criminal records on dockets books from 1921; on computer back to 9/2000.

General Information: No juvenile, adoption, sexual, mental health or expunged records released. Copy fee: $1.00 for first page, $.25 each add'l. Cert fee: $2.50 for 1st page; $.50 each add'l page. Payee: Court Clerk. Personal checks accepted. Prepayment required. Will bill copy fees.

Magistrate Court 121 Roberta Dr, #B, Barnesville, GA 30204; 770-358-5154; Fax: 770-358-5214. Hours: 8AM-5PM (EST). *Civil Actions Under $15,000, Eviction, Small Claims.*

Probate Court 326 Thomaston St, Barnesville, GA 30204; 770-358-5155; Fax: 770-358-5348. Hours: 8AM-5PM (EST). *Probate.*

Lanier County

Superior Court County Courthouse, 100 Main St, Lakeland, GA 31635; 229-482-3594; Fax: 229-482-8333. Hours: 8AM-Noon, 1-5PM (EST). *Felony, Misdemeanor, Civil.*

Civil Records: Access: In person only. Visitors must perform in person searches for themselves. No search fee. Required to search: name, years to search. Civil cases indexed by defendant, plaintiff. Civil records on dockets books from 1921; on computer back to 1995.

Criminal Records: Access: In person only. Visitors must perform in person searches for themselves. No search fee. Required to search: name, years to search, DOB, signed release. Criminal records on dockets books from 1921; on computer back to 1995.

General Information: No juvenile, adoption, sexual, mental health or expunged records released. Copy fee: $.25 per page. Cert fee: $3.00. Payee: Court Clerk. Personal checks accepted. Prepayment required.

Magistrate Court 100 Main St, County Courthouse, Lakeland, GA 31635; 229-482-2207; Fax: 229-482-8333. Hours: 8AM-Noon; 1PM-5PM (EST). *Civil Actions Under $15,000, Eviction, Small Claims.*

Probate Court County Courthouse, 100 Main St, Lakeland, GA 31635; 229-482-3668; Fax: 229-482-8333. Hours: 8AM-5PM, closed for noon hour (EST). *Probate.*
https://www.gaprobate.org/counties/lanier/index.html

Laurens County

Superior & Magistrate Court PO Box 2028, Dublin, GA 31040; 478-272-3210; Fax: 478-275-2595. Hours: 8:30AM-5:30PM (EST). *Felony, Misdemeanor, Civil, Eviction, Small Claims.*

Civil Records: Access: In person only. Visitors must perform in person searches for themselves. No search fee. Required to search: name, years to search. Civil cases indexed by defendant, plaintiff. Civil records on computer from 1992, dockets books from 1800s.

Criminal Records: Access: In person only. Visitors must perform in person searches for themselves. No search fee. Required to search: name, years to search;

also helpful: SSN. Criminal records on computer from 1992, dockets books from 1800s.

General Information: Public Access terminal is available. No juvenile, adoption, sexual, mental health or expunged records released. Copy fee: $.25 per page. Cert fee: $2.50 plus $.50 per page after first. Payee: Court Clerk. Personal checks accepted. Prepayment required.

Probate Court PO Box 2098, County Courthouse, Rm 108, Dublin, GA 31040; 478-272-2566; Fax: 478-277-2932. Hours: 8:30AM-5:30PM (EST). *Probate.*
https://www.gaprobate.org/counties/laurens/index.html

Lee County

Superior Court PO Box 597, Leesburg, GA 31763; 229-759-6018. Hours: 8AM-5PM (EST). *Felony, Misdemeanor, Civil.*

Civil Records: Access: Mail, in person. Both court and visitors may perform in person searches. No search fee. Required to search: name, years to search. Civil cases indexed by defendant, plaintiff. Civil records on docket books from 1850.

Criminal Records: Access: Mail, in person. Both court and visitors may perform in person searches. Search fee: $5.00. Required to search: name, years to search, DOB; also helpful: SSN, race, sex. Criminal records on docket books from 1850, computerized since 1996.

General Information: No juvenile, adoption, sexual, mental health or expunged records released. Will fax results to local or toll free line. Copy fee: $1.00 per page. Cert fee: $2.00. Payee: Court Clerk. Personal checks accepted. Prepayment required. Mail requests: SASE required. Mail turnaround time 1 week.

Magistrate Court PO Box 522, Leesburg, GA 31763; 229-759-6016; Fax: 229-759-3303. Hours: 8AM-5PM (EST). *Civil Actions Under $15,000, Eviction, Small Claims.*

Probate Court PO Box 592, Leesburg, GA 31763; 229-759-6005; Fax: 229-759-3345. Hours: 8AM-5PM (EST). *Probate, Traffic.*

Liberty County

Superior & State Court PO Box 50, Hinesville, GA 31313-0050; 912-876-3625; Civil phone: 912-876-7276; Criminal phone: 912-876-7289; Fax: 912-876-7394. Hours: 8AM-5PM (EST). *Felony, Misdemeanor, Civil.*
www.libertyco.com

Civil Records: Access: Fax, mail, in person. Both court and visitors may perform in person searches. Search fee: $5.00. Required to search: name, years to search, signed release. Civil cases indexed by defendant, plaintiff. Civil records on computer from 1986, dockets books from 1700s.

Criminal Records: Access: Mail, in person. Both court and visitors may perform in person searches. Search fee: $5.00 per name. Required to search: name, years to search, DOB, signed release; also helpful: SSN, race, sex. Criminal records on computer from 1986, dockets books from 1700s.

General Information: Public Access terminal is available. No juvenile, adoption, sexual, mental health or expunged records released. Will fax results for $5.00 1st 5 pages, $1.00 each add'l page. Need prepaid account for fax retrieval. Copy fee: $1.00 per page. Cert fee: $2.50 plus $.50 per page after first. Payee: Court Clerk. Business checks accepted. Prepayment required. Mail requests: SASE not required. Mail turnaround time 1-3 days.

Magistrate Court PO Box 912, Hinesville, GA 31310; 912-368-2063; Fax: 912-876-2474. Hours: 8AM-12;00,1-5PM (EST). *Civil Actions Under $15,000, Eviction, Small Claims.*

www.libertyco.com

Probate Court PO Box 28, Hinesville, GA 31310; 912-876-3635; Fax: 912-876-3589. Hours: 8AM-5PM (EST). *Probate.*

Lincoln County

Superior Court PO Box 340, Lincolnton, GA 30817; 706-359-5505. Hours: 9AM-5PM (EST). *Felony, Misdemeanor, Civil.*
Civil Records: Access: In person only. Visitors must perform in person searches for themselves. No search fee. Required to search: name, years to search. Civil cases indexed by defendant, plaintiff. Civil records on index books from 1796, computerized since 1992. There is no public terminal, must search in the books.
Criminal Records: Access: In person only. Visitors must perform in person searches for themselves. No search fee. Required to search: name, years to search. Criminal records on index books from 1796, records are not computerized.
General Information: Public Access terminal is available. No adoption or juvenile records released. Copy fee: $.25 per page. Cert fee: $2.50. Payee: Superior Court Clerk. Personal checks accepted. Prepayment required.

Magistrate & Probate Court PO Box 205, 210 Humphrey St, Lincolnton, GA 30817; 706-359-5519; Probate phone: 706-359-5528; Fax: 706-359-5520. Hours: 9AM-5PM (EST). *Civil Actions Under $15,000, Eviction, Small Claims, Probate.*
Note: Probate fax is 706-359-4729. Court also has jurisdiction for bad checks, arrest warrants, preliminary hearings, and county ordinance violations.

Long County

Superior & State Court PO Box 458, Ludowici, GA 31316; 912-545-2123; Fax: 912-545-2020. Hours: 8:30AM-5PM (EST). *Felony, Misdemeanor, Civil.*
Civil Records: Access: Mail, fax, in person. Only the court performs in person searches; visitors may not. Search fee: $5.00 per name. Required to search: name, years to search. Civil cases indexed by defendant, plaintiff. Civil records on docket books, archived from 1921.
Criminal Records: Access: Mail, fax, in person. Only the court performs in person searches; visitors may not. Search fee: $5.00 per name. Required to search: name, years to search, DOB; also helpful: SSN, race, sex. Criminal records on docket books, archived from 1921.
General Information: Public Access terminal is available. No juvenile, adoption, sealed, sexual, mental health, expunged or confidential records released. Copy fee: $.25 per page. Cert fee: $2.50 for 1st page, $.50 each add'l. Payee: Court Clerk. Business checks accepted. Prepayment required. Mail requests: SASE required. Mail turnaround time 1 week.

Magistrate & Probate Court PO Box 426, Ludowici, GA 31316; 912-545-2131; Probate phone: 912-545-2315; Fax: 912-545-2150. Hours: 8:30AM-4:30PM (EST). *Civil Actions Under $15,000, Eviction, Small Claims, Probate.*

Lowndes County

Superior & State Court PO Box 1349, Valdosta, GA 31603; 229-333-5127. Hours: 8AM-5PM (EST). *Felony, Misdemeanor, Civil.*
http://www2.state.ga.us/courts/superior/dca/dca2sohp.htm
Civil Records: Access: Mail, in person. Both court and visitors may perform in person searches. Search fee: $3.00 per name for mail requests. Required to search: name, years to search. Civil cases indexed by

defendant, plaintiff. Civil records on computer from 1990, prior on dockets books.
Criminal Records: Access: In person only. Visitors must perform in person searches for themselves. No search fee. Required to search: name, years to search, DOB; also helpful: SSN, race, sex. Criminal records on computer back to 1984; prior records on docket books.
General Information: Public Access terminal is available. No juvenile, adoption, sexual, mental health or expunged records released. Fee to fax results is $.25 per page. Copy fee: $.25 per page. Cert fee: $2.50 plus $.50 per page after 1st; $5.00 minimum. Payee: Court Clerk. Only cashiers checks and money orders accepted. Prepayment required.

Magistrate Court PO Box 1349, Valdosta, GA 31603; 229-671-2610; Fax: 229-671-3442. Hours: 8AM-5PM (EST). *Civil Actions Under $15,000, Eviction, Small Claims.*

Probate Court PO Box 72, Valdosta, GA 31603; 229-333-5103; Fax: 229-333-7646. Hours: 8AM-5PM (EST). *Probate.* www.lowndescounty.com

Lumpkin County

Superior, Juvenile & Magistrate Court 99 Courthouse Hill, #D, Dahlonega, GA 30533-0541; 706-864-3736; Fax: 706-864-5298. Hours: 8AM-5PM (EST). *Felony, Misdemeanor, Civil, Eviction, Small Claims.*
Note: For Magistrate Court criminal records info, call 706-864-7760.
Civil Records: Access: In person only. Visitors must perform in person searches for themselves. No search fee. Required to search: name, years to search; also helpful: address. Civil cases indexed by defendant, plaintiff. Civil records on computer from 1988, prior on dockets books to 1833.
Criminal Records: Access: In person only. Visitors must perform in person searches for themselves. No search fee. Required to search: name, years to search, DOB; also helpful: address, SSN, race, sex. Criminal records on computer from 1988, prior on dockets books to 1833.
General Information: Public Access terminal is available. No juvenile, adoption, sealed records released. Copy fee: $1.00 per page; $.25 if in person. Cert fee: $2.50 plus $.50 per page after first. Payee: Court Clerk. Personal checks accepted. Prepayment required.

Probate Court 99 Courthouse Hill, #C, Dahlonega, GA 30533; 706-864-3847; Fax: 706-864-9271. Hours: 8AM-5PM (EST). *Probate.*

Macon County

Superior Court PO Box 337, Oglethorpe, GA 31068; 478-472-7661. Hours: 8AM-5PM (EST). *Felony, Misdemeanor, Civil.*
Civil Records: Access: Mail, in person. Both court and visitors may perform in person searches. No search fee. Civil cases indexed by defendant, plaintiff. Civil records on dockets books from 1800s.
Criminal Records: Access: In person only. Both court and visitors may perform in person searches. No search fee. Criminal records on dockets books from 1800s.
General Information: Public Access terminal is available. No juvenile, adoption, sexual, mental health or expunged records released. Copy fee: $.25 per page. Cert fee: $2.00. Payee: Court Clerk. Business checks accepted. Prepayment required.

Magistrate Court PO Box 605, Oglethorpe, GA 31068; 478-472-8509; Fax: 478-472-5643. Hours: 8AM-Noon, 1-5PM (EST). *Civil Actions Under $15,000, Eviction, Small Claims.*

Probate Court PO Box 216, 100 Sumter St, Oglethorpe, GA 31068; 478-472-7685; Fax: 478-472-5643. Hours: 8AM-Noon, 1-5PM (EST). *Probate.*
https://www.gaprobate.org/counties/macon/index.html

Madison County

Superior Court PO Box 247, Danielsville, GA 30633; 706-795-3352; Fax: 706-795-2209. Hours: 8AM-5PM (EST). *Felony, Misdemeanor, Civil.*
Civil Records: Access: In person only. Visitors must perform in person searches for themselves. No search fee. Required to search: name, years to search. Civil cases indexed by defendant. Civil records on computer since 07/96, archived since 1811.
Criminal Records: Access: In person only. Visitors must perform in person searches for themselves. No search fee. Required to search: name, years to search, DOB; also helpful: SSN, race, sex. Criminal records on computer since 07/96, archived since 1811.
General Information: Public Access terminal is available. No juvenile, adoption, sexual, mental health or expunged records released. Copy fee: $.25 per page. Cert fee: $2.50 plus $.50 per page after first. Payee: Court Clerk. No personal checks accepted. Prepayment required.

Magistrate Court PO Box 6, Danielsville, GA 30633; 706-795-5679; Fax: 706-795-2222. Hours: 8AM-5PM (EST). *Civil Actions Under $15,000, Eviction, Small Claims.*

Probate Court PO Box 207, Danielsville, GA 30633; 706-795-6365; Fax: 706-795-5933. Hours: 8AM-5PM (EST). *Probate.*

Marion County

Superior Court PO Box 41, Buena Vista, GA 31803; 229-649-7321; Fax: 229-649-7931. Hours: 8:30AM-5PM (EST). *Felony, Misdemeanor, Civil.*
Civil Records: Access: In person only. Visitors must perform in person searches for themselves. No search fee. Required to search: name, years to search. Civil cases indexed by defendant, plaintiff. Civil records on books.
Criminal Records: Access: In person only. Visitors must perform in person searches for themselves. No search fee. Required to search: name, years to search; also helpful: SSN. Criminal records on books.
General Information: No juvenile, adoption, sexual, mental health or expunged records released. Copy fee: $.25 per page. Cert fee: $2.50 plus $.50 per page after first. Payee: Court Clerk. Personal checks accepted. Prepayment required.

Magistrate & Probate Court PO Box 207, Buena Vista, GA 31803; 229-649-5542; Fax: 229-649-2059. Hours: 8:30AM-5PM (EST). *Civil Under $15,000, Eviction, Small Claims, Probate.*

McDuffie County

Superior Court PO Box 158, 337 Main St, Rm 101, Thomson, GA 30824; 706-595-2134. Hours: 8AM-5PM (EST). *Felony, Misdemeanor, Civil.*
Civil Records: Access: In person only. Visitors must perform in person searches for themselves. No search fee. Required to search: name, years to search. Civil cases indexed by defendant, plaintiff. Civil records on computer from 1991, dockets books from 1871.
Criminal Records: Access: In person only. Visitors must perform in person searches for themselves. No search fee. Required to search: name, years to search, signed release; also helpful: DOB. Civil records on computer from 1991, dockets books from 1800s.
General Information: Public Access terminal is available. No juvenile or adoption records released. Copy fee: $.25 per page self; $1.00 per page assisted. Cert fee: $2.50 plus $.50 per page after first. Payee:

Clerk Superior Court. Personal checks accepted. Prepayment required.

Magistrate Court PO Box 252, Thomson, GA 30824; 706-597-2618; Fax: 706-595-2041. Hours: 8AM-5PM (EST). *Civil Actions Under $15,000, Eviction, Small Claims.*

Probate Court PO Box 2028, Thomson, GA 30824; 706-595-2124; Fax: 706-597-2644. Hours: 8AM-5PM (EST). *Probate.*

McIntosh County

Superior & State Court PO Box 1661, Darien, GA 31305; 912-437-6641; Fax: 912-437-6673. 8AM-4:30PM (EST). *Felony, Misdemeanor, Civil.*
Civil Records: Access: In person only. Visitors must perform in person searches for themselves. No search fee. Required to search: name, years to search. Civil cases indexed by defendant, plaintiff. Civil records on computer from 1991, dockets books from 1872.
Criminal Records: Access: In person only. Visitors must perform in person searches for themselves. No search fee. Required to search: name, years to search, DOB; also helpful: SSN, race, sex. Criminal records on computer from 1991, dockets books from 1872.
General Information: Public Access terminal is available. No juvenile, adoption, sexual, or expunged records released. Copy fee: $.25 per pg unassisted; $.50 if helped. Cert fee: $2.50. Payee: Court Clerk. Personal checks accepted. Prepayment required.

Magistrate Court PO Box 459, Darien, GA 31305; 912-437-4888; Fax: 912-437-2768. Hours: 8AM-4:30PM (EST). *Civil Actions Under $15,000, Eviction, Small Claims.*

Probate Court PO Box 453, Darien, GA 31305; 912-437-6636; Fax: 912-437-6635. Hours: 8AM-5PM (EST). *Probate.*
www.darientel.net/~pcourt

Meriwether County

Superior Court PO Box 160, Greenville, GA 30222; 706-672-4416; Fax: 706-672-9465. Hours: 8;30AM-5PM (EST). *Felony, Misdemeanor, Civil.*
Civil Records: Access: In person only. Visitors must perform in person searches for themselves. Search fee: none. Required to search: name, years to search. Civil cases indexed by defendant, plaintiff. Civil records on microfilm and computer from 1990, prior on writ and minute books to 1827.
Criminal Records: Access: In person only. Visitors must perform in person searches for themselves. No search fee. Required to search: name, years to search, DOB, SSN. Criminal records go back to 1827; on computer back to 1991.
General Information: Public Access terminal is available. No juvenile, adoption, sexual, mental health or expunged records released. Copy fee: $.25 per page self serve $1.00. Cert fee: $2.50 plus $.50 per page after first. Payee: Court Clerk. Business checks accepted. Prepayment required.

Magistrate Court PO Box 702, 124 N Court Sq, Greenville, GA 30222; 706-672-1247; Fax: 706-672-1172. Hours: 8:30AM-Noon; 1PM-4:30PM (EST). *Civil Actions Under $15,000, Eviction, Small Claims.*

Probate Court PO Box 608, Greenville, GA 30222; 706-672-4952; Probate phone: 706-672-1817; Fax: 706-672-6660. Hours: 8:30AM-5PM (EST). *Probate.*

Miller County

Superior & State Court PO Box 66, Colquitt, GA 39837; 229-758-4102. Hours: 8AM-5PM (EST). *Felony, Misdemeanor, Civil.*
Civil Records: Access: In person only. Visitors must perform in person searches for themselves. No search fee. Required to search: name, years to search. Civil cases indexed by defendant, plaintiff. Civil records on dockets books from 1800s, computerized from 1995.
Criminal Records: Access: In person only. Visitors must perform in person searches for themselves. No search fee. Required to search: name, years to search. Criminal records on dockets books from 1800s, computerized from 1995.
General Information: Public Access terminal is available. No juvenile or adoption records released. Copy fee: $1.00 per page. Cert fee: $2.50 plus $1.00 per page after first. Payee: Court Clerk. Business checks accepted. Prepayment required.

Magistrate & Probate Court 155 S 1st St, Box 1, Rm 110, Colquitt, GA 39837; 229-758-4110; Fax: 229-758-8133. Hours: 9AM-5PM (EST). *Civil Actions Under $15,000, Small Claims, Probate.*

Mitchell County

Superior & State Court PO Box 427, Camilla, GA 31730; 229-336-2022. Hours: 8:30AM-5PM (EST). *Felony, Misdemeanor, Civil.*
Civil Records: Access: In person only. Visitors must perform in person searches for themselves. No search fee. Required to search: name, years to search. Civil cases indexed by defendant. Civil records on dockets books from 1800s.
Criminal Records: Access: In person only. Visitors must perform in person searches for themselves. No search fee. Required to search: name, years to search, DOB; also helpful: SSN, race, sex. Criminal records on dockets books from 1800s.
General Information: No juvenile, adoption, sexual, mental health or expunged records released. Copy fee: $.25 per page. Cert fee: $2.50 plus $.50 per page after first. Payee: Court Clerk. Only cashiers checks and money orders accepted. Prepayment required.

Magistrate Court PO Box 626, Camilla, GA 31730-0626; 229-336-2077; Fax: 229-336-2039. Hours: 8:30AM-Noon; 1PM-5PM (EST). *Civil Actions Under $15,000, Eviction, Small Claims.*

Probate Court PO Box 229, Camilla, GA 31730; 229-336-2016; Fax: 229-336-2354. Hours: 8:30AM-5PM (EST). *Probate.*
https://www.gaprobate.org/counties/mitchell/index.html

Monroe County

Superior Court PO Box 450, Forsyth, GA 31029; 478-994-7022; Fax: 478-994-7053. Hours: 8AM-5PM (EST). *Felony, Misdemeanor, Civil.*
Civil Records: Access: Mail, in person. Visitors must perform in person searches for themselves. No search fee. Required to search: name, years to search. Civil cases indexed by defendant, plaintiff. Civil records on computer from 1986, dockets books from 1800s.
Criminal Records: Access: Mail, in person. Both court and visitors may perform in person searches. No search fee. Required to search: name, years to search, signed release. Criminal records on computer from 1989.
General Information: Public Access terminal is available. No juvenile, adoption, sexual, mental health or expunged records released. Will not fax results. Copy fee: $1.00 per page $.25 self serve. Cert fee: $2.50 plus $.50 per page after first. Payee: Court Clerk. Personal checks accepted. Prepayment required. Mail requests: SASE required. Mail turnaround time 3 days.

Magistrate Court PO Box 974, Forsyth, GA 31029; 478-994-7018; Fax: 478-994-7284. Hours: 8:30AM-Noon, 1:30-5:00PM (EST). *Civil Actions Under $15,000, Eviction, Small Claims.*

Probate Court PO Box 187, Forsyth, GA 31029; 478-994-7036; Fax: 478-994-7054. Hours: 8AM-5:00PM (EST). *Probate.*

Montgomery County

Superior Court PO Box 311, Mt Vernon, GA 30445; 912-583-4401. Hours: 8AM-5PM (EST). *Felony, Misdemeanor, Civil.*
Civil Records: Access: In person only. Visitors must perform in person searches for themselves. No search fee. Required to search: name, years to search. Civil cases indexed by defendant, plaintiff. Civil records on computer from 1993, on dockets from 1793.
Criminal Records: Access: In person only. Visitors must perform in person searches for themselves. No search fee. Required to search: name, years to search, DOB; also helpful: SSN, race, sex. Criminal records on computer from 1993, on dockets from 1793.
General Information: Public Access terminal is available. No juvenile or adoption records released. Copy fee: $1.00 per page. Cert fee: $2.50 per page. Payee: Superior Court Clerk. Personal checks accepted.

Magistrate Court PO Box 174, Mt Vernon, GA 30445; 912-583-2170; Fax: 912-583-4343. Hours: 8:30AM-4:30PM (EST). *Civil Actions Under $15,000, Eviction, Small Claims.*

Probate Court PO Box 444, 400 Railroad Ave, Mt Vernon, GA 30445; 912-583-2681; Fax: 912-583-4343. Hours: 9AM-5PM (EST). *Probate.*
https://www.gaprobate.org/counties/montgomery/index.html

Morgan County

Superior Court PO Box 130, 149 E Jefferson St, Madison, GA 30650; 706-342-3605. Hours: 9AM-5PM (EST). *Felony, Misdemeanor, Civil.*
Civil Records: Access: In person only. Visitors must perform in person searches for themselves. No search fee. Required to search: name, years to search. Civil cases indexed by defendant, plaintiff. Civil records on computer from 1986, on dockets from 1900s.
Criminal Records: Access: In person only. Visitors must perform in person searches for themselves. No search fee. Required to search: name, years to search, signed release. Criminal records on computer from 1986, on dockets from 1900s.
General Information: Public Access terminal is available. No juvenile, adoption, sexual, mental health or expunged records released. Copy fee: $.25 per page. Cert fee: $2.50 plus $.50 per page after first. Payee: Superior Court Clerk. Personal checks accepted. Prepayment required.

Magistrate Court PO Box 589, Madison, GA 30650; 706-342-3088; Fax: 706-343-6364. Hours: 9AM-5PM (EST). *Civil Actions Under $15,000, Eviction, Small Claims.*
www.morganga.org

Probate Court PO Box 857, Madison, GA 30650; 706-343-6500; Fax: 706-343-6465. Hours: 9AM-5PM (EST). *Probate.* Note: This court also has Misdemeanor and Traffic cases.

Murray County

Superior Court PO Box 1000, Chatsworth, GA 30705; 706-695-2932. Hours: 8:30AM-5PM (EST). *Felony, Misdemeanor, Civil.*
Civil Records: Access: In person only. Visitors must perform in person searches for themselves. No search fee. Required to search: name, years to search. Civil

cases indexed by defendant, plaintiff. Civil records on dockets from 1940, prior to 1940 archived; computerized records since 2000.

Criminal Records: Access: In person only. Visitors must perform in person searches for themselves. No search fee. Required to search: name, years to search, signed release. Criminal records on dockets from 1940, prior to 1940 archived; computerized records since 2000.

General Information: Public Access terminal is available. No juvenile, adoption, sexual, mental health or expunged records released. Copy fee: $.25 per page. Cert fee: $2.50 plus $.50 per page after first. Payee: Superior Court Clerk. Personal checks accepted. Prepayment required.

Magistrate Court 121 N 4th Ave, Chatsworth, GA 30705; 706-695-3021; Fax: 706-695-7525. Hours: 8AM-Noon, 1-5PM (EST). *Civil Actions Under $15,000, Eviction, Small Claims.*

Probate Court 115 Fort St, Chatsworth, GA 30705; 706-695-3812; Fax: 706-517-1340. Hours: 8:30AM-5PM (EST). *Probate.*
https://www.gaprobate.org/counties/murray/index.html

Muscogee County

Superior & State Court PO Box 2145, Columbus, GA 31902; 706-653-4351; Fax: 706-653-4359. Hours: 8:30AM-5PM (EST). *Felony, Misdemeanor, Civil.*

Civil Records: Access: Mail, in person. Both court and visitors may perform in person searches. Search fee: $30.00 per name. Required to search: name, years to search. Civil cases indexed by defendant, plaintiff. Civil records on computer from 1989, on dockets from 1919 to 1989.

Criminal Records: Access: Mail, in person. Both court and visitors may perform in person searches. Search fee: $30.00 per name. Required to search: name, years to search, DOB; also helpful: SSN. Criminal records on computer since 1989, on dockets from 1989 to 1957.

General Information: Public Access terminal is available. No adoption, sealed or first offender records released. Copy fee: $.25 per page. Cert fee: $2.50 plus $.50 per page after first. Payee: Superior Court Clerk. Business checks accepted. Prepayment required. Mail requests: SASE requested. Turnaround time 1 week.

Magistrate Court Box 1340, Columbus, GA 31902; 706-653-4390; Fax: 706-653-4559. Hours: 8:30AM-5PM (EST). *Civil Actions Under $15,000, Eviction, Small Claims.*

Probate Court PO Box 1340, Columbus, GA 31902; 706-653-4333. 8:30AM-4PM (EST). *Probate.*

Newton County

Superior Court 1132 Usher St, Covington, GA 30014; 770-784-2035; Probate phone: 770-784-2045; Fax: 770-385-8930. Hours: 8AM-5PM (EST). *Felony, Misdemeanor, Civil.*

Civil Records: Access: Mail, in person. Visitors must perform in person searches for themselves. Search fee: $1.00 (for mailing). Required to search: name, years to search. Civil cases indexed by defendant, plaintiff. Civil records on computer from 1991, on dockets from 1900s.

Criminal Records: Access: Mail, in person. Visitors must perform in person searches for themselves. Search fee: $1.00 (for mailing). Required to search: name, years to search, signed release. Criminal records on computer from 1991, on dockets from 1900s.

General Information: Public Access terminal is available. No adoption, sexual, mental health or expunged records released. Copy fee: $.25 per page. Cert fee: $2.50 plus $.50 per page after first. Payee:

Superior Court Clerk. Personal checks accepted. Prepayment required. Mail turnaround time is two weeks.

Magistrate & Probate Court 1132 Usher St, Rm 148, Covington, GA 30014; 770-784-2045 or 770-784-2050; Fax: 770-784-2145. Hours: 8AM-5PM (EST). *Civil Actions Under $15,000, Eviction, Small Claims, Probate.*

Oconee County

Superior & Magistrate Courts PO Box 1099, Watkinsville, GA 30677; 706-769-3940; Fax: 706-769-3948. Hours: 8AM-5PM (EST). *Felony, Misdemeanor, Civil, Eviction, Small Claims.*

Civil Records: Access: In person only. Visitors must perform in person searches for themselves. No search fee. Required to search: name, years to search. Civil cases indexed by defendant, plaintiff. Civil records on computer from 1989, on dockets from 1875.

Criminal Records: Access: In person only. Visitors must perform in person searches for themselves. No search fee. Required to search: name, years to search; also helpful: DOB, SSN. Criminal records on computer from 1989, on dockets from 1875.

General Information: Public Access terminal is available. No juvenile, adoption, sexual, mental health or expunged records released. Copy fee: $.25 per page. Cert fee: $2.50 plus $.50 per page after first. Payee: Superior Court Clerk. Personal checks accepted. Prepayment required.

Probate Court PO Box 54, Watkinsville, GA 30677; 706-769-3936; Fax: 706-769-3934. Hours: 8AM-5PM (EST). *Probate.*
www.oconeecounty.net

Oglethorpe County

Superior Court PO Box 68, Lexington, GA 30648; 706-743-5731; Fax: 706-743-5335. Hours: 8AM-5PM (EST). *Felony, Misdemeanor, Civil.*
www.gsccca.org/Clerks/default.asp

Civil Records: Access: Mail, in person. Visitors must perform in person searches for themselves. Search fee: $25.00. Required to search: name, years to search. Civil cases indexed by defendant. Civil records on computer from 1992, on dockets from 1900s.

Criminal Records: Access: In person only. Visitors must perform in person searches for themselves. No search fee. Required to search: name, years to search, DOB; also helpful: SSN, race, sex. Criminal records on computer from 1992, on dockets from 1900s.

General Information: Public Access terminal is available. No juvenile or adoption records released. Will fax results for $2.50 per page. Copy fee: $.25 per page. Cert fee: $2.50 plus $.50 per page after first. Payee: Superior Court Clerk. Personal checks accepted. Prepayment required. Mail turnaround time 2-3 days.

Magistrate Court Box 356, Lexington, GA 30648; 706-743-8321; Fax: 706-743-3177. Hours: 8AM-5PM (EST). *Civil Actions Under $15,000, Eviction, Small Claims.*

Probate Court PO Box 70, 111 W Main St, Lexington, GA 30648; 706-743-5350; Fax: 706-743-3514. Hours: 7:30AM-5PM (EST). *Probate.*
https://www.gaprobate.org/counties/oglethorpe/index.html

Paulding County

Superior Court 11 Courthouse Sq, Rm G2, Dallas, GA 30132; 770-443-7527; Civil phone: 770-443-7529; Criminal phone: 770-505-6582. Hours: 8AM-5PM (EST). *Felony, Misdemeanor, Civil.*

Civil Records: Access: In person only. Visitors must perform in person searches for themselves. No search fee. Required to search: name, years to search. Civil

cases indexed by defendant, plaintiff. Civil records on computer from 1990, archived from 1850.

Criminal Records: Access: In person only. Visitors must perform in person searches for themselves. No search fee. Required to search: name, years to search, DOB; also helpful: SSN, race, sex. Criminal records on docket books.

General Information: Public Access terminal is available. No juvenile, adoption, sexual, mental health or expunged records released. Copy fee: $.25 per page; $1 per page if office assists. Cert fee: $2.50 plus $.50 per page after first. Payee: Court Clerk. Personal checks accepted. Prepayment required.

Magistrate Court 25 Courthouse Sq, Rm 402, Dallas, GA 30132; 770-443-7532; Probate phone: 770-443-7541. 8AM-5PM (EST). *Civil Actions Under $15,000, Eviction, Small Claims, Probate.*

Probate Court 25 Courthouse Sq. Annex, Rm 102, Dallas, GA 30132; 770-443-7541; Fax: 770-443-7631. Hours: 8AM-5PM (EST). *Probate.*
https://www.gaprobate.org/counties/paulding/index.html

Peach County

Superior Court PO Box 389, Ft Valley, GA 31030; 478-825-5331. Hours: 8:30AM-5PM (EST). *Felony, Misdemeanor, Civil.*

Civil Records: Access: Mail, in person. Both court and visitors may perform in person searches. No search fee. Required to search: name, years to search. Civil cases indexed by defendant, plaintiff. Civil records on computer back to 1997; on dockets from 1925.

Criminal Records: Access: Mail, in person. Both court and visitors may perform in person searches. No search fee. Required to search: name, years to search, DOB; also helpful: SSN, race, sex. Criminal records on computer back to 1997; on dockets from 1925.

General Information: No juvenile, adoption, sexual, mental health or expunged records released. Copy fee: $.25 per page. Cert fee: $3.00. Payee: Court Clerk. Personal checks accepted. Prepayment required. Mail requests: SASE required. Mail turnaround time 1 week.

Magistrate Court 700 Spruce St, Bldg A, Ft Valley, GA 31030; 478-825-2060; Fax: 478-825-1893. Hours: 8AM-5PM (EST). *Civil Actions Under $15,000, Eviction, Small Claims.*

Probate Court PO Box 327, Ft Valley, GA 31030; 478-825-2313; Fax: 478-825-2678. Hours: 8AM-5PM (EST). *Probate.*

Pickens County

Superior Court 52 N Main St # 102, Jasper, GA 30143; 706-253-8763. Hours: 8AM-5PM (EST). *Felony, Misdemeanor, Civil.*
http://9thjudicialdistrict-ga.org/dca9apphp.shtml

Civil Records: Access: In person only. Visitors must perform in person searches for themselves. No search fee. Required to search: name, years to search. Civil cases indexed by defendant, plaintiff. Civil records on computer from 1988, dockets from 1854.

Criminal Records: Access: In person only. Visitors must perform in person searches for themselves. No search fee. Required to search: name, years to search, DOB, signed release; also helpful: SSN, race, sex. Criminal records on computer from 1988, dockets from 1854.

General Information: Public Access terminal is available. No juvenile, adoption, sexual, mental health or expunged records released. Copy fee: $.25 per page. $1.00 per page if the court makes the copies. Cert fee: $2.50 plus $.50 per page after first. Payee: Court Clerk. Personal checks accepted. Prepayment required.

Magistrate Court 50 N Main St #105, Jasper, GA 30143; 706-253-8747; Fax: 706-253-8750. Hours: 8AM-5PM (EST). *Civil Actions Under $15,000, Eviction, Small Claims.*

Probate Court 50 N Main St, #203, Jasper, GA 30143; 706-253-8756; Fax: 706-253-8760. Hours: 8AM-Noon, 1-5PM (EST). *Probate.*
https://www.gaprobate.org/counties/pickens/index.html

Pierce County

Superior & State Court PO Box 588, 312 Nichols St, Blackshear, GA 31516; 912-449-2020. Hours: 9AM-5PM (EST). *Felony, Misdemeanor, Civil.*

Civil Records: Access: In person only. Visitors must perform in person searches for themselves. No search fee. Required to search: name, years to search. Civil cases indexed by defendant. Civil records on computer from 1991, on index from 1800s.

Criminal Records: Access: In person only. Visitors must perform in person searches for themselves. No search fee. Required to search: name, years to search. Criminal records on computer from 1991, on index from 1800s.

General Information: Public Access terminal is available. (Civil records only on terminal.) Copy fee: $.25 per page. Cert fee: $2.50 for 1st page, $.50 each add'l. Payee: Superior Court Clerk. Personal checks accepted. Prepayment required.

Magistrate Court 312 Nichols St, # 3, Blackshear, GA 31516-1926; 912-449-2027, 449-2007; Fax: 912-449-2103. 9AM-5PM *Civil Actions Under $15,000, Eviction, Small Claims.*

Probate Court PO Box 406, 312 Nichols St, Blackshear, GA 31516; 912-449-2029; Fax: 912-449-1417. Hours: 9AM-5PM (EST). *Probate.*

Pike County

Superior Court PO Box 10, Zebulon, GA 30295; 770-567-2000. Hours: 8AM-5PM (EST). *Felony, Misdemeanor, Civil.*

Civil Records: Access: In person only. Visitors must perform in person searches for themselves. No search fee. Required to search: name, years to search. Civil cases indexed by defendant, plaintiff. Civil records on dockets books from 1823.

Criminal Records: Access: In person only. Visitors must perform in person searches for themselves. No search fee. Required to search: name, years to search. Criminal records on dockets books from 1823.

General Information: No juvenile, adoption, sexual, mental health or expunged records released. Copy fee: $.25 per page. Cert fee: $2.00 plus $1.00 per page after first. Payee: Court Clerk. Personal checks accepted. Prepayment required.

Magistrate Court PO Box 466, Zebulon, GA 30295; 770-567-2004; Fax: 770-567-2023. Hours: 8AM-5PM (EST). *Civil Actions Under $15,000, Eviction, Small Claims.*

Probate Court PO Box 324, Zebulon, GA 30295; 770-567-8734; Fax: 770-567-2019. Hours: 8:30AM--12;00-1PM-5PM (EST). *Probate.*

Polk County

Superior Court PO Box 948, 100 Proir St, Rm 106, Cedartown, GA 30125; 770-749-2114; Fax: 770-749-2148. Hours: 9AM-5PM (EST). *Felony, Misdemeanor, Civil.*

Civil Records: Access: In person only. Visitors must perform in person searches for themselves. No search fee. Required to search: name, years to search. Civil cases indexed by defendant, plaintiff. Civil records on computer from 1991, alpha indexes from 1930.

Criminal Records: Access: Mail, in person. Visitors must perform in person searches for themselves. No search fee. Required to search: name, years to search, DOB, signed release; also helpful: SSN, race, sex. Criminal records on computer from 1991, alpha indexes from 1930.

General Information: Public Access terminal is available. No juvenile, adoption, sexual, mental health or expunged records released. Fee to fax results is $2.00 per page. Copy fee: $.25 per page. Cert fee: $2.50 plus $.50 per page after first. Payee: Court Clerk. Personal checks accepted. Prepayment required.

Magistrate Court 100 Prior St, Courthouse 2, Cedartown, GA 30125; 770-749-2187; Civil phone: 770-749-2130; Fax: 770-749-2189. Hours: 9AM-5PM (EST). *Civil Actions Under $15,000, Eviction, Small Claims.*
Note: Rockmart, GA ofice: 200 S Marble St, Rockmart, GA 30153; 770-684-4718. Court also has jurisdiction for bad checks, arrest warrants, preliminary hearings, and county ordinance violations.

Probate Court Polk County Courthouse. Rm 102, Cedartown, GA 30125; 770-749-2128; Probate phone: 770-749-2129; Fax: 770-749-2150. Hours: 9AM-4:45PM (EST). *Probate.*
www.polkcountygeorgia.us/courts.html

Pulaski County

Superior Court PO Box 60, Hawkinsville, GA 31036; 478-783-1911; Fax: 478-892-3308. Hours: 8AM-5PM (EST). *Felony, Misdemeanor, Civil.*

Civil Records: Access: Mail, in person. Visitors must perform in person searches for themselves. No search fee. Required to search: name, years to search. Civil cases indexed by defendant, plaintiff. Civil records on computer from 1986, alpha index from early 1800s.

Criminal Records: Access: In person. Visitors must perform in person searches themselves. No search fee. Required to search: name, years to search, signed release; also helpful: DOB, SSN. Criminal records on computer from 1986, alpha index from early 1800s.

General Information: Public Access terminal is available. No juvenile or adoption records released. Copy fee: $1.00 per page. Cert fee: $2.00 plus $.50 per page. Payee: Court Clerk. Personal checks accepted. Prepayment required.

Magistrate Court PO Box 667, Hawkinsville, GA 31036; 478-783-1357; Fax: 478-783-0696. Hours: 8AM-5PM (EST). *Civil Actions Under $15,000, Eviction, Small Claims.*

Probate Court Pulaski County Courthouse, PO Box 156, Hawkinsville, GA 31036; 478-783-2061; Fax: 478-783-9219. 8AM-5PM (EST). *Probate.*

Putnam County

Superior & State Court County Courthouse, Eatonton, GA 31024; 706-485-4501; Fax: 706-485-2875. Hours: 8AM-5PM (EST). *Felony, Misdemeanor, Civil.*

Civil Records: Access: In person only. Visitors must perform in person searches for themselves. No search fee. Required to search: name, years to search. Civil cases indexed by defendant, plaintiff. Civil records on computer since 1997; prior records on dockets to early 1900s.

Criminal Records: Access: In person only. Visitors must perform in person searches for themselves. No search fee. Required to search: name, years to search, DOB; also helpful: SSN, race, sex. Criminal records on computer since 1997; prior records on dockets to early 1930s.

General Information: Public Access terminal is available. No juvenile, adoption, sexual, mental health or expunged records released. Will not fax results. Copy fee: $1.00 per page. Cert fee: $2.50 +$.50 add'l pages. Payee: Court Clerk. Personal checks accepted. Prepayment required.

Magistrate Court 108 S Madison Ave, #101, Eatonton, GA 31024; 706-485-4306; Fax: 706-484-1814. Hours: 8AM-5PM (EST). *Civil Actions Under $15,000, Eviction, Small Claims.*

Probate Court County Courthouse, 100 S Jefferson Ave, Eatonton, GA 31024; 706-485-5476/9761; Fax: 706-485-2515. Hours: 8AM-5PM (EST). *Probate.*
https://www.gaprobate.org/counties/putnam/index.html

Quitman County

Superior Court PO Box 307, Georgetown, GA 39854; 229-334-2578. Hours: 8AM-Noon, 1-5PM (EST). *Felony, Misdemeanor, Civil.*

Civil Records: Access: In person only. Visitors must perform in person searches for themselves. No search fee. Required to search: name, years to search. Civil records go back to 1920s.

Criminal Records: Access: In person only. Visitors must perform in person searches for themselves. No search fee. Required to search: name, years to search, DOB; also helpful: SSN, race, sex. Records go back to 1930s. The court asks mail requesters to mail the sheriff's office with a $10.00 fee and signed, notarized (subject) request.

General Information: Public Access terminal is available. No juvenile, adoption, sexual, mental health or expunged records released. Copy fee: $.50 per page. Cert fee: $2.50 for 1st page, $.50 each add'l. Payee: Clerk of Superior Court. Personal checks accepted. Prepayment required.

Magistrate & Probate Court PO Box 7, Georgetown, GA 39854; 229-334-2224; Fax: 229-334-6826. Hours: 8:AM-5PM (EST). *Civil Actions Under $15,000, Eviction, Small Claims, Probate.*

Rabun County

Superior Court 25 Courthouse Sq, #105, Clayton, GA 30525; 706-782-3615; Fax: 706-782-1391. Hours: 8:30AM-5PM (EST). *Felony, Misdemeanor, Civil.*

Civil Records: Access: Mail, in person. Visitors must perform in person searches for themselves. No search fee. Required to search: name, years to search. Civil cases indexed by defendant, plaintiff. Civil records on dockets from 1949; on computer since.

Criminal Records: Access: Mail, in person. Visitors must perform in person searches for themselves. No search fee. Required to search: name, years to search, DOB, signed release; also helpful: SSN, race, sex. Criminal records on dockets from 1949; on computer since.

General Information: Public Access terminal is available. No juvenile, adoption, sexual, mental health or expunged records released. Will fax results for $.25 per copy. Payment must be made in advance. Copy fee: $.25 per page. Cert fee: $5.00. Payee: Court Clerk. Personal checks accepted. Prepayment required.

Magistrate Court 25 Courthouse Sq, #105, Clayton, GA 30525; 706-782-2285; Fax: 706-782-1391. Hours: 8:30AM-5PM (EST). *Civil Actions Under $15,000, Eviction, Small Claims.*

Probate Court 25 Courthouse Sq, #215, Clayton, GA 30525; 706-782-3614; Fax: 706-782-9278. Hours: 8:30AM-5:00PM (EST). *Probate.*
www.rabuncountygov.com/contactus.htm

Randolph County

Superior Court PO Box 98, Cuthbert, GA 39840; 229-732-2216; Fax: 229-732-5881. Hours: 8AM-5PM (EST). *Felony, Misdemeanor, Civil.*

Civil Records: Access: In person only. Visitors must perform in person searches for themselves. No search fee. Required to search: name, years to search. Civil cases indexed by defendant. Civil records on index from 1835.

Criminal Records: Access: In person only. Visitors must perform in person searches for themselves. No search fee. Required to search: name, years to search, DOB; also helpful: SSN, race, sex. Criminal records on index from 1835.

General Information: No juvenile, adoption, sexual, mental health or expunged records released. Copy fee: $.25 per page. Cert fee: $2.00 plus $.50 per page after first. Payee: Court Clerk. Personal checks accepted. Prepayment required.

Magistrate Court PO Box 6, 113 W Pearl St, Cuthbert, GA 39840; 229-732-6182; Fax: 229-732-5635. Hours: 8AM-5PM-W;8AM-12;00 (EST). *Civil Actions Under $15,000, Eviction, Small Claims.*

Probate Court PO Box 424, Cuthbert, GA 39840; 229-732-2671; Fax: 229-732-5781. Hours: 8AM-5PM (EST). *Probate.*

Richmond County

Superior Court 530 Greene St, Augusta, GA 30911; 706-821-2460; Fax: 706-821-2448. Hours: 8:30AM-5PM (EST). *Felony, Misdemeanor, Civil.*
www.augustaga.gov/departments/clerk_sup/default.htm

Civil Records: Access: Mail, in person, online. Visitors must perform in person searches for themselves. No search fee. Required to search: name, years to search. Civil cases indexed by defendant, plaintiff. Civil records on docket books and microfilm from 1940s, real estate from 1986 on computer. Name search at www.augustaga.gov/departments/clerk_sup/disclaim.htm for records 2001 forward.

Criminal Records: Access: Mail, in person, online. Visitors must perform in person searches for themselves. No search fee. Required to search: name, years to search. Criminal records on docket books and microfilm from 1940s, real estate from 1986 on computer. Name searching online at www.augustaga.gov/departments/clerk_sup/disclaim.htm for records 2001 forward.

General Information: No juvenile, adoption, sexual, mental health or expunged records released. Copy fee: $.25 per page. Cert fee: $2.50 plus $.50 per page after first. Payee: Superior Court Clerk. Business and local checks accepted. Prepayment required. Mail requests: SASE requested. Turnaround time 1 week.

State Court 401 Walton Way, #218A, Augusta, GA 30911; 706-821-1233. Hours: 8:30AM-5PM (EST). *Misdemeanor, Civil.*
www.augustaga.gov

Civil Records: Access: In person, online. Visitors must perform in person searches for themselves. No search fee. Required to search: name, years to search. Civil cases indexed by defendant, plaintiff. Civil records on docket books and microfilm from 1940s, prior archived; computerized records since 2001. Name search at www.augustaga.gov/departments/clerk_sup/disclaim.htm.

Criminal Records: Access: In person only. Visitors must perform in person searches for themselves. No search fee. Required to search: name, years to search, DOB; also helpful: SSN, race, sex. Criminal records on docket books and microfilm from 1940s, prior archived; computerized records since 2001.

General Information: Public Access terminal is available. No juvenile, adoption, sexual, mental health or expunged records released. Copy fee: $.25 per page. Cert fee: $2.50 plus $.50 per page after first. Payee: Court Clerk. Only cashiers checks and money orders accepted. Prepayment required.

Civil & Magistrate Court 530 Greene St, Rm 705, Augusta, GA 30911; 706-821-2370; Fax: 706-821-2381. Hours: 8:30AM-5PM (EST). *Civil Actions Under $45,000, Eviction, Small Claims.*
Note: The Magistrate Court does have some misdemeanor records, related to violations of city ordinances.

Civil Records: Access: Phone, mail, in person. Both court and visitors may perform in person searches. No search fee. Required to search: name, years to search. Civil cases indexed by defendant, plaintiff. Civil records on dockets back to 1970s.

General Information: Copy fee: $.25 per page. Cert fee: $5.00. Payee: Magistrate Court. Business checks accepted. Prepayment required. Mail requests: SASE requested. Turnaround time 1 day.

Probate Court 530 Greene St, Rm 401, Augusta, GA 30911; 706-821-2434; Fax: 706-821-2442. Hours: 8:30AM-5PM (EST). *Probate.*

Rockdale County

Superior Court PO Box 937, 922 Court St, Conyers, GA 30012; 770-929-4021. Hours: 8AM-4:45PM (EST). *Felony, Civil.*

Civil Records: Access: In person only. Visitors must perform in person searches for themselves. No search fee. Required to search: name, years to search. Civil cases indexed by defendant, plaintiff. Civil records on computer back to 1990, in books from 1900.

Criminal Records: Access: In person only. Visitors must perform in person searches for themselves. No search fee. Required to search: name, years to search, signed release. Criminal records on computer back to 1990, in books from 1900.

General Information: Public Access terminal is available. No juvenile, adoption, sexual, mental health or expunged records released. Copy fee: $.25 per page. Cert fee: $2.50 plus $.50 per page after first. Payee: Clerk Superior Court. Personal checks accepted. Prepayment required.

State Court PO Box 938, Conyers, GA 30012; 770-929-4019. Hours: 8AM-4:45PM (EST). *Misdemeanor, Civil.*

Civil Records: Access: In person only. Visitors must perform in person searches for themselves. No search fee. Required to search: name, years to search. Civil cases indexed by defendant, plaintiff. Civil records on computer from 1994, on dockets to 1994.

Criminal Records: Access: In person only. Visitors must perform in person searches for themselves. No search fee. Required to search: name, years to search. Criminal records on computer from 1990, on dockets from 1987-1990.

General Information: Public Access terminal is available. No juvenile, adoption, sexual, mental health or expunged records released. Copy fee: $.25 per page. Cert fee: $2.50 plus $.50 per page after first. Payee: Rockdale State Court. Business checks accepted. Prepayment required.

Magistrate Court PO Box 289, Conyers, GA 30012; 770-929-4014; Fax: 770-785-2496. Hours: 8:30AM-4:30PM (EST). *Civil Actions Under $15,000, Eviction, Small Claims.*

Probate Court 922 Court St NE, Rm 107, Conyers, GA 30012; 770-929-4058; Fax: 770-918-6463. Hours: 8:30AM-4:30PM (EST). *Probate.*
https://www.gaprobate.org/counties/rockdale/index.html

Schley County

Superior Court PO Box 7, 14 S Broad St., Ellaville, GA 31806; 229-937-5581; Fax: 229-937-5588. Hours: 8AM-Noon,1-5PM (EST). *Felony, Misdemeanor, Civil.*
www.gsccca.org/clerks

Civil Records: Access: In person only. Visitors must perform in person searches for themselves. No search fee. Required to search: name, years to search. Civil cases indexed by defendant. Civil records in books from 1885.

Criminal Records: Access: In person only. Visitors must perform in person searches for themselves. No search fee. Required to search: name, years to search, DOB, signed release; also helpful: SSN, race, sex. Criminal records in books from 1934.

General Information: Public Access terminal is available. No adoption records released. Copy fee: $.25 per page. Cert fee: $2.50 plus $.50 per page after first. Payee: Clerk Superior Court. Personal checks accepted. Prepayment required.

Magistrate Court PO Box 372, Ellaville, GA 31806; 229-937-5587; Fax: 229-937-5588. Hours: 8AM-5PM (EST). *Civil Actions Under $15,000, Eviction, Small Claims.*

Probate Court PO Box 385, Ellaville, GA 31806; 229-937-2905; Fax: 229-937-5588. Hours: 8:30AM-Noon, 1-5PM (EST). *Probate.*
https://www.gaprobate.org/counties/schley/index.html

Screven County

Superior Court PO Box 156, Sylvania, GA 30467; 912-564-2614; Fax: 912-564-2622. Hours: 8:30AM-5PM (EST). *Felony, Misdemeanor, Civil.*

Civil Records: Access: In person only. Visitors must perform in person searches for themselves. No search fee. Required to search: name, years to search. Civil cases indexed by defendant, plaintiff. Civil records on dockets from 1793.

Criminal Records: Access: In person only. Visitors must perform in person searches for themselves. No search fee. Required to search: name, years to search, DOB; also helpful: SSN, race, sex. Criminal records on dockets from 1793.

General Information: No juvenile or adoption records released. Copy fee: $.25 per page. Cert fee: $3.00. Payee: Court Clerk. Personal checks accepted. Prepayment required.

State Court PO Box 156, Sylvania, GA 30467; 912-564-2614; Fax: 912-564-2622. Hours: 8:00AM-5PM (EST). *Misdemeanor, Civil.*

Civil Records: Access: In person only. Visitors must perform in person searches for themselves. No search fee. Required to search: name, years to search. Civil cases indexed by defendant, plaintiff. Civil records on dockets from 1793; computerized records since 1991.

Criminal Records: Access: In person only. Visitors must perform in person searches for themselves. No search fee. Required to search: name, years to search, DOB; also helpful: SSN, race, sex. Criminal records on dockets from 1793; computerized records since 1991.

General Information: Public Access terminal is available. No juvenile, adoption, sexual, mental health or expunged records released. Copy fee: $.25 per page. Cert fee: $3.00. Payee: Court Clerk. Personal checks accepted. Prepayment required.

Magistrate Court PO Box 64, Sylvania, GA 30467; 912-564-7375; Fax: 912-564-5618. Hours: 8AM-5PM (EST). *Civil Actions Under $15,000, Eviction, Small Claims.*

Probate Court 216 Mims Rd, #107, Sylvania, GA 30467; 912-564-2783; Fax: 912-564-9139. Hours: 8AM-5PM (EST). *Probate.*

Seminole County

Superior Court PO Box 672, Main St, Donalsonville, GA 39845; 229-524-2525; Fax: 229-524-8883. Hours: 8:30AM-5PM (EST). *Felony, Misdemeanor, Civil.*
Civil Records: Access: Fax, in person. Both court and visitors may perform in person searches. Search fee: $1.00 per name per year. Required to search: name, years to search. Civil cases indexed by defendant, plaintiff. Civil records on computer from 1994, on dockets from 1921.
Criminal Records: Access: Fax, mail, in person. Both court and visitors may perform in person searches. Search fee: $1.00 per name per year. Required to search: name, years to search, DOB, signed release; also helpful: SSN, race, sex. Criminal records on computer from 1994, on dockets from 1921.
General Information: No juvenile, adoption, sexual, mental health or expunged records released. Will fax results $1.00 per page. Copy fee: $1.00 per page. Copy fees are $.25 per page in person. Cert fee: $2.50. Payee: Court Clerk. Personal checks accepted. Prepayment required. Mail requests: SASE required. Mail turnaround time 1 day.

Magistrate & Probate Court Seminole County Courthouse, 200 S Knox Ave, Donalsonville, GA 39845; 229-524-5256; Fax: 229-524-8644. Hours: 8;30AM-5PM (EST). *Civil Actions Under $15,000, Eviction, Small Claims.*
https://www.gaprobate.org/counties/seminole/index.html

Spalding County

Superior Court PO Box 1046, Griffin, GA 30224; Civil phone: 770-467-4746; Criminal phone: 770-467-4745. Hours: 8AM-5PM (EST). *Felony, Misdemeanor, Civil.*
Civil Records: Access: Mail, in person. Visitors must perform in person searches for themselves. No search fee. Required to search: name, years to search. Civil cases indexed by defendant, plaintiff. Civil records on computer from 1991, on dockets from 1852. Mail for specific case info only, the court will not do name searches.
Criminal Records: Access: Mail, in person. Visitors must perform in person searches for themselves. No search fee. Required to search: name, years to search; also helpful: DOB, SSN, race, sex. Criminal records on computer from 1991, on dockets from 1852. Court will not do name searches, will only do specific case files.
General Information: Public Access terminal is available. No juvenile, adoption, sexual, mental health or expunged records released. Copy fee: $.25 per page. Cert fee: $2.00 per document; $.50 per page. Payee: Court Clerk. Personal checks accepted. Prepayment required. Mail requests: SASE required. Mail turnaround time 2 days.

State Court PO Box 1046, Griffin, GA 30224; 770-467-4745; Civil phone: 770-467-4746; Criminal phone: 770-467-4745; Probate phone: 770-467-4340. Hours: 8AM-5PM (EST). *Misdemeanor, Civil.*
Civil Records: Access: In person only. Visitors must perform in person searches for themselves. No search fee. Required to search: name, years to search. Civil cases indexed by defendant, plaintiff. Civil records on computer back to 1995; prior records on dockets from 1852. Mail access only for specific case information, no name searching.
Criminal Records: Access: Mail, in person. Visitors must perform in person searches for themselves. No search fee. Required to search: name, years to search,

DOB; also helpful: SSN, race, sex. Criminal records on computer back to 1995; prior records on dockets from 1852. Mail access for specific case information only, no name searching by the court.
General Information: Public Access terminal is available. No juvenile, adoption, sexual, mental health or expunged records released. Copy fee: $.25 per page. Cert fee: $2.00. Payee: Court Clerk. Business checks accepted. Prepayment required. Mail requests: SASE required. Mail turnaround time 2 days.

Magistrate Court 132 E Solomon St, Griffin, GA 30223; 770-467-4320; Fax: 770-467-0081. Hours: 8AM-5PM (EST). *Civil Actions Under $15,000, Eviction, Small Claims.*

Probate Court 132 E Solomon St, Griffin, GA 30223; 770-467-4340; Fax: 770-467-4243. Hours: 8AM-5PM (EST). *Probate.*
https://www.gaprobate.org/counties/spalding/index.html

Stephens County

Superior Court 205 Alexander St N, #202, Toccoa, GA 30577; 706-886-9496; Fax: 706-886-5710. Hours: 8AM-5PM (EST). *Felony, Misdemeanor, Civil.*
Civil Records: Access: Mail, in person. Both court and visitors may perform in person searches. Search fee: $7.50 per name. Required to search: name, years to search. Civil cases indexed by defendant, plaintiff. Civil records on computer back to 1988, on dockets from 1906.
Criminal Records: Access: In person only. Only the court performs in person searches; visitors may not. Search fee: $7.50 per name. Required to search: name, years to search, DOB, signed release; also helpful: SSN, race, sex. Criminal records on computer back to 1988, on dockets from 1906.
General Information: Public Access terminal is available. No juvenile, adoption, sexual, mental health or expunged records released. Fee to fax results pre-paid: $2.00 1st page, $1.00 each add'l. Copy fee: $1.00 per page. Cert fee: $2.50 plus $.50 per page after first. Payee: Court Clerk. Personal checks accepted. Prepayment required. Mail turnaround time 1 day.

State Court 205 N Alexander St Rm 202, County Government Bldg, Toccoa, GA 30577; 706-886-3598/9496. Hours: 8AM-5PM (EST). *Misdemeanor, Civil.*
Civil Records: Access: In person only. Visitors must perform in person searches for themselves. No search fee. Required to search: name, years to search. Civil cases indexed by defendant, plaintiff. Civil records on computer back to 1991, on dockets from 1906.
Criminal Records: Access: In person only. Visitors must perform in person searches for themselves. No search fee. Required to search: name, years to search, DOB; also helpful: SSN, race, sex. Criminal records on computer back to 1990, on dockets from 1906.
General Information: Public Access terminal is available. No juvenile, adoption, sexual, mental health or expunged records released. Will not fax results. Copy fee: $1.00 per page. Cert fee: $2.50 plus $.50 per page after first. Payee: Court Clerk. Personal checks accepted. Prepayment required.

Magistrate Court 205 N Alexander St, Rm 107, Toccoa, GA 30577; 706-886-6205; Fax: 706-886-5569. Hours: 8:30AM-5:00Pm (EST). *Civil Actions Under $15,000, Eviction, Small Claims.*

Probate Court 205 N Alexander, # 108, Toccoa, GA 30577; 706-886-2828; Fax: 706-886-2631. Hours: 8AM-5PM M-F, closed for lunch hour (EST). *Probate.*

Stewart County

Superior Court PO Box 910, Main St, Lumpkin, GA 31815; 229-838-6220. Hours: 8AM-4:30PM (EST). *Felony, Misdemeanor, Civil.*
Civil Records: Access: In person only. Visitors must perform in person searches for themselves. No search fee. Required to search: name, years to search; also helpful: address. Civil cases indexed by defendant. Civil records in index books.
Criminal Records: Access: In person only. Visitors must perform in person searches for themselves. No search fee. Required to search: name, years to search; also helpful: address, DOB, SSN. Criminal records in index books to 1840s.
General Information: Public Access terminal is available. No juvenile, adoption, sexual, mental health or sealed records are released. Copy fee: $.25 per page. Cert fee: $2.50 plus $.50 per page after first. Payee: Clerk of Superior Court. Personal checks accepted. Prepayment required.

Magistrate Court PO Box 712, Lumpkin, GA 31815; 229-838-0505; Fax: 229-838-0015. Hours: 8AM-5PM (EST). *Civil Actions Under $15,000, Eviction, Small Claims.*

Probate Court PO Box 876, Lumpkin, GA 31815; 229-838-4394; Fax: 229-838-9084. Hours: 8AM-Noon, 1-4:30PM (EST). *Probate.*
https://www.gaprobate.org/counties/stewart/index.html

Sumter County

State Court PO Box 333, Americus, GA 31709; 229-928-4537. Hours: 9AM-5PM (EST). *Misdemeanor, Civil.*
Civil Records: Access: In person only. Visitors must perform in person searches for themselves. No search fee. Required to search: name, years to search. Civil cases indexed by defendant, plaintiff. Civil records on dockets from late 1800s.
Criminal Records: Access: In person only. Visitors must perform in person searches for themselves. No search fee. Required to search: name, years to search, DOB; also helpful: SSN, race, sex. Criminal records on dockets from late 1800s.
General Information: No juvenile, adoption, sealed, sexual, mental health or expunged records released. Copy fee: $.25 per page. Cert fee: $2.50 plus $.50 per page. Payee: Court Clerk. Prepayment required.

Magistrate Court PO Box 563, Americus, GA 31709; 229-928-4524; Fax: 229-928-4527. Hours: 9AM-5PM (EST). *Civil Actions Under $15,000, Eviction, Small Claims.*

Probate Court PO Box 246, Americus, GA 31709; 229-928-4551; Fax: 229-928-4622. Hours: 8AM-5PM (EST). *Probate.*

Talbot County

Superior Court PO Box 325, Talbotton, GA 31827; 706-665-3239; Fax: 706-665-8637. Hours: 9AM-5PM (EST). *Felony, Misdemeanor, Civil.*
Civil Records: Access: In person only. Visitors must perform in person searches for themselves. No search fee. Required to search: name, years to search. Civil cases indexed by defendant, plaintiff. Civil records on dockets from 1827.
Criminal Records: Access: In person only. Visitors must perform in person searches for themselves. No search fee. Required to search: name, years to search. Criminal records are computerized. Historical documents are indexed in docket books.
General Information: No juvenile, adoption, sexual, mental health or expunged records released. Copy fee: $.25 per page. Cert fee: $2.00 plus $.50 per page after first. Payee: Superior Court. Business checks accepted. Prepayment required.

Magistrate & Probate Court PO Box 157, Talbotton, GA 31827; 706-665-8866; Fax: 706-665-8240. Hours: 8AM-5PM (EST). *Civil Actions Under $15,000, Eviction, Small Claims, Probate.*
https://www.gaprobate.org/counties/talbot/index.html

Taliaferro County

Superior Court PO Box 182, Crawfordville, GA 30631; 706-456-2123. Hours: 9AM-5PM (EST). *Felony, Misdemeanor, Civil.*
Civil Records: Access: In person only. Visitors must perform in person searches for themselves. No search fee. Required to search: name, years to search. Civil cases indexed by defendant, plaintiff. Civil records on dockets from 1825.
Criminal Records: Access: In person only. Visitors must perform in person searches for themselves. No search fee. Required to search: name, years to search, DOB; also helpful: SSN, race, sex. Criminal records on dockets from 1825.
General Information: Public Access terminal is available. No juvenile, adoption, sexual, mental health or expunged records released. Copy fee: $.25 per page. Cert fee: $2.00. Payee: Court Clerk. Personal checks accepted. Prepayment required.

Magistrate & Probate Court PO Box 264, Crawfordville, GA 30631; 706-456-2253; Fax: 706-456-3550. Hours: 9AM-5PM (EST). *Civil Actions Under $15,000, Eviction, Small Claims, Probate.*

Tattnall County

Superior & State Court PO Box 39, Reidsville, GA 30453; 912-557-6716; Fax: 912-557-4861. Hours: 8AM-5PM (EST). *Felony, Misdemeanor, Civil.*
Civil Records: Access: In person only. Visitors must perform in person searches for themselves. No search fee. Required to search: name, years to search; also helpful: address. Civil cases indexed by defendant, plaintiff. Civil records on computer back to 1990; on dockets from 1800s.
Criminal Records: Access: In person only. Visitors must perform in person searches for themselves. No search fee. Required to search: name, years to search, DOB; also helpful: address, SSN, race, sex. Criminal records on computer back to 1990; on dockets from 1800s.
General Information: Public Access terminal is available. No juvenile, adoption, sexual, mental health or expunged records released. Copy fee: $.25 per page. Cert fee: $3.00 plus $.50 per page after first. Payee: Court Clerk. Business checks accepted. Prepayment required.

Magistrate Court PO Box 513, Reidsville, GA 30453; 912-557-4372; Fax: 912-557-3136. Hours: 8AM-5PM (EST). *Civil Actions Under $15,000, Eviction, Small Claims.*

Probate Court PO Box 699, Reidsville, GA 30453; 912-557-6719; Fax: 912-557-3976. Hours: 8:30AM-5PM (EST). *Probate.*

Taylor County

Superior Court PO Box 248, Courthouse Sq, Butler, GA 31006; 478-862-5594; Fax: 478-862-5334. Hours: 8AM-5PM (EST). *Felony, Misdemeanor, Civil.*
Civil Records: Access: In person only. Both court and visitors may perform in person searches. Search fee: Copy fee only. Required to search: name, years to search. Civil cases indexed by defendant, plaintiff. Civil records on computer from 1991, dockets from 1852.
Criminal Records: Access: In person only. Visitors must perform in person searches for themselves. Search fee: Copy fee only. Required to search: name,

years to search, DOB; also helpful: SSN, race, sex. Criminal records on computer from 1991, dockets from 1852.
General Information: Public Access terminal is available. No juvenile, adoption, sexual, mental health or expunged records released. Copy fee: $.25 per page. $1.00 minimum. Cert fee: $2.00 plus $.50 per page. Payee: Court Clerk. Personal checks accepted. Prepayment required.

Magistrate & Probate Court PO Box 536, 1 Courthouse Sq, Butler, GA 31006; 478-862-3357; Fax: 478-862-9447. Hours: 8AM-5PM (EST). *Civil Actions Under $15,000, Eviction, Small Claims, Probate.*
https://www.gaprobate.org/counties/taylor/index.html

Telfair County

Superior Court Courthouse, 128 Oak St, #2, McRae, GA 31055; 229-868-6525; Fax: 229-868-7956. Hours: 8:30AM-4:30PM (EST). *Felony, Misdemeanor, Civil.*
Civil Records: Access: Phone, mail, in person. Visitors must perform in person searches for themselves. No search fee. Required to search: name, years to search. Civil cases indexed by defendant. Civil records on dockets from early 1900s.
Criminal Records: Access: Phone, in person. Visitors must perform in person searches for themselves. No search fee. Required to search: name, years to search, DOB, signed release; also helpful: SSN, race, sex. Criminal records on dockets from early 1900s.
General Information: No juvenile, adoption, sexual, mental health or expunged records released. Copy fee: $.25 per page. Cert fee: $3.00. Payee: Court Clerk. Personal checks accepted. Prepayment required. Mail requests: SASE requested. Turnaround time 1 week.

Magistrate Court 128 E Oak St, #5, McRae, GA 31055; 229-868-6772; Fax: 229-868-6902. Hours: 8:30AM-4:30PM (EST). *Civil Actions Under $15,000, Eviction, Small Claims.*

Probate Court 128 E Oak St, #1, McRae, GA 31055; 229-868-6038; Fax: 229-868-7620. Hours: 8:30AM-Noon, 1-4:30PM (EST). *Probate.*

Terrell County

Superior Court PO Box 189, 513 S Main St, Dawson, GA 39842; 229-995-2631. Hours: 8:30AM-5PM (EST). *Felony, Misdemeanor, Civil.*
Civil Records: Access: In person only. Visitors must perform in person searches for themselves. No search fee. Required to search: name, years to search. Civil cases indexed by defendant. Civil records on computer from 1988, dockets books from 1900s.
Criminal Records: Access: In person only. Visitors must perform in person searches for themselves. No search fee. Required to search: name, years to search, DOB, signed release; also helpful: SSN, race, sex. Criminal records on computer from 1988, dockets books from 1900s.
General Information: Public Access terminal is available. No juvenile, adoption, sexual, mental health or expunged records released. Copy fee: $.25 per page. Cert fee: $2.50 plus $.50 per page after first. Payee: Court Clerk. Business checks accepted. Prepayment required.

Magistrate Court PO Box 793, Dawson, GA 39842; 229-995-3757; Fax: 229-995-4496. Hours: 8AM-5PM (EST). *Civil Actions Under $15,000, Eviction, Small Claims, Misdemeanors.*

Probate Court PO Box 67, Dawson, GA 39842; 229-995-5515; Fax: 229-995-4301. *Probate.*
https://www.gaprobate.org/counties/terrell/index.html

Thomas County

Superior & State Court PO Box 1995, Thomasville, GA 31799; 229-225-4108; Fax: 229-225-4110. Hours: 8AM-5PM (EST). *Felony, Misdemeanor, Civil.*
www.thomascoclerkofcourt.org
Civil Records: Access: In person only. Visitors must perform in person searches for themselves. No search fee. Required to search: name, years to search. Civil cases indexed by defendant, plaintiff. Civil records on computer from 1989, archived from 1826.
Criminal Records: Access: In person only. Visitors must perform in person searches for themselves. No search fee. Required to search: name, years to search, DOB; also helpful: SSN, race, sex. Criminal records computerized since 1989.
General Information: Public Access terminal is available. No juvenile, adoption, sexual, mental health or expunged records released. Copy fee: $1.00 per page. Cert fee: $2.00. Payee: Court Clerk. Personal checks accepted. Prepayment required.

Magistrate Court PO Box 879, Thomasville, GA 31799; 229-225-3334; Fax: 229-225-3342. Hours: 8AM-5PM (EST). *Civil Actions Under $15,000, Eviction, Small Claims.*

Probate Court PO Box 1582, Thomasville, GA 31799; 229-225-4116; Fax: 229-227-1698. Hours: 8AM-5PM (EST). *Probate.*

Tift County

Superior & State Court PO Box 354, Tifton, GA 31793; 229-386-7810. Hours: 8AM-5PM (EST). *Felony, Misdemeanor, Civil.*
Note: Call 229-786-7815 to reach the Superior Court.

Civil Records: Access: In person only. Visitors must perform in person searches for themselves. No search fee. Required to search: name, years to search. Civil cases indexed by defendant. Civil records on dockets books from 1905.
Criminal Records: Access: In person only. Visitors must perform in person searches for themselves. No search fee. Required to search: name, years to search, DOB; also helpful: SSN, race, sex. Criminal records on dockets books from 1905.
General Information: Public Access terminal is available. No juvenile, adoption, sexual, mental health or expunged records released. Copy fee: $.25 per page. Cert fee: $2.50 plus $.50 per page after first. Payee: Court Clerk. Personal checks accepted. Prepayment required.

Magistrate Court PO Box 214, Tifton, GA 31793; 229-386-7907; Fax: 229-386-7978. Hours: 8AM-5PM (EST). *Civil Actions Under $15,000, Eviction, Small Claims.*

Probate Court PO Box 792, 225 Tift Ave, Rm 117 (physical address), Tifton, GA 31793; 229-386-7936, 229-386-7914; Fax: 229-386-7926. Hours: 9AM-5PM (EST). *Probate.*

Toombs County

Superior & State Court PO Drawer 530, Lyons, GA 30436; 912-526-3501; Fax: 912-526-1015. Hours: 8:30AM-5PM (EST). *Felony, Misdemeanor, Civil.*
Civil Records: Access: In person only. Visitors must perform in person searches for themselves. No search fee. Required to search: name, years to search. Civil cases indexed by defendant, plaintiff. Civil records on dockets books from 1908, on computer since 1995.
Criminal Records: Access: In person only. Visitors must perform in person searches for themselves. No search fee. Required to search: name, years to search,

DOB; also helpful: SSN, race, sex. Criminal records on dockets books from 1908, on computer since 1995.
General Information: Public Access terminal is available. No juvenile, adoption, sexual, mental health or expunged records released. Copy fee: $1.00 per page. Cert fee: $2.50 plus $1.00 per page after first. Payee: Court Clerk. No personal checks accepted. Prepayment required.

Magistrate Court PO Box 1460, Lyons, GA 30436; 912-526-8984; Fax: 912-526-8985. Hours: 8:30AM-5PM (EST). *Civil Actions Under $15,000, Eviction, Small Claims.*

Probate Court Toombs County Courthouse, PO Box 1370, Lyons, GA 30436; 912-526-8696; Fax: 912-526-1008. Hours: 8:30AM-5PM (EST). *Probate.*

Towns County

Superior Court 48 River St #E, Hiawassee, GA 30546; 706-896-2130. Hours: 8:30AM-4:30PM (EST). *Felony, Misdemeanor, Civil.*
Civil Records: Access: In person only. Visitors must perform in person searches for themselves. No search fee. Required to search: name, years to search. Civil cases indexed by plaintiff. Civil records on dockets books from 1923, records computerized 2002 forward.
Criminal Records: Access: In person only. Visitors must perform in person searches for themselves. No search fee. Required to search: name, years to search, DOB, signed release; also helpful: SSN, race, sex. Criminal records on docket books to 1945, indexed by defendant; records computerized 2002 forward.
General Information: No juvenile, adoption, sexual, mental health or expunged records released. Copy fee: $.25 per page. Cert fee: $2.50 per page. Payee: Court Clerk. Personal checks accepted. Prepayment required.

Magistrate & Probate Court 48 River St. # C, Hiawassee, GA 30546; 706-896-3467; Fax: 706-896-1772. Hours: 8:30AM-4:30PM (EST). *Civil Actions Under $15,000, Eviction, Small Claims, Probate.*

Treutlen County

Superior & State Court PO Box 356, Soperton, GA 30457; 912-529-4215; Probate phone: 912-529-3342. Hours: 8AM-5PM (EST). *Felony, Misdemeanor, Civil.*
Civil Records: Access: Mail, in person. Both court and visitors may perform in person searches. No search fee. Required to search: name, years to search. Civil cases indexed by defendant, plaintiff. Civil records on computer from 1991, dockets books from 1919.
Criminal Records: Access: Mail, in person. Both court and visitors may perform in person searches. No search fee. Required to search: name, years to search, DOB; also helpful: SSN, race, sex. Criminal records on computer from 1991, dockets books from 1919.
General Information: Public Access terminal is available. No juvenile, adoption, sexual, mental health or expunged records released. Copy fee: $.25 per page. Cert fee: $2.50 plus $.50 per page after first. Payee: Court Clerk. Personal checks accepted. Prepayment required. Mail turnaround time 1-2 days.

Magistrate & Probate Court 114 2nd St South, Courthouse Annex, Soperton, GA 30457; 912-529-3342; Fax: 912-529-6838. Hours: 9AM-12; 1-5PM (EST). *Civil Actions Under $15,000, Eviction, Small Claims, Probate.*

Troup County

Superior & State Court 900 Dallas St., LaGrange, GA 30240; 706-883-1740. Hours: 8AM-5PM (EST). *Felony, Misdemeanor, Civil.*
Civil Records: Access: In person only. Visitors must perform in person searches for themselves. No search fee. Required to search: name, years to search. Civil cases indexed by defendant, plaintiff. Civil records on computer from 1996, on docket books from 1940s.
Criminal Records: Access: In person only. Visitors must perform in person searches for themselves. No search fee. Required to search: name, years to search, DOB; also helpful: SSN, race, sex. Criminal records on computer from 1996, on docket books from 1940s.
General Information: No juvenile, adoption, sexual, mental health or expunged records released. Will not fax results. Copy fee: $.25 per page. Cert fee: $2.50 plus $.50 per page. Payee: Court Clerk. Personal checks accepted. Prepayment required.

Magistrate Court 119 Ridley Ave, #101, LaGrange, GA 30240; 706-883-1695; Fax: 706-883-1632. Hours: 8AM-5PM (EST). *Civil Actions Under $15,000, Eviction, Small Claims.*

Probate Court 900 Dallis St, County Admin. Bldg., LaGrange, GA 30240; 706-883-1690; Fax: 706-812-7933. Hours: 8AM-5PM (EST). *Probate.*
www.georgiacourts.org/counties/troup

Turner County

Superior Court PO Box 106, 219 E College Ave, Ashburn, GA 31714; 229-567-2011; Fax: 229-567-0450. Hours: 8AM-5PM (EST). *Felony, Misdemeanor, Civil.*
Civil Records: Access: In person only. Visitors must perform in person searches for themselves. No search fee. Required to search: name, years to search. Civil cases indexed by defendant, plaintiff. Civil records on docket books, archived from 1905.
Criminal Records: Access: In person only. Visitors must perform in person searches for themselves. No search fee. Required to search: name, years to search, DOB, signed release; also helpful: SSN, race, sex. Criminal records on docket books, archived from 1905.
General Information: No juvenile, adoption, sexual, mental health or expunged records released. Copy fee: $1.00 by court, $.25 if do it yourself. Cert fee: $2.50 plus $1.00 per page after first. Payee: Court Clerk. Personal checks accepted. Prepayment required.

Magistrate Court 219 E College, Ashburn, GA 31714; 229-567-3155. Hours: 8:30AM-4:30PM (EST). *Civil Actions Under $15,000, Eviction, Small Claims.*

Probate Court PO Box 2506, Ashburn, GA 31714; 229-567-2151; Fax: 229-567-0358. Hours: 8AM-5PM (EST). *Probate.*

Twiggs County

Superior Court PO Box 243, Jeffersonville, GA 31044; 478-945-3350. Hours: 8AM-5PM (EST). *Felony, Misdemeanor, Civil.*
Civil Records: Access: In person only. Visitors must perform in person searches for themselves. No search fee. Required to search: name, years to search. Civil cases indexed by defendant, plaintiff. Civil records on computer from 1991, dockets books to 1901.
Criminal Records: Access: In person only. Visitors must perform in person searches for themselves. No search fee. Required to search: name, years to search, DOB, signed release; also helpful: SSN, race, sex. Criminal records on computer from 1991, dockets books to 1901.
General Information: Public Access terminal is available. No juvenile, adoption, sexual, mental health

or expunged records released. Copy fee: $.25 per page. Cert fee: $2.50 plus $.50 per page after first. Payee: Court Clerk. Personal checks accepted. Prepayment required.

Magistrate Court PO Box 146, Jeffersonville, GA 31044; 478-945-3428; Fax: 478-945-2083. Hours: 9AM-5PM (EST). *Civil Actions Under $15,000, Eviction, Small Claims.*

Probate Court PO Box 186, Jeffersonville, GA 31044; 478-945-3390/3252; Fax: 478-945-6070. 9AM-5PM (EST). *Probate, Misdemeanor Traffic.*

Union County

Superior Court 114 Courthouse St, Box 5, Blairsville, GA 30512; 706-439-6022; Fax: 706-439-6026. Hours: 8AM-5PM (EST). *Felony, Misdemeanor, Civil.*
Civil Records: Access: In person only. Both court and visitors may perform in person searches. No search fee. Required to search: name, years to search. Civil cases indexed by defendant, plaintiff. Civil records on computer from 1993, on dockets from 1936.
Criminal Records: Access: In person only. Both court and visitors may perform in person searches. No search fee. Required to search: name, years to search, DOB, signed release; also helpful: SSN, race, sex. Criminal records on docket books from 1930; computerized records since 1997.
General Information: Public Access terminal is available. No juvenile, adoption, sexual, mental health or expunged records released. Copy fee: $.25 per page. Cert fee: $2.50 plus $.25 per page after first. Payee: Court Clerk. Personal checks accepted. Prepayment required.

Magistrate Court 114 Courthouse St, #10, Blairsville, GA 30512; 706-439-6008; Fax: 706-439-6104. Hours: 8AM-4:30PM (EST). *Civil Actions Under $15,000, Eviction, Small Claims.*

Probate Court 114 Courthouse St, #8, Blairsville, GA 30512; 706-439-6005; Fax: 706-439-6009. Hours: 8AM-4:30PM (EST). *Probate.*

Upson County

Superior Court PO Box 469, Thomaston, GA 30286; 706-647-7835; Probate phone: 706-647-7015; Fax: 706-647-8999. Hours: 8AM-5PM (EST). *Felony, Misdemeanor, Civil.*
Civil Records: Access: Mail, in person. Visitors must perform in person searches for themselves. Search fee: $5.00. Required to search: name, years to search. Civil cases indexed by defendant, plaintiff. Civil records on dockets books from 1927; on computer back to 1990.
Criminal Records: Access: Mail, in person. Visitors must perform in person searches for themselves. No search fee. Required to search: name, years to search, DOB; also helpful: SSN, race, sex. Criminal records on docket books from 1937; on computer back to 1990.
General Information: Public Access terminal is available. No juvenile, adoption, sexual, mental health or expunged records released. Copy fee: $.25 per page. Cert fee: $2.50 plus $.50 per page after first. Payee: Court Clerk. Personal checks accepted. Prepayment required. Mail turnaround time is 15 days.

Magistrate Court PO Box 890, Thomaston, GA 30286; 706-647-6891; Fax: 706-647-1248. Hours: 8AM-4:45PM (EST). *Civil Actions Under $15,000, Eviction, Small Claims.*

Probate Court PO Box 906, Thomaston, GA 30286; 706-647-7015; Fax: 706-646-3341. Hours: 8AM-5PM (EST). *Probate.*

Walker County

Superior & State Court PO Box 448, LaFayette, GA 30728; 706-638-1772. Hours: 8AM-5PM (EST). *Felony, Misdemeanor, Civil.*

Civil Records: Access: In person only. Visitors must perform in person searches for themselves. No search fee. Required to search: name, years to search. Civil cases indexed by defendant, plaintiff. Civil records on dockets books from 1883; computerized since 2000.

Criminal Records: Access: In person only. Visitors must perform in person searches for themselves. No search fee. Required to search: name, years to search, DOB; also helpful: SSN, race, sex. Criminal records on dockets books from 1883.

General Information: No juvenile, adoption, sexual, mental health or expunged records released. Copy fee: $.25 per page. Cert fee: $2.00. Payee: Court Clerk. Personal checks accepted.

Magistrate Court 102 Napier St, LaFayette, GA 30728; 706-638-1217; Fax: 706-638-1218. Hours: 8AM-5PM (EST). *Civil Actions Under $15,000, Eviction, Small Claims.*

Probate Court PO Box 436, LaFayette, GA 30728; 706-638-2852; Fax: 706-638-2869. Hours: 8AM-5PM (EST). *Probate.*
www.walkercounty.org

Walton County

Superior Court PO Box 745, Monroe, GA 30655; 770-267-1307; Fax: 770-267-1441. Hours: 8:30AM-5PM (EST). *Felony, Misdemeanor, Civil.*

Civil Records: Access: In person only. Visitors must perform in person searches for themselves. No search fee. Required to search: name, years to search. Civil cases indexed by defendant, plaintiff. Civil records on computer from 1990, dockets books from 1900s.

Criminal Records: Access: In person only. Visitors must perform in person searches for themselves. No search fee. Required to search: name, years to search; also helpful: DOB, race, sex. Criminal records on computer from 1990, dockets books from 1900s.

General Information: Public Access terminal is available. No juvenile, adoption, sexual, mental health or expunged records released. Copy fee: $.25 per page. Cert fee: $2.50 plus $.50 per page after first. Payee: Court Clerk. Personal checks accepted. Prepayment required.

Magistrate Court PO Box 1188, Monroe, GA 30655; 770-267-1385; Fax: 770-266-1512. Hours: 8:30AM-5PM (EST). *Civil Actions Under $15,000, Eviction, Small Claims, Criminal warrants, Bad check warrants, County ordinance violations.*

Probate Court PO Box 629, Monroe, GA 30655; 770-267-1345, 267-1387; Fax: 770-267-1417. Hours: 8:30AM-5PM (EST). *Probate.*

https://www.gaprobate.org/counties/walton/index.html

Note: This location also has traffic and misdemeanor records.

Ware County

Superior & State Court PO Box 776, Waycross, GA 31502; 912-287-4340. Hours: 9AM-5PM (EST). *Felony, Misdemeanor, Civil.*

Civil Records: Access: In person only. Visitors must perform in person searches for themselves. No search fee. Required to search: name, years to search. Civil cases indexed by defendant. Civil records on computer since 1995; prior records on dockets books from 1874.

Criminal Records: Access: In person only. Visitors must perform in person searches for themselves. No search fee. Required to search: name, years to search, DOB; also helpful: SSN, race, sex. Criminal records on computer since 1995; prior records on dockets books from 1874.

General Information: No juvenile, adoption, sexual, mental health or expunged records released. Copy fee: $.25 per page; $1.00 if court assists. Cert fee: $2.50 plus $.50 per page after first. Payee: Court Clerk. Personal checks accepted. Prepayment required.

Magistrate Court PO Box 17, 201 State St, Rm 102, Waycross, GA 31501; 912-287-4373; Fax: 912-287-4377. Hours: 9AM-5PM (EST). *Civil Actions Under $15,000, Eviction, Small Claims.*

Probate Court Ware County Courthouse, #123, 800 Church St, Waycross, GA 31501; 912-287-4315/6; Probate phone: 912-287-4316; Fax: 912-287-4317. Hours: 9AM-5PM (EST). *Probate.*

Warren County

Superior Court PO Box 227, 100 Main St, Warrenton, GA 30828; 706-465-2262; Fax: 706-465-0232. Hours: 8AM-5PM (EST). *Felony, Misdemeanor, Civil.*

Civil Records: Access: Mail, in person. Visitors must perform in person searches for themselves. No search fee. Required to search: name, years to search. Civil cases indexed by defendant, plaintiff. Civil records on docket books to 1950.

Criminal Records: Access: Mail, in person. Visitors must perform in person searches for themselves. No search fee. Required to search: name, years to search, DOB, signed release; also helpful: SSN, race, sex. Criminal records on docket books to 1950, computerized since 2000.

General Information: No juvenile, adoption, sexual, mental health or expunged records released. Copy fee: $.25 per page. Cert fee: $2.50 for 1st page, $.50 each add'l. Payee: Court Clerk. Only cashiers checks and money orders accepted. Prepayment required.

Magistrate Court PO Box 203, Warrenton, GA 30828; 706-465-3123; Fax: 706-465-1300. Hours: 8AM-5PM (EST). *Civil Actions Under $15,000, Eviction, Small Claims.*

Probate Court PO Box 364, Warrenton, GA 30828; 706-465-2227; Fax: 706-465-1300. Hours: 8AM-4:30PM (EST). *Probate.*

Washington County

Superior & State Court PO Box 231, Sandersville, GA 31082; 478-552-3186. Hours: 9AM-5PM (EST). *Felony, Misdemeanor, Civil.*

Civil Records: Access: Mail, in person. Visitors must perform in person searches for themselves. No search fee. Required to search: name, years to search. Civil cases indexed by defendant, plaintiff. Civil records on dockets books to 1869.

Criminal Records: Access: Mail, in person. Visitors must perform in person searches for themselves. No search fee. Required to search: name, years to search. Criminal records on dockets books to 1869.

General Information: Public Access terminal is available. No juvenile, adoption, sexual, mental health or expunged records released. Will fax results to local or toll free line, as long as copy fee paid. Copy fee: $.25 per page. Cert fee: $2.50. Payee: Court Clerk. Personal checks not accepted. Prepayment required.

Magistrate Court PO Box 1053, Sandersville, GA 31082; 478-552-3591. Hours: 9AM-5PM (EST). *Civil Actions Under $15,000, Eviction, Small Claims.*

Probate Court PO Box 669, Sandersville, GA 31082; 478-552-3304; Fax: 478-552-7424. Hours: 9AM-Noon, 1-5PM (EST). *Probate.*

Wayne County

Superior & State Court PO Box 920, Jesup, GA 31598; 912-427-5930; Fax: 912-427-5939. Hours: 8:30AM-5PM (EST). *Felony, Misdemeanor, Civil.*

Civil Records: Access: In person only. Visitors must perform in person searches for themselves. No search fee. Required to search: name, years to search. Civil cases indexed by defendant, plaintiff. Civil records on computer, on docket books from 1810.

Criminal Records: Access: In person only. Visitors must perform in person searches for themselves. No search fee. Required to search: name, years to search, DOB. Criminal records on computer, on docket books from 1810.

General Information: Public Access terminal is available. No juvenile, adoption, sexual, mental health or expunged records released. Copy fee: $.25 per page. Cert fee: $2.50 plus $.50 per page after first. Payee: Superior Court Clerk. Personal checks accepted. Prepayment required.

Magistrate Court PO Box 27, Jesup, GA 31598; 912-427-5960; Fax: 912-427-5944. Hours: 8:30AM-Noon; 1PM-5PM (EST). *Civil Actions Under $15,000, Eviction, Small Claims.*

Probate Court 174 N Brunswick St, Jesup, GA 31598; 912-427-5940; Fax: 912-427-5944. Hours: 8:30AM-5PM (EST). *Probate.*

Webster County

Superior Court PO Box 117, Preston, GA 31824; 229-828-3525. Hours: 8AM-4:30PM (EST). *Felony, Misdemeanor, Civil.*

Civil Records: Access: In person only. Visitors must perform in person searches for themselves. No search fee. Required to search: name, years to search. Civil cases indexed by defendant, plaintiff. Civil records on docket books from 1860; computerized records since 2000.

Criminal Records: Access: In person only. Visitors must perform in person searches for themselves. No search fee. Required to search: name, years to search, signed release. Criminal records on docket books from 1860; computerized records since 2000.

General Information: Public Access terminal is available. No juvenile, adoption, sexual, mental health or expunged records released. Copy fee: $.25 per page. Cert fee: $2.50 plus $.50 per page after 1st page. Payee: Clerk Superior Court. Personal checks accepted. Prepayment required.

Magistrate & Probate Court PO Box 135, Preston, GA 31824; 229-828-3615; Fax: 229-828-3616. Hours: 8:00AM-4:30PM (EST). *Civil Actions Under $15,000, Eviction, Small Claims, Probate.*

Note: This court will not give out SSNs. Court also has jurisdiction for bad checks, arrest warrants, preliminary hearings, and county ordinance violations

Wheeler County

Superior Court PO Box 38, Alamo, GA 30411; 912-568-7137. Hours: 8AM-4PM (EST). *Felony, Misdemeanor, Civil.*

Civil Records: Access: In person only. Visitors must perform in person searches for themselves. No search fee. Required to search: name, years to search. Civil cases indexed by defendant. Civil records on docket books from 1913.

Criminal Records: Access: In person only. Visitors must perform in person searches for themselves. No search fee. Required to search: name, years to search. Criminal records on docket books from 1913.

General Information: No juvenile or adoption records released. Copy fee: $.25 per page. Cert fee: $2.50 plus $.50 each add'l page. Payee: Superior Court Clerk. Personal checks accepted. Prepayment required.

Magistrate & Probate Court PO Box 477, 119 W Pearl St, Alamo, GA 30411; 912-568-7133; Fax: 912-568-1743. Hours: 8AM-4PM (EST). *Civil Actions Under $15,000, Eviction, Small Claims, Probate.*

White County

Superior Court 59 S Main St, # B, Cleveland, GA 30528; 706-865-2613; Fax: 706-865-7749. Hours: 8:30AM-5PM (EST). *Felony, Misdemeanor, Civil.*

Civil Records: Access: In person only. Visitors must perform in person searches for themselves. No search fee. Required to search: name, years to search. Civil cases indexed by defendant, plaintiff. Civil records on computer from 1996, on docket books from 1857. Will accept mail requests only if a case number is provided.

Criminal Records: Access: In person only. Visitors must perform in person searches for themselves. No search fee. Required to search: name, years to search. Criminal records on computer from 1996, on docket books from 1857. Will accept mail requests only if a case number is provided.

General Information: Public Access terminal is available. No juvenile, adoption, sexual, mental health or expunged records released. Copy fee: $1.00 per page. Cert fee: $2.50 plus $.50 per page after first. Payee: Superior Court Clerk. Business checks accepted. Prepayment required.

Magistrate Court 59 S Main St, #D, Cleveland, GA 30528; 706-865-6636; Fax: 706-865-7738. Hours: 8:30AM-5PM (EST). *Civil Actions Under $15,000, Misdemeanor, Eviction, Small Claims.*

Probate Court 59 S Main St, #H, Cleveland, GA 30528; 706-865-4141; Fax: 706-865-1324. Hours: 8:30AM-5PM (EST). *Probate, Misdemeanor.*

Whitfield County

Superior Court PO Box 868, 300 W Crawford St, Dalton, GA 30722; 706-275-7450; Fax: 706-275-7462. Hours: 8AM-5PM (EST). *Felony, Misdemeanor, Civil.*

Civil Records: Access: In person only. Visitors must perform in person searches for themselves. No search fee. Required to search: name, years to search. Civil cases indexed by defendant, plaintiff. Civil records on computer from 1988, on docket books from 1852.

Criminal Records: Access: In person only. Visitors must perform in person searches for themselves. No search fee. Required to search: name, years to search, offense, date of offense. Criminal records on computer from 1988, on docket books from 1852.

General Information: Public Access terminal is available. No juvenile, adoption, sexual, mental health or expunged records released. Copy fee: $.50 per page. Cert fee: $3.00. Payee: Superior Court Clerk. Business checks accepted. Prepayment required.

Magistrate Court PO Box 386, Dalton, GA 30722-0386; 706-278-5052; Fax: 706-278-8810. Hours: 8AM-5PM M-W, F; 9AM-5PM Th (EST). *Civil Actions Under $15,000, Eviction, Small Claims.*

Probate Court 301 Crawford St, Dalton, GA 30720; 706-275-7400; Fax: 706-281-1735. Hours: 8AM-4:45PM (EST). *Probate.*

Wilcox County

Superior & Magistrate Courts 103 N Broad St, Abbeville, GA 31001; 229-467-2442; Probate phone: 229-467-2220; Fax: 229-467-2886. Hours: 9AM-5PM (EST). *Felony, Misdemeanor, Civil, Eviction, Small Claims.*

Civil Records: Access: Mail, in person. Both court and visitors may perform in person searches. No search fee. Required to search: name, years to search. Civil cases indexed by defendant, plaintiff. Civil records on computer since 1995; prior records on docket books from 1950s.

Criminal Records: Access: Mail, in person. Both court and visitors may perform in person searches. No search fee. Required to search: name, years to search, DOB; also helpful: SSN. Criminal records on computer since 1995; prior records on docket books from 1950s.

General Information: Public Access terminal is available. No juvenile, adoption, sexual, mental health or expunged records released. Copy fee: $.25 per page. Cert fee: $2.50 per page. Payee: Superior Court Clerk. Personal checks accepted. Prepayment required. Mail turnaround time 1 week.

Probate Court 103 N Broad St, Abbeville, GA 31001; 229-467-2220; Fax: 229-467-2000. Hours: 9AM-5PM (EST). *Probate.*

Wilkes County

Superior Court 23 E Court St, Rm 205, Washington, GA 30673; 706-678-2423. Hours: 9AM-5PM (EST). *Felony, Misdemeanor, Civil.*

Civil Records: Access: In person only. Visitors must perform in person searches for themselves. No search fee. Required to search: name, years to search. Civil cases indexed by defendant, plaintiff. Civil records on docket books from 1700s, computerized from 1998.

Criminal Records: Access: In person only. Visitors must perform in person searches for themselves. No search fee. Required to search: name, years to search. Criminal records on docket books from 1700s, computerized from 1998.

General Information: Public Access terminal is available. No juvenile or adoption records released. Copy fee: $.25 per page self-serve. Cert fee: $2.50 plus $.50 per page after first. Payee: Superior Court Clerk. Personal checks accepted. Prepayment required.

Magistrate Court 23 E Court St, Rm 427, Washington, GA 30673; 706-678-1881; Fax: 706-678-1865. Hours: 8:30AM-5PM (EST). *Civil Actions Under $15,000, Eviction, Small Claims.*

Probate Court 23 E Court St, Rm 422, Washington, GA 30673; 706-678-2523; Fax: 706-678-4854. Hours: 8:30AM-5PM (EST). *Probate.* https://www.gaprobate.org/counties/wilkes/index.html

Wilkinson County

Superior Court PO Box 250, Irwinton, GA 31042; 478-946-2221; Fax: 478-946-1497. Hours: 8AM-5PM (EST). *Felony, Misdemeanor, Civil.*

Civil Records: Access: In person only. Visitors must perform in person searches for themselves. No search fee. Required to search: name, years to search. Civil cases indexed by defendant, plaintiff. Civil records on computer from 1991, on docket books from 1900s.

Criminal Records: Access: In person only. Visitors must perform in person searches for themselves. No search fee. Required to search: name, years to search, DOB. Criminal records on computer from 1991, on docket books from 1900s. The court will not do searches.

General Information: Public Access terminal is available. No juvenile, adoption, sexual, mental health or expunged records released. Copy fee: $.25 per page. Cert fee: $2.50 per page. Payee: Superior Court Clerk. Personal checks accepted. Prepayment required.

Magistrate & Probate Court PO Box 201, Irwinton, GA 31042; 478-946-2222/2439; Fax: 478-946-3810. Hours: 8AM-5PM (EST). *Civil Actions Under $15,000, Eviction, Small Claims, Probate.*

Worth County

Superior & State Court 201 N Main St, Rm 13, Sylvester, GA 31791; 229-776-8205; Fax: 229-776-8237. Hours: 8AM-5PM (EST). *Felony, Misdemeanor, Civil, Small Claims.*

Civil Records: Access: In person only. Visitors must perform in person searches for themselves. No search fee. Required to search: name, years to search. Civil cases indexed by defendant, plaintiff. Civil records computerized since 1995, on books since 1880, real estate records from 9/93.

Criminal Records: Access: In person only. Visitors must perform in person searches for themselves. No search fee. Required to search: name, years to search; also helpful: SSN. Criminal records computerized since 1995.

General Information: Public Access terminal is available. No juvenile, adoption, sexual, mental health or expunged records released. Copy fee: $.25 per page. Cert fee: $2.50 plus $.50 per page after first. Payee: Superior Court Clerk. Personal checks accepted. Prepayment required.

Magistrate Court PO Box 64, 201 N Main St, Sylvester, GA 31791; 229-776-8210. Hours: 9AM-5PM (EST). *Civil Actions Under $15,000, Eviction, Small Claims.*
Note: All records are maintained at the Superior Court, not here

Probate Court 201 N Main St, Rm 12, Sylvester, GA 31791; 229-776-8207; Fax: 229-776-1540. Hours: 8AM-5PM (EST). *Probate.* https://www.gaprobate.org/counties/worth/index.html

Georgia Recording Offices

ORGANIZATION: 159 counties, 159 recording offices. The recording officer is Clerk of Superior Court. All transactions are recorded in a "General Execution Docket." The entire state is in the Eastern Time Zone (EST).

REAL ESTATE RECORDS: Most counties will not perform real estate searches. Copy fees are the same as for UCC. Certification fees are usually $2.00-$2.50 per document - $1.00 for seal and $1.00 for stamp - plus $.50 per page.

UCC RECORDS: There is no central state agency office for UCC. Financing statements are filed only with the Clerk of Superior Court and one can file in any county. Their system, as of January 1, 1995, merges all new UCC filings into a central statewide database, and allows statewide searching for new filings only from any county office. However, filings prior to that date will remain at the county offices. Only a few counties will perform local UCC searches. Use search request form UCC-11 for local searches. Search fees vary from $2.50 to $25.00 per debtor name. UCC copies usually cost $.25 per page if you make it and $1.00 per page if the county makes it.

TAX LIEN RECORDS: All tax liens on personal property are filed with the county Clerk of Superior Court in a "General Execution Docket" (grantor/grantee) or "Lien Index." Most counties will not perform tax lien searches. Copy fees are the same as for UCC.

OTHER LIENS: Judgments, hospital, materialman, county tax, lis pendens, child support, labor, mechanics.

ONLINE ACCESS: The Georgia Superior Court Clerk's Cooperative Authority (GSCCCA) at www.gsccca.org/search offers free access to three state indices. The Real Estate Index contains property transactions from all counties since 01/01/99. The Lien Index includes lines filed on real and personal property. Almost all counties are on on this system; eventually this will be statewide. Throughput varies, but is generally from 01/10/2002 forward. The UCC Index contains UCC financing statement data from all counties since 1/1995, and can be searched by name, taxpayer ID, file date and file number. Additionally, the actual image of the corresponding UCC statement can be downloaded for a fee. Go to the website for details.

Appling County

County Superior Court Clerk, PO Box 269, Baxley, GA 31513. **Phone-**912-367-8126; fax-912-367-8180; hours 8AM-5PM Will search UCC records. UCC search per debtor- 10 for 1st page; $2.00 each add'l pg. UCC copy- $.25 per page. Will not search real estate or tax lien records. RE copy- $.50 per page. Cert fee: $2.50 per cert. Payee: County Clerk of Superior Court. **Online Access to RE Deed, Lien, UCC records:** See www.gsccca.org **Other phones:** Assessor-912-367-8109; Treasurer-912-367-8100.

Atkinson County

County Superior Court Clerk, PO Box 6, Pearson, GA 31642. **Phone-**912-422-3343; fax-912-422-7025; hours 8AM-Noon, 1-5PM. Will not search records. Record copy- $.25 per page. Cert fee: $2.50 per cert. Payee: Atkinson County Clerk of Superior Court. **Online Access to RE Deed, UCC records:** See www.gsccca.org for Deed and UCC indexes. **Other phones:** Assessor-912-422-7382.

Bacon County

County Superior Court Clerk, PO Box 376, Alma, GA 31510. **Phone-**County Superior Court Clerk, R/E & UCC Recording- 912-632-4915; fax-912-632-6545; hours 9AM-5PM. Will not search records. UCC copy- $1.00 per page. RE record copy- $.25 per page. Cert fee: $2.00 per doc, $.50 per page. Payee: Bacon County Clerk of Superior Court. **Online Access to RE Deed, Lien, UCC records:** See www.gsccca.org **Other phones:** Assessor-912-632-5215; Treasurer-912-632-5214; Elections-912-632-7661; Vital Records-912-632-7661.

Baker County

County Superior Court Clerk, PO Box 10, Newton, GA 39870. **Phone-**229-734-3004; fax-229-734-7770; hours 9AM-5PM. Will not search records. Record copy-$1.00 per page. Cert fee: $2.00 per cert. Payee: County Clerk of Superior Court. **Online Access to RE Deed, Lien, UCC records:** See www.gsccca.org **Other phones:** Assessor-229-734-3012.

Baldwin County

County Superior Court Clerk, PO Drawer 987, Milledgeville, GA 31059. **Phone-**478-445-4007, R/E Recording- 478-445-4008, UCC Recording- 478-445-5754; fax-478-445-1404; hours 8:30AM-5PM
Will not search records. UCC copy- $1.00 per page. RE record copy- $.25 per page. Cert fee: $2.50 per cert. Payee: Baldwin County Clerk of Superior Court. **Online Access to RE Deed, Lien, UCC records:** See www.gsccca.org **Other phones:** Assessor-Appraiser-478-453-5300; Treasurer-478-434-4791; Elections-478-445-4526; Vital Records-478-445-4807; Sheriff-478-445-4893.

Banks County

County Superior Court Clerk, 144 Yonah Homer Rd #8, Homer, GA 30547-2614. **Phone-**706-677-6243, R/E Recording- 706-677-6240, UCC Recording- 706-677-6240; fax-706-677-6294; hours 8AM-5PM
Will not search records. UCC copy- $1.00 per page. Cert fee: $3.75 per doc, $.50 per page. Payee: County Clerk of Superior Court. **Online Access to RE Deed, UCC, Lien records:** See www.gsccca.org **Other phones:** Assessor-706-677-2320; Treasurer-706-677-6200; Elections-706-677-6250.

Barrow County

County Superior Court Clerk, PO Box 1280, Winder, GA 30680. **Phone-**770-307-3035; hours 8AM-5PM
Will not search records. UCC copy- $1.00 per page. Cert fee: $2.50 per doc, $.50 per page. Payee: Barrow County Clerk of Superior Court. **Online Access to RE Deed, Lien, UCC records:** See www.gsccca.org **Other phones:** Assessor-770-307-3108; Treasurer-770-307-3106.

Bartow County

County Superior Court Clerk, 135 W. Cherokee Ave., #233, Cartersville, GA 30120. **Phone-**770-387-5025; hours 8AM-5PM. Will not search records. Record copy- $.25 per page. Cert fee: $2.50 1st pg., $.25 each add'l pg. Payee: Bartow County Clerk of Superior Court. **Online Access to RE Deed, UCC,**

Lien records: See www.gsccca.org **Other phones:** Assessor-770-387-5090.

Ben Hill County

County Superior Court Clerk, PO Box 1104, Fitzgerald, GA 31750-1104. **Phone-**County Superior Court Clerk, R/E & UCC Recording- 229-426-5135; fax-229-426-5487; hours 8:30AM-4:30PM. Will not search records. UCC copy- $1.00 per page. Cert fee: $2.00 per doc. Payee: Ben Hill County Clerk of Superior Court. **Online Access to RE Deed, UCC, Lien records:** See www.gsccca.org **Other phones:** Assessor-229-426-5147; Elections-229-426-5151.

Berrien County

County Superior Court Clerk, 101 E. Marion Ave. #3, Nashville, GA 31639. **Phone-**County Superior Court Clerk, R/E & UCC Recording- 229-686-5506; hours 8AM-5PM. Will not search records. UCC copy-$1.00 per page. Cert fee: $2.00 per doc, $.50 per page. Payee: County Clerk of Superior Court. **Online Access to RE Deed, Lien, UCC records:** See www.gsccca.org **Other phones:** Assessor-229-686-2149; Treasurer-229-686-7461 (Tax Commissioner); Appraiser-229-686-5213; Elections-229-686-5213.

Bibb County

County Superior Court Clerk, PO Box 1015, Macon, GA 31202-1015. **Phone-**478-621-6527; fax-478-621-6033; hours 8:30AM-5PM. Will search UCC records. Search per debtor-$10.00. Copy fee-$.25 per page. Will not search tax liens. Will search real estate records. RE record copy- $.25 per page. Cert fee: $2.50 per doc, $.50 per page. Payee: Bibb County Clerk of Superior Court. **Online Access to RE Deed, UCC, Property, Lien, Finance Statement records:** See www.gsccca.org for Deed and UCC indexes. Also, search land, financing statements and liens on the Superior Court clerk search page for free at http://68.109.200.12/resolution. Also, search the assessors' property tax records for free at www.qpublic.net/bibb/digest_search1.html. Search for property ownership for free at www.co.bibb.ga.us/engineering/property/search.htm. **Other phones:** Assessor-478-742-2254; Treasurer-478-621-6310.

Bleckley County

County Superior Court Clerk, 306 SE 2nd St, Cochran, GA 31014. **Phone**-478-934-3210; fax-478-934-6671; hours 8:30AM-5PM

Will not search records. Record copy- $.25 per page. Cert fee: $2.50 1st pg., $.50 for every add'l pg. Payee: Bleckley County Clerk of Superior Court. **Online Access to RE Deed, Lien, UCC records:** See www.gsccca.org **Other phones:** Assessor-478-934-3209; Treasurer-478-934-3200.

Brantley County

County Superior Court Clerk, PO Box 1067, Nahunta, GA 31553. **Phone**-912-462-5635, R/E Recording- 912-462-7682, UCC Recording- 912-462-7682; fax-912-462-5538; 8AM-5PM. Will search UCC records. UCC copy- $1.00 per page. Will not search real estate or tax lien records. Cert fee: $2.00 per doc, $.50 per page. Payee: Brantley County Clerk of Superior Court. **Online Access to RE Deed, Lien, UCC records:** See www.gsccca.org **Other phones:** Assessor-912-462-5251; Treasurer-912-462-5256.

Brooks County

County Superior Court Clerk, PO Box 630, Quitman, GA 31643. **Phone**-County Superior Court Clerk, R/E & UCC Recording- 229-263-4747; fax-229-263-5050; hours 8AM-5PM. Will search UCC records. UCC copy- $1.00 per page. Will not search real estate or tax lien records. Cert fee: $2.00 per doc, $.50 per page. Payee: Brooks County Clerk of Superior Court. **Online Access to RE Deed, Lien, UCC records:** See www.gsccca.org **Other phones:** Assessor-229-263-7920; Elections-229-2635567; Vital Records-229-263-7585.

Bryan County

County Superior Court Clerk, PO Box 670, Pembroke, GA 31321. **Phone**-912-653-3872, R/E Recording- 912-653-3872 option #4, UCC Recording- 912-653-3872 option #4; fax-912-653-3805; hours 8AM-5PM

Will not search records. UCC copy- $1.00 per page. RE copy- $.25 per page. Cert fee: $2.50 per cert. Payee: Bryan County Clerk of Superior Court. **Online Access to RE Deed, UCC, Lien, Notaries, Plat records:** See www.gsccca.org **Other phones:** Assessor-912-653-3889; Treasurer-912-653-3839; Appraiser-912-653-3889; Elections-912-653-3859; Vital Records-912-653-3856.

Bulloch County

County Superior Court Clerk, 20 Siebald St, Judicial Annex, Statesboro, GA 30458. **Phone**-912-764-9009; fax-912-764-5953; hours 8AM-5PM

Will not search records. UCC copy- $1.00 per page. Cert fee: $2.50 per cert. Payee: County Clerk of Superior Court. **Online Access to RE Deed, Lien, UCC records:** See www.gsccca.org **Other phones:** Assessor-912-764-2181; Treasurer-912-764-6285.

Burke County

County Superior Court Clerk, PO Box 803, Waynesboro, GA 30830-0803. **Phone**-County Superior Court Clerk, R/E & UCC Recording- 706-554-2279; fax-706-554-7887; hours 9AM-5PM

Will not search records. UCC copy- $1.00 per page. RE record copy- $.25 per page. Cert fee: $2.00 per doc, $.50 per page. Payee: Burke County Clerk of Superior Court. **Online Access to RE Deed, UCC, Lien, Plat records:** See www.gsccca.org **Other phones:** Assessor-706-554-2607; Treasurer-706-554-2324; Appraiser-706-554-2607; Elections-706-554-7457; Vital Records-706-554-3000.

Butts County

County Superior Court Clerk, PO Box 320, Jackson, GA 30233. **Phone**-770-775-8215; fax-770-504-1359;

hours 8AM-5PM. Will not search records. UCC copy fee- $1.00 per page. Cert fee: $2.50 per cert. Payee: Butts County Clerk of Superior Court. **Online Access to RE Deed, UCC, Lien records:** See www.gsccca.org **Other phones:** Assessor-770-775-8207; Treasurer-770-775-8200.

Calhoun County

County Superior Court Clerk, PO Box 69, Morgan, GA 39866. **Phone**-229-849-2715; fax-229-849-0072; hours 8AM-5PM. Will search UCC records. No fee for UCC record search. UCC copy- $1.00 per page. Will do tax lien search, but they do not maintain hard-copy records. Will not search real estate records. RE record copy- $.25 per page. Cert fee: 5.00 per doc. Payee: County Clerk Superior Court. **Online Access to RE Deed, UCC records:** See www.gsccca.org for Deed, and UCCs. **Other phones:** Assessor-229-849-4685; Treasurer-229-849-2970.

Camden County

County Superior Court Clerk, PO Box 578, Woodbine, GA 31569-0578. **Phone**-912-576-5622, UCC Recording- 915-576-5622; hours 9AM-5PM

Will not search records. Record copy- $.25 per page. Cert fee: $2.00 1st pg, $.50 each add'l. Payee: Camden County Clerk of Superior Court. **Online Access to RE Deed, Lien, UCC records:** See www.gsccca.org **Other phones:** Assessor-912-576-3241; Treasurer-912-576-5601.

Candler County

County Superior Court Clerk, PO Drawer 830, Metter, GA 30439. **Phone**-912-685-5257; fax-912-685-2160; hours 8:30AM-5PM. Will search UCC records. UCC copy- $.25 per page. Will not search real estate or tax lien records. RE record copy- $1.00 per page. Cert fee: $2.00 per doc, $.50 per page. Payee: Candler County Clerk of Superior Court. **Online Access to RE Deed, Lien, UCC records:** See www.gsccca.org **Other phones:** Assessor-912-685-6346; Treasurer-912-685-5257; Elections-912-685-6687; Vital Records-912-685-2357.

Carroll County

County Superior Court Clerk, PO Box 1620, Carrollton, GA 30112. **Phone**-770-830-5830, R/E Recording- 770-830-5835, UCC Recording- 770-830-5835 x2255; fax-770-214-3584; hours 8AM-5PM. Will not search records. Record copy- $1.00 per page. Cert fee: $2.50 per cert. Payee: Carroll County Clerk of Superior Court. **Online Access to RE Deed, UCC, Notary Public, Lien records:** See www.gsccca.org **Other phones:** Assessor-770-830-5812; Treasurer-770-830-5801; Appraiser-770-830-5843; Elections-770-830-5824; Vital Records-770-836-6667.

Catoosa County

County Superior Court Clerk, 875 Lafayette St, Courthouse, Ringgold, GA 30736. **Phone**-706-935-4231; fax-none; hours 8:30AM-5PM

Will not search records. Record copy- $1.00 per page. Cert fee: $2.50 per doc, $.50 per page. Payee: Catoosa County Clerk of Superior Court. **Online Access to RE Deed, Lien, UCC records:** See www.gsccca.org **Other phones:** Assessor-706-965-3772; Treasurer-706-935-2500.

Charlton County

County Superior Court Clerk, PO Box 760, Folkston, GA 31537. **Phone**-912-496-2354; fax-912-496-3882; hours 8AM-5PM. Will search UCC records. UCC copy- $1.00 per page. Will not search real estate or tax lien records. Cert fee: $.50 per doc, + $.50 per page. Payee: Charlton County Clerk of Superior Court. **Online Access to RE Deed, Lien, UCC records:** See www.gsccca.org **Other phones:** Assessor-912-496-7437.

Chatham County

County Superior Court Clerk, PO Box 10227, Savannah, GA 31412. **Phone**-County Superior Court Clerk, R/E & UCC Recording- 912-652-7214, UCC Recording- 912-652-7219; fax-912-652-7380; hours 8AM-5PM www.chathamcourts.org Will not search records. Copy fee- $.25 per page. Cert fee: $2.00 per doc + $.50 per page. Payee: Chatham County Clerk of Superior Court. **Online Access to RE Deed, Lien, UCC records:** See www.gsccca.org **Other phones:** Assessor-912-652-7127; Elections-912-652-7494; Vital Records-912-356-2108.

Chattahoochee County

County Superior Court Clerk, PO Box 120, Cusseta, GA 31805-0120. **Phone**-706-989-3424, R/E Recording- 709-989-3424; fax-706-989-0396; hours 8AM-5PM. Will search UCC records. UCC copy fee- $1.00 per page. Will not search real estate or tax lien records. Cert fee: $2.50 per cert. Payee: Chattahoochee County Clerk of Superior Court. **Online Access to RE Deed, Lien, UCC records:** See www.gsccca.org **Other phones:** Assessor-706-989-3249; Elections-706-989-3602; Vital Records-706-989-3603.

Chattooga County

County Superior Court Clerk, PO Box 159, Summerville, GA 30747. **Phone**-706-857-0706; fax-706-857-0686; hours 8:30AM-5PM

Will not search records. Copy fee- $.25 per page. Cert fee: $2.00 per doc, $.50 per page. Payee: Chattooga County Clerk of Superior Court. **Online Access to RE Deed, Lien, UCC records:** See www.gsccca.org **Other phones:** Assessor-706-857-3819; Treasurer-706-857-0703.

Cherokee County

County Superior Court Clerk, 90 North St, #G-170, Canton, GA 30114. **Phone**-County Superior Court Clerk, R/E & UCC Recording- 678-493-6531, UCC Recording- 678-493-6527; hours 8AM-5PM www.cherokeega.org

Will not search records. Copy fee- $1.00 per page. Cert fee: $2.00 per doc, $.50 per page. Payee: Cherokee County Clerk of Superior Court. **Online Access to RE Deed, UCC, Sex Offender, Inmate records:** See www.gsccca.org for Deed and UCC indexes. Also, search the sheriff's sex offender list at www.cherokeega-sheriff.org/offender/offender.htm Also, search inmate info on private company website at www.vinelink.com/index.jsp. **Other phones:** Elections-770-479-0407; Vital Records-678-493-6160; Tax Assessor-678-493-6120.

Clarke County

County Superior Court Clerk, PO Box 1805, Athens, GA 30603. **Phone**-706-613-3196, R/E Recording- 706-613-3190; fax-706-613-3189; hours 8AM-5PM

Will not search records. Copy fee- $1.00 per page. Cert fee: $3.00 + $1.00 per page. Payee: Clerk of Superior Court. **Online Access to RE Deed, UCC, Property, Inmate records:** See www.gsccca.org for Deed and UCC indexes. Also, you may view property information for free at https://athens-clarke.ga.ezgov.com/ezproperty/review_search.jsp; however, there is no name searching. Also, search inmate info on private company website at www.vinelink.com/index.jsp. **Other phones:** Assessor-706-613-3140; Treasurer-706-613-3040.

Clay County

County Superior Court Clerk, PO Box 550, Fort Gaines, GA 39851-0550. **Phone**-229-768-2631; fax-229-768-3047; hours 8AM-4:30PM

Will not search records. UCC copy- $1.00 per page. Cert fee: $3.00 1st pg, $.50 each add'l. Payee:

Clay County Clerk of Superior Court. **Online Access to RE Deed, UCC, Lien records:** See www.gsccca.org **Other phones:** Assessor-229-768-2000; Treasurer-229-768-3238; Elections-229-768-2915; Vital Records-229-768-2915.

Clayton County

County Superior Court Clerk, 9151 Tara Blvd, Rm 202, Jonesboro, GA 30236. **Phone-**770-477-3395; fax-770-477-3490; hours-8AM-5PM www.co.clayton.ga.us/superior_court/clerk_of_courts/ Will not search records. UCC copy- $1.00 per page. RE record copy- $.25 per page. Cert fee: $2.00 per doc, $.50 per page. Payee: Clayton County Clerk of Superior Court. **Online Access to Real Estate, UCC, Lien, Property Tax records:** See www.gsccca.org Also, search tax assessor records for free at www.qpublic.net/clayton/search.html. **Other phones:** Assessor-770-447-3285; Tax Commissioner-770-477-3311; Probate Court-770-477-3301.

Clinch County

County Superior Court Clerk, PO Box 433, Homerville, GA 31634. **Phone-**912-487-5854, R/E Recording- 912-481-5854; fax-912-487-3083; hours 8AM-5PM Will not search records. Copy fee- $.25 per page. Cert fee: $3.00 per doc. Payee: Clinch County Clerk of Superior Court. **Online Access to RE Deed, Lien, UCC records:** See www.gsccca.org **Other phones:** Assessor-912-487-2561.

Cobb County

County Superior Court Clerk, PO Box 3490, Marietta, GA 30061. **Phone-**770-528-1363; fax-770-528-1325; hours 8AM-5PM www.cobbgasupctclk.com Will not search records. UCC copy- $1.00 per page. Cert fee: $2.00 1st pg, $.50 each add'l. Payee: Cobb County Clerk of Superior Court. **Online Access to Real Estate, Grantor/Grantee, UCC, Deed, Property Tax records:** Property records on the County Superior Court Clerk website are free at www.cobbgasupctclk.com/index.htm. Search by name, address, land description, instrument type, or book & page. You may also search court records. Also, see www.gsccca.org for online access to Deed and UCC indexes. Also, search property tax records for free at www.cobbtax.org. Click on "Property Taxes". No name searching. **Other phones:** Assessor-770-528-3100; Treasurer-770-528-8600.

Coffee County

County Superior Court Clerk, 101 S. Peterson Ave., Courthouse, Douglas, GA 31533. **Phone-**912-384-2865, R/E Recording- 912-384-2865 x239, UCC Recording- 912-384-2865 x239; hours 8:30AM-5PM Will not search records. UCC copy- $1.00 per page. Cert fee: $3.00 per cert. Payee: County Clerk of Superior Court. **Online Access to RE Deed, Lien, UCC records:** See www.gsccca.org **Other phones:** Assessor-912-384-2136; Treasurer-912-384-4799; Appraiser-912-384-2136; Elections-912-384-5213 or 384-7018; Vital Records-912-389-4458.

Colquitt County

County Superior Court Clerk, PO Box 2827, Moultrie, GA 31776-2827. **Phone-**229-616-7420, R/E Recording- 229-616-7063; fax-229-616-7029; hours 8AM-5PM. Will not search records. UCC copy- $1.00 per page. Cert fee: $2.00 per doc, $.50 per page. Payee: Colquitt County Clerk of Superior Court. **Online Access to RE Deed, UCC, Lien, Notary, Public records:** See www.gsccca.org **Other phones:** Assessor-229-616-7425.

Columbia County

County Superior Court Clerk, PO Box 2930, Evans, GA 30809. **Phone-**706-312-7139; hours 8AM-5PM

Will not search records. UCC copy- $1.00 per page. Cert fee: $2.00 per doc, $.50 per page. Payee: Columbia County Clerk of Superior Court. **Online Access to RE Deed, UCC, Lien, Sex Offender, Property records:** See www.gsccca.org Also, search the registered sex offender list at www.columbiacountyso.org/offenders.html. Also, search the GIS-mapping site for property information for free at http://64.89.116.248/default.htm. **Other phones:** Assessor-706-541-0920.

Cook County

County Superior Court Clerk, 212 N. Hutchinson Ave, Adel, GA 31620-2497. **Phone-**County Superior Court Clerk, R/E & UCC Recording- 229-896-7717; hours 8:30AM-4:30PM This agency only records real estate transactions, not UCC. UCC copy fee- $1.00 per page. Will not search real estate records. RE record copy- $1.00 per page. Cert fee: $2.00 per doc, $.50 per page. Payee: Cook County Clerk of Superior Court. **Online Access to RE Deed, Lien, UCC records:** See www.gsccca.org **Other phones:** Assessor-229-896-3665; Elections-229-896-3941.

Coweta County

County Superior Court Clerk, 200 Court Sq, Courthouse, 1st Fl, Newnan, GA 30263. **Phone-**County Superior Court Clerk, R/E & UCC Recording- 770-254-2690, UCC Recording- 770-254-2696; fax-770-254-3700; hours 8AM-5PM. Will not search records. UCC copy- $1.00 per page. Cert fee: $2.50 1st page, $.50 each add'l. Payee: Coweta County Clerk of Superior Court. **Online Access to RE Deed, UCC, Lien records:** See www.gsccca.org **Other phones:** Assessor-770-254-2680.

Crawford County

County Superior Court Clerk, PO Box 1037, Roberta, GA 31078-1037. **Phone-**County Superior Court Clerk, R/E & UCC Recording- 478-836-3328; hours 9AM-5PM. Will not search records. Copy fee- $1.00 per page. Cert fee: $2.50 per doc + $.50 per page. Payee: County Clerk of Superior Court. **Online Access to RE Deed, Lien, UCCs:** See www.gsccca.org **Other phones:** Assessor-478-836-2800; Treasurer-478-836-3575; Elections-478-836-3575; Vital Records-478-836-3313.

Crisp County

County Superior Court Clerk, PO Box 747, Cordele, GA 31010-0747. **Phone-**County Superior Court Clerk, R/E & UCC Recording- 229-276-2616; fax-229-273-5730; hours 8:30AM-5PM Will not search records. Record copy- $1.00 per page. Cert fee: $2.50 1st pg, $.50 each add'l. Payee: Crisp County Clerk of Superior Court. **Online Access to RE Deed, Lien, UCC records:** See www.gsccca.org **Other phones:** Assessor-229-276-2635; Treasurer-229-276-2672; Appraiser-229-276-2635; Elections-229-276-2611; Tax Commissioner-229-276-2630.

Dade County

County Superior Court Clerk, PO Box 417, Trenton, GA 30752. **Phone-**County Superior Court Clerk, R/E & UCC Recording- 706-657-4778; fax-706-657-8284; hours 8:30AM-5PM Will not search records. Record copy- $1.00 per page. Cert fee: $2.00 per doc, $.50 per page. Payee: Dade County Clerk of Superior Court. **Online Access to RE Deed, Lien, UCC records:** See www.gsccca.org **Other phones:** Assessor-706-657-6341; Treasurer-706-657-4625; Appraiser-706-657-6341; Elections-706-657-4414; Vital Records-706-657-4414; Tax Commission-706-657-7563; Small Claims-706-657-4113.

Dawson County

County Superior Court Clerk, 25 Tucker Ave, #106, Dawsonville, GA 30534-0222. **Phone-**706-344-3510, R/E Recording- 706-344-3510 x229, UCC Recording-706-344-3510 x227; fax-706-344-3511; hours 8AM-5PM. Will not search records. UCC copy- $1.00 per page. Cert fee: $2.50 per doc, $.25 per page. Payee: Dawson County Clerk of Superior Court. **Online Access to RE Deed, UCC, Lien records:** See www.gsccca.org Also, search the assessor property data for free at www.dawsontaxassessors.org/page2.html.

De Kalb County

County Superior Court Clerk, 556 N. McDonough St, Courthouse, Rm 208, Decatur, GA 30030. **Phone-**404-371-2836, R/E Recording- 404-371-2836 x3741, UCC Recording- 404-371-2836 x3735; hours 7:30AM-6PM Will search UCC records. UCC copy- $1.00 per page. Will not search real estate or tax lien records. Office will not make copies for you. Cert fee: $2.50 per doc, $.50 per page. Payee: De Kalb County Clerk of Superior Court. **Online Access to RE Deed, UCC, Property Tax, records:** See www.gsccca.org for Deed and UCC indexes. Also, search tax commissioner property tax data for free at https://dklbweb.dekalbga.org/taxcommissioner/Property TaxMain2.htm. Click on "Make/View Property Tax Payment." No name searching. Search registered sex offender list at www.dekalbsheriff.org/regnames3.html. **Other phones:** Assessor-404-371-4938.

Decatur County

County Superior Court Clerk, PO Box 336, Bainbridge, GA 39818. **Phone-**County Superior Court Clerk, R/E & UCC Recording- 229-248-3025; fax-229-248-3029; hours 8AM-5PM Will not search records. UCC copy- $1.00 per page. RE record copy- $.25 per page. Cert fee: $2.00 per doc, $.50 per page. Payee: Decatur County Clerk of Superior Court. **Online Access to RE Deed, Lien, UCC records:** See www.gsccca.org **Other phones:** Assessor-229-248-3008; Treasurer-229-248-3030; Appraiser-229-248-3008; Elections-229-248-3021; Vital Records-229-248-3055.

Dodge County

County Superior Court Clerk, PO Box 4276, Eastman, GA 31023-4276. **Phone-**478-374-2871; fax-478-374-3035; hours 9AM-Noon,1-5PM Will not search records. UCC copy- $1.00 per page. RE copy- $.25 per page. Cert fee: $2.50 per doc, + $.50 per page. Payee: Dodge County Clerk of Superior Court. **Online Access to RE Deed, Lien, UCC records:** See www.gsccca.org **Other phones:** Assessor-478-374-8122; Treasurer-478-374-3775; Elections-478-378-8123; Vital Records-478-374-3775.

Dooly County

County Superior Court Clerk, PO Box 326, Vienna, GA 31092-0326. **Phone-**County Superior Court Clerk, R/E & UCC Recording- 229-268-4234; fax-229-268-6142; hours 8:30AM-5PM. Will not search records. UCC copy- $1.00 per page. Cert fee: $2.50 per doc, $1.00 per page. Payee: Dooly County Clerk of Superior Court. **Online Access to RE Deed, Lien, UCC records:** See www.gsccca.org **Other phones:** Assessor-229-268-4719; Treasurer-229-268-4228.

Dougherty County

County Superior Court Clerk, PO Box 1827, Albany, GA 31701. **Phone-**County Superior Court Clerk, R/E & UCC Recording- 229-431-2198; fax-229-431-2850; hours 8:30AM-5PM www.albany.ga.us Will not search records. UCC copy- $1.00 per page. Cert fee: $2.00 per doc, $1.00 per page. Payee: Dougherty County Clerk of Superior Court. **Online Access to Real Estate, Personal Property, Tax,**

Courts, Deed, Mortgage, Tax Assessor, Personal Property, UCC, Death, Divorce, Trade Name records: Access to the clerk of courts Dept. of Deeds public menu is at www.albany.ga.us/doco/clerk_court_rec.htm. Click on "clerk of courts records." Also, the searchable tax records system at www.albany.ga.us/doco/tax_tag.htm has personal property, deeds, assessments. Click on "County/City Tax Record System." Call 229-431-2130 during business hours for help navigating this system. Also, see www.gsccca.org for online access to Deed and UCC indexes. **Other phones:** Assessor-229-431-2130; Treasurer-229-431-2130; Elections-229-431-3247.

Douglas County

County Superior Court Clerk, 8700 Hospital Dr., Douglas County Courthouse, Douglasville, GA 30134. **Phone-**770-920-7449, R/E Recording- 770-920-7257; hours 8AM-5PM. Will not search records. UCC copy-$1.00 per page. RE record copy- $.50 per page. Cert fee: $2.50 1st 2 pages, $.50 each add'l. Payee: Douglas County Clerk of Superior Court. **Online Access to RE Deed, Lien, UCC records:** See www.gsccca.org **Other phones:** Assessor-770-920-7228; Appraiser-770-920-7228; Elections-770-920-7236; Vital Records-770-920-7249.

Early County

County Superior Court Clerk, PO Box 849, Blakely, GA 39823. **Phone-**County Superior Court Clerk, R/E & UCC Recording- 229-723-3033; fax-229-723-4411; hours 8AM-5PM. Will not search records. Record copy- $1.00 per page. Cert fee: $2.50 per doc, $.50 per page. Payee: Early County Clerk of Superior Court. **Online Access to RE Deed, Lien, UCC records:** See www.gsccca.org **Other phones:** Assessor-229-723-3088; Treasurer-229-723-4024.

Echols County

County Superior Court Clerk, PO Box 213, Statenville, GA 31648. **Phone-**County Superior Court Clerk, R/E & UCC Recording- 229-559-5642; fax-229-559-5792; hours 8AM-Noon, 1-4:30PM. Will not search records. Record copy- $1.00 per page. Cert fee: $2.50 1st page, $.50 each add'l. Payee: Echols County Clerk of Superior Court. **Online Access to RE Deed, Lien, UCC records:** See www.gsccca.org **Other phones:** Assessor-229-559-7370; Treasurer-229-559-5253; Elections-229-559-7526.

Effingham County

County Superior Court Clerk, PO Box 387, Springfield, GA 31329-0387. **Phone-**912-754-2118, R/E Recording- 912-754-2145; hours 8:30AM-5PM Will not search records. Cert fee: $2.00 per doc, $.50 per page. Payee: Effingham County Clerk of Superior Court. **Online Access to RE Deed, UCC, Lien records:** See www.gsccca.org **Other phones:** Assessor-912-754-2125; Elections-912-754-2115; Vital Records-912-754-2112; Tax Commissioner-912-754-2121; Zoning-912-754-2128.

Elbert County

County Superior Court Clerk, PO Box 619, Elberton, GA 30635. **Phone-**County Superior Court Clerk, R/E & UCC Recording- 706-283-2005; fax-706-213-7286; hours 8AM-5PM Will not search records. Record copy- $1.00 per page. Cert fee: $2.00 per doc, $.50 per page. Payee: Elbert County Clerk of Superior Court. **Online Access to RE Deed, UCC, Lien Records, Plat recording records:** See www.gsccca.org **Other phones:** Assessor-706-283-2008; Treasurer-706-283-2018; Elections-706-283-2016.

Emanuel County

County Superior Court Clerk, PO Box 627, Swainsboro, GA 30401. **Phone-**County Superior Court

Clerk, R/E & UCC Recording- 478-237-8911; fax-478-237-2173; hours 8AM-5PM. Will not search records. UCC copy- $1.00 per page. Cert fee: $2.00 per doc, $.50 per page. Payee: Emanuel County Clerk of Superior Court. **Online Access to RE Deed, UCC records:** See www.gsccca.org for Deed and UCC indexes. **Other phones:** Assessor-478-237-3424; Treasurer-478-237-3881.

Evans County

County Superior Court Clerk, PO Box 845, Claxton, GA 30417. **Phone-**912-739-3868; fax-912-739-2504; hours 8AM-5PM. Will not search UCC records or tax liens. UCC copy- $1.00 per page. Will search real estate records. Cert fee: $2.00 per doc, $.50 per page. Payee: Evans County Clerk of Superior Court. **Online Access to RE Deed, Lien, UCC records:** See www.gsccca.org **Other phones:** Assessor-912-739-3424; Treasurer-912-739-1147; Elections-912-739-0708.

Fannin County

County Superior Court Clerk, PO Box 1300, Blue Ridge, GA 30513. **Phone-**County Superior Court Clerk, R/E & UCC Recording- 706-632-2039; hours 9AM-5PM. Will not search records. Cert fee: $2.50 per doc, $.50 per page. Payee: Fannin County Clerk of Superior Court. **Online Access to RE Deed, Lien, UCC records:** See www.gsccca.org **Other phones:** Assessor-706-632-5954; Treasurer-706-632-2645; Appraiser-706-632-5954; Elections-706-632-7740; Vital Records-706-623-3011.

Fayette County

County Superior Court Clerk, PO Box 130, Fayetteville, GA 30214. **Phone-**770-716-4290, R/E Recording- 770-716-4291, UCC Recording- 770-716-4291; fax-770-716-4868; hours 8AM-4:30PM www.admin.co.fayette.ga.us Will not search records. UCC copy- $1.00 per page. Cert fee: $2.00 per doc, $.50 per page. Payee: Fayette County Clerk of Superior Court. **Online Access to Assessor, Real Estate, UCC, Lien records:** Records on the County Assessor database are free on the GIS-mapping site at www.fayettecountymaps.com/disclaimer.htm. See www.gsccca.org for Deed and UCC indexes. **Other phones:** Assessor-770-460-5730 x5402; Tax Commissioner-770-461-3652.

Floyd County

County Superior Court Clerk, PO Box 1110, Rome, GA 30162-1110. **Phone-**706-291-5190, R/E Recording- 706-291-5158, UCC Recording- 706-291-5206; fax-706-233-0035; hours 8AM-5PM Will not search records. UCC copy- $1.00 per page. RE record copy- $.50 per page. Cert fee: $2.00 per doc, $.50 per page. Payee: Floyd County Clerk of Superior Court. **Online Access to RE Deed, Lien, UCC records:** See www.gsccca.org **Other phones:** Assessor-706-291-5143; Treasurer-706-291-5148; Appraiser-706-291-5144; Elections-706-291-5168; Tax Office-706-291-5147.

Forsyth County

County Superior Court Clerk, 100 Courthouse Sq, Rm 010, Cumming, GA 30040. **Phone-**County Superior Court Clerk, R/E & UCC Recording- 770-781-2120, UCC Recording- 770-781-2120 x 2690 or 2681; fax-770-886-2858; 8:30AM-5PM www.forsythco.com Will not search records. UCC copy- $1.00 per page. Cert fee: $2.50 per doc + $.50 per page. Payee: Forsyth County Clerk of Superior Court. **Online Access to RE Deed, Lien, UCC records:** See www.gsccca.org **Other phones:** Assessor-770-781-2106; Treasurer-770-781-2110; Elections-770-781-2118; Vital Records-770-781-2140.

Franklin County

County Superior Court Clerk, PO Box 70, Carnesville, GA 30521. **Phone-**706-384-2514; fax-706-384-4384; hours 8AM-5PM. Will not search records. UCC copy-$1.00 per page. RE copy- $.25 per page. Cert fee: $2.50 per doc, $.50 per page. Payee: Franklin County Clerk of Superior Court. **Online Access to RE Deed, Lien, UCC records:** See www.gsccca.org Other phones: Assessor-706-384-4896.

Fulton County

County Superior Court Clerk, 136 Pryor St, Atlanta, GA 30303. **Phone-**404-730-5300, R/E Recording- 404-730-5371, UCC Recording- 404-730-5553; hours 8:30AM-5PM www.fcclk.org Will not search records. Copy fee-$1.00 per page. For questions on current real estate records, call 404-730-5305 Cert fee: $2.00 per doc, $.50 per page. Payee: Fulton County Clerk of Superior Court. **Online Access to RE Deed, Lien, UCC records:** See www.gsccca.org **Other phones:** Assessor-404-730-6440; Treasurer-404-730-6100; Tax Lien Records-404-730-5305; Copy requests-404-730-5286.

Gilmer County

County Superior Court Clerk, 1 West Side Sq, Courthouse, Box #30, Ellijay, GA 30540. **Phone-**County Superior Court Clerk, R/E & UCC Recording- 706-635-4462; fax-706-635-1462; hours 8:30AM-5PM. Will not search records. UCC copy- $1.00 per page. Cert fee: $2.50 per doc, $.50 per page. Payee: Gilmer County Clerk of Superior Court. **Online Access to RE Deed, Lien, UCC records:** See www.gsccca.org **Other phones:** Assessor-706-635-2703; Treasurer-706-635-4361.

Glascock County

County Superior Court Clerk, PO Box 231, Gibson, GA 30810. **Phone-**County Superior Court Clerk, R/E & UCC Recording- 706-598-2084; fax-706-598-2577; hours 8AM-Noon,1-5PM Will not search records. Cert fee: $2.00 per doc, $.50 per page. Payee: Glascock County Clerk of Superior Court. **Online Access to RE Deed, UCC, Lien records:** See www.gsccca.org **Other phones:** Assessor-706-598-2863; Treasurer-706-598-2671; Elections-706-598-3241.

Glynn County

County Superior Court Clerk, PO Box 1355, Brunswick, GA 31521-1355. **Phone-**County Superior Court Clerk, R/E & UCC Recording- 912-554-7313; fax-912-267-5625; hours 8:30AM-5PM Will not search real estate or UCC records. UCC copy-$1.00 per page. Will search tax liens. RE record copy- $.25 per copy. Cert fee: $2.50 per doc, $.50 per page. Payee: Glynn County Clerk of Superior Court. **Online Access to Assessor, Property, Recording, UCC, Lien records:** Access the assessor property tax records free on the GIS mapping site at http://mapit.binarybus.com/glynn/a_pp/default.htm. See www.gsccca.org for online access to Deed, Lien and UCC indexes. **Other phones:** Assessor-912-554-7093; Treasurer-912-554-7120; Elections-912-554-7060.

Gordon County

County Superior Court Clerk, 100 Wall St., Courthouse, #102, Calhoun, GA 30701. **Phone-**County Superior Court Clerk, R/E & UCC Recording- 706-629-9533; fax-706-629-2139; hours 8:30AM-5PM Will not search records. UCC copy- $1.00 per page. RE record copy- $.50 per page. Cert fee: $2.50 per doc, $.50 per page. Payee: Gordon County Clerk of Superior Court. **Online Access to RE Deed, Lien, UCC records:** See www.gsccca.org **Other phones:** Assessor-706-629-6812; Treasurer-706-629-9242; Elections-706-629-7781; Vital Records-706-629-7314.

Grady County

Superior Court Clerk, Box 8, 250 N. Broad St, Cairo, GA 39828. **Phone-**Superior Court Clerk, R/E & UCC Recording- 229-377-2912; hours 8:30AM-5PM Will not search records. Public Access terminal is available. Clerk will assist visitors. UCC copy-$1.00 per page. RE record copy- $.25 per page. Cert fee: $2.00 per doc, $.50 per page. Payee: Grady County Clerk of Superior Court. **Online Access to RE Deed, Lien, UCC:** See www.gsccca.org **Other phones:** Registrar-229-377-1897.

Greene County

County Superior Court Clerk, 113 N Main St, Courthouse, #109, Greensboro, GA 30642-1107. **Phone-**706-453-3340; fax-706-453-9179; hours 8AM-5PM. Will not search records. UCC copy- $.25 per page. Cert fee: $2.50 1st page, $.25 each add'l. Payee: County Clerk of Superior Court. **Online Access to RE Deed, UCC, Lien:** See www.gsccca.org **Other phones:** Assessor-706-453-3355.

Gwinnett County

County Superior Court Clerk, PO Box 880, Lawrenceville, GA 30046. **Phone-**County Superior Court Clerk, R/E & UCC Recording- 770-822-8100; hours 8AM-5PM www.gwinnettcourts.com Will search UCC records. UCC copy- $1.00 per page. Will not search real estate or tax lien records. Cert fee: $2.50 per doc, $.25 per page. Payee: Gwinnett County Clerk of Superior Court. **Online Access to Property, Deed, UCC, Judgment, Lien records:** See www.gsccca.org for Deed, Plat and UCC indexes. Deed records go back to 1999; UCCs to1995. Also, search civil court judgments at www.gwinnettcourts.com/misc/casendx.htm. **Other phones:** Assessor-770-822-7233; Treasurer-770-822-8000.

Habersham County

County Superior Court Clerk, 555 Monroe St, Unit 35, Clarkesville, GA 30523. **Phone-**County Superior Court Clerk, R/E & UCC Recording- 706-754-2923; fax-706-754-8779; hours 8AM-5PM. Will not search records. Record copy- $.25 per page. Cert fee: $2.50 per doc, $.50 per page. Payee: Habersham County Clerk of Superior Court. **Online Access to RE Deed, UCC, Lien records:** See www.gsccca.org **Other phones:** Assessor-706-754-2557; Treasurer-706-754-6264; Appraiser-706-754-2557; Elections-706-754-2013; Vital Records-706-754-2013.

Hall County

County Superior Court Clerk, PO Box 1336, Gainesville, GA 30503-1336. **Phone-**770-531-7052, R/E Recording- 770-531-7058; fax-770-536-0702; hours 8AM-5PM www.hallcounty.org Will not search records. Record copy- $1.00 per page. Cert fee: $2.00 per doc, $.50 per page. Payee: Hall County Clerk of Superior Court. **Online Access to RE Deed, UCC, Lien, Plat records:** See www.gsccca.org **Other phones:** Assessor-770-531-6720; Treasurer-770-531-6950.

Hancock County

County Superior Court Clerk, PO Box 451, Sparta, GA 31087. **Phone-**706-444-6644; fax-706-444-5685; hours 9AM-5PM. Will not search records. Record copy-$.25 per page. Cert fee: $2.50 1st page, $.50 each add'l. Payee: Hancock County Clerk of Superior Court. **Online Access to RE Deed, Lien, UCC records:** See www.gsccca.org **Other phones:** Assessor-706-444-5721.

Haralson County

County Superior Court Clerk, PO Drawer 849, Buchanan, GA 30113. **Phone-**County Superior Court Clerk, R/E & UCC Recording- 770-646-2005; fax-770-646-2035; hours 8:30AM-5PM Will not search records. UCC copy- $1.00 per page. Cert fee: $2.00 per doc, $.50 per page. Payee: Haralson County Clerk of Superior Court. **Online Access to RE Deed, Lien, UCC records:** See www.gsccca.org **Other phones:** Assessor-770-646-2022; Treasurer-770-646-2022; Appraiser-770-646-2022; Vital Records-770-646-2008.

Harris County

County Superior Court Clerk, PO Box 528, Hamilton, GA 31811. **Phone-**County Superior Court Clerk, R/E & UCC Recording- 706-628-5570; fax-706-628-7039; hours 8AM-5PM Will not search records. UCC copy- $1.00 per page. Cert fee: $2.50 per doc, $.50 per page. Payee: Harris County Clerk of Superior Court. **Online Access to RE Deed, Lien, UCC records:** See www.gsccca.org **Other phones:** Assessor-706-628-5171; Treasurer-706-628-4958; Elections-706-628-5210; Tax Commissioner-706-628-4843.

Hart County

County Superior Court Clerk, PO Box 386, Hartwell, GA 30643. **Phone-**County Superior Court Clerk, R/E & UCC Recording- 706-376-7189; fax-706-376-1277; hours 8:30AM-5PM. Will not search records. Record copy- $1.00 per page. Cert fee: $2.00 per doc, $.50 per page. Payee: Hart County Clerk of Superior Court. **Online Access to RE Deed, Lien, UCC records:** See www.gsccca.org **Other phones:** Assessor-706-376-3997; Treasurer-706-376-2024; Appraiser-706-376-3997; Elections-706-376-2565; Vital Records-706-376-2565.

Heard County

County Superior Court Clerk, PO Box 249, Franklin, GA 30217. **Phone-**706-675-3301; fax-706-675-0819; hours 8:30AM-5PM. Will not search records. UCC copy- $1.00 per page. RE copy- $.25 per page. Cert fee: $2.50 per doc. Payee: Heard County Clerk of Superior Court. **Online Access to RE Deed, Lien, UCC records:** See www.gsccca.org **Other phones:** Assessor-706-675-3786.

Henry County

County Superior Court Clerk, Courthouse, #1 Courthouse Sq, McDonough, GA 30253. **Phone-**County Superior Court Clerk, R/E & UCC Recording-770-954-2121; hours 8AM-5PM www.co.henry.ga.us Will not search records. UCC copy- $1.00 per page. Cert fee: $2.50 1st page, $.50 each add'l. Payee: Henry County Clerk of Superior Court. **Online Access to RE Deed, UCC, Property Tax, Assessor:** www.gsccca.org. Search tax assessor records for free at www.co.henry.ga.us/TaxAssessors/Disclaimer.htm. **Other phones:** Assessor-770-954-2420; Treasurer-770-954-2470; Elections-770-954-2069; Vital Records-770-954-2303.

Houston County

County Superior Court Clerk, 201 N Perry Pkwy, Perry, GA 31069. **Phone-**478-987-2170, R/E Recording- 478-218-4720, UCC Recording- 478-218-4720; fax-478-987-3252; hours-8:30AM-5PM www.houstoncountyga.com Will not search records. Record copy- $1.00 per page. Cert fee: $2.00 per doc, $.50 per page. Payee: Houston County Clerk of Superior Court. **Online Access to Assessor, Real Estate, Plat, Lien, records:** Access to the assessor's Mapguide database is free at www.assessor.houstoncountyga.org. Download the Autodesk MapGuide viewer. Also, real Estate indexes back to 9/1972 are at www.houstoncounty.org. Also, the clerks recording indices of plats, land records, liens is free at http://67.32.12.213/resolution/. Pre-1998 real estate and pre-1994 financing statements are also available. See www.gsccca.org for online access to Deed, Lien and UCC indexes. **Other phones:** Assessor-478-218-4750; Appraiser-478-218-4750; Elections-478-987-1973; Vital Records-478-218-4710; Marriage/Death/Birth Records-478-218-4710; Divorce Records-478-218-4740.

Irwin County

County Superior Court Clerk, 113 N Irwin Ave, Ocilla, GA 31774. **Phone-**229-468-5356; fax-229-468-9753; hours 8AM-5PM. Will not search records. Record copy- $1.00 per page. Cert fee: $2.50 per doc, $.50 per page. Payee: Irwin County Clerk of Superior Court. **Online Access to RE Deed, Lien, UCC records:** See www.gsccca.org for Deed and UCC indexes. **Other phones:** Assessor-229-468-5514; Treasurer-229-468-5505.

Jackson County

County Superior Court Clerk, PO Box 7, Jefferson, GA 30549. **Phone-**706-367-6360, R/E Recording- 706-367-6362; fax-706-367-2468; hours 8AM-5PM Will search UCC records. UCC copy- $1.00 per page. Will not search real estate or tax lien records. Cert fee: $2.00 per doc, $.50 per page. Payee: Jackson County Clerk of Superior Court. **Online Access to RE Deed, Lien, UCC:** See www.gsccca.org **Other phones:** Appraiser-706-367-6330; Elections-706-367-6377; Vital Records-706-367-6366.

Jasper County

County Superior Court Clerk, Courthouse, Monticello, GA 31064. **Phone-**706-468-4901, R/E Recording- 706-468-4901 x226, UCC Recording- 706-468-4901 x226; fax-706-468-4946; hours 8AM-5PM Will not search records. UCC copy- $1.00 per page. Cert fee: $2.50 per doc, + $.50 per page. Payee: Jasper County Clerk of Superior Court. **Online Access to RE Deed, UCC, Lien:** See www.gsccca.org **Other phones:** Assessor-706-468-4904; Treasurer-706-468-4900; Appraiser-706-468-4904; Elections-706-468-4903; Vital Records-706-468-4903.

Jeff Davis County

County Superior Court Clerk, PO Box 429, Hazlehurst, GA 31539. **Phone-**County Superior Court Clerk, R/E & UCC Recording- 912-375-6615; fax-912-375-6637; hours 8AM-5PM Will not search records. Record copy- $1.00 per page. Cert fee: $2.00 per doc, $.50 per page. Payee: Jeff Davis County Clerk of Superior Court. **Online Access to RE Deed, Lien, UCC:** See www.gsccca.org **Other phones:** Assessor-912-375-6624; Treasurer-912-375-6611; Appraiser-912-375-6624; Elections-912-375-6625; Vital Records-912375-6626.

Jefferson County

County Superior Court Clerk, PO Box 151, Louisville, GA 30434. **Phone-**478-625-7922; fax-478-625-9589; hours 9AM-5PM. Will not search records. Record copy- $.25 per page. Cert fee: $2.50 per doc, + $.50 per page. Payee: Jefferson County Clerk of Superior Court. **Online Access to RE Deed, Lien, UCC records:** See www.gsccca.org **Other phones:** Assessor-478-625-8209; Treasurer-478-625-7736.

Jenkins County

County Superior Court Clerk, PO Box 659, Millen, GA 30442. **Phone-**County Superior Court Clerk, R/E & UCC Recording- 478-982-4683; fax-478-982-1274; hours 8:30AM-1-5PM Will not search records. UCC copy- $1.00 per page. RE record copy- $.25 per page. Cert fee: $2.50 per doc. Payee: Jenkins County Clerk of Superior Court. **Online Access to RE Deed, Lien, UCC records:** See www.gsccca.org **Other phones:** Assessor-478-982-4939; Treasurer-478-982-4925.

Johnson County

County Superior Court Clerk, PO Box 321, Wrightsville, GA 31096. **Phone-**478-864-3484; fax-478-864-1343; hours 9AM-5PM. Will not search records. UCC copy- $.25 per page. Cert fee: $3.00 per doc. Payee: Johnson County Clerk of Superior Court. **Online Access to RE Deed, Lien, UCC records:** See www.gsccca.org **Other phones:** Assessor-478-864-3325; Treasurer-478-864-2565.

Jones County

County Superior Court Clerk, PO Box 39, Gray, GA 31032. **Phone-**478-986-6671; hours 8:30AM-4:30PM Will not search records. UCC copy- $.50 per page. RE copy- $.25 per page. Cert fee: $2.50 per doc. Payee: Jones County Clerk of Superior Court. **Online Access to RE Deed, Lien, UCC records:** See www.gsccca.org **Other phones:** Assessor-478-986-6300; Treasurer-478-986-6538.

Lamar County

County Superior Court Clerk, 326 Thomaston St, Courthouse, Barnesville, GA 30204-1669. **Phone-**770-358-5145; fax-770-358-5814; hours 8AM-5PM Will not search records. Record copy- $1.00 for 1st page, $.25 each add'l. Cert fee: $2.50 per doc, $.50 per page. Payee: Lamar County Clerk of Superior Court. **Online Access to RE Deed, Lien, UCC records:** See www.gsccca.org **Other phones:** Assessor-770-358-5161; Treasurer-770-358-5162.

Lanier County

County Superior Court Clerk, 100 Main St, County Courthouse, Lakeland, GA 31635. **Phone-**229-482-3594; fax-229-482-8333; hours 8AM-Noon,1-5PM Will not search records. UCC copy- $1.00 per page. Cert fee: $3.00 per cert. Payee: Lanier County Clerk of Superior Court. **Online Access to RE Deed, Lien, UCC records:** See www.gsccca.org **Other phones:** Assessor-229-482-2090; Treasurer-229-482-3795.

Laurens County

County Superior Court Clerk, PO Box 2028, Dublin, GA 31040. **Phone-**County Superior Court Clerk, R/E & UCC Recording- 478-272-3210; fax-478-275-2595; hours 8:30AM-5:30PM
Will not search records. UCC copy- $1.00 per page. Cert fee: $2.50 per doc, $.50 per page. Payee: Laurens County Clerk of Superior Court. **Online Access to RE Deed, Lien, UCC records:** See www.gsccca.org **Other phones:** Assessor-478-272-6443; Treasurer-478-272-6994; Elections-478-272-2566; Vital Records-478-272-2051.

Lee County

County Superior Court Clerk, PO Box 49, Leesburg, GA 31763. **Phone-**County Superior Court Clerk, R/E & UCC Recording- 229-759-6018; fax-229-759-6049; hours 8AM-5PM. Will not search records. UCC copy- $1.00 per page. Cert fee: $2.00 per doc, $1.00 per page. Payee: Lee County Clerk of Superior Court. **Online Access to RE Deed, UCC, Lien records:** See www.gsccca.org **Other phones:** Assessor-229-759-6010; Treasurer-229-759-6000.

Liberty County

County Superior Court Clerk, PO Box 50, Hinesville, GA 31310. **Phone-**County Superior Court Clerk, R/E & UCC Recording- 912-876-3625; fax-912-369-5463; hours 8AM-5PM www.libertyco.com
Will not search records. UCC copy- $1.00 per page. Cert fee: $2.50 per doc, $.50 per page. Payee: County Clerk of Superior Court. **Online Access to RE Deed, UCC, Lien records:** See www.gsccca.org **Other phones:** Assessor-912-876-2823; Treasurer-912-876-3389; Vital Records-912-876-3625.

Lincoln County

County Superior Court Clerk, PO Box 340, Lincolnton, GA 30817. **Phone-**County Superior Court Clerk, R/E & UCC Recording- 706-359-5505; hours 9AM-Noon, 1PM-5PM. Will not search records. RE record copy- $1.00 per page. Cert fee: $2.00 per doc, $1.00 per page. Payee: Lincoln County Clerk of Superior Court. **Online Access to RE Deed, UCC records:** See www.gsccca.org for Deed and UCC indexes. **Other phones:** Assessor-706-359-5502; Appraiser-706-359-5502; Elections-706-359-6126; Vital Records-706-359-5528.

Long County

County Superior Court Clerk, PO Box 458, Ludowici, GA 31316. **Phone-**County Superior Court Clerk, R/E & UCC Recording- 912-545-2123; fax-912-545-2020; hours 8:30AM-5PM
Will not search records. UCC copy- $.25 per page. RE record copy- $1.00 per page. Cert fee: $2.50 1st page; $.50 each add'l. Payee: Long County Clerk of Superior Court. **Online Access to RE Deed, Lien, UCC records:** See www.gsccca.org **Other phones:** Assessor-912-545-9111; Treasurer-912-545-2127; Elections-912-545-2234; Vital Records-912-545-2131; Sheriffs Dept.-912-545-2118.

Lowndes County

County Superior Court Clerk, PO Box 1349, Valdosta, GA 31601-1349. **Phone-**County Superior Court Clerk, R/E & UCC Recording- 229-333-5125, UCC Recording- 229-333-5183; fax-229-333-7637; hours 8AM-5PM. Will not search records. Record copy- $.25 per page. Cert fee: $2.00 per doc + $.50 per page. Payee: Lowndes County Clerk of Superior Court. **Online Access to RE Deed, Lien, UCC records:** See www.gsccca.org **Other phones:** Assessor-229-671-2540; Treasurer-229-671-2570.

Lumpkin County

County Superior Court Clerk, 99 Courthouse Hill, #D, Dahlonega, GA 30533-0541. **Phone-**County Superior Court Clerk, R/E & UCC Recording- 706-864-3736; fax-706-864-5298; hours 8AM-5PM. Will not search records. Record copy- $.25 per page. Cert fee: $2.00 per doc, $.50 per page. Payee: Lumpkin County Clerk of Superior Court. **Online Access to RE Deed, UCC, Lien records:** See www.gsccca.org **Other phones:** Assessor-706-864-2433; Treasurer-706-864-3742; Appraiser-706-864-2433; Elections-706-864-3847; Vital Records-706-864-3847.

Macon County

County Superior Court Clerk, PO Box 337, Oglethorpe, GA 31068. **Phone-**County Superior Court Clerk, R/E & UCC Recording- 478-472-7661; fax-478-472-4775; hours 8:30AM-5PM
Will not search records. UCC copy- $1.00 per page. Cert fee: $2.00 per cert. Payee: Macon County Clerk of Superior Court. **Online Access to RE Deed, Lien, UCC records:** See www.gsccca.org **Other phones:** Assessor-478-472-6560; Treasurer-478-472-7031; Appraiser-478-472-6560; Elections-478-472-7685; Vital Records-478-472-7685.

Madison County

County Superior Court Clerk, PO Box 247, Danielsville, GA 30633. **Phone-**County Superior Court Clerk, R/E & UCC Recording- 706-795-3352; fax-706-795-2209; hours 8AM-5PM
Will not search records. UCC copy fee- $1.00 per page. Cert fee: $2.50 per cert + $.50 per page. Payee: Madison County Clerk of Superior Court. **Online Access to RE Deed, Lien, UCC records:** See www.gsccca.org

Marion County

County Superior Court Clerk, PO Box 41, Buena Vista, GA 31803. **Phone-**County Superior Court Clerk, R/E & UCC Recording- 229-649-7321; fax-229-649-7931; hours 9AM-5PM. Will not search records. UCC copy- $1.00 per page. Cert fee: $2.50 per doc, $.50 per page. Payee: Marion County Clerk of Superior Court. **Online Access to RE Deed, Lien, UCC records:** See www.gsccca.org **Other phones:** Assessor-229-649-5504; Treasurer-229-649-2603; Appraiser-229-649-5504; Elections-229-649-2603; Vital Records-229-649-5542.

McDuffie County

County Superior Court Clerk, PO Box 158, Thomson, GA 30824-0150. **Phone-**County Superior Court Clerk, R/E & UCC Recording- 706-595-2134; fax-706-595-9150; hours 8AM-5PM
Will not search records. UCC copy- $1.00 per page. $.25 for self-serve copies. Cert fee: $2.00 per doc, $.50 per page. Payee: McDuffie County Clerk of Superior Court. **Online Access to RE Deed, Lien, UCC records:** See www.gsccca.org **Other phones:** Assessor-706-595-2128; Treasurer-706-595-2100; Appraiser-706-595-2128; Elections-706-595-2105; Vital Records-706-595-2124.

McIntosh County

County Superior Court Clerk, PO Box 1661, Darien, GA 31305. **Phone-**County Superior Court Clerk, R/E & UCC Recording- 912-437-6641; fax-912-437-6673; hours 8AM-4:30PM
Will not search records. UCC copy- $1.00 per page. RE record copy- $.50 per page. Cert fee: $2.00 per doc, $.50 per page. Payee: McIntosh County Clerk of Superior Court. **Online Access to Deed (2000-present), UCC, Notary, Lien records:** Call 800-304-5175 to subscribe to UCCs and Deed indexes online service. See www.gsccca.org for online access to Deed, Lien and UCC indexes. **Other phones:** Assessor-912-437-6663; Treasurer-912-437-6641; Appraiser-912-437-6663; Vital Records-912-437-6636.

Meriwether County

County Superior Court Clerk, PO Box 160, Greenville, GA 30222-0160. **Phone-**County Superior Court Clerk, R/E & UCC Recording- 706-672-4416; fax-706-672-9465; hours 8:30AM-5PM. Will search UCC records. UCC copy- $1.00 per page. Will not search real estate or tax lien records. Cert fee: $2.00 per doc, $.50 per page. Payee: Meriwether County Clerk of Superior Court. **Online Access to RE Deed, Lien, UCC records:** See www.gsccca.org **Other phones:** Assessor-706-672-4222; Treasurer-706-672-4219; Appraiser-706-672-4222; Elections-706-672-4952; Vital Records-706-672-4974.

Miller County

County Superior Court Clerk, PO Box 66, Colquitt, GA 39837. **Phone-**County Superior Court Clerk, R/E & UCC Recording- 229-758-4102; fax-229-758-6585; hours 9AM-5PM
Will not search records. Record copy- $1.00 per page. Cert fee: $2.50 per cert. Payee: Miller County Clerk of Superior Court. **Online Access to RE Deed, Lien, UCC records:** See www.gsccca.org **Other phones:** Assessor-229-758-4100; Treasurer-229-758-4101; Appraiser-229-758-4100; Elections-229-758-4118; Vital Records-229-758-4110.

Mitchell County

County Superior Court Clerk, PO Box 427, Camilla, GA 31730. **Phone-**County Superior Court Clerk, R/E & UCC Recording- 229-336-2022; fax-229-336-2003; hours 8:30AM-5PM
Will not search records. Record copy- $.25 per page. Cert fee: $2.50 1st page, $.50 each add'l. Payee:

Mitchell County Clerk of Superior Court. **Online Access to RE Deed, Lien, UCC records:** See www.gsccca.org **Other phones:** Assessor-229-336-2005; Treasurer-229-336-2010; Elections-229-336-2016; Vital Records-229-336-2016.

Monroe County

County Superior Court Clerk, PO Box 450, Forsyth, GA 31029-0450. **Phone-**478-994-7022; fax-478-994-7053; hours 8:30AM-4:30PM

Will not search records. Record copy- $1.00 per page. Cert fee: $2.00 per doc, $.50 per page. Payee: Monroe County Clerk of Superior Court. **Online Access to RE Deed, UCC, Lien records:** See www.gsccca.org **Other phones:** Assessor-478-994-7038; Appraiser-478-994-7038; Elections-478-994-7036; Vital Records-478-994-7036.

Montgomery County

County Superior Court Clerk, PO Box 311, Mount Vernon, GA 30445. **Phone-**912-583-4401; hours 9AM-5PM. Will not search records. Record copy-$1.00 per page. Cert fee: $2.00 per doc, $.50 per page. **Online Access to RE Deed, Lien, UCC records:** See www.gsccca.org **Other phones:** Assessor-912-583-4131; Elections-912-583-2681; Vital Records-912-583-2681.

Morgan County

County Superior Court Clerk, PO Box 130, Madison, GA 30650. **Phone-**706-342-3605; hours 9AM-5PM Temporary location; 259 2nd St. Madison, GaA30650. Will not search records. UCC copy- $1.00 per page. Cert fee: $2.50 per doc, $.50 per page. Payee: County Clerk of Superior Court. **Online Access to RE Deed, Lien, UCCs:** See www.gsccca.org **Other phones:** Assessor-706-342-0551.

Murray County

County Superior Court Clerk, PO Box 1000, Chatsworth, GA 30705. **Phone-**706-695-2932; fax-706-517-9672; hours 8:30AM-5PM

Will not search records. UCC copy- $.25 per page. Cert fee: $2.50 1st page; $.25 each add'l. Payee: Murray County Clerk of Superior Court. **Online Access to RE Deed, Lien, UCC records:** See www.gsccca.org **Other phones:** Assessor-706-695-2521; Treasurer-706-695-3423.

Muscogee County

County Superior Court Clerk, PO Box 2145, Columbus, GA 31902-2145. **Phone-**706-653-4358, R/E Recording- 706-653-4356, UCC Recording- 706-653-4356; fax-706-653-4359; hours 8:30AM-5PM

Will not search records. UCC copy- $.25 per page. Cert fee: $3.00 per cert $.50 add'l. Payee: Muscogee County Clerk of Superior Court. **Online Access to RE Deed, Lien, UCC records:** See www.gsccca.org **Other phones:** Assessor-706-653-4398; Treasurer-706-653-4100.

Newton County

County Superior Court Clerk, 1132 Usher St, 3rd Fl, Newton County Judicial Ctr, Covington, GA 30014. **Phone-**770-784-2035, R/E Recording- 770-784-2040, UCC Recording- 770-784-2040; hours 8AM-5PM

Will not search records. UCC copy- $1.00 per page. Cert fee: $2.50 1st page, $.50 each add'l. Payee: County Clerk of Superior Court. **Online Access to RE Deed, Lien, UCCs:** See www.gsccca.org **Other phones:** Assessor-770-784-2000.

Oconee County

County Superior Court Clerk, PO Box 1099, Watkinsville, GA 30677. **Phone-**706-769-3940; fax-706-769-3948; hours 8AM-5PM. Will not search records. UCC copy- $1.00 per page. Cert fee: $2.50 per doc, $.50 per page. Payee: Oconee County

Clerk of Superior Court. **Online Access to RE Deed, UCC, Lien records:** See www.gsccca.org **Other phones:** Assessor-706-769-3921.

Oglethorpe County

County Superior Court Clerk, PO Box 68, Lexington, GA 30648-0068. **Phone-**County Superior Court Clerk, R/E & UCC Recording- 706-743-5731; fax-706-743-5335; hours 8AM-5PM

Will not search real estate or UCC records. UCC copy-$.50 per page. Will search tax liens. Tax lien search fee- $2.00 per debtor. Cert fee: $2.00 per doc, $.50 per page. Payee: Oglethorpe County Clerk of Superior Court. **Online Access to UCC, Real Estate records:** UCC and real estate records are online from the Oglethorpe County Clerk for a monthly subscription fee of $9.95 + $.25 per printed page. Guest accounts are available. For information and to open an account, call 404-327-9058. See www.gsccca.org for online access to Deed, Lien and UCC indexes. **Other phones:** Assessor-706-743-5166.

Paulding County

County Superior Court Clerk, 11 Courthouse Sq., Rm G-2, Dallas, GA 30132. **Phone-**770-443-7527, R/E Recording- 770-443-7528; hours 8AM-5PM. Will not search records. UCC copy- $1.00 per page. Cert fee: $2.00 per doc, $.50 per page. Payee: Paulding County Clerk of Superior Court. **Online Access to RE Deed, Lien, UCCs:** See www.gsccca.org **Other phones:** Assessor-770-443-7606.

Peach County

County Superior Court Clerk, PO Box 389, Fort Valley, GA 31030. **Phone-**478-825-5331; hours 8:30AM-5PM. Will not search records. UCC copy- $1.00 per page. Cert fee: $2.00 per doc, $.50 per page. Payee: Peach County Clerk of Superior Court. **Online Access to RE Deed, Lien, UCC records:** See www.gsccca.org **Other phones:** Assessor-478-825-5924; Treasurer-478-825-2535.

Pickens County

County Superior Court Clerk, PO Box 130, Jasper, GA 30143. **Phone-**706-253-8763; hours 8AM-5PM Will not search records. UCC copy- $1.00 per page. RE copy- $.25 per page. Cert fee: $2.50 per doc, $.50 per page. Payee: Pickens County Clerk of Superior Court. **Online Access to RE Deed, Lien, UCC records:** See www.gsccca.org **Other phones:** Assessor-706-253-8700.

Pierce County

County Superior Court Clerk, PO Box 588, Blackshear, GA 31516. **Phone-**County Superior Court Clerk, R/E & UCC Recording- 912-449-2020; fax-912-449-2106; hours 9AM-5PM

Will not search records. UCC copy- $1.00 per page. RE record copy- $.50 per page. Cert fee: $2.50 per doc, $.50 per page. Payee: Pierce County Clerk of Superior Court. **Online Access to RE Deed, Lien, UCC records:** See www.gsccca.org **Other phones:** Assessor-912-449-2025; Appraiser-912-449-2025; Elections-912-449-2028.

Pike County

County Superior Court Clerk, PO Box 10, Zebulon, GA 30295. **Phone-**770-567-2000; hours 8AM-5PM Will not search records. UCC copy- $1.00 per page. Cert fee: $2.00 per doc, $.50 per page. Payee: Pike County Clerk of Superior Court. **Online Access to RE Deed, UCC, Liens:** See www.gsccca.org

Polk County

County Superior Court Clerk, PO Box 948, Cedartown, GA 30125. **Phone-**770-749-2114; fax-770-749-2148; hours 9AM-5PM. Will not search records. Record copy- $.25 per page. Cert fee: $2.50 per page.

Payee: Polk County Clerk of Superior Court. **Online Access to RE Deed, Lien, UCC records:** See www.gsccca.org **Other phones:** Assessor-770-749-2125; Treasurer-770-749-2108.

Pulaski County

Superior Court Clerk, PO Box 60, Hawkinsville, GA 31036. **Phone-**Superior Court Clerk, R/E & UCC Recording- 478-783-1911; fax-478-892-3308; hours 8AM-5PM. Will not search records. UCC copy- $1.00 per page. Cert fee: $2.00 per doc, $.50 per page. Payee: Pulaski County Clerk of Superior Court. **Online Access to RE Deed, Lien, UCC records:** See www.gsccca.org **Other phones:** Assessor-478-783-4154; Treasurer-478-783-2811; Elections-478-783-2061; Vital Records-478-783-2061.

Putnam County

County Superior Court Clerk, 100 S Jefferson St, Courthouse, Eatonton, GA 31024-1087. **Phone-**County Superior Court Clerk, R/E & UCC Recording- 706-485-4501; fax-706-485-2875; hours 8AM-5PM

Will not search records. Record copy- $1.00 per page if assisted, $.25 per page if unassisted. Cert fee: $3.00 per doc + $1.00 per page. Payee: Putnam County Clerk of Superior Court. **Online Access to RE Deed, UCC, Lien records:** See www.gsccca.org **Other phones:** Assessor-706-485-6376; Treasurer-706-485-5441; Elections-706-485-8683; Vital Records-706-485-5476.

Quitman County

County Superior Court Clerk, PO Box 307, Georgetown, GA 39854. **Phone-**County Superior Court Clerk, R/E & UCC Recording- 229-334-2578; fax-229-334-3991; hours 8AM-Noon, 1-5PM. Will not search UCC records. UCC copy- $1.00 per page. Separate federal/state combined tax lien search- $10.00 per debtor. Will not search real estate records. RE record copy- $.50 per page. Cert fee: $2.50 1st pg., $.50 each add'l pg. Payee: Quitman County Clerk of Superior Court. **Online Access to RE Deed, Lien, UCC records:** See www.gsccca.org **Other phones:** Assessor-229-334-2159; Treasurer-229-334-0903; Appraiser-229-334-2159; Elections-229-334-2224; Vital Records-229-334-2224.

Rabun County

County Superior Court Clerk, 25 Courthouse Sq #105, Clayton, GA 30525. **Phone-**County Superior Court Clerk, R/E & UCC Recording- 706-782-3615; fax-706-782-7588; hours 8:30AM-5PM

Will not search UCC records. UCC copy- $.25 per page. Will not search tax liens. Real estate owner, mortgage, and property transfer searches available. RE copy- $.25 per page. Cert fee: $5.00 per doc. Payee: Rabun County Clerk of Superior Court. **Online Access to RE Deed, Lien, UCC records:** See www.gsccca.org **Other phones:** Assessor-706-782-5068; Treasurer-706-782-3813; Elections-706-782-2657; Vital Records-706-782-3614.

Randolph County

County Superior Court Clerk, PO Box 98, Cuthbert, GA 39840. **Phone-**229-732-2216; fax-229-732-5881; hours 8AM-5PM

Will not search records. UCC copy- $.50 per page. RE copy- $.25 per page. Cert fee: $2.50 per doc. Payee: Randolph County Clerk of Superior Court. **Online Access to RE Deed, Lien, UCC records:** See www.gsccca.org **Other phones:** Assessor-229-732-2522; Treasurer-229-732-6440.

Richmond County

County Superior Court Clerk, PO Box 2046, Augusta, GA 30903. **Phone-**706-821-2460, R/E Recording- 706-821-2468, UCC Recording- 706-821-1296; fax-706-821-2448; hours 8:30AM-5PM

Will not search records. Record copy- $1.00 per page. Cert fee: $2.50 per doc, + $50 per page. Payee: Richmond County Clerk of Superior Court. **Online Access to RE Deed, Lien, UCC records:** See www.gsccca.org **Other phones:** Assessor-706-821-2310; Treasurer-706-821-2391.

Rockdale County

County Superior Court Clerk, PO Box 937, Conyers, GA 30012. **Phone-**County Superior Court Clerk, R/E & UCC Recording- 770-929-4068, UCC Recording-770-929-4069; fax-770-860-0381; hours 8:15AM-4:45PM. Will not search records. UCC copy- $1.00 per page. Cert fee: $2.50 per doc, $.50 per page. Payee: Rockdale County Clerk of Superior Court. **Online Access to RE Deed, UCC, Lien records:** See www.gsccca.org **Other phones:** Assessor-770-929-4024; Treasurer-770-929-4009.

Schley County

County Superior Court Clerk, PO Box 7, Ellaville, GA 31806-0007. **Phone-**County Superior Court Clerk, R/E & UCC Recording- 229-937-5581; fax-229-937-5588; hours 8AM-Noon,1-5PM

Will not search records. UCC copy- $1.00 per page. RE record copy- $.25 per page. Cert fee: $2.00 per doc, $.35 per page. Payee: Schley County Clerk of Superior Court. **Online Access to RE Deed, Lien, UCC records:** See www.gsccca.org **Other phones:** Assessor-229-937-9169; Appraiser-229-937-9169; Elections-229-937-2905; Vital Records-229-937-2905; Tax Commissioner-229-937-2689.

Screven County

County Superior Court Clerk, PO Box 156, Sylvania, GA 30467. **Phone-**912-564-2614; fax-912-564-2622; hours 8AM-5PM. Will not search records. UCC copy- $.25 per page. Cert fee: $3.00 1st page; $1.50 each add'l. Payee: Screven County Clerk of Superior Court. **Online Access to RE Deed, Lien, UCC records:** See www.gsccca.org **Other phones:** Assessor-912-564-7918.

Seminole County

County Superior Court Clerk, PO Box 672, Donalsonville, GA 39845. **Phone-**County Superior Court Clerk, R/E & UCC Recording- 229-524-2525; fax-229-524-8883; hours 9AM-5PM. Will not search records. UCC copy- $1.00 per page. Cert fee: $2.00 per doc, $.50 per page. Payee: Seminole County Clerk of Superior Court. **Online Access to RE Deed, Lien, UCC records:** See www.gsccca.org **Other phones:** Assessor-229-524-5831.

Spalding County

County Superior Court Clerk, PO Box 1046, Griffin, GA 30224. **Phone-**770-467-4356; hours 8AM-5PM Will not search records. Record copy- $.25 per page. Cert fee: $2.00 per doc, $.50 per page. Payee: Spalding County Clerk of Superior Court. **Online Access to RE Deed, UCC, Lien records:** See www.gsccca.org Plats will soon be available. **Other phones:** Assessor-770-228-9900 x350.

Stephens County

County Superior Court Clerk, 205 N. Alexander St, Rm 202, Stephens County Courthouse, Toccoa, GA 30577-2310. **Phone-**County Superior Court Clerk, R/E & UCC Recording- 706-886-9496; fax-706-886-5710; hours 8AM-5PM. Will not search records. UCC copy- $1.00 per page. Cert fee: $2.50 1st page, $.50 each add'l. Payee: Stephens County Clerk of Superior Court. **Online Access to RE Deed, UCC, Lien records:** See www.gsccca.org **Other phones:** Assessor-706-886-4753; Elections-706-886-8954; Vital Records-706-886-2828.

Stewart County

County Superior Court Clerk, PO Box 910, Lumpkin, GA 31815-0910. **Phone-**229-838-6220; fax-229-838-4505; hours 8AM-4:30PM

Will not search records. UCC copy- $1.00 per page. RE record copy- $.25 per page. Cert fee: $2.00 per doc, $.50 per page. Payee: Stewart County Clerk of Superior Court. **Online Access to RE Deed, Lien, UCC records:** See www.gsccca.org

Sumter County

Superior Court Clerk, PO Box 333, Americus, GA 31709. **Phone-**Superior Court Clerk, R/E & UCC Recording- 229-928-4537; hours 9AM-5PM

Will not search records. UCC copy- $1.00 per page. Cert fee: $2.00 per doc, $.50 per page. Payee: Sumter County Clerk of Superior Court. **Online Access to RE Deed, UCC, Lien records:** See www.gsccca.org **Other phones:** Assessor-229-928-4513; Appraiser-229-928-4513; Elections-229-928-4580; Vital Records-229-924-3637 (Health Dept).

Talbot County

County Superior Court Clerk, PO Box 325, Talbotton, GA 31827-0325. **Phone-**706-665-3239; fax-706-665-8637; hours 9AM-5PM

Will not search records. UCC copy- $1.00 per page. Cert fee: $2.00 per doc, $.50 per page. Payee: Talbot County Clerk of Superior Court. **Online Access to RE Deed, Lien, UCC records:** See www.gsccca.org **Other phones:** Assessor-706-665-3377; Treasurer-706-665-3240.

Taliaferro County

County Superior Court Clerk, PO Box 182, Crawfordville, GA 30631. **Phone-**County Superior Court Clerk, R/E & UCC Recording- 706-456-2123; fax-706-456-2749; hours 9AM-Noon, 1-5PM

Will not search records. UCC copy- $1.00 per page. Cert fee: $2.00 per doc + $.25 per page. Payee: Taliaferro County Clerk of Superior Court. **Online Access to RE Deed, Lien, UCC records:** See www.gsccca.org **Other phones:** Assessor-706-456-2717; Elections-706-456-2253; Vital Records-706-456-2316.

Tattnall County

County Superior Court Clerk, PO Box 39, Reidsville, GA 30453. **Phone-**County Superior Court Clerk, R/E & UCC Recording- 912-557-6716; fax-912-557-4552; hours 8AM-4:30PM

Will not search records. UCC copy- $1.00 per page. Cert fee: $3.00 per cert. Payee: Tattnall County Clerk of Superior Court. **Online Access to RE Deed, Lien, UCC records:** See www.gsccca.org **Other phones:** Assessor-912-557-4010; Appraiser-912-557-4010; Probate Court-912-557-6917.

Taylor County

County Superior Court Clerk, PO Box 248, Butler, GA 31006. **Phone-**County Superior Court Clerk, R/E & UCC Recording- 478-862-5594; fax-478-862-5334; hours 8AM-5PM. Will not search records. UCC copy- $1.00 per page. RE record copy- $.25 per page. Cert fee: $2.00 per doc, $.50 per page. Payee: Taylor County Clerk of Superior Court. **Online Access to RE Deed, Lien, UCC records:** See www.gsccca.org **Other phones:** Assessor-478-862-3802; Vital Records-478-862-3357.

Telfair County

County Superior Court Clerk, 128 E Oak St, #2, Courthouse, McRae, GA 31055-1604. **Phone-**County Superior Court Clerk, R/E & UCC Recording- 229-868-6525; fax-229-868-7956; hours 8:30AM-4:30PM Will not search records. Record copy- $.25 per page. Cert fee: $3.00 per doc + $.25 per page. Payee:

Telfair County Clerk of Superior Court. **Online Access to RE Deed, UCC records:** See www.gsccca.org for Deed and UCC indexes. **Other phones:** Assessor-229-868-6772; Appraiser-229-868-2896; Elections-229-868-6038.

Terrell County

County Superior Court Clerk, PO Box 189, Dawson, GA 39842. **Phone-**229-995-2631; hours 8:30AM-5PM. Will not search records. UCC copy- $1.00 per page. Cert fee: $3.00 1st page, $.50 each add'l. Payee: Terrell County Clerk of Superior Court. **Online Access to RE Deed, Lien, UCC records:** See www.gsccca.org **Other phones:** Assessor-229-995-5210; Treasurer-229-995-5151.

Thomas County

County Superior Court Clerk, PO Box 1995, Thomasville, GA 31799. **Phone-**229-225-4108; fax-229-225-4110; hours-8AM-5PM www.thomascoclerkofcourt.org

Will not search records. UCC copy- $1.00 per page. Cert fee: $2.00 per cert. Payee: Thomas County Clerk of Superior Court. **Online Access to RE Deed, UCC, Lien records:** See www.gsccca.org **Other phones:** Assessor-229-225-4133; Treasurer-229-225-4133; Appraiser-229-225-4133; Elections-229-225-4101; Vital Records-229-226-4241.

Tift County

County Superior Court Clerk, PO Box 354, Tifton, GA 31793. **Phone-**229-386-7810; fax-229-386-7807; hours 9AM-5PM. Will not search records. Record copy- $.25 per page. Cert fee: $2.50 per cert. Payee: Tift County Clerk of Superior Court. **Online Access to RE Deed, Lien, UCCs:** See www.gsccca.org **Other phones:** Assessor-229-386-7840.

Toombs County

County Superior Court Clerk, PO Drawer 530, Lyons, GA 30436. **Phone-**County Superior Court Clerk, R/E & UCC Recording- 912-526-3501; fax-912-526-1015; hours 8:30AM-5PM. Will not search records. Record copy- $1.00 per page. Cert fee: $2.00 per doc, $.50 per page. Payee: Toombs County Clerk of Superior Court. **Online Access to RE Deed, Lien, UCC records:** See www.gsccca.org **Other phones:** Assessor-912-526-6291; Treasurer-912-526-8575; Appraiser-912-526-6291; Elections-912-526-8696.

Towns County

County Superior Court Clerk, 48 River St., Courthouse, #E, Hiawassee, GA 30546. **Phone-**County Superior Court Clerk, R/E & UCC Recording- 706-896-2130; hours 8:30AM-4:30PM. Will not search records. UCC copy- $1.00 per page. Cert fee: $2.00 per doc, $.50 per page. Payee: Towns County Clerk of Superior Court. **Online Access to Real Estate, Deed, UCC records:** See www.gsccca.org **Other phones:** Assessor-706-896-3984; Treasurer-706-896-2276; Appraiser-706-896-3984; Elections-706-896-4353; Vital Records-706-896-3467.

Treutlen County

County Superior Court Clerk, PO Box 356, Soperton, GA 30457. **Phone-**County Superior Court Clerk, R/E & UCC Recording- 912-529-4215; fax-none; hours 8AM-5PM. Will not search records. Record copy- $.25 per page. Cert fee: $2.00 per doc, $.50 per page. Payee: Treutlen County Clerk of Superior Court. **Online Access to RE Deed, Lien, UCC records:** See www.gsccca.org **Other phones:** Assessor-912-529-4343; Elections-912-529-3098.

Troup County

County Superior Court Clerk, PO Box 866, LaGrange, GA 30241-0866. **Phone-**County Superior Court Clerk, R/E & UCC Recording- 706-883-1740; hours 8AM-

5PM. Will not search records. UCC copy- $1.00 per page. Cert fee: $2.50 per doc, $.50 per page. Payee: Troup County Clerk of Superior Court. **Online Access to RE Deed, Lien, UCC records:** See www.gsccca.org **Other phones:** Assessor-706-883-1625; Treasurer-706-883-1620.

Turner County

County Superior Court Clerk, PO Box 106, Ashburn, GA 31714. **Phone**-County Superior Court Clerk, R/E & UCC Recording- 229-567-2011; fax-229-567-0450; hours 8AM-5PM. Will not search records. UCC copy- $1.00 per page. Cert fee: $2.50 1st page, $.50 each add'l. Payee: Turner County Clerk of Superior Court. **Online Access to RE Deed, UCC records:** See www.gsccca.org for Deed and UCC indexes. **Other phones:** Assessor-229-567-2334; Treasurer-229-567-4313; Appraiser-229-567-2334.

Twiggs County

County Superior Court Clerk, PO Box 228, Jeffersonville, GA 31044-0228. **Phone**-County Superior Court Clerk, R/E & UCC Recording- 478-945-3350; fax-478-945-6751; hours 8AM-5PM Will not search records. Record copy- $.25 per copy. Cert fee: $2.00 per doc, $.50 per page. Payee: Twiggs County Clerk of Superior Court. **Online Access to RE Deed, UCC records:** See www.gsccca.org for Deed and UCC indexes. **Other phones:** Assessor-478-945-3663; Treasurer-478-945-3629; Appraiser-478-945-3663; Elections-478-945-3639; Vital Records-478-945-3390.

Union County

County Superior Court Clerk, 114 Courthouse St #5, Blairsville, GA 30512. **Phone**-706-439-6022; fax-706-439-6026; hours 8AM-5PM. Will not search records. UCC copy- $.25 per page. Cert fee: $2.50 per cert. Payee: Union County Clerk of Superior Court. **Online Access to RE Deed, Lien, UCC records:** See www.gsccca.org **Other phones:** Assessor-706-439-6011; Treasurer-706-439-6000.

Upson County

County Superior Court Clerk, PO Box 469, Thomaston, GA 30286. **Phone**-706-647-7835; fax-706-647-8999; hours 8AM-5PM. Will search UCC records. UCC copy- $1.00 per page. Will not search real estate or tax lien records. Cert fee: $2.00 per doc, $.50 per page. Payee: Upson County Clerk of Superior Court. **Online Access to RE Deed, Lien, UCC records:** See www.gsccca.org **Other phones:** Assessor-706-647-8176; Elections-706-647-7015.

Walker County

County Superior Court Clerk, PO Box 448, La Fayette, GA 30728. **Phone**-706-638-1742, R/E Recording- 706-638-1780, UCC Recording- 706-638-1757; fax-706-638-1779; hours 8AM-5PM Will search UCC records. UCC copy- $1.00 per page. Will not search real estate or tax lien records. RE record copy- $1.00 per page. Cert fee: $2.00 per cert. Payee: Walker County Clerk of Superior Court. **Online Access to RE Deed, Lien, UCC records:** See www.gsccca.org **Other phones:** Assessor-706-638-2929; Treasurer-706-638-2929.

Walton County

County Superior Court Clerk, PO Box 745, Monroe, GA 30655. **Phone**-County Superior Court Clerk, R/E & UCC Recording- 770-267-1304, UCC Recording- 770-267-1305; fax-770-267-1441; hours 8:30AM-5PM. Will not search records. UCC copy- $1.00 per page. Cert fee: $3.00per cert. Payee: County Clerk of Superior Court. **Online Access to RE Deed, UCC, Lien records:** See www.gsccca.org **Other phones:** Assessor-770-267-1477.

Ware County

County Superior Court Clerk, PO Box 776, Waycross, GA 31502-0776. **Phone**-912-287-4340; fax-912-287-2498; hours 9AM-5PM. Will not search records. UCC copy- $1.00 per page. Cert fee: $2.50 per cert. Payee: Ware County Clerk of Superior Court. **Online Access to RE Deed, Lien, UCC records:** See www.gsccca.org **Other phones:** Assessor-912-287-4383; Treasurer-912-287-4305.

Warren County

County Superior Court Clerk, PO Box 227, Warrenton, GA 30828. **Phone**-County Superior Court Clerk, R/E & UCC Recording- 706-465-2262; fax-706-465-0232; hours 8AM-Noon, 1-5PM. Will search UCC records. UCC copy- $1.00 per page. Will not search real estate or tax lien records. RE record copy- $.25 per page. Cert fee: $2.50 per doc, $.50 per page. Payee: Warren County Clerk of Superior Court. **Online Access to RE Deed, Lien, UCC records:** See www.gsccca.org **Other phones:** Assessor-706-465-3321; Treasurer-706-465-2171.

Washington County

County Superior Court Clerk, PO Box 231, Sandersville, GA 31082-0231. **Phone**-County Superior Court Clerk, R/E & UCC Recording- 478-552-3186; hours 9AM-5PM Will search UCC records. Search per debtor- $5.00. UCC copy- $1.00 per page. Will not search real estate or tax lien records. RE record copy- $.25 per page. Cert fee: $2.00 per doc, $.50 per page. Payee: Washington County Clerk of Superior Court. **Online Access to RE Deed, Lien, UCC records:** See www.gsccca.org **Other phones:** Assessor-478-552-2937.

Wayne County

County Superior Court Clerk, PO Box 920, Jesup, GA 31598-0920. **Phone**-County Superior Court Clerk, R/E & UCC Recording- 912-427-5930; fax-912-427-5939; hours 8:30AM-5PM. Will not search records. UCC copy- $1.00 per page. RE record copy- $.25 per page. Cert fee: $2.00 per doc, $.50 per page. Payee: Wayne County Clerk of Superior Court. **Online Access to RE Deed, Lien, UCC records:** See www.gsccca.org **Other phones:** Assessor-912-427-5920; Treasurer-912-427-5900.

Webster County

County Superior Court Clerk, PO Box 117, Preston, GA 31824. **Phone**-229-828-3525; fax-229-828-6961; 8AM-Noon, 12:30PM-4:30PM. Will not search records. Record copy- $.25 per page. Cert fee: $2.50 1st page, $.50 each add'l. Payee: Webster County Clerk of Superior Court. **Online Access to RE Deed, UCC, Lien records:** See www.gsccca.org **Other phones:** Assessor-229-828-3690.

Wheeler County

County Superior Court Clerk, PO Box 38, Alamo, GA 30411-0038. **Phone**-County Superior Court Clerk, R/E & UCC Recording- 912-568-7137; fax-912-568-7453; hours 8AM-4PM. Will not search records. UCC copy- $1.00 per page. Cert fee: $2.00 per doc, $.50 per page. Payee: Wheeler County Clerk of Superior Court. **Online Access to RE Deed, Lien, UCC records:** See www.gsccca.org **Other phones:** Assessor-912-568-7924; Treasurer-912-568-7131; Elections-912-568-7133; Vital Records-912-568-7161.

White County

County Superior Court Clerk, 59 S. Main St, Courthouse, #B, Cleveland, GA 30528. **Phone**-County Superior Court Clerk, R/E & UCC Recording- 706-865-2613; fax-706-865-2613; hours 8:30AM-5PM

Will not search records. UCC copy- $1.00 per page. Cert fee: $2.00 per doc, $.50 per page. Payee: White County Clerk of Superior Court. **Online Access to RE Deed, Lien, UCC records:** See www.gsccca.org **Other phones:** Assessor-706-865-5328; Treasurer-706-865-2225; Appraiser-706-865-5328; Elections-706-865-4141; Vital Records-706-865-4141; County Commissioner-706-865-2235.

Whitfield County

County Superior Court Clerk, PO Box 868, Dalton, GA 30722. **Phone**-706-275-7450; fax-706-275-7456; hours 8AM-5PM. Will not search records. UCC copy- $.25 per page. Cert fee: $3.00 per cert. Payee: Whitfield County Clerk of Superior Court. **Online Access to RE Deed, Lien, UCC records:** See www.gsccca.org **Other phones:** Assessor-706-275-7410; Treasurer-706-275-7510.

Wilcox County

County Superior Court Clerk, 103 N Broad StCourthouse, Courthouse, Abbeville, GA 31001-1000. **Phone**-County Superior Court Clerk, R/E & UCC Recording- 229-467-2442; fax-229-467-2886; hours 9AM-5PM. Will not search records. UCC copy- $1.00 per page. RE record copy- $.25 per page. Cert fee: $2.50 per doc, $.50 per add'l. Payee: Wilcox County Clerk of Superior Court. **Online Access to RE Deed, UCC, Lien records:** See www.gsccca.org **Other phones:** Assessor-229-467-2428; Appraiser-229-467-2028; Elections-229-467-2300; Vital Records-229-467-2220.

Wilkes County

County Superior Court Clerk, 23 E. Court St, Rm 205, Washington, GA 30673. **Phone**-County Superior Court Clerk, R/E & UCC Recording- 706-678-2423; fax-706-678-2115; hours 9AM-5PM Will not search records. UCC copy- $1.00 per page. Real estate in-person copies $.25 each. Cert fee: $2.00 per doc and $.50 per page. Payee: Wilkes County Superior Court Clerk. **Online Access to RE Deed, Lien, UCC records:** See www.gsccca.org for Deed, UCC indexes, liens and plats. **Other phones:** Assessor-706-678-7732; Elections-706-678-2523; Vital Records-706-678-2523.

Wilkinson County

County Superior Court Clerk & Juvenile Court, PO Box 250, Irwinton, GA 31042-0250. **Phone**-County Superior Court Clerk & Juvenile Court, R/E & UCC Recording- 478-946-2221; fax-478-946-1497; hours 8AM-5PM Will not search records. Record copy- $1.00 per page. Cert fee: $2.00 per doc, $.50 per page. Payee: Wilkinson County Clerk of Superior Court. **Online Access to RE Deed, Lien, UCC:** See www.gsccca.org **Other phones:** Assessor-478-946-2076; Treasurer-478-946-2236 (County Commissioner); Appraiser-478-946-2076; Elections-478-946-2188; Vital Records-478-946-2222; Tax Commisioner-478-946-2232.

Worth County

County Superior Court Clerk, 201 N. Main St, Courthouse, Rm 13, Sylvester, GA 31791. **Phone**-County Superior Court Clerk, R/E & UCC Recording-229-776-8205; fax-229-776-8237; hours 8AM-5PM Will not search records. Record copy- $1.00 per page. Cert fee: $2.50 per doc, $.50 per page. Payee: Worth County Clerk of Superior Court. **Online Access to RE Deed, Lien, UCC records:** See www.gsccca.org **Other phones:** Assessor-229-776-8203; Treasurer-229-776-8204; Elections-229-776-8208; Vital Records-229-776-8207.

Georgia County Locator

You will usually be able to find the city name in the City/County Cross Reference below. In that case, it is a simple matter to determine the county from the cross reference. However, only the official US Postal Service city names are included in this index. There are an additional 40,000 place names that people use in their addresses. Therefore, we have also included a ZIP/City Cross Reference immediately following the City/County Cross Reference.

If you know the ZIP Code but the city name does not appear in the City/County Cross Reference index, look up the ZIP Code in the ZIP/City Cross Reference, find the city name, then look up the city name in the City/County Cross Reference. For example, you want to know the county for an address of Menands, NY 12204. There is no "Menands" in the City/County Cross Reference. The ZIP/City Cross Reference shows that ZIP Codes 12201-12288 are for the city of Albany. Looking back in the City/County Cross Reference, Albany is in Albany County.

Georgia City/County Cross Reference

ABBEVILLE Wilcox
ACWORTH (30102) Cherokee(53), Bartow(25), Cobb(21)
ACWORTH (30101) Cobb(71), Paulding(23), Bartow(4)
ADAIRSVILLE (30103) Bartow(66), Gordon(25), Floyd(8)
ADEL Cook
ADRIAN (31002) Emanuel(54), Johnson(25), Laurens(14), Treutlen(6)
AILEY Montgomery
ALAMO (30411) Wheeler(69), Laurens(30)
ALAPAHA (31622) Berrien(95), Irwin(4)
ALBANY (31701) Dougherty(96), Lee(3)
ALBANY (31705) Dougherty(89), Worth(5), Mitchell(4)
ALBANY (31721) Dougherty(87), Lee(8), Baker(2), Terrell(1)
ALBANY Dougherty
ALLENHURST (31301) Liberty(76), Long(23)
ALLENTOWN Wilkinson
ALMA (31510) Bacon(95), Pierce(4)
ALPHARETTA (30005) Fulton(81), Forsyth(18)
ALPHARETTA Fulton
ALSTON Montgomery
ALTO (30510) Habersham(62), Banks(30), Hall(6)
ALTO Habersham
AMBROSE Coffee
AMERICUS (31719) Sumter(91), Schley(8)
AMERICUS Sumter
ANDERSONVILLE (31711) Macon(80), Sumter(16), Schley(2)
APPLING Columbia
ARABI (31712) Crisp(82), Turner(11), Worth(6)
ARAGON (30104) Polk(72), Floyd(24), Bartow(3)
ARGYLE Clinch
ARLINGTON (39813) Calhoun(58), Early(40)
ARMUCHEE (30105) Floyd(67), Chattooga(32)
ARNOLDSVILLE (30619) Oglethorpe(91), Oconee(8)
ASHBURN (31714) Turner(96), Worth(2)
ATHENS (30601) Clarke(95), Madison(3), Jackson(1)
ATHENS (30606) Clarke(88), Oconee(11)
ATHENS (30607) Jackson(59), Clarke(40)
ATHENS Clarke
ATLANTA (30339) Cobb(96), Fulton(3)
ATLANTA (30338) De Kalb(98), Fulton(1)
ATLANTA (30360) De Kalb(79), Gwinnett(20)
ATLANTA (30324) Fulton(83), De Kalb(16)
ATLANTA (30349) Fulton(65), Clayton(34)
ATLANTA (30350) Fulton(97), De Kalb(2)
ATLANTA (30354) Fulton(91), Clayton(8)
ATLANTA De Kalb
ATLANTA Fulton
ATTAPULGUS Decatur

AUBURN (30011) Barrow(78), Gwinnett(21)
AUBURN Barrow
AUGUSTA (30907) Columbia(73), Richmond(26)
AUGUSTA (30909) Richmond(98), Columbia(1)
AUGUSTA Columbia
AUGUSTA Richmond
AUSTELL (30168) Cobb(90), Douglas(9)
AVERA (30803) Jefferson(92), Glascock(7)
AVONDALE ESTATES De Kalb
AXSON (31624) Atkinson(68), Coffee(23), Ware(8)
BACONTON Mitchell
BAINBRIDGE Decatur
BALDWIN Banks
BALL GROUND (30107) Cherokee(80), Pickens(14), Forsyth(5)
BARNESVILLE (30204) Lamar(95), Upson(3)
BARNEY Brooks
BARTOW (30413) Jefferson(71), Washington(27), Johnson(1)
BARWICK Brooks
BAXLEY Appling
BELLVILLE Evans
BERLIN Colquitt
BETHLEHEM (30620) Barrow(73), Gwinnett(19), Walton(6)
BISHOP (30621) Oconee(73), Morgan(26)
BLACKSHEAR Pierce
BLAIRSVILLE (30512) Union(98), Fannin(1)
BLAIRSVILLE Union
BLAKELY (39823) Early(97), Miller(2)
BLOOMINGDALE (31302) Chatham(55), Effingham(44)
BLUE RIDGE (30513) Fannin(89), Gilmer(10)
BLUFFTON (31724) Clay(89), Early(10)
BLUFFTON (39824) Early(54), Clay(45)
BLYTHE (30805) Burke(54), Richmond(45)
BOGART (30622) Oconee(61), Clarke(30), Jackson(8)
BOLINGBROKE Monroe
BONAIRE Houston
BONEVILLE McDuffie
BOSTON (31626) Thomas(82), Brooks(17)
BOSTWICK Morgan
BOWDON (30108) Carroll(95), Heard(4)
BOWDON JUNCTION Carroll
BOWERSVILLE Hart
BOWMAN (30624) Elbert(74), Hart(14), Madison(10)
BOX SPRINGS (31801) Talbot(58), Marion(39), Muscogee(1)
BRASELTON (30517) Jackson(63), Gwinnett(14), Hall(13), Barrow(8)
BREMEN (30110) Haralson(92), Carroll(7)
BRINSON (39825) Decatur(90), Seminole(9)
BRINSON Decatur
BRISTOL (31518) Appling(56), Pierce(26), Wayne(14), Bacon(2)

BRONWOOD Terrell
BROOKFIELD Tift
BROOKLET Bulloch
BROOKS (30205) Spalding(52), Fayette(47)
BROXTON (31519) Coffee(97), Jeff Davis(2)
BRUNSWICK Glynn
BUCHANAN (30113) Haralson(87), Polk(12)
BUCKHEAD (30625) Morgan(95), Putnam(4)
BUENA VISTA (31803) Marion(94), Schley(4)
BUFORD (30519) Gwinnett(93), Hall(6)
BUFORD Gwinnett
BUTLER Taylor
BYROMVILLE Dooly
BYRON (31008) Peach(67), Crawford(23), Houston(9)
CADWELL Laurens
CAIRO Grady
CALHOUN (30701) Gordon(98), Floyd(1)
CALHOUN Gordon
CALVARY Grady
CAMAK Warren
CAMILLA (31730) Mitchell(98), Decatur(1)
CANON (30520) Hart(60), Franklin(39)
CANTON Cherokee
CARLTON (30627) Madison(71), Oglethorpe(28)
CARNESVILLE (30521) Franklin(96), Banks(3)
CARROLLTON Carroll
CARTERSVILLE Bartow
CASSVILLE Bartow
CATAULA Harris
CAVE SPRING Floyd
CECIL Cook
CEDAR SPRINGS Early
CEDARTOWN (30125) Polk(98), Floyd(1)
CENTERVILLE Houston
CHATSWORTH Murray
CHAUNCEY (31011) Dodge(98), Laurens(1)
CHERRYLOG (30522) Gilmer(57), Fannin(42)
CHESTER (31012) Dodge(89), Bleckley(9), Laurens(1)
CHESTNUT MOUNTAIN Hall
CHICKAMAUGA (30707) Walker(97), Catoosa(2)
CHULA (31733) Tift(54), Irwin(44)
CISCO Murray
CLARKDALE Cobb
CLARKESVILLE (30523) Habersham(89), Rabun(10)
CLARKSTON De Kalb
CLAXTON (30417) Evans(89), Tattnall(10)
CLAYTON (30525) Rabun(98), Towns(1)
CLERMONT (30527) Hall(89), White(10)
CLEVELAND (30528) White(96), Lumpkin(3)
CLIMAX Decatur
CLINCHFIELD Houston

CLYO Effingham
COBB Sumter
COBBTOWN (30420) Tattnall(92), Candler(6)
COCHRAN (31014) Bleckley(85), Twiggs(11), Dodge(2)
COCHRAN Putnam
COHUTTA Whitfield
COLBERT (30628) Madison(93), Oglethorpe(6)
COLEMAN (39836) Clay(68), Randolph(31)
COLEMAN (31736) Randolph(80), Clay(19)
COLLINS Tattnall
COLQUITT (31737) Miller(96), Baker(2)
COLQUITT (39837) Miller(80), Early(13), Decatur(3), Baker(2)
COLUMBUS Muscogee
COMER (30629) Madison(91), Oglethorpe(8)
COMMERCE (30530) Jackson(41), Banks(26), Madison(22), Franklin(9)
COMMERCE Jackson
CONCORD Pike
CONLEY (30288) De Kalb(52), Clayton(47)
CONLEY Clayton
CONYERS (30012) Rockdale(97), De Kalb(1)
CONYERS (30013) Rockdale(93), Newton(6)
CONYERS Rockdale
COOLIDGE (31738) Thomas(88), Colquitt(11)
COOSA Floyd
CORDELE Crisp
CORNELIA Habersham
COTTON Mitchell
COVINGTON (30014) Newton(89), Walton(9)
COVINGTON Newton
CRANDALL Murray
CRAWFORD Oglethorpe
CRAWFORDVILLE (30631) Taliaferro(91), Wilkes(7), Greene(1)
CRESCENT McIntosh
CULLODEN (31016) Monroe(52), Upson(28), Crawford(14), Lamar(4)
CUMMING (30040) Forsyth(95), Cherokee(4)
CUMMING Forsyth
CUSSETA (31805) Chattahoochee(98), Stewart(1)
CUTHBERT (39840) Randolph(89), Calhoun(10)
CUTHBERT Randolph
DACULA (30019) Gwinnett(98), Walton(1)
DACULA Gwinnett
DAHLONEGA Lumpkin
DAISY Evans
DALLAS (30157) Paulding(98), Cobb(1)
DALLAS Paulding
DALTON Whitfield
DAMASCUS (31741) Early(73), Baker(19), Miller(6)
DAMASCUS (39841) Early(95), Miller(2), Baker(1)

DANIELSVILLE (30633) Madison(98), Franklin(1)
DANVILLE (31017) Twiggs(76), Wilkinson(19), Bleckley(4)
DARIEN McIntosh
DAVISBORO Washington
DAWSON (39842) Terrell(93), Calhoun(6)
DAWSON Terrell
DAWSONVILLE (30534) Dawson(86), Lumpkin(10), Forsyth(2)
DE SOTO (31743) Sumter(65), Lee(34)
DEARING (30808) McDuffie(97), Warren(2)
DECATUR De Kalb
DEMOREST Habersham
DENTON (31532) Jeff Davis(97), Coffee(2)
DEWY ROSE (30634) Elbert(55), Hart(44)
DEXTER Laurens
DILLARD Rabun
DIXIE Brooks
DOERUN (31744) Colquitt(66), Worth(29), Mitchell(4)
DONALSONVILLE Seminole
DOUGLAS Coffee
DOUGLASVILLE (30134) Douglas(62), Paulding(37)
DOUGLASVILLE Douglas
DOVER Screven
DRY BRANCH (31020) Twiggs(95), Bibb(4)
DU PONT (31630) Clinch(74), Echols(25)
DUBLIN Laurens
DUDLEY (31022) Laurens(97), Bleckley(1), Dodge(1)
DULUTH (30097) Gwinnett(48), Fulton(45), Forsyth(5)
DULUTH Fulton
DULUTH Gwinnett
EAST ELLIJAY Gilmer
EASTANOLLEE (30538) Stephens(72), Franklin(27)
EASTMAN Dodge
EATONTON Putnam
EDEN Effingham
EDISON (39846) Calhoun(95), Clay(4)
ELBERTON (30635) Elbert(98), Hart(1)
ELKO Houston
ELLABELL (31308) Bryan(77), Bulloch(22)
ELLAVILLE (31806) Schley(90), Macon(8)
ELLENTON Colquitt
ELLENWOOD (30294) De Kalb(42), Clayton(34), Henry(23)
ELLENWOOD Gwinnett
ELLERSLIE Harris
ELLIJAY (30536) Gilmer(98), Dawson(1)
ELLIJAY Gilmer
EMERSON Bartow
ENIGMA (31749) Berrien(65), Tift(32), Irwin(1)
EPWORTH Fannin
ESOM HILL Polk
ETON Murray
EVANS Columbia
EXPERIMENT Spalding
FAIRBURN (30213) Fulton(86), Fayette(13)
FAIRMOUNT (30139) Gordon(60), Pickens(33), Bartow(5)
FARGO (31631) Clinch(78), Charlton(13), Echols(8)
FARMINGTON Oconee
FAYETTEVILLE (30215) Fayette(92), Clayton(7)
FAYETTEVILLE Fayette
FELTON Haralson
FITZGERALD (31750) Ben Hill(86), Irwin(13)
FLEMING Liberty
FLINTSTONE Walker
FLOVILLA Butts
FLOWERY BRANCH Hall
FOLKSTON (31537) Charlton(93), Camden(6)
FOREST PARK Clayton
FORSYTH Monroe

FORT BENNING (31905) Chattahoochee(59), Muscogee(40)
FORT BENNING Muscogee
FORT GAINES Clay
FORT OGLETHORPE Catoosa
FORT STEWART (31314) Liberty(97), Bryan(1)
FORT STEWART Liberty
FORT VALLEY (31030) Peach(76), Crawford(20), Macon(2), Houston(1)
FORTSON (31808) Harris(65), Muscogee(34)
FOWLSTOWN Decatur
FRANKLIN Heard
FRANKLIN SPRINGS Franklin
FUNSTON Colquitt
GAINESVILLE (30506) Hall(95), Forsyth(4)
GAINESVILLE Hall
GARFIELD (30425) Emanuel(38), Bulloch(38), Jenkins(23)
GAY Meriwether
GENEVA Talbot
GEORGETOWN (39854) Clay(51), Quitman(48)
GEORGETOWN (31754) Quitman(89), Clay(11)
GIBSON (30810) Glascock(86), Warren(11), Jefferson(1)
GILLSVILLE (30543) Hall(59), Banks(24), Jackson(15)
GIRARD (30426) Burke(81), Screven(18)
GLENN Heard
GLENNVILLE (30427) Tattnall(98), Long(1)
GLENWOOD (30428) Wheeler(73), Laurens(26)
GOOD HOPE (30641) Walton(82), Morgan(16)
GORDON (31031) Wilkinson(65), Twiggs(21), Baldwin(7), Jones(5)
GOUGH Burke
GRACEWOOD Richmond
GRANTVILLE (30220) Meriwether(54), Coweta(45)
GRAY Jones
GRAYSON Gwinnett
GRAYSVILLE Catoosa
GREENSBORO Greene
GREENVILLE (30222) Meriwether(98), Troup(1)
GRIFFIN (30224) Spalding(91), Pike(6), Lamar(2)
GRIFFIN Spalding
GROVETOWN (30813) Columbia(95), Richmond(4)
GUYTON Effingham
HADDOCK (31033) Jones(86), Baldwin(13)
HAGAN Evans
HAHIRA (31632) Lowndes(58), Cook(41)
HAMILTON Harris
HAMPTON (30228) Henry(60), Clayton(34), Spalding(4)
HARALSON Coweta
HARDWICK Baldwin
HARLEM (30814) Columbia(98), McDuffie(1)
HARRISON Washington
HARTSFIELD Colquitt
HARTWELL Hart
HAWKINSVILLE (31036) Pulaski(86), Houston(13)
HAZLEHURST (31539) Jeff Davis(94), Appling(4)
HELEN White
HELENA (31037) Telfair(88), Wheeler(9), Dodge(1)
HEPHZIBAH (30815) Richmond(79), Burke(20)
HIAWASSEE Towns
HIGH SHOALS Morgan
HILLSBORO (31038) Jasper(74), Jones(23), Putnam(2)
HINESVILLE (31313) Liberty(98), Long(1)
HINESVILLE Liberty

HIRAM (30141) Paulding(96), Cobb(3)
HOBOKEN Brantley
HOGANSVILLE (30230) Troup(64), Heard(17), Meriwether(17), Coweta(1)
HOLLY SPRINGS Cherokee
HOMER Banks
HOMERVILLE Clinch
HORTENSE (31543) Wayne(50), Brantley(43), Glynn(5)
HOSCHTON (30548) Jackson(78), Gwinnett(10), Barrow(8), Hall(2)
HOWARD Taylor
HULL (30646) Madison(97), Jackson(1), Clarke(1)
IDEAL Macon
ILA Madison
INMAN Fayette
IRON CITY (39859) Seminole(96), Miller(3)
IRWINTON Wilkinson
IRWINVILLE Irwin
JACKSON (30233) Butts(82), Monroe(10), Henry(3), Lamar(2)
JACKSONVILLE Telfair
JAKIN Early
JASPER (30143) Pickens(98), Cherokee(1)
JEFFERSON Jackson
JEFFERSONVILLE (31044) Twiggs(98), Wilkinson(1)
JEKYLL ISLAND Glynn
JEKYLL ISLAND BRANCH Glynn
JENKINSBURG (30234) Butts(84), Henry(14)
JERSEY Walton
JESUP Wayne
JEWELL (31045) Warren(96), Hancock(3)
JONESBORO (30236) Clayton(94), Henry(5)
JONESBORO (30238) Clayton(94), Fayette(5)
JONESBORO Clayton
JULIETTE (31046) Monroe(88), Jones(11)
JUNCTION CITY Talbot
KATHLEEN Houston
KENNESAW Cobb
KEYSVILLE (30816) Burke(73), Jefferson(26)
KINGS BAY Camden
KINGSLAND Camden
KINGSTON (30145) Bartow(56), Floyd(43)
KITE (31049) Johnson(60), Emanuel(39)
KNOXVILLE Crawford
LA FAYETTE Walker
LAGRANGE (30240) Troup(98), Heard(1)
LAGRANGE Troup
LAKE PARK (31636) Lowndes(60), Echols(39)
LAKELAND Lanier
LAKEMONT Rabun
LAVONIA (30553) Franklin(63), Hart(36)
LAWRENCEVILLE Gwinnett
LEARY (31762) Baker(50), Calhoun(50)
LEARY (39862) Calhoun(96), Baker(3)
LEBANON Cherokee
LEESBURG Lee
LENOX (31637) Cook(88), Colquitt(5), Berrien(3), Tift(1)
LESLIE (31764) Sumter(92), Lee(7)
LEXINGTON Oglethorpe
LILBURN Gwinnett
LILLY Dooly
LINCOLNTON (30817) Lincoln(96), McDuffie(1), Wilkes(1)
LINDALE (30147) Floyd(94), Polk(5)
LITHIA SPRINGS Douglas
LITHONIA De Kalb
LIZELLA (31052) Bibb(55), Crawford(44)
LOCUST GROVE (30248) Henry(93), Spalding(4), Butts(1)
LOGANVILLE (30052) Walton(57), Gwinnett(40), Rockdale(1)
LOGANVILLE Gwinnett
LOOKOUT MOUNTAIN (30750) Walker(66), Dade(33)

LOUISVILLE (30434) Jefferson(96), Burke(3)
LOUVALE Stewart
LOVEJOY Clayton
LUDOWICI (31316) Long(98), Liberty(1)
LULA (30554) Hall(59), Banks(40)
LUMBER CITY (31549) Telfair(82), Wheeler(17)
LUMPKIN Stewart
LUTHERSVILLE Meriwether
LYERLY Chattooga
LYONS (30436) Toombs(89), Emanuel(5), Tattnall(5)
MABLETON Cobb
MACON (31210) Bibb(90), Monroe(9)
MACON (31211) Bibb(58), Jones(41)
MACON (31217) Bibb(51), Twiggs(37), Jones(10)
MACON (31220) Bibb(80), Monroe(19)
MACON Bibb
MADISON (30650) Morgan(93), Greene(5), Walton(1)
MANASSAS Tattnall
MANCHESTER (31816) Meriwether(90), Talbot(9)
MANOR Ware
MANSFIELD (30055) Jasper(49), Newton(44), Morgan(5)
MANSFIELD Jasper
MARBLE HILL (30148) Pickens(70), Dawson(29)
MARIETTA Cobb
MARSHALLVILLE Macon
MARTIN (30557) Franklin(55), Stephens(44)
MATTHEWS Jefferson
MAUK (31058) Taylor(47), Marion(45), Schley(6)
MAXEYS Oglethorpe
MAYSVILLE (30558) Jackson(53), Banks(46)
MC CAYSVILLE Fannin
MC INTYRE Wilkinson
MC RAE Telfair
MCDONOUGH (30252) Henry(98), Rockdale(1)
MCDONOUGH Henry
MEANSVILLE (30256) Pike(57), Upson(40), Lamar(2)
MEIGS (31765) Mitchell(42), Thomas(33), Colquitt(24)
MELDRIM Effingham
MENLO (30731) Chattooga(60), Walker(25), Dade(14)
MERIDIAN McIntosh
MERSHON (31551) Pierce(58), Bacon(41)
MESENA Warren
METTER Candler
MIDLAND (31820) Muscogee(65), Harris(34)
MIDVILLE (30441) Burke(49), Emanuel(49), Jenkins(1)
MIDWAY Liberty
MILAN (31060) Dodge(76), Telfair(23)
MILLEDGEVILLE (31061) Baldwin(94), Putnam(3), Wilkinson(1), Hancock(1)
MILLEDGEVILLE Baldwin
MILLEN (30442) Jenkins(93), Burke(4), Screven(1)
MILLWOOD (31552) Ware(67), Atkinson(28), Coffee(4)
MILNER (30257) Lamar(87), Pike(12)
MINERAL BLUFF Fannin
MITCHELL (30820) Glascock(47), Warren(45), Washington(6)
MOLENA (30258) Pike(72), Upson(27)
MONROE Walton
MONTEZUMA (31063) Dooly(67), Macon(32)
MONTICELLO Jasper
MONTROSE (31065) Laurens(87), Bleckley(8), Wilkinson(3)
MOODY A F B Lowndes

MORELAND Coweta
MORGAN Calhoun
MORGANTON (30560) Fannin(83), Union(16)
MORRIS (39867) Clay(83), Randolph(8), Quitman(5), Stewart(2)
MORRIS (31767) Quitman(60), Clay(29), Randolph(4), Stewart(4)
MORROW Clayton
MORVEN Brooks
MOULTRIE Colquitt
MOUNT AIRY Habersham
MOUNT BERRY Floyd
MOUNT VERNON Montgomery
MOUNT ZION Carroll
MOUNTAIN CITY Rabun
MURRAYVILLE (30564) Lumpkin(61), Hall(33), White(5)
MUSELLA (31066) Crawford(94), Monroe(3), Bibb(2)
MYSTIC Irwin
NAHUNTA (31553) Brantley(97), Charlton(2)
NASHVILLE Berrien
NAYLOR (31641) Lowndes(78), Lanier(21)
NELSON Cherokee
NEWBORN (30056) Jasper(56), Newton(22), Morgan(20)
NEWBORN Newton
NEWINGTON (30446) Screven(67), Effingham(32)
NEWNAN Coweta
NEWTON Baker
NICHOLLS (31554) Coffee(67), Bacon(22), Ware(9)
NICHOLSON (30565) Jackson(85), Madison(14)
NORCROSS (30092) Gwinnett(97), Fulton(2)
NORCROSS Gwinnett
NORMAN PARK (31771) Colquitt(97), Worth(2)
NORRISTOWN Emanuel
NORTH METRO Gwinnett
NORWOOD Warren
NUNEZ Emanuel
OAKFIELD Worth
OAKMAN Gordon
OAKWOOD Hall
OCHLOCKNEE (31773) Thomas(79), Grady(18), Colquitt(1)
OCILLA Irwin
OCONEE Washington
ODUM (31555) Wayne(85), Appling(14)
OFFERMAN Pierce
OGLETHORPE Macon
OLIVER Screven
OMAHA Stewart
OMEGA (31775) Colquitt(58), Tift(24), Worth(17)
ORCHARD HILL Spalding
OXFORD (30054) Newton(84), Walton(15)
OXFORD Newton
PALMETTO (30268) Fulton(81), Coweta(18)
PARROTT (31777) Terrell(81), Webster(18)
PARROTT (39877) Webster(81), Terrell(18)
PATTERSON (31557) Pierce(95), Appling(3)
PAVO (31778) Brooks(69), Thomas(28), Colquitt(1)
PEACHTREE CITY Fayette
PEARSON (31642) Atkinson(91), Coffee(5), Clinch(2)
PELHAM (31779) Mitchell(82), Grady(16)
PEMBROKE (31321) Bryan(54), Bulloch(45)
PENDERGRASS (30567) Jackson(74), Hall(25)
PERKINS (30822) Jenkins(96), Burke(3)
PERRY (31069) Houston(97), Peach(2)

PINE LAKE De Kalb
PINE MOUNTAIN (31822) Harris(67), Troup(24), Meriwether(8)
PINE MOUNTAIN VALLEY Harris
PINEHURST Dooly
PINEVIEW (31071) Wilcox(94), Pulaski(5)
PITTS (31072) Crisp(52), Wilcox(47)
PLAINFIELD Dodge
PLAINS (31780) Sumter(74), Webster(25)
PLAINVILLE (30733) Gordon(93), Floyd(6)
POOLER Chatham
PORTAL (30450) Bulloch(98), Emanuel(1)
PORTERDALE Fayette
PORTERDALE Newton
POULAN Worth
POWDER SPRINGS (30127) Cobb(80), Paulding(19)
POWDER SPRINGS Cobb
PRESTON Webster
PULASKI Candler
PUTNEY Dougherty
QUITMAN Brooks
RABUN GAP Rabun
RANGER (30734) Gordon(76), Pickens(23)
RAY CITY (31645) Berrien(51), Lowndes(26), Lanier(22)
RAYLE (30660) Wilkes(80), Oglethorpe(16), Taliaferro(3)
REBECCA (31783) Turner(60), Irwin(30), Ben Hill(9)
RED OAK Fulton
REDAN De Kalb
REGISTER (30452) Bulloch(97), Evans(1)
REIDSVILLE Tattnall
RENTZ Laurens
RESACA (30735) Gordon(63), Murray(22), Whitfield(14)
REX (30273) Clayton(92), Henry(7)
REYNOLDS (31076) Macon(69), Taylor(30)
RHINE (31077) Dodge(94), Telfair(5)
RICEBORO (31323) Liberty(94), McIntosh(5)
RICHLAND (31825) Webster(74), Stewart(24)
RICHMOND HILL Bryan
RINCON Effingham
RINGGOLD (30736) Catoosa(97), Walker(2)
RISING FAWN (30738) Dade(69), Walker(30)
RIVERDALE (30296) Clayton(81), Fulton(11), Fayette(6)
RIVERDALE Clayton
ROBERTA Crawford
ROCHELLE Wilcox
ROCK SPRING (30739) Walker(82), Catoosa(17)
ROCKLEDGE Laurens
ROCKMART (30153) Polk(65), Paulding(30), Haralson(4)
ROCKY FACE (30740) Whitfield(87), Walker(12)
ROCKY FORD (30455) Screven(98), Jenkins(1)
ROME Floyd
ROOPVILLE (30170) Heard(62), Carroll(37)
ROSSVILLE (30741) Walker(66), Catoosa(33)
ROSWELL (30075) Fulton(82), Cobb(15), Cherokee(1)
ROSWELL Fulton
ROYSTON (30662) Franklin(56), Hart(27), Madison(14), Elbert(1)
RUPERT (31081) Taylor(96), Macon(1), Schley(1)
RUTLEDGE Morgan
RYDAL (30171) Bartow(79), Gordon(20)
SAINT GEORGE Charlton
SAINT MARYS Camden
SAINT SIMONS ISLAND Glynn
SALE CITY (31784) Mitchell(95), Colquitt(4)

SANDERSVILLE Washington
SAPELO ISLAND McIntosh
SARDIS Burke
SARGENT Coweta
SASSER Terrell
SAUTEE NACOOCHEE (30571) White(97), Habersham(2)
SAVANNAH Chatham
SCOTLAND Telfair
SCOTTDALE De Kalb
SCREVEN Wayne
SEA ISLAND Glynn
SEA ISLAND BRANCH Glynn
SENOIA (30276) Coweta(82), Meriwether(12), Fayette(5)
SEVILLE Wilcox
SHADY DALE Jasper
SHANNON Floyd
SHARON Taliaferro
SHARPSBURG Coweta
SHELLMAN (31786) Randolph(95), Terrell(2), Calhoun(1)
SHELLMAN (39886) Randolph(63), Calhoun(34), Terrell(1)
SHILOH (31826) Talbot(63), Harris(36)
SILOAM Greene
SILVER CREEK (30173) Floyd(92), Polk(7)
SMARR Monroe
SMITHVILLE (31787) Lee(60), Sumter(39)
SMYRNA Cobb
SNELLVILLE (30039) Gwinnett(95), De Kalb(2), Rockdale(1)
SNELLVILLE Gwinnett
SOCIAL CIRCLE (30025) Walton(74), Newton(25)
SOCIAL CIRCLE Walton
SOPERTON (30457) Treutlen(94), Montgomery(3), Emanuel(1)
SPARKS Cook
SPARTA (31087) Hancock(95), Baldwin(3), Washington(1)
SPRINGFIELD Effingham
STAPLETON (30823) Warren(50), Jefferson(48)
STATENVILLE Echols
STATESBORO Bulloch
STATHAM (30666) Barrow(66), Oconee(25), Jackson(7)
STEPHENS Oglethorpe
STILLMORE Emanuel
STOCKBRIDGE (30281) Henry(88), Rockdale(5), Clayton(5)
STOCKTON (31649) Lanier(77), Echols(17), Clinch(5)
STONE MOUNTAIN (30087) De Kalb(57), Gwinnett(42)
STONE MOUNTAIN De Kalb
SUCHES (30572) Union(75), Fannin(24)
SUGAR VALLEY (30746) Gordon(96), Walker(3)
SUMMERTOWN Emanuel
SUMMERVILLE (30747) Chattooga(96), Walker(3)
SUMNER Worth
SUNNY SIDE Spalding
SURRENCY Appling
SUWANEE (30024) Gwinnett(72), Forsyth(25), Fulton(2)
SUWANEE Gwinnett
SWAINSBORO Emanuel
SYCAMORE (31790) Turner(98), Irwin(1)
SYLVANIA Screven
SYLVESTER (31791) Worth(98), Dougherty(1)
TALBOTTON Talbot
TALKING ROCK (30175) Pickens(62), Gilmer(37)
TALLAPOOSA Haralson
TALLULAH FALLS Rabun
TALMO (30575) Jackson(74), Hall(25)
TARRYTOWN (30470) Montgomery(83), Treutlen(16)
TATE Pickens

TAYLORSVILLE (30178) Bartow(81), Polk(17), Paulding(1)
TEMPLE (30179) Carroll(50), Paulding(32), Haralson(17)
TENNGA Murray
TENNILLE (31089) Washington(98), Johnson(1)
THE ROCK (30285) Upson(61), Pike(20), Lamar(18)
THOMASTON Upson
THOMASVILLE (31792) Thomas(97), Grady(2)
THOMASVILLE Thomas
THOMSON (30824) McDuffie(96), Warren(1), Columbia(1)
TIFTON Tift
TIGER Rabun
TIGNALL (30668) Wilkes(82), Lincoln(17)
TOCCOA (30577) Stephens(69), Franklin(22), Habersham(6), Banks(1)
TOCCOA Stephens
TOOMSBORO Wilkinson
TOWNSEND McIntosh
TRENTON Dade
TRION (30753) Chattooga(77), Walker(22)
TUCKER (30084) De Kalb(78), Gwinnett(21)
TUCKER De Kalb
TUNNEL HILL (30755) Whitfield(53), Catoosa(46)
TURIN Coweta
TURNERVILLE Habersham
TWIN CITY (30471) Emanuel(85), Bulloch(13), Candler(1)
TY TY (31795) Worth(56), Tift(43)
TYBEE ISLAND Chatham
TYRONE Fayette
UNADILLA (31091) Dooly(98), Houston(1)
UNION CITY Fulton
UNION POINT (30669) Greene(88), Oglethorpe(10)
UPATOI (31829) Muscogee(71), Harris(28)
UVALDA (30473) Toombs(61), Montgomery(38)
VALDOSTA (31605) Lowndes(97), Brooks(2)
VALDOSTA Lowndes
VALONA McIntosh
VARNELL Whitfield
VIDALIA (30474) Toombs(87), Montgomery(11), Emanuel(1)
VIDALIA Toombs
VIENNA (31092) Dooly(96), Crisp(3)
VILLA RICA (30180) Carroll(70), Douglas(20), Paulding(8)
WACO (30182) Carroll(62), Haralson(37)
WADLEY Jefferson
WALESKA Cherokee
WALTHOURVILLE Liberty
WARESBORO Ware
WARM SPRINGS (31830) Meriwether(96), Harris(3)
WARNER ROBINS Houston
WARRENTON Warren
WARTHEN Washington
WARWICK (31796) Worth(98), Crisp(1)
WASHINGTON Wilkes
WATKINSVILLE (30677) Oconee(96), Greene(3)
WAVERLY Camden
WAVERLY HALL (31831) Talbot(55), Harris(44)
WAYCROSS (31503) Ware(94), Brantley(4), Pierce(1)
WAYCROSS Ware
WAYNESBORO Burke
WAYNESVILLE (31566) Brantley(56), Camden(38), Glynn(4)
WEST GREEN (31567) Jeff Davis(58), Coffee(41)
WEST POINT (31833) Troup(70), Harris(29)
WESTON Webster

WHIGHAM Grady
WHITE (30184) Bartow(70), Cherokee(29)
WHITE OAK Camden
WHITE PLAINS (30678) Greene(96), Hancock(1), Taliaferro(1)
WHITESBURG (30185) Carroll(95), Douglas(4)
WILDWOOD Dade
WILEY Rabun

WILLACOOCHEE (31650) Coffee(70), Atkinson(28)
WILLIAMSON (30292) Pike(68), Spalding(31)
WINDER (30680) Barrow(98), Oconee(1)
WINSTON Douglas
WINTERVILLE (30683) Clarke(60), Oglethorpe(37), Madison(2)
WOODBINE Camden

WOODBURY Meriwether
WOODLAND Talbot
WOODSTOCK (30188) Cherokee(97), Cobb(2)
WOODSTOCK Cherokee
WRAY (31798) Irwin(50), Coffee(41), Ben Hill(7)
WRENS Jefferson

WRIGHTSVILLE (31096) Johnson(84), Washington(10), Laurens(5)
YATESVILLE (31097) Upson(89), Lamar(7), Monroe(3)
YOUNG HARRIS (30582) Towns(78), Union(21)
ZEBULON (30295) Pike(97), Lamar(2))

Georgia ZIP/City Cross Reference

Note: In 2003, a number of Georgia Zip Codes were changed. This change affected 31 Zip Codes (listed below) beginning with 317. These 31 Zip Codes now begin with 398. The locations (and county in parenthesis) are: ARLINGTON (Calhoun), ATTAPULGUS (Decatur), BAINBRIDGE (Decatur), BLAKELY (Early), BLUFFTON (Clay), BRINSON (Decatur), BRONWOOD (Terrell), CAIRO (Grady), CALVARY (Grady), CEDAR SPRINGS (Early), CLIMAX (Decatur), COLEMAN (Randolph), COLQUITT (Miller), CUTHBERT (Randolph), DAMASCUS (Early), DAWSON (Terrell), DONALSONVILLE (Seminole), EDISON (Calhoun), FORT GAINES (Clay), FOWLSTOWN (Decatur), GEORGETOWN (Quitman), IRON CITY (Seminole), JAKIN (Early), LEARY (Calhoun), MORGAN (Calhoun), MORRIS (Quitman), NEWTON (Baker), PARROTT (Terrell), SASSER (Terrell), SHELLMAN (Randolph), WHIGHAM (Grady). There is one new Zip Code for Atlanta - 39901.

30001-30001 AUSTELL	30094-30094 CONYERS	30171-30171 RYDAL	30255-30255 MANSFIELD
30002-30002 AVONDALE ESTATES	30095-30099 DULUTH	30172-30172 SHANNON	30256-30256 MEANSVILLE
30003-30003 NORCROSS	30101-30102 ACWORTH	30173-30173 SILVER CREEK	30257-30257 MILNER
30004-30005 ALPHARETTA	30103-30103 ADAIRSVILLE	30174-30174 SUWANEE	30258-30258 MOLENA
30006-30008 MARIETTA	30104-30104 ARAGON	30175-30175 TALKING ROCK	30259-30259 MORELAND
30009-30009 ALPHARETTA	30105-30105 ARMUCHEE	30176-30176 TALLAPOOSA	30260-30260 MORROW
30010-30010 NORCROSS	30106-30106 AUSTELL	30177-30177 TATE	30261-30261 LAGRANGE
30011-30011 AUBURN	30107-30107 BALL GROUND	30178-30178 TAYLORSVILLE	30262-30262 NEWBORN
30012-30013 CONYERS	30108-30108 BOWDON	30179-30179 TEMPLE	30263-30265 NEWNAN
30014-30016 COVINGTON	30109-30109 BOWDON JUNCTION	30180-30180 VILLA RICA	30266-30266 ORCHARD HILL
30017-30017 GRAYSON	30110-30110 BREMEN	30182-30182 WACO	30267-30267 OXFORD
30018-30018 JERSEY	30111-30111 CLARKDALE	30183-30183 WALESKA	30268-30268 PALMETTO
30019-30019 DACULA	30112-30112 CARROLLTON	30184-30184 WHITE	30269-30269 PEACHTREE CITY
30020-30020 CLARKDALE	30113-30113 BUCHANAN	30185-30185 WHITESBURG	30270-30270 PORTERDALE
30021-30021 CLARKSTON	30114-30115 CANTON	30187-30187 WINSTON	30270-30270 PEACHTREE CITY
30022-30023 ALPHARETTA	30116-30116 CARROLLTON	30188-30189 WOODSTOCK	30271-30271 NEWNAN
30024-30024 SUWANEE	30120-30121 CARTERSVILLE	30195-30199 DULUTH	30272-30272 RED OAK
30025-30025 SOCIAL CIRCLE	30122-30122 LITHIA SPRINGS	30201-30202 ALPHARETTA	30273-30273 REX
30026-30026 DULUTH	30123-30123 CASSVILLE	30203-30203 AUBURN	30274-30274 RIVERDALE
30026-30026 NORTH METRO	30124-30124 CAVE SPRING	30204-30204 BARNESVILLE	30275-30275 SARGENT
30027-30027 CONLEY	30125-30125 CEDARTOWN	30205-30205 BROOKS	30276-30276 SENOIA
30028-30028 CUMMING	30126-30126 MABLETON	30206-30206 CONCORD	30277-30277 SHARPSBURG
30029-30029 DULUTH	30127-30127 POWDER SPRINGS	30207-30208 CONYERS	30278-30278 SNELLVILLE
30029-30029 NORTH METRO	30128-30128 CUMMING	30209-30210 COVINGTON	30279-30279 SOCIAL CIRCLE
30030-30037 DECATUR	30129-30129 COOSA	30211-30211 DACULA	30281-30281 STOCKBRIDGE
30038-30038 LITHONIA	30130-30131 CUMMING	30212-30212 EXPERIMENT	30284-30284 SUNNY SIDE
30039-30039 SNELLVILLE	30132-30132 DALLAS	30213-30213 FAIRBURN	30285-30285 THE ROCK
30040-30041 CUMMING	30133-30135 DOUGLASVILLE	30214-30215 FAYETTEVILLE	30286-30286 THOMASTON
30042-30046 LAWRENCEVILLE	30136-30136 DULUTH	30216-30216 FLOVILLA	30287-30287 MORROW
30047-30048 LILBURN	30137-30137 EMERSON	30217-30217 FRANKLIN	30288-30288 CONLEY
30049-30049 ELLENWOOD	30138-30138 ESOM HILL	30218-30218 GAY	30289-30289 TURIN
30049-30049 LAWRENCEVILLE	30139-30139 FAIRMOUNT	30219-30219 GLENN	30290-30290 TYRONE
30050-30051 FOREST PARK	30140-30140 FELTON	30220-30220 GRANTVILLE	30291-30291 UNION CITY
30052-30052 LOGANVILLE	30141-30141 HIRAM	30221-30221 GRAYSON	30292-30292 WILLIAMSON
30054-30054 OXFORD	30142-30142 HOLLY SPRINGS	30222-30222 GREENVILLE	30293-30293 WOODBURY
30055-30055 MANSFIELD	30143-30143 JASPER	30223-30224 GRIFFIN	30294-30294 ELLENWOOD
30056-30056 NEWBORN	30144-30144 KENNESAW	30226-30226 LILBURN	30295-30295 ZEBULON
30057-30057 LITHIA SPRINGS	30145-30145 KINGSTON	30227-30227 LAWRENCEVILLE	30296-30296 RIVERDALE
30058-30058 LITHONIA	30146-30146 LEBANON	30228-30228 HAMPTON	30297-30298 FOREST PARK
30059-30059 MABLETON	30147-30147 LINDALE	30229-30229 HARALSON	30301-30399 ATLANTA
30060-30069 MARIETTA	30148-30148 MARBLE HILL	30230-30230 HOGANSVILLE	30401-30401 SWAINSBORO
30070-30070 PORTERDALE	30149-30149 MOUNT BERRY	30232-30232 INMAN	30410-30410 AILEY
30071-30071 NORCROSS	30150-30150 MOUNT ZION	30233-30233 JACKSON	30411-30411 ALAMO
30072-30072 PINE LAKE	30151-30151 NELSON	30234-30234 JENKINSBURG	30412-30412 ALSTON
30073-30073 POWDER SPRINGS	30152-30152 KENNESAW	30235-30235 JERSEY	30413-30413 BARTOW
30074-30074 REDAN	30153-30153 ROCKMART	30236-30238 JONESBORO	30414-30414 BELLVILLE
30075-30077 ROSWELL	30154-30154 DOUGLASVILLE	30239-30239 ALPHARETTA	30415-30415 BROOKLET
30078-30078 SNELLVILLE	30155-30155 DULUTH	30240-30241 LAGRANGE	30417-30417 CLAXTON
30079-30079 SCOTTDALE	30156-30156 KENNESAW	30243-30246 LAWRENCEVILLE	30420-30420 COBBTOWN
30080-30082 SMYRNA	30157-30157 DALLAS	30247-30247 LILBURN	30421-30421 COLLINS
30083-30083 STONE MOUNTAIN	30158-30159 NORTH METRO	30248-30248 LOCUST GROVE	30423-30423 DAISY
30084-30085 TUCKER	30160-30160 KENNESAW	30249-30249 LOGANVILLE	30424-30424 DOVER
30086-30088 STONE MOUNTAIN	30161-30165 ROME	30250-30250 LOVEJOY	30425-30425 GARFIELD
30089-30089 DECATUR	30168-30168 AUSTELL	30251-30251 LUTHERSVILLE	30426-30426 GIRARD
30090-30090 MARIETTA	30169-30169 CANTON	30252-30253 MCDONOUGH	30427-30427 GLENNVILLE
30091-30093 NORCROSS	30170-30170 ROOPVILLE	30254-30254 NEWNAN	30428-30428 GLENWOOD

30429-30429 HAGAN	30571-30571 SAUTEE NACOOCHEE	30753-30753 TRION	31057-31057 MARSHALLVILLE
30434-30434 LOUISVILLE	30572-30572 SUCHES	30755-30755 TUNNEL HILL	31058-31058 MAUK
30436-30436 LYONS	30573-30573 TALLULAH FALLS	30756-30756 VARNELL	31059-31059 MILLEDGEVILLE
30438-30438 MANASSAS	30575-30575 TALMO	30757-30757 WILDWOOD	31060-31060 MILAN
30439-30439 METTER	30576-30576 TIGER	30802-30802 APPLING	31061-31062 MILLEDGEVILLE
30441-30441 MIDVILLE	30577-30577 TOCCOA	30803-30803 AVERA	31063-31063 MONTEZUMA
30442-30442 MILLEN	30580-30580 TURNERVILLE	30805-30805 BLYTHE	31064-31064 MONTICELLO
30445-30445 MOUNT VERNON	30581-30581 WILEY	30806-30806 BONEVILLE	31065-31065 MONTROSE
30446-30446 NEWINGTON	30582-30582 YOUNG HARRIS	30807-30807 CAMAK	31066-31066 MUSELLA
30447-30447 NORRISTOWN	30596-30596 ALTO	30808-30808 DEARING	31067-31067 OCONEE
30448-30448 NUNEZ	30597-30597 DAHLONEGA	30809-30809 EVANS	31068-31068 OGLETHORPE
30449-30449 OLIVER	30598-30598 TOCCOA	30810-30810 GIBSON	31069-31069 PERRY
30450-30450 PORTAL	30599-30599 COMMERCE	30811-30811 GOUGH	31070-31070 PINEHURST
30451-30451 PULASKI	30601-30613 ATHENS	30812-30812 GRACEWOOD	31071-31071 PINEVIEW
30452-30452 REGISTER	30619-30619 ARNOLDSVILLE	30813-30813 GROVETOWN	31072-31072 PITTS
30453-30453 REIDSVILLE	30620-30620 BETHLEHEM	30814-30814 HARLEM	31073-31073 PLAINFIELD
30454-30454 ROCKLEDGE	30621-30621 BISHOP	30815-30815 HEPHZIBAH	31075-31075 RENTZ
30455-30455 ROCKY FORD	30622-30622 BOGART	30816-30816 KEYSVILLE	31076-31076 REYNOLDS
30456-30456 SARDIS	30623-30623 BOSTWICK	30817-30817 LINCOLNTON	31077-31077 RHINE
30457-30457 SOPERTON	30624-30624 BOWMAN	30818-30818 MATTHEWS	31078-31078 ROBERTA
30458-30461 STATESBORO	30625-30625 BUCKHEAD	30819-30819 MESENA	31079-31079 ROCHELLE
30464-30464 STILLMORE	30627-30627 CARLTON	30820-30820 MITCHELL	31081-31081 RUPERT
30466-30466 SUMMERTOWN	30628-30628 COLBERT	30821-30821 NORWOOD	31082-31082 SANDERSVILLE
30467-30467 SYLVANIA	30629-30629 COMER	30822-30822 PERKINS	31083-31083 SCOTLAND
30470-30470 TARRYTOWN	30630-30630 CRAWFORD	30823-30823 STAPLETON	31084-31084 SEVILLE
30471-30471 TWIN CITY	30631-30631 CRAWFORDVILLE	30824-30824 THOMSON	31085-31085 SHADY DALE
30473-30473 UVALDA	30633-30633 DANIELSVILLE	30828-30828 WARRENTON	31086-31086 SMARR
30474-30475 VIDALIA	30634-30634 DEWY ROSE	30830-30830 WAYNESBORO	31087-31087 SPARTA
30477-30477 WADLEY	30635-30635 ELBERTON	30833-30833 WRENS	31088-31088 WARNER ROBINS
30499-30499 REIDSVILLE	30638-30638 FARMINGTON	30900-30999 AUGUSTA	31089-31089 TENNILLE
30501-30501 GAINESVILLE	30639-30639 FRANKLIN SPRINGS	31001-31001 ABBEVILLE	31090-31090 TOOMSBORO
30502-30502 CHESTNUT MOUNTAIN	30641-30641 GOOD HOPE	31002-31002 ADRIAN	31091-31091 UNADILLA
30503-30507 GAINESVILLE	30642-30642 GREENSBORO	31003-31003 ALLENTOWN	31092-31092 VIENNA
30510-30510 ALTO	30643-30643 HARTWELL	31004-31004 BOLINGBROKE	31093-31093 WARNER ROBINS
30511-30511 BALDWIN	30645-30645 HIGH SHOALS	31005-31005 BONAIRE	31094-31094 WARTHEN
30512-30512 BLAIRSVILLE	30646-30646 HULL	31006-31006 BUTLER	31095-31095 WARNER ROBINS
30513-30513 BLUE RIDGE	30647-30647 ILA	31007-31007 BYROMVILLE	31096-31096 WRIGHTSVILLE
30514-30514 BLAIRSVILLE	30648-30648 LEXINGTON	31008-31008 BYRON	31097-31097 YATESVILLE
30515-30515 BUFORD	30650-30650 MADISON	31009-31009 CADWELL	31098-31099 WARNER ROBINS
30516-30516 BOWERSVILLE	30655-30656 MONROE	31010-31010 CORDELE	31106-31199 ATLANTA
30517-30517 BRASELTON	30660-30660 RAYLE	31011-31011 CHAUNCEY	31200-31299 MACON
30518-30519 BUFORD	30662-30662 ROYSTON	31012-31012 CHESTER	31301-31301 ALLENHURST
30520-30520 CANON	30663-30663 RUTLEDGE	31013-31013 CLINCHFIELD	31302-31302 BLOOMINGDALE
30521-30521 CARNESVILLE	30664-30664 SHARON	31014-31014 COCHRAN	31303-31303 CLYO
30522-30522 CHERRYLOG	30665-30665 SILOAM	31015-31015 CORDELE	31304-31304 CRESCENT
30523-30523 CLARKESVILLE	30666-30666 STATHAM	31016-31016 CULLODEN	31305-31305 DARIEN
30525-30525 CLAYTON	30667-30667 STEPHENS	31017-31017 DANVILLE	31307-31307 EDEN
30527-30527 CLERMONT	30668-30668 TIGNALL	31018-31018 DAVISBORO	31308-31308 ELLABELL
30528-30528 CLEVELAND	30669-30669 UNION POINT	31019-31019 DEXTER	31309-31309 FLEMING
30529-30530 COMMERCE	30671-30671 MAXEYS	31020-31020 DRY BRANCH	31310-31310 HINESVILLE
30531-30531 CORNELIA	30673-30673 WASHINGTON	31021-31021 DUBLIN	31312-31312 GUYTON
30533-30533 DAHLONEGA	30677-30677 WATKINSVILLE	31022-31022 DUDLEY	31313-31313 HINESVILLE
30534-30534 DAWSONVILLE	30678-30678 WHITE PLAINS	31023-31023 EASTMAN	31314-31315 FORT STEWART
30535-30535 DEMOREST	30680-30680 WINDER	31024-31024 EATONTON	31316-31316 LUDOWICI
30536-30536 ELLIJAY	30683-30683 WINTERVILLE	31025-31025 ELKO	31318-31318 MELDRIM
30537-30537 DILLARD	30701-30703 CALHOUN	31026-31026 COCHRAN	31319-31319 MERIDIAN
30538-30538 EASTANOLLEE	30705-30705 CHATSWORTH	31026-31026 EATONTON	31320-31320 MIDWAY
30539-30539 EAST ELLIJAY	30707-30707 CHICKAMAUGA	31027-31027 DUBLIN	31321-31321 PEMBROKE
30540-30540 ELLIJAY	30708-30708 CISCO	31028-31028 CENTERVILLE	31322-31322 POOLER
30541-30541 EPWORTH	30710-30710 COHUTTA	31029-31029 FORSYTH	31323-31323 RICEBORO
30542-30542 FLOWERY BRANCH	30711-30711 CRANDALL	31030-31030 FORT VALLEY	31324-31324 RICHMOND HILL
30543-30543 GILLSVILLE	30719-30722 DALTON	31031-31031 GORDON	31326-31326 RINCON
30544-30544 DEMOREST	30724-30724 ETON	31032-31032 GRAY	31327-31327 SAPELO ISLAND
30545-30545 HELEN	30725-30725 FLINTSTONE	31033-31033 HADDOCK	31328-31328 TYBEE ISLAND
30546-30546 HIAWASSEE	30726-30726 GRAYSVILLE	31034-31034 HARDWICK	31329-31329 SPRINGFIELD
30547-30547 HOMER	30728-30728 LA FAYETTE	31035-31035 HARRISON	31331-31331 TOWNSEND
30548-30548 HOSCHTON	30730-30730 LYERLY	31036-31036 HAWKINSVILLE	31332-31332 VALONA
30549-30549 JEFFERSON	30731-30731 MENLO	31037-31037 HELENA	31333-31333 WALTHOURVILLE
30552-30552 LAKEMONT	30732-30732 OAKMAN	31038-31038 HILLSBORO	31400-31499 SAVANNAH
30553-30553 LAVONIA	30733-30733 PLAINVILLE	31039-31039 HOWARD	31501-31503 WAYCROSS
30554-30554 LULA	30734-30734 RANGER	31040-31040 DUBLIN	31510-31510 ALMA
30555-30555 MC CAYSVILLE	30735-30735 RESACA	31041-31041 IDEAL	31512-31512 AMBROSE
30557-30557 MARTIN	30736-30736 RINGGOLD	31042-31042 IRWINTON	31513-31515 BAXLEY
30558-30558 MAYSVILLE	30738-30738 RISING FAWN	31044-31044 JEFFERSONVILLE	31516-31516 BLACKSHEAR
30559-30559 MINERAL BLUFF	30739-30739 ROCK SPRING	31045-31045 JEWELL	31518-31518 BRISTOL
30560-30560 MORGANTON	30740-30740 ROCKY FACE	31046-31046 JULIETTE	31519-31519 BROXTON
30562-30562 MOUNTAIN CITY	30741-30741 ROSSVILLE	31047-31047 KATHLEEN	31520-31521 BRUNSWICK
30563-30563 MOUNT AIRY	30742-30742 FORT OGLETHORPE	31049-31049 KITE	31522-31522 SAINT SIMONS ISLAND
30564-30564 MURRAYVILLE	30746-30746 SUGAR VALLEY	31050-31050 KNOXVILLE	31523-31525 BRUNSWICK
30565-30565 NICHOLSON	30747-30747 SUMMERVILLE	31051-31051 LILLY	31527-31527 JEKYLL ISLAND
30566-30566 OAKWOOD	30750-30750 LOOKOUT MOUNTAIN	31052-31052 LIZELLA	31527-31527 JEKYLL ISLAND BRANCH
30567-30567 PENDERGRASS	30751-30751 TENNGA	31054-31054 MC INTYRE	31532-31532 DENTON
30568-30568 RABUN GAP	30752-30752 TRENTON	31055-31055 MC RAE	31533-31535 DOUGLAS

31537-31537 FOLKSTON	31735-31735 COBB	31830-31830 WARM SPRINGS
31539-31539 HAZLEHURST	31736-31736 COLEMAN	31831-31831 WAVERLY HALL
31542-31542 HOBOKEN	31737-31737 COLQUITT	31832-31832 WESTON
31543-31543 HORTENSE	31738-31738 COOLIDGE	31833-31833 WEST POINT
31544-31544 JACKSONVILLE	31739-31739 COTTON	31836-31836 WOODLAND
31545-31546 JESUP	31740-31740 CUTHBERT	31900-31904 COLUMBUS
31547-31547 KINGS BAY	31741-31741 DAMASCUS	31905-31905 FORT BENNING
31548-31548 KINGSLAND	31742-31742 DAWSON	31906-31994 COLUMBUS
31549-31549 LUMBER CITY	31743-31743 DE SOTO	31995-31995 FORT BENNING
31550-31550 MANOR	31744-31744 DOERUN	31997-31999 COLUMBUS
31551-31551 MERSHON	31745-31745 DONALSONVILLE	39813-39813 ARLINGTON
31552-31552 MILLWOOD	31746-31746 EDISON	39815-39815 ATTAPULGUS
31553-31553 NAHUNTA	31747-31747 ELLENTON	39817-39819 BAINBRIDGE
31554-31554 NICHOLLS	31749-31749 ENIGMA	39823-39823 BLAKELY
31555-31555 ODUM	31750-31750 FITZGERALD	39824-39824 BLUFFTON
31556-31556 OFFERMAN	31751-31751 FORT GAINES	39825-39825 BRINSON
31557-31557 PATTERSON	31752-31752 FOWLSTOWN	39826-39826 BRONWOOD
31558-31558 SAINT MARYS	31753-31753 FUNSTON	39827-39828 CAIRO
31560-31560 SCREVEN	31754-31754 GEORGETOWN	39829-39829 CALVARY
31561-31561 SEA ISLAND	31756-31756 HARTSFIELD	39832-39832 CEDAR SPRINGS
31561-31561 SEA ISLAND BRANCH	31757-31758 THOMASVILLE	39834-39834 CLIMAX
31562-31562 SAINT GEORGE	31759-31759 IRON CITY	39836-39836 COLEMAN
31563-31563 SURRENCY	31760-31760 IRWINVILLE	39837-39837 COLQUITT
31564-31564 WARESBORO	31761-31761 JAKIN	39840-39840 CUTHBERT
31565-31565 WAVERLY	31762-31762 LEARY	39841-39841 DAMASCUS
31566-31566 WAYNESVILLE	31763-31763 LEESBURG	39842-39842 DAWSON
31567-31567 WEST GREEN	31764-31764 LESLIE	39845-39845 DONALSONVILLE
31568-31568 WHITE OAK	31765-31765 MEIGS	39846-39846 EDISON
31569-31569 WOODBINE	31766-31766 MORGAN	39851-39851 FORT GAINES
31598-31599 JESUP	31767-31767 MORRIS	39852-39852 FOWLSTOWN
31601-31606 VALDOSTA	31768-31768 MOULTRIE	39854-39854 GEORGETOWN
31620-31620 ADEL	31769-31769 MYSTIC	39859-39859 IRON CITY
31622-31622 ALAPAHA	31770-31770 NEWTON	39861-39861 JAKIN
31623-31623 ARGYLE	31771-31771 NORMAN PARK	39862-39862 LEARY
31624-31624 AXSON	31772-31772 OAKFIELD	39866-39866 MORGAN
31625-31625 BARNEY	31773-31773 OCHLOCKNEE	39867-39867 MORRIS
31626-31626 BOSTON	31774-31774 OCILLA	39870-39870 NEWTON
31627-31627 CECIL	31775-31775 OMEGA	39877-39877 PARROTT
31629-31629 DIXIE	31776-31776 MOULTRIE	39885-39885 SASSER
31630-31630 DU PONT	31777-31777 PARROTT	39886-39886 SHELLMAN
31631-31631 FARGO	31778-31778 PAVO	39897-39897 WHIGHAM
31632-31632 HAHIRA	31779-31779 PELHAM	39901-39901 ATLANTA
31634-31634 HOMERVILLE	31780-31780 PLAINS	
31635-31635 LAKELAND	31781-31781 POULAN	
31636-31636 LAKE PARK	31782-31782 PUTNEY	
31637-31637 LENOX	31783-31783 REBECCA	
31638-31638 MORVEN	31784-31784 SALE CITY	
31639-31639 NASHVILLE	31785-31785 SASSER	
31641-31641 NAYLOR	31786-31786 SHELLMAN	
31642-31642 PEARSON	31787-31787 SMITHVILLE	
31643-31643 QUITMAN	31788-31788 MOULTRIE	
31645-31645 RAY CITY	31789-31789 SUMNER	
31646-31646 SAINT GEORGE	31790-31790 SYCAMORE	
31647-31647 SPARKS	31791-31791 SYLVESTER	
31648-31648 STATENVILLE	31792-31792 THOMASVILLE	
31649-31649 STOCKTON	31793-31794 TIFTON	
31650-31650 WILLACOOCHEE	31795-31795 TY TY	
31698-31699 VALDOSTA	31796-31796 WARWICK	
31699-31699 MOODY A F B	31797-31797 WHIGHAM	
31700-31708 ALBANY	31798-31798 WRAY	
31709-31710 AMERICUS	31799-31799 THOMASVILLE	
31711-31711 ANDERSONVILLE	31801-31801 BOX SPRINGS	
31712-31712 ARABI	31803-31803 BUENA VISTA	
31713-31713 ARLINGTON	31804-31804 CATAULA	
31714-31714 ASHBURN	31805-31805 CUSSETA	
31715-31715 ATTAPULGUS	31806-31806 ELLAVILLE	
31716-31716 BACONTON	31807-31807 ELLERSLIE	
31717-31718 BAINBRIDGE	31808-31808 FORTSON	
31719-31719 AMERICUS	31810-31810 GENEVA	
31720-31720 BARWICK	31811-31811 HAMILTON	
31721-31721 ALBANY	31812-31812 JUNCTION CITY	
31722-31722 BERLIN	31814-31814 LOUVALE	
31723-31723 BLAKELY	31815-31815 LUMPKIN	
31724-31724 BLUFFTON	31816-31816 MANCHESTER	
31725-31725 BRINSON	31820-31820 MIDLAND	
31726-31726 BRONWOOD	31821-31821 OMAHA	
31727-31727 BROOKFIELD	31822-31822 PINE MOUNTAIN	
31728-31728 CAIRO	31823-31823 PINE MOUNTAIN VALLEY	
31729-31729 CALVARY	31824-31824 PRESTON	
31730-31730 CAMILLA	31825-31825 RICHLAND	
31732-31732 CEDAR SPRINGS	31826-31826 SHILOH	
31733-31733 CHULA	31827-31827 TALBOTTON	
31734-31734 CLIMAX	31829-31829 UPATOI	

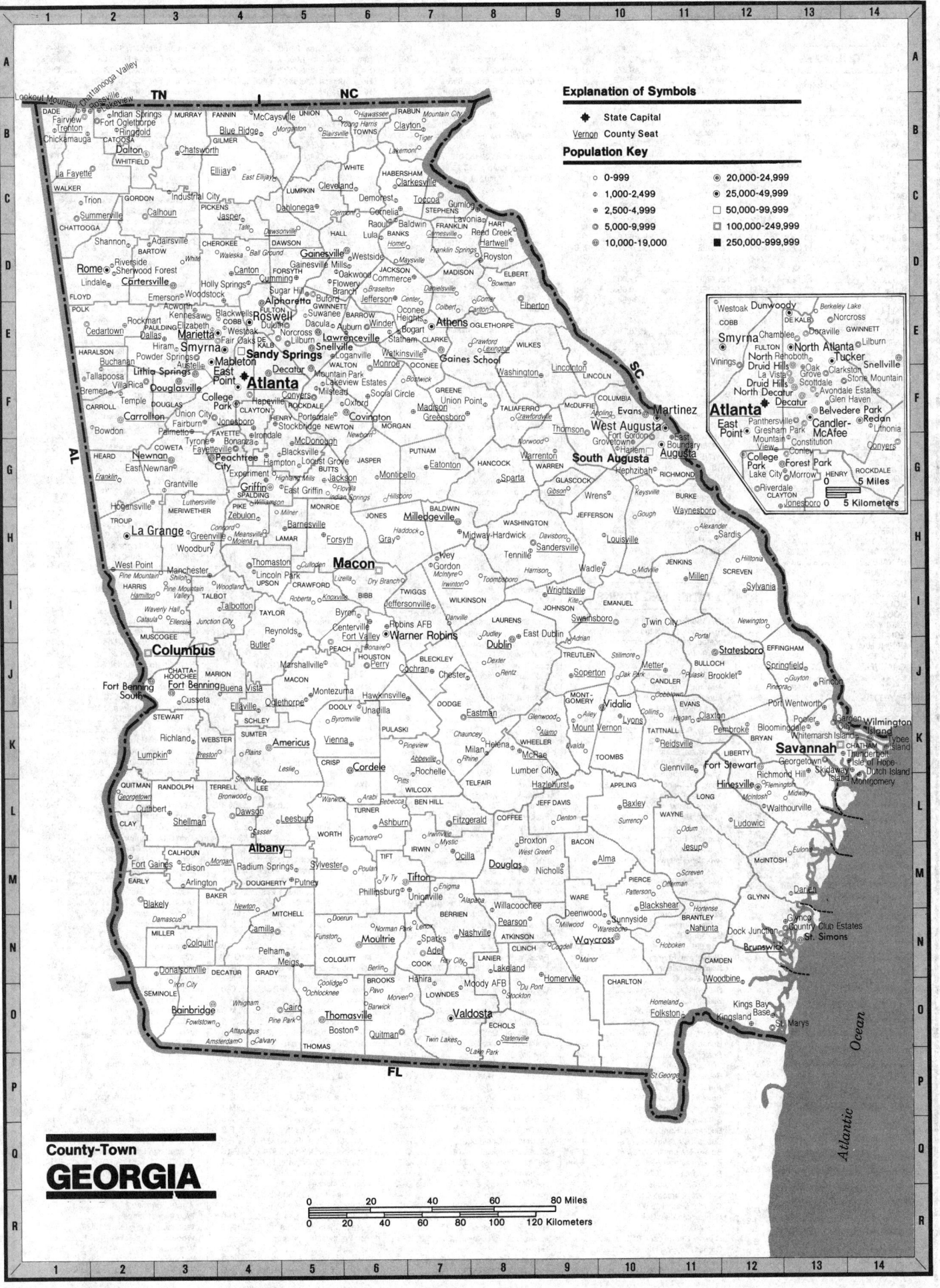

County-Town

GEORGIA

COUNTIES

(159 Counties)

Name of County	Population	Location on Map
APPLING	15,744	L-10
ATKINSON	6,213	N-8
BACON	9,566	L-9
BAKER	3,615	M-3
BALDWIN	39,530	H-7
BANKS	10,308	D-6
BARROW	29,721	E-6
BARTOW	55,911	D-2
BEN HILL	16,245	L-7
BERRIEN	14,153	N-7
BIBB	149,967	I-6
BLECKLEY	10,430	J-7
BRANTLEY	11,077	N-11
BROOKS	15,398	N-6
BRYAN	15,438	K-12
BULLOCH	43,125	J-11
BURKE	20,579	G-11
BUTTS	15,326	G-5
CALHOUN	5,013	M-3
CAMDEN	30,167	N-11
CANDLER	7,744	J-10
CARROLL	71,422	F-2
CATOOSA	42,464	B-2
CHARLTON	8,496	O-10
CHATHAM	216,935	K-13
CHATTAHOOCHEE	16,934	J-3
CHATTOOGA	22,242	C-1
CHEROKEE	90,204	D-3
CLARKE	87,594	E-7
CLAY	3,364	L-2
CLAYTON	182,052	F-4
CLINCH	6,160	N-8
COBB	447,745	E-4
COFFEE	29,592	L-8
COLQUITT	36,645	N-5
COLUMBIA	66,031	F-10
COOK	13,456	N-7
COWETA	53,853	G-3
CRAWFORD	8,991	I-5
CRISP	20,011	K-5
DADE	13,147	B-1
DAWSON	9,429	D-5
DEKALB	545,837	E-4
DECATUR	25,511	N-4
DODGE	17,607	J-7
DOOLY	9,901	J-5
DOUGHERTY	96,311	M-4
DOUGLAS	71,120	F-3
EARLY	11,854	M-2
ECHOLS	2,334	O-8
EFFINGHAM	25,687	J-12
ELBERT	18,949	D-8
EMANUEL	20,546	I-10
EVANS	8,724	J-11
FANNIN	15,992	B-4
FAYETTE	62,415	F-4
FLOYD	81,251	D-1
FORSYTH	44,083	D-5
FRANKLIN	16,650	C-7
FULTON	648,951	E-4
GILMER	13,368	B-4
GLASCOCK	2,357	G-9
GLYNN	62,496	M-12
GORDON	35,072	C-2
GRADY	20,279	N-4
GREENE	11,793	F-7
GWINNETT	352,910	E-5
HABERSHAM	27,621	C-6
HALL	95,428	D-5
HANCOCK	8,908	G-8
HARALSON	21,966	E-1
HARRIS	17,788	I-2
HART	19,712	C-8
HEARD	8,628	G-2
HENRY	58,741	F-4
HOUSTON	89,208	J-6
IRWIN	8,649	M-7
JACKSON	30,005	D-6
JASPER	8,453	G-6
JEFF DAVIS	12,032	L-9
JEFFERSON	17,408	H-9
JENKINS	8,247	H-11
JOHNSON	8,329	I-9
JONES	20,739	H-6
LAMAR	13,038	H-5
LANIER	5,531	N-8
LAURENS	39,988	I-8
LEE	16,250	L-4
LIBERTY	52,745	K-12
LINCOLN	7,442	F-9
LONG	6,202	L-11
LOWNDES	75,981	O-7
LUMPKIN	14,573	C-5
MACON	13,114	J-5
MADISON	21,050	D-7
MARION	5,590	J-3
MCDUFFIE	20,119	F-9
MCINTOSH	8,634	M-12
MERIWETHER	22,411	H-3
MILLER	6,280	N-3
MITCHELL	20,275	N-4
MONROE	17,113	H-5
MONTGOMERY	7,163	J-9
MORGAN	12,883	F-6
MURRAY	26,147	B-3
MUSCOGEE	179,278	I-2
NEWTON	41,808	F-5
OCONEE	17,618	E-6
OGLETHORPE	9,763	E-8
PAULDING	41,611	E-3
PEACH	21,189	J-5
PICKENS	14,432	C-3
PIERCE	13,328	M-10
PIKE	10,224	H-4
POLK	33,815	E-1
PULASKI	8,108	K-6
PUTNAM	14,137	G-7
QUITMAN	2,209	L-2
RABUN	11,648	B-7
RANDOLPH	8,023	L-3
RICHMOND	189,719	G-11
ROCKDALE	54,091	F-5
SCHLEY	3,588	K-4
SCREVEN	13,842	I-12
SEMINOLE	9,010	O-2
SPALDING	54,457	G-4
STEPHENS	23,257	C-7
STEWART	5,654	K-3
SUMTER	30,228	K-4
TALBOT	6,524	I-3
TALIAFERRO	1,915	F-8
TATTNALL	17,722	K-10
TAYLOR	7,642	I-4
TELFAIR	11,000	L-8
TERRELL	10,653	L-3
THOMAS	38,986	O-5
TIFT	34,998	M-6
TOOMBS	24,072	K-10
TOWNS	6,754	B-6
TREUTLEN	5,994	J-9
TROUP	55,536	H-2
TURNER	8,703	L-6
TWIGGS	9,806	I-7
UNION	11,993	B-5
UPSON	26,300	I-4
WALKER	58,340	C-1
WALTON	38,586	E-6
WARE	35,471	M-9
WARREN	6,078	G-9
WASHINGTON	19,112	H-8
WAYNE	22,356	L-11
WEBSTER	2,263	K-3
WHEELER	4,903	K-8
WHITE	13,006	C-6
WHITFIELD	72,462	B-2
WILCOX	7,008	L-7
WILKES	10,597	E-8
WILKINSON	10,228	I-7
WORTH	19,745	L-5
TOTAL	6,478,216	

CITIES AND TOWNS

Note: The first name is that of the city or town, second, that of the county in which it is located, then the population and location on the map.

Abbeville, Dodge/Wilcox, 907 .... K-7
Acworth, Cobb, 4,519 .... E-3
Adairsville, Bartow, 2,131 .... D-3
Adel, Cook, 5,093 .... N-7
Alamo, Wheeler, 855 .... K-8
Albany, Dougherty, 78,122 .... M-5
Alma, Bacon, 3,663 .... M-9
Alpharetta, Fulton, 13,002 .... E-4
Americus, Sumter, 16,512 .... K-4
Appling, Columbia F-10
Arlington, Calhoun/Early, 1,513 .... M-3
Ashburn, Turner, 4,827 .... L-6
Athens, Clarke, 45,734 .... E-7
Atlanta, DeKalb/Fulton, 394,017 .... F-4
Auburn, Barrow/Gwinnett, 3,139 .... E-6
Augusta, Richmond, 44,639 .... G-11
Austell, Cobb/Douglas, 4,173 .... E-3
Avondale Estates, DeKalb, 2,209 .... F-13
Bainbridge, Decatur, 10,712 .... O-3
Baldwin, Banks/Habersham, 1,439 .... C-6
Barnesville, Lamar, 4,747 .... H-5
Baxley, Appling, 3,841 .... L-10
• Belvedere Park, DeKalb, 18,089 .... F-13
Blackshear, Pierce, 3,263 .... M-10
• Blacksville, Henry, 1,112 .... G-5
Blackwells, Cobb E-4
Blairsville, Union, 564 .... B-5
Blakely, Early, 5,595 .... M-2
Bloomingdale, Chatham, 2,271 .... K-13
Blue Ridge, Fannin, 1,336 .... B-4
Bogart, Clarke/Oconee, 1,018 .... E-6
• Bonanza, Clayton, 2,010 .... G-4
Boston, Thomas, 1,395 .... O-6
Bowdon, Carroll, 1,981 .... F-2
Bremen, Carroll/Haralson, 4,356 .... F-2
Brooklet, Bulloch, 1,013 .... J-12
Broxton, Coffee, 1,211 .... M-8
Brunswick, Glynn, 16,433 .... N-13
Buchanan, Haralson, 1,009 .... E-2
Buena Vista, Marion, 1,472 .... J-4
Buford, Gwinnett/Hall, 8,771 .... D-5
Butler, Taylor, 1,673 .... I-4
Byron, Peach, 2,276 .... I-6
Cairo, Grady, 9,035 .... O-5
Calhoun, Gordon, 7,135 .... C-3
Camilla, Mitchell, 5,008 .... N-4
• Candler-McAfee, DeKalb, 29,491 .... F-13
Canton, Cherokee, 4,817 .... D-4
Carnesville, Franklin, 514 .... D-7
Carrollton, Carroll, 16,029 .... F-2
Cartersville, Bartow, 12,035 .... D-3
Cedartown, Polk, 7,978 .... F-2
Centerville, Houston, 3,251 .... I-6
Chamblee, DeKalb, 7,668 .... E-13
Chatsworth, Murray, 2,865 .... B-3
• Chattanooga Valley, Walker, 4,088 .... B-2
Chester, Dodge, 1,072 .... J-8
Chickamauga, Walker, 2,149 .... B-2
Clarkesville, Habersham, 1,151 .... C-6
Clarkston, DeKalb, 5,385 .... F-13
Claxton, Evans, 2,464 .... K-11
Clayton, Rabun, 1,613 .... B-7
Cleveland, White, 1,653 .... C-6
Cochran, Bleckley, 4,390 .... J-7
College Park, Clayton/Fulton, 20,457 .... F-4
Colquitt, Miller, 1,991 .... N-3
Columbus, Muscogee, 178,681 .... J-2
Commerce, Jackson, 4,108 .... D-7
• Conley, Clayton, 5,528 .... G-13
Constitution, DeKalb G-13
Conyers, Rockdale, 7,380 .... F-5
Cordele, Crisp, 10,321 .... K-6
Cornelia, Habersham, 3,219 .... C-7
• Country Club Estates, Glynn, 7,500 .... N-13
Covington, Newton, 10,026 .... F-6
Crawfordville, Taliaferro, 577 .... F-8
Cumming, Forsyth, 2,828 .... D-5
Cusseta, Chattahoochee, 1,107 .... J-3
Cuthbert, Randolph, 3,730 .... L-3
Dacula, Gwinnett, 2,217 .... E-5
Dahlonega, Lumpkin, 3,086 .... C-5
Dallas, Paulding, 2,810 .... E-3
Dalton, Whitfield, 21,761 .... B-2
Danielsville, Madison, 318 .... D-7
Darien, McIntosh, 1,783 .... M-13
Dawson, Terrell, 5,295 .... L-4
Dawsonville, Dawson, 467 .... C-5
Decatur, DeKalb, 17,336 .... F-4
• Deenwood, Ware, 2,055 .... N-10
Demorest, Habersham, 1,088 .... C-6
• Dock Junction, Glynn, 7,094 .... N-13
Donalsonville, Seminole, 2,761 .... N-3
Doraville, DeKalb, 7,626 .... F-13
Douglas, Coffee, 10,464 .... M-8
Douglasville, Douglas, 11,635 .... F-3
• Druid Hills, DeKalb, 12,174 .... F-13
Dublin, Laurens, 16,312 .... J-8
Duluth, Gwinnett, 9,029 .... E-5
• Dunwoody, DeKalb, 26,302 .... E-13
• East Boundary, Richmond, 3,271 .... G-11
East Dublin, Laurens, 2,524 .... I-8
• East Griffin, Spalding, 1,746 .... G-5
• East Newnan, Coweta, 1,173 .... G-3
East Point, Fulton, 34,402 .... F-4
Eastman, Dodge, 5,153 .... K-7
Eatonton, Putnam, 4,737 .... G-7
Edison, Calhoun, 1,182 .... M-3
Elberton, Elbert, 5,682 .... E-8
Elizabeth, Cobb E-4
Ellaville, Schley, 1,724 .... K-4
Ellijay, Gilmer, 1,178 .... B-4
Emerson, Bartow, 1,201 .... D-3
• Evans, Columbia, 13,713 .... F-10
• Experiment, Spalding, 3,762 .... G-4
• Fair Oaks, Cobb, 6,996 .... E-4
Fairburn, Fulton, 4,013 .... F-3
• Fairview, Walker, 6,444 .... B-2
Fayetteville, Fayette, 5,827 .... G-4
Fitzgerald, Ben Hill/Irwin, 8,612 .... L-7
Flowery Branch, Hall, 1,251 .... D-5
Folkston, Charlton, 2,285 .... O-11
Forest Park, Clayton, 16,925 .... G-13
Forsyth, Monroe, 4,268 .... H-5
• Fort Benning South, Chattahoochee, 14,617 .... J-3
Fort Gaines, Clay, 1,248 .... M-2
• Fort Gordon, Richmond, 9,140 .... G-10
Fort Oglethorpe, Catoosa/Walker, 5,880 .... B-2
• Fort Stewart, Liberty, 13,774 .... K-12
Fort Valley, Peach, 8,198 .... J-5
Franklin, Heard, 876 .... G-2
• Gaines School, Clarke, 11,354 .... E-7
Gainesville, Hall, 17,885 .... D-6
• Gainesville Mills, Hall, 1,329 .... D-6
Garden City, Chatham, 7,410 .... K-13
• Georgetown, Chatham, 5,554 .... K-13
Gibson, Glascock, 679 .... G-9
Glen Haven, DeKalb F-13
Glennville, Tattnall, 3,676 .... K-11
Glynco, Glynn N-13
Gordon, Wilkinson, 2,468 .... H-7
Grantville, Coweta, 1,180 .... G-3
Gray, Jones, 2,189 .... H-6
Greensboro, Greene, 2,860 .... F-8
Greenville, Meriwether, 1,167 .... H-3
• Gresham Park, DeKalb, 9,000 .... F-13
Griffin, Spalding, 21,347 .... G-4
Grovetown, Columbia, 3,596 .... G-10
• Gumlog, Franklin, 1,470 .... C-7
Hahira, Lowndes, 1,353 .... O-7
Hamilton, Harris, 454 .... I-3
Hampton, Henry, 2,694 .... G-4
Hapeville, Fulton, 5,483 .... F-4
Harlem, Columbia, 2,199 .... G-10
Hartwell, Hart, 4,555 .... D-8
Hawkinsville, Pulaski, 3,527 .... J-7
Hazlehurst, Jeff Davis, 4,202 .... L-9
Helena, Telfair/Wheeler, 1,256 .... K-8
Hephzibah, Richmond, 2,466 .... G-10
Hiawassee, Towns, 547 .... B-6
Hinesville, Liberty, 21,603 .... L-12
Hiram, Paulding, 1,389 .... E-3
Hogansville, Troup, 2,976 .... G-3
Holly Springs, Cherokee, 2,406 .... D-4
Homer, Banks, 742 .... D-7
Homerville, Clinch, 2,560 .... N-9
• Indian Springs, Catoosa, 1,273 .... B-2
Industrial City, Gordon/Murry C-3
• Irondale, Clayton, 3,352 .... F-4
Irwinton, Wilkinson, 641 .... I-7
• Isle of Hope-Dutch Island, Chatham, 2,637 .... K-14
Ivey, Wilkinson, 1,053 .... H-7
Jackson, Butts, 4,076 .... G-5
Jasper, Pickens, 1,772 .... C-4
Jefferson, Jackson, 2,763 .... E-6
Jeffersonville, Twiggs, 1,545 .... I-7
Jesup, Wayne, 8,958 .... M-11
Jonesboro, Clayton, 3,635 .... F-4
Kennesaw, Cobb, 8,936 .... F-3
• Kings Bay Base, Camden, 3,463 .... O-12
Kingsland, Camden, 4,699 .... O-12
Knoxville, Crawford I-5
La Fayette, Walker, 6,313 .... C-2
La Grange, Troup, 25,597 .... H-2
La Vista, DeKalb F-13
Lake City, Clayton, 2,733 .... G-13
Lakeland, Lanier, 2,467 .... N-8
• Lakeview, Catoosa/Walker, 5,237 .... B-2
• Lakeview Estates, Rockdale, 1,477 .... F-5
Lavonia, Franklin, 1,840 .... C-8
Lawrenceville, Gwinnett, 16,848 .... E-5
Leesburg, Lee, 1,452 .... L-5
Lexington, Oglethorpe, 230 .... E-8
Lilburn, Gwinnett, 9,301 .... E-5
Lincoln Park, Upson H-4
Lincolnton, Lincoln, 1,476 .... E-9
• Lindale, Floyd, 4,187 .... D-2
• Lithia Springs, Douglas, 11,403 .... F-3
Lithonia, DeKalb, 2,448 .... F-14
Locust Grove, Henry, 1,681 .... G-5
Loganville, Gwinnett/Walton, 3,180 .... E-5
Lookout Mountain, Walker, 1,636 .... B-1
Louisville, Jefferson, 2,429 .... H-10
Ludowici, Long, 1,291 .... L-12
Lula, Banks/Hall, 1,018 .... D-6
Lumber City, Telfair, 1,429 .... K-9
Lumpkin, Stewart, 1,250 .... K-3
Lyons, Toombs, 4,502 .... K-10
• Mableton, Cobb, 25,725 .... E-4
Macon, Bibb/Jones, 106,612 .... H-6
Madison, Morgan, 3,483 .... F-7
Manchester, Meriwether/Talbot, 4,104 .... H-3
Marietta, Cobb, 44,129 .... E-4
Marshallville, Macon, 1,457 .... J-5
• Martinez, Columbia/Richmond, 33,731 .... F-11
McCaysville, Fannin, 1,065 .... B-4
McDonough, Henry, 2,929 .... G-5
McRae, Telfair, 3,007 .... K-8
Meigs, Mitchell/Thomas, 1,120 .... N-5
Metter, Candler, 3,707 .... J-11
• Midway-Hardwick, Baldwin, 4,910 .... H-7
Milan, Dodge/Telfair, 1,056 .... K-8
Milledgeville, Baldwin, 17,727 .... H-7
Millen, Jenkins, 3,808 .... I-11
Milstead, Rockdale F-5
Monroe, Walton, 9,759 .... F-6
Montezuma, Macon, 4,506 .... J-5
• Montgomery, Chatham, 4,327 .... K-14
Monticello, Jasper, 2,289 .... G-6
• Moody AFB, Lowndes, 1,288 .... O-7
Morgan, Calhoun, 252 .... M-3
Morrow, Clayton, 5,168 .... G-13
Moultrie, Colquitt, 14,865 .... N-6
Mount Vernon, Montgomery, 1,914 .... K-9
Mountain View, Clayton G-12
Nahunta, Brantley, 1,049 .... N-11
Nashville, Berrien, 4,782 .... N-7
Newnan, Coweta, 12,497 .... G-3
Newton, Baker, 703 .... M-4
Nicholls, Coffee, 1,003 .... M-9
Norcross, Gwinnett, 5,947 .... E-5
• North Atlanta, DeKalb, 27,812 .... E-13
• North Decatur, DeKalb, 13,936 .... F-13
• North Druid Hills, DeKalb, 14,170 .... F-13
Oak Grove, DeKalb F-13
Oakwood, Hall, 1,464 .... D-5
Ocilla, Irwin, 3,182 .... M-7
Oglethorpe, Macon, 1,302 .... J-5
Oxford, Newton, 1,945 .... F-6
Palmetto, Coweta/Fulton, 2,612 .... F-3
• Panthersville, DeKalb, 9,874 .... F-13
Peachtree City, Fayette, 19,027 .... G-4
Pearson, Atkinson, 1,714 .... N-8
Pelham, Mitchell, 3,869 .... N-5
Pembroke, Bryan, 1,503 .... K-12
Perry, Houston/Peach, 9,452 .... J-6
• Phillipsburg, Tift, 1,044 .... M-6
Pooler, Chatham, 4,453 .... K-13
Port Wentworth, Chatham, 4,012 .... K-13
Porterdale, Newton, 1,278 .... F-5
Powder Springs, Cobb, 6,893 .... E-3
Preston, Webster, 388 .... K-3
• Putney, Dougherty, 3,108 .... M-5
Quitman, Brooks, 5,292 .... O-6
Radium Springs, Dougherty M-5
• Raoul, Habersham, 1,666 .... C-6
• Redan, DeKalb, 24,376 .... F-14
• Reed Creek, Hart, 1,854 .... D-8
Rehoboth, DeKalb E-13
Reidsville, Tattnall, 2,469 .... K-11
Reynolds, Taylor, 1,166 .... I-5
Richland, Stewart, 1,668 .... K-3
Richmond Hill, Bryan, 2,934 .... K-13
Rincon, Effingham, 2,697 .... J-13
Ringgold, Catoosa, 1,675 .... B-2
Riverdale, Clayton, 9,359 .... G-12
Riverside, Floyd D-2
• Robins AFB, Houston, 3,092 .... I-6
Rochelle, Wilcox, 1,510 .... K-7
Rockmart, Polk, 3,356 .... E-2
Rome, Floyd, 30,326 .... D-2
Rossville, Walker, 3,601 .... B-2
Roswell, Fulton, 47,923 .... E-4
Royston, Franklin/Hart/Madison, 2,758 .... D-8
Saint Marys, Camden, 8,187 .... O-12
• Saint Simons, Glynn, 12,026 .... N-13
Sandersville, Washington, 6,290 .... H-9
• Sandy Springs, Fulton, 67,842 .... E-4
Sardis, Burke, 1,116 .... H-11
Savannah, Chatham, 137,560 .... K-13
• Scottdale, DeKalb, 8,636 .... F-13
• Shannon, Floyd, 1,703 .... D-2
Shellman, Randolph, 1,162 .... L-3
Sherwood Forest, Floyd D-2
• Skidaway Island, Chatham, 4,495 .... K-14
Smyrna, Cobb, 30,981 .... E-4
Snellville, Gwinnett, 12,084 .... E-5
Social Circle, Newton/Walton, 2,755 .... F-6
• Soperton, Treutlen, 2,797 .... J-9
• South Augusta, Richmond, 55,998 .... G-10
Sparks, Cook, 1,205 .... N-7
Sparta, Hancock, 1,710 .... G-8
Springfield, Effingham, 1,415 .... J-13
Statenville, Echols O-8
Statesboro, Bulloch, 15,854 .... J-11
Statham, Barrow, 1,360 .... E-6
Stockbridge, Henry, 3,359 .... F-5
Stone Mountain, DeKalb, 6,494 .... F-13
Sugar Hill, Gwinnett, 4,557 .... D-5
Summerville, Chattooga, 5,025 .... C-1
• Sunnyside, Ware, 1,506 .... N-10
Suwanee, Gwinnett, 2,412 .... E-5
Swainsboro, Emanuel, 7,361 .... I-10
Sylvania, Screven, 2,871 .... I-12
Sylvester, Worth, 5,702 .... M-6
Talbotton, Talbot, 1,046 .... I-4
Tallapoosa, Haralson, 2,805 .... F-1
Temple, Carroll, 1,870 .... F-2
Tennille, Washington, 1,552 .... H-9
Thomaston, Upson, 9,127 .... H-4
Thomasville, Thomas, 17,457 .... O-5
Thomson, McDuffie, 6,862 .... F-9
Thunderbolt, Chatham, 2,786 .... K-14
Tifton, Tift, 14,215 .... M-7
Toccoa, Stephens, 8,266 .... C-7
Trenton, Dade, 1,994 .... B-1
Trion, Chattooga, 1,661 .... C-1
• Tucker, DeKalb, 25,781 .... E-13
Twin City, Emanuel, 1,466 .... I-10
Tybee Island, Chatham, 2,842 .... K-14
Tyrone, Fayette, 2,724 .... G-4
Unadilla, Dooly, 1,620 .... J-6
Union City, Fulton, 8,375 .... F-4
Union Point, Greene, 1,753 .... F-8
• Unionville, Tift, 2,710 .... M-7
Valdosta, Lowndes, 39,806 .... O-7
Vidalia, Montgomery/Toombs, 11,078 .... J-10
Vienna, Dooly, 2,708 .... K-6
Villa Rica, Carroll/Douglas, 6,542 .... F-2
• Vinings, Cobb, 7,417 .... F-12
Wadley, Jefferson, 2,473 .... H-10
Walthourville, Liberty, 2,024 .... L-12
Warner Robins, Houston, 43,726 .... I-6
Warrenton, Warren, 2,056 .... G-9
Washington, Wilkes, 4,279 .... F-9
Watkinsville, Oconee, 1,600 .... E-7
Waycross, Pierce/Ware, 16,410 .... N-10
Waynesboro, Burke, 5,701 .... H-11
• West Augusta, Richmond, 27,637 .... F-11
West Point, Harris/Troup, 3,571 .... H-2
Westoak, Cobb E-4
• Westside, Hall, 2,180 .... D-6
• Whitemarsh Island, Chatham, 2,824 .... K-14
Willacoochee, Atkinson, 1,205 .... M-8
• Wilmington Island, Chatham, 11,230 .... K-14
Winder, Barrow, 7,373 .... E-6
Woodbine, Camden, 1,212 .... O-12
Woodbury, Meriwether, 1,429 .... H-3
Woodstock, Cherokee, 4,361 .... E-4
Wrens, Jefferson, 2,414 .... G-10
Wrightsville, Johnson, 2,331 .... I-9
Zebulon, Pike, 1,035 .... H-4

Explanation of symbols: •– Census Designated Place (CDP)

Hawaii

General Help Numbers:

Governor's Office
State Capitol
415 S Beretania St
Honolulu, HI 96813
http://gov.state.hi.us

808-586-0034
Fax 808-586-0006
7:45AM-5PM

Attorney General's Office
425 Queen St
Honolulu, HI 96813
www.state.hi.us/ag

808-586-1500
Fax 808-586-1239
7:45AM-4:30PM

Legislative Records
Hawaii Legislature
415 S Beretania St
Honolulu, HI 96813
www.capitol.hawaii.gov

808-587-0700
Fax 808-586-3584
9AM-5PM

State Archives
Iolani Palace Grounds
Honolulu, HI 96813
www.state.hi.us/dags/archives

808-586-0329
Fax 808-586-0330
9AM-4PM

State Specifics:

Capital:	Honolulu
	Honolulu County
Time Zone:	HT (Hawaii Standard Time)
Number of Counties:	4
Population:	1,257,608
Web Site:	www.state.hi.us

State Agencies

Criminal Records

Hawaii Criminal Justice Data Center, Liane Moriyama, Administrator, 465 S King St, Room 101, Honolulu, HI 96813; 808-587-3106, 8AM-4PM.

www.state.hi.us/hcjdc/

Indexing & Storage: Records are available from the 1930's. It takes 1 to 20 days before new records are available for inquiry. Records are indexed on in an electronic statewide repository of criminal history records.

Searching: Include the following in your request-any aliases. Also helpful are gender, date of birth, Social Security Number. Submission of fingerprints is an option. 99% of the records are fingerpirnt-supported.

Access by: mail, in person.

Fee & Payment: The search fee for a name-based criminal record search is $15.00. A fingerprint-based search is $25.00. A public access (convictions only) printout, available only in-person at this office or at main police stations, is $10.00. Certification fee: $10.00. Fee payee: Director of Finance, State of Hawaii. Prepayment

required. Money orders and cashiers' checks are the only acceptable methods of payment. No credit cards accepted.

Mail search: Turnaround time: 5 to 7 days. A SASE is requested.

In person search: The public may access conviction information by computer on-site.

Statewide Court Records

Administrative Director of Courts, 417 S. King St, Honolulu, HI 96813; 808-539-4900, 808-539-4909 (Public Affairs Office), 808-539-4855 (Fax), 7:45AM-4:30PM.

www.courts.state.hi.us/index.jsp

Note: Except for certain online research capabilities, all court record access must be done at the local level.

Access by: online.

Online search: Free online access to Circuit Court and Family Court records is available at www.courts.state.hi.us (click on "Search Court Records"). Search by name or case number. These records are not considered "official" for FCRA compliant searches. Also, opinions from the appellate court are available from the home web page site.

Sexual Offender Registry

Access to Records is Restricted

Hawaii Criminal Justice Data Center, Sexual Offender Registry, 465 S King St, Room 101, Honolulu, HI 96813; 808-587-3106, 8AM-4PM.

www.state.hi.us/hcjdc/

Note: The sexual offender registration database is not available for name searches. The court will decide if the offender's information is necessary to protect the public.

Incarceration Records

Hawaii Department of Public Safety, Hawaii Criminal Justice Data Center, 465 South King Street, Room 101, Honolulu, HI 96813; 808-587-3100, 7:45AM-4:30PM.

www.hawaii.gov/hcjdc/

Indexing & Storage: Records are available on current and former inmates. It takes 1 to 20 days before new records are available for inquiry.

Searching: Include the following in your request-name; DOB and SSN helpful.

Access by: mail.

Fee & Payment: Fee for search is $15.00. Fee payee: Department of Public Safety Money orders and cashiers' checks are the only acceptable methods of payment.

Mail search: Turnaround time: 7 to 10 days. A SASE is requested.

Corporation, Trade Name, Limited Partnership, Assumed Name, Limited Liability Company, Limited Liability Partnerships Trademarks, Servicemarks,

Business Registration Division, PO Box 40, Honolulu, HI 96810 (Courier: 1010 Richard St, 1st Floor, Honolulu, HI 96813); 808-586-2727, 808-586-2733 (Fax), 7:45AM-4:30PM.

www.businessregistrations.com

Indexing & Storage: Records are available from 1859 to present for active entities, 1900 to present for inactive entities. New records are available for inquiry immediately.

Searching: There are no access restrictions. Records are open to the public. Include the following in your request-full name of business. In addition to the articles of incorporation, corporation records include the following information: Annual Reports, Officers, Directors,

DBAs, Prior (merged) names, Inactive and Reserved names.

Access by: mail, phone, fax, in person, online.

Fee & Payment: There is no search fee. The copy fee is $.25 per page. Fee payee: Business Registration Division. Prepayment required. Personal checks accepted. No credit cards accepted.

Mail search: Turnaround time: 2 weeks. A SASE is requested.

Phone search: They will confirm data over the phone or let you know how many copies to prepay.

Fax search: Same criteria as mail searches.

In person search: Turnaround time is while you wait.

Online search: Online access to business names is available through the Internet at www.businessregistrations.com. There are no fees, the system is open 24 hours. For assistance during business hours, call 808-586-2727. Tax license searching is available free at www.ehawaiigov.org/serv/taxpayer. Search by name, ID number of DBA name.

Other access: Bulk data can be purchased online through ehawaiigov.com. Visit the website or call 808-587-4220 for more information.

Uniform Commercial Code, Federal and State Tax Liens, Real Estate Recordings

UCC Division, Bureau of Conveyances, PO Box 2867, Honolulu, HI 96803 (Courier: Dept. of Land & Natural Resources, 1151 Punchbowl St, Honolulu, HI 96813); 808-587-0154, 808-587-4380 (Fax), 7:45AM-4:30PM.

www.state.hi.us/dlnr/bc/bc.html

Indexing & Storage: Records are available from 1845. Records are on microfiche from 1976 through 02/28/02. It takes 1 day before new records are available for inquiry.

Searching: Use search request form UCC-11. Include the following in your request-debtor name. A UCC record does not include tax liens; a separate search is required.

Access by: mail, in person, online.

Fee & Payment: Fees are $25.00 per debtor name plus $5.00 for each financing statement and statement of assignment reported. Copies cost $1.00 per page. Fee payee: Bureau of Conveyances. Prepayment required. An initial fee of $25.00 must be paid in advance, additional fees will be invoiced. Personal checks accepted. No credit cards accepted.

Mail search: Turnaround time: 1 week. A SASE is requested.

In person search: There is self-service in the public reference room.

Online search: Search the indices from 1976 forward at http://166.122.230.66/boc/. Search by grantor, grantee, business name. Includes real estate recordings.

Sales Tax Registrations

State does not impose sales tax.

Birth Certificates

State Department of Health, Vital Records Section, PO Box 3378, Honolulu, HI 96801 (Courier: 1250

Punchbowl St, Room 103, Honolulu, HI 96813); 808-586-4533, 7:45AM-2:30PM.

www.hawaii.gov/doh

Indexing & Storage: Records are available from mid 1800's to present. It takes 10-20 days before new records are available for inquiry. Records are indexed on inhouse computer.

Searching: Must have a signed release from person of record or immediate family member. Include the following in your request-full name, names of parents, mother's maiden name, date of birth, place of birth, relationship to person of record, reason for information request. Include a daytime phone number in your request. The Vital Records office will call you collect to verify information, if required. If your record is prior to July, 1909, you must know the Island and District of event.

Access by: mail, in person, online.

Fee & Payment: Fees are $10.00 for first copy and $4.00 for each subsequent copy of same record. Fee payee: State Department of Health. Prepayment required. Money orders, certified checks, and cashier's checks are accepted. No credit cards accepted.

Mail search: Turnaround time: 4 to 6 weeks. No SASE is required.

In person search: Turnaround time is 10 days or more.

Online search: Records may requested from https://www.ehawaiigov.org/doh/vitrec/html/down.html. The turnaround time is the same as mail requests.

Expedited service: Expedited service is available for mail searches. Turnaround time: 5 to 7 days. You must inclose a return pre-paid, self-addressed envelope.

Death Records

State Department of Health, Vital Records Section, PO Box 3378, Honolulu, HI 96801 (Courier: 1250 Punchbowl St, Room 103, Honolulu, HI 96813); 808-586-4533, 7:45AM-2:30PM.

www.hawaii.gov/doh

Indexing & Storage: Records are available from mid 1800's on, but early records are not complete. It takes 10-20 days before new records are available for inquiry. Records are indexed on inhouse computer.

Searching: Must have a signed release from immediate family member. Include the following in your request-full name, date of death, place of death, names of parents, relationship to person of record, reason for information request. Include a daytime phone number in your request. The agency will return requests if not. For records prior to July 1909, you must include the Island and District of the event.

Access by: mail, in person.

Fee & Payment: The fee is $10.00 per record and $4.00 for each subsequent copy of same record. Fee payee: State Department of Health. Prepayment required. Cashier's checks and money orders accepted. No credit cards accepted.

Mail search: Turnaround time: 4 to 6 weeks.

In person search: Turnaround time is 10 days or more.

Expedited service: Expedited service is available for mail searches. Turnaround time: 5 to 7 days.

You must inclose a return pre-paid, self-addressed envelope.

Marriage Certificates

State Department of Health, Vital Records Section, PO Box 3378, Honolulu, HI 96801 (Courier: 1250 Punchbowl St, Room 103, Honolulu, HI 96813); 808-586-4533, 7:45AM-2:30PM.

www.hawaii.gov/doh

Indexing & Storage: Records are available from mid 1800's to present. It takes 3-5 days before new records are available for inquiry. Records are indexed on inhouse computer.

Searching: Must have a signed release from person of record or immediate family member. Include the following in your request-names of husband and wife, wife's maiden name, date of marriage, place or county of marriage, names of parents, relationship to person of record, reason for information request. Include a daytime phone number. The office will return requests otherwise. For records prior to July 1909, include the Island of the event.

Access by: mail, in person, online.

Fee & Payment: Fee is $10.00 per record and $4.00 for subsequent copy of same record. Fee payee: State Department of Health. Prepayment required. Cashier's check and money orders accepted. No credit cards accepted.

Mail search: Turnaround time: 4 to 6 weeks. No SASE is required.

In person search: Turnaround time is 10 days or more.

Online search: Records may requested from https://www.ehawaiigov.org/doh/vitrec/html/down .html. The turnaround time is the same as mail requests.

Expedited service: Expedited service is available for mail searches. Turnaround time: 5 to 7 days. You must inclose a return pre-paid, self-addressed envelope.

Divorce Records

State Department of Health, Vital Records Section, PO Box 3378, Honolulu, HI 96801 (Courier: 1250 Punchbowl St, Room 103, Honolulu, HI 96813); 808-586-4533, 7:45AM-2:30PM.

www.hawaii.gov/health

Indexing & Storage: Records are available from July 1951 to Dec 2002. Prior records and those from Jan.2003 forward are held by the clerk of the court granting the decree. Records are indexed on manually.

Searching: Must have a signed release from person of record or immediate family member. Include the following in your request-names of husband and wife, date of divorce, place of divorce, relationship to person of record, reason for information request. Include a daytime phone number in your request. This office will call you collect to verify information, if required.

Access by: mail, in person.

Fee & Payment: The fee is $10.00 per record and $4.00 each additional copy of same record. Fee payee: State Department of Health. Prepayment required. Cashier's check and money orders accepted. No credit cards accepted.

Mail search: Turnaround time: 4 to 6 weeks.

In person search: Results are mailed. Turnaround time is 10 days or more.

Expedited service: Expedited service is available for mail searches. Turnaround time: 5 to 7 days. You must inclose a return pre-paid, self-addressed envelope.

Workers' Compensation Records

Labor & Industrial Relations, Disability Compensation Division, 830 Punchbowl St, Room 209, Honolulu, HI 96813; 808-586-9174, 808-586-9219 (Fax), 7:45AM-4:30PM.

www.state.hi.us/hrd/workcmp.html

Indexing & Storage: Records are available for the past 8 years. Prior records are in the State Archives but still must be requested through the Disability Compensation Division. It takes 2 to 7 days from receipt before new records are available for inquiry. Records are indexed on inhouse computer. Records are normally destroyed after 40 years.

Searching: Must have a signed release from injured party or HI circuit court order signed by a judge. Include the following in your request-claimant name, Social Security Number, claim number.

Access by: mail, fax, in person.

Fee & Payment: There is no search fee, copy fee is $.05 per page. Fee payee: Director of Finance. Prepayment required. Personal checks accepted. No credit cards accepted.

Mail search: Turnaround time: 6 to 12 weeks. A SASE is requested.

Fax search: Same criteria as mail searches.

In person search: In person requests only saves mail time; results are mailed.

Driver Records

Traffic Violations Bureau, Abstract Section, 1111 Alakea St, 2nd Fl, Honolulu, HI 96813; 808-538-5530, 808-961-7470 (Hawaii Court), 808-244-2800 (Maui Court), 808-246-3330 (Kauai Court), 808-538-5520 (Fax), 7:45AM-9:PM.

www.hawaii.gov/dot/highways/

Note: The TVB issues two types of abstracts. The Public Abstract shows moving violation convictions, but not juvenile reocrds unless signed for. The Court Abstract shows all action, whether convicted or dismissed.

Indexing & Storage: Records are available for three years for moving violations, five years for no-faults, and ten years for DUIs. Accidents are only listed if a citation is issued for the accident. The driver's address is screened from the record. It takes less than 2 weeks before new records are available for inquiry. Records are normally destroyed after 5 years.

Searching: The Public Abstract is given to insurers and employers. Casual requesters can obtain records; however, personal information is not released. The driver's full name, DOB and either license number or SSN are needed when ordering. The webpage for the courts is www.courts.state.hi.us/index.jsp.

Access by: mail, in person.

Fee & Payment: The fee is $7.00 per request. There is a full charge even if no record is found. Copies of tickets are only available from the court where ticket was issued. The fees are $1.00 for first copy, $.50 each additional copy. Fee payee: District Court. Prepayment required. The state requires a money order or cashier's check for mail-in requests; in-person requesters may use cash, credit cards, or business checks. Visa/MC and JCB accepted.

Mail search: Turnaround time: 2 - 5 days.

In person search: Walk-in requests can be processed in five to twenty minutes at any county district traffic court or at the Traffic Violations Bureau Office in Honolulu.

Other access: Magnetic tape ordering is available in Hawaii for frequent or large orders. The fee is $7.00 per request. Turnaround time is 48 hours. Call the Abstracts Section at 808-538-5530 for more information.

Expedited service: Will expedite delivery if a pre-paid envelope is provided.

Vehicle Ownership, Vehicle Identification

Access to Records is Restricted

Accident Reports

Records not maintained by a state level agency.

Note: Accident reports are not available from the state. Records are maintained at the county level at the police departments and are only available to those involved.

Vessel Ownership, Vessel Registration

Land & Natural Resources, Division of Boating & Recreation, 333 Queen St Rm 300, Honolulu, HI 96813; 808-587-1970, 808-587-1977 (Fax), 7:45AM-4:30PM.

www.hawaii.gov/dlnr/dbor/dbor.html

Indexing & Storage: Records are available 1950s, computerized since 1994, and on microfiche from 1987 to 1994. It takes 30 days or less before new records are available for inquiry.

Searching: Requests must be made in writing and must include a statement revealing the purpose for which the information will be used. Name or hull ID number or registration number is required for search. The following data is not released: addresses or phone numbers.

Access by: mail, fax, in person.

Fee & Payment: There is no search fee.

Mail search: Turnaround time: 1 to 2 days. No SASE is required.

Fax search: Same criteria as mail searching.

In person search: Turnaround time is usually the same day.

Voter Registration

Records not maintained by a state level agency.

Note: Voter information is maintained by the County Clerks. Here are contact numbers. City and County of Honolulu 808-523-4293; County of Hawaii 808-961-8277; County of Maui 808-270-7749; County of Kauai 808-241-6350.

GED Certificates

Department of Education, GED Records, 634 Pensacola, #222, Honolulu, HI 96814; 808-594-0170, 808-594-0181 (Fax), 8AM-4PM.

Note: GED certificates are not issued by this agency. Instead, high school diplomas are issued to qualified individuals. This office in moving in late 2004.

Searching: Include the following in your request-signed release, date of birth, Social Security Number. Knowing the approximate date and location of the test is helpful. The requirements are for both verifications and copies of transcripts.

Access by: mail, fax, in person.

Fee & Payment: Fees will vary, depending on the record location site.

Mail search: Turnaround time: 5 to 10 days. A SASE is required.

Fax search: Same criteria as mail search.

In person search: Same criteria as mail search.

Hunting and Fishing License Information

Access to Records is Restricted

Land & Natural Resources Department, 1151 Punchbowl St, Kalanimokui Bldg, Honolulu, HI 96813; 808-587-0100 (Fishing), 808-587-0166 (Hunting), 7:45AM-4:30PM.

www.state.hi.us/dlnr

Note: Fishing information is kept by the Aquatic Resources Division; Hunting information by the Division of Forestry & Wildlife. 808-587-0115 is fax for Fishing; 808-587-0160 is fax for Hunting. Limited record information is released to the public. Generally, this department's information is only released to law enforcement agencies. There is no "search engine" here.

Hawaii State Licensing Agencies

Licenses Searchable Online

Acupuncturist #4 .... www.ehawaiigov.org/serv/pvl
Architect #19 .... www.ehawaiigov.org/serv/pvl
Auction #42 .... www.ehawaiigov.org/serv/pvl
Bank/Bank Agencies/Offices #28 .... www.hawaii.gov/dcca/dfi/regulated.html
Barber Shop/Barber/Barber Apprentice #5 ..... www.ehawaiigov.org/serv/pvl
Beauty Instructor #5 .... www.ehawaiigov.org/serv/pvl
Beauty Operator/School/Shop #5 .... www.ehawaiigov.org/serv/pvl
Cemetery #42 .... www.ehawaiigov.org/serv/pvl
Certified Public Accountant - CPA #21 .... www.ehawaiigov.org/serv/pvl
Chiropractor #6 .... www.ehawaiigov.org/serv/pvl
Collection Agency #42 .... www.ehawaiigov.org/serv/pvl
Condominium Mgr. Agent/Hotel Operator #34 . www.ehawaiigov.org/serv/pvl
Contractor #27 .... www.ehawaiigov.org/serv/pvl
Credit Union #28 .... www.hawaii.gov/dcca/dfi/regulated.html
Dental Hygienist #7 .... www.ehawaiigov.org/serv/pvl
Dentist #7 .... www.ehawaiigov.org/serv/pvl
Drug (Prescription) Dist./Whlse. #16 .... www.ehawaiigov.org/serv/pvl
Elected Officials Financial Disclosure #41 ...... www.state.hi.us/ethics/noindex/pubrec.htm
Electrician #29 .... www.ehawaiigov.org/serv/pvl
Electrologist #42 .... www.ehawaiigov.org/serv/pvl
Elevator Mechanic #29 .... www.ehawaiigov.org/serv/pvl
Emergency Medical Personnel #13 .... www.hawaii.gov.dcca.pvi
Employment Agency #42 .... www.ehawaiigov.org/serv/pvl
Engineer #19 .... www.ehawaiigov.org/serv/pvl
Escrow Company #28 .... www.hawaii.gov/dcca/dfi/regulated.html
Financial Services Loan Company #28 .... www.hawaii.gov/dcca/dfi/regulated.html
Hearing Aid Dealer/Fitter #30 .... www.ehawaiigov.org/serv/pvl
Insurance Adjuster #31 .... www.ehawaiigov.org/serv/hils
Insurance Agent #31 .... www.ehawaiigov.org/serv/hils
Insurance Producer/Solicitor #31 .... www.ehawaiigov.org/serv/hils
Landscape Architect #19 .... www.ehawaiigov.org/serv/pvl
Lobbyist #41 .... www.state.hi.us/ethics/noindex/pubrec.htm
Marriage & Family Therapist #42 .... www.ehawaiigov.org/serv/pvl
Massage Therapist/Establishment #42 .... www.ehawaiigov.org/serv/pvl
Mechanic #42 .... www.ehawaiigov.org/serv/pvl
Medical Doctor #13 .... www.hawaii.gov.dcca.pvi
Mortgage Broker/Solicitor #42 .... www.ehawaiigov.org/serv/pvl
Motor Vehicle Dealer/Broker/Seller #42 .... www.ehawaiigov.org/serv/pvl
Motor Vehicle Repair Dealer #42 .... www.ehawaiigov.org/serv/pvl
Naturopathic Physician #10 .... www.ehawaiigov.org/serv/pvl
Nurse #14 .... www.ehawaiigov.org/serv/pvl
Nursing Home Administrator #12 .... www.ehawaiigov.org/serv/pvl
Occupational Therapist #17 .... www.ehawaiigov.org/serv/pvl
Optician, Dispensing #8 .... www.ehawaiigov.org/serv/pvl
Optometrist #11 .... www.ehawaiigov.org/serv/pvl
Osteopathic Physician #13 .... www.hawaii.gov.dcca.pvi
Pest Control Field Rep./Operator #32 .... www.ehawaiigov.org/serv/pvl
Pharmacist #16 .... www.ehawaiigov.org/serv/pvl
Pharmacy #16 .... www.ehawaiigov.org/serv/pvl
Physical Therapist #17 .... www.ehawaiigov.org/serv/pvl
Physician Assistant #13 .... www.hawaii.gov.dcca.pvi
Pilot, Port #42 .... www.ehawaiigov.org/serv/pvl
Plumber #29 .... www.ehawaiigov.org/serv/pvl
Podiatrist #13 .... www.hawaii.gov.dcca.pvi
Private Detective/Investigation Agency #18 .... www.ehawaiigov.org/serv/pvl
Psychologist #20 .... www.ehawaiigov.org/serv/pvl
Public Accountant - PA #21 .... www.ehawaiigov.org/serv/pvl
Real Estate Agent/Broker/Sales #34 .... www.ehawaiigov.org/serv/pvl
Real Estate Appraiser #9 .... www.ehawaiigov.org/serv/pvl

Savings & Loan Association #28 .... www.hawaii.gov/dcca/dfi/regulated.html
Savings Bank #28 .... www.hawaii.gov/dcca/dfi/regulated.html
Security Guard/Agency #18 .... www.ehawaiigov.org/serv/pvl
Social Worker #42 .... www.ehawaiigov.org/serv/pvl
Speech Pathologist/Audiologist #22 .... www.ehawaiigov.org/serv/pvl
Surveyor, Land #19 .... www.ehawaiigov.org/serv/pvl
Timeshare #42 .... www.ehawaiigov.org/serv/pvl
Travel Agency #42 .... www.ehawaiigov.org/serv/pvl
Trust Company #28 .... www.hawaii.gov/dcca/dfi/regulated.html
Veterinarian #23 .... www.ehawaiigov.org/serv/pvl

Hawaii Licensing Quick Finder

Acupuncturist #4 808-586-3000
Airport-related Occupation #37 808-836-6533
Architect #19 808-586-3000
Attorney #38 808-537-1868
Auction #42 808-586-2699
Bank/Bank Agencies/Offices #28 808-586-2820
Barber Shop/Barber/Barber Appren. #5 808-586-3000
Beauty Instructor #5 808-586-3000
Beauty Operator/School/Shop #5 808-586-3000
Boxer #24 808-586-2701
Boxing Mgr./Matchmaker/Physician #24 808-586-2701
Boxing Professional (Promoter) #24 808-586-2701
Boxing Second #24 808-586-2701
Boxing Timekeeper/Judge/Referee #24 808-586-2701
Cable Franchise #26 808-586-2620
Cemetery #42 808-586-2699
Certified Public Accountant - CPA #21.808-586-3000
Chiropractor #6 808-586-3000
Clinical Lab Technician #40 808-453-6653
Clinical Lab Cytotechnologist #40 808-453-6653
Clinical Lab Director #40 808-453-6653
Clinical Lab Technologist/Spec. #40 808-453-6653
Collection Agency #42 808-586-2699
Condominium Agent/hotel operator#34. 808-587-3222
Condominium Managing Agent #34 808-587-3222
Contractor #27 808-586-3000
Credit Union #28 808-586-2820
Dental Hygienist #7 808-586-3000
Dentist #7 808-586-3000
Drivers License #39 808-532-7730
Drug (Prescription) Dist./Whlse. #16 808-586-2694
Educational Administrator #35 808-586-3420
Elected Officials Fin'l Disclosure #41 ... 808-587-0460
Electrician #29 808-586-3000

Electrologist #42 808-586-2699
Elevator Mechanic #29 808-586-3000
Embalmer #43 808-586-8000
Emergency Medical Personnel #13 808-586-3000
Employment Agency #42 808-586-2699
Engineer #19 808-586-3000
Escrow Company #28 808-586-2820
Financial Services Loan Company #28. 808-586-2820
Hearing Aid Dealer/Fitter #30 808-586-3000
Insurance Adjuster #31 808-586-2788
Insurance Agent #31 808-586-2788
Insurance Producer/Solicitor #31 808-586-2788
Investment Advisor/Rep. #25 808-586-2730
Landscape Architect #19 808-586-3000
Lobbyist #41 808-587-0460
Marine License, Commercial #36 808-587-0100
Marriage & Family Therapist #42 808-586-2693
Massage Therapist/Establishm't #42 ... 808-586-2699
Mechanic #42 808-586-2701
Medical Doctor #13 808-586-3000
Mortgage Broker/Solicitor #42 808-586-3000
Motor Vehicle Dealer/Broker/Seller #42 808-586-2699
Motor Vehicle Repair Dealer #42 808-586-2699
Naturopathic Physician #10 808-586-3000
Notary Public #3 808-586-1216
Nuclear Medicine Technologist #44 808-586-4700
Nurse / Nurses' Aide #14 808-586-3000
Nursing Home Administrator #12 808-586-3000
Occupational Therapist #17 808-586-2698
Optician, Dispensing #8 808-586-3000
Optometrist #11 808-586-2694
Osteopathic Physician #13 808-586-3000
Pest Control Field Rep./Operator #32. 808-586-3000
Pesticide Applicator #2 808-973-9409

Pesticide Applicator, Private #2 808-973-9424
Pesticide Dealer #2 808-973-9413
Pesticide Product #2 808-973-9414
Pharmacist #16 808-586-2694
Pharmacy #16 808-586-2694
Physical Therapist #17 808-586-2694
Physician Assistant #13 808-586-3000
Pilot, Port #42 808-586-2699
Plumber #29 808-586-3000
Podiatrist #13 808-586-2708
Private Detective #18 808-586-3000
Private Detective/Inv. Agency #18 808-586-3000
Psychologist #20 808-586-3000
Public Accountant - PA #21 808-586-3000
Radiation Therapist #44 808-586-4700
Radiographer #44 808-586-4700
Real Estate Agent/Broker/Sales #34 ... 808-587-3222
Real Estate Appraiser #9 808-586-3000
Sanitarian #43 808-586-4576
Savings & Loan Association #28 808-586-2820
Savings Bank #28 808-586-2820
Securities Salesperson #25 808-586-2730
Security Guard/Agency #18 808-586-3000
Shorthand Reporter #1 808-539-4226
Social Worker #42 808-586-2696
Speech Pathologist/Audiologist #22 808-586-3000
Surveyor, Land #19 808-586-3000
Tattoo Artist #43 808-586-8000
Taxi Certifications #39 808-532-7730
Teacher #35 808-586-3392
Timeshare #42 808-586-2699
Travel Agency #42 808-586-2699
Trust Company #28 808-586-2820
Veterinarian #23 808-586-3000

Hawaii Licensing Agency Information

1 Board of Certified Shorthand Reporters, 777 Punchbowl St, Honolulu, HI 96813; 808-539-4226, Fax: 808-539-4149. Email: csrhi@maui.net

2 Department of Agriculture, 1428 S. King St., Honolulu, HI 96814; 808-973-9401, Fax: 808-973-9418. www.hawaiiag.org/hdoa Email: hdoa.info@hawaii.gov

3 Department of Attorney General, Notary Public Office, 425 Queen St, Honolulu, HI 96813; 808-586-1216, Fax: 808-586-1205. www.state.hi.us/ag/notary_unit.htm

4 Department of Commerce & Consumer Affairs, Board of Acupuncture, PO Box 3469 (335 Merchant St., 96813), Honolulu, HI 96801; 808-586-2698, Fax: 808-586-2689. www.hawaii.gov/dcca/pvl/areas_acupuncture.html Email: acupuncture@dcca.hawaii.gov Search Database at www.ehawaiigov.org/serv/pvl

5 Department of Commerce & Consumer Affairs, Board of Barbering & Cosmetology, PO Box 3469

(1010 Richards St, 96813), Honolulu, HI 96801; 808-586-2696. www.state.hi.us/dcca/pvl/areas_barbering.html Email: barber_cosm@dcca.hawaii.gov Search Database at www.ehawaiigov.org/serv/pvl Note: Rosters are available for sale, however do not include personal info or addresses.

6 Department of Commerce & Consumer Affairs, Board of Chiropractic Examiners, PO Box 3469 (335 Merchant St., 96813), Honolulu, HI 96801; 808-586-2698, Fax: 808-586-2689. www.hawaii.gov/dcca/pvl/areas_chiropractor.html Email: chiropractor@dcca.hawaii.gov Search Database at www.ehawaiigov.org/serv/pvl

7 Department of Commerce & Consumer Affairs, Board of Dental Examiners, PO Box 3469 (1010 Richards St 96813), Honolulu, HI 96801; 808-586-2702. www.hawaii.gov/dcca/pvl/areas_dentist.html Email: dental@dcca.hawaii.gov Search Database at www.ehawaiigov.org/serv/pvl

8 Department of Commerce & Consumer Affairs, Dispensing Optician Program, PO Box 3469 (1010 Richards St, 96813), Honolulu, HI 96801; 808-586-3000, Fax: 808-586-3031. www.state.hi.us/dcca/pvl/areas_optometry.html Email: optician@dcca.state.hi.us Search Database at www.ehawaiigov.org/serv/pvl

9 Department of Commerce & Consumer Affairs, Professional & Vocational Licensing, Attn:REA, PO Box 3469, Honolulu, HI 96801; 808-586-2704. www.state.hi.us/dcca/pvl/areas_real_estate_appraiser.html Email: appraiser@dcca.state.hi.us Search Database at www.ehawaiigov.org/serv/pvl

10 Department of Commerce & Consumer Affairs, Board of Examiners in Naturopathy, PO Box 3469 (1010 Richards St, 96813), Honolulu, HI 96801; 808-586-2704, Fax: 808-586-3031. www.state.hi.us/dcca/pvl/areas_natropathy.html Email: naturopathy@dcca.state.hi.us Search Database at www.ehawaiigov.org/serv/pvl

11 Department of Commerce & Consumer Affairs, Board of Examiners in Optometry, PO Box 3469 (335 Merchant St. 3rd Fl, 96813), Honolulu, HI 96801; 808-586-2694. www.state.hi.us/dcca/pvl/areas_optometry.html Email: optometry@dcca.state.hi.us Search Database at www.ehawaiigov.org/serv/pvl

12 Department of Commerce & Consumer Affairs, Nursing Home Administrators Program, PO Box 3469 (335 Merchant St, 96813), Honolulu, HI 96801; 808-586-2695. www.hawaii.gov/dcca/pvl/areas_nursing_home.html Email: nursing_home@dcca.hawaii.gov Search Database at www.ehawaiigov.org/serv/pvl

13 Department of Commerce & Consumer Affairs, Board of Medical Examiners, PO Box 3469 (335 Merchant, 96813), Honolulu, HI 96801; 808-586-2708. www.hawaii.gov/dcca/pvl/areas_medical.html Email: medical@dcca.hawaii.gov Search Database at www.hawaii.gov.dcca.pvi

14 Department of Commerce & Consumer Affairs, Board of Nursing, PO Box 3469 (335 Merchant St, 96813), Honolulu, HI 96801; 808-586-2695. www.hawaii.gov/dcca/pvl/areas_nurse.html Email: nursing@dcca.hawaii.gov Search Database at www.ehawaiigov.org/serv/pvl

16 Department of Commerce & Consumer Affairs, Board of Pharmacy, PO Box 3469 (335 Merchant St. 3rd Fl, 96813), Honolulu, HI 96801; 808-586-2694. www.state.hi.us/dcca/pvl/areas_pharmacy.html Email: pharmacy@dcca.state.hi.us Search Database at www.ehawaiigov.org/serv/pvl

17 Department of Commerce & Consumer Affairs, Board of Physical Therapy, PO Box 3469 (335 Merchant St. 3rd Fl, 96813), Honolulu, HI 96801; 808-586-2694. www.state.hi.us/dcca/pvl/areas_physical_therapy.html Email: phys_therapy@dcca.state.hi.us Search Database at www.ehawaiigov.org/serv/pvl

18 Department of Commerce & Consumer Affairs, Board of Private Detectives & Guards, PO Box 3469 (335 Merchant St, 96813), Honolulu, HI 96801; 808-586-2701, Fax: 808-586-2589. www.hawaii.gov/dcca/pvl/areas_private_detective.html Email: detective@dcca.hawaii.gov Search Database at www.ehawaiigov.org/serv/pvl

19 Department of Commerce & Consumer Affairs, Architects & Surveyors, Board of Prof. Engineers, PO Box 3469 (1010 Richards St, 96813), Honolulu, HI 96801; 808-586-2702. www.hawaii.gov/dcca/pvl/areas_engineer.html Email: easla@dcca.hawaii.gov Search Database at www.ehawaiigov.org/serv/pvl

20 Department of Commerce & Consumer Affairs, Board of Psychology, PO Box 3469 (335 Merchant St Rm 301, 96813), Honolulu, HI 96801; 808-586-2693. www.hawaii.gov/dcca./pvl Email: psychology@hawaii.gov Search Database at www.ehawaiigov.org/serv/pvl

21 Department of Commerce & Consumer Affairs, Board of Public Accountancy, PO Box 3469 (1010 Richards St, 96813), Honolulu, HI 96801; 808-586-2696, Fax: 808-586-2874. www.hawaii.gov/dcca/pvl Email: accountancy@dcca.hawaii.gov

Search Database at www.ehawaiigov.org/serv/pvl Note: Search for CPA or PA. Also, they do sell/provide lists or other means of verification at (1) www.ehawaii.gov/pvllistbuilder (2) www.ehawaii.gov/subscription/html/.

22 Department of Commerce & Consumer Affairs, Board of Speech Pathology & Audiology, PO Box 3469 (335 Merchant St Rm 301, 96813), Honolulu, HI 96801; 808-586-2698. www.hawaii.gov/dcca/pvl Email: speech@dcca.hawaii.gov Search Database at www.ehawaiigov.org/serv/pvl

23 Department of Commerce & Consumer Affairs, Board of Veterinary Examiners, PO Box 3469 (1010 Richards St, 96813), Honolulu, HI 96801; 808-586-2696. www.state.hi.us/dcca/pvl/areas_veterinary.html Email: veterinary@dcca.hawaii.gov Search Database at www.ehawaiigov.org/serv/pvl Note: Rosters are available for sale, however do not include personal info or addresses.

24 Department of Commerce & Consumer Affairs, Boxing Commission, PO Box 3469 (1010 Richards St, 96813), Honolulu, HI 96801; 808-586-2701, Fax: 808-586-2689. Email: boxing@dcca.state.hi.us

25 Department of Commerce & Consumer Affairs, Business Registration Division, Securities Compliance Branch, PO Box 3469 (1010 Richards St, 96813), Honolulu, HI 96801; 808-586-2722, Fax: 808-586-2733. www.hawaii.gov/dcca/ocp/

26 Department of Commerce & Consumer Affairs, Cable TV Division, PO Box 541, Honolulu, HI 96809; 808-586-2620, Fax: 808-586-2625. www.hawaii.gov/dcca/catv

27 Department of Commerce & Consumer Affairs, Contractors License Board, PO Box 3469 335 Merchant St. (96813), Honolulu, HI 96801; 808-586-2700, Fax: 808-586-3031. www.state.hi.us/dcca/pvl/areas_contractor.html Email: contractor@dcca.hawaii.gov Search Database at www.ehawaiigov.org/serv/pvl

28 Department of Commerce & Consumer Affairs, Division of Financial Institutions, PO Box 2054 (335 Merchant St Rm 221), Honolulu, HI 96805; 808-586-2820, Fax: 808-586-2818. www.hawaii.gov/dcca/dfi Email: dfi@dcca.hawaii.gov Search Database at www.hawaii.gov/dcca/dfi/regulated.html

29 Department of Commerce & Consumer Affairs, Board of Electricians, Plumbers & Elevator Mechanics Licensing, PO Box 3469 (335 Merchant St., 96813), Honolulu, HI 96801; 808-586-2705. www.hawaii.gov/dcca/pvl/areas_electrician.html Email: elect_plumb@dcca.hawaii.gov Search Database at www.ehawaiigov.org/serv/pvl

30 Department of Commerce & Consumer Affairs, Hearing Aid Dealers & Fitters Program, PO Box 3469 (335 Merchant St., 96813), Honolulu, HI 96801; 808-586-2698, Fax: 808-586-2689. www.hawaii.gov/dcca/pvl/areas_hearing_aid.html Email: hearingaid@dcca.hawaii.gov Search Database at www.ehawaiigov.org/serv/pvl

31 Department of Commerce & Consumer Affairs, Insurance Division, Licensing Branch, 335 Merchant St #333, Honolulu, HI 96813; 808-586-2790, Fax: 808-587-6714.

www.ehawaiigov.org Email: inslic@dcca.hawaii.gov Search Database at www.ehawaiigov.org/serv/hils

32 Department of Commerce & Consumer Affairs, Pest Control Board, PO Box 3469 (335 Merchant St, 96813), Honolulu, HI 96801; 808-586-2705. www.hawaii.gov/dcca/pvl/areas_pest_control.html Email: pest_control@dcca.hawaii.gov Search Database at www.ehawaiigov.org/serv/pvl

34 Department of Commerce & Consumer Affairs, Real Estate Commission, 335 Merchant Street Rm 333, Honolulu, HI 96813; 808-586-2643. www.state.hi.us/hirec Email: hirec@dcca.state.hi.us Search Database at www.ehawaiigov.org/serv/pvl

35 Department of Education, Board of Education, PO Box 2360, Honolulu, HI 96804; 808-586-3332, Fax: 808-586-3433.

36 Department of Land & Natural Resources, Division of Aquatic Resources, 1151 Punch Bowl St Rm 330, Honolulu, HI 96813; 808-587-0100, Fax: 808-587-0115. www.state.hi.us/dlnr/dar Email: dlnr_aquatics@exec.state.hi.us

37 Department of Transportation, Airports Division, Airport District Manager, 300 Rodgers Blvd. # 12, Honolulu, HI 96819-1897; 808-836-6533, Fax: 808-836-6682. www.state.hi.us/dot/airports

38 Hawaii State Bar Association, 1132 Bishop St #906, Honolulu, HI 96813-2814; 808-537-1868, Fax: 808-521-7936. www.hsba.org

39 Motor Vehicle Licensing Division, City Square Driver License, 1199 Dillingham St Rm A101, Honolulu, HI 96817; 808-532-7730, Fax: 808-832-2904. Note: School Bus and Regular Bus Drivers are now part of the general "commercial drivers' license." No longer something that can be verified separately.

40 Department of Health, Laboratory Licensing, 2725 Waimano Home Rd, Pearl City, HI 96782; 808-453-6653, Fax: 808-453-6662.

41 State Ethics Commission, 1001 Bishop St, Pacific Tower #970, Honolulu, HI 96813; 808-587-0460, Fax: 808-587-0470. www.state.hi.us/ethics Email: ethics@hawaiiethics.org Search Database at www.state.hi.us/ethics/noindex/pubrec.htm

42 Department of Commerce & Consumer Affairs, Professional & Vocational Licensing Div-Programs, 1010 Richards St 1st Fl, Honolulu, HI 96813; 808-587-3295. www.state.hi.us/dcca/pvl/ Search Database at www.ehawaiigov.org/serv/pvl

43 Department of Health, Sanitation Branch, 591 Ala Moana Blvd, Honolulu, HI 96813; 808-586-8000, Fax: 808-586-4729. www.hawaii.gov/doh Email: san_info@ehsdmail.health.state.hi.us

44 Department of Health, Radiologic Technology Board, 591 Ala Moana Blvd, Honolulu, HI 96813-4921; 808-586-4700, Fax: 808-586-5838. Email: rtakata@sdmail.health.state.hi.us

Hawaii Federal Courts

The following list indicates the district and division name for each county in the state.

County/Court Cross Reference

Hawaii...Honolulu
Honolulu..Honolulu
Kalawao...Honolulu
Kauai..Honolulu
Maui...Honolulu

US District Court

District of Hawaii

Honolulu Division 300 Ala Moana Blvd, Rm C-338, Honolulu, HI 96850 (courier address: Use mail address for courier delivery) 808-541-1300, Fax: 808-541-1303. www.hid.uscourts.gov

Counties: All counties.

Indexing & Storage: New cases available in the index immediately after filing date. A microfiche index is also maintained.

Fee & Payment: Payment may be made by money order, cashier check, personal check. Payee: Clerk, U.S. District Court.

Phone Search: No searching by telephone.

In Person Search: Fee charged if court conducts your in person search for you.

PACER: PACER is available online at http://pacer.hid.uscourts.gov. Case records go back to October 1991. Records never purged. New civil records are online after 1 day. New criminal records online after 3 days.

U.S. Bankruptcy Court

District of Hawaii

Honolulu Division 1132 Bishop St, Suite 250-L, Honolulu, HI 96813 (courier address: Use mail address for courier delivery) 808-522-8100, Fax: 800-522-8120. www.hib.uscourts.gov

Counties: All counties.

Indexing & Storage: Cases indexed by debtor as well as by case number. New cases available in the index 24 hours after filing date.

Fee & Payment: Payment may be made by money order, cashier check, personal check. Debtor's checks are not accepted. Payee: U.S. Bankruptcy Court.

Phone Search: Only docket information available by phone. Automated voice case information service (VCIS) is available. Call VCIS at 808-522-8122.

In Person Search: Fee charged if court conducts your in person search for you.

PACER: PACER now on new ECF system at https://ecf.hib.uscourts.gov. No need to access old webRACER system. Case records go back to 1987. Records purged varies. New civil records are online after 1 day.

Electronic Filing: Electronic filing information online at https://ecf.hib.uscourts.gov

Standards for Federal Courts: The search fee is $20.00 per item (one party name or case number). Certification fee is $7.00 per document. Copy fee is $.50 per page. All fees standard unless noted in profile. Mail Search: always enclose a stamped self addressed envelope unless otherwise noted. Most courts accept fax requests or will suggest a copying/search vendor. Before releasing records, all courts require prepayment unless noted in profile.

Open records are located at the court unless otherwise noted. District courts index by defendant and plaintiff as well as by case number. Bankruptcy courts usually index by debtor and case number. While most courts now have their indexes on computer, many still maintain index card files as well.

The universal PACER sign-up number is 800-676-6856. Find PACER and the Party/Case Index on the Web at http://pacer.psc.uscourts.gov. PACER dial-up access is $.60 per minute. Also, courts offering internet access via RACER, PACER, Web-PACER or the new CM-ECF charge $.07 per page fee unless noted as free.

Hawaii County Courts

Court	Jurisdiction	No. of Courts	How Organized
Circuit Courts*	General	4	4 Circuits
District Courts*	Limited	7	4 Circuits

* Profiled in this Sourcebook.

CIVIL									
Court	Tort	Contract	Real Estate	Min. Claim	Max. Claim	Small Claims	Estate	Eviction	Domestic Relations
Circuit Courts*	X	X	X	$5000/ $10,000	No Max		X		X
District Courts*	X	X	X	$0	$20,000	$3500		X	

CRIMINAL					
Court	Felony	Misdemeanor	DWI/DUI	Preliminary Hearing	Juvenile
Circuit Courts*	X	X	X		X
District Courts*		X	X	X	

ADMINISTRATION

Administrative Director of Courts, Judicial Branch, 417 S King St, Honolulu, HI, 96813; 808-539-4900, Fax: 808-539-4855. www.courts.state.hi.us/index.jsp

COURT STRUCTURE

Hawaii's trial level is comprised of Circuit Courts (with Family Courts) and District Courts. These trial courts function in four judicial circuits: First (Oahu), Second (Maui/Molokai/Lanai), Third (Hawaii County), and Fifth (Kauai/Niihau). The Fourth Circuit was merged with the Third in 1943.

Circuit Courts are general jurisdiction and handle all jury trials, felony cases, and civil cases over $20,000, also probate and guardianship. The District Court handles criminal cases punishable by a fine and/or less then 1-yr imprisonment and some civil cases up to $20,000, also landlord/tenant and DUI cases.

ONLINE ACCESS

Free online access to all Circuit Court and family court records, and civil records from the District courts is available at the web site www.courts.state.hi.us (click on "Search Court Records"). Search by name or case number. These records are not considered "official" for FCRA compliant searches. Most courts have access back to mid 1980's. Also, opinions from the Appellate Court are available from the home page url.

ADD'L INFORMATION

Most Hawaii state courts offer a public access terminal to search records at the courthouse.

Civil cases down to $5000 minimum are found at the Circuit Court if a jury is involved.

Hawaii County

3rd Circuit Court Legal Documents Section PO Box 1007, Hilo, HI 96721-1007; 808-961-7404; Fax: 808-961-7416. Hours: 7:45AM-4:30PM (HT). *Felony, Misdemeanor, Civil Actions Over $5,000, Probate.* www.courts.state.hi.us

Civil Records: Access: Mail, fax, in person, online. Both court and visitors may perform in person searches. Search fee: $5.00 per name. Required to search: name, years to search. Civil cases indexed by defendant, plaintiff. Civil records on computer from 1988, index card system prior to 1988. Free record searching is at www.courts.state.hi.us/index.jsp. Click on "Search Court Records." Search by name or case number. Records go back to early 1900s.

Criminal Records: Access: Mail, fax, in person, online. Both court and visitors may perform in person searches. Search fee: $5.00 per name. Required to search: name, years to search. Criminal records on computer from 1988, index card system prior to 1988. Online access to criminal records is the same as civil.

General Information: Public Access terminal is available. No adoption, juvenile, dependencies,

confidential records released without court's approval. Will fax results to local or toll free line. Copy fee: $1.00 for first page, $.50 each add'l. Microfilm copy is $1.00 per page. Cert fee: $2.00. Payee: Clerk, 3rd Circuit Court. Personal checks accepted. Prepayment required. SASE required. Mail turnaround time 2 days depending upon staff coverage.

District Court PO Box 4879, Hilo, HI 96720; 808-961-7470; Fax: 808-961-7447. Hours: 7:45AM-4:30PM (HT). *Misdemeanor, Civil Actions Under $20,000, Eviction, Small Claims.* www.courts.state.hi.us/index.jsp

Civil Records: Access: Phone, fax, mail, in person, online. Both the court and visitors may perform in person searches. Search fee: $5.00 per name. Required to search: name, years to search, case number; also helpful: address. Civil cases indexed by defendant. Civil records on ledgers from statehood. Search records at www.courts.state.hi.us/index.jsp. Click on "Search Court Records."

Criminal Records: Access: Phone, fax, mail, in person, online. Both the court and visitors may perform in person searches. Search fee: $5.00 per name. Required to search: name, years to search, case

number; also helpful: address, DOB, SSN. Criminal records on computer since March 1996. Public access terminal available for criminal abstracts. Free record searching at www.courts.state.hi.us/index.jsp. Click on "Search Court Records."

General Information: Public Access terminal is available. (Available for criminal abstract record only.) No family court records released. Will fax results $2.00 1st page, $1.00 each add'l. Extra fee for out of state faxing. Copy fee: $1.00 for first page, $.50 each add'l. Off site storage- usual copy fees plus $5.00. Cert fee: $2.00. Payee: Clerk of the District Court. Personal checks accepted. Visa, MC accepted. Prepayment required. Mail requests: SASE requested. Turnaround time 1 week.

Honolulu County

1st Circuit Court Legal Documents Branch, 777 Punchbowl St, 1st Fl, Honolulu, HI 96813; 808-539-4300; Fax: 808-539-4314. 7:45AM-4:30PM (HT). *Felony, Civil Actions Over $5,000, Probate, Family.* www.courts.state.hi.us/index.jsp

Civil Records: Access: Mail, in person, online. Both court and visitors may perform in person searches. Search fee: $5.00 per name. Required to search:

name, years to search. Civil cases indexed by defendant, plaintiff. Civil records on computer from 1983, on microfiche and archived from 1900. Online access to Circuit Court & family court records free at http://166.122.201.55/jud/Hoohiki/index.htm?spawn= 1 Search by name or case #. Records go back to 1984.

Criminal Records: Access: Mail, in person, online. Both court and visitors may perform in person searches. Search fee: $5.00 per name. Required to search: name, years to search, DOB; also helpful: SSN. Criminal records on computer from 1983, on microfiche and archived from 1900. Online access to criminal records is the same as civil.

General Information: Public Access terminal is available. No adoptions, paternity or sealed records released. Copy fee: $1.00 for first page, $.50 each add'l. Microfilm service fee $5.00; cost of copies $1.00 per page. Cert fee: $2.00. Payee: 1st Circuit Court. Business checks accepted. Prepayment, SASE required. Mail turnaround time same day.

District Court - Civil Division
1111 Alakea St, 3rd Fl, Honolulu, HI 96813; 808-538-5151; Fax: 808-538-5444. Hours: 7:45AM-4:30PM (HT). *Civil Actions Under $20,000, Eviction, Small Claims.* www.courts.state.hi.us/index.jsp

Civil Records: Access: Phone, mail, in person, online. Both court and visitors may perform in person searches. Search fee: $5.00 per name. Required to search: name, years to search. Civil cases indexed by defendant. Civil records on computer from 1990; plaintiff index only on computer records. Free record searching is at www.courts.state.hi.us/index.jsp. Click on "Search Court Records."

General Information: Public Access terminal is available. No sealed records released. Call for fax back fee. No cert fee. Payee: District Court of the 1st Circuit. Personal checks accepted. Visa, MC, Discover accepted. Prepayment required. Mail requests: SASE required. Mail turnaround: 1 week.

District Court - Criminal Division
1111 Alakea St, 3rd Fl Judicial Services, Honolulu, HI 96813; 808-538-5100; Fax: 808-538-5111. Hours: 8AM-4:15PM (HT). *Misdemeanor, Traffic.* www.courts.state.hi.us/index.jsp

Criminal Records: Access: Fax, mail, in person, online. Only the court performs in person searches; visitors may not. Search fee: $5.00 per name. Required to search: name, years to search, SSN, signed release, aliases; also helpful: address, DOB. Free record searching at www.courts.state.hi.us/index.jsp. Click on "Search Court Records."

General Information: No sealed records released. No copy fee. No cert fee. Payee: District Court of the 1st Judicial Circuit. Business checks accepted. Prepayment required. Mail requests: SASE required. Mail turnaround time 1 week.

Kauai County

5th Circuit Court 3059 Umi St, Rm #101, Lihue, HI 96766; 808-246-3300; Fax: 808-246-3310. 7:45AM-4:30PM *elony, Misdemeanor, Civil Actions Over $20,000, Probate.* www.courts.state.hi.us

Civil Records: Access: Mail, in person, online. Both court and visitors may perform in person searches. Search fee: $5.00 per name. Required to search: name, years to search. Civil cases indexed by plaintiff & defendant. Civil records on computer from 1987, microfiche from 1960. Free record searching at www.courts.state.hi.us/index.jsp. Click on "Search Court Records." Search by name or case number. Records go back to 1900s.

Criminal Records: Access: Mail, in person, online. Both court and visitors may perform in person searches. Search fee: $5.00 per name. Required to search: name, years to search, DOB; also helpful: SSN. Criminal records on computer from 1987,

microfiche from 1960. Online access to criminal records is the same as civil.

General Information: Public Access terminal is available. No juvenile, dependencies records released. Copy fee: $1.00 for first page, $.50 each add'l. Cert fee: $2.00. Payee: 5th Circuit Court. Only cashiers checks, money orders or cash accepted. Prepayment required. Mail requests: SASE required. Mail turnaround time approx. 1 week.

District Court of the 5th Circuit - Civil
4357 Rice St, #101, Lihue, HI 96766; 808-246-3301; Fax: 808-241-7103. 7:45AM-4:30PM (HT). *Civil Actions Under $20,000, Eviction, Small Claims.* www.courts.state.hi.us/index.jsp

Civil Records: Access: Phone, fax, mail, in person, online. Both court and visitors may perform in person searches. Search fee: $5.00 per case. Required to search: name, years to search. Civil cases indexed by defendant. Civil records on index books. Free record searching is at www.courts.state.hi.us/index.jsp. Click on "Search Court Records."

General Information: No juvenile records released. Will fax results for $2.00 1st page, $1.00 each add'l. Copy fee: $1.00 for first page, $.50 each add'l. No cert fee. Payee: District Court of the Fifth Circuit. Personal in state personal checks accepted; no third party checks. Visa, MasterCard accepted. Prepayment required. Mail requests: SASE requested. Turnaround time 1-7 days.

District Court of the 5th Circuit - Criminal
3059 Umi St, Rm 111, Lihue, HI 96766; 808-246-3330; Fax: 808-246-3309. 7:45AM-4:30PM (HT). *Misdemeanor.* www.courts.state.hi.us/index.jsp

Criminal Records: Access: Phone, fax, mail, in person, online. Only the court performs in person searches; visitors may not. Search fee: $10.00. Required to search: name, years to search, DOB; also helpful: SSN. Free record searching at www.courts.state.hi.us/index.jsp. Click on "Search Court Records."

General Information: Will fax results for $2.00 1st page, $1.00 each add'l page. Copy fee: $1.00 for first page, $.50 each add'l. Cert fee: $2.00. Payee: District Court. Turnaround time is within 1 week.

Maui County

2nd Circuit Court 2145 Main St, #106, Wailuku, HI 96793; 808-244-2929; Fax: 808-244-2932. Hours: 7:45AM-4:30PM (HT). *Felony, Misdemeanor, Civil Actions Over $5,000, Probate.* www.courts.state.hi.us

Court also covers the counties of Lanai and Molokai.

Civil Records: Access: Mail, in person, online. Both court and visitors may perform in person searches. Search fee: $5.00 per name. Required to search: name, years to search. Civil cases indexed by defendant, plaintiff. Civil records on computer from 10/88, some prior on microfiche. Online access to Circuit Court & family court records is free at www.courts.state.hi.us/index.jsp. Click on "Search Court Records." Records go back to 1984.

Criminal Records: Access: Mail, in person, online. Both court and visitors may perform in person searches. Search fee: $5.00 per name. Required to search: name, years to search; also helpful: DOB, SSN. Criminal records on computer from 10/88, some prior on microfiche. Online access to criminal records is the same as civil.

General Information: Public Access terminal is available. No juvenile or paternity records released. Fee to fax results is $5.00 1st page, $2.00 each add'l in USA; $2.00 for first and $1.00 each add'l in Hawaii. Copy fee: File marked pages are $1.00 per page; non-file marked are $.50. Cert fee: $2.00. Payee: Clerk, 2nd Circuit Court. Personal checks

accepted. Prepayment required. Mail requests: SASE required. Mail turnaround time 1 week.

Lanai District Court
PO Box 631376, Lanai City, HI 96763; 808-565-6447. 7:45AM-4:30PM (HT). *Misdemeanor, Civil Actions Under $20,000, Eviction, Small Claims.* www.courts.state.hi.us/index.jsp

Civil Records: Access: Mail, online, in person. Only the court performs in person searches; visitors may not. Search fee: $5.00 per search. Required to search: name, years to search. Civil cases indexed by defendant, plaintiff. Civil records on index and docket books back to statehood. Free record searching is at www.courts.state.hi.us/index.jsp. Click on "Search Court Records." Records go back to 12/03.

Criminal Records: Access: Mail, in person, online. Only the court performs in person searches; visitors may not. Search fee: $5.00 per search. Required to search: name, years to search; also helpful: DOB, SSN. Criminal records on computer since 1997. Online access to criminal records is the same as civil.

General Information: Copy fee: $1.00 for first page, $.50 each add'l. Cert fee: $1.00. Payee: Lanai District Court. Personal checks accepted. Credit cards accepted if paid through Wailuka Dist. Court. Prepayment required. Mail turnaround: 2-3 weeks.

Molokai District Court
PO Box 284, Kaunakakai, HI 96748; 808-553-5451; Fax: 808-553-3374. 7:45AM-4:30PM (HT). *Misdemeanor, Civil Actions Under $20,000, Eviction, Small Claims.* www.courts.state.hi.us

Civil Records: Access: In person, online. Only the court performs in person searches; visitors may not. Search fee: $5.00 per name. Required to search: name, years to search. Civil records on index and docket books back to statehood. Free record searching is at www.courts.state.hi.us/index.jsp. Click on "Search Court Records."

Criminal Records: Access: In person, online. Only the court performs in person searches; visitors may not. Search fee: $5.00 per name. Required to search: name, years to search, DOB, SSN. Criminal records on computer since 1980. Online access to criminal records is the same as civil.

General Information: No juvenile or paternity records released. Copy fee: $1.00 for first page, $.50 each add'l. Cert fee: $5.00. Payee: Molokai District Court. Business checks okay. Prepayment required.

Wailuku District Court
2145 Main St, # 137, Wailuku, HI 96793; 808-244-2800; Fax: 808-244-2849. 7:45AM-4:30PM (HT). *Misdemeanor, Civil Actions Under $20,000, Eviction, Small Claims.* www.courts.state.hi.us

Civil Records: Access: Mail, in person, online. Only the court performs in person searches; visitors may not. Search fee: $5.00 per name. Required to search: name, years to search; also helpful: address. Civil cases indexed by defendant, plaintiff. Civil records on index and docket books. Free record searching is at www.courts.state.hi.us/index.jsp. Click on "Search Court Records."

Criminal Records: Access: Mail, in person, online. Only the court performs in person searches; visitors may not. Search fee: $5.00 per name. Required to search: name, years to search, DOB, SSN. Criminal records on computer since 1980. Online access to criminal records is the same as civil.

General Information: Will fax results $5.00 1st page, $2.00 each add'l. Within HI; $2.00 1st page, $1.00 each add'l. Copy fee: $1.00 for first page, $.50 each add'l. No cert fee. Payee: District Court 2nd Circuit. Personal checks accepted. Visa, MC accepted. Prepayment required. Mail requests: SASE required. Mail turnaround time 2-3 weeks.

Hawaii Recording Offices

ORGANIZATION: All UCC financing statements, tax liens, and real estate documents are filed centrally with the Bureau of Conveyances located in Honolulu. The entire state is in the Hawaii Time Zone (HT).

Bureau of Conveyances

Bureau of Conveyances, PO Box 2867, Honolulu, HI 96803. **Phone**-808-587-0154, R/E Recording-808-587-0134; fax-808-587-4380; hours 7:45AM-4:30PM www.hawaii.gov/dlnr/bc

The Honolulu property assessor is located at 842 Bethel St, Honolulu, Hawaii 96813. Will search UCC records. Search per debtor- $25.00 min.; add'l charges for found records. UCC copy- $1.00 per page. Tax liens not included in UCC search. Will not search real estate records. Cert fee: $1.00 per page. Payee: Bureau of Conveyances. **Online Access to Property records:** Property records on the Hawaii County property assessor records are free at www.hawaiipropertytax.com. Also, search Honolulu real estate records at www.honolulupropertytax.com. No name searching. Maui Assessor Property records are free at www.mauipropertytax.com. There is also a Maui property lookup at http://gil.co.maui.hi.us/kivanet/2/land/lookup/index.cfm?fa=dslladdr. Indices to all documents recorded in the Bureau of Conveyances from 1976 to current are online at www.hawaii.gov.dlnr/bc. Certified copies of documents may also be ordered. **Other phones:** Assessor-808-527-5541/5511; Land Court-808-587-0138.

Hawaii County Locator

You will usually be able to find the city name in the City/County Cross Reference below. In that case, it is a simple matter to determine the county from the cross reference. However, only the official US Postal Service city names are included in this index. There are an additional 40,000 place names that people use in their addresses. Therefore, we have also included a ZIP/City Cross Reference immediately following the City/County Cross Reference.

If you know the ZIP Code but the city name does not appear in the City/County Cross Reference index, look up the ZIP Code in the ZIP/City Cross Reference, find the city name, then look up the city name in the City/County Cross Reference. For example, you want to know the county for an address of Menands, NY 12204. There is no "Menands" in the City/County Cross Reference. The ZIP/City Cross Reference shows that ZIP Codes 12201-12288 are for the city of Albany. Looking back in the City/County Cross Reference, Albany is in Albany County.

Hawaii City/County Cross Reference

AIEA Honolulu	HONOMU Hawaii	KULA Maui	PAPAIKOU Hawaii
ANAHOLA Kauai	HOOLEHUA Maui	KUNIA Honolulu	PEARL CITY Honolulu
BARBERS POINT Honolulu	KAAAWA Honolulu	KURTISTOWN Hawaii	PEARL HARBOR Honolulu
BARBERS POINT N A S Honolulu	KAHUKU Honolulu	LAHAINA Maui	PEPEEKEO Hawaii
CAMP H M SMITH Honolulu	KAHULUI Maui	LAIE Honolulu	PRINCEVILLE Kauai
CAPTAIN COOK Hawaii	KAILUA Honolulu	LANAI CITY Maui	PUKALANI Maui
ELEELE Kauai	KAILUA KONA Hawaii	LAUPAHOEHOE Hawaii	PUUNENE Maui
EWA BEACH Honolulu	KALAHEO Kauai	LAWAI Kauai	SCHOFIELD BARRACKS Honolulu
FORT SHAFTER Honolulu	KALAUPAPA Maui	LIHUE Kauai	TAMC Honolulu
HAIKU Maui	KAMUELA Hawaii	M C B H KANEOHE BAY Honolulu	TRIPLER ARMY MEDICAL CTR Honolulu
HAKALAU Hawaii	KANEOHE Honolulu	MAKAWAO Maui	VOLCANO Hawaii
HALEIWA Honolulu	KAPAA Kauai	MAKAWELI Kauai	WAHIAWA Honolulu
HANA Maui	KAPAAU Hawaii	MAUNALOA Maui	WAIALUA Honolulu
HANALEI Kauai	KAPOLEI Honolulu	MILILANI Honolulu	WAIANAE Honolulu
HANAMAULU Kauai	KAUMAKANI Kauai	MOUNTAIN VIEW Hawaii	WAIKOLOA Hawaii
HANAPEPE Kauai	KAUNAKAKAI Maui	NAALEHU Hawaii	WAILUKU Maui
HAUULA Honolulu	KEAAU Hawaii	NINOLE Hawaii	WAIMANALO Honolulu
HAWAII NATIONAL PARK Hawaii	KEALAKEKUA Hawaii	OCEAN VIEW Hawaii	WAIMEA Kauai
HAWI Hawaii	KEALIA Kauai	OOKALA Hawaii	WAIPAHU Honolulu
HICKAM AFB Honolulu	KEAUHOU Hawaii	PAAUHAU Hawaii	WAKE ISLAND Honolulu
HILO Hawaii	KEKAHA Kauai	PAAUILO Hawaii	WHEELER ARMY AIRFIELD Honolulu
HOLUALOA Hawaii	KIHEI Maui	PAHALA Hawaii	
HONAUNAU Hawaii	KILAUEA Kauai	PAHOA Hawaii	
HONOKAA Hawaii	KOLOA Kauai	PAIA Maui	
HONOLULU Honolulu	KUALAPUU Maui	PAPAALOA Hawaii	

ZIP/City Cross Reference

96701-96701 AIEA	96732-96733 KAHULUI	96762-96762 LAIE	96789-96789 MILILANI
96703-96703 ANAHOLA	96734-96734 KAILUA	96763-96763 LANAI CITY	96790-96790 KULA
96704-96704 CAPTAIN COOK	96737-96737 OCEAN VIEW	96764-96764 LAUPAHOEHOE	96791-96791 WAIALUA
96705-96705 ELEELE	96738-96738 WAIKOLOA	96765-96765 LAWAI	96792-96792 WAIANAE
96706-96706 EWA BEACH	96739-96739 KEAUHOU	96766-96766 LIHUE	96793-96793 WAILUKU
96707-96707 KAPOLEI	96740-96740 KAILUA KONA	96767-96767 LAHAINA	96795-96795 WAIMANALO
96708-96708 HAIKU	96741-96741 KALAHEO	96768-96768 MAKAWAO	96796-96796 WAIMEA
96709-96709 KAPOLEI	96742-96742 KALAUPAPA	96769-96769 MAKAWELI	96797-96797 WAIPAHU
96710-96710 HAKALAU	96743-96743 KAMUELA	96770-96770 MAUNALOA	96800-96850 HONOLULU
96712-96712 HALEIWA	96744-96744 KANEOHE	96771-96771 MOUNTAIN VIEW	96853-96853 HICKAM AFB
96713-96713 HANA	96745-96745 KAILUA KONA	96772-96772 NAALEHU	96854-96854 WHEELER ARMY
96714-96714 HANALEI	96746-96746 KAPAA	96773-96773 NINOLE	AIRFIELD
96715-96715 HANAMAULU	96747-96747 KAUMAKANI	96774-96774 OOKALA	96857-96857 SCHOFIELD BARRACKS
96716-96716 HANAPEPE	96748-96748 KAUNAKAKAI	96775-96775 PAAUHAU	96858-96858 FORT SHAFTER
96717-96717 HAUULA	96749-96749 KEAAU	96776-96776 PAAUILO	96859-96859 TRIPLER ARMY MED CTR
96718-96718 HAWAII NATIONAL PARK	96750-96750 KEALAKEKUA	96777-96777 PAHALA	96859-96859 TAMC
96719-96719 HAWI	96751-96751 KEALIA	96778-96778 PAHOA	96860-96860 PEARL HARBOR
96720-96721 HILO	96752-96752 KEKAHA	96779-96779 PAIA	96861-96861 CAMP H M SMITH
96722-96722 PRINCEVILLE	96753-96753 KIHEI	96780-96780 PAPAALOA	96862-96862 BARBERS POINT N A S
96725-96725 HOLUALOA	96754-96754 KILAUEA	96781-96781 PAPAIKOU	96862-96862 BARBERS POINT
96726-96726 HONAUNAU	96755-96755 KAPAAU	96782-96782 PEARL CITY	96863-96863 M C B H KANEOHE BAY
96727-96727 HONOKAA	96756-96756 KOLOA	96783-96783 PEPEEKEO	96898-96898 WAKE ISLAND
96728-96728 HONOMU	96757-96757 KUALAPUU	96784-96784 PUUNENE	
96729-96729 HOOLEHUA	96759-96759 KUNIA	96785-96785 VOLCANO	
96730-96730 KAAAWA	96760-96760 KURTISTOWN	96786-96786 WAHIAWA	
96731-96731 KAHUKU	96761-96761 LAHAINA	96788-96788 PUKALANI	

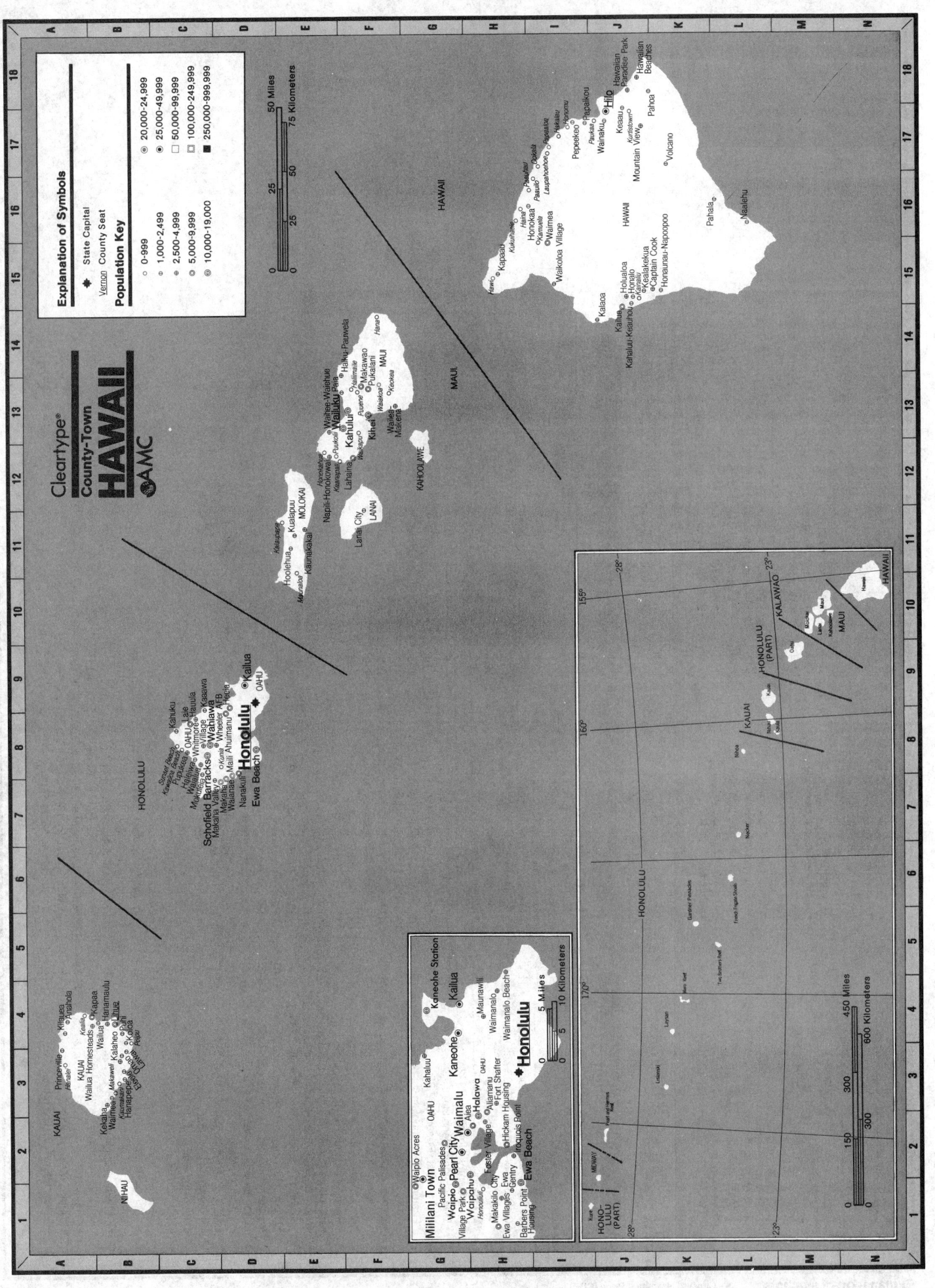

COUNTIES

(5 Counties)

Name of County	Population	Location on Map
HAWAII	120,317	G-16
HONOLULU	836,231	B-7
KALAWAO	130	D-11
KAUAI	51,177	A-2
MAUI	100,374	G-13
TOTAL	1,108,229	

CITIES AND TOWNS

Note: The first name is that of the city or town, second, that of the county in which it is located, then the population and location on the map.

- Ahuimanu, Honolulu, 8,387 ... D-8
- Aiea, Honolulu, 8,906 ... H-2
- Aliamanu, Honolulu, 8,835 ... H-3
- Anahola, Kauai, 1,181 ... A-4
- Barbers Point Housing, Honolulu, 2,218 ... H-1
- Captain Cook, Hawaii, 2,595 ... J-15
- Eleele, Kauai, 1,489 ... B-3
- Ewa Beach, Honolulu, 14,315 ... D-8
- Ewa Gentry, Honolulu, 1,992 ... H-1
- Ewa Villages, Honolulu, 3,780 ... H-1
- Fort Shafter, Honolulu, 2,952 ... H-3
- Foster Village, Honolulu ... H-2
- Haiku-Pauwela, Maui, 4,509 ... F-13
- Halawa, Honolulu, 13,408 ... H-2
- Haleiwa, Honolulu, 2,442 ... C-8
- Hanamaulu, Kauai, 3,611 ... B-4
- Hanapepe, Kauai, 1,395 ... B-3
- Hauula, Honolulu, 3,479 ... C-8
- Hawaiian Beaches, Hawaii, 2,846 ... J-18
- Hawaiian Paradise Park, Hawaii, 3,389 ... J-17
- Heeia, Honolulu, 5,010 ... D-9
- Hickam Housing, Honolulu, 6,553 ... H-2
- Hilo, Hawaii, 37,808 ... J-17
- Holualoa, Hawaii, 3,834 ... J-15
- Honalo, Hawaii, 1,926 ... J-15
- Honaunau-Napoopoo, Hawaii, 2,373 ... K-15
- Honokaa, Hawaii, 2,186 ... I-16
- Honolulu, Honolulu, 365,272 ... D-9
- Hoolehua, Maui ... E-11
- Iroquois Point, Honolulu, 4,188 ... H-2
- Kaaawa, Honolulu, 1,138 ... C-8
- Kahaluu, Honolulu, 3,068 ... G-3
- Kahaluu-Keauhou, Hawaii, 1,990 ... J-15
- Kahuku, Honolulu, 2,063 ... C-8
- Kahului, Maui, 16,889 ... F-13
- Kailua, Hawaii, 9,126 ... J-14
- Kailua, Honolulu, 36,818 ... D-9
- Kalaheo, Kauai, 3,592 ... B-3
- Kalaoa, Hawaii, 4,490 ... J-14
- Kaneohe, Honolulu, 35,448 ... G-4
- Kapaa, Kauai, 8,149 ... A-4
- Kapaau, Hawaii, 1,083 ... H-15
- Kaunakakai, Maui, 2,658 ... E-11
- Keaau, Hawaii, 1,584 ... J-17
- Kealakekua, Hawaii, 1,453 ... J-15
- Kekaha, Kauai, 3,506 ... B-3
- Kihei, Maui, 11,107 ... F-13
- Kilauea, Kauai, 1,685 ... A-4
- Koloa, Kauai, 1,791 ... B-4
- Kualapuu, Maui, 1,661 ... E-11
- Lahaina, Maui, 9,073 ... F-12
- Laie, Honolulu, 5,577 ... C-8
- Lanai City, Maui, 2,400 ... F-11
- Lawai, Kauai, 1,787 ... B-3
- Lihue, Kauai, 5,536 ... B-4
- Maili, Honolulu, 6,059 ... D-8
- Makaha, Honolulu, 7,990 ... C-7
- Makaha Valley, Honolulu, 1,012 ... C-7
- Makakilo City, Honolulu, 9,828 ... H-1
- Makawao, Maui, 5,405 ... F-13
- Maunawili, Honolulu, 4,847 ... H-4
- Mililani Town, Honolulu, 29,359 ... G-2
- Mokuleia, Honolulu, 1,776 ... C-8
- Mountain View, Hawaii, 3,075 ... J-17
- Naalehu, Hawaii, 1,027 ... L-16
- Nanakuli, Honolulu, 9,575 ... D-8
- Napili-Honokowai, Maui, 4,332 ... E-12
- Omao, Kauai, 1,142 ... B-3
- Pacific Palisades, Honolulu ... G-2
- Pahala, Hawaii, 1,520 ... L-16
- Pahoa, Hawaii, 1,027 ... K-18
- Paia, Maui, 2,091 ... F-13
- Papaikou, Hawaii, 1,634 ... I-17
- Pearl City, Honolulu, 30,993 ... G-2
- Pepeekeo, Hawaii, 1,813 ... I-17
- Princeville, Kauai, 1,244 ... A-3
- Puhi, Kauai, 1,210 ... B-4
- Pukalani, Maui, 5,879 ... F-13
- Pupukea, Honolulu, 4,111 ... C-8
- Schofield Barracks, Honolulu, 19,597 ... C-8
- Village Park, Honolulu, 7,407 ... G-1
- Volcano, Hawaii, 1,516 ... K-16
- Wahiawa, Honolulu, 17,386 ... C-8
- Waialua, Honolulu, 3,943 ... C-8
- Waianae, Honolulu, 8,758 ... D-7
- Waihee-Waiehu, Maui, 4,004 ... E-13
- Waikoloa Village, Hawaii, 2,248 ... I-15
- Wailea-Makena, Maui, 3,799 ... F-13
- Wailua, Kauai, 2,018 ... B-4
- Wailua Homesteads, Kauai, 3,870 ... A-4
- Wailuku, Maui, 10,688 ... E-13
- Waimalu, Honolulu, 29,967 ... H-2
- Waimanalo, Honolulu, 3,508 ... H-4
- Waimanalo Beach, Honolulu, 4,185 ... H-5
- Waimea, Hawaii, 5,972 ... I-15
- Waimea, Kauai, 1,840 ... B-3
- Wainaku, Hawaii, 1,243 ... J-17
- Waipahu, Honolulu, 31,435 ... G-2
- Waipio, Honolulu, 11,812 ... G-2
- Waipio Acres, Honolulu, 5,304 ... D-8
- Wheeler AFB, Honolulu, 2,600 ... D-8
- Whitmore Village, Honolulu, 3,373 ... C-8

Explanation of symbols: ● – Census Designated Place (CDP)

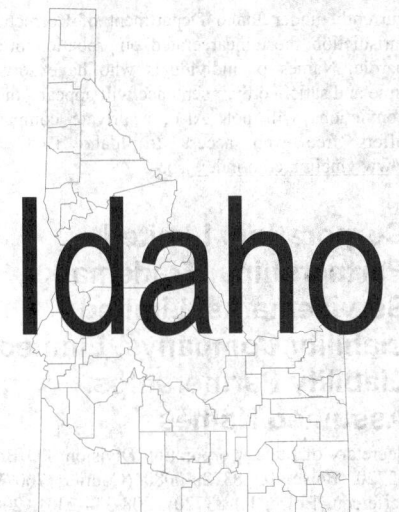

Idaho

General Help Numbers:

Governor's Office
PO Box 83720
Boise, ID 83720-0034
http://www2.state.id.us/gov/index.htm

208-334-2100
Fax 208-334-2175
8AM-6PM

Attorney General's Office
PO Box 83720
Boise, ID 83720-0010
http://www2.state.id.us/ag

208-334-2400
Fax 208-334-2530
8AM-5PM

Legislative Records
PO Box 83720
Boise, ID 83720-0054
http://www2.state.id.us/legislat/legislat.html

208-334-2475
Fax 208-334-2125
8AM-5PM

State Archives
Historical Library & Archives
450 N 4th Street
Boise, ID 83702-6027
http://idahohistory.net

208-334-3356
Fax 208-334-3198
9AM-5PM

State Specifics:

Capital:
Boise
Ada County

Time Zone:
MST*

** Idaho's ten northwestern-most counties are PST:
They are: Benewah, Bonner, Boundary, Clearwater,
Idaho, Kootenai, Latah, Lewis, Nez Perce, Shoshone.*

Number of Counties:
44

Population:
1,366,332

Web Site:
www.state.id.us

State Agencies

Criminal Records

State Repository, Bureau of Criminal Identification, PO Box 700, Meridian, ID 83680-0700 (Courier: 700 S Stratford Dr, Meridian, ID 83642); 208-884-7130, 208-884-7193 (Fax), 8AM-4PM.

www.isp.state.id.us

Indexing & Storage: Records are available from 1960 on. It takes about 3 days before new records are available for inquiry. Records are normally destroyed after subject reaches 99th year.

Searching: Include the following in your request-name, DOB. SSN and alias will aid in identification. Fingerprints are optional but may be required to establish positive identification.

Fingerprint searches take 5-7 days. 100% of records are fingerprint-supported.

Access by: mail, in person.

Fee & Payment: The $10.00 fee per person is applicable for either a name search or a fingerprint search. Fee payee: Idaho State Police. Prepayment required. Cashier check or money order is preferred form of payment. No credit cards accepted.

Mail search: Turnaround time: 10 to 15 days.

In person search: You may request information in person, but results are still mailed.

Statewide Court Records

Administrative Director of the Courts, PO Box 83720, Boise, ID 83720-0101 (Courier: 451 W State St, Boise, ID 83720); 208-334-2246, 208-334-2146 (Fax), 9AM-5PM.

www.isc.idaho.gov/

Note: Except for certain online research capabilities, all court record access must be done at the local level. For tribal court information, visit www.isc.idaho.gov/tribalmn.htm.

Access by: online.

Online search: Although appellate and supreme court opinions are available from the web, there is no statewide computer system offering external access. ISTARS is a statewide intra-court/intra-agency system for all counties, enabling all courts to provide public access terminals on-site.

Sexual Offender Registry

State Repository, Central Sexual Offender Registry, PO Box 700, Meridian, ID 83680-0700 (Courier: 700 S Stratford Dr, Meridian, ID 83642); 208-884-7305, 208-884-7193 (Fax), 8AM-5PM.

www.isp.state.id.us

Indexing & Storage: Records are available from 07/01/93. It takes about 3 days before new records are available for inquiry.

Searching: Any person may inquire by submitting a completed SOR-4 Form to the central registry or a local sheriff. Photos may be requested using SOR-5 Form. Include the following in your request-name and either DOB or address. Requests may be made on a named individual or a list of registered sex offenders by ZIP Code or county.

Access by: mail, in person, online.

Fee & Payment: There is a $5.00 fee, plus an additional $5.00 if photo needed. Schools and nonprofit organizations working with youth, women, or other vulnerable populations are exempt from payment of the fee. Fee payee: BCI. Prepayment required. Cashier check or money order is preferred form of payment. But personal checks are accepted. No credit cards accepted.

Mail search: Turnaround time: 5 to 7 days.

In person search: You may request information from this agency or from any local sheriff's office.

Online search: Access from the web page is available to the public. Inquires can be made by name, address, or by county or ZIP Code.

Incarceration Records

Idaho Department of Corrections, Records Bureau, 1299 N. Orchard Street, Suite 110, Boise, ID 83706; 208-658-2000, 208-327-7444 (Fax), 8AM-5PM.

www.corrections.state.id.us

Indexing & Storage: Records are available on current and former inmates. It takes 3 days before new records are available for inquiry. Records are normally destroyed after 2 years if probation only and not convicted of sex crime. All other records not destroyed but sent to state storage.

Searching: Include the following in your request-first and last name. DOB, SSN, DOC number are helpful.

Access by: mail, phone, fax, in person, online.

Fee & Payment: Cost is $2.00 for pulling from state storage, if required. Copies are $.10 per page after 5 pages.

Mail search: Turnaround time: 5 to 7 days. Requests in writing must be specific about information requested. Use SASE or you will be charged for postage.

Phone search: Limited searching by phone, "is subject there or not."

Fax search: Only if just needing an inmate location.

In person search: The public has right to view records in person upon making a written request to schedule an appointment with records custodian.

Online search: This database search at https://www.accessidaho.org/public/corr/offender/search.html provides information about offenders

currently under Idaho Department of Correction jurisdiction: those incarcerated, on probation, or on parole. Names of individuals who have served time and satisfied their sentence will appear - their convictions will not. Also, a private company offers free web access to Idaho DOC at www.vinelink.com/index.jsp.

Corporation, Limited Partnerships, Trademarks, Servicemarks, Limited Liability Companys, Limited Liability Partnerships, Assumed Names

Secretary of State, Corporation Division, PO Box 83720, Boise, ID 83720-0080 (Courier: 700 W Jefferson, Boise, ID 83720); 208-334-2301, 208-334-2080 (Fax), 8AM-5PM.

www.idsos.state.id.us

Note: Effective 1/1/97, fictitious or assumed names are found at this office. (Previously they had recorded at the county level.) Not-for-profits records are located here, also.

Indexing & Storage: Records are available for all entities. New records are available for inquiry immediately. Records are indexed on computer.

Searching: Ongoing requesters should establish a pre-paid account. Include the following in your request-full name of business, specific records that you need copies of. In addition to the articles of incorporation, corporation records include the following information: Annual Reports, Officers, Directors, Prior names, Inactive and Reserved names, and Filing History. Cross reference of owners/officers is not avail.

Access by: mail, phone, fax, in person, online.

Fee & Payment: There is no search fee. The fee for copies is $.25 per page. Certification is $10.00 as is a Certification of Existence. Fee payee: Secretary of State. Prepayment required. Agency will invoice for payment. Personal checks accepted. No credit cards accepted.

Mail search: Turnaround time: 1 to 2 days. No SASE is required.

Phone search: There is a limit of 3 entities per call.

Fax search: Copies cost an additional $.50 each if returned by fax.

In person search: Call first to make an appointment so that they can pull file.

Online search: Business Entity Searches at www.accessidaho.org/public/sos/corp/search.html ?SearchFormstep=crit. This is a free Internet service open 24 hours daily. Includes not-for-profit entities.

Other access: There are a variety of formats and media available for bulk purchase requesters. Requesters can subscribers to a monthly CD update.

Expedited service: Expedited service is available for mail, phone and in person searches. Turnaround time: 1 day. Add $20.00 per document.

Uniform Commercial Code, Federal and State Tax Liens

UCC Division, Secretary of State, PO Box 83720, Boise, ID 83720-0080 (Courier: 700 W Jefferson, Boise, ID 83720); 208-334-3191, 208-334-2847 (Fax), 8AM-5PM.

www.idsos.state.id.us

Indexing & Storage: Records are available from 1967. It takes 1 to 2 days before new records are available for inquiry. Records are indexed on inhouse computer.

Searching: The search includes federal tax liens, farm filings, and seed and labor filings. There is also an agricultural commodity lien search. Federal tax liens on individuals are filed at the county level. Include the following in your request-debtor name. For state tax liens that closed prior to 01/07/98, one must search at the county. On that date, the state took over the filing and database of state tax liens.

Access by: mail, phone, fax, in person, online.

Fee & Payment: Information search request is $12.00 per name. Copies are $1.00 per page if no file number given and $.25 per page if file name given. Fee payee: Secretary of State. Prepayment is not required, but preferred. Personal checks accepted. No credit cards accepted.

Mail search: Turnaround time: 1 to 2 days. No SASE is required.

Phone search: They will tell if a filing exists.

Fax search: Searches can be invoiced. There is an additional fee of $.50 per page.

In person search: You may request information in person, time permitting.

Online search: There is a free limited search at https://www.accessidaho.org/secure/sos/liens/search.html. We recommend professional searchers to subscribe to the extensive commercial service at this site. There is a $75 annual fee and possible transaction fees.

Other access: A summary data file on current filing is available on 4mm data tape.

Sales Tax Registrations

Revenue Operations Division, Records Management, PO Box 36, Boise, ID 83722 (Courier: 800 Park, Boise, ID 83722); 208-334-7660, 208-334-7792 (Records Management), 208-334-7650 (Fax), 8AM-5:00PM.

http://tax.idaho.gov/SalesUseTaxRate.htm

Indexing & Storage: Records are available from 1983. The agency maintains records on computer since 1998 and on microfiche from 1983 to present. It takes 90 days before new records are available for inquiry. Records are normally destroyed after 3 years.

Searching: This agency will only confirm that a business is registered if a tax permit number is provided. They will provide no other information. The only information released is that within public domain. They will also search if provided with a tax permit number, a DBA or an EIN.

Access by: mail, phone, fax, in person, email.

Fee & Payment: There is no search fee, but there is a fee for postage for mail requests or for faxing. Fee payee: ISTC, PO Box 36, Boise, ID 83732. Prepayment required. Personal checks accepted. No credit cards accepted.

Mail search: Turnaround time: 1 to 3 days. The copy fee is $.10 per page, after 20 pages. No SASE is required.

Phone search: No fee for telephone request. Only general information is released.

Fax search: The fee is $1.00 per page. Turnaround time 24 hours.

In person search: Copy fees apply.

Online search: Email requests are accepted at rmcmichael@tax.state.id.us.

Birth Certificates

Vital Records, PO Box 83720, Boise, ID 83720-0036 (Courier: 450 W State St, 1st Floor, Boise, ID 83702); 208-334-5988, 208-389-9096 (Fax), 8AM-5PM.

www.healthandwelfare.idaho.gov/

Indexing & Storage: Records are available on computer from July 1911 to present.

Searching: Records are confidential for 100 years. Only immediate family or legal representative may receive records as well as those who have a notarized release from persons of record or an immediate family member. Include the following in your request-full name, names of parents, mother's maiden name, date of birth, city of birth, relationship to person of record, reason for information request. Also include a copy of a photo ID and sign the request. The following data is not released: adoption records or sealed records.

Access by: mail, fax.

Fee & Payment: Requesters must include their signature and a copy of a driver's license or photo ID. Fee is $13.00 per name, add $13.00 per name requested for additional copies. Fee payee: Vital Records. Prepayment required. Credit cards accepted for fax requests only. Personal checks accepted. Major credit cards accepted.

Mail search: Turnaround time: 2 to 3 weeks. No SASE is required.

Fax search: See Expedited Service.

Expedited service: Expedited service is available for fax requests. The fee is $23.50 plus cost of return by FedEx or mail. Requests received by noon (MT) will be processed within 2 working days if requesting Federal Express delivery; otherwise 1 week turnaround.

Death Records

Vital Records, PO Box 83720, Boise, ID 83720-0036 (Courier: 450 W State St, 1st Floor, Boise, ID 83702); 208-334-5988, 208-389-9096 (Fax), 8AM-5PM.

www.healthandwelfare.idaho.gov/

Indexing & Storage: Records are available from July 1911 to present. Records are indexed on microfilm, inhouse computer.

Searching: Records are confidential for 50 years and are available only to immediate family members or legal representatives or a person who has a notarized release from persons of record or an immediate family member. Include the following in your request-full name, date of death, city of death, relationship to person of record, reason for information request.

Access by: mail, fax, online.

Fee & Payment: Include a copy of your driver's license or photo ID and signature with request. The fee is $13.00 per name or additional copy. Fee

payee: Vital Records. Prepayment required. Credit cards are accepted with fax requests only. Personal checks accepted. Major credit cards accepted.

Mail search: Turnaround time: 2 to 3 weeks. No SASE is required.

Fax search: See Expedited Services.

Online search: The agency has made the death index of records older than 50 available at http://abish.byui.edu/specialCollections/fhc/Death/searchForm.cfm. There is no fee.

Expedited service: Expedited service is available for fax requests. The fee is $23.50 plus cost of return by FedEx.

Marriage Certificates

Vital Records, PO Box 83720, Boise, ID 83720-0036 (Courier: 450 W State St, 1st Floor, Boise, ID 83702); 208-334-5988, 208-389-9096 (Fax), 8AM-5PM.

www.healthandwelfare.idaho.gov/

Indexing & Storage: Records are available from May 1947 to present.

Searching: Records are confidential for 50 years. Only immediate family members and legal representatives may obtain recent records, others may obtain records with a notarized release from a family member or person of record. Include the following in your request-names of husband and wife, date of marriage, city of marriage, relationship.

Access by: mail, fax.

Fee & Payment: Include a copy of a photo ID or driver's license and a signature with request. The fee is $13.00 per name and per each additional copy. Fee payee: Vital Records. Prepayment required. Major credit cards accepted with fax requests only. Personal checks accepted.

Mail search: Turnaround time: 2 to 3 weeks. No SASE is required.

Fax search: See Expedited Services.

Expedited service: Expedited service is available for fax requests. The fee is $23.50 plus cost of return by FedEx, Postal Express, or Priority Mail.

Divorce Records

Vital Records, PO Box 83720, Boise, ID 83720-0036; 208-334-5988, 208-389-9096 (Fax), 8AM-5PM.

www.healthandwelfare.idaho.gov/

Note: This agency only maintains certificates of divorce; copies of decrees are available through the court system.

Indexing & Storage: Records are available from May 1947 to present. New records are available for inquiry immediately. Records are indexed on microfilm, inhouse computer.

Searching: Records are confidential for 50 years and are available only to immediate family members, legal representatives, and a person with a notarized signed release from persons of record or immediate family. Include the following in your request-names of husband and wife, date of divorce, city of divorce, relationship.

Access by: mail, fax.

Fee & Payment: Include a copy of a driver's license or photo ID and include a signature with request. The fee is $13.00 per name. Fee payee: Vital Records. Prepayment required. Credit cards

are accepted with fax requests only. Personal checks accepted. Major credit cards accepted.

Mail search: Turnaround time: 2 to 3 weeks. No SASE is required.

Fax search: See Expedited Services.

Expedited service: Expedited service is available for fax requests. The fee is $23.50 plus cost of return by FedEx, Postal Express, or Priority Mail.

Workers' Compensation Records

Industrial Commission of Idaho, Attn: Records Management, PO Box 83720, Boise, ID 83720-0041; 208-334-6000, 208-334-2321 (Fax), 8AM-5PM.

http://www2.state.id.us/iic

RMR-1 is used by parties on an open claim. RMR-2 is used by employers and prospective employers subject to ADA. RMR-3 is used by employers and prospective employers not subject to ADA. RMR-4 is subject's release for other parties.

Indexing & Storage: Records are available from 1917 on. New records are available for inquiry immediately. Records are indexed on microfilm, index cards, inhouse computer. Records are normally destroyed after microfilming.

Searching: RMR-2 form requires notarized signature. If not subject to ADA, then form RMR-3 is used which requires non-notarized signature. Include the following in your request-claimant name, Social Security Number, date of accident and claim number. The following data is not released: psychiatric information.

Access by: mail, fax, in person.

Fee & Payment: Copy costs depend upon file size which are those that exceed 100 copied pages or 50 microfilmed pages. Larger files cost $.05 per page on paper and $.10 per page on microfilm. If file is off site, shipping fees of $2.00 per file apply. Fee payee: Industrial Commission. Charges that total under $5.00 are waived. Personal checks accepted. No credit cards accepted.

Mail search: Turnaround time: 3 days. There is a charge for postage. A SASE is required.

Fax search: Fax searching available, except RMR-2 Form.

In person search: One may request information in person. However, not all files are available the same day because some files are not on site and must be ordered from storage.

Driver Records

Idaho Transportation Department, Driver's Services, PO Box 34, Boise, ID 83731-0034 (Courier: 3311 W State, Boise, ID 83703); 208-334-8736, 208-334-8739 (Fax), 8:30AM-5PM.

www.itd.idaho.gov/dmv/

Indexing & Storage: Records are available for at least 3 years for moving violations, DUIs and suspensions. Accidents are not shown on the record. It takes 1 day from receipt before new records are available for inquiry. Records are normally destroyed after 7 years and archived to tape.

Searching: Personal information is not released to casual requesters unless the requestor claims a valid authorization. The driver's license number and DOB are used for the primary search. If no record is found, a secondary search is performed using the name and DOB, or name and license number. The following data is not released: SSNs, medical information, signature, address.

Access by: mail, fax, in person, online.

Fee & Payment: The fee is $4.00 per record. Convenience fees are added for online and batch searches. Fee payee: Idaho Transportation Department. Prepayment required. Ongoing requesters can set up an account. Personal checks accepted. Credit cards accepted: MasterCard, Visa.

Mail search: Turnaround time: 3 to 5 days. Mail-in requesters are asked to use the state form. No SASE is required.

Fax search: Fax requests for records are accepted, if paid by a credit card or by account. Call 208-334-8761 to set up an account.

In person search: Walk-in requesters may receive up to ten records while they wait, the rest are processed overnight.

Online search: Idaho offers online access (CICS) to the driver license files through its portal provider, Access Idaho. Fee is $5.50 per record. For more information, call 208-332-0102 or visit www.accessidaho.org.

Other access: Idaho offers bulk retrieval of basic drivers license information with a signed contract. For information, call 208-334-860.

Vehicle and Vessel Ownership and Regustration

Idaho Transportation Department, Vehicle Services, PO Box 34, Boise, ID 83731-0034; 208-334-8773, 208-334-8663, 208-334-8542 (Fax), 8:30AM-5PM.

www.itd.idaho.gov/dmv/

Note: Model year vessels 2000 or newer that have either a motor or are longer than 12 feet must be titled. If a lien is placed on a model year older than 2000, then that vessel must be titled.

Indexing & Storage: Records are available from 1981. It takes 1 day before new records are available for inquiry.

Searching: Personal information is not released to casual requesters unless the requestor claims a valid authorization. Submit the name, VIN, license plate number for search, current address is also helpful. The following data is not released: Social Security Numbers or medical records.

Access by: mail, fax, in person, online.

Fee & Payment: The fee is $4.00 for current title with lien information or for a registration search. A complete title history (using the microfilm) is $8.00. Convenience fees are added for online and batch searches. Fee payee: Idaho Transportation Department. Prepayment required. Motor vehicle record accounts may be established by calling 208-334-8761. Personal checks accepted. Credit cards accepted: MasterCard, Visa.

Mail search: Turnaround time: 5 to 10 days. Information request forms are available. No SASE is required.

Fax search: You may fax a request with a major credit card. Results, except for history records, can returned by fax for no additional fee. Turnaround time is three days.

In person search: You may request information in person here or at any County Assessor auto licensing location statewide.

Online search: Idaho offers online and batch access to registration and title files through its portal provider, Access Idaho. Records are $4.00 each plus an additional $1.50 convenience fee. For more information, call 208-332-0102 ro visit www.accessidaho.org.

Other access: Idaho offers bulk retrieval of registration, ownership, and vehicle information with a signed contract. For more information, call 208-334-8601.

Accident Reports

Idaho Transportation Department, Office of Highway Safety-Accident Records, PO Box 7129, Boise, ID 83707-1129; 208-334-8100, 208-334-4430 (Fax), 8AM-12:00PM; 1PM-5PM.

Indexing & Storage: Records are available from 1970's (on microfilm) to present. It takes 1 day for electronic reports, 3 months if paper before new records are available for inquiry. Records are normally destroyed after microfilming.

Searching: Include the following in your request-full name, date of accident, location of accident, driver's license number.

Access by: mail, phone, fax, in person.

Fee & Payment: The fee is $4.00 per report plus handling and tax. Fee payee: Idaho Transportation Department, Financial Control. Do not send a check with a request, you will be billed. Personal checks accepted. No credit cards accepted.

Mail search: Turnaround time: 2 weeks. A SASE is requested.

Phone search: Fee charged if copies sent. Turnaround time is 2 weeks.

Fax search: Turnaround time 2 weeks.

In person search: It is suggested that walk-in requesters call first before going to department should the state have to locate the records on microfilm.

Other access: Computer files may be purchased with prepaid deposit plus computer charges. However, the file will not contain addresses, citation information, or drivers' license numbers and other personal information. Annual databases may be purchased.

Vessel Registration

Idaho Parks & Recreation, PO Box 83720, Boise, ID 83720-0065; 208-334-4197, 208-334-2639 (Fax), 8AM-5PM.

www.idahoparks.org

Note: Liens are not recorded on registration and must be searched with either UCCs or at the DOT where vessels are titled.

Indexing & Storage: Records are available from 1987 to present. Older records are available, but to search them, you must know the registration #. Records are indexed on computer. All boats with motors and/or sails must be registered.

Searching: Registration records are open to the public. Phone numbers and addresses not are released. To search, provide one of the following: owner's name, hull #, or registration #.

Access by: mail, phone, fax, in person.

Fee & Payment: There is no search fee.

Mail search: Turnaround time: 10 working days.

Phone search: Name searching is permitted.

Fax search: Searching for pre-approved accounts.

In person search: Counter service available.

Voter Registration

Records not maintained by a state level agency.

Note: Records are maintained by the County Clerks. The counties will generally release name, address, and voting precinct on individual request. Lists may be purchased, but not for commercial purposes.

GED Certificates

Department of Education, GED Testing, PO Box 83720, Boise, ID 83720-0027; 208-332-6980, 208-334-4664 (Fax), 8AM-5PM.

www.sde.state.id.us

Indexing & Storage: It takes 1 week before new records are available for inquiry. Records are normally destroyed after (records not destroyed).

Searching: Include the following in your request-Social Security Number, date of birth. A signed release is necessary for copies of transcripts or for scores. Will not expedite requests.

Access by: mail, phone, fax, in person.

Mail search: Turnaround time: 2 to 3 days. No SASE is required. No fee for mail request.

Phone search: No fee for telephone request. Verification only over the phone.

Fax search: Turnaround time is 1 day.

In person search: No fee for request. Information is released immediately.

Hunting and Fishing License Information

ID Department of Fish & Game, Licenses Division, PO Box 25, Boise, ID 83707-0025. 208-334-3717 (License Department), 208-334-3736 (Enforcement Office), 208-334-2148 (Fax), 8AM-5PM.

http://fishandgame.idaho.gov/

Note: The license division says that if you want an individual name, you must call the Enforcement Office. This office will not release individual records with addresses, they will only confirm is there is a license issued.

Indexing & Storage: Records are available from January 1992 to present.

Searching: Use of their request form is required. Include signature and copy of valid ID.

Access by: mail, phone, in person.

Fee & Payment: There is no fee unless the search is extensive.

Mail search: Turnaround time: variable. No SASE is required.

Phone search: They will only confirm.

In person search: Turnaround time: variable.

Idaho State Licensing Agencies
Licenses Searchable Online

Applicator, Commercial/Private #20 .... www.agri.state.id.us/agresource/_agtechlookup/querylic.asp

Attorney #29 .... http://www2.state.id.us/isb/mem/attorney_roster.asp

Bank #21.. http://finance.state.id.us/industry/bank_info.asp

Boiler Inspector #10 .... www.accessidaho.org/public/dbs/safety/search.html

Collection Agency/Collector #21 .... http://finance.state.id.us/industry/CA_List.asp

Community Action Program #27 .... www.puc.state.id.us/consumer/helplist.pdf

Consumer Loan Company & Credit Sale #21 .... http://finance.state.id.us/industry/ICC_List.asp

Contractor, Public Works #31 .... www.accessidaho.org/public/dbs/pubworks/search.html

Credit Union #21... http://finance.state.id.us/industry/creditunion_section.asp

Dental Hygienist #13... http://www2.state.id.us/isbd/search.htm

Dentist #13.. http://www2.state.id.us/isbd/search.htm

Elections & Campaign Disclosure #28 .... www.idsos.state.id.us/notary/npindex.htm

Electrical Apprentice/Journeyman #10 .... www.accessidaho.org/public/dbs/electrical/search.html

Electrical Inspector/Contractor #10.................... www.accessidaho.org/public/dbs/electrical/search.html

Engineer #17 .... http://www2.state.id.us/ipels/pelsnumb.htm

Finance Company #21... http://finance.state.id.us/industry/ICC_List.asp

Geologist #18.. http://www2.state.id.us/ibpg/search.htm

Guide #15 .... http://www2.state.id.us/oglb/oglbhome.htm

Insurance Agent Licensure Examination #24 ..... www.doi.state.id.us/insurance/search.asp

Insurance Agent/Corp./Partnership #24 .... www.doi.state.id.us/insurance/search.asp

Insurance Broker #24 .... www.doi.state.id.us/insurance/search.asp

Insurer, Domestic/Mutual/Foreign/Alien #24....... www.doi.state.id.us/insurance/search.asp

Investment Advisor #21 .... http://finance.state.id.us/industry/securities_resources.asp?resource=IARR

Lobbyist #28 .... www.idsos.state.id.us/elect/lobbyist/lobinfo.htm

Manufactured Commercial Building #10.............. www.accessidaho.org/public/dbs/building/search.html

Manufactured Homes & Housing #10.................. www.accessidaho.org/public/dbs/building/search.html

Manufactured Housing Dealer/Broker/Mfg. #10 . www.accessidaho.org/public/dbs/building/search.html

Mortgage Broker/Banker #21.............................. http://finance.state.id.us/industry/mortgage_list.asp

Mortgage Company #21 .... http://finance.state.id.us/industry/mortgage_section.asp

Mortician/Mortician Resident Trainee #3 .... https://www.ibol.idaho.gov/eIBOLPublic/LPRBrowserl.aspx

Notary Public #28 .... www.idsos.state.id.us/notary/npindex.htm

Optometrist #19 .... www.arbo.org/odfinder/LicSearch.asp

Oral Surgeon #13 .... http://www2.state.id.us/isbd/search.htm

Orthodontist #13... http://www2.state.id.us/isbd/search.htm

Outfitter #15.. http://www2.state.id.us/oglb/oglbhome.htm

Pesticide Applicator/Operator/Dealer/Mfg #6 ..... www.agri.state.id.us/agresource/_agtechlookup/querylic.asp

Plumbing Apprentice/Journeyman #10................ www.accessidaho.org/public/dbs/plumbing/search.html

Plumbing Inspector/Contractor #10 .... www.accessidaho.org/public/dbs/plumbing/search.html

Public Accountant Firm #12................................ http://www2.state.id.us/boa/HTM/firmsearch.htm

Public Accountant-CPA #12 .... http://www2.state.id.us/boa/HTM/accountantsearch.htm

Public Accountant-LPA #12................................. http://www2.state.id.us/boa/HTM/accountantsearch.htm

Real Estate Agent/Broker/Company #34............. www.accessidaho.org/public/irec/licensing/search.html

Real Estate Appraiser #19.................................. www.asc.gov/content/category1/appr_by_state.asp

Savings & Loan Association #21 .... http://finance.state.id.us/industry/bank_info.asp

Securities Broker/Dealer/Seller/Issuer #21......... http://finance.state.id.us/industry/securities.asp

Surveyor, Land #17 .... http://www2.state.id.us/ipels/pelsnumb.htm

Trust Company #21 .... http://finance.state.id.us/consumer/bank_info.asp

Utility Pay Station #27... www.puc.state.id.us/consumer/paystations.htm

Idaho Licensing Quick Finder

Applicator, Commercial/Private #20	208-332-8500
Aquaculture, Commercial #20	208-332-8500
Architect #19	208-334-3233
Artificial Inseminator #20	208-332-8500
Asbestos Worker #10	208-334-2129
Athletic Trainer #30	208-327-7000
Attorney #29	208-344-4500
Bakery #11	208-327-7499
Bank #21	208-332-8005
Barber School Instructor #19	208-334-3233
Barber/Barber Shop/Barber School #19	208-334-3233
Bed & Breakfast #11	208-327-7499
Beekeeper #20	208-332-8500
Beer & Wine License, Whlse/Retail #25	208-884-7060
Boiler Inspector #10	208-334-2129
Boiler Safety Code #10	208-334-2129
Bottling Plant #11	208-327-7499
Boxer #32	208-221-6534
Boxing/Wrestling Event #32	208-221-6534
Boxing/Wrestling Professional #32	208-221-6534
Brewery #25	208-884-7060
Brokerage Dealer #12	208-334-2490
Building Inspector #10	208-334-3896
Chemigator #20	208-332-8500
Child Care Institution/Agency #7	208-334-5700
Child Care Licensure #7	208-334-5700
Chiropractor #19	208-334-3233
Clinical Laboratory Registration #2	208-334-2235
Clinical Nurse Specialist #14	208-334-3110 X21
Collection Agency/Collector #21	208-332-8002
Commission Merchant #20	208-332-8500
Commodity Dealer #20	208-332-8500
Communication Disorders School Specialist #5	208-332-6800
Community Action Program #27	208-334-0300
Construction Manager #31	208-334-4057
Consumer Loan Company & Credit Sale #21	208-332-8002
Contractor, Public Works #31	208-334-4057
Controlled Substance Registrant #16	208-334-2356
Cosmetologist/Cosmetology Salon #19	208-334-3233
Cosmetology School/Instructor #19	208-334-3233
Counselor #19	208-334-3233
Counselor, Professional #19	208-334-3233
Credit Union #21	208-332-8003
Crematory #3	208-334-3233
Dairy Farm/Dairy Product Processor #20	208-332-8500
Day Care Center Inspector #11	208-327-7499
Day Care Center/Home #7	208-334-5700
Dental Assistant #13	208-334-2369
Dental Hygienist #13	208-334-2369
Dentist #13	208-334-2369
Denturist #19	208-334-3233
Dietitian #30	208-327-7000
Driller, Rotary #26	208-327-7900
Drug Mfg./Repackager/Whlse. #16	208-334-2356
Drug Outlet (i.e. Nursing Home) #16	208-334-2356
Drug Sales, Non-Pharmacy (i.e. Grocery Store) #16	208-334-2356
Egg Distributor/Grader #20	208-332-8500
Elections & Campaign Disclosure #28	208-334-2852
Electrical Apprentice/Journeyman #10	208-334-2183
Electrical Inspector/Contractor #10	208-334-2183
Electrolysis #19	208-334-3233
Elevator Installation/Repairmen #10	208-334-2129
Emergency Medical Technician #9	208-334-4000
Engineer #17	208-334-3860
Environmental Health Specialist #19	208-334-3233
Esthetician #19	208-334-3233
Euthanasia Agency #1	208-332-8588

Euthanasia Technician #1	208-332-8588
Exceptional Child School Program Advisor #5	208-332-6800
Farm Produce Dealer/Broker #20	208-332-8500
Feed Manufacturer, Commercial #20	208-332-8500
Fertilizer Mfg., Commercial #20	208-332-8500
Finance Company #21	208-332-8002
Fire Inspector #23	208-334-4370
Fire Sprinkler Fitter #23	208-334-4370
Fire Sprinkler System Contractor #23	208-334-4370
Fireworks License #23	208-334-4370
Fishing, Commercial #22	208-334-3717
Florist/Nurseryman #20	208-332-8620
Food Establishment Studied #11	208-327-7499
Food Processing/Mfg. Plant #11	208-327-7499
Food Warehouse, Cold Storage #11	208-327-7499
Foster Home #7	208-334-5700
Funeral Director #3	208-334-3233
Funeral Director Trainee #3	208-334-3233
Funeral Establishment #3	208-334-3233
Fur Buyer #22	208-334-3717
Game Farm (Commercial Wildlife) #22	208-334-3717
Geologist #18	208-334-2268
Grocery Store #11	208-327-7499
Guide #15	208-327-7380
Hearing Aid Dealer/Fitter #19	208-334-3233
Horse Racing Event/Occupation #33	208-884-7080
Hospital (Child or Elderly) #8	208-334-6626
Insurance Agent Licensure Examination #24	208-334-4250
Insurance Agent/Corp./Partnership #24	208-334-4250
Insurance Broker #24	208-334-4250
Insurer, Domestic/Mutual/Foreign/Alien #24	208-334-4250
Intermediate Care Facility for the Mentally Retarded #8	208-334-6626
Investment Advisor #21	208-332-8004
Landscape Architect #19	208-334-3233
Liquor License, Retail #25	208-884-7060
Livestock Auction Market #20	208-332-8500
Livestock Brand #25	208-884-7070
Loan Agent #12	208-334-2490
Loan Collection Officer #12	208-334-2490
Lobbyist #28	208-334-2852
Logging #10	208-334-6000
Mammography #2	208-334-2235
Manufactured Commercial Bldg. #10	208-334-3896
Manufactured Homes & Housing #10	208-334-3896
Manufactured Housing Dealer/Broker/Mfg. #10	208-334-3896
Medical Doctor #30	208-327-7000
Medical Resident #30	208-327-7000
Midwife Nurse #14	208-334-3110 X21
Milk & Dairy Product Storage/Hauling/Handling #20	208-332-8500
Mine Safety Training #10	208-334-2129
Mixer-Loader #20	208-332-8500
Mortgage Broker/Banker #21	208-332-8002
Mortgage Company #21	208-332-8002
Mortician/Mortician Trainee #3	208-334-3233
Notary Public #28	208-334-2810
Nurse #14	208-334-3110 X21
Nurse Anesthetist #14	208-334-3110 X21
Nurse Practitioner-Div of Medicaid #14	208-334-3110 x21
Nurse-LPN #14	208-334-3110 X21
Nursing Assistant #14	800-748-2480
Nursing Care (Skilled) Facility #8	208-334-6626
Nursing Home Administrator #19	208-334-3233
Occupational Therapist/Assistant #30	208-327-7000

Optometrist #19	208-334-3233
Oral Surgeon #13	208-334-2369
Organic Certification #20	208-332-8620
Orthodontist #13	208-334-2369
Osteopathic Physician #30	208-327-7000
Outfitter #15	208-327-7380
Paramedic (EMT) #9	208-334-4000
Pest Control Consultant #6	208-332-8600
Pesticide Applicator/Operator/Dealer/Mfg. #6	208-332-8600
Pharmacist/Phamacist Intern/Preceptor #16	208-334-2356
Pharmacy Mail Svc. #16	208-334-2356
Pharmacy/Drug Store #16	208-334-2356
Physical Therapist/Assistant #30	208-327-7000
Physician Assistant #30	208-327-7000
Plumbing Apprentice/Journeyman #10	208-334-3442
Plumbing Inspector/Contractor #10	208-334-3442
Podiatrist #19	208-334-3233
Police (Peace) Officer #25	208-884-7250
Polysomnography Tech./Trainee #30	208-327-7000
Polysomnography Technologist #30	208-327-7000
Psychologist #19	208-334-3233
Public Accountant Firm #12	208-334-2490
Public Accountant-CPA -LPA #12	208-334-2490
Public Commodity Warehouse #20	208-332-8500
Real Estate Agent/Broker/Company #34	208-334-3285
Real Estate Appraiser #19	208-334-3233
Recreational Vehicle Manufacturer #10	208-334-3896
Rehabilitation Facility #8	208-334-6626
Residential Care Administrator #19	208-334-3233
Residential Care Facility #8	208-334-6626
Residential School #7	208-334-5700
Respiratory Therapist #30	208-327-7000
Restaurant Sanitation Standard #11	208-327-7499
Savings & Loan Association #21	208-332-8005
School Counselor #5	208-332-6800
School Nurse #5	208-332-6800
School Principal/Superintendent #5	208-332-6800
Securities Broker/Dealer/Seller/Issuer #21	208-332-8004
Seed Company #20	208-332-8620
Septic Suptom Permit #11	208-327-7499
Septic Tank Pumper #11	208-327-7499
Shooting Preserve #22	208-334-3717
Shorthand Reporter #4	208-334-2517
Social Worker #19	208-334-3233
Soil & Plant Amendment Mfg. #20	208-332-8620
Solicitor (Financial) #21	208-332-8002
Special Education Director #5	208-332-6800
Subdivision Approval #11	208-327-7499
Substance Abuse Treatment Ctr. #7	208-334-5700
Subsurface Sewage License #11	208-327-7499
Surveyor, Land #17	208-334-3860
Swimming Pool License #11	208-327-7499
Taxidermist #22	208-334-3717
Teacher #5	208-332-6800
Trapper/Junior Trapper #22	208-334-3717
Trust Company #21	208-332-8005
Utility Pay Station #27	208-334-0300
Utility - Regulated #27	208-334-0300
Veterinarian/Veterinary Technician #1	208-332-8588
Veterinary Drug Outlet/Technician #16	208-334-2356
Water Laboratory #2	208-334-2235
Water Rights Examiner #26	208-327-7900
Water Well Driller #26	208-327-7900
Weighmaster #20	208-332-8500
Winery #25	208-884-7060
Wrestler #32	208-221-6534
X-ray Equipment #2	208-334-2235

Idaho Licensing Agency Information

1 Board of Veterinary Medicine, PO Box 7249, Boise, ID 83707; 208-332-8588, Fax: 208-334-4062. Email: sjensen@agri.state.id.us

2 Bureau of Laboratories, 2220 Old Penitentiary Rd, Boise, ID 83712; 208-334-2235, Fax: 208-334-2382.

3 Bureau of Occupational Licenses, Mortician Board of Examiners, 1109 Main St, #220, Boise, ID 83702-5642; 208-334-3233, Fax: 208-334-3945. http://www2.state.id.us/ibol/mor.htm Email: ibol@ibol.state.id.us Search Database at http://www2.state.id.us/ibol/ibollicense_Search.cfm

4 Certified Shorthand Reporters Board, 550 W State St, Boise, ID 83720-0017; 208-334-2517, Fax: 208-334-5211. Email: modedo@ibpg.state.id.us

5 Department of Education, Teacher Certification, PO Box 83720, Boise, ID 83720-0027; 208-332-6800, Fax: 208-334-2094. www.sde.state.id.us/certification Email: kpotter@sde.state.id.us

6 Department of Agriculture, Pesticides Division - Licensing, 2270 Old Penitentiary Rd, Boise, ID 83712; 208-332-8600, Fax: 208-334-3547. www.agri.state.id.us Email: ar_app_licensing@agri.state.id.us Search Database at www.agri.state.id.us/agre source/_agtechlookup/querylic.asp

7 Department of Health & Welfare, Division of Family and Community Services, 450 W State St, 5th Fl, Boise, ID 83720; 208-334-5700, Fax: 208-334-6699. http://www2.state.id.us/dhw/facs/index_facs.htm

8 Department of Health & Welfare, Bureau of Facility Standards, PO Box 83720 (450 W. State St, 10th Fl), Boise, ID 83720; 208-373-0502, Fax: 208-334-6558. http://www2.state.id.us/dhw/

9 Department of Health & Welfare, Bureau of Emergency Medical Services, 590 W Washington, Boise, ID 83702; 208-334-4000, Fax: 208-334-4015. http://www2.state.id.us/dhw/index.htm

10 Division of Building Safety, 1090 E. Watertower St., Meridian, ID 83642; 208-334-3950, Fax: 208-334-2683; Elect. 208-855-2165; Plumb. 208-855-9339. http://www2.state.id.us/dbs/dbs_index.html Email: swallace@dbs.state.id.us Search Database at http://www2.state.id.us/dbs/dbs_index.html

11 Environmental Health Department, Bakery & Related Licensing, 707 N Armstrong Place, Boise, ID 83704; 208-327-7499, Fax: 208-327-8553. www.cdhd.org/EnvironmentalHealth/

12 Board of Accountancy, 1109 Main #470, Boise, ID 83702-0002; 208-334-2490, Fax: 208-334-2615. http://www2.state.id.us/boa Email: isba@boa.state.id.us Search Database at http://www2.state.id.us/boa

13 Board of Dentistry, PO Box 83720 (708½ W. Franklin St), Boise, ID 83720-0021; 208-334-2369, Fax: 208-334-3247. http://www2.state.id.us/isbd Email: smiller@isbd.state.id.us Search Database at http://www2.state.id.us/isbd/search.htm

14 Board of Nursing, 280 N 8th St #210, Boise, ID 83720; 208-334-3110, Fax: 208-334-3262. http://www2.state.id.us/ibn/ibnhome.htm Email: lcoley@ibn.state.id.us

15 Board of Outfitters & Guides, 1365 N Orchard St, Rm 172, Boise, ID 83706; 208-327-7380, Fax: 208-327-7382. http://www2.state.id.us/oglb/oglbhome.htm Email: dsangrey@oglb.state.id.us Search Database at http://www2.state.id.us/oglb/oglbhome.htm Note: Scroll to the bottom of the page to find the appropriate links for searching.

16 Board of Pharmacy, 3380 Americana Terr #320, PO Box 83720, Boise, ID 83720-0067; 208-334-2356, Fax: 208-334-3536. www.state.id.us/bop Email: rmarkuson@bop.state.id.us Note: List are available for $53.00 each; written request and prepayment required. Applications are available online.

17 Board of Professional Engineers & Surveyors, 600 S Orchard, #A, Boise, ID 83705; 208-334-3860, Fax: 208-334-2008. http://www2.state.id.us/ipels/index.htm Email: dcurtis@ipels.state.id.us Search Database at http://www2.state.id.us/ipels/pelsnumb.htm

18 Board of Professional Geologists, P.O. Box 83720, Boise, ID 83720-0033; 208-334-2268. http://www2.state.id.us/ibpg/ Email: ibpg@ibpg.state.id.us Search Database at http://www2.state.id.us/ibpg/search.htm

19 Bureau of Occupational Licenses, 1109 Main St, Owyhee Plaza, #220, Boise, ID 83702; 208-334-3233, Fax: 208-334-3945. http://www2.state.id.us/ibol/ Email: ibol@ibol.state.id.us

20 Department of Agriculture, Inspections/Registrations, 2270 Old Penitentiary Rd, Boise, ID 83712; 208-332-8500, Fax: 208-334-2170. www.agri.state.id.us

21 Department of Finance, Financial Bureau, 700 W State St, 2nd Fl, Boise, ID 83720-0031; 208-332-8000, Fax: 208-332-8098. www.idahofinance.com Email: finance@fin.state.id.us

22 Department of Fish & Game, PO Box 25, Boise, ID 83707; 208-334-3700, Fax: 208-334-2114. http://www2.state.id.us/fishgame Email: idfginfo@idfg.state.id.us

23 Department of Insurance, State Fire Marshall, 700 W State St, 3rd Fl, Boise, ID 83720-0043; 208-334-4370, Fax: 208-334-4375. www.doi.state.id.us/sfm/firemars.aspx Email: mlarson@doi.state.id.us

24 Department of Insurance, 700 W State St 3rd floor, Boise, ID 83720-0043; 208-334-4250, Fax: 208-334-4398. www.doi.state.id.us Search Database at www.doi.state.id.us/insurance/search.asp

25 State Police, PO Box 700, Meridian, ID 83680-0700; 208-884-7000, Fax: 208-884-7090. www.isp.state.id.us

26 Department of Water Resources, 1301 N Orchard St, Boise, ID 83706; 208-327-7900, Fax: 208-327-7866. www.idwr.state.id.us Email: dlarsen@idwr.state.id.us

27 Public Utilities Commission, 472 W Washington St, Boise, ID 83702; 208-334-0300, Fax: 208-334-3762. www.puc.state.id.us

28 Secretary of State, Rm 203, Statehouse, PO Box 83720, Boise, ID 83720; 208-334-2300, Fax: 208-334-2282. www.idsos.state.id.us Email: sosinfo@idsos.state.id.us Search Database at www.idsos.state.id.us

29 State Bar, PO Box 895, Boise, ID 83701; 208-334-4500, Fax: 208-334-4515. http://www2.state.id.us/isb/ Search Database at http://www2.state.id.us/is b/mem/attorney_roster.asp

30 Board of Medicine, PO Box 83720, Boise, ID 83720-0058; 208-327-7000, Fax: 208-327-7005. www.bom.state.id.us Email: info@bom.state.id.us Search Database at www.bom.state.id.us

31 Division of Building Safety, Public Works Contractors Board, PO Box 83720 (1090 Watertower St, Meridian, ID), Boise, ID 83720-0073; 208-334-4057, Fax: 208-855-9666. http://www2.state.id.us/dbs/dbs_index.html

32 State Athletic Department, 7600 W. Katsilometes Dr., Pocatello, ID 83201; 208-221-6534.

33 Horse Racing Commission, 700 Stratford Dr, Meridian, ID 83642; 208-884-7080, Fax: 208-884-7098. www.in.gov/ihrc/ Email: ardie.noyes@isp.state.id.us

34 Real Estate Commission, PO Box 83720 (633 N 4th St), Boise, ID 83720-0077; 208-334-3285, Fax: 208-334-2050. www.idahorealestatecommission.com Email: djones@irec.state.id.us Search Database at www.accessidaho.org/public/irec/licensing/search.html

Idaho Federal Courts

The following list indicates the district and division name for each county in the state. If the bankruptcy court location is different from the district court, then the location of the bankruptcy court appears in parentheses.

County/Court Cross Reference

County	Court		County	Court
Ada	Boise		Gem	Boise
Adams	Boise		Gooding	Boise
Bannock	Pocatello		Idaho	Pocatello (Moscow)
Bear Lake	Pocatello		Jefferson	Pocatello
Benewah	Coeur d' Alene		Jerome	Boise
Bingham	Pocatello		Kootenai	Coeur d' Alene
Blaine	Boise		Latah	Moscow
Boise	Boise		Lemhi	Pocatello
Bonner	Coeur d' Alene		Lewis	Moscow
Bonneville	Pocatello		Lincoln	Boise
Boundary	Coeur d' Alene		Madison	Pocatello
Butte	Pocatello		Minidoka	Boise
Camas	Boise		Nez Perce	Moscow
Canyon	Boise		Oneida	Pocatello
Caribou	Pocatello		Owyhee	Boise
Cassia	Boise		Payette	Boise
Clark	Pocatello		Power	Pocatello
Clearwater	Moscow		Shoshone	Coeur d' Alene
Custer	Pocatello		Teton	Pocatello
Elmore	Boise		Twin Falls	Boise
Franklin	Pocatello		Valley	Boise
Fremont	Pocatello		Washington	Boise

Standards for Federal Courts: The search fee is $20.00 per item (one party name or case number). Certification fee is $7.00 per document. Copy fee is $.50 per page. All fees standard unless noted in profile. Mail Search: always enclose a stamped self addressed envelope unless otherwise noted. Most courts accept fax requests or will suggest a copying/search vendor. Before releasing records, all courts require prepayment unless noted in profile.

Open records are located at the court unless otherwise noted. District courts index by defendant and plaintiff as well as by case number. Bankruptcy courts usually index by debtor and case number. While most courts now have their indexes on computer, many still maintain index card files as well.

The universal PACER sign-up number is 800-676-6856. Find PACER and the Party/Case Index on the Web at http://pacer.psc.uscourts.gov. PACER dial-up access is $.60 per minute. Also, courts offering internet access via RACER, PACER, Web-PACER or the new CM-ECF charge $.07 per page fee unless noted as free.

US District Court

District of Idaho

Boise Division MSC 039, Federal Bldg, 550 W Fort St, Room 400, Boise, ID 83724 (courier address: Use mail address for courier delivery) 208-334-1361 1-800-448-6172, Fax: 208-334-9362. www.id.uscourts.gov

Counties: Ada, Adams, Blaine, Boise, Camas, Canyon, Cassia, Elmore, Gem, Gooding, Jerome, Lincoln, Minidoka, Owyhee, Payette, Twin Falls, Valley, Washington.

Indexing & Storage: New cases available in the index immediately after filing date.

Fee & Payment: Payment may be made by money order, cashier check, personal check. Prepayment is only required for large requests. Payee: U.S. District Court Clerk.

Phone Search: All public information will be released over the phone.

Mail Search: A SASE not required.

In Person Search: Fee charged if court conducts your in person search for you. Copying available from Court Copy Service, a private vendor.

PACER: There is no PACER access to this court.

Opinions Online: Court opinions are online at www.id.uscourts.gov

Other Online Access: Search records online using RACER. Currently the system is FREE; visit www.id.uscourts.gov/doc.htm. Court does not participate in the U.S. party case index.

Coeur d' Alene Division c/o Boise Division, MSD 039, Federal Bldg, 550 W Fort St, Room 400, Boise, ID 83724 (courier address: Use mail address for courier delivery) 208-334-1361, Fax: 208-334-9386. www.id.uscourts.gov

Counties: Benewah, Bonner, Boundary, Kootenai, Shoshone.

Indexing & Storage: Cases indexed by as well as by case number. New cases available in the index after filing date. Open records are located at the Boise Division.

Fee & Payment: Payment may be made by money order, cashier check. Business checks are not accepted. Personal checks are not accepted.

Phone Search: No searching by telephone.

In Person Search: Permitted.

PACER: There is no PACER access to this court.

Opinions Online: Court opinions are online at www.id.uscourts.gov

Other Online Access: Search records online using RACER. Currently the system is FREE; visit www.id.uscourts.gov/doc.htm. Court does not participate in the U.S. party case index.

Moscow Division c/o Boise Division, PO Box 039, Federal Bldg, 550 W Fort St, Boise, ID 83724 (courier address: Use mail address for courier delivery) 208-334-1074, Fax: 208-883-1576. www.id.uscourts.gov

Counties: Clearwater, Latah, Lewis, Nez Perce.

Indexing & Storage: Cases indexed by as well as by case number. New cases available in the index after filing date. Open records are located at the Boise Division.

Fee & Payment: Payment may be made by money order, cashier check. Business checks are not accepted. Personal checks are not accepted.

Phone Search: No searching by telephone.

In Person Search: Permitted.

PACER: There is no PACER access to this court.

Opinions Online: Court opinions are online at www.id.uscourts.gov

Other Online Access: Search records online using RACER. Currently the system is FREE; visit www.id.uscourts.gov/doc.htm. Court does not participate in the U.S. party case index.

Pocatello Division c/o Boise Division, 801 E Sherman, Pocatello, ID 83201 (courier address: Use mail address for courier delivery) 208-334-1074 1-800-448-6172. www.id.uscourts.gov

Counties: Bannock, Bear Lake, Bingham, Bonneville, Butte, Caribou, Clark, Custer, Franklin, Fremont, Idaho, Jefferson, Lemhi, Madison, Oneida, Power, Teton.

Indexing & Storage: Cases indexed by as well as by case number. New cases available in the index after filing date. Open records are located at the Boise Division.

Fee & Payment: Payment may be made by money order, cashier check. Business checks are not accepted. Personal checks are not accepted.

Phone Search: No searching by telephone.

In Person Search: Permitted.

PACER: There is no PACER access to this court.

Opinions Online: Court opinions are online at www.id.uscourts.gov

Other Online Access: Search records online using RACER. Currently the system is FREE; visit www.id.uscourts.gov/doc.htm. Court does not participate in the U.S. party case index.

U.S. Bankruptcy Court

District of Idaho

Boise Division MSC 042, U.S. Courthouse, 550 W Fort St, Room 400, Boise, ID 83724 (courier address: Use mail address for courier delivery) 208-334-1074, Fax: 208-334-9362. www.id.uscourts.gov

Counties: Ada, Adams, Blaine, Boise, Camas, Canyon, Cassia, Elmore, Gem, Gooding, Jerome, Lincoln, Minidoka, Owyhee, Payette, Twin Falls, Valley, Washington.

Indexing & Storage: Cases indexed by debtor as well as by case number. New cases available in the index immediately after filing date.

Fee & Payment: Payment may be made by money order, cashier check. Business checks are not accepted. Personal checks are not accepted. Make all search and copy arrangements with private vendor Court Copy Services, 208-334-9463.

Phone Search: Only docket information available by phone. Automated voice case information service (VCIS) is available. VCIS: 208-334-9386.

Mail Search: A SASE not required.

In Person Search: Fee charged if court conducts your in person search for you.

PACER: No PACER online. There is no PACER access to this court.

Opinions Online: Court opinions are online at www.id.uscourts.gov

Other Online Access: Search records online using RACER. Currently the system is FREE; visit www.id.uscourts.gov/doc.htm. Court does not participate in the U.S. party case index.

Coeur d' Alene Division 205 N 4th St, 2nd Floor, Coeur d'Alene, ID 83814 (courier address: Use mail address for courier delivery) 208-664-4925, Fax: 208-765-0270. www.id.uscourts.gov

Counties: Benewah, Bonner, Boundary, Kootenai, Shoshone.

Indexing & Storage: Cases indexed by debtor as well as by case number. New cases available in the index immediately after filing date.

Fee & Payment: Payment may be made by money order, cashier check, business check. Personal checks are not accepted. Payee: U.S. Bankruptcy Court.

Phone Search: Only docket information available by phone. Automated voice case information service (VCIS) is available. Call VCIS at 208-334-9386.

In Person Search: Fee charged if court conducts your in person search for you.

PACER: No PACER online. There is no PACER access to this court.

Opinions Online: Court opinions are online at www.id.uscourts.gov

Other Online Access: Search records online using RACER. Currently the system is FREE; visit www.id.uscourts.gov/doc.htm. Court does not participate in the U.S. party case index.

Moscow Division 220 E 5th St, Moscow, ID 83843 (courier address: Use mail address for courier delivery) 208-882-7612, Fax: 208-883-1576. www.id.uscourts.gov

Counties: Clearwater, Idaho, Latah, Lewis, Nez Perce.

Indexing & Storage: Cases indexed by debtor as well as by case number. New cases available in the index immediately after filing date.

Fee & Payment: Payment may be made by money order, cashier check, business check. Personal checks are not accepted. Payee: U.S. Bankruptcy Court.

Phone Search: Only docket information available by phone. Automated voice case information service (VCIS) is available. VCIS: 208-334-9386.

In Person Search: Fee charged if court conducts your in person search for you.

PACER: No PACER online. There is no PACER access to this court.

Opinions Online: Court opinions are online at www.id.uscourts.gov

Other Online Access: Search records online using RACER. Currently the system is FREE; visit www.id.uscourts.gov/doc.htm. Court does not participate in the U.S. party case index.

Pocatello Division 801 E Sherman, Pocatello, ID 83201 (courier address: Use mail address for courier delivery) 208-478-4123, Fax: 208-478-4106. www.id.uscourts.gov

Counties: Bannock, Bear Lake, Bingham, Bonneville, Butte, Caribou, Clark, Custer, Franklin, Fremont, Jefferson, Lemhi, Madison, Oneida, Power, Teton.

Indexing & Storage: Cases indexed by debtor as well as by case number. New cases available in the index immediately after filing date. No cases have been sent to the Federal Records Center yet.

Fee & Payment: Payment may be made by money order, cashier check, business check. Personal checks are not accepted. Copy service will bill after first order. Payee: U.S. Bankruptcy Court. Copy service will fax results for $.50 per page.

Phone Search: Only docket information available by phone. Automated voice case information service (VCIS) is available. Call VCIS at 208-334-9386. Copy service will fax results for $.50 per page.

In Person Search: Fee charged if court conducts your in person search for you.

PACER: No PACER online. There is no PACER access to this court.

Opinions Online: Court opinions are online at www.id.uscourts.gov

Other Online Access: Search records online using RACER. Currently the system is FREE; visit www.id.uscourts.gov/doc.htm. Court does not participate in the U.S. party case index.

Idaho County Courts

Court	Jurisdiction	No. of Courts	How Organized
District Courts*	General	Comb.	7 Districts
Magistrates Division*	Limited	2	7 Districts
Combined Courts*		44	

* Profiled in this Sourcebook.

Court	CIVIL								
	Tort	Contract	Real Estate	Min. Claim	Max. Claim	Small Claims	Estate	Eviction	Domestic Relations
District Courts*	X	X	X	$0	No Max				
Magistrates Division*	X	X	X	$0	$10,000	$4000	X	X	X

Court	CRIMINAL				
	Felony	Misdemeanor	DWI/DUI	Preliminary Hearing	Juvenile
District Courts*	X	X	X	X	
Magistrates. Division*			X	X	X

ADMINISTRATION

Administrative Director of Courts, Supreme Court Building, PO Box 83720, Boise, ID, 83720-0101; 208-334-2246, Fax: 208-334-2146. www.isc.idaho.gov//

COURT STRUCTURE

District judges hear felony criminal cases and civil actions if the amount involved is more than $10,000, and appeals of decisions of the Magistrate Division. The Magistrate Division hears probate matters, divorce proceedings, juvenile proceedings, initial felony proceedings through the preliminary hearing, criminal misdemeanors, infractions, civil cases when the amount in dispute does not exceed $10,000, and cases in Small Claims Court, established for disputes of $4,000 or less.

ONLINE ACCESS

Although appellate and supreme court opinions are available from the web site, but there is no statewide computer system offering external access. ISTARS is a statewide intra-court/intra-agency system run and managed by the State Supreme Court. All counties are on ISTARS, and all courts provide public access terminals on-site.

ADDITIONAL INFORMATION

A statewide court administrative rule states that record custodians do not have a duty to "compile or summarize information contained in a record, nor ... to create new records for the requesting party." Under this rule, some courts will not perform searches.

Many courts require a signed release for employment record searches.

The following fees are mandated statewide: Search Fee - none; Certification Fee - $1.00 per document plus copy fee; Copy Fee - $1.00 per page. Not all jurisdictions currently follow these guidelines. Some counties charge $5.00 or $6.00 to do a name search.

A detailed description of the court rules regarding access to records may be found in Idaho Court Administrative Rule 32.

Ada County

Ada County Criminal Court 200 W Front St, Rm 1190, Boise, ID 83702-5931; 208-287-6900; Criminal phone: Ext 2. Hours: 8AM-5PM (MST). *Felony, Misdemeanor, Traffic.* http://www2.state.id.us/fourthjudicial
Criminal Records: Access: Mail, in person. Both court and visitors may perform in person searches. No search fee. Required to search: name, years to search; also helpful: address, DOB, SSN. Criminal records on computer from 1985, microfiche from 1983, docket books back to statehood.
General Information: Public Access terminal is available. No alcohol level or confidential evaluation records released. Will fax results to local or toll free line. Copy fee: $1.00 per page. Cert fee: $1.50. Payee: Ada County. Personal checks accepted. Prepayment required. Mail requests: SASE required. Mail turnaround time up to 1-2 weeks.

District & Magistrate Courts 200 W Front, Rm 1155, Boise, ID 83702-5931; 208-287-6900. Hours: 8:30AM-5PM (MST). *Civil, Eviction, Small Claims, Probate.* http://www2.state.id.us/fourthjudicial
Civil Records: Access: Mail, in person. Both court and visitors may perform in person searches. No search fee. Required to search: name, years to search; also helpful: address. Civil cases indexed by defendant, plaintiff. Civil records on computer since 1985, microfiche and docket books from 1860s.
Criminal Records: Access: Mail, in person. Both court and visitors may perform in person searches. No search fee. Required to search: name, years to search; also helpful: address, DOB, SSN. Criminal records on computer since 1985, microfiche and docket books from 1860s.
General Information: Public Access terminal is available. No juvenile, adoption, child protection records released. Will fax results to local or toll free line. Copy fee: $1.00 per page. Cert fee: $1.50 per page. Payee: Ada County. Personal checks accepted. Prepayment required. Mail requests: SASE required. Mail turnaround time 1-7 days.

Adams County

District & Magistrate Courts PO Box 48, Council, ID 83612; 208-253-4561/4233; Fax: 208-253-4880. 8AM-5PM (MST). *Felony, Misdemeanor, Civil, Eviction, Small Claims, Probate.*

Civil Records: Access: Fax, mail, in person. Both court and visitors may perform in person searches. No search fee. Required to search: name, years to search. Civil cases indexed by defendant, plaintiff. Civil records on computer back to 1993, microfiche from 1972, docket books from 1911.

Criminal Records: Access: Fax, mail, in person. Both court and visitors may perform in person searches. No search fee. Required to search: name, years to search, signed release, DOB or SSN. Criminal records on computer back to 1993, microfiche from 1972, docket books from 1911. Include DOB and/or SSN.

General Information: Public Access terminal is available. No juvenile, sealed cases records released. Will fax results $4.00 per page. Copy fee: $1.00 per page. Cert fee: $1.00. Payee: Adams County. Personal checks accepted. Prepayment required. Mail requests: SASE requested. Turnaround time 2 days.

Bannock County

District & Magistrate Courts 624 E Center, Rm 220, Pocatello, ID 83201; 208-236-7351; Civil phone: 208-236-7350; Criminal phone: 208-236-7352; Probate phone: 208-236-7351; Fax: 208-236-7013. 8AM-5PM (MST). *Felony, Misdemeanor, Civil, Eviction, Small Claims, Probate.*
www.co.bannock.id.us/clkcrt1.htm Note: The phone number for Misdemeanors is 208-236-7272.

Civil Records: Access: Fax, mail, in person. Both court and visitors may perform in person searches. Search fee: None, unless extensive research involved. Required to search: name, years to search. Civil cases indexed by defendant, plaintiff. Civil records on computer from 1986, on docket books from 1970s.

Criminal Records: Access: Fax, mail, in person. Both court and visitors may perform in person searches. Search fee: None, unless extensive research involved. Required to search: name, years to search; also helpful: DOB, SSN. Criminal records on computer from 1986, on docket books from 1970s.

General Information: Public Access terminal is available. No adoption, mental, juvenile, termination, domestic violence records released. Will fax results $1.00 per page. Copy fee: $1.00 per page. Cert fee: $.50 per page. Payee: Bannock County District Court. Personal checks accepted. Prepayment required. Mail requests: SASE required. Mail turnaround time 1 day to 2 weeks.

Bear Lake County

District & Magistrate Courts PO Box 190, Paris, ID 83261; 208-945-2208; Fax: 208-945-2780. Hours: 8:30AM-5PM (MST). *Felony, Misdemeanor, Civil, Eviction, Small Claims, Probate.*

Civil Records: Access: Fax, mail, in person. Only the court performs in person searches; visitors may not. No search fee. Required to search: name, years to search. Civil cases indexed by defendant, plaintiff. Civil records on computer back to 1991, docket books from early 1900s.

Criminal Records: Access: Fax, mail, in person. Only the court performs in person searches; visitors may not. No search fee. Required to search: name, years to search, DOB; also helpful: SSN, signed release. Criminal records on computer back to 1991, docket books from early 1900s.

General Information: No juvenile, CPA, divorce records released. Will fax results $1.00 per page. Copy fee: $1.00 per page. Cert fee: $1.50. Payee: Clerk of Court. Business checks accepted.

Prepayment required. Mail requests: SASE required. Mail turnaround time 2-3 days.

Benewah County

District & Magistrate Courts Courthouse, 701 College Ave, St Maries, ID 83861; 208-245-3241; Fax: 208-245-3046. Hours: 9AM-5PM (PST). *Felony, Misdemeanor, Civil, Eviction, Small Claims, Probate.*

Civil Records: Access: Fax, mail, in person. Only the court performs in person searches; visitors may not. Search fee: $5.00 per name. Required to search: name, years to search. Civil cases indexed by defendant, plaintiff. Civil records on computer from 1991, index cards and docket books from early 1900s. Fax requests must include copy of fees check.

Criminal Records: Access: Mail, fax, in person. Only the court performs in person searches; visitors may not. Search fee: $5.00 per name. If printout required $.15 per page. Required to search: name, years to search. Criminal records on computer from 1991, index cards and docket books from early 1900s. Fax requests must include copy of fees check.

General Information: No juvenile, adoptions, mental commitments or sealed records released. No fee to fax results if search fee paid. Copy fee: $1.00 per page. Cert fee: $1.00. Payee: Clerk of Court. Personal checks accepted. Prepayment required. Mail requests: SASE required. Mail turnaround: 3-5 days.

Bingham County

District & Magistrate Courts 501 N Maple St, #402, Blackfoot, ID 83221-1700; 208-785-8040 X3124 (Dist) X3121 (Magis); Civil phone: X3123 or X3124; Criminal phone: X3118, X3117 or X3122; Probate phone: X3123 or X3124; Fax: 208-785-8057 (Dist) 208-782-3167 (Magist). Hours: 8AM-Noon, 1-5PM (MST). *Felony, Misdemeanor, Civil, Eviction, Small Claims, Probate.* Note: Small Claims X3120

Civil Records: Access: Phone, fax, mail, in person. Both court and visitors may perform in person searches. No search fee. Required to search: name, years to search; also helpful: address. Civil cases indexed by defendant, plaintiff. Civil records on computer from 1989, from microfiche from 1865.

Criminal Records: Access: Phone, fax, mail, in person. Visitors must perform in person searches for themselves. No search fee. Required to search: name, years to search, signed release; also helpful: address, DOB, SSN. Criminal records on computer from 1989, from microfiche from 1865.

General Information: Public Access terminal is available. (Criminal only.) No juvenile, adoption, mental records released. Will fax results for $1.25 per page. Copy fee: $1.00 per page. Cert fee: $1.00. Payee: Clerk of Court. Personal checks accepted. Prepayment required. Mail requests: SASE required. Mail turnaround time 1-2 weeks.

Blaine County

District & Magistrate Courts 201 2nd Ave S, #106, Hailey, ID 83333; 208-788-5548; Fax: 208-788-5527. 9AM-5PM (MST). *Felony, Misdemeanor, Civil, Eviction, Small Claims, Probate.*
Note: The Magistrate Court (Misdemeanor, Small Claims, Eviction, Probate); Magistrate Court phone is 208-788-5525; fax 208-788-5527.

Civil Records: Access: In person only. Visitors must perform in person searches. No search fee. Required to search: name, years to search. Civil cases indexed by defendant, plaintiff. Civil records on computer from 1992.

Criminal Records: Access: In person only. Visitors must perform in person searches. No search fee. Required to search: name, years to search, DOB, SSN. Criminal records on computer since 1988.

General Information: Public Access terminal is available. No juvenile records released. Copy fee: $1.00 per page. Cert fee: $1.00 per document. Payee: Clerk of Court. Personal checks accepted. Prepayment required.

Boise County

District & Magistrate Courts PO Box 126, Idaho City, ID 83631; 208-392-4452; Fax: 208-392-6712. 8AM-5PM (MST). *Felony, Misdemeanor, Civil, Eviction, Small Claims, Probate.*

Civil Records: Access: In person only. Visitors must perform in person searches for themselves. No search fee. Required to search: name, years to search. Civil cases indexed by defendant, plaintiff. Civil records on computer from 6/90, on docket books from 1863.

Criminal Records: Access: In person only. Visitors must perform in person searches for themselves. No search fee. Required to search: name, years to search, SSN; also helpful: DOB. Criminal records on computer from 6/90, on docket books from 1863.

General Information: Public Access terminal is available. No juvenile, adoption records released. Copy fee: $1.00 per page. Cert fee: $1.50 per page. Payee: Boise County. Personal checks accepted. Prepayment required.

Bonner County

District & Magistrate Courts 215 S. 1st Ave, Bonner Courthouse, Sandpoint, ID 83864; 208-265-1432; Fax: 208-265-1447. Hours: 9AM-5PM (PST). *Felony, Misdemeanor, Civil, Eviction, Small Claims, Probate.*

Civil Records: Access: In person only. Visitors must perform in person searches for themselves. No search fee. Required to search: name, years to search; also helpful: address. Civil cases indexed by defendant, plaintiff. Civil records on computer from 1990, index and docket books from 1907.

Criminal Records: Access: In person only. Visitors must perform in person searches for themselves. No search fee. Required to search: name, years to search; also helpful: address, DOB, SSN. Criminal records on computer from 1990, index and docket books before.

General Information: Public Access terminal is available. No juvenile records released. Will fax results for $3.00 per page. Copy fee: $1.00 per page. Cert fee: $1.00. Payee: Bonner County Clerk. Personal checks accepted. Prepayment required.

Bonneville County

District & Magistrate Courts 605 N Capital, Idaho Falls, ID 83402; 208-529-1350; Fax: 208-529-1300. 8AM-5PM (MST). *Felony, Misdemeanor, Civil, Eviction, Small Claims, Probate.*
www.co.bonneville.id.us

Civil Records: Access: In person only. Visitors must perform in person searches for themselves. No search fee. Required to search: name, years to search. Civil cases indexed by defendant, plaintiff. Civil records on computer from civil from 1991. Docket books by case number ongoing. Actual case records are archived before 10/91.

Criminal Records: Access: In person only. Visitors must perform in person searches for themselves. No search fee. Required to search: name, years to search, DOB, signed release; also helpful: SSN. Criminal misdemeanor records on computer from 1983, felony on computer from 1991, civil from 1991. Criminal on microfiche from 1977, civil from 1923. Docket books by case number ongoing. Actual case records are archived before 10/91.

General Information: Public Access terminal is available. No child protective, protection orders, juvenile, sanity, adoption or termination records released. Copy fee: $1.00 per page. Cert fee: $1.00. Payee: Bonneville County. Personal checks accepted.

For criminal and traffic records only. Prepayment required.

Boundary County

District & Magistrate Courts Boundary County Courthouse, PO Box 419, Bonners Ferry, ID 83805; 208-267-5504; Fax: 208-267-7814. Hours: 9AM-5PM (PST). *Felony, Misdemeanor, Civil, Eviction, Small Claims, Probate.*
www.boundary-idaho.com

Civil Records: Access: In person only. Visitors must perform in person searches for themselves. No search fee. Required to search: name, years to search; also helpful: address. Civil cases indexed by defendant, plaintiff. Civil records on computer from 1989; by case number, index books, cards or microfiche by name from early 1900s.

Criminal Records: Access: In person only. Visitors must perform in person searches for themselves. No search fee. Required to search: name, years to search, SSN; also helpful: DOB. Criminal records on computer from 1989; by case number, index books, cards or microfiche by name from early 1900s.

General Information: Public Access terminal is available. No sealed records released. Copy fee: $1.00 per page. Cert fee: $1.00 per page. Payee: Clerk of Court. Personal checks accepted. Prepayment required.

Butte County

District & Magistrate Courts 326 W. Grano Ave, Arco, ID 83213; 208-527-8259; Fax: 208-527-3448. Hours: 9AM-Noon; 1PM-5PM (MST). *Felony, Misdemeanor, Civil, Eviction, Small Claims, Probate.*

Civil Records: Access: Phone, fax, mail, in person. Both court and visitors may perform in person searches. No search fee. Required to search: name, years to search; also helpful: address. Civil cases indexed by defendant, plaintiff. Civil records on computer from 1989, archives prior. Docket books by case number from early 1910s.

Criminal Records: Access: Phone, fax, mail, in person. Both court and visitors may perform in person searches. No search fee. Required to search: name, years to search; also helpful: address, DOB, SSN. Criminal records on computer from 1992 archives prior. Docket books by case number from early 1910s.

General Information: Public Access terminal is available. No juvenile records released. Fee to fax results is $1.00 per page. Copy fee: $1.00 per page. Cert fee: $2.50. Payee: Butte County Magistrate Court. Personal checks accepted. Prepayment required. Mail requests: SASE required. Mail turnaround time 1 week.

Camas County

District & Magistrate Courts PO Box 430, Fairfield, ID 83327; 208-764-2238; Fax: 208-764-2349. Hours: 8:30AM-Noon, 1-5PM (MST). *Felony, Misdemeanor, Civil, Eviction, Small Claims, Probate.*

Civil Records: Access: Mail, in person. Both court and visitors may perform in person searches. No search fee. Required to search: name, years to search; also helpful: address. Civil cases indexed by defendant, plaintiff. Civil records from archives from 1917. Register of actions by case number.

Criminal Records: Access: Mail, in person. Both court and visitors may perform in person searches. No search fee. Required to search: name, years to search; also helpful: address, DOB, SSN. Criminal records from archives from 1917. Register of actions by case number.

General Information: Public Access terminal is available. No juvenile or domestic violence records

released. Will fax results to local or toll free line. Copy fee: $1.00 per page. Cert fee: $1.00. Payee: Camas County Courthouse. Personal checks accepted. Prepayment required. Mail requests: SASE required. Mail turnaround time 1 day.

Canyon County

District & Magistrate Courts 1115 Albany, Caldwell, ID 83605; Civil phone: 208-454-7570; Criminal phone: 208-454-7571. Hours: 8:30AM-5PM (MST). *Felony, Misdemeanor, Civil, Eviction, Small Claims, Probate.* www.the3rdjudicialdistrict.com
Note: Small claims phone is 208-454-7577

Civil Records: Access: In person only. Visitors must perform in person searches for themselves. Search fee: none. Required to search: name, years to search. Civil cases indexed by defendant, plaintiff. Civil records on computer from 1989, microfiche from 1800s, and docket books. A daily court calendar is at www.the3rdjudicialdistrict.com.

Criminal Records: Access: In person only. Visitors must perform in person searches for themselves. Search fee: none. Required to search: name, years to search; also helpful: DOB. Criminal records on computer from 1989, microfiche from 1800s, and docket books. A daily court calendar is at www.the3rdjudicialdistrict.com.

General Information: Public Access terminal is available. No adoption, mental, domestic violence records not released. Copy fee: $1.00 per page. Cert fee: $1.00. Payee: Clerk of Court. Only cashiers checks and money orders accepted. Prepayment required.

Caribou County

District & Magistrate Courts 159 S.Main, Soda Springs, ID 83276; 208-547-4342; Fax: 208-547-4759. 9AM-5PM (MST). *Felony, Misdemeanor, Civil, Eviction, Small Claims, Probate.*

Civil Records: Access: Phone, fax, mail, in person. Both court and visitors may perform in person searches. No search fee. Required to search: name, years to search. Civil cases indexed by defendant, plaintiff. Civil records on computer from 1989, from archives from 1919 by case number.

Criminal Records: Access: Phone, fax, mail, in person. Both court and visitors may perform in person searches. No search fee. Required to search: name, years to search, DOB, SSN; also helpful: address. Criminal records on computer from 1989, from archives from 1919 by case number.

General Information: Public Access terminal is available. No adoption, guardianship records released. Will fax results $2.00 1st page, $1.00 each add'l. Copy fee: $1.00 per page. Cert fee: $1.00. Payee: Clerk of Court. Business checks accepted. Out of state checks not accepted. Prepayment required. Mail requests: SASE required. Mail turnaround time up to 1 week.

Cassia County

District & Magistrate Courts 1459 Overland, Burley, ID 83318; 208-878-7351 Magistrate; 878-4367 Dist; Fax: 208-878-1003. Hours: 8:30AM-5PM (MST). *Felony, Misdemeanor, Civil, Eviction, Small Claims, Probate.*
www.cassiacounty.org/judicial/default.htm

Civil Records: Access: Phone, fax, mail, in person. Both court and visitors may perform in person searches. No search fee. Required to search: name, years to search; also helpful: address. Civil cases indexed by defendant, plaintiff. Civil records on computer from 1990, archives from 1900s.

Criminal Records: Access: Fax, mail, in person. Both court and visitors may perform in person searches. No search fee. Required to search: name,

years to search; also helpful: address, DOB, SSN. Criminal records on computer from 1990, archives from 1900s.

General Information: Public Access terminal is available. No juvenile, adoption, mental commitment, child protection records released. Will fax results $2.50 per page. Copy fee: $1.00 per page. Cert fee: $1.50. Payee: Clerk of Court. Personal checks accepted. Prepayment required. Mail requests: SASE required. Mail turnaround time 1-2 days.

Clark County

District & Magistrate Courts PO Box 205, DuBois, ID 83423; 208-374-5402; Fax: 208-374-5609. 9AM-5PM (MST). *Felony, Misdemeanor, Civil, Eviction, Small Claims, Probate.*

Civil Records: Access: In person only. Both court and visitors may perform in person searches. No search fee. Required to search: name, years to search; also helpful: address. Civil cases indexed by defendant, plaintiff. Civil records on computer from 1985, on microfiche for civil judgments and from archives from 1919.

Criminal Records: Access: In person only. Visitors must perform in person searches. No search fee. Required to search: name, years to search; also helpful: address, DOB, SSN. Criminal records on computer from 1985, on microfiche for civil judgments and from archives from 1919.

General Information: Public Access terminal is available. No juvenile, adoption records released. Will fax results $.50 per page. Copy fee: $1.00 per page. Cert fee: $2.00. Payee: Clerk of Court. Personal checks accepted. Prepayment required.

Clearwater County

District & Magistrate Courts PO Box 586, Orofino, ID 83544; 208-476-5596; Fax: 208-476-5159. 8AM-5PM (PST). *Felony, Misdemeanor, Civil, Eviction, Small Claims, Probate.*

Civil Records: Access: Phone, fax, mail, in person. Only the court performs in person searches; visitors may not. No search fee. Required to search: name, years to search. Civil cases indexed by defendant, plaintiff. Civil records on computer from 8/91, in docket books prior to 1911.

Criminal Records: Access: Phone, fax, mail, in person. Only the court performs in person searches; visitors may not. No search fee. Required to search: name or case number, years to search. Criminal records on computer from 8/91, in docket books prior to 1911.

General Information: No juvenile, domestic violence, adoption, social records released. Will fax results $1.00 per page. Copy fee: $1.00 per page. Cert fee: $1.00. Payee: Clerk of Court. Business checks accepted. Prepayment required. Mail requests: SASE requested. Turnaround time 7 days.

Custer County

District & Magistrate Courts PO Box 385, Challis, ID 83226; 208-879-2359; Fax: 208-879-6412. 8AM-5PM (MST). *Felony, Misdemeanor, Civil, Eviction, Small Claims, Probate.*

Civil Records: Access: Phone, mail, in person. Both court and visitors may perform in person searches. Search fee: $5.00 per name. Required to search: name, years to search. Civil cases indexed by defendant. Civil records on computer from 1989, archived from early 1900s.

Criminal Records: Access: Phone, mail, in person. Both court and visitors may perform in person searches. Search fee: $5.00 per name. Required to search: name, years to search, DOB, signed release; also helpful: SSN. Criminal records on computer from 1989, archived from early 1900s.

General Information: Public Access terminal is available. No juvenile, adoption records released. Will not fax results. Copy fee: $1.00 per page. Cert fee: $1.00 per page. Payee: Custer County. Personal checks accepted. Prepayment required. Mail turnaround time 1 week.

Elmore County

District & Magistrate Courts 150 S 4th E, # 5, Mountain Home, ID 83647; 208-587-2133 x208; Fax: 208-587-2134. Hours: 9AM-5PM (MST). *Felony, Misdemeanor, Civil, Eviction, Small Claims, Probate.*

Civil Records: Access: In person only. Visitors must perform in person searches for themselves. No search fee. Required to search: name; also helpful: years to search. Civil cases indexed by defendant, plaintiff. Civil records on computer from 1992, on microfiche from 1972, archived from early 1900s.

Criminal Records: Access: In person only. Visitors must perform in person searches for themselves. No search fee. Required to search: name, DOB, signed release; also helpful: years to search, SSN. Criminal records on computer from 1992, on microfiche from 1972, archived from early 1900s.

General Information: Public Access terminal is available. No juvenile, adoption, domestic violence, mental commitment records released. Will fax results for $1.00 per page. Copy fee: $1.00 per page. Cert fee: $1.00 per page. Payee: Elmore County. Personal checks accepted. Prepayment required.

Franklin County

District & Magistrate Courts 39 W Oneida, Preston, ID 83263; 208-852-0877; Fax: 208-852-2926. 9AM-5PM (MST). *Felony, Misdemeanor, Civil, Eviction, Small Claims, Probate.*

Civil Records: Access: Phone, fax, mail, in person. Only the court may perform in person searches. Search fee: $5.00 per name. Fee is for years prior to 1990. No fee for 1990 to present. Required to search: name, years to search. Civil cases indexed by defendant, plaintiff. Civil records on computer from 1987, on microfiche from 1983, archived from 1920.

Criminal Records: Access: Phone, fax, mail, in person. Only the court may perform in person searches. Search fee: $5.00 per name. Fee is for years prior to 1990. No fee for 1990 to present. Required to search: name, years to search; also helpful: DOB, SSN. Criminal records on computer from 1987, on microfiche from 1977, archived from 1920.

General Information: No adoption records released. No fee to fax results. Local faxing only. Copy fee: $1.00 per page. Cert fee: $1.00. Payee: Clerk of Court. Personal checks accepted. Prepayment required. Mail requests: SASE required. Mail turnaround: 2-3 days.

Fremont County

District & Magistrate Courts 151 W 1st N, St Anthony, ID 83445; 208-624-7401; Fax: 208-624-4607. 9AM-5PM (MST). *Felony, Misdemeanor, Civil, Eviction, Small Claims, Probate.*

Civil Records: Access: Phone, fax, mail, in person. Both court and visitors may perform in person searches. No search fee. Required to search: name, years to search; also helpful: address. Civil cases indexed by defendant, plaintiff. Civil records on computer back to 1990, microfiche for last 20 years, prior archives. Thursday is the best day for in person searches.

Criminal Records: Access: Fax, mail, in person. Both court and visitors may perform in person searches. No search fee. Required to search: name, years to search, DOB; also helpful: SSN. Criminal records on computer back to 1990, microfiche for last 20 years, prior archives. Thursday is the best day for in person searches.

Gem County

District & Magistrate Courts 415 E Main St, Emmett, ID 83617; 208-365-4561-District Court 208-365-4221-Magistrate Court; Fax: 208-365-6172. Hours: 8AM-5PM (MST). *Felony, Misdemeanor, Civil, Eviction, Small Claims, Probate.*
www.co.gem.id.us/judicial/default.htm

Civil Records: Access: Mail, in person. Both court and visitors may perform in person searches. Search fee: $5.00 per name. Required to search: name, years to search; also helpful: address. Civil cases indexed by defendant, plaintiff. Civil records on computer from 1990, on microfiche and archived from 1916.

Criminal Records: Access: Mail, in person. Both court and visitors may perform in person searches. Search fee: $5.00 per name per court. Required to search: name, years to search, DOB, SSN; also helpful: address. Criminal records on computer from 1990, on microfiche and archived from 1972.

General Information: Public Access terminal is available. No juvenile, adoption records or domestic violence released. Will fax results to local or toll free line. Copy fee: $1.00 per page. Cert fee: $1.00 plus $.50 per page. Payee: Gem County. Personal checks accepted. Prepayment required. Mail requests: SASE required. Mail turnaround time 10 days.

Gooding County

District & Magistrate Courts PO Box 27, Gooding, ID 83330; Civil phone: 208-934-4261; Criminal phone: 208-934-4861; Fax: 208-934-4408. Hours: 8AM-5PM (MST). *Felony, Misdemeanor, Civil, Eviction, Small Claims, Probate.*
Note: Magistrate Court can be reached at 208-934-4261. Magistrate Court address is PO Box 477. Only felony reocrds are available at District Court.

Civil Records: Access: Phone, fax, mail, in person. Visitors must perform in person searches for themselves. No search fee. Required to search: name, years to search. Civil cases indexed by defendant, plaintiff. Civil records on computer from 1994, on microfiche, docket books from 1860s.

Criminal Records: Access: In person only. Visitors must perform in person searches for themselves. No search fee. Required to search: name, years to search, DOB, SSN. Criminal records on computer from 1994, on microfiche, docket books from 1860s.

General Information: Public Access terminal is available. No juvenile, adoption, domestic violence records released. Fee to fax results is $1.00 per page. Copy fee: $1.00 per page. Cert fee: $1.00. Payee: Gooding County Clerk. Personal checks accepted. Prepayment required. Mail requests: SASE required. Mail turnaround time 5-10 days.

Idaho County

District & Magistrate Courts 320 W Main, Grangeville, ID 83530; 208-983-2776; Fax: 208-983-2376. 8:30AM-5PM (PST). *Felony, Misdemeanor, Civil, Eviction, Small Claims, Probate.*

Civil Records: Access: Phone, fax, mail, in person. Only the court performs in person searches; visitors may not. No search fee. Required to search: name, years to search. Civil cases indexed by defendant, plaintiff. Civil records on computer from 1989, on microfiche and archived from late 1800s.

Criminal Records: Access: Phone, fax, mail, in person. Only the court performs in person searches; visitors may not. No search fee. Required to search: name, years to search. Criminal records on computer from 1989, microfiche and archived from late 1800s.

General Information: No domestic violence, juvenile, hospitalization, adoption, termination records released. Will fax results for $1.00 per page. Copy fee: $1.00 per page. Cert fee: $1.00. Payee: Idaho County. Personal checks accepted. Prepayment required. Mail requests: SASE not required. Mail turnaround time same week.

Jefferson County

District & Magistrate Courts PO Box 71, Rigby, ID 83442; 208-745-7736; Fax: 208-745-6636. Hours: 9AM-5PM (MST). *Felony, Misdemeanor, Civil, Eviction, Small Claims, Probate.*

Civil Records: Access: In person only. Both court and visitors may perform in person searches. No search fee. Required to search: name, years to search. Civil cases indexed by defendant, plaintiff. Civil records archived from early 1900s; on computer back to 8/1992. Type of case also helpful with request. This information is on the public access computer. Please use this first.

Criminal Records: Access: In person only. Both court and visitors may perform in person searches. No search fee. Required to search: name, years to search, DOB. Criminal records archived from early 1900s; on comptuer back to 8/1992. Type of case also helpful with request. This information is on the public access computer. Please use this first before requesting from the Deputy Clerks.

General Information: Public Access terminal is available. No juvenile, adoption, some domestic records released. Copy fee: $1.00 per page. Cert fee: $1.00 per page. Payee: Clerk of Court. Personal checks accepted. Prepayment required.

Jerome County

District & Magistrate Courts 300 N Lincoln St, Jerome, ID 83338; 208-324-8811; Fax: 208-324-2719. 8:30AM-5PM (MST). *Felony, Misdemeanor, Civil, Eviction, Small Claims, Probate.*

Civil Records: Access: Fax, mail, in person. Both court and visitors may perform in person searches. No search fee. Required to search: name, years to search. Civil cases indexed by defendant, plaintiff. Civil records on computer from 1989, prior on microfiche.

Criminal Records: Access: Fax, mail, in person. Visitors must perform in person searches for themselves. No search fee. Required to search: name, years to search, address, DOB, SSN. Criminal records on computer from 1989, civil from 1988, prior on microfiche. Will not do background searches.

General Information: Public Access terminal is available. No juvenile records released. Will fax results $3.00 1st page, $2.50 each add'l. Copy fee: $1.00 per page. Cert fee: $1.50 per page. Payee: Clerk of Court. Personal checks accepted. Prepayment required. SASE required. Mail turnaround: 2 days.

Kootenai County

District & Magistrate Court 324 W Garden Ave (PO Box 9000), Coeur d'Alene, ID 83816-9000; 208-446-1180; Civil phone: 208-446-1160; Criminal phone: 208-446-1170; Fax: 208-446-1188. Hours: 9AM-5PM (PST). *Felony, Misdemeanor, Civil, Eviction, Small Claims, Probate.*
www.co.kootenai.id.us/departments/districtcourt

Civil Records: Access: Mail, in person. Visitors must perform in person searches for themselves. No search fee. Required to search: name, years to search. Civil cases indexed by defendant, plaintiff. Civil records on computer from 1989, on microfiche from 1881, archived from 1819.

Criminal Records: Access: Mail, in person. Visitors must perform in person searches for themselves. No search fee. Required to search: name, years to search;

also helpful: DOB, SSN. Criminal records on computer from 1989, on microfiche from 1881.

General Information: Public Access terminal is available. No sealed, adoption, parental termination, mentally incapacitated records released. Will fax results to local or toll free line. Copy fee: $1.00 per page. Cert fee: $1.00. Payee: Clerk of Court. Personal checks accepted. Credit cards accepted through Official Payments 800-530-8189. Prepayment required. Mail turnaround time in 2 days.

Latah County

District & Magistrate Courts PO Box 8068, Moscow, ID 83843; 208-883-2255; Fax: 208-883-2259. Hours: 8:30AM-5PM M-W, 8AM-5PM TH,F (PST). *Felony, Misdemeanor, Civil, Eviction, Small Claims, Probate.*

Civil Records: Access: Phone, fax, mail, in person. Both court and visitors may perform in person searches. Search fee: $4.00 per name. Required to search: name, years to search; also helpful: address. Civil cases indexed by defendant, plaintiff. Civil records on computer from 1986, archived before.

Criminal Records: Access: Phone, fax, mail, in person. Both court and visitors may perform in person searches. Search fee: $4.00 per name. Required to search: name, years to search; also helpful: address, DOB, SSN. Criminal records on computer from 1986, archived from May 1888.

General Information: Public Access terminal is available. No adoption, juvenile, hospitalization records released. Will fax results to local or toll free line. Copy fee: $1.00 per page. Cert fee: $1.00. Payee: Clerk of Court. Personal checks accepted. Prepayment required. Mail turnaround time 1-2 days.

Lemhi County

District & Magistrate Courts 206 Courthouse Dr, Salmon, ID 83467; 208-756-2815; Civil phone: x225; Criminal phone: x225; Probate phone: x242; Fax: 208-756-8424. Hours: 8AM-5PM (MST). *Felony, Misdemeanor, Civil, Eviction, Small Claims, Probate.*

Civil Records: Access: Phone, fax, mail, in person. Both court and visitors may perform in person searches. Search fee: $5.00 per name. Required to search: name, years to search; also helpful: address. Civil cases indexed by defendant, plaintiff. Civil records on computer from 1991.

Criminal Records: Access: Phone, fax, mail, in person. Both court and visitors may perform in person searches. Search fee: $5.00 per name. Required to search: name, years to search; also helpful: address, DOB, SSN. Criminal records on computer from 1991, on microfiche from 1964, archives from 1869.

General Information: Public Access terminal is available. No PSI, sealed records released. Fee to fax results is $1.00 per page. Copy fee: $1.00 per page. Cert fee: $1.00. Payee: Lemhi County Clerk. Personal checks accepted. Will not accept credit cards. Prepayment required. Mail requests: SASE requested. Turnaround time 1 day.

Lewis County

District & Magistrate Courts 510 Oak St (PO Box 39), Nezperce, ID 83543; 208-937-2251; Fax: 208-937-9233. 9AM-5PM (PST). *Felony, Misde.,, Civil, Eviction, Small Claims, Probate.*

Civil Records: Access: Phone, fax, mail, in person. Both court and visitors may perform in person searches. No search fee. Required to search: name, years to search. Civil cases indexed by defendant, plaintiff. Civil records on computer from 1991, archived from late 1911.

Criminal Records: Access: Phone, fax, mail, in person. Both court and visitors may perform in person searches. No search fee. Required to search: name,

years to search; also helpful: DOB, SSN. Criminal records on computer from 1991, archived before.

General Information: No juvenile, adoption records released. Will fax results $1.00 per page. Copy fee: $1.00 per page. Cert fee: $1.00. Payee: Clerk of Court. Two-party checks not accepted. Prepayment required. Mail requests: SASE required. Mail turnaround: 1 wk.

Lincoln County

District & Magistrate Courts Drawer A, Shoshone, ID 83352; 208-886-2173; Fax: 208-886-2458. Hours: 8:30AM-5PM (MST). *Felony, Misdemeanor, Civil, Eviction, Small Claims, Probate.*

Civil Records: Access: In person, mail fax. Both the court and visitors may perform in person searches for themselves. No search fee. Required to search: name, years to search. Civil cases indexed by defendant, plaintiff. Civil records on computer from 1992, archives from 1800s.

Criminal Records: Access: In person, mail fax. Both the court and visitors may perform in person searches. No search fee. Required to search: name, years to search; also helpful: DOB, SSN. Criminal records on computer from 1992, archives from 1800s.

General Information: Public Access terminal is available. No juvenile, domestic violence, sealed records released. Copy fee: $1.00 per page. Cert fee: $1.00. Payee: Lincoln County Courts. Personal checks accepted. Prepayment required. Mail requests: SASE required. Mail turnaround time 5 days.

Madison County

District & Magistrate Courts PO Box 389, Rexburg, ID 83440; 208-356-9383; Fax: 208-356-5425. 9AM-5PM (MST). *Felony, Misdemeanor, Civil, Eviction, Small Claims, Probate.*

Civil Records: Access: In person only. Both court and visitors may perform in person searches. No search fee. Required to search: name, years to search; also helpful: address. Civil cases indexed by defendant, plaintiff. Civil records on computer from 1991, microfiche and archives from early 1900s.

Criminal Records: Access: In person only. Visitors must perform in person searches for themselves. No search fee. Required to search: name, years to search; also helpful: address, DOB, SSN. Criminal records on computer from 1991, microfiche and archives from early 1900s.

General Information: Public Access terminal is available. No juvenile records released. Copy fee: $1.00 per page. Cert fee: $1.00. Payee: Clerk of Court. Personal checks accepted. Prepayment required.

Minidoka County

District & Magistrate Courts PO Box 368, Rupert, ID 83350; 208-436-9041 (Dist) 436-7186 (Magis); Fax: 208-436-5857. Hours: 8:30AM-5PM (MST). *Felony, Misdemeanor, Civil, Eviction, Small Claims, Probate.*

Civil Records: Access: Fax, mail, in person. Both the court and visitors may perform in person searches. No search fee. Required to search: name, years to search. Civil cases indexed by defendant, plaintiff. Civil records on computer from 1989, archives from early 1900s.

Criminal Records: Access: Fax, mail, in person. Both the court and visitors may perform in person searches. No search fee. Required to search: name, years to search, DOB, SSN, signed release. Criminal records on computer from 1989, archives early 1900s.

General Information: Public Access terminal is available. Juvenile records released with a signed relase. Will fax results $.50 per page. Copy fee: $1.00 per page. Cert fee: $.50 per page. Payee: Clerk of Court. Personal checks accepted. Prepayment required. Mail turnaround time 1-3 days.

Nez Perce County

District & Magistrate Court PO Box 896 (1230 Main St), Lewiston, ID 83501; 208-799-3040; Fax: 208-799-3058. Hours: 8AM-5PM (PST). *Felony, Misdemeanor, Civil, Eviction, Small Claims, Probate.*

www.co.nezperce.id.us/clerk/clerk.htm

Civil Records: Access: Phone, fax, mail, in person. Both court and visitors may perform in person searches. No search fee. Required to search: name; also helpful: years to search. Civil cases indexed by defendant, plaintiff. Civil records on computer from 1990, microfiche from 1970 and archives from late 1800s.

Criminal Records: Access: Phone, fax, mail, in person. Both court and visitors may perform in person searches. No search fee. Required to search: name, DOB; also helpful: years to search, aliases, SSN. Criminal records on computer from 1990, microfiche from 1970 and archives from late 1800s.

General Information: Public Access terminal is available. Will fax results $1.00 per doc, $1.00 1st page, plus (if long-distance) $.50 each add'l minute. Copy fee: $1.00 per page. Cert fee: $1.00 per document. Payee: Clerk of Court. Personal checks accepted. Prepayment required. Mail requests: SASE required. Mail turnaround time 10 day waiting period.

Oneida County

District & Magistrate Courts 10 Court St, Malad City, ID 83252; 208-766-4285 X111,112,114,105; Fax: 208-766-2990. Hours: 9AM-5PM (MST). *Felony, Misdemeanor, Civil, Eviction, Small Claims, Probate.*

Civil Records: Access: Phone, fax, mail, in person. Both court and visitors may perform in person searches. No search fee. Required to search: name, years to search; also helpful: address. Civil cases indexed by case number, defendant, plaintiff. Civil records on computer from 07/90, archives from 1886.

Criminal Records: Access: Phone, fax, mail, in person. Both court and visitors may perform in person searches. No search fee. Required to search: name, years to search; also helpful: address, DOB, SSN. Criminal records on computer from 07/90, archives from 1886.

General Information: No juvenile, adoption records released. Will fax results $1.00 per page. Copy fee: $1.00 per page. Cert fee: $1.00. Payee: Clerk of Court. Personal checks accepted. Prepayment required. Mail requests: SASE requested. Turnaround time 1-2 days.

Owyhee County

District & Magistrate Courts-I Courthouse, PO Box 128, Murphy, ID 83650; 208-495-2806; Fax: 208-495-1226. Hours: 8:30AM-5PM (MST). *Felony, Misdemeanor, Civil, Eviction, Small Claims, Probate.* http://owyheecounty.net/court/index.htm

Civil Records: Access: Mail, in person. Both court and visitors may perform in person searches. Search fee: $6.00 per name found. Required to search: name, years to search. Civil cases indexed by defendant, plaintiff. Civil records on computer from 1992.

Criminal Records: Access: Fax, mail, in person. Both court and visitors may perform in person searches. Search fee: $6.00 per name found. Required to search: name, years to search; also helpful: DOB. Criminal records on computer from 1992, archives from 1800s. Signed release required for search of juvenile records.

General Information: No adoption, juvenile (except for some that are open), domestic violence records released. Fee to fax results is $1.00 per page (copies) and $5.00 per document. Copy fee: $1.00 per page. Cert fee: $1.00 per page. Payee: Owyhee County. Only cashiers checks and money orders accepted.

Prepayment required. Mail requests: Include $.37 for return postage. Turnaround time 5-10 days, longer if records archived.

Homedale Magistrate Court
31 W Wyoming, Homedale, ID 83628-3402; 208-337-4540; Fax: 208-337-3035. Hours: 8:30AM-5PM (MST). *Misdemeanor, Civil Actions Under $10,000, Eviction, Small Claims.*
http://owyheecounty.net/court/index.htm
Civil Records: Access: Mail, in person. Only the court performs in person searches; visitors may not. No search fee. Required to search: name, years to search; also helpful: address. Civil cases indexed by defendant. Civil records on computer from 1992, archives from 1975.
Criminal Records: Access: Mail, in person. Only the court performs in person searches; visitors may not. No search fee. Required to search: name, years to search; also helpful: address, DOB, SSN. Criminal records on computer from 1992, archives from 1975.
General Information: No juvenile or mental records released. Will fax results $5.00 each 1st 2 pages, $2.00 pages 3-10; $.75 each add'l. Copy fee: $1.00 per page. Cert fee: $1.00 per document. Payee: Clerk of Court. Prepayment required. Mail turnaround time is 2 days.

Payette County

District & Magistrate Courts
1130 3rd Ave N, #104, Payette, ID 83661; 208-642-6000 (Dist) 642-6010(Magis); Fax: 208-642-6011. Hours: 9AM-5PM (MST). *Felony, Misdemeanor, Civil, Eviction, Small Claims, Probate.* Note: Rm #104 - District Court; Rm #106 - Magistrate Court
Civil Records: Access: Fax, mail, in person. Both court and visitors may perform in person searches. Search fee: $5.00 per name. Required to search: name, years to search; also helpful: address. Civil cases indexed by defendant, plaintiff. Civil records on computer back to 1992, prior on microfiche or archived from 1917.
Criminal Records: Access: Fax, mail, in person. Both court and visitors may perform in person searches. Search fee: $5.00 per name. Required to search: name, years to search, signed release; also helpful: address, DOB, SSN. Criminal records on computer back to 1992, prior microfiche or archived.
General Information: Public Access terminal is available. No juvenile, adoption records released. Will fax results $3.00 1st page, $.50 each add'l. Copy fee: $1.00 per page. Cert fee: $1.00. Payee: Clerk of Court. Personal checks accepted. Prepayment required. Mail requests: SASE required. Mail turnaround time 1 day.

Power County

District & Magistrate Courts
543 Bannock Ave, American Falls, ID 83211; 208-226-7611 (Dist) 226-7618(Magistrate); Fax: 208-226-7612. Hours: 9AM-5PM (MST). *Felony, Misdemeanor, Civil, Eviction, Small Claims, Probate.*
Civil Records: Access: Phone, fax, mail, in person. Both the court and visitors may perform in person searches. Search fee: $5.00 per name found. Required to search: name, years to search. Civil cases indexed by defendant. Civil records on computer from 1986, prior archived from early 1900s.
Criminal Records: Access: Phone, fax, mail, in person. Both the court and visitors may perform in person searches. Search fee: $5.00 per name found. Required to search: name, years to search, DOB, SSN, signed release. Criminal records on computer from 1986, prior archived from early 1900s.

General Information: Public Access terminal is available. No juvenile, mental commitment records released. Fee to fax results is $1.00 per page. Copy fee: $1.00 per page. Cert fee: $1.50. Payee: Power County Magistrate Court. Personal checks accepted. Prepayment required. Mail requests: SASE required. Mail turnaround time 10 days.

Shoshone County

District & Magistrate Courts
700 Bank St, Wallace, ID 83873; 208-752-1266; Fax: 208-753-0921. 9AM-5PM (PST). *Felony, Misdemeanor, Civil, Eviction, Small Claims, Probate.*
Civil Records: Access: Phone, fax, mail, in person. Both court and visitors may perform in person searches. No search fee. Required to search: name, years to search; also helpful: address. Civil cases indexed by defendant, plaintiff. Civil records on computer from 1988, archived from late 1880s. Juvenile case information not available by fax.
Criminal Records: Access: Phone, mail, in person. Both court and visitors may perform in person searches. No search fee. Required to search: name, years to search; also helpful: address, DOB, SSN. Criminal records on computer from 1988, archived from late 1880s.
General Information: Public Access terminal is available. (Has records since 1995.) No special proceeding, juvenile records released. Will fax results $2.00 1st page, $1.00 each add'l. Add $1.00 1st page if long distance. Copy fee: $1.00 per page. Cert fee: $1.00. Payee: Clerk of Court. Personal checks accepted. Prepayment required. Mail requests: SASE required. Mail turnaround time 1-2 days.

Teton County

District & Magistrate Courts
89 N Main, #5, Driggs, ID 83422; 208-354-2239; Fax: 208-354-8496. Hours: 9AM-5PM (MST). *Felony, Misdemeanor, Civil, Eviction, Small Claims, Probate.*
Note: Address and telephone given above are for District Court. If you wish to access only the Magistrate Court and call 208-354-2239.
Civil Records: Access: Phone, fax, mail, in person. Both court and visitors may perform in person searches. Search fee: $5.00 per name. Required to search: name, years to search; also helpful: address. Civil cases indexed by defendant, plaintiff. Civil records on computer from 1992, archives from 1974, I-Star since 1992.
Criminal Records: Access: Phone, fax, mail, in person. Both court and visitors may perform in person searches. Search fee: $5.00 per name. Required to search: name, years to search; also helpful: address, DOB, SSN. Criminal records on computer from 1992, archives from 1974, I-Star since 1993.
General Information: Public Access terminal is available. No juvenile, DV records released. Will fax results $2.00 per page. Copy fee: $1.00 per page. Cert fee: $1.00. Payee: Clerk of Court. Personal checks accepted. Prepayment required. Mail requests: SASE required. Mail turnaround time 3 days.

Twin Falls County

District & Magistrate Courts
PO Box 126, Twin Falls, ID 83303-0126; 208-736-4013; Fax: 208-736-4155. 8AM-5PM (MST). *Felony, Misdemeanor, Civil, Eviction, Small Claims, Probate.*
www.co.twin-falls.id.us/5thdistrict
Civil Records: Access: In person only. Visitors must perform searches for themselves. No search fee. Required to search: name, years to search; also helpful: address. Civil cases indexed by defendant,

plaintiff. Civil records on computer from 1989, archives from early 1900s.
Criminal Records: Access: In person only. Visitors must perform searches for themselves. No search fee. Required to search: name, years to search; also helpful: address, DOB, SSN. Criminal records on computer from 1989, archives from early 1900s.
General Information: Public Access terminal is available. No adoption, termination, juvenile records released. Will fax results $2.50 per page. Copy fee: $1.00 per page. Cert fee: $1.00 per page. Payee: Court Services. Personal checks accepted. Prepayment required.

Valley County

District & Magistrate Courts-I
PO Box 1350, Cascade, ID 83611; 208-382-7178; Fax: 208-382-7184. 8AM-5PM (MST). *Felony, Misdemeanor, Civil, Eviction, Small Claims, Probate.*
Note: There is a Courthouse Annex in MaCall that handles Misdemeanors, Small Claims and Juvenile. However, the McCall Court does not do any background checks and forwards all of its closed cases to the court in Cascade.
Civil Records: Access: Phone, fax, mail, in person. Both court and visitors may perform in person searches. Search fee: $5.00. Required to search: name, years to search; also helpful: address. Civil cases indexed by defendant, plaintiff. Civil records on computer from 1990, microfiche and archives from early 1900s.
Criminal Records: Access: Phone, fax, mail, in person. Both court and visitors may perform in person searches. Search fee: $5.00. Required to search: name, years to search; also helpful: address, DOB, SSN. Criminal records on computer from 1990, microfiche and archives from early 1900s.
General Information: Public Access terminal is available. No juvenile records released. No fee to fax results. Copy fee: $1.00 per page. Cert fee: $.50 per document. Payee: Valley County. Two-party or out of country (w/o printed-stamped US Funds) checks not accepted. Prepayment required. Mail requests: SASE required. Mail turnaround time 1-3 days.

Washington County

District & Magistrate Courts
PO Box 670, Weiser, ID 83672; 208-414-2092; Fax: 208-414-3925. Hours: 8:30AM-5PM (MST). *Felony, Misdemeanor, Civil, Eviction, Small Claims, Probate.* www.the3rdjudicialdistrict.com
Note: This court will only perform searches for probate records, and these requests must be in writing. Turnaround time on probate records is 3-10 days.
Civil Records: Access: In person, mail. Visitors must perform in person searches for themselves. No search fee. Required to search: name. Civil cases indexed by defendant, plaintiff. Civil records on computer from 02/90, archives from late 1800s.
Criminal Records: Access: In person only. Visitors must perform in person searches for themselves. No search fee. Required to search: name, years to search, DOB. Criminal records on computer from 02/90, archives from late 1800s.
General Information: Public Access terminal is available. No juvenile, adoption, hospitalization, child protection-termination of parental rights records released. Copy fee: $1.00 per page. Cert fee: $1.00. Payee: Washington County. Business checks accepted, if local. Prepayment required.

Idaho Recording Offices

ORGANIZATION: 44 counties, 44 recording offices. The recording officer is County Recorder. Many counties utilize a grantor/grantee index containing all transactions recorded with them. 34 counties are in the Mountain Time Zone (MST), and the uppermost 10 are in the Pacific Time Zone (PST).

REAL ESTATE RECORDS: Most counties will not perform real estate name searches. Certification of copies usually costs $1.00 per document.

UCC RECORDS: Financing statements are filed at the state level except for real estate related filings. All counties will perform UCC searches. Use search request form UCC-4. Search fees are usually $6.00 per debtor name for a listing of filings and $12.00 per debtor name for a listing plus copies at no additional charge. Separately ordered copies usually cost $1.00 per page.

TAX LIEN RECORDS: Until 07/01/98, state tax liens were filed at the local county recorder. Now they are filed with the Secretary of State who has all active case files. Federal tax liens on personal property of businesses are filed with the Secretary of State. Other federal tax liens are filed with the county recorder. Some counties will perform a combined tax lien search for $5.00 while others will not perform tax lien searches.

OTHER LIENS: Judgments, hospital, labor, mechanics.

ONLINE ACCESS: Two counties have web access to assessor records. The Secretary of State's office offers online access to UCCs.

Ada County

County Clerk & Recorder, 200 W Front St, Rm 1207, Boise, ID 83702. **Phone**-208-287-6845, UCC Recording- 208-287-6855; fax-208-287-6459; hours 8:30AM-4:30PM. Will search UCC records; search only- $6.00 per debtor. Info + copy request - $12.00. UCC copy- $1.00 per page after 10 pages. UCC search includes tax liens if requested. Separate federal/state combined tax lien search- $10.00 per debtor. Will not search real estate records. Cert fee: $1.00 per doc. Payee: Ada County Clerk & Recorder. **Online Access to Assessor, Property, Inmate records:** Search the property assessor database for free at www.adacountyassessor.org. Click on "Online Property Information System". No name searching. Also, search inmate info on private company website www.vinelink.com/index.jsp. **Other phones:** Assessor-208-287-7200; Treasurer-208-287-6800; Elections-208-287-6860; Vital Records-208-334-5980.

Adams County

County Clerk & Recorder, PO Box 48, Council, ID 83612. **Phone**-208-253-4561; fax-208-253-4880; hours 8AM-Noon, 1-5PM. Will not search records. Record copy- $1.00 per page. Cert fee: $1.00 per cert. Payee: County Clerk and Recorder. **Other phones:** Assessor-208-253-4271; Treasurer-208-253-4263.

Bannock County

County Clerk & Recorder, 624 E. Center, Courthouse, Rm 211, Pocatello, ID 83201. **Phone**-County Clerk & Recorder, R/E & UCC Recording- 208-236-7340; fax-208-236-7345; hours 8AM-5PM Will search UCC records; search only- $6.00 per debtor. Info + copy request - $12.00. UCC copy fee- $1.00 per page. UCC search includes tax liens if requested. Separate federal/state combined tax lien search- $5.00 per debtor. Will not search real estate records. Cert fee: $1.00 per page. Payee: Bannock County Clerk and Recorder. **Other phones:** Assessor-208-236-7260.

Bear Lake County

County Clerk & Recorder, PO Box 190, Paris, ID 83261. **Phone**-County Clerk & Recorder, R/E & UCC Recording- 208-945-2212; fax-208-945-2780; hours 8:30AM-5PM. Will search UCC records; search only- $6.00 per debtor. Info + copy request - $12.00. UCC copy fee- $1.00 per page. Tax liens not included in UCC search. Separate federal/state combined tax lien search- $5.00 per debtor. Mortgage searches available. RE record copy- $1.00 per page. Cert fee: $1.00 per doc. Payee: Bear Lake County Clerk and Recorder. **Other phones:** Assessor-208-945-2155; Treasurer-208-945-2130; Elections-208-945-2212; Vital Records-208-945-2212.

Benewah County

County Clerk & Recorder, 701 College, St. Maries, ID 83861. **Phone**-County Clerk & Recorder, R/E & UCC Recording- 208-245-3212; fax-208-245-3046; hours 9AM-5PM. Will search UCC records; search only- $6.00 per debtor. Info + copy request - $12.00. Will do a limited tax lien search. Will not search real estate records. RE record copy- $1.06 per page. Cert fee: $1.00 per cert. Payee: Benewah County Clerk and Recorder. **Other phones:** Assessor-208-245-2821; Treasurer-208-245-2421.

Bingham County

County Clerk & Recorder, 501 N. Maple #205, Blackfoot, ID 83221. **Phone**-208-785-5005, R/E Recording- 208-785-5005 x3163, UCC Recording-208-785-5005 x3157; fax-208-785-4131; hours 8AM-5PM. Will search UCC records; search only- $6.00 per debtor. Info + copy request - $12.00. UCC copy- $1.00 per page. UCC search includes tax liens if requested. Separate federal/state combined tax lien search- $5.00 per debtor. Will not search real estate records. RE record copy- $1.00 per page. Cert fee: $1.00 per page. Payee: Bingham County Clerk and Recorder. **Other phones:** Assessor-208-785-5005 x3017; Treasurer-208-785-5005 x3090; Appraiser-208-785-5005 x3024; Elections-208-785-5005 x3164; Vital Records-208-334-5988.

Blaine County

County Clerk & Recorder, 206 1st Ave. South #200, Hailey, ID 83333. **Phone**-County Clerk & Recorder, R/E & UCC Recording- 208-788-5505; fax-208-788-5501; hours 9AM-5PM www.co.blaine.id.us Will search UCC records; search only- $6.00 per debtor. Info + copy request - $12.00. UCC copy fee- $1.00 per page. Will search federal tax liens. Tax lien search fee- $5.00 per debtor. Mortgage searches available. RE record copy- $1.00 per page. Cert fee: $1.00 per cert. Payee: Blaine County Recorder. **Other phones:** Assessor-208-788-5535; Treasurer-208-788-5530; Appraiser-208-788-5535; Elections-208-788-5510.

Boise County

County Clerk & Recorder, PO Box 1300, Idaho City, ID 83631. **Phone**-County Clerk & Recorder, R/E & UCC Recording- 208-392-4431; fax-208-392-4473; hours 8AM-5PM. Will search UCC records; search only- $6.00 per debtor. Info + copy request - $12.00. Will not search tax liens. Real estate owner, mortgage, and property transfer searches available. RE record copy- $1.00 per page. Cert fee: $1.50 per doc. Payee: Boise County Clerk and Recorder. **Other phones:** Assessor-208-392-4415; Treasurer-208-392-4441; Appraiser-208-392-4415; Elections-208-392-4431; 208-392-6636.

Bonner County

County Clerk & Recorder, 215 S. 1st, Sandpoint, ID 83864. **Phone**-208-265-1432, R/E Recording- 208-265-1490, UCC Recording- 208-265-1490; fax-208-265-1447; hours 9AM-5PM. Will search UCC records; search only- $6.00 per debtor. Info + copy request - $12.00. UCC copy- $1.00 per page. Will not search real estate or tax lien records. RE record copy- $1.00 per page. Cert fee: $1.00 per cert. Payee: Bonner County Clerk and Recorder. **Other phones:** Assessor-208-265-1440; Treasurer-208-265-1433; Elections-208-265-1490.

Bonneville County

County Clerk & Recorder, 605 N. Capital Ave, Idaho Falls, ID 83402-3582. **Phone**-208-529-1350, R/E Recording- 208-529-1350 x1350, UCC Recording-208-529-1350 x1350; fax-208-529-1353; hours 8AM-5PM www.co.bonneville.id.us Will search UCC records; search only- $6.00 per debtor. Info + copy request - $12.00. UCC copy- $1.00 per page. Tax liens not included in UCC search. Separate federal/state combined tax lien search- $5.00 per debtor. Will search real estate records. Cert fee: $1.00 per cert. Payee: Bonneville County. **Other phones:** Assessor-208-529-1350 x1320; Treasurer-208-529-1350 x1380; Appraiser-208-529-1350 x1361; Elections-208-529-1350 x1363; Vital Records-208-529-1350 x1350.

Boundary County

County Clerk & Recorder, PO Box 419, Bonners Ferry, ID 83805. **Phone**-County Clerk & Recorder, R/E & UCC Recording- 208-267-2242; fax-208-267-7814; hours 9AM-5PM www.boundary-idaho.com

Will search UCC records; search only- $6.00 per debtor. Info + copy request - $12.00. UCC copy fee- $1.00 per page. Will not search real estate or tax lien records. RE record copy- $1.00 per page. Cert fee: $1.00 per cert. Payee: County Clerk and Recorder. **Other phones:** Assessor-208-267-3301; Treasurer-208-267-3291; Appraiser-208-267-3301; Elections-208-267-2242; Vital Records-208-267-2242.

Butte County

County Clerk & Recorder, PO Box 737, Arco, ID 83213. **Phone-**County Clerk & Recorder, R/E & UCC Recording- 208-527-3021, UCC Recording- 208-527-3012; fax-208-527-3295; hours 9AM-5PM. Will not search UCC records. Record copy fee- $1.00 per page. Real estate owner, mortgage, and property transfer searches available. Cert fee: $1.00 per page. Payee: County Clerk and Recorder. **Other phones:** Assessor-208-527-8288; Treasurer-208-527-3047.

Camas County

County Clerk & Recorder, PO Box 430, Fairfield, ID 83327-0430. **Phone-**County Clerk & Recorder, R/E & UCC Recording- 208-764-2242; fax-208-764-2349; hours 8:30AM-Noon, 1-5PM
Will search UCC records; search only-$6.00. UCC copy fee- $6.00 per name. Will search tax liens. Tax lien search fee- $5.00 per debtor. Will not search real estate records. Cert fee: $1.00 per cert. Payee: Camas County Clerk and Recorder. **Other phones:** Assessor-208-764-2370; Treasurer-208-764-2126; Appraiser-208-764-2370; Elections-208-764-2242; Vital Records-208-764-2242.

Canyon County

County Recorder, 1115 Albany St, Caldwell, ID 83605. **Phone-**County Recorder, R/E & UCC Recording- 208-454-7556; 8:30AM-5PM www.canyoncounty.org
Will search UCC records; search only- $6.00 per debtor. Info + copy request - $12.00. UCC copy fee- included in search fee. Tax liens not included in UCC search. Tax lien search fee- $5.00 per debtor. Will search real estate records. RE record copy- $1.00 per page. Cert fee: $1.00 per doc. Payee: Canyon County Recorder. **Online Access to Assessor, Property records:** Access to the Assessor and Treasurer's databases requires $35 registration/setup fee and 150 yearly fee. For subscription info, email clane@canyoncounty.org or call 208-454-7401 or visit the website. **Other phones:** Assessor-208-454-7431; Treasurer-208-454-7354; Elections-208-454-7562; Vital Records-208-334-5980.

Caribou County

County Clerk & Recorder, PO Box 775, Soda Springs, ID 83276-0775. **Phone-**County Clerk & Recorder, R/E & UCC Recording- 208-547-4324; fax-208-547-4759; hours 9AM-5PM. Will search UCC records; search only-$13.48hr. UCC copy fee- $1.00 per page. UCC search includes tax liens if requested. Will not search real estate records. Cert fee: $1.00 per cert. Payee: County Clerk and Recorder. **Other phones:** Assessor-208-547-4749; Treasurer-208-547-3726.

Cassia County

County Clerk & Recorder, 1459 Overland Ave, Rm 105, Burley, ID 83318. **Phone-**County Clerk & Recorder, R/E & UCC Recording- 208-878-5240; fax-208-878-1003; hours 8:30AM-5PM
Will not search UCC records. Record copy- $1.00 per page. Separate federal/state combined tax lien search- $5.00 per debtor. Will not search real estate records. Cert fee: $1.00 per doc. Payee: Cassia County Clerk and Recorder. **Other phones:** Assessor-208-878-3540; Treasurer-208-878-7202; Appraiser-208-878-3540; Elections-208-878-5240; Vital Records-208-878-5240.

Clark County

County Clerk & Recorder, PO Box 205, Dubois, ID 83423. **Phone-**208-374-5304; fax-208-374-5609; hours 9AM-5PM. Will not search records. Cert fee: $1.00 per page. Payee: Clark County Clerk and Recorder. **Other phones:** Assessor-208-374-5404.

Clearwater County

County Clerk & Recorder, PO Box 586, Orofino, ID 83544-0586. **Phone-**County Clerk & Recorder, R/E & UCC Recording- 208-476-5615; fax-208-476-9315; hours 8AM-5PM www.clearwatercounty.org
Will search UCC records; search only- $6.00 per debtor. Info + copy request - $12.00. UCC copy fee- $1.00 per page. Will not search real estate or tax lien records. RE record copy- $1.00 per page. Cert fee: $1.00 per cert. Payee: County Clerk and Recorder. **Other phones:** Assessor-208-476-4912; Treasurer-208-476-5213; Appraiser-208-476-4912; Elections-208-476-5615; Vital Records-208-476-5615.

Custer County

County Clerk & Recorder, PO Box 385, Challis, ID 83226. **Phone-**208-879-2360; fax-208-879-5246; hours 8AM-5PM. Will search UCC records. Fee per debtor- $1.00 per page copy fee. Record copy fee- $1.00 per page. Will not search real estate or tax lien records. Cert fee: $1.00 per doc. Payee: Custer County Clerk and Recorder. **Other phones:** Assessor-208-879-2325; Treasurer-208-879-2330.

Elmore County

County Clerk & Recorder, 150 S. 4th East, ##3, Mountain Home, ID 83647-3097. **Phone-**County Clerk & Recorder, R/E & UCC Recording- 208-587-2130; fax-208-587-2159; 9AM-5PM www.elmoreco.org
Will search UCC records; search only- $6.00 per debtor. Info + copy request - $12.00. UCC copy- $6.00 per name. Will search tax liens including federal tax liens. Will not search real estate records. RE record copy- $1.00 per page. Cert fee: $1.00 per cert. Payee: Elmore County. **Other phones:** Assessor-208-587-2126; Treasurer-208-587-2138; Appraiser-208-587-2126; Elections-208-587-2130; Vital Records-208-587-2130.

Franklin County

County Clerk & Recorder, 39 W. Oneida, Preston, ID 83263. **Phone-**County Clerk & Recorder, R/E & UCC Recording- 208-852-1090; fax-208-852-1094; hours 9AM-5PM
Will search UCC records for Franklin County only. Information request only- $6.00 per debtor. Info + copy request - $12.00. UCC copy fee- $1.00 per page. Will not search real estate or tax lien records. RE record copy- $1.00 per page. Cert fee: $1.00 per page. Payee: Franklin County Clerk and Recorder. **Other phones:** Assessor-208-852-1091; Treasurer-208-852-1095; Appraiser-208-852-1091; Elections-208-852-1090; Vital Records-208-852-1090.

Fremont County

County Clerk & Recorder, 151 W. 1st N. Rm12, St. Anthony, ID 83445. **Phone-**County Clerk & Recorder, R/E & UCC Recording- 208-624-3148; fax-208-624-7335; hours-9AM-5PM www.co.fremont.id.us/departments/index.htm
Will not search UCC records. Record copy- $1.00 per page. Separate federal/state combined tax lien search- $5.00 per debtor. Will not search real estate records. Cert fee: $1.00 per cert. Payee: Fremont County Clerk and Recorder. **Other phones:** Assessor-208-624-7894; Treasurer-208-624-3361; Appraiser-208-624-7984; Elections-208-624-7332; Vital Records-208-624-3148; Commissioners-208-624-4271.

Gem County

County Clerk & Recorder, 415 E. Main, Emmett, ID 83617. **Phone-**County Clerk & Recorder, R/E & UCC Recording- 208-365-4561; fax-208-365-7795; hours 8AM-5PM. Will search fixture filings only. Information request only- $6.00 per debtor. Info + copy request - $12.00. Tax liens not included in UCC search. Separate federal/state combined tax lien search- $5.00 per debtor. Will not search real estate records. RE record copy- $1.00 per page. Cert fee: $1.00 per page. Payee: Gem County Clerk and Recorder. **Other phones:** Assessor-208-365-2982; Treasurer-208-365-3272; Appraiser-208-365-2982; Elections-208-365-4561; Vital Records-208-334-5980.

Gooding County

County Clerk & Recorder, PO Box 417, Gooding, ID 83330. **Phone-**County Clerk & Recorder, R/E & UCC Recording- 208-934-4841; fax-208-934-5085; hours 9AM-5PM. Will search UCC records; search only- $12.00. UCC copy fee- $1.00 per page. Tax liens not included in UCC search. Separate federal/state combined tax lien search- $5.00 per debtor. Will not search real estate records. RE record copy- $1.00 per page. Cert fee: $1.00 per page. Payee: Gooding County Clerk and Recorder. **Other phones:** Assessor-208-934-5666; Treasurer-208-935-5673; Elections-208-934-4841.

Idaho County

County Clerk & Recorder, 320 W. Main, Rm 5, Grangeville, ID 83530. **Phone-**208-983-2751; fax-208-983-1428; hours 8:30AM-5PM
Will search UCC records; search only- $6.00 per debtor. Info + copy request - $12.00. Record copy fee- $1.00 per page. Will not search real estate or tax lien records. Cert fee: $1.00 per page. Payee: Idaho County Recorder. **Other phones:** Assessor-208-983-2742; Treasurer-208-983-2801.

Jefferson County

County Clerk & Recorder, PO Box 275, Rigby, ID 83442. **Phone-**County Clerk & Recorder, R/E & UCC Recording- 208-745-7756; fax-208-745-6636; hours 9AM-5PM. Will not search records. Cert fee: $1.00 per page. Payee: County Clerk and Recorder. **Other phones:** Assessor-208-745-9215; Treasurer-208-745-9219.

Jerome County

County Clerk & Recorder, 300 N. Lincoln, Courthouse, Rm 301, Jerome, ID 83338. **Phone-**208-324-8811, R/E Recording- 208-324-8811 x114, UCC Recording- 208-324-8811 x114; fax-208-324-2719; hours 8:30AM-4:30PM. Will not search UCC records. Record copy fee- $1.00 per page. Tax lien search fee- $5.00 per debtor. Will not search real estate records. RE record copy- $1.00 per page. Cert fee: $1.00. Payee: Jerome County Clerk and Recorder. **Other phones:** Assessor-208-324-7508 X139; Treasurer-208-324-7594; Appraiser-208-324-7507 x138; Elections-208-324-8811 x113.

Kootenai County

County Clerk & Recorder, PO Box 9000, Coeur d'Alene, ID 83816-9000. **Phone-**208-446-1480; hours 9AM-5PM www.co.kootenai.id.us/default.asp
Will search UCC records; search only- $6.00 per debtor. Info + copy request - $12.00. UCC copy- $1.00 per page. Non-standard forms $4.00 add'l. Will not search real estate or tax lien records. RE record copy- $1.00 per page. Cert fee: $1.00 per cert. Payee: County Recorder's Office. **Online Access to Property, Recording, Unclaimed Property records:** the county mapping/recording database is free at www.co.kootenai.id.us/departm ents/mapping.

No name searching. **Other phones:** Assessor-208-446-1500 x1500; Treasurer-208-446-1005 x1005.

Latah County

County Clerk & Recorder, PO Box 8068, Moscow, ID 83843-0568. **Phone-**County Clerk & Recorder, R/E & UCC Recording- 208-882-8580 x3379; fax-208-883-7203; hours 8AM-5PM www.latah.id.us
Will search UCC records; search only- $6.00 per debtor. Info + copy request - $12.00. UCC copy fee- $1.00 per page. Will not search tax liens. Will do very limited searches real estate records. RE record copy- $1.00 per page. Cert fee: $1.00 per doc. Payee: County Recorder. **Other phones:** Assessor-208-882-8580 x3306; Treasurer-208-882-8580 x3343; Appraiser-208-882-8580 x3516; Elections-208-883-2278; Vital Records-208-334-5980 (Boise).

Lemhi County

County Clerk & Recorder, 206 Courthouse Drive, Salmon, ID 83467. **Phone-**208-756-2815, R/E Recording-208-756-2815 x224, UCC Recording- 208-756-2815 x224; fax-208-756-8424; hours 8AM-5PM
Will search UCC records; search only- $6.00 per debtor. Info + copy request - $12.00. UCC copy fee- $1.00 per page. UCC search includes tax liens if requested. Separate federal/state combined tax lien search- $10.00 per debtor. Will not search real estate records. RE record copy- $1.00 per page. Cert fee: $1.00 per cert. Payee: Lemhi County Clerk and Recorder. **Other phones:** Assessor-208-756-3116 x236; Treasurer-208-756-2816 x227; Appraiser-208-756-3116 x236; Elections-208-756-2815 x221; Vital Records-208-756-2815 x224.

Lewis County

County Clerk & Recorder, PO Box 39, Nezperce, ID 83543. **Phone-**208-937-2661; fax-208-937-9234; hours 9AM-5PM. Will search UCC records; search only- $6.00 per debtor. Info + copy request - $12.00. UCC copy fee- $1.00 per page. Tax liens not included in UCC search. Separate federal/state combined tax lien search- $5.00 per debtor. Will not search real estate records. Cert fee: $1.00 per cert. Payee: Lewis County Clerk and Recorder. **Other phones:** Assessor-208-937-2261; Treasurer-208-937-2341; Elections-208-937-2661.

Lincoln County

County Clerk & Recorder, PO Drawer A, Shoshone, ID 83352-2774. **Phone-**County Clerk & Recorder, R/E & UCC Recording- 208-886-7641; fax-208-886-2707; hours 8:30AM-5PM. Will search UCC records; search only- $6.00 per debtor. Info + copy request - $12.00. UCC copy fee- $6.00 per 2 copies. Will not search real estate or tax lien records. Cert fee: $1.00 per cert. Payee: Lincoln County Clerk and Recorder. **Other phones:** Assessor-208-886-2161; Treasurer-208-886-7681; Appraiser-208-886-2161; Elections-208-886-7641; Vital Records-208-886-7641.

Madison County

County Clerk & Recorder, PO Box 389, Rexburg, ID 83440. **Phone-**208-359-6200 x1, R/E Recording- 208-356-3662, UCC Recording- 208-356-3662; fax-208-356-8396; hours 9AM-5PM www.co.madison.id.us
Will search UCC records; search only- $6.00 per debtor. Info + copy request - $12.00. UCC copy fee- $1.00 per page. UCC search includes tax liens. Separate federal/state combined tax lien search- $10.00 per debtor. Will not search real estate records. RE record copy- $1.00 per page. Cert fee: $1.00 per cert. Payee: Madison County Clerk and Recorder. **Other phones:** Assessor-208-356-3071; Treasurer-208-356-6871.

Minidoka County

County Clerk & Recorder, PO Box 368, Rupert, ID 83350-0474. **Phone-**County Clerk & Recorder, R/E & UCC Recording- 208-436-9511; fax-208-436-0737; hours 8:30AM-5PM. Will search UCC records; search only- $6.00 per debtor. Info + copy request - $12.00. UCC copy fee- $1.00 per page. Will not search real estate or tax lien records. RE record copy- $1.00 per page. Cert fee: $1.00 per cert. Payee: Minidoka County Recorder. **Other phones:** Assessor-208-436-7181; Treasurer-208-436-7188; Appraiser-208-436-7181; Elections-208-436-9511; Vital Records-208-334-5980.

Nez Perce County

County Clerk & Recorder, PO Box 896, Lewiston, ID 83501-0896. **Phone-**208-799-3020; fax-208-799-3070; hours 8AM-5PM www.co.nezperce.id.us
Will search UCC records; search only- $6.00 per debtor. Info + copy request - $12.00. Record copy fee- $1.00 per page. Will not search real estate or tax liens. Cert fee: $1.00 per cert. Payee: Nez Perce County Auditor and Recorder. **Other phones:** Assessor-208-799-3010; Treasurer-208-799-3030; Elections-208-799-3023; Vital Records-208-799-3020.

Oneida County

County Clerk & Recorder, 10 Court St, Malad, ID 83252. **Phone-**208-766-4116 x100, R/E Recording- 208-76-4116 x100 or 102, UCC Recording- 208-76-4116 x100 or 102; fax-208-766-2448; hours 9AM-5PM. Will search UCC records; search only- $6.00 per debtor. Info + copy request - $12.00. UCC copy fee- $1.00 per page. Will not search real estate or tax lien records. RE record copy- $1.00 per page. Cert fee: $1.00 per cert. Payee: Oneida County Clerk and Recorder. **Other phones:** Assessor-208-766-2954; Treasurer-208-766-2962; Appraiser-208-766-4116 x109, 106 or 116; Elections-208-76-4116 x100 or 102.

Owyhee County

County Clerk & Recorder, PO Box 128, Murphy, ID 83650. **Phone-**County Clerk & Recorder, R/E & UCC Recording- 208-495-2421; fax-208-495-1173; hours 8:30AM-5PM. Will search UCC records; search only-$6.00. UCC copy- $1.00 per page. UCC search includes tax liens if requested. Separate federal/state combined tax lien search- $6.00 per debtor. Will not research real estate records. RE record copy- $1.00 per page. Cert fee: $1.00 per page. Payee: Owyhee County Clerk and Recorder. **Other phones:** Assessor-208-495-2817; Treasurer-208-495-1158; Appraiser-208-495-2817; Elections-208-495-2421; Vital Records-208-495-2421.

Payette County

County Clerk & Recorder, 1130 3rd Ave. North, #104, Payette, ID 83661. **Phone-**County Clerk & Recorder, R/E & UCC Recording- 208-642-6000; fax-208-642-6011; hours 9AM-5PM. Will search UCC records; search only- $6.00 per debtor. Info + copy request - $12.00. Will not search real estate or tax lien records. RE record copy- $1.00 per page. Cert fee: $1.00 per cert. Payee: County Clerk and Recorder. **Other phones:** Assessor-208-642-6012; Treasurer-208-642-6005; Appraiser-208-642-6012; Elections-208-642-6000.

Power County

County Clerk & Recorder, 543 Bannock, American Falls, ID 83211. **Phone-**County Clerk & Recorder, R/E & UCC Recording- 208-226-7611; fax-208-226-7612; hours 9AM-5PM www.co.power.id.us
Will search UCC records; search only- $6.00 per debtor. Info + copy request - $12.00. UCC copy fee- $.50 per page. Will search tax liens. Tax lien search fee- $5.00 per search. Will not search real estate records. RE record copy- $.50 per page. Cert fee: $1.00 per cert. Payee: Power County Clerk and Recorder. **Other phones:** Assessor-208-226-7616; Treasurer-208-226-7614; Elections-208-226-7611; Vital Records-208-226-7611.

Shoshone County

County Clerk & Recorder, 700 Bank St, Courthouse, #120, Wallace, ID 83873-2348. **Phone-**County Clerk & Recorder, R/E & UCC Recording- 208-752-1264; fax-208-753-2711; hours 9AM-5PM. UCC records that cover fixtures, mineral and timber still filed here. UCC search per debtor-$6.00 per name; $12.00 if a copy is required. UCC copy fee- $1.00 per page. Will not search real estate or tax lien records. RE record copy- $1.00 per page. Cert fee: $1.00 per doc. Payee: Shoshone County Clerk and Recorder. **Other phones:** Assessor-208-752-1202; Treasurer-208-752-1261; Appraiser-208-752-1202; Elections-208-752-1264; Vital Records-208-752-1264.

Teton County

County Clerk & Recorder, 89 N. Main #1, Driggs, ID 83422. **Phone-**County Clerk & Recorder, R/E & UCC Recording- 208-354-2905; fax-208-354-8410; hours 9AM-5PM. Will search UCC records; search only-$5.00 per debtor. Copy fee is $1.00 per page. UCC search includes tax liens. Real estate owner, mortgage, and property transfer searches available. RE record copy- $1.00 per page. Cert fee: $1.50 per cert. Payee: Teton County Clerk and Recorder. **Other phones:** Assessor-208-354-3507; Treasurer-208-354-2254; Appraiser-208-354-3507; Elections-208-354-2905.

Twin Falls County

County Clerk & Recorder, PO Box 126, Twin Falls, ID 83303-0126. **Phone-**County Clerk & Recorder, R/E & UCC Recording- 208-736-4004; fax-208-736-4182; hours 8AM-5PM www.twinfallscounty.org
May or may not search UCC records. Information request only- $6.00 per debtor. Info + copy request - $12.00. UCC copy fee- $1.00 per page. Tax liens not included in UCC search. Separate federal/state combined tax lien search- $5.00 per debtor. Will not search real estate records. Cert fee: $1.00 per cert. Payee: County Clerk and Recorder. **Other phones:** Assessor-208-736-4010; Treasurer-208-736-4008; Elections-208-736-4004; Vital Records-208-334-5980.

Valley County

County Clerk & Recorder, PO Box 1350, Cascade, ID 83611-1350. **Phone-**208-382-7100; fax-208-382-7107; hours 9AM-5PM
Will search UCC records; search only- $6.00 per debtor. Info + copy request - $12.00. UCC copy fee- $1.00 per page. Will not search real estate or tax lien records. Cert fee: $1.00 per cert. Payee: Valley County Clerk and Recorder. **Other phones:** Assessor-208-382-7126; Treasurer-208-382-7110.

Washington County

County Clerk & Recorder, PO Box 670, Weiser, ID 83672-0670. **Phone-**208-549-2092, R/E Recording- 208-414-2092, UCC Recording- 208-414-2092; fax-208-549-3925; hours 8:30AM-5PM
Will search UCC records; search only- $6.00 per debtor. Info + copy request - $12.00. UCC copy-$1.00 per page. Federal/state combined tax lien search- $10.00 per debtor. Will not search real estate records. RE record copy- $1.00 per page. Cert fee: $1.00 per doc. Payee: County Clerk and Recorder. **Other phones:** Assessor-208-414-2000; Treasurer-208-414-0324; Appraiser-208-414-2000; Elections-208-414-2092; Vital Records-208-414-2092 (1907-1911 only); Vital Statistics (Boise, ID)-288-334-5988.

Idaho County Locator

You will usually be able to find the city name in the City/County Cross Reference below. In that case, it is a simple matter to determine the county from the cross reference. However, only the official US Postal Service city names are included in this index. We have also included a ZIP/City Cross Reference immediately following the City/County Cross Reference. If you know the ZIP Code but the city name does not appear in the City/County Cross Reference index, look up the ZIP Code in the ZIP/City Cross Reference, find the city name, then look up the city name in the City/County Cross Reference.

Idaho City/County Cross Reference

ABERDEEN Bingham
AHSAHKA Clearwater
ALBION Cassia
ALMO Cassia
AMERICAN FALLS Power
ARBON Power
ARCO Butte
ARIMO Bannock
ASHTON Fremont
ATHOL (83801) Kootenai(87), Bonner(12)
ATLANTA Elmore
ATOMIC CITY Bingham
AVERY Shoshone
BANCROFT Caribou
BANKS Boise
BASALT Bingham
BAYVIEW (83803) Kootenai(93), Bonner(6)
BELLEVUE Blaine
BERN Bear Lake
BLACKFOOT Bingham
BLANCHARD Bonner
BLISS Gooding
BLOOMINGTON Bear Lake
BOISE (83716) Ada(69), Boise(28), Elmore(2)
BOISE Ada
BONNERS FERRY Boundary
BOVILL Latah
BRUNEAU Owyhee
BUHL Twin Falls
BURLEY Cassia
CALDER Shoshone
CALDWELL (83607) Canyon(94), Payette(4), Gem(1)
CALDWELL Canyon
CAMBRIDGE Washington
CAREY Blaine
CAREYWOOD Bonner
CARMEN Lemhi
CASCADE Valley
CASTLEFORD Twin Falls
CATALDO (83810) Kootenai(97), Shoshone(2)
CHALLIS (83226) Custer(98), Lemhi(1)
CHESTER Fremont
CLARK FORK Bonner
CLARKIA Shoshone
CLAYTON Custer
CLIFTON Franklin
COBALT Lemhi
COCOLALLA Bonner
COEUR D ALENE Kootenai
COLBURN Bonner
CONDA Caribou
COOLIN Bonner
CORRAL Camas
COTTONWOOD Idaho
COUNCIL Adams
CRAIGMONT Lewis
CULDESAC (83524) Nez Perce(96), Lewis(3)
DAYTON Franklin
DEARY Latah
DECLO Cassia
DESMET Benewah
DIETRICH Lincoln
DINGLE Bear Lake
DONNELLY Valley
DOVER Bonner
DOWNEY Bannock

DRIGGS Teton
DUBOIS Clark
EAGLE Ada
EASTPORT Boundary
EDEN Jerome
ELBA Cassia
ELK CITY Idaho
ELK RIVER Clearwater
ELLIS (83235) Custer(82), Lemhi(17)
EMMETT Gem
FAIRFIELD Camas
FELT Teton
FENN Idaho
FERDINAND Idaho
FERNWOOD (83830) Benewah(94), Shoshone(5)
FILER Twin Falls
FIRTH Bingham
FISH HAVEN Bear Lake
FORT HALL Bingham
FRANKLIN Franklin
FRUITLAND Payette
FRUITVALE Adams
GARDEN VALLEY Boise
GENESEE (83832) Latah(67), Nez Perce(32)
GENEVA Bear Lake
GEORGETOWN Bear Lake
GIBBONSVILLE Lemhi
GLENNS FERRY Elmore
GOODING Gooding
GRACE Caribou
GRAND VIEW Owyhee
GRANGEVILLE Idaho
GREENCREEK Idaho
GREENLEAF Canyon
HAGERMAN (83332) Gooding(82), Twin Falls(17)
HAILEY Blaine
HAMER Jefferson
HAMMETT (83627) Elmore(98), Owyhee(1)
HANSEN Twin Falls
HARRISON Kootenai
HARVARD Latah
HAYDEN Kootenai
HAZELTON Jerome
HEADQUARTERS Clearwater
HEYBURN (83336) Minidoka(72), Cassia(27)
HILL CITY Camas
HOLBROOK Oneida
HOMEDALE Owyhee
HOPE Bonner
HORSESHOE BEND (83629) Boise(91), Gem(8)
HOWE Butte
HUSTON Canyon
IDAHO CITY Boise
IDAHO FALLS Bonneville
INDIAN VALLEY (83632) Adams(90), Washington(9)
INKOM Bannock
IONA Bonneville
IRWIN Bonneville
ISLAND PARK Fremont
JEROME (83338) Jerome(98), Gooding(1)
JULIAETTA (83535) Latah(92), Nez Perce(7)
KAMIAH (83536) Idaho(68), Lewis(31)
KELLOGG Shoshone

KENDRICK (83537) Nez Perce(76), Latah(23)
KETCHUM (83340) Blaine(98), Custer(1)
KIMBERLY Twin Falls
KING HILL Elmore
KINGSTON Shoshone
KOOSKIA Idaho
KOOTENAI Bonner
KUNA (83634) Ada(95), Canyon(4)
LACLEDE Bonner
LAKE FORK Valley
LAPWAI Nez Perce
LAVA HOT SPRINGS Bannock
LEADORE (83464) Lemhi(98), Clark(1)
LEMHI Lemhi
LENORE (83541) Nez Perce(52), Clearwater(47)
LETHA Gem
LEWISTON Nez Perce
LEWISVILLE Jefferson
LOWMAN Boise
LUCILE Idaho
MACKAY Custer
MACKS INN Fremont
MALAD CITY Oneida
MALTA Cassia
MARSING Owyhee
MAY (83253) Lemhi(86), Custer(13)
MC CALL (83638) Valley(96), Adams(2)
MC CAMMON Bannock
MCCALL (83638) Valley(96), Adams(2)
MEDIMONT Kootenai
MELBA (83641) Canyon(50), Owyhee(41), Ada(8)
MENAN (83434) Jefferson(91), Madison(8)
MERIDIAN Ada
MESA Adams
MIDDLETON Canyon
MIDVALE Washington
MINIDOKA Minidoka
MONTEVIEW Jefferson
MONTPELIER Bear Lake
MOORE Butte
MORELAND Bingham
MOSCOW Latah
MOUNTAIN HOME Elmore
MOUNTAIN HOME A F B Elmore
MOYIE SPRINGS Boundary
MULLAN Shoshone
MURPHY Owyhee
MURRAY Shoshone
MURTAUGH (83344) Twin Falls(78), Cassia(21)
NAMPA (83687) Canyon(98), Ada(1)
NAMPA Canyon
NAPLES Boundary
NEW MEADOWS (83654) Adams(98), Idaho(1)
NEW PLYMOUTH Payette
NEWDALE (83436) Madison(57), Teton(28), Fremont(13)
NEZPERCE Lewis
NORDMAN Bonner
NORTH FORK Lemhi
NOTUS Canyon
OAKLEY Cassia
OLA Gem
OLDTOWN Bonner
OROFINO Clearwater
OSBURN Shoshone

OVID Bear Lake
PALISADES Bonneville
PARIS Bear Lake
PARKER Fremont
PARMA (83660) Canyon(89), Payette(10)
PAUL (83347) Lincoln(73), Jerome(18), Minidoka(8)
PAYETTE Payette
PECK Nez Perce
PICABO Blaine
PIERCE Clearwater
PINEHURST Shoshone
PINGREE Bingham
PLACERVILLE Boise
PLUMMER Benewah
POCATELLO (83202) Bannock(96), Bingham(3)
POCATELLO (83204) Bannock(94), Power(5)
POCATELLO Bannock
POLLOCK (83547) Idaho(80), Adams(20)
PONDERAY Bonner
PORTHILL Boundary
POST FALLS Kootenai
POTLATCH Latah
PRESTON Franklin
PRIEST RIVER Bonner
PRINCETON Latah
RATHDRUM Kootenai
REUBENS (83548) Nez Perce(65), Lewis(34)
REXBURG Madison
RICHFIELD Lincoln
RIGBY Jefferson
RIGGINS Idaho
RIRIE (83443) Bonneville(54), Jefferson(45)
ROBERTS Jefferson
ROCKLAND Power
ROGERSON Twin Falls
RUPERT Minidoka
SAGLE Bonner
SAINT ANTHONY Fremont
SAINT CHARLES Bear Lake
SAINT MARIES (83861) Benewah(88), Kootenai(11)
SALMON Lemhi
SAMUELS Bonner
SANDPOINT Bonner
SANTA Benewah
SHELLEY (83274) Bingham(98), Bonneville(1)
SHOSHONE Lincoln
SHOUP Lemhi
SILVERTON Shoshone
SMELTERVILLE Shoshone
SODA SPRINGS (83276) Caribou(91), Bear Lake(8)
SPALDING Nez Perce
SPENCER Clark
SPIRIT LAKE (83869) Kootenai(73), Bonner(26)
SPRINGFIELD Bingham
SQUIRREL Fremont
STANLEY Custer
STAR (83669) Ada(90), Canyon(9)
STITES Idaho
STONE Oneida
SUGAR CITY (83448) Madison(76), Fremont(23)

SUN VALLEY Blaine
SWAN VALLEY Bonneville
SWANLAKE Bannock
SWEET (83670) Gem(92), Boise(7)
TENDOY Lemhi
TENSED Benewah
TERRETON Jefferson

TETON (83451) Fremont(64), Madison(35)
TETONIA Teton
THATCHER Franklin
TROY Latah
TWIN FALLS Twin Falls
UCON Bonneville
VICTOR Teton

VIOLA Latah
WALLACE Shoshone
WARREN Idaho
WAYAN (83285) Caribou(50), Bonneville(49)
WEIPPE Clearwater
WEISER Washington

WENDELL Gooding
WESTON Franklin
WHITE BIRD Idaho
WILDER Canyon
WINCHESTER Lewis
WORLEY Kootenai
YELLOW PINE Valley

Idaho ZIP/City Cross Reference

ZIP	City	ZIP	City	ZIP	City	ZIP	City
83201-83202	POCATELLO	83327-83327	FAIRFIELD	83531-83531	FENN	83672-83672	WEISER
83203-83203	FORT HALL	83328-83328	FILER	83533-83533	GREENCREEK	83676-83676	WILDER
83204-83209	POCATELLO	83330-83330	GOODING	83534-83534	HEADQUARTERS	83677-83677	YELLOW PINE
83210-83210	ABERDEEN	83332-83332	HAGERMAN	83535-83535	JULIAETTA	83680-83680	MERIDIAN
83211-83211	AMERICAN FALLS	83333-83333	HAILEY	83536-83536	KAMIAH	83686-83687	NAMPA
83212-83212	ARBON	83334-83334	HANSEN	83537-83537	KENDRICK	83700-83799	BOISE
83213-83213	ARCO	83335-83335	HAZELTON	83538-83538	COTTONWOOD	83801-83801	ATHOL
83214-83214	ARIMO	83336-83336	HEYBURN	83539-83539	KOOSKIA	83802-83802	AVERY
83215-83215	ATOMIC CITY	83337-83337	HILL CITY	83540-83540	LAPWAI	83803-83803	BAYVIEW
83217-83217	BANCROFT	83338-83338	JEROME	83541-83541	LENORE	83804-83804	BLANCHARD
83218-83218	BASALT	83340-83340	KETCHUM	83542-83542	LUCILE	83805-83805	BONNERS FERRY
83220-83220	BERN	83341-83341	KIMBERLY	83543-83543	NEZPERCE	83806-83806	BOVILL
83221-83221	BLACKFOOT	83342-83342	MALTA	83544-83544	OROFINO	83808-83808	CALDER
83223-83223	BLOOMINGTON	83343-83343	MINIDOKA	83545-83545	PECK	83809-83809	CAREYWOOD
83226-83226	CHALLIS	83344-83344	MURTAUGH	83546-83546	PIERCE	83810-83810	CATALDO
83227-83227	CLAYTON	83346-83346	OAKLEY	83547-83547	POLLOCK	83811-83811	CLARK FORK
83228-83228	CLIFTON	83347-83347	PAUL	83548-83548	REUBENS	83812-83812	CLARKIA
83229-83229	COBALT	83348-83348	PICABO	83549-83549	RIGGINS	83813-83813	COCOLALLA
83230-83230	CONDA	83349-83349	RICHFIELD	83551-83551	SPALDING	83814-83816	COEUR D ALENE
83231-83231	MOORE	83350-83350	RUPERT	83552-83552	STITES	83821-83821	COOLIN
83232-83232	DAYTON	83352-83352	SHOSHONE	83553-83553	WEIPPE	83822-83822	OLDTOWN
83233-83233	DINGLE	83353-83354	SUN VALLEY	83554-83554	WHITE BIRD	83823-83823	DEARY
83234-83234	DOWNEY	83355-83355	WENDELL	83555-83555	WINCHESTER	83824-83824	DESMET
83235-83235	ELLIS	83401-83406	IDAHO FALLS	83601-83601	ATLANTA	83825-83825	DOVER
83236-83236	FIRTH	83415-83415	IDAHO FALLS	83602-83602	BANKS	83826-83826	EASTPORT
83237-83237	FRANKLIN	83420-83420	ASHTON	83604-83604	BRUNEAU	83827-83827	ELK RIVER
83238-83238	GENEVA	83421-83421	CHESTER	83605-83607	CALDWELL	83830-83830	FERNWOOD
83239-83239	GEORGETOWN	83422-83422	DRIGGS	83610-83610	CAMBRIDGE	83832-83832	GENESEE
83241-83241	GRACE	83423-83423	DUBOIS	83611-83611	CASCADE	83833-83833	HARRISON
83243-83243	HOLBROOK	83424-83424	FELT	83612-83612	COUNCIL	83834-83834	HARVARD
83244-83244	HOWE	83425-83425	HAMER	83615-83615	DONNELLY	83835-83835	HAYDEN
83245-83245	INKOM	83427-83427	IONA	83616-83616	EAGLE	83836-83836	HOPE
83246-83246	LAVA HOT SPRINGS	83428-83428	IRWIN	83617-83617	EMMETT	83837-83837	KELLOGG
83250-83250	MC CAMMON	83429-83429	ISLAND PARK	83619-83619	FRUITLAND	83839-83839	KINGSTON
83251-83251	MACKAY	83431-83431	LEWISVILLE	83620-83620	FRUITVALE	83840-83840	KOOTENAI
83252-83252	MALAD CITY	83433-83433	MACKS INN	83622-83622	GARDEN VALLEY	83841-83841	LACLEDE
83253-83253	MAY	83434-83434	MENAN	83623-83623	GLENNS FERRY	83842-83842	MEDIMONT
83254-83254	MONTPELIER	83435-83435	MONTEVIEW	83624-83624	GRAND VIEW	83843-83844	MOSCOW
83255-83255	MOORE	83436-83436	NEWDALE	83626-83626	GREENLEAF	83845-83845	MOYIE SPRINGS
83256-83256	MORELAND	83437-83437	PALISADES	83627-83627	HAMMETT	83846-83846	MULLAN
83260-83260	OVID	83438-83438	PARKER	83628-83628	HOMEDALE	83847-83847	NAPLES
83261-83261	PARIS	83440-83441	REXBURG	83629-83629	HORSESHOE BEND	83848-83848	NORDMAN
83262-83262	PINGREE	83442-83442	RIGBY	83630-83630	HUSTON	83849-83849	OSBURN
83263-83263	PRESTON	83443-83443	RIRIE	83631-83631	IDAHO CITY	83850-83850	PINEHURST
83271-83271	ROCKLAND	83444-83444	ROBERTS	83632-83632	INDIAN VALLEY	83851-83851	PLUMMER
83272-83272	SAINT CHARLES	83445-83445	SAINT ANTHONY	83633-83633	KING HILL	83852-83852	PONDERAY
83274-83274	SHELLEY	83446-83446	SPENCER	83634-83634	KUNA	83853-83853	PORTHILL
83276-83276	SODA SPRINGS	83447-83447	SQUIRREL	83635-83635	LAKE FORK	83854-83854	POST FALLS
83277-83277	SPRINGFIELD	83448-83448	SUGAR CITY	83636-83636	LETHA	83855-83855	POTLATCH
83278-83278	STANLEY	83449-83449	SWAN VALLEY	83637-83637	LOWMAN	83856-83856	PRIEST RIVER
83280-83280	STONE	83450-83450	TERRETON	83638-83638	MC CALL	83857-83857	PRINCETON
83281-83281	SWANLAKE	83451-83451	TETON	83638-83638	MCCALL	83858-83858	RATHDRUM
83283-83283	THATCHER	83452-83452	TETONIA	83639-83639	MARSING	83860-83860	SAGLE
83285-83285	WAYAN	83454-83454	UCON	83641-83641	MELBA	83861-83861	SAINT MARIES
83286-83286	WESTON	83455-83455	VICTOR	83642-83642	MERIDIAN	83862-83862	SAMUELS
83287-83287	FISH HAVEN	83460-83460	REXBURG	83643-83643	MESA	83864-83864	SANDPOINT
83301-83301	TWIN FALLS	83462-83462	CARMEN	83644-83644	MIDDLETON	83865-83865	COLBURN
83302-83302	ROGERSON	83463-83463	GIBBONSVILLE	83645-83645	MIDVALE	83866-83866	SANTA
83303-83303	TWIN FALLS	83464-83464	LEADORE	83647-83647	MOUNTAIN HOME	83867-83867	SILVERTON
83311-83311	ALBION	83465-83465	LEMHI	83648-83648	MOUNTAIN HOME A F B	83868-83868	SMELTERVILLE
83312-83312	ALMO	83466-83466	NORTH FORK	83650-83650	MURPHY	83869-83869	SPIRIT LAKE
83313-83313	BELLEVUE	83467-83467	SALMON	83651-83653	NAMPA	83870-83870	TENSED
83314-83314	BLISS	83468-83468	TENDOY	83654-83654	NEW MEADOWS	83871-83871	TROY
83316-83316	BUHL	83469-83469	SHOUP	83655-83655	NEW PLYMOUTH	83872-83872	VIOLA
83318-83318	BURLEY	83501-83501	LEWISTON	83656-83656	NOTUS	83873-83873	WALLACE
83320-83320	CAREY	83520-83520	AHSAHKA	83657-83657	OLA	83874-83874	MURRAY
83321-83321	CASTLEFORD	83522-83522	COTTONWOOD	83660-83660	PARMA	83876-83876	WORLEY
83322-83322	CORRAL	83523-83523	CRAIGMONT	83661-83661	PAYETTE	83877-83877	POST FALLS
83323-83323	DECLO	83524-83524	CULDESAC	83666-83666	PLACERVILLE	83888-83888	SANDPOINT
83324-83324	DIETRICH	83525-83525	ELK CITY	83669-83669	STAR		
83325-83325	EDEN	83526-83526	FERDINAND	83670-83670	SWEET		
83326-83326	ELBA	83530-83530	GRANGEVILLE	83671-83671	WARREN		

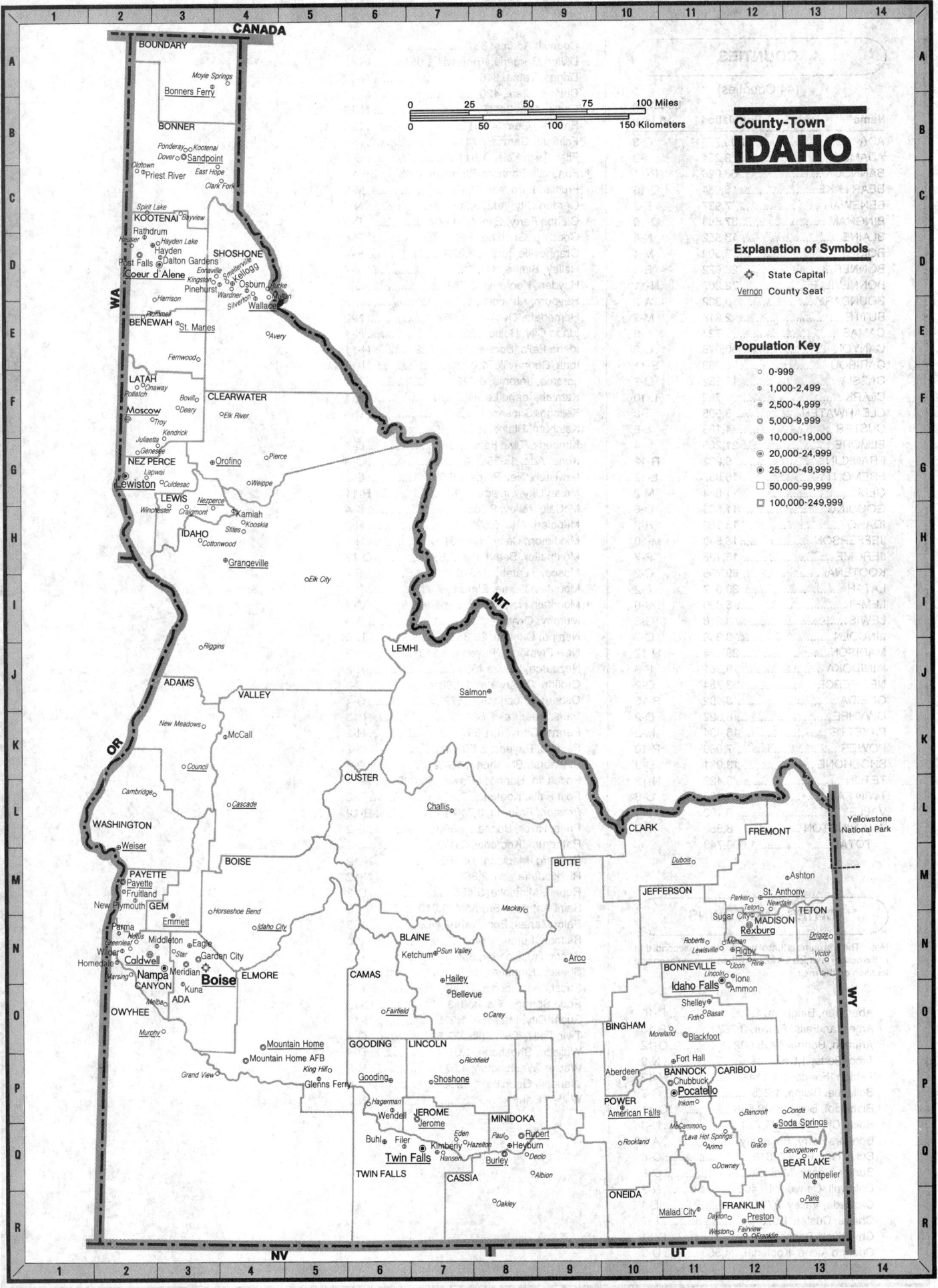

County-Town
IDAHO

Explanation of Symbols

◇ State Capital
Vernon County Seat

Population Key

○ 0-999
⊙ 1,000-2,499
⊕ 2,500-4,999
⊕ 5,000-9,999
⊗ 10,000-19,000
⊛ 20,000-24,999
⊛ 25,000-49,999
□ 50,000-99,999
▣ 100,000-249,999

COUNTIES

(44 Counties)

Name	Population	Location on Map
ADA	205,775	O-3
ADAMS	3,254	J-3
BANNOCK	66,026	P-11
BEAR LAKE	6,084	Q-13
BENEWAH	7,937	E-2
BINGHAM	37,583	O-10
BLAINE	13,552	N-6
BOISE	3,509	M-4
BONNER	26,622	B-3
BONNEVILLE	72,207	N-11
BOUNDARY	8,332	A-2
BUTTE	2,918	M-9
CAMAS	727	N-6
CANYON	90,076	O-2
CARIBOU	6,963	P-11
CASSIA	19,532	Q-7
CLARK	762	L-10
CLEARWATER	8,505	F-3
CUSTER	4,133	L-6
ELMORE	21,205	N-4
FRANKLIN	9,232	R-12
FREMONT	10,937	L-12
GEM	11,844	M-2
GOODING	11,633	O-6
IDAHO	13,783	H-3
JEFFERSON	16,543	M-10
JEROME	15,138	P-7
KOOTENAI	69,795	C-2
LATAH	30,617	F-2
LEMHI	6,899	J-6
LEWIS	3,516	G-3
LINCOLN	3,308	O-7
MADISON	23,674	N-12
MINIDOKA	19,361	P-8
NEZ PERCE	33,754	G-2
ONEIDA	3,492	R-10
OWYHEE	8,392	O-2
PAYETTE	16,434	M-2
POWER	7,086	P-10
SHOSHONE	13,931	D-3
TETON	3,439	N-13
TWIN FALLS	53,580	Q-6
VALLEY	6,109	J-4
WASHINGTON	8,550	L-2
TOTAL	**1,006,749**	

CITIES AND TOWNS

Note: The first name is that of the city or town, second, that of the county in which it is located, then the population and location on the map.

Aberdeen, Bingham, 1,406 .... P-10
American Falls, Power, 3,757 .... P-10
Ammon, Bonneville, 5,002 .... O-12
Arco, Butte, 1,016 .... N-9
Ashton, Fremont, 1,114 .... M-13
Bellevue, Blaine, 1,275 .... O-7
Blackfoot, Bingham, 9,646 .... O-11
Boise City, Ada, 125,738 .... N-3
Bonners Ferry, Boundary, 2,193 .... A-3
Buhl, Twin Falls, 3,516 .... Q-6
Burley, Cassia/Minidoka, 8,702 .... Q-8
Caldwell, Canyon, 18,400 .... N-2
Cascade, Valley, 877 .... L-4
Challis, Custer, 1,073 .... L-7
Chubbuck, Bannock, 7,791 .... P-11
Coeur d'Alene, Kootenai, 24,563 .... D-3

Council, Adams, 831 .... K-3
Dalton Gardens, Kootenai, 1,951 .... D-3
Driggs, Teton, 846 .... N-13
Dubois, Clark, 420 .... M-11
Eagle, Ada, 3,327 .... N-13
Emmett, Gem, 4,601 .... N-3
Fairfield, Camas, 371 .... O-6
Filer, Twin Falls, 1,511 .... Q-6
• Fort Hall, Bannock/Bingham, 2,681 ..... P-11
Fruitland, Payette, 2,400 .... M-2
Garden City, Ada, 6,369 .... N-3
Glenns Ferry, Elmore, 1,304 .... P-5
Gooding, Gooding, 2,820 .... P-6
Grangeville, Idaho, 3,226 .... H-4
Hailey, Blaine, 3,687 .... N-7
Hayden, Kootenai, 3,744 .... D-2
Heyburn, Minidoka, 2,714 .... Q-8
Homedale, Owyhee, 1,963 .... N-2
Idaho City, Boise, 322 .... N-4
Idaho Falls, Bonneville, 43,929 .... N-11
Iona, Bonneville, 1,049 .... N-12
Jerome, Jerome, 6,529 .... P-7
Kamiah, Idaho/Lewis, 1,157 .... H-4
Kellogg, Shoshone, 2,591 .... D-4
Ketchum, Blaine, 2,523 .... N-7
Kimberly, Twin Falls, 2,367 .... Q-7
Kuna, Ada, 1,955 .... O-3
Lewiston, Nez Perce, 28,082 .... G-2
Malad City, Oneida, 1,946 .... R-11
McCall, Valley, 2,005 .... K-4
Meridian, Ada, 9,596 .... N-3
Middleton, Canyon, 1,851 .... N-2
Montpelier, Bear Lake, 2,656 .... Q-13
Moscow, Latah, 18,519 .... F-2
Mountain Home, Elmore, 7,913 .... P-4
• Mountain Home AFB, Elmore, 5,936 ... O-4
Murphy, Owyhee O-2
Nampa, Canyon, 28,365 .... N-3
New Plymouth, Payette, 1,313 .... M-2
Nezperce, Lewis, 453 .... H-3
Orofino, Clearwater, 2,868 .... G-3
Osburn, Shoshone, 1,579 .... D-4
Paris, Bear Lake, 581 .... R-13
Parma, Canyon, 1,597 .... N-2
Payette, Payette, 5,592 .... M-2
Pinehurst, Shoshone, 1,722 .... D-4
Pocatello, Bannock/Power, 46,080 ...... P-11
Post Falls, Kootenai, 7,349 .... D-2
Preston, Franklin, 3,710 .... R-12
Priest River, Bonner, 1,560 .... C-2
Rathdrum, Kootenai, 2,000 .... D-2
Rexburg, Madison, 14,302 .... N-12
Rigby, Jefferson, 2,681 .... N-12
Rupert, Minidoka, 5,455 .... Q-8
Saint Anthony, Fremont, 3,010 .... M-12
Saint Maries, Benewah, 2,442 .... E-3
Salmon, Lemhi, 2,941 .... J-8
Sandpoint, Bonner, 5,203 .... B-3
Shelley, Bingham, 3,536 .... O-11
Shoshone, Lincoln, 1,249 .... P-7
Soda Springs, Caribou, 3,111 .... Q-12
Sugar City, Madison, 1,275 .... N-12
Twin Falls, Twin Falls, 27,591 .... Q-7
Wallace, Shoshone, 1,010 .... D-4
Weiser, Washington, 4,571 .... M-2
Wendell, Gooding, 1,963 .... P-6
Wilder, Canyon, 1,232 .... N-2

Explanation of symbols: ●– Census Designated Place (CDP)

Illinois

General Help Numbers:

Governor's Office
222 S College, 1st Fl
Springfield, IL 62706
http://www.illinois.gov/gov/

217-782-0244
Fax 217-524-4049
8:30AM-5PM

Attorney General's Office
500 S 2nd St
Springfield, IL 62706
www.ag.state.il.us

217-782-1090
Fax 217-524-4701
8:45AM-4:45PM

Legislative Records
Illinois General Assembly
House (or Senate) Bills Division
Springfield, IL 62706
www.legis.state.il.us

217-782-3944
217-782-7017
Fax 217-524-6059
8AM-4:30PM

State Archives
Archives Division
Norton Bldg, Capitol Complex
Springfield, IL 62756
www.sos.state.il.us/departments
/archives/archives.html

217-782-4682
Fax 217-524-3930
8AM-4:30PM M-F,
8AM-3:30PM SA

State Specifics:

Capital: Springfield
Sangamon County

Time Zone: CST

Number of Counties: 102

Population: 12,653,544

Web Site: http://www100.state.il.us

State Agencies

Criminal Records

Illinois State Police, Bureau of Identification, 260 N Chicago St, Joliet, IL 60432-4075; 815-740-5216 x5184, 815-740-5215 (Fax), 8AM-4PM M-F.

www.isp.state.il.us

Indexing & Storage: Records are available from 1930's on. It takes 1 to 5 days before new records are available for inquiry. Records are indexed on microfilm, index cards, inhouse computer.

Searching: Requester must use the Uniform Conviction Information Form ISP6-405B. Personal requests are honored per Illinois statute.

Include the following in your request: name, date of birth, sex, race. Fingerprint cards are an option; a fingerprint search using Form ISP6-404B is recommended in order to assure proper identification. All forms can be ordered (but not downloaded) at the website. The following data is not released: records with warrants only, juvenile records unless juvenile convicted by an adult court of law.

Access by: mail, in person, online.

Fee & Payment: The search fee is $16.00 per form. A fingerprint search is $20.00. Fee payee: Illinois State Police. Prepayment required. Modem

users and ongoing UCIA requesters must prepay for records in groups of 35 at a time. Personal checks accepted. No credit cards accepted.

Mail search: Turnaround time: 3 to 4 weeks. No SASE is required.

In person search: An in person search saves mailing time only.

Online search: Online access costs $10.00 per name. Upon signing an interagency agreement with ISP and establishing an escrow account, users can submit inquiries by email. Responses are sent back in 24 to 48 hours by either email or fax.

Statewide Court Records

Administrative Office of Courts, 222 N. LaSalle - 13th Floor, Chicago, IL 60601; 312-793-3250, 312-793-1335 (Fax), 8AM-5PM.

www.state.il.us/court/

Note: Except for certain online research capabilities, all court record access must be done at the local level.

Access by: online.

Online search: The web page offers access to supreme and appellate opinions. There is no statewide public online system for local court records. A few Circuit Courts offer online access. A vendor, Judici.com, offers free searching for a few counties with a fee service for multi-county searching.

Sexual Offender Registry

Illinois State Police, SOR Unit, 400 Iles Park Place, #140, Springfield, IL 62703-2978; 217-785-0653, 8AM-4PM M-F.

www.isp.state.il.us/sor/frames.htm

Note: Persons required to register as Sex Offenders are persons who have been charged of an offense listed in Illinois Compiled Statutes 730 ILCS 150/2(B).

Indexing & Storage: It takes 1 to 5 days before new records are available for inquiry.

Searching: Illinois Compiled Statutes (730 ILCS 152/115 (a) and (b)) mandate that the Illinois State Police ("ISP") establish and maintain a statewide Sex Offender Database, accessible on the Internet. A status fileld indicates if offender listed as "COMPLIANT" are in good standing with the Sex Offender Registration Laws. Offenders listed as "NON-COMPLIANT" have failed to maintain accurate registration information.

Access by: online.

Online search: The website provides an online listing of sex offenders required to register in the State of Illinois. The database is updated daily and allows searching by name, city, county, and ZIP Code. The City of Chicago provides its own search site at http://12.17.79.4.

Incarceration Records

Illinois Department of Corrections, Public Information Office, PO Box 19277, Springfield, IL 62794-9277 (Courier: 1301 Concordia Court, Springfield, IL 62794); 217-522-2666 x2008, 217-522-3568 (Fax), 8:30AM-5PM M-F.

www.idoc.state.il.us

Note: Offender information is available to the general public and private organizations.

Indexing & Storage: Records are available on current and former inmates, except online is current only. It takes 1 to 5 days before new records are available for inquiry.

Searching: Records are never destroyed, but are archived. Include the following in your request-full name and DOB, IBOC #, gender, race helpful. For a online search, you can provide name or DOB or IDOC #. Location, conviction information, physical identifiers, and release dates are reported.

Access by: mail, phone, online.

Mail search: Turnaround time: 1 to 2 weeks. No SASE is required.

Phone search: Name searching available by phone.

Online search: Click on Inmate Search at the website. Also, a private company offers free web access at www.vinelink.com/index.jsp. Includes state, DOC, and county jails.

Other access: A CD of the inmate database can be purchased for $45.00.

Corporation, Limited Partnership, Trade Names, Assumed Name, Limited Liability Company Records

Department of Business Services, Corporate Department, 330 Howlett Bldg, 3rd Floor, Copy Section, Springfield, IL 62756 (Courier: 501 S 2nd St, Springfield, IL 62756); 217-782-7880, 217-782-9521 (Name Availability), 217-524-5248 (Expedited Srv), 217-782-4528 (Fax), 8AM-4:30PM.

www.ilsos.net/

Indexing & Storage: Records are available from mid-1800's on. Closed records are stored at the State Archives. Only limited information is available for corporations dissolved before 1986. New records are available for inquiry immediately. Records are indexed on inhouse computer.

Searching: Records are on micro-film from 1984. In-house computer has name of agent, state and date of incorporation, etc. Include the following in your request-full name of business, corporation file number. In addition to the articles of incorporation, corporation records include the following information: Annual Reports, Officers, Directors, Prior (merged) names, Assumed names, and Inactive names.

Access by: mail, phone, in person, online.

Fee & Payment: The search fee is $5.00 per name. Certification is $10.00 which includes search fee. Copies are $.50 per page after the initial $5.00. Fee payee: Secretary of State. Prepayment required. There is an additional $.50 charge to use a credit card. Personal checks accepted. Credit cards accepted: MasterCard, Visa, Discover.

Mail search: Turnaround time: 5 to 7 days. A SASE is requested.

Phone search: Expedited copy service is available using a credit card.

In person search: Turnaround time: variable.

Online search: The website gives free access to Corporate/LLC records at www.cyberdriveillinois.com/departments/business_services/corpstart.html. A commercial access program is also available. Fees vary. Potential users must submit in writing the purpose of the request. Submit your request to become involved in this program to the Director's office.

Other access: List or bulk file purchases are available. Contact the Director's Office for details.

Expedited service: Expedited service is available for mail, phone and fax searches. Turnaround time: 24 hours. Add $5.00 per business name.

Uniform Commercial Code, Federal Tax Liens

Secretary of State, UCC Division, 2nd & Edwards St, Howlett Bldg, Room 350 West, Springfield, IL 62756; 217-782-7518, 8AM-4:30PM.

www.cyberdriveillinois.com

Indexing & Storage: Records are available from 1962. Records are computerized since 1972. It takes 48 hours before new records are available for inquiry. Records are normally destroyed after 1 year after lapsing.

Searching: Use search request form UCC-11. Request searches for federal tax liens on businesses since 1988 separately with a fee of $5.00. Federal tax liens on individuals and all state tax liens are filed at the county level. Include the following in your request-debtor name and address.

Access by: mail, in person.

Fee & Payment: A UCC search is $10.00 per debtor name. A federal tax lien search only is available for $5.00 plus $.50 per page of copies. Copies are $1.00 per page. Fee payee: Secretary of State. Prepayment required. Personal checks accepted. Credit cards accepted: MasterCard, Visa, Discover.

Mail search: Turnaround time: 48 hours. A SASE is requested.

In person search: Documents can be viewed at no charge.

Other access: The entire database can be purchased and This agency offers a CD update service for $250 per month.

State Tax Liens

Records not maintained by a state level agency.

Note: All state tax liens are filed at the county.

Sales Tax Registrations

Revenue Department, Taxpayer Services, PO Box 19041, Springfield, IL 62794-9041 (Courier: 101 W Jefferson, Springfield, IL 62702); 800-732-8866, 217-782-7897, 217-782-4217 (Fax), 8AM-5PM.

www.iltax.com/Businesses/

Indexing & Storage: Records are available for all active businesses with the state, records can go back to the 1930s.

Searching: This agency will only confirm that a business is registered. They provide no other information. Include the following in your request-tax number or business name. The state tax permit or federal tax ID is also helpful.

Access by: mail, phone, in person.

Fee & Payment: The fee is $5.00 per return.

Mail search: Turnaround time: 7 to 10 days. A SASE is requested.

Phone search: Will do up to 5 confirmations at a time.

In person search: Turnaround time: variable.

Birth Certificates

IL Department of Public Health, Division of Vital Records, 605 W Jefferson St, Springfield, IL 62702-5097; 217-782-6554, 217-782-6553

(Instructions), 217-523-2648 (Fax), 8:30AM-5PM M-F.

www.idph.state.il.us/vitalrecords/index.htm

Indexing & Storage: Records are available from 1916 to present. It takes up to one month before new records are available for inquiry. Records are indexed on microfiche, inhouse computer.

Searching: Birth records are not considered public records. Copies are available to subject if 18 years old, parents, or legal guardian (with court order). Include the following in your request-full name, date of birth, place of birth, relationship to person of record, names of parents, mother's maiden name, signature of requester and photo ID with daytime phone. Place of birth can be city or county. Include name of hospital, if known. The following data is not released: sealed records.

Access by: mail, phone, fax, in person, online.

Fee & Payment: Fees are $10.00 per name for a computer abstract and $15.00 per name for a certified copy of original. Add $2.00 for each additional copy. Add $8.50 service fee to use a credit card. Fee payee: Illinois Department of Public Health. Prepayment required. Personal checks accepted. Credit cards accepted: MasterCard, Visa, AmEx, Discover.

Mail search: Turnaround time: 15 days. No SASE is required.

Phone search: Use of credit card is required for extra fee of $8.50. Normal turnaround time is 2 days.

Fax search: Same criteria as phone searching.

In person search: Turnaround time less than 1/2 hour, must show picture ID.

Online search: Records may requested from www.vitalchek.com, a state-endorsed vendor.

Expedited service: Expedited service is available for mail, phone and fax searches. Add $8.50 for using a credit card, $14.50 for express delivery.

Death Records

IL Department of Public Health, Division of Vital Records, 605 W Jefferson St, Springfield, IL 62702-5097; 217-782-6554, 217-782-6553 (Instructions), 217-523-2648 (Fax), 8AM-4:30PM.

www.idph.state.il.us/vitalrecords/index.htm

Indexing & Storage: Records are available from 1916 to present. New records are available for inquiry immediately. Records are indexed on microfiche.

Searching: Death records are not considered public documents. Copies are available to person with property rights interest in the record. Once records are 20 years old, they are open for genealogical searches. Include the following in your request-full name, date of death, place of death, relationship to person of record, parents' names, reason for request, photo ID and signature of requester.

Access by: mail, fax, in person, online.

Fee & Payment: Fees are $17.00 for a certified Death Certificate, or $10.00 if for genealogy (archived) records. Fee payee: Illinois Department of Public Health. Prepayment required. Personal checks accepted. Credit cards accepted: MasterCard, Visa, AmEx, Discover.

Mail search: Turnaround time: 8 to 10 weeks. No SASE is required.

Fax search: See expedited service.

In person search: There is one day waiting period. If ordered by 2PM, will be available the next day after 10AM.

Online search: No online access available from this agency. However, the state archives database of Illinois Death Certificates 1916-1950 is available free at www.cyberdriveillinois.com/departments/archives/genealogy/forms/idphdeathsrch.html. Also, records may requested from www.vitalchek.com, a state-endorsed vendor.

Expedited service: Expedited service is available for mail, online, and fax searches. The fee is $8.50 for the credit card use and $14.50 for express delivery. If you send your request in by express delivery, they will turnaround in two days.

Marriage Certificates, Divorce Records

Records not maintained by a state level agency.

Note: State will verify marriage or divorce from 1962-present, but will not issue certificate. Verification requests must be in writing and there is a fee of $5.00 per event requested. Records of marriage and divorce are found at the county of issue. There is a free online search of a statewide Marriage Index for 1763-1900 found at the Illinois State Archives website at www.cyberdriveillinois.com/departments/archives/marriage.html.

Workers' Compensation Records

Industrial Commission, 100 W Randolph, 8th Floor, Chicago, IL 60601; 312-814-6611, 8:30AM-5PM.

www.state.il.us/agency/iic

Note: The website lists cases that are up for a hearing status.

Indexing & Storage: Records are available on computer from 1982 to present, on microfiche from 1927 to 1981. Settled file copies are stored in Springfield, but must be requested from Chicago. Data is indexed by name and file number. It takes 3 months before new records are available for inquiry. Records are indexed on file folders. Records are normally destroyed after five years.

Searching: Include the following in your request-claimant name, Social Security Number, date of accident. Include case number and company name.

Access by: mail, phone, in person, online.

Fee & Payment: There is no charge for a small file. For "large files," the office will contact you and suggest you use a record retrieval service. If your request is large enough to warrant the use of a copy service, the service will have its own fees that must be paid by you. Personal checks are accepted.

Mail search: Turnaround time: 2 weeks. Send a name as well as any other information you may have, such as company name and date of accident, to determine if any files exist. A SASE is requested.

Phone search: Information about a case is accessed by the file number. The staff will do a name search if you have enough information for them to do so.

In person search: There are several public access terminals available in the office.

Online search: Case information status for active cases only is available at the webpage. Click on the IIC box on the right side of the screen.

Driver Records

Abstract Information Unit, Drivers Services Department, 2701 S Dirksen Prky, Springfield, IL 62723; 217-782-2720, 8AM-4:30PM.

www.sos.state.il.us

Note: No personal identifiable information is provided on record unless requester is exempt. Exempt requesters include business representatives with a legitimate business need (e.g. insurance, financial institutions, employers, etc.).

Indexing & Storage: Records are available for 4 years for moving violations; 7 years for suspension; lifetime for DWI. Commercial Driver records can go back 10 years for serious violations. It takes 2 weeks before new records are available for inquiry.

Searching: Non-exempt requesters, with no consent, may receive records without personal information, but there is a 10 day waiting period while the state notifies the subject. Include the following in your request-full name, date of birth, sex. Exempt requesters qualify per DPPA guidelines and receive full record information.

Access by: mail, in person, online.

Fee & Payment: The fee is $12.00 per record, which includes certification. There is a full charge for a "no record found." Fee payee: Secretary of State. Prepayment required. Personal checks accepted. No credit cards accepted.

Mail search: Turnaround time: 10 days. No SASE is required.

In person search: Up to five requests will be processed immediately if requester meets the access requirement (see above). Requests are available from any full-time Driver Services Facility statewide.

Online search: A program for high volume, approved users is available. Records are $12.00 each. Call 217-785-2384 for further information.

Other access: Overnight cartridge batch processing is available to high volume users (there is a 200 request minimum per day). Call 217-785-2384 for more information.

Vehicle Ownership, Vehicle Identification

Vehicle Services Department, Vehicle Record Inquiry, 501 S 2nd Street #408, Springfield, IL 62756; 217-782-6992, 217-524-0122 (Fax), 8AM-4:30PM.

www.sos.state.il.us

Indexing & Storage: Records are available generally for 10 years to present. It takes 1 to 2 weeks before new records are available for inquiry. Records are normally destroyed after 10 years.

Searching: Personal information is not released for non-business purposes. Bulk sales are not permitted for solicitation purposes. Include the following in your request-name, reason for search. Records are open to "Exempt" requesters include courts, law enforcment, legal representatives (including licensed IL PIs) the insurance industry and others designated per DPPA. A non-exempt requester receives data without personal information.

Access by: mail, in person.

Fee & Payment: The fee is $5.00 per record search. Fee payee: Secretary of State. Prepayment required. Personal checks accepted. MasterCard, Visa, Discover accepted.

Mail search: Turnaround time: 4 to 7 days. You may search by mail, but there is a 10 day delay if the requester is not "exempt." A SASE is requested.

In person search: Walk-in requesters may retrieve data immediately; however, if requester is not exempt there is a 10 day delay.

Other access: This agency will sell customized, bulk requests upon approval of purpose and with a signed contract. Contact the Data Processing Division in Room 400.

Accident Reports (Crash Reports)

Illinois State Police, Patrol Records Unit, 500 Iles Park Place, Ste 200, Springfield, IL 62703-2982; 217-785-0614, 217-785-2325 (Fax), 8AM-5PM.

www.isp.state.il.us

Note: To request report if crash occurred on IL Tollway System, send check or money order payable to: IL Toll Highway Authority, Attn: State Police District 15, One Authority Drive, Downers Grove, IL 60515.

Indexing & Storage: Records are available from 1976 to present. It takes 2-4 weeks before new records are available for inquiry. Records are normally destroyed after 2 years but maintained on microfilm for 50 years.

Searching: Crash reports are considered public record and are available without restriction. Items needed by the requester include date, names of drivers involved, report number, and an exact location.

Access by: mail, phone, in person, online.

Fee & Payment: The fee is $5.00 per report or $20.00 for a reconstruction report. Fee payee:

Illinois State Police. Prepayment required. Personal checks accepted. No credit cards accepted.

Mail search: Turnaround time: 7 to 10 days. If requester provides prepaid express envelope & label, the request will be returned quicker. A SASE is requested.

Phone search: You may call to get information, but copies of records are only released with written requests.

In person search: Turnaround time is immediate if report is on file.

Online search: Records can be requested and paid for online via E-Pay at the webpage. The fee is $6.00 per report.

Vessel Ownership, Vessel Registration

Department of Natural Resources, 1natural Resources Way, Springfield, IL 62702; 800-382-1696, 217-557-0180, 217-782-5016 (Fax), 8AM-5PM.

http://dnr.state.il.us

Note: Lien information will show on the history report.

Indexing & Storage: Records are available from 1982 to the present. Snow mobile records are also available. Records are indexed on computer. All boats must be titled and registered unless if only used on a private lake. Records are normally destroyed after 4 years.

Searching: To search, one of the following is required: name, hull ID, or registration #.

Access by: mail, phone.

Fee & Payment: There is a $5.00 fee for any search, including a title history search. Fee payee: IL Dept of Natural Resources. Prepayment required. Personal checks accepted. No credit cards accepted.

Mail search: Turnaround time: 4 to 6 weeks. No SASE is required.

Phone search: They will give very limited name search and verification information, time permitting.

Voter Registration

Access to Records is Restricted

Board of Elections, 1020 S Spring, Springfield, IL 62704; 217-782-4141, 217-782-5959 (Fax), 8AM-4:30PM.

www.elections.state.il.us

Note: The data is not considered public record at the state level and is only available in bulk format to political committees and government agencies. County Clerks control the information at the local level.

GED Certificates

Access to Records is at County Level

State Board of Education, GED Testing, 100 N 1st St S-230, Springfield, IL 62777; 217-782-2948 (Main Number).

Note: All GED information is kept at the county level. You must contact the county where the test was taken. If you need assistance determining which county, contact the State Board of Education at the number listed here.

Hunting and Fishing License Information

Access to Records is Restricted

IL Dept of Natural Resources, License Section, PO Box 19459, Springfield, IL 62794; 217-782-2965, 217-782-5016 (Fax), 8:30AM-5PM.

http://dnr.state.il.us

Note: They are just now creating a central database. At this time, records are not available. The vendors hold license records for years prior to 2002. Vendors can be searched at http://dnr.state.il.us/admin/systems/vendor.htm.

Illinois State Licensing Agencies

Licenses Searchable Online

Acupuncturist #11	www.ildpr.com/licenselookup/default.asp
Architect #11	www.ildpr.com/licenselookup/default.asp
Asbestos Contractor #17	www.idph.state.il.us/
Athletic Trainer #11	www.ildpr.com/licenselookup/default.asp
ATM Privately Owned #29	www.obre.state.il.us/CBT/REGENTY/ATMREG.pdf
Attorney #1	www.iardc.org/lawyersearch.asp
Auctioneer #29	www.obrelookupclear.state.il.us/default.asp
Audiologist #11	www.ildpr.com/licenselookup/default.asp
Bank #29	www.obrelookupclear.state.il.us/default.asp
Barber #11	www.ildpr.com/licenselookup/default.asp
Bilingual Teacher, Transitional #35	https://isbes1.isbe.net/otis
Check Seller/Distributor #29	www.obrelookupclear.state.il.us/default.asp
Chiropractor #11	www.ildpr.com/licenselookup/default.asp
Collection Agency #11	www.ildpr.com/licenselookup/default.asp
Controlled Substance Registrant #11	www.ildpr.com/licenselookup/default.asp
Corporate Fiduciary #29	www.obre.state.il.us/CBT/REGENTY/usa.asp?State=N
Cosmetologist #11	www.ildpr.com/licenselookup/default.asp
Counselor/Clinical Professional Counselor #11	www.ildpr.com/licenselookup/default.asp
Dentist/Dental Hygienist #11	www.ildpr.com/licenselookup/default.asp
Dietitian/Nutrition Counselor #11	www.ildpr.com/licenselookup/default.asp
Doctor/Physician #11	www.ildpr.com/licenselookup/default.asp
Drug Distributor, Wholesale #11	www.ildpr.com/licenselookup/default.asp
Early Childhood Teacher #35	https://isbes1.isbe.net/otis
Engineer/Engineer, Structural #11	www.ildpr.com/licenselookup/default.asp
Environmental Health Practitioner #11	www.ildpr.com/licenselookup/default.asp
Esthetician #11	www.ildpr.com/licenselookup/default.asp
Funeral Director/Embalmer #11	www.ildpr.com/licenselookup/default.asp
Geologist #11	www.ildpr.com/licenselookup/default.asp
HMO #4	www.ins.state.il.us/healthInsurance/HMO_by_County.htm
Home Inspector #29	www.obrelookupclear.state.il.us/default.asp
Insurance Producer #4	http://neonwebh.cmcf.state.il.us:8080/ins/imsfor
Interior Designer #11	www.ildpr.com/licenselookup/default.asp
Landscape Architect #11	www.ildpr.com/licenselookup/default.asp
Lead Contractor #17	http://app.idph.state.il.us/Envhealth/Lead/Leadcnt.asp
Lead Risk Assessor/Insp./Supervisor #17	http://app.idph.state.il.us/Envhealth/lead/Leadinsp.asp
Lead Training Provider #17	http://app.idph.state.il.us/Envhealth/lead/Leadinsp.asp
Liquor License, Retail/Dist./Mfg. #25	http://www2.state.il.us/lcc/license_search.asp
Lobbyist #32	www.cyberdriveillinois.com/departments/index/lobbyist/home.html
Locksmith #11	www.ildpr.com/licenselookup/default.asp
Long Term Care Insurance Company #4	http://neonwebh.cmcf.state.il.us:8080/ins/imsfor
Marriage & Family Therapist #11	www.ildpr.com/licenselookup/default.asp
Medical Corporation #11	www.ildpr.com/licenselookup/default.asp
Medical Doctor #11	www.ildpr.com/licenselookup/default.asp
Mortgage Banker/Broker #29	www.obre.state.il.us/MBLookup/MBList.htm
Nail Technician #11	www.ildpr.com/licenselookup/default.asp
Naprapath #11	www.ildpr.com/licenselookup/default.asp
Notary Public #32	www.cyberdriveillinois.com/departments/index/notary/home.html
Nurse #11	www.ildpr.com/licenselookup/default.asp
Nursing Home Administrator #17	www.medicare.gov/Nursing/Overview.asp
Occupational Therapist #11	www.ildpr.com/licenselookup/default.asp
Optometrist #11	www.ildpr.com/licenselookup/default.asp
Orthotist #11	www.ildpr.com/licenselookup/default.asp
Osteopathic Physician #11	www.ildpr.com/licenselookup/default.asp
Pawnbroker #29	www.obrelookupclear.state.il.us/default.asp
Pest Control Technician/Business #17	www.idph.state.il.us/
Pesticide Applicator #17	www.idph.state.il.us/
Pharmacist/Pharmacy #11	www.ildpr.com/licenselookup/default.asp
Physical Therapist #11	www.ildpr.com/licenselookup/default.asp
Physician Assistant #11	www.ildpr.com/licenselookup/default.asp
Podiatrist #11	www.ildpr.com/licenselookup/default.asp

Polygraph - Deception Detection Examiner #11............www.ildpr.com/licenselookup/default.asp
Private Detective #11............www.ildpr.com/licenselookup/default.asp
Private Security Contractor #11............www.ildpr.com/licenselookup/default.asp
Psychologist #11............www.ildpr.com/licenselookup/default.asp
Public Accountant-CPA #11............www.ildpr.com/licenselookup/default.asp
Real Estate Agent/Broker/Appraiser #29............www.obrelookupclear.state.il.us/default.asp
Roofer #11............www.ildpr.com/licenselookup/default.asp
Savings & Loan Association #29............www.obrelookupclear.state.il.us/default.asp
Savings Bank #29............www.obrelookupclear.state.il.us/default.asp
Securities Salesperson/Dealer #33............www.nasdr.com
Sewage System Contractor #17............www.idph.state.il.us/
Shorthand Reporter #11............www.ildpr.com/licenselookup/default.asp
Social Worker #11............www.ildpr.com/licenselookup/default.asp
Special Teacher #35............https://isbes1.isbe.net/otis
Speech-Language Pathologist #11............www.ildpr.com/licenselookup/default.asp
Stock Broker #33............www.nasdr.com
Substitute Teacher #35............https://isbes1.isbe.net/otis
Surveyor, Land #11............www.ildpr.com/licenselookup/default.asp
Teacher #35............https://isbes1.isbe.net/otis
Timeshare/Land Sales #29............www.obrelookupclear.state.il.us/default.asp
Trust Company #29............www.obre.state.il.us/CBT/REGENTY/Institution.asp?Inst=2
Veterinarian #11............www.dpr.state.il.us/licenselookup/default.asp
Water Well & Pump Installation Contractor/IDPH #17............www.idph.state.il.us/

Illinois Licensing Quick Finder

Accident Reconstruction Specialist #19 217-782-4540
Acupuncturist #11............217-785-0800
Alcohol Abuse Counselor #21............217-698-8110
Ambulance Service #13............217-785-2080
Amusement Ride #37............217-782-9347
Animal Breeder #6............217-785-3423
Aquaculturist #6............217-785-3423
Architect #11............217-785-0800
Asbestos Contractor #17............217-782-3517
Athletic Trainer #11............217-785-0800
ATM Privately Owned #29............312-793-3000
Attorney #1............217-522-6838
Auctioneer #29............312-793-8704
Auctioneer, Vehicle #30............217-782-7817
Audiologist #11............217-785-0800
Automotive Parts Recycler #30............217-782-7817
Bank #29............312-793-3000
Barber #11............217-785-0800
Bilingual Teacher, Transitional #35............800-845-8749
Bingo Operation #18............217-785-5864
Blacksmith #26............312-814-2600
Blaster #7............217-782-4970
Boat Operator #6............217-782-2138
Boiler Inspector #36............217-782-2696
Boxing/Wrestling Event/Professibn'l #11217-785-0800
Breath Analyzer Operator #13............217-782-1571
Business Broker #33............217-785-4923
Business Opportunity #33............217-785-7371
Charitable Game #18............217-785-5864
Check Seller/Distributor #29............312-793-3000
Child Care Facility #2............217-785-2688
Chiropractor #11............217-785-0800
Coal Mine Worker #8............217-782-6791
Collection Agency #11............217-785-0800
Controlled Substance Registrant #11............217-785-0800
Coroner (County) #19............217-782-4540
Corporate Fiduciary #29............312-793-3000
Correction Officer (County) #19............217-782-4540
Cosmetologist #11............217-785-0800
Counselor/Clinical Prof. Counselor #11 217-785-0800
Criminal Elec. Surveillance Officer #19.217-782-4540
Cross-Connection Control Device Inspector #24
............217-782-1020
Day Care #2............217-785-2688
Dentist/Dental Hygienist #11............217-785-0800
Dietitian/Nutrition Counselor #11............217-785-0800

Distribution System (Public Utility) Operator #24
............217-782-9720
Doctor/Physician #11............217-785-0800
Driving Instructor #31............847-437-3953
Drug Distributor, Wholesale #11............217-785-0800
Early Childhood Teacher #35............800-845-8749
Emergency Medical Technician #13............217-785-2080
Employee Leasing Company #4............217-782-6366
Employment Agency #23............312-793-2810
Engineer #11............217-785-0800
Engineer, Structural #11............217-785-0800
Environmental Health Practitioner #11..217-785-0800
Esthetician #11............217-785-0800
Explosive Magazine Storage #8............217-782-9976
Explosive, General Use #8............217-782-9976
Firearms Regulation (Firearm Owner's Reg.) #27
............217-782-7980
Fish Dealer #6............217-785-3423
Fisherman, Commercial #6............217-785-3423
Food Processing Plant/Warehouse #13 217-785-2439
Food Service Sanitation Manager #13.217-785-2439
Funeral Director/Embalmer #11............217-785-0800
Fur Buyer/Tanner/Dyer #6............217-785-3423
Gambling Addiction Counselor #21............217-698-8110
Gambling Employee #20............312-814-4702
Geologist #11............217-785-0800
Hearing Instrument Dispenser #15............217-782-4733
Hearing Screening Technician #15............217-782-4733
HMO #4............217-782-6366
Home Health Aide #13............217-782-7412
Home Health Care Agency #13............217-782-7412
Home Inspector #29............217-782-3000
Horseshoer #26............312-814-2600
Hospital #13............217-782-7412
Hunting Area Operator #6............217-785-3423
Industrial Radiographer #9............217-785-9913
Insurance Producer #4............217-782-6366
Interior Designer #11............217-785-0800
Investment Adviser #33............217-785-4929
Investment Adviser Rep, #33............217-557-4609
Laboratory Analysis Technician #13............217-785-8820
Land Sale #11............217-785-0800
Landfill Chief Operator #24............217-782-9877
Landscape Architect #11............217-785-0800
Lead Contractor #17............217-782-3517
Lead Risk Assessor/Inspct./Supv'r #17. 217-782-3517
Lead Training Provider #17............217-782-3517

Liquor License, Retail/Dist./Mfg. #25 ... 312-814-3930
Loan Broker #33............217-785-4923
Lobbyist #32............217-782-0705
Locksmith #11............217-785-0800
Long Term Care Insurance Co. #4............217-782-6366
Marriage & Family Therapist #11............217-785-0800
Medical Corporation #11............217-785-0800
Medical Doctor #11............217-785-0800
Mental Health Counselor #21............217-698-8110
Mine Engineer/Foreman #8............217-782-6791
Mine Rescue Supervisor/Assistant #8. 217-782-6791
Mine Supervisor #8............217-782-6791
Mortgage Banker/Broker #29............217-793-1409
Motor Vehicle Dealer, New #30............217-782-7817
Nail Technician #11............217-785-0800
Naprapath #11............217-785-0800
Notary Public #32............217-782-0705
Nuclear Medicine Technologist #9............217-785-9913
Nurse #11............217-785-0800
Nurses' Aide #13............217-785-5133
Nursing Agency #23. 312-793-1718 or 312-793-2810
Nursing Home #12............217-702-0545
Nursing Home Administrator #17............217-782-0514
Occupational Aide #12............217-782-0545
Occupational Therapist #11............217-785-0800
Optometrist #11............217-785-0800
Orthotist #11............217-785-0800
Osteopathic Physician #11............217-785-0800
Pari-Mutuel Employee #26............312-814-2600
Pawnbroker #29............312-793-3000
Pest Control Technician/Business #17. 217-782-4674
Pesticide Applicator #17............217-782-5830
Pharmacist/Pharmacy #11............217-785-0800
Physical Aide #12............217-782-0545
Physical Therapist #11............217-785-0800
Physician Assistant #11............217-785-0800
Podiatrist #11............217-785-0800
Polygraph - Deception Detection Examiner #11
............217-785-0800
Private Detective #11............217-785-0800
Private Security Contractor #11............217-785-0800
Psychologist #11............217-785-0800
Public Accountant-CPA #11............217-785-0800
Pull Tab Operator #18............217-785-5864
Racetrack #26............312-814-2600

Radiation Therapist #10	217-785-9913	School Principal/Super./Admin. #35	800-845-8749
Radiographer #10	217-785-9913	School Psychologist #35	800-845-8749
Radon Measurement Specialist #10	217-785-9935	Scrap Processor #30	217-782-7817
Real Estate Agent/Broker/Sales #29	312-793-8704	Securities Salesperson/Dealer #33	217-782-2256
Real Estate Appraiser #29	312-793-8704	Sewage System Contractor #17	217-782-5830
Rehabilitation Aide #12	217-782-0545	Sheriff Law Enforcement Officer #19	217-782-4540
Restaurant & Retail Food Store #17	217-785-2439	Shorthand Reporter #11	217-785-0800
Riverboat Employee #20	312-814-4702	Social Worker #11	217-785-0800
Roofer #11	217-785-0800	Special Teacher #35	800-845-8749
Salvage Firm #13	217-785-2439	Speech-Language Pathologist #11	217-785-0800
Savings & Loan Association #29	217-782-9043	Stock Broker #33	217-782-2256
Savings Bank #29	217-782-9043	Substance Abuse Counselor #21	217-698-8110
School Business Official #35	800-845-8749	Substitute Teacher #35	800-845-8749
School Guidance Counselor #35	800-845-8749	Surveyor, Land #11	217-785-0800
School Media Specialist/Librarian #35	800-845-8749	Tanning Facility #17	217-785-2439
School Nurse #35	800-845-8749	Taxidermist #6	217-785-3423

Teacher #35	800-845-8749
Timber Buyer #3	217-782-6431
Timeshare #11	217-785-0800
Timeshare/Land Sales #29	312-793-8704
Trust Company #29	312-793-3000
Underground Shot Firer #8	217-782-6791
Used Vehicle Dealer #30	217-782-7817
Vehicle Rebuilder/Repair #30	217-782-7817
Veterinarian #11	217-785-0800
Vision Screening Technician #15	217-782-4733
Waste Water Plant Operator #24	217-782-9720
Water Supply Operator #24	217-782-9720
Water Well/Pump Installation Contr.#17	217-782-5830
Water Well Contractor/IDPH #17	217-782-5830
Weighing/Measuring Device Serviceman #22	
	217-782-3817

Illinois Licensing Agency Information

1 Attorney Registration & Disciplinary Commission of Supreme Court of IL, 1 N. Old Capitol Plaza #333, Springfield, IL 62701; 217-522-6838, Fax: 217-522-2417. www.iardc.org   Search Database at www.iardc.org/lawyersearch.asp

2 Department of Children & Family Services, 406 E Monroe St, Springfield, IL 62701; 217-785-2509, Fax: 217-785-1052. www.state.il.us/dcfs

3 Department of Natural Resources, Division of Forest Services, 1 Natural Resources Way, Springfield, IL 62702; 217-782-6431, Fax: 217-785-8405. www.dnr.state.il.us

4 Department of Insurance, 320 W Washington, Springfield, IL 62767-0001; 217-782-4515, Fax: 217-782-5020. www.ins.state.il.us Email: director@ins.state.il.us

6 Department of Natural Resources, Commercial Permits, One Natural Resources Way, Springfield, IL 62702-1271; 217-785-3423, Fax: 217-782-5016. http://dnr.state.il.us

8 Department of Natural Resources, Office of Mine & Minerals, One Natural Resources Way, Springfield, IL 62702-1271; 217-782-6791, Fax: 217-524-4819. http://dnr.state.il.us/mines/

9 Emergency Management Agency, 1035 Outer Park Dr, Springfield, IL 62704; 217-785-9900, Fax: 217-785-9962. www.state.il.us/iema/ Email: webmaster@iema.state.il.us

11 Department of Professional Regulation, Professions/Occupations/Entities, 320 W Washington, 3rd Fl, Springfield, IL 62786; 217-785-0800, Fax: 217-782-7645. www.dpr.state.il.us   Email: netinfo@dpr084rl.state.il.us Search Database at www.ildpr.com/licenselookup/default.asp

12 Department of Public Aid, Bureau of Long-Term Care, 201 S. Grand Ave, Springfield, IL 62763-0001; 217-782-0545, Fax: 217-524-7114. www.state.il.us/dpa/medical_programs.htm Email: aidd2011@mail.idpa.state.il.us

13 Department of Public Health, Education & Training Section, 525 W Jefferson St 4th Fl, Springfield, IL 62761; 217-782-4977, Fax: 217-782-3987. www.idph.state.il.us

15 Department of Public Health, Division of Health Assessment & Screening, 500 E. Monroe, 1st Floor, Springfield, IL 62701; 217-782-4733, Fax: 217-557-5324. www.idph.state.il.us Email: gtanner@idph.state.il.us

17 Department of Public Health, Environmental Health, 525 W Jefferson St, 3rd Fl, Springfield, IL 62761; 217-782-5830, Fax: 217-785-0253. www.idph.state.il.us Email: mailus@idph.state.il.us

18 Department of Revenue, Bingo Division, 101 W Jefferson RM3011, Springfield, IL 62794; 217-785-5864. www.iltax.com

19 Law Enforcement & Standards Training Board, 600 S 2nd St, #300, Springfield, IL 62704; 217-782-4540, Fax: 217-524-5350. www.ptb.state.il.us   Email: ptb@pop.state.il.us

20 Gaming Board, 160 N Lasalle #300, Chicago, IL 60601; 312-814-4700, Fax: 312-814-4602. www.igb.state.il.us

21 Counselor Certification Department, IAODAPCA, 1305 Wabash Ave #L, Springfield, IL 62704-4938; 217-698-8110, Fax: 217-698-8234. www.iaodapca.org Email: IAODAPCA@aol.com.

22 Department of Agriculture, State Fairgrounds, PO Box 19281, Springfield, IL 62794-9281; 217-782-2172, Fax: 217-524-7801. www.agr.state.il.us

23 Department of Labor, State of Illinois Bldg., 160 N LaSalle, 13th Fl, #C1300, Chicago, IL 60601; 312-793-2800, Fax: 312-793-5257. www.state.il.us/agency/idol Email: idol@pop.state.il.us

24 Environmental Protection Agency, PO Box 19276 (1021 N Grand Ave E), Springfield, IL 62794-9276; 217-782-1020, Fax: 217-782-0075. www.epa.state.il.us/water/index.html

25 Freedom of Information Compliance Officer, Liquor Control Commission, 100 W Randolph, #5-300, Chicago, IL 60601; 312-814-2206, Fax: 312-814-2241. www.state.il.us/lcc/default.htm Email: ilcc_info@mail.state.il.us Search Database at http://www2.state.il.us/lcc/license_search.asp

26 Racing Board, 100 W Randolph, #11-100, Chicago, IL 60601; 312-814-2600, Fax: 312-814-5062. www.state.il.us/agency/irb Email: irb@pop.state.il.us

27 State Police, FOID, 100 Iles Park Pl, 103 Armory Bldg, Springfield, IL 62708; 217-782-7980, Fax: 217-782-9139. www.isp.state.il.us

29 Office of Banks & Real Estate, Bureaus of Res. Finance; Banks & Trusts; Real Estate Professions, 500 E Monroe, Springfield, IL 62701-1509; 217-782-3000, Fax: 217-524-5941. www.obre.state.il.us/AGENCY/licenseinfo.htm Email: obr_webmaster@pop.state.il.us Search Database at www.obrelookupclear.state.il.us/default.asp

30 Secretary of State, Vehicle Services, Dealers/Remitters, Howlett Bldg, Rm 069, Springfield, IL 62756; 217-782-7817, Fax: 217-524-0120. www.sos.state.il.us Email: secwhite@ccgate.sos.state.il.us

31 Secretary of State, Commercial Driver Training, 650 Roppolo Dr, Elk Grove, IL 60007; 847-437-3953, Fax: 847-437-3911.

32 Secretary of State, Index Department, 111 E Monroe St, Springfield, IL 62756; 217-782-7017, Fax: 217-524-0930. www.sos.state.il.us/departments/index/dept_index.html

33 Secretary of State, Securities Department, 520 S 2nd St, Lincoln Tower, #200, Springfield, IL 62701; 217-782-2256, Fax: 217-524-2172. www.cyberdriveillinois.com/departments/securities/securities.html Search Database at www.nasdr.com

35 Division of Professional Certification, Board of Education, 100 N 1st St, Springfield, IL 62777; 800-845-8749, 217 782-4321, Fax: 217 524-4928. www.isbe.state.il.us/teachers/ Search Database at https://isbes1.isbe.net/otis

36 State Fire Marshall, 1035 Stevenson Dr, Springfield, IL 62703; 217-785-0969, Fax: 217-782-1062. www.state.il.us/osfm

37 Department of Labor, Carnival & Amusement Ride Safety Division, 1 West Old State Capitol Plaza, #300, Springfield, IL 62701; 217-782-9347, Fax: 217-785-8776. www.state.il.us/agency/idol/

Illinois Federal Courts

The following list indicates the district and division name for each county in the state. If the bankruptcy court location is different from the district court, then the location of the bankruptcy court appears in parentheses.

County/Court Cross Reference

County	District	Division
Adams	Central	Springfield
Alexander	Southern	Benton
Bond	Southern	East St Louis
Boone	Northern	Rockford
Brown	Central	Springfield
Bureau	Central	Peoria
Calhoun	Southern	East St Louis
Carroll	Northern	Rockford
Cass	Central	Springfield
Champaign	Central	Danville/Urbana (Danville)
Christian	Central	Springfield
Clark	Southern	Benton (East St Louis)
Clay	Southern	Benton (East St Louis)
Clinton	Southern	East St Louis
Coles	Central	Danville/Urbana (Danville)
Cook	Northern	Chicago (Eastern)
Crawford	Southern	Benton (East St Louis)
Cumberland	Southern	Benton
De Kalb	Northern	Rockford
De Witt	Central	Springfield
Douglas	Central	Danville/Urbana (Danville)
Du Page	Northern	Chicago (Eastern)
Edgar	Central	Danville/Urbana (Danville)
Edwards	Southern	Benton
Effingham	Southern	Benton (East St Louis)
Fayette	Southern	East St Louis
Ford	Central	Danville/Urbana (Danville)
Franklin	Southern	Benton
Fulton	Central	Peoria
Gallatin	Southern	Benton
Greene	Central	Springfield
Grundy	Northern	Chicago (Eastern)
Hamilton	Southern	Benton
Hancock	Central	Peoria
Hardin	Southern	Benton
Henderson	Central	Rock Island (Peoria)
Henry	Central	Rock Island (Peoria)
Iroquois	Central	Danville/Urbana (Danville)
Jackson	Southern	Benton
Jasper	Southern	Benton (East St Louis)
Jefferson	Southern	Benton
Jersey	Southern	East St Louis
Jo Daviess	Northern	Rockford
Johnson	Southern	Benton
Kane	Northern	Chicago (Eastern)
Kankakee	Central	Danville/Urbana (Danville)
Kendall	Northern	Chicago (Eastern)
Knox	Central	Peoria
La Salle	Northern	Chicago (Eastern)
Lake	Northern	Chicago (Eastern)
Lawrence	Southern	Benton (East St Louis)
Lee	Northern	Rockford
Livingston	Central	Peoria (Danville)
Logan	Central	Springfield
Macon	Central	Danville/Urbana (Sprngfld)
Macoupin	Central	Springfield
Madison	Southern	East St Louis
Marion	Southern	East St Louis
Marshall	Central	Peoria
Mason	Central	Springfield
Massac	Southern	Benton
McDonough	Central	Peoria
McHenry	Northern	Rockford
McLean	Central	Peoria (Springfield)
Menard	Central	Springfield
Mercer	Central	Rock Island (Peoria)
Monroe	Southern	East St Louis
Montgomery	Central	Springfield
Morgan	Central	Springfield
Moultrie	Central	Danville/Urbana (Danville)
Ogle	Northern	Rockford
Peoria	Central	Peoria
Perry	Southern	Benton
Piatt	Central	Danville/Urbana (Danville)
Pike	Central	Springfield
Pope	Southern	Benton
Pulaski	Southern	Benton
Putnam	Central	Peoria
Randolph	Southern	East St Louis
Richland	Southern	Benton (East St Louis)
Rock Island	Central	Rock Island (Peoria)
Saline	Southern	Benton
Sangamon	Central	Springfield
Schuyler	Central	Springfield
Scott	Central	Springfield
Shelby	Central	Springfield
St. Clair	Southern	East St Louis
Stark	Central	Peoria
Stephenson	Northern	Rockford
Tazewell	Central	Peoria
Union	Southern	Benton
Vermilion	Central	Danville/Urbana (Danville)
Wabash	Southern	Benton
Warren	Central	Rock Island (Peoria)
Washington	Southern	East St Louis (Benton)
Wayne	Southern	Benton
White	Southern	Benton
Whiteside	Northern	Rockford
Will	Northern	Chicago (Eastern)
Williamson	Southern	Benton
Winnebago	Northern	Rockford
Woodford	Central	Peoria

Standards for Federal Courts: The search fee is $20.00 per item (one party name or case number). Certification fee is $7.00 per document. Copy fee is $.50 per page. All fees standard unless noted in profile. Mail Search: always enclose a stamped self addressed envelope unless otherwise noted. Most courts accept fax requests or will suggest a copying/search vendor. Before releasing records, all courts require prepayment unless noted in profile.

Open records are located at the court unless otherwise noted. District courts index by defendant and plaintiff as well as by case number. Bankruptcy courts usually index by debtor and case number. While most courts now have their indexes on computer, many still maintain index card files as well.

The universal PACER sign-up number is 800-676-6856. Find PACER and the Party/Case Index on the Web at http://pacer.psc.uscourts.gov. PACER dial-up access is $.60 per minute. Also, courts offering internet access via RACER, PACER, Web-PACER or the new CM-ECF charge $.07 per page fee unless noted as free.

US District Court

Central District of Illinois

Danville/Urbana Division 201 S Vine, Room 218, Urbana, IL 61802 (courier address: Use mail address for courier delivery) 217-373-5830, Fax: 217-373-5834. www.ilcd.uscourts.gov

Counties: Champaign, Coles, Douglas, Edgar, Ford, Iroquois, Kankakee, Macon, Moultrie, Piatt, Vermilion.

Indexing & Storage: New cases available in the index immediately after filing date. District wide searches are availabile for civil records from October 1989 and criminal records from April 1992 from this court.

Fee & Payment: Payment may be made by money order, cashier check, business check. Personal checks are not accepted. Payee: Clerk, U.S. District Court.

Phone Search: Only docket information available by phone.

Mail Search: A SASE not required.

In Person Search: Fee charged if court conducts your in person search for you. Exemplification fee is $10.00.

PACER: PACER is available online at http://pacer.ilcd.uscourts.gov. Records purged after 5-7 years. New records are online after 1 day.

Electronic Filing: Electronic filing information online at https://ecf.ilcd.uscourts.gov

Peoria Division U.S. District Clerk's Office, 309 Federal Bldg, 100 NE Monroe St, Peoria, IL 61602 (courier address: Use mail address for courier delivery) 309-671-7117, Fax: 309-671-0780. www.ilcd.uscourts.gov

Counties: Bureau, Fulton, Hancock, Knox, Livingston, McDonough, McLean, Marshall, Peoria, Putnam, Stark, Tazewell, Woodford.

Indexing & Storage: New cases available in the index immediately after filing date. District-wide searches are available for civil cases from November 1989 and for criminal records from April 1994.

Fee & Payment: Payment may be made by money order, cashier check. Business checks are not accepted. Personal checks are not accepted. Law firm checks are accepted. Payee: Clerk, U.S. District Court.

Phone Search: No searching by telephone.

In Person Search: Fee charged if court conducts your in person search for you.

PACER: PACER is available online at http://pacer.ilcd.uscourts.gov. Records purged after 5-7 years. New records are online after 1 day.

Electronic Filing: Electronic filing information online at https://ecf.ilcd.uscourts.gov

Rock Island Division U.S. District Clerk's Office, Room 40, U.S. Court House, 211 19th St, Rock Island, IL 61201 (courier address: Use mail address for courier delivery) 309-793-5778, Fax: 309-793-5878. www.ilcd.uscourts.gov

Counties: Henderson, Henry, Mercer, Rock Island, Warren.

Indexing & Storage: New cases available in the index immediately after filing date.

Fee & Payment: Payment may be made by money order, cashier check, business check. Personal checks are not accepted. Payee: Clerk of U.S. District Court.

Phone Search: All information that is not sealed is available for release over the phone.

In Person Search: Fee charged if court conducts your in person search for you.

PACER: PACER is available online at http://pacer.ilcd.uscourts.gov. Records purged after 5-7 years. New records are online after 1 day.

Electronic Filing: Electronic filing information online at https://ecf.ilcd.uscourts.gov

Springfield Division Clerk, 151 U.S. Courthouse, 600 E Monroe, Springfield, IL 62701 (courier address: Use mail address for courier delivery) 217-492-4020, Fax: 217-492-4028. www.ilcd.uscourts.gov

Counties: Adams, Brown, Cass, Christian, De Witt, Greene, Logan, Macoupin, Mason, Menard, Montgomery, Morgan, Pike, Sangamon, Schuyler, Scott, Shelby.

Indexing & Storage: New cases available in the index immediately after filing date. District wide searches are available for civil records from November 1989 and criminal records from 1992 from this court.

Fee & Payment: Payment may be made by money order, cashier check, business check. Personal checks are not accepted. Payee: U.S. District Court Clerk.

Phone Search: No searching by telephone.

Mail Search: A SASE not required.

In Person Search: Fee charged if court conducts your in person search for you.

PACER: PACER is available online at http://pacer.ilcd.uscourts.gov. Records purged after 5-7 years. New records are online after 1 day.

Electronic Filing: Electronic filing information online at https://ecf.ilcd.uscourts.gov

U.S. Bankruptcy Court

Central District of Illinois

Danville Division 201 N Vermilion #130, Danville, IL 61832-4733 (courier address: Use mail address for courier delivery) 217-431-4820, Fax: 217-431-2694. www.ilcb.uscourts.gov

Counties: Champaign, Coles, Douglas, Edgar, Ford, Iroquois, Kankakee, Livingston, Moultrie, Piatt, Vermilion.

Indexing & Storage: Cases indexed by debtor as well as by case number. New cases available in the index 24 hours after filing date.

Fee & Payment: Payment may be made by money order, cashier check, business check. Personal checks are not accepted. Payee: U.S. Bankruptcy Court. Will fax results $25.00 if records in Chicago. Will fax results for $15.00.

Phone Search: Docket information available by phone. Automated voice case information service (VCIS) is available. Call VCIS at 800-827-9005 or 217-492-4550. Will fax results $25.00 if records in Chicago. Will fax results for $15.00.

In Person Search: Fee charged if court conducts your in person search for you.

PACER: PACER is available online at http://pacer.ilcb.uscourts.gov. Records purged immediately when case is closed. New civil records are online after 2 days.

Electronic Filing: Electronic filing information online at https://ecf.ilcb.uscourts.gov

Peoria Division Room 216, 100 NE Monroe, Peoria, IL 61602 (courier address: Use mail address for courier delivery) 309-671-7035, Fax: 309-671-7076. www.ilcb.uscourts.gov

Counties: Bureau, Fulton, Hancock, Henderson, Henry, Knox, Marshall, McDonough, Mercer, Peoria, Putnam, Rock Island, Stark, Tazewell, Warren, Woodford.

Indexing & Storage: Cases indexed by debtor as well as by case number. New cases available in the index 24 hours after filing date.

Fee & Payment: Payment may be made by money order, cashier check, business check. Personal checks are not accepted. Will invoice for copy fees only. Payee: U.S. Bankruptcy Court.

Phone Search: Automated voice case information service (VCIS) is available. Call VCIS at 800-827-9005 or 217-492-4550.

In Person Search: Fee charged if court conducts your in person search for you.

PACER: PACER is available online at http://pacer.ilcb.uscourts.gov. Records purged immediately when case is closed. New civil records are online after 2 days.

Electronic Filing: Electronic filing information online at https://ecf.ilcb.uscourts.gov

Springfield Division 226 U.S. Courthouse, Springfield, IL 62701 (courier: 600 E Monroe St., #226, Springfield, IL 62701), 217-492-4551, Fax: 217-492-4556. www.ilcb.uscourts.gov

Counties: Adams, Brown, Cass, Christian, De Witt, Greene, Logan, Macon, Macoupin, Mason, McLean, Menard, Montgomery, Morgan, Pike, Sangamon, Schuyler, Scott, Shelby.

Indexing & Storage: Cases indexed by debtor as well as by case number. New cases available in the index 24 hours after filing date.

Fee & Payment: Payment may be made by money order, cashier check, business check. Personal checks are not accepted. Will invoice for copy fees only. Payee: U.S. Bankruptcy Court.

Phone Search: Automated voice case information service (VCIS) is available. Call VCIS at 800-827-9005 or 217-492-4550.

In Person Search: Fee charged if court conducts your in person search for you.

PACER: PACER is available online at http://pacer.ilcb.uscourts.gov. Records purged immediately when case is closed. New civil records are online after 2 days.

Electronic Filing: Electronic filing information online at https://ecf.ilcb.uscourts.gov

U.S. District Court

Northern District of Illinois

Chicago (Eastern) Division 20th Floor, 219 S Dearborn St, Chicago, IL 60604 (Use mail address for courier delivery) 312-435-5698, Fax: 312-554-8512. www.ilnd.uscourts.gov

Counties: Cook, Du Page, Grundy, Kane, Kendall, Lake, La Salle, Will.

Indexing & Storage: New cases available in the index 2 days after filing date. Records are also indexed on microfiche.

Fee & Payment: Payment may be made by money order, cashier check, personal check, Visa, Mastercard. Except for criminal bail bonds, all types of checks or money orders are accepted. Credit cards are only accepted in person. Payee: Clerk, U.S. District Court.

Phone Search: No searching by telephone. Only docket information available by phone. Phone inquiries may be made from 8:15AM-5PM.

In Person Search: Fee charged if court conducts your in person search for you.

PACER: PACER is available online at http://pacer.ilnd.uscourts.gov. Document images available in RACER section. Records purged varies. New records are online after 1-2 days.

Electronic Filing: Currently in the process of implementing CM/ECF.

Rockford Division Room 211, 211 S Court St, Rockford, IL 61101 (courier address: Use mail address for courier delivery) 815-987-4355, Fax: 815-987-4291. www.ilnd.uscourts.gov

Counties: Boone, Carroll, De Kalb, Jo Daviess, Lee, McHenry, Ogle, Stephenson, Whiteside, Winnebago.

Indexing & Storage: New cases available in the index 1-3 days after filing date.

Fee & Payment: Payment may be made by money order, cashier check, personal check. Payee: Clerk, U.S. District Court.

Phone Search: No searching by telephone.

Mail Search: Any indictments, pending information, case numbers and docket sheets (if specifically requested) will be released. A SASE not required.

In Person Search: Permitted.

PACER: PACER is available online at http://pacer.ilnd.uscourts.gov. Document images available in RACER section. Records purged varies. New records are online after 1-2 days.

Electronic Filing: Currently in the process of implementing CM/ECF.

U.S. Bankruptcy Court

Northern District of Illinois

Chicago (Eastern) Division 219 S Dearborn St, Chicago, IL 60604-1802 (Use mail address for courier delivery) 312-435-5694, Fax: 312-408-7750. www.ilnb.uscourts.gov

Counties: Cook, Du Page, Grundy, Kane, Kendall, La Salle, Lake, Will.

Indexing & Storage: Cases indexed by debtor as well as by case number. New cases available in the index 1 day after filing date.

Fee & Payment: Payment may be made by money order, cashier check, business check. Personal checks are not accepted. Payee: Clerk, U.S. Bankruptcy Court.

Phone Search: If the searcher has a case number, any information contained on the docket will be released. Automated voice case information service (VCIS) is available. Call VCIS at 888-232-6814 or 312-408-5089.

In Person Search: Fee charged if court conducts your in person search for you. Copying available via Ikon Copy Svc, 312-913-9508.

PACER: Access to PACER/RACER is available at the website. Document images available. Case records go back to July 1, 1993. Records never purged. New civil records are online after 1 day.

Electronic Filing: Electronic filing information online at https://ecf.ilnb.uscourts.gov

Other Online Access: Case Image Viewing is available from 5AM to 11:59 p.m. CST at www.ilnb.uscourts.gov/casenotice.htm. Access fee is $.07 per page.

Rockford Division Room 110, 211 S Court St, Rockford, IL 61101 (courier address: Use mail address for courier delivery) 815-987-4350, Fax: 815-987-4205. www.ilnb.uscourts.gov

Counties: Boone, Carroll, De Kalb, Jo Daviess, Lee, McHenry, Ogle, Stephenson, Whiteside, Winnebago.

Indexing & Storage: Cases indexed by debtor and creditors as well as by case number. New cases available in the index immediately after filing date.

Fee & Payment: Payment may be made by money order, cashier check, personal check. Debtor's checks are not accepted. Payee: Clerk, U.S. Bankruptcy Court.

Phone Search: Only docket information available by phone. Automated voice case information service (VCIS) is available. VCIS: 888-232-6814.

In Person Search: Fee charged if court conducts your in person search for you.

PACER: Access to PACER/RACER is available at the website. Document images available. New civil records are online after 1 day.

Electronic Filing: Electronic filing information online at https://ecf.ilnb.uscourts.gov

Other Online Access: Case Image Viewing is available from 5AM to 11:59PM CST at

www.ilnb.uscourts.gov/casenotice.htm. Access fee is $.07 per page.

U.S. District Court

Southern District of Illinois

Benton Division 301 W Main St, Benton, IL 62812 (Use mail address for courier delivery) 618-439-7760. www.ilsd.uscourts.gov

Counties: Alexander, Clark, Clay, Crawford, Cumberland, Edwards, Effingham, Franklin, Gallatin, Hamilton, Hardin, Jackson, Jasper, Jefferson, Johnson, Lawrence, Massac, Perry, Pope, Pulaski, Richland, Saline, Union, Wabash, Wayne, White, Williamson. Cases mayalso be allocated to the Benton Division.

Indexing & Storage: New cases available in the index immediately after filing date. The name and date are required to search for records. Records are also indexed on microfiche.

Fee & Payment: Payment may be made by money order, cashier check, personal check. Except in an emergency, Payee: Clerk, U.S. District Court.

Phone Search: Docket information available.

In Person Search: Fee charged if court conducts your in person search for you.

PACER: PACER is available online at http://pacer.ilsd.uscourts.gov. Records purged when deemed necessary. New civil records are online after 1 day. New criminal records online after 1-2 days.

Electronic Filing: Electronic filing information online at https://ecf.ilsd.uscourts.gov

East St Louis Division PO Box 249, East St Louis, IL 62202 (courier address: 750 Missouri Ave, East St Louis, IL 62201), 618-482-9371. www.ilsd.uscourts.gov

Counties: Bond, Calhoun, Clinton, Fayette, Jersey, Madison, Marion, Monroe, Randolph, St. Clair, Washington. Cases for these counties may also be allocated to the Benton Division.

Indexing & Storage: New cases available in the index immediately after filing date. Name and date are required to search for records. Records are also indexed on microfiche.

Fee & Payment: Payment may be made by money order, cashier check, personal check. Except in an emergency, Cash is also accepted. Payee: Clerk, U.S. District Court.

Phone Search: Docket information available by phone.

In Person Search: Fee charged if court conducts your in person search for you. You may make copies only if arrangement made with bonded vendor.

PACER: PACER is available online at http://pacer.ilsd.uscourts.gov. Records purged when deemed necessary. New civil records are online after 1 day. New criminal records online after 1-2 days.

Electronic Filing: Electronic filing information online at https://ecf.ilsd.uscourts.gov

U.S. Bankruptcy Court

Southern District of Illinois

Benton Division 301 W Main, Benton, IL 62812 (Use mail address for courier delivery) 618-435-2200. www.ilsb.uscourts.gov

Counties: Alexander, Edwards, Franklin, Gallatin, Hamilton, Hardin, Jackson, Jefferson, Johnson, Massac, Perry, Pope, Pulaski, Randolph, Saline, Union, Wabash, Washington, Wayne, White, Williamson.

Indexing & Storage: Cases indexed by debtor as well as by case number. New cases available in the index immediately after filing date.

Fee & Payment: Payment may be made by money order, cashier check, business check. Personal checks are not accepted. Payee: Clerk, U.S. Bankruptcy Court.

Phone Search: Automated voice case information service (VCIS) is available. Call VCIS at 800-726-5622 or 618-482-9365.

In Person Search: Fee charged if court conducts your in person search for you.

PACER: PACER is available online at http://pacer.ilsb.uscourts.gov. Records purged as deemed necessary. New civil records are online after 1 day.

Electronic Filing: Electronic filing information online at https://ecf.ilsb.uscourts.gov

East St Louis Division PO Box 309, East St Louis, IL 62202-0309 (courier address: 750 Missouri Ave, East St Louis, IL 62201), 618-482-9400. www.ilsb.uscourts.gov

Counties: Bond, Calhoun, Clark, Clay, Clinton, Crawford, Cumberland, Effingham, Fayette, Jasper, Jersey, Lawrence, Madison, Marion, Monroe, Richland, St. Clair.

Indexing & Storage: Cases indexed by debtor as well as by case number. New cases available in the index 1 working day after filing date. Records are also indexed on microfiche. District wide searches are available from this court.

Fee & Payment: Payment may be made by money order, cashier check, personal check. Debtor's checks are not accepted. Payee: Clerk, U.S. Bankruptcy Court.

Phone Search: Automated voice case information service (VCIS) is available. Call VCIS at 800-726-5622 or 618-482-9365.

Mail Search: A SASE not required.

In Person Search: Fee charged if court conducts your in person search for you.

PACER: PACER is available online at http://pacer.ilsb.uscourts.gov. Records purged as deemed necessary. New civil records are online after 1 day.

Electronic Filing: Electronic filing information online at https://ecf.ilsb.uscourts.gov

Illinois County Courts

Court	Jurisdiction	No. of Courts	How Organized
Circuit Courts*	General	106	22 Circuits

* Profiled in this Sourcebook.

Court	CIVIL								
	Tort	Contract	Real Estate	Min. Claim	Max. Claim	Small Claims	Estate	Eviction	Domestic Relations
Circuit Courts*	X	X	X	$0	No Max	$5000	X	X	X

Court	CRIMINAL				
	Felony	Misdemeanor	DWI/DUI	Preliminary Hearing	Juvenile
Circuit Courts*	X	X	X	X	X

ADMINISTRATION   Administrative Office of Courts, 222 N LaSalle 13th Floor, Chicago, IL, 60601; 312-793-3250, Fax: 312-793-1335. www.state.il.us/court/

COURT STRUCTURE   Illinois is divided into 22 judicial circuits; 3 are single county: Cook, Du Page (18th Circuit) and Will (12th Circuit). The other 19 circuits consist of 2 or more contiguous counties. The Circuit Court of Cook County is the largest unified court system in the world. Its 2300-person staff handles approximately 2.4 million cases each year. The civil part of the various Circuit Courts in Cook County is divided as follows: under $30,000 are "civil cases" and over $30,000 are "civil law division cases."

Probate is handled by the Circuit Court in all counties.

ONLINE ACCESS   While there is no statewide public online system available, other than appellate and supreme court opinions from the web site. A number of Illinois Circuit Courts offer online access, many through a vendor at www.judici.com.

ADDITIONAL INFORMATION   The search fee is set by statute and has three levels based on the county population. The higher the population, the larger the fee. In most courts, both civil and criminal data is on computer from the same starting date. In most Illinois courts the search fee is charged on a per name per year basis.

Adams County

Circuit Court 521 Vermont St, Quincy, IL 62301; 217-277-2100; Fax: 217-277-2116. Hours: 8:15AM-4:30PM (CST). *Felony, Misdemeanor, Civil, Eviction, Small Claims, Probate.*
www.co.adams.il.us
Civil Records: Access: Phone, mail, fax, in person, online, email. Both court and visitors may perform in person searches. Search fee: $2.00 per name. Fee is $4.00 for years prior to 1987. Required to search: name, years to search. Civil cases indexed by defendant, plaintiff. Civil records on computer from 1987, books and index cards from 1920. Online access to 8th Circuit Clerk of Court records is free at www.judici.com/courts/cases/case_search.jsp?court=IL001025J. Search by name, case or docket number back to 1987.
Criminal Records: Access: Phone, mail, fax, in person, online, email. Both court and visitors may perform in person searches. Search fee: $2.00 per name. Fee is $4.00 for years prior to 1987. Required to search: name, years to search, DOB. Criminal records on computer from 1987, books and index cards from 1920. Online access to criminal records is the same as civil. The county inmate list and warrant list is at the home page.
General Information: Public Access terminal is available. No juvenile or adoption records released.
Copy fee: $.50 each add'l. Cert fee: $6.00. Payee: Clerk of Circuit Court. Personal checks accepted. Prepayment required. Mail requests: SASE required. Mail turnaround time 2-3 days.

Alexander County

Circuit Court 2000 Washington Ave, Cairo, IL 62914; 618-734-0107; Fax: 618-734-7003. Hours: 8AM-Noon-1-4PM (CST). *Felony, Misdemeanor, Civil, Eviction, Small Claims, Probate.*
Civil Records: Access: Fax, mail, in person. Only the court may perform in person searches. Search fee: $4.00 per name per year. Required to search: name, years to search. Civil cases indexed by defendant, plaintiff. Civil records on computer from 1987, books and index cards from 1800s.
Criminal Records: Access: Fax, mail, in person. Only the court may perform in person searches. Search fee: $6.00 per name per year. Required to search: name. Criminal records on computer from 1987, books and index cards from 1800s.
General Information: No juvenile or adoption records released. Will fax results to local or toll free line. Copy fee: $2.00 for first page, $.50 each add'l. Cert fee: $6.00. Payee: Clerk of Circuit Court. Personal checks not accepted. Prepayment required. Mail requests: SASE required. Mail turnaround time 1 day.

Bond County

Circuit Court 200 W College Ave, Greenville, IL 62246; 618-664-3208; Fax: 618-664-2257. Hours: 8AM-4:30PM (CST). *Felony, Misdemeanor, Civil, Small Claims, Probate.*
www.johnkking.com
Civil Records: Access: Mail, in person. Both court and visitors may perform in person searches. Search fee: $5.00 per name per year. Required to search: name, years to search. Civil cases indexed by defendant, plaintiff. Civil records on computer back to 1/87 (and are limited); in index books from 1900s.
Criminal Records: Access: Mail, in person. Both court and visitors may perform in person searches. Search fee: $5.00 per name per year. Required to search: name, years to search, DOB. Criminal records on computer back to 1964; index books from 1900s.
General Information: Public Access terminal is available. No juvenile or adoption records released. Will not fax results. Copy fee: $.50 per page. Cert fee: $5.00 plus $.50 per page. Payee: Clerk of Circuit Court. Personal checks accepted. Prepayment required. Mail requests: SASE required. Mail turnaround time 1-2 weeks.

Boone County

Circuit Court 601 N Main, #303, Belvidere, IL 61008; 815-544-0371. Hours: 8:30AM-5PM (CST). *Felony, Misdemeanor, Civil, Eviction, Small Claims, Probate.*

Civil Records: Access: Mail, in person. Both court and visitors may perform in person searches. Search fee: $6.00 per name per year. Required to search: name, years to search. Civil cases indexed by defendant, plaintiff. Civil records on computer since August, 1993, on index books from 1800s.

Criminal Records: Access: Mail, in person. Both court and visitors may perform in person searches. Search fee: $6.00 per name per year. Required to search: name, years to search, DOB; also helpful: SSN, signed release. Records on computer since August, 1993, on index books from 1800s.

General Information: Public Access terminal is available. No juvenile or adoption records released. Copy fee: $2.00 for first page, $.50 each add'l. Cert fee: $6.00. Payee: Clerk of Circuit Court. Personal checks may be accepted. Prepayment required. Mail requests: SASE required. Mail turnaround: 1-2 days.

Brown County

Circuit Court Brown County Courthouse, 200 Court St, Rm 5, Mt Sterling, IL 62353; 217-773-2713. 8:30AM-4:30PM (CST). *Felony, Misdemeanor, Civil, Eviction, Small Claims, Probate.*

Civil Records: Access: Phone, fax, mail, in person. Both court and visitors may perform in person searches. Search fee: $4.00 per name per year. Required to search: name, years to search. Civil cases indexed by defendant, plaintiff. Civil records on computer since 1994, on index books from 1830s.

Criminal Records: Access: Phone, fax, mail, in person. Both court and visitors may perform in person searches. Search fee: $4.00 per name per year. Required to search: name, years to search, DOB, signed release. Criminal records on computer since 1994, on index books from 1830s.

General Information: Public Access terminal is available. No juvenile or adoption records released. Will fax results $3.00 per page. Copy fee: $.35 per page. Cert fee: $2.00. Payee: Clerk of Circuit Court. Only cashiers checks and money orders accepted. Prepayment required. Mail requests: SASE required. Mail turnaround time 1 week.

Bureau County

Circuit Court 702 S Main, Princeton, IL 61356; 815-872-2001; Fax: 815-872-0027. Hours: 8AM-4PM (CST). *Felony, Misdemeanor, Civil, Eviction, Small Claims, Probate.*
www.bccirclk.gov
Civil Records: Access: Online, in person. Both court and visitors may perform in person searches. Search fee: $4.00 per name per year. Required to search: name, years to search. Civil cases indexed by defendant, plaintiff. Civil records on computer from 8/1988, prior on index books. Online access to judicial circuit records is free at www.bccirclk.gov/remote.htm. Click on "JIMS". Index includes dates, defendants, record sheets and dispositions and goes back to 8/1988.

Criminal Records: Access: Mail, in person, online. Both court and visitors may perform in person searches. Search fee: $6.00 per name per year. Required to search: name, years to search, DOB. Criminal records on computer from 8/1988, prior on index books. Online access to criminal records is the same as civil.

General Information: Public Access terminal is available. No juvenile or adoption records released. Fee to fax results is $2.00 1st pg; $1.00 each add'l. Copy fee: $.50 per page. Cert fee: $6.00. Payee:

Bureau County Circuit Clerk. Personal checks accepted. Prepayment required. Mail requests: SASE required. Mail turnaround time 1 week.

Calhoun County

Circuit Court PO Box 486, Hardin, IL 62047; 618-576-2451; Fax: 618-576-9541. Hours: 8:30AM-4:30PM (CST). *Felony, Misdemeanor, Civil, Eviction, Small Claims, Probate.*

Civil Records: Access: Phone, fax, mail, in person. Both court and visitors may perform in person searches. Search fee: $6.00 per name. Required to search: name, years to search. Civil cases indexed by defendant, plaintiff. Civil records on index books from 1800s, computerized since 07/98.

Criminal Records: Access: Phone, fax, mail, in person. Both court and visitors may perform in person searches. Search fee: $6.00 per name. Required to search: name, years to search, DOB. Criminal records on index books from 1800s, computerized since 07/98.

General Information: No juvenile or adoption records released. No fee to fax results. Copy fee: $2.00 for first page. $.50 per page, pages 2-19; $.25 each additional page. Cert fee: $2.00. Payee: Clerk of Circuit Court. Only cashiers checks and money orders accepted. Prepayment required. Mail requests: SASE required. Mail turnaround time 1 day.

Carroll County

Circuit Court 301 N Main St, PO Box 32, Mt Carroll, IL 61053; 815-244-0230; Fax: 815-244-3869. 8:30AM-4:30PM (CST). *Felony, Misdemeanor, Civil, Eviction, Small Claims, Probate.*

Civil Records: Access: Mail, in person, online. Both court and visitors may perform in person searches. Search fee: $6.00 per name per year. Required to search: name, years to search. Civil cases indexed by defendant. Civil records on computer from 1988, prior on index books. Access is free to civil, small claims, probate and traffic records at www.judici.com/courts/index.jsp?court=IL008015J. Records go back to 1988.

Criminal Records: Access: Mail, in person, online. Both court and visitors may perform in person searches. Search fee: $6.00 per name per year. Required to search: name, years to search, DOB. Criminal records on computer from 1988, prior on index books. Criminal records access is free at www.judici.com/courts/index.jsp?court=IL008015J. Records go back to 1988. Will respond by fax if possible.

General Information: Public Access terminal is available. No juvenile, mental health or adoption records released. Will not fax results. Copy fee: $2.00 for first page, $.50 each add'l. Cert fee: $10.00. Payee: Clerk of Circuit Court. Personal checks accepted. Prepayment required. Mail requests: SASE required. Mail turnaround time 2-3 days.

Cass County

Circuit Court PO Box 203, Virginia, IL 62691; 217-452-7225. Hours: 8:30AM-4:30PM (CST). *Felony, Misdemeanor, Civil, Eviction, Small Claims, Probate.*

Civil Records: Access: Mail, fax, in person. Visitors must perform in person searches for themselves. Search fee: $6.00 per name per year, for search conducted by staff. Required to search: name, years to search. Civil cases indexed by defendant, plaintiff. Civil records on index books from 1800s.

Criminal Records: Access: Mail, fax, in person. Visitors must perform in person searches for themselves. Search fee: $6.00 per name per year, for search performed by staff. Required to search: name, years to search, DOB; also helpful: SSN. Criminal

records on index books from 1800s, on computer back to 1998.

General Information: Public Access terminal is available. No juvenile or adoption records released. Will not fax results. Copy fee: $1.00 for first page, $.50 each add'l. Cert fee: $5.00 for up to 19 pages. Payee: Cass County Circuit Clerk. Personal checks accepted. No credit cards accepted. Prepayment required. Mail requests: SASE required. Mail turnaround time 1-2 weeks.

Champaign County

Circuit Court 101 E Main, Urbana, IL 61801; Civil phone: 217-384-3725; Criminal phone: 217-384-3727; Fax: 217-384-3879. Hours: 8:30AM-4:30PM (CST). *Felony, Misdemeanor, Civil, Eviction, Small Claims, Probate.*
www.cccircuitclerk.com
Civil Records: Access: Mail, online, in person. Both court and visitors may perform in person searches. Search fee: $4.00 per name per year. Required to search: name, years to search. Civil cases indexed by defendant, plaintiff. Civil records on computer from 1986, index books from 1800s. Access to the circuit clerk's case query online system formerly called PASS is now free at https://secure.jtsmith.com/clerk/clerk.asp. Online case records go back to '92.

Criminal Records: Access: Mail, online, in person. Both court and visitors may perform in person searches. Search fee: $4.00 per name per year. Required to search: name, years to search; also helpful: DOB, SSN. Criminal records on computer from 1988, index books from 1800s. Online access to criminal records is the same as civil.

General Information: Public Access terminal is available. No juvenile or adoption records released. Will fax results for $1.00 1st page, $.50 ea add'l. Copy fee: $1.50 1st page, $.50 add'l page. Cert fee: $2.00. Payee: Clerk of Circuit Court. Personal checks accepted. Prepayment required. Mail requests: SASE required. Mail turnaround time 1-2 weeks.

Christian County

Circuit Court PO Box 617, Taylorville, IL 62568; 217-824-4966; Fax: 217-824-5030. Hours: 8AM-4PM (CST). *Felony, Misdemeanor, Civil, Eviction, Small Claims, Probate.*

Civil Records: Access: Phone, mail, in person. Both court and visitors may perform in person searches. Search fee: $5.00 per name per year. Required to search: name; also helpful: years to search. Civil cases indexed by defendant, plaintiff. Civil records on computer from 1988, index books from 1840.

Criminal Records: Access: Phone, mail, in person. Both court and visitors may perform in person searches. Search fee: $5.00 per name per year. Required to search: name; also helpful: years to search, DOB. Criminal records on computer from 1988, index books from 1840.

General Information: No juvenile or adoption records released. Will fax results to toll free or local number. Copy fee: $1.00 for first page, $.50 each add'l. Cert fee: $2.00. Payee: Clerk of Circuit Court. Business checks accepted. Prepayment required. Mail requests: SASE required. Mail turnaround: 1-2 days.

Clark County

Circuit Court PO Box 187, Marshall, IL 62441; 217-826-2811; Criminal phone: 217-826-2811. Hours: 8AM-4PM (CST). *Felony, Misdemeanor, Civil, Eviction, Small Claims, Probate.*

Civil Records: Access: Mail, in person. Both court and visitors may perform in person searches. Search fee: $6.00 per name per year. Required to search: name, years to search; also helpful: address. Civil cases indexed by defendant, plaintiff. Civil records on computer from 1989, index books from 1800s.

Criminal Records: Access: Mail, in person. Both court and visitors may perform in person searches. Search fee: $6.00 per name per year. Required to search: name, years to search, DOB, signed release; also helpful: address, SSN. Criminal records on computer from 1989, index books from 1800s.

General Information: Public Access terminal is available. No juvenile, maternity, or adoption records released. Copy fee: $2.00 for first page, $.50 each add'l. After 20 pages, fee is $.25 per page. Cert fee: $6.00. Payee: Clerk of Circuit Court. Only cashiers checks and money orders accepted. Prepayment required. Mail requests: SASE required. Mail turnaround time 1 week.

Clay County

Circuit Court PO Box 100, Louisville, IL 62858; 618-665-3523; Fax: 618-665-3543. Hours: 8AM-4PM (CST). *Felony, Misdemeanor, Civil, Eviction, Small Claims, Probate.*

Civil Records: Access: Fax, mail, in person. Both court and visitors may perform in person searches. Search fee: $5.00 per name. Fee is $5.00 per year prior to 1988. Required to search: name, years to search. Civil cases indexed by defendant. Civil records on computer from 1988, index books prior.

Criminal Records: Access: Fax, mail, in person. Both court and visitors may perform in person searches. Search fee: $5.00 per name. Fee is $5.00 per year prior to 1988. Required to search: name, years to search; also helpful: DOB. Criminal records on computer from 1988, index books from 1850s.

General Information: Public Access terminal is available. No juvenile or adoption records released. Will fax results for $1.00 1st page, $.50 each add'l. Copy fee: $1.00 for first page, $.50 each add'l 19; $.25 each thereafter. Cert fee: $6.00. Payee: Clerk of Circuit Court. No personal checks accepted. Prepayment required. Mail requests: SASE required. Mail turnaround time 2-3 days.

Clinton County

Circuit Court County Courthouse, PO Box 407, Carlyle, IL 62231; 618-594-2464. Hours: 8AM-4PM (CST). *Felony, Misdemeanor, Civil, Eviction, Small Claims, Probate.*

Civil Records: Access: Mail, in person. Both court and visitors may perform in person searches. Search fee: $10.00 per name. Fee is for 10 year search. Required to search: name, years to search. Civil cases indexed by defendant, plaintiff. Civil records on computer from 1988, index books from 1825.

Criminal Records: Access: Mail, in person. Both court and visitors may perform in person searches. Search fee: $10.00 per name. Flat fee for 10 year search. Required to search: name, years to search, DOB. Criminal records on computer from 1988, index books from 1825.

General Information: Public Access terminal is available. No juvenile or adoption records released. Will not fax results. Copy fee: $.50 per page. Cert fee: $6.00. Payee: Clerk of Circuit Court. Personal checks accepted. Prepayment required. Mail requests: SASE required. Mail turnaround time 2-4 days.

Coles County

Circuit Court PO Box 48, Charleston, IL 61920; 217-348-0516. Hours: 8:30AM-4:30PM (CST). *Felony, Misdemeanor, Civil, Eviction, Small Claims, Probate.*

Civil Records: Access: Fax, mail, in person, online. Both court and visitors may perform in person searches. Search fee: $5.00 per name. Required to search: name, years to search. Civil cases indexed by defendant, plaintiff. Civil records on computer from 1989, index books from 1800s. Access is free to civil, small claims, probate and traffic records at

www.judici.com/courts/index.jsp?court=IL015025J, to 1989.

Criminal Records: Access: Fax, mail, in person, online. Both court and visitors may perform in person searches. Search fee: $6.00 per name. Required to search: name, years to search, DOB; also helpful: SSN. Criminal records on computer from 1989, index books from 1800s. Criminal records access is free at www.judici.com/courts/index.jsp?court=IL015025J.

General Information: Public Access terminal is available. No juvenile or adoption records released. Will fax results to local or toll free line. Copy fee: $2.00 1st, $.50 per page. Cert fee: $6.00. Payee: Clerk of Circuit Court. Personal checks accepted. Prepayment required. Mail requests: SASE required. Mail turnaround time 1-2 days.

Cook County

Circuit Court - Criminal Division 2650 S California Ave, Chicago, IL 60608; 773-869-3140 Admin; Criminal phone: 773-869-3677; Fax: 773-869-4444. Hours: 8:30AM-4:30PM (CST). *Felony.* www.cookcountyclerkofcourt.org

Note: Cases are heard in six district courts within the county and each court has a central index. This location houses criminal records only.

Criminal Records: Access: Mail, in person. Both court and visitors may perform in person searches. Search fee: $9.00 per name per year. Required to search: name, years to search, DOB; also helpful: SSN. Criminal records on computer since 1964; prior records on microfiche from 1800s. A search or record request form is online at http://198.173.15.31/forms/pdf_files/CriminalForm.pdf.

General Information: Public Access terminal is available. (Public terminal for criminal in person searchers.) No juvenile or adoption records released. Copy fee: $2.00 for first page, $.50 each add'l. $.25 per page after 20. Cert fee: $9.00. Payee: Clerk of Circuit Court. Personal checks accepted with drivers license number or attorney code. Prepayment required. Mail requests: SASE required. Mail turnaround time is 7-10 days.

Circuit Court - Chicago District 1 50 W Washington, Rm 601, Chicago, IL 60602; 312-603-5030; Civil phone: 312-603-5145; Criminal phone: 312-603-4641; Probate phone: 312-603-6441; Fax: 312-603-3659 (crim). Hours: 8:30AM-4:30PM (CST). *Misdemeanor, Civil Action Under $100,000, Eviction, Small Claims, Probate.* www.cookcountyclerkofcourt.org

Note: Cases are heard in six district courts within the county. Each court has a central index. Eventually all case files are maintained here. Probate is a separate division at this same address, Rm 1202.

Civil Records: Access: Phone, mail, online, in person. Both court and visitors may perform in person searches. Search fee: $9.00 per year. Required to search: name, years to search. Civil cases indexed by defendant, plaintiff. Civil records on computer from 1983, index books from 1800s. Online case searching for limited case information - case snapshots - is free at www.cookcountyclerkofcourt.org/Terms/terms.htm Search by name, case number or court date. Information includes parties (up to 3), attorneys, case type, the filing date, the ad damnum (amount of damages sought), division/district, and most current court date. A online search request form is at http://198.173.15.31/forms/pdf_files/CivilForm.pdf. Phone inquiries to court to check status only. Phone record requests can be directed to the Computer Center at 312-603-7586 or 7.

Criminal Records: Access: Phone, mail, online, in person. Visitors must perform in person searches for themselves. Search fee: $9.00 per year. Required to search: name, years to search, DOB. Access to

criminal records is the same as civil. Criminal records online are misdemeanor records only. Phone record requests can be directed to the Computer Center at 312-603-7586 or 7. Search misdemeanors in person in Rm 1006.

General Information: Public Access terminal is available. No juvenile or adoption records released. Copy fee: $2.00 for first page, $.50 each add'l. Cert fee: $9.00. Payee: Clerk of Circuit Court. Personal checks accepted. Prepayment required. Mail requests: SASE required. Mail turnaround time 1 week.

Bridgeview District 5 10220 S 76th Ave, Rm 121, Bridgeview Court Bldg, Bridgeview, IL 60453; Civil phone: 708-974-6500; Criminal phone: 708-974-6422. Hours: 8;30-4;30PM (CST). *Felony, Civil Action Under $100,000, Eviction, Small Claims.* www.cookcountyclerkofcourt.org

Note: Alsip, Bridgeview, Burbank, Countryside, Evergreen Pk, Forest View, Hickory Hills, Hinsdale, Hodgkins, Hometown, Justice, Lagrange, Lemont, Lyons, McCook, Oak Lawn, Orland Hills, Palos Park, Stickney, Summit, West Haven, Willow Springs, Worth.

Civil Records: Access: Online, in person. Visitors must perform in person searches for themselves. No search fee. Required to search: name, years to search. Civil cases indexed by defendant, plaintiff. Civil records computerized since 1985, microfiche to early 1970s. Limited online case information is available; see Circuit Court - Chicago Division for details.

Criminal Records: Access: Online, in person. Visitors must perform in person searches for themselves. No search fee. Required to search: name. Online access to criminal records is the same as civil. Mail searches are directed to the Criminal Bureau, 2650 S California, Chicago 60608.

General Information: Public Access terminal is available. Copy fee: $2.00 for first page, $.50 each add'l. Cert fee: $9.00. Payee: Clerk of Circuit Court. Personal checks accepted.

Markham District 6 16501 S Kedzie Pkwy, Rm119, Markham, IL 60426-5509; 708-210-4262; Civil phone: 708-210-4227; Criminal phone: 708-210-4588. Hours: 8:30AM-4:30PM (CST). *Felony, Misdemeanor, Civil Action Under $30,000, Eviction, Small Claims, Traffic.* www.cookcountyclerkofcourt.org

Note: Blue Is, Burnham, Calumet, Chicago Hgts, Crestwood, Crete, Dixmoor, Dolton, Flossmoor, Glenwood, Harvey, Hazelcrest, Homewood, Lansing, Lynwood, Markham, Matteson, Midlothian, Oak Forest, Posen, Riverdale, Robbins, Sauk Village, Tinley Pk.

Civil Records: Access: Online, in person. Visitors must perform in person searches for themselves. No search fee. Required to search: name. Civil cases indexed by defendant, plaintiff. Civil records computerized since 1989. Limited online case information is available; see Circuit Court - Chicago Division for details.

Criminal Records: Access: Mail, online, in person. Visitors must perform in person searches for themselves. Search fee: $9.00 per name per division. Required to search: name, years to search. Misdemeanor records go back 10 years. Online access to criminal records is the same as civil. Mail searches are directed to the Criminal Bureau, 2650 S California, Chicago 60608.

General Information: Public Access terminal is available. Will not fax results. Copy fee: $2.00 for first page, $.50 each add'l. Cert fee: $9.00. Payee: Clerk of Circuit Court. Personal checks accepted. Prepayment required. Mail requests: SASE required. Mail turnaround time 2 weeks.

Maywood District 4 1500 S Maybrook Dr, Rm 236, Maywood, IL 60153-2410; 708-865-4937; Civil phone: 708-865-4973; Criminal phone: 708-865-5517. Hours: 8;30AM-4;30PM (CST). *Felony, Civil Action Under $100,000, Eviction, Small Claims.* www.cookcountyclerkofcourt.org
Note: Bellwood, Berkeley, Berwyn, Broadview, Brookfield, Cicero, Elmwood Park, Forest Park, Franklin Park, Hillside, La Grange Park, Maywood, Melrose Park, Northlake, North Riverside, Oak Park, River Forest, River Grove, Riverside, Stone Park, Westchester.

Civil Records: Access: Mail, online, in person. Visitors must perform in person searches for themselves. Search fee: $9.00 per name per division. Required to search: name; also helpful: years to search. Civil cases indexed by defendant, plaintiff. Civil records computerized since 1982, docket books to 1970s, prior archived. Limited online case information is available; see Circuit Court - Chicago Division for details.

Criminal Records: Access: Online, in person. Visitors must perform in person searches for themselves. No search fee. Required to search: name, years to search, DOB. Online access to criminal records is the same as civil. Mail searches are directed to the Criminal Bureau, 2650 S California, Chicago 60608.

General Information: Public Access terminal is available. Copy fee: $2.00 for first page, $.50 each add'l. Cert fee: $9.00. Payee: Clerk of Circuit Court. Personal checks accepted. Prepayment required. Mail turnaround time 1 week.

Rolling Meadows District 3 2121 Euclid Ave, Rolling Meadows, IL 60008-1566; 847-818-3000; Civil phone: 847-818-2300; Criminal phone: 847-818-2928. Hours: 8:30AM-4:30PM (CST). *Felony, Civil Action Under $100,000, Eviction, Small Claims.* www.cookcountyclerkofcourt.org
Note: Arlington Hgts, Barrington, Bartlett, Bensonville, Buffalo Grove, Elgin, Elk Grove Village, Hanover Pk, Harwood Hgts, Inverness, Mt. Prospect, Norridge, Palatine, Prospect Hgts, Rolling Meadows, Roselle, Rosemont, Schaumburg, Schiller Pk, Wheeling.

Civil Records: Access: Mail, online, in person. Visitors must perform in person searches for themselves. Search fee: $9.00 per name per division. Required to search: name; also helpful: years to search. Civil cases indexed by defendant, plaintiff. Civil records are computerized since 1986. Limited online case information is available; see Circuit Court - Chicago Division for details.

Criminal Records: Access: Online, in person. Visitors must perform in person searches for themselves. No search fee. Required to search: name, years to search; also helpful: DOB, SSN. Online access to criminal records is the same as civil. Mail searches are directed to the Criminal Bureau, 2650 S California, Chicago 60608.

General Information: Public Access terminal is available. Copy fee: $2.00 for first page, $.50 each add'l. Cert fee: $9.00. Payee: Clerk of Circuit Court. Personal checks accepted. Turnaround time 2 weeks.

Skokie District 2 Skokie Court Bldg, Rm 136, 5600 Old Orchard Rd, Skokie, IL 60076-1023; 847-470-7250. Hours: 8:30AM-4:30PM (CST). *Misdemeanor, Civil Action Under $100,000, Eviction, Small Claims.* www.cookcountyclerkofcourt.org
Note: Deerfield, Des Plaines, Evanston, Glencoe, Glenview, Golf, Kenilworth, Lincolnwood, Morton Grove, Niles, Northbrook, Northfield, Park Ridge, Prospect Heights, Skokie, Wilmette, Winnetka.

Civil Records: Access: Phone, mail, online, in person. Visitors must perform in person searches for themselves. Search fee: $10.00 per name per year. Required to search: name, years to search. Civil cases indexed by defendant, plaintiff. Civil records computerized since 1983. Limited online case information is available; see Circuit Court - Chicago Division for details.

Criminal Records: Access: Mail, online, in person. Both court and visitors may perform in person searches. Search fee: $9.00 per name per year. Required to search: name, years to search; also helpful: DOB, SSN. Online access to criminal records is the same as civil. Mail searches are directed to the Criminal Bureau, 2650 S California, Chicago 60608.

General Information: Public Access terminal is available. All records are public. Copy fee: $2.00 for first page, $.50 each add'l. Cert fee: $9.00. Payee: Clerk of Circuit Court. Personal checks accepted. Prepayment required. Mail requests: SASE not required. Mail turnaround time 1 week to 1 month.

Crawford County

Circuit Court PO Box 655, Robinson, IL 62454-0655; 618-544-3512; Fax: 618-546-5628. Hours: 8AM-4PM (CST). *Felony, Misdemeanor, Civil, Eviction, Small Claims, Probate.*
Civil Records: Access: Fax, mail, in person. Both court and visitors may perform in person searches. Search fee: $4.00 per name per year. Required to search: name, years to search. Civil cases indexed by defendant, plaintiff. Civil records on computer from 1989, index books from 1800s.
Criminal Records: Access: Fax, mail, in person. Both court and visitors may perform in person searches. Search fee: $4.00 per name per year. Required to search: name, years to search, DOB. Criminal records on computer from 1989, index books from 1800s.
General Information: Public Access terminal is available. No juvenile or adoption records released. Will fax results $2.00 1st page, $.25 each add'l. Copy fee: $1.00 for first page, $.50 each add'l. Cert fee: $5.00. Payee: Circuit Clerk. Personal checks accepted. Prepayment required. Mail requests: SASE required. Mail turnaround time up to 1 week.

Cumberland County

Circuit Court PO Box 145, Toledo, IL 62468; 217-849-3601; Fax: 217-849-2655. Hours: 8AM-4PM (CST). *Felony, Misdemeanor, Civil, Eviction, Small Claims, Probate.*
Civil Records: Access: Phone, fax, mail, in person. Both court and visitors may perform in person searches. Search fee: $6.00 per name per year. Required to search: name, years to search. Civil cases indexed by defendant, plaintiff. Civil records on computer from 1990, index books from 1885.
Criminal Records: Access: Phone, fax, mail, in person. Both court and visitors may perform in person searches. Search fee: $6.00 per name per year. Required to search: name, years to search; also helpful: DOB, SSN. Criminal records on computer from 1990, index books from 1885.
General Information: Public Access terminal is available. No juvenile or adoption records released. Will fax results. Copy fee: $1.00 for 1st page, $.50 per page next 19, then $.25 per page. Cert fee: $10.00. Payee: Clerk of Circuit Court. Only cashiers checks and money orders accepted. Prepayment required. Mail requests: SASE required. Mail turnaround time up to 1 week.

De Kalb County

Circuit Court 133 W State St, Sycamore, IL 60178; Civil phone: 815-895-7131; Criminal phone: 815-895-7138; Fax: 815-895-7140. Hours: 8:30AM-4:30PM (CST). *Felony, Misdemeanor, Civil, Eviction, Small Claims, Probate.*
www.co.kane.il.us/judicial
Civil Records: Access: Mail, in person, online. Both court and visitors may perform in person searches. Search fee: $4.00 per name per year. Required to search: name, years to search; also helpful: address. Civil cases indexed by defendant, plaintiff. Civil records on computer since 1987, records go back to 1858. Online access to court records is via a internet subscription system. Fee is $240 per year for this county or $300 for Will, Madison, Sangamon, Winnebago, Kane, Kendall, DeKalb courts. For info, email bmulticourt@janojustice.com or call 866-511-2892.
Criminal Records: Access: Mail, in person, online. Both court and visitors may perform in person searches. Search fee: $4.00 per name per year. Required to search: name, years to search, signed release; also helpful: address, DOB. Criminal records on computer since 9/91, on index books back 60 years. Online access to court records is via a internet subscription system. Fee is $240 per year for this county or $300 for Will, Madison, Sangamon, Winnebago, Kane, Kendall, DeKalb courts. For info, email bmulticourt@janojustice.com or call 866-511-2892.
General Information: Public Access terminal is available. No juvenile or adoption records released. Copy fee: $1.00 for first page, $.50 each add'l. After 20 pages, copies are $.25 each. Cert fee: $5.00. Payee: DeKalb County Circuit Clerk. Personal checks accepted. Visa, MC accepted. Accepted in person only. Prepayment required. Mail requests: SASE required. Mail turnaround time 2 weeks.

De Witt County

Circuit Court 201 Washington St, Clinton, IL 61727; 217-935-2195; Fax: 217-935-3310. Hours: 8:30AM-4:30PM (CST). *Felony, Misdemeanor, Civil, Eviction, Small Claims, Probate.*
Civil Records: Access: Mail, fax, in person. Both court and visitors may perform in person searches. Search fee: $4.00 per name per year. Required to search: name, years to search. Civil cases indexed by defendant. Civil records on computer from 1989, index books from 1839.
Criminal Records: Access: Mail, fax, in person. Both court and visitors may perform in person searches. Search fee: $4.00 per name per year. Required to search: name, years to search, DOB. Criminal records on computer from 1989, index books from 1839.
General Information: Public Access terminal is available. No juvenile or adoption records released. Will fax results to local or toll free line. Copy fee: $.2.00 for first page, $.50 each add'l, if over 20 then $.25 per page. Cert fee: $10.00. Payee: Clerk of Circuit Court. Only cashiers checks and money orders accepted. Prepayment required. Mail requests: SASE required. Mail turnaround time 1-2 weeks.

Douglas County

Circuit Court PO Box 50, Tuscola, IL 61953; 217-253-2352; Criminal phone: 217-253-2353 - Traffic. Hours: 8:30AM-4:30PM (CST). *Felony, Misdemeanor, Civil, Eviction, Small Claims, Probate.*
Civil Records: Access: Phone, fax, mail, in person. Both court and visitors may perform in person searches. Search fee: $5.00 per name per year. Required to search: name, years to search. Civil cases

indexed by defendant, plaintiff. Civil records on computer from 1989, index books from 1859.

Criminal Records: Access: Mail, in person. Both court and visitors may perform in person searches. Search fee: $5.00 per name per year. Required to search: name, years to search: also helpful: DOB, SSN. Criminal records on computer from 1989, index books from 1859.

General Information: Public Access terminal is available. No juvenile or adoption records released. Will fax results $5.00 for 1st 4 pages; $1.00 each add'l. Copy fee: $1.00 for first page, $.50 each add'l. $.25 per pg after 20 pages. Cert fee: $2.00. Payee: Douglas County Circuit Clerk. Personal checks accepted. Prepayment required. Mail requests: SASE required. Mail turnaround time 1 week.

Du Page County

Circuit Court 505 N County Farm Rd, Wheaton, IL 60187; 630-407-8700; Civil phone: 630-682-7100; Criminal phone: 630-682-7080/630-407-8600; Fax: 630-682-7082. Hours: 8:30AM-4:30PM (CST). *Felony, Misdemeanor, Civil, Eviction, Small Claims, Probate.*

www.co.dupage.il.us/courtclerk

Civil Records: Access: Mail, in person. Both court and visitors may perform in person searches. Search fee: $6.00 per name per year. Required to search: name, years to search. Civil cases indexed by defendant, plaintiff. Civil records online from 1976, microfilm records back to 1939, index records back to 1839. All document files after 01/01/92 are on optical disk.

Criminal Records: Access: Mail, in person. Both court and visitors may perform in person searches. Search fee: $6.00 per name per year. Required to search: name, years to search, DOB. Criminal records online from 1976, microfilm records back to 1939, index records back to 1839. All document files after 01/01/92 are on optical disk.

General Information: Public Access terminal is available. No juvenile or adoption records released. Copy fee: $2.00 for first page, $.50 each add'l. Cert fee: $6.00. Payee: Clerk of Circuit Court. Personal checks accepted. Visa, MC accepted. Prepayment required. Mail requests: SASE required. Mail turnaround time 1 week.

Edgar County

Circuit Court County Courthouse, 115 W Court, Paris, IL 61944; 217-466-7447. Hours: 8AM-4PM (CST). *Felony, Misdemeanor, Civil, Eviction, Small Claims, Probate.*

Civil Records: Access: Phone, mail, in person. Both court and visitors may perform in person searches. Search fee: $4.00 per name per year. Required to search: Name, years to search. Civil cases indexed by defendant, plaintiff. Civil records on computer from 1992, index books from 1823.

Criminal Records: Access: In person only. Both court and visitors may perform in person searches. Search fee: $4.00 per name per year. Required to search: Name, years to search, DOB. Criminal records on computer from 1992, index books from 1880.

General Information: Public Access terminal is available. No juvenile or adoption records released. Will not fax results. Copy fee: $2.00 first page; $.50 per page thereafter. Cert fee: $2.00. Payee: Janis K Nebergall, Circuit Clerk. Personal checks accepted. Prepayment required. Mail requests: SASE required. Mail turnaround time 1 week.

Edwards County

Circuit Court County Courthouse, Albion, IL 62806; 618-445-2016; Fax: 618-445-4943. Hours: 8AM-4PM (CST). *Felony, Misdemeanor, Civil, Eviction, Small Claims, Probate.*

Civil Records: Access: Mail, in person. Both court and visitors may perform in person searches. Search fee: $4.00 per name per year. Required to search: name, years to search. Civil cases indexed by defendant. Civil records on computer from 1988, books and index cards from 1815.

Criminal Records: Access: Mail, in person. Both court and visitors may perform in person searches. Search fee: $4.00 per name per year. Required to search: name, years to search, DOB. Criminal records on computer from 1988, index books from 1815.

General Information: Public Access terminal is available. No juvenile or adoption records released. Copy fee: $.50 per page. Cert fee: $2.00. Payee: Clerk of Circuit Court. Only cashiers checks and money orders accepted. Prepayment required. Mail requests: SASE required. Mail turnaround time 1 week.

Effingham County

Circuit Court 100 E Jefferson, PO Box 586, Effingham, IL 62401; 217-342-4065; Fax: 217-342-6183. Hours: 8AM-4PM (CST). *Felony, Misdemeanor, Civil, Small Claims, Probate.*

Civil Records: Access: Mail, in person. Both court and visitors may perform in person searches. Search fee: $5.00 per name; also $5.00 per year if prior to 1988; $5.00 per page for computer generated info. Required to search: name, years to search; also helpful: address. Civil cases indexed by defendant, plaintiff. Civil records on computer from 1988, index books from 1800s.

Criminal Records: Access: Mail, in person. Both court and visitors may perform in person searches. Search fee: $5.00 per name; also $5.00 per year if prior to 1988; $5.00 per page for computer generated info. Required to search: name, years to search, DOB; also helpful: address. Criminal records on computer from 1988, index books from 1800s.

General Information: Public Access terminal is available. No juvenile or adoption records released. Copy fee: $1.00 for first page, $.50 each add'l. $.25 per page after 20. Cert fee: $6.00. Payee: Effingham County Circuit Clerk. Business checks accepted. Prepayment required. Mail requests: SASE required. Mail turnaround time 1 week.

Fayette County

Circuit Court 221 S 7th St, Vandalia, IL 62471; 618-283-5009. Hours: 8AM-4PM (CST). *Felony, Misdemeanor, Civil, Eviction, Small Claims, Probate.*

Civil Records: Access: Phone, mail, fax, in person. Both court and visitors may perform in person searches. Search fee: $5.00 per name per year. Required to search: name, years to search. Civil cases indexed by defendant. Civil records on computer from 1988, index books from 1800s.

Criminal Records: Access: Phone, mail, fax, in person. Both court and visitors may perform in person searches. Search fee: $5.00 per name per year. Required to search: name, years to search, DOB. Criminal records on computer from 1988, index books from 1800s.

General Information: Public Access terminal is available. No juvenile, impounded or adoption records released. Copy fee: $1.00 for first page, $.50 each add'l. Cert fee: $2.00. Payee: Clerk of Circuit Court. Business checks accepted. Prepayment required. Mail requests: SASE required. Mail turnaround time 1 month.

Ford County

Circuit Court 200 W State St, Paxton, IL 60957; 217-379-2641; Fax: 217-379-3445. Hours: 8:30AM-4:30PM (CST). *Felony, Misdemeanor, Civil, Eviction, Small Claims, Probate.*

Civil Records: Access: Mail, fax, in person. Both court and visitors may perform in person searches. Search fee: $4.00 per name per year. Required to search: name, years to search. Civil cases indexed by defendant. Civil records on index books from 1800s; on computer back to 3/2000.

Criminal Records: Access: Mail, fax, in person. Both court and visitors may perform in person searches. Search fee: $4.00 per name per year. Required to search: name, years to search, DOB (signed release if for juvenile). Criminal records on index books from 1800s; on computer back to 3/2000.

General Information: Public Access terminal is available. No juvenile or adoption records released. Will fax results to local or toll free line. Copy fee: $1.00 for first page, $.50 each add'l. after 20 pages then $.25 per page. Cert fee: $4.00. Payee: Clerk of Circuit Court. Personal checks accepted. Prepayment required. Mail requests: SASE required. Mail turnaround time 2 days.

Franklin County

Circuit Court County Courthouse, PO Box 485, Benton, IL 62812; Civil phone: 618-439-2011. Hours: 8AM-4PM (CST). *Felony, Misdemeanor, Civil, Small Claims, Probate, Entry and Detainer, Traffic.* Note: Traffic 618-438-6731

Civil Records: Access: Mail, in person. Both court and visitors may perform in person searches. Search fee: $4.00 per name per year. Required to search: name, years to search. Civil cases indexed by defendant, plaintiff. Civil records on computer from 1987, index books from 1843.

Criminal Records: Access: Mail, in person. Both court and visitors may perform in person searches. Search fee: $4.00 per name per year. Required to search: name, years to search, DOB. Criminal records on computer from 1987, index books from 1843.

General Information: Public Access terminal is available. No juvenile or adoption records released. Will not fax results. Copy fee: $1.00 for first page, $.50 each add'l. Cert fee: $5.00. Payee: Franklin County Circuit Clerk. Only cashiers checks and money orders accepted. Prepayment required. Mail requests: SASE required. Mail turnaround: 1 week.

Fulton County

Circuit Court PO Box 152, Lewistown, IL 61542; 309-547-3041; Fax: 309-547-3674. Hours: 8AM-4PM (CST). *Felony, Misdemeanor, Civil, Eviction, Small Claims, Probate.*

Civil Records: Access: Phone, mail, fax, in person. Both court and visitors may perform in person searches. Search fee: $5.00 per name per year. Required to search: name, years to search. Civil cases indexed by defendant, plaintiff. Civil records on computer back to 1990, index books from 1900.

Criminal Records: Access: Mail, in person. Both court and visitors may perform in person searches. Search fee: $5.00 per name per year. Required to search: name, years to search; also helpful: DOB. Criminal records on computer back to 1990, index books from 1879.

General Information: Public Access terminal is available. No juvenile, impounded or adoption records released. Copy fee: $2.00 for first page, $.50 each add'l. Cert fee: $3.00. Payee: Fulton County Circuit Clerk. Business checks accepted. Prepayment required. Mail requests: SASE required. Mail turnaround time 1-2 days; older, archived records require add'l 2-3 days.

Gallatin County

Circuit Court County Courthouse, PO Box 249, Shawneetown, IL 62984; 618-269-3140; Fax: 618-269-4324. Hours: 8AM-N, 1-4PM (CST). *Felony, Misdemeanor, Civil, Eviction, Small Claims, Probate.*

Civil Records: Access: Fax, mail, in person. Both the court and visitors may perform in person searches. Search fee: $6.00 per name, per year. Required to search: name, years to search. Civil cases indexed by defendant. Civil records on index books from 1800s; computerized records since 1992.

Criminal Records: Access: Fax, mail, in person. Both the court and visitors may perform in person searches. Search fee: $6.00 per name, per year. Required to search: name, years to search, DOB, signed release. Criminal records on index books from 1800s; computerized records since 1992.

General Information: Public Access terminal is available. (Public terminal may be temporarily down.) No juvenile or adoption records released. Will fax results $1.00 per page. Copy fee: $.25 per page. Cert fee: $4.00. Payee: Clerk of Circuit Court. Business checks accepted. Prepayment required. Mail requests: SASE required. Mail turnaround time 1 week.

Greene County

Circuit Court 519 N Main, County Courthouse, Carrollton, IL 62016; 217-942-3421; Fax: 217-942-5431. 8AM-4PM (CST). *Felony, Misdemeanor, Civil, Eviction, Small Claims, Probate.*

Civil Records: Access: Phone, mail, in person. Both court and visitors may perform in person searches. Search fee: $5.00 per name. Required to search: name, years to search. Civil cases indexed by defendant, plaintiff. Civil records on index books from 1830s; computerized since 2002.

Criminal Records: Access: Phone, fax, mail, in person. Both court and visitors may perform in person searches. Search fee: $5.00 per name. Required to search: name, years to search, DOB. Criminal records on index books from 1875; computerized since 2002. No felonies by phone. Include signed release with felony search requests.

General Information: Public Access terminal is available. No juvenile or adoption records released. Will fax results for $.25 per page. Copy fee: $.25 per page. Cert fee: $2.00. Payee: Clerk of Circuit Court. Personal checks accepted. Prepayment required. Mail requests: SASE required. Mail turnaround: 1-2 days.

Grundy County

Circuit Court PO Box 707, Morris, IL 60450; 815-941-3256; Fax: 815-941-3265. Hours: 8AM-4:30PM (CST). *Felony, Misdemeanor, Civil, Eviction, Small Claims, Probate.*

Civil Records: Access: Mail, in person. Both court and visitors may perform in person searches. Search fee: $5.00 per name per year. Required to search: name, years to search. Civil cases indexed by defendant, plaintiff. Civil records on computer back to 1988. Online access to judicial circuit records should be in late 2004 (or when funding available) for local attorney firms and retrievers.

Criminal Records: Access: Mail, in person. Both court and visitors may perform in person searches. Search fee: $5.00 per name per year. Required to search: name, years to search, DOB, signed release. Criminal records on computer back to 1988.

General Information: Public Access terminal is available. No juvenile or adoption records released. Copy fee: $.50 per page. Cert fee: $2.00. Payee: Clerk of Circuit Court. Personal checks accepted. Prepayment required. Mail requests: SASE required. Mail turnaround time 1-2 days.

Hamilton County

Circuit Court County Courthouse, McLeansboro, IL 62859; 618-643-3224; Fax: 618-643-3455. Hours: 8AM-4:30PM (CST). *Felony, Misdemeanor, Civil, Eviction, Small Claims, Probate.*

Civil Records: Access: Mail, in person. Both court and visitors may perform in person searches. Search fee: $4.00 per name per year. Required to search: name, years to search. Civil cases indexed by defendant, plaintiff. Civil records on index books from 1800s; computer records go back to 1990.

Criminal Records: Access: Mail, in person. Both court and visitors may perform in person searches. Search fee: $4.00 per name per year. Required to search: name, years to search, DOB. Criminal records on index books from 1800s; computer records go back to 1990.

General Information: No juvenile or adoption records released. Will fax results. Copy fee: $.50 per page. Cert fee: $5.00 plus $1.00 per page 1st 19 pages, $.50 per page for next 19 pages; additional pages $.25. Payee: Clerk of Circuit Court. No personal checks accepted. Prepayment required. Mail requests: SASE required. Mail turnaround time 1-2 days.

Hancock County

Circuit Court PO Box 189, 500 Main St, #8, Carthage, IL 62321; 217-357-2616; Fax: 217-357-2231. Hours: 8AM-4PM (CST). *Felony, Misdemeanor, Civil, Eviction, Small Claims, Probate.*

Civil Records: Access: Phone, fax, mail, in person. Both court and visitors may perform in person searches. Search fee: $5.00 per name per year. Required to search: name, years to search. Civil cases indexed by defendant, plaintiff. Civil records on computer from 1992, index books from 1800s. For phone and fax searches, they will only search to determine if a record exists.

Criminal Records: Access: Phone, fax, mail, in person. Both court and visitors may perform in person searches. Search fee: $5.00 per name per year. Required to search: name, years to search, DOB; also helpful: SSN. Criminal records on computer from 1990, index books from 1970, archived to 1800s. For phone and fax searches, they will only search to determine if a record exists.

General Information: Public Access terminal is available. No juvenile or adoption records released. Will fax results no fee. Copy fee: $2.00 for first page, $1.00 each add'l. Cert fee: $3.00. Payee: Clerk of Circuit Court. Personal checks accepted. Prepayment required. Mail requests: SASE required. Mail turnaround time 1 week.

Hardin County

Circuit Court PO Box 308, County Courthouse, Main & Market Sts, Elizabethtown, IL 62931; 618-287-2735; Fax: 618-287-2713. Hours: 8AM-4PM (CST). *Felony, Misdemeanor, Civil, Eviction, Small Claims, Probate.*

Civil Records: Access: Mail, fax, in person. Both court and visitors may perform in person searches. Search fee: $6.00 per name per year. Required to search: name, years to search. Civil cases indexed by defendant, plaintiff. Civil records on computer back to 9/1992; on index books from 1800s.

Criminal Records: Access: Mail, fax, in person. Both court and visitors may perform in person searches. Search fee: $6.00 per name per year. Required to search: name, years to search, DOB. Criminal records on computer back to 9/1992; on index books from 1800s.

General Information: No juvenile or adoption records released. Fee to fax results is $2.00 for 1st 2 pages; $.50 each add'l page. Copy fee: $.25 per page.

Cert fee: $1.00 plus $.50 each add'l page. Payee: Circuit Clerk. Business checks, cashiers checks and money orders accepted. Prepayment required. Mail requests: SASE required. Mail turnaround time 1 week.

Henderson County

Circuit Court County Courthouse, PO Box 546, Oquawka, IL 61469; 309-867-3121; Fax: 309-867-3207. 8AM-4PM (CST). *Felony, Misdemeanor, Civil, Eviction, Small Claims, Probate.*

www.9thjudicial.org

Civil Records: Access: Phone, mail, in person. Both court and visitors may perform in person searches. Search fee: $5.00 per name per year. Required to search: name, years to search. Civil cases indexed by defendant, plaintiff. Civil records on computer from 1991, index books from 1800s.

Criminal Records: Access: Phone, mail, in person. Both court and visitors may perform in person searches. Search fee: $5.00 per name per year. Required to search: name, years to search, DOB; also helpful: SSN. Criminal records on computer from 1991, index books from 1800s.

General Information: Public Access terminal is available. No juvenile or adoption records released. Will not fax results. Copy fee: $2.00 plus $.50 each add'l page till 20, then $.25 per page. Cert fee: $3.00 plus $.50 each add'l page. Payee: Clerk of Circuit Court. Personal checks accepted. Prepayment required. Mail requests: SASE required. Mail turnaround time 1 day to 1 week.

Henry County

Circuit Court PO Box 9, Henry County Courthouse, Cambridge, IL 61238; 309-937-3572. Hours: 8AM-4:30PM (CST). *Felony, Misdemeanor, Civil, Eviction, Small Claims, Probate.*

Civil Records: Access: Mail, in person, online. Both court and visitors may perform in person searches. Search fee: $6.00 per name per year. Required to search: name, years to search. Civil cases indexed by defendant. Civil records on computer from 1989, index books from 1800s. Access is free to civil, small claims, probate and traffic records at www.judici.com/courts/index.jsp?court=IL037015J.

Criminal Records: Access: Mail, in person, online. Both court and visitors may perform in person searches. Search fee: $6.00 per name per year. Required to search: name, middle initial, years to search, DOB; also helpful-last known address. Criminal records on computer from 1989, index books from 1800s. Criminal records access is free at www.judici.com/courts/index.jsp?court=IL037015J.

General Information: Public Access terminal is available. No juvenile or adoption records released. Will fax results to local or toll free line. Copy fee: $1.50 for first page, $.50 each add'l. Cert fee: $4.00. Payee: Clerk of Circuit Court. Only cashiers checks and money orders accepted. Prepayment required. Mail requests: SASE not required. Mail turnaround time 2 weeks.

Iroquois County

Circuit Court 550 S 10th St, Watseka, IL 60970; 815-432-6950 (6952 Traff) (6991 Ch Supp); Fax: 815-432-6953. Hours: 8:30AM-4:30PM (CST). *Felony, Misdemeanor, Civil, Eviction, Small Claims, Probate.*

Civil Records: Access: Fax, mail, in person. Both court and visitors may perform in person searches. Search fee: $6.00 per name per year. Required to search: name, years to search. Civil cases indexed by defendant. Civil records on index books from 1900, computerized since 1989.

Criminal Records: Access: Fax, mail, in person. Both court and visitors may perform in person

searches. Search fee: $6.00 per name per year. Required to search: name, years to search, DOB. Criminal records on index books from 1820, computerized since 1989.

General Information: Public Access terminal is available. No juvenile or adoption records released. Fee to fax results is $6.00 per document. Copy fee: $.50 per page. Cert fee: $2.00. Payee: Clerk of Circuit Court. Personal checks accepted. Prepayment required. Mail requests: SASE required. Mail turnaround time 1-2 days.

Jackson County

Circuit Court PO Drawer 730, County Courthouse, 1001 Walnut, Murphysboro, IL 62966; 618-687-7300. Hours: 8AM-4PM (CST). *Felony, Misdemeanor, Civil, Eviction, Small Claims, Probate.* www.circuitclerk.co.jackson.il.us

Civil Records: Access: Mail, in person, online. Both court and visitors may perform in person searches. Search fee: $4.00 per name per year. Required to search: name, years to search. Civil records indexed by defendant, plaintiff. Civil records on computer from 1986, index books from 1860. Access is free to civil, small claims, and traffic records at http://circuitclerk.co.jackson.il.us/. Probate records are at www.iltrails.org/jackson/prodex.htm.

Criminal Records: Access: Mail, in person, online. Both court and visitors may perform in person searches. Search fee: $4.00 per name per year. Required to search: name, years to search. Criminal records on computer from 1986, index books from 1860. Criminal records access is free at http://circuitclerk.co.jackson.il.us/. Click on "Case information."

General Information: Public Access terminal is available. No juvenile or adoption records released. May fax back results if specifically requested; may depend on how busy the clerks are. Copy fee: $1.00 1st page, $.50 each add'l. Cert fee: $2.50. Payee: Circuit Clerk. Personal checks accepted. Prepayment required. Mail requests: SASE required. Mail turnaround time 1-2 weeks.

Jasper County

Circuit Court 100 W Jourdan St, Newton, IL 62448; 618-783-2524. Hours: 8AM-4PM (CST). *Felony, Misdemeanor, Civil, Eviction, Small Claims, Probate.*

Civil Records: Access: Mail, in person. Both court and visitors may perform person searches. Search fee: $5.00 per name. Required to search: name, years to search; also helpful: address. Civil cases indexed by defendant, plaintiff. Civil records on computer from 1988, index books from 1835.

Criminal Records: Access: Mail, in person. Both court and visitors may perform in person searches. Search fee: $5.00 per name. Required to search: name, years to search, DOB, sex, signed release. Criminal records on computer from 1988, index books from 1835.

General Information: No juvenile or adoption records released. Fee to fax results is $2.00 per document. Copy fee: $1.00 1st page; $.50 each add'l page. Cert fee: $6.00. Payee: Clerk of Circuit Court. Personal checks accepted. Prepayment required. Mail requests: SASE required. Mail turnaround: 1 week.

Jefferson County

Circuit Court PO Box 1266, Mt Vernon, IL 62864; 618-244-8008; Fax: 618-244-8029. Hours: 8AM-5PM (CST). *Felony, Misdemeanor, Civil, Eviction, Small Claims, Probate.*

Civil Records: Access: Phone, fax, mail, in person. Both court and visitors may perform in person searches. Search fee: $8.00. Required to search: name, years to search. Civil cases indexed by defendant.

Civil records on computer back to 1988, index books from 1800s. Fax requests must be followed by original by mail before being processed.

Criminal Records: Access: Phone, fax, mail, in person. Both court and visitors may perform in person searches. Search fee: $8.00. Required to search: name, years to search, DOB, SSN. Criminal records on computer back to 1988, index books from 1800s.

General Information: Sealed records not released. Will fax results $.25 per page plus phone charge. Copy fee: $.25 per page. No cert fee. Payee: Clerk of Circuit Court. Only cashiers checks and money orders accepted. Prepayment required. Mail requests: SASE required. Mail turnaround time 1-2 weeks.

Jersey County

Circuit Court 201 W Pearl St, Jerseyville, IL 62052; 618-498-5571; Fax: 618-498-6128. Hours: 8:30AM-4:30PM (CST). *Felony, Misdemeanor, Civil, Eviction, Small Claims, Probate.*

Civil Records: Access: Fax, mail, in person. Both court and visitors may perform in person searches. Search fee: $5.00 per name. Required to search: name, years to search. Civil cases indexed by defendant. Civil records on computer from 1991, index books from 1800s.

Criminal Records: Access: Fax, mail, in person. Both court and visitors may perform in person searches. Search fee: $5.00 per name. Required to search: name, years to search, DOB. Criminal records on computer back to 1991, index books from 1800s.

General Information: No juvenile or adoption records released. Will fax results. Copy fee: $.50 per page. Cert fee: $2 for 1st 2 pages; $.50 each add'l. Payee: Clerk of Circuit Court. Personal checks accepted. Prepayment required. Mail requests: SASE required. Mail turnaround time 1 week.

Jo Daviess County

Circuit Court 330 N Bench St, Galena, IL 61036; 815-777-2295/0037. Hours: 8AM-4PM (CST). *Felony, Misdemeanor, Civil, Eviction, Small Claims, Probate.*

Civil Records: Access: Mail, in person, online. Visitors must perform in person searches for themselves. Search fee: $6.00. Required to search: name, years to search. Civil cases indexed by defendant, plaintiff. Civil records on computer since 1992, on index books from 1960; will and probate back to 1850. Access is free to civil, small claims, probate and traffic records at www.judici.com/courts/index.jsp?court=IL043015J.

Criminal Records: Access: Mail, in person, online. Both court and visitors may perform in person searches. Search fee: $6.00 per name. Fee is for 1992 to present. Prior to 1992 $6.00 per name per year. Required to search: name, years to search, DOB. Criminal records on computer since 1992, on index books from 1960. Online access to criminal records is at www.judici.com/courts/index.jsp?court=IL043015J.

General Information: Public Access terminal is available. No juvenile or adoption records released. Will fax results for copy fee charge, if to toll- free line. Copy fee: $.50 per page. Cert fee: $10.00. Payee: Circuit Clerk. Business checks accepted. Prepayment required. Mail requests: SASE required. Mail turnaround time 1 week.

Johnson County

Circuit Court PO Box 517, Vienna, IL 62995; 618-658-4751; Fax: 618-658-2908. Hours: 8AM-4PM (CST). *Felony, Misdemeanor, Civil, Eviction, Small Claims, Probate.*

Civil Records: Access: Mail, in person. Both court and visitors may perform in person searches. Search fee: $4.00 per name per year. Required to search: name, years to search. Civil cases indexed by

defendant, plaintiff. Civil records on computer from 1987, index books from 1930s.

Criminal Records: Access: Mail, in person. Both court and visitors may perform in person searches. Search fee: $4.00 per name per year. Required to search: name, years to search, DOB. Criminal records on computer from 1987, index books from 1930s.

General Information: Public Access terminal is available. No juvenile or adoption records released. Will fax results with advance payment. Copy fee: $.50. Cert fee: $3.00. Payee: Circuit Clerk. Business checks accepted. Prepayment required. Mail requests: SASE required. Mail turnaround time 1 week.

Kane County

Circuit Court PO Box 112, Geneva, IL 60134; 630-232-3413; Civil phone: 630-208-3323; Criminal phone: 630-208-3319; Fax: 630-208-2172. Hours: 8:30AM-4:30PM (CST). *Felony, Misdemeanor, Civil, Eviction, Small Claims, Probate.* www.cic.co.kane.il.us

Civil Records: Access: Phone, fax, mail, in person, online. Both court and visitors may perform in person searches. Search fee: $4.00 per name per year. Required to search: name, years to search. Civil cases indexed by defendant, plaintiff. Civil records on computer from 1986, index books from 1800s. Online access to court records is via a internet subscription system. Fee is $240 per year for this county or $300 for Will, Madison, Sangamon, Winnebago, Kane, Kendall, DeKalb courts. For info, email bmulticourt@janojustice.com or call 866-511-2892.

Criminal Records: Access: Phone, fax, mail, in person, online. Both court and visitors may perform in person searches. Search fee: $4.00 per name per year. Required to search: name, years to search, DOB. Criminal records on computer from 1986, index books from 1800s. Online access to court records is via a internet subscription system. Fee is $240 per year for this county or $300 for Will, Madison, Sangamon, Winnebago, Kane, Kendall, DeKalb courts. For info, email bmulticourt@janojustice.com or call 866-511-2892.

General Information: Public Access terminal is available. No juvenile, mental health or adoption records released. Will fax results $2.00 1st page, $.50 each add'l. Copy fee: $2.00 for first page, $.50 each next 19, then $.25 each add'l. Cert fee: $4.00. Judgment orders certification fee $10.00. Payee: Clerk of Circuit Court. Personal checks accepted. Visa, MC, Discover accepted. Prepayment required. Mail requests: SASE required. Mail turnaround: 1 week.

Kankakee County

Circuit Court 450 E Court St, County Courthouse, Kankakee, IL 60901; 815-937-2905; Fax: 815-939-8830. 8:30AM-4:30PM *Felony, Misdemeanor, Civil, Eviction, Small Claims, Probate.*

Civil Records: Access: Mail, in person. Both court and visitors may perform in person searches. Search fee: $5.00 per name per year. Required to search: name, years to search. Civil cases indexed by defendant, plaintiff. Civil records on computer from 1990, index books from 1800s.

Criminal Records: Access: Mail, in person. Both court and visitors may perform in person searches. Search fee: $5.00 per name per year. Required to search: name, years to search, DOB. Criminal records on computer from 1990, index books from 1800s.

General Information: Public Access terminal is available. No juvenile, impounded, mental health, expunged or adoption records released. Will not fax results. Copy fee: $2.00 for first page, $.50 each add'l. Cert fee: $5.00. Payee: Clerk of Circuit Court. Personal checks accepted. Prepayment required. Mail requests: SASE required. Mail turnaround: 1-2 weeks.

Kendall County

Circuit Court PO Drawer M, 807 W John St, Yorkville, IL 60560; 630-553-4183; Civil phone: 630-553-4183; Criminal phone: 630-553-4184. Hours: 8AM-4:30PM (CST). *Felony, Misdemeanor, Civil, Eviction, Small Claims, Probate.*
Note: Traffic/DUI at 630-553-4185.

Civil Records: Access: Mail, in person, online. Both court and visitors may perform in person searches. Search fee: $6.00 per name per year. Required to search: name, years to search. Civil cases indexed by defendant, plaintiff. Civil records on computer since 1992, on index books from 1800s. Online access to court records is via a internet subscription system. Fee is $240 per year for this county or $300 for Will, Madison, Sangamon, Winnebago, Kane, Kendall, DeKalb courts. For info, email bmulticourt@janojustice.com or call 866-511-2892.

Criminal Records: Access: Mail, in person, online. Both court and visitors may perform in person searches. Search fee: $6.00 per name per year. Required to search: name, years to search, DOB. Criminal records on computer since 1992, on index books from 1800s. Online access to court records is via a internet subscription system. Fee is $240 per year for this county or $300 for Will, Madison, Sangamon, Winnebago, Kane, Kendall, DeKalb courts. For info, email bmulticourt@janojustice.com or call 866-511-2892.

General Information: Public Access terminal is available. No juvenile or adoption records released. Copy fee: $2.00 for first page, $.50 each add'l. $4.00 per page when hard copy printouts when cases are maintained on an automated medium. Cert fee: $4.00. Payee: Clerk of Circuit Court. Only cashiers checks and money orders accepted. Prepayment required. Mail requests: SASE required. Mail turnaround time 2-3 days.

Knox County

Circuit Court County Courthouse, Galesburg, IL 61401; 309-345-3817; Fax: 309-345-0098. Hours: 8:30AM-4:30PM (CST). *Felony, Misdemeanor, Civil, Eviction, Small Claims, Probate.*
Civil Records: Access: Fax, mail, in person. Both court and visitors may perform in person searches. Search fee: $5.00 per year per name. Required to search: name, years to search. Civil cases indexed by defendant, plaintiff. Civil records on index books from 1800s.
Criminal Records: Access: Fax, mail, in person. Both court and visitors may perform in person searches. Search fee: $5.00 per year per name. Required to search: name, years to search, DOB, sex. Criminal records on index books from 1800s.
General Information: Public Access terminal is available. No juvenile or adoption records released. Will fax results same as copy schedule. Copy fee: $2.00 for first page, $.50 each add'l. Cert fee: $3.00. Payee: Clerk of Circuit Court. Personal checks accepted. Prepayment required. Mail requests: SASE not required. Mail turnaround time 1 week.

La Salle County

Circuit Court - Civil Division PO Box 617, 111 W Madison St, Ottawa, IL 61350-0617; Civil phone: 815-434-8671; Criminal phone: 815-434-8271; Fax: 815-433-9198. Hours: 8AM-4:30PM (CST). *Civil, Eviction, Small Claims, Probate.*
Civil Records: Access: Mail, fax, online, in person. Both court and visitors may perform in person searches. No search fee. Required to search: name, years to search. Civil cases indexed by defendant, plaintiff. Some records on computer since late 1980s; prior records on index books from 1800s. Online access to Judicial Circuit records requires a $200

setup fee (waived for not-for-profits) and $.10 per minute usage fee. Call the Clerk's office at 815-434-8671 for details.
General Information: Public Access terminal is available. No juvenile or adoption records released. Will not fax results. Copy fee: $2.00 for first page, $1.00 each add'l. Cert fee: $2.00. Payee: Clerk of Circuit Court. Personal checks accepted. Visa, MC accepted. Prepayment required. Mail requests: SASE required. Mail turnaround time 1-2 weeks.

Circuit Court - Criminal Division 707 Etna Rd, #141, Ottawa, IL 61360; 815-434-8271; Civil phone: 815-434-8671; Fax: 815-434-8299. Hours: 8AM-4:30PM (CST). *Felony, Misdemeanor.*
www.lasallecounty.com
Criminal Records: Access: In person only. Visitors must perform in person searches for themselves. No search fee. Required to search: name, years to search; also helpful: DOB. Online access to Judicial Circuit records requires a $200 setup fee (waived for not-for-profits) and $.10 per minute usage fee. Call the Clerk's office at 815-434-8671 for details.
General Information: Public Access terminal is available. No juvenile or adoption records released. No fee to fax results. Copy fee: $2.00 for first page, $1.00 each add'l. Cert fee: $2.00. Payee: Clerk of Circuit Court. Personal checks accepted. Visa, MC accepted. Prepayment required. Mail requests: SASE required. Mail turnaround time 1-2 weeks.

Lake County

Circuit Court 18 N County St, Waukegan, IL 60085; 847-377-3600 (Admin.); Civil phone: 847-377-3209; Criminal phone: 847-377-3211. Hours: 8:30AM-5PM (CST). *Felony, Misdemeanor, Civil, Eviction, Small Claims, Probate.*
www.19thcircuitcourt.state.il.us
Civil Records: Access: Mail, in person. Both court and visitors may perform in person searches. Search fee: $5.00 per name per year. Required to search: name, years to search. Civil cases indexed by defendant, plaintiff. Civil records on computer or microfiche from 1968, index books from 1800s.
Criminal Records: Access: Masil, in person. Mail, in person. Both court and visitors may perform in person searches. Search fee: $5.00 per name per year. Required to search: name, years to search, DOB. Criminal records on computer or microfiche from 1968, index books from 1800s.
General Information: Public Access terminal is available. No juvenile or adoption records released. Copy fee: $2.00 for 1st page, $.50 each add'l. Cert fee: $5.00. Payee: Circuit Clerk. No personal checks accepted. Discover cards accepted. Prepayment required. Mail requests: SASE required. Mail turnaround time 1-2 days.

Lawrence County

Circuit Court County Courthouse, 1100 State St, Lawrenceville, IL 62439; 618-943-2815; Fax: 618-943-5205. 8AM-4PM (CST). *Felony, Misdemeanor, Civil, Eviction, Small Claims, Probate.*
Civil Records: Access: Mail, in person. Both court and visitors may perform in person searches. Search fee: $4.00 per name per year. Required to search: name, years to search, address. Civil cases indexed by defendant, plaintiff. Civil records on computer from 10/99, index books from 1800s.
Criminal Records: Access: Mail, in person. Both court and visitors may perform in person searches. Search fee: $4.00 per name per year. Required to search: name, years to search, address, DOB, SSN, signed release. Criminal records on computer from 10/99, index books from 1800s.
General Information: No juvenile or adoption records released. Will fax results for $1.00 1st page,

$.50 each add'l; after 20 pages, will copy for $.25 per page. Copy fee: $1.00 for first page, $.50 each add'l; after 20 pages, will copy for $.25 per page. Cert fee: $5.00. Payee: Clerk of Circuit Court. Only cashiers checks and money orders accepted. Prepayment required. Mail requests: SASE required. Mail turnaround time 2-3 days.

Lee County

Circuit Court 309 S Galena, #320, Dixon, IL 61021; 815-284-5234. Hours: 8:30AM-4:30PM (CST). *Felony, Misdemeanor, Civil, Eviction, Small Claims, Probate.*
Civil Records: Access: Mail, in person, online. Both court and visitors may perform in person searches. Search fee: $6.00 per name per year. Required to search: name, years to search. Civil cases indexed by defendant, plaintiff. Civil records on computer from 1989, index books from 1800s. Access is free to civil, small claims, probate and traffic records at www.judici.com/courts/index.jsp?court=IL052025J.
Criminal Records: Access: Mail, in person, online. Both court and visitors may perform in person searches. Search fee: $6.00 per name per year. Required to search: name, years to search, DOB; also helpful: SSN. Criminal records on computer from 1989, index books from 1800s. Criminal records access is free at www.judici.com/courts/index.jsp?court=IL052025J.
General Information: Public Access terminal is available. (Not available Summer, 2004.) No juvenile, impounded or adoption records released. Copy fee: $.50 per page. Cert fee: $2.00. Payee: Clerk of Circuit Court. Personal checks accepted. Prepayment required. Mail requests: SASE required. Mail turnaround time 1 week.

Livingston County

Circuit Court 112 W Madison St, Pontiac, IL 61764; 815-844-2602. Hours: 8AM-4:30PM (CST). *Felony, Misdemeanor, Civil, Eviction, Small Claims, Probate.*
Civil Records: Access: Mail, in person. Both court and visitors may perform in person searches. Search fee: $5.00 per name per year. Required to search: name, years to search; also helpful: address. Civil cases indexed by defendant, plaintiff. Civil records on computer from 1989 (child support since 1988), index books from 1837. Search probate index (1837 - 1958) www.cyberdriveillinois.com/departments/archives/pontiac.html.
Criminal Records: Access: Mail, in person. Both court and visitors may perform in person searches. Search fee: $4.00 per name per year. Required to search: name, years to search, DOB, SSN; also helpful: address. Criminal records on computer from 1989 (child support since 1988), index books from 1837. Signed release required for juvenile cases.
General Information: Public Access terminal is available. No juvenile, impound or adoption records released. Fee to fax results is $3.00 per fax. Copy fee: $1.00 for 1st pg; $.50 per pg, pages 2-19; $.25 each additional page. Cert fee: $2.00. Payee: Livingston County Circuit Clerk. Personal checks accepted. Prepayment required. Mail requests: SASE required. Mail turnaround time 3-5 days.

Logan County

Circuit Court County Courthouse, PO Box 158, Lincoln, IL 62656; 217-732-2376; Civil phone: 217-735-1163; Fax: 217-732-1231; 732-1232 civ.fax. 8:30AM-4:30PM (CST). *Felony, Misdemeanor, Civil, Eviction, Small Claims, Probate.*
www.co.logan.il.us/circuit_clerk
Civil Records: Access: Mail, fax, in person, online. Both court and visitors may perform in person searches. Search fee: $5.00 per name per year.

Required to search: name, years to search. Civil cases indexed by defendant, plaintiff. Civil records on computer back to 1990, index books from 1857. Online access to civil, small claims, probate and traffic records is free at http://co.logan.il.us/circuit_clerk/. Click on search court cases.

Criminal Records: Access: Mail, fax, in person, online. Both court and visitors may perform in person searches. Search fee: $5.00 per name per year. Required to search: name, years to search, DOB; also helpful: sex. Criminal records on computer back to 1990, index books from 1857. Criminal records access is free at http://co.logan.il.us/circuit_clerk/. Click on search court cases.

General Information: Public Access terminal is available. No juvenile or adoption records released. Copy fee: $2.00 for first page, $.50 each add'l. After 20 pages, the fee is $.25 per page. Cert fee: $5.00. Payee: Carla Bender, Circuit Clerk. Business checks accepted. Prepayment required. Mail requests: SASE not required. Mail turnaround time 1 week.

Macon County

Circuit Court 253 E Wood St, Decatur, IL 62523; Civil phone: 217-424-1454; Criminal phone: 217-421-0272; Probate phone: 217-424-1455; Fax: 217-424-1350. Hours: 8AM-4:30PM (CST). *Felony, Misdemeanor, Civil, Eviction, Small Claims, Probate.*

www.court.co.macon.il.us

Civil Records: Access: Phone, fax, mail, online, in person. Both court and visitors may perform in person searches. Search fee: $4.00 per name per year. Required to search: name, years to search; also helpful: address. Civil cases indexed by defendant, plaintiff. Civil records on computer from 1989, index books from 1800s. Access to court records is free online at www.court.co.macon.il.us/Templates/SearchCaseInfo.htm. Search docket information back to 04/96. Includes traffic, probate, family, small claims.

Criminal Records: Access: Fax, mail, online, in person. Both court and visitors may perform in person searches. Search fee: $4.00 per name per year. Required to search: name, years to search; also helpful: address, DOB, SSN. Criminal records on computer from 1989, index books from 1800s. Access to court records is free online at www.court.co.macon.il.us/Templates/SearchCaseInfo.htm. Search docket information back to 04/96.

General Information: Public Access terminal is available. No juvenile or adoption records released. Will fax results to local or toll free line, if not certified copy. Copy fee: $2.00 for first page, $.50 each add'l. Cert fee: $2.00. Payee: Macon County Circuit Clerk. Business checks accepted. Prepayment required. Mail requests: SASE required. Mail turnaround: 1 week.

Macoupin County

Circuit Court PO Box 197, Carlinville, IL 62626; 217-854-3211; Fax: 217-854-7361. Hours: 8:30AM-4:30PM (CST). *Felony, Misdemeanor, Civil, Eviction, Small Claims, Probate.*
Civil Records: Access: Mail, in person. Both court and visitors may perform in person searches. Search fee: $6.00 per name per year. Required to search: name, years to search. Civil cases indexed by defendant, plaintiff. Civil records on computer from 1994, index books from 1837.

Criminal Records: Access: Mail, in person. Both court and visitors may perform in person searches. Search fee: $6.00 per name per year. Required to search: name, years to search; also helpful: DOB, SSN. Criminal records on computer from 1994, index books from 1837.

General Information: Public Access terminal is available. No juvenile or adoption records released.

Will fax results for same fee structure as copy fees. Copy fee: $2.00 for first page, $.50 each add'l; $.25 for 20+ pages. Cert fee: $6.00. Payee: Mike Mathis Circuit Clerk. Personal checks accepted. Prepayment required. Mail requests: SASE required. Mail turnaround time 1 month to 6 weeks.

Madison County

Circuit Court 155 N Main St, Edwardsville, IL 62025; 618-692-6240; Fax: 618-692-0676. Hours: 8:30AM-4:30PM (CST). *Felony, Misdemeanor, Civil, Eviction, Small Claims, Probate.*
www.co.madison.il.us

Civil Records: Access: Mail, in person, online. Both court and visitors may perform in person searches. Search fee: $4.00 per name per year. Required to search: name, years to search. Civil cases indexed by defendant, plaintiff. Civil cases on computer from 1990, index books from 1800s. Online access to court records is via a internet subscription system. Fee is $240 per year for this county or $300 for Will, Sangamon, Madison, Winnebago, Kane, Kendall, DeKalb courts. For info, email bmulticourt@janojustice.com or call 866-511-2892.

Criminal Records: Access: Mail, in person, online. Both court and visitors may perform in person searches. Search fee: $4.00 per name per year. Required to search: name, years to search, DOB. Criminal records on computer from 1990, index books from 1800s. Online access to court records is via a internet subscription system. Fee is $240 per year for this county or $300 for Will, Sangamon, Madison, Winnebago, Kane, Kendall, DeKalb courts. For info, email bmulticourt@janojustice.com or call 866-511-2892.

General Information: Public Access terminal is available. No juvenile, mental health, adoption records released. Will fax results to local or toll free line. Copy fee: $2.00 for 1st pg; $.50 per pg for pgs 2-19; $.25 ea add'l pg. Cert fee: $4.00. Payee: Clerk of Circuit Court. Personal checks accepted. Prepayment required. Mail requests: SASE required. Mail turnaround time 2-3 days.

Marion County

Circuit Court PO Box 130, 100 E Main, Salem, IL 62881; 618-548-3856; Fax: 618-548-2358. Hours: 8AM-4PM (CST). *Felony, Misdemeanor, Civil, Eviction, Small Claims, Probate.*
Civil Records: Access: In person only. Visitors must perform in person searches for themselves. No search fee. Required to search: name, years to search. Civil cases indexed by defendant, plaintiff. Civil records on computer from 1988, index books from 1800s.

Criminal Records: Access: In person only. Visitors must perform in person searches for themselves. No search fee. Required to search: name, years to search; also helpful: DOB, SSN. Criminal records on computer from 1988, index books from 1800s.

General Information: Public Access terminal is available. No juvenile or adoption records released. Copy fee: $1.00 for 1st page, $.50 each add'l. Cert fee: $2.00. Payee: Clerk of Circuit Court. Only cashiers checks and money orders accepted. Prepayment required. Will bill to attorneys.

Marshall County

Circuit Court PO Box 328, Lacon, IL 61540-0328; 309-246-6435; Fax: 309-246-2173. Hours: 8:30AM-Noon, 1-4:30PM (CST). *Felony, Misdemeanor, Civil, Eviction, Small Claims, Probate.*
Civil Records: Access: Mail, in person. Both court and visitors may perform in person searches. Search fee: $6.00 per name per year. Required to search: name, years to search. Civil cases indexed by defendant, plaintiff. Civil records on computer from

1988, microfiche since 1964, index books from 1800s.

Criminal Records: Access: Mail, in person. Both court and visitors may perform in person searches. Search fee: $6.00 per name per year. Required to search: name, years to search, DOB. Criminal records on computer from 1988, microfiche since 1964, index books from 1800s.

General Information: Public Access terminal is available. No juvenile or adoption records released. Will fax results to local or toll free line. Copy fee: $.50 per page. Cert fee: $4.00. Payee: Clerk of Circuit Court. Personal checks accepted. Prepayment required. Mail requests: SASE required. Mail turnaround time 1 week.

Mason County

Circuit Court 125 N Plum, Havana, IL 62644; 309-543-6619; Fax: 309-543-4214. Hours: 8AM-4PM (CST). *Felony, Misdemeanor, Civil, Eviction, Small Claims, Probate.* www.masoncountyil.org
Civil Records: Access: Mail, in person. Both court and visitors may perform in person searches. Search fee: $4.00 per name per year. Required to search: name, years to search. Civil cases indexed by defendant, plaintiff. Civil records on computer from 1989, index books from 1800s.

Criminal Records: Access: Mail, in person. Both court and visitors may perform in person searches. Search fee: $4.00 per name per year. Required to search: name, years to search, DOB. Criminal records on computer from 1989, index books from 1800s.

General Information: Public Access terminal is available. No juvenile or adoption records released. Will fax results for $5.00 per fax. Copy fee: $1.00 for first page, $.50 each add'l. Cert fee: $2.00. Payee: Clerk of Circuit Court. Only cashiers checks and money orders accepted. Prepayment required. Mail requests: SASE required. Mail turnaround time 1 week.

Massac County

Circuit Court PO Box 152, Courthouse Sq, Metropolis, IL 62960; 618-524-9359; Fax: 618-524-4850. Hours: 8AM-Noon, 1-4PM (CST). *Felony, Misdemeanor, Civil, Eviction, Small Claims, Probate.*
Civil Records: Access: Mail, in person. Both court and visitors may perform in person searches. Search fee: $6.00 per name per year. Required to search: name, years to search. Civil cases indexed by defendant. Civil records on computer from 1986, index books from 1800s.

Criminal Records: Access: Mail, in person. Both court and visitors may perform in person searches. Search fee: $6.00 per name per year. Required to search: name, years to search, DOB, signed release. Criminal records on computer from 1986, index books from 1800s.

General Information: Public Access terminal is available. No juvenile or adoption records released. Copy fee: $.10 per page. Cert fee: $3.00. Payee: Clerk of Circuit Court. Only cashiers checks and money orders accepted. Prepayment required. Mail requests: SASE required. Mail turnaround time 5 business days.

McDonough County

Circuit Court County Courthouse, #1 Courthouse Sq, Macomb, IL 61455; 309-837-4889; Fax: 309-833-4493. 8AM-4PM (CST). *Felony, Misdemeanor, Civil, Eviction, Small Claims, Probate.*
Civil Records: Access: Phone, fax, mail, in person. Both court and visitors may perform in person searches. Search fee: $5.00 per name per year. Required to search: name, years to search. Civil cases indexed by defendant, plaintiff. Civil records on computer from 1991, index books from 1800s.

Criminal Records: Access: Phone, fax, mail, in person. Both court and visitors may perform in person searches. Search fee: $5.00 per name per year. Required to search: name, years to search; also helpful: SSN. Criminal records on computer from 1991, index books from 1800s.

General Information: Public Access terminal is available. No juvenile or adoption records released. Fee to fax results is $2.00 per page. Copy fee: $2.00 1st pg; $.50 each add'l 19pgs; $.25 over 20 pgs. Cert fee: $3.00. Payee: Clerk of Circuit Court. Personal checks accepted. Prepayment required. Mail requests: SASE required. Mail turnaround time 1 week.

McHenry County

Circuit Court 2200 N Seminary Ave, Woodstock, IL 60098; 815-334-4307; Fax: 815-338-8583. Hours: 8AM-4:30PM (CST). *Felony, Misdemeanor, Civil, Eviction, Small Claims, Probate.*

www.mchenrycircuitclerk.org

Civil Records: Access: Phone, fax, mail, online, in person. Both court and visitors may perform in person searches. Search fee: $4.00 per name per year. Required to search: name, years to search. Civil cases indexed by defendant, plaintiff. Civil records on computer from 1991, index books from 1800s. Access to records on the remote online system requires $750 license fee and $53.50 access fee, plus $50 per month. Records date back to 1991. Civil, criminal, probate, traffic, and domestic records are available. For more information, call 815-334-4193.

Criminal Records: Access: Phone, fax, mail, online, in person. Both court and visitors may perform in person searches. Search fee: $4.00 per name per year. Required to search: name, years to search, DOB; also helpful: SSN. Criminal records on computer from 1990, index books from 1800s. Access to records on the remote online system requires $750 license fee and $53.50 access fee, plus $50 per month. Records date back to 1990. Civil, criminal, probate, traffic, and domestic records are available. For more information, call 815-334-4193. Phone searches are limited to one only.

General Information: Public Access terminal is available. No juvenile or adoption records released. Copy fee: $2.00 for first page, $.50 each add'l. Over 20 copies then fee is $.25 per page. Cert fee: $4.00. Payee: Clerk of Circuit Court. Personal checks accepted. Visa, MC, Discover accepted. Prepayment required. Mail requests: SASE required. Mail turnaround time 1 week; criminal requests processed same day.

McLean County

Circuit Court Attn: Clerk, PO Box 2420, Bloomington, IL 61702-2420; 309-888-5301; Civil phone: 309-888-5341; Criminal phone: 309-888-5321. 8:30AM-4:30PM *Felony, Misdemeanor, Civil, Eviction, Small Claims, Probate.*

www.mcleancountyil.gov

Civil Records: Access: Mail, in person, online. Both court and visitors may perform in person searches. Search fee: $6.00 per name per year. Required to search: name, years to search. Civil cases indexed by defendant, plaintiff. Civil records on computer from 1991, index books from 1800s. Public access is free at www.mcleancountyil.gov/circuitclerk/PA_main.htm.

Criminal Records: Access: Mail, online. Both court and visitors may perform in person searches. Search fee: $6.00 per name per year. Required to search: name, years to search, DOB; also helpful: address, SSN. Criminal records on computer from 1991, index books from 1800s. Access is free at www.mcleancountyil.gov/circuitclerk/PA_main.htm.

General Information: Public Access terminal is available. (Criminal only.) No juvenile or adoption records released. Copy fee: $1.00 for first page, $.50

each add'l. Cert fee: $6.00. Payee: McLean County Circuit Clerk. Personal checks accepted. Prepayment required. Mail requests: SASE required. Mail turnaround time 10 days.

Menard County

Circuit Court PO Box 466, Petersburg, IL 62675; 217-632-2615. Hours: 8:30AM-4:30PM (CST). *Felony, Misdemeanor, Civil, Eviction, Small Claims, Probate.*

Civil Records: Access: Mail, in person. Both court and visitors may perform in person searches. Search fee: $4.00 per name per year. Required to search: name, years to search. Civil cases indexed by defendant. Civil records on computer from March, 1994, on index books from 1839.

Criminal Records: Access: Mail, in person. Both court and visitors may perform in person searches. Search fee: $4.00 per name per year. Required to search: name, years to search, DOB. Criminal records on computer from March, 1994, on index books from 1839.

General Information: No juvenile or adoption records released. Copy fee: $1.00 for first page, $.50 each add'l. Cert fee: $1.00. Payee: Clerk of Circuit Court. Only cashiers checks and money orders accepted. Prepayment required. Mail requests: SASE required. Mail turnaround time 2 days.

Mercer County

Circuit Court PO Box 175, Aledo, IL 61231; 309-582-7122; Fax: 309-582-7121. Hours: 8AM-4PM (CST). *Felony, Misdemeanor, Civil, Eviction, Small Claims, Probate.*

www.mercercountyil.org

Civil Records: Access: Fax, mail, in person, online. Both the court and visitors may perform in person searches. No search fee. Required to search: name, years to search. Civil cases indexed by defendant, plaintiff. Civil records on computer from 1988, index books from 1800s. Access is free to civil, small claims, probate and traffic records at www.judici.com/courts/index.jsp?court=IL066015J.

Criminal Records: Access: Phone, fax, mail, in person, online. Both the court and visitors may perform in person searches. Search fee: $5.00 per name per year. Required to search: name, years to search, DOB. Criminal records on computer from 1988, index books from 1800s. Criminal records access is free at www.judici.com/courts/index.jsp?court=IL066015J.

General Information: Public Access terminal is available. (Records go back to 1988.) No juvenile or adoption records released. Fee to fax results is $1.00 per page. Copy fee: $.25 per page. Cert fee: $3.50. Payee: Clerk of Circuit Court. Business checks accepted. Prepayment required. Mail requests: SASE required. Mail turnaround time 2-3 days.

Monroe County

Circuit Court 100 S Main St, Waterloo, IL 62298; 618-939-8681; Civil phone: x274; Criminal phone: x273; Probate phone: x274; Fax: 618-939-1929. Hours: 8AM-4:30PM (CST). *Felony, Misdemeanor, Civil, Eviction, Small Claims, Probate.*

Civil Records: Access: Phone, fax, mail, in person. Both court and visitors may perform in person searches. Search fee: $6.00 per name per year. Required to search: name, years to search, DOB. Civil cases indexed by defendant, plaintiff. Civil records on computer from 1992, index books from 1818.

Criminal Records: Access: Phone, fax, mail, in person. Both court and visitors may perform in person searches. Search fee: $6.00 per name per year. Required to search: name, years to search, DOB. Criminal records on computer from 1992, index books from 1818.

General Information: Public Access terminal is available. No juvenile or adoption records released. No fee to fax results. Copy fee: $1.00 for first page, $.50 each add'l. If over 20 pages, fee is $.25 per page (from 20 on). Cert fee: $5.00. Payee: Circuit Clerk. Business checks accepted. Mail requests: SASE required. Mail turnaround time 1 week.

Montgomery County

Circuit Court County Courthouse, PO Box C, Hillsboro, IL 62049; 217-532-9546. Hours: 8AM-4PM (CST). *Felony, Misdemeanor, Civil, Eviction, Small Claims, Probate.*

www.courts.montgomery.k12.il.us

Civil Records: Access: Mail, online, in person. Both court and visitors may perform in person searches. Search fee: $5.00 per name per year. Required to search: name, years to search. Civil cases indexed by defendant, plaintiff. Civil records on computer from 1988, index books from 1821, microfiche (probate only) since 1939. Online access to court records is at www.courts.montgomery.k12.il.us/CaseInfo.htm. Search by name or case number.

Criminal Records: Access: Mail, online, in person. Both court and visitors may perform in person searches. Search fee: $5.00 per name per year. Required to search: name, years to search, DOB. Criminal records on computer from 1988, index books from 1821, microfiche (probate only) since 1939. Online access to court records is at www.courts.montgomery.k12.il.us/CaseInfo.htm. Search by name or case number.

General Information: Public Access terminal is available. No juvenile or adoption records released. Will not fax results. Copy fee: $1.00 for first page, $.50 each add'l. Cert fee: $10.00. Payee: Clerk of Circuit Court. Only cashiers checks and money orders accepted. Prepayment required. Mail requests: SASE required. Mail turnaround time 1 week.

Morgan County

Circuit Court 300 W State St, Jacksonville, IL 62650; 217-243-5419; Fax: 217-243-2009. Hours: 8:30AM-4:30PM (CST). *Felony, Misdemeanor, Civil, Eviction, Small Claims, Probate.*

Civil Records: Access: Mail, in person. Both court and visitors may perform in person searches. Search fee: $5.00 per name per year. Required to search: name, years to search. Civil cases indexed by defendant and plaintiff. Civil records on computer from 1990, index books from mid 1800s.

Criminal Records: Access: Mail, in person. Both court and visitors may perform in person searches. Search fee: $5.00 per name per year. Required to search: name, years to search, DOB. Criminal records on computer from 1990, index books from mid 1800s.

General Information: Public Access terminal is available. No juvenile or adoption records released. Will fax results for $1.50 1st page, $.50 each add'l. Copy fee: $1.00 first page, $.50 per page thereafter. Cert fee: $4.00. Payee: Clerk of Circuit Court. Only cashiers checks and money orders accepted. Prepayment required. Mail requests: SASE required. Mail turnaround time 1 week.

Moultrie County

Circuit Court 10 S Main, #7, Moultrie County Courthouse, Sullivan, IL 61951; 217-728-4622. Hours: 8:30AM-4:30PM (CST). *Felony, Misdemeanor, Civil, Eviction, Small Claims, Probate.*

www.circuit-clerk.moultrie.il.us

Civil Records: Access: Mail, in person. Both court and visitors may perform in person searches. Search fee: $4.00 per name per year. Required to search: name, years to search. Civil cases indexed by defendant. Civil records on computer from 1990, index books from 1850.

Criminal Records: Access: Mail, in person. Both court and visitors may perform in person searches. Search fee: $4.00 per name per year. Required to search: name, years to search, DOB. Criminal records on computer from 1990, index books from 1850.

General Information: No juvenile or adoption records released. Copy fee: $.25 per page. Cert fee: $2.00. Payee: Clerk of Circuit Court. Business checks accepted. Prepayment required. Mail requests: SASE required. Mail turnaround time 1 week.

Ogle County

Circuit Court PO Box 337, Oregon, IL 61061; 815-732-1130; Civil phone: 815-732-1130; Criminal phone: 815-732-1140. Hours: 8:30AM-4:30PM (CST). *Felony, Misdemeanor, Civil, Eviction, Small Claims, Probate.*

www.oglecounty.org/marty/circuitclerk.html

Civil Records: Access: Mail, in person, online. Both court and visitors may perform in person searches. Search fee: $6.00 per name per year. Required to search: name, years to search. Civil cases indexed by defendant, plaintiff. Civil records on computer back to 1994; prior records on microfiche last 10 years, index books from 1836. Access is free to civil, small claims, probate and traffic records at www.oglecounty.org. Click on "Search for Case Information."

Criminal Records: Access: Mail, online, in person. Both court and visitors may perform in person searches. Search fee: $6.00 per name per year. Required to search: name, years to search, DOB. Criminal records on computer back to 1989; prior records on microfiche last 10 years, index books from 1836. Criminal records access is free at www.oglecounty.org. Click on "Search for Case Information."

General Information: Public Access terminal is available. No juvenile or adoption records released. Will not fax results. Copy fee: $2.00 for first page, $.50 each add'l. $.25 per page after 20. Cert fee: $10.00. Payee: Clerk of Circuit Court. Only cashiers checks and money orders accepted. Prepayment required. Mail requests: SASE required. Mail turnaround time 2-3 weeks.

Peoria County

Circuit Court 324 Main St, Peoria, IL 61602; 309-672-6953; Fax: 309-677-6228. Hours: 8:30AM-5PM (CST). *Felony, Misdemeanor, Civil, Eviction, Small Claims, Probate.*

Civil Records: Access: Phone, mail, in person. Both court and visitors may perform in person searches. Search fee: $6.00 per name per year. Required to search: name, years to search. Civil cases indexed by defendant, plaintiff. Civil records on computer from 1986 (traffic), from 1987 (civil), archived from 1800s.

Criminal Records: Access: Phone, mail, in person. Both court and visitors may perform in person searches. Search fee: $6.00 per name per year, Additional $10.00 to mail. Required to search: name, years to search, DOB; also helpful: SSN. Criminal records on computer from 1978, archived from 1800s.

General Information: Public Access terminal is available. No juvenile or adoption records released. Copy fee: $2.00 for first page, $.50 each add'l. Cert fee: $6.00. Payee: Clerk of Circuit Court. Personal checks accepted. Visa, MC accepted. Prepayment required. Mail requests: SASE required. Mail turnaround time 1 week.

Perry County

Circuit Court PO Box 219, Pinckneyville, IL 62274; 618-357-6726. Hours: 8AM-4PM (CST). *Felony, Misdemeanor, Civil, Eviction, Small Claims, Probate.*

Civil Records: Access: Mail, in person. Both court and visitors may perform in person searches. Search fee: $4.00 per name per year. Required to search: name, years to search. Civil cases indexed by defendant, plaintiff. Civil records on computer from 1990, index books from 1800s.

Criminal Records: Access: Mail, in person. Both court and visitors may perform in person searches. Search fee: $4.00 per name per year. Required to search: name, years to search; also helpful: DOB. Criminal records on computer from 1990, index books from 1800s.

General Information: Public Access terminal is available. No juvenile or adoption records released. Will not fax results. Copy fee: $1.00 for first page; $.50 for next 19 pages; $.25 per page thereafter. Cert fee: $2.00. Payee: Clerk of Circuit Court. Only cashiers checks and money orders accepted. Prepayment required. Mail requests: SASE required. Mail turnaround time 1 week.

Piatt County

Circuit Court PO Box 288, Monticello, IL 61856; 217-762-4966; Fax: 217-762-8394. Hours: 8:30AM-4:30PM (CST). *Felony, Misdemeanor, Civil, Eviction, Small Claims, Probate.*

www.chittendensuperiorcourt.com

Civil Records: Access: Phone, fax, mail, in person. Both court and visitors may perform in person searches. No search fee. Required to search: name, years to search. Civil cases indexed by defendant, plaintiff. Civil records on computer since 1988, index books from 1800s.

Criminal Records: Access: Phone, fax, mail, in person. Both court and visitors may perform in person searches. No search fee. Required to search: name, years to search, DOB; also helpful: SSN. Criminal records on computer since 1988, index books from 1800s.

General Information: Public Access terminal is available. No juvenile or adoption records released. Will fax results $1.00 1st page, $.50 each add'l. Copy fee: $1.00 for first page, $.50 each add'l. Cert fee: $1.00 plus $.50 each add'l page. Payee: Clerk of Circuit Court. Business checks accepted. Prepayment required. Mail requests: SASE not required. Mail turnaround time 2-3 days.

Pike County

Circuit Court Pike County Courthouse, 100 E Washington St, Pittsfield, IL 62363; 217-285-6612; Fax: 217-285-4726. Hours: 8:30AM-4:30PM (CST). *Felony, Misdemeanor, Civil, Eviction, Small Claims, Probate.*

Civil Records: Access: Mail, in person, online. Both court and visitors may perform in person searches. Search fee: $6.00 per name per year. Required to search: name, years to search. Civil cases indexed by defendant, plaintiff. Civil records on computer since 1992, index books from 1800s. Access is free to civil, small claims, probate and traffic records at www.judici.com/courts/index.jsp?court=IL075015J.

Criminal Records: Access: Mail, in person, online. Both court and visitors may perform in person searches. Search fee: $6.00 per name per year. Required to search: name, years to search; also helpful: SSN. Criminal records on computer since 1992, index books from 1800s. Criminal records access is free at www.judici.com/courts/index.jsp?court=IL075015J.

General Information: Public Access terminal is available. No juvenile or adoption records released. Copy fee: $2.00 for first page, $.50 each add'l. $.25 per page after 19 pages. Cert fee: $10.00 judgements; $6.00 othr documents. Payee: Circuit Clerk. No personal checks accepted; money order or cash only. Prepayment required. Mail requests: SASE required. Mail turnaround time ASAP.

Pope County

Circuit Court PO Box 438, Golconda, IL 62938; 618-683-3941; Fax: 618-683-3018. Hours: 8AM-4PM (CST). *Felony, Misdemeanor, Civil, Eviction, Small Claims, Probate.*

Civil Records: Access: Phone, fax, mail, in person. Both court and visitors may perform in person searches. Search fee: $6.00 per name per year. Required to search: name, years to search. Civil cases indexed by defendant. Civil records on computer from 1989, index books from 1800s.

Criminal Records: Access: Phone, fax, mail, in person. Both court and visitors may perform in person searches. Search fee: $6.00 per name per year. Required to search: name, years to search, DOB. Criminal records on computer from 1989, index books from 1800s.

General Information: Public Access terminal is available. No juvenile or adoption records released. Will fax results $.50 per page. Copy fee: $.25 per page. Cert fee: $6.00. Payee: Circuit Clerk. Business checks accepted. Prepayment required. Mail requests: SASE required. Mail turnaround time 2-3 days.

Pulaski County

Circuit Court PO Box 88, 500 Illinois Ave, Rm C, Mound City, IL 62963; 618-748-9300; Fax: 618-748-9329. 8AM-4PM (CST). *Felony, Misdemeanor, Civil, Eviction, Small Claims, Probate.*

Civil Records: Access: Mail, in person. Both court and visitors may perform in person searches. Search fee: $6.00 per name. Required to search: name, years to search. Civil cases indexed by defendant, plaintiff. Civil records on computer since 1989, on books prior.

Criminal Records: Access: Mail, in person. Both court and visitors may perform in person searches. Search fee: $6.00 per name per year. Required to search: name, years to search, signed release; also helpful: DOB, SSN. Criminal records on computer since 1989, on books prior.

General Information: No juvenile, adoption records released. Copy fee: $1.00 for first page, $.50 each add'l. If over 20 pages, fee becomes $.25 per copy. Cert fee: $2.00. Payee: Clerk of Circuit Court. Only cashiers checks and money orders accepted. Prepayment required. Mail requests: SASE required. Mail turnaround time 1 week.

Putnam County

Circuit Court 120 N 4th St, Hennepin, IL 61327; 815-925-7016; Fax: 815-925-7492. Hours: 9AM-4PM (CST). *Felony, Misdemeanor, Civil, Eviction, Small Claims, Probate.*

Civil Records: Access: Mail, in person. Both court and visitors may perform in person searches. Search fee: $5.00 per name. Fee is per 5 years searched. Required to search: name, years to search. Civil cases indexed by defendant. Civil records on computer from 1991, index books from 1836.

Criminal Records: Access: Mail, in person. Both court and visitors may perform in person searches. Search fee: $5.00 per name. Fee is per 5 years searched. Required to search: name, years to search, DOB. Criminal records on computer from 1991, index books from 1836. No criminal searches performed on Thursdays.

General Information: Public Access terminal is available. No juvenile or adoption records released.

Copy fee: $.50 per page. $.25 per page after 20. Cert fee: $2.00. Payee: Clerk of Circuit Court. Only cashiers checks and money orders accepted. Prepayment required. Mail requests: SASE required. Mail turnaround time 3 days.

Randolph County

Circuit Court County Courthouse, Rm 302, Chester, IL 62233; 618-826-5000 X194; Fax: 618-826-3761. 8AM-4PM (CST). *Felony, Misdemeanor, Civil, Eviction, Small Claims, Probate.*
Civil Records: Access: Mail, in person. Both court and visitors may perform in person searches. Search fee: $4.00 per name per year. Required to search: name, years to search. Civil cases indexed by defendant, plaintiff. Civil records on computer from 1992, index books from 1800s. Visitors can search both.
Criminal Records: Access: Mail, in person. Both court and visitors may perform in person searches. Search fee: $4.00 per name per year. Required to search: name, years to search, DOB. Criminal records on computer from 1992, index books from 1800s. Visitors can search both.
General Information: Public Access terminal is available. No juvenile or adoption records released. Copy fee: $.25 per page. Cert fee: $2.00 for seal and $1.00 1st page and $.50 each add'l page. Payee: Clerk of Circuit Court. Business checks accepted. Prepayment required. Mail requests: SASE required. Mail turnaround time 1-2 days.

Richland County

Circuit Court 103 W Main, #21, Olney, IL 62450; 618-392-2151; Fax: 618-392-5041. Hours: 8AM-4PM (CST). *Felony, Misdemeanor, Civil, Eviction, Small Claims, Probate.*
Civil Records: Access: Phone, mail, fax, in person. Both court and visitors may perform in person searches. Search fee: $4.00 per name per year. Required to search: name, years to search. Civil cases indexed by defendant. Civil records on index books from 1867; on computer back to 1999.
Criminal Records: Access: Mail, in person. Both court and visitors may perform in person searches. Search fee: $4.00 per name per year. Required to search: name, years to search, DOB. Criminal records on index books from 1867; on computer back to 1986.
General Information: Public Access terminal is available. No juvenile or adoption records released. Will fax results for $0.25 per page. Copy fee: $1.00 for first page, $.50 each add'l. Cert fee: $.50. Payee: Clerk of Circuit Court. Only cashiers checks and money orders accepted. Prepayment required. Mail requests: SASE required. Mail turnaround: 1-2 weeks.

Rock Island County

Circuit Court PO Box 5230 (210 15th St), Rock Island, IL 61204-5230; 309-786-4451; Fax: 309-786-3029. 8AM-4:30PM (CST). *Felony, Misdemeanor, Civil, Eviction, Small Claims, Probate.*
www.co.rock-island.il.us/Government/CircuitClk/CircuitClk.html
Civil Records: Access: Mail, online, in person. Both court and visitors may perform in person searches. Search fee: $6.00 per name per year. Required to search: name, years to search. Civil cases indexed by defendant, plaintiff. Civil records on computer from 1989, index books from 1950s. Full access to court records on the remote online system requires $300 setup fee plus a $1.00 per minute for access. Civil, criminal, probate, traffic, and domestic records can be accessed by name or case number. Also, access to civil, small claims, probate and traffic records free at www.judici.com/courts/cases/index.jsp?court=IL081025J

Criminal Records: Access: Mail, online, in person. Both court and visitors may perform in person searches. Search fee: $6.00 per name per year. Required to search: name, years to search, DOB; also helpful: SSN. Criminal records on computer from 1989, index books from 1950s. Online access to criminal records is the same as civil - there are two methods.
General Information: Public Access terminal is available. No juvenile or adoption records released. Will fax results $1.50 1st page, $.50 each add'l. Copy fee: $1.50 for first page, $.50 each add'l. Cert fee: $4.00. Payee: Circuit Clerks Office. Money orders accepted. Prepayment required. Mail requests: SASE required. Mail turnaround time 1 week.

Saline County

Circuit Court County Courthouse, Harrisburg, IL 62946; 618-253-5096; Fax: 618-252-3904. Hours: 8AM-4PM (CST). *Felony, Misdemeanor, Civil, Eviction, Small Claims, Probate.*
Civil Records: Access: Fax, mail, in person. Both court and visitors may perform in person searches. Search fee: $5.00 per name per year. Required to search: name, years to search. Civil cases indexed by defendant, plaintiff. Civil records on computer back to 1986, index books archived from 1886.
Criminal Records: Access: Fax, mail, in person. Both court and visitors may perform in person searches. Search fee: $5.00 per name per year. Required to search: name, years to search, DOB. Criminal records on computer back to 1986, index books archived from 1800s.
General Information: Public Access terminal is available. No juvenile or adoption records released. Fee to fax results is $2.00 1st page, $1.00 each add'l. Copy fee: $1.00 for first page, $.50 each add'l. Cert fee: $5.00. Payee: Clerk of Circuit Court. Business checks accepted. Prepayment required. Mail requests: SASE required. Mail turnaround time 1-2 weeks.

Sangamon County

Circuit Court 200 S 9th St Rm 405, Springfield, IL 62701; 217-753-6674; Fax: 217-753-6665. Hours: 8:30AM-4:30PM (CST). *Felony, Misdemeanor, Civil, Eviction, Small Claims, Probate.*
www.co.sangamon.il.us/court
Civil Records: Access: Fax, mail, in person, online. Both court and visitors may perform in person searches. Search fee: $4.00 per name per year. Required to search: name, years to search. Civil cases indexed by defendant, plaintiff. Civil records on computer from 1982, index books from 1800s. Online access to court records is via a internet subscription system. Fee is $240 per year for this county or $300 for Will, Madison, Sangamon, Winnebago, Kane, Kendall, DeKalb courts. For info, email bmulticourt@janojustice.com or call 866-511-2892.
Criminal Records: Access: Fax, mail, in person, online. Both court and visitors may perform in person searches. Search fee: $4.00 per name per year. Required to search: name, years to search, DOB. Criminal records on computer from 1982, index books from 1800s. Online access to court records is via a internet subscription system. Fee is $240 per year for this county or $300 for Will, Madison, Sangamon, Winnebago, Kane, Kendall, DeKalb courts. For info, email bmulticourt@janojustice.com or call 866-511-2892.
General Information: Public Access terminal is available. No juvenile, mental health, adoption records released. No fee to fax results. Copy fee: $2.00 for first page, $.50 each add'l. $.25 per page after 19. Cert fee: $4.00. Payee: Circuit Clerk. Personal checks accepted. Prepayment required. Mail requests: SASE required. Mail turnaround: 1-2 weeks.

Schuyler County

Circuit Court PO Box 80, Rushville, IL 62681; 217-322-4633; Fax: 217-322-6164. Hours: 8AM-4PM (CST). *Felony, Misdemeanor, Civil, Eviction, Small Claims, Probate.*
Civil Records: Access: Mail, in person. Both court and visitors may perform in person searches. Search fee: $6.00 per name per year. Required to search: name, years to search. Civil cases indexed by defendant. Civil records on computer from 1988, index books from 1800s.
Criminal Records: Access: Mail, in person. Both court and visitors may perform in person searches. Search fee: $6.00 per name per year. Required to search: name, years to search, DOB. Criminal records on computer from 1988, index books from 1800s.
General Information: No juvenile or adoption records released. Fee to fax results is $1.00 per page. Copy fee: $2.00 for first page, $.50 each add'l. $.25 after 20. Cert fee: $10.00. Payee: Clerk of Circuit Court. Only cashiers checks and money orders accepted. Prepayment required. Mail requests: SASE required. Mail turnaround time 1 week.

Scott County

Circuit Court 35 E Market St, Winchester, IL 62694; 217-742-5217; Fax: 217-742-5853. Hours: 8AM-Noon, 1-4PM (CST). *Felony, Misdemeanor, Civil, Eviction, Small Claims, Probate.*
Civil Records: Access: Mail, in person. Both court and visitors may perform in person searches. Search fee: $5.00 per name per year. Required to search: name, years to search. Civil cases indexed by defendant, plaintiff. Civil records on index books from 1800s.
Criminal Records: Access: Mail, in person. Both court and visitors may perform in person searches. Search fee: $5.00 per name per year. Required to search: name, years to search, DOB. Criminal records on index books from 1800s.
General Information: No juvenile or adoption records released. Will not fax results. Copy fee: $1.00 for first page, $.50 each add'l. After 20 pages, copies are $.25 each. Cert fee: $2.00. Payee: Clerk of Circuit Court. Only cashiers checks and money orders accepted. Prepayment required. Mail requests: SASE required. Mail turnaround time 1 week.

Shelby County

Circuit Court County Courthouse, PO Box 469, Shelbyville, IL 62565; 217-774-4212; Fax: 217-774-4109. 8AM-4PM (CST). *Felony, Misdemeanor, Civil, Eviction, Small Claims, Probate.*
Civil Records: Access: Fax, mail, in person. Both court and visitors may perform in person searches. Search fee: $4.00 per name. Required to search: name, years to search. Civil cases indexed by defendant, plaintiff. Civil records on computer from 1988, index books from 1848.
Criminal Records: Access: Fax, mail, in person. Both court and visitors may perform in person searches. Search fee: $4.00 per name. Required to search: name, years to search, DOB. Criminal records on computer from 1988, index books from 1848.
General Information: Public Access terminal is available. No juvenile or adoption records released. Will fax results for $5.00 per name or year. Copy fee: $1.00 for first page, $.50 each add'l. Cert fee: $2.00. Payee: Circuit Clerk. Prepayment required. Mail requests: SASE required. Mail turnaround: 1-2 weeks.

St. Clair County

Circuit Court 10 Public Sq, Belleville, IL 62220-1623; 618-277-6832; Criminal phone: Extension #4 for felony. 8AM-4PM (CST). *Felony, Misdemeanor, Civil, Eviction, Small Claims, Probate.*

Civil Records: Access: Mail, in person. Both court and visitors may perform in person searches. Search fee: $6.00 per name per year. Required to search: name, years to search; also helpful: address. Civil cases indexed by defendant, plaintiff. Civil records on computer from 1990, microfiche from 1800s.

Criminal Records: Access: Mail, in person. Both court and visitors may perform in person searches. Search fee: $6.00 per name per year. Required to search: name, years to search, DOB. Criminal records on computer from 1990, microfiche from 1800s.

General Information: Public Access terminal is available. No juvenile or adoption records released. Will not fax results. Copy fee: $2.00 for first page, $.50 each add'l. $.25 per pg after 19. Cert fee: $6.00. Payee: Clerk of Circuit Court. Personal checks accepted. Prepayment required. Mail requests: SASE required. Mail turnaround time 1-2 days.

Stark County

Circuit Court 130 W Main St, Toulon, IL 61483; 309-286-5941. 8:30AM-4:30PM *Felony, Misde., Civil, Eviction, Small Claims, Probate.*

Civil Records: Access: Mail, in person. Both court and visitors may perform in person searches. Search fee: $6.00 per name per year. Required to search: name, years to search. Civil cases indexed by defendant. Civil records on index books from 1800s.

Criminal Records: Access: Mail, in person. Both court and visitors may perform in person searches. Search fee: $6.00 per name per year. Required to search: name, years to search, DOB. Criminal records on index books from 1800s.

General Information: Public Access terminal is available. No juvenile or adoption records released. Copy fee: $1.00 for first page, $.50 each add'l. Cert fee: $4.00. Payee: Clerk of Circuit Court. Personal checks accepted. Prepayment required. Mail requests: SASE required. Mail turnaround time 2-3 days.

Stephenson County

Circuit Court PO Box 785, Freeport, IL 61032; 815-235-8266. 8:30AM-4:30PM *Felony, Misde., Civil, Eviction, Small Claims, Probate.* www.judici.com

Civil Records: Access: Mail, in person, online. Both court and visitors may perform in person searches. Search fee: $6.00 per name per year. Required to search: name, years to search. Civil cases indexed by defendant, plaintiff. Civil records on computer from 8/1989, index books from 1875. Access is free to civil, small claims, probate and traffic records at www.judici.com/courts/index.jsp?court=IL089015J.

Criminal Records: Access: Mail, in person, online. Both court and visitors may perform in person searches. Search fee: $6.00 per name per year. Required to search: name, years to search, DOB. Criminal records on computer from 8/1989, index books from 1875. Criminal records access is free at www.judici.com/courts/index.jsp?court=IL089015J.

General Information: Public Access terminal is available. No juvenile or adoption records released. Copy fee: $2.00 for first page, $.50 each add'l. Cert fee: $10.00. Payee: Clerk of Circuit Court. Business checks accepted. Prepayment required. Mail requests: SASE required. Mail turnaround time 5-15 days.

Tazewell County

Circuit Court Courthouse, 4th & Court Sts, Pekin, IL 61554; 309-477-2214. 8:30AM-5PM (CST). *Felony, Misdemeanor, Civil, Small Claims, Probate.*

Civil Records: Access: Mail, in person. Both court and visitors may perform in person searches. Search fee: $6.00 per name per year. Required to search: name, years to search. Civil cases indexed by defendant, plaintiff. Civil records on computer from 02/89 index books from 1800s.

Criminal Records: Access: Mail, in person. Both court and visitors may perform in person searches. Search fee: $6.00 per name per year. Required to search: name, years to search, DOB, signed release. Criminal records on computer from 02/89 index books from 1800s.

General Information: Public Access terminal is available. No juvenile or adoption records released. Copy fee: $2.00 for first page, $.50 each add'l. After 20 pages, $.25 per page. Cert fee: $6.00. Payee: Clerk of Circuit Court. Only cashiers checks and money orders accepted. Prepayment required. Mail requests: SASE required. Mail turnaround time 3-4 days.

Union County

Circuit Court Union County Courthouse, 309 W Market, Rm 101, Jonesboro, IL 62952; 618-833-5913; Fax: 618-833-5223. Hours: 8AM-Noon,1-4PM (CST). *Felony, Misdemeanor, Civil, Eviction, Small Claims, Probate.*

Civil Records: Access: Fax, mail, in person, online. Both court and visitors may perform in person searches. Search fee: $6.00 per name per year. Required to search: name, years to search. Civil cases indexed by defendant, plaintiff. Civil records on computer from 1986, index books from 1800s. Access is free to civil, small claims, probate and traffic records at www.judici.com/courts/index.jsp?court=IL091015J. Public can only search paper records up to 1986. Only court personnel have access to computer records.

Criminal Records: Access: Fax, mail, in person, online. Both court and visitors may perform in person searches. Search fee: $6.00 per name per year. Required to search: name, years to search; also helpful: DOB. Criminal records on computer from 1986, index books from 1800s. Criminal records access is free at www.judici.com/courts/index.jsp?court=IL091015J. In person criminal record search procedures are the same as civil.

General Information: No juvenile or adoption records released. Fee to fax results is $5.00. Copy fee: $2.00 first page, $.50 2-19th copy, $.25 thereafter. Cert fee: $5.00. Payee: Lorraine Moreland, Circuit Clerk. Business checks accepted. Prepayment required. Mail requests: SASE required. Mail turnaround time 1 week.

Vermilion County

Circuit Court 7 N Vermilion, Danville, IL 61832; 217-554-7700; Fax: 217-554-7728. Hours: 8:30AM-4:30PM (CST). *Felony, Misdemeanor, Civil, Eviction, Small Claims, Probate.*

Civil Records: Access: Phone, mail, in person, online. Both court and visitors may perform in person searches. Search fee: $4.00 per name per year. Required to search: name, years to search. Civil cases indexed by defendant, plaintiff. Civil records on computer from 1989; microfilm from March 1949 to May 1989; index books from 1800s. Search the index at www.judici.com/courts/cases/case_search.jsp?court=IL092015J. Records are current to 1989.

Criminal Records: Access: Phone, mail, in person, online. Both court and visitors may perform in person searches. Search fee: $4.00 per name per year. Required to search: name, years to search, DOB; also

helpful: SSN. Criminal records on computer from 1989; microfilm from March 1949 to May 1989; index books from 1800s. Search the index at www.judici.com/courts/cases/case_search.jsp?court=IL092015J. Records are current to 1989.

General Information: Public Access terminal is available. No juvenile, impounded, mental health or adoption records released. Copy fee: $1.00 for first page, $.50 each add'l. Cert fee: $4.00. Payee: Clerk of Circuit Court. Business checks accepted. Prepayment required. Mail requests: SASE required. Mail turnaround time 1 week.

Wabash County

Circuit Court PO Box 997, 401 Market St, Mt Carmel, IL 62863; 618-262-5362; Fax: 618-263-4441. 8AM-5PM (CST). *Felony, Misdemeanor, Civil, Eviction, Small Claims, Probate.*

Civil Records: Access: Mail, in person. Both court and visitors may perform in person searches. Search fee: $4.00 per name per year. Required to search: name, years to search. Civil cases indexed by defendant, plaintiff. Civil records on computer from 1988, index books from 1800s.

Criminal Records: Access: Mail, in person. Both court and visitors may perform in person searches. Search fee: $4.00 per name per year. Required to search: name, years to search, DOB. Criminal records on computer from 1988, index books from 1800s.

General Information: Public Access terminal is available. No juvenile or adoption records released. Will fax if all fees prepaid. Copy fee: $.50 for 1st 20 pages; $.25 each add'l. Cert fee: $5.00. Payee: Clerk of Circuit Court. Only cashiers checks and money orders accepted. Prepayment required. Mail requests: SASE required. Mail turnaround time 5 days.

Warren County

Circuit Court 100 W Broadway, Monmouth, IL 61462; 309-734-5179. Hours: 8AM-4:30PM (CST). *Felony, Misdemeanor, Civil, Eviction, Small Claims, Probate.*

Civil Records: Access: Mail, in person. Both court and visitors may perform in person searches. Search fee: $5.00 per name per year. Required to search: name, years to search. Civil cases indexed by defendant. Civil records on computer from 2000, index books from 1800s.

Criminal Records: Access: Mail, in person. Both court and visitors may perform in person searches. Search fee: $5.00 per name per year. Required to search: name, years to search, DOB. Criminal records on computer from 2000, index books from 1800s.

General Information: Public Access terminal is available. No juvenile or adoption records released. Copy fee: $.50 per page. Cert fee: $3.00. Payee: Clerk of Circuit Court. Only cashiers checks and money orders accepted. Prepayment required. Mail requests: SASE required. Mail turnaround time 1-2 weeks.

Washington County

Circuit Court 101 E St Louis St, Nashville, IL 62263; 618-327-4800 X305; Fax: 618-327-3583. Hours: 8AM-4PM (CST). *Felony, Misdemeanor, Civil, Eviction, Small Claims, Probate.*

Civil Records: Access: Mail, in person. Both court and visitors may perform in person searches. Search fee: $5.00 per name per year. Required to search: name, years to search. Civil cases indexed by defendant, plaintiff. Civil records on computer since 1998; 1988 for child support; prior records on index books from 1800s.

Criminal Records: Access: Mail, in person. Both court and visitors may perform in person searches. Search fee: $5.00 per name per year. Required to search: name, years to search; also helpful: DOB.

Criminal records on computer since 1998; 1988 for child support; prior records on index books.

General Information: Public Access terminal is available. No juvenile or adoption records released. Will fax results to local or toll free line. Copy fee: $1.00 per page. Cert fee: $3.00. Payee: Washington County Circuit Clerk. No personal checks accepted. Prepayment required. Will bill to attorneys. Mail requests: SASE required. Mail turnaround: 3-5 days.

Wayne County

Circuit Court County Courthouse, 307 E Main St, Fairfield, IL 62837; 618-842-7684; Fax: 618-842-2556. Hours: 8AM-4:30PM (CST). *Felony, Misdemeanor, Civil, Small Claims, Probate.*

Civil Records: Access: Mail, fax, in person. Both court and visitors may perform in person searches. Search fee: $4.00 per name per year. Required to search: name, years to search. Civil cases indexed by defendant, plaintiff. Civil records on computer back to 11/88, index books from 1800s.

Criminal Records: Access: Mail, fax, in person. Both court and visitors may perform in person searches. Search fee: $4.00 per name per year. Required to search: name, years to search, DOB. Criminal records computerized back 1/1990.

General Information: Public Access terminal is available. No juvenile or adoption records released. Will fax results. Copy fee: $1.00 1st page, $.50 each add'l. Cert fee: $5.00. Payee: Clerk of Circuit Court. Only cashiers checks and money orders accepted. Prepayment required. Mail requests: SASE required. Mail turnaround time 1 week.

White County

Circuit Court PO Box 310, 301 E Main, County Courthouse, Carmi, IL 62821; 618-382-2321 x4; Fax: 618-382-2322. Hours: 8AM-4PM (CST). *Felony, Misdemeanor, Civil, Small Claims, Probate.*

Civil Records: Access: Fax, mail, in person. Both court and visitors may perform in person searches. Search fee: $4.00 per name per year. Required to search: name, years to search. Civil cases indexed by defendant, plaintiff. Civil records on computer from 1991, index books from 1800s.

Criminal Records: Access: Fax, mail, in person. Both court and visitors may perform in person searches. Search fee: $4.00 per name per year. Required to search: name, years to search; also helpful: DOB. Criminal records on computer from 1991, index books from 1800s.

General Information: Public Access terminal is available. No juvenile or adoption records released. Will fax results $2.00 per page. Copy fee: $.50 per page. Cert fee: $5.00 plus $.50 per add'l page. Payee: Clerk of Circuit Court. Personal checks accepted. Prepayment required. Mail requests: SASE required. Mail turnaround time 1-2 weeks.

Whiteside County

Circuit Court 200 E Knox St, Morrison, IL 61270-2698; 815-772-5188; Fax: 815-772-5187. 8:30AM-4:30PM (CST). *Felony, Misdemeanor, Civil, Eviction, Small Claims, Probate.*

Civil Records: Access: Phone, fax, mail, in person, online. Both court and visitors may perform in person searches. Search fee: $6.00 per name. Required to search: name, years to search. Civil cases indexed by defendant. Civil records on computer from 1989, index books from 1800s. Access is free to civil, small claims, probate and traffic records at

www.judici.com/courts/cases/case_search.jsp?court=IL098015J.

Criminal Records: Access: Phone, fax, mail, in person, online. Both court and visitors may perform in person searches. Search fee: $6.00 per name. Required to search: name, years to search, DOB. Criminal records on computer from 1988, index books from 1800s. Access to criminal records is the same as civil.

General Information: Public Access terminal is available. No juvenile or adoption records released. No fee to fax results. Local faxing only. Copy fee: $.25 per page. Cert fee: $4.00. Payee: Clerk of Circuit Court. Personal checks accepted. Prepayment required. Mail requests: SASE required. Mail turnaround time 1 week.

Will County

Circuit Court 14 W Jefferson St, #212, Joliet, IL 60432; 815-727-8592; Fax: 815-727-8896. Hours: 8:30AM-4:30PM (CST). *Felony, Misdemeanor, Civil, Eviction, Small Claims, Probate.*

www.willcountycircuitcourt.com

Civil Records: Access: Fax, mail, in person, online. Both court and visitors may perform in person searches. Search fee: $4.00 per name per year. Required to search: name, years to search. Civil cases indexed by defendant, plaintiff. Civil records on computer from 1989, index books from 1800s. Online access to court records is via a internet subscription system. Fee is $240 per year for Will County or $300 for Will, Sangamon, Madison, Winnebago, Kane, Kendall, DeKalb courts. For info, email benright@willcountyillinois.com or 815-727-8592.

Criminal Records: Access: Fax, mail, in person, online. Both court and visitors may perform in person searches. Search fee: $4.00 per name per year. Required to search: name, years to search, DOB. Criminal records on computer from 1989, index books from 1800s. Online access to court records is via a internet subscription system. Fee is $240 per year for Will County or $300 for Will,Sangamon,Madison,Winnebago,Kane,Kendall,DeKalb courts. For info, email benright@willcountyillinois.com or call 815-727-8592. Only attorneys can fax in requests.

General Information: Public Access terminal is available. No juvenile, adoption, mental health records released. Will not fax results. Copy fee: $2.00 for first page, $.50 each add'l. Cert fee: $4.00. Payee: Pamela J McGuire Clerk of Circuit Court. Only cashiers checks and money orders accepted. Prepayment required. Mail requests: SASE required. Mail turnaround time 2 weeks.

Williamson County

Circuit Court 200 W Jefferson St, Marion, IL 62959; 618-997-1301 X153. Hours: 8AM-4PM (CST). *Felony, Misdemeanor, Civil, Eviction, Small Claims, Probate.*

Civil Records: Access: Mail, in person. Both court and visitors may perform in person searches. Search fee: $4.00 per name per year. Required to search: name, years to search. Civil cases indexed by defendant, plaintiff. Civil records on computer from 07/86, index books from 1800s.

Criminal Records: Access: Mail, in person. Both court and visitors may perform in person searches. Search fee: $4.00 per name per year. Required to search: name, years to search, DOB. Criminal records on computer from 07/86, index books from 1800s.

General Information: Public Access terminal is available. No juvenile or adoption records released. Copy fee: $1.00 for first page, $.50 each add'l. Cert fee: $2.00. Payee: Clerk of Circuit Court. Business checks accepted. Prepayment required. Mail requests: SASE required. Mail turnaround time 1 week.

Winnebago County

Circuit Court 400 W State St, Rockford, IL 61101; 815-978-3031 (records); Civil phone: 815-987-2510; Criminal phone: 815-987-3079/3175; Fax: 815-987-3012. 8AM-5PM *Felony, Misdemeanor, Civil, Eviction, Small Claims, Probate.*

www.cc.co.winnebago.il.us

Note: Criminal records is in Rm 108. Civil is Rm 104.

Civil Records: Access: Phone, mail, in person, online. Both court and visitors may perform in person searches. Search fee: $6.00 per page. Required to search: name, years to search. Civil cases indexed by defendant, plaintiff. Civil records on computer back to 1983; prior records on index books from 1800s. Online access to court records is free at www.cc.co.winnebago.il.us/caseinfo.asp?P=I; Registration, username and password is required. Includes Civil, Probate, Traffic but not juvenile back to 1980s. Call Craig at 815-987-2532 for information.

Criminal Records: Access: Phone, mail, in person, online. Both court and visitors may perform in person searches. Search fee: $6.00 per name per year. Required to search: name, years to search, DOB. Criminal records on computer back to 1983; prior records on index books from 1800s. Online access to court records is free at www.cc.co.winnebago.il.us/caseinfo.asp?P=I; Registration, username and password is required. Includes Felony and Misdemeanor but not juvenile back to 1980s. Call Craig at 815-987-2532 for information.

General Information: Public Access terminal is available. No juvenile, mental or adoption records released. Will fax results to local or toll free line. Copy fee: $2.00 for first page, $.50 each add'l. After 20 pgs, fee is $.25 per pg. Cert fee: $8.00. Payee: Clerk of Circuit Court. Personal checks accepted. Prepayment required. Mail requests: SASE required. Mail turnaround time 1 week.

Woodford County

Circuit Court County Courthouse, PO Box 284, 115 N Main, #201, Eureka, IL 61530; 309-467-3312. Hours: 8AM-5PM (CST). *Felony, Misdemeanor, Civil, Eviction, Small Claims, Probate.*

Civil Records: Access: Mail, in person. Both court and visitors may perform in person searches. Search fee: $5.00 per name per year. Required to search: name, years to search. Civil cases indexed by defendant, plaintiff. Civil records on computer from 1990, index books from 1800s.

Criminal Records: Access: Mail, in person. Both court and visitors may perform in person searches. Search fee: $5.00 per name per year. Required to search: name, years to search, DOB. Criminal records on computer from 1990, index books from 1800s.

General Information: Public Access terminal is available. No juvenile or adoption records released. Copy fee: $.50 per page. Cert fee: $4.00. Payee: Woodford County Circuit Clerk. Personal checks accepted. Prepayment required. Mail requests: SASE required. Mail turnaround time 2-3 days

Illinois Recording Offices

ORGANIZATION: 102 counties, 103 recording offices. Cook County had separate offices for real estate recording and UCC filing until June 30, 2001. As of that date the UCC filing office only searches for -- and no longer takes new -- UCC filings. The recording officer is Recorder of Deeds. Many counties utilize a grantor/grantee index containing all transactions. The entire state is in the Central Time Zone (CST).

REAL ESTATE RECORDS: Most counties will not perform real estate searches. Cost of certified copies varies widely, but many counties charge the same as the cost of recording the document. Tax records are usually located at the Treasurer's Office.

UCC RECORDS: Financing statements are filed at the state level except for real estate related filings which are filed with the County Recorder. (See above regarding Cook County.) Most counties will perform UCC searches. Use search request form UCC-11. Search fees are usually $10.00 per debtor name/address combination. Copies usually cost $1.00 per page.

TAX LIEN RECORDS: Federal tax liens on personal property of businesses are filed with the Secretary of State. Other federal and all state tax liens on personal property are filed with the County Recorder. Some counties will perform tax lien searches for $5.00-$10.00 per name (state and federal are separate searches in many of these counties) and $1.00 per page of copy.

OTHER LIENS: Judgments, mechanics, contractor, medical, lis pendens, oil & gas, mobile home.

ONLINE ACCESS: A limited number of counties offer online access. There is no statewide system.

Adams County

County Recorder, PO Box 1067, Quincy, IL 62306. **Phone-**County Recorder, R/E & UCC Recording- 217-277-2125; hours 8:30AM-4:30PM

Will not search records. Record copy- $1.00 per page. Cert fee: $12.00 per cert + $1.00 per page after 4 pages. Payee: Adams County Recorder. **Online Access to Assessor, Real Estate records:** sist www.emapsplus.com/ILAdams/maps/. Includes name searching. **Other phones:** Assessor-217-277-2136; Treasurer-217-277-2248; Elections-217-277-2157; Vital Records-217-277-2158.

Alexander County

County Recorder, 2000 Washington Ave, Cairo, IL 62914. **Phone-**618-734-7000; fax-618-734-7002; hours 8AM-Noon, 1-4PM

Will not search records. RE record copy- $1.00 per page. Cert fee: Same as original recording fee. Payee: Alexander County Recorder. **Other phones:** Assessor-618-734-7006; Treasurer-618-734-7009; Elections-618-734-7000; Vital Records-618-734-7000.

Bond County

County Recorder, 203 W. College Ave, Greenville, IL 62246. **Phone-**618-664-0449; fax-618-664-9414; hours 8AM-4PM

Will search UCC records. Search per debtor/address- $10.00. UCC copy- $1.00 per page. UCC search includes tax liens if requested. Separate federal/state combined tax lien search- $10.00 per debtor. Will not search real estate records. Cert fee: $25.00 1st 4 pages, $1.00 each add'l. Payee: Bond County Recorder. **Other phones:** Assessor-618-664-2848; Treasurer-618-664-0618.

Boone County

County Recorder, 601 N. Main St, #202, Belvidere, IL 61008. **Phone-**815-544-3103; fax-815-547-8701; hours 8:30AM-5PM www.boonecountyil.org

Will search UCC records. Search per debtor/address- $10.00. UCC copy- $1.00 per page. Will not search real estate or tax lien records. Cert fee: Same as original recording fee. Payee: Boone County Recorder. **Online Access to Real Estate records:** A commercial system - PropertyMax - is at

http://booneilpropertymax.governmaxa.com/propertymax/rover30.asp. Fee is PropertyMax allows the user to search for a property in a variety of ways, including owner, address, parcel identification number, alternate identification number, property description, and GIS map. Subscribers have the option of choosing from any of the three $10.00 per month packages. **Other phones:** Assessor-815-544-2958; Treasurer-815-544-2666; Elections-815-544-3103; Vital Records-815-544-3103.

Brown County

County Recorder, Courthouse - Rm4, #1 Court St, Mount Sterling, IL 62353-1285. **Phone-**County Recorder, R/E & UCC Recording- 217-773-3421; fax-217-773-2233; hours 8:30AM-4:30PM

Will search UCC records. Search per debtor/address- $13.00. UCC copy- $1.00 per page. UCC search includes tax liens if requested. Tax lien search fee- $11.00 per debtor. Will not search real estate records. RE record copy- $1.00 per page. Cert fee: $25.00 per cert, + $1.00 peraddtl page. Payee: Brown County Recorder. **Other phones:** Assessor-217-773-3415; Treasurer-217-773-3133; Elections-217-773-3421; Vital Records-217-773-3421.

Bureau County

County Recorder, 700 S. Main St., Courthouse, Princeton, IL 61356. **Phone-**County Recorder, R/E & UCC Recording- 815-875-3239; fax-815-879-4803; hours 8AM-4PM

Will search UCC records. Search per debtor/address- $10.00. UCC copy- $1.00 per page. Will not search real estate or tax lien records. Cert fee: Same as current recording fee. Payee: Bureau County Recorder. **Other phones:** Assessor-815-875-6478; Treasurer-815-875-3241; Elections-815-875-2014; Vital Records-815-875-3239.

Calhoun County

County Clerk & Recorder, PO Box 187, Hardin, IL 62047. **Phone-**618-576-2351; fax-618-576-2895; hours 8:30AM-4:30PM

Will search UCC records. Search per debtor/address- $10.00. UCC copy- $.50 per page. UCC search includes tax liens. Mortgage searches available. RE record copy- $.50 per page. Cert fee: $2.00 per cert. Payee: Calhoun County Clerk and Recorder.

Other phones: Assessor-618-576-8041; Treasurer-618-576-2421.

Carroll County

County Recorder, PO Box 152, Mount Carroll, IL 61053. **Phone-**815-244-0223; fax-815-244-3709; hours 8:30AM-4:30AM

Will not search records. UCC copy fee- $2.00 per page. Cert fee: Same as original recording fee. Payee: Carroll County Recorder. **Other phones:** Assessor-815-244-0238; Treasurer-815-244-0243.

Cass County

County Recorder, 100 E Springfield St, Virginia, IL 62691. **Phone-**217-452-7217; fax-217-452-7219; hours 8:30AM-4:30PM

Will not search records. UCC copy- $1.00 per page. Cert fee: $35.00 add'l $1.00 per page. Payee: Cass County Recorder. **Other phones:** Assessor-217-452-7249; Treasurer-217-452-7721.

Champaign County

County Recorder, 1776 E. Washington, Urbana, IL 61802. **Phone-**217-384-3774; fax-217-344-1663; hours 8AM-4:30PM. Will search UCC records. Search per debtor/address- $10.00. UCC copy- $1.00 per page. UCC search does not include state tax liens. Will not search real estate records. RE record copy- $1.50 per page. Cert fee: $12.00 per cert + $1.00 per page after 4 pages. Payee: Champaign County Recorder. **Online Access to Property records:** Access to property information is from a private company at https://www.landrecords.net. You may subscribe or search using credit card payment for $3.99 per search. **Other phones:** Assessor-217-384-3760; Treasurer-217-384-3743.

Christian County

County Recorder, PO Box 647, Taylorville, IL 62568. **Phone-**County Recorder, R/E & UCC Recording- 217-824-4960; fax-217-824-5105; hours 8AM-4PM

Will search UCC records. Search per debtor/address- $10.00. UCC copy- $1.00 per page. Will not search real estate or tax lien records. RE record copy- $1.00 per copy. Cert fee: $31.00 per cert. Payee: Christian County Recorder. **Online Access to UCC, Property records:** Access to property and

UCC records from 1990 to present is via a private company at https://www.landrecords.net/. Subscription or pay-per search service available. **Other phones:** Assessor-217-824-5900; Treasurer-217-824-4889; Elections-217-824-4969; Vital Records-217-824-4969.

Clark County

County Recorder, Courthouse, Marshall, IL 62441. **Phone-**County Recorder, R/E & UCC Recording- 217-826-8311; hours 8AM-4PM

Will search UCC records. Search per debtor/address-$10.00. UCC copy- $1.00 per page. Will not search real estate or tax lien records. RE record copy- $.50 per copy. Cert fee: $14.00 per cert. Payee: Clark County Recorder. **Other phones:** Assessor-217-826-5815; Treasurer-217-826-5721; Elections-217-826-8311; Vital Records-217-826-8311.

Clay County

County Recorder, PO Box 160, Louisville, IL 62858-0160. **Phone-**County Recorder, R/E & UCC Recording- 618-665-3626; fax-618-665-3607; hours 8AM-4PM

Will search UCC records. UCC search per debtor-$10.00 per name per 5 yrs. Copy fee is $.25 per page. Will search tax liens including federal tax liens. Real estate owner, mortgage, and property transfer searches available. Copy fee-$.25 per page. Payee: Clay County Recorder. **Other phones:** Assessor-618-665-3370; Treasurer-618-665-3727; Elections-618-665-3626; Vital Records-618-665-3626.

Clinton County

County Recorder, PO Box 308, Carlyle, IL 62231. **Phone-**County Recorder, R/E & UCC Recording- 618-594-2464, UCC Recording- 618-594-0142; fax-618-594-0195; hours 8AM-4PM www.clintonco.org

Will not search UCC records. Will search tax liens. Tax lien search fee- $10.00 per debtor. Will not search real estate records. Record copy- $1.00 per page. Cert fee: $3.00 per cert. Payee: Clinton County Recorder. **Online Access to Property records:** Access to property information is from a private company at https://www.landrecords.net.You may subscribe or search using credit card payment for $3.99 per search. Index goes back to 1988; images to 1992. **Other phones:** Assessor-618-594-3221; Treasurer-618-594-2464; Elections-618-594-2464; Vital Records-618-594-2464.

Coles County

County Recorder, 651 Jackson Ave, Rm 122, Charleston, IL 61920. **Phone-**County Recorder, R/E & UCC Recording- 217-348-7325; fax-217-348-7337; hours 8:30AM-4:30PM

Will search UCC records. Search per debtor/address-$10.00. UCC copy- $1.00 per page. Will not search real estate or tax lien records. Cert fee: $5.00. Payee: County Recorder. **Other phones:** Assessor-217-348-0508; Treasurer-217-348-0511; Elections-217-348-0524; Vital Records-217-348-0501.

Cook County

Recorder of Deeds, 118 N. Clark St, Rm 120, Chicago, IL 60602-1387. **Phone-**312-603-7524, R/E Recording-312-603-5066; fax-312-603-5063; hours 9AM-5PM www.ccrd.info

Will search UCC records. Search per debtor/address-$10.00. UCC copy- $1.00 per page. Will not search tax liens. See Recorder for real estate records. Cert fee: $6.00. Payee: Cook County Recorder. **Online Access to Property Tax records:**. **Other phones:** Assessor-312-443-7550; Treasurer-312-603-4436; Vital Records-312-603-7790.

Cook County Recorder

County Recorder, 118 N. Clark St. #120, Rm 230, Chicago, IL 60602. **Phone-**312-603-5134, 312-603-5050, R/E Recording- 312-603-5066, UCC Recording-312-603-5050; fax-312-603-5063; hours 8AM-4:55PM www.ccrd.info

There are no filings recorded at this office after June 30, 2001. Only records prior to this date can be searched. Will search UCC records, but only real estate related UCC filed here. Search per debtor- $20 certified; $10.00 uncertified. UCC copy fee- $1.00 per page. Federal tax lien copies-$2.00 uncertified, $5.00 certified. Will not search real estate records. Cert fee: double the uncertified doc cost. Payee: Cook County Recorder. **Online Access to Real Estate, Recorder, Deed, Grantor/Grantee, Heir records:** Search Grantor/Grantee index and locate property data at www.ccrd.info. Fee for documents. Search the DIMS database of the recordings since 10/1985; registration and fees apply. Includes Treasurer's Current Year Tax System (APIN) and DuPageCounty Recorder. Sign-up information is at www.cookctyrecorder.com/new.htm. Also, you may purchase the real estate transfer list; $100 per year on disk ($50 if you pick-up at agency.) Also, search the treasurer's heirs database free at www.cookcountytreasurer.com/inheritance/search/. Search assessor data for free at www.cookcountyassessor.com/startsearch.html, however, there is no name searching. **Other phones:** Assessor-312-443-7550; Treasurer-312-443-4436.

Crawford County

County Recorder, PO Box 616, Robinson, IL 62454-0602. **Phone-**County Recorder, R/E & UCC Recording- 618-546-1212; fax-618-546-0140; hours 8AM-4PM www.crawfordcountyclerk.com

Will search UCC records. Search per debtor/address-$10.00. UCC copy- $.50 per page. Will not search tax liens. Will search for specific real estate records only; no lengthy searches performed. RE record copy-$.50 per page. Cert fee: $13.00 per cert. Payee: Crawford County Recorder. **Other phones:** Assessor-618-544-8221; Treasurer-618-544-2614; Elections-618-546-2590; Vital Records-618-546-1212.

Cumberland County

County Recorder, PO Box 146, Toledo, IL 62468. **Phone-**County Recorder, R/E & UCC Recording- 217-849-2631; fax-217-849-2968; hours 8AM-4PM

Will search UCC records. Search per debtor/address-$10.00. UCC copy- $.50 per page. Will not search real estate or tax lien records. Cert fee: $12.00 per cert. Payee: County Recorder. **Other phones:** Assessor-217-849-3831; Treasurer-217-849-2321; Elections-217-849-2631; Vital Records-217-849-2631.

De Kalb County

County Recorder, 110 E. Sycamore St, Sycamore, IL 60178. **Phone-**815-895-7156; hours 8:30AM-4:30PM Will search UCC records. Search per debtor/address-$10.00. UCC copy- $1.00 per page. Will not search real estate or tax lien records. RE record copy- $1.00 per page. Cert fee: $18.00 per page + $1.00 add'l. Payee: De Kalb County Recorder. **Online Access to Real Estate, Lien records:** The De Kalb County online system requires a $350 subscription fee, with a per minute charge of $.25, $.50 if printing. Records date back to 1980. Lending agency information is available. For further information, contact Sheila Larson at 815-895-7152. **Other phones:** Assessor-815-895-7120; Treasurer-815-895-7112.

De Witt County

County Recorder, PO Box 439, Clinton, IL 61727-0439. **Phone-**County Recorder, R/E & UCC Recording- 217-935-2119; fax-217-935-4596; hours 8:30AM-4:30PM. Will search UCC records. Search fee per name is $10.00. UCC copy- $1.00 per page. Will not search real estate or tax lien records. RE record copy- $.50 per page. Cert fee: $2.00 per doc. Payee: De Witt County Recorder. **Other phones:** Assessor-217-935-2242; Treasurer-217-935-2359; Appraiser/ Auditor-217-935-2242; Elections-217-935-2119; Vital Records-217-935-2119.

Douglas County

County Recorder, PO Box 467, Tuscola, IL 61953-0467. **Phone-**County Recorder, R/E & UCC Recording- 217-253-4410; fax-217-253-2233; hours 8:30AM-4:30PM. Will not search records. UCC copy- $1.00 per page. RE record copy- $2.00 per doc. Cert fee: $8.00 per cert. Payee: Douglas County Recorder. **Other phones:** Assessor-217-253-3031; Treasurer-217-253-4011; Elections-217-253-2411; Vital Records-217-253-2411.

Du Page County

County Recorder, PO Box 936, Wheaton, IL 60189. **Phone-**County Recorder, R/E & UCC Recording- 630-407-5400; fax-630-407-5300; hours 8AM-4:30PM www.dupageco.org/recorder/

Will search UCC records. Search per debtor/address-$10.00. UCC copy- $1.00 per page. Will not search real estate or tax lien records. RE record copy- $.50 per page. Cert fee: $5.00 per cert. Payee: Du Page County Recorder. **Online Access to Real Estate, Lien, Tax Assessor records:** For access to the Du Page County database one must lease a live interface telephone line from a carrier to establish a connection. There is a fee of $.05 per transaction. Records date back to 1977. For info, contact Fred Kieltcka at 630-682-7030. Free internet access may soon be available. Access to sheriff's sex offenders, most wanted, and deadbeat parents lists are free at www.co.dupage.il.us/sheriff. Search Wayne Township property records at www.waynetownshipassessor.com/disclaimer.html Search Bloomingdale Township property records at www.bloomingdaletownshipassessor.com/OPID/opid.asp. Search Wheatland Township records at www.wheatlandtownship.com/Assessor/disclaim.html. No name searching in either Town. **Other phones:** Assessor-630-407-5858; Treasurer-630-407-5900; Elections-630-407-5600; Vital Records-630-407-5500.

Edgar County

County Clerk and Recorder, 115 W. Court St, Rm J, Paris, IL 61944-1785. **Phone-**County Clerk and Recorder, R/E & UCC Recording- 217-466-7433; fax-217-466-7430; hours 8AM-4PM

Will search UCC records. Search per debtor/address-$10.00. UCC copy- $1.00 per page. Tax liens not included in UCC search. Tax lien search fee-$10.00 per debtor. Limited real estate owner, mortgage, and property transfer searches available. RE record copy- $1.00 per page. Cert fee: $12.00 1st 4 pages; $1.00 each add'l. Payee: Edgar County Recorder. **Other phones:** Assessor-217-466-7418; Treasurer-217-466-7446; Elections-217-466-7433; Vital Records-217-466-7433.

Edwards County

County Recorder, 50 E. Main St, Courthouse, Albion, IL 62806-1294. **Phone-**County Recorder, R/E & UCC Recording- 618-445-2115; fax-618-445-4941; hours 8AM-4PM. Will search UCC records. Search per debtor/address- $10.00 for 5 year search. UCC copy- $1.00 per copy. Tax liens not included in UCC search. Tax lien search fee- $10.00 per debtor. Will search real estate records. RE record copy- $1.00 per copy. Cert fee: $10.00 per cert. Payee: Edwards County Recorder. **Other phones:** Assessor-618-445-3591; Treasurer-618-445-3581; Elections-618-445-2115; Vital Records-618-445-2115.

Effingham County

County Clerk & Recorder, PO Box 628, Effingham, IL 62401-0628. **Phone-**County Clerk & Recorder, R/E & UCC Recording- 217-342-6535; fax-217-342-3577; hours 8AM-4PM http://co.effingham.il.us
Will search UCC records. Search per debtor/address- $10.00. UCC copy- $1.00 per page. Tax liens not included in UCC search. Separate federal/state combined tax lien search- $10.00 per debtor. Will not search real estate records. RE record copy- $1.00 per doc, not exeeding 4 pages, $.50 per add'l. Cert fee: $5.00 per cert. Payee: Effingham County Clerk and Recorder. **Other phones:** Assessor-217-324-6711; Treasurer-217-342-6844; Elections-217-342-6535; Vital Records-217-342-6535.

Fayette County

County Recorder, PO Box 401, Vandalia, IL 62471-0401. **Phone-**County Recorder, R/E & UCC Recording- 618-283-5000; fax-618-283-5004; hours 8AM-4PM
Will search UCC records. Search per debtor/address- $10.00. UCC copy- $1.00 per page. Will not search real estate or tax lien records. RE record copy- $1.00 per page. Cert fee: $12.00 for 1st 4 pages; $1.00 per each add'l pg. Payee: Fayette County Recorder. **Other phones:** Assessor-618-283-5020; Treasurer-618-283-5022; Elections-618-283-5000; Vital Records-618-283-5000.

Ford County

County Recorder, 200 W. State St, Rm 101, Paxton, IL 60957. **Phone-**County Recorder, R/E & UCC Recording- 217-379-2721; fax-217-379-3258; hours 8:30AM-4:30PM www.prairienet.org
Will search UCC records. Search per debtor/address- $10.00. UCC copy- $1.00 per page. Will not search real estate or tax lien records. RE record copy- $1.00 per page. Cert fee: $22.00 1st 4 pg, then $1.00. Payee: Ford County Recorder. **Other phones:** Assessor-217-379-4132; Treasurer-217-379-2532; Elections-217-379-2721; Vital Records-217-379-2721.

Franklin County

County Clerk & Recorder, PO Box 607, Benton, IL 62812. **Phone-**County Clerk & Recorder, R/E & UCC Recording- 618-438-3221; fax-618-435-3405; hours 8AM-4PM. Will search UCC records. Search per debtor/address- $10.00. UCC copy- $1.00 per page. Tax liens not included in UCC search. Must have written request for searches. Separate federal/state combined tax lien search- $10.00 per debtor. Real estate record owner and mortgage searches available. RE record copy- $.50 per page. Must have a written request for copies with money included. Cert fee: $1.00 per cert. Payee: Franklin County Clerk & Recorder. **Other phones:** Assessor-618-438-4331; Treasurer-618-438-7311; Elections-618-438-3403; Vital Records-618-438-3221.

Fulton County

County Recorder, PO Box 226, Lewistown, IL 61542. **Phone-**309-547-3041, R/E Recording- 309-547-3041 x43, UCC Recording-309-547-3041 x43; 8AM-4PM
Will search UCC records. Search per debtor/address- $10.00. UCC copy- $.50 per page. Will not search real estate or tax lien records. Cert fee: $5.00. Payee: Fulton County Recorder. **Other phones:** Assessor-309-547-3041 x58; Treasurer-309-547-3041 x25; Elections-309-547-3041 x704; Vital Records-309-547-3041 x 42.

Gallatin County

County Recorder, PO Box 550, Shawneetown, IL 62984. **Phone-**County Recorder, R/E & UCC Recording- 618-269-3025; fax-618-269-3343; hours 8AM-4PM. Will search UCC records. Search per debtor/address- $10.00. UCC copy- $1.00 per page. Will not search real estate or tax lien records. RE record copy- $.25 per page. Cert fee: $10.00 per cert. Payee: Gallatin County Recorder. **Online Access to Property records:** Search for propety information on the GIS-mapping site for free at www.co.gallatin.mt.us/GIS/index.htm. No name searching. **Other phones:** Assessor-618-269-3791; Treasurer-618-269-3022; Appraiser/ Auditor-618-269-3791; Elections-618-269-3025; Vital Records-618-269-3025.

Greene County

County Recorder, 519 N. Main St, Courthouse, Carrollton, IL 62016-1033. **Phone-**County Recorder, R/E & UCC Recording- 217-942-5443; fax-217-942-9323; hours 8AM-4PM
Will not search UCC records. UCC copy- $1.00 per page. Separate federal/state combined tax lien search- $10.00 per debtor. Will not search real estate records. RE record copy- $.25 per page. Payee: Greene County Recorder. **Other phones:** Assessor-217-942-6412; Treasurer-217-942-5124; Elections-217-942-5443; Vital Records-217-942-5443.

Grundy County

County Recorder, PO Box 675, Morris, IL 60450-0675. **Phone-**815-941-3224; fax-815-942-2222; hours 8AM-4:30PM. Will search UCC records. Search per debtor/address- $10.00. UCC copy- $1.00 per page. UCC search includes tax liens if requested. Will not search real estate records. Cert fee: Same as original recording fee. Payee: Grundy County Recorder. **Other phones:** Assessor-815-941-3269; Treasurer-815-941-3215; Elections-815-941-3221; Vital Records-815-941-3222.

Hamilton County

County Recorder, Courthouse, 100 S Jackson St, Rm 2, McLeansboro, IL 62859-1489. **Phone-**County Recorder, R/E & UCC Recording- 618-643-2721; hours 8AM-4:30PM
Will search UCC records. Search per debtor/address- $10.00. UCC copy- $1.00 per page. Will search tax liens. Tax lien search fee- $10.00 per search. Will search real estate records. Cert fee: $5.00 1st 4 pages; $1.00 each add'l. Payee: Hamilton County Recorder. **Other phones:** Treasurer-618-643-3313; Vital Records-618-643-2721.

Hancock County

County Recorder, PO Box 39, Carthage, IL 62321-0039. **Phone-**County Recorder, R/E & UCC Recording- 217-357-3911; hours 8AM-4PM
Will search UCC records. Search per debtor/address- $10.00. UCC copy- $1.00 per page. Will not search tax liens. Will search real estate records. RE record copy- $.50 per copy if off computer; $1.00 per page if off microfiche. Cert fee: $15.00 per doc. Payee: Hancock County Recorder. **Other phones:** Assessor-217-357-2615; Treasurer-217-357-2624; Appraiser/ Auditor-217-357-3519; Elections-217-357-3911; Vital Records-217-357-3911.

Hardin County

County Recorder, PO Box 187, Elizabethtown, IL 62931. **Phone-**County Recorder, R/E & UCC Recording- 618-287-2251; fax-618-287-2661; hours 8AM-4PM
Will search UCC records. Search per debtor/address- $10.00. UCC copy- $1.00 per doc. UCC search includes tax liens if requested. Separate federal/state combined tax lien search- $10.00 per debtor. Will search real estate records. RE record copy- $1.00 per doc. Cert fee: $5.00 per cert. Payee: Hardin County Recorder. **Other phones:** Assessor-618-287-3551; Treasurer-618-287-2053;

Elections-618-287-2251; Vital Records-618-287-2251; Other fax-618-287-2661.

Henderson County

County Recorder, PO Box 308, Oquawka, IL 61469-0308. **Phone-**County Recorder, R/E & UCC Recording- 309-867-2911; fax-309-867-2033; hours 8AM-4PM. Will search UCC records. Search per debtor/address- $10.00. UCC copy- $1.00 per page. Will not search real estate or tax lien records. RE record copy- $.50 per page. Cert fee: $15.00 per cert. Payee: Henderson County Recorder. **Other phones:** Assessor-309-867-3291; Treasurer-309-867-3121; Appraiser/ Auditor-309-867-3291; Elections-309-867-2911; Vital Records-309-867-2911.

Henry County

County Recorder, 307 W Center St, Henry County Courthouse, Cambridge, IL 61238. **Phone-**309-937-3486; fax-309-937-2796; hours 8AM-4:30PM www.henrycty.com/recorder/index.html
Will search UCC records. Search per debtor/address- $10.00. UCC copy- $1.00 per page. Will not search real estate or tax liens records. Cert fee: $12.00 per doc. Payee: Henry County Recorder. **Online Access to Assessor, Most Wanted records:** Access to the assessor database is free at www.henrycty.com/assessor/search.asp. Also, county most wanted/fugitive list is at www.henrycty.com/sheriff/fugitives.html. **Other phones:** Assessor-309-937-3570; Treasurer-309-937-3576; Elections-309-937-3492; Vital Records-309-937-3575.

Iroquois County

County Recorder, 1001 E. Grant St, Watseka, IL 60970. **Phone-**815-432-6962; fax-815-432-3894; hours 8:30AM-4:30PM. Will search UCC records. Search per debtor/address- $10.00. UCC copy- $3.00 1st 4 pages, $1.00 each add'l. UCC search includes tax liens if requested. Will not search real estate records. RE record copy- $3.00 1st 4 pages, $1.00 each add'l. Cert fee: $5.00 per cert. Payee: Iroquois County Recorder. **Other phones:** Assessor-815-432-6978; Treasurer-815-432-6985; Elections-815-432-6960; Vital Records-815-432-6960.

Jackson County

County Recorder, 1001 Walnut, The Courthouse, Murphysboro, IL 62966. **Phone-**618-687-7360; hours 8AM-4PM. Will search UCC records prior to 7/2001. Search per debtor/address- $10.00. UCC copy- $.50 per page. Will not search real estate or tax lien records. RE copy- $.50 per page. Payee: Jackson County Recorder. **Other phones:** Assessor-618-687-7220; Treasurer-618-687-3555.

Jasper County

County Recorder, 204 W Washington St #2, Newton, IL 62448. **Phone-**County Recorder, R/E & UCC Recording- 618-783-3124; fax-618-783-4137; hours 8AM-4:30PM. Will search UCC records. Search per debtor/address- $10.00. UCC copy- $.50 per page. Will not search real estate or tax lien records. RE record copy- $.50 per page. Cert fee: $7.00 per cert for 1st 2 pages, $1.00 each add'l pg. Payee: Jasper County Recorder. **Other phones:** Assessor-618-783-8042; Treasurer-618-783-3211; Elections-618-783-3124; Vital Records-618-783-3124.

Jefferson County

County Recorder, 100 S. 10th St, Rm 105, Courthouse, Mount Vernon, IL 62864. **Phone-**618-244-8020; hours 8AM-5PM. Will search UCC records. Search per debtor/address- $10.00. UCC copy- $2.00 per page. Will not search real estate or tax lien records. Cert fee: $5.00 per cert. Payee: Jefferson County Recorder. **Other phones:** Assessor-618-244-8016; Treasurer-618-244-8011.

Jersey County

County Recorder, 200 N Lafayette #2, Jerseyville, IL 62052. **Phone-**County Recorder, R/E & UCC Recording- 618-498-5571 x117/8; fax-618-498-6128; hours 8:30AM-4:30PM

Will search UCC records. Search per debtor/address- $10.00. UCC copy- $1.00 per page. Tax liens not included in UCC search. Separate federal/state combined tax lien search- $10.00 per debtor. Will not search real estate records. RE record copy- $1.00 if after 6/1985; $2.00 each if before. Cert fee: $10.00 per cert. Payee: Jersey County Recorder. **Other phones:** Assessor-618-498-5571 x126; Treasurer-618-498-5571 x110; Elections-618-498-5571 x112; Vital Records-618-498-5571 x113.

Jo Daviess County

County Recorder, 330 N. Bench St, Galena, IL 61036. **Phone-**County Recorder, R/E & UCC Recording- 815-777-9694; fax-815-777-3688; hours 8AM-4PM

Will search UCC records. Search per debtor/address- $10.00. UCC copy- $1.00 per page. Will not search tax liens. Will do 20-year search regarding to liens for genealogy purposes. RE record copy- $1.00 per page. Cert fee: Same as original recording fee. Payee: Jo Daviess County Recorder. **Other phones:** Assessor-815-777-1016; Treasurer-815-777-0355; Elections-815-777-0161; Vital Records-815-777-0161.

Johnson County

County Recorder, PO Box 96, Vienna, IL 62995. **Phone-**County Recorder, R/E & UCC Recording- 618-658-3611; fax-618-658-2908; hours 8AM-Noon,1-4PM. Will search UCC records. Search per debtor book/name- $10.00. UCC copy- $1.00 per page. Will search tax liens including federal tax liens. Will search real estate records. RE record copy- $1.00 per instrument. Cert fee: $7.00 per cert. Payee: Johnson County Recorder. **Other phones:** Assessor-618-658-8010; Treasurer-618-658-8042; Elections-618-658-3611; Vital Records-618-658-3611.

Kane County

County Recorder, PO Box 71, Geneva, IL 60134. **Phone-**County Recorder, R/E & UCC Recording- 630-232-5935; fax-630-232-5945; hours 8:30AM-4:30PM www.co.kane.il.us

Will search UCC records. Search per debtor/address- $10.00. UCC copy- $1.00 per page. Will not search real estate or tax lien records. Payee: Kane County Recorder. **Online Access to Real Estate records:** Search property tax records free at www.co.kane.il.us/webapps/colapp1/txinq.htm, search by parcel number only; no name searching. **Other phones:** Assessor-630-232-3818; Treasurer-630-232-3565.

Kankakee County

County Recorder, 189 E. Court St, Kankakee, IL 60901. **Phone-**County Recorder, R/E & UCC Recording- 815-937-2980; fax-815-937-3657; hours 8:30AM-4:30PM. Will search UCC records. Search per debtor/address- $10.00. UCC copy- $1.00 per page. Will not search real estate or tax lien records. RE record copy- $.25 per page. Cert fee: Same as original recording fee. Payee: Kankakee County Recorder. **Other phones:** Assessor-815-937-2945; Treasurer-815-937-2960; Elections-815-937-2990; Vital Records-815-937-2990.

Kendall County

County Recorder, 111 W. Fox St, Yorkville, IL 60560. **Phone-**County Recorder, R/E & UCC Recording- 630-553-4112; fax-630-553-5283; hours 8AM-4:30PM Will not search records. UCC copy- $1.00 per page. Cert fee: $24.00 for 1st 4 pages; $1.00 each add'l. Payee: Kendall County Recorder. **Online Access to**

Real Estate records: Search property information at www.co.kendall.il.us/cidnet/public.htm. Search tax information by name or parcel number. **Other phones:** Assessor-630-553-4146; Treasurer-630-553-4124; Appraiser/ Auditor-630-553-4146; Elections-630-553-4105; Vital Records-630-553-4105.

Knox County

County Recorder, 200 S. Cherry, County Courthouse, Galesburg, IL 61401. **Phone-**309-345-3818; fax-309-343-3842; hours 8:30AM-4:30PM. Will search UCC records. Search per debtor/address- $10.00. UCC copy- $.25 per page. Will not search real estate or tax lien records. RE copy- $.25 per page. Cert fee: $18.00 per 4 pages. Payee: Knox County Recorder. **Other phones:** Assessor-309-345-3806; Treasurer-309-345-3863; Elections-309-345-3815.

La Salle County

County Recorder, PO Box 189, Ottawa, IL 61350. **Phone-**County Recorder, R/E & UCC Recording- 815-434-8226; fax-815-434-8260; hours 8AM-4:30PM www.lasallecounty.org/Final/contents2.htm Will search UCC records. Search per debtor/address- $10.00. UCC copy- $1.00 per page. Will not search real estate or tax lien records. RE record copy- $1.00 per page. Cert fee: $10.00 per doc. Payee: La Salle County Recorder. **Online Access to Real Estate, Assessor records:** Assessor/property records on the County Assessor database are online at www.lasallecounty.org/cidnet/asrpfull.htm. Registration and password required; there is a $200.00 per year fee, plus per minute charges. For information, phone 815-434-8233. Also, last 2 years assessment data can be accessed free at www.lasallecounty.org/contents3.htm. Parcel number is required. **Other phones:** Assessor-815-434-8280; Treasurer-815-434-8220; Elections-815-434-8202; Vital Records-815-434-8202.

Lake County

County Recorder, 18 N. County St, Courthouse - 2nd Fl, Waukegan, IL 60085-4358. **Phone-**County Recorder, R/E & UCC Recording- 847-377-2575; fax-847-625-7200; hours-8:30AM-5PM www.co.lake.il.us/recorder Will search UCC records. Search per debtor/address- $10.00. UCC copy- $1.00 per page. Will not search real estate or tax lien records. RE record copy- $1.00 per page. Cert fee: $1.00 per page. Payee: Lake County Recorder. **Online Access to Real Estate records:** Search the tax assessor's data at www.co.lake.il.us/assessor/assessments/default.asp. No name searching. **Other phones:** Assessor-847-377-2050; Treasurer-847-377-2323; Elections-847-377-3610; Vital Records-847-377-3610.

Lawrence County

County Recorder, 1100 State St, Courthouse, Lawrenceville, IL 62439. **Phone-**County Recorder, R/E & UCC Recording- 618-943-5126; fax-618-943-5205; hours 9AM-5PM

Will search UCC records. Search per debtor/address- $10.00. UCC copy- $1.00 per page. UCC search includes tax liens if requested. Separate federal/state combined tax lien search- $15.00 per debtor. Will not search real estate records. Cert fee: $1.50 per doc,same as fee chrgd. Payee: Lawrence County Recorder. **Other phones:** Assessor-618-943-2719; Treasurer-618-943-2016; Elections-618-943-2346; Vital Records-618-943-2346.

Lee County

County Recorder, PO Box 329, Dixon, IL 61021-0329. **Phone-**815-288-3309; fax-815-288-6492; hours 8:30AM-4:30PM

Will search UCC records. Search per debtor/address- $16.00. UCC copy- $1.00 per page. Will not search tax liens. Will search real estate records. RE

record copy- $1.00 per page. Cert fee: Same as original recording fee. Payee: Lee County Recorder. **Other phones:** Assessor-815-288-4483; Treasurer-815-288-4477.

Livingston County

County Recorder, 112 W. Madison, Courthouse, Pontiac, IL 61764-1871. **Phone-**County Recorder, R/E & UCC Recording- 815-844-2006; fax-815-842-1844; hours 8AM-4:30PM www.livingstoncounty-il.org Will search UCC records. Search per debtor/address- $10.00. UCC copy- $1.00 per page. Tax liens not included in UCC search. Separate federal/state combined tax lien search- $10.00 per debtor. Will not search real estate records. RE record copy- $1.00 per page. Cert fee: $5.00 per doc. Payee: Livingston County Recorder. **Other phones:** Assessor-815-844-7214; Treasurer-815-844-2306; Elections-815-842-9318; Vital Records-815-844-2006.

Logan County

County Recorder, PO Box 278, Lincoln, IL 62656. **Phone-**County Recorder, R/E & UCC Recording- 217-732-4148; fax-217-732-6064; hours 8:30AM-4:30PM www.co.logan.il.us/county_clerk/ Will search UCC records. Search per debtor/address- $10.00. UCC copy fee- $1.00 per page. Will not search real estate or tax lien records. RE record copy- $.25 per page. Cert fee: $30.00 per doc. Payee: Logan County Recorder. **Online Access to Property records:** Search the tax assessor database at http://loganilpropertymax.governmaxa.com/propertyma x/rover30.asp?sid=671F91267FEE4E1CA02DA85876 98C606. **Other phones:** Assessor-217-732-9635; Treasurer-217-732-3761; Elections-217-732-4148; Vital Records-217-732-4148.

Macon County

County Recorder, 141 S. Main St, Rm 201, Decatur, IL 62523-1293. **Phone-**County Recorder, R/E & UCC Recording- 217-424-1359; fax-217-428-2908; hours 8:30AM-4:30PM

Will search UCC records. Search per debtor/address- $15.00. UCC copy- $1.00 per page. UCC search includes tax liens if requested. Separate federal/state combined tax lien search- $10.00 per debtor. Will not search real estate records. RE record copy- $1.00 per page. Cert fee: Same as original recording fee. Payee: Macon County Recorder. **Other phones:** Assessor-217-424-1364; Treasurer-217-424-1426; Elections-217-424-1309; Vital Records-217-424-1305.

Macoupin County

County Recorder, PO Box 107, Carlinville, IL 62626. **Phone-**217-854-3214; fax-217-854-7347; hours 8:30AM-4:30PM. Will not search records. Record copy- $1.00 per page. Cert fee: $10.00 per cert. Payee: Macoupin County Recorder. **Other phones:** Assessor-217-854-8281; Treasurer-217-854-4014.

Madison County

County Recorder, PO Box 308, Edwardsville, IL 62025-0308. **Phone-**County Recorder, R/E & UCC Recording- 618-692-7040 x4775; fax-618-692-9843; hours 8AM-5PM

Will search UCC records. Search per debtor/address- $10.00. UCC copy- $1.00 per page. Will search tax liens. Will not search real estate records. RE copy- $1.00 per page. Cert fee: $12.00 per doc + $1 per page beyond 4. Payee: Madison County Recorder. **Other phones:** Assessor-618-692-6270; Treasurer-618-692-6260; Appraiser/ Auditor-618-692-7040 x4569; Elections-618-692-7040 x4682; Vital Records-618-692-7040 x4685.

Marion County

County Recorder, PO Box 637, Salem, IL 62881. **Phone**-618-548-3400, R/E Recording- 618-548-3852, UCC Recording- 618-548-3852; fax-618-548-2226; hours 8AM-4PM. Will search UCC records. Search per debtor- $10.00. UCC copy- $1.00 per page; $.50 each add'l. Tax liens not included in UCC search. Separate tax lien search fee- $10.00 per debtor. Will not search real estate records. Cert fee: $12.00 per cert and $1.00 per page. Payee: Marion County Recorder. **Other phones:** Assessor-618-548-3853; Treasurer-618-548-3858; Elections-618-548-3400; Vital Records-618-548-3850.

Marshall County

County Recorder, PO Box 328, Lacon, IL 61540. **Phone**-County Recorder, R/E & UCC Recording- 309-246-6325; fax-309-246-3667; hours 8:30AM-4:30PM Will search UCC records. Search per debtor/address- $10.00. UCC copy- $1.00 per page. Will not search real estate or tax lien records. Cert fee: $25.00-1st 4 pages, $1.00 per add'l. Payee: Marshall County Recorder. **Other phones:** Assessor-309-246-2350; Treasurer-309-246-6085; Elections-309-246-6325; Vital Records-309-246-6325.

Mason County

County Recorder, PO Box 77, Havana, IL 62644. **Phone**-County Recorder, R/E & UCC Recording- 309-543-6661; fax-309-543-2085; hours 8AM-4PM Will search UCC records. Search per debtor/address- $10.00. UCC copy- $1.00 per page. Will not search real estate or tax lien records. RE record copy- $.50 per page. Cert fee: $5.00 per doc. Payee: Mason County Recorder. **Other phones:** Assessor-309-543-4775; Treasurer-309-543-3359; Elections-309-543-6661; Vital Records-309-543-6661.

Massac County

County Recorder, PO Box 429, Metropolis, IL 62960. **Phone**-County Recorder, R/E & UCC Recording- 618-524-5213; fax-618-524-8514; hours 8AM-4PM Will not search records. UCC copy- $1.00 per page. RE record copy- $.25 per page. Cert fee: $5.00 per cert. Payee: Massac County Recorder. **Other phones:** Assessor-618-524-9632; Treasurer-618-524-5121; Elections-618-524-5213; Vital Records-618-524-5213.

McDonough County

County Recorder, 1 Courthouse Sq, Macomb, IL 61455. **Phone**-County Recorder, R/E & UCC Recording- 309-833-2474; fax-309-836-3368; hours 8AM-4PM. Will not search records. Record copy- $1.50 per page. Cert fee: Same as original recording fee. Payee: McDonough County Recorder. **Other phones:** Assessor-309-833-5305; Treasurer-309-833-2032; Elections-309-833-4649; Vital Records-309-833-2474.

McHenry County

County Recorder, 2200 N. Seminary Ave, Rm A280, Woodstock, IL 60098. **Phone**-815-334-4110; fax-815-338-9612; hours-8AM-4:30PM www.co.mchenry.il.us/countydpt/recorder Will search UCC records. Search per debtor/address- $10.00. UCC copy- $1.00 per page. Will do tax lien search. Will not search real estate records. RE record copy- $1.50 per page, $.50 each add'l. Cert fee: $12.00 for 1st 4 pages, $1.00 each add'l. Payee: McHenry County Recorder. **Online Access to Assessor/Treasurer, Property, Foreclosure records:** Records on the County Treasurer Inquiry site are free at http://taxweb2k.co.mchenry.il.us/cidnet/publictreasurer.htm. Also, access to real estate records is via a private company at https://www.landrecords.net/. Subscription or pay-per

search service available. The sheriff's foreclosure list is free at www.co.mchenry.il.us.

McLean County

County Recorder, PO Box 2400, Bloomington, IL 61702-2400. **Phone**-County Recorder, R/E & UCC Recording- 309-888-5170; fax-309-888-5927; hours 8AM-4:30PM www.mclean.gov/ Will not search records. Record copy- $1.00 per page. Cert fee: $18.00 1st 4 pg, then $1.00. Payee: McLean County Recorder. **Online Access to Recorder, Deed, UCC, Lien, Vital Statistic, Assessor, Property, Treasurer Tax Bill, Sex Offender, Assumed Name, Elected Official records:** Access to recorder official records and UCCs is free at www.mclean.gov/resolution/. Also, the county parcel is atwww.mclean.gov/tax/taxlookup_search.asp. No name searching. Also, access to the Township of Normal assessor database is free at www.normaltownship.org/Assessor/ParcelSearch.php. No name searching; parcel number or address required. Also, search the sex offender data at www.mclean.gov/sheriff/SexOffenderPage.htm. Also, search the assumed named list at www.mclean.gov/CountyClerk/CountyClerkAssumed NamesMain.asp. Search election officials by precinct at the website. **Other phones:** Assessor-309-888-5130; Treasurer-309-888-5180; Elections-309-888-5190.

Menard County

County Recorder, PO Box 465, Petersburg, IL 62675. **Phone**-217-632-2415, R/E Recording- 217-632-3201, UCC Recording- 217-632-3201; fax-217-632-4301; hours 8:30AM-4:30PM Will search UCC records. Search per debtor/address- $10.00. UCC copy- $1.00 per page. Will not search real estate or tax lien records. RE record copy- $1.00 per page. Cert fee: $7.00 per doc. Payee: Menard County Recorder. **Other phones:** Assessor-217-632-4461; Treasurer-217-632-2333; Appraiser/ Auditor-217-632-4461; Elections-217-632-3201; Vital Records-217-632-3201.

Mercer County

County Recorder, PO Box 66, Aledo, IL 61231. **Phone**-County Recorder, R/E & UCC Recording- 309-582-7021; fax-309-582-7022; hours 8AM-4PM Will search UCC records. Search per debtor/address- $10.00. UCC copy- $1.00 per page. Will not search real estate or tax lien records. Payee: Mercer County Recorder. **Other phones:** Assessor-309-582-7814; Treasurer-309-582-2524.

Monroe County

County Recorder, 100 S. Main, Courthouse, Waterloo, IL 62298-1399. **Phone**-618-939-9681; fax-618-939-8639; hours 8AM-4:30PM Will not search records. Record copy- $1.00 per page. Cert fee: $2.50 per doc + $1.00 per page. Payee: Monroe County Recorder. **Other phones:** Assessor-618-939-9681 x211; Treasurer-618-939-8681 x213.

Montgomery County

County Recorder, 1 Courthouse Sq, Historic Courthouse, Hillsboro, IL 62049-1196. **Phone**-County Recorder, R/E & UCC Recording- 217-532-9532; fax-217-532-9581; hours-8AM-4PM www.montgomeryco.com Will search UCC records. Search per debtor/address- $10.00. UCC copy- $1.00 per page. UCC search includes tax liens if requested. Separate federal/state combined tax lien search- $10.00 per debtor. Real estate owner, mortgage, and property transfer searches available. RE record copy- $1.00 per page. Cert fee: $29.00 per doc. Payee: Montgomery County Recorder. **Other phones:** Assessor-217-532-9595; Treasurer-217-532-9521; Elections-217-532-9530; Vital Records-217-532-9537.

Morgan County

County Recorder, PO Box 1387, Jacksonville, IL 62651. **Phone**-County Recorder, R/E & UCC Recording- 217-243-8581; fax-217-243-8368; hours 8:30AM-4:30PM Will search UCC records. Search per debtor/address- $10.00. UCC copy- $1.00 per page. UCC search includes tax liens if requested. Separate federal/state combined tax lien search- $10.00 per debtor. Will not search real estate records. RE record copy- $1.00 per page. Cert fee: $5.00 per cert. Payee: Morgan County Recorder. **Other phones:** Assessor-217-243-8557; Treasurer-217-243-8581; Elections-217-243-8581; Vital Records-217-243-8581.

Moultrie County

County Recorder, 10 S Main, #6, Courthouse, Sullivan, IL 61951. **Phone**-County Recorder, R/E & UCC Recording- 217-728-4389; fax-217-728-8178; hours 8:30AM-4:30PM. Will search UCC records. Search per debtor/address- $10.00. UCC copy- $1.00 per page. Tax liens not included in UCC search. Separate federal/state combined tax lien search- $10.00 per debtor. Will not search real estate records. Cert fee: $14.00 per cert. Payee: Moultrie County Recorder. **Other phones:** Assessor-217-728-4951; Treasurer-217-728-4032; Elections-217-728-4389; Vital Records-217-728-4389.

Ogle County

County Recorder, PO Box 357, Oregon, IL 61061. **Phone**-815-732-1115 x269/1, R/E Recording- 815-732-1115 x269/270/271, UCC Recording- 815-732-1115 x269/270/271; hours 8:30AM-4:30PM Will search UCC records. Search per debtor/address- $10.00. UCC copy- $1.00 per page. UCC search includes tax liens if requested. Tax lien search fee- $5.00 per debtor. Will not search real estate records. RE record copy- $1.00 per page. Cert fee: Same as original recording fee. Payee: Ogle County Recorder. **Online Access to Land, Recorder, Deed, UCC records:** Access to recorder data is free at www.landaccess.com/proi/county.jsp?county=ilogle,. **Other phones:** Assessor-815-732-1150 x239, 256, 257, 258 & 305; Treasurer-815-732-1100 x202/201/310 & 286; Elections-815-732-1110 x012/213/281/214 & 215; Vital Records-815-732-1110 x012/213/281/214 & 215.

Peoria County

County Recorder, 324 Main St, County Courthouse, Rm G04, Peoria, IL 61602. **Phone**-County Recorder, R/E & UCC Recording- 309-672-6090; hours 9AM-5PM www.co.peoria.il.us/ Will search UCC records. Search per debtor/address- $10.00. UCC copy- $1.00 per page. Will not search real estate or tax lien records. RE record copy- $.50 per page. Cert fee: Same as current recording fee. Payee: Peoria County Recorder. **Online Access to Assessor records:** View tax assessor records at www.co.peoria.il.us/frame.php?destination=209.251.115.194%2Fassessor%2Frealasp1.asp. The recorder's office has a subscritpion servce with web access. Call the recorder for details (none are posted on webpage). **Other phones:** Assessor-309-672-6910; Treasurer-309-672-6065.

Perry County

County Recorder, PO Box 438, Pinckneyville, IL 62274. **Phone**-County Recorder, R/E & UCC Recording- 618-357-5116; fax-618-357-3194; hours 8AM-4PM www.perrycountyil.org Will search UCC records. Search per debtor/address- $10.00. UCC copy- $5.00 per doc. Tax liens not included in UCC search. Tax lien search fee- $10.00. Will search real estate records. RE record copy- $5.00 per doc. Cert fee: $2.00 per cert.

Payee: Perry County Recorder. **Other phones:** Assessor-618-357-2209; Treasurer-618-357-5002; Elections-618-357-5116; Vital Records-618-357-5116.

Piatt County

County Recorder, PO Box 558, Monticello, IL 61856-0558. **Phone-**County Recorder, R/E & UCC Recording- 217-762-9487; fax-217-762-7563; hours 8:30AM-4:30PM www.piattcounty.org
Will search UCC records. Search per debtor/address-$10.00. UCC copy- $1.00 per page. Will not search real estate or tax lien records. RE record copy- $.50 per page. Cert fee: $8.00 per file + $.50 per page. Payee: Piatt County Recorder. **Other phones:** Assessor-217-762-4266; Treasurer-217-762-4866; Elections-217-762-9487; Vital Records-217-762-9487.

Pike County

County Recorder, 100 E. Washington St., Courthouse, Pittsfield, IL 62363. **Phone-**County Recorder, R/E & UCC Recording- 217-285-6812; fax-217-285-5820; hours 8:30AM-4PM
Will search UCC records. Search per debtor/address-$10.00. UCC copy- $1.00 per page. Will search tax liens. Tax lien search fee- $10.00 per debtor. Will not search real estate records. RE record copy-$1.00 per deed. Cert fee: $10.00 per doc. Payee: Pike County Recorder. **Other phones:** Assessor-217-285-2382; Treasurer-217-285-4218; Elections-217-285-6812; Vital Records-217-285-6812.

Pope County

County Recorder, PO Box 216, Golconda, IL 62938. **Phone-**618-683-4466; fax-618-683-4466; hours 8AM-Noon, 1-4PM
Will search UCC records. Search per debtor/address-$10.00. UCC copy- $1.00 per page. UCC search includes tax liens if requested. Will not search real estate records. Cert fee: $5.00 per cert. Payee: Pope County Recorder. **Other phones:** Assessor-618-683-6231; Treasurer-618-683-5501.

Pulaski County

County Recorder, PO Box 118, Mound City, IL 62963. **Phone-**618-748-9360; fax-618-748-9305; hours 8AM-Noon, 1-4PM
Will search UCC records. Search per debtor/address-$10.00. UCC copy- $.50 per page. Will not search real estate or tax lien records. RE copy- $.50 per page. Cert fee: $7.00 per doc. Payee: Pulaski County Recorder. **Other phones:** Assessor-618-748-9321; Treasurer-618-748-9322.

Putnam County

County Recorder, PO Box 236, Hennepin, IL 61327. **Phone-**County Recorder, R/E & UCC Recording- 815-925-7129; fax-815-925-7549; hours 9AM-4PM
Will search UCC records. Search per debtor/address-$10.00. UCC copy- $1.00 per page. Will not search real estate or tax lien records. RE record copy- $.50 per page (non-certified). Cert fee: $27.00 per doc; includes 4 pages, $1.00 each add'l. Payee: Putnam County Recorder. **Other phones:** Assessor-815-925-7238; Treasurer-815-925-7226; Appraiser/ Auditor-815-925-7238; Elections-815-925-7129; Vital Records-815-925-7129.

Randolph County

County Recorder, 1 Taylor St, Rm 202, Chester, IL 62233-0309. **Phone-**618-826-5000 x191, R/E Recording- 618-826-5000 x117, UCC Recording- 618-826-5000 x117; fax-618-826-3750; hours 8AM-4:00PM
Will search UCC records. Search per debtor/address-$10.00 for 5 year. UCC copy- $1.00 per page. Tax liens not included in UCC search. Tax lien search fee- $10.00 per debtor. Will not search real estate

records. Records back to 1989 on computer Cert fee: $26.00 for 4 pages, $1.00 each add'l. Payee: Randolph County Recorder. **Online Access to Property records:** Access to real estate records is via a private company at https://www.landrecords.net/. Subscription or pay-per search service available. Images go back to 1995; index to 1989. **Other phones:** Assessor-618-826-5000 x192; Treasurer-618-826-5000 x224; Elections-618-826-5000 x116; Vital Records-618-826-5000 x112.

Richland County

County Recorder, 103 W. Main, Courthouse, Olney, IL 62450. **Phone-**618-392-3111; fax-618-393-4005; hours 8AM-4PM
Will search UCC records. Search per debtor/address-$10.00. UCC copy- $1.00 per page. Will not search real estate or tax lien records. RE record copy- $3.00 per doc. Cert fee: $12.00 1st 4 pg, then $1.00. Payee: Richland County Recorder. **Other phones:** Assessor-618-395-4387; Treasurer-618-392-8341; Elections-618-392-3111; Vital Records-618-392-3111.

Rock Island County

County Recorder, PO Box 3067, Rock Island, IL 61204. **Phone-**309-558-3360; fax-309-558-3642; hours 8AM-4:30PM www.co.rock-island.il.us
Will search UCC records. Search per debtor/address-$10.00. UCC copy- $1.00 per page. Tax liens included in UCC search. Federal/state combined tax lien search- $10.00 per debtor Will not search real estate records. RE copy- $.25 per page; $2.00 each if mailed. Cert fee: Does not certify. Payee: County Recorder. **Online Access to Property, Assessor records:** Access to real estate records is via a private company at https://www.landrecords.net/. Subscription or pay-per search service available. Index goes back to 1982, images back to 1992, subdivisions to 1995. Also, Moline Town assessor records are free at www.molinetownship.com/Assessor/disclaimer.html. For the application for certified copy of vital records go to http://ricoclerk.revealed.net/. **Other phones:** Assessor-309-786-4451; Treasurer-309-786-4451.

Saline County

County Recorder, 10 E. Poplar, #17, Harrisburg, IL 62946. **Phone-**618-253-8197, R/E Recording- 618-253-3073, UCC Recording- 618-253-3073; fax-618-252-3073; hours 8AM-4PM
Will search UCC records that are not in land records. Search per debtor/address- $10.00. UCC copy-$1.00 per page. Will not search real estate or tax lien records. RE record copy- $1.00 per page for deeds, all other real estate records are $.25 per page. Cert fee: $5.00 per doc. Payee: Saline County Recorder. **Other phones:** Assessor-618-252-0691; Treasurer-618-253-6915; Elections-618-253-8197; Vital Records-618-253-8197.

Sangamon County

County Recorder, PO Box 669, Springfield, IL 62705-0669. **Phone-**217-535-3150; fax-217-535-3159; hours 8:30AM-5PM www.co.sangamon.il.us
Will search UCC records. Search per debtor/address-$10.00. UCC copy- $1.00 per page. UCC search includes tax liens if requested. Will not search real estate records. RE record copy- $2.00 1st page, $.50 each add'l. Cert fee: $26.00. Payee: Sangamon County Recorder. **Online Access to Property records:** Access to real estate records is via a private company at https://www.landrecords.net/. Subscription or pay-per search service available. Records go back to 1992. **Other phones:** Assessor-217-753-6615; Treasurer-217-753-6800.

Schuyler County

County Recorder, PO Box 200, Rushville, IL 62681. **Phone-**County Recorder, R/E & UCC Recording- 217-322-4734; fax-217-322-6164; hours 8AM-4PM
Will search UCC records. Search per debtor/address-$10.00. UCC copy- $1.00 per page. Tax liens not included in UCC search. Tax lien search fee-$10.00 per debtor. Will not search real estate records. RE record copy- $.50 per page. Cert fee: $7.00 per cert. Payee: Schuyler County Recorder. **Other phones:** Assessor-217-322-4432; Treasurer-217-322-3830; Elections-217-322-4734; Vital Records-217-322-4734.

Scott County

County Recorder, Courthouse, Winchester, IL 62694. **Phone-**County Recorder, R/E & UCC Recording- 217-742-3178; fax-217-742-5853; hours 8AM-4PM
Will search UCC records. Search per debtor/address-$10.00. UCC copy- $1.00 per page. UCC search does not include tax liens. Real estate owner, mortgage, and property transfer searches available. RE record copy- $1.00 per page. Cert fee: $45.00 per cert. Payee: Scott County Recorder. **Other phones:** Assessor-217-742-5751; Treasurer-217-742-3368; Elections-217-742-3178; Vital Records-217-742-3178.

Shelby County

County Recorder, PO Box 230, Shelbyville, IL 62565. **Phone-**217-774-4421; fax-217-774-5291; hours 8AM-4PM. Will not search records. UCC copy- $1.00 per page. Cert fee: $34.00 per cert. Payee: Shelby County Recorder. **Other phones:** Assessor-217-774-5579; Treasurer-217-774-3841.

St. Clair County

County Recorder, PO Box 543, Belleville, IL 62220. **Phone-**618-277-6600, UCC Recording- 618-277-6600 x2484; 8:30AM-5PM www.stclaircountyrecorder.com
Will search UCC records. Search per debtor/address-$13.00. UCC copy- $1.00 per page. Tax liens not included in UCC search. Tax lien search fee-$10.00 per debtor. Will not search real estate records. RE record copy- $2.00 per page. Payee: St. Clair County Recorder. **Online Access to Recorder, Grantor/Grantee, Real Estate, Divorce, Lien, Judgment records:** Access to the county recorder records is free at www.stclaircountyrecorder.com/cgi-bin/display.cgi?file=search. Three search methods are available. **Other phones:** Assessor-618-277-6600 x2509; Treasurer-618-277-6600 x2448; Elections-770-531-6600 x2363.

Stark County

County Recorder, PO Box 97, Toulon, IL 61483. **Phone-**County Recorder, R/E & UCC Recording- 309-286-5911; fax-309-286-4039; hours 8:30AM-4:30PM www.starkcourt.org
Will search UCC records. Search per debtor/address-$10.00. UCC copy- $1.00 per page. Will search tax liens. Will not search real estate records. RE record copy- $.50 per page. Cert fee: $5.00 per copy. Payee: Stark County Recorder. **Online Access to Unclaimed Fund records:** Access the county clerk of courts unclaimed funds database at www.starkcourt.org (click on "Unclaimed Funds"). File is in pdf format. **Other phones:** Assessor-309-286-7172; Treasurer-309-286-5901; Elections-309-286-5911; Vital Records-309-286-5911.

Stephenson County

County Recorder, 15 N. Galena Ave, #1, Freeport, IL 61032. **Phone-**815-235-8385; fax-none; hours 8:30AM-4:30PM
Will search UCC records. Search per debtor/address-$10.00. UCC copy- $1.00 per page. Will not search real estate or tax lien records. RE copy-

$1.00 per page. Cert fee: $12.00. Payee: Stephenson County Recorder. **Other phones:** Assessor-815-235-8260; Treasurer-815-235-8264.

Tazewell County

County Recorder, PO Box 36, Pekin, IL 61555-0036. **Phone**-309-477-2210; fax-309-477-2321; hours 8:30AM-5PM

Will search UCC records. Search per debtor/address-$12.00. Copy fee is $.50 per page. Will not search real estate or tax lien records. RE record copy-$.50 per page. Cert fee: $12.00 1st 4 pages; $1.00 each add'l. Payee: Tazewell County Recorder. **Other phones:** Assessor-309-477-2275; Treasurer-309-477-2284.

Union County

County Recorder, Jonesboro, IL 62952. **Phone**-618-833-5711; fax-618-833-8712; hours 8AM-4PM

Will search UCC records. Search per debtor/address-$10.00. UCC copy- $.50 per page. Will not search real estate or tax lien records. RE copy- $.50 per page. Cert fee: $5.00 per cert. Payee: Union County Recorder. **Other phones:** Assessor-618-833-8051; Treasurer-618-833-5621.

Vermilion County

County Recorder, 6 N. Vermilion St, Danville, IL 61832-5877. **Phone**-217-554-6041; fax-217-554-6047; hours 8AM-4:30PM

Will search UCC records. Search per debtor/address-$10.00. UCC copy- $1.00 per page. Will not search real estate or tax lien records. RE record copy- $1.00 1st page, $.50 each add'l. Cert fee: $12.00 per cert up to 4 pages, $1.00 for add'l pages per doc. Payee: Vermilion County Recorder. **Other phones:** Assessor-217-554-1941; Treasurer-217-554-6081.

Wabash County

County Recorder, PO Box 277, Mount Carmel, IL 62863. **Phone**-County Recorder, R/E & UCC Recording-618-262-4561; hours 8AM-5PM

Will search UCC records. Search per debtor/address-$10.00. UCC copy- $1.00 per page. Tax liens not included in UCC search. Will not search real estate records. RE record copy- $.50 per page. Cert fee: $12.00 1st 4 pg, then $1.00. Payee: Wabash County Recorder. **Other phones:** Assessor-618-262-4463; Treasurer-618-262-5262; Elections-618-262-4561; Vital Records-618-262-4561.

Warren County

County Recorder, 100 W Broadway, Courthouse, Monmouth, IL 61462-1797. **Phone**-309-734-8592; fax-309-734-7406; hours 8AM-4:30PM

Will search UCC records. Search per debtor/address-$10.00. UCC copy- $.50 per page. Will not search real estate or tax lien records. RE record copy-$.50 per page. Payee: Warren County Recorder. **Other phones:** Assessor-309-734-8561; Treasurer-309-734-8536; Elections-309-734-4612; Vital Records-309-734-8592.

Washington County

County Recorder, 101 E. St. Louis St, County Courthouse, Nashville, IL 62263-1105. **Phone**-County Recorder, R/E & UCC Recording- 618-327-4800 x300; fax-618-327-3582; hours 8AM-4PM

Will search UCC records. Search per debtor/address-$10.00. UCC copy- $1.00 per page. UCC search includes tax liens if requested. Real estate owner, mortgage, and property transfer searches available. RE record copy- $1.00 per page. Cert fee: $5.00 per cert + $1.00 per page. Payee: Washington County Recorder. **Other phones:** Assessor-618-327-4800 x325; Treasurer-618-327-4800 x315; Elections-618-327-4800 x300; Vital Records-618-327-4800 x300.

Wayne County

County Recorder, PO Box 187, Fairfield, IL 62837. **Phone**-County Recorder, R/E & UCC Recording- 618-842-5182; fax-618-842-6427; hours 8AM-4:30PM http://assessor.wayne.il.us

Will search UCC records. Search per debtor/address-$10.00. UCC copy- $1.00 per page. Tax liens not included in UCC search. Federal/state combined tax lien search- $10.00 + $1.00 per page. Will search real estate records. RE record copy- $1.00 per page. Cert fee: $5.00 per cert + $1.00 per page. Payee: Wayne County Recorder. **Online Access to Assessor, Property records:** Records on the Wayne Township Assessor Office database are free at http://assessor.wayne.il.us/OPID.html. Also, you may subscribe to the advanced search feature for a fee. Access includes legal, assessment, sales history, buildings and other information. **Other phones:** Assessor-618-842-2582; Treasurer-618-842-5087; Elections-618-842-5182; Vital Records-618-842-5182.

White County

County Recorder, PO Box 339, Carmi, IL 62821. **Phone**-County Recorder, R/E & UCC Recording- 618-382-7211; hours 8AM-4PM

Will search UCC records. Search per debtor/address-$10.00. UCC copy- $1.00 per page. UCC search includes tax liens if requested. Tax lien search fee-$2.00 1st 4 pages, $.50 add'l. Will not search real estate records. RE record copy- $2.00 per doc. Cert fee: $15.00 1st 4 pg, then $1.00. Payee: White County Recorder. **Other phones:** Assessor-618-618-382-721182-2332; Treasurer-618-382-8122; Elections-618-382-7211; Vital Records-618-382-7211.

Whiteside County

County Recorder, 200 E. Knox, Morrison, IL 61270. **Phone**-815-772-5241, R/E Recording- 815-772-5192; UCC Recording- 815-772-5192; fax-815-772-5244; hours 8:30AM-4:30PM www.whiteside.org

Will search UCC records. Search per debtor/address-$10.00. UCC copy- $.50 per page. Will not search real estate or tax lien records. RE record copy-$.50 per page. Payee: Whiteside County Recorder. **Other phones:** Assessor-815-772-5195; Treasurer-815-772-5196.

Will County

County Recorder, 58 E Clinton, #100, Joliet, IL 60432. **Phone**-815-740-4637; fax-815-740-4697; hours 8:30AM-4:30PM

Will search UCC records. Search per debtor/address-$10.00. UCC copy- $1.00 per page. Will not search real estate or tax lien records. RE record copy- $1.00 per page. Cert fee: Same as original recording fee. Payee: Will County Recorder. **Online Access to Assessor, Appraiser, Property, Voter Registration, Deed, Lien, Mortgage records:** Access to the Recorder's real estate and lien records is free at www.willcountydata.com/rec/searchselect.htm Access to voter registration data is free at https://www.willcountydata.com/voterstatus/Voter_lookup_input.htm. The assessor offers a free parcel number inquiry at http://66.158.72.248:2080/cics/cwba/ccalm03; no name searching. Also, access to Town of Manhattan assessor records is free at www.manhattantownship.net. No name searching.

Williamson County

County Recorder, PO Box 1108, Marion, IL 62959-1108. **Phone**-618-997-1301 X121, R/E Recording-618-997-1301 x 121; fax-618-993-2071; hours 8AM-4PM

Will search UCC records. Search per debtor/address-$10.00. UCC copy- $1.00 per page. Will not search tax liens. Will search real estate records. RE record copy- $1.00 per page. Cert fee: $5.00 per cert. Payee: Williamson County Recorder. **Other phones:** Assessor-618-997-1301 x164; Treasurer-618-997-1301 x129; Elections-618-997-1301 x102; Vital Records-618-997-1301 x102.

Winnebago County

County Recorder, 404 Elm St, Rm 405, Rockford, IL 61101. **Phone**-815-987-3100; fax-815-961-3261; hours 8AM-4PM

Will search UCC records. Search per debtor/address-$13.75. UCC copy fee- $.10 per page. UCC search includes tax liens if requested. Separate federal/state combined tax lien search- $5.00 per debtor. Will not search real estate records. Cert fee: $25.00 add'l $1.00 per page. Payee: Winnebago County Recorder. **Online Access to Property, UCC records:** Access to county land and UCC records is free at www.landaccess.com/proi/county.jsp?county=ilwinnebago. **Other phones:** Assessor-815-987-3025; Treasurer-815-987-3010.

Woodford County

County Recorder, 115 N. Main, Courthouse, Rm 202, Eureka, IL 61530-1273. **Phone**-County Recorder, R/E & UCC Recording- 309-467-2822; hours 8AM-5PM

Will search UCC records. Search per debtor/address-$10.00. UCC copy- $1.00 per page. Will not search real estate or tax lien records. Cert fee: $28 per 1st 4 pages. Payee: Woodford County Recorder. **Other phones:** Assessor-309-467-3708; Treasurer-309-467-4621; Elections-309-467-2822; Vital Records-309-467-2822.

Illinois County Locator

You will usually be able to find the city name in the City/County Cross Reference below. In that case, it is a simple matter to determine the county from the cross reference. However, only the official US Postal Service city names are included in this index. There are an additional 40,000 place names that people use in their addresses. Therefore, we have also included a ZIP/City Cross Reference immediately following the City/County Cross Reference.

If you know the ZIP Code but the city name does not appear in the City/County Cross Reference index, look up the ZIP Code in the ZIP/City Cross Reference, find the city name, then look up the city name in the City/County Cross Reference. For example, you want to know the county for an address of Menands, NY 12204. There is no "Menands" in the City/County Cross Reference. The ZIP/City Cross Reference shows that ZIP Codes 12201-12288 are for the city of Albany. Looking back in the City/County Cross Reference, Albany is in Albany County.

Illinois City/County Cross Reference

ABINGDON (61410) Knox(97), Warren(2)
ADAIR McDonough
ADDIEVILLE Washington
ADDISON Du Page
ADRIAN Hancock
AKIN Franklin
ALBANY Whiteside
ALBERS Clinton
ALBION Edwards
ALDEN McHenry
ALEDO Mercer
ALEXANDER (62601) Morgan(93),
   Sangamon(6)
ALEXIS (61412) Mercer(83), Warren(16)
ALGONQUIN (60102) McHenry(82),
   Kane(17)
ALHAMBRA Madison
ALLENDALE Wabash
ALLERTON (61810) Vermilion(71),
   Douglas(14), Edgar(12), Champaign(1)
ALMA Marion
ALPHA Henry
ALSEY Scott
ALSIP Cook
ALTAMONT (62411) Effingham(98),
   Fayette(1)
ALTO PASS (62905) Union(79),
   Jackson(20)
ALTON (62002) Madison(98), Macoupin(1)
ALTONA (61414) Knox(68), Henry(31)
ALVIN Vermilion
AMBOY Lee
AMF OHARE Cook
ANCHOR (61720) McLean(91), Ford(8)
ANCONA Livingston
ANDALUSIA Rock Island
ANDOVER Henry
ANNA Union
ANNAPOLIS (62413) Crawford(93),
   Clark(6)
ANNAWAN Henry
ANTIOCH Lake
APPLE RIVER Jo Daviess
ARCOLA (61910) Douglas(86), Coles(13)
ARENZVILLE (62611) Cass(83),
   Morgan(16)
ARGENTA Macon
ARLINGTON Bureau
ARLINGTON HEIGHTS Cook
ARMINGTON (61721) Tazewell(92),
   Logan(7)
ARMSTRONG Vermilion
AROMA PARK Kankakee
ARROWSMITH McLean
ARTHUR (61911) Douglas(54),
   Moultrie(41), Coles(4)
ASHKUM Iroquois
ASHLAND (62612) Cass(76), Morgan(22)
ASHLEY (62808) Washington(81),
   Jefferson(18)
ASHMORE Coles
ASHTON (61006) Lee(78), Ogle(21)
ASSUMPTION (62510) Christian(86),
   Shelby(13)
ASTORIA Fulton

ATHENS (62613) Menard(95), Logan(3)
ATKINSON Henry
ATLANTA (61723) Logan(98), McLean(1)
ATWATER Macoupin
ATWOOD (61913) Douglas(64), Piatt(34),
   Moultrie(1)
AUBURN Sangamon
AUGUSTA (62311) Hancock(90),
   Schuyler(5), Adams(3)
AURORA (60504) Du Page(76), Kane(12),
   Will(9), Kendall(2)
AURORA Du Page
AURORA Kane
AVA Jackson
AVISTON (62216) Clinton(97), Madison(2)
AVON (61415) Fulton(80), Warren(19)
BAILEYVILLE (61007) Ogle(69),
   Stephenson(30)
BALDWIN Randolph
BARDOLPH McDonough
BARNHILL Wayne
BARRINGTON (60010) Lake(57),
   Cook(36), McHenry(4)
BARRINGTON Lake
BARRY (62312) Pike(85), Adams(14)
BARSTOW Rock Island
BARTELSO Clinton
BARTLETT (60103) Du Page(50),
   Cook(49)
BASCO Hancock
BATAVIA Kane
BATCHTOWN Calhoun
BATH Mason
BAYLIS (62314) Pike(76), Adams(22)
BEARDSTOWN Cass
BEASON (62512) Logan(93), De Witt(6)
BEAVERVILLE (60912) Kankakee(56),
   Iroquois(43)
BECKEMEYER Clinton
BEDFORD PARK Cook
BEECHER (60401) Will(97), Kankakee(2)
BEECHER CITY (62414) Effingham(63),
   Fayette(27), Shelby(9)
BELKNAP (62908) Massac(53),
   Johnson(46)
BELLE RIVE (62810) Jefferson(95),
   Hamilton(3), Wayne(1)
BELLEVILLE St. Clair
BELLFLOWER McLean
BELLMONT Wabash
BELLWOOD Cook
BELVIDERE Boone
BEMENT Piatt
BENLD Macoupin
BENSENVILLE Du Page
BENSON Woodford
BENTON Franklin
BERKELEY Cook
BERWICK Warren
BERWYN Cook
BETHALTO Madison
BETHANY (61914) Moultrie(97), Macon(2)
BIG ROCK (60511) Kane(94), De Kalb(5)
BIGGSVILLE Henderson
BINGHAM Fayette

BIRDS Lawrence
BISHOP HILL Henry
BISMARCK Vermilion
BLACKSTONE Livingston
BLANDINSVILLE (61420) McDonough(91),
   Hancock(8)
BLOOMINGDALE Du Page
BLOOMINGTON McLean
BLUE ISLAND Cook
BLUE MOUND (62513) Macon(76),
   Christian(23)
BLUFF SPRINGS Cass
BLUFFS (62621) Scott(94), Morgan(5)
BLUFORD (62814) Jefferson(98),
   Wayne(1)
BOLES Johnson
BOLINGBROOK (60440) Will(97), Du
   Page(2)
BOLINGBROOK Will
BONDVILLE Champaign
BONE GAP Edwards
BONFIELD Kankakee
BONNIE Jefferson
BOODY Macon
BOURBONNAIS Kankakee
BOWEN (62316) Hancock(97), Adams(2)
BRACEVILLE (60407) Grundy(51), Will(47)
BRADFORD (61421) Stark(58),
   Bureau(34), Marshall(6)
BRADLEY Kankakee
BRAIDWOOD Will
BREESE Clinton
BRIDGEPORT Lawrence
BRIDGEVIEW Cook
BRIGHTON (62012) Jersey(46),
   Macoupin(45), Madison(7)
BRIMFIELD Peoria
BRISTOL Kendall
BROADLANDS (61816) Champaign(97),
   Douglas(2)
BROADVIEW Cook
BROCTON (61917) Edgar(95), Douglas(4)
BROOKFIELD Cook
BROOKPORT (62910) Massac(96),
   Pope(3)
BROUGHTON Hamilton
BROWNING (62624) Schuyler(97),
   Fulton(2)
BROWNS (62818) Wabash(61),
   Edwards(38)
BROWNSTOWN Fayette
BRUSSELS Calhoun
BRYANT Fulton
BUCKINGHAM (60917) Kankakee(90),
   Livingston(8)
BUCKLEY Iroquois
BUCKNER Franklin
BUDA Bureau
BUFFALO Sangamon
BUFFALO GROVE (60089) Lake(57),
   Cook(42)
BUFFALO PRAIRIE Rock Island
BULPITT Christian
BUNCOMBE (62912) Johnson(55),
   Union(44)

BUNKER HILL Macoupin
BURBANK Cook
BUREAU Bureau
BURLINGTON Kane
BURNSIDE Hancock
BURNT PRAIRIE (62820) White(86),
   Wayne(13)
BUSHNELL McDonough
BUTLER Montgomery
BYRON Ogle
CABERY (60919) Kankakee(43), Ford(31),
   Livingston(25)
CACHE Alexander
CAIRO Alexander
CALEDONIA (61011) Boone(70),
   Winnebago(29)
CALHOUN Richland
CALUMET CITY Cook
CAMARGO Douglas
CAMBRIA Williamson
CAMBRIDGE Henry
CAMDEN Schuyler
CAMERON Warren
CAMP GROVE Marshall
CAMP POINT Adams
CAMPBELL HILL (62916) Jackson(77),
   Randolph(12), Perry(10)
CAMPUS Livingston
CANTON Fulton
CANTRALL Sangamon
CAPRON Boone
CARBON CLIFF Rock Island
CARBONDALE (62902) Jackson(70),
   Williamson(27)
CARBONDALE Jackson
CARLINVILLE Macoupin
CARLOCK (61725) McLean(70),
   Woodford(29)
CARLYLE Clinton
CARMAN Henderson
CARMI White
CAROL STREAM Cook
CAROL STREAM Du Page
CARPENTERSVILLE Kane
CARRIER MILLS (62917) Saline(88),
   Williamson(11)
CARROLLTON Greene
CARTERVILLE Williamson
CARTHAGE Hancock
CARY (60013) McHenry(94), Lake(5)
CASEY (62420) Clark(85),
   Cumberland(11), Coles(1)
CASEYVILLE St. Clair
CASTLETON Stark
CATLIN Vermilion
CAVE IN ROCK Hardin
CEDAR POINT La Salle
CEDARVILLE Stephenson
CENTRALIA (62801) Marion(67),
   Clinton(22), Washington(6), Jefferson(4)
CERRO GORDO (61818) Piatt(77),
   Macon(22)
CHADWICK (61014) Carroll(82),
   Whiteside(17)

CHAMBERSBURG (62323) Pike(91), Brown(8)
CHAMPAIGN Champaign
CHANA Ogle
CHANDLERVILLE (62627) Cass(71), Mason(28)
CHANNAHON (60410) Will(94), Grundy(5)
CHAPIN (62628) Morgan(87), Scott(12)
CHARLESTON Coles
CHATHAM Sangamon
CHATSWORTH Livingston
CHEBANSE (60922) Kankakee(62), Iroquois(37)
CHENOA (61726) McLean(94), Livingston(5)
CHERRY Bureau
CHERRY VALLEY (61016) Winnebago(88), Boone(11)
CHESTER Randolph
CHESTERFIELD (62630) Macoupin(97), Greene(1)
CHESTNUT Logan
CHICAGO Cook
CHICAGO HEIGHTS Cook
CHICAGO RIDGE Cook
CHILLICOTHE (61523) Peoria(97), Marshall(2)
CHRISMAN Edgar
CHRISTOPHER Franklin
CICERO Cook
CISCO (61830) Piatt(70), Macon(29)
CISNE Wayne
CISSNA PARK Iroquois
CLARE De Kalb
CLAREMONT (62421) Richland(97), Crawford(1), Lawrence(1)
CLARENDON HILLS Du Page
CLAY CITY (62824) Clay(95), Wayne(4)
CLAYTON (62324) Adams(97), Brown(2)
CLAYTONVILLE Iroquois
CLIFTON Iroquois
CLINTON De Witt
COAL CITY Grundy
COAL VALLEY (61240) Rock Island(75), Henry(24)
COATSBURG Adams
COBDEN Union
COELLO Franklin
COFFEEN Montgomery
COLCHESTER (62326) McDonough(97), Hancock(2)
COLETA Whiteside
COLFAX McLean
COLLINSVILLE (62234) Madison(90), St. Clair(9)
COLLISON Vermilion
COLMAR McDonough
COLONA Henry
COLP Williamson
COLUMBIA (62236) Monroe(94), St. Clair(5)
COLUSA Hancock
COMPTON Lee
CONCORD Morgan
CONGERVILLE (61729) Woodford(96), McLean(3)
COOKSVILLE McLean
CORDOVA Rock Island
CORNELL Livingston
CORNLAND Logan
CORTLAND De Kalb
COTTAGE HILLS Madison
COULTERVILLE (62237) Randolph(46), Washington(27), Perry(26)
COUNTRY CLUB HILLS Cook
COWDEN (62422) Shelby(74), Fayette(25)
CREAL SPRINGS (62922) Williamson(71), Johnson(28)
CRESCENT CITY Iroquois
CRESTON Ogle
CRETE Will
CREVE COEUR Tazewell

CROPSEY (61731) McLean(67), Ford(31), Livingston(1)
CROSSVILLE White
CRYSTAL LAKE McHenry
CUBA Fulton
CULLOM (60929) Livingston(89), Ford(10)
CUTLER (62238) Perry(95), Randolph(4)
CYPRESS (62923) Johnson(85), Pulaski(8), Union(5)
DAHINDA Knox
DAHLGREN (62828) Hamilton(97), Wayne(2)
DAKOTA Stephenson
DALE Hamilton
DALLAS CITY (62330) Hancock(93), Henderson(6)
DALTON CITY (61925) Macon(57), Moultrie(42)
DALZELL Bureau
DANA (61321) La Salle(87), Livingston(4), Woodford(4), Marshall(3)
DANFORTH Iroquois
DANVERS (61732) McLean(63), Tazewell(36)
DANVILLE Vermilion
DARIEN Du Page
DAVIS (61019) Stephenson(65), Winnebago(34)
DAVIS JUNCTION (61020) Ogle(94), Winnebago(5)
DAWSON Sangamon
DE KALB De Kalb
DE LAND Piatt
DE SOTO (62924) Jackson(80), Williamson(19)
DECATUR Macon
DEER CREEK Tazewell
DEER GROVE (61243) Whiteside(89), Bureau(5), Lee(5)
DEERE CO GROUP CLAIMS Rock Island
DEERFIELD (60015) Lake(95), Cook(4)
DEERFIELD Cook
DEKALB De Kalb
DELAVAN Tazewell
DENNISON (62423) Clark(90), Edgar(9)
DEPUE Bureau
DES PLAINES Cook
DEWEY (61840) Champaign(97), Ford(2)
DEWITT De Witt
DIETERICH (62424) Effingham(90), Jasper(9)
DIVERNON Sangamon
DIX (62830) Jefferson(95), Marion(4)
DIXON (61021) Lee(91), Ogle(8)
DOLTON Cook
DONGOLA (62926) Union(90), Pulaski(9)
DONNELLSON (62019) Montgomery(52), Bond(47)
DONOVAN Iroquois
DORSEY (62021) Madison(93), Macoupin(6)
DOVER Bureau
DOW Jersey
DOWELL Jackson
DOWNERS GROVE Du Page
DOWNS McLean
DU BOIS (62831) Washington(91), Perry(8)
DU QUOIN (62832) Perry(96), Jackson(3)
DUNDAS (62425) Richland(86), Jasper(13)
DUNDEE Kane
DUNFERMLINE Fulton
DUNLAP Peoria
DUPO St. Clair
DURAND Winnebago
DWIGHT (60420) Livingston(93), Grundy(6)
EAGARVILLE Macoupin
EARLVILLE (60518) La Salle(72), De Kalb(22), Lee(4)
EAST ALTON Madison
EAST CARONDELET (62240) St. Clair(97), Monroe(2)
EAST DUBUQUE Jo Daviess
EAST GALESBURG Knox

EAST LYNN Vermilion
EAST MOLINE Rock Island
EAST PEORIA (61611) Tazewell(86), Woodford(13)
EAST SAINT LOUIS St. Clair
EASTON Mason
EDDYVILLE Pope
EDELSTEIN (61526) Peoria(90), Marshall(8), Stark(1)
EDGEWOOD (62426) Effingham(58), Clay(37), Fayette(4)
EDINBURG Christian
EDWARDS Peoria
EDWARDSVILLE Madison
EFFINGHAM Effingham
EL PASO (61738) Woodford(96), McLean(2)
ELBURN Kane
ELCO Alexander
ELDENA Lee
ELDORADO (62930) Saline(98), Gallatin(1)
ELDRED Greene
ELEROY Stephenson
ELGIN (60120) Kane(56), Cook(43)
ELGIN Du Page
ELGIN Kane
ELIZABETH (61028) Jo Daviess(98), Carroll(1)
ELIZABETHTOWN (62931) Hardin(82), Gallatin(17)
ELK GROVE VILLAGE (60007) Cook(96), Du Page(3)
ELK GROVE VILLAGE Cook
ELKHART Logan
ELKVILLE Jackson
ELLERY (62833) Edwards(56), Wayne(43)
ELLIOTT Ford
ELLIS GROVE Randolph
ELLISVILLE Fulton
ELLSWORTH McLean
ELMHURST Du Page
ELMWOOD Peoria
ELMWOOD PARK Cook
ELSAH Jersey
ELVASTON Hancock
ELWIN Macon
ELWOOD Will
EMDEN (62635) Tazewell(94), Logan(5)
EMINGTON Livingston
EMMA White
ENERGY Williamson
ENFIELD (62835) White(94), Hamilton(5)
EOLA Du Page
EQUALITY (62934) Gallatin(68), Saline(31)
ERIE (61250) Whiteside(94), Henry(5)
ESMOND (60129) Ogle(53), De Kalb(46)
ESSEX (60935) Kankakee(98), Will(1)
EUREKA Woodford
EVANSTON Cook
EVANSVILLE Randolph
EVERGREEN PARK Cook
EWING (62836) Franklin(98), Jefferson(1)
FAIRBURY (61739) Livingston(97), McLean(2)
FAIRFIELD Wayne
FAIRMOUNT Vermilion
FAIRVIEW Fulton
FAIRVIEW HEIGHTS St. Clair
FARINA (62838) Fayette(55), Clay(29), Marion(13), Effingham(1)
FARMER CITY (61842) De Witt(89), McLean(9), Piatt(1)
FARMERSVILLE Montgomery
FARMINGTON (61531) Fulton(92), Peoria(5), Knox(1)
FENTON (61251) Whiteside(95), Rock Island(5)
FERRIS Hancock
FIATT Fulton
FIDELITY Jersey
FIELDON (62031) Jersey(97), Greene(2)
FILLMORE Montgomery
FINDLAY Shelby

FISHER (61843) Champaign(94), McLean(5)
FITHIAN Vermilion
FLANAGAN Livingston
FLAT ROCK (62427) Crawford(93), Lawrence(6)
FLORA Clay
FLOSSMOOR Cook
FOOSLAND (61845) Champaign(76), Ford(14), McLean(9)
FOREST CITY Mason
FOREST PARK Cook
FORREST Livingston
FORRESTON Ogle
FORSYTH Macon
FORT SHERIDAN Lake
FOWLER Adams
FOX LAKE Lake
FOX RIVER GROVE (60021) McHenry(96), Lake(3)
FOX VALLEY Du Page
FRANKFORT Will
FRANKFORT HEIGHTS Franklin
FRANKLIN (62638) Morgan(98), Macoupin(1)
FRANKLIN GROVE (61031) Lee(96), Ogle(3)
FRANKLIN PARK Cook
FRANKLIN PARK Du Page
FREDERICK Schuyler
FREEBURG St. Clair
FREEMAN SPUR Williamson
FREEPORT Stephenson
FULTON Whiteside
FULTS Monroe
GALATIA (62935) Saline(97), Hamilton(1)
GALATIA Saline
GALENA Jo Daviess
GALESBURG Knox
GALT Whiteside
GALVA (61434) Henry(97), Knox(1)
GARDEN PRAIRIE (61038) Boone(89), McHenry(10)
GARDNER Grundy
GAYS (61928) Moultrie(75), Coles(16), Shelby(7)
GEFF Wayne
GENESEO Henry
GENEVA Kane
GENOA De Kalb
GEORGETOWN Vermilion
GERLAW Warren
GERMAN VALLEY (61039) Stephenson(69), Ogle(30)
GERMANTOWN Clinton
GIBSON CITY (60936) Ford(98), Champaign(1)
GIFFORD Champaign
GILBERTS Kane
GILLESPIE Macoupin
GILMAN Iroquois
GILSON Knox
GIRARD (62640) Macoupin(89), Montgomery(10)
GLADSTONE Henderson
GLASFORD (61533) Peoria(82), Fulton(17)
GLEN CARBON Madison
GLEN ELLYN Du Page
GLENARM Sangamon
GLENCOE Cook
GLENDALE HEIGHTS Du Page
GLENVIEW Cook
GLENVIEW NAS Cook
GLENWOOD Cook
GODFREY (62035) Madison(87), Jersey(12)
GOLCONDA (62938) Pope(90), Hardin(5), Massac(4)
GOLDEN Adams
GOLDEN EAGLE Calhoun
GOLDEN GATE Wayne
GOLF Cook
GOOD HOPE McDonough

GOODFIELD Woodford
GOODWINE Iroquois
GOREVILLE (62939) Johnson(92), Williamson(4), Union(3)
GORHAM Jackson
GRAFTON Jersey
GRAND CHAIN (62941) Pulaski(61), Massac(38)
GRAND RIDGE La Salle
GRAND TOWER Jackson
GRANITE CITY Madison
GRANT PARK (60940) Kankakee(95), Will(4)
GRANTSBURG (62943) Johnson(76), Massac(19), Pope(4)
GRANVILLE Putnam
GRAYMONT Livingston
GRAYSLAKE Lake
GRAYVILLE (62844) White(57), Edwards(42)
GREAT LAKES Lake
GREEN VALLEY Tazewell
GREENFIELD (62044) Greene(87), Macoupin(12)
GREENUP Cumberland
GREENVIEW Menard
GREENVILLE Bond
GRIDLEY (61744) McLean(91), Livingston(8)
GRIGGSVILLE Pike
GROVELAND Tazewell
GURNEE Lake
HAGARSTOWN Fayette
HAMBURG Calhoun
HAMEL Madison
HAMILTON Hancock
HAMLETSBURG Pope
HAMMOND (61929) Piatt(97), Moultrie(2)
HAMPSHIRE (60140) Kane(98), De Kalb(1)
HAMPTON Rock Island
HANNA CITY Peoria
HANOVER Jo Daviess
HANOVER PARK (60133) Cook(57), Du Page(42)
HARDIN Calhoun
HARMON (61042) Lee(98), Whiteside(1)
HARRISBURG Saline
HARRISTOWN Macon
HARTFORD Madison
HARTSBURG (62643) Montgomery(60), Logan(40)
HARVARD McHenry
HARVEL (62538) Montgomery(83), Christian(16)
HARVEY Cook
HARWOOD HEIGHTS Cook
HAVANA (62644) Mason(94), Fulton(5)
HAZEL CREST Cook
HEBRON McHenry
HECKER Monroe
HENDERSON Knox
HENNEPIN Putnam
HENNING Vermilion
HENRY Marshall
HERALD White
HEROD (62947) Saline(43), Hardin(31), Pope(25)
HERRICK (62431) Shelby(53), Fayette(46)
HERRIN Williamson
HERSCHER (60941) Kankakee(96), Iroquois(2), Ford(1)
HETTICK Macoupin
HEYWORTH (61745) McLean(96), De Witt(3)
HICKORY HILLS Cook
HIDALGO Jasper
HIGHLAND (62249) Madison(94), Clinton(4)
HIGHLAND PARK Lake
HIGHWOOD Lake
HILLSBORO Montgomery
HILLSDALE Rock Island
HILLSIDE Cook

HILLVIEW Greene
HINCKLEY De Kalb
HINDSBORO (61930) Douglas(81), Coles(18)
HINES Cook
HINSDALE (60527) Du Page(91), Cook(8)
HINSDALE Du Page
HOFFMAN Clinton
HOFFMAN ESTATES Cook
HOLCOMB Ogle
HOMER (61849) Champaign(84), Vermilion(15)
HOMETOWN Cook
HOMEWOOD Cook
HOOPESTON (60942) Vermilion(91), Iroquois(8)
HOOPPOLE Henry
HOPEDALE Tazewell
HOPKINS PARK Kankakee
HOYLETON Washington
HUDSON (61748) McLean(98), Woodford(1)
HUEY Clinton
HULL (62343) Pike(89), Adams(10)
HUMBOLDT Coles
HUME Edgar
HUNTLEY (60142) McHenry(76), Kane(23)
HUNTSVILLE Schuyler
HURST Williamson
HUTSONVILLE Crawford
ILLINOIS CITY (61259) Rock Island(98), Mercer(1)
ILLIOPOLIS (62539) Sangamon(94), Macon(5)
INA (62846) Jefferson(98), Franklin(1)
INDIANOLA (61850) Vermilion(98), Edgar(1)
INDUSTRY (61440) McDonough(97), Schuyler(2)
INGLESIDE Lake
INGRAHAM (62434) Jasper(84), Clay(15)
IOLA Clay
IPAVA Fulton
IROQUOIS Iroquois
IRVING Montgomery
IRVINGTON Washington
ISLAND LAKE (60042) Lake(51), McHenry(48)
ITASCA Du Page
IUKA Marion
IVESDALE (61851) Champaign(89), Piatt(8), Douglas(2)
JACKSONVILLE Morgan
JACOB Jackson
JANESVILLE Cumberland
JEFFERSON BANK Peoria
JERSEYVILLE Jersey
JEWETT (62436) Jasper(59), Cumberland(40)
JOHNSONVILLE Wayne
JOHNSTON CITY Williamson
JOLIET Will
JONESBORO Union
JOPPA Massac
JOY (61260) Mercer(94), Rock Island(5)
JUNCTION Gallatin
JUSTICE Cook
KAMPSVILLE (62053) Calhoun(97), Pike(2)
KANE (62054) Greene(58), Jersey(41)
KANEVILLE Kane
KANKAKEE Kankakee
KANSAS (61933) Edgar(85), Clark(12), Coles(2)
KARBERS RIDGE Hardin
KARNAK (62956) Pulaski(50), Massac(48)
KASBEER Bureau
KEENES (62851) Wayne(65), Jefferson(27), Marion(7)
KEENSBURG Wabash
KEITHSBURG (61442) Mercer(95), Henderson(4)
KELL (62853) Marion(98), Jefferson(1)

KEMPTON (60946) Ford(81), Livingston(18)
KENILWORTH Cook
KENNEY (61749) De Witt(72), Logan(15), Macon(12)
KENT (61044) Stephenson(65), Jo Daviess(35)
KEWANEE Henry
KEYESPORT (62253) Bond(59), Clinton(37), Fayette(3)
KILBOURNE Mason
KINCAID Christian
KINDERHOOK Pike
KINGS Ogle
KINGSTON (60145) De Kalb(93), Boone(6)
KINGSTON MINES Peoria
KINMUNDY (62854) Marion(97), Clay(1), Fayette(1)
KINSMAN (60437) Grundy(97), La Salle(2)
KIRKLAND (60146) De Kalb(89), Boone(8), Ogle(1), Winnebago(1)
KIRKWOOD (61447) Warren(92), Henderson(7)
KNOXVILLE Knox
LA FAYETTE (61449) Knox(53), Stark(46)
LA GRANGE Cook
LA GRANGE PARK Cook
LA HARPE (61450) Hancock(56), McDonough(41), Henderson(1)
LA MOILLE (61330) Bureau(52), Lee(47)
LA PLACE Piatt
LA PRAIRIE (62346) Adams(63), Schuyler(22), Hancock(14)
LA ROSE Marshall
LA SALLE La Salle
LACON Marshall
LADD Bureau
LAFOX Kane
LAKE BLUFF Lake
LAKE FOREST Lake
LAKE FORK Logan
LAKE IN THE HILLS McHenry
LAKE VILLA Lake
LAKE ZURICH Lake
LAKEWOOD Shelby
LANARK Carroll
LANCASTER Wabash
LANE De Witt
LANSING Cook
LATHAM (62543) Logan(82), Macon(17)
LAURA (61451) Peoria(92), Stark(7)
LAWNDALE Logan
LAWRENCEVILLE Lawrence
LE ROY McLean
LEAF RIVER (61047) Ogle(96), Winnebago(2), Stephenson(1)
LEBANON St. Clair
LEE (60530) Lee(56), De Kalb(43)
LEE CENTER Lee
LELAND (60531) La Salle(64), De Kalb(35)
LEMONT (60439) Cook(51), Du Page(44), Will(4)
LENA (61048) Stephenson(96), Jo Daviess(3)
LENZBURG (62255) St. Clair(92), Washington(7)
LEONORE La Salle
LERNA (62440) Coles(72), Cumberland(27)
LEWISTOWN Fulton
LEXINGTON McLean
LIBERTY Adams
LIBERTYVILLE Lake
LIMA Adams
LINCOLN Logan
LINCOLN'S NEW SALEM Menard
LINCOLNSHIRE Lake
LINCOLNWOOD Cook
LINDENWOOD Ogle
LISLE Du Page
LITCHFIELD (62056) Montgomery(93), Macoupin(6)
LITERBERRY Morgan

LITTLE YORK (61453) Warren(87), Henderson(12)
LITTLETON (61452) Schuyler(83), McDonough(16)
LIVERPOOL Fulton
LIVINGSTON Madison
LOAMI Sangamon
LOCKPORT Will
LODA (60948) Iroquois(95), Ford(4)
LOGAN Franklin
LOMAX Henderson
LOMBARD Du Page
LONDON MILLS (61544) Fulton(86), Knox(13)
LONG GROVE Lake
LONG POINT Livingston
LONGVIEW (61852) Champaign(82), Douglas(17)
LOOGOOTEE Fayette
LORAINE (62349) Adams(94), Hancock(5)
LOSTANT (61334) La Salle(89), Putnam(9)
LOUISVILLE Clay
LOVEJOY St. Clair
LOVES PARK (61111) Winnebago(97), Boone(2)
LOVES PARK Winnebago
LOVINGTON (61937) Moultrie(94), Macon(3), Piatt(1)
LOWDER Sangamon
LOWPOINT Woodford
LUDLOW (60949) Champaign(90), Ford(9)
LYNDON Whiteside
LYNN CENTER (61262) Henry(92), Mercer(7)
LYONS Cook
MACEDONIA (62860) Franklin(88), Hamilton(11)
MACHESNEY PARK Winnebago
MACKINAW Tazewell
MACOMB McDonough
MACON Macon
MAEYSTOWN Monroe
MAGNOLIA (61336) Putnam(96), Marshall(3)
MAHOMET Champaign
MAKANDA (62958) Jackson(69), Williamson(15), Union(14)
MALDEN Bureau
MALTA De Kalb
MANCHESTER Scott
MANHATTAN Will
MANITO (61546) Mason(83), Tazewell(16)
MANLIUS Bureau
MANSFIELD (61854) Piatt(95), McLean(4)
MANTENO (60950) Kankakee(98), Will(1)
MAPLE PARK (60151) Kane(81), De Kalb(18)
MAPLETON Peoria
MAQUON Knox
MARENGO McHenry
MARIETTA (61459) Fulton(60), McDonough(39)
MARINE Madison
MARION Williamson
MARISSA (62257) St. Clair(70), Washington(27), Randolph(1)
MARK Putnam
MARKHAM Cook
MAROA Macon
MARSEILLES La Salle
MARSHALL (62441) Clark(98), Edgar(1)
MARTINSVILLE (62442) Clark(98), Crawford(1)
MARTINTON Iroquois
MARYVILLE Madison
MASCOUTAH St. Clair
MASON (62443) Effingham(90), Clay(9)
MASON CITY Mason
MATHERVILLE Mercer
MATTESON Cook
MATTOON Coles
MAUNIE White
MAYWOOD Cook

MAZON Grundy
MC CLURE (62957) Alexander(65), Union(34)
MC CONNELL Stephenson
MC HENRY McHenry
MC LEAN (61754) McLean(96), Logan(3)
MC LEANSBORO Hamilton
MC NABB Putnam
MCHENRY (60051) McHenry(89), Lake(10)
MCHENRY Cook
MCHENRY McHenry
MECHANICSBURG (62545) Sangamon(63), Christian(36)
MEDIA (61460) Henderson(95), Warren(4)
MEDINAH Du Page
MEDORA (62063) Jersey(58), Macoupin(41)
MELROSE PARK Cook
MELVIN (60952) Ford(95), Livingston(4)
MENARD Randolph
MENDON (62351) Adams(85), Hancock(14)
MENDOTA (61342) La Salle(97), Bureau(1), Lee(1)
MEREDOSIA (62665) Morgan(95), Scott(2), Cass(2)
MERNA McLean
METAMORA Woodford
METCALF Edgar
METROPOLIS Massac
MICHAEL Calhoun
MIDDLETOWN (62666) Logan(85), Menard(14)
MIDLOTHIAN Cook
MILAN Rock Island
MILFORD Iroquois
MILL SHOALS White
MILLBROOK Kendall
MILLCREEK Union
MILLEDGEVILLE (61051) Carroll(94), Ogle(3), Whiteside(2)
MILLER CITY Alexander
MILLINGTON Kendall
MILLSTADT St. Clair
MILMINE Piatt
MILTON Pike
MINERAL Bureau
MINIER Tazewell
MINONK (61760) Woodford(93), Marshall(6)
MINOOKA (60447) Grundy(48), Kendall(26), Will(24)
MOBIL OIL CREDIT CORP Du Page
MODE Shelby
MODESTO (62667) Macoupin(98), Morgan(1)
MODOC Randolph
MOKENA Will
MOLINE Rock Island
MOMENCE Kankakee
MONEE Will
MONMOUTH Warren
MONROE CENTER (61052) Ogle(94), Winnebago(2), De Kalb(2)
MONTGOMERY (60538) Kendall(61), Kane(38)
MONTGOMERY WARD Du Page
MONTICELLO Piatt
MONTROSE (62445) Jasper(55), Cumberland(33), Effingham(11)
MOOSEHEART Kane
MORO Madison
MORRIS Grundy
MORRISON Whiteside
MORRISONVILLE (62546) Christian(90), Montgomery(9)
MORTON Tazewell
MORTON GROVE Cook
MOSSVILLE Peoria
MOUND CITY Pulaski
MOUNDS Pulaski
MOUNT AUBURN (62547) Christian(97), Macon(2)

MOUNT CARMEL Wabash
MOUNT CARROLL (61053) Carroll(92), Jo Daviess(7)
MOUNT ERIE Wayne
MOUNT MORRIS Ogle
MOUNT OLIVE (62069) Macoupin(97), Montgomery(2)
MOUNT PROSPECT Cook
MOUNT PULASKI Logan
MOUNT STERLING Brown
MOUNT VERNON Jefferson
MOWEAQUA (62550) Shelby(63), Christian(36)
MOZIER Calhoun
MT ZION Macon
MUDDY Saline
MULBERRY GROVE (62262) Bond(87), Fayette(11), Montgomery(1)
MULKEYTOWN Franklin
MUNCIE Vermilion
MUNDELEIN Lake
MURDOCK Douglas
MURPHYSBORO Jackson
MURRAYVILLE Morgan
NACHUSA Lee
NAPERVILLE (60565) Du Page(65), Will(34)
NAPERVILLE (60564) Will(81), Du Page(18)
NAPERVILLE Du Page
NASHVILLE Washington
NASON Jefferson
NATIONAL STOCK YARDS St. Clair
NAUVOO Hancock
NEBO (62355) Pike(62), Calhoun(37)
NELSON Lee
NEOGA (62447) Cumberland(87), Shelby(11), Coles(1)
NEPONSET (61345) Bureau(97), Stark(2)
NEW ATHENS (62264) St. Clair(97), Monroe(2)
NEW BADEN (62265) Clinton(91), St. Clair(8)
NEW BEDFORD Bureau
NEW BERLIN Sangamon
NEW BOSTON Mercer
NEW BURNSIDE (62967) Johnson(88), Williamson(11)
NEW CANTON Pike
NEW DOUGLAS (62074) Madison(90), Bond(4), Macoupin(3), Montgomery(1)
NEW HAVEN (62867) Gallatin(59), White(40)
NEW HOLLAND (62671) Logan(95), Mason(4)
NEW LENOX Will
NEW MEMPHIS Clinton
NEW SALEM Pike
NEW WINDSOR (61465) Mercer(88), Henry(11)
NEWARK (60541) Kendall(91), Grundy(6), La Salle(2)
NEWMAN (61942) Douglas(91), Edgar(8)
NEWTON (62448) Jasper(97), Richland(2)
NIANTIC Macon
NILES Cook
NILWOOD Macoupin
NIOTA Hancock
NOBLE (62868) Richland(94), Clay(4), Wayne(1)
NOKOMIS (62075) Montgomery(95), Christian(4)
NORA Jo Daviess
NORMAL McLean
NORRIS Fulton
NORRIS CITY (62869) White(94), Gallatin(3), Hamilton(1)
NORTH AURORA Kane
NORTH CHICAGO Lake
NORTH HENDERSON (61466) Mercer(96), Warren(4)
NORTHBROOK Cook
O FALLON St. Clair

OAK FOREST Cook
OAK LAWN Cook
OAK PARK Cook
OAKDALE (62268) Washington(94), Perry(5)
OAKFORD (62673) Cass(51), Menard(48)
OAKLAND (61943) Coles(78), Douglas(14), Edgar(6)
OAKLEY Macon
OAKWOOD Vermilion
OBLONG (62449) Crawford(90), Jasper(8)
OCONEE (62553) Shelby(50), Christian(29), Montgomery(20)
ODELL Livingston
ODIN Marion
OGDEN (61859) Champaign(88), Vermilion(11)
OGLESBY La Salle
OHIO (61349) Bureau(77), Lee(21), Cass(1)
OHLMAN Montgomery
OKAWVILLE Washington
OLIVE BRANCH Alexander
OLMSTED Pulaski
OLNEY Richland
OLYMPIA FIELDS Cook
OMAHA Gallatin
ONARGA Iroquois
ONEIDA Knox
OPDYKE Jefferson
OPHEIM Henry
OPHIEM Henry
OQUAWKA Henderson
ORANGEVILLE Stephenson
ORAVILLE Jackson
OREANA Macon
OREGON Ogle
ORIENT Franklin
ORION (61273) Henry(83), Rock Island(16)
ORLAND PARK Cook
OSCO Henry
OSWEGO Kendall
OTTAWA La Salle
OWANECO (62555) Christian(91), Macon(8)
OZARK Johnson
PALATINE (60074) Cook(98), Lake(1)
PALATINE Cook
PALESTINE Crawford
PALMER Christian
PALMYRA Macoupin
PALOMA Adams
PALOS HEIGHTS Cook
PALOS HILLS Cook
PALOS PARK Cook
PANA (62557) Christian(92), Shelby(5), Montgomery(1)
PANAMA Montgomery
PAPINEAU Iroquois
PARIS Edgar
PARK FOREST (60466) Cook(54), Will(45)
PARK RIDGE Cook
PARKERSBURG Richland
PATOKA (62875) Marion(94), Fayette(5)
PATTERSON Greene
PAW PAW Lee
PAWNEE (62558) Sangamon(88), Christian(8), Montgomery(2)
PAXTON (60957) Ford(96), Champaign(2)
PAYSON Adams
PEARL (62361) Pike(97), Calhoun(2)
PEARL CITY (61062) Stephenson(96), Jo Daviess(2)
PECATONICA (61063) Winnebago(91), Stephenson(8)
PEKIN Tazewell
PENFIELD (61862) Champaign(79), Vermilion(20)
PEORIA Peoria
PEORIA HEIGHTS Peoria
PEOTONE (60468) Will(97), Kankakee(2)
PERCY (62272) Randolph(80), Perry(19)
PERKS Pulaski

PERRY Pike
PERU (61354) La Salle(98), Bureau(1)
PESOTUM Champaign
PETERSBURG Menard
PHILO Champaign
PIASA (62079) Macoupin(66), Jersey(33)
PIERRON Bond
PINCKNEYVILLE Perry
PIPER CITY (60959) Ford(93), Livingston(5)
PITTSBURG Williamson
PITTSFIELD Pike
PLAINFIELD (60544) Will(98), Kendall(1)
PLAINVIEW Macoupin
PLAINVILLE Adams
PLANO Kendall
PLATO CENTER Kane
PLEASANT HILL (62366) Pike(98), Calhoun(1)
PLEASANT PLAINS Sangamon
PLYMOUTH (62367) Hancock(50), McDonough(41), Schuyler(7)
POCAHONTAS (62275) Bond(68), Madison(22), Clinton(8)
POLO Ogle
POMONA Jackson
PONTIAC Livingston
POPLAR GROVE Boone
PORT BYRON Rock Island
POSEN Cook
POTOMAC Vermilion
PRAIRIE CITY McDonough
PRAIRIE DU ROCHER (62277) Randolph(57), Monroe(42)
PREEMPTION Mercer
PRINCETON Bureau
PRINCEVILLE (61559) Peoria(97), Stark(2)
PROPHETSTOWN (61277) Whiteside(80), Henry(19)
PROSPECT HEIGHTS Cook
PULASKI Pulaski
PUTNAM (61560) Putnam(93), Bureau(4), Marshall(2)
QUINCY Adams
RADOM Washington
RALEIGH Saline
RAMSEY (62080) Fayette(92), Montgomery(6), Shelby(1)
RANKIN (60960) Vermilion(72), Ford(21), Iroquois(3), Champaign(2)
RANSOM (60470) La Salle(90), Grundy(6), Livingston(2)
RANTOUL Champaign
RAPIDS CITY Rock Island
RARITAN Henderson
RAYMOND (62560) Montgomery(90), Macoupin(9)
RED BUD (62278) Randolph(68), Monroe(31)
REDDICK (60961) Kankakee(83), Livingston(13), Grundy(2)
REDMON Edgar
RENAULT Monroe
REYNOLDS (61279) Rock Island(73), Mercer(26)
RICHMOND McHenry
RICHTON PARK Cook
RICHVIEW (62877) Washington(97), Jefferson(2)
RIDGE FARM (61870) Vermilion(95), Edgar(4)
RIDGWAY Gallatin
RIDOTT Stephenson
RINARD Wayne
RINGWOOD McHenry
RIO (61472) Knox(98), Mercer(1)
RIVER FOREST Cook
RIVER GROVE Cook
RIVERDALE Cook
RIVERSIDE Cook
RIVERTON Sangamon
ROANOKE Woodford
ROBBINS Cook

ROBERTS (60962) Ford(97), Livingston(2)
ROBINSON Crawford
ROCHELLE (61068) Ogle(97), Lee(1)
ROCHESTER (62563) Sangamon(96), Christian(3)
ROCK CITY Stephenson
ROCK FALLS Whiteside
ROCK ISLAND Rock Island
ROCKBRIDGE (62081) Greene(98), Jersey(2)
ROCKFORD (61102) Winnebago(98), Ogle(1)
ROCKFORD (61114) Winnebago(96), Boone(3)
ROCKFORD Winnebago
ROCKPORT Pike
ROCKTON Winnebago
ROCKWOOD (62280) Jackson(58), Randolph(41)
ROLLING MEADOWS Cook
ROME Peoria
ROMEOVILLE Will
ROODHOUSE (62082) Greene(88), Scott(9), Morgan(1)
ROSAMOND (62083) Christian(61), Montgomery(38)
ROSCOE (61073) Winnebago(98), Boone(1)
ROSELLE (60172) Du Page(81), Cook(18)
ROSEVILLE (61473) McDonough(69), Warren(30)
ROSICLARE Hardin
ROSSVILLE Vermilion
ROUND LAKE Lake
ROXANA Madison
ROYAL Champaign
ROYALTON Franklin
RUSHVILLE Schuyler
RUSSELL Lake
RUTLAND (61358) La Salle(75), Marshall(24)
SADORUS (61872) Champaign(90), Douglas(9)
SAILOR SPRINGS Clay
SAINT ANNE (60964) Kankakee(93), Iroquois(6)
SAINT AUGUSTINE (61474) Knox(93), Warren(5), Fulton(1)
SAINT CHARLES Kane
SAINT DAVID Fulton
SAINT ELMO (62458) Fayette(91), Effingham(8)
SAINT FRANCISVILLE (62460) Lawrence(89), Wabash(10)
SAINT JACOB Madison
SAINT JOSEPH Champaign
SAINT LIBORY St. Clair
SAINT PETER Fayette
SAINTE MARIE Jasper
SALEM Marion
SAN JOSE (62682) Mason(82), Tazewell(9), Logan(8)
SANDOVAL (62882) Marion(92), Clinton(7)
SANDWICH (60548) De Kalb(77), La Salle(19), Kendall(3)
SAUNEMIN Livingston
SAVANNA Carroll
SAVOY Champaign
SAWYERVILLE Macoupin
SAYBROOK McLean
SCALES MOUND Jo Daviess
SCHAUMBURG Cook
SCHELLER (62883) Jefferson(62), Franklin(29), Perry(7)
SCHILLER PARK Cook
SCIOTA (61475) McDonough(87), Warren(11)
SCIOTO MILLS Stephenson
SCIOTO MILLSX Stephenson
SCOTT AIR FORCE BASE St. Clair
SCOTTVILLE Macoupin
SEATON (61476) Mercer(88), Henderson(10), Warren(1)

SEATONVILLE Bureau
SECOR Woodford
SENECA (61360) La Salle(83), Grundy(16)
SERENA La Salle
SESSER Franklin
SEWARD Winnebago
SEYMOUR Champaign
SHABBONA De Kalb
SHANNON (61078) Carroll(84), Stephenson(8), Ogle(7)
SHATTUC Clinton
SHAWNEETOWN Gallatin
SHEFFIELD Bureau
SHELBYVILLE Shelby
SHELDON Iroquois
SHERIDAN La Salle
SHERMAN Sangamon
SHERRARD Mercer
SHIPMAN Macoupin
SHIRLAND Winnebago
SHIRLEY McLean
SHOBONIER (62885) Fayette(95), Marion(4)
SHUMWAY (62461) Effingham(93), Shelby(6)
SIBLEY Ford
SIDELL (61876) Vermilion(84), Edgar(15)
SIDNEY Champaign
SIGEL (62462) Cumberland(59), Shelby(39), Effingham(1)
SILVIS Rock Island
SIMPSON (62985) Johnson(86), Pope(13)
SIMS Wayne
SKOKIE Cook
SMITHBORO Bond
SMITHFIELD Fulton
SMITHSHIRE (61478) Warren(94), Henderson(5)
SMITHTON St. Clair
SOLON MILLS McHenry
SOMONAUK (60552) De Kalb(58), La Salle(41)
SORENTO (62086) Bond(81), Montgomery(16), Madison(1)
SOUTH BELOIT (61080) Winnebago(96), Boone(3)
SOUTH ELGIN Kane
SOUTH HOLLAND Cook
SOUTH PEKIN Tazewell
SOUTH ROXANA Madison
SOUTH WILMINGTON Grundy
SPARLAND (61565) Marshall(95), Peoria(4)
SPARTA Randolph
SPEER Stark
SPRING GROVE (60081) McHenry(79), Lake(20)
SPRING VALLEY Bureau
SPRINGERTON (62887) White(78), Hamilton(21)
SPRINGFIELD Sangamon
STANDARD Putnam
STANDARD CITY Macoupin
STANFORD McLean
STAUNTON (62088) Macoupin(85), Madison(14)
STEELEVILLE Randolph
STEGER (60475) Will(56), Cook(43)
STERLING (61081) Whiteside(98), Lee(1)
STEWARD (60553) Lee(98), De Kalb(1)
STEWARDSON Shelby
STILLMAN VALLEY (61084) Ogle(95), Winnebago(4)
STOCKLAND Iroquois
STOCKTON Jo Daviess
STONE PARK Cook
STONEFORT (62987) Saline(57), Williamson(34), Pope(7)
STONINGTON Christian
STOY Crawford
STRASBURG Shelby
STRAWN (61775) Livingston(90), Ford(9)
STREAMWOOD Cook

STREATOR (61364) La Salle(91), Livingston(8)
STRONGHURST Henderson
SUBLETTE Lee
SUGAR GROVE Kane
SULLIVAN Moultrie
SUMMER HILL Pike
SUMMERFIELD St. Clair
SUMMIT ARGO Cook
SUMNER (62466) Lawrence(88), Crawford(6), Richland(5)
SUTTER (62373) Hancock(94), Adams(5)
SYCAMORE (60178) De Kalb(97), Kane(2)
TABLE GROVE (61482) Fulton(52), Knox(25), McDonough(21)
TALLULA Menard
TAMAROA Perry
TAMMS Alexander
TAMPICO (61283) Whiteside(49), Bureau(48), Henry(2)
TAYLOR RIDGE Rock Island
TAYLOR SPRINGS Montgomery
TAYLORVILLE Christian
TECHNY Cook
TENNESSEE (62374) McDonough(58), Hancock(41)
TEUTOPOLIS (62467) Effingham(86), Jasper(8), Cumberland(5)
TEXICO (62889) Jefferson(69), Marion(30)
THAWVILLE (60968) Iroquois(56), Ford(41), Livingston(1)
THAYER Sangamon
THEBES Alexander
THOMASBORO Champaign
THOMPSONVILLE (62890) Franklin(67), Williamson(24), Saline(6), Hamilton(1)
THOMSON Carroll
THORNTON Cook
TILDEN Randolph
TILTON Vermilion
TIMEWELL (62375) Brown(97), Adams(2)
TINLEY PARK (60477) Cook(95), Will(4)
TISKILWA Bureau
TOLEDO Cumberland
TOLONO Champaign
TOLUCA Marshall
TONICA (61370) La Salle(98), Putnam(1)
TOPEKA Mason
TOULON (61483) Stark(61), Henry(38)
TOVEY Christian
TOWANDA McLean
TOWER HILL Shelby
TREMONT Tazewell
TRENTON (62293) Clinton(73), St. Clair(16), Madison(9)
TRILLA (62469) Cumberland(76), Coles(23)
TRIUMPH La Salle
TRIVOLI (61569) Peoria(97), Fulton(2)
TROY Madison
TROY GROVE La Salle
TUNNEL HILL Johnson
TUSCOLA Douglas
ULLIN (62992) Pulaski(97), Alexander(2)
UNION McHenry
UNION HILL Kankakee
UNITY Alexander
URBANA Champaign
URSA Adams
UTICA La Salle
VALIER Franklin
VALMEYER Monroe
VAN ORIN Bureau
VANDALIA Fayette
VARNA Marshall
VENEDY Washington
VENICE (62090) Madison(97), St. Clair(2)
VERGENNES Jackson
VERMILION Edgar
VERMONT (61484) McDonough(64), Fulton(34), Schuyler(1)
VERNON (62892) Marion(90), Fayette(9)
VERNON HILLS Lake

VERONA Grundy
VERSAILLES Brown
VICTORIA Knox
VIENNA Johnson
VILLA GROVE (61956) Douglas(95), Champaign(4)
VILLA PARK Du Page
VILLA RIDGE Pulaski
VIOLA Mercer
VIRDEN (62690) Macoupin(89), Montgomery(5), Sangamon(4)
VIRGIL Kane
VIRGINIA Cass
WADSWORTH Lake
WAGGONER (62572) Macoupin(58), Montgomery(41)
WALNUT (61376) Bureau(92), Lee(7)
WALNUT HILL (62893) Marion(57), Jefferson(42)
WALSH Randolph
WALSHVILLE Montgomery
WALTONVILLE Jefferson
WAPELLA De Witt
WARREN (61087) Jo Daviess(98), Stephenson(1)
WARRENSBURG Macon
WARRENVILLE Du Page
WARSAW (62379) Hancock(95), Adams(4)
WASCO Kane
WASHBURN (61570) Woodford(77), Marshall(22)
WASHINGTON Tazewell
WATAGA Knox
WATERLOO (62298) Monroe(92), St. Clair(7)
WATERMAN De Kalb
WATSEKA Iroquois
WATSON Effingham
WAUCONDA Lake
WAUKEGAN Lake
WAVERLY (62692) Morgan(76), Sangamon(23)
WAYNE (60184) Du Page(59), Kane(40)
WAYNE CITY (62895) Wayne(95), Hamilton(4)
WAYNESVILLE De Witt
WEDRON La Salle
WELDON (61882) De Witt(91), Macon(7)
WELLINGTON Iroquois
WENONA (61377) Marshall(88), La Salle(11)
WEST BROOKLYN Lee
WEST CHICAGO (60185) Du Page(98), Kane(1)
WEST CHICAGO Du Page
WEST FRANKFORT (62896) Franklin(94), Williamson(5)
WEST LIBERTY Jasper
WEST POINT Hancock
WEST SALEM (62476) Edwards(77), Wabash(19), Lawrence(1), Richland(1)
WEST UNION Clark
WEST YORK (62478) Clark(55), Crawford(44)
WESTCHESTER Cook
WESTERN SPRINGS Cook
WESTERVELT Shelby
WESTFIELD (62474) Clark(90), Coles(9)
WESTMONT Du Page
WESTVILLE Vermilion
WHEATON Du Page
WHEELER (62479) Jasper(97), Effingham(2)
WHEELING (60090) Cook(98), Lake(1)
WHITE HALL Greene
WHITE HEATH (61884) Piatt(77), Champaign(22)
WHITTINGTON Franklin
WILLIAMSFIELD (61489) Knox(89), Peoria(10)
WILLIAMSVILLE (62693) Sangamon(88), Logan(11)
WILLISVILLE Perry

WILLOW HILL Jasper
WILLOW SPRINGS Cook
WILLOWBROOK (60527) Du Page(91), Cook(8)
WILMETTE Cook
WILMINGTON (60481) Will(98), Grundy(1)
WILSONVILLE Macoupin
WINCHESTER (62694) Scott(86), Morgan(13)
WINDSOR (61957) Shelby(93), Moultrie(6)

WINFIELD Du Page
WINNEBAGO Winnebago
WINNETKA Cook
WINSLOW Stephenson
WINTHROP HARBOR Lake
WITT Montgomery
WOLF LAKE Union
WONDER LAKE McHenry
WOOD DALE Du Page
WOOD RIVER Madison

WOODHULL (61490) McDonough(47), Henry(47), Knox(4)
WOODLAND Iroquois
WOODLAWN Jefferson
WOODRIDGE Du Page
WOODSON Morgan
WOODSTOCK McHenry
WOOSUNG Ogle
WORDEN Madison
WORTH Cook

WRIGHTS Greene
WYANET Bureau
WYOMING (61491) Stark(96), Marshall(3)
XENIA (62899) Clay(96), Marion(3)
YALE (62481) Jasper(97), Cumberland(2)
YATES CITY Knox
YORKVILLE Kendall
ZEIGLER Franklin
ZION Lake

Illinois ZIP/City Cross Reference

60000-60000	PALATINE	60085-60085	WAUKEGAN	60156-60156	LAKE IN THE HILLS	60439-60439	LEMONT
60001-60001	ALDEN	60086-60086	NORTH CHICAGO	60157-60157	MEDINAH	60440-60440	BOLINGBROOK
60002-60002	ANTIOCH	60087-60087	WAUKEGAN	60158-60158	CAROL STREAM	60441-60441	LOCKPORT
60004-60006	ARLINGTON HEIGHTS	60088-60088	GREAT LAKES	60159-60159	SCHAUMBURG	60442-60442	MANHATTAN
60007-60007	ELK GROVE VILLAGE	60089-60089	BUFFALO GROVE	60160-60161	MELROSE PARK	60443-60443	MATTESON
60008-60008	ROLLING MEADOWS	60090-60090	WHEELING	60162-60162	HILLSIDE	60444-60444	MAZON
60009-60009	ELK GROVE VILLAGE	60091-60091	WILMETTE	60163-60163	BERKELEY	60445-60445	MIDLOTHIAN
60010-60011	BARRINGTON	60092-60092	LIBERTYVILLE	60164-60164	MELROSE PARK	60446-60446	ROMEOVILLE
60012-60012	CRYSTAL LAKE	60093-60093	WINNETKA	60165-60165	STONE PARK	60447-60447	MINOOKA
60013-60013	CARY	60094-60095	PALATINE	60168-60168	SCHAUMBURG	60448-60448	MOKENA
60014-60014	CRYSTAL LAKE	60096-60096	WINTHROP HARBOR	60170-60170	PLATO CENTER	60449-60449	MONEE
60015-60015	DEERFIELD	60097-60097	WONDER LAKE	60171-60171	RIVER GROVE	60450-60450	MORRIS
60016-60019	DES PLAINES	60098-60098	WOODSTOCK	60172-60172	ROSELLE	60451-60451	NEW LENOX
60020-60020	FOX LAKE	60099-60099	ZION	60173-60173	SCHAUMBURG	60452-60452	OAK FOREST
60021-60021	FOX RIVER GROVE	60100-60100	CAROL STREAM	60174-60175	SAINT CHARLES	60453-60454	OAK LAWN
60022-60022	GLENCOE	60101-60101	ADDISON	60176-60176	SCHILLER PARK	60455-60455	BRIDGEVIEW
60025-60025	GLENVIEW	60102-60102	ALGONQUIN	60177-60177	SOUTH ELGIN	60456-60456	HOMETOWN
60026-60026	GLENVIEW NAS	60103-60103	BARTLETT	60178-60178	SYCAMORE	60457-60457	HICKORY HILLS
60029-60029	GOLF	60104-60104	BELLWOOD	60179-60179	HOFFMAN ESTATES	60458-60458	JUSTICE
60030-60030	GRAYSLAKE	60105-60106	BENSENVILLE	60180-60180	UNION	60459-60459	BURBANK
60031-60031	GURNEE	60107-60107	STREAMWOOD	60181-60181	VILLA PARK	60460-60460	ODELL
60033-60033	HARVARD	60108-60108	BLOOMINGDALE	60182-60182	VIRGIL	60461-60461	OLYMPIA FIELDS
60034-60034	HEBRON	60109-60109	BURLINGTON	60183-60183	WASCO	60462-60462	ORLAND PARK
60035-60035	HIGHLAND PARK	60110-60110	CARPENTERSVILLE	60184-60184	WAYNE	60463-60463	PALOS HEIGHTS
60037-60037	FORT SHERIDAN	60111-60111	CLARE	60185-60186	WEST CHICAGO	60464-60464	PALOS PARK
60038-60038	PALATINE	60112-60112	CORTLAND	60187-60187	WHEATON	60465-60465	PALOS HILLS
60039-60039	CRYSTAL LAKE	60113-60113	CRESTON	60188-60188	CAROL STREAM	60466-60466	PARK FOREST
60040-60040	HIGHWOOD	60114-60114	ADDISON	60189-60189	WHEATON	60467-60467	ORLAND PARK
60041-60041	INGLESIDE	60115-60115	DE KALB	60190-60190	WINFIELD	60468-60468	PEOTONE
60042-60042	ISLAND LAKE	60115-60115	DEKALB	60191-60191	WOOD DALE	60469-60469	POSEN
60043-60043	KENILWORTH	60116-60116	CAROL STREAM	60192-60196	SCHAUMBURG	60470-60470	RANSOM
60044-60044	LAKE BLUFF	60117-60117	BLOOMINGDALE	60197-60197	CAROL STREAM	60471-60471	RICHTON PARK
60045-60045	LAKE FOREST	60118-60118	DUNDEE	60201-60209	EVANSTON	60472-60472	ROBBINS
60046-60046	LAKE VILLA	60119-60119	ELBURN	60251-60251	PALATINE	60473-60473	SOUTH HOLLAND
60047-60047	LAKE ZURICH	60120-60122	ELGIN	60296-60297	MCHENRY	60474-60474	SOUTH WILMINGTON
60048-60048	LIBERTYVILLE	60122-60122	CAROL STREAM	60301-60304	OAK PARK	60475-60475	STEGER
60049-60049	LONG GROVE	60123-60123	ELGIN	60305-60305	RIVER FOREST	60476-60476	THORNTON
60050-60050	MC HENRY	60125-60125	CAROL STREAM	60351-60351	CAROL STREAM	60477-60477	TINLEY PARK
60050-60050	MCHENRY	60126-60126	ELMHURST	60352-60352	MOBIL OIL CREDIT CORP	60478-60478	COUNTRY CLUB HILLS
60051-60051	MC HENRY	60128-60128	CAROL STREAM	60353-60353	CAROL STREAM	60479-60479	VERONA
60051-60051	MCHENRY	60129-60129	ESMOND	60398-60398	FRANKLIN PARK	60480-60480	WILLOW SPRINGS
60053-60053	MORTON GROVE	60130-60130	FOREST PARK	60399-60399	BENSENVILLE	60481-60481	WILMINGTON
60055-60055	PALATINE	60131-60131	FRANKLIN PARK	60401-60401	BEECHER	60482-60482	WORTH
60056-60056	MOUNT PROSPECT	60132-60132	CAROL STREAM	60402-60402	BERWYN	60490-60490	BOLINGBROOK
60060-60060	MUNDELEIN	60133-60133	HANOVER PARK	60406-60406	BLUE ISLAND	60491-60491	LOCKPORT
60061-60061	VERNON HILLS	60134-60134	GENEVA	60407-60407	BRACEVILLE	60499-60499	BEDFORD PARK
60062-60062	NORTHBROOK	60135-60135	GENOA	60408-60408	BRAIDWOOD	60501-60501	SUMMIT ARGO
60063-60063	DEERFIELD	60136-60136	GILBERTS	60409-60409	CALUMET CITY	60504-60507	AURORA
60064-60064	NORTH CHICAGO	60137-60138	GLEN ELLYN	60410-60410	CHANNAHON	60510-60510	BATAVIA
60065-60065	NORTHBROOK	60139-60139	GLENDALE HEIGHTS	60411-60412	CHICAGO HEIGHTS	60511-60511	BIG ROCK
60067-60067	PALATINE	60140-60140	HAMPSHIRE	60415-60415	CHICAGO RIDGE	60512-60512	BRISTOL
60068-60068	PARK RIDGE	60141-60141	HINES	60416-60416	COAL CITY	60513-60513	BROOKFIELD
60069-60069	LINCOLNSHIRE	60142-60142	HUNTLEY	60417-60417	CRETE	60514-60514	CLARENDON HILLS
60070-60070	PROSPECT HEIGHTS	60143-60143	ITASCA	60419-60419	DOLTON	60515-60516	DOWNERS GROVE
60071-60071	RICHMOND	60144-60144	KANEVILLE	60420-60420	DWIGHT	60517-60517	WOODRIDGE
60072-60072	RINGWOOD	60145-60145	KINGSTON	60421-60421	ELWOOD	60518-60518	EARLVILLE
60073-60073	ROUND LAKE	60146-60146	KIRKLAND	60422-60422	FLOSSMOOR	60519-60519	EOLA
60074-60074	PALATINE	60147-60147	LAFOX	60423-60423	FRANKFORT	60520-60520	HINCKLEY
60075-60075	RUSSELL	60148-60148	LOMBARD	60424-60424	GARDNER	60521-60523	HINSDALE
60076-60077	SKOKIE	60149-60149	MONTGOMERY WARD	60425-60425	GLENWOOD	60525-60525	LA GRANGE
60078-60078	PALATINE	60150-60150	MALTA	60426-60426	HARVEY	60526-60526	LA GRANGE PARK
60079-60079	WAUKEGAN	60151-60151	MAPLE PARK	60428-60428	MARKHAM	60527-60527	HINSDALE
60080-60080	SOLON MILLS	60152-60152	MARENGO	60429-60429	HAZEL CREST	60527-60527	WILLOWBROOK
60081-60081	SPRING GROVE	60153-60153	MAYWOOD	60430-60430	HOMEWOOD	60530-60530	LEE
60082-60082	TECHNY	60154-60154	WESTCHESTER	60431-60436	JOLIET	60531-60531	LELAND
60083-60083	WADSWORTH	60155-60155	CAROL STREAM	60437-60437	KINSMAN	60532-60532	LISLE
60084-60084	WAUCONDA	60155-60155	BROADVIEW	60438-60438	LANSING	60534-60534	LYONS

60536-60536 MILLBROOK	60948-60948 LODA	61077-61077 SEWARD	61329-61329 LADD
60537-60537 MILLINGTON	60949-60949 LUDLOW	61078-61078 SHANNON	61330-61330 LA MOILLE
60538-60538 MONTGOMERY	60950-60950 MANTENO	61079-61079 SHIRLAND	61331-61331 LEE CENTER
60539-60539 MOOSEHEART	60951-60951 MARTINTON	61080-61080 SOUTH BELOIT	61332-61332 LEONORE
60540-60540 NAPERVILLE	60952-60952 MELVIN	61081-61081 STERLING	61333-61333 LONG POINT
60541-60541 NEWARK	60953-60953 MILFORD	61084-61084 STILLMAN VALLEY	61334-61334 LOSTANT
60542-60542 NORTH AURORA	60954-60954 MOMENCE	61085-61085 STOCKTON	61335-61335 MC NABB
60543-60543 OSWEGO	60955-60955 ONARGA	61087-61087 WARREN	61336-61336 MAGNOLIA
60544-60544 PLAINFIELD	60956-60956 PAPINEAU	61088-61088 WINNEBAGO	61337-61337 MALDEN
60545-60545 PLANO	60957-60957 PAXTON	61089-61089 WINSLOW	61338-61338 MANLIUS
60546-60546 RIVERSIDE	60959-60959 PIPER CITY	61091-61091 WOOSUNG	61340-61340 MARK
60548-60548 SANDWICH	60960-60960 RANKIN	61100-61110 ROCKFORD	61341-61341 MARSEILLES
60549-60549 SERENA	60961-60961 REDDICK	61111-61111 LOVES PARK	61342-61342 MENDOTA
60550-60550 SHABBONA	60962-60962 ROBERTS	61112-61112 ROCKFORD	61344-61344 MINERAL
60551-60551 SHERIDAN	60963-60963 ROSSVILLE	61115-61115 MACHESNEY PARK	61345-61345 NEPONSET
60552-60552 SOMONAUK	60964-60964 SAINT ANNE	61125-61126 ROCKFORD	61346-61346 NEW BEDFORD
60553-60553 STEWARD	60966-60966 SHELDON	61130-61132 LOVES PARK	61348-61348 OGLESBY
60554-60554 SUGAR GROVE	60967-60967 STOCKLAND	61201-61206 ROCK ISLAND	61349-61349 OHIO
60555-60555 WARRENVILLE	60968-60968 THAWVILLE	61230-61230 ALBANY	61350-61350 OTTAWA
60556-60556 WATERMAN	60969-60969 UNION HILL	61231-61231 ALEDO	61353-61353 PAW PAW
60557-60557 WEDRON	60970-60970 WATSEKA	61232-61232 ANDALUSIA	61354-61354 PERU
60558-60558 WESTERN SPRINGS	60973-60973 WELLINGTON	61233-61233 ANDOVER	61356-61356 PRINCETON
60559-60559 WESTMONT	60974-60974 WOODLAND	61234-61234 ANNAWAN	61358-61358 RUTLAND
60560-60560 YORKVILLE	61001-61001 APPLE RIVER	61235-61235 ATKINSON	61359-61359 SEATONVILLE
60561-60561 DARIEN	61006-61006 ASHTON	61236-61236 BARSTOW	61360-61360 SENECA
60563-60567 NAPERVILLE	61007-61007 BAILEYVILLE	61237-61237 BUFFALO PRAIRIE	61361-61361 SHEFFIELD
60568-60568 AURORA	61008-61008 BELVIDERE	61238-61238 CAMBRIDGE	61362-61362 SPRING VALLEY
60570-60570 HINSDALE	61010-61010 BYRON	61239-61239 CARBON CLIFF	61363-61363 STANDARD
60572-60572 AURORA	61011-61011 CALEDONIA	61240-61240 COAL VALLEY	61364-61364 STREATOR
60597-60597 FOX VALLEY	61012-61012 CAPRON	61241-61241 COLONA	61367-61367 SUBLETTE
60598-60598 AURORA	61013-61013 CEDARVILLE	61242-61242 CORDOVA	61368-61368 TISKILWA
60599-60599 FOX VALLEY	61014-61014 CHADWICK	61243-61243 DEER GROVE	61369-61369 TOLUCA
60600-60626 CHICAGO	61015-61015 CHANA	61244-61244 EAST MOLINE	61370-61370 TONICA
60627-60627 RIVERDALE	61016-61016 CHERRY VALLEY	61249-61249 DEERE CO GROUP CLAIMS	61371-61371 TRIUMPH
60628-60634 CHICAGO	61017-61017 COLETA	61250-61250 ERIE	61372-61372 TROY GROVE
60635-60635 ELMWOOD PARK	61018-61018 DAKOTA	61251-61251 FENTON	61373-61373 UTICA
60636-60649 CHICAGO	61019-61019 DAVIS	61252-61252 FULTON	61374-61374 VAN ORIN
60650-60650 CICERO	61020-61020 DAVIS JUNCTION	61254-61254 GENESEO	61375-61375 VARNA
60651-60665 CHICAGO	61021-61021 DIXON	61256-61256 HAMPTON	61376-61376 WALNUT
60666-60666 AMF OHARE	61024-61024 DURAND	61257-61257 HILLSDALE	61377-61377 WENONA
60667-60701 CHICAGO	61025-61025 EAST DUBUQUE	61258-61258 HOOPPOLE	61378-61378 WEST BROOKLYN
60706-60706 HARWOOD HEIGHTS	61027-61027 ELEROY	61259-61259 ILLINOIS CITY	61379-61379 WYANET
60707-60707 ELMWOOD PARK	61028-61028 ELIZABETH	61260-61260 JOY	61401-61402 GALESBURG
60712-60712 LINCOLNWOOD	61030-61030 FORRESTON	61261-61261 LYNDON	61410-61410 ABINGDON
60714-60714 NILES	61031-61031 FRANKLIN GROVE	61262-61262 LYNN CENTER	61411-61411 ADAIR
60799-60799 CHICAGO	61032-61032 FREEPORT	61263-61263 MATHERVILLE	61412-61412 ALEXIS
60803-60803 ALSIP	61036-61036 GALENA	61264-61264 MILAN	61413-61413 ALPHA
60804-60804 CICERO	61037-61037 GALT	61265-61266 MOLINE	61414-61414 ALTONA
60805-60805 EVERGREEN PARK	61038-61038 GARDEN PRAIRIE	61270-61270 MORRISON	61415-61415 AVON
60827-60827 RIVERDALE	61039-61039 GERMAN VALLEY	61272-61272 NEW BOSTON	61416-61416 BARDOLPH
60901-60902 KANKAKEE	61041-61041 HANOVER	61273-61273 ORION	61417-61417 BERWICK
60910-60910 AROMA PARK	61042-61042 HARMON	61274-61274 OSCO	61418-61418 BIGGSVILLE
60911-60911 ASHKUM	61043-61043 HOLCOMB	61275-61275 PORT BYRON	61419-61419 BISHOP HILL
60912-60912 BEAVERVILLE	61044-61044 KENT	61276-61276 PREEMPTION	61420-61420 BLANDINSVILLE
60913-60913 BONFIELD	61045-61045 KINGS	61277-61277 PROPHETSTOWN	61421-61421 BRADFORD
60914-60914 BOURBONNAIS	61046-61046 LANARK	61278-61278 RAPIDS CITY	61422-61422 BUSHNELL
60915-60915 BRADLEY	61047-61047 LEAF RIVER	61279-61279 REYNOLDS	61423-61423 CAMERON
60917-60917 BUCKINGHAM	61048-61048 LENA	61281-61281 SHERRARD	61424-61424 CAMP GROVE
60918-60918 BUCKLEY	61049-61049 LINDENWOOD	61282-61282 SILVIS	61425-61425 CARMAN
60919-60919 CABERY	61050-61050 MC CONNELL	61283-61283 TAMPICO	61426-61426 CASTLETON
60920-60920 CAMPUS	61051-61051 MILLEDGEVILLE	61284-61284 TAYLOR RIDGE	61427-61427 CUBA
60921-60921 CHATSWORTH	61052-61052 MONROE CENTER	61285-61285 THOMSON	61428-61428 DAHINDA
60922-60922 CHEBANSE	61053-61053 MOUNT CARROLL	61299-61299 ROCK ISLAND	61430-61430 EAST GALESBURG
60924-60924 CISSNA PARK	61054-61054 MOUNT MORRIS	61301-61301 LA SALLE	61431-61431 ELLISVILLE
60926-60926 CLAYTONVILLE	61057-61057 NACHUSA	61310-61310 AMBOY	61432-61432 FAIRVIEW
60927-60927 CLIFTON	61058-61058 NELSON	61311-61311 ANCONA	61433-61433 FIATT
60928-60928 CRESCENT CITY	61059-61059 NORA	61312-61312 ARLINGTON	61434-61434 GALVA
60929-60929 CULLOM	61060-61060 ORANGEVILLE	61313-61313 BLACKSTONE	61435-61435 GERLAW
60930-60930 DANFORTH	61061-61061 OREGON	61314-61314 BUDA	61436-61436 GILSON
60931-60931 DONOVAN	61062-61062 PEARL CITY	61315-61315 BUREAU	61437-61437 GLADSTONE
60932-60932 EAST LYNN	61063-61063 PECATONICA	61316-61316 CEDAR POINT	61438-61438 GOOD HOPE
60933-60933 ELLIOTT	61064-61064 POLO	61317-61317 CHERRY	61439-61439 HENDERSON
60934-60934 EMINGTON	61065-61065 POPLAR GROVE	61318-61318 COMPTON	61440-61440 INDUSTRY
60935-60935 ESSEX	61067-61067 RIDOTT	61319-61319 CORNELL	61441-61441 IPAVA
60936-60936 GIBSON CITY	61068-61068 ROCHELLE	61320-61320 DALZELL	61442-61442 KEITHSBURG
60938-60938 GILMAN	61070-61070 ROCK CITY	61321-61321 DANA	61443-61443 KEWANEE
60939-60939 GOODWINE	61071-61071 ROCK FALLS	61322-61322 DEPUE	61447-61447 KIRKWOOD
60940-60940 GRANT PARK	61072-61072 ROCKTON	61323-61323 DOVER	61448-61448 KNOXVILLE
60941-60941 HERSCHER	61073-61073 ROSCOE	61324-61324 ELDENA	61449-61449 LA FAYETTE
60942-60942 HOOPESTON	61074-61074 SAVANNA	61325-61325 GRAND RIDGE	61450-61450 LA HARPE
60944-60944 HOPKINS PARK	61075-61075 SCALES MOUND	61326-61326 GRANVILLE	61451-61451 LAURA
60945-60945 IROQUOIS	61076-61076 SCIOTO MILLS	61327-61327 HENNEPIN	61452-61452 LITTLETON
60946-60946 KEMPTON	61076-61076 SCIOTO MILLSX	61328-61328 KASBEER	61453-61453 LITTLE YORK

Zip Range	City
61454-61454	LOMAX
61455-61455	MACOMB
61458-61458	MAQUON
61459-61459	MARIETTA
61460-61460	MEDIA
61462-61462	MONMOUTH
61465-61465	NEW WINDSOR
61466-61466	NORTH HENDERSON
61467-61467	ONEIDA
61468-61468	OPHEIM
61468-61468	OPHIEM
61469-61469	OQUAWKA
61470-61470	PRAIRIE CITY
61471-61471	RARITAN
61472-61472	RIO
61473-61473	ROSEVILLE
61474-61474	SAINT AUGUSTINE
61475-61475	SCIOTA
61476-61476	SEATON
61477-61477	SMITHFIELD
61478-61478	SMITHSHIRE
61479-61479	SPEER
61480-61480	STRONGHURST
61482-61482	TABLE GROVE
61483-61483	TOULON
61484-61484	VERMONT
61485-61485	VICTORIA
61486-61486	VIOLA
61488-61488	WATAGA
61489-61489	WILLIAMSFIELD
61490-61490	WOODHULL
61491-61491	WYOMING
61501-61501	ASTORIA
61516-61516	BENSON
61517-61518	BRIMFIELD
61519-61519	BRYANT
61520-61520	CANTON
61523-61523	CHILLICOTHE
61524-61524	DUNFERMLINE
61525-61525	DUNLAP
61526-61526	EDELSTEIN
61528-61528	EDWARDS
61529-61529	ELMWOOD
61530-61530	EUREKA
61531-61531	FARMINGTON
61532-61532	FOREST CITY
61533-61533	GLASFORD
61534-61534	GREEN VALLEY
61535-61535	GROVELAND
61536-61536	HANNA CITY
61537-61537	HENRY
61539-61539	KINGSTON MINES
61540-61540	LACON
61541-61541	LA ROSE
61542-61542	LEWISTOWN
61543-61543	LIVERPOOL
61544-61544	LONDON MILLS
61545-61545	LOWPOINT
61546-61546	MANITO
61547-61547	MAPLETON
61548-61548	METAMORA
61550-61550	MORTON
61552-61552	MOSSVILLE
61553-61553	NORRIS
61554-61558	PEKIN
61559-61559	PRINCEVILLE
61560-61560	PUTNAM
61561-61561	ROANOKE
61562-61562	ROME
61563-61563	SAINT DAVID
61564-61564	SOUTH PEKIN
61565-61565	SPARLAND
61567-61567	TOPEKA
61568-61568	TREMONT
61569-61569	TRIVOLI
61570-61570	WASHBURN
61571-61571	WASHINGTON
61572-61572	YATES CITY
61600-61607	PEORIA
61610-61610	CREVE COEUR
61611-61611	EAST PEORIA
61612-61615	PEORIA
61616-61616	PEORIA HEIGHTS
61625-61644	PEORIA
61649-61649	JEFFERSON BANK
61650-61656	PEORIA
61701-61710	BLOOMINGTON
61720-61720	ANCHOR
61721-61721	ARMINGTON
61722-61722	ARROWSMITH
61723-61723	ATLANTA
61724-61724	BELLFLOWER
61725-61725	CARLOCK
61726-61726	CHENOA
61727-61727	CLINTON
61728-61728	COLFAX
61729-61729	CONGERVILLE
61730-61730	COOKSVILLE
61731-61731	CROPSEY
61732-61732	DANVERS
61733-61733	DEER CREEK
61734-61734	DELAVAN
61735-61735	DEWITT
61736-61736	DOWNS
61737-61737	ELLSWORTH
61738-61738	EL PASO
61739-61739	FAIRBURY
61740-61740	FLANAGAN
61741-61741	FORREST
61742-61742	GOODFIELD
61743-61743	GRAYMONT
61744-61744	GRIDLEY
61745-61745	HEYWORTH
61747-61747	HOPEDALE
61748-61748	HUDSON
61749-61749	KENNEY
61750-61750	LANE
61751-61751	LAWNDALE
61752-61752	LE ROY
61753-61753	LEXINGTON
61754-61754	MC LEAN
61755-61755	MACKINAW
61756-61756	MAROA
61758-61758	MERNA
61759-61759	MINIER
61760-61760	MINONK
61761-61761	NORMAL
61764-61764	PONTIAC
61769-61769	SAUNEMIN
61770-61770	SAYBROOK
61771-61771	SECOR
61772-61772	SHIRLEY
61773-61773	SIBLEY
61774-61774	STANFORD
61775-61775	STRAWN
61776-61776	TOWANDA
61777-61777	WAPELLA
61778-61778	WAYNESVILLE
61790-61790	NORMAL
61791-61799	BLOOMINGTON
61801-61803	URBANA
61810-61810	ALLERTON
61811-61811	ALVIN
61812-61812	ARMSTRONG
61813-61813	BEMENT
61814-61814	BISMARCK
61815-61815	BONDVILLE
61816-61816	BROADLANDS
61817-61817	CATLIN
61818-61818	CERRO GORDO
61820-61826	CHAMPAIGN
61830-61830	CISCO
61831-61831	COLLISON
61832-61832	DANVILLE
61833-61833	TILTON
61834-61834	DANVILLE
61839-61839	DE LAND
61840-61840	DEWEY
61841-61841	FAIRMOUNT
61842-61842	FARMER CITY
61843-61843	FISHER
61844-61844	FITHIAN
61845-61845	FOOSLAND
61846-61846	GEORGETOWN
61847-61847	GIFFORD
61848-61848	HENNING
61849-61849	HOMER
61850-61850	INDIANOLA
61851-61851	IVESDALE
61852-61852	LONGVIEW
61853-61853	MAHOMET
61854-61854	MANSFIELD
61855-61855	MILMINE
61856-61856	MONTICELLO
61857-61857	MUNCIE
61858-61858	OAKWOOD
61859-61859	OGDEN
61862-61862	PENFIELD
61863-61863	PESOTUM
61864-61864	PHILO
61865-61865	POTOMAC
61866-61868	RANTOUL
61870-61870	RIDGE FARM
61871-61871	ROYAL
61872-61872	SADORUS
61873-61873	SAINT JOSEPH
61874-61874	SAVOY
61875-61875	SEYMOUR
61876-61876	SIDELL
61877-61877	SIDNEY
61878-61878	THOMASBORO
61880-61880	TOLONO
61882-61882	WELDON
61883-61883	WESTVILLE
61884-61884	WHITE HEATH
61910-61910	ARCOLA
61911-61911	ARTHUR
61912-61912	ASHMORE
61913-61913	ATWOOD
61914-61914	BETHANY
61917-61917	BROCTON
61919-61919	CAMARGO
61920-61920	CHARLESTON
61924-61924	CHRISMAN
61925-61925	DALTON CITY
61928-61928	GAYS
61929-61929	HAMMOND
61930-61930	HINDSBORO
61931-61931	HUMBOLDT
61932-61932	HUME
61933-61933	KANSAS
61936-61936	LA PLACE
61937-61937	LOVINGTON
61938-61938	MATTOON
61940-61940	METCALF
61941-61941	MURDOCK
61942-61942	NEWMAN
61943-61943	OAKLAND
61944-61944	PARIS
61949-61949	REDMON
61951-61951	SULLIVAN
61953-61953	TUSCOLA
61955-61955	VERMILION
61956-61956	VILLA GROVE
61957-61957	WINDSOR
62001-62001	ALHAMBRA
62002-62002	ALTON
62006-62006	BATCHTOWN
62009-62009	BENLD
62010-62010	BETHALTO
62011-62011	BINGHAM
62012-62012	BRIGHTON
62013-62013	BRUSSELS
62014-62014	BUNKER HILL
62015-62015	BUTLER
62016-62016	CARROLLTON
62017-62017	COFFEEN
62018-62018	COTTAGE HILLS
62019-62019	DONNELLSON
62021-62021	DORSEY
62022-62022	DOW
62023-62023	EAGARVILLE
62024-62024	EAST ALTON
62025-62026	EDWARDSVILLE
62027-62027	ELDRED
62028-62028	ELSAH
62030-62030	FIDELITY
62031-62031	FIELDON
62032-62032	FILLMORE
62033-62033	GILLESPIE
62034-62034	GLEN CARBON
62035-62035	GODFREY
62036-62036	GOLDEN EAGLE
62037-62037	GRAFTON
62040-62040	GRANITE CITY
62044-62044	GREENFIELD
62045-62045	HAMBURG
62046-62046	HAMEL
62047-62047	HARDIN
62048-62048	HARTFORD
62049-62049	HILLSBORO
62050-62050	HILLVIEW
62051-62051	IRVING
62052-62052	JERSEYVILLE
62053-62053	KAMPSVILLE
62054-62054	KANE
62056-62056	LITCHFIELD
62058-62058	LIVINGSTON
62059-62059	LOVEJOY
62060-62060	MADISON
62061-62061	MARINE
62062-62062	MARYVILLE
62063-62063	MEDORA
62065-62065	MICHAEL
62067-62067	MORO
62069-62069	MOUNT OLIVE
62070-62070	MOZIER
62071-62071	NATIONAL STOCK YARDS
62074-62074	NEW DOUGLAS
62075-62075	NOKOMIS
62076-62076	OHLMAN
62077-62077	PANAMA
62078-62078	PATTERSON
62079-62079	PIASA
62080-62080	RAMSEY
62081-62081	ROCKBRIDGE
62082-62082	ROODHOUSE
62083-62083	ROSAMOND
62084-62084	ROXANA
62085-62085	SAWYERVILLE
62086-62086	SORENTO
62087-62087	SOUTH ROXANA
62088-62088	STAUNTON
62089-62089	TAYLOR SPRINGS
62090-62090	VENICE
62091-62091	WALSHVILLE
62092-62092	WHITE HALL
62093-62093	WILSONVILLE
62094-62094	WITT
62095-62095	WOOD RIVER
62097-62097	WORDEN
62098-62098	WRIGHTS
62201-62207	EAST SAINT LOUIS
62208-62208	FAIRVIEW HEIGHTS
62214-62214	ADDIEVILLE
62215-62215	ALBERS
62216-62216	AVISTON
62217-62217	BALDWIN
62218-62218	BARTELSO
62219-62219	BECKEMEYER
62220-62223	BELLEVILLE
62224-62224	MASCOUTAH
62225-62225	SCOTT AIR FORCE BASE
62226-62226	BELLEVILLE
62230-62230	BREESE
62231-62231	CARLYLE
62232-62232	CASEYVILLE
62233-62233	CHESTER
62234-62234	COLLINSVILLE
62236-62236	COLUMBIA
62237-62237	COULTERVILLE
62238-62238	CUTLER
62239-62239	DUPO
62240-62240	EAST CARONDELET
62241-62241	ELLIS GROVE
62242-62242	EVANSVILLE
62243-62243	FREEBURG
62244-62244	FULTS
62245-62245	GERMANTOWN
62246-62246	GREENVILLE
62247-62247	HAGARSTOWN
62248-62248	HECKER

ZIP	Place	ZIP	Place	ZIP	Place	ZIP	Place
62249-62249	HIGHLAND	62358-62358	NIOTA	62512-62512	BEASON	62663-62663	MANCHESTER
62250-62250	HOFFMAN	62359-62359	PALOMA	62513-62513	BLUE MOUND	62664-62664	MASON CITY
62252-62252	HUEY	62360-62360	PAYSON	62514-62514	BOODY	62665-62665	MEREDOSIA
62253-62253	KEYESPORT	62361-62361	PEARL	62515-62515	BUFFALO	62666-62666	MIDDLETOWN
62254-62254	LEBANON	62362-62362	PERRY	62517-62517	BULPITT	62667-62667	MODESTO
62255-62255	LENZBURG	62363-62363	PITTSFIELD	62518-62518	CHESTNUT	62668-62668	MURRAYVILLE
62256-62256	MAEYSTOWN	62365-62365	PLAINVILLE	62519-62519	CORNLAND	62670-62670	NEW BERLIN
62257-62257	MARISSA	62366-62366	PLEASANT HILL	62520-62520	DAWSON	62671-62671	NEW HOLLAND
62258-62258	MASCOUTAH	62367-62367	PLYMOUTH	62521-62527	DECATUR	62672-62672	NILWOOD
62259-62259	MENARD	62370-62370	ROCKPORT	62530-62530	DIVERNON	62673-62673	OAKFORD
62260-62260	MILLSTADT	62372-62372	SUMMER HILL	62531-62531	EDINBURG	62674-62674	PALMYRA
62261-62261	MODOC	62373-62373	SUTTER	62532-62532	ELWIN	62675-62675	PETERSBURG
62262-62262	MULBERRY GROVE	62374-62374	TENNESSEE	62533-62533	FARMERSVILLE	62676-62676	PLAINVIEW
62263-62263	NASHVILLE	62375-62375	TIMEWELL	62534-62534	FINDLAY	62677-62677	PLEASANT PLAINS
62264-62264	NEW ATHENS	62376-62376	URSA	62535-62535	FORSYTH	62681-62681	RUSHVILLE
62265-62265	NEW BADEN	62378-62378	VERSAILLES	62536-62536	GLENARM	62682-62682	SAN JOSE
62266-62266	NEW MEMPHIS	62379-62379	WARSAW	62537-62537	HARRISTOWN	62683-62683	SCOTTVILLE
62268-62268	OAKDALE	62380-62380	WEST POINT	62538-62538	HARVEL	62684-62684	SHERMAN
62269-62269	O FALLON	62401-62401	EFFINGHAM	62539-62539	ILLIOPOLIS	62685-62685	SHIPMAN
62271-62271	OKAWVILLE	62410-62410	ALLENDALE	62540-62540	KINCAID	62686-62686	STANDARD CITY
62272-62272	PERCY	62411-62411	ALTAMONT	62541-62541	LAKE FORK	62688-62688	TALLULA
62273-62273	PIERRON	62413-62413	ANNAPOLIS	62543-62543	LATHAM	62689-62689	THAYER
62274-62274	PINCKNEYVILLE	62414-62414	BEECHER CITY	62544-62544	MACON	62690-62690	VIRDEN
62275-62275	POCAHONTAS	62415-62415	BIRDS	62545-62545	MECHANICSBURG	62691-62691	VIRGINIA
62277-62277	PRAIRIE DU ROCHER	62417-62417	BRIDGEPORT	62546-62546	MORRISONVILLE	62692-62692	WAVERLY
62278-62278	RED BUD	62418-62418	BROWNSTOWN	62547-62547	MOUNT AUBURN	62693-62693	WILLIAMSVILLE
62279-62279	RENAULT	62419-62419	CALHOUN	62548-62548	MOUNT PULASKI	62694-62694	WINCHESTER
62280-62280	ROCKWOOD	62420-62420	CASEY	62549-62549	MT ZION	62695-62695	WOODSON
62281-62281	SAINT JACOB	62421-62421	CLAREMONT	62550-62550	MOWEAQUA	62700-62796	SPRINGFIELD
62282-62282	SAINT LIBORY	62422-62422	COWDEN	62551-62551	NIANTIC	62801-62801	CENTRALIA
62283-62283	SHATTUC	62423-62423	DENNISON	62552-62552	OAKLEY	62803-62803	HOYLETON
62284-62284	SMITHBORO	62424-62424	DIETERICH	62553-62553	OCONEE	62805-62805	AKIN
62285-62285	SMITHTON	62425-62425	DUNDAS	62554-62554	OREANA	62806-62806	ALBION
62286-62286	SPARTA	62426-62426	EDGEWOOD	62555-62555	OWANECO	62807-62807	ALMA
62288-62288	STEELEVILLE	62427-62427	FLAT ROCK	62556-62556	PALMER	62808-62808	ASHLEY
62289-62289	SUMMERFIELD	62428-62428	GREENUP	62557-62557	PANA	62809-62809	BARNHILL
62292-62292	TILDEN	62431-62431	HERRICK	62558-62558	PAWNEE	62810-62810	BELLE RIVE
62293-62293	TRENTON	62432-62432	HIDALGO	62560-62560	RAYMOND	62811-62811	BELLMONT
62294-62294	TROY	62433-62433	HUTSONVILLE	62561-62561	RIVERTON	62812-62812	BENTON
62295-62295	VALMEYER	62434-62434	INGRAHAM	62563-62563	ROCHESTER	62814-62814	BLUFORD
62296-62296	VENEDY	62435-62435	JANESVILLE	62565-62565	SHELBYVILLE	62815-62815	BONE GAP
62297-62297	WALSH	62436-62436	JEWETT	62567-62567	STONINGTON	62816-62816	BONNIE
62298-62298	WATERLOO	62438-62438	LAKEWOOD	62568-62568	TAYLORVILLE	62817-62817	BROUGHTON
62301-62306	QUINCY	62439-62439	LAWRENCEVILLE	62570-62570	TOVEY	62818-62818	BROWNS
62310-62310	ADRIAN	62440-62440	LERNA	62571-62571	TOWER HILL	62819-62819	BUCKNER
62311-62311	AUGUSTA	62441-62441	MARSHALL	62572-62572	WAGGONER	62820-62820	BURNT PRAIRIE
62312-62312	BARRY	62442-62442	MARTINSVILLE	62573-62573	WARRENSBURG	62821-62821	CARMI
62313-62313	BASCO	62443-62443	MASON	62574-62574	WESTERVELT	62822-62822	CHRISTOPHER
62314-62314	BAYLIS	62444-62444	MODE	62601-62601	ALEXANDER	62823-62823	CISNE
62316-62316	BOWEN	62445-62445	MONTROSE	62610-62610	ALSEY	62824-62824	CLAY CITY
62318-62318	BURNSIDE	62446-62446	MOUNT ERIE	62611-62611	ARENZVILLE	62825-62825	COELLO
62319-62319	CAMDEN	62447-62447	NEOGA	62612-62612	ASHLAND	62827-62827	CROSSVILLE
62320-62320	CAMP POINT	62448-62448	NEWTON	62613-62613	ATHENS	62828-62828	DAHLGREN
62321-62321	CARTHAGE	62449-62449	OBLONG	62615-62615	AUBURN	62829-62829	DALE
62323-62323	CHAMBERSBURG	62450-62450	OLNEY	62617-62617	BATH	62830-62830	DIX
62324-62324	CLAYTON	62451-62451	PALESTINE	62618-62618	BEARDSTOWN	62831-62831	DU BOIS
62325-62325	COATSBURG	62452-62452	PARKERSBURG	62621-62621	BLUFFS	62832-62832	DU QUOIN
62326-62326	COLCHESTER	62454-62454	ROBINSON	62622-62622	BLUFF SPRINGS	62833-62833	ELLERY
62327-62327	COLMAR	62458-62458	SAINT ELMO	62624-62624	BROWNING	62834-62834	EMMA
62328-62328	QUINCY	62459-62459	SAINTE MARIE	62625-62625	CANTRALL	62835-62835	ENFIELD
62329-62329	COLUSA	62460-62460	SAINT FRANCISVILLE	62626-62626	CARLINVILLE	62836-62836	EWING
62330-62330	DALLAS CITY	62461-62461	SHUMWAY	62627-62627	CHANDLERVILLE	62837-62837	FAIRFIELD
62332-62332	PITTSFIELD	62462-62462	SIGEL	62628-62628	CHAPIN	62838-62838	FARINA
62334-62334	ELVASTON	62463-62463	STEWARDSON	62629-62629	CHATHAM	62839-62839	FLORA
62336-62336	FERRIS	62464-62464	STOY	62630-62630	CHESTERFIELD	62840-62840	FRANKFORT HEIGHTS
62338-62338	FOWLER	62465-62465	STRASBURG	62631-62631	CONCORD	62841-62841	FREEMAN SPUR
62339-62339	GOLDEN	62466-62466	SUMNER	62633-62633	EASTON	62842-62842	GEFF
62340-62340	GRIGGSVILLE	62467-62467	TEUTOPOLIS	62634-62634	ELKHART	62843-62843	GOLDEN GATE
62341-62341	HAMILTON	62468-62468	TOLEDO	62635-62635	EMDEN	62844-62844	GRAYVILLE
62343-62343	HULL	62469-62469	TRILLA	62638-62638	FRANKLIN	62845-62845	HERALD
62344-62344	HUNTSVILLE	62471-62471	VANDALIA	62639-62639	FREDERICK	62846-62846	INA
62345-62345	KINDERHOOK	62473-62473	WATSON	62640-62640	GIRARD	62847-62847	IOLA
62346-62346	LA PRAIRIE	62474-62474	WESTFIELD	62642-62642	GREENVIEW	62848-62848	IRVINGTON
62347-62347	LIBERTY	62475-62475	WEST LIBERTY	62643-62643	HARTSBURG	62849-62849	IUKA
62348-62348	LIMA	62476-62476	WEST SALEM	62644-62644	HAVANA	62850-62850	JOHNSONVILLE
62349-62349	LORAINE	62477-62477	WEST UNION	62649-62649	HETTICK	62851-62851	KEENES
62351-62351	MENDON	62478-62478	WEST YORK	62650-62651	JACKSONVILLE	62852-62852	KEENSBURG
62352-62352	MILTON	62479-62479	WHEELER	62655-62655	KILBOURNE	62853-62853	KELL
62353-62353	MOUNT STERLING	62480-62480	WILLOW HILL	62656-62656	LINCOLN	62854-62854	KINMUNDY
62354-62354	NAUVOO	62481-62481	YALE	62659-62659	LINCOLN'S NEW SALEM	62855-62855	LANCASTER
62355-62355	NEBO	62501-62501	ARGENTA	62660-62660	LITERBERRY	62856-62856	LOGAN
62356-62356	NEW CANTON	62510-62510	ASSUMPTION	62661-62661	LOAMI	62857-62857	LOOGOOTEE
62357-62357	NEW SALEM	62511-62511	ATWATER	62662-62662	LOWDER	62858-62858	LOUISVILLE

62859-62859 MC LEANSBORO	62860-62860 MACEDONIA	62861-62861 MAUNIE	62964-62964 MOUNDS
62862-62862 MILL SHOALS	62894-62894 WALTONVILLE	62931-62931 ELIZABETHTOWN	62965-62965 MUDDY
62863-62863 MOUNT CARMEL	62895-62895 WAYNE CITY	62932-62932 ELKVILLE	62966-62966 MURPHYSBORO
62864-62864 MOUNT VERNON	62896-62896 WEST FRANKFORT	62933-62933 ENERGY	62967-62967 NEW BURNSIDE
62865-62865 MULKEYTOWN	62897-62897 WHITTINGTON	62934-62934 EQUALITY	62969-62969 OLIVE BRANCH
62866-62866 NASON	62898-62898 WOODLAWN	62935-62935 GALATIA	62970-62970 OLMSTED
62867-62867 NEW HAVEN	62899-62899 XENIA	62938-62938 GOLCONDA	62971-62971 ORAVILLE
62868-62868 NOBLE	62901-62903 CARBONDALE	62939-62939 GOREVILLE	62972-62972 OZARK
62869-62869 NORRIS CITY	62905-62905 ALTO PASS	62940-62940 GORHAM	62973-62973 PERKS
62870-62870 ODIN	62906-62906 ANNA	62941-62941 GRAND CHAIN	62974-62974 PITTSBURG
62871-62871 OMAHA	62907-62907 AVA	62942-62942 GRAND TOWER	62975-62975 POMONA
62872-62872 OPDYKE	62908-62908 BELKNAP	62943-62943 GRANTSBURG	62976-62976 PULASKI
62874-62874 ORIENT	62909-62909 BOLES	62944-62944 HAMLETSBURG	62977-62977 RALEIGH
62875-62875 PATOKA	62910-62910 BROOKPORT	62945-62945 GALATIA	62979-62979 RIDGWAY
62876-62876 RADOM	62912-62912 BUNCOMBE	62946-62946 HARRISBURG	62982-62982 ROSICLARE
62877-62877 RICHVIEW	62913-62913 CACHE	62947-62947 HEROD	62983-62983 ROYALTON
62878-62878 RINARD	62914-62914 CAIRO	62948-62948 HERRIN	62984-62984 SHAWNEETOWN
62879-62879 SAILOR SPRINGS	62915-62915 CAMBRIA	62949-62949 HURST	62985-62985 SIMPSON
62880-62880 SAINT PETER	62916-62916 CAMPBELL HILL	62950-62950 JACOB	62987-62987 STONEFORT
62881-62881 SALEM	62917-62917 CARRIER MILLS	62951-62951 JOHNSTON CITY	62988-62988 TAMMS
62882-62882 SANDOVAL	62918-62918 CARTERVILLE	62952-62952 JONESBORO	62990-62990 THEBES
62883-62883 SCHELLER	62919-62919 CAVE IN ROCK	62953-62953 JOPPA	62991-62991 TUNNEL HILL
62884-62884 SESSER	62920-62920 COBDEN	62954-62954 JUNCTION	62992-62992 ULLIN
62885-62885 SHOBONIER	62921-62921 COLP	62955-62955 KARBERS RIDGE	62993-62993 UNITY
62886-62886 SIMS	62922-62922 CREAL SPRINGS	62956-62956 KARNAK	62994-62994 VERGENNES
62887-62887 SPRINGERTON	62923-62923 CYPRESS	62957-62957 MC CLURE	62995-62995 VIENNA
62888-62888 TAMAROA	62924-62924 DE SOTO	62958-62958 MAKANDA	62996-62996 VILLA RIDGE
62889-62889 TEXICO	62926-62926 DONGOLA	62959-62959 MARION	62997-62997 WILLISVILLE
62890-62890 THOMPSONVILLE	62927-62927 DOWELL	62960-62960 METROPOLIS	62998-62998 WOLF LAKE
62891-62891 VALIER	62928-62928 EDDYVILLE	62961-62961 MILLCREEK	62999-62999 ZEIGLER
62892-62892 VERNON	62929-62929 ELCO	62962-62962 MILLER CITY	
62893-62893 WALNUT HILL	62930-62930 ELDORADO	62963-62963 MOUND CITY	

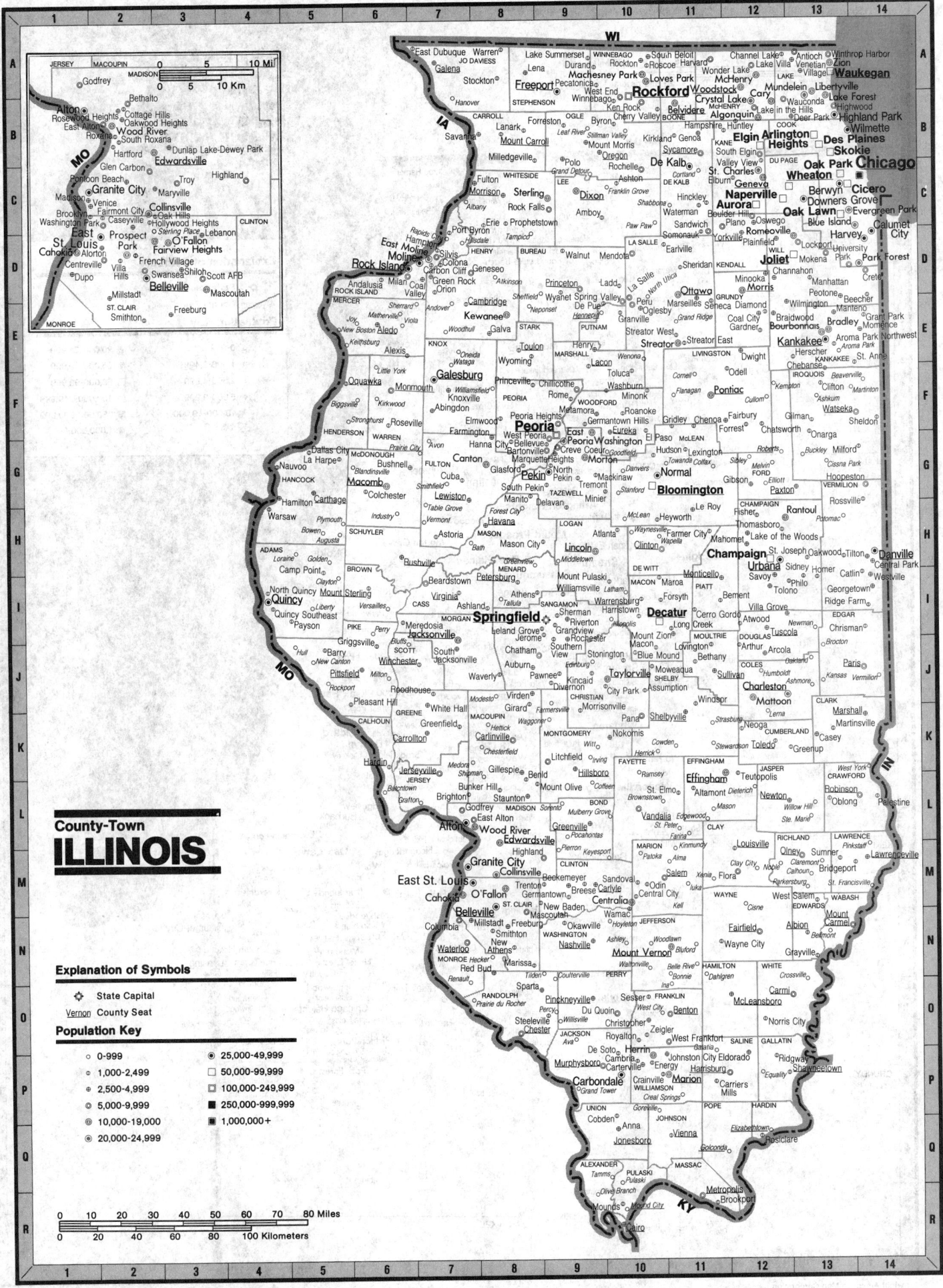

County-Town
ILLINOIS

Explanation of Symbols

⬦ State Capital

Vernon County Seat

Population Key

○ 0-999	⊛ 25,000-49,999
○ 1,000-2,499	□ 50,000-99,999
⊙ 2,500-4,999	▢ 100,000-249,999
◉ 5,000-9,999	■ 250,000-999,999
⊚ 10,000-19,000	■ 1,000,000+
⊚ 20,000-24,999	

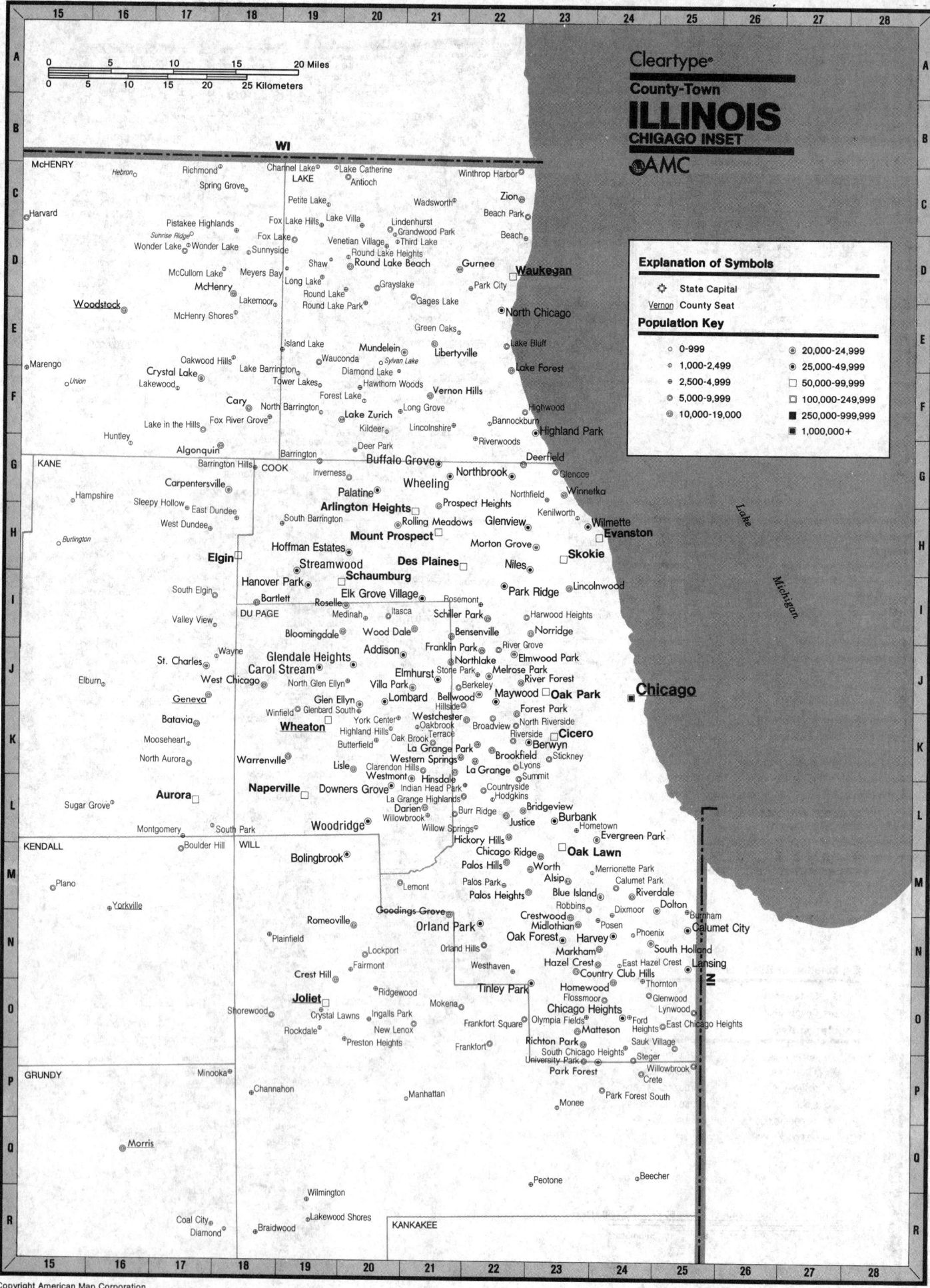

Cleartype®
County-Town
ILLINOIS
CHIGAGO INSET
⊛AMC

Explanation of Symbols

✧	State Capital
Vernon	County Seat

Population Key

○	0-999	⊙	20,000-24,999
⊙	1,000-2,499	⊛	25,000-49,999
⊕	2,500-4,999	□	50,000-99,999
⊘	5,000-9,999	▢	100,000-249,999
⊛	10,000-19,000	■	250,000-999,999
		■	1,000,000+

Explanation of symbols: ● – Census Designated Place (CDP)

Jerseyville, Jersey, 7,382 ... K-7
Johnston City, Williamson, 3,706 ... P-11
Joliet, Will, 76,836 ... D-13
Jonesboro, Union, 1,728 ... Q-10
Justice, Cook, 11,137 ... L-22
Kankakee, Kankakee, 27,575 ... E-13
Ken Rock, Winnebago ... B-10
Kenilworth, Cook, 2,402 ... H-23
Kewanee, Henry, 12,969 ... E-8
Kildeer, Lake, 2,257 ... F-20
Kincaid, Christian, 1,353 ... J-9
Kirkland, DeKalb, 1,011 ... B-11
Knoxville, Knox, 3,243 ... F-7
La Grange, Cook, 15,362 ... K-22
La Grange Highlands, Cook ... L-21
La Grange Park, Cook, 12,861 ... K-22
La Harpe, Hancock, 1,407 ... G-5
La Salle, La Salle, 9,717 ... D-10
Lacon, Marshall, 1,986 ... E-9
Ladd, Bureau, 1,283 ... D-10
Lake Barrington, Lake, 3,855 ... F-19
Lake Bluff, Lake, 5,513 ... E-22
• Lake Catherine, Lake, 1,515 ... C-19
Lake Forest, Lake, 17,836 ... B-13
• Lake Summerset, Stephenson/Winnebago, 1,296 ... A-9
Lake Villa, Lake, 2,857 ... A-13
Lake Zurich, Lake, 14,947 ... F-19
Lake in the Hills, McHenry, 5,866 ... B-12
• Lake of the Woods, Champaign, 2,748 ... H-12
Lakemoor, Lake/McHenry, 1,322 ... D-18
Lakewood, McHenry, 1,609 ... F-17
• Lakewood Shores, Will, 1,606 ... R-19
Lanark, Carroll, 1,382 ... B-8
Lansing, Cook, 28,086 ... N-25
Lawrenceville, Lawrence, 4,897 ... M-14
Le Roy, McLean, 2,777 ... H-11
Lebanon, St. Clair, 3,688 ... D-3
Leland Grove, Sangamon, 1,679 ... I-9
Lemont, Cook, 7,348 ... M-21
Lena, Stephenson, 2,605 ... A-8
Lewistown, Fulton, 2,572 ... G-7
Lexington, McLean, 1,809 ... G-11
Libertyville, Lake, 19,174 ... A-13
Lichtfield, Montgomery ... K-9
Lincoln, Logan, 15,418 ... H-9
Lincolnshire, Lake, 4,931 ... F-21
Lincolnwood, Cook, 11,365 ... I-23
Lindenhurst, Lake, 8,038 ... C-20
Lisle, DuPage, 19,512 ... K-20
Litchfield, Montgomery, 6,883 ... K-4
Lockport, Will, 9,401 ... D-13
Lombard, DuPage, 39,408 ... J-20
Long Creek, Macon, 1,250 ... I-10
Long Grove, Lake, 4,740 ... F-20
• Long Lake, Lake, 2,888 ... D-19
Louisville, Clay, 1,098 ... M-12
Loves Park, Winnebago, 15,462 ... A-10
Lovington, Moultrie, 1,143 ... J-11
Lynwood, Cook, 6,535 ... O-25
Lyons, Cook, 9,828 ... K-22
Machesney Park, Winnebago, 19,033 ... A-10
Mackinaw, Tazewell, 1,331 ... G-9
Macomb, McDonough, 19,952 ... G-6
Macon, Macon, 1,282 ... J-10
Madison, Limestone/Madison, 4,629 ... C-1
Mahomet, Champaign, 3,103 ... H-12
Manhattan, Will, 2,059 ... D-13
Manito, Mason, 1,711 ... G-8
Manteno, Kankakee, 3,488 ... E-13
Marengo, McHenry, 4,768 ... F-15
Marion, Williamson, 14,545 ... P-10
Marissa, St. Clair, 2,375 ... N-8
Markham, Cook, 13,136 ... N-24
Maroa, Macon, 1,602 ... I-10
Marquette Heights, Tazewell, 3,077 ... G-9
Marseilles, La Salle, 4,811 ... E-11
Marshall, Clark, 3,555 ... K-14
Martinsville, Clark, 1,161 ... K-13
Maryville, Madison, 2,576 ... C-3
Mascoutah, St. Clair, 5,511 ... N-8
Mason City, Mason, 2,323 ... H-9
Matteson, Cook, 11,378 ... O-23
Mattoon, Coles, 18,441 ... J-12
Maywood, Cook, 27,139 ... J-22
McCullom Lake, McHenry, 1,033 ... D-18
McHenry, McHenry, 16,177 ... A-12
McHenry Shores, McHenry ... E-18
McLeansboro, Hamilton, 2,677 ... O-12
• Medinah, DuPage, 2,512 ... I-20
Melrose Park, Cook, 20,859 ... J-22
Mendota, La Salle, 7,018 ... D-10
Meredosia, Morgan, 1,134 ... I-6
Merrionette Park, Cook, 2,065 ... M-24
Metamora, Woodford, 2,520 ... F-9
Metropolis, Massac, 6,734 ... R-11
Meyers Bay, Lake ... D-19
Midlothian, Cook, 14,372 ... N-23
Milan, Rock Island, 5,831 ... D-6
Milford, Iroquois, 1,512 ... G-14
Milledgeville, Carroll, 1,076 ... B-8
Millstadt, St. Clair, 2,566 ... N-7
Minier, Tazewell, 1,155 ... G-10
Minonk, Woodford, 1,982 ... F-10
Minooka, Grundy/Will, 2,561 ... D-12
Mokena, Will, 6,128 ... D-13
Moline, Rock Island, 43,202 ... D-7
Momence, Kankakee, 2,968 ... E-14
Monee, Will, 1,044 ... P-23
Monmouth, Warren, 9,489 ... F-6
Montgomery, Kane/Kendall, 4,267 ... L-17
Monticello, Piatt, 4,549 ... I-11
Mooseheart, Kane ... K-17
Morris, Grundy, 10,270 ... D-12
Morrison, Whiteside, 4,363 ... C-8
Morrisonville, Christian, 1,113 ... K-9
Morton, Tazewell, 13,799 ... G-9
Morton Grove, Cook, 22,408 ... H-23
Mound City, Pulaski, 765 ... R-10
Mounds, Pulaski, 1,407 ... R-10
Mount Carmel, Wabash, 8,287 ... N-13
Mount Carroll, Carroll, 1,726 ... B-8
Mount Morris, Ogle, 2,919 ... B-9
Mount Olive, Macoupin, 2,126 ... L-8
Mount Prospect, Cook, 53,170 ... H-21
Mount Pulaski, Logan, 1,610 ... I-10
Mount Sterling, Brown, 1,922 ... I-6
Mount Vernon, Jefferson, 16,988 ... N-11
Mount Zion, Macon, 4,522 ... I-11
Moweaqua, Christian/Shelby, 1,785 ... J-10
Mundelein, Lake, 21,215 ... E-20
Murphysboro, Jackson, 9,176 ... P-9
Naperville, DuPage/Will, 85,351 ... C-12
Nashville, Washington, 3,202 ... N-9
Nauvoo, Hancock, 1,108 ... G-4
Neoga, Cumberland, 1,678 ... K-12
New Athens, St. Clair, 2,010 ... N-8
New Baden, Clinton/St. Clair, 2,602 ... M-9
New Lenox, Will, 9,627 ... O-21
Newton, Jasper, 3,154 ... L-12
Niles, Cook, 28,284 ... H-22
Nokomis, Montgomery, 2,534 ... K-10
Normal, McLean, 40,023 ... G-10
Norridge, Cook, 14,459 ... I-23
Norris City, White, 1,341 ... O-12
North Aurora, Kane, 5,940 ... K-17
North Barrington, Lake, 1,787 ... F-19
North Chicago, Lake, 34,978 ... E-22
North Glen Ellyn, DuPage ... J-20
North Lake, Cook ... J-21
North Pekin, Tazewell, 1,556 ... G-9
North Quincy, Adams ... I-4
North Riverside, Cook, 6,005 ... K-22
Northbrook, Cook, 32,308 ... G-22
Northfield, Cook, 4,635 ... G-23
Northlake, Cook, 12,505 ... J-21
Oak Brook, Cook/DuPage, 9,178 ... K-21
Oak Forest, Cook, 26,203 ... N-23
Oak Hills, St. Clair ... C-3
Oak Lawn, Cook, 56,182 ... C-13
Oak Park, Cook, 53,648 ... C-13
Oakbrook Terrace, DuPage, 1,907 ... K-21
Oakwood, Vermilion, 1,533 ... H-13
Oakwood Heights, Madison ... B-2
Oakwood Hills, McHenry, 1,498 ... E-18
Oblong, Crawford, 1,616 ... L-13
Odell, Livingston, 1,030 ... F-12
Odin, Marion, 1,150 ... M-10
O'Fallon, St. Clair, 16,073 ... D-3
Oglesby, La Salle, 3,619 ... E-10
Okawville, Washington, 1,274 ... N-9
Olney, Richland, 8,664 ... M-13
Olympia Fields, Cook, 4,248 ... O-23
Onarga, Iroquois, 1,281 ... F-13
Oquawka, Henderson, 1,442 ... F-6
Oregon, Ogle, 3,891 ... B-10
Orion, Henry, 1,821 ... D-7
Orland Hills, Cook, 5,510 ... N-22
Orland Park, Cook, 35,720 ... N-22
Oswego, Kendall, 3,876 ... C-12
Ottawa, La Salle, 17,451 ... D-11
Palatine, Cook, 39,253 ... G-20
Palestine, Crawford, 1,619 ... L-14
Palos Heights, Cook, 11,478 ... M-22
Palos Hills, Cook, 17,803 ... M-22
Palos Park, Cook, 4,199 ... M-22
Pana, Christian, 5,796 ... K-10
Paris, Edgar, 8,987 ... J-14
Park City, Lake, 4,677 ... D-22
Park Forest, Cook/Will, 24,656 ... D-14
Park Forest South, Cook/Will ... P-24
Park Ridge, Cook, 36,175 ... I-22
Pawnee, Sangamon, 2,384 ... J-9
Paxton, Ford, 4,289 ... G-13
Payson, Adams, 1,114 ... I-5
Pecatonica, Winnebago, 1,760 ... A-9
Pekin, Peoria/Tazewell, 32,254 ... G-9
Peoria, Peoria, 113,504 ... F-9
Peoria Heights, Peoria/Tazewell/Woodford, 6,930 ... F-9
Peotone, Will, 2,947 ... E-13
Peru, La Salle, 9,302 ... E-10
Petersburg, Menard, 2,261 ... I-8
Petite Lake, Lake ... C-19
Philo, Champaign, 1,028 ... I-12
Phoenix, Cook, 2,217 ... N-24
Pinckneyville, Perry, 3,372 ... O-9
• Pistakee Highlands, McHenry, 3,848 ... C-18
Pittsfield, Pike, 4,231 ... J-6
Plainfield, Will, 4,557 ... D-12
Plano, Kendall, 5,104 ... C-12
Pleasant Hill, Pike, 1,030 ... J-6
Polo, Ogle, 2,514 ... B-9
Pontiac, Livingston, 11,428 ... F-11
Pontoon Beach, Madison, 4,013 ... C-2
Port Byron, Rock Island, 1,002 ... D-7
Posen, Cook, 4,226 ... N-24
• Preston Heights, Will, 2,750 ... O-19
Princeton, Bureau, 7,197 ... D-9
Princeville, Peoria, 1,421 ... F-8
Prophetstown, Whiteside, 1,749 ... C-8
Prospect Heights, Cook, 15,239 ... G-21
Quincy, Adams, 39,681 ... I-4
Quincy Southeast, Adams ... I-4
Rantoul, Champaign, 17,212 ... H-12
Red Bud, Randolph, 2,918 ... N-8
Richmond, McHenry, 1,016 ... C-18
Richton Park, Cook, 10,523 ... O-23
Ridgewood, Will ... O-20
Ridgway, Gallatin, 1,103 ... P-12
River Forest, Cook, 11,669 ... J-22
River Grove, Cook, 9,961 ... J-22
Riverdale, Cook, 13,671 ... M-24
Riverside, Cook, 8,774 ... K-22
Riverton, Sangamon, 2,638 ... I-9
Riverwoods, Lake, 2,868 ... G-22
Roanoke, Woodford, 1,910 ... F-10
Robbins, Cook, 7,498 ... M-23
Robinson, Crawford, 6,740 ... L-14
Rochelle, Ogle, 8,769 ... C-10
Rochester, Sangamon, 2,676 ... J-9
Rock Falls, Whiteside, 9,654 ... C-9
Rock Island, Rock Island, 40,552 ... D-6
Rockdale, Will, 1,709 ... O-19
Rockford, Winnebago, 139,426 ... B-10
Rockton, Winnebago, 2,928 ... A-10
Rolling Meadows, Cook, 22,591 ... H-20
• Rome, Peoria, 1,902 ... F-9
Romeoville, Will, 14,074 ... D-13
Roodhouse, Greene, 2,139 ... J-7
Roscoe, Winnebago, 2,079 ... A-10
Roselle, Cook/DuPage, 20,819 ... I-20
Rosemont, Cook, 3,995 ... I-22
Roseville, Warren, 1,151 ... F-6
• Rosewood Heights, Madison, 4,821 ... B-2
Rosiclare, Hardin, 1,378 ... Q-12
Rossville, Vermilion, 1,334 ... H-14
Round Lake, Lake, 3,550 ... D-20
Round Lake Beach, Lake, 16,434 ... D-20
Round Lake Heights, Lake, 1,251 ... D-20
Round Lake Park, Lake, 4,045 ... E-20
Roxana, Madison, 1,562 ... B-2
Royalton, Franklin, 1,191 ... O-10
Rushville, Schuyler, 3,229 ... H-6
Saint Anne, Kankakee, 1,153 ... E-14
Saint Charles, DuPage/Kane, 22,501 ... C-12
Saint Elmo, Fayette, 1,473 ... L-11
Saint Joseph, Champaign, 2,052 ... H-13
Salem, Marion, 7,470 ... M-10
Sandoval, Marion, 1,535 ... M-10
Sandwich, DeKalb/Kendall, 5,567 ... D-11
Sauk Village, Cook/Will, 9,926 ... O-25
Savanna, Carroll, 3,819 ... B-8
Savoy, Champaign, 2,674 ... I-12
Schaumburg, Cook/DuPage, 68,586 ... I-20
Schiller Park, Cook, 11,189 ... I-22
• Scott AFB, St. Clair, 7,245 ... D-3
Seneca, Grundy/La Salle, 1,878 ... E-11
Sesser, Franklin, 2,087 ... O-10
Shaw, Lake ... D-19
Shawneetown, Gallatin, 1,575 ... P-12
Shelbyville, Shelby, 4,943 ... K-11
Sheldon, Iroquois, 1,109 ... F-14
Sheridan, La Salle, 1,288 ... D-11
Sherman, Sangamon, 2,080 ... I-9
Shiloh, St. Clair, 2,655 ... D-3
Shorewood, Will, 6,264 ... O-18
Sidney, Champaign, 1,027 ... I-13
Silvis, Rock Island, 6,926 ... D-7
Skokie, Cook, 59,432 ... B-13
Sleepy Hollow, Kane, 3,241 ... H-17
Smithton, St. Clair, 1,587 ... N-8
Somonauk, DeKalb/La Salle, 1,263 ... D-11
South Barrington, Cook, 2,937 ... H-19
South Beloit, Winnebago, 4,072 ... A-10
South Chicago Heights, Cook, 3,597 ... O-24
South Elgin, Kane, 7,474 ... B-12
South Holland, Cook, 22,105 ... N-24
South Jacksonville, Morgan, 3,187 ... J-7
South Park, Kane ... L-17
South Pekin, Tazewell, 1,184 ... G-9
South Roxana, Madison, 1,961 ... B-2
Southern View, Sangamon, 1,906 ... J-9
Sparta, Randolph, 4,853 ... O-8
Spring Grove, McHenry, 1,066 ... C-18
Spring Valley, Bureau, 5,246 ... E-10
Springfield, Sangamon, 105,227 ... I-9
Staunton, Macoupin, 4,806 ... L-8
Steeleville, Randolph, 2,059 ... O-9
Steger, Cook/Will, 8,584 ... P-24
Sterling, Whiteside, 15,132 ... C-9
Stickney, Cook, 5,678 ... K-23
Stockton, Jo Daviess, 1,871 ... A-8
Stone Park, Cook, 4,383 ... J-22
Stonington, Christian, 1,006 ... J-10
Streamwood, Cook, 30,987 ... H-19
Streator, La Salle/Livingston, 14,121 ... E-11
Streator East, La Salle ... E-11
Streator West, La Salle ... E-11
Sugar Grove, Kane, 2,005 ... L-16
Sullivan, Moultrie, 4,354 ... J-11
Summit, Cook, 9,971 ... L-22
Sumner, Lawrence, 1,083 ... M-13
Sunnyside, McHenry, 1,529 ... D-18
Swansea, St. Clair, 8,201 ... D-2
Sycamore, DeKalb, 9,708 ... B-11
Taylorville, Christian, 11,133 ... J-10
Teutopolis, Effingham, 1,417 ... L-12
Third Lake, Lake, 1,248 ... D-20
Thomasboro, Champaign, 1,250 ... H-12
Thornton, Cook, 2,778 ... N-24
Tilton, Vermilion, 2,729 ... H-14
Tinley Park, Cook/Will, 37,121 ... O-23
Toledo, Cumberland, 1,199 ... K-12
Tolono, Champaign, 2,605 ... I-12
Toluca, Marshall, 1,315 ... F-10
Toulon, Stark, 1,328 ... E-8
Tower Lakes, Lake, 1,333 ... F-19
Tremont, Tazewell, 2,088 ... G-9
Trenton, Clinton, 2,481 ... M-9
Troy, Madison, 6,046 ... C-3
Tuscola, Douglas, 4,155 ... I-12
University Park, Cook/Will, 6,204 ... D-23
Urbana, Champaign, 36,344 ... H-12
Valley View, Kane ... C-12
Vandalia, Fayette, 6,114 ... L-10
• Venetian Village, Lake, 3,133 ... A-13
Venice, Madison, 3,571 ... C-2
Vernon Hills, Lake, 15,319 ... F-21
Vienna, Johnson, 1,446 ... Q-11
Villa Grove, Douglas, 2,734 ... I-12
Villa Hills, St. Clair ... D-2
Villa Park, DuPage, 22,253 ... J-21
Virden, Macoupin/Sangamon, 3,635 ... J-8
Virginia, Cass, 1,767 ... I-7
Wadsworth, Lake, 1,826 ... C-21
Walnut, Bureau, 1,463 ... D-9
Wamac, Clinton/Marion/Washington, 1,501 ... N-10
Warren, Jo Daviess, 1,550 ... A-8
Warrensburg, Macon, 1,274 ... I-10
Warrenville, DuPage, 11,333 ... K-19
Warsaw, Hancock, 1,882 ... H-4
Washburn, Marshall/Woodford, 1,075 ... F-10
Washington, Tazewell, 10,099 ... G-9
Washington Park, St. Clair, 7,431 ... C-2
Waterloo, Monroe, 5,072 ... N-7
Waterman, DeKalb, 1,074 ... C-11
Watseka, Iroquois, 5,424 ... F-14
Wauconda, Lake, 6,294 ... B-13
Waukegan, Lake, 69,392 ... A-13
Waverly, Morgan, 1,402 ... J-8
Wayne, DuPage/Kane, 1,541 ... H-4
Wayne City, Wayne, 1,099 ... N-11
West Chicago, DuPage, 14,796 ... J-18
West Dundee, Kane, 3,728 ... H-17
West End, Winnebago ... B-10
West Frankfort, Franklin, 8,526 ... O-11
• West Peoria, Peoria, 5,314 ... G-9
West Salem, Edwards, 1,042 ... M-13
Westchester, Cook, 17,301 ... K-22
Western Springs, Cook, 11,984 ... K-21
Westhaven, Cook ... N-22
Westmont, DuPage, 21,228 ... L-21
Westville, Vermilion, 3,387 ... I-14
Wheaton, DuPage, 51,464 ... C-13
Wheeling, Cook/Lake, 29,911 ... G-21
White Hall, Greene, 2,814 ... J-7
Williamsville, Sangamon, 1,140 ... I-9
Willow Springs, Cook/DuPage, 4,509 ... L-22
Willowbrook, DuPage, 8,598 ... L-21
• Willowbrook, Will, 1,808 ... P-25
Wilmette, Cook, 26,690 ... B-14
Wilmington, Will, 4,743 ... E-13
Winchester, Scott, 1,769 ... J-7
Windsor, Shelby, 1,143 ... J-11
Winfield, DuPage, 7,096 ... K-19
Winnebago, Winnebago, 1,840 ... B-10
Winnetka, Cook, 12,174 ... G-23
Winthrop Harbor, Lake, 6,240 ... A-13
Wonder Lake, McHenry, 1,024 ... D-17
• Wonder Lake, McHenry, 6,664 ... A-12
Wood Dale, DuPage, 12,425 ... I-21
Wood River, Madison, 11,490 ... L-7
Woodridge, DuPage/Will, 26,256 ... L-20
Woodstock, McHenry, 14,353 ... A-12
Worth, Cook, 11,208 ... M-23
Wyanet, Bureau, 1,017 ... D-9
Wyoming, Stark, 1,462 ... E-8
• York Center, DuPage, 4,818 ... K-20
Yorkville, Kendall, 3,925 ... D-12
Zeigler, Franklin, 1,746 ... O-10
Zion, Lake, 19,775 ... A-13

Explanation of symbols: •– Census Designated Place (CDP)

Indiana

General Help Numbers:

Governor's Office
206 State House
Indianapolis, IN 46204-2797
www.in.gov/gov

317-232-4567
Fax 317-232-3443
8AM-5PM

Attorney General's Office
402 W Washington
Indianapolis, IN 46204
www.in.gov/attorneygeneral

317-232-6201
8:30AM-5PM

Legislative Records
Legislative Services Agency
200 W Washington, Room 301
Indianapolis, IN 46204-2789
www.in.gov/legislative

317-232-9856
8:15AM-4:45PM

State Archives
Commission on Public Records
6400 E 30th St
Indianapolis, IN 46219
www.in.gov/icpr

317-591-5222
Fax 317-591-5324
8AM-4:30PM

State Specifics:

Capital:

Indianapolis
Marion County

Time Zone:

EST*

* Indiana's eleven northwestern-most counties are CST:
They are: Gibson, Jasper, Laporte, Lake, Newton, Porter, Posey, Spencer, Starke,
Vanderburgh, Warrick.

Number of Counties:

92

Population:

6,195,643

Web Site:

www.state.in.us

State Agencies

Criminal Records

Indiana State Police, Central Records, IGCN - 100
N Senate Ave, Rm N302, Indianapolis, IN 46204-
2259; 317-232-8266, 317-233-8813 (Fax), 8AM-
4PM.

www.IN.gov/isp/

Indexing & Storage: Records are available from
1935. It takes 10 days before new records are
available for inquiry. Records are indexed on
inhouse computer. Records are normally destroyed
after 99 years.

Searching: The release of records is governed by
IC 5-2-5. A "Limited Criminal History" is
available to designated entites including
employers, licensing agencies, schools, and certain
other designates. Use State Form 8053. Include the
following in your request-full name, date of birth,
sex, race. Submitting fingerprints is an option.
100% of the records are fingerprint-supported.

Access by: mail, in person, online.

Fee & Payment: The fee for employers is $7.00
per name for a limited criminal history, and if no
fingerprints used. The fee for a fingerprint search
is $10.00. If subject requests own record, fee is

$10.00, and this is for a FULL record. Fee payee:
State of Indiana. Prepayment required. Cash,
money orders, and certified checks are accepted.
Ongoing requesters may open a monthly billing
account. No bills over $10.00 accepted. Credit
cards accepted online only.

Mail search: Turnaround time: Two weeks. Use
State Form 8053, which can be downloaded from
the   web   site   at
www.in.gov/isp/lch/LCHrequest.pdf.

In person search: Requester must have picture
ID, turnaround time is 15-20 minutes, but the full
record is mailed out 24 hours later.

Online search: The standard online search fee is $17.50 at www.in.gov/isp/lch/. Subcribers to accessIndiana can obtain records for $15.00 per search or for no charge if you are statuatorily exempt, or $7.00 if you have a government exemption.

Statewide Court Records

State Court Administrator, 200 W Washington St, #1080, Indianapolis, IN 46204; 317-232-2542, 317-233-6586 (Fax), 8:30AM-4:30PM.

www.in.gov/judiciary/

Note: Except for certain online research capabilities, all court record access must be done at the local level.

Access by: online.

Online search: The website gives free access to an index of docket information for Supreme, Appeals, and Tax Court cases. There is no statewide trial court records service available.

Sexual Offender Registry

Sex and Violent Offender Directory Manager, Indiana Criminal Justice Institute, One North Capitol, Suite 1000, Indianapolis, IN 46204-2038; 317-232-1233, 317-232-4979 (Fax).

https://secure.in.gov/serv/cji_sor

Note: Indiana law requires the Indiana Criminal Justice Institute to maintain a directory of individuals who have been convicted of one or more of the sex and violent offenses requiring registration with local sheriff departments.

Indexing & Storage: Records are available from 04/01/89.

Searching: While this state agency will help requesters to a point, most searchers are directed to the local sheriffs' offices or to the web page.

Access by: mail, phone, in person, online.

Mail search: Turnaround time: 3 - 5 days.

Phone search: Limited phone searching is available.

In person search: No searching in person at this agency, but you may search at any of the local sheriff's offices in the state.

Online search: The website has a searching capabilities by name and city or county. Also, an excellent search site is maintained by the Indiana Sheriff's Association at www.indianasheriffs.org/default.asp. The Indiana Sheriffs' Sex Offender Registry presents photographs, addresses, and identifiers of registered sex and violent offenders.

Incarceration Records

Indiana Department of Corrections, IGCS, Supervisor of Records, Room E-334, 302 W. Washington Street, Indianapolis, IN 46204; 317-232-5765, 317-232-5728 (Fax), 8AM-4:30PM.

www.in.gov/indcorrection

Indexing & Storage: Records are available on current and former inmates. It takes 10 days before new records are available for inquiry. Records are normally destroyed after 10 years.

Searching: Computerized records go back to 1989. Include the following in your request-first and last name; the DOB and SSN helpful. To search online provide either full name or inmate number. Location, DOC number, physical identifiers, sentencing and conviction information, and release dates are released.

Access by: mail, phone, fax, online.

Fee & Payment: Fee is $.10 per page. Fee payee: Department of Corrections

Mail search: Turnaround time: 5 to 10 working days.

Phone search: Limited searching available by phone.

Fax search: Fax requests are accepted.

Online search: At the website, click on Offender Search.

Corporation, Limited Partnerships, Limited Liability Company, Limited Liability Partnerships, Fictitious Name, Assumed Name,

Corporation Division, Secretary of State, 302 W Washington St, Room E018, Indianapolis, IN 46204; 317-232-6576, 317-233-3387 (Fax), 8AM-5:30PM M-F.

www.IN.gov/sos/

Note: This agency also holds Agricultural Cooperative and Business Trust records.

Indexing & Storage: Records are available for all active entities. It takes 1-3 days before new records are available for inquiry. Records are indexed on microfilm, inhouse computer, and paper.

Searching: There are no restrictions, all information is public record. Include the following in your request-full name of business, specific records that you need copies of. Other records available include: Annual or Bi-annual Reports, Officers (when applicable), Prior (merged) names, Inactive and Reserved names, Assumed Business names, and Registered Agent and address.

Access by: mail, phone, in person, online.

Fee & Payment: There is no search fee. Copies cost $1.00 per page plus $15.00 for document certification. Due & Diligent Searches may be ordered for information that cannot be found initially. Fee payee: Secretary of State. Prepayment required. The state will allow pre-paid accounts for filing only. Personal checks accepted. Credit cards accepted online.

Mail search: Turnaround time: 3 to 5 days. No pre-payments accepted for mail requests. Due & Diligent searches take 10 business days. A SASE is welcomed.

Phone search: Limited verification information is available.

In person search: Requests submitted by noon are ready by noon the next day. Requests after 12 noon are ready within 2 business days.

Online search: You can conduct Business Entity Name Searches, Name Availability Checks and acquire official Certificates of Existence or Authorization at the website. The site also gives access to UCC records. Frequent users of Business Services Online should subscribe to accessIndiana at www.ai.org/ai/business/.

Other access: Monthly lists of all new businesses are available online, as are bulk data and specialized searches. Look for Special Business Entity Search Orders at the website.

Trademarks/Servicemarks

Secretary of State, Trademark Division, 302 W Washington St, IGC-South, Room E018, Indianapolis, IN 46204; 317-232-6540, 317-233-3675 (Fax), 8:AM-4:30PM.

www.in.gov/sos/business/trademarks.html

Note: These records are considered public and are available with no restrictions.

Indexing & Storage: Records are available for active trademarks. It takes 2 to 3 days before new records are available for inquiry. Records are normally destroyed after 3 years after expiration of mark.

Searching: Search requires trademark/servicemark name or file ID number. It generally takes 2 to 3 days to search for logo/designs, but name of mark searches can be done immediately. If you have the file ID number, it will help. Cannot search by owner of trademark.

Access by: mail, phone, fax, in person.

Fee & Payment: Copies cost $1.00 per page, copies returned by fax are an additional $1.00. Fee payee: Secretary of State. Prepayment required. Cash is not accepted. Personal checks accepted. No credit cards accepted.

Mail search: Turnaround time: 2 to 3 days. A SASE is requested.

Phone search: Limited searching by telephone; will do 2 or 3 names only.

Fax search: Limited searching by fax; will do 2 or 3 names only.

In person search: You may request information in person, however, the search clerk is not available full-time.

Uniform Commercial Code

UCC Division, Secretary of State, 302 West Washington St, Room E-018, Indianapolis, IN 46204; 317-233-3984, 317-233-3387 (Fax), 8AM-5:30PM.

www.in.gov/sos/business/ucc.html

Indexing & Storage: Records are available 1964, indexed on computer. It takes 3 days before new records are available for inquiry.

Searching: Use the state request form. All tax liens are filed at the county level. Include the following in your request-debtor name.

Access by: mail, in person, online.

Fee & Payment: The search fee of $5.00 per debtor name, which includes all copies. Fee payee: Secretary of State. Personal checks accepted. No credit cards accepted.

Mail search: Turnaround time: 2 days.

In person search: Turnaround time is 2 days

Online search: You may browse lien records at https://www.ai.org/sos/bus_service/online_ucc/browse/default.asp. There is no charge. An official search may be performed for $4.40. If requester is subscriber to AccessIndiana then fee to obtain record is $3.00. Plans are underway to offer filing services also.

Federal Tax Liens, State Tax Liens

Records not maintained by a state level agency.

Note: All tax liens are found at the county level.

Sales Tax Registrations

In Dept of Revenue, Sales Tax Registrations, PO Box 7218, Indianapolis, IN 46207; 317-233-4015, 317-232-2103 (Fax), 8:15AM-4:45PM.

www.in.gov/dor/

Searching: This agency will only confirm whether a company is registered. No other information will be given about the company. The database is not available for purchase. Include the following in your request-legal name or Indiana Tax ID or Federal Tax ID.

Access by: mail, phone.

Mail search: Turnaround time: 6 to 12 weeks. No fee for mail request.

Phone search: No fee for telephone request. This is very limited, only one search permitted.

Birth Certificates

State Department of Health, Vital Records Office, PO Box 7125, Indianapolis, IN 46206-7125 (Courier: 2 N. Meridian, Indianapolis, IN 46204); 317-233-2700, 317-233-7210 (Fax), 8:15AM-4:45PM.

www.in.gov/isdh/index.htm

Note: The information is also available at each local county health department.

Indexing & Storage: Records are available from October 1907 on and are computerized since 1978. It takes 12 weeks before new records are available for inquiry. Records are indexed on microfilm, index cards, books (volumes).

Searching: Must have a signed release from person of record or be immediate family member or show direct need. Include the following in your request-full name, names of parents, mother's maiden name, date of birth, place of birth, relationship to person of record, reason for information request.

Access by: mail, fax, in person, online.

Fee & Payment: Search is $10.00 per name. If exact date of birth is not known there is an additional fee of $10.00 for each 5 years searched. Add $4.00 per name requested for each additional copy of same record. Fee payee: Indiana State Department of Health. Prepayment required. Personal checks accepted. Credit cards accepted: MasterCard, Visa, AmEx, Discover.

Mail search: Turnaround time: 3 to 4 weeks. Must include a copy of a signature ID with your request. No SASE is required.

Fax search: See expedited service.

In person search: Only available between 10AM-2PM, it takes about 30 minutes to process the request.

Online search: Records may be ordered online via the website, but the requester must still fax a photo copy of an ID before the record request is processed. Also, records may requested from www.vitalchek.com, a state-endorsed vendor.

Expedited service: Expedited service is available for mail, online and fax searches. Turnaround time: 3 to 5 days. The expedited service requires use of a credit card (extra $5.50) and a $12.85 payment for overnight service.

Death Records

State Department of Health, Vital Records Office, PO Box 7125, Indianapolis, IN 46206-7125 (Courier: 2 N. Meridian, Indianapolis, IN 46204); 317-233-2700, 317-233-7210 (Fax), 8:15AM-4:45PM.

www.in.gov/isdh/index.htm

Indexing & Storage: Records are available from 1900 on. It takes 12 weeks before new records are available for inquiry. Records are indexed on microfilm, index cards, books (volumes).

Searching: This index is not for public review. You must have a signed release from immediate family member. Include a copy of your photo ID with your request. Include the following in your request-full name, date of death, place of death, relationship to person of record, reason for information request.

Access by: mail, fax, in person, online.

Fee & Payment: Fee is $8.00 per name. If exact date of death is not known, there is a $8.00 fee for each 5 years searched. Add $4.00 per name requested for each additional copy of same record. Fee payee: Indiana State Department of Health. Prepayment required. Personal checks accepted. Credit cards accepted: MasterCard, Visa, AmEx, Discover.

Mail search: Turnaround time: 1 month. No SASE is required.

Fax search: See expedited service.

In person search: Available from 10AM-2PM.

Online search: Records may requested from www.vitalchek.com, a state-endorsed vendor.

Expedited service: Expedited service is available for fax searches. Turnaround time: 3 to 5 days. The expedited service requires use of a credit card fee ($5.50) and $12.85 payment for express delivery.

Marriage Certificates, Divorce Records

Records not maintained by a state level agency.

Note: Marriage and divorce records are found at county of issue. This agency tells us that the index can also be found at the Indiana State Library.

Workers' Compensation Records

Workers Compensation Board, 402 W Washington St, Room W196, Indianapolis, IN 46204-2753; 317-232-3808, 317-233-5493 (Fax), 8AM-4:30PM.

www.in.gov/workcomp/index.html

Note: Claims information for disputes that require a hearing are available online, those are the only online records available.

Indexing & Storage: Records are available for past 9 years. It takes 48 hours before new records are available for inquiry. Records are indexed on inhouse computer. Records are normally destroyed after 12 years.

Searching: Must have a notarized authorization release from claimant or a subpoena to obtain records from this agency. Requests are reviewed by the Executive Secretary who decides whether to release the information. Include the following in your request-claimant name, Social Security Number, date of accident, reason for information request.

Access by: mail.

Fee & Payment: Copies are $.10 per page, there is no search fee. Fee payee: Workers Compensation Board. Personal checks accepted. No credit cards accepted.

Mail search: Turnaround time: variable. A SASE is required.

Driver Records

BMV-Driving Records, 100 N Senate Ave, Indiana Government Center North, Room N405, Indianapolis, IN 46204; 317-232-6000 x2, 8:15AM-4:30PM.

www.IN.gov/bmv/

Note: Copies of tickets are available at the address listed above for a fee of $8.00 per ticket.

Indexing & Storage: Records are available for 7 years (10 years for habitual violators) for moving violations; 10 years for DWIs and suspensions. Accidents reported to the state police appear on the record. It takes 1-3 weeks before new records are available for inquiry.

Searching: Personal information is not disclosed to casual requesters. Further, a driver's SSN, driver's license number or Federal ID number is not disclosed to all non-governmental requesters. Include the following in your request-State Form 48430, ID of requester. The license number or name and DOB are required when ordering a record.

Access by: mail, in person, online.

Fee & Payment: The fee is $4.00 per record, except for online requests. The fee is $8.00 for a certified record. The fee is $12.00 for certified "complete" record and history. Turnaround time is 4 to 6 weeks for certified records. Fee payee: Bureau of Motor Vehicles. Prepayment required. Personal checks accepted. No credit cards accepted.

Mail search: Turnaround time: 7 to 10 days. No SASE is required.

In person search: Up to seven requests are processed at one time for a walk-in requester at the Customer Service Center located at 531 Virginia Ave, Indianapolis or at any of the Regional Service Centers.

Online search: Access Indiana Information Network (AIIN) is the state owned interactive information and communication system which provides batch and interactive access to driving records. There is an annual $50.00 fee. Online access costs $6.00 per record. For more information, call AIIN at 317-233-2010 or go to www.in.gov.

Vehicle and Vessel Ownership and Registration

Bureau of Motor Vehicles, Records, 100 N Senate Ave, Room N404, Indianapolis, IN 46204; 317-233-2513 (Titles), 317-233-6000 (Registration), 8:15AM-4:45PM.

www.in.gov/bmv/

Indexing & Storage: Records are available for 3 years on computer and up to ten years on microfilm. All motor boats that were valued over $3,000 when new must be titled and registered.

Searching: Casual requesters can obtain records, but no personal information is released on subjects without consent. Vehicle owner's SSN, driver's license number, and Federal ID number cannot be disclosed to all non-governmental requesters. There are five types of records available for search; title inquiry, title history, registration inquiry, registration history, and registration copy. The title history will show liens. The title inquiry will show current listed lienholder, also.

Access by: mail, in person, online.

Fee & Payment: For vehicle, the fee is $4.00 per "inquiry" and $8.00 per "history." For watercraft, the fee is $4.00 for all title and registration searches. Fee payee: Bureau of Motor Vehicles. Prepayment required. Personal checks accepted. No credit cards accepted.

Mail search: Turnaround time: within 2 weeks. No SASE is required.

In person search: The walk-in address for the Customer Service Center is 531 Virginia Ave, Indianapolis. Turnaround time depends on availability of personnel. Title histories are not provided on an immediate basis, they must be returned by mail or picked up later.

Online search: The Access Indiana Information network (AIIN) at 317-233-2010 is the state appointed vendor. Visit www.in.gov for more information. Search the Indiana Bureau of Motor Vehicles database for title and lien information by VIN number, title number, or social security number. Salvage titles included. The fee is $5.00 per record plus an annual fee of $50.00.

Other access: Bulk record requests are not available from Indiana.

Accident Reports

State Police Department, Vehicle Crash Records Sections, Room N301, Indiana Government Center, Indianapolis, IN 46204; 317-232-8286, 317-232-0652 (Fax), 8AM-4PM.

Note: The only reports released are those of the officers. Indiana operator report forms are not released.

Indexing & Storage: Records are available from 20 years to present. Older records are archived on microfiche. It takes 2 weeks before new records are available for inquiry.

Searching: Include the following in your request- full name, date of accident, location of accident.

Access by: mail, phone, in person.

Fee & Payment: The fee is $3.00 per report. If you are requesting all reports on a per-name basis, there is a $6.81 per hour search fee in addition. Fee payee: Indiana State Police. Prepayment required. Personal checks accepted. No credit cards accepted.

Mail search: Turnaround time: 10 days. No SASE is required.

Phone search: You can phone to see if a report is on file before the fee is sent.

In person search: Normal turnaround time is while you wait. If you are requesting all accidents on a "name," this request should be in writing and will take longer.

Other access: For information about bulk file purchasing, contact the Data Section at 317-232-8289.

Voter Registration

Access to Records is Restricted

Election Division, 302 Washington, Room E-204, Indianapolis, IN 46204-2767; 317-232-3939, 317-233-6793 (Fax), 8AM-4:30PM.

www.IN.gov/sos/elections/

Note: This agency will not sell records for commercial or investigative reasons, but will sell data in bulk format for political purposes for $5,000. In general, the Circuit Court has records locally. Campaign finance reports are searchable at the website, which is full of good information about elections in IN.

GED Certificates

Division of Adult Education, GED Testing, State House Rm 229, Indianapolis, IN 46204-2798; 317-232-0522, 317-233-0859 (Fax), 8AM-4:30PM.

www.doe.state.in.us/adulted/

Note: The suggested Release Form is available online at the website. This agency also releases diplomas and transcripts of scores.

Indexing & Storage: It takes six weeks before new records are available for inquiry.

Searching: To search, all of the following are required: a signed release, name, date/year of test, date of birth, SSN, city of test, and a phone number where you can be reached.

Access by: mail, fax.

Fee & Payment: There is no fee. Email requests are accepted, but, like all requests, a signed release is required.

Mail search: Turnaround time: 5 to 7 days. Records are available by mail.

Fax search: Records are available by fax.

Hunting and Fishing License Information

Records not maintained by a state level agency.

Note: There is not a true statewide centralized database. The licenses purchased online are warehoused by www.accessIndiana.com. Vendors throughout the state keep all hard copies of their records. This agency and accessindiana will not do look-ups on the system and will not make lists available.

Indiana State Licensing Agencies

Licenses Searchable Online

Acupuncturist #9 .... https://extranet.in.gov/WebLookup/Search.aspx

Appraiser, Residential/General/Trainee/Temp #18 .... https://extranet.in.gov/WebLookup/Search.aspx

Architect #18 .... https://extranet.in.gov/WebLookup/Search.aspx

Asbestos Contractor #4 .... www.in.gov/idem/air/compliance/index.html

Asbestos Disposal Manager/Worker #4 .... www.in.gov/idem/air/compliance/index.html

Asbestos Inspector/Supervisor/Project Designer #4 .... www.in.gov/idem/air/compliance/index.html

Asbestos Training Course Provider #4 .... www.in.gov/idem/air/compliance/index.html

Athletic Trainer #9 .... https://extranet.in.gov/WebLookup/Search.aspx

Attorney #15 .... http://hostpub.courts.state.in.us/HostPublisher/rollatty/roa1_inp.jsp

Auctioneer #18 .... https://extranet.in.gov/WebLookup/Search.aspx

Audiologist #9 .... https://extranet.in.gov/WebLookup/Search.aspx

Bailbondsman/Agent #7 .... www.in.gov/idoi/bailbond/

Barber/Barber Instructor #18 .... https://extranet.in.gov/WebLookup/Search.aspx

Boxer #18 .... https://extranet.in.gov/WebLookup/Search.aspx

Boxing Occupation #18 .... https://extranet.in.gov/WebLookup/Search.aspx

Child Care Center/Child Care Home/Provider #10 .... www.carefinderindiana.org/carefinder/LicStatus.htm

Chiropractor #9 .... https://extranet.in.gov/WebLookup/Search.aspx

Clinical Nurse Specialist #9 .... https://extranet.in.gov/WebLookup/Search.aspx

Collection Agency #19 .... www.in.gov/sos/securities/

Cosmetologist #18 .... https://extranet.in.gov/WebLookup/Search.aspx

CPA-Public Accountant #18 .... https://extranet.in.gov/WebLookup/Search.aspx

Dental Anesthetist #9 .... https://extranet.in.gov/WebLookup/Search.aspx

Dental Hygienist #9 .... https://extranet.in.gov/WebLookup/Search.aspx

Dentist #9 .... https://extranet.in.gov/WebLookup/Search.aspx

Dietitian #9 .... https://extranet.in.gov/WebLookup/Search.aspx

Electrologist #18 .... https://extranet.in.gov/WebLookup/Search.aspx

Embalmer #18 .... https://extranet.in.gov/WebLookup/Search.aspx

Emergency Medical Technician #22 .... www.in.gov/sema/ems

Engineer #18 .... https://extranet.in.gov/WebLookup/Search.aspx

Engineering Intern #18 .... https://extranet.in.gov/WebLookup/Search.aspx

Environmental Health Specialist #9 .... https://extranet.in.gov/WebLookup/Search.aspx

Esthetician #18 .... https://extranet.in.gov/WebLookup/Search.aspx

Funeral/Cemetery Director #18 .... https://extranet.in.gov/WebLookup/Search.aspx

Hazardous Waste Facility/Handler #5 .... www.in.gov/idem/land/permits/lists/index.html

Health Services Administrator #9 .... https://extranet.in.gov/WebLookup/Search.aspx

Hearing Aid Dealer #9 .... https://extranet.in.gov/WebLookup/Search.aspx

Hypnotist #9 .... https://extranet.in.gov/WebLookup/Search.aspx

Insurance Agent/Consultant #7 .... www.in.gov/idoi/agent_licensing/

Investment Advisor #19 .... www.in.gov/sos/securities/

Landscape Architect #18 .... https://extranet.in.gov/WebLookup/Search.aspx

Loan Broker #19 .... www.in.gov/sos/securities/

Lottery Retailer #16 .... www.in.gov/hoosierlottery/games/retailerlocator.asp

Manicurist #18 .... https://extranet.in.gov/WebLookup/Search.aspx

Marriage & Family Therapist #9 .... https://extranet.in.gov/WebLookup/Search.aspx

Medical Doctor #9 .... https://extranet.in.gov/WebLookup/Search.aspx

Medical Residency Permit #9 .... https://extranet.in.gov/WebLookup/Search.aspx

Mental Health Counselor #9 .... https://extranet.in.gov/WebLookup/Search.aspx

Midwife Nurse #9 .... https://extranet.in.gov/WebLookup/Search.aspx

Notary Public #17 .... www.ai.org/serv/sos_notary

Nurse Midwife #9 .... https://extranet.in.gov/WebLookup/Search.aspx

Nurse-RN/LPN #9 .... https://extranet.in.gov/WebLookup/Search.aspx

Nursing Home Administrator #9 .... https://extranet.in.gov/WebLookup/Search.aspx

Occupational Therapist /Therapy Assistant #9 .... https://extranet.in.gov/WebLookup/Search.aspx

Optometrist #9 .... https://extranet.in.gov/WebLookup/Search.aspx

Optometrist Drug Certification #9 .... https://extranet.in.gov/WebLookup/Search.aspx
Osteopathic Physician #9 .... https://extranet.in.gov/WebLookup/Search.aspx
Pharmacist/Pharmacist Intern/Pharmacy Technician #9 .. https://extranet.in.gov/WebLookup/Search.aspx
Physical Therapist/Therapist Assistant #9 .... https://extranet.in.gov/WebLookup/Search.aspx
Physician/Physician Assistant #9 .... https://extranet.in.gov/WebLookup/Search.aspx
PI Company Employee #18 .... https://extranet.in.gov/WebLookup/Search.aspx
Placement Officer #14 .... http://mustang.doe.state.in.us/TEACH/teach_inq.cfm
Plumber #18 .... https://extranet.in.gov/WebLookup/Search.aspx
Plumbing Contractor #18 .... https://extranet.in.gov/WebLookup/Search.aspx
Podiatrist #9 .... https://extranet.in.gov/WebLookup/Search.aspx
Polygraph Examiner #21 .... www.polygraphorganizations.org/IPA/members.html
Private Detective #18 .... https://extranet.in.gov/WebLookup/Search.aspx
Psychologist #9 .... https://extranet.in.gov/WebLookup/Search.aspx
Public Accountant #18 .... https://extranet.in.gov/WebLookup/Search.aspx
Real Estate Agent/Broker/Seller #18 .... https://extranet.in.gov/WebLookup/Search.aspx
Real Estate Appraiser #18 .... https://extranet.in.gov/WebLookup/Search.aspx
Recovery Agent #7 .... www.in.gov/idoi/bailbond/
Respiratory Care Practitioner #9 .... https://extranet.in.gov/WebLookup/Search.aspx
School Administrator/Principal #14 .... http://mustang.doe.state.in.us/TEACH/teach_inq.cfm
School Counselor/Director #14 .... http://mustang.doe.state.in.us/TEACH/teach_inq.cfm
School Nurse #14 .... http://mustang.doe.state.in.us/TEACH/teach_inq.cfm
Securities Broker/Dealer/Sales Agent #19 .... www.in.gov/sos/securities/
Shampoo Operator #18 .... https://extranet.in.gov/WebLookup/Search.aspx
Social Worker #9 .... https://extranet.in.gov/WebLookup/Search.aspx
Social Worker, Clinical #9 .... https://extranet.in.gov/WebLookup/Search.aspx
Solid Waste Facility #5 .... www.in.gov/idem/land/permits/lists/index.html
Speech Pathologist #9 .... https://extranet.in.gov/WebLookup/Search.aspx
Surveyor, Land #18 .... https://extranet.in.gov/WebLookup/Search.aspx
Teacher #14 .... http://mustang.doe.state.in.us/TEACH/teach_inq.cfm
Veterinarian/Veterinary Tech #9 .... https://extranet.in.gov/WebLookup/Search.aspx
Waste Tire Processor/Transporter #5 .... www.in.gov/idem/land/permits/lists/index.html
Yard Waste Composting Facility #5 .... www.in.gov/idem/land/permits/lists/index.html

Indiana Licensing Quick Finder

Acupuncturist #9 317-232-2960
Alcoholic Beverage Dealer/Manufacturer #1
.... 317-232-2430
Alcoholic Beverage Dist./Retailer/Employee #1
.... 317-232-2430
Animal (Dead) Rendering #2 317-227-0300
Appraiser, Residential/General #18 317-232-2980
Appraiser, Trainee/Temp #18 317-232-2980
Architect #18 317-232-2980
Asbestos Contractor #4 317-232-4861
Asbestos Disposal Mgr./Worker #4 317-232-8232
Asbestos Inspector/Spvr./Designer #4 . 317-232-8232
Asbestos Management Planner #4 317-232-8232
Asbestos Training Course Provider #4.. 317-232-8219
Athletic Trainer #9 317-232-2960
Attorney #15 317-232-5861
Auctioneer #18 317-232-2980
Audiologist #9 317-232-2960
Bailbondsman/Agent #7 317-232-5249
Bank & Trust Company #6 317-232-5846
Barber/Barber Instructor #18 317-232-2980
Boiler & Pressure Vessel Inspector #8 .. 317-232-1921
Boxer #18 317-232-2980
Boxing Occupation #18 317-232-2980
Brands, Livestock #2 317-227-0300
Building & Loan #6 317-232-5851
Check Casher #6 317-232-3955
Child Care Center #10 317-232-4469
Child Care Home/Provider #10 317-232-4521
Chiropractor #9 317-232-2960

Clinical Nurse Specialist #9 317-232-2960
Collection Agency #19 317-232-0093
Consumer Credit Grantor #6 317-232-5849
Cosmetologist #18 317-232-2980
CPA-Public Accountant #18 317-232-2980
Credit Union #6 317-232-5851
Dairy-related Occupation #2 317-227-0300
Dental Anesthetist #9 317-232-2960
Dental Hygienist #9 317-232-2960
Dentist #9 317-232-2960
Dietitian #9 317-232-2960
Electrologist #18 317-232-2980
Elevator Safety Contractor #8 317-232-6609
Embalmer #18 317-232-2980
Emergency Medical Technician #22 ... 317-233-6545
Engineer #18 317-232-2980
Engineering Intern #18 317-232-2980
Environmental Health Specialist #9 317-232-2960
Esthetician #18 317-232-2980
Funeral/Cemetery Director #18 317-232-2980
Grain Bank/Warehouse #12 317-232-1358
Grain Buyer #12 317-232-1360
Hazardous Waste Facility/Handler #5 .. 317-232-8603
Health Services Administrator #9 317-232-2960
Hearing Aid Dealer #9 317-232-2960
Horse Racing Occupation #13 317-233-3119
Hypnotist #9 317-232-2960
Insurance Adjuster #7 317-232-2414
Insurance Agent/Consultant #7 317-232-2414
Investment Advisor #19 317-232-6681

Landscape Architect #18 317-232-2980
Lead Contractor #4 317-232-4861
Lead Inspector #4 317-233-6514
Lead Project Designer #4 317-233-6514
Lead Project Supervisor #4 317-233-6514
Lead Risk Assessor #4 317-233-6514
Lead Training Course Provider #4 317-232-8219
Lead Worker #4 317-233-6514
Lender #6 317-232-3955
Livestock Dealer/market #2 317-227-0300
Livestock Transportation #2 317-227-0300
Loan Broker #19 317-232-6681
Lottery Retailer #16 317-264-4800
Manicurist #18 317-232-2980
Manufactured Home Builder #8 317-232-1408
Marriage & Family Therapist #9 317-232-2960
Meat & Poultry #2 317-227-0300
Medical Doctor #9 317-232-2960
Medical Residency Permit #9 317-232-2960
Mental Health Counselor #9 317-232-2960
Midwife Nurse #9 317-232-2960
Money Transmitter #6 317-232-3955
Notary Public #17 317-232-6542
Nurse #9 317-232-2960
Nurse Midwife #9 317-232-2960
Nurse-RN/LPN #9 317-232-2960
Nursing Home Administrator #9 317-232-2960
Occupational Therapist #9 317-232-2960
Occupational Therapy Assistant #9 317-232-2960
Optometrist #9 317-232-2960

Optometrist Drug Certification #9	317-232-2960
Osteopathic Physician #9	317-232-2960
Pawnbroker #6	317-232-3955
Pesticide Applicator #3	765-494-1594
Pesticide Technician/Consultant #3	765-494-1594
Pharmacist/Pharmacist Intern #9	317-232-2960
Pharmacy Technician #9	317-232-2960
Physical Therapist/Therapist Asst #9	317-233-2960
Physician #9	317-232-2960
Physician Assistant #9	317-232-2960
PI Company Employee #18	317-232-2980
Placement Officer #14	317-232-9010
Plumber #18	317-232-2980
Plumbing Contractor #18	317-232-2980
Podiatrist #9	317-232-2960

Polygraph Examiner #21	317-232-8263
Private Detective #18	317-232-2980
Psychologist #9	317-232-2960
Public Accountant #18	317-232-2980
Radiologic Technologist #20	317-233-7565
Real Estate Agent/Broker/Seller #18	317-232-2980
Real Estate Appraiser #18	317-232-2980
Recovery Agent #7	317-232-5249
Respiratory Care Practitioner #9	317-232-2960
School Administrator/Principal #14	317-232-9010
School Counselor #14	317-232-9010
School Director #14	317-232-9010
School Nurse #14	317-232-9010
Securities Broker/Dealer #19	317-232-6690
Securities Sales Agent #19	317-232-6690

Shampoo Operator #18	317-232-2980
Social Worker #9	317-232-2960
Social Worker, Clinical #9	317-232-2960
Solid Waste Facility #5	317-232-8603
Speech Pathologist #9	317-232-2960
Surveyor, Land #18	317-232-2980
Teacher #14	317-232-9010
Underground Storage Tank #8	317-233-3560
Veterinarian #9	317-232-2960
Veterinary Tech #9	317-232-2960
Warehouse, Agricultural, etc. #12	317-232-1358
Waste Tire Processor/Transporter #5	317-232-8603
Waste Water Treatment Plant Operator #5	317-232-8666
Yard Waste Composting Facility #5	317-232-8603

Indiana Licensing Agency Information

1 Alcohol and Tobacco Commission, 302 W Washington St, Rm E114, Indianapolis, IN 46204; 317-233-3940, Fax: 317-233-6114.
www.in.gov/atc   Email: kchew@atc.state.in.us

2 Licensing & Compliance, Board of Animal Health, 805 Beachway Dr #50, Indianapolis, IN 46224; 317-227-0300, Fax: 317-227-0330.
www.state.in.us/boah/   Email: dderrer@boah.in.gov

3 Department of Biochemistry, Office of Indiana State Chemist, Purdue University,175 S. University Street, West Lafayette, IN 47907-2063; 765-494-1492, Fax: 765-494-4331.
www.isco.purdue.edu   Email: walshm@isco.purdue.edu

4 Department of Environmental Management, Asbestos/Lead Program, 100 N. Senate, Indianapolis, IN 46204-6015; 317-233.3257, Fax: 317-232-8406.
www.IN.gov/idem/   Search Database at www.in.gov/idem/air/compliance/index.html

5 Department of Environmental Management, Office of Land Quality, PO Box 6015, Indianapolis, IN 46204-6015; 317-232-8603, Fax: 317-232-8406.
www.in.gov/idem/land/
Email: webmaster@dem.state.in.us   Search Database at www.in.gov/idem/land/permits/lists/index.html

6 Department of Financial Institutions, 30 S Meridian St #300, Indianapolis, IN 46204-2759; 317-232-3955, Fax: 317-232-7655.
www.dfi.state.in.us

7 Department of Insurance, 311 W Washington St #300, Indianapolis, IN 46204-2787; 317-232-2385, Fax: 317-232-5251.
www.in.gov/idoi   Email: doi@state.in.us
Search Database at www.in.gov/idoi/

8 Fire & Building Services, 402 W Washington St, IGS-S, Rm W246, Indianapolis, IN 46204; 317-232-2222, Fax: 317-232-0146.
www.in.gov/sema/osfm/

9 Health Professions Bureau, 402 W Washington St Rm W066, Indianapolis, IN 46204-2758; 317-232-2960, Fax: 317-233-4236.
www.ai.org/hpb   Email: kburch@hpb.state.in.us
Search Database at
https://extranet.in.gov/WebLookup/Search.aspx
Note: To search online, you have to subscribe to AIIN. For more info on AIIN, visit
www.state.in.us/premium/about.html.

10 Family and Social Services Administration, Bureau of Child Development, 402 W. Washington St., Rm W386, Indianapolis, IN 46201; 317-232-1144.
www.ai.org/fssa/children
Email: cbigsbee2@fssa.state.in.us/
Search Database at www.carefinderindiana.org

12 Grain Buyers & Warehouse Licensing Agency, 150 W Market St, Rm 416, Indianapolis, IN 46204-2810; 317-232-1356, Fax: 317-232-1362.
www.IN.gov/igbwla/
Email: dhenry@commerce.state.in.us Note:
Confidentiality Clause in governing statute prevents giving listing of licensees.

13 Horse Racing Licensing, 150 W Market St, Indianapolis, IN 46204; 317-233-3119, Fax: 317-233-4470.
www.IN.gov/ihrc/   Email: hrc@state.in.us

14 Professional Standards Board, 101 W Ohio St, #300, Indianapolis, IN 46204; 317-232-9010, 1-866-542-3672, Fax: 317-232-9023.
www.state.in.us/psb
Email: helpdesk@psb.state.in.us

15 Clerk of the Indiana Supreme Court, Roll of Attoneys Clerk, 217 State House, 20th Fl, Indianapolis, IN 46204; 317-232-1930, Fax: 317-232-8365. www.IN.gov/judiciary/
Search Database at http://hostpub.courts.state.in.us/HostPublisher/rollatty/roa1_inp.jsp

16 Lottery Commission of Indiana, 201 S Capitol Av #1100, Indianapolis, IN 46225; 317-264-4800, Fax: 317-264-4908.
www.in.gov/hoosierlottery
Email: playersupport@hoosierlottery.com

17 Business Services Division - Notary, Office of Secretary of State, Statehouse, #201, Indianapolis, IN 46204; 317-232-6542, Fax: 317-233-3283.
www.in.gov/sos/notary/
Email: notary@sos.in.gov
Search Database at www.ai.org/serv/sos_notary

18 Professional Licensing Agency, Boards & Commissions, 302 W Washington St, Rm E034, Indianapolis, IN 46204; 317-232-2980, Fax: 317-232-2312. www.IN.gov/pla/
Email: jsmall@hpb.in.gov   Search Database at https://extranet.in.gov/WebLookup/Search.aspx

19 Secretary of State, Securities Division, 302 W Washington Rm E-111, Indianapolis, IN 46204; 317-232-6681, Fax: 317-233-3675.
www.in.gov/sos/securities/index.html
Search Database at
www.in.gov/serv/sos_securities

20 Division of End. & Radiologic Health, Board of Health, 2 N Meridian St, 5F, Indianapolis, IN 46204-3010; 317-233-7150, Fax: 317-233-7154.

21 State Police, 100 N Senate Ave, Government Center N, #302, Indianapolis, IN 46204-2259; 317-232-8263.
www.indianapolygraphassociation.com
Search Database at www.polygraphorganizations.org/IPA/members.html

22 Emergency Medical Svcs, EMS Certification, 302 W Washington St, IGCS #E208, Indianapolis, IN 46204; 317-233-6545, Fax: 317-233-8394.
www.in.gov/sema   Search Database at www.in.gov/sema/ems Note: The toll free number EMS number is 800-666-7784.

Indiana Federal Courts

The following list indicates the district and division name for each county in the state. If the bankruptcy court location is different from the district court, then the location of the bankruptcy court appears in parentheses.

County/Court Cross Reference

County	District	Division
Adams	Northern	Fort Wayne
Allen	Northern	Fort Wayne
Bartholomew	Southern	Indianapolis
Benton	Northern	Lafayette (Hammond at Lafayette)
Blackford	Northern	Fort Wayne
Boone	Southern	Indianapolis
Brown	Southern	Indianapolis
Carroll	Northern	Lafayette (Hammond at Lafayette)
Cass	Northern	South Bend
Clark	Southern	New Albany
Clay	Southern	Terre Haute
Clinton	Southern	Indianapolis
Crawford	Southern	New Albany
Daviess	Southern	Evansville
DeKalb	Northern	Fort Wayne
Dearborn	Southern	New Albany
Decatur	Southern	Indianapolis
Delaware	Southern	Indianapolis
Dubois	Southern	Evansville
Elkhart	Northern	South Bend
Fayette	Southern	Indianapolis
Floyd	Southern	New Albany
Fountain	Southern	Indianapolis
Franklin	Southern	Indianapolis
Fulton	Northern	South Bend
Gibson	Southern	Evansville
Grant	Northern	Fort Wayne
Greene	Southern	Terre Haute
Hamilton	Southern	Indianapolis
Hancock	Southern	Indianapolis
Harrison	Southern	New Albany
Hendricks	Southern	Indianapolis
Henry	Southern	Indianapolis
Howard	Southern	Indianapolis
Huntington	Northern	Fort Wayne
Jackson	Southern	New Albany
Jasper	Northern	Lafayette (Hammond at Lafayette)
Jay	Northern	Fort Wayne
Jefferson	Southern	New Albany
Jennings	Southern	New Albany
Johnson	Southern	Indianapolis
Knox	Southern	Terre Haute
Kosciusko	Northern	South Bend
La Porte	Northern	South Bend
LaGrange	Northern	Fort Wayne
Lake	Northern	Hammond (Hammond. at Gary)
Lawrence	Southern	New Albany
Madison	Southern	Indianapolis
Marion	Southern	Indianapolis
Marshall	Northern	South Bend
Martin	Southern	Evansville
Miami	Northern	South Bend
Monroe	Southern	Indianapolis
Montgomery	Southern	Indianapolis
Morgan	Southern	Indianapolis
Newton	Northern	Lafayette (Hammond at Lafayette)
Noble	Northern	Fort Wayne
Ohio	Southern	New Albany
Orange	Southern	New Albany
Owen	Southern	Terre Haute
Parke	Southern	Terre Haute
Perry	Southern	Evansville
Pike	Southern	Evansville
Porter	Northern	Hammond (Hammond. at Gary)
Posey	Southern	Evansville
Pulaski	Northern	South Bend
Putnam	Southern	Terre Haute
Randolph	Southern	Indianapolis
Ripley	Southern	New Albany
Rush	Southern	Indianapolis
Scott	Southern	New Albany
Shelby	Southern	Indianapolis
Spencer	Southern	Evansville
St. Joseph	Northern	South Bend
Starke	Northern	South Bend
Steuben	Northern	Fort Wayne
Sullivan	Southern	Terre Haute
Switzerland	Southern	New Albany
Tippecanoe	Northern	Lafayette (Hammond at Lafayette)
Tipton	Southern	Indianapolis
Union	Southern	Indianapolis
Vanderburgh	Southern	Evansville
Vermillion	Southern	Terre Haute
Vigo	Southern	Terre Haute
Wabash	Northern	South Bend
Warren	Northern	Lafayette (Hammond at Lafayette)
Warrick	Southern	Evansville
Washington	Southern	New Albany
Wayne	Southern	Indianapolis
Wells	Northern	Fort Wayne
White	Northern	Lafayette (Hammond at Lafayette)
Whitley	Northern	Fort Wayne

Standards for Federal Courts: The search fee is $20.00 per item (one party name or case number). Certification fee is $7.00 per document. Copy fee is $.50 per page. All fees standard unless noted in profile. Mail Search: always enclose a stamped self addressed envelope unless otherwise noted. Most courts accept fax requests or will suggest a copying/search vendor. Before releasing records, all courts require prepayment unless noted in profile.

Open records are located at the court unless otherwise noted. District courts index by defendant and plaintiff as well as by case number. Bankruptcy courts usually index by debtor and case number. While most courts now have their indexes on computer, many still maintain index card files as well.

The universal PACER sign-up number is 800-676-6856. Find PACER and the Party/Case Index on the Web at http://pacer.psc.uscourts.gov. PACER dial-up access is $.60 per minute. Also, courts offering internet access via RACER, PACER, Web-PACER or the new CM-ECF charge $.07 per page fee unless noted as free.

US District Court

Northern District of Indiana

Fort Wayne Division Room 1108, Federal Bldg, 1300 S Harrison St, Fort Wayne, IN 46802 (courier address: Use mail address for courier delivery) 260-424-7360. www.innd.uscourts.gov

Counties: Adams, Allen, Blackford, DeKalb, Grant, Huntington, Jay, Lagrange, Noble, Steuben, Wells, Whitley.

Indexing & Storage: New cases available in the index 1-2 days after filing date.

Fee & Payment: Payment may be made by money order, cashier check, personal check. Payee: Clerk, U.S. District Court.

Phone Search: Only case names and numbers will be released over the phone.

In Person Search: Fee charged if court conducts your in person search for you. Only the court may search the card index.

PACER: PACER is available online at http://pacer.innd.uscourts.gov. Records purged as deemed necessary. New records are online after 2 days.

Electronic Filing: Electronic filing information at https://ecf.innd.uscourts.gov/cgi-bin/login.pl

Hammond Division Room 101, 507 State St, Hammond, IN 46320 (courier address: Use mail address for courier delivery) 219-937-5235. www.innd.uscourts.gov

Counties: Lake, Porter.

Indexing & Storage: New cases available in the index 1-3 days after filing date.

Fee & Payment: Payment may be made by money order, cashier check, personal check. Payee: Clerk, U.S. District Court.

Phone Search: Only docket information available.

In Person Search: Fee charged if court conducts your in person search for you.

PACER: PACER is available online at http://pacer.innd.uscourts.gov. Records purged as deemed necessary. New records are online after 2 days.

Electronic Filing: Electronic filing information at https://ecf.innd.uscourts.gov/cgi-bin/login.pl

Lafayette Division PO Box 1498, Lafayette, IN 47902 (courier: 230 N 4th St, Lafayette, IN 47901), 765-420-6250. www.innd.uscourts.gov

Counties: Benton, Carroll, Jasper, Newton, Tippecanoe, Warren, White.

Indexing & Storage: New cases available in the index 24 hours after filing date. Microfiche is also available.

Fee & Payment: Payment may be made by money order, cashier check, personal check. Payee: Clerk, U.S. District Court.

Phone Search: Only docket information available.

In Person Search: Fee charged if court conducts your in person search for you.

PACER: PACER is available online at http://pacer.innd.uscourts.gov. Records purged as deemed necessary. New records are online after 2 days.

Electronic Filing: Electronic filing information at https://ecf.innd.uscourts.gov/cgi-bin/login.pl

South Bend Division Room 102, 204 S Main, South Bend, IN 46601 (courier address: Use mail address for courier delivery) 574-246-8000, Fax: 574-246-8002. www.innd.uscourts.gov

Counties: Cass, Elkhart, Fulton, Kosciusko, La Porte, Marshall, Miami, Pulaski, St. Joseph, Starke, Wabash.

Indexing & Storage: New cases available in the index 2 days after filing date.

Fee & Payment: Payment may be made by money order, cashier check, personal check. Payee: Clerk, U.S. District Court.

Phone Search: Only docket information available.

In Person Search: Fee charged if court conducts your in person search for you.

PACER: PACER is available online at http://pacer.innd.uscourts.gov. Document images are available in the RACER section. Records purged as deemed necessary. New records are online after 2 days.

Electronic Filing: Electronic filing information at https://ecf.innd.uscourts.gov/cgi-bin/login.pl

U.S. Bankruptcy Court

Northern District of Indiana

Fort Wayne Division PO Box 2547, Fort Wayne, IN 46801-2547 (courier address: 1188 Federal Bldg, 1300 S Harrison St, Fort Wayne, IN 46802), 260-420-5100. www.innb.uscourts.gov

Counties: Adams, Allen, Blackford, DeKalb, Grant, Huntington, Jay, Lagrange, Noble, Steuben, Wells, Whitley.

Indexing & Storage: Cases indexed by debtor and creditors as well as by case number. New cases available in the index 24 hours after filing date. A card index of debtor names is also maintained. Records in closed cases are only kept locally for a

brief period. Records are shipped to the Chicago FRC annually. At the time a case is closed, both the date of filing and the date of closing are factors in determining when the case is shipped.

Fee & Payment: Payment may be made by money order, cashier check, personal check. Debtor's checks are not accepted. Payee: Clerk, U.S. Bankruptcy Court.

Phone Search: Only docket information available by phone. Automated voice case information service (VCIS) is available. Call VCIS at 800-755-8393 or 574-236-8814.

In Person Search: Fee charged if court conducts your in person search for you.

PACER: PACER is available online at http://pacer.innb.uscourts.gov. Records purged every 6 months. New civil records are online after 2 days.

Electronic Filing: Electronic filing information online at https://ecf.innb.uscourts.gov

Hammond at Gary Division U.S. Bankruptcy Court, Northern District of Indiana, 5400 Federal Plaza, Hammond, Indiana 46320 (courier address: Use mail address for courier delivery) 219-852-3480, Fax: 219-881-3307. www.innb.uscourts.gov

Counties: Lake, Porter.

Indexing & Storage: Cases indexed by debtor and creditors as well as by case number. New cases available in the index 24 hours after filing date. Records in closed cases are only kept locally for a brief period. Records are shipped to the FRC twice a year. At the time a case is closed, both the date of filing and the date of closing are factors in determining when the case is shipped.

Fee & Payment: Payment may be made by money order, cashier check, personal check, Vis/MC. Debtor's checks and credit cards are not accepted. Payee: Clerk, U.S. Bankruptcy Court.

Phone Search: Only docket information available by phone. Automated voice case information service (VCIS) is available. Call VCIS at 800-755-8393 or 574-236-8814.

In Person Search: Fee charged if court conducts your in person search for you.

PACER: PACER is available online at http://pacer.innb.uscourts.gov. Records purged every 6 months. New civil records are online after 2 days.

Electronic Filing: Electronic filing information online at https://ecf.innb.uscourts.gov

Hammond at Lafayette Division c/o Fort Wayne Division, PO Box 2547, Fort Wayne, IN 46801-2547 (courier address: U.S. Court House, 1300 South Harrison St, Ft. Wayne, Indiana 46802), 260-420-5100. www.innb.uscourts.gov

Counties: Benton, Carroll, Jasper, Newton, Tippecanoe, Warren, White.

Indexing & Storage: Cases indexed by debtor and collector as well as by case number. New cases available in the index after filing date. All the files for the Hammond Division at Lafayette are physically kept in the Fort Wayne office. All papers pertaining to Hammond Division at Lafayette cases after the initial filing, including claims, should be sent to the Fort Wayne office. Open records located at the Ft. Wayne Division.

Fee & Payment: Payment may be made by money order, cashier check. Business checks are not accepted. Personal checks are not accepted.

Phone Search: Automated voice case information service (VCIS) is available. Call VCIS at 800-755-8393 or 574-236-8814.

In Person Search: Permitted.

PACER: PACER is available online at http://pacer.innb.uscourts.gov. Records purged every 6 months. New civil records are online after 2 days.

Electronic Filing: Electronic filing information online at https://ecf.innb.uscourts.gov

South Bend Division PO Box 7003, South Bend, IN 46634-7003 (courier address: 401 S Michigan St, South Bend, IN 46601), 574-968-2100, Fax: 574-968-2205. www.innb.uscourts.gov

Counties: Cass, Elkhart, Fulton, Kosciusko, La Porte, Marshall, Miami, Pulaski, St. Joseph, Starke, Wabash.

Indexing & Storage: Cases indexed by debtor and creditors as well as by case number. New cases available in the index 24 hours after filing date. Records in closed cases are only kept locally for a brief period. Records are shipped to the Chicago FRC semi-annually. At the time a case is closed, both the date of filing and the date of closing are factors in determining when the case is shipped.

Fee & Payment: Payment may be made by money order, cashier check, personal check, Visa or Mastercard. Debtor's checks are not accepted. Payee: Clerk, U.S. Bankruptcy Court.

Phone Search: Only docket information available by phone. Automated voice case information service (VCIS) is available. Call VCIS at 800-755-8393 or 574-236-8814.

In Person Search: Fee charged if court conducts your in person search for you. Self service copy machine available.

PACER: PACER is available online at http://pacer.innb.uscourts.gov. Records purged every 6 months. New civil records are online after 2 days.

Electronic Filing: Electronic filing information online at https://ecf.innb.uscourts.gov

U.S. District Court

Southern District of Indiana

Evansville Division 304 Federal Bldg, 101 NW Martin Luther King Blvd, Evansville, IN 47708 (courier address: Use mail address for courier delivery) 812-434-6410, Fax: 812-434-6418. www.insd.uscourts.gov

Counties: Daviess, Dubois, Gibson, Martin, Perry, Pike, Posey, Spencer, Vanderburgh, Warrick.

Indexing & Storage: New cases available in the index immediately after filing date. Cases prior to 1992 are indexed by name only on index cards.

Fee & Payment: Payment may be made by money order, cashier check, personal check. Payee: Clerk, U.S. District Court.

Phone Search: No searching by telephone.

Mail Search: A SASE not required.

In Person Search: Fee charged if court conducts your in person search for you. Court search covers a period of 10 years.

PACER: There is no PACER access to this court.

Electronic Filing: Electronic filing information online at https://ecf.insd.uscourts.gov

Other Online Access: Search records free on the Internet; www.insd.uscourts.gov/casesearch.htm to search. Court does not participate in the U.S. party case index.

Indianapolis Division Clerk, Room 105, 46 E Ohio St, Indianapolis, IN 46204 (Use mail address for courier delivery) 317-229-3700, Fax: 317-229-3959. www.insd.uscourts.gov

Counties: Bartholomew, Boone, Brown, Clinton, Decatur, Delaware, Fayette, Fountain, Franklin, Hamilton, Hancock, Hendricks, Henry, Howard, Johnson, Madison, Marion, Monroe, Montgomery, Morgan, Randolph, Rush, Shelby, Tipton, Union, Wayne.

Indexing & Storage: New cases available in the index 24 hours after filing date. District wide searches are available from this court for cases from 1996 to the present.

Fee & Payment: Payment may be made by money order. Business checks are not accepted, Visa, Mastercard. Personal checks are not accepted. Payee: Clerk, U.S. District Court.

Phone Search: Only information contained on the face of the docket sheet will be released over the phone. Anything from the remaining pages requires that the search fee be paid.

Mail Search: A SASE not required.

In Person Search: Fee charged if court conducts your in person search for you. Public access terminal available.

PACER: There is no PACER access to this court.

Electronic Filing: Electronic filing information online at https://ecf.insd.uscourts.gov

Other Online Access: Search records free on the Internet; www.insd.uscourts.gov/casesearch.htm to search. Court does not participate in the U.S. party case index.

New Albany Division Room 210, 121 W Spring St, New Albany, IN 47150 (Use mail address for courier delivery) 812-542-4510, Fax: 812-542-4515. www.insd.uscourts.gov

Counties: Clark, Crawford, Dearborn, Floyd, Harrison, Jackson, Jefferson, Jennings, Lawrence, Ohio, Orange, Ripley, Scott, Switzerland, Washington.

Indexing & Storage: New cases available in the index immediately after filing date. Files may also be in Indianapolis or Evansville.

Fee & Payment: Payment may be made by money order, cashier check, personal check. Payee: Clerk, U.S. District Court.

Phone Search: No searching by telephone.

In Person Search: Fee charged if court conducts your in person search for you.

PACER: There is no PACER access to this court.

Electronic Filing: Electronic filing information online at https://ecf.insd.uscourts.gov

Other Online Access: Search records free on the Internet; www.insd.uscourts.gov/casesearch.htm to search. Court does not participate in the U.S. party case index.

Terre Haute Division 210 Federal Bldg, Terre Haute, IN 47808 (courier address: Use mail

PACER: There is no PACER access to this court.

Electronic Filing: Electronic filing information online at https://ecf.insd.uscourts.gov

Other Online Access: Search records free on the Internet; www.insd.uscourts.gov/casesearch.htm to search. Court does not participate in the U.S. party case index.

address for courier delivery) 812-234-9484, Fax: 812-238-1831. www.insd.uscourts.gov

Counties: Clay, Greene, Knox, Owen, Parke, Putnam, Sullivan, Vermillion, Vigo.

Indexing & Storage: New cases available in the index immediately after filing date.

Fee & Payment: Payment may be made by money order, cashier check, personal check. Payee: Clerk, U.S. District Court.

Phone Search: All information that is not sealed is available for release over the phone.

In Person Search: Fee charged if court conducts your in person search for you.

PACER: There is no PACER access to this court.

Electronic Filing: Electronic filing information online at https://ecf.insd.uscourts.gov

Other Online Access: Search records free on the Internet; www.insd.uscourts.gov/casesearch.htm to search. Court does not participate in the U.S. party case index.

U.S. Bankruptcy Court

Southern District of Indiana

Evansville Division 352 Federal Building, 101 NW Martin Luther King Blvd, Evansville, IN 47708 (courier: Use mail address for courier delivery) 812-434-6470, Fax: 812-434-6471. www.insb.uscourts.gov

Counties: Daviess, Dubois, Gibson, Martin, Perry, Pike, Posey, Spencer, Vanderburgh, Warrick.

Indexing & Storage: Cases indexed by debtor as well as by case number. New cases available in the index 1-2 days after filing date.

Fee & Payment: Payment may be made by money order, cashier check, personal check. Debtor's checks are not accepted. Payee: Clerk, U.S. Bankruptcy Court.

Phone Search: Only docket information available by phone. Automated voice case information service (VCIS) is available. Call VCIS at 800-335-8003.

In Person Search: Fee charged if court conducts your in person search for you.

PACER: PACER is now available at www.insb.uscourts.gov. Click on "Case Search." Registration and fees required. Document images available. The free case lookup system is no longer found. Records purged every 3 months. New civil records are online after 2-3 days.

Other Online Access: Court does not participate in the U.S. party case index.

Indianapolis Division U.S. Courthouse, Rm 116, 46 E Ohio St, Indianapolis, IN 46204 (Use mail address for courier delivery) 317-229-3800, Fax: 317-229-3801. www.insb.uscourts.gov

Counties: Bartholomew, Boone, Brown, Clinton, Decatur, Delaware, Fayette, Fountain, Franklin, Hamilton, Hancock, Hendricks, Henry, Howard, Johnson, Madison, Marion, Monroe, Montgomery, Morgan, Randolph, Rush, Shelby, Tipton, Union, Wayne.

Indexing & Storage: Cases indexed by debtor as well as by case number. New cases available in the index 48 hours after filing date. Records are stored electronically since 1986.

Fee & Payment: Payment may be made by money order, cashier check, personal check. Debtor's checks are not accepted. Payee: Clerk, U.S. Bankruptcy Court (SDIN).

Phone Search: Only docket information available by phone. Automated voice case information service (VCIS) is available. VCIS: 800-335-8003.

In Person Search: Fee charged if court conducts your in person search for you.

PACER: PACER is now available at www.insb.uscourts.gov. Click on "Case Search." Registration and fees required. Document images available. The free case lookup system is no longer found. Records purged every 3 months. New civil records are online after 2-3 days.

Other Online Access: Court does not participate in the U.S. party case index.

New Albany Division U.S. Courthouse, Rm 110, 121 W Spring St, New Albany, IN 47150 (courier address: Use mail address for courier delivery) 812-452-4540, Fax: 812-542-4541. www.insb.uscourts.gov

Counties: Clark, Crawford, Dearborn, Floyd, Harrison, Jackson, Jefferson, Jennings, Lawrence, Ohio, Orange, Ripley, Scott, Switzerland, Washington.

Indexing & Storage: Cases indexed by debtor as well as by case number. New cases available in the index 48 hours after filing date.

Fee & Payment: Payment may be made by money order, cashier check, personal check. Debtor's checks are not accepted. Payee: Clerk, U.S. Bankruptcy Court (SDIN).

Phone Search: Only docket information available by phone. Automated voice case information service (VCIS) is available. VCIS: 800-335-8003.

In Person Search: Fee charged if court conducts your in person search for you.

PACER: PACER is now available at www.insb.uscourts.gov. Click on "Case Search." Registration and fees required. Document images available. The free case lookup system is no longer found. Records purged every 3 months. New civil records are online after 2-3 days.

Other Online Access: Court does not participate in the U.S. party case index.

Terre Haute Division Federal Bldg Rm 207, 30 N 7th St, Terre Haute, IN 47808 (Use mail address for courier delivery) 812-238-1550, Fax: 812-238-1831. www.insb.uscourts.gov

Counties: Clay, Greene, Knox, Owen, Parke, Putnam, Sullivan, Vermillion, Vigo.

Indexing & Storage: Cases indexed by debtor as well as by case number. New cases available in the index 48 hours after filing date. Records are stored electronically since 1986.

Fee & Payment: Payment may be made by money order, cashier check, personal check. A search fee will only be charged if a detailed search is required. Personal checks are not accepted from debtors. Payee: Clerk, U.S. Bankruptcy Court.

Phone Search: Only docket information available by phone. Automated voice case information service (VCIS) is available. Call VCIS at 800-335-8003.

In Person Search: Fee charged if court conducts your in person search for you.

PACER: PACER is now available at www.insb.uscourts.gov. Click on "Case Search." Registration and fees required. Document images available. The free case lookup system is no longer found. Records purged every 3 months. New civil records are online after 2-3 days.

Other Online Access: Court does not participate in the U.S. party case index.

Indiana County Courts

Court	Jurisdiction	No. of Courts	How Organized
Circuit Courts*	General	24	88 Circuits
Superior Courts*	General	4	
Combined Courts*		68	
County Courts*	Limited	Comb	
Combined Circuit/County*		4	
City Courts	Limited	48	
Small Claims -Marion County	Special	9	
Town Courts	Municipal	27	
Probate Court	Special	1	St. Joseph County

* Profiled in this Sourcebook.

Court	CIVIL								
	Tort	Contract	Real Estate	Min. Claim	Max. Claim	Small Claims	Estate	Eviction	Domestic Relations
Circuit Courts*	X	X	X	$0	No Max	$3000	X		X
Superior Courts*	X	X	X	$0	No Max	$3000	X		X
County Courts*	X	X	X	$0	$10,000	$3000		X	X
City Courts	X	X		$0	$2500			X	X
Small Claims - Marion County						$3000			
Town Courts									X
Probate Court							X		

Court	CRIMINAL				
	Felony	Misdemeanor	DWI/DUI	Preliminary Hearing	Juvenile
Circuit Courts*	X	X	X	X	X
Superior Courts*	X	X	X	X	X
County Courts*	X	X	X	X	
City Courts		X	X	X	
Small Claims - Marion County					
Town Courts		X	X	X	
Probate Court					X

ADMINISTRATION State Court Administrator, 115 W Washington St, #1080, Indianapolis, IN, 46204; 317-232-2542, Fax: 317-232-8372. www.in.gov/judiciary

COURT STRUCTURE There are 92 judicial circuits with Circuit Courts or Combined Circuit and Superior Courts. In addition, there are 48 City Courts and 27 Town Courts. County courts are gradually being restructured into divisions of the Superior Courts. Note that Small Claims in Marion County are heard at the township and records are maintained at that level. The phone number for the township offices are indicated in Marion County.

ONLINE ACCESS There is no statewide trial court records service available. However, the web site above gives free access to an index of docket information for Supreme, Appeals, and Tax Court cases.

ADDITIONAL INFORMATION The Circuit Court Clerk/County Clerk in a county is the same individual and is responsible for keeping all county judicial records. However, we recommend that, when requesting a record, the request indicate which court heard the case (Circuit, Superior, or County).

Many courts are no longer performing searches, especially criminal searches, based on a 7/8/96 statement by the State Board of Accounts.

Certification and copy fees are set by statute as $1.00 per document plus copy fee for certification and $1.00 per page for copies.

Adams County

Circuit & Superior Court 112 S 2nd St, Decatur, IN 46733; 260-724-5309; Fax: 260-724-5313. 8AM-4:30PM (EST). *Felony, Misdemeanor, Civil, Eviction, Small Claims, Probate.*
Civil Records: Access: In person only. Visitors must perform in person searches for themselves. No search fee. Required to search: name, years to search. Civil cases indexed by defendant, plaintiff. Civil records on computer from 1992, archived from 1876. Some records on index cards.
Criminal Records: Access: In person only. Visitors must perform in person searches for themselves. No search fee. Required to search: name, years to search, DOB; also helpful: SSN. Criminal records on computer from 1992, archived from 1876. Some records on index cards.
General Information: Public Access terminal is available. (Limited data available.) No juvenile, adoption, mental health or sealed records released. Copy fee: $1.00 per page. Cert fee: $2.00 per page. Payee: Adams County Clerk. Only cashiers checks and money orders accepted. Prepayment required.

Allen County

Circuit & Superior Court 715 S Calhoun St. Rm 200 Courthouse, Ft Wayne, IN 46802; 260-449-7245. 8AM-4:30PM (EST). *Felony, Misdemeanor, Civil, Eviction, Small Claims, Probate.*
www.co.allen.in.us
Civil Records: Access: In person only. Visitors must perform in person searches for themselves. No search fee. Required to search: name, years to search. Civil cases indexed by defendant, plaintiff. Recent civil cases on computer; prior records on microfiche, archived and index from 1824.
Criminal Records: Access: In person only. Visitors must perform in person searches for themselves. No search fee. Required to search: name, years to search; also helpful: DOB, SSN. Recent cases on computer; prior records on microfiche, archived and index prior..
General Information: Public Access terminal is available. No juvenile, adoption or sealed records released. Copy fee: $1.00 per page. Cert fee: $1.00 per page. Payee: Clerk of Allen Circuit Court. Business checks accepted. Prepayment required.

Bartholomew County

Circuit & Superior Court PO Box 924, Columbus, IN 47202-0924; 812-379-1600; Fax: 812-379-1675. 8AM-5PM (EST). *Felony, Misdemeanor, Civil, Eviction, Small Claims, Probate.*
www.bartholomewco.com
Civil Records: Access: In person, online. Visitors must perform in person searches for themselves. No search fee. Required to search: name. Civil cases indexed by plaintiff. Civil records on computer from 1985, on microfilm from 1940, on index from 1821. An online subscription service is at www.doxpop.com. Fees are involved. Records date from 05/85. A limited free search is at www.doxpop.com/prod/court/CourtQuery.
Criminal Records: Access: Fax, mail, in person, online. Only the court performs in person searches; visitors may not. No search fee. Required to search: name, years to search, DOB; also helpful: SSN, race, sex. Criminal records on computer from 1985, on

microfilm from 1940, on index from 1821. Online access to criminal records is the same as civil.
General Information: Public Access terminal is available. No juvenile, mental health, adoption or sealed released. All searches 1985 to present. Will fax results $5.00 per page; no fee to toll-free number. Copy fee: $0.25 per page. Cert fee: $1.00. Payee: Bartholomew County Clerk. Personal checks accepted. Prepayment required. Mail requests: SASE required. Mail turnaround time 1 day.

Benton County

Circuit Court 706 E 5th St, #37, Fowler, IN 47944-1556; 765-884-0930; Fax: 765-884-0322. Hours: 8:30AM-4PM (EST). *Felony, Misdemeanor, Civil, Eviction, Small Claims, Probate.*
www.bentoncounty.org
Civil Records: Access: In person only. Visitors must perform in person searches for themselves. No search fee. Required to search: name, years to search. Civil cases indexed by defendant, plaintiff. Civil records on computer from 1992, on index books from 1860.
Criminal Records: Access: Mail, in person,fax. Visitors must perform in person searches for themselves. Search fee: $5.00 per name; send search requests to attention of Melissa Williams in Clerk's office. Required to search: name, years to search, DOB. Criminal records on computer from 1992, on index books from 1860.
General Information: Public Access terminal is available. No juvenile, mental, adoption or sealed released. Will fax results to local or toll free line. Copy fee: $1.00 per page. Cert fee: $1.00. Payee: Benton County Clerk. Only cashiers checks and money orders accepted. Prepayment required. Mail requests: SASE required. Mail turnaround: 2-3 days.

Blackford County

Circuit & Superior Court 110 W Washington St, Hartford City, IN 47348; 765-348-1130. Hours: 8AM-4PM (EST). *Felony, Misdemeanor, Civil, Eviction, Small Claims, Probate.*
Civil Records: Access: Mail, in person. Visitors must perform in person searches for themselves. No search fee. Required to search: name, years to search. Civil cases indexed by defendant, plaintiff. Civil records on computer from 1991, on index from 1800.
Criminal Records: Access: Mail, in person. Visitors must perform in person searches for themselves. No search fee. Required to search: name, years to search, DOB; also helpful: SSN. court records on computer from 1991, on index from 1800.
General Information: Public Access terminal is available. No juvenile, mental, adoption or sealed released. Fee to fax results is $1.00 per page. Copy fee: $1.00 per page. Cert fee: $2.00. Payee: Clerk of Blackford County. Business checks accepted. Prepayment required. Mail turnaround time 1 week.

Boone County

Circuit & Superior Court I & II Rm 212, Courthouse Sq, Lebanon, IN 46052; 765-482-3510. Hours: 7AM-4PM (EST). *Felony, Misdemeanor, Civil, Eviction, Small Claims, Probate.*
www.bccn.boone.in.us/bccn/Boone_Clerk.html
Civil Records: Access: Mail, in person. Both court and visitors may perform in person searches. No search fee. Required to search: name, years to search.

Civil cases indexed by defendant, plaintiff. Civil records on index from 1900.
Criminal Records: Access: Mail, in person. Both court and visitors may perform in person searches. No search fee. Required to search: name, years to search; also helpful: SSN. Criminal records on index from 1900.
General Information: Public Access terminal is available. No juvenile, mental, adoption or sealed released. Will fax results to local or toll free line. Copy fee: $1.00 per page. Cert fee: $1.00. Payee: Boone County Clerk. Business checks accepted. Prepayment required. Mail requests: SASE required. Mail turnaround time 1 week.

Brown County

Circuit Court Box 85, Nashville, IN 47448; 812-988-5510; Fax: 812-988-5515. Hours: 8AM-4PM (EST). *Felony, Misdemeanor, Civil, Eviction, Small Claims, Probate.*
Civil Records: Access: In person only. Visitors must perform in person searches for themselves. No search fee. Required to search: name, years to search. Civil cases indexed by defendant, plaintiff. Civil records on open cases on computer from 1993, in entry books from early 1800s. Records are not indexed by SSN, but SSNs can be viewed.
Criminal Records: Access: In person only. Visitors must perform in person searches for themselves. No search fee. Required to search: name, years to search, DOB; also helpful: SSN. Criminal records on open cases on computer from 1993, in entry books from early 1800s. Records are not indexed by SSN, but SSNs can be viewed.
General Information: Public Access terminal is available. No juvenile, mental, adoption or sealed records released. Copy fee: $1.00 per page. Cert fee: $2.00. Payee: County Clerk. Personal checks accepted. Prepayment required.

Carroll County

Circuit & Superior Court Courthouse, 101 W Main, Delphi, IN 46923; 765-564-4485; Fax: 765-564-1835. Hours: 8AM-5PM M,T,Th,F; 8AM-Noon W (EST). *Felony, Misdemeanor, Civil, Eviction, Small Claims, Probate.*
Civil Records: Access: In person only. Visitors must perform in person searches for themselves. No search fee. Required to search: name, years to search. Civil cases indexed by defendant, plaintiff. Civil records archived from 1981, on index from 1828.
Criminal Records: Access: In person only. Visitors must perform in person searches for themselves. No search fee. Required to search: name, years to search. Criminal records archived from 1981, on index prior
General Information: No juvenile, mental, adoption or sealed released. Copy fee: $1.00 per page. Cert fee: $1.00. Payee: Carroll County Clerk. Personal checks are not accepted. Prepayment required.

Cass County

Circuit & Superior Court 200 Court Park, Logansport, IN 46947; 574-753-7730. Hours: 8AM-4PM (EST). *Felony, Misdemeanor, Civil, Eviction, Small Claims, Probate.*
Civil Records: Access: Mail, in person. Both court and visitors may perform in person searches. No search fee. Required to search: name, years to search.

Civil cases indexed by defendant, plaintiff. Civil records on computer from 1989, on index from 1830s.
Criminal Records: Access: Mail, in person. Both court and visitors may perform in person searches. No search fee. Required to search: name, years to search, DOB; also helpful: SSN, signed release. Criminal records on computer from 1989, on index from 1830s.
General Information: Public Access terminal is available. No juvenile, mental, adoption or sealed released. Will fax results for $1.00 per page. Copy fee: $1.00 per page. Cert fee: $3.00. Payee: Cass County Clerk. Personal checks not accepted; use money order. Prepayment required. Mail requests: SASE requested. Turnaround time 2 weeks.

Clark County

Circuit, Superior & County Court 501 E Court, Rm 137, Jeffersonville, IN 47130; 812-285-6244. Hours: 8:30AM-4:30PM M-F, 8:30-Noon S (EST). *Felony, Misdemeanor, Civil, Eviction, Small Claims, Probate.*
www.clarkprosecutor.org/html/courts/courts.htm
Civil Records: Access: In person only. Visitors must perform in person searches for themselves. No search fee. Required to search: name, years to search; also helpful: address. Civil cases indexed by defendant, plaintiff. Civil records on computer since 8/92, on index cards from 1900.
Criminal Records: Access: In person only. Visitors must perform in person searches for themselves. No search fee. Required to search: name, years to search; also helpful: DOB, SSN. Criminal records on computer since 8/92, on index cards from 1900.
General Information: Public Access terminal is available. No juvenile, mental, adoption or sealed released. Copy fee: $1.00 per page. Cert fee: $1.00. Payee: County Clerk. Business checks accepted. Prepayment required.

Clay County

Circuit & Superior Court 609 E National Ave, #213, Brazil, IN 47834; 812-448-9024. Hours: 8AM-4PM (EST). *Felony, Misdemeanor, Civil, Eviction, Small Claims, Probate.*
Civil Records: Access: Mail, in person. Visitors must perform in person searches for themselves. No search fee. Required to search: name, years to search; also helpful: address. Civil cases indexed by defendant, plaintiff. Civil records on index from 1850; on computer back to 1995.
Criminal Records: Access: Mail, in person. Visitors must perform in person searches for themselves. No search fee. Required to search: name, years to search, address, DOB; also helpful-SSN, signed release. Criminal records on index from 1850; on computer back to 1995.
General Information: Public Access terminal is available. No juvenile, mental, adoption or sealed released. Copy fee: $1.00 per page. Cert fee: $1.00. Payee: County Clerk. Business checks accepted. Prepayment required. Mail requests: SASE required. Mail turnaround time 1 week.

Clinton County

Circuit & Superior Court 265 Courthouse Sq, Frankfort, IN 46041; 765-659-6335. Hours: 8AM-4PM M-TH,8AM-5PM F; 8/AM-12PM Thur (EST). *Felony, Misdemeanor, Civil, Eviction, Small Claims, Probate.*
Civil Records: Access: In person, online. Visitors must perform in person searches for themselves. No search fee. Required to search: name, years to search. Civil cases indexed by defendant, plaintiff. Civil records on computer from 1991, on microfiche and index from 1900s. An online subscription service is at www.doxpop.com. Fees are involved. Records date

from 01/91. A limited free search is at www.doxpop.com/prod/court/CourtQuery.
Criminal Records: Access: In person, online. Visitors must perform in person searches for themselves. No search fee. Required to search: name, years to search, signed release; also helpful: DOB. Criminal records on computer from 1991, on microfiche and index from 1900s. Online access to criminal records is the same as civil.
General Information: Public Access terminal is available. No juvenile, mental, adoption or sealed released. Will not fax results. Copy fee: $1.00 per page. Cert fee: $1.00. Payee: County Clerk. Business checks accepted. Prepayment required.

Crawford County

Circuit Court Box 375, English, IN 47118; 812-338-2565; Fax: 812-338-2507. Hours: 8AM-4PM M,F; 8AM-6PM T-Th (EST). *Felony, Misdemeanor, Civil, Eviction, Small Claims, Probate.*
Civil Records: Access: In person only. Visitors must perform in person searches for themselves. No search fee. Required to search: name, years to search. Civil cases indexed by defendant, plaintiff. Civil records on index from 1900s.
Criminal Records: Access: Fax, mail, in person. Only the court performs in person searches; visitors may not. Search fee: $5.00 per name. Required to search: name, years to search, DOB, SSN, signed release. Criminal records on index from 1900s.
General Information: No juvenile, mental, adoption or sealed released. No fee to fax results. Copy fee: $1.00 per page. Fee is for criminal division only. Cert fee: $2.00. Payee: County Clerk. Business checks accepted. Prepayment required. Mail requests: SASE required. Mail turnaround time 1 week.

Daviess County

Circuit & Superior Court PO Box 739, Washington, IN 47501; 812-254-8664; Civil phone: 812-254-8664; Criminal phone: 812-254-8669; Probate phone: 812-254-8664; Fax: 812-254-8698. Hours: 8AM-4PM (EST). *Felony, Misdemeanor, Civil, Eviction, Small Claims, Probate.*
Civil Records: Access: Mail, in person, online. Both court and visitors may perform in person searches. No search fee. Required to search: name, years to search. Civil cases indexed by defendant, plaintiff. Civil records on index from 1900s; recent on computer since 1993. An online subscription service is at www.doxpop.com. Fees are involved. Records date from 02/94. A limited free search is at www.doxpop.com/prod/court/CourtQuery.
Criminal Records: Access: Mail, in person, online. Both court and visitors may perform in person searches. No search fee. Required to search: name, years to search. Criminal records on index from 1900s; recent on computer since 1993. Online access to criminal records is the same as civil.
General Information: Public Access terminal is available. No juvenile, mental, adoption or sealed records released. Copy fee: $1.00 per page. Cert fee: $1.00. Payee: Daviess County Clerk. Business checks accepted. Prepayment required. Mail requests: SASE required. Mail turnaround time varies.

Dearborn County

Circuit & Superior Court Courthouse, 215 W High St, Lawrenceburg, IN 47025; 812-537-8867; Fax: 812-532-2021. Hours: 8:30AM-4:30PM (EST). *Felony, Misdemeanor, Civil, Eviction, Small Claims, Probate.*
www.dearborncounty.org/datafiles/judges.html
Civil Records: Access: In person only. Visitors must perform in person searches for themselves. No search fee. Required to search: name, years to search. Civil

cases indexed by defendant, plaintiff. Civil records on computer from 1992, on index from 1970s.
Criminal Records: Access: In person only. Visitors must perform in person searches for themselves. No search fee. Required to search: name, years to search, DOB; also helpful: SSN. Criminal records on computer from 1992, on index from 1970s, archived to 1930.
General Information: Public Access terminal is available. No juvenile, mental, adoption or sealed records released. Copy fee: $1.00 per page. Cert fee: $1.00. Payee: Circuit Court Clerk. Only cashiers checks and money orders accepted. Prepayment required.

Decatur County

Circuit & Superior Court 150 Courthouse Sq, #244, Greensburg, IN 47240; 812-663-8223/8642; Fax: 812-663-8642. Hours: 8AM-4PM, 8AM-5PM F (EST). *Felony, Misdemeanor, Civil, Eviction, Small Claims, Probate.* www.decaturcounty.in.gov
Civil Records: Access: Phone, mail, in person. Visitors must perform in person searches for themselves. No search fee. Required to search: name, years to search. Civil cases indexed by defendant, plaintiff. Civil records on index from 1823; on computer back to 1998.
Criminal Records: Access: Mail, in person. Visitors must perform in person searches for themselves. No search fee. Required to search: name, years to search, DOB; also helpful: SSN. Criminal records on index from 1823; on computer back to 1998.
General Information: Public Access terminal is available. No juvenile, mental, adoption or sealed released. Copy fee: $1.00 per page. Cert fee: $1.00. Payee: Decatur County Clerk. Personal checks accepted. Prepayment required. Mail turnaround time 2-7 days.

DeKalb County

Circuit & Superior Court PO Box 230, Auburn, IN 46706; 219-925-0912; Fax: 219-925-5126. Hours: 8:30AM-4:30PM (EST). *Felony, Misdemeanor, Civil, Eviction, Small Claims, Probate.*
Civil Records: Access: In person only. Visitors must perform in person searches for themselves. No search fee. Required to search: name, years to search. Civil cases indexed by defendant, plaintiff. Civil records on computer back to 1987, on index from 1913.
Criminal Records: Access: In person only. Visitors must perform in person searches for themselves. No search fee. Required to search: name, years to search, DOB. Criminal records on computer back to 1987, on index from 1913. Will send case files if case number known.
General Information: Public Access terminal is available. No juvenile, mental, adoption or sealed released. Copy fee: $1.00 per page. Cert fee: $1.00. Payee: Court Clerk. Only cashiers checks and money orders accepted. Prepayment required. Mail turnaround time is 3 days if case number provided.

Delaware County

Circuit Court Box 1089, Muncie, IN 47308; 765-747-7726; Fax: 765-747-7768. Hours: 8:30AM-4:30PM (EST). *Felony, Misdemeanor, Civil, Small Claims, Probate.* www.dcclerk.org
Civil Records: Access: Fax, mail, in person, online. Both court and visitors may perform in person searches. No search fee. Required to search: name, years to search. Civil cases indexed by defendant, plaintiff. Civil records on computer from 1989, on microfiche, archived and on index from 1800. An online subscription service is at www.doxpop.com. Fees are involved. Records date from 01/89. A limited

free search is available at www.doxpop.com/prod/court/CourtQuery.

Criminal Records: Access: In person, online. Visitors must perform in person searches for themselves. No search fee. Required to search: name, years to search, DOB, SSN. Criminal records on computer from 1989, on microfiche, archived and on index from 1800. Online access to criminal records from 1850 to 1950 only is free at www.munpl.org/Main_Pages/documents.htm, the Muncie Public Library website. Also, an online subscription service is at www.doxpop.com. Fees are involved. Records date from 01/89.

General Information: Public Access terminal is available. No juvenile, mental, adoption or sealed released. Fee to fax results is $2.00. Copy fee: $.10 per page. Cert fee: $1.00. Payee: Court Clerk. Business checks accepted. Prepayment required. Mail turnaround time 1-2 days.

Dubois County

Circuit & Superior Court 1 Courthouse Sq, Jasper, IN 47546; 812-481-7070/7035/7020; Fax: 812-481-7030. Hours: 8AM-4PM (EST). *Felony, Misdemeanor, Civil, Eviction, Small Claims, Probate.*

Civil Records: Access: In person only. Visitors must perform in person searches for themselves. No search fee. Required to search: name; also helpful: years to search. Civil cases indexed by defendant, plaintiff. Civil records on computer from 8\93, on index books from 1930.

Criminal Records: Access: In person only. Visitors must perform in person searches for themselves. No search fee. Required to search: name; also helpful: years to search. Criminal records on computer from 8\93, on index books from 1930.

General Information: Public Access terminal is available. No juvenile, mental, adoption or sealed records released. Copy fee: $.25 per page. Cert fee: $1.00. Payee: Court Clerk. Personal checks accepted. Prepayment required.

Elkhart County

Elkhart Superior Courts 1, 2, 5, 6 315 S 2nd St, Elkhart, IN 46516; 574-523-2233/2305/2007; Fax: 574-523-2323. Hours: 8AM-4PM T-F, 8AM-5PM M (EST). *Felony, Misdemeanor, Civil, Eviction, Small Claims, Probate.*
www.elkhartcountyindiana.com/administrative/clerk.html
Civil Records: Access: In person, online. Visitors must perform in person searches for themselves. No search fee. Required to search: name, years to search. Civil cases indexed by defendant, plaintiff. Civil records archived from 1830; on computer since 1996. Some records on index books. An online subscription service is at www.doxpop.com. Fees are involved. Records date from 01/92. A limited free search is at www.doxpop.com/prod/court/CourtQuery.
Criminal Records: Access: In person, online. Visitors must perform in person searches for themselves. No search fee. Required to search: name, years to search, DOB; also helpful: SSN. Criminal records archived from 1830; on computer since 1996. Some records on index books. Online access to criminal records is the same as civil.
General Information: Public Access terminal is available. No juvenile, mental, adoption or sealed records released. Copy fee: $1.00 per page. Cert fee: $2.00. Payee: Court Clerk. Personal checks not accepted. Prepayment required.

Goshen Circuit & Superior Courts 3, 4

Courthouse, 101 N Main St, Goshen, IN 46526; 574-535-6431; Fax: 574-535-6471. Hours: 8AM-5PM M, 8AM-4PM T-F (EST). *Felony, Misdemeanor, Civil, Eviction, Small Claims, Probate.*
www.elkhartcountyindiana.com/administrative/clerk.html Note: Includes Circuit Court (Rm 204) and Superior Court 3 (Rm 205, 535-6438) and 4 (Rm 105, 535-6403).
Civil Records: Access: In person, online. Visitors must perform in person searches for themselves. No search fee. Required to search: name, years to search. Civil cases indexed by defendant, plaintiff. Civil records archived from 1830; on computer since 1996. Some records on index books. An online subscription service is at www.doxpop.com. Fees are involved; $39.00 per month. Records date from 01/92. A limited free search is available at www.doxpop.com/prod/court/CourtQuery.
Criminal Records: Access: In person, online. Visitors must perform in person searches for themselves. No search fee. Required to search: name, years to search, DOB; also helpful: SSN. Criminal records archived from 1830; on computer since 1996. Some records on index books. Online access to criminal records is the same as civil.
General Information: Public Access terminal is available. No juvenile, mental, adoption or sealed records released. Will not fax results. Copy fee: $1.00 per page. Cert fee: $1.00. Payee: Court Clerk. No personal checks accepted. Prepayment required.

Fayette County

Circuit & Superior Court PO Box 607, Connersville, IN 47331-0607; 765-825-1813. Hours: 8:30AM-4PM (5PM on Wed) (EST). *Felony, Misdemeanor, Civil, Eviction, Small Claims, Probate.*
www.co.fayette.in.us
Civil Records: Access: In person only. Visitors must perform in person searches for themselves. No search fee. Required to search: name, years to search. Civil cases indexed by defendant, plaintiff. Civil records on computer from 1988 (Circuit), 1992 (Superior).
Criminal Records: Access: In person only. Visitors must perform in person searches for themselves. No search fee. Required to search: name, years to search. Criminal records on computer from 1988 (Circuit), 1992 (Superior).
General Information: Public Access terminal is available. No juvenile, mental, adoption or sealed released. Copy fee: $1.00 per page. Cert fee: $1.00. Payee: Fayette County Clerk. Only cashiers checks and money orders accepted. Prepayment required.

Floyd County

Circuit, Superior & County Court Box 1056, City County Bldg, New Albany, IN 47150; 812-948-5414; Fax: 812-948-4711. Hours: 8AM-4PM (EST). *Felony, Misdemeanor, Civil, Eviction, Small Claims, Probate.*
Civil Records: Access: Mail, in person. Visitors must perform in person searches for themselves. No search fee. Required to search: name, years to search. Civil cases indexed by defendant, plaintiff. Civil records on computer from 1988, archived from 1978, on index from 1819.
Criminal Records: Access: Mail, in person. Visitors must perform in person searches for themselves. Search fee: $5.00. Required to search: name, years to search; also helpful: SSN. Criminal records on computer from 1988, archived from 1978, on index from 1819.
General Information: Public Access terminal is available. No juvenile, mental, adoption or sealed released. Copy fee: $.10 per page. Cert fee: $1.00. Payee: Court Clerk. Personal checks accepted.

Prepayment required. Mail requests: SASE required. Mail turnaround time 1-2 days.

Fountain County

Circuit Court Box 183, Covington, IN 47932; 765-793-2192; Fax: 765-793-5002. Hours: 8AM-4PM (EST). *Felony, Misdemeanor, Civil, Eviction, Small Claims, Probate.*
Civil Records: Access: Mail, in person. Both court and visitors may perform in person searches. No search fee. Required to search: name, years to search. Civil cases indexed by defendant, plaintiff. Civil records on computer from 1995.
Criminal Records: Access: Mail, in person. Both court and visitors may perform in person searches. No search fee. Required to search: name, years to search. Criminal records on computer from 1995.
General Information: Public Access terminal is available. No juvenile, mental, adoption or sealed released. Will not fax results. Copy fee: $1.00 per page. Cert fee: $2.00. Payee: Court Clerk. Personal checks not accepted. Prepayment required. Mail requests: SASE required. Mail turnaround time 1-2 days if records after 1989, 4-5 days if prior.

Franklin County

Circuit Court 459 Main, Brookville, IN 47012; 765-647-5111; Fax: 765-647-3224. Hours: 8:30AM-4PM (EST). *Felony, Misdemeanor, Civil, Eviction, Small Claims, Probate.*
Civil Records: Access: In person only. Visitors must perform in person searches for themselves. No search fee. Required to search: name, years to search. Civil cases indexed by defendant, plaintiff. Civil records on index.
Criminal Records: Access: In person only. Visitors must perform in person searches for themselves. No search fee. Required to search: name, years to search. Criminal records on index.
General Information: No juvenile, mental, adoption or sealed released. Copy fee: $1.00 per page. Cert fee: $1.00. Payee: Court Clerk. Personal checks accepted. Prepayment required.

Fulton County

Circuit Court 815 Main St, PO Box 524, Rochester, IN 46975; 574-223-2911; Fax: 574-223-8304. Hours: 8AM-4PM M-TH, 8AM-5PM F (EST). *Felony, Misdemeanor, Civil, Eviction, Small Claims, Probate.*
Civil Records: Access: Mail, in person. Both court and visitors may perform in person searches. No search fee. Required to search: name, years to search. Civil cases indexed by defendant, plaintiff. Civil records on computer from 1989, on microfiche, archived and on index from 1845.
Criminal Records: Access: Mail, in person. Both court and visitors may perform in person searches. No search fee. Required to search: name, years to search. Criminal records on computer from 1989, on microfiche, archived and on index from 1845.
General Information: Public Access terminal is available. No juvenile, mental, adoption or sealed released. Will fax results for $4.00 per page. Copy fee: $1.00 per page. Cert fee: $1.00. Payee: Court Clerk. Business checks accepted. Prepayment required. Mail requests: SASE Required. Mail turnaround time 3-4 days.

Gibson County

Circuit & Superior Court Courthouse, PO Box 630, Princeton, IN 47670; 812-386-6474; Fax: 812-386-5025. 8AM-4PM (CST). *Felony, Misdemeanor, Civil, Eviction, Small Claims, Probate.*
Civil Records: Access: In person only. Visitors must perform in person searches for themselves. No search

fee. Required to search: name, years to search. Civil cases indexed by defendant, plaintiff. Civil records on computer from 1996, on microfiche from 1940, on index from 1813.

Criminal Records: Access: In person only. Visitors must perform in person searches for themselves. No search fee. Required to search: name, years to search. Criminal records on computer from 1996, on microfiche from 1940, on index from 1813.

General Information: Public Access terminal is available. No juvenile, mental, adoption or sealed records released. Copy fee: $1.00 per page. Cert fee: $1.00. Payee: Court Clerk. Only cashiers checks and money orders accepted. Prepayment required.

Grant County

Circuit & Superior Court Courthouse 101 E 4th St, Marion, IN 46952; 765-668-8121; Fax: 765-668-6541. 8AM-4PM (EST). *Felony, Misdemeanor, Civil, Eviction, Small Claims, Probate.* www.grantcounty.net

Civil Records: Access: In person only. Visitors must perform in person searches for themselves. No search fee. Required to search: name, years to search; also helpful: address. Civil cases indexed by defendant, plaintiff. Civil records on computer from 1989, on index from 1881.

Criminal Records: Access: In person only. Visitors must perform in person searches for themselves. No search fee. Required to search: name, years to search; also helpful: DOB, SSN. Criminal records on computer from 1989, on index from 1881.

General Information: Public Access terminal is available. No juvenile, adoption, mental health or sealed records released. Copy fee: $.10 per page. Cert fee: $1.00. Payee: Court Clerk. Personal checks accepted. Prepayment required.

Greene County

Circuit & Superior Court PO Box 229, Bloomfield, IN 47424; 812-384-8532; Fax: 812-384-8458. Hours: 8AM-4PM (EST). *Felony, Misdemeanor, Civil, Eviction, Small Claims, Probate.*

Civil Records: Access: In person only. Visitors must perform in person searches for themselves. No search fee. Required to search: name, years to search. Civil cases indexed by defendant, plaintiff. Civil records on computer back to 1989, all other records in books.

Criminal Records: Access: In person only. Visitors must perform in person searches for themselves. No search fee. Required to search: name, years to search. Criminal records on computer back to 1989; prior in books.

General Information: Public Access terminal is available. No juvenile, mental, adoption or sealed released. Copy fee: $1.00 per page. Cert fee: $1.00. Payee: Court Clerk. Only cashiers checks and money orders accepted. Prepayment required.

Hamilton County

Circuit & Superior Court One Hamilton County Sq, #106, Noblesville, IN 46060-2233; 317-776-9629; Fax: 317-776-9727. Hours: 8AM-4:30PM (EST). *Felony, Misdemeanor, Civil, Eviction, Small Claims, Probate.* www.co.hamilton.in.us

Civil Records: Access: In person only. Visitors must perform in person searches for themselves. No search fee. Required to search: name, years to search. Civil cases indexed by defendant, plaintiff. Civil indices on computer from 1987, on index from 1840s.

Criminal Records: Access: In person only. Visitors must perform in person searches for themselves. No search fee. Required to search: name, years to search. Criminal records on computer from 1987, on index from 1840s.

General Information: Public Access terminal is available. No juvenile, mental, adoption or sealed released. Copy fee: $.50 per page. Cert fee: $1.00 plus $.50 per page. Payee: Court Clerk. Business checks accepted. Prepayment required.

Hancock County

Circuit & Superior Court 9 E Main St, Rm 201, Greenfield, IN 46140; 317-477-1109; Fax: 317-462-1163. Hours: 8AM-4PM (EST). *Felony, Misdemeanor, Civil, Eviction, Small Claims, Probate.*

Civil Records: Access: In person only. Both court and visitors may perform in person searches. No search fee. Required to search: name, years to search. Civil cases indexed by defendant, plaintiff. Civil records on computer from 07/88, on index and archived from 1883.

Criminal Records: Access: In person only. Both court and visitors may perform in person searches. No search fee. Required to search: name, years to search, DOB; also helpful: SSN. Criminal records on computer from 07/88, index and archived from 1883.

General Information: Public Access terminal is available. No juvenile, mental, adoption or sealed released. Copy fee: $1.00 per page for case history, otherwise $.25 per page. Cert fee: $1.00. Payee: Court Clerk. Only cashier checks or money orders accepted. Prepayment required.

Harrison County

Circuit Court 300 N Capitol, Corydon, IN 47112; 812-738-4289. Hours: 8AM-4:30PM (EST). *Civil, Eviction, Probate.*

Civil Records: Access: Mail, in person. Visitors must perform in person searches for themselves. No search fee. Required to search: name, years to search. Civil cases indexed by defendant, plaintiff. Civil records on index from 1900. Court personnel will only do record searching when they have time, strongly urge using a retriever.

Criminal Records: Access: Mail, in person. Visitors must perform in person searches for themselves. No search fee. Required to search: name, years to search, DOB; also helpful-SSN. Criminal records on index from 1900; on computer back to 1992. Court personnel only do record searching when they have time, suggest to use a retriever.

General Information: No juvenile, mental, adoption or sealed released. Fee to fax results is $1.00 per page. Copy fee: $1.00 per page. Cert fee: $1.00 per document plus $1.00 per page. Payee: Court Clerk. Only cashiers checks and money orders accepted. Prepayment required. Mail turnaround time: as time permits.

Superior Court 1445 Gardner Ln #3126, Corydon, IN 47112; 812-738-8149; Fax: 812-738-2459. Hours: 8AM-4:30PM (EST). *Felony, Misdemeanor, Small Claims.*

Civil Records: Access: In person only. Visitors must perform in person searches for themselves. No search fee. Required to search: name, years to search. Civil cases indexed by defendant, plaintiff. Civil records on index from 1900; on computer back to 1992.

Criminal Records: Access: In person only. Visitors must perform in person searches for themselves. No search fee. Required to search: name, years to search, DOB; also helpful-SSN. Criminal records on index from 1900; on computer back to 1992.

General Information: Public Access terminal is available. No juvenile, mental, adoption or sealed released. Copy fee: $1.00 per page. Cert fee: $1.00 per document plus $1.00 per page. Payee: Court Clerk. Only cashiers checks and money orders accepted. Prepayment required.

Hendricks County

Circuit & Superior Court PO Box 599, Danville, IN 46122; 317-745-9231; Fax: 317-745-9306. 8AM-4PM (EST). *Felony, Misdemeanor, Civil, Eviction, Small Claims, Probate.*

Civil Records: Access: In person only. Visitors must perform in person searches for themselves. No search fee. Required to search: name, years to search. Civil cases indexed by defendant, plaintiff. Civil records on computer since late 1992, on index from 1800s. Will do Mail request if out of state-turnaround time 72 Hrs.

Criminal Records: Access: In person only. Visitors must perform in person searches for themselves. No search fee. Required to search: name, years to search; also helpful: DOB, SSN. Criminal records on computer since late 1992, on index from 1800s. Will do Mail request if out of state-turnaround time 72 Hrs.

General Information: No juvenile, mental, adoption or sealed released. Copy fee: $1.00 per page. Cert fee: $1.00. Payee: Court Clerk. Business checks accepted. Prepayment required.

Henry County

Circuit & Superior Courts I & II PO Box B, New Castle, IN 47362; 765-529-6401. Hours: 8AM-4PM (EST). *Felony, Misdemeanor, Civil, Eviction, Small Claims, Probate.*

Civil Records: Access: In person only. Visitors must perform in person searches for themselves. No search fee. Required to search: name, years to search. Civil cases indexed by plaintiff. Civil records on computer from 2003, archived from 1979, on index from 1976.

Criminal Records: Access: In person only. Visitors must perform in person searches for themselves. No search fee. Required to search: name, years to search. Criminal records on computer from 2003, archived from 1979, on index from 1976.

General Information: Public Access terminal is available. No juvenile, mental, protective orders, adoption or any other confidential records. Copy fee: $1.00 per page. Cert fee: $1.00. Payee: Henry County Clerk. Only cashiers checks and money orders accepted. Prepayment required.

Howard County

Circuit & Superior Court PO Box 9004, Kokomo, IN 46904; 765-456-2204; Civil phone: 765-456-2000; Criminal phone: 765-456-2000; Fax: 765-456-2267. Hours: 8AM-4PM (EST). *Felony, Misdemeanor, Civil, Eviction, Small Claims, Probate.* http://co.howard.in.us/clerk1

Note: Small Claims 765-456-2204

Civil Records: Access: In person, online. Visitors must perform in person searches for themselves. No search fee. Required to search: name, years to search. Civil cases indexed by defendant, plaintiff. Civil records on computer since 1992 on microfiche from early 1800s. An online subscription service is at www.doxpop.com. Fees are involved. Records date from 07/94. A limited free search is at www.doxpop.com/prod/court/CourtQuery.

Criminal Records: Access: In person, online. Visitors must perform in person searches for themselves. No search fee. Required to search: name, years to search; also helpful: DOB, SSN. Criminal records on computer since 1992, on microfiche from early 1800s. Online access to criminal records is the same as civil.

General Information: Public Access terminal is available. No juvenile, mental, adoption or sealed records released. Copy fee: $.20 per page for any page printed. Cert fee: $1.00. Payee: County Clerk. Only cashiers checks and money orders accepted. Prepayment required.

Huntington County

Circuit & Superior Court PO Box 228, Huntington, IN 46750; 260-358-4817; Fax: 260-358-4880. Hours: 8AM-4:30PM (EST). *Felony, Misdemeanor, Civil, Eviction, Small Claims, Probate.*

Civil Records: Access: Fax, phone, mail, in person. Both court and visitors may perform in person searches. No search fee. Required to search: name, years to search. Civil cases indexed by defendant, plaintiff. Civil records on computer from 1990, on microfiche from 1970, index & archived from 1800s.

Criminal Records: Access: In person only. Visitors must perform in person searches for themselves. No search fee. Required to search: name, years to search. Criminal records on computer from 1990, on microfiche from 1970, on index and archived from 1800s.

General Information: Public Access terminal is available. No juvenile, mental, adoption or sealed released. Will fax results to local or toll free line. Copy fee: $1.00 per page. Cert fee: $1.00. Payee: County Clerk. Personal checks not accepted. Prepayment required. Mail requests: SASE not required. Mail turnaround time 1-2 days.

Jackson County

Circuit Court PO Box 318, Brownstown, IN 47220; 812-358-6117; Fax: 812-358-6187. Hours: 8AM-4:30PM (EST). *Felony, Misdemeanor, Civil, Eviction, Small Claims, Probate.*

Note: Will not perform searches for private companies.

Civil Records: Access: Fax, mail, in person. Both court and visitors may perform in person searches. Search fee: $5.00 per name. Required to search: name, years to search. Civil cases indexed by defendant, plaintiff. Civil records on computer from 1989, on index from 1800s.

Criminal Records: Access: In person only. Visitors must perform in person searches for themselves. No search fee. Required to search: name, years to search; also helpful: DOB, SSN. Criminal records on computer from 1989, on index from 1800s. Will recommend local document retrievers to do searches for you.

General Information: Public Access terminal is available. No juvenile, mental, adoption or sealed released. Will fax results $5.00 per doc; no fee to toll-free number. Copy fee: $1.00 per page. Cert fee: $2.00. Payee: Jackson County Clerk. Personal checks accepted. Prepayment required. Mail requests: SASE required. Mail turnaround time is 2-3 weeks.

Superior Court PO Box 788, Seymour, IN 47274; 812-522-9676; Fax: 812-523-6065. Hours: 8AM-4:30PM (EST). *Felony, Misdemeanor, Civil, Eviction, Small Claims.*

Civil Records: Access: Mail, in person. Visitors must perform in person searches for themselves. No search fee. Required to search: name, years to search. Civil cases indexed by defendant, plaintiff. Civil records on computer from 1989, on index from 1800s.

Criminal Records: Access: In person only. Visitors must perform in person searches for themselves. No search fee. Required to search: name, years to search; also helpful: DOB, SSN. Criminal records on computer from 1989, on index from 1800s.

General Information: No juvenile, mental, adoption or sealed released. Will fax results $5.00 per doc; no fee to toll-free number. Copy fee: $1.00 per page. Cert fee: $2.00. Payee: Jackson County Clerk. Only cashiers checks and money orders accepted. Prepayment required.

Jasper County

Circuit Court 115 W Washington, Rensselaer, IN 47978; 219-866-4941; Civil phone: 219-866-4926; Criminal phone: 219-866-4926; Probate phone: 218-866-4929. 8AM-4PM (CST). *Felony, Misdemeanor, Civil, Eviction, Small Claims, Probate.*

Note: This court also handles juvenile, paternity and adoption.

219-866-4909 Traffic; 219-866-4928 Child Support

Civil Records: Access: Mail, in person. Both court and visitors may perform in person searches. No search fee. Required to search: name, years to search. Civil cases indexed by defendant, plaintiff. County records on computer from 1976, circuit from 1989. Some records on index from 1900s.

Criminal Records: Access: Mail, in person. Both court and visitors may perform in person searches. No search fee. Required to search: name, years to search; also helpful: DOB, SSN. County records on computer from 1976, circuit from 1989. Some records on index from 1900s.

General Information: Public Access terminal is available. No juvenile, mental, adoption or sealed released. Copy fee: $1.00 per page. Cert fee: $.50 per page. Payee: Jasper County Clerk. Business checks accepted. Prepayment required. Mail requests: SASE required. Mail turnaround time 1 day.

Superior Court 115 W Washington St, Rensselaer, IN 47978; 219-866-4922; Civil phone: 219-866-4922; Criminal phone: 21-866-4922; Probate phone: 219-866-4912. Hours: 8AM-4PM (CST). *Felony, Misdemeanor, Civil, Probate.*

Civil Records: Access: Mail, in person. Both court and visitors may perform in person searches. No search fee. Required to search: name, years to search. Civil cases indexed by defendant, plaintiff. County records on computer from 1976, circuit from 1989. Some records on index from 1800s.

Criminal Records: Access: Mail, in person. Both court and visitors may perform in person searches. No search fee. Required to search: name, years to search. County records on computer from 1976, circuit from 1989. Some records on index from 1800s.

General Information: Public Access terminal is available. No juvenile, mental, adoption or sealed released. Copy fee: $.50 per page. Non-case related copies are $.10 per page. Cert fee: $1.00 per page. Payee: County Clerk. Only cashiers checks and money orders accepted. Prepayment required. Mail requests: SASE required. Mail turnaround time 1 day to 1 week.

Jay County

Circuit & Superior Court Courthouse, Portland, IN 47371; 260-726-4951. Hours: 8:30AM-4:30PM (EST). *Felony, Misdemeanor, Civil, Eviction, Small Claims, Probate.*

www.co.jay.in.us

Civil Records: Access: Mail, in person, online. Visitors must perform in person searches for themselves. No search fee. Required to search: name, years to search; also helpful: address. Civil cases indexed by defendant, plaintiff. Civil records on computer from 8\94, prior on microfiche from 1979, on index books from 1900. An online subscription service is at www.doxpop.com. Fees are involved. Records date from 03/94. A limited free search is at www.doxpop.com/prod/court/CourtQuery.

Criminal Records: Access: Mail, in person, online. Visitors must perform in person searches for themselves. No search fee. Required to search: name, years to search, DOB; also helpful: SSN, address. Criminal records on computer from 8\94, prior on microfiche from 1979, on index books from 1900. Online access to criminal records is the same as civil.

Jefferson County

Circuit & Superior Court Courthouse 300 E Main St Rm 203, Madison, IN 47250; 812-265-8923; Fax: 812-265-8950. Hours: 8AM-4PM (EST). *Felony, Misdemeanor, Civil, Eviction, Small Claims, Probate.*

Civil Records: Access: In person only. Visitors must perform in person searches for themselves. No search fee. Required to search: name, years to search. Civil cases indexed by plaintiff, defendant. Civil records on index from 1975, computerized since 1995.

Criminal Records: Access: In person only. Visitors must perform in person searches for themselves. No search fee. Required to search: Name, years to search, address, DOB, SSN, signed release. Criminal records on index from 1975, computerized since 1995.

General Information: Public Access terminal is available. No juvenile, mental, adoption or sealed released. Copy fee: $1.00 per page. Cert fee: $1.00. Payee: County Clerk. Only cashiers checks and money orders accepted. Prepayment required.

Jennings County

Circuit Court Courthouse, PO Box 385, Vernon, IN 47282; 812-352-3070. Hours: 8AM-4PM (EST). *Felony, Misdemeanor, Civil, Eviction, Small Claims, Probate.*

Civil Records: Access: In person. Visitors must perform in person searches for themselves. No search fee. Required to search: name, years to search. Civil cases indexed by defendant, plaintiff. Civil records on index from 1930; computerized since 2000.

Criminal Records: Access: In person only. Visitors must perform in person searches for themselves. No search fee. Required to search: name, years to search, DOB; also helpful: SSN. Criminal records on index from 1930; computerized since 2000.

General Information: Public Access terminal is available. No juvenile, mental, adoption or sealed released. Copy fee: $.25 per page. Cert fee: $1.00. Payee: County Clerk. Personal checks accepted. Prepayment required.

Johnson County

Circuit & Superior Court Courthouse, PO Box 368, Franklin, IN 46131; 317-736-3708; Civil phone: 3177363708; Criminal phone: 317-736-3986; Probate phone: 317-736-3913; Fax: 317-736-3749. Hours: 8AM-4:30PM (EST). *Felony, Misdemeanor, Civil, Eviction, Small Claims, Probate.*

Civil Records: Access: Phone, fax, mail, in person, online. Both court and visitors may perform in person searches. No search fee. Required to search: name, years to search. Civil cases indexed by defendant, plaintiff. Civil records on computer back 10 years. An online subscription service is at www.doxpop.com. Fees are involved. Records date from 08/89. A limited free search is at www.doxpop.com/prod/court/CourtQuery.

Criminal Records: Access: Phone, fax, mail, in person, online. Both court and visitors may perform in person searches. No search fee. Required to search: name, years to search; also helpful: DOB, SSN. Criminal records on computer back 15 years.

General Information: Public Access terminal is available. No juvenile, mental, adoption or sealed released. Long distance fee for faxing only. Copy fee: $1.00 per page. Cert fee: $1.00. Payee: County Clerk.

Business checks accepted. Prepayment required. Mail turnaround time 1-2 days.

Knox County

Circuit & Superior Court 101 N 7th St, Vincennes, IN 47591; 812-885-2521. Hours: 8AM-4PM (EST). *Felony, Misdemeanor, Civil, Eviction, Small Claims, Probate.*

Civil Records: Access: Mail, in person. Visitors must perform in person searches for themselves. No search fee. Required to search: name, years to search. Civil cases indexed by defendant, plaintiff. Civil records on index books from 1800s.

Criminal Records: Access: Mail, in person. Visitors must perform in person searches for themselves. No search fee. Required to search: name, years to search. Criminal records on index books from 1800s.

General Information: No juvenile, mental, adoption or sealed released. Copy fee: $1.00 per page. Cert fee: $1.00. Payee: Knox County Clerk. Personal checks accepted. Prepayment required. Mail turnaround time 1 week.

Kosciusko County

Circuit & Superior Court 121 N Lake, Warsaw, IN 46580; 574-372-2331; Civil phone: 57-372-2331; Criminal phone: 574-372-2457 (1st), 372-2453 (2nd & 3rd); Fax: 574-372-2338. Hours: 8AM-4:30PM (EST). *Felony, Misdemeanor, Civil, Eviction, Small Claims, Probate.*

Civil Records: Access: Fax, in person. Both court and visitors may perform in person searches. No search fee. Required to search: name, years to search. Civil cases indexed by defendant, plaintiff. Civil records on computer from 10/1/93, general index from 1908.

Criminal Records: Access: Fax, in person. Both court and visitors may perform in person searches. No search fee. Required to search: name, years to search; also helpful-DOB, SSN. DL#. Criminal records on computer from 10/1/93, general index from 1908.

General Information: Public Access terminal is available. No juvenile, mental, adoption or sealed released. Will fax results to toll free number only. Copy fee: $.50 per page after 1st 20 pages. Cert fee: $1.00. Payee: County Clerk. Personal checks accepted. Prepayment required.

La Porte County

Circuit & Superior Court 813 Lincolnway, La Porte, IN 46350; 219-326-6808; Fax: 219-326-6626. Hours: 8:00AM-4PM (CST). *Felony, Misdemeanor, Civil, Eviction, Probate.*

Civil Records: Access: In person only. Visitors must perform in person searches for themselves. No search fee. Required to search: name, years to search. Civil cases indexed by defendant, plaintiff. Civil records on microfiche and index from 1900.

Criminal Records: Access: In person only. Visitors must perform in person searches for themselves. No search fee. Required to search: name, years to search. Criminal records on microfiche and index from 1900.

General Information: Public Access terminal is available. No juvenile, mental, adoption or sealed released. Copy fee: $1.00 per page. Cert fee: $1.00 per page. Payee: Court Clerk. Business checks accepted. Prepayment required.

LaGrange County

Circuit & Superior Court 105 N Detroit St, Courthouse, LaGrange, IN 46761; 260-463-3442; Fax: 260-463-2187. Hours: 8AM-4PM M-TH, 8AM-5PM F (EST). *Felony, Misdemeanor, Civil, Eviction, Small Claims, Probate.*

Civil Records: Access: Phone, mail, in person. Visitors must perform in person searches for themselves. No search fee. Required to search: name, years to search. Civil cases indexed by defendant, plaintiff. Civil records on computer from 1990, on books from 1900.

Criminal Records: Access: Phone, mail, in person. Visitors must perform in person searches for themselves. No search fee. Required to search: name, years to search; also helpful: DOB, SSN. Criminal records on computer from 1990, on books from 1900.

General Information: Public Access terminal is available. No juvenile, mental, adoption or sealed released. Copy fee: $1.00 per page. Cert fee: $1.00. Payee: LaGrange County Clerk. Personal checks accepted. Prepayment required. Mail requests: SASE requested. Turnaround time 1-2 days from 1/1/90; 30 days if prior to 1/1/90.

Lake County

Circuit & Superior Court 2293 N Main St, Courthouse, Crown Point, IN 46307; 219-755-3460; Fax: 219-755-3520. Hours: 8:30AM-4PM (CST). *Felony, Misdemeanor, Civil, Eviction, Small Claims, Probate.* www.lakecountyin.org/index.jsp

Civil Records: Access: Mail, fax, in person. Both court and visitors may perform in person searches. No search fee. Required to search: name, years to search; also helpful: address. Civil cases indexed by defendant, plaintiff. Civil records go back to 1920s; on microfiche back to 1983; on computer back to 1990s. Fax requests must be on letterhead.

Criminal Records: Access: Mail, in person. Both court and visitors may perform in person searches. Search fee: $7.00. Required to search: name, years to search, DOB, SSN; also helpful: address. Criminal records go back to 1900s; on microfiche back to 1983; on computer back to 1990s. Search requests for background checks are forwarded to the County Bureau of Identification, 219-755-3316. Authorization required.

General Information: Public Access terminal is available. No juvenile, mental, adoption or sealed released. Copy fee: $1.00 per page. Cert fee: $2.00. Payee: Lake County Clerk. Business checks accepted. Prepayment required. Mail turnaround time 1 week.

Lawrence County

Circuit, Superior & County Court 31 Courthouse, 916 15th St RM31, Bedford, IN 47421; 812-275-7543; Fax: 812-277-2024. Hours: 8:30AM-4:30PM (EST). *Felony, Misdemeanor, Civil, Eviction, Small Claims, Probate.*

Note: Superior Court I is located at 1410 I St, 812-275-3124. Superior Court II is located at 1420 I St, 812-275-4161. All small claims are filed in Superior II.

Civil Records: Access: In person only. Visitors must perform in person searches for themselves. No search fee. Required to search: name, years to search. Civil cases indexed by plaintiff. Civil records on computer from 1987, on index from 1817.

Criminal Records: Access: In person only. Visitors must perform in person searches for themselves. No search fee. Required to search: name, years to search, DOB; also helpful: SSN. Criminal records on computer from 1987, on index from 1817.

General Information: Public Access terminal is available. No juvenile, mental, adoption or sealed released. Copy fee: $1.00 per page. Cert fee: $1.00. Payee: Lawrence County Clerk. Only cashiers checks and money orders accepted. Prepayment required.

Madison County

Circuit, Superior & County Court PO Box 1277, Anderson, IN 46015-1277; 765-641-9443; Fax: 765-640-4203. Hours: 8AM-4PM (EST). *Felony, Misdemeanor, Civil, Eviction, Small Claims, Probate.*

http://madisoncty.com/courts/index.html

Civil Records: Access: In person only. Visitors must perform in person searches for themselves. No search fee. Required to search: name, years to search. Civil cases indexed by defendant. Civil records on microfiche and archived from 1950, on index from 1900.

Criminal Records: Access: In person only. Visitors must perform in person searches for themselves. No search fee. Required to search: name, years to search, signed release. Criminal records on microfiche and archived from 1950, on index from 1900.

General Information: Public Access terminal is available. No juvenile, mental, adoption or sealed released. Copy fee: $1.00 per page. Cert fee: $1.00. Payee: County Clerk. Business checks accepted. Prepayment required.

Marion County

Circuit & Superior Court 200 E Washington St, Indianapolis, IN 46204; 317-327-4740; Civil phone: 317-327-4733; Criminal phone: 317-327-4733. 8AM-4:30PM (EST). *Felony, Misdemeanor, Civil, Probate.* www.indygov.org/clerk

Note: The Municipal Court of Marion County, once separate, is now part of Superior Court. All records are merged with the Superior Court.

Civil Records: Access: Mail, online, in person. Both court and visitors may perform in person searches. No search fee. Required to search: name, years to search. Civil cases indexed by defendant, plaintiff. Civil records on computer back to 1981, on microfiche, archived and on index from 1912. Small claims records are held by the township in which they were filed; the phone numbers are listed below. Perform an online name search for free at www.civicnet.net. There is a $7.50 charge assessed to view each Case Summary. Records go back to 1991.

Criminal Records: Access: Mail, online, in person. Both court and visitors may perform in person searches. Search fee: $10.00 per name. Required to search: name, years to search, DOB; also helpful: SSN. Criminal records on computer back to 1981, on microfiche, archived and on index from 1912. Small claims records are held by the township in which they were filed; the phone numbers are listed below. Access to online criminal records at https://www.civicnet.net/criminal/ requires a subscription or you may search at rate of $4.50 per name and pay with credit card. Criminal records go back to 1988.

General Information: Public Access terminal is available. No juvenile, mental, adoption or sealed released. Copy fee: $1.00 per page. Cert fee: $1.00. Payee: County Clerk. Personal checks accepted. Prepayment required. Mail requests: SASE not required. Mail turnaround time 1-2 days.

Marshall County

Circuit & Superior Court 1 & 2 211 W Madison St, Plymouth, IN 46563; 574-936-8922; Fax: 574-936-8893. Hours: 8AM-4PM (EST). *Felony, Misdemeanor, Civil, Eviction, Small Claims, Probate.*

Civil Records: Access: In person, online. Visitors must perform in person searches for themselves. No search fee. Required to search: name, years to search; also helpful: address. Civil cases indexed by defendant, plaintiff. Civil records on computer from 1989, on microfiche, archived and on index from

1835. An online subscription service is at www.doxpop.com. Fees are involved. Records date from 09/88. A limited free search is at www.doxpop.com/prod/court/CourtQuery.

Criminal Records: Access: In person, online. Visitors must perform in person searches for themselves. No search fee. Required to search: name, years to search, signed release; also helpful: address, DOB, SSN. Criminal records on computer from 1989, on microfiche, archived and on index from 1835. Online access to criminal records is the same as civil.

General Information: Public Access terminal is available. No juvenile, mental, adoption or sealed released. Fee to fax results is $5.00 per page; $1.00 each addl, not to exceed $10.00. Copy fee: $1.00 per page. Cert fee: $2.00. Payee: County Clerk. Business checks accepted. Prepayment required.

Martin County

Circuit Court PO Box 120 (111 Main St), Shoals, IN 47581; 812-247-3651; Fax: 812-247-2791. Hours: 8AM-4PM (EST). *Felony, Misdemeanor, Civil, Eviction, Small Claims, Probate.*

Civil Records: Access: Mail, fax, in person. Both court and visitors may perform in person searches. No search fee. Required to search: name, years to search. Civil cases indexed by defendant, plaintiff. Civil records on index books.

Criminal Records: Access: Mail, fax, in person. Both court and visitors may perform in person searches. No search fee. Required to search: name, years to search, DOB or SSN. Criminal records on index books.

General Information: No juvenile, mental, adoption, or sealed records released. Will fax results to local or toll free line. Copy fee: $1.00 per page. Cert fee: $2.00. Payee: County Clerk. Business checks accepted. Prepayment required. Mail turnaround time 4 days.

Miami County

Circuit & Superior Court PO Box 184, Peru, IN 46970; 765-472-3901; Fax: 765-472-1778. Hours: 8AM-4PM (EST). *Felony, Misdemeanor, Civil, Eviction, Small Claims, Probate.*

Civil Records: Access: Fax, mail, in person, online. Both court and visitors may perform in person searches. Search fee: $10.00 per name per page. Required to search: name, years to search. Civil cases indexed by defendant, plaintiff. Civil records on computer back to 4/1998, archived from 1900s. Some records on docket books by case number and alpha. An online subscription service is at www.doxpop.com. Fees are involved. Records date from 03/98. A limited free search is at www.doxpop.com/prod/court/CourtQuery.

Criminal Records: Access: Fax, mail, in person, online. Both court and visitors may perform in person searches. Search fee: $10.00 per name per page. Required to search: name, years to search, DOB, SSN, signed release. Criminal records on computer back to 4/1998; archived from 1900s. Some records on docket books by case number and alpha. Online access to criminal records is the same as civil.

General Information: Public Access terminal is available. No juvenile, mental, adoption, or sealed released. Will fax results $1.00 per page; no fee for toll free or local call. Copy fee: $1.00 per page. Cert fee: $1.00. Payee: Miami County Clerk. Personal checks accepted. Prepayment required. Mail turnaround time 1-2 days.

Monroe County

Circuit Court PO Box 547, Bloomington, IN 47402; 812-349-2614; Fax: 812-349-2610. Hours: 8AM-4PM (EST). *Felony, Misdemeanor, Civil, Eviction, Small Claims, Probate.*
www.co.monroe.in.us

Civil Records: Access: Mail, fax, in person, online. Both court and visitors may perform in person searches. No search fee. Required to search: name, years to search. Civil cases indexed by defendant, plaintiff. Civil records on computer from 1993. Some records on docket books by case number and alpha. In the process of putting records on microfilm. An online subscription service is at www.doxpop.com. Fees are involved. Records date from 08/93. A limited free search is www.doxpop.com/prod/court/CourtQuery.

Criminal Records: Access: Mail, fax, in person, online. Both court and visitors may perform in person searches. No search fee. Required to search: name, years to search, DOB; also helpful: SSN. Criminal records on computer from 1993. Some records on docket books by case number and alpha. In the process of putting records on microfilm. Online access to criminal records is the same as civil.

General Information: Public Access terminal is available. No juvenile, mental, adoption or sealed released. Fee to fax results is $1.00 per page. Copy fee: $1.00 per page. Cert fee: $1.00. Payee: Monroe County Clerk. Personal checks accepted. Prepayment required. Mail turnaround time 48 hours.

Montgomery County

Circuit, Superior & County Court PO Box 768, Crawfordsville, IN 47933; 765-364-6430; Fax: 765-364-6355. Hours: 8:30AM-4:30PM (EST). *Felony, Misdemeanor, Civil, Eviction, Small Claims, Probate.* www.montgomeryco.net

Civil Records: Access: Phone, fax, mail, in person, online. Both court and visitors may perform in person searches. No search fee. Required to search: name, years to search. Civil cases indexed by defendant, plaintiff. Civil records on computer from 1990, some on microfiche and docket books, and archived from 1800s. An online subscription service is at www.doxpop.com. Fees are involved. Records date from 01/90. A limited free search is at www.doxpop.com/prod/court/CourtQuery. Indicate type(s) of cases sought in mail search request.

Criminal Records: Access: Mail, fax, in person, online. Both court and visitors may perform in person searches. No search fee. Required to search: name, years to search, DOB; also helpful: SSN. Criminal records on computer from 1990, some on microfiche and docket books, and archived from 1800s. Online access to criminal records is the same as civil.

General Information: Public Access terminal is available. No juvenile, mental, adoption or sealed released. Will fax results $1.00 per page plus $3.25 fax fee. Copy fee: $1.00 per page. Cert fee: $2.00. Payee: Montgomery County Clerk. Business checks accepted. Prepayment required. Mail requests: SASE required. Mail turnaround time 1 week.

Morgan County

Circuit & Superior Court PO Box 1556, Martinsville, IN 46151; 765-342-1025; Fax: 765-342-1111. 8AM-4PM (EST). *Felony, Misdemeanor, Civil, Eviction, Small Claims, Probate.*

Civil Records: Access: In person only. Visitors must perform in person searches for themselves. No search fee. Required to search: name, years to search. Civil cases indexed by defendant, plaintiff. Civil records archived from 1970; on computer back to 1993. Some records on index cards. In some instances, limited information is given over the phone if the docket number is known.

Criminal Records: Access: In person only. Visitors must perform in person searches for themselves. No search fee. Required to search: name, years to search, DOB; also helpful: SSN, signed release. Criminal records archived from 1970; on microfilm 1992-95, on computer back to 1993.

General Information: Public Access terminal is available. No juvenile, mental, adoption or sealed released. Copy fee: $.05 per page. Cert fee: $1.00 per page. Payee: Morgan County Clerk. Personal checks accepted. Prepayment required.

Newton County

Circuit & Superior Court PO Box 49, Kentland, IN 47951; 219-474-6081. Hours: 8AM-4PM (CST). *Felony, Misdemeanor, Civil, Eviction, Small Claims, Probate.*

Civil Records: Access: Mail, in person. Both court and visitors may perform in person searches. Search fee: $3.00 per name. Required to search: name, years to search. Civil cases indexed by defendant, plaintiff. Civil records on index from 1937, partial on microfiche; on computer back to 1996.

Criminal Records: Access: Mail, in person. Both court and visitors may perform in person searches. Search fee: $3.00 per name. Required to search: name, years to search, DOB, signed release; also helpful: SSN. Criminal records on index from 1937, partial on microfiche; on computer back to 1996.

General Information: Public Access terminal is available. No juvenile, mental, adoption or sealed records released. Will fax results to local or toll free line. Copy fee: $.25 per page. Cert fee: $1.25. Payee: Clerk of Newton Circuit Court. Business checks accepted. Prepayment required. Mail requests: SASE required. Mail turnaround time 1-2 weeks.

Noble County

Circuit, Superior I & Superior II Court 101 N Orange St, Albion, IN 46701; 260-636-2736; Fax: 260-636-4000. Hours: 8AM-4PM (EST). *Felony, Misdemeanor, Civil, Eviction, Small Claims, Probate.*

Civil Records: Access: Fax, mail, in person. Both court and visitors may perform in person searches. No search fee. Required to search: name, years to search. Civil cases indexed by defendant, plaintiff. Civil records on index cards and docket books to 1856; on computer back to 1992.

Criminal Records: Access: Fax, mail, in person. Both court and visitors may perform in person searches. No search fee. Required to search: name, years to search; also helpful: DOB, SSN. Criminal records on index cards and docket books to 1856; on computer back to 1992. Criminal record searches are 10-year only.

General Information: Public Access terminal is available. No juvenile, mental, adoption or sealed released. Will fax results to toll-free number. Copy fee: $1.00 per page. Cert fee: $1.00. Payee: Noble County Clerk. No personal checks accepted. Prepayment required. Mail requests: SASE required. Mail turnaround time 1 week.

Ohio County

Circuit & Superior Court PO Box 185, Rising Sun, IN 47040; 812-438-2610; Fax: 812-438-1215. Hours: 9AM-4PM M,T,Th,F 9AM-Noon S (EST). *Felony, Misdemeanor, Civil, Eviction, Small Claims, Probate.*

Civil Records: Access: Phone, fax, mail, in person. Both court and visitors may perform in person searches. No search fee. Required to search: name, years to search. Civil cases indexed by defendant, plaintiff. Civil records archived from 1844; on computer back to 8/1999.

Criminal Records: Access: In person only. Visitors must perform in person searches for themselves. No search fee. Required to search: name, years to search. Criminal records on computer back to 8/1999.

General Information: Public Access terminal is available. No juvenile, mental, adoption or sealed released. Fee to fax results is $3.00 1st page, $1.00 each add'l paid in advance. Copy fee: $1.00 per page. Cert fee: $2.00. Payee: Ohio County Clerk. Personal checks accepted. Prepayment required.

Orange County

Circuit & County Court Courthouse, Court St, Paoli, IN 47454; 812-723-2649; Fax: 812-723-0239. Hours: 8AM-4PM (EST). *Felony, Civil, Eviction, Small Claims, Probate.*

Note: The Superior Court handles misdemeanors and Class D (minor) felonies.

Civil Records: Access: Mail, fax, in person. Both court and visitors may perform in person searches. No search fee. Required to search: name, years to search. Civil cases indexed by defendant, plaintiff. Civil records archived from 1874. Some records on docket books.

Criminal Records: Access: Mail, fax, in person. Both court and visitors may perform in person searches. No search fee. Required to search: name, years to search. Criminal records archived from 1874. Some records on docket books.

General Information: No juvenile, mental, adoption or sealed released. Copy fee: $1.00 per page. Cert fee: $2.00 per document. Payee: Orange Circuit Clerk. Only cashiers checks and money orders accepted. Prepayment required. Mail requests: SASE required. Mail turnaround time 2 weeks.

Superior Court 205 E Main St, Paoli, IN 47454; 812-723-7134. Hours: 8AM-Noon, 1-4PM (EST). *Felony (Class D), Misdemeanor.*

Note: The Circuit and County Court handles felonies, eviction, and small claims.

Criminal Records: Access: In person. Both court and visitors may perform in person searches. No search fee. Required to search: name, years to search. Criminal records archived from 1874. Some records on docket books. Direct mail search requests to the Circuit and County Court.

General Information: No juvenile, mental, adoption or sealed released. Copy fee: $1.00 per page. Cert fee: $2.00 per document. Only cashiers checks and money orders accepted. Prepayment required.

Owen County

Circuit Court PO Box 146, Courthouse, Spencer, IN 47460; 812-829-5015; Fax: 812-829-5147. Hours: 8AM-4PM (EST). *Felony, Misdemeanor, Civil, Eviction, Small Claims, Probate.*

Civil Records: Access: In person only. Visitors must perform in person searches for themselves. Search fee: none. Required to search: name, years to search. Civil cases indexed by defendant, plaintiff. Civil records archived from 1800s. Some records on docket books.

Criminal Records: Access: In person only. Visitors must perform in person searches for themselves. Search fee: none. Required to search: name, years to search. Criminal records archived from 1800s. Some records on docket books.

General Information: No juvenile, mental, adoption or sealed records released. Copy fee: $1.00 per page. Cert fee: $1.00. Payee: Owen County Clerk. Business checks accepted. Prepayment required.

Parke County

Circuit Court 116 W High St, Rm 204, Rockville, IN 47872; 765-569-5132. Hours: 8AM-4PM (EST). *Felony, Misdemeanor, Civil, Eviction, Small Claims, Probate.*

Civil Records: Access: In person only. Visitors must perform in person searches for themselves. No search fee. Required to search: name, years to search. Civil cases indexed by defendant, plaintiff. Civil records archived from 1880s. Some records on docket books.

Criminal Records: Access: In person only. Visitors must perform in person searches for themselves. No search fee. Required to search: name, years to search. Criminal records archived from 1880s. Some records on docket books.

General Information: No juvenile, mental, adoption or sealed released. Copy fee: $1.00 per page. Cert fee: $2.00. Payee: Parke County Clerk. Personal checks not accepted. Prepayment required.

Perry County

Circuit Court 2219 Payne St, #219, Courthouse, #219, Tell City, IN 47586; 812-547-3741. Hours: 8AM-4PM (EST). *Felony, Misdemeanor, Civil, Eviction, Small Claims, Probate.*

Civil Records: Access: In person only. Both court and visitors may perform in person searches. No search fee. Required to search: name, years to search. Civil cases indexed by defendant, plaintiff. Civil records archived from 1900s. Some records on dockets.

Criminal Records: Access: In person only. Both court and visitors may perform in person searches. No search fee. Required to search: name, years to search. Criminal records archived from 1900s. Some records on dockets.

General Information: No juvenile, mental, adoption or sealed released. Copy fee: $.50 per page. Cert fee: $1.00. Payee: Perry County Clerk. Business checks accepted. Prepayment required.

Pike County

Circuit Court PO Box 407, Petersburg, IN 47567; 812-354-6025; Fax: 812-354-3552. Hours: 8AM-4PM (EST). *Felony, Misdemeanor, Civil, Eviction, Small Claims, Probate.*

Civil Records: Access: Mail, in person. Both court and visitors may perform in person searches. No search fee. Required to search: name, years to search. Civil cases indexed by defendant, plaintiff. Civil records archived from 1817. Some records on docket books and index file; on computer since 7/99.

Criminal Records: Access: Mail, in person. Both court and visitors may perform in person searches. No search fee. Required to search: name, years to search, DOB. Criminal records archived from 1817. Some records on docket books and index file; on computer since 7/99.

General Information: No juvenile, mental, adoption or sealed released. Copy fee: $1.00 per page. Cert fee: $2.00. Payee: Pike County Clerk. Only cashiers checks and money orders accepted. Prepayment required. Mail requests: SASE required. Mail turnaround time 1-2 days.

Porter County

Circuit Court Records Division, Courthouse, 16 E Lincolnway Rm 217, Valparaiso, IN 46383-5659; 219-465-3453; Fax: 219-465-3592. Hours: 8:30AM-4:30PM (CST). *Felony, Misdemeanor, Civil, Eviction, Small Claims, Probate.*

www.porterco.org

Civil Records: Access: Mail, in person. Both court and visitors may perform in person searches. No search fee. Required to search: name, years to search. Civil cases indexed by defendant, plaintiff. Civil

records on computer index from 1990. Circuit Court records kept from 1844, Superior Court records from 1895. Probate records from Circuit Court kept from 1853, Superior Court from 1900.

Criminal Records: Access: Mail, in person. Both court and visitors may perform in person searches. No search fee. Required to search: name, years to search. Criminal records on computer index since 1990. Circuit Court criminal records kept from 1877, Superior Court from 1895.

General Information: Public Access terminal is available. No juvenile, mental, adoption or sealed released. Copy fee: $1.00 per page. Cert fee: $1.00. Payee: Porter County Clerk. Only cashiers checks and money orders accepted. Prepayment required. Mail requests: SASE required. Mail turnaround time 1-2 weeks.

Superior Court 3560 Willow Creek Dr, Portage, IN 46368; 219-759-2501. Hours: 8:30AM-4:30PM (CST). *Misdemeanor, Civil, Small Claims, Probate.*

Civil Records: Access: Mail, in person. Both court and visitors may perform in person searches. No search fee. Required to search: name, years to search. Civil cases indexed by defendant, plaintiff. Civil records on computer since 1991; prior records on manual index.

Criminal Records: Access: Mail, in person. Both court and visitors may perform in person searches. No search fee. Required to search: name, years to search; also helpful: DOB, SSN. Criminal records on computer since 1991; prior records on manual index.

General Information: Public Access terminal is available. No juvenile, mental, adoption or sealed records released. Fee to fax results is $.79 per page. Copy fee: $2.00 per page. Cert fee: $1.00. Payee: Porter County Clerk. Only cashiers checks and money orders accepted. Prepayment required.

Posey County

Circuit & Superior Court PO Box 606, 300 Main St, Mount Vernon, IN 47620-0606; 812-838-1306; Fax: 812-838-1307. Hours: 8AM-4PM (CST). *Felony, Misdemeanor, Civil, Eviction, Small Claims, Probate.*

http://members.sigecom.net/pcc

Civil Records: Access: In person only. Visitors must perform in person searches for themselves. No search fee. Required to search: name, years to search; also helpful: address. Civil cases indexed by defendant, plaintiff. Civil records on computer since 8/88, prior on docket books.

Criminal Records: Access: In person only. Visitors must perform in person searches for themselves. No search fee. Required to search: name, years to search; also helpful: DOB, SSN. Criminal records on computer since 8/88, prior on docket books.

General Information: Public Access terminal is available. (Available in Superior Court.) No juvenile, mental, adoption or sealed released. Copy fee: $1.00 per page. Cert fee: $1.00. Payee: Posey County Clerk. Only cashiers checks and money orders accepted. Prepayment required.

Pulaski County

Circuit & Superior Court 112 E Main, Rm 230, Winamac, IN 46996; 574-946-3313; Fax: 574-946-4953. Hours: 8AM-4PM (EST). *Felony, Misdemeanor, Civil, Eviction, Small Claims, Probate.*

Civil Records: Access: In person only. Visitors must perform in person searches for themselves. No search fee. Required to search: name, years to search. Civil cases indexed by defendant. Civil records archived from 1850s. Some records on docket books. On computer back to 1998.

Criminal Records: Access: In person only. Visitors must perform in person searches for themselves. No search fee. Required to search: name, years to search; also helpful: SSN. Criminal records archived from 1850s. Some records on docket books. On computer back to 1998.

General Information: Public Access terminal is available. No juvenile, mental, adoption or sealed records released. Copy fee: $.50 per page. Cert fee: $2.00. Payee: Pulaski County Clerk. Only cashiers checks and money orders accepted. Prepayment required.

Putnam County

Circuit & Superior Court PO Box 546, Greencastle, IN 46135; 765-653-2648. Hours: 8AM-4PM (EST). *Felony, Misdemeanor, Civil, Eviction, Small Claims, Probate.*

Civil Records: Access: Mail, in person, online. Visitors must perform in person searches for themselves. No search fee. Required to search: name, years to search. Civil cases indexed by defendant, plaintiff. Civil records on index books from 1991, archived from 1800s. Some records on docket books. An online subscription service is at www.doxpop.com. Fees are involved. Records date from 01/93. A limited free search is at www.doxpop.com/prod/court/CourtQuery.

Criminal Records: Access: In person, online. Visitors must perform in person searches for themselves. No search fee. Required to search: name, years to search; also helpful: DOB, SSN. Criminal records on index books from 1991, archived from 1800s. Some records on docket books. Online access to criminal records is the same as civil.

General Information: Public Access terminal is available. No juvenile, mental, adoption or sealed records released. Copy fee: $1.00 per page. Cert fee: $1.00. Payee: Putnam County Clerk. Business checks accepted. Prepayment required. Mail turnaround time 1 week.

Randolph County

Circuit & Superior Court PO Box 230 Courthouse, Winchester, IN 47394-0230; 765-584-7070 X231; Fax: 765-584-2958. Hours: 8AM-4PM (EST). *Felony, Misdemeanor, Civil, Eviction, Small Claims, Probate.*

Civil Records: Access: Fax, mail, in person, online. Visitors must perform in person searches for themselves. No search fee. Required to search: name, years to search. Civil cases indexed by defendant, plaintiff. Civil records archived from early 1800s, computerized from 1994. Records on docket books and microfiche. An online subscription service is at www.doxpop.com. Fees are involved. Records date from 03/94. A limited free search is at www.doxpop.com/prod/court/CourtQuery.

Criminal Records: Access: Fax, mail, in person, online. Visitors must perform in person searches for themselves. No search fee. Required to search: name, years to search. Criminal records archived from early 1800s, computerized since 1994. Records on docket books and microfiche. Online access to criminal records is the same as civil.

General Information: Public Access terminal is available. No juvenile, mental, adoption or sealed records released. Will fax results $4.00 for 1st page, $.75 each add'l. Copy fee: $1.00 per page. Cert fee: $1.00. Payee: Randolph County Clerk. Checks and money orders accepted. Prepayment required. Mail requests: SASE required. Mail turnaround time 3 days.

Ripley County

Circuit Court PO Box 177, Versailles, IN 47042; 812-689-6115. Hours: 8AM-4PM (EST). *Felony, Misdemeanor, Civil, Eviction, Small Claims, Probate.*

Civil Records: Access: Phone, mail, in person. Both court and visitors may perform in person searches. No search fee. Required to search: name, years to search. Civil cases indexed by defendant, plaintiff. Civil records on computer since 1993, archived from 1800s. Some records on docket books.

Criminal Records: Access: Mail, in person. Both court and visitors may perform in person searches. No search fee. Required to search: name, years to search, DOB, signed release; also helpful: SSN. Criminal records on computer since 1993, archived from 1800s. Some records on docket books.

General Information: Public Access terminal is available. No juvenile, mental, adoption or sealed records released. Will fax results for $1.00 per page. Payments must be mailed in first. Copy fee: $1.00 per page. Cert fee: $3.00. Payee: Clerk of Ripley Circuit Court. Personal checks accepted. Prepayment required. Mail turnaround time 1 week.

Rush County

Circuit & Superior Court PO Box 429, Rushville, IN 46173; 765-932-2086; Fax: 765-932-4165. 8AM-4PM (EST). *Felony, Misdemeanor, Civil, Eviction, Small Claims, Probate.*

Note: This office will not conduct general searches, but will pull files if the specific case number is given.

Civil Records: Access: In person only. Visitors must perform in person searches for themselves. No search fee. Required to search: name, years to search. Civil cases indexed by defendant, plaintiff. Civil records archived from 1822. Some records on docket books.

Criminal Records: Access: In person only. Visitors must perform in person searches for themselves. No search fee. Required to search: name, years to search, DOB; also helpful: SSN, cause number. Criminal records archived from 1822. Some records on docket books. Court will only search the status of an open case, and you need to provide the case number of it.

General Information: No juvenile, mental, adoption or sealed records released. Copy fee: $1.00 per page. Cert fee: $1.00. Payee: Rush County Clerk. Business checks accepted. Prepayment required.

Scott County

Circuit & Superior Court 1 E McClain Ave, #120, Scottsburg, IN 47170; 812-752-8420; Fax: 812-752-5459. Hours: 8:30AM-4:30PM (EST). *Felony, Misdemeanor, Civil, Eviction, Small Claims, Probate.*

Civil Records: Access: In person only. Visitors must perform in person searches for themselves. No search fee. Required to search: name, years to search; also helpful: address. Civil cases indexed by defendant, plaintiff. Civil records on computer from 2/90, on docket books from 1970.

Criminal Records: Access: In person only. Visitors must perform in person searches for themselves. No search fee. Required to search: name, years to search; also helpful: DOB, SSN. Criminal records on computer from 2/90, on docket books from 1970.

General Information: Public Access terminal is available. No juvenile, mental, adoption or sealed records released. Copy fee: $1.00 per page. Cert fee: $2.00. Payee: Scott County Clerk. Business checks accepted. Prepayment required.

Shelby County

Circuit & Superior Court 407 S Harrison St, Rm 206, Shelbyville, IN 46176; 317-392-6320. Hours: 8AM-4PM (EST). *Felony, Misdemeanor, Civil, Eviction, Small Claims, Probate.*

Civil Records: Access: In person only. Visitors must perform in person searches for themselves. No search fee. Required to search: name, years to search. Civil cases indexed by defendant, plaintiff. Civil records on computer since 07/95.

Criminal Records: Access: In person only. Visitors must perform in person searches for themselves. No search fee. Required to search: name, years to search. Criminal records on computer since 07/95.

General Information: Public Access terminal is available. No juvenile, mental, adoption or sealed released. Copy fee: $1.00 per page. Cert fee: $1.00. Payee: Clerk of Court. Personal checks not accepted. Prepayment required.

Spencer County

Circuit Court PO Box 12, Rockport, IN 47635; 812-649-6027; Fax: 812-649-6030. Hours: 8AM-4PM (CST). *Felony, Misdemeanor, Civil, Eviction, Small Claims, Probate.*

Civil Records: Access: In person only. Visitors must perform in person searches for themselves. No search fee. Required to search: name, years to search. Civil cases indexed by defendant, plaintiff. Civil records archived from early 1900s. Some records on docket books. Child support cases on computer. Starting 02/02 all new cases are computerized.

Criminal Records: Access: In person only. Visitors must perform in person searches for themselves. No search fee. Required to search: name, years to search. Criminal records archived from early 1900s. Some records on docket books. Starting 02/02 all new cases are computerized.

General Information: Public Access terminal is available. No juvenile, mental, adoption or sealed released. Copy fee: $1.00 per page. Cert fee: $1.00. Payee: Spencer Circuit Court. Only cashiers checks and money orders accepted. Prepayment required.

St. Joseph County

Circuit & Superior Court 101 S Main St, South Bend, IN 46601; 574-235-9635; Fax: 574-235-9838. 8AM-4:30PM (EST). *Felony, Misdemeanor, Civil, Eviction, Small Claims, Probate.*

Civil Records: Access: Mail, in person. Both court and visitors may perform in person searches. No search fee. Required to search: name, years to search. Civil cases indexed by defendant, plaintiff. Civil records on general index from 1962, computerized since 1992.

Criminal Records: Access: In person only. Visitors must perform in person searches for themselves. No search fee. Required to search: name, years to search; also helpful: address, DOB, SSN. Criminal records on general index from 1962, computerized since 1984.

General Information: Public Access terminal is available. No juvenile, mental, adoption or sealed released. Copy fee: $.05 per page. Cert fee: $1.00. Payee: St Joseph County Clerk. Business checks accepted. Prepayment required. Mail requests: SASE required. Mail turnaround time 1-2 days.

Starke County

Circuit Court Courthouse, 53 E Washington St, Knox, IN 46534; 574-772-9128. Hours: 8:30AM-4PM (CST). *Felony, Misdemeanor, Civil, Eviction, Small Claims, Probate.*

Civil Records: Access: In person only. Both the court and visitors may perform in person searches. No search fee. Required to search: name, years to search. Civil cases indexed by defendant, plaintiff. Civil records archived from 1850s. Some records on docket books.

Criminal Records: Access: In person only. Both the court and visitors may perform in person searches. No search fee. Required to search: name, years to search, DOB; also helpful: SSN. Criminal records archived from 1850s. Some records on docket books.

General Information: No juvenile, mental, adoption or sealed released. Copy fee: $1.00 per page. Cert fee: $2.00. Payee: Clerk of Stark Circuit Court. Business checks accepted. Prepayment required.

Steuben County

Circuit & Superior Court Courthouse, 55 S Public Sq, Angola, IN 46703; 260-668-1000 X2240. Hours: 8AM-4:30PM (EST). *Felony, Misdemeanor, Civil, Eviction, Small Claims, Probate.*

Civil Records: Access: In person only. Visitors must perform in person searches for themselves. No search fee. Required to search: name, years to search. Civil cases indexed by defendant, plaintiff. Civil records archived from 1800s. Some records on docket books.

Criminal Records: Access: In person only. Visitors must perform in person searches for themselves. No search fee. Required to search: name, years to search. Criminal records archived from 1800s, computerized since 06/94. Some records on docket books.

General Information: Public Access terminal is available. No juvenile, mental, adoption, some probate, or sealed released. Copy fee: $1.00 per page. Cert fee: $2.00. Payee: Steuben County Clerk. Only cashiers checks and money orders accepted. Prepayment required.

Sullivan County

Circuit & Superior Court Courthouse, Rm 304, PO Box 370, Sullivan, IN 47882-0370; 812-268-4657. 8AM-4PM (EST). *Felony, Misdemeanor, Civil, Eviction, Small Claims, Probate.*

Civil Records: Access: In person, online. Visitors must perform in person searches for themselves. No search fee. Required to search: name, years to search; also helpful: address. Civil cases indexed by defendant, plaintiff. Civil records on docket books or general index from late 1850's; computerized from 1999. An online subscription service is at www.doxpop.com. Fees are involved. Records date from 06/98. A limited free search is at www.doxpop.com/prod/court/CourtQuery.

Criminal Records: Access: In person, online. Visitors must perform in person searches for themselves. No search fee. Required to search: name, years to search, DOB, signed release; also helpful: address, SSN. Criminal records on docket books or general index from late 1850's; computerized from 1999. Online access to criminal records same as civil.

General Information: Public Access terminal is available. No juvenile, mental, adoption or sealed released. Copy fee: $1.00 per page. Cert fee: $1.00 per page. Payee: Sullivan County. No personal checks accepted. Prepayment required.

Switzerland County

Circuit & Superior Court Courthouse, 212 W Main St, Vevay, IN 47043; 812-427-3175; Fax: 812-427-2017. Hours: 8-3:30PM M-W & F; 8AM-Noon Th (EST). *Felony, Misdemeanor, Civil, Eviction, Small Claims, Probate.*

Civil Records: Access: in person only. Visitors must perform in person searches for themselves. No search fee. Required to search: name, years to search, DOB. Civil cases indexed by defendant, plaintiff. Civil records archived from 1900s. All records on docket books or general index.

Criminal Records: Access: In person only. Visitors must perform in person searches for themselves. No search fee. Required to search: name, years to search,

DOB. Criminal records archived from 1900s. All records on docket books or general index.

General Information: No juvenile, mental, adoption or sealed records released. Copy fee: $1.00 per page. Cert fee: $1.00. Payee: Switzerland County Clerk. Only cashiers checks and money orders accepted. Prepayment required.

Tippecanoe County

Circuit, Superior & County Court PO Box 1665, Lafayette, IN 47902; 765-423-9326; Fax: 765-423-9194. Hours: 8AM-4:30PM (EST). *Felony, Misdemeanor, Civil, Eviction, Small Claims, Probate.* www.county.tippecanoe.in.us

Civil Records: Access: In person, mail, online. Visitors must perform in person searches for themselves. No search fee. Required to search: name, years to search. Civil cases indexed by defendant, plaintiff. Civil records on computer from 1987, on microfiche from 1900. Some records on index and docket books. Online access to court records through CourtView are free online at www.county.tippecanoe.in.us/court/pa.htm.

Criminal Records: Access: In person, mail, online. Visitors must perform in person searches for themselves. No search fee. Required to search: name, years to search; also helpful: DOB, SSN, sex, signed release. Criminal records on computer from 1987, on microfiche from 1900. Some records on index and docket books. Online access to criminal records is the same as civil.

General Information: Public Access terminal is available. No juvenile, mental, adoption or sealed released. Will fax results for $2.00 pe page. Copy fee: $1.00 per page. Cert fee: $1.00. Payee: Tippecanoe County Clerk. Business checks accepted. Prepayment required.

Tipton County

Circuit Court Tipton County Courthouse, Tipton, IN 46072; 765-675-2791; Fax: 765-675-7797. Hours: 8AM-4PM M-Th, 8AM-5PM F (EST). *Felony, Misdemeanor, Civil, Eviction, Small Claims, Probate.*

Civil Records: Access: In person only. Visitors must perform in person searches for themselves. No search fee. Required to search: name, years to search. Civil cases indexed by defendant, plaintiff. Civil records on card file and archived from 1930s.

Criminal Records: Access: In person only. Visitors must perform in person searches for themselves. No search fee. Required to search: name, years to search. Criminal records on card file and archived from 1930s.

General Information: No juvenile, mental, adoption or sealed released. Copy fee: $1.00 per page. Cert fee: $1.00. Payee: Tipton County Clerk. Personal checks accepted. Prepayment required.

Union County

Circuit Court 26 W Union St, Liberty, IN 47353; 765-458-6121; Fax: 765-458-5263. Hours: 8AM-4PM (EST). *Felony, Misdemeanor, Civil, Eviction, Small Claims, Probate.*

Civil Records: Access: In person only. Both court and visitors may perform in person searches. Search fee: None. Required to search: name, years to search. Civil cases indexed by defendant, plaintiff. Civil records archived from 1821. Some records on docket books or entry books.

Criminal Records: Access: In person only. Both court and visitors may perform in person searches. Search fee: None. Required to search: name, years to search; also helpful: DOB, SSN. Criminal records archived from 1821. Some records on docket books or entry books.

General Information: No juvenile, mental, adoption or sealed records released. Copy fee: $.25 per page. Cert fee: $2.00. Payee: Union County Clerk. Only cashiers checks and money orders accepted. Prepayment required.

Vanderburgh County

Circuit & Superior Court PO Box 3356 (Civic Center Courts Bldg - Rm 216), Evansville, IN 47732-3356; 812-435-5160; Civil phone: 812-435-5722; Criminal phone: 812-435-5169; Probate phone: 812-435-5377; Fax: 812-435-5849. Hours: 8AM-5PM (CST). *Felony, Misdemeanor, Civil, Eviction, Small Claims, Probate.* www.vanderburghgov.org/vander/countyclerk/index.htm

Civil Records: Access: In person only. Visitors must perform in person searches for themselves. No search fee. Required to search: name, years to search. Civil cases indexed by defendant, plaintiff. Civil records on computer back to 1991, archived from 1900s. Some records on index books.

Criminal Records: Access: In person only. Visitors must perform in person searches for themselves. No search fee. Required to search: name, years to search, DOB, SSN. Criminal records on computer back to 1991, archived from 1900s. Some records on books.

General Information: Public Access terminal is available. No juvenile, mental, adoption or sealed released. Copy fee: $1.00 per page. Cert fee: $1.00. Payee: Vanderburgh County Clerk. Business checks accepted. Prepayment required.

Vermillion County

Circuit Court PO Box 10, Newport, IN 47966-0010; 765-492-3500. Hours: 8AM-4PM (EST). *Felony, Misdemeanor, Civil, Eviction, Small Claims, Probate.*

Civil Records: Access: mail, in person. Both court and visitors may perform in person searches. Search fee: none. Required to search: name. Civil cases indexed by defendant, plaintiff. Records on computer go back to 1994; archived from 1824. Some records on docket books.

Criminal Records: Access: In person only. Both court and visitors may perform in person searches. Search fee: none. Required to search: name. Records on computer go back to 1994; archived from 1825. Some records on docket books.

General Information: No juvenile, mental, adoption or sealed released. Copy fee: $1.00 per page. Cert fee: $2.00. Payee: Vermillion County Clerk. Business checks accepted. Prepayment required.

Vigo County

Circuit Court 2nd Fl, Courthouse, PO Box 8449, Terre Haute, IN 47807-8449; 812-462-3211. Hours: 8AM-4PM (EST). *Felony, Misdemeanor, Civil, Eviction, Small Claims, Probate.* http://vigocountyin.com

Civil Records: Access: In person, online. Visitors must perform in person searches for themselves. No search fee. Required to search: name, years to search. Civil cases indexed by defendant, plaintiff. Civil records on index books; on computer back to 8/1996. An online subscription service is at www.doxpop.com. Fees are involved. Records date from 04/96. A limited free search is at www.doxpop.com/prod/court/CourtQuery.

Criminal Records: Access: In person, online. Visitors must perform in person searches for themselves. No search fee. Required to search: name, years to search; also helpful: DOB, SSN. Criminal records on index books; on computer back to 8/1996. Online access to criminal records is the same as civil.

General Information: Public Access terminal is available. No juvenile, mental, adoption or sealed released. Copy fee: $1.00 per page. Cert fee: $1.00.

Payee: Vigo County Clerk. Only cashiers checks and money orders accepted. Prepayment required.

Wabash County

Circuit & Superior Court 69 W Hill St, Wabash, IN 46992; 260-563-0661 X230; Fax: 260-569-1352. 8AM-4PM (EST). *Felony, Misdemeanor, Civil, Eviction, Small Claims, Probate.*
Civil Records: Access: In person, online. Visitors must perform in person searches for themselves. No search fee. Required to search: name, years to search. Civil cases indexed by defendant, plaintiff. Civil records archived from 1800s; on computer since 1989. Some judgments on fee books. An online subscription service is at www.doxpop.com. Fees are involved. Records date from 08/89. A limited free search is www.doxpop.com/prod/court/CourtQuery.
Criminal Records: Access: In person, online. Visitors must perform in person searches for themselves. No search fee. Required to search: name, years to search, DOB; also helpful: SSN. Criminal records archived from 1800s; on computer since 1989. Some judgments on fee books. Online access to criminal records is the same as civil.
General Information: Public Access terminal is available. No juvenile, mental, adoption or sealed records released. Copy fee: $1.00 per page. Cert fee: $1.00. Payee: Wabash County Clerk. Business checks accepted. Prepayment required.

Warren County

Circuit Court #11, 125 N Monroe, Williamsport, IN 47993; 765-762-3510; Fax: 765-762-7251. Hours: 8AM-4PM (EST). *Felony, Misdemeanor, Civil, Eviction, Small Claims, Probate.*
Civil Records: Access: In person only. Both court and visitors may perform in person searches. No search fee. Required to search: name, years to search. Civil cases indexed by defendant, plaintiff. Civil records archived from 1828. Some records on docket books.
Criminal Records: Access: In person only. Both court and visitors may perform in person searches. No search fee. Required to search: name, years to search, DOB; also helpful: SSN. Criminal records archived from 1828. Some records on docket books.
General Information: No juvenile, mental, adoption or sealed released. Fee to fax specific documents is $1.00 per page. Copy fee: $1.00 per page. Cert fee: $1.00. Payee: Warren County Clerk. Personal checks accepted. Prepayment required.

Warrick County

Circuit & Superior Court One County Sq, #200, Boonville, IN 47601; 812-897-6160. Hours: 8AM-4PM (CST). *Felony, Misdemeanor, Civil, Eviction, Small Claims, Probate.*
Civil Records: Access: In person only. Both court and visitors may perform in person searches. No search fee. Required to search: name, years to search. Civil cases indexed by defendant, plaintiff. Civil records on computer from 1987, archived from 1900s. Some records on index books.
Criminal Records: Access: In person only. Both court and visitors may perform in person searches. No search fee. Required to search: name, years to search; also helpful: DOB, SSN. Criminal records on computer from 1987, archived from 1900s. Some records on index books.
General Information: Public Access terminal is available. No juvenile, mental, adoption or sealed released. Will not fax results. Copy fee: $1.00 per

page. Cert fee: $1.00. Payee: Warrick County Clerk. Business checks accepted. Prepayment required.

Washington County

Circuit & Superior Court Courthouse, 99 Public Sq, #102, Salem, IN 47167; 812-883-1634/5748; Fax: 812-883-8108. Hours: 8:30AM-4PM M-Th, 8:30AM-6PM F (EST). *Felony, Misdemeanor, Civil, Small Claims, Probate.*
Note: Will only return calls to toll-free numbers.
Civil Records: Access: In person only. Visitors may perform in person searches. No search fee. Required to search: name, years to search; also helpful: address. Civil cases indexed by defendant, plaintiff. Civil records on books, archived from 1820. Some records on docket books.
Criminal Records: Access: In person only. Both court and visitors may perform in person searches. No search fee. Required to search: name, years to search, DOB; also helpful: address, SSN. Criminal index on computer from 1980, docket books & archived prior.
General Information: No juvenile, mental, adoption or sealed released; no information given out via telephone. Will not fax results. Copy fee: $1.00 per page. Cert fee: $1.00. Payee: Washington County Clerk. Only cashiers checks and money orders accepted. Prepayment required.

Wayne County

Circuit & Superior Court Courthouse, 301 E Main St, Richmond, IN 47374; 765-973-9200; Fax: 765-973-9490. Hours: 8:30AM-5PM M; 8:30AM-4:30PM T-F (EST). *Felony, Misdemeanor, Civil, Eviction, Small Claims, Probate.*
www.co.wayne.in.us/courts
Civil Records: Access: Mail, fax, in person, online. Visitors must perform in person searches themselves. No search fee. Required to search: name, years to search. Civil cases indexed by defendant, plaintiff. Civil records on computer from 4/90, circuit on microfiche from 1957, superior on microfiche from 1960 to 1971, all archived from 1800s. Some records on dockets. An online subscription service is at www.doxpop.com. Fees are involved. Records date from 03/90. A limited free search is at www.doxpop.com/prod/court/CourtQuery. Fax request must be on letterhead.
Criminal Records: Access: Mail, fax, in person, online. Both court and visitors may perform in person searches. No search fee. Required to search: name, years to search, fax request on letterhead. Criminal records on computer from 4/90, circuit on microfiche from 1957, superior on microfiche from 1960 to 1971, all archived from 1800s. Some records on dockets. Online access to criminal records is the same as civil. Fax request must be on letterhead.
General Information: Public Access terminal is available. No juvenile, mental, adoption or sealed released. Will not fax results. Copy fee: $1.00 per page. Cert fee: $1.00. Payee: Wayne County Clerk. Personal checks accepted. Prepayment required. Mail requests: SASE required. Mail turnaround: 2-3 days.

Wells County

Circuit & Superior Court 102 W Market, Rm 201, Bluffton, IN 46714; 260-824-6479. Hours: 8AM-4:30PM (EST). *Civil, Probate.*
Civil Records: Access: In person only. Visitors must perform in person searches for themselves. No search fee. Required to search: name, years to search. Civil cases indexed by defendant, plaintiff. Civil records archived from 1837. Some records on docket books.

Criminal Records: Access: In person only. Visitors must perform in person searches for themselves. No search fee. Required to search: name, years to search, DOB; also helpful: SSN. Criminal records archived from 1837. Some records on docket books.
General Information: No juvenile, mental, adoption or sealed released. Copy fee: $1.00 per page. Cert fee: $2.00. Payee: Wells County Clerk. Personal checks accepted. Prepayment required.

White County

Circuit Court PO Box 350, 110 N Main, Monticello, IN 47960; 574-583-7032; Fax: 574-583-1532. Hours: 8AM-4PM (EST). *Civil, Probate.*
Civil Records: Access: In person only. Visitors must perform in person searches for themselves. No search fee. Required to search: name, years to search. Civil cases indexed by defendant, plaintiff. Civil records on indexes and files, some records on docket books back to 1950s.
General Information: No juvenile, mental, adoption or sealed released. Copy fee: $1.00 per page. Cert fee: $1.00. Payee: White County Clerk. Personal checks accepted. Prepayment required.

Superior Court PO Box 1005, 110 N Main, Monticello, IN 47960; 574-583-9520; Fax: 574-583-2437. Hours: 8AM-4PM (EST). *Felony, Misdemeanor, Eviction, Small Claims.*
Civil Records: Access: In person only. Both court and visitors may perform in person searches. Court will search only if a date is provided No search fee. Required to search: name, years to search. Civil cases indexed by defendant, plaintiff. Civil records on indexes and files, some records on docket books.
Criminal Records: Access: In person only. Both court and visitors may perform in person searches. Court will search only if a date is provided. No search fee. Required to search: name, years to search. Criminal records on indexes and files, some records on docket books.
General Information: No juvenile, mental, adoption or sealed released. Copy fee: $1.00 per page. Cert fee: $1.00. Payee: White County Clerk. Personal checks accepted. Prepayment required.

Whitley County

Circuit & Superior Court 101 W Van Buren, Rm 10, Columbia City, IN 46725; 260-248-3102; Fax: 260-248-3137. Hours: 8AM-4:30PM (EST). *Felony, Misdemeanor, Civil, Eviction, Small Claims, Probate.*
Civil Records: Access: In person only. Visitors must perform in person searches for themselves. No search fee. Required to search: name, years to search. Civil cases indexed by defendant, plaintiff. Civil records on computer from 1999. Some records on docket books.
Criminal Records: Access: In person only. Visitors must perform in person searches for themselves. No search fee. Required to search: name, years to search; also helpful: DOB. Criminal records on computer from 1999. Some records on docket books back to 1900.
General Information: Public Access terminal is available. No juvenile, mental, adoption or sealed released. Copy fee: $1.00 per page. Cert fee: $1.00. Payee: Whitley County Clerk. Only cashiers checks and money orders accepted. Prepayment required.

Indiana Recording Offices

ORGANIZATION: 92 counties, 92 recording offices. The recording officer is County Recorder (Circuit Clerk for state tax liens on personal property). Many counties utilize a "Miscellaneous Index" for tax and other liens. 81 counties are in the Eastern Time Zone (EST), and 11 are in the Central Time Zone (CST).

REAL ESTATE RECORDS: Most counties will not perform real estate name searches. Copies usually cost $1.00 per page, and certification usually costs $5.00 per document.

UCC RECORDS: Financing statements are filed at the state level, except for real estate related collateral, which are filed with the County Recorder. However, prior to 07/2001, consumer goods collateral were also filed at the County Recorder and these older records can be searched there. Starting 07/2002, farm collateral will change from local to state centralized filing. All counties will perform UCC searches. Use search request form UCC-11. Search fees are usually $8.00 per debtor name and $5.00 for each add'l name. Copies are usually included in the search fee. Most counties also charge $.50 for a financing statement reported on a search.

TAX LIEN RECORDS: All federal tax liens on personal property are filed with the County Recorder. State tax liens on personal property are filed with the Circuit Clerk, who is in a different office from the Recorder. Refer to the County Court section for information about Indiana Circuit Courts. Most counties will not perform tax lien searches.

OTHER LIENS: Judgments, mechanics, hospital, sewer, utility, innkeeper.

ONLINE ACCESS: A growing number of agencies offer online access. The most notable is the subscription service offered by Marion County at www.civicnet.net

Adams County

County Recorder, 313 W. Jefferson, Rm 240, Adams County Service Complex, Decatur, IN 46733. **Phone-** County Recorder, R/E & UCC Recording- 260-724-5343; fax-260-724-5344; hours 8AM-4:30PM

Will search UCC records by mail only. Search per debtor- $8.00; $5.00 each add'l. UCC copy- included in search fee. Will not do federal tax lien search. Will not search real estate records. RE record copy- $1.00 per page. Cert fee: $5.00 per doc. Payee: Adams County Recorder. **Other phones:** Assessor-260-724-5301; Treasurer-260-724-5353; Auditor-260-724-5300.

Allen County

County Recorder, 1 E. Main St, City County Bldg, Rm 206, Fort Wayne, IN 46802-1890. **Phone-**County Recorder, R/E & UCC Recording- 260-449-7165; fax-260-449-3261; hours 8AM-4:30PM

Will search UCC records. Search per debtor- $8.00; $5.00 each add'l. UCC copy- included in search fee. Will not do federal tax lien search. Will not search real estate records. RE record copy- $1.00 per page. Cert fee: $5.00 per doc. Payee: Allen County Recorder. **Other phones:** Assessor-260-428-7123; Treasurer-260-428-7693; Elections-260-449-7329; Vital Records-260-449-7147.

Bartholomew County

County Recorder, PO Box 1121, Columbus, IN 47202-1121. **Phone-**812-379-1520; fax-812-375-5440; hours 8AM-5PM www.bartholomewco.com

Will search UCC records. Search per debtor- $8.00; $5.00 each add'l. UCC copy fee- $1.00 per page. Will not do federal tax lien search. Will not search real estate records. RE record copy- $1.00 per page. Cert fee: $5.00 per doc. Payee: Bartholomew County Recorder. **Online Access to Property, GIS records:** Access to PAGIS, the county Public Access Geographic Information System, is free at www.bartholomewco.com/login.phtml; you must have an email for free registration. **Other phones:** Assessor-812-379-1505; Treasurer-812-379-1530; Elections-812-379-1604; Vital Records-812-379-1550.

Benton County

County Recorder, 706 E. 5th St, #24, Fowler, IN 47944-1556. **Phone-**County Recorder, R/E & UCC Recording- 765-884-1630; fax-765-884-2013; hours 8:30AM-4PM

Will search UCC records. Search per debtor- $8.00; $5.00 each add'l. UCC copy- included in search fee. Will not search real estate or tax lien records. RE record copy- $1.00 per page. Cert fee: $5.00 per doc. Payee: Benton County Recorder. **Other phones:** Assessor-765-884-1205; Treasurer-765-884-1070; Elections-765-884-0930; Vital Records-765-884-1728.

Blackford County

County Recorder, 110 W. Washington St, Courthouse, Hartford City, IN 47348. **Phone-**County Recorder, R/E & UCC Recording- 765-348-2207; fax-765-348-7222; hours 8AM-4PM

Will search UCC records. Search per debtor- $8.00; $5.00 each add'l. Copy fee is $1.00 per page. Will not do federal tax lien search. Will not search real estate records. RE record copy- $1.00 per page. Cert fee: $5.00 per doc. Payee: Blackford County Recorder. **Other phones:** Assessor-765-348-1707; Treasurer-765-348-2504; Elections-765-348-1130; Vital Records-765-348-2207.

Boone County

County Recorder, 202 Courthouse Sq, Lebanon, IN 46052. **Phone-**765-482-3070, R/E Recording- 765-482-2940; hours 8AM-4PM

Will search UCC records. Search per debtor- $8.00. $5.00 per extra name. UCC copy- included in search fee. Will not do federal tax lien search. Will not search real estate records. RE record copy- $1.00 per page. Cert fee: $5.00 per doc + $1.00 per copy. Payee: Boone County Recorder. **Other phones:** Assessor-765-482-0140; Treasurer-765-482-2880; Elections-765-482-3510.

Brown County

County Recorder, PO Box 86, Nashville, IN 47448. **Phone-**County Recorder, R/E & UCC Recording- 812-988-5462; fax-812-988-5520; hours 8AM-4PM

Will search UCC records. Search per debtor- $8.00; $5.00 each add'l. UCC copy- included in search fee. Will not do federal tax lien search. Will not search real estate records. RE record copy- $1.00 per page. Cert fee: $5.00 per doc. Payee: Brown County Recorder. **Other phones:** Assessor-812-988-5466; Treasurer-812-988-5458.

Carroll County

County Recorder, 101 W. Main St, Court House, Delphi, IN 46923-1522. **Phone-**County Recorder, R/E & UCC Recording- 765-564-2124; fax-765-564-2576; hours 8AM-5PM M,T,Th,F; 8AM-Noon W

Will search UCC records. Search per debtor- $8.00; $5.00 each add'l. UCC copy- included in search fee. Will not search real estate or tax lien records. RE record copy- $1.00 per page. Cert fee: $5.00 per doc. Payee: County Recorder. **Other phones:** Assessor-765-564-3444; Treasurer-765-564-3446; Elections-765-564-4485; Vital Records-765-564-3420.

Cass County

County Recorder, 102 Cass County Gov't Bldg., Logansport, IN 46947. **Phone-**574-753-7810; hours 8AM-4PM M-TH; 8AM-5PM F www.in-map.net/counties/CASS/recorder/

Will search UCC records. Search per debtor- $8.00; $5.00 each add'l. UCC copy- included in search fee. Will not do federal tax lien search. Will not search real estate records. RE record copy- $1.00 per page. Cert fee: $5.00 per doc. Payee: Cass County Recorder. **Other phones:** Assessor-574-753-7720; Treasurer-574-753-7720.

Clark County

County Recorder, 501 E. Court Ave, Rm 105, Jeffersonville, IN 47130. **Phone-**812-285-6236; hours 8;30AM-4:30PM. Will search UCC records. Search per debtor- $8.00, $5.00 add'l. UCC copy- included in search fee. Will not search real estate or tax lien records. RE record copy- $1.00 per page. Cert fee: $6.00 per doc; no fee to certify UCCs. Payee: Clark County Recorder. **Other phones:** Assessor-812-285-6224; Treasurer-812-285-6205.

Clay County

County Recorder, 609 E National Ave., Courthouse, Rm 111, Brazil, IN 47834. **Phone-**County Recorder, R/E & UCC Recording- 812-448-9005; fax-812-446-5095; hours 8AM-4PM
Will search UCC records. Search per debtor- $8.00; $5.00 each add'l. UCC copy- included in search fee. Will not do federal tax lien search. Will not search real estate records. RE record copy- $1.00 per page. Cert fee: $5.00 per doc. Payee: Clay County Recorder. **Other phones:** Assessor-812-448-9013; Treasurer-812-448-9009; Elections-812-448-9023; Vital Records-812-448-9018.

Clinton County

County Recorder, 270 Courthouse Sq, Frankfort, IN 46041-1957. **Phone-**County Recorder, R/E & UCC Recording- 765-659-6320; fax-765-659-6391; hours 8AM-4PM (till noon on Thur)
Will search UCC records. Search per debtor- $8.00; $5.00 each add'l. UCC copy- included in search fee. Will not do federal tax lien search. Will not search real estate records. RE record copy- $1.00 per page. Cert fee: $5.00 per doc. Payee: Clinton County Recorder. **Other phones:** Assessor-765-659-6315; Treasurer-765-659-6325; Elections-765-659-6335; Vital Records-765-659-6385.

Crawford County

County Recorder, PO Box 214, English, IN 47118-0214. **Phone-**County Recorder, R/E & UCC Recording- 812-338-2615; fax-812-338-2507; hours 8AM-4PM M & F; 8AM-6PM T & Th; Closed W
Will search UCC records. Search per debtor- $8.00; $5.00 each add'l. UCC copy- included in search fee. Will not do federal tax lien search. Will not search real estate records. RE record copy- $1.00 per page. Cert fee: $5.00 per doc. Payee: Crawford County Recorder. **Other phones:** Assessor-812-338-2402; Treasurer-812-338-2651.

Daviess County

County Recorder, PO Box 793, Washington, IN 47501. **Phone-**812-254-8675; fax-812-254-8647; hours 8AM-4PM. Will search UCC records. Search per debtor- $8.00; $5.00 each add'l. UCC copy- included in search fee. Will not search real estate or tax lien records. RE record copy- $1.00 per page. Cert fee: $5.00 per doc; $5.00 to certify UCCs. Payee: Daviess County Recorder. **Other phones:** Assessor-812-254-8660; Treasurer-812-254-8677.

Dearborn County

County Recorder, 215 B, W. High St, Lawrenceburg, IN 47025. **Phone-**County Recorder, R/E & UCC Recording- 812-537-8837; fax-none; hours 8:30AM-4:30PM. Will search UCC records. Search per debtor- $8.00; $5.00 each add'l. UCC copy-included in search fee. Will not search real estate or tax lien records. RE record copy- $1.00 per page. Cert fee: $5.00 per doc. Payee: Dearborn County Recorder. **Other phones:** Assessor-812-537-8809; Treasurer-812-537-8811.

Decatur County

County Recorder, 150 Courthouse Sq, #121, Greensburg, IN 47240. **Phone-**County Recorder, R/E & UCC Recording- 812-663-4681; fax-812-663-2407; hours 8AM-4PM (F open until 5PM)
Will search UCC records. Search per debtor- $8.00; $5.00 each add'l. UCC copy- included in search fee. Will not search tax liens. Will search real estate records. RE record copy- $1.00 per page. Cert fee:

$5.00 per doc. Payee: Decatur County Recorder. **Other phones:** Assessor-812-663-4860; Treasurer-812-663-4190.

DeKalb County

County Recorder, PO Box 810, Auburn, IN 46706. **Phone-**County Recorder, R/E & UCC Recording- 260-925-2112; fax-260-925-5126; hours 8:30AM-4:30PM
Will search UCC records. Search per debtor- $8.00; $5.00 each add'l. UCC copy- included in search fee. Will not do federal tax lien search. Will not search real estate records. RE record copy- $1.00 per page. Cert fee: $5.00 per doc. Payee: DeKalb County Recorder. **Other phones:** Assessor-260-925-1824; Treasurer-260-925-2712; Elections-260-925-0912; Vital Records-260-925-2220.

Delaware County

County Recorder, PO Box 1008, Muncie, IN 47308. **Phone-**765-747-7804; fax-765-284-1875; hours 8:30AM-4:30PM. Will search UCC records. Search per debtor- $8.00; $5.00 each add'l. UCC copy-included in search fee. Will not search real estate or tax lien records. RE record copy- $1.00 per page. Cert fee: $5.00 per doc; no fee to certify UCCs. Payee: Delaware County Recorder. **Other phones:** Assessor-765-747-7715; Treasurer-765-747-7808; Vital Records-765-747-7804.

Dubois County

County Recorder, 1 Courthouse Sq, Rm 101, Jasper, IN 47546. **Phone-**County Recorder, R/E & UCC Recording- 812-481-7067; fax-812-481-7044; hours 8AM-4PM
Will search UCC records. Search per debtor- $8.00; $5.00 each add'l. UCC copy- included in search fee. Will not do federal tax lien search. Will not search real estate records. RE record copy- $1.00 per page. Cert fee: $5.00 per page. Payee: Dubois County Recorder. **Other phones:** Assessor-812-481-7010; Treasurer-812-481-7080.

Elkhart County

County Recorder, PO Box 837, Goshen, IN 46527. **Phone-**574-535-6754, R/E Recording- 574-535-6756; hours 8AM-5PM M-Th, 8AM-4PM F www.elkhartcountygov.com/administrative
Will search UCC records. Search per debtor- $8.00; $5.00 each add'l. Copy fee-$1.00 per page. Will not do federal tax lien search. Will not search real estate records. RE record copy- $1.00 per page. Cert fee: $5.00 per doc. Payee: Elkhart County Recorder. **Online Access to Real Estate, Lien, Tax Assessor records:** Access Elkhart County records for an annual fee of $50.00 plus a min. of $20.00 per month of use. The min. fee allows for 2 hours access, and add'l use is billed at $10 per hour. Lending agency data available. For information, call at 574-535-6777. **Other phones:** Assessor-574-535-6702; Treasurer-574-535-6759; Elections-574-535-6469; Vital Records-574-523-2107; Voter Registration-574-535-6775.

Fayette County

County Recorder, PO Box 324, Connersville, IN 47331-0324. **Phone-**765-825-3051; hours 8:30AM-4PM www.co.fayette.in.us
Will search UCC records; request on written standard form only. Search per debtor- $8.00; $5.00 each add'l. UCC copy- included in search fee. Will not do federal tax lien search. Will not search real estate records. RE record copy- $1.00 per page. Cert fee: $5.00 per doc. Payee: Fayette County Recorder. **Other phones:** Assessor-765-825-4931; Treasurer-765-825-1013; Elections-765-825-1813; Recorder-765-825-3051; Health Dept-765-825-4013.

Floyd County

County Recorder, PO Box 878, New Albany, IN 47151-0878. **Phone-**County Recorder, R/E & UCC Recording- 812-948-5430; fax-812-949-7727; hours 8AM-4PM
Will search UCC records. Search per debtor- $8.00; $5.00 each add'l. UCC copy- included in search fee. Will not search real estate or tax lien records. RE record copy- $1.00 per page. Cert fee: $5.00 per doc. Payee: Floyd County Recorder. **Online Access to Recording, Real Estate records:** Computerized versions of microfiche cards will be on the internet sometime in 2004; call clerk at 812-948-5430 for update information. **Other phones:** Assessor-812-948-5420; Treasurer-812-948-5477.

Fountain County

County Recorder, PO Box 55, Covington, IN 47932. **Phone-**County Recorder, R/E & UCC Recording- 765-793-2431; fax-765-793-6211; hours 8AM-4PM
Will search UCC records. Search per debtor- $8.00; $5.00 each add'l name. UCC copy- included in search fee. Will not do federal tax lien search. Will not search real estate records. RE record copy- $1.00 per page. Cert fee: $5.00 per doc. Payee: Fountain County Recorder. **Other phones:** Assessor-765-793-3481; Treasurer-765-793-3691; Elections-765-793-2192; Vital Records-765-793-3035.

Franklin County

County Recorder, 459 Main St, Brookville, IN 47012-1486. **Phone-**County Recorder, R/E & UCC Recording- 765-647-5131; hours 8:30AM-4PM
Will search UCC records. Search per debtor- $8.00; $5.00 each add'l. UCC copy- included in search fee. Will not search real estate or tax lien records. RE record copy- $1.00 per page. Cert fee: $5.00 per doc. Payee: County Recorder. **Other phones:** Assessor-765-647-4921; Treasurer-765-647-5121; Elections-765-647-5111; Vital Records-765-647-4322.

Fulton County

County Recorder, 125 E 9th St, Rochester, IN 46975. **Phone-**County Recorder, R/E & UCC Recording- 574-223-2914; fax-574-223-4734; hours 8AM-4PM (F 8AM-5PM)
Will search UCC records. Search per debtor- $8.00; $5.00 each add'l. UCC copy- included in search fee. Will not do federal tax lien search. Will not search real estate records. RE record copy- $1.00 per page. Cert fee: $5.00 per doc. Payee: County Recorder. **Other phones:** Assessor-574-223-2801; Treasurer-574-223-7705; Vital Records-574-223-2881.

Gibson County

County Recorder, PO Box 1078, Princeton, IN 47670. **Phone-**County Recorder, R/E & UCC Recording- 812-385-3332; fax-812-386-9502; hours 8AM-4PM
Will search UCC records. Search per debtor-$8.00 1st name and $5.00 each add'l name on same UCC. UCC copy- included in search fee. Will not do federal tax lien search. Will not search real estate records. RE record copy- $1.00 per page. Cert fee: $5.00 per doc. Payee: Gibson County Recorder. **Other phones:** Assessor-812-385-5286; Treasurer-812-385-2540; Appraiser/ Auditor-812-385-4927; Elections-812-385-8401; Vital Records-812-385-3831.

Grant County

County Recorder, 401 S. Adams St, Marion, IN 46953. **Phone-**County Recorder, R/E & UCC Recording- 765-668-8871; hours 8AM-4PM www.grantcounty.net
Will search UCC records. Search per debtor- $8.00; $5.00 each add'l. UCC copy- included in search fee. Will not search real estate or tax lien records. RE record copy- $1.00 per page. Cert fee: $5.00 per doc; no fee to certify UCCs. Payee: Grant

County Recorder. **Online Access to Recorder, Deed, UCC, Mortgage, Assessor, Property Tax, Voter Registration, Sex Offender records:** Access to recorder data is free at www.grantcounty.net/grant/grant.fwx?D04LIST. Tax information is at www.grantcounty.net/grant/grant.fwx?D03LIST Access to assessor property information is free at www.grantcounty.net/grant/grant.fwx?D01LIST. The sheriff's sex offender list is available at www.grantcounty.net/grant/grant.fwx?D14SEXLIST. **Other phones:** Assessor-765-668-8871; Treasurer-765-668-8871; Appraiser/ Auditor-765-668-8871; Elections-765-668-8871; Vital Records-765-668-8871.

Greene County

County Recorder, PO Box 309, Bloomfield, IN 47424. **Phone-**812-384-2020, R/E Recording- 812-384-2020 & 812-384-2023, UCC Recording- 812-384-2021 & 812-384-2023; fax-812-384-2044; hours 8AM-4PM www.co.greene.in.us
Will search UCC records. Search per debtor- $8.00; $5.00 each add'l. UCC copy- included in search fee. Will not search tax liens. Real estate owner, mortgage, and property transfer searches available. RE record copy- $1.00 per page. Cert fee: $5.00 per doc. Payee: Greene Co. Recorder. **Other phones:** Assessor-812-384-2003; Treasurer-812-384-4378; Elections-812-384-2015; Vital Records-812-384-2016.

Hamilton County

County Recorder, 33 N. 9th St, #309, Courthouse, Noblesville, IN 46060. **Phone-**County Recorder, R/E & UCC Recording- 317-776-9618, UCC Recording- 317-776-9688; fax-317-776-8200; hours 8AM-4:30PM
Will search UCC records. Search per debtor- $8.00; $5.00 each add'l. UCC copy fee- $1.00 per page. Will not do federal tax lien search. Will not search real estate records. RE record copy- $1.00 per page. Cert fee: $5.00 per doc. Payee: Hamilton County Recorder. **Online Access to Inmate, Offender records:** Search inmate information for free on private company website at www.vinelink.com/index.jsp. **Other phones:** Assessor-317-776-9614; Treasurer-317-776-9620.

Hancock County

County Recorder, 9 E. Main St, Courthouse, Rm 204, Greenfield, IN 46140. **Phone-**317-477-1142; hours 8AM-4PM www.hancockcoingov.org/recorder
Will search UCC records. Search per debtor- $8.00; $5.00 each add'l. UCC copy- included in search fee. Will not search real estate or tax lien records. RE record copy- $1.00 per page. Cert fee: $5.00 per doc. Payee: Hancock County Recorder. **Online Access to Sale Disclosure records:** Access to the assessor's sales desclosure data is free at www.hancockcoingov.org/assessor/sales_disclosure_search.asp. **Other phones:** Assessor-317-477-1102; Treasurer-317-462-1152; Elections-317-477-1171; Vital Records-317-477-1125.

Harrison County

County Recorder, 300 Capitol Ave, Courthouse, Rm 204, Corydon, IN 47112. **Phone-**County Recorder, R/E & UCC Recording- 812-738-3788; fax-812-738-1153; hours 8AM-4PM M,T,Th,F; 8AM-Noon W & Sat
Will search UCC records. Search per debtor- $8.00; $5.00 each add'l name. UCC copy- included in search fee. Will not do federal tax lien search. Will not search real estate records. RE record copy- $1.00 per page. Cert fee: $5.00 per doc. Payee: Harrison County Recorder. **Other phones:** Assessor-812-738-4280; Treasurer-812-738-2348; Elections-812-738-3126; Vital Records-812-738-3237.

Hendricks County

County Recorder, 355 S Washington, Danville, IN 46122. **Phone-**County Recorder, R/E & UCC Recording- 317-745-9224; hours 8AM-4PM www.co.hendricks.in.us
Will search UCC records. Search per debtor- $8.00; $5.00 each add'l. UCC copy- included in search fee. Will not search real estate or tax lien records. RE record copy- $1.00 per page. Cert fee: $5.00 per doc. Payee: Hendricks County Recorder. **Online Access to Property, GIS-Mapping records:** Access to county property data on the GIS mapping site is free at http://in32.plexisgroup.com/map/index.html. Click on "Query" to select query by owner name. **Other phones:** Assessor-317-745-9207; Treasurer-317-745-9220; Appraiser/ Auditor-317-745-9206.

Henry County

County Recorder, PO Box K, New Castle, IN 47362. **Phone-**County Recorder, R/E & UCC Recording- 765-529-4304; fax-765-521-7017; hours 8AM-4PM
Will search UCC records. Search per debtor- $8.00; $5.00 each add'l. UCC copy- included in search fee. Will not do federal tax lien search. Will not search real estate records. RE record copy- $1.00 per page. Cert fee: $5.00 per doc. Payee: Henry County Recorder. **Other phones:** Assessor-765-529-2104; Treasurer-765-529-4404; Elections-765-529-6401; Vital Records-765-521-7058; Auditor-765-529-2800.

Howard County

County Recorder, PO Box 733, Kokomo, IN 46903-0733. **Phone-**765-456-2210; fax-765-456-2056; hours 8AM-4PM
Will not search records. RE record copy- $1.00 per page. Cert fee: $5.00 per doc. Payee: Howard County Recorder. **Other phones:** Assessor-317-456-2211; Treasurer-317-456-2213.

Huntington County

County Recorder, 201 N. Jefferson St., Rm 101, Huntington, IN 46750-2841. **Phone-**County Recorder, R/E & UCC Recording- 260-358-4848; hours 8AM-4:30PM
Will search UCC records. Search per debtor- $8.00; $5.00 each add'l. UCC copy- $.50 per page. Will not do federal tax lien search. Will not search real estate records. RE record copy- $1.00 per page. Cert fee: $5.00 per doc. Payee: Huntington County Recorder. **Other phones:** Assessor-260-358-4802; Treasurer-260-358-4860.

Jackson County

County Recorder, PO Box 75, Brownstown, IN 47220. **Phone-**812-358-6113; hours 8AM-4:30PM. Will search UCC records. Search per debtor- $8.00; $5.00 each add'l. UCC copy- included in search fee. Will not search real estate or tax lien records. RE record copy- $1.00 per page. Cert fee: $5.00 per doc. Payee: Jackson County Recorder. **Other phones:** Assessor-812-358-6111; Treasurer-812-358-6125.

Jasper County

County Recorder, 115 W. Washington, Courthouse Box 4, Rensselaer, IN 47978-2891. **Phone-**219-866-4923, R/E Recording- 219-866-4930 (Auditor), UCC Recording- 219-866-4923 (Recorder); hours 8AM-4PM
Will search UCC records. Search per debtor- $8.00; $5.00 each add'l name. UCC copy- included in search fee. Tax liens not included in UCC search. We do no search work other than UCCs. Will not search real estate records. RE record copy- $1.00 per page. Cert fee: $5.00 per doc. Payee: Jasper County Recorder. **Other phones:** Assessor-219-866-4914; Treasurer-219-866-4938.

Jay County

County Recorder, 120 W. Main St, Portland, IN 47371. **Phone-**County Recorder, R/E & UCC Recording- 260-726-6940; hours 8:30AM-4:30PM
Will search UCC records. Search per debtor- $8.00; $5.00 each add'l. UCC copy- included in search fee. Will not do federal tax lien search. Will not search real estate records. RE record copy- $1.00 per page. Cert fee: $5.00 per cert. Payee: Jay County Recorder. **Other phones:** Assessor-260-726-6929; Treasurer-260-726-6925.

Jefferson County

County Recorder, 300 E Main St, Courthouse - Rm 104, Madison, IN 47250. **Phone-**County Recorder, R/E & UCC Recording- 812-265-8902; hours 8AM-4PM
Will search UCC records. Search per debtor- $8.00; $5.00 each add'l. UCC copy- included in search fee. Will not search real estate or tax lien records. RE record copy- $1.00 per page. Cert fee: $5.00 per doc. Payee: Jefferson County Recorder. **Other phones:** Assessor-812-265-8905; Treasurer-812-265-8910; Elections-812-265-8926; Health Dept-812-273-1942.

Jennings County

County Recorder, PO Box 397, Vernon, IN 47282-0397. **Phone-**County Recorder, R/E & UCC Recording- 812-352-3053; fax-812-352-3000; hours 8AM-4PM
Will search UCC records. Search per debtor- $8.00; $5.00 each add'l. UCC copy- included in search fee. Will not search real estate or tax lien records. RE record copy- $1.00 per page. Cert fee: $5.00 per doc. Payee: Jennings County Recorder. **Other phones:** Assessor-812-352-3013; Treasurer-812-352-3060; Appraiser/ Auditor-812-352-3021; Elections-812-352-3080; Vital Records-812-352-3024; Auditors Phones-812-352-3016; Clerks Phone-812-352-3070.

Johnson County

County Recorder, PO Box 489, Franklin, IN 46131. **Phone-**County Recorder, R/E & UCC Recording- 317-736-3718; fax-317-736-4776; hours 8AM-4:30PM
Will search UCC records. Search per debtor- $8.00; $5.00 each add'l. (The $5.00 add'l is only for Husband and Wife-not different corporate endinges, etc). UCC copy- included in search fee. Will not do federal tax lien search. Will not search real estate records. RE record copy- $1.00 per page. Cert fee: $5.00 per doc. Payee: Johnson County Recorder. **Other phones:** Assessor-317-736-3030; Treasurer-317-736-3711; Elections-317-736-3789; Vital Records-317-736-3775; Assessor County-317-736-3715.

Knox County

County Recorder, 101 N 7th St, Courthouse, Vincennes, IN 47591. **Phone-**812-885-2508; fax-812-886-2414; hours 8AM-4PM
Will search UCC records. Search per debtor-$8.00; $5.00 each add'l. UCC copy- included in search fee. Will not search real estate or tax lien records. RE copy- $1.00 per page. Cert fee: $5.00 per doc. Payee: Knox County Recorder. **Other phones:** Assessor-812-885-2513; Treasurer-812-885-2506.

Kosciusko County

County Recorder, 100 W. Center St, Courthouse Rm 14, Warsaw, IN 46580. **Phone-**County Recorder, R/E & UCC Recording- 574-372-2360; fax-574-372-2469; hours 8AM-4:30PM http://kcgov.com
Will search UCC records. Search per debtor- $8.00; $5.00 each add'l. UCC copy- included in search fee. Will not do federal tax lien search. Will not search real estate records. RE record copy- $1.00 per copy. Cert fee: $5.00 per cert. Payee: Kosciusko

County Recorder. **Online Access to Property, GIS Mapping records:** Access to proeprty records on the searchable GIS mapping site is free at http://kcgov.com/application/gis/viewer.htm. Click on "Search" to get to name search mode. **Other phones:** Assessor-574-372-2310; Treasurer-574-372-2370; Elections-574-372-2329; Vital Records-574-372-2329.

La Porte County

County Recorder, 813 Lincolnway, La Porte, IN 46350-3488. **Phone**-219-326-6808, R/E Recording- 219-326-6808 x267, UCC Recording- 219-326-6808 x234; fax-219-326-0828; hours 8:00AM-4PM (Recording hours 8:00AM-3PM) www.laportecounty.org
Will search UCC records. Search per debtor- $8.00; $5.00 each add'l. UCC copy- included in search fee. Tax liens not included in UCC search. Will not search real estate records. RE record copy- $1.00 per page. Cert fee: $5.00 per doc. Payee: La Porte County Recorder. **Online Access to Property records:** Access to real estate records is via a private company at https://www.landrecords.net/. Subscription or pay-per search service available. Index goes back to 8/1988; images back to 8/1999. **Other phones:** Assessor-219-326-6808 x233; Treasurer-219-326-6808 x268; Elections-219-326-6808 x465; Vital Records-219-326-6808 x200.

LaGrange County

County Recorder, PO Box 214, LaGrange, IN 46761. **Phone**-County Recorder, R/E & UCC Recording- 260-499-6320; hours 8AM-4PM M-Th; 8AM-5PM F
Will search UCC records. Search per debtor- $8.00; $5.00 each add'l. UCC copy- included in search fee. Will not search real estate or tax lien records. RE record copy- $1.00 per page. Cert fee: $5.00 per doc. Payee: LaGrange County Recorder. **Other phones:** Assessor-260-499-6319; Treasurer-260-499-6316.

Lake County

County Recorder, 2293 N Main St, Bldg. A, 2nd Fl, Crown Point, IN 46307. **Phone**-219-755-3730; fax-219-755-3257; hours 8:30AM-4:30PM
Will search UCC records. Search per debtor- $8.00; $5.00 each add'l. UCC copy- included in search fee. UCC search does not include federal tax liens. Real estate owner, mortgage, and property transfer searches available. RE record copy- $1.00 per page. Cert fee: $5.00 per doc. Payee: Lake County Recorder. **Other phones:** Assessor-219-755-3200; Treasurer-219-755-3760.

Lawrence County

County Recorder, 916 15th St, Rm 21, Rm 21, Bedford, IN 47421. **Phone**-County Recorder, R/E & UCC Recording- 812-275-3245; fax-812-275-4138; hours 8:30AM-4:30PM
Will search UCC records. Search per debtor- $8.00; $5.00 each add'l. UCC copy- included in search fee. Will not do federal tax lien search. Will not search real estate records. RE record copy- $1.00 per page. Cert fee: $5.00 per doc. Payee: Lawrence County Recorder. **Other phones:** Assessor-812-275-5695; Treasurer-812-275-2431.

Madison County

County Recorder, 16 E. 9th St, Anderson, IN 46016. **Phone**-765-641-9618, R/E Recording- 765-641-9615, UCC Recording- 765-608-7828; fax-765-641-9617; hours 8AM-4PM
Will search UCC records. Search per debtor- $1.00 + $3.00 per each supplemental fee and $.50 per page. UCC copy- $.50 per page. Will not search real estate or tax lien records. RE record copy- $1.00 per page. Cert fee: $5.00 per doc. Payee: Madison County Recorder. **Other phones:** Assessor-

765-641-9401; Treasurer-765-641-9645; Elections-765-641-9459; Vital Records-765-641-9433.

Marion County

County Recorder, 200 E. Washington, City-County Bldg, #721, Indianapolis, IN 46204. **Phone**-317-327-4020, R/E Recording- 317-327-4018, UCC Recording-317-327-4015; fax-317-327-3942; hours 8AM-4:30PM www.indygov.org/recorder
Will search UCC records. Search per debtor- $8.00; $5.00 each add'l. UCC copy- included in search fee. UCC search includes federal tax liens if requested. Property transfer searches available. RE record copy- $1.00 per page. Cert fee: $5.00 per doc. Payee: Marion County Recorder. **Online Access to Real Estate, Lien, Deed, UCC, Inmate records:** Access to Marion County online records requires a $200 set up fee, plus an escrow balance of at least $100 must be maintained. add'l charges are $.25 per minute, $.05 display charge for 1st page; $.05 each add'l. Records date back to 1987; images from 2/24/93. Federal tax liens and UCC information are available. For information, contact Mike Kerner at 317-327-4587. Also, acquire recording information on customized CD-rom and in specialized online reports. Also, search inmate info on private company website at www.vinelink.com/index.jsp. **Other phones:** Assessor-317-327-4907; Treasurer-317-327-4040; Auditor-317-327-4646.

Marshall County

County Recorder, 112 W. Jefferson St, Rm 201, Plymouth, IN 46563. **Phone**-County Recorder, R/E & UCC Recording- 574-935-8515; fax-574-935-5099; hours 8AM-4PM
Will search UCC records. Search per debtor- $8.00; $5.00 each add'l. UCC copy- included in search fee. Will not do federal tax lien search. Will not search real estate records. RE record copy- $1.00 per page. Cert fee: $5.00 per doc. Payee: Marshall County Recorder. **Other phones:** Assessor-574-935-8525; Treasurer-574-935-8518.

Martin County

County Recorder, PO Box 147, Shoals, IN 47581. **Phone**-County Recorder, R/E & UCC Recording- 812-247-2420; fax-812-247-2756; hours 8AM-4PM
Will not search records. RE record copy- $1.00 per page. Cert fee: $5.00 per doc. Payee: Martin County Recorder. **Other phones:** Assessor-812-247-2070; Treasurer-812-247-3701.

Miami County

County Recorder, 25 N. Broadway #205, Peru, IN 46970. **Phone**-765-472-3901; fax-765-472-1412; hours 8AM-4PM
Will search UCC records. Search per debtor- $8.00;$5.00 add'l. UCC copy- included in search fee. Will not do federal tax lien search. Will not search real estate records. RE record copy- $1.00 per page. Cert fee: $5.00 per doc. Payee: Miami County Recorder.

Monroe County

County Recorder, PO Box 1634, Bloomington, IN 47402. **Phone**-County Recorder, R/E & UCC Recording- 812-349-2520; hours 8AM-4PM
Will search UCC records. UCC search per debtor- $8.00 1st name; $5.00 each add'l name per search. UCC copy fee- $1.00 per page. Will not do federal tax lien search. Will not search real estate records. RE record copy- $1.00 per page. Cert fee: $5.00 per cert. Payee: Monroe County Recorder. **Other phones:** Assessor-812-349-2502; Treasurer-812-349-2530; Elections-812-349-2615; Vital Records-812-349-2543.

Montgomery County

County Recorder, PO Box 865, Crawfordsville, IN 47933. **Phone**-765-364-6415; fax-765-364-6404; hours 8AM-4PM. Will search UCC records. Search per debtor- $8.00; $5.00 each add'l. UCC copy-included in search fee. Will not search real estate or tax lien records. RE record copy- $1.00 per page. Cert fee: $5.00 per doc. Payee: Montgomery County Recorder. **Other phones:** Assessor-765-364-6420; Treasurer-765-364-6410.

Morgan County

County Recorder, PO Box 1653, Martinsville, IN 46151. **Phone**-County Recorder, R/E & UCC Recording- 765-342-1077; hours 8AM-4PM (8AM-5PM F) Will search UCC records. Search per debtor- $8.00; $5.00 each add'l. UCC copy-included in search fee. Will not do federal tax lien search. Will not search real estate records. RE record copy- $1.00 per page. Cert fee: $5.00 per doc. Payee: Morgan County Recorder. **Other phones:** Assessor-765-342-1065; Treasurer-765-342-1048; Elections-765-342-1029; Vital Records-765-342-6621.

Newton County

County Recorder, 201 N 3rd St, Kentland, IN 47951. **Phone**-219-474-6081; hours 8AM-4PM
Will search UCC records. Search per debtor- $8.00; $5.00 each add'l. UCC copy- included in search fee. Will not do federal tax lien search. Mortgage searches available. RE record copy- $1.00 per page. Cert fee: $5.00 per doc. Payee: Newton County Recorder. **Other phones:** Assessor-219-474-6081; Treasurer-219-474-6081.

Noble County

County Recorder, 101 N. Orange St, Rm 210, Albion, IN 46701. **Phone**-County Recorder, R/E & UCC Recording- 260-636-2672; fax-260-636-3264; hours 8AM-4PM www.noblecountyrecorder.com
Will search UCC records. Search per debtor- $5.00 per search. UCC copy- included in search fee. Will not search real estate or tax lien records. RE record copy- $1.00 per page. Cert fee: $5.00 per doc. Payee: Noble County Recorder. **Other phones:** Assessor-260-636-2297; Treasurer-260-636-2644.

Ohio County

County Recorder, 413 Main St, Courthouse, Rising Sun, IN 47040. **Phone**-County Recorder, R/E & UCC Recording- 812-438-3369; fax-812-438-4590; hours 9AM-4PM M,T,Th,F; 9AM-12 Sat; Closed W
Will search UCC records. Search per debtor- $8.00; $5.00 each add'l. UCC copy- included in search fee. Will not do federal tax lien search. Will not search real estate records. RE record copy- $1.00 per page. Cert fee: $5.00 1st pg, $1.00 each add'l. Payee: Ohio County Recorder. **Other phones:** Assessor-812-438-3264; Treasurer-812-438-2724; Elections-812-438-2610; Vital Records-812-438-2551.

Orange County

County Recorder, 205 E Main St, Courthouse, Paoli, IN 47454. **Phone**-812-723-3600; hours 8AM-4PM
Will search UCC records. Search per debtor- $8.00; $5.00 each add'l. UCC copy- included in search fee. Will not search real estate or tax lien records. RE record copy- $1.00 per page. Cert fee: $5.00 per doc. Payee: Orange County Recorder. **Other phones:** Assessor-812-723-3600.

Owen County

County Recorder, Courthouse, Spencer, IN 47460. **Phone**-812-829-5013; fax-812-829-5014; hours 8AM-4PM. Will search UCC records. Search per debtor- $8.00; $5.00 each add'l. UCC copy- included in search fee. Will not search real estate or tax lien records. RE record copy- $1.00 per page. Cert fee: $5.00 per doc. Payee: Owen County Recorder. **Other phones:** Assessor-812-829-5018; Treasurer-812-829-5011.

Parke County

County Recorder, 116 W. High St., Rm 102, Rockville, IN 47872-1787. **Phone-**County Recorder, R/E & UCC Recording- 765-569-3419; fax-765-569-4037; hours 8AM-4PM. Will search UCC records. Search per debtor- $8.00; $5.00 each add'l. UCC copy-included in search fee. Will not do federal tax lien search. Will not search real estate records. RE record copy- $1.00 per page. Cert fee: $5.00 per doc. Payee: Parke County Recorder. **Other phones:** Assessor-765-569-4036; Treasurer-765-569-3437.

Perry County

County Recorder, 2219 Payne St, Rm W2, Tell City, IN 47586-2830. **Phone-**County Recorder, R/E & UCC Recording- 812-547-4261; fax-812-547-6428; hours 8AM-4PM. Will search UCC records. Search per debtor- $8.00; $5.00 each add'l. UCC copy-included in search fee. Will not search real estate or tax lien records. RE record copy- $1.00 per page. Cert fee: $5.00 per doc. Payee: Perry County Recorder. **Other phones:** Assessor-812-547-5531; Treasurer-812-547-4816; Elections-812-547-3741; Vital Records-812-547-2746.

Pike County

County Recorder, 801 E Main St, Courthouse, Petersburg, IN 47567-1298. **Phone-**812-354-6747; fax-812-354-9431; hours 8AM-4PM

Will search UCC records. Search per debtor- $8.00; $5.00 each add'l. UCC copy- included in search fee. Will not do federal tax lien search. Will not search real estate records. RE record copy- $1.00 per page. Cert fee: $5.00 per doc. Payee: Pike County Recorder. **Other phones:** Assessor-812-354-6584; Treasurer-812-354-6363; Elections-812-354-6025; Vital Records-812-354-8797.

Porter County

County Recorder, 155 Indiana Ave, #210, Valparaiso, IN 46383. **Phone-**County Recorder, R/E & UCC Recording- 219-465-3465, UCC Recording- 219-465-3374; fax-219-465-3592; hours 8:30AM-4:30PM

Will search UCC records. Search per debtor- $8.00; $5.00 each add'l. UCC copy- included in search fee. Will not do federal tax lien search. Will not search real estate records. RE record copy- $1.00 per page. Cert fee: $5.00 per doc. Payee: Porter County Recorder. **Other phones:** Assessor-219-465-3460; Treasurer-219-465-3470.

Posey County

County Recorder, 126 E 3rd St #215, Mount Vernon, IN 47620. **Phone-**County Recorder, R/E & UCC Recording- 812-838-1314; fax-812-838-8563; hours 8AM-4PM

Will search UCC records. Search fee is $8.00 for 1 name, $5.00 each additional name. UCC copy-included in search fee. Will not search real estate or tax lien records. RE record copy- $1.00 per page. Cert fee: $5.00 per doc. Payee: Posey County Recorder. **Other phones:** Assessor-812-838-1309; Treasurer-812-838-1316; Elections-812-838-1339; Vital Records-812-838-8561.

Pulaski County

County Recorder, 112 E Main St, Courthouse - Rm 220, Winamac, IN 46996. **Phone-**County Recorder, R/E & UCC Recording- 574-946-3844; hours 8AM-4PM. Will search UCC records. Search per debtor-$8.00; $5.00 each add'l. UCC copy- included in search fee. There is no copy fee if clerk does search. Will not do a state tax lien search. Will not

search real estate records. RE record copy- $1.00 per page. Cert fee: $5.00 per doc. Payee: Pulaski County Recorder. **Other phones:** Assessor-574-946-3845; Treasurer-574-946-3632; Elections-574-946-3313; Vital Records-574-946-6080.

Putnam County

County Recorder, Courthouse Sq, Rm 25, Greencastle, IN 46135. **Phone-**765-653-5613; hours 8AM-4PM Will search UCC records. Search per debtor- $8.00; $5.00 each add'l. UCC copy- included in search fee. Will not search real estate or tax lien records. RE record copy- $1.00 per page. Cert fee: $5.00 per doc. Payee: Putnam County Recorder. **Other phones:** Assessor-765-653-4312; Treasurer-765-653-4510.

Randolph County

County Recorder, 100 S Main St, Courthouse, Rm 101, Winchester, IN 47394-1899. **Phone-**County Recorder, R/E & UCC Recording- 765-584-7300; hours 8AM-4PM. Will search UCC records. Search per debtor-$8.00; $5.00 for each add'l name. UCC copy-included in search fee. Will not do federal tax lien search. Will not search real estate records. RE record copy- $1.00 per page. Cert fee: $5.00 per doc. Payee: Randolph County Recorder. **Other phones:** Assessor-765-584-2427; Treasurer-765-584-0704; Appraiser/ Auditor-765-584-7407; Elections-765-584-1155; Vital Records-765-584-1155.

Ripley County

County Recorder, PO Box 404, Versailles, IN 47042. **Phone-**812-689-5808, R/E Recording- 812-934-9498, UCC Recording- 812-934-9498; fax-812-689-0048; hours 8AM-4PM. Will search UCC records. Search per debtor- $8.00 per search.$5.00 add'l. UCC copy- included in search fee. Will not search real estate or tax lien records. RE record copy- $1.00 per page. Cert fee: $5.00 per doc. Payee: Ripley County Recorder. **Other phones:** Assessor-812-689-5656; Treasurer-812-689-6352.

Rush County

County Recorder, Courthouse, Rm 208, Rushville, IN 46173. **Phone-**765-932-2388; hours 8AM-4PM Will search UCC records. Search per debtor- $8.00; $5.00 each add'l. UCC copy- included in search fee. Will not do federal tax lien search. Will not search real estate records. RE record copy- $1.00 per page. Cert fee: $5.00 per doc. Payee: Rush County Recorder. **Other phones:** Assessor-765-932-3242; Treasurer-765-932-2386.

Scott County

County Recorder, 1 E. McClain St, #100, Scottsburg, IN 47170. **Phone-**812-752-8442; fax-812-752-2678; hours 8:30AM-4:30PM. Will search UCC records. Search per debtor- $8.00; $5.00 each add'l. UCC copy- included in search fee. Will not search real estate or tax lien records. RE record copy- $1.00 per page. Cert fee: $5.00 per doc. Payee: Scott County Recorder. **Other phones:** Assessor-812-752-8436; Treasurer-812-752-8414.

Shelby County

County Recorder, 407 S. Harrison, Courthouse, Shelbyville, IN 46176. **Phone-**County Recorder, R/E & UCC Recording- 317-392-6370; fax-317-392-6393; hours 8AM-4PM

Will search UCC records. Search per debtor- $8.00; $5.00 each add'l. UCC copy- included in search fee. Will not do federal tax lien search. Will not search real estate records. RE record copy- $1.00 per page. Cert fee: $5.00 per doc. Payee: Shelby County Recorder. **Other phones:** Assessor-317-392-5481; Treasurer-317-392-6375.

Spencer County

County Recorder, 200 Main, Courthouse, Rockport, IN 47635. **Phone-**812-649-6013; fax-812-649-6005; hours 8AM-4PM

Will search UCC records. Search per debtor- $8.00; $5.00 each add'l. UCC copy- included in search fee. Self-serve copies are $.50 per page. Will not search real estate or tax lien records. RE record copy- $1.00 per page. Cert fee: $5.00 per doc. Payee: Spencer County Recorder. **Other phones:** Assessor-812-649-2381; Treasurer-812-649-4556.

St. Joseph County

County Recorder, 227 W Jefferson, Rm 321, South Bend, IN 46601. **Phone-**County Recorder, R/E & UCC Recording- 574-235-9525; fax-574-235-5170; hours 8AM-4:30PM. Will search UCC records. Search per debtor- $8.00; $5.00 each add'l. UCC copy-included in search fee. Will not do federal tax lien search. Will not search real estate records. RE record copy- $1.00 per page. Cert fee: $5.00 per doc. Payee: St. Joseph County Recorder. **Online Access to Land, Most Wanted records:** Access to county land information is via a private company using Tapestry at https://www.landrecords.net/. Registration and credit card required; casual requesters permitted. Index goes back to 12/1992; images to 9/2000. Also, access to the county sheriff most wanted list is at www.skyenet.net/cstoppers/mostwanted/mostwant.html . **Other phones:** Assessor-574-235-9523; Treasurer-574-235-9531; Elections-574-235-9635; Vital Records-574-235-6719.

Starke County

County Recorder, PO Box 1, Knox, IN 46534. **Phone-**574-772-9110, R/E Recording- 574-772-9109, UCC Recording- 574-772-9109; fax-574-772-9178; hours 8:30AM-4PM. Will search UCC records. Search per debtor- $8.00; $5.00 each add'l. UCC copy-included in search fee. Will not do federal tax lien search. Will not search real estate records. RE record copy- $1.00 per page. Cert fee: $5.00 per doc. Payee: Starke County Recorder. **Other phones:** Assessor-574-772-9107; Treasurer-574-772-9113.

Steuben County

County Recorder, PO Box 397, Angola, IN 46703. **Phone-**County Recorder, R/E & UCC Recording- 260-668-1000 x1700; fax-260-665-8483; hours 8AM-4:30PM. Will search UCC records. Search per debtor- $8.00; $5.00 each add'l. UCC copy-included in search fee. Will not do federal tax lien search. Will not search real estate records. RE record copy- $1.00 per page. Cert fee: $5.00 per doc. Payee: Steuben County Recorder. **Other phones:** Assessor-260-668-1000 x1000; Treasurer-260-668-1000 x1900; Elections-260-668-1000 x2220; Vital Records-260-668-1000 x1500.

Sullivan County

County Recorder, 100 Court House Sq, Rm 205, Sullivan, IN 47882-1565. **Phone-**812-268-4844; fax-812-268-0521; hours 8AM-4PM

Will search UCC records. Search per debtor- $8.00; $5.00 each add'l. UCC copy- included in search fee. Will not search real estate or tax lien records. RE record copy- $1.00 Per Page. Cert fee: $5.00 per doc. Payee: Sullivan County Recorder. **Other phones:** Assessor-812-268-4657; Treasurer-812-268-6410; Vital Records-812-268-4029.

Switzerland County

County Recorder, 212 W Main, Courthouse, Vevay, IN 47043. **Phone-**812-427-2544; hours 8AM-3:30PM Will search UCC records. UCC search per debtor-$1.00 per copy. UCC copy fee- $1.00 per copy. Will not search real estate or tax lien records. RE record copy- $1.00 per page. Cert fee: $5.00 per doc. Payee: Switzerland County Recorder. **Other phones:** Assessor-812-427-3379; Treasurer-812-427-3369; Auditor-812-427-3302.

Tippecanoe County

County Recorder, 20 N. 3rd St, Lafayette, IN 47901. **Phone**-765-423-9353, R/E Recording- 765-423-9352; fax-765-423-9158; hours-8AM-4:30PM http://county.tippecanoe.in.us
Will search UCC records. Search per debtor- $5.00 per name + $3.00 supplemental per season. UCC copy- included in search fee. Will do a federal tax lien search. Tax lien search fee- $1.00 per page. Will not search real estate records. RE record copy-$1.00 per page. Cert fee: $5.00 per doc. Payee: Tippecanoe County Recorder. **Online Access to Property records:** Access to property information on the county gis-mapping site is free at http://gis.county.tippecanoe.in.us/gis/app12/index.html. **Other phones:** Assessor-765-423-9255.

Tipton County

County Recorder, 101 E. Jefferson St., Courthouse, Tipton, IN 46072. **Phone**-765-675-4614; fax-765-675-3893; hours 8AM-4PM. Will search UCC records. Search per debtor- $8.00; $5.00 each add'l. UCC copy- included in search fee. Will not search real estate or tax lien records. RE record copy- $1.00 per page. Cert fee: $5.00 per doc. Payee: Tipton County Recorder. **Other phones:** Assessor-765-675-2465; Treasurer-765-675-2742.

Union County

County Recorder, 26 W. Union St, Liberty, IN 47353. **Phone**-County Recorder, R/E & UCC Recording- 765-458-5434; fax-765-458-5263; hours 8AM-4PM
Will search UCC records. Search per debtor- $8.00; $5.00 each add'l. UCC copy- included in search fee. Will not do federal tax lien search. Will not search real estate records. RE record copy- $1.00 per page. Cert fee: $5.00 per doc. Payee: Union County Recorder. **Other phones:** Assessor-317-458-5331; Treasurer-317-458-6491.

Vanderburgh County

County Recorder, PO Box 1037, Evansville, IN 47708. **Phone**-County Recorder, R/E & UCC Recording- 812-435-5215; fax-812-435-5580; hours 8AM-4:30PM www.assessor.evansville.net
Will search UCC records. Search per debtor- $8.00; $5.00 each add'l. No UCC copy fee. Will not search real estate or tax lien records. Copy fee-$1.00 per page. Cert fee: $5.00 per doc. Payee: Vanderburgh County Recorder. **Online Access to Property records:** Records on the Assessor Property database are free at www.assessor.evansville.net/disclaim.htm. **Other phones:** Assessor-812-435-5273; Treasurer-812-435-5248; Elections-812-435-5160; Vital Records-812-435-5681.

Vermillion County

County Recorder, PO Box 145, Newport, IN 47966-0145. **Phone**-765-492-5003; hours 8AM-4PM
Will search UCC records. Search per debtor-$8.00,1st,$5.00 add'l. UCC copy fee- $1.00 per page. Will not search real estate or tax lien records. RE record copy- $1.00 per page. Cert fee: $5.00 per doc. Payee: Vermillion County Recorder. **Other phones:** Assessor-765-492-5004.

Vigo County

County Recorder, 199 Oak St, Terre Haute, IN 47807. **Phone**-County Recorder, R/E & UCC Recording- 812-462-3301; fax-812-232-2219; hours 8AM-4PM
Will not search records. RE record copy- $1.00 per page. Cert fee: $5.00 per doc. Payee: Vigo County Recorder. **Other phones:** Assessor-812-462-3358; Treasurer-812-462-3251; Vital Records-812-462-2442.

Wabash County

County Recorder, One W. Hill St., Courthouse, Wabash, IN 46992. **Phone**-County Recorder, R/E & UCC Recording- 260-563-0661 x253; hours 8AM-4PM
Will search UCC records if their request form is used. Search per debtor- $8.00; $5.00 each add'l name. UCC copy- included in search fee. Will not do federal tax lien search. Will not search real estate records. RE record copy- $1.00 per page. Cert fee: $5.00 per doc + $1.00 per page copy fee. Payee: Wabash County Recorder. **Other phones:** Assessor-260-563-0661 x227; Treasurer-260-563-0661 x259.

Warren County

County Recorder, 125 N. Monroe, Courthouse - #10, Williamsport, IN 47993-1162. **Phone**-765-762-3174; fax-765-762-7222; hours 8AM-4PM
Will search UCC records. Search per debtor- $8.00; $5.00 each add'l. UCC copy- included in search fee. Will not search real estate or tax lien records. RE record copy- $1.00 per page. Cert fee: $5.00 per doc. Payee: Warren County Recorder. **Other phones:** Assessor-765-762-4528; Treasurer-765-762-3562; Elections-765-762-3510.

Warrick County

County Recorder, PO Box 28, Boonville, IN 47601-0028. **Phone**-County Recorder, R/E & UCC Recording- 812-897-6165; fax-812-897-6168; hours 8AM-4PM www.warrickcounty.gov/departments/recorder.htm
Will search UCC records. Search per debtor- $8.00; $5.00 each add'l. UCC copy fee- $1.00 per page. Will not do federal tax lien search. Will not search real estate records. RE record copy- $1.00 per page. Cert fee: $5.00 per doc. Payee: Warrick County Recorder. **Online Access to Assessor, Property, Tax Bill records:** Access to the assessors proerpty tax data is free at www.pvdnetwork.com/Search/Search.asp. Also, access to tax bill records is free at www.pvdnetwork.com/Search/TaxSearch.asp. **Other phones:** Assessor-812-897-6125; Treasurer-812-897-6166; Elections-812-897-6161.

Washington County

County Recorder, Courthouse, Salem, IN 47167. **Phone**-812-883-4001; fax-812-883-4020; hours 8:30AM-4PM (F 8:30AM-6PM)
Will search UCC records. Search per debtor- $8.00; $5.00 each add'l. UCC copy- $1.00 per page. Will not do federal tax lien search. Will not search real estate records. RE record copy- $1.00 per page. Cert fee: $5.00 per doc. Payee: Washington County Recorder. **Other phones:** Assessor-812-883-4000; Treasurer-812-883-3307.

Wayne County

County Recorder, 401 E Main St, County Admin. Bldg, Richmond, IN 47374. **Phone**-County Recorder, R/E & UCC Recording- 765-973-9235; fax-765-973-9341; hours 8:30AM-5PM M; 8:30AM-4:30 PM T-F www.co.wayne.in.us/offices
Will search UCC records. Search per debtor- $8.00; $5.00 each add'l. UCC copy- included in search fee. Will not search real estate or tax lien records. RE record copy- $1.00 per page. Cert fee: $5.00 per doc. Payee: Wayne County Recorder. **Online Access to Property, Assessor, Marriage records:** Access to the county property records database is free at http://prc.co.wayne.in.us. Marriage records are being added irregularly to the website at www.co.wayne.in.us/marriage/retrieve.cgi. Records are from 1811 forward, with recent years being added. **Other phones:** Assessor-765-973-9254; Treasurer-765-973-9238; Elections-765-973-9226; Vital Records-765-973-9245.

Wells County

County Recorder, 102 W Market St, Courthouse - #203, Bluffton, IN 46714. **Phone**-County Recorder, R/E & UCC Recording- 260-824-6507; fax-260-824-1238; hours 8AM-4:30PM. Will search UCC records. Search per debtor- $8.00; $5.00 each add'l. UCC copy- included in search fee. Will not search real estate or tax lien records. RE record copy- $1.00 per page. Cert fee: $5.00 per doc. Payee: Wells County Recorder. **Other phones:** Assessor-260-824-6476; Treasurer-260-824-6514; Appraiser/ Auditor-260-824-6476; Elections-260-824-6482; Vital Records-260-824-6489; Auditor-260-824-6474.

White County

County Recorder, PO Box 127, Monticello, IN 47960. **Phone**-574-583-5912; fax-574-583-1521; hours 8AM-4PM. Will search UCC records. Search per debtor-$8.00; $5.00 each add'l. UCC copy- included in search fee. Will not search real estate or tax lien records. RE record copy- $1.00 per page. Cert fee: $6.00 per doc. Payee: White County Recorder. **Other phones:** Assessor-574-583-7755.

Whitley County

County Recorder, Courthouse, 2nd Fl - Rm 18, Columbia City, IN 46725. **Phone**-County Recorder, R/E & UCC Recording- 260-248-3106; fax-260-248-3163; hours 8AM-4:30PM M-Th; 8AM-6PM F
Will search UCC records. Search per debtor- $8.00; $5.00 each add'l. UCC copy- included in search fee. Will not do federal tax lien search. Will not search real estate records. RE record copy- $1.00 per page. Cert fee: $5.00 per doc. Payee: Whitley County Recorder. **Other phones:** Assessor-260-248-3109; Treasurer-260-248-3105; Elections-260-248-3102.

Indiana County Locator

You will usually be able to find the city name in the City/County Cross Reference below. In that case, it is a simple matter to determine the county from the cross reference. However, only the official US Postal Service city names are included in this index. There are an additional 40,000 place names that people use in their addresses. Therefore, we have also included a ZIP/City Cross Reference immediately following the City/County Cross Reference.

If you know the ZIP Code but the city name does not appear in the City/County Cross Reference index, look up the ZIP Code in the ZIP/City Cross Reference, find the city name, then look up the city name in the City/County Cross Reference. For example, you want to know the county for an address of Menands, NY 12204. There is no "Menands" in the City/County Cross Reference. The ZIP/City Cross Reference shows that ZIP Codes 12201-12288 are for the city of Albany. Looking back in the City/County Cross Reference, Albany is in Albany County.

Indiana City/County Cross Reference

ADVANCE Boone
AKRON (46910) Fulton(58), Kosciusko(31), Miami(9)
ALAMO Montgomery
ALBANY (47320) Delaware(92), Randolph(7)
ALBION Noble
ALEXANDRIA (46001) Madison(97), Delaware(2)
AMBIA (47917) Warren(51), Benton(48)
AMBOY (46911) Miami(89), Wabash(10)
AMO Hendricks
ANDERSON (46017) Madison(96), Delaware(3)
ANDERSON Madison
ANDREWS (46702) Huntington(91), Wabash(8)
ANGOLA Steuben
ARCADIA Hamilton
ARCOLA Allen
ARGOS (46501) Marshall(96), Fulton(3)
ARLINGTON (46104) Rush(98), Shelby(1)
ASHLEY (46705) DeKalb(70), Steuben(29)
ATHENS Fulton
ATLANTA (46031) Hamilton(62), Tipton(37)
ATTICA (47918) Fountain(81), Warren(17), Tippecanoe(1)
ATWOOD Kosciusko
AUBURN (46706) DeKalb(98), Allen(1)
AURORA Dearborn
AUSTIN (47102) Scott(85), Jackson(14)
AVILLA (46710) Noble(96), DeKalb(3)
AVOCA Lawrence
AVON Hendricks
BAINBRIDGE Putnam
BARGERSVILLE (46106) Johnson(96), Morgan(3)
BATESVILLE (47006) Franklin(58), Ripley(40)
BATH (47010) Franklin(69), Union(30)
BATTLE GROUND (47920) Tippecanoe(79), White(14), Carroll(6)
BEDFORD Lawrence
BEECH GROVE Marion
BELLMORE Parke
BENNINGTON (47011) Switzerland(55), Ohio(44)
BENTONVILLE Fayette
BERNE Adams
BETHLEHEM Clark
BEVERLY SHORES Porter
BICKNELL Knox
BIPPUS Huntington
BIRDSEYE (47513) Dubois(78), Crawford(15), Perry(4), Orange(1)
BLANFORD Vermillion
BLOOMFIELD Greene
BLOOMINGDALE Parke
BLOOMINGTON (47404) Monroe(98), Owen(1)
BLOOMINGTON Monroe
BLUFFTON (46714) Wells(96), Adams(3)
BOGGSTOWN (46110) Shelby(94), Johnson(5)

BOONE GROVE Porter
BOONVILLE (47601) Warrick(98), Spencer(1)
BORDEN (47106) Clark(90), Washington(5), Floyd(4)
BOSTON Wayne
BOSWELL (47921) Benton(81), Warren(18)
BOURBON (46504) Marshall(96), Kosciusko(3)
BOWLING GREEN (47833) Owen(51), Clay(48)
BRADFORD Harrison
BRANCHVILLE Perry
BRAZIL (47834) Clay(89), Vigo(6), Parke(4)
BREMEN (46506) Marshall(88), St. Joseph(11)
BRIDGETON Parke
BRIMFIELD Noble
BRINGHURST Carroll
BRISTOL Elkhart
BRISTOW Perry
BROOK (47922) Newton(94), Jasper(5)
BROOKLYN Morgan
BROOKSTON (47923) White(87), Carroll(12)
BROOKVILLE Franklin
BROWNSBURG Hendricks
BROWNSTOWN Jackson
BROWNSVILLE (47325) Union(78), Fayette(19), Wayne(2)
BRUCEVILLE Knox
BRYANT (47326) Jay(96), Adams(2)
BUCK CREEK Tippecanoe
BUCKSKIN Gibson
BUFFALO White
BUNKER HILL Miami
BURKET Kosciusko
BURLINGTON Carroll
BURNETTSVILLE (47926) White(67), Carroll(29), Cass(2)
BURNEY Decatur
BURROWS Carroll
BUTLER DeKalb
BUTLERVILLE Jennings
CAMBRIDGE CITY (47327) Wayne(94), Henry(4)
CAMBY (46113) Morgan(55), Marion(29), Hendricks(15)
CAMDEN (46917) Carroll(98), Cass(1)
CAMPBELLSBURG (47108) Washington(91), Orange(8)
CANAAN (47224) Jefferson(98), Switzerland(1)
CANNELBURG Daviess
CANNELTON Perry
CARBON (47837) Parke(66), Clay(33)
CARLISLE Sullivan
CARMEL Hamilton
CARTERSBURG Hendricks
CARTHAGE (46115) Rush(94), Hancock(5)
CAYUGA Vermillion
CEDAR GROVE Franklin
CEDAR LAKE Lake

CELESTINE Dubois
CENTERPOINT (47840) Clay(95), Putnam(4)
CENTERVILLE Wayne
CENTRAL Harrison
CHALMERS White
CHANDLER Warrick
CHARLESTOWN Clark
CHARLOTTESVILLE (46117) Hancock(89), Henry(10)
CHESTERTON Porter
CHRISNEY Spencer
CHURUBUSCO (46723) Whitley(63), Allen(23), Noble(12)
CICERO Hamilton
CLARKS HILL (47930) Tippecanoe(73), Montgomery(14), Clinton(11)
CLARKSBURG Decatur
CLARKSVILLE Clark
CLAY CITY (47841) Clay(98), Owen(1)
CLAYPOOL Kosciusko
CLAYTON (46118) Hendricks(97), Morgan(2)
CLEAR CREEK Monroe
CLIFFORD Bartholomew
CLINTON Vermillion
CLOVERDALE (46120) Putnam(74), Owen(20), Morgan(4)
COAL CITY (47427) Owen(86), Clay(13)
COALMONT Clay
COATESVILLE (46121) Hendricks(56), Putnam(43)
COLBURN Tippecanoe
COLFAX (46035) Clinton(69), Boone(26), Montgomery(3)
COLUMBIA CITY (46725) Whitley(96), Noble(2)
COLUMBUS (47201) Bartholomew(95), Brown(4)
COLUMBUS Bartholomew
COMMISKEY (47227) Jennings(80), Jefferson(15)
CONNERSVILLE Fayette
CONVERSE (46919) Grant(53), Miami(37), Howard(8), Wabash(1)
CORTLAND Jackson
CORUNNA (46730) DeKalb(97), Noble(2)
CORY (47846) Clay(98), Vigo(1)
CORYDON Harrison
COVINGTON (47932) Fountain(89), Warren(5), Vermillion(4)
CRAIGVILLE (46731) Wells(90), Adams(9)
CRANDALL Harrison
CRANE Martin
CRAWFORDSVILLE Montgomery
CROMWELL (46732) Noble(57), Kosciusko(42)
CROSS PLAINS Ripley
CROTHERSVILLE (47229) Jackson(89), Jennings(10)
CROWN POINT (46307) Lake(98), Porter(1)
CROWN POINT Lake

CULVER (46511) Marshall(77), Starke(10), Fulton(10), Pulaski(1)
CUTLER (46920) Carroll(98), Clinton(1)
CYNTHIANA (47612) Posey(79), Gibson(20)
DALE (47523) Spencer(37), Dubois(33), Warrick(29)
DALEVILLE (47334) Delaware(98), Henry(1)
DANA Vermillion
DANVILLE Hendricks
DARLINGTON Montgomery
DAYTON Tippecanoe
DECATUR Adams
DECKER Knox
DEEDSVILLE Miami
DELONG Fulton
DELPHI Carroll
DEMOTTE (46310) Jasper(82), Newton(17)
DENHAM Pulaski
DENVER (46926) Miami(95), Cass(3)
DEPAUW Harrison
DEPUTY (47230) Jefferson(91), Jennings(8)
DERBY Perry
DILLSBORO (47018) Dearborn(97), Ohio(2)
DONALDSON Marshall
DUBLIN Wayne
DUBOIS (47527) Dubois(97), Orange(1)
DUGGER (47848) Sullivan(96), Greene(3)
DUNKIRK (47336) Jay(63), Blackford(20), Delaware(16)
DUNREITH Henry
DUPONT (47231) Jefferson(74), Jennings(25)
DYER Lake
EARL PARK (47942) Benton(96), Newton(3)
EARL PARK Benton
EAST CHICAGO Lake
EAST ENTERPRISE Switzerland
EATON (47338) Delaware(98), Blackford(1)
ECKERTY Crawford
ECONOMY Wayne
EDINBURGH (46124) Johnson(54), Bartholomew(26), Shelby(19)
EDWARDSPORT (47528) Knox(98), Sullivan(2)
ELBERFELD (47613) Warrick(91), Gibson(7)
ELIZABETH (47117) Harrison(97), Floyd(2)
ELIZABETHTOWN (47232) Bartholomew(69), Jennings(30)
ELKHART Elkhart
ELLETTSVILLE Monroe
ELNORA (47529) Daviess(96), Greene(3)
ELWOOD (46036) Madison(91), Tipton(7)
EMINENCE Morgan
EMISON Knox
ENGLISH (47118) Crawford(67), Orange(27), Perry(5)
ETNA GREEN (46524) Kosciusko(97), Marshall(2)

EVANSTON Spencer
EVANSVILLE (47712) Vanderburgh(86), Posey(13)
EVANSVILLE Vanderburgh
FAIR OAKS (47943) Jasper(55), Newton(45)
FAIRBANKS Sullivan
FAIRLAND Shelby
FAIRMOUNT (46928) Grant(97), Madison(2)
FALMOUTH (46127) Rush(75), Fayette(24)
FARMERSBURG (47850) Sullivan(76), Vigo(23)
FARMLAND Randolph
FERDINAND (47532) Dubois(69), Spencer(27), Perry(2)
FILLMORE Putnam
FINLY Hancock
FISHERS Hamilton
FLAT ROCK (47234) Shelby(92), Bartholomew(7)
FLORA (46929) Carroll(91), Howard(8)
FLORENCE Switzerland
FLOYDS KNOBS (47119) Floyd(95), Clark(4)
FOLSOMVILLE Warrick
FONTANET Vigo
FOREST Clinton
FORT BRANCH Gibson
FORT RITNER Lawrence
FORT WAYNE (46818) Allen(98), Whitley(1)
FORT WAYNE Allen
FORTVILLE (46040) Hancock(73), Hamilton(19), Madison(6)
FOUNTAIN CITY (47341) Wayne(97), Randolph(2)
FOUNTAINTOWN (46130) Shelby(72), Hancock(27)
FOWLER Benton
FOWLERTON Grant
FRANCESVILLE (47946) Pulaski(83), Jasper(15)
FRANCISCO Gibson
FRANKFORT (46041) Clinton(98), Carroll(1)
FRANKLIN Johnson
FRANKTON Madison
FREDERICKSBURG (47120) Washington(97), Harrison(2)
FREEDOM Owen
FREELANDVILLE Knox
FREETOWN (47235) Jackson(71), Brown(28)
FREMONT Steuben
FRENCH LICK (47432) Orange(87), Dubois(11), Martin(1)
FRIENDSHIP Ripley
FULDA Spencer
FULTON Fulton
GALVESTON (46932) Cass(90), Howard(5), Miami(4)
GARRETT DeKalb
GARY (46403) Lake(98), Porter(1)
GARY Lake
GAS CITY Grant
GASTON (47342) Delaware(97), Grant(1)
GENEVA (46740) Adams(93), Wells(4), Jay(2)
GENTRYVILLE (47537) Spencer(68), Warrick(31)
GEORGETOWN (47122) Floyd(62), Harrison(37)
GLENWOOD (46133) Fayette(57), Rush(42)
GOLDSMITH Tipton
GOODLAND (47948) Newton(72), Jasper(15), Benton(12)
GOSHEN Elkhart
GOSPORT (47433) Owen(72), Monroe(16), Morgan(10)
GRABILL Allen
GRAMMER Bartholomew

GRANDVIEW Spencer
GRANGER (46530) St. Joseph(95), Elkhart(4)
GRANTSBURG Crawford
GRASS CREEK Fulton
GRAYSVILLE Sullivan
GREENCASTLE (46135) Putnam(98), Parke(1)
GREENFIELD Hancock
GREENS FORK Wayne
GREENSBORO Henry
GREENSBURG Decatur
GREENTOWN Howard
GREENVILLE (47124) Floyd(74), Harrison(25)
GREENWOOD Johnson
GRIFFIN (47616) Posey(85), Gibson(14)
GRIFFITH Lake
GRISSOM AFB Miami
GRISSOM ARB Miami
GROVERTOWN (46531) Starke(97), Marshall(2)
GUILFORD Dearborn
GWYNNEVILLE Shelby
HAGERSTOWN (47346) Wayne(96), Henry(3)
HAMILTON (46742) Steuben(84), DeKalb(15)
HAMLET (46532) Starke(60), La Porte(39)
HAMMOND Lake
HANNA La Porte
HANOVER Jefferson
HARDINSBURG (47125) Orange(56), Washington(43)
HARLAN Allen
HARMONY Clay
HARRODSBURG Monroe
HARTFORD CITY Blackford
HARTSVILLE (47244) Bartholomew(74), Decatur(25)
HATFIELD Spencer
HAUBSTADT (47639) Gibson(76), Vanderburgh(21), Warrick(1)
HAYDEN Jennings
HAZLETON (47640) Gibson(70), Pike(29)
HEBRON (46341) Porter(79), Lake(17), Jasper(1)
HELMSBURG Brown
HELTONVILLE (47436) Lawrence(92), Monroe(7)
HEMLOCK Howard
HENRYVILLE (47126) Clark(95), Washington(3), Scott(1)
HIGHLAND Lake
HILLISBURG Clinton
HILLSBORO (47949) Fountain(97), Montgomery(2)
HILLSDALE Vermillion
HOAGLAND (46745) Allen(97), Adams(2)
HOBART (46342) Lake(98), Porter(1)
HOBBS Tipton
HOLLAND (47541) Dubois(74), Pike(18), Warrick(4), Spencer(2)
HOLTON Ripley
HOMER Rush
HOPE Bartholomew
HOWE LaGrange
HUDSON (46747) Steuben(77), LaGrange(13), DeKalb(8)
HUNTERTOWN (46748) Allen(96), DeKalb(2), Noble(1)
HUNTINGBURG (47542) Dubois(97), Pike(2)
HUNTINGTON Huntington
HURON Lawrence
HYMERA Sullivan
IDAVILLE (47950) White(91), Carroll(8)
INDIANAPOLIS (46229) Marion(92), Hancock(7)
INDIANAPOLIS (46234) Marion(67), Hendricks(32)
INDIANAPOLIS (46239) Marion(98), Hancock(1)

INDIANAPOLIS (46256) Marion(93), Hamilton(6)
INDIANAPOLIS (46259) Marion(91), Shelby(4), Johnson(3)
INDIANAPOLIS (46278) Marion(94), Hendricks(5)
INDIANAPOLIS Hamilton
INDIANAPOLIS Marion
INGALLS Madison
INGLEFIELD Vanderburgh
IRELAND Dubois
JAMESTOWN (46147) Boone(91), Hendricks(8)
JASONVILLE (47438) Greene(70), Clay(24), Sullivan(5)
JASPER Dubois
JEFFERSONVILLE Clark
JONESBORO Grant
JONESVILLE Bartholomew
JUDSON Parke
KEMPTON (46049) Tipton(91), Clinton(8)
KENDALLVILLE Noble
KENNARD Henry
KENTLAND Newton
KEWANNA (46939) Fulton(93), Pulaski(6)
KEYSTONE Wells
KIMMELL Noble
KINGMAN (47952) Fountain(84), Parke(15)
KINGSBURY La Porte
KINGSFORD HEIGHTS La Porte
KIRKLIN (46050) Clinton(73), Boone(22), Tipton(3)
KNIGHTSTOWN (46148) Henry(84), Rush(15)
KNIGHTSVILLE Clay
KNOX Starke
KOKOMO (46901) Howard(98), Miami(1)
KOKOMO Howard
KOLEEN Greene
KOUTS Porter
KURTZ Jackson
LA CROSSE (46348) La Porte(98), Porter(1)
LA FONTAINE (46940) Wabash(87), Huntington(8), Grant(3)
LA PORTE La Porte
LACONIA Harrison
LADOGA (47954) Montgomery(94), Putnam(4)
LAFAYETTE Tippecanoe
LAGRANGE (46761) LaGrange(95), Steuben(4)
LAGRO Wabash
LAKE CICOTT Cass
LAKE STATION Lake
LAKE VILLAGE Newton
LAKETON Wabash
LAKEVILLE (46536) St. Joseph(92), Marshall(7)
LAMAR Spencer
LANDESS Grant
LANESVILLE (47136) Harrison(81), Floyd(18)
LAOTTO (46763) Noble(85), DeKalb(14)
LAPAZ Marshall
LAPEL Madison
LAPORTE La Porte
LARWILL (46764) Whitley(92), Noble(7)
LAUREL Franklin
LAWRENCEBURG Dearborn
LEAVENWORTH (47137) Crawford(96), Perry(2)
LEBANON Boone
LEESBURG Kosciusko
LEITERS FORD Fulton
LEO Allen
LEOPOLD Perry
LEROY Lake
LEWIS (47858) Vigo(48), Clay(37), Sullivan(14)
LEWISVILLE (47352) Rush(52), Henry(46), Fayette(1)

LEXINGTON (47138) Jefferson(52), Scott(46)
LIBERTY (47353) Union(94), Franklin(5)
LIBERTY CENTER (46766) Wells(98), Huntington(1)
LIBERTY MILLS Wabash
LIGONIER (46767) Noble(96), Elkhart(1), LaGrange(1)
LINCOLN CITY Spencer
LINDEN (47955) Montgomery(97), Tippecanoe(2)
LINN GROVE Adams
LINTON Greene
LITTLE YORK Washington
LIZTON Hendricks
LOGANSPORT (46947) Cass(98), Carroll(1)
LOOGOOTEE (47553) Martin(79), Daviess(20)
LOSANTVILLE (47354) Randolph(72), Henry(16), Delaware(6), Wayne(4)
LOWELL Lake
LUCERNE (46950) Cass(96), Fulton(3)
LYNN Randolph
LYNNVILLE (47619) Warrick(92), Gibson(6)
LYONS Greene
MACKEY Gibson
MACY (46951) Miami(70), Fulton(29)
MADISON (47250) Jefferson(96), Ripley(2), Switzerland(1)
MAGNET Perry
MANILLA (46150) Rush(92), Shelby(7)
MARENGO (47140) Orange(53), Crawford(46)
MARIAH HILL Spencer
MARION Grant
MARKLE (46770) Wells(73), Huntington(26)
MARKLEVILLE (46056) Madison(82), Hancock(14), Henry(3)
MARSHALL Parke
MARTINSVILLE Morgan
MARYSVILLE (47141) Clark(92), Scott(7)
MATTHEWS Grant
MAUCKPORT Harrison
MAXWELL Hancock
MAYS Rush
MC CORDSVILLE (46055) Hancock(75), Hamilton(24)
MECCA Parke
MEDARYVILLE (47957) Pulaski(89), Jasper(10)
MEDORA (47260) Jackson(98), Lawrence(1)
MELLOTT Fountain
MEMPHIS Clark
MENTONE (46539) Kosciusko(91), Fulton(6), Marshall(2)
MEROM Sullivan
MERRILLVILLE Lake
METAMORA Franklin
MEXICO Miami
MIAMI Miami
MICHIGAN CITY (46360) La Porte(94), Porter(5)
MICHIGAN CITY La Porte
MICHIGANTOWN Clinton
MIDDLEBURY (46540) Elkhart(90), LaGrange(9)
MIDDLETOWN (47356) Henry(92), Madison(5), Delaware(2)
MIDLAND Greene
MILAN Ripley
MILFORD (46542) Kosciusko(95), Elkhart(4)
MILL CREEK La Porte
MILLERSBURG (46543) Elkhart(71), LaGrange(27), Noble(1)
MILLHOUSEN Decatur
MILLTOWN (47145) Crawford(96), Washington(3)
MILROY (46156) Rush(95), Decatur(4)

MILTON (47357) Wayne(71), Fayette(22), Madison(5)
MISHAWAKA St. Joseph
MITCHELL Lawrence
MODOC (47358) Randolph(98), Wayne(1)
MONGO LaGrange
MONON (47959) White(87), Jasper(9), Pulaski(2)
MONROE Adams
MONROE CITY Knox
MONROEVILLE (46773) Allen(89), Adams(10)
MONROVIA Morgan
MONTEREY (46960) Pulaski(62), Starke(30), Fulton(6)
MONTEZUMA Parke
MONTGOMERY Daviess
MONTICELLO (47960) White(88), Carroll(11)
MONTMORENCI Tippecanoe
MONTPELIER (47359) Blackford(87), Wells(11)
MOORELAND (47360) Henry(94), Wayne(3), Randolph(1)
MOORES HILL Dearborn
MOORESVILLE (46158) Morgan(90), Hendricks(9)
MORGANTOWN (46160) Brown(53), Morgan(29), Johnson(16)
MOROCCO Newton
MORRIS Ripley
MORRISTOWN (46161) Shelby(74), Hancock(17), Rush(7)
MOUNT AYR Newton
MOUNT PLEASANT Perry
MOUNT SAINT FRANCIS Floyd
MOUNT SUMMIT Henry
MOUNT VERNON Posey
MULBERRY (46058) Clinton(97), Tippecanoe(2)
MUNCIE Delaware
MUNSTER Lake
NABB (47147) Clark(42), Scott(31), Jefferson(25)
NAPOLEON Ripley
NAPPANEE (46550) Elkhart(84), Kosciusko(10), Marshall(4)
NASHVILLE (47448) Brown(98), Monroe(1)
NEBRASKA Jennings
NEEDHAM (46162) Johnson(57), Shelby(42)
NEW ALBANY Floyd
NEW CARLISLE (46552) La Porte(56), St. Joseph(43)
NEW CASTLE Henry
NEW GOSHEN Vigo
NEW HARMONY Posey
NEW HAVEN Allen
NEW LEBANON Sullivan
NEW LISBON Henry
NEW MARKET Montgomery
NEW MIDDLETOWN Harrison
NEW PALESTINE (46163) Hancock(94), Shelby(4)
NEW PARIS Elkhart
NEW POINT Decatur
NEW RICHMOND (47967) Montgomery(92), Tippecanoe(7)
NEW ROSS (47968) Montgomery(86), Boone(8), Hendricks(4)
NEW SALISBURY Harrison
NEW TRENTON Franklin
NEW WASHINGTON Clark
NEW WAVERLY Cass
NEWBERRY (47449) Greene(93), Daviess(5), Martin(1)
NEWBURGH Warrick
NEWPORT Vermillion
NEWTOWN Fountain
NINEVEH (46164) Brown(69), Johnson(30)
NOBLESVILLE Hamilton
NORMAN (47264) Jackson(72), Lawrence(24), Monroe(3)

NORTH JUDSON (46366) Starke(96), Pulaski(3)
NORTH LIBERTY (46554) St. Joseph(97), La Porte(2)
NORTH MANCHESTER (46962) Wabash(94), Kosciusko(5)
NORTH SALEM (46165) Hendricks(98), Putnam(1)
NORTH VERNON Jennings
NORTH WEBSTER Kosciusko
NOTRE DAME St. Joseph
OAKFORD Howard
OAKLAND CITY (47660) Gibson(85), Pike(13)
OAKTOWN (47561) Knox(93), Sullivan(6)
OAKVILLE Delaware
ODON Daviess
OLDENBURG Franklin
ONWARD Cass
OOLITIC Lawrence
ORA Starke
ORESTES Madison
ORLAND (46776) Steuben(76), LaGrange(23)
ORLEANS (47452) Orange(82), Lawrence(16)
OSCEOLA (46561) St. Joseph(87), Elkhart(12)
OSGOOD Ripley
OSSIAN (46777) Wells(93), Allen(3), Adams(2)
OSSIAN Steuben
OSSIAN Wells
OTISCO Clark
OTTERBEIN (47970) Benton(45), Warren(34), Tippecanoe(18)
OTWELL (47564) Pike(87), Dubois(12)
OWENSBURG Greene
OWENSVILLE Gibson
OXFORD Benton
PALMYRA (47164) Harrison(72), Washington(27)
PAOLI Orange
PARAGON (46166) Morgan(89), Owen(10)
PARIS CROSSING (47270) Jennings(93), Jefferson(6)
PARKER CITY (47368) Randolph(84), Delaware(15)
PATOKA Gibson
PATRICKSBURG Owen
PATRIOT Switzerland
PAXTON Sullivan
PEKIN (47165) Washington(96), Clark(1), Floyd(1)
PENCE Warren
PENDLETON (46064) Madison(94), Hancock(4)
PENNVILLE (47369) Jay(95), Blackford(4)
PERRYSVILLE Vermillion
PERSHING Wayne
PERU (46970) Miami(93), Cass(3), Wabash(2)
PETERSBURG Pike
PETROLEUM Wells
PIERCETON (46562) Kosciusko(85), Noble(8), Whitley(6)
PIERCEVILLE Ripley
PIMENTO (47866) Vigo(96), Sullivan(3)
PINE VILLAGE (47975) Warren(93), Benton(6)
PITTSBORO (46167) Hendricks(98), Boone(1)
PLAINFIELD Hendricks
PLAINVILLE Daviess
PLEASANT LAKE Steuben
PLEASANT MILLS Adams
PLYMOUTH Marshall
POLAND (47868) Owen(83), Clay(13), Putnam(2)
PONETO Wells
PORTAGE Porter
PORTLAND Jay

POSEYVILLE (47633) Posey(93), Gibson(4), Vanderburgh(1)
PRAIRIE CREEK Vigo
PRAIRIETON Vigo
PREBLE Adams
PRINCETON Gibson
PUTNAMVILLE Putnam
QUINCY (47456) Owen(60), Morgan(35), Putnam(4)
RAGSDALE Knox
RAMSEY Harrison
REDKEY (47373) Jay(82), Randolph(17)
REELSVILLE Putnam
REMINGTON (47977) Jasper(79), Benton(19), White(1)
RENSSELAER Jasper
REYNOLDS White
RICHLAND Spencer
RICHMOND Wayne
RIDGEVILLE (47380) Randolph(91), Jay(8)
RILEY Vigo
RISING SUN Ohio
ROACHDALE (46172) Putnam(97), Montgomery(2)
ROANN (46974) Wabash(61), Miami(38)
ROANOKE (46783) Huntington(50), Allen(39), Whitley(8), Wells(2)
ROCHESTER Fulton
ROCKFIELD Carroll
ROCKPORT Spencer
ROCKVILLE Parke
ROLLING PRAIRIE La Porte
ROME Perry
ROME CITY Noble
ROMNEY (47981) Tippecanoe(88), Montgomery(11)
ROSEDALE (47874) Parke(51), Vigo(33), Clay(14)
ROSELAWN Newton
ROSSVILLE (46065) Clinton(59), Carroll(40)
ROYAL CENTER (46978) Cass(93), Pulaski(3), White(3)
RUSHVILLE Rush
RUSSELLVILLE (46175) Putnam(89), Parke(7), Montgomery(3)
RUSSIAVILLE (46979) Howard(83), Clinton(10), Tipton(3), Carroll(1)
SAINT ANTHONY Dubois
SAINT BERNICE Vermillion
SAINT CROIX (47576) Perry(95), Crawford(4)
SAINT JOE DeKalb
SAINT JOHN Lake
SAINT MARY OF THE WOODS Vigo
SAINT MEINRAD (47577) Spencer(93), Perry(6)
SAINT PAUL (47272) Decatur(69), Shelby(28), Rush(2)
SALAMONIA Jay
SALEM Washington
SAN PIERRE (46374) Starke(95), Pulaski(3)
SANDBORN (47578) Knox(81), Greene(17)
SANDFORD Vigo
SANTA CLAUS Spencer
SARATOGA Randolph
SCHERERVILLE Lake
SCHNEIDER Lake
SCHNELLVILLE Dubois
SCIPIO Jennings
SCOTLAND Greene
SCOTTSBURG (47170) Scott(84), Washington(14)
SEDALIA Clinton
SEELYVILLE Vigo
SELLERSBURG (47172) Clark(92), Floyd(7)
SELMA Delaware
SERVIA Wabash
SEYMOUR (47274) Jackson(93), Bartholomew(3), Jennings(2)

SHARPSVILLE (46068) Tipton(90), Howard(9)
SHELBURN Sullivan
SHELBY Lake
SHEPARDSVILLE Vigo
SHERIDAN (46069) Hamilton(68), Boone(27), Clinton(4)
SHIPSHEWANA LaGrange
SHIRLEY (47384) Henry(72), Hancock(27)
SHOALS Martin
SIDNEY Kosciusko
SILVER LAKE (46982) Kosciusko(75), Wabash(20), Fulton(3)
SIMS Grant
SMITHVILLE Monroe
SOLSBERRY (47459) Greene(87), Owen(11)
SOMERSET Wabash
SOMERVILLE Gibson
SOUTH BEND St. Joseph
SOUTH MILFORD LaGrange
SOUTH WHITLEY (46787) Whitley(91), Kosciusko(7)
SPENCER Owen
SPENCERVILLE (46788) Allen(64), DeKalb(35)
SPICELAND Henry
SPRINGPORT (47386) Henry(97), Delaware(2)
SPRINGVILLE (47462) Lawrence(82), Greene(8), Monroe(8)
SPURGEON Pike
STANFORD Monroe
STAR CITY (46985) Pulaski(96), White(3)
STATE LINE Warren
STAUNTON Clay
STENDAL Pike
STILESVILLE (46180) Morgan(56), Hendricks(43)
STINESVILLE Monroe
STOCKWELL Tippecanoe
STRAUGHN (47387) Henry(98), Fayette(1)
STROH LaGrange
SULLIVAN Sullivan
SULPHUR Crawford
SULPHUR SPRINGS Henry
SUMAVA RESORTS Newton
SUMMITVILLE (46070) Madison(94), Delaware(3), Grant(2)
SUNMAN (47041) Ripley(61), Dearborn(38)
SWAYZEE (46986) Grant(98), Howard(1)
SWEETSER Grant
SWITZ CITY Greene
SYRACUSE (46567) Kosciusko(96), Elkhart(3)
TALBOT Benton
TANGIER Parke
TASWELL (47175) Crawford(92), Orange(7)
TAYLORSVILLE Bartholomew
TEFFT Jasper
TELL CITY Perry
TEMPLETON Benton
TENNYSON (47637) Warrick(87), Spencer(12)
TERRE HAUTE Vigo
THAYER Newton
THORNTOWN Boone
TIPPECANOE (46570) Marshall(88), Fulton(11)
TIPTON Tipton
TOBINSPORT Perry
TOPEKA (46571) LaGrange(98), Noble(1)
TRAFALGAR (46181) Johnson(84), Brown(15)
TROY (47588) Spencer(89), Perry(10)
TUNNELTON Lawrence
TWELVE MILE (46988) Cass(97), Fulton(2)
TYNER Marshall
UNDERWOOD (47177) Scott(57), Clark(42)
UNION CITY (47390) Randolph(95), Jay(4)

UNION MILLS (46382) La Porte(98), Lake(1)
UNIONDALE Wells
UNIONVILLE (47468) Monroe(59), Brown(40)
UNIVERSAL Vermillion
UPLAND (46989) Grant(96), Blackford(2), Delaware(1)
URBANA Wabash
VALLONIA (47281) Jackson(58), Washington(41)
VALPARAISO Porter
VAN BUREN (46991) Grant(85), Huntington(12), Wells(2)
VEEDERSBURG Fountain
VELPEN (47590) Pike(86), Dubois(13)
VERNON Jennings
VERSAILLES Ripley
VEVAY (47043) Switzerland(97), Jefferson(2)
VINCENNES Knox
WABASH Wabash
WADESVILLE Posey
WAKARUSA (46573) Elkhart(74), St. Joseph(25)

WALDRON (46182) Shelby(81), Rush(18)
WALKERTON (46574) St. Joseph(38), Marshall(22), Starke(21), La Porte(17)
WALLACE Fountain
WALTON Cass
WANATAH La Porte
WARREN (46792) Huntington(82), Wells(17)
WARSAW Kosciusko
WASHINGTON Daviess
WATERLOO (46793) DeKalb(98), Steuben(1)
WAVELAND (47989) Montgomery(81), Parke(15), Putnam(3)
WAWAKA Noble
WAYNETOWN (47990) Montgomery(86), Fountain(13)
WEBSTER Wayne
WEST BADEN SPRINGS Orange
WEST COLLEGE CORNER (47003) Franklin(86), Union(13)
WEST HARRISON (47060) Dearborn(72), Franklin(27)
WEST LAFAYETTE Tippecanoe
WEST LEBANON Warren

WEST MIDDLETON Howard
WEST NEWTON Marion
WEST TERRE HAUTE Vigo
WESTFIELD Hamilton
WESTPHALIA Knox
WESTPOINT Tippecanoe
WESTPORT (47283) Decatur(92), Bartholomew(4), Jennings(2)
WESTVILLE (46391) La Porte(76), Porter(23)
WHEATFIELD Jasper
WHEATLAND Knox
WHEELER Porter
WHITELAND Johnson
WHITESTOWN Boone
WHITING Lake
WILKINSON (46186) Hancock(96), Henry(3)
WILLIAMS (47470) Lawrence(97), Martin(2)
WILLIAMSBURG (47393) Wayne(71), Randolph(28)
WILLIAMSPORT Warren
WILLOW BRANCH Hancock
WINAMAC Pulaski

WINCHESTER Randolph
WINDFALL (46076) Tipton(94), Howard(5)
WINGATE (47994) Montgomery(77), Fountain(18), Tippecanoe(3)
WINONA LAKE Kosciusko
WINSLOW Pike
WOLCOTT (47995) White(96), Jasper(2)
WOLCOTTVILLE (46795) LaGrange(89), Noble(9)
WOLFLAKE Noble
WOODBURN Allen
WORTHINGTON (47471) Greene(81), Owen(18)
WYATT St. Joseph
YEOMAN Carroll
YODER (46798) Allen(92), Wells(7)
YORKTOWN Delaware
YOUNG AMERICA Cass
ZANESVILLE Allen
ZIONSVILLE (46077) Boone(91), Hamilton(7), Marion(1)

Indiana ZIP/City Cross Reference

46001-46001 ALEXANDRIA	46117-46117 CHARLOTTESVILLE	46200-46298 INDIANAPOLIS	46405-46405 LAKE STATION
46011-46018 ANDERSON	46118-46118 CLAYTON	46301-46301 BEVERLY SHORES	46406-46409 GARY
46030-46030 ARCADIA	46120-46120 CLOVERDALE	46302-46302 BOONE GROVE	46410-46411 MERRILLVILLE
46031-46031 ATLANTA	46121-46121 COATESVILLE	46303-46303 CEDAR LAKE	46501-46501 ARGOS
46032-46033 CARMEL	46122-46122 DANVILLE	46304-46304 CHESTERTON	46502-46502 ATWOOD
46034-46034 CICERO	46123-46123 AVON	46307-46308 CROWN POINT	46504-46504 BOURBON
46035-46035 COLFAX	46124-46124 EDINBURGH	46310-46310 DEMOTTE	46506-46506 BREMEN
46036-46036 ELWOOD	46125-46125 EMINENCE	46311-46311 DYER	46507-46507 BRISTOL
46038-46038 FISHERS	46126-46126 FAIRLAND	46312-46312 EAST CHICAGO	46508-46508 BURKET
46039-46039 FOREST	46127-46127 FALMOUTH	46319-46319 GRIFFITH	46510-46510 CLAYPOOL
46040-46040 FORTVILLE	46128-46128 FILLMORE	46320-46320 HAMMOND	46511-46511 CULVER
46041-46041 FRANKFORT	46129-46129 FINLY	46321-46321 MUNSTER	46513-46513 DONALDSON
46044-46044 FRANKTON	46130-46130 FOUNTAINTOWN	46322-46322 HIGHLAND	46514-46517 ELKHART
46045-46045 GOLDSMITH	46131-46131 FRANKLIN	46323-46327 HAMMOND	46524-46524 ETNA GREEN
46046-46046 HILLISBURG	46133-46133 GLENWOOD	46340-46340 HANNA	46526-46528 GOSHEN
46047-46047 HOBBS	46135-46135 GREENCASTLE	46341-46341 HEBRON	46530-46530 GRANGER
46048-46048 INGALLS	46140-46140 GREENFIELD	46342-46342 HOBART	46531-46531 GROVERTOWN
46049-46049 KEMPTON	46142-46143 GREENWOOD	46345-46345 KINGSBURY	46532-46532 HAMLET
46050-46050 KIRKLIN	46144-46144 GWYNNEVILLE	46346-46346 KINGSFORD HEIGHTS	46534-46534 KNOX
46051-46051 LAPEL	46146-46146 HOMER	46347-46347 KOUTS	46536-46536 LAKEVILLE
46052-46052 LEBANON	46147-46147 JAMESTOWN	46348-46348 LA CROSSE	46537-46537 LAPAZ
46055-46055 MC CORDSVILLE	46148-46148 KNIGHTSTOWN	46349-46349 LAKE VILLAGE	46538-46538 LEESBURG
46056-46056 MARKLEVILLE	46149-46149 LIZTON	46350-46350 LA PORTE	46539-46539 MENTONE
46057-46057 MICHIGANTOWN	46150-46150 MANILLA	46350-46350 LAPORTE	46540-46540 MIDDLEBURY
46058-46058 MULBERRY	46151-46151 MARTINSVILLE	46351-46352 LA PORTE	46542-46542 MILFORD
46060-46062 NOBLESVILLE	46154-46154 MAXWELL	46352-46352 LAPORTE	46543-46543 MILLERSBURG
46063-46063 ORESTES	46155-46155 MAYS	46355-46355 LEROY	46544-46546 MISHAWAKA
46064-46064 PENDLETON	46156-46156 MILROY	46356-46356 LOWELL	46550-46550 NAPPANEE
46065-46065 ROSSVILLE	46157-46157 MONROVIA	46360-46361 MICHIGAN CITY	46552-46552 NEW CARLISLE
46067-46067 SEDALIA	46158-46158 MOORESVILLE	46365-46365 MILL CREEK	46553-46553 NEW PARIS
46068-46068 SHARPSVILLE	46160-46160 MORGANTOWN	46366-46366 NORTH JUDSON	46554-46554 NORTH LIBERTY
46069-46069 SHERIDAN	46161-46161 MORRISTOWN	46367-46367 LA PORTE	46555-46555 NORTH WEBSTER
46070-46070 SUMMITVILLE	46162-46162 NEEDHAM	46368-46368 PORTAGE	46556-46556 NOTRE DAME
46071-46071 THORNTOWN	46163-46163 NEW PALESTINE	46371-46371 ROLLING PRAIRIE	46561-46561 OSCEOLA
46072-46072 TIPTON	46164-46164 NINEVEH	46372-46372 ROSELAWN	46562-46562 PIERCETON
46074-46074 WESTFIELD	46165-46165 NORTH SALEM	46373-46373 SAINT JOHN	46563-46563 PLYMOUTH
46075-46075 WHITESTOWN	46166-46166 PARAGON	46374-46374 SAN PIERRE	46565-46565 SHIPSHEWANA
46076-46076 WINDFALL	46167-46167 PITTSBORO	46375-46375 SCHERERVILLE	46566-46566 SIDNEY
46077-46077 ZIONSVILLE	46168-46168 PLAINFIELD	46376-46376 SCHNEIDER	46567-46567 SYRACUSE
46082-46082 CARMEL	46170-46170 PUTNAMVILLE	46377-46377 SHELBY	46570-46570 TIPPECANOE
46102-46102 ADVANCE	46171-46171 REELSVILLE	46379-46379 SUMAVA RESORTS	46571-46571 TOPEKA
46103-46103 AMO	46172-46172 ROACHDALE	46380-46380 TEFFT	46572-46572 TYNER
46104-46104 ARLINGTON	46173-46173 RUSHVILLE	46381-46381 THAYER	46573-46573 WAKARUSA
46105-46105 BAINBRIDGE	46175-46175 RUSSELLVILLE	46382-46382 UNION MILLS	46574-46574 WALKERTON
46106-46106 BARGERSVILLE	46176-46176 SHELBYVILLE	46383-46385 VALPARAISO	46580-46582 WARSAW
46107-46107 BEECH GROVE	46180-46180 STILESVILLE	46390-46390 WANATAH	46590-46590 WINONA LAKE
46110-46110 BOGGSTOWN	46181-46181 TRAFALGAR	46391-46391 WESTVILLE	46595-46595 WYATT
46111-46111 BROOKLYN	46182-46182 WALDRON	46392-46392 WHEATFIELD	46600-46699 SOUTH BEND
46112-46112 BROWNSBURG	46183-46183 WEST NEWTON	46393-46393 WHEELER	46701-46701 ALBION
46113-46113 CAMBY	46184-46184 WHITELAND	46394-46394 WHITING	46702-46702 ANDREWS
46114-46114 CARTERSBURG	46186-46186 WILKINSON	46399-46399 LOWELL	46703-46703 ANGOLA
46115-46115 CARTHAGE	46187-46187 WILLOW BRANCH	46400-46404 GARY	46704-46704 ARCOLA

46705-46705 ASHLEY	46929-46929 FLORA	47043-47043 VEVAY	47272-47272 SAINT PAUL
46706-46706 AUBURN	46930-46930 FOWLERTON	47060-47060 WEST HARRISON	47273-47273 SCIPIO
46710-46710 AVILLA	46931-46931 FULTON	47102-47102 AUSTIN	47274-47274 SEYMOUR
46711-46711 BERNE	46932-46932 GALVESTON	47104-47104 BETHLEHEM	47280-47280 TAYLORSVILLE
46713-46713 BIPPUS	46933-46933 GAS CITY	47106-47106 BORDEN	47281-47281 VALLONIA
46714-46714 BLUFFTON	46935-46935 GRASS CREEK	47107-47107 BRADFORD	47282-47282 VERNON
46720-46720 BRIMFIELD	46936-46936 GREENTOWN	47108-47108 CAMPBELLSBURG	47283-47283 WESTPORT
46721-46721 BUTLER	46937-46937 HEMLOCK	47110-47110 CENTRAL	47302-47308 MUNCIE
46723-46723 CHURUBUSCO	46938-46938 JONESBORO	47111-47111 CHARLESTOWN	47320-47320 ALBANY
46725-46725 COLUMBIA CITY	46939-46939 KEWANNA	47112-47112 CORYDON	47322-47322 BENTONVILLE
46730-46730 CORUNNA	46940-46940 LA FONTAINE	47114-47114 CRANDALL	47324-47324 BOSTON
46731-46731 CRAIGVILLE	46941-46941 LAGRO	47115-47115 DEPAUW	47325-47325 BROWNSVILLE
46732-46732 CROMWELL	46942-46942 LAKE CICOTT	47116-47116 ECKERTY	47326-47326 BRYANT
46733-46733 DECATUR	46943-46943 LAKETON	47117-47117 ELIZABETH	47327-47327 CAMBRIDGE CITY
46737-46737 FREMONT	46944-46944 LANDESS	47118-47118 ENGLISH	47330-47330 CENTERVILLE
46738-46738 GARRETT	46945-46945 LEITERS FORD	47119-47119 FLOYDS KNOBS	47331-47331 CONNERSVILLE
46740-46740 GENEVA	46946-46946 LIBERTY MILLS	47120-47120 FREDERICKSBURG	47334-47334 DALEVILLE
46741-46741 GRABILL	46947-46947 LOGANSPORT	47122-47122 GEORGETOWN	47335-47335 DUBLIN
46742-46742 HAMILTON	46950-46950 LUCERNE	47123-47123 GRANTSBURG	47336-47336 DUNKIRK
46743-46743 HARLAN	46951-46951 MACY	47124-47124 GREENVILLE	47337-47337 DUNREITH
46744-46744 OSSIAN	46952-46953 MARION	47125-47125 HARDINSBURG	47338-47338 EATON
46745-46745 HOAGLAND	46957-46957 MATTHEWS	47126-47126 HENRYVILLE	47339-47339 ECONOMY
46746-46746 HOWE	46958-46958 MEXICO	47129-47129 CLARKSVILLE	47340-47340 FARMLAND
46747-46747 HUDSON	46959-46959 MIAMI	47130-47134 JEFFERSONVILLE	47341-47341 FOUNTAIN CITY
46748-46748 HUNTERTOWN	46960-46960 MONTEREY	47135-47135 LACONIA	47342-47342 GASTON
46750-46750 HUNTINGTON	46961-46961 NEW WAVERLY	47136-47136 LANESVILLE	47344-47344 GREENSBORO
46755-46755 KENDALLVILLE	46962-46962 NORTH MANCHESTER	47137-47137 LEAVENWORTH	47345-47345 GREENS FORK
46759-46759 KEYSTONE	46965-46965 OAKFORD	47138-47138 LEXINGTON	47346-47346 HAGERSTOWN
46760-46760 KIMMELL	46967-46967 ONWARD	47139-47139 LITTLE YORK	47348-47348 HARTFORD CITY
46761-46761 LAGRANGE	46968-46968 ORA	47140-47140 MARENGO	47351-47351 KENNARD
46763-46763 LAOTTO	46970-46970 PERU	47141-47141 MARYSVILLE	47352-47352 LEWISVILLE
46764-46764 LARWILL	46971-46971 GRISSOM AFB	47142-47142 MAUCKPORT	47353-47353 LIBERTY
46765-46765 LEO	46971-46971 GRISSOM ARB	47143-47143 MEMPHIS	47354-47354 LOSANTVILLE
46766-46766 LIBERTY CENTER	46974-46974 ROANN	47144-47144 JEFFERSONVILLE	47355-47355 LYNN
46767-46767 LIGONIER	46975-46975 ROCHESTER	47145-47145 MILLTOWN	47356-47356 MIDDLETOWN
46769-46769 LINN GROVE	46977-46977 ROCKFIELD	47146-47146 MOUNT SAINT FRANCIS	47357-47357 MILTON
46770-46770 MARKLE	46978-46978 ROYAL CENTER	47147-47147 NABB	47358-47358 MODOC
46771-46771 MONGO	46979-46979 RUSSIAVILLE	47150-47151 NEW ALBANY	47359-47359 MONTPELIER
46772-46772 MONROE	46980-46980 SERVIA	47160-47160 NEW MIDDLETOWN	47360-47360 MOORELAND
46773-46773 MONROEVILLE	46982-46982 SILVER LAKE	47161-47161 NEW SALISBURY	47361-47361 MOUNT SUMMIT
46774-46774 NEW HAVEN	46983-46983 SIMS	47162-47162 NEW WASHINGTON	47362-47362 NEW CASTLE
46776-46776 ORLAND	46984-46984 SOMERSET	47163-47163 OTISCO	47366-47366 NEW LISBON
46777-46777 OSSIAN	46985-46985 STAR CITY	47164-47164 PALMYRA	47367-47367 OAKVILLE
46778-46778 PETROLEUM	46986-46986 SWAYZEE	47165-47165 PEKIN	47368-47368 PARKER CITY
46779-46779 PLEASANT LAKE	46987-46987 SWEETSER	47166-47166 RAMSEY	47369-47369 PENNVILLE
46780-46780 PLEASANT MILLS	46988-46988 TWELVE MILE	47167-47167 SALEM	47370-47370 PERSHING
46781-46781 PONETO	46989-46989 UPLAND	47170-47170 SCOTTSBURG	47371-47371 PORTLAND
46782-46782 PREBLE	46990-46990 URBANA	47172-47172 SELLERSBURG	47373-47373 REDKEY
46783-46783 ROANOKE	46991-46991 VAN BUREN	47174-47174 SULPHUR	47374-47375 RICHMOND
46784-46784 ROME CITY	46992-46992 WABASH	47175-47175 TASWELL	47380-47380 RIDGEVILLE
46785-46785 SAINT JOE	46994-46994 WALTON	47177-47177 UNDERWOOD	47381-47381 SALAMONIA
46786-46786 SOUTH MILFORD	46995-46995 WEST MIDDLETON	47199-47199 JEFFERSONVILLE	47382-47382 SARATOGA
46787-46787 SOUTH WHITLEY	46996-46996 WINAMAC	47201-47203 COLUMBUS	47383-47383 SELMA
46788-46788 SPENCERVILLE	46998-46998 YOUNG AMERICA	47220-47220 BROWNSTOWN	47384-47384 SHIRLEY
46789-46789 STROH	47001-47001 AURORA	47222-47222 BURNEY	47385-47385 SPICELAND
46790-46790 OSSIAN	47003-47003 WEST COLLEGE CORNER	47223-47223 BUTLERVILLE	47386-47386 SPRINGPORT
46791-46791 UNIONDALE	47006-47006 BATESVILLE	47224-47224 CANAAN	47387-47387 STRAUGHN
46792-46792 WARREN	47010-47010 BATH	47225-47225 CLARKSBURG	47388-47388 SULPHUR SPRINGS
46793-46793 WATERLOO	47011-47011 BENNINGTON	47226-47226 CLIFFORD	47390-47390 UNION CITY
46794-46794 WAWAKA	47012-47012 BROOKVILLE	47227-47227 COMMISKEY	47392-47392 WEBSTER
46795-46795 WOLCOTTVILLE	47016-47016 CEDAR GROVE	47228-47228 CORTLAND	47393-47393 WILLIAMSBURG
46796-46796 WOLFLAKE	47017-47017 CROSS PLAINS	47229-47229 CROTHERSVILLE	47394-47394 WINCHESTER
46797-46797 WOODBURN	47018-47018 DILLSBORO	47230-47230 DEPUTY	47396-47396 YORKTOWN
46798-46798 YODER	47019-47019 EAST ENTERPRISE	47231-47231 DUPONT	47401-47408 BLOOMINGTON
46799-46799 ZANESVILLE	47020-47020 FLORENCE	47232-47232 ELIZABETHTOWN	47420-47420 AVOCA
46800-46899 FORT WAYNE	47021-47021 FRIENDSHIP	47234-47234 FLAT ROCK	47421-47421 BEDFORD
46901-46904 KOKOMO	47022-47022 GUILFORD	47235-47235 FREETOWN	47424-47424 BLOOMFIELD
46910-46910 AKRON	47023-47023 HOLTON	47236-47236 GRAMMER	47426-47426 CLEAR CREEK
46911-46911 AMBOY	47024-47024 LAUREL	47240-47240 GREENSBURG	47427-47427 COAL CITY
46912-46912 ATHENS	47025-47025 LAWRENCEBURG	47243-47243 HANOVER	47429-47429 ELLETTSVILLE
46913-46913 BRINGHURST	47030-47030 METAMORA	47244-47244 HARTSVILLE	47430-47430 FORT RITNER
46914-46914 BUNKER HILL	47031-47031 MILAN	47245-47245 HAYDEN	47431-47431 FREEDOM
46915-46915 BURLINGTON	47032-47032 MOORES HILL	47246-47246 HOPE	47432-47432 FRENCH LICK
46916-46916 BURROWS	47033-47033 MORRIS	47247-47247 JONESVILLE	47433-47433 GOSPORT
46917-46917 CAMDEN	47034-47034 NAPOLEON	47249-47249 KURTZ	47434-47434 HARRODSBURG
46919-46919 CONVERSE	47035-47035 NEW TRENTON	47250-47250 MADISON	47435-47435 HELMSBURG
46920-46920 CUTLER	47036-47036 OLDENBURG	47260-47260 MEDORA	47436-47436 HELTONVILLE
46921-46921 DEEDSVILLE	47037-47037 OSGOOD	47261-47261 MILLHOUSEN	47437-47437 HURON
46922-46922 DELONG	47038-47038 PATRIOT	47262-47262 NEBRASKA	47438-47438 JASONVILLE
46923-46923 DELPHI	47039-47039 PIERCEVILLE	47263-47263 NEW POINT	47439-47439 KOLEEN
46925-46925 DENHAM	47040-47040 RISING SUN	47264-47264 NORMAN	47441-47441 LINTON
46926-46926 DENVER	47041-47041 SUNMAN	47265-47265 NORTH VERNON	47443-47443 LYONS
46928-46928 FAIRMOUNT	47042-47042 VERSAILLES	47270-47270 PARIS CROSSING	47445-47445 MIDLAND

47446-47446	MITCHELL
47448-47448	NASHVILLE
47449-47449	NEWBERRY
47451-47451	OOLITIC
47452-47452	ORLEANS
47453-47453	OWENSBURG
47454-47454	PAOLI
47455-47455	PATRICKSBURG
47456-47456	QUINCY
47457-47457	SCOTLAND
47458-47458	SMITHVILLE
47459-47459	SOLSBERRY
47460-47460	SPENCER
47462-47462	SPRINGVILLE
47463-47463	STANFORD
47464-47464	STINESVILLE
47465-47465	SWITZ CITY
47467-47467	TUNNELTON
47468-47468	UNIONVILLE
47469-47469	WEST BADEN SPRINGS
47470-47470	WILLIAMS
47471-47471	WORTHINGTON
47490-47490	BLOOMINGTON
47501-47501	WASHINGTON
47512-47512	BICKNELL
47513-47513	BIRDSEYE
47514-47514	BRANCHVILLE
47515-47515	BRISTOW
47516-47516	BRUCEVILLE
47519-47519	CANNELBURG
47520-47520	CANNELTON
47521-47521	CELESTINE
47522-47522	CRANE
47523-47523	DALE
47524-47524	DECKER
47525-47525	DERBY
47527-47527	DUBOIS
47528-47528	EDWARDSPORT
47529-47529	ELNORA
47530-47530	EMISON
47531-47531	EVANSTON
47532-47532	FERDINAND
47535-47535	FREELANDVILLE
47536-47536	FULDA
47537-47537	GENTRYVILLE
47541-47541	HOLLAND
47542-47542	HUNTINGBURG
47545-47545	IRELAND
47546-47549	JASPER
47550-47550	LAMAR
47551-47551	LEOPOLD
47552-47552	LINCOLN CITY
47553-47553	LOOGOOTEE
47555-47555	MAGNET
47556-47556	MARIAH HILL
47557-47557	MONROE CITY
47558-47558	MONTGOMERY
47559-47559	MOUNT PLEASANT
47561-47561	OAKTOWN
47562-47562	ODON
47564-47564	OTWELL
47567-47567	PETERSBURG
47568-47568	PLAINVILLE
47573-47573	RAGSDALE
47574-47574	ROME
47575-47575	SAINT ANTHONY
47576-47576	SAINT CROIX
47577-47577	SAINT MEINRAD
47578-47578	SANDBORN
47579-47579	SANTA CLAUS
47580-47580	SCHNELLVILLE
47581-47581	SHOALS
47584-47584	SPURGEON
47585-47585	STENDAL
47586-47586	TELL CITY
47587-47587	TOBINSPORT
47588-47588	TROY
47590-47590	VELPEN
47591-47591	VINCENNES
47596-47596	WESTPHALIA
47597-47597	WHEATLAND
47598-47598	WINSLOW
47601-47601	BOONVILLE
47610-47610	CHANDLER
47611-47611	CHRISNEY
47612-47612	CYNTHIANA
47613-47613	ELBERFELD
47614-47614	FOLSOMVILLE
47615-47615	GRANDVIEW
47616-47616	GRIFFIN
47617-47617	HATFIELD
47618-47618	INGLEFIELD
47619-47619	LYNNVILLE
47620-47620	MOUNT VERNON
47629-47630	NEWBURGH
47631-47631	NEW HARMONY
47633-47633	POSEYVILLE
47634-47634	RICHLAND
47635-47635	ROCKPORT
47637-47637	TENNYSON
47638-47638	WADESVILLE
47639-47639	HAUBSTADT
47640-47640	HAZLETON
47647-47647	BUCKSKIN
47648-47648	FORT BRANCH
47649-47649	FRANCISCO
47654-47654	MACKEY
47660-47660	OAKLAND CITY
47665-47665	OWENSVILLE
47666-47666	PATOKA
47670-47671	PRINCETON
47683-47683	SOMERVILLE
47700-47750	EVANSVILLE
47801-47814	TERRE HAUTE
47830-47830	BELLMORE
47831-47831	BLANFORD
47832-47832	BLOOMINGDALE
47833-47833	BOWLING GREEN
47834-47834	BRAZIL
47836-47836	BRIDGETON
47837-47837	CARBON
47838-47838	CARLISLE
47840-47840	CENTERPOINT
47841-47841	CLAY CITY
47842-47842	CLINTON
47845-47845	COALMONT
47846-47846	CORY
47847-47847	DANA
47848-47848	DUGGER
47849-47849	FAIRBANKS
47850-47850	FARMERSBURG
47851-47851	FONTANET
47852-47852	GRAYSVILLE
47853-47853	HARMONY
47854-47854	HILLSDALE
47855-47855	HYMERA
47856-47856	JUDSON
47857-47857	KNIGHTSVILLE
47858-47858	LEWIS
47859-47859	MARSHALL
47860-47860	MECCA
47861-47861	MEROM
47862-47862	MONTEZUMA
47863-47863	NEW GOSHEN
47864-47864	NEW LEBANON
47865-47865	PAXTON
47866-47866	PIMENTO
47868-47868	POLAND
47869-47869	PRAIRIE CREEK
47870-47870	PRAIRIETON
47871-47871	RILEY
47872-47872	ROCKVILLE
47874-47874	ROSEDALE
47875-47875	SAINT BERNICE
47876-47876	SAINT MARY OF THE WOODS
47877-47877	SANDFORD
47878-47878	SEELYVILLE
47879-47879	SHELBURN
47880-47880	SHEPARDSVILLE
47881-47881	STAUNTON
47882-47882	SULLIVAN
47884-47884	UNIVERSAL
47885-47885	WEST TERRE HAUTE
47901-47905	LAFAYETTE
47906-47907	WEST LAFAYETTE
47909-47909	LAFAYETTE
47916-47916	ALAMO
47917-47917	AMBIA
47918-47918	ATTICA
47920-47920	BATTLE GROUND
47921-47921	BOSWELL
47922-47922	BROOK
47923-47923	BROOKSTON
47924-47924	BUCK CREEK
47925-47925	BUFFALO
47926-47926	BURNETTSVILLE
47928-47928	CAYUGA
47929-47929	CHALMERS
47930-47930	CLARKS HILL
47931-47931	COLBURN
47932-47932	COVINGTON
47933-47939	CRAWFORDSVILLE
47940-47940	DARLINGTON
47941-47941	DAYTON
47942-47942	EARL PARK
47943-47943	FAIR OAKS
47944-47944	FOWLER
47946-47946	FRANCESVILLE
47948-47948	GOODLAND
47949-47949	HILLSBORO
47950-47950	IDAVILLE
47951-47951	KENTLAND
47952-47952	KINGMAN
47954-47954	LADOGA
47955-47955	LINDEN
47957-47957	MEDARYVILLE
47958-47958	MELLOTT
47959-47959	MONON
47960-47960	MONTICELLO
47962-47962	MONTMORENCI
47963-47963	MOROCCO
47964-47964	MOUNT AYR
47965-47965	NEW MARKET
47966-47966	NEWPORT
47967-47967	NEW RICHMOND
47968-47968	NEW ROSS
47969-47969	NEWTOWN
47970-47970	OTTERBEIN
47971-47971	OXFORD
47973-47973	PENCE
47974-47974	PERRYSVILLE
47975-47975	PINE VILLAGE
47976-47976	EARL PARK
47977-47977	REMINGTON
47978-47978	RENSSELAER
47980-47980	REYNOLDS
47981-47981	ROMNEY
47982-47982	STATE LINE
47983-47983	STOCKWELL
47984-47984	TALBOT
47985-47985	TANGIER
47986-47986	TEMPLETON
47987-47987	VEEDERSBURG
47988-47988	WALLACE
47989-47989	WAVELAND
47990-47990	WAYNETOWN
47991-47991	WEST LEBANON
47992-47992	WESTPOINT
47993-47993	WILLIAMSPORT
47994-47994	WINGATE
47995-47995	WOLCOTT
47996-47996	WEST LAFAYETTE
47997-47997	YEOMAN

County-Town
INDIANA

COUNTIES

(92 Counties)

CITIES AND TOWNS

Note: The first name is that of the city or town, second, that of the county in which it is located, then the population and location on the map.

Explanation of symbols: • – Census Designated Place (CDP)

General Help Numbers:

Governor's Office
State Capitol Bldg
Des Moines, IA 50319
www.governor.state.ia.us/

515-281-5211
Fax 515-281-6611
8AM-4:30PM

Attorney General's Office
Hoover Bldg
1305 E Walnut St
Des Moines, IA 50319
www.state.ia.us/government/ag

515-281-5164
Fax 515-281-4209
8AM-4:30PM

Legislative Records
Legislative Information Office
State Capitol
Des Moines, IA 50319
www.legis.state.ia.us

515-281-5129

8AM-4:30PM

State Archives
Library/Archives
600 E. Locust
Des Moines, IA 50319-0290
www.iowahistory.org

515-281-5111
Fax 515-282-0502
9AM-4:30PM TU-SA
& M (June-Aug)

State Specifics:

Capital:	Des Moines Polk County
Time Zone:	CST
Number of Counties:	99
Population:	2,944,062
Web Site:	www.iowa.gov/state/main/index.html

State Agencies

Criminal Records

Division of Criminal Investigations, Bureau of Identification, Wallace State Office Bldg, 502 E. 9th, Des Moines, IA 50319-0041; 515-281-4776, 515-242-6876 (Fax), 8AM-4:30PM.

www.state.ia.us/government/dps/dci/crimhist.htm

Note: Ongoing requesters can order records via e-mail.

Indexing & Storage: Records are available until the person is 80 years old or passes away, then records are deleted. There is a computerized index

going back to 1935. It takes up to 10 days before new records are available for inquiry. Records are indexed on in house computer (100%). Records are normally destroyed after 4 years if there is no disposition.

Searching: A signed release or waiver is not required, nor are fingerprints. But if release (Form A) is included, the reports will show any arrest over 18 months old without a disposition, otherwise if no release is presented then only up to 18 months. Include the following in your request-date of birth, sex. The Social Security Number and

middle name are helpful. A signed release is an option. Be sure to give the full name. Request Form A is required for each surname. This form can be obtained from the website, by fax, mail, or in person.

Access by: mail, fax, in person.

Fee & Payment: The fee for a record search is $13.00 per surname checked. If married and maiden names are checked, the fee would be $26.00. Iowa law requires employers to pay the fee for potential employees' record checks. Fee payee: Iowa Division of Criminal Investigation. Payment is required unless pre-arranged billing has been arranged. Ongoing requesters can set up an account with a $500 deposit. Personal checks accepted. Credit cards accepted: MasterCard, Visa.

Mail search: Turnaround time: 2 to 5 days. No SASE is required.

Fax search: See expedited service.

In person search: Only the subject or their attorney will receive the record while they wait, within 15 minutes.

Other access: Although this agency does not offer online access, there is online free access to the statewide Iowa Judicial System courts database at www.judicial.state.ia.us/online_records/.

Expedited service: Expedited service is available for fax searches. Account is required, request must be prepaid or a credit card is required. Turnaround time: 1 to 3 days. Add $2.00 per record to receive back by fax.

Statewide Court Records

State Court Administrator, Judicial Branch Bldg, 111 East Court Ave, Des Moines, IA 50319; 515-281-5241, 515-242-0014 (Fax), 8AM-4:30PM.

www.judicial.state.ia.us/courtadmin

Access by: online. No searching by mail.

Online search: Criminal, civil, probate, traffic and appellate information is available from all 99 counties in Iowa at www.judicial.state.ia.us/online_records/. There is no fee for basic information, and a pay system is available for more detailed requests. Name searches are available on a statewide or specific county basis. Although records are updated daily, the historical records offered are not from the same starting date on a county-by-county basis. Also, from the home page one may access supreme and apppellate court opinions.

Sexual Offender Registry

Division of Criminal Investigations, SOR Unit, Wallace State Office Bldg, Des Moines, IA 50319; 515-281-8716, 515-242-6297 (Fax), 8AM-4:30PM.

www.iowasexoffenders.com/

Note: The Iowa Sex Offender Registry became law on July 1, 1995 and is found in Chapter 692A Code of Iowa.

Indexing & Storage: Records are available from 07/01/95, if online back to 1999. It takes up to 2 days before new records are available for inquiry.

Searching: Include the following in your request- date of birth, address if known, SSN helpful. This office will not permit walk-in requesters, it is suggested to visit the local police of sheriff office.

Access by: mail, online.

Mail search: Turnaround time: 1 to 2 days. No SASE is required.

Online search: The website does not contain the entire list of sex offenders registered in Iowa. In accordance with Iowa law, only those registrants who have been assessed as "at risk" to re-offend can be listed.

Incarceration Records

Iowa Department of Corrections, 420 Watson Powell Jr. Way, Des Moines, IA 50309-1639; 515-242-5710, 515-281-4062 (Second fax number), 515-281-7345 (Fax), 8AM-4:30PM.

www.doc.state.ia.us

Indexing & Storage: Records are available on current and former inmates. It takes up to 10 days before new records are available for inquiry. Records are normally destroyed after Never.

Searching: Computer records go back to 1986. Include the following in your request-full name and DOB or SSN. Location, physical identifiers, county of conviction, and conviction information details are released. Deeper records - sentencing information - are also available; please include details of reason for request. The following data is not released: medical or home address data.

Access by: mail, phone, online.

Fee & Payment: Search fee is $12.00 per hour plus postage fee. Copy fee is $.20 per page. Fee payee: Treasurer, State of Iowa, Dept. of Corrections. Prepayment required. Personal checks accepted. No credit cards accepted.

Mail search: Turnaround time: 1 to 10 days. Turnaround time on archived records is significantly longer. No SASE is required.

Phone search: Name searching for basic information is available by phone.

Online search: Click on Public Info for an inmate search. This site seems to be under construction at times.

Other access: Bulk records are not available, but should be in the future.

Corporation, Limited Liability Company, Fictitious Name, Limited Partnership Trademarks/Servicemarks

Secretary of State - Corporation Division, 321 E 12th Street, 1st Floor, Lucas Bldg, Des Moines, IA 50319; 515-281-5204, 515-242-5953 (Fax), 8AM-4:30PM.

www.sos.state.ia.us

Indexing & Storage: Records are available from the late 1800s. New records are available for inquiry immediately. Records are indexed on microfilm, inhouse computer, on-line.

Searching: Include the following in your request- full name of business or filing number, specific records that you need copies of. In addition to the articles of incorporation, the following information is released: Annual/Biennial Reports, Officers, Directors, DBAs, Prior (merged) names, Inactive and Reserved names.

Access by: mail, phone, fax, in person, online.

Fee & Payment: Copies are $1.00 each, certificataion is $5.00. Fee payee: Secretary of State. Prepayment required. A charge account may be established for ongoing requesters. Call 515-281-5204 for more details. Personal checks accepted. Credit cards accepted: MasterCard, Visa.

Mail search: Turnaround time: 2 to 3 days. A SASE is requested. No fee for mail request.

Phone search: No fee for telephone request. You are restricted to 3 requests per call.

Fax search: Add $1.00 for each page that is faxed. Turnaround time is 2 days.

In person search: No fee for request.

Online search: For free searching, go to www.sos.state.ia.us/corp/corp_search.asp.

Other access: This agency will sell the records in database format. Call the number listed above and ask for Karen Ubaldo for more information.

Uniform Commercial Code, Federal Tax Liens

UCC Division, Secretary of State, 1st Floor, Lucas Bldg, Des Moines, IA 50319; 515-281-5204, 515-242-5953 (Other Fax Line), 515-242-6556 (Fax), 8AM-4:30PM.

www.sos.state.ia.us

Indexing & Storage: Records are available from 1966 and are computerized. All current records are on optical disk. It takes 1 to 3 days before new records are available for inquiry.

Searching: Use search request form UCC-11. Specify if you also want federal tax liens and include another search fee. Federal tax liens on individuals and all state tax liens are filed at the county level. Include the following in your request-debtor name or filing number. Copies of filings may be requested at time of search, but do not ask for copies with your initial request unless you have a charge account.

Access by: mail, phone, fax, in person, online.

Fee & Payment: The fee is $5.00 per debtor name, $6.00 for federal liens. Copies are $1.00 per page. Fee payee: Secretary of State. Prepayment required. Personal checks accepted. Credit cards accepted: MasterCard, Visa.

Mail search: Turnaround time: 1 to 2 days. A SASE is requested.

Phone search: A telephone search is available with a prepaid or charge account, or with credit card.

Fax search: Turnaround time usually same day, fee is $1.00 per page.

In person search: Simple requests may be processed while you wait.

Online search: All computerized information on or before June 30, 2001 is available online at www.sos.state.ia.us/Ucc_Search/UccOld_Search.html. There is no fee at this "UCC Archive" site. For computerized records online from July 1, 2001 to present, search at www.sos.state.ia.us/UCC_Search/UCC_Search.asp.

State Tax Liens

Records not maintained by a state level agency.

Note: Records are found at the county recorder's offices.

Sales Tax Registrations

Department of Revenue, Taxpayer Services Division, Hoover State Office Bldg, Des Moines, IA 50306-0465; 515-281-3114, 515-242-6487 (Fax), 8AM-4PM.

www.state.ia.us/tax

Indexing & Storage: Records are available for 3 years. Records are indexed on computer, microfiche. Records are normally destroyed after 3 years.

Searching: This agency will provide any information found on the face of the Tax Permit- business name, business address, and tax permit number. Information not released includes telephone numbers, tax liabilities, taxes collected, officers, federal ID#s, etc. Include the following in your request-business name. They will also search by tax permit number. Requests are accepted by email at idrf@idrf.state.ia.us.

Access by: mail, phone, fax, email.

Fee & Payment: There is no search fee; however, there is a $5.00 copy fee per document. Fee payee: Treasurer State of Iowa. Prepayment required. Personal checks accepted. No credit cards accepted.

Mail search: Turnaround time: 14 to 21 days. No SASE is required.

Phone search: Limited information is available by phone.

Fax search: Records are available by fax.

Other access: The agency will provide the database on lists, fees vary from $20.00 to $45.00.

Birth Certificates

Iowa Department of Public Health, Bureau of Vital Records, 321 E 12th St, Lucas Bldg, Des Moines, IA 50319-0075; 515-281-4944, 515-281-5871 (Message Recording), 7AM-4:45PM.

www.idph.state.ia.us

Note: All vital records are open for inspection at the county level, usually for a $10.00 fee.

Indexing & Storage: Records are available from 1880 to present. It takes 30 days to 6 weeks before new records are available for inquiry. Records are indexed on microfiche, inhouse computer.

Searching: Adoption records are not released. Include the following in your request-full name, names of parents, mother's maiden name, date of birth, place of birth, relationship to person of record, reason for information request. Must have copy of a photo ID (mail) or a photo ID (in person) to search.

Access by: mail, phone, in person.

Fee & Payment: The search fee is $10.00. There is an additional $5.50 fee to use a credit card. For records 1880 to 1915, a $10.00 per year fee is charged. The agency may raise fees in 2005 to $15.00 per record. Fee payee: Iowa Department of Public Health. Prepayment required. Personal checks accepted. Credit cards accepted: MasterCard, Visa, AmEx, Discover.

Mail search: Turnaround time: within 1 month.

Phone search: Records are available by phone with use of credit card.

In person search: Same day service is not available. Turnaround time is 48 hours.

Expedited service: Expedited mail service is available for phone searches. Add $11.00 per package for faster shipping. Must use a credit card which is an extra $5.50. Normal turnaround time is 10-14 days.

Death Records

Iowa Department of Public Health, Vital Records, 321 E 12th St, Lucas Bldg, Des Moines, IA 50319-0075; 515-281-4944, 515-281-5871 (Message Recording), 7AM-4:45PM.

www.idph.state.ia.us

Indexing & Storage: Records are available from 1880 to present. From 1880 to 1895 there is no index. It takes up to 60 days before new records

are available for inquiry. Records are indexed on microfiche, inhouse computer.

Searching: Include the following in your request-full name, date of death, place of death, relationship to person of record, reason for information request. Must have a copy of a photo ID (mail) or a photo ID (in person) to search.

Access by: mail, phone, in person.

Fee & Payment: The search fee is $10.00 for each index searched. There is an additional $5.50 fee when using a credit card. The agency may raise fees in 2005 to $15.00 per record. Fee payee: Iowa Department of Public Health. Prepayment required. Personal checks accepted. Credit cards accepted: MasterCard, Visa, AmEx, Discover.

Mail search: Turnaround time: within 1 month.

Phone search: Record requests are available by phone with use of credit card.

In person search: Same day service in not available. Turnaround time is 48 hours.

Expedited service: Expedited mail service is available phone searches. Add fee for express delivery. Also, be sure to include the extra credit card fee. Turnaround time is 7-10 days.

Marriage Certificates

Iowa Department of Public Health, Vital Records, 321 E 12th St, Lucas Bldg, Des Moines, IA 50319-0075; 515-281-4944, 515-281-5871 (Message Recording), 7AM-4:45PM.

www.idph.state.ia.us

Indexing & Storage: Records are available from 1880. Records from 1880 to 1915 have to be searched by year. 1916 forward are indexed. It takes up to 1 week before new records are available for inquiry. Records are indexed on microfiche, inhouse computer.

Searching: Include the following in your request-names of husband and wife, date of marriage, place or county of marriage.

Access by: mail, phone, in person.

Fee & Payment: The search fee is $10.00 per index searched. There is an additional $5.50 fee when using a credit card. The agency may raise fees in 2005 to $15.00 per record. Fee payee: Iowa Department of Public Health. Prepayment required. Personal checks accepted. Credit cards accepted: MasterCard, Visa, AmEx, Discover.

Mail search: Turnaround time: within 1 month.

Phone search: Record requests are available by phone with use of credit card.

In person search: Same day service is not available. Turnaround time is 48 hours.

Expedited service: Expedited mail service is available for phone searches. Add fee for express delivery. Also, there is an additional $5.50 for use of credit card. Turnaround time is 7-10 days.

Divorce Records

Records not maintained by a state level agency.

Note: Divorce records are found at the county court issuing the decree. In general, records are available from 1880.

Workers' Compensation Records

Iowa Workforce Development, Division of Workers' Compensation, 1000 E Grand Ave, Des Moines, IA 50319; 515-281-5387, 515-281-6501 (Fax), 8AM-4:30PM.

www.iowaworkforce.org/wc

Note: Regular, ongoing requesters may apply for charge accounts.

Indexing & Storage: Records are available from 1985 to present. It takes 2 weeks before new records are available for inquiry.

Searching: Include the following in your request-claimant name, Social Security Number, place of employment at time of accident. Older records may take as long as 6 weeks to research.

Access by: mail, fax, in person.

Fee & Payment: The search fee is $20.00 per hour, with a $5.00 minimum. Photo copies are $.50 per page, fax copies $.75 per page. Fee payee: Workers' Compensation. Prepayment required. Personal checks accepted. No credit cards accepted.

Mail search: Turnaround time: 3 to 5 days. A SASE is requested.

Fax search: Response to fax requests is made by mail.

In person search: Files are available for personal viewing only if requested in advance.

Other access: This agency sells its entire database or can sell data transmissions of pages ($.045 per page).

Driver Records

Department of Transportation, Driver Service Records Section, PO Box 9204, Des Moines, IA 50306-9204 (Courier: Park Fair Mall, 100 Euclid, Des Moines, IA 50306); 515-244-9124, 800-532-1121 (Iowa only), 515-237-3152 (Fax), 8AM-4:30PM.

www.dot.state.ia.us/mvd

Note: Copies of tickets can be requested from this address for $.50 per copy.

Indexing & Storage: Records are available for 5 to 7 years for moving violations; 12 years for DWIs; 3 to 7 years after closed for suspensions. The driver's address is shown on the record. Accidents are listed, but fault is not shown. It takes 2 to 3 days before new records are available for inquiry. Records are normally destroyed after 5 years.

Searching: Casual requesters receive records without personal information, unless written consent of the subject is presented. Include the following in your request-full name, driver's license number, date of birth. Will not expedite requests. County sheriffs in Iowa are authorized to furnish copies of driving records, but not all do.

Access by: mail, fax, in person, online.

Fee & Payment: The fee for certified mail-in or walk-in requests is $5.50 per record. Electronic records are $8.50 each. There is no charge for a no record found. Fee payee: Treasurer, State of Iowa. Prepayment required. Personal checks accepted. No credit cards accepted.

Mail search: Turnaround time: 5 to 10 days. An account can be established for on-going requesters. No SASE is required.

Fax search: Pre-approved accounts may be able to fax to IowaAccess, but not to this agency.

In person search: The public access terminal is no longer available. Records must be ordered from personnel.

Online search: The state requires that all ongoing requesters/users access records via IowaAccess. The fee is $8.50 per record, the service is interactive or batch. Requesters must be approved and open an account. The records contain personal information, so requesters must comply with DPPA. For more information, contact IowaAccess at 515-323-3468 or 866-492-3468.

Vehicle Ownership, Vehicle Identification

Department of Transportation, Office of Vehicle Services, PO Box 9278, Des Moines, IA 50306-9278 (Courier: Park Fair Mall, 100 Euclid, Des Moines, IA 50306); 515-237-3148, 515-237-3049, 515-237-3181 (Fax), 8AM-4:30PM.

www.dot.state.ia.us/mvd/

Note: Vehicle lien information is not maintained by this department.

Indexing & Storage: Records are available for 7 years for titile; for 3 years for registration. It takes 30 days before new records are available for inquiry. Records are normally destroyed after 7 years.

Searching: Vehicle registration information is released to casual requesters, but personal information is not given without written consent of the subject. The state is in compliance with DPPA. Records may be accessed by VIN, name, title no. and plate - subject to DPPA and Iowa Code 321.11.

Access by: mail, fax, in person, online.

Fee & Payment: Fees: $.50 per certified record. Computer printout is $1.00. Record search-$2.70 per quarter hour or fraction thereof. Fee payee: Iowa Department of Transportation. Prepayment required. Personal checks accepted. No credit cards accepted.

Mail search: Turnaround time: within 14 days. No SASE is required.

Fax search: Fax searching available.

In person search: You may request information in person, but results may still be mailed, depending on workload.

Online search: Online access is available to dealers, Iowa licensed investigators and security companies. There is no fee. All accounts must register and be pre-approved. Write to the Office of Motor Vehicle, explaining purpose/use of records.

Other access: Iowa makes the entire vehicle file or selected data available for purchase. Weekly updates are also available for those purchasers. Requesters subject to DPPA reuqirements. For more information, call 515-237-3110.

Accident Reports

Department of Transportation, Office of Driver Services, Park Fair Mall, 100 Euclid, Des Moines, IA 50306; 515-244-9124, 800-532-1121, 515-239-1837 (Fax), 8AM-4:30PM.

www.dot.state.ia.us/mvd/ods/index.htm

Indexing & Storage: Records are available for five years. It takes three days before new records are available for inquiry. Records are normally destroyed after 5 years.

Searching: Accident reports are available only to the person involved in accident or the person's insurance company or attorney. Will not expedite requests.

Include the following in your request-full name, date of accident, location of accident.

Access by: mail, fax, in person.

Fee & Payment: The fee is $4.00 per officer report. Fee payee: Treasurer, State of Iowa. Prepayment required. The state allows regular, ongoing requesters to open a deposit account. Personal checks accepted. No credit cards accepted.

Mail search: Turnaround time: 2 to 3 weeks. No SASE is required.

Fax search: Same criteria as mail searches.

In person search: Turnaround time for walk-in requesters is generally immediate.

Vessel Ownership, Vessel Registration

Records not maintained by a state level agency.

Note: Vessels are registered at the county level.

Voter Registration

Secretary of State, Voter Registration Division, Lucas State Office Building, 1st Fl, Des Moines, IA 50319; 515-281-5781, 515-242-5953 (Fax), 8AM-4:30PM.

www.sos.state.ia.us

Indexing & Storage: Records are available for active records and two elections back for inactive. It takes two weeks before new records are available for inquiry.

Searching: E-mail requests to sos@sos.state.ia.us. The following data is not released: Social Security Numbers or bulk information or lists for commercial purposes.

Access by: phone, fax, in person.

Fee & Payment: There is no fee for confirmation. No searching by mail.

Phone search: Will only confirm.

Fax search: Fax requests are accepted if request list is short.

In person search: Records may be viewed.

Other access: Information is available on cartridge, disk or CD for political purposes only. Data can be sorted by any field on the registration file. Fees are determined by cost of production.

GED Certificates

Department of Education, GED Records, Grimes State Office Building, Des Moines, IA 50319-0146; 515-281-7308, 515-281-3636, 515-281-6544 (Fax), 8AM-5PM.

Indexing & Storage: It takes 1 month before new records are available for inquiry.

Searching: Include the following in your request-Social Security Number, date of birth. A signed release form is required for a copy of a diploma or transcript. The year and city of test are also helpful.

Access by: mail, phone, fax, in person.

Fee & Payment: There is a $5.00 fee for a copy of a transcript or a diploma, $3.00 for a second copy. There is no fee for a verification. Fee payee: IA Department of Education. Prepayment required. Money orders are accepted. No personal checks accepted. No credit cards accepted.

Mail search: Turnaround time: 1 to 3 days. A SASE is requested.

Phone search: Limited information is available.

Fax search: They will return verification data by fax to local or toll-free numbers.

In person search: Limited information given across-the-counter.

Other access: There are several different statewide GED databases available.

Hunting and Fishing License Information

Department of Natural Resources, Wallace Building, 502 E 9th Street, Des Moines, IA 50319-0034; 515-281-8688, 515-281-6794 (Fax), 8AM-4PM.

www.state.ia.us

Indexing & Storage: Records are available for current year on computer, past years on microfiche. It takes six months before new records are available for inquiry. Records are indexed on inhouse computer. Records are normally destroyed after 3 years.

Searching: Include the following in your request-full name, date of birth, Social Security Number. This agency only maintains records for deer (except bow & free landowners) and turkey.

Access by: mail, phone, fax, in person.

Fee & Payment: There is no charge for a search of one record for personal use. Lists will incur a fee based on length and how search must be done. Fee payee: Iowa Department of Natural Resources. Personal checks accepted. No credit cards accepted.

Mail search: Turnaround time: 7 days. No SASE is required.

Phone search: You may call for information.

Fax search: Fax requests accepted with signature of the requester.

In person search: You may request information in person.

Other access: Bulk data is released on CD.

Iowa State Licensing Agencies

Licenses Searchable Online

Acupuncturist #14 .... www.docboard.org/ia/df/iasearch.htm
Anesthesiologist #14 .... www.docboard.org/ia/df/iasearch.htm
Architect #10 .... www.state.ia.us/government/com/prof/search/index.html
Bank #4 .... www.idob.state.ia.us
Credit Union #6 .... www.iacudiv.state.ia.us/Public/fieldofmembership/membersearch.htm
Debt Management Company #4 .... www.idob.state.ia.us/license/lic_default.htm
Delayed Deposit Service Business #4 .... www.idob.state.ia.us/license/lic_default.htm
Doctor #14 .... www.docboard.org/ia/df/iasearch.htm
Engineer #10 .... www.state.ia.us/government/com/prof/search/index.html
Excursion Gambling Boat #19 .... http://www3.state.ia.us/irgc/
Finance Company #4 .... www.idob.state.ia.us/license/lic_default.htm
Hypnotist #14 .... www.docboard.org/ia/df/iasearch.htm
Landscape Architect #10 .... www.state.ia.us/government/com/prof/search/index.html
Lobbyist #8 .... www.legis.state.ia.us/Lobbyist.html
Medical Doctor #14 .... www.docboard.org/ia/df/iasearch.htm
Money Transmitter #4 .... www.idob.state.ia.us/license/lic_default.htm
Mortgage Banker/Broker/Loan Service #4 .... www.idob.state.ia.us/license/lic_default.htm
Notary Public #31 .... www.sos.state.ia.us/notaries/notary_search.asp
Nurse - Nurse, Advance Registered -LPN #15 .... www.state.ia.us/nursing/Licensure.html
Optometrist #22 .... www.arbo.org/odfinder/LicSearch.asp
Orthopedic Doctor #14 .... www.docboard.org/ia/df/iasearch.htm
Osteopathic Physician #14 .... www.docboard.org/ia/df/iasearch.htm
Pari-Mutuel Race Ttrack Enclosure #19 .... http://www3.state.ia.us/irgc/
Pediatrician #14 .... www.docboard.org/ia/df/iasearch.htm
Pesticide Dealer/Applicator #3 .... www.kellysolutions.com/ia/dealers/index.asp
Psychiatrist #14 .... www.docboard.org/ia/df/iasearch.htm
Real Estate Agent/Broker/Sales #10 .... www.state.ia.us/government/com/prof/search/index.html
Real Estate Appraiser #32 .... www.state.ia.us/government/com/prof/search/index.html
Surveyor, Land #10 .... www.state.ia.us/government/com/prof/search/index.html

Iowa Licensing Quick Finder

Acupuncturist #14 515-281-5171
Adoption Investigator #18 515-281-6220
Alcoholic Beverage Retail/Whlse./Mfg. #5
.... 515-281-7430
Amusement Ride Inspection #27 515-281-5415
Anesthesiologist #14 515-281-5171
Appraiser #10 515-281-7393
Architect #10 515-281-7393
Asbestos Abatement Contractor/Worker #27
.... 515-281-6175
Asbestos Inspector #27 515-281-6175
Asbestos Project Designer/Mgmt. Planner #27
.... 515-281-6175
Athletic Agent #31 515-281-5204
Athletic Trainer #22 515-281-4401
Attorney #30 515-281-5911
Audiologist #22 515-281-4408
Bail Enforcement Agent #25 515-281-7610
Bank #4 515-281-4014
Barber #22 515-281-4416
Boiler Inspector #27 515-281-6533
Bus Driver #34 515-237-3079
Chiropractor #22 515-281-4287
Contractor #27 515-242-5870
Controlled Substance Registrant #16 ... 515-281-5944
Cosmetologist #22 515-281-4416
Cosmetology Instructor #22 515-281-4416
Cosmetology Salon/School #22 515-281-4416
Credit Union #6 515-281-6514
Crematory #22 515-281-4287

Day Care #17 515-283-9106
Debt Management Company #4 515-281-4014
Delayed Deposit Service Business #4 .. 515-281-4014
Dental Hygienist #13 515-281-5047
Dentist #13 515-281-5047
Dietitian #22 515-281-6959
Doctor #14 515-281-5171
Drug Distributor/Whlse./Mfg. #16 515-281-5944
Electrologist #22 515-281-4416
Elevator Inspection #27 515-281-5415
Emergency Medical Technician-Paramedic #27
.... 515-281-3239
Engineer #10 515-281-4126
Esthetician #33 515-281-4031
Esthetician #22 515-281-4416
Excursion Gambling Boat #19 515-281-7352
Family Foster Care #17 515-283-9106
Finance Company #4 515-281-4014
First Response Paramedic #27 515-281-4958
Funeral Director/Home #22 515-281-4287
Group Foster Care #17 515-283-9106
Hearing Aid Dispenser/Dealer #22 515-281-6959
Hypnotist #14 515-281-5171
Instructional Schools #31 515-281-5204
Instructor, Com. College or Voc./Tech. School #12
.... 800-788-7856
Insurance Agency #7 515-281-7757
Insurance Company #7 515-281-7367
Insurance Producer #7 515-281-7757
Landfill Operator #20 515-281-5918

Landscape Architect #10 515-281-4126
Lobbyist #8 515-281-5381
Lottery Retailer #26 515-281-7900
Manicurist #33 515-281-4031
Manicurist/Nail Technician #22 515-281-4416
Marriage & Family Therapist #22 515-281-4422
Massage Therapist #22 515-281-6959
Medical Doctor #14 515-281-5171
Mental Health Counselor #22 515-281-4422
Money Transmitter #4 515-281-4014
Mortgage Banker/Broker #4 515-281-4014
Mortgage Loan Service #4 515-281-4014
Mortuary Science #22 515-281-4287
Nail Technologist #33 515-281-4031
Notary Public #31 515-281-5204
Nuclear Medicine Technologist #29 515-725-0306
Nurse #15 515-281-3255
Nurse, Advance Register'd Practice #15 ... 515-281-3255
Nurse-LPN #15 515-281-3255
Nursing Home Administrator #22 515-281-4401
Occupational Therapist/Assistant #22 . 515-281-4401
Optometrist #22 515-281-4287
Orthopedic Doctor #14 515-281-5171
Osteopathic Physician #14 515-281-5171
Pari-Mutuel Race Track Enclosure #19 ... 515-281-7352
Pediatrician #14 515-281-5171
Pesticide Dealer/Applicator #3 515-281-5601
Pesticide Private Applicator #3 515-281-4339
Pharmacist/Pharmacy Tech/Intern #16 ... 515-281-5944
Pharmacy #16 515-281-5944

Physical Therapist/Assistant #22 515-281-4401	Real Estate Appraiser #32 515-281-7393	Tattoo Artist #22 515-242-5149
Physician Assistant #22 515-242-4408	Respiratory Therapist #22 515-281-4501	Taxi Driver #34 515-237-3079
Podiatrist #22 515-242-4422	School Coach #12 800-788-7856	Teacher #12 800-788-7856
Post-Secondary School #31 515-281-5204	School Counselor #12 800-788-7856	Transient Merchant #31 515-281-5204
Private Inv./Security Guard #25 515-281-7610	School Principal/Superintendent #12 ... 800-788-7856	Travel Agency #31 515-281-5204
Psychiatrist #14 515-281-5171	Securities Agent/Broker/Dealer #7 515-281-4441	Truck Driver #34 515-237-3079
Psychologist #22 515-281-4401	Sheep Dealer #2 515-281-8601	Veterinarian #2 515-281-8617
Public Accountant-CPA #10 515-281-4126	Shorthand Reporter #30 515-725-8029	Veterinary Technician #2 515-281-8617
Radiation Therapist #29 515-281-4942	Social Worker #22 515-281-4422	Voting Booth/Equipment #1 515-281-0145
Radioactive Material #29 515-281-3478	Solid Waste Compost Facility Operator #20	Waste Water Lagoon/Treatment Operator #20
Radiographer, Medical #29 515-725-0306	 515-281-5918	 515-725-0284
Radon Measurement Specialist #29 515-281-4928	Solid Waste Incinerator Operator #20 .. 515-281-5918	Water Distribution Operator #20 515-725-0284
Radon Mitigation Specialist #29 515-281-4928	Speech Pathologist/Audiologist #22 515-281-3031	Water Treatment Operator #20 515-725-0284
Real Estate Agent/Broker/Sales #10 515-281-7393	Surveyor, Land #10 515-281-4126	Well Driller #20 515-725-0284

Iowa Licensing Agency Information

1 Attn: Sandy Steinbach, Secretary of State's Office, Board of Voting Systems Examiners, Hoover Bldg, 2nd Fl, Des Moines, IA 50319; 515-281-0145, Fax: 515-242-2953.
www.sos.state.ia.us

2 Department of Agriculture, Animal Industry Bureau, CP & RA, E 9th & Grand Ave, Wallace Bldg, 2nd Fl, Des Moines, IA 50319; 515-281-5305, Fax: 515-281-4282.
www.agriculture.state.ia.us/animalIndustry.htm

3 Department of Agriculture, Pesticide Division, Wallace State Office Bldg, Des Moines, IA 50319; 515-281-5601, Fax: 515-242-6497.
www.agriculture.state.ia.us/pesticidebureau.htm
Email: chuck.eckermann@idals.state.ia.us
Search Database at
www.kellysolutions.com/ia/dealers/index.asp

4 Department of Commerce, Iowa Division of Banking, 200 E Grand Ave, Des Moines, IA 50309; 515-281-4014, Fax: 515-281-4862.
www.idob.state.ia.us
Email: www.idob.state.ia.us/./email/email_form.asp
Search Database at
www.idob.state.ia.us/license/lic_default.htm

5 Department of Commerce, Alcoholic Beverage Division, 1918 SE Hulsizer Ave, Ankeny, IA 50021; 515-281-7432, Fax: 515-281-7375.
www.iowaabd.com   Email: freund@iowaabd.com

6 Department of Commerce, Credit Union Division, 200 E Grand Ave #370, Des Moines, IA 50309; 515-281-6514, Fax: 515-281-7595.
www.iacudiv.state.ia.us   Search Database at
www.iacudiv.state.ia.us/Public/fieldofmembership/membersearch.htm

7 IA Insurance Division, 330 Maple St, Des Moines, IA 50319-0065; 515-281-5705, Fax: 515-281-3059.   www.iid.state.ia.us
Email: producer.licensing@iid.state.ia.us

8 Lobby1st Registration, Chief Clerk of the House, Statehouse, Des Moines, IA 50319; 515-281-5381.   www.legis.state.ia.us/
Search Database at
www.legis.state.ia.us/Lobbyist.html
Note: You may also search at
http://coolice.legis.state.ia.us/Cool-ICE/default.asp?Category=Matt&Service=Lobby.

10 Department of Commerce, Professional Licensing Division, 1920 SE Hulsizer Ave, Ankeny, IA 50021;
515-281-7393, Fax: 515-281-7411.
www.state.ia.us/proflic   Search Database at
www.state.ia.us/government/com/prof/search/

12 Department of Education, Board of Education Examiners, Grimes State Office Bldg, Des Moines, IA 50319-0147;
515-281-5849, Fax: 515-281-7669.
www.state.ia.us/educate/programs/boee

13 Board of Dental Examiners, 400 SW 8th St, #D, Des Moines, IA 50309-4687; 515-281-5157, Fax: 515-281-7969.   www.state.ia.us/dentalboard
Email: ibde@bon.state.ia.us   Note: Telephone verifications accepted, call 515-281-5047.

14 Board of Medical Examiners, 400 SW 8th #C, Des Moines, IA 50309-4686; 515-281-5171, Fax: 515-242-5908.   www.docboard.org/ia
Email: ibme@bon.state.ia.us   Search Database at
www.docboard.org/ia/df/iasearch.htm   Note: Automated phone system verifications, call 515-281-5171. There is also direct access to their database (for a fee) at
https://www.info.state.ia.us/sing/medicalmain.htm.

15 Board of Nursing, River Point Business Park, 400 SW 8th St. #B, Des Moines, IA 50309-4685; 515-281-3255, Fax: 515-281-4825.
www.state.ia.us/nursing/
Email: ibon@bon.state.ia.us   Search Database at
www.state.ia.us/nursing/Licensure.html
Note: Rosters available. Forms available at
www.state.ia.us/nursing/, select general info.

16 Board of Pharmacy Examiners, 400 SW 8th St. # E, Des Moines, IA 50308; 515-281-5944, Fax: 515-281-4609.   www.state.ia.us/ibpe

17 Department of Human Services, Adult & Family Services, Hoover State Office Bldg, 5th Fl, Des Moines, IA 50319-0114; 515-281-5521, Fax: 515-281-4597.   www.dhs.state.ia.us

18 Department of Human Services, Divison of B.D.P.S., 1305 E Walnut, Des Moines, IA 50319-0114; 515-281-6220, Fax: 515-242-6036.

19 Department of Inspections & Appeals, Racing & Gaming Commission, 717 E Court Av #B, Des Moines, IA 50309;
515-281-7352, Fax: 515-242-6560.
http://www3.state.ia.us/irgc/
Search Database at http://www3.state.ia.us/irgc/

20 Department of Natural Resources, 502 E 9th St, Wallace State Office Bldg, Des Moines, IA 50319-0034; 515-281-5918, Fax: 515-281-6794.
www.iowadnr.com.
Email: elonda.bacon@dnr.state.ia.us

22 Department of Public Health, Division of Professional Licensing, Lucas State Office Bldg, Des Moines, IA 50319; 515-281-7074, Fax: 515-281-3121.
www.idph.state.ia.us/licensure

25 Department of Public Safety, Wallace State Office Bldg, Des Moines, IA 50319;
515-281-7610, Fax: 515-281-8921.
www.dps.state.ia.us   Email: piinfo@dps.state.ia.us

26 Department of Revenue & Finance, Lottery Board, 2015 Grand Av, Des Moines, IA 50312; 515-281-7900, Fax: 515-281-7882.
www.ialottery.com   Email: Web.Master@ilot.state.ia.us

27 Division of Labor, Workforce Development, 1000 E Grand Ave, Des Moines, IA 50319-0209; 515-281-6175, Fax: 515-281-7995.
www.iowaworkforce.org

29 Department of Public Health, Bureau of Radiological Health, 401 SW 7th St. #D, Des Moines, IA 50309-4611;
515-281-3478, Fax: 515-725-0318.
http://idph.state.ia.us/

30 Supreme Court Clerk's Office, Legal Boards, 1111 E Court Ave, Des Moines, IA 50319; 515-281-5911, Fax: 515-242-6164.
www.judicial.state.ia.us/regs

31 Secretary of State, Lucas Bldg, 1st Fl, 321 E. 12th St., Des Moines, IA 50319; 515-281-5204, Fax: 515-242-5953 or 6556.
www.sos.state.ia.us
Email: sos@sos.state.ia.us

32 Real Estate Appraiser Board, 1918 SE Hulsizer, Ankeny, IA 50021-3941; 515-281-7393, Fax: 515-281-7411.
www.state.ia.us/government/com/prof/appraiser/home.html
Email: IAPP@max.state.ia.us   Search Database at
www.state.ia.us/government/com/prof/search/

33 Bureau of Professional Licensure, Board of Cosmetology Arts & Sciences Examiners, 321 E 12th St, Lucas State Office Bldg 5th Fl, Des Moines, IA 50319-0075; 515-281-4287, Fax: 515-281-3121.
www.idph.state.ia.us/licensure

34 Department of Transportation, Motor Vehicle Division, Office of Driver Svcs, PO Box 9204, 100 Euclid, Park Fair Mall, Des Moines, IA 50306-9204; 515-237-3079, Fax: 515-237-3152.
www.dot.state.ia.us/mvd/ods/
Email: ods@dot.iowa.gov.

Iowa Federal Courts

The following list indicates the district and division name for each county in the state. If the bankruptcy court location is different from the district court, then the location of the bankruptcy court appears in parentheses.

County/Court Cross Reference

County	District	Division
Adair	Southern	Council Bluffs (Des Moines)
Adams	Southern	Council Bluffs (Des Moines)
Allamakee	Northern	Cedar Rapids
Appanoose	Southern	Des Moines (Central)
Audubon	Southern	Council Bluffs (Des Moines)
Benton	Northern	Cedar Rapids
Black Hawk	Northern	Cedar Rapids
Boone	Southern	Des Moines (Central)
Bremer	Northern	Cedar Rapids
Buchanan	Northern	Cedar Rapids
Buena Vista	Northern	Sioux Cty (Cedar Rapids)
Butler	Northern	Sioux Cty (Cedar Rapids)
Calhoun	Northern	Sioux Cty (Cedar Rapids)
Carroll	Northern	Sioux Cty (Cedar Rapids)
Cass	Southern	Council Bluffs (Des Moines)
Cedar	Northern	Cedar Rapids
Cerro Gordo	Northern	Cedar Rapids
Cherokee	Northern	Sioux Cty (Cedar Rapids)
Chickasaw	Northern	Cedar Rapids
Clarke	Southern	Council Bluffs (Des Moines)
Clay	Northern	Sioux Cty (Cedar Rapids)
Clayton	Northern	Cedar Rapids
Clinton	Southern	Council Bluffs (Des Moines)
Crawford	Northern	Sioux Cty (Cedar Rapids)
Dallas	Southern	Des Moines (Central)
Davis	Southern	Des Moines (Central)
Decatur	Southern	Council Bluffs (Des Moines)
Delaware	Northern	Cedar Rapids
Des Moines	Southern	Des Moines (Central)
Dickinson	Northern	Sioux Cty (Cedar Rapids)
Dubuque	Northern	Cedar Rapids
Emmet	Northern	Sioux Cty (Cedar Rapids)
Fayette	Northern	Cedar Rapids
Floyd	Northern	Cedar Rapids
Franklin	Northern	Sioux Cty (Cedar Rapids)
Fremont	Southern	Council Bluffs (Des Moin
Greene	Southern	Des Moines (Central)
Grundy	Northern	Cedar Rapids
Guthrie	Southern	Des Moines (Central)
Hamilton	Northern	Sioux Cty (Cedar Rapids)
Hancock	Northern	Sioux Cty (Cedar Rapids)
Hardin	Northern	Cedar Rapids
Harrison	Southern	Council Bluffs (Des Moines)
Henry	Southern	Davenport (Des Moines)
Howard	Northern	Cedar Rapids
Humboldt	Northern	Sioux Cty (Cedar Rapids)
Ida	Northern	Sioux Cty (Cedar Rapids)
Iowa	Northern	Cedar Rapids
Jackson	Northern	Cedar Rapids
Jasper	Southern	Des Moines (Central)
Jefferson	Southern	Des Moines (Central)
Johnson	Southern	Davenport (Des Moines)
Jones	Northern	Cedar Rapids
Keokuk	Southern	Des Moines (Central)
Kossuth	Northern	Sioux Cty (Cedar Rapids)
Lee	Southern	Davenport (Des Moines)
Linn	Northern	Cedar Rapids
Louisa	Southern	Davenport (Des Moines)
Lucas	Southern	Council Bluffs (Des Moines)
Lyon	Northern	Sioux Cty (Cedar Rapids)
Madison	Southern	Des Moines (Central)
Mahaska	Southern	Des Moines (Central)
Marion	Southern	Des Moines (Central)
Marshall	Southern	Des Moines (Central)
Mills	Southern	Council Bluffs (Des Moines)
Mitchell	Northern	Cedar Rapids
Monona	Northern	Sioux Cty (Cedar Rapids)
Monroe	Southern	Des Moines (Central)
Montgomery	Southern	Council Bluffs (Des Moines)
Muscatine	Southern	Davenport (Des Moines)
O'Brien	Northern	Sioux Cty (Cedar Rapids)
Osceola	Northern	Sioux Cty (Cedar Rapids)
Page	Southern	Council Bluffs (Des Moines)
Palo Alto	Northern	Sioux Cty (Cedar Rapids)
Plymouth	Northern	Sioux Cty (Cedar Rapids)
Pocahontas	Northern	Sioux Cty (Cedar Rapids)
Polk	Southern	Des Moines (Central)
Pottawattamie	Southern	Council Bluffs (Des Moines)
Poweshiek	Southern	Des Moines (Central)
Ringgold	Southern	Council Bluffs (Des Moines)
Sac	Northern	Sioux Cty (Cedar Rapids)
Scott	Southern	Davenport (Des Moines)
Shelby	Southern	Council Bluffs (Des Moines)
Sioux	Northern	Sioux Cty (Cedar Rapids)
Story	Southern	Des Moines (Central)
Tama	Northern	Cedar Rapids
Taylor	Southern	Council Bluffs (Des Moines)
Union	Southern	Council Bluffs (Des Moines)
Van Buren	Southern	Davenport (Des Moines)
Wapello	Southern	Des Moines (Central)
Warren	Southern	Des Moines (Central)
Washington	Southern	Davenport (Des Moines)
Wayne	Southern	Council Bluffs (Des Moines)
Webster	Northern	Sioux Cty (Cedar Rapids)
Winnebago	Northern	Sioux Cty (Cedar Rapids)
Winneshiek	Northern	Cedar Rapids
Woodbury	Northern	Sioux Cty (Cedar Rapids)
Worth	Northern	Sioux Cty (Cedar Rapids)
Wright	Northern	Sioux Cty (Cedar Rapids)

Standards for Federal Courts: The search fee is $20.00 per item (one party name or case number). Certification fee is $7.00 per document. Copy fee is $.50 per page. All fees standard unless noted in profile. Mail Search: always enclose a stamped self addressed envelope unless otherwise noted. Most courts accept fax requests or will suggest a copying/search vendor. Before releasing records, all courts require prepayment unless noted in profile.

Open records are located at the court unless otherwise noted. District courts index by defendant and plaintiff as well as by case number. Bankruptcy courts usually index by debtor and case number. While most courts now have their indexes on computer, many still maintain index card files as well.

The universal PACER sign-up number is 800-676-6856. Find PACER and the Party/Case Index on the Web at http://pacer.psc.uscourts.gov. PACER dial-up access is $.60 per minute. Also, courts offering internet access via RACER, PACER, Web-PACER or the new CM-ECF charge $.07 per page fee unless noted as free.

US District Court
Northern District of Iowa

Cedar Rapids (Eastern) Division Court Clerk, PO Box 74710, Cedar Rapids, IA 52407-4710 (courier address: Federal Bldg, U.S. Courthouse, 101 1st St SE, Room 313, Cedar Rapids, IA 52401), 319-286-2300. www.iand.uscourts.gov

Counties: Allamakee, Benton, Black Hawk, Bremer, Buchanan, Cedar, Chickasaw, Clayton, Delaware, Dubuque, Fayette, Floyd, Grundy, Hardin, Howard, Iowa, Jackson, Jones, Linn, Mitchell, Tama, Winneshiek. This court also has records for the Dubuque Branch.

Indexing & Storage: New cases available in the index immediately after filing date.

Fee & Payment: Payment may be made by money order, cashier check, personal check. Payee: Clerk, U.S. District Court.

Phone Search: Anything that is public record will be released over the phone, but only for one name per call.

Mail Search: A SASE not required.

In Person Search: Fee charged if court conducts your in person search for you.

PACER: PACER is available online at http://pacer.iand.uscourts.gov. New records are online after 1 day.

Electronic Filing: Electronic filing information online at https://ecf.iand.uscourts.gov

Sioux City (Western) Division Room 301, Federal Bldg, 320 6th St, Sioux City, IA 51101 (courier address: Use mail address for courier delivery) 712-233-3900. www.iand.uscourts.gov

Counties: Buena Vista, Butler, Calhoun, Carroll, Cerro Gordo, Cherokee, Clay, Crawford, Dickinson, Emmet, Franklin, Hamilton, Hancock, Humboldt, Ida,Kossuth, Lyon, Monona, O'Brien, Osceola, Palo Alto, Plymouth, Pocahontas, Sac, Sioux, Webster, Winnebago, Woodbury, Worth, Wright. This court also has records for the Ft. Dodge, Independence, and Mason City Divisions. Court is held occasionally held in Ft. Dodge, but records are here at Sioux City.

Indexing & Storage: New cases available in the index immediately after filing date.

Fee & Payment: Payment may be made by money order, cashier check, personal check. Payee: Clerk, U.S. District Court.

Phone Search: Only docket information available.

In Person Search: Fee charged if court conducts your in person search for you.

PACER: PACER is available online at http://pacer.iand.uscourts.gov. New records are online after 1 day.

Electronic Filing: Electronic filing information online at https://ecf.iand.uscourts.gov

U.S. Bankruptcy Court
Northern District of Iowa

Cedar Rapids (Eastern) Division PO Box 74890, Cedar Rapids, IA 52407-4890 (courier address: 8th Floor, 425 2nd St SE, Cedar Rapids, IA 52401), 319-286-2200, Fax: 319-286-2280. www.ianb.uscourts.gov

Counties: Allamakee, Benton, Black Hawk, Bremer, Buchanan, Cedar, Chickasaw, Clayton, Delaware, Dubuque, Fayette, Floyd, Grundy, Howard, Iowa, Jackson, Jones, Linn, Mitchell, Tama, Winneshiek. Also has electronic records of cases from the Sioux City Division.

Indexing & Storage: Cases indexed by debtor and creditors as well as by case number. New cases available in the index immediately after filing date. District wide searches are available for information from 1988 to the present from this court. This court handles records for the Sioux City division.

Fee & Payment: Payment may be made by money order, cashier check, business check, Visa or Mastercard. Personal checks are not accepted. Checks are accepted from in-state law firms only. Payee: Clerk, U.S. Bankruptcy Court.

Phone Search: Only minimal information will be released over the phone. Not all docket information will be released. Automated voice case information service (VCIS) is available. Call VCIS at 800-249-9859 or 319-362-9906.

In Person Search: Permitted.

PACER: PACER is available online at http://pacer.ianb.uscourts.gov. Document images available.

Electronic Filing: Electronic filing information online at https://ecf.ianb.uscourts.gov

Sioux City (Western) Division PO Box 3857, Sioux City, IA 51102-3857 (courier address: Federal Bldg., 320 6th St., Sioux City, IA 51101), 712-233-3939, Fax: 712-233-3942. www.ianb.uscourts.gov

Counties: Buena Vista, Calhoun, Carroll, Cerro Gordo, Cherokee, Clay, Crawford, Dickinson, Emmet, Floyd, Franklin, Hamilton, Hancock, Hardin,Humboldt, Ida, Kossuth, Lyon, Mitchell, Monona, O'Brien, Osceola, Palo Alto, Plymouth, Pocahontas, Sac, Sioux, Webster, Winnebago, Woodbury, Worth, Wright. Case records are also available electronically at the Cedar Rapids Division.

Indexing & Storage: Cases indexed by debtor and creditors as well as by case number. New cases available in the index immediately after filing date. District wide searches available for information from 1988 to the present from this court.

Fee & Payment: Payment may be made by money order, cashier check, business check, Visa or Mastercard. Personal checks are not accepted. Checks are accepted from in-state law firms only. Payee: Clerk, U.S. Bankruptcy Court.

Phone Search: Only minimal information will be released over the phone. Not all docket information will be released. Automated voice case information service (VCIS) is available. Call VCIS at 800-249-9859 or 319-362-9906.

In Person Search: Permitted.

PACER: PACER is available online at http://pacer.ianb.uscourts.gov. Document images available.

Electronic Filing: Electronic filing information online at https://ecf.ianb.uscourts.gov

U.S. District Court

Southern District of Iowa

Council Bluffs (Western) Division PO Box 307, Council Bluffs, IA 51502 (courier address: Room 313, 8 S 6th St, Council Bluffs, IA 51502), 712-328-0283, Fax: 712-328-1241. www.iasd.uscourts.gov

Counties: Audubon, Cass, Fremont, Harrison, Mills, Montgomery, Page, Pottawattamie, Shelby.

Indexing & Storage: New cases available in the index immediately after filing date.

Fee & Payment: Payment may be made by money order, cashier check, personal check. The search fee will be charged only if the clerk's staff is required to spend more than 5 minutes searching. Payee: Clerk, U.S. District Court. Will fax results for $3.00 for up to 9 pages; $5.00 if more, plus copy fee.

Phone Search: All information available will be released over the phone. Will fax results for $3.00 for up to 9 pages; $5.00 if more, plus copy fee.

In Person Search: Fee charged if court conducts your in person search for you.

PACER: PACER is available online at http://pacer.iasd.uscourts.gov. Document images available. Records purged every six months. New records are online after 3 days.

Other Online Access: The RACER system is now administered by PACER. Fee is $.07 per page.

Davenport (Eastern) Division PO Box 256, Davenport, IA 52805 (courier address: Room 215, 131 E 4th St, Davenport, IA 52801), 563-322-3223, Fax: 563-322-2962. www.iasd.uscourts.gov

Counties: Henry, Johnson, Lee, Louisa, Muscatine, Scott, Van Buren, Washington.

Indexing & Storage: New cases available in the index 1 week after filing date. All criminal cases are handled in Des Moines Division. Civil cases are handled here.

Fee & Payment: Payment may be made by money order, cashier check, personal check. Will bill fees. Payee: Clerk, U.S. District Court. Will fax back for $3.00 up to 9 pages; $5.00 if more, plus copy fees.

Phone Search: Docket information available by phone. Will fax back for $3.00 up to 9 pages; $5.00 if more, plus copy fees.

Mail Search: A SASE not required.

In Person Search: Fee charged if court conducts your in person search for you. You may only search the index cards.

PACER: PACER is available online at http://pacer.iasd.uscourts.gov. Document images available. Records purged every six months. New records are online after 3 days.

Other Online Access: The RACER system is now administered by PACER. Fee of $.07 per page is now charged.

Des Moines (Central) Division PO Box 9344, Des Moines, IA 50306-9344 (courier address: 123 E. Walnut St., Rm. 300, Des Moines, IA 50306-9344), 515-284-6248, Fax: 515-284-6418. www.iasd.uscourts.gov

Counties: Adair, Adams, Appanoose, Boone, Clarke, Clinton, Dallas, Davis, Decatur, Des Moines, Greene, Guthrie, Jasper, Jefferson, Keokuk, Lucas, Madison, Mahaska, Marion, Marshall, Monroe, Polk, Poweshiek, Ringgold, Story, Taylor, Union, Wapello, Warren, Wayne.

Indexing & Storage: New cases available in the index immediately after filing date. Records are stored by date filed and closed.

Fee & Payment: Payment may be made by money order, cashier check, personal check. A bill can be sent by mail. Payee: Clerk, U.S. District Court. Will fax back for $3.00 up to 9 pages; $5.00 if more, plus copy fee.

Phone Search: No searching by telephone. Requests for searches must be in writing. Will fax back for $3.00 up to 9 pages; $5.00 if more, plus copy fee.

Mail Search: A SASE not required.

In Person Search: Fee charged if court conducts your in person search for you. Only the clerk can conduct criminal searches.

PACER: PACER is available online at http://pacer.iasd.uscourts.gov. Document images available. Records purged every six months. New records are online after 3 days.

Other Online Access: The RACER system is now administered by PACER. Fee is $.07 per page.

U.S. Bankruptcy Court

Southern District of Iowa

Des Moines Division PO Box 9264, Des Moines, IA 50306-9264 (courier address: 300 U.S. Courthouse Annex, 110 East Court Ave, Des Moines, IA 50309), 515-284-6230, Fax: 515-284-6404. www.iasb.uscourts.gov

Counties: Adair, Adams, Appanoose, Audubon, Boone, Cass, Clarke, Clinton, Dallas, Davis, Decatur, Des Moines, Fremont, Greene, Guthrie, Harrison, Henry, Jasper, Jefferson, Johnson, Keokuk, Lee, Louisa, Lucas, Madison, Mahaska, Marion, Marshall, Mills, Monroe, Montgomery, Muscatine, Page, Polk, Pottawattamie, Poweshiek, Ringgold, Scott, Shelby, Story, Taylor, Union, Van Buren, Wapello, Warren, Washington, Wayne.

Indexing & Storage: Cases indexed by debtor as well as by case number. New cases available in the index immediately after filing date.

Fee & Payment: Payment may be made by money order, cashier check, business check. Personal checks are not accepted. Payee: CopyCat Photocopy Center.

Phone Search: The information released over the phone is: name, case number, chapter date file, assets, attorney, attorney's telephone number, trustee, judge, status and discharge. Information is available from June 1987. Automated voice case information service (VCIS) is available. Call VCIS at 888-219-5534 or 515-284-6427.

In Person Search: Fee charged if court conducts your in person search for you. Copies made at court for $.50 per page.

PACER: New CM/ECF online system access only. Records purged every six months. New civil records are online after 1 day.

Electronic Filing: Electronic filing information online at https://ecf.iasb.uscourts.gov

Other Online Access: The RACER system has been replaced by the ECF/PACER system. Access fee is $.07 per page.

Iowa County Courts

Court	Jurisdiction	No. of Courts	How Organized
District Courts*	General	100	8 Districts

* Profiled in this Sourcebook.

CIVIL								
Court	Tort	Contract	Real Estate	Min. Claim	Max. Claim	Small Claims	Estate	Eviction	Domestic Relations
District Courts*	X	X	X	$0	No Max	$4000	X	X	X

CRIMINAL					
Court	Felony	Misdemeanor	DWI/DUI	Preliminary Hearing	Juvenile
District Courts*	X	X	X	X	X

ADMINISTRATION — State Court Administrator, Judicial Branch Bldg, 1111 East Court Ave, Des Moines, IA, 50319; 515-281-5241, Fax: 515-242-0014. www.judicial.state.ia.us

COURT STRUCTURE — The District Court is the court of general jurisdiction. Effective 7/1/95, the Small Claims limit increased to $4000 from $3000.

Vital records were moved from courts to the County Recorder's office in each county.

ONLINE ACCESS — Criminal, civil, probate, traffic and appellate information is now available from all 99 counties in Iowa at www.judicial.state.ia.us/online_records. There is no fee for basic information, and a pay system is offered for more detailed requests. Name searches are available on a statewide or specific county basis. While this is an excellent site with much information, there is one important consideration to keep in mind. Although records are updated daily, the historical records offered are not from the same starting date on a county-by-county basis. Also, from the home page one may access supreme and apppellate court opinions.

ADDITIONAL INFORMATION — In most courts, the Certification Fee is $10.00 plus copy fee. Copy Fee is $.50 per page. Most courts do not do searches and recommend either in person searches or use of a record retriever.

Courts that accept written search requests usually require an SASE.

Most courts have a Public access terminal for access to that court's records.

Adair County

5th District Court PO Box L, Greenfield, IA 50849; 641-743-2445; Fax: 641-743-2974. Hours: 8AM-4:30PM (CST). *Felony, Misdemeanor, Civil, Eviction, Small Claims, Probate.*
Civil Records: Access: In person, online. Both court and visitors may perform in person searches. No search fee. Required to search: name, years to search. Civil cases indexed by defendant, plaintiff. Civil records on docket books from late 1800s, computerized since 11/1996. Civil, probate, and appellate information is at www.judicial.state.ia.us/online_records.
Criminal Records: Access: In person, online. Both court and visitors may perform in person searches. No search fee. Required to search: name, years to search, DOB, signed release; also helpful: SSN. Criminal records on docket books from late 1800s, computerized since 11/1996. Criminal, traffic, and appellate information is online at www.judicial.state.ia.us/online_records.
General Information: Public Access terminal is available. No juvenile, sealed, dissolution of marriage, mental health domestic abuse or deferred records released. Copy fee: $.50 per page. Cert fee: $10.00. Payee: Clerk of Court. Personal checks accepted. Prepayment required.

Adams County

5th District Court Courthouse, PO Box 484, Corning, IA 50841; 641-322-4711; Fax: 641-322-4523. 8AM-4:30PM (CST). *Felony, Misdemeanor, Civil, Eviction, Small Claims, Probate.*
Civil Records: Access: In person, online. Visitors must perform in person searches for themselves. No search fee. Required to search: name, years to search. Civil cases indexed by defendant, plaintiff. Civil records on docket books from late 1800s, on computer back to 11/96. Civil, probate, and appellate data is at www.judicial.state.ia.us/online_records.
Criminal Records: Access: In person, online. Visitors must perform in person searches for themselves. No search fee. Required to search: name, years to search, signed release. Criminal records on docket books from late 1800s, on computer back to 11/96. Criminal, traffic, and appellate information is online at www.judicial.state.ia.us/online_records.
General Information: Public Access terminal is available. No sealed, dissolution of marriage, mental health, sealed or expunged records released. Copy fee: $.50 per page. Cert fee: $10.00. Payee: Clerk of Court. Personal checks accepted. Prepayment required.

Allamakee County

1st District Court PO Box 248, Waukon, IA 52172; 563-568-6351. Hours: 8AM-4:30PM Monday - Friday (CST). *Felony, Misdemeanor, Civil, Eviction, Small Claims, Probate.*
www.iowacourtsonline.org
Civil Records: Access: In person, online. Visitors must perform in person searches for themselves. No search fee. Required to search: name, years to search. Civil cases indexed by defendant, plaintiff. All judgments on computer back to 4/1997; on index books back to 1880, probate back to 1852. Civil, probate, and appellate information is at www.judicial.state.ia.us/online_records.
Criminal Records: Access: In person, online. Visitors must perform in person searches for themselves. No search fee. Required to search: name, years to search, signed release. Criminal records on docket books from 1800s; on computer back to 4/1997. Criminal, traffic, and appellate information is online at www.judicial.state.ia.us/online_records.
General Information: Public Access terminal is available. No juvenile, adoption, sealed, pending dissolution of marriage, mental health, domestic abuse or deferred records released. Copy fee: $.50 per page. Cert fee: $10.00. Payee: Clerk of Court. Personal checks accepted. Prepayment required.

Appanoose County

8th District Court PO Box 400, Centerville, IA 52544; 641-856-6101; Fax: 641-856-2282. Hours: 8AM-4:30 PM (CST). *Felony, Misdemeanor, Civil, Eviction, Small Claims, Probate.*
Civil Records: Access: In person, online. Visitors must perform in person searches for themselves. No search fee. Required to search: name, years to search. Civil cases indexed by defendant, plaintiff. Civil records on docket books from 1847, on computer back to 2/96. Civil, probate, and appellate information is at www.judicial.state.ia.us/online_records.
Criminal Records: Access: In person, online. Visitors must perform in person searches for themselves. No search fee. Required to search: name, years to search, signed release. Criminal records on docket books from 1847, on computer back to 2/96. Criminal, traffic, and appellate information is online at www.judicial.state.ia.us/online_records.
General Information: Public Access terminal is available. No juvenile, sealed, dissolution of marriage, mental health, domestic abuse or deferred records released. Copy fee: $.25 per page. Cert fee: $10.00. Payee: Clerk of Court. Personal checks accepted. Prepayment required.

Audubon County

4th District Court 318 Leroy St, #6, Audubon, IA 50025; 712-563-4275; Fax: 712-563-4276. Hours: 8AM-4:30PM (CST). *Felony, Misdemeanor, Civil, Eviction, Small Claims, Probate.*
Civil Records: Access: In person, online. Visitors must perform in person searches for themselves. No search fee. Required to search: name, years to search; also helpful: address. Civil cases indexed by defendant, plaintiff. Civil records on docket books from 1930s, computerized since 1996. Civil, probate, and appellate information is at www.judicial.state.ia.us/online_records.
Criminal Records: Access: In person, online. Visitors must perform in person searches for themselves. No search fee. Required to search: name, years to search; also helpful: DOB, SSN, address. Criminal records on docket books from late 1800s. Criminal, traffic, and appellate information is online at www.judicial.state.ia.us/online_records.
General Information: Public Access terminal is available. No juvenile, sealed, dissolution of marriage, mental health, domestic abuse or deferred records released. Copy fee: $.50 per page. Cert fee: $10.00. Payee: Clerk of Court. Prepayment required.

Benton County

6th District Court PO Box 719, Vinton, IA 52349; 319-472-2766; Fax: 319-472-2747. Hours: 8AM-4:30PM (CST). *Felony, Misdemeanor, Civil, Eviction, Small Claims, Probate.*
www.iowacourtsonline.org
Civil Records: Access: In person, online. Visitors must perform in person searches for themselves. No search fee. Required to search: name, years to search. Civil cases indexed by defendant, plaintiff. Civil records on original record books from 1800s, index is on computer since 06/95. Civil, probate, and appellate data is at www.judicial.state.ia.us/online_records.
Criminal Records: Access: In person, online. Visitors must perform in person searches for themselves. No search fee. Required to search: name, years to search. Criminal records on original record books from 1800s, index is on computer since 06/95. Criminal, traffic, and appellate information is online at www.judicial.state.ia.us/online_records.
General Information: Public Access terminal is available. No juvenile, sealed, dissolution of marriage, mental health, domestic abuse or deferred records released. Copy fee: $.50 per page. Cert fee: $10.00.

Payee: Clerk of Court. Personal checks accepted. Prepayment required.

Black Hawk County

1st District Court 316 E 5th St, Waterloo, IA 50703; 319-833-3331. Hours: 8AM-4:30PM (CST). *Felony, Misdemeanor, Civil, Eviction, Small Claims, Probate.*
Civil Records: Access: In person, online. Visitors must perform in person searches for themselves. No search fee. Required to search: name, years to search. Civil cases indexed by defendant, plaintiff. Civil records on computer from 1992, docket books from early 1900s. Civil, probate, and appellate information is at www.judicial.state.ia.us/online_records.
Criminal Records: Access: In person, online. Visitors must perform in person searches for themselves. No search fee. Required to search: name, years to search; also helpful: DOB, SSN. Criminal records on computer from 1992, docket books from early 1900s. Criminal, traffic, and appellate data is online at www.judicial.state.ia.us/online_records.
General Information: Public Access terminal is available. No juvenile, sealed, dissolution of marriage, mental health, domestic abuse or deferred records released. Copy fee: $.50 per page. Cert fee: $10.00. Payee: District Court. Personal checks accepted. Prepayment required.

Boone County

2nd District Court 201 State St, Boone, IA 50036; 515-433-0561; Fax: 515-433-0563. Hours: 8AM-4:30PM (CST). *Felony, Misdemeanor, Civil, Eviction, Small Claims, Probate.*
Civil Records: Access: In person, online. Visitors must perform in person searches for themselves. No search fee. Required to search: name, years to search. Civil cases indexed by defendant, plaintiff. Civil records on docket books from 1890s; computerized records go back to 1996. Civil, probate, and appellate data is at www.judicial.state.ia.us/online_records.
Criminal Records: Access: In person, online. Visitors must perform in person searches for themselves. No search fee. Required to search: name, years to search, offense, date of offense. Criminal records on docket books from 1890s; computerized records go back to 1996. Criminal, traffic, and appellate information is online at www.judicial.state.ia.us/online_records.
General Information: Public Access terminal is available. No juvenile, sealed, dissolution of marriage, mental health, domestic abuse or deferred records released. Copy fee: $.50 per page. Cert fee: $10.00. Payee: Clerk of Court. Personal checks accepted. Prepayment required.

Bremer County

2nd District Court PO Box 328, Waverly, IA 50677; 319-352-5661; Fax: 319-352-1054. Hours: 8AM-4:30PM (CST). *Felony, Misdemeanor, Civil, Eviction, Small Claims, Probate.*
www.co.bremer.ia.us
Public access terminal has records since 1996 only.
Civil Records: Access: In person, online. Visitors must perform in person searches for themselves. No search fee. Required to search: name, years to search. Civil cases indexed by defendant, plaintiff. Civil records on computer since 07/97; prior records on docket books from 1900s. Civil, probate, and appellate information is at www.judicial.state.ia.us/online_records.
Criminal Records: Access: In person, online. Visitors must perform in person searches for themselves. No search fee. Required to search: name, years to search. Criminal records go back to 1900s; computerized records go back to 1996. Criminal,

traffic, and appellate information is online at www.judicial.state.ia.us/online_records.
General Information: Public Access terminal is available. No juvenile, sealed, dissolution of marriage, mental health, domestic abuse or deferred records released. Copy fee: $.50 per page. Cert fee: $10.00. Payee: Clerk of Court. Personal checks accepted. Visa, MC accepted. Prepayment required.

Buchanan County

1st District Court PO Box 259, Independence, IA 50644; 319-334-2196; Fax: 319-334-7455. Hours: 8AM-4:30PM (CST). *Felony, Misdemeanor, Civil, Eviction, Small Claims, Probate.*
Civil Records: Access: In person, online. Both court and visitors may perform in person searches. No search fee. Required to search: name, years to search. Civil cases indexed by defendant, plaintiff. Civil records on docket books from 1800s; computerized since 1996. Civil, probate, and appellate information is at www.judicial.state.ia.us/online_records.
Criminal Records: Access: Mail, in person, online. Both court and visitors may perform in person searches. No search fee. Required to search: name, years to search. Criminal records on docket books from 1800s; computerized since 1996. Criminal, traffic, and appellate information is online at www.judicial.state.ia.us/online_records.
General Information: Public Access terminal is available. No juvenile, sealed, dissolution of marriage, mental health, domestic abuse or deferred records released. Will fax results; fee is $.50 per page. Copy fee: $.50 per page. Cert fee: $10.00. Payee: Clerk of Court. Personal checks accepted. Visa, MC accepted. Prepayment required. Mail requests: SASE required. Mail turnaround time 2 days.

Buena Vista County

3rd District Court PO Box 1186, Storm Lake, IA 50588; 712-749-2546; Fax: 712-749-2700. Hours: 8AM-4:30PM (CST). *Felony, Misdemeanor, Civil, Eviction, Small Claims, Probate.*
Civil Records: Access: In person, online. Visitors must perform in person searches for themselves. No search fee. Required to search: name, years to search. Civil cases indexed by defendant, plaintiff. Civil records on index cards from early 1900s; on computer back to 1996. Civil, probate, and appellate data is at www.judicial.state.ia.us/online_records.
Criminal Records: Access: In person, online. Visitors must perform in person searches for themselves. No search fee. Required to search: name, years to search. Criminal records on index cards from early 1900s; on computer back to 1994. Criminal, traffic, and appellate information is online at www.judicial.state.ia.us/online_records.
General Information: Public Access terminal is available. No juvenile, sealed, dissolution of marriage, mental health, domestic abuse or deferred records released. Copy fee: $.50 per page. Cert fee: $10.00 per document. Payee: Clerk of Court. Personal checks accepted. Prepayment required.

Butler County

2nd District Court PO Box 307, Allison, IA 50602; 319-267-2487; Fax: 319-267-2488. Hours: 9AM-3:30PM (CST). *Felony, Misdemeanor, Civil, Eviction, Small Claims, Probate.*
Civil Records: Access: In person, online. Visitors must perform in person searches for themselves. No search fee. Required to search: name, years to search. Civil cases indexed by defendant, plaintiff. Civil records on docket books from 1800s, on computer back to 4/97. Civil, probate, and appellate information is at www.judicial.state.ia.us/online_records.
Criminal Records: Access: In person, online. Visitors must perform in person searches for

themselves. No search fee. Required to search: name, years to search. Criminal records on docket books from 1800s, on computer back to 4/97. Criminal, traffic, and appellate information is online at www.judicial.state.ia.us/online_records.

General Information: Public Access terminal is available. No juvenile, sealed, dissolution of marriage, mental health, domestic abuse or deferred records released. Copy fee: $1.00 for first page, $.50 each add'l. Cert fee: $10.00. Payee: Clerk of Court. Personal checks accepted. Prepayment required.

Calhoun County

2nd District Court Box 273, Rockwell City, IA 50579; 712-297-8122; Fax: 712-297-5082. Hours: 8AM-4:30PM (CST). *Felony, Misdemeanor, Civil, Eviction, Small Claims, Probate.*

Civil Records: Access: In person, online. Visitors must perform in person searches for themselves. No search fee. Required to search: name, years to search. Civil cases indexed by defendant, plaintiff. Civil records on docket books from 1880s, computerized since 07/97. Civil, probate, and appellate information is at www.judicial.state.ia.us/online_records.

Criminal Records: Access: In person, online. Visitors must perform in person searches for themselves. No search fee. Required to search: name, years to search, DOB, signed release; also helpful: SSN. Criminal records on docket books from 1880s, computerized since 07/97. Criminal, traffic, and appellate information is online at www.judicial.state.ia.us/online_records.

General Information: Public Access terminal is available. No juvenile, sealed, pending dissolution of marriage, mental health, domestic abuse or deferred records released. Copy fee: $.50 per page. Cert fee: $10.00. Payee: Clerk of the Court. Personal checks accepted. Visa, MC accepted. Prepayment required.

Carroll County

2nd District Court PO Box 867, Carroll, IA 51401; 712-792-4327; Fax: 712-792-4328. Hours: 8AM-4:30PM (CST). *Felony, Misdemeanor, Civil, Eviction, Small Claims, Probate.*

Civil Records: Access: In person, online. Visitors must perform in person searches for themselves. No search fee. Required to search: name, years to search. Civil cases indexed by defendant, plaintiff. Civil records on index books from 1800s; computerized records go back to 1993 on a limited basis. Everything from September 1997 to present. Civil, probate, and appellate information is at www.judicial.state.ia.us/online_records.

Criminal Records: Access: In person, online. Visitors must perform in person searches for themselves. No search fee. Required to search: name, years to search. Criminal records on computer from June 1993, index books from 1800s. Criminal, traffic, and appellate information is online at www.judicial.state.ia.us/online_records.

General Information: Public Access terminal is available. No juvenile, sealed, dissolution of marriage, mental health, domestic abuse or deferred records released. Will fax specifc case file requests for $1.00 per page. Copy fee: $.50 per page. Cert fee: $10.00. Payee: Clerk of Court. Personal checks accepted. Credit cards accepted. Prepayment required.

Cass County

4th District Court 5 W 7th St, Courthouse, Atlantic, IA 50022; 712-243-2105. Hours: 8AM-4:30PM (CST). *Felony, Misdemeanor, Civil, Eviction, Small Claims, Probate.*

Civil Records: Access: In person, online. Visitors must perform in person searches for themselves. No search fee. Required to search: name, years to search. Civil cases indexed by defendant, plaintiff. Civil

records on docket books from early 1900s; on computer back to 11/1996. Civil, probate, and appellate information is at www.judicial.state.ia.us/online_records.

Criminal Records: Access: In person, online. Visitors must perform in person searches for themselves. No search fee. Required to search: name, years to search, signed release; also helpful: DOB, SSN. Criminal records on docket books from 1880s; on computer back to 11/1996. Criminal, traffic, and appellate information is online at www.judicial.state.ia.us/online_records.

General Information: Public Access terminal is available. No juvenile, sealed, dissolution of marriage, mental health, domestic abuse or deferred records released. Copy fee: $.25 per page. Cert fee: $10.00. Payee: Clerk of Court. Personal checks accepted. Prepayment required.

Cedar County

7th District Court 400 Cedar St, Attn: Cedar County Clerk of Court, Tipton, IA 52772; 563-886-2101. 8AM-4:30PM (CST). *Felony, Misdemeanor, Civil, Eviction, Small Claims, Probate.*

Civil Records: Access: In person, online. Visitors must perform in person searches for themselves. No search fee. Required to search: name, years to search. Civil cases indexed by defendant, plaintiff. Civil records on computer since Dec.1996; on microfiche and docket books from 1839. Civil, probate, and appellate information is at www.judicial.state.ia.us/online_records.

Criminal Records: Access: In person, online. Visitors must perform in person searches for themselves. No search fee. Required to search: name, years to search; also helpful: DOB, SSN, signed release. Criminal records on computer since July 1992; on microfiche and docket books from 1839. Criminal, traffic, and appellate information is online at www.judicial.state.ia.us/online_records.

General Information: Public Access terminal is available. No juvenile, sealed, dissolution of marriage, mental health, domestic abuse or deferred records released. Copy fee: $.50 per page. Cert fee: $10.00. Payee: Clerk of Court. Only cashiers checks and money orders accepted. Prepayment required.

Cerro Gordo County

2nd District Court 220 W Washington, Mason City, IA 50401; 641-424-6431. Hours: 8AM-4:30PM (CST). *Felony, Misdemeanor, Civil, Eviction, Small Claims, Probate.*

Civil Records: Access: In person only. Visitors must perform in person searches for themselves. No search fee. Required to search: name, years to search. Civil cases indexed by defendant, plaintiff. Civil records on computer since 1996; prior records on docket books from early 1900s. Civil, probate, and appellate data is at www.judicial.state.ia.us/online_records.

Criminal Records: Access: In person, online. Visitors must perform in person searches for themselves. No search fee. Required to search: name, years to search; also helpful: DOB, SSN. Criminal records on computer since 4/95; prior records on index cards from 1977. Criminal, traffic, and appellate information is online at www.judicial.state.ia.us/online_records.

General Information: Public Access terminal is available. No Sealed, dissolution of marriage, mental health, domestic abuse or deferred records released. Copy fee: $.50 per page. Cert fee: $10.00. Payee: Clerk of Court. Personal checks accepted. Credit cards accepted. Prepayment required.

Cherokee County

3rd District Court Courthouse Drawer F, Cherokee, IA 51012; 712-225-6744; Fax: 712-225-6749. Hours: 8AM-4:30PM (CST). *Felony, Misdemeanor, Civil, Eviction, Small Claims, Probate.*

Civil Records: Access: In person, online. Visitors must perform in person searches for themselves. No search fee. Required to search: name, years to search. Civil cases indexed by defendant, plaintiff. Civil records on docket books from 1800s, indexed on computer since 1997. Civil, probate, and appellate information is at www.judicial.state.ia.us/online_records.

Criminal Records: Access: In person, online. Visitors must perform in person searches for themselves. No search fee. Required to search: name, years to search. Criminal records index is computerized since 1997. Criminal, traffic, and appellate information is online at www.judicial.state.ia.us/online_records.

General Information: Public Access terminal is available. No juvenile, sealed, dissolution of marriage, mental health, domestic abuse or deferred records released. Copy fee: $.50 per page. Cert fee: $10.00. Payee: Clerk of Court. Personal checks accepted. Prepayment required.

Chickasaw County

1st District Court County Courthouse, 8 E Prospect, New Hampton, IA 50659; 641-394-2106; Fax: 641-394-5106. Hours: 8AM-4:30PM (CST). *Felony, Misdemeanor, Civil, Eviction, Small Claims, Probate.*

Civil Records: Access: In person, online. Visitors must perform in person searches for themselves. No search fee. Required to search: name, years to search. Civil cases indexed by defendant, plaintiff. Civil records on docket books from late 1800s; on computer back to 1996. Civil, probate, and appellate information is at www.judicial.state.ia.us/online_records.

Criminal Records: Access: In person, online. Visitors must perform in person searches for themselves. No search fee. Required to search: name, years to search, signed release. Criminal records on docket books from late 1800s; on computer back to 1996. Criminal, traffic, and appellate information is online at www.judicial.state.ia.us/online_records.

General Information: Public Access terminal is available. No juvenile, sealed, dissolution of marriage, adoption, mental health, domestic abuse or deferred records released. Copy fee: $.50. $.25 per page after first 10. Cert fee: $10.00. Payee: Clerk of District Court. Personal checks accepted.

Clarke County

5th District Court 100 S Main St, Clarke County Courthouse, Osceola, IA 50213; 641-342-6096; Fax: 641-342-2463. Hours: 8AM-4:30PM (CST). *Felony, Misdemeanor, Civil, Eviction, Small Claims, Probate.*

Civil Records: Access: In person, online. Both court and visitors may perform in person searches. No search fee. Required to search: name, years to search. Civil cases indexed by defendant, plaintiff. Civil records on docket books from early 1900s, on computer back to 7/96. Civil, probate, and appellate data is at www.judicial.state.ia.us/online_records.

Criminal Records: Access: In person, online. Both court and visitors may perform in person searches. No search fee. Required to search: name, years to search; also helpful: SSN. Criminal records on docket books from early 1900s, on computer back to 7/96. Criminal, traffic, and appellate information is online at www.judicial.state.ia.us/online_records.

General Information: Public Access terminal is available. No juvenile, sealed, dissolution of marriage, mental health, domestic abuse or deferred records released. Copy fee: $.50 per page. Cert fee: $10.00. Payee: Clerk of Court. Personal checks accepted. Prepayment required.

Clay County

3rd District Court Courthouse, 215 W 4th St, Spencer, IA 51301; 712-262-4335. Hours: 8 AM-4:30 PM (CST). *Felony, Misdemeanor, Civil, Eviction, Small Claims, Probate.*

Civil Records: Access: In person, online. Visitors must perform in person searches for themselves. No search fee. Required to search: name, years to search. Civil cases indexed by defendant, plaintiff. Civil records on microfilm from to 1972 to 1995, docket books from 1800s, on computer back to 8/18/97. Civil, probate, and appellate information is at www.judicial.state.ia.us/online_records.

Criminal Records: Access: In person, online. Visitors must perform in person searches for themselves. No search fee. Required to search: name, years to search. Criminal records on microfilm from to 1972 to 1995, docket books from 1800s, on comptuer back to 1/7/97. Criminal, traffic, and appellate information is online at www.judicial.state.ia.us/online_records.

General Information: Public Access terminal is available. No juvenile, sealed, pending dissolution of marriage, mental health, sealed domestic abuse or deferred records released. Copy fee: $.50 per page. Cert fee: $10.00. Payee: Clerk of Court. Personal checks accepted. Visa, MC accepted.

Clayton County

1st District Court PO Box 418, Clayton County Courthouse, Elkader, IA 52043; 563-245-2204; Fax: 563-245-2825. Hours: 8AM-4:30PM (CST). *Felony, Misdemeanor, Civil, Eviction, Small Claims, Probate.*

Civil Records: Access: In person, online. Visitors must perform in person searches for themselves. No search fee. Required to search: name, years to search. Civil cases indexed by defendant, plaintiff. Civil records on docket books from late 1880s, on computer back to 4/97. Civil, probate, and appellate information is at www.judicial.state.ia.us/online_records.

Criminal Records: Access: In person, online. Visitors must perform in person searches for themselves. No search fee. Required to search: name, years to search. Criminal records on docket books from late 1880s, on computer back to 4/97. Criminal, traffic, and appellate information is online at www.judicial.state.ia.us/online_records.

General Information: Public Access terminal is available. No juvenile unless child is age 10 or older and offense is considered a public offense, sealed, dissolution of marriage, mental health, domestic abuse or deferred records released. Copy fee: $.50 per page. Cert fee: $10.00. Payee: Clerk of Court. Personal checks accepted. Prepayment required.

Clinton County

7th District Court Courthouse (PO Box 2957), Clinton, IA 52733; 563-243-6213; Fax: 563-243-3655. 8AM-4:30PM (CST). *Felony, Misdemeanor, Civil, Eviction, Small Claims, Probate.*

Civil Records: Access: In person, online. Visitors must perform in person searches for themselves. No search fee. Required to search: name, years to search. Civil cases indexed by defendant. Civil records on computer since 1993, on docket books prior. Civil, probate, and appellate information is at www.judicial.state.ia.us/online_records.

Criminal Records: Access: In person, online. Visitors must perform in person searches for

themselves. No search fee. Required to search: name, years to search, DOB, signed release. Criminal records on computer since 1980, on docket books prior. Criminal, traffic, and appellate information is online at www.judicial.state.ia.us/online_records.

General Information: Public Access terminal is available. No juvenile, adoption, sealed, dissolution of marriage before decree, mental health, domestic abuse or deferred records released. Copy fee: $.50 per page. Cert fee: $10.00. Payee: Clerk of Court. Personal checks accepted. Visa, MC accepted. Prepayment required.

Crawford County

3rd District Court 1202 Broadway, Denison, IA 51442; 712-263-2242; Fax: 712-263-5753. Hours: 8AM-4:30 (CST). *Felony, Misdemeanor, Civil, Eviction, Small Claims, Probate.*

Civil Records: Access: In person, online. Visitors must perform in person searches for themselves. No search fee. Required to search: name, years to search. Civil cases indexed by defendant, plaintiff. Civil records available since 1937, on docket books from 1869, on computer back to 1/96. Civil, probate, and appellate information is at www.judicial.state.ia.us/online_records.

Criminal Records: Access: In person, online. Visitors must perform in person searches for themselves. No search fee. Required to search: name, years to search. Criminal records available since 1937, on docket books from 1869, on computer back to 1/96. Criminal, traffic, and appellate information is online at www.judicial.state.ia.us/online_records.

General Information: Public Access terminal is available. No juvenile, sealed, dissolution of marriage, mental health, domestic abuse or deferred records released. Copy fee: $.50 per page. Cert fee: $10.00. Payee: Clerk of Court. Personal checks accepted. Prepayment required.

Dallas County

5th District Court 801 Court St, Adel, IA 50003; 515-993-5816; Fax: 515-993-6991. Hours: 8AM-4:30PM (CST). *Felony, Misdemeanor, Civil, Eviction, Small Claims, Probate.*

Civil Records: Access: In person, mail, online. Visitors must perform in person searches for themselves. No search fee. Required to search: name, years to search. Civil cases indexed by defendant, plaintiff. Civil records on docket books from 1800s; computerized records since 1996. Civil, probate, and appellate information is at www.judicial.state.ia.us/online_records.

Criminal Records: Access: In person, mail, online. Visitors must perform in person searches for themselves. No search fee. Required to search: name, years to search. Criminal records on docket books from 1800s; computerized records since 1994. Criminal, traffic, and appellate information is online at www.judicial.state.ia.us/online_records.

General Information: Public Access terminal is available. No juvenile, sealed, dissolution of marriage, mental health, domestic abuse or deferred records released. Copy fee: $.50 per page. Cert fee: $10.00. Payee: Clerk of Court. Personal checks accepted. Turnaround time is 1 week.

Davis County

8th District Court Davis County Courthouse, Bloomfield, IA 52537; 641-664-2011; Fax: 641-664-2041. 8AM-4:30PM (CST). *Felony, Misdemeanor, Civil, Eviction, Small Claims, Probate.*

Civil Records: Access: In person, online. Visitors must perform in person searches for themselves. No search fee. Required to search: name, years to search. Civil cases indexed by defendant, plaintiff. Civil records on docket books from late 1800s;

computerized since 1997. Civil, probate, and appellate data is at www.judicial.state.ia.us/online_records.

Criminal Records: Access: In person, online. Visitors must perform in person searches for themselves. No search fee. Required to search: name, years to search, DOB. Criminal records on docket books from late 1800s; computerized since 1997. Criminal, traffic, and appellate information is online at www.judicial.state.ia.us/online_records.

General Information: Public Access terminal is available. (Records go back to 1997.) No juvenile, sealed, dissolution of marriage, mental health, domestic abuse or deferred records released. Copy fee: $.25 per page. Cert fee: $10.00. Payee: Clerk of Court. Personal checks accepted. Prepayment required.

Decatur County

5th District Court 207 N Main St, Leon, IA 50144; 641-446-4331; Fax: 641-446-3759. Hours: 8AM-4:30PM (CST). *Felony, Misdemeanor, Civil, Eviction, Small Claims, Probate.*

Civil Records: Access: In person, online. Visitors must perform in person searches for themselves. No search fee. Required to search: name, years to search. Civil cases indexed by defendant, plaintiff. Civil records on docket books since 1880; on computer back to 1996. Civil, probate, and appellate data is at www.judicial.state.ia.us/online_records.

Criminal Records: Access: In person, online. Visitors must perform in person searches themselves. No search fee. Required to search: name, years to search, DOB or SSN. Criminal records on docket books since 1880; on computer back to 1996. Criminal, traffic, and appellate information is online at www.judicial.state.ia.us/online_records.

General Information: Public Access terminal is available. No juvenile, sealed, dissolution of marriage, mental health, domestic abuse or deferred records released. Copy fee: $.50 per page. Cert fee: $10.00. Payee: Clerk of Court. Personal checks accepted. Prepayment required.

Delaware County

District Court Delaware County Courthouse, PO Box 527, Manchester, IA 52057; 563-927-4942; Fax: 563-927-3074. Hours: 8AM-4:30PM (CST). *Felony, Misdemeanor, Civil, Eviction, Small Claims, Probate.*

Civil Records: Access: In person, online. Visitors must perform in person searches for themselves. No search fee. Required to search: name, years to search. Civil cases indexed by defendant, plaintiff. Civil records on docket books from late 1800s; on computer back to 1996. Civil, probate, and appellate data is at www.judicial.state.ia.us/online_records.

Criminal Records: Access: In person, online. Visitors must perform in person searches for themselves. No search fee. Required to search: name, years to search. Criminal records on docket books from late 1800s; on computer back to 1996. Criminal, traffic, and appellate information is online at www.judicial.state.ia.us/online_records.

General Information: Public Access terminal is available. No juvenile, sealed, dissolution of marriage, mental health, domestic abuse or deferred records released. Copy fee: $.50 per page. Cert fee: $10.00. Payee: Clerk of Court. Personal checks accepted. Prepayment required.

Des Moines County

8th District Court 513 Main St, PO Box 158, Burlington, IA 52601; 319-753-8262/8262; Fax: 319-753-8253. Hours: 8AM-4:30PM (CST). *Felony, Misdemeanor, Civil, Eviction, Small Claims, Probate.*
www.judicial.state.ia.us/district/d8.asp

Note: City of Des Moines is not located here; see Polk county.

Civil Records: Access: In person, online. Visitors must perform in person searches for themselves. No search fee. Required to search: name, years to search; also helpful: address. Civil cases indexed by defendant, plaintiff. Civil records on computer from July, 1992, docket books prior. Civil, probate, and appellate information is at www.judicial.state.ia.us/online_records.

Criminal Records: Access: In person, online. Visitors must perform in person searches for themselves. No search fee. Required to search: name, years to search, aliases; also helpful: DOB, SSN. Criminal records on computer from July, 1992, docket books prior. Criminal, traffic, and appellate information is online at www.judicial.state.ia.us/online_records. Records go back to 1992.

General Information: Public Access terminal is available. No juvenile, sealed, dissolution of marriage, mental health, domestic abuse or deferred records released. Copy fee: $.25 per page. Cert fee: $10.00. Payee: Clerk of Court. Personal checks accepted. Visa, MC accepted. Prepayment required.

Dickinson County

3rd District Court PO Drawer O N, Spirit Lake, IA 51360; 712-336-1138; Fax: 712-336-4005. Hours: 8AM-4:30PM (CST). *Felony, Misdemeanor, Civil, Eviction, Small Claims, Probate.*

Civil Records: Access: In person, online. Visitors must perform in person searches for themselves. No search fee. Required to search: name, years to search. Civil cases indexed by defendant, plaintiff. Early information on microfiche, docket books from 1800s; computerized back to 1992. Civil, probate, and appellate information is at www.judicial.state.ia.us/online_records.

Criminal Records: Access: In person, online. Visitors must perform in person searches for themselves. No search fee. Required to search: name, years to search. Criminal records early information on microfiche, docket books from 1800s; computerized back to 1992. Criminal, traffic, and appellate information is online at www.judicial.state.ia.us/online_records.

General Information: Public Access terminal is available. No juvenile, sealed, dissolution of marriage, mental health, domestic abuse or deferred records released. Copy fee: $.50 per page. Cert fee: $10.00. Payee: Clerk of Court. Personal checks accepted. Prepayment required.

Dubuque County

1st District Court 720 Central, Dubuque, IA 52001; 563-589-4418. Hours: 8AM-4:30PM (CST). *Felony, Misdemeanor, Civil, Eviction, Small Claims, Probate.*

Civil Records: Access: In person, online. Visitors must perform in person searches for themselves. No search fee. Required to search: name, years to search. Civil cases indexed by defendant, plaintiff. Civil records on computer since July, 1994, on docket books from 1900s. Civil, probate, and appellate information is at www.judicial.state.ia.us/online_records.

Criminal Records: Access: In person, online. Visitors must perform in person searches for themselves. No search fee. Required to search: name, years to search; also helpful: DOB, SSN. Criminal records on computer since July, 1994, on docket books from 1900s. Criminal, traffic, and appellate information is online at www.judicial.state.ia.us/online_records.

General Information: Public Access terminal is available. No juvenile, sealed, dissolution of marriage, mental health, domestic abuse or expunged records released. Copy fee: $.50 per page. Cert fee: $10.00. Payee: Clerk of District Court. Local checks accepted. Visa, MC accepted. Prepayment required.

Emmet County

3rd District Court Emmet County, 609 1st Ave N, Estherville, IA 51334; 712-362-3325. Hours: 8AM-4:30PM (CST). *Felony, Misdemeanor, Civil, Eviction, Small Claims, Probate.*

Civil Records: Access: In person, online. Visitors must perform in person searches for themselves. No search fee. Required to search: name, years to search. Civil cases indexed by defendant, plaintiff. Civil records on docket books from 1900s, on computer back to 2/96. Civil, probate, and appellate information is at www.judicial.state.ia.us/online_records.

Criminal Records: Access: In person, online. Visitors must perform in person searches for themselves. No search fee. Required to search: name, years to search. Criminal records on docket books from 1900s, on computer back to 2/96. Criminal, traffic, and appellate information is online at www.judicial.state.ia.us/online_records.

General Information: Public Access terminal is available. (Records go back to 1996.) No juvenile, sealed, dissolution of marriage, mental health, domestic abuse or deferred records released. Copy fee: $.50 per page. Cert fee: $10.00. Payee: Clerk of Court. Personal checks accepted. Prepayment required.

Fayette County

Fayette County District Court PO Box 458, West Union, IA 52175; 563-422-5694; Fax: 563-422-3137. Hours: 8AM-Noon, 4:30PM (CST). *Felony, Misdemeanor, Civil, Eviction, Small Claims, Probate, Traffic.*

Civil Records: Access: In person, online. Visitors must perform in person searches for themselves. Search fee: none. Required to search: name, years to search. Civil cases indexed by defendant, plaintiff. Civil records on docket books from 1900s, on computer back to 8/96. Civil, probate, and appellate data is at www.judicial.state.ia.us/online_records.

Criminal Records: Access: In person, online. Visitors must perform in person searches for themselves. Search fee: none. Required to search: name, years to search. Criminal records on docket books from 1900s; 1940-1960 on CD-ROM, on computer back to 8/96. Criminal, traffic, and appellate information is online at www.judicial.state.ia.us/online_records.

General Information: Public Access terminal is available. No juvenile, sealed, dissolution of marriage, mental health, domestic abuse or deferred records released. Copy fee: $.50 per page. Cert fee: $10.00. Payee: Clerk of Court. Personal checks accepted. Prepayment required.

Floyd County

2nd District Court 101 S Main St, Charles City, IA 50616; 641-228-7777; Fax: 641-228-7772. Hours: 8AM-4:30PM (CST). *Felony, Misdemeanor, Civil, Eviction, Small Claims, Probate.*
http://www.iowacourtsonline.org

Civil Records: Access: In person, online. Visitors must perform in person searches for themselves. No search fee. Required to search: name, years to search. Civil cases indexed by defendant, plaintiff. Civil records in docket books, are computerized since 1996. Civil, probate, and appellate information is at www.judicial.state.ia.us/online_records.

Criminal Records: Access: In person, online. Visitors must perform in person searches for

themselves. No search fee. Required to search: name, years to search, DOB, signed release; also helpful: SSN. Criminal records in docket books, are computerized since 1996. Criminal, traffic, and appellate information is online at www.judicial.state.ia.us/online_records.

General Information: Public Access terminal is available. No juvenile, sealed, dissolution of marriage, mental health, domestic abuse or deferred records released. Will not fax results. Copy fee: $.50 per page. Cert fee: $10.00. Payee: Clerk of Court. Personal checks accepted. Credit cards accepted. Prepayment required.

Franklin County

2nd Judicial District Court 12 1st Ave NW, PO Box 28, Hampton, IA 50441; 641-456-5626; Fax: 641-456-5628. Hours: 8AM-4PM (CST). *Felony, Misdemeanor, Civil, Eviction, Small Claims, Probate.*

Civil Records: Access: In person, online. Visitors must perform in person searches for themselves. No search fee. Required to search: name, years to search. Civil cases indexed by defendant, plaintiff. Civil records on microfiche and/or microfilm from 1860 to 1984, on docket books from 1984 to present. Civil, probate, and appellate information is at www.judicial.state.ia.us/online_records.

Criminal Records: Access: In person, online. Visitors must perform in person searches for themselves. No search fee. Required to search: name, years to search. Criminal records on microfiche and/or microfilm from 1860 to 1984, on docket books from 1984 to present. Criminal, traffic, and appellate information is online at www.judicial.state.ia.us/online_records.

General Information: Public Access terminal is available. No juvenile, sealed, dissolution of marriage, mental health, domestic abuse or deferred records released. Will fax specifc case file requests for $1.00 per page. Copy fee: $.50 per page. Cert fee: $10.00. Payee: Clerk of District Court. Personal checks accepted. Visa, MC accepted. Credit cards accepted for traffic fees only. Prepayment required.

Fremont County

4th District Court PO Box 549, Sidney, IA 51652; 712-374-2232; Fax: 712-374-3330. Hours: 8:00AM-4:30PM (CST). *Felony, Misdemeanor, Civil, Eviction, Small Claims, Probate.*
www.co.fremont.ia.us

Civil Records: Access: In person, online. Visitors must perform in person searches for themselves. No search fee. Required to search: name. Civil cases indexed by defendant, plaintiff. Computerized from 11/96, civil records in docket books and microfiche from the 1930's. Civil, probate, and appellate data is at www.judicial.state.ia.us/online_records.

Criminal Records: Access: In person, online. Visitors must perform in person searches for themselves. No search fee. Required to search: name. Computerized from 11/96, criminal records in docket books and microfiche from the 1930's. Criminal, traffic, and appellate information is online at www.judicial.state.ia.us/online_records.

General Information: Public Access terminal is available. No juvenile, sealed, dissolution of marriage, mental health, domestic abuse or deferred records released. Copy fee: $.25 per page. Cert fee: $10.00. Payee: Clerk of Court. Personal checks accepted. Prepayment required.

Greene County

2nd District Court Greene County Courthouse, 114 N Chestnut, Jefferson, IA 50129; 515-386-2516. Hours: 8AM-4:30PM (CST). *Felony, Misdemeanor, Civil, Eviction, Small Claims, Probate.*
Civil Records: Access: In person, online. Visitors must perform in person searches for themselves. No search fee. Required to search: name, years to search. Civil cases indexed by defendant, plaintiff. Civil records on microfiche from 1981 back to establishment of court, docket books from 1800s, on computer back to 7/97. Civil, probate, and appellate information is at www.judicial.state.ia.us/online_records.
Criminal Records: Access: In person, online. Visitors must perform in person searches for themselves. No search fee. Required to search: name, years to search. Criminal records on microfiche from 1981 back to establishment of court, docket books from 1800s, on computer back to 7/97. Criminal, traffic, and appellate information is online at www.judicial.state.ia.us/online_records.
General Information: Public Access terminal is available. No juvenile, sealed, dissolution of marriage, mental health, domestic abuse or deferred records released. Copy fee: $.50 per page. Cert fee: $10.00. Payee: Clerk of Court. Personal checks accepted. Visa, MC accepted. Credit cards accepted for traffic fees only. Prepayment required.

Grundy County

1st District Court Grundy County Courthouse, 706 G Ave, Grundy Center, IA 50638; 319-824-5229; Fax: 319-824-3447. Hours: 8AM-4:30PM (CST). *Felony, Misdemeanor, Civil, Eviction, Small Claims, Probate.*
www.grundycounty.org/clerkofcourt/index.asp
Civil Records: Access: In person, online. Visitors must perform in person searches for themselves. No search fee. Required to search: name, years to search. Civil cases indexed by defendant, plaintiff. Civil records on docket books from 1881, on computer back to 4/97. Civil, probate, and appellate information is at www.judicial.state.ia.us/online_records. Records complete back to 4/97.
Criminal Records: Access: In person, online. Visitors must perform in person searches for themselves. No search fee. Required to search: name, years to search. Criminal records on docket books from 1881, on computer back to 4/97. Criminal, traffic, and appellate information is online at www.judicial.state.ia.us/online_records.
General Information: Public Access terminal is available. No pending, confidential, juvenile, sealed, dissolution of marriage, mental health, or expunged records released. Copy fee: $.50 per page. Cert fee: $10.00. Payee: Clerk of Court. Personal checks accepted. Visa, MC accepted. Prepayment required.

Guthrie County

5th District Court Courthouse, 200 N 5th St, Guthrie Center, IA 50115; 641-747-3415. Hours: 8AM-4:30PM (CST). *Felony, Misdemeanor, Civil, Eviction, Small Claims, Probate.*
Civil Records: Access: In person, online. Visitors must perform in person searches for themselves. No search fee. Required to search: name, years to search. Civil cases indexed by defendant, plaintiff. Civil records on computer since 11/96; prior records on docket books from 1880s. Civil, probate, and appellate information is at www.judicial.state.ia.us/online_records.
Criminal Records: Access: In person, online. Visitors must perform in person searches for themselves. No search fee. Required to search: name, years to search. Criminal records on computer since

11/96; prior records on docket books from 1880s. Criminal, traffic, and appellate information is online at www.judicial.state.ia.us/online_records.
General Information: Public Access terminal is available. No juvenile, sealed, dissolution of marriage, mental health, domestic abuse or deferred records released. Copy fee: $.50 per page. Cert fee: $10.00. Payee: Clerk of Court. Personal checks accepted. Prepayment required.

Hamilton County

2nd District Court Courthouse, PO Box 845, Webster City, IA 50595; 515-832-9600. Hours: 8:30AM-4:30PM (CST). *Felony, Misdemeanor, Civil, Eviction, Small Claims, Probate.*
Civil Records: Access: In person, online. Visitors must perform in person searches for themselves. No search fee. Required to search: name, years to search. Civil cases indexed by defendant, plaintiff. Civil records on microfiche from 1939, docket books from 1880s. Civil, probate, and appellate information is at www.judicial.state.ia.us/online_records.
Criminal Records: Access: In person, online. Visitors must perform in person searches for themselves. No search fee. Required to search: name, years to search. Criminal records go back to 1996. Criminal, traffic, and appellate information is online at www.judicial.state.ia.us/online_records.
General Information: Public Access terminal is available. No juvenile, sealed, dissolution of marriage, mental health, domestic abuse records released. Will fax specifc case file requests for $1.00 per page. Copy fee: $.50 per page. Cert fee: $10.00. Payee: Clerk of Court. Personal checks accepted. Credit cards accepted. Prepayment required.

Hancock County

2nd District Court 855 State St, Garner, IA 50438; 641-923-2532; Fax: 641-923-3521. Hours: 9AM-3:30PM (CST). *Felony, Misdemeanor, Civil, Eviction, Small Claims, Probate.*
Civil Records: Access: In person, online. Visitors must perform in person searches for themselves. No search fee. Required to search: name, years to search. Civil cases indexed by defendant, plaintiff. Civil records on docket books from 1880s; on computer since 1997. Civil, probate, and appellate information is at www.judicial.state.ia.us/online_records.
Criminal Records: Access: In person, online. Visitors must perform in person searches for themselves. No search fee. Required to search: name, years to search. Criminal records on docket books from 1880s; on computer since 1997. Criminal, traffic, and appellate information is online at www.judicial.state.ia.us/online_records.
General Information: Public Access terminal is available. No juvenile, sealed, dissolution of marriage, mental health, domestic abuse or deferred records released. Copy fee: $.50 per page. Cert fee: $10.00. Payee: Clerk of Court. Personal checks accepted. Prepayment required.

Hardin County

2nd District Court Courthouse, PO Box 495, Eldora, IA 50627; 641-858-2328; Fax: 641-858-2320. Hours: 9AM-3:30PM (CST). *Felony, Misdemeanor, Civil, Eviction, Small Claims, Probate.*
Civil Records: Access: In person, online. Visitors must perform in person searches for themselves. No search fee. Required to search: name, years to search. Civil cases indexed by defendant, plaintiff. Civil records on docket books from 1880s, on computer back to 2/96. Civil, probate, and appellate information is at www.judicial.state.ia.us/online_records.
Criminal Records: Access: In person, online. Visitors must perform in person searches for themselves. No search fee. Required to search: name,

years to search. Criminal records on docket books from 1880s, on computer back to 2/96. Criminal, traffic, and appellate information is online at www.judicial.state.ia.us/online_records.
General Information: Public Access terminal is available. No juvenile, sealed, dissolution of marriage, mental health, domestic abuse or deferred records released. Copy fee: $.50 per page. Cert fee: $10.00. Payee: Clerk of Court. Personal checks accepted. Visa, MC accepted. Prepayment required.

Harrison County

District Court Court House, Logan, IA 51546; 712-644-2665. Hours: 8:30AM-3:30PM (CST). *Felony, Misdemeanor, Civil, Eviction, Small Claims, Probate.*
Civil Records: Access: In person, online. Visitors must perform in person searches for themselves. No search fee. Required to search: name, years to search. Civil cases indexed by defendant, plaintiff. Civil records on computer since 11/96; prior on docket books since 1840s in Clerk's office. Recent death and birth certificates on microfiche. Civil, probate, and appellate information is at www.judicial.state.ia.us/online_records.
Criminal Records: Access: In person, online. Visitors must perform in person searches for themselves. No search fee. Required to search: name, years to search. Criminal records on computer since 11/96, prior on docket books from 1840s in Clerk's office. Criminal, traffic, and appellate information is online at www.judicial.state.ia.us/online_records.
General Information: Public Access terminal is available. No juvenile, sealed, confidential, dissolution of marriage, mental health, domestic abuse or deferred records released. Copy fee: $.25 per page. Cert fee: $10.00. Payee: Clerk of Court. Personal checks accepted. Prepayment required.

Henry County

8th District Court Clerk of Court, PO Box 176, Mount Pleasant, IA 52641; Civil phone: 319-385-2632; Criminal phone: 319-385-3150/319-385-4203; Fax: 319-385-4144. Hours: 8AM-4:30PM (CST). *Felony, Misdemeanor, Civil, Eviction, Small Claims, Probate.*
Civil Records: Access: In person, online. Visitors must perform in person searches for themselves. No search fee. Required to search: name, years to search. Civil cases indexed by defendant, plaintiff. Civil records on docket books from 1880s, on computer back to 10/1986. Civil, probate, and appellate information is at www.judicial.state.ia.us/online_records.
Criminal Records: Access: In person, online. Visitors must perform in person searches for themselves. No search fee. Required to search: name, years to search, DOB; also helpful: address, SSN. Criminal records on docket books from early 1900s, on computer back to 2/96. Criminal, traffic, and appellate information is online at www.judicial.state.ia.us/online_records.
General Information: Public Access terminal is available. No juvenile, sealed, dissolution of marriage, mental health, domestic abuse or deferred records released. Copy fee: $.25 per page. Cert fee: $10.00. Payee: Clerk of Court. Personal checks accepted. Prepayment required.

Howard County

1st District Court Courthouse, 137 N Elm St, Cresco, IA 52136; 563-547-2661. Hours: 8AM-4:30PM (CST). *Felony, Misdemeanor, Civil, Eviction, Small Claims, Probate.*
www.judicial.state.ia.us/district/d1.asp
Civil Records: Access: In person, online. Visitors must perform in person searches for themselves. No

search fee. Required to search: name, years to search. Civil cases indexed by defendant, plaintiff. Civil records on docket books from 1900s, on computer back to 4/97. Civil, probate, and appellate information is at www.judicial.state.ia.us/online_records.

Criminal Records: Access: In person, online. Visitors must perform in person searches for themselves. No search fee. Required to search: name, years to search, DOB. Criminal records on docket books from 1900s, on computer back to 4/97. Criminal, traffic, and appellate information is online at www.judicial.state.ia.us/online_records.

General Information: Public Access terminal is available. No juvenile, sealed, pending, dissolution of marriage, mental health, domestic abuse or deferred records released. Copy fee: $.50 per page. Cert fee: $10.00. Payee: Clerk of Court. Personal checks accepted. Prepayment required.

Humboldt County

2nd District Court PO Box 100, Dakota City, IA 50529; 515-332-1806; Fax: 515-332-7100. Hours: 8AM-4:30PM (CST). *Felony, Misdemeanor, Civil, Eviction, Small Claims, Probate.*

Civil Records: Access: In person, online. Visitors must perform in person searches for themselves. No search fee. Required to search: name, years to search. Civil cases indexed by defendant, plaintiff. Civil records on docket books from early 1900s; computerized records since 7/97. Civil, probate, and appellate information is at www.judicial.state.ia.us/online_records.

Criminal Records: Access: In person, online. Visitors must perform in person searches for themselves. No search fee. Required to search: name, years to search. Criminal records on docket books from early 1900s; computerized records since 7/97. Criminal, traffic, and appellate information is online at www.judicial.state.ia.us/online_records.

General Information: Public Access terminal is available. No juvenile, sealed, dissolution of marriage, mental health, domestic abuse or deferred records released. Copy fee: $.50 per page. Cert fee: $10.00. Payee: Clerk of Court. Personal checks accepted. Prepayment required.

Ida County

3rd District Court Courthouse, 401 Moorehead St, Ida Grove, IA 51445; 712-364-2628; Fax: 712-364-2699. Hours: 8AM-4:30PM T, TH, F (CST). *Felony, Misdemeanor, Civil, Eviction, Small Claims, Probate.*

Civil Records: Access: In person, online. Visitors must perform in person searches for themselves. No search fee. Required to search: name, years to search. Civil cases indexed by defendant, plaintiff. Civil records on docket books from early 1800s, computerized since 07/97. Civil, probate, and appellate information is at www.judicial.state.ia.us/online_records.

Criminal Records: Access: In person, online. Visitors must perform in person searches for themselves. No search fee. Required to search: name, years to search. Criminal records on docket books from early 1800s, computerized since 07/97. Criminal, traffic, and appellate information is online at www.judicial.state.ia.us/online_records.

General Information: Public Access terminal is available. No juvenile, sealed, dissolution of marriage, mental health, domestic abuse or deferred records released. Copy fee: $.50 per page. Cert fee: $10.00. Payee: Clerk of Court. Personal checks accepted. Prepayment required.

Iowa County

6th District Court PO Box 266, Marengo, IA 52301; 319-642-3914. Hours: 8AM-4:30PM (CST). *Felony, Misdemeanor, Civil, Eviction, Small Claims, Probate.*

Civil Records: Access: In person, online. Visitors must perform in person searches for themselves. No search fee. Required to search: name, years to search. Civil cases indexed by defendant, plaintiff. Civil records on docket books from early 1800s; on computer back to 2/97. Civil, probate, and appellate information is at www.judicial.state.ia.us/online_records.

Criminal Records: Access: Mail, in person, online. Visitors must perform in person searches for themselves. No search fee. Required to search: name, years to search. Criminal records on docket books from early 1800s; on computer back to 2/1997. Criminal, traffic, and appellate information is online at www.judicial.state.ia.us/online_records.

General Information: Public Access terminal is available. No juvenile, sealed, dissolution of marriage, mental health, domestic abuse or deferred records released. Copy fee: $.50 per page. Cert fee: $10.00. Payee: Clerk of Court. Personal checks accepted. Prepayment required. Mail requests: Turnaround is as time permits.

Jackson County

7th District Court 201 W Platt, Maquoketa, IA 52060; 563-652-4946; Fax: 563-652-2708. Hours: 8AM-4:30PM (CST). *Felony, Misdemeanor, Civil, Eviction, Small Claims, Probate.*

Civil Records: Access: In person, online. Visitors must perform in person searches for themselves. No search fee. Required to search: name, years to search. Civil cases indexed by defendant, plaintiff. Civil records on computer since 1994, on docket books from 1900s. Civil, probate, and appellate information is at www.judicial.state.ia.us/online_records.

Criminal Records: Access: In person, online. Visitors must perform in person searches for themselves. No search fee. Required to search: name, years to search, DOB; also helpful: SSN. Criminal records on computer since 1994, on docket books from 1900s. Criminal, traffic, and appellate information is online at www.judicial.state.ia.us/online_records.

General Information: Public Access terminal is available. No juvenile, sealed, dissolution of marriage, mental health, domestic abuse or deferred records released. Copy fee: $.50 per page. Cert fee: $10.00. Payee: Clerk of Court. Personal checks accepted. Prepayment required.

Jasper County

5th District Court 101 1st St North, Rm 104, Newton, IA 50208; 641-792-3255; Civil phone: 641-792-3255; Criminal phone: 641-792-9161; Fax: 641-792-2818. Hours: 8AM-4:30PM (CST). *Felony, Misdemeanor, Civil, Eviction, Small Claims, Probate.*
www.judicial.state.ia.us/decisions/district/d5.asp

Civil Records: Access: In person, online. Visitors must perform in person searches for themselves. Court will pull file if given case number. No search fee. Required to search: name, years to search. Civil cases indexed by defendant, plaintiff. Civil records on computer since 1994, docket books from 1900s. Civil, probate, and appellate information is at www.judicial.state.ia.us/online_records.

Criminal Records: Access: In person, online. Visitors must perform in person searches for themselves. Court will pull file if given case number. No search fee. Required to search: name, years to search. Criminal records on computer since 1994,

docket books from 1900s. Criminal, traffic, and appellate information is online at www.judicial.state.ia.us/online_records.

General Information: Public Access terminal is available. No juvenile, sealed, dissolution of marriage, mental health, or deferred records released. Juvenile delinquency is public record, not CINA< FINA termination of adoption. Copy fee: $.50 per page. Cert fee: $10.00 per document. Payee: Clerk of Court. Personal checks accepted. Prepayment required.

Jefferson County

8th District Court PO Box 984, Fairfield, IA 52556; 641-472-3454; Fax: 641-472-9472. Hours: 8AM-4:30PM M-F (CST). *Felony, Misdemeanor, Civil, Eviction, Small Claims, Probate.*

Civil Records: Access: In person, online. Visitors must perform in person searches for themselves. No search fee. Required to search: name, years to search. Civil cases indexed by defendant, plaintiff. Civil records on docket books from 1800s, on computer back to 2/96. Civil, probate, and appellate information is at www.judicial.state.ia.us/online_records.

Criminal Records: Access: In person, online. Visitors must perform in person searches for themselves. No search fee. Required to search: name, years to search, DOB. Criminal records on docket books from 1800s, on computer back to 2/96. Criminal, traffic, and appellate information is online at www.judicial.state.ia.us/online_records.

General Information: Public Access terminal is available. No juvenile, sealed, dissolution of marriage, mental health, domestic abuse or deferred records released. Copy fee: $.25 per page. Cert fee: $10.00. Payee: Clerk of Court. Personal checks accepted. Prepayment required.

Johnson County

6th District Court PO Box 2510, Iowa City, IA 52244; 319-356-6060. Hours: 8AM-4:30PM (CST). *Felony, Misdemeanor, Civil, Eviction, Small Claims, Probate.*

Civil Records: Access: In person, online. Visitors must perform in person searches for themselves. No search fee. Required to search: name, years to search. Civil cases indexed by defendant, plaintiff. Civil records on docket books and microfilm from 1880s, on computer back to 4/93. Civil, probate, and appellate information is at www.judicial.state.ia.us/online_records.

Criminal Records: Access: In person, online. Visitors must perform in person searches for themselves. No search fee. Required to search: name, years to search; also helpful: address, DOB, SSN. Criminal records on docket books and microfilm from 1880s, on computer back to 4/93. Criminal, traffic, and appellate information is online at www.judicial.state.ia.us/online_records.

General Information: Public Access terminal is available. No juvenile, sealed, dissolution of marriage, mental health, domestic abuse or deferred records released. Copy fee: $.50 per page. Cert fee: $10.00. Payee: Clerk of Court. Personal checks accepted. Prepayment required.

Jones County

6th District Court PO Box 19, Attn: Clerk of District Court, Anamosa, IA 52205; 319-462-4341. Hours: 8AM-4:30PM (CST). *Felony, Misdemeanor, Civil, Eviction, Small Claims, Probate.*

Civil Records: Access: In person, online. Visitors must perform in person searches for themselves. No search fee. Required to search: name, years to search. Civil cases indexed by defendant, plaintiff. Civil records on docket books from mid 1800s; dockets on computer back to 6/1997. Civil, probate, and appellate

information is at www.judicial.state.ia.us/online_records.
Criminal Records: Access: In person, online. Visitors must perform in person searches for themselves. No search fee. Required to search: name, years to search. Criminal records on docket books from early 1900s; dockets on computer back to 11/1996. Criminal, traffic, and appellate information is online at www.judicial.state.ia.us/online_records.
General Information: Public Access terminal is available. No juvenile, sealed, dissolution of marriage (prior to decree), mental health or deferred records released. Copy fee: $.50 per page. Cert fee: $10.00. Payee: Clerk of Court. Personal checks accepted. Prepayment required.

Keokuk County

8th District Court 101 S Main, Courthouse, Sigourney, IA 52591; 641-622-2210; Fax: 641-622-2171. Hours: 8AM-4:30PM (CST). *Felony, Misdemeanor, Civil, Eviction, Small Claims, Probate.*
Civil Records: Access: In person, online. Visitors must perform in person searches for themselves. No search fee. Required to search: name, years to search. Civil cases indexed by defendant, plaintiff. Civil records on docket books from 1888; on computer back to 2/1997. Civil, probate, and appellate information is at www.judicial.state.ia.us/online_records.
Criminal Records: Access: In person, online. Visitors must perform in person searches for themselves. No search fee. Required to search: name, years to search. Criminal records on docket books from 1888; on computer back to 2/1997. Criminal, traffic, and appellate information is online at www.judicial.state.ia.us/online_records.
General Information: Public Access terminal is available. No juvenile, sealed, dissolution of marriage, mental health, domestic abuse or deferred records released. Copy fee: $.25 per page. Cert fee: $10.00. Payee: Clerk of Court. Personal checks accepted. Prepayment required.

Kossuth County

3rd District Court Kossuth County Courthouse, 114 W State St, Algona, IA 50511; 515-295-3240. Hours: 8AM-4;30PM (CST). *Felony, Misdemeanor, Civil, Eviction, Small Claims, Probate.*
Civil Records: Access: In person, online. Visitors must perform in person searches for themselves. No search fee. Required to search: name, years to search. Civil cases indexed by defendant, plaintiff. Civil records on computer since 09/97; prior records on dockets. Civil, probate, and appellate information is at www.judicial.state.ia.us/online_records.
Criminal Records: Access: In person, online. Visitors must perform in person searches for themselves. No search fee. Required to search: name, years to search. Criminal records on computer since 09/97; prior records on dockets. Criminal, traffic, and appellate information is online at www.judicial.state.ia.us/online_records.
General Information: Public Access terminal is available. No juvenile, sealed, dissolution of marriage, mental health, domestic abuse or deferred records released. Copy fee: $.50 per page. Cert fee: $10.00. Payee: Clerk of Court. Personal checks accepted. Prepayment required.

Lee County

8th District Court PO Box 1443, Ft Madison, IA 52627; 319-372-3523. Hours: 8AM-4:30PM (CST). *Felony, Misdemeanor, Civil, Eviction, Small Claims, Probate.*
Civil Records: Access: In person, online. Visitors must perform in person searches for themselves. No

search fee. Required to search: name, years to search. Civil cases indexed by defendant, plaintiff. Civil records on docket books from early 1800s; computerized from 1996. Civil, probate, and appellate information is at www.judicial.state.ia.us/online_records.
Criminal Records: Access: In person, online. Visitors must perform in person searches for themselves. No search fee. Required to search: name, years to search. Criminal records on docket books from early 1800s; computerized from 1996. Criminal, traffic, and appellate information is online at www.judicial.state.ia.us/online_records.
General Information: Public Access terminal is available. No juvenile, sealed, pending dissolution of marriage, mental health, domestic abuse or deferred records released. Copy fee: $.25 per page. Cert fee: $10.00. Payee: Clerk of Court. Personal checks accepted. Prepayment required.

Linn County

District Court Linn County Courthouse, PO Box 1468, Cedar Rapids, IA 52406-1468; 319-398-3411; Fax: 319-398-3449. Hours: 8AM-4:30PM (CST). *Felony, Misdemeanor, Civil, Eviction, Small Claims, Probate.*
Civil Records: Access: In person, online. Visitors must perform in person searches for themselves. No search fee. Required to search: name, years to search. Civil cases indexed by defendant, plaintiff. Civil records on computer from 1995, docket books from early 1900s. Civil, probate, and appellate information is at www.judicial.state.ia.us/online_records.
Criminal Records: Access: In person, online. Visitors must perform in person searches for themselves. No search fee. Required to search: name, years to search; also helpful: address, DOB. Criminal records on computer since 1993. Criminal, traffic, and appellate information is online at www.judicial.state.ia.us/online_records.
General Information: Public Access terminal is available. No juvenile, sealed, pending dissolution of marriage, mental health, domestic abuse or deferred records released. Copy fee: $.50 per page. Cert fee: $10.00. Payee: Clerk of Court. Personal checks accepted. Prepayment required.

Louisa County

8th District Court PO Box 268, Wapello, IA 52653; 319-523-4541; Fax: 319-523-4542. Hours: 8AM-4;30PM (CST). *Felony, Misdemeanor, Civil, Eviction, Small Claims, Probate.*
Civil Records: Access: In person, online. Both court and visitors may perform in person searches. No search fee. Required to search: name, years to search. Civil cases indexed by defendant, plaintiff. Civil records on docket books from 1920s, on computer since 02/97. Civil, probate, and appellate information is at www.judicial.state.ia.us/online_records.
Criminal Records: Access: In person, online. Both court and visitors may perform in person searches. No search fee. Required to search: name, years to search, DOB, signed release; also helpful: SSN. Criminal records on docket books from 1920s, on computer since 02/97. Criminal, traffic, and appellate information is online at www.judicial.state.ia.us/online_records.
General Information: Public Access terminal is available. No juvenile, sealed, dissolution of marriage, mental health, domestic abuse or deferred records released. Copy fee: $.25 per page. Cert fee: $10.00. Payee: Clerk of Court. Personal checks accepted. Prepayment required.

Lucas County

5th District Court Courthouse, 916 Braden, Chariton, IA 50049; 641-774-4421; Fax: 641-774-8669. Hours: 8AM-4:30PM M-F (CST). *Felony, Misdemeanor, Civil, Eviction, Small Claims, Probate.*
Civil Records: Access: In person, online. Visitors must perform in person searches for themselves. No search fee. Required to search: name, years to search. Civil cases indexed by defendant, plaintiff. Civil records on docket books from 1880s; on computer back to 1997. Civil, probate, and appellate information is at www.judicial.state.ia.us/online_records.
Criminal Records: Access: In person, online. Visitors must perform in person searches for themselves. No search fee. Required to search: name, years to search, signed release; also helpful: SSN. Criminal records on docket books from 1880s; on computer back to 1997. Criminal, traffic, and appellate information is online at www.judicial.state.ia.us/online_records.
General Information: Public Access terminal is available. No juvenile, adoption, sealed, dissolution of marriage, mental health, domestic abuse or deferred records released. Will fax back results for $1.00 per page. Copy fee: $.50 per page. Cert fee: $10.00. Payee: Clerk of District Court. Personal checks accepted. Visa, MC accepted. Prepayment required.

Lyon County

3rd District Court Courthouse, Rock Rapids, IA 51246; 712-472-2623; Fax: 712-472-2422. Hours: 8AM-4:30PM (CST). *Felony, Misdemeanor, Civil, Eviction, Small Claims, Probate.*
Civil Records: Access: In person, online. Visitors must perform in person searches for themselves. No search fee. Required to search: name, years to search. Civil cases indexed by defendant, plaintiff. Civil records on docket books from 1880s, on computer back to 9/97. Civil, probate, and appellate information is at www.judicial.state.ia.us/online_records.
Criminal Records: Access: In person, online. Visitors must perform in person searches for themselves. No search fee. Required to search: name, years to search. Criminal records on docket books from 1880s, on computer back to 9/97. Criminal, traffic, and appellate information is online at www.judicial.state.ia.us/online_records.
General Information: Public Access terminal is available. No juvenile, sealed, dissolution of marriage, mental health, domestic abuse or deferred records released. Copy fee: $.50 per page. Cert fee: $10.00. Payee: Clerk of Court. Personal checks accepted. Prepayment required.

Madison County

5th District Court PO Box 152, Winterset, IA 50273; 515-462-4451; Fax: 515-462-9825. Hours: 8AM-4:30PM (CST). *Felony, Misdemeanor, Civil, Eviction, Small Claims, Probate.*
Civil Records: Access: In person, online. Visitors must perform in person searches for themselves. No search fee. Required to search: name, years to search. Civil cases indexed by plaintiff. Civil records on docket books from 1880s; computerized records since 1996. Misdemeanor records from 1974 to present. Other criminal same record keeping as civil. Civil, probate, and appellate information is at www.judicial.state.ia.us/online_records.
Criminal Records: Access: In person, online. Visitors must perform in person searches for themselves. No search fee. Required to search: name, years to search; also helpful: DOB. Criminal records on docket books from 1880s; computerized records since 1996. Misdemeanor records from 1974 to

present. Other criminal same record keeping as civil. Criminal, traffic, and appellate information is online at www.judicial.state.ia.us/online_records.

General Information: Public Access terminal is available. No juvenile, sealed, dissolution of marriage, mental health, domestic abuse of deferred records released. Copy fee: $.50 per page. Cert fee: $10.00. Payee: Clerk of Court. Personal checks accepted. Prepayment required.

Mahaska County

8th District Court Courthouse, 106 S 1st St, Oskaloosa, IA 52577; 641-673-7786; Fax: 641-672-1256. 8AM-4:30PM (CST). *Felony, Misdemeanor, Civil, Eviction, Small Claims, Probate.*

Civil Records: Access: In person, online. Visitors must perform in person searches for themselves. No search fee. Required to search: name, years to search. Civil cases indexed by defendant, plaintiff. Civil records on docket books from 1880s; computerized records since 1995. Civil, probate, and appellate data is at www.judicial.state.ia.us/online_records.

Criminal Records: Access: In person, online. Visitors must perform in person searches for themselves. No search fee. Required to search: name, years to search. Criminal records on docket books from 1880s; computerized records since 1995. Criminal, traffic, and appellate information is online at www.judicial.state.ia.us/online_records.

General Information: Public Access terminal is available. No juvenile, sealed, dissolution of marriage, mental health, domestic abuse or deferred records released. Copy fee: $.50 per page. Docket Copy Fee: $1.00 per page. Cert fee: $10.00. Payee: Clerk of Court. Personal checks accepted. Prepayment required.

Marion County

5th District Court PO Box 497, Knoxville, IA 50138; 641-828-2207; Fax: 641-828-7580. Hours: 8AM-4:30PM (CST). *Felony, Misdemeanor, Civil, Eviction, Small Claims, Probate.*

Civil Records: Access: In person, online. Visitors must perform in person searches for themselves. No search fee. Required to search: name, years to search. Civil cases indexed by defendant, plaintiff. Civil records on computer since 1992, docket books from 1896. Civil, probate, and appellate information is at www.judicial.state.ia.us/online_records.

Criminal Records: Access: In person, online. Visitors must perform in person searches for themselves. No search fee. Required to search: name, years to search. Criminal records on computer since 1992, docket books from 1896. Criminal, traffic, and appellate information is online at www.judicial.state.ia.us/online_records.

General Information: Public Access terminal is available. Delinquencies are public, not CINA, FINA, Termination or adoptions. No juvenile, sealed, dissolution of marriage, or mental health records released. Copy fee: $.50 per page. Cert fee: $10.00. Payee: Clerk of Court. Personal checks accepted. Prepayment required.

Marshall County

2nd District Court Courthouse, 17 E Main St., Marshalltown, IA 50158; 641-754-1603; Fax: 641-754-1600. Hours: 8AM-4:30PM (CST). *Felony, Misdemeanor, Civil, Eviction, Small Claims, Probate.*

Note: This court alos handles traffic, child support, and liens.

Civil Records: Access: In person, online. Visitors must perform in person searches for themselves. No search fee. Required to search: name, years to search. Civil cases indexed by defendant, plaintiff. Civil

records on computer since June, 1994, docket books from late 1800s. Civil, probate, and appellate information is at www.judicial.state.ia.us/online_records.

Criminal Records: Access: In person, online. Visitors must perform in person searches for themselves. No search fee. Required to search: name, years to search; also helpful: DOB, SSN. Criminal records on computer since August, 1992, docket books from late 1800s. Criminal, traffic, and appellate data is at www.judicial.state.ia.us/online_records.

General Information: Public Access terminal is available. No juvenile, sealed, pending dissolution of marriage, mental health, sealed domestic abuse and deferred records released. Copy fee: $.50 per page. Cert fee: $10.00. Payee: Clerk of Court. Personal checks accepted. Credit cards accepted. Prepayment required.

Mills County

4th District Court 418 Sharp St, Courthouse, Glenwood, IA 51534; 712-527-4880; Fax: 712-527-4936. 8AM-4:30PM (CST). *Felony, Misdemeanor, Civil, Eviction, Small Claims, Probate.*

Civil Records: Access: In person, online. Both court and visitors may perform in person searches. No search fee. Required to search: name, years to search. Civil cases indexed by defendant, plaintiff. Civil records on docket books since 1880s; computerized records since 1992. Civil, probate, and appellate information is at www.judicial.state.ia.us/online_records.

Criminal Records: Access: In person, online. Both court and visitors may perform in person searches. No search fee. Required to search: name, years to search, DOB; also helpful: SSN. Criminal records on docket books since 1880s; computerized records since 02/96. Criminal, traffic, and appellate information is online at www.judicial.state.ia.us/online_records.

General Information: Public Access terminal is available. No juvenile, sealed, dissolution of marriage, mental health, domestic abuse or deferred records released. Copy fee: $.25 per page. Cert fee: $10.00. Payee: Clerk of Court. Personal checks accepted. Prepayment required.

Mitchell County

2nd District Court 508 State St, Osage, IA 50461; 641-732-3726; Fax: 641-732-3728. Hours: 9AM-3:30PM (CST). *Felony, Misdemeanor, Civil, Eviction, Small Claims, Probate.*

Civil Records: Access: In person, online. Visitors must perform in person searches for themselves. No search fee. Required to search: name, years to search. Civil cases indexed by defendant, plaintiff. Civil records on docket books from 1880s, computerized since 1997. Civil, probate, and appellate information is at www.judicial.state.ia.us/online_records.

Criminal Records: Access: In person, online. Visitors must perform in person searches for themselves. No search fee. Required to search: name, years to search, signed release. Criminal records on docket books from 1880s, computerized since 1997. Criminal, traffic, and appellate information is online at www.judicial.state.ia.us/online_records.

General Information: Public Access terminal is available. No juvenile, sealed, dissolution of marriage, mental health, domestic abuse or deferred records released. Copy fee: $.50 per page. Cert fee: $10.00 plus copy fee. Payee: Clerk of Court. Personal checks accepted. Prepayment required.

Monona County

3rd District Court 610 Iowa Ave, Attn: Clerk of Court, Onawa, IA 51040; 712-423-2491. Hours: 8AM-4:30PM (CST). *Felony, Misdemeanor, Civil, Eviction, Small Claims, Probate.*

www.iowacourtsonline.org

Civil Records: Access: In person, online. Visitors must perform in person searches for themselves. No search fee. Required to search: name, years to search. Civil cases indexed by defendant, plaintiff. Civil records on computer since 07/97; prior records on microfiche and docket books from 1880s. Civil, probate, and appellate information is at www.judicial.state.ia.us/online_records.

Criminal Records: Access: In person, online. Visitors must perform in person searches for themselves. No search fee. Required to search: name, years to search. Criminal records on computer since 07/97; prior records on microfiche and docket books from 1880s. Criminal, traffic, and appellate data is online at www.judicial.state.ia.us/online_records.

General Information: Public Access terminal is available. No juvenile, sealed, dissolution of marriage, mental health, or deferred records released. Copy fee: $.50 per page. Cert fee: $10.00. Payee: Clerk of Court. Personal checks accepted. Prepayment required.

Monroe County

8th District Court Courthouse, 10 Benton Ave E, Albia, IA 52531; 641-932-5212; Fax: 641-932-3245. 8AM-4:30PM (CST). *Felony, Misdemeanor, Civil, Eviction, Small Claims, Probate.*

Civil Records: Access: In person, online. Visitors must perform in person searches for themselves. No search fee. Required to search: name, years to search. Civil cases indexed by defendant, plaintiff. Civil records on docket books from late 1800s, on computer back to 2/97. Civil, probate, and appellate information is at www.judicial.state.ia.us/online_records.

Criminal Records: Access: In person, online. Visitors must perform in person searches for themselves. No search fee. Required to search: name, years to search, DOB, signed release; also helpful: SSN. Criminal records on docket books from late 1800s, on computer back to 2/97. Criminal, traffic, and appellate information is online at www.judicial.state.ia.us/online_records.

General Information: Public Access terminal is available. No juvenile, sealed, dissolution of marriage, mental health, domestic abuse or deferred records released. Copy fee: $.50 per page. Cert fee: $10.00. Payee: Clerk of Court. Personal checks accepted. Prepayment required.

Montgomery County

4th District Court PO Box 469, Red Oak, IA 51566; 712-623-4986. Hours: 8:30AM-4:30PM (CST). *Felony, Misdemeanor, Civil, Eviction, Small Claims, Probate.*

Civil Records: Access: In person, online. Visitors must perform in person searches for themselves. Search fee: none. Required to search: name, years to search. Civil cases indexed by defendant, plaintiff. Civil records on docket books from 1940, microfiche prior, on computer back to 6/96. Civil, probate, and appellate information is at www.judicial.state.ia.us/online_records.

Criminal Records: Access: In person, online. Visitors must perform in person searches for themselves. Search fee: none. Required to search: name, years to search. Criminal records on docket books from 1940, microfiche prior, on computer back to 6/96. Criminal, traffic, and appellate information is online at www.judicial.state.ia.us/online_records.

General Information: Public Access terminal is available. No juvenile, sealed, dissolution of marriage, mental health or deferred records released. Copy fee: $.25 per page. Cert fee: $10.00. Payee: Clerk of Court. Personal checks accepted. Prepayment required.

Muscatine County

7th District Court PO Box 8010, Courthouse, Muscatine, IA 52761; 563-263-6511; Criminal phone: 563-263-2447; Fax: 563-264-3622. Hours: 8AM-4:30PM (CST). *Felony, Misdemeanor, Civil, Eviction, Small Claims, Probate.*

Civil Records: Access: In person, online. Visitors must perform in person searches for themselves. No search fee. Required to search: name, years to search. Civil cases indexed by defendant, plaintiff. Civil records on docket books, on computer since 10/95. Civil, probate, and appellate information is at www.judicial.state.ia.us/online_records.

Criminal Records: Access: In person, online. Visitors must perform in person searches for themselves. No search fee. Required to search: name, years to search. Criminal Records are computerized since 04/94. Criminal, traffic, and appellate data is online at www.judicial.state.ia.us/online_records.

General Information: Public Access terminal is available. No juvenile, sealed, dissolutions of marriage, mental health, domestic abuse or deferred records released. Copy fee: $.50 per page. Cert fee: $10.00. Payee: Clerk of Court. Personal checks accepted. Prepayment required.

O'Brien County

3rd District Court Courthouse, Criminal Records, Primghar, IA 51245; 712-757-3255; Fax: 712-757-2965. Hours: 8AM-4:30PM (CST). *Felony, Misdemeanor, Civil, Eviction, Small Claims, Probate.*

Civil Records: Access: In person, online. Visitors must perform in person searches for themselves. No search fee. Required to search: name, years to search. Civil cases indexed by defendant, plaintiff. Civil records on docket books from late 1800s; computerized since 1997. Civil, probate, and appellate data is at www.judicial.state.ia.us/online_records.

Criminal Records: Access: In person, online. Visitors must perform in person searches for themselves. No search fee. Required to search: name, years to search; also helpful: DOB, SSN. Criminal records on docket books from late 1800s; computerized since 1997. Criminal, traffic, and appellate information is online at www.judicial.state.ia.us/online_records.

General Information: Public Access terminal is available. No juvenile, sealed, dissolution of marriage, mental health records released. Copy fee: $.50 per page. Cert fee: $10.00. Payee: Clerk of Court. Personal checks accepted. Prepayment required.

Osceola County

3rd District Court Courthouse, Criminal Records, Sibley, IA 51249; 712-754-3595; Fax: 712-754-2480. Hours: 8AM-4:30PM (may be closed Monday & Wednesday) (CST). *Felony, Misdemeanor, Civil, Eviction, Small Claims, Probate.*

Civil Records: Access: In person, online. Visitors must perform in person searches for themselves. No search fee. Required to search: name, years to search. Civil cases indexed by defendant, plaintiff. Civil records on docket books from 1883; on computer back to 1997. Civil, probate, and appellate data is at www.judicial.state.ia.us/online_records.

Criminal Records: Access: In person, online. Visitors must perform in person searches for themselves. No search fee. Required to search: name, years to search. Criminal records on docket books from 1883; on computer back to 1997. Criminal,

traffic, and appellate information is online at www.judicial.state.ia.us/online_records.

General Information: Public Access terminal is available. No juvenile, sealed, dissolution of marriage, mental health, domestic abuse or deferred records released. Copy fee: $.50 per page. Cert fee: $10.00. Payee: Clerk of Court. Personal checks accepted. Prepayment required.

Page County

4th District Court 112 E Main, Box 263, Clarinda, IA 51632; 712-542-3214; Fax: 712-542-5460. 8AM-4:30PM (CST). *Felony, Misdemeanor, Civil, Eviction, Small Claims, Probate.*

Civil Records: Access: In person, online. Visitors must perform in person searches for themselves. No search fee. Required to search: name, years to search. Civil cases indexed by defendant, plaintiff. Civil records on docket books; on computer back to 1995. Civil, probate, and appellate information is at www.judicial.state.ia.us/online_records.

Criminal Records: Access: In person, online. Visitors must perform in person searches for themselves. No search fee. Required to search: name, years to search, DOB, SSN, signed release. Criminal records on docket books; on computer back to 1995. Criminal, traffic, and appellate information is online at www.judicial.state.ia.us/online_records.

General Information: Public Access terminal is available. No juvenile, sealed dissolution of marriage, mental health or deferred records released. Will fax specifc case file requests for $2.00. Copy fee: $.25 per page. Cert fee: $10.00. Payee: Clerk of District Court. Personal checks accepted. Prepayment required.

Palo Alto County

3rd District Court PO Box 387, Emmetsburg, IA 50536; 712-852-3603. Hours: 8AM-4:30PM (CST). *Felony, Misdemeanor, Civil, Eviction, Small Claims, Probate.*

Civil Records: Access: In person, online. Visitors must perform in person searches for themselves. No search fee. Required to search: name, years to search. Civil cases indexed by defendant, plaintiff. Civil records on docket books from 1800s; computerized from 1997. Civil, probate, and appellate information is at www.judicial.state.ia.us/online_records.

Criminal Records: Access: In person, online. Visitors must perform in person searches for themselves. No search fee. Required to search: name, years to search, DOB, SSN. Criminal records on docket books from 1800s; computerized from 1997. Criminal, traffic, and appellate information is online at www.judicial.state.ia.us/online_records.

General Information: Public Access terminal is available. No juvenile, sealed, dissolution of marriage, mental health, domestic abuse or deferred records released. Copy fee: $.50 per page. Cert fee: $10.00. Payee: Clerk of Court. Personal checks accepted. Prepayment required.

Plymouth County

3rd Judicial District Plymouth County Clerk of District Court, Courthouse 215-4th Ave SE, Le Mars, IA 51031; 712-546-4215. Hours: 8AM-4:30PM (CST). *Felony, Misdemeanor, Civil, Eviction, Small Claims, Probate.*

Civil Records: Access: In person, online. Visitors must perform in person searches for themselves. No search fee. Required to search: name, years to search. Civil cases indexed by defendant, plaintiff. Civil records on docket books from 1895 to 11/92, docket cards from 11/92 to 7/97, on computer back to 7/97. Civil, probate, and appellate information is at www.judicial.state.ia.us/online_records.

Criminal Records: Access: In person, online. Visitors must perform in person searches for

themselves. No search fee. Required to search: name, years to search. Criminal records on docket books from 1895 to 11/92, docket cards from 11/92 to 7/97, on computer back to 7/97. Criminal, traffic, and appellate information is online at www.judicial.state.ia.us/online_records.

General Information: Public Access terminal is available. No juvenile, (sealed, dissolution of marriage), mental health, domestic abuse or deferred records released. Will fax specifc case file requests for $.50 per page. Copy fee: $.50 per page. Cert fee: $10.00. Payee: Clerk of Court. Personal checks accepted. Prepayment required.

Pocahontas County

2nd District Court Courthouse, 99 Court Sq, Pocahontas, IA 50574; 712-335-4208; Fax: 712-335-5045. 9AM-3:30PM (CST). *Felony, Misdemeanor, Civil, Eviction, Small Claims, Probate.*

Civil Records: Access: In person, online. Visitors must perform in person searches for themselves. No search fee. Required to search: name, years to search. Civil cases indexed by defendant, plaintiff. Civil records on docket books from 1880s, on computer back to 7/97. Civil, probate, and appellate information is at www.judicial.state.ia.us/online_records.

Criminal Records: Access: In person, online. Visitors must perform in person searches for themselves. No search fee. Required to search: name, years to search, DOB. Criminal records on docket books from 1880s, on computer back to 7/97. Criminal, traffic, and appellate information is online at www.judicial.state.ia.us/online_records.

General Information: Public Access terminal is available. No juvenile, sealed, dissolution of marriage, mental health, domestic abuse or deferred records released. Copy fee: $.50 per page. Cert fee: $10.00. Payee: Clerk of Court. Personal checks accepted. Prepayment required.

Polk County

District Court 500 Mulberry St, Rm 201, Des Moines, IA 50309; 515-286-3772; Fax: 515-286-3172 (Civil) 323-5250 (Criminal). Hours: 8AM-4:30PM (CST). *Felony, Misdemeanor, Civil, Eviction, Small Claims, Probate.*

www.judicial.state.ia.us

Civil Records: Access: Mail, in person, online. Visitors must perform in person searches for themselves. No search fee. Required to search: name, years to search; also helpful: address. Civil cases indexed by defendant, plaintiff. Civil records on computer back to 1990; docket books and index cards from 1880s and microfilm prior to 1970. Civil, probate, and appellate information is at www.judicial.state.ia.us/online_records. Mail search requests are not recommended.

Criminal Records: Access: Mail, in person, online. Visitors must perform in person searches for themselves. No search fee. Required to search: name, years to search, address, DOB; also helpful: SSN. Criminal records on computer back to 1990; docket books and index cards from 1880s and microfilm prior to 1970. Criminal, traffic, and appellate information is online at www.judicial.state.ia.us/online_records. Mail search requests are not recommended.

General Information: Public Access terminal is available. No juvenile, child, sealed, pending dissolution of marriage, mental health, expunged, domestic abuse or deferred records released. Copy fee: $.50 per page. Microfilm copy fee: $.50 per page. Cert fee: $10.00. Payee: Clerk of Court. Personal checks accepted. Credit cards accepted: Visa. Prepayment required.

Pottawattamie County

4th District Court 227 S 6th St, Council Bluffs, IA 51501; 712-328-5604. Hours: 8:30AM-4:30PM (CST). *Felony, Misdemeanor, Civil, Eviction, Small Claims, Probate.*
Civil Records: Access: In person, online. Visitors must perform in person searches for themselves. No search fee. Required to search: name, years to search. Civil cases indexed by defendant, plaintiff. Civil records on computer from 1978, index books prior. Records are being microfilmed as load permits. Civil, probate, and appellate information is at www.judicial.state.ia.us/online_records.
Criminal Records: Access: In person, online. Visitors must perform in person searches for themselves. No search fee. Required to search: name, years to search. Criminal records on computer from 1978, index books prior. Records are being microfilmed as load permits. Criminal, traffic, and appellate information is online at www.judicial.state.ia.us/online_records.
General Information: Public Access terminal is available. No juvenile, sealed, pending dissolution of marriage, mental health, domestic abuse or deferred records released. Copy fee: $.25 per page. Cert fee: $10.00. Payee: Clerk of Court. Personal checks accepted. Prepayment required.

Poweshiek County

8th District Court PO Box 218, Montezuma, IA 50171; 641-623-5644; Fax: 641-623-5320. Hours: 8AM-4:30PM (CST). *Felony, Misdemeanor, Civil, Eviction, Small Claims, Probate.*
Civil Records: Access: In person, online. Visitors must perform in person searches for themselves. No search fee. Required to search: name, years to search. Civil cases indexed by defendant, plaintiff. Civil records on index cards from 1980, docket books from early 1900s, computer since 7/95. Civil, probate, and appellate information is at www.judicial.state.ia.us/online_records.
Criminal Records: Access: In person, online. Visitors must perform in person searches for themselves. No search fee. Required to search: name, years to search. Criminal records on computer since 1995, index cards since 1980, docket books from early 1900s. Criminal, traffic, and appellate information is online at www.judicial.state.ia.us/online_records.
General Information: Public Access terminal is available. No juvenile, sealed, dissolution of marriage, mental health, domestic abuse or deferred records released. Copy fee: $.25 per page. Cert fee: $10.00. Payee: Clerk of Court. Personal checks accepted. Prepayment required.

Ringgold County

5th District Court 109 W Madison (PO Box 523), Mount Ayr, IA 50854; 641-464-3234; Fax: 641-464-2478. Hours: 8AM-4:30PM (CST). *Felony, Misdemeanor, Civil, Small Claims, Probate, Traffic.*
Civil Records: Access: In person, online. Visitors must perform in person searches for themselves. No search fee. Required to search: name, years to search. Civil cases indexed by defendant, plaintiff. Civil records on docket books; on computer back to 11/06. Civil, probate, and appellate information is at www.judicial.state.ia.us/online_records.
Criminal Records: Access: In person, online. Visitors must perform in person searches for themselves. No search fee. Required to search: name, years to search. Criminal records on docket books; on computer back to 11/96. Criminal, traffic, and appellate information is online at www.judicial.state.ia.us/online_records.

General Information: Public Access terminal is available. No juvenile, sealed, pending dissolution of marriage, mental health or deferred records released. Copy fee: $.50 per page. Cert fee: $10.00. Payee: Clerk of Court. Personal checks accepted.

Sac County

2nd District Court PO Box 368, Sac City, IA 50583; 712-662-7791; Fax: 712-662-7978. Hours: 8AM-4:30PM (CST). *Felony, Misdemeanor, Civil, Eviction, Small Claims, Probate.*
www.iowacourtsonline.org
Civil Records: Access: In person, online. Visitors must perform in person searches for themselves. No search fee. Required to search: name. Civil cases indexed by defendant, plaintiff. Civil records go back to 1888; on computer back to 7/1997. Civil, probate, and appellate information is at www.judicial.state.ia.us/online_records.
Criminal Records: Access: In person, online. Visitors must perform in person searches for themselves. Court may assist in search, if necessary. No search fee. Required to search: name, approximate date. Criminal records go back to 1888; on comptuer back to 7/1997. Criminal, traffic, and appellate information is online at www.judicial.state.ia.us/online_records.
General Information: Public Access terminal is available. No juvenile, sealed, pending dissolution of marriage, mental health, domestic abuse or deferred records released. Will not fax results. Copy fee: $.50 per page. Cert fee: $10.00. Payee: Clerk of Court. Personal checks accepted. Prepayment required.

Scott County

7th District Court 416 W 4th St, Davenport, IA 52801; 563-326-8786. Hours: 8AM-4:30PM (CST). *Felony, Misdemeanor, Civil, Eviction, Small Claims, Probate.* courtsonline org
Civil Records: Access: In person, online. Visitors must perform in person searches for themselves. No search fee. Required to search: name, years to search. Civil cases indexed by defendant, plaintiff. Civil records on computer back to 11/1993, docket books prior. Civil, probate, and appellate information is at www.judicial.state.ia.us/online_records.
Criminal Records: Access: In person, online. Visitors must perform in person searches for themselves. No search fee. Required to search: name, years to search, DOB; also helpful: SSN. Criminal records on computer back to 1992, printouts and docket books prior. Criminal, traffic, and appellate information is online at www.judicial.state.ia.us/online_records.
General Information: Public Access terminal is available. No juvenile, sealed, dissolution of marriage, mental health, domestic abuse or deferred records released. Copy fee: $.50 per page. Cert fee: $10.00. Payee: Clerk of Court. Personal checks accepted. Prepayment required.

Shelby County

4th District Court PO Box 431, Harlan, IA 51537; 712-755-5543; Fax: 712-755-2667. Hours: 8:30AM-3:30PM (CST). *Felony, Misdemeanor, Civil, Eviction, Small Claims, Probate.*
www.shco.org
Note: The court will not perform name searches.
Civil Records: Access: In person, online. Visitors must perform in person searches for themselves. No search fee. Required to search: name, years to search. Civil cases indexed by defendant, plaintiff. Civil records on original files back to 1969, microfilm prior, on computer back to 10/95. Civil, probate, and appellate information is at www.judicial.state.ia.us/online_records.

Criminal Records: Access: In person, online. Visitors must perform in person searches for themselves. No search fee. Required to search: name, years to search; also helpful: DOB. Criminal records on original files back to 1980, microfilm prior, on computer back to 10/95. Criminal, traffic, and appellate information is online at www.judicial.state.ia.us/online_records.
General Information: Public Access terminal is available. No juvenile, sealed, dissolution of marriage, mental health, domestic abuse or deferred records released. Copy fee: $.25 per page. Cert fee: $10.00. Payee: Clerk of Court. Personal checks accepted. Prepayment required.

Sioux County

3rd District Court PO Box 47, Courthouse, Orange City, IA 51041; 712-737-2286; Fax: 712-737-8908. Hours: 8AM-4:30PM (CST). *Felony, Misdemeanor, Civil, Eviction, Small Claims, Probate.*
Civil Records: Access: In person, online. Visitors must perform in person searches for themselves. No search fee. Required to search: name, years to search. Civil cases indexed by defendant, plaintiff. Civil records on docket books from 1800s; computerized records since 9/97. Civil, probate, and appellate data is at www.judicial.state.ia.us/online_records.
Criminal Records: Access: In person, online. Visitors must perform in person searches for themselves. No search fee. Required to search: name, years to search, signed release. Criminal records on docket books from 1800s; computerized records since 9/97. Criminal, traffic, and appellate information is online at www.judicial.state.ia.us/online_records.
General Information: Public Access terminal is available. No juvenile, sealed, dissolution of marriage, mental health, domestic abuse or deferred records released. Copy fee: $.50 per page. Cert fee: $10.00. Payee: Clerk of Court. Personal checks accepted. Prepayment required.

Story County

2nd District Court PO Box 408, 1315 S B Ave, Nevada, IA 50201; 515-382-7410; Probate phone: 515-382-7420. Hours: 8AM-4:30PM (CST). *Felony, Misdemeanor, Civil, Probate.*
Note: Also has a branch in Ames that handles minor misdemeanors, traffic, and small claims.
Civil Records: Access: In person, online. Visitors must perform in person searches for themselves. No search fee. Required to search: name, years to search. Civil cases indexed by defendant, plaintiff. Civil records on docket books from 1900s; on computer back to 1995. Civil, probate, and appellate data is at www.judicial.state.ia.us/online_records.
Criminal Records: Access: In person, online. Visitors must perform in person searches for themselves. No search fee. Required to search: name, years to search. Criminal records on computer since 1992, prior on docket books. Criminal, traffic, and appellate information is online at www.judicial.state.ia.us/online_records.
General Information: Public Access terminal is available. No sealed, pending dissolution of marriage, mental health, or expunged records released. Will not fax results. Copy fee: $.50 per page. Cert fee: $10.00. Payee: Clerk of Court. Personal checks accepted. Prepayment required.

Ames Associate District Court PO Box 748, 515 Clark St, Ames, IA 50010; 515-239-5140. Hours: 8AM-4:30PM (CST). *Misdemeanor (Minor), Small Claims, Eviction.*
Note: A branch of the District Court in Nevada.
Civil Records: Access: In person, online. Visitors must perform in person searches for themselves. No

search fee. Required to search: name, years to search. Civil cases indexed by defendant, plaintiff. Civil records on docket books from 1900s; on computer back to 1995. Civil, probate, and appellate data is at www.judicial.state.ia.us/online_records.

Criminal Records: Access: In person, online. Visitors must perform in person searches for themselves. No search fee. Required to search: name, years to search. Criminal records on computer since 1992, prior on docket books. Criminal, traffic, and appellate information is online at www.judicial.state.ia.us/online_records.

General Information: Public Access terminal is available. No sealed or expunged records released. Will not fax results. Copy fee: $.50 per page. Cert fee: $10.00. Payee: Clerk of Court. Personal checks accepted. Prepayment required.

Tama County

6th Judicial District Court PO Box 306, Toledo, IA 52342; 641-484-3721; Fax: 641-484-6403. 8AM-4:30PM (CST). *Felony, Misdemeanor, Civil, Eviction, Small Claims, Probate.*

Civil Records: Access: In person, online. Visitors must perform in person searches for themselves. No search fee. Required to search: name, years to search. Civil cases indexed by defendant, plaintiff. Civil records on docket books from 1880s; computerized records since 1997. Magistrate dockets to 1972, prior to 1972, Justice of the Peace. Civil, probate, and appellate information is at www.judicial.state.ia.us/online_records.

Criminal Records: Access: In person, online. Visitors must perform in person searches for themselves. No search fee. Required to search: name, years to search. Criminal records on docket books from 1880s; computerized records since 1995. Magistrate dockets to 1972, prior to 1972, Justice of the Peace. Criminal, traffic, and appellate information is online at www.judicial.state.ia.us/online_records.

General Information: Public Access terminal is available. No juvenile, sealed, dissolution of marriage, mental health, domestic abuse or deferred records released. Copy fee: $.50 per page. Cert fee: $10.00. Payee: Clerk of Court. Personal checks accepted. Prepayment required.

Taylor County

5th District Court Courthouse, Bedford, IA 50833; 712-523-2095; Fax: 712-523-2936. Hours: 8AM-4:30PM (CST). *Felony, Misdemeanor, Civil, Eviction, Small Claims, Probate.*

Civil Records: Access: In person, online. Visitors must perform in person searches for themselves. No search fee. Required to search: name, years to search. Civil cases indexed by defendant, plaintiff. Civil records on computer since 11/01/96; prior to 1880s. Civil, probate, and appellate information is at www.judicial.state.ia.us/online_records.

Criminal Records: Access: In person, online. Visitors must perform in person searches for themselves. No search fee. Required to search: name, years to search. Criminal records on computer since 11/01/96; prior to 1880s. Criminal, traffic, and appellate information is online at www.judicial.state.ia.us/online_records.

General Information: Public Access terminal is available. No juvenile, sealed, dissolution of marriage, mental health, domestic abuse or deferred records released. Will fax results to local or toll free line. Copy fee: $.50 per page. Cert fee: $10.00. Payee: Clerk of Court. Personal checks accepted. Prepayment required.

Union County

5th District Court Courthouse, Creston, IA 50801; 641-782-7315; Fax: 641-782-8241. Hours: 8AM-4:30PM (CST). *Felony, Misdemeanor, Civil, Eviction, Small Claims, Probate.*

Civil Records: Access: In person, mail, online. Visitors must perform in person searches for themselves. No search fee. Required to search: name, years to search. Civil cases indexed by defendant, plaintiff. Civil records on docket books from 1900s; computerized back to 9/1996. Civil, probate, and appellate information is at www.judicial.state.ia.us/online_records.

Criminal Records: Access: In person, mail, online. Visitors must perform in person searches for themselves. No search fee. Required to search: name, years to search. Criminal records on docket books from 1900s; computerized back to 9/996. Criminal, traffic, and appellate information is online at www.judicial.state.ia.us/online_records.

General Information: Public Access terminal is available. No juvenile, sealed, pending dissolution of marriage, mental health, domestic abuse or deferred records released. No fee to fax results. Copy fee: $.50 per page. Cert fee: $10.00. Payee: Clerk of Court. Personal checks accepted. Prepayment required. Mail turnaround time 1-2 days.

Van Buren County

8th District Court Courthouse Criminal Records, Keosauqua, IA 52565; 319-293-3108; Fax: 319-293-3811. 8AM-4:30PM (CST). *Felony, Misdemeanor, Civil, Eviction, Small Claims, Probate.*

Civil Records: Access: In person, online. Visitors must perform in person searches for themselves. Search fee: none. Required to search: name, years to search. Civil cases indexed by defendant, plaintiff. Civil records on docket books from 1837, computerized since 1997. Civil, probate, and appellate information back to 1997 is at www.judicial.state.ia.us/online_records.

Criminal Records: Access: In person, online. Visitors must perform in person searches for themselves. No search fee. Required to search: name, years to search, DOB. Criminal records on docket books from 1837, computerized since 1997. Criminal, traffic, and appellate information is online at www.judicial.state.ia.us/online_records.

General Information: Public Access terminal is available. No sealed, mental health, or sealed records released; will release un-sealed juvenile, marriage dissolution or DA records if after July, 2000. Copy fee: $.25 per page. Cert fee: $10.00. Payee: Clerk of Court. Personal checks accepted. Prepayment required.

Wapello County

8th District Court 101 W 4th, Ottumwa, IA 52501; 641-683-0060; Fax: 641-683-0064. Hours: 8AM-3:30PM (CST). *Felony, Misdemeanor, Civil, Eviction, Small Claims, Probate.*

Note: SSNs are only maintained on a confidential sheet not available to the public.

Civil Records: Access: In person, online. Visitors must perform in person searches for themselves. No search fee. Required to search: name, years to search. Civil cases indexed by defendant, plaintiff. Civil records on computer (child support), docket books prior; computerized records since 5/1994. Civil, probate, and appellate information is at www.judicial.state.ia.us/online_records.

Criminal Records: Access: In person, online. Visitors must perform in person searches for themselves. No search fee. Required to search: name, years to search, DOB; also helpful: SSN. Criminal records on computer (for 6 months prior), docket

books prior; computerized records since 5/1994. Criminal, traffic, and appellate information is online at www.judicial.state.ia.us/online_records.

General Information: Public Access terminal is available. No juvenile, sealed, dissolution of marriage, mental health, domestic abuse or deferred records released. Copy fee: $.25 per page. Cert fee: $10.00. Payee: Clerk of Court. Personal checks accepted. Prepayment required.

Warren County

5th District Court PO Box 379, Indianola, IA 50125; 515-961-1033; Civil phone: 515-961-1027; Criminal phone: 515-961-1033; Probate phone: 515-961-1037; Fax: 515-961-1071. Hours: 8AM-4:30PM (CST). *Felony, Misdemeanor, Civil, Eviction, Small Claims, Probate.*

Civil Records: Access: In person, online. Visitors must perform in person searches for themselves. No search fee. Required to search: name, years to search. Civil cases indexed by defendant, plaintiff. Civil records on computer back to 10/1995; prior on docket books to 1925. Civil, probate, and appellate data is at www.judicial.state.ia.us/online_records.

Criminal Records: Access: In person, online. Visitors must perform in person searches for themselves. No search fee. Required to search: name, years to search. Criminal records on computer back to 10/1995; prior on docket books to 1945. Criminal, traffic, and appellate information is online at www.judicial.state.ia.us/online_records.

General Information: Public Access terminal is available. No juvenile, sealed, dissolution of marriage, mental health, domestic abuse or deferred records released. Will not fax results. Copy fee: $.50 per page. Cert fee: $10.00. Payee: Clerk of Court. Personal checks accepted. Credit cards accepted. Prepayment required.

Washington County

8th District Court PO Box 391, Washington, IA 52353; 319-653-7741; Fax: 319-653-7787. Hours: 8AM-4:30PM (CST). *Felony, Misdemeanor, Civil, Eviction, Small Claims, Probate.*

Civil Records: Access: In person, online. Visitors must perform in person searches for themselves. No search fee. Required to search: name, years to search. Civil cases indexed by defendant, plaintiff. Civil records on computer back to 1997, microfilm from 1940, docket books since court inception. Civil, probate, and appellate information is at www.judicial.state.ia.us/online_records.

Criminal Records: Access: In person, online. Visitors must perform in person searches for themselves. No search fee. Required to search: name, years to search. Criminal records on computer back to 1997, microfilm from 1940, docket books since court inception. Criminal, traffic, and appellate information is online at www.judicial.state.ia.us/online_records.

General Information: Public Access terminal is available. No juvenile, sealed, dissolution of marriage, mental health, domestic abuse or deferred records released. Copy fee: $.25 per page. Cert fee: $10.00. Payee: Clerk of Court. Personal checks accepted. Prepayment required.

Wayne County

5th District Court PO Box 424, Corydon, IA 50060; 641-872-2264; Fax: 641-872-2431. Hours: 8AM-4:30PM (CST). *Felony, Misdemeanor, Civil, Eviction, Small Claims, Probate.*

Civil Records: Access: In person, online. Visitors must perform in person searches for themselves. No search fee. Required to search: name, years to search. Civil cases indexed by defendant, plaintiff. Civil records on dockets from 1890, on computer back to

2/97. Civil, probate, and appellate information is at www.judicial.state.ia.us/online_records.

Criminal Records: Access: In person, online. Visitors must perform in person searches for themselves. No search fee. Required to search: name, years to search, DOB. Criminal records on dockets from 1890, on computer back to 2/97. Criminal, traffic, and appellate information is online at www.judicial.state.ia.us/online_records.

General Information: Public Access terminal is available. No juvenile, sealed, dissolution of marriage, mental health, domestic abuse or deferred records released. Copy fee: $.50 per page. Cert fee: $10.00. Payee: Clerk of Court. Personal checks accepted. Prepayment required.

Webster County

2nd District Court 701 Central Ave, Courthouse, Ft Dodge, IA 50501; 515-576-7115. Hours: 8AM-4:30PM (CST). *Felony, Misdemeanor, Civil, Eviction, Small Claims, Probate.*

Civil Records: Access: In person, online. Visitors must perform in person searches for themselves. No search fee. Required to search: name, years to search. Civil cases indexed by defendant, plaintiff. Civil records on docket books from 1800s, on computer since 1995. Civil, probate, and appellate information is at www.judicial.state.ia.us/online_records.

Criminal Records: Access: In person, online. Visitors must perform in person searches for themselves. No search fee. Required to search: name, years to search, signed release. Criminal records on docket books from 1800s, on computer since 1995. Criminal, traffic, and appellate information is online at www.judicial.state.ia.us/online_records.

General Information: Public Access terminal is available. No juvenile, sealed, dissolution of marriage, mental health, domestic abuse or deferred records released. Copy fee: $.50 per page. Cert fee: $10.00. Payee: Clerk of Court. Personal checks accepted. Prepayment required.

Winnebago County

2nd District Court 126 S Clark, Box 468, Forest City, IA 50436; 641-585-4520; Fax: 641-585-2615. Hours: 9AM-3:30PM (CST). *Felony, Misdemeanor, Civil, Eviction, Small Claims, Probate.* www.iowacourtsonline.org

Civil Records: Access: In person, online. Visitors must perform in person searches for themselves. No search fee. Required to search: name, years to search; also helpful: address. Civil cases indexed by defendant, plaintiff. Civil records on dockets from 1880s; on computer since 9/1997. Civil, probate, and appellate information is at www.judicial.state.ia.us/online_records.

Criminal Records: Access: In person, online. Visitors must perform in person searches for themselves. No search fee. Required to search: name, years to search, offense, date of offense; also helpful: address, DOB, aliases. Criminal records on dockets from 1940s; on computer since 9/1997. Criminal, traffic, and appellate information is online at www.judicial.state.ia.us/online_records.

General Information: Public Access terminal is available. No juvenile, pending or dismissed dissolution of marriage, mental health, criminal deferred or substance abuse records released.

Domestic abuse law change states that parts of the file may be public, depending on Judge's order. Will not fax results. Copy fee: $.50 per page. Cert fee: $10.00. Payee: Clerk of Court. Personal checks accepted. Visa, MC accepted. Prepayment required.

Winneshiek County

1st District Court 201 W Main St, Decorah, IA 52101; 563-382-2469; Fax: 563-382-0603. Hours: 8AM-4:30PM (CST). *Felony, Misdemeanor, Civil, Eviction, Small Claims, Probate.*

Civil Records: Access: In person, online. Visitors must perform in person searches for themselves. No search fee. Required to search: name, years to search. Civil cases indexed by defendant, plaintiff. Civil records on computer since 1994, docket books since 1860s. Civil, probate, and appellate information is at www.judicial.state.ia.us/online_records.

Criminal Records: Access: In person, online. Visitors must perform in person searches for themselves. No search fee. Required to search: name, years to search, signed release. Criminal records on computer since 1992, docket books since 1860s. Criminal, traffic, and appellate information is online at www.judicial.state.ia.us/online_records.

General Information: Public Access terminal is available. No juvenile, sealed, dissolution of marriage, mental health, domestic abuse or deferred records released. Copy fee: $.50 per page. Cert fee: $10.00. Payee: Clerk of Court. Personal checks accepted. Prepayment required.

Woodbury County

3rd District Court Woodbury County Courthouse, 620-Douglas, Rm 101, Sioux City, IA 51101-1248; 712-279-6611; Fax: 712-279-6021. 8AM-4:30PM *Felony, Civil, Eviction, Probate.*

Civil Records: Access: In person, online. Visitors must perform in person searches for themselves. No search fee. Required to search: name, years to search. Civil cases indexed by defendant, plaintiff. Civil records on index books from early 1900; on computer from 7/95. Civil, probate, and appellate information is at www.judicial.state.ia.us/online_records.

Criminal Records: Access: In person, online. Visitors must perform in person searches for themselves. No search fee. Required to search: name, years to search. Criminal records on index books from early 1900; on computer from 10/95. Criminal, traffic, and appellate information is online at www.judicial.state.ia.us/online_records.

General Information: Public Access terminal is available. No sealed, pending dissolution of marriage, mental health records released. Copy fee: $.50 per page. Cert fee: $10.00. Payee: Clerk of Court. Personal checks accepted. Prepayment required.

Associate District Court 407 7th St, County Clerk at Law Enforcement Ctr, Sioux City, IA 51101; 712-279-6624. Hours: 8AM-4:30PM (CST). *Misdemeanor, Civil, Eviction, Small Claims.*

Civil Records: Access: In person, online. Visitors must perform in person searches for themselves. No search fee. Required to search: name, years to search. Civil cases indexed by defendant, plaintiff. Civil records on docket books from early 1900; on computer from 7/95. Civil, probate, and appellate data is at www.judicial.state.ia.us/online_records.

Criminal Records: Access: In person, online. Visitors must perform in person searches for themselves. No search fee. Required to search: name, years to search. Criminal Records indexed on computer since 1992; on computer from 7/92. Criminal, traffic, and appellate information is online at www.judicial.state.ia.us/online_records.

General Information: Public Access terminal is available. No juvenile records released. Copy fee: $.50 per page. Cert fee: $10.00. Payee: Clerk of Court. Personal checks accepted. Prepayment required.

Worth County

2nd District Court 1000 Central Ave, Northwood, IA 50459; 641-324-2840; Fax: 641-324-2360. 9AM-3:30PM (CST). *Felony, Misdemeanor, Civil, Eviction, Small Claims, Probate.*

Case # Required for documents; will fax back results.

Civil Records: Access: In person, online. Visitors must perform in person searches for themselves. No search fee. Required to search: name, years to search. Civil cases indexed by defendant, plaintiff. Civil records on computer and docket books, on computer back to 4/97. Civil, probate, and appellate information is at www.judicial.state.ia.us/online_records.

Criminal Records: Access: In person, online. Visitors must perform in person searches for themselves. No search fee. Required to search: name, years to search. Criminal records on computer and docket books, on computer back to 4/97. Criminal, traffic, and appellate information is online at www.judicial.state.ia.us/online_records.

General Information: Public Access terminal is available. No juvenile, sealed, dissolution of marriage, mental health, domestic abuse, dismissed, or deferred records released. Copy fee: $.50 per page. Cert fee: $10.00. Payee: Clerk of Court. Personal checks accepted. Prepayment required.

Wright County

2nd District Court PO Box 306, Clarion, IA 50525; 515-532-3113; Fax: 515-532-2343. Hours: 9AM-3:30PM (CST). *Felony, Misdemeanor, Civil, Eviction, Small Claims, Probate.*

Civil Records: Access: In person, online. Visitors must perform in person searches for themselves. No search fee. Required to search: name, years to search. Civil cases indexed by defendant, plaintiff. Civil records on docket books from 1880; on computer since 1997. Civil, probate, and appellate information is at www.judicial.state.ia.us/online_records.

Criminal Records: Access: In person, online. Visitors must perform in person searches for themselves. No search fee. Required to search: name, years to search; also helpful: DOB, SSN. Criminal records on docket books from 1880s; on computer since 1997. Criminal, traffic, and appellate information is online at www.judicial.state.ia.us/online_records.

General Information: Public Access terminal is available. No juvenile, sealed, dissolution of marriage, mental health, domestic abuse or deferred records released. Copy fee: $.50 per page. Cert fee: $10.00. Payee: Clerk of Court. Personal checks accepted. Prepayment required.

Iowa Recording Offices

ORGANIZATION: 99 counties, 100 recording offices. Lee County has two recording offices. The recording officer is the County Recorder. Many counties utilize a grantor/grantee index containing all transactions recorded with them. See the notes under the county for how to determine which office is appropriate to search. The entire state is in the Central Time Zone (CST).

REAL ESTATE RECORDS: Most counties are hesitant to perform real estate searches, but some will provide a listing from the grantor/grantee index with the understanding that it is not certified in the sense that a title search is. Certification of copies usually costs $2.00-5.00 per document.

UCC RECORDS: Financing statements are filed at the state level except for real estate related collateral, which are filed with the County Recorder. However, prior to 07/2001, consumer goods were also filed at the County Recorder and these older records can be searched there. Most Iowa counties will perform UCC searches; see county profiles for exceptions. Use search request form UCC-11. Search fees are usually $5.00 per debtor name ($6.00 if the standard UCC-11 form is not used). Copies usually cost $1.00 per page.

TAX LIEN RECORDS: Federal tax liens on personal property of businesses are filed with the Secretary of State. Other federal and all state tax liens on personal property are filed with the County Recorder. County search practices vary widely, but most provide some sort of tax lien search for $6.00 per name.

OTHER LIENS: Home improvement, job service.

ONLINE ACCESS: There is no statewide access to county recorder data, however assessor records for 40 counties, plus cities of Ames, Cedar Rapids, Iowa City, and Souix City are available free at www.iowaassessors.com.

A statewide Property Tax lookup and payment page is available at www.iowatreasurers.org/county_locator.cfm?ID=1. First, select the county, then follow prompts to the search page where you can first look-up the name, then parcel info.

Adair County

County Recorder, 400 Public Sq, Courthouse, Greenfield, IA 50849. **Phone**-641-743-2411; fax-641-743-2565; hours 8AM-4:30PM
Will not search records. Record copy- $1.00 per page. Cert fee: $5.00 per doc. Payee: Adair County Recorder. **Other phones:** Assessor-641-745-2531; Treasurer-641-743-2312; Elections-641-743-2546; Vital Records-641-743-2411.

Adams County

County Recorder, PO Box 28, Corning, IA 50841. **Phone**-County Recorder, R/E & UCC Recording- 641-322-3744; fax-641-322-3744; hours 8:30AM-4:30PM
Will search UCC records. Search per debtor- $5.00. UCC copy- $1.00 per page. Tax liens not included in UCC search. Tax lien search- $6.00 per debtor. Will not search real estate records. RE record copy- $.25 per page. Cert fee: $5.00 per doc. Payee: Adams County Recorder. **Other phones:** Assessor-641-322-4312; Treasurer-641-322-3210; Elections-641-322-3340; Vital Records-641-322-3744; Clerk of Court-641-322-4711.

Allamakee County

County Recorder, 110 Allamakee St, Courthouse, Waukon, IA 52172-1794. **Phone**-County Recorder, R/E & UCC Recording- 563-568-2364; fax-319-568-6419; hours 8AM-4PM
Will search UCC records. Search per debtor- $5.00. UCC copy- $1.00 per page. UCC search includes tax liens. Separate federal/state combined tax lien search- $6.00 per doc. Will not search real estate records. RE record copy- $.50 per page. Cert fee: $5.00 per doc. Payee: Allamakee County Recorder. **Other phones:** Assessor-563-568-3145; Treasurer-563-568-3793.

Appanoose County

County Recorder, Courthouse, Centerville, IA 52544. **Phone**-County Recorder, R/E & UCC Recording- 641-856-6103; fax-641-856-8023; hours 8:30AM-4:30PM
Will search UCC records. Search per debtor- $5.00. UCC copy- $1.00 per page. UCC search includes tax liens if requested. Separate federal/state combined tax lien search- $5.00 per debtor. Will not search real estate records. RE record copy- $.25 per page. Cert fee: $5 per doc. Will not certify UCCs. Payee: Appanoose County Recorder. **Other phones:** Assessor-641-437-4529; Treasurer-641-856-3097; Vital Records-641-856-6103.

Audubon County

County Recorder, 318 Leroy St. #7, Audubon, IA 50025-1255. **Phone**-County Recorder, R/E & UCC Recording- 712-563-2119; fax-712-563-4766; hours 8AM-4:30PM. Will not search UCC records. Separate federal/state combined tax lien search- $6.00 per debtor. Will not search real estate records. Record copy- $1.00 per page. Cert fee: $5.00. Payee: Audubon County Recorder of Deeds. **Other phones:** Assessor-712-563-3418; Treasurer-712-563-2293; Vital Records-712-563-2119.

Benton County

County Recorder, Courthouse, Vinton, IA 52349. **Phone**-319-472-3309; fax-319-472-3309; hours 8AM-4:30PM. Will not search records. UCC copy- $1.00 per page. RE record- $.50 per page. Cert fee: $5.00 per doc. Payee: County Recorder. **Other phones:** Assessor-319-472-5211; Treasurer-319-472-2450.

Black Hawk County

County Recorder, 316 E. 5th St, Courthouse, Rm 208, Waterloo, IA 50703-4774. **Phone**-319-833-3171, R/E Recording- 319-833-3012, UCC Recording- 319-833-3012; fax-319-833-3170; hours 8AM-5PM

Will search UCC records; fixture filings only. Search per debtor- $5.00. UCC copy- $1.00 per page. Will search tax liens. Separate federal tax lien search- $6.00 per debtor. State lein search- $2.00 per debtor. Real estate owner, mortgage, and property transfer searches available. RE record copy- $.75 per page. Cert fee: $5.00 per doc. Payee: Black Hawk County Recorder. **Online Access to Assessor, Property records:** Access to the assessor database of property and sales data is available free at www.iowaassessors.com. **Other phones:** Assessor-319-833-3006; Treasurer-319-833-3013; Elections-319-833-3007; Vital Records-319-833-3012.

Boone County

County Recorder, 201 State St, Boone, IA 50036-3987. **Phone**-County Recorder, R/E & UCC Recording- 515-433-0514; fax-515-432-8102; hours 8AM-4:30PM
Will search UCC records prior to 7/1/2001. UCC copy fee- $1.00 per page. Will not search real estate or tax lien records. RE record copy- $.50 per page. Cert fee: $5.00 per doc. Payee: Boone County Recorder. **Online Access to Assessor, Property records:** Access to the assessor database of property and sales data is free at www.iowaassessors.com. **Other phones:** Assessor-515-433-0508; Treasurer-515-433-0510; Elections-515-433-0502; Vital Records-515-433-0514.

Bremer County

County Recorder, 415 E Bremer Ave, Waverly, IA 50677. **Phone**-County Recorder, R/E & UCC Recording- 319-352-0401; fax-319-352-0518; hours 8AM-4:30PM. Will search UCC records. Search per debtor- $5.00. UCC copy- $1.00 per page. Tax liens not included in UCC search. Separate federal/state combined tax lien search- $6.00 per debtor. Real estate owner, mortgage, and property transfer searches available. RE record copy- $.50 per page. Cert fee: $5.00 per cert. Payee: Bremer County Recorder. **Other phones:** Assessor-319-352-

0145; Treasurer-319-352-0242; Elections-319-352-0340; Vital Records-319-352-0401.

Buchanan County

County Recorder, PO Box 298, Independence, IA 50644-0298. **Phone**-County Recorder, R/E & UCC Recording- 319-334-4259; fax-319-334-7453; hours 8AM-4:30PM. Will search UCC records. Search per debtor- $5.00. UCC copy- $1.00 per page. UCC search includes tax liens if requested. Tax lien search fee- $5.00 per page. Will not search real estate records. RE record copy- $.50 per page. Cert fee: $5.00 per cert. Payee: Buchanan County Recorder. **Other phones:** Assessor-319-334-2706; Treasurer-319-334-4340; Elections-319-334-4109; Vital Records-319-334-4259.

Buena Vista County

County Recorder, PO Box 454, Storm Lake, IA 50588. **Phone**-712-749-2539; fax-712-749-2539; hours 8AM-4:30PM. Will search UCC records. Search per debtor- $5.00. UCC copy- $1.00 per page. UCC search includes tax liens. Separate federal/state combined tax lien search- $5.00 per debtor. Will not search real estate records. RE record copy- $.50 per page. Cert fee: $5.00 1st page, $.50 each add'l. Payee: Buena Vista County Recorder. **Online Access to Property Assessor, Ag Sale, Inmate, Accident, Incident records:** Search the property assessor and Ag sales databases for free at www.co.buena-vista.ia.us/assessors/. No name searching. Also, search the jail inmates list for free at www.bvsheriff.com/jailroster/index.html. Also, search accident/incident reports for free at www.bvsheriff.com/accident-incident/index.html. **Other phones:** Assessor-712-749-2543; Treasurer-712-749-5533.

Butler County

County Recorder, PO Box 346, Allison, IA 50602. **Phone**-319-267-2735; fax-319-267-2675; hours 8AM-4PM. Will search UCC records. Search per debtor- $5.00. UCC copy- $1.00 per page. Will not search real estate or tax lien records. RE record copy- $.50 per page. Cert fee: $10.00 per doc. Payee: Butler County Recorder. **Other phones:** Assessor-319-267-2264.

Calhoun County

County Recorder, 416 4th St. #3, Calhoun County Courthouse, Rockwell City, IA 50579. **Phone**-County Recorder, R/E & UCC Recording- 712-297-8121; hours 8:30AM-4:30PM
Will do fixture filing document number UCC record searches only. Search per debtor- $5.00. UCC copy- $1.00 per page. Tax liens not included in UCC search. Tax lien search fee- $5.00 per debtor. Will not search real estate records. RE record copy- $.25 per page. Cert fee: $5.00 per doc. Payee: Calhoun County Recorder. **Online Access to Treasurer, Property, Death, Assessor, Real Estate Sale records:** Access the treasurers property database at https://www.iowatreasurers.net/propertytax/index.php. Also, access Death records from genealogists for free at www.rootsweb.com/~usgenweb/ia/calhoun/death.htm. Access to the assessor database of property and sales data is free at www.iowaassessors.com and at http://calhoun.iowaassessors.com/search.php?mode=search. **Other phones:** Assessor-712-297-7500; Treasurer-712-297-7111; Vital Records-712-297-8121.

Carroll County

County Recorder, PO Box 782, Carroll, IA 51401-0782. **Phone**-County Recorder, R/E & UCC Recording- 712-792-3328; fax-712-792-9493; hours 8AM-4:30PM
Will search UCC records. Search per debtor- $5.00. UCC copy- $1.00 per page. Tax liens not included

in UCC search. Tax lien search- $6.00 per debtor. Will not search real estate records. RE record copy- $.50 per page. Cert fee: $5.00 per doc. Payee: Carroll County Recorder of Deeds. **Online Access to Assessor, Property records:** Access to the assessor database of property and sales data is free at www.iowaassessors.com. **Other phones:** Assessor-712-792-9973; Treasurer-712-792-1200; Vital Records-712-792-3328.

Cass County

County Recorder, 5 W. 7th, Atlantic, IA 50022-1492. **Phone**-712-243-1692; fax-712-243-6660; hours 8AM-4:30PM. Will not search records. Record copy- $1.00 per page. Cert fee: $5.00 per doc. Payee: Cass County Recorder. **Other phones:** Assessor-712-243-2005; Treasurer-712-243-5503; Elections-712-243-4570; Vital Records-712-243-1692.

Cedar County

County Recorder, 400 Cedar St, Courthouse, Tipton, IA 52772-1752. **Phone**-County Recorder, R/E & UCC Recording- 563-886-2230; fax-563-886-2120; hours 8AM-4PM
Will search UCC records. Search per debtor- $5.00. UCC copy- $1.00 per page. Separate federal/state combined tax lien search- $6.00 per debtor. Will not search real estate records. RE record copy- $.25 per page, $1.00 min. Cert fee: $5.00 per doc. Payee: Cedar County Recorder. **Other phones:** Assessor-563-886-6413; Treasurer-563-886-2557; Elections-563-886-3168; Vital Records-563-886-2230.

Cerro Gordo County

County Recorder, 220 N. Washington, Mason City, IA 50401. **Phone**-County Recorder, R/E & UCC Recording- 641-421-3056; fax-641-421-3154; hours 8AM-4:30PM www.co.cerro-gordo.ia.us
Will search UCC records. Search per debtor- $5.00. UCC copy- $1.00 per page. Tax liens not included in UCC search. Tax lien search- $6.00 per debtor. Real estate owner, mortgage, and property transfer searches available. RE record copy- $.50 per page. Cert fee: $5.00 per doc. Payee: Cerro Gordo County Recorder of Deeds. **Online Access to Real Estate, Property, Assessor records:** Access to the County and Mason City property records is free at www.co.cerro-gordo.ia.us/parcel_inquiry/parcel_inquiry.cfm. No name searching. Also, access to the assessor database of property and sales data is free at www.iowaassessors.com. **Other phones:** Assessor-641-421-3065 (county); -3061 (city); Treasurer-641-421-3037; Elections-641-421-3027; Vital Records-641-421-3062.

Cherokee County

County Recorder, Drawer G, Cherokee, IA 51012. **Phone**-County Recorder, R/E & UCC Recording- 712-225-6735; fax-712-225-6754; hours 8AM-4:30PM
Will search UCC records. Search per debtor- $5.00. UCC copy- $.50 per page. UCC search includes tax liens if requested. Separate federal/state combined tax lien search- $5.00 per debtor. Real estate owner, mortgage, and property transfer searches available. RE record copy- $.50 per page. Cert fee: $5.00 per doc. Payee: Cherokee County Recorder of Deeds. **Other phones:** Assessor-712-225-6701; Treasurer-712-225-6740; Appraiser/ Auditor-712-225-6701; Elections-712-225-6704; Vital Records-712-225-6735.

Chickasaw County

County Recorder, PO Box 14, New Hampton, IA 50659. **Phone**-County Recorder, R/E & UCC Recording- 641-394-2336; fax-641-394-2816; hours 8:30AM-4:30PM www.chickasawcoia.org
Will search UCC records. Search per debtor- $5.00. UCC copy- $1.00 per page. UCC search includes

tax liens if requested. Separate federal/state combined tax lien search- $6.00 per debtor. Real estate owner and property transfer searches available. RE record copy- $.50 per page. Cert fee: $5.00 per doc, plu $.50 each add'l pg. Payee: Chickasaw County Recorder. **Other phones:** Assessor-641-394-2813; Treasurer-641-394-2107; Elections-641-394-2100; Vital Records-641-394-2336.

Clarke County

County Recorder, 100 S Main, Courthouse, Osceola, IA 50213. **Phone**-641-342-3313; fax-641-342-3313; hours 8:30AM-4:30PM. Will search UCC records. Search per debtor- $5.00. UCC copy- $1.00 per page. Tax liens not included in UCC search. Separate combined tax lien search available. Tax lien search fee- $6.00 1st name, $5.00 per add'l. Mortgage searches available. RE record copy- $.25 per page. Cert fee: $5.00 per doc. Payee: Clarke County Recorder. **Other phones:** Assessor-641-342-3817; Treasurer-641-342-3311.

Clay County

County Recorder, 300 W. 4th St, #3, Admin. Bldg, Spencer, IA 51301-3806. **Phone**-County Recorder, R/E & UCC Recording- 712-262-1081; fax-712-264-3983; hours 8AM-4:30PM www.co.clay.ia.us
Will not search UCC records. Tax lien search- $5.00 per debtor. Will not search real estate records. Record copy- $1.00 per page. Cert fee: $5.00 per doc. Payee: Clay County Recorder of Deeds. **Online Access to Real Estate, Recording, Grantor/Grantee, Tax Sale Certificate, Mortgage, Assessor, Property records:** At the main website, click to choose database to search; name search on all except the real estate/tax inquiry. Access to the assessor database of property and sales data is free at www.iowaassessors.com. **Other phones:** Assessor-712-262-1986; Treasurer-712-262-2179; Appraiser/ Auditor-712-262-1986; Elections-712-262-1569; Vital Records-712-262-1081.

Clayton County

County Recorder, PO Box 278, Elkader, IA 52043. **Phone**-County Recorder, R/E & UCC Recording- 563-245-2710; fax-319-245-2353; hours 8AM-4:30PM www.claytoncountyiowa.net
Will search UCC records. Search per debtor- $5.00. UCC copy- $1.00 per page. Tax liens not included in UCC search. Separate federal/state combined tax lien search- $6.00 per debtor. Real estate owner, mortgage, and property transfer searches available. RE record copy- $1.00 per page. Cert fee: $5.00 per doc. Payee: Clayton County Recorder. **Other phones:** Assessor-563-245-2533; Treasurer-563-245-1807; Appraiser/ Auditor-563-245-2533; Elections-563-245-1106; Vital Records-563-245-2710; Clerk of Court-563-245-2204.

Clinton County

County Recorder, PO Box 2957, Clinton, IA 52733-2957. **Phone**-563-244-0565 x0544; fax-563-242-8412; hours 8AM-4:30PM www.clintoncountyiowa.com
Will search UCC records. Search per debtor- $5.00. UCC copy- $1.00 per page. Tax lien search fee- $5.00 per debtor. Will not search real estate records. RE record copy- $1.00 per page. Cert fee: $5.00 per doc. Payee: Clinton County Recorder of Deeds. **Other phones:** Assessor-563-242-0569; Treasurer-563-242-0573; Vital Records-563-244-0565 /0544.

Crawford County

County Recorder, 1202 Broadway, Denison, IA 51442. **Phone**-County Recorder, R/E & UCC Recording- 712-263-3643; fax-712-263-3413; hours 8AM-4:30PM http://crawfordcounty.org
Will search UCC records. Search per debtor- $5.00. UCC copy- $1.00 per page. UCC search includes

tax liens if requested. Separate federal/state combined tax lien search- $6.00 per debtor. Will not search real estate records. RE record copy- $.25 per page. Cert fee: $5.00 per doc plus copy fee. Payee: Crawford County Recorder. **Other phones:** Assessor-712-263-3447; Treasurer-712-263-2648; Elections-712-263-3045; Vital Records-712-263-3643; no info given over the phone.

Dallas County

County Recorder, PO Box 38, Adel, IA 50003-0038. **Phone-**County Recorder, R/E & UCC Recording- 515-993-5804; fax-515-933-5970; hours 8AM-4:30PM Will search UCC records. Search per debtor- $5.00. UCC copy- $1.00 per page. UCC search includes tax liens if requested. Separate federal/state combined tax lien search- $6.00 per debtor. Real estate owner, mortgage, and property transfer searches available. RE record copy- $.50 per page. Cert fee: $5.00 per doc. Payee: Dallas County Recorder. **Online Access to Assessor, Property records:** Access to the assessor database of property and sales data is free at www.iowaassessors.com. **Other phones:** Assessor-515-993-5802; Treasurer-515-993-5808; Vital Records-515-993-5804.

Davis County

County Recorder, 100 Courthouse Sq #7, Bloomfield, IA 52537. **Phone-**County Recorder, R/E & UCC Recording- 641-664-2321; fax-641-664-3082; hours 7:30AM-4:30PM www.daviscountyassessor.org Will search UCC records. Search per debtor- $5.00. UCC copy- $1.00 per page. UCC search includes tax liens if requested. Separate federal/state combined tax lien search- $6.00 per debtor. Will not name search real estate records. RE record copy- $.30 per page. Cert fee: $5.00 per doc. Payee: Davis County Recorder. **Online Access to Real Estate, Assessor, Property Tax records:** Access to county real estate data is free on the GIS system at www.daviscountyassessor.org/pmc/. Also, access to the assessor database of property and sales data is free at www.iowaassessors.com. **Other phones:** Assessor-641-664-3101; Treasurer-641-664-2155; Elections-641-664-2101; Vital Records-641-664-2321.

Decatur County

County Recorder, 207 N. Main St, Leon, IA 50144. **Phone-**641-446-4322; fax-641-446-7159; hours 8AM-4:30PM. Will search UCC records. Search per debtor- $5.00. UCC copy- $1.00 per page. Will not search real estate records. RE record copy- $.25 per page. Cert fee: $4.00 per cert. Payee: County Recorder. **Other phones:** Assessor-641-446-4314.

Delaware County

County Recorder, 301 E Main, Courthouse, Manchester, IA 52057. **Phone-**563-927-4665; fax-319-927-3641; hours 8AM-4:30PM Will search UCC records. Search per debtor- $12.00. Search request using non-standard form (per name)- $13.00. UCC copy- $1.00 per page. Tax liens not included in UCC search. Will not search real estate records. RE record copy- $.25 per page. Cert fee: $5.00 per doc + $1.00 per page. Payee: Delaware County Recorder. **Other phones:** Assessor-563-927-2526; Treasurer-563-927-2845.

Des Moines County

County Recorder, PO Box 277, Burlington, IA 52601-0277. **Phone-**County Recorder, R/E & UCC Recording- 319-753-8221; fax-319-753-8721; hours 8AM-4:30PM www.co.des-moines.ia.us/ Will search UCC records. Search per debtor- $5.00. UCC copy- $1.00 per page. UCC search includes tax liens if requested. Will not search real estate records. RE record copy- $1.00 per page if on micro film; $2.00 if faxed. Cert fee: $5.00 per doc.

Payee: Des Moines County Recorder. **Other phones:** Assessor-319-753-8224; Treasurer-319-753-8252; Appraiser/ Auditor-319-753-8255; Elections-319-753-8266; Vital Records-319-753-8221; Motor Vehicle-319-753-8273.

Dickinson County

County Recorder, PO Box O.E., Spirit Lake, IA 51360. **Phone-**County Recorder, R/E & UCC Recording- 712-336-1495; fax-712-336-2677; hours 8AM-4:30PM Will not search records. UCC copy- $1.00 per page. Cert fee: $5.00 per doc. Payee: Dickinson County Recorder. **Online Access to Assessor, Property records:** Access to the assessor database of property and sales data is free at www.iowaassessors.com. **Other phones:** Assessor-712-336-2687; Treasurer-712-336-1205; Vital Records-712-336-1495.

Dubuque County

County Recorder, 720 Central #9, Courthouse, Dubuque, IA 52001. **Phone-**County Recorder, R/E & UCC Recording- 563-589-4434; fax-319-589-4484; hours 8:30AM-5PM www.dubuquecounty.org Will search UCC records. Search per debtor- $5.00. UCC copy- $1.00 per page. Will not search real estate or tax lien records. RE record copy- $1.00 per page. Cert fee: $2.00 per doc. Payee: Dubuque County Recorder. **Online Access to Assessor, Property records:** Access to the assessor database of property and sales data is free at www.iowaassessors.com. **Other phones:** Assessor-563-589-4432; Treasurer-563-589-4436; Elections-563-589-4458; Vital Records-563-589-4434.

Emmet County

County Recorder, 609 1st Ave North, Estherville, IA 51334. **Phone-**County Recorder, R/E & UCC Recording- 712-362-4115; fax-712-362-7454; hours 8AM-4:30PM Will not search UCC records. UCC copy- $1.00 per page. Separate federal/state combined tax lien search- $5.00 per debtor. Will not search real estate records. RE record copy- $.50 per page. Cert fee: $5.00 per doc. Payee: Emmet County Recorder. **Online Access to Real Estate, Assessor, Property records:** Access to real estate records on the county database are free at www.emmet.org/pmc. Also, the GIS mapping database may be searched. Includes parcel report, survey section grid, parcel maps, and more. Search the "Parcel Data" link by owner name, parcel ID, or address. Search Page or Disclamer Page is: www.record32@netins.net. Also, access to the assessor database of property and sales data is free at www.iowaassessors.com. **Other phones:** Assessor-712-362-2609; Treasurer-712-362-3824; Appraiser/ Auditor-712-362-2609; Elections-712-362-4261; Vital Records-712-362-4115; Clerk of Court-712-362-3325.

Fayette County

County Recorder, PO Box 226, West Union, IA 52175-0226. **Phone-**563-422-3687; fax-563-422-3739; hours 8AM-4PM. Will search UCC records. Search per debtor- $5.00. UCC copy- $1.00 per page. Tax liens not included in UCC search. Tax lien search- $5.00 per debtor. Will not search real estate records. RE record copy- $.50 per page. Cert fee: $5.00 1st page, $.50 each add'l. Payee: Fayette County Recorder. **Other phones:** Assessor-563-422-3397; Treasurer-563-422-3787.

Floyd County

County Recorder, 101 S Main, Courthouse, Charles City, IA 50616. **Phone-**County Recorder, R/E & UCC Recording- 641-257-6154; fax-641-228-6458; hours 8AM-4:30PM Will search UCC records. Search per debtor- $5.00. UCC copy- $1.00 per page. Separate federal/state combined tax lien search- $6.00 per debtor. Real

estate record owner and mortgage searches available. RE record copy- $.25 per page. Cert fee: $5.00 per doc. Payee: Floyd County Recorder. **Online Access to Assessor, Property records:** Also, access to the assessor database of property and sales data is free at www.iowaassessors.com. **Other phones:** Assessor-641-257-6152; Treasurer-641-257-6118; Elections-641-257-6131; Vital Records-641-257-6154.

Franklin County

County Recorder, PO Box 26, Hampton, IA 50441. **Phone-**641-456-5675; fax-641-456-6009; hours 8AM-4PM. Will search UCC records. Search per debtor- $5.00. UCC copy- $1.00 per page. UCC search includes tax liens if requested. Separate federal/state combined tax lien search- $6.00 per debtor. Real estate owner, mortgage, and property transfer searches available. RE record copy- $.25 per page. Cert fee: $5.00 per doc. Payee: Franklin County Recorder. **Other phones:** Assessor-641-456-5118; Treasurer-641-456-5678.

Fremont County

County Recorder, PO Box 295, Sidney, IA 51652. **Phone-**County Recorder, R/E & UCC Recording- 712-374-2315; fax-712-374-2826; hours 8AM-4:30PM Will search UCC records. Search per debtor- $5.00. UCC copy- $1.00 per page. Tax liens not included in UCC search. Tax lien search- $5.00 per debtor. Will not search real estate records. RE record copy- $.50 per page. Cert fee: $5.00 per doc. Payee: Fremont County Recorder. **Other phones:** Assessor-712-374-2631; Treasurer-712-374-2122; Elections-712-374-2031; Vital Records-712-374-2315.

Greene County

County Recorder, 114 N. Chestnut, Courthouse, Jefferson, IA 50129. **Phone-**515-386-3716, R/E Recording- 515-386-5670, UCC Recording- 515-386-5670; fax-515-386-5274; hours 8AM-4:30PM Will search UCC records. Search per debtor- $5.00. UCC copy- $1.00 per page. UCC search includes tax liens if requested. Separate federal/state combined tax lien search- $6.00 per debtor. Will not search real estate records. RE record copy- $.25 per page. Cert fee: $5.00 per doc. Payee: Greene County Recorder. **Online Access to Assessor, Property records:** Also, access to the assessor database of property and sales data is free at www.iowaassessors.com. **Other phones:** Assessor-515-386-5660; Treasurer-515-386-5675; Appraiser/ Auditor-515-386-5680; Elections-515-386-5680; Vital Records-515-386-5670.

Grundy County

County Recorder, 706 G Ave, Grundy Center, IA 50638-1447. **Phone-**County Recorder, R/E & UCC Recording- 319-824-3234; hours 8AM-4:30PM Will search UCC records. Search per debtor- $5.00. UCC copy- $1.00 per page. Tax liens not included in UCC search. Separate federal/state combined tax lien search- $6.00 per debtor. Will not search real estate records. Cert fee: $5.00 per doc. Payee: Grundy County Recorder. **Online Access to Assessor, Property records:** Access to the assessor database of property and sales data is free at www.iowaassessors.com. **Other phones:** Assessor-319-824-6216; Treasurer-319-824-3412; Elections-319-824-3122; Vital Records-319-824-3234.

Guthrie County

County Recorder, 200 N. 5th, Courthouse, Guthrie Center, IA 50115. **Phone-**County Recorder, R/E & UCC Recording- 641-747-3412; fax-641-747-3081; hours 8AM-4:30PM Will search UCC records. Search per debtor- $5.00. UCC copy- $1.00 per page. UCC search includes tax liens. Tax lien search fee $5.00 per doc. Will not search real estate records. RE record copy- $.25 per page. Cert fee: $5.00 per doc. Payee: Guthrie County Recorder. **Other phones:** Assessor-641-747-3319; Treasurer-641-747-3414; Appraiser/ Auditor-641-747-3319; Elections-641-747-3619; Vital Records-641-747-3412.

Hamilton County

County Recorder, PO Box 126, Webster City, IA 50595-0126. **Phone**-515-832-9535; fax-515-832-8620; hours 8AM-4:30PM
Will search UCC records. Search per debtor- $5.00. UCC copy- $1.00 per page. UCC search includes federal tax liens if requested. RE record copy- $.50 per page. Cert fee: $5.00 1st page, $.50 each add'l. Payee: Hamilton County Recorder. **Online Access to Assessor, Property records:** Access to the assessor database of property and sales data is free at www.iowaassessors.com. **Other phones:** Assessor-515-832-9505; Treasurer-515-832-9542.

Hancock County

County Recorder, 855 State St, Garner, IA 50438. **Phone**-County Recorder, R/E & UCC Recording- 641-923-2464, UCC Recording- 641-923-2404; fax-641-923-3912; hours 8AM-4PM
Will not search UCC records. UCC copy- $1.00 per page. Separate federal/state combined tax lien search- $5.00 per debtor. Will not search real estate records. RE record copy- $.50 per page. Cert fee: $5.00 per doc. Payee: Hancock County Recorder. **Other phones:** Assessor-641-923-2269; Treasurer-641-923-3122; Appraiser/ Auditor-641-923-2269; Vital Records-641-923-2464.

Hardin County

County Recorder, PO Box 443, Eldora, IA 50627. **Phone**-641-939-8178; fax-641-939-8245; hours 8AM-4:30PM. Will search UCC records. Search per debtor- $5.00. UCC copy- $1.00 per page. Will not search tax liens. Real estate owner, mortgage, and property transfer searches available. RE record copy- $.25 per page. Cert fee: $5.00 per cert. Payee: Hardin County Recorder. **Other phones:** Assessor-641-939-8100; Treasurer-641-939-8226; Appraiser/ Auditor-641-939-8230; Drivers License-641-939-8328.

Harrison County

County Recorder, Courthouse, Logan, IA 51546. **Phone**-County Recorder, R/E & UCC Recording- 712-644-2545; fax-712-644-3157; hours 8AM-4:30PM
Will search UCC records. Search per debtor- $5.00. UCC copy- $1.00 per page. Tax liens not included in UCC search. Tax lien search fee- $5.00 per debtor. Will not search real estate records. RE record copy- $.50 per page. Cert fee: $5.00 per doc. Payee: Harrison County Recorder. **Online Access to Assessor, Property records:** Access to the assessor database of property and sales data is free at www.iowaassessors.com. **Other phones:** Assessor-712-644-3101; Treasurer-712-644-2750; Elections-712-644-2401; Vital Records-712-644-2545.

Henry County

County Recorder, PO Box 106, Mount Pleasant, IA 52641. **Phone**-319-385-0765; fax-319-385-3601; hours 8AM-4:30PM
Will search UCC records. Search per debtor- $5.00. UCC copy- $1.00 per page. Tax liens not included in UCC search. Separate federal tax lien search- $6.00 per debtor. Will not search real estate records. Cert fee: $5.00 per page. Payee: Henry County Recorder. **Other phones:** Assessor-319-385-0750; Treasurer-319-385-0763; Elections-319-385-0756; Vital Records-319-385-0765.

Howard County

County Recorder, 137 N Elm, Court House, Cresco, IA 52136. **Phone**-563-547-3621; fax-319-547-1103; hours 8AM-4:30PM
Will search UCC records. Search per debtor- $5.00. UCC copy- $1.00 per page. Will not search tax liens. Real estate owner, mortgage, and property transfer searches available. RE record copy- $.50 per page. Cert fee: $5.00 per doc. Payee: Howard County Recorder. **Other phones:** Assessor-563-547-3409; Treasurer-563-547-3860; Vital Records-563-547-3621.

Humboldt County

County Recorder, PO Box 100, Dakota City, IA 50529-0100. **Phone**-515-332-3693; fax-515-332-1738; hours 8AM-4:30PM
Will not search records. UCC copy- $1.00 per page. RE record- $.25 per page. Cert fee: $5.00 1st page, $1.00 each add'l. Payee: Humboldt County Recorder. **Other phones:** Assessor-515-332-1463; Treasurer-515-332-1681.

Ida County

County Recorder, 401 Moorehead, Courthouse, Ida Grove, IA 51445. **Phone**-County Recorder, R/E & UCC Recording- 712-364-2220; fax-712-364-3939; hours 8AM-4:30PM. Will search UCC records. Search per debtor- $5.00. UCC copy- $1.00 per page. Tax liens not included in UCC search. Separate federal/state combined tax lien search- $6.00 per debtor. Will not search real estate records. RE record copy- $.25 per page. Cert fee: $5.00 per doc. Payee: Ida County Recorder. **Other phones:** Assessor-712-364-3622; Treasurer-712-364-2287; Elections-712-364-2620; Vital Records-712-364-2220.

Iowa County

County Recorder, PO Box 185, Marengo, IA 52301. **Phone**-County Recorder, R/E & UCC Recording- 319-642-3622; fax-319-642-5562; hours 7;30AM-4:30PM
Will search UCC records. Search per debtor- $5.00. UCC copy- $1.00 per page. UCC search includes tax liens if requested. Will not search real estate records. Cert fee: $5.00 per doc & $1.00 per page. Payee: Iowa County Recorder. **Other phones:** Assessor-319-642-3851; Treasurer-319-642-3672; Elections-319-642-3923; Vital Records-319-642-3622.

Jackson County

County Recorder, 201 W. Platt, Courthouse, Maquoketa, IA 52060. **Phone**-County Recorder, R/E & UCC Recording- 563-652-2504; fax-563-652-6460; 8:00AM-4:30PM www.jacksoncountyiowa.com
Will not search records. UCC copy- $1.00 per page. RE record- $.50 per page. Cert fee: $5.00 and $1.00 per page for real estate filings, Vital records cert $10.00 each. Payee: Jackson County Recorder. **Other phones:** Assessor-563-652-4935; Treasurer-563-652-5649; Elections-563-652-3144; Vital Records-563-652-2504.

Jasper County

County Recorder, PO Box 665, Newton, IA 50208. **Phone**-641-792-5442, R/E Recording- 647-792-5442, UCC Recording- 647-792-5442; fax-641-791-3680; hours 8AM-5PM
Will search UCC records. Search per debtor- $5.00. UCC copy- $1.00 per page. Will search federal tax liens. Will not search real estate records. RE record copy- $.25 per page by mail, $2.00 per page by fax. Cert fee: $5.00 per doc, up to 10 pages, $.25 each add'l. Payee: Jasper County Recorder. **Online Access to Assessor, Property records:** Access to the assessor database of property and sales data is free at www.iowaassessors.com. **Other phones:** Assessor-

641-792-6195; Treasurer-641-792-6115; Elections-641-792-7350; Vital Records-647-792-5442.

Jefferson County

County Recorder, 51 W. Briggs, Fairfield, IA 52556-2820. **Phone**-641-472-4331; fax-641-472-6695; hours 8AM-4:30PM
Will search UCC records. Search per debtor- $5.00. UCC copy- $1.00 per page. UCC search includes tax liens if requested. State tax lien searches are uncertified and performed at no charge. Will not search real estate records. RE record copy- $.50 per page. Cert fee: $2.00 per doc + $.50 per page. Payee: Jefferson County Recorder. **Online Access to Assessor, Property records:** Access to the assessor database of property and sales data is free at www.iowaassessors.com. **Other phones:** Assessor-641-472-2849; Treasurer-641-472-2349.

Johnson County

County Recorder, 913 S. Dubuque St, #202, Iowa City, IA 52240-4207. **Phone**-319-356-6093; fax-319-339-6181; hours 8AM-4PM M,W,F; 8AM-5:30PM T,Th www.johnson-county.com
Will search UCC records. Search per debtor- $5.00. UCC copy- $1.00 per page. Tax lien search fee- $5.00 per debtor. Will not search real estate records. Copy fee-$.25 per page. Cert fee: $2.00 per doc. Payee: Johnson County Recorder. **Online Access to Assessor, Property records:** Access to the assessor database of property and sales data is free at www.iowaassessors.com. Iowa City is in a separate database. **Other phones:** Assessor-319-356-6078; Treasurer-319-356-6087; Elections-319-356-6004; Vital Records-319-356-6093.

Jones County

County Recorder, 500 W Main, Courthouse, Rm 116, Anamosa, IA 52205-1632. **Phone**-County Recorder, R/E & UCC Recording- 319-462-2477; fax-319-462-5802; hours-8AM-4:30PM www.co.jones.ia.us/recorder.html
Will search UCC records. Search per debtor- $5.00. UCC copy- $1.00 per page. Will not search tax liens. Owner, mortgage, and property transfer self-searches available. RE record copy- $.50 per page. Cert fee: $5.00 per doc and $.50 per page. Payee: Jones County Recorder. **Other phones:** Assessor-319-462-2671; Treasurer-319-462-3550; Elections-319-462-2282; Vital Records-319-462-2477.

Keokuk County

County Recorder, 101 S. Main St., Courthouse, Sigourney, IA 52591. **Phone**-County Recorder, R/E & UCC Recording- 641-622-2540; fax-641-622-3789; hours 8AM-4:30PM www.keokukcountyia.com
Will search UCC records. Search per debtor- $5.00. UCC copy- $1.00 per page. UCC search includes tax liens if requested. Will not search real estate records. RE record copy- $1.00 per page. Cert fee: $5.00 1st page; $1.00 each add'l. Payee: Keokuk County Recorder. **Other phones:** Assessor-641-622-2560; Treasurer-641-622-2421; Elections-641-622-2320; Vital Records-641-622-2540.

Kossuth County

County Recorder, 114 W. State, Algona, IA 50511. **Phone**-515-295-5660; fax-515-295-3071; 8AM-4PM
Will not search UCC records. UCC copy- $1.00 per page. Separate federal/state tax lien search- $10.00 per debtor. Will not search real estate records. RE record copy- $.50 per page. Cert fee: $5.00 1st page, $2.50 each add'l. Payee: Kossuth County Recorder. **Online Access to Assessor, Property records:** Access to the assessor database of property and sales data is free at www.iowaassessors.com. **Other phones:** Assessor-515-295-3857; Treasurer-515-295-3404.

Lee County (Northern District)

County Recorder, PO Box 322, Fort Madison, IA 52627-0322. **Phone-**County Recorder, R/E & UCC Recording- 319-372-4662; fax-319-372-7033; hours 8:30AM-4:30PM www.leecounty.org
Will search UCC records. Search per debtor- $5.00. UCC copy- $1.00 per page. Tax liens not included in UCC search. Will not search real estate records. RE record copy- $.35 per page. Cert fee: $5.00 per cert. Payee: Lee County Recorder. **Other phones:** Assessor-319-372-6302; Treasurer-319-372-3405; Elections-319-372-3705; Vital Records-319-372-4662.

Lee County (Southern District)

County Recorder, PO Box 160, Keokuk, IA 52632. **Phone-**County Recorder, R/E & UCC Recording- 319-524-1126; fax-319-524-1544; hours 8:30AM-4:30PM www.leecounty.org
Will search UCC records; request must be on correct form. Search per debtor- $5.00. UCC copy- $1.00 per page. Will not search real estate records. RE record copy- $.35 per page. Cert fee: $5.00 per doc. Payee: Lee County Recorder. **Other phones:** Assessor-319-524-1375; Treasurer-319-524-1550; Appraiser/ Auditor-319-524-2482; Elections-319-524-2482; Vital Records-319-524-1126.

Linn County

County Recorder, PO Box 1406, Cedar Rapids, IA 52406-1406. **Phone-**County Recorder, R/E & UCC Recording- 319-892-5420; fax-319-892-5459; hours 8AM-5PM www.linncountyrecorder.com
Will search UCC records. Search per debtor- $5.00. UCC copy- $1.00 per page. Separate federal/state combined tax lien search- $6.00 per debtor. Will not search real estate records. Cert fee: $5.00 per doc. Payee: Linn County Recorder. **Online Access to Assessor, Property records:** Access to City of Cedar Rapids property information is free at www.cedar-rapids-assessor.org/pmc/. No name searching. Also, cccess to the assessor database of property and sales data is free at www.iowaassessors.com. **Other phones:** Assessor-319-892-5220; Treasurer-319-892-5550; Elections-319-892-5400; Vital Records-319-892-5445.

Louisa County

County Recorder, PO Box 264, Wapello, IA 52653-0264. **Phone-**319-523-5361; fax-319-523-5362; hours 8AM-4:30PM
Will search UCC records. Search per debtor- $6.00, $5.00 for add'l. Search request using non-standard form (per name)- $6.00. UCC copy- $1.00 per page. Will not search real estate or tax lien records. Cert fee: $5.00. Payee: Louisa County Recorder.

Lucas County

County Recorder, 916 Braden, Courthouse, Chariton, IA 50049. **Phone-**641-774-2413; fax-641-774-1619; hours 8AM-4PM
Will not search UCC records. UCC copy- $1.00 per page. Will not search tax liens. RE record copy- $.25 per page. Cert fee: $5.00 per doc + $1.00 per page. Payee: County Recorder. **Other phones:** Assessor-641-774-4411; Treasurer-641-774-5213.

Lyon County

County Recorder, 206 Second Ave, Courthouse, Rock Rapids, IA 51246. **Phone-**County Recorder, R/E & UCC Recording- 712-472-2381; fax-712-472-2381; hours 8AM-4:30PM. Will search UCC records. Search per debtor- $5.00. UCC copy- $1.00 per page. UCC search includes tax liens if requested. Will not search real estate records. Cert fee: $5.00 per doc. Payee: Lyon County Recorder. **Online Access to Assessor, Property records:** Access to the assessor property and sales data is free at www.iowaassessors.com. **Other phones:** Assessor-

712-472-3592; Treasurer-712-472-3703; Elections-712-472-3713; Vital Records-712-472-2381.

Madison County

County Recorder, PO Box 152, Winterset, IA 50273-0152. **Phone-**County Recorder, R/E & UCC Recording- 515-462-3771; fax-515-462-5881; hours 8AM-4:30PM; 9AM-Noon Last Sat of the month www.madisoncoia.us
Will search UCC records. Search per debtor- $5.00. UCC copy- $1.00 per page. Tax liens not included in UCC search. Federal tax lien search- $6.00; $5.00 for state tax lien. Will not search real estate records. RE record copy- $.50 per page. Cert fee: $5.00 per doc + $.50 per page. Payee: Madison County Recorder. **Online Access to Assessor, Property records:** Access to the assessor database of property and sales data is free at www.iowaassessors.com. **Other phones:** Assessor-515-462-4303; Treasurer-515-462-1542; Elections-515-462-3914; Vital Records-515-462-3771.

Mahaska County

County Recorder, 106 S.1st. St,Courthouse, Oskaloosa, IA 52577. **Phone-**County Recorder, R/E & UCC Recording- 641-673-8187; hours 8AM-4:30PM
Will not search UCC records. UCC copy- $1.00 per page. Will not search real estate records. Cert fee: $10.00 per doc. Payee: Mahaska County Recorder. **Online Access to Assessor, Property records:** Access to the assessor database of property and sales data is free at www.iowaassessors.com. **Other phones:** Assessor-641-673-5805; Treasurer-641-673-5482; Vital Records-641-673-8187.

Marion County

County Recorder, 214 E. Main St., Knoxville, IA 50138. **Phone-**County Recorder, R/E & UCC Recording- 641-828-2211; fax-641-828-3538; hours 8AM-4:30PM. May or may not search UCC records. UCC Search per debtor- $5.00. UCC copy- $1.00 per page. UCC search includes tax liens if requested. Separate federal/state combined tax lien search- $6.00 per debtor. Will not search real estate records. Cert fee: $5.00 per doc. Payee: Marion County Recorder. **Online Access to Assessor, Property records:** Access to assessor property and sales data is free at www.iowaassessors.com. **Other phones:** Assessor-641-828-2215; Treasurer-641-828-2211; Vital Records-641-828-2211.

Marshall County

County Recorder, PO Box 573, Marshalltown, IA 50158-0573. **Phone-**641-754-6355; fax-641-754-6349; hours 8AM-4:30PM www.co.marshall.ia.us
Will search UCC records. Search per debtor- $5.00. UCC copy- $1.00 per page. UCC search includes tax liens if requested. Will not search real estate records. RE record copy- $.50 per page; $1.00 per page to mail. Cert fee: $2.00 per doc. Payee: Marshall County Recorder. **Online Access to Assessor, Property records:** Access to the assessor's property record card system is free at www.co.marshall.ia.us/departments/assessor/disclaimer_html. Also, access to the assessor database of property and sales data is free at www.iowaassessors.com. **Other phones:** Assessor-641-754-6305; Treasurer-641-754-6366; Elections-641-754-6323; Vital Records-641-754-6355; Auditor-641-754-6323.

Mills County

County Recorder, 418 Sharp St, Courthouse, Glenwood, IA 51534. **Phone-**712-527-9315; hours 8AM-4:30PM
Will search UCC records. Search per debtor- $5.00. Will not search tax liens. Record copy- $1.00 per page. Cert fee: $5.00 per doc + $1.00 per page. Payee: Mills County Recorder. **Online Access to**

Assessor, Property records: Access to the assessor database of property and sales data is free at www.iowaassessors.com. **Other phones:** Assessor-712-527-4883; Treasurer-712-527-4419.

Mitchell County

County Recorder, 508 State St, Osage, IA 50461-1250. **Phone-**County Recorder, R/E & UCC Recording- 641-732-5861; fax-641-732-5218; hours 8AM-4:30PM
Will search UCC records. Search per debtor- $5.00. UCC copy- $1.00 per page. Tax liens not included in UCC search. Will not search real estate records. RE record copy- $.50 per page. Cert fee: $5.00 per doc. Payee: County Recorder. **Other phones:** Assessor-641-732-5861; Treasurer-641-732-5861.

Monona County

County Recorder, PO Box 53, Onawa, IA 51040. **Phone-**County Recorder, R/E & UCC Recording- 712-423-2575; fax-712-423-3034; hours 8AM-4:30PM
Will not search records. UCC copy- $1.00 per page. RE record- $.50 per page. Cert fee: $5.00 per page. Payee: Monona County Recorder. **Other phones:** Assessor-712-423-2271; Treasurer-712-423-2271; Elections-712-423-2191; Vital Records-712-423-2575.

Monroe County

County Recorder, 10 Benton Ave. East, Courthouse, Albia, IA 52531. **Phone-**641-932-5164; fax-641932-2863; hours 8AM-4PM. Will search UCC records. Search per debtor- $5.00. UCC copy- $1.00 per page. Will not search tax liens. Real estate owner, mortgage, and property transfer searches available. RE record copy- $.25-1.00 per page. Cert fee: $5.00 per doc + $.25 per page. Payee: Monroe County Recorder. **Other phones:** Assessor-641-932-2180; Treasurer-641-932-5011.

Montgomery County

County Recorder, PO Box 469, Red Oak, IA 51566. **Phone-**County Recorder, R/E & UCC Recording- 712-623-4363; fax-712-623-8915; hours 8AM-4:30PM
Will search UCC records. Search per debtor- $5.00. UCC Information request $6.00 if recorder has to provide form. UCC copy- $1.00 per page. Tax liens not included in UCC search. Separate federal tax lien search- $6.00 per debtor. Will not search real estate records. RE record copy- $.50 per page. Cert fee: $5.00 per cert. Payee: Montgomery County Recorder. **Online Access to Assessor, Property records:** Access to the assessor database of property and sales data is free at www.iowaassessors.com. **Other phones:** Assessor-712-623-4171; Treasurer-712-623-2392; Appraiser/ Auditor-712-623-4171; Elections-712-623-5127; Vital Records-712-623-4363.

Muscatine County

County Recorder, 401 E. 3rd St, Courthouse, Muscatine, IA 52761-4166. **Phone-**County Recorder, R/E & UCC Recording- 563-263-7741; fax-563-263-7248; hours 8AM-4:30PM www.co.muscatine.ia.us
Will search UCC records. Search per debtor- $5.00. Tax liens not included in UCC search. Separate federal tax lien search- $6.00 per debtor. Real estate owner, mortgage, and property transfer searches available. Record copy- $1.00 per page; fee to fax results is $1.50 per page. Cert fee: $5.00 per doc. Payee: Muscatine County Recorder. **Online Access to Property, GIS-mapping records:** Access to property data on the GIS service is free at www.magic-gis.org/pmc/main.asp?page=query. No name searching. **Other phones:** Assessor-563-263-7061; Treasurer-563-263-7113; Elections-563-263-5821; Vital Records-563-263-7741.

O'Brien County

County Recorder, PO Box 340, Primghar, IA 51245-0340. **Phone-**County Recorder, R/E & UCC Recording- 712-957-3045; fax-712-957-3046; hours 8AM-4:30PM www.obriencounty.com/government/recorder.htm Will do verbal record searches on computer back to 1988, but will not guarantee results. Will not search UCC records. UCC copy- $1.00 per page. Federal/state combined tax lien search fee- $5.00 per page. Will not search real estate records. RE record copy- $.50 per page or $1.00 per page in older books. Cert fee: $5.00 per doc. Payee: O'Brien County Recorder. **Other phones:** Assessor-712-957-3205; Treasurer-712-957-3210 or 4185; Elections-712-957-3225; Vital Records-712-957-3045.

Osceola County

County Recorder, 300 7th St, Courthouse, Sibley, IA 51249-1695. **Phone-**County Recorder, R/E & UCC Recording- 712-754-3345; fax-712-754-3743; hours 8AM-4:30PM www.osceolaclerkcourt.org Will search UCC records. Search per debtor- $5.00. UCC search includes tax liens if requested. Separate federal/state combined tax lien search- $12.00 per debtor. Will not search real estate records. Record copy- $1.00 per page. Cert fee: $5.00 per cert + $1.00 per page. Payee: Osceola County Recorder. **Other phones:** Assessor-712-754-3438; Treasurer-712-754-3217; Elections-712-754-2241; Vital Records-712-754-3345; Assessor-712-754-3438.

Page County

County Recorder, 112 E. Main St., Courthouse, Clarinda, IA 51632. **Phone-**712-542-3130; fax-712-542-3636; hours 8AM-4:30PM. Will not search UCC records. UCC copy- $1.00 per page. Separate federal/state combined tax lien search- $11.00 per debtor. Real estate owner, mortgage, and property transfer searches available. RE record- $.50 per page. Cert fee: $5.00 per doc + $1.00 per page. Payee: Page County Recorder. **Other phones:** Assessor-712-542-2516; Treasurer-712-542-5322.

Palo Alto County

County Recorder, PO Box 248, Emmetsburg, IA 50536. **Phone-**County Recorder, R/E & UCC Recording- 712-852-3701; fax-712-852-3704; hours 8AM-4PM. Will search UCC records; ritten requests only. Search per debtor- $5.00. UCC copy- $1.00 per page. Tax liens not included in UCC search. Separate federal/state combined tax lien search- $6.00 per debtor. Will not search real estate records. RE record- $.50 per page. Cert fee: $5.00 per cert + $.50 per page. Payee: Palo Alto County Recorder. **Other phones:** Assessor-712-852-3823; Treasurer-712-852-3844; Elections-712-852-2924; Vital Records-712-852-3701.

Plymouth County

County Recorder, 215 4th Ave. SE, Courthouse, Le Mars, IA 51031. **Phone-**712-546-4020; hours 8AM-5PM. Will search UCC records. Search per debtor- $5.00. UCC copy- $1.00 per page. Tax liens not included in UCC search. Tax lien search fee- $6.00 per debtor. Will not search real estate records. Cert fee: $5.00 per certification; add'l $.50 per page. Payee: Plymouth County Recorder. **Online Access to Assessor, Property records:** Access to the assessor database of property and sales data is free at www.iowaassessors.com. **Other phones:** Treasurer-712-546-4020.

Pocahontas County

County Recorder, 99 Court Sq, Pocahontas, IA 50574-1621. **Phone-**County Recorder, R/E & UCC Recording- 712-335-4404; fax-712-335-4502; hours

8AM-4PM. Will search UCC records. Search per debtor- $5.00. UCC copy- $1.00 per page. Federal/state combined tax lien search- $6.00 per debtor. Real estate owner, mortgage, and property transfer searches available. RE record- $.25 per page. Cert fee: $5.00 per cert. Payee: Pocahontas County Recorder. **Other phones:** Assessor-712-335-5016; Treasurer-712-335-4334; Vital Records-712-335-4404.

Polk County

County Recorder, 111 Court Ave, Rm 250, County Admin. Bldg., Des Moines, IA 50309. **Phone-**County Recorder, R/E & UCC Recording- 515-286-3160, UCC Recording- 515-286-2241; fax-515-323-5393; hours 8AM-4:30PM www.co.polk.ia.us Will search UCC records. Search per debtor- $5.00. UCC copy- $1.00 per page. Tax liens not included in UCC search. Separate federal/state combined tax lien search- $11.00 per debtor. Will not search real estate records. RE record- $.50 per page. Cert fee: $5.00 per doc. Payee: Polk County Recorder. **Online Access to Assessor, Property, Real Estate Sale, Recording, Deed, Lien, UCC records:** Access to the Recorder's Index Search is free at http://recorder.co.polk.ia.us. Also includes trade names, financing statements, and plats as well as recordings. Also, access to the Polk County assessor database is free at www.assess.co.polk.ia.us/web/basic/search.htm. Search by property or by sales. Also, access to the assessor database of property and sales data is free at www.iowaassessors.com. **Other phones:** Assessor-515-286-3014; Treasurer-515-286-3041; Elections-515-286-3247; Vital Records-515-286-3781.

Pottawattamie County

County Recorder, 227 S. Sixth St, Council Bluffs, IA 51501. **Phone-**County Recorder, R/E & UCC Recording- 712-328-5612; fax-712-328-4738; hours 8AM-4PM www.pottcounty.com Will search UCC records. Search per debtor- $5.00. UCC copy- $1.00 per page. Tax liens not included in UCC search. Federal tax line search- $6.00; state lien- $$2.00 per debtor. Will not search real estate records. RE record copy- $.75 per page. Cert fee: $2.00 per doc. Payee: Pottawattamie County Recorder. **Online Access to Real Estate, Property, Residential Sale, Assessor records:** Records on the Pottawattamie County Courthouse/Council Bluffs property database are free at www.pottco.org. Search by owner name, address, or parcel number. Records since 7/1/89, images since 10/20/2002. Records of the County Assessor "Residential Sales" and property database are free at www.pottco.org/htdocs/assessor.html. Also, access to the assessor database of property and sales data is free at www.iowaassessors.com. **Other phones:** Assessor-712-328-5617; Treasurer-712-328-5627; Elections-712-328-5700 (Auditor); Vital Records-712-328-5612; Recorder's Office Info Line-712-328-5725.

Poweshiek County

County Recorder, PO Box 656, Montezuma, IA 50171-0656. **Phone-**County Recorder, R/E & UCC Recording- 641-623-5434; fax-641-623-2875; hours 8AM-4PM Will not search records. UCC copy- $2.00 per page. Cert fee: $5.00 per doc. Payee: Poweshiek County Recorder. **Online Access to Assessor, Property records:** Access to the assessor database of property and sales data is free at www.iowaassessors.com. **Other phones:** Assessor-641-623-5445; Treasurer-641-623-5128; Elections-641-623-5434.

Ringgold County

County Recorder, 109 W Madison #204, Mount Ayr, IA 50854. **Phone-**County Recorder, R/E & UCC Recording- 641-464-3231; fax-641-464-2568; hours 8AM-4PM. Will search UCC records. Search per debtor- $5.00. UCC copy- $1.00 per page. UCC

search includes tax liens if requested. Will not search real estate records. RE record copy- $.50 per page. Cert fee: $6.00 per doc. Payee: County Recorder. **Other phones:** Assessor-641-464-3233; Treasurer-641-464-3230; Vital Records-641-464-3231.

Sac County

County Recorder, 100 NW State St., Sac City, IA 50583. **Phone-**County Recorder, R/E & UCC Recording- 712-662-7789; fax-712-662-6298; hours 8AM-4:30PM www.saccounty.org Will search UCC records. Search per debtor- $5.00. UCC copy- $1.00 per page. Tax liens not included in UCC search. Will not search real estate records. RE record copy- $.50 per page. Cert fee: $5.00 per cert. Payee: Sac County Recorder. **Other phones:** Assessor-712-662-4492; Treasurer-712-662-7411; Elections-712-662-7310; Vital Records-712-662-7789.

Scott County

County Recorder, 428 Western Ave, 5th Fl, Davenport, IA 52801-1187. **Phone-**County Recorder, R/E & UCC Recording- 563-326-8621; fax-563-328-3225; hours 8AM-4:30PM www.scottcountyiowa.com Will search UCC records. Search per debtor- $5.00. UCC copy- $1.00 per page. Will search tax liens. Tax lien search fee- $5.00 per debtor. Will not search real estate records. Cert fee: $5.00 per doc. Payee: Scott County Recorder. **Online Access to Assessor, Property, Restaurant Inspection, Most Wanted records:** Access to assessor property records is available free at www.scottcountyiowa.com/assessor/query.asp. Also search restaurant inspections at www.scottcountyiowa.com/health/food.html. Also, view the sheriff's most wanted list at www.scottcountyiowa.com/sheriff/mostwanted.html. **Other phones:** Assessor-563-326-8635; Treasurer-563-326-8664; Elections-563-326-8631; Vital Records-563-326-8650.

Shelby County

County Recorder, PO Box 67, Harlan, IA 51537-0067. **Phone-**County Recorder, R/E & UCC Recording- 712-755-5640; fax-712-755-7556; hours 8AM-4:30PM www.shco.org Will search UCC records. Search per debtor- $5.00. Tax liens not included in UCC search. Separate federal tax lien search- $6.00 per debtor. Will not search real estate records. Record copy- $1.00 per page. Cert fee: $2.00 per doc. Payee: Shelby County Recorder. **Online Access to Real Estate Recording, Assessor, Property records:** Access to the county GIS parcel search is free at http://maps.shco.org/pmc/main.asp?page=query. You can do a name search, fees involved. Call 870-856-3055 for subscription information. Also, access to the assessor database of property and sales data is free at www.iowaassessors.com. **Other phones:** Assessor-712-755-5718; Treasurer-712-755-5898; Elections-712-755-3831; Vital Records-712-755-5640.

Sioux County

County Recorder, PO Box 48, Orange City, IA 51041. **Phone-**County Recorder, R/E & UCC Recording- 712-737-2229; fax-712-737-2230; hours 8AM-4:30PM www.siouxcounty.org Will search UCC records. Search per debtor- $5.00. UCC copy- $1.00 per page. Tax liens not included in UCC search. Tax lien search fee- $6.00 per debtor. Will not search real estate records. RE record copy- $.25 per page. Cert fee: $2.00 per page. Payee: Sioux County Recorder. **Online Access to Property Tax records:** Search the treasurer's property tax records online by subscriptin; for information please contact Micah Van Maanen at 712-737-6818, http://siouxcounty.org/treasurer.htm. **Other phones:** Assessor-712-737-4274; Treasurer-712-737-3505;

Appraiser/ Auditor-712-737-4274; Elections-712-737-2216; Vital Records-712-737-2229.

Story County

County Recorder, PO Box 55, Nevada, IA 50201-0055. **Phone-**County Recorder, R/E & UCC Recording- 515-382-7230; fax-515-382-7326; hours 8AM-5PM (No recording after 3:30PM) www.storycounty.com/departments.html
Will search UCC records. Search per debtor- $5.00. Tax liens not included in UCC search. Federal tax lien search- $6.00 per debtor (state tax liens included). Will not search real estate records. Record copy- $1.00 per page. Cert fee: $5.00 per doc. Payee: Story County Recorder. **Online Access to Assessor, Property Tax, Grantor/Grantee, Deed, Mortgage, UCC, Sheriff Sale, Most Wanted records:** Records on the assessor database are free at www.storyassessor.org/pmc/main.asp?page=query. No name searching. Also, land records on the recorder's database are free at https://www.landaccess.com. Also, City of Ames property assessor data is free at www.amesassessor.org/pmc/ but no name searching. Also, the sheriff's sale and most wanted lists are at www.storycounty.com/SheriffWeb.nsf/index.htm.
Also, access to the assessor database of property and sales data is free at www.iowaassessors.com. **Other phones:** Assessor-515-382-7320; Treasurer-515-382-7330; Appraiser/ Auditor-515-382-7322; Elections-515-382-7217; Vital Records-515-382-7237; Deputy Assessor-515-382-7322.

Tama County

County Recorder, PO Box 82, Toledo, IA 52342. **Phone-**641-484-3320; hours 8AM-4:30PM
Will search UCC records. Search per debtor- $5.00. UCC copy- $1.00 per page. Will not search real estate or tax lien records. RE copy- $1.00 per page. Cert fee: $5.00 per doc + $.25 per page. Payee: Tama County Recorder. **Other phones:** Assessor-641-484-3545; Treasurer-641-484-3141.

Taylor County

County Recorder, 405 Jefferson St., Courthouse, Bedford, IA 50833. **Phone-**712-523-2275; fax-712-523-2274; hours 8AM-4:30PM. Will not search UCC records. Federal/state combined tax lien search- $11.00 per page. Will not search real estate records. Record copy- $1.00 per page. Cert fee: $2.00 per page. Payee: County Recorder. **Other phones:** Assessor-712-523-2444; Treasurer-712-523-2080.

Union County

County Recorder, 300 N. Pine St, Creston, IA 50801. **Phone-**641-782-1725; fax-641-782-1709; hours 8:30AM-4:30PM. Will search UCC records. Search per debtor- $5.00. UCC copy- $1.00 per page. Will not search tax liens. Real estate owner and property transfer searches available; no mortgage searches. RE record copy- $.50 per page. Cert fee: $5.00 per doc + $.50 per page. Payee: Union County Recorder. **Other phones:** Assessor-641-782-1735; Treasurer-641-782-1710.

Van Buren County

County Recorder, PO Box 455, Keosauqua, IA 52565. **Phone-**County Recorder, R/E & UCC Recording- 319-293-3240; fax-319-293-3828; hours 8AM-4:30PM
Will search UCC records. Search per debtor- $5.00. UCC copy- $1.00 per page. Will not search real estate or tax lien records. RE record copy- $.25 per page. Cert fee: $2.00 per doc. Payee: Van Buren County Recorder. **Other phones:** Assessor-319-293-3001; Treasurer-319-293-3110; Elections-319-293-3129; Vital Records-319-293-3240.

Wapello County

County Recorder, 101 W. 4th St, Ottumwa, IA 52501. **Phone-**County Recorder, R/E & UCC Recording- 641-683-0045; fax-641-683-0019; hours 8AM-4:30PM
Will search UCC records. Search per debtor- $5.00. UCC copy- $1.00 per page. UCC search includes tax liens if requested. Separate federal/state combined tax lien search- $6.00 per debtor. Will not search real estate records. RE copy- $1.00 per page. Cert fee: $5.00 per doc. Payee: County Recorder. **Other phones:** Assessor-641-683-0088; Treasurer-641-683-0040; Vital Records-641-683-0045.

Warren County

County Recorder, 301 N Buxton, #109, Indianola, IA 50125. **Phone-**515-961-1089; hours 8AM-4:30PM
Will search UCC records up to July 1, 2001. Mail requests must include a SASE. Search per debtor- $5.00. Federal tax liens not included in UCC search. Separate federal/state tax lien search- $6.00 per debtor. Will not search real estate records. Record copy- $1.00 per page. Cert fee: $5.00 per doc. Payee: Warren County Recorder. **Online Access to Assessor, Property records:** Access to the assessor database of property and sales data is free at www.iowaassessors.com. **Other phones:** Assessor-515-961-1010; Treasurer-515-961-1110.

Washington County

County Recorder, PO Box 889, Washington, IA 52353-0889. **Phone-**County Recorder, R/E & UCC Recording- 319-653-7727; hours 8AM-4:30PM
Will not search UCC records. UCC copy- $1.00 per page. Tax lien search fee- $6.00 per debtor. Mortgage searches available. RE record copy- min. $1.00 + $.40 per page. Cert fee: $5.00 per doc + copy fee of $.30 per page. Payee: Washington County Recorder. **Online Access to Assessor, Property records:** Access to the assessor database of property and sales data is free at www.iowaassessors.com. **Other phones:** Assessor-319-653-7709; Treasurer-319-653-7726; Elections-319-653-7777; Vital Records-319-653-7727.

Wayne County

County Recorder, PO Box 435, Corydon, IA 50060. **Phone-**County Recorder, R/E & UCC Recording- 641-872-1676; fax-641-872-2843; hours 8AM-4PM
Will search UCC records. Search per debtor- $5.00. UCC copy- $1.00 per page. Will not search tax liens. Real estate owner, mortgage, and property transfer searches available. RE record copy- $.50 per page. Cert fee: $5.00 1st page; $1.00 each add'l. Payee: Wayne County Recorder. **Other phones:** Assessor-641-872-2663; Treasurer-641-872-2515; Vital Records-641-872-1676.

Webster County

County Recorder, PO Box 1253, Fort Dodge, IA 50501. **Phone-**County Recorder, R/E & UCC Recording- 515-576-2401; fax-515-574-3723; hours 8AM-4:30PM www.webstercountyia.org
Will search UCC records. Search per debtor- $5.00. UCC search includes tax liens if requested. Will not search real estate records. Record copy- $1.00 per page. Cert fee: $6.00 per doc. Payee: Webster County Recorder. **Online Access to Assessor, Property, Real Estate records:** Access to the assessor database of property and sales data is free at www.iowaassessors.com. Also, property data is free at www.webstercountyia.org. **Other phones:** Assessor-515-576-4721; Treasurer-515-576-2731; Elections-515-573-7175; Vital Records-515-576-2401.

Winnebago County

County Recorder, 126 S. Clark St #1, Courthouse, Forest City, IA 50436-1706. **Phone-**County Recorder, R/E & UCC Recording- 641-585-2094; fax-641-585-2891; hours 8AM-4:30PM. Will not search UCC records. UCC copy- $1.00 per page. Will not search real estate records. RE record copy- $.50 per page. Cert fee: $5.00 per doc. Payee: Winnebago County Recorder. **Other phones:** Assessor-641-585-2163; Treasurer-641-585-2322; Appraiser/ Auditor-641-585-3412; Vital Records-641-585-2094.

Winneshiek County

County Recorder, 201 W. Main St, Decorah, IA 52101. **Phone-**563-382-3486; fax-319-387-4083; hours 8AM-4PM. Will search UCC records. Search per debtor- $5.00. UCC search includes tax liens if requested. Will not search real estate records. Record copy- $1.00 per page. Cert fee: $2.00 per doc + $1.00 per page. Payee: Winneshiek County Recorder. **Other phones:** Assessor-563-382-5356; Treasurer-563-382-3753; Vital Records-563-382-3486.

Woodbury County

County Auditor & Recorder, 620 Douglas St, Rm 106, Sioux City, IA 51101. **Phone-**County Auditor & Recorder, R/E & UCC Recording- 712-279-6528; fax-712-233-8946; hours 8AM-4:30PM
Will search UCC records. Search per debtor- $5.00. UCC copy- $1.00 per page. Separate federal/state combined tax lien search- $12.00 per debtor. Will not search real estate records. RE record copy- $.50 per page. Cert fee: $5.00 per doc. Payee: Woodbury County Auditor & Recorder. **Online Access to Assessor, Property, Real Estate records:** Access to the assessor database of property and sales data is free at www.iowaassessors.com. Also, search Sioux City property data for free at http://sidwellmaps.com/website/siouxcity/eula1.asp. No name searching. **Other phones:** Assessor-712-279-6505 or 712-279-6535; Treasurer-712-279-6495; Elections-712-279-6465; Vital Records-712-279-6266.

Worth County

County Recorder, 1000 Central Ave, Northwood, IA 50459. **Phone-**County Recorder, R/E & UCC Recording- 641-324-2734; fax-641-324-3682; hours 8AM-4PM. Will search UCC records. Search per debtor- $5.00. UCC copy- $1.00 per page. Tax liens not included in UCC search. Tax lien search fee- $5.00 per debtor. Will not search real estate records. RE record copy- $.50 per page if picked up, $1.00 per page if mailed, $1.50 per page if faxed. Cert fee: $5.00 per doc. Payee: Worth County Recorder. **Other phones:** Assessor-641-324-1198; Treasurer-641-324-2942; Elections-641-324-2316; Vital Records-641-324-2734.

Wright County

County Recorder, PO Box 187, Clarion, IA 50525. **Phone-**County Recorder, R/E & UCC Recording- 515-532-3204; fax-515-532-2669; hours 8AM-4PM www.wrightcounty.org/county_offices.htm
Will search UCC records. Search per debtor- $5.00. UCC copy- $1.00 per page. Tax liens not included in UCC search. Separate federal/state combined tax lien search- $6.00 per debtor. Real estate record owner and mortgage searches available. RE record copy- $.50 per page. Cert fee: $5.00 per doc. Payee: Wright County Recorder. **Other phones:** Assessor-515-532-3737; Treasurer-515-532-2691.

Iowa County Locator

You will usually be able to find the city name in the City/County Cross Reference below. In that case, it is a simple matter to determine the county from the cross reference. However, only the official US Postal Service city names are included in this index. We have also included a ZIP/City Cross Reference immediately following the City/County Cross Reference.

Iowa City/County Cross Reference

A C NIELSEN CO Clinton
ACKLEY (50601) Hardin(71), Franklin(11),
    Butler(9), Grundy(7)
ACKWORTH Warren
ADAIR (50002) Adair(68), Guthrie(30),
    Audubon(1)
ADEL Dallas
AFTON Union
AGENCY Wapello
AINSWORTH Washington
AKRON Plymouth
ALBERT CITY (50510) Buena Vista(84),
    Pocahontas(15)
ALBIA Monroe
ALBION Marshall
ALBURNETT Linn
ALDEN (50006) Hardin(84), Franklin(14)
ALEXANDER (50420) Franklin(84),
    Wright(10), Story(4)
ALGONA Kossuth
ALLEMAN Polk
ALLENDORF Osceola
ALLERTON Wayne
ALLISON Butler
ALPHA Fayette
ALTA Buena Vista
ALTA VISTA (50603) Chickasaw(85),
    Howard(13)
ALTON (51003) Sioux(98), Plymouth(1)
ALTOONA Polk
ALVORD Lyon
AMANA (52203) Iowa(84), Johnson(14)
AMANA Iowa
AMES (50014) Story(96), Boone(3)
AMES Story
ANAMOSA Jones
ANDOVER Clinton
ANDREW Jackson
ANITA (50020) Cass(87), Adair(6),
    Audubon(5)
ANKENY Polk
ANTHON Woodbury
APLINGTON (50604) Butler(85),
    Grundy(14)
ARCADIA Carroll
ARCHER O'Brien
AREDALE (50605) Butler(69), Franklin(30)
ARGYLE Lee
ARION Crawford
ARISPE Union
ARLINGTON (50606) Fayette(94),
    Clayton(5)
ARMSTRONG (50514) Emmet(79),
    Kossuth(20)
ARNOLDS PARK Dickinson
ARTHUR (51431) Ida(87), Sac(12)
ASHTON (51232) Osceola(76), Lyon(19),
    O'Brien(2)
ASPINWALL Crawford
AT AND T Pottawattamie
ATALISSA (52720) Muscatine(78),
    Cedar(21)
ATKINS Benton
ATLANTIC (50022) Cass(98), Audubon(1)
AUBURN (51433) Sac(59), Calhoun(39),
    Carroll(1)
AUDUBON Audubon
AURELIA (51005) Cherokee(87), Buena
    Vista(12)
AURORA (50607) Buchanan(60),
    Fayette(39)
AUSTINVILLE Butler

AVOCA (51521) Pottawattamie(91),
    Shelby(8)
AYRSHIRE (50515) Palo Alto(81), Clay(18)
BADGER (50516) Webster(88),
    Humboldt(11)
BAGLEY (50026) Guthrie(71), Greene(28)
BALDWIN (52207) Jackson(90), Clinton(9)
BANCROFT Kossuth
BARNES CITY (50027) Mahaska(97),
    Poweshiek(2)
BARNUM Webster
BARTLETT Fremont
BATAVIA (52533) Jefferson(71),
    Wapello(28)
BATTLE CREEK (51006) Ida(90),
    Woodbury(9)
BAXTER Jasper
BAYARD (50029) Guthrie(96), Greene(3)
BEACON Mahaska
BEACONSFIELD Ringgold
BEAMAN (50609) Grundy(73),
    Marshall(20), Tama(5)
BEAVER Boone
BEDFORD Taylor
BELLE PLAINE (52208) Benton(93),
    Iowa(3), Tama(1)
BELLEVUE Jackson
BELMOND Wright
BENNETT Cedar
BENTON Ringgold
BERNARD (52032) Dubuque(59),
    Jackson(36), Jones(4)
BERWICK Polk
BETTENDORF Scott
BEVINGTON Madison
BIG ROCK Scott
BIRMINGHAM (52535) Van Buren(96),
    Jefferson(3)
BLAIRSBURG (50034) Hamilton(85),
    Wright(14)
BLAIRSTOWN (52209) Benton(96), Iowa(3)
BLAKESBURG (52536) Wapello(88),
    Monroe(9), Davis(2)
BLANCHARD Page
BLENCOE (51523) Monona(95),
    Harrison(4)
BLOCKTON (50836) Taylor(90),
    Ringgold(9)
BLOOMFIELD (52537) Davis(95),
    Wapello(4)
BLUE GRASS (52726) Scott(91),
    Muscatine(8)
BODE (50519) Humboldt(71), Kossuth(28)
BONAPARTE Van Buren
BONDURANT Polk
BOONE Boone
BOONEVILLE Dallas
BOUTON (50039) Dallas(96), Boone(3)
BOXHOLM Boone
BOYDEN (51234) Sioux(97), Lyon(2)
BRADDYVILLE Page
BRADFORD Franklin
BRADGATE (50520) Humboldt(95),
    Pocahontas(4)
BRANDON Buchanan
BRAYTON (50042) Audubon(92), Cass(7)
BREDA (51436) Carroll(75), Sac(13),
    Crawford(10)
BRIDGEWATER (50837) Adair(74),
    Cass(18), Adams(6)
BRIGHTON (52540) Jefferson(50),
    Washington(49)

BRISTOW Butler
BRITT Hancock
BRONSON Woodbury
BROOKLYN Poweshiek
BRUNSVILLE Plymouth
BRYANT Clinton
BUCKEYE Hardin
BUCKINGHAM Tama
BUFFALO Scott
BUFFALO CENTER (50424)
    Winnebago(88), Kossuth(11)
BURLINGTON Des Moines
BURNSIDE Webster
BURR OAK Winneshiek
BURT Kossuth
BUSSEY (50044) Marion(73),
    Mahaska(19), Monroe(7)
CALAMUS Clinton
CALLENDER Webster
CALMAR (52132) Winneshiek(86),
    Howard(13)
CALUMET O'Brien
CAMANCHE Clinton
CAMBRIDGE (50046) Story(81), Polk(18)
CANTRIL Van Buren
CARBON Adams
CARLISLE (50047) Warren(87), Polk(12)
CARNARVON Sac
CARPENTER Mitchell
CARROLL Carroll
CARSON Pottawattamie
CARTER LAKE Pottawattamie
CASCADE (52033) Dubuque(70),
    Jones(30)
CASEY (50048) Guthrie(73), Adair(26)
CASTALIA (52133) Winneshiek(72),
    Fayette(27)
CASTANA Monona
CEDAR Mahaska
CEDAR FALLS (50613) Black Hawk(97),
    Grundy(1)
CEDAR FALLS Black Hawk
CEDAR RAPIDS Linn
CENTER JUNCTION Jones
CENTER POINT (52213) Linn(90),
    Benton(7), Scott(1)
CENTERVILLE Appanoose
CENTRAL CITY Linn
CHAPIN Franklin
CHARITON Lucas
CHARLES CITY Floyd
CHARLOTTE (52731) Clinton(91),
    Jackson(8)
CHARTER OAK Crawford
CHATSWORTH Sioux
CHELSEA (52215) Tama(83),
    Poweshiek(17)
CHEROKEE Cherokee
CHESTER Howard
CHILLICOTHE Wapello
CHURDAN (50050) Greene(95),
    Calhoun(3), Carroll(1)
CHURDAN Greene
CINCINNATI Appanoose
CLARE (50524) Webster(94),
    Pocahontas(2), Humboldt(1)
CLARENCE (52216) Cedar(86), Jones(13)
CLARINDA Page
CLARION Wright
CLARKSVILLE Butler
CLEAR LAKE Cerro Gordo

CLEARFIELD (50840) Taylor(80),
    Ringgold(19)
CLEGHORN (51014) Cherokee(98),
    O'Brien(1)
CLEMONS Marshall
CLERMONT (52135) Fayette(97),
    Clayton(2)
CLIMBING HILL Woodbury
CLINTON Clinton
CLIO Wayne
CLIVE (50325) Polk(87), Dallas(12)
CLUTIER Tama
COGGON (52218) Linn(86), Delaware(13)
COIN Page
COLESBURG (52035) Clayton(71),
    Delaware(18), Dubuque(10)
COLFAX Jasper
COLLEGE SPRINGS Page
COLLINS (50055) Story(69), Jasper(28),
    Marshall(2)
COLO Story
COLUMBIA Marion
COLUMBUS CITY Louisa
COLUMBUS JUNCTION (52738)
    Louisa(95), Washington(4)
COLWELL Floyd
CONESVILLE (52739) Louisa(65),
    Muscatine(34)
CONRAD (50621) Grundy(92), Marshall(7)
CONROY Iowa
COON RAPIDS (50058) Carroll(80),
    Guthrie(11), Audubon(5), Greene(3)
COOPER Greene
CORALVILLE Johnson
CORNING (50841) Adams(94), Taylor(5)
CORRECTIONVILLE (51016)
    Woodbury(93), Ida(6)
CORWITH (50430) Hancock(64),
    Kossuth(29), Humboldt(2), Wright(2)
CORYDON Wayne
COULTER Franklin
COUNCIL BLUFFS (51503)
    Pottawattamie(98), Mills(1)
COUNCIL BLUFFS Pottawattamie
CRAIG Plymouth
CRAWFORDSVILLE (52621)
    Washington(69), Louisa(29), Henry(1)
CRESCENT Pottawattamie
CRESCO (52136) Howard(92),
    Winneshiek(7)
CRESTON (50801) Union(96), Adair(1),
    Adams(1)
CROMWELL Union
CRYSTAL LAKE Hancock
CUMBERLAND (50843) Cass(96),
    Adams(3)
CUMMING (50061) Warren(60),
    Madison(15), Dallas(11), Polk(11)
CURLEW Palo Alto
CUSHING (51018) Woodbury(60), Ida(39)
CYLINDER Palo Alto
DAKOTA CITY Humboldt
DALLAS Marion
DALLAS CENTER Dallas
DANA (50064) Greene(94), Boone(6)
DANBURY (51019) Woodbury(79), Ida(8),
    Monona(6), Crawford(5)
DANVILLE (52623) Des Moines(91),
    Henry(8)
DAVENPORT Scott
DAVIS CITY Decatur
DAWSON Dallas

DAYTON (50530) Webster(96), Boone(3)
DE SOTO Dallas
DE WITT Clinton
DECATUR Decatur
DECORAH Winneshiek
DEDHAM (51440) Carroll(97), Audubon(2)
DEEP RIVER (52222) Poweshiek(73),
   Iowa(26)
DEFIANCE (51527) Shelby(84),
   Crawford(16)
DELAWARE Delaware
DELHI Delaware
DELMAR (52037) Clinton(93), Jackson(6)
DELOIT Crawford
DELPHOS Ringgold
DELTA (52550) Keokuk(98), Mahaska(1)
DENISON Crawford
DENMARK Lee
DENVER Bremer
DERBY (50068) Wayne(64), Lucas(35)
DES MOINES (50320) Polk(89),
   Warren(10)
DES MOINES Polk
DEWAR Black Hawk
DEXTER (50070) Dallas(34), Guthrie(25),
   Madison(23), Adair(17)
DIAGONAL (50845) Ringgold(97), Union(2)
DICKENS (51333) Clay(97), Dickinson(2)
DIKE Grundy
DIXON Scott
DOLLIVER Emmet
DONAHUE Scott
DONNELLSON Lee
DOON (51235) Lyon(96), Sioux(3)
DORCHESTER (52140) Allamakee(94),
   Winneshiek(5)
DOUDS (52551) Van Buren(96), Davis(3)
DOUGHERTY (50433) Cerro Gordo(53),
   Floyd(18), Franklin(18), Butler(9)
DOW CITY Crawford
DOWS (50071) Wright(53), Franklin(46)
DRAKESVILLE (52552) Davis(94),
   Wapello(5)
DUBUQUE Dubuque
DUMONT (50625) Butler(92), Franklin(7)
DUNCOMBE (50532) Webster(94),
   Hamilton(4)
DUNDEE Delaware
DUNKERTON Black Hawk
DUNLAP (51529) Harrison(81),
   Crawford(8), Monona(6), Shelby(2)
DURANGO Dubuque
DURANT (52747) Cedar(63), Scott(24),
   Muscatine(12)
DYERSVILLE (52040) Dubuque(94),
   Delaware(5)
DYSART (52224) Tama(71), Benton(27)
EAGLE GROVE (50533) Wright(96),
   Humboldt(2), Webster(1)
EARLHAM (50072) Madison(77),
   Dallas(22)
EARLING Shelby
EARLVILLE Delaware
EARLY Sac
EDDYVILLE (52553) Wapello(47),
   Mahaska(41), Monroe(11)
EDGEWOOD (52042) Clayton(75),
   Delaware(24)
ELBERON (52225) Tama(82), Benton(17)
ELDON (52554) Wapello(88), Davis(4),
   Jefferson(3), Van Buren(3)
ELDORA (50627) Hardin(95), Grundy(4)
ELDRIDGE Scott
ELGIN (52141) Fayette(71), Clayton(28)
ELK HORN (51531) Shelby(86),
   Audubon(13)
ELKADER Clayton
ELKHART Polk
ELKPORT Clayton
ELLIOTT (51532) Montgomery(55),
   Pottawattamie(38), Cass(6)
ELLSTON (50074) Ringgold(97), Union(2)

ELLSWORTH (50075) Hamilton(88),
   Pocahontas(11)
ELMA (50628) Howard(97), Mitchell(2)
ELWOOD Clinton
ELY (52227) Linn(97), Johnson(2)
EMERSON (51533) Mills(68),
   Montgomery(31)
EMMETSBURG Palo Alto
EPWORTH Dubuque
ESSEX (51638) Page(97), Montgomery(2)
ESTHERVILLE (51334) Emmet(98),
   Dickinson(1)
EVANSDALE Black Hawk
EVERLY (51338) Clay(82), Dickinson(17)
EXIRA (50076) Audubon(98), Guthrie(1)
EXLINE Appanoose
FAIRBANK (50629) Buchanan(44),
   Fayette(28), Black Hawk(15),
   Bremer(10)
FAIRFAX (52228) Linn(80), Benton(11),
   Johnson(7)
FARLEY Dubuque
FARMERSBURG Clayton
FARMINGTON (52626) Van Buren(75),
   Lee(24)
FARNHAMVILLE (50538) Calhoun(91),
   Webster(8)
FARRAGUT Fremont
FAYETTE Fayette
FENTON (50539) Kossuth(81), Palo
   Alto(18)
FERGUSON Marshall
FERTILE (50434) Cerro Gordo(87),
   Worth(11)
FESTINA Winneshiek
FLORIS Davis
FLOYD Floyd
FONDA (50540) Pocahontas(82),
   Calhoun(14), Buena Vista(1), Sac(1)
FONDA Pocahontas
FONTANELLE Adair
FOREST CITY (50436) Winnebago(91),
   Hancock(8)
FORT ATKINSON (52144) Winneshiek(78),
   Fayette(12), Chickasaw(8)
FORT DODGE Webster
FORT MADISON Lee
FOSTORIA Clay
FREDERICKSBURG (50630)
   Chickasaw(92), Bremer(7)
FREDERIKA Bremer
FREMONT (52561) Mahaska(73),
   Keokuk(15), Benton(11)
FRUITLAND Muscatine
GALT Wright
GALVA (51020) Ida(66), Sac(17),
   Cherokee(15)
GARBER Clayton
GARDEN CITY Hardin
GARDEN GROVE Decatur
GARNAVILLO Clayton
GARNER Hancock
GARRISON Benton
GARWIN (50632) Tama(83), Marshall(16)
GENEVA Franklin
GEORGE Lyon
GIBSON (50104) Keokuk(82),
   Poweshiek(12), Mahaska(5)
GIFFORD Hardin
GILBERT Story
GILBERTVILLE Black Hawk
GILLETT GROVE Clay
GILMAN (50106) Marshall(71), Jasper(15),
   Tama(9), Poweshiek(3)
GILMORE CITY (50541) Pocahontas(50),
   Humboldt(49)
GLADBROOK (50635) Tama(94),
   Marshall(5)
GLENWOOD Mills
GLIDDEN (51443) Carroll(98), Greene(1)
GOLDFIELD (50542) Wright(80),
   Humboldt(19)
GOODELL Hancock

GOOSE LAKE Clinton
GOWRIE (50543) Webster(94), Greene(5)
GRAETTINGER (51342) Palo Alto(81),
   Emmet(18)
GRAFTON (50440) Worth(98), Mitchell(1)
GRAND JUNCTION (50107) Greene(95),
   Boone(3)
GRAND MOUND Clinton
GRAND RIVER (50108) Decatur(90),
   Clarke(8)
GRANDVIEW Louisa
GRANGER (50109) Polk(61), Dallas(38)
GRANT Montgomery
GRANVILLE (51022) Sioux(59),
   O'Brien(39)
GRAVITY Taylor
GRAY Audubon
GREELEY (52050) Delaware(87),
   Clayton(12)
GREEN MOUNTAIN Marshall
GREENE (50636) Butler(83), Floyd(16)
GREENFIELD Adair
GREENVILLE Clay
GRIMES (50111) Polk(95), Dallas(4)
GRINNELL (50112) Poweshiek(89),
   Jasper(10)
GRINNELL Poweshiek
GRISWOLD (51535) Cass(52),
   Pottawattamie(47)
GRUNDY CENTER Grundy
GRUVER Emmet
GUERNSEY (52221) Poweshiek(88),
   Iowa(11)
GUTHRIE CENTER Guthrie
GUTTENBERG (52052) Clayton(93),
   Dubuque(6)
HALBUR Carroll
HALE Jones
HAMBURG Fremont
HAMLIN (50117) Audubon(98), Guthrie(1)
HAMPTON Franklin
HANCOCK Pottawattamie
HANLONTOWN (50444) Worth(80), Cerro
   Gordo(18), Winnebago(1)
HANSELL Franklin
HARCOURT (50544) Webster(98),
   Greene(1)
HARDY Humboldt
HARLAN Shelby
HARPER Keokuk
HARPERS FERRY Allamakee
HARRIS (51345) Osceola(94), Dickinson(5)
HARTFORD Warren
HARTLEY (51346) O'Brien(89), Osceola(6),
   Clay(4)
HARTWICK (52232) Poweshiek(85),
   Iowa(14)
HARVEY Marion
HASTINGS Mills
HAVELOCK (50546) Pocahontas(97), Palo
   Alto(2)
HAVERHILL Marshall
HAWARDEN Sioux
HAWKEYE Fayette
HAYESVILLE Keokuk
HAZLETON Buchanan
HEDRICK (52563) Keokuk(67),
   Wapello(31), Jefferson(1)
HENDERSON (51541) Mills(71),
   Pottawattamie(19), Montgomery(9)
HIAWATHA Linn
HIGHLANDVILLE Winneshiek
HILLS Johnson
HILLSBORO (52630) Van Buren(55),
   Henry(26), Lee(17)
HINTON Plymouth
HOLLAND Grundy
HOLSTEIN (51025) Ida(86), Cherokee(7),
   Woodbury(5)
HOLY CROSS (52053) Dubuque(83),
   Clayton(16)
HOMESTEAD (52236) Iowa(98),
   Johnson(2)

HONEY CREEK Pottawattamie
HOPKINTON (52237) Delaware(94),
   Dubuque(3), Jones(1)
HORNICK (51026) Woodbury(75),
   Monona(24)
HOSPERS (51238) Sioux(64), O'Brien(35)
HOUGHTON Lee
HUBBARD (50122) Hardin(98), Story(1)
HUDSON (50643) Black Hawk(93),
   Grundy(6)
HULL Sioux
HUMBOLDT (50548) Humboldt(98),
   Webster(1)
HUMESTON (50123) Wayne(78),
   Lucas(10), Decatur(8), Clarke(1)
HUXLEY (50124) Story(93), Polk(6)
IDA GROVE Ida
IMOGENE (51645) Fremont(53), Mills(36),
   Page(6), Montgomery(2)
INDEPENDENCE Buchanan
INDIANOLA Warren
INWOOD (51240) Lyon(90), Sioux(9)
IONIA (50645) Chickasaw(97), Floyd(2)
IOWA CITY Johnson
IOWA FALLS (50126) Hardin(97),
   Franklin(2)
IRA Jasper
IRETON (51027) Sioux(81), Plymouth(18)
IRWIN Shelby
JACKSON JUNCTION Winneshiek
JAMAICA (50128) Guthrie(63), Greene(24),
   Dallas(12)
JANESVILLE (50647) Bremer(54), Black
   Hawk(45)
JEFFERSON Greene
JESUP (50648) Buchanan(90), Black Hawk(9)
JEWELL Hamilton
JOHNSTON Polk
JOICE (50446) Worth(81), Winnebago(19)
JOLLEY Calhoun
KALONA (52247) Washington(66),
   Johnson(33)
KAMRAR Hamilton
KANAWHA (50447) Hancock(76),
   Wright(23)
KELLERTON (50133) Ringgold(97),
   Decatur(2)
KELLEY (50134) Story(78), Boone(21)
KELLOGG Jasper
KENSETT Worth
KENT (50850) Adams(50), Union(49)
KEOKUK Lee
KEOSAUQUA Van Buren
KEOTA (52248) Keokuk(72),
   Washington(27)
KESLEY Butler
KESWICK (50136) Keokuk(95), Iowa(3)
KEYSTONE Benton
KILLDUFF Jasper
KIMBALLTON (51543) Audubon(84),
   Shelby(15)
KINGSLEY (51028) Plymouth(82),
   Woodbury(17)
KINROSS Keokuk
KIRKMAN Shelby
KIRKVILLE Wapello
KIRON (51448) Crawford(65), Sac(18),
   Ida(15)
KLEMME (50449) Cerro Gordo(65),
   Hancock(34)
KNIERIM Calhoun
KNOXVILLE Marion
LA MOTTE (52054) Jackson(97),
   Dubuque(2)
LA PORTE CITY (50651) Black Hawk(93),
   Benton(6)
LACONA (50139) Warren(69), Lucas(20),
   Marion(9)
LADORA Iowa
LAKE CITY (51449) Calhoun(96), Carroll(3)
LAKE MILLS (50450) Winnebago(94),
   Worth(5)
LAKE PARK Dickinson

LAKE VIEW Sac
LAKOTA Kossuth
LAMONI (50140) Decatur(91), Ringgold(8)
LAMONT (50650) Buchanan(71), Fayette(26), Delaware(2)
LANESBORO Carroll
LANGWORTHY Jones
LANSING Allamakee
LARCHWOOD Lyon
LARRABEE (51029) Cherokee(95), O'Brien(4)
LATIMER Franklin
LAUREL (50141) Marshall(53), Jasper(46)
LAURENS (50554) Pocahontas(96), Palo Alto(2), Buena Vista(1)
LAWLER (52154) Chickasaw(94), Howard(5)
LAWTON Woodbury
LE CLAIRE Scott
LE GRAND Marshall
LE MARS Plymouth
LEDYARD Kossuth
LEHIGH Webster
LEIGHTON (50143) Mahaska(97), Marion(2)
LELAND Winnebago
LENOX (50851) Taylor(77), Adams(11), Union(8), Ringgold(2)
LEON Decatur
LESTER Lyon
LETTS (52754) Louisa(77), Muscatine(22)
LEWIS (51544) Cass(77), Pottawattamie(22)
LIBERTY CENTER Warren
LIBERTYVILLE (52567) Jefferson(83), Van Buren(16)
LIDDERDALE Carroll
LIME SPRINGS Howard
LINCOLN Tama
LINDEN (50146) Dallas(88), Guthrie(11)
LINEVILLE (50147) Wayne(85), Marion(14)
LINN GROVE (51033) Buena Vista(60), Clay(39)
LISBON (52253) Linn(71), Cedar(13), Jones(10), Johnson(4)
LISCOMB (50148) Marshall(88), Grundy(11)
LITTLE CEDAR Mitchell
LITTLE ROCK (51243) Lyon(91), Osceola(8)
LITTLE SIOUX (51545) Harrison(89), Monona(10)
LITTLEPORT Clayton
LIVERMORE (50558) Humboldt(54), Kossuth(45)
LOCKRIDGE (52635) Jefferson(74), Henry(25)
LOGAN Harrison
LOHRVILLE (51453) Calhoun(91), Carroll(7), Greene(1)
LONE ROCK Kossuth
LONE TREE (52755) Johnson(87), Louisa(10), Muscatine(1)
LONG GROVE (52756) Scott(98), Clinton(1)
LORIMOR (50149) Union(68), Madison(31)
LOST NATION Clinton
LOVILIA (50150) Monroe(98), Marion(1)
LOW MOOR Clinton
LOWDEN (52255) Cedar(97), Clinton(2)
LU VERNE (50560) Kossuth(81), Humboldt(18)
LUANA (52156) Clayton(83), Allamakee(16)
LUCAS (50151) Lucas(55), Warren(43), Clarke(1)
LUTHER Boone
LUXEMBURG Dubuque
LUZERNE (52257) Benton(98), Iowa(1)
LYNNVILLE (50153) Jasper(91), Mahaska(5), Poweshiek(2)
LYTTON (50561) Calhoun(58), Sac(41)
MACEDONIA Pottawattamie

MACKSBURG (50155) Madison(94), Adair(4), Union(1)
MADRID (50156) Boone(96), Polk(2), Dallas(1)
MAGNOLIA Harrison
MALCOM Poweshiek
MALLARD (50562) Palo Alto(88), Pocahontas(11)
MALOY Ringgold
MALVERN Mills
MANCHESTER Delaware
MANILLA (51454) Crawford(70), Shelby(29)
MANLY (50456) Worth(96), Cerro Gordo(3)
MANNING (51455) Carroll(85), Crawford(7), Audubon(5), Shelby(1)
MANSON (50563) Calhoun(81), Pocahontas(15), Webster(2)
MAPLETON (51034) Monona(92), Woodbury(5), Crawford(1)
MAQUOKETA (52060) Jackson(98), Clinton(1)
MARATHON Buena Vista
MARBLE ROCK Floyd
MARCUS (51035) Cherokee(93), Plymouth(5)
MARENGO (52301) Iowa(98), Benton(1)
MARION Linn
MARNE (51552) Cass(78), Shelby(20), Pottawattamie(1)
MARQUETTE Clayton
MARSHALLTOWN Marshall
MARTELLE (52305) Jones(86), Linn(13)
MARTENSDALE Warren
MARTINSBURG Keokuk
MASON CITY Cerro Gordo
MASONVILLE (50654) Delaware(64), Buchanan(35)
MASSENA (50853) Cass(96), Adams(3)
MATLOCK Sioux
MAURICE Sioux
MAXWELL (50161) Story(58), Polk(40), Jasper(1)
MAY CITY Osceola
MAYNARD Fayette
MC CALLSBURG (50154) Story(90), Hardin(9)
MC CAUSLAND Scott
MC CLELLAND Pottawattamie
MC GREGOR Clayton
MC INTIRE Mitchell
MECHANICSVILLE (52306) Cedar(78), Jones(21)
MEDIAPOLIS Des Moines
MELBOURNE (50162) Marshall(97), Jasper(2)
MELCHER Marion
MELROSE (52569) Monroe(68), Appanoose(17), Wayne(9), Lucas(3)
MELVIN (51350) Osceola(96), O'Brien(3)
MENLO (50164) Guthrie(70), Adair(29)
MERIDEN Cherokee
MERRILL Plymouth
MESERVEY (50457) Cerro Gordo(51), Hancock(22), Franklin(18), Wright(8)
MIDDLE AMANA Iowa
MIDDLETOWN Des Moines
MILES (52064) Jackson(93), Clinton(6)
MILFORD Dickinson
MILLERSBURG Iowa
MILLERTON Wayne
MILO Warren
MILTON (52570) Van Buren(84), Davis(15)
MINBURN Dallas
MINDEN Pottawattamie
MINEOLA Mills
MINGO (50168) Jasper(95), Polk(4)
MISSOURI VALLEY (51555) Harrison(80), Pottawattamie(19)
MITCHELLVILLE (50169) Polk(81), Jasper(18)
MODALE Harrison
MONDAMIN Harrison

MONMOUTH (52309) Jackson(74), Jones(25)
MONONA (52159) Clayton(75), Allamakee(24)
MONROE (50170) Jasper(87), Marion(12)
MONTEZUMA (50171) Poweshiek(98), Mahaska(1)
MONTEZUMA Poweshiek
MONTICELLO Jones
MONTOUR Tama
MONTPELIER Muscatine
MONTROSE Lee
MOORHEAD (51558) Monona(92), Harrison(7)
MOORLAND (50566) Webster(98), Calhoun(1)
MORAVIA (52571) Appanoose(90), Monroe(9)
MORLEY Jones
MORNING SUN (52640) Louisa(74), Des Moines(25)
MORRISON Grundy
MOSCOW (52760) Muscatine(62), Cedar(37)
MOULTON (52572) Appanoose(92), Davis(7)
MOUNT AUBURN Benton
MOUNT AYR Ringgold
MOUNT PLEASANT (52641) Henry(96), Washington(2)
MOUNT STERLING Van Buren
MOUNT UNION (52644) Henry(70), Des Moines(29)
MOUNT VERNON Linn
MOVILLE Woodbury
MURRAY (50174) Clarke(97), Union(2)
MUSCATINE (52761) Muscatine(96), Louisa(2)
MYSTIC Appanoose
NASHUA (50658) Chickasaw(85), Floyd(12), Bremer(2)
NEMAHA Sac
NEOLA (51559) Pottawattamie(96), Harrison(3)
NEVADA Story
NEW ALBIN Allamakee
NEW HAMPTON Chickasaw
NEW HARTFORD (50660) Butler(84), Grundy(15)
NEW LIBERTY (52765) Scott(87), Cedar(12)
NEW LONDON (52645) Henry(86), Des Moines(13)
NEW MARKET (51646) Taylor(97), Page(2)
NEW PROVIDENCE (50206) Hardin(88), Marshall(7), Story(4)
NEW SHARON (50207) Mahaska(98), Poweshiek(1)
NEW VIENNA (52065) Dubuque(89), Delaware(10)
NEW VIRGINIA (50210) Warren(91), Clarke(8)
NEWELL (50568) Buena Vista(90), Sac(8)
NEWHALL Benton
NEWTON Jasper
NICHOLS (52766) Muscatine(93), Johnson(6)
NODAWAY (50857) Adams(76), Taylor(19), Montgomery(3)
NORA SPRINGS (50458) Floyd(64), Cerro Gordo(31), Mitchell(4)
NORTH BUENA VISTA Clayton
NORTH ENGLISH (52316) Iowa(88), Keokuk(11)
NORTH LIBERTY Johnson
NORTH WASHINGTON Chickasaw
NORTHBORO (51647) Page(80), Fremont(19)
NORTHWOOD Worth
NORWALK Warren
NORWAY (52318) Benton(75), Iowa(24)
NUMA Appanoose

OAKDALE Johnson
OAKLAND Pottawattamie
OAKVILLE (52646) Louisa(53), Des Moines(46)
OCHEYEDAN Osceola
ODEBOLT Sac
OELWEIN Fayette
OGDEN Boone
OKOBOJI Dickinson
OLDS Henry
OLIN (52320) Jones(93), Cedar(6)
OLLIE (52576) Keokuk(98), Jefferson(1)
ONAWA Monona
ONSLOW Jones
ORAN Fayette
ORANGE CITY Sioux
ORCHARD (50460) Mitchell(75), Floyd(24)
ORIENT Adair
OSAGE Mitchell
OSCEOLA Clarke
OSKALOOSA Mahaska
OSSIAN (52161) Winneshiek(84), Fayette(15)
OTHO Webster
OTLEY (50214) Marion(98), Jasper(1)
OTO Woodbury
OTTOSEN (50570) Humboldt(60), Kossuth(37), Pocahontas(1)
OTTUMWA Wapello
OXFORD (52322) Johnson(97), Iowa(2)
OXFORD JUNCTION (52323) Jones(83), Clinton(7), Linn(4), Cedar(4)
OYENS Plymouth
PACIFIC JUNCTION Mills
PACKWOOD (52580) Jefferson(95), Keokuk(4)
PALMER Pocahontas
PALO (52324) Linn(85), Benton(14)
PANAMA (51562) Shelby(97), Harrison(2)
PANORA Guthrie
PARKERSBURG (50665) Butler(76), Grundy(23)
PARNELL (52325) Iowa(85), Johnson(14)
PATON (50217) Greene(79), Boone(14), Webster(5)
PATTERSON Madison
PAULLINA (51046) O'Brien(96), Cherokee(3)
PELLA (50219) Marion(94), Mahaska(5)
PEOSTA Dubuque
PERCIVAL Fremont
PERRY (50220) Dallas(93), Boone(5)
PERSHING Marion
PERSIA (51563) Harrison(97), Shelby(2)
PERU (50222) Madison(98), Clarke(1)
PETERSON (51047) Clay(70), Buena Vista(16), Cherokee(9), O'Brien(4)
PIERSON (51048) Woodbury(71), Cherokee(28)
PILOT GROVE Lee
PILOT MOUND Boone
PISGAH Harrison
PLAINFIELD (50666) Bremer(73), Butler(26)
PLANO (52581) Appanoose(95), Wayne(4)
PLEASANT VALLEY Scott
PLEASANTVILLE (50225) Marion(71), Warren(28)
PLOVER Pocahontas
PLYMOUTH (50464) Cerro Gordo(77), Worth(20), Mitchell(2)
POCAHONTAS Pocahontas
POLK CITY (50226) Polk(97), Boone(2)
POMEROY (50575) Calhoun(66), Pocahontas(33)
POPEJOY Franklin
PORTSMOUTH (51565) Shelby(79), Harrison(20)
POSTVILLE (52162) Allamakee(55), Clayton(32), Winneshiek(8), Fayette(3)
PRAIRIE CITY (50228) Jasper(96), Polk(1), Marion(1)
PRAIRIEBURG Linn

PRESCOTT (50859) Adams(97), Adair(2)
PRESTON (52069) Jackson(94), Clinton(5)
PRIMGHAR O'Brien
PRINCETON Scott
PROLE (50229) Warren(89), Madison(10)
PROMISE CITY Wayne
PROTIVIN Howard
PULASKI Davis
QUASQUETON Buchanan
QUIMBY Cherokee
RADCLIFFE (50230) Hardin(70), Hamilton(27), Story(1)
RAKE Winnebago
RALSTON Carroll
RANDALIA Fayette
RANDALL Hamilton
RANDOLPH (51649) Fremont(98), Mills(1)
RAYMOND Black Hawk
READLYN Bremer
REASNOR Jasper
RED OAK Montgomery
REDDING Ringgold
REDFIELD (50233) Dallas(88), Guthrie(11)
REINBECK (50669) Grundy(90), Tama(7), Black Hawk(1)
REMBRANDT Buena Vista
REMSEN (51050) Plymouth(98), Cherokee(1)
RENWICK (50577) Humboldt(69), Wright(30)
RHODES (50234) Marshall(77), Jasper(22)
RICEVILLE (50466) Howard(51), Mitchell(48)
RICHLAND (52585) Keokuk(59), Washington(30), Jefferson(9)
RICKETTS Crawford
RIDGEWAY Winneshiek
RINARD Calhoun
RINGSTED (50578) Emmet(93), Palo Alto(3), Kossuth(3)
RIPPEY (50235) Greene(91), Boone(5), Dallas(2)
RIVERSIDE (52327) Washington(68), Johnson(28), Louisa(2)
RIVERTON Fremont
ROBINS Linn
ROCK FALLS Cerro Gordo
ROCK RAPIDS Lyon
ROCK VALLEY (51247) Sioux(98), Lyon(1)
ROCKFORD (50468) Floyd(86), Cerro Gordo(13)
ROCKWELL Cerro Gordo
ROCKWELL CITY Calhoun
RODMAN Palo Alto
RODNEY (51051) Monona(92), Woodbury(7)
ROLAND (50236) Story(97), Hamilton(2)
ROLFE (50581) Pocahontas(98), Palo Alto(1)
ROME Henry
ROSE HILL (52586) Mahaska(92), Keokuk(7)
ROWAN (50470) Wright(96), Franklin(3)
ROWLEY Buchanan
ROYAL Clay
RUDD (50471) Floyd(94), Mitchell(5)
RUNNELLS (50237) Polk(92), Jasper(4), Marion(2)
RUSSELL (50238) Lucas(92), Wayne(7)
RUTHVEN (51358) Palo Alto(80), Clay(19)
RUTLAND Humboldt
RYAN Delaware
SABULA (52070) Jackson(89), Clinton(10)
SAC CITY Sac
SAINT ANSGAR (50472) Mitchell(95), Worth(4)
SAINT ANTHONY (50239) Marshall(87), Story(12)
SAINT CHARLES (50240) Warren(60), Madison(39)
SAINT DONATUS Jackson
SAINT LUCAS Fayette
SAINT MARYS Warren

SAINT OLAF Clayton
SAINT PAUL Lee
SALEM (52649) Henry(86), Lee(13)
SALIX Woodbury
SANBORN O'Brien
SCARVILLE Winnebago
SCHALLER (51053) Sac(91), Ida(6), Buena Vista(2)
SCHLESWIG (51461) Crawford(94), Ida(5)
SCOTCH GROVE Jones
SCRANTON (51462) Greene(97), Carroll(2)
SEARSBORO (50242) Poweshiek(94), Jasper(5)
SELMA (52588) Van Buren(73), Davis(25), Jefferson(1)
SERGEANT BLUFF Woodbury
SEYMOUR (52590) Wayne(90), Appanoose(9)
SHAMBAUGH Page
SHANNON CITY (50861) Union(76), Ringgold(23)
SHARPSBURG Taylor
SHEFFIELD (50475) Franklin(76), Cerro Gordo(23)
SHELBY (51570) Shelby(56), Pottawattamie(36), Harrison(6)
SHELDAHL Polk
SHELDON (51201) O'Brien(89), Sioux(9)
SHELL ROCK Butler
SHELLSBURG Benton
SHENANDOAH (51603) Page(85), Fremont(14)
SHENANDOAH Page
SHERRILL (52073) Dubuque(97), Clayton(2)
SIBLEY Osceola
SIDNEY Fremont
SIGOURNEY Keokuk
SILVER CITY (51571) Mills(53), Pottawattamie(46)
SIOUX CENTER Sioux
SIOUX CITY (51109) Woodbury(87), Plymouth(12)
SIOUX CITY Woodbury
SIOUX RAPIDS (50585) Buena Vista(71), Clay(28)
SLATER (50244) Story(72), Polk(25), Boone(2)
SLOAN (51055) Woodbury(66), Monona(33)
SMITHLAND (51056) Woodbury(92), Monona(7)
SOLDIER Monona
SOLON Johnson
SOMERS (50586) Calhoun(89), Webster(10)
SOUTH AMANA Iowa
SOUTH ENGLISH Keokuk
SPENCER Clay
SPERRY Des Moines
SPILLVILLE Winneshiek
SPIRIT LAKE Dickinson
SPRAGUEVILLE Jackson
SPRINGBROOK Jackson
SPRINGVILLE Linn
STACYVILLE Mitchell
STANHOPE Hamilton
STANLEY (50671) Fayette(72), Buchanan(27)
STANTON Montgomery
STANWOOD Cedar
STATE CENTER (50247) Marshall(94), Story(5)
STEAMBOAT ROCK (50672) Hardin(91), Grundy(8)
STOCKPORT (52651) Van Buren(93), Jefferson(6)
STOCKTON (52769) Scott(66), Muscatine(31), Henry(1)
STORM LAKE Buena Vista
STORY CITY (50248) Story(87), Hamilton(10), Boone(2)

STOUT Grundy
STRATFORD (50249) Hamilton(77), Webster(14), Boone(7)
STRAWBERRY POINT (52076) Clayton(95), Delaware(3), Fayette(1)
STRUBLE Plymouth
STUART (50250) Guthrie(74), Adair(25)
SULLY Jasper
SUMNER (50674) Bremer(72), Fayette(21), Chickasaw(6)
SUPERIOR Dickinson
SUTHERLAND (51058) O'Brien(95), Clay(2), Cherokee(1)
SWALEDALE Cerro Gordo
SWAN (50252) Warren(68), Marion(31)
SWEA CITY Kossuth
SWEDESBURG Henry
SWISHER (52338) Johnson(94), Linn(5)
TABOR (51653) Fremont(64), Mills(35)
TAINTOR Mahaska
TAMA Tama
TEEDS GROVE Clinton
TEMPLETON (51463) Carroll(98), Audubon(1)
TENNANT Shelby
TERRIL (51364) Dickinson(75), Clay(16), Emmet(8)
THAYER (50254) Union(97), Clarke(3)
THOMPSON Winnebago
THOR (50591) Humboldt(84), Webster(15)
THORNBURG Keokuk
THORNTON (50479) Cerro Gordo(89), Franklin(10)
THURMAN Fremont
TIFFIN Johnson
TINGLEY Ringgold
TIPTON Cedar
TITONKA (50480) Kossuth(94), Hancock(3), Winnebago(1)
TODDVILLE Linn
TOETERVILLE Mitchell
TOLEDO Tama
TORONTO Clinton
TRACY (50256) Marion(75), Mahaska(24)
TRAER Tama
TREYNOR Pottawattamie
TRIPOLI Bremer
TROY MILLS Linn
TRUESDALE Buena Vista
TRURO (50257) Madison(69), Warren(16), Clarke(14)
TURIN Monona
UDELL Appanoose
UNDERWOOD Pottawattamie
UNION (50258) Hardin(78), Marshall(20), Grundy(1)
UNIONVILLE (52594) Appanoose(68), Davis(31)
UNIVERSITY PARK Mahaska
URBANA Benton
URBANDALE (50323) Polk(59), Dallas(40)
URBANDALE Polk
UTE (51060) Monona(85), Crawford(14)
VAIL Crawford
VAN HORNE Benton
VAN METER (50261) Dallas(55), Madison(44)
VAN WERT Decatur
VARINA Pocahontas
VENTURA (50482) Cerro Gordo(87), Hancock(12)
VICTOR (52347) Iowa(79), Poweshiek(20)
VILLISCA (50864) Montgomery(85), Page(9), Taylor(2), Cass(1)
VINCENT Webster
VINING Tama
VINTON Benton
VIOLA Linn
VOLGA Clayton
WADENA (52169) Fayette(95), Clayton(4)
WALCOTT (52773) Scott(98), Muscatine(1)
WALFORD Benton
WALKER (52352) Linn(98), Buchanan(1)

WALL LAKE (51466) Sac(93), Carroll(3), Crawford(3)
WALLINGFORD Emmet
WALNUT (51577) Pottawattamie(74), Shelby(24)
WAPELLO Louisa
WASHINGTON Washington
WASHTA (51061) Cherokee(79), Ida(19)
WATERLOO Black Hawk
WATERVILLE Allamakee
WATKINS Benton
WAUCOMA (52171) Fayette(70), Chickasaw(15), Winneshiek(13)
WAUKEE Dallas
WAUKON (52172) Allamakee(98), Winneshiek(1)
WAVERLY Bremer
WAYLAND (52654) Henry(84), Washington(14)
WEBB (51366) Clay(92), Buena Vista(7)
WEBSTER (52355) Keokuk(94), Iowa(5)
WEBSTER CITY Hamilton
WELDON (50264) Decatur(66), Clarke(33)
WELLMAN (52356) Washington(78), Johnson(11), Iowa(8)
WELLSBURG (50680) Grundy(98), Hardin(1)
WELTON Clinton
WESLEY (50483) Kossuth(78), Hancock(21)
WEST AMANA Iowa
WEST BEND (50597) Kossuth(55), Palo Alto(41), Humboldt(1)
WEST BRANCH (52358) Cedar(84), Johnson(15)
WEST BURLINGTON Des Moines
WEST CHESTER Washington
WEST DES MOINES (50266) Polk(75), Dallas(25)
WEST DES MOINES Polk
WEST GROVE Davis
WEST LIBERTY Muscatine
WEST POINT (52656) Lee(98), Henry(1)
WEST UNION Fayette
WESTFIELD Plymouth
WESTGATE Fayette
WESTPHALIA Shelby
WESTSIDE (51467) Crawford(72), Carroll(27)
WEVER (52658) Lee(87), Des Moines(12)
WHAT CHEER (50268) Keokuk(93), Mahaska(6)
WHEATLAND (52777) Clinton(94), Cedar(5)
WHITING Monona
WHITTEMORE (50598) Kossuth(76), Palo Alto(23)
WHITTEN Hardin
WILLIAMS (50271) Hamilton(91), Wright(8)
WILLIAMSBURG Iowa
WILLIAMSON Lucas
WILTON (52778) Muscatine(56), Cedar(43)
WINFIELD (52659) Henry(84), Louisa(15)
WINTERSET Madison
WINTHROP Buchanan
WIOTA Cass
WODEN (50484) Winnebago(49), Hancock(47), Kossuth(3)
WOODBINE Harrison
WOODBURN (50275) Clarke(86), Lucas(13)
WOODWARD (50276) Dallas(72), Boone(27)
WOOLSTOCK (50599) Wright(80), Hamilton(19)
WORTHINGTON (52078) Dubuque(79), Delaware(20)
WYOMING Jones
YALE (50277) Guthrie(84), Dallas(15)
YARMOUTH Des Moines
YORKTOWN Page
ZEARING Story
ZWINGLE (52079) Dubuque(50), Jackson(50)

Iowa ZIP/City Cross Reference

50001-50001 ACKWORTH	50119-50119 HARVEY	50233-50233 REDFIELD	50460-50460 ORCHARD
50002-50002 ADAIR	50120-50120 HAVERHILL	50234-50234 RHODES	50461-50461 OSAGE
50003-50003 ADEL	50122-50122 HUBBARD	50235-50235 RIPPEY	50464-50464 PLYMOUTH
50005-50005 ALBION	50123-50123 HUMESTON	50236-50236 ROLAND	50465-50465 RAKE
50006-50006 ALDEN	50124-50124 HUXLEY	50237-50237 RUNNELLS	50466-50466 RICEVILLE
50007-50007 ALLEMAN	50125-50125 INDIANOLA	50238-50238 RUSSELL	50467-50467 ROCK FALLS
50008-50008 ALLERTON	50126-50126 IOWA FALLS	50239-50239 SAINT ANTHONY	50468-50468 ROCKFORD
50009-50009 ALTOONA	50127-50127 IRA	50240-50240 SAINT CHARLES	50469-50469 ROCKWELL
50010-50014 AMES	50128-50128 JAMAICA	50241-50241 SAINT MARYS	50470-50470 ROWAN
50015-50015 ANKENY	50129-50129 JEFFERSON	50242-50242 SEARSBORO	50471-50471 RUDD
50020-50020 ANITA	50130-50130 JEWELL	50243-50243 SHELDAHL	50472-50472 SAINT ANSGAR
50021-50021 ANKENY	50131-50131 JOHNSTON	50244-50244 SLATER	50473-50473 SCARVILLE
50022-50022 ATLANTIC	50132-50132 KAMRAR	50246-50246 STANHOPE	50475-50475 SHEFFIELD
50025-50025 AUDUBON	50133-50133 KELLERTON	50247-50247 STATE CENTER	50476-50476 STACYVILLE
50026-50026 BAGLEY	50134-50134 KELLEY	50248-50248 STORY CITY	50477-50477 SWALEDALE
50027-50027 BARNES CITY	50135-50135 KELLOGG	50249-50249 STRATFORD	50478-50478 THOMPSON
50028-50028 BAXTER	50136-50136 KESWICK	50250-50250 STUART	50479-50479 THORNTON
50029-50029 BAYARD	50137-50137 KILLDUFF	50251-50251 SULLY	50480-50480 TITONKA
50030-50030 BEACONSFIELD	50138-50138 KNOXVILLE	50252-50252 SWAN	50481-50481 TOETERVILLE
50031-50031 BEAVER	50139-50139 LACONA	50253-50253 TAINTOR	50482-50482 VENTURA
50032-50032 BERWICK	50140-50140 LAMONI	50254-50254 THAYER	50483-50483 WESLEY
50033-50033 BEVINGTON	50141-50141 LAUREL	50255-50255 THORNBURG	50484-50484 WODEN
50034-50034 BLAIRSBURG	50142-50142 LE GRAND	50256-50256 TRACY	50501-50501 FORT DODGE
50035-50035 BONDURANT	50143-50143 LEIGHTON	50257-50257 TRURO	50510-50510 ALBERT CITY
50036-50037 BOONE	50144-50144 LEON	50258-50258 UNION	50511-50511 ALGONA
50038-50038 BOONEVILLE	50145-50145 LIBERTY CENTER	50259-50259 GIFFORD	50514-50514 ARMSTRONG
50039-50039 BOUTON	50146-50146 LINDEN	50261-50261 VAN METER	50515-50515 AYRSHIRE
50040-50040 BOXHOLM	50147-50147 LINEVILLE	50262-50262 VAN WERT	50516-50516 BADGER
50041-50041 BRADFORD	50148-50148 LISCOMB	50263-50263 WAUKEE	50517-50517 BANCROFT
50042-50042 BRAYTON	50149-50149 LORIMOR	50264-50264 WELDON	50518-50518 BARNUM
50043-50043 BUCKEYE	50150-50150 LOVILIA	50265-50266 WEST DES MOINES	50519-50519 BODE
50044-50044 BUSSEY	50151-50151 LUCAS	50268-50268 WHAT CHEER	50520-50520 BRADGATE
50046-50046 CAMBRIDGE	50152-50152 LUTHER	50269-50269 WHITTEN	50521-50521 BURNSIDE
50047-50047 CARLISLE	50153-50153 LYNNVILLE	50271-50271 WILLIAMS	50522-50522 BURT
50048-50048 CASEY	50154-50154 MC CALLSBURG	50272-50272 WILLIAMSON	50523-50523 CALLENDER
50049-50049 CHARITON	50155-50155 MACKSBURG	50273-50273 WINTERSET	50524-50524 CLARE
50050-50050 CHURDAN	50156-50156 MADRID	50274-50274 WIOTA	50525-50526 CLARION
50051-50051 CLEMONS	50157-50157 MALCOM	50275-50275 WOODBURN	50527-50527 CURLEW
50052-50052 CLIO	50158-50158 MARSHALLTOWN	50276-50276 WOODWARD	50528-50528 CYLINDER
50054-50054 COLFAX	50160-50160 MARTENSDALE	50277-50277 YALE	50529-50529 DAKOTA CITY
50055-50055 COLLINS	50161-50161 MAXWELL	50278-50278 ZEARING	50530-50530 DAYTON
50056-50056 COLO	50162-50162 MELBOURNE	50300-50321 DES MOINES	50531-50531 DOLLIVER
50057-50057 COLUMBIA	50163-50163 MELCHER	50322-50323 URBANDALE	50532-50532 DUNCOMBE
50058-50058 COON RAPIDS	50164-50164 MENLO	50325-50325 CLIVE	50533-50533 EAGLE GROVE
50059-50059 COOPER	50165-50165 MILLERTON	50327-50397 DES MOINES	50535-50535 EARLY
50060-50060 CORYDON	50166-50166 MILO	50398-50398 WEST DES MOINES	50536-50536 EMMETSBURG
50061-50061 CUMMING	50167-50167 MINBURN	50401-50402 MASON CITY	50538-50538 FARNHAMVILLE
50062-50062 DALLAS	50168-50168 MINGO	50420-50420 ALEXANDER	50539-50539 FENTON
50063-50063 DALLAS CENTER	50169-50169 MITCHELLVILLE	50421-50421 BELMOND	50540-50540 FONDA
50064-50064 DANA	50170-50170 MONROE	50423-50423 BRITT	50541-50541 GILMORE CITY
50065-50065 DAVIS CITY	50171-50172 MONTEZUMA	50424-50424 BUFFALO CENTER	50542-50542 GOLDFIELD
50066-50066 DAWSON	50173-50173 MONTOUR	50426-50426 CARPENTER	50543-50543 GOWRIE
50067-50067 DECATUR	50174-50174 MURRAY	50427-50427 CHAPIN	50544-50544 HARCOURT
50068-50068 DERBY	50177-50177 GRINNELL	50428-50428 CLEAR LAKE	50545-50545 HARDY
50069-50069 DE SOTO	50197-50198 KNOXVILLE	50430-50430 CORWITH	50546-50546 HAVELOCK
50070-50070 DEXTER	50201-50201 NEVADA	50431-50431 COULTER	50548-50548 HUMBOLDT
50071-50071 DOWS	50206-50206 NEW PROVIDENCE	50432-50432 CRYSTAL LAKE	50551-50551 JOLLEY
50072-50072 EARLHAM	50207-50207 NEW SHARON	50433-50433 DOUGHERTY	50552-50552 KNIERIM
50073-50073 ELKHART	50208-50208 NEWTON	50434-50434 FERTILE	50553-50553 FONDA
50074-50074 ELLSTON	50210-50210 NEW VIRGINIA	50435-50435 FLOYD	50554-50554 LAURENS
50075-50075 ELLSWORTH	50211-50211 NORWALK	50436-50436 FOREST CITY	50556-50556 LEDYARD
50076-50076 EXIRA	50212-50212 OGDEN	50438-50438 GARNER	50557-50557 LEHIGH
50077-50077 CHURDAN	50213-50213 OSCEOLA	50439-50439 GOODELL	50558-50558 LIVERMORE
50078-50078 FERGUSON	50214-50214 OTLEY	50440-50440 GRAFTON	50559-50559 LONE ROCK
50101-50101 GALT	50216-50216 PANORA	50441-50441 HAMPTON	50560-50560 LU VERNE
50102-50102 GARDEN CITY	50217-50217 PATON	50444-50444 HANLONTOWN	50561-50561 LYTTON
50103-50103 GARDEN GROVE	50218-50218 PATTERSON	50446-50446 JOICE	50562-50562 MALLARD
50104-50104 GIBSON	50219-50219 PELLA	50447-50447 KANAWHA	50563-50563 MANSON
50105-50105 GILBERT	50220-50220 PERRY	50448-50448 KENSETT	50565-50565 MARATHON
50106-50106 GILMAN	50221-50221 PERSHING	50449-50449 KLEMME	50566-50566 MOORLAND
50107-50107 GRAND JUNCTION	50222-50222 PERU	50450-50450 LAKE MILLS	50567-50567 NEMAHA
50108-50108 GRAND RIVER	50223-50223 PILOT MOUND	50451-50451 LAKOTA	50568-50568 NEWELL
50109-50109 GRANGER	50225-50225 PLEASANTVILLE	50452-50452 LATIMER	50569-50569 OTHO
50110-50110 GRAY	50226-50226 POLK CITY	50453-50453 LELAND	50570-50570 OTTOSEN
50111-50111 GRIMES	50227-50227 POPEJOY	50454-50454 LITTLE CEDAR	50571-50571 PALMER
50112-50112 GRINNELL	50228-50228 PRAIRIE CITY	50455-50455 MC INTIRE	50573-50573 PLOVER
50115-50115 GUTHRIE CENTER	50229-50229 PROLE	50456-50456 MANLY	50574-50574 POCAHONTAS
50116-50116 HAMILTON	50230-50230 RADCLIFFE	50457-50457 MESERVEY	50575-50575 POMEROY
50117-50117 HAMLIN	50231-50231 RANDALL	50458-50458 NORA SPRINGS	50576-50576 REMBRANDT
50118-50118 HARTFORD	50232-50232 REASNOR	50459-50459 NORTHWOOD	50577-50577 RENWICK

50578-50578 RINGSTED	50674-50674 SUMNER	51047-51047 PETERSON	51451-51451 LANESBORO
50579-50579 ROCKWELL CITY	50675-50675 TRAER	51048-51048 PIERSON	51452-51452 LIDDERDALE
50580-50580 RODMAN	50676-50676 TRIPOLI	51049-51049 QUIMBY	51453-51453 LOHRVILLE
50581-50581 ROLFE	50677-50677 WAVERLY	51050-51050 REMSEN	51454-51454 MANILLA
50582-50582 RUTLAND	50680-50680 WELLSBURG	51051-51051 RODNEY	51455-51455 MANNING
50583-50583 SAC CITY	50681-50681 WESTGATE	51052-51052 SALIX	51458-51458 ODEBOLT
50585-50585 SIOUX RAPIDS	50682-50682 WINTHROP	51053-51053 SCHALLER	51459-51459 RALSTON
50586-50586 SOMERS	50700-50706 WATERLOO	51054-51054 SERGEANT BLUFF	51460-51460 RICKETTS
50587-50587 RINARD	50707-50707 EVANSDALE	51055-51055 SLOAN	51461-51461 SCHLESWIG
50588-50588 STORM LAKE	50799-50799 WATERLOO	51056-51056 SMITHLAND	51462-51462 SCRANTON
50590-50590 SWEA CITY	50801-50801 CRESTON	51057-51057 STRUBLE	51463-51463 TEMPLETON
50591-50591 THOR	50830-50830 AFTON	51058-51058 SUTHERLAND	51465-51465 VAIL
50592-50592 TRUESDALE	50831-50831 ARISPE	51059-51059 TURIN	51466-51466 WALL LAKE
50593-50593 VARINA	50833-50833 BEDFORD	51060-51060 UTE	51467-51467 WESTSIDE
50594-50594 VINCENT	50835-50835 BENTON	51061-51061 WASHTA	51501-51503 COUNCIL BLUFFS
50595-50595 WEBSTER CITY	50836-50836 BLOCKTON	51062-51062 WESTFIELD	51510-51510 CARTER LAKE
50597-50597 WEST BEND	50837-50837 BRIDGEWATER	51063-51063 WHITING	51519-51519 AT AND T
50598-50598 WHITTEMORE	50839-50839 CARBON	51100-51111 SIOUX CITY	51520-51520 ARION
50599-50599 WOOLSTOCK	50840-50840 CLEARFIELD	51201-51201 SHELDON	51521-51521 AVOCA
50601-50601 ACKLEY	50841-50841 CORNING	51230-51230 ALVORD	51523-51523 BLENCOE
50602-50602 ALLISON	50842-50842 CROMWELL	51231-51231 ARCHER	51525-51525 CARSON
50603-50603 ALTA VISTA	50843-50843 CUMBERLAND	51232-51232 ASHTON	51526-51526 CRESCENT
50604-50604 APLINGTON	50844-50844 DELPHOS	51234-51234 BOYDEN	51527-51527 DEFIANCE
50605-50605 AREDALE	50845-50845 DIAGONAL	51235-51235 DOON	51528-51528 DOW CITY
50606-50606 ARLINGTON	50846-50846 FONTANELLE	51237-51237 GEORGE	51529-51529 DUNLAP
50607-50607 AURORA	50847-50847 GRANT	51238-51238 HOSPERS	51530-51530 EARLING
50608-50608 AUSTINVILLE	50848-50848 GRAVITY	51239-51239 HULL	51531-51531 ELK HORN
50609-50609 BEAMAN	50849-50849 GREENFIELD	51240-51240 INWOOD	51532-51532 ELLIOTT
50611-50611 BRISTOW	50850-50850 KENT	51241-51241 LARCHWOOD	51533-51533 EMERSON
50612-50612 BUCKINGHAM	50851-50851 LENOX	51242-51242 LESTER	51534-51534 GLENWOOD
50613-50614 CEDAR FALLS	50852-50852 MALOY	51243-51243 LITTLE ROCK	51535-51535 GRISWOLD
50616-50616 CHARLES CITY	50853-50853 MASSENA	51244-51244 MATLOCK	51536-51536 HANCOCK
50619-50619 CLARKSVILLE	50854-50854 MOUNT AYR	51245-51245 PRIMGHAR	51537-51537 HARLAN
50620-50620 COLWELL	50857-50857 NODAWAY	51246-51246 ROCK RAPIDS	51540-51540 HASTINGS
50621-50621 CONRAD	50858-50858 ORIENT	51247-51247 ROCK VALLEY	51541-51541 HENDERSON
50622-50622 DENVER	50859-50859 PRESCOTT	51248-51248 SANBORN	51542-51542 HONEY CREEK
50623-50623 DEWAR	50860-50860 REDDING	51249-51249 SIBLEY	51543-51543 KIMBALLTON
50624-50624 DIKE	50861-50861 SHANNON CITY	51250-51250 SIOUX CENTER	51544-51544 LEWIS
50625-50625 DUMONT	50862-50862 SHARPSBURG	51301-51301 SPENCER	51545-51545 LITTLE SIOUX
50626-50626 DUNKERTON	50863-50863 TINGLEY	51330-51330 ALLENDORF	51546-51546 LOGAN
50627-50627 ELDORA	50864-50864 VILLISCA	51331-51331 ARNOLDS PARK	51548-51548 MC CLELLAND
50628-50628 ELMA	50936-50981 DES MOINES	51333-51333 DICKENS	51549-51549 MACEDONIA
50629-50629 FAIRBANK	51001-51001 AKRON	51334-51334 ESTHERVILLE	51550-51550 MAGNOLIA
50630-50630 FREDERICKSBURG	51002-51002 ALTA	51338-51338 EVERLY	51551-51551 MALVERN
50631-50631 FREDERIKA	51003-51003 ALTON	51340-51340 FOSTORIA	51552-51552 MARNE
50632-50632 GARWIN	51004-51004 ANTHON	51341-51341 GILLETT GROVE	51553-51553 MINDEN
50633-50633 GENEVA	51005-51005 AURELIA	51342-51342 GRAETTINGER	51554-51554 MINEOLA
50634-50634 GILBERTVILLE	51006-51006 BATTLE CREEK	51343-51343 GREENVILLE	51555-51555 MISSOURI VALLEY
50635-50635 GLADBROOK	51007-51007 BRONSON	51344-51344 GRUVER	51556-51556 MODALE
50636-50636 GREENE	51008-51008 BRUNSVILLE	51345-51345 HARRIS	51557-51557 MONDAMIN
50637-50637 GREEN MOUNTAIN	51009-51009 CALUMET	51346-51346 HARTLEY	51558-51558 MOORHEAD
50638-50638 GRUNDY CENTER	51010-51010 CASTANA	51347-51347 LAKE PARK	51559-51559 NEOLA
50640-50640 HANSELL	51011-51011 CHATSWORTH	51349-51349 MAY CITY	51560-51560 OAKLAND
50641-50641 HAZLETON	51012-51012 CHEROKEE	51350-51350 MELVIN	51561-51561 PACIFIC JUNCTION
50642-50642 HOLLAND	51014-51014 CLEGHORN	51351-51351 MILFORD	51562-51562 PANAMA
50643-50643 HUDSON	51015-51015 CLIMBING HILL	51354-51354 OCHEYEDAN	51563-51563 PERSIA
50644-50644 INDEPENDENCE	51016-51016 CORRECTIONVILLE	51355-51355 OKOBOJI	51564-51564 PISGAH
50645-50645 IONIA	51017-51017 CRAIG	51357-51357 ROYAL	51565-51565 PORTSMOUTH
50647-50647 JANESVILLE	51018-51018 CUSHING	51358-51358 RUTHVEN	51566-51566 RED OAK
50648-50648 JESUP	51019-51019 DANBURY	51360-51360 SPIRIT LAKE	51570-51570 SHELBY
50649-50649 KESLEY	51020-51020 GALVA	51363-51363 SUPERIOR	51571-51571 SILVER CITY
50650-50650 LAMONT	51022-51022 GRANVILLE	51364-51364 TERRIL	51572-51572 SOLDIER
50651-50651 LA PORTE CITY	51023-51023 HAWARDEN	51365-51365 WALLINGFORD	51573-51573 STANTON
50652-50652 LINCOLN	51024-51024 HINTON	51366-51366 WEBB	51574-51574 TENNANT
50653-50653 MARBLE ROCK	51025-51025 HOLSTEIN	51401-51401 CARROLL	51575-51575 TREYNOR
50654-50654 MASONVILLE	51026-51026 HORNICK	51430-51430 ARCADIA	51576-51576 UNDERWOOD
50655-50655 MAYNARD	51027-51027 IRETON	51431-51431 ARTHUR	51577-51577 WALNUT
50657-50657 MORRISON	51028-51028 KINGSLEY	51432-51432 ASPINWALL	51578-51578 WESTPHALIA
50658-50658 NASHUA	51029-51029 LARRABEE	51433-51433 AUBURN	51579-51579 WOODBINE
50659-50659 NEW HAMPTON	51030-51030 LAWTON	51436-51436 BREDA	51591-51591 RED OAK
50660-50660 NEW HARTFORD	51031-51031 LE MARS	51437-51437 CARNARVON	51593-51593 HARLAN
50661-50661 NORTH WASHINGTON	51033-51033 LINN GROVE	51439-51439 CHARTER OAK	51601-51603 SHENANDOAH
50662-50662 OELWEIN	51034-51034 MAPLETON	51440-51440 DEDHAM	51630-51630 BLANCHARD
50664-50664 ORAN	51035-51035 MARCUS	51441-51441 DELOIT	51631-51631 BRADDYVILLE
50665-50665 PARKERSBURG	51036-51036 MAURICE	51442-51442 DENISON	51632-51632 CLARINDA
50666-50666 PLAINFIELD	51037-51037 MERIDEN	51443-51443 GLIDDEN	51636-51636 COIN
50667-50667 RAYMOND	51038-51038 MERRILL	51444-51444 HALBUR	51637-51637 COLLEGE SPRINGS
50668-50668 READLYN	51039-51039 MOVILLE	51445-51445 IDA GROVE	51638-51638 ESSEX
50669-50669 REINBECK	51040-51040 ONAWA	51446-51446 IRWIN	51639-51639 FARRAGUT
50670-50670 SHELL ROCK	51041-51041 ORANGE CITY	51447-51447 KIRKMAN	51640-51640 HAMBURG
50671-50671 STANLEY	51044-51044 OTO	51448-51448 KIRON	51645-51645 IMOGENE
50672-50672 STEAMBOAT ROCK	51045-51045 OYENS	51449-51449 LAKE CITY	51646-51646 NEW MARKET
50673-50673 STOUT	51046-51046 PAULLINA	51450-51450 LAKE VIEW	51647-51647 NORTHBORO

51648-51648 PERCIVAL	52154-52154 LAWLER	52308-52308 MILLERSBURG	52553-52553 EDDYVILLE
51649-51649 RANDOLPH	52155-52155 LIME SPRINGS	52309-52309 MONMOUTH	52554-52554 ELDON
51650-51650 RIVERTON	52156-52156 LUANA	52310-52310 MONTICELLO	52555-52555 EXLINE
51651-51651 SHAMBAUGH	52157-52157 MC GREGOR	52312-52312 MORLEY	52556-52557 FAIRFIELD
51652-51652 SIDNEY	52158-52158 MARQUETTE	52313-52313 MOUNT AUBURN	52560-52560 FLORIS
51653-51653 TABOR	52159-52159 MONONA	52314-52314 MOUNT VERNON	52561-52561 FREMONT
51654-51654 THURMAN	52160-52160 NEW ALBIN	52315-52315 NEWHALL	52562-52562 HAYESVILLE
51655-51655 BARTLETT	52161-52161 OSSIAN	52316-52316 NORTH ENGLISH	52563-52563 HEDRICK
51656-51656 YORKTOWN	52162-52162 POSTVILLE	52317-52317 NORTH LIBERTY	52565-52565 KEOSAUQUA
51693-51693 SHENANDOAH	52163-52163 PROTIVIN	52318-52318 NORWAY	52566-52566 KIRKVILLE
52001-52004 DUBUQUE	52164-52164 RANDALIA	52319-52319 OAKDALE	52567-52567 LIBERTYVILLE
52030-52030 ANDREW	52165-52165 RIDGEWAY	52320-52320 OLIN	52568-52568 MARTINSBURG
52031-52031 BELLEVUE	52166-52166 SAINT LUCAS	52321-52321 ONSLOW	52569-52569 MELROSE
52032-52032 BERNARD	52168-52168 SPILLVILLE	52322-52322 OXFORD	52570-52570 MILTON
52033-52033 CASCADE	52169-52169 WADENA	52323-52323 OXFORD JUNCTION	52571-52571 MORAVIA
52035-52035 COLESBURG	52170-52170 WATERVILLE	52324-52324 PALO	52572-52572 MOULTON
52036-52036 DELAWARE	52171-52171 WAUCOMA	52325-52325 PARNELL	52573-52573 MOUNT STERLING
52037-52037 DELMAR	52172-52172 WAUKON	52326-52326 QUASQUETON	52574-52574 MYSTIC
52038-52038 DUNDEE	52175-52175 WEST UNION	52327-52327 RIVERSIDE	52575-52575 NUMA
52039-52039 DURANGO	52201-52201 AINSWORTH	52328-52328 ROBINS	52576-52576 OLLIE
52040-52040 DYERSVILLE	52202-52202 ALBURNETT	52329-52329 ROWLEY	52577-52577 OSKALOOSA
52041-52041 EARLVILLE	52203-52204 AMANA	52330-52330 RYAN	52580-52580 PACKWOOD
52042-52042 EDGEWOOD	52205-52205 ANAMOSA	52331-52331 SCOTCH GROVE	52581-52581 PLANO
52043-52043 ELKADER	52206-52206 ATKINS	52332-52332 SHELLSBURG	52583-52583 PROMISE CITY
52044-52044 ELKPORT	52207-52207 BALDWIN	52333-52333 SOLON	52584-52584 PULASKI
52045-52045 EPWORTH	52208-52208 BELLE PLAINE	52334-52334 SOUTH AMANA	52585-52585 RICHLAND
52046-52046 FARLEY	52209-52209 BLAIRSTOWN	52335-52335 SOUTH ENGLISH	52586-52586 ROSE HILL
52047-52047 FARMERSBURG	52210-52210 BRANDON	52336-52336 SPRINGVILLE	52588-52588 SELMA
52048-52048 GARBER	52211-52211 BROOKLYN	52337-52337 STANWOOD	52590-52590 SEYMOUR
52049-52049 GARNAVILLO	52212-52212 CENTER JUNCTION	52338-52338 SWISHER	52591-52591 SIGOURNEY
52050-52050 GREELEY	52213-52213 CENTER POINT	52339-52339 TAMA	52593-52593 UDELL
52052-52052 GUTTENBERG	52214-52214 CENTRAL CITY	52340-52340 TIFFIN	52594-52594 UNIONVILLE
52053-52053 HOLY CROSS	52215-52215 CHELSEA	52341-52341 TODDVILLE	52595-52595 UNIVERSITY PARK
52054-52054 LA MOTTE	52216-52216 CLARENCE	52342-52342 TOLEDO	52601-52601 BURLINGTON
52055-52055 LITTLEPORT	52217-52217 CLUTIER	52343-52343 TORONTO	52619-52619 ARGYLE
52056-52056 LUXEMBURG	52218-52218 COGGON	52344-52344 TROY MILLS	52620-52620 BONAPARTE
52057-52057 MANCHESTER	52219-52219 PRAIRIEBURG	52345-52345 URBANA	52621-52621 CRAWFORDSVILLE
52060-52060 MAQUOKETA	52220-52220 CONROY	52346-52346 VAN HORNE	52623-52623 DANVILLE
52064-52064 MILES	52221-52221 GUERNSEY	52347-52347 VICTOR	52624-52624 DENMARK
52065-52065 NEW VIENNA	52222-52222 DEEP RIVER	52348-52348 VINING	52625-52625 DONNELLSON
52066-52066 NORTH BUENA VISTA	52223-52223 DELHI	52349-52349 VINTON	52626-52626 FARMINGTON
52068-52068 PEOSTA	52224-52224 DYSART	52350-52350 VIOLA	52627-52627 FORT MADISON
52069-52069 PRESTON	52225-52225 ELBERON	52351-52351 WALFORD	52630-52630 HILLSBORO
52070-52070 SABULA	52226-52226 ELWOOD	52352-52352 WALKER	52631-52631 HOUGHTON
52071-52071 SAINT DONATUS	52227-52227 ELY	52353-52353 WASHINGTON	52632-52632 KEOKUK
52072-52072 SAINT OLAF	52228-52228 FAIRFAX	52354-52354 WATKINS	52635-52635 LOCKRIDGE
52073-52073 SHERRILL	52229-52229 GARRISON	52355-52355 WEBSTER	52637-52637 MEDIAPOLIS
52074-52074 SPRAGUEVILLE	52230-52230 HALE	52356-52356 WELLMAN	52638-52638 MIDDLETOWN
52075-52075 SPRINGBROOK	52231-52231 HARPER	52357-52357 WEST AMANA	52639-52639 MONTROSE
52076-52076 STRAWBERRY POINT	52232-52232 HARTWICK	52358-52358 WEST BRANCH	52640-52640 MORNING SUN
52077-52077 VOLGA	52233-52233 HIAWATHA	52359-52359 WEST CHESTER	52641-52641 MOUNT PLEASANT
52078-52078 WORTHINGTON	52235-52235 HILLS	52361-52361 WILLIAMSBURG	52642-52642 ROME
52079-52079 ZWINGLE	52236-52236 HOMESTEAD	52362-52362 WYOMING	52644-52644 MOUNT UNION
52099-52099 DUBUQUE	52237-52237 HOPKINTON	52400-52499 CEDAR RAPIDS	52645-52645 NEW LONDON
52101-52101 DECORAH	52240-52240 IOWA CITY	52501-52501 OTTUMWA	52646-52646 OAKVILLE
52130-52130 ALPHA	52241-52241 CORALVILLE	52530-52530 AGENCY	52647-52647 OLDS
52131-52131 BURR OAK	52242-52246 IOWA CITY	52531-52531 ALBIA	52648-52648 PILOT GROVE
52132-52132 CALMAR	52247-52247 KALONA	52533-52533 BATAVIA	52649-52649 SALEM
52133-52133 CASTALIA	52248-52248 KEOTA	52534-52534 BEACON	52650-52650 SPERRY
52134-52134 CHESTER	52249-52249 KEYSTONE	52535-52535 BIRMINGHAM	52651-52651 STOCKPORT
52135-52135 CLERMONT	52250-52250 KINROSS	52536-52536 BLAKESBURG	52652-52652 SWEDESBURG
52136-52136 CRESCO	52251-52251 LADORA	52537-52537 BLOOMFIELD	52653-52653 WAPELLO
52140-52140 DORCHESTER	52252-52252 LANGWORTHY	52538-52538 WEST GROVE	52654-52654 WAYLAND
52141-52141 ELGIN	52253-52253 LISBON	52540-52540 BRIGHTON	52655-52655 WEST BURLINGTON
52142-52142 FAYETTE	52254-52254 LOST NATION	52542-52542 CANTRIL	52656-52656 WEST POINT
52143-52143 FESTINA	52255-52255 LOWDEN	52543-52543 CEDAR	52657-52657 SAINT PAUL
52144-52144 FORT ATKINSON	52257-52257 LUZERNE	52544-52544 CENTERVILLE	52658-52658 WEVER
52146-52146 HARPERS FERRY	52301-52301 MARENGO	52548-52548 CHILLICOTHE	52659-52659 WINFIELD
52147-52147 HAWKEYE	52302-52302 MARION	52549-52549 CINCINNATI	52660-52660 YARMOUTH
52149-52149 HIGHLANDVILLE	52305-52305 MARTELLE	52550-52550 DELTA	52701-52701 ANDOVER
52150-52150 JACKSON JUNCTION	52306-52306 MECHANICSVILLE	52551-52551 DOUDS	52720-52720 ATALISSA
52151-52151 LANSING	52307-52307 MIDDLE AMANA	52552-52552 DRAKESVILLE	52721-52721 BENNETT
52722-52722 BETTENDORF	52737-52737 COLUMBUS CITY	52753-52753 LE CLAIRE	52767-52767 PLEASANT VALLEY
52725-52725 BIG ROCK	52739-52739 CONESVILLE	52754-52754 LETTS	52768-52768 PRINCETON
52726-52726 BLUE GRASS	52742-52742 DE WITT	52755-52755 LONE TREE	52769-52769 STOCKTON
52727-52727 BRYANT	52745-52745 DIXON	52756-52756 LONG GROVE	52771-52771 TEEDS GROVE
52728-52728 BUFFALO	52746-52746 DONAHUE	52757-52757 LOW MOOR	52772-52772 TIPTON
52729-52729 CALAMUS	52747-52747 DURANT	52758-52758 MC CAUSLAND	52773-52773 WALCOTT
52730-52730 CAMANCHE	52748-52748 ELDRIDGE	52759-52759 MONTPELIER	52774-52774 WELTON
52731-52731 CHARLOTTE	52749-52749 FRUITLAND	52760-52760 MOSCOW	52776-52776 WEST LIBERTY
52732-52733 CLINTON	52750-52750 GOOSE LAKE	52761-52761 MUSCATINE	52777-52777 WHEATLAND
52734-52734 A C NIELSEN CO	52751-52751 GRAND MOUND	52765-52765 NEW LIBERTY	52778-52778 WILTON
52736-52736 CLINTON	52752-52752 GRANDVIEW	52766-52766 NICHOLS	52800-52809 DAVENPORT

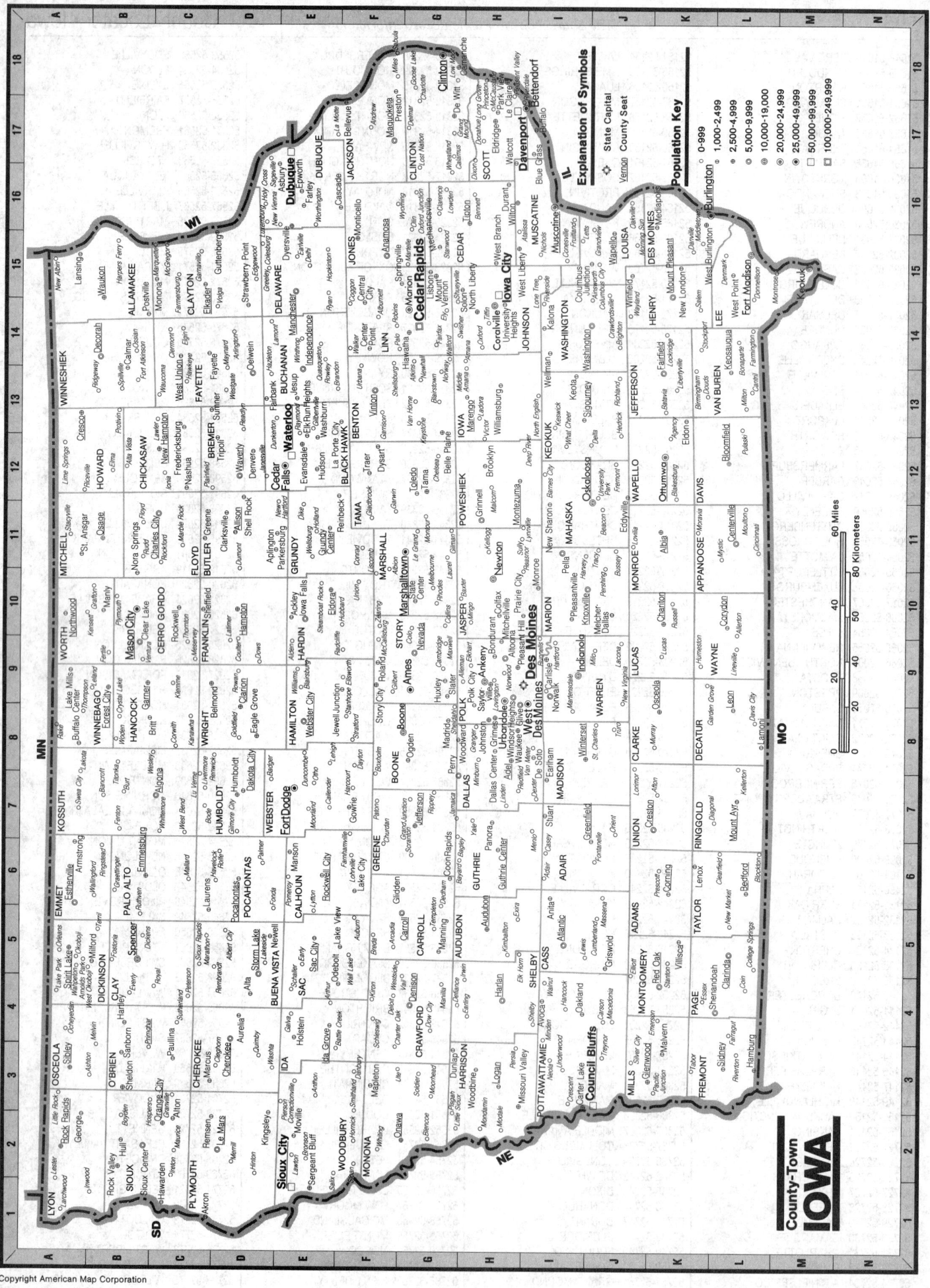

County-Town
IOWA

Copyright American Map Corporation

Explanation of symbols: ● – Census Designated Place (CDP)

Kansas

General Help Numbers:

Governor's Office

State Capitol Bldg, Room 212S   785-296-3232
Topeka, KS 66612-1590   Fax 785-296-7973
http://www.ksgovernor.org/   8AM-5PM

Attorney General's Office

Memorial Hall   785-296-2215
120 SW 10th Ave   Fax 785-296-6296
Topeka, KS 66612-1597   8AM-5PM
http://www.accesskansas.org/ksag/

Legislative Records

Kansas State Library, Capitol Bldg   785-296-2149
300 SW 10th Ave   Fax 785-296-6650
Topeka, KS 66612   8AM-5PM
www.kslegislature.org or http://skways.lib.ks.us/ksl

State Archives

Library and Archives Division   785-272-8681
6425 SW 6th Ave   Fax 785-272-8682
Topeka, KS 66615-1099   9AM-4:30PM M-SA
www.kshs.org/

State Specifics:

Capital:
Topeka
Shawnee County

Time Zone:
CST*
* Kansas' five western-most counties are MST:
They are: Greeley, Hamilton, Kearny, Sherman, Wallace,

Number of Counties:
105

Population:
2,723,507

Web Site:
www.accesskansas.org

State Agencies

Criminal Records

Kansas Bureau of Investigation, Criminal Records Division, 1620 SW Tyler, Crim. History Record Sec., Topeka, KS 66612-1837; 785-296-8200, 785-368-7162 (Fax), 8AM-5PM.

www.accesskansas.org/kbi/

Note: Agencies dealing with children, the elderly or disabled clientele may qualify for reduced fees. These accounts are known as Caretaker accounts.

Indexing & Storage: Records are available from 1939 to present. It takes up to 4 days before new records are available for inquiry. Records are indexed on Kansas Central Repository database, which is synchronized with the automated fingerprint ID system database. Records are normally destroyed after court-ordered expungement or if subject reaches 100 years old.

Searching: The criminal history information maintained by the KBI includes felony and misdemeanor arrests, prosecution data, court dispositions and information of incarceration in state-operated confinement facilities. Include the following in your request-full name, sex, race, date of birth, SSN. Each request must be on a separate "Records Check Request Form." Fingerprints are optional. Approximately 85% of records are fingerprint supported. Turnaround time may be several weeks if the record is not currently automated; approximately 46% of records are automated. The following data is not released: expunged records, non-convictions or juvenile records except to Criminal justice agencies and agencies required by law.

Access by: mail, fax, online.

Fee & Payment: Fees: $17.50 for a name check, $25.00 if certified; $30.00 for fingerprint search, $40.00 if certified. Check your own record or be a caregiver and fee is $12.50. Caretaker fingerpirnt check is $20.00. Fee payee: KBI Records Fees Fund. Prepayment required. Personal checks and credit cards are accepted.

Mail search: Turnaround time: 2 to 4 weeks. A SASE is requested.

Fax search: Prior arrangement is required, same criteria as mail.

Online search: Anyone may obtain non-certified criminal records online at www.accesskansas.org/kbi/criminalhistory/. The system is also available for premium subscribers of accessKansas. The fee is $17.50 per record; credit cards accepted online. The system is unavailable between the hours of midnight and 4 AM daily. A Kansas "Mosted Wanted" list is available at www.accesskansas.org/kbi/mw.htm.

Statewide Court Records

Judicial Administrator, Kansas Judicial Center, 301 SW 10th St, Topeka, KS 66612-1507; 785-296-4873, 785-296-7076 (Fax), 8AM-5PM.

www.kscourts.org

Note: There is no statewide access to all county trial courts.

Online search: The website above offers free online access to published opinions of the Supreme and Appellate courts, as well as case information for the Appellate courts.

Sexual Offender Registry

Kansas Bureau of Investigation, Sexual Offender Registry, 1620 SW Tyler, Topeka, KS 66612-1837; 785-296-8200, 785-296-6781 (Fax), 8AM-5PM.

www.accesskansas.org/kbi/ro.shtml

Indexing & Storage: Records are available from 4/14/1994 forward. It takes 5 to 10 days before new records are available for inquiry.

Searching: Further information on any registered offender in the file can be obtained from the sheriff's office in the registrant's county of residence. Include the following in your request-name, DOB. SSN is helpful.

Access by: mail, fax, in person, online.

Mail search: Turnaround time: 1 to 2 days. A SASE is requested.

Fax search: Prior arrangement is required, same criteria as mail.

In person search: Search in person at this office or at local law enforcement offices in the state.

Online search: Searching is available at the website. All open registrants are searchable.

Incarceration Records

Kansas Department of Corrections, Public Information Officer, 900 SW Jackson, 4th floor, Topeka, KS 66612-1284; 785-296-3310, 785-296-7023 (Fax), 8AM-5PM.

http://docnet.dc.state.ks.us

Indexing & Storage: Records are available on current and former inmates. It takes up to 4 days before new records are available for inquiry. Records are normally destroyed after 30 years.

Searching: Include the following in your request-full name. The date of birth and SSN are helpful. Location, KDOC number, physical identifiers, sentencing and conviction information, disciplinary record, and custody or supervision level are released. The following is not released: medical, mental health, substance abuse

Access by: mail, phone, fax, online.

Mail search: Turnaround time: 2 to 4 weeks. SASE is required.

Phone search: Name searching permitted.

Fax search: Same criteria as mail.

Online search: Web access to the database known as KASPER gives information on offenders who are: currently incarcerated; under post-incarceration supervision; and, who have been discharged from a sentence. The database does not have information available about inmates sent to Kansas under the provisions of the interstate compact agreement. Go to http://docnet.dc.state.ks.us/kasper2/default.asp.

Corporation, Limited Partnerships, Limited Liability Company Records

Secretary of State, Memorial Hall, 1st Floor, 120 SW 10th Ave, Topeka, KS 66612-1594; 785-296-4564, 785-296-4570 (Fax), 8AM-5PM.

www.kssos.org/main.html

Indexing & Storage: Records are available since the applicable laws have been in effect. All Annual Reports before 1995 are at the Historical Society. New records are available for inquiry immediately. Records are indexed on inhouse computer.

Searching: Items not released include confidential annual report balance sheets and copies of extensions. Include the following in your request-full name of business, specific records that you need copies of. In addition to the articles of incorporation, corporation records include the following information: Annual Reports, Officers, Directors and Prior (merged) names. They do not keep Inactive or Reserved names.

Access by: mail, phone, fax, in person, online.

Fee & Payment: There is no search fee. Plain copies are $1.00 per page. A certificate of good standing is $15.00, $12.50, if electronic. A letter of good standing is $10.00. Fee payee: Secretary of State. Prepayment required. When requesting by mail, send check for $5.00 or $10.00. They will refund any excess. Prepaid accounts are available. Personal checks accepted. Credit cards accepted: MasterCard, Visa.

Mail search: Turnaround time: 2 to 3 days.

Phone search: General information is given without charge.

Fax search: Items can be returned by fax for an additional $2.00 for the first page and $1.00 each additional page.

In person search: No fee for request.

Online search: Free entity searching is available at www.accesskansas.org/apps/corporations.html. Search by individual or company name, key word, date, or organizational number. There is no fee to search records, but there is a fee to order copies of certificates of good standings.

Trademarks/Servicemarks

Secretary of State, Trademarks/Servicemarks Division, 120 SW 10th Ave, Rm 100, Topeka, KS 66612-1240; 785-296-4564, 785-296-4570 (Fax), 8AM-5PM.

www.kssos.org

Indexing & Storage: Records are available from the 1950s, all on computer. It takes 2 to 3 days before new records are available for inquiry.

Searching: All information recorded is available to the public. However, Kansas law prohibits the use of names and/or addresses derived from public record for solicitation purposes. Include the following in your request-trademark/servicemark name, name of owner. The search provides the

names and addresses of owners, date of filing, and class code of filing.

Access by: mail, phone, fax, in person.

Fee & Payment: There is no search fee. Copies are $1.00 per page. Certification is $15.00 plus the copy fees. Fee payee: Secretary of State. Prepayment required. The Secretary of State's office offers prepaid accounts for all regular, ongoing requesters. Personal checks accepted. Credit cards accepted: MasterCard, Visa.

Mail search: Turnaround time: 1 to 2 days. A mail request must include the name of trademark/servicemark and/or the owner's name.

Phone search: They will give you limited information from the computer index.

Fax search: Turnaround time 24 hours.

In person search: No fee for request.

Other access: For bulk file purchase call Ann at 785-296-6271.

Uniform Commercial Code, Federal and State Tax Liens

Secretary of State - UCC Searches, Memorial Hall, 1st Fl, 120 SW 10th Ave, Topeka, KS 66612; 785-296-4564, 785-296-3659 (Fax), 8AM-5PM.

www.kssos.org/business/business_ucc.html

Indexing & Storage: Records are available from 1966 on computer, from 1966 to present on microfiche with exception of electronic filings. These images available from July 30, 2001.

Searching: Use search request form UCC-11. The search includes federal tax liens on businesses. Federal tax liens on individuals can be filed here or at county, all state tax liens are filed at the county level. Include the following in your request-debtor name. You must order copies to receive collateral information. No collateral data is given over the phone.

Access by: mail, phone, fax, in person, online.

Fee & Payment: The search fee is $20.00 per name, $10.00 if searched online, and copies are $1.00 per page. Fee payee: Secretary of State. Prepayment required. Personal checks accepted. Credit cards accepted: MasterCard, Visa.

Mail search: Turnaround time: 3 days. A SASE is requested.

Phone search: Search fee applies.

Fax search: Same criteria as mail searching. You can have data returned by fax for an additional $2.00 for 1ˢᵗ page and $1.00 each additional page.

In person search: Unless extensive list given, data available while you wait.

Online search: Online service is provided by accessKansas at www.accesskansas.org. The system is open 24 hours daily. There is an annual fee. UCC records are $10.00 per record. This is the same online system used for corporation records. For more information, call at 800-4-KANSAS.

Other access: Records in a bulk or database format is available from accessKansas.com.

Sales Tax Registrations

Access to Records is Restricted

Kansas Department of Revenue, Record requests, Docking State Office Bldg, 915 SW Harrison, Topeka, KS 66625-3570; 785-296-3081, 785-296-7928 (Fax), 7AM-5PM.

www.ksrevenue.org/

Note: Sales tax registration information is considered confidential and not public record.

Birth Certificates

Kansas Department of Health & Environment, Office of Vital Statistics, 1000 SW Jackson, #120, Topeka, KS 66612-2221; 785-296-1400, 785-296-3253 (Phone Credit Card Orders), 785-357-4332 (Fax), 8AM-5PM.

www.kdhe.state.ks.us/vital

Note: Vital records are not considered public records in Kansas. Uncertified copies or verifications are not provided to the public. Birth certificates began being filed with the Office July 1, 1911.

Indexing & Storage: Records are available from July 1911 to present. Delayed birth registrations from the late-1800s are available. It takes approximately 2 weeks before new records are available for inquiry. Records are indexed on microfiche, inhouse computer.

Searching: Must have a signed release from person of record or have direct interest for personal or property right. You must also include photocopy of your government-issued photo ID (DL, for instance). Include the following in your request-full name, names of parents, mother's maiden name, date of birth, place of birth, relationship to person of record, reason for information request. Include a daytime phone number.

Access by: mail, phone, fax, in person.

Fee & Payment: The fee is $12.00 for first certified copy, includes search of 5 years. Additional fee required for additional years searched. Add $7.00 for each additional copy of same record. Fee payee: Vital Statistics. There is an additional $9.00 VitalChek fee with the use of a credit card. Money orders, personal checks and major Credit cards accepted.

Mail search: Turnaround time: 5-10 business days. Include copy of your government-issued photo ID. A SASE is requested.

Phone search: You must use a credit card for an additional $9.00 fee. Turnaround time is within 3 business days. Phone service from 8am to 4pm.

Fax search: The fee must include $9.00 for use of a credit card. Turnaround time is within 3 business days.

In person search: Available 9AM to 4PM. You must complete an application and provide your photo ID. Turnaround time: 20 to 30 minutes.

Expedited service: Expedited service is available for credit card searches. Turnaround time: overnight delivery. Overnight mail services for return of documents is available for an additional fee. Requests may require up to 24 business hours to process. Use of credit card required.

Death Records

Kansas State Department of Health & Environment, Office of Vital Statistics, 1000 SW Jackson, #120, Topeka, KS 66612-2221; 785-296-1400, 785-296-3253 (Phone Credit Card Orders), 785-357-4332 (Fax), 8AM-5PM.

www.kdhe.state.ks.us/vital

Note: Vital records are not considered public records in Kansas. Uncertified copies or verifications are not provided to the public.

Indexing & Storage: Records are available from July 1, 1911 to present. New records are available for inquiry immediately. Records are indexed on microfiche, inhouse computer.

Searching: Must have a signed release from immediate family member or show direct interest for personal or property right. You must also include photocopy of your government-issued photo ID (DL, for instance). Include the following in your request-full name, date of death, place of death, relationship to person of record, reason for information request. Please include a daytime phone number.

Access by: mail, phone, fax, in person.

Fee & Payment: The fee is $13.00 for first certified copy, includes search of 5 years. Additional fee required for additional years searched. Add $7.00 for each additional copy of same record. Fee payee: Vital Statistics. Prepayment required. Money orders, personal checks and major Credit cards accepted. There is a $9.00 VitalChek fee for the use of a credit card.

Mail search: Turnaround time: 5-10 business days. Must include a personal ID. A SASE is requested.

Phone search: Use a credit card required for an additional $9.00 fee. Turnaround time is within 3 business days.

Fax search: Same criteria as phone searches.

In person search: Available 9AM to 4PM. Must complete an application and provide your personal photo ID. Turnaround time: 20 to 30 minutes.

Expedited service: Expedited service is available for credit card requests. Overnight service is available for an additional fee. Use of credit card required.

Marriage Certificates

Kansas State Department of Health & Environment, Office of Vital Statistics, 1000 SW Jackson, #120, Topeka, KS 66612-2221; 785-296-1400, 785-296-3253 (Phone Credit Card Orders), 785-357-4332 (Fax), 8AM-5PM.

www.kdhe.state.ks.us/vital

Note: Vital records are not considered public records in Kansas. Uncertified copies or verifications are not provided to the public.

Indexing & Storage: Records are available from May 1, 1913 to present. Records prior to 1913 are found at county of issue. Records are computerized from 1993. It takes 2 months before new records are available for inquiry. Records are indexed on microfiche, inhouse computer

Searching: Must have a signed release from person of record or have direct interest in personal or property right. You must also include photocopy of your government-issued photo ID (DL, for instance). Include the following in your request-names of husband and wife, date of marriage, place or county of marriage, relationship to person of record, reason for information request, wife's maiden name. Include a daytime phone number.

Access by: mail, phone, fax, in person.

Fee & Payment: The fee is $12.00 for first certified copy, includes search of 5 years. Additional fee required for additional years searched. Add $7.00 for each additional copy of same record. Fee payee: Vital Statistics. Prepayment required. Money orders, personal checks and major Credit cards accepted.

Mail search: Turnaround time: 5-10 business days. Must include a personal ID number. A SASE is requested.

Phone search: You must use a credit card for an additional $9.00 fee. Turnaround time is within 3 business days.

Fax search: Same criteria as phone searches.

In person search: You must complete an application and provide your photo ID. Available 9AM to 4PM. Turnaround time 20 to 30 minutes.

Expedited service: Expedited service is available for credit card requests. Overnight mail service is available for an additional fee. Overnight requests may require up to 24 business hours to process. Use of credit card required.

Divorce Records

Kansas State Department of Health & Environment, Office of Vital Statistics, 1000 SW Jackson, #120, Topeka, KS 66612-2221; 785-296-1400, 785-296-3253 (Phone Credit Card Orders), 785-357-4332 (Fax), 8AM-5PM.

www.kdhe.state.ks.us/vital

Note: The agency will issue a divorce certificate, but a copy of the decree must be ordered from the county of issue. Vital records are not considered public records in Kansas. Uncertified copies or verifications are not provided to the public.

Indexing & Storage: Records are available from July 1, 1951 to present. Records prior to July 1, 1951 are found at county of issue. It takes the second month after the divorce is filed before new records are available for inquiry. Records are indexed on microfiche, inhouse computer

Searching: Must have a signed release from person of record or show direct interest in personal or property right. You must also include photocopy of your government-issued photo ID (DL, for instance). Include the following in your request-names of husband and wife, date of divorce, county of divorce, relationship to person of record, reason for information request. Include your daytime telephone number.

Access by: mail, phone, fax, in person.

Fee & Payment: The fee is $12.00 for first certified copy, includes search of 5 years. Additional fee required for additional years searched. Add $7.00 for each additional copy of same record. Fee payee: Vital Statistics. Prepayment required. Money orders are accepted. Personal checks accepted. Credit cards accepted: MasterCard, Visa, AmEx, Discover.

Mail search: Turnaround time: 5-10 business days. A SASE is requested.

Phone search: Must use a credit card for an additional $9.00 fee. Turnaround time is within 3 business days.

Fax search: Same criteria as phone searches.

In person search: You must complete an application and provide your photo ID. Available 9AM to 4PM. Turnaround time is 20-30 minutes.

Expedited service: Expedited service is available for credit card requests. Overnight mail service is available for an additional fee and may require up to 24 business hours to process. Use of credit card required.

Workers' Compensation Records

Human Resources Department, Workers Compensation Division, 800 SW Jackson, Suite 600, Topeka, KS 66612-1227; 785-296-6762, 785-296-3430 (Fax), 8AM-5PM.

www.dol.ks.gov/index.html

Indexing & Storage: Records are available from the mid-1970's on. New records are available for inquiry immediately. Records are indexed on inhouse computer, file folders.

Searching: Information not released includes financial information submitted by employer, peer review records, and records related to safety inspections. Medical records are only released to those authorized by law, and are not open to the general public. Include the following in your request-claimant name, SSN. All requests must be on Division Forms. Employers may receive medical records if a job has been conditionally offered and there is a signed release by the subject.

Access by: mail, phone, fax, in person.

Fee & Payment: There is no search fee.

Mail search: Turnaround time: 1 week to 10 days.

Phone search: Some records are available for verification by phone.

Fax search: Fax searching available.

In person search: Requests maintained off premises will take 2 days to obtain.

Driver Records, Accident Reports

Department of Revenue, Driver Control Bureau, PO Box 12021, Topeka, KS 66612-202; 785-296-3671, 785-296-6851 (Fax), 8AM-4:45PM.

www.ksrevenue.org/vehicle.htm

Indexing & Storage: Records are available for 3 years for minor violations and lifetime for DWIs. The state does not record speeding violations of 10 mph or less over in a 55 to 75 speed zone. It takes 2 to 21 days before new records are available for inquiry. Records are normally destroyed after 4 to 6 years, then are microfilmed.

Searching: Permissible use requesters should use Form TR/DL 302. Casual requesters must secure written consent from subject before any records are released and use Form TR/DL 301. The DL number and either full name or DOB are required when ordering a driving record. The driver's address will show on the record. For an accident report, include the full name, DOB and/or VIN number, and date of accident. The following data is not released: medical information.

Access by: mail, in person, online.

Fee & Payment: The fee is $6.00 for a walk-in or mail-in request for a driving record. An accident report is available for $6.00 per page and copies of tickets $6.00 each. Fee payee: Department of Revenue. Prepayment required. Personal checks accepted. No credit cards accepted.

Mail search: Turnaround time: 2 to 5 days. A SASE is requested.

In person search: Walk-in requests are usually processed within 30 minutes. Local law enforcement agencies may also honor driving record requests at a higher cost.

Online search: Kansas has contracted with the AccessKansas (800-452-6727) to service all electronic media requests of driver license

histories at www.accesskansas.org. The fee per record is $6.00 for batch requests or $6.50 for immediate inquiry. There is an initial $75 subscription fee and an annual $60 fee. The system is open 24 hours a day, 7 days a week. Batch requests are available at 7:30 am (if ordered by 10 pm the previous day).

Vehicle Ownership, Vehicle Identification

Division of Vehicles, Title and Registration Bureau, 915 Harrison, Rm 155, Topeka, KS 66626-0001; 785-296-3621, 785-296-3852 (Fax), 8AM-4:45PM.

www.ksrevenue.org/vehicle.htm

Indexing & Storage: Records are available from approximately 1940. Older records are on microfilm, on microfiche from 1970-1987, and computerized since 1988. It takes 8 weeks from application date before new records are available for inquiry.

Searching: Casual requesters can only obtain records with consent of subject. Records are restricted from purchase for the purpose of obtaining address mail lists for selling property or services. Include the following in your request-Form TR/DL302.

Access by: mail, in person, online.

Fee & Payment: The fee for a title/registration verification depends on the request mode, noted as below. Fee payee: Kansas Department of Revenue. Prepayment required. Personal checks accepted. No credit cards accepted.

Mail search: Turnaround time: 2 days. The fee for a title or registration verification is $6.00. The fee for a title application copy of a vehicle title history is $10.00 .A SASE is requested.

In person search: Inquires are processed while you wait; however, requests must include form mentioned above. Same fees as by mail.

Online search: Online batch inquires are $6.00 per record; online interactive requests are $6.50 per record. Visit www.accesskansas.org for a complete description of accessKansas (800-452-6727), the state authorized vendor. There is an initial $75 subscription fee and an annual $60 fee to access records from AccessKansas.

Other access: This agency has several programs available to sell data in bulk format. Contact Donnita Thoma at the Dept of Revenue's Bureau of Policy and Research.

Vessel Ownership, Vessel Registration

Kansas Department of Wildlife & Parks, Boat Registration, 512 SE 25th Ave, Pratt, KS 67124-8174; 620-672-5911, 620-672-3013 (Fax), 8AM-5PM M-F.

www.kdwp.state.ks.us

Note: Liens must be searched at the county level.

Indexing & Storage: Records are available from 1967 to present. Records are indexed on computer. Titles are not required. All motorized or sailboats must be registered. It takes 1 week before new records are available for inquiry. Records are normally destroyed after 3 years.

Searching: All requests must be submitted in writing with specific reason given for the request. Data not is released for solicitation use. Include

the following in your request-name, either KA# or hull #, and name of person making request.

Access by: mail, fax, in person.

Fee & Payment: There is no search fee, unless extensive searching is requested.

Mail search: Turnaround time: 1-3 days.

Fax search: Same criteria as mail searching.

In person search: Inquires are processed while you wait; however, requests must be in writing.

Voter Registration

Access to Records is Restricted

Secretary of State - Elections Division, Memorial Hall, 1st Floor, 120 SW 10th Ave, Topeka, KS 66612-1594; 785-296-4564, 8AM-5PM.

www.kssos.org

Note: Individual records must be searched at the county level. This agency will sell the database on disk or CD only for political purposes.

GED Certificates

Kansas Board of Regents, GED Records, 1000 SW jackson St #520, Topeka, KS 66612-1368; 785-296-3191, 785-296-0983 (Fax), 8AM-4:30PM.

www.kansasregents.org

Indexing & Storage: It takes 3 weeks before new records are available for inquiry.

Searching: Include the following in your request-name at time of test, DOB, SSN, signed release and requester phone number. Also include the date of the test.

Access by: mail.

Fee & Payment: There is a $10.00 fee for a verification, transcript, or a duplicate diploma. Fee payee: Kansas Board of Regents. Prepayment required. Cash and money orders are accepted. Personal checks and credit cards not accepted.

Mail search: Turnaround time: 1 week.

Hunting and Fishing License Information

Dept of Wildlife & Parks, Licensing and Permits, 512 SE 25th Ave, Pratt, KS 67124-8174; 620-672-5911, 620-672-3013 (Fax), 8AM-5PM.

www.kdwp.state.ks.us

Note: The database of fishing licenses consists only of those licenses issued by this agency. Many vendors throughout the state also issue licenses and their data is not forwarded to this agency.

Searching: You can get big game information only. Requester must indicate what information is required and its intended use. Requests for information to be used for the sale of products or services will not be answered. Include the following in your request-full name, date of birth. Request may require an Open Records Certification to be completed. Suggest to call first.

Access by: mail, in person.

Fee & Payment: The agency reserves the right to recover costs for voluminous requests.

Mail search: Turnaround time: 1 to 3 days.

In person search: You may request information in person.

Kansas State Licensing Agencies

Licenses Searchable Online

Alcohol/Drug Counselor #3	www.ksbsrb.org/verification.html
Architect #14	www.accesskansas.org/roster-search/index.html
Athletic Trainer #10	www.ksbha.org
Body Piercer #6	www.accesskansas.org/kboc/
Charity Organization #27	www.kscharitycheck.org/search.asp
Chiropractor #10	www.ksbha.org
Cosmetic Facility #6	www.accesskansas.org/kboc/
Cosmetologist / Cosmetology School Instructor #6	www.accesskansas.org/kboc/
Counselor, Professional #3	www.ksbsrb.org/verification.html
Crematories #11	www.accesskansas.org/ksbma/listings.html
Dentist/Dental Hygienist #19	www.accesskansas.org/dental-verification/index.html
Electrologist #6	www.accesskansas.org/kboc/
Embalmer #11	www.accesskansas.org/ksbma/listings.html
Engineer #14	www.accesskansas.org/roster-search/index.html
Esthetician #6	www.accesskansas.org/kboc/
Funeral Establishment or Related Occupation #11	www.accesskansas.org/ksbma/listings.html
Geologist #14	www.accesskansas.org/roster-search/index.html
Insurance Company #22	www.ksinsurance.org/company/main.html
Landscape Architect #14	www.accesskansas.org/roster-search/index.html
Lobbyist #27	www.kssos.org/elections/elections_lobbyists.html
Marriage & Family Therapist #3	www.ksbsrb.org/verification.html
Medical Doctor #10	www.ksbha.org
Nail Technician #6	www.accesskansas.org/kboc/
Nurse #12	https://www.accesskansas.org/app/nursing/verification/
Occupational Therapist/Assistant #10	www.ksbha.org
Optometrist #26	www.arbo.org/odfinder/LicSearch.asp
Osteopathic Physician #10	www.ksbha.org
Permanent Cosmetic Technician #6	www.accesskansas.org/kboc/
Pharmacist #13	https://www.accesskansas.org/pharmacy_verification/index.html
Physical Therapist/Assistant #10	www.ksbha.org
Physician Assistant #10	www.ksbha.org
Podiatrist #10	www.ksbha.org
Private Investigator #23	https://www.accesskansas.org/kbi-pi-verify/index.html
Psychologist #3	www.ksbsrb.org/verification.html
Psychologist(Masters Level) #3	www.ksbsrb.org/verification.html
Public Accountant-CPA #4	www.ksboa.org/permit_list.htm
Real Estate Agent/Broker/Salesperson #31	https://www.accesskansas.org/krec/verification/index.html
Real Estate Appraiser #28	www.accesskansas.org
Respiratory Therapist #10	www.ksbha.org
Social Worker #3	www.ksbsrb.org/verification.html
Surveyor, Land #14	www.accesskansas.org/roster-search/index.html
Tanning Facility #6	www.accesskansas.org/kboc/
Tattoo Artist #6	www.accesskansas.org/kboc/
Teacher #7	www.ksbe.state.ks.us/cert/cert_search.html

Kansas Licensing Quick Finder

Abstractor #1	316-544-2311	Child Care Attendant #30 ... 785-296-1270	Engineer #14 ... 785-296-3054
Adult Care Home Administrator #16 785-296-0061	Chiropractor #10 ... 785-296-7413	Esthetician #6 ... 785-296-3155
Alcohol Vendor License #20 ... 785-296-7015	Contractor, General #21 ... 785-296-4460	Fundraiser/Prof. Solicitor #27 800-432-2310
Alcohol/Drug Counselor #3 ... 785-296-3240	Cosmetic Facility #6 ... 785-296-3155	Funeral Director/Assistant Financial Director #11
Ambulance Attendant/Service #8 785-296-7299	Cosmetologist #6 ... 785-296-3155	 785-296-3980
Animal Facility Inspector #2 ... 785-296-2326	Cosmetology School Instructor #6 785-296-3155	Funeral Establishm't/Branches #11 785-296-3980
Architect #14 ... 785-296-3054	Counselor, Professional #3 ... 785-296-3240	Geologist #14 ... 785-296-3054
Athletic Trainer #10 ... 785-296-7413	Crematories #11 ... 785-296-3980	Hearing Aid Dispenser #9 ... 316-263-0774
Attorney #18 ... 785-296-8409	Dental Hygienist #19 ... 785-296-6400	Home Health Aide #16 ... 785-296-6877
Audiologist #16 ... 785-296-0061	Dentist #19 ... 785-296-6400	Insurance Agent #22 ... 785-296-7859
Barber #5 ... 785-296-2211	Dietitian #16 ... 785-296-0061	Insurance Company #22 ... 785-296-7859
Barber College #5 ... 785-296-2211	Drug Tax Stamp #20 ... 785-296-7015	Investment Advisor #29 ... 785-296-3307
Barber Shop #5 ... 785-296-2211	Electrologist #6 ... 785-296-3155	Landscape Architect #14 ... 785-296-3054
Body Piercer #6 ... 785-296-3155	Embalmer #11 ... 785-296-3980	Livestock Inspector #2 ... 785-296-2326
Charity Organization #27 ... 800-432-2310	Emergency Medical Technician #8 785-296-7299	Lobbyist #27 ... 785-296-3488

Marriage & Family Therapist #3 785-296-3240	Physician Assistant #10 785-296-7413	School Counselor #7 785-296-2288
Medical Doctor #10 785-296-7413	Podiatrist #10 785-296-7413	School Library Media Specialist #7 785-296-2288
Medication Aide #16 785-296-6877	Private Investigator #23 785-296-4436	School Nurse #7 785-296-2288
Nail Technician #6 785-296-3155	Psychologist #3 785-296-3240	Securities Agent #29 785-296-3307
Notary Public #27 785-296-2239	Psychologist(Masters Level) #3 785-296-3240	Securities Broker/Dealer #29 785-296-3307
Nurse #12 785-296-4929	Public Accountant-CPA #4 785-296-2162	Shorthand Reporter #17 785-296-3299
Nurses' Aide #16 785-296-6877	RacingWagering Equipment/Svcs #25.. 785-296-5800	Social Worker #3 785-296-3240
Nursing Home Administrator #16 785-296-0061	Racing Facility Owner/Mgr. #25 785-296-5800	Special Investigator #2 785-296-2326
Occupational Therapist/Assistant #10.. 785-296-7413	Racing Occupation License #25 785-296-5800	Speech/Language Pathologist #16 785-296-0061
Optometrist #26 785-832-9986	Racing Organization #25 785-296-5800	Surveyor, Land #14 785-296-3054
Osteopathic Physician #10 785-296-7413	Real Estate Agent/Broker/Seller #31 ... 785-296-3411	Tanning Facility #6 785-296-3155
Permanent Cosmetic Technician #6 785-296-3155	Real Estate Appraiser #28 785-271-3373	Tattoo Artist #6 785-296-3155
Pesticide Applicator/Dealer #24 785-296-2263	Respiratory Therapist #10 785-296-7413	Teacher #7 785-296-2288
Pharmacist #13 785-296-8420	Salon #5 785-296-2211	Tobacco Registration #20 785-296-7015
Physical Therapist/Assistant #10 785-296-7413	School Administrator #7 785-296-2288	Veterinarian #15 785-456-8781

Kansas Licensing Agency Information

1 Abstracters Board of Examiners, 521 S. Main - PO Box 549, Hugoton, KS 67951-0549; 316-544-2311, Fax: 316-544-8029. Email: glen@pld.com

2 Animal Health Department, 708 S Jackson, Topeka, KS 66603-3714; 785-296-2326, Fax: 785-296-1765.

3 Behavioral Sciences Regulatory Board, 712 S Kansas, Topeka, KS 66603; 785-296-3240, Fax: 785-296-3112. www.ksbsrb.org   Email: leslie.allen@bsrb.state.ks.us Search Database at www.ksbsrb.org/verification.html

4 Board of Accountancy, 900 SW Jackson #556, Topeka, KS 66612-1239; 785-296-2162, Fax: 785-291-3501. www.ksboa.org   Email: info@ksboa.state.ks.us Search Database at www.ksboa.org/permit_list.htm

5 Board of Barbering, 700 SW Jackson #1002, Topeka, KS 66603; 785-296-2211, Fax: 785-368-7071. Email: barber@yahoo.com

6 Board of Cosmetology, 714 SW Jackson #100, Topeka, KS 66603; 785-296-3155, Fax: 785-296-3002. www.ink.org/public/kboc Search Database at www.accesskansas.org/kboc/

7 Board of Education, 120 SE 10th Ave, Topeka, KS 66612-1182; 785-296-3201, Fax: 785-296-7933. www.ksbe.state.ks.us/Welcome.html Search Database at www.ksbe.state.ks.us/cert/cert_search.html Note: Check status and verify via telephone at 785-296-2288.

8 Board of Emergency Medical Services, Landon State Office Building 900SW Jackson #10315, Topeka, KS 66603-3826; 785-296-7299, Fax: 785-296-6212.   www.ksbems.org

9 Board of Examiners for Hearing Aid Dispensers, 600 N St Francis, Wichita, KS 67201-0252; 316-263-0774, Fax: 316-264-2681. Email: sherry@mid-stateslabs.com

10 Board of Healing Arts, 235 S Topeka Blvd, Topeka, KS 66603-3068; 785-296-7413, Fax: 785-296-0852. www.ksbha.org Email: cabbot@ink.org

11 Board of Mortuary Arts, 700 SW Jackson, #904, Topeka, KS 66603-3733; 785-296-3980, Fax: 785-296-0891. www.accesskansas.org/ksbma Email: bomal@ksbma.state.ks.us Search Database at www.accesskansas.org/ksbma/listings.html

12 Board of Nursing, Landon State Office Bldg. 900 SW Jackson, Rm 1051, Topeka, KS 66612-1230; 785-296-4929, Fax: 785-296-3929. www.ksbn.org Email: info@ksbn.state.ks.us Search Database at https://www.accesskansas.org/app/nursing/verification/ Note: Registered users of INK (Information Network of Kansas) can subscribe and get license verifications for $.25; Non-subscribers fee is $1.00 each.

13 Board of Pharmacy, 900 Jackson, Landon State Office Bldg, Rm 560, Topeka, KS 66612-1231; 785-296-4056, Fax: 785-296-8420. Email: pharmacy@pharmacy.state.ks.us Search Database at https://www.accesskansas.org/pharmacy_verification/index.html

14 Board of Technical Professions, 900 SW Jackson, Rm 507, Topeka, KS 66612-1257; 785-296-3053. www.accesskansas.org/ksbtp/ Search Database at www.accesskansas.org/roster-search/index.html

15 Board of Veterinary Examiners, PO Box 242 (1003 Lincoln), Wamego, KS 66547-0242; 785-456-8781, Fax: 785-456-8782. www.accesskansas.org/veterinary/

16 Department of Health & Environment, Bureau of Health Facilities, 900 SW Jackson #1051-S, Topeka, KS 66612-1290; 785-296-1240, Fax: 785-296-3075. www.kdhe.state.ks.us/hoc/index.html Email: mpetty@kdhe.state.ks.us

17 Clerk of Appellate Court, 301 S.W. 10th Avenue Rm. 374, Topeka, KS 66612-1507; 785-296-3299, Fax: 785-296-1028. www.kscourts.org   Email: green@kscourts.org

18 Clerk of the Supreme Court, 301 SW 10th Ave, Rm 374, Topeka, KS 66612; 785-296-8409, Fax: 785-296-1028. www.kscourts.org   Email: registration@kscourts.org

19 Dental Board, 900 SW Jackson St Rm 564S, Topeka, KS 66612-1220; 785-296-6400, Fax: 785-296-3116. www.accesskansas.org/kdb Email: info@dental.state.ks.us Search at www.accesskansas.org/dental-verification/index.html

20 Department of Revenue, Alcoholic Beverage Control, 915 SW Harrison St, Rm 214, Topeka, KS 66625-3512; 785-296-7015, Fax: 785-296-7185. www.ksrevenue.org/abc.htm Email: abc@kdor.state.ks.us

21 Department of Revenue, Robert B Docking, State Office Bldg, 915 SW Harrison St, Topeka, KS 66625-0001; 877-526-7738. www.ksrevenue.org

22 Insurance Department, 420 SW 9th, Topeka, KS 66612-1678; 785-296-7859, Fax: 785-368-7019. www.ksinsurance.org Search Database at www.ksinsurance.org/company/main.html

23 Bureau of Investigation, Private Detective Licensing Unit, 1620 SW Tyler, Topeka, KS 66612-1837; 785-296-4436, Fax: 785-296-6781. www.accesskansas.org/kbi/ Email: corrina.clements@kbi.state.ks.us Search Database at https://www.accesskansas.org/kbi-pi-verify/index.html

24 Department of Agriculture, Records Ctr, 109 SW 9th St, Topeka, KS 66612; 785-296-2263, Fax: 785-296-0673. www.accesskansas.org/kda

25 Racing Commission, 3400 SW Van Buren, Topeka, KS 66611-2228; 785-296-5800, Fax: 785-296-0900. www.accesskansas.org/krc Email: kracing@ynetworks.com

26 Board of Examiners in Optometry, 3109 W. 6th St. #D, Lawrence, KS 66049; 785-832-9986, Fax: 785-832-9986. www.terraworld.net/kssbeo Email: kssbeo@terraworld.net Search Database at www.arbo.org/odfinder/LicSearch.asp

27 Office of Secretary of State, Memorial Hall, 1st Floor, 120 SW 10th Av, Topeka, KS 66612-1594; 785-296-4504, Fax: 785-296-4570. www.kssos.org/main.html Email: kssos@kssos.org

28 Office of the Commissioner of Banks, Real Estate Appraisal Board, 1100 SW Wanamaker #104, Topeka, KS 66604-3805; 785-271-3373, Fax: 785-271-3370. www.accesskansas.org/kreab Email: kreab@cjnetworks.com Search Database at www.accesskansas.org

29 Securities Commissioner of Kansas, 618 S Kansas 2nd Fl, Topeka, KS 66603-3804; 785-296-3307, Fax: 785-296-6872. www.securities.state.ks.us Email: securities@securities.state.ks.us

30 Child Care Licensing & Registration, 1000 SW Jackson #200, Topeka, KS 66612; 785-296-1240, Fax: 785-296-0803.

31 Real Estate Commission, Licensing Board, 3 Townsite Plaza #200, 120 SE 6th, Topeka, KS 66603-3511; 785-296-3411, Fax: 785-296-1771. www.accesskansas.org/krec/ Email: krec@krec.state.ks.us Search at https://www.accesskansas.org/krec/verification/index.html Note: Search results are limited to 15 results at one time if a general name or city search is requested.

Kansas Federal Courts

The following list indicates the district and division name for each county in the state. If the bankruptcy court location is different from the district court, then the location of the bankruptcy court appears in parentheses.

County/Court Cross Reference

Allen................Topeka	Greenwood................Wichita	Pawnee................Wichita
Anderson................Topeka	Hamilton................Wichita	Phillips................Wichita
Atchison................Kansas City	Harper................Wichita	Pottawatomie................Topeka
Barber................Wichita	Harvey................Wichita	Pratt................Wichita
Barton................Wichita	Haskell................Wichita	Rawlins................Wichita
Bourbon................Kansas City	Hodgeman................Wichita	Reno................Wichita
Brown................Kansas City	Jackson................Topeka	Republic................Topeka
Butler................Wichita	Jefferson................Wichita	Rice................Wichita
Chase................Topeka	Jewell................Topeka	Riley................Topeka
Chautauqua................Wichita	Johnson................Kansas City	Rooks................Wichita
Cherokee................Kansas City	Kearny................Wichita	Rush................Wichita
Cheyenne................Wichita	Kingman................Wichita	Russell................Wichita
Clark................Wichita	Kiowa................Wichita	Saline................Topeka
Clay................Topeka	Labette................Kansas City	Scott................Wichita
Cloud................Topeka	Lane................Wichita	Sedgwick................Wichita
Coffey................Topeka	Leavenworth................Kansas City	Seward................Wichita
Comanche................Kansas City (Wichita)	Lincoln................Topeka	Shawnee................Topeka
Cowley................Wichita	Linn................Kansas City	Sheridan................Wichita
Crawford................Kansas City	Logan................Wichita	Sherman................Wichita
Decatur................Wichita	Lyon................Topeka	Smith................Wichita
Dickinson................Topeka	Marion................Topeka	Stafford................Wichita
Doniphan................Kansas City	Marshall................Kansas City	Stanton................Wichita
Douglas................Topeka	McPherson................Wichita	Stevens................Wichita
Edwards................Wichita	Meade................Wichita	Sumner................Wichita
Elk................Wichita	Miami................Kansas City	Thomas................Wichita
Ellis................Wichita	Mitchell................Topeka	Trego................Wichita
Ellsworth................Wichita	Montgomery................Wichita	Wabaunsee................Topeka
Finney................Wichita	Morris................Topeka	Wallace................Wichita
Ford................Wichita	Morton................Wichita	Washington................Topeka
Franklin................Topeka	Nemaha................Kansas City	Wichita................Wichita
Geary................Topeka	Neosho................Topeka	Wilson................Topeka
Gove................Wichita	Ness................Wichita	Woodson................Topeka
Graham................Wichita	Norton................Wichita	Wyandotte................Kansas City
Grant................Wichita	Osage................Topeka	
Gray................Wichita	Osborne................Wichita	
Greeley................Wichita	Ottawa................Topeka	

Standards for Federal Courts: The search fee is $20.00 per item (one party name or case number). Certification fee is $7.00 per document. Copy fee is $.50 per page. All fees standard unless noted in profile. Mail Search: always enclose a stamped self addressed envelope unless otherwise noted. Most courts accept fax requests or will suggest a copying/search vendor. Before releasing records, courts require prepayment unless noted in profile.

Open records are located at the court unless otherwise noted. District courts index by defendant and plaintiff as well as by case number. Bankruptcy courts usually index by debtor and case number. While most courts now have their indexes on computer, many still maintain index card files as well.

The universal PACER sign-up number is 800-676-6856. Find PACER and the Party/Case Index on the Web at http://pacer.psc.uscourts.gov. PACER dial-up access is $.60 per minute. Also, courts offering internet access via RACER, PACER, Web-PACER or the new CM-ECF charge $.07 per page fee unless noted as free.

US District Court

District of Kansas

Kansas City Division Clerk, 500 State Ave, Kansas City, KS 66101 (courier address: Use mail address for courier delivery) 913-551-6719. www.ksd.uscourts.gov

Counties: Atchison, Bourbon, Brown, Cherokee, Crawford, Doniphan, Johnson, Labette, Leavenworth, Linn, Marshall, Miami, Nemaha, Wyandotte.

Indexing & Storage: New cases available in the index immediately after filing date. Records are also indexed on microfiche.

Fee & Payment: Payment may be made by money order, cashier check, personal check. No search fee is charged unless certification is required. All certification searches are conducted by the Wichita office. Payee: Clerk, U.S. District Court.

Phone Search: No searching by telephone. Only docket information will be released over the phone if you have a case number.

Mail Search: A SASE not required.

In Person Search: Permitted.

PACER: PACER is available online at http://pacer.ksd.uscourts.gov. Case records go back to 1994. Records never purged. New civil records are online after 2 days. New criminal records online after 3 days.

Electronic Filing: Electronic filing information online at https://ecf.ksd.uscourts.gov

Topeka Division Clerk, U.S. District Court, Room 490, 444 SE Quincy, Topeka, KS 66683 (courier address: Use mail address for courier delivery) 785-295-2610. www.ksd.uscourts.gov

Counties: Allen, Anderson, Chase, Clay, Cloud, Coffey, Dickinson, Douglas, Franklin, Geary, Jackson, Jewell, Lincoln, Lyon, Marion, Mitchell, Morris, Neosho, Osage, Ottawa, Pottawatomie,

Republic, Riley, Saline, Shawnee, Wabaunsee, Washington, Wilson, Woodson.

Indexing & Storage: New cases available in the index 24 hours after filing date. A full name, the case number and a date are very helpful to obtain records.

Fee & Payment: Payment may be made by money order, cashier check, personal check. Payee: Clerk of U.S. District Court.

Phone Search: Docket information available by phone.

In Person Search: Fee charged if court conducts your in person search for you. If the case is on the computer, in person searchers may search free.

PACER: PACER is available online at http://pacer.ksd.uscourts.gov. Case records go back to 1994. Records never purged. New civil records are online after 2 days. New criminal records online after 3 days.

Electronic Filing: Electronic filing information online at https://ecf.ksd.uscourts.gov

Wichita Division 204 U.S. Courthouse, 401 N Market, Wichita, KS 67202-2096 (courier address: Use mail address for courier delivery) 316-269-6491. www.ksd.uscourts.gov

Counties: All counties in Kansas. Cases may be heard from counties in the other division.

Indexing & Storage: New cases available in the index immediately after filing date. Records are indexed on the computer since 1990. Prior records are indexed on microfiche or index cards. District wide searches are available from this court.

Fee & Payment: Payment may be made by money order, cashier check, personal check. Payee: Clerk, U.S. District Court.

Phone Search: Will do computer search on one name over the phone.

In Person Search: Fee charged if court conducts your in person search for you.

PACER: PACER is available online at http://pacer.ksd.uscourts.gov. Case records go back to 1994. Records never purged. New civil records are online after 2 days. New criminal records online after 3 days.

Electronic Filing: Electronic filing information online at https://ecf.ksd.uscourts.gov

U.S. Bankruptcy Court

District of Kansas

Kansas City Division 500 State Ave, Room 161, Kansas City, KS 66101 (courier address: Use mail address for courier delivery) 913-551-6732, Fax: 913-551-6715. www.ksb.uscourts.gov

Counties: Atchison, Bourbon, Brown, Cherokee, Comanche, Crawford, Doniphan, Johnson, Labette, Leavenworth, Linn, Marshall, Miami, Nemaha, Wyandotte.

Indexing & Storage: Cases indexed by debtor as well as by case number. New cases available in the index 1 day after filing date. Approximate year of filing will also help in the search for files. Bankruptcy searches can be performed from any bankruptcy court in the district for case files from 1989 forward; master listing for pre-1989 cases are available from the Topeka Office.

Fee & Payment: Payment may be made by money order, cashier check, personal check. Debtor's checks are not accepted. Payee: Clerk of U.S. Bankruptcy Court.

Phone Search: Only docket information available by phone. Automated voice case information service (VCIS) is available. Call VCIS at 800-827-9028 or 316-269-6668.

In Person Search: Fee charged if court conducts your in person search for you.

PACER: PACER is available online at http://pacer.ksb.uscourts.gov. Document images available. Records purged every 6 months. New civil records are online after 1 day.

Electronic Filing: Electronic filing information at https://ecf.ksb.uscourts.gov (attorneys only)

Topeka Division 240 U.S. Courthouse, 444 SE Quincy, Topeka, KS 66683 (courier address: Use mail address for courier delivery) 785-295-2750, Fax: 785-295-2964. www.ksb.uscourts.gov

Counties: Allen, Anderson, Chase, Clay, Cloud, Coffey, Dickinson, Douglas, Franklin, Geary, Jackson, Jewell, Lincoln, Lyon, Marion, Mitchell, Morris, Neosho, Osage, Ottawa, Pottawatomie, Republic, Riley, Saline, Shawnee, Wabaunsee, Washington, Wilson, Woodson.

Indexing & Storage: Cases indexed by debtor as well as by case number. New cases available in the index 1 day after filing date. Approximate year of filing will also help in the search for files.

Fee & Payment: Payment may be made by money order, cashier check, personal check. Debtor's

checks are not accepted. Payee: Clerk, U.S. Bankruptcy Court.

Phone Search: Only docket information available by phone. Automated voice case information service (VCIS) is available. Call VCIS at 800-827-9028 or 316-269-6668.

Mail Search: A SASE not required.

In Person Search: Fee charged if court conducts your in person search for you.

PACER: PACER is available online at http://pacer.ksb.uscourts.gov. Document images available. Records purged every 6 months. New civil records are online after 1 day.

Electronic Filing: Electronic filing information at https://ecf.ksb.uscourts.gov (attorneys only)

Wichita Division 167 U.S. Courthouse, 401 N Market, Wichita, KS 67202 (courier address: Use mail address for courier delivery) 316-269-6486, Fax: 316-269-6181. www.ksb.uscourts.gov

Counties: Barber, Barton, Butler, Chautauqua, Cheyenne, Clark, Comanche, Cowley, Decatur, Edwards, Elk, Ellis, Ellsworth, Finney, Ford, Gove, Graham, Grant, Gray, Greeley, Greenwood, Hamilton, Harper, Harvey, Haskell, Hodgeman, Jefferson, Kearny, Kingman, Kiowa,Lane, Logan, Mcpherson, Meade, Montgomery, Morton, Ness, Norton, Osborne, Pawnee, Phillips, Pratt, Rawlins, Reno, Rice, Rooks, Rush, Russell, Scott, Sedgwick, Seward, Sheridan, Smith, Stafford, Stanton, Stevens, Sumner, Thomas, Trego, Wallace, Wichita.

Indexing & Storage: Cases indexed by debtor as well as by case number. New cases available in the index 1 day after filing date. Records are also indexed on microfiche. District wide searches are available from this division.

Fee & Payment: Payment may be made by money order, cashier check, personal check. Payee: Clerk, U.S. Bankruptcy Court.

Phone Search: Only the attorneys, trustees, hearing dates and file dates will be released over the phone. Automated voice case information service (VCIS) is available. Call VCIS at 800-827-9028 or 316-269-6668.

Mail Search: A SASE not required.

In Person Search: Permitted.

PACER: PACER is available online at http://pacer.ksb.uscourts.gov. Document images available. Records purged every 6 months. New civil records are online after 1 day.

Electronic Filing: Electronic filing information at https://ecf.ksb.uscourts.gov (attorneys only)

Kansas County Courts

Court	Jurisdiction	No. of Courts	How Organized
District Courts*	General	109	31 Districts
Municipal Courts	Municipal	350	

* Profiled in this Sourcebook.

Court		CIVIL							
	Tort	Contract	Real Estate	Min. Claim	Max. Claim	Small Claims	Estate	Eviction	Domestic Relations
District Courts*	X	X	X	$0	No Max	$1800	X	X	
Municipal Courts									

Court	CRIMINAL				
	Felony	Misdemeanor	DWI/DUI	Preliminary Hearing	Juvenile
District Courts*	X	X	X	X	X
Municipal Courts			X		

ADMINISTRATION

Judicial Administrator, Kansas Judicial Center, 301 SW 10th St, Topeka, KS, 66612; 785-296-4873, Fax: 785-296-7076. www.kscourts.org

COURT STRUCTURE

The District Court is the court of general jurisdiction. There are 110 courts in 31 districts in 105 counties. If an individual in Municipal Court wants a jury trial, the request must be filed de novo in a District Court.

ONLINE ACCESS

Commercial online access is available for District Court Records in 4 counties - Johnson, Sedgwick, Shawnee, and Wyandotte - through Access Kansas, part of the Information Network of Kansas (INK) Services. Franklin and Finney counties may be available in 2004. A user may access INK at www.accesskansas.org or via a dial-up system. The INK subscription fee is $75.00, and the annual renewal fee is $60.00. There is no per minute connect charge, but there is a transaction fee. Other information from INK includes Drivers License, Title, Registration, Lien, and UCC searches. For additional information or a registration packet, call 800-4-KANSAS (800-452-6727).

The Kansas Appellate Courts offer free online access to case information at www.kscourts.org. Published opinions from the Appellate and Supreme courts are also available.

ADDITIONAL INFORMATION

Five counties - Cowley, Crawford, Labette, Montgomery, and Neosho - have two hearing locations but only one record center, which is the location included in this Sourcebook.

Many Kansas courts do not do criminal record searches and will refer any criminal requests to the Kansas Bureau of Investigation. The Kansas Legislature's Administrative Order 156 (Fall, 2000) allows Courts to charge up to $12.00 per hour for search services, though courts may set their own search fees, if any.

Allen County

District Court PO Box 630, 1 N. Washington St, Iola, KS 66749; 620-365-1425; Fax: 620-365-1429. Hours: 8AM-5PM (CST). *Felony, Misdemeanor, Civil, Eviction, Small Claims, Probate.*
Civil Records: Access: Fax, mail, in person. Both court and visitors may perform in person searches. Search fee: $12.00 per hour. Required to search: name, years to search. Civil cases indexed by defendant, plaintiff. Civil records on computer from 1993, manual index from 1800s.
Criminal Records: Access: Fax, mail, in person. Both court and visitors may perform in person searches. Search fee: $12.00 per hour. Required to search: name, years to search. Criminal records on computer from 1993, manual index from 1800s.
General Information: Public Access terminal is available. No juvenile (under the age of 15), mental health, sealed or expunged records released. Accepts requests via email, but cannot return results by email. Fee to fax results is $1.00 per page. Copy fee: $.50 per page. Cert fee: $1.00. Payee: Clerk of Court. Personal checks accepted. Prepayment required. Mail requests: SASE required. Mail turnaround time 1 week.

Anderson County

District Court PO Box 305, Garnett, KS 66032; 785-448-6886; Fax: 785-448-3230. Hours: 8AM-N, N-4PM (CST). *Felony, Misdemeanor, Civil, Eviction, Small Claims, Probate.*
www.kscourts.org/dstcts/4dstct.htm
Civil Records: Access: Fax, mail, in person, online. Both court and visitors may perform in person searches. Search fee: $12.50 per hour plus copy fee. Required to search: name, years to search. Civil cases indexed by defendant, plaintiff. Civil records on computer from 1977, index books from 1800s. Current court calendars are free online at www.kscourts.org/dstcts/4andckt.htm. Also, access to probate court records is free at www.kscourts.org/dstcts/4anprrec.htm.
Criminal Records: Access: Fax, mail, in person, online. Visitors must perform in person searches for themselves. Search fee: $12.50 per hour plus copy fee. Required to search: name, years to search. Criminal records on computer from 1977, index books from 1800s. Online access to criminal calendars is the same as civil. For criminal record searches, the court urges requesters to contact the KS Bureau of Investigations.
General Information: Public Access terminal is available. (This court is not on statewide system.) No juvenile, mental health, sealed or expunged records released. Will fax results $2.00 1st page, $.50 each add'l. Copy fee: $.25 per page. Cert fee: $1.00. Payee: District Court. Personal checks accepted. Mail requests: SASE required. Mail turnaround time within 3 days.

Atchison County

District Court PO Box 408, Atchison, KS 66002; 913-367-7400; Fax: 913-367-1171. Hours: 8AM-5PM (CST). *Felony, Misdemeanor, Civil, Eviction, Small Claims, Probate.*
Civil Records: Access: Fax, mail, in person. Both court and visitors may perform in person searches.

Search fee: $12.00 per hour. Required to search: name, years to search. Civil cases indexed by defendant, plaintiff. Civil records on computer from 1991, index books from 1900s, archives from 1860s.
Criminal Records: Access: In person only. Visitors must perform in person searches for themselves. No search fee. Required to search: name, years to search; also helpful: SSN. Criminal records on computer from 1991, index books from 1900s, archives from 1860s.
General Information: Public Access terminal is available. No juvenile, mental health, sealed or expunged records released. Will fax results for $1.25 per page. Copy fee: $.25 per page. Cert fee: $1.00. Payee: District Court. Personal checks accepted. Prepayment required. Mail requests: SASE required. Mail turnaround time 1-5 days.

Barber County

District Court 118 E Washington, Medicine Lodge, KS 67104; 620-886-5639; Fax: 620-886-5854. Hours: 8AM-Noon,1-5PM (CST). *Felony, Misdemeanor, Civil, Eviction, Small Claims, Probate.*
Civil Records: Access: In person only. Visitors must perform in person searches for themselves. No search fee. Required to search: name, years to search. Civil cases indexed by defendant, plaintiff. Civil records on computer from 1990, microfiche from 1900-1976, index cards from 1800s.
Criminal Records: Access: In person only. Visitors must perform in person searches for themselves. No search fee. Required to search: name, years to search, SSN; also helpful: DOB. Criminal records on computer from 1990, microfiche from 1900-1976, index cards from 1800s.
General Information: Public Access terminal is available. No juvenile, mental health, sealed or expunged records released. Copy fee: $.25 per page. Cert fee: $1.00. Payee: District Court. Personal checks accepted. Prepayment required.

Barton County

District Court 1400 Main, Rm 306, Great Bend, KS 67530; 620-793-1856; Fax: 620-793-1860. Hours: 8AM-5PM (CST). *Felony, Misdemeanor, Civil, Eviction, Small Claims, Probate.*
Civil Records: Access: Fax, mail, in person. Both court and visitors may perform in person searches. Search fee: $12.00 per hour. Required to search: name, years to search. Civil cases indexed by defendant, plaintiff. Civil records on computer 1990, microfiche and archives from 1800s, index from 1987.
Criminal Records: Access: Fax, mail, in person. Both court and visitors may perform in person searches. Search fee: $12.00 per hour. Required to search: name, years to search. Criminal records on computer 1990, microfiche and archives from 1800s, index from 1987. Court prefers that screening firm and employment-related searches be performed through the state criminal record agency.
General Information: Public Access terminal is available. No juvenile, mental health, sealed or expunged records released. No fee to fax results. Copy fee: $.35 per page; $.50 for microfilm copies. No cert fee. Payee: Clerk of Court. Personal checks accepted. Prepayment required. Mail requests: SASE required. Mail turnaround time 3 days.

Bourbon County

District Court PO Box 868, Ft Scott, KS 66701; 620-223-0780; Fax: 620-223-5303. Hours: 8:30AM-4:30PM (CST). *Felony, Misdemeanor, Civil, Eviction, Small Claims, Probate.*
Civil Records: Access: In person only. Visitors must perform in person searches for themselves. No search fee. Required to search: name, years to search. Civil

cases indexed by defendant, plaintiff. Civil records on computer since 1990, index on computer since 1985.
Criminal Records: Access: In person only. Visitors must perform in person searches for themselves. No search fee. Required to search: name, years to search; also helpful: SSN. Criminal records on computer since 1990, index on computer since 1985.
General Information: Public Access terminal is available. No juvenile, mental health, sealed or expunged records released. Copy fee: $.25 per page. Cert fee: $1.00. Payee: Clerk of Court. Personal checks accepted. Prepayment required.

Brown County

District Court PO Box 417, Hiawatha, KS 66434; 785-742-7481; Fax: 785-742-3506. Hours: 8AM-5PM (CST). *Felony, Misdemeanor, Civil, Eviction, Small Claims, Probate.*
Civil Records: Access: Phone, fax, mail, in person. Both court and visitors may perform in person searches. Search fee: $12.00 per hour. Required to search: name, years to search. Civil cases indexed by defendant, plaintiff. Civil records on computer from 1982, microfiche from 1900s, index books prior.
Criminal Records: Access: Phone, fax, mail, in person. Both court and visitors may perform in person searches. Search fee: $12.00 per hour. Required to search: name, years to search; also helpful: SSN. Criminal records on computer from 1982, microfiche and index books from 1900s.
General Information: Public Access terminal is available. No juvenile, mental health, sealed or expunged records released. Fee to fax results is $1.00 per page. Copy fee: $.50 for first page, $.25 each add'l. Cert fee: $1.00. Payee: District Court. Personal checks accepted. Prepayment required. Mail requests: SASE required. Mail turnaround time 1-2 days.

Butler County

District Court 201 W Pine, #101, El Dorado, KS 67042; 316-322-4370; Fax: 316-321-9486. Hours: 8AM-5PM (CST). *Felony, Misdemeanor, Civil, Eviction, Small Claims, Probate.*
Civil Records: Access: In person only. Visitors must perform in person searches for themselves. No search fee. Required to search: name, years to search. Civil cases indexed by defendant, plaintiff. Civil records on computer from 1992, index cards from 1800s.
Criminal Records: Access: In person, fax. Visitors must perform in person searches for themselves. Search fee: $12.00 per hour. Required to search: name, years to search, SSN. Criminal records on computer from 1992, index cards from 1800s.
General Information: Public Access terminal is available. No juvenile, mental health, sealed or expunged records released. Will fax results to local or toll free line. Copy fee: $.50 per page. Cert fee: $1.00. Payee: Clerk of District Court. Personal checks accepted. Prepayment required.

Chase County

District Court PO Box 529, Cottonwood Falls, KS 66845; 620-273-6319; Fax: 620-273-6890. Hours: 8AM-5PM (CST). *Felony, Misdemeanor, Civil, Eviction, Small Claims, Probate.*
Civil Records: Access: In person only. Visitors must perform in person searches for themselves. No search fee. Required to search: name, years to search. Civil cases indexed by defendant, plaintiff. Civil records on computer from late 1990, microfiche from 1860, index books from 1860; visitors may search the printed index desk copy.
Criminal Records: Access: In person only. Visitors must perform in person searches for themselves. No search fee. Required to search: name, years to search. Criminal records on computer from late 1990,

microfiche from 1860, index books from 1860; visitors may search the printed index desk copy.
General Information: No juvenile, mental health, sealed or expunged records released. Copy fee: $.50 per page. Cert fee: $2.00. Payee: District Court. Personal checks accepted. Prepayment required.

Chautauqua County

District Court 215 N Chautauqua, PO Box 306, Sedan, KS 67361; 620-725-5870; Fax: 620-725-3027. 8:30AM-4:30PM (CST). *Felony, Misdemeanor, Civil, Eviction, Small Claims, Probate.*
www.14thjudicialdistrict-ks.org
Civil Records: Access: Mail, in person. Both court and visitors may perform in person searches. Search fee: $12.00 per hour. Required to search: name, years to search. Civil cases indexed by defendant, plaintiff. Civil records on computer from 1990, archives from 1950, index cards from 1870.
Criminal Records: Access: Mail, in person. Both court and visitors may perform in person searches. Search fee: $12.00 per hour. Required to search: name, years to search; also helpful: DOB. Criminal records on computer from 1990, archives from 1950, index cards from 1870.
General Information: Public Access terminal is available. No juvenile, mental health, sealed or expunged records released. Will fax results. Copy fee: $.25 per page. Cert fee: $1.00. Payee: District Court. Personal checks accepted. Mail requests: SASE required. Mail turnaround time 1-2 weeks.

Cherokee County

District Court PO Box 189, Columbus, KS 66725; 620-429-3880; Fax: 620-429-1130. Hours: 8AM-5PM (CST). *Felony, Misdemeanor, Civil, Eviction, Small Claims, Probate.*
Civil Records: Access: Mail, fax, in person. Visitors must perform in person searches for themselves. Search fee: $12.00 per hour. Required to search: name, years to search. Civil cases indexed by defendant, plaintiff. Civil records on computer back 14 years, index books from 1867.
Criminal Records: Access: Mail, fax, in person. Visitors must perform in person searches for themselves. Search fee: $12.00 per hour. Required to search: name, years to search; also helpful: SSN. Criminal records on computer back 14 years, index books from 1867.
General Information: Public Access terminal is available. No juvenile, mental health, sealed or expunged records released. Will not fax results. Copy fee: $.25/page. Cert fee: $1.00. Payee: District Court. Personal checks accepted. Prepayment required. Mail turnaround time is 3 days.

Cheyenne County

District Court PO Box 646, St Francis, KS 67756; 785-332-8850; Fax: 785-332-8851. Hours: 8AM-Noon,1-5PM (CST). *Felony, Misdemeanor, Civil, Eviction, Small Claims, Probate.*
Civil Records: Access: Fax, mail, in person. Both court and visitors may perform in person searches. No search fee. Required to search: name, years to search. Civil cases indexed by defendant, plaintiff. Civil records on strip index from 1989, index cards from 1870.
Criminal Records: Access: Fax, mail, in person. Both court and visitors may perform in person searches. No search fee. Required to search: name, years to search. Criminal records on strip index from 1989, index cards from 1870.
General Information: No juvenile, adoptions, mental health, sealed or expunged records released. Will fax results $1.00 per page unless toll free line used. Copy fee: $.25 per page. Cert fee: $1.00. Payee: Clerk of Court. Personal checks accepted. Prepayment

required. Mail requests: SASE not required. Mail turnaround time 2 days.

Clark County

District Court PO Box 790, Ashland, KS 67831; 620-635-2753; Fax: 620-635-2155. Hours: 8AM-5PM (CST). *Felony, Misdemeanor, Civil, Eviction, Small Claims, Probate.*

www.kscourts.org/dstcts/16dstct.htm

Civil Records: Access: Mail, fax, in person. Both court and visitors may perform in person searches. Search fee: $12.00 per hour. Required to search: name, years to search. Civil cases indexed by defendant, plaintiff. Civil records on computer from 1992 (Child support only), microfiche and archives from 1800s, index cards from 1800s.

Criminal Records: Access: Mail, fax, in person. Both court and visitors may perform in person searches. Search fee: $12.00 per hour (may be no fee if short and a name search). Required to search: name, years to search; also helpful: SSN. Criminal records on index cards.

General Information: No juvenile, mental health, sealed or expunged records released. Will fax results. Copy fee: $.25 per page. Cert fee: $1.00. Payee: District Court. Personal checks accepted. Prepayment required. Mail requests: SASE required. Mail turnaround time 1 day.

Clay County

District Court PO Box 203, Clay Center, KS 67432; 785-632-3443; Fax: 785-632-2651. Hours: 8AM-5PM (CST). *Felony, Misdemeanor, Civil, Eviction, Small Claims, Probate.*

www.co.riley.ks.us/districtcourt

Civil Records: Access: Mail, in person. Visitors must perform in person searches for themselves. Search fee: $12.00 per hour. Required to search: name, years to search. Civil cases indexed by defendant, plaintiff. Civil records on computer from July, 1994, index books from late 1800s.

Criminal Records: Access: Mail, in person. Visitors must perform in person searches for themselves. Search fee: $12.00 per hour. Required to search: name. Criminal records on computer from July, 1994, index books from late 1800s.

General Information: Public Access terminal is available. No juvenile, adoption, mental health, sealed or expunged records released. Will fax results for $2.00 per page. Copy fee: $.25 per page. Cert fee: $1.00. Payee: Clerk of District Court. Personal checks accepted. Prepayment required. Mail requests: SASE required. Mail turnaround time 2 days.

Cloud County

District Court 811 Washington, Concordia, KS 66901; 785-243-8124; Fax: 785-243-8188. Hours: 8:00AM-5PM (CST). *Felony, Misdemeanor, Civil, Eviction, Small Claims, Probate.*

www.kscourts.org/dstcts/12dstct.htm

Civil Records: Access: Phone, fax, mail, in person. Visitors must perform in person searches for themselves. Search fee: $12.00 per hour. Required to search: name, years to search. Civil cases indexed by defendant, plaintiff. Civil records in print indexes from 1992, index books prior to 1992.

Criminal Records: Access: Fax, mail, in person. Both court and visitors may perform in person searches. Search fee: $12.00 per hour. Required to search: name, years to search; also helpful: SSN. Criminal records in print indexes from 1992, index books prior to 1992.

General Information: Public Access terminal is available. No juvenile, mental health, sealed or expunged records released. Will fax results $2.00 per page. Copy fee: $.25 per page. Cert fee: $1.00. Payee:

Clerk of Court. Personal checks accepted. Prepayment required. Mail requests: SASE required. Mail turnaround time 3-4 days.

Coffey County

District Court PO Box 330, Burlington, KS 66839; 620-364-8628; Fax: 620-364-8535. Hours: 8AM-4PM (CST). *Felony, Misdemeanor, Civil, Eviction, Small Claims, Probate.*

www.kscourts.org/dstct/4dstct.htm

Civil Records: Access: Mail, fax, in person, email, online. Both court and visitors may perform in person searches. Search fee: $12.00 per hour. Required to search: name, years to search. Civil cases indexed by defendant, plaintiff. Civil records on computer back to 1800s. Current court calendars are free online at www.franklincoks.org/4thdistrict/coffeybydate.html. Probate and marriage records are accessible at this website. Also, access to probate court records is free at www.kscourts.org/dstcts/4coprrec.htm.

Criminal Records: Access: Mail, fax, in person, email. Both court and visitors may perform in person searches. Search fee: $12.00 per hour. Required to search: name, years to search, DOB. Criminal records on computer back to 1800s. Online access to criminal court calendar is the same as civil, but records or index are not online.

General Information: Public Access terminal is available. No juvenile, mental health, sealed or expunged records released. Fee to fax results is $2.00 1st page; $.50 each add'l. Copy fee: $.25 per page. Cert fee: $1.00. Payee: Clerk of District Court. Personal checks accepted. Prepayment required. Mail requests: SASE required. Mail turnaround time 3 days.

Comanche County

District Court PO Box 722, Coldwater, KS 67029; 620-582-2182; Fax: 620-582-2603. Hours: 8AM-5PM (CST). *Felony, Misdemeanor, Civil, Eviction, Small Claims, Probate.*

www.kscourts.org/dstcts/16dstct.htm

Civil Records: Access: In person only. Both court and visitors may perform in person searches. No search fee. Required to search: name, years to search. Civil cases indexed by defendant, plaintiff. Civil records on computer since 1992 (child support only), index cards from 1886.

Criminal Records: Access: In person only. Both court and visitors may perform in person searches. No search fee. Required to search: name, years to search; also helpful: SSN. Criminal records on index cards from 1886.

General Information: Public Access terminal is available. No juvenile, mental health, sealed or expunged records released. Copy fee: $.25 per page. Cert fee: $1.00. Payee: District Court. Personal checks accepted. Prepayment required.

Cowley County

Arkansas City District Court PO Box 1152, Arkansas City, KS 67005; 620-441-4520; Fax: 620-442-7213. Hours: 8AM-Noon,1-4PM (CST). *Felony, Misdemeanor, Civil, Eviction, Small Claims, Probate.*

Note: This court covers the southern part of the county. All felony records are kept at Winfield.

Civil Records: Access: Mail, in person. Both court and visitors may perform in person searches. Search fee: $12.00 per hour. Required to search: name, years to search. Civil cases indexed by defendant, plaintiff. Civil records from 1977. This Court facility has only been in existence since 1977, so no records prior to that date, index cards only. Computer records commencing 1994.

Criminal Records: Access: Mail, in person. Both court and visitors may perform in person searches. Search fee: $12.00. Required to search: name, years to search, SSN. Criminal records from 1977. This Court facility has only been in existence since 1977, so no records prior to that date. Computer records commencing 1994.

General Information: Public Access terminal is available. No juvenile, mental health, sealed or expunged records released. Copy fee: $.50 per page. Cert fee: $1.00. Payee: Clerk of Court. Personal checks accepted. Prepayment required. Mail requests: SASE helpful. Turnaround time 1 week.

Winfield District Court PO Box 472, Winfield, KS 67156; 620-221-5470; Fax: 620-221-1097. Hours: 8AM-Noon,1-4PM (CST). *Felony, Misdemeanor, Civil, Eviction, Small Claims, Probate.*

Note: This court covers northern part of county.

Civil Records: Access: Fax, mail, in person. Both court and visitors may perform in person searches. Search fee: $12.00 per hour. Required to search: name, years to search. Civil cases indexed by defendant, plaintiff. Civil records on computer since 1994, index cards from 1874.

Criminal Records: Access: Fax, mail, in person. Both court and visitors may perform in person searches. Search fee: $12.00 per hour. Required to search: name, years to search. Criminal records on computer since 1994, index cards from 1874.

General Information: Public Access terminal is available. No juvenile, mental health, sealed or expunged records released. Copy fee: $.50 per page. Cert fee: $1.00. Payee: Clerk of Court. Personal checks accepted. Prepayment required. Mail requests: SASE not required. Mail turnaround time 1 week.

Crawford County

Girard District Court PO Box 69, Girard, KS 66743; 620-724-6211; Fax: 620-724-4987. 8AM-5PM (CST). *Felony, Misdemeanor, Civil, Probate.*

Note: Records on computer are maintained here for the Pittsburg District Court as well since 8/92. For prior cases, search both courts separately.

Civil Records: Access: Fax, mail, in person. Both court and visitors may perform in person searches. Search fee: $12.00 per hour. Required to search: name, years to search. Civil cases indexed by defendant, plaintiff. Civil records on computer since August, 1992, microfiche from 1977, index cards from 1977.

Criminal Records: Access: Phone, fax, in person. Both court and visitors may perform in person searches. Search fee: $12.00 per hour. Required to search: name, years to search. Criminal records on computer since August, 1992, microfiche from 1977, index cards from 1977. Employment/work-related mail inquires are referred to the Kansas Bureau of Investigation.

General Information: Public Access terminal is available. No juvenile, mental health, sealed or expunged records released. Will fax results $2.50 per page. Copy fee: $.25 per page. Cert fee: $1.00. Payee: Clerk of Court. Personal checks accepted. Prepayment required. Mail requests: SASE required. Mail turnaround time 3 days.

Pittsburg District Court 602 N Locust, Pittsburg, KS 66762; 620-231-0391; Fax: 620-231-0316. Hours: 8AM-5PM (CST). *Misdemeanor, Civil, Eviction, Small Claims, Probate.*

Note: Records back to 8/92 can be searched at Girard District Court as well; Girard and Pittsburg share a computer system. For cases prior to 8/92, search both courts separately.

Civil Records: Access: Fax, mail, in person. Both court and visitors may perform in person searches.

Search fee: $12.00 per hour. Required to search: name, years to search. Civil cases indexed by defendant, plaintiff. Civil records on computer since August, 1992, microfiche from 1977, index cards from 1977.

Criminal Records: Access: In person, mail. Both court and visitors may perform in person searches. Search fee: $12.00 per hour. Required to search: name, years to search. Criminal records on computer since August, 1992, microfiche from 1977, index cards from 1977. Employment/work-related mail inquires are referred to the Kansas Bureau of Investigation. Mail requests must be on courts form, call court for form and they will fax it to you.

General Information: Public Access terminal is available. No juvenile, mental health, sealed or expunged records released. Will fax results $2.50 per page. Copy fee: $.25 per page. Cert fee: $1.00. Payee: Clerk of Court. Personal checks accepted. Prepayment required. Mail requests: SASE required. Mail turnaround time 3 days.

Decatur County

District Court PO Box 89, Oberlin, KS 67749; 785-475-8107; Fax: 785-475-8170. Hours: 8AM-5PM (CST). *Felony, Misdemeanor, Civil, Eviction, Small Claims, Probate.*

Civil Records: Access: In person only. Visitors must perform in person searches for themselves. No search fee. Required to search: name, years to search. Civil cases indexed by defendant, plaintiff. Civil records on index books from 1870.

Criminal Records: Access: In person only. Visitors must perform in person searches for themselves. No search fee. Required to search: name, years to search. Criminal records on index books from 1870.

General Information: Public Access terminal is available. No adoption, juvenile, mental health, sealed or expunged records released. Copy fee: $.25 per page. Cert fee: $1.00. Payee: Clerk of District Court. Prepayment required.

Dickinson County

District Court PO Box 127, Abilene, KS 67410; 785-263-3142; Fax: 785-263-4407. Hours: 9AM-5PM (CST). *Felony, Misdemeanor, Civil, Eviction, Small Claims, Probate.*

Civil Records: Access: Mail, fax, in person, email. Both court and visitors may perform in person searches. Search fee: $12.00 per hour. Required to search: name, years to search. Civil cases indexed by defendant, plaintiff. Civil records on computer since 7/92, on index books prior.

Criminal Records: Access: Mail, fax, in person, email. Both court and visitors may perform in person searches. Search fee: $12.00 per hour. Required to search: name, years to search; also helpful: SSN. Criminal records on computer since 7/92, on index books prior.

General Information: Public Access terminal is available. No juvenile, mental health, sealed or expunged records released. Will fax results for $1.00 per page. Copy fee: $1.00. Fee for first 4 pages. Add $.25 per page thereafter. Cert fee: $1.00. Payee: Clerk of District Court. Personal checks accepted. Prepayment required. Mail requests: SASE required. Mail turnaround time 1 week.

Doniphan County

District Court PO Box 295, Troy, KS 66087; 785-985-3582; Fax: 785-985-2402. Hours: 8AM-5PM (CST). *Felony, Misdemeanor, Civil, Eviction, Small Claims, Probate.*

Civil Records: Access: Phone, fax, mail, in person. Both court and visitors may perform in person searches. Search fee: $12.00 per hour. Required to search: name, years to search. Civil cases indexed by

defendant, plaintiff. Civil records on computer since 1992; index cards from 1856.

Criminal Records: Access: Phone, fax, mail, in person. Only the court performs in person searches; visitors may not. Search fee: $12.00 per hour. Required to search: name, years to search; also helpful: address, DOB. Criminal records on computer since 1992; index cards from 1852.

General Information: Public Access terminal is available. No juvenile, mental health, sealed or expunged records released. Fee to fax results is $2.00 per page. Copy fee: $.50 for first page, $.25 each add'l. Cert fee: $1.00. Payee: Clerk of Court. Personal checks accepted. Prepayment required. Mail requests: SASE required. Mail turnaround time 1-2 days.

Douglas County

District Court 111 E 11th St, Rm 144, Lawrence, KS 66044-2966; 785-832-5256; Fax: 785-832-5174. Hours: 8AM-4PM (CST). *Felony, Misdemeanor, Civil, Eviction, Small Claims, Probate.* www.douglas-county.com/District_Court/dc.asp

Civil Records: Access: Phone, fax, mail, in person, online. Both court and visitors may perform in person searches. Search fee: $12.00 per hour. Required to search: name, years to search. Civil cases indexed by defendant, plaintiff. Civil records on index cards from 1863, archived from 1865 on film, indexed on computer since 1989. Online access via Internet to district court records is $180.00 annual fee and $60.00 set-up fee. For further information and registration, contact Beverly at 785-832-5299. All written requests must include a phone number.

Criminal Records: Access: Phone, fax, mail, in person, online. Both court and visitors may perform in person searches. Search fee: $12.00 per hour. Required to search: name, years to search; also helpful: DOB, SSN. Criminal records on computer from 1989, index cards 1860, archived from 1865. Online access to criminal records is the same as civil. All other background check requests must be in writing.

General Information: Public Access terminal is available. No juvenile, mental health, sealed or expunged records released. Will fax results for $2.00 per document. Copy fee: $.25 per page. Cert fee: $1.00. Authentications are $2.00 each. Payee: Clerk of Court. Personal checks accepted. Prepayment required. Mail requests: SASE not required. Mail turnaround time 3 days.

Edwards County

District Court PO Box 232, Kinsley, KS 67547; 620-659-2442; Fax: 620-659-2998. Hours: 8AM-5PM (CST). *Felony, Misdemeanor, Civil, Eviction, Small Claims, Probate.* www.kscourts.org/dstcts/24dstct.htm

Civil Records: Access: Mail, in person. Both court and visitors may perform in person searches. Search fee: $12.00 per hour. Required to search: name, years to search. Civil cases indexed by defendant, plaintiff. Civil records on index books from 1800s.

Criminal Records: Access: In person only. Visitors must perform in person searches for themselves. No search fee. Required to search: name, years to search. Criminal records on index books from 1800s.

General Information: Public Access terminal is available. No juvenile, adoption, mental health, sealed or expunged records released. Will fax results to local or toll free line. Copy fee: $.25 per page. Cert fee: $1.00. Payee: Clerk District Court. Personal checks accepted. Prepayment required. Mail requests: SASE required. Mail turnaround time 1-2 days.

Elk County

District Court PO Box 306, Howard, KS 67349; 620-374-2370; Fax: 620-374-3531. Hours: 8AM-4:30PM (CST). *Felony, Misdemeanor, Civil, Eviction, Small Claims, Probate.*

Civil Records: Access: Mail, in person. Both court and visitors may perform in person searches. Search fee: Depending on difficulty, clerk may charge $12 per hr search fee. Required to search: name, years to search. Civil cases indexed by defendant, plaintiff. Civil records on index books from 1907.

Criminal Records: Access: Mail, in person. Both court and visitors may perform in person searches. Search fee: Depending on difficulty, clerk may charge $12 per hr search fee. Required to search: name, years to search. Criminal records on index books from 1907; on comptuer back to 1984.

General Information: Public Access terminal is available. No juvenile, mental health, sealed or expunged records released. Fee to fax results is $2 plus $.50 per page. Copy fee: $.50 per page. Cert fee: $1.00. Payee: Clerk of District Court. Personal checks accepted. Prepayment required. Mail turnaround time 1-2 days.

Ellis County

District Court PO Box 8, Hays, KS 67601; 785-628-9415; Fax: 785-628-8415. Hours: 8AM-5PM (CST). *Felony, Misdemeanor, Civil, Eviction, Small Claims, Probate.* www.23rdjudicial.org

Civil Records: Access: Mail, in person. Both court and visitors may perform in person searches. Search fee: $12.00 per hour. Required to search: name, years to search. Civil cases indexed by defendant, plaintiff. Civil records on computer from 1991, microfiche from 1900s, index cards from 1800s, archives from 1800s.

Criminal Records: Access: In person only. Visitors must perform in person searches for themselves. No search fee. Required to search: name, years to search. Criminal records on computer from 1991, microfiche from 1900s, index cards from 1800s, archives from 1800s.

General Information: Public Access terminal is available. No juvenile, mental health, sealed or expunged records released. Copy fee: $.25 per page. Cert fee: $1.00. Payee: Clerk of Court. Personal checks accepted. Prepayment required. Mail requests: SASE required. Mail turnaround time 7 days.

Ellsworth County

District Court 210 N Kansas, Ellsworth, KS 67439-3118; 785-472-3832; Fax: 785-472-5712. Hours: 8AM-5PM (CST). *Felony, Misdemeanor, Civil, Eviction, Small Claims, Probate.*

Civil Records: Access: Phone, fax, mail, in person. Both court and visitors may perform in person searches. No search fee. Required to search: name, years to search. Civil cases indexed by defendant, plaintiff. Civil records on computer from 1994, microfiche from 1900s, books from late 1800s.

Criminal Records: Access: Phone, fax, mail, in person. Both court and visitors may perform in person searches. No search fee. Required to search: name, years to search; also helpful: SSN. Criminal records on computer from 1994, microfiche from 1900s, books from late 1800s.

General Information: No juvenile, mental health, sealed or expunged records released. Will fax results $.50 per page. Copy fee: $.35 per page. No cert fee. Payee: District Court. Personal checks accepted. Prepayment required. Mail requests: SASE required. Mail turnaround time 1-2 days.

Finney County

District Court PO Box 798, Garden City, KS 67846; Civil phone: 620-271-6121; Criminal phone: 620-271-6132; Fax; 620-271-6140. Hours: 8AM-4:30PM (CST). *Felony, Misdemeanor, Civil, Eviction, Small Claims, Probate.*

Civil Records: Access: In person only. Visitors must perform in person searches for themselves. No search fee. Required to search: name, years to search. Civil cases indexed by defendant, plaintiff. Civil records on computer from 1991, microfiche from 1900s, index books from 1900s.

Criminal Records: Access: In person only. Visitors must perform in person searches for themselves. No search fee. Required to search: name, years to search. Criminal records on computer from 1991, microfiche from 1900s, index books from 1900s.

General Information: Public Access terminal is available. No juvenile, Mental health, sealed or expunged records released. Copy fee: $.25 per page, $1.00 minimum. Cert fee: $1.00. Payee: District Court. Personal checks accepted. Prepayment required.

Ford County

District Court 101 W Spruce, Dodge City, KS 67801; 620-227-4609; Civil phone: 620-227-4610; Criminal phone: 620-227-4608; Fax: 620-227-6799. Hours: 8AM-5PM (CST). *Felony, Misdemeanor, Civil, Eviction, Small Claims, Probate.*
www.kscourts.org/dstcts/16dstct.htm

Civil Records: Access: Fax, mail, in person. Both court and visitors may perform in person searches. Search fee: $12.00 per hour. Required to search: name, years to search. Civil cases indexed by defendant, plaintiff. Civil records on computer back to 10/1991, microfiche/film from 1900s, index books from 1900s.

Criminal Records: Access: Fax, mail, in person. Both court and visitors may perform in person searches. Search fee: $12 per hour. Required to search: name, years to search, DOB; also helpful: SSN. Criminal records on computer back to 10/1991, microfiche/film from 1900s, index books from 1900s.

General Information: Public Access terminal is available. No juvenile, mental health, sealed or expunged records released. Fee to fax results is $1.00 per page. Copy fee: $.25 per page. Cert fee: $1.00. Payee: Clerk of District Court. Personal checks accepted. Prepayment required. Mail requests: SASE required. Mail turnaround time 3 days.

Franklin County

District Court PO Box 637 (301 S Main), Ottawa, KS 66067; 785-242-6000; Fax: 785-242-5970. Hours: 8AM-12, 1PM-4PM (CST). *Felony, Misdemeanor, Civil, Eviction, Small Claims, Probate.*
www.kscourts.org/dstcts/4dstct.htm

Civil Records: Access: Mail, fax, in person, online. Both court and visitors may perform in person searches. Search fee: $12.00 per hour. Required to search: name, years to search. Civil cases indexed by defendant, plaintiff. Civil records on computer back to 1979, index books from 1800s. Current court calendars are free online at www.franklincoks.org/4thdistrict/franklinbydate.html. Also, access to probate court records is free at www.kscourts.org/dstcts/4frprrec.htm.

Criminal Records: Access: In person, online. Visitors must perform in person searches for themselves. No search fee. Required to search: name, years to search, SSN. Criminal records on computer back to 1980, index books from 1800s. Online access to criminal calendars is the same as civil.

General Information: Public Access terminal is available. No juvenile, mental health, sealed or expunged records released. Will fax results to local or toll free line. Copy fee: $.25 per page. Cert fee: $1.00. Payee: Clerk of District Court. Personal checks accepted. Prepayment required. Mail requests: SASE required. Mail turnaround time 3-5 days.

Geary County

District Court PO Box 1147, Junction City, KS 66441; 785-762-5221; Fax: 785-762-4420. Hours: 8AM-5PM (CST). *Felony, Misdemeanor, Civil, Eviction, Small Claims, Probate.*

Civil Records: Access: Mail, in person, email. Both court and visitors may perform in person searches. Search fee: $12.00 per hour. Required to search: name, years to search. Civil cases indexed by defendant, plaintiff. Civil records on computer from 1992, microfiche, index books and archives from 1894.

Criminal Records: Access: Mail, in person, email. Both court and visitors may perform in person searches. Search fee: $12.00 per hour. Required to search: name, years to search; also helpful: SSN. Criminal records on computer from 1992, microfiche, index books and archives from 1894.

General Information: Public Access terminal is available. No juvenile, adoption, mental health, sealed or expunged records released. Fee to fax results is $2.00 per page. Copy fee: $.25 per page. Cert fee: $1.00. Payee: Clerk of Court. Personal checks accepted. Prepayment required. Mail requests: SASE not required. Mail turnaround time 3 days.

Gove County

District Court PO Box 97, Gove, KS 67736; 785-938-2310; Fax: 785-938-2312. Hours: 8AM-Noon, 1-5PM (CST). *Felony, Misdemeanor, Civil, Eviction, Small Claims, Probate.*

Civil Records: Access: Fax, mail, in person. Both court and visitors may perform in person searches. Search fee: $9.00 per hour. Required to search: name, years to search. Civil cases indexed by defendant, plaintiff. Civil records on computer from 1992, index books from 1890 through present.

Criminal Records: Access: Fax, mail, in person. Both court and visitors may perform in person searches. Search fee: $9.00 per hour. Required to search: name, years to search. Criminal records on computer from 1992, index books also.

General Information: No juvenile, mental health, sealed or expunged records released. Fee to fax results is $1.00 per page. Copy fee: $.25 per page. Cert fee: $1.00. Payee: Clerk of District Court. Personal checks accepted. Prepayment required. Mail requests: SASE required. Mail turnaround time 1-2 days.

Graham County

District Court 410 N Pomeroy, Hill City, KS 67642; 785-421-3458; Fax: 785-421-5463. Hours: 8AM-5PM (CST). *Felony, Misdemeanor, Civil, Eviction, Small Claims, Probate.*

Civil Records: Access: In person. Visitors must perform in person searches for themselves. No search fee. Civil cases indexed by defendant, plaintiff. Civil records on index books from 1880s; computerized records go back to 2000.

Criminal Records: Access: Mail, in person. Visitors must perform in person searches for themselves. Search fee: $12.00 per hour. Required to search: name, years to search, DOB; also helpful: SSN, signed release. Criminal records on index books from 1880s; computerized records go back to 2000.

General Information: No juvenile, mental health, sealed or expunged records released. Will fax results to local or toll free line. Copy fee: $.25 per page. Cert fee: $1.00. Payee: Clerk of District Court. Personal checks accepted. Prepayment required.

Grant County

District Court 108 S Glenn, Ulysses, KS 67880; 620-356-1526; Fax: 620-353-2131. Hours: 8:30AM-5PM (CST). *Felony, Misdemeanor, Civil, Eviction, Small Claims, Probate.*

Civil Records: Access: In person, mail. Visitors must perform in person searches for themselves. Search fee: $12.80 per hour. Required to search: name, years to search. Civil cases indexed by defendant, plaintiff. Civil records on computer from 1977, microfiche index from 1880s.

Criminal Records: Access: In person, mail. Visitors must perform in person searches for themselves. Search fee: $12.80 per hour. Required to search: name, years to search. Criminal records on computer from 1977, microfiche index from 1880s. The court refers all searchers to the state Bureau of investigations, including in-person searchers.

General Information: Public Access terminal is available. No juvenile, mental health, sealed or expunged records released. Will not fax results. Copy fee: $.50 per page. Cert fee: $1.00. Payee: District Court. Personal checks accepted. Prepayment required. Mail requests: SASE required. Mail turnaround time same day.

Gray County

District Court PO Box 487, Cimarron, KS 67835; 620-855-3812; Fax: 620-855-7037. Hours: 8AM-5PM (CST). *Felony, Misdemeanor, Civil, Eviction, Small Claims, Probate.*
www.kscourts.org/dstcts/16dstct.htm

Civil Records: Access: Fax, mail, in person. Visitors must perform in person searches for themselves. Search fee: $12.00 per hour. Required to search: name; also helpful: years to search. Civil cases indexed by defendant, plaintiff. Civil records on computer from 1990, index books from 1800s. Fax requests must be pre-paid.

Criminal Records: Access: Fax, mail, in person. Visitors must perform in person searches for themselves. Search fee: $12.00 per hour. Required to search: name, years to search; also helpful: address, DOB. Criminal records on computer from 1990, index books from 1800s. Fax requests must be pre-paid.

General Information: Public Access terminal is available. No juvenile, mental health, sealed or expunged records released. Will fax results for $1.00 per page. Copy fee: $.50 per page. Cert fee: $1.00. Payee: Clerk of District Court. Personal checks accepted. Prepayment required.

Greeley County

District Court PO Box 516, Tribune, KS 67879; 620-376-4292. Hours: 8AM-Noon, 1-5PM (MST). *Felony, Misdemeanor, Civil, Eviction, Small Claims, Probate.*

Civil Records: Access: Mail, in person. Both court and visitors may perform in person searches. No search fee. Required to search: name, years to search. Civil cases indexed by defendant, plaintiff. Civil records on hardcopy index from beginning.

Criminal Records: Access: Mail, in person. Both court and visitors may perform in person searches. No search fee. Required to search: name, years to search; also helpful: SSN. Criminal records on hardcopy index from beginning.

General Information: Public Access terminal is available. No juvenile, mental health, sealed or expunged records released. Will fax results for $1.00 per page. Copy fee: $.50 per page. Cert fee: $1.00. Payee: Clerk of the District Court. Personal checks accepted. Prepayment required. Mail turnaround time is 3 days.

Greenwood County

District Court 311 N Main, Eureka, KS 67045; 620-583-8153; Fax: 620-583-6818. Hours: 8AM-5PM (CST). *Felony, Misdemeanor, Civil, Eviction, Small Claims, Probate.*

Civil Records: Access: Mail, in person. Both court and visitors may perform in person searches. Search fee: $12.00 per hour if search is conducted by court personnel. Required to search: name, years to search. Civil cases indexed by defendant, plaintiff. Civil records on computer from 1993, index cards from 1800s.

Criminal Records: Access: Mail, in person. Both court and visitors may perform in person searches. Search fee: $12.00 per hour if search is performed by court personnel. Required to search: name, years to search. Criminal records on computer from 1993, index cards from 1800s.

General Information: Public Access terminal is available. No juvenile, mental health, sealed or expunged records released, Will fax results to local or toll free line. Copy fee: $.50 per page. Cert fee: $1.00. Payee: Clerk of Court. Personal checks accepted. Prepayment required. Mail requests: SASE required. Mail turnaround time 1-2 days.

Hamilton County

District Court PO Box 745, Syracuse, KS 67878; 620-384-5159; Fax: 620-384-7806. Hours: 8AM-5PM (MST). *Felony, Misdemeanor, Civil, Eviction, Small Claims, Probate.*

Civil Records: Access: In person only. Visitors must perform in person searches for themselves. No search fee. Required to search: name, years to search. Civil cases indexed by defendant, plaintiff. Civil records on computer from 1985, microfiche, archives and index cards from 1880s.

Criminal Records: Access: In person only. Visitors must perform in person searches for themselves. No search fee. Required to search: name, years to search. Criminal records on computer from 1985, microfiche, archives and index cards from 1880s.

General Information: Public Access terminal is available. No juvenile, mental health, sealed or expunged records released. Copy fee: $.25 per page. Cert fee: $1.00. Payee: Clerk of District Court. Personal checks accepted. Prepayment required.

Harper County

District Court PO Box 467, Anthony, KS 67003; 620-842-3721; Fax: 620-842-6025. Hours: 8AM-Noon, 1-5PM (CST). *Felony, Misdemeanor, Civil, Eviction, Small Claims, Probate.*

Civil Records: Access: Fax, mail, in person. Both court and visitors may perform in person searches. Search fee: $12.00 per hour. Required to search: name, years to search. Civil cases indexed by defendant, plaintiff. Civil records on computer from 1976, microfiche, index books and archives from 1887.

Criminal Records: Access: In person only. Visitors must perform in person searches for themselves. No search fee. Required to search: name, years to search, SSN. Criminal records on computer from 1976, microfiche, index books and archives from 1887.

General Information: Public Access terminal is available. No juvenile, mental health, sealed or expunged records released. Will fax results $1.00 per page. Copy fee: $.25 per page. Cert fee: $1.00. Payee: Clerk of District Court. Personal checks accepted. Prepayment required.

Harvey County

District Court PO Box 665, Newton, KS 67114-0665; 316-284-6890; Civil phone: 316-284-6894; Criminal phone: 316-284-6896; Fax: 316-283-4601.

Hours: 9AM-5PM (CST). *Felony, Misdemeanor, Civil, Eviction, Small Claims, Probate.*

Civil Records: Access: Mail, fax, in person, email. Both court and visitors may perform in person searches. Search fee: $12.00 per hour. Required to search: name, years to search. Civil cases indexed by defendant, plaintiff. Civil records on index books from 1800s; on computer back to mid 1970s.

Criminal Records: Access: Mail, fax, in person. Both court and visitors may perform in person searches. Search fee: $12.00 per name. Required to search: name, years to search, DOB; also helpful-SSN, signed release. Criminal records computerized since 1960s, archived from 1800s. Call KBI for thorough search.

General Information: Public Access terminal is available. No juvenile, mental health, sealed or expunged records released. Copy fee: $.50 per page. Cert fee: $1.00. Payee: Clerk of District Court. Personal checks accepted. Prepayment required. Mail requests: SASE helpful. Turnaround time 3-5 days.

Haskell County

District Court PO Box 146, Sublette, KS 67877; 620-675-2671; Fax: 620-675-8599. Hours: 8AM-5PM (CST). *Felony, Misdemeanor, Civil, Eviction, Small Claims, Probate.*

Civil Records: Access: Phone, mail, fax, in person. Both court and visitors may perform in person searches. Search fee: $12.00 per hour. Required to search: name, years to search. Civil cases indexed by defendant, plaintiff. Civil records on computer from 1990, index books from 1874.

Criminal Records: Access: Phone, mail, fax, in person. Visitors must perform in person searches for themselves. Search fee: $12.00 per hour. Required to search: name, years to search. Criminal records on computer from 1990, index books from 1874,

General Information: Public Access terminal is available. No juvenile, mental health, sealed or expunged records released. Will fax results for $.25 per page or $3.00 per document. Copy fee: $.25 per page. Cert fee: $1.00. Payee: Clerk of District Court. Personal checks accepted. Prepayment required. Mail requests: SASE not required. Mail turnaround time same day.

Hodgeman County

District Court PO Box 187, Jetmore, KS 67854; 620-357-6522; Fax: 620-357-6216. Hours: 8:30AM-5PM (CST). *Felony, Misdemeanor, Civil, Eviction, Small Claims, Probate.*

www.kscourts.org/dstcts/24dstct.htm

Civil Records: Access: Phone, fax, mail, in person. Both court and visitors may perform in person searches. Search fee: $12.00 per hour. Required to search: name, years to search. Civil cases indexed by defendant, plaintiff. Civil records on index cards and books from 1800s.

Criminal Records: Access: In person only. Visitors must perform in person searches for themselves. No search fee. Required to search: name, years to search; also helpful: SSN. Criminal records on index cards and books from 1800s.

General Information: No juvenile, mental health, sealed or expunged records released. Will fax results $.50 per page. Copy fee: $.25 per page. Cert fee: $1.00. Payee: Clerk of Court. Personal checks accepted. Prepayment required. Must prepay for mail and fax. Mail requests: SASE not required. Mail turnaround time 1-2 days.

Jackson County

District Court 400 New York Ave #311, Holton, KS 66436; 785-364-2191; Fax: 785-364-3804. Hours: 8AM-4:30PM (CST). *Felony, Misdemeanor, Civil, Eviction, Small Claims, Probate.*

Civil Records: Access: In person only. Visitors must perform in person searches for themselves. No search fee. Required to search: name, years to search. Civil cases indexed by defendant, plaintiff. Civil records on index cards from 1800s, recent records computerized.

Criminal Records: Access: In person only. Visitors must perform in person searches for themselves. No search fee. Required to search: name, years to search. Criminal records on index cards from 1800s, recent records computerized.

General Information: No juvenile, mental health, sealed or expunged records released. Copy fee: $.25 per page. Cert fee: $1.00. Payee: Clerk of District Court. Personal checks accepted. Prepayment required.

Jefferson County

District Court PO Box 327, Oskaloosa, KS 66066; 785-863-2461; Fax: 785-863-2369. Hours: 8AM-4:30PM (CST). *Felony, Misdemeanor, Civil, Eviction, Small Claims, Probate.*

Civil Records: Access: In person only. Visitors must perform in person searches for themselves. No search fee. Required to search: name, years to search. Civil cases indexed by defendant, plaintiff. Civil records on computer since 01/77, on index books from 1855.

Criminal Records: Access: In person only. Visitors must perform in person searches for themselves. No search fee. Required to search: name, years to search; also helpful: SSN. Criminal records on index books from 1855, computerized since 01/77.

General Information: Public Access terminal is available. No juvenile, mental health, sealed or expunged records released. Copy fee: $.25 per page. Cert fee: $1.00. Payee: District Court. Personal checks accepted. Prepayment required.

Jewell County

District Court 307 N Commercial, Mankato, KS 66956; 785-378-4030; Fax: 785-378-4035. Hours: 8AM-5PM (CST). *Felony, Misdemeanor, Civil, Eviction, Small Claims, Probate.*

www.kscourts.org/dstcts/12dstct.htm

Civil Records: Access: Phone, fax, mail, in person. Both court and visitors may perform in person searches. Search fee: $12.00 per hour. Required to search: name, years to search. Civil cases indexed by defendant, plaintiff. Civil records on index books from 1871.

Criminal Records: Access: Phone, fax, mail, in person. Both court and visitors may perform in person searches. Search fee: $12.00 per hour. Required to search: name, years to search. Criminal records on index books from 1871.

General Information: No juvenile, mental health, sealed or expunged records released. Will fax results $3.00 per page. Copy fee: $.25 per page. Cert fee: $1.00. Payee: District Court. Personal checks accepted. Prepayment required. Mail requests: SASE required. Mail turnaround time 1-2 days.

Johnson County

District Court 100 N Kansas, Olathe, KS 66061; 913-715-3500; Civil phone: 913-715-3400; Criminal phone: 913-715-3460; Fax: 913-715-3481. Hours: 8:30AM-4PM (CST). *Felony, Misdemeanor, Civil, Eviction, Small Claims, Probate.*

www.jocoks.com/countyclerk/

Note: Search requests should be made to the Records Center, phone 913-715-3480.

Civil Records: Access: Fax, mail, online, in person. Both court and visitors may perform in person searches. Search fee: $12.00 per hour. Required to search: name, years to search. Civil cases indexed by defendant, plaintiff. Civil records on computer from 1980, microfiche, archives and index prior. Index

online through Access Kansas. See www.accesskansas.org for subscription information.
Criminal Records: Access: Fax, mail, in person. Both court and visitors may perform in person searches. Search fee: $12.00 per hour. Required to search: name, years to search. Criminal records on computer from 1980, microfiche, archives and index prior. Criminal fax number is 913-715-3481.
General Information: Public Access terminal is available. No juvenile, mental health, sealed or expunged records released. No employment searches. Will fax results $2.50 per page. Copy fee: $.50 per page. Copy fee for records prior to 1997 $10.00 flat fee. Cert fee: $1.00. Payee: Clerk of the District Court. Only cashiers checks and money orders accepted. Prepayment required. Mail requests: SASE required. Mail turnaround time 1-2 days if current records; 1-2 weeks for very old document.

Kearny County

District Court PO Box 64, Lakin, KS 67860; 620-355-6481; Fax: 620-355-7462. Hours: 8AM-Noon,1-5PM (CST). *Felony, Misdemeanor, Civil, Eviction, Small Claims, Probate.*
Civil Records: Access: Mail, in person. Visitors must perform in person name searches for themselves. Search fee: $12.00 per hour; but court will only search if you provide a case number. Required to search: name, years to search. Civil cases indexed by defendant, plaintiff. Civil records on computer from 1991, index books from 1900s. A case number must be provided with mail search requests.
Criminal Records: Access: Mail, in person. Visitors must perform in person name searches for themselves. Search fee: $12.00 per hour, but court will only search if you provide a case number. Required to search: name, years to search. Criminal records on computer from 1991, index books from 1900s. A case number must be provided with mail search requests.
General Information: Public Access terminal is available. No juvenile, mental health, adoption, sealed or expunged records released. Will fax results for $1.00 per page prepaid. Copy fee: $.25 per page. Cert fee: $1.00. Payee: District Court. Personal checks accepted. Prepayment required. Mail requests: SASE required. Mail turnaround time 3 days.

Kingman County

District Court PO Box 495 (130 N Spruce St), Kingman, KS 67068; 620-532-5151; Fax: 620-532-2952. Hours: 8AM-Noon, 1-5PM (CST). *Felony, Misdemeanor, Civil, Eviction, Small Claims, Probate.*
Civil Records: Access: Mail, fax, in person. Both court and visitors may perform in person searches. Search fee: $12.00 per hour. Required to search: name, years to search. Civil cases indexed by defendant, plaintiff. Civil records on computer from 1990, microfiche, archives and index cards prior.
Criminal Records: Access: Mail, fax, in person. Both court and visitors may perform in person searches. Search fee: $12.00 per hour. Required to search: name, years to search; also helpful: case type. Criminal records on computer from 1990, microfiche, archives and index cards from 1800s.
General Information: Public Access terminal is available. No juvenile, mental health, sealed or expunged records released. Fee to fax results is $1.00 per page. Copy fee: $.25 per page. Cert fee: $1.00. Payee: Clerk of Court. Personal checks accepted. Prepayment required. Mail requests: SASE required. Mail turnaround time 1-2 days.

Kiowa County

District Court 211 E Florida, Greensburg, KS 67054; 620-723-3317; Fax: 620-723-2970. Hours: 8AM-5PM (CST). *Felony, Misdemeanor, Civil, Eviction, Small Claims, Probate.*
www.kscourts.org/dstcts/16dstct.htm
Civil Records: Access: Fax, mail, in person. Both court and visitors may perform in person searches. Search fee: $12.00 per hour. Required to search: name, years to search. Civil cases indexed by defendant, plaintiff. Civil records archived and on index books from 1800s; computerized back to 1980.
Criminal Records: Access: Fax, mail, in person. Both court and visitors may perform in person searches. Search fee: $12.00 per hour. Required to search: name, years to search, signed release; also helpful: DOB. Criminal records archived and on index books from 1800s; computerized back to 1940.
General Information: Public Access terminal is available. No juvenile, mental health, sealed or expunged records released. Fee to fax results is $1.00 per page. Copy fee: $.25 per page. Cert fee: $1.00. Payee: Clerk of District Court. Personal checks accepted. Prepayment required. Mail requests: SASE required. Mail turnaround time 7 days.

Labette County

District Court Courthouse, 501 Merchant, 3rd Fl, Oswego, KS 67356; 620-795-4533 X 245 (620-421-4120 Parsons); Fax: 620-795-3056 (316-421-3633 Parsons). 8AM-5PM (CST). *Felony, Misdemeanor, Civil, Eviction, Small Claims, Probate.*
Civil Records: Access: In person. Visitors must perform in person searches for themselves. No search fee. Required to search: name, years to search. Civil cases indexed by defendant, plaintiff. Civil records on computer since 1992.
Criminal Records: Access: In person. Visitors must perform in person searches for themselves. No search fee. Required to search: name, years to search; also helpful: DOB, SSN. Criminal records on computer since 1992.
General Information: Public Access terminal is available. no juvenile, adoption, mental health, sealed or expunged records released. Copy fee: $.25 per page. Cert fee: $1.00. Payee: Clerk of District Court. Personal checks accepted. Prepayment required.

District Court 201 S Central, Parsons, KS 67357; 620-421-4120; Fax: 620-421-3633. Hours: 8AM-5PM (CST). *Felony, Misdemeanor, Civil, Eviction, Small Claims, Probate.*
Civil Records: Access: Mail, in person. Both court and visitors may perform in person searches. No search fee. Required to search: name, years to search. Civil cases indexed by defendant, plaintiff. Civil records on computer from 1992, index books prior.
Criminal Records: Access: Mail, in person. Both court and visitors may perform in person searches. Search fee: $12.00 per hr ($6.00 min). Required to search: name, years to search. Criminal records on computer from 1992, index books from 1874.
General Information: Public Access terminal is available. No juvenile, adoption, mental health, sealed or expunged records released. Copy fee: $.25 per page. Cert fee: $1.00. Payee: Clerk of District Court. Personal checks accepted. Prepayment required. Mail requests: SASE required. Mail turnaround: 1-2 days.

Lane County

District Court PO Box 188, Dighton, KS 67839; 620-397-2805; Fax: 620-397-5526. Hours: 8AM-5PM (CST). *Felony, Misdemeanor, Civil, Eviction, Small Claims, Probate.*
www.kscourts.org/dstcts/24dstct.htm

Civil Records: Access: Mail, in person. Both court and visitors may perform in person searches. Search fee: $12.00 per hour. Required to search: name, years to search. Civil cases indexed by defendant, plaintiff. Civil records on computer since 1993; prior records from 1800s.
Criminal Records: Access: Mail, in person. Visitors must perform in person searches for themselves. Search fee: $12.00 per name. Required to search: name, years to search; also helpful: SSN. Criminal records on computer since 1993; prior records from 1800s.
General Information: No juvenile, mental health, sealed or expunged records released. Copy fee: $.25 per page. Cert fee: $1.00. Payee: Clerk of Court. Personal checks accepted. Prepayment required. Mail requests: SASE required. Mail turnaround time 1-2 weeks.

Leavenworth County

District Court 601 S 3rd St, Leavenworth, KS 66048; 913-684-0700; Civil phone: 913-684-0701; Criminal phone: 913-684-0704; Fax: 913-684-0492. Hours: 8AM-5PM (CST). *Felony, Misdemeanor, Civil, Eviction, Small Claims, Probate.*
Civil Records: Access: Mail, in person. Both court and visitors may perform in person searches. Search fee: $12.00 per hour, if extensive. Required to search: name, years to search. Civil cases indexed by defendant, plaintiff. Civil records on computer from 1990, microfiche to 1952 and index books from 1901.
Criminal Records: Access: Mail, in person. Both court and visitors may perform in person searches. Search fee: $12.00 per hour, if extensive. Required to search: name, years to search; also helpful: SSN. Criminal records on computer from 1990, microfiche and index books from 1960.
General Information: Public Access terminal is available. No juvenile, mental health, sealed or expunged records released. Will fax results if local call. Copy fee: $.25 per page. Cert fee: $1.00. Payee: Clerk of District Court. Personal checks accepted. Mail requests: SASE required. Mail turnaround time 3-4 days.

Lincoln County

District Court 216 E Lincoln Ave, Lincoln, KS 67455; 785-524-4057; Fax: 785-524-3204. Hours: 8AM-12, 1-5PM (CST). *Felony, Misdemeanor, Civil, Eviction, Small Claims, Probate.*
www.kscourts.org/dstcts/12dstct.htm
Civil Records: Access: Fax, mail, in person. Only the court performs in person searches; visitors may not. No search fee. Required to search: name; also helpful: years to search. Civil cases indexed by defendant, plaintiff. All records on computer.
Criminal Records: Access: In person only. Only the court performs in person searches; visitors may not. No search fee. Required to search: name; also helpful: years to search, DOB, SSN. Criminal records on computer since 1980, on index cards from 1880. Will search 1 name by phone only, maybe.
General Information: No juvenile, mental health, sealed or expunged records released. Will fax results $3.00 per page. Copy fee: $.25 per page. Cert fee: $1.00. Payee: Clerk of Court. Personal checks accepted. Prepayment required.

Linn County

District Court PO Box 350, 318 Chestnut St., Mound City, KS 66056-0350; 913-795-2660; Fax: 913-795-2004. Hours: 8AM-4:30PM (CST). *Felony, Misdemeanor, Civil, Eviction, Small Claims, Probate.*
Civil Records: Access: In person only. Visitors must perform in person searches for themselves. No search fee. Required to search: name, years to search. Civil

cases indexed by defendant, plaintiff. Civil records on computer from 1990, archives and index books prior.

Criminal Records: Access: In person only. Visitors must perform in person searches for themselves. No search fee. Required to search: name, years to search. Criminal records on computer from 1990, archives and index books from 1886.

General Information: Public Access terminal is available. No juvenile, mental health, sealed or expunged records released. Copy fee: $.25 per page. Cert fee: $1.25. Payee: Clerk of District Court. Personal checks accepted. Prepayment required.

Logan County

District Court 710 W 2nd St, Oakley, KS 67748-1233; 785-672-3654; Fax: 785-672-3517. 8:30AM-Noon, 1-5PM (CST). *Felony, Misdemeanor, Civil, Eviction, Small Claims, Probate.*

Civil Records: Access: In person only. Visitors must perform in person searches for themselves. No search fee. Required to search: name; also helpful: years to search. Civil cases indexed by defendant, plaintiff. Civil records on computer from 1927, index cards from 1887.

Criminal Records: Access: In person only. Visitors must perform in person searches for themselves. No search fee. Required to search: name; also helpful: SSN, years to search. Criminal records on computer from 1927 index cards from 1887.

General Information: Public Access terminal is available. No juvenile, mental health, sealed or expunged records released. Copy fee: $.25 per page. Cert fee: $1.00. Payee: Clerk of District Court. Personal checks accepted. Prepayment required.

Lyon County

District Court 430 Commercial St, Emporia, KS 66801; 620-341-3281; Fax: 620-341-3497. Hours: 8AM-4PM (CST). *Felony, Misdemeanor, Civil, Eviction, Small Claims, Probate.*

www.lyoncounty.org/MV2Base.asp?VarCN=115

Civil Records: Access: Fax, mail, in person. Both court and visitors may perform in person searches. Search fee: $12.00 per hour. Required to search: name, years to search. Civil cases indexed by defendant, plaintiff. Records maintained since 1859.

Criminal Records: Access: Fax, mail, in person. Both court and visitors may perform in person searches. Search fee: $12.00 per hour. Required to search: name, years to search. Records maintained since 1859.

General Information: Public Access terminal is available. (Has records 1998 to present.) No mental health, sealed or expunged records released. Will fax results $1.00 per page. Copy fee: $.50 per page. Cert fee: $2.00. Payee: Clerk of District Court. Personal checks accepted. Prepayment required. Mail turnaround time 3 days maximum.

Marion County

District Court PO Box 298, Marion, KS 66861; 620-382-2104; Fax: 620-382-2259. Hours: 8AM-5PM; 9AM-5PM (open to public) (CST). *Felony, Misdemeanor, Civil, Eviction, Small Claims, Probate.*

Civil Records: Access: In person only. Visitors must perform in person searches for themselves. No search fee. Required to search: name, years to search. Civil cases indexed by defendant, plaintiff. Civil records on computer from July, 1992, on index cards from 1800s.

Criminal Records: Access: In person only. Visitors must perform in person searches for themselves. No search fee. Required to search: name, years to search. Criminal records on computer from July, 1992, on index cards from 1800s.

General Information: Public Access terminal is available. No juvenile, mental health, sealed or expunged records released. Copy fee: $1.00 per page. Cert fee: $1.00. Payee: District Court. Personal checks accepted. Prepayment required.

Marshall County

District Court PO Box 86, 1201 Broadway, Office #5, Marysville, KS 66508; 785-562-5301; Fax: 785-562-2458. Hours: 8AM-5PM; Search hours: 8:30AM-4:30PM (CST). *Felony, Misdemeanor, Civil, Eviction, Small Claims, Probate.*

Note: Actual marriage licenses from 1860 through June 18, 1942 may be viewed and copied from 1:00PM - 4:00PM. Records are located in old historical courthouse located next door .

Civil Records: Access: Fax, mail, in person. Both court and visitors may perform in person searches. Search fee: $12.00 per hour. Required to search: name, years to search. Civil cases indexed by defendant, plaintiff. Civil records on computer from 1990, microfiche from 1977 (earlier records on roll-marriage licenses on computer index 1860s, forward/naturalizations on computer index).

Criminal Records: Access: Fax, mail, in person. Both court and visitors may perform in person searches. Search fee: $12.00 per hour. Required to search: name, years to search. Criminal records on computer from 1986, microfiche from 1977.

General Information: Public Access terminal is available. No juvenile, offender under 14 years of age, no child in need of care, mental health, sealed or expunged records released. Will fax results for $2.00 1st page, $1.00 each add'l. Prepayment required. Copy fee: $.50 for first page, $.25 each add'l. Cert fee: $1.00. Payee: Clerk of Court. Personal checks accepted. Prepayment required. Mail requests: SASE required. Mail turnaround time 1-2 days.

McPherson County

District Court PO Box 1106, McPherson, KS 67460; 620-241-3422; Fax: 620-241-1372. Hours: 8AM-5PM (CST). *Felony, Misdemeanor, Civil, Eviction, Small Claims, Probate.*

Civil Records: Access: Mail, in person. Both court and visitors may perform in person searches. Search fee: $12.00 per hour. Required to search: name, years to search. Civil cases indexed by defendant, plaintiff. Civil records on microfilm from 1953, index cards from 1900s.

Criminal Records: Access: Mail, in person. Both court and visitors may perform in person searches. Search fee: $12.00 per hour. Required to search: name, years to search; also helpful: SSN. Criminal records on microfilm from 1953, index cards from 1900s.

General Information: Public Access terminal is available. No juvenile, mental health, sealed or expunged records released. Will fax results for $1.00 per page. Copy fee: $.50 per page. Cert fee: $1.00. Payee: District Court. Personal checks accepted. Prepayment required. Mail requests: SASE required. Mail turnaround time 1-3 days.

Meade County

Meade County District Court PO Box 623, Meade, KS 67864; 620-873-8750; Fax: 620-873-8759. 8AM-5PM (CST). *Felony, Misdemeanor, Civil, Eviction, Small Claims, Probate.*

www.kscourts.org/dstcts/16dstct.htm

Note: All employment background checks requested by mail, phone, or fax are referred to the KBI (state agency for criminal records).

Civil Records: Access: Mail, in person. Both court and visitors may perform in person searches. Search fee: $12.00 per hour. Required to search: name, years

to search. Civil cases indexed by defendant, plaintiff. Civil records on computer from 1990, index cards from 1896.

Criminal Records: Access: Mail, in person. Both court and visitors may perform in person searches. Search fee: $12.00 per hour. Required to search: name, years to search. Criminal records on computer from 1990, index cards from 1896.

General Information: Public Access terminal is available. No juvenile, mental health, sealed or expunged records released. Copy fee: $.25 per page. Cert fee: $1.00. Payee: Clerk of Court. Only cashiers checks and money orders accepted. Prepayment required. Mail requests: SASE required. Mail turnaround time 1-2 days.

Miami County

District Court PO Box 187, Paola, KS 66071; 913-294-3326; Fax: 913-294-2535. Hours: 8AM-4:30PM (CST). *Felony, Misdemeanor, Civil, Eviction, Small Claims, Probate.*

Civil Records: Access: In person only. Both court and visitors may perform in person searches. No search fee. Required to search: name, years to search. Civil cases indexed by defendant, plaintiff. Civil records on computer from 1984, index cards from 1890s.

Criminal Records: Access: In person only. Both court and visitors may perform in person searches. No search fee. Required to search: name, years to search; also helpful: SSN. Criminal records on computer from 1984, index cards from 1890s.

General Information: Public Access terminal is available. No juvenile, mental health, sealed or expunged records released. Will fax specific document for $.50 per page. Copy fee: $.50 per page. Cert fee: $1.00. Payee: District Court. Personal checks accepted. Prepayment required.

Mitchell County

District Court 115 S Hersey, Beloit, KS 67420; 785-738-3753; Fax: 785-738-4101. Hours: 8AM-5PM (CST). *Felony, Misdemeanor, Civil, Eviction, Small Claims, Probate.*

www.kscourts.org/dstcts/12dstct.htm

Civil Records: Access: Mail, in person. Both court and visitors may perform in person searches. Search fee: $10.00 per hour. Required to search: name, years to search. Civil cases indexed by defendant, plaintiff. Civil records on index cards from 1876.

Criminal Records: Access: Mail, in person. Both court and visitors may perform in person searches. Search fee: $10.00 per hour. Required to search: name, years to search. Criminal records on index cards from 1977, archived to 1870.

General Information: No juvenile, mental health, sealed or expunged records released. Copy fee: $.25 per page. Cert fee: $1.25. Payee: Clerk of Court. Personal checks accepted. Prepayment required. Mail requests: SASE required. Mail turnaround: 1-2 days.

Montgomery County

Independence District Court 300 E Main St, #201, Independence, KS 67301; 620-330-1070; Fax: 620-331-6120. 8AM-5PM *Felony, Misdemeanor, Civil, Eviction, Small Claims, Probate.*

Civil Records: Access: Fax, mail, in person. Both court and visitors may perform in person searches. Search fee: $12.80 per hour. $6.00 minimum. Required to search: name, years to search. Civil cases indexed by defendant, plaintiff. Civil records on computer since 1992, on microfiche from 1870-1930, archives 1930-1992, index cards from 1870. This court covers civil cases for the northern part of the county. It is suggested to search both courts.

Criminal Records: Access: Fax, mail, in person. Both court and visitors may perform in person

searches. Search fee: $12.80 per hour. $6.00 minimum. Required to search: name, years to search; also helpful: SSN. Criminal records on computer since 1992, on microfiche from 1870-1930, archives 1930-1992, index cards from 1870.

General Information: Public Access terminal is available. No juvenile, adoptions, mental health, sealed or expunged records released. Will fax results for $5.00 1st page, $1.00 each add'l. Copy fee: $.25 per page. Cert fee: $1.00. Payee: Clerk of Court. Personal checks accepted. Prepayment required. Mail requests: SASE not required. Mail turnaround time 72 hours.

Coffeyville District Court 102 W 7th St, #A, Coffeyville, KS 67337; 620-251-1060; Fax: 620-251-2734. Hours: 8AM-5PM (CST). *Civil, Eviction, Small Claims, Probate.*

Note: This court covers civil cases for the southern part of the county, although cases can be filed in either court. It is recommended to search both courts

Civil Records: Access: Fax, mail, in person. Both court and visitors may perform in person searches. Search fee: $12.80 per hour; $6.00 minimum. Required to search: name, years to search. Civil cases indexed by defendant, plaintiff. Civil records on computer back to 1992, on paper, fiche, etc. since 1924.

General Information: Public Access terminal is available. No juvenile, mental health, sealed, adoption, or expunged records released. Fee to fax results is $1.00 per page. Copy fee: $.25 per page. Cert fee: $1.25. Payee: Clerk of Court. Personal checks accepted. Prepayment required. Mail requests: SASE requested. Turnaround time 72 hours.

Morris County

District Court County Courthouse, Council Grove, KS 66846; 620-767-6838; Fax: 620-767-6488. Hours: 8AM-5PM (CST). *Felony, Misdemeanor, Civil, Eviction, Small Claims, Probate.*

Civil Records: Access: Fax, mail, in person. Both court and visitors may perform in person searches. Search fee: $12.00 per hour. Required to search: name, years to search. Civil cases indexed by defendant, plaintiff. Civil records on computer since 1992, on microfiche, archives and index cards from 1860.

Criminal Records: Access: Fax, mail, in person. Both court and visitors may perform in person searches. Search fee: $12.00 per hour. Required to search: name, years to search. Criminal records on computer since 1992, on microfiche, archives and index cards from 1860.

General Information: Public Access terminal is available. Will fax results $1.00 per page. Copy fee: $.25 per page. Cert fee: $1.00. Payee: Clerk of Court. Personal checks accepted. Prepayment required. Mail requests: SASE required. Mail turnaround time 1-2 days.

Morton County

District Court PO Box 825, Elkhart, KS 67950; 620-697-2563; Fax: 620-697-4289. Hours: 8AM-Noon, 1-5PM (CST). *Felony, Misdemeanor, Civil, Eviction, Small Claims, Probate.*

Civil Records: Access: Mail, fax, in person. Both court and visitors may perform in person searches. Search fee: $12.00 per hour. Required to search: name, years to search. Civil cases indexed by defendant, plaintiff. Civil records on computer from 1992, index cards from 1800s.

Criminal Records: Access: In person only. Visitors must perform in person searches for themselves. No search fee. Required to search: name, years to search. Criminal records on computer from 1977, index cards from 1800s.

General Information: Public Access terminal is available. No juvenile, mental health, sealed or expunged records released. Fee to fax results is $2.50 1st pg.; $.50 each add'l. Copy fee: $.25 per page. Cert fee: $1.00. Payee: Clerk of Court. Two party checks not accepted. Prepayment required.

Nemaha County

District Court PO Box 213, Seneca, KS 66538; 785-336-2146; Fax: 785-336-6450. Hours: 8AM-5PM (CST). *Felony, Misdemeanor, Civil, Eviction, Small Claims, Probate.*

Civil Records: Access: Phone, mail, in person. Both court and visitors may perform in person searches. Search fee: $12.00 per hour. Required to search: name, years to search. Civil cases indexed by defendant, plaintiff. Civil records on computer from 1977, index cards from 1870.

Criminal Records: Access: Phone, mail, in person. Both court and visitors may perform in person searches. Search fee: $12.00 per hour. Required to search: name, years to search, SSN. Criminal records on computer from 1977, index cards from 1870.

General Information: Public Access terminal is available. No juvenile, mental health, sealed or expunged records released. Will fax results for $2.00 1st page, $1.00 each add'l. Copy fee: $.25 per page. Cert fee: $1.00. Payee: Clerk of District Court. Business checks accepted. Prepayment required. Mail requests: SASE required. Mail turnaround: 1-2 days.

Neosho County

Chanute District Court 102 S Lincoln, PO Box 889, Chanute, KS 66720; 620-431-5700; Fax: 620-431-5710. Hours: 8AM-5PM (CST). *Felony, Misdemeanor, Civil, Eviction, Small Claims.*

Note: This is a branch court of Erie.

Civil Records: Access: Mail, in person. Both court and visitors may perform in person searches. Search fee: $12.00 per hour. Required to search: name, years to search. Civil cases indexed by defendant, plaintiff. Civil records on computer since 1993; prior to 1955.

Criminal Records: Access: In person only. Both court and visitors may perform in person searches. Search fee: $12.00 per hour per name. Required to search: name, years to search. Criminal records on computer since 1993; prior to 1955.

General Information: Public Access terminal is available. No juvenile, mental health, sealed or expunged records released. Fee to fax results is $1.00 per page. Copy fee: $.50 per page. Cert fee: $1.00. Payee: Clerk of District Court. Personal checks accepted. Prepayment required. Mail turnaround time 1-3 days.

Erie District Court Neosho County Courthouse, PO Box 19, Erie, KS 66733; 620-244-3831; Criminal phone: 620-431-5700; Fax: 620-244-3830. Hours: 8AM-noon, 1-4:30PM (CST). *Felony, Misdemeanor, Civil, Eviction, Small Claims, Probate.*

Note: This is the main court for the county.

Civil Records: Access: Fax, mail, in person. Both court and visitors may perform in person searches. Search fee: $12.00 per hour. Required to search: name, years to search. Civil cases indexed by defendant, plaintiff. Civil records on index cards from 1900s; on computer back to 1993.

Criminal Records: Access: Mail, in person. Visitors must perform in person searches for themselves. Search fee: $12.00 per record. Required to search: name, years to search, DOB. Criminal records on index cards from 1900s; on computer back to 1993. Limited mail searches are okay, lists should be sent to the central state agency.

General Information: Public Access terminal is available. No juvenile, mental health, sealed or expunged records released. Fee to fax results is $1.00 per page. Copy fee: $.50 per page. Cert fee: $1.00. Payee: Clerk of Court. Personal checks accepted. Prepayment required. Mail turnaround time 1-3 days.

Ness County

District Court PO Box 445, Ness City, KS 67560; 785-798-3693; Fax: 785-798-3348. Hours: 8AM-5PM (CST). *Felony, Misdemeanor, Civil, Eviction, Small Claims, Probate.*

Civil Records: Access: Fax, mail, in person. Both court and visitors may perform in person searches. Search fee: $12.00 per hour. Required to search: name, years to search. Civil cases indexed by defendant, plaintiff. Civil records on index books from 1885.

Criminal Records: Access: In person only. Visitors must perform in person searches for themselves. No search fee. Required to search: name, years to search. Criminal records on index books from 1885.

General Information: Public Access terminal is available. No juvenile, mental health, sealed or expunged records released. Fee to fax results is $1.00 per page. Copy fee: $.25 per page. Cert fee: $1.00. Payee: Clerk of Court. Personal checks accepted. Prepayment required. Mail requests: SASE not required. Mail turnaround time 3 days.

Norton County

District Court PO Box 70, Norton, KS 67654; 785-877-5720; Fax: 785-877-5722. Hours: 8AM-5PM (CST). *Felony, Misdemeanor, Civil, Eviction, Small Claims, Probate.*

Civil Records: Access: Mail, in person. Both court and visitors may perform in person searches. Search fee: $12.00 per hour. Required to search: name, years to search. Civil cases indexed by defendant, plaintiff. Civil records on index from 1900s.

Criminal Records: Access: Mail, in person. Both court and visitors may perform in person searches. Search fee: $12.00 per hour. Required to search: name, years to search. Criminal records on index from 1900s.

General Information: No juvenile, mental health, sealed or expunged records released. Will fax results to local or toll free line. Copy fee: $.25 per page. Cert fee: $1.00. Payee: Clerk of District Court. Personal checks accepted. Prepayment required. Mail requests: SASE required. Mail turnaround time 1 week.

Osage County

District Court PO Box 549, Lyndon, KS 66451; 785-828-4514; Fax: 785-828-4704. Hours: 8AM-Noon,1-4PM (CST). *Felony, Misdemeanor, Civil, Eviction, Small Claims, Probate.*
www.kscourts.org/dstct/4dstct.htm

Civil Records: Access: In person, online. Visitors must perform in person searches for themselves. Search fee: $12.00 per hour. Required to search: name, years to search. Civil cases indexed by defendant, plaintiff. Civil records on computer from 1980. Current court calendars are free online at www.franklincoks.org/4thdistrict/osagebydate.html. Also, access to probate court records is free at www.kscourts.org/dstcts/4osprrec.htm.

Criminal Records: Access: In person, online. Visitors must perform in person searches for themselves. Search fee: $12.00 per hour. Required to search: name, years to search. Criminal records on computer from 1980. Online access to criminal records is the same as civil.

General Information: Public Access terminal is available. No juvenile, mental health, sealed or expunged records released. Copy fee: $.25 per page. Cert fee: $1.00. Payee: Clerk of Court. Business checks accepted. Prepayment required.

Osborne County

District Court 423 W Main, PO Box 160, Osborne, KS 67473; 785-346-5911; Fax: 785-246-5992. 8AM-5PM (CST). *Felony, Misdemeanor, Civil, Eviction, Small Claims, Probate.*

Civil Records: Access: In person only. Visitors must perform in person searches for themselves. No search fee. Required to search: name, years to search. Civil cases indexed by defendant, plaintiff. Civil records on microfiche from 1872-1980, index books from 1981, index cards from 1872.

Criminal Records: Access: In person, fax, mail. Both court and visitors may perform in person searches. Search fee: $12.00 per hr. Required to search: name, years to search; also helpful: SSN. Criminal records on microfiche from 1872-1980, index books from 1981, index cards from 1872.

General Information: No juvenile, mental health, sealed or expunged records released. Copy fee: $.25 per page. Cert fee: $1.00. Payee: Clerk of District Court. Personal checks accepted. Prepayment required. Mail requests: SASE requested. Turnaround time is 3 days.

Ottawa County

District Court 307 N Concord, Minneapolis, KS 67467; 785-392-2917; Fax: 785-392-3626. Hours: 8AM-12;00-1-5PM (CST). *Felony, Misdemeanor, Civil, Eviction, Small Claims, Probate.*

Civil Records: Access: Mail, fax, in person. Both court and visitors may perform in person searches. Search fee: $9.00 per hour. Required to search: name, years to search. Civil cases indexed by defendant, plaintiff. Civil records on index from 1800s; computerized records since 1990.

Criminal Records: Access: In person only. No search fee. Required to search: name, years to search; also helpful: SSN. Criminal records on index from 1800s; computerized records since 1990.

General Information: Public Access terminal is available. No juvenile, mental health, sealed or expunged records released. Copy fee: $.25. Cert fee: $1.00. Payee: Clerk of District Court. Personal checks accepted. Prepayment required.

Pawnee County

District Court PO Box 270, Larned, KS 67550; 620-285-6937; Fax: 620-285-3665. Hours: 8AM-5PM (CST). *Felony, Misdemeanor, Civil, Eviction, Small Claims, Probate.*

www.kscourts.org/dstcts/24dstct.htm

Civil Records: Access: Fax, mail, in person. Both court and visitors may perform in person searches. Search fee: $12.00 an hour if done by court. Required to search: name, years to search. Civil cases indexed by defendant, plaintiff. Civil records on computer from 1991, index cards from 1900s.

Criminal Records: Access: Fax, mail, in person. Visitors must perform in person searches for themselves. Search fee: $12.00 an hour if done by court. Required to search: name, years to search; also helpful: SSN. Criminal records on computer from 1991, index cards from 1900s.

General Information: No juvenile, mental health, sealed or expunged records released. Will fax results $.50 per page. Copy fee: $.25 per page. Cert fee: $1.00. Payee: Clerk of District Court. Personal checks accepted. Prepayment required. Mail requests: SASE not required. Mail turnaround time 1-2 days.

Phillips County

District Court PO Box 564, Phillipsburg, KS 67661; 785-543-6830; Fax: 785-543-6832. Hours: 8AM-5PM (CST). *Felony, Misdemeanor, Civil, Eviction, Small Claims, Probate.*

Civil Records: Access: Mail, in person. Visitors must perform in person searches for themselves. Search fee: $12.00 per hour. Required to search: name, years to search. Civil cases indexed by defendant, plaintiff. Civil records on index from 1900s; on computer back to 1994.

Criminal Records: Access: In person, mail. Visitors must perform in person searches for themselves. Search fee: $12.00 per hour. Required to search: name, years to search; also helpful: DOB, SSN. Criminal records on index from 1900s; on computer back to 1994.

General Information: No juvenile, mental health, sealed or expunged records released. Will fax results for $.50 per page. Copy fee: $.25 per page. Cert fee: $1.00. Payee: Clerk of District Court. Personal checks accepted. Prepayment required. Mail turnaround time 2 days.

Pottawatomie County

District Court PO Box 129, Westmoreland, KS 66549; 785-457-3392; Fax: 785-457-2107. Hours: 8AM-4:30PM (CST). *Felony, Misdemeanor, Civil, Eviction, Small Claims, Probate.*

Civil Records: Access: In person only. Visitors must perform in person searches for themselves. No search fee. Required to search: name, years to search. Civil cases indexed by defendant, plaintiff. Civil records computerized since 1998, on microfiche from 1800s, index from 1800s.

Criminal Records: Access: In person only. Visitors must perform in person searches for themselves. No search fee. Required to search: name, years to search; also helpful: SSN. Criminal records computerized since 1998, on microfiche from 1800s, index from 1800s.

General Information: Public Access terminal is available. (Records go back to 1995.) No juvenile, mental health, sealed or expunged records released. Copy fee: $.25 per page. Cert fee: $2.00. Payee: Clerk of District Court. Personal checks accepted. Prepayment required.

Pratt County

District Court PO Box 984, Pratt, KS 67124; 620-672-4100; Fax: 620-672-2902. Hours: 8AM-Noon, 1-5PM (CST). *Felony, Misdemeanor, Civil, Eviction, Small Claims, Probate.*

www.prattcounty.org

Civil Records: Access: Mail, fax, in person. Both court and visitors may perform in person searches. Search fee: $12.00 per hour. Required to search: name, years to search. Civil cases indexed by defendant, plaintiff. Civil records on computer back to 1988, microfiche, archives, index from 1878.

Criminal Records: Access: Mail, fax, in person. Only the court performs in person searches; visitors may not. Search fee: $12.00 per hour. Required to search: name, years to search, DOB; also helpful: SSN, signed release. Criminal records on computer back to 1988, microfiche, archives, index from 1878.

General Information: Public Access terminal is available. No juvenile, mental health, sealed or expunged records released. Fee to fax results is $1.00 per page. Copy fee: $.25 per page. Cert fee: $1.00. Payee: Clerk of District Court. Personal checks accepted. Prepayment required. Mail requests: SASE required. Mail turnaround time 1-2 days.

Rawlins County

District Court 607 Main, #F, Atwood, KS 67730; 785-626-3465; Fax: 785-626-3350. Hours: 9AM-5PM (CST). *Felony, Misdemeanor, Civil, Eviction, Small Claims, Probate.*

Civil Records: Access: In person only. Visitors must perform in person searches for themselves. No search fee. Required to search: name, years to search. Civil cases indexed by defendant, plaintiff. Civil records on index from 1900s.

Criminal Records: Access: In person only. Visitors must perform in person searches for themselves. No search fee. Required to search: name, years to search; also helpful: SSN. Criminal records on index from 1900s. This agency refers requesters to the Kansas Bureau of Investigations.

General Information: No juvenile, mental health, sealed or expunged records released. Copy fee: $.25 per page. Cert fee: $1.00. Payee: Clerk of District Court. Only in state checks accepted. Prepayment required.

Reno County

District Court 206 W 1st, Hutchinson, KS 67501; 620-694-2956; Fax: 620-694-2958. Hours: 8AM-Noon, 1-5PM (CST). *Felony, Misdemeanor, Civil, Eviction, Small Claims, Probate.*

Civil Records: Access: Mail, in person. Only the court performs in person searches; visitors may not. Search fee: $12.00 per hour. Required to search: name, years to search. Civil cases indexed by defendant, plaintiff. Civil records on computer from 1992, index cards from 1900s.

Criminal Records: Access: Mail, in person. Only the court performs in person searches; visitors may not. Search fee: $12.00 per hour. Required to search: name, years to search, DOB, signed release; also helpful: address, SSN. Criminal records on computer from 1992, index cards from 1900s.

General Information: No mental health, juvenile (some), sealed or expunged records released. Copy fee: $.25 per page. Cert fee: $1.00. Payee: Clerk of District Court. Only cashiers checks and money orders accepted. Prepayment required. Mail requests: SASE required. Mail turnaround time 3-5 days (in-state); 3-10 days (out-of-state).

Republic County

District Court PO Box 8, Belleville, KS 66935; 785-527-7234; Fax: 785-527-5029. Hours: 8AM-5PM (CST). *Felony, Misdemeanor, Civil, Eviction, Small Claims, Probate.*

www.kscourts.org/dstcts/12dstct.htm

Civil Records: Access: Mail, in person. Both court and visitors may perform in person searches. Search fee: $8.00 per hour. Required to search: name, years to search. Civil cases indexed by defendant, plaintiff. Civil records on computer from 1990, index cards from 1869 for probate.

Criminal Records: Access: In person only. Visitors must perform in person searches for themselves. No search fee. Required to search: name, years to search. Criminal records on computer from 1990, index cards from 1869 for probate.

General Information: No juvenile, mental health, sealed or expunged records released. Will fax results to local or toll free line or for $3.00 per page. Copy fee: $.25 per page. Cert fee: $1.00. Payee: Clerk of Court. Personal checks accepted. Prepayment required. Mail requests: SASE required. Mail turnaround time 2-4 weeks.

Rice County

District Court 101 W Commercial, Lyons, KS 67554; 620-257-2383; Fax: 620-257-3826. Hours: 8:00AM-5PM (CST). *Felony, Misdemeanor, Civil, Eviction, Small Claims, Probate.*

Civil Records: Access: Fax, mail, in person. Both the court and visitors may perform in person searches. Search fee: $9.00 per hour. Required to search: name, years to search. Civil cases indexed by defendant, plaintiff. Civil records on computer from 1980, index cards from 1880.

Criminal Records: Access: Fax, mail, in person. Visitors must perform in person searches for themselves. Search fee: $12.00 per hour. Required to search: name, years to search; also helpful: SSN. Criminal records on computer from 1980, index cards from 1880. All criminal searches are referred to the KBI, 1620 SW Tyler, Topeka KS 66601.

General Information: Public Access terminal is available. No juvenile, mental health, sealed or expunged records released. Fee to fax results is $.50 per page. Copy fee: $1.00 for first page, $.25 each add'l. No cert fee. Payee: Clerk of Court. Personal checks accepted. Prepayment required. Mail requests: SASE required. Mail turnaround time 1-3 days.

Riley County

District Court PO Box 158, Manhattan, KS 66505-0158; 785-537-6364. Hours: 8:30AM-5PM (CST). *Felony, Misdemeanor, Civil, Eviction, Small Claims, Probate.* www.co.riley.ks.us/districtcourt

Civil Records: Access: In person only. Visitors must perform in person searches for themselves. No search fee. Required to search: name, years to search. Civil cases indexed by defendant, plaintiff. Civil records on computer back to 10/93; prior records in index journals.

Criminal Records: Access: In person only. Visitors must perform in person searches for themselves. No search fee. Required to search: name, years to search; also helpful: DOB, SSN. Criminal records on computer back to 1986, microfiche, archives and index cards from 1900s.

General Information: Public Access terminal is available. No mental health, sealed or expunged records released. Copy fee: $.25 per page. Cert fee: $1.00. Payee: Clerk of Court. Personal checks accepted. Prepayment required.

Rooks County

District Court 115 N Walnut, PO Box 532, Stockton, KS 67669; 785-425-6718; Fax: 785-425-6568. 8AM-5PM (CST). *Felony, Misdemeanor, Civil, Eviction, Small Claims, Probate.*

Civil Records: Access: Mail, in person. Both court and visitors may perform in person searches. Search fee: $12.00 per hour. Required to search: name, years to search. Civil cases indexed by defendant, plaintiff. Civil records on index cards from 1888; on computer since.

Criminal Records: Access: Mail, in person. Both court and visitors may perform in person searches. Search fee: $12.00 per hour. Required to search: name, years to search; also helpful: DOB, SSN. Criminal records on index cards from 1888; on computer since.

General Information: Public Access terminal is available. No juvenile, adoption, mental health, sealed or expunged records released. Fee to fax results is $1.00 per page. Copy fee: $.25 per page. Cert fee: $2.00. Payee: Clerk of Court. Personal checks accepted. Prepayment required. Mail requests: SASE required. Mail turnaround time 1-3 days.

Rush County

District Court PO Box 387, La Crosse, KS 67548; 785-222-2718; Fax: 785-222-2748. Hours: 8AM-5PM (CST). *Felony, Misdemeanor, Civil, Eviction, Small Claims, Probate.* www.kscourts.org/dstcts/24dstct.htm

Civil Records: Access: Phone, fax, mail, in person. Both court and visitors may perform in person searches. Search fee: $12.00 per hour. Required to search: name, years to search. Civil cases indexed by defendant, plaintiff. Civil records on computer from April, 1994, on index from 1800s.

Criminal Records: Access: In person only. Visitors must perform in person searches for themselves. No search fee. Required to search: name, years to search; also helpful: SSN. Criminal records on computer from April, 1994, on index from 1800s.

General Information: Public Access terminal is available. No juvenile, mental health, sealed or expunged records released. Will fax results for $.50 per page. Copy fee: $.25 per page. Cert fee: $1.00. Payee: Clerk of District Court. Personal checks accepted. Prepayment required. Mail requests: SASE required. Mail turnaround time 3 days.

Russell County

District Court PO Box 876, Russell, KS 67665; 785-483-5641; Fax: 785-483-2448. Hours: 8AM-5PM (CST). *Felony, Misdemeanor, Civil, Eviction, Small Claims, Probate.*

Civil Records: Access: Fax, mail, in person. Both court and visitors may perform in person searches. Search fee: $12.00 per hour. Required to search: name, years to search. Civil cases indexed by defendant, plaintiff. Civil records on computer from 1990, index cards from 1900s.

Criminal Records: Access: Fax, mail, in person. Both court and visitors may perform in person searches. Search fee: $12.00 per hour. Required to search: name, years to search, DOB. Criminal records on computer from 1990, index cards from 1900s.

General Information: Public Access terminal is available. No juvenile, mental health, sealed or expunged records released. Fee to fax results is $.50 per page. Copy fee: $.50 per page. No cert fee. Payee: Clerk of Court. Personal checks accepted. Prepayment required. Mail requests: SASE required. Mail turnaround time 3 days.

Saline County

District Court PO Box 1760, Salina, KS 67402-1760; 785-309-5831; Fax: 785-309-5845. Hours: 8:30AM-4PM (CST). *Felony, Misdemeanor, Civil, Eviction, Small Claims, Probate.*

Civil Records: Access: Mail, in person. Both court and visitors may perform in person searches. Search fee: $12.00 per hour. Required to search: name, years to search, address. Civil cases indexed by defendant, plaintiff. Civil records on computer from 1990, index from early 1900s.

Criminal Records: Access: Mail, in person. Both court and visitors may perform in person searches. Search fee: $12.00 per hour. Required to search: name, years to search, address, DOB, SSN, signed release. Criminal records on computer from 1990, index from early 1900s.

General Information: Public Access terminal is available. No juvenile, mental health, sealed or expunged records released. Copy fee: $.25 per page. Cert fee: $1.00. Payee: Clerk of District Court. Personal checks accepted. Prepayment required. Mail requests: SASE not required. Mail turnaround 1 week.

Scott County

District Court 303 Court, Scott City, KS 67871; 620-872-7208. Hours: 8AM-Noon, 1-5PM (CST). *Felony, Misdemeanor, Civil, Eviction, Small Claims, Probate.*

Civil Records: Access: Mail, in person. No search fee. Required to search: name, years to search. Civil cases indexed by defendant, plaintiff. Civil records on computer back to 1992, index cards from 1980s.

Criminal Records: Access: In person only. Visitors must perform in person searches for themselves. No search fee. Required to search: name, years to search, DOB. Criminal records on computer back to 1992, index cards from 1980s.

General Information: Public Access terminal is available. No juvenile, mental health, sealed or expunged records released. Fee to fax results is $1.00 per page. Copy fee: $.25 per page. Cert fee: $1.00. Payee: Clerk of Court. Personal checks accepted. Prepayment required. Mail requests: SASE required. Mail turnaround time 1-2 days.

Sedgwick County

District Court 525 N Main, Wichita, KS 67203; 316-383-7302; Civil phone: 316-660-5719; Criminal phone: 316-660-5719; Probate phone: 316-660-5721; Fax: 316-660-5780. Hours: 8AM-4PM (CST). *Felony, Misdemeanor, Civil, Eviction, Small Claims, Probate.* http://distcrt18.state.ks.us/

Note: Phone numbers above are for records department; direct numbers for the divisions are: criminal-316-660-5720 (fax-660-5777); civil-316-660-5690 (fax-660-5775

Civil Records: Access: Fax, mail, online, in person. Both court and visitors may perform in person searches. Search fee: $12.00 per hour. Fee charged if more than 15 minutes. Required to search: name, years to search. Civil cases indexed by defendant, plaintiff. Civil records on computer from 1983, microfiche from 1982, archives from 1977 and index cards from 1900s. Access to the remote online system via AccessKansas requires a $225 setup fee, $49 monthly fee and small transaction fee. The system also includes probate, traffic, domestic, and criminal cases. For more information, call 316-383-7563 or visit www.accesskansas.org/online-services.html.

Criminal Records: Access: Fax, mail, online, in person. Both court and visitors may perform in person searches. Search fee: $12.00 per hour. Fee charged if more than 15 minutes. Required to search: name, years to search. Criminal records on computer from 1983, microfiche from 1982, archives from 1977 and index cards from 1900s. Online access to criminal records is the same as civil.

General Information: Public Access terminal is available. No juvenile, adoption, mental health, sealed or expunged records released. Will fax results $5.00 1st page, $2.00 each add'l. Copy fee: $.25 per page. Cert fee: $1.00. Payee: Clerk of Court. Personal checks accepted. Prepayment required. Mail requests: SASE required. Mail turnaround time 7-10 days.

Seward County

District Court 415 N Washington, #103, Liberal, KS 67901; 620-626-3234; Civil phone: 620-626-3391; Criminal phone: 620-626-3234; Probate phone: 620-626-3232; Fax: 620-626-3302. Hours: 8:30AM-5PM (CST). *Felony, Misdemeanor, Civil, Eviction, Small Claims, Probate.* Note: Court will do searches on occasion, fee is $12.00 per hour. The Small Claims Court can be reached at 620-626-3232.

Civil Records: Access: In person only. Visitors must perform in person searches for themselves. No search fee. Required to search: name, years to search. Civil cases indexed by defendant, plaintiff. Civil records on computer back to 1977, index from 1900s.

Criminal Records: Access: In person only. Visitors must perform in person searches for themselves. No search fee. Required to search: name, years to search; also helpful: SSN. Criminal records on computer back to 1977, index from 1900s.

General Information: Public Access terminal is available. No juvenile, mental health, sealed or expunged records released. Will fax results for $2.00 1st page; $.50 each add'l page. Copy fee: $.25 per page. Cert fee: $1.25. Payee: Clerk of District Court. Personal checks accepted. Prepayment required.

Shawnee County

District Court 200 E 7th, Rm 209, Topeka, KS 66603; 785-233-8200 X4327; Civil phone: x5158; Criminal phone: x5157; Probate phone: x4358; Fax: 785-291-4911. Hours: 8AM-5PM (CST). *Felony, Misdemeanor, Civil, Eviction, Small Claims, Probate.* www.shawneecourt.org

Civil Records: Access: Fax, mail, in person, online. Both court and visitors may perform in person searches. Search fee: $12.00 per hour. Required to search: name, years to search. Civil cases indexed by defendant, plaintiff. Civil records on computer from 1980, microfiche from 1950, archives and index from 1800s. Index online through INK of Kansas. See www.ink.org for subscription information. Also, access to county court records is free at www.shawneecourt.org/doc/index.html. Also, online access to court record images is free at www.shawneecourt.org/img_temp.htm. Also find "viewing restricted" domestic documents here.

Criminal Records: Access: Fax, mail, in person, online. Both court and visitors may perform in person searches. Search fee: $12.00 per hour. Required to search: name, years to search, DOB. Criminal records on computer from 1980, microfiche from 1950, archives and index from 1800s. Online access to criminal records is the same as civil.

General Information: Public Access terminal is available. No juvenile, mental health, sealed or expunged records released. Will fax results to local or toll free line. Copy fee: $.50 per page. $1.50 per pg for microfilm copies. Cert fee: $2.25. Payee: Clerk of District Court. Personal checks accepted. Prepayment required. Mail requests: SASE not required. Mail turnaround time 3-4 days.

Sheridan County

District Court PO Box 753, Hoxie, KS 67740; 785-675-3451; Fax: 785-675-2256. Hours: 8AM-Noon, 1PM-5PM (CST). *Felony, Misdemeanor, Civil, Eviction, Small Claims, Probate.*

Civil Records: Access: Phone, fax, mail, in person. Both court and visitors may perform in person searches. Search fee: $12.00 per hour. Required to search: name, years to search. Civil cases indexed by defendant, plaintiff. Civil records on strip index from 1885. Mail requests require use of a special form.

Criminal Records: Access: Phone, fax, mail, in person. Both court and visitors may perform in person searches. Search fee: $12.00 per hour. Required to search: name, years to search, signed release. Criminal records on index from 1885; on computer since 1995.

General Information: Public Access terminal is available. No juvenile, mental health, sealed or expunged records released. Will fax results to local or toll free line. Copy fee: $.25 per page. Cert fee: $1.00. Payee: Clerk of Court. Personal checks accepted. Prepayment required. Mail requests: SASE required. Mail turnaround time 1-2 days.

Sherman County

District Court 813 Broadway, Rm 201, Goodland, KS 67735; 785-899-4850; Fax: 785-899-4858. 8:30AM-5PM (MST). *Felony, Misdemeanor, Civil, Eviction, Small Claims, Probate.*

Civil Records: Access: In person only. Visitors must perform in person searches for themselves. No search fee. Required to search: name, years to search. Civil cases indexed by defendant, plaintiff. Civil records on docket books from 1900s.

Criminal Records: Access: In person only. Visitors must perform in person searches for themselves. No search fee. Required to search: name, years to search; also helpful: SSN. Criminal records on docket books from 1900s.

General Information: No juvenile, mental health, sealed or expunged records released. Copy fee: $.25 per page. Cert fee: $1.00. Payee: Clerk of District Court. Personal checks accepted. Prepayment required.

Smith County

District Court PO Box 273, Smith Center, KS 66967; 785-282-5140/41; Fax: 785-282-5145. Hours: 8AM-5PM (CST). *Felony, Misdemeanor, Civil, Eviction, Small Claims, Probate.*

Civil Records: Access: In person only. Visitors must perform in person searches for themselves. No search fee. Required to search: name, years to search. Civil cases indexed by defendant, plaintiff. Civil records on index cards from 1873.

Criminal Records: Access: In person only. Visitors must perform in person searches for themselves. No search fee. Required to search: name, years to search; also helpful: SSN. Criminal records on index cards from 1873.

General Information: No juvenile, mental health, sealed or expunged records released. Copy fee: $.25 per page. Cert fee: $1.00. Payee: Clerk of Court. Personal checks accepted. Prepayment required.

Stafford County

District Court PO Box 365, St John, KS 67576; 620-549-3295; Fax: 620-549-3298. Hours: 8AM-5PM (CST). *Felony, Misdemeanor, Civil, Eviction, Small Claims, Probate.* www.staffordcounty.org

Civil Records: Access: Phone, mail, fax, in person, email. Both court and visitors may perform in person searches. Search fee: $12.00 per hour, 15 minutes minimum. Required to search: name, years to search. Civil cases indexed by defendant, plaintiff. Civil records on computer from 1988, microfiche and index from 1900s.

Criminal Records: Access: In person only. Visitors must perform in person searches for themselves. Search fee: $12.00 per hour, 15 minutes minimum. Required to search: name, years to search; also helpful: signed release. Criminal records on computer from 1988, microfiche and index from 1900s. All mail request mmust go to the Kansas Bureau of Investigations.

General Information: Public Access terminal is available. No juvenile, mental health, sealed or expunged records released. Will not fax results. Copy fee: $.25 per page. No cert fee. Payee: Clerk of District Court. Personal checks accepted. Prepayment required. Mail requests: SASE required. Mail turnaround time 1-3 days.

Stanton County

District Court PO Box 913, Johnson, KS 67855; 620-492-2180; Fax: 620-492-6410. Hours: 8AM-5PM (CST). *Felony, Misdemeanor, Civil, Eviction, Small Claims, Probate.*

Civil Records: Access: Phone, fax, mail, in person. Both court and visitors may perform in person

searches. Search fee: $12.00 per hour. Required to search: name, years to search. Civil cases indexed by defendant, plaintiff. Civil records on computer from 1977, index from 1887.

Criminal Records: Access: Phone, fax, mail, in person. Both court and visitors may perform in person searches. Search fee: $12.00 per hour. Required to search: name, years to search, DOB, SSN. Criminal records on computer from 1977, index from 1887.

General Information: Public Access terminal is available. No juvenile, mental health, sealed or expunged records released. Will fax results $2.50 1st page, $.50 each add'l. Copy fee: $.25 per page. Cert fee: $1.00. Payee: Clerk of District Court. Personal checks accepted. Prepayment required. Mail requests: SASE required. Mail turnaround time 1-3 days.

Stevens County

District Court 200 E 6th, Hugoton, KS 67951; 620-544-2484; Fax: 620-544-2528. Hours: 8AM-5PM closed noon-1 (CST). *Felony, Misdemeanor, Civil, Eviction, Small Claims, Probate.*

Civil Records: Access: Mail, in person. Both court and visitors may perform in person searches. Search fee: $12.50 per hour. Required to search: name, years to search. Civil cases indexed by defendant, plaintiff. Civil records on computer from 1991, microfiche, archives and index from 1887.

Criminal Records: Access: In person only. Visitors must perform in person searches for themselves. No search fee. Required to search: name, years to search; also helpful: SSN. Criminal records on computer from 1991, microfiche, archives and index from 1887.

General Information: Public Access terminal is available. No juvenile, mental health, sealed or expunged records released. Fee to fax results is $3.00 plus $.25 per page. Copy fee: $.25 per page. Cert fee: $1.25. Payee: Clerk of District Court. Personal checks accepted. Prepayment required. Must prepay for fax and mail. Mail requests: SASE required. Mail turnaround time 1-3 days.

Sumner County

District Court PO Box 399, Sumner County Courthouse, Wellington, KS 67152; 620-326-5936; Fax: 620-326-5365. Hours: 8AM-Noon, 1-5PM (CST). *Felony, Misdemeanor, Civil, Eviction, Small Claims, Probate.*

Note: Court will not perform searches for "employment purposes" nor do they perform lien searches. The court prefers that you summit requests on their request form.

Civil Records: Access: Mail, fax, in person. Both court and visitors may perform in person searches. Search fee: $12.00 per hour. Required to search: name, years to search. Civil cases indexed by defendant, plaintiff. Civil records on computer back to 1991, index cards from 1800s for probate.

Criminal Records: Access: Mail, fax, in person. Both court and visitors may perform in person searches. Search fee: $12.00 per hour. Required to search: name, years to search; also helpful: case number. Criminal records on computer back to 1991, index cards from 1800s for probate.

General Information: Public Access terminal is available. No juvenile, mental health, sealed or expunged records released. Will fax results for $1.00 per page up to 10 pages. Copy fee: $.25 per page. Cert fee: $2.00. Payee: Clerk of Court. Personal checks accepted. Prepayment required. Mail requests: SASE not required. Mail turnaround time 1-3 days.

Thomas County

District Court PO Box 805, Colby, KS 67701; 785-462-4540; Fax: 785-462-2291. Hours: 8:30AM-5PM (CST). *Felony, Misdemeanor, Civil, Eviction, Small Claims, Probate.*
Civil Records: Access: Fax, mail, in person. Both court and visitors may perform in person searches. Search fee: $12.00 per hour. Required to search: name, years to search. Civil cases indexed by defendant, plaintiff. Civil records on index from 1887.
Criminal Records: Access: Fax, mail, in person. Both court and visitors may perform in person searches. Search fee: $12.00 per hour. Required to search: name, years to search, DOB, sex; also helpful: SSN. Criminal records on index from 1887.
General Information: Public Access terminal is available. No juvenile, mental health, sealed or expunged records released. Will fax results $1.00 per page. Copy fee: $.25 per page. Cert fee: $1.00. Payee: Clerk. Personal checks accepted. Prepayment , SASE required. Mail requests: Mail turnaround time varies.

Trego County

District Court 216 N Main, Wakeeney, KS 67672; 785-743-2148; Fax: 785-743-2726. Hours: 8:30AM-5PM (CST). *Felony, Misdemeanor, Civil, Eviction, Small Claims, Probate.*
Civil Records: Access: Phone, mail, fax, in person. Both court and visitors may perform in person searches. Search fee: $12.00 per hour. Required to search: name, years to search. Civil cases indexed by defendant, plaintiff. Civil records on computer since 1996; prior records on card index.
Criminal Records: Access: Mail, in person. Only the court performs in person searches; visitors may not. Search fee: $12.00 per hour. Required to search: name, years to search; also helpful: DOB, SSN, sex. Criminal records on computer since 1996; prior records on card index.
General Information: Public Access terminal is available. No juvenile, mental health, sealed or expunged records released. Fee to fax results is $2.00 1st page; $.50 each add'l page. Copy fee: $.25 per page. Cert fee: $2.00. Payee: Clerk of Court. Personal checks accepted. Prepayment required. Mail requests: SASE required. Mail turnaround time 1-2 weeks.

Wabaunsee County

District Court Courthouse, PO Box 278, Alma, KS 66401; 785-765-2406; Fax: 785-765-2487. Hours: 8AM-4:30PM (CST). *Felony, Misdemeanor, Civil, Eviction, Small Claims, Probate.*
Civil Records: Access: In person only. Visitors must perform in person searches for themselves. No search fee. Required to search: name, years to search. Civil cases indexed by defendant, plaintiff. Civil records on book index from 1800s; on computer back to 1996.
Criminal Records: Access: In person only. Visitors must perform in person searches for themselves. No search fee. Required to search: name, years to search; also helpful: SSN. Criminal records on book index from 1800s; on computer back to 1996.
General Information: Public Access terminal is available. No juvenile, mental health, sealed or expunged records released. Copy fee: $.50 per page. Cert fee: $1.25. Payee: Clerk of District Court. Personal checks accepted. Prepayment required.

Wallace County

District Court PO Box 8, Sharon Springs, KS 67758; 785-852-4289; Fax: 785-852-4271. Hours: 8AM-Noon,1-5PM (MST). *Felony, Misdemeanor, Civil, Eviction, Small Claims, Probate.*
Civil Records: Access: Mail, in person, fax. Both court and visitors may perform in person searches.

Search fee: $12.00 per hour. Required to search: name; also helpful: years to search. Civil cases indexed by defendant, plaintiff. Civil records on index from 1887. By mail only if requested for a particular case, court will not do name searches.
Criminal Records: Access: In person only. Visitors must perform in person searches for themselves. No search fee. Required to search: name; also helpful: years to search. Criminal records on index from 1887.
General Information: No juvenile offender (under 14 years old), juvenile in need of care, adoption, mental health, sealed or expunged records released. Will fax results to local or toll free line. Copy fee: $.25 per page. Cert fee: $1.00. Payee: Clerk of Court. Personal checks accepted. Prepayment required. Mail requests: SASE not required. Mail turnaround time 1-2 days.

Washington County

District Court Courthouse, 214 C St, Washington, KS 66968; 785-325-2381; Fax: 785-325-2557. Hours: 8AM-Noon,1-5PM (CST). *Felony, Misdemeanor, Civil, Eviction, Small Claims, Probate.*
www.kscourts.org/dstcts/12dstct.htm
Civil Records: Access: Fax, mail, in person. Both court and visitors may perform in person searches. Search fee: $12.00 per hour. Required to search: name, years to search. Civil cases indexed by defendant, plaintiff. Civil records on card index from 1887; on computer back to 1995.
Criminal Records: Access: Fax, mail, in person. Both court and visitors may perform in person searches. Search fee: $12.00 per hour. Required to search: name, years to search. Criminal records on card index from 1887; on computer back to 1995.
General Information: No juvenile, mental health, sealed or expunged records released. Fee to fax results is $3.00 per page. Copy fee: $.25 per page. Cert fee: $1.00. Payee: Clerk of Court. Personal checks accepted. Prepayment required. Mail requests: SASE required. Mail turnaround time 1-3 days.

Wichita County

District Court 206 S 4th St, PO Box 968, Leoti, KS 67861; 620-375-4454; Fax: 620-375-2999. Hours: 8AM-5PM (CST). *Felony, Misdemeanor, Civil, Eviction, Small Claims, Probate.*
Note: This court is not in Wichita, KS. Wichita, KS is in Sedgwick County.
Civil Records: Access: Mail, in person. Both court and visitors may perform in person searches. Search fee: $12.00 per hour. Required to search: name, years to search. Civil cases indexed by defendant, plaintiff. Civil records on computer back to 1986, on index from 1900.
Criminal Records: Access: In person only. Visitors must perform in person searches for themselves. No search fee. Required to search: name, years to search. Criminal records on computer back to 1986, on index from 1900. Criminal records are through the KBI.
General Information: Public Access terminal is available. (Index goes back to 1991.) No juvenile, mental health, sealed or expunged records released. Copy fee: $.20 per page. Cert fee: $1.00. Payee: Clerk of District Court. Personal checks accepted. Prepayment required. Mail requests: SASE required. Mail turnaround time 1 week.

Wilson County

District Court PO Box 246, Fredonia, KS 66736; 620-378-4533; Fax: 620-378-4531. Hours: 8:30AM-5PM (CST). *Felony, Misdemeanor, Civil, Eviction, Small Claims, Probate.*
Civil Records: Access: Fax, mail, in person. Both court and visitors may perform in person searches.

Search fee: $12.00 per hour. Required to search: name, years to search. Civil cases indexed by defendant, plaintiff. Civil records on computer since 1993, index cards from 1864.
Criminal Records: Access: Fax, mail, in person. Both court and visitors may perform in person searches. Search fee: $12.00 per hour. Required to search: name, years to search; also helpful: SSN. Criminal records on computer since 1993, index cards from 1864.
General Information: Public Access terminal is available. No juvenile, mental health, sealed or expunged records released. Fee to fax results is $1.00 per page. Copy fee: $.25 per page. Cert fee: $1.00. Payee: Clerk of Court. Personal checks accepted. Prepayment required. Mail requests: SASE required. Mail turnaround time 1-3 weeks.

Woodson County

District Court PO Box 228, Yates Center, KS 66783; 620-625-8610; Fax: 620-625-8674. Hours: 8AM-Noon,1-5PM (CST). *Felony, Misdemeanor, Civil, Eviction, Small Claims, Probate.*
Civil Records: Access: Fax, mail, in person. Both court and visitors may perform in person searches. Search fee: $12.00 per hour. Required to search: name, years to search. Civil cases indexed by defendant, plaintiff. Civil records on index from 1880s, on computer since 1993.
Criminal Records: Access: In person only. Visitors must perform in person searches for themselves. No search fee. Required to search: name, years to search. Criminal records on index from 1880s, on computer since 1993. Refer phone inquires to KBI at 785-296-8200.
General Information: Public Access terminal is available. No juvenile (under age 14 years), mental health, sealed or expunged records released. Fee to fax results is $1.00 per page. Copy fee: $.50 per page. Cert fee: $1.00. Payee: District Court. Business checks accepted. Prepayment required. Mail requests: SASE required. Mail turnaround time 1 day.

Wyandotte County

District Court 710 N 7th St, Kansas City, KS 66101; Civil phone: 913-573-2901; Criminal phone: 913-573-2905. Hours: 8AM-5PM (CST). *Felony, Misdemeanor, Civil, Eviction, Small Claims, Probate.* Note: Crminal fax is 913-573-8177, civil fax is 813-573-4134.
Civil Records: Access: Phone, mail, online, in person. Both court and visitors may perform in person searches. No search fee. Required to search: name, years to search. Civil cases indexed by defendant, plaintiff. Civil records on computer from 1975, microfiche, archives and index from 1900s. Access to the remote online system requires specific software and $20 setup fee. Transactions are $.05 each. For more information call 913-573-2885.
Criminal Records: Access: Online, in person. Visitors must perform in person searches for themselves. No search fee. Required to search: name, years to search, DOB, SSN. Criminal records on computer from 1972, microfiche, archives and index from early 1900s. Online access to criminal records is the same as civil. Refer phone inquires to KBI at 785-296-8200.
General Information: Public Access terminal is available. No juvenile, mental health, sealed or expunged records released. Copy fee: $.25 per page. Cert fee: $1.00. Payee: Clerk of District Court. Personal checks accepted. Prepayment required. Mail requests: SASE required. Mail turnaround: 1-3 days.

Kansas Recording Offices

ORGANIZATION: 105 counties, 105 recording offices. The recording officer is Register of Deeds. Many counties utilize a "Miscellaneous Index" for tax and other liens, separate from real estate records. 100 counties are in the Central Time Zone (CST) and 5 are in the Mountain Time Zone (MST).

REAL ESTATE RECORDS: Most counties will not perform real estate searches, although some will do as an accommodation with the understanding that they are not "certified." Some counties will also do a search based upon legal description to determine owner. Copy fees vary, and certification fees are usually $1.00 per document. Tax records are located at the Appraiser's Office.

UCC RECORDS: Financing statements are filed at the state level, except for real estate related collateral, which are filed with the Register of Deeds. However, prior to 07/2001, consumer goods collateral were also filed at the Register of Deeds and these older records can be searched there. All counties will perform UCC searches. Use search request form UCC-3. Search fees are usually $15.00 per debtor name. Copies usually cost $1.00 per page.

TAX LIEN RECORDS: Federal tax liens on personal property of businesses are filed with the Secretary of State. Other federal tax liens and all state tax liens on personal property are filed with the county Register of Deeds. Most counties automatically include tax liens on personal property with a UCC search. Tax liens on personal property may usually be searched separately for $8.00 per name.

OTHER LIENS: Mechanics, harvesters, lis pendens, threshers.

ONLINE ACCESS: A few counties have online access to recorder records; there is no statewide system.

Allen County

County Register of Deeds, 1 N. Washington Ave, Iola, KS 66749. **Phone-**County Register of Deeds, R/E & UCC Recording- 620-365-1412; fax-620-365-1414; hours 8AM-5PM www.ksrods.org

UCC record search per debtor- $15.00. UCC copy- $1.00 per page. UCC search includes tax liens. Tax lien search fee- $15.00 per debtor. Will not search real estate records. RE record copy- $.50 per page if mailed; $1.00 if faxed. Cert fee: $1.00 per doc. Payee: County Register of Deeds. **Other phones:** Assessor-620-365-1415; Treasurer-620-365-1409; Appraiser-620-365-1415; Elections-620-365-1407; Vital Records-785-296-1400 (Topeka); Clerk of District Court (Marriage, etc.)-620-365-1425; City of Iola Clerk (Birth & Death before 1911)-620-365-4910.

Anderson County

County Register of Deeds, 100 E 4th St, Courthouse, Garnett, KS 66032-1503. **Phone-**County Register of Deeds, R/E & UCC Recording- 785-448-3715; fax-785-448-5621; hours 8AM-5PM

UCC record search per debtor- $15.00. UCC copy- $1.00 per page. UCC search includes tax liens. Separate tax lien search fee- $15.00 per debtor. Will not search real estate records. RE record copy- $1.00 per page. Cert fee: $1.00 per page. Payee: County Register of Deeds. **Online Access to Marriage records:** free access to marriage records is by alpha search at www.kscourts.org/dstcts/4anmarec.htm. **Other phones:** Assessor-appraiser-785-448-6844; Treasurer-785-448-5824; Elections-785-448-6841.

Atchison County

County Register of Deeds, 423 N. 5th St., Courthouse, Atchison, KS 66002-1861. **Phone-**County Register of Deeds, R/E & UCC Recording- 913-367-2568; fax-913-367-8441; hours 8:30AM-5PM. UCC record search per debtor- $15.00. UCC copy- $1.00 per page. UCC search includes tax liens if requested. Separate federal/state combined tax lien search- $15.00 per debtor. Real estate owner, mortgage, and property transfer searches available. RE record copy- $.50 per page. Cert fee: $1.00 per page. Payee: County Register of Deeds. **Other phones:** Assessor-913-367-4400; Treasurer-913-367-5332; Elections-913-367-1653; Vital Records-913-367-1653.

Barber County

County Register of Deeds, 120 E. Washington St, Courthouse, Medicine Lodge, KS 67104. **Phone-**620-886-3981; fax-620-886-5045; hours 8:30AM-5PM

UCC record search per debtor- $15.00. UCC copy- $1.00 per page. UCC search includes tax liens. Separate federal/state combined tax lien search- $8.00 per debtor. Will search real estate records on a limited basis. RE record copy- $.25 per page standard fee; may vary. Cert fee: $1.00 per cert. Payee: County Register of Deeds. **Other phones:** Assessor-620-886-3795; Treasurer-620-886-3775; Appraiser-620-886-3723; Elections-620-886-3961.

Barton County

County Register of Deeds, 1400 Main St, Courthouse, #205, Great Bend, KS 67530-4037. **Phone-**County Register of Deeds, R/E & UCC Recording- 620-793-1849; fax-620-793-1981; hours 8AM-5PM www.bartoncounty.org

UCC record search per debtor- $15.00. UCC search includes tax liens. Tax lien search fee- $5.00 per debtor. Will not search real estate records. Record copy- $1.00 per page. Cert fee: $1.00 per cert. Payee: Barton County Register of Deeds. **Online Access to Assessor records:** Access to the County 2002 Property value list by address and name is at www.bartoncounty.org/values/Propvalues.htm. **Other phones:** Assessor-appraiser-620-793-1821; Treasurer-620-793-1827; Elections-620-793-1835.

Bourbon County

County Register of Deeds, 210 S. National, Fort Scott, KS 66701. **Phone-**County Register of Deeds, R/E & UCC Recording- 620-223-3800 x17; fax-620-223-5241; hours 8:30AM-4:30PM

Will not search UCC records. UCC copy- $1.00 per page. Separate federal/state combined tax lien search- $15.00 per debtor. Will not search real estate records. RE record copy- $.35 to $1.00 per page. Cert fee: $1.00 per cert. Payee: Bourbon County Register of Deeds. **Other phones:** Assessor-620-223-3800 x16; Treasurer-620-223-3800 x29.

Brown County

County Register of Deeds, 601 Oregon, Courthouse, Hiawatha, KS 66434. **Phone-**County Register of Deeds, R/E & UCC Recording- 785-742-3741; fax-785-742-3255; hours-8AM-5PM www.brown.kansasgov.com

UCC record search per debtor- $15.00. UCC copy- $1.00 per page. UCC search includes tax liens. Separate federal/state combined tax lien search- $8.00 per debtor. Real estate record owner and mortgage searches available. RE record copy- $.30 per page. Cert fee: $1.00 per cert. Payee: County Register of Deeds. **Other phones:** Assessor-785-742-7232; Treasurer-785-742-2051; Appraiser-785-742-7232; Elections-785-742-2581.

Butler County

County Register of Deeds, 205 W. Central, Courthouse, #104, El Dorado, KS 67042. **Phone-**County Register of Deeds, R/E & UCC Recording- 316-322-4113, UCC Recording- 316-322-4111; fax-316-321-1011; hours 8AM-5PM www.bucoks.com

UCC record search per debtor- $15.00. UCC copy- $1.00 per page. UCC search includes tax liens if requested. Separate federal/state combined tax lien search- $15.00 per debtor. Will not search real estate records. Cert fee: $1.00 per cert. Payee: Butler County Register of Deeds. **Online Access to Appraiser, Real Estate Value records:** Access to the appraiser's Real Estate Market Values data is free at www.bucoks.com/depts/appr/values/values.htm. No name searching. **Other phones:** Assessor-316-321-4220; Treasurer-316-322-4210; Appraiser-316-322-4220; Elections-316-322-4233; Vital Records-785-296-1400 (State of Kansas).

Chase County

County Register of Deeds, PO Box 529, Cottonwood Falls, KS 66845-0529. **Phone-**County Register of Deeds, R/E & UCC Recording- 620-273-6398; fax-620-273-6617; hours 8AM-5PM

UCC record search per debtor- $15.00. UCC copy- $1.00 per page. UCC search includes tax liens if requested. Separate federal/state combined tax lien search- $15.00 per debtor. Will search real estate records. RE record copy- $.50 or $1.00 per page. Cert fee: $1.00 per cert. Payee: County Register of Deeds. **Other phones:** Assessor-620-273-6423;

Treasurer-620-273-6493; Appraiser-620-273-6306; Elections-620-273-6423; Vital Records-620-273-6398.

Chautauqua County

County Register of Deeds, 215 N. Chautauqua, Courthouse, Sedan, KS 67361. **Phone**-620-725-5830; fax-620-725-5831; hours 8AM-Noon,1-4PM

UCC record search per debtor- $15.00. UCC copy-$1.00 per page. UCC search includes tax liens. Separate federal/state combined tax lien search-$8.00 per debtor. Will not search real estate records. RE record copy- $.50-$1.00 per page. Cert fee: $1.00 per cert. Payee: Chautauqua County Register of Deeds. **Other phones**: Assessor-620-725-3127; Treasurer-620-725-3666.

Cherokee County

County Register of Deeds, PO Box 228, Columbus, KS 66725. **Phone**-County Register of Deeds, R/E & UCC Recording- 620-429-3777; fax-620-429-1362; hours 9AM-5PM. UCC record search per debtor- $15.00. UCC copy- $1.00 per page. UCC search includes tax liens. Separate federal/state combined tax lien search- $15.00 per debtor. Will not search real estate records. RE record copy- $.50 per page; $1.00 min. Cert fee: $1.00 per cert. Payee: Cherokee County Register of Deeds. **Other phones**: Assessor-620-429-3984; Treasurer-620-429-2418; Appraiser-620-429-3984; Elections-620-429-8043.

Cheyenne County

County Register of Deeds, PO Box 907, St. Francis, KS 67756-0907. **Phone**-County Register of Deeds, R/E & UCC Recording- 785-332-8820; fax-785-332-8825; hours 8AM-Noon,1-5PM

UCC record search per debtor- $15.00. UCC copy-$1.00 per page. UCC search includes tax liens. Will not search real estate records. RE record copy-$.35 per page. Cert fee: $1.00 per cert. Payee: Cheyenne County Register of Deeds. **Other phones**: Assessor-785-332-8830; Treasurer-785-332-8810; Appraiser-785-332-8830; Elections-785-332-8800; Vital Records-785-332-8850.

Clark County

County Register of Deeds, PO Box 222, Ashland, KS 67831-0222. **Phone**-County Register of Deeds, R/E & UCC Recording- 620-635-2812; fax-620-635-2393; hours 8:30AM-4:30PM

UCC record search per debtor- $15.00. UCC copy-$1.00 per page. UCC search includes tax liens. Separate federal/state combined tax lien search-$8.00 per debtor. Will not search real estate records. RE record copy- $.25 per page, plus postage. Cert fee: $1.00 per cert. Payee: Clark County Register of Deeds. **Other phones**: Assessor-620-635-2142; Treasurer-620-635-2745; Appraiser-620-635-2142; Elections-620-635-2813.

Clay County

County Register of Deeds, PO Box 63, Clay Center, KS 67432. **Phone**-785-632-3811; fax-785-632-2736; hours 8AM-5PM

UCC record search per debtor- $15.00. UCC copy-$1.00 per page. UCC search includes tax liens. Separate federal/state combined tax lien search-$15.00 per debtor. Real estate owner, mortgage, and property transfer searches available. RE record copy-$.50 per page. Cert fee: $1.00 per cert. Payee: Clay County Register of Deeds. **Other phones**: Assessor-785-632-2800; Treasurer-785-632-3282.

Cloud County

County Register of Deeds, PO Box 96, Concordia, KS 66901-0096. **Phone**-County Register of Deeds, R/E & UCC Recording- 785-243-8121; fax-785-243-8123; hours 8AM-4:30PM www.cloudcountyks.org

UCC record search per debtor- $15.00. UCC copy-$1.00 per page. UCC search includes tax liens. Separate federal/state combined tax lien search-$15.00 per debtor. Will not search real estate records. Cert fee: $3.00 per cert. Payee: Cloud County Register of Deeds. **Online Access to Assessor, Property records**: Access assessor property data at www.cloudcountyks.org/V2RunLev2.asp?submit1=OK. You may search by registering or without. **Other phones**: Assessor-appraiser-785-243-8100; Treasurer-785-243-8115; Elections-785-243-8110.

Coffey County

County Register of Deeds, 110 S 6th St, Rm 205 - Courthouse, Burlington, KS 66839. **Phone**-620-364-2423; hours 8AM-5PM

UCC record search per debtor- $15.00. UCC copy-$1.00 per page. UCC search includes tax liens. Separate federal/state combined tax lien search-$8.00 per debtor. Will not search real estate records. RE record copy- $.50 per page. Cert fee: $1.00 per cert. Payee: Coffey County Register of Deeds. **Online Access to Marriage records**: Access to marriage records is by alpha search up to 1/18/2001 for free at www.kscourts.org/dstcts/4osmarec.htm. **Other phones**: Assessor-620-364-8426; Treasurer-620-364-5532.

Comanche County

County Register of Deeds, PO Box 576, Coldwater, KS 67029-0576. **Phone**-County Register of Deeds, R/E & UCC Recording- 620-582-2152; fax-620-582-2390; hours 9AM-Noon,1-5PM

UCC record search per debtor- $15.00. UCC search includes tax liens. Will not search real estate records but will help walk-ins. Record copy- $1.00 per page. Cert fee: $1.00 per cert. Payee: Comanche County Register of Deeds. **Other phones**: Assessor-620-582-2544; Treasurer-620-582-2964; Appraiser-620-582-2544; Elections-620-582-2361.

Cowley County

County Register of Deeds, PO Box 741, Winfield, KS 67156-0471. **Phone**-620-221-5461; fax-620-221-5463; hours 8AM-Noon,1-5PM

UCC record search per debtor- $15.00. UCC search includes tax liens. Separate federal/state combined tax lien search- $15.00 per debtor. Will not search real estate records. Record copy- $1.00 per page. Cert fee: $1.00 per cert. Payee: Cowley County Register of Deeds. **Other phones**: Assessor-620-221-5430; Treasurer-620-221-5412.

Crawford County

County Register of Deeds, PO Box 44, Girard, KS 66743. **Phone**-County Register of Deeds, R/E & UCC Recording- 620-724-8218; fax-620-724-8823; hours 8:30AM-4:30PM

UCC record search per debtor- $15.00. UCC copy-$1.00 per page. UCC search includes tax liens. Separate federal/state combined tax lien search-$8.00 per debtor. Real estate record owner and mortgage searches available. RE record- $.25 per page. Cert fee: $1.00 per cert. Payee: Crawford County Register of Deeds. **Other phones**: Assessor-620-724-6431; Treasurer-620-724-8222.

Decatur County

County Register of Deeds, PO Box 167, Oberlin, KS 67749-0167. **Phone**-County Register of Deeds, R/E & UCC Recording- 785-475-8105; fax-785-475-8150; hours 8AM-Noon,1-5PM

UCC record search per debtor- $15.00. UCC copy-$1.00 per page. UCC search includes tax liens. Will not search real estate records. RE record copy-$.25 per page. Cert fee: $1.00 per cert. Payee: Decatur County Register of Deeds. **Other phones**: Assessor-785-475-8109; Treasurer-785-475-8103;

Appraiser-785-475-8109; Elections-785-475-8102; Vital Records-785-475-8105; Clerk of District Court-785-475-8107; Decatur County Clerk-785-475-8102.

Dickinson County

County Register of Deeds, PO Box 517, Abilene, KS 67410. **Phone**-County Register of Deeds, R/E & UCC Recording- 785-263-3073; fax-785-263-0428; hours 8AM-5PM. UCC record search per debtor- $15.00. UCC copy- $1.00 per page. UCC search includes tax liens if requested. Separate federal/state combined tax lien search- $8.00 per debtor. Real estate owner, mortgage, and property transfer searches available. RE record copy- $.50 per page. Cert fee: $1.00 per cert. Payee: Dickinson County Register of Deeds. **Online Access to Property, Assessor records**: Access to county property tax data is free at www.dickinson.kansasgov.com/disclaimerlev2.asp. **Other phones**: Assessor-785-263-4418; Treasurer-785-263-3231.

Doniphan County

County Register of Deeds, PO Box 73, Troy, KS 66087. **Phone**-County Register of Deeds, R/E & UCC Recording- 785-985-3932; fax-785-985-3723; hours 8AM-5PM www.dpcountyks.com

UCC record search per debtor- $15.00. UCC copy-$1.00 per page. UCC search includes tax liens if requested. Separate federal/state combined tax lien search- $15.00 per debtor. Real estate owner, mortgage, and property transfer searches available. RE record copy- $.50 per page. Cert fee: $1.00 per cert. Payee: Doniphan County Register of Deeds. **Other phones**: Assessor-785-985-3977; Treasurer-785-985-3831; Appraiser-785-985-3977; Elections-785-985-3513.

Douglas County

County Register of Deeds, 1100 Massachusetts, Courthouse, Lawrence, KS 66044-3097. **Phone**-785-832-5283, R/E Recording- 785-832-5282; fax-785-330-2807; hours 8AM-5PM www.douglas-county.com

UCC record search per debtor- $15.00. UCC copy-$1.00 per page. Will search tax liens. Federal/state combined tax lien search- $15.00 per tax lien. Will not search real estate records. RE record copy- $.50 per page. Cert fee: $1.00 per cert. Payee: Douglas County Register of Deeds. **Online Access to Property Appraiser, Real Estate, Recording, Deed, Lien records**: Two non-government sites provide free access to records from the Douglas County Assessor. Find County Property Appraiser records at www.douglas-county.com/value. Douglas County property valuations can be found at http://hometown.lawrence.com/valuation/valuation.cgi. Also, Register of Deeds records data is by subscription, phone number for info and subscription-785-832-5183. **Other phones**: Assessor-785-841-7700 x107; Treasurer-785-841-7700; Appraiser-785-832-5290; Elections-785-832-5147.

Edwards County

County Register of Deeds, PO Box 264, Kinsley, KS 67547-0364. **Phone**-620-659-3131; fax-620-659-2583; hours 8AM-5PM. UCC record search per debtor-$15.00. Will not search real estate records. Record copy- $1.00 per page. Cert fee: $1.00 per cert. Payee: County Register of Deeds. **Other phones**: Assessor-620-659-3100; Treasurer-620-659-3132.

Elk County

County Register of Deeds, PO Box 476, Howard, KS 67349-0476. **Phone**-County Register of Deeds, R/E & UCC Recording- 620-374-2472; fax-620-374-2771; hours 8AM-4:30PM

UCC record search per debtor- $15.00. UCC copy-$1.00 per page. UCC search includes tax liens. Will not search real estate records. RE record copy-

$.25 per page. Cert fee: $1.00 per cert. Payee: Elk County Register of Deeds. **Other phones:** Assessor-620-374-2832; Treasurer-620-374-2256; Elections-620-374-2490; Vital Records-620-374-2370.

Ellis County

County Register of Deeds, PO Box 654, Hays, KS 67601. **Phone**-785-628-9450; R/E Recording- 785-628-9452; fax- 785-628-9451; hours-8AM-5PM www.ksrods.org
UCC record search per debtor- $15.00. UCC copy-$1.00 per page. UCC search includes tax liens if requested. Separate federal/state combined tax lien search- $15.00 per debtor. Will search real estate records. RE record copy- $.25 per page. Cert fee: $1.00 per cert. Payee: Ellis County Register of Deeds. **Other phones:** Assessor-785-628-9400; Treasurer-785-628-9466; Appraiser-785-628-9400; Elections-785-628-9410; Vital Records-785-628-9450; Second Line-785-628-9452.

Ellsworth County

County Register of Deeds, 210 N. Kansas #7, Courthouse, Ellsworth, KS 67439-3110. **Phone**-785-472-3022; fax-785-472-4912; hours 8AM-5PM
UCC record search per debtor- $15.00. UCC copy-$1.00 per page. UCC search includes tax liens. Separate federal/state combined tax lien search-$15.00 per debtor. Real estate owner, mortgage, and property transfer searches available. Cert fee: $1.00 per cert. Payee: Ellsworth County Register of Deeds. **Other phones:** Assessor-785-472-3165; Treasurer-785-472-4152.

Finney County

County Register of Deeds, PO Box M, Garden City, KS 67846. **Phone**-County Register of Deeds, R/E & UCC Recording- 620-272-3520; fax-620-272-3624; hours 8AM-5PM www.finneycounty.org
UCC record search per debtor- $15.00. UCC copy-$1.00 per sheet. Will search tax liens. Separate federal/state combined tax lien search- $15.00 per debtor. Will not search real estate records. RE record copy- $.25 per page. Cert fee: $1.00 per cert. Payee: County Register of Deeds. **Other phones:** Assessor-620-272-3517; Treasurer-620-373-3526; Appraiser-620-272-3585; Elections-620-272-3523.

Ford County

County Register of Deeds, PO Box 1352, Dodge City, KS 67801-1352. **Phone**-County Register of Deeds, R/E & UCC Recording- 620-227-4565; fax-620-227-4568; fax-620-227-4566; hours 9AM-5PM
UCC record search per debtor- $15.00. UCC copy-$1.00 per page. UCC search includes tax liens. Real estate owner, mortgage, and property transfer searches available. RE record copy- $.75 per page. Cert fee: $1.00 per cert. Payee: Ford County Register of Deeds. **Other phones:** Assessor-620-227-4516; Treasurer-620-227-4535; Appraiser-620-227-4570; Elections-620-227-4553.

Franklin County

County Register of Deeds, 315 S. Main, Courthouse, Rm 103, Ottawa, KS 66067-2335. **Phone**-785-229-3440; fax-785-229-3419; hours 8AM-4:30PM
UCC record search per debtor- $15.00. UCC copy-$1.00 per page. UCC search includes tax liens. Separate federal/state combined tax lien search-$8.00 per debtor. Real estate record owner searches available. RE record copy- $.25 per page after the 1st. Cert fee: $1.00 per cert and $.25 per page. Payee: Franklin County Register of Deeds. **Online Access to Marriage records:** Access to county marriage records is by alpha search for free at www.kscourts.org/dstcts/4frmarec.htm. **Other phones:** Assessor-785-242-2573; Treasurer-785-242-4201.

Geary County

County Register of Deeds, PO Box 927, Junction City, KS 66441-2591. **Phone**-785-238-5531; fax-785-762-2642; hours 8:30AM-5PM. UCC record search per debtor- $15.00. UCC copy- $1.00 per page. UCC search includes tax liens. Separate federal/state combined tax lien search- $15.00 per debtor. Will not search real estate records. Cert fee: $1.00 per cert. Payee: County Register of Deeds. **Other phones:** Assessor-785-238-4407; Treasurer-785-238-3912.

Gove County

County Register of Deeds, PO Box 116, Gove, KS 67736. **Phone**-County Register of Deeds, R/E & UCC Recording- 785-938-4465; fax-785-938-4486; hours 8AM-Noon, 1PM-5PM. UCC record search per debtor- $15.00. UCC copy- $1.00 per page. UCC search includes tax liens if requested. Separate federal/state combined tax lien search- (no set fee). Will search real estate records, time permitting. RE record copy- $.50 per page. Cert fee: $1.00 per cert. Payee: Gove County Register of Deeds. **Other phones:** Assessor-785-938-2301; Treasurer-785-938-2275; Appraiser-785-938-2301; Elections-785-938-2300; Vital Records-785-938-4465.

Graham County

County Register of Deeds, 410 N. Pomeroy, Hill City, KS 67642. **Phone**-785-421-2551; fax-785-421-2784; hours 8AM-5PM. UCC record search per debtor-$15.00. UCC copy- $1.00 per page. UCC search includes tax liens. Separate federal/state combined tax lien search- $8.00 per debtor. Will not search real estate records. Cert fee: $1.00 per cert. Payee: Graham County Register of Deeds. **Other phones:** Assessor-785-674-2196; Treasurer-785-674-2331.

Grant County

County Register of Deeds, 108 S. Glenn, Lower Level, Courthouse, Ulysses, KS 67880. **Phone**-County Register of Deeds, R/E & UCC Recording- 620-356-1538; fax-620-356-5379; hours 9AM-5PM
UCC record search per debtor- $15.00. UCC search includes tax liens. Separate federal/state combined tax lien search- $15.00 per debtor. Will not search real estate records. Record copy- $1.00 per page. Cert fee: $1.00 per cert. Payee: Grant County Register of Deeds. **Other phones:** Assessor-620-356-3362; Treasurer-620-356-1551; Appraiser-620-356-3362; Elections-620-356-1335.

Gray County

County Register of Deeds, PO Box 487, Cimarron, KS 67835-0487. **Phone**-620-855-3835; fax-620-855-3107; hours 8AM-5PM. UCC record search per debtor-$15.00. UCC copy- $1.00 per page. Will not search tax liens. Real estate owner, mortgage, and property transfer searches available. RE record copy-$.50 per page. Cert fee: $1.00 per cert. Payee: Gray County Register of Deeds. **Other phones:** Assessor-620-855-3858; Treasurer-620-855-3861; Appraiser-620-855-3858; Elections-620-855-3618.

Greeley County

County Register of Deeds, PO Box 12, Tribune, KS 67879. **Phone**-620-376-4275; fax-620-376-2294; hours 9AM-5PM. UCC record search per debtor- $15.00. UCC copy- $1.00 per page. UCC search includes tax liens. Separate federal/state combined tax lien search- $8.00 per debtor. Will not search real estate records. Cert fee: No charge. Payee: Greeley County Register of Deeds. **Other phones:** Assessor-620-376-4057; Treasurer-620-376-4413.

Greenwood County

County Register of Deeds, 311 N Main, Courthouse, Eureka, KS 67045-1311. **Phone**-620-583-8162; fax-620-583-8178; hours 8AM-5PM
UCC record search per debtor- $15.00. UCC copy-$1.00 per page. UCC search includes tax liens. Separate federal & state combined tax lien search-$15.00 Will search real estate by legal description. Cert fee: $1.00 per cert. Payee: Greenwood County Register of Deeds. **Other phones:** Assessor-620-583-7431; Treasurer-620-583-8146.

Hamilton County

County Register of Deeds, PO Box 1167, Syracuse, KS 67878. **Phone**-County Register of Deeds, R/E & UCC Recording- 620-384-6925; fax-620-384-5853; hours 8AM-Noon, 1-4:30PM
UCC record search per debtor- $15.00. UCC copy-$1.00 per page. Will not search real estate or tax lien records. RE record copy- $.25 per page. Cert fee: $1.00 per doc. Payee: Hamilton County Register of Deeds. **Other phones:** Treasurer-620-384-5522; Appraiser-620-384-5451.

Harper County

County Register of Deeds, 201 N Jennings, Courthouse, Anthony, KS 67003. **Phone**-County Register of Deeds, R/E & UCC Recording- 620-842-5336; fax-620-842-3455; hours-8AM-Noon,1-5PM www.harpercounty.org/departments.htm
UCC record search per debtor- $15.00. UCC search includes tax liens. Will search real estate by record owner as a courtesy. Record copy- $1.00 per page. Cert fee: $1.00 per cert. Payee: County Register of Deeds. **Other phones:** Assessor-620-842-3718; Treasurer-620-842-5191; Elections-620-842-5555.

Harvey County

County Register of Deeds, PO Box 687, Newton, KS 67114-0687. **Phone**-County Register of Deeds, R/E & UCC Recording- 316-284-6950; fax-316-284-6951; hours 8AM-5PM. UCC record search per debtor-$15.00. UCC search includes tax liens if requested. Separate federal/state combined tax lien search-$15.00 per debtor. Real estate owner, mortgage, and property transfer searches available. Record copy-$1.00 per page. Cert fee: $1.00 per cert. Payee: Harvey County Register of Deeds. **Other phones:** Assessor-316-284-6815; Treasurer-316-284-6976; Appraiser-316-284-6815; Elections-316-284-6842.

Haskell County

County Register of Deeds, PO Box 656, Sublette, KS 67877. **Phone**-620-675-8343; 9AM-Noon,1-5PM
UCC record search per debtor- $15.00. UCC copy-$1.00 per page. Tax liens included in UCC search and will search separately. Separate federal/state combined tax lien search- $15.00 per debtor. Will not search real estate records. Cert fee: $1.00 per cert. Payee: County Register of Deeds. **Other phones:** Assessor-620-675-8269; Treasurer-620-675-2265.

Hodgeman County

County Register of Deeds, PO Box 505, Jetmore, KS 67854-0505. **Phone**-620-357-8536; fax-620-357-6161; hours 9AM-12;00-1-5PM. UCC record search per debtor- $15.00. UCC copy- $1.00 per page. UCC search includes tax liens. Separate federal/state combined tax lien search- $8.00 per debtor. Will not search real estate records. Cert fee: $1.00 per cert. Payee: County Register of Deeds. **Other phones:** Assessor-620-357-8366; Treasurer-620-357-6236.

Jackson County

County Register of Deeds, 415 New York, Courthouse, Rm 203, Holton, KS 66436. **Phone-**County Register of Deeds, R/E & UCC Recording- 785-364-3591; fax-785-364-3420; hours 8AM-4:30PM

UCC record search per debtor- $15.00. UCC copy-$1.00 per page. Will search tax liens. Tax lien search fee- $15.00 per debtor. Will look up real estate last owner or mortgagor. RE record copy- $.25 per page after the 1st. Cert fee: $1.00 per cert. Payee: County Register of Deeds. **Other phones:** Assessor-785-364-5256; Treasurer-785-364-3791; Appraiser-785-364-5256; Elections-785-364-5200.

Jefferson County

County Register of Deeds, PO Box 352, Oskaloosa, KS 66066-0352. **Phone-**County Register of Deeds, R/E & UCC Recording- 785-863-2243; fax-785-863-2602; hours 8AM-6:30PM M; 8AM-4PM T-F

UCC record search per debtor- $15.00. UCC search includes tax liens. Separate federal/state combined tax lien search- $8.00 per debtor. Real estate record owner searches, but indexed by location. Record copy-$1.00 per page. Cert fee: $1.00 per cert. Payee: Jefferson County Register of Deeds. **Other phones:** Assessor-785-863-2080; Treasurer-785-863-2691; Appraiser-785-863-2552; Elections-785-863-2272.

Jewell County

County Register of Deeds, 307 N. Commercial St, Courthouse, Mankato, KS 66956-2093. **Phone-**County Register of Deeds, R/E & UCC Recording- 785-378-4070; fax-785-378-4075; hours 8:30AM-Noon, 1-4:30PM. UCC record search per debtor- $15.00. UCC search includes tax liens. Separate federal/state combined tax lien search- $15.00 Will search real estate records. Record copy- $1.00 per page. Cert fee: $1.00 per cert. Payee: Jewell County Register of Deeds. **Other phones:** Assessor-785-378-4000; Treasurer-785-378-4090; Appraiser-785-378-4000; Elections-785-378-4020.

Johnson County

County Register of Deeds, PO Box 700, Olathe, KS 66051. **Phone-**913-715-2300 x5375; fax-913-715-2310; hours 8AM-5PM www.jocoks.com

UCC record search per debtor- $20.00. UCC copy-$1.00 per page. UCC search includes tax liens. Separate federal/state combined tax lien search-$8.00 per debtor. Will not search real estate records. RE record copy- $.50 per page. Cert fee: $1.00 per cert. Payee: Johnson County Register of Deeds. **Online Access to Property Appraiser, Tax Sale, Land records:** Records on the Johnson County Kansas Land Records database are free at http://appraiser.jocogov.org/disclaimer.htm. At the bottom of the Disclaimer page, click on "Yes". No name searching. Also, search the tax sales list for free at www.jocoks.com/countyclerk/taxsale/salenone.htm. **Other phones:** Assessor-913-829-9500; Treasurer-913-715-2600.

Kearny County

County Register of Deeds, PO Box 42, Lakin, KS 67860. **Phone-**County Register of Deeds, R/E & UCC Recording- 620-355-6241; fax-620-355-7382; hours 8AM-5PM. UCC record search per debtor- $15.00. UCC copy-$1.00 per page. Will search limited tax liens. Will not search real estate records. RE record copy- $.25 per page. Cert fee: $1.00 per cert. Payee: Kearny County Register of Deeds. **Other phones:** Assessor-appraiser-620-355-6427; Treasurer-620-355-6372; Elections-620-355-6422.

Kingman County

County Register of Deeds, 130 N Spruce, Kingman, KS 67068. **Phone-**County Register of Deeds, R/E & UCC Recording- 620-532-3211; fax-620-532-2037; hours 8AM-Noon,1-5PM

UCC record search per debtor- $15.00. UCC copy-$1.00 per page. UCC search includes tax liens. Separate federal/state combined tax lien search-$8.00 per debtor. Will not search real estate records. Cert fee: $1.00 per cert. Payee: Kingman County Register of Deeds. **Other phones:** Assessor-620-532-2256; Treasurer-620-532-3461; Appraiser-620-532-2256; Elections-620-532-2521.

Kiowa County

County Register of Deeds, 211 E Florida, Greensburg, KS 67054. **Phone-**620-723-2441; fax-620-723-1033; hours 8:30AM-Noon, 1-5PM www.kiowacounty.us

UCC record search per debtor- $15.00. UCC search includes tax liens. Separate federal/state or combined tax lien search- $15.00 per debtor. Will not search real estate records. Record copy- $1.00 per page. Cert fee: $1.00 per cert. Payee: Kiowa County Register of Deeds. **Other phones:** Assessor-620-723-3366; Treasurer-620-723-2681; Appraiser-620-723-3301.

Labette County

County Register of Deeds, 521 Merchant, Courthouse, Oswego, KS 67356. **Phone-**County Register of Deeds, R/E & UCC Recording- 620-795-4931; fax-620-795-2928; hours 8:30AM-5PM

UCC record search per debtor- $15.00. UCC copy-$1.00 per page. Tax liens not included in UCC search. Tax lien search fee- fee for copies. Will not search real estate records. RE record copy- $.25 per page. Cert fee: $1.50 per cert. Payee: Labette County Register of Deeds. **Other phones:** Assessor-620-795-2548; Treasurer-620-795-2918; Appraiser-620-795-2548; Elections-620-795-2138.

Lane County

County Register of Deeds, PO Box 805, Dighton, KS 67839-0805. **Phone-**County Register of Deeds, R/E & UCC Recording- 620-397-2803; fax-620-397-5937; hours 8AM-Noon,1-5PM

UCC record search per debtor- $15.00, $1.00 copy fee. UCC search includes tax liens. Separate federal/state combined tax lien search- $15.00 per debtor. Real estate owner, mortgage, and property transfer searches available. Record copy- $1.00 per page. Cert fee: $2.00 per cert. Payee: Lane County Register of Deeds. **Other phones:** Assessor-620-397-2804; Treasurer-620-397-2802; Appraiser-620-397-2804; Elections-620-397-5356.

Leavenworth County

County Register of Deeds, 300 Walnut, Rm 103, Courthouse, Leavenworth, KS 66048. **Phone-**County Register of Deeds, R/E & UCC Recording- 913-684-0424; fax-913-684-0406; hours 8AM-5PM

UCC record search per debtor- $15.00. UCC search includes tax liens if requested. Separate federal/state combined tax lien search- $8.00 per debtor. Will not search real estate records. Record copy- $1.00 per page. Cert fee: $1.00 per cert. Payee: Leavenworth County Register of Deeds. **Other phones:** Assessor-913-684-0440; Treasurer-913-684-0430; Appraiser-913-684-0440; Elections-913-684-0421.

Lincoln County

County Register of Deeds, 216 E. Lincoln, Lincoln, KS 67455-2056. **Phone-**785-524-4657; fax-785-524-5008; hours 8AM-Noon,12:30-4:30PM

UCC record search per debtor- $15.00. UCC copy-$1.00 per page. UCC search includes tax liens.

Separate federal/state combined tax lien search-$8.00 per debtor. Will not search real estate records. RE record copy- $.35 per page. Cert fee: $1.00 per cert. Payee: Lincoln County Register of Deeds. **Other phones:** Treasurer-785-524-4190; Appraiser-785-524-4958; Elections-785-524-4757.

Linn County

County Register of Deeds, PO Box 350, Mound City, KS 66056-0350. **Phone-**913-795-2226, R/E Recording-913-352-2226, UCC Recording- 913-352-2226; fax-913-795-2889; hours 8AM-Noon, 12:30-4:30PM

UCC record search per debtor- $15.00. UCC copy-$1.00 per page. UCC search includes tax liens if requested. Separate federal/state combined tax lien search- $8.00 per debtor. Will not search real estate records. RE record copy- $1.50 1st page, then $.15 per page. Cert fee: $1.00 per cert. Payee: Linn County Register of Deeds. **Other phones:** Assessor-913-795-2536; Treasurer-913-795-2227.

Logan County

County Register of Deeds, 710 W. 2nd St, Courthouse, Oakley, KS 67748. **Phone-**County Register of Deeds, R/E & UCC Recording- 785-672-4224; fax-785-672-3517; hours 8AM-5PM

UCC record search per debtor- $15.00. UCC copy-$1.00 per page. Tax liens not included in UCC search. Separate federal/state combined tax lien search- $15.00 per debtor. Will not search real estate records. RE record copy- $.25 per page, $1.00 per page mailed or faxed. Cert fee: $1.00 per cert. Payee: Logan County Register of Deeds. **Other phones:** Assessor-785-672-4821; Treasurer-785-672-3216; Appraiser-785-672-4821; Elections-785-672-4244; County Clerk-785-672-4244.

Lyon County

County Register of Deeds, 430 Commercial St, Emporia, KS 66801. **Phone-**County Register of Deeds, R/E & UCC Recording- 620-341-3241; fax-620-341-3438; hours 8AM-5PM. UCC record search per debtor- $15.00. UCC search includes tax liens. Separate federal/state combined tax lien search-$8.00 per debtor. Real estate record owner and mortgage searches available. Record copy- $1.00 per page. Cert fee: $1.00 per cert. Payee: Lyon County Register of Deeds.

Marion County

County Register of Deeds, PO Box 158, Marion, KS 66861-0158. **Phone-**620-382-2151; fax-620-382-3420; hours 8:30AM-5PM

UCC record search per debtor- $15.00. UCC copy-$1.00 per page. UCC search includes tax liens if requested. Separate federal/state combined tax lien search- $8.00 per debtor. Will not search real estate records. RE record copy- $.25 per page; $.50 if on microfilm. Cert fee: $1.00 per cert. Payee: Marion County Register of Deeds. **Other phones:** Assessor-620-382-3715; Treasurer-620-382-2180; Appraiser-620-382-3778; Elections-620-382-2185.

Marshall County

County Register of Deeds, 1201 Broadway, Courthouse, Marysville, KS 66508. **Phone-**County Register of Deeds, R/E & UCC Recording- 785-562-3226; fax-785-562-5685; hours 8:30AM-5PM

UCC record search per debtor- $15.00. UCC copy-$1.00 per page. UCC search includes tax liens. Separate federal/state combined tax lien search-$6.00 per debtor. Will not search real estate records. Copy fee-$1.00 per doc. Cert fee: $2.00 per cert. Payee: County Register of Deeds. **Other phones:** Assessor-785-562-3301; Treasurer-785-562-5363; Appraiser-785-562-3301; Elections-785-562-5361.

McPherson County

County Register of Deeds, PO Box 86, McPherson, KS 67460. **Phone**-County Register of Deeds, R/E & UCC Recording- 620-241-5050; fax-620-245-0749; hours 8AM-5PM www.mcphersoncountyks.us
UCC record search per debtor- $15.00. UCC search includes tax liens. Separate federal/state combined tax lien search- $15.00 per debtor. Real estate record owner and mortgage searches available. Record copy- $1.00 1st page and $.50 each add'l. Cert fee: $1.00 per cert. Payee: McPherson County Register of Deeds. **Other phones:** Assessor-620-241-5870; Treasurer-620-241-3664; Elections-620-241-3656.

Meade County

County Register of Deeds, PO Box 399, Meade, KS 67864-0399. **Phone**-620-873-8705, R/E Recording-602-873-8705; fax-620-873-8713; hours 8AM-5PM
UCC record search per debtor- $15.00. UCC copy- $1.00 per page. UCC search includes tax liens. Separate federal/state combined tax lien search- $8.00 per debtor. Will not search real estate records. RE record copy- $.50 per page. Cert fee: $1.00 per cert. Payee: Meade County Register of Deeds. **Other phones:** Assessor-620-873-8710; Treasurer-620-873-8740; Appraiser-620-873-8710; Elections-620-873-8700.

Miami County

County Register of Deeds, 201 S. Pearl St. #101, Paola, KS 66071. **Phone**-913-294-3716; fax-913-294-9515; hours 8AM-4:30PM
UCC record search per debtor- $15.00. UCC copy- $1.00 per page. Will not search real estate or tax lien records. Cert fee: $1.00 per cert. Payee: Miami County Register of Deeds. **Other phones:** Assessor-913-294-9311; Treasurer-913-294-2353.

Mitchell County

County Register of Deeds, PO Box 6, Beloit, KS 67420. **Phone**-785-738-3854; fax-785-738-5844; hours 8:30AM-5PM
UCC record search per debtor- $15.00. UCC copy- $1.00 per page. UCC search includes tax liens if requested. Separate federal/state combined tax lien search- $8.00 per debtor. Will search real estate by legal description. Cert fee: $1.00 per cert. Payee: Mitchell County Register of Deeds. **Other phones:** Assessor-785-738-5061; Treasurer-785-738-3411.

Montgomery County

County Register of Deeds, PO Box 647, Independence, KS 67301. **Phone**-620-330-1140; fax-620-330-1144; hours 8:30AM-5PM. UCC record search per debtor- $15.00. UCC copy- $1.00 per page. Will not search real estate or tax lien records. Cert fee: $1.00 per cert. Payee: Montgomery County Register of Deeds. **Other phones:** Assessor-620-331-4510; Treasurer-620-331-3040.

Morris County

County Register of Deeds, Courthouse, Council Grove, KS 66846. **Phone**-620-767-5614; fax-620-767-6712; hours 8AM-5PM. UCC record search per debtor- $15.00. UCC search includes tax liens if requested. Separate federal/state combined tax lien search- $8.00 per debtor. Will not search real estate records. Record copy- $1.00 per page. Cert fee: $1.00 per cert. Payee: Morris County Register of Deeds. **Other phones:** Assessor-620-767-5617; Treasurer-620-767-5614; Appraiser-620-767-5533; Elections-620-767-5518.

Morton County

County Register of Deeds, PO Box 756, Elkhart, KS 67950-0756. **Phone**-County Register of Deeds, R/E & UCC Recording- 620-697-2561; fax-620-697-4386;

hours 9AM-5PM. UCC record search per debtor- $15.00. UCC search includes tax liens if requested. Separate federal/state combined tax lien search- $8.00 per debtor. Will not search real estate records. Record copy- $1.00 per page. Cert fee: $1.00 per doc/$.25 per page. Payee: Morton County Register of Deeds. **Other phones:** Assessor-620-697-2106; Treasurer-620-697-2560; Appraiser-620-697-2106; Elections-620-697-2157.

Nemaha County

County Register of Deeds, PO Box 211, Seneca, KS 66538. **Phone**-County Register of Deeds, R/E & UCC Recording- 785-336-2120; fax-785-336-3373; hours 8AM-4:30PM
UCC record search per debtor- $15.00. UCC copy- $1.00 per page. UCC search includes tax liens if requested. Separate federal/state combined tax lien search- $8.00 per debtor. Will search real estate records. RE record copy- $.50 per page. Cert fee: $1.00 per cert. Payee: Nemaha County Register of Deeds. **Other phones:** Assessor-785-336-2179; Treasurer-785-336-2106.

Neosho County

County Register of Deeds, PO Box 138, Erie, KS 66733-0138. **Phone**-620-244-3858; fax-620-244-3860; hours 8AM-4:30PM. UCC record search per debtor- $15.00. UCC copy- $1.00 per page. UCC search includes tax liens if requested. Separate federal/state combined tax lien search- $8.00 per debtor. Will not search real estate records. RE record copy- $.25 per page. Cert fee: $1.00 per cert. Payee: County Register of Deeds. **Other phones:** Assessor-620-244-3821; Treasurer-620-244-3800.

Ness County

County Register of Deeds, PO Box 127, Ness City, KS 67560. **Phone**-785-798-3127; fax-785-798-3829; hours 8AM-Noon, 1PM-5PM. UCC record search per debtor- $15.00. UCC copy- $1.00 per page. UCC search includes tax liens. Separate federal/state combined tax lien search- $15.00 per debtor. Will not search real estate records. Cert fee: $2.00 for 1st 2 pages. Payee: Ness County Register of Deeds. **Other phones:** Assessor-785-798-2777.

Norton County

County Register of Deeds, PO Box 70, Norton, KS 67654. **Phone**-County Register of Deeds, R/E & UCC Recording- 785-877-5765; fax-785-877-5703; hours 8AM-Noon, 1-5PM
UCC record search per debtor- $15.00. UCC copy- $1.00 per page. UCC search includes tax liens. Separate federal/state combined tax lien search- $8.00 per debtor. Real estate owner, mortgage, and property transfer searches available. Cert fee: $1.00 per cert. Payee: Norton County Register of Deeds. **Other phones:** Assessor-785-877-5700; Treasurer-785-877-5795; Appraiser-785-877-5700; Elections-785-877-5710.

Osage County

County Register of Deeds, PO Box 265, Lyndon, KS 66451-0265. **Phone**-785-828-4523; fax-785-828-4749; hours 8AM-5PM www.osageco.org
UCC record search per debtor- $15.00. UCC copy- $1.00 per page. UCC search includes tax liens if requested. Separate federal/state combined tax lien search- $8.00 per debtor. Will not search real estate records. RE record copy- $1.00 for 1st page, $.25 each add'l. This fee is for each instruments you want a copy of. Cert fee: $1.00 per cert + $1.00 for the 1st page and $.25 per add'l. Payee: Osage County Register of Deeds. **Online Access to Appraiser, Property records:** access to property appraiser data is free at www.osageco.org/MV2Base.asp?VarCN=34. There are two levels- public and

registered user. The latter can see sales information as well as property data. **Other phones:** Assessor-913-828-3124; Treasurer-913-828-4923.

Osborne County

County Register of Deeds, PO Box 160, Osborne, KS 67473-0160. **Phone**-785-346-2452; fax-785-346-5252; 8:30AM-Noon, 1-5PM www.osbornecounty.org
UCC record search per debtor- $15.00. UCC copy- $1.00 per page. UCC search includes tax liens. Separate federal/state combined tax lien search- $8.00 per debtor. Real estate owner, mortgage, and property transfer searches available. RE record copy- $.25 per page. Cert fee: $1.00 per cert. Payee: Osborne County Register of Deeds. **Online Access to Property, Appraiser records:** Access to property appraisal land data is free at www.osbornecounty.org. Search field is at bottom right of page. CAMA Records found at www.osbornecounty.org. **Other phones:** Assessor-785-346-2310; Treasurer-785-346-2251; Appraiser-785-346-2310.

Ottawa County

County Register of Deeds, 307 N Concord, Courthouse - #220, Minneapolis, KS 67467-2140. **Phone**-County Register of Deeds, R/E & UCC Recording- 785-392-2078; fax-785-392-3605; hours 8AM-Noon, 1-5PM www.ottawacounty.org
UCC record search per debtor- $15.00. UCC copy- $1.00 per page. Separate federal/state combined tax lien search- $8.00 per debtor. Will search real estate by name or legal description. RE record copy- $.25 per page. Cert fee: $1.00 per cert. Payee: Ottawa County Register of Deeds. **Online Access to Appraiser, Property Tax records:** Access to the appraiser property tax data is free at www.ottawacounty.org/index.asp?DocumentID=283. **Other phones:** Assessor-785-392-3037; Treasurer-785-392-3129; Appraiser-785-392-3037; Elections-785-392-2279.

Pawnee County

County Register of Deeds, 715 Broadway St., Courthouse, 2nd Fl, Larned, KS 67550-3097. **Phone**-County Register of Deeds, R/E & UCC Recording- 620-285-3276; fax-620-285-3802; 8:30AM-5PM. UCC record search per debtor- $15.00. UCC search includes tax liens. Request must be in writing, using the proper form. Separate federal/state combined tax lien search- $5.00 per debtor, copy fee is $.25 per page. Will look up last deed of record and do a simple name search. RE record and UCC copy- $1.00 per page. Cert fee: $1.00 per cert. Payee: Pawnee County. **Other phones:** Assessor-620-285-2915; Treasurer-620-285-3746; Appraiser-620-285-2915; Elections-620-285-3721; Vital Records-620-285-6937.

Phillips County

County Register of Deeds, 310 State St, Courthouse, Phillipsburg, KS 67661. **Phone**-785-543-6875; fax-785-999-9999; hours 8AM-5PM
UCC record search per debtor- $15.00. UCC copy- $1.00 per page. UCC search includes tax liens. Separate federal/state combined tax lien search- $8.00 per debtor. Will not search real estate records. RE record copy- $.25 per page. Cert fee: $1.00 per cert. Payee: Phillips County Register of Deeds. **Other phones:** Assessor-785-543-6810; Treasurer-785-543-6895.

Pottawatomie County

County Register of Deeds, PO Box 186, Westmoreland, KS 66549. **Phone**-785-457-3471; fax-785-457-3577; hours 8AM-4:30PM www.pottcounty.org
UCC record search per debtor- $15.00. UCC copy- $1.00 per page. UCC search includes tax liens. Separate federal/state combined tax lien search-

$15.00 per debtor. Will not search real estate records. RE record copy- $.50 per copy. Cert fee: $1.50 per cert. Payee: Pottawatomie County Register of Deeds. **Other phones:** Assessor-785-457-3500; Treasurer-785-457-3681.

Pratt County

County Register of Deeds, PO Box 873, Pratt, KS 67124. **Phone-**County Register of Deeds, R/E & UCC Recording- 620-672-4140; fax-620-672-9541; hours 8AM-Noon,1-5PM www.prattcounty.org
Will search UCC records; written requests only. Search per debtor- $15.00. UCC copy- $1.00 per page. Will not search real estate records. RE record copy- $.50 per page. Cert fee: $1.00 per cert. Payee: Pratt County Register of Deeds. **Other phones:** Assessor-620-672-4112; Treasurer-620-672-4116; Appraiser-620-672-4112; Elections-620-672-4110; District Court (probates & state tax liens)-620-672-4100.

Rawlins County

County Register of Deeds, PO Box 201, Atwood, KS 67730. **Phone-**County Register of Deeds, R/E & UCC Recording- 785-626-3172; fax-785-626-9481; hours 9AM-Noon,1-5PM
UCC record search per debtor- $15.00. UCC copy- $1.00 per page. Will not search real estate or tax lien records. Cert fee: $1.00 per page. Payee: Rawlins County Register of Deeds. **Other phones:** Assessor-785-626-3101; Treasurer-785-626-3331.

Reno County

County Register of Deeds, 206 W. First, Hutchinson, KS 67501. **Phone-**620-694-2942; fax-620-694-2944; hours 8AM-5PM. UCC record search per debtor- $15.00. UCC copy- $1.00 per page. UCC search includes tax liens. Separate federal/state combined tax lien search- $8.00 per debtor. Will not search real estate records. Cert fee: $1.00 per cert. Payee: Reno County Register of Deeds. **Other phones:** Assessor-620-694-2915; Treasurer-620-694-2938.

Republic County

County Register of Deeds, PO Box 429, Belleville, KS 66935. **Phone-**785-527-7238; fax-785-527-2659; hours 8AM-5PM
UCC record search per debtor- $15.00. UCC copy- $.25 per page. UCC search includes tax liens. Separate federal/state combined tax lien search- $15.00 per debtor. Real estate record owner and mortgage searches available. RE record copy- $.25 per page. Cert fee: $1.00 per cert. Payee: Republic County Register of Deeds. **Other phones:** Assessor-785-527-5691; Treasurer-785-527-5691.

Rice County

County Register of Deeds, 101 W. Commercial, Lyons, KS 67554. **Phone-**County Register of Deeds, R/E & UCC Recording- 620-257-2931; fax-620-257-3039; hours 8:00AM-5PM
UCC record search per debtor- $15.00. UCC copy- $1.00 per page. UCC search includes tax liens. Separate federal/state combined tax lien search- $8.00 per debtor. Real estate owner, mortgage, and property transfer searches available. RE record copy- $1.00 1st page, then $.25 per page. Cert fee: $1.00 per cert. Payee: Rice County Register of Deeds. **Other phones:** Assessor-620-257-3611; Treasurer-620-257-2852.

Riley County

County Register of Deeds, 5th & Humboldt Sts., 110 Courthouse Plaza, Manhattan, KS 66502-6018. **Phone-**County Register of Deeds, R/E & UCC Recording-785-537-6340; fax-785-537-6343; hours 8AM-5PM www.co.riley.ks.us/register/
UCC record search per debtor- $15.00. UCC search includes tax liens. Separate federal/state combined

tax lien search- $15.00 per debtor. Will not search real estate records. Record copy- $1.00 per page. Cert fee: $1.00 per cert. Payee: County Register of Deeds. **Other phones:** Assessor-785-537-6310; Treasurer-785-537-6320; Appraiser-785-537-6310.

Rooks County

County Register of Deeds, 115 N. Walnut St., Stockton, KS 67669. **Phone-**785-425-6291; fax-785-425-6497; hours 8AM-Noon,1-5PM
UCC record search per debtor- $15.00. UCC copy- $1.00 per page. Tax liens not included in UCC search. Separate federal/state combined tax lien search- $8.00 per debtor. Will not search real estate records. Cert fee: $1.00 per cert. Payee: Rooks County Register of Deeds. **Other phones:** Assessor-785-425-6262; Treasurer-785-425-6291.

Rush County

County Register of Deeds, PO Box 117, La Crosse, KS 67548. **Phone-**785-222-3312; fax-785-222-3559; hours 8:30AM-Noon, 1-5PM
UCC record search per debtor- $15.00. UCC copy- $1.00 per page. Will not search tax liens. Will give owner for a property. Cert fee: $2.00 per cert. Payee: Rush County Register of Deeds. **Other phones:** Assessor-785-222-2659; Treasurer-785-222-3416.

Russell County

County Register of Deeds, PO Box 191, Russell, KS 67665. **Phone-**County Register of Deeds, R/E & UCC Recording- 785-483-4612; fax-785-483-5725; hours 8AM-5PM. UCC record search per debtor- $15.00. UCC copy- $1.00 per page. UCC search includes tax liens. Separate federal/state combined tax lien search- $15.00 per debtor. Will not search real estate records. RE record copy- $.50 per page. Cert fee: $1.00 per cert. Payee: Russell County Register of Deeds. **Other phones:** Assessor-785-483-5551; Treasurer-785-483-2251; Appraiser-785-483-5551; Elections-785-483-4641.

Saline County

County Register of Deeds, PO Box 5040, Salina, KS 67402-5040. **Phone-**785-309-5855; fax-785-309-5856; hours 8AM-5PM www.co.saline.ks.us
UCC record search per debtor- $15.00. UCC copy- $1.00 per page. UCC search includes tax liens. Separate federal/state combined tax lien search- $15.00 per debtor. Will not search real estate records. RE record copy- $.25 per page + $1.00 mailing fee. Cert fee: $1.00 per cert. Payee: Saline County Register of Deeds. **Other phones:** Assessor-785-309-5800; Treasurer-785-309-5860.

Scott County

County Register of Deeds, 303 Court St., Courthouse, Scott City, KS 67871. **Phone-**County Register of Deeds, R/E & UCC Recording- 620-872-3155; fax-620-872-7145; hours-8AM-5PM www.scott.kansasgov.com
UCC record search per debtor- $15.00. UCC copy- $1.00 per page. UCC search includes tax liens. Separate federal/state combined tax lien search- $8.00 per debtor. Will do limited real estate searches. RE record copy- $.50 per page. Cert fee: $1.00 per cert. Payee: Scott County Register of Deeds. **Other phones:** Assessor-620-872-5446; Treasurer-620-872-2640; Appraiser-620-872-5446; Elections-620-872-2420.

Sedgwick County

County Register of Deeds, PO Box 3326, Wichita, KS 67201-3326. **Phone-**County Register of Deeds, R/E & UCC Recording- 316-660-9400; fax-316-383-8066; hours 8AM-5PM www.sedgwickcounty.org/deeds/
UCC record search per debtor- $15.00. UCC copy- $1.00 per page. UCC search includes tax liens if

requested. Separate federal/state combined tax lien search- $15.00 per debtor. Will not search real estate records. Cert fee: $1.00 per cert. Payee: Sedgwick County Register of Deeds. **Online Access to Real Estate, Lien, Recorder, Assessor, Property Sale, Property Tax, Treasurer, Delinquent Tax records:** Access to the exhaustive County online system (all departments) require a $225 set up fee, $49 monthly fee and a per transaction fee of $.09. For information on this and county record access generally, call Cindy Kirkland at 316-660-9860. Also free access recorder deeds is at http://205.172.12.40/rmis/. Also, Property Appraisal/Tax Information is available at www.sedgwickcounty.org/realpropertyinfo/realproperty.html. **Other phones:** Assessor-316-660-9110; Treasurer-316-660-9100; Appraiser-316-660-9110; Elections-316-660-7100; County Clerk-316-660-9200.

Seward County

County Register of Deeds, 415 N. Washington, #105, Courthouse, Liberal, KS 67901. **Phone-**County Register of Deeds, R/E & UCC Recording- 620-626-3220, UCC Recording- 620-626-3223; fax-620-626-3362; hours 8AM-5PM www.seward.kansasgov.com
This office will do limited real estate searches. Involved ones need to be done by a title company. UCC record search per debtor- $15.00. UCC search includes tax liens. Separate federal/state combined tax lien search- $15.00 per debtor. Record copy- $1.00 per page. Cert fee: $1.00 per cert. Payee: Seward County Register of Deeds. **Other phones:** Treasurer-620-626-3219; Appraiser-620-626-3252; Elections-620-626-3201; Vital Records-913-296-1400.

Shawnee County

County Register of Deeds, 200 E. 7th St, #108, Topeka, KS 66603-3932. **Phone-**County Register of Deeds, R/E & UCC Recording- 785-233-8200 x4020, UCC Recording- 785-233-8200 x4021; fax-785-291-4950; hours 8AM-4:30PM www.co.shawnee.ks.us
UCC record search per debtor- $15.00. Tax liens included in UCC search. Separate federal & state combined tax lien search- $15.00 per debtor. Will not search real estate records. Record copy- $1.50 per page. Cert fee: $1.00 per doc. Payee: Shawnee County Register of Deeds. **Online Access to Property Appraiser, Personal Property records:** Search residential or commercial property appraisal data at www.co.shawnee.ks.us/Appraiser/appr_home.shtm. Search residential by name; commercial by address. **Other phones:** Assessor-785-233-8200 x5151; Treasurer-785-233-8200 x5161; Appraiser-785-233-2882 x6000; Elections-785-266-0285.

Sheridan County

County Register of Deeds, PO Box 899, Hoxie, KS 67740-0899. **Phone-**785-675-3741; fax-785-675-3050; hours 8AM-Noon,1-5PM
UCC record search per debtor- $15.00. UCC copy- $1.00 per page. UCC search includes tax liens if requested. Real estate record owner searches available. Cert fee: $1.00 per cert. Payee: Sheridan County Register of Deeds. **Other phones:** Assessor-785-675-3932; Treasurer-785-675-3622.

Sherman County

County Register of Deeds, 813 Broadway, Rm 104, Goodland, KS 67735-3097. **Phone-**County Register of Deeds, R/E & UCC Recording- 785-899-4845; fax-785-899-4848; hours 7AM-Noon,1-4PM.UCC record search per debtor- $15.00. UCC copy- $1.00 per page; $2.00 per page if over 8 1/2 X 14 inches. UCC search includes tax liens. Will not perform name searches of real estate records. RE record copy- $1.00 per page. Cert fee: $1.00 per cert. Payee: Sherman County Register of Deeds. **Other phones:** Assessor-785-899-4825; Treasurer-785-899-4810; Appraiser-785-899-4825; Elections-785-899-4800.

Smith County

County Register of Deeds, 218 S. Grant, Smith Center, KS 66967. **Phone-**County Register of Deeds, R/E & UCC Recording- 785-282-5160; fax-785-282-6257; hours 8AM-Noon, 1-5PM. UCC record search per debtor- $15.00. UCC copy- $2.00 per page. Tax liens not included in UCC search. Separate federal/state combined tax lien search- $8.00 per debtor. Real estate owner, mortgage, and property transfer searches available. RE record copy- $1.00 per page. Cert fee: $1.00 per page. Payee: Smith County Register of Deeds. **Other phones:** Assessor-785-282-5100; Treasurer-785-282-5170; Appraiser-785-282-5100; Elections-785-282-5110.

Stafford County

County Register of Deeds, 209 N. Broadway, Stafford County Courthouse, St. John, KS 67576. **Phone-**620-549-3505; hours 8AM-Noon,1-5PM
UCC record search per debtor- $15.00. UCC copy- $1.00 per page. UCC search includes tax liens. Will not search real estate records. Cert fee: $1.00 per cert + copy fee. Payee: Stafford County Register of Deeds. **Other phones:** Assessor-620-549-3540; Treasurer-620-549-3508; Appraiser-620-549-3540.

Stanton County

County Register of Deeds, PO Box 716, Johnson, KS 67855. **Phone-**620-492-2190; fax-620-492-2688; hours 8:30AM-Noon, 1-5PM
UCC record search per debtor- $15.00. UCC copy- $1.00 per page. UCC search includes tax liens. Separate federal/state combined tax lien search- $8.00 per debtor. Will not search real estate records. RE record copy- $1.00 1st page, then $.50 per page. Cert fee: $1.00 per cert. Payee: Stanton County Register of Deeds. **Other phones:** Assessor-620-492-6896; Treasurer-620-492-2160.

Stevens County

County Register of Deeds, 200 E. 6th, Hugoton, KS 67951. **Phone-**County Register of Deeds, R/E & UCC Recording- 620-544-2630; fax-620-544-4081; hours 9AM-5PM. UCC record search per debtor- $15.00. UCC copy- $1.00 per page. Will not search real estate or tax lien records. RE record copy- $.25 per page. Cert fee: $1.00 per cert. Payee: Stevens County Register of Deeds. **Other phones:** Assessor-620-544-2993; Treasurer-620-544-2542; Appraiser-620-544-2693; Elections-620-544-2541.

Sumner County

County Register of Deeds, PO Box 469, Wellington, KS 67152. **Phone-**County Register of Deeds, R/E & UCC Recording- 620-326-2041; fax-620-326-8172; hours 8AM-5PM. UCC record search per debtor- $15.00. UCC copy- $1.00 per page. UCC search includes tax liens if requested. Real estate owner, mortgage, and property transfer searches available. Cert fee: $1.00 per cert. Payee: Sumner County Register of Deeds. **Other phones:** Assessor-appraiser-620-326-8986; Treasurer-620-326-3371; Elections-620-326-3395.

Thomas County

County Register of Deeds, 300 N. Court, Colby, KS 67701. **Phone-**County Register of Deeds, R/E & UCC Recording- 785-462-4535; fax-785-462-4512; hours 8AM-Noon, 1PM-5PM
UCC record search per debtor- $15.00. UCC copy- $1.00 per page. UCC search includes tax liens. Separate federal/state combined tax lien search-

$8.00 per debtor. Will confirm property owner from legal description. RE record copy- $.25 per page; $1.00 fax fee for long distance request. Cert fee: $1.00 per cert. Payee: Thomas County Register of Deeds. **Other phones:** Assessor-785-462-4525; Treasurer-785-462-4520; Elections-785-462-4500.

Trego County

County Register of Deeds, 216 Main, WaKeeney, KS 67672-2189. **Phone-**County Register of Deeds, R/E & UCC Recording- 785-743-6622; fax-785-743-2461; hours 8:30AM-5PM. UCC record search per debtor- $15.00. UCC copy- $1.00 per page. UCC search includes tax liens. Separate tax lien search fee- $15.00. Will give last owner name from legal description. RE record copy- $1.00 1st page, $.25 each add'l. Cert fee: $1.00 per cert. Payee: Trego County Register of Deeds. **Other phones:** Assessor-785-743-5758; Treasurer-785-743-2001; Appraiser-785-743-5758; Elections-785-743-5773.

Wabaunsee County

County Register of Deeds, PO Box 278, Alma, KS 66401-0278. **Phone-**County Register of Deeds, R/E & UCC Recording- 785-765-3822; fax-785-765-3824; hours 8AM-4:30PM www.wabaunsee.kansasgov.com UCC record search per debtor- $20.00. UCC copy- $1.00 per page. UCC search includes tax liens. Will not search real estate records. RE record copy- $.50 per page. Cert fee: $1.00 per cert + $.50 per page. Payee: Wabaunsee County Register of Deeds. **Online Access to Property Tax, Treasurer, Property, Assessor records:** Access to the treasurer's property tax data is available free at www.wabaunsee.kansasgov.com/TaxSearch.asp. Also, access to the assessor parcel search data is at www.wabaunsee.kansasgov.com/v2loginreg.asp; registration is asked for, but you may search basic data for free. To subscribe, phone 785-765-3508. **Other phones:** Assessor-785-765-3508; Treasurer-785-765-3812; Appraiser-785-765-3508; Elections-785-765-2421; Vital Records-785-765-3822.

Wallace County

County Register of Deeds, PO Box 10, Sharon Springs, KS 67758-9998. **Phone-**County Register of Deeds, R/E & UCC Recording- 785-852-4283; fax-785-852-4783; hours 8AM-Noon, 1-5PM. UCC record search per debtor- $15.00. UCC copy- $1.00 per page. UCC search includes tax liens. Separate federal/state combined tax lien search- $8.00 per debtor. Will not search real estate records. Cert fee: $1.00 per cert. Payee: County Register of Deeds. **Other phones:** Assessor-785-852-4206; Treasurer-785-852-4281; Appraiser-785-852-4206; Elections-785-852-4282.

Washington County

County Register of Deeds, 214 C St, Courthouse, Washington, KS 66968-1928. **Phone-**County Register of Deeds, R/E & UCC Recording- 785-325-2286; fax-785-325-2830; hours 8AM-5PM
UCC record search per debtor- $15.00. UCC copy- $1.00 per page. UCC search includes tax liens. Separate federal/state combined tax lien search- $8.00 per debtor. Will give real estate information at no charge. RE record copy- $.25 per page. Their old bound books are $.50. Cert fee: $1.00 per cert. Payee: Washington County Register of Deeds. **Other phones:** Assessor-785-325-2236; Treasurer-785-325-2461; Appraiser-785-325-2236; Elections-785-325-2974.

Wichita County

County Register of Deeds, PO Box 472, Leoti, KS 67861-0472. **Phone-**County Register of Deeds, R/E & UCC Recording- 620-375-2733; fax-316-375-4350; hours 8AM-Noon,1-5PM. Will search UCC records by mail only. Search per debtor- $15.00. UCC search includes tax liens. Separate federal/state combined tax lien search- $15.00 per debtor. Will not search real estate records. Record copy- $1.00 per page. Cert fee: $1.00 per cert. Payee: Wichita County Register of Deeds. **Other phones:** Assessor-620-375-4242; Treasurer-620-375-2713; Appraiser-620-375-4242; Elections-620-375-2731.

Wilson County

County Register of Deeds, Courthouse, Rm 106, Fredonia, KS 66736-1396. **Phone-**County Register of Deeds, R/E & UCC Recording- 620-378-3662; fax-620-378-4762; hours 8:30AM-5PM
UCC record search per debtor- $15.00. UCC copy- $1.00 per page. UCC search includes tax liens. Separate federal/state combined tax lien search- $15.00 per debtor. Real estate record owner and mortgage searches available. RE record copy- $.40 per page; $1.00 per page for big bound books. Cert fee: $1.00 per cert. Payee: Wilson County Register of Deeds. **Other phones:** Assessor-620-378-2187.

Woodson County

County Register of Deeds, 105 W. Rutledge, Rm 101, Yates Center, KS 66783-1499. **Phone-**620-625-8635; fax- 620-625-8670; hours 8AM-Noon,1-5PM www.woodsoncounty.net
UCC record search per debtor- $15.00. UCC copy- $1.00 per page. UCC search includes tax liens. Separate federal/state combined tax lien search- $8.00 per debtor. Will not search real estate records. RE record copy- $.50 per page. Cert fee: $1.00 per cert. Payee: Woodson County Register of Deeds. **Other phones:** Assessor-620-625-8600; Treasurer-620-625-8650.

Wyandotte County

County Register of Deeds, 710 N. 7th St., Courthouse, Kansas City, KS 66101-3084. **Phone-**County Register of Deeds, R/E & UCC Recording- 913-573-2841; fax-913-321-3075; hours 8AM-5PM
UCC record search per debtor- $15.00. UCC copy- $1.00 per page. UCC search includes tax liens. Separate federal/state combined tax lien search- $15.00 per debtor. Will not search real estate records. RE record copy- $1.00 1st page, $.50 each add'l. Cert fee: $1.00 per cert. Payee: Wyandotte County Register of Deeds. **Online Access to Real Estate, Lien, Property Appraisal, Personal Property, Recording, Deed, Judgment records:** County records are online and property tax records are on dial-up. The property dial-up services requires a $20 set up fee, with $5 monthly min. and $.05 each transaction (enter key). Lending agency information is also available. For information, contact Louise Sachen at 913-573-2885. Also, the Register has an Internet subscription service named Laredo; index goes back to 1975, images to 1991. Online late in 2003. Records from the County Treasurer Tax database are free at https://www.accesskansas.org/apps/wyandotteProperty Tax. Name search for personal property only, other property searches require street number and name; no name searching. **Other phones:** Assessor-913-287-2641; Treasurer-913-573-2823; Appraiser-913-573-2889; Elections-913-334-1414.

Kansas County Locator

You will usually be able to find the city name in the City/County Cross Reference below. In that case, it is a simple matter to determine the county from the cross reference. However, only the official US Postal Service city names are included in this index. There are an additional 40,000 place names that people use in their addresses. Therefore, we have also included a ZIP/City Cross Reference immediately following the City/County Cross Reference.

If you know the ZIP Code but the city name does not appear in the City/County Cross Reference index, look up the ZIP Code in the ZIP/City Cross Reference, find the city name, then look up the city name in the City/County Cross Reference. For example, you want to know the county for an address of Menands, NY 12204. There is no "Menands" in the City/County Cross Reference. The ZIP/City Cross Reference shows that ZIP Codes 12201-12288 are for the city of Albany. Looking back in the City/County Cross Reference, Albany is in Albany County.

City/County Cross Reference

ABBYVILLE Reno
ABILENE Dickinson
ADA (67414) Ottawa(94), Lincoln(5)
ADMIRE Lyon
AGENDA Republic
AGRA Phillips
ALBERT (67511) Barton(56), Rush(43)
ALDEN (67512) Rice(90), Reno(9)
ALEXANDER (67513) Rush(90), Pawnee(9)
ALLEN Lyon
ALMA Wabaunsee
ALMENA (67622) Norton(98), Phillips(1)
ALTA VISTA (66834) Wabaunsee(52), Morris(19), Jackson(17), Geary(10)
ALTAMONT Labette
ALTON (67623) Osborne(96), Smith(3)
ALTOONA Wilson
AMERICUS Lyon
AMES Cloud
ANDALE Sedgwick
ANDOVER Butler
ANTHONY Harper
ARCADIA (66711) Crawford(96), Bourbon(3)
ARCADIA Bourbon
ARGONIA (67004) Sumner(86), Harper(12)
ARKANSAS CITY Cowley
ARLINGTON Reno
ARMA Crawford
ARNOLD (67515) Ness(75), Trego(24)
ASHLAND Clark
ASSARIA (67416) Saline(97), McPherson(2)
ATCHISON (66002) Atchison(93), Leavenworth(5), Jefferson(1)
ATHOL Smith
ATLANTA (67008) Cowley(69), Butler(30)
ATTICA (67009) Harper(97), Barber(2)
ATWOOD Rawlins
AUBURN (66402) Shawnee(98), Osage(1)
AUGUSTA Butler
AURORA Cloud
AXTELL (66403) Marshall(93), Nemaha(6)
BAILEYVILLE (66404) Nemaha(94), Marshall(5)
BALDWIN CITY (66006) Douglas(95), Franklin(4)
BARNARD (67418) Lincoln(91), Mitchell(8)
BARNES (66933) Washington(93), Riley(6)
BARTLETT Labette
BASEHOR Leavenworth
BAXTER SPRINGS Cherokee
BAZINE Ness
BEATTIE Marshall
BEAUMONT Butler
BEAVER Barton
BEELER (67518) Ness(74), Lane(25)
BELLE PLAINE Sumner
BELLEVILLE Republic
BELOIT (67420) Mitchell(97), Cloud(1)
BELPRE (67519) Edwards(90), Pawnee(10)
BELVIDERE Kiowa

BELVUE (66407) Wabaunsee(70), Pottawatomie(29)
BENDENA Doniphan
BENEDICT Wilson
BENNINGTON Ottawa
BENTLEY Sedgwick
BENTON (67017) Butler(89), Sedgwick(10)
BERN Nemaha
BERRYTON (66409) Shawnee(91), Douglas(6), Osage(2)
BEVERLY (67423) Lincoln(98), Ellsworth(1)
BIRD CITY Cheyenne
BISON Rush
BLUE MOUND (66010) Linn(96), Bourbon(2)
BLUE RAPIDS (66411) Marshall(97), Riley(2)
BLUFF CITY (67018) Harper(91), Sumner(8)
BOGUE Graham
BONNER SPRINGS (66012) Wyandotte(65), Leavenworth(34)
BREMEN (66412) Marshall(93), Washington(6)
BREWSTER (67732) Thomas(59), Sherman(32), Rawlins(7)
BRONSON (66716) Bourbon(94), Allen(5)
BROOKVILLE (67425) Saline(58), Ellsworth(40), Lincoln(1)
BROWNELL (67521) Ness(89), Trego(10)
BUCKLIN (67834) Ford(92), Clark(6)
BUCYRUS (66013) Johnson(52), Miami(47)
BUFFALO (66717) Wilson(96), Woodson(3)
BUHLER (67522) Reno(91), Harvey(8)
BUNKER HILL Russell
BURDEN Cowley
BURDETT (67523) Pawnee(92), Hodgeman(7)
BURDICK (66838) Morris(93), Marion(4), Chase(1)
BURLINGAME (66413) Osage(95), Lyon(3), Wabaunsee(1)
BURLINGTON Coffey
BURNS (66840) Butler(58), Marion(36), Chase(5)
BURR OAK Jewell
BURRTON (67020) Harvey(58), Reno(37), Sedgwick(3)
BUSHTON (67427) Rice(81), Ellsworth(16), Barton(2)
BYERS (67021) Pratt(94), Stafford(5)
CALDWELL Sumner
CAMBRIDGE Cowley
CANEY Montgomery
CANTON (67428) McPherson(93), Marion(6)
CARBONDALE Osage
CARLTON Dickinson
CASSODAY Butler
CATHARINE Ellis
CAWKER CITY (67430) Mitchell(75), Jewell(17), Osborne(4), Smith(2)
CEDAR Smith

CEDAR POINT (66843) Chase(97), Marion(2)
CEDAR VALE (67024) Chautauqua(77), Cowley(22)
CENTERVILLE (66014) Anderson(52), Linn(47)
CENTRALIA Nemaha
CHANUTE (66720) Neosho(96), Wilson(3)
CHAPMAN Dickinson
CHASE Rice
CHAUTAUQUA Chautauqua
CHENEY (67025) Sedgwick(72), Kingman(26)
CHEROKEE Crawford
CHERRYVALE (67335) Montgomery(87), Labette(12)
CHETOPA (67336) Labette(75), Cherokee(24)
CIMARRON (67835) Gray(73), Finney(22), Hodgeman(3)
CIRCLEVILLE Jackson
CLAFLIN (67525) Barton(96), Rice(3)
CLAY CENTER (67432) Clay(98), Ottawa(1)
CLAYTON (67629) Norton(81), Decatur(18)
CLEARVIEW CITY Johnson
CLEARWATER (67026) Sedgwick(96), Sumner(3)
CLIFTON (66937) Washington(83), Clay(16)
CLYDE (66938) Cloud(80), Washington(11), Republic(4), Clay(3)
COATS (67028) Pratt(60), Kiowa(25), Barber(13)
CODELL Rooks
COFFEYVILLE (67337) Montgomery(95), Labette(4)
COLBY Thomas
COLDWATER (67029) Comanche(97), Kiowa(2)
COLLYER (67631) Trego(73), Graham(22), Gove(3), Sheridan(1)
COLONY (66015) Anderson(79), Coffey(20)
COLUMBUS Cherokee
COLWICH Sedgwick
CONCORDIA (66901) Cloud(97), Republic(2)
CONWAY SPRINGS (67031) Sumner(96), Sedgwick(3)
COOLIDGE Hamilton
COPELAND (67837) Haskell(55), Gray(39), Meade(5)
CORNING Nemaha
COTTONWOOD FALLS Chase
COUNCIL GROVE (66846) Morris(94), Lyon(4)
COURTLAND (66939) Republic(92), Jewell(7)
COYVILLE Wilson
CRESTLINE Cherokee
CUBA (66940) Republic(98), Washington(1)
CUMMINGS Atchison

CUNNINGHAM (67035) Kingman(71), Pratt(18), Reno(9)
DAMAR (67632) Rooks(73), Graham(26)
DANVILLE Harper
DE SOTO Johnson
DEARING Montgomery
DEERFIELD (67838) Kearny(62), Finney(37)
DELIA Jackson
DELPHOS (67436) Ottawa(84), Cloud(15)
DENISON (66419) Jackson(87), Jefferson(12)
DENNIS Labette
DENNIS THE MENACE Sedgwick
DENTON Doniphan
DERBY Sedgwick
DEXTER Cowley
DIGHTON (67839) Lane(92), Gove(6)
DODGE CITY Ford
DORRANCE (67634) Russell(98), Barton(1)
DOUGLASS (67039) Butler(97), Cowley(1)
DOVER Shawnee
DOWNS (67437) Osborne(95), Smith(4)
DRESDEN (67635) Decatur(70), Sheridan(29)
DURHAM Marion
DWIGHT (66849) Morris(63), Geary(36)
EASTON Leavenworth
EDGERTON (66021) Johnson(71), Miami(26), Douglas(2)
EDMOND (67636) Norton(82), Graham(17)
EDNA Labette
EDSON Sherman
EDWARDSVILLE Wyandotte
EFFINGHAM Atchison
EL DORADO Butler
ELBING Butler
ELK CITY (67344) Montgomery(65), Chautauqua(21), Elk(13)
ELK FALLS Elk
ELKHART Morton
ELLINWOOD (67526) Barton(94), Rice(4), Stafford(1)
ELLIS (67637) Ellis(87), Trego(12)
ELLSWORTH Ellsworth
ELMDALE Chase
ELSMORE Allen
ELWOOD Doniphan
EMMETT (66422) Pottawatomie(54), Jackson(45)
EMPORIA Lyon
ENGLEWOOD Clark
ENSIGN (67841) Gray(80), Ford(19)
ENTERPRISE Dickinson
ERIE Neosho
ESBON Jewell
ESKRIDGE Wabaunsee
EUDORA (66025) Douglas(76), Johnson(22)
EUREKA Greenwood
EVEREST (66424) Brown(89), Atchison(10)
FAIRVIEW Brown

FALL RIVER (67047) Greenwood(67), Elk(20), Wilson(11)
FALUN (67442) Saline(97), McPherson(2)
FARLINGTON Crawford
FLORENCE Marion
FONTANA Miami
FORD Ford
FORMOSO (66942) Jewell(98), Republic(1)
FORT DODGE Ford
FORT LEAVENWORTH Leavenworth
FORT RILEY Geary
FORT SCOTT Bourbon
FOSTORIA Pottawatomie
FOWLER (67844) Meade(80), Ford(13), Gray(5)
FRANKFORT (66427) Marshall(97), Pottawatomie(2)
FRANKLIN Crawford
FREDONIA Wilson
FREEPORT (67049) Harper(90), Sumner(10)
FRONTENAC Crawford
FULTON (66738) Bourbon(97), Linn(2)
GALENA Cherokee
GALESBURG Neosho
GALVA McPherson
GARDEN CITY Finney
GARDEN PLAIN Sedgwick
GARDNER Johnson
GARFIELD Pawnee
GARLAND Bourbon
GARNETT Anderson
GAS Allen
GAYLORD (67638) Smith(98), Osborne(1)
GEM (67734) Thomas(52), Rawlins(47)
GENESEO (67444) Rice(65), Ellsworth(34)
GEUDA SPRINGS (67051) Sumner(83), Cowley(16)
GIRARD Crawford
GLADE (67639) Phillips(96), Rooks(3)
GLASCO (67445) Cloud(92), Ottawa(7)
GLEN ELDER (67446) Mitchell(91), Jewell(8)
GODDARD Sedgwick
GOESSEL Marion
GOFF Nemaha
GOODLAND Sherman
GORHAM (67640) Russell(73), Ellis(26)
GOVE Gove
GRAINFIELD (67737) Gove(75), Sheridan(25)
GRANTVILLE Jefferson
GREAT BEND (67530) Barton(98), Stafford(1)
GREELEY (66033) Anderson(62), Franklin(35), Linn(2)
GREEN (67447) Clay(61), Riley(38)
GREENLEAF Washington
GREENSBURG Kiowa
GREENWICH Sedgwick
GRENOLA (67346) Elk(75), Chautauqua(25)
GRIDLEY (66852) Coffey(82), Greenwood(10), Woodson(6)
GRINNELL (67738) Gove(73), Sheridan(26)
GYPSUM (67448) Saline(47), McPherson(26), Dickinson(22), Marion(3)
HADDAM (66944) Washington(96), Republic(3)
HALSTEAD Harvey
HAMILTON Greenwood
HANOVER Washington
HANSTON (67849) Hodgeman(97), Ness(2)
HARDTNER Barber
HARLAN Smith
HARPER (67058) Harper(97), Kingman(2)
HARTFORD (66854) Lyon(78), Coffey(21)
HARVEYVILLE (66431) Wabaunsee(91), Shawnee(8)

HAVANA (67347) Montgomery(67), Chautauqua(32)
HAVEN Reno
HAVENSVILLE (66432) Pottawatomie(78), Jackson(20), Nemaha(1)
HAVILAND (67059) Kiowa(75), Edwards(16), Pratt(7)
HAYS Ellis
HAYSVILLE Sedgwick
HAZELTON (67061) Barber(68), Harper(31)
HEALY (67850) Lane(84), Scott(10), Gove(4)
HEPLER (66746) Crawford(91), Bourbon(8)
HERINGTON (67449) Dickinson(81), Morris(17)
HERNDON (67739) Rawlins(95), Decatur(4)
HESSTON Harvey
HIAWATHA Brown
HIGHLAND Doniphan
HILL CITY Graham
HILLSBORO Marion
HILLSDALE Miami
HOISINGTON Barton
HOLCOMB (67851) Finney(95), Kearny(2), Scott(1)
HOLLENBERG Washington
HOLTON (66436) Jackson(97), Atchison(2)
HOLYROOD (67450) Ellsworth(84), Barton(14), Russell(1)
HOME Marshall
HOPE (67451) Dickinson(98), Marion(1)
HORTON (66439) Brown(84), Jackson(10), Atchison(5)
HOWARD Elk
HOXIE (67740) Sheridan(97), Graham(2)
HOYT (66440) Jackson(98), Shawnee(1)
HUDSON Stafford
HUGOTON Stevens
HUMBOLDT Allen
HUNTER (67452) Lincoln(54), Mitchell(45)
HUTCHINSON Reno
INDEPENDENCE Montgomery
INGALLS (67853) Gray(90), Finney(9)
INMAN (67546) McPherson(86), Rice(6), Reno(5)
IOLA Allen
ISABEL (67065) Barber(59), Pratt(38), Kingman(1)
IUKA Pratt
JAMESTOWN (66948) Cloud(81), Republic(18)
JENNINGS (67643) Decatur(94), Sheridan(5)
JETMORE Hodgeman
JEWELL Jewell
JOHNSON (67855) Stanton(96), Grant(2), Morton(1)
JUNCTION CITY Geary
KALVESTA Finney
KANOPOLIS Ellsworth
KANORADO (67741) Sherman(95), Cheyenne(2), Wallace(1)
KANSAS CITY (66109) Wyandotte(97), Leavenworth(2)
KANSAS CITY Wyandotte
KECHI Sedgwick
KENDALL (67857) Hamilton(55), Kearny(44)
KENSINGTON (66951) Smith(75), Phillips(24)
KINCAID (66039) Anderson(89), Allen(10)
KINGMAN (67068) Kingman(98), Reno(1)
KINGSDOWN (67858) Ford(90), Clark(9)
KINSLEY (67547) Edwards(97), Hodgeman(1)
KIOWA Barber
KIRWIN (67644) Phillips(91), Smith(5), Rooks(3)
KISMET Seward
LA CROSSE Rush
LA CYGNE Linn

LA HARPE Allen
LAKE CITY Barber
LAKIN Kearny
LAMONT Greenwood
LANCASTER Atchison
LANE Franklin
LANSING Leavenworth
LARNED (67550) Pawnee(97), Stafford(1)
LATHAM (67072) Butler(87), Cowley(12)
LAWRENCE (66044) Douglas(92), Jefferson(4), Leavenworth(3)
LAWRENCE Douglas
LE ROY Coffey
LEAVENWORTH Leavenworth
LEBANON (66952) Smith(98), Jewell(1)
LEBO (66856) Coffey(70), Osage(29)
LECOMPTON Douglas
LEHIGH Marion
LENEXA Johnson
LENORA (67645) Norton(73), Graham(26)
LEON Butler
LEONARDVILLE Riley
LEOTI (67861) Wichita(96), Logan(3)
LEVANT Thomas
LEWIS Edwards
LIBERAL Seward
LIBERTY (67351) Montgomery(85), Labette(14)
LIEBENTHAL Rush
LINCOLN Lincoln
LINCOLNVILLE (66858) Marion(97), Chase(2)
LINDSBORG (67456) McPherson(89), Saline(10)
LINN Washington
LINWOOD Leavenworth
LITTLE RIVER Rice
LOGAN (67646) Phillips(78), Rooks(9), Graham(7), Norton(4)
LONG ISLAND Phillips
LONGFORD (67458) Clay(83), Ottawa(15)
LONGTON (67352) Elk(96), Chautauqua(3)
LORRAINE Ellsworth
LOST SPRINGS (66859) Marion(86), Morris(13)
LOUISBURG Miami
LOUISVILLE Pottawatomie
LUCAS (67648) Russell(75), Osborne(18), Lincoln(6)
LUDELL Rawlins
LURAY (67649) Russell(65), Osborne(34)
LYNDON Osage
LYONS Rice
MACKSVILLE (67557) Stafford(59), Pratt(19), Pawnee(14), Edwards(6)
MADISON (66860) Greenwood(58), Lyon(41)
MAHASKA (66955) Washington(98), Republic(1)
MAIZE Sedgwick
MANCHESTER Dickinson
MANHATTAN (66503) Riley(98), Pottawatomie(1)
MANHATTAN Riley
MANKATO Jewell
MANTER (67862) Stanton(75), Morton(24)
MAPLE CITY Cowley
MAPLE HILL Wabaunsee
MAPLETON (66754) Bourbon(96), Linn(3)
MARIENTHAL Wichita
MARION Marion
MARQUETTE (67464) McPherson(75), Ellsworth(24)
MARYSVILLE Marshall
MATFIELD GREEN Chase
MAYETTA Jackson
MAYFIELD Sumner
MC CONNELL A F B Sedgwick
MC CRACKEN (67556) Rush(67), Ellis(16), Ness(15)
MC CUNE (66753) Crawford(96), Labette(4)

MC DONALD (67745) Rawlins(75), Cheyenne(25)
MC FARLAND Wabaunsee
MC LOUTH (66054) Jefferson(69), Leavenworth(30)
MCCONNELL AFB Sedgwick
MCPHERSON McPherson
MEADE Meade
MEDICINE LODGE Barber
MELVERN Osage
MENTOR Saline
MERIDEN (66512) Jefferson(90), Jackson(6), Shawnee(3)
MILAN Sumner
MILFORD Geary
MILTON (67106) Sumner(62), Sedgwick(35), Kingman(2)
MILTONVALE (67466) Cloud(60), Ottawa(25), Clay(14)
MINNEAPOLIS Ottawa
MINNEOLA (67865) Ford(65), Clark(34)
MISSION Johnson
MOLINE (67353) Elk(75), Chautauqua(24)
MONTEZUMA (67867) Gray(96), Meade(3)
MONUMENT (67747) Logan(90), Thomas(9)
MORAN (66755) Allen(98), Bourbon(1)
MORGANVILLE Clay
MORLAND Graham
MORRILL Brown
MORROWVILLE Washington
MOSCOW Stevens
MOUND CITY Linn
MOUND VALLEY Labette
MOUNDRIDGE (67107) McPherson(68), Harvey(31)
MOUNT HOPE (67108) Sedgwick(59), Reno(40)
MULBERRY Crawford
MULLINVILLE Kiowa
MULVANE (67110) Sedgwick(68), Sumner(30), Cowley(1)
MUNDEN Republic
MURDOCK Kingman
MUSCOTAH (66058) Jackson(66), Atchison(33)
NARKA (66960) Republic(97), Washington(2)
NASHVILLE (67112) Kingman(86), Barber(13)
NATOMA (67651) Osborne(66), Rooks(26), Ellis(5), Russell(1)
NEAL Greenwood
NEKOMA (67559) Rush(84), Pawnee(15)
NEODESHA (66757) Wilson(92), Montgomery(7)
NEOSHO FALLS (66758) Coffey(54), Woodson(40), Anderson(2), Allen(1)
NEOSHO RAPIDS (66864) Lyon(90), Coffey(9)
NESS CITY Ness
NETAWAKA (66516) Jackson(78), Brown(21)
NEW ALBANY Wilson
NEW ALMELO Norton
NEW CAMBRIA (67470) Saline(89), Ottawa(10)
NEW CENTURY Johnson
NEWTON (67114) Harvey(95), Butler(2), Marion(1)
NICKERSON Reno
NIOTAZE Chautauqua
NORCATUR (67653) Decatur(70), Norton(29)
NORTH NEWTON Harvey
NORTON Norton
NORTONVILLE (66060) Jefferson(51), Atchison(48)
NORWAY Republic
NORWICH (67118) Kingman(94), Sedgwick(2), Harper(1), Sumner(1)
OAKHILL (67472) Clay(70), Ottawa(29)

OAKLEY (67748) Logan(83), Thomas(11), Gove(4)
OBERLIN (67749) Decatur(98), Rawlins(1)
ODIN Barton
OFFERLE (67563) Edwards(56), Ford(38), Hodgeman(4)
OGALLAH (67656) Trego(92), Graham(7)
OGDEN Riley
OKETO Marshall
OLATHE Johnson
OLMITZ Barton
OLPE Lyon
OLSBURG Pottawatomie
ONAGA (66521) Pottawatomie(94), Nemaha(5)
ONEIDA Nemaha
OPOLIS Crawford
OSAGE CITY Osage
OSAWATOMIE (66064) Miami(96), Franklin(3)
OSBORNE Osborne
OSKALOOSA Jefferson
OSWEGO (67356) Labette(98), Cherokee(1)
OTIS (67565) Rush(87), Barton(10), Russell(1)
OTTAWA Franklin
OVERBROOK (66524) Osage(58), Douglas(28), Shawnee(9), Franklin(2)
OVERLAND PARK Johnson
OXFORD (67119) Sumner(67), Cowley(32)
OZAWKIE Jefferson
PALCO (67657) Rooks(60), Graham(37), Trego(2)
PALMER (66962) Washington(88), Clay(11)
PAOLA Miami
PARADISE (67658) Russell(67), Osborne(32)
PARK (67751) Gove(69), Sheridan(30)
PARKER (66072) Linn(94), Miami(4)
PARSONS (67357) Labette(93), Neosho(6)
PARTRIDGE Reno
PAWNEE ROCK (67567) Barton(61), Pawnee(24), Stafford(9), Rush(5)
PAXICO Wabaunsee
PEABODY (66866) Marion(93), Harvey(5)
PECK (67120) Sedgwick(70), Sumner(29)
PENOKEE Graham
PERRY Jefferson
PERU Chautauqua
PFEIFER Ellis
PHILLIPSBURG Phillips
PIEDMONT (67122) Greenwood(65), Elk(34)
PIERCEVILLE Finney
PIQUA Woodson
PITTSBURG (66762) Crawford(97), Cherokee(2)
PLAINS (67869) Meade(86), Seward(13)
PLAINVILLE Rooks
PLEASANTON Linn
PLEVNA Reno
POMONA Franklin
PORTIS (67474) Osborne(72), Smith(27)
POTTER Atchison
POTWIN Butler
POWHATTAN Brown
PRAIRIE VIEW (67664) Phillips(92), Norton(7)
PRATT Pratt

PRESCOTT Linn
PRETTY PRAIRIE (67570) Reno(90), Kingman(9)
PRINCETON Franklin
PROTECTION (67127) Comanche(88), Clark(11)
QUENEMO Osage
QUINTER (67752) Gove(91), Sheridan(8)
RAGO Kingman
RAMONA (67475) Marion(63), Dickinson(36)
RANDALL Jewell
RANDOLPH Riley
RANSOM (67572) Ness(81), Trego(18)
RANTOUL (66079) Franklin(94), Miami(5)
RAYMOND Rice
READING (66868) Lyon(88), Osage(10)
REDFIELD Bourbon
REPUBLIC Republic
REXFORD (67753) Thomas(63), Sheridan(30), Rawlins(5)
RICHFIELD Morton
RICHMOND (66080) Franklin(77), Anderson(22)
RILEY Riley
RIVERTON Cherokee
ROBINSON (66532) Brown(72), Doniphan(27)
ROCK (67131) Cowley(98), Butler(1)
ROLLA (67954) Morton(74), Stevens(25)
ROSALIA Butler
ROSE HILL (67133) Butler(98), Sedgwick(1)
ROSSVILLE (66533) Shawnee(97), Jackson(3)
ROXBURY McPherson
ROZEL Pawnee
RUSH CENTER (67575) Rush(96), Pawnee(3)
RUSSELL (67665) Russell(98), Barton(1)
RUSSELL SPRINGS Logan
SABETHA (66534) Nemaha(92), Brown(7)
SAINT FRANCIS Cheyenne
SAINT GEORGE Pottawatomie
SAINT JOHN (67576) Stafford(96), Pratt(3)
SAINT MARYS (66536) Pottawatomie(94), Wabaunsee(2), Shawnee(2)
SAINT PAUL Neosho
SALINA Saline
SATANTA (67870) Haskell(78), Grant(16), Seward(5)
SAVONBURG (66772) Allen(97), Bourbon(2)
SAWYER (67134) Pratt(89), Barber(10)
SCAMMON Cherokee
SCANDIA Republic
SCHOENCHEN Ellis
SCOTT CITY (67871) Scott(97), Finney(1)
SCRANTON Osage
SEDAN Chautauqua
SEDGWICK (67135) Harvey(60), Sedgwick(39)
SELDEN (67757) Sheridan(57), Decatur(38), Thomas(4)
SENECA Nemaha
SEVERY (67137) Greenwood(88), Elk(11)
SEWARD Stafford
SHARON (67138) Barber(97), Harper(2)
SHARON SPRINGS Wallace
SHAWNEE Johnson
SHAWNEE MISSION Johnson

SHIELDS (67874) Lane(86), Gove(13)
SILVER LAKE (66539) Shawnee(97), Jackson(2)
SIMPSON Mitchell
SMITH CENTER Smith
SMOLAN Saline
SOLDIER (66540) Jackson(96), Nemaha(3)
SOLOMON (67480) Dickinson(59), Saline(20), Ottawa(19)
SOUTH HAVEN Sumner
SOUTH HUTCHINSON Reno
SPEARVILLE (67876) Ford(91), Hodgeman(8)
SPIVEY Kingman
SPRING HILL (66083) Johnson(62), Miami(37)
STAFFORD Stafford
STARK (66775) Neosho(98), Bourbon(1)
STERLING (67579) Rice(81), Reno(18)
STILWELL Johnson
STOCKTON Rooks
STRONG CITY Chase
STUDLEY (67759) Sheridan(89), Graham(10)
STUTTGART Phillips
SUBLETTE (67877) Haskell(93), Seward(6)
SUMMERFIELD Marshall
SUN CITY Barber
SYCAMORE Montgomery
SYLVAN GROVE (67481) Lincoln(96), Russell(3)
SYLVIA Reno
SYRACUSE (67878) Hamilton(85), Stanton(14)
TALMAGE Dickinson
TAMPA Marion
TECUMSEH Shawnee
TESCOTT (67484) Ottawa(80), Saline(15), Lincoln(3)
THAYER (66776) Neosho(82), Wilson(15)
TIMKEN (67582) Rush(98), Pawnee(1)
TIPTON (67485) Osborne(53), Mitchell(46)
TONGANOXIE Leavenworth
TOPEKA (66615) Shawnee(87), Wabaunsee(12)
TOPEKA (66617) Shawnee(90), Jefferson(8)
TOPEKA Shawnee
TORONTO (66777) Woodson(87), Greenwood(11), Wilson(1)
TOWANDA Butler
TREECE Cherokee
TRIBUNE Greeley
TROY Doniphan
TURON (67583) Reno(49), Pratt(41), Stafford(9)
TURON Pratt
TYRO Montgomery
UDALL (67146) Cowley(93), Sumner(6)
ULYSSES (67880) Grant(98), Kearny(1)
UNIONTOWN Bourbon
UTICA (67584) Ness(56), Gove(23), Lane(10), Trego(9)
VALLEY CENTER (67147) Sedgwick(97), Harvey(2)
VALLEY FALLS (66088) Jefferson(97), Atchison(2)
VASSAR Osage
VERMILLION (66544) Marshall(95), Nemaha(4)
VICTORIA Ellis

VIOLA Sedgwick
VIRGIL (66870) Greenwood(97), Woodson(2)
VLIETS Marshall
WA KEENEY (67672) Trego(96), Graham(3)
WAKARUSA (66546) Shawnee(86), Osage(13)
WAKEFIELD (67487) Clay(90), Dickinson(7), Geary(2)
WALDO (67673) Russell(82), Osborne(17)
WALDRON Harper
WALKER Ellis
WALLACE (67761) Wallace(70), Logan(26), Wichita(2)
WALNUT (66780) Bourbon(78), Crawford(20), Neosho(1)
WALTON (67151) Harvey(89), Marion(10)
WAMEGO (66547) Pottawatomie(88), Wabaunsee(11)
WATERVILLE (66548) Marshall(95), Washington(2), Riley(1)
WATHENA Doniphan
WAVERLY (66871) Coffey(96), Osage(3)
WEBBER Jewell
WEIR Cherokee
WELDA (66091) Anderson(97), Franklin(2)
WELLINGTON Sumner
WELLS Ottawa
WELLSVILLE (66092) Franklin(66), Miami(25), Douglas(7)
WESKAN (67762) Wallace(98), Greeley(1)
WEST MINERAL Cherokee
WESTMORELAND Pottawatomie
WESTPHALIA (66093) Anderson(56), Coffey(43)
WETMORE (66550) Nemaha(80), Jackson(10), Brown(8)
WHEATON (66551) Pottawatomie(98), Marshall(1)
WHITE CITY (66872) Morris(96), Geary(3)
WHITE CLOUD (66094) Doniphan(98), Brown(1)
WHITEWATER (67154) Butler(94), Harvey(5)
WHITING Jackson
WICHITA (67230) Sedgwick(96), Butler(3)
WICHITA Sedgwick
WILLIAMSBURG (66095) Franklin(88), Anderson(10)
WILMORE (67155) Comanche(84), Kiowa(15)
WILSEY Morris
WILSON (67490) Ellsworth(82), Russell(10), Lincoln(6)
WINCHESTER (66097) Jefferson(98), Leavenworth(1)
WINDOM (67491) McPherson(77), Rice(22)
WINFIELD Cowley
WINONA (67764) Logan(88), Thomas(11)
WOODBINE Dickinson
WOODSTON Rooks
WRIGHT Ford
YATES CENTER Woodson
YODER Reno
ZENDA (67159) Kingman(83), Harper(16)
ZURICH (67676) Rooks(90), Ellis(9)

Kansas ZIP/City Cross Reference

66002-66002 ATCHISON	66403-66403 AXTELL	66712-66712 ARMA	66871-66871 WAVERLY
66006-66006 BALDWIN CITY	66404-66404 BAILEYVILLE	66713-66713 BAXTER SPRINGS	66872-66872 WHITE CITY
66007-66007 BASEHOR	66406-66406 BEATTIE	66714-66714 BENEDICT	66873-66873 WILSEY
66008-66008 BENDENA	66407-66407 BELVUE	66716-66716 BRONSON	66901-66901 CONCORDIA
66010-66010 BLUE MOUND	66408-66408 BERN	66717-66717 BUFFALO	66930-66930 AGENDA
66012-66012 BONNER SPRINGS	66409-66409 BERRYTON	66720-66720 CHANUTE	66931-66931 AMES
66013-66013 BUCYRUS	66411-66411 BLUE RAPIDS	66724-66724 CHEROKEE	66932-66932 ATHOL
66014-66014 CENTERVILLE	66412-66412 BREMEN	66725-66725 COLUMBUS	66933-66933 BARNES
66015-66015 COLONY	66413-66413 BURLINGAME	66727-66727 COYVILLE	66935-66935 BELLEVILLE
66016-66016 CUMMINGS	66414-66414 CARBONDALE	66728-66728 CRESTLINE	66936-66936 BURR OAK
66017-66017 DENTON	66415-66415 CENTRALIA	66732-66732 ELSMORE	66937-66937 CLIFTON
66018-66018 DE SOTO	66416-66416 CIRCLEVILLE	66733-66733 ERIE	66938-66938 CLYDE
66019-66019 CLEARVIEW CITY	66417-66417 CORNING	66734-66734 FARLINGTON	66939-66939 COURTLAND
66020-66020 EASTON	66418-66418 DELIA	66735-66735 FRANKLIN	66940-66940 CUBA
66021-66021 EDGERTON	66419-66419 DENISON	66736-66736 FREDONIA	66941-66941 ESBON
66023-66023 EFFINGHAM	66420-66420 DOVER	66738-66738 FULTON	66942-66942 FORMOSO
66024-66024 ELWOOD	66422-66422 EMMETT	66739-66739 GALENA	66943-66943 GREENLEAF
66025-66025 EUDORA	66423-66423 ESKRIDGE	66740-66740 GALESBURG	66944-66944 HADDAM
66026-66026 FONTANA	66424-66424 EVEREST	66741-66741 GARLAND	66945-66945 HANOVER
66027-66027 FORT LEAVENWORTH	66425-66425 FAIRVIEW	66741-66741 ARCADIA	66946-66946 HOLLENBERG
66030-66030 GARDNER	66426-66426 FOSTORIA	66742-66742 GAS	66948-66948 JAMESTOWN
66031-66031 NEW CENTURY	66427-66427 FRANKFORT	66743-66743 GIRARD	66949-66949 JEWELL
66032-66032 GARNETT	66428-66428 GOFF	66746-66746 HEPLER	66951-66951 KENSINGTON
66033-66033 GREELEY	66429-66429 GRANTVILLE	66748-66748 HUMBOLDT	66952-66952 LEBANON
66035-66035 HIGHLAND	66431-66431 HARVEYVILLE	66749-66749 IOLA	66953-66953 LINN
66036-66036 HILLSDALE	66432-66432 HAVENSVILLE	66751-66751 LA HARPE	66955-66955 MAHASKA
66039-66039 KINCAID	66433-66433 MARYSVILLE	66753-66753 MC CUNE	66956-66956 MANKATO
66040-66040 LA CYGNE	66434-66434 HIAWATHA	66754-66754 MAPLETON	66958-66958 MORROWVILLE
66041-66041 LANCASTER	66436-66436 HOLTON	66755-66755 MORAN	66959-66959 MUNDEN
66042-66042 LANE	66438-66438 HOME	66756-66756 MULBERRY	66960-66960 NARKA
66043-66043 LANSING	66439-66439 HORTON	66757-66757 NEODESHA	66961-66961 NORWAY
66044-66047 LAWRENCE	66440-66440 HOYT	66758-66758 NEOSHO FALLS	66962-66962 PALMER
66048-66048 LEAVENWORTH	66441-66441 JUNCTION CITY	66759-66759 NEW ALBANY	66963-66963 RANDALL
66049-66049 LAWRENCE	66442-66442 FORT RILEY	66760-66760 OPOLIS	66964-66964 REPUBLIC
66050-66050 LECOMPTON	66449-66449 LEONARDVILLE	66761-66761 PIQUA	66966-66966 SCANDIA
66051-66051 OLATHE	66450-66450 LOUISVILLE	66762-66762 PITTSBURG	66967-66967 SMITH CENTER
66052-66052 LINWOOD	66451-66451 LYNDON	66763-66763 FRONTENAC	66968-66968 WASHINGTON
66053-66053 LOUISBURG	66501-66501 MC FARLAND	66767-66767 PRESCOTT	66970-66970 WEBBER
66054-66054 MC LOUTH	66502-66506 MANHATTAN	66769-66769 REDFIELD	67001-67001 ANDALE
66056-66056 MOUND CITY	66507-66507 MAPLE HILL	66770-66770 RIVERTON	67002-67002 ANDOVER
66058-66058 MUSCOTAH	66508-66508 MARYSVILLE	66771-66771 SAINT PAUL	67003-67003 ANTHONY
66060-66060 NORTONVILLE	66509-66509 MAYETTA	66772-66772 SAVONBURG	67004-67004 ARGONIA
66061-66063 OLATHE	66510-66510 MELVERN	66773-66773 SCAMMON	67005-67005 ARKANSAS CITY
66064-66064 OSAWATOMIE	66512-66512 MERIDEN	66775-66775 STARK	67008-67008 ATLANTA
66066-66066 OSKALOOSA	66514-66514 MILFORD	66776-66776 THAYER	67009-67009 ATTICA
66067-66067 OTTAWA	66515-66515 MORRILL	66777-66777 TORONTO	67010-67010 AUGUSTA
66070-66070 OZAWKIE	66516-66516 NETAWAKA	66778-66778 TREECE	67012-67012 BEAUMONT
66071-66071 PAOLA	66517-66517 OGDEN	66779-66779 UNIONTOWN	67013-67013 BELLE PLAINE
66072-66072 PARKER	66518-66518 OKETO	66780-66780 WALNUT	67015-67015 BELVIDERE
66073-66073 PERRY	66520-66520 OLSBURG	66781-66781 WEIR	67016-67016 BENTLEY
66075-66075 PLEASANTON	66521-66521 ONAGA	66782-66782 WEST MINERAL	67017-67017 BENTON
66076-66076 POMONA	66522-66522 ONEIDA	66783-66783 YATES CENTER	67018-67018 BLUFF CITY
66077-66077 POTTER	66523-66523 OSAGE CITY	66801-66801 EMPORIA	67019-67019 BURDEN
66078-66078 PRINCETON	66524-66524 OVERBROOK	66830-66830 ADMIRE	67020-67020 BURRTON
66079-66079 RANTOUL	66526-66526 PAXICO	66833-66833 ALLEN	67021-67021 BYERS
66080-66080 RICHMOND	66527-66527 POWHATTAN	66834-66834 ALTA VISTA	67022-67022 CALDWELL
66083-66083 SPRING HILL	66528-66528 QUENEMO	66835-66835 AMERICUS	67023-67023 CAMBRIDGE
66085-66085 STILWELL	66531-66531 RILEY	66838-66838 BURDICK	67024-67024 CEDAR VALE
66086-66086 TONGANOXIE	66532-66532 ROBINSON	66839-66839 BURLINGTON	67025-67025 CHENEY
66087-66087 TROY	66533-66533 ROSSVILLE	66840-66840 BURNS	67026-67026 CLEARWATER
66088-66088 VALLEY FALLS	66534-66534 SABETHA	66842-66842 CASSODAY	67028-67028 COATS
66090-66090 WATHENA	66535-66535 SAINT GEORGE	66843-66843 CEDAR POINT	67029-67029 COLDWATER
66091-66091 WELDA	66536-66536 SAINT MARYS	66845-66845 COTTONWOOD FALLS	67030-67030 COLWICH
66092-66092 WELLSVILLE	66537-66537 SCRANTON	66846-66846 COUNCIL GROVE	67031-67031 CONWAY SPRINGS
66093-66093 WESTPHALIA	66538-66538 SENECA	66849-66849 DWIGHT	67032-67032 CALDWELL
66094-66094 WHITE CLOUD	66539-66539 SILVER LAKE	66850-66850 ELMDALE	67035-67035 CUNNINGHAM
66095-66095 WILLIAMSBURG	66540-66540 SOLDIER	66851-66851 FLORENCE	67036-67036 DANVILLE
66097-66097 WINCHESTER	66541-66541 SUMMERFIELD	66852-66852 GRIDLEY	67037-67037 DERBY
66100-66112 KANSAS CITY	66542-66542 TECUMSEH	66853-66853 HAMILTON	67038-67038 DEXTER
66113-66113 EDWARDSVILLE	66543-66543 VASSAR	66854-66854 HARTFORD	67039-67039 DOUGLASS
66115-66160 KANSAS CITY	66544-66544 VERMILLION	66855-66855 LAMONT	67041-67041 ELBING
66200-66201 SHAWNEE MISSION	66545-66545 VLIETS	66856-66856 LEBO	67042-67042 EL DORADO
66201-66201 MISSION	66546-66546 WAKARUSA	66857-66857 LE ROY	67045-67045 EUREKA
66202-66222 SHAWNEE MISSION	66547-66547 WAMEGO	66858-66858 LINCOLNVILLE	67047-67047 FALL RIVER
66222-66222 MISSION	66548-66548 WATERVILLE	66859-66859 LOST SPRINGS	67049-67049 FREEPORT
66223-66251 SHAWNEE MISSION	66549-66549 WESTMORELAND	66860-66860 MADISON	67050-67050 GARDEN PLAIN
66251-66251 OVERLAND PARK	66550-66550 WETMORE	66861-66861 MARION	67051-67051 GEUDA SPRINGS
66262-66283 SHAWNEE MISSION	66551-66551 WHEATON	66862-66862 MATFIELD GREEN	67052-67052 GODDARD
66283-66283 OVERLAND PARK	66552-66552 WHITING	66863-66863 NEAL	67053-67053 GOESSEL
66285-66285 SHAWNEE MISSION	66554-66554 RANDOLPH	66864-66864 NEOSHO RAPIDS	67054-67054 GREENSBURG
66285-66285 LENEXA	66555-66555 MARYSVILLE	66865-66865 OLPE	67055-67055 GREENWICH
66286-66286 SHAWNEE MISSION	66600-66699 TOPEKA	66866-66866 PEABODY	67056-67056 HALSTEAD
66286-66286 SHAWNEE	66701-66701 FORT SCOTT	66868-66868 READING	67057-67057 HARDTNER
66401-66401 ALMA	66710-66710 ALTOONA	66869-66869 STRONG CITY	67058-67058 HARPER
66402-66402 AUBURN	66711-66711 ARCADIA	66870-66870 VIRGIL	67059-67059 HAVILAND

67060-67060	HAYSVILLE
67061-67061	HAZELTON
67062-67062	HESSTON
67063-67063	HILLSBORO
67065-67065	ISABEL
67066-67066	IUKA
67067-67067	KECHI
67068-67068	KINGMAN
67070-67070	KIOWA
67071-67071	LAKE CITY
67072-67072	LATHAM
67073-67073	LEHIGH
67074-67074	LEON
67101-67101	MAIZE
67102-67102	MAPLE CITY
67103-67103	MAYFIELD
67104-67104	MEDICINE LODGE
67105-67105	MILAN
67106-67106	MILTON
67107-67107	MOUNDRIDGE
67108-67108	MOUNT HOPE
67109-67109	MULLINVILLE
67110-67110	MULVANE
67111-67111	MURDOCK
67112-67112	NASHVILLE
67114-67114	NEWTON
67117-67117	NORTH NEWTON
67118-67118	NORWICH
67119-67119	OXFORD
67120-67120	PECK
67122-67122	PIEDMONT
67123-67123	POTWIN
67124-67124	PRATT
67127-67127	PROTECTION
67128-67128	RAGO
67131-67131	ROCK
67132-67132	ROSALIA
67133-67133	ROSE HILL
67134-67134	SAWYER
67135-67135	SEDGWICK
67137-67137	SEVERY
67138-67138	SHARON
67140-67140	SOUTH HAVEN
67142-67142	SPIVEY
67143-67143	SUN CITY
67144-67144	TOWANDA
67146-67146	UDALL
67147-67147	VALLEY CENTER
67149-67149	VIOLA
67150-67150	WALDRON
67151-67151	WALTON
67152-67152	WELLINGTON
67154-67154	WHITEWATER
67155-67155	WILMORE
67156-67156	WINFIELD
67159-67159	ZENDA
67200-67220	WICHITA
67221-67221	MC CONNELL A F B
67221-67221	MCCONNELL AFB
67223-67236	WICHITA
67240-67240	DENNIS THE MENACE
67251-67278	WICHITA
67301-67301	INDEPENDENCE
67330-67330	ALTAMONT
67332-67332	BARTLETT
67333-67333	CANEY
67334-67334	CHAUTAUQUA
67335-67335	CHERRYVALE
67336-67336	CHETOPA
67337-67337	COFFEYVILLE
67340-67340	DEARING
67341-67341	DENNIS
67342-67342	EDNA
67344-67344	ELK CITY
67345-67345	ELK FALLS
67346-67346	GRENOLA
67347-67347	HAVANA
67349-67349	HOWARD
67351-67351	LIBERTY
67352-67352	LONGTON
67353-67353	MOLINE
67354-67354	MOUND VALLEY
67355-67355	NIOTAZE
67356-67356	OSWEGO
67357-67357	PARSONS
67360-67360	PERU
67361-67361	SEDAN
67363-67363	SYCAMORE
67364-67364	TYRO
67401-67402	SALINA
67410-67410	ABILENE
67414-67414	ADA
67416-67416	ASSARIA
67417-67417	AURORA
67418-67418	BARNARD
67420-67420	BELOIT
67422-67422	BENNINGTON
67423-67423	BEVERLY
67425-67425	BROOKVILLE
67427-67427	BUSHTON
67428-67428	CANTON
67429-67429	CARLTON
67430-67430	CAWKER CITY
67431-67431	CHAPMAN
67432-67432	CLAY CENTER
67436-67436	DELPHOS
67437-67437	DOWNS
67438-67438	DURHAM
67439-67439	ELLSWORTH
67441-67441	ENTERPRISE
67442-67442	FALUN
67443-67443	GALVA
67444-67444	GENESEO
67445-67445	GLASCO
67446-67446	GLEN ELDER
67447-67447	GREEN
67448-67448	GYPSUM
67449-67449	HERINGTON
67450-67450	HOLYROOD
67451-67451	HOPE
67452-67452	HUNTER
67454-67454	KANOPOLIS
67455-67455	LINCOLN
67456-67456	LINDSBORG
67457-67457	LITTLE RIVER
67458-67458	LONGFORD
67459-67459	LORRAINE
67460-67460	MCPHERSON
67463-67463	MANCHESTER
67464-67464	MARQUETTE
67465-67465	MENTOR
67466-67466	MILTONVALE
67467-67467	MINNEAPOLIS
67468-67468	MORGANVILLE
67469-67469	ENTERPRISE
67470-67470	NEW CAMBRIA
67472-67472	OAKHILL
67473-67473	OSBORNE
67474-67474	PORTIS
67475-67475	RAMONA
67476-67476	ROXBURY
67478-67478	SIMPSON
67479-67479	SMOLAN
67480-67480	SOLOMON
67481-67481	SYLVAN GROVE
67482-67482	TALMAGE
67483-67483	TAMPA
67484-67484	TESCOTT
67485-67485	TIPTON
67487-67487	WAKEFIELD
67488-67488	WELLS
67490-67490	WILSON
67491-67491	WINDOM
67492-67492	WOODBINE
67501-67504	HUTCHINSON
67505-67505	SOUTH HUTCHINSON
67510-67510	ABBYVILLE
67511-67511	ALBERT
67512-67512	ALDEN
67513-67513	ALEXANDER
67514-67514	ARLINGTON
67515-67515	ARNOLD
67516-67516	BAZINE
67517-67517	BEAVER
67518-67518	BEELER
67519-67519	BELPRE
67520-67520	BISON
67521-67521	BROWNELL
67522-67522	BUHLER
67523-67523	BURDETT
67524-67524	CHASE
67525-67525	CLAFLIN
67526-67526	ELLINWOOD
67529-67529	GARFIELD
67530-67530	GREAT BEND
67543-67543	HAVEN
67544-67544	HOISINGTON
67545-67545	HUDSON
67546-67546	INMAN
67547-67547	KINSLEY
67548-67548	LA CROSSE
67550-67550	LARNED
67552-67552	LEWIS
67553-67553	LIEBENTHAL
67554-67554	LYONS
67556-67556	MC CRACKEN
67557-67557	MACKSVILLE
67559-67559	NEKOMA
67560-67560	NESS CITY
67561-67561	NICKERSON
67562-67562	ODIN
67563-67563	OFFERLE
67564-67564	OLMITZ
67565-67565	OTIS
67566-67566	PARTRIDGE
67567-67567	PAWNEE ROCK
67568-67568	PLEVNA
67569-67569	TURON
67570-67570	PRETTY PRAIRIE
67572-67572	RANSOM
67573-67573	RAYMOND
67574-67574	ROZEL
67575-67575	RUSH CENTER
67576-67576	SAINT JOHN
67577-67577	SEWARD
67578-67578	STAFFORD
67579-67579	STERLING
67581-67581	SYLVIA
67582-67582	TIMKEN
67583-67583	TURON
67584-67584	UTICA
67585-67585	YODER
67601-67601	HAYS
67621-67621	AGRA
67622-67622	ALMENA
67623-67623	ALTON
67625-67625	BOGUE
67626-67626	BUNKER HILL
67627-67627	CATHARINE
67628-67628	CEDAR
67629-67629	CLAYTON
67630-67630	CODELL
67631-67631	COLLYER
67632-67632	DAMAR
67634-67634	DORRANCE
67635-67635	DRESDEN
67636-67636	EDMOND
67637-67637	ELLIS
67638-67638	GAYLORD
67639-67639	GLADE
67640-67640	GORHAM
67641-67641	HARLAN
67642-67642	HILL CITY
67643-67643	JENNINGS
67644-67644	KIRWIN
67645-67645	LENORA
67646-67646	LOGAN
67647-67647	LONG ISLAND
67648-67648	LUCAS
67649-67649	LURAY
67650-67650	MORLAND
67651-67651	NATOMA
67652-67652	NEW ALMELO
67653-67653	NORCATUR
67654-67654	NORTON
67656-67656	OGALLAH
67657-67657	PALCO
67658-67658	PARADISE
67659-67659	PENOKEE
67660-67660	PFEIFER
67661-67661	PHILLIPSBURG
67663-67663	PLAINVILLE
67664-67664	PRAIRIE VIEW
67665-67665	RUSSELL
67667-67667	SCHOENCHEN
67669-67669	STOCKTON
67670-67670	STUTTGART
67671-67671	VICTORIA
67672-67672	WA KEENEY
67673-67673	WALDO
67674-67674	WALKER
67675-67675	WOODSTON
67676-67676	ZURICH
67701-67701	COLBY
67730-67730	ATWOOD
67731-67731	BIRD CITY
67732-67732	BREWSTER
67733-67733	EDSON
67734-67734	GEM
67735-67735	GOODLAND
67736-67736	GOVE
67737-67737	GRAINFIELD
67738-67738	GRINNELL
67739-67739	HERNDON
67740-67740	HOXIE
67741-67741	KANORADO
67743-67743	LEVANT
67744-67744	LUDELL
67745-67745	MC DONALD
67747-67747	MONUMENT
67748-67748	OAKLEY
67749-67749	OBERLIN
67751-67751	PARK
67752-67752	QUINTER
67753-67753	REXFORD
67755-67755	RUSSELL SPRINGS
67756-67756	SAINT FRANCIS
67757-67757	SELDEN
67758-67758	SHARON SPRINGS
67759-67759	STUDLEY
67761-67761	WALLACE
67762-67762	WESKAN
67764-67764	WINONA
67801-67801	DODGE CITY
67831-67831	ASHLAND
67834-67834	BUCKLIN
67835-67835	CIMARRON
67836-67836	COOLIDGE
67837-67837	COPELAND
67838-67838	DEERFIELD
67839-67839	DIGHTON
67840-67840	ENGLEWOOD
67841-67841	ENSIGN
67842-67842	FORD
67843-67843	FORT DODGE
67844-67844	FOWLER
67846-67846	GARDEN CITY
67849-67849	HANSTON
67850-67850	HEALY
67851-67851	HOLCOMB
67853-67853	INGALLS
67854-67854	JETMORE
67855-67855	JOHNSON
67856-67856	KALVESTA
67857-67857	KENDALL
67858-67858	KINGSDOWN
67859-67859	KISMET
67860-67860	LAKIN
67861-67861	LEOTI
67862-67862	MANTER
67863-67863	MARIENTHAL
67864-67864	MEADE
67865-67865	MINNEOLA
67867-67867	MONTEZUMA
67868-67868	PIERCEVILLE
67869-67869	PLAINS
67870-67870	SATANTA
67871-67871	SCOTT CITY
67874-67874	SHIELDS
67876-67876	SPEARVILLE
67877-67877	SUBLETTE
67878-67878	SYRACUSE
67879-67879	TRIBUNE
67880-67880	ULYSSES
67882-67882	WRIGHT
67901-67905	LIBERAL
67950-67950	ELKHART
67951-67951	HUGOTON
67952-67952	MOSCOW
67953-67953	RICHFIELD
67954-67954	ROLLA

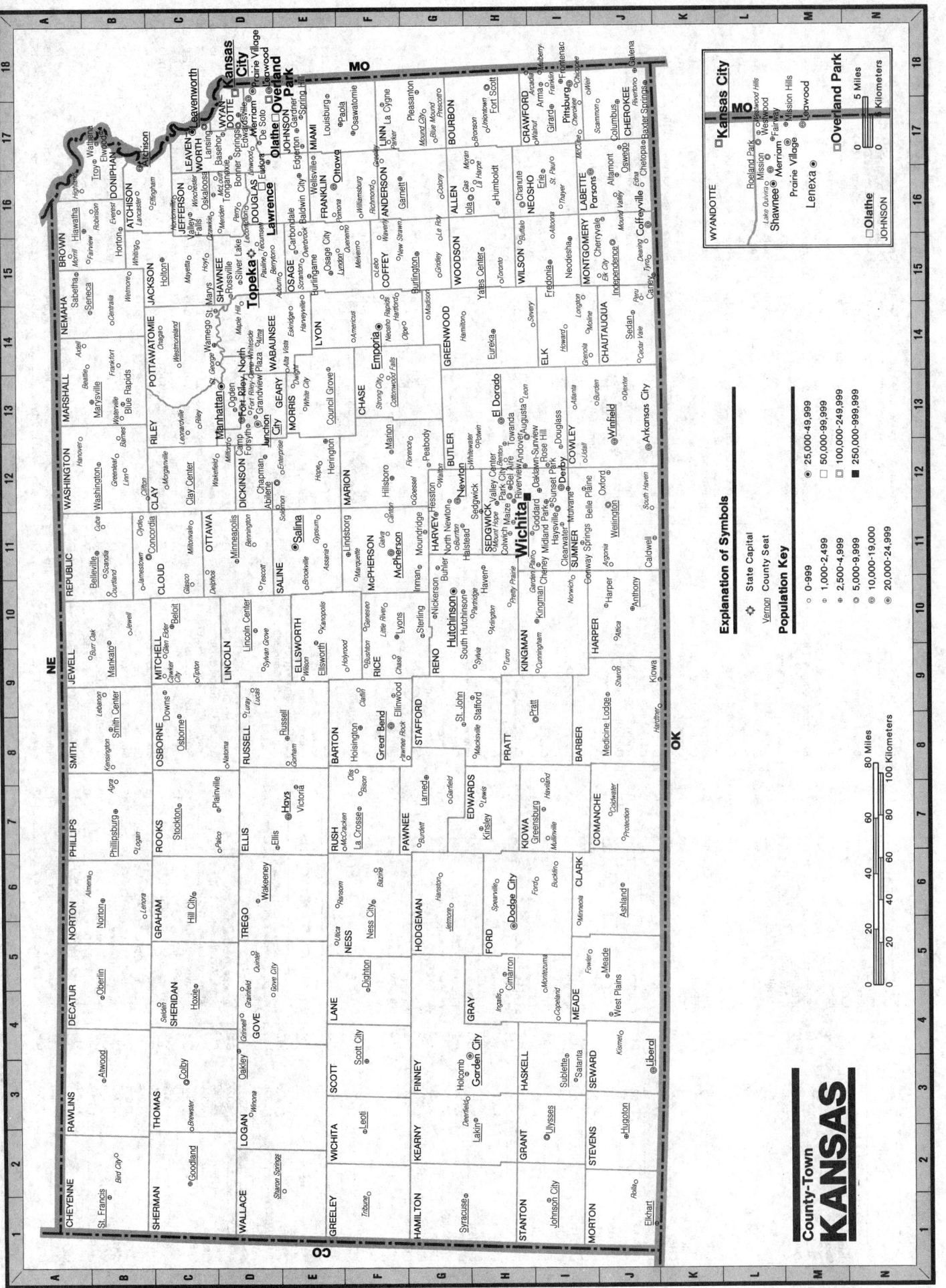

County-Town
KANSAS

CITIES AND TOWNS

Note: The first name is that of the city or town, second, that of the county in which it is located, then the population and location on the map.

Explanation of symbols: • – Census Designated Place (CDP)

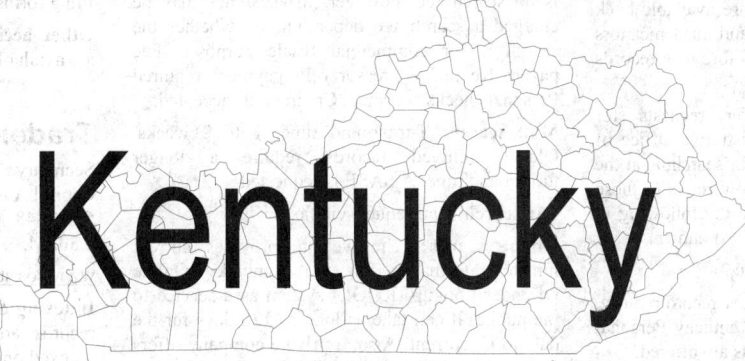

Kentucky

General Help Numbers:

Governor's Office

700 Capitol Ave, Room 100
Frankfort, KY 40601
http://gov.state.ky.us

502-564-2611
Fax 502-564-2517
7:30AM-5PM

Attorney General's Office

700 Capitol Ave, Ste. 118
Frankfort, KY 40601
www..law.state.ky.us

502-696-5300
Fax 502-564-2894
8AM-5PM

Legislative Records

Kentucky General Assembly, Research Commission
700 Capitol Ave, Room 300
Frankfort, KY 40601
www.lrc.state.ky.us

502-372-7181
Fax 502-223-5094
8AM-4:30PM

State Archives

300 Coffee Tree Rd
Frankfort, KY 40601
www.kdla.ky.gov/index.htm

502-564-8300
Fax 502-564-5773
8AM-4PM T-SA

State Specifics:

Capital:

Frankfort
Franklin County

Time Zone:

EST*

* Kentucky's forty western-most counties are CST: They are: Adair, Allen, Ballard, Barren, Breckinridge, Butler, Caldwell, Calloway, Carlisle, Christian, Clinton, Crittenden, Cumberland, Daviess, Edmonson, Fulton, Graves, Grayson, Hancock, Hart, Henderson, Hickman, Hopkins, Livingstone, Logan, Marshall, McCracken, McLean, Metcalfe, Monroe, Muhlenberg, Ohio,Russell, Simpson, Todd, Trigg, Union, Warren, Wayne, Webster.

Number of Counties:

120

Population:

4,117,827

Web Site:

www.kentucky.gov/

State Agencies

Criminal Records

Kentucky State Police, Criminal Identification and Records Branch, 1250 Louisville Rd, Frankfort, KY 40601; 502-227-8713, 502-226-7422 (Fax), 8AM-4PM.

www.kentuckystatepolice.org

Note: Interestingly, local Kentucky courts will not do criminal searches. They refer all requesters to the Administrative Office of Courts in Frankfort, KY; phone 502-573-2350. This office will also suggest to check the court system.

Indexing & Storage: Records are available from 1952 on for criminal records. It takes a minimum of 30 days before new records are available for inquiry. Records are indexed on inhouse computer,

fingerprint cards. Nearly 75% of records are automated.

Searching: Records are available to all requesters as long as a signed release is submitted. Special forms are suggested for certain employment purposes such as nursing, schools, lottery, EMT, YMCA, daycare, and adoptive/foster parent background searches. Include the following in your request-signed release from subject, full name, date of birth, Social Security Number, reason for information request. Fingerprints are not requested. Statistical information about criminal offenses and accidents is available from 1971 on. The following data is not released: juvenile records.

Access by: mail, in person.

Fee & Payment: The fee is $10.00 per name. Fee payee: Kentucky State Treasurer. Prepayment required. Personal checks accepted. No credit cards accepted.

Mail search: Turnaround time: 2 to 3 weeks. A SASE is requested.

In person search: Turnaround time is while you wait. There is a limit of 5 searches.

Statewide Court Records

Administrative Office of Courts, Pre-trail Services Records Division, 100 Mill Creek Park, Frankfort, KY 40601; 502-573-1682, 800-928-6381, 502-573-1669 (Fax), 7:30AM-5PM.

www.kycourts.net

Indexing & Storage: Records are available back to 1978 for felony convictions, and misdemeanors back five years. It takes 1 day before new records are available for inquiry.

Searching: Many courts refer requests for criminal searches to the Administrative Office of Courts due to lack of personnel for searching at the court level. The information below refers to these criminal record requests. Include the following in your request-name, DOB and SSN if known.

Access by: mail, in person, online.

Fee & Payment: Fee is $10.00 per record request. Fee payee: State Treasurer of Kentucky Personal checks accepted. Prepaid accounts are offered.

Mail search: Turnaround time: 1-2 days. A SASE is required. No searching by mail.

In person search: Walk-in hours are above, drive-through until 12:30PM.

Online search: Searching is limited. You may search six days of daily court calendars by county for free at http://dockets.kycourts.net/. From the website above search Supreme Court and appellate opinions.

Sexual Offender Registry

Kentucky State Police, Criminal identification and Records Branch, 1250 Louisville Rd, Frankfort, KY 40601; 502-227-8718, 866-564-5652 (Alert Line), 502-226-7419 (Fax), 8AM-4PM.

www.kentuckystatepolice.org/sor.htm

Indexing & Storage: Records are available from 7/15/94 forward.

Searching: Only offenders convicted of statutorily covered crimes who are convicted after July 15, 1994 or incarcerated or sentenced after July 15, 1998 are listed.

Access by: phone, online. No written requests accepted.

Phone search: Serach requests can be placed 24/7 on the Alert Line. Provide your telephone number and up to three ZIP Codes to monitor. You will be notifed if registered sex offender is moving into one of the ZIP Code areas that you entered.

Online search: Access is available via the website. Search by City, ZIP, or County.

Incarceration Records

Kentucky Department of Corrections, Offender Information Services, PO Box 2400, Frankfort, KY 40602-2400 (Courier: 275 E. Main, Room 619, Frankfort, KY 40602); 502-564-2433, 800-511-1670 (Victim Notification Line), 502-564-1471 (Fax), 8AM-4:30PM.

www.corrections.ky.gov

Indexing & Storage: Records are available on current and former inmates. It takes approximately 30 days before new records are available for inquiry. Records are indexed on computer back to 1981; prior in archives on paper. Records are normally destroyed after 5 years after release (institutional versions) and after 75 years after release from the central office file.

Searching: Include the following in your request-full name. DOB and SSN are helpful. Index does not include alias or other names used. Location, physical identifiers, conviction and sentencing information, and release dates are reported.

Access by: mail, fax, online.

Fee & Payment: Copy fee is $.10 per page. There is no search fee, however, list searches may be charged a search fee depending on whether the search is for commercial resale purposes. Fee payee: Kentucky Treasurer Prepayment required Personal checks accepted. Credit cards accepted.

Mail search: Turnaround time: 1 to 2 weeks. Older, archived records require a longer turnaround time. A SASE is requested.

Fax search: Can request via fax.

Online search: The website provides current inmate information on the Kentucky Online Offender Lookup (KOOL) system as a service to the public. It can take as long as 120 days for the data to be current. Also, a private company offers free web access at www.vinelink.com/index.jsp. Include state, DOC, and county jails

Other access: The IT Department has the database on magnetic tape; this is available to users with compatible systems. For information on tape access, call 502-564-4360.

Expedited service: Will expedite processing if reason is given for delivering the record in a timely manner.

Corporation, Limited Partnerships, Assumed Name, Limited Liability Company Records

Secretary of State, Corporate Records, PO Box 718, Frankfort, KY 40602-0718 (Courier: 700 Capitol Ave, Room 156, Frankfort, KY 40601); 502-564-7330, 502-564-4075 (Fax), 8AM-4PM.

www.sos.state.ky.us

Indexing & Storage: Records are available from the 1977 forward on computer index. Hard copies are on microfilm. Records inactive by 1976 are archived and it takes 2 weeks to research. New records are available for inquiry immediately. Records are normally destroyed after they have been microfilmed.

Searching: Computer records are limited, they contain name, dates, current registered agent and initial incorporators and initial directors. They do contain current lists of officers and directors when available. Include the following in your request-full name of business.

Access by: mail, phone, fax, in person, online.

Fee & Payment: There is no search fee, but there is a $5.00 certification fee. Copies are $1.00 (minimum) for up to first to 10 pages, and $.10 per each additional page. Pages can be certified for $.50 each. A Certificate of Good Standing is $10.00. Fee payee: Secretary of State. Prepayment required. Send at least $1.00 in the mail for copies. If certified copies are needed, call first. Personal checks accepted. Credit cards accepted, minimum $5.00.

Mail search: Turnaround time: 2 to 3 days. No SASE is required.

Phone search: Only information on the computer system is released over the phone.

Fax search: Fax requests accepted with a credit card.

In person search: Turnaround time while you wait. If you order 5 or more, they will mail the records to you.

Online search: The Internet site, open 24 hours, has a searchable database with over 340,000 KY

businesses. The site also offers downloading of filing forms.

Other access: Monthly lists of new corporations are available for $50.00 per month.

Trademarks/Servicemarks

Secretary of State, Trademarks Section, 700 Capitol Ave, Suite 152, Frankfort, KY 40601; 502-564-2848 x442, 502-564-1484 (Fax), 8AM-4:30PM.

www.sos.state.ky.us

Indexing & Storage: It takes minutes before new records are available for inquiry. Records are indexed on original documents on file in the office and online access to database. Records are normally destroyed after three years.

Searching: Include the trademark/servicemark name or applicant name or certification number. Also, wordmark and description helps.

Access by: mail, phone, fax, in person, online.

Fee & Payment: There is no fee.

Mail search: Turnaround time: 1 week. A SASE is requested.

Phone search: Ask for Johnna Ballinger.

Fax search: Fax requests accepted.

In person search: Turnaround time while you wait.

Online search: Free, searchable database at www.kysos.com/trademarks/tmstart.asp.

Uniform Commercial Code

UCC Division, Secretary of State, PO Box 1470, Frankfort, KY 40602-1470 (Courier: 363C Versailles Rd, Mare Manor, Frankfort, KY 40601); 502-573-0265, 502-573-0259 (Fax), 8AM-4:30PM.

www.kysos.com

Note: The state adopted Revised Article 9 effective July 1, 2001.

Indexing & Storage: It takes 24 hours before new records are available for inquiry.

Searching: The Secretary of State maintains a searchable index for all active UCC records that provides for the retrieval of a record by the name of the debtor and by the file number of the initial financing statement to which the record relates. Include the following in your request-full debtor name. No partial name searches are permitted, except at website. The agency advises requesters to use Form UCC-11.

Access by: mail, in person, online.

Fee & Payment: $5.00 for a certified search. $.10 per page for copies of UCC records. Fee payee: KY State Treasurer. Personal checks accepted. No credit cards accepted.

Mail search: Turnaround time: 1-3 business days. Full names are required.

In person search: Turnaround time while you wait. If you order extensive records, they will mail the results to you.

Online search: UCC record searching is offered free of charge at the website. Search by debtor name, or file number. SSNs are withheld from the online system. Pre-paid accounts may be established for those requiring copies or certified documents.

Federal Tax Liens, State Tax Liens

Records not maintained by a state level agency.

Note: All tax liens are at the county level.

Sales Tax Registrations

Revenue Cabinet, Tax Compliance Department, Sales Tax Section, Station 53, PO Box 181, Frankfort, KY 40602-0181 (Courier: 200 Fair Oaks, Bldg 2, Frankfort, KY 40602); 502-564-5170, 502-564-2041 (Fax), 8AM-4:30PM.

http://revenue.ky.gov

Note: This agency will only confirm if a tax permit exists. The agency will NOT confirm if a business is registered. They will provide no other information.

Indexing & Storage: Records are available from the 1970's. Records are indexed on computer from 1996 to present, and on microfilm from 1985 to 1995.

Searching: Include the following in your request- tax permit number.

Access by: mail, in person.

Mail search: Turnaround time: 2 to 3 months. A SASE is requested. No fee for mail request.

In person search: No fee for request.

Birth Certificates

Department for Public Health, Vital Statistics, 275 E Main St - IE-A, Frankfort, KY 40621-0001; 502-564-4212, 502-227-0032 (Fax), 8AM-4PM.

http://chs.ky.gov/publichealth/vital.htm

Indexing & Storage: Records are available from 1911 to present. It takes 1 month before new records are available for inquiry. Records are indexed on microfiche, inhouse computer, books (volumes).

Searching: Include the following in your request- full name, names of parents, mother's maiden name, date of birth, place of birth. Provide a daytime phone number.

Access by: mail, phone, fax, in person, online.

Fee & Payment: Searches are $10.00 per name. Add $10.50 if using a credit card. Fee payee: Kentucky State Treasurer. Prepayment required. Personal checks accepted. Credit cards accepted: MasterCard, Visa, AmEx, Discover.

Mail search: Turnaround time: 3 to 4 weeks. No SASE is required.

Phone search: Must use a credit card (add $10.50 fee) for a phone request. Turnaround time is 3 to 5 days.

Fax search: Same fees as telephone search.

In person search: Turnaround time 1 1/2 hour.

Online search: Records may be ordered online via a state designated vendor at www.vitalchek.com.

Expedited service: Expedited service is available for mail, phone, online and fax orders. Turnaround time: overnight delivery. Add $12.75 per package for shipping. Also, be sure to include extra credit card use fee.

Death Records

Department for Public Health, Vital Statistics, 275 E Main St - IE-A, Frankfort, KY 40621-0001; 502-564-4212, 502-227-0032 (Fax), 8AM-3PM.

http://chs.ky.gov/publichealth/vital.htm

Indexing & Storage: Records are available from 1911 on. It takes 1 month before new records are available for inquiry. Records are indexed on microfiche, inhouse computer, books (volumes).

Searching: Include the following in your request- full name, date of death, place of death. Provide a daytime phone number.

Access by: mail, phone, fax, in person, online.

Fee & Payment: The fee is $6.00 per name. Fee payee: Kentucky State Treasurer. Prepayment required. Personal checks accepted. Credit cards accepted: MasterCard, Visa, AmEx, Discover.

Mail search: Turnaround time: 3 to 4 weeks. No SASE is required.

Phone search: Must use a credit card (add $10.50 fee) to make phone request. Turnaround time is 2-3 days.

Fax search: Same fees and turnaround time as telephone requests.

In person search: Turnaround time 1 1/2 hour.

Online search: In cooperation with the University of Kentucky, there is a searchable death index at http://ukcc.uky.edu:80/~vitalrec/. This is for non-commercial use only. Records are from 1911 through 1992. Also, there is a free genealogy site at http://vitals.rootsweb.com/ky/death/search.cgi. Death Indexes from 1911-2000 are available. You may search by surname, given name, place of death, residence, or year. Records may be ordered online via a state designated vendor at www.vitalchek.com.

Expedited service: Expedited service is available for mail, phone, online and fax orders. Turnaround time: overnight delivery. Add $12.75 per package for shipping. Also, be sure to include extra credit card use fee.

Marriage Certificates

Department for Public Health, Vital Statistics, 275 E Main St - IE-A, Frankfort, KY 40621-0001; 502-564-4212, 502-227-0032 (Fax), 8AM-3PM.

http://chs.ky.gov/publichealth/vital.htm

Indexing & Storage: Records are available from June 1958 to present. It takes 1 to 2 months before new records are available for inquiry. Records are indexed on microfiche, inhouse computer, books (volumes).

Searching: Include the following in your request- names of husband and wife, date of marriage, place or county of marriage. Must also include where marriage license was obtained and a daytime phone number.

Access by: mail, phone, fax, in person, online.

Fee & Payment: The fee is $6.00 per name. Fee payee: Kentucky State Treasurer. Prepayment required. Personal checks accepted. Credit cards accepted: MasterCard, Visa, AmEx, Discover.

Mail search: Turnaround time: 3 to 4 weeks. No SASE is required.

Phone search: Must use a credit card (add $10.50 fee) for a phone request. Turnaround time is 3 to 5 days.

Fax search: Same criteria as phone orders.

In person search: Turnaround time 1 1/2 hour.

Online search: In cooperation with the University of Kentucky, a searchable index is available on the Internet at http://ukcc.uky.edu:80/~vitalrec/. The index runs from 1973 through 1993. This is for non-commercial use only. Records may be ordered online via a state designated vendor at www.vitalchek.com.

Other access: Contact Libraries and Archives.

Expedited service: Expedited service is available for mail, phone, online and fax orders. Turnaround time: overnight delivery. Add $12.75 per package for shipping. Also, be sure to include extra credit card use fee.

Divorce Records

Department for Public Health, Vital Statistics, 275 E Main St - IE-A, Frankfort, KY 40621-0001; 502-564-4212, 502-227-0032 (Fax), 8AM-3PM.

http://chs.ky.gov/publichealth/vital.htm

Indexing & Storage: Records are available from June, 1958 to present. It takes 1 to 2 months before new records are available for inquiry. Records are indexed on microfiche, inhouse computer, books (volumes).

Searching: Include the following in your request- names of husband and wife, date of divorce, place of divorce. Provide a daytime phone number.

Access by: mail, phone, fax, in person, online.

Fee & Payment: The fee is $6.00 per name. Fee payee: Kentucky State Treasurer. Prepayment required. Personal checks accepted. Credit cards accepted: MasterCard, Visa, AmEx, Discover.

Mail search: Turnaround time: 3 to 4 weeks. No SASE is required.

Phone search: Must use a credit card (add $10.50 fee) for a phone request. Turnaround time 3-5 days.

Fax search: Same criteria as phone requests.

In person search: Turnaround time 1 1/2 hour.

Online search: In cooperation with the University of Kentucky, there is a searchable index on the Internet at http://ukcc.uky.edu:80/~vitalrec/. This is for non-commercial use only. The index is for 1973-1993. Records may be ordered online via a state designated vendor at www.vitalchek.com.

Other access: Contact Libraries and Archives.

Expedited service: Expedited service is available for mail, phone, online and fax orders. Turnaround time: overnight delivery. Add $12.75 per package for shipping. Also, be sure to include extra credit card use fee.

Workers' Compensation Records

Kentucky Office of Workers' Claims, Prevention Park, 657 To Be Announced Ave, Frankfort, KY 40601; 502-564-5550, 502-564-5732 (Fax), 8AM-4:30PM.

http://labor.ky.gov/dwc

Indexing & Storage: Records are available from 1982 to present on computer. New records are available for inquiry immediately. Records are normally destroyed after 75 years.

Searching: Must have a signed release from claimant only for copies of first report. Otherwise, information is open to the public per KRS 61.870 through 61.884. Include the following in your request-claimant name, Social Security Number, date of accident, place of employment at time of accident. The following data is not released: Social Security Numbers, addresses or personal information (height, weight, sex, eye color, etc.).

Access by: mail, fax, in person.

Fee & Payment: Fees are $.50 per page from microfilm and photocopies are $.10 per page. Fee payee: Kentucky State Treasurer. Payment may be submitted at the time records are picked up. Otherwise, an invoice will be mailed at the end of the month. Personal checks accepted. No credit cards accepted.

Mail search: Turnaround time: 2 to 4 weeks. Requests are processed in order by the date received.A SASE is requested.

Fax search: Fax requests are processed by date of receipt same as requests that are mailed.

In person search: The office will have the records ready for you if you call ahead first and make an appointment.

Other access: A listing of file contents may be requested. Call for details.

Driver Records

Division of Driver Licensing, KY Transportation Cabinet, 200 Mero Street, Frankfort, KY 40622; 502-564-6800 x2250, 502-564-5787 (Fax), 8AM-4:30PM.

www.kytc.state.ky.us/drlic/

Note: Requests for copies of tickets must be submitted in writing to Cabinets Record Custodian, Department of Administrative Services, State Office Building, Frankfort 40622. There is a $.10 fee per document.

Indexing & Storage: Records are available for 3 years for moving violations, DWIs and suspensions. Accidents are not reported on 3 years records. It takes 5 to 10 days before new records are available for inquiry. Records are normally destroyed after five years.

Searching: Casual requesters can obtain record information, but personal information is "cloaked" unless written consent by subject is provided. The SSN or DL, the full name and DOB are needed when ordering. The driver's address is not included as part of the search report without a release from the driver.

Access by: mail, in person, online.

Fee & Payment: The fee is $3.00 per record, $4.50 if online. Fee payee: Kentucky State Treasurer. Credit cards accepted. Business checks accepted.

Mail search: Turnaround time: 3 days.

In person search: Walk-in requesters may receive records immediately at the address listed above or at any one of 11 field offices in the state.

Online search: There are 2 systems. Permissible use requesters who need personal information can order by batch, minimum order is 150 requests per batch. Input received by 3 PM will be available the next morning. Fee is $4.50 per record and billing is monthly. Call for details to subscribe. Records without personal information can be obtained at https://dhr.ky.gov/DHRWeb/RS?AC=2. The same fee applies and up to 50 records can be ordered and received immediately.

Vehicle Ownership, Vehicle Identification

Department of Motor Vehicles, Division of Motor Vehicle Licensing, PO Box 2014, Frankfort, KY 40622; 502-564-4076 (Title History), 502-564-3298 (Other Requests), 502-564-2737 (Questions), 502-564-1686 (Fax), 8AM-4:30PM.

www.kytc.state.ky.us

Note: The state adopted all 14 permissible uses per DPPA guidelines.

Indexing & Storage: Records are available from 1978 years to present, but generally only last 10 years released. Records are indexed on computer from 1989 to present, and on microfiche from 1989 to present. It takes 1-4 weeks before new records are available for inquiry. Records are normally destroyed after 20 years.

Searching: Vehicle and ownership records are not to the public without consent of subject. Vendors must submit either TC96-16 or TC96-325 when requesting data. This agency will not do a search by SSN.

Access by: mail, in person, online.

Fee & Payment: The fee is $2.00 per record request. The state reports current lien information. There is a full charge for a "no record found." Fee payee: Kentucky State Treasurer Prepayment required. Cash and money orders are accepted. Personal checks accepted. No credit cards accepted.

Mail search: Turnaround time: 5 to 10 days. A SASE is requested.

In person search: Turnaround time is while you wait (typically, 15 minutes to 1 hour).

Online search: Online access costs $2.00 per record. The online mode is interactive. Title, lien and registration searches are available. Records include those for mobile homes. For more information, contact Gail Warfield at 502-564-4076.

Other access: Kentucky has the ability to supply customized bulk delivery of vehicle registration information. The request must be in writing with the intended use outlined. For more information, call 502-564-3298.

Expedited service: Expedited service is available for walk-ins only. You must set up an account. For more information, call 502-564-5301.

Accident Reports

State Police, Criminal Ident. & Records Branch, 1250 Louisville Rd, Frankfort, KY 40601; 502-226-2169, 502-226-7418 (Fax), 8AM-4:30PM.

www.kentuckystatepolice.org

Indexing & Storage: Records are available from 1998 at this location. It takes less than 1 day before new records are available for inquiry.

Searching: Requests must be made through "open records." Statistical detailed listing of accidents at specific locations without personal identifying information is available for a fee with a written request. For more information phone 502-226-2169 for details. Search requirements include the date, driver's name and location.

Access by: mail, fax, in person.

Fee & Payment: The charge is $.10 per page. Fee payee: KY State Treasurer. Prepayment required. Personal checks accepted. No credit cards accepted.

Mail search: Turnaround time: 1 to 2 weeks. A SASE is requested.

Fax search: Fax requests accepted.

In person search: Counter service is available.

Other access: Specific accident statistics may be obtained by phoning the statistics coordinator.

Vessel Ownership, Vessel Registration

Division of Motor Vehicle Licensing, Vessel Titles and Registration, State Office Building, 3rd Floor, Frankfort, KY 40622; 502-564-2737 (Registration), 8AM-5PM.

www.kytc.state.ky.us

Indexing & Storage: Records are available for titles from 1990, for registration from 1985. Prior records are kept by Circuit Clerks. Only motorized vessels must be titled and registered.

Searching: Personal information is not released to casual requesters. The hull number, title number or KY number must be submitted.

Access by: mail, in person.

Fee & Payment: The fee is $2.00 per record. Fee payee: Kentucky State Treasurer. Prepayment required. No credit cards accepted.

Mail search: Turnaround time: 1 week.

In person search: Most of the time results will be mailed.

Voter Registration

State Board of Elections, 140 Walnut, Frankfort, KY 40601; 502-573-7100, 502-573-4369 (Fax), 8AM-4:30PM.

www.kysos.com/index/main/elecdiv.asp

Note: Written requests are always required; agency is required to respond within 3 days. Bulk data is available for political purposes or specific research purposes only. For individual searches, it is best to go to the county level.

Searching: The agency will provide verification of records and voting histories upon receipt of a written request. For questions, contact natalie.jensen@mail.state.ky.us. The SSN or DOB is required when doing a verification. The following data is not released: Social Security Numbers, bulk information or information to ineligible persons, pursuant to state statutes.

Access by: mail, fax, in person.

Fee & Payment: There is no search fee. There is a $.10 per page copy fee.

Mail search: Turnaround time: 3 business days. Turnaround time is longer for information exempted by statute.

Fax search: Records are available by fax.

In person search: Records may be ordered (with written request) and picked up in person. Law allows for 3 business day turnaround.

Other access: Data is available on CD-rom, labels or lists for eligible persons, pursuant to state statutes

GED Certificates

Dept for Adult Education and Literacy, GED Program, Capitol Plaza Tower, 500 Mero St, 3rd Fl, Frankfort, KY 40601; 502-573-5114 x2, 502-573-5436 (Fax).

http://adulted.state.ky.us

Indexing & Storage: It takes 4 weeks after test before new records are available for inquiry.

Searching: To verify or to get copy of transcript or diploma, all of the following is required: a signed release, name, date/year of test, date of birth, SSN, and city of test.

Access by: mail, in person.

Fee & Payment: The fee for verification or a copy of transcript or duplicate diplomas is $5.00 each. Fee payee: KY State Treasurer. Prepayment required. Money orders are accepted, personal checks are not. No credit cards accepted.

Mail search: Turnaround time: 1 week or less. No SASE is required.

In person search: In person searchers must bring a photo ID. Turnaround time is same day.

Hunting and Fishing License Information

Fish & Wildlife Resources Department, Division of Administrative Services, 1 Game Farm Rd, Arnold Mitchell Bldg, Frankfort, KY 40601; 502-564-4224, 502-564-6508 (Fax), 8AM-4:30PM.

www.kdfwr.state.ky.us

Note: A database has been created, starting in 1996. Records are not released without written request and for good reason. Records are not available for commercial mail lists. Older records are archived in boxes. Record retrieval extremely difficult.

Indexing & Storage: Records are available for the past two years (actual copies). Prior records are archived and not readily available. It takes 16 days before new records are available for inquiry. Records are indexed on hard copy. Records are normally destroyed after 5 years, in general.

Searching: Requests must be in writing and addressed to the Commissioner's Office. The general public cannot receive records, beyond the type of license issued. Include the following in your request-full name, Social Security Number. By law, the agency will respond to all search requests within three days.

Access by: mail, fax, in person.

Fee & Payment: Fees are $.10 per page plus cost of postage. Prepayment required. Personal checks accepted.

Mail search: Records are available by mail.

Fax search: Records may be requested by fax.

In person search: Limited information available in person, extensive lists will be mailed.

Kentucky State Licensing Agencies

Licenses Searchable Online

Addiction Psychiatrist MD #41 ....http://weba.state.ky.us/genericsearch/LicenseSearch.asp?AGY=5
Agent of Issuer, Securities #18..............................http://dfi.ky.gov/scr/ifs/old/sec/
Alcohol/Drug Counselor #15..................................https://kyeasupt1.state.ky.us/OPB/BrdWebSearch.asp?BRD=4
Anesthesiologist #41...http://weba.state.ky.us/genericsearch/LicenseSearch.asp?AGY=5
Architect #7 ....http://kybera.com/roster.shtml
Art Therapist #15...https://kyeasupt1.state.ky.us/OPB/BrdWebSearch.asp?BRD=5
Athlete Agent #15 ....https://kyeasupt1.state.ky.us/OPB/BrdWebSearch.asp?BRD=19
Athletic Trainer, Medical #41 ....http://weba.state.ky.us/genericsearch/LicenseSearch.asp?AGY=5
Attorney #2 ....www.kybar.org/Default.aspx?tabid=26
Auctioneer/Auctioneer Apprentice #4 ....http://weba.state.ky.us/genericsearch/LicenseSearch.asp?AGY=3
Bank #18...http://dfi.ky.gov/scr/ifs/old/fi/
Check Casher #18 ....http://dfi.ky.gov/whoweregulate/check%20casher%20recap.pdf
Counselor, Pastoral #15 ....https://kyeasupt1.state.ky.us/OPB/BrdWebSearch.asp?BRD=3
Counselor, Professional #15...................................https://kyeasupt1.state.ky.us/OPB/BrdWebSearch.asp?BRD=6
Credit Union #18 ....http://dfi.ky.gov/scr/ifs/old/fi/
Dentist/Dental Hygienist #6 ....http://dentistry.ky.gov/
Dental Laboratory #6 ....http://dentistry.ky.gov/
Dietitian/Nutritionist #15..https://kyeasupt1.state.ky.us/OPB/BrdWebSearch.asp?BRD=8
Drinking Water Treatment/Dist. System Operator #29 ..www.water.ky.gov/optcert/
EDP Servicer #18 ....http://dfi.ky.gov/scr/ifs/old/fi/
Engineer #39 ....http://kyboels.ky.gov/SearchRoster.asp
Engineer/Land Surveyor Firm #39..........................http://kyboels.ky.gov/SearchRoster.asp
Geologist #15...https://kyeasupt1.state.ky.us/OPB/BrdWebSearch.asp?BRD=1
Hearing Instrument Specialist #15..........................https://kyeasupt1.state.ky.us/OPB/BrdWebSearch.asp?BRD=15
Insurance Agent #21..www.doi.state.ky.us/kentucky/search/agent/
Insurance CE Provider #21.....................................www.doi.state.ky.us/kentucky/search/provider/
Insurance Company/Insurer #21 ....www.doi.state.ky.us/kentucky/search/company/
Interior Designer #7 ....www.kybera.com/idlist.shtml
Investment Advisor/Company #18...........................http://dfi.ky.gov/scr/ifs/old/sec/
Legislative Employers of Lobbyists #40 ....www.lrc.state.ky.us/otherweb/ethics/agents.htm
Loan Company, Comm./Industrial #18 ....http://dfi.ky.gov/whoweregulate/Small%20Industrial%20Loan%20Recap.pdf
Lobbyist #40 ....www.lrc.state.ky.us/otherweb/ethics/agents.txt
Marriage & Family Therapist #15............................https://kyeasupt1.state.ky.us/OPB/BrdWebSearch.asp?BRD=9
Medical Doctor/Surgeon/Medical Specialist MD #41....http://weba.state.ky.us/genericsearch/LicenseSearch.asp?AGY=5
Mortgage Broker #18 ....http://dfi.ky.gov/whoweregulate/mort_brokers.asp
Mortgage Loan Company #18 ....http://dfi.ky.gov/whoweregulate/mort_company.asp
Nurse-RN/LPN/ Specialized Nurses (Midwife, Anes., Clinical, SANE, etc. #9   https://ssla.state.ky.us/KBN/kbnknar.asp
Nurses Aide #9 ....https://ssla.state.ky.us/KBN/kbnknar.asp
Nursing Home Administrator #15.............................https://kyeasupt1.state.ky.us/OPB/BrdWebSearch.asp?BRD=10
Occupational Therapist/Assistant #15 ....https://kyeasupt1.state.ky.us/OPB/BrdWebSearch.asp?BRD=16
Ophthalmic Dispenser/Optician/Apprentice #10 ....https://kyeasupt1.state.ky.us/OPB/BrdWebSearch.asp?BRD=11
Optometrist #11 ....http://weba.state.ky.us/GenericSearch/LicenseSearch.asp?AGY=8
Osteopathic Physician #41 ....http://weba.state.ky.us/genericsearch/LicenseSearch.asp?AGY=5
Physical Therapist /Therapist Assistant #38.................http://weba.state.ky.us/genericsearch/LicenseSearch.asp?AGY=4
Physician Assistant #41...http://weba.state.ky.us/genericsearch/LicenseSearch.asp?AGY=5
Proprietary Education School #15 ....https://kyeasupt1.state.ky.us/OPB/BrdWebSearch.asp?BRD=18
Psychiatrist (MD) #41 ....http://weba.state.ky.us/genericsearch/LicenseSearch.asp?AGY=5
Psychologist #15..https://kyeasupt1.state.ky.us/OPB/BrdWebSearch.asp?BRD=7
Public Accountant-CPA #3 ....http://cpa.state.ky.us/Locate.html
Radiation Operator #44 ....http://weba.state.ky.us/genericsearch/LicenseSearch.asp?AGY=5
Real Estate Agent/Broker/Sales #33 ....http://weba.state.ky.us/realestate/LicenseeLookUp.asp
Real Estate Appraiser #32......................................www.kreab.ky.gov/
Real Estate Brokerage/Firm #33 ....http://weba.state.ky.us/realestate/FirmLookUp.asp
Savings & Loan #18..http://dfi.ky.gov/scr/ifs/old/fi/
School Administrator #25..www.kyepsb.net
School Guidance Counselor/Media Librarian #25 ....www.kyepsb.net
School Nurse #25 ....www.kyepsb.net
School Social Worker/Psychologist #25..................www.kyepsb.net
Securities Agent/Broker/Dealer #18 ....http://dfi.ky.gov/scr/ifs/old/sec/
Social Worker #15 ....https://kyeasupt1.state.ky.us/OPB/BrdWebSearch.asp?BRD=2

Speech-Language Pathologist/Audiologist #15 .... https://kyeasupt1.state.ky.us/OPB/BrdWebSearch.asp?BRD=13
Surveyor, Land #39 .... http://kyboels.ky.gov/SearchRoster.asp
Teacher #25 .... www.kyepsb.net
Trust Company #18 .... http://dfi.ky.gov/scr/ifs/old/fi/
Veterinarian #15 .... https://kyeasupt1.state.ky.us/OPB/BrdWebSearch.asp?BRD=14
Waste Water System Operator #29 .... www.water.ky.gov/optcert/
Water Well Driller #29 .... www.water.ky.gov/gw/gwdb/

Kentucky Licensing Quick Finder

Addiction Psychiatrist MD #41 502-429-8046
Agent of Issuer, Securities #18 502-573-3370
Alcohol/Drug Counselor #15 .... 502-564-3296 x226
Ambulance Provider #14 502-564-8963
Anesthesiologist #41 502-429-8046
Animal Technician #15 502-564-3296
Architect #7 859-246-2069
Art Therapist #15 .... 502-564-3296 x230
Athlete Agent #15 .... 502-564-3296 x222
Athletic Trainer, Medical #41 502-429-8046
Attorney #2 502-564-3795
Auctioneer/Auctioneer Apprentice #4 ... 502-339-9453
Bank #18 502-573-3390
Barber #5 502-429-8841
Blacksmith #31 859-246-2040
Boiler Contractor/Insp./Installer #26 502-564-8142
Building Inspector #26 502-564-8090
Check Casher #18 502-573-3390
Check Seller/Casher #18 502-573-3390
Child Care Facility #13 502-564-2800
Chiropractor #35 270-651-2522
Compost Operator #24 502-565-6716
Coroner #17 859-622-1328
Cosmetologist #37 502-564-4262
Counselor, Pastoral #15 .... 502-564-3296 x226
Counselor, Professional #15 .... 502-564-3296 x226
Credit Union #18 502-573-3390
Dental Hygienist #6 502-423-0573
Dental Laboratory #6 502-423-0573
Dental Laboratory Technician #6 502-423-0573
Dentist #6 502-423-0573
Dietitian/Nutritionist #15 .... 502-564-3296 x227
Drinking Water Treatment/Dist. System Operator #29
.... 502-564-3410
Driver Training Instructor #42 502-226-7404
Drug Manufacturer/Wholesaler #12 502-573-1580
EDP Servicer #18 502-573-3390
Electrical Contractor/Inspector #26 502-564-8370
Elevator Inspector #26 502-564-8499
Embalmer #36 502-241-3918
EMS Instructor #14 502-564-8963
EMT #14 502-564-8963
Engineer #39 502-573-2680
Engineer/Land Surveyor Firm #39 502-573-2680
Exterminator #16 502-564-7274
Fire Alarm System Inspector #26 502-564-3626
Fire Protection Sprinkler Installer #26 .. 502-564-3626
Fire Suppression System Insp. #26 502-564-8090
Fishing, Commercial #20 800-858-1549
Funeral Director #36 502-241-3918
Fur Buyer/Processor #20 800-858-1549
Geologist #15 .... 502-564-3296 x227

Guide, Hunting & Fishing #20 800-858-1549
Health Care Facility #13 502-564-2800
Hearing Instrument Special't #15 . 502-564-3296 x240
Horse Claiming License #31 859-246-2040
Horse Farm Manager/Agent #31 859-246-2040
Horse Owner/Trainer/Asst. Trainer #31 829-246-2040
Horse Racing Occupation License #31.. 859-246-2040
Horse Racing Official/Auth. Agent #31.. 859-246-2040
Horse Veterinarian/Veterinary Asst. #31859-246-2040
Horse Veterinary Dental Tech. #31 859-246-2040
HVAC Journeyman/Master/Mechanic/Contr. #26
.... 502-564-1436
Insurance Adjuster #21 502-564-3630
Insurance Agent /CE Provider #21....... 502-564-3630
Insurance Company/Insurer #21 502-564-3630
Insurance Consultant/Solicitor #21 502-564-3630
Interior Designer #7 859-246-2069
Interpreters for the Deaf #15 .... 502-564-3296 x239
Investment Advisor/Company #18 502-573-3370
Investment Advisor/Rep. #18 502-573-3390
Jockey Agent #31 859-246-2040
Jockey/Jockey Apprentice #31 859-246-2040
Lake Operator #20 800-858-1549
Landfarm Operator #24 502-564-6716
Landfill Operator/Manager #24 502-564-6716
Law Enforcement Training Instruct. #17 859-622-1328
Legislative Employers of Lobbyists #40 502-573-2863
Liquor License #1 502-564-4850
Loan Company, Comm./Industrial #18.. 502-573-3390
Lobbyist #40 502-573-2863
Malt Beverage Distributor #1 502-564-4850
Marriage & Family Therapist #15 . 502-564-3296 x239
Medical Doctor/Surgeon #41 502-429-8046
Medical Specialist MD #41 502-429-8046
Midwife Nurse #9 502-329-7000
Milk Sampler/Weigher/Tester #43 859-257-2785
Mining related occupation #22 502-573-0140
Mortgage Broker #18 502-573-3390
Mortgage Loan Company #18 502-573-3390
Nail Technician #37 502-564-4262
Notary Public #30 502-564-3490
Nurse Anesthetist #9 502-329-7000
Nurse-RN/LPN/Clinical Spec. SANE #9 502-329-7000
Nurses Aide /Nurses' Aide Instruct'r #9 502-329-7048
Nurse Midwife #9 502-329-7000
Nursing Home Administrator #15 . 502-564-3296 x222
Occupational Therapist/Assistant #15... 502-564-3296
Ophthalmic Dispenser/Optician/Apprentice #10
.... 502-564-3296 x227
Optometrist #11 859-246-2744
Osteopathic Physician #41 502-429-8046
Paramedic #14 502-564-8963

Pari-Mutuel Employee #31 859-246-2040
Pesticide Applicator #16 502-564-7274
Pesticide Dealer #16 502-564-7274
Pharmacist #12 502-573-1580
Pharmacy #12 502-573-1580
Physical Therapist #38 502-327-8497
Physical Therapist Assistant #38 502-327-8497
Physician Assistant #41 502-429-8046
Plans & Specifications Inspector #26... 502-564-8090
Plumber #26 502-564-3580
Podiatrist #27 270-759-0007
Police Officer #17 859-622-1328
Polygraph Examiner/Examiner Trainee #28
.... 502-564-4756
Property Valuation Administrator #34 .. 502-564-8338
Proprietary Education School #15 502-564-4233
Psychiatris (MD #41 502-429-8046
Psychologist #15 .... 502-564-3296 x225
Public Accountant-CPA #3 502-595-3037
Racetrack Occupation (vendors, etc.) #31
.... 859-246-2040
Racing Association Employee #31 859-246-2040
Racing Vendor/Vendor Employee #31.. 859-246-2040
Radiation Operator #44 502-564-3700
Radiation Producing Machine #44 502-564-3700
Radioactive Material Licensee #44 502-564-3700
Real Estate Agent/Broker/Sales #33 ... 502-425-4273
Real Estate Appraiser #32 859-543-8943
Real Estate Brokerage/Firm #33.......... 502-425-4273
Rehabilitation Counselor #23 502-564-6745
Sanitarian #45 502-564-7398
Savings & Loan #18 502-573-3390
School Administrator #25 502-564-4606
School Bus Driver #46 502-564-4718
School Counselor /Media Librarian #25 502-564-4606
School Nurse #25 502-564-4606
School Social Worker/Psychologist #25 502-564-4606
Securities Agent/Broker/Dealer #18 502-573-3370
Septic System Installer, Onsite #45 502-564-4856
Sexual Assault Nurse Examiner #9 502-329-7000
Social Worker #15 .... 502-564-3296 x230
Speech-Language Pathologist/Audiologist #15
.... 502-564-3296 x240
Stable Employee #31 859-246-2040
Surveyor, Land #39 502-573-2680
Taxidermist #20 800-858-1549
Teacher #25 502-564-4606
Trust Company #18 502-573-3390
Veterinarian #15 .... 502-564-3296 x223
Waste Water System Operator #29 502-564-3410
Water Well Driller #29 502-564-3410

Kentucky Licensing Agency Information

1 Alcoholic Beverage Control Department, 1003 Twilight Trail, #A2, Frankfort, KY 40601; 502-564-4850, Fax: 502-564-1442.

2 Bar Association, 514 W Main St, Frankfort, KY 40601-1883; 502-564-3795, Fax: 502-564-3225. www.kybar.org Email: webmaster@kybar.org Search Database at www.kybar.org/Default.aspx?tabid=26

3 Board of Accountancy, 332 W Broadway, #310, Louisville, KY 40202; 502-595-3037, Fax: 502-595-4281. http://cpa.state.ky.us Email: debby.abell@mail.state.ky.us Search Database at http://cpa.state.ky.us/Locate.html

4 Board of Auctioneers, 9112 Leesgate Rd #5, Louisville, KY 40222-5089; 502-339-9453, Fax: 502-423-1854. http://auctioneers.ky.gov Email: auctioneers@mail.state.ky.us

5 Board of Barbering, 9114 Leesgate Rd, #6, Louisville, KY 40222-5055; 502-429-8841, Fax: 502-429-5223.

6 Board of Dentistry, 10101 Linn Station Rd, #540, Louisville, KY 40223; 502-423-0573, Fax: 502-423-1239. http://dentistry.ky.gov Search Database at http://dentistry.ky.gov

7 Board of Examiners & Registration of Architects, 301 E Main St #860, Lexington, KY 40507; 859-246-2069, Fax: 859-246-2431. http://kybera.com/ Email: kybera@iglou.com Search Database at http://kybera.com/roster.shtml

9 Board of Nursing, 312 Whittington Pky, #300, Louisville, KY 40222-5172; 502-329-7000, Fax: 502-329-7011. http://kbn.ky.gov/index-old.htm Email: kbn.webmaster@mail.state.ky.us Search at https://ssla.state.ky.us/KBN/kbnknar.asp Note: Social security number required to search; there is $.70 fee per name.

10 Division of Occupations and Professions, Board of Ophthalmic Dispensers, PO Box 1360, Frankfort, KY 40602; 502-564-3296 x227, Fax: 502-564-4818. http://occupations.ky.gov/ophthalmicdispensers/ Search Database at https://kyeasupt1.state.ky.us/OPB/BrdWebSearch.asp?BRD=11 Note: You may also search ophthamoloy licenses at http://weba.state.ky.us/genericsearch/LicenseSearch.asp?AGY=5.

11 Board of Optometric Examiners, 301 E Main St #850, Lexington, KY 40507-1578; 859-246-2744, Fax: 859-246-2746. http://optometry.state.ky.us Email: ky.optometry@mail.state.ky.us Search Database at http://weba.state.ky.us/GenericSearch/LicenseSearch.asp?AGY=8

12 Board of Pharmacy, 23 Millcreek Park, Frankfort, KY 40601; 502-573-1580, Fax: 502-573-1582. www.state.ky.us/boards/pharmacy/ Note: Oral verification is limited to status and expiration date. Requests for add'l information must be in writing accompanied by a $5.00 fee. Copies of discipline orders/detailed searches may be more costly.

13 Division of Licensing & Regulations, Cabinet for Health Services, CHR Bldg, 5th Fl East, Frankfort, KY 40621-0001; 502-564-2800, Fax: 502-564-6546. http://chs.state.ky.us Email: fparrish@mail.state.ky.us

14 Board of Emergency Medical Services, 275 East Main Street, HS1E-F, Frankfort, KY 40621; 502-564-8963, Fax: 502-564-4687. www.kbems.org

15 Department of Administration, Division of Occupations & Professions, PO Box 1360, Frankfort, KY 40602; 502-564-3296, Fax: 502-564-4818. www.state.ky.us/agencies/finance/occupations

16 Department of Agriculture, Division of Pesticide Regulation, 100 Fair Oak Ln, 2nd Fl., Frankfort, KY 40601; 502-564-7274, Fax: 502-564-3773. www.kyagr.com Email: BillyRay.Smith@kyagr.com

17 Department of Criminal Justice Training, 521 Lancaster Ave, Richmond, KY 40475; 859-622-1328, Fax: 859-622-2740. http://docjt.jus.state.ky.us Email: pops@docjt.jus.state.ky.us

18 Department of Financial Institutions, Division of Law & Regulatory Compliance, 1025 Capitol Center Dr #200, Frankfort, KY 40601; 800-223-3390, Fax: 502-573-8787. www.dfi.state.ky.us

Email: Becky.Mills@mail.state.ky.us Search Database at http://dfi.ky.gov/whoweregulate.htm

20 Department of Fish & Wildlife, 1 Game Farm Rd, Frankfort, KY 40601; 800-858-1549, Fax: 502-564-9136. www.kdfwr.state.ky.us

21 Department of Insurance, Licensing Division, PO Box 517, 215 W Main St (40601), Frankfort, KY 40602-0517; 502-564-3630. www.doi.state.ky.us/kentucky/ Email: Randy.Donahue@mail.state.ky.us Search Database at www.doi.state.ky.us/kentucky

22 Department of Mines & Minerals, PO Box 2244, Frankfort, KY 40602-2244; 502-573-0140, Fax: 502-573-0152. http://dmm.ppr.ky.gov Email: JohnFranklin@mail.state.ky.us

23 Department of Vocational Rehabilitation, 209 St Clair St, Frankfort, KY 40601; 502-564-4440, Fax: 502-564-6742. http://kydvr.state.ky.us Email: flemingb@ihdi.uky.edu

24 Division of Waste Management, 14 Reilly Rd, Frankfort, KY 40601; 502-564-6716, Fax: 502-564-4049. www.waste.ky.gov Email: ron.gruzesky@ky.gov

25 Education Professional Standards Board, 100 Airport Rd 3rd Fl, Frankfort, KY 40601; 502-564-4606, Fax: 502-564-7080. www.kyepsb.net Email: sherry.paul@ky.gov Search Database at www.kyepsb.net

26 Department of Housing, Buildings, and Construction, 1047 US 127 S, #1, Frankfort, KY 40601; 502-564-8044, Fax: 502-564-6799. www.state.ky.us/agencies/cppr/dhbc/ Email: charlene.slemp@mail.state.ky.us

27 Kentucky Board of Podiatry, 908 B South 12th St, Murray, KY 42071-2949; 270-759-0007, Fax: 270-753-0684.

28 State Police, Polygraph Unit, 1250 Louisville Rd, Frankfort, KY 40601; 502-564-4756, Fax: 502-564-5956. www.kentuckystatepolice.org Email: kpayne@mail.state.ky.us

29 Division of Water, Natural Resources & Environmental Protection, 14 Reilly Rd, Frankfort Office Park, Frankfort, KY 40601; 502-564-3410, Fax: 502-564-9720. www.water.ky.gov

30 Office of Secretary of State, Notary Commissions, PO Box 821, Frankfort, KY 40602-0821; 502-564-3490 x413, Fax: 502-564-4075. www.kysos.com/admin/notary/mainpage.asp Email: Kbagwell@mail.sos.state.ky.us

31 Kentucky Racing Commission, 4063 Iron Works Pike, Lexington, KY 40511; 859-246-2040, Fax: 859-246-2039. http://krc.ppr.ky.gov

32 Real Estate Appraisers Board, 2480 Fortune Dr #120, Lexington, KY 40509; 859-543-8943, Fax: 859-543-0028. www.kreab.ky.gov Email: larry.disney@ky.gov Search Database at www.kreab.ky.gov

33 Real Estate Commission, 10200 Linn Station Rd, #201, Louisville, KY 40223; 502-425-4273, Fax: 502-426-2717. http://krec.ky.gov Email: krecweb@uky.edu Search Database at http://krec.ky.gov

34 Department of Property Taxation, Revenue Cabinet, 200 Fair Oaks Lane, Frankfort, KY 40620; 502-564-8338, Fax: 502-564-8368. www.revenue.state.ky.us/contact.htm Email: revweb@mail.state.ky.us

35 Board of Chiropractic Examiners, 209 S Green St (PO Box 183), Glasgow, KY 42142-0183; 270-651-2522, Fax: 270-651-8784. Email: kychiro@glasgow-ky.com

36 Board of Embalmers & Funeral Directors, PO Box 324, Crestwood, KY 40014; 502-241-3918, Fax: 502-241-4297.

37 Board of Hairdressers & Cosmetologists, 111 St James Court #A, Frankfort, KY 40601; 502-564-4262, Fax: 502-564-0481.

38 Board of Physical Therapy, 9110 Leesgate Rd, #6, Louisville, KY 40222-5159; 502-327-8497, Fax: 502-423-0934. http://pt.ky.gov Email: kybpt@ky.gov Search at http://weba.state.ky.us/genericsearch/LicenseSearch.asp?AGY=4

39 Professional Engineers & Land Surveyors, Board of Licensure, 160 Democrat Dr, Frankfort, KY 40601; 502-573-2680, Fax: 502-573-6687. http://kyboels.state.ky.us Email: larry.perkins@mail.state.ky.us Search Database at http://kyboels.ky.gov/SearchRoster.asp

40 Legislative Ethics Commission, 22 Mill Creek Park, Frankfort, KY 40601; 502-573-2863, Fax: 502-573-2929. www.lrc.state.ky.us/otherweb/ethics/ Search Database at www.lrc.state.ky.us/otherweb/ethics/

41 Board of Medical Licensure, 310 Whittington Pky, #1B, Louisville, KY 40222; 502-429-8046, Fax: 502-429-9923. www.kbml.org Search Database at http://weba.state.ky.us/genericsearch/LicenseSearch.asp?AGY=5 Note: Use the fee dialup service only if you have a license or certification number.

42 State Police Driver Testing Section, 919 Versailles Rd, Frankfort, KY 40601; 502-226-7404, Fax: 502-226-7412.

43 Division of Regulatory Services, 103 Regulatory Service Bldg, Lexington, KY 40546-0275; 859-257-2785, Fax: 859-323-9931. www.rs.uky.edu Email: cthompso@ca.uky.edu

44 Radiation Health & Toxic Agents Branch, Department of Public Health, 275 E Main St, Frankfort, KY 40621; 502-564-3700, Fax: 502-564-1492. http://publichealth.state.ky.us/radiation.htm

45 Department for Public Health, Registered Sanitarian Examining Committee, 275 E Main, 2nd Fl E, HS 2EA, Frankfort, KY 40621; 502-564-7398, Fax: 502-564-6533. http://chs.state.ky.us/publichealth/registered_sanitariancontent.htm Email: guy.delius@mail.state.ky.us

46 Department of Education, Pupil Transportation, 500 Mero St 15th Fl, Frankfort, KY 40601; 502-564-4718, Fax: 502-564-9574. www.kde.state.ky.us

Kentucky Federal Courts

The following list indicates the district and division name for each county in the state. If the bankruptcy court location is different from the district court, then the location of the bankruptcy court appears in parentheses.

County/Court Cross Reference

County	District	Division
Adair	Western	Bowling Green (Louisville)
Allen	Western	Bowling Green (Louisville)
Anderson	Eastern	Frankfort (Lexington)
Ballard	Western	Paducah (Louisville)
Barren	Western	Bowling Green (Louisville)
Bath	Eastern	Lexington
Bell	Eastern	London (Lexington)
Boone	Eastern	Covington (Lexington)
Bourbon	Eastern	Lexington
Boyd	Eastern	Ashland (Lexington)
Boyle	Eastern	Lexington
Bracken	Eastern	Covington (Lexington)
Breathitt	Eastern	Pikeville (Lexington)
Breckinridge	Western	Louisville
Bullitt	Western	Louisville
Butler	Western	Bowling Green (Louisville)
Caldwell	Western	Paducah (Louisville)
Calloway	Western	Paducah (Louisville)
Campbell	Eastern	Covington (Lexington)
Carlisle	Western	Paducah (Louisville)
Carroll	Eastern	Frankfort (Lexington)
Carter	Eastern	Ashland (Lexington)
Casey	Western	Bowling Green (Louisville)
Christian	Western	Paducah (Louisville)
Clark	Eastern	Lexington
Clay	Eastern	London (Lexington)
Clinton	Western	Bowling Green (Louisville)
Crittenden	Western	Paducah (Louisville)
Cumberland	Western	Bowling Green (Louisville)
Daviess	Western	Owensboro (Louisville)
Edmonson	Western	Bowling Green (Louisville)
Elliott	Eastern	Ashland (Lexington)
Estill	Eastern	Lexington
Fayette	Eastern	Lexington
Fleming	Eastern	Lexington
Floyd	Eastern	Pikeville (Lexington)
Franklin	Eastern	Frankfort (Lexington)
Fulton	Western	Paducah (Louisville)
Gallatin	Eastern	Covington (Lexington)
Garrard	Eastern	Lexington
Grant	Eastern	Covington (Lexington)
Graves	Western	Paducah (Louisville)
Grayson	Western	Owensboro (Louisville)
Green	Western	Bowling Green (Louisville)
Greenup	Eastern	Ashland (Lexington)
Hancock	Western	Owensboro (Louisville)
Hardin	Western	Louisville
Harlan	Eastern	London (Lexington)
Harrison	Eastern	Lexington
Hart	Western	Bowling Green (Louisville)
Henderson	Western	Owensboro (Louisville)
Henry	Eastern	Frankfort (Lexington)
Hickman	Western	Paducah (Louisville)
Hopkins	Western	Owensboro (Louisville)
Jackson	Eastern	London (Lexington)
Jefferson	Western	Louisville
Jessamine	Eastern	Lexington
Johnson	Eastern	Pikeville (Lexington)
Kenton	Eastern	Covington (Lexington)
Knott	Eastern	Pikeville (Lexington)
Knox	Eastern	London (Lexington)
Larue	Western	Louisville
Laurel	Eastern	London (Lexington)
Lawrence	Eastern	Ashland (Lexington)
Lee	Eastern	Lexington
Leslie	Eastern	London (Lexington)
Letcher	Eastern	Pikeville (Lexington)
Lewis	Eastern	Ashland (Lexington)
Lincoln	Eastern	Lexington
Livingston	Western	Paducah (Louisville)
Logan	Western	Bowling Green (Louisville)
Lyon	Western	Paducah (Louisville)
Madison	Eastern	Lexington
Magoffin	Eastern	Pikeville (Lexington)
Marion	Western	Louisville
Marshall	Western	Paducah (Louisville)
Martin	Eastern	Pikeville (Lexington)
Mason	Eastern	Covington (Lexington)
McCracken	Western	Paducah (Louisville)
McCreary	Eastern	London (Lexington)
McLean	Western	Owensboro (Louisville)
Meade	Western	Louisville
Menifee	Eastern	Lexington
Mercer	Eastern	Lexington
Metcalfe	Western	Bowling Green (Louisville)
Monroe	Western	Bowling Green (Louisville)
Montgomery	Eastern	Lexington
Morgan	Eastern	Ashland (Lexington)
Muhlenberg	Western	Owensboro (Louisville)
Nelson	Western	Louisville
Nicholas	Eastern	Lexington
Ohio	Western	Owensboro (Louisville)
Oldham	Western	Louisville
Owen	Eastern	Frankfort (Lexington)
Owsley	Eastern	London (Lexington)
Pendleton	Eastern	Covington (Lexington)
Perry	Eastern	Pikeville (Lexington)
Pike	Eastern	Pikeville (Lexington)
Powell	Eastern	Lexington
Pulaski	Eastern	London (Lexington)
Robertson	Eastern	Covington (Lexington)
Rockcastle	Eastern	London (Lexington)
Rowan	Eastern	Ashland (Lexington)
Russell	Western	Bowling Green (Louisville)
Scott	Eastern	Lexington
Shelby	Eastern	Frankfort (Lexington)
Simpson	Western	Bowling Green (Louisville)
Spencer	Western	Louisville
Taylor	Western	Bowling Green (Louisville)
Todd	Western	Bowling Green (Louisville)
Trigg	Western	Paducah (Louisville)
Trimble	Eastern	Frankfort (Lexington)
Union	Western	Owensboro (Louisville)
Warren	Western	Bowling Green (Louisville)
Washington	Western	Louisville
Wayne	Eastern	London (Lexington)
Webster	Western	Owensboro (Louisville)
Whitley	Eastern	London (Lexington)
Wolfe	Eastern	Lexington
Woodford	Eastern	Lexington

Standards for Federal Courts: The search fee is $20.00 per item (one party name or case number). Certification fee is $7.00 per document. Copy fee is $.50 per page. All fees standard unless noted in profile. Mail Search: always enclose a stamped self addressed envelope unless otherwise noted. Most courts accept fax requests or will suggest a copying/search vendor. Before releasing records, all courts require prepayment unless noted in profile.

Open records are located at the court unless otherwise noted. District courts index by defendant and plaintiff as well as by case number. Bankruptcy courts usually index by debtor and case number. While most courts now have their indexes on computer, many still maintain index card files as well.

The universal PACER sign-up number is 800-676-6856. Find PACER and the Party/Case Index on the Web at http://pacer.psc.uscourts.gov. PACER dial-up access is $.60 per minute. Also, courts offering internet access via RACER, PACER, Web-PACER or the new CM-ECF charge $.07 per page fee unless noted as free.

US District Court

Eastern District of Kentucky

Ashland Division Suite 336, 1405 Greenup Ave, Ashland, KY 41101 (courier address: Use mail address for courier delivery) 606-329-8652. www.kyed.uscourts.gov

Counties: Boyd, Carter, Elliott, Greenup, Lawrence, Lewis, Morgan, Rowan.

Indexing & Storage: New cases available in the index 1-2 days after filing date. Lexington Division has a master index for the district. The index is computerized from 1992.

Fee & Payment: Payment may be made by money order, cashier check, personal check. Payee: Clerk, USDC.

Phone Search: Only docket information from active cases will be released over the phone.

Mail Search: A SASE not required.

In Person Search: Fee charged if court conducts your in person search for you.

PACER: PACER is available online at http://pacer.kyed.uscourts.gov. Case records go back to September 1991. Records never purged. New records are online after 1 day.

Electronic Filing: Electronic filing information at https://ecf.kyed.uscourts.gov/cgi-bin/login.pl

Covington Division Clerk, PO Box 1073, Covington, KY 41012 (courier: U.S. Courthouse, Room 201, 35 W 5th St, Covington, KY 41011), 859-392-7925. www.kyed.uscourts.gov

Counties: Boone, Bracken, Campbell, Gallatin, Grant, Kenton, Mason, Pendleton, Robertson.

Indexing & Storage: New cases available in the index immediately after filing date.

Fee & Payment: Payment may be made by money order, cashier check, personal check. The

turnaround time for written requests varies. Payee: Clerk, U.S. District Court.

Phone Search: No searching by telephone.

In Person Search: Fee charged if court conducts your in person search for you.

PACER: PACER is available online at http://pacer.kyed.uscourts.gov. Case records go back to September 1991. Records never purged. New records are online after 1 day.

Electronic Filing: Electronic filing information at https://ecf.kyed.uscourts.gov/cgi-bin/login.pl

Frankfort Division Room 313, 330 W Broadway, Frankfort, KY 40601 (courier address: Use mail address for courier delivery) 502-223-5225. www.kyed.uscourts.gov

Counties: Anderson, Carroll, Franklin, Henry, Owen, Shelby, Trimble.

Indexing & Storage: New cases available in the index immediately after filing date. Records have been indexed on computer since January, 1993.

Fee & Payment: Payment may be made by money order, cashier check, personal check. Payee: Clerk, U.S. District Court.

Phone Search: Only docket information available.

Mail Search: A SASE not required.

In Person Search: Fee charged if court conducts your in person search for you.

PACER: PACER is available online at http://pacer.kyed.uscourts.gov. Case records go back to September 1991. Records never purged. New records are online after 1 day.

Electronic Filing: Electronic filing information at https://ecf.kyed.uscourts.gov/cgi-bin/login.pl

Lexington Division PO Box 3074, Lexington, KY 40588 (courier address: Room 206, 101 Barr St, Lexington, KY40588-3074), 859-233-2503. www.kyed.uscourts.gov

Counties: Bath, Bourbon, Boyle, Clark, Estill, Fayette, Fleming, Garrard, Harrison, Jessamine, Lee, Lincoln, Madison, Menifee, Mercer, Montgomery, Nicholas, Powell, Scott, Wolfe, Woodford. Lee and Wolfe counties were part of the Pikeville Divisionbefore 10/31/92. Perry became part of Pikeville after 1992.

Indexing & Storage: New cases available in the index 24 hours after filing date. Civil cases filed after October 1, 1992 are on the computer. Cases prior to October 1992 are on index cards.

Fee & Payment: Payment may be made by money order, cashier check, personal check. Payee: Clerk, USDC.

Phone Search: Only docket information from active cases will be released over the phone.

Mail Search: A SASE not required.

In Person Search: Fee charged if court conducts your in person search for you.

PACER: PACER is available online at http://pacer.kyed.uscourts.gov. Case records go back to September 1991. Records never purged. New records are online after 1 day.

Electronic Filing: Electronic filing information at https://ecf.kyed.uscourts.gov/cgi-bin/login.pl

London Division PO Box 5121, London, KY 40745-5121 (courier address: 124 U.S. Courthouse, 310 S Main, London, KY 40741), 606-877-7910. www.kyed.uscourts.gov

Counties: Bell, Clay, Harlan, Jackson, Knox, Laurel, Leslie, McCreary, Owsley, Pulaski, Rockcastle, Wayne, Whitley.

Indexing & Storage: New cases available in the index 1 day after filing date.

Fee & Payment: Payment may be made by money order, cashier check, personal check. Payee: Clerk, USDC.

Phone Search: Only docket information available.

In Person Search: Fee charged if court conducts your in person search for you.

PACER: PACER is available online at http://pacer.kyed.uscourts.gov. Case records go back to September 1991. Records never purged. New records are online after 1 day.

Electronic Filing: Electronic filing information at https://ecf.kyed.uscourts.gov/cgi-bin/login.pl

Pikeville Division Office of the clerk, 203 Federal Bldg, 110 Main St, Pikeville, KY 41501 (courier address: Use mail address for courier delivery) 606-437-6160. www.kyed.uscourts.gov

Counties: Breathitt, Floyd, Johnson, Knott, Letcher, Magoffin, Martin, Perry, Pike. Lee and Wolfe Counties were part of this division until 10/31/92, when they were moved to the Lexington Division.

Indexing & Storage: New cases available in the index immediately after filing date.

Fee & Payment: Payment may be made by money order, cashier check, personal check. Prepayment required except for Kentucky attorneys. Payee: Clerk, U.S. District Court.

Phone Search: Only the date the case was filed and the status of the case will be released over the phone.

Mail Search: A SASE not required.

In Person Search: Fee charged if court conducts your in person search for you.

PACER: PACER is available online at http://pacer.kyed.uscourts.gov. Case records go back to September 1991. Records never purged. New records are online after 1 day.

Electronic Filing: Electronic filing information at https://ecf.kyed.uscourts.gov/cgi-bin/login.pl

U.S. Bankruptcy Court

Eastern District of Kentucky

Lexington Division PO Box 1111, Lexington, KY 40589-1111 (courier address: Community Trust Bldg, Suite 202, 100 E Vine St, Lexington, KY 40507), 859-233-2608. www.kyeb.uscourts.gov

Counties: Anderson, Bath, Bell, Boone, Bourbon, Boyd, Boyle, Bracken, Breathitt, Campbell, Carroll, Carter, Clark, Clay, Elliott, Estill, Fayette, Fleming, Floyd, Franklin, Gallatin, Garrard, Grant, Greenup, Harlan, Harrison, Henry, Jackson, Jessamine, Johnson,Kenton, Knott, Knox, Laurel, Lawrence, Lee, Leslie, Letcher, Lewis, Lincoln, Madison, Magoffin, Martin, Mason, McCreary, Menifee, Mercer, Montgomery, Morgan, Nicholas, Owen, Owsley, Pendleton, Perry, Pike, Powell, Pulaski, Robertson, Rockcastle, Rowan,Scott, Shelby, Trimble, Wayne, Whitley, Wolfe, Woodford.

Indexing & Storage: Cases indexed by debtor as well as by case number. New cases available in the index 3 days after filing date.

Fee & Payment: Payment may be made by money order, cashier check, business check. Personal checks are not accepted. Prepayment is required (excluding pauper filings). Payee: Clerk, U.S. Bankruptcy Court.

Phone Search: Only docket information available by phone. Automated voice case information service (VCIS) is available. Call VCIS at 800-998-2650 or 606-233-2657.

In Person Search: Fee charged if court conducts your in person search for you.

PACER: PACER is available online at http://pacer.kyeb.uscourts.gov. Records purged every six months. New civil records are online after 1 day.

Electronic Filing: Electronic filing information online at https://ecf.kyeb.uscourts.gov

U.S. District Court

Western District of Kentucky

Bowling Green Division U.S. District Court, 241 E Main St, Room 120, Bowling Green, KY 42101-2175 (courier address: Use mail address for courier delivery) 270-389-2500, Fax: 270-393-2519. www.kywd.uscourts.gov

Counties: Adair, Allen, Barren, Butler, Casey, Clinton, Cumberland, Edmonson, Green, Hart, Logan, Metcalfe, Monroe, Russell, Simpson, Taylor, Todd, Warren.

Indexing & Storage: New cases available in the index 1-2 days after filing date.

Fee & Payment: Payment may be made by money order, cashier check, personal check. Payee: Clerk, U.S. District Court.

Phone Search: Only docket information available by phone.

In Person Search: Fee charged if court conducts your in person search for you.

PACER: Court converted the online WebPACER service over to nationwide PACER standards; click on "Court Records." Registration and fee required. New records are online after 1 day.

Electronic Filing: Electronic filing information at www.kywd.uscourts.gov/CMECFWelcome.php

Opinions Online: Court opinions are online at www.kywd.uscourts.gov

Louisville Division Clerk, U.S. District Court, 601 Broadway, Rm106, Louisville, KY 40202 (courier address: Use mail address for courier delivery) 502-625-3500, Fax: 502-625-3880. www.kywd.uscourts.gov

Counties: Breckinridge, Bullitt, Hardin, Jefferson, Larue, Marion, Meade, Nelson, Oldham, Spencer, Washington.

Indexing & Storage: New cases available in the index immediately after filing date. Records are indexed on index cards from 1938 to 1979. Records are indexed on microfiche from 1979 to 4/92. Records after 4/92 are on the automated system. District wide searches are available from this court for information from 1938.

Fee & Payment: Payment may be made by money order, cashier check, personal check. Payee: Clerk, U.S. District Court.

Phone Search: No searching by telephone. Only docket information available by phone.

In Person Search: Fee charged if court conducts your in person search for you.

PACER: Court has converted the online WebPACER service over to nationwide PACER standards; click on "Court Records" Registration and fee required. New records are online after 1 day.

Electronic Filing: Electronic filing information at www.kywd.uscourts.gov/CMECFWelcome.php

Opinions Online: Court opinions are online at www.kywd.uscourts.gov

Owensboro Division Federal Bldg, Room 126, 423 Frederica St, Owensboro, KY 42301 (courier address: Use mail address for courier delivery) 270-689-4400, Fax: 207-689-4419. www.kywd.uscourts.gov

Counties: Daviess, Grayson, Hancock, Henderson, Hopkins, McLean, Muhlenberg, Ohio, Union, Webster.

Indexing & Storage: New cases available in the index 1-2 days after filing date. The court needs the correct name, date and/or criminal or civil case number to search for a record.

Fee & Payment: Payment may be made by money order, cashier check, personal check. The court will only bill to in state searchers. Payee: Clerk, U.S. District Court.

Phone Search: Only docket information available.

Mail Search: A SASE not required.

In Person Search: Fee charged if court conducts your in person search for you.

PACER: Court converted the online WebPACER service over to nationwide PACER standards; click on "Court Records." Registration and fee required. Case records go back to 1994. New records are online after 1 day.

Electronic Filing: Electronic filing information at www.kywd.uscourts.gov/CMECFWelcome.php

Opinions Online: Court opinions are online at www.kywd.uscourts.gov

Paducah Division 501 Broadway, Ste127, Paducah, KY 42001 (courier address: Use mail address for courier delivery) 270-415-6400, Fax: 270-415-6419. www.kywd.uscourts.gov

Counties: Ballard, Caldwell, Calloway, Carlisle, Christian, Crittenden, Fulton, Graves, Hickman, Livingston, Lyon, McCracken, Marshall, Trigg.

Indexing & Storage: New cases available in the index 1-2 days after filing date.

Fee & Payment: Payment may be made by money order, cashier check, personal check. Payee: Clerk, U.S. District Court.

Phone Search: Only docket information available by phone.

In Person Search: Fee charged if court conducts your in person search for you.

PACER: Court converted the online WebPACER service over to nationwide PACER standards; click on "Court Records." Registration and fee required. New records are online after 1 day.

Electronic Filing: Electronic filing information at www.kywd.uscourts.gov/CMECFWelcome.php

Opinions Online: Court opinions are online at www.kywd.uscourts.gov

U.S. Bankruptcy Court

Western District of Kentucky

Louisville Division 546 U.S. Courthouse, 601 W Broadway, Louisville, KY 40202 (courier address: Use mail address for courier delivery) 502-627-5800. www.kywb.uscourts.gov

Counties: Adair, Allen, Ballard, Barren, Breckinridge, Bullitt, Butler, Caldwell, Calloway, Carlisle, Casey, Christian, Clinton, Crittenden, Cumberland, Daviess, Edmonson, Fulton, Graves, Grayson, Green, Hancock, Hardin, Hart, Henderson, Hickman, Hopkins, Jefferson, Larue, Livingston, Logan, Lyon, Marion, Marshall, McCracken, McLean, Meade, Metcalfe, Monroe, Muhlenberg, Nelson, Ohio, Oldham, Russell, Simpson, Spencer, Taylor, Todd, Trigg, Union, Warren, Washington, Webster.

Indexing & Storage: Cases indexed by debtor as well as by case number. New cases available in the index 1-2 days after filing date. District wide searches are available from this division. This division maintains records for all of the divisions in this district.

Fee & Payment: Payment may be made by money order, cashier check. Business checks are not accepted. Personal checks are not accepted. Payee: Clerk, U.S. Bankruptcy Court. Will fax back in an emergency, $.50 per page.

Phone Search: Only docket information available by phone. Automated voice case information service (VCIS) is available. Call VCIS at 800-263-9385 or 502-625-7391. Will fax back in an emergency, $.50 per page.

In Person Search: Fee charged if court conducts your in person search for you.

PACER: PACER is available online at http://pacer.kywb.uscourts.gov. Records purged every six months. New civil records are online after 1-2 days.

Electronic Filing: Electronic filing information online at https://ecf.kywb.uscourts.gov

Kentucky County Courts

Court	Jurisdiction	No. of Courts	How Organized
Circuit Courts*	General	19	57 Judicial Circuits
District Courts*	Limited	19	60 Judicial Districts
Combined*		102	

* Profiled in this Sourcebook.

Court	CIVIL								
	Tort	Contract	Real Estate	Min. Claim	Max. Claim	Small Claims	Estate	Eviction	Domestic Relations
Circuit Courts*	X	X	X	$4000	No Max				X
District Courts*	X	X	X	$0	$4000	$1500	X	X	X

Court	CRIMINAL				
	Felony	Misdemeanor	DWI/DUI	Preliminary Hearing	Juvenile
Circuit Courts*	X				
District Courts*		X	X	X	X

ADMINISTRATION Administrative Office of Courts, 100 Mill Creek Park, Frankfort, KY, 40601; 502-573-1682, Fax: 502-573-1669. www.kycourts.net

COURT STRUCTURE The Circuit Court is the court of general jurisdiction and the District Court is the limited jurisdiction court. Most of Kentucky's counties combined the courts into one location and records are co-mingled. Circuit courts have jurisdiction over cases involving capital offenses and felonies, divorces, adoptions, terminations of parental rights, land dispute title problems and contested probates of will. Juvenile matters, city and county ordinances, misdemeanors, traffic offenses, probate of wills, felony preliminary hearings, and civil cases involving $4,000 or less are heard in District Court. Ninety percent of all Kentuckians involved in court proceedings appear in District Court.

ONLINE ACCESS There are statewide, online computer systems called SUSTAIN and KyCourts available for internal judicial/state agency use only, and KY Bar attorneys may register to use the KCOJ court records data at http://courtnetpublic.kycourts.net. No courts offer online access to records. However, you may search daily court calendars by county for free at http://dockets.kycourts.net. Also, you may search online for open dockets (limited) of the supreme court at http://162.114.20.136/dockets.

ADDITIONAL INFORMATION Until 1978, county judges handled all cases; therefore, in many cases, District and Circuit Court records go back only to 1978. Records prior to that time are archived.

Many courts refer requests for criminal searches to the Administrative Office of Courts (AOC - 502-573-1682 or 800-928-6381) due to lack of personnel for searching at the court level. AOC maintains records on an internal system called COURTNET, which contains information on opening, closing, proceedings, disposition, and parties to including individual defendants. Felony convictions are accessible back to 1978, and Misdemeanors back five years. The required Release Form is available from the AOC at the numbers above. A check or money order for the search fee of $10.00 per requested individual ($5.00 fee if non-profit or if you are the individual) is payable to the State Treasurer of Kentucky. A SASE and a second postage-attached envelope must accompany the request.

Adair County

Circuit & District Court 500 Public Sq, #6, Columbia, KY 42728; 270-384-2626; Fax: 270-384-4299. 8AM-4PM (CST). *Felony, Misdemeanor, Civil, Eviction, Small Claims, Probate.*
Civil Records: Access: In person only. Visitors must perform in person searches for themselves. No search fee. Required to search: name, years to search. Civil records on computer since June 1993, prior records on docket books since 1978.

Criminal Records: Access: Mail, in person. Visitors must perform in person searches for themselves. No search fee. Required to search: name, years to search, SSN. Criminal records on computer since June 1993, prior records on docket books since 1978. Mail requests must be made to Pretrial Services, 100 Millcreek Pk, Frankfort KY 40601, 800-928-6381.
General Information: Public Access terminal is available. No adoption, mental, juvenile, or sealed records released. Copy fee: $.25 per page. No cert fee. Payee: Circuit Clerk. Personal checks accepted.

Prepayment required. Mail requests: SASE required. Mail turnaround time same day.

Allen County

Circuit & District Court Box 477, Scottsville, KY 42164; 270-237-3561. Hours: 8AM-4:30PM (CST). *Felony, Misdemeanor, Civil, Eviction, Small Claims, Probate.*
Civil Records: Access: In person only. Visitors must perform in person searches for themselves. Search fee: none. Required to search: name, years to search.

Civil cases indexed by defendant, plaintiff. Civil records on computer since 1992, records on index cards from 1980 to 1992, prior records on books.

Criminal Records: Access: In person only. Visitors must perform in person searches for themselves. Search fee: none. Required to search: name, years to search; also helpful: SSN. Criminal records on computer back to 1992, records on index cards from 1978 to 1992, prior records on books. Court recommends that criminal search requests be directed to the State of Kentucky AOC, 502-573-2350.

General Information: Public Access terminal is available. No adoption, mental, juvenile, or sealed records released. Copy fee: $.25 per page. Cert fee: $5.00. Payee: Circuit Clerk. Personal checks accepted. Prepayment required.

Anderson County

Circuit Court Courthouse 151 S Main St, Lawrenceburg, KY 40342; 502-839-3508. 8:30AM-5PM (EST). *Felony, Civil Actions Over $4,000.*

Civil Records: Access: In person only. Only the court performs in person searches; visitors may not. No search fee. Required to search: name, years to search. Civil cases indexed by defendant, plaintiff. Civil records on computer since August 1994, prior records on docket books since 1978.

Criminal Records: Access: In person only. Visitors must perform in person searches for themselves. No search fee. Required to search: name, years to search; also helpful: DOB, SSN. All record requests are referred to the state agency at 502-573-2350.

General Information: No adoption, mental, juvenile, or sealed records released. Copy fee: $.25 per page. Cert fee: $5.00. Payee: Clerk of Circuit Clerk. Personal checks accepted. Prepayment required.

District Court 151 S Main, Lawrenceburg, KY 40342; 502-839-5445. Hours: 8:30AM-Noon-1--5PM M-TH, 8:30AM-6PM F (EST). *Misdemeanor, Civil Actions Under $4,000, Eviction, Small Claims, Probate.*

Civil Records: Access: Phone, mail, fax, in person. Only the court performs in person searches; visitors may not. Search fee: None. Required to search: name, years to search. Civil cases indexed by defendant, plaintiff. Civil records on computer since 8/1994, prior records on index cards back to 1978.

Criminal Records: Access: In person only. No search fee. Required to search: name, years to search; also helpful: DOB, SSN. Criminal records on computer back to 1994; prior records on index cards back to 1978. The court will not do searches and offers no means to look up a name in an index. You must have the exact case number, but there is no way to get the case number. All requests are referred to Pre-trial Services at 800-928-6381. You may call them to perform the search for you.

General Information: No adoption, mental, juvenile, or sealed records released. Copy fee: $.1.00 per page. Cert fee: $5.00. Payee: County District Court. Business checks accepted. Prepayment required.

Ballard County

Circuit & District Court Box 265, Wickliffe, KY 42087; 270-335-5123; Fax: 270-335-3849. Hours: 8AM-4PM (CST). *Felony, Misdemeanor, Civil, Eviction, Small Claims, Probate.*

Civil Records: Access: Mail, fax, in person. Both court and visitors may perform in person searches. No search fee. Required to search: name, years to search. Civil cases indexed by defendant, plaintiff. Civil records on computer since 1992, prior records on books to 1978.

Criminal Records: Access: In person only. Visitors must perform in person searches for themselves. No search fee. Required to search: name, years to search,

DOB. Criminal records on computer since 1992, prior records on books to 1978.

General Information: Public Access terminal is available. No adoption, mental, juvenile, or sealed records released. Fee to fax results is $2.00 1st page, $1.00 each addl. Copy fee: $.25 per page. Cert fee: $5.00. Payee: Circuit Clerk. Only cashiers checks and money orders accepted. Prepayment required. Mail requests: SASE required. Mail turnaround: 2 days.

Barren County

Circuit & District Court PO Box 1359, Glasgow, KY 42142-1359; 270-651-3763; Fax: 270-651-6203. Hours: 8AM-4:30PM (CST). *Felony, Misdemeanor, Civil, Eviction, Small Claims, Probate.*

Civil Records: Access: In person only. Visitors must perform in person searches for themselves. No search fee. Required to search: name, years to search. Civil cases indexed by defendant, plaintiff. Civil records on computer back to 10/1991, prior records on index books since 1800s.

Criminal Records: Access: In person only. Visitors must perform in person searches for themselves. No search fee. Required to search: name, years to search, DOB; also helpful: SSN. Criminal records on computer back to 10/1991, prior records on index books since 1800s. Criminal record search requests should be directed to AOC Pre-Trial Services in Frankfort, 800-928-6381.

General Information: Public Access terminal is available. No adoption, mental, juvenile, or sealed records released. Copy fee: $.25 per page. Cert fee: $5.00. Payee: Circuit Clerk. Personal checks accepted. Prepayment required.

Bath County

Circuit & District Court Box 558, Owingsville, KY 40360; 606-674-2186 X6821; Fax: 606-674-3996. 8AM-4PM (EST). *Felony, Misdemeanor, Civil, Eviction, Small Claims, Probate.*

Civil Records: Access: In person only. Visitors must perform in person searches for themselves. No search fee. Required to search: name, years to search. Civil cases indexed by defendant, plaintiff. Civil records computerized since 1994, on docket books since 1978, prior records archived.

Criminal Records: Access: In person only. Visitors must perform in person searches for themselves. No search fee. Required to search: name, years to search, DOB, SSN. Criminal records computerized since 1994, on docket books since 1978, prior archived.

General Information: Public Access terminal is available. No adoption, mental, juvenile, or sealed records released. Copy fee: $.25 per page. Cert fee: $5.00. Payee: Circuit Clerk. Personal checks accepted. Prepayment required.

Bell County

Circuit & District Court Box 307, Pineville, KY 40977; 606-337-2942/9900; Fax: 606-337-8850. Hours: 8:30AM-4PM (EST). *Felony, Misdemeanor, Civil, Eviction, Small Claims, Probate.*

Civil Records: Access: Phone, mail, in person. Both court and visitors may perform in person searches. No search fee. Required to search: name, years to search. Civil cases indexed by defendant, plaintiff. Civil records on computer since 08/91, prior records on docket books since 1978.

Criminal Records: Access: In person only. Visitors must perform in person searches for themselves. No search fee. Required to search: name, years to search. Criminal records on computer since 08/91, prior records on docket books since 1978. Direct written criminal records checks to Pretrial Services Records Division, 100 Millcreek Pk, Frankfort, KY, 40601; for info call 502-573-1682 or 800-928-6381.

General Information: Public Access terminal is available. No adoption, mental, juvenile, or sealed records released. Copy fee: $.25 per page. Cert fee: $5.00. Payee: Circuit Clerk. Personal checks accepted. Prepayment required. Mail requests: SASE required.

Boone County

Circuit & District Court 6025 Rogers Ln #141, Burlington, KY 41005; 859-334-2286; Civil phone: 859-334-2287 District; Criminal phone: 859-334-3536 District; Fax: 859-334-3650. Hours: 8:30AM-4:30PM (EST). *Felony, Misdemeanor, Civil, Eviction, Small Claims, Probate.*

Civil Records: Access: Mail, in person. Both court and visitors may perform in person searches. No search fee. Required to search: name, years to search. Civil cases indexed by defendant, plaintiff. Civil records on computer since July 1990, on index card file since 1978, prior records on books.

Criminal Records: Access: In person only. Visitors must perform in person searches for themselves. No search fee. Required to search: name, years to search, DOB; also helpful: SSN. Criminal records on computer since July 1990, on index card file since 1978, prior records on books.

General Information: Public Access terminal is available. No adoption, mental, juvenile, or sealed records released. Fee to fax results is $3.00 per page. Copy fee: $.25 per page. Cert fee: $5.00. Payee: Circuit Clerk. Only cashiers checks and money orders accepted. Prepayment required. Mail requests: SASE required.

Bourbon County

Circuit & District Court Box 740, Paris, KY 40361; 859-987-2624; Fax: 859-987-6049. Hours: 8:30AM-4:30PM M-TH, 8:30AM-6PM F (EST). *Felony, Misdemeanor, Civil, Eviction, Small Claims, Probate.*

Civil Records: Access: In person only. Visitors must perform in person searches for themselves. No search fee. Required to search: name, years to search. Civil cases indexed by defendant, plaintiff. Civil records on computer since November 1991, prior on books.

Criminal Records: Access: In person only. Visitors must perform in person searches for themselves. No search fee. Required to search: name, years to search; also helpful: SSN. Criminal records on computer since November 1991, prior records on books.

General Information: Public Access terminal is available. No adoption, mental, juvenile, or sealed records released. Copy fee: $.25 per page. Cert fee: $5.00. Payee: Circuit Clerk. Personal checks accepted. Prepayment required.

Boyd County

Circuit & District Court Box 694, Catlettsburg, KY 41129-0694; 606-739-4131; Fax: 606-739-6330. Hours: 8:30AM-4PM (EST). *Felony, Misdemeanor, Civil, Eviction, Small Claims, Probate.*

Civil Records: Access: In person only. Visitors must perform in person searches for themselves. No search fee. Required to search: name, years to search. Civil cases indexed by defendant, plaintiff. Civil records on computer since 1991, prior records on index cards since 1975.

Criminal Records: Access: In person only. Only the court performs in person searches; visitors may not. No search fee. Required to search: name, years to search, signed release; also helpful: DOB, SSN. Criminal records on computer since 1991, on index cards since 1978; misdemeanor & traffic from 1987.

General Information: Public Access terminal is available. No adoption, mental, juvenile, or sealed records released. Copy fee: $.25 per page. Cert fee: $5.00. Payee: Circuit Clerk. Personal checks accepted. Prepayment required.

Boyle County

Circuit Court Courthouse, 321 Main St, Danville, KY 40422; 859-239-7442; Fax: 859-239-7000. Hours: 8AM-5PM (EST). *Felony, Civil Actions Over $4,000.*

Civil Records: Access: Fax, mail, in person. Both court and visitors may perform in person searches. No search fee. Required to search: name, years to search. Civil cases indexed by defendant, plaintiff. Civil records on computer since 08/91, prior records on index cards. Note that civil case records do not contain SSN or DOBs. Therefore a truly accurate search cannot be done at this court, per the court.

Criminal Records: Access: In person only. Visitors must perform in person searches for themselves. No search fee. Required to search: name, years to search, DOB, SSN. Criminal records on computer since 08/91, prior records on index cards. This office will not perform criminal name checks.

General Information: Public Access terminal is available. No adoption, mental, juvenile, or sealed records released. Will fax civil record searches only, $2.00 1st page, $1.00 ea add'l. Copy fee: $.25 per page. Cert fee: $5.00. Payee: Circuit Clerk. Personal checks accepted. Prepayment required. Mail requests: SASE required. Mail turnaround time 2-4 days.

District Court Courthouse, 3rd Fl, Danville, KY 40422; 859-239-7362; Civil phone: 859-239-7394; Fax: 859-239-7807. Hours: 8AM-4:30PM (EST). *Misdemeanor, Civil Actions Under $4,000, Eviction, Small Claims, Probate.*

Civil Records: Access: Mail, fax, in person. Both court and visitors may perform in person searches. No search fee. Required to search: name, years to search. Civil cases indexed by defendant, plaintiff. Civil records on computer since 08/91, prior records on index cards since 1977.

Criminal Records: Access: Mail, fax, in person. Both court and visitors may perform in person searches. No search fee. Required to search: name, DOB, SSN. Criminal records on computer since 08/91; prior records on card index.

General Information: Public Access terminal is available. No adoption, mental, juvenile, or sealed records released. Fee to fax results is $2.00 per page. Copy fee: $.25 per page. Cert fee: $5.00. Payee: District Clerk. Personal checks accepted. Prepayment required. Mail requests: SASE required. Mail turnaround time 3-4 days.

Bracken County

Circuit & District Court PO Box 205, Brooksville, KY 41004-0205; 606-735-3328; Fax: 606-735-3900. 8AM-4:30PM M,T,TH,F, 8:30AM-Noon W & Sat (EST). *Felony, Misdemeanor, Civil, Eviction, Small Claims, Probate.*

Civil Records: Access: Mail, in person. Both court and visitors may perform in person searches. No search fee. Required to search: name, years to search. Civil cases indexed by defendant, plaintiff. Civil records on computer since 1993, prior records on docket books since the 1800s.

Criminal Records: Access: In person only. Visitors must perform in person searches for themselves. No search fee. Required to search: name, years to search. Criminal records on computer since 1993, prior records on docket books since the 1800s.

General Information: Public Access terminal is available. No adoption, mental, juvenile, or sealed records released. Will not fax results. Copy fee: $.25 per page. Cert fee: $5.00. Payee: Circuit Clerk. Prepayment required. Mail requests: SASE required.

Breathitt County

Circuit & District Court 1137 Main St, Jackson, KY 41339; 606-666-5768; Fax: 606-666-4893. Hours: 8AM-4PM M,T,TH,F; 9AM-Noon W; 9AM-Noon Sat (EST). *Felony, Misdemeanor, Civil, Eviction, Small Claims, Probate.*

Civil Records: Access: Mail, in person. Both court and visitors may perform in person searches. No search fee. Required to search: name, years to search. Civil cases indexed by defendant, plaintiff. Civil records in files since 1987.

Criminal Records: Access: Mail, in person. Both court and visitors may perform in person searches. No search fee. Required to search: name, years to search, DOB, SSN, signed release. Criminal records in files since 1987.

General Information: Public Access terminal is available. No adoption, mental, juvenile, or sealed records released. Copy fee: $.25 per page. Cert fee: $5.00. Payee: Circuit Clerk. Personal checks accepted. Prepayment required. Mail requests: SASE required. Mail turnaround time 2-3 days.

Breckinridge County

Circuit & District Court Box 111, Hardinsburg, KY 40143; 270-756-2239; Fax: 270-756-1129. Hours: 8AM-4PM (CST). *Felony, Misdemeanor, Civil, Eviction, Small Claims, Probate.*

Civil Records: Access: In person only. Visitors must perform in person searches for themselves. No search fee. Required to search: name, years to search. Civil cases indexed by defendant, plaintiff. Civil records on computer back to 8/1994, on index cards since 1978, prior records on docket books since the 1800s.

Criminal Records: Access: In person only. Visitors must perform in person searches for themselves. No search fee. Required to search: name, years to search, DOB, SSN. Criminal records on computer back to 8/1994, on index cards since 1978, prior records on docket books since the 1800s.

General Information: Public Access terminal is available. No adoption, mental, juvenile, or sealed records released. Copy fee: $.25 per page. Cert fee: $5.00. Payee: Circuit Clerk. Personal checks accepted. Prepayment required.

Bullitt County

Circuit & District Court Box 746, Shepardsville, KY 40165; 502-543-7104; Fax: 502-543-7158. 8AM-4PM (EST). *Felony, Misdemeanor, Civil, Eviction, Small Claims, Probate.*

Note: This office no longer conducts name searches.

Civil Records: Access: In person only. Visitors must perform in person searches for themselves. No search fee. Required to search: name. Civil cases indexed by defendant, plaintiff. Civil records on computer since 11/91, prior records on index cards since the 1800s.

Criminal Records: Access: In person only. Visitors must perform in person searches for themselves. No search fee. Required to search: name, years to search, DOB, SSN. Criminal records on computer since 11/91, prior records on index cards since the 1800s.

General Information: Public Access terminal is available. No adoption, mental, juvenile, or sealed records released. Fee to fax case file is $1.00 per page. Copy fee: $.25 per page. Cert fee: $5.00. Payee: Circuit Clerk. Personal checks accepted. Prepayment required.

Butler County

Circuit & District Court Box 625, Morgantown, KY 42261; 270-526-5631. Hours: 8AM-4:30PM M-F; 9AM-Noon Sat (CST). *Felony, Misdemeanor, Civil, Eviction, Small Claims, Probate.*

Civil Records: Access: Mail, in person. No search fee. Required to search: name, years to search. Civil cases indexed by defendant, plaintiff. Civil records on computer since 1993, prior records on index cards since the 1800s.

Criminal Records: Access: Mail, in person. Both court and visitors may perform in person searches. No search fee. Required to search: name, years to search, DOB; also helpful: SSN. Criminal records on computer since 1993, prior records on index cards since the 1800s.

General Information: Public Access terminal is available. No adoption, mental, juvenile, or sealed records released. Copy fee: $.25 per page. No cert fee. Payee: Circuit Clerk. Personal checks accepted. Prepayment required. Mail requests: SASE required. Mail turnaround time 1 week.

Caldwell County

Circuit & District Court 105 West Court Sq, Princeton, KY 42445; 270-365-6884; Fax: 270-365-9171. 8AM-4PM (CST). *Felony, Misdemeanor, Civil, Eviction, Small Claims, Probate.*

Civil Records: Access: Mail, fax, in person. Visitors must perform in person searches for themselves. No search fee. Required to search: name, years to search. Civil cases indexed by defendant, plaintiff. Civil records on index cards; on computer back to 9/94.

Criminal Records: Access: In person only. Visitors must perform in person searches for themselves. No search fee. Required to search: name, years to search, DOB; also helpful: SSN. Criminal records on index cards; on computer back to 9/94.

General Information: Public Access terminal is available. No adoption, mental, juvenile, or sealed records released. Fee to fax results is $2.00 for 1st page, $1.00 each add'l. Copy fee: $.25 per page. Copy request must include postage. Certification fee: $5.00. Payee: Circuit Clerk. Personal checks accepted. Prepayment required. Mail requests: SASE required. Mail turnaround time 2 days.

Calloway County

Circuit & District Court 312 N 4th St, Murray, KY 42071; 270-753-2714; Fax: 270-759-9822. Hours: 8AM-4:30PM (CST). *Felony, Misdemeanor, Civil, Eviction, Small Claims, Probate.*

Note: Circuirt court civil and criminal phone number is 270-753-2773.

Civil Records: Access: Mail, in person. Both court and visitors may perform in person searches. No search fee. Required to search: name, years to search. Civil cases indexed by defendant, plaintiff. Civil records on computer since 06/92, on index cards since 1978. Prior to 1978 records are archived in Frankfort.

Criminal Records: Access: In person only. Visitors must perform in person searches for themselves. No search fee. Required to search: name, years to search, DOB; also helpful: SSN. Criminal records on computer since 06/92, on index cards since 1978. Prior to 1978 records are archived in Frankfort.

General Information: Public Access terminal is available. No adoption, mental, juvenile, or sealed records released. Copy fee: $.25 per page. Certification fee: $5.00. Payee: Circuit Clerk. Personal checks accepted. Prepayment required. Mail requests: SASE required. Mail turnaround time 2-4 days.

Campbell County

Circuit Court 330 York St, Rm 8, Newport, KY 41071; 859-292-6314. Hours: 8:30AM-4PM (EST). *Felony, Civil Actions Over $4,000.*

www.kycourts.net/clerks/campbellclerk.shtm

Civil Records: Access: In person only. Visitors must perform in person searches for themselves. No search fee. Required to search: name, years to search. Civil

cases indexed by defendant, plaintiff. Civil records on computer since 1992, prior records on index cards since 1978.

Criminal Records: Access: In person only. Visitors must perform in person searches for themselves. No search fee. Required to search: name, years to search; also helpful: SSN. Criminal records on computer since 1992, prior records on index cards since 1978.

General Information: Public Access terminal is available. No adoption, mental, juvenile, or sealed records released. Copy fee: $.25 per page. Certification fee: $5.00. Payee: Circuit Court. Personal checks accepted. Prepayment required.

District Court 600 Columbia St, Newport, KY 41071-1816; 859-292-6305; Fax: 859-292-6593. 8:30AM-4PM (EST). *Misdemeanor, Civil Actions Under $4,000, Eviction, Small Claims, Probate.*
www.kycourts.net/clerks/campbellclerk.shtm
Civil Records: Access: Mail, in person. Both court and visitors may perform in person searches. Search fee: $10.00 (probate searches only). Required to search: name, years to search. Civil cases indexed by defendant, plaintiff. Civil records on computer back to 1992, prior records on index cards to 1978.

Criminal Records: Access: In person only. Visitors must perform in person searches for themselves. Search fee: none. Required to search: name, years to search. Criminal records on computer back to 1992, prior records on index cards to 1978.

General Information: Public Access terminal is available. No adoption, mental, juvenile, or sealed records released. Copy fee: $.25 per page. Certification fee: $5.00. Payee: Campbell Circuit Clerk. Business checks accepted. Prepayment required. Mail requests: SASE required. Mail turnaround time 7 days.

Carlisle County

Circuit & District Court Box 337, Bardwell, KY 42023; 270-628-5425; Fax: 270-628-5456. Hours: 8AM-4PM (CST). *Felony, Misdemeanor, Civil, Eviction, Small Claims, Probate.*
Civil Records: Access: Phone, fax, mail, in person. Both court and visitors may perform in person searches. No search fee. Required to search: name, years to search. Civil cases indexed by defendant, plaintiff. Civil records on computer since May 1993, records on docket books since 1978, prior records archived.

Criminal Records: Access: Phone, fax, mail, in person. Both court and visitors may perform in person searches. No search fee. Required to search: name, years to search. Criminal records on computer since May 1993, records on docket books since 1978, prior records archived.

General Information: Public Access terminal is available. No adoption, mental, juvenile, or sealed records released. Will fax results for $2.00 per page. Copy fee: $.25 per page. Certification fee: $5.00. Payee: Circuit Clerk. Personal checks accepted. Prepayment required. Mail requests: SASE required. Mail turnaround time 1-5 days.

Carroll County

Circuit & District Court 802 Clay St, Carrollton, KY 41008; 502-732-4305; Fax: 502-732-8138. 8AM-4:30PM (EST). *Felony, Misdemeanor, Civil, Eviction, Small Claims, Probate.*
Civil Records: Access: In person only. Visitors must perform in person searches. No search fee. Required to search: name, years to search. Civil cases indexed by defendant, plaintiff. Civil records on computer since 1994, on docket books since 1980. Records before 1980 are archived in Frankfort.

Criminal Records: Access: In person only. Visitors must perform in person searches. No search fee.

Required to search: name, years to search, DOB; also helpful: SSN. Criminal records on computer since 1994, on docket books since 1980. Records before 1980 are archived in Frankfort.

General Information: Public Access terminal is available. No adoption, mental, juvenile, or sealed records released. Copy fee: $.25 per page. Certification fee: $5.00. Payee: Circuit Clerk. Personal checks accepted. Prepayment required.

Carter County

Circuit Court 100 E. Main St, Grayson, KY 41143; 606-474-5191; Fax: 606-474-8826. Hours: 8:30AM-4PM M-F; 9AM-Noon Sat (EST). *Felony, Civil Actions Over $4,000.*
Civil Records: Access: Mail, in person. Both court and visitors may perform in person searches. No search fee. Required to search: name, years to search. Civil cases indexed by defendant, plaintiff. Civil records on computer since 1994, records archived since 1978, prior records are archived.

Criminal Records: Access: In person only. Both court and visitors may perform in person searches. No search fee. Required to search: name, years to search, DOB, SSN. Criminal records on computer since 1994, records archived since 1978, prior records are archived.

General Information: Public Access terminal is available. No adoption, mental, juvenile, or sealed records released. Will not fax results. Copy fee: $.25 per page. Certification fee: $5.00. Payee: Carter County Circuit Clerk. Prepayment required. Mail requests: SASE required. Mail turnaround: 1-2 days.

District Court Courthouse, Rm 203, 300 West Main, Grayson, KY 41143; 606-474-6572; Fax: 606-474-8584. Hours: 8AM-4PM (EST). *Misdemeanor, Civil Actions Under $4,000, Eviction, Small Claims, Probate.*
Civil Records: Access: Mail, in person. Both court and visitors may perform in person searches. No search fee. Required to search: name, years to search. Civil cases indexed by defendant, plaintiff. Civil records on computer since 1994, prior records on index cards.

Criminal Records: Access: In person only. Visitors must perform in person searches for themselves. No search fee. Required to search: name, years to search, DOB; also helpful: SSN. Criminal records on computer since 1994, prior records on index cards.

General Information: Public Access terminal is available. No adoption, mental, juvenile, or sealed records released. Copy fee: $.25 per page. Certification fee: $5.00. Payee: District Clerk. Personal checks accepted. Prepayment required. Mail requests: SASE required. Mail turnaround: 2-4 days.

Casey County

Circuit & District Court PO Box 147, Liberty, KY 42539; 606-787-6510. Hours: 8AM-4:30PM M, Tu & F, 8AM-4PM W-Th, 8AM-Noon Sat (EST). *Felony, Misdemeanor, Civil, Eviction, Small Claims, Probate.*
Note: This court asks all pre-trial record requests go to the Administrative office of the Courts in Frankfort.

Civil Records: Access: In person. Visitors must perform in person searches for themselves. No search fee. Required to search: name, years to search. Civil cases indexed by defendant, plaintiff. Civil records on index cards since 1978, prior records archived, computerized from 1995.

Criminal Records: Access: In person only. Visitors must perform in person searches for themselves. No search fee. Required to search: name, years to search, DOB, SSN, signed release. Criminal records on index cards since 1978, prior records archived,

computerized from 1995.

General Information: Public Access terminal is available. No adoption, mental, juvenile, or sealed records released. Copy fee: $.25 per page. Certification fee: $5.00. Payee: Circuit Clerk. Personal checks accepted. Prepayment required.

Christian County

Circuit & District Court Christian County Justice Center, 100 Justice Way, Hopkinsville, KY 42240; 270-889-6539; Fax: 270-889-6564. Hours: 8AM-4:30PM (CST). *Felony, Misdemeanor, Civil, Eviction, Small Claims, Probate.*
Civil Records: Access: Mail, in person. Both court and visitors may perform in person searches. No search fee. Required to search: name, years to search. Civil cases indexed by defendant, plaintiff. Civil records on computer since 1991, prior records on index cards since 1978.

Criminal Records: Access: In person only. Visitors must perform in person searches for themselves. No search fee. Required to search: name, years to search; also helpful: DOB, SSN. Criminal records on computer since 1991, prior records on index cards since 1978.

General Information: Public Access terminal is available. No adoption, mental, juvenile, or sealed records released. Copy fee: $.25 per page. Certification fee: $5.00. Payee: Circuit Clerk. Personal checks accepted. Prepayment required. Mail requests: SASE required. Mail turnaround time 2-4 days.

Clark County

Circuit Court Box 687, Winchester, KY 40392; 859-737-7264. Hours: 8AM-4PM (EST). *Felony, Civil Actions Over $4,000.*
Civil Records: Access: Mail, in person. Both court and visitors may perform in person searches. No search fee. Required to search: name, years to search; also helpful: address. Civil cases indexed by defendant, plaintiff. Civil records on computer since 1989, on index cards since 1950, prior records archived since the 1700s.

Criminal Records: Access: In person only. Visitors must perform in person searches for themselves. No search fee. Required to search: name, years to search; also helpful: address, DOB, SSN. Criminal records on computer since 1989, on index cards since 1950, prior records archived since the 1700s.

General Information: Public Access terminal is available. No adoption, mental, juvenile, or sealed records released. Copy fee: $.25 per page. Certification fee: $5.00. Payee: Circuit Clerk. Personal checks accepted. Prepayment required. Mail requests: SASE required. Mail turnaround time 2-4 days.

District Court PO Box 687, Winchester, KY 40392-0687; 859-737-7141; Fax: 859-737-7005. 8AM-4PM (EST). *Misdemeanor, Civil Actions Under $4,000, Eviction, Small Claims, Probate.*
Civil Records: Access: Mail, in person. Both court and visitors may perform in person searches. No search fee. Required to search: name, years to search. Civil cases indexed by defendant, plaintiff. Civil records on computer since 1989, on docket books since 1978, prior records on archived.

Criminal Records: Access: Mail, in person. Both court and visitors may perform in person searches. No search fee. Required to search: name, years to search; also helpful: DOB, SSN. Criminal records on computer since 1989, on docket books since 1978, prior records on archived.

General Information: Public Access terminal is available. No adoption, mental, juvenile, or sealed records released. Copy fee: $.25 per page. Certification fee: $5.00. Payee: District Clerk.

Personal checks accepted. Prepayment required. Mail requests: SASE required. Mail turnaround: 1-3 days.

Clay County

Circuit & District Court 79 Highway 80, #3, Manchester, KY 40962; 606-598-3663; Fax: 606-598-4047. Hours: 7:30AM-4:30PM (EST). *Felony, Misdemeanor, Civil, Eviction, Small Claims, Probate.*

Civil Records: Access: In person only. Visitors must perform in person searches for themselves. No search fee. Required to search: name, years to search. Civil cases indexed by defendant, plaintiff. Civil records on computer back to 1992, on index cards since 1978, records through 1986 in archives.

Criminal Records: Access: In person only. Visitors must perform in person searches for themselves. No search fee. Required to search: name, years to search, DOB; also helpful: SSN. Criminal records on computer back to 1992, on index cards since 1978, records through 1986 in archives.

General Information: Public Access terminal is available. No adoption, mental, juvenile, or sealed records released. Copy fee: $.25 per page. Certification fee: $5.00. Payee: Circuit Clerk. Personal checks accepted. Prepayment required.

Clinton County

Circuit & District Court Courthouse 2nd Fl, 100 S Cross St, Albany, KY 42602; 606-387-6424; Fax: 606-387-8154. Hours: 8AM-4;30PM M-F; 8AM-Noon Sat (CST). *Felony, Misdemeanor, Civil, Eviction, Small Claims, Probate.*

Civil Records: Access: Phone, mail, in person. Both court and visitors may perform in person searches. No search fee. Required to search: name, years to search. Civil cases indexed by defendant, plaintiff. Civil records on computer since 08/92, on docket books since 1978, prior records archived to 1865.

Criminal Records: Access: Phone, mail, in person. Visitors must perform in person searches for themselves No search fee. Required to search: name, years to search, SSN; also helpful: DOB. Criminal records on computer since 08/92, on docket books since 1978, prior records archive to 1865.

General Information: Public Access terminal is available. No adoption, mental, juvenile, or sealed records released. Copy fee: $.25 per page. Certification fee: $5.00. Payee: Circuit Clerk. Personal checks accepted. Prepayment required. Mail requests: SASE required. Mail turnaround time 5 days.

Crittenden County

Circuit & District Court 107 S Main, Marion, KY 42064; 270-965-4200 (and) 270-965-4046. Hours: 8AM-4:30PM (CST). *Felony, Misdemeanor, Civil, Eviction, Small Claims, Probate, Traffic.*

Civil Records: Access: Mail, in person. Visitors must perform in person searches for themselves. No search fee. Required to search: name, years to search. Civil cases indexed by defendant, plaintiff. Civil records on index cards since 1977; on computer back to 9/94.

Criminal Records: Access: In person only. Visitors must perform in person searches for themselves. No search fee. Required to search: name, years to search. Circuit criminal records on index cards since 1977; on computer back to 9/94; District Criminal 1994 to present.

General Information: Public Access terminal is available. No adoption, mental, juvenile, or sealed records released. Fee to fax results is $2.00 1st page; $1.00 each add'l. Copy fee: $.25 per page. Certification fee: $5.00. Payee: Circuit Clerk. Personal checks not accepted. Prepayment required. Mail requests: SASE required. Mail turnaround time 10 days.

Cumberland County

Circuit & District Court Box 395, Burkesville, KY 42717; 270-864-2611. Hours: 8AM-4PM (CST). *Felony, Misdemeanor, Civil, Eviction, Small Claims, Probate.*

Civil Records: Access: Mail, fax, in person. Both court and visitors may perform in person searches. No search fee. Required to search: name, years to search. Civil cases indexed by defendant, plaintiff. Civil records on computer back to 06/93, on docket cards from 1978, prior records archived.

Criminal Records: Access: Mail, fax, in person. Both court and visitors may perform in person searches. No search fee. Required to search: name, years to search, DOB; also helpful: SSN. Criminal records on computer back to 06/93, on docket cards from 1978, prior records archived.

General Information: Public Access terminal is available. No adoption, mental, juvenile, or sealed records released. Fee to fax results is $2.00 and $1.00 per page. Copy fee: $.25 per page. Certification fee: $5.00. Payee: Circuit Clerk. Personal checks accepted. Prepayment required. Mail requests: SASE required. Mail turnaround time 3-5 days.

Daviess County

Circuit & District Court Box 277 (100 E Second St), Owensboro, KY 42302; 270-687-7330 (Circuit Crim); Civil phone: 270-687-7220 (Circuit Civil); 270-687-7205 (District Civil); Criminal phone: 270-687-7330 (Circuit Crim); 270-687-7200 (District Crim); Probate phone: 270-687-7207. Hours: 8AM-4PM (CST). *Felony, Misdemeanor, Civil, Eviction, Small Claims, Probate.*

Civil Records: Access: In person only. Visitors must perform in person searches for themselves. No search fee. Required to search: name, years to search. Civil cases indexed by defendant, plaintiff. Civil records on computer since 04/91, on index cards since 1978, prior records on docket books since 1809. Search in person only on Tuesday or Thursday.

Criminal Records: Access: In person only. Visitors must perform in person searches for themselves. No search fee. Required to search: name, years to search, DOB, SSN. Criminal records on computer since 04/91, on index cards since 1978, prior records on docket books since 1809. Search in person only on Tuesday or Thursday.

General Information: Public Access terminal is available. No adoption, mental, juvenile, or sealed records released. Copy fee: $.25 per page. Certification fee: $5.00. Payee: Circuit Clerk. Business checks accepted. Prepayment required.

Edmonson County

Circuit & District Court Box 739, 110 Cross Main St., Brownsville, KY 42210; 270-597-2584; Fax: 270-597-2884. Hours: 8AM-4:30PM M-W,F; 8AM-Noon Th,S (CST). *Felony, Misdemeanor, Civil, Eviction, Small Claims, Probate.*

Civil Records: Access: In person only. Visitors must perform in person searches for themselves. No search fee. Required to search: name, years to search, address. Civil cases indexed by defendant, plaintiff. Civil records computerized since 1995, on index cards and docket books from 1800s.

Criminal Records: Access: In person only. Visitors must perform in person searches for themselves. No search fee. Required to search: name, years to search, DOB, SSN. Criminal records computerized since 1995, on index cards and docket books from 1800s.

General Information: No adoption, mental, juvenile, or sealed records released. Copy fee: $.25 per page. Certification fee: $5.00. Payee: Circuit Clerk. Personal checks accepted. Prepayment required.

Elliott County

Circuit & District Court Box 788, Sandy Hook, KY 41171; 606-738-5238; Fax: 606-738-6962. Hours: 8AM-4PM M-F; 9AM-Noon Sat (EST). *Felony, Misdemeanor, Civil, Eviction, Small Claims, Probate.*

Civil Records: Access: In person only. Both court and visitors may perform in person searches. No search fee. Required to search: name, years to search. Civil cases indexed by defendant, plaintiff. Civil records on computer since October 1992, prior records on index cards since 1978.

Criminal Records: Access: In person only. Both court and visitors may perform in person searches. No search fee. Required to search: name, years to search; also helpful: SSN. Criminal records on computer since October 1992, prior records on index cards since 1978. Mail requests for criminal searches may be made to the state AOC.

General Information: Public Access terminal is available. No adoption, mental, juvenile, or sealed records released. Will fax results for $2.00 1st page; $1.00 each add'l page (for specific case documents). Copy fee: $.25 per page. Certification fee: $5.00. Payee: Circuit Clerk. Personal checks accepted. Prepayment required.

Estill County

Circuit & District Court 130 Main St, Rm 207, Irvine, KY 40336; 606-723-3970; Fax: 606-723-1158. Hours: 8AM-4PM (EST). *Felony, Misdemeanor, Civil, Eviction, Small Claims, Probate.*

Civil Records: Access: Phone, fax, mail, in person. Both court and visitors may perform in person searches. No search fee. Required to search: name, years to search. Civil cases indexed by defendant, plaintiff. Civil records on index cards back to 1965; on computer back to 1994.

Criminal Records: Access: Phone, fax, mail, in person. Both court and visitors may perform in person searches. No search fee. Required to search: name, years to search, DOB, SSN. Criminal records on computer back to 1994.

General Information: Public Access terminal is available. No adoption, mental, juvenile, or sealed records released. Fee to fax results is $1.00 per page. Copy fee: $.25 per page. Certification fee: $5.00. Payee: Circuit Clerk. Personal checks accepted. Prepayment required. Mail requests: SASE required. Mail turnaround time 2-4 days.

Fayette County

Circuit Court - Criminal & Civil Divisions 120 N Limestone, Lexington, KY 40507; Civil phone: 859-246-2141; Criminal phone: 859-246-2224; Fax: 859-246-2146. Hours: 8:30AM-4:30PM (EST). *Felony, Civil Actions Over $4,000.*

Civil Records: Access: Mail, in person. Both court and visitors may perform in person searches. Search fee: $5.00 per name. Required to search: name, years to search. Civil cases indexed by defendant, plaintiff. Civil records on computer since April 1993, on index cards since 1978, prior records on books and archived.

Criminal Records: Access: Mail, in person. Both court and visitors may perform in person searches. Search fee: $5.00 per name. Required to search: name, years to search; also helpful: DOB, SSN. Criminal records on computer since April 1993, on index cards since 1978, prior records on books and archived.

General Information: Public Access terminal is available. No adoption, juvenile, mental, or sealed records released. Copy fee: $.25 per page. Certification fee: $5.00. Payee: Fayette County Circuit Clerk. No personal checks accepted. Prepayment required. Mail requests: SASE required. Mail turnaround time 1-2 days.

District Court - Criminal & Civil 150 N Limestone #D112, Lexington, KY 40507; Civil phone: 859-246-2240; Criminal phone: 859-246-2228. Hours: 8AM-4PM (EST). *Misdemeanor, Civil Actions Under $4,000, Eviction, Small Claims, Probate.*

Civil Records: Access: Mail, in person. Both court and visitors may perform in person searches. Search fee: $5.00 per name. Required to search: name, years to search. Civil cases indexed by defendant, plaintiff. Civil records on computer since 1992, prior records on index cards since 1977.

Criminal Records: Access: In person only. Visitors must perform in person searches for themselves. No search fee. Required to search: name, years to search, DOB; also helpful: SSN. Criminal records on computer since 1977.

General Information: Public Access terminal is available. No adoption, mental, juvenile, or sealed records released. Copy fee: $.25 per page. Certification fee: $1.00. Payee: District Clerk. Personal checks accepted. Prepayment required. Mail requests: SASE required. Mail turnaround: 3 days.

Fleming County

Circuit & District Court Courthouse 100 Court Square, Flemingsburg, KY 41041; 606-845-7011; Fax: 606-849-2400. Hours: 8AM-4:30PM (EST). *Felony, Misdemeanor, Civil, Eviction, Small Claims, Probate.*

Civil Records: Access: Phone, fax, mail, in person. Both court and visitors may perform in person searches. No search fee. Required to search: name, years to search. Civil cases indexed by defendant, plaintiff. Civil records on computer since May 1994, prior records on index cards since 1978.

Criminal Records: Access: In person only. Both court and visitors may perform in person searches. No search fee. Required to search: name, years to search, DOB; also helpful: SSN. Criminal records on computer since May 1994, prior records on index cards since 1978.

General Information: Public Access terminal is available. No adoption, mental, juvenile, or sealed records released. Fee to fax results is $1.00 per page. Copy fee: $.25 per page. Certification fee: $5.00. Payee: Circuit Clerk. Personal checks accepted. Prepayment required. Mail requests: SASE required. Mail turnaround time 1-2 days.

Floyd County

Circuit Court 127 S Lake Dr, Prestonsburg, KY 41653-3368; 606-886-3090; Civil phone: 606-886-2124; Criminal phone: 606-886-9114; Probate phone: 606-886-2124; Fax: 606-886-9075. Hours: 8AM-4PM (EST). *Felony, Civil Actions Over $4,000.*

Civil Records: Access: Mail, in person. Both court and visitors may perform in person searches. No search fee. Required to search: name, years to search. Civil cases indexed by defendant, plaintiff. Civil records on computer since September 1991, prior records on index cards since 1978.

Criminal Records: Access: Mail, in person. Both court and visitors may perform in person searches. No search fee. Required to search: name, years to search, DOB, SSN. Criminal records on computer since September 1991, prior records on index cards since 1978.

General Information: Public Access terminal is available. No adoption, mental, juvenile, or sealed records released. Will fax results for $2.00 1st page; $1.00 per add'l page. Copy fee: $.25 per page. Certification fee: $5.00. Payee: Clerk of Circuit Court. Personal checks accepted. Prepayment required. Mail

requests: SASE required. Mail turnaround time 2-4 days.

District Court 127 S Lake Dr, Prestonsburg, KY 41653; 606-886-9114. Hours: 8AM-4PM (EST). *Misdemeanor, Small Claims.*

Note: Small claims can be reached at 606-886-2124

Criminal Records: Access: Phone, mail, in person. Only the court performs in person searches; visitors may not. No search fee. Required to search: name, years to search; also helpful: SSN. Criminal records on computer since 1991, prior records in index cards since 1989. Records are only kept for five years in this office.

General Information: No adoption, mental, juvenile, or sealed records released. Copy fee: $.25 per page. Certification fee: $5.00. Payee: Floyd District Court. Personal checks accepted. Prepayment required. Mail requests: SASE required. Mail turnaround: 2-4 days.

Franklin County

Circuit Court Box 678 (214 St Clair St), Frankfort, KY 40602; 502-564-8380; Criminal phone: 502-573-2350/Adm; Fax: 502-564-8188. Hours: 8AM-4:30PM (EST). *Felony, Civil Actions Over $4,000.*

Note: Criminal records located at; 100 Mill Creek Park, Frankfort KY 40601- walkin 7am-3pm, or drive thru 7am -10pm

Civil Records: Access: In person. Visitors must perform in person searches for themselves. No search fee. Required to search: name, years to search. Civil cases indexed by defendant, plaintiff. Civil records on computer since 1990, prior records on index cards since 1978.

Criminal Records: Access: In person, mail. Visitors must perform in person searches for themselves. Search fee: $10.00 per name. Required to search: name, years to search, DOB, SSN. Criminal records on computer since 1990, prior records on index cards since 1978. All requests are referred to the state Administrator's Office of Courts.

General Information: No adoption, mental, juvenile, or sealed records released. Will fax results $15.00. Copy fee: $10.00. Payee: Circuit Clerk. Personal checks accepted. Prepayment required. Mail requests: SASE required. Mail turnaround time is 2-3 days.

District Court Box 678, Frankfort, KY 40601; 502-564-7013; Fax: 502-564-8188. Hours: 8AM-4:30PM (EST). *Misdemeanor, Civil Actions Under $4,000, Eviction, Small Claims, Probate.*

Civil Records: Access: In person only. Visitors must perform in person searches for themselves. No search fee. Required to search: name, years to search. Civil cases indexed by defendant, plaintiff. Civil records on computer since 1990, records on index cards since 1978, prior records archived.

Criminal Records: Access: In person only. Visitors must perform in person searches for themselves. No search fee. Required to search: name, years to search, DOB. Criminal records on computer since 1990, records on index cards since 1978, prior records archived.

General Information: Public Access terminal is available. No adoption, mental, juvenile, or sealed records released. Copy fee: $.25 per page. Certification fee: $5.00. Payee: Franklin Circuit Clerk. Personal checks accepted. Prepayment required.

Fulton County

Circuit & District Court Box 198, Hickman, KY 42050; 270-236-3944; Fax: 270-236-3729. Hours: 8AM-4PM (CST). *Felony, Misdemeanor, Civil, Eviction, Small Claims, Probate.*

Note: 6 days of the court docket information can be found at www.kycourts.com.

Civil Records: Access: Mail, in person. Both court and visitors may perform in person searches. No search fee. Required to search: name, years to search. Civil cases indexed by defendant, plaintiff. Civil records on index from 1980, computerized from 1995, and archived since 1843.

Criminal Records: Access: In person only. Visitors must perform in person searches for themselves. No search fee. Required to search: name, years to search. Criminal records on index from 1980, computerized from 1995, and archived since 1843.

General Information: Public Access terminal is available. No adoption, mental, juvenile, or sealed records released. Copy fee: $.25 per page. Certification fee: $5.00. Payee: Circuit Clerk. Personal checks accepted. Prepayment required. Mail requests: SASE required.

Gallatin County

Circuit Court Box 256 (100 Main St), Warsaw, KY 41095; 859-567-5241. Hours: 8AM-4:30PM M,T,Th,F; Closed W (EST). *Felony, Civil Actions Over $4,000.*

Civil Records: Access: Mail, in person. Both court and visitors may perform in person searches. No search fee. Required to search: name, years to search. Civil cases indexed by defendant, plaintiff. Civil records go back to 1990. Computerized records go to 1993.

Criminal Records: Access: Mail, in person. Both court and visitors may perform in person searches. No search fee. Required to search: name, years to search; also helpful: SSN. Criminal records go back to 1990. Computerized records to 1993.

General Information: Public Access terminal is available. No adoption, mental, juvenile, or sealed records released. Will fax results for $2.00 per page, $3.00 per document. Copy fee: $.25 per page. Certification fee: $5.00. Payee: Circuit Clerk. Personal checks accepted. Prepayment required. Mail requests: SASE required. Mail turnaround time 4 days.

District Court Box 256, Warsaw, KY 41095; 859-567-2388; Probate phone: 859-567-2388 x1. Hours: 8AM-4:30PM T,Th,F; 8AM-6PM M; 8AM-Noon Sat (EST). *Misdemeanor, Civil Actions Under $4,000, Eviction, Small Claims, Probate.*

Civil Records: Access: Mail, in person. Both court and visitors may perform in person searches. No search fee. Required to search: name, years to search. Civil cases indexed by defendant, plaintiff. Civil records on computer since November 1993, prior records on index cards since 1978.

Criminal Records: Access: Mail, in person. Both court and visitors may perform in person searches. No search fee. Required to search: name, years to search, DOB; also helpful: SSN. Criminal records on computer since November 1993, prior records on index cards since 1978.

General Information: Public Access terminal is available. No adoption, mental, juvenile, or sealed records released. Fee to fax results is $2.00 per page, $3.00 per document. Copy fee: $.25 per page. Certification fee: $5.00. Payee: District Clerk. Personal checks accepted. Prepayment required. Mail turnaround time 1-2 days.

Garrard County

Circuit & District Court 7 Public Square, Courthouse Annex, Lancaster, KY 40444; 859-792-6032; Fax: 859-792-6414. Hours: 8AM-4PM M,T,TH,F, 8AM-Noon Wed & Sat (EST). *Felony, Misdemeanor, Civil, Eviction, Small Claims, Probate.*

Note: Circuit Clerk can be reached at 859-792-2961.

Civil Records: Access: In person only. Visitors must perform in person searches for themselves. Search fee: none. Required to search: name, years to search. Civil cases indexed by defendant, plaintiff. Civil records in index since 1978.

Criminal Records: Access: In person only. Visitors must perform in person searches for themselves. No search fee. Required to search: name, years to search; also helpful: address, DOB, SSN. Criminal records in index since 1978.

General Information: Public Access terminal is available. No adoption, mental, juvenile, or sealed records released. Copy fee: $.25 per page. Certification fee: $5.00. Payee: Circuit Clerk. Personal checks accepted. Prepayment required.

Grant County

Circuit & District Court Courthouse 101 N Main, Williamstown, KY 41097; 859-824-4467 (Circuit) 859-823-5251 (District). Hours: 8AM-4PM (EST). *Felony, Misdemeanor, Civil, Eviction, Small Claims, Probate.*

Civil Records: Access: In person only. Visitors must perform in person searches for themselves. No search fee. Required to search: name, years to search. Civil cases indexed by defendant, plaintiff. Civil records on computer back to 1992, prior records on index cards for District Court since 1978; Circuit Court since 1988.

Criminal Records: Access: In person only. Visitors must perform in person searches for themselves. No search fee. Required to search: name, years to search, DOB; also helpful: SSN. Criminal records on computer back to 1992, prior records on index cards since 1988.

General Information: Public Access terminal is available. No adoption, mental, juvenile, or sealed records released. Will fax specific docket for $2.00 for 1st page; $1.00 each add'l page. Copy fee: $.25 per page. Certification fee: $5.00. Payee: Circuit Clerk. Personal checks accepted. Prepayment required.

Graves County

Circuit & District Court Courthouse 100 E Broadway, Mayfield, KY 42066; 270-247-1733; Fax: 270-247-7358. Hours: 8AM-4:30PM (CST). *Felony, Misdemeanor, Civil, Eviction, Small Claims, Probate.*

Civil Records: Access: In person only. Visitors must perform in person searches for themselves. No search fee. Required to search: name, years to search. Civil cases indexed by defendant, plaintiff. Civil records on computer since June, 1994, prior records on index cards since 1978.

Criminal Records: Access: In person only. Visitors must perform in person searches for themselves. No search fee. Required to search: name, years to search, DOB; also helpful: SSN. Criminal records on computer since June, 1994, prior records on index cards since 1978.

General Information: Public Access terminal is available. No adoption, mental, juvenile, or sealed records released. Will fax results $3.00 plus $1.00 per page if specific case docket requested. Copy fee: $.25 per page. Certification fee: $5.00. Payee: Circuit Clerk. Personal checks accepted. Prepayment required.

Grayson County

Circuit & District Court 125 E White Oak, Leitchfield, KY 42754; 270-259-3040; Fax: 270-259-9866. Hours: 8AM-5PM M-F (CST). *Felony, Misdemeanor, Civil, Eviction, Small Claims, Probate.*

Civil Records: Access: Mail, in person. Both court and visitors may perform in person searches. Search

fee: $10.00 per name. Required to search: name, years to search. Civil cases indexed by defendant, plaintiff. Civil records on computer since 05/94, prior records on index cards since 1978.

Criminal Records: Access: Mail, in person. Both court and visitors may perform in person searches. Search fee: $10.00. Required to search: name, years to search; also helpful: DOB, SSN. Criminal records on computer since 05/94, prior records on index cards since 1978.

General Information: Public Access terminal is available. No adoption, mental, juvenile, or sealed records released. Copy fee: $.25 per page. Certification fee: $5.00. Payee: Circuit Clerk. Personal checks accepted. Prepayment required. Mail requests: SASE required. Mail turnaround time 2 days.

Green County

Circuit & District Court 203 W Court St, Greensburg, KY 42743; 270-932-5631; Fax: 270-932-6468. Hours: 8AM-4PM M-W, F; 8AM-12:30PM Sat (EST). *Felony, Misdemeanor, Civil, Eviction, Small Claims, Probate.*

Civil Records: Access: Fax, mail, in person. Both court and visitors may perform in person searches. No search fee. Required to search: name, years to search; also helpful: address. Civil cases indexed by defendant, plaintiff. Civil records on index cards since 1978; computerized records since 1978.

Criminal Records: Access: Fax, mail, in person. Both court and visitors may perform in person searches. No search fee. Required to search: name, years to search; also helpful: address, DOB, SSN. Criminal records on index cards since 1978; computerized records since 1978.

General Information: Public Access terminal is available. No adoption, mental, juvenile, or sealed records released. No fee to fax results; will fax to toll-free numbers only. Copy fee: $.25 per page. No certification fee. Payee: Circuit Clerk. Personal checks accepted. Prepayment required. Mail requests: SASE required. Mail turnaround time 1-2 days.

Greenup County

Circuit & District Court Courthouse Annex, 301 Main St, Greenup, KY 41144; 606-473-9869; Fax: 606-473-7388. Hours: 9AM-4:30PM M-F (EST). *Felony, Misdemeanor, Civil, Eviction, Small Claims, Probate.*

Civil Records: Access: In person only. Both court and visitors may perform in person searches. No search fee. Required to search: name, years to search. Civil cases indexed by defendant, plaintiff. Civil records on computer since 1990, prior records on index cards since 1978.

Criminal Records: Access: In person only. Visitors must perform in person searches for themselves. No search fee. Required to search: name, years to search, DOB; also helpful: SSN. Criminal records on computer since 1990, prior records on index cards since 1978.

General Information: Public Access terminal is available. No adoption, mental, juvenile, or sealed records released. Copy fee: $.25 per page. Certification fee: $5.00. Payee: Circuit Clerk. Personal checks accepted. Prepayment required.

Hancock County

Circuit & District Court Courthouse, PO Box 250, Hawesville, KY 42348; 270-927-8144; Fax: 270-927-8629. Hours: 8AM-4PM M,T,W,F; 8AM-5:30PM Th (CST). *Felony, Misdemeanor, Civil, Eviction, Small Claims, Probate.*

Civil Records: Access: In person only. Both court and visitors may perform in person searches. No search fee. Required to search: name, years to search.

Civil cases indexed by defendant, plaintiff. Civil records on computer since August, 1994, prior records on index cards.

Criminal Records: Access: In person only. Both court and visitors may perform in person searches. No search fee. Required to search: name, years to search, DOB; also helpful: SSN. Criminal records on computer since August, 1994, prior records on index cards. Court recommends that you do searches through the state AOC in Frankfort.

General Information: Public Access terminal is available. No adoption, mental, juvenile, or sealed records released. Fee to fax specifc case file is $2.00 for 1st page; $1.00 each add'l. Copy fee: $.25 per page. Certification fee: $5.00. Payee: Circuit Clerk. Personal checks accepted. Prepayment required.

Hardin County

Circuit & District Court Hardin County Justice Center, 120 E Dixie Ave, Elizabethtown, KY 42701; 270-766-5000; Fax: 270-766-5243. Hours: 8AM-4:30PM; (EST). *Felony, Misdemeanor, Civil, Eviction, Small Claims, Probate.*

Civil Records: Access: In person only. Visitors must perform in person searches for themselves. No search fee. Required to search: name, years to search. Civil cases indexed by defendant, plaintiff. Civil records on computer since 03/28/94, prior records on index cards since 1978.

Criminal Records: Access: In person only. Visitors must perform in person searches for themselves. No search fee. Required to search: name, years to search, DOB. Criminal records on computer since 03/28/94, prior records on index cards since 1978.

General Information: Public Access terminal is available. No adoption, mental, juvenile, motor vehicle or sealed records released. Will fax specific document for $2.00 per page, payable in advance by money order only. Copy fee: $.25 per page. Certification fee: $5.00. Payee: Circuit Clerk. Money orders only accepted. Prepayment required.

Radcliff District Court 220 Freedom Way, Radcliff, KY 40160; 270-351-1299/4799; Fax: 270-351-1301. Hours: 8:30AM-12, 12:00-4PM (EST). *Probate, Eviction.*

Harlan County

Circuit & District Court Box 190, Harlan, KY 40831; 606-573-2680. Hours: 8AM-4:30PM (EST). *Felony, Misdemeanor, Civil, Eviction, Small Claims, Probate.*

Civil Records: Access: In person only. Visitors must perform in person searches for themselves. No search fee. Required to search: name, years to search. Civil cases indexed by defendant, plaintiff. Civil records on computer since August, 1991, on index cards since 1978, records prior to 1991 are archived in Frankfort.

Criminal Records: Access: In person only. Visitors must perform in person searches for themselves. No search fee. Required to search: name, years to search, DOB; also helpful: SSN. Criminal records on computer since August, 1991, on index cards since 1978, records prior to 1991 are archived in Frankfort.

General Information: Public Access terminal is available. No adoption, mental, juvenile, sealed or domestic violence records released. Copy fee: $.25 per page. Certification fee: $5.00. Payee: Circuit Clerk. Only local personal checks accepted. Prepayment required.

Harrison County

Circuit & District Court 115 Court St #1, Cynthiana, KY 41031; 859-234-1914; Fax: 859-234-6787. Hours: 8:30AM-4:30PM M-F, 9AM-12PM Sat (EST). *Felony, Misdemeanor, Civil, Eviction, Small Claims, Probate.*
Civil Records: Access: Mail, in person. Both court and visitors may perform in person searches. No search fee. Required to search: name, years to search. Civil cases indexed by defendant, plaintiff. Civil records on index cards since 1978 (circuit only); on computer back to 1995; others back to 1953.
Criminal Records: Access: In person only. Visitors must perform in person searches for themselves. No search fee. Required to search: name, years to search, DOB; also helpful: SSN. Criminal records on index cards since 1978 (circuit only); on computer back to 1995; others back to 1953.
General Information: Public Access terminal is available. No adoption, mental, juvenile, or sealed records released. Copy fee: $.25 per page. Certification fee: $5.00. Payee: Circuit Clerk. Personal checks accepted. Prepayment required. Mail requests: SASE required. Mail turnaround time 2-4 days.

Hart County

Circuit & District Court Box 248, Munfordville, KY 42765; 270-524-5181. Hours: 8AM-4PM M-F (CST). *Felony, Misdemeanor, Civil, Eviction, Small Claims, Probate.*
Civil Records: Access: In person only. Visitors must perform in person searches for themselves. No search fee. Required to search: name, years to search; also helpful: address. Civil cases indexed by defendant, plaintiff. Civil records on index cards since 1978, computerized since 03/95.
Criminal Records: Access: In person only. Visitors must perform in person searches for themselves. No search fee. Required to search: name, years to search, DOB, SSN; also helpful: address. Criminal records on index cards since 1978, computerized since 03/95.
General Information: Public Access terminal is available. No adoption, mental, juvenile, or sealed records released. Copy fee: $.25 per page. Certification fee: $5.00. Payee: Circuit Clerk. Business checks accepted. Prepayment required.

Henderson County

Circuit & District Court PO Box 675, Henderson, KY 42420; 270-826-2405/1566; Fax: 270-831-2710 (District). Hours: 8AM-6PM M; 8AM-4:30PM T-F (CST). *Felony, Civil Actions Over $4,000.*
Civil Records: Access: In person only. Visitors must perform in person searches for themselves. No search fee. Required to search: name, years to search. Civil cases indexed by defendant, plaintiff. Civil records on computer from March, 1991, records on index cards from 1978 to March, 1991.
Criminal Records: Access: In person only. Visitors must perform in person searches for themselves. No search fee. Required to search: name, years to search, DOB. Criminal records on computer from March, 1991, records on index cards from 1978 to March, 1991.
General Information: Public Access terminal is available. No adoption, mental, juvenile, or sealed records released. Copy fee: $.25 per page. Certification fee: $5.00. Payee: Circuit Clerk. Personal checks accepted. Prepayment required.

Henry County

Circuit & District Court PO Box 359 (30 Main St), New Castle, KY 40050; 502-845-7551; Fax: 502-845-2969. Hours: 8AM-4:30PM M-F (EST). *Felony, Misdemeanor, Civil, Eviction, Small Claims, Probate.*
Civil Records: Access: In person only. Visitors must perform in person searches for themselves. No search fee. Required to search: name, years to search. Civil cases indexed by defendant, plaintiff. Civil records on computer since May, 1994, records on docket books since 1800s.
Criminal Records: Access: In person only. Visitors must perform in person searches for themselves. No search fee. Required to search: name, years to search; also helpful: SSN. Criminal records on computer since May, 1994, records on docket books since 1800s.
General Information: Public Access terminal is available. No adoption, mental, juvenile, or sealed records released. Copy fee: $.25 per page. Certification fee: $5.00. Payee: Circuit Clerk. Personal checks accepted. Prepayment required.

Hickman County

Circuit & District Court 109 S Washington St, Clinton, KY 42031; 270-653-3901; Fax: 270-653-3989. Hours: 8AM-4PM (CST). *Felony, Misdemeanor, Civil, Eviction, Small Claims, Probate.*
Civil Records: Access: Mail, in person. Both court and visitors may perform in person searches. No search fee. Required to search: name, years to search. Civil cases indexed by defendant, plaintiff. Civil records on computer from 06/94 to present, on index from 1978 to 06/94. If court does search, request must be in writing.
Criminal Records: Access: Mail, in person. Both court and visitors may perform in person searches. No search fee. Required to search: name, years to search, DOB; also helpful: SSN. Criminal records on computer from 06/94 to present, on index from 1978 to 06/94. Requests must be in writing.
General Information: Public Access terminal is available. No adoption, mental, juvenile, or sealed records released. Fee to fax results is $2.00 1st pg; $1.00 each add'l. Copy fee: $.25 per page. Certification fee: $5.00. Payee: Circuit Clerk. Personal checks accepted. Prepayment required. Mail requests: SASE required. Mail turnaround time same day.

Hopkins County

Circuit & District Court Courthouse 30 S Main St, Madisonville, KY 42431; 270-824-7502; Fax: 270-824-7032. Hours: 7:30AM-4PM (CST). *Felony, Misdemeanor, Civil, Eviction, Small Claims, Probate.*
Civil Records: Access: In person only. Visitors must perform in person searches for themselves. No search fee. Required to search: name, years to search. Civil cases indexed by defendant, plaintiff. Civil records on computer back to 6/1991; on index cards from 1978 to 1991.
Criminal Records: Access: In person only. Visitors must perform in person searches for themselves. No search fee. Required to search: name, years to search, signed release; also helpful: DOB, SSN. Criminal records on computer back to 6/1991, on index cards from 1978 to 1991, archived since 1800s.
General Information: Public Access terminal is available. No adoption, mental, juvenile, or sealed records released. Copy fee: $.25 per page. Certification fee: $5.00. Payee: Circuit Clerk. Personal checks accepted. Prepayment required.

Jackson County

Circuit Court PO Box 84, McKee, KY 40447; 606-287-7783; Fax: 606-287-3277. Hours: 8AM-4PM M-F 8AM-Noon Sat (EST). *Felony, Civil Actions Over $4,000.*
Civil Records: Access: Fax, mail, in person. Both court and visitors may perform in person searches. No search fee. Required to search: name, years to search; also helpful: address. Civil cases indexed by defendant, plaintiff. Civil records on computer from May, 1993 to present, on index cards from 1978 to 1993.
Criminal Records: Access: Fax, mail, in person. Both court and visitors may perform in person searches. No search fee. Required to search: name, years to search, DOB; also helpful: SSN. Criminal records on computer from May, 1993 to present, on index cards from 1990 to 1993.
General Information: Public Access terminal is available. No adoption, mental, juvenile, or sealed records released. Fee to fax results is $1.00 per page. Copy fee: $.25 per page. Certification fee: $5.00. Payee: Jackson County Circuit Clerk. Personal checks accepted. Prepayment required. Mail requests: SASE required. Mail turnaround time 2 days.

District Court PO Box 84, McKee, KY 40447; 606-287-8651; Fax: 606-287-3277. Hours: 8AM-4PM M-F; 8AM-Noon Sat (EST). *Misdemeanor, Civil Actions Under $4,000, Eviction, Small Claims, Probate.*
Civil Records: Access: Fax, mail, in person. Both court and visitors may perform in person searches. No search fee. Required to search: name, years to search. Civil cases indexed by defendant, plaintiff. Civil records on computer back to May, 1993, on index cards from 1978.
Criminal Records: Access: Fax, mail, in person. Both court and visitors may perform in person searches. No search fee. Required to search: name, years to search, DOB; also helpful: SSN. Criminal records on computer back to May, 1993; on index cards from 1990.
General Information: Public Access terminal is available. No adoption, mental, juvenile, or sealed records released. Copy fee: $.25 per page. Certification fee: $5.00. Payee: Jackson County District Clerk. Personal checks accepted. Prepayment required. Mail requests: SASE required. Mail turnaround time 1 week.

Jefferson County

Circuit & District Court Hall of Justice 600 W Jefferson St, Louisville, KY 40202; 502-595-3064; Civil phone: 502-595-3015; Criminal phone: 502-595-3042; Fax: 502-595-4629. *Felony, Misdemeanor, Civil, Eviction, Small Claims, Probate.*
Civil Records: Access: Phone, mail, in person. Visitors must perform in person searches for themselves. No search fee. Required to search: name, years to search. Civil cases indexed by defendant, plaintiff. Civil records on computer from 1988 to present, on index cards from 1978 to 1988.
Criminal Records: Access: Mail, in person. Visitors must perform in person searches for themselves. No search fee. Required to search: name, years to search; also helpful: DOB, SSN. Criminal records on computer from 1988 to present, on index cards from 1978 to 1988.
General Information: Public Access terminal is available. No adoption, mental, juvenile, or sealed records released. Copy fee: $.25 per page. Certification fee: $5.00. Payee: Circuit Clerk. Personal checks accepted. Credit cards accepted for District

Criminal Traffic. Prepayment required. Mail requests: SASE not required. Mail turnaround time 3 days.

Jessamine County

Circuit Court 107 N Main St, Nicholasville, KY 40356; 859-885-4531. Hours: 8AM-4:30PM M-W, F; 8AM-12PM TH (EST). *Felony, Civil Actions Over $4,000.*
Civil Records: Access: Mail, in person. Visitors must perform in person searches for themselves. No search fee. Required to search: name, years to search. Civil cases indexed by defendant, plaintiff. Civil records on computer from June, 1992 to present, on index cards from 1978 to 1992.
Criminal Records: Access: Mail, in person. Visitors must perform in person searches for themselves. No search fee. Required to search: name, years to search, DOB; also helpful: SSN. Criminal records on computer from June, 1992 to present, on index cards from 1978 to 1992.
General Information: Public Access terminal is available. No adoption, mental, juvenile, or sealed records released. Copy fee: $.25 per page. Certification fee: $5.00. Payee: Jessamine Circuit Clerk. Personal checks accepted. Prepayment required. Mail requests: SASE required. Mail turnaround time 1-2 days.

District Court 107 N Main St, Nicholasville, KY 40356; 859-887-1005; Fax: 859-887-0425. Hours: 8AM-4:30PM M-W; 8AM-Noon TH; 8AM-4:30PM F (EST). *Misdemeanor, Civil Actions Under $4,000, Eviction, Small Claims, Probate.*
Civil Records: Access: Mail, in person. Both court and visitors may perform in person searches. No search fee. Required to search: name, years to search. Civil cases indexed by defendant, plaintiff. Civil records on computer since 1992, on file cards prior.
Criminal Records: Access: Mail, in person. Both court and visitors may perform in person searches. No search fee. Required to search: name, years to search; also helpful: DOB, SSN. Criminal records on computer since 1992, on file cards prior.
General Information: Public Access terminal is available. No adoption, mental, juvenile, or sealed records released. Copy fee: $.25 per page. Certification fee: $5.00. Payee: District Clerk. Personal checks accepted. Prepayment required. Mail requests: SASE required. Mail turnaround: 2-4 days.

Johnson County

Circuit & District Court Box 1405, Paintsville, KY 41240; 606-789-5181; Fax: 606-789-4192. Hours: 8AM-4:30PM; 8:30AM-Noon Sat Driver's license only (EST). *Felony, Misdemeanor, Civil, Eviction, Small Claims, Probate.*
Civil Records: Access: Phone, mail, in person. Visitors must perform in person searches for themselves. No search fee. Required to search: name, years to search. Civil cases indexed by defendant, plaintiff. Civil records on computer since 09/88, on index cards from 1978 to 1988, books from 1843 to 1978. From 1988 and prior files are at the archives in Frankfort.
Criminal Records: Access: In person only. Visitors must perform in person searches for themselves. No search fee. Required to search: name, years to search, DOB, SSN. Criminal records on computer since 09/88, on index cards from 1978 to 1988, books from 1843 to 1978. From 1988 and prior files are at the archives in Frankfort. Court will not conduct searches. Contact AOC for statewide search by mail.
General Information: Public Access terminal is available. No adoption, mental, juvenile, or sealed records released. Copy fee: $.25 per page. Certification fee: $5.00. Payee: Circuit Clerk. Personal

checks accepted. Prepayment required. Mail requests: SASE required. Mail turnaround time at least 3 days.

Kenton County

Circuit Court 230 Madison Ave (PO Box 669), Covington, KY 41011; 859-292-6521; Fax: 859-292-6611. Hours: 8AM-5PM (EST). *Felony, Civil Actions Over $4,000.*
www.aoc.state.ky.us/kenton
Civil Records: Access: Mail, in person. Both court and visitors may perform in person searches. Search fee: none. Required to search: name, years to search. Civil cases indexed by defendant, plaintiff. Civil records on computer back to 06/89, on index cards from 1800s.
Criminal Records: Access: In person only. Visitors must perform in person searches for themselves. No search fee. Required to search: name, years to search, DOB or SSN. Criminal records on computer back to 6/89.
General Information: Public Access terminal is available. No adoption, mental, juvenile, or sealed records released. Will not fax results. Copy fee: $.25 per page. Video of hearings are $15.00, turnaround time 7-14 days. Certification fee: $5.00. Payee: Kenton Circuit Clerk. Prepayment required. Mail requests: SASE required. Mail turnaround time 1-2 days.

District Court 230 Madison Ave, 3rd Fl, Covington, KY 41011; 859-292-6523; Fax: 859-292-6611. 7AM-5PM (EST). *Misdemeanor, Civil Actions Under $4,000, Eviction, Small Claims, Probate.*
www.aoc.state.ky.us/kenton
Civil Records: Access: Mail, in person. Only the court performs in person searches; visitors may not. No search fee. Required to search: name, years to search. Civil cases indexed by defendant, plaintiff. Civil records on computer from 1991 to present, on index cards from 1985.
Criminal Records: Access: In person only. Visitors must perform in person searches for themselves. No search fee. Required to search: name, years to search DOB; also helpful: SSN. Criminal records on computer from 05/91 to present, index cards held since 1996.
General Information: Public Access terminal is available. No adoption, mental, juvenile, or sealed records released. Fee to fax results is $3.00 per document. Copy fee: $.25 per page. Certification fee: $5.00. Payee: District Clerk. Business checks accepted. Prepayment required. Mail requests: SASE required. Mail turnaround time 1 week.

Knott County

Circuit & District Court PO Box 1317, Hindman, KY 41822; 606-785-5021. Hours: 8AM-4PM; 8AM-noon Sat. (EST). *Felony, Misdemeanor, Civil, Eviction, Small Claims, Probate.*
Civil Records: Access: Fax, mail, in person. Visitors must perform in person searches for themselves. No search fee. Required to search: name, years to search. Civil cases indexed by defendant, plaintiff. Civil records in index files, computerized since 11/94.
Criminal Records: Access: Phone, fax, mail, in person. Visitors must perform in person searches themselves. No search fee. Required to search: name, years to search, DOB; also helpful: SSN. Criminal records in index files; on computer back to 11/1994.
General Information: Public Access terminal is available. No adoption, mental, juvenile, or sealed records released. Will fax results to local or toll free line. Copy fee: $.25 per page. Certification fee: $5.00. Payee: Circuit Clerk. Personal checks accepted. Prepayment required. Mail requests: SASE required. Mail turnaround time 2-4 days.

Knox County

Circuit & District Court PO Box 760 (401 Court Sq #202, Barbourville, KY 40906; 606-546-3075 (Circuit) 546-3232 (Dist); Fax: 606-546-7949. Hours: 8AM-4:30PM M-F; 8:30AM-noon Sat (EST). *Felony, Misdemeanor, Civil, Eviction, Small Claims, Probate.*
Civil Records: Access: In person only. Visitors must perform in person searches for themselves. No search fee. Required to search: name, years to search. Civil cases indexed by defendant, plaintiff. Civil records go back to 1978; on computer back to 07/92.
Criminal Records: Access: In person only. Visitors must perform in person searches for themselves. No search fee. Required to search: name, years to search, DOB; also helpful: SSN. Criminal records go back to 1978; on computer back to 07/92.
General Information: Public Access terminal is available. No adoption, mental, juvenile, or sealed records released. Copy fee: $.25 per page. Certification fee: $5.00. Payee: Circuit Clerk. Personal checks accepted. Prepayment required.

Larue County

Circuit & District Court Courthouse Annex, PO Box 191 (209 W High St), Hodgenville, KY 42748; 270-358-3421; Fax: 270-358-3731. Hours: 8AM-4PM (EST). *Felony, Misdemeanor, Civil, Eviction, Small Claims, Probate.*
Civil Records: Access: In person only. Both court and visitors may perform in person searches. No search fee. Required to search: name, years to search. Civil cases indexed by defendant, plaintiff. Civil records on computer since 1995.
Criminal Records: Access: In person only. Both court and visitors may perform in person searches. No search fee. Required to search: name, years to search, DOB; also helpful: SSN. Criminal records on computer since 1995.
General Information: Public Access terminal is available. No adoption, mental, juvenile, or sealed records released. No fee to fax results. Copy fee: $.25 per page. No certification fee. Payee: Circuit Clerk. Personal checks accepted. Prepayment required.

Laurel County

Circuit & District Court Box 1798, London, KY 40743-1798; 606-864-2863; Fax: 606-864-8264. Hours: 8AM-4:30PM (EST). *Felony, Misdemeanor, Civil, Eviction, Small Claims, Probate.*
Civil Records: Access: In person only. Visitors must perform in person searches for themselves. No search fee. Required to search: name, years to search. Civil cases indexed by defendant, plaintiff. Civil records on computer from 07/94, and index books from 1992.
Criminal Records: Access: In person only. Visitors must perform in person searches for themselves. No search fee. Required to search: name, years to search, DOB, SSN. Criminal records on computer from 07/94, and index books from 1987.
General Information: Public Access terminal is available. No adoption, mental, juvenile, or sealed records released. Copy fee: $.25 per page. Certification fee: $5.00. Payee: Circuit Clerk. Personal checks accepted. Prepayment required.

Lawrence County

Circuit & District Court Courthouse, PO Box 212, Louisa, KY 41230; 606-638-4215; Fax: 606-638-0264. Hours: 8:30AM-4:30PM M-F, 8:30AM-Noon Sat (EST). *Felony, Misdemeanor, Civil, Eviction, Small Claims, Probate.*
Note: Current docket information is online on the statewide system at www.dockets.kycourts.net.

Civil Records: Access: Mail, fax, in person. Both court and visitors may perform in person searches. No search fee. Required to search: name, years to search. Civil cases indexed by defendant, plaintiff. Civil records on computer from 11/94, index cards from 1978.

Criminal Records: Access: Mail, in person. Both court and visitors may perform in person searches. No search fee. Required to search: name, years to search; also helpful: DOB, SSN. Criminal records on computer from 11/94, index cards from 1978.

General Information: Public Access terminal is available. No adoption, mental, juvenile, or sealed records released. Fee to fax results is $2.00 per page. Copy fee: $.25 per page. Certification fee: $5.00. Payee: Circuit Clerk. Personal checks accepted. Prepayment required. Mail requests: SASE required. Mail turnaround time within 1 week.

Lee County

Circuit & District Court Box E, Beattyville, KY 41311; 606-464-8400; Fax: 606-464-0144. Hours: 8AM-4PM M-F; 8:30AM-11:30AM Sat (EST). *Felony, Misdemeanor, Civil, Eviction, Small Claims, Probate.*

Civil Records: Access: In person only. Visitors must perform in person searches for themselves. No search fee. Required to search: name, years to search. Civil cases indexed by defendant, plaintiff. Civil records on computer from 09/94 to present, on index cards from 1978.

Criminal Records: Access: In person only. Visitors must perform in person searches for themselves. No search fee. Required to search: name, years to search, DOB; also helpful: SSN. Criminal records on computer from 09/94 to present, on index cards from 1978.

General Information: Public Access terminal is available. No adoption, mental, juvenile, or sealed records released. Copy fee: $.25 per page. Certification fee: $5.00. Payee: Circuit Clerk. Only cashiers checks, money orders and attorney checks accepted. Prepayment required.

Leslie County

Circuit & District Court Box 1750, Hyden, KY 41749; 606-672-2505; Fax: 606-672-5128. Hours: 8AM-4PM M-gaF; 8AM-Noon Sat (EST). *Felony, Misdemeanor, Civil, Eviction, Small Claims, Probate.*

Civil Records: Access: In person. Visitors must perform in person searches for themselves. No search fee. Required to search: name, years to search. Civil cases indexed by plaintiff. Civil records on computer and index books.

Criminal Records: Access: In person only. Visitors must perform in person searches for themselves. No search fee. Required to search: name, years to search; also helpful: address, DOB, SSN. Criminal records on computer and index books.

General Information: Public Access terminal is available. No adoption, mental, juvenile, or sealed records released. Copy fee: $.25 per page. Certification fee: $5.00. Payee: Circuit Clerk. Personal checks accepted. Prepayment required.

Letcher County

Circuit & District Court 156 W Main St, #201, Whitesburg, KY 41858; 606-633-7559/8810; Fax: 606-633-5864. Hours: 8:30AM-4PM M-F; 8:30AM-12PM first Sat of month (EST). *Felony, Misdemeanor, Civil, Eviction, Small Claims, Probate.*

Civil Records: Access: Fax, mail, in person. Both court and visitors may perform in person searches. Search fee: none. Required to search: name, years to

search; also helpful: address. Civil cases indexed by defendant, plaintiff. Civil records on computer go back to 11/1991; on index books from 1986 to 1991. Files maintained in office. Records from 1985 to 1800s in archives in Frankfort.

Criminal Records: Access: In person only. Visitors must perform in person searches for themselves. Search fee: none. Required to search: name, years to search, DOB, SSN; also helpful: address. Criminal records on computer go back to 11/1991; on index cards from 1986 to 1991. Files maintained in office. Records from 1985 to 1800s in archives in Frankfort. Contact AOC 800-928-6381 for statewide search by mail.

General Information: Public Access terminal is available. No adoption, mental, juvenile, or sealed records released. Fee to fax results is $2.00 1st page, $1.00 each add'l. Copy fee: $.25 per page. Certification fee: $5.00. Payee: Circuit Clerk. Personal checks accepted. Prepayment required. Mail requests: SASE required. Mail turnaround time 2-4 days.

Lewis County

Circuit & District Court PO Box 70, Vanceburg, KY 41179; 606-796-3053; Fax: 606-796-3030. Hours: 8AM-4:30PM M,T,Th,F 8:30-Noon W,Sat (EST). *Felony, Misdemeanor, Civil, Eviction, Small Claims, Probate.*

Civil Records: Access: Phone, mail, in person. Both court and visitors may perform in person searches. No search fee. Required to search: name, years to search. Civil cases indexed by defendant, plaintiff. Computerized from 1994, civil records on index cards back to 1955.

Criminal Records: Access: Mail, in person. Both court and visitors may perform in person searches. No search fee. Required to search: name, years to search, DOB; also helpful: SSN. Computerized from 1994, criminal records on index cards back to 1960s.

General Information: Public Access terminal is available. No adoption, mental, juvenile, or sealed records released. Copy fee: $.25 per page. Certification fee: $5.00. Payee: Circuit Clerk. Personal checks accepted. Prepayment required. Mail requests: SASE required. Mail turnaround time within 1 week.

Lincoln County

Circuit & District Court 101 E Main, Stanford, KY 40484; 606-365-2535; Fax: 606-365-3389. Hours: 8AM-4PM; 9AM-12PM Sat. (EST). *Felony, Misdemeanor, Civil, Eviction, Small Claims, Probate.*

Civil Records: Access: In person only. Visitors must perform in person searches for themselves. No search fee. Required to search: name, years to search. Civil cases indexed by defendant, plaintiff. Civil records on computer from 05/94, index cards prior, archived from 1978 to 1900.

Criminal Records: Access: In person only. Visitors must perform in person searches for themselves. No search fee. Required to search: name, years to search; also helpful: SSN. Criminal records on computer from 05/94, index cards prior, archived from 1978 to 1900.

General Information: Public Access terminal is available. No adoption, mental, juvenile, or sealed records released. Copy fee: $.25 per page. No certification fee. Payee: Circuit Clerk. Personal checks accepted. Prepayment required.

Livingston County

Circuit & District Court PO Box 160, Smithland, KY 42081; 270-928-2172. 8AM-6PM M 8AM-4PM T-F (CST). *Felony, Misdemeanor, Civil, Eviction, Small Claims, Probate.*

Civil Records: Access: In person only. Visitors must perform in person searches for themselves. No search

fee. Required to search: name, years to search. Civil cases indexed by defendant, plaintiff. Civil records on computer from 1993 to present, index cards prior, archived from 1799 to 1851.

Criminal Records: Access: In person only. Visitors must perform in person searches for themselves. No search fee. Required to search: name, years to search, DOB; also helpful: SSN. Criminal records on computer from 1993 to present, index cards prior, archived from 1799 to 1851.

General Information: Public Access terminal is available. No adoption, mental, juvenile, or sealed records released. Copy fee: $.25 per page. Certification fee: $5.00. Payee: Circuit Clerk. Personal checks accepted. Prepayment required.

Logan County

Circuit Court Box 420 (W 4th St), Russellville, KY 42276-0420; 270-726-2424; Fax: 270-726-7893. Hours: 8AM-4:30PM M-Th; 8AM-5PM F (CST). *Felony, Civil Actions Over $4,000.*

Civil Records: Access: In person only. Visitors must perform in person searches for themselves. No search fee. Required to search: name, years to search. Civil cases indexed by defendant, plaintiff. Civil records on computer from April, 1992 to present, on index card from 1978 to 1992.

Criminal Records: Access: In person only. Visitors must perform in person searches for themselves. No search fee. Required to search: name, years to search, DOB, SSN. Criminal records on computer from April, 1992 to present, on index card from 1978 to 1992.

General Information: Public Access terminal is available. No adoptions, mental, juvenile or sealed records released. Copy fee: $.25 per page. Certification fee: $5.00. Payee: Circuit Clerk. Only cashiers checks and money orders accepted. Prepayment required.

District Court Box 420, Russellville, KY 42276; 270-726-3107; Fax: 270-726-7893. Hours: 8AM-4:30PM (CST). *Misdemeanor, Civil Actions Under $4,000, Eviction, Small Claims, Probate.*

Civil Records: Access: In person only. Visitors must perform in person searches for themselves. No search fee. Required to search: name, years to search. Civil cases indexed by defendant, plaintiff. Civil records on computer since 1992, index cards from 1978 to 1992.

Criminal Records: Access: In person only. Visitors must perform in person searches for themselves. No search fee. Required to search: name, years to search, DOB; also helpful: SSN. Criminal records on computer since 1992, index cards from 1978 to 1991.

General Information: Public Access terminal is available. No adoption, mental, juvenile, or sealed records released. Copy fee: $.25 per page. Certification fee: $5.00. Payee: Logan District Court. Personal checks accepted. Prepayment required.

Lyon County

Circuit & District Court Box 565, Eddyville, KY 42038; 270-388-7231. Hours: 8AM-4PM (CST). *Felony, Misdemeanor, Civil, Eviction, Small Claims, Probate.*

Note: This court also handles domestic violence, traffic, and juvenile cases.

Civil Records: Access: In person only. Visitors must perform in person searches for themselves. No search fee. Required to search: name, years to search. Civil cases indexed by defendant, plaintiff. Civil records on computer from 11/94 to present, on index cards from 1978 to 1994.

Criminal Records: Access: In person only. Visitors must perform in person searches for themselves. No search fee. Required to search: name, years to search,

DOB; also helpful: SSN. Criminal records on computer from 11/94 to present. Circuit court records are on index cards from 1978 to 1994, but not District court records.

General Information: Public Access terminal is available. No adoption, mental, juvenile, or sealed records released. Copy fee: $.25 per page. Certification fee: $5.00. Payee: Circuit Clerk. Personal checks not accepted. Prepayment required.

Madison County

Circuit Court PO Box 813 (101 W Main St), Madison County Courthouse, Richmond, KY 40476-0813; 859-624-4793. Hours: 8AM-4PM (EST). *Felony, Civil Actions Over $4,000.*
www.kycourts.net/Circuit/Circuit_Intro.shtm
Civil Records: Access: In person only. Visitors must perform in person searches for themselves. Search fee: none. Required to search: name, years to search. Civil cases indexed by defendant, plaintiff. Civil records on computer back to 10/1990 to present, on index cards from 1978 to 1990.
Criminal Records: Access: In person only. Visitors must perform in person searches for themselves. No search fee. Required to search: name, years to search; also helpful: DOB, SSN. Criminal records on computer back to 10/1990 to present, on index cards from 1978 to 1990. Contact AOC for statewide searches by mail.
General Information: Public Access terminal is available. No adoption, mental, juvenile, or sealed records released. Copy fee: $.25 per page. Certification fee: $5.00. Payee: Circuit Clerk. Personal checks accepted. Prepayment required.

District Court Madison Hall of Justice, 351 West Main St, Richmond, KY 40475; 859-624-4722; Fax: 859-624-4746. Hours: 8AM-4PM (EST). *Misdemeanor, Civil Actions Under $4,000, Eviction, Small Claims, Probate.*
Civil Records: Access: Fax, mail, in person. Visitors must perform in person searches themselves. No search fee. Required to search: name, years to search. Civil cases indexed by defendant, plaintiff. Civil records go back to 11/90; computerized records go back to 11/90.
Criminal Records: Access: In person only. Visitors must perform in person searches themselves. No search fee. Required to search: name, years to search, DOB; also helpful: SSN. Criminal records go back to 11/90; computerized records go back to 11/90.
General Information: Public Access terminal is available. No adoption, mental, juvenile, or sealed records released. Fee to fax results is $2.00 per page. Copy fee: $.25 per page. Certification fee: $5.00. Payee: District Court. Personal checks accepted. Prepayment required. Mail requests: SASE required. Mail turnaround time 1 week.

Magoffin County

Circuit & District Court Box 147, Salyersville, KY 41465; 606-349-2215; Fax: 606-349-2209. Hours: 8AM-4PM (EST). *Felony, Misdemeanor, Civil, Eviction, Small Claims, Probate.*
Civil Records: Access: Fax, mail, in person. Both court and visitors may perform in person searches. No search fee. Required to search: name, years to search. Civil cases indexed by defendant, plaintiff. Civil records on computer from March, 1993 to present, on index cards from 1978 to 1993. Cases before 1990 are in archives.
Criminal Records: Access: Fax, mail, in person. Both court and visitors may perform in person searches. No search fee. Required to search: name, years to search, DOB; also helpful: SSN. Criminal records on computer from March, 1993 to present, on

index cards from 1978 to 1993. Cases before 1990 are in archives.
General Information: Public Access terminal is available. No adoption, mental, juvenile, or sealed records released. Fee to fax results is $2.00 for 1st page, $1.00 each add'l. Copy fee: $.25 per page. Certification fee: $5.00; Seal $1.00 extra. Payee: Circuit Clerk. Personal checks accepted. Prepayment required. Mail requests: SASE required. Mail turnaround time 3 days.

Marion County

Circuit & District Court 120 W Main St, #6, Lebanon, KY 40033; 270-692-2681. Hours: 8:30AM-4:30PM M-F; 8:30AM-Noon Sat (EST). *Felony, Misdemeanor, Civil, Eviction, Small Claims, Probate.*
Civil Records: Access: In person only. Visitors must perform in person searches for themselves. No search fee. Required to search: name, years to search. Civil cases indexed by defendant, plaintiff. Civil records on computer from May, 1993 to present, on index cards from 1978 to 1993.
Criminal Records: Access: In person only. Visitors must perform in person searches for themselves. No search fee. Required to search: name, years to search; also helpful: SSN. Criminal records on computer from May, 1993 to present, on index cards from 1978 to 1993.
General Information: Public Access terminal is available. No adoption, mental, juvenile, or sealed records released. Copy fee: $.25 per page. Certification fee: $5.00. Payee: Circuit Clerk. Personal checks accepted. Prepayment required.

Marshall County

Circuit & District Court 80 Judicial Dr, Unit #101, Benton, KY 42025; 270-527-3883/1721; Fax: 270-527-5865. Hours: 8AM-4:30PM (CST). *Felony, Misdemeanor, Civil, Eviction, Small Claims, Probate.*
Civil Records: Access: Phone, fax, mail, in person. Both court and visitors may perform in person searches. No search fee. Required to search: name, years to search. Civil cases indexed by defendant, plaintiff. Civil records on computer since August, 1992 to present, on index books from 1978 to 1992.
Criminal Records: Access: Phone, fax, mail, in person. Both court and visitors may perform in person searches. No search fee. Required to search: name, years to search, DOB; also helpful: SSN. Criminal records on computer since August, 1992 to present, on index books from 1978 to 1992.
General Information: Public Access terminal is available. No adoption, mental, juvenile, or sealed records released. Fee to fax results is $2.00 for 1st page, $1.00 each add'l. Copy fee: $.25 per page. Certification fee: $5.00. Payee: Circuit Clerk. Personal checks accepted. Prepayment required. Mail requests: SASE required. Mail turnaround time 3 days.

Martin County

Circuit & District Court Box 430, Inez, KY 41224; 606-298-3508; Fax: 606-298-4202. Hours: 8AM-4PM except 1st & 3rd Th 8AM-7PM (EST). *Felony, Misdemeanor, Civil, Eviction, Small Claims, Probate.*
Civil Records: Access: Mail, in person. Both court and visitors may perform in person searches. No search fee. Required to search: name, years to search. Civil cases indexed by defendant, plaintiff. Civil records on computer since April, 1994, District on index books since 1987, Circuit on index books since 1978, prior records on docket books.
Criminal Records: Access: In person only. Visitors must perform in person searches for themselves. No

search fee. Required to search: name, years to search; also helpful: DOB, SSN. Criminal records on computer since April, 1994, District on index books since 1987, Circuit on index books since 1978, prior records on docket books.
General Information: Public Access terminal is available. No adoption, mental, juvenile, or sealed records released. Copy fee: $.25 per page. Return postage required. Certification fee: $5.00. Payee: Circuit Clerk. Personal checks accepted. Prepayment required.

Mason County

Circuit Court 100 W 3rd St, Maysville, KY 41056; 606-564-4340; Fax: 606-564-0932. Hours: 8:30AM-4:30PM (EST). *Felony, Civil Actions Over $4,000.*
Civil Records: Access: In person only. Visitors must perform in person searches for themselves. Search fee: none. Required to search: name, years to search. Civil cases indexed by defendant, plaintiff. Civil records on computer back to 4/1994, records on index books since 1929, prior records archived from 1798.
Criminal Records: Access: In person only. Visitors must perform in person searches for themselves. Search fee: none. Required to search: name, years to search, DOB. Criminal records on computer back to 4/1994, records on index books since 1929, prior records archived from 1798.
General Information: Public Access terminal is available. No adoption, mental, juvenile, or sealed records released. Copy fee: $.25 per page. Certification fee: $5.00. Payee: Kentucky State Treasurer. Personal checks or money order accepted. Prepayment required.

District Court 100 W 3rd St, Maysville, KY 41056; 606-564-4011; Fax: 606-564-0932. Hours: 8:30AM-4:30PM (EST). *Misdemeanor, Civil Actions Under $4000, Eviction, Small Claims, Probate.*
Civil Records: Access: In person only. Visitors must perform in person searches for themselves. No search fee. Required to search: name, years to search. Civil cases indexed by defendant, plaintiff. Civil records on computer since April, 1994, prior records on index books from 1994.
Criminal Records: Access: In person only. Visitors must perform in person searches for themselves. No search fee. Required to search: name, years to search. Criminal records on computer since April, 1994, prior records on index books from 1983.
General Information: Public Access terminal is available. No adoption, mental, juvenile, or sealed records released. Copy fee: $.25 per page. Certification fee: $5.00. Payee: KY State Treasurer. Personal checks accepted. Prepayment required.

McCracken County

Circuit Court Box 1455 (301 S 6th St), Paducah, KY 42002-1455; 270-575-7280. Hours: 8:30AM-4:30PM M, 8:30AM-4:30PM T-F (CST). *Felony, Civil Actions Over $4,000.* Note: Visitors may only search from 2PM-4PM on Thursday.
Civil Records: Access: In person. Both court and visitors may perform in person searches. No search fee. Required to search: name, years to search. Civil cases indexed by defendant, plaintiff. Civil records on computer since September 1991, prior records on index cards since 1978.
Criminal Records: Access: In person. Both court and visitors may perform in person searches. No search fee. Required to search: name, years to search; also helpful: DOB, SSN. Criminal records on computer since September 1991, prior records on index cards since 1978.
General Information: Public Access terminal is available. No adoption, mental, juvenile, or sealed

records released. Copy fee: $.25 per page. Certification fee: $5.00. Payee: Circuit Clerk. Personal checks accepted. Prepayment required.

District Court Box 1436, Paducah, KY 42002; 270-575-7270. Hours: 8:30AM-4:30PM (CST). *Misdemeanor, Civil Actions Under $4,000, Eviction, Small Claims, Probate.*

Civil Records: Access: In person only. Visitors must perform in person searches for themselves. No search fee. Required to search: name, years to search. Civil cases indexed by defendant, plaintiff. Civil records on computer since 09/91, on index books since 1978, prior records archived from the 1900s. Visitors may search only from 2PM to 4PM on Thursday.

Criminal Records: Access: In person only. Visitors must perform in person searches for themselves. No search fee. Required to search: name, years to search; also helpful: SSN. Criminal records on computer since 09/91, on index books since 1982, prior records archived from the 1900s.

General Information: Public Access terminal is available. No adoption, mental, juvenile, or sealed records released. Copy fee: $.25 per page. Certification fee: $5.00. Payee: District Clerk. Personal checks accepted. Prepayment required.

McCreary County

Circuit & District Court Box 40, Whitley City, KY 42653; 606-376-5041; Fax: 606-376-8844. 8;30AM-4:30PM (EST). *Felony, Misdemeanor, Civil, Eviction, Small Claims, Probate.*

Civil Records: Access: Mail, in person. Both court and visitors may perform in person searches. No search fee. Required to search: name, years to search; also helpful: address. Civil cases indexed by defendant, plaintiff. Civil records go back to 1992; on computer back to 1995.

Criminal Records: Access: In person only. Both court and visitors may perform in person searches. No search fee. Required to search: name, years to search, DOB, SSN; also helpful: address. Criminal records go back to 1992; on computer back to 1995.

General Information: Public Access terminal is available. No adoption, mental, juvenile, or sealed records released. Copy fee: $.25 per page. Certification fee: $5.00 per document. Payee: Circuit Clerk. Personal checks accepted. Prepayment required.

McLean County

Circuit & District Court Box 145 (210 E Main St), Calhoun, KY 42327; 270-273-3966; Fax: 270-273-5918. Hours: 8AM-4:30PM M-F; open till 6PM F (CST). *Felony, Misdemeanor, Civil, Eviction, Small Claims, Probate.*

Civil Records: Access: Mail, in person. Only the court performs in person searches; visitors may not. No search fee. Required to search: name, years to search. Civil cases indexed by defendant, plaintiff. Civil records on computer since 1991, prior records on index cards since 1978.

Criminal Records: Access: In person only. Visitors must perform in person searches for themselves. No search fee. Required to search: name, years to search, DOB; also helpful: SSN. Criminal records on computer since 1991, prior records on index cards since 1978. The court refers all written requests to the Administrative Office of Courts in Frankfort.

General Information: Public Access terminal is available. No adoption, mental, juvenile, or sealed records released. Will fax results to local or toll free line. Copy fee: $.25 per page. Certification fee: $5.00. Payee: Circuit Clerk. Personal checks accepted. Prepayment required.

Meade County

Circuit & District Court Courthouse 516 Fairway Dr, Brandenburg, KY 40108; 270-422-4961; Fax: 270-422-2147. Hours: 8AM-4:30AM except Thurs. 8AM-6:30PM (EST). *Felony, Misdemeanor, Civil, Eviction, Small Claims, Probate.*

Note: This court asks all record requests go to the Administrative office of the Courts in Frankfort.

Civil Records: Access: In person, mail, fax. Visitors must perform in person searches for themselves. No search fee. Required to search: name, years to search. Civil cases indexed by defendant, plaintiff. Civil records on computer since 2/95, prior on index cards.

Criminal Records: Access: In person only. Visitors must perform in person searches for themselves. No search fee. Required to search: name, years to search. Criminal records on computer since 2/95, prior on index cards.

General Information: Public Access terminal is available. No adoption, mental, juvenile, or sealed records released. Will not fax results. Copy fee: $.25 per page. Certification fee: $5.00. Payee: Circuit Clerk. Personal checks accepted. Prepayment required.

Menifee County

Circuit & District Court Box 172, Frenchburg, KY 40322; 606-768-2461; Fax: 606-768-2462. Hours: 8:30AM-4PM (EST). *Felony, Misdemeanor, Civil, Eviction, Small Claims, Probate.*

Civil Records: Access: In person. Visitors must perform in person searches for themselves. No search fee. Required to search: name, years to search. Civil cases indexed by defendant, plaintiff. Civil records on index cards from 1978 to 1994.

Criminal Records: Access: In person only. Visitors must perform in person searches for themselves. No search fee. Required to search: name, years to search. Criminal records on index cards from 1978 to 1994.

General Information: Public Access terminal is available. No adoption, mental, juvenile, or sealed records released. Copy fee: $.25 per page. Certification fee: $5.00. Payee: Circuit Clerk. Prepayment required.

Mercer County

Circuit & District Court Courthouse, 224 Main St S, Harrodsburg, KY 40330-1696; 859-734-6306; Civil phone: 859-734-6305; Criminal phone: 859-734-6307; Probate phone: 859-734-6305; Fax: 859-734-9159. Hours: 8AM-4:30PM (EST). *Felony, Misdemeanor, Civil, Eviction, Small Claims, Probate.*

Note: Circuit Civil & Criminal 859-734-6306

Civil Records: Access: In person only. Visitors must perform in person searches for themselves. No search fee. Required to search: name, years to search. Civil cases indexed by defendant, plaintiff. Civil records on computer back to 1993; prior in index books.

Criminal Records: Access: In person only. Visitors must perform in person searches for themselves. No search fee. Required to search: name, years to search; also helpful: DOB, SSN. Criminal records on computer back to 1993; prior in index books.

General Information: Public Access terminal is available. No adoption, mental, juvenile, or sealed records released. Copy fee: $.25 per page. Certification fee: $5.00. Payee: Circuit Clerk. Personal checks accepted. Prepayment required.

Metcalfe County

Circuit & District Court Box 485, Edmonton, KY 42129; 270-432-3663; Fax: 270-432-4437. Hours: 8AM-4PM (CST). *Felony, Misdemeanor, Civil, Eviction, Small Claims, Probate.*

Civil Records: Access: Phone, fax, mail, in person. Both court and visitors may perform in person searches. No search fee. Required to search: name, years to search. Civil cases indexed by defendant, plaintiff. Civil records on computer back to 1992, prior records on index cards since 1978.

Criminal Records: Access: Phone, fax, mail, in person. Both court and visitors may perform in person searches. No search fee. Required to search: name, years to search, DOB, SSN, signed release. Criminal records on computer back to 1992, prior records on index cards since 1980.

General Information: Public Access terminal is available. No adoption, mental, juvenile, or sealed records released. Fee to fax results is $2.00 1st page; $1.00 each add'l. Copy fee: $.25 per page. Certification fee: $5.00. Payee: Circuit Clerk. Personal checks accepted. Prepayment required. Mail requests: SASE required. Mail turnaround time 1-2 days.

Monroe County

Circuit & District Court 200 N Main St #B, Tompkinsville, KY 42167; 270-487-5480; Fax: 270-487-0068. 8AM-4PM (CST). *Felony, Misdemeanor, Civil, Eviction, Small Claims, Probate.*

Civil Records: Access: Phone, mail, in person. Both court and visitors may perform in person searches. No search fee. Required to search: name, years to search. Civil cases indexed by defendant, plaintiff. Civil records kept in files.

Criminal Records: Access: In person only. Both court and visitors may perform in person searches. No search fee. Required to search: name, years to search. Criminal records kept in files.

General Information: Public Access terminal is available. No adoption, mental, juvenile, or sealed records released. Copy fee: $.25 per page. Certification fee: $5.00. Payee: Circuit Clerk. Personal checks accepted. Prepayment required. Mail requests: SASE required. Mail turnaround time 1 week.

Montgomery County

Circuit & District Court Courthouse, One Court St (PO Box 327), Mt Sterling, KY 40353; 859-498-5966; Fax: 859-498-9341. Hours: 8:30AM-4PM (EST). *Felony, Misdemeanor, Civil, Eviction, Small Claims, Probate.*

Civil Records: Access: Mail, in person. Both court and visitors may perform in person searches. No search fee. Required to search: name, years to search. Civil cases indexed by defendant, plaintiff. Civil records on computer since August, 1991, on index cards from 1978-1991, prior records on docket books.

Criminal Records: Access: In person only. Visitors must perform in person searches for themselves. No search fee. Required to search: name, years to search. Criminal records on computer since August, 1991, on index cards from 1978-1991, prior records on docket books.

General Information: Public Access terminal is available. No adoption, mental, juvenile, or sealed records released. Copy fee: $.25 per page. Certification fee: $5.00. Payee: Circuit Clerk. Personal checks accepted. Prepayment required.

Morgan County

Circuit & District Court Box 85, West Liberty, KY 41472; 606-743-3763; Fax: 606-743-2633. Hours: 8AM-4PM (EST). *Felony, Misdemeanor, Civil, Eviction, Small Claims, Probate.*

Civil Records: Access: Mail, in person. Both court and visitors may perform in person searches. No search fee. Required to search: name, years to search. Civil cases indexed by defendant, plaintiff. Civil records on computer back to 9/1993; index books back to 1921.

Criminal Records: Access: Mail, in person. Both court and visitors may perform in person searches. No search fee. Required to search: name, years to search. Criminal records on computer back to 9/1993; index books back to 1921.

General Information: Public Access terminal is available. No adoption, mental, juvenile, or sealed records released. Copy fee: $.25 per page. Certification fee: $5.00. Payee: Circuit Clerk. Personal checks accepted. Prepayment required. Mail turnaround time 1 day.

Muhlenberg County

Circuit Court Box 776 (109 E Main St), Greenville, KY 42345; 270-338-4850 (Felony); Fax: 270-338-0177. Hours: 8AM-4PM (CST). *Felony, Civil Actions Over $4,000.*

Note: Direct mail felony record requests to state AOC.

Civil Records: Access: In person only. Visitors must perform in person searches for themselves. No search fee. Required to search: name, years to search. Civil cases indexed by defendant, plaintiff. Civil records on computer since May, 1992, records on index since 1932, prior records archived since 1940.

Criminal Records: Access: In person only. Visitors must perform in person searches for themselves. No search fee. Required to search: name, years to search, SSN; also helpful: DOB. Criminal records on computer since May, 1992, records on index since 1932, prior records archived since 1940.

General Information: Public Access terminal is available. No adoption, mental, juvenile, or sealed records released. Copy fee: $.25 per page. Certification fee: $5.00. Payee: Circuit Clerk. Personal checks accepted. Prepayment required.

District Court Box 776, Greenville, KY 42345; 270-338-0995; Fax: 270-338-0177. Hours: 8AM-4PM (CST). *Misdemeanor, Civil Actions Under $4,000, Eviction, Small Claims, Probate.*

Civil Records: Access: In person only. Both court and visitors may perform in person searches. No search fee. Required to search: name, years to search. Civil cases indexed by defendant, plaintiff. Civil records on computer since 1992, prior records on index books.

Criminal Records: Access: In person only. Visitors must perform in person searches for themselves. No search fee. Required to search: name, years to search. Criminal records on computer since 1992, prior records on index books. The court recommends all requesters go to the State Admin. Office of the Courts.

General Information: Public Access terminal is available. No adoption, mental, juvenile, or sealed records released. Copy fee: $.25 per page. Certification fee: $5.00. Payee: District Clerk. Personal checks accepted. Prepayment required.

Nelson County

Circuit & District Court Box 845, Bardstown, KY 40004; 502-348-3648. Hours: 8:30AM-4:30PM (EST). *Felony, Misdemeanor, Civil, Eviction, Small Claims, Probate.*

Civil Records: Access: Mail, in person. Both court and visitors may perform in person searches. No

search fee. Required to search: name, years to search. Civil cases indexed by defendant, plaintiff. Civil records on computer since 1990, on index since 1978, prior records archived from 1940.

Criminal Records: Access: Mail, in person. Both court and visitors may perform in person searches. No search fee. Required to search: name, years to search, DOB; also helpful: SSN. Criminal records on computer since 1990, on index since 1978, prior records archived from 1940.

General Information: Public Access terminal is available. No adoption, mental, juvenile, domestic violence or sealed records released. Copy fee: $.25 per page. Certification fee: $5.00. Payee: Circuit Clerk. Personal checks accepted. Prepayment required. Mail turnaround time 2 weeks.

Nicholas County

Circuit & District Court PO Box 109, Carlisle, KY 40311; 859-289-2336; Fax: 859-289-6141. 8:30AM-4:30PM M-F (EST). *Felony, Misdemeanor, Civil, Eviction, Small Claims, Probate.*

Civil Records: Access: Fax, mail, in person. Both court and visitors may perform in person searches. No search fee. Required to search: name, years to search, written request. Civil cases indexed by defendant, plaintiff. Civil records on computer since March, 1993, prior records on index cards.

Criminal Records: Access: Fax, mail, in person. Both court and visitors may perform in person searches. No search fee. Required to search: name, years to search, written request. Criminal records on computer since 3/1993, prior records on index cards.

General Information: Public Access terminal is available. No adoption, mental, juvenile, or sealed records released. No fee to fax results. Copy fee: $.25 per page. Certification fee: $5.00. Payee: Circuit Clerk. Personal checks accepted. Prepayment required. Mail requests: SASE required. Mail turnaround time 1-2 days.

Ohio County

Circuit & District Court PO Box 67 (130 E Washington, #300), Hartford, KY 42347; 270-298-3671; Fax: 270-298-9565. Hours: 8:30AM-4:30PM (CST). *Felony, Misdemeanor, Civil, Eviction, Small Claims, Probate.*

Civil Records: Access: In person only. Visitors must perform in person searches for themselves. No search fee. Required to search: name, years to search. Civil cases indexed by defendant, plaintiff. Civil records on computer since 10/91, Circuit court on index books since the 1800s, District court on index books since 1987 and prior records are archived.

Criminal Records: Access: In person only. Visitors must perform in person searches for themselves. No search fee. Required to search: name, years to search. Criminal records on computer since 10/91, Circuit court on index books since the 1800s, District court on index books since 1987 and prior records are archived.

General Information: Public Access terminal is available. No adoption, mental, juvenile, or sealed records released. Copy fee: $.25 per page. Certification fee: $5.00. Payee: Circuit Clerk. No personal checks accepted. Prepayment required.

Oldham County

Circuit & District Court 100 W Main St, La Grange, KY 40031; 502-222-9837; Fax: 502-222-3047. 8AM-4PM (EST). *Felony, Misdemeanor, Civil, Eviction, Small Claims, Probate.*

Note: Criminal record requests are referred to the Administrative office of the Courts in Frankfort.

Civil Records: Access: In person only. Visitors must perform in person searches for themselves. No search

fee. Required to search: name, years to search. Civil cases indexed by defendant, plaintiff. Civil records on computer since 1991, on index books since 1978, prior records archived since 1800s.

Criminal Records: Access: In person only. Visitors must perform in person searches for themselves. No search fee. Required to search: name, years to search; also helpful: SSN. Criminal records on computer since 1991, on index books since 1978, prior records archived since 1800s.

General Information: Public Access terminal is available. No adoption, mental, juvenile, or sealed records released. Will fax specifc case file $1.00 per doc plus $.20 per page. Copy fee: $.25 per page. Certification fee: $5.00. Payee: Circuit Clerk. Personal checks accepted. Prepayment required.

Owen County

Circuit & District Court Box 473, Owenton, KY 40359; 502-484-2232; Fax: 502-484-0625. Hours: 8AM-4PM (EST). *Felony, Misdemeanor, Civil, Eviction, Small Claims, Probate.*

Civil Records: Access: Fax, mail, in person. Both court and visitors may perform in person searches. No search fee. Required to search: name, years to search. Civil cases indexed by defendant, plaintiff. Civil records on computer since 1992, prior records on index books since 1946. Cases before 1978 transferred to state archives.

Criminal Records: Access: Fax, mail, in person. Both court and visitors may perform in person searches. No search fee. Required to search: name, years to search, DOB, SSN. Criminal records on computer since 1992, prior records on index books since 1946. Cases before 1978 transferred to state archives. Court suggests statewide search through A.O.C. at 502-573-2350.

General Information: Public Access terminal is available. No adoption, mental, juvenile, or sealed records released. Copy fee: $.25 per page. Certification fee: $5.00. Payee: Circuit Clerk. Personal checks accepted. Prepayment required. Mail turnaround time 1 week.

Owsley County

Circuit & District Court Box 130 (N Court St), Booneville, KY 41314; 606-593-6226; Fax: 606-593-6343. Hours: 8AM-4PM M-F, 8AM-Noon Sat (EST). *Felony, Misdemeanor, Civil, Eviction, Small Claims, Probate.*

Civil Records: Access: In person only. Visitors must perform in person searches for themselves. No search fee. Required to search: name, years to search. Civil cases indexed by defendant, plaintiff. Civil records on computer since 10/1994, prior records on index cards since 1967.

Criminal Records: Access: In person only. Visitors must perform in person searches for themselves. No search fee. Required to search: name, years to search, DOB or SSN. Criminal records on computer since 10/1994, prior records on index cards since 1967.

General Information: Public Access terminal is available. No adoption, mental, juvenile, or sealed records released. Will fax specific documents for $2.00 1st page; $1.00 ea add'l. Copy fee: $.25 per page. Certification fee: $5.00. Payee: Circuit Clerk. Personal checks accepted. Prepayment required.

Pendleton County

Circuit & District Court PO Box 69, (223 Main St.), Falmouth, KY 41040; 859-654-3347. Hours: 8AM-4PM (EST). *Felony, Misdemeanor, Civil, Eviction, Small Claims, Probate.*

Civil Records: Access: Mail, in person. Both court and visitors may perform in person searches. No search fee. Required to search: name, years to search.

Civil cases indexed by defendant, plaintiff. Civil records on computer since July, 1994, prior records on index books since 1978.

Criminal Records: Access: In person only. Both court and visitors may perform in person searches. No search fee. Required to search: name, years to search. Criminal records on computer since July, 1994, prior records on index books since 1978.

General Information: Public Access terminal is available. No adoption, mental, juvenile, or sealed records released. Copy fee: $.25 per page. Certification fee: $5.00. Payee: Circuit Clerk. Personal checks accepted. Prepayment required. Mail requests: SASE not required.

Perry County

Circuit Court Box 7433, Hazard, KY 41701; 606-435-6000; Fax: 606-435-6143. Hours: 8AM-4PM (EST). *Felony, Civil Actions Over $4,000.*

Civil Records: Access: In person only. Visitors must perform in person searches only. No search fee. Required to search: name, years to search. Civil cases indexed by defendant, plaintiff. Civil records on computer since October, 1991, prior records on index cards since 1978.

Criminal Records: Access: In person only. Visitors must perform in person searches only. No search fee. Required to search: name, years to search. Criminal records on computer since October, 1991, prior records on index cards since 1978.

General Information: Public Access terminal is available. No adoption, mental, juvenile, or sealed records released. Copy fee: $.25 per page. Certification fee: $5.00. Payee: Circuit Clerk. Personal checks accepted. Prepayment required.

District Court PO Box 7433, Hazard, KY 41702; 606-435-6002. Hours: 8AM-4PM (EST). *Misdemeanor, Civil Actions Under $4,000, Eviction, Small Claims, Probate.*

Civil Records: Access: In person. No search fee. Required to search: name, years to search. Civil cases indexed by defendant, plaintiff. Civil records on computer since 1991, records on index books since 1978, prior records archived since 1900s.

Criminal Records: Access: In person. Visitors must perform in person searches for themselves. No search fee. Required to search: name, years to search. Criminal records on computer since 1991, records on index books since 1978, prior records archived since 1900s.

General Information: Public Access terminal is available. No adoption, mental, juvenile, or sealed records released. Copy fee: $.25 per page. Certification fee: $5.00. Payee: District Clerk. Personal checks accepted. Prepayment required.

Pike County

Circuit & District Court PO Box 1002, Pikeville, KY 41502; 606-433-7557; Fax: 606-433-7044. 8AM-4:30PM (EST). *Felony, Misdemeanor, Civil, Eviction, Small Claims, Probate.*

Civil Records: Access: Mail, in person. Both court and visitors may perform in person searches. No search fee. Required to search: name, years to search. Civil cases indexed by defendant, plaintiff. Civil records on computer since March, 1994, prior records on index cards from 1978.

Criminal Records: Access: In person only. Both the court and visitors may perform in person searches. No search fee. Required to search: name, years to search. Criminal records on computer since March, 1994, prior records on index cards from 1978.

General Information: Public Access terminal is available. No adoption, mental, juvenile, or sealed records released. Will not fax results. Copy fee: $.25 per page. Certification fee: $5.00. Payee: Circuit

Clerk. Personal checks accepted. Prepayment required. Mail requests: SASE required. Mail turnaround time 3 days.

Powell County

Circuit & District Court Box 578, Stanton, KY 40380; 606-663-4141; Fax: 606-663-2710. Hours: 8AM-4PM M,T,W,F, 8AM-Noon Th & Sat (EST). *Felony, Misdemeanor, Civil, Eviction, Small Claims, Probate.*

Civil Records: Access: Mail, in person. Both court and visitors may perform in person searches. No search fee. Required to search: name, years to search. Civil cases indexed by defendant, plaintiff. Civil records on computer since 1993, prior records on index cards since 1978.

Criminal Records: Access: In person only. Visitors must perform in person searches for themselves. No search fee. Required to search: name, years to search, DOB; also helpful: SSN. Criminal records on computer since 1993, prior records on index cards since 1978. This office will not provide criminal record checks.

General Information: Public Access terminal is available. No adoption, mental, juvenile, or sealed records released. Copy fee: $.25 per page. Certification fee: $5.00. Payee: Circuit Clerk. Personal checks not accepted; money orders preferred. Prepayment required. Mail requests: SASE required. Mail turnaround time varies.

Pulaski County

Circuit & District Court Box 664, 100 N Maine, Courthouse Sq 3rd Fl, Somerset, KY 42502; 606-677-4029; Fax: 606-677-4002. Hours: 8AM-4:30PM M-F, 8AM-Noon Sat (EST). *Felony, Misdemeanor, Civil, Eviction, Small Claims, Probate.*

Civil Records: Access: In person only. Visitors must perform in person searches for themselves. No search fee. Required to search: name, years to search. Civil cases indexed by defendant, plaintiff. Civil records on computer since 1991, prior records on index books from 1978.

Criminal Records: Access: In person only. Visitors must perform in person searches for themselves. No search fee. Required to search: name, years to search. Criminal records on computer since 1991, prior records on index books from 1978.

General Information: Public Access terminal is available. No adoption, mental, juvenile, or sealed records released. Copy fee: $.25 per page. Certification fee: $5.00. Payee: Circuit Clerk. Personal checks accepted. Prepayment required.

Robertson County

Circuit & District Court PO Box 63, 211 Court St, Mt Olivet, KY 41064; 606-724-5993; Fax: 606-724-5721. Hours: 8:30AM-4:30PM (EST). *Felony, Misdemeanor, Civil, Eviction, Small Claims, Probate.*

Civil Records: Access: In person only. Visitors must perform in person searches for themselves. No search fee. Required to search: name, years to search. Civil cases indexed by defendant, plaintiff. Civil records on computer to 1995, previous on index cards.

Criminal Records: Access: In person only. Visitors must perform in person searches for themselves. No search fee. Required to search: name, years to search; also helpful: DOB, SSN. Criminal records on computer to 1995, previous on index cards.

General Information: Public Access terminal is available. No adoption, mental, juvenile, or sealed records released. Copy fee: $.25 per page. Certification fee: $5.00. Payee: Circuit Clerk. Personal checks accepted. Prepayment required.

Rockcastle County

Circuit & District Court Courthouse Annex, 1st Fl, 205 E Main St., Rm 102, Mt Vernon, KY 40456; 606-256-2581. 8AM-4PM M-W & F; 8AM-6PM Th; 8:30AM-Noon Sat (EST). *Felony, Misdemeanor, Civil, Eviction, Small Claims, Probate.*

Civil Records: Access: In person. Visitors must perform in person searches for themselves. No search fee. Required to search: name, years to search. Civil cases indexed by defendant, plaintiff. Civil records on computer since 1991, index cards from 1978 to 1990, prior are archived at Frankfort.

Criminal Records: Access: In person only. Visitors must perform in person searches for themselves. No search fee. Required to search: name, years to search, DOB; also helpful: SSN. Criminal Records from 1991 to present are available. A form is available to request a criminal history through AOC Retrieval Services. This court provides the form via mail if you provide them a SASE.

General Information: Public Access terminal is available. No adoption, mental, juvenile, or sealed records released. Copy fee: $.25 per page. Certification fee: $5.00. Payee: Circuit Clerk. Personal checks accepted. Prepayment required.

Rowan County

Circuit & District Court 627 E Main, Morehead, KY 40351-1398; 606-784-4574; Fax: 606-784-1899. Hours: 8:30AM-4:30PM M-F 8:30AM-12PM SAT (EST). *Felony, Misdemeanor, Civil, Eviction, Small Claims, Probate.*
www.kycourts.net

Civil Records: Access: In person only. Visitors must perform in person searches for themselves. No search fee. Required to search: name, years to search. Civil cases indexed by defendant, plaintiff. Civil records on computer from 1991, index cards from 1989, archived from 1900.

Criminal Records: Access: In person only. Visitors must perform in person searches for themselves. No search fee. Required to search: name, years to search. Criminal records on computer from 1991, index cards from 1989, archived from 1900.

General Information: Public Access terminal is available. No adoption, mental, juvenile, or sealed records released. Copy fee: $.50 per page. No certification fee. Payee: Circuit Clerk. Only cashiers checks and money orders accepted. Prepayment required.

Russell County

Circuit & District Court 410 Monument Square, #203, Jamestown, KY 42629; 270-343-2185; Fax: 270-343-5808. Hours: 7:30AM-5PM (CST). *Felony, Misdemeanor, Civil, Eviction, Small Claims, Probate.*

Civil Records: Access: In person only. Visitors must perform in person searches for themselves. No search fee. Required to search: name, years to search. Civil cases indexed by defendant, plaintiff. Civil records on computer from August, 1994, index cards from 1978-1994, prior archived at Frankfort.

Criminal Records: Access: In person only. Visitors must perform in person searches for themselves. No search fee. Required to search: name, years to search. Criminal records on computer from August, 1994, index cards from 1978-1994, prior archived at Frankfort.

General Information: Public Access terminal is available. No adoption, mental, juvenile, or sealed records released. Copy fee: $.25 per page. Certification fee: $5.00. Payee: Circuit Clerk. Personal checks accepted. Prepayment required.

Scott County

Circuit & District Court 119 N Hamilton, Georgetown, KY 40324; 502-863-0474. Hours: 8:30-4:30PM (EST). *Felony, Misdemeanor, Civil, Eviction, Small Claims, Probate.*

Civil Records: Access: Mail, in person. Both court and visitors may perform in person searches. No search fee. Required to search: name, years to search. Civil cases indexed by defendant, plaintiff. Civil records on computer since 1992, index cards from 1978 to 1992, in books prior.

Criminal Records: Access: Mail, in person. Both court and visitors may perform in person searches. No search fee. Required to search: name, years to search; also helpful: SSN. Criminal records on computer since 1992, index cards from 1978 to 1992, in books prior.

General Information: Public Access terminal is available. No adoption, mental, juvenile, paternity and domestic violence records released. Copy fee: $.25 per page. Certification fee: $5.00. Payee: Circuit Clerk. Personal checks accepted. Prepayment required. Mail requests: SASE required. Mail turnaround time varies.

Shelby County

Circuit & District Court 501 Main St, Shelbyville, KY 40065; 502-633-1287; Civil phone: 502-633-4736 (Dist Ct); Fax: 502-633-0146 (633-6421 Dist Ct fax). Hours: 8:30AM-4:30PM (EST). *Felony, Misdemeanor, Civil, Eviction, Small Claims, Probate.*

Civil Records: Access: Fax, mail, in person. Both court and visitors may perform in person searches. No search fee. Required to search: name, years to search. Civil cases indexed by defendant, plaintiff. Civil records on computer back to 1991; index cards from 1978 to 1991.

Criminal Records: Access: In person only. Visitors must perform in person searches for themselves. No search fee. Required to search: name, years to search, DOB. Criminal records on computer back to 1991; index cards from 1978 to 1991.

General Information: Public Access terminal is available. No adoption, mental, juvenile, or sealed records released. Copy fee: $.25 per page. Certification fee: $5.00. Payee: Circuit Clerk. Personal checks accepted. Prepayment required. Mail requests: SASE required. Mail turnaround time 3-5 days.

Simpson County

Circuit & District Court Box 261, Franklin, KY 42135-0261; 270-586-8910/4241; Fax: 270-586-0265. 8AM-4PM (CST). *Felony, Misdemeanor, Civil, Eviction, Small Claims, Probate.*
www.dockets.kycourts.net

Civil Records: Access: In person. Both court and visitors may perform in person searches. No search fee. Required to search: name, years to search. Civil cases indexed by defendant, plaintiff. Civil records on computer since 11/92, manual prior to 1978.

Criminal Records: Access: In person. Visitors must perform in person searches themselves No search fee. Required to search: name, years to search, DOB, SSN. Criminal records on computer since 11/92, card index back to 1978.

General Information: Public Access terminal is available. No adoption, mental, juvenile, or sealed records released. Copy fee: $.25 per page. Certification fee: $5.00. Payee: Circuit Clerk. Only cashiers checks and money orders accepted. Prepayment required.

Spencer County

Circuit & District Court Box 282, Taylorsville, KY 40071; 502-477-3220; Fax: 502-477-9368. Hours: 7:45AM-4PM (EST). *Felony, Misdemeanor, Civil, Eviction, Small Claims, Probate.*

Civil Records: Access: Mail, in person. Visitors must perform in person searches for themselves. No search fee. Required to search: name, years to search. Civil cases indexed by defendant, plaintiff. Civil records on computer from 08/94 to present, index cards from 1978 to 1994.

Criminal Records: Access: Mail, in person. Visitors must perform in person searches for themselves. No search fee. Required to search: name, years to search, DOB; also helpful: SSN. Criminal records on computer from 08/94 to present, index cards from 1978 to 1994.

General Information: Public Access terminal is available. No adoption, mental, juvenile, or sealed records released. Copy fee: $.25 per page. Certification fee: $5.00. Payee: Circuit Clerk. Personal checks accepted. Prepayment required. Mail requests: SASE required. Mail turnaround time 1-4 days.

Taylor County

Circuit & District Court 203 N Court Courthouse, Campbellsville, KY 42718; 270-465-6686; Fax: 270-789-4356. Hours: 8AM-4:30PM (EST). *Felony, Misdemeanor, Civil, Eviction, Small Claims, Probate.*

Civil Records: Access: In person only. Both court and visitors may perform in person searches. No search fee. Required to search: name, years to search. Civil cases indexed by defendant, plaintiff. Civil records on computer from 1993 to present, index cards from 1978 to 1993.

Criminal Records: Access: In person only. Visitors must perform in person searches for themselves. No search fee. Required to search: name, years to search, DOB, SSN. Criminal records on computer from 1993 to present, index cards from 1978 to 1993.

General Information: Public Access terminal is available. No adoption, mental, juvenile, or sealed records released. Copy fee: $.25 per page. Certification fee: $5.00. Payee: Circuit Clerk. Personal checks accepted. Prepayment required.

Todd County

Circuit & District Court Box 337 (202 E. Washington St), Elkton, KY 42220; 270-265-5631; Fax: 270-265-2122. Hours: 8AM-4:30PM (CST). *Felony, Misdemeanor, Civil, Eviction, Small Claims, Probate.*

Civil Records: Access: In person only. Visitors must perform in person searches for themselves. No search fee. Required to search: name, years to search. Civil cases indexed by defendant, plaintiff. Civil records on computer since January, 1993, index cards from 1978-1993, index books prior to 1978.

Criminal Records: Access: In person only. Visitors must perform in person searches for themselves. No search fee. Required to search: name, years to search. Criminal records on computer since January, 1993, index cards from 1978-1993, index books prior.

General Information: Public Access terminal is available. No adoption, mental, juvenile, or sealed records released. Copy fee: $.25 per page. Certification fee: $5.00. Payee: Circuit Clerk. Personal checks accepted. Prepayment required.

Trigg County

Circuit & District Court Box 673, Cadiz, KY 42211; 270-522-6270. Hours: 8AM-4PM (CST). *Felony, Misdemeanor, Civil, Eviction, Small Claims, Probate.*

Note: District Court can be reached at 270-522-7070.

Civil Records: Access: In person only. Visitors must perform in person searches for themselves. No search fee. Required to search: name, years to search. Civil cases indexed by defendant, plaintiff. Civil records on computer from 4/1993 to present, index cards from 1978 to 1993.

Criminal Records: Access: In person only. Visitors must perform in person searches for themselves. Search fee: none. Required to search: name, years to search, DOB; also helpful: SSN. Criminal records on computer from 4/1993 to present, index cards from 1978 to 1993.

General Information: Public Access terminal is available. No adoption, mental, juvenile, or sealed records released. Copy fee: $.25 per page. Certification fee: $5.00. Payee: Circuit Clerk. Only cashiers checks and money orders accepted. Prepayment required.

Trimble County

Circuit & District Court Box 248, Bedford, KY 40006; 502-255-3213, 502-255-3525 (District); Fax: 502-255-4953. Hours: 8AM-4:30PM M,T,Th,F 8AM-Noon Sat (EST). *Felony, Misdemeanor, Civil, Eviction, Small Claims, Probate.*

Civil Records: Access: Mail, in person. Both court and visitors may perform in person searches. No search fee. Required to search: name, years to search. Civil cases indexed by defendant, plaintiff. Civil records on computer and in folders from 1993 to present, folders 1978 to 1992, archives prior to 1978.

Criminal Records: Access: In person only. Visitors must perform in person searches for themselves. No search fee. Required to search: name, years to search, DOB; also helpful: SSN. Criminal records on computer and in folders from 1993 to present, folders 1978 to 1992, archives prior to 1978.

General Information: Public Access terminal is available. No adoption, mental, juvenile, or sealed records released. Will not fax results. Copy fee: $.25 per page. Certification fee: $5.00. Payee: Circuit Clerk. Only cashiers checks and money orders accepted. Prepayment required. Mail requests: SASE required. Mail turnaround time 2-4 days.

Union County

Circuit & District Court Box 59, Morganfield, KY 42437; 270-389-0800/0804; Fax: 270-389-9887. Hours: 8AM-4PM (CST). *Felony, Misdemeanor, Civil, Eviction, Small Claims, Probate.*

Note: No searches performed on Thursday.

Civil Records: Access: Mail, in person. Both court and visitors may perform in person searches. No search fee. Required to search: name, years to search. Civil cases indexed by defendant, plaintiff. Civil records on computer since June, 1994 (new records only); prior on index cards and archived.

Criminal Records: Access: In person only. Visitors must perform in person searches for themselves. No search fee. Required to search: name, years to search, DOB, SSN. Criminal records on computer since June, 1994 (new records only); prior on index cards and archived. Contact AOC for statewide search by mail (criminal requests to be acquired through Pre-Trial Svcs, Frankfort).

General Information: Public Access terminal is available. No adoption, mental, juvenile, or sealed records released. Copy fee: $.25 per page. Certification fee: $5.00. Payee: Circuit Clerk.

Business checks accepted. Prepayment required. Mail requests: SASE required. Mail turnaround: 2-4 days.

Warren County

Circuit & District Court 1001 Center St #102, Bowling Green, KY 42101-2184; 270-746-7400; Fax: 270-746-7501. Hours: 8:AM-4:30PM (CST). *Felony, Misdemeanor, Civil, Eviction, Small Claims, Probate.*

Civil Records: Access: In person only. Visitors must perform in person searches for themselves. No search fee. Required to search: name, years to search. Civil cases indexed by defendant, plaintiff. Civil records on computer since 1989.

Criminal Records: Access: In person only. Visitors must perform in person searches for themselves. No search fee. Required to search: name, years to search; also helpful: DOB, SSN. Criminal records on computer since 1990.

General Information: Public Access terminal is available. No adoption, mental, juvenile, or sealed records released. Copy fee: $.25 per page. Certification fee: $5.00. Payee: Circuit Clerk. Personal checks accepted. Prepayment required.

Washington County

Circuit & District Court PO Box 346, Springfield, KY 40069; 859-336-3761; Fax: 859-336-9824. Hours: 8AM-4:30PM; 8:30-12 on Sat (EST). *Felony, Misdemeanor, Civil, Eviction, Small Claims, Probate.*

Civil Records: Access: In person only. Both court and visitors may perform in person searches. No search fee. Required to search: name, years to search. Civil cases indexed by defendant, plaintiff. Civil records on computer, index cards and archived.

Criminal Records: Access: In person only. Both court and visitors may perform in person searches. No search fee. Required to search: name, years to search, DOB. Criminal records on computer, index cards and archived. Mail requests must be made to Pretrial Services, 100 Millcreek Park., Frankfort, KY 40602, 800-928-6381.

General Information: Public Access terminal is available. No adoption, mental, juvenile, or sealed records released. Copy fee: $.25 per page. Return postage required. Certification fee: $5.00. Payee: Circuit Clerk. Personal checks accepted. Prepayment required.

Wayne County

Circuit & District Court 109 N Main St, Monticello, KY 42633-1458; 606-348-5841; Fax: 606-348-4225. Hours: 8AM-4:15PM M-F; 8:30AM-Noon Sat (CST). *Felony, Misdemeanor, Civil, Eviction, Small Claims, Probate.*

Civil Records: Access: Mail, in person. Visitors must perform in person searches for themselves. No search fee. Required to search: name, years to search. Civil cases indexed by defendant, plaintiff. Civil records on computer from 10/92 to present, index cards from 1978 to 1992.

Criminal Records: Access: Mail, in person. Visitors must perform in person searches for themselves. No search fee. Required to search: name, years to search;

also helpful: DOB, SSN. Criminal records on computer from 10/92 to present, index cards from 1978 to 1992.

General Information: Public Access terminal is available. No adoption, mental, juvenile, or sealed records released. Copy fee: $.25 per page. Certification fee: $5.00. Payee: Circuit Clerk. Personal checks accepted. Prepayment required. Mail requests: SASE required. Mail turnaround time 5 days.

Webster County

Circuit & District Court Box 290 (25 US Hiway 41A South), Dixon, KY 42409; 270-639-9160; Fax: 270-639-6757. Hours: 8AM-4PM (CST). *Felony, Misdemeanor, Civil, Eviction, Small Claims, Probate.*

Civil Records: Access: Fax, mail, in person. Both court and visitors may perform in person searches. No search fee. Required to search: name, years to search. Civil cases indexed by defendant, plaintiff. Civil records in office from 1987 to present, prior records are at Frankfort archives.

Criminal Records: Access: Fax, mail, in person. Both court and visitors may perform in person searches. No search fee. Required to search: name, years to search. Criminal records in office from 1987 to present, prior records are at Frankfort archives.

General Information: Public Access terminal is available. No adoption, mental, juvenile, or sealed records released. Fee to fax results is $2.00 for 1st page, $1.00 each add'l. Copy fee: $.25 per page. Certification fee: $5.00. Payee: Circuit Clerk. Personal checks accepted. Prepayment required. Mail requests: SASE required. Mail turnaround time 1 day.

Whitley County

Corbin Circuit & District Court 805 S Main St #10, Corbin, KY 40701; 606-523-1085; Fax: 606-523-2049. Hours: 8AM-4PM (EST). *Felony, Misdemeanor, Civil, Eviction, Small Claims, Probate.*

Civil Records: Access: In person only. Visitors must perform in person searches for themselves. No search fee. Required to search: name, years to search. Civil cases indexed by defendant, plaintiff. Civil records on computer from 1993 to present, index books prior.

Criminal Records: Access: In person only. Visitors must perform in person searches for themselves. No search fee. Required to search: name, years to search. Criminal records on computer from 1993 to present, index books prior.

General Information: Public Access terminal is available. No adoption, mental, juvenile or sealed records released. Copy fee: $.25 per page. Certification fee: $5.00. Payee: District Court. Personal checks accepted. Prepayment required.

Williamsburg Circuit & District Court Box 329, Williamsburg, KY 40769; 606-549-2973. Hours: 8AM-4PM (EST). *Felony, Misdemeanor, Civil, Eviction, Small Claims, Probate.*

Note: Circuit court can be reached at 606-549-2973. District court can be reached at 606-549-5162.

Civil Records: Access: In person only. Visitors must perform in person searches for themselves. No search fee. Required to search: name, years to search. Civil

cases indexed by defendant, plaintiff. Civil records on computer from 1993 to present, index cards from 1978 to 1993.

Criminal Records: Access: In person only. Visitors must perform in person searches for themselves. No search fee. Required to search: name, years to search; also helpful: DOB, SSN. Criminal records on computer from 1993 to present, index cards from 1978 to 1993.

General Information: Public Access terminal is available. No adoption, mental, juvenile, or sealed records released. Copy fee: $.25 per page. Certification fee: $5.00. Payee: Whitley Circuit Clerk. Personal checks accepted. Prepayment required.

Wolfe County

Circuit & District Court Box 296, Campton, KY 41301; 606-668-3736; Fax: 606-668-3198. 8:30AM-4:30PM (EST). *Felony, Misdemeanor, Civil, Eviction, Small Claims, Probate.* www.kycourts.net/clerks/wolfeclerk.shtm

Civil Records: Access: Mail, in person. Both court and visitors may perform in person searches. No search fee. Required to search: name, years to search. Civil cases indexed by defendant, plaintiff. Civil records on computer from 1992 to present, index books prior.

Criminal Records: Access: Mail, in person. Both court and visitors may perform in person searches. No search fee. Required to search: name, years to search; also helpful: DOB, SSN. Criminal records on computer from 1992 to present, index books prior. Mail requests should be directed to Pretrial Services, 100 Millcreek Park, Frankfort, KY 40601, 502-573-2350.

General Information: Public Access terminal is available. No adoption, mental, juvenile, or sealed records released. Copy fee: $.25 per page. Certification fee: $5.00. Payee: Circuit Clerk. Personal checks accepted. Prepayment required. Mail requests: SASE required. Mail turnaround time same day.

Woodford County

Circuit & District Court 130 Court St, Versailles, KY 40383; 859-873-3711; Fax: 859-879-8531. Hours: 8AM-4PM M-Th; 8AM-6PM F (EST). *Felony, Misdemeanor, Civil, Eviction, Small Claims, Probate.*

Civil Records: Access: In person only. Visitors must perform in person searches for themselves. No search fee. Required to search: name, years to search. Civil cases indexed by defendant, plaintiff. Civil records on computer from 02/91 to present, index cards from 1978 to 1991.

Criminal Records: Access: In person only. Visitors must perform in person searches for themselves. No search fee. Required to search: name, years to search; also helpful: SSN. Criminal records on computer from 02/91 to present, index cards from 1978 to 1991.

General Information: Public Access terminal is available. No adoption, mental, juvenile, or sealed records released. Copy fee: $.25 per page. Certification fee: $5.00. Payee: Circuit Clerk. Personal checks accepted. Prepayment required.

Kentucky Recording Offices

ORGANIZATION: 120 counties, 122 recording offices. The recording officer is County Clerk. Kenton County has two recording offices. Jefferson County has a separate office for UCC filing until June 30, 2001; that office now only searches for filings up to that date. 80 counties are in the Eastern Time Zone (EST) and 40 are in the Central Time Zone (CST). Many offices are open until Noon on Saturdays.

REAL ESTATE RECORDS: Most counties will not perform real estate searches. Copy fees vary. Certification fee is usually $5 per document. Tax records are maintained by the Property Valuation Administrator, designated "Assessor" in this section.

UCC RECORDS: Under revised Article 9, Kentucky changes from a "local filing state" to a "central filing state" with the Secretary of State's office. Collateral on non-resident debtors were always filed at the state level. Real estate related UCCs are still found at the County Clerk's offcie. Many counties will not perform UCC searches. Use search request form UCC-11. Search fees are usually $5.00 per debtor name. Copy fees vary widely.

TAX LIEN RECORDS: All federal and state tax liens on personal property are filed with the County Clerk, often in an "Encumbrance Book." Most counties will not perform tax lien searches.

OTHER LIENS: Judgments, motor vehicle, mechanics, lis pendens, bail bond

ONLINE ACCESS: Five counties offer free access to assessor or real estate records. Several other counties offer commercial systems. There is no statewide system.

Adair County

County Clerk, 424 Public Sq, Columbia, KY 42728. **Phone**-County Clerk, R/E & UCC Recording- 270-384-2801; fax-270-384-4805; hours 7:30AM-4PM Will not search records. Record copy- $1.00 per page. Cert fee: $5.00 per cert. Payee: Adair County Clerk. **Other phones:** Elections-270-384-2801; Vital Records-270-384-2801.

Allen County

County Clerk, 201 W. Main St, Rm 6, Scottsville, KY 42164. **Phone**-County Clerk, R/E & UCC Recording- 270-237-3706; fax-270-237-9206; hours 8:00AM-4:30PM, 8:00AM-Noon Sat Will search UCC records. UCC search per debtor- $5.00. Will not search real estate or tax lien records. Record copy- $.25 per page. Cert fee: $5.00 per doc. Payee: Allen County Clerk. **Other phones:** Assessor-270-237-3711.

Anderson County

County Clerk, 151 S. Main, Lawrenceburg, KY 40342. **Phone**-County Clerk, R/E & UCC Recording- 502-839-3041; fax-502-839-3043; hours 8:30AM-5PM M-Th; 8:30AM-6PM F UCC record search per debtor- $5.00. Copy fee is $.25 per page. Will not search real estate records. Cert fee: $5.00 per doc. Payee: Anderson County Clerk. **Other phones:** Assessor-502-839-4061; Treasurer-502-839-3471; Appraiser/ Auditor-502-839-4061; Elections-502-839-3041; Vital Records-502-564-4212.

Ballard County

County Clerk, PO Box 145, Wickliffe, KY 42087. **Phone**-County Clerk, R/E & UCC Recording- 270-335-5168; fax-270-335-3081; hours 8AM-4PM M-F; 8AM-5:30PM Last Friday of month UCC record search per debtor- $5.00. UCC search includes tax liens if requested. Mortgage searches available. Record copy- $.50 per page. Cert fee: $5.00 per cert. Payee: Ballard County Clerk. **Other phones:** Assessor-270-335-3400; Treasurer-270-335-5176; Elections-270-335-5168; Vital Records-270-335-5123.

Barren County

County Clerk, 117 N Public Sq #1A, Glasgow, KY 42141-2869. **Phone**-County Clerk, R/E & UCC Recording- 270-651-5200; fax-270-651-1083; hours 8AM-4:30AM. UCC record search per debtor- $5.00. UCC copy- $1.00 per page. Will not search real estate or tax lien records. RE record copy- $.25 per page. Cert fee: $6.00 per cert. Payee: County Clerk. **Other phones:** Assessor-270-651-2026; Treasurer-270-651-3338; Elections-270-651-5200.

Bath County

County Clerk, PO Box 609, Owingsville, KY 40360. **Phone**-606-674-2613; fax-606-674-9526; hours 8AM-4PM. Will not search UCC records. UCC copy fee- $1.00 per page. Will not search tax liens. Real estate record owner and mortgage searches available. Cert fee: $3.50 per doc. Payee: Bath County Clerk. **Other phones:** Assessor-606-674-6382.

Bell County

County Clerk, PO Box 156, Pineville, KY 40977. **Phone**-County Clerk, R/E & UCC Recording- 606-337-6143; fax-606-337-5415; hours 8AM-4PM M-F; 8AM-Noon Sat. UCC record search per debtor- $5.00. UCC copy- $2.00 per page. Will not search real estate or tax lien records. RE record copy- $2.00 per doc. Cert fee: $3.50 per cert. Payee: Bell County Clerk. **Other phones:** Assessor-606-337-2720; Treasurer-606-337-2497; Elections-606-337-6143.

Boone County

County Clerk, PO Box 874, Burlington, KY 41005. **Phone**-859-334-2137; fax-859-334-2193; hours 8:30AM-4:30PM M, W-F; 8:30AM-6PM T www.boonecountyclerk.com Will search UCC records. UCC copy- $1.00 per page. Will not search real estate or tax lien records. RE record copy- $.50 per page. Cert fee: $3.50 per cert. Payee: County Clerk. **Online Access to Real Estate, Lien, UCC, Assessor, Marriage records:** Access the county clerk database through eCCLIX, a fee-based service; $200.00 sign-up and $65.00 monthly. Records go back to 1989; images to 1998. For information, see the website or call 502-266-9445. **Other phones:** Assessor-859-334-2236; Treasurer-859-334-2150.

Bourbon County

County Clerk, PO Box 312, Paris, KY 40362-0312. **Phone**-County Clerk, R/E & UCC Recording- 859-987-2142; fax-859-987-5660; hours 8:30AM-4:30PM M-Th; 8:30AM-6PM F Will not search records. UCC copy- $2.00 per page. RE record- $3.50 per doc. Cert fee: $5.00 per cert. Payee: Bourbon County Clerk. **Other phones:** Assessor-859-987-2152; Treasurer-859-987-2139; Elections-859-987-2142; Vital Records-502-564-4212.

Boyd County

County Clerk, PO Box 523, Catlettsburg, KY 41129. **Phone**-606-739-5116; fax-606-739-6357; hours 8:30AM-4PM main office; 9AM-4:30PM & 9AM-Noon Sat. Will not search records. Record copy- $.50 per page. Cert fee: $5.00 per doc. Payee: Boyd County Clerk. **Online Access to Real Estate, Lien records:** Access to the County Clerk online records requires a $10 monthly usage fee. The system operates 24 hours daily; records date back to 1/1979. Lending agency information is available. For information, contact Doris Stephen Hallan-Clerk or Kathy Fisher at 606-739-5116. **Other phones:** Assessor-606-739-5173; Treasurer-606-739-4242.

Boyle County

County Clerk, 321 W. Main St., Rm 123, Danville, KY 40422-1837. **Phone**-County Clerk, R/E & UCC Recording- 859-238-1112; fax-859-238-1114; hours 8:30AM-5PM M; 8:30AM-4PM T-F UCC record search per debtor- $1.00 for computer page. UCC copy- $1.00 per page. Will not search real estate or tax lien records. RE record copy- $.50 per page. Cert fee: $5.00 per cert. Payee: Boyle County Clerk. **Other phones:** Assessor-859-238-1104; Treasurer-859-238-1118; Vital Records-502-564-4212 (Frankfort, KY).

Bracken County

County Clerk, PO Box 147, Brooksville, KY 41004-0147. **Phone**-County Clerk, R/E & UCC Recording- 606-735-2952; fax-606-735-2687; hours 8AM-4PM M,T,Th,F; 8AM-Noon W,Sat Will not search records. UCC copy- $.25 per page. Cert fee: $5.00 per cert. Payee: Bracken County Clerk. **Other phones:** Assessor-606-735-2228;

Treasurer-606-735-2125; Appraiser/ Auditor-606-735-2228; Elections-606-735-2952606-735-2952.

Breathitt County

County Clerk, 1137 Main St, Jackson, KY 41339. **Phone-**County Clerk, R/E & UCC Recording- 606-666-3810; fax-606-666-3807; hours 8AM-4PM M,T,Th,F; 8AM-Noon W; 9AM-Noon Sat

UCC record search per debtor- $5.00. UCC copy-$1.00 per page. Will not search tax liens. Will only search real estate records if deed book and page number provided. RE record copy- $.50 per page. Cert fee: $5.00 per record. Payee: Breathitt County Clerk. **Other phones:** Treasurer-606-666-4268; Elections-606-666-3810.

Breckinridge County

County Clerk, PO Box 538, Hardinsburg, KY 40143. **Phone-**County Clerk, R/E & UCC Recording- 270-756-6166, UCC Recording- 270-756-2246; fax-270-756-1569; hours 8AM-4PM, 8AM-Noon Sat

Will not search records. Record copy- $1.00 per page. Cert fee: $5.00 per cert. Payee: County Clerk. **Other phones:** Assessor-270-756-5154; Treasurer-270-756-2269; Elections-270-756-2246.

Bullitt County

County Clerk, PO Box 6, Shepherdsville, KY 40165-0006. **Phone-**County Clerk, R/E & UCC Recording-502-543-2513; fax-502-543-9121;

hours 8AM-4PM M,T,W,F; 8AM-6PM Th www.bullittcountyclerk.ky.gov

UCC record search per debtor- $5.00. UCC copy-$5.00 per doc. Will not search real estate or tax lien records. RE record copy- $.30 per page walkin or $1.50 per page by mail. Cert fee: $5.00 per cert. Payee: Bullitt County Clerk. **Other phones:** Assessor-502-543-7480; Treasurer-502-543-2262; Elections-502-543-2513; Vital Records-502-543-2415; Tax Collector-502-543-2514.

Butler County

County Clerk, PO Box 449, Morgantown, KY 42261. **Phone-**270-526-5676; fax-270-526-2658; hours 8AM-4:30PM. Will not search records. Record copy fee-$.25 per page. Cert fee: $5.00 per cert. Payee: Butler County Clerk.

Caldwell County

County Clerk, 100 E Market St, Rm 3, Courthouse - Rm 3, Princeton, KY 42445. **Phone-**County Clerk, R/E & UCC Recording- 270-365-6754; fax-270-365-7447; hours 8AM-4PM. UCC record search per debtor-$5.00. UCC copy- $1.00 per page. Will not search real estate or tax lien records. RE record copy-$.25 per page. Fee to fax results is $5.00 per doc. Cert fee: $5.00 per cert. Payee: Caldwell County Clerk. **Other phones:** Assessor-270-365-7227; Treasurer-270-365-9776; Elections-270-365-6754.

Calloway County

County Clerk, 101 S. 5th St, Murray, KY 42071-2569. **Phone-**270-753-3923; fax-270-759-9611; hours 8AM-4:30PM

UCC record search per debtor- $5.00. UCC copy-$1.00 per page. Will not search real estate or tax lien records. RE record copy- $.10 per page. Cert fee: 5.00 per cert. Payee: Calloway County Clerk. **Other phones:** Assessor-270-753-3482.

Campbell County

County Clerk, 4th & York Sts, Courthouse, Newport, KY 41071. **Phone-**859-292-3850, R/E Recording- 859-292-3845; fax-859-292-3887; hours 8:30AM-6PM M; 8:30AM-4PM T-F; 9AM-Noon Sat

UCC record search per debtor- $5.00. UCC copy-$1.00 per page. Will not search real estate or tax lien records. RE record copy- $.50 per page. Cert

fee: $5.00 1st 3 pages; $.25 each add'l. Payee: Campbell County Clerk. **Online Access to Property, Appraiser records:** Access to the Property Valuation Administrator property value is free at http://campbellpropertymax.governmax.com/propertymax/rover30.asp. **Other phones:** Assessor-859-292-3871; Treasurer-859-292-3838; Appraiser/ Auditor-859-292-3871; Elections-859-292-3885.

Carlisle County

County Clerk, PO Box 176, Bardwell, KY 42023. **Phone-**County Clerk, R/E & UCC Recording- 270-628-3233; fax-270-628-0191; hours 8:30AM-4PM Will not search records. UCC copy- $1.00 per page. Separate federal/state combined tax lien search-$5.00 per debtor. RE record copy- $.10 per page. Cert fee: $5.00 per cert. Payee: Carlisle County Clerk. **Other phones:** Assessor-270-628-5498; Treasurer-270-628-3922.

Carroll County

County Clerk, 440 Main St, Court House, Carrollton, KY 41008. **Phone-**County Clerk, R/E & UCC Recording- 502-732-7005; fax-502-732-7007; hours 8:30AM-4:30PM M,T,Th,F; 8:30AM-Noon W,Sat UCC record search per debtor- $5.00. Tax liens not included in UCC search. Will not search real estate records. Record copy- $.25 per page. Cert fee: $5.00 per cert. Payee: Carroll County Clerk. **Other phones:** Assessor-502-732-5448; Treasurer-502-732-7000; Elections-502-732-7005.

Carter County

County Clerk, 300 W. Main St, Rm 232, Grayson, KY 41143. **Phone-**County Clerk, R/E & UCC Recording-606-474-5188; fax-606-474-6883; hours 8:30AM-4PM; 8:30AM-Noon Sat

UCC record search per debtor- $5.00. Will not search real estate or tax lien records. Record copy- $.50 per page. Cert fee: $5.00 per doc. Payee: Carter County Clerk. **Other phones:** Assessor-606-474-5663; Treasurer-606-474-9551; Elections-606-474-5188; Vital Records-606-474-5188.

Casey County

County Clerk, Box 310, Liberty, KY 42539. **Phone-**606-787-6471; fax-606-787-9155; hours 8AM-4:30PM M-F; 8AM-Noon Sat

UCC record search per debtor- $5.00. UCC copy fee-$.25 per page. Will not search real estate or tax lien records. RE record copy- $.25 per page. Cert fee: $5.00 per cert. Payee: Casey County Clerk. **Other phones:** Assessor-606-787-7621; Treasurer-606-787-6154; Appraiser/ Auditor-606-787-7621; Elections-606-787-6471.

Christian County

County Clerk, 511 S. Main, Hopkinsville, KY 42240. **Phone-**270-887-4105, R/E Recording- 270-887-4109; fax-270-887-4186; hours 8AM-4:30PM

UCC record search per debtor- $5.00. UCC copy-$1.00 per page. Will not search real estate or tax lien records. RE record copy- $.50 per page. Cert fee: $5.00 per cert. Payee: Christian County Clerk. **Other phones:** Assessor-270-887-4115; Treasurer-270-887-4103; Appraiser/ Auditor-270-887-4115; Elections-270-887-4105.

Clark County

County Clerk, PO Box 4060, Winchester, KY 40392. **Phone-**859-745-0280, R/E Recording- 859-745-0282; fax-859-745-4251; hours 8AM-5PM M; 8AM-4PM T-F

UCC record search per debtor- $5.00. Will not search real estate or tax lien records. Record copy- $.25 per page. Cert fee: $5.00 per cert. Payee: Clark County Clerk. **Other phones:** Assessor-859-745-

0270; Treasurer-859-745-0200; Elections-859-745-0280; Vital Records-859-745-0282.

Clay County

County Clerk, 123 Town Sq #3, Manchester, KY 40962. **Phone-**606-598-2544; fax-606-599-0603; hours 8AM-4:30PM; 8AM-Noon Sat

Will not search records. UCC copy- $.50 per page. Cert fee: $5.00 per cert. Payee: Clay County Clerk. **Other phones:** Assessor-606-598-3832; Treasurer-606-598-2071.

Clinton County

County Clerk, 212 Washington St, Courthouse, Albany, KY 42602. **Phone-**County Clerk, R/E & UCC Recording- 606-387-5943; fax-606-387-5258; hours 8AM-4:30PM; 8AM-Noon Sat

UCC record search per debtor- $5.00. Will only search as time allows. Will do tax lien search as time allows. Will not search real estate records. Record copy- $1.00 per page. Cert fee: $3.50 per cert. Payee: Clinton County Clerk. **Other phones:** Assessor-606-387-5938; Treasurer-606-387-5234; Elections-606-387-5943; Vital Records-606-387-5943.

Crittenden County

County Clerk, 107 S. Main, Courthouse, #203, Marion, KY 42064. **Phone-**County Clerk, R/E & UCC Recording- 270-965-3403; fax-270-965-3447; hours 8AM-4:30PM M,T,Th,F; 8AM-Noon W,Sat

Will search UCC records. UCC copy- $.50 per page. Will not search real estate or tax lien records. Cert fee: $5.00. Payee: Crittenden County Clerk. **Other phones:** Assessor-270-965-4598; Treasurer-270-965-5251; Elections-270-965-3404.

Cumberland County

County Clerk, PO Box 275, Burkesville, KY 42717. **Phone-**County Clerk, R/E & UCC Recording- 270-864-3726; fax-270-864-5884; hours 8AM-4:30PM; 8AM-Noon Sat

UCC record search per debtor- $5.00. Will not search real estate or tax lien records. Record copy- $.50 per page. Cert fee: $3.50 per cert. Payee: Cumberland County Clerk. **Other phones:** Assessor-270-864-5161; Treasurer-270-864-3444; Elections-270-864-3726.

Daviess County

County Clerk, PO Box 609, Owensboro, KY 42302. **Phone-**270-685-8420, R/E Recording- 270-685-8434; fax-270-685-2431; hours 8AM-4PM M-Th; 8AM-6PM F

UCC record search per debtor- $5.00. Will not search real estate or tax lien records. Record copy- $.25 per page. Cert fee: $5.50 per cert. Payee: Daviess County Clerk. **Other phones:** Assessor-270-685-8474; Treasurer-270-685-8424; Elections-270-685-8434.

Edmonson County

County Clerk, PO Box 830, Brownsville, KY 42210-0830. **Phone-**County Clerk, R/E & UCC Recording-270-597-2624; fax-270-597-9714; hours 8AM-5PM M,T,W,F; 8AM-Noon Sat

Will not search records. Record copy- $.50 per page. Cert fee: $5.00 per cert. Payee: Edmonson County Clerk. **Other phones:** Assessor-270-597-2381; Treasurer-270-597-2819; Elections-270-597-2624; Vital Records-270-597-2624.

Elliott County

County Clerk, PO Box 225, Sandy Hook, KY 41171-0225. **Phone-**County Clerk, R/E & UCC Recording-606-738-5421; fax-606-738-4462; hours 8AM-4PM; 9AM-Noon Sat

UCC record search per debtor- $5.00. UCC copy-$1.00 per page. Tax liens not included in UCC search. Will not search real estate records. RE record copy- $.50 per sheet. Cert fee: $5.00 per page. Payee: Elliott County Clerk. **Other phones:** Assessor-606-738-5090; Treasurer-606-738-5821; Elections-606-738-5421; Vital Records-606-738-5421.

Estill County

County Clerk, PO BOX 59, Irvine, KY 40336. **Phone-**606-723-5156; fax-606-723-5108; hours 8AM-12;00-1-4PM M,T,Th,F; 8AM-Noon W,Sat
UCC record search per debtor- $5.00. UCC copy- $.25 per page. UCC search includes tax liens if requested. Separate federal/state combined tax lien search- $3.50 per debtor. Real estate owner, mortgage, and property transfer searches available. Cert fee: $5.00 per cert. Payee: Estill County Clerk. **Other phones:** Assessor-606-723-4569.

Fayette County

County Clerk, 162 E. Main St, Lexington, KY 40507-1334. **Phone-**859-253-3344; hours 8AM-4:30PM
UCC record search per debtor- $5.00. UCC copy- $.50 per page. Will not search real estate or tax lien records. Cert fee: $5.00 for doc. Payee: Fayette County Clerk. **Online Access to Property, Crime Map records:** Search the GIS-property mapping site for free by address at http://arcims.lfucg.com/maps/zoning/viewer.htm. No name searching. Also, search the interactive crime map at http://crimewatch.lfucg.com. **Other phones:** Assessor-859-254-2722; Treasurer-859-258-3300.

Fleming County

County Clerk, Court Sq, Rm 101, Flemingsburg, KY 41041. **Phone-**County Clerk, R/E & UCC Recording-606-845-8461; fax-606-845-0212; hours 8:30AM-4:30PM M-F; 8:30AM-Noon Sat
UCC record search per debtor- $5.00. UCC copy- $1.00 per page. Will not search real estate or tax lien records. RE record copy- $2.00 per page. Cert fee: $5.00 per cert. Payee: Fleming County Clerk. **Other phones:** Assessor-606-845-8801; Treasurer-606-845-8801; Elections-606-845-8461; Vital Records-606-845-8461.

Floyd County

County Clerk, PO Box 1089, Prestonsburg, KY 41653-5089. **Phone-**606-886-3816; fax-606-886-8089; hours 8AM-4:30PM M,T,W,Th; 8AM-6PM F;9AM-Noon Sat
Will not search records. Record copy- $.50 per page. Cert fee: $5.00 per doc. Payee: Floyd County Clerk. **Other phones:** Assessor-606-886-9622.

Franklin County

County Clerk, PO Box 338, Frankfort, KY 40602. **Phone-**502-875-8703, R/E Recording- 502-875-8710; fax-502-875-8718; hours 8AM-4:30PM www.franklincountyclerk.org
UCC record search per debtor- $5.00. UCC copy- $1.00 per page. Will not search real estate or tax lien records. RE record copy- $.25 per page. Cert fee: $5.00 per cert. Payee: Franklin County Clerk. **Other phones:** Assessor-502-875-878-; Treasurer-502-875-8747; Elections-502-875-8704; Vital Records-502-564-4212.

Fulton County

County Clerk, PO Box 126, Hickman, KY 42050. **Phone-**270-236-2061; fax-270-236-2522; 8AM-4PM
UCC record search per debtor- $5.00. UCC copy- $1.00 per page. Real estate owner, mortgage, and property transfer searches available. Cert fee: $5.00 per cert. Payee: Fulton County Clerk. **Other phones:** Assessor-270-236-2548; Treasurer-270-236-2594.

Gallatin County

County Clerk, PO Box 1309, Warsaw, KY 41095. **Phone-**859-567-5411; fax-859-567-5444; hours 8AM-6PM M; 8AM-4:30PM T-F; 8AM-12 Sat.
Will search UCC records. UCC copy- $2.00 per page. Will not search real estate or tax lien records. RE record copy- $.25 per page. Cert fee: $5.00 per cert. Payee: Gallatin County Clerk. **Other phones:** Assessor-859-567-5621; Treasurer-859-567-5691; Elections-859-567-5411.

Garrard County

County Clerk, 15 Public Sq, #5, Courthouse Bldg., Lancaster, KY 40444. **Phone-**County Clerk, R/E & UCC Recording- 859-792-3071; fax-859-792-6751; hours 8AM-4PM M,T,Th,F; 8AM-Noon W,Sat
Berea, KY addresses may be in Madison County, and parts of Crab Orchard are in Lincoln County. UCC record search per debtor- $5.00. UCC search includes tax liens if requested. Separate federal/state combined tax lien search- $6.50 per debtor. Real estate owner, mortgage, and property transfer searches available. Record copy- $5.00 per doc. Cert fee: $5.00 per cert. Payee: Garrard County Clerk. **Other phones:** Assessor-859-792-3291; Treasurer-859-792-4178; Appraiser/ Auditor-859-792-3291; Elections-859-792-3071; Vital Records-859-792-3071.

Grant County

County Clerk, 101 N Main St, Courthouse Basement, Rm 15, Williamstown, KY 41097. **Phone-**859-824-3321; fax-859-824-3367; hours 8:30AM-4PM M-F; 8:30AM-Noon Sat
UCC record search per debtor- $5.00. Will not search real estate or tax lien records. Record copy- $.25 per page. Cert fee: $5.00 per cert. Payee: Grant County Clerk. **Other phones:** Assessor-859-824-6511; Treasurer-859-824-7561.

Graves County

County Clerk, Courthouse, Mayfield, KY 42066. **Phone-**270-247-1676, R/E Recording- 270-247-1697; fax-270-247-1274; hours 8AM-4:30PM M-Th; 8AM-6PM F
UCC record search per debtor- $5.00. UCC copy- $2.00 per page. Will not search real estate or tax lien records. RE record copy- $.50 per page. Cert fee: $5.00 per doc. Payee: Graves County Clerk. **Other phones:** Assessor-270-247-3301; Treasurer-270-247-3626; Elections-270-247-1676.

Grayson County

County Clerk, 10 Public Sq, Leitchfield, KY 42754. **Phone-**County Clerk, R/E & UCC Recording- 270-259-5295, UCC Recording- 270-259-3201; fax-270-230-0881; hours 8AM-5PM M,T,W,F; 8AM-Noon Th,Sat
UCC record search per debtor- $5.00. Will not search real estate or tax lien records. Record copy- $.25 per page. Cert fee: $5.00 per cert. Payee: Grayson County Clerk. **Other phones:** Assessor-270-259-4838; Treasurer-270-259-5000; Elections-270-259-3201; Vital Records-270-259-5295.

Green County

County Clerk, 203 W. Court St, Greensburg, KY 42743. **Phone-**270-932-5386; fax-270-932-6241; hours 8AM-4PM M-W,F; 8AM-Noon Th,Sat.
Will search UCC records. Record copy- $1.50 per instrument; $.50 per page generally. Will search state/federal tax liens. Will not search real estate records. Cert fee: $5.00 per cert. Payee: Green County Clerk. **Other phones:** Assessor-270-932-7518; Treasurer-270-932-4024.

Greenup County

County Clerk, PO Box 686, Greenup, KY 41144-0686. **Phone-**County Clerk, R/E & UCC Recording- 606-473-7396; fax-606-473-5354; hours 9AM-4:30PM M-F
UCC record search per debtor- $5.00. UCC copy- $1.00 per page. Will not search real estate or tax lien records. RE record copy- $.50 per page. Cert fee: $5.00 per cert. Payee: Greenup County Clerk. **Other phones:** Assessor-606-473-9984; Treasurer-606-473-5350; Elections-606-473-7396; Vital Records-606-473-7396.

Hancock County

County Clerk, PO Box 146, Hawesville, KY 42348. **Phone-**County Clerk, R/E & UCC Recording- 270-927-6117; fax-270-927-8639; hours 8AM-4PM M-W,F; 8AM-5:30PM Th . Will not search records. Cert fee: $5.00 per cert. Payee: Hancock County Clerk. **Other phones:** Assessor-270-927-6846; Treasurer-270-927-8101; Elections-270-927-6117.

Hardin County

County Clerk, PO Box 1030, Elizabethtown, KY 42702. **Phone-**270-765-4116, R/E Recording- 270-765-2171; fax-270-769-2682; hours 8AM-4:30PM www.hccoky.org
UCC record search per debtor- $5.00. UCC copy- $1.00 per page. Will search tax liens. Will not search real estate records. RE record copy- $.25 per page. Cert fee: $5.00 per doc. Payee: Hardin County Clerk. **Online Access to Recording, Will, Deed, Mortgage, Real Estate, Marriage, Assumed Name records:** Access to the County Clerk's records search page is free at www.hccoky.org/search/search.asp. Deeds go back to 1983; mortgages to 1976; most other records all available. **Other phones:** Assessor-270-765-2129; Treasurer-270-765-2350; Appraiser/ Auditor-270-765-2129; Elections-270-765-6762; Vital Records-270-765-2171.

Harlan County

County Clerk, PO Box 670, Harlan, KY 40831-0670. **Phone-**County Clerk, R/E & UCC Recording- 606-573-3636; fax-606-573-0064; hours 8:30AM-4:30PM M-W & F; 8:30AM-6PM Th
UCC record search per debtor- $5.00. UCC copy- $1.00 per page. Will not search real estate or tax lien records. RE record copy- $.50 per page. Cert fee: $5.00 per cert. Payee: Harlan County Clerk. **Other phones:** Assessor-606-573-1990; Treasurer-606-573-4771.

Harrison County

County Clerk, 313 Oddville Rd, Cynthiana, KY 41031. **Phone-**859-234-7130, R/E Recording- 859-235-0513; fax-859-234-8049; hours 8:30AM-4:30PM M T W F; 8:30AM-6PM T Th
Deed Room phone #: 859-235-0513. UCC record search per debtor- $5.00. Will not search real estate or tax lien records. Record copy- $.25 per page. Cert fee: $5.00 per doc. Payee: Harrison County Clerk. **Other phones:** Assessor-859-234-7113; Treasurer-859-234-7136.

Hart County

County Clerk, PO Box 277, Munfordville, KY 42765. **Phone-**County Clerk, R/E & UCC Recording- 270-524-2751; fax-270-524-0458; hours 8AM-4PM (8AM-Noon Sat)
Will not search records. UCC copy- $1.00 per page. Cert fee: $3.50 per cert. Payee: Hart County Clerk. **Other phones:** Assessor-270-524-2321; Treasurer-270-524-9474.

Henderson County

County Clerk, PO Box 374, Henderson, KY 42419-0374. **Phone-**County Clerk, R/E & UCC Recording-270-826-3906; fax-270-826-9677; hours 8AM-4:30PM M-Th; 8AM-6PM F
Will not search records. UCC copy fee- $.50 per file. RE record copy- $.25 per page. Cert fee: $5.00 per cert. Payee: Henderson County Clerk. **Other phones:** Assessor-270-827-6024; Treasurer-270-826-3233; Appraiser/ Auditor-270-826-6024; Elections-270-826-3906.

Henry County

County Clerk, PO Box 615, New Castle, KY 40050-0615. **Phone-**502-845-5705; fax-502-845-5708; hours 8AM -5PM; M ; 8AM-4PM,T,W,Th F
UCC record search per debtor- $5.00. UCC copy-$1.00 per page. Will not search real estate or tax lien records. Cert fee: $5.00. Payee: Henry County Clerk.

Hickman County

County Clerk, 110 E Clay, Courthouse, Clinton, KY 42031-1296. **Phone-**270-653-2131; fax-270-653-4248; hours 8:30AM-4PM
Will not search records. Record copy- $.25 per page. Cert fee: $5.00 per cert. Payee: Hickman County Clerk. **Other phones:** Assessor-270-653-5521; Treasurer-270-653-6195; Elections-270-653-2131; Vital Records-270-653-6110.

Hopkins County

County Clerk, 10 S Main St, Madisonville, KY 42431. **Phone-**County Clerk, R/E & UCC Recording- 270-821-7361, UCC Recording- 270-825-5001; fax-270-825-7000; hours 8AM-4PM
UCC record search per debtor- $5.00. UCC copy-$1.00 per page. Will not search real estate or tax lien records. Cert fee: $5.00. Payee: Hopkins County Clerk. **Other phones:** Assessor-270-825-3092; Treasurer-270-825-2666.

Jackson County

County Clerk, PO Box 339, McKee, KY 40447. **Phone-**606-287-7800; fax-606-287-4505; hours 8AM-4PM; 8:30AM-Noon Sat
Will not search records. UCC copy fee- $.25 per page. Cert fee: $5.00 per cert. Payee: Jackson County Clerk. **Other phones:** Assessor-606-287-7634; Treasurer-606-287-8562.

Jefferson County Clerk

County Clerk, PO Box 35339, Louisville, KY 40232-5339. **Phone-**502-574-6427, R/E Recording- 502-574-6220; fax-502-574-6041; hours 8AM-4:30PM
UCC record search per debtor- $5.00. UCC copy fee-$2.00 per file number. Will not search tax liens. See Recorder for real estate records. Cert fee: $5.00 per cert. Payee: Jefferson County Clerk. **Online Access to Property, Assessor records:** Access to the county property valuation administrator's assessment roll is free at www.pvalouky.org/. **Other phones:** Assessor-502-574-6380.

Jefferson County Recorder

County Clerk, 527 W Jefferson St, Rm 204, Louisville, KY 40202. **Phone-**County Clerk, R/E & UCC Recording- 502-574-5785, UCC Recording- 502-574-6130; fax-502-574-8130; hours 8AM-4:45PM www.countyclerk.jefferson.ky.us
Will search UCC records, but only real estate related UCC filed here. Search per debtor- $5.00.Will not search real estate or tax lien records. Payee: Jefferson County Clerk. **Online Access to Land records:** Online land records system found at www.jccorecords.ky.gov/.

Jessamine County

County Clerk, 101 N. Main St, Nicholasville, KY 40356-1270. **Phone-**County Clerk, R/E & UCC Recording- 859-885-4161; fax-859-885-5837; hours 8AM-5PM M; 8AM-4PM T,W,F; 8AM-Noon Th; 9am-Noon Sa
Will not search records. UCC copy- $1.00 per page. Payee: Jessamine County Clerk. **Other phones:** Assessor-859-885-4931; Treasurer-859-885-4500; Elections-859-885-4161.

Johnson County

County Clerk, 230 Court St. Courthouse, Paintsville, KY 41240. **Phone-**606-789-2557; fax-606-789-2559; hours 8AM-4;30PM, 8:30AM-Noon Sat
Will not search UCC records. UCC copy- $.25 per page. Will not search tax liens. Real estate owner, mortgage, and property transfer searches available. Cert fee: $5.00 per cert. Payee: Johnson County Clerk. **Other phones:** Assessor-606-789-2564.

Kenton County (1st District)

County Clerk, PO Box 1109, Covington, KY 41012. **Phone-**859-392-1600, R/E Recording- 859-392-1653, UCC Recording- 859-392-1650; fax-859-392-1639; hours 8:30AM-4PM M-Th; 8:30AM-6PM F www.kentonpva.com
UCC record search per debtor- $5.00. UCC copy-$1.00 per page. Will not search real estate or tax lien records. RE record copy- $.25 per page. Cert fee: $5.00 per cert. Payee: Kenton County Clerk. **Online Access to Property Appraiser records:** Access the county Property Valuation database at www.kentonpva.com. Click on "Property Data." Search for free by using "Guest Access." For full, professional property data you may subscribe; fee for user name/password is $50. per month. **Other phones:** Assessor-859-392-1750; Treasurer-859-392-1420; Elections-859-392-1620; Vital Records-859-392-1650 (Marriage License Only).

Kenton County (2nd District)

County Clerk, PO Box 38, Independence, KY 41051. **Phone-**859-392-1692, R/E Recording- 859-392-1619; fax-859-392-1681; hours 8:30AM-4PM M,T,Th,F; 8:30AM-6PM W www.kentonpva.com
2nd District includes property south of Banklick Creek. 1st District includes property north of Banklick Creek. UCC record search per debtor- $5.00. UCC copy-$1.00 per page. Will not search real estate or tax lien records. RE record copy- $.50 per page. Cert fee: $5.00 per cert. Payee: Kenton County Clerk. **Online Access to Property Appraiser records:** Access to the county Property Valuation database is free at www.kentonpva.com/pvacat/catsearch.htm. **Other phones:** Assessor-859-392-1750; Treasurer-859-392-1420.

Knott County

County Clerk, PO Box 446, Hindman, KY 41822. **Phone-**606-785-5651; fax-606-785-0996; hours 8AM-4PM, 8AM-Noon Sat
UCC record search per debtor- $5.00. UCC copy-$1.00 per page. UCC search includes tax liens if requested with extra fee. Real estate owner, mortgage, and property transfer searches available. RE record copy- $.25 per page. Cert fee: $5.50 per cert. Payee: Knott County Clerk. **Other phones:** Assessor-606-785-5569; Treasurer-606-785-5592.

Knox County

County Clerk, 401 Court Sq, #102, Barbourville, KY 40906. **Phone-**County Clerk, R/E & UCC Recording-606-546-3568; fax-606-546-3589; 8:30AM-4PM
UCC record search per debtor- $5.00. UCC copy-$1.00 per page. Will not search real estate or tax lien records. Cert fee: $5.00 per cert. Payee: Knox

County Clerk. **Other phones:** Assessor-606-546-4113; Treasurer-606-546-6192; Elections-606-546-3568; Vital Records-606-564-4212.

Larue County

County Clerk, 209 W. High St., Hodgenville, KY 42748. **Phone-**270-358-3544; fax-270-358-4528; hours 8AM-4:30PM M,T,Th,F; 8AM-Noon W,Sat
Will search UCC records. UCC copy- $1.00 per page. Tax liens not included in UCC search. Separate federal/state combined tax lien search-$1.00 per debtor. Real estate owner, mortgage, and property transfer searches available. Cert fee: $3.50 per cert. Payee: County Clerk. **Other phones:** Assessor-270-358-4202; Treasurer-270-358-4400.

Laurel County

County Clerk, 101 S. Main, Rm 203, Courthouse, London, KY 40741. **Phone-**606-864-5158; fax-606-864-7369; hours 8AM-4:30PM; 8:30AM-Noon Sat
Will not search records. UCC copy- $2.00 per page. Cert fee: $5.00 per cert. Payee: Laurel County Clerk. **Online Access to Property Appraiser records:** county Property Valuation database is free at www.pvdnetwork.com/PVDNet.asp?SiteID=107. **Other phones:** Assessor-606-864-2889.

Lawrence County

County Clerk, 122 S. Main Cross St, Louisa, KY 41230. **Phone-**County Clerk, R/E & UCC Recording-606-638-4108, UCC Recording- 606-638-0504; fax-606-638-0638; hours 8:30AM-4PM; 8:30AM-Noon Sat. UCC record search per debtor- $5.00. Will not search real estate or tax lien records. Record copy-$.50 per page. Cert fee: $5.00 per cert. Payee: Lawrence County Clerk. **Other phones:** Assessor-606-638-4743; Treasurer-606-638-4102; Appraiser/ Auditor-606-638-4743; Elections-606-638-4108; Vital Records-606-638-4188.

Lee County

County Clerk, PO Box 551, Beattyville, KY 41311. **Phone-**County Clerk, R/E & UCC Recording- 606-464-4115; fax-606-464-4102; hours 8AM-4PM
UCC record search per debtor- $5.00. Copy fee is $.25 per page. Will not search tax liens. Will search real estate records. Copy fee-$.25 per page. Cert fee: $5.00 per cert. Payee: Lee County Clerk. **Other phones:** Assessor-606-464-4105; Treasurer-606-464-4100; Elections-606-464-4115; Vital Records-606-464-4115; 2nd Main Number-606-464-4116.

Leslie County

County Clerk, PO Box 916, Hyden, KY 41749-0916. **Phone-**606-672-2193; fax-606-672-4264; hours 8AM-5PM; 8AM-Noon Sat. UCC record search per debtor-$5.00. UCC copy- $.50 per page. Will not search real estate or tax lien records. Cert fee: $5.00 per cert. Payee: Leslie County Clerk. **Other phones:** Assessor-606-672-2456.

Letcher County

County Clerk, 156 Main St. #102, Whitesburg, KY 41858. **Phone-**606-633-2432; fax-606-632-9282; hours 8:30AM-4PM; 8:30AM-Noon 1st Sat of month
UCC record search per debtor- $20.00. UCC copy-$1.00 per page. Will not search real estate or tax lien records. Cert fee: $5.00 per cert. Payee: Letcher County Clerk. **Other phones:** Assessor-606-633-2182.

Lewis County

County Clerk, PO Box 129, Vanceburg, KY 41179-0129. **Phone-**County Clerk, R/E & UCC Recording-606-796-3062; fax-606-796-6511; hours 8:30AM-4:30PM M T Th F; 8:30AM-Noon W
Will not search UCC records. Federal/state combined tax lien search- $5.00 per debtor. Real estate record

owner and mortgage searches available. Cert fee: $5.00 per cert. Payee: Lewis County Clerk. **Other phones:** Assessor-606-796-2622; Treasurer-606-796-2722; Elections-606-796-2311; Vital Records-606-796-3062.

Lincoln County

County Clerk, 102 E. Main, Courthouse, Stanford, KY 40484. **Phone-**606-365-4570, R/E Recording- 606-365-4520; fax-606-365-4572; hours 8AM-4PM M-F; 9AM-Noon Sat
Will not search records. UCC copy- $2.00 per page. RE record - $.25 per page. Cert fee: $5.00 per cert. Payee: Lincoln County Clerk. **Other phones:** Assessor-606-365-4550; Treasurer-606-365-4590; Elections-606-365-4570.

Livingston County

County Clerk, PO Box 400, Smithland, KY 42081-0400. **Phone-**County Clerk, R/E & UCC Recording-270-928-2162; fax-270-928-2162; hours 8AM-4PM; 8AM-6PM M
UCC record search per debtor- $5.00. UCC copy- $.50 per page. Will not search real estate or tax lien records. RE record copy- $.25 per page. Cert fee: $5.00 per cert. Payee: Livingston County Clerk. **Other phones:** Assessor-270-928-2524.

Logan County

County Clerk, PO Box 358, Russellville, KY 42276-0358. **Phone-**County Clerk, R/E & UCC Recording-270-726-6061; fax-270-726-4355; 8:30AM-4:30PM
UCC record search per debtor- $5.00. UCC copy- $1.00 per page. UCC search includes tax liens if requested. Will not search real estate records. RE record copy- $.25 per page. Cert fee: $5.00 per cert. Payee: Logan County Clerk. **Other phones:** Assessor-270-726-8334; Treasurer-270-726-2167.

Lyon County

County Clerk, PO Box 310, Eddyville, KY 42038. **Phone-**County Clerk, R/E & UCC Recording- 270-388-2331; fax-270-388-0634; hours 8:30AM-4PM
UCC record search per debtor- $5.00. UCC copy- $1.00 per page. Will not search real estate or tax lien records. Cert fee: $3.50 per cert. Payee: Lyon County Clerk. **Other phones:** Assessor-270-388-7271; Treasurer-270-388-7193; Elections-270-388-2331.

Madison County

County Clerk, 101 W. Main St, County Court House, Richmond, KY 40475-1415. **Phone-**859-624-4704; fax-859-624-8474; hours 8AM-4PM M-F; 8AM-6;30PM Th
UCC record search per debtor- $5.00. UCC copy- $1.00 per page. Will not search real estate or tax lien records. Cert fee: $10.00. Payee: Madison County Clerk. **Other phones:** Assessor-859-624-4704.

Magoffin County

County Clerk, PO Box 530, Salyersville, KY 41465. **Phone-**County Clerk, R/E & UCC Recording- 606-349-2216; fax-606-349-2328; hours 8:30AM-4PM; 8:30AM-Noon Sat
UCC record search per debtor- $9.00. Will not search real estate or tax lien records. Record copy- $1.00 per page. Cert fee: $3.50 per cert. Payee: Magoffin County Clerk. **Other phones:** Assessor-606-349-6198; Treasurer-606-349-2313; Elections-606-349-6194; Vital Records-606-349-2216.

Marion County

County Clerk, 120 W Main St, Courthouse, #3, Lebanon, KY 40033. **Phone-**270-692-2651; fax-270-692-9811; hours 8:30AM-4:30PM; 8:30AM-Noon Sat. UCC record search per debtor- $5.00. Will not

search real estate or tax lien records. Record copy- $.25 per page. Cert fee: $5.00 per doc. Payee: Marion County Clerk. **Other phones:** Assessor-270-692-3401; Treasurer-270-692-3451.

Marshall County

County Clerk, 1101 Main St, Courthouse, Benton, KY 42025. **Phone-**270-527-4740; fax-270-527-4738; hours 8AM-4:30PM
Will not search records. UCC copy- $1.00 per page. Cert fee: $5.00 per cert. Payee: Marshall County Clerk. **Other phones:** Assessor-270-527-4728.

Martin County

County Clerk, PO Box 460, Inez, KY 41224-0485. **Phone-**County Clerk, R/E & UCC Recording- 606-298-2810; fax-606-298-0143; hours 8AM-5PM; 8AM-Noon Sat
UCC record search per debtor- $5.00. UCC copy- $.50 per page. Will not search real estate or tax lien records. Cert fee: $5.00 per cert. Payee: Martin County Clerk. **Other phones:** Assessor-606-298-2808; Treasurer-606-298-2800; Elections-606-298-2810; Vital Records-606-298-7752.

Mason County

County Clerk, PO Box 234, Maysville, KY 41056. **Phone-**606-564-3341; fax-606-564-8979; hours 9AM-5PM; 9-11:30AM Sat
UCC record search per debtor- $5.00. UCC copy fee- $.25 per page. Will not search real estate or tax lien records. Cert fee: $5.00 per cert. Payee: Mason County Clerk. **Other phones:** Assessor-606-564-3700; Treasurer-606-564-6381.

McCracken County

County Clerk, PO Box 609, Paducah, KY 42002-0609. **Phone-**270-444-4700; fax-270-444-4704; hours 8:30AM-4:30PM (M open until 5:30PM)
Will search UCC records. UCC search per debtor- $5.00 per search. UCC copy- $1.00 per page. Will not search real estate or tax lien records. RE record copy- $5.00 for 4 pages or less, $2.00 each add'l. Cert fee: $5.00 per cert. Payee: McCracken County Clerk. **Other phones:** Assessor-270-444-4712; Treasurer-270-444-4725.

McCreary County

County Clerk, PO Box 699, Whitley City, KY 42653. **Phone-**606-376-2411; fax-606-376-3898; hours 8:30AM-4:30PM M-F; 9AM-Noon Sat
UCC record search per debtor- $5.00. Will not search real estate or tax lien records. Record copy- $1.00 per page. Cert fee: $3.50 per cert. Payee: McCreary County Clerk. **Other phones:** Assessor-606-376-2514.

McLean County

County Clerk, PO Box 57, Calhoun, KY 42327-0057. **Phone-**County Clerk, R/E & UCC Recording- 270-273-3082; fax-270-273-5084; hours 8AM-4:30PM; 9AM-Noon Sat
Will search UCC records only in their office. Search per debtor- $5.00. Will not search real estate or tax lien records. Record copy- $.25 per page. Cert fee: $5.00 per instrument. Payee: McLean County Clerk. **Other phones:** Assessor-270-273-3291; Treasurer-270-273-9964; Elections-270-273-3082.

Meade County

County Clerk, PO Box 614, Brandenburg, KY 40108. **Phone-**270-422-2152; fax-270-422-2158; hours 8AM-4:30PM; 9AM-Noon Sat
They are planning to offer internet access to records late in 2003. Call for information. UCC record search per debtor- $5.00. UCC copy- $.50 per page. Will not search real estate or tax lien records. Cert fee:

$5.00 per cert. Payee: Meade County Clerk. **Other phones:** Assessor-270-422-2178.

Menifee County

County Clerk, PO Box 123, Frenchburg, KY 40322-0123. **Phone-**County Clerk, R/E & UCC Recording-606-768-3512; fax-606-768-6738; hours 8:30AM-4PM M,T,W,F; 8:30-11:30AM Th,Sat
Will not search records. UCC copy- $1.00 per page. RE record copy- $.25 per page. Cert fee: $5.00 per cert. Payee: Menifee County Clerk. **Other phones:** Assessor-606-768-3514; Treasurer-606-768-2931; Elections-606-768-3512; Vital Records-606-768-3512.

Mercer County

County Clerk, PO Box 426, Harrodsburg, KY 40330. **Phone-**859-734-6313; fax-859-734-6309; hours 8AM-4:30PM. UCC record search per debtor- $5.00. UCC copy- $.50 per page. UCC search includes tax liens if requested. Separate federal/state combined tax lien search- $5.00 per debtor. Will not search real estate records. Cert fee: $5.00 per cert. Payee: Mercer County Clerk. **Other phones:** Assessor-859-734-6330.

Metcalfe County

County Clerk, PO Box 25, Edmonton, KY 42129. **Phone-**270-432-4821; fax-270-432-5176; 8AM-4PM
UCC record search per debtor- $20.00. UCC copy- $1.00 per page. Will not search real estate or tax lien records. RE record copy- $.50 per page. Cert fee: $5.00 per cert. Payee: Metcalfe County Clerk. **Other phones:** Assessor-270-432-3162; Treasurer-270-432-3181.

Monroe County

County Clerk, 200 N. Main St. #D, Tompkinsville, KY 42167-1548. **Phone-**County Clerk, R/E & UCC Recording- 270-487-5471; fax-270-487-5976; hours 8AM-4:30PM M-F; 8AM-Noon Sat. Will not search records. UCC copy fee- $.25 per page. Cert fee: $5.00 per cert. Payee: Monroe County Clerk. **Other phones:** Assessor-270-487-6401; Treasurer-270-487-5505; Elections-270-487-5471.

Montgomery County

County Clerk, PO Box 414, Mount Sterling, KY 40353. **Phone-**County Clerk, R/E & UCC Recording- 859-498-8700; fax-859-498-8729 or 498-8738; hours 8:30AM-4PM M-TH; 8:30-6PM F
UCC record search per debtor- $5.00. UCC copy- $.50 per page. Will search tax liens including federal tax liens. Will not search real estate records. RE record copy- $.25 per page. Cert fee: $5.00 per cert. Payee: County Clerk. **Other phones:** Assessor-859-498-8710; Treasurer-859-498-8703; Elections-859-498-8700; Vital Records-859-498-8700.

Morgan County

County Clerk, PO Box 26, West Liberty, KY 41472. **Phone-**County Clerk, R/E & UCC Recording- 606-743-3949; fax-606-743-2111; hours 8AM-4PM; 8AM-Noon Sat
UCC record search per debtor- $5.00. UCC copy- $1.00 per page. Will search tax liens including federal tax liens. Will search real estate records. RE record copy- $.50 per page. Cert fee: $1.50 per cert. Payee: Morgan County Clerk. **Other phones:** Assessor-606-743-3349; Treasurer-606-743-3195; Appraiser/ Auditor-606-743-3349; Elections-606-743-3949; Vital Records-606-743-3949.

Muhlenberg County

County Clerk, PO Box 525, Greenville, KY 42345. **Phone-**270-338-1441; fax-270-338-1774; hours 8AM-4PM; 8AM-6PM F
Record copy fee-$.25 per page; $5.00 to fax back. $1.00 for research per book. UCC record search per debtor-

$5.00.UCC search includes tax liens if requested. Will not search real estate records. Cert fee: $2.00 per cert. Payee: Muhlenberg County Clerk. **Other phones:** Assessor-270-338-4664.

Nelson County

County Clerk, PO Box 312, Bardstown, KY 40004. **Phone-**County Clerk, R/E & UCC Recording- 502-348-1830, UCC Recording- 502-348-1828; fax-502-348-1822; hours 8:30AM-4:30PM M-F; 8AM-11:45AM Sat

UCC record search per debtor- $5.00. UCC copy- $.25 per page. Will not search real estate or tax lien records. Cert fee: $5.00 per cert. Payee: Nelson County Clerk. **Other phones:** Assessor-502-348-1810; Treasurer-502-348-1800; Appraiser/ Auditor-502-348-1810; Elections-502-348-1829; Vital Records-502-564-4212.

Nicholas County

County Clerk, PO Box 227, Carlisle, KY 40311. **Phone-**859-289-3730; fax-859-289-3709; hours 8AM-4:30PM; 8-11:30AM Sat

UCC record search per debtor- $5.00. UCC search includes tax liens if requested. Will search real estate records. Record copy- $1.00 per page. Cert fee: $5.00 per cert. Payee: Nicholas County Clerk. **Other phones:** Assessor-859-289-3735; Treasurer-859-289-3725; Elections-859-289-3730.

Ohio County

County Clerk, PO Box 85, Hartford, KY 42347. **Phone-**270-298-4422; fax-270-298-4425; hours 8AM-4:30PM M-Th; 8AM-6PM F; 8AM-Noon Sat

Will not search records. UCC copy fee- $.25 per page. Cert fee: $5.00 per cert. Payee: Ohio County Clerk. **Other phones:** Assessor-270-298-3692.

Oldham County

County Clerk, 100 W. Jefferson St, LaGrange, KY 40031. **Phone-**County Clerk, R/E & UCC Recording- 502-222-9311; fax-502-222-3208; hours 8:30AM-4PM M-W,F; 8:30AM-6PM Th http://oldhamcounty.state.ky.us

UCC record search per debtor- $5.00. Copy fee included in search. Will not search real estate or tax lien records. Cert fee: $5.00 per cert. Payee: Oldham County Clerk. **Online Access to Real Estate, Lien, UCC, Assessor, Marriage records:** Access to the database is through eCCLIX database, a fee-based service; $200.00 sign-up & $65.00 monthly. Records go back, to 1980. UCC images to 2/97. Real estate instruments back to 1/95. Marriages back to 1980. For information, see the website http://oldhamcounty.state.ky.us/ecclix.stm or call 502-266-9445. **Other phones:** Assessor-502-222-9320; Elections-502-222-0047.

Owen County

County Clerk, 135 W Bryan St, Owenton, KY 40359-0338. **Phone-**County Clerk, R/E & UCC Recording- 502-484-2213; fax-502-484-1002; hours 8AM-4PM M T TH F; 8am-Noon W SAT, Closed on WED

Will not search records. Record copy- $.25 per page. Cert fee: $5.00 per instrument. Payee: Owen County Clerk. **Other phones:** Assessor-502-484-5172; Treasurer-502-484-3557; Elections-502-484-2213; Vital Records-502-484-2213.

Owsley County

County Clerk, PO Box 500, Booneville, KY 41314. **Phone-**606-593-5735; fax-606-593-5737; hours 8AM-4PM; 8AM-12 Sat

Will search UCC records. UCC search per debtor- $5.00.UCC search includes tax liens if requested. Will not search real estate records. Cert fee: $6.00 per cert. Payee: Owsley County Clerk. **Other phones:** Assessor-606-593-6265; Treasurer-606-593-6202.

Pendleton County

County Clerk, PO Box 112, Falmouth, KY 41040. **Phone-**County Clerk, R/E & UCC Recording- 859-654-3380; fax-859-654-5600; hours 8:30AM-4PM M-F; 8:30AM-Noon Sat. Will search UCC records. UCC copy- $2.00 per page. UCC search includes tax liens if requested. Separate federal/state combined tax lien search- $5.00 per doc. Will not search real estate records. RE record copy- $.25 per page. Cert fee: $5.00 per cert. Payee: Pendleton County Clerk. **Other phones:** Assessor-859-654-6055; Treasurer-859-654-4321; Appraiser/ Auditor-859-654-3380; Elections-859-654-3380.

Perry County

County Clerk, PO Box 150, Hazard, KY 41702. **Phone-**County Clerk, R/E & UCC Recording- 606-436-4614; fax-606-439-0557; hours 8AM-4PM

Will fax back for $1.00 per page. UCC record search per debtor- $5.00. Tax liens not included in UCC search. Tax lien search fee- $5.00 per debtor. Will not search real estate records. Cert fee: $5.00 per cert. Payee: Perry County Clerk. **Other phones:** Assessor-606-436-4914; Treasurer-606-436-1816.

Pike County

County Clerk, PO Box 631, Pikeville, KY 41502-0631. **Phone-**606-432-6240; fax-606-432-6222; hours 8:30AM-4:30 M,T,W,Th; 8:30-6PM F; 8:30AM-Noon Sat.

UCC record search per debtor- $5.00. UCC copy- $.50 per page. Will not search real estate or tax lien records. Cert fee: $5.00. Payee: Pike County Clerk. **Other phones:** Assessor-606-432-6201.

Powell County

County Clerk, PO Box 548, Stanton, KY 40380. **Phone-**County Clerk, R/E & UCC Recording- 606-663-6444; fax-606-663-6406; hours 9AM-4PM M-W; 9AM-Noon Th; 9AM-4PM F; 9AM-Noon Sat

Will not search records. UCC copy fee- $.25 per page. RE record- $.10 per page. Cert fee: $5.00 per cert. Payee: Powell County Clerk. **Other phones:** Assessor-606-663-4184; Treasurer-606-663-2834; Appraiser/ Auditor-606-663-4184; Vital Records-502-564-4212.

Pulaski County

County Clerk, PO Box 724, Somerset, KY 42502. **Phone-**606-679-3652, R/E Recording- 606-679-2042, UCC Recording- 606-679-2042; fax-606-678-0073; hours 8AM-4:30PM

UCC record search per debtor- $5.00. UCC copy- $.50 per page. Will not search real estate or tax lien records. Cert fee: $5.00 per cert. Payee: Pulaski County Clerk. **Other phones:** Assessor-606-679-1812; Treasurer-606-679-1311; Elections-606-679-3652; Vital Records-606-679-3652.

Robertson County

County Clerk, PO Box 75, Mount Olivet, KY 41064. **Phone-**606-724-5212; fax-606-724-5022; hours 8:30-Noon, 1-4PM M,T,Th,F; 8:30AM-Noon W, Sat

Will not search records. UCC copy fee- $1.00 per page. Cert fee: $6.50 per cert, no copy fee. Payee: Robertson County Clerk. **Other phones:** Assessor-606-724-5213; Treasurer-606-724-5403.

Rockcastle County

County Clerk, 205 E Main St #6, Mount Vernon, KY 40456. **Phone-**606-256-2831; fax-606-256-4302; hours 8:30-4PM; 8;30-Noon Sat

UCC record search per debtor- $5.00. UCC copy fee- $1.00 per page. Will not search real estate or tax lien records. Cert fee: $5.00. Payee: Rockcastle County Clerk. **Other phones:** Assessor-606-256-4194; Treasurer-606-256-3623.

Rowan County

County Clerk, 627 E. Main St, Courthouse - 2nd Fl, Morehead, KY 40351. **Phone-**County Clerk, R/E & UCC Recording- 606-784-5212; fax-606-784-2923; hours 8AM-4PM M-TH; 8AM-6PM F

UCC record search per debtor- $5.00. Copy fee is $1.00 per copy. Will not search real estate or tax lien records. RE record copy- $.25 per page. Cert fee: $5.00 per cert. Payee: Rowan County Clerk. **Other phones:** Assessor-606-784-5512; Treasurer-606-784-4211; Vital Records-502-564 4212.

Russell County

County Clerk, PO Box 579, Jamestown, KY 42629-0579. **Phone-**270-343-2125; fax-270-343-4700; hours 8AM-4PM; 8AM-11;00 Sat

UCC record search per debtor- $5.00. Search request using non-standard form (per name)- $6.00. UCC copy- $1.00 per page. Will not search real estate or tax lien records. Cert fee: $5.00 per cert. Payee: Russell County Clerk. **Other phones:** Assessor-270-343-4395; Treasurer-270-343-2112.

Scott County

County Clerk, 101 E Main St, Courthouse, Georgetown, KY 40324-1794. **Phone-**502-863-7875; fax-502-863-7898; hours 8:30AM-4:30PM M-Th; 8:30AM-6PM F. UCC record search per debtor- $5.00. UCC copy- $1.00 per page. Will not search real estate or tax lien records. Cert fee: $5.00 per cert. Payee: Scott County Clerk. **Other phones:** Assessor-502-863-7885; Treasurer-502-863-7850.

Shelby County

County Clerk, PO Box 819, Shelbyville, KY 40066-0819. **Phone-**County Clerk, R/E & UCC Recording- 502-633-4410, UCC Recording- 502-513-0265; fax-502-633-7887; hours 8:30AM-4:30PM M,T,W,F; 8:30AM-6PM Th www.shelbycountyclerk.com

Will search UCC records. UCC copy- $1.00 per page. Will not search real estate or tax lien records. RE record copy- $.10 per page. Cert fee: $5.00 per cert. Payee: Shelby County Clerk. **Online Access to Real Estate, Deed, Recording records:** Access is via the eCCLIX subsciption system at www.shelbycountyclerk.com/ecclix.stm. Images go back to 1998; index to 1995. Sign-up fee is $100 + $65 per month for unlimited access. For information, phone 502-266-9445 or email sales@softwaremanagementinc.com. **Other phones:** Assessor-502-633-4403; Treasurer-502-633-1220; Elections-502-633-4410; Vital Records-502-564-4212.

Simpson County

County Clerk, PO Box 268, Franklin, KY 42135-0268. **Phone-**270-586-8161; fax-270-586-6464; hours 8AM-4PM. UCC record search per debtor- $5.00. UCC copy- $.50 per page. Will not search real estate or tax lien records. Cert fee: $5.00 per cert. Payee: Simpson County Clerk. **Other phones:** Assessor-502-586-4261; Treasurer-502-586-7184.

Spencer County

County Clerk, PO Box 544, Taylorsville, KY 40071. **Phone-**502-477-3215; fax-502-477-3216; hours 8AM-4:30PM M-F; 8AM-11;30 Sat

UCC record search per debtor- $5.00. UCC copy fee- $.25 per page. Will not search real estate or tax lien records. Cert fee: $5.00 per cert. Payee: Spencer County Clerk. **Other phones:** Assessor-502-477-3207; Treasurer-502-477-3211.

Taylor County

County Clerk, 203 N. Court St, ## 5, Campbellsville, KY 42718-2298. **Phone-**County Clerk, R/E & UCC Recording- 270-465-6677; fax-270-789-1144; hours 8AM-4:30PM M-Th; 8AM-5PM F

Will not search records. Cert fee: $5.00. Payee: Taylor County Clerk. **Other phones:** Assessor-270-465-5811; Treasurer-270-789-1008.

Todd County

County Clerk, PO Box 307, Elkton, KY 42220. **Phone-**270-265-2363; fax-270-265-2588; 8AM-4:30PM
Will not search records. Record copy- $.25 per page. Cert fee: $5.00 per cert. Payee: Todd County Clerk. **Other phones:** Assessor-270-265-5614; Treasurer-270-265-2451.

Trigg County

County Clerk, PO Box 1310, Cadiz, KY 42211. **Phone-**270-522-6661; fax-270-522-6662; hours 8AM-4PM M-Th; 8AM-5PM F. UCC record search per debtor- $3.50. UCC copy- $1.00 per page. Will search tax liens. Tax lien search fee- $3.00 per debtor. Will not search real estate records. Cert fee: $3.50 per cert. Payee: Trigg County Clerk. **Other phones:** Assessor-270-522-6661; Treasurer-270-522-8459; Elections-270-522-6661.

Trimble County

County Clerk, PO Box 262, Bedford, KY 40006-0262. **Phone-**County Clerk, R/E & UCC Recording- 502-255-7174; fax-502-255-7045; hours 8:30AM-4:30PM M,T,Th,F; 8:30AM-Noon Sat
Will not search records. Record copy- $.25 per page. Cert fee: $5.00 per cert. Payee: Trimble County Clerk. **Other phones:** Assessor-502-255-3592; Elections-502-255-7174; Vital Records-502-255-7174.

Union County

County Clerk, PO Box 119, Morganfield, KY 42437-0119. **Phone-**270-389-1334; fax-270-389-9135; hours 8AM-4PM. Will search UCC records. UCC search per debtor- $5.00. UCC copy- $.50 per page. Will not search real estate or tax lien records. Cert fee: $5.00. Payee: Union County Clerk. **Other phones:** Assessor-270-389-1933.

Warren County

County Clerk, PO Box 478, Bowling Green, KY 42102-0478. **Phone-**County Clerk, R/E & UCC Recording- 270-842-9416; fax-270-843-5319; hours 8:30AM-4:30PM http://warrencounty.state.ky.us
UCC record search per debtor- $5.00. Will not search real estate or tax lien records. RE record copy- $.25 per page. Cert fee: $5.00 per cert. Payee: Warren County Clerk. **Online Access to Real Estate, Lien, UCC, Assessor, Marriage records:** Access the county clerk database through eCCLIX, a fee-based service; $200.00 sign-up and $65.00 monthly. Records go back to 1989; images to 1998. For information, see the website or call 502-266-9445. **Other phones:** Assessor-270-842-3268; Treasurer-270-842-5805; Elections-270-842-5306; Vital Records-270-842-9416.

Washington County

County Clerk, PO Box 446, Springfield, KY 40069. **Phone-**859-336-5425; fax-859-336-5408; hours 9AM-4:30PM; 9AM-Noon Sat. UCC record search per debtor- $5.00. UCC copy fee- $.25 per copy. Tax liens not included in UCC search. Separate federal/state combined tax lien search- $10.00 per debtor. Real estate record owner and mortgage searches available. Cert fee: $5.00 per cert. Payee: Washington County Clerk. **Other phones:** Assessor-859-336-5420; Elections-859-336-5425.

Wayne County

County Clerk, PO Box 565, Monticello, KY 42633. **Phone-**County Clerk, R/E & UCC Recording- 606-348-6661; fax-606-348-8303; hours 8AM-4:30PM; 8AM-Noon Sat
UCC record search per debtor- $5.00. Will not search real estate or tax lien records. Cert fee: $5.00 per cert. Payee: Wayne County Clerk. **Other phones:** Assessor-606-348-6621; Treasurer-606-348-8411.

Webster County

County Clerk, PO Box 19, Dixon, KY 42409-0019. **Phone-**County Clerk, R/E & UCC Recording- 270-639-7006; fax-270-639-7029; hours 8AM-4PM M; 8AM-4PM T-F. Will search UCC records. Search per instrument- $5.00 per instrument, if copies required. UCC copy- $.25 per page. Tax liens not included in UCC search. Tax lien search fee- $5.00 per debtor. Will not search real estate records. RE record copy- $.50 per page. Cert fee: $5.00 per cert. Payee: Webster County Clerk. **Other phones:** Assessor-270-639-7016; Treasurer-270-639-5042.

Whitley County

County Clerk, PO Box 8, Williamsburg, KY 40769. **Phone-**County Clerk, R/E & UCC Recording- 606-549-6002; fax-606-549-2790; hours 7:30AM-4PM; 7:30AM-Noon Sat. UCC record search per debtor- $3.50. UCC copy- $.50 per page. Fee is $2.50 per page to fax results. Will not search real estate or tax lien records. RE record copy- $.25 per page. Cert fee: $5.00 per cert. Payee: Whitley County Clerk. **Other phones:** Assessor-606-549-6008.

Wolfe County

County Clerk, PO Box 400, Campton, KY 41301. **Phone-**County Clerk, R/E & UCC Recording- 606-668-3515; fax-606-668-3492; hours 8AM-4PM M,T,Th,F; 8AM-Noon Sat
UCC record search per debtor- $5.00. UCC copy- $1.00 per page. Will not search real estate or tax lien records. Payee: Wolfe County Clerk. **Other phones:** Assessor-606-668-6923; Treasurer-606-668-4060; Appraiser/ Auditor-606-668-6925; Elections-606-668-3515; Vital Records-606-668-4212.

Woodford County

County Clerk, 103 S Main St, Courthouse - Rm 120, Versailles, KY 40383. **Phone-**859-873-3421; fax-859-873-6985; hours 8AM-4PM M,T,W,Th; 8AM-5:45PM F. Will not search records. Cert fee: $5.00 per cert. Payee: Woodford County Clerk. **Other phones:** Assessor-859-873-4101; Treasurer-859-873-6122; Elections-859-873-3421.

Kentucky County Locator

You will usually be able to find the city name in the City/County Cross Reference below. In that case, it is a simple matter to determine the county from the cross reference. However, only the official US Postal Service city names are included in this index. There are an additional 40,000 place names that people use in their addresses. Therefore, we have also included a ZIP/City Cross Reference immediately following the City/County Cross Reference.

If you know the ZIP Code but the city name does not appear in the City/County Cross Reference index, look up the ZIP Code in the ZIP/City Cross Reference, find the city name, then look up the city name in the City/County Cross Reference.

Kentucky City/County Cross Reference

AARON (42601) Clinton(97), Russell(2)
ABERDEEN Butler
ACORN Pulaski
ADAIRVILLE (42202) Logan(98), Simpson(1)
ADAMS Lawrence
ADOLPHUS Allen
AGES BROOKSIDE Harlan
ALBANY Clinton
ALEXANDRIA Campbell
ALLEGRE Todd
ALLEN Floyd
ALLENSVILLE (42204) Todd(78), Logan(21)
ALLOCK Perry
ALMO Calloway
ALPHA (42603) Clinton(69), Wayne(30)
ALTRO Breathitt
ALVATON (42122) Warren(94), Allen(5)
AMBURGEY Knott
ANNVILLE (40402) Jackson(95), Clay(4)
ARGILLITE Greenup
ARJAY Bell
ARLINGTON (42021) Carlisle(92), Hickman(7)
ARTEMUS Knox
ARY Perry
ASHCAMP Pike
ASHER Leslie
ASHLAND (41102) Boyd(93), Greenup(6)
ASHLAND Boyd
ATHOL Breathitt
AUBURN (42206) Logan(92), Simpson(6), Warren(1)
AUGUSTA Bracken
AUSTIN Barren
AUXIER Floyd
AVAWAM Perry
AXTEL Breckinridge
BAGDAD (40003) Shelby(83), Franklin(16)
BAKERTON Cumberland
BANDANA Ballard
BANNER Floyd
BARBOURVILLE Knox
BARDSTOWN Nelson
BARDWELL Carlisle
BARLOW Ballard
BASKETT Henderson
BATTLETOWN Meade
BAXTER Harlan
BAYS Breathitt
BEAR BRANCH Leslie
BEATTYVILLE Lee
BEAUMONT Metcalfe
BEAUTY Martin
BEAVER Floyd
BEAVER DAM (42320) Ohio(98), Butler(1)
BEDFORD (40006) Trimble(97), Carroll(2)
BEE SPRING Edmonson
BEECH CREEK Muhlenberg
BEECH GROVE McLean
BEECHMONT Muhlenberg
BELCHER Pike
BELFRY Pike
BELLEVUE Campbell
BELTON Muhlenberg
BENHAM Harlan

BENTON (42025) Marshall(98), Calloway(1)
BEREA (40403) Madison(87), Garrard(10), Rockcastle(2)
BEREA Madison
BERRY (41003) Harrison(67), Grant(19), Pendleton(12)
BETHANY Wolfe
BETHEL Bath
BETHELRIDGE Casey
BETHLEHEM Henry
BETSY LAYNE (41605) Floyd(89), Pike(10)
BEULAH HEIGHTS McCreary
BEVERLY (40913) Bell(57), Clay(42)
BEVINSVILLE Floyd
BIG CLIFTY (42712) Grayson(60), Hardin(39)
BIG CREEK Clay
BIG LAUREL (40808) Harlan(50), Leslie(50)
BIG SPRING (40106) Breckinridge(80), Hardin(20)
BIGHILL Madison
BIMBLE Knox
BLACKEY Letcher
BLACKFORD Webster
BLAINE Lawrence
BLANDVILLE Ballard
BLEDSOE (40810) Harlan(87), Leslie(12)
BLOOMFIELD (40008) Nelson(89), Spencer(9)
BLUE RIVER Floyd
BLUEHOLE Clay
BOAZ (42027) Graves(80), McCracken(19)
BOND Jackson
BONNIEVILLE Hart
BONNYMAN Perry
BOONEVILLE (41314) Breathitt(56), Owsley(43)
BOONS CAMP Johnson
BOSTON Nelson
BOW (42714) Cumberland(92), Clinton(7)
BOWEN Powell
BOWLING GREEN (42101) Warren(96), Edmonson(2)
BOWLING GREEN Warren
BRADFORDSVILLE (40009) Marion(78), Taylor(16), Casey(5)
BRANDENBURG Meade
BREEDING (42715) Adair(94), Metcalfe(4), Cumberland(1)
BREMEN Muhlenberg
BRINKLEY Knott
BRODHEAD (40409) Rockcastle(90), Lincoln(9)
BRONSTON (42518) Pulaski(96), Wayne(3)
BROOKLYN Butler
BROOKS (40109) Bullitt(97), Jefferson(2)
BROOKSVILLE Bracken
BROWDER Muhlenberg
BROWNS FORK Perry
BROWNSVILLE Edmonson
BRUIN Elliott
BRYANTS STORE Knox
BRYANTSVILLE Garrard
BUCKHORN (41721) Perry(94), Breathitt(5)

BUCKNER Oldham
BUFFALO (42716) Larue(75), Green(20), Taylor(3)
BULAN (41722) Perry(65), Knott(34)
BURDINE Letcher
BURGIN Mercer
BURKESVILLE Cumberland
BURKHART Wolfe
BURLINGTON Boone
BURNA Livingston
BURNSIDE Pulaski
BURNWELL Pike
BUSH Laurel
BUSKIRK Morgan
BUSY (41723) Perry(76), Leslie(23)
BUTLER Pendleton
BYPRO Floyd
CADIZ Trigg
CALHOUN (42327) McLean(97), Daviess(2)
CALIFORNIA Campbell
CALVERT CITY Marshall
CALVIN Bell
CAMP DIX Lewis
CAMPBELLSBURG (40011) Henry(76), Trimble(18), Carroll(4)
CAMPBELLSVILLE (42718) Taylor(92), Marion(3), Green(2), Larue(1)
CAMPBELLSVILLE Taylor
CAMPTON (41301) Wolfe(93), Breathitt(3), Lee(2)
CANADA Pike
CANE VALLEY Adair
CANEY Morgan
CANEYVILLE (42721) Grayson(89), Butler(7), Edmonson(3)
CANMER Hart
CANNEL CITY Morgan
CANNON Knox
CANOE Breathitt
CANTON Trigg
CARLISLE (40311) Nicholas(90), Bourbon(8)
CARRIE Knott
CARTER Carter
CARVER Magoffin
CASEY CREEK (42723) Adair(61), Taylor(31), Casey(6)
CASEY CREEKG (42723) Adair(61), Taylor(31), Casey(6)
CATLETTSBURG (41129) Boyd(87), Lawrence(12)
CAVE CITY (42127) Barren(92), Hart(7)
CAWOOD Harlan
CECILIA Hardin
CENTER (42214) Metcalfe(70), Green(29)
CENTERTOWN Ohio
CENTRAL CITY Muhlenberg
CERULEAN (42215) Christian(52), Trigg(47)
CHAPLIN Nelson
CHAPPELL Leslie
CHAVIES Perry
CINDA Leslie
CISCO Magoffin
CLARKSON Grayson
CLAY (42404) Webster(90), Union(9)

CLAY CITY Powell
CLAYHOLE Breathitt
CLEARFIELD Rowan
CLEATON Muhlenberg
CLERMONT Bullitt
CLIFTY Todd
CLINTON Hickman
CLOSPLINT Harlan
CLOVERPORT Breckinridge
COALGOOD Harlan
COBHILL Estill
COLDIRON Harlan
COLUMBIA Adair
COLUMBUS Hickman
COMBS Perry
CONCORD Lewis
CONFLUENCE Leslie
CONLEY Magoffin
CONSTANCE Boone
CONSTANTINE Breckinridge
CONWAY Rockcastle
COOPERSVILLE Wayne
CORBIN (40701) Whitley(51), Knox(24), Laurel(24)
CORBIN Whitley
CORINTH (41010) Grant(59), Owen(30), Harrison(7), Scott(1)
CORNETTSVILLE (41731) Perry(68), Letcher(31)
CORYDON Henderson
COTTLE Morgan
COVINGTON Kenton
COXS CREEK (40013) Nelson(78), Spencer(13), Bullitt(7)
CRAB ORCHARD (40419) Lincoln(70), Garrard(17), Rockcastle(8), Pulaski(4)
CRANKS Harlan
CRAYNE Crittenden
CRAYNOR Floyd
CRESTWOOD Oldham
CRITTENDEN (41030) Grant(70), Boone(28), Kenton(1)
CROCKETT Morgan
CROFTON Christian
CROMONA Letcher
CROMWELL (42333) Ohio(87), Butler(12)
CROWN Letcher
CRYSTAL (40420) Lee(83), Estill(16)
CUB RUN (42729) Hart(70), Edmonson(29)
CULVER Elliott
CUMBERLAND (40823) Harlan(97), Letcher(2)
CUNDIFF Adair
CUNNINGHAM (42035) Carlisle(82), Graves(17)
CURDSVILLE Daviess
CUSTER Breckinridge
CUTSHIN Leslie
CYNTHIANA (41031) Harrison(97), Nicholas(1), Bourbon(1)
DABOLT Jackson
DAISY Perry
DANA Floyd
DANVILLE (40422) Boyle(98), Lincoln(1)
DANVILLE Boyle
DAVID Floyd

DAWSON SPRINGS (42408) Hopkins(86), Caldwell(10), Christian(3)
DAYHOIT Harlan
DAYTON Campbell
DE MOSSVILLE Pendleton
DEANE (41812) Letcher(81), Knott(18)
DEBORD Martin
DECOY (41321) Knott(80), Breathitt(20)
DEFOE Henry
DELPHIA Perry
DELTA Wayne
DEMA Knott
DENNISTON Menifee
DENTON (41132) Carter(75), Lawrence(22), Boyd(1)
DENVER Johnson
DEWITT Knox
DEXTER (42036) Calloway(98), Marshall(1)
DICE Perry
DINGUS Morgan
DIXON Webster
DIZNEY Harlan
DORTON Pike
DOVER (41034) Mason(97), Bracken(2)
DRAFFIN Pike
DRAKE Warren
DRAKESBORO Muhlenberg
DREYFUS Madison
DRIFT Floyd
DRY RIDGE Grant
DUBRE (42731) Cumberland(74), Metcalfe(25)
DUNBAR Butler
DUNDEE Ohio
DUNMOR (42339) Muhlenberg(92), Butler(7)
DUNNVILLE (42528) Casey(93), Russell(4), Adair(1)
DWALE Floyd
DWARF Perry
DYCUSBURG Crittenden
EARLINGTON Hopkins
EAST BERNSTADT Laurel
EAST POINT (41216) Floyd(52), Johnson(47)
EASTERN Floyd
EASTVIEW Hardin
EASTWOOD Jefferson
EDDYVILLE Lyon
EDMONTON (42129) Metcalfe(93), Adair(6)
EDNA Magoffin
EGYPT Jackson
EIGHTY EIGHT Barren
EKRON Meade
ELIZABETHTOWN Hardin
ELIZAVILLE Fleming
ELK HORN (42733) Taylor(79), Casey(17), Adair(3)
ELKFORK Morgan
ELKHORN CITY Pike
ELKTON (42220) Todd(97), Muhlenberg(1)
ELLIOTTVILLE Rowan
ELSIE Magoffin
EMERSON Lewis
EMINENCE (40019) Henry(97), Shelby(2)
EMLYN Whitley
EMMA Floyd
EMMALENA Knott
ENDICOTT Floyd
EOLIA Letcher
ERILINE Clay
ERLANGER Kenton
ERMINE Letcher
ESSIE Leslie
ESTILL Floyd
ETOILE Barren
EUBANK (42567) Pulaski(89), Lincoln(10)
EVARTS Harlan
EWING Fleming
EZEL Morgan
FAIRDALE Jefferson

FAIRFIELD Nelson
FAIRPLAY Adair
FAIRVIEW Christian
FALCON Magoffin
FALL ROCK Clay
FALLS OF ROUGH (40119) Grayson(61), Breckinridge(36), Ohio(2)
FALMOUTH Pendleton
FANCY FARM (42039) Graves(45), Carlisle(34), Hickman(20)
FARMERS Rowan
FARMINGTON (42040) Graves(76), Calloway(23)
FAUBUSH (42532) Pulaski(58), Russell(35), Wayne(6)
FEDSCREEK Pike
FERGUSON Pulaski
FILLMORE Lee
FINCHVILLE Shelby
FINLEY (42736) Taylor(56), Marion(43)
FIREBRICK Lewis
FISHERVILLE (40023) Spencer(51), Jefferson(47)
FISTY Knott
FLAT FORK Magoffin
FLAT LICK Knox
FLATGAP (41219) Johnson(98), Lawrence(1)
FLATWOODS Greenup
FLEMINGSBURG Fleming
FLORENCE Boone
FOGERTOWN Clay
FORD Clark
FORDS BRANCH Pike
FORDSVILLE (42343) Ohio(71), Hancock(28)
FOREST HILLS Pike
FORT CAMPBELL Christian
FORT KNOX (40121) Hardin(75), Meade(24)
FORT THOMAS Campbell
FOSTER Bracken
FOUNTAIN RUN (42133) Monroe(51), Barren(31), Allen(17)
FOURMILE (40939) Knox(71), Bell(28)
FRAKES (40940) Whitley(67), Bell(32)
FRANKFORT (40601) Franklin(96), Woodford(1), Shelby(1)
FRANKFORT Franklin
FRANKLIN (42134) Simpson(94), Allen(5)
FRANKLIN Simpson
FRAZER Wayne
FREDONIA (42411) Caldwell(60), Crittenden(34), Lyon(5)
FREDVILLE Magoffin
FREEBURN Pike
FRENCHBURG Menifee
FRITZ Magoffin
FT MITCHELL Kenton
FUGET Johnson
FULTON (42041) Fulton(71), Graves(16), Hickman(11)
GALVESTON Floyd
GAMALIEL Monroe
GAPVILLE Magoffin
GARFIELD (40140) Breckinridge(98), Hardin(1)
GARNER Knott
GARRARD Clay
GARRETT (41630) Floyd(52), Knott(47)
GARRISON (41141) Greenup(90), Lewis(5), Carter(3)
GAYS CREEK Perry
GEORGETOWN Scott
GERMANTOWN (41044) Mason(82), Bracken(17)
GHENT Carroll
GILBERTSVILLE Marshall
GILLMORE Wolfe
GIRDLER Knox
GLASGOW Barren
GLENCOE (41046) Grant(84), Gallatin(15)
GLENDALE Hardin

GLENS FORK (42741) Adair(94), Russell(5)
GLENVIEW Jefferson
GOODY Pike
GOOSE ROCK Clay
GORDON Letcher
GOSHEN Oldham
GRACEY (42232) Christian(71), Trigg(28)
GRADYVILLE Adair
GRAHAM Muhlenberg
GRAHN Carter
GRAND RIVERS Livingston
GRATZ Owen
GRAVEL SWITCH (40328) Boyle(40), Marion(38), Casey(19), Washington(1)
GRAY (40734) Knox(97), Laurel(2)
GRAY HAWK Jackson
GRAYS KNOB Harlan
GRAYSON (41143) Carter(90), Greenup(9)
GREEN HALL Owsley
GREEN ROAD Knox
GREENSBURG (42743) Green(98), Adair(1)
GREENUP Greenup
GREENVILLE Muhlenberg
GRETHEL Floyd
GULSTON Harlan
GUNLOCK Magoffin
GUSTON (40142) Meade(95), Breckinridge(4)
GUTHRIE Todd
GYPSY Magoffin
HADDIX Breathitt
HADLEY Warren
HAGERHILL Johnson
HALDEMAN Rowan
HALFWAY Allen
HALLIE Letcher
HALO Floyd
HAMLIN Calloway
HAMPTON Livingston
HANSON Hopkins
HAPPY Perry
HARDBURLY Perry
HARDIN (42048) Marshall(96), Calloway(3)
HARDINSBURG Breckinridge
HARDY Pike
HARDYVILLE (42746) Hart(78), Metcalfe(13), Green(7), Barren(1)
HARLAN Harlan
HARNED Breckinridge
HAROLD Floyd
HARRODS CREEK Jefferson
HARRODSBURG (40330) Mercer(95), Washington(4)
HARTFORD Ohio
HAWESVILLE (42348) Hancock(97), Daviess(2)
HAZARD (41701) Perry(90), Knott(9)
HAZARD Perry
HAZEL Calloway
HAZEL GREEN (41332) Morgan(62), Wolfe(37)
HEBRON Boone
HEIDELBERG Lee
HEIDRICK Knox
HELLIER Pike
HELTON (40840) Leslie(78), Harlan(21)
HENDERSON Henderson
HENDRICKS Magoffin
HERD Jackson
HERNDON (42236) Christian(87), Trigg(12)
HESTAND (42151) Monroe(91), Metcalfe(8)
HI HAT Floyd
HICKMAN Fulton
HICKORY Graves
HILLSBORO Fleming
HILLVIEW Bullitt
HIMA Clay
HINDMAN Knott
HINKLE Knox
HIPPO Floyd

HISEVILLE Barren
HITCHINS Carter
HODGENVILLE Larue
HOLLAND Allen
HOLLYBUSH Knott
HOLMES MILL Harlan
HONAKER Floyd
HOPE (40334) Bath(92), Montgomery(7)
HOPKINSVILLE Christian
HORSE BRANCH (42349) Ohio(82), Grayson(17)
HORSE CAVE (42749) Hart(90), Metcalfe(7), Barren(2)
HOSKINSTON Leslie
HOWARDSTOWN (40028) Nelson(84), Larue(16)
HUDDY Pike
HUDSON Breckinridge
HUEYSVILLE (41640) Knott(66), Floyd(33)
HUFF Edmonson
HULEN Bell
HUNTER Floyd
HUNTSVILLE Butler
HUSTONVILLE (40437) Lincoln(67), Casey(32)
HYDEN Leslie
INDEPENDENCE Kenton
INEZ Martin
INGLE Pulaski
INGRAM Bell
INSKO Morgan
IRVINE (40336) Estill(98), Lee(1)
IRVINGTON Breckinridge
ISLAND McLean
ISLAND CITY Owsley
ISOM Letcher
ISONVILLE Elliott
IVEL Floyd
IVYTON Magoffin
JACKHORN Letcher
JACKSON (41339) Breathitt(97), Knott(2)
JACOBS Carter
JAMBOREE Pike
JAMESTOWN Russell
JEFF Perry
JEFFERSONVILLE Montgomery
JENKINS (41537) Letcher(93), Pike(6)
JEREMIAH Letcher
JETSON Butler
JOB Martin
JOHNS RUN Carter
JONANCY Pike
JONESVILLE Grant
JUNCTION CITY (40440) Boyle(97), Lincoln(2)
KEATON Johnson
KEAVY Laurel
KEENE Jessamine
KEITH Harlan
KENTON Kenton
KENVIR Harlan
KERBY KNOB Jackson
KETTLE Cumberland
KETTLE ISLAND Bell
KEVIL (42053) McCracken(57), Ballard(42)
KIMPER Pike
KINGS MOUNTAIN (40442) Lincoln(50), Casey(49)
KIRKSEY (42054) Calloway(79), Marshall(14), Graves(5)
KITE Knott
KNIFLEY Adair
KNOB LICK (42154) Metcalfe(87), Barren(12)
KONA Letcher
KRYPTON (41754) Perry(97), Leslie(2)
KUTTAWA Lyon
LA CENTER Ballard
LA FAYETTE Christian
LA GRANGE (40031) Oldham(94), Henry(5)
LA GRANGE Oldham
LACKEY (41643) Knott(88), Floyd(11)

LAMB (42155) Barren(60), Monroe(39)
LAMBRIC Breathitt
LAMERO Rockcastle
LANCASTER (40444) Garrard(98), Lincoln(1)
LANCASTER Garrard
LANGLEY Floyd
LATONIA Kenton
LAWRENCEBURG Anderson
LEANDER Johnson
LEATHERWOOD Perry
LEBANON Marion
LEBANON JUNCTION (40150) Bullitt(97), Hardin(2)
LEBURN Knott
LEDBETTER Livingston
LEE CITY Wolfe
LEECO Lee
LEITCHFIELD (42754) Grayson(91), Breckinridge(8)
LEITCHFIELD Grayson
LEJUNIOR Harlan
LENOX Morgan
LEROSE Owsley
LETCHER Letcher
LEWISBURG (42256) Logan(74), Butler(13), Todd(11)
LEWISPORT (42351) Hancock(90), Daviess(9)
LEXINGTON (40509) Fayette(98), Clark(1)
LEXINGTON (40511) Fayette(97), Scott(1)
LEXINGTON (40515) Fayette(95), Jessamine(3)
LEXINGTON (40516) Fayette(89), Bourbon(10)
LEXINGTON Fayette
LIBERTY Casey
LICK CREEK Pike
LILY Laurel
LINDSEYVILLE Edmonson
LINEFORK Letcher
LITTCARR Knott
LITTLE Breathitt
LIVERMORE (42352) McLean(93), Ohio(6)
LIVINGSTON Rockcastle
LLOYD Greenup
LOCKPORT Henry
LOLA Livingston
LONDON Laurel
LONE Lee
LOOKOUT Pike
LORETTO (40037) Marion(75), Washington(13), Nelson(10)
LOST CREEK (41348) Breathitt(91), Perry(8)
LOUISA Lawrence
LOUISVILLE (40229) Jefferson(63), Bullitt(36)
LOUISVILLE (40241) Jefferson(98), Oldham(1)
LOUISVILLE (40245) Jefferson(90), Shelby(8)
LOUISVILLE (40299) Jefferson(98), Bullitt(1)
LOUISVILLE Jefferson
LOVELACEVILLE Ballard
LOVELY Martin
LOWES Graves
LOWMANSVILLE (41232) Lawrence(72), Johnson(27)
LOYALL Harlan
LUCAS Barren
LYNCH Harlan
LYNNVILLE Graves
MACEDONIA Breathitt
MACEO Daviess
MACKVILLE Washington
MADISONVILLE Hopkins
MAGNOLIA (42757) Larue(48), Hart(45), Green(6)
MAJESTIC Pike
MALLIE Knott
MALONE Morgan

MAMMOTH CAVE Edmonson
MANCHESTER Clay
MANITOU Hopkins
MANNSVILLE Taylor
MAPLE MOUNT Daviess
MARIBA Menifee
MARION (42064) Crittenden(98), Caldwell(1)
MARROWBONE Cumberland
MARSHALLVILLE Magoffin
MARSHES SIDING McCreary
MARTHA (41159) Lawrence(97), Johnson(2)
MARTIN Floyd
MARY ALICE Harlan
MARYDELL Laurel
MASON Grant
MASONIC HOME Jefferson
MAYFIELD Graves
MAYKING Letcher
MAYSLICK (41055) Mason(86), Fleming(13)
MAYSVILLE Mason
MAZIE Lawrence
MC ANDREWS Pike
MC CARR Pike
MC COMBS (41545) Pike(90), Floyd(10)
MC DANIELS Breckinridge
MC DOWELL Floyd
MC HENRY Ohio
MC KEE (40447) Jackson(96), Rockcastle(1), Estill(1)
MC KINNEY Lincoln
MC QUADY Breckinridge
MC ROBERTS Letcher
MC VEIGH Pike
MEALLY Johnson
MEANS (40346) Menifee(79), Bath(12), Montgomery(8)
MELBER (42069) Graves(80), McCracken(17), Carlisle(2)
MELBOURNE Campbell
MELVIN Floyd
MIDDLEBURG Casey
MIDDLESBORO Bell
MIDWAY (40347) Woodford(90), Franklin(5), Scott(3)
MIGRATE Fayette
MILBURN Carlisle
MILFORD Bracken
MILL SPRINGS Wayne
MILLERSBURG Bourbon
MILLS Knox
MILLSTONE Letcher
MILLTOWN Adair
MILLWOOD Grayson
MILTON (40045) Trimble(85), Carroll(14)
MIMA Morgan
MINERVA Mason
MINNIE Floyd
MIRACLE Bell
MISTLETOE Owsley
MITCHELLSBURG Boyle
MIZE Morgan
MONTICELLO Wayne
MONTPELIER Adair
MOON Morgan
MOOREFIELD Nicholas
MOORMAN Muhlenberg
MOREHEAD (40351) Rowan(98), Elliott(1)
MORGANFIELD (42437) Union(97), Webster(2)
MORGANTOWN Butler
MORNING VIEW Kenton
MORRILL Jackson
MORTONS GAP Hopkins
MOUNT EDEN (40046) Spencer(78), Anderson(14), Shelby(7)
MOUNT HERMON Monroe
MOUNT OLIVET Robertson
MOUNT SHERMAN (42764) Green(57), Larue(39), Hart(3)

MOUNT STERLING (40353) Montgomery(97), Clark(1)
MOUNT VERNON Rockcastle
MOUNT WASHINGTON Bullitt
MOUSIE Knott
MOUTHCARD Pike
MOZELLE Leslie
MULDRAUGH Meade
MUNFORDVILLE Hart
MURRAY Calloway
MUSES MILLS Fleming
MYRA Pike
NANCY (42544) Pulaski(75), Wayne(17), Russell(7)
NARROWS Ohio
NAZARETH Nelson
NEAFUS Grayson
NEBO (42441) Hopkins(96), Webster(3)
NELSE Pike
NEON Letcher
NERINX Marion
NEVISDALE Whitley
NEW CONCORD Calloway
NEW HAVEN (40051) Nelson(80), Larue(19)
NEW HOPE (40052) Nelson(77), Marion(17), Larue(5)
NEW LIBERTY Owen
NEWPORT Campbell
NICHOLASVILLE Jessamine
NOCTOR Breathitt
NORTH MIDDLETOWN Bourbon
NORTONVILLE (42442) Hopkins(96), Christian(3)
OAK GROVE Christian
OAKLAND Warren
OAKVILLE Logan
OFFUTT Johnson
OIL SPRINGS Johnson
OLATON (42361) Ohio(89), Grayson(10)
OLD LANDING Lee
OLDTOWN Greenup
OLIVE HILL (41164) Carter(97), Elliott(1)
OLLIE Edmonson
OLMSTEAD (42265) Logan(88), Todd(11)
OLYMPIA Bath
ONEIDA Clay
OPHIR Morgan
ORLANDO Rockcastle
OVEN FORK Letcher
OWENSBORO Daviess
OWENTON Owen
OWINGSVILLE (40360) Bath(93), Montgomery(6)
PADUCAH McCracken
PAINT LICK (40461) Garrard(61), Madison(38)
PAINTSVILLE Johnson
PARIS Bourbon
PARK CITY (42160) Barren(74), Edmonson(25)
PARKERS LAKE McCreary
PARKSVILLE (40464) Boyle(86), Casey(13)
PARROT Jackson
PARTRIDGE Letcher
PATHFORK Harlan
PAW PAW Pike
PAYNEVILLE Meade
PELLVILLE Hancock
PEMBROKE (42266) Christian(92), Todd(7)
PENDLETON (40055) Trimble(42), Henry(37), Oldham(20)
PENROD Muhlenberg
PEOPLES Jackson
PERRY PARK Owen
PERRYVILLE (40468) Boyle(88), Washington(6), Mercer(4)
PETERSBURG Boone
PEWEE VALLEY Oldham
PEYTONSBURG Cumberland
PHELPS Pike

PHILPOT (42366) Daviess(95), Hancock(3), Ohio(1)
PHYLLIS Pike
PIKEVILLE Pike
PILGRIM Martin
PINE KNOT McCreary
PINE RIDGE (41360) Wolfe(92), Powell(7)
PINE TOP Knott
PINEVILLE Bell
PINSONFORK Pike
PIPPA PASSES Knott
PITTSBURG Laurel
PLANK Clay
PLEASUREVILLE (40057) Henry(72), Shelby(27)
PLUMMERS LANDING Fleming
POMEROYTON Menifee
POOLE Webster
PORT ROYAL Henry
POWDERLY Muhlenberg
PREMIUM Letcher
PRESTON Bath
PRESTONSBURG Floyd
PRIMROSE Lee
PRINCETON (42445) Caldwell(93), Lyon(2), Hopkins(2), Trigg(1)
PRINTER Floyd
PROSPECT (40059) Jefferson(56), Oldham(43)
PROVIDENCE (42450) Webster(88), Hopkins(7), Crittenden(4)
PROVO Butler
PRYSE Estill
PUTNEY Harlan
QUALITY (42268) Butler(72), Logan(27)
QUICKSAND Breathitt
QUINCY Lewis
RACCOON Pike
RADCLIFF Hardin
RANSOM Pike
RAVEN Knott
RAVENNA Estill
RAYWICK Marion
REDFOX Knott
REED Henderson
REGINA Pike
RENFRO VALLEY Rockcastle
REVELO McCreary
REYNOLDS STATION (42368) Hancock(74), Ohio(25)
RHODELIA (40161) Meade(92), Breckinridge(8)
RICETOWN Owsley
RICHARDSON Lawrence
RICHARDSVILLE Warren
RICHMOND Madison
RINEYVILLE Hardin
RIVER (41254) Johnson(88), Lawrence(11)
ROARK (40979) Leslie(82), Clay(17)
ROBARDS (42452) Henderson(88), Webster(11)
ROBINSON CREEK Pike
ROCHESTER Butler
ROCKFIELD (42274) Warren(93), Logan(6)
ROCKHOLDS (40759) Whitley(85), Knox(14)
ROCKHOUSE Pike
ROCKPORT Ohio
ROCKY HILL Edmonson
ROCKYBRANCH Wayne
ROGERS Wolfe
ROSINE Ohio
ROUNDHILL (42275) Butler(66), Edmonson(33)
ROUSSEAU Breathitt
ROWDY Perry
ROWLETTS Hart
ROXANA Letcher
ROYALTON Magoffin
RUMSEY McLean
RUSH (41168) Boyd(64), Carter(34)
RUSSELL Greenup

RUSSELL SPRINGS (42642) Russell(93), Adair(5), Casey(1)
RUSSELLVILLE Logan
SACRAMENTO (42372) McLean(56), Muhlenberg(43)
SADIEVILLE (40370) Harrison(58), Scott(41)
SAINT CATHARINE Washington
SAINT CHARLES Hopkins
SAINT FRANCIS Marion
SAINT HELENS Lee
SAINT JOSEPH Daviess
SAINT MARY Marion
SAINT PAUL Lewis
SALDEE Breathitt
SALEM (42078) Livingston(64), Crittenden(35)
SALT LICK (40371) Bath(90), Menifee(9)
SALVISA (40372) Mercer(94), Anderson(5)
SALYERSVILLE Magoffin
SANDERS Carroll
SANDGAP Jackson
SANDY HOOK Elliott
SASSAFRAS Knott
SAUL Perry
SAWYER McCreary
SCALF Knox
SCIENCE HILL Pulaski
SCOTTSVILLE Allen
SCUDDY Perry
SE REE Breckinridge
SEBREE Webster
SECO Letcher
SEDALIA Graves
SEITZ Magoffin
SEXTONS CREEK (40983) Clay(91), Owsley(8)
SHARON GROVE Todd
SHARPSBURG (40374) Bath(86), Nicholas(11), Bourbon(2)
SHELBIANA Pike
SHELBY GAP Pike
SHEPHERDSVILLE Bullitt
SHOPVILLE Pulaski
SIDNEY Pike
SILER (40763) Whitley(84), Bell(15)
SILVER GROVE Campbell
SILVERHILL Morgan
SIMPSONVILLE Shelby
SITKA Johnson
SIZEROCK Leslie
SLADE Powell
SLAUGHTERS (42456) Webster(68), Hopkins(31)
SLEMP Perry
SLOANS VALLEY Pulaski
SMILAX Leslie
SMITH Harlan
SMITH MILLS Henderson
SMITHFIELD (40068) Henry(79), Shelby(10), Oldham(9)
SMITHLAND Livingston
SMITHS GROVE (42171) Warren(42), Edmonson(32), Barren(24)
SOLDIER Carter
SOMERSET Pulaski
SONORA (42776) Hardin(72), Larue(27)

SOUTH CARROLLTON Muhlenberg
SOUTH PORTSMOUTH (41174) Greenup(97), Lewis(2)
SOUTH SHORE Greenup
SOUTH UNION Logan
SOUTH WILLIAMSON Pike
SPARTA (41086) Owen(86), Gallatin(13)
SPEIGHT Pike
SPOTTSVILLE Henderson
SPRING LICK Grayson
SPRINGFIELD (40069) Washington(98), Marion(1)
STAB Pulaski
STAFFORDSVILLE Johnson
STAMBAUGH Johnson
STAMPING GROUND (40379) Scott(77), Owen(19), Franklin(3)
STANFORD (40484) Lincoln(94), Garrard(4)
STANLEY Daviess
STANTON (40380) Powell(95), Estill(4)
STANVILLE (41659) Floyd(93), Pike(6)
STEARNS McCreary
STEELE Pike
STEFF Grayson
STEPHENS Elliott
STEPHENSBURG Hardin
STEPHENSPORT Breckinridge
STEUBENVILLE Wayne
STINNETT Leslie
STONE Pike
STONEY FORK (40988) Harlan(53), Bell(46)
STOPOVER Pike
STRUNK McCreary
STURGIS (42459) Union(93), Crittenden(6)
SULLIVAN Union
SULPHUR Henry
SUMMER SHADE (42166) Metcalfe(67), Monroe(18), Barren(14)
SUMMERSVILLE (42782) Green(93), Hart(6)
SUMMIT Hardin
SUNFISH Edmonson
SWAMP BRANCH Johnson
SWEEDEN Edmonson
SYMSONIA (42082) Graves(72), Marshall(23), McCracken(4)
TALBERT Breathitt
TALCUM (41765) Knott(85), Perry(14)
TALLEGA Lee
TATEVILLE Pulaski
TAYLORSVILLE (40071) Spencer(90), Bullitt(8)
TEABERRY Floyd
THELMA Johnson
THORNTON Letcher
THOUSANDSTICKS Leslie
THREEFORKS Martin
TILINE Livingston
TOLER Pike
TOLLESBORO Lewis
TOLU Crittenden
TOMAHAWK Martin
TOMPKINSVILLE Monroe
TOPMOST Knott
TOTZ Harlan

TRAM Floyd
TRENTON (42286) Todd(96), Christian(3)
TROSPER Knox
TURKEY CREEK (41570) Pike(96), Martin(3)
TURNERS STATION (40075) Henry(77), Carroll(22)
TUTOR KEY Johnson
TYNER Jackson
TYPO Perry
ULYSSES Lawrence
UNION Boone
UNION STAR (40171) Meade(86), Breckinridge(13)
UNIONTOWN (42461) Union(95), Henderson(4)
UPTON (42784) Hardin(48), Larue(29), Hart(22)
UTICA (42376) Daviess(72), Ohio(20), McLean(7)
VAN LEAR Johnson
VANCEBURG (41179) Lewis(96), Carter(3)
VANCLEVE Breathitt
VARNEY Pike
VENTRESS Hardin
VERONA Boone
VERSAILLES (40383) Woodford(96), Jessamine(3)
VERSAILLES Woodford
VERTREES Hardin
VEST Knott
VICCO (41773) Perry(63), Knott(36)
VINCENT Owsley
VINE GROVE (40175) Hardin(53), Meade(45), Breckinridge(1)
VIPER Perry
VIRGIE Pike
VOLGA Johnson
WACO (40385) Madison(98), Estill(1)
WADDY (40076) Shelby(80), Franklin(12), Anderson(6)
WALKER Knox
WALLINGFORD (41093) Fleming(97), Lewis(2)
WALLINS CREEK Harlan
WALNUT GROVE Pulaski
WALTON Boone
WANETA Jackson
WARBRANCH (40874) Leslie(94), Clay(5)
WARFIELD Martin
WARSAW Gallatin
WASHINGTON Mason
WATER VALLEY (42085) Graves(68), Hickman(31)
WATERVIEW Cumberland
WAVERLY (42462) Union(90), Henderson(9)
WAX Grayson
WAYLAND Floyd
WAYNESBURG (40489) Lincoln(89), Casey(10)
WEBBVILLE (41180) Lawrence(90), Carter(9)
WEBSTER (40176) Breckinridge(95), Meade(4)
WEEKSBURY Floyd
WELCHS CREEK Butler

WELLINGTON (40387) Menifee(91), Morgan(7), Wolfe(1)
WENDOVER Leslie
WEST LIBERTY (41472) Morgan(98), Elliott(1)
WEST LOUISVILLE Daviess
WEST PADUCAH McCracken
WEST POINT (40177) Hardin(80), Bullitt(13), Jefferson(6)
WEST PRESTONSBURG Floyd
WEST SOMERSET Pulaski
WEST VAN LEAR Johnson
WESTPORT Oldham
WESTVIEW Breckinridge
WHEATCROFT Webster
WHEATLEY Owen
WHEELWRIGHT Floyd
WHICK Breathitt
WHITE MILLS Hardin
WHITE OAK Morgan
WHITE PLAINS (42464) Hopkins(72), Muhlenberg(15), Christian(11)
WHITEHOUSE Johnson
WHITESBURG Letcher
WHITESVILLE (42378) Daviess(55), Ohio(44)
WHITLEY CITY McCreary
WICKLIFFE Ballard
WIDECREEK Breathitt
WILDIE Rockcastle
WILLARD Carter
WILLIAMSBURG (40769) Whitley(98), McCreary(1)
WILLIAMSPORT Johnson
WILLIAMSTOWN Grant
WILLISBURG (40078) Washington(97), Mercer(1), Anderson(1)
WILLOW SHADE Metcalfe
WILMORE (40390) Jessamine(98), Woodford(1)
WINCHESTER Clark
WIND CAVE Jackson
WINDSOR Casey
WINDY Wayne
WINGO (42088) Graves(84), Hickman(15)
WINSTON Estill
WITTENSVILLE Johnson
WOODBINE (40771) Knox(86), Whitley(13)
WOODBURN (42170) Warren(62), Simpson(37)
WOODBURY Butler
WOODMAN Pike
WOOLLUM (40999) Knox(98), Clay(1)
WOOTON Leslie
WORTHINGTON Greenup
WORTHVILLE (41098) Owen(96), Carroll(3)
WRIGLEY Morgan
YEADDISS Leslie
YERKES Perry
YOSEMITE Casey
ZACHARIAH Lee
ZOE Lee

Kentucky ZIP/City Cross Reference

40003-40003	BAGDAD	40018-40018	EASTWOOD	40037-40037	LORETTO	40056-40056	PEWEE VALLEY
40004-40004	BARDSTOWN	40019-40019	EMINENCE	40040-40040	MACKVILLE	40057-40057	PLEASUREVILLE
40006-40006	BEDFORD	40020-40020	FAIRFIELD	40041-40041	MASONIC HOME	40058-40058	PORT ROYAL
40007-40007	BETHLEHEM	40022-40022	FINCHVILLE	40045-40045	MILTON	40059-40059	PROSPECT
40008-40008	BLOOMFIELD	40023-40023	FISHERVILLE	40046-40046	MOUNT EDEN	40060-40060	RAYWICK
40009-40009	BRADFORDSVILLE	40025-40025	GLENVIEW	40047-40047	MOUNT WASHINGTON	40061-40061	SAINT CATHARINE
40010-40010	BUCKNER	40026-40026	GOSHEN	40048-40048	NAZARETH	40062-40062	SAINT FRANCIS
40011-40011	CAMPBELLSBURG	40027-40027	HARRODS CREEK	40049-40049	NERINX	40063-40063	SAINT MARY
40012-40012	CHAPLIN	40028-40028	HOWARDSTOWN	40050-40050	NEW CASTLE	40065-40066	SHELBYVILLE
40013-40013	COXS CREEK	40031-40032	LA GRANGE	40051-40051	NEW HAVEN	40067-40067	SIMPSONVILLE
40014-40014	CRESTWOOD	40033-40033	LEBANON	40052-40052	NEW HOPE	40068-40068	SMITHFIELD
40017-40017	DEFOE	40036-40036	LOCKPORT	40055-40055	PENDLETON	40069-40069	SPRINGFIELD

Zip Range	City
40070-40070	SULPHUR
40071-40071	TAYLORSVILLE
40075-40075	TURNERS STATION
40076-40076	WADDY
40077-40077	WESTPORT
40078-40078	WILLISBURG
40103-40103	AXTEL
40104-40104	BATTLETOWN
40106-40106	BIG SPRING
40107-40107	BOSTON
40108-40108	BRANDENBURG
40109-40109	BROOKS
40110-40110	CLERMONT
40111-40111	CLOVERPORT
40114-40114	CONSTANTINE
40115-40115	CUSTER
40117-40117	EKRON
40118-40118	FAIRDALE
40119-40119	FALLS OF ROUGH
40121-40121	FORT KNOX
40129-40129	HILLVIEW
40140-40140	GARFIELD
40142-40142	GUSTON
40143-40143	HARDINSBURG
40144-40144	HARNED
40145-40145	HUDSON
40146-40146	IRVINGTON
40150-40150	LEBANON JUNCTION
40152-40152	MC DANIELS
40153-40153	MC QUADY
40155-40155	MULDRAUGH
40157-40157	PAYNEVILLE
40159-40160	RADCLIFF
40161-40161	RHODELIA
40162-40162	RINEYVILLE
40164-40164	SE REE
40165-40165	SHEPHERDSVILLE
40170-40170	STEPHENSPORT
40171-40171	UNION STAR
40175-40175	VINE GROVE
40176-40176	WEBSTER
40177-40177	WEST POINT
40178-40178	WESTVIEW
40200-40299	LOUISVILLE
40306-40306	BETHEL
40309-40309	BOWEN
40310-40310	BURGIN
40311-40311	CARLISLE
40312-40312	CLAY CITY
40313-40313	CLEARFIELD
40316-40316	DENNISTON
40317-40317	ELLIOTTVILLE
40319-40319	FARMERS
40320-40320	FORD
40322-40322	FRENCHBURG
40324-40324	GEORGETOWN
40327-40327	GRATZ
40328-40328	GRAVEL SWITCH
40329-40329	HALDEMAN
40330-40330	HARRODSBURG
40334-40334	HOPE
40336-40336	IRVINE
40337-40337	JEFFERSONVILLE
40339-40339	KEENE
40340-40340	NICHOLASVILLE
40341-40341	LAMERO
40342-40342	LAWRENCEBURG
40345-40345	MARIBA
40346-40346	MEANS
40347-40347	MIDWAY
40348-40348	MILLERSBURG
40350-40350	MOOREFIELD
40351-40351	MOREHEAD
40353-40353	MOUNT STERLING
40355-40355	NEW LIBERTY
40356-40356	NICHOLASVILLE
40357-40357	NORTH MIDDLETOWN
40358-40358	OLYMPIA
40359-40359	OWENTON
40360-40360	OWINGSVILLE
40361-40362	PARIS
40363-40363	PERRY PARK
40365-40365	POMEROYTON
40366-40366	PRESTON
40370-40370	SADIEVILLE
40371-40371	SALT LICK
40372-40372	SALVISA
40374-40374	SHARPSBURG
40376-40376	SLADE
40379-40379	STAMPING GROUND
40380-40380	STANTON
40383-40384	VERSAILLES
40385-40385	WACO
40386-40386	VERSAILLES
40387-40387	WELLINGTON
40389-40389	WHEATLEY
40390-40390	WILMORE
40391-40392	WINCHESTER
40402-40402	ANNVILLE
40403-40404	BEREA
40405-40405	BIGHILL
40407-40407	BOND
40409-40409	BRODHEAD
40410-40410	BRYANTSVILLE
40415-40415	COBHILL
40417-40417	CONWAY
40419-40419	CRAB ORCHARD
40420-40420	CRYSTAL
40421-40421	DABOLT
40422-40423	DANVILLE
40426-40426	DREYFUS
40430-40430	EGYPT
40434-40434	GRAY HAWK
40435-40435	HERD
40437-40437	HUSTONVILLE
40440-40440	JUNCTION CITY
40441-40441	KERBY KNOB
40442-40442	KINGS MOUNTAIN
40444-40444	LANCASTER
40445-40445	LIVINGSTON
40446-40446	LANCASTER
40447-40447	MC KEE
40448-40448	MC KINNEY
40452-40452	MITCHELLSBURG
40455-40455	MORRILL
40456-40456	MOUNT VERNON
40460-40460	ORLANDO
40461-40461	PAINT LICK
40464-40464	PARKSVILLE
40465-40465	PARROT
40467-40467	PEOPLES
40468-40468	PERRYVILLE
40471-40471	PRYSE
40472-40472	RAVENNA
40473-40473	RENFRO VALLEY
40475-40476	RICHMOND
40481-40481	SANDGAP
40484-40484	STANFORD
40486-40486	TYNER
40488-40488	WANETA
40489-40489	WAYNESBURG
40492-40492	WILDIE
40494-40494	WIND CAVE
40495-40495	WINSTON
40500-40598	LEXINGTON
40601-40622	FRANKFORT
40701-40702	CORBIN
40724-40724	BUSH
40729-40729	EAST BERNSTADT
40730-40730	EMLYN
40734-40734	GRAY
40737-40737	KEAVY
40740-40740	LILY
40741-40748	LONDON
40751-40751	MARYDELL
40754-40754	NEVISDALE
40755-40755	PITTSBURG
40759-40759	ROCKHOLDS
40763-40763	SILER
40769-40769	WILLIAMSBURG
40771-40771	WOODBINE
40801-40801	AGES BROOKSIDE
40803-40803	ASHER
40806-40806	BAXTER
40807-40807	BENHAM
40808-40808	BIG LAUREL
40810-40810	BLEDSOE
40813-40813	CALVIN
40815-40815	CAWOOD
40816-40816	CHAPPELL
40818-40818	COALGOOD
40819-40819	COLDIRON
40820-40820	CRANKS
40823-40823	CUMBERLAND
40824-40824	DAYHOIT
40825-40825	DIZNEY
40826-40826	EOLIA
40827-40827	ESSIE
40828-40828	EVARTS
40829-40829	GRAYS KNOB
40830-40830	GULSTON
40831-40831	HARLAN
40840-40840	HELTON
40843-40843	HOLMES MILL
40844-40844	HOSKINSTON
40845-40845	HULEN
40846-40846	KEITH
40847-40847	KENVIR
40849-40849	LEJUNIOR
40854-40854	LOYALL
40855-40855	LYNCH
40856-40856	MIRACLE
40858-40858	MOZELLE
40861-40861	OVEN FORK
40862-40862	PARTRIDGE
40863-40863	PATHFORK
40865-40865	PUTNEY
40867-40867	SMITH
40868-40868	STINNETT
40870-40870	TOTZ
40873-40873	WALLINS CREEK
40874-40874	WARBRANCH
40902-40902	ARJAY
40903-40903	ARTEMUS
40906-40911	BARBOURVILLE
40913-40913	BEVERLY
40914-40914	BIG CREEK
40915-40915	BIMBLE
40917-40917	BLUEHOLE
40921-40921	BRYANTS STORE
40923-40923	CANNON
40927-40927	CLOSPLINT
40930-40930	DEWITT
40931-40931	ERILINE
40932-40932	FALL ROCK
40935-40935	FLAT LICK
40936-40936	FOGERTOWN
40939-40939	FOURMILE
40940-40940	FRAKES
40941-40941	GARRARD
40943-40943	GIRDLER
40944-40944	GOOSE ROCK
40946-40946	GREEN ROAD
40949-40949	HEIDRICK
40951-40951	HIMA
40953-40953	HINKLE
40955-40955	INGRAM
40958-40958	KETTLE ISLAND
40962-40962	MANCHESTER
40964-40964	MARY ALICE
40965-40965	MIDDLESBORO
40970-40970	MILLS
40972-40972	ONEIDA
40977-40977	PINEVILLE
40978-40978	PLANK
40979-40979	ROARK
40981-40981	SAUL
40982-40982	SCALF
40983-40983	SEXTONS CREEK
40988-40988	STONEY FORK
40995-40995	TROSPER
40997-40997	WALKER
40999-40999	WOOLLUM
41001-41001	ALEXANDRIA
41002-41002	AUGUSTA
41003-41003	BERRY
41004-41004	BROOKSVILLE
41005-41005	BURLINGTON
41006-41006	BUTLER
41007-41007	CALIFORNIA
41008-41008	CARROLLTON
41009-41009	CONSTANCE
41010-41010	CORINTH
41011-41014	COVINGTON
41015-41015	LATONIA
41016-41016	COVINGTON
41017-41017	FT MITCHELL
41018-41018	ERLANGER
41019-41019	COVINGTON
41022-41022	FLORENCE
41030-41030	CRITTENDEN
41031-41031	CYNTHIANA
41033-41033	DE MOSSVILLE
41034-41034	DOVER
41035-41035	DRY RIDGE
41037-41037	ELIZAVILLE
41039-41039	EWING
41040-41040	FALMOUTH
41041-41041	FLEMINGSBURG
41042-41042	FLORENCE
41043-41043	FOSTER
41044-41044	GERMANTOWN
41045-41045	GHENT
41046-41046	GLENCOE
41048-41048	HEBRON
41049-41049	HILLSBORO
41051-41051	INDEPENDENCE
41052-41052	JONESVILLE
41053-41053	KENTON
41054-41054	MASON
41055-41055	MAYSLICK
41056-41056	MAYSVILLE
41059-41059	MELBOURNE
41061-41061	MILFORD
41062-41062	MINERVA
41063-41063	MORNING VIEW
41064-41064	MOUNT OLIVET
41065-41065	MUSES MILLS
41071-41072	NEWPORT
41073-41073	BELLEVUE
41074-41074	DAYTON
41075-41075	FORT THOMAS
41076-41076	NEWPORT
41080-41080	PETERSBURG
41081-41081	PLUMMERS LANDING
41083-41083	SANDERS
41085-41085	SILVER GROVE
41086-41086	SPARTA
41091-41091	UNION
41092-41092	VERONA
41093-41093	WALLINGFORD
41094-41094	WALTON
41095-41095	WARSAW
41096-41096	WASHINGTON
41097-41097	WILLIAMSTOWN
41098-41098	WORTHVILLE
41099-41099	NEWPORT
41101-41114	ASHLAND
41121-41121	ARGILLITE
41124-41124	BLAINE
41125-41125	BRUIN
41127-41127	CAMP DIX
41128-41128	CARTER
41129-41129	CATLETTSBURG
41131-41131	CONCORD
41132-41132	DENTON
41135-41135	EMERSON
41137-41137	FIREBRICK
41139-41139	FLATWOODS
41141-41141	GARRISON
41142-41142	GRAHN
41143-41143	GRAYSON
41144-41144	GREENUP
41146-41146	HITCHINS
41149-41149	ISONVILLE
41150-41150	JACOBS
41152-41152	JOHNS RUN
41156-41156	LLOYD
41159-41159	MARTHA
41160-41160	MAZIE
41163-41163	OLDTOWN
41164-41164	OLIVE HILL

41166-41166	QUINCY
41168-41168	RUSH
41169-41169	RUSSELL
41170-41170	SAINT PAUL
41171-41171	SANDY HOOK
41173-41173	SOLDIER
41174-41174	SOUTH PORTSMOUTH
41175-41175	SOUTH SHORE
41177-41177	STEPHENS
41179-41179	VANCEBURG
41180-41180	WEBBVILLE
41181-41181	WILLARD
41183-41183	WORTHINGTON
41189-41189	TOLLESBORO
41201-41201	ADAMS
41203-41203	BEAUTY
41204-41204	BOONS CAMP
41211-41211	CULVER
41214-41214	DEBORD
41215-41215	DENVER
41216-41216	EAST POINT
41219-41219	FLATGAP
41220-41220	FUGET
41222-41222	HAGERHILL
41224-41224	INEZ
41225-41225	JOB
41226-41226	KEATON
41228-41228	LEANDER
41230-41230	LOUISA
41231-41231	LOVELY
41232-41232	LOWMANSVILLE
41234-41234	MEALLY
41237-41237	OFFUTT
41238-41238	OIL SPRINGS
41240-41240	PAINTSVILLE
41250-41250	PILGRIM
41253-41253	RICHARDSON
41254-41254	RIVER
41255-41255	SITKA
41256-41256	STAFFORDSVILLE
41257-41257	STAMBAUGH
41258-41258	SWAMP BRANCH
41260-41260	THELMA
41261-41261	THREEFORKS
41262-41262	TOMAHAWK
41263-41263	TUTOR KEY
41264-41264	ULYSSES
41265-41265	VAN LEAR
41266-41266	VOLGA
41267-41267	WARFIELD
41268-41268	WEST VAN LEAR
41269-41269	WHITEHOUSE
41271-41271	WILLIAMSPORT
41274-41274	WITTENSVILLE
41301-41301	CAMPTON
41306-41306	ALTRO
41307-41307	ATHOL
41310-41310	BAYS
41311-41311	BEATTYVILLE
41313-41313	BETHANY
41314-41314	BOONEVILLE
41315-41315	BURKHART
41316-41316	CANOE
41317-41317	CLAYHOLE
41321-41321	DECOY
41323-41323	FILLMORE
41327-41327	GILLMORE
41328-41328	GREEN HALL
41331-41331	HADDIX
41332-41332	HAZEL GREEN
41333-41333	HEIDELBERG
41338-41338	ISLAND CITY
41339-41339	JACKSON
41340-41340	LAMBRIC
41342-41342	LEE CITY
41343-41343	LEECO
41344-41344	LEROSE
41346-41346	LITTLE
41347-41347	LONE
41348-41348	LOST CREEK
41351-41351	MISTLETOE
41352-41352	MIZE
41357-41357	NOCTOR
41358-41358	OLD LANDING
41360-41360	PINE RIDGE
41362-41362	PRIMROSE
41363-41363	QUICKSAND
41364-41364	RICETOWN
41365-41365	ROGERS
41366-41366	ROUSSEAU
41367-41367	ROWDY
41368-41368	SAINT HELENS
41369-41369	SALDEE
41370-41370	MACEDONIA
41377-41377	TALBERT
41378-41378	TALLEGA
41385-41385	VANCLEVE
41386-41386	VINCENT
41390-41390	WHICK
41391-41391	WIDECREEK
41396-41396	ZACHARIAH
41397-41397	ZOE
41406-41406	BUSKIRK
41407-41407	CANEY
41408-41408	CANNEL CITY
41409-41409	CARVER
41410-41410	CISCO
41411-41411	CONLEY
41412-41412	COTTLE
41413-41413	CROCKETT
41417-41417	DINGUS
41419-41419	EDNA
41421-41421	ELKFORK
41422-41422	ELSIE
41425-41425	EZEL
41426-41426	FALCON
41427-41427	FLAT FORK
41430-41430	FREDVILLE
41431-41431	FRITZ
41433-41433	GAPVILLE
41438-41438	GYPSY
41441-41441	HENDRICKS
41443-41443	INSKO
41444-41444	IVYTON
41447-41447	LENOX
41451-41451	MALONE
41452-41452	MARSHALLVILLE
41456-41456	MIMA
41457-41457	MOON
41459-41459	OPHIR
41464-41464	ROYALTON
41465-41465	SALYERSVILLE
41466-41466	SEITZ
41467-41467	SILVERHILL
41472-41472	WEST LIBERTY
41474-41474	WHITE OAK
41477-41477	WRIGLEY
41501-41502	PIKEVILLE
41503-41503	SOUTH WILLIAMSON
41512-41512	ASHCAMP
41513-41513	BELCHER
41514-41514	BELFRY
41517-41517	BURDINE
41518-41518	BURNWELL
41519-41519	CANADA
41520-41520	DORTON
41521-41521	DRAFFIN
41522-41522	ELKHORN CITY
41524-41524	FEDSCREEK
41526-41526	FORDS BRANCH
41527-41527	FOREST HILLS
41528-41528	FREEBURN
41529-41529	GOODY
41531-41531	HARDY
41534-41534	HELLIER
41535-41535	HUDDY
41536-41536	JAMBOREE
41537-41537	JENKINS
41538-41538	JONANCY
41539-41539	KIMPER
41540-41540	LICK CREEK
41542-41542	LOOKOUT
41543-41543	MC ANDREWS
41544-41544	MC CARR
41545-41545	MC COMBS
41546-41546	MC VEIGH
41547-41547	MAJESTIC
41548-41548	MOUTHCARD
41549-41549	MYRA
41550-41550	NELSE
41551-41551	PAW PAW
41553-41553	PHELPS
41554-41554	PHYLLIS
41555-41555	PINSONFORK
41557-41557	RACCOON
41558-41558	RANSOM
41559-41559	REGINA
41560-41560	ROBINSON CREEK
41561-41561	ROCKHOUSE
41562-41562	SHELBIANA
41563-41563	SHELBY GAP
41564-41564	SIDNEY
41565-41565	SPEIGHT
41566-41566	STEELE
41567-41567	STONE
41568-41568	STOPOVER
41569-41569	TOLER
41570-41570	TURKEY CREEK
41571-41571	VARNEY
41572-41572	VIRGIE
41574-41574	WOODMAN
41601-41601	ALLEN
41602-41602	AUXIER
41603-41603	BANNER
41604-41604	BEAVER
41605-41605	BETSY LAYNE
41606-41606	BEVINSVILLE
41607-41607	BLUE RIVER
41612-41612	BYPRO
41614-41614	CRAYNOR
41615-41615	DANA
41616-41616	DAVID
41619-41619	DRIFT
41621-41621	DWALE
41622-41622	EASTERN
41625-41625	EMMA
41626-41626	ENDICOTT
41627-41627	ESTILL
41629-41629	GALVESTON
41630-41630	GARRETT
41631-41631	GRETHEL
41632-41632	GUNLOCK
41633-41633	HALO
41635-41635	HAROLD
41636-41636	HI HAT
41637-41637	HIPPO
41639-41639	HONAKER
41640-41640	HUEYSVILLE
41641-41641	HUNTER
41642-41642	IVEL
41643-41643	LACKEY
41645-41645	LANGLEY
41647-41647	MC DOWELL
41649-41649	MARTIN
41650-41650	MELVIN
41651-41651	MINNIE
41653-41653	PRESTONSBURG
41655-41655	PRINTER
41659-41659	STANVILLE
41660-41660	TEABERRY
41663-41663	TRAM
41666-41666	WAYLAND
41667-41667	WEEKSBURY
41668-41668	WEST PRESTONSBURG
41669-41669	WHEELWRIGHT
41701-41702	HAZARD
41710-41710	ALLOCK
41712-41712	ARY
41713-41713	AVAWAM
41714-41714	BEAR BRANCH
41719-41719	BONNYMAN
41720-41720	BROWNS FORK
41721-41721	BUCKHORN
41722-41722	BULAN
41723-41723	BUSY
41725-41725	CARRIE
41727-41727	CHAVIES
41728-41728	CINDA
41729-41729	COMBS
41730-41730	CONFLUENCE
41731-41731	CORNETTSVILLE
41732-41732	CUTSHIN
41733-41733	DAISY
41735-41735	DELPHIA
41736-41736	DICE
41739-41739	DWARF
41740-41740	EMMALENA
41743-41743	FISTY
41745-41745	GAYS CREEK
41746-41746	HAPPY
41747-41747	HARDBURLY
41749-41749	HYDEN
41751-41751	JEFF
41754-41754	KRYPTON
41756-41756	LEATHERWOOD
41759-41759	SASSAFRAS
41760-41760	SCUDDY
41762-41762	SIZEROCK
41763-41763	SLEMP
41764-41764	SMILAX
41765-41765	TALCUM
41766-41766	THOUSANDSTICKS
41771-41771	TYPO
41772-41772	VEST
41773-41773	VICCO
41774-41774	VIPER
41775-41775	WENDOVER
41776-41776	WOOTON
41777-41777	YEADDISS
41778-41778	YERKES
41801-41801	AMBURGEY
41804-41804	BLACKEY
41805-41805	BRINKLEY
41810-41810	CROMONA
41811-41811	CROWN
41812-41812	DEANE
41815-41815	ERMINE
41817-41817	GARNER
41819-41819	GORDON
41821-41821	HALLIE
41822-41822	HINDMAN
41823-41823	HOLLYBUSH
41824-41824	ISOM
41825-41825	JACKHORN
41826-41826	JEREMIAH
41828-41828	KITE
41829-41829	KONA
41831-41831	LEBURN
41832-41832	LETCHER
41833-41833	LINEFORK
41834-41834	LITTCARR
41835-41835	MC ROBERTS
41836-41836	MALLIE
41837-41837	MAYKING
41838-41838	MILLSTONE
41839-41839	MOUSIE
41840-41840	NEON
41843-41843	PINE TOP
41844-41844	PIPPA PASSES
41845-41845	PREMIUM
41847-41847	REDFOX
41848-41848	ROXANA
41849-41849	SECO
41855-41855	THORNTON
41858-41858	WHITESBURG
41859-41859	DEMA
41861-41861	RAVEN
41862-41862	TOPMOST
41901-41906	MIGRATE
42001-42003	PADUCAH
42020-42020	ALMO
42021-42021	ARLINGTON
42022-42022	BANDANA
42023-42023	BARDWELL
42024-42024	BARLOW
42025-42025	BENTON
42026-42026	BLANDVILLE
42027-42027	BOAZ
42028-42028	BURNA
42029-42029	CALVERT CITY
42031-42031	CLINTON
42032-42032	COLUMBUS

ZIP Range	City
42033-42033	CRAYNE
42035-42035	CUNNINGHAM
42036-42036	DEXTER
42037-42037	DYCUSBURG
42038-42038	EDDYVILLE
42039-42039	FANCY FARM
42040-42040	FARMINGTON
42041-42041	FULTON
42044-42044	GILBERTSVILLE
42045-42045	GRAND RIVERS
42046-42046	HAMLIN
42047-42047	HAMPTON
42048-42048	HARDIN
42049-42049	HAZEL
42050-42050	HICKMAN
42051-42051	HICKORY
42053-42053	KEVIL
42054-42054	KIRKSEY
42055-42055	KUTTAWA
42056-42056	LA CENTER
42058-42058	LEDBETTER
42059-42059	LOLA
42060-42060	LOVELACEVILLE
42061-42061	LOWES
42063-42063	LYNNVILLE
42064-42064	MARION
42066-42066	MAYFIELD
42069-42069	MELBER
42070-42070	MILBURN
42071-42071	MURRAY
42076-42076	NEW CONCORD
42078-42078	SALEM
42079-42079	SEDALIA
42081-42081	SMITHLAND
42082-42082	SYMSONIA
42083-42083	TILINE
42084-42084	TOLU
42085-42085	WATER VALLEY
42086-42086	WEST PADUCAH
42087-42087	WICKLIFFE
42088-42088	WINGO
42101-42104	BOWLING GREEN
42120-42120	ADOLPHUS
42122-42122	ALVATON
42123-42123	AUSTIN
42124-42124	BEAUMONT
42127-42127	CAVE CITY
42128-42128	DRAKE
42129-42129	EDMONTON
42130-42130	EIGHTY EIGHT
42131-42131	ETOILE
42133-42133	FOUNTAIN RUN
42134-42134	FRANKLIN
42140-42140	GAMALIEL
42141-42142	GLASGOW
42150-42150	HALFWAY
42151-42151	HESTAND
42152-42152	HISEVILLE
42153-42153	HOLLAND
42154-42154	KNOB LICK
42155-42155	LAMB
42156-42156	LUCAS
42157-42157	MOUNT HERMON
42159-42159	OAKLAND
42160-42160	PARK CITY
42163-42163	ROCKY HILL
42164-42164	SCOTTSVILLE
42166-42166	SUMMER SHADE
42167-42167	TOMPKINSVILLE
42169-42169	WILLOW SHADE
42170-42170	WOODBURN
42171-42171	SMITHS GROVE
42201-42201	ABERDEEN
42202-42202	ADAIRVILLE
42203-42203	ALLEGRE
42204-42204	ALLENSVILLE
42206-42206	AUBURN
42207-42207	BEE SPRING
42209-42209	BROOKLYN
42210-42210	BROWNSVILLE
42211-42211	CADIZ
42212-42212	CANTON
42214-42214	CENTER
42215-42215	CERULEAN
42216-42216	CLIFTY
42217-42217	CROFTON
42219-42219	DUNBAR
42220-42220	ELKTON
42221-42221	FAIRVIEW
42223-42223	FORT CAMPBELL
42232-42232	GRACEY
42234-42234	GUTHRIE
42235-42235	HADLEY
42236-42236	HERNDON
42240-42241	HOPKINSVILLE
42250-42250	HUFF
42251-42251	HUNTSVILLE
42252-42252	JETSON
42254-42254	LA FAYETTE
42256-42256	LEWISBURG
42257-42257	LINDSEYVILLE
42259-42259	MAMMOTH CAVE
42261-42261	MORGANTOWN
42262-42262	OAK GROVE
42263-42263	OAKVILLE
42264-42264	OLLIE
42265-42265	OLMSTEAD
42266-42266	PEMBROKE
42267-42267	PROVO
42268-42268	QUALITY
42270-42270	RICHARDSVILLE
42273-42273	ROCHESTER
42274-42274	ROCKFIELD
42275-42275	ROUNDHILL
42276-42276	RUSSELLVILLE
42280-42280	SHARON GROVE
42283-42283	SOUTH UNION
42284-42284	SUNFISH
42285-42285	SWEEDEN
42286-42286	TRENTON
42287-42287	WELCHS CREEK
42288-42288	WOODBURY
42301-42304	OWENSBORO
42320-42320	BEAVER DAM
42321-42321	BEECH CREEK
42322-42322	BEECH GROVE
42323-42323	BEECHMONT
42324-42324	BELTON
42325-42325	BREMEN
42326-42326	BROWDER
42327-42327	CALHOUN
42328-42328	CENTERTOWN
42330-42330	CENTRAL CITY
42332-42332	CLEATON
42333-42333	CROMWELL
42334-42334	CURDSVILLE
42337-42337	DRAKESBORO
42338-42338	DUNDEE
42339-42339	DUNMOR
42343-42343	FORDSVILLE
42344-42344	GRAHAM
42345-42345	GREENVILLE
42347-42347	HARTFORD
42348-42348	HAWESVILLE
42349-42349	HORSE BRANCH
42350-42350	ISLAND
42351-42351	LEWISPORT
42352-42352	LIVERMORE
42354-42354	MC HENRY
42355-42355	MACEO
42356-42356	MAPLE MOUNT
42357-42357	MOORMAN
42358-42358	NARROWS
42361-42361	OLATON
42364-42364	PELLVILLE
42365-42365	PENROD
42366-42366	PHILPOT
42367-42367	POWDERLY
42368-42368	REYNOLDS STATION
42369-42369	ROCKPORT
42370-42370	ROSINE
42371-42371	RUMSEY
42372-42372	SACRAMENTO
42373-42373	SAINT JOSEPH
42374-42374	SOUTH CARROLLTON
42375-42375	STANLEY
42376-42376	UTICA
42377-42377	WEST LOUISVILLE
42378-42378	WHITESVILLE
42402-42402	BASKETT
42403-42403	BLACKFORD
42404-42404	CLAY
42406-42406	CORYDON
42408-42408	DAWSON SPRINGS
42409-42409	DIXON
42410-42410	EARLINGTON
42411-42411	FREDONIA
42413-42413	HANSON
42419-42420	HENDERSON
42431-42431	MADISONVILLE
42436-42436	MANITOU
42437-42437	MORGANFIELD
42440-42440	MORTONS GAP
42441-42441	NEBO
42442-42442	NORTONVILLE
42444-42444	POOLE
42445-42445	PRINCETON
42450-42450	PROVIDENCE
42451-42451	REED
42452-42452	ROBARDS
42453-42453	SAINT CHARLES
42455-42455	SEBREE
42456-42456	SLAUGHTERS
42457-42457	SMITH MILLS
42458-42458	SPOTTSVILLE
42459-42459	STURGIS
42460-42460	SULLIVAN
42461-42461	UNIONTOWN
42462-42462	WAVERLY
42463-42463	WHEATCROFT
42464-42464	WHITE PLAINS
42501-42503	SOMERSET
42510-42510	ACORN
42516-42516	BETHELRIDGE
42518-42518	BRONSTON
42519-42519	BURNSIDE
42528-42528	DUNNVILLE
42532-42532	FAUBUSH
42533-42533	FERGUSON
42536-42536	INGLE
42539-42539	LIBERTY
42541-42541	MIDDLEBURG
42544-42544	NANCY
42553-42553	SCIENCE HILL
42554-42554	SHOPVILLE
42555-42555	SLOANS VALLEY
42557-42557	STAB
42558-42558	TATEVILLE
42563-42563	WALNUT GROVE
42564-42564	WEST SOMERSET
42565-42565	WINDSOR
42566-42566	YOSEMITE
42567-42567	EUBANK
42601-42601	AARON
42602-42602	ALBANY
42603-42603	ALPHA
42607-42607	BEULAH HEIGHTS
42611-42611	COOPERSVILLE
42613-42613	DELTA
42618-42618	FRAZER
42629-42629	JAMESTOWN
42631-42631	MARSHES SIDING
42632-42632	MILL SPRINGS
42633-42633	MONTICELLO
42634-42634	PARKERS LAKE
42635-42635	PINE KNOT
42638-42638	REVELO
42640-42640	ROCKYBRANCH
42642-42642	RUSSELL SPRINGS
42643-42643	SAWYER
42647-42647	STEARNS
42648-42648	STEUBENVILLE
42649-42649	STRUNK
42653-42653	WHITLEY CITY
42655-42655	WINDY
42701-42702	ELIZABETHTOWN
42711-42711	BAKERTON
42712-42712	BIG CLIFTY
42713-42713	BONNIEVILLE
42714-42714	BOW
42715-42715	BREEDING
42716-42716	BUFFALO
42717-42717	BURKESVILLE
42718-42719	CAMPBELLSVILLE
42720-42720	CANE VALLEY
42721-42721	CANEYVILLE
42722-42722	CANMER
42723-42723	CASEY CREEKG
42723-42723	CASEY CREEK
42724-42724	CECILIA
42726-42726	CLARKSON
42728-42728	COLUMBIA
42729-42729	CUB RUN
42730-42730	CUNDIFF
42731-42731	DUBRE
42732-42732	EASTVIEW
42733-42733	ELK HORN
42735-42735	FAIRPLAY
42736-42736	FINLEY
42740-42740	GLENDALE
42741-42741	GLENS FORK
42742-42742	GRADYVILLE
42743-42743	GREENSBURG
42746-42746	HARDYVILLE
42748-42748	HODGENVILLE
42749-42749	HORSE CAVE
42752-42752	KETTLE
42753-42753	KNIFLEY
42754-42755	LEITCHFIELD
42757-42757	MAGNOLIA
42758-42758	MANNSVILLE
42759-42759	MARROWBONE
42761-42761	MILLTOWN
42762-42762	MILLWOOD
42763-42763	MONTPELIER
42764-42764	MOUNT SHERMAN
42765-42765	MUNFORDVILLE
42766-42766	NEAFUS
42768-42768	PEYTONSBURG
42772-42772	ROWLETTS
42776-42776	SONORA
42779-42779	SPRING LICK
42780-42780	STEFF
42781-42781	STEPHENSBURG
42782-42782	SUMMERSVILLE
42783-42783	SUMMIT
42784-42784	UPTON
42785-42785	VENTRESS
42785-42785	VERTREES
42786-42786	WATERVIEW
42787-42787	WAX
42788-42788	WHITE MILLS

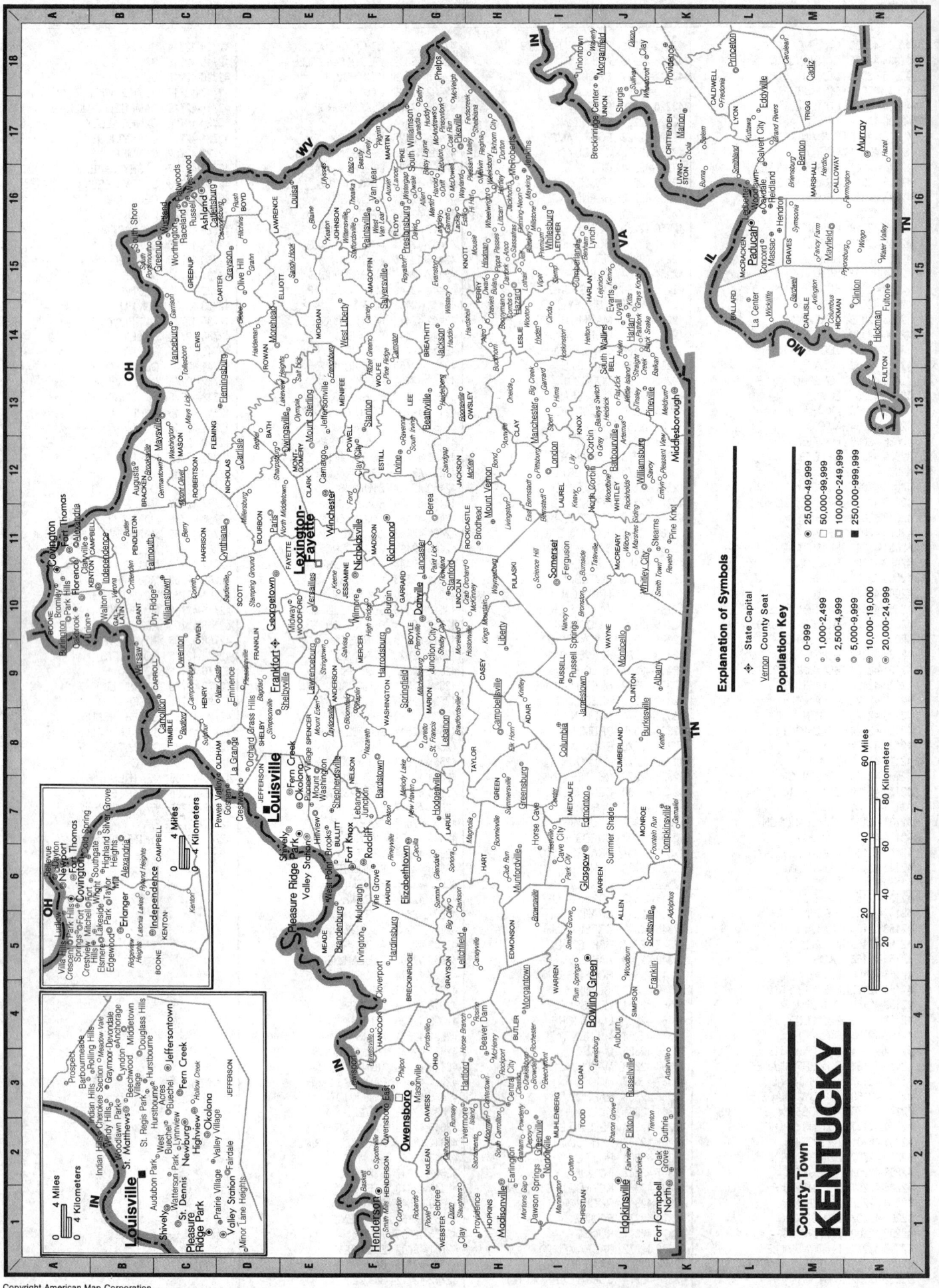

Explanation of Symbols

◉ State Capital
Vernon County Seat

Population Key

Symbol	Population
◌	0-999
◦	1,000-2,499
⊙	2,500-4,999
◎	5,000-9,999
⊕	10,000-19,000
⊕	20,000-24,999
◉	25,000-49,999
□	50,000-99,999
▢	100,000-249,999
■	250,000-999,999

County-Town
KENTUCKY

COUNTIES

(120 Counties)

Name of County	Population	Location on Map
ADAIR	15,360	I-8
ALLEN	14,628	J-5
ANDERSON	14,571	E-9
BALLARD	7,902	L-14
BARREN	34,001	J-6
BATH	9,692	D-13
BELL	31,506	J-13
BOONE	57,589	B-10
BOURBON	19,236	D-11
BOYD	51,150	D-16
BOYLE	25,641	G-9
BRACKEN	7,766	B-12
BREATHITT	15,703	G-14
BRECKINRIDGE	16,312	G-4
BULLITT	47,567	E-7
BUTLER	11,245	H-4
CALDWELL	13,232	K-17
CALLOWAY	30,735	M-16
CAMPBELL	83,866	B-11
CARLISLE	5,238	M-14
CARROLL	9,292	C-9
CARTER	24,340	D-15
CASEY	14,211	H-9
CHRISTIAN	68,941	I-1
CLARK	29,496	E-12
CLAY	21,746	H-13
CLINTON	9,135	J-9
CRITTENDEN	9,196	K-17
CUMBERLAND	6,784	J-8
DAVIESS	87,189	G-3
EDMONSON	10,357	H-5
ELLIOTT	6,455	E-15
ESTILL	14,614	F-12
FAYETTE	225,366	E-11
FLEMING	12,292	C-12
FLOYD	43,586	F-15
FRANKLIN	43,781	D-9
FULTON	8,271	N-13
GALLATIN	5,393	B-10
GARRARD	11,579	G-10
GRANT	15,737	B-10
GRAVES	33,550	M-15
GRAYSON	21,050	G-4
GREEN	10,371	H-7
GREENUP	36,742	C-15
HANCOCK	7,864	F-4
HARDIN	89,240	F-6
HARLAN	36,574	I-15
HARRISON	16,248	C-11
HART	14,890	H-6
HENDERSON	43,044	F-1
HENRY	12,823	C-9
HICKMAN	5,566	M-14
HOPKINS	46,126	H-1
JACKSON	11,955	G-12
JEFFERSON	664,937	D-7
JESSAMINE	30,508	F-10
JOHNSON	23,248	E-15
KENTON	142,031	B-10
KNOTT	17,906	H-15
KNOX	29,676	I-13
LARUE	11,679	G-7
LAUREL	43,438	I-12
LAWRENCE	13,998	D-16
LEE	7,422	G-13
LESLIE	13,642	H-14
LETCHER	27,000	I-15
LEWIS	13,029	C-14
LINCOLN	20,045	G-10
LIVINGSTON	9,062	K-16
LOGAN	24,416	I-3
LYON	6,624	L-17
MADISON	57,508	F-11
MAGOFFIN	13,077	F-15
MARION	16,499	G-8
MARSHALL	27,205	M-16
MARTIN	12,526	F-17
MASON	16,666	C-12
MCCRACKEN	62,879	L-15
MCCREARY	15,603	J-11
MCLEAN	9,628	G-2
MEADE	24,170	E-5
MENIFEE	5,092	F-13
MERCER	19,148	F-9
METCALFE	8,963	I-7
MONROE	11,401	J-7
MONTGOMERY	19,561	E-12
MORGAN	11,648	E-14
MUHLENBERG	31,318	I-2
NELSON	29,710	F-7
NICHOLAS	6,725	D-12
OHIO	21,105	G-3
OLDHAM	33,263	D-8
OWEN	9,035	C-9
OWSLEY	5,036	H-13
PENDLETON	12,036	B-11
PERRY	30,283	H-14
PIKE	72,583	F-17
POWELL	11,686	F-12
PULASKI	49,489	H-10
ROBERTSON	2,124	C-12
ROCKCASTLE	14,803	H-11
ROWAN	20,353	D-14
RUSSELL	14,716	I-9
SCOTT	23,867	D-10
SHELBY	24,824	D-8
SIMPSON	15,145	J-4
SPENCER	6,801	E-8
TAYLOR	21,146	H-8
TODD	10,940	I-2
TRIGG	10,361	M-17
TRIMBLE	6,090	C-8
UNION	16,557	J-17
WARREN	76,673	I-4
WASHINGTON	10,441	F-8
WAYNE	17,468	J-9
WEBSTER	13,955	G-1
WHITLEY	33,326	J-11
WOLFE	6,503	F-13
WOODFORD	19,955	E-10
TOTAL	3,685,296	

CITIES AND TOWNS

Note: The first name is that of the city or town, second, that of the county in which it is located, then the population and location on the map.

Albany, Clinton, 2,062 ... K-9
Alexandria, Campbell, 5,592 ... A-11
Anchorage, Jefferson, 2,082 ... B-4
Ashland, Boyd, 23,622 ... C-16
Auburn, Logan, 1,273 ... J-4
Audubon Park, Jefferson, 1,520 .. C-2
Augusta, Bracken, 1,336 ... B-12
Barbourmeade, Jefferson, 1,402 . A-3
Barbourville, Knox, 3,658 ... J-13
Bardstown, Nelson, 6,801 ... F-8
Bardwell, Carlisle, 819 ... M-14
Beattyville, Lee, 1,131 ... G-13
Beaver Dam, Ohio, 2,904 ... H-3
Bedford, Trimble, 761 ... C-8
Beechwood Village, Jefferson, 1,263 ... B-3
Bellevue, Campbell, 6,997 ... A-6
Benton, Marshall, 3,899 ... M-16
Berea, Madison, 9,126 ... G-11
Booneville, Owsley, 232 ... G-13
Bowling Green, Warren, 40,641 ... I-5
Brandenburg, Meade, 1,857 ... A-6
• Breckinridge Center, Union, 2,375 ... J-18
Brodhead, Rockcastle, 1,140 ... H-11
Bromley, Kenton, 1,137 ... A-10
• Brooks, Bullitt, 2,464 ... E-7
Brooksville, Bracken, 670 ... B-12
Brownsville, Edmonson, 897 ... I-5
• Buechel, Jefferson, 7,081 ... C-3
Burgin, Mercer, 1,009 ... F-10
Burkesville, Cumberland, 1,815 ... J-8
• Burlington, Boone, 6,070 ... A-10
Cadiz, Trigg, 2,148 ... M-18
Calhoun, McLean, 854 ... G-2
Calvert City, Marshall, 2,531 ... L-17
Camargo, Montgomery, 1,022 .. E-12
Campbellsville, Taylor, 9,577 ... H-8
Campton, Wolfe, 484 ... F-14
Carlisle, Nicholas, 1,639 ... D-12
Carrollton, Carroll, 3,715 ... C-9
Catlettsburg, Boyd, 2,231 ... C-16
Cave City, Barren, 1,953 ... I-6
Central City, Muhlenberg, 4,979 . H-3
• Claryville, Campbell, 2,038 ... B-11
Clay, Webster, 1,173 ... G-1
Clay City, Powell, 1,258 ... F-12
Clinton, Hickman, 1,547 ... N-14
Cloverport, Breckinridge, 1,207 ... F-4
Cold Spring, Campbell, 2,880 ... A-6
Columbia, Adair, 3,845 ... I-8
• Concord, McCracken, 1,560 ... L-15
Corbin, Knox/Whitley, 7,419 ... I-12
Covington, Kenton, 43,264 ... A-11
Crescent Springs, Kenton, 2,179 A-5
Crestview Hills, Kenton, 2,546 ... B-5
Crestwood, Oldham, 1,435 ... D-8
Cumberland, Harlan, 3,112 ... I-15
Cynthiana, Harrison, 6,497 ... D-11
Danville, Boyle, 12,420 ... D-10
Dawson Springs, Hopkins, 3,129 .. I-1
Dayton, Campbell, 6,576 ... A-6
Dixon, Webster, 552 ... G-1
Douglass Hills, Jefferson, 5,549 .. B-3
Dry Ridge, Grant, 1,601 ... B-10
Earlington, Hopkins, 1,833 ... H-1
Eddyville, Lyon, 1,889 ... L-17
Edgewood, Kenton, 8,143 ... B-5
Edmonton, Metcalfe, 1,477 ... I-7
Elizabethtown, Hardin, 18,167 ... G-7
Elkton, Todd, 1,789 ... J-3
Elsmere, Kenton, 6,847 ... B-5
Eminence, Henry, 2,055 ... D-9
Erlanger, Kenton, 15,979 ... B-5
Evarts, Harlan, 1,063 ... J-15
• Fairdale, Jefferson, 6,563 ... D-2
Falmouth, Pendleton, 2,378 ... C-11
• Fern Creek, Jefferson, 16,406 ... E-7
Flatwoods, Greenup, 7,799 ... C-16
Flemingsburg, Fleming, 3,071 ... D-13
Flemming-Neon, Letcher ... H-16
Florence, Boone, 18,624 ... A-10
• Fort Campbell North, Christian, 18,861 ... K-2
• Fort Knox, Hardin/Meade, 21,495 ... F-6
Fort Mitchell, Kenton, 7,438 ... A-5
Fort Thomas, Campbell, 16,032 ... A-11
Fort Wright, Kenton, 6,570 ... A-6
Frankfort, Franklin, 25,968 ... D-9
Franklin, Simpson, 7,607 ... K-4
Frenchburg, Menifee, 625 ... E-13
Fulton, Fulton, 3,078 ... N-15
Georgetown, Scott, 11,414 ... D-10
Glasgow, Barren, 12,351 ... I-6
• Goshen, Oldham, 2,447 ... D-7
Graymoor-Devondale, Jefferson, 2,911 ... B-3
Grayson, Carter, 3,510 ... D-15
Greensburg, Green, 1,990 ... H-8
Greenup, Greenup, 1,158 ... C-15
Greenville, Muhlenberg, 4,689 ... I-3
Guthrie, Todd, 1,504 ... K-3
Hardinsburg, Breckinridge, 1,906 ... F-5
Harlan, Harlan, 2,686 ... J-14
Harrodsburg, Mercer, 7,335 ... F-10
Hartford, Ohio, 2,532 ... H-3
Hawesville, Hancock, 998 ... F-4
Hazard, Perry, 5,416 ... H-15
Henderson, Henderson, 25,945 ... F-2
• Hendron, McCracken, 3,712 ... L-15
Hickman, Fulton, 2,689 ... N-14
Highland Heights, Campbell, 4,223 ... B-6
• Highview, Jefferson, 14,814 ... C-3
Hillview, Bullitt, 6,119 ... E-7
Hindman, Knott, 798 ... H-15
Hodgenville, Larue, 2,721 ... G-7
Hopkinsville, Christian, 29,809 ... J-2
Horse Cave, Hart, 2,284 ... I-6
Hurstbourne, Jefferson, 4,420 ... B-3
Hurstbourne Acres, Jefferson, 1,072 ... B-3
Hyden, Leslie, 375 ... I-14
Independence, Kenton, 10,444 .. B-10
Indian Hills, Jefferson, 1,074 ... B-2
Indian Hills Cherokee Section, Jefferson, 1,005 ... B-3
Inez, Martin, 511 ... F-17
Irvine, Estill, 2,836 ... F-12
Irvington, Breckinridge, 1,180 ... F-5
Jackson, Breathitt, 2,466 ... G-14
Jamestown, Russell, 1,641 ... I-9
Jeffersontown, Jefferson, 23,221 ... C-3
Jeffersonville, Montgomery, 1,854 ... E-13
Jenkins, Letcher, 2,751 ... H-16
Junction City, Boyle/Lincoln, 1,983 ... D-10
La Center, Ballard, 1,040 ... L-14
La Grange, Oldham, 3,853 ... D-8
Lakeside Park, Kenton, 3,131 ... B-5
Lancaster, Garrard, 3,421 ... G-10
Lawrenceburg, Anderson, 5,911 ... E-9
Lebanon, Marion, 5,695 ... G-8
Lebanon Junction, Bullitt, 1,741 ... F-7
• Ledbetter, Livingston, 1,694 ... L-16
Leitchfield, Grayson, 4,965 ... G-5
Lewisport, Hancock, 1,778 ... I-3
Lexington-Fayette, Fayette, 225,366 ... E-11
Liberty, Casey, 1,937 ... H-9
Livermore, McLean, 1,534 ... G-3
London, Laurel, 5,757 ... I-12
Louisa, Lawrence, 1,990 ... E-16
Louisville, Jefferson, 269,063 ... D-7
Loyall, Harlan, 1,100 ... J-14
Ludlow, Kenton, 4,736 ... A-5
Lynch, Harlan, 1,166 ... I-16
Lyndon, Jefferson, 8,037 ... B-3
Lynnview, Jefferson, 1,017 ... C-2
Madisonville, Hopkins, 16,200 ... H-2
Manchester, Clay, 1,634 ... I-13
Marion, Crittenden, 3,320 ... K-17
• Masonville, Daviess, 1,119 ... G-3
• Massac, McCracken, 3,733 ... M-15
Mayfield, Graves, 9,935 ... M-16
Maysville, Mason, 7,169 ... C-13
McKee, Jackson, 870 ... H-12
• McRoberts, Letcher, 1,101 ... H-16
Middlesborough, Bell, 11,328 ... K-13
Middletown, Jefferson, 5,016 ... B-4
Midway, Woodford, 1,290 ... E-10
Minor Lane Heights, Jefferson, 1,675 ... D-1
Monticello, Wayne, 5,357 ... J-9
Morehead, Rowan, 8,357 ... D-14
Morganfield, Union, 3,776 ... J-18
Morgantown, Butler, 2,284 ... H-4
Mount Olivet, Robertson, 384 ... C-12
Mount Sterling, Montgomery, 5,362 ... E-12
Mount Vernon, Rockcastle, 2,654 ... H-11
Mount Washington, Bullitt, 5,226 ... E-7
Muldraugh, Hardin/Meade, 1,376 ... F-6
Munfordville, Hart, 1,556 ... H-6
Murray, Calloway, 14,439 ... N-17
New Castle, Henry, 893 ... D-9
• Newburg, Jefferson, 21,647 ... C-2
Newport, Campbell, 18,871 ... A-6
Nicholasville, Jessamine, 13,603 ... F-10
• North Corbin, Knox/Laurel, 1,601 ... I-12
Nortonville, Hopkins, 1,209 ... I-2
Oak Grove, Christian, 2,863 ... K-2
• Oakbrook, Boone, 4,113 ... A-10
• Okolona, Jefferson, 18,902 ... E-7
Olive Hill, Carter, 1,809 ... D-15
Orchard Grass Hills, Oldham, 1,058 ... D-8
Owensboro, Daviess, 53,549 ... F-3
Owensboro East, Daviess ... F-3
Owenton, Owen, 1,306 ... C-10
Owingsville, Bath, 1,491 ... E-13
Paducah, McCracken, 27,256 ... L-16
Paintsville, Johnson, 4,354 ... F-16
Paris, Bourbon, 8,730 ... D-11
Park Hills, Kenton, 3,321 ... A-10
Pewee Valley, Oldham, 1,283 ... D-7
• Phelps, Pike, 1,298 ... G-18
Pikeville, Pike, 6,324 ... G-17
• Pine Knot, McCreary, 1,549 ... K-11
Pineville, Bell, 2,198 ... J-13
Pioneer Village, Bullitt, 1,130 ... E-7
• Pleasure Ridge Park, Jefferson, 25,131 ... E-7
Prairie Village, Jefferson ... D-1
Prestonsburg, Floyd, 3,558 ... G-16
Princeton, Caldwell, 6,940 ... L-18
Prospect, Jefferson, 2,788 ... A-3
Providence, Webster, 4,123 ... J-1
Raceland, Greenup, 2,256 ... C-16
Radcliff, Hardin, 19,772 ... F-6
• Reidland, McCracken, 4,054 ... L-16
Richmond, Madison, 21,155 ... F-11
Rolling Hills, Jefferson, 1,135 ... B-3
Russell, Greenup, 4,014 ... C-16
Russell Springs, Russell, 2,363 ... I-9
Russellville, Logan, 7,454 ... J-3
• Saint Dennis, Jefferson, 10,326 .. C-1
Saint Matthews, Jefferson, 15,800 ... B-3
Saint Regis Park, Jefferson, 1,756 ... B-3
Salyersville, Magoffin, 1,917 ... F-15
Sandy Hook, Elliott, 548 ... E-15
Scottsville, Allen, 4,278 ... J-6
Sebree, Webster, 1,510 ... G-1
Shelbyville, Shelby, 6,238 ... E-8
Shepherdsville, Bullitt, 4,805 ... E-7
Shively, Jefferson, 15,535 ... E-7
Silver Grove, Campbell, 1,102 ... B-7
Smithland, Livingston, 384 ... L-16
Somerset, Pulaski, 10,733 ... I-10
South Shore, Greenup, 1,318 ... B-15
• South Wallins, Harlan, 1,022 ... J-14
Southgate, Campbell, 3,266 ... B-6
Springfield, Washington, 2,875 ... G-8
Stanford, Lincoln, 2,686 ... G-10
Stanton, Powell, 2,795 ... F-13
• Stearns, McCreary, 1,550 ... K-11
Sturgis, Union, 2,184 ... J-18
Summer Shade, Metcalfe ... J-7
Taylor Mill, Kenton, 5,530 ... B-6
Taylorsville, Spencer, 774 ... E-8
Tompkinsville, Monroe, 2,861 ... K-7
Union, Boone, 1,001 ... B-10
Uniontown, Union, 1,008 ... I-18
• Valley Station, Jefferson, 22,840 ... E-7
Valley Village, Jefferson ... C-2
• Van Lear, Johnson, 1,050 ... F-16
Vanceburg, Lewis, 1,713 ... C-14
Versailles, Woodford, 7,269 ... E-10
Villa Hills, Kenton, 7,739 ... A-5
Vine Grove, Hardin, 3,586 ... F-6
Walton, Boone, 2,034 ... B-10
Warsaw, Gallatin, 1,202 ... B-9
Watterson Park, Jefferson, 1,542 ... C-2
West Buechel, Jefferson, 1,587 .. C-2
West Liberty, Morgan, 1,887 ... F-14
West Point, Hardin, 1,216 ... E-6
• Westwood, Boyd, 5,300 ... C-16
Whitesburg, Letcher, 1,636 ... I-16
• Whitley City, McCreary, 1,133 ... J-11
Wickliffe, Ballard, 851 ... L-14
Williamsburg, Whitley, 5,493 ... J-12
Williamstown, Grant, 3,023 ... C-10
Wilmore, Jessamine, 4,215 ... F-10
Winchester, Clark, 15,799 ... E-12
Windy Hills, Jefferson, 2,452 ... B-3
Woodlawn Park, Jefferson, 1,099 ... B-3
• Woodlawn-Oakdale, McCracken, 4,954 ... L-16
Worthington, Greenup, 1,751 ... C-15
Wurtland, Greenup, 1,221 ... C-15

Explanation of symbols: • – Census Designated Place (CDP)

Louisiana

General Help Numbers:

Governor's Office
PO Box 94004
Baton Rouge, LA 70804-9004
www.gov.state.la.us

225-342-0991
Fax 225-342-7099
8AM-5PM

Attorney General's Office
LA Department of Justice
PO Box 94005
Baton Rouge, LA 70804-9005
www.ag.state.la.us

225-342-7013
Fax 225-342- 8703
8:30AM-5PM

Legislative Records
State Capitol, 2nd Floor
PO Box 44486
Baton Rouge, LA 70804
www.legis.state.la.us

225-342-2456

8AM-5PM

State Archives
Records Mgt, & History
3851 Essen Lane
Baton Rouge, LA 70809-2137
www.sec.state.la.us/archives/
archives/archives-index.htm

225-922-1000
Fax 225-922-0433
8AM-4:30PM,
9-5 SA 1-5 SU

State Specifics:

Capital: Baton Rouge
East Baton Rouge Parish

Time Zone: CST

Number of Parishes: 64

Population: 4,496,334

Web Site: www.state.la.us

State Agencies

Criminal Records

Access to Records is Restricted

State Police, Bureau of Criminal Identification, 7979 Independence Blvd, Baton Rouge, LA 70806-6409; 225-925-6095, 225-925-7005 (Fax), 8AM-4:30PM.

www.lsp.org

Note: Records ARE RESTRICTED and are not available to the public in general. Records are available for employment or licensing purposes as state law dictates. Authorized forms are available from this department.

Statewide Court Records

Judicial Administrator, Judicial Council of the Supreme Court, 400 Royal Street, Suite 1190, New Orleans, LA 70130-8101; 504-310-2550, 504-310-2587 (Fax), 9AM-5PM.

www.lasc.org

Indexing & Storage: It takes 24 hours before new records are available for inquiry. Records are normally destroyed after no less than 3 years.

Searching: Include the following in your request- name; also helpful-specific information such as DOB, years to search. Include your name and contact information.

Access by: mail, online.

Fee & Payment: There is no search fee

Mail search: Turnaround time: 72 hours. Records are available by mail.

Online search: Search opinions from the state Supreme Court at www.lasc.org/opinion_search.asp. Online records go back to 1995.

Sexual Offender Registry

State Police, Sex Offender and Child Predator Registry, PO Box 66614, Box A-6, Baton Rouge, LA 70896; 225-925-6100, 800-858-0551, 225-925-7005 (Fax), 8AM-4:30PM.

www.lasocpr.lsp.org/socpr/

Note: The Sex Offender and Child Predator Registry program is statutorily provided through La. R. S. 15:542 & 15:542.1, et. seq., of the Louisiana Criminal Code.

Indexing & Storage: Records are available from 6/18/92. It takes 1 to 3 days before new records are available for inquiry. Records are normally destroyed after the registration term expires (varies by nature of record).

Access by: mail, phone, fax, in person, online.

Mail search: Turnaround time: 30 days. No SASE is required.

Phone search: You must supply name, race, sex, DOB in a phone request. Request can be delayed due to limited staff.

Fax search: Same criteria as phone search.

In person search: This office and local law enforcement will perform searches.

Online search: Search by name, ZIP Code, or view the entire list at the website. Also search by city, school area or parish.

Expedited service: Will try to expedite request, if requested.

Incarceration Records

Department of Public Safety and Corrections, P.O. Box 94304, Attn: Office of Adult Services, Baton Rouge, LA 70804-9304; 225-342-6642, 225-342-9711 (Locator), 225-342-3349 (Fax), 8AM-4:30PM.

www.corrections.state.la.us

Indexing & Storage: Records are available on current and former inmates. It takes approximately 1 to 3 days before new records are available for inquiry.

Searching: Include the following in your request-full name. DOC number is helpful. Index does not include alias or other names used. Location, physical identifiers, conviction and sentencing information, and release dates are reported.

Access by: mail, fax, online.

Fee & Payment: There is no search fee.

Mail search: Turnaround time 30 days. A SASE is not requested.

Fax search: Can request via fax.

Online search: Access is limited to schedules for upcoming Parole Board hearings, as well as decisions from previous Parole Board hearings. Go to http://www.corrections.state.la.us/Offices/parolebo ard/paroledockets.htm. Also, a private company offers free web access at www.vinelink.com/index.jsp.

Corporation, Limited Partnership, Limited Liability Company Records, Trademarks/Servicemarks

Commercial Division, Corporation Department, PO Box 94125, Baton Rouge, LA 70804-9125 (Courier: 8549 United Plaze Blvd, Baton Rouge, LA 70809); 225-925-4704, 225-925-4726 (Fax), 8AM-4:30PM.

www.sos.louisiana.gov

Note: Fictitious Names and Assumed Names are found at the parish level.

Indexing & Storage: Records are available from mid-1800s. New records are available for inquiry immediately. Records are indexed on microfilm, inhouse computer, index cards, on-line.

Searching: Include the following in your request-full name of business. In addition to the articles of incorporation, corporation records include the following information: Annual Reports, Officers, Directors, Prior (merged) names, Inactive names, Reserved names and (possibly) US Tax ID number.

Access by: mail, phone, fax, in person, online.

Fee & Payment: The search fee is $1.00. Copies cost $15.00 without amendments and $25.00 with amendments and $10.00 plus a fee of $.25 per page after 40 pages for specific query searches on computer. Fee payee: Secretary of State. Prepayment required. Personal checks accepted. Credit cards accepted: MasterCard, Visa, AmEx, Discover.

Mail search: Turnaround time: 5 to 10 working days. No SASE is required.

Phone search: You may call for information; however, only limited information is available.

Fax search: There is an additional $1.00 per page fee if returned by fax. Turnaround time is 5 to 10 working days.

In person search: There is a free public access terminal.

Online search: There are 2 ways to go: free on the Internet or pay. To view limited information on the website, go to "Commercial Division, Corporations Section," then "Search Corporations Database." The pay system is $360 per year for unlimited access. Almost any communications software will work. The system is open from 6:30 am to 11pm. For more information, call Carolyn Vogelaar at 225-925-4792.

Other access: This agency offers corporation, LLC, partnership, and trademark information on tape cartridges. For more info, call 225-925-4792.

Expedited service: Expedited service is available for mail and phone searches. Turnaround time: 1 day. Add $30.00 per business name.

Uniform Commercial Code

Secretary of State, UCC Records, PO Box 94125, Baton Rouge, LA 70804-9125; 800-256-3758, 225-342-7011 (Fax), 8AM-4:30PM.

www.sec.state.la.us/comm/ucc/ucc-index.htm

Note: The statewide index of UCC filings is available in each parish office. All tax liens and financial statements are filed at the parish level. IRS liens show up on UCC records. Records CANNOT be obtained from this office, except via the online system.

Indexing & Storage: Records are available for all active listings. Records are indexed on computer since 1990. It takes 2 days before new records are available for inquiry. Records are normally destroyed after 1 year after laspe date.

Searching: All filing information including debtor names, property descriptions, and subsequent filings and amendments are available. Mail-in requests are sent to any parish, as all searches reflect statewide information.

Access by: online.

Fee & Payment: Fees are only for the online service. Fee payee: Secretary of State. Prepayment required. The payment information outlined here applies only to online access. Personal checks accepted. Credit cards accepted: MasterCard, Visa.

Online search: An annual $400 fee gives unlimited access to UCC filing information. The dial-up service is open from 6:30 AM to 11 PM daily. Most any software communications program can be configured to work. For further information, call Carolyn Vogelaar at 225-925-4792, or e-mail cvogelaar@sos.louisiana.gov or visit the website.

Federal Tax Liens, State Tax Liens

Records not maintained by a state level agency.

Note: Records are filed with the Clerk of Court at the parish level.

Sales Tax Registrations

Access to Records is Restricted

Revenue Department, Taxpayer Services Division, PO Box 201, Baton Rouge, LA 70821-0201 (Courier: 617 N 3rd St, Baton Rouge, LA 70802); 225-219-7356, 225-219-2210 (Fax), 8AM-4:30PM.

www.rev.state.la.us

Note: This agency will confirm is an entity has a sales tax permit. It will only provide registration information to the registrant itself.

Birth Certificates

Vital Records Registry, Office of Public Health, PO Box 60630, New Orleans, LA 70160 (Courier: 325 Loyola Ave Room 102, New Orleans, LA 70112); 504-568-5152, 504-568-8353, 800-454-9570, 866-761-1855 (Fax), 8AM-4PM.

www.oph.dhh.state.la.us/recordsstatistics/vitalreco rds/

Note: Some certificates (all types of vital records) contain information at the bottom of the document that is confidential and not released to anyone. This information is used for statistical purposes and varies depending on legislative action.

Indexing & Storage: Records are available from 1914 on. Birth records for only the City of New Orleans are available for 100 years. Records older than 100 years should be ordered from the State Archives. New records are available for inquiry immediately. Records are indexed on microfiche, index cards, inhouse computer.

Searching: Birth certificates are considered confidential for 100 years. Requesters must be related to the person of record or have a signed release. Include the following in your request-full name, names of parents, mother's maiden name, date of birth, place of birth, relationship to person of record, reason for information request. Older records must be searched at the State Archives 225-922-1184.

Access by: mail, fax, in person, online.

Fee & Payment: A "long form" birth certificate is $15.00, while a "birth card" is $9.00. Fee payee: Vital Records Registry. Prepayment required. Credit cards are not accepted for mail requests. Personal checks accepted. Credit cards accepted: MasterCard, Visa.

Mail search: Turnaround time: 4-6 weeks. No SASE is required.

Fax search: Fax requests accepted, use of credit card required.

In person search: Photo ID required, turnaround time immediate.

Online search: Orders can be placed online at www.vitalchek, a state-approved vendor.

Expedited service: If ordered from state, based on only an urgent need basis. You must provide documentation of the emergency with plane tickets, verifications of reservations, or official letters requesting documents by a specific date. A fee of $15.50 is charged for overnight delivery. Phone and online service from vitalchek includes a $12.95 fee for using a credit card. Turnaround time is 10 days via this agency, 2-3 days via vitalchek.

Death Records

Vital Records Registry, Office of Public Health, PO Box 60630, New Orleans, LA 70160 (Courier: 325 Loyola Ave Room 102, New Orleans, LA 70112); 504-568-5152, 504-568-8353, 800-454-9570, 866-761-1855 (Fax), 8AM-4PM.

www.oph.dhh.state.la.us/recordsstatistics/vitalrecords/

Note: This agency refers to expedited service as emergency service

Indexing & Storage: Records are available from 1950 on. Records over 50 years old must be obtained from the State Archives. New records are available for inquiry immediately. Records are indexed on microfiche, index cards, inhouse computer.

Searching: Death records are considered confidential for 50 years. Must show how related or have a signed release from immediate family member if for investigative purposes. Include the following in your request-full name, date of death, place of death, relationship to person of record, reason for information request, photo ID. Records older than 50 years must be searched at the State Archives 225-922-1184.

Access by: mail, fax, in person, online.

Fee & Payment: The search fee is $7.00. Fee payee: Department of Vital Records. Prepayment required. Credit cards accepted for fax and in person requests only. Personal checks accepted. Credit cards accepted: MasterCard, Visa.

Mail search: Turnaround time: 4-6 weeks. No SASE is required.

Fax search: Fax requests accepted. Use of credit card required.

In person search: In person search requires a photo ID. Turnaround time usually 45 minutes.

Online search: Orders can be placed online at www.vitalchek.com, a state-appoved vendor.

Expedited service: If ordered from state, based on only an urgent need basis. You must provide documentation of the emergency with plane tickets, verifications of reservations, or official letters requesting documents by a specific date. A fee of $15.50 is charged for overnight delivery. Phone and online service from vitalchek includes a $12.95 fee for using a credit card. Turnaround time is 10 days via this agency, 2-3 days via vitalchek.

Marriage Certificates, Divorce Records

Records not maintained by a state level agency.

Note: Only Orleans Parish marriage records are available from 1948 on at the VR Registry for a $5.00 fee, same search criteria as others. Include bride name (maiden), groom and date of marriage. Other marriage & all divorce records are found at parish of event. Marriage Records older than 50 years are open to the public.

Workers' Compensation Records

Department of Labor, Office of Workers' Compensation, PO Box 94040, Baton Rouge, LA 70804-9040 (Courier: LA Department of Labor, Office of Workers' Compensation, Baton Rouge, LA 70802); 800-201-3457, 225-342-7582 (Fax), 8AM-5PM.

www.laworks.net

Note: For partial information, and to determine if a record exists, and if you have the name and SSN, see the Other Access section below.

Indexing & Storage: Records are available from 1983 to present on microfilm. Only cases on file are those where the employee lost 7 days or more of work and/or had disputed issues resolved or settlements approved. New records are available for inquiry immediately. Records are indexed on microfilm. Records are normally destroyed after 10 years.

Searching: Most records are considered confidential. Public records include decisions, awards, or orders in disputed cases. No records are released until "copy" charges are paid. Include the following in your request-claimant name, Social Security Number, date of accident, reason for information request, specific records that you need copies of. Otherwise, signed release required. All record requests must be in writing. The following data is not released: pending records.

Access by: mail, phone, fax, in person.

Fee & Payment: Copies are $.25 per page, $1.00 to certify, there is no fee to search. Fee payee: Workers' Compensation Administrative Fund. Prepayment required. Cash is not accepted. Personal checks accepted. No credit cards accepted.

Mail search: Turnaround time: 3 days.

Phone search: With a name and SSN (required), you may use the "Easy Call" Interactive Voice Response System at 225-342-8731 for partial public information, especially to determine if a record exists.

Fax search: Records can be requested by fax at no extra fee.

In person search: If you request in person, the turnaround time is shortened only by the mail time.

Other access: With a name and SSN (required), you may use the "Easy Call" Interactive Voice Response System at 225-342-8731 for partial public information, especially to determine if a record exists. Enter 1-4-1-2-2 after the phone answers.

Driver Records

Dept of Public Safety and Corrections, Office of Motor Vehicles, PO Box 64886, Baton Rouge, LA 70896 (Courier: 109 S Foster Dr, Baton Rouge, LA 70806); 877-368-5463, 225-925-6388, 225-925-6915 (Fax), 8AM-4:30PM.

www.expresslane.org

Note: Copies of tickets may be obtained from the address listed above. The fee is $5.00 per document.

Indexing & Storage: Records are available for 3 yrs for moving violations, 10 yrs from DWI conviction date, and 5 or 10 yrs for suspensions. Pre-8/15/01 accidents are displayed 3 yrs from accident date, no fault shown. Accidents after 8/01 shown only if license is suspended. It takes 2 to 3 weeks before new records are available for inquiry. Records are normally destroyed after 3, 5, or 10 years according to the type of violation.

Searching: Casual requesters can obtain driving records with proper release form signed by subject. Include the following in your request-driver's license number, full name, date of birth. It is sometimes helpful to include the race or sex when requesting a record.

Access by: mail, phone, fax, in person, online.

Fee & Payment: The fee for mail-in or walk-in requests is $15.00 per name. The fee for vendor online or tape requests is $6.00. Fee payee: Office of Motor Vehicles. Prepayment required. Personal Checks not accepted. Credit cards accepted at web site only.

Mail search: Turnaround time: 10 working days. No SASE is required.

Phone search: No searching by telephone unless authorized under DPPA.

Fax search: No searching by fax unless authorized under DPPA.

In person search: Walk-in requesters may "view" a record for no charge. Casual requesters must present signed form. The fee is for the hard copy. Records can be requested from the Motor Vehicle Offices in New Orleans, Lake Charles, Monroe, Baton Rouge, Shreveport, and Alexandria.

Online search: There are two methods. The commercial requester, interactive mode is available from 7 AM to 9:30 PM daily. There is a minimum order requirement of 2,000 requests per month. A bond or large deposit is required. Fee is $6.00 per record. For more information, call 225-925-6032. The 2nd method is for individuals to order their own record from the Internet site at www.expresslane.org. The fee is $16.40 and requires a credit card.

Other access: Tape ordering is available for batch delivery. Bulk database sales are available to permissible users.

Vehicle Ownership, Vehicle Identification

Department of Public Safety & Corrections, Office of Motor Vehicles, PO Box 64886, Baton Rouge, LA 70896 (Courier: 7979 Independence Blvd, Baton Rouge, LA 70806); 225-925-4955, 877-368-5463, 225-925-4256 (Fax), 8AM-4PM.

www.dps.state.la.us/omv/home.html

Indexing & Storage: Records are available for 7 years. Records are normally destroyed after 7 years.

Searching: Casual requesters can obtain records, but personal information is not released without consent of subject. The agency requires a written request stating the nature of the inquiry. The following data is not released: Social Security Numbers.

Access by: mail.

Fee & Payment: The current fee for VIN, registration, and plate checks is $10.00 per record, which includes certification. Fee payee: Office of Motor Vehicles. Prepayment required. Personal checks accepted. No credit cards accepted.

Mail search: Turnaround time: 2 - 4 weeks. Mail searches require license plate number or vehicle identification number (VIN).

Accident Reports

Louisiana State Police, Traffic Records Unit - A27, PO Box 66614, Baton Rouge, LA 70896 (Courier: 7919 Independence Blvd, Baton Rouge, LA 70806); 225-925-6157, 225-925-4922 (Fax), 8AM-4PM.

www.lsp.org/safety_crash.html

Note: Send questions to ehardin@dps.state.la.us.

Indexing & Storage: Records are available from 1990's to present. It takes 2 to 3 weeks before new records are available for inquiry. Records are normally destroyed after 8 years.

Searching: If photos needed, usesame PO Box but attention Photo Lab D-3 or call 225-925-3518. The driver name(s), date of accident and parish are needed when ordering.

Access by: mail, phone, in person.

Fee & Payment: The fee is $7.50 per record. Fee payee: Louisiana State Police. Prepayment

required. Personal checks are not accepted. No credit cards accepted.

Mail search: Turnaround time: 10 working days. A SASE is requested.

Phone search: Sarching by telephone available for ongoing accounts.

In person search: Turnaround time is while you wait, if personnel not busy.

Vessel Ownership, Vessel Registration

Department of Wildlife & Fisheries, Vessel Records, PO Box 14796, Baton Rouge, LA 70898 (Courier: 2000 Quail Dr, Baton Rouge, LA 70808); 225-765-2898, 225-763-5421 (Fax), 8:15AM-4:15PM.

www.wlf.state.la.us/apps/netgear/page3.asp

Note: Lien information is found at the parish level.

Indexing & Storage: Records are available from 1960 to present. Record are indexed on computer from the 1970s to present. All motorized boats and sailboats over 12 ft must be registered.

Searching: The hull ID # is not released. To search, one of the following is required: Louisiana #, name, or hull ID #, and from whom boat was acquired. Records are subject to DPPA and 14 permissible uses. Records not released to the public unless subject has given permission or by subpoena.

Access by: mail.

Fee & Payment: There is no fee.

Mail search: Turnaround time: 7 to 10 days. No SASE is required.

Other access: Records can be purchased in bulk in a variety of media formats. There is a $100.00 minimum deposit, the fee is $.05 per record.

Voter Registration

Louisiana Secretary of State, Elections Division, PO Box 94125, Baton Rouge, LA 70804-9125; 225-922-0900, 225-219-9608 (Fax), 8AM-5PM.

www.sos.louisiana.gov/elections/elections-index.htm

Note: Although the information is public record, individual searching must be done at the parish level through the Parish Registrar of Voters.

Indexing & Storage: Records are available for all currently registered voters.

Searching: The agency will sell the database statewide or by parish. Media formats include email, labels, CD, and lists. There are no restrictions regarding purchasing for marketing purposes. The following data is not released: Social Security Numbers.

GED Certificates

Div of Family, Career, and Technical Education, PO Box 94064, Baton Rouge, LA 70804-9064; 225-342-0444 (Main Number), 225-219-4439 (Fax), 8AM - 4:30PM.

Searching: You may verify a GED. To search, you must use their form, which may be requested via phone, fax, or mail. Include the following in your request-name at time of test, DOB, SSN.

Access by: mail, fax, in person.

Fee & Payment: There is no fee.

Mail search: Turnaround time 2 weeks. No SASE is required.

Fax search: Results of a fax search will be mailed, same criteria as mail searches.

In person search: In person searchers must have a photo ID. Turnaround time: Immediate.

Hunting and Fishing License Information

Access to Records is Restricted

Wildlife & Fisheries Department, License Division, PO Box 98000, Baton Rouge, LA 70898-9000 (Courier: 2000 Quail Dr, Baton Rouge, LA 70808); 225-765-2881, 225-765-3150 (Fax), 8:AM-4:30PM.

www.wlf.state.la.us/

Note: All license information is subject to the DPPA under US Code 18. At present, not all 14 permissible uses are readily available and use of a subpoena is suggested.

Louisiana State Licensing Agencies

Licenses Searchable Online

Acupuncturist #20	www.lsbme.org/verifications.htm
Architect/Architectural Firm #50	www.lastbdarchs.com/roster.htm
Athletic Trainer #20	www.lsbme.org/verifications.htm
Bank #32	www.ofi.state.la.us
Bond For Deed Agency #32	www.ofi.state.la.us
Check Casher #32	www.ofi.state.la.us
Chemical Engineer #40	www.lapels.com/indiv_search.asp
Child Residential Care #35	www.dss.state.la.us/departments/os/child_care_facilities_by_parish.html
Chiropractor #7	www.lachiropracticboard.com/lic-drs.htm
Clinical Lab Personnel #20	www.lsbme.org/verifications.htm
Collection Agency #32	www.ofi.state.la.us
Consumer Credit Grantor #32	www.ofi.state.la.us
Contractor, Commercial/Resi./General #30	www.lslbc.state.la.us/findcontractor.asp
Counselor, Professional (LPC) #46	www.lpcboard.org/lpc_alpha_list.htm
Credit Repair Agency #32	www.ofi.state.la.us
Credit Union #32	www.ofi.state.la.us
Day Care Facility #35	www.dss.state.la.us/departments/os/child_care_facilities_by_parish.html
Dentist/Dental Hygienist #9	http://docs.lsbd.org:8080/dentistsearch.asp
Dietitian #13	www.lbedn.org/licensee_database.asp
Drug Distributor, Wholesale #64	www.lsbwdd.org
Electrical Engineer #40	www.lapels.com/indiv_search.asp
Emergency Shelter #35	www.dss.state.la.us/departments/os/child_care_facilities_by_parish.html
Engineer/Engineer Intern #40	www.lapels.com/indiv_search.asp
Engineering Firm #40	www.lapels.com/firm_search.asp
Environmental Engineer #40	www.lapels.com/indiv_search.asp
Exercise Physiologist, Clinical #20	www.lsbme.org/verifications.htm
Family Support #35	www.dss.state.la.us/departments/os/child_care_facilities_by_parish.html
Foster Care/Adoption Care #35	www.dss.state.la.us/departments/os/child_care_facilities_by_parish.html
Infant Intervention Service #35	www.dss.state.la.us/departments/os/child_care_facilities_by_parish.html
Insurance Agent, LHA/PC #33	www.ldi.state.la.us/search_forms/searchforms.htm
Insurance Agent/Broker/Producer #33	www.ldi.state.la.us/search_forms/searchforms.htm
Land Surveyor Firm #40	www.lapels.com/firm_search.asp
Land Surveyor/Surveyor Intern #40	www.lapels.com/indiv_search.asp
Lender #32	www.ofi.state.la.us
Lobbyist #66	www.ethics.state.la.us/lobs.htm
Medical Doctor #20	www.lsbme.org/verifications.htm
Midwife #20	www.lsbme.org/verifications.htm
Mortgage Lender/Broker, Residential #32	www.ofi.state.la.us/newrml.htm
Notary Public #54	www.sos.louisiana.gov/
Notification Filer #32	www.ofi.state.la.us/newnotif.htm
Nuclear Engineer #40	www.lapels.com/indiv_search.asp
Nutritionist #13	www.lbedn.org/licensee_database.asp
Occupational Therapist/Technologist #20	www.lsbme.org/verifications.htm
Optometrist #22	www.arbo.org/odfinder/LicSearch.asp
Osteopathic Physician #20	www.lsbme.org/verifications.htm
Pawnbroker #32	www.ofi.state.la.us/newpawn.htm
Pharmacist/Pharmacy/Pharm.Technician #23	www.labp.com/pbs.html
Pharmacy Interns (College) #23	www.labp.com/pbs.html
Pharmacy/Hospital #23	www.labp.com/pbs.html
Physician Assistant #20	www.lsbme.org/verifications.htm
Podiatrist #20	www.lsbme.org/verifications.htm
Psychologist #15	www.onesimuswebs.com/lsbep_db.asp
Radiologic Technologist, Private #20	www.lsbme.org/verifications.htm
Real Estate Appraiser #29	www.lreasbc.state.la.us/appraiserinfo.htm
Respiratory Therapist/Therapy Technician #20	www.lsbme.org/verifications.htm
Savings & Loan #32	www.ofi.state.la.us/newcus.htm
Solicitor #33	www.ldi.state.la.us/search_forms/searchforms.htm
Speech Pathologist/Audiologist #18	www.lbespa.org
Thrift & Loan Company #32	www.ofi.state.la.us/newthrift.htm
Vocational Rehabilitation Counselor #63	www.lrcboard.org/licensee_database.asp

Louisiana Licensing Quick Finder

Acupuncturist #20 504-568-6820
Adult Day Care #35 225-022-0015
Adult Education Instructor #42 225-342-3490
Adult Residential Care #35 225-022-0015
Agricultural Consultant #56 225-925-3787
Alarm/Security Company #26 225-272-2310
Alcoholic Beverage Vendor #3 225-925-4041
Amusement Ride/Attraction Inspector #55
.... 225-925-7045
Amusement Ride/Attraction Owner/Operator #55
.... 225-925-7045
Arborist/Utility Arborist #39 225-952-8100
Architect/Architectural Firm #50 225-925-4802
Art Therapist #42 225-342-3490
Athletic Trainer #20 504-568-6820
Attorney #49 504-566-1600
Auctioneer/Auction Company #44 225-922-2329
Bank #32 225-925-4660
Barber/Barber Shop/Instructor/School #4
.... 225-925-1701
Boiler Inspector/Installer #55 225-925-4344
Bond For Deed Agency #32 225-925-4660
Boxing/Wrestling Personnel #27 337-439-8308
Burglar Alarm Contractor #55 225-925-6766
Cemetery #2 504-838-5267
Check Casher #32 225-925-4660
Check Seller #32 225-925-4660
Chemical Engineer #40 225-925-6291
Child Nutrition Program Supv'r #42 225-342-3490
Child Residential Care #35 225-022-0015
Chiropractor #7 225-765-2322
Clinical Lab Personnel #20 504-568-6820
Collection Agency #32 225-925-4660
Compulsive Gambler Counselor #28 ... 225-927-7600
Construction Projects,Commercial +$50,000 #41
.... 225-765-2301
Consumer Credit Grantor #32 225-925-4667
Contractor, Commercial/Resid'l #30 504-736-7125
Contractor, General/Subcontractor #41 225-765-2301
Cosmetologist/Cosmetology Instruct. #8 225-756-3404
Counselor, Professional (LPC) #46 225-765-2515
Court Reporter #37 225-342-2668
Credit Repair Agency #32 225-925-4660
Credit Union #32 225-925-4660
Day Care Facility #35 225-922-0015
Dental Hygienist #9 504-568-8574
Dentist #9 504-568-8574
Dietitian #13 225-756-3490
Drug Distributor, Wholesale #64 225-295-8567
Electrical Engineer #40 225-925-6291
Electrologist #10 318-463-6180
Electronics Repairman #34 225-231-4710
Embalmer #12 504-838-5109
Emergency Medical Technician #20 504-568-6820
Emergency Shelter #35 225-922-0015
Engineer/Engineer Intern #40 225-925-6291
Engineering Firm #40 225-925-6291
Environmental Engineer #40 225-925-6291
Equine Dentist #45 225-342-2176
Esthetician #8 225-756-3404
Euthanasia Technician #45 225-342-2176

Exercise Physiologist, Clinical #20 504-568-6820
Explosives Dealer/Handler #38 225-925-6113
Family Support #35 225-022-0015
Fire Alarm Contractor #55 225-925-6766
Fire Extinguisher Contractor #55 225-925-6766
Fire Protection Sprinkler Contr. #55 225-925-6766
Fire Suppression Contractor #55 225-925-6766
Florist, Retail/Wholesale #39 225-952-8100
Foster Care/Adoption Care #35 225-922-0015
Funeral Director/Establishment #12 504-838-5109
Funeral Home Internship/Work Permit #12
.... 504-838-5109
Guidance Counselor #42 225-342-3490
Hearing Aid Dealer #19 318-362-3014
Horse Owner/Trainer #52 504-483-4000
Horse Racing #52 504-483-4000
Horse Racing-related Profession #52 ... 504-483-4000
Horticulturist #39 225-952-8100
Infant Intervention Service #35 225-022-0015
Insurance Agent, LHA/PC #33 225-342-0860
Insurance Agent/Broker #33 225-342-0860
Insurance Producer #33 225-342-0860
Interior Designer #14 225-298-1283
Investment Advisor #53 225-925-4660
Jockey/Apprentice/Jockey Agent #52 .. 504-483-4000
Juvenile Detention #35 225-022-0015
Land Surveyor Firm #40 225-925-6291
Land Surveyor/Surveyor Intern #40 225-925-6291
Landscape Architect #39 225-952-8100
Landscape Contractor #39 225-952-8100
Lender #32 225-925-4660
Livestock Branding #43 225-925-3962
Loan Broker #32 225-925-4660
Lobbyist #66 225-763-8777
Lottery #47 225-297-2000
Lottery Claims Center #48 504-889-0031
Manicurist #8 225-756-3404
Massage Therapist #62 225-771-4090
Maternity Home #35 225-922-0015
Medical Doctor #20 504-568-6820
Medical Gas Piping Installer #51 504-826-2382
Midwife #20 504-568-6820
Montessori Teacher #42 225-342-3490
Mortgage Lender/Broker, Resid'l #32 .. 225-925-4662
Motor Vehicle Agent/Salesman #59 504-838-5207
Motor Vehicle Dealer; New/Used #59 . 504-838-5207
Motor Vehicle Inspector #1 225-667-1927
Motor Vehicle Leasing/Rental Co. #59. 504-838-5207
Motor Vehicle Sales Finance Co. #59.. 504-838-5207
Music Therapist #42 225-342-3490
Notary Public #54 225-922-0507
Notification Filer #32 225-992-0634
Nuclear Engineer #40 225-925-6291
Nuclear Medicine Technologist #16 504-838-5231
Nurse (Practical) School #25 504-838-5791
Nurse, RN/PRRN #21 504-838-5332
Nurse, Student #21 504-838-5332
Nurse-LPN #25 504-838-5791
Nurses' Aide #36 225-925-4132
Nursing Home Administrator #36 225-922-0009
Nursing School #21 504-838-5332

Nutritionist #13 225-756-3490
Occupational Therapist/Techn'gist #20. 504-568-6820
Optometrist #22 318-335-2989
Osteopathic Physician #20 504-568-6820
Pari-Mutuel Employee #52 504-483-4000
Pawnbroker #32 225-925-4660
Payday Lender #32 225-925-4660
Personal Care Attendant #35 225-922-0015
Pesticide Applicator #56 225-925-3796
Pesticide Dealer/Operator #56 225-925-3796
Pharmacist/Pharmacy #23 225-925-6496
Pharmacy Interns (College) #23 225-925-6496
Pharmacy Tech #23 225-925-6496
Pharmacy/Hospital #23 225-925-6496
Physical Therapist/Therapist Asst #24. 337-262-1043
Physician Assistant #20 504-568-6820
Plumber Journeyman/Master #51 504-826-2382
Podiatrist #20 504-568-6820
Polygraph Examiner #57 225-389-3836
Prevention Specialist, Social Work #28 225-927-7600
Private Investigator/PI Company #58 .. 225-763-3556
Private Security #26 225-272-2310
Psychologist #15 225-763-3935
Public Accountant-CPA #5 504-566-1244
Radiation Therapy Technologist #16 .. 504-838-5231
Radiographer #16 504-838-5231
Radiologic Technologist #16 504-838-5231
Radiologic Technologist, Private #20 ... 504-568-6820
Reading Specialist #42 225-342-3490
Real Estate Agent/Broker/Sales #60 ... 225-925-4771
Real Estate Appraiser #29 225-925-4771
Respiratory Therapist/Therapy Technologist #20
.... 504-568-6820
Respite Care #35 225-022-0015
Sanitarian #17 225-925-7204
Satellite Technician #34 225-231-4710
Savings & Loan #32 225-925-4660
School Counselor/Librarian/Nurse/Principal #42
.... 225-342-3490
School Psychologist #42 225-342-3490
School Superintendent, Parish/City #42 225-342-3490
School Therapist #42 225-342-3490
Securities Salesperson/Dealer #53 225-925-4660
Security Guard #26 225-272-2310
Shorthand Reporter #37 225-342-2668
Social Worker #6 .... 225.756.3470
Solicitor #33 225-342-0860
Speech Pathologist/Audiologist #18 225-763-5480
Speech/Language/Hearing Teacher #42
.... 225-342-3490
Substance Abuse Counselor #28 225-927-7600
Supervised Independent Living #35 225-022-0015
Teacher, Temporary #42 225-342-3490
Teacher/Teacher's Aide #11 225-342-3490
Thrift & Loan Company #32 225-925-4660
Timeshare Interest Salesperson #60 ... 225-925-4771
TV-Radio Technician #34 225-231-4710
Used Vehicle Salesperson #61 225-925-3870
Veterinarian/Veterinary Technician #45 225-342-2176
Vocational Rehab. Counselor #63 225-922-1435
Water Supply Piping #51 504-826-2382

Louisiana Licensing Agency Information

1 State Police Safety & Enforcement, PO Box 66614, Baton Rouge, LA 70896; 225-667-1927, Fax: 225-925-3966.

2 Cemetery Board, 2901 Ridgelake Dr, #101, Metairie, LA 70002-4946; 504-838-5267, Fax: 504-838-5289. www.lcb.state.la.us

3 Board of Alcohol & Tobacco, 8549 United Plaza Blvd, Baton Rouge, LA 70809; 225-925-4041, Fax: 225-925-3975. www.atc.rev.state.la.us/atcweb/home.htm Email: info@atcla.com

4 Board of Barber Examiners, PO Box 14029, Baton Rouge, LA 70898-4029; 225-925-1701, Fax: 225-925-1703.

5 Board of Certified Public Accountants, 601 Poydras St, #1770, New Orleans, LA 70130; 504-566-1244, Fax: 504-566-1252. www.cpaboard.state.la.us/ Email: sitemaster@cpaboard.state.la.us Note: They do sell lists.

6 Board of Certified Social Work Examiners, 18550 Highland Rd Suite B, Baton Rouge, LA 70809; 225.756.3470, Fax: 225.756.3472. www.labswe.org Email: socialwork@labswe.org

7 Board of Chiropractic Examiners, 8621 Summa Ave, Baton Rouge, LA 70809; 225-765-2322, Fax: 225-765-2640. www.lachiropracticboard.com/lic-drs.htm Email: lsbce@eatel.net Search Database at www.lachiropracticboard.com/lic-drs.htm

8 Board of Cosmetology, 11622 Sunbelt Court, Baton Rouge, LA 70809; 225-756-3404, Fax: 225-756-3410/3109.

9 Board of Dentistry, 365 Canal Street, #2680, New Orleans, LA 70112; 504-568-8574, Fax: 504-568-8598. www.lsbd.org Email: carolyn@lsbd.org Search Database at http://docs.lsbd.org:8080/dentistsearch.asp Note: Lists of all dentists is sold for $500.00; list of denatal hygienists is also available for $500.00.

10 Board of Electrolysis Examiners, PO Box 67, DeRidder, LA 70634-0067; 318-463-6180, Fax: 318-463-3991. Email: istatebrdee@aol.com

11 Board of Elementary & Secondary Education, 626 N 4th St, Baton Rouge, LA 70804-9064; 225-342-3490, 877-453-2721, Fax: 225-342-3499. www.doe.state.la.us

12 Board of Embalmers & Funeral Directors, P.O. Box 8757, Metairie, LA 70011; 504-838-5109, Fax: 504-838-5112. www.lsbefd.state.la.us Email: labefd@bellsouth.net

13 Board of Examiners of Dietitics & Nutrition, 18550 Highland Rd, Baton Rouge, LA 70809; 225-756-3490, Fax: 225-756-3472. www.lbedn.org Email: admin@lbedn.org

14 Board of Examiners of Interior Designers, 2900 Westfork Dr #200, Baton Rouge, LA 70827-0004; 225-298-1283, Fax: 225-925-1892.

15 Board of Examiners of Psychologists, 8280 YMCA Plaza Dr, Bldg 8B, Baton Rouge, LA 70810; 225-763-3935, Fax: 225-763-3968. www.lsbep.org Email: lsbep@cmq.net Search Database at www.onesimuswebs.com/lsbep_db.asp

16 Board of Examiners of Radiologic Technologists, 3108 Cleary Ave, #207, Metairie, LA 70002; 504-838-5231, Fax: 504-780-1740. Email: larabrd@bellsouth.net

17 Board of Examiners of Sanitarians, 1772 Wooddale Blvd, Baton Rouge, LA 70806; 225-925-7204, Fax: 225-925-7245. www.lsbes.org Email: dkuhns@dhh.state.la.us

18 Board of Examiners of Speech/Language Pathology & Audiology, 18550 Highland Rd Suite B, Baton Rouge, LA 70810; 225-763-3480, Fax: 225-763-3472. www.lbespa.org/ Email: speech@ibespa.org Search Database at www.lbespa.org

19 Board of Hearing Aid Dealers, 2200 Justice St, Monroe, LA 71201; 318-362-3014, Fax: 318-362-3019.

20 Executive Director, Board of Medical Examiners, 630 Camp St, New Orleans, LA 70130; 504-568-6820, auto response: dial 1, Fax: 504-568-8893. www.lsbme.org Email: lsbmever@lsbme.org Search Database at www.lsbme.org/verifications.htm

21 Board of Nursing, 3510 N Causeway Blvd, #601, Metairie, LA 70002; 504-838-5332, Fax: 504-838-5349. www.lsbn.state.la.us Email: lsbn@lsbn.state.la.us

22 Board of Optometry Examiners, 115 B N 13th St, Oakdale, LA 71463; 318-335-2989, Fax: 318-335-2989. Email: labor@yahoo.com Search Database at www.arbo.org/odfinder/LicSearch.asp

23 Board of Pharmacy, 5615 Corporate Blvd, #8E, Baton Rouge, LA 70808; 225-925-6496, Fax: 225-925-6499. www.labp.com Email: labp@labp.com Search Database at www.labp.com/pbs.html

24 Board of Physical Therapy Examiners, 104 Fairlane Dr, Lafayette, LA 70507-5307; 337-262-1043, Fax: 337-262-1054. www.laptboard.org Email: lsbpte@iamerica.net

25 Board of Practical Nurse Examiners, 3421 N Causeway Blvd #203, Metairie, LA 70002-3711; 504-838-5791, Fax: 504-838-5279. www.lsbpne.com

26 Board of Private Security Examiners, 15703 Old Hammond Hwy, Baton Rouge, LA 70816; 225-272-2310, Fax: 225-272-5816.

27 Boxing & Wrestling Commission, PO Box 251, Franklin, LA 70538; 337-439-8308.

28 Board of Certification for Substance Abuse Counselors, 8738 Quarters Lake Rd, Baton Rouge, LA 70809; 225-922-7700, Fax: 225-922-7701. www.lsbcsac.org Email: admin@lsbcsac.org

29 Real Estate Appraisers State Board of Certification, 5222 Summa Ct, Baton Rouge, LA 70809-3727; 225-925-4771, 800-821-4529, Fax: 225-925-4431. www.lreasbc.state.la.us Email: info@lreasbc.state.la.us Search Database at www.lreasbc.state.la.us/appraiserinfo.htm

30 Contractors Licensing Board (New Orleans), 1221 Elmwood Pk Blvd, New Orleans, LA 70141; 504-736-7125, Fax: 504-736-7125 *Key. www.lslbc.state.la.us Search Database at www.lslbc.state.la.us/findcontractor.asp

32 Office of Financial Institutions, 8660 United Plaza Blvd, 2nd Floor, Baton Rouge, LA 70809; 225-925-4660, Fax: 225-925-4548. www.ofi.state.la.us Email: ofila@ofi.state.la.us

33 Department of Insurance, Agent's License Division, 1702 N. 3rd Street, Baton Rouge, LA 70802; 225-342-0860, Fax: 225-219-9322. www.ldi.state.la.us Search Database at www.ldi.state.la.us/search_forms/searchforms.htm

34 Radio And Television Technicians Board, 6554 Florida Boulevard #109, Baton Rouge, LA 70806; 225-231-4710, Fax: 225-231-4711.

35 Department of Social Services, Bureau of Licensing, PO Box 3078, Baton Rouge, LA 70821; 225-922-0015, Fax: 225-922-0014. www.dss.state.la.us

36 Examiners of Nursing Facility Administrators, 5647 Superior Dr, Baton Rouge, LA 70816-6049; 225-922-0009, Fax: 225-922-0006. Email: kempwright@compuserve.com

37 Examiners of Certified Shorthand Reporters, PO Box 3257, Baton Rouge, LA 70821-3257; 225-342-2668, Fax: 225-342-2698. Email: courtreporter@lacourtreporterboard.com

38 Explosives Control Unit, PO Box 66614, Mail Stop 21, Baton Rouge, LA 70896; 225-925-6113, Fax: 225-925-4048. www.lsp.org/tess.html#materials

39 Department of Agriculture, Horticulture Commission, PO Box 3596, Baton Rouge, LA 70821-3596; 225-952-8100, Fax: 225-952-3760. www.ldaf.state.la.us

40 Professional Engineers & Land Surveying Board, 9643 Brookline Ave #121, Baton Rouge, LA 70809-1433; 225-925-6291, Fax: 225-925-6292. www.lapels.com Search Database at www.lapels.com/indiv_search.asp Note: Will sell list of licensees.

41 Licensing Board for Contractors, PO Box 14419, Baton Rouge, LA 70898-4419; 225-765-2301, Fax: 225-765-2431. www.lslbc.louisiana.gov Email: info@lslbc.state.la.us Search Database at www.lslbc.louisiana.gov

42 Department of Education, Licensing Bureau of Higher Education Certification, 626 N 4th St, Baton Rouge, LA 70804-9064; 225-342-3490, Fax: 225-342-3499.
www.doe.state.la.us

43 LA Dept of Agriculture & Forestry, Livestock Brand Commission, PO Box 1951 (5825 Florida Blvd, 70806), Baton Rouge, LA 70821; 225-925-3962, Fax: 225-925-4103.
www.ldaf.state.la.us
Email: linfo@ldaf.state.la.us

44 Auctioneers Licensing Board, 8017 Jefferson Hwy, #A-2, Baton Rouge, LA 70809; 225-922-2329, Fax: 225-925-1892.
www.lalb.org/
Email: auctionboard@eatel.net

45 Board of Veterinary Medicine, 263 3rd St, #104, Baton Rouge, LA 70801; 225-342-2176, Fax: 225-342-2142.
www.lsbvm.org
Email: lbvm@eatel.net Note: They do sell lists.

46 Licensed Professional Counselors, Board of Examiners, 8631 Summa Ave, #A, Baton Rouge, LA 70809; 225-765-2515, Fax: 225-765-2514.
www.lpcboard.org
Email: lpcboard@eatel.net Search Database at www.lpcboard.org/lpc_alpha_list.htm

47 Lottery Corporation, State Headquarters, 555 Laurel St., Baton Rouge, LA 70801; 225-297-2000, Fax: 225-297-2005.
www.lalottery.com

48 Lottery Corporation, 2222 Clearview Parkway, Metairie, LA 70001; 504-889-0031, Fax: 504-889-0490.
www.louisianalottery.com

49 State Bar Association, 601 St Charles Av, New Orleans, LA 70130; 504-566-1600, Fax: 504-566-0930.
www.lsba.org
Email: lsbainfo@lsba.org

50 Board of Architectural Examiners, 9625 Fenway Ave #B, Baton Rouge, LA 70809-1413; 225-925-4802, Fax: 225-925-4804.
www.lastbdarchs.com
Email: bd@lsbae.brcoxmail.com
Search Database at www.lastbdarchs.com/roster.htm

51 Plumbing Board, 2714 Canal St, #512, New Orleans, LA 70119; 504-826-2382, Fax: 504-826-2175.

52 Louisiana State Racing Commission, 320 N Carrollton Ave, #2B, New Orleans, LA 70119-5100; 504-483-4000, Fax: 504-483-4898.
http://horseracing.la.gov/
Email: webmaster@lre.state.la.us

53 Securities Division, Office of Financial Institutions, PO Box 94095 (8660 United Plaza Blvd, 2nd Fl), Baton Rouge, LA 70804; 225-925-4660, Fax: 225-925-4548.
www.ofi.state.la.us

54 Office of Secretary of State, PO Box 94125, Baton Rouge, LA 70804-9125; 225-922-0507, Fax: 225-922-0945.
www.sos.louisiana.gov/notary-pub/notary-index.htm
Email: notaries@sos.louisiana.gov
Search Database at www.sos.louisiana.gov/

55 Office of the State Fire Marshall, 8181 Independence Blvd, Baton Rouge, LA 70806; 225-925-4911; 800-256-5452, Fax: 225-925-3813.
www.dps.state.la.us/sfm

56 Agricultural & Environmental Sciences, Pest Control Commission, PO Box 3596 (5825 Florida Blvd), Baton Rouge, LA 70821; 225-925-3796, 225-925-3770, Fax: 225-925-3760.
www.ldaf.state.la.us/divisions/aes/default.asp
Email: info@ldaf.state.la.us

57 Baton Rouge Police Dept., Polygraph Board, PO Box 2406, Baton Rouge, LA 70821; 225-389-3836.

58 Board of Private Investigators Examiners, 2051 Silverside Dr. #109, Baton Rouge, LA 70808; 225-763-3556, Fax: 225-763-3536.
www.lsbpie.com/
Email: lsbpie@intersurf.com

59 Motor Vehicle Commission, 3519 12th Street, Metairie, LA 70002-3427; 504-838-5207.
www.lmvc.state.la.us/

60 Real Estate Commission, P.O. Box 14785, Baton Rouge, LA 70898-4785; 225-925-4771, Fax: 225-925-4431.
www.lrec.state.la.us
Email: info@lrec.state.la.us

61 Used Motor Vehicle & Parts Commission, 3132 Valley Creek Drive, Baton Rouge, LA 70808; 225-925-3870, Fax: 225-925-3869.
www.lumvpc.state.la.us

62 Professional Licensing Boards, Board of Massage Therapy, 12022 Plank Road, Baton Rouge, LA 70811; 225-771-4090, Fax: 225-771-4021.
www.lsbmt.org
Email: lsbmt@eatel.net

63 Board of Examiners, Board of Vocational Rehabilitation Counselors, PO Box 41594, Baton Rouge, LA 70835; 225-922-1435, Fax: 225-922-1352.
www.lrcboard.org
Email: lrcboard@eatel.net

64 Board of Wholesale Drug Distributors, 12046 Justice Ave, #C, Baton Rouge, LA 70816; 225-295-8567, Fax: 225-295-8568.
www.lsbwdd.org
Email: lsbwdd@bellsouth.net
Search Database at www.lsbwdd.org

66 Supervisory Committee on Campaign Finance Disclosure, Louisiana Board of Ethics, 2415 Quail Dr #314, Baton Rouge, LA 70808-0110; 225-763-8777; 800-842-6630, Fax: 225-763-8780.
www.ethics.state.la.us Search Database at www.ethics.state.la.us/lobs.htm

Louisiana Federal Courts

The following list indicates the district and division name for each Parish in the state. If the bankruptcy court location is different from the district court, then the location of the bankruptcy court appears in parentheses.

Parish/Court Cross Reference

Parish	District	Division
Acadia Parish	Western	Lafayette (Lafayette-Opelousas)
Allen Parish	Western	Lake Charles
Ascension Parish	Middle	Baton Rouge
Assumption Parish	Eastern	New Orleans
Avoyelles Parish	Western	Alexandria
Beauregard Parish	Western	Lake Charles
Bienville Parish	Western	Shreveport
Bossier Parish	Western	Shreveport
Caddo Parish	Western	Shreveport
Calcasieu Parish	Western	Lake Charles
Caldwell Parish	Western	Monroe
Cameron Parish	Western	Lake Charles
Catahoula Parish	Western	Alexandria
Claiborne Parish	Western	Shreveport
Concordia Parish	Western	Alexandria
De Soto Parish	Western	Shreveport
East Baton Rouge Parish	Parish	Middle Baton Rouge
East Carroll Parish	Western	Monroe
East Feliciana Parish	Middle	Baton Rouge
Evangeline Parish	Western	Lafayette (Lafayette-Opelousas)
Franklin Parish	Western	Monroe
Grant Parish	Western	Alexandria
Iberia Parish	Western	Lafayette (Lafayette-Opelousas)
Iberville Parish	Middle	Baton Rouge
Jackson Parish	Western	Monroe
Jefferson Davis Parish	Western	Lake Charles
Jefferson Parish	Eastern	New Orleans
La Salle Parish	Western	Alexandria
Lafayette Parish	Western	Lafayette (Lafayette-Opelousas)
Lafourche Parish	Eastern	New Orleans
Lincoln Parish	Western	Monroe
Livingston Parish	Middle	Baton Rouge
Madison Parish	Western	Monroe
Morehouse Parish	Western	Monroe
Natchitoches Parish	Western	Alexandria
Orleans Parish	Eastern	New Orleans
Ouachita Parish	Western	Monroe
Plaquemines Parish	Eastern	New Orleans
Pointe Coupee Parish	Middle	Baton Rouge
Rapides Parish	Western	Alexandria
Red River Parish	Western	Shreveport
Richland Parish	Western	Monroe
Sabine Parish	Western	Shreveport
St. Bernard Parish	Eastern	New Orleans
St. Charles Parish	Eastern	New Orleans
St. Helena Parish	Middle	Baton Rouge
St. James Parish	Eastern	New Orleans
St. John the Baptist Parish	Parish	EasternNew Orleans
St. Landry Parish	Western	Lafayette (Lafayette-Opelousas)
St. Martin Parish	Western	Lafayette (Lafayette-Opelousas)
St. Mary Parish	Western	Lafayette (Lafayette-Opelousas)
St. Tammany Parish	Eastern	New Orleans
Tangipahoa Parish	Eastern	New Orleans
Tensas Parish	Western	Monroe
Terrebonne Parish	Eastern	New Orleans
Union Parish	Western	Monroe
Vermilion Parish	Western	Lafayette (Lafayette-Opelousas)
Vernon Parish	Western	Alexandria
Washington Parish	Eastern	New Orleans
Webster Parish	Western	Shreveport
West Baton Rouge Parish	Parish	Middle Baton Rouge
West Carroll Parish	Western	Monroe
West Feliciana Parish	Middle	Baton Rouge
Winn Parish	Western	Alexandria

Standards for Federal Courts: The search fee is $20.00 per item (one party name or case number). Certification fee is $7.00 per document. Copy fee is $.50 per page. All fees standard unless noted in profile. Mail Search: always enclose a stamped self addressed envelope unless otherwise noted. Most courts accept fax requests or will suggest a copying/search vendor. Before releasing records, all courts require prepayment unless noted in profile.

Open records are located at the court unless otherwise noted. District courts index by defendant and plaintiff as well as by case number. Bankruptcy courts usually index by debtor and case number. While most courts now have their indexes on computer, many still maintain index card files as well.

The universal PACER sign-up number is 800-676-6856. Find PACER and the Party/Case Index on the Web at http://pacer.psc.uscourts.gov. PACER dial-up access is $.60 per minute. Also, courts offering internet access via RACER, PACER, Web-PACER or the new CM-ECF charge $.07 per page fee unless noted as free.

US District Court

Eastern District of Louisiana

New Orleans Division Clerk, 500 Poydras St, New Orleans, LA 70130 (courier address: Use mail address for courier pdelivery) 504-589-7650, Fax: 504-589-7189. www.laed.uscourts.gov

Parishes: Assumption Parish, Jefferson Parish, Lafourche Parish, Orleans Parish, Plaquemines Parish, St. Bernard Parish, St. Charles Parish, St. James Parish, St. John the Baptist Parish, St. Tammany Parish, Tangipahoa Parish, Terrebonne Parish, Washington Parish.

Indexing & Storage: New cases available in the index 1-2 days after filing date.

Fee & Payment: Payment may be made by money order, cashier check, personal check. Payee: Clerk, U.S. District Court.

Phone Search: No searching by telephone. Only docket information available by phone.

In Person Search: Fee charged if court conducts your in person search for you.

PACER: PACER is available online at http://pacer.laed.uscourts.gov. Document images available. Records purged every six months. New records are online after 1-2 days.

U.S. Bankruptcy Court

Eastern District of Louisiana

New Orleans Division Clerk, 500 Poydras St, New Orleans, LA 70130 (courier address: Use mail address for courier delivery) 504-589-7878. www.laeb.uscourts.gov

Parishes: Assumption Parish, Jefferson Parish, Lafourche Parish, Orleans Parish, Plaquemines Parish, St. Bernard Parish, St. Charles Parish, St. James Parish, St. John the Baptist Parish, St. Tammany Parish, Tangipahoa Parish, Terrebonne Parish, Washington Parish.

Indexing & Storage: Cases indexed by debtor as well as by case number. New cases available in the index 2 days after filing date. Records are also indexed on microfiche. District wide searches are available from this court from November 1985 for information in the computer and from 1979 to 1985 on card index.

Fee & Payment: Payment may be made by money order, cashier check, business check. Personal checks are not accepted. Payee: Clerk, U.S. Bankruptcy Court.

Phone Search: Information is available from 9:00 to 10:30 a.m. and 1:00 to 2:30 p.m. over the phone. There is no fee for case status information. Only docket information will be released. Automated voice case information service (VCIS) is available. Call VCIS at 504-589-7879.

In Person Search: Fee charged if court conducts your in person search for you.

PACER: PACER is available online at http://pacer.laeb.uscourts.gov. Records purged every six months. New civil records are online after 2 days.

Electronic Filing: Electronic filing information online at https://ecf.laeb.uscourts.gov

U.S. District Court

Middle District of Louisiana

Baton Rouge Division PO Box 2630, Baton Rouge, LA 70821-2630 (courier: 777 Florida St., #139, Baton Rouge, LA 70801), 225-389-3500, Fax: 225-389-3501. www.lamd.uscourts.gov

Parishes: Ascension Parish, East Baton Rouge Parish, East Feliciana Parish, Iberville Parish, Livingston Parish, Pointe Coupee Parish, St. Helena Parish, West Baton Rouge Parish, West Feliciana Parish.

Indexing & Storage: New cases available in the index immediately after filing date. Index prior to 1992 is on microfiche and computer.

Fee & Payment: Payment may be made by money order, cashier check, business check, Visa/MC. Personal checks not accepted. Court has no billing procedures. Payee: Clerk U.S. District Court.

Phone Search: Only docket information available by phone. If the information is at the Federal Records Center, the court will provide the information needed to review a record.

Mail Search: A SASE not required.

In Person Search: Fee charged if court conducts your in person search for you. A coin operated copier is available.

PACER: PACER is available online at http://pacer.lamd.uscourts.gov. Document images available. New records are online after 1 day.

U.S. Bankruptcy Court

Middle District of Louisiana

Baton Rouge Division Room 119, 707 Florida St, Baton Rouge, LA 70801 (courier address: Use mail address for courier delivery) 225-389-0211. www.lamb.uscourts.gov

Parishes: Ascension Parish, East Baton Rouge Parish, East Feliciana Parish, Iberville Parish, Livingston Parish, Pointe Coupee Parish, St. Helena Parish, West Baton Rouge Parish, West Feliciana Parish.

Indexing & Storage: Cases indexed by debtor and creditors as well as by case number. New cases available in the index immediately after filing date.

Fee & Payment: Payment may be made by money order, cashier check, business check. Personal checks are not accepted. Payee: Clerk, U.S. Bankruptcy Court.

Phone Search: Only docket information available by phone. Automated voice case information service (VCIS) is available. Call VCIS at 225-382-2175.

In Person Search: Fee charged if court conducts your in person search for you.

PACER: PACER is available online at http://pacer.lamb.uscourts.gov. New civil records are online after 1 day.

Electronic Filing: Electronic filing information online at https://ecf.lamb.uscourts.gov

U.S. District Court

Western District of Louisiana

Alexandria Division PO Box 1269, Alexandria, LA 71309 (courier address: 515 Murray, Alexandria, LA 71301), 318-473-7415, Fax: 318-473-7345. www.lawd.uscourts.gov

Parishes: Avoyelles Parish, Catahoula Parish, Concordia Parish, Grant Parish, La Salle Parish, Natchitoches Parish, Rapides Parish, Winn Parish.

Indexing & Storage: New cases available in the index 3 days after filing date.

Fee & Payment: Payment may be made by money order, cashier check, personal check. Payee: Clerk, U.S. District Court.

Phone Search: Only docket information available by phone.

In Person Search: Fee charged if court conducts your in person search for you.

PACER: PACER is available online at https://pacer.lawd.uscourts.gov. Document images available. Records purged as deemed necessary. New records are online after 1 day.

Electronic Filing: Electronic filing information online at https://ecf.lawd.uscourts.gov

Lafayette Division Room 113, Federal Bldg, 705 Jefferson St, Lafayette, LA 70501 (courier address: Use mail address for courier delivery) 337-593-5000. www.lawd.uscourts.gov

Parishes: Acadia Parish, Evangeline Parish, Iberia Parish, Lafayette Parish, St. Landry Parish, St. Martin Parish, St. Mary Parish, Vermilion Parish.

Indexing & Storage: New cases available in the index 1 day after filing date.

Fee & Payment: Payment may be made by money order, cashier check, business check. Personal checks are not accepted. Payee: Clerk, U.S. District Court.

Phone Search: Only docket information available.

Mail Search: Certified name searches can only be performed from the Shreveport office. A SASE not required.

In Person Search: Permitted. Certified name searches only available at Shreveport office.

PACER: PACER is available online at https://pacer.lawd.uscourts.gov. Document images available. Records purged as deemed necessary. New records are online after 1 day.

Electronic Filing: Electronic filing information online at https://ecf.lawd.uscourts.gov

Lake Charles Division 611 Broad St, Suite 188, Lake Charles, LA 70601 (courier address: Use mail address for courier delivery) 337-437-3870. www.lawd.uscourts.gov

Parishes: Allen Parish, Beauregard Parish, Calcasieu Parish, Cameron Parish, Jefferson Davis Parish, Vernon Parish.

Indexing & Storage: New cases available in the index 3 days after filing date.

Fee & Payment: Payment may be made by money order, cashier check, business check. Personal checks are not accepted. Payee: Clerk, U.S. District Court.

Phone Search: Only docket information available by phone.

In Person Search: Fee charged if court conducts your in person search for you.

PACER: PACER is available online at https://pacer.lawd.uscourts.gov. Document images available. Records purged as deemed necessary. New records are online after 1 day.

Electronic Filing: Electronic filing information online at https://ecf.lawd.uscourts.gov

Monroe Division PO Drawer 3087, Monroe, LA 71210 (courier address: Room 215, 201 Jackson St, Monroe, LA 71201), 318-322-6740. www.lawd.uscourts.gov

Parishes: Caldwell Parish, East Carroll Parish, Franklin Parish, Jackson Parish, Lincoln Parish, Madison Parish, Morehouse Parish, Ouachita Parish, Richland Parish, Tensas Parish, Union Parish, West Carroll Parish.

Indexing & Storage: New cases available in the index 3 days after filing date. The Shreveport computerized index is used for searching. This division has been without a judge since 1996, and may not be getting one. Therefore, there are very few case records held here any longer. It is recommended to search at the Shreveport division.

Fee & Payment: Payment may be made by money order, cashier check, business check. Personal checks are not accepted. Payee: Clerk, U.S. District Court.

Phone Search: Only docket information available.

In Person Search: Fee charged if court conducts your in person search for you.

PACER: PACER is available online at https://pacer.lawd.uscourts.gov. Document images available. Records purged as deemed necessary. New records are online after 1 day.

Electronic Filing: Electronic filing information online at https://ecf.lawd.uscourts.gov

Shreveport Division U.S. Courthouse, Suite 1167, 300 Fannin St, Shreveport, LA 71101-3083 (courier address: Use mail address for courier delivery) 318-676-4273. www.lawd.uscourts.gov

Parishes: Bienville Parish, Bossier Parish, Caddo Parish, Claiborne Parish, De Soto Parish, Red River Parish, Sabine Parish, Webster Parish.

Indexing & Storage: New cases available in the index immediately after filing date. On computer are cases that were filed in 1977 or later. Copies from closed records in cases filed in 1977 or later are available from microfiche located at this court.

Fee & Payment: Payment may be made by money order, cashier check, business check. Personal checks are not accepted. Payee: Clerk, U.S. District Court.

Phone Search: Only docket information available by phone. If the information is at the Federal Records Center, the court will provide the information needed to review a record.

Mail Search: A SASE not required.

In Person Search: Fee charged if court conducts your in person search for you.

PACER: PACER is available online at https://pacer.lawd.uscourts.gov. Document images available. Records purged as deemed necessary. New records are online after 1 day.

Electronic Filing: Electronic filing information online at https://ecf.lawd.uscourts.gov

U.S. Bankruptcy Court

Western District of Louisiana

Alexandria Division 300 Jackson St, Suite 116, Alexandria, LA 71301-8357 (courier address: Hemenway Bldg, 300 Jackson St, Alexandria, LA 71301), 318-445-1890. www.lawb.uscourts.gov

Parishes: Avoyelles Parish, Catahoula Parish, Concordia Parish, Grant Parish, La Salle Parish, Natchitoches Parish, Rapides Parish, Vernon Parish, Winn Parish.

Indexing & Storage: Cases indexed by debtor as well as by case number. New cases available in the index 1 day after filing date. Chapter 7 and 11 cases from the Monroe Division are now at this court. Chapter 12 and Chapter 13 continue to be handled by Shreveport.

Fee & Payment: Payment may be made by money order, cashier check, personal check. A copy service will also do the search and copies for fee plus cost of postage. The copy service will bill law firms. Payee: Clerk, U.S. Bankruptcy Court or copy service.

Phone Search: Only docket information available by phone. Automated voice case information service (VCIS) is available. Call VCIS at 800-326-4026 or 318-676-4234.

Mail Search: A SASE not required.

In Person Search: Fee charged if court conducts your in person search for you.

PACER: PACER is available online at http://pacer.lawb.uscourts.gov. Document images available. New civil records are online after 1 day.

Electronic Filing: Electronic filing information online at https://ecf.lawb.uscourts.gov

Lafayette-Opelousas Division PO Box J, Opelousas, LA 70571-1909 (courier: Room 205, 231 S Union, Opelousas, LA 70570), 318-948-3451, Fax: 318-948-4426. www.lawb.uscourts.gov

Parishes: Acadia Parish, Evangeline Parish, Iberia Parish, Lafayette Parish, St. Landry Parish, St. Martin Parish, St. Mary Parish, Vermilion Parish.

Indexing & Storage: Cases indexed by debtor as well as by case number. New cases available in the index 1 day after filing date. Records are indexed on index cards for pre-1987 files only. Records are also indexed on microfiche. District wide searches are available for information from January 1, 1986 from this division. This office handles case records for the Lake Charles Division also.

Fee & Payment: Payment may be made by money order, cashier check, business check. Personal checks are not accepted. Payee: Clerk, U.S. Bankruptcy Court. Will fax back to toll-free numbers.

Phone Search: Only docket information available by phone. Automated voice case information service (VCIS) is available. Call VCIS at 800-326-4026 or 318-676-4234. Will fax back to toll-free numbers.

Mail Search: A SASE not required.

In Person Search: Fee charged if court conducts your in person search for you. Court personnel will assist searchers at no charge.

PACER: PACER is available online at http://pacer.lawb.uscourts.gov. New civil records are online after 1 day.

Electronic Filing: Electronic filing information online at https://ecf.lawb.uscourts.gov

Lake Charles Division c/o Lafayette-Opelousas Division, PO Box J, Opelousas, LA 70571-1909 (courier address: Room 205, 250 S Union, Opelousas, LA 70570), 318-948-3451. www.lawb.uscourts.gov

Parishes: Allen Parish, Beauregard Parish, Calcasieu Parish, Cameron Parish, Jefferson Davis Parish.

Indexing & Storage: Cases indexed by as well as by case number. New cases available in the index after filing date. Open records are located at the Division.

Fee & Payment: Payment may be made by money order, cashier check. Business checks are not accepted. Personal checks are not accepted.

Phone Search: Automated voice case information service (VCIS) is available. Call VCIS at 800-326-4026 or 318-676-4234.

Mail Search: A SASE not required.

In Person Search: Permitted.

PACER: PACER is available online at http://pacer.lawb.uscourts.gov. Document images available. New civil records are online after 1 day.

Electronic Filing: Electronic filing information online at https://ecf.lawb.uscourts.gov

Monroe Division c/o Shreveport Division, Suite 2201, 300 Fannin St, Shreveport, LA 71101 (courier address: Use mail address for courier delivery) 318-676-4267. www.lawb.uscourts.gov

Parishes: Caldwell Parish, East Carroll Parish, Franklin Parish, Jackson Parish, Lincoln Parish, Madison Parish, Morehouse Parish, Ouachita Parish, Richland Parish, Tensas Parish, Union Parish, West Carroll Parish.

Indexing & Storage: Cases indexed by as well as by case number. New cases available in the index after filing date. This court is an unmanned office. Cases are housed as follows: Chapter 7 and Chapter 11 cases to Alexandria; Chapter 12 and Chapter 13 cases to Shreveport. Open records are located at the Shreveport Division.

Fee & Payment: Payment may be made by money order. Business checks are not accepted. Personal checks are not accepted.

Phone Search: Automated voice case information service (VCIS) is available. Call VCIS at 800-326-4026 or 318-676-4234.

In Person Search: Permitted.

PACER: PACER is available online at http://pacer.lawb.uscourts.gov. New civil records are online after 1 day.

Electronic Filing: Electronic filing information online at https://ecf.lawb.uscourts.gov

Shreveport Division Suite 2201, 300 Fannin St, Shreveport, LA 71101-3089 (courier address: Use mail address for courier delivery) 318-676-4267. www.lawb.uscourts.gov

Parishes: Bienville Parish, Bossier Parish, Caddo Parish, Claiborne Parish, De Soto Parish, Red River Parish, Sabine Parish, Webster Parish.

Indexing & Storage: Cases indexed by as well as by case number. New cases available in the index immediately after filing date.

Fee & Payment: Payment may be made by money order, business check. Personal checks are not accepted. Debtor's checks are not accepted. Payee: Clerk, U.S. Bankruptcy Court.

Phone Search: Automated voice case information service (VCIS) is available. Call VCIS at 800-326-4026 or 318-676-4234.

In Person Search: Fee charged if court conducts your in person search for you.

PACER: PACER is available online at http://pacer.lawb.uscourts.gov. New civil records are online after 1 day.

Electronic Filing: Electronic filing information online at https://ecf.lawb.uscourts.gov

Louisiana Parish Courts

Court	Jurisdiction	No. of Courts	How Organized
District Courts*	General	65	42 Districts
City Courts*	Limited	50	City Boundaries
Parish Courts	Limited	3	
Justice of the Peace Courts	Municipal	390	
Mayor's Courts	Municipal	250	
Family Court	Special	1	East Baton Rouge
Juvenile Courts	Special	5	

* Profiled in this Sourcebook.

Court	CIVIL								
	Tort	Contract	Real Estate	Min. Claim	Max. Claim	Small Claims	Estate	Eviction	Domestic Relations
District Courts*	X	X	X	$0	No Max		X		X
City Courts*	X	X	X	$0	$15,000	$3000			X
Parish Courts	X	X	X	$0	$10,000	$3000		X	X
Justice of the Peace Courts	X	X	X	$0	$3000	$3000		X	
Family Court									X
Juvenile Courts									X

Court	CRIMINAL				
	Felony	Misdemeanor	DWI/DUI	Preliminary Hearing	Juvenile
District Courts*	X	X	X		X
City Courts*		X	X	X	X
Parish Courts		X	X	X	X
Justice of the Peace Courts					
Mayor's Courts					
Family Court					X
Juvenile Courts					X

ADMINISTRATION   Judicial Administrator, Judicial Council of the Supreme Court, 400 Royal Street, Suite 1190, New Orleans, LA, 70130; 504-310-2550, Fax: 504-310-2587; www.lasc.org

COURT STRUCTURE   The trial court of general jurisdiction in Louisiana is the district court. A District Court Clerk in each Parish holds all the records for that Parish. Each Parish has its own clerk and courthouse. City courts are courts of record and generally exercise concurrent jurisdiction with the district court in civil cases where the amount in controversy does not exceed $15,000. In criminal matters, they generally have jurisdiction over ordinance violations and misdemeanor violations of state law. City judges also handle a large number of traffic cases. Parish courts exercise jurisdiction in civil cases worth up to $10,000 and criminal cases punishable by fines of $1,000 or less, or imprisonment of six months or less. Cases are appealable from the parish courts directly to the courts of appeal. A municipality may have a Mayor's Court; the mayor may hold trials, but nothing over $30.00, and there are no records.

ONLINE ACCESS   The online computer system, Case Management Information System (CMIS), is operating and development is continuing. It is for internal use only; there is no plan to permit online public access. However, Supreme Court and Appellate opinions are currently available.

There are a number of Parishes that offer a means of remote online access to the public.

Acadia Parish

15th District Court PO Box 922, Crowley, LA 70527; 337-788-8881; Fax: 337-788-1048. Hours: 8:30AM-4:30PM (CST). *Felony, Misdemeanor, Civil, Probate.*
www.acadiaparishclerk.com
Civil Records: Access: Phone, fax, mail, in person. Both court and visitors may perform in person searches. Search fee: $11.00 per name per year. Required to search: name, years to search. Civil cases indexed by defendant, plaintiff. Civil records on computer from 1979, archived from 1800s.
Criminal Records: Access: Phone, fax, mail, in person. Both court and visitors may perform in person searches. Search fee: $11.00 per name per year. Required to search: name, years to search, DOB; also helpful: SSN. Criminal records on computer from 1979, archived from 1800s. Copy of check must be included in the fax request. Copy of check must be faxed with request.
General Information: Public Access terminal is available. No adoption or juvenile records released. Fee to fax results is $6.00 1st page, $2.00 for any add'l pages. Copy fee: $2.00 per page. Certification fee: $6.00. Payee: Acadia Parish Clerk of Court. Personal checks accepted. Prepayment required. Mail requests: SASE required. Mail turnaround time 1-2 days.

Allen Parish

33rd District Court PO Box 248, Oberlin, LA 70655; 337-639-4351; Fax: 337-639-2030. Hours: 8AM-4:30PM (CST). *Felony, Misdemeanor, Civil, Probate.*
Civil Records: Access: Fax, mail, in person. Both court and visitors may perform in person searches. Search fee: $10.00 per name. Fee is for a 10 year search. Required to search: name, years to search. Civil cases indexed by defendant, plaintiff. Civil records archived back to 1913; on computer back to 1985.
Criminal Records: Access: Mail, in person. Both court and visitors may perform in person searches. Search fee: $10.00 per name. Fee is for a 10 year search. Required to search: name, years to search, DOB, SSN. Criminal records archived back to 1913; on computer back to 7/94.
General Information: Public Access terminal is available. No adoption or juvenile records released. Fee to fax results is $2.00 per page. Copy fee: $1.00 per page. Certification fee: $5.00. Payee: Allen Parish Clerk of Court. Personal checks accepted. Prepayment required. Mail requests: SASE requested. Turnaround time 2 days.

Ascension Parish

23rd District Court PO Box 192, Donaldsonville, LA 70346; 225-473-9866; Fax: 225-473-8641 civ; 473-9287 crim. Hours: 8:30AM-4:30PM (CST). *Felony, Misdemeanor, Civil, Probate.*
www.eatel.net/~apcc/Clerk_of_Court/indexx.html
Civil Records: Access: Fax, mail, in person. Both court and visitors may perform in person searches. Search fee: $10.00 per name; add $5.00 on search fee if request made by fax. Required to search: name, years to search. Civil cases indexed by defendant, plaintiff. Civil records on computer from 1987, index books back to 1800s, property tax since 1994, mortgage since 11/77.
Criminal Records: Access: Fax, mail, in person. Both court and visitors may perform in person searches. Search fee: $10.00 per name; add $5.00 on search fee if request made by fax. Required to search: name, years to search, DOB; also helpful: SSN.

Criminal Records go back to 1800s; computerized records since 11/86.
General Information: Public Access terminal is available. No adoption or juvenile records released. Will fax results $5.00 1st page, $1.00 each add'l. Copy fee: $1.00 per page. Certification fee: $3.00. Payee: Ascension Parish Clerk of Court. Personal checks accepted. Prepayment required. Mail requests: SASE requested. Turnaround time 2 days.

Assumption Parish

23rd District Court PO Box 249, Napoleonville, LA 70390; 985-369-6653; Fax: 985-369-2032. Hours: 8:30AM-4:30PM (CST). *Felony, Misdemeanor, Civil, Probate.*
Civil Records: Access: Fax, mail, in person. Both court and visitors may perform in person searches. Search fee: $10.00 per name per 10 years. Required to search: name, years to search. Civil cases indexed by defendant, plaintiff. Civil records archived back to 1800s; on computer back to 1990.
Criminal Records: Access: Fax, mail, in person. Both court and visitors may perform in person searches. Search fee: $10.00 per name per 10 years. Required to search: name, years to search, DOB. Criminal records archived back to 1800s; on computer back to 1994.
General Information: Public Access terminal is available. No adoption or juvenile records released. Will fax results $2.00 1st page, $1.00 each add'l. Copy fee: $1.00 per page. Certification fee: $5.00. Payee: Assumption Parish Clerk of Court. Personal checks accepted. Prepayment required. Mail requests: SASE requested. Turnaround time 1 day.

Avoyelles Parish

12th District Court PO Box 219, Marksville, LA 71351; 318-253-7523. Hours: 8:30AM-4:30PM (CST). *Felony, Misdemeanor, Civil, Probate.*
Civil Records: Access: Mail, in person. Both court and visitors may perform in person searches. Search fee: $10.00 per name. Required to search: name, years to search. Civil cases indexed by defendant, plaintiff. Civil records on computer from 1985, microfiche back to 1800s.
Criminal Records: Access: Mail, in person. Both court and visitors may perform in person searches. Search fee: $10.00 per name. Required to search: name, years to search, DOB; also helpful: SSN. Criminal records on computer from 1985, microfiche back to 1800s.
General Information: No adoption or juvenile records released. Copy fee: $1.00 per page. Certification fee: $3.00 per page. Payee: Clerk of Court. Personal checks accepted. Prepayment required. Mail requests: SASE not required. Mail turnaround time 1 day.

Beauregard Parish

36th District Court PO Box 100, DeRidder, LA 70634; 337-463-8595; Fax: 337-462-3916. Hours: 8AM-4:30PM (CST). *Felony, Misdemeanor, Civil, Probate.*
Civil Records: Access: Mail, in person. Both court and visitors may perform in person searches. Search fee: $15.00 per name. Fee is per 10 years searched. Required to search: name, years to search. Civil cases indexed by defendant, plaintiff. Civil records on computer since 1985, archived from 1913.
Criminal Records: Access: Mail, in person. Both court and visitors may perform in person searches. Search fee: $15.00 per name. Fee is per 10 years searched. Required to search: name, years to search, DOB; also helpful: SSN. Criminal record index in books.

General Information: No adoption or juvenile records released. Copy fee: $1.25 per page. Certification fee: $5.00. Payee: Clerk of Court. Personal checks accepted. Prepayment required. Mail requests: SASE required. Mail turnaround time 1 week.

Bienville Parish

2nd District Court 100 Courthouse Dr, Rm 100, Arcadia, LA 71001; 318-263-2123; Fax: 318-263-7426. Hours: 8:30AM-4:30PM (CST). *Felony, Misdemeanor, Civil, Probate.*
www.bienvilleparish.org/clerk
Civil Records: Access: Fax, mail, in person. Both court and visitors may perform in person searches. Search fee: $10.00 per name. Required to search: name, years to search. Civil cases indexed by defendant, plaintiff. Civil records on computer from 1991, index books prior.
Criminal Records: Access: Fax, mail, in person. Both court and visitors may perform in person searches. Search fee: $10.00 per name. Required to search: name, years to search, DOB; also helpful: SSN. Criminal records on computer from 1991, index books prior.
General Information: Public Access terminal is available. (Terminal only has civil records, no criminal.) No adoption or juvenile records released. Will fax results $3.00 plus $1.00 per page. Copy fee: $1.00 per page. Certification fee: $5.00. Payee: Clerk of Court. Personal checks accepted. Prepayment required. Mail requests: SASE required. Mail turnaround time 2-3 days.

Bossier Parish

26th District Court PO Box 430, Benton, LA 71006; 318-965-2336; Fax: 318-965-2713. Hours: 8:30AM-4:30PM (CST). *Felony, Misdemeanor, Civil, Probate.*
www.bossierclerk.com
Civil Records: Access: Mail, online, in person. Both court and visitors may perform in person searches. Search fee: $15.00 per name. Required to search: name, years to search. Civil cases indexed by defendant, plaintiff. Civil records on computer from 1987, index books back to 1843. Access to the Parish Clerk of Court online records requires $50 setup fee and a $35 monthly flat fee. Civil, criminal, probate (1982 forward), traffic and domestic index information is by name or case number. Call 318-965-2336 for more information.
Criminal Records: Access: Mail, online, in person. Both court and visitors may perform in person searches. Search fee: $15.00 per name. Required to search: name, years to search. Criminal records on computer since 1982. Online access to criminal records is the same as civil.
General Information: Public Access terminal is available. No adoption or juvenile records released. Will not fax results. Copy fee: $.50 per page. Certification fee: $2.00. Payee: Clerk of Court. Business checks accepted. Prepayment required. Mail requests: SASE requested. Turnaround time 4-5 days.

Caddo Parish

1st District Court 501 Texas St, Rm 103, Shreveport, LA 71101-5408; 318-226-6786; Civil phone: 318-226-6778; Criminal phone: 318-226-6786; Fax: 318-677-5371. Hours: 8:30AM-5PM (CST). *Felony, Misdemeanor, Civil, Probate.*
www.caddoclerk.com
Civil Records: Access: Mail, in person, online. Both court and visitors may perform in person searches. Search fee: $10.00 per name. Required to search: name, years to search. Civil cases indexed by defendant, plaintiff. Civil records on computer from

1984. Online access to civil records back to 1994 and name index back to 1984 is through county dial-up service. Registration and $50 set-up fee and $30 monthly usage fee is required. Marriage and recording information is also available. For information and sign-up, call 318-226-6523.

Criminal Records: Access: Mail, in person, online. Both court and visitors may perform in person searches. Search fee: $10.00 per name. For criminal computer printouts, fee is $2.00 for first page and $1.00 each add'l. Required to search: name, years to search, DOB; also helpful: SSN. Criminal records on computer from 1984. Online access to criminal records is the same as civil. Online criminal name index goes back to '80; minutes to '84. Current calendar is also available.

General Information: Public Access terminal is available. No adoption or juvenile records released. Copy fee: $.50 per page (in person); $1.25 per page (mail). Certification fee: $2.00. Payee: Clerk of Court. Personal checks accepted. Prepayment required. Mail requests: SASE required. Mail turnaround time 1-2 days.

Shreveport City Court 1244 Texas, Shreveport, LA 71101; 318-673-5800. Hours: 8AM-5PM (CST). *Civil Actions Under $15,000, Small Claims.*

Civil Records: Access: Mail, in person. Visitors must perform in person searches for themselves. No search fee. Required to search: name, years to search. Civil cases indexed by defendant, plaintiff. Civil records on computer back to 1965. Must have case number for mail searches.

General Information: Public Access terminal is available. No sealed records released. Copy fee: $.50 per page. Certification fee: $2.50. Payee: Shreveport City Court. Personal checks accepted. Prepayment required. Mail requests: SASE required. Mail turnaround time 2-4 days.

Calcasieu Parish

14th District Court PO Box 1030, Lake Charles, LA 70602; 337-437-3550; Fax: 337-437-3350/3833. Hours: 8:30AM-4:30PM (CST). *Felony, Misdemeanor, Civil, Probate.*
www.calclerkofcourt.com
Civil Records: Access: Fax, mail, in person. Both court and visitors may perform in person searches. Search fee: $15.00 per name. Additional fee of $1.00 per year after 1st 10 years. Required to search: name, years to search. Civil cases indexed by defendant, plaintiff. Civil records on computer since 1987.

Criminal Records: Access: Mail, in person. Both court and visitors may perform in person searches. Search fee: $15.00 per name. Additional fee of $2.00 per year after 1st 10 years. Required to search: name, years to search, DOB; also helpful: SSN. Criminal records on computer since 1987.

General Information: Public Access terminal is available. No adoption or juvenile records released. Will fax results $7.00 1st page, $2.00 each add'l. Fax available for civil division only. Copy fee: $1.00 per page. Certification fee: $10.00. Payee: Clerk of Court. Personal checks accepted. Prepayment required. Mail requests: SASE required. Mail turnaround time 1 week.

Lake Charles City Court PO Box 1664, Lake Charles, LA 70602; 337-491-1564. Hours: 8:30AM-4PM (CST). *Civil Actions Under $25,000, Small Claims.*
www.lakecharlescitycourt.com
Civil Records: Access: Mail, in person. Visitors must perform in person searches for themselves. No search fee. Required to search: name, years to search. Civil cases indexed by defendant, plaintiff. Civil records

kept on paper for 10 years, older records archived on computer.

General Information: Public Access terminal is available. No sealed records released. Will not fax results. Copy fee: $1.50 per page. Certification fee: $1.50. Payee: Lake Charles City Court. Personal checks accepted. Prepayment required. Mail turnaround time 2-5 days.

Caldwell Parish

37th District Court PO Box 1327, Columbia, LA 71418; 318-649-2272; Fax: 318-649-2037. Hours: 8AM-4:30PM (CST). *Felony, Misdemeanor, Civil, Probate.*
Note: All record requests must be in writing.

Civil Records: Access: Fax, mail, in person. Both court and visitors may perform in person searches. Search fee: $10.00 per name if court does search. Required to search: name, years to search. Civil cases indexed by defendant, plaintiff. Civil records on books from 1838, computerized since 11/84.

Criminal Records: Access: Mail, in person. Both court and visitors may perform in person searches. Search fee: $10.00 per name if court does search. Required to search: name, years to search, DOB; also helpful: SSN. Note that some criminal records don't contain DOB or SSN. Criminal Records kept on books since 1970.

General Information: Public Access terminal is available. No adoption or juvenile records released. Will fax results $3.00 1st page, $1.00 each add'l plus costs for the copies. Copy fee: $1.00 per page. Certification fee: $5.00 plus $1.00 per page. Payee: Clerk of Court. Personal checks accepted. Prepayment required. Mail requests: SASE not required. Mail turnaround time 1 week.

Cameron Parish

38th District Court PO Box 549, Cameron, LA 70631; 337-775-5316; Fax: 337-775-7172. Hours: 8:30AM-4:30PM (CST). *Felony, Misdemeanor, Civil, Probate.*
Civil Records: Access: Phone, mail, fax, in person. Both court and visitors may perform in person searches. Search fee: $10.00. Required to search: name, years to search. Civil cases indexed by defendant, plaintiff. Civil records from 1874; on computer back to 7/1994.

Criminal Records: Access: Fax, mail, in person. Both court and visitors may perform in person searches. Search fee: $10.00 per name. Required to search: name, years to search, DOB. Criminal records from 1874; on computer back to 1968.

General Information: Public Access terminal is available. No adoption, interdiction or juvenile records released. Fee to fax results is $1.00 per page, plus cert fee. Copy fee: $1.00 per page. Certification fee: $5.00. Payee: Cameron Parish Clerk of Court. Personal checks accepted. Prepayment required. Mail requests: SASE required. Mail turnaround time 2 days.

Catahoula Parish

7th District Court PO Box 654, Harrisonburg, LA 71340; 318-744-5497; Fax: 318-744-5488. Hours: 8AM-4:30PM (CST). *Felony, Misdemeanor, Civil, Probate.*
Civil Records: Access: Mail, in person. Both court and visitors may perform in person searches. Search fee: $2.00 per name; $2.00 per year. Required to search: name, years to search. Civil cases indexed by defendant, plaintiff. Civil records minute entries back to 1800s.

Criminal Records: Access: Mail, in person. Both court and visitors may perform in person searches. Search fee: $2.00 per name; $2.00 per year. Required

to search: name, years to search, DOB. Criminal records minute entries back to 1800s.

General Information: No adoption or juvenile records released. Will fax results for $5.00 plus $1.00 per page. Copy fee: $1.00 per page. Certification fee: $5.00. Payee: Clerk of Court. Personal checks accepted. Prepayment required. Mail requests: SASE required. Mail turnaround time 1-2 weeks.

Claiborne Parish

2nd District Court PO Box 330, Homer, LA 71040; 318-927-9601; Fax: 318-927-2345. Hours: 8:30AM-4:30PM (CST). *Felony, Misdemeanor, Civil, Probate.*
Civil Records: Access: Mail, in person. Both court and visitors may perform in person searches. Search fee: $10.00 per name. Required to search: name, years to search. Civil cases indexed by defendant, plaintiff. Civil records on index books back to early 1900s.

Criminal Records: Access: Mail, in person. Both court and visitors may perform in person searches. Search fee: $10.00 per name. Required to search: name, years to search, DOB; also helpful: SSN. Criminal records on computer 1993 forward.

General Information: No adoption or juvenile records released. Fee to fax results is $10.00 per document. Copy fee: $1.00 per page. Certification fee: $5.00. Payee: Clerk of Court. Personal checks accepted. Prepayment required. Mail requests: SASE required. Mail turnaround time 1-2 days.

Concordia Parish

7th District Court PO Box 790, Vidalia, LA 71373; 318-336-4204; Fax: 318-336-8777. Hours: 8:30AM-4:30PM (CST). *Felony, Misdemeanor, Civil, Probate.*
www.concordiaclerk.org
Civil Records: Access: Mail, in person. Visitors must perform in person searches for themselves. Search fee: $25.00 per name. Required to search: name, years to search. Civil cases indexed by defendant, plaintiff. Civil records on computer from 1983, index books back to 1800s.

Criminal Records: Access: Mail, in person. Visitors must perform in person searches for themselves. Search fee: $15.00 per name. Required to search: name, years to search, DOB; also helpful: SSN. Criminal records on computer from 1983, index books back to 1800s.

General Information: Public Access terminal is available. No adoption or juvenile records released. Will fax results $5.00 per document plus $1.00 per page. Copy fee: $1.00 per page. Certification fee: $5.50. Payee: Clerk of Court. Personal checks accepted. Prepayment required. Mail requests: SASE not required. Mail turnaround time 3-4 days.

De Soto Parish

11th District Court PO Box 1206, Mansfield, LA 71052; 318-872-3110; Criminal phone: 318-872-3181; Fax: 318-872-4202. Hours: 8AM-4:30PM (CST). *Felony, Misdemeanor, Civil, Probate.*
Civil Records: Access: Mail, in person. Both court and visitors may perform in person searches. Search fee: $10.00 per name. Required to search: name, years to search. Civil cases indexed by defendant, plaintiff. Civil records on computer from 1991, index books back to 1843.

Criminal Records: Access: Mail, in person. Both court and visitors may perform in person searches. Search fee: $10.00 per name. Required to search: name, years to search, DOB. Criminal records on computer since 1991, archived or in books to 1950s.

General Information: Public Access terminal is available. No adoption or juvenile records released. Fee to fax results is $5.00 plus $1.00 per page. Copy fee: $1.00 per page. Certification fee: $3.50 plus $1.00 per page. Payee: Clerk of Court. Prepayment required. Mail requests: SASE Required. Mail turnaround time 1-2 days.

East Baton Rouge Parish

19th District Court PO Box 1991, Baton Rouge, LA 70821; 225-389-3950; Criminal phone: 225-389-3964; Fax: 225-389-3392. Hours: 7:30AM-5:30PM (CST). *Felony, Misdemeanor, Civil, Probate.* www.ebrclerkofcourt.org

Civil Records: Access: Fax, mail, online, in person. Both court and visitors may perform in person searches. Search fee: Search fee is determined by the years searched. Required to search: name, years to search. Civil cases indexed by defendant, plaintiff. Civil records in index books from 1942. Online access to the clerk's database is by subscription. Civil record indexes go back to '88; case tracking of civil and probate back to 1991. Setup fee is $100.00 plus $15.00 per month plus per-minute usage charges. VS Com software required. Call the MIS Dept at 225-389-5295 for information or visit the website.

Criminal Records: Access: Mail, online, in person. Both court and visitors may perform in person searches. Search fee: $20.00 per name. Required to search: name, years to search, DOB; also helpful: SSN. Criminal records in index books from 1942; on computer back to 1990. Online access to criminal records is the same as civil. Criminal case tracking goes back to 8/1990.

General Information: Public Access terminal is available. No adoption or juvenile records released. Fee to fax results is $5.00 per document and $.50 per page. Copy fee: $.50 per page. Criminal record copy fee is $1.00 per page. Certification fee: $1.00. Payee: East Baton Rouge Parish. Only cashiers checks, business checks, and money orders accepted. Prepayment required. Mail requests: SASE helpful. Turnaround time is 3-5 days.

Baton Rouge City Court 233 St Louis St, Baton Rouge, LA 70802; 225-389-5279; Civil phone: 225-389-3017; Criminal phone: 225-389-5294; Fax: 225-389-5260. Hours: 8AM-5PM (CST). *Civil Actions Under $20,000, Small Claims, Criminal Traffic.* www.brgov.com/dept/citycourt

Civil Records: Access: Mail, in person, fax, online. Visitors must perform in person searches for themselves. No search fee. Required to search: name, years to search. Civil cases indexed by defendant, plaintiff. Civil records on computer back to 1985, microfiche to 1980. Access to the city court's database, including attorneys and warrants, is free at http://brcc.ci.baton-rouge.la.us/.

General Information: Public Access terminal is available. No sealed records released. Copy fee: $.50 per page. Certification fee: $1.00. Payee: Baton Rouge City Court. Personal checks accepted. Credit cards accepted: Visa, MC, with 5% surcharge. Prepayment required. Mail turnaround time 2-5 days.

East Carroll Parish

6th District Court 400 1st St, Lake Providence, LA 71254; 318-559-2399. Hours: 8:30AM-4:30PM (CST). *Felony, Misdemeanor, Civil, Probate.*

Civil Records: Access: Mail, in person. Both court and visitors may perform in person searches. Search fee: $10.00 per name. Required to search: name, years to search. Civil cases indexed by defendant, plaintiff. Civil records on index books back to 1832.

Criminal Records: Access: Mail, in person. Both court and visitors may perform in person searches. Search fee: $20.00 for 10 yr check. Required to search: name, years to search, DOB; also helpful: SSN. Criminal records on index books back to 1832.

General Information: No adoption or juvenile records released. Copy fee: $2.00 per page. Certification fee: $5.00. Payee: Clerk of Court. Personal checks not accepted. Prepayment required. Mail requests: SASE required. Mail turnaround time same day.

East Feliciana Parish

20th District Court PO Box 599, Clinton, LA 70722; 225-683-5145; Fax: 225-683-3556. Hours: 8:30AM-4:30PM (CST). *Felony, Misdemeanor, Civil, Probate.* www.eastfelicianaclerk.com/court.html

Civil Records: Access: Mail, in person, online. Both court and visitors may perform in person searches. Search fee: $10.00 per name per ten years. Required to search: name, years to search; also helpful: address. Civil cases indexed by defendant, plaintiff. Civil records on computer from 1980, index books back to 1825. A web subscription service is available. $400.00 per quarter permits access to viewable documents; $250 per quarter permits access in indices. This database also includes recordings, conveyances, mortgages, and marriage records.

Criminal Records: Access: Fax, mail, in person. Both court and visitors may perform in person searches. Search fee: $10.00 per name. Required to search: name, years to search, DOB, SNN. Criminal records on computer from 1990, index books back to 1825. State which years to search.

General Information: Public Access terminal is available. No adoption or juvenile records released. Will fax results $5.00 1st page, $1.00 each add'l. Copy fee: $1.00 per page. Certification fee: $5.00. Payee: Clerk of Court. Personal checks accepted. Prepayment required. Mail requests: SASE required. Mail turnaround time 1-2 days.

Evangeline Parish

13th District Court PO Drawer 347, Ville Platte, LA 70586; 337-363-5671; Fax: 337-363-5780. Hours: 8AM-4:30PM (CST). *Felony, Misdemeanor, Civil, Probate.*

Civil Records: Access: Fax, mail, in person. Both court and visitors may perform in person searches. Search fee: $10.00 per name. Fee is for first 7 years searched. Add $2.00 per additional year. Required to search: name, years to search. Civil cases indexed by defendant, plaintiff. Civil records on computer back to 1989; prior records archived from 1911.

Criminal Records: Access: Fax, mail, in person. Both court and visitors may perform in person searches. Search fee: $10.00 per name. Fee is for first 7 years searched. Add $2.00 per additional year. Required to search: name, years to search; also helpful: DOB, SSN. Criminal records on computer back to 1989, prior records archived from 1911.

General Information: Public Access terminal is available. No adoption or juvenile records released. Will fax results $5.00 1st page, $2.00 each add'l. Copy fee: $.75 per page; $5.00 minimum. Certification fee: $2.00 per page. Payee: Clerk of Court. Personal checks accepted. Prepayment required. Mail turnaround time 1-2 days.

Franklin Parish

5th District Court PO Box 1564, Winnsboro, LA 71295; 318-435-5133; Fax: 318-435-5134. Hours: 8:30AM-4:30PM (CST). *Felony, Misdemeanor, Civil, Probate.*

Civil Records: Access: Mail, in person. Both court and visitors may perform in person searches. Search fee: $10.00 per name. Required to search: name, years to search. Civil cases indexed by defendant, plaintiff. Civil records on computer from 1989, index books back to 1843.

Criminal Records: Access: Mail, in person. Both court and visitors may perform in person searches. Search fee: $10.00 per name. Fee includes 10 year search. Required to search: name, years to search, DOB; also helpful: SSN. Criminal records on computer since 1995.

General Information: No adoption or juvenile records released. Will fax results $5.00 1st page, $1.00 each add'l. Copy fee: $1.00 per page. Certification fee: $5.00. Payee: Clerk of Court. Business checks accepted. Prepayment required. Mail requests: SASE required. Mail turnaround time 1-2 days.

Grant Parish

35th District Court PO Box 263, Colfax, LA 71417; 318-627-3246; Fax: 318-627-3201. Hours: 8:30AM-4:30PM (CST). *Felony, Misdemeanor, Civil, Probate.*

Civil Records: Access: Phone, fax, mail, in person. Both court and visitors may perform in person searches. Search fee: $5.00 per name. Required to search: name, years to search. Civil cases indexed by defendant, plaintiff. Civil records on computer back to 1990; index books back to 1878.

Criminal Records: Access: Phone, fax, mail, in person. Both court and visitors may perform in person searches. Search fee: $5.00 per name. Required to search: name, years to search, DOB; also helpful: SSN. Criminal index goes back to 1904; on computer back to 1996.

General Information: No adoption or juvenile records released without approval of a judge. Will fax results for a prepaid fee of $5.00. Copy fee: $1.00 per page. Certification fee: $5.00. Payee: Grant Parish Clerk of Court. Personal checks accepted. Prepayment required. Mail requests: SASE required. Mail turnaround time 1-2 days.

Iberia Parish

16th District Court PO Drawer 12010, New Iberia, LA 70562-2010; 337-365-7282; Fax: 337-365-0737. Hours: 8:30AM-4:30PM (CST). *Felony, Misdemeanor, Civil, Probate.*

Civil Records: Access: In person. Visitors must perform in person searches for themselves. No search fee. Required to search: name, years to search; also helpful: address. Civil cases indexed by defendant, plaintiff. Civil records on computer back to 1974, index books back to 1868.

Criminal Records: Access: In person. Visitors must perform in person searches for themselves. No search fee. Required to search: name, years to search, DOB; also helpful: address, SSN. Criminal records on computer back to 1994, index books back to 1868.

General Information: Public Access terminal is available. No adoption or juvenile records released. Will fax specific case file data to local or toll-free number. Copy fee: $.75 per page. Certification fee: $5.50. Payee: Clerk of Court. Personal checks accepted. Prepayment required.

Iberville Parish

18th District Court PO Box 423, Plaquemine, LA 70764; 225-687-5160; Fax: 225-687-5260. Hours: 8:30AM-4:30PM (CST). *Felony, Misdemeanor, Civil, Probate.*

Civil Records: Access: Fax, mail, in person. Both court and visitors may perform in person searches. Search fee: $10.00 per name. Required to search: name, years to search. Civil cases indexed by defendant, plaintiff. Civil records on books back to 1800s.

Criminal Records: Access: Mail, in person. Both court and visitors may perform in person searches. Search fee: $10.00 per name. Required to search:

name, years to search, DOB; also helpful: SSN. Criminal records on books back to 1800s.

General Information: Public Access terminal is available. No adoption or juvenile records released. Fee to fax results is $5.00 1st page, $2.00 each add'l. Copy fee: $1.00 per page. Certification fee: $5.00. Payee: Clerk of Court. Personal checks accepted. Prepayment required. Mail requests: SASE required. Mail turnaround time 1-2 days.

Jackson Parish

2nd District Court PO Drawer 730, Jonesboro, LA 71251; 318-259-2424; Fax: 318-395-0386. Hours: 8:30AM-4:30PM (CST). *Felony, Misdemeanor, Civil, Probate.*

Civil Records: Access: Phone, mail, in person. Both court and visitors may perform in person searches. Search fee: $10.00 per name. Fee is per 10 years searched. Required to search: name, years to search. Civil cases indexed by defendant, plaintiff. Civil records on index books from 1880 and on computer since 1988.

Criminal Records: Access: Phone, mail, in person. Both court and visitors may perform in person searches. Search fee: $10.00 per name. Fee is per 10 years searched. Required to search: name, years to search, DOB; also helpful: SSN. Criminal records on computer since 1988.

General Information: Public Access terminal is available. No adoption or juvenile records released. Will fax results for $5.00. Copy fee: $1.00 per page. Certification fee: $2.50. Payee: Clerk of Court. Personal checks accepted. Prepayment required. Mail requests: SASE required. Mail turnaround time 1-2 days.

Jefferson Davis Parish

31st District Court PO Box 799, Jennings, LA 70546; 337-824-8340; Fax: 337-824-1354. Hours: 8:30AM-4:30PM (CST). *Felony, Misdemeanor, Civil, Probate.*

Civil Records: Access: Mail, in person. Both court and visitors may perform in person searches. Search fee: $10.00 per name for 10 years. Required to search: name, years to search; also helpful: address. Civil cases indexed by defendant, plaintiff. Civil records archived from 1913, on computer back to 1991.

Criminal Records: Access: Mail, in person. Both court and visitors may perform in person searches. Search fee: $10.00 per name for 10 years. Required to search: name, years to search; also helpful: DOB, SSN. Criminal records archived from 1913, on computer back to 1991. Include city of residence of subject in your search request.

General Information: Public Access terminal is available. No adoption or juvenile records released. Will fax results for $1.00 per page plus a $10.00 fax fee. Copy fee: $1.00 per page. Certification fee: $5.00. Payee: Clerk of Court. Personal checks accepted. Prepayment required. Mail requests: SASE not required. Mail turnaround time 2 days.

Jefferson Parish

24th District Court PO Box 10, Gretna, LA 70053; Civil phone: 504-364-2611; Criminal phone: 504-364-2992; Fax: 504-364-3797. Hours: 8:30AM-4:30PM (CST). *Felony, Misdemeanor, Civil, Probate.*
www.jpclerkofcourt.us

Civil Records: Access: Fax, mail, online, in person. Both court and visitors may perform in person searches. Search fee: $20.00 per name per year. Required to search: name, years to search. Civil cases indexed by defendant, plaintiff. Civil records on computer from 1986, in index books back to 1972, prior records archived. Online access is through dial-

up service; initiation fee is $200, plus $85.00 monthly and $.25 per minute usage. Includes recordings, marriage index, and assessor rolls. For further information and sign-up, call 504-364-2908 or visit the website and click on "Jeffnet.".

Criminal Records: Access: Mail, online, in person. Both court and visitors may perform in person searches. Search fee: $10.00 per name. Required to search: name, years to search, DOB; also helpful: SSN. Criminal records on computer from 1994 to present, active cases are in books from 1972. Online access is via a dial-up service, see civil.

General Information: Public Access terminal is available. No adoption, juvenile or grand jury records released. Will fax results $5.00 1st page, $1.00 each add'l. Copy fee: $1.00 per page. Certification fee: $2.00 per page (copy machine), $1.50 if from computer. Payee: Clerk of Court. Only cashiers checks and money orders accepted. Prepayment required. Mail requests: SASE required. Mail turnaround time 1-2 days.

La Salle Parish

28th District Court PO Box 1316, Jena, LA 71342; 318-992-2158; Fax: 318-992-2157. Hours: 8:30AM-4:30PM (CST). *Felony, Misdemeanor, Civil, Probate.*

Civil Records: Access: Phone, fax, mail, in person. Both court and visitors may perform in person searches. Search fee: $20.00 1st name, $10.00 additional name. Fee is for 10 year search per name with certificate. Required to search: name, years to search. Civil cases indexed by defendant, plaintiff. Civil records archived from 1916; on computer since 06/95.

Criminal Records: Access: Phone, fax, mail, in person. Both court and visitors may perform in person searches. Search fee: $20.00 1st name, $10.00 additional name. Fee is for 10 year search per name with certificate. Required to search: name, years to search, DOB; also helpful: SSN. Criminal records archived from 1936; on computer since 1999.

General Information: No adoption or juvenile records released. Fee to fax results is $10.00 per document. Copy fee: $1.00 per page. Certification fee: $5.00 per page. Payee: Clerk of Court. Personal checks accepted. Prepayment required. Mail requests: SASE not required. Mail turnaround time 1-2 weeks; will release results sooner by phone.

Lafayette Parish

15th District Court PO Box 2009, c/o Clerk of Court, Lafayette, LA 70502; 337-291-6400; Fax: 337-291-6392. Hours: 8:30AM-4:30PM (CST). *Felony, Misdemeanor, Civil, Probate.*
www.lafayetteparishclerk.com

Civil Records: Access: Phone, fax, mail, online, in person. Both court and visitors may perform in person searches. Search fee: $20.00 per name. Required to search: name, years to search. Civil cases indexed by defendant, plaintiff. Civil records archived from 1923; on computer back to 1986. Access to the remote online system requires $100 setup fee plus $15 per month and $.50 per minute. Civil index goes back to 1986. For more information, call Derek Comeaux at 337-291-6433.

Criminal Records: Access: Phone, fax, mail, in person. Both court and visitors may perform in person searches. Search fee: $20.00 per name. Required to search: name, years to search, DOB. Criminal records archived from 1966; on computer back to 1983. Online access to criminal records is the same as civil.

General Information: Public Access terminal is available. No adoption or juvenile records released. Will fax results to local or toll free line for $1.00 per page fee, 2 page minimum. Copy fee: $1.00 per page.

Certification fee: The fee is $1.00 for criminal records and $5.50 for civil. Payee: Clerk of Court. Personal checks accepted. Prepayment required. Mail requests: SASE not required. Mail turnaround time 1-2 days.

Lafourche Parish

17th District Court PO Box 818, Thibodaux, LA 70302; 985-447-4841; Fax: 985-447-5800. Hours: 8:30AM-4:30PM (CST). *Felony, Misdemeanor, Civil, Probate.*

Civil Records: Access: Fax, mail, in person. Both court and visitors may perform in person searches. Search fee: $20.00 per name. Fee is for 10 year search. Required to search: name, years to search. Civil cases indexed by defendant, plaintiff. Civil records on computer back to 7/1982, microfiche from 1968, index books back to 1800s.

Criminal Records: Access: Fax, mail, in person. Both court and visitors may perform in person searches. Search fee: $20.00 per name. Fee is for 10 year search. Required to search: name, years to search, DOB; also helpful: SSN, race, sex. Criminal records on computer back to 7/1982, microfiche from 1968, index books back to 1800s.

General Information: Public Access terminal is available. No adoption or juvenile records released. Fee to fax results is $2.00 per page. Copy fee: $1.00 per page. Certification fee: Minimum certification fee with copies is $5.00. Payee: Lafourche Parish Clerk of Court. Personal checks accepted. Prepayment required. Mail requests: SASE requested. Turnaround time 7 days.

Lincoln Parish

3rd District Court PO Box 924, Ruston, LA 71273-0924; 318-251-5130; Fax: 318-255-6004. Hours: 8:30AM-4:30PM (CST). *Felony, Misdemeanor, Civil, Probate.*

Civil Records: Access: Mail, in person. Both court and visitors may perform in person searches. Search fee: $10.00 per name. Fee is per 10 years searched. Required to search: name, years to search. Civil cases indexed by defendant, plaintiff. Civil records on computer since 1985, index books back to 1800s.

Criminal Records: Access: Mail, in person. Both court and visitors may perform in person searches. Search fee: $10.00 per name. Fee is per 10 years searched. Required to search: name, years to search, DOB; also helpful: SSN. Criminal records on computer since 1992.

General Information: Public Access terminal is available. No adoption or juvenile records released. Fee to fax results is $5.00 for 1st page, $1.00 each add'l. Copy fee: $1.00 per page $.50 self serve. Certification fee: $5.00. Payee: Clerk of Court. Personal checks accepted. Prepayment required. Mail requests: SASE not required. Mail turnaround time 1-2 days.

Livingston Parish

21st District Court PO Box 1150, Livingston, LA 70754; 225-686-2216. Hours: 8AM-4:30PM (CST). *Felony, Misdemeanor, Civil, Probate.*

Civil Records: Access: Mail, In person. Visitors must perform in person searches for themselves. Search fee: $25.00. Required to search: name, years to search. Civil cases indexed by defendant, plaintiff. Civil records on index books since 1800s; computerized records past 10 years.

Criminal Records: Access: In person, mail. Visitors must perform in person searches for themselves. Search fee: $25.00. Required to search: name, years to search, DOB; also helpful: SSN, race, sex. Criminal records on index books since 1800s; computerized records past 10 years.

General Information: Public Access terminal is available. No adoption or juvenile records released. Copy fee: $1.00 per page. Certification fee: $5.00. Payee: 21st District Court. Personal checks accepted. Prepayment required.

Madison Parish

6th District Court PO Box 1710, Tallulah, LA 71282; 318-574-0655; Fax: 318-574-3961. Hours: 8:30AM-4:30PM (CST). *Felony, Misdemeanor, Civil, Probate.*

Civil Records: Access: Phone, mail, in person. Both court and visitors may perform in person searches. Search fee: $10.00 per name. Required to search: name, years to search. Civil cases indexed by defendant, plaintiff. Civil records kept on computer since 7/93.

Criminal Records: Access: Phone, mail, in person, fax. Both court and visitors may perform in person searches. Search fee: $10.00 per name. Required to search: name, years to search, DOB; also helpful: SSN. Criminal records on index, computerized since 1999.

General Information: No adoption or juvenile records released. Copy fee: $2.00 per page. Certification fee: $5.50. Fee does not include any copy fees. Payee: Clerk of Court. Personal checks accepted. Prepayment required. Mail requests: SASE required. Mail turnaround time 1-2 days.

Morehouse Parish

4th District Court PO Box 1543, Bastrop, LA 71221; 318-281-3343; Fax: 318-281-3775. Hours: 8:30AM-4:30PM (CST). *Felony, Misdemeanor, Civil, Probate.*

Civil Records: Access: Phone, fax, mail, in person. Both court and visitors may perform in person searches. Search fee: $15.00 per name. Fee is per 10 years searched. Required to search: name, years to search; also helpful: address. Civil cases indexed by defendant, plaintiff. Civil records on computer since 1987, in books since 1898, some on microfilm.

Criminal Records: Access: Phone, fax, mail, in person. Both court and visitors may perform in person searches. Search fee: $15.00 per name. Fee is per 10 years searched. Required to search: name, years to search, DOB; also helpful: address, SSN. Criminal records in books since 1926 and on microfilm since 1974; computerized records go back to 1994.

General Information: Public Access terminal is available. No adoption, juvenile or judicial commitment records released. Will fax results $5.00 1st page, $1.00 each add'l. Copy fee: $1.00 per page. Certification fee: $5.00. Payee: Clerk of Court. Personal checks accepted. Prepayment required. Mail requests: SASE required. Mail turnaround time 2-3 days.

Natchitoches Parish

10th District Court PO Box 476, Natchitoches, LA 71458; 318-352-8152; Fax: 318-352-9321. Hours: 8:30AM-4:30PM (CST). *Felony, Misdemeanor, Civil, Probate, Small Claims.*

Civil Records: Access: Phone, fax, mail, in person. Both court and visitors may perform in person searches. Search fee: $10.00 per name. Required to search: name, years to search. Civil cases indexed by defendant, plaintiff. Civil records on computer back to 6/1991, archived from 1950, index books back to 1800s.

Criminal Records: Access: Phone, mail, in person. Both court and visitors may perform in person searches. Search fee: $10.00 per name. Required to search: name, years to search, DOB; also helpful: SSN. Criminal records on computer back to 6/1991, archived from 1950, index books back to 1800s.

General Information: Public Access terminal is available. No adoption or juvenile records released. Will fax results $5.00 1st page, $2.00 each add'l. Fax available for civil division only. Copy fee: $1.00 per page. Certification fee: $5.00. Payee: Clerk of Court. Personal checks accepted. Prepayment required. Mail requests: SASE required. Mail turnaround time 1 week.

Orleans Parish

Civil District Court 421 Loyola Ave, Rm 402, Attn: Clerk of Civil Dist. Ct., New Orleans, LA 70112; 504-592-9100; Fax: 504-592-9128. Hours: 8AM-6PM (CST). *Civil, Probate, Domestic Relations.*
www.orleanscdc.gov

Civil Records: Access: Phone, mail, online, in person. Both court and visitors may perform in person searches. No search fee. Required to search: name, years to search. Civil cases indexed by defendant, plaintiff. Civil records on computer since 1985, in books back to early 1800s. CDC Remote provides access to civil cases from 1985 and First City Court cases as well as parish mortgage and conveyance indexes. The fee is $250 or $300 per year. Call 504-592-9264 for more information.

General Information: Public Access terminal is available. No adoptions or juvenile released. Will not fax results. Copy fee: $1.00 per page. Certification fee: $2.00 per document. Payee: Clerk of Court. Only attorneys' checks, cashiers checks and money orders accepted. Prepayment required. Mail requests: SASE required. Mail turnaround time 1-2 days.

Criminal District Court 2700 Tulane Ave, Rm 115, New Orleans, LA 70119; 504-827-3546; Fax: 504-827-3385. Hours: 8:15AM-3PM (CST). *Felony, Misdemeanor.*

Criminal Records: Access: Mail, fax, in person. Both court and visitors may perform in person searches. Search fee: $10.00 per name. Required to search: name, DOB, SSN. SNN must be included. If you do not specify the years to search, then the search will include their complete records. Criminal records on computer past 8 years, books and files go back to early 1900s. Only government agencies and companies using their letterhead may fax in requests.

General Information: No adoption or juvenile records released. No copy fee. No certification fee. Payee: Clerk of Court. Business checks accepted. Prepayment required. Mail requests: SASE required. Mail turnaround time 2 days.

New Orleans City Court 421 Loyola Ave, Rm 201, New Orleans, LA 70112; 504-592-9155; Fax: 504-592-9281. Hours: 8:30AM-4PM (CST). *Civil Actions Under $20,000, Small Claims.*
www.orleanscdc.gov

Civil Records: Access: Mail, online, in person. Both court and visitors may perform in person searches. No search fee. Required to search: name, years to search. Civil cases indexed by defendant, plaintiff. Civil records on computer back to 1988. CDC Remote provides access to First City Court cases from 1988 as well as civil cases, parish mortgage and conveyance indexes. The fee is $250 or $300 per year. Call 504-592-9264 for more information.

General Information: Public Access terminal is available. No sealed records released. Copy fee: $1.00 per page. Certification fee: $2.00 plus copy fee. Payee: New Orleans First City Court. Personal checks accepted. Visa, MasterCard accepted. Checks are not accepted for Small Claims. Prepayment required. Mail requests: SASE requested. Turnaround time 5-10 days.

Ouachita Parish

4th District Court PO Box 1862, Monroe, LA 71210-1862; 318-327-1444; Fax: 318-327-1462. Hours: 8:30AM-5PM (CST). *Felony, Misdemeanor, Civil, Probate.*

Civil Records: Access: Fax, mail, in person. Both court and visitors may perform in person searches. Search fee: $10.00 per name. Required to search: name, years to search. Civil cases indexed by defendant, plaintiff. Civil records on computer from 1991, index books back to 1800s.

Criminal Records: Access: Fax, mail, in person. Both court and visitors may perform in person searches. Search fee: $10.00 per name. Required to search: name, years to search, DOB; also helpful: SSN. Criminal records on computer from 1991, index books back to 1800s.

General Information: Public Access terminal is available. No adoption or juvenile records released. Will fax results $2.00 1st page, $1.00 each add'l. Copy fee: $.50 per page. Certification fee: $1.00. Payee: Clerk of Court. Business checks accepted. Checks accepted up to $50.00. Prepayment required. Mail requests: SASE requested. Turnaround time 1-2 days.

Plaquemines Parish

25th District Court PO Box 40, (301 Maine St), Belle Chasse, LA 70037; 504-392-4969. Hours: 8:30AM-4:30PM (CST). *Felony, Misdemeanor, Civil, Probate.*

Civil Records: Access: In person only. Visitors must perform in person searches for themselves. No search fee. Required to search: name, years to search. Civil cases indexed by defendant, plaintiff. Civil records on index books back to 1800s; computerized since 1/91. Court will search probate records for $10 per name.

Criminal Records: Access: In person only. Visitors must perform in person searches for themselves. No search fee. Required to search: name, years to search, DOB. Criminal records on index books back to 1966; computerized records go back to 1/91. The county sex offender database is free at www.lasocpr.lsp.org/Static/Search.htm. Contact the Plaquemines Sheriff's Office (18039 Hwy 15, Pointe-a-LaHache 70082) for a criminal search, 985-333-5002, fax-985-333-9238.

General Information: Public Access terminal is available. No adoption or juvenile records released. Copy fee: $.50 per page. Certification fee: $5.00. Payee: Clerk of Court. Personal checks accepted. Prepayment required.

Pointe Coupee Parish

18th District Court PO Box 86, New Roads, LA 70760; 225-638-9596; Fax: 225-638-9590. Hours: 8:30AM-4:30PM (CST). *Felony, Misdemeanor, Civil, Probate.*

Civil Records: Access: Mail, in person. Both court and visitors may perform in person searches. Search fee: $10.00 per name. Required to search: name, years to search. Civil cases indexed by defendant, plaintiff. Civil records on index books back to 1800s.

Criminal Records: Access: In person only. Visitors must perform in person searches for themselves. No search fee. Required to search: name, years to search, DOB; also helpful: SSN. Criminal records on index books back to 1800s.

General Information: Public Access terminal is available. No adoption or juvenile records released. Will fax results to local or toll free line. Copy fee: $1.25 per page. Certification fee: $5.00. Payee: Clerk of Court. Personal checks accepted. Prepayment required. Mail requests: SASE not required. Mail turnaround time 2 weeks.

Rapides Parish

9th District Court PO Box 952, Alexandria, LA 71309; 318-473-8153; Fax: 318-473-4667. Hours: 8:30AM-4:30PM (CST). *Felony, Misdemeanor, Civil, Probate.*
www.rapidesclerk.org
Civil Records: Access: Mail, in person. Both court and visitors may perform in person searches. Search fee: $11.00 per name. Fee is per separate index. Required to search: name, years to search. Civil cases indexed by defendant, plaintiff. Civil records on index books since 1864, civil in computer since 10/84.
Criminal Records: Access: Mail, in person. Both court and visitors may perform in person searches. Search fee: $11.00 per name. Fee is per separate index. Required to search: name, years to search, DOB; also helpful: SSN. Criminal records on computer since 1984; prior records in index books back to 1864.
General Information: Public Access terminal is available. No adoption, juvenile, or judicial commitment records released. Will fax results to local or toll free line. Copy fee: $1.00 per page. Certification fee: $5.00. Payee: Rapides Parish Clerk of Court. Personal checks accepted. Prepayment required. Mail requests: SASE not required. Mail turnaround time 2-4 days.

Red River Parish

39th District Court PO Box 485, Coushatta, LA 71019; 318-932-6741. Hours: 8:30AM-4:30PM (CST). *Felony, Misdemeanor, Civil, Probate.*
Civil Records: Access: Mail, in person. Both court and visitors may perform in person searches. Search fee: $10.00 per name. Required to search: name, years to search. Civil cases indexed by defendant, plaintiff. Civil records on index books.
Criminal Records: Access: Mail, in person. Only the court performs in person searches; visitors may not. Search fee: $10.00 per name. Required to search: name, years to search, DOB; also helpful: SSN. The index is kept in the DA's office.
General Information: Public Access terminal is available. No adoption or juvenile records released. Will fax results to local or toll free line. Copy fee: $1.00 per page. Certification fee: $5.00. Payee: Clerk of Court. Personal checks accepted. Prepayment required. Mail requests: SASE required. Mail turnaround time 1-2 days.

Richland Parish

5th District Court PO Box 119, Rayville, LA 71269; 318-728-4171. Hours: 8:30AM-4:30PM (CST). *Felony, Misdemeanor, Civil, Probate.*
Civil Records: Access: Mail, in person. Both court and visitors may perform in person searches. Search fee: $10.00 per name. Required to search: name, years to search. Civil cases indexed by defendant, plaintiff. Civil records on since 1/94, prior on books to 1800s.
Criminal Records: Access: Mail, in person. Both court and visitors may perform in person searches. Search fee: $10.00 per name. Required to search: name, years to search, DOB, SSN. Criminal records on since 1/94, prior on books to 1800s.
General Information: No adoption or juvenile records released. Will fax results to local or toll free line. Copy fee: $1.00 per page. Certification fee: $5.00. Payee: Clerk of Court. Personal checks accepted. Prepayment required. Mail requests: SASE required. Mail turnaround time 1-2 days.

Sabine Parish

11th District Court Sabine Clerk of Court, PO Box 419, Many, LA 71449; 318-256-6223; Fax: 318-256-9037. Hours: 8AM-4:30PM (CST). *Felony, Misdemeanor, Civil, Probate.*
Civil Records: Access: Fax, mail, in person. Both court and visitors may perform in person searches. Search fee: $20.00 per name. Required to search: name, years to search. Civil cases indexed by defendant, plaintiff. Civil records on index books back to 1843.
Criminal Records: Access: Fax, mail, in person. Both court and visitors may perform in person searches. Search fee: $20.00 per name. Required to search: name, years to search.
General Information: Public Access terminal is available. No adoption or juvenile records released. Will fax results $5.00 1st page, $2.00 each add'l. Copy fee: $1.25 per page. Certification fee: $5.00. Payee: Sabine Parish Clerk. Personal checks accepted. Prepayment required. Mail requests: SASE required. Mail turnaround time 5-10 days.

St. Bernard Parish

34th District Court PO Box 1746, Chalmette, LA 70044; 504-271-3434. Hours: 8:30AM-4:30PM (CST). *Felony, Misdemeanor, Civil, Probate.*
Civil Records: Access: Mail, in person. Both court and visitors may perform in person searches. Search fee: $10.00 per name. Fee is per 10 years searched. Required to search: name, years to search. Civil cases indexed by defendant, plaintiff. Civil records on index books back to 1800s, on computer since 1989.
Criminal Records: Access: Mail, in person. Both court and visitors may perform in person searches. Search fee: $10.00 per name. Fee is per 10 years searched. Required to search: name, years to search, DOB; also helpful: SSN. Criminal records on index books back to 1800s, on computer since 1989.
General Information: Public Access terminal is available. No adoption or juvenile. Will not fax results. Copy fee: $1.00 per page. Certification fee: $5.00. Payee: Clerk of Court. No Personal checks accepted. Prepayment required. Mail requests: SASE required. Mail turnaround time 2-3 days.

St. Charles Parish

29th District Court PO Box 424, Hahnville, LA 70057; 985-783-6632; Fax: 985-783-2005. Hours: 8:30AM-4:30PM (CST). *Felony, Misdemeanor, Civil, Probate.*
Civil Records: Access: Mail, in person. Both court and visitors may perform in person searches. Search fee: $10.00 per name. Required to search: name, years to search. Civil cases indexed by defendant, plaintiff. Civil records on computer back to 1982, on index books back to 1890.
Criminal Records: Access: Mail, in person. Both court and visitors may perform in person searches. Search fee: $10.00 per name. Required to search: name, years to search, DOB; also helpful: SSN, race, sex. Criminal records on computer back to 1981, on index books back to 1900s.
General Information: Public Access terminal is available. No adoption or juvenile records released. Fee to fax results is $4.00 per document. Copy fee: $.50 per page. Certification fee: $2.00 per page. Payee: Clerk of Court. Personal checks accepted. Prepayment required. Mail turnaround time 1 day.

St. Helena Parish

21st District Court PO Box 308, Greensburg, LA 70441; 225-222-4514. Hours: 8:30AM-4:30PM (CST). *Felony, Misdemeanor, Civil, Probate.*
Civil Records: Access: Phone, mail, fax, in person. Both court and visitors may perform in person searches. Search fee: $10.00 per name. Required to search: name, years to search. Civil cases indexed by defendant, plaintiff. Civil records on index books back to 1800s.
Criminal Records: Access: Mail, in person. Both court and visitors may perform in person searches. Search fee: $10.00 per name. Required to search: name, years to search, DOB; also helpful: SSN. Criminal records on index books back to 1800s.
General Information: No adoption or juvenile records released. Fee to fax results is $2.00 per page. No copy fee. Certification fee: $5.00. Payee: Clerk of Court. Personal checks accepted. Prepayment required. Mail requests: SASE required. Mail turnaround time 1-2 days.

St. James Parish

23rd District Court PO Box 63, Convent, LA 70723; 225-562-7496; Fax: 504-562-2383. Hours: 8AM-4:30PM (CST). *Felony, Misdemeanor, Civil, Probate.*
Civil Records: Access: Mail, in person. Both court and visitors may perform in person searches. Search fee: $15.00 per name. Required to search: name, years to search. Civil cases indexed by defendant, plaintiff. Civil records on index books back to early 1900s; on computer back to 1988.
Criminal Records: Access: Mail, in person. Both court and visitors may perform in person searches. Search fee: $15.00 per name. Required to search: name, years to search, DOB. Criminal records on index books back to early 1900s; on computer back to 1988.
General Information: Public Access terminal is available. No adoption or juvenile records released. Copy fee: $1.00 per page. Certification fee: $5.00. Payee: Clerk of Court. Only cashiers checks and money orders accepted. Prepayment required. Mail requests: SASE required. Mail turnaround time 1-2 days.

St. John the Baptist Parish

40th District Court PO Box 280, Edgard, LA 70049; 985-497-3331; Fax: 985-497-3972. Hours: 8:30AM-4:30PM (CST). *Felony, Misdemeanor, Civil, Probate.*
www.stjohnclerk.org
Civil Records: Access: Mail, fax, in person. Both court and visitors may perform in person searches. Search fee: $15.00 per name. Fee is for first 15 years. Add $1.00 per add'l year. Required to search: name, years to search. Civil cases indexed by defendant, plaintiff. Civil records on computer since 1982.
Criminal Records: Access: Mail, fax, in person. Both court and visitors may perform in person searches. Search fee: $15.00 per name. Fee is for first 15 years. Add $1.00 per add'l year. Required to search: name, years to search, DOB; also helpful: SSN. Felony records on computer since 1983, misdemeanors since 3/91.
General Information: Public Access terminal is available. No adoption or juvenile records released. Fee to fax results is $5.00 per page. Copy fee: $2.00 per page. Certification fee: $5.00 plus copy fee. Payee: Clerk of Court. Personal checks accepted. Prepayment required. Mail requests: SASE required. Mail turnaround time 3-4 days.

St. Landry Parish

27th District Court PO Box 750, Courthouse, Opelousas, LA 70570; 337-942-5606; Fax: 337-948-1653. Hours: 8AM-4:30PM (CST). *Felony, Misdemeanor, Civil, Probate.*
www.stlandry.org
Civil Records: Access: Mail, fax, in person, online. Both court and visitors may perform in person searches. Search fee: $15.00 per name. Additional $1.00 fee per year after 1st 10 years. Required to search: name, years to search. Civil cases indexed by defendant, plaintiff. Civil records on index books back to 1800s, on computer back to 1992. Access to civil cases is at www.stlandry.org/html/remote. Fee is $60.00 per month. Includes civil court records back to 1998, also land indexes and images.
Criminal Records: Access: Mail, fax, in person. Both court and visitors may perform in person searches. Search fee: $15.00 per name. Additional $1.00 fee per year after 1st 10 years. Required to search: name, years to search, DOB; also helpful: SSN. Criminal records on index books back to 1800s, on computer back to 1992.
General Information: Public Access terminal is available. (Public terminal only has civil records.) No adoption or juvenile records released. Fee to fax results is $5.00 1st page, $1.00 each add'l. Copy fee: $.75 per page. Certification fee: $5.50. Payee: Clerk of Court. Personal checks accepted. Prepayment required. Mail requests: SASE required. Mail turnaround time 1-2 days.

St. Martin Parish

16th District Court PO Box 308, St. Martinville, LA 70582; 337-394-2210; Fax: 337-394-7772. Hours: 8:30AM-4:30PM (CST). *Felony, Misdemeanor, Civil, Probate.*
Civil Records: Access: In person. Both court and visitors may perform in person searches. No search fee. Required to search: name, years to search; also helpful: address. Civil cases indexed by defendant, plaintiff. Civil records archived from 1760, on computer since 1990.
Criminal Records: Access: In person. Both court and visitors may perform in person searches. Search fee: $10.00 per name. Required to search: name, years to search, DOB; also helpful: address, SSN. Criminal records archived from 1760, on computer since 1990.
General Information: Public Access terminal is available. No adoption, sealed records, expunged or juvenile records released. Will fax results $.75 per page. Copy fee: $.50 per page. Certification fee: $6.00. Payee: Clerk of Court. Personal checks accepted. Prepayment required.

St. Mary Parish

16th Judicial District Court PO Box 1231, Franklin, LA 70538; 337-828-4100 X200; Fax: 337-828-2509. Hours: 8:30AM-4:30PM (CST). *Felony, Misdemeanor, Civil, Probate.*
Civil Records: Access: In person only. Visitors must perform in person searches for themselves. No search fee. Required to search: name, years to search. Civil cases indexed by defendant, plaintiff. Civil records on index books back to 1800s.
Criminal Records: Access: In person only. Visitors must perform in person searches for themselves. No search fee. Required to search: name, years to search, DOB; also helpful: SSN. Criminal records on index books back to 1800s.
General Information: No adoption or juvenile records released. Copy fee: $1.00 per page. Certification fee: $5.00. Payee: St. Mary Parish Clerk of Court. Personal checks accepted. Prepayment required.

St. Tammany Parish

22nd District Court PO Box 1090, Covington, LA 70434; 985-809-8700. Hours: 8:30AM-4:30PM (CST). *Felony, Misdemeanor, Civil, Probate.*
www.stpgov.org/othergov/clerk/index.html
Civil Records: Access: Mail, in person, online. Both court and visitors may perform in person searches. Search fee: $10.00 per name. Required to search: name, years to search. Civil cases indexed by defendant, plaintiff. Civil records on index books back to 1800s, on computer since 1967. Remote online access to civil records is from the Clerk of Court. $50 initial setup fee, $50.00 per month and $.20 to print a page. For information, call Kristie Howell at 985-809-8787.
Criminal Records: Access: Mail, in person, online. Both court and visitors may perform in person searches. Search fee: $10.00 per name. Required to search: name, years to search, DOB; also helpful: SSN. Criminal records on computer since 10/87. Remote online access to criminal records is the same as civil.
General Information: Public Access terminal is available. No adoption or juvenile records released. Copy fee: $.25 per page. Certification fee: $2.00 per document. Payee: Clerk of Court. Personal checks accepted. Prepayment required. Mail requests: SASE required. Mail turnaround time 2-3 days.

Tangipahoa Parish

21st District Court PO Box 667, Amite, LA 70422; 985-748-4146; Fax: 985-748-6503; civ is 748-6746; crim is 747-3387. Hours: 8:30AM-4:30PM (CST). *Felony, Misdemeanor, Civil, Probate.*
www.tangiclerk.org
Civil Records: Access: Mail, in person, online. Both court and visitors may perform in person searches. Search fee: $10.00 per name per 10 years. Required to search: name, years to search. Civil cases indexed by defendant, plaintiff. Civil records archived back to early 1900s; on computer back to 1980s. Online access to Parish notarial index records is by free subscription (subject to change); fee is $1.00 to print a document. Images go back to 1/1990; index to 1974. Visit www.tangiclerk.org/OnlineServices/onlineservices.asp for information or call Alison Theard: 985-748-4146.
Criminal Records: Access: Mail, in person. Both court and visitors may perform in person searches. Search fee: $10.00 per name. Required to search: name, years to search, DOB, SSN. Criminal records archived back to early 1900s; on computer back to 1993.
General Information: Public Access terminal is available. No adoption or juvenile records released. Fee to fax results is $5.00 1st page, $1.00 each add'l. Copy fee: $1.00 per page. Certification fee: $5.50. Payee: Clerk of Court. Personal checks accepted. Prepayment required. Mail requests: SASE required. Mail turnaround time 3-4 days.

Tensas Parish

6th District Court PO Box 78, 201 Courthouse Sq, St. Joseph, LA 71366; 318-766-3921. Hours: 8:30AM-4:30PM (CST). *Felony, Misdemeanor, Civil, Probate.*
Civil Records: Access: In person only. Visitors must perform in person searches for themselves. No search fee. Required to search: name, years to search. Civil cases indexed by defendant, plaintiff. Civil records archived back to 1800s, on computer since mid-1998.
Criminal Records: Access: In person only. Visitors must perform in person searches for themselves. No search fee. Required to search: name, years to search;

also helpful: DOB, SSN. Criminal records on computer since 1998; archived back to 1800s.
General Information: No adoption or juvenile records released. Certification fee: $5.50. Payee: Clerk of Court. Personal checks accepted. Prepayment required.

Terrebonne Parish

32nd District Court PO Box 1569, Houma, LA 70361; 985-868-5660. Hours: 8:30AM-4:30PM (CST). *Felony, Misdemeanor, Civil, Probate.*
Civil Records: Access: Mail, in person. Both court and visitors may perform in person searches. Search fee: $20.00 per name. Required to search: name, years to search. Civil cases indexed by defendant, plaintiff. Civil records on computer since 1986, in books to 1823.
Criminal Records: Access: Mail, in person. Both court and visitors may perform in person searches. Search fee: $20.00 per name. Required to search: name, years to search, DOB; also helpful: SSN, race, sex. Criminal records archived to 1800s.
General Information: No adoption or juvenile records released. Fee to fax results is $2.00 per page. Copy fee: $.75 per page. Certification fee: $6.00. Payee: Terrebonne Parish Clerk of Court. Personal checks accepted. Prepayment required. Mail requests: SASE required. Mail turnaround time 2-3 days.

Union Parish

3rd District Court Courthouse Bldg, 100 E Bayou #105, Farmerville, LA 71241; 318-368-3055; Fax: 318-368-3861. Hours: 8:30AM-4:30PM (CST). *Felony, Misdemeanor, Civil, Probate.*
Civil Records: Access: Mail, in person. Search fee: $5.00 per name. Required to search: name, years to search. Civil cases indexed by defendant, plaintiff. Civil records on index books back to 1839.
Criminal Records: Access: Mail, fax, in person. Both court and visitors may perform in person searches. Search fee: $10.00 per name. Required to search: name, years to search, SSN. Criminal records on index books back to 1839; computerized records go back to 1982.
General Information: No adoption or juvenile records released. Will fax results $5.00 per doc. Copy fee: $.75 per page. Certification fee: $3.00. Payee: Clerk of Court. Personal checks accepted. Prepayment required. Mail requests: SASE required. Mail turnaround time 2-3 days.

Vermilion Parish

15th District Court 100 N. State St, #101, Abbeville, LA 70511-0790; 337-898-1992; Fax: 337-898-0404. Hours: 8:30AM-4:30PM (CST). *Felony, Misdemeanor, Civil, Probate.*
Civil Records: Access: Phone, fax, mail, in person. Both court and visitors may perform in person searches. Search fee: $12.00 per name. Fee for second name on same search request is $6.50. Required to search: name, years to search. Civil cases indexed by defendant, plaintiff. Civil records on computer since 1982, in books since 1885, on microfilm since 1885.
Criminal Records: Access: Phone, fax, mail, in person. Both court and visitors may perform in person searches. Search fee: $12.00 per name. Fee for second name on same search request is $6.50. Required to search: name, years to search, DOB; also helpful: SSN, race, sex. Criminal records on computer since 1982, in books since 1885, on microfilm since 1885.
General Information: Public Access terminal is available. No adoption or juvenile records released. Will fax results $2.00 1st page, $1.00 each add'l. Copy fee: $1.00 per page. Certification fee: $5.00. Payee: Vermilion Parish Clerk of Court. Personal checks accepted. Prepayment required. Mail requests:

SASE required. Mail turnaround time 1-2 days after payment.

Vernon Parish

30th District Court PO Box 40, Leesville, LA 71496; 337-238-1384; Fax: 337-238-9902. Hours: 8AM-4:30PM (CST). *Felony, Misdemeanor, Civil, Probate.*

Civil Records: Access: Mail, fax, in person. Both court and visitors may perform in person searches. Search fee: $10.00 per name. Required to search: name, years to search. Civil cases indexed by defendant, plaintiff. Civil records on computer from November 1985, archived back to 1900.

Criminal Records: Access: Mail, in person. Both court and visitors may perform in person searches. Search fee: $10.00 per name. Required to search: name, years to search, DOB, SNN. Criminal records on computer from November 1985, archived back to 1900.

General Information: Public Access terminal is available. No adoption or juvenile records released. Will fax results to local or toll free line. Copy fee: $1.25 per page. Certification fee: $5.00. Payee: Clerk of Court. Personal checks accepted. Prepayment required. Mail requests: SASE required. Mail turnaround time same day.

Washington Parish

22nd District Court PO Box 607, Franklinton, LA 70438; 985-839-4663/7821. Hours: 8AM-4:30PM (CST). *Felony, Misdemeanor, Civil, Probate.*

Civil Records: Access: Mail, in person. Both court and visitors may perform in person searches. Search fee: $10.00 per name. Required to search: name, years to search. Civil cases indexed by defendant, plaintiff. Civil records on computer from 1993, archived April 1967, index books back to 1800s.

Criminal Records: Access: Mail, in person. Both court and visitors may perform in person searches. Search fee: $10.00 per name. Required to search: name, years to search, DOB, SSN. Criminal records on computer from 1993, archived April 1967, index books back to 1800s.

General Information: Public Access terminal is available. No adoption or juvenile records released. Copy fee: $1.00 per page. Certification fee: $5.00. Payee: Washington Parish Clerk of Court. Personal checks accepted. Prepayment required. Mail requests: SASE requested. Turnaround time 1-2 days.

Webster Parish

26th District Court PO Box 370, Minden, LA 71058-0370; 318-371-0366; Fax: 318-371-0226. Hours: 8:30AM-4:30PM (CST). *Felony, Misdemeanor, Civil, Probate.*

Civil Records: Access: Fax, mail, in person. Both court and visitors may perform in person searches. Search fee: $10.00 per name. Required to search:

name, years to search. Civil cases indexed by defendant, plaintiff. Civil records archived back to 1800s, on computer since 1986.

Criminal Records: Access: Fax, mail, in person. Both court and visitors may perform in person searches. Search fee: $10.00 per name. Required to search: name; also helpful: years to search. Criminal records not on computer, in books to 1800s.

General Information: Public Access terminal is available. No adoption or juvenile records released. Will fax results $5.00 per page. Copy fee: $1.00 per page. Certification fee: $5.00. Payee: Clerk of Court. Personal checks accepted. Prepayment required. Mail requests: SASE not required. Mail turnaround time 2-3 days.

West Baton Rouge Parish

18th District Court PO Box 107, Port Allen, LA 70767; 225-383-0378. Hours: 8:30AM-4:30PM (CST). *Felony, Misdemeanor, Civil, Probate.*

Civil Records: Access: Phone, mail, in person. Both court and visitors may perform in person searches. Search fee: $10.00 per name. Required to search: name, years to search. Civil cases indexed by defendant, plaintiff. Civil records on computer from 1983.

Criminal Records: Access: Phone, mail, in person. Both court and visitors may perform in person searches. Search fee: $10.00 per name. Required to search: name, years to search, DOB; also helpful: SSN. Criminal records on computer from 1983.

General Information: Public Access terminal is available. No adoption or juvenile records released. Copy fee: $1.00 per page. Certification fee: $2.00. Payee: Clerk of Court. Personal checks accepted. Prepayment required. Mail requests: SASE required. Mail turnaround time 1-2 days.

West Carroll Parish

5th District Court PO Box 1078, Oak Grove, LA 71263; 318-428-3281. Hours: 8:30AM-4:30PM (CST). *Felony, Misdemeanor, Civil, Probate.*

Civil Records: Access: Mail, in person. Both court and visitors may perform in person searches. Search fee: $1.00 per name per year. Required to search: name, years to search. Civil cases indexed by defendant, plaintiff. Civil records on index books back to 1800s.

Criminal Records: Access: Mail, in person. Both court and visitors may perform in person searches. Search fee: $1.00 per name per year. Required to search: name, years to search, DOB. Criminal records on index books back to 1800s.

General Information: Public Access terminal is available. No adoption or juvenile records released. Will fax results to local or toll free line. Copy fee: $1.00 per page. Certification fee: $5.00. Payee: Clerk of Court. Only cashiers checks and money orders accepted. Prepayment required. Mail requests: SASE required. Mail turnaround time 1-2 days.

West Feliciana Parish

20th District Court PO Box 1843, St Francisville, LA 70775; 225-635-3794; Fax: 225-635-3770. Hours: 8:30AM-4:30PM (CST). *Felony, Misdemeanor, Civil, Probate.*

Civil Records: Access: Mail, in person. Both court and visitors may perform in person searches. Search fee: $10.00 per name. Fee is per 5 years searched. Required to search: name, years to search; also helpful: address. Civil cases indexed by defendant, plaintiff. Civil records on computer from 1984, index books back to 1800s.

Criminal Records: Access: Mail, in person. Both court and visitors may perform in person searches. Search fee: $10.00 per name. Fee is per 5 years searched. Required to search: name, years to search, DOB; also helpful: address. Criminal records on computer since 1992; prior on cards and dockets back to 1800s.

General Information: Public Access terminal is available. No adoption, juvenile or juvenile records released. Copy fee: $1.00 per page. Certification fee: $5.00. Payee: Clerk of Court. Business checks accepted. Prepayment required. Mail requests: SASE required. Mail turnaround time 3-5 days.

Winn Parish

8th District Court 100 Main St, #103, Winnfield, LA 71483; 318-628-3515; Fax: 318-628-3527. Hours: 8AM-4:30PM (CST). *Felony, Misdemeanor, Civil, Probate.*

Civil Records: Access: Mail, in person. Both court and visitors may perform in person searches. Search fee: $20.00 per name; $10.00 for second name. Fee is for 10 year search. Required to search: name, years to search, address. Civil cases indexed by defendant, plaintiff. Civil records on books from 1886 to present, on computer from 1988, mortgages since 1981, conveyances since 1993.

Criminal Records: Access: Mail, in person. Both court and visitors may perform in person searches. Search fee: $20.00 per name; $10.00 for second name. Fee is for 10 year search. Required to search: name, years to search, address, DOB; also helpful: SSN. Criminal records in books since 1886, computerized since 1997.

General Information: No adoption or juvenile records released. Fee to fax results is $5.00 per document and $1.00 per page. Copy fee: $1.00 per page. Certification fee: $5.00. Payee: Winn Parish Clerk of Court. Personal checks accepted. Prepayment required. Mail requests: SASE required. Mail turnaround time 2-3 days.

Louisiana Recording Offices

ORGANIZATION: 64 parishes (not counties), 64 recording offices. One parish, St. Martin, has two non-contiguous segments. The recording officer is the Clerk of Court. Many parishes include tax and other non-UCC liens in their mortgage records. The entire state is in the Central Time Zone (CST).

REAL ESTATE RECORDS: Most parishes will perform a mortgage search. Some will provide a record owner search. Copy and certification fees vary widely.

UCC RECORDS: Financing statements are filed with the Clerk of Court in any parish in the state and are entered onto a statewide computerized database of UCC financing statements available for searching at any parish office. All parishes perform UCC searches for $30.00 per debtor name. Use search request form UCC-11. Copy fees are $1.00 to $1.25 per page.

TAX LIEN RECORDS: All federal and state tax liens are filed with the Clerk of Court. Parishes usually file tax liens on personal property in their UCC or mortgage records, and most will perform tax lien searches for varying fees. Some parishes will automatically include tax liens on personal property in a mortgage certificate search.

OTHER LIENS: Judgments, labor, material, hospital.

ONLINE ACCESS: A number of Parishes offer online access to recorded documents. Most are commercial fee systems.

Acadia Parish

Clerk of Court, PO Box 922, Crowley, LA 70526. **Phone**-Clerk of Court, R/E & UCC Recording- 337-788-8881; fax-337-788-1048; hours 8:30AM-4:30PM www.acadiaparishclerk.com
UCC record search per debtor- $30.00. Tax liens not included in UCC search. Federal/state combined tax lien search- $20.00 per debtor (11 year search). Will provide mortgage certificates. Record copy- $1.00 per page. Cert fee: $5.50 per cert + $1.00 per page. Payee: Acadia Parish Clerk of Court. **Other phones:** Assessor-337-788-8871; Treasurer-337-788-8800; Elections-337-788-8881; Vital Records-337-788-8881.

Allen Parish

Clerk of Court, PO Box 248, Oberlin, LA 70655. **Phone**-Clerk of Court, R/E & UCC Recording- 337-639-4351; fax-337-639-2030; hours 8AM-4:30PM
UCC record search per debtor- $30.00. Tax liens: request in writing with fees and file number, book and page. Tax lien search fee- $20.00 1st name, $10.00 each add'l name. Will not search real estate records. Record copy- $1.00 per page. Cert fee: $2.00 per cert. Payee: Parish Clerk of Court. **Other phones:** Assessor-337-639-4391; Elections-337-639-4351; Vital Records-337-639-4351.

Ascension Parish

Clerk of Court, PO Box 192, Donaldsonville, LA 70346. **Phone**-Clerk of Court, R/E & UCC Recording-225-473-9866; fax-225-473-8641; 8:30AM-4:30PM
UCC record search per debtor- $30.00. UCC search includes tax liens if requested. Separate federal/state combined tax lien search- $12.00 per debtor. Real estate record owner and mortgage searches available. Record copy- $1.00 per page. Cert fee: $5.00 per cert. Payee: Parish Clerk of Court. **Other phones:** Assessor-225-473-9239.

Assumption Parish

Clerk of Court, PO Drawer 249, Napoleonville, LA 70390. **Phone**-985-369-6653; fax-985-369-2032; hours 8:30AM-4:30PM
UCC record search per debtor- $30.00. UCC search includes tax liens if requested. Separate federal/state combined tax lien search- $20.00 per debtor. Real estate record owner and mortgage searches available. Record copy- $1.00 per page. Cert fee: $5.00 per cert. Payee: Assumption Parish Clerk of Court. **Other phones:** Assessor-985-369-6385; Register of Voters-985-369-7347.

Avoyelles Parish

Clerk of Court, PO Box 196, Marksville, LA 71351. **Phone**-Clerk of Court, R/E & UCC Recording- 318-253-7523; fax-318-253-4614; hours 8:30AM-4:30PM
UCC record search per debtor- $30.00. UCC copy-$1.00 per page. UCC search includes tax liens if requested. Separate federal/state combined tax lien search- $21.00 per debtor. Will not search real estate records. Cert fee: $5.00 per cert. Payee: Parish Clerk of Court. **Other phones:** Assessor-318-253-4507; Treasurer-318-253-9208.

Beauregard Parish

Clerk of Court, PO Box 100, De Ridder, LA 70634. **Phone**-337-463-8595; fax-337-462-3916; hours 8AM-4:30PM. UCC record search per debtor- $30.00. Tax liens not included in UCC search. Real estate owner, mortgage, and property transfer searches available. Record copy- $1.00 per page. Cert fee: $2.25 per cert. Payee: Parish Clerk of Court. **Other phones:** Assessor-337-463-8945.

Bienville Parish

Clerk of Court, 100 Courthouse Dr, Rm 100, Arcadia, LA 71001-3600. **Phone**-Clerk of Court, R/E & UCC Recording- 318-263-2123; fax-318-263-7426; hours 8:30AM-4:30PM www.bienvilleparish.org/clerk
UCC record search per debtor- $30.00. UCC copy-$2.00 per page. Tax liens not included in UCC search. Tax lien search fee- $20.00 1st name, $10.00 each add'l. Will search real estate records. RE record copy- $1.00 per page. Cert fee: $5.00 per cert. Payee: Bienville Parish Clerk of Court. **Other phones:** Assessor-318-263-2214; Treasurer-318-263-2019.

Bossier Parish

Clerk of Court, PO Box 430, Benton, LA 71006. **Phone**-318-965-2336; fax-318-965-2713; hours 8:30AM-4:30PM www.bossierclerk.com
UCC record search per debtor- $30.00. UCC copy-$1.00 per page. UCC search includes tax liens. Separate federal/state combined tax lien search-$15.00 per debtor. Mortgage searches available. RE record copy- $.50 per page. Cert fee: $2.00 per cert. Payee: Bossier Parish Clerk of Court. **Other phones:** Assessor-318-965-2213.

Caddo Parish

Clerk of Court, 501 Texas St, Shreveport, LA 71101-5408. **Phone**-318-226-6780, R/E Recording- 318-226-6790, UCC Recording- 318-226-6783; fax-318-227-9080; hours 8:30AM-5PM www.caddoclerk.com
UCC record search per debtor- $30.00. UCC copy-$1.25 per page. Tax liens not included in UCC search. Separate federal/state combined tax lien search- $10.00 per debtor. Will not search real estate records. Cert fee: $2.00. Payee: Caddo Parish Clerk of Court. **Online Access to Real Estate, Lien, Marriage records:** Access to the Parish online records requires a $50 set up fee plus a $30 monthly fee. Mortgages and indirect conveyances date back to 1981; direct conveyances date back to 1914. Lending agency information available. UCCs are at Sec. of State. Marriage licenses go back to 1937. For system information, contact Susan Twohig at 318-226-6523. Also, an assessor property search is free at www.caddoassessor.org/cgi-bin/pub_search.pl, but no name searching for free. **Other phones:** Assessor-318-226-6702; Treasurer-318-226-6900; Elections-318-226-6788.

Calcasieu Parish

Clerk of Court, PO Box 1030, Lake Charles, LA 70601-1030. **Phone**-337-437-3550; fax-337-437-3350; hours 8:30AM-4:30PM
UCC record search per debtor- $30.00. UCC copy-$1.00 per page. UCC search includes tax liens. Separate federal/state combined tax lien search-$14.00 per debtor. Real estate record owner and mortgage searches available. Cert fee: $5.00 per cert. Payee: Parish Clerk of Court. **Other phones:** Assessor-337-437-3461; Treasurer-337-437-3680.

Caldwell Parish

Clerk of Court, PO Box 1327, Columbia, LA 71418. **Phone**-Clerk of Court, R/E & UCC Recording- 318-649-2272; fax-318-649-2037; hours 8AM-4:30PM
Will search UCC records through the LA Sec of State Computer in their office. Search per debtor- $30.00. Tax liens not included in UCC search. Federal/state combined tax lien search- $20.00 per debtor. Mortgage searches available. Record copy-$1.00 per page. Cert fee: $5.00 per cert. Payee: Caldwell Parish Clerk of Court. **Other phones:** Assessor-318-649-2636; Treasurer-318-649-2681.

Cameron Parish

Clerk of Court, PO Box 549, Cameron, LA 70631. **Phone-**Clerk of Court, R/E & UCC Recording- 337-775-5316; fax-337-775-7172; hours 8:30AM-4:30PM UCC record search per debtor- $30.00 per search up to 10 statements. Will search tax liens. Separate federal/state combined tax lien search- $15.00 per debtor. Real estate owner, mortgage, and property transfer searches available. Record copy- $1.00 per page. Cert fee: $5.00 per cert. Payee: Parish Clerk of Court. **Other phones:** Assessor-337-775-5416; Treasurer-337-775-5718; Elections-337-775-5316; Vital Records-337-775-5316.

Catahoula Parish

Clerk of Court, PO Box 654, Harrisonburg, LA 71340. **Phone-**318-744-5497; fax-318-744-5488; hours 8:30AM-4:30PM. UCC record search per debtor- $30.00. UCC copy- $1.00 per page. Tax liens not included in UCC search. Separate federal/state combined tax lien search- $20.00 per debtor. Will not search real estate records. Cert fee: $5.00 per cert. Payee: Catahoula Parish Clerk of Court. **Other phones:** Assessor-318-744-5291.

Claiborne Parish

Clerk of Court, PO Box 330, Homer, LA 71040. **Phone-**Clerk of Court, R/E & UCC Recording- 318-927-9601; fax-318-927-2345; hours 8:30AM-4:30PM UCC record search per debtor- $30.00. Record copy fee- $1.00 per page. Will not search tax liens. Mortgage certificate searches including tax liens available. Cert fee: $5.00 per cert. Payee: Claiborne Parish Clerk of Court. **Other phones:** Assessor-318-927-3022; Treasurer-318-927-2222; Elections-318-927-9601; Vital Records-318-927-9601.

Concordia Parish

Clerk of Court, PO Box 790, Vidalia, LA 71373. **Phone-**Clerk of Court, R/E & UCC Recording- 318-336-4204; fax-318-336-8777; hours 8:30AM-4:30PM UCC record search per debtor- $30.00. Will not search tax liens. Mortgage searches available. Record copy- $2.00 per copy. Cert fee: $5.50 per cert. Payee: Concordia Parish Clerk of Court. **Other phones:** Assessor-318-336-5122; Treasurer-318-336-2151; Appraiser/ Auditor-318-336-5122; Elections-318-336-4204.

De Soto Parish

Clerk of Court, PO Box 1206, Mansfield, LA 71052. **Phone-**Clerk of Court, R/E & UCC Recording- 318-872-3110; fax-318-872-4202; hours 8AM-4:30PM UCC record search per debtor- $30.00. UCC search includes tax liens if requested. Separate federal/state combined tax lien search- $17.00 per debtor Real estate owner, mortgage, and property transfer searches available. Record copy- $1.00 per page. Cert fee: $3.50 per cert. Payee: De Soto Parish Clerk of Court. **Other phones:** Assessor-318-872-3610; Elections-318-872-3110; Criminal-318-872-3181.

East Baton Rouge Parish

Clerk of Court, PO Box 1991, Baton Rouge, LA 70821-1991. **Phone-**225-389-3960; fax-225-389-3392; hours 7:30AM-5:30PM www.ebrclerkofcourt.org UCC record search per debtor- $30.00. Tax liens not included in UCC search. Federal/state combined tax lien search- $23.10 per debtor. Real estate owner, mortgage, and property transfer searches available. Record copy- $.50 per page. Cert fee: $5.00 per cert. Payee: East Baton Rouge Parish Clerk of Court. **Online Access to Real Estate, Lien records:** Access to online records requires a $100 set up fee with a $5 monthly fee and $.33 per minute of use. Four years worth of data is kept active on the

system. Lending agency information is available. For information, contact Wendy Gibbs at 225-398-5295. UCC information is located at the Sec. of State. **Other phones:** Assessor-225-389-3920.

East Carroll Parish

Clerk of Court, 400 1st St, Lake Providence, LA 71254. **Phone-**Clerk of Court, R/E & UCC Recording- 318-559-2399; fax-318-559-1502; hours 8:30AM-4:30PM UCC record search per debtor- $30.00. Tax liens not included in UCC search. Federal/state combined tax lien search- $20.00 per debtor per 10 years. Real estate owner, mortgage, and property transfer searches available. Record copy- $2.00 per page. Cert fee: $5.00 per cert. Payee: East Carroll Parish Clerk of Court. **Other phones:** Assessor-318-559-2850; Treasurer-318-559-2000.

East Feliciana Parish

Clerk of Court, PO Drawer 599, Clinton, LA 70722. **Phone-**Clerk of Court, R/E & UCC Recording- 225-683-5145; fax-225-683-3556; hours 8:30AM-4:30PM www.eastfelicianaclerk.com/
UCC record search per debtor- $30.00. Tax liens not included in UCC search. Separate federal/state combined tax lien search- $20.00 per debtor. Mortgage searches available. Property description and names exactly required. Record copy- $1.00 per page. Cert fee: $5.00 per cert if copy provided. Payee: East Feliciana Parish Clerk of Court. **Online Access to Real Estate, Lien, Mortgage, Marriage, Civil Court records:** Access to online records requires a subscription, $100 set up fee with a $50 monthly usage fee for indices or $100.00 per month for indices plus images. Conveyances go back to 1962, mortgages to 1981. Marriages go back to 1987 and miscellaneous back to 1984. For information, contact clerk's office at 225-683-5145 or visit www.eastfelicianaclerk.com/. **Other phones:** Assessor-225-683-8945; Elections-225-683-5145.

Evangeline Parish

Clerk of Court, PO Drawer 347, Ville Platte, LA 70586. **Phone-**Clerk of Court, R/E & UCC Recording- 337-363-5671; fax-337-363-5780; hours 8AM-4:30PM UCC record search per debtor- $30.00. UCC copy- $1.00 per page. Tax liens not included in UCC search. Separate federal/state combined tax lien search- $15.00 per debtor. Mortgage searches available. RE record copy- $.75 per page. Cert fee: $2.00 per page. Payee: Parish Clerk of Court. **Other phones:** Assessor-337-363-4310; Treasurer-337-363-5651; Elections-337-363-5671.

Franklin Parish

Clerk of Court, PO Box 1564, Winnsboro, LA 71295. **Phone-**Clerk of Court, R/E & UCC Recording- 318-435-5133; fax-318-435-5134; hours 8:30AM-4:30PM UCC record search per debtor- $30.00. UCC copy- $2.00 per page. Tax liens not included in UCC search. Tax lien search fee- $20.00 per debtor. Mortgage searches available. Property description required. RE record copy- $1.00 per page. Cert fee: $5.00 per cert. Payee: Parish Clerk of Court. **Other phones:** Assessor-318-435-5390.

Grant Parish

Clerk of Court, PO Box 263, Colfax, LA 71417. **Phone-**Clerk of Court, R/E & UCC Recording- 318-627-3246; fax-318-627-3201; hours 8:30AM-4:30PM UCC record search per debtor- $30.00. Tax liens not included in UCC search. Separate federal/state combined tax lien search- $20.00; $10.00 add'l name. Mortgage searches available. Record copy- $1.00 per page. Cert fee: $5.00 per cert. Payee: Grant Parish Clerk of Court. **Other phones:** Assessor-318-627-5471; Treasurer-318-627-3157; Elections-318-627-3246.

Iberia Parish

Clerk of Court, PO Drawer 12010, New Iberia, LA 70562-2010. **Phone-**337-365-7282; fax-337-365-0737; hours 8:30AM-4:30PM
Will search UCC records using a UCC search form. Search per debtor- $30.00. UCC copy- $1.00 per page. Tax liens not included in UCC search. Federal/state combined tax lien search- $16.40 per 1st name. Real estate owner, mortgage, and property transfer searches available. RE record copy- $.75 per page. Cert fee: $5.50 per cert. Payee: Iberia Parish Clerk of Court. **Online Access to Real Estate, Lien, Marriage, Divorce records:** Access to the Parish online records requires a $50 monthly usage fee. Records date back to 1959. Lending agency information is available. For information, call 337-365-7282. **Other phones:** Assessor-337-369-4415.

Iberville Parish

Clerk of Court, PO Box 423, Plaquemine, LA 70765-0423. **Phone-**225-687-5160; fax-225-687-5260; hours 8:30AM-4:30PM
UCC record search per debtor- $30.00. UCC copy- $1.00 per page. Tax liens not included in UCC search. Mortgage searches available. RE record copy- $.75 per page. Cert fee: $2.00 per cert. Payee: Iberville Parish Clerk of Court. **Other phones:** Assessor-225-687-3568.

Jackson Parish

Clerk of Court, PO Drawer 370, Jonesboro, LA 71251. **Phone-**Clerk of Court, R/E & UCC Recording- 318-259-2424; fax-318-395-0386; hours 8:30AM-4:30PM UCC record search per debtor- $30.00. Tax liens will automatically show on a mortgage certificate search. Separate federal/state combined tax lien search- $20.00 per debtor. Mortgage certificate searches available. Record copy- $1.00 per page. Cert fee: $2.50 per cert. Payee: Parish Clerk of Court. **Other phones:** Assessor-318-259-2151; Elections-318-259-2424; Police Jury-318-259-2361.

Jefferson Davis Parish

Clerk of Court, PO Box 799, Jennings, LA 70546-0799. **Phone-**337-824-1160/1161, R/E Recording- 337-824-1160, UCC Recording- 337-824-1160; fax-337-824-1354; hours 8:30AM-4:30PM. UCC record search per debtor- $30.00. UCC copy- $2.00 per page. Tax liens not included in UCC search. Tax lien search fee- $20.00 per debtor. Real estate record owner and mortgage searches available. RE record copy- $1.00 per page. Cert fee: $5.00 per cert. Payee: Jefferson Davis Parish Clerk of Court. **Other phones:** Assessor-337-824-3451; Treasurer-337-824-4792; Elections-337-824-1160; Vital Records-337-824-1161; 337-824-8340-Civil Dept.

Jefferson Parish

Clerk of Court, PO Box 10, Gretna, LA 70054-0010. **Phone-**504-364-2900; fax-504-364-3780; hours 7:30AM-4:30PM www.clerkofcourt.co.jefferson.la.us UCC record search per debtor- $30.00. UCC copy- $1.00 per page. Tax liens not included in UCC search, but tax liens are included with other lien searches. Separate federal/state combined tax lien search- $20.00 per debtor. Mortgage and property transfer searches available. Cert fee: $2.00 per page. Payee: Jefferson Parish Clerk of Court. **Online Access to Real Estate, Assessor, Marriage, Civil records:** Access to the clerk's JeffNet database is by subscription; set-up fee is $200.00 + $8.50 monthly and $.25 per minute. Mortgage and conveyance images go back to 1967; index to 1967. Marriage and assessor records go back to 1992. For information, visit https://ssl.jpclerkofcourt.us/JeffnetSetup/default.asp.

La Salle Parish

Clerk of Court, PO Box 1316, Jena, LA 71342. **Phone-**Clerk of Court, R/E & UCC Recording- 318-992-2158; fax-318-992-2157; hours 8:30AM-4:30PM

UCC record search per debtor- $30.00. UCC search includes tax liens if requested. Separate federal/state combined tax lien search- $20.00 first name, $10.00 per add'l name. Real estate record owner and mortgage searches available. Record copy- $1.00 per page. Cert fee: $5.00 per cert; $1.00 per page. Payee: La Salle Parish Clerk of Court. **Other phones:** Assessor-318-992-8256; Appraiser/ Auditor-318-992-2211; Elections-318-992-2158; Vital Records-318-992-2158.

Lafayette Parish

Clerk of Court, PO Box 2009, Lafayette, LA 70502. **Phone-**337-291-6400, R/E Recording- 337-291-6310, UCC Recording- 337-291-6310; fax-337-291-6392; hours   8:30AM-4:30PM www.lafayetteparishclerk.com

UCC record search per debtor- $30.00. Separate federal/state combined tax lien search- $20.00 per debtor. Mortgage searches available. Record copy- $1.00 per page. Cert fee: $5.50 + copy fees. Payee: Lafayette Parish Clerk of Court. **Online Access to Real Estate, Lien records:** Access to Parish online records requires a $100 set up fee + $15 per month and $.50 per minute. Conveyances date back to 1936; mortgages to 1948; other records to 1986. Lending agency information is available. For information, contact Derek Comeaux at 337-291-6433. Tax and UCC lien information is for this parish only. Also, assessor property data is free at www.lafayetteassessor.com/search.html, but no name searching. **Other phones:** Assessor-337-291-7080; Elections-337-291-6454; Vital Records-337-262-5616 x139.

Lafourche Parish

Clerk of Court, PO Box 818, Thibodaux, LA 70302. **Phone-**Clerk of Court, R/E & UCC Recording- 985-447-4841; fax-985-447-5800; hours 8:30AM-4:30PM

UCC record search per debtor- $30.00. UCC copy- $2.00 per page. Tax liens not included in UCC search. Will not search real estate records but will provide mortgage certificates. RE record copy- $1.00 per page. Cert fee: $5.00 per cert. Payee: Lafourche Parish Clerk of Court. **Other phones:** Assessor-985-447-7242;   Treasurer-985-447-4841; Elections-985-447-4841.

Lincoln Parish

Clerk of Court, PO Box 924, Ruston, LA 71273-0924. **Phone-**Clerk of Court, R/E & UCC Recording- 318-251-5130; fax-318-255-6004; hours 8:30AM-4:30PM

UCC record search per debtor- $30.00. UCC copy- $1.00 per page. Tax liens not included in UCC search. Separate tax lien search-$20.00 first name, $10.00 per each add'l name. Mortgage searches available. RE record copy- $1.00 per page. Cert fee: $3.00 per cert. Payee: Lincoln Parish Clerk of Court. **Other phones:** Assessor-318-251-5140.

Livingston Parish

Clerk of Court, PO Box 1150, Livingston, LA 70754. **Phone-**225-686-2216; fax-225-686-1867; hours 8AM-4:30PM

UCC record search per debtor- $30.00. UCC search includes tax liens if requested. Separate federal/state combined tax lien search- $22.00 per debtor. Will not search real estate records. Record copy- $1.00 per page. Cert fee: $6.00 per page. Payee: Livingston Parish Clerk of Court. **Other phones:** Assessor-225-686-7278.

Madison Parish

Clerk of Court, PO Box 1710, Tallulah, LA 71282. **Phone-**Clerk of Court, R/E & UCC Recording- 318-574-0655; fax-318-574-3961; hours 8:30AM-4:30PM UCC record search per debtor- $30.00. UCC copy- $1.00 per page. Will search tax liens including federal tax liens. Mortgage searches available. RE record copy- $2.00 per page. Cert fee: $5.50 per cert. Payee: Madison Parish Clerk of Court. **Other phones:** Assessor-318-574-0117; Elections-318-574-0655.

Morehouse Parish

Clerk of Court, PO Box 1543, Bastrop, LA 71221-1543. **Phone-**Clerk of Court, R/E & UCC Recording- 318-281-3343; fax-318-281-3775; hours 8:30AM-4:30PM

UCC record search per debtor- $30.00. Tax liens not included in UCC search. Separate federal/state combined tax lien search- $20.00 per debtor. Real estate record owner and mortgage searches available. Record copy- $1.00 per page. Cert fee: $5.00 per cert. Payee: Morehouse Parish Clerk of Court. **Other phones:** Assessor-318-281-1802; Vital Records-318-568-5050.

Natchitoches Parish

Clerk of Court, PO Box 476, Natchitoches, LA 71458-0476. **Phone-**318-352-8152; fax-318-352-9321; hours 8:30AM-4:30PM

UCC record search per debtor- $30.00. UCC copy- $1.00 per page. Tax liens not included in UCC search. Separate federal/state combined tax lien search- $24.00 per debtor. Real estate owner, mortgage, and property transfer searches available. Cert fee: $5.00 per cert. Payee: Natchitoches Parish Clerk of Court. **Other phones:** Assessor-318-352-2377; Vital Records-318-357-2243; Civil-318-357-2293 or 2294.

Orleans Parish

Clerk of Court, 421 Loyola Ave, New Orleans, LA 70112. **Phone-**504-592-9100, R/E Recording- 504-592-9176, UCC Recording- 504-592-9189; fax-504-592-9128; hours 9AM-4PM www.orleanscdc.gov UCC record search per debtor- $30.00. UCC copy- $2.00 per page. UCC search, add add'l $5.00 for federal and/or state tax lien search. Separate federal/state combined tax lien search- $30.00 per debtor. Real estate record owner and property transfer searches available. RE record copy- $1.00 per page. Cert fee: $5.00 per page for UCC; $3.00 for real estate records. Payee: Orleans Parish Recorder of Mortgages. **Online Access to Real Estate, Mortgage, Lien, Birth, Death records:** Access to the Parish online records requires a $300 yearly subscription fee. Records date back to 1989. Access includes real estate, liens, civil and 1st city court records. For information, contact at 504-592-9264. Also, unofficial birth records to 1900 and death records to 1950 are free at www.rootsweb.com/~usgenweb/la/orleans.htm. Also includes limited marriage lists. **Other phones:** Assessor-504-592-7050; Vital Records-504-568-5152.

Ouachita Parish

Clerk of Court, PO Box 1862, Monroe, LA 71210-1862. **Phone-**318-327-1444; fax-318-327-1462; hours 8:30AM-5PM

UCC record search per debtor- $30.00. UCC copy- $1.00 per page. UCC search includes tax liens. Separate federal or state tax lien search- $20.00 1st name $10.00 per debtor thereafter. Mortgage searches available. Cert fee: $3.50 per cert. Payee: Ouachita Parish Clerk of Court. **Other phones:** Assessor-318-327-1300.

Plaquemines Parish

Clerk of Court, PO Box 40, Belle Chasse, LA 70037-0040. **Phone-**504-392-4969, R/E Recording- 504-297-5180, UCC Recording- 504-297-5180; hours 8:30AM-4:30PM

UCC record search per debtor- $30.00. UCC copy- $2.00 per page. UCC search includes tax liens. Separate federal/state combined tax lien search- $20.00 per debtor. Real estate record owner and property searches available. RE record copy- $.50 per page. Cert fee: $3.00 per cert. Payee: Plaquemines Parish Clerk of Court. **Other phones:** Assessor-504-297-5250; Elections-504-297-5180.

Pointe Coupee Parish

Clerk of Court, PO Box 86, New Roads, LA 70760. **Phone-**Clerk of Court, R/E & UCC Recording- 225-638-9596; fax-225-638-9590; hours 8:30AM-4:30PM UCC record search per debtor- $30.00. Tax liens not included in UCC search. Separate federal tax lien search- $12.00 first name, $6.50 each add'l name. Real estate owner, mortgage, and property transfer searches available. Record copy- $1.00 per page. Cert fee: $5.00 per cert. Payee: Pointe Coupee Parish Clerk of Court. **Other phones:** Assessor-225-638-7077; Treasurer-504-638-9556.

Rapides Parish

Clerk of Court, PO Box 952, Alexandria, LA 71309. **Phone-**Clerk of Court, R/E & UCC Recording- 318-473-8153; fax-318-473-4667; hours 8:30AM-4:30PM UCC record search per debtor- $30.00. UCC copy- $1.00 per page. UCC search includes tax liens if requested. Separate federal/state combined tax lien search- $20.00 per debtor. Real estate record owner and mortgage searches available. Cert fee: $5.00 per cert. Payee: Rapides Parish Clerk of Court. **Other phones:** Assessor-318-448-8511; Elections-318-473-6770.

Red River Parish

Clerk of Court, PO Box 485, Coushatta, LA 71019-0485. **Phone-**Clerk of Court, R/E & UCC Recording- 318-932-6741; fax-318-932-3126; hours 8:30AM-4:30PM

Will search UCC records. Certificate search per debtor- $30.00. UCC search does not include tax liens. Separate federal/state combined tax lien search- $20.00 per debtor. Mortgage searches available; includes tax liens. Record copy- $1.25 per page. Cert fee: $5.00 per cert. Payee: Red River Parish Clerk of Court. **Other phones:** Assessor-318-932-4922; Elections-318-932-6741.

Richland Parish

Clerk of Court, PO Box 119, Rayville, LA 71269. **Phone-**318-728-4171; fax-318-728-7020; hours 8:30AM-4:30PM

UCC record search per debtor- $30.00. UCC search includes tax liens if requested. Mortgage searches available. Record copy- $1.00 per page. Cert fee: $5.00 per cert. Payee: Richland Parish Clerk of Court. **Other phones:** Assessor-318-728-4491.

Sabine Parish

Clerk of Court, PO Box 419, Many, LA 71449. **Phone-**Clerk of Court, R/E & UCC Recording- 318-256-6223; fax-318-256-9037; hours 8AM-4:30PM

UCC record search per debtor- $30.00. Will search tax liens. Federal/state combined tax lien search- $30.00 per debtor. Real estate owner, mortgage, and property transfer searches available. Record copy- $1.25 per page. Cert fee: $5.00 per cert. Payee: Sabine Parish Clerk of Court. **Other phones:** Assessor-318-256-3482;   Treasurer-318-256-5637; Sheriff-318-256-9241.

St. Bernard Parish

Clerk of Court, PO Box 1746, Chalmette, LA 70044. **Phone**-Clerk of Court, R/E & UCC Recording- 504-271-3434; hours 8:30AM-4:30PM

UCC record search per debtor- $30.00. UCC copy-$1.00 per page. UCC search includes tax liens if requested. Mortgage and property transfer searches available. Cert fee: $2.00 per cert. Payee: St. Bernard Parish Clerk of Court. **Other phones:** Assessor-504-279-6379; Elections-504-271-3434.

St. Charles Parish

Clerk of Court, PO Box 424, Hahnville, LA 70057. **Phone**-Clerk of Court, R/E & UCC Recording- 985-783-6632; fax-985-783-2005; hours 8:30AM-4:30PM UCC record search per debtor- $30.00. UCC copy-$1.00 per page. UCC search includes tax liens if requested. Separate federal & state combined tax lien search- $20.00 1st name, $10.00 per add'l name. Mortgage searches available. RE record copy-$.50 per page. Cert fee: $20.00 1st name, $10.00 per add'l name. Payee: St. Charles Parish Clerk of Court. **Other phones:** Assessor-985-783-6281.

St. Helena Parish

Clerk of Court, PO Box 308, Greensburg, LA 70441-0308. **Phone**-225-222-4514, R/E Recording- 225-222-4521; fax-225-222-3443; hours 8:30AM-4:30PM UCC record search per debtor- $30.00. UCC search includes tax liens if requested. Separate federal/state combined tax lien search- $10.00 per debtor. Real estate record owner searches available. Record copy- $1.00 per page. Cert fee: $5.00 per cert. Payee: Parish Clerk of Court. **Other phones:** Assessor-225-222-4540; Appraiser/ Auditor-225-222-4553; Elections-225-222-4440.

St. James Parish

Clerk of Court, PO Box 63, Convent, LA 70723. **Phone**-Clerk of Court, R/E & UCC Recording- 225-562-7496; fax-225-562-2383; hours 8AM-4:30PM Will search UCC records. Certificate per debtor-$30.00. Tax liens not included in UCC search. Separate federal/state combined tax lien search- $15.00 per debtor. Real estate owner, mortgage, and property transfer searches available. Record copy-$1.00 per page. Cert fee: $5.00 per cert. Payee: St. James Parish Clerk of Court. **Other phones:** Assessor-225-562-2250; Treasurer-504-562-2300; Elections-225-562-7496.

St. John the Baptist Parish

Clerk of Court, PO Box 280, Edgard, LA 70049-0280. **Phone**-985-497-3331, R/E Recording- 985-497-8836 x246, UCC Recording- 985-497-8836 x242; fax-985-497-3972; hours 8:30AM-4:30PM UCC record search per debtor- $30.00. Record copy-$2.00 per page. (fax back $3.00 per page). Tax liens not included in UCC search. Separate tax lien search-$12.00 first name, $6.00 each add'l name. Real estate owner, mortgage, and property transfer searches available. Cert fee: $5.00 per cert. Payee: St. John the Baptist Parish Clerk of Court. **Other phones:** Assessor-985-497-8788.

St. Landry Parish

Clerk of Court, PO Box 750, Opelousas, LA 70571-0750. **Phone**-337-942-5606, R/E Recording- 337-942-5606 x121, UCC Recording- 337-942-5606 x122; fax-337-948-7265; hours-8AM-4:30PM www.stlandry.org/index.htm UCC record search per debtor- $30.00. UCC copy-$2.00 per page. Tax liens not included in UCC search. Federal/state combined tax lien search-$20.00 1st name, $10.00 each add'l name. Real estate owner, mortgage, and property transfer searches available. RE record copy- $.75 per page. Cert fee:

$1.00 per page. Payee: St. Landry Parish Clerk of Court. **Other phones:** Assessor-337-942-2316; Treasurer-337-948-6516; Elections-337-942-5606 x133; Vital Records-337-942-5606 x122.

St. Martin Parish

Clerk of Court, PO Box 308, St. Martinville, LA 70582. **Phone**-337-394-2210; fax-337-394-7772; 8:30AM-4:30PM. UCC record search per debtor- $30.00. UCC copy- $2.00 per page. Tax liens not included in UCC search. Real estate owner, mortgage, and property transfer searches available. RE record copy-$.75 per page. Cert fee: $5.00 per cert. Payee: St. Martin Parish Clerk of Court. **Other phones:** Assessor-337-394-2208; Treasurer-337-394-2200; Elections-337-394-2210; Vital Records-337-394-2210.

St. Mary Parish

Clerk of Court, PO Drawer 1231, Franklin, LA 70538. **Phone**-318-828-4100 x200, R/E Recording- 337-828-4100 x200, UCC Recording- 337-828-4100 x200; fax-318-828-2509; hours 8:30AM-4:30PM UCC record search per debtor- $30.00. UCC copy-$2.00 per page. Will search tax liens. Separate federal/state combined tax lien search- $20.00 per debtor. Real estate owner, mortgage, and property transfer searches available. RE record copy- $1.00 per page. Cert fee: $5.00 per cert. Payee: St. Mary Parish Clerk of Court. **Other phones:** Assessor-337-828-4100 x250.

St. Tammany Parish

Clerk of Court, PO Box 1090, Covington, LA 70434. **Phone**-985-898-2430, R/E Recording- 985-809-8740, UCC Recording- 985-809-8740 x27840; hours 8:30AM-4:30PM www.sttammanyclerk.org/main/index.asp UCC record search per debtor- $30.00. Tax liens not included in UCC search. Separate tax lien search-$12.00 first name, $6.50 each add'l name. Real estate owner, mortgage, and property transfer searches available. Record copy- $.25 per page. Cert fee: $2.00 per cert. Payee: St. Tammany Parish Clerk of Court. **Online Access to Recorder, Real Estate, Mortgage, Lien, Assessor, Property Tax records:** Access to online records requires a $50 per month + $.20 per printed page. Records date back to 1961; viewable images on conveyances back to 1985; mortgages to 8/93. For information, call 985-809-8787. Free public access is also available at https://www.sttammanyclerk.org/liveapp/default.asp; includes marriages, land, and court cases. UCC lien data is with the Secretary of State. **Other phones:** Assessor-985-809-8180; Elections-985-809-8743.

Tangipahoa Parish

Clerk of Court, PO Box 667, Amite, LA 70422. **Phone**-985-748-4146, R/E Recording- 985-549-1612; fax-985-748-6746; 8:30AM-4:30PM www.tangiclerk.org UCC record search per debtor- $30.00. UCC copy-$1.00 per page. Tax liens not included in UCC search. Separate tax lien search-$12.50 1st name, $6.50 each add'l name. Mortgage searches available. Cert fee: $5.50 per cert. Payee: Tangipahoa Parish Clerk of Court. **Online Access to Real Estate, Lien, Recording, Civil, Marriage, Mortgage records:** Access to Parish online records requires registration and a trial membership. Print documents for $1.00 each. They may later charge a $55 monthly fee. Record dates vary though most indexes go back before 1990. Lending agency information is available. For information, contact Alison Carona at 504-549-1611. Also, a mapping feature is being developed that includes assessor basic information; access will be free.

Tensas Parish

Clerk of Court, PO Box 78, St. Joseph, LA 71366. **Phone**-318-766-3921; fax-318-766-3926.

UCC record search per debtor- $30.00. UCC copy-$1.00 per page. Tax liens not included in UCC search. Real estate owner, mortgage, and property transfer searches available. RE record copy- $.75 per page. Cert fee: $4.00 per cert. Payee: Tensas Parish Clerk of Court. **Other phones:** Assessor-225-766-3501.

Terrebonne Parish

Clerk of Court, PO Box 1569, Houma, LA 70361. **Phone**-985-868-5660, UCC Recording- 985-868-5660 x15; fax-985-868-5143; hours 8:30AM-4:30PM UCC record search per debtor- $30.00. UCC copy-$1.00 per page. Tax liens not included in UCC search. Real estate owner, mortgage, and property transfer searches available. RE record copy- $.75 per page. Cert fee: $5.00 per cert. Payee: Parish Clerk of Court. **Other phones:** Assessor-985-876-6620.

Union Parish

Clerk of Court, 100 E. Bayou St, #105, Courthouse, Farmerville, LA 71241. **Phone**-318-368-3055; fax-318-368-3861; hours 8:30AM-4:30PM UCC record search per debtor- $30.00. Tax liens not included in UCC search. Separate federal/state combined tax lien search- $20.00 per debtor per 10 year period. Real estate record owner and mortgage searches available. Record copy- $1.00 per page. Cert fee: $3.00 per cert. Payee: Union Parish Clerk of Court. **Other phones:** Assessor-318-368-3232.

Vermilion Parish

Clerk of Court, 100 N State St #101, Courthouse Bldg, Abbeville, LA 70510. **Phone**-Clerk of Court, R/E & UCC Recording- 337-898-1992; fax-337-898-0404; hours 8:30AM-4:30PM UCC record search per debtor- $30.00. UCC search includes tax liens. Separate tax lien search fee-$12.00 per debtor, $6.50 each add'l. Real estate owner, mortgage, and property transfer searches available. Record copy- $1.00 per page. Cert fee: $5.00 per cert. Payee: Parish Clerk of Court. **Other phones:** Assessor-337-893-2837; Treasurer-337-898-4300; Appraiser/ Auditor-337-898-2837; Elections-337-898-1992; Vital Records-337-898-1992.

Vernon Parish

Clerk of Court, PO Box 40, Leesville, LA 71496-0040. **Phone**-337-238-1384, R/E Recording- 337-238-4824; fax-337-238-9902; hours 8AM-4:30PM UCC record search per debtor- $30.00. UCC copy-$2.00 per page. Tax liens not included in UCC search. Tax lien search fee- $20.00 per debtor. Will search real estate records. RE record copy- $1.25 per page. Cert fee: $5.00 per cert. Payee: Vernon Parish Clerk of Court. **Other phones:** Assessor-337-239-2167; Elections-337-238-1384.

Washington Parish

Clerk of Court, PO Box 607, Franklinton, LA 70438. **Phone**-985-839-7821; fax-985-839-7851; hours 8AM-4:30PM. UCC record search per debtor- $30.00. UCC copy- $1.00 per page. Tax liens not included in UCC search. Real estate owner, mortgage, and property transfer searches available. Cert fee: $3.50 per cert. Payee: Washington Parish Clerk of Court. **Other phones:** Assessor-985-839-2280.

Webster Parish

Clerk of Court, PO Box 370, Minden, LA 71058-0370. **Phone**-Clerk of Court, R/E & UCC Recording- 318-371-0366; fax-318-371-0226; hours 8:30AM-4:30PM UCC record search per debtor- $30.00. Will search federal tax liens. Real estate record owner searches available. Record copy- $1.00 per page. Cert fee: $5.00 per cert. Payee: Webster Parish Clerk of Court. **Other phones:** Assessor-318-377-9311; Elections-318-371-0366.

West Baton Rouge Parish

Clerk of Court, PO Box 107, Port Allen, LA 70767. **Phone-**Clerk of Court, R/E & UCC Recording- 225-383-0378; fax-225-383-3694; hours 8:30AM-4:30PM UCC record search per debtor- $30.00. Record copy fee- $1.00 per page by clerk; $.50 self serve. Tax liens not included in UCC search. Real estate owner, mortgage, and property transfer searches available. Cert fee: $5.00 per item + $2.00 per page. Payee: West Baton Rouge Parish Clerk of Court. **Other phones:** Assessor-225-344-6777.

West Carroll Parish

Clerk of Court, PO Box 1078, Oak Grove, LA 71263. **Phone-**318-428-2369, R/E Recording- 318-428-3281, UCC Recording- 318-428-3281; fax-318-428-9896; hours 8:30AM-4:30PM
UCC record search per debtor- $30.00. Will search tax liens. Federal/state combined tax lien search- $20.00 per 10 years. Mortgage searches available only. Record copy- $1.00 per page. Cert fee: $5.00 per cert. Payee: West Carroll Parish Clerk of Court. **Other phones:** Assessor-318-428-2371.

West Feliciana Parish

Clerk of Court, PO Box 1843, St. Francisville, LA 70775. **Phone-**225-635-3794; fax-225-635-3770; hours 8:30AM-4:30PM
UCC record search per debtor- $30.00. UCC copy- $1.00 per page. Tax liens not included in UCC search. Real estate owner, mortgage, and property transfer searches available. Cert fee: $5.00 per cert. Payee: West Feliciana Parish Clerk of Court. **Other phones:** Assessor-225-635-3350.

Winn Parish

Clerk of Court, PO Box 137, Winnfield, LA 71483. **Phone-**Clerk of Court, R/E & UCC Recording- 318-628-3515; fax-318-628-3527; hours 8AM-4:30PM
UCC record search per debtor- $30.00. Tax liens not included in UCC search. Separate federal & state combined tax lien search- $20.00 per debtor. Real estate owner, mortgage, and property transfer searches available. Record copy- $1.00 per page. Cert fee: $5.00 per cert. Payee: Winn Parish Clerk of Court. **Other phones:** Assessor-318-628-3267; Treasurer-318-628-5824.

Louisiana County Locator

You will usually be able to find the city name in the City/Parish Cross Reference below. In that case, it is a simple matter to determine the county from the cross reference. However, only the official US Postal Service city names are included in this index. There are an additional 40,000 place names that people use in their addresses. Therefore, we have also included a ZIP/City Cross Reference immediately following the City/Parish Cross Reference.

If you know the ZIP Code but the city name does not appear in the City/Parish Cross Reference index, look up the ZIP Code in the ZIP/City Cross Reference, find the city name, then look up the city name in the City/Parish Cross Reference. For example, you want to know the county for an address of Menands, NY 12204. There is no "Menands" in the City/Parish Cross Reference. The ZIP/City Cross Reference shows that ZIP Codes 12201-12288 are for the city of Albany. Looking back in the City/Parish Cross Reference, Albany is in Albany Parish.

Louisiana City/Parish Cross Reference

ABBEVILLE Vermilion Parish
ABITA SPRINGS St. Tammany Parish
ACME Concordia Parish
ADDIS West Baton Rouge Parish
AIMWELL Catahoula Parish
AKERS Tangipahoa Parish
ALBANY Livingston Parish
ALEXANDRIA Rapides Parish
AMA St. Charles Parish
AMELIA St. Mary Parish
AMITE (70422) Tangipahoa Parish(71), St. Helena Parish(28)
ANACOCO (71403) Vernon Parish(97), Sabine Parish(2)
ANGIE Washington Parish
ANGOLA West Feliciana Parish
ARABI St. Bernard Parish
ARCADIA (71001) Bienville Parish(80), Lincoln Parish(9), Claiborne Parish(9)
ARCHIBALD Richland Parish
ARNAUDVILLE (70512) St. Landry Parish(59), St. Martin Parish(40)
ASHLAND Natchitoches Parish
ATHENS Claiborne Parish
ATLANTA (71404) Grant Parish(50), Winn Parish(49)
AVERY ISLAND Iberia Parish
BAKER East Baton Rouge Parish
BALDWIN St. Mary Parish
BALL Rapides Parish
BARATARIA Jefferson Parish
BARKSDALE AFB Bossier Parish
BASILE (70515) Acadia Parish(59), Evangeline Parish(40)
BASKIN Franklin Parish
BASTROP Morehouse Parish
BATCHELOR Pointe Coupee Parish
BATON ROUGE East Baton Rouge Parish
BAYOU GOULA Iberville Parish
BELCHER Caddo Parish
BELL CITY (70630) Calcasieu Parish(67), Cameron Parish(32)
BELLE CHASSE Plaquemines Parish
BELLE ROSE Assumption Parish
BELMONT Sabine Parish
BENTLEY Grant Parish
BENTON Bossier Parish
BERNICE (71222) Union Parish(81), Claiborne Parish(18)
BERWICK St. Mary Parish
BETHANY Caddo Parish
BIENVILLE Bienville Parish
BIG BEND Avoyelles Parish
BLANCHARD Caddo Parish
BLANKS Pointe Coupee Parish
BOGALUSA (70427) Washington Parish(97), St. Tammany Parish(2)
BOGALUSA Washington Parish
BONITA Morehouse Parish
BOOTHVILLE Plaquemines Parish
BORDELONVILLE Avoyelles Parish
BOSSIER CITY Bossier Parish
BOURG (70343) Terrebonne Parish(82), Lafourche Parish(17)

BOUTTE St. Charles Parish
BOYCE Rapides Parish
BRAITHWAITE Plaquemines Parish
BRANCH Acadia Parish
BREAUX BRIDGE St. Martin Parish
BRITTANY Ascension Parish
BROUSSARD (70518) Lafayette Parish(89), St. Martin Parish(6), Iberia Parish(3)
BRUSLY West Baton Rouge Parish
BRYCELAND Bienville Parish
BUCKEYE Rapides Parish
BUECHE West Baton Rouge Parish
BUNKIE (71322) Avoyelles Parish(86), St. Landry Parish(12), Rapides Parish(1)
BURAS Plaquemines Parish
BURNSIDE Ascension Parish
BUSH St. Tammany Parish
CADE St. Martin Parish
CALHOUN Ouachita Parish
CALVIN Winn Parish
CAMERON Cameron Parish
CAMPTI Natchitoches Parish
CARENCRO (70520) Lafayette Parish(98), St. Landry Parish(1)
CARLISLE Plaquemines Parish
CARVILLE Iberville Parish
CASTOR Bienville Parish
CECILIA St. Martin Parish
CENTER POINT (71323) Avoyelles Parish(98), Rapides Parish(1)
CENTERVILLE St. Mary Parish
CHALMETTE St. Bernard Parish
CHARENTON St. Mary Parish
CHASE Franklin Parish
CHATAIGNIER Evangeline Parish
CHATHAM Jackson Parish
CHAUVIN Terrebonne Parish
CHENEYVILLE (71325) Rapides Parish(67), Evangeline Parish(32)
CHOPIN Natchitoches Parish
CHOUDRANT (71227) Lincoln Parish(65), Jackson Parish(27), Ouachita Parish(6)
CHURCH POINT (70525) Acadia Parish(82), St. Landry Parish(17)
CLARENCE Natchitoches Parish
CLARKS Caldwell Parish
CLAYTON (71326) Catahoula Parish(65), Concordia Parish(33)
CLINTON (70722) East Feliciana Parish(96), East Baton Rouge Parish(3)
CLOUTIERVILLE Natchitoches Parish
COLFAX Grant Parish
COLLINSTON (71229) Morehouse Parish(82), Ouachita Parish(17)
COLUMBIA (71418) Caldwell Parish(86), Richland Parish(8), Ouachita Parish(3), Catahoula Parish(1)
CONVENT St. James Parish
CONVERSE (71419) Sabine Parish(85), De Soto Parish(14)
COTTON VALLEY (71018) Webster Parish(87), Bossier Parish(12)
COTTONPORT Avoyelles Parish

COUSHATTA (71019) Red River Parish(88), Natchitoches Parish(11)
COVINGTON St. Tammany Parish
CREOLE Cameron Parish
CRESTON Natchitoches Parish
CROWLEY Acadia Parish
CROWVILLE Franklin Parish
CULLEN Webster Parish
CUT OFF Lafourche Parish
CYPRESS Natchitoches Parish
DARROW Ascension Parish
DAVANT Plaquemines Parish
DELCAMBRE (70528) Vermilion Parish(77), Iberia Parish(22)
DELHI (71232) Richland Parish(61), Franklin Parish(19), Madison Parish(19)
DELTA Madison Parish
DENHAM SPRINGS (70706) Livingston Parish(89), St. Helena Parish(10)
DENHAM SPRINGS Livingston Parish
DEQUINCY Calcasieu Parish
DERIDDER (70634) Beauregard Parish(91), Vernon Parish(8)
DERRY Natchitoches Parish
DES ALLEMANDS (70030) St. Charles Parish(88), Lafourche Parish(11)
DESTREHAN St. Charles Parish
DEVILLE (71328) Rapides Parish(86), Avoyelles Parish(13)
DODSON Winn Parish
DONALDSONVILLE Ascension Parish
DONNER Terrebonne Parish
DOWNSVILLE (71234) Union Parish(80), Ouachita Parish(14), Lincoln Parish(5)
DOYLINE Webster Parish
DRY CREEK (70637) Beauregard Parish(72), Allen Parish(27)
DRY PRONG (71423) Grant Parish(96), Rapides Parish(3)
DUBACH (71235) Lincoln Parish(98), Claiborne Parish(1)
DUBBERLY (71024) Webster Parish(89), Bienville Parish(10)
DULAC Terrebonne Parish
DUPLESSIS Ascension Parish
DUPONT Avoyelles Parish
DUSON Lafayette Parish
EAST POINT Red River Parish
ECHO Rapides Parish
EDGARD St. John the Baptist Parish
EFFIE (71331) Avoyelles Parish(97), Catahoula Parish(2)
EGAN Acadia Parish
ELIZABETH Allen Parish
ELM GROVE Bossier Parish
ELMER Rapides Parish
ELTON (70532) Jefferson Davis Parish(79), Allen Parish(20)
EMPIRE Plaquemines Parish
ENTERPRISE (71425) Catahoula Parish(68), Rapides Parish(31)
EPPS (71237) West Carroll Parish(83), Madison Parish(13), East Carroll Parish(3)

ERATH Vermilion Parish
EROS (71238) Ouachita Parish(53), Jackson Parish(46)
ERWINVILLE (70729) West Baton Rouge Parish(97), Pointe Coupee Parish(2)
ESTHERWOOD Acadia Parish
ETHEL East Feliciana Parish
EUNICE (70535) St. Landry Parish(94), Acadia Parish(4), Evangeline Parish(1)
EVANGELINE Acadia Parish
EVANS Vernon Parish
EVERGREEN Avoyelles Parish
EXTENSION Franklin Parish
FAIRBANKS Ouachita Parish
FARMERVILLE Union Parish
FENTON Jefferson Davis Parish
FERRIDAY Concordia Parish
FISHER Sabine Parish
FLATWOODS (71427) Rapides Parish(75), Natchitoches Parish(24)
FLORA Natchitoches Parish
FLORIEN Sabine Parish
FLUKER (70436) Tangipahoa Parish(85), St. Helena Parish(14)
FOLSOM St. Tammany Parish
FORDOCHE Pointe Coupee Parish
FOREST West Carroll Parish
FOREST HILL Rapides Parish
FORT NECESSITY Franklin Parish
FRANKLIN St. Mary Parish
FRANKLINTON Washington Parish
FRENCH SETTLEMENT Livingston Parish
FRIERSON De Soto Parish
FROGMORE Concordia Parish
FULLERTON Vernon Parish
GALLIANO Lafourche Parish
GARDEN CITY St. Mary Parish
GARDNER Rapides Parish
GARYVILLE St. John the Baptist Parish
GEISMAR Ascension Parish
GEORGETOWN Grant Parish
GHEENS Lafourche Parish
GIBSLAND Bienville Parish
GIBSON Terrebonne Parish
GILBERT Franklin Parish
GILLIAM Caddo Parish
GLENMORA (71433) Rapides Parish(98), Allen Parish(1)
GLOSTER De Soto Parish
GLYNN (70736) Pointe Coupee Parish(98), West Baton Rouge Parish(1)
GOLDEN MEADOW Lafourche Parish
GOLDONNA (71031) Natchitoches Parish(53), Winn Parish(46)
GONZALES Ascension Parish
GORUM Natchitoches Parish
GOUDEAU Avoyelles Parish
GRAMBLING Lincoln Parish
GRAMERCY St. James Parish
GRAND CANE De Soto Parish
GRAND CHENIER Cameron Parish
GRAND COTEAU St. Landry Parish
GRAND ISLE Jefferson Parish
GRANT Allen Parish

GRAY Terrebonne Parish
GRAYSON (71435) Caldwell Parish(98), Catahoula Parish(1)
GREENSBURG St. Helena Parish
GREENWELL SPRINGS East Baton Rouge Parish
GREENWOOD Caddo Parish
GRETNA Jefferson Parish
GROSSE TETE Iberville Parish
GUEYDAN (70542) Vermilion Parish(95), Cameron Parish(4)
HACKBERRY Cameron Parish
HAHNVILLE St. Charles Parish
HALL SUMMIT Red River Parish
HAMBURG Avoyelles Parish
HAMMOND (70403) Tangipahoa Parish(95), Livingston Parish(4)
HAMMOND Tangipahoa Parish
HARMON Red River Parish
HARRISONBURG Catahoula Parish
HARVEY Jefferson Parish
HAUGHTON Bossier Parish
HAYES Calcasieu Parish
HAYNESVILLE Claiborne Parish
HEBERT Caldwell Parish
HEFLIN (71039) Webster Parish(80), Bienville Parish(19)
HESSMER Avoyelles Parish
HESTER St. James Parish
HICKS Vernon Parish
HINESTON (71438) Rapides Parish(82), Vernon Parish(17)
HODGE Jackson Parish
HOLDEN (70744) Livingston Parish(95), St. Helena Parish(4)
HOMER Claiborne Parish
HORNBECK (71439) Vernon Parish(78), Sabine Parish(21)
HOSSTON Caddo Parish
HOUMA (70364) Terrebonne Parish(81), Lafourche Parish(18)
HOUMA Terrebonne Parish
HUSSER Tangipahoa Parish
IDA Caddo Parish
INDEPENDENCE (70443) Tangipahoa Parish(52), Livingston Parish(29), St. Helena Parish(17)
INNIS Pointe Coupee Parish
IOTA Acadia Parish
IOWA Calcasieu Parish
JACKSON (70748) East Feliciana Parish(76), West Feliciana Parish(21), East Baton Rouge Parish(2)
JAMESTOWN Bienville Parish
JARREAU Pointe Coupee Parish
JEANERETTE (70544) Iberia Parish(84), St. Mary Parish(15)
JENA La Salle Parish
JENNINGS (70546) Jefferson Davis Parish(97), Acadia Parish(2)
JIGGER Franklin Parish
JONES Morehouse Parish
JONESBORO (71251) Jackson Parish(94), Bienville Parish(5)
JONESVILLE (71343) Catahoula Parish(88), Concordia Parish(11)
JOYCE Winn Parish
KAPLAN Vermilion Parish
KEATCHIE De Soto Parish
KEITHVILLE Caddo Parish
KELLY (71441) Caldwell Parish(82), La Salle Parish(17)
KENNER Jefferson Parish
KENTWOOD (70444) Tangipahoa Parish(82), St. Helena Parish(15), Washington Parish(1)
KILBOURNE West Carroll Parish
KILLONA St. Charles Parish
KINDER (70648) Allen Parish(98), Jefferson Davis Parish(1)
KRAEMER Lafourche Parish
KROTZ SPRINGS St. Landry Parish
KURTHWOOD Vernon Parish

LA PLACE (70068) St. John the Baptist Parish(95), St. Charles Parish(4)
LA PLACE St. John the Baptist Parish
LABADIEVILLE Assumption Parish
LABARRE Pointe Coupee Parish
LACAMP Vernon Parish
LACASSINE Jefferson Davis Parish
LACOMBE St. Tammany Parish
LAFAYETTE Lafayette Parish
LAFITTE Jefferson Parish
LAKE ARTHUR (70549) Jefferson Davis Parish(97), Cameron Parish(2)
LAKE CHARLES (70607) Calcasieu Parish(90), Cameron Parish(9)
LAKE CHARLES Calcasieu Parish
LAKE PROVIDENCE East Carroll Parish
LAKELAND Pointe Coupee Parish
LAROSE Lafourche Parish
LARTO Catahoula Parish
LAWTELL St. Landry Parish
LE MOYEN St. Landry Parish
LEANDER Vernon Parish
LEBEAU St. Landry Parish
LEBLANC Allen Parish
LECOMPTE Rapides Parish
LEESVILLE Vernon Parish
LENA (71447) Rapides Parish(54), Natchitoches Parish(45)
LEONVILLE St. Landry Parish
LETTSWORTH Pointe Coupee Parish
LIBUSE Rapides Parish
LILLIE (71256) Union Parish(94), Claiborne Parish(5)
LISBON Claiborne Parish
LIVINGSTON Livingston Parish
LIVONIA Pointe Coupee Parish
LOCKPORT Lafourche Parish
LOGANSPORT De Soto Parish
LONGLEAF Rapides Parish
LONGSTREET De Soto Parish
LONGVILLE Beauregard Parish
LORANGER Tangipahoa Parish
LOREAUVILLE Iberia Parish
LOTTIE Pointe Coupee Parish
LULING St. Charles Parish
LUTCHER St. James Parish
LYDIA Iberia Parish
MADISONVILLE St. Tammany Parish
MAMOU Evangeline Parish
MANDEVILLE St. Tammany Parish
MANGHAM Richland Parish
MANSFIELD De Soto Parish
MANSURA Avoyelles Parish
MANY Sabine Parish
MARINGOUIN Iberville Parish
MARION Union Parish
MARKSVILLE Avoyelles Parish
MARRERO Jefferson Parish
MARTHAVILLE (71450) Natchitoches Parish(68), Sabine Parish(31)
MATHEWS Lafourche Parish
MAUREPAS (70449) Livingston Parish(95), Ascension Parish(4)
MAURICE (70555) Vermilion Parish(96), Lafayette Parish(3)
MELDER Rapides Parish
MELROSE Natchitoches Parish
MELVILLE St. Landry Parish
MER ROUGE Morehouse Parish
MERAUX St. Bernard Parish
MERMENTAU Acadia Parish
MERRYVILLE Beauregard Parish
METAIRIE Jefferson Parish
MILTON Lafayette Parish
MINDEN (71055) Webster Parish(96), Claiborne Parish(2)
MINDEN Webster Parish
MIRA Caddo Parish
MITTIE Allen Parish
MODESTE Ascension Parish
MONROE Ouachita Parish
MONTEGUT (70377) Terrebonne Parish(89), Lafourche Parish(10)

MONTEREY Concordia Parish
MONTGOMERY (71454) Grant Parish(82), Winn Parish(17)
MOORINGSPORT Caddo Parish
MORA (71455) Rapides Parish(98), Natchitoches Parish(1)
MOREAUVILLE Avoyelles Parish
MORGAN CITY (70380) St. Mary Parish(91), Assumption Parish(8)
MORGAN CITY St. Mary Parish
MORGANZA Pointe Coupee Parish
MORROW (71356) St. Landry Parish(57), Avoyelles Parish(42)
MORSE Acadia Parish
MOUNT AIRY St. John the Baptist Parish
MOUNT HERMON Washington Parish
NAPOLEONVILLE Assumption Parish
NATALBANY Tangipahoa Parish
NATCHEZ Natchitoches Parish
NATCHITOCHES (71457) Natchitoches Parish(97), Winn Parish(2)
NATCHITOCHES Natchitoches Parish
NEGREET Sabine Parish
NEW IBERIA Iberia Parish
NEW ORLEANS (70146) Orleans Parish(91), Plaquemines Parish(8)
NEW ORLEANS Jefferson Parish
NEW ORLEANS Orleans Parish
NEW ROADS Pointe Coupee Parish
NEW SARPY St. Charles Parish
NEWELLTON Tensas Parish
NEWLLANO Vernon Parish
NOBLE Sabine Parish
NORCO St. Charles Parish
NORWOOD East Feliciana Parish
OAK GROVE West Carroll Parish
OAK RIDGE (71264) Morehouse Parish(77), Richland Parish(22)
OAKDALE (71463) Allen Parish(88), Evangeline Parish(6), Rapides Parish(4)
OBERLIN Allen Parish
OIL CITY Caddo Parish
OLLA (71465) La Salle Parish(87), Winn Parish(9), Caldwell Parish(2)
OPELOUSAS St. Landry Parish
OSCAR Pointe Coupee Parish
OTIS Rapides Parish
PAINCOURTVILLE Assumption Parish
PALMETTO St. Landry Parish
PARADIS St. Charles Parish
PATTERSON St. Mary Parish
PAULINA St. James Parish
PEARL RIVER St. Tammany Parish
PELICAN De Soto Parish
PERRY Vermilion Parish
PIERRE PART (70339) Assumption Parish(92), St. Martin Parish(7)
PILOTTOWN Plaquemines Parish
PINE GROVE (70453) St. Helena Parish(85), Livingston Parish(14)
PINE PRAIRIE Evangeline Parish
PINEVILLE (71360) Rapides Parish(96), Avoyelles Parish(2), Grant Parish(1)
PINEVILLE Rapides Parish
PIONEER West Carroll Parish
PITKIN (70656) Vernon Parish(62), Rapides Parish(18), Allen Parish(18)
PLAIN DEALING Bossier Parish
PLAQUEMINE Iberville Parish
PLATTENVILLE Assumption Parish
PLAUCHEVILLE Avoyelles Parish
PLEASANT HILL (71065) Sabine Parish(98), Natchitoches Parish(1)
POINTE A LA HACHE Plaquemines Parish
POLLOCK Grant Parish
PONCHATOULA Tangipahoa Parish
PORT ALLEN West Baton Rouge Parish
PORT BARRE St. Landry Parish
PORT SULPHUR Plaquemines Parish
POWHATAN Natchitoches Parish
PRAIRIEVILLE Ascension Parish
PRIDE East Baton Rouge Parish
PRINCETON Bossier Parish

PROVENCAL Natchitoches Parish
QUITMAN (71268) Jackson Parish(79), Bienville Parish(20)
RACELAND Lafourche Parish
RAGLEY (70657) Beauregard Parish(85), Allen Parish(14)
RAYNE (70578) Acadia Parish(90), Vermilion Parish(5), Lafayette Parish(4)
RAYVILLE Richland Parish
REDDELL Evangeline Parish
REEVES Allen Parish
RESERVE St. John the Baptist Parish
RHINEHART Catahoula Parish
RINGGOLD (71068) Bienville Parish(93), Red River Parish(6)
ROANOKE Jefferson Davis Parish
ROBELINE (71469) Natchitoches Parish(75), Sabine Parish(24)
ROBERT Tangipahoa Parish
RODESSA Caddo Parish
ROSA St. Landry Parish
ROSEDALE Iberville Parish
ROSELAND Tangipahoa Parish
ROSEPINE Vernon Parish
ROUGON Pointe Coupee Parish
RUBY Rapides Parish
RUSTON (71270) Lincoln Parish(94), Jackson Parish(5)
RUSTON Lincoln Parish
SAINT AMANT Ascension Parish
SAINT BENEDICT St. Tammany Parish
SAINT BERNARD St. Bernard Parish
SAINT FRANCISVILLE West Feliciana Parish
SAINT GABRIEL Iberville Parish
SAINT JAMES St. James Parish
SAINT JOSEPH Tensas Parish
SAINT LANDRY Evangeline Parish
SAINT MARTINVILLE St. Martin Parish
SAINT MAURICE Winn Parish
SAINT ROSE St. Charles Parish
SALINE (71070) Natchitoches Parish(59), Bienville Parish(40)
SAREPTA (71071) Webster Parish(95), Bossier Parish(4)
SCHRIEVER Terrebonne Parish
SCOTT (70583) Lafayette Parish(94), Acadia Parish(5)
SHONGALOO Webster Parish
SHREVEPORT (71107) Caddo Parish(98), Bossier Parish(1)
SHREVEPORT (71115) Caddo Parish(95), Red River Parish(4)
SHREVEPORT Caddo Parish
SIBLEY Webster Parish
SICILY ISLAND (71368) Catahoula Parish(98), Franklin Parish(1)
SIEPER Rapides Parish
SIKES Winn Parish
SIMMESPORT Avoyelles Parish
SIMPSON Vernon Parish
SIMSBORO (71275) Lincoln Parish(85), Bienville Parish(14)
SINGER Beauregard Parish
SLAGLE Vernon Parish
SLAUGHTER East Feliciana Parish
SLIDELL St. Tammany Parish
SONDHEIMER East Carroll Parish
SORRENTO Ascension Parish
SPEARSVILLE Union Parish
SPRINGFIELD (70462) Livingston Parish(97), Tangipahoa Parish(2)
SPRINGHILL (71075) Webster Parish(96), Bossier Parish(3)
STARKS Calcasieu Parish
START Richland Parish
STERLINGTON (71280) Ouachita Parish(55), Union Parish(44)
STONEWALL De Soto Parish
SUGARTOWN Beauregard Parish
SULPHUR Calcasieu Parish
SUMMERFIELD Claiborne Parish
SUN St. Tammany Parish

SUNSET St. Landry Parish
SUNSHINE Iberville Parish
SWARTZ Ouachita Parish
TALISHEEK St. Tammany Parish
TALLULAH Madison Parish
TANGIPAHOA Tangipahoa Parish
TAYLOR Bienville Parish
THERIOT Terrebonne Parish
THIBODAUX (70301) Lafourche
   Parish(95), Terrebonne Parish(3)
THIBODAUX Lafourche Parish
TICKFAW Tangipahoa Parish
TIOGA Rapides Parish
TORBERT Pointe Coupee Parish

TRANSYLVANIA East Carroll Parish
TROUT La Salle Parish
TULLOS (71479) Winn Parish(62), La Salle
   Parish(37)
TUNICA West Feliciana Parish
TURKEY CREEK Evangeline Parish
UNCLE SAM St. James Parish
URANIA La Salle Parish
VACHERIE (70090) St. James Parish(81),
   St. John the Baptist Parish(18)
VENICE Plaquemines Parish
VENTRESS Pointe Coupee Parish
VERDA Grant Parish
VICK Avoyelles Parish

VIDALIA Concordia Parish
VILLE PLATTE Evangeline Parish
VINTON Calcasieu Parish
VIOLET St. Bernard Parish
VIVIAN Caddo Parish
WAKEFIELD West Feliciana Parish
WALKER Livingston Parish
WASHINGTON (70589) St. Landry
   Parish(92), Evangeline Parish(7)
WATERPROOF Tensas Parish
WATSON Livingston Parish
WELSH Jefferson Davis Parish
WEST MONROE Ouachita Parish
WESTLAKE Calcasieu Parish

WESTWEGO Jefferson Parish
WEYANOKE West Feliciana Parish
WHITE CASTLE Iberville Parish
WILDSVILLE Concordia Parish
WILSON East Feliciana Parish
WINNFIELD Winn Parish
WINNSBORO Franklin Parish
WISNER Franklin Parish
WOODWORTH Rapides Parish
YOUNGSVILLE (70592) Lafayette
   Parish(81), Vermilion Parish(11), Iberia
   Parish(6)
ZACHARY East Baton Rouge Parish
ZWOLLE Sabine Parish

Louisiana ZIP/City Cross Reference

70001-70011 METAIRIE	70357-70357 GOLDEN MEADOW	70517-70517 BREAUX BRIDGE	70642-70642 FULLERTON
70030-70030 DES ALLEMANDS	70358-70358 GRAND ISLE	70518-70518 BROUSSARD	70643-70643 GRAND CHENIER
70031-70031 AMA	70359-70359 GRAY	70519-70519 CADE	70644-70644 GRANT
70032-70032 ARABI	70360-70364 HOUMA	70520-70520 CARENCRO	70645-70645 HACKBERRY
70033-70033 METAIRIE	70371-70371 KRAEMER	70521-70521 CECILIA	70646-70646 HAYES
70036-70036 BARATARIA	70372-70372 LABADIEVILLE	70522-70522 CENTERVILLE	70647-70647 IOWA
70037-70037 BELLE CHASSE	70373-70373 LAROSE	70523-70523 CHARENTON	70648-70648 KINDER
70038-70038 BOOTHVILLE	70374-70374 LOCKPORT	70524-70524 CHATAIGNIER	70650-70650 LACASSINE
70039-70039 BOUTTE	70375-70375 MATHEWS	70525-70525 CHURCH POINT	70651-70651 LEBLANC
70040-70040 BRAITHWAITE	70376-70376 MODESTE	70526-70527 CROWLEY	70652-70652 LONGVILLE
70041-70041 BURAS	70377-70377 MONTEGUT	70528-70528 DELCAMBRE	70653-70653 MERRYVILLE
70042-70042 CARLISLE	70380-70381 MORGAN CITY	70529-70529 DUSON	70654-70654 MITTIE
70043-70044 CHALMETTE	70390-70390 NAPOLEONVILLE	70531-70531 EGAN	70655-70655 OBERLIN
70046-70046 DAVANT	70391-70391 PAINCOURTVILLE	70532-70532 ELTON	70656-70656 PITKIN
70047-70047 DESTREHAN	70392-70392 PATTERSON	70533-70533 ERATH	70657-70657 RAGLEY
70049-70049 EDGARD	70393-70393 PLATTENVILLE	70534-70534 ESTHERWOOD	70658-70658 REEVES
70050-70050 EMPIRE	70394-70394 RACELAND	70535-70535 EUNICE	70659-70659 ROSEPINE
70051-70051 GARYVILLE	70395-70395 SCHRIEVER	70537-70537 EVANGELINE	70660-70660 SINGER
70052-70052 GRAMERCY	70397-70397 THERIOT	70538-70538 FRANKLIN	70661-70661 STARKS
70053-70054 GRETNA	70401-70404 HAMMOND	70540-70540 GARDEN CITY	70662-70662 SUGARTOWN
70055-70055 METAIRIE	70420-70420 ABITA SPRINGS	70541-70541 GRAND COTEAU	70663-70665 SULPHUR
70056-70056 GRETNA	70421-70421 AKERS	70542-70542 GUEYDAN	70668-70668 VINTON
70057-70057 HAHNVILLE	70422-70422 AMITE	70543-70543 IOTA	70669-70669 WESTLAKE
70058-70059 HARVEY	70426-70426 ANGIE	70544-70544 JEANERETTE	70704-70704 BAKER
70060-70060 METAIRIE	70427-70429 BOGALUSA	70546-70546 JENNINGS	70706-70706 DENHAM SPRINGS
70062-70065 KENNER	70431-70431 BUSH	70548-70548 KAPLAN	70707-70707 GONZALES
70066-70066 KILLONA	70433-70435 COVINGTON	70549-70549 LAKE ARTHUR	70710-70710 ADDIS
70067-70067 LAFITTE	70436-70436 FLUKER	70550-70550 LAWTELL	70711-70711 ALBANY
70068-70069 LA PLACE	70437-70437 FOLSOM	70551-70551 LEONVILLE	70712-70712 ANGOLA
70070-70070 LULING	70438-70438 FRANKLINTON	70552-70552 LOREAUVILLE	70714-70714 BAKER
70071-70071 LUTCHER	70441-70441 GREENSBURG	70554-70554 MAMOU	70715-70715 BATCHELOR
70072-70073 MARRERO	70442-70442 HUSSER	70555-70555 MAURICE	70716-70716 BAYOU GOULA
70075-70075 MERAUX	70443-70443 INDEPENDENCE	70556-70556 MERMENTAU	70717-70717 BLANKS
70076-70076 MOUNT AIRY	70444-70444 KENTWOOD	70558-70558 MILTON	70718-70718 BRITTANY
70078-70078 NEW SARPY	70445-70445 LACOMBE	70559-70559 MORSE	70719-70719 BRUSLY
70079-70079 NORCO	70446-70446 LORANGER	70560-70563 NEW IBERIA	70720-70720 BUECHE
70080-70080 PARADIS	70447-70447 MADISONVILLE	70569-70569 LYDIA	70721-70721 CARVILLE
70081-70081 PILOTTOWN	70448-70448 MANDEVILLE	70570-70571 OPELOUSAS	70722-70722 CLINTON
70082-70082 POINTE A LA HACHE	70449-70449 MAUREPAS	70575-70575 PERRY	70723-70723 CONVENT
70083-70083 PORT SULPHUR	70450-70450 MOUNT HERMON	70576-70576 PINE PRAIRIE	70725-70725 DARROW
70084-70084 RESERVE	70451-70451 NATALBANY	70577-70577 PORT BARRE	70726-70727 DENHAM SPRINGS
70085-70085 SAINT BERNARD	70452-70452 PEARL RIVER	70578-70578 RAYNE	70728-70728 DUPLESSIS
70086-70086 SAINT JAMES	70453-70453 PINE GROVE	70580-70580 REDDELL	70729-70729 ERWINVILLE
70087-70087 SAINT ROSE	70454-70454 PONCHATOULA	70581-70581 ROANOKE	70730-70730 ETHEL
70090-70090 VACHERIE	70455-70455 ROBERT	70582-70582 SAINT MARTINVILLE	70732-70732 FORDOCHE
70091-70091 VENICE	70456-70456 ROSELAND	70583-70583 SCOTT	70733-70733 FRENCH SETTLEMENT
70092-70092 VIOLET	70457-70457 SAINT BENEDICT	70584-70584 SUNSET	70734-70734 GEISMAR
70094-70096 WESTWEGO	70458-70461 SLIDELL	70585-70585 TURKEY CREEK	70736-70736 GLYNN
70100-70195 NEW ORLEANS	70462-70462 SPRINGFIELD	70586-70586 VILLE PLATTE	70737-70737 GONZALES
70301-70310 THIBODAUX	70463-70463 SUN	70589-70589 WASHINGTON	70738-70738 BURNSIDE
70339-70339 PIERRE PART	70464-70464 TALISHEEK	70591-70591 WELSH	70739-70739 GREENWELL SPRINGS
70340-70340 AMELIA	70465-70465 TANGIPAHOA	70592-70592 YOUNGSVILLE	70740-70740 GROSSE TETE
70341-70341 BELLE ROSE	70466-70466 TICKFAW	70593-70598 LAFAYETTE	70743-70743 HESTER
70342-70342 BERWICK	70467-70467 ANGIE	70601-70629 LAKE CHARLES	70744-70744 HOLDEN
70343-70343 BOURG	70468-70469 SLIDELL	70630-70630 BELL CITY	70747-70747 INNIS
70344-70344 CHAUVIN	70470-70471 MANDEVILLE	70631-70631 CAMERON	70748-70748 JACKSON
70345-70345 CUT OFF	70501-70509 LAFAYETTE	70632-70632 CREOLE	70749-70749 JARREAU
70346-70346 DONALDSONVILLE	70510-70511 ABBEVILLE	70633-70633 DEQUINCY	70750-70750 KROTZ SPRINGS
70352-70352 DONNER	70512-70512 ARNAUDVILLE	70634-70634 DERIDDER	70751-70751 LABARRE
70353-70353 DULAC	70513-70513 AVERY ISLAND	70637-70637 DRY CREEK	70752-70752 LAKELAND
70354-70354 GALLIANO	70514-70514 BALDWIN	70638-70638 ELIZABETH	70753-70753 LETTSWORTH
70355-70355 GHEENS	70515-70515 BASILE	70639-70639 EVANS	70754-70754 LIVINGSTON
70356-70356 GIBSON	70516-70516 BRANCH	70640-70640 FENTON	70755-70755 LIVONIA

Range	Name	Range	Name	Range	Name	Range	Name
70756-70756	LOTTIE	71071-71071	SAREPTA	71340-71340	HARRISONBURG	71457-71458	NATCHITOCHES
70757-70757	MARINGOUIN	71072-71072	SHONGALOO	71341-71341	HESSMER	71459-71459	LEESVILLE
70759-70759	MORGANZA	71073-71073	SIBLEY	71342-71342	JENA	71460-71460	NEGREET
70760-70760	NEW ROADS	71075-71075	SPRINGHILL	71343-71343	JONESVILLE	71461-71461	NEWLLANO
70761-70761	NORWOOD	71078-71078	STONEWALL	71344-71344	LARTO	71462-71462	NOBLE
70762-70762	OSCAR	71079-71079	SUMMERFIELD	71345-71345	LEBEAU	71463-71463	OAKDALE
70763-70763	PAULINA	71080-71080	TAYLOR	71346-71346	LECOMPTE	71465-71465	OLLA
70764-70765	PLAQUEMINE	71082-71082	VIVIAN	71347-71347	LE MOYEN	71466-71466	OTIS
70767-70767	PORT ALLEN	71101-71109	SHREVEPORT	71348-71348	LIBUSE	71467-71467	POLLOCK
70769-70769	PRAIRIEVILLE	71110-71110	BARKSDALE AFB	71350-71350	MANSURA	71468-71468	PROVENCAL
70770-70770	PRIDE	71111-71113	BOSSIER CITY	71351-71351	MARKSVILLE	71469-71469	ROBELINE
70772-70772	ROSEDALE	71115-71166	SHREVEPORT	71353-71353	MELVILLE	71471-71471	SAINT MAURICE
70773-70773	ROUGON	71171-71172	BOSSIER CITY	71354-71354	MONTEREY	71472-71472	SIEPER
70774-70774	SAINT AMANT	71201-71213	MONROE	71355-71355	MOREAUVILLE	71473-71473	SIKES
70775-70775	SAINT FRANCISVILLE	71218-71218	ARCHIBALD	71356-71356	MORROW	71474-71474	SIMPSON
70776-70776	SAINT GABRIEL	71219-71219	BASKIN	71357-71357	NEWELLTON	71475-71475	SLAGLE
70777-70777	SLAUGHTER	71220-71221	BASTROP	71358-71358	PALMETTO	71477-71477	TIOGA
70778-70778	SORRENTO	71222-71222	BERNICE	71359-71361	PINEVILLE	71479-71479	TULLOS
70780-70780	SUNSHINE	71223-71223	BONITA	71362-71362	PLAUCHEVILLE	71480-71480	URANIA
70781-70781	TORBERT	71225-71225	CALHOUN	71363-71363	RHINEHART	71481-71481	VERDA
70782-70782	TUNICA	71226-71226	CHATHAM	71364-71364	ROSA	71483-71483	WINNFIELD
70783-70783	VENTRESS	71227-71227	CHOUDRANT	71365-71365	RUBY	71485-71485	WOODWORTH
70784-70784	WAKEFIELD	71229-71229	COLLINSTON	71366-71366	SAINT JOSEPH	71486-71486	ZWOLLE
70785-70785	WALKER	71230-71230	CROWVILLE	71367-71367	SAINT LANDRY	71496-71496	LEESVILLE
70786-70786	WATSON	71232-71232	DELHI	71368-71368	SICILY ISLAND	71497-71497	NATCHITOCHES
70787-70787	WEYANOKE	71233-71233	DELTA	71369-71369	SIMMESPORT		
70788-70788	WHITE CASTLE	71234-71234	DOWNSVILLE	71371-71371	TROUT		
70789-70789	WILSON	71235-71235	DUBACH	71372-71372	VICK		
70791-70791	ZACHARY	71237-71237	EPPS	71373-71373	VIDALIA		
70792-70792	UNCLE SAM	71238-71238	EROS	71375-71375	WATERPROOF		
70800-70898	BATON ROUGE	71239-71239	EXTENSION	71377-71377	WILDSVILLE		
71001-71001	ARCADIA	71240-71240	FAIRBANKS	71378-71378	WISNER		
71002-71002	ASHLAND	71241-71241	FARMERVILLE	71401-71401	AIMWELL		
71003-71003	ATHENS	71242-71242	FOREST	71403-71403	ANACOCO		
71004-71004	BELCHER	71243-71243	FORT NECESSITY	71404-71404	ATLANTA		
71006-71006	BENTON	71245-71245	GRAMBLING	71405-71405	BALL		
71007-71007	BETHANY	71247-71247	HODGE	71406-71406	BELMONT		
71008-71008	BIENVILLE	71249-71249	JIGGER	71407-71407	BENTLEY		
71009-71009	BLANCHARD	71250-71250	JONES	71409-71409	BOYCE		
71014-71014	BRYCELAND	71251-71251	JONESBORO	71410-71410	CALVIN		
71016-71016	CASTOR	71253-71253	KILBOURNE	71411-71411	CAMPTI		
71018-71018	COTTON VALLEY	71254-71254	LAKE PROVIDENCE	71412-71412	CHOPIN		
71019-71019	COUSHATTA	71256-71256	LILLIE	71414-71414	CLARENCE		
71020-71020	CRESTON	71259-71259	MANGHAM	71415-71415	CLARKS		
71021-71021	CULLEN	71260-71260	MARION	71416-71416	CLOUTIERVILLE		
71023-71023	DOYLINE	71261-71261	MER ROUGE	71417-71417	COLFAX		
71024-71024	DUBBERLY	71263-71263	OAK GROVE	71418-71418	COLUMBIA		
71025-71025	EAST POINT	71264-71264	OAK RIDGE	71419-71419	CONVERSE		
71027-71027	FRIERSON	71266-71266	PIONEER	71420-71420	CYPRESS		
71028-71028	GIBSLAND	71268-71268	QUITMAN	71421-71421	DERRY		
71029-71029	GILLIAM	71269-71269	RAYVILLE	71422-71422	DODSON		
71030-71030	GLOSTER	71270-71273	RUSTON	71423-71423	DRY PRONG		
71031-71031	GOLDONNA	71275-71275	SIMSBORO	71424-71424	ELMER		
71032-71032	GRAND CANE	71276-71276	SONDHEIMER	71425-71425	ENTERPRISE		
71033-71033	GREENWOOD	71277-71277	SPEARSVILLE	71426-71426	FISHER		
71034-71034	HALL SUMMIT	71279-71279	START	71427-71427	FLATWOODS		
71036-71036	HARMON	71280-71280	STERLINGTON	71428-71428	FLORA		
71037-71037	HAUGHTON	71281-71281	SWARTZ	71429-71429	FLORIEN		
71038-71038	HAYNESVILLE	71282-71284	TALLULAH	71430-71430	FOREST HILL		
71039-71039	HEFLIN	71286-71286	TRANSYLVANIA	71431-71431	GARDNER		
71040-71040	HOMER	71291-71294	WEST MONROE	71432-71432	GEORGETOWN		
71043-71043	HOSSTON	71295-71295	WINNSBORO	71433-71433	GLENMORA		
71044-71044	IDA	71301-71315	ALEXANDRIA	71434-71434	GORUM		
71045-71045	JAMESTOWN	71316-71316	ACME	71435-71435	GRAYSON		
71046-71046	KEATCHIE	71318-71318	BIG BEND	71436-71436	HEBERT		
71047-71047	KEITHVILLE	71320-71320	BORDELONVILLE	71437-71437	HICKS		
71048-71048	LISBON	71321-71321	BUCKEYE	71438-71438	HINESTON		
71049-71049	LOGANSPORT	71322-71322	BUNKIE	71439-71439	HORNBECK		
71050-71050	LONGSTREET	71323-71323	CENTER POINT	71440-71440	JOYCE		
71051-71051	ELM GROVE	71324-71324	CHASE	71441-71441	KELLY		
71052-71052	MANSFIELD	71325-71325	CHENEYVILLE	71443-71443	KURTHWOOD		
71055-71058	MINDEN	71326-71326	CLAYTON	71444-71444	LACAMP		
71059-71059	MIRA	71327-71327	COTTONPORT	71445-71445	LEANDER		
71060-71060	MOORINGSPORT	71328-71328	DEVILLE	71446-71446	LEESVILLE		
71061-71061	OIL CITY	71329-71329	DUPONT	71447-71447	LENA		
71063-71063	PELICAN	71330-71330	ECHO	71448-71448	LONGLEAF		
71064-71064	PLAIN DEALING	71331-71331	EFFIE	71449-71449	MANY		
71065-71065	PLEASANT HILL	71333-71333	EVERGREEN	71450-71450	MARTHAVILLE		
71066-71066	POWHATAN	71334-71334	FERRIDAY	71451-71451	MELDER		
71067-71067	PRINCETON	71335-71335	FROGMORE	71452-71452	MELROSE		
71068-71068	RINGGOLD	71336-71336	GILBERT	71454-71454	MONTGOMERY		
71069-71069	RODESSA	71338-71338	GOUDEAU	71455-71455	MORA		
71070-71070	SALINE	71339-71339	HAMBURG	71456-71456	NATCHEZ		

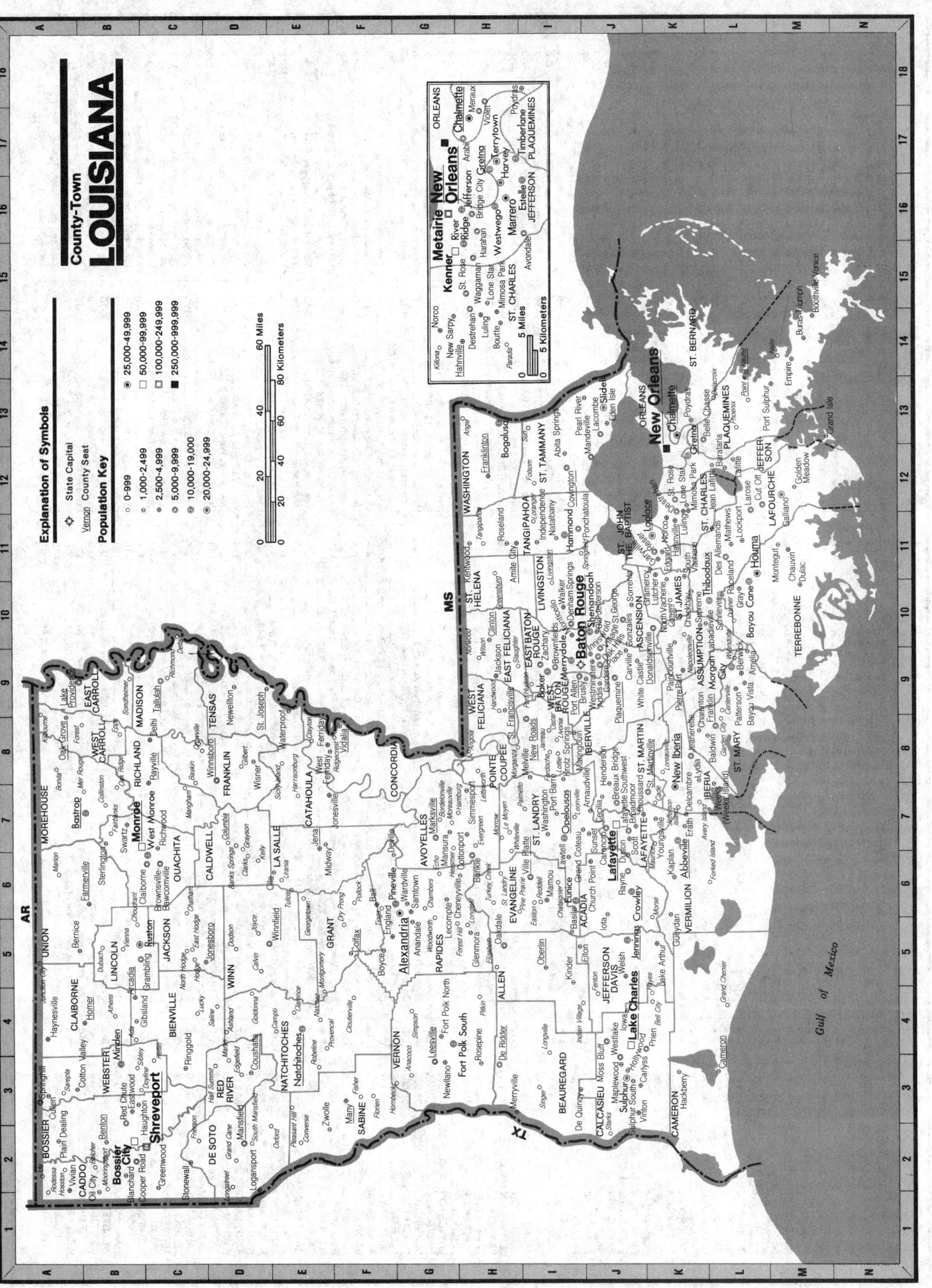

LOUISIANA

County-Town

Explanation of Symbols

✪ State Capital

Vernon County Seat

Population Key

⊙ 0-999
⊕ 1,000-2,499
⊛ 2,500-4,999
◉ 5,000-9,999
◉ 10,000-19,000
□ 20,000-24,999
◉ 25,000-49,999
□ 50,000-99,999
□ 100,000-249,999
■ 250,000-999,999

Explanation of symbols: ● – Census Designated Place (CDP)

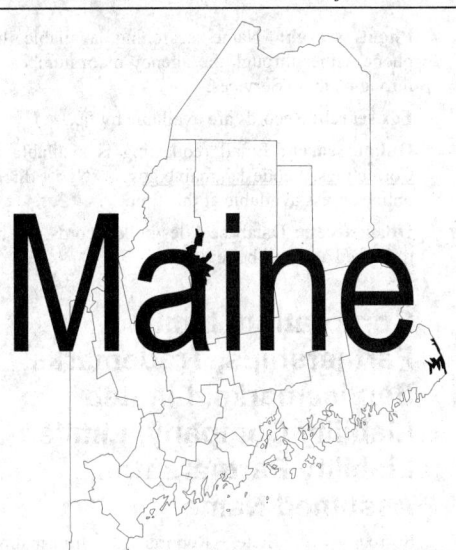

Maine

General Help Numbers:

Governor's Office
1 State House Station, Room 236
Augusta, ME 04333-0001
www.state.me.us/governor

207-287-3531
Fax 207-287-1034
7:30AM-5:30PM

Attorney General's Office
6 State House Station
Augusta, ME 04333
www.state.me.us/ag

207-626-8800
Fax 207-626-8828
8AM-5PM

Legislative Records
Maine Legislature, 2 State House Station
Legislative Document Room
Augusta, ME 04333-0002
http://janus.state.me.us/legis

207-287-1692
Fax 207-287-1456
8AM-5PM

State Archives
84 State House Station
Augusta, ME 04333-0084
www.state.me.us/sos/arc

207-287-5795
Fax 207-287-5739
8:30AM-4PM

State Specifics:

Capital:	Augusta Kennebec County
Time Zone:	EST
Number of Counties:	16
Population:	1,305,728
Web Site:	www.state.me.us

State Agencies

Criminal Records

Maine State Police, State Bureau of Identification, 500 Civic Center Dr, Augusta, ME 04333; 207-624-7240, 207-287-3421 (Fax), 8AM-5PM.

www.informe.org/PCR/

Indexing & Storage: Records are available from 1937 on. It takes 1 to 2 days before new records are available for inquiry. Records are indexed on computer (43%) and court index cards. Records are normally destroyed after 99 years, if no activity within last five years.

Searching: Requests must be in writing. Will only do FBI fingerprint checks as authorized by Maine Statutes. Records are updated as often as courts submit records. Include the following in request-name, date of birth, any aliases, purpose of the inquiry and name and address of requester. Fingerprints are optional. Include maiden name for females. 63% of the records are fingerprint-supported. Fingerprints generally are submitted with arrest information by the police. The following data is not released: juvenile records.

Access by: mail, fax, in person, online.

Fee & Payment: The search fee is $25.00 (unless requester is Maine resident ordering online). Fee payee: Treasurer, State of Maine. Personal checks accepted. Credit cards accepted at website.

Mail search: Turnaround time: 1 week.

Fax search: Records may be requested by fax, but only in approved emergency situations.

In person search: This only saves mail-in time; records are returned by mail.

Online search: One may request a record search at www.informe.org/PCR/. Results are usually returned via e-mail in 2 hours. Fee is $25.00, unless requester is an in-state subscriber to InforME, then fee is $15.00 per record. There is a $75.00 annual fee to be a subscriber.

Statewide Court Records

State Court Administrator, PO Box 4820, Portland, ME 04112; 207-822-0792, 207-822-0781 (Fax), 8AM-4PM.

www.courts.state.me.us

Note: Access to trial court records is not available from a central location. Except for certain online research capabilities, all court record access must be done at the local level.

Access by: online.

Online search: The website offers access to Maine Supreme Court opinions and administrative orders, but not all documents are available online. Also, the site offers online access to trial court schedules by region and case type.

Sexual Offender Registry

State Bureau of Investigation, 36 Hospital St., Attn: SOR, Augusta, ME 04333; 207-624-7009, 207-624-7088 (Fax), 8AM-5PM.

www.state.me.us/dps/

Indexing & Storage: Records are available from 06/30/92 to present. It takes 1 to 2 days before new records are available for inquiry.

Searching: Include the following in your request-name, date of birth, any aliases. The following data is not released: juvenile records.

Access by: mail, phone, fax, in person, online.

Fee & Payment: There is no fee.

Mail search: Turnaround time: 1-2 days. A SASE is requested.

Phone search: Will confirm by phone.

Fax search: Records are available by fax for ongoing requesters with lists.

In person search: Record information released for small request amounts.

Online search: Search at www.informe.org/sor/. Search by name, town or ZIP Code. Information is only provided for those individuals that are required to register pursuant to Title 34-A MRSA, Chapter 15. Records date to 06/30/92 forward. The date of the last address verification is indicated next to the registrant's address.

Other access: The entire database is for sale.

Incarceration Records

Maine Department of Corrections, Inmate Records, 111 State House Station, Augusta, ME 04333; 207-287-2711, 207-287-4381 (Probation info), 800-968-6909 (Victim Services/Inmate info), 207-287-4370 (Fax), 8AM-4:30PM.

www.state.me.us/corrections

Indexing & Storage: Records are available on current and former inmates. It takes 1 to 2 days before new records are available for inquiry. Records are normally destroyed after never - archived seven years after release.

Searching: One may also do a search by sending an email to Corrections.Webdesk@maine.gov. Include your full name, address, and reasons for the search. Public information is provided. Include the following in your request-name, date of birth, any aliases. Fingerprints are optional.

Access by: mail, phone, fax, email.

Fee & Payment: There is no fee.

Mail search: Turnaround time: 1-2 weeks. A SASE is requested.

Phone search: Name searching available by phone, either through the agency main number or through Victim Services.

Fax search: Records are available by fax.

Online search: Email requesting is available at Corrections.Webdesk@maine.gov. No direct online access available at this time.

Other access: Database sales/bulk records can be requested and will be reviewed.

Corporation, Limited Partnerships, Trademarks, Servicemarks, Limited Liability Company, Limited Liability Partnerships, Assumed Name,

Secretary of State, Reports & Information Division, 101 State House Station, Augusta, ME 04333-0101; 207-624-7752, 207-624-7736 (Main Number), 207-287-5874 (Fax), 8AM-5PM.

www.state.me.us/sos/cec/corp

Indexing & Storage: Records are available from 1700's on. The older records are in law books. Records on the in-house computer are for all active and some inactive corporations. New records are available for inquiry immediately. Records are indexed on index cards, inhouse computer.

Searching: Include the following in your request-full name of business, specific records that you need copies of. In addition to the articles of incorporation, corporation records include the following information: Annual Reports (back to 1972), Officers, Directors, Prior (merged) names, Inactive and Reserved names.

Access by: mail, phone, fax, in person, online.

Fee & Payment: Copies are $2.00 per page if plain and $5.00 if certified. A Certificate of Existence is $30.00 and $10.00 if not for profit. Fee payee: Secretary of State. They will invoice for copies. Personal checks accepted. MasterCard and Visa accepted.

Mail search: Turnaround time: 1 week. No SASE is required.

Phone search: They will provide names and addresses of officers and directors over the phone.

Fax search: Records are available by fax.

In person search: See expedited service.

Online search: Basic information about the entity including address, corp ID, agent, and status is found at www.informe.org/icrs/ICRS. A commercial subscriber account gives extensive information and ability to download files.

Other access: Lists of new entities filed with this office are available monthly.

Expedited service: Expedited service is available for mail and phone searches. Turnaround time: 24 hours. Add $50.00 per business name. For immediate service, the fee is $100.00.

Uniform Commercial Code, Federal and State Tax Liens

Secretary of State, UCC Records Section, 101 State House Station, Augusta, ME 04333-0101 (Courier: Burton McCross State Office Bldg, 109 Sewell St, 4th Fl, Augusta, ME 04333); 207-624-7760, 207-287-5874 (Fax), 8AM-5PM.

www.maine.gov/sos/cec/corp/ucc.htm

Indexing & Storage: Records are available from 1964. Records are computerized since 1993. It takes 3 to 4 days before new records are available for inquiry. Records are indexed on computer. Records are normally destroyed after 5 years.

Searching: Use search request form UCC-11 when needed for certification or a form fabricated by this office. The search includes both federal and state tax liens. Searching is done by index number or debtor name only. Try to include a middle initial in your request. They will not search by address or collateral or secured party.

Access by: mail, phone, fax, in person, online.

Fee & Payment: Searches cost $20.00 per name, $12.00 if online. Certification is $5.00. Fee payee: Secretary of State. Prepayment required. Ongoing requesters may make arrangements for invoicing. Personal checks accepted. No credit cards accepted.

Mail search: Turnaround time: a maximum of 5 days. If update or certain dates requested, state boldly. No SASE is required.

Phone search: Limited information is available by phone. Usually this is limited to only those listed on the filing.

Fax search: Same criteria as mail requests. Up to 15 pages will be returned as long as request is in writing.

In person search: There are 2 public access terminals. If copies are needed, written request required and fees apply, see expedited services below.

Online search: Online access for official records is available at www.sosonline.org. Fees are involved. There is a free search of the index to find names or name variations at this site.

Other access: Farm products - buyers reports, secured party available in bulk.

Expedited service: Expedited service is available for mail searches. The Maine specific UCC-11 request form has a box to check if expedited service requested. Add $10.00 per name for overnight, $25.00 if immediate. If by mail, write and highlight the word "Expedite" on request.

Sales Tax Registrations

Maine Revenue Services, Sales, Fuel & Special Tax Division, 24 State House Station, Augusta, ME 04333; 207-624-9693, 207-287-6628 (Fax), 8AM-4PM.

www.maine.gov/revenue

Indexing & Storage: Records are available from 1993, on computer. It takes up to 2 months before new records are available for inquiry.

Searching: This agency will only confirm that a business is registered. They will provide no other information. Include the following in your request-business name. They will also search by tax permit number or federal ID.

Access by: mail, phone, fax, in person.

Mail search: Turnaround time: 7 to 10 days. A SASE is requested. No fee for mail request.

Phone search: No fee for telephone request.

Fax search: Same criteria as mail searching.

In person search: No fee for request.

Birth Certificates

Maine Department of Human Services, Vital Records, 221 State St, Station 11, Augusta, ME

04333-0011; 207-287-3181, 877-523-2659 (VitalChek), 207-287-1093 (Fax), 8AM-5PM.

www.state.me.us/dhs/vitalrecords.htm

Note: The website has a link to VitalChek for online ordering.

Indexing & Storage: Records are available from 1923 to present. Maine State Archives has records prior to 1923 (call 207-287-5795). Records are indexed on computer from 1975 to present, and on microfiche from 1892 to present. It takes up to one month before new records are available for inquiry. Records are indexed on books (volumes).

Searching: Must give relationship to person of record and reason for request. Confidential information will not be released except to the person listed on the birth certificate. Include the following in your request-full name, names of parents, mother's maiden name, date of birth, place of birth. Also include your daytime phone number with the request. The following data is not released: illegitimate births or adoption records.

Access by: mail, phone, in person.

Fee & Payment: $10.00 fee for certified copy, add $4.00 per name for additional copy of same record. Fee payee: Treasurer, State of Maine. Prepayment required. Personal checks accepted. Major credit cards accepted.

Mail search: Turnaround time: 1 to 2 weeks. Specific dates are needed to search as well as names (if available).

Phone search: See expedited service.

In person search: Turnaround time immediate.

Other access: Physical birth lists are available for purchase, excluding restricted information.

Expedited service: Expedited service is available for mail, phone and fax searches. Turnaround time: 1-5 days. Use of credit card is required. Add fee of $26.95 for 1-3 days service or $19.95 for 3-5 days service.

Death Records

Maine Department of Human Services, Vital Records, 221 State St, Station 11, Augusta, ME 04333-0011; 207-287-3181, 877-523-2659 (VitalChek), 207-287-1093 (Fax), 8AM-5PM.

www.state.me.us/dhs/vitalrecords.htm

Note: The website has a link to VitalChek for online ordering.

Indexing & Storage: Records are available from 1923 to present. Maine State Archives has records prior to 1923 (call 207-287-5795). Records are indexed on computer from 1975 to present, and on microfiche from 1892 to present. It takes up to 1 month before new records are available for inquiry. Records are indexed on books (volumes).

Searching: Access to cause of death is restricted to those with a legitimate interest in the information. All information on certificate of death is confidential, except name, age, date of death, as well as city/town where death occurred. Include the following in your request-full name, date of death, place of death, relationship to person of record.

Access by: mail, phone, in person, online.

Fee & Payment: $10.00 fee for certified copy, add $4.00 per name for additional copy of same record. Fee payee: Treasurer, State of Maine. Prepayment required. Personal checks accepted. Major credit cards accepted.

Mail search: Turnaround time: 1 to 2 weeks. When requesting a search, keep in mind that records are filed by the date of the death, and then by name. SASE required.

Phone search: See expedited service.

In person search: Turnaround time immediate.

Online search: A free genealogy site at http://vitals.rootsweb.com/me/death/search.cgi has Death Indexes from 1960-1997. Search by surname, given name, place or year. Also Search death records 1960 thru 1996 at www.state.me.us/sos/arc/geneology/homepage.html.

Other access: Bulk file purchases are available, with the exclusion of restricted data.

Expedited service: Expedited service is available for mail, phone and fax searches. Turnaround time: 1-5 days. Use of credit card is required. Add fee of $26.95 for 1-3 days service or $19.95 for 3-5 days service.

Marriage Certificates

Maine Department of Human Services, Vital Records, 221 State St, Station 11, Augusta, ME 04333-0011; 207-287-3181, 877-523-2659 (VitalChek), 207-287-1093 (Fax), 8AM-5PM.

www.state.me.us/dhs/vitalrecords.htm

Note: The website has a link to VitalChek for online ordering.

Indexing & Storage: Records are available from 1923 to present. Maine State Archives has records prior to 1923 (call 207-287-5795). Records are indexed on microfiche from 1892 to present. It takes up to one month before new records are available for inquiry. Records are indexed on books (volumes).

Searching: Must give relationship to persons of record and reason for request. Data recorded in the section of the certificate specified as confidential is not released (i.e. race, education, etc.). Include the following in your request-names of husband and wife, date of marriage, place or county of marriage.

Access by: mail, phone, in person, online.

Fee & Payment: $10.00 fee for certified copy, add $4.00 per name for additional copy of same record. Fee payee: Treasurer, State of Maine. Prepayment required. Personal checks accepted. Major credit cards accepted.

Mail search: Turnaround time: 1 to 2 weeks.

Phone search: See expedited service.

In person search: Turnaround time is immediate.

Online search: Records are available at www.state.me.us/sos/arc/geneology/homepage.html from 1892-1966 and 1976-1996. Marriage History records from the Maine State Archives are available at http://thor.dafs.state.me.us/pls/archives/archdev.marriage_archive.search_form.

Other access: Bulk file purchasing is available, with restricted data excluded.

Expedited service: Expedited service is available for mail, phone and fax searches. Turnaround time: 1-5 days. Use of credit card is required. Add fee of $26.95 for 1-3 days service or $19.95 for 3-5 days service.

Divorce Records

Maine Department of Human Services, Office of Vital Records, 221 State St, Station 11, Augusta, ME 04333-0011; 207-287-3181, 877-523-2659 (VitalChek), 207-287-1093 (Fax), 8AM-5PM.

www.state.me.us/dhs/vitalrecords.htm

Note: The website has a link to VitalChek for online ordering.

Indexing & Storage: Records are available from 1892 to present. Maine State Archives has records prior to 1923, call 207-287-5795. It takes up to 1 month before new records are available for inquiry. Records are indexed on books (volumes).

Searching: Must give relationship to persons of record and reason for request. Include the following in your request-names of husband and wife, date of divorce, place of divorce.

Access by: mail, phone, in person.

Fee & Payment: $10.00 fee for certified copy, add $4.00 per name for additional copy of same record. Fee payee: Treasurer, State of Maine. Prepayment required. Personal checks accepted. Major credit cards accepted.

Mail search: Turnaround time: 1 to 2 weeks.

Phone search: See expedited service.

In person search: Turnaround time is while you wait for up to 2 requests.

Other access: Index information is available for bulk purchase.

Expedited service: Expedited service is available for phone requests. Turnaround time: 1-5 days. Use of credit card is required. Add fee of $26.95 for 1-3 days service or $19.95 for 3-5 days service.

Workers' Compensation Records

Workers Compensation Board, 27 State House Station, Augusta, ME 04333-0027; 207-287-7071, 207-287-5895 (Fax), 7:30AM-5PM.

www.state.me.us/

Note: Both pre AND post employment checks are not permitted.

Indexing & Storage: Records are available from 1984, indexed on computer. It takes 1 month before new records are available for inquiry. Records are normally destroyed after 6 years.

Searching: Records are considered confidential and are released "on a need-to-know basis." Include the following in your request-claimant name, Social Security Number, reason for information request. The following data is not released: personal information (height, weight, sex, eye color, etc.) or Social Security Numbers.

Access by: mail, in person.

Fee & Payment: The research fee is $5.00. Copies are $.50 per page. Fee payee: Trea. State of Maine, Workers' Compensation Board. When remitting payment, please include invoice number on your check. Personal checks accepted. No credit cards accepted.

Mail search: Turnaround time: 3 to 4 weeks. Requests should be addressed to: Linda Larrabee, Workers' Compensation Board, 27 State House Station, Augusta, ME 04333-0027. A SASE is requested.

In person search: Requests must still be in writing and prior approval is suggested.

Other access: Computer data is available, but requests are screened for purpose.

Driver Records

BMV - Driver License Services, 101 Hospital Street, 29 State House Station, Augusta, ME 04333-0029; 207-624-9000 x52116, 207-624-9090 (Fax), 8AM-5PM.

www.state.me.us/sos/bmv

Indexing & Storage: Records are available for 3 years for moving violations, DWIs and 3 years after the reinstatement of suspensions. Accidents are indicated on the record. It takes up to 30 days before new records are available for inquiry. Records are normally destroyed after filming.

Searching: Driving records and ticket information is released per DPPA guidelines. Personal information is not available to the general public unless the subject opts in, or a signed release is presented. The full name and DOB are required for a search. The driver's license number is optional. The following data is not released: medical information.

Access by: mail, fax, in person, online.

Fee & Payment: The fee is $5.00 for a non-certified record and $6.00 for a certified record, and $7.00 if accessed online. A "no record found" incurs a full charge, except for walk-in requesters. Fee payee: Secretary of State. Prepayment required. Personal checks accepted. No credit cards accepted.

Mail search: Turnaround time: 3 days. No SASE is required.

Fax search: Add $2.00 and results are returned by mail.

In person search: Up to 5 requests can be obtained in-person immediately; additional requests are available the next day.

Online search: Access is through InforME via the Internet. There is a $50.00 annual fee and records are $7.00 per request. Visit the website for details and sign-up or call 207-621-2600. The state offers "Driver Cross Check" - a program for employers, to provide notification when activity occurs on a specific record.

Vehicle Ownership, Vehicle Identification

Department of Motor Vehicles, Registration Section, 29 State House Station, Augusta, ME 04333-0029; 207-624-9000 x52149, 207-624-9204 (Fax), 8AM-5PM M-F.

www.state.me.us/sos/bmv/

Indexing & Storage: Records are available from 1982. It takes up to 30 days before new records are available for inquiry. Records are normally destroyed after three years.

Searching: Casual requesters can obtain records, but personal information is not included unless the subject gives authorization. Opt-in is available. Include the following in your request-full name and DOB, or by VIN or by license plate number. It is suggested to become an account holder.

Access by: mail, phone, fax, in person, online.

Fee & Payment: Fees: $6.00 for certified record; $5.00 for uncertified record. Will also fax record back for an additional $2.00. Fee payee: Secretary of State. Prepayment required. Personal checks accepted. Credit cards accepted.

Mail search: Turnaround time: 5 days. No SASE is required.

Phone search: Telephone searching is available for parties who establish an account. They are billed monthly.

Fax search: Established accounts may order by fax, and then have data returned by fax for an additional $2.00.

In person search: Immediate service limited to simple requests.

Online search: Maine offers online access to title and registration records through InfoMe. Fee is $5.00 per record. Records are available as interactive online, FTP or on CD. Contact InfoMe at info@informe.org.

Accident Reports

Maine State Police, Traffic Division, Station 20, Augusta, ME 04333-0020 (Courier: 397 Water St, Gardiner, ME 04345); 207-624-8944, 207-624-8945 (Fax), 8AM-5PM.

www.state.me.us/dps/msp

Note: Accidents must be reported involving death, injury, or property damage in excess of $1000.00.

Indexing & Storage: Records are available from 1975. Most records are on microfilm. It takes up to 30 days before new records are available for inquiry.

Searching: Most accident records are public information. All requests must be in writing. If a fatality is involved, the fatility report is not released until the court case is concluded. Include the following in your request-full name, date of birth, date of accident, location of accident. Be sure to order by the operator's name, not by vehicle owner name.

Access by: mail, in person.

Fee & Payment: The fee is $5.00 per copy for Police Traffic report, $10.00 for an Officers Investigative Report (fatality involved), $10.00 for an Accident Reconstruction Report, and $10.00 for a Vehicle Autopsy Report. Fee payee: Maine State Police. Prepayment required. Personal checks accepted. No credit cards accepted.

Mail search: Turnaround time: 7 days. No SASE is required.

In person search: Turnaround time is usually immediate for walk-in requesters.

Vessel Ownership, Vessel Registration

Dept of Inland Fisheries & Wildlife, Vessel Records, 41 State House Station, 284 State St, Augusta, ME 04333-0041; 207-287-5231, 207-287-8094 (Fax), 8AM-5PM.

www.state.me.us/ifw

Note: Liens are not recorded here and must be searched with UCCs.

Indexing & Storage: Records are available from 1987 to present for registrations that have been continuously renewed. There are no titles, all motorized boats must be registered. Records are indexed on computer. Records are normally destroyed after 7 years and number is re-issued.

Searching: Include the following in your request-name or registration number.

Access by: mail, phone, fax, in person.

Fee & Payment: The search fee is $5.00 per record for a name search. A boat history fee is $25.00. Fee payee: Treasurer, State of Maine. Prepayment required. Credit cards accepted: MasterCard, Visa, Discover.

Mail search: Turnaround time: 1 to 2 weeks. No SASE is required.

Phone search: Results will only be given verbally, if payment is arranged using a credit card.

Fax search: Turnaround time is within 72 hours. A credit card must be used for all fax searches.

In person search: Counter service available.

Voter Registration

Records not maintained by a state level agency.

Note: The data is considered public record in Maine, but can only be accessed at the municipality level.

GED Certificates

Dept of Education, Attn: GED, 23 State House Station, Augusta, ME 04333; 207-624-6752, 207-624-6731 (Fax), 8AM-5PM.

http://janus.state.me.us/education

Indexing & Storage: It takes 2 dyas before new records are available for inquiry.

Searching: Requests for transcripts must be in writing. To verify, all of the following is required: name, date of birth, and SSN. For transcripts, a signed release is required.

Access by: mail, phone, fax, in person, email.

Fee & Payment: There are no fees for verification or copy of transcript, but $13.00 for copy of the GED.

Mail search: Turnaround time 1-2 days. No SASE is required.

Phone search: You can do a verification over the phone.

Fax search: Turnaround time 1-2 days.

In person search: Turnaround time is immediate.

Online search: Email requests can be made by sending email to: lisa.taylor@maine.gov

Hunting and Fishing License Information

Inland Fisheries & Wildlife Department, Licensing Division, 284 State St, Augusta, ME 04333; 207-287-5209, 207-287-8094 (Fax), 8AM-5PM.

www.state.me.us/ifw

Note: The state is in the process of computerizing license data. Licenses are issued online at the website. Also, licenses are issued by Town Clerks and approved businesses and forwarded monthly to this department.

Indexing & Storage: Records are available from 1996 to present. It takes at least 3 months, if not online before new records are available for inquiry. Records are indexed on inhouse computer.

Searching: All information is considered open to the public. Include the following in your request-full name, date of birth, address.

Access by: mail, phone, in person.

Fee & Payment: Individual searches are completed for $5.00 each. Fee payee: Treasurer, State of Maine. Prepayment required. Credit cards accepted: MasterCard, Visa.

Mail search: Turnaround time: 7 business days. No SASE is required.

Phone search: Credit card required.

In person search: Immediate service limited to simple requests.

Other access: Bulk data purchases are available at a cost of $.05 per name. Call InforME at 207-621-2600.

Maine State Licensing Agencies
Licenses Searchable Online

Acupuncturist #13	http://pfr.informe.org/webquery/LicLookup.aspx
Adult Day Service #9	www.state.me.us/dhs/beas/facilities/fac_main.php
Advanced Practice Registered Nurse #8	www.maine.gov/boardofnursing
Aesthetician #13	http://pfr.informe.org/webquery/LicLookup.aspx
Alcohol/Drug Abuse Counselor #13	http://pfr.informe.org/webquery/LicLookup.aspx
Ambulatory Surgical Center #9	http://licert.dhs.state.me.us
Animal Medical Technician #13	http://pfr.informe.org/webquery/LicLookup.aspx
Appraiser, Residential Real Estate #13	http://pfr.informe.org/webquery/LicLookup.aspx
Architect #13	http://pfr.informe.org/webquery/LicLookup.aspx
Assisted Living Facility #9	www.state.me.us/dhs/beas/facilities/fac_main.php
Athletic Trainer #13	http://pfr.informe.org/webquery/LicLookup.aspx
ATV-All-Terrain Vehicle #11	www.state.me.us/ifw/index.html
Auctioneer #13	http://pfr.informe.org/webquery/LicLookup.aspx
Barber #13	http://pfr.informe.org/webquery/LicLookup.aspx
Body Piercer #19	www.state.me.us/dhs/eng/el/index.html
Boiler #13	http://pfr.informe.org/webquery/LicLookup.aspx
Boxer #13	http://pfr.informe.org/webquery/LicLookup.aspx
Charitable Solicitation #13	http://pfr.informe.org/webquery/LicLookup.aspx
Child Care Resource #7	www.state.me.us/dhs/choosingbrochure.pdf
Chiropractor #13	http://pfr.informe.org/webquery/LicLookup.aspx
Cosmetologist #13	http://pfr.informe.org/webquery/LicLookup.aspx
Counselor #13	http://pfr.informe.org/webquery/LicLookup.aspx
Dental Hygienist #16	www.mainedental.org/search.htm
Dental Radiographer #16	www.mainedental.org/search.htm
Dentist #16	www.mainedental.org/search.htm
Denturist #16	www.mainedental.org/search.htm
Dietitian #13	http://pfr.informe.org/webquery/LicLookup.aspx
Electrician #13	http://pfr.informe.org/webquery/LicLookup.aspx
Elevator/Tramway #13	http://pfr.informe.org/webquery/LicLookup.aspx
Employee Leasing Company #15	www.state.me.us/pfr/ins/emplease.htm
Engineer #17	http://professionals.maineusa.com/engineers/database.html
Forester #13	http://pfr.informe.org/webquery/LicLookup.aspx
Fund Raiser #13	http://pfr.informe.org/webquery/LicLookup.aspx
Funeral Service #13	http://pfr.informe.org/webquery/LicLookup.aspx
Geologist #13	http://pfr.informe.org/webquery/LicLookup.aspx
Hearing Aid Dealer/Fitter #13	http://pfr.informe.org/webquery/LicLookup.aspx
HMO #15	www.state.me.us/pfr/ins/inshmo.htm
Home Health Agency #9	http://licert.dhs.state.me.us
Home Health Care Service Agency #9	http://licert.dhs.state.me.us
Hospice #9	http://licert.dhs.state.me.us
Hospital #9	http://licert.dhs.state.me.us
Insurance Adjuster #15	http://pfr.informe.org/webquery/LicLookup.aspx
Insurance Advisor #13	http://pfr.informe.org/webquery/LicLookup.aspx
Insurance Agency #15	http://pfr.informe.org/webquery/LicLookup.aspx
Insurance Agent/Company #13	http://pfr.informe.org/webquery/LicLookup.aspx
Insurance Company #15	http://pfr.informe.org/webquery/LicLookup.aspx
Insurance Consultant #15	http://pfr.informe.org/webquery/LicLookup.aspx
Insurance Producer #15	http://pfr.informe.org/webquery/LicLookup.aspx
Interior Designer #13	http://pfr.informe.org/webquery/LicLookup.aspx
Intermediate Care Facility for the Mentally Retarded #9	http://licert.dhs.state.me.us
Interpreter #13	http://pfr.informe.org/webquery/LicLookup.aspx
Investment Advisor #12	http://pfr.informe.org/webquery/LicLookup.aspx
Kickboxer #13	http://pfr.informe.org/webquery/LicLookup.aspx
Landscape Architect #13	http://pfr.informe.org/webquery/LicLookup.aspx

Licensed Practical Nurse #8	www.maine.gov/boardofnursing
Lobbyist #1	www.mainecampaignfinance.com/public/entity_list.asp?TYPE=LOB
Manicurist #13	http://pfr.informe.org/webquery/LicLookup.aspx
Manufactured Housing #13	http://pfr.informe.org/webquery/LicLookup.aspx
Marriage & Family Therapist #13	http://pfr.informe.org/webquery/LicLookup.aspx
Massage Therapist #13	http://pfr.informe.org/webquery/LicLookup.aspx
Medical Doctor #23	www.docboard.org/me/df/mesearch.htm
Naturopathic Physician #13	http://pfr.informe.org/webquery/LicLookup.aspx
Notary Public #24	www.state.me.us/sos/cec/rcn/notary/notlist.htm
Nurse #8	www.maine.gov/boardofnursing
Nursing Home #9	http://licert.dhs.state.me.us
Nursing Home Administrator #13	http://pfr.informe.org/webquery/LicLookup.aspx
Occupational Therapist #13	http://pfr.informe.org/webquery/LicLookup.aspx
Oil & Solid Fuel Professional/Company #13	http://pfr.informe.org/webquery/LicLookup.aspx
Optometrist #18	http://pfr.informe.org/webquery/LicLooKup.aspx
Osteopathic Physician/Phys. Assist. #26	www.docboard.org/me-osteo/df/index.htm
Osteopathic Resident/Intern #26	www.docboard.org/me-osteo/df/index.htm
Pastoral Counselor #13	http://pfr.informe.org/webquery/LicLookup.aspx
Pharmacist #13	http://pfr.informe.org/webquery/LicLookup.aspx
Physical Therapist #13	http://pfr.informe.org/webquery/LicLookup.aspx
Physician Assistant #23	www.docboard.org/me/df/mesearch.htm
Plumber #13	http://pfr.informe.org/webquery/LicLookup.aspx
Podiatrist #13	http://pfr.informe.org/webquery/LicLookup.aspx
Preferred Provider Organization #15	www.state.me.us/pfr/ins/insppo.htm
Psychologist #13	http://pfr.informe.org/webquery/LicLookup.aspx
Public Accountant-CPA #13	http://pfr.informe.org/webquery/LicLookup.aspx
Radiologic Technician #13	http://pfr.informe.org/webquery/LicLookup.aspx
Real Estate Appraiser, General #13	http://pfr.informe.org/webquery/LicLookup.aspx
Real Estate Appraiser/Trainee #13	http://pfr.informe.org/webquery/LicLookup.aspx
Real Estate Broker #13	http://pfr.informe.org/webquery/LicLookup.aspx
Registered Professional Nurse #8	www.maine.gov/boardofnursing
Reinsurance Intermediary #15	http://pfr.informe.org/webquery/LicLookup.aspx
Re-insurer, Approved #15	http://pfr.informe.org/webquery/LicLookup.aspx
Renal Disease (End Stage) Facility #9	http://licert.dhs.state.me.us
Respiratory Care Therapist #13	http://pfr.informe.org/webquery/LicLookup.aspx
Risk Purchasing Group #15	www.state.me.us/pfr/ins/meriskpurchasinggroups.htm
Risk Retention Group #15	www.state.me.us/pfr/ins/meriskretentiongroups.htm
Securities Agent/Broker #12	http://pfr.informe.org/webquery/LicLookup.aspx
Snowmobile #11	www.state.me.us/ifw/index.html
Social Worker #13	http://pfr.informe.org/webquery/LicLookup.aspx
Soil Scientist #13	http://pfr.informe.org/webquery/LicLookup.aspx
Speech Pathologist/Audiologist #13	http://pfr.informe.org/webquery/LicLookup.aspx
Substance Abuse Counselor #13	http://pfr.informe.org/webquery/LicLookup.aspx
Surplus Lines Company #15	http://pfr.informe.org/webquery/LicLookup.aspx
Surveyor, Land #13	http://pfr.informe.org/webquery/LicLookup.aspx
Third Party Adminstrator #15	http://pfr.informe.org/webquery/LicLookup.aspx
Utilization Review Entity #15	www.state.me.us/pfr/ins/insmedur.htm
Vendor, Itinerant/Transient #13	http://pfr.informe.org/webquery/LicLookup.aspx
Veterinarian/Veterinary Technician #13	http://pfr.informe.org/webquery/LicLookup.aspx
Viatical Settlements Provider #15	www.state.me.us/pfr/ins/viaticalsettlementproviders.htm
Watercraft #11	www.state.me.us/ifw/index.html
Wrestler #13	http://pfr.informe.org/webquery/LicLookup.aspx

Maine Licensing Quick Finder

Acupuncturist #13	207-624-8603
Adoption Agency #7	207-287-5060
Adult Day Service #9	207-287-9250
Adult/Child Homes, Inspection #20	207-624-8744
Aesthetician #13	207-624-8603
Air Quality Control Business #5	207-287-2437
Alcohol/Drug Abuse Counselor #13	207-624-8603
Alcoholic Beverage Distributor #21	207-624-8745
Ambulance Attendant #10	207-287-3953
Ambulatory Surgical Center #9	207-287-9300
Animal Medical Technician #13	207-624-8603
Appraiser, Resident'l Real Estate #13	207-624-8616
Architect #13	207-624-8522
Assisted Living Facility #9	207-287-9250
Athletic Trainer #13	207-624-8624
Attorney #22	207-623-1121
ATV-All-Terrain Vehicle #11	207-287-2043
Auctioneer #13	207-624-8521
Bank #14	207-624-8648
Barber #13	207-624-8579
Beekeeper #3	207-287-3117
Body Piercer #19	207-287-5671
Boiler #13	207-624-8606
Bottle Club #21	207-624-8745
Boxer #13	207-624-8603
Brewery/Winery #21	207-624-8745
Campground #19	207-287-5671
Charitable Solicitation #13	207-624-8624
Child Care Resource #7	207-287-5060
Children's Camp #19	207-287-5671
Chiropractor #13	207-624-8634
Circus/Carnival #20	207-624-8735
Commercial Shellfish #27	207-624-6550
Compressed Air Producer (Breathing) #19	207-287-5671
Construction Plan Review #20	207-624-8735
Cosmetologist #13	207-624-8620
Counselor #13	207-624-8626
Credit Union #14	207-624-8648
Dance Hall, Inspection #20	207-624-8744
Day Care #7	207-287-5060
Dental Hygienist #16	207-287-4746
Dental Radiographer #16	207-287-4746
Dentist #16	207-287-4746
Denturist #16	207-287-4746
Dietitian #13	207-624-8611
Eating Place #19	207-287-5671
Electrician #13	207-624-8611
Electrologist #19	207-287-5671
Elevator/Tramway #13	207-624-8672
Emergency Medical Technician #10	207-287-3953
Employee Leasing Company #15	207-624-8475
Engineer #17	207-287-3236
Explosive #20	207-624-8744
Firearm Permit, Concealed #25	207-624-8775
Fireworks #20	207-624-8744
First Responder #10	207-287-3953
Forester #13	207-624-8521
Foster Care #7	207-287-5060

Fund Raiser #13	207-624-8624
Funeral Service #13	207-624-8623
Games of Chance	
Games of Chance #25	207-624-8775
Geologist #13	207-624-8627
Hazardous Material/Solid Waste Operator #6	207-287-2651
Hearing Aid Dealer/Fitter #13	207-624-8674
HMO #15	207-624-8475
Home Health Agency #9	207-287-9300
Home Health Care Svc Agency #9	207-287-9300
Hospice #9	207-287-9300
Hospital #9	207-287-9300
Insurance Adjuster #15	207-624-8475
Insurance Advisor #13	207-624-8545
Insurance Agency #15	207-624-8475
Insurance Agent/Company #13	207-624-8545
Insurance Company #15	207-624-8475
Insurance Consultant #15	207-624-8475
Insurance Producer #15	207-624-8475
Interior Designer #13	207-624-8522
Intermediate Care Facility for the Mentally Retarded #9	207-287-9300
Interpreter #13	207-624-8624
Investment Advisor #12	207-624-8551
Kickboxer #13	207-624-8603
Landscape Architect #13	207-624-8522
Library Media Specialist #4	207-624-6603
Limited Purpose Bank #14	207-624-8648
Liquor Salesperson #21	207-624-8745
Liquor Store #21	207-624-8745
Liquor Wholesaler #21	207-624-8745
Lobbyist #1	207-287-6221
Lobster Harvester #27	207-624-6550
Lottery Retailer #2	207-287-3721
Manicurist #13	207-624-8603
Manufactured Housing #13	207-624-8612
Marine Worm Digger #27	207-624-6550
Marriage & Family Therapist #13	207-624-8626
Massage Therapist #13	207-624-8613
Mechanical Ride, Inspection #20	207-624-8735
Medical Doctor #23	207-287-3601
Micropigmentation Practitioner #19	207-287-5671
Motor Vehicle Race #20	207-624-8735
Naturopathic Physician #13	207-624-8603
Notary Public #24	207-624-7650
Nursery School, Inspection #20	207-624-8744
Nursing Home #9	207-287-9300
Nursing Home Administrator #13	207-624-8623
Occupational Therapist #13	207-624-8626
Oil & Solid Fuel Professional/Company #13	207-624-8672
On & Off Premise Liquor License #21	207-624-8745
Optometrist #18	207-624-8691
Osteopathic Physician Extender #26	207-287-2480
Osteopathic Physician/Phys.Assist.#26	207-287-2480
Osteopathic Resident/Intern #26	207-287-2480
Paramedic #10	207-287-3953
Pastoral Counselor #13	207-624-8626

Pesticide Applicator #3	207-287-2731
Pesticide Dealer #3	207-287-2731
Pharmacist #13	207-624-8620
Physical Therapist #13	207-624-8628
Physician Assistant #23	207-287-3601
Pilot #13	207-624-8620
Plumber #13	207-624-8628
Podiatrist #13	207-624-8626
Polygraph Examiner #20	207-624-7074
Preferred Provider Organization #15	207-624-8475
Private Investigator #25	207-624-8775
Propane/LPGas Operator/Delivery #13	207-624-8610
Propane/LPGas Technician #13	207-624-8610
Psychologist #13	207-624-8628
Public Accountant-CPA #13	207-582-8627
Radiologic Technician #13	207-624-8628
Real Estate Appraiser, General #13	207-624-8616
Real Estate Appraiser/Trainee #13	207-624-8616
Real Estate Broker #13	207-624-8603
Reinsurance Intermediary #15	207-624-8475
Re-insurer, Approved #15	207-624-8475
Renal Disease (End Stage) Facility #9	207-287-9300
Residential Child Care Provider #7	207-287-5060
Respiratory Care Therapist #13	207-624-8616
Risk Purchasing Group #15	207-624-8475
Risk Retention Group #15	207-624-8475
Savings & Loan #14	207-624-8648
School Guidance Counselor #4	207-624-6603
School Library Media Specialist #4	207-624-6603
School Principal/Superintendent #4	207-624-6603
Sea Urchin Harvester #27	207-624-6550
Seaweed Harvester #27	207-624-6550
Securities Agent/Broker #12	207-624-8551
Security Company, Guard/Alarm #25	207-624-8775
Self Insurance Company #15	207-624-8475
Snowmobile #11	207-287-2043
Social Worker #13	207-624-8631
Soil Scientist #13	207-624-8603
Special Catering Permit (Liquor) #21	207-624-8745
Speech Pathologist/Audiologist #13	207-624-8634
Storage Tanks, Above Ground #20	207-624-8735
Substance Abuse Counselor #13	207-624-8634
Surplus Lines Company #15	207-624-8475
Surveyor, Land #13	207-624-8611
Swimming Pool #19	207-287-5671
Tattoo Artist #19	207-287-5671
Taxidermist #11	207-287-2751
Teacher #4	207-624-6603
Theatre #20	207-624-8744
Third Party Adminstrator #15	207-624-8475
Tobacco Retailer #19	207-287-5671
Trust Company #14	207-624-8648
Utilization Review Entity #15	207-624-8475
Vendor, Itinerant/Transient #13	207-624-8624
Veterinarian/Veterinary Technician #13	207-624-8628
Viatical Settlements Provider #15	207-624-8475
Watercraft #11	207-287-2043
Wrestler #13	207-624-8603

Maine Licensing Agency Information

1 Registrar, Commission on Governmental Ethics & Elections, State House Station 135, Augusta, ME 04333; 207-287-6221, Fax: 207-287-6775. www.state.me.us/ethics
Search Database at www.mainecampaig nfinance.com/public/entity_list.asp?TYPE=LOB

2 Department of Administrative & Financial Services, Bureau of Alcoholic Beverages & Lottery Operations, 8 State House Station, Augusta, ME 04333-0008; 207-287-3721, Fax: 207-287-6769. www.mainelottery.com

3 Department of Agriculture, Food & Rural Resources, Board of Pesticides Control, 280 State House Station, Augusta, ME 04332-0028; 207-287-2731, Fax: 207-287-7548. www.state.me.us/agriculture/pesticides/ Email: gary.fish@maine.gov

4 Department of Education, Certification Office, 23 State House Station, Augusta Complex, Augusta, ME 04333-0023; 207-624-6603, Fax: 207-624-6604. www.state.me.us/education/homepage.htm Email: Pat.Julien@state.me.us
Note: Make labels for school mailing lists at www.state.me.us/education/labels/labels.htm.

5 Department of Environmental Protection, Bureau of Air Quality Control, 17 State House Station, Augusta, ME 04333-0017; 207-287-2437, Fax: 207-287-7641. www.maine.gov/dep/air/

6 Department of Environmental Protection, Bureau/Hazardous Materials & Solid Waste Control, State House Station 17, Augusta, ME 04333; 207-287-2651, Fax: 207-287-7826. www.state.me.us/dep/staff.htm

7 Department of Human Services, Office of Child Care, 221 State St, 11 State House Station, Augusta, ME 04333-0011; 207-287-5060, Fax: 207-287-5282. www.state.me.us/dhs/occhs.htm Email: childcare.info@state.me.us

8 Department of Professional & Financial Regulation, Maine State Board of Nursing, # 158 State House Station, Augusta, ME 04333-0158; 207-287-1133, Fax: 207-287-1149. www.maine.gov/boardofnursing Email: virginia.e.delormier@state.me.us

9 Department of Human Services, Division of Licensing and Certification, 11 SHS, Augusta, ME 04333; 207-287-9300, Fax: 207-287-9304. www.state.me.us/bms/ Search Database at http://licert.dhs.state.me.us

10 Department of Public Safety, Main Emergency Medical Svcs, 16 Edison Dr, Augusta, ME 04333; 207-287-3953, Fax: 207-289-6251. www.state.me.us/dps/ems Email: maine.ems@state.me.us

11 Department of Inland Fisheries & Wildlife, Licensing & Registration Division, 284 State St, 41 Statehouse Station, Augusta, ME 04333-0041; 207-287-8000, Fax: 207-287-8094. www.state.me.us/ifw/index.html Email: ifw@state.me.us   Search Database at www.state.me.us/ifw/index.html

12 Department of Professional & Financial Regulation, Office of Securities, 121 State House Station, Augusta, ME 04333; 207-624-8551, Fax: 207-624-8590. www.state.me.us/pfr/sec/sec_index.htm
Search Database at http://pfr.informe.org/webquery/LicLookup.aspx

13 Department of Professional & Financial Regulation, Office of Licensing & Registration, 35 State House Station, Augusta, ME 04333-0035; 207-624-8603, Fax: 207-624-8637. www.maineprofessionalreg.org   Search Database at www.state.me.us/pfr/olr/olr_disclaimer.htm

14 Department of Professional & Financial Regulation, Bureau of Financial Institutions, 36 State House Station, Augusta, ME 04333-0036; 207-624-8570, Fax: 207-624-8590. www.mainebankingreg.org

15 Department of Professional & Financial Regulation, Bureau of Insurance, State House Station 34, Augusta, ME 04333-0034; 207-624-8475, 624-8545, Fax: 207-624-8599. Email: webmaster_pfr@state.me.us

16 Board of Dental Examiners, 143 Statehouse Station, 2 Bangor St, Augusta, ME 04333-0143; 207-287-3333/4746, Fax: 207-287-8140. www.mainedental.org Email: anita.c.merrow@maine.gov
Search at www.mainedental.org/search.htm Note: To obtain lists of the above, contact Kim Haggan at 207-287-5459.

17 Professional Engineers Reg. Board, 92 State House Station, Augusta, ME 04333; 207-287-3236, Fax: 207-626-2309. Email: prexar.com   Search Database at http://profe ssionals.maineusa.com/engineers/database.html

18 Department of Professional & Financial Regulation, Board of Optometry, 113 State House Station, Augusta, ME 04333; 207-624-8691, Fax: 207-624-8691. www.state.me.us/pfr/auxboards/optometry/ Email: susan.a.giampetruzzi@maine.gov
Search Database at http://pfr.informe.org/webquery/LicLooKup.aspx

Note: The alternative search site is www.odfinder.org/LicSearch.asp.

19 Department of Human Services, Health Engineering, Eating & Lodging Program, 11 State House Station (161 Capitol St), Augusta, ME 04333-0011; 207-287-5671, Fax: 207-287-3165. www.state.me.us/dhs/eng/el/index.html Email: david.l.libby@maine.gov Note: Written requests may be mailed or faxed, only.

20 Department of Public Safety, Administrative Licensing & Permits, 18 Meadow Rd, 104 State House Station, Augusta, ME 04333-0042; 207-287-3619, Fax: 207-287-3042. www.state.me.us/dps

21 Department of Public Safety, Licensing & Inspection-Liquor, 164 State House Station, Augusta, ME 04333; 207-624-8745, Fax: 207-624-8767.

22 Board of Overseers of the Bar, PO Box 527 (97 Winthrop St), Augusta, ME 04332; 207-623-1121, Fax: 207-623-4175. www.mebaroverseers.org Email: board@mebaroverseers.org

23 Medical Doctor & Physician Assistant Licensing & Investigation, Board of Licensure in Medicine, 137 State House Station, 2 Bangor St, Augusta, ME 04333; 207-287-3601, Fax: 207-287-6590. www.docboard.org/me/me_home.htm Email: Tim.E.Terranova@state.me.us
Search at www.docboard.org/me/df/mesearch.htm

24 Secretary of State, Div of Elections & Commissions, Notary Public Section, 101 State House Station, Augusta, ME 04333-0101; 207-624-7650, Fax: 207-287-6545. www.state.me.us/sos/cec/rcn/notary/not.htm
Search Database at www.state.me.us/sos/cec/rcn/notary/not.htm

25 State Police Licensing Division, Department of Public Safety, 164 State House Station, Augusta, ME 04333; 207-624-8775, Fax: 207-624-8767.

26 State of Maine, Board of Osteopathic Licensure, 142 State House Station, Augusta, ME 04333-0142; 207-287-2480, Fax: 207-287-3015. www.docboard.org/me-osteo/ Email: susan.e.strout@maine.gov
Search Database at www.docboard.org/me-osteo/df/index.htm

27 Department of Marine Resources, Bureau of Marine Patrol, Licensing Division, 21 State House Station, Hallowell Annex-Baker Bldg, Augusta, ME 04333-0021; 207-624-6550, Fax: 207-624-6550.

Maine Federal Courts

The following list indicates the district and division name for each county in the state. If the bankruptcy court location is different from the district court, then the location of the bankruptcy court appears in parentheses.

County/Court Cross Reference

Androscoggin	Portland
Aroostook	Bangor
Cumberland	Portland
Franklin	Bangor
Hancock	Bangor
Kennebec	Bangor
Knox	Portland (Bangor)
Lincoln	Portland (Bangor)
Oxford	Portland
Penobscot	Bangor
Piscataquis	Bangor
Sagadahoc	Portland
Somerset	Bangor
Waldo	Bangor
Washington	Bangor
York	Portland

Standards for Federal Courts: The search fee is $20.00 per item (one party name or case number). Certification fee is $7.00 per document. Copy fee is $.50 per page. All fees standard unless noted in profile. Mail Search: always enclose a stamped self addressed envelope unless otherwise noted. Most courts accept fax requests or will suggest a copying/search vendor. Before releasing records, all courts require prepayment unless noted in profile.

Open records are located at the court unless otherwise noted. District courts index by defendant and plaintiff as well as by case number. Bankruptcy courts usually index by debtor and case number. While most courts now have their indexes on computer, many still maintain index card files as well.

The universal PACER sign-up number is 800-676-6856. Find PACER and the Party/Case Index on the Web at http://pacer.psc.uscourts.gov. PACER dial-up access is $.60 per minute. Also, courts offering internet access via RACER, PACER, Web-PACER or the new CM-ECF charge $.07 per page fee unless noted as free.

US District Court

District of Maine

Bangor Division Court Clerk, PO Box 1007, Bangor, ME 04402-1007 (courier: Room 357, 202 Harlow St, Bangor, ME 04401), 207-945-0575, Fax: 207-945-0362. www.med.uscourts.gov

Counties: Aroostook, Franklin, Hancock, Kennebec, Penobscot, Piscataquis, Somerset, Waldo, Washington.

Indexing & Storage: New cases available in the index immediately after filing date. Records are indexed and stored by year, then docket number for case files and by name for electronic index system.

Fee & Payment: Payment may be made by money order, cashier check, personal check. Payee: Clerk, U.S. District Court.

Phone Search: Any public record information will be released over the phone including the accession number.

Mail Search: A SASE not required.

In Person Search: Fee charged if court conducts your in person search for you.

PACER: PACER is available online at https://pacer.med.uscourts.gov. Records purged every 6 months. New records online after 1 day.

Electronic Filing: Electronic filing information online at https://ecf.med.uscourts.gov

Portland Division Court Clerk, 156 Federal St, Portland, ME 04101 (courier address: Use mail address for courier delivery) 207-780-3356, Fax: 207-780-3772. www.med.uscourts.gov

Counties: Androscoggin, Cumberland, Knox, Lincoln, Oxford, Sagadahoc, York.

Indexing & Storage: New cases available in the index immediately after filing date. Records are indexed and stored by year, then docket number for case files and by name for electronic index system.

Fee & Payment: Payment may be made by money order, cashier check, personal check. Payee: Clerk, U.S. District Court.

Phone Search: Any public record information will be released over the phone including accession numbers.

Mail Search: A SASE not required.

In Person Search: Fee charged if court conducts your in person search for you.

PACER: PACER is available online at https://pacer.med.uscourts.gov. Records purged every 6 months. New records online after 1 day.

Electronic Filing: Electronic filing information online at https://ecf.med.uscourts.gov

U.S. Bankruptcy Court

District of Maine

Bangor Division PO Box 1109, Bangor, ME 04402-1109 (courier address: 202 Harlow St, Bangor, ME 04401), 207-945-0348, Fax: 207-945-0304. www.meb.uscourts.gov

Counties: Aroostook, Franklin, Hancock, Kennebec, Knox, Lincoln, Penobscot, Piscataquis, Somerset, Waldo, Washington.

Indexing & Storage: Cases indexed by debtor as well as by case number. New cases available in the index immediately after filing date. Archived records are available within 2 weeks of shipment to the archives. The length of time records are retained depends on space; files are usually retained 3 years before being sent to the Boston Federal Records Center.

Fee & Payment: Payment may be made by money order, cashier check, business check. Personal checks are not accepted. Payee: United States Courts.

Phone Search: Automated voice case information service (VCIS) is available. Call VCIS at 800-650-7253 or 207-780-3755.

Mail Search: A SASE not required.

In Person Search: Fee charged if court conducts your in person search for you. There is no charge for docket data.

PACER: PACER is available online at http://pacer.meb.uscourts.gov. Records purged every two years. New civil records are online after 1 day.

Electronic Filing: Electronic filing information online at https://ecf.meb.uscourts.gov

Portland Division 537 Congress St, Portland, ME 04101 (courier address: P.O. Box 17575, Portland, ME 04112-8575), 207-780-3482, Fax: 207-780-3679. www.meb.uscourts.gov

Counties: Androscoggin, Cumberland, Oxford, Sagadahoc, York.

Indexing & Storage: Cases indexed by debtor as well as by case number. New cases available in the index immediately after filing date. Searches for cases filed prior to 1988 require the debtor's name. Automated searches require either the case number or debtor's name. Records from the court are available from the court immediately after docketing. Information through VCIS and Pacer is available 24 hours after docketing.

Fee & Payment: Payment may be made by money order, cashier check, business check. Personal checks are not accepted. Prepayment is required for individual requesters. Payee: U.S. Bankruptcy Court.

Phone Search: Only docket information available by phone. Automated voice case information service (VCIS) is available. Call VCIS at 800-650-7253 or 207-780-3755.

In Person Search: Fee charged if court conducts your in person search for you.

PACER: PACER is available online at http://pacer.meb.uscourts.gov. Records purged every two years. New civil records are online after 1 day.

Electronic Filing: Electronic filing information online at https://ecf.meb.uscourts.gov

Maine County Courts

Court	Jurisdiction	No. of Courts	How Organized
Superior Courts*	General	17	16 Counties
District Courts*	Limited	31	13 Districts
Probate Courts*	Special	16	

* Profiled in this Sourcebook.

Court	CIVIL								
	Tort	Contract	Real Estate	Min. Claim	Max. Claim	Small Claims	Estate	Eviction	Domestic Relations
Superior Courts*	X	X	X	No Min	No Max				X
District Courts*	X	X	X	No Min	No Max	$4500		X	X
Probate Courts*							X		X

Court	CRIMINAL				
	Felony	Misdemeanor	DWI/DUI	Preliminary Hearing	Juvenile
Superior Courts*	X	X	X	X	
District Courts*	X	X	X	X	X
Probate Courts*					

ADMINISTRATION

State Court Administrator, PO Box 4820, Portland, ME, 04112; 207-822-0792, Fax: 207-822-0781. www.state.me.us/courts

COURT STRUCTURE

One Superior Court, the court of general jurisdiction is located in each of Maine's sixteen counties, except for Aroostook County, which has two Superior Courts. Both Superior and District Courts handle misdemeanor and felony cases, with jury trials being held in Superior Court only. The District Court hears both civil and criminal and always sits without a jury.

Within the District Court is the Family Division, which hears all divorce and family matters, including child support and paternity cases. The District Court also hears child protection cases, and serves as Maine's juvenile court. Actions for protection from abuse or harassment, mental health, small claims cases and money judgments are filed in the District Court. Traffic violations are processed primarily through a centralized Violations Bureau, part of the District Court system. Prior to year 2001, District Courts accepted civil cases involving claims less than $30,000. Now, District Courts have jurisdiction concurrent with that of the Superior Court for all civil actions except cases vested in the Superior Court by statute.

ONLINE ACCESS

The website offers access to Maine Supreme Court opinions and administrative orders, but not all documents are available online. Also, the site offers online access to trial court schedules by region and case type. Some county level courts are online through a private vendor.

ADDITIONAL INFORMATION

Per administrative order, Maine Superior and District courts increased their search fees effective September 1st, 2003 as follows: 1) $15.00 for a search. Previously, most courts charged $0 for a search; 2) Copy fee: 1st page is $2.00, $1.00 each additional; 3) If mail requests do not include a self-addressed stamped envelope, then add an additional $5.00.

Most mail requests of a name search for full criminal history record information are returned to the sender, referring them to the State Bureau of Investigation. Mail requests that make a specific inquiry related to an identified case are responded to in writing, with appropriate copy and attestation fees.

PROBATE COURTS

Probate Courts are part of the county court system, not the state system. Even though the Probate Court may be housed with other state courts, it is on a different phone system and calls may not be transferred.

Androscoggin County

Androscoggin Superior Court PO Box 3660, Auburn, ME 04212-3660; 207-783-5450. Hours: 8AM-4:30PM (EST). *Felony, Misdemeanor, Civil Actions.*
Note: Effective 09/01/03, the search fees and copy fees listed are mandatory per adminstrative rule. Further, if a SASE is not supplied for mail searches, the court may charge an add'l $5.00.
Civil Records: Access: Phone, mail, in person. Only the court performs in person searches; visitors may not. Search fee: $15.00, includes both civil and criminal. Required to search: name, years to search; also helpful: address. Civil cases indexed by defendant, plaintiff. Civil records on index cards since 1977.
Criminal Records: Access: Mail, in person. Only the court performs in person searches; visitors may not. Search fee: $15.00, includes both civil and criminal. Required to search: name, years to search; also helpful: DOB. Criminal records go back to 1920s; on computer back to 1997.
General Information: No adoption, juvenile, impounded by judge, certain domestic matters. Copy fee: $2.00 1st page, $1.00 each add'l. Certification fee: $5.00. Payee: Androscoggin Superior Court. Personal checks accepted. Prepayment required. Mail requests: SASE required. Mail turnaround: 1 week.

Lewiston District Court - South 8 PO Box 1345, 71 Lisbon St., Lewiston, ME 04243-1345; Civil phone: 207-795-4801; Criminal phone: 207-795-4800. Hours: 8AM-4PM (EST). *Misdemeanor, Civil Actions, Eviction, Small Claims.*
Note: Effective 09/01/03, the search fees and copy fees listed are mandatory per adminstrative rule. Further, if a SASE is not supplied for mail searches, the court may charge an add'l $5.00.
Civil Records: Access: Mail, in person. Both court and visitors may perform in person searches. Search fee: $15.00, includes both civil and criminal. Required to search: name, years to search; also helpful: address. Civil cases indexed by defendant. Civil records on docket books from 1956-1987; on computer back to 1987.
Criminal Records: Access: Mail, in person. Both court and visitors may perform in person searches. Search fee: $15.00, includes both civil and criminal. Required to search: name, years to search, DOB; also helpful: address, SSN. Criminal records on computer back to 1987, docket books from 1956-1987.
General Information: No juvenile, protective custody records released. Copy fee: $2.00 1st page, $1.00 each add'l. Certification fee: $5.00. Payee: Maine District Court. Personal checks accepted. Prepayment required. Mail requests: SASE required. Mail turnaround time 1-2 days.

North Androscoggin District Court 11 2 Main St, Livermore Falls, ME 04254; 207-897-3800. Hours: 8AM-4PM T-Th (EST). *Misdemeanor, Civil Actions, Eviction, Small Claims.*
Note: Effective 09/01/03, the search fees and copy fees listed are mandatory per adminstrative rule. Further, if a SASE is not supplied for mail searches, the court may charge an add'l $5.00.
Civil Records: Access: Mail, in person. Both court and visitors may perform in person searches. Search fee: $15.00, includes both civil and criminal. Required to search: name, years to search, DOB. Civil cases indexed by defendant. Civil records on docket books, computerized since 12/01.
Criminal Records: Access: Mail, in person. Only the court performs in person searches; visitors may not. Search fee: $15.00, includes both civil and criminal. Required to search: name, years to search; also

helpful: DOB. Criminal records on computer since 1988, prior on docket books.
General Information: No juvenile, protective custody records released. Copy fee: $2.00 1st page, $1.00 each add'l. Certification fee: $5.00. Payee: Maine District Court. Personal checks accepted. Prepayment required. Mail requests: SASE required. Mail turnaround time up to 1 week.

Probate Court 2 Turner St, Auburn, ME 04210; 207-782-0281; Fax: 207-782-1135. Hours: 8:30AM-5PM (EST). *Probate.*

Aroostook County

Caribou Superior Court 144 Sweden St, #101, Caribou, ME 04736; 207-498-8125. Hours: 8AM-4PM (EST). *Felony, Misdemeanor, Civil Actions.*
Note: Effective 09/01/03, the search fees and copy fees listed are mandatory per adminstrative rule. Further, if a SASE is not supplied for mail searches, the court may charge an add'l $5.00.
Civil Records: Access: Mail, in person. Only the court performs in person searches; visitors may not. Search fee: $15.00, includes both civil and criminal. Required to search: name, years to search. Civil cases indexed by defendant, plaintiff. Civil records on docket books since 1960. All cases 1990 forward stored in Caribou Court.
Criminal Records: Access: Mail, in person. Only the court performs in person searches; visitors may not. Search fee: $15.00, includes both civil and criminal. Required to search: name, years to search; also helpful: DOB. Criminal records on docket books since 1960. All cases 1990 forward stored in Caribou Court.
General Information: No juvenile, protective custody records released. Copy fee: $2.00 1st page, $1.00 each add'l. Certification fee: $5.00. Payee: Treasurer, State of Maine or Superior Court. Personal checks accepted. Prepayment required. Mail requests: SASE required. Mail turnaround time 1 week.

Houlton Superior Court PO Box 457, Houlton, ME 04730; 207-532-6563. Hours: 8AM-4PM (EST). *Felony, Misdemeanor, Civil Actions.*
Note: The Court only holds record prior to 1990 and is open only on occasion. All cases since are located at the Superior Court in Caribou.

Caribou District Court - East 1 144 Sweden St, Caribou, ME 04736; 207-493-3144. Hours: 8AM-4PM (EST). *Misdemeanor, Civil Actions, Eviction, Small Claims.*
Note: Effective 09/01/03, the search fees and copy fees listed are mandatory per adminstrative rule. Further, if a SASE is not supplied for mail searches, the court may charge an add'l $5.00.
Civil Records: Access: Mail, in person. Only the court performs in person searches; visitors may not. Search fee: $15.00, includes both civil and criminal. Required to search: name, years to search. Civil cases indexed by defendant. Civil records on docket books since 1963, on computer from 10/01.
Criminal Records: Access: Mail, in person. Visitors must perform in person searches for themselves. Search fee: $15.00, includes both civil and criminal. Required to search: name, years to search; also helpful: DOB. Criminal records on computer since 1987 (includes traffic), docket books since 1963.
General Information: Public Access terminal is available. (Public access for criminal records only.) No juvenile or child protective records released. Copy fee: $2.00 1st page, $1.00 each add'l. Payee: Maine District Court. Personal checks accepted. Prepayment required. Mail requests: SASE required. Mail turnaround time 1 week.

District Court 2 PO Box 794 (27 Riverside Dr), Presque Isle, ME 04769; 207-764-2055. Hours: 8AM-4PM (EST). *Misdemeanor, Civil Actions, Eviction, Small Claims.*
Note: Effective 09/01/03, the search fees and copy fees listed are mandatory per adminstrative rule. Further, if a SASE is not supplied for mail searches, the court may charge an add'l $5.00.
Civil Records: Access: Mail, in person. Both court and visitors may perform in person searches. Search fee: $15.00, includes both civil and criminal. Required to search: name, years to search. Civil cases indexed by defendant. Civil records on computer since 1999, docket books since 1963.
Criminal Records: Access: Mail, in person. Visitors must perform in person searches for themselves. Search fee: $15.00, includes both civil and criminal. Required to search: name, years to search; also helpful: DOB. Criminal records on computer since 1987, docket books since 1963.
General Information: Public Access terminal is available. (Records go back to 1999.) No juvenile or child protective records released. Copy fee: $2.00 1st page, $1.00 each add'l. Certification fee: $5.00. Payee: Maine District Court. Personal checks accepted. Prepayment required. Mail requests: SASE required. Mail turnaround time 1 week.

Fort Kent District Court - District 1 Division of Western Aroostook, PO Box 473, Fort Kent, ME 04743; 207-834-5003. 8AM-4PM (EST). *Misdemeanor, Civil Actions, Eviction, Small Claims.*
Note: Effective 09/01/03, the search fees and copy fees listed are mandatory per adminstrative rule. Further, if a SASE is not supplied for mail searches, the court may charge an add'l $5.00.
Civil Records: Access: Phone, mail, in person. Only the court performs in person searches; visitors may not. Search fee: $15.00, includes both civil and criminal. Required to search: name, years to search. Civil cases indexed by defendant, plaintiff. Civil records are computerized since 08/01.
Criminal Records: Access: Phone, mail, in person. Only the court performs in person searches; visitors may not. Search fee: $15.00, includes both civil and criminal. Required to search: name, years to search. Criminal records on computer from 1988, on docket books from 1960-1988.
General Information: No juvenile, protective custody, impounded, mental health records released. Copy fee: $2.00 1st page, $1.00 each add'l. Certification fee: $5.00. Payee: Maine District Court. Personal checks accepted. Prepayment required. Mail requests: SASE required. Mail turnaround: 2-3 days.

Houlton District Court - South 2 PO Box 457, Houlton, ME 04730; 207-532-2147. Hours: 8AM-4PM (EST). *Misdemeanor, Civil Actions, Eviction, Small Claims.*
Note: Effective 09/01/03, the search fees and copy fees listed are mandatory per adminstrative rule. Further, if a SASE is not supplied for mail searches, the court may charge an add'l $5.00.
Civil Records: Access: Mail, in person. Both court and visitors may perform in person searches. Search fee: $15.00, includes both civil and criminal. Required to search: name, years to search; also helpful: address. Civil cases indexed by defendant, plaintiff. Civil records on docket books since 1960.
Criminal Records: Access: Mail, in person. Only the court performs in person searches; visitors may not. Search fee: $15.00, includes both civil and criminal. Required to search: name, years to search; also helpful: address, DOB. Criminal records on computer since June 1987, docket books since 1960.
General Information: No Juvenile or protective custody records released. Copy fee: $2.00 1st page,

$1.00 each add'l. Certification fee: $5.00. Payee: Maine District Court. Personal checks accepted. Prepayment required. Mail requests: SASE required. Mail turnaround time 2-3 days.

Madawaska District Court - West
PO Box 127, 645 E Main St, Madawaska, ME 04756; 207-728-4700. Hours: 8AM-4PM M,T,F (EST). *Misdemeanor, Civil Actions, Eviction, Small Claims.*
Note: Effective 09/01/03, the search fees and copy fees listed are mandatory per adminstrative rule. Further, if a SASE is not supplied for mail searches, the court may charge an add'l $5.00.
Civil Records: Access: Phone, mail, in person. Only the court performs in person searches; visitors may not. Search fee: $15.00, includes both civil and criminal. Required to search: name, years to search. Civil cases indexed by defendant, plaintiff. Civil records on docket books from 1967; on comptuer back to 8/2001.
Criminal Records: Access: Phone, mail, in person. Only the court performs in person searches; visitors may not. Search fee: $15.00, includes both civil and criminal. Required to search: name, years to search, DOB. Criminal records on computer back to 1988, docket books from 1965.
General Information: No juvenile, protected custody, impounded or mental health records released. Copy fee: $2.00 1st page, $1.00 each add'l. Payee: Maine District Court. Personal checks accepted. Prepayment required. Mail requests: SASE required. Mail turnaround time 2-3 days.

Probate Court
26 Court St #103, Houlton, ME 04730; 207-532-1502. 8AM-4:30PM (EST). *Probate.*

Cumberland County

Superior Court - Civil
142 Federal St, Portland, ME 04101; 207-822-4105; Civil phone: 207-822-4105; Criminal phone: 207-822-4113. Hours: 8AM-4:30PM (EST). *Civil Actions.*
Note: Effective 09/01/03, the search fees and copy fees listed are mandatory per adminstrative rule. Further, if a SASE is not supplied for mail searches, the court may charge an add'l $5.00.
Civil Records: Access: In person. Both court and visitors may perform in person searches. Search fee: $15.00 per name. Required to search: name, years to search. Civil cases indexed by defendant, plaintiff. Civil records on index cards since 1975, prior records archived. They will only answer general questions on filing and hearing dates by phone or mail.
General Information: No juvenile, medical malpractice, impounded records released. Will not fax results. Copy fee: $2.00 1st page, $1.00 each add'l. Certification fee: $5.00. Payee: Superior Court. Personal checks accepted. Prepayment required. Mail requests: SASE required. Mail turnaround time varies by number of requests presented.

Superior Court - Criminal
142 Federal St, Portland, ME 04101; 207-822-4113. Hours: 8AM-4:30PM (EST). *Felony, Misdemeanor.*
Note: Effective 09/01/03, the search fees and copy fees listed are mandatory per adminstrative rule. Further, if a SASE is not supplied for mail searches, the court may charge an add'l $5.00.
Criminal Records: Access: In person only. Both court and visitors may perform in person searches. Search fee: $15.00, includes both civil and criminal. Required to search: name, years to search, DOB. Criminal records on index cards since 1900s, some records form 08/98 to present are computerized.
General Information: No juvenile records released. Copy fee: $2.00 1st page, $1.00 each add'l. Certification fee: $5.00. Payee: Clerk of Courts.

Personal checks accepted. Prepayment required. Mail requests: SASE required. Mail turnaround: 2-3 days.

Portland District Court - South 9 Civil
PO Box 412, 205 Newbury St, Portland, ME 04112; 207-822-4200. Hours: 8AM-4:30PM (EST). *Civil Actions, Eviction, Small Claims.*
Note: Also see Sagadahoc District Court, which handles cases from eastern Cumberland County. Also see Brighton District Court which handles cases from western Cumberland County.
Civil Records: Access: In person. Both court and visitors may perform in person searches. Search fee: $15.00, includes both civil and criminal. Required to search: name, years to search. Civil cases indexed by defendant. Civil records go back ten years, small claims and eviction five years. Effective 09/01/03, the search fees and copy fees listed are mandatory per adminstrative rule. Further, if a SASE is not supplied for mail searches, the court may charge add'l $5.00.
General Information: No child custody records released. Copy fee: $2.00 1st page, $1.00 each add'l. Certification fee: $5.00. Payee: Maine District Court. Personal checks accepted. Prepayment required. Mail requests: SASE required. Mail turnaround: 1 week.

Portland District Court - South 9 Criminal
PO Box 412, Portland, ME 04112; 207-822-4204. 8AM-4:30PM (EST). *Misdemeanor.*
Note: Effective 09/01/03, the search fees and copy fees listed are mandatory per adminstrative rule. Further, if a SASE is not supplied for mail searches, the court may charge an add'l $5.00.
Criminal Records: Access: In person,mail. Only the court performs in person searches; visitors may not. Search fee: $15.00 per name. Required to search: name, years to search, DOB, offense, date of offense. Criminal records on computer back to 09/86, prior records archived.
General Information: No impounded records released. Copy fee: $1.00 per page. Certification fee: $1.00. Payee: Maine District Court. Personal checks accepted. Prepayment required. Mail requests: SASE required. Mail turnaround time 3-4 days.

Bath District Court - East 6
147 New Meadows Rd, Bath, ME 04530; 207-442-0200. Hours: 8AM-4PM. *Misdemeanor, Civil Actions, Eviction, Small Claims.*
Note: Combined with West Bath District Court 6 in Sagadahoc County.

Bridgton District Court - North 9
2 Chase Common, Bridgton, ME 04009; 207-647-3535. Hours: 8AM-4PM (EST). *Misdemeanor, Civil Actions, Eviction, Small Claims.*
Note: Effective 09/01/03, the search fees and copy fees listed are mandatory per adminstrative rule. Further, if a SASE is not supplied for mail searches, the court may charge an add'l $5.00.
Civil Records: Access: Phone, mail, in person. Visitors must perform in person searches for themselves. Search fee: $15.00, includes both civil and criminal. Required to search: name, years to search. Civil cases indexed by defendant. Civil records go back to 1965; on computer back to 2001.
Criminal Records: Access: Phone, mail, in person. Visitors must perform in person searches for themselves. Search fee: $15.00, includes both civil and criminal. Required to search: name, years to search; also helpful: DOB. Criminal records on computer back to 1986, records go back to 1965.
General Information: Public Access terminal is available. (Criminal only.) No juvenile, protective custody, financial affidavits, impounded or domestic records released. Will not fax results. Copy fee: $2.00 1st page, $1.00 each add'l. Payee: Maine District Court. Personal checks accepted. Prepayment

required. Mail requests: SASE required. Mail turnaround time 5 days.

Probate Court
PO Box 15277, Portland, ME 04101-4196; 207-871-8382; Fax: 207-791-2658. Hours: 8:30AM-4:30PM (EST). *Probate.*
www.cumberlandcounty.org

Franklin County

Superior Court
140 Main St, Farmington, ME 04938; 207-778-3346. Hours: 8AM-4PM (EST). *Felony, Misdemeanor, Civil Actions.*
Note: Effective 09/01/03, the search fees and copy fees listed are mandatory per adminstrative rule. Further, if a SASE is not supplied for mail searches, the court may charge an add'l $5.00.
Civil Records: Access: Mail, in person. Both court and visitors may perform in person searches. Search fee: $15.00, includes both civil and criminal. Required to search: name, years to search. Civil cases indexed by defendant, plaintiff. Civil records on docket books and index cards since 1900s.
Criminal Records: Access: Mail, in person. Only the court performs in person searches; visitors may not. Search fee: $15.00, includes both civil and criminal. Required to search: name, years to search; also helpful: DOB, SSN. Criminal records on docket books and index cards since 1900s.
General Information: No juvenile, impounded or medical malpractice records released. Copy fee: $2.00 1st page, $1.00 each add'l. Certification fee: $5.00. Payee: Superior Court. Personal checks accepted. Prepayment required. Mail requests: SASE required. Mail turnaround time is 1 week.

Franklin District Court 12
129 Main St, Farmington, ME 04938; 207-778-8200. Hours: 8AM-4PM (EST). *Misdemeanor, Civil Actions, Eviction, Small Claims.*
Note: Effective 09/01/03, the search fees and copy fees listed are mandatory per adminstrative rule.
Civil Records: Access: Mail, in person. Visitors must perform in person searches for themselves. Search fee: $15.00 if request for more than name. Required to search: name, years to search. Civil cases indexed by defendant. Civil records on docket books since 1965 (index cards in front).
Criminal Records: Access: Mail, in person. Only the court performs in person searches; visitors may not. Search fee: $15.00 if request for more than name. Required to search: name, years to search, DOB. Criminal records on computer since 1987, on docket books since 1965 (index cards in front).
General Information: No impounded records released. Copy fee: $2.00 1st page, $1.00 each add'l. Certification fee: $5.00. Payee: Maine District Court. Personal checks accepted. Prepayment required. Mail turnaround time is 1 week.

Probate Court
County Courthouse, 140 Main St, Farmington, ME 04938; 207-778-5888; Fax: 207-778-5899. Hours: 8:30AM-4PM (EST). *Probate.*

Hancock County

Superior Court
50 State St, Ellsworth, ME 04605-1926; 207-667-7176. Hours: 8AM-4PM (EST). *Felony, Misdemeanor, Civil Actions.*
Note: Effective 09/01/03, the search fees and copy fees listed are mandatory per adminstrative rule.
Civil Records: Access: In person only. Only the court performs in person searches; visitors may not. Search fee: $15.00 per name, if multiples. Required to search: name, years to search. Civil cases indexed by defendant, plaintiff. Civil records on card files since 1960.
Criminal Records: Access: In person only. Only the court performs in person searches; visitors may not.

Search fee: $15.00 per name, if multiples. Required to search: name, years to search, DOB. Criminal records on card files since 1960.

General Information: No protective custody records released. Copy fee: $2.00 1st page, $1.00 each add'l. Certification fee: $5.00. Payee: State of Maine. Personal checks accepted. Prepayment required.

Bar Harbor District Court - South 5 93

Cottage St, Bar Harbor, ME 04609; 207-288-3082. Hours: 8AM-4PM (EST). *Misdemeanor, Civil Actions, Eviction, Small Claims.*

Note: Effective 09/01/03, the search fees and copy fees listed are mandatory per adminstrative rule.

Civil Records: Access: Mail, in person. Court may perform in person searches. Search fee: $15.00, includes both civil and criminal. Required to search: name, years to search. Civil cases indexed by defendant, plaintiff. Civil records on docket books since 1970.

Criminal Records: Access: Mail, in person. Court may perform in person searches. Search fee: $15.00, includes both civil and criminal. Required to search: name, years to search, DOB. Criminal records on computer since 1987, on docket books since 1970.

General Information: No juvenile or impounded records released. Copy fee: $2.00 1st page, $1.00 each add'l. Certification fee: $5.00 per cert. Payee: Maine District Court. Personal checks accepted. Prepayment required. Mail requests: SASE required. Mail turnaround time 2-3 days.

Ellsworth District Court - Central 5 50

State St #2, Ellsworth, ME 04605; 207-667-7141. Hours: 8AM-4PM (EST). *Misdemeanor, Civil Actions, Eviction, Small Claims.*

Note: Effective 09/01/03, the search fees and copy fees listed are mandatory per adminstrative rule.

Civil Records: Access: Mail, in person. Both court and visitors may perform in person searches. Search fee: $15.00, includes both civil and criminal. Required to search: name, years to search. Civil cases indexed by defendant, plaintiff. Need to know names of both parties to search. Civil records on docket books since 1965; on computer back to 10/01.

Criminal Records: Access: Mail, in person. Only the court performs in person searches, visitors may not. Search fee: $15.00, includes both civil and criminal. Required to search: name, years to search, DOB. Criminal records on computer back to 1987, docket books since 1965.

General Information: Public access terminal has criminal only. No juvenile, child protection, adoption or mental health records released. Copy fee: $2.00 1st page, $1.00 each add'l. Certification fee: $5.00. Payee: Maine District Court. Personal checks accepted. Prepayment required. Mail turnaround time 1 week.

Probate Court 50 State St, #6, Ellsworth, ME 04605; 207-667-8434; Probate phone: 207-667-9098; Fax: 207-667-5316. 8:30AM-4PM (EST). *Probate.*

Kennebec County

Superior Court 95 State St, Clerk of Court, Augusta, ME 04330; 207-624-5800. Hours: 8AM-4PM (EST). *Felony, Misdemeanor, Civil Actions.*

Note: Effective 09/01/03, the search fees and copy fees listed are mandatory per adminstrative rule.

Civil Records: Access: In person only. Only the court performs in person searches; visitors may not. Search fee: $15.00. Required to search: name, years to search. Civil cases indexed by defendant, plaintiff. Civil records on index cards since 1977, docket books since 1970, on computer 2 years.

Criminal Records: Access: In person only. Only the court performs in person searches; visitors may not.

Search fee: $15.00. Required to search: name, years to search; also helpful: DOB, docket number. Criminal records on index cards since 1977, docket books since 1978, on computer 5 years.

General Information: No protective custody records released. Copy fee: $2.00 1st page, $1.00 each add'l. Payee: Treasurer State of Maine. Personal checks and credit cards accepted. Prepayment required.

Maine District Court 7 Division of Southern Kennebec, 145 State St, Augusta, ME 04330-7495; 207-287-8075. Hours: 8AM-4PM (EST). *Misdemeanor, Civil Actions, Eviction, Small Claims.*

Note: Effective 09/01/03, the search fees and copy fees listed are mandatory per adminstrative rule. Further, if a SASE is not supplied for mail searches, the court may charge an add'l $5.00.

Civil Records: Access: Mail, in person. Both court and visitors may perform in person searches. Search fee: $15.00, includes both civil and criminal. Required to search: name, years to search. Civil cases indexed by defendant. Civil records kept 10 years.

Criminal Records: Access: Mail, in person. Only the court may perform in person searches. Search fee: $15.00, includes both civil and criminal. Required to search: name, years to search, DOB; also helpful: SSN. Criminal records on computer back to 1987, docket books since 1963.

General Information: No juvenile, mental health, protective custody and closed proceeding case records released. Copy fee: $2.00 1st page, $1.00 each add'l. Certification fee: $5.00. Payee: Maine District Court. Personal checks accepted. Prepayment required. Mail requests: SASE required. Mail turnaround: 1 week.

Waterville District Court - District 7 18

Colby St, PO Box 397, Waterville, ME 04903; 207-873-2103. Hours: 8AM-4PM (EST). *Misdemeanor, Civil Actions, Eviction, Small Claims.*

Note: Effective 09/01/03, the search fees and copy fees listed are mandatory per adminstrative rule. Further, if a SASE is not supplied for mail searches, the court may charge an add'l $5.00.

Civil Records: Access: Mail, in person. Both court and visitors may perform in person searches. Search fee: $15.00, includes both civil and criminal. Required to search: name, years to search; also helpful: address. Civil cases indexed by defendant. Civil records on docket books from 1979-1998; on computer since 2001.

Criminal Records: Access: Mail, in person. Both court and visitors may perform in person searches. Search fee: $15.00, includes both civil and criminal. Required to search: name, years to search, DOB; also helpful: address, SSN. Criminal records on computer since 1999, docket books from 1979-1987.

General Information: No juvenile, protective custody records released. Court reserves the right to restrict the number of record requests. Copy fee: $2.00 1st page, $1.00 each add'l. Certification fee: $5.00 per doc. Payee: Maine District Court. Personal checks accepted. Prepayment required. Mail requests: SASE required. Mail turnaround time 1 week.

Probate Court 95 State St, Augusta, ME 04330; 207-622-7558 or 207-622-7559; Fax: 207-621-1639. Hours: 8AM-4PM (EST). *Probate.* www.datamaine.com/probate

Knox County

Superior Court 62 Union St, Rockland, ME 04841-2836; 207-594-2576. Hours: 8AM-4PM (EST). *Felony, Misdemeanor, Civil Actions.*

Note: Effective 09/01/03, the search fees and copy fees listed are mandatory per adminstrative rule. Further, if a SASE is not supplied for mail searches, the court may charge an add'l $5.00.

Civil Records: Access: Phone, mail, in person. Both court and visitors may perform in person searches. Search fee: $15.00, includes both civil and criminal. Required to search: name, years to search. Civil cases indexed by defendant, plaintiff. Civil records on docket books since 1930s, index cards (in office) since mid-1970s; on computer back to 1999.

Criminal Records: Access: Mail, in person. Only the court performs in person searches; visitors may not. Search fee: $15.00, includes both civil and criminal. Required to search: name, years to search; also helpful: DOB. Criminal records on docket books since 1930s, index cards (in office) since mid-1970s; on computer back to 1999.

General Information: No Impounded or pre-sentence records released. Copy fee: $2.00 1st page, $1.00 each add'l. Certification fee: $5.00. Payee: State Treasurer. Personal checks accepted. Visa, MC accepted. Prepayment required. Mail requests: SASE required. Mail turnaround time 1 week.

District Court 6 62 Union St, Rockland, ME 04841; 207-596-2240; Probate phone: 207-594-0427. Hours: 8AM-4PM (EST). *Misdemeanor, Civil Actions, Eviction, Small Claims.*

Note: Effective 09/01/03, the search fees and copy fees listed are mandatory per adminstrative rule. Further, if a SASE is not supplied for mail searches, the court may charge an add'l $5.00.

Civil Records: Access: In person, mail. Court may perform in person searches. Search fee: $15.00 per name. Required to search: name, years to search. Civil cases indexed by defendant, plaintiff. Civil records on docket books.

Criminal Records: Access: In person, mail. Only the court performs in person searches; visitors may not. Search fee: $15.00 per name. Required to search: name, years to search, DOB. Criminal records on docket books.

General Information: No impounded records released. Copy fee: $2.00 1st page, $1.00 each add'l. Certification fee: $5.00. Payee: Maine District Court. Personal checks accepted. Prepayment required. Mail requests: SASE required. Mail turnaround: 2-3 weeks.

Probate Court 62 Union St, Rockland, ME 04841; 207-594-0427; Fax: 207-594-0443. Hours: 8AM-4PM (EST). *Probate.* http://knoxcounty.midcoast.com

Lincoln County

Lincoln County Superior Court High St, PO Box 249, Wiscasset, ME 04578; 207-882-7517; Fax: 207-882-7741. Hours: 8AM-4PM (EST). *Felony, Misdemeanor, Civil Actions.*

www.co.lincoln.me.us

Note: Effective 09/01/03, the search fees and copy fees listed are mandatory per adminstrative rule. Further, if a SASE is not supplied for mail searches, the court may charge an add'l $5.00.

Civil Records: Access: Mail, in person. Only the court performs in person searches; visitors may not. Search fee: $15.00, includes both civil and criminal. Required to search: name, years to search. Civil cases indexed by defendant, plaintiff. Civil records on docket books and index cards since 1960s.

Criminal Records: Access: Mail, in person. Only the court performs in person searches; visitors may not. Search fee: $15.00, includes both civil and criminal. Required to search: name, years to search, DOB. Criminal records on docket books and index cards since 1960s.

General Information: No protective custody records released. Copy fee: $2.00 1st page, $1.00 each add'l. Certification fee: $5.00. Payee: Lincoln County Superior Court. Personal checks accepted.

Prepayment required. Mail requests: SASE required. Mail turnaround time is 1-2 days.

District Court 6 32 High St, PO Box 249, Wiscasset, ME 04578; 207-882-6363; Fax: 207-882-5980. Hours: 8AM-4PM (EST). *Misdemeanor, Civil Actions, Eviction, Small Claims.*
www.co.lincoln.me.us
Note: Effective 09/01/03, the search fees and copy fees listed are mandatory per adminstrative rule. Further, if a SASE is not supplied for mail searches, the court may charge an add'l $5.00.

Civil Records: Access: Phone, mail, in person. Both court and visitors may perform in person searches. Search fee: $15.00, includes both civil and criminal. Required to search: name, years to search. Civil cases indexed by defendant, plaintiff. Civil records on docket books since 1965; on computer back to 1987.
Criminal Records: Access: Mail, in person. Only the court performs in person searches; visitors may not. Search fee: $15.00, includes both civil and criminal. Required to search: name, years to search, DOB or SSN. Criminal records on computer back to 1987, docket books since 1960.
General Information: No juvenile, child protective or impounded records released. Will fax results to local or toll free line. Copy fee: $2.00 1st page, $1.00 each add'l. Certification fee: $5.00. Payee: Maine District Court. Personal checks accepted. Prepayment required. Mail requests: SASE required. Mail turnaround time 1 week.

Probate Court 32 High St, PO Box 249, Wiscasset, ME 04578; 207-882-7392; Fax: 207-882-4324. Hours: 8AM-4PM (EST). *Probate.*
www.co.lincoln.me.us/dep.html

Oxford County

Superior Court Courthouse, 26 Western Ave, PO Box 179, South Paris, ME 04281-0179; 207-743-8936. Hours: 8AM-4PM (EST). *Felony, Misdemeanor, Civil Actions.*
Note: Effective 09/01/03, the search fees and copy fees listed are mandatory per adminstrative rule. Further, if a SASE is not supplied for mail searches, the court may charge an add'l $5.00.

Civil Records: Access: Mail, in person. Visitors must perform in person searches for themselves. Search fee: $15.00, includes both civil and criminal. Required to search: name, years to search, DOB. Civil cases indexed by defendant, plaintiff. Criminal records on computer back to 1998; on docket books since 1980.
Criminal Records: Access: Mail, in person. Visitors must perform in person searches for themselves. Search fee: $15.00, includes both civil and criminal. Required to search: name, years to search, DOB. Criminal records on docket books since 1960.
General Information: No protective custody or protection from abuse records released. Copy fee: $2.00 1st page, $1.00 each add'l. Payee: Clerk of Superior Court. Personal checks accepted. Prepayment required. Mail requests: SASE required. Mail turnaround time 3-4 days.

Rumford District Court - Div. of North Oxford Municipal Bldg, 145 Congress St, Rumford, ME 04276; 207-364-7171. Hours: 8AM-4PM (EST). *Misdemeanor, Civil Actions, Eviction, Small Claims.*
Note: Effective 09/01/03, the search fees and copy fees listed are mandatory per adminstrative rule. Further, if a SASE is not supplied for mail searches, the court may charge an add'l $5.00.

Civil Records: Access: Mail, in person. Both court and visitors may perform in person searches. Search fee: $15.00 for two or more searches. Required to search: name, years to search. Civil cases indexed by

defendant, plaintiff. Civil records on docket books since 1966.
Criminal Records: Access: Mail, in person. Both court and visitors may perform in person searches. Search fee: $15.00 for two or more searches. Required to search: name, years to search, DOB. Criminal records on computer since March 1988, docket books since 1966.
General Information: No impounded records released. Will not fax results. Copy fee: $2.00 1st page, $1.00 each add'l. Payee: Maine District Court. Personal checks accepted. Prepayment required. Mail requests: SASE required. Mail turnaround: 1 week.

South Paris District Court - South 11 26 Western Ave, South Paris, ME 04281; 207-743-8942. Hours: 8AM-4PM (EST). *Misdemeanor, Civil Actions, Eviction, Small Claims.*
Note: Effective 09/01/03, the search fees and copy fees listed are mandatory per adminstrative rule. Further, if a SASE is not supplied for mail searches, the court may charge an add'l $5.00.

Civil Records: Access: Mail, in person. Only the court performs in person searches; visitors may not. Search fee: $15.00, includes both civil and criminal. Required to search: name, years to search. Civil cases indexed by defendant. Civil records on docket books back 5 years.
Criminal Records: Access: Mail, in person. Both court and visitors may perform in person searches. Search fee: $15.00, includes both civil and criminal. Required to search: name, years to search; also helpful: DOB. Criminal records on computer since 04/99, docket books back to 1966. Records after 4/99 cannot be accessed on the public access computer; request a search in writing.
General Information: Public Access terminal is available. (Criminal only, and only for years stated above.) No juvenile or child protective records released. Copy fee: $2.00 1st page, $1.00 each add'l. Payee: Maine District Court. Personal checks accepted. Prepayment required. Mail requests: SASE required. Mail turnaround time 1-2 days.

Probate Court 26 Western Ave, PO Box 179, South Paris, ME 04281; 207-743-6671; Fax: 207-743-2656. Hours: 8AM-4PM (EST). *Probate.*
www.oxfordcounty.org/probate.htm

Penobscot County

Superior Court 97 Hammond St, Bangor, ME 04401; 207-561-2300. Hours: 8AM-4:30PM (EST). *Felony, Misdemeanor, Civil Actions.*
Note: The search fees and copy fees listed are mandatory per adminstrative rule. Further, if a SASE is not supplied for mail searches, the court may charge an add'l $5.00. There is no charge for a single search.

Civil Records: Access: Mail, in person. Only the court performs in person searches; visitors may not. Search fee: $15.00 per name multiple searches only (otherwise no fee for single case) includes both civil and criminal. Required to search: name, years to search. Civil cases indexed by defendant, plaintiff. Civil records on docket books since 1976; on computer back to 2002; archived back to 1927.
Criminal Records: Access: Mail, in person. Only the court performs in person searches; visitors may not. Search fee: $15.00 per name multiple searches only (otherwise no fee for single case) includes both civil and criminal. Required to search: name, years to search, DOB. Criminal records on docket books since 1976; on computer back to 1998; archived to 1927.
General Information: No impounded records released. Will not fax results. Copy fee: $2.00 1st page, $1.00 each add'l. Certification fee: $5.00 per doc. Payee: Treasurer, State of Maine. Personal

checks accepted. Prepayment required. Mail requests: SASE required.

Bangor District Court 73 Hammond St, Bangor, ME 04401; 207-941-3040. Hours: 8AM-4PM (EST). *Misdemeanor, Civil Actions, Eviction, Small Claims.*
Note: Effective 09/01/03, the search fees and copy fees listed are mandatory per adminstrative rule. Further, if a SASE is not supplied for mail searches, the court may charge an add'l $5.00.

Civil Records: Access: Mail, in person. Both court and visitors may perform in person searches. Search fee: $15.00, includes both civil and criminal. Required to search: name, years to search. Civil cases indexed by defendant. Civil records on docket books since 1962. Court suggests using central state repository.
Criminal Records: Access: Mail, in person. Both court and visitors may perform in person searches. Search fee: $15.00, includes both civil and criminal. Required to search: name, years to search; also helpful: DOB. Criminal records on computer since late 1986, docket books since 1962.
General Information: Public Access terminal is available. (Criminal only.) No protective custody records released. Copy fee: $2.00 1st page, $1.00 each add'l. Payee: Maine District Court. Personal checks accepted. Prepayment required. Mail requests: SASE required. Mail turnaround time 1 week.

Central District Court - Central 13 66 Maine St, Lincoln, ME 04457; 207-794-8512. Hours: 8AM-4PM (EST). *Misdemeanor, Civil Actions, Eviction, Small Claims.*
Note: Effective 09/01/03, the search fees and copy fees listed are mandatory per adminstrative rule. Further, if a SASE is not supplied for mail searches, the court may charge an add'l $5.00.

Civil Records: Access: In person only. Only the court performs in person searches; visitors may not. Search fee: $15.00. Required to search: name, years to search. Civil cases indexed by defendant. Civil records on docket books since 1964.
Criminal Records: Access: In person only. Only the court performs in person searches; visitors may not. Search fee: $15.00. Required to search: name, years to search, DOB. Criminal records on computer since 1987, docket books since 1964.
General Information: No juvenile or protective custody records released. Copy fee: $2.00 1st page, $1.00 each add'l. Certification fee: $5.00. Payee: Maine District Court. Personal checks accepted. Prepayment required.

Millinocket District Court - North 13 207 Penobscot Ave, Millinocket, ME 04462; 207-723-4786. Hours: 8AM-4PM (EST). *Misdemeanor, Civil Actions, Eviction, Small Claims.*
Note: Effective 09/01/03, the search fees and copy fees listed are mandatory per adminstrative rule. Further, if a SASE is not supplied for mail searches, the court may charge an add'l $5.00.

Civil Records: Access: In person only. Both the court and visitors may perform in person searches. No search fee. Required to search: name, years to search. Civil cases indexed by defendant, plaintiff. Civil records on docket books since 1964; computerized records since 1987.
Criminal Records: Access: Mail, in person. Both court and visitors may perform in person searches. Search fee: $15.00 per name. No charge if you provide docket numbers. Required to search: name, years to search, DOB. Criminal records on computer since 1987, docket books since 1964.
General Information: No juvenile or protective custody records released. Will not fax results. Copy fee: $2.00 1st page, $1.00 each add'l. Certification fee: $5.00. Payee: Maine District Court. Personal

checks accepted. Prepayment required. Mail requests: SASE requested. Turnaround time 3-6 days.

Newport District Court - West 3 12 Water St, Newport, ME 04953; 207-368-5778; Hours: 8AM-4PM (EST). *Misdemeanor, Civil Actions, Eviction, Small Claims.*

Note: Effective 09/01/03, the search fees and copy fees listed are mandatory per adminstrative rule. Further, if a SASE is not supplied for mail searches, the court may charge an add'l $5.00.

Civil Records: Access: Mail, in person. Both court and visitors may perform in person searches. Search fee: $15.00, includes both civil and criminal. Required to search: name, years to search. Civil cases indexed by defendant, plaintiff. Civil records on docket books back to 1965; computerized back to 2001.

Criminal Records: Access: Mail, in person. Both court and visitors may perform in person searches. Search fee: $15.00, includes both civil and criminal. Required to search: name, years to search, DOB. Criminal records on computer for 5 years, on docket books since 1987.

General Information: Public Access terminal is available. No impounded records released. Copy fee: $2.00 1st page, $1.00 each add'l. Certification fee: $5.00 per cert. Payee: Maine District Court. Personal checks accepted. Prepayment required. Mail requests: SASE required. Mail turnaround time 1 week.

Probate Court 97 Hammond St, Bangor, ME 04401-4996; 207-942-8769; Fax: 207-941-8499. Hours: 8AM-4:30PM (EST). *Probate.*

Piscataquis County

Superior Court 159 E Main St, Dover-Foxcroft, ME 04426; 207-564-8419; Fax: 207-564-3363. Hours: 8AM-4PM (EST). *Felony, Misdemeanor, Civil Actions.*

Note: Effective 09/01/03, the search fees and copy fees listed are mandatory per adminstrative rule. Further, if a SASE is not supplied for mail searches, the court may charge an add'l $5.00.

Civil Records: Access: Mail, in person. Only the court performs in person searches; visitors may not. Search fee: $15.00, includes both civil and criminal. Required to search: name, years to search. Civil cases indexed by defendant, plaintiff. Civil records on docket books since 1960; computerized records since 1998.

Criminal Records: Access: Mail, in person. Only the court performs in person searches; visitors may not. Search fee: $15.00, includes both civil and criminal. Required to search: name, years to search; also helpful: DOB. Criminal records on docket books since 1960; computerized records since 1998.

General Information: No pre-sentence report records released. Copy fee: $2.00 1st page, $1.00 each add'l. Payee: State of Maine Superior Court. Personal checks accepted. Prepayment required. Mail requests: SASE required. Mail turnaround time 1 week.

District Court 13 163 E Main St, Dover-Foxcroft, ME 04426; 207-564-2240. Hours: 8AM-4PM (EST). *Misdemeanor, Civil Actions, Eviction, Small Claims.*

Note: Effective 09/01/03, the search fees and copy fees listed are mandatory per adminstrative rule. Further, if a SASE is not supplied for mail searches, the court may charge an add'l $5.00.

Civil Records: Access: Mail, in person. Both court and visitors may perform in person searches. Search fee: $15.00, includes both civil and criminal. Required to search: name, years to search. Civil cases indexed by defendant, plaintiff. Civil records on docket books since 1963.

Criminal Records: Access: Mail, in person. Both court and visitors may perform in person searches. Search fee: $15.00, includes both civil and criminal. Required to search: name, years to search; also helpful: DOB. Criminal records on computer since 1987, docket books since 1963.

General Information: No protective custody or juvenile records released. Copy fee: $2.00 1st page, $1.00 each add'l. Payee: Maine District Court. Personal checks accepted. Prepayment required. Mail requests: SASE required. Mail turnaround: 1 week.

Probate Court 159 E Main St, Dover-Foxcroft, ME 04426; 207-564-2431; Fax: 207-564-2431. Hours: 8:30AM-4PM (EST). *Probate.*

Sagadahoc County

Superior Court 752 High St, PO Box 246, Bath, ME 04530; 207-443-9733. Hours: 8AM-4:30PM (EST). *Felony, Misdemeanor, Civil Actions.*

Note: Effective 09/01/03, the search fees and copy fees listed are mandatory per adminstrative rule. Further, if a SASE is not supplied for mail searches, the court may charge an add'l $5.00.

Civil Records: Access: Mail, in person. Both court and visitors may perform in person searches. Search fee: $15.00, includes both civil and criminal. Required to search: name, years to search. Civil cases indexed by defendant, plaintiff. Civil records on docket books since 1900s; on comptuer back to 1999.

Criminal Records: Access: Mail, in person. Both court and visitors may perform in person searches. Search fee: $15.00, includes both civil and criminal. Required to search: name, years to search, DOB. Criminal records on docket books since 1900s; on computer back to 1999.

General Information: No impounded records released. Copy fee: $2.00 1st page, $1.00 each add'l. Certification fee: $5.00. Payee: Clerk of Superior Court. Cash, checks and money orders accepted. Prepayment required. Mail requests: SASE required. Mail turnaround time 2 days.

West Bath District Court 6 147 New Meadows Rd, West Bath, ME 04530; 207-442-0200. Hours: 8AM-4PM (EST). *Misdemeanor, Civil Actions, Eviction, Small Claims.*

Note: This court handles the eastern part of Cumberland County and all of Sagadahoc County.

Civil Records: Access: In person only. Both court and visitors may perform in person searches. Search fee: $15.00, includes both civil and criminal. Required to search: name, years to search. Civil cases indexed by defendant, plaintiff. Civil records on docket books since 1980s; prior archived. Effective 09/01/03, the search fees and copy fees listed are mandatory per adminstrative rule. Further, if a SASE is not supplied for mail searches, the court may charge an add'l $5.00.

Criminal Records: Access: In person only. Both court and visitors may perform in person searches. Search fee: $15.00, includes both civil and criminal. Required to search: name, years to search; also helpful: DOB. Criminal records on computer since 1987, docket books back to 1975; prior archived. Effective 09/01/03, the search fees and copy fees listed are mandatory per adminstrative rule.

General Information: No protective custody or juvenile records released. Copy fee: $2.00 1st page, $1.00 each add'l. Certification fee: $5.00. Payee: Maine District Court. Personal checks accepted. Prepayment required.

Probate Court 752 High St, Bath, ME 04530; 207-443-8218; Fax: 207-443-8217. Hours: 8:30AM-4:30PM (EST). *Probate.*

Somerset County

Superior Court PO Box 725, Skowhegan, ME 04976; 207-474-5161; Probate phone: 207-474-3322. Hours: 8AM-4PM (EST). *Felony, Misdemeanor, Civil Actions.*

Note: Effective 09/01/03, the search fees and copy fees listed are mandatory per adminstrative rule.

Civil Records: Access: In person only. Only the court performs in person searches; visitors may not. Search fee: $5.00 per name. There is no fee for searching one name only. Required to search: name, years to search. Civil cases indexed by defendant, plaintiff. Civil records archived in Augusta back to 1800s, docket books and index cards back to 1900s.

Criminal Records: Access: In person only. Only the court performs in person searches; visitors may not. Search fee: $5.00 per name. There is no fee for searching one name only. Required to search: name, years to search; also helpful: DOB. Criminal records archived in Augusta back to 1800s, docket books and index cards back to 1900s; on computer back to 1998.

General Information: No impounded, present investigations, psychological evaluations or child support records released. Copy fee: $2.00 1st page, $1.00 each add'l. Certification fee: $5.00. Payee: Clerk of Superior Court. Personal checks accepted. Prepayment required.

District Court 12 PO Box 525, 47 Court St, Skowhegan, ME 04976; 207-474-9518. Hours: 8AM-4PM (EST). *Misdemeanor, Civil Actions, Eviction, Small Claims.*

Note: Effective 09/01/03, the search fees and copy fees listed are mandatory per adminstrative rule. Further, if a SASE is not supplied for mail searches, the court may charge an add'l $5.00.

Civil Records: Access: Mail, in person. Both court and visitors may perform in person searches. Search fee: $15.00, includes both civil and criminal. Required to search: name, years to search. Civil cases indexed by defendant. Civil records on docket books since 1960s, divorces since 1970s.

Criminal Records: Access: Mail, in person. Both court and visitors may perform in person searches. Search fee: $15.00, includes both civil and criminal. Required to search: name, years to search; also helpful: DOB. Criminal records on computer since 1987, docket books since 1960s.

General Information: Public Access terminal is available. (Criminal only.) No juvenile records released. Copy fee: $2.00 1st page, $1.00 each add'l. Certification fee: $5.00. Payee: Maine District Court. Personal checks accepted. Prepayment required. Mail requests: SASE required. Mail turnaround: 2-4 weeks.

Probate Court 41 Court St, Skowhegan, ME 04976; 207-474-3322. Hours: 8:30AM-4:30PM (EST). *Probate.*

Waldo County

Superior Court 137 Church St, PO Box 188, Belfast, ME 04915; 207-338-1940. Hours: 8AM-4PM (EST). *Felony, Misdemeanor, Civil Actions.*

Note: Effective 09/01/03, the search fees and copy fees listed are mandatory per adminstrative rule. Further, if a SASE is not supplied for mail searches, the court may charge an add'l $5.00.

Civil Records: Access: Mail, in person. Only the court performs in person searches; visitors may not. Search fee: $15.00, includes both civil and criminal. Required to search: name, years to search. Civil cases indexed by defendant, plaintiff. Civil records archived back to 1980 (not in office), on docket books since 1980; on computer back to 1998.

Criminal Records: Access: Mail, in person. Only the court performs in person searches; visitors may not.

Search fee: $15.00, includes both civil and criminal. Required to search: name, years to search, DOB. Criminal records archived back to 1975 (not in office), on docket books since 1975; on computer back to 1998.

General Information: No protective custody records released. Will not fax results. Copy fee: $2.00 1st page, $1.00 each add'l. Payee: State Treasurer. Personal checks accepted. Prepayment required. Mail requests: SASE required. Mail turnaround: 1 week.

District Court 5 PO Box 382, 103 Church St, Belfast, ME 04915; 207-338-3107. 8AM-4PM (EST). *Misdemeanor, Civil Actions, Eviction, Small Claims.* Note: Effective 09/01/03, the search fees and copy fees listed are mandatory per adminstrative rule. Further, if a SASE is not supplied for mail searches, the court may charge an add'l $5.00.

Civil Records: Access: Mail, in person. Both court and visitors may perform in person searches. Search fee: $15.00, includes both civil and criminal. Required to search: name, years to search. Civil cases indexed by defendant, plaintiff. Civil records on docket books since 1966, computerized since 2001.

Criminal Records: Access: Mail, in person. Both court and visitors may perform in person searches. Search fee: $15.00, includes both civil and criminal. Required to search: name, years to search, DOB. Criminal records on computer since 1987, docket books since 1966.

General Information: No juvenile or impounded records released. Will not fax results. Copy fee: $2.00 1st page, $1.00 each add'l. Certification fee: $5.00. Payee: Maine District Court. Personal checks accepted. Prepayment required. Mail requests: SASE required. Mail turnaround time 1 week.

Probate Court 39A Spring St, PO Box 323, Belfast, ME 04915-0323; 207-338-2780/2963; Fax: 207-338-2360. Hours: 8AM-4PM (EST). *Probate.*

Washington County

Superior Court Clerk of Court, PO Box 526, Machias, ME 04654; 207-255-3326. Hours: 8AM-4PM (EST). *Felony, Misdemeanor, Civil.* Note: Effective 09/01/03, the search fees and copy fees listed are mandatory per adminstrative rule. Further, if a SASE is not supplied for mail searches, the court may charge an add'l $5.00.

Civil Records: Access: Mail, in person. Both court and visitors may perform in person searches. Search fee: $15.00, includes both civil and criminal. Required to search: name, years to search. Civil cases indexed by defendant, plaintiff. Civil records on docket books and index cards since 1930s.

Criminal Records: Access: Mail, in person. Both court and visitors may perform in person searches. Search fee: $15.00, includes both civil and criminal. Required to search: name, years to search, DOB. Criminal records on docket books and index cards since 1930s.

General Information: No impounded records released. Will not fax results. Copy fee: $2.00 1st page, $1.00 each add'l. Certification fee: $5.00. Payee: Treasurer, State of Maine. Personal checks accepted. Prepayment required. Mail requests: SASE required. Mail turnaround time 1 week.

Calais District Court - North 4 PO Box 929, Calais, ME 04619; 207-454-2055; TTY# 207-454-0085. 8AM-4PM (EST). *Misdemeanor, Civil Actions, Eviction, Small Claims.* Note: Effective 09/01/03, the search fees and copy fees listed are mandatory per adminstrative rule.

Civil Records: Access: In person only. Visitors must perform in person searches for themselves. No search fee. Required to search: name, years to search. Civil

cases indexed by defendant, plaintiff. Civil records on docket books since 1964.

Criminal Records: Access: In person only. Visitors must perform in person searches for themselves. No search fee. Required to search: name, years to search, DOB. Criminal records on computer since 1987, docket books since 1964.

General Information: Public Access terminal is available. No juvenile or protective custody records released. Copy fee: $2.00 1st page, $1.00 each add'l. Payee: Maine District Court. Personal checks accepted. Prepayment required.

Maine District Court 4 47 Court St, PO Box 297, Machias, ME 04654; 207-255-3044. Hours: 8AM-4PM (EST). *Misdemeanor, Civil Actions, Eviction, Small Claims.* Note: Effective 09/01/03, the search fees and copy fees listed are mandatory per adminstrative rule. Further, if a SASE is not supplied for mail searches, the court may charge an add'l $5.00.

Civil Records: Access: Mail, in person. Both court and visitors may perform in person searches. Search fee: 1st name free add'l $15.00. Required to search: name, years to search. Civil cases indexed by defendant, plaintiff. Civil records on docket books since 1964; on computer 1987-1999.

Criminal Records: Access: Mail, in person. Both court and visitors may perform in person searches. Search fee: 1st name free add'l $15.00. Required to search: name, years to search, DOB. Criminal records on computer 1987-1999, docket books since 1964.

General Information: Public Access terminal is available. (Public terminal for civil in person searches.) No protective custody or juvenile records released. Copy fee: $2.00 1st page, $1.00 each add'l. Certification fee: $5.00. Payee: Maine District Court. Personal checks accepted. Prepayment required. Mail requests: SASE required. Mail turnaround: 4 days.

Probate Court PO Box 297, Machias, ME 04654; 207-255-6591. Hours: 8AM-4PM (EST). *Probate.*

York County

Superior Court Clerk of Court, PO Box 160, Alfred, ME 04002; 207-324-5122; Probate phone: 207-324-5117. Hours: 8AM-4:30PM (EST). *Felony, Misdemeanor, Civil Actions.* Effective 09/01/03, the search fees and copy fees listed are mandatory per adminstrative rule. Further, if a SASE is not supplied for mail searches, court may charge an add'l $5.00.

Civil Records: Access: Mail, in person. Only the court performs in person searches; visitors may not. Search fee: $15.00, includes both civil and criminal. Required to search: name, years to search. Civil cases indexed by defendant, plaintiff. Civil records on docket books since 1960; computerized records go back to 2002.

Criminal Records: Access: Mail, in person. Only the court performs in person searches; visitors may not. Search fee: $15.00, includes both civil and criminal. Required to search: name, years to search, DOB. Criminal records on docket books since 1966; computerized records go back to 1998.

General Information: No juvenile, or protective custody records released. Will not fax results. Copy fee: $2.00 1st page, $1.00 each add'l. Payee: Clerk of Courts. Only cashiers checks and money orders accepted. Prepayment required. Mail turnaround time: 1-5 names is 5 days; 6-10 names 30 working days.

Biddeford District Court - East 10 25 Adams St, Biddeford, ME 04005; 207-283-1147. Hours: 8AM-4PM (EST). *Misdemeanor, Civil Actions, Eviction, Small Claims.* Note: Effective 09/01/03, the search fees and copy fees listed are mandatory per adminstrative rule.

Further, if a SASE is not supplied for mail searches, the court may charge an add'l $5.00.

Civil Records: Access: mail, in person. Visitors must perform in person searches for themselves. Search fee: $15.00, includes both civil and criminal. Required to search: name, years to search. Civil cases indexed by defendant. Civil records on docket books since 1989. Court will do up to 3 searches.

Criminal Records: Access: Mail, in person. Visitors must perform in person searches for themselves. Search fee: $15.00, includes both civil and criminal. Required to search: name, years to search; also helpful: DOB. Criminal records on computer since 1986. Court will do up to 3 searches.

General Information: No child protection or juvenile records released. Copy fee: $2.00 1st page, $1.00 each add'l. Payee: Maine District Court. Personal checks accepted. Prepayment required. Mail requests: SASE required.

Springvale District Court - West 10 447 Main St, Springvale, ME 04083; 207-459-1400. Hours: 8AM-4PM (EST). *Misdemeanor, Civil Actions, Eviction, Small Claims.* Note: Effective 09/01/03, the search fees and copy fees listed are mandatory per adminstrative rule. Further, if a SASE is not supplied for mail searches, the court may charge an add'l $5.00.

Civil Records: Access: Mail, in person. Both court and visitors may perform in person searches. Search fee: $15.00, includes both civil and criminal. Required to search: name, years to search. Civil cases indexed by defendant. Civil records on computer since 1985, docket books since 1985.

Criminal Records: Access: Mail, in person. Both court and visitors may perform in person searches. Search fee: $15.00, includes both civil and criminal. Required to search: name, years to search, DOB. Criminal records on computer since 1997, dockets books since 1980.

General Information: No impounded, juvenile, mental health or protective custody records released. Copy fee: $2.00 1st page, $1.00 each add'l. Certification fee: $5.00. Payee: Maine District Court. Personal checks accepted. Prepayment required. Mail requests: SASE required. Mail turnaround: 3-4 days.

York District Court - South 10 PO Box 770, Chase's Pond Rd, York, ME 03909-0770; 207-363-1230. Hours: 8AM-4PM (EST). *Misdemeanor, Civil Actions, Eviction, Small Claims.* Note: Effective 09/01/03, the search fees and copy fees listed are mandatory per adminstrative rule. Further, if a SASE is not supplied for mail searches, the court may charge an add'l $5.00.

Civil Records: Access: Mail, in person. Visitors must perform in person searches for themselves. Search fee: $15.00, includes both civil and criminal. Required to search: name, years to search. Civil cases indexed by defendant, plaintiff. Civil records on docket books since 1975; on computer back to 1987.

Criminal Records: Access: Mail, in person. Visitors must perform in person searches for themselves. Search fee: $15.00, includes both civil and criminal. Required to search: name, years to search, DOB. Criminal records on computer back to 1987, docket books since 1975.

General Information: No impounded, juvenile and protective custody records released. Will not fax results. Copy fee: $2.00 1st page, $1.00 each add'l. Certification fee: $5.00. Payee: Maine District Court. Personal checks accepted. Prepayment required. Mail turnaround: 2-4 days.

Probate Court PO Box 399, 45 Kennebunk Rd, Alfred, ME 04002; 207-324-1577; Fax: 207-324-0163. Hours: 8:30AM-4:30PM (EST). *Probate.*

Maine Recording Offices

ORGANIZATION: 16 counties, 17 recording offices. The recording officer is County Register of Deeds. Counties maintain a general index of all transactions recorded. Aroostock and Oxford Counties each have two recording offices. There are no county assessors; each town has its own. The entire state is in the Eastern Time Zone (EST).

REAL ESTATE RECORDS: Counties do not usually perform real estate name searches, but some will look up a name informally. Copy and certification fees vary widely. Assessor and tax records are located at the town/city level.

UCC RECORDS: Financing statements are filed at the state level, except for real estate related filings, which are filed only with the Register of Deeds. Counties do not perform UCC searches. Copy fees are usually $1.00 per page.

TAX LIEN RECORDS: All tax liens on personal property are filed with the Secretary of State. All tax liens on real property are filed with the Register of Deeds.

OTHER LIENS: Municipal, bail bond, mechanics.

ONLINE ACCESS: There is no statewide system. However, a private vendor has placed assessor records from a number of towns on the Internet. Visit http://data.visionappraisal.com

Androscoggin County

County Register of Deeds, 2 Turner St, Courthouse, Auburn, ME 04210-5978. **Phone-**County Register of Deeds, R/E & UCC Recording- 207-782-0191; fax-207-784-3163; 8AM-5PM http://142.167.64.12/alis/ww400r.pgm Will not search records. UCC copy- $1.00 per page. Cert fee: No charge. Payee: Androscoggin County Register of Deeds. **Online Access to Real Estate, Tax Lien, Assessor records:** Access the Registry index by subscription for a $140.00 annual fee + $1.00 per page/image printed. Indexes go back to 1976. For information and sign-up contact Jeanine at 207-782-0191. Also, Town of Lisbon Assessor data is free at www.lisbonme.org/clerk/index.htm. No name searching. Also, the City of Auburn tax assessor data is searchable free at www.auburnmaine.org/html/webgis.htm. **Other phones:** Treasurer-207-784-7491.

Aroostook County (Northern District)

County Register of Deeds, PO Box 47, Fort Kent, ME 04743. **Phone-**County Register of Deeds, R/E & UCC Recording- 207-834-3925; fax-207-834-3138; hours-8AM-4:30PM www.aroostook.me.us/deeds.html Will not search records. UCC copy- $1.00 per page. Real estate copies- $.50 per page if county does, $.25 per page self-serve. Cert fee: $2.00 per doc. Payee: Northern Aroostook County Register of Deeds. **Online Access to Deed records:** There is a commercial system available. $50.00 per year fee and $.25 per minute when online. Call for details. **Other phones:** Assessor-207-834-3090; Treasurer-207-834-3090; Elections-207-834-3090; Vital Records-207-834-3090.

Aroostook County (Southern District)

County Register of Deeds, 26 Court St, #102, Houlton, ME 04730. **Phone-**207-532-1500, R/E Recording- 207-834-3925; fax-207-532-7319; hours 8AM-4:30PM www.aroostook.me.us/indexhome.html All locations from New Sweden south file in this office. Will not search records. UCC copy- $1.00 per page. RE record copy- $.25 per page, $.50 if register makes copy. Payee: Aroostook County Register of Deeds.

Cumberland County

County Register of Deeds, PO Box 7230, Portland, ME 04112. **Phone-**County Register of Deeds, R/E & UCC Recording- 207-871-8389; fax-207-772-4162; hours 8:30AM-4:30PM Will not search records. UCC copy- $1.50 per page. Cert fee: $2.00 per doc. Payee: Register of Deeds. **Online Access to Assessor, Property Sale records:** Cape Elizabeth Town Assessor data is free www.capeelizabeth.com/taxdata.html. Town of Gray assessor data is at www.graymaine.org/vclerk/index.htm. No name searching. Raymond Town assessor data at www.raymondmaine.org/government/assessing/. Freeport Town Assessor- www.freeportmaine.co /assessor/sendform.html. Portland assessor-www.portlandassessor.com. So. Portland assessor-http://data.visionappraisal.com/SouthPortlandME. Scarborough Town data is searchable at www.scarborough.me.us/townhall/assessing/searc h.html Cumberland town assessor, also Gorham town assessor, Standish town assessor, all at http://data.visionappraisal.com. Falmouth '02 data: www.town.falmouth.me.us/assessing/home.html. Yarmouth property info: www.yarmouth.me.us. **Other phones:** Assessor-207-874-8486; Treasurer-207-871-8392.

Franklin County

County Register of Deeds, 140 Main St, Courthouse, Farmington, ME 04938-1818. **Phone-**207-778-5889; fax-207-778-5899; hours 8:30AM-4PM. Will not search records. UCC copy- $1.00 per financing statement. RE record copy- $1.00 per page. Cert fee: $.50 per cert. Payee: Franklin County Register of Deeds.

Hancock County

County Register of Deeds, 50 State St #9, Ellsworth, ME 04605. **Phone-**County Register of Deeds, R/E & UCC Recording- 207-667-8353; fax-207-667-1410; hours-8:30AM-4PM www.co.hancock.me.us Will not search UCC records. UCC copy- $2.00 per page. Will not search real estate or tax lien records. Cert fee: $1.00 per doc. Payee: Hancock County Registry of Deeds. **Online Access to Real Estate, Lien, UCC, Recording records:** Access to the county registry of deeds database at www.registryofdeeds.com requires registration. Viewing of records back to 1790 is

free, but $1.25 per page to print. Register online. For information, visit www.registryofdeeds.com or call 888-833-3979. Also, City of Ellsworth real estate data is available free at www.ci.ellsworth.me.us/realestatedb.html. Also, access to Bar Harbor property data is at www.visionappraisal.com/databases/ct/index.htm. Free registration required.

Kennebec County

County Register of Deeds, PO Box 1053, Augusta, ME 04332-1053. **Phone-**207-622-0431; fax-207-622-1598; hours 8AM-4PM Will not search records. UCC copy- $1.00 per financing statement. RE record copy- $1.00 per page. Cert fee: $.50 per cert. Payee: Kennebec County Register of Deeds. **Online Access to Assessor, Property records:** Records on the Winslow Town Property Records database are free at www.winslowmaine.org. Records on Town of Waterville Assessor's database are free at http://data.visionappraisal.com/WatervilleME/. For full data, user ID is required; registration is free. Also, search the City of Augusta assessor database at http://data.visionappraisal.com/AugustaME/. Free registration for full data.

Knox County

County Register of Deeds, PO Box 943, Rockland, ME 04841. **Phone-**207-594-0422; fax-207-594-0446; hours-8AM-4PM www.knoxcounty.midcoast.com Will not search records. UCC copy- $1.00 per financing statement. Cert fee: $1.00 per doc. Payee: Knox County Register of Deeds. **Online Access to Property records:** Search only the Town of Camden tax/property map page for free at http://maps.k2bh.com. Select "search by name" to search by name. Also, search the Camden town assessor data at http://data.visionappraisal.com/CamdenME/.

Lincoln County

County Register of Deeds, PO Box 249, Wiscasset, ME 04578-0249. **Phone-**207-882-7515; fax-207-882-4061; hours 8AM-4PM Will not search records. Record copy- $1.00 per page. Cert fee: $.50 per doc. Payee: Lincoln County Register of Deeds. **Online Access to Property records:** Only Town of Boothbay property data is available free at www.town.boothbay.me.us/bbaytop.htm.

Oxford County

County Register of Deeds, PO Box 179, South Paris, ME 04281-0179. **Phone-**207-743-6211; fax-207-743-2656; hours 8AM-4PM

File in this office for all towns EXCEPT the following: Brownfield, Denmark, Fryeburg, Hiram, Lovell, Porter, Stoneham, Stow, and Sweden. Will not search records. Record copy-$1.00 per page. Cert fee: $1.00 per doc. Payee: Oxford County Register of Deeds.

Penobscot County

County Register of Deeds, PO Box 2070, Bangor, ME 04402-2070. **Phone-**207-942-8797; fax-207-945-4920; hours 8AM-4:30PM

Will not search records. UCC copy- $1.00 per page. Cert fee: $1.00 per doc. Payee: Penobscot County Register of Deeds. **Online Access to Assessor, Property records:** Search the City of Old Town real estate database for free at www.old-town.me.us/assessor/rev.asp. May view indexes and documents for free at www.penobscotdeeds.com. Must contact Registery for copies.

Piscataquis County

County Register of Deeds, 159 E. Main St, Dover-Foxcroft, ME 04426. **Phone-**207-564-2411; fax-207-564-7708; hours 8:30AM-4PM

Will not search records. They still record furnaces, equipment and mobile homes UCCs. UCC copy-$1.00 per financing statement. RE record copy- $1.00 per page. Cert fee: $0.00. Payee: Piscataquis County Register of Deeds. **Online Access to Deed, Land, Judgment records:** In the process of developing a searchable website. Online searching expected in late 2005.

Sagadahoc County

County Register of Deeds, PO Box 246, Bath, ME 04530. **Phone-**207-443-8214; fax-207-443-8216; hours 8:30AM-4:30PM www.cityofbath.com

Will not search records. Will check a name for recent recording. UCC copy- $1.00 per financing statement. RE record copy- $1.00 per page. Cert fee: No charge. Payee: Sagadahoc County Register of Deeds. **Online Access to Recording, Grantor/Grantee, Real Estate, Assessor, Most Wanted records:** Register of Deeds records are online for a $50.00 per year fee + $.25 per minute access fee. Records go back to 1964 on the index, Grantor/Grantee. For information and registration, call the Register of Deeds. Also, records on City of Bath Assessor database are available free at www.cityofbath.com/assessdb/search.asp. The county sheriff's most wanted list is at www.clinic.net/sheriff/mostwant.htm.

Somerset County

County Register of Deeds, PO Box 248, Skowhegan, ME 04976-0248. **Phone-**207-474-3421; fax-207-474-2793; hours 8:30AM-4:30PM

All tax info and vital records are done at the municipal level. Will not search UCC records. Will make copies- provide book and page number. UCC copy- $1.00 per page; $2.00 if faxed. Will not search real estate or tax lien records. RE record copy- $1.00 per page; $2.00 per page if faxed. Cert fee: $1.00 per docu. Payee: Register of Deeds.

Waldo County

County Register of Deeds, PO Box D, Belfast, ME 04915. **Phone-**207-338-1710; fax-207-338-6360; hours 8AM-4PM

Will not search records. Record copy- $1.00 per page. Cert fee: $1.00 per cert. Payee: Waldo County Register of Deeds.

Washington County

County Register of Deeds, PO Box 297, Machias, ME 04654-0297. **Phone-**207-255-6512; fax-207-255-3838; hours 8AM-4PM

Will not search records. Record copy- $1.00 per page. Cert fee: $1.00 per doc. Payee: Washington County Register of Deeds. **Other phones:** Assessor-207-255-6621 (Machias area only); Treasurer-207-255-8354; County Clerk-207-255-3127.

York County

County Register of Deeds, PO Box 339, Alfred, ME 04002-0339. **Phone-**207-324-1576; fax-207-324-2886; hours 8:30AM-4:30PM

Will not search records. Record copy- $1.25 per page. Cert fee: $1.00 per doc. Payee: York County Register of Deeds. **Online Access to Assessor, Property records:** Search the Town of Kennebunk assessor data available free at www.kennebunkmaine.org; click on Departments, then Tax Assessment, then choose desired data file. Search the Town of Elliot assessor data at http://data.visionappraisal.com/EliotME. Register & search Town of York assessor data at http://data.visionappraisal.com/yorkme/. Town of York assessor at http://data.visionappraisal.com/YorkME. Free registration is required. Town of Arundel assessor data is available at http://data.visionappraisal.com/ArundelME/. Same for Town of Old Orchard Beach at http://data.visionappraisal.com/OldorchardbeachME/, Saco at http://data.visionappraisal.com/SacoME/, and Town of Kittery assessor data at http://data.visionappraisal.com/KitteryME/. **Other phones:** Treasurer-207-324-1571.

Maine County Locator

You will usually be able to find the city name in the City/County Cross. Reference below. In that case, it is a simple matter to determine the county from the cross reference. However, only the official US Postal Service city names are included in this index. There are an additional 40,000 place names that people use in their addresses. Therefore, we have also included a ZIP/City Cross. Reference immediately following the City/County Cross. Reference.

If you know the ZIP Code but the city name does not appear in the City/County Cross. Reference index, look up the ZIP Code in the ZIP/City Cross. Reference, find the city name, then look up the city name in the City/County Cross. Reference. For example, you want to know the county for an address of Menands, NY 12204. There is no "Menands" in the City/County Cross. Reference. The ZIP/City Cross. Reference shows that ZIP Codes 12201-12288 are for the city of Albany. Looking back in the City/County Cross. Reference, Albany is in Albany County.

Maine City/County Cross Reference

ABBOT Piscataquis
ABBOT VILLAGE Piscataquis
ACTON York
ADDISON Washington
ALBION Kennebec
ALFRED York
ALNA Lincoln
ANDOVER Oxford
ANSON Somerset
ASHLAND Aroostook
ATHENS Somerset
ATLANTIC Hancock
AUBURN Androscoggin
AUGUSTA Kennebec
AURORA Hancock
BAILEY ISLAND Cumberland
BAILEYVILLE Washington
BANGOR Penobscot
BAR HARBOR Hancock
BAR MILLS York
BASS HARBOR Hancock
BATH Sagadahoc
BAYVILLE Lincoln
BEALS Washington
BELFAST Waldo
BELGRADE Kennebec
BELGRADE LAKES Kennebec
BENEDICTA Aroostook
BERNARD Hancock
BERWICK York
BETHEL Oxford
BIDDEFORD York
BIDDEFORD POOL York
BINGHAM Somerset
BIRCH HARBOR Hancock
BLAINE Aroostook
BLUE HILL Hancock
BLUE HILL FALLS Hancock
BOOTHBAY Lincoln
BOOTHBAY HARBOR Lincoln
BOWDOIN Sagadahoc
BOWDOINHAM Sagadahoc
BRADFORD Penobscot
BRADLEY Penobscot
BREMEN Lincoln
BREWER Penobscot
BRIDGEWATER Aroostook
BRIDGTON Cumberland
BRISTOL Lincoln
BROOKLIN Hancock
BROOKS Waldo
BROOKSVILLE Hancock
BROOKTON Washington
BROWNFIELD Oxford
BROWNVILLE Piscataquis
BROWNVILLE JUNCTION Piscataquis
BRUNSWICK Cumberland
BRYANT POND Oxford
BUCKFIELD Oxford
BUCKS HARBOR Washington
BUCKSPORT Hancock
BURLINGTON Penobscot
BURNHAM Waldo

BUSTINS ISLAND Cumberland
BUXTON York
CALAIS Washington
CAMBRIDGE Somerset
CAMDEN Knox
CANAAN Somerset
CANTON Oxford
CAPE ELIZABETH Cumberland
CAPE NEDDICK York
CAPE PORPOISE York
CARATUNK Somerset
CARDVILLE Penobscot
CARIBOU Aroostook
CARMEL Penobscot
CASCO Cumberland
CASTINE Hancock
CENTER LOVELL Oxford
CHAMBERLAIN Lincoln
CHARLESTON Penobscot
CHEBEAGUE ISLAND Cumberland
CHERRYFIELD Washington
CHINA Kennebec
CHINA VILLAGE Kennebec
CLAYTON LAKE Aroostook
CLIFF ISLAND Cumberland
CLINTON Kennebec
COLUMBIA FALLS Washington
COOPERS MILLS Lincoln
COREA Hancock
CORINNA Penobscot
CORINTH Penobscot
CORNISH York
COSTIGAN Penobscot
CRANBERRY ISLES Hancock
CROUSEVILLE Aroostook
CUMBERLAND CENTER Cumberland
CUMBERLAND FORESIDE Cumberland
CUSHING Knox
CUTLER Washington
DAMARISCOTTA Lincoln
DANFORTH Washington
DANVILLE Androscoggin
DEER ISLE Hancock
DENMARK Oxford
DENNYSVILLE Washington
DETROIT Somerset
DEXTER (04930) Penobscot(97),
    Somerset(2)
DIXFIELD Oxford
DIXMONT Penobscot
DOVER FOXCROFT Piscataquis
DRESDEN Lincoln
DRYDEN Franklin
DURHAM Androscoggin
EAGLE LAKE Aroostook
EAST ANDOVER Oxford
EAST BALDWIN Cumberland
EAST BLUE HILL Hancock
EAST BOOTHBAY Lincoln
EAST CORINTH Penobscot
EAST DIXFIELD Franklin
EAST LIVERMORE Androscoggin
EAST MACHIAS Washington

EAST MILLINOCKET Penobscot
EAST NEWPORT Penobscot
EAST ORLAND Hancock
EAST PARSONFIELD York
EAST POLAND Androscoggin
EAST STONEHAM Oxford
EAST VASSALBORO Kennebec
EAST WATERBORO York
EAST WATERFORD Oxford
EAST WILTON Franklin
EAST WINTHROP Kennebec
EASTON Aroostook
EASTPORT Washington
EDDINGTON Penobscot
EDGECOMB Lincoln
ELIOT York
ELLSWORTH Hancock
ENFIELD Penobscot
ESTCOURT STATION Aroostook
ETNA Penobscot
EUSTIS Franklin
EXETER Penobscot
FAIRFIELD (04937) Kennebec(97),
    Somerset(2)
FALMOUTH Cumberland
FARMINGDALE Kennebec
FARMINGTON Franklin
FARMINGTON FALLS Franklin
FORT FAIRFIELD Aroostook
FORT KENT Aroostook
FORT KENT MILLS Aroostook
FRANKFORT Waldo
FRANKLIN Hancock
FREEDOM Waldo
FREEPORT Cumberland
FRENCHBORO Hancock
FRENCHVILLE Aroostook
FRIENDSHIP Knox
FRYE Oxford
FRYEBURG Oxford
GARDINER Kennebec
GARLAND Penobscot
GEORGETOWN Sagadahoc
GLEN COVE Knox
GORHAM Cumberland
GOULDSBORO Hancock
GRAND ISLE Aroostook
GRAND LAKE STREAM Washington
GRAY Cumberland
GREENBUSH Penobscot
GREENE Androscoggin
GREENVILLE Piscataquis
GREENVILLE JUNCTION (04442)
    Piscataquis(86), Somerset(13)
GREENWOOD Oxford
GROVE Washington
GUILFORD Piscataquis
HALLOWELL Kennebec
HAMPDEN Penobscot
HANCOCK Hancock
HANOVER Oxford
HARBORSIDE Hancock
HARMONY Somerset

HARPSWELL Cumberland
HARRINGTON Washington
HARRISON Cumberland
HARTLAND Somerset
HAYNESVILLE Aroostook
HEBRON Oxford
HINCKLEY Somerset
HIRAM Oxford
HOLDEN (04429) Penobscot(98),
    Hancock(1)
HOLLIS CENTER York
HOPE Knox
HOULTON Aroostook
HOWLAND Penobscot
HUDSON Penobscot
HULLS COVE Hancock
ISLAND FALLS Aroostook
ISLE AU HAUT Knox
ISLE OF SPRINGS Lincoln
ISLESBORO Waldo
ISLESFORD Hancock
JACKMAN Somerset
JAY Franklin
JEFFERSON Lincoln
JONESBORO Washington
JONESPORT Washington
KENDUSKEAG Penobscot
KENNEBUNK York
KENNEBUNKPORT York
KENTS HILL Kennebec
KINGFIELD Franklin
KINGMAN Penobscot
KITTERY York
KITTERY POINT York
LAGRANGE (04453) Penobscot(98),
    Piscataquis(1)
LAMBERT LAKE Washington
LEBANON York
LEE Penobscot
LEEDS Androscoggin
LEVANT Penobscot
LEWISTON Androscoggin
LIBERTY Waldo
LILLE Aroostook
LIMERICK York
LIMESTONE Aroostook
LIMINGTON York
LINCOLN Penobscot
LINCOLN CENTER Penobscot
LINCOLNVILLE Waldo
LINCOLNVILLE CENTER Waldo
LISBON Androscoggin
LISBON CENTER Androscoggin
LISBON FALLS Androscoggin
LITCHFIELD Kennebec
LITTLE DEER ISLE Hancock
LIVERMORE Androscoggin
LIVERMORE FALLS Androscoggin
LOCKE MILLS Oxford
LONG ISLAND Cumberland
LOVELL Oxford
LUBEC Washington
MACHIAS Washington

MACHIASPORT Washington
MADAWASKA Aroostook
MADISON Somerset
MANCHESTER Kennebec
MANSET Hancock
MAPLETON Aroostook
MARS HILL Aroostook
MASARDIS Aroostook
MATINICUS Knox
MATTAWAMKEAG Penobscot
MECHANIC FALLS Androscoggin
MEDDYBEMPS Washington
MEDWAY Penobscot
MEREPOINT Cumberland
MEXICO Oxford
MILBRIDGE Washington
MILFORD Penobscot
MILLINOCKET Penobscot
MILO Piscataquis
MINOT Androscoggin
MINTURN Hancock
MONHEGAN Lincoln
MONMOUTH Kennebec
MONROE Waldo
MONSON Piscataquis
MONTICELLO Aroostook
MOODY York
MORRILL Waldo
MOUNT DESERT Hancock
MOUNT VERNON Kennebec
NAPLES Cumberland
NEW GLOUCESTER Cumberland
NEW HARBOR Lincoln
NEW LIMERICK Aroostook
NEW PORTLAND Somerset
NEW SHARON Franklin
NEW SWEDEN Aroostook
NEW VINEYARD Franklin
NEWAGEN Lincoln
NEWCASTLE Lincoln
NEWFIELD York
NEWPORT Penobscot
NEWRY Oxford
NOBLEBORO Lincoln
NORRIDGEWOCK Somerset
NORTH AMITY Aroostook
NORTH ANSON Somerset
NORTH BERWICK York
NORTH BRIDGTON Cumberland
NORTH BROOKLIN Hancock
NORTH FRYEBURG Oxford
NORTH HAVEN Knox
NORTH JAY Franklin
NORTH MONMOUTH Kennebec
NORTH NEW PORTLAND Somerset
NORTH SHAPLEIGH York
NORTH TURNER Androscoggin
NORTH VASSALBORO Kennebec
NORTH WATERBORO York
NORTH WATERFORD Oxford
NORTH YARMOUTH Cumberland
NORTHEAST HARBOR Hancock
NORWAY Oxford
OAKFIELD Aroostook
OAKLAND Kennebec
OCEAN PARK York
OGUNQUIT York
OLAMON Penobscot

OLD ORCHARD BEACH York
OLD TOWN Penobscot
OQUOSSOC Franklin
ORIENT Aroostook
ORLAND Hancock
ORONO Penobscot
ORRINGTON Penobscot
ORRS ISLAND Cumberland
OTTER CREEK Hancock
OWLS HEAD Knox
OXBOW Aroostook
OXFORD Oxford
PALERMO Waldo
PALMYRA Somerset
PARIS Oxford
PARSONSFIELD York
PASSADUMKEAG Penobscot
PATTEN Penobscot
PEAKS ISLAND Cumberland
PEJEPSCOT Sagadahoc
PEMAQUID Lincoln
PEMBROKE Washington
PENOBSCOT Hancock
PERHAM Aroostook
PERRY Washington
PERU Oxford
PHILLIPS Franklin
PHIPPSBURG Sagadahoc
PITTSFIELD Somerset
PLAISTED Aroostook
PLYMOUTH Penobscot
POLAND Androscoggin
PORT CLYDE Knox
PORTAGE Aroostook
PORTER Oxford
PORTLAND Cumberland
POWNAL Cumberland
PRESQUE ISLE Aroostook
PRINCETON Washington
PROSPECT HARBOR Hancock
QUIMBY Aroostook
RANDOLPH Kennebec
RANGELEY Franklin
RAYMOND Cumberland
READFIELD Kennebec
RICHMOND Sagadahoc
ROBBINSTON Washington
ROCKLAND Knox
ROCKPORT Knox
ROCKWOOD (04478) Somerset(86),
    Piscataquis(13)
ROUND POND Lincoln
ROXBURY Oxford
RUMFORD Oxford
RUMFORD CENTER Oxford
RUMFORD POINT Oxford
SABATTUS Androscoggin
SACO York
SAINT AGATHA Aroostook
SAINT ALBANS Somerset
SAINT DAVID Aroostook
SAINT FRANCIS Aroostook
SAINT GEORGE Knox
SALSBURY COVE Hancock
SANDY POINT Waldo
SANFORD York
SANGERVILLE Piscataquis
SARGENTVILLE Hancock

SCARBOROUGH Cumberland
SEAL COVE Hancock
SEAL HARBOR Hancock
SEARSMONT Waldo
SEARSPORT Waldo
SEBAGO Cumberland
SEBAGO LAKE Cumberland
SEBASCO ESTATES Sagadahoc
SEBEC Piscataquis
SEBEC LAKE Piscataquis
SEDGWICK Hancock
SHAPLEIGH York
SHAWMUT Somerset
SHERIDAN Aroostook
SHERMAN Aroostook
SHERMAN MILLS Aroostook
SHERMAN STATION (04777)
    Penobscot(90), Aroostook(9)
SHIRLEY MILLS Piscataquis
SINCLAIR Aroostook
SKOWHEGAN Somerset
SMALL POINT Sagadahoc
SMITHFIELD Somerset
SMYRNA MILLS Aroostook
SOLDIER POND Aroostook
SOLON Somerset
SORRENTO Hancock
SOUTH BERWICK York
SOUTH BRISTOL Lincoln
SOUTH CASCO Cumberland
SOUTH CHINA Kennebec
SOUTH FREEPORT Cumberland
SOUTH GARDINER Kennebec
SOUTH GOULDSBORO Hancock
SOUTH HIRAM Oxford
SOUTH PARIS Oxford
SOUTH PORTLAND Cumberland
SOUTH THOMASTON Knox
SOUTH WATERFORD Oxford
SOUTH WINDHAM Cumberland
SOUTHPORT Lincoln
SOUTHWEST HARBOR Hancock
SPRINGFIELD Penobscot
SPRINGVALE York
SPRUCE HEAD Knox
SQUIRREL ISLAND Lincoln
STACYVILLE (04777) Penobscot(90),
    Aroostook(9)
STACYVILLE Penobscot
STANDISH Cumberland
STEEP FALLS Cumberland
STETSON Penobscot
STEUBEN Washington
STILLWATER Penobscot
STOCKHOLM Aroostook
STOCKTON SPRINGS Waldo
STONEHAM Oxford
STONINGTON Hancock
STRATTON Franklin
STRONG Franklin
SULLIVAN Hancock
SUMNER Oxford
SUNSET Hancock
SURRY Hancock
SWANS ISLAND Hancock
TEMPLE Franklin
TENANTS HARBOR Knox
THOMASTON Knox

THORNDIKE Waldo
TOPSFIELD Washington
TOPSHAM Sagadahoc
TREVETT Lincoln
TROY Waldo
TURNER Androscoggin
TURNER CENTER Androscoggin
UNION Knox
UNITY Waldo
UPPER FRENCHVILLE Aroostook
VAN BUREN Aroostook
VANCEBORO Washington
VASSALBORO Kennebec
VIENNA Kennebec
VINALHAVEN Knox
WAITE Washington
WALDOBORO Lincoln
WALLAGRASS Aroostook
WALPOLE Lincoln
WARREN Knox
WASHBURN Aroostook
WASHINGTON Knox
WATERBORO York
WATERFORD Oxford
WATERVILLE Kennebec
WAYNE Kennebec
WEEKS MILLS Kennebec
WELD Franklin
WELLS York
WESLEY Washington
WEST BALDWIN Cumberland
WEST BETHEL Oxford
WEST BOOTHBAY HARBOR Lincoln
WEST BOWDOIN Sagadahoc
WEST BUXTON York
WEST ENFIELD Penobscot
WEST FARMINGTON Franklin
WEST FORKS Somerset
WEST KENNEBUNK York
WEST MINOT Androscoggin
WEST NEWFIELD York
WEST PARIS Oxford
WEST POLAND Androscoggin
WEST ROCKPORT Knox
WEST SOUTHPORT Lincoln
WEST TREMONT Hancock
WESTBROOK Cumberland
WESTFIELD Aroostook
WHITEFIELD Lincoln
WHITING Washington
WHITNEYVILLE Washington
WILEYS CORNER Knox
WILTON Franklin
WINDHAM Cumberland
WINDSOR Kennebec
WINN Penobscot
WINTER HARBOR Hancock
WINTERPORT Waldo
WINTERVILLE Aroostook
WINTHROP Kennebec
WISCASSET Lincoln
WOODLAND Washington
WOOLWICH Sagadahoc
WYTOPITLOCK Aroostook
YARMOUTH Cumberland
YORK York
YORK BEACH York
YORK HARBOR York

Maine ZIP/City Cross Reference

03901-03901 BERWICK	04085-04085 STEEP FALLS	04286-04286 WEST BETHEL	04461-04461 MILFORD
03902-03902 CAPE NEDDICK	04086-04086 TOPSHAM	04287-04287 WEST BOWDOIN	04462-04462 MILLINOCKET
03903-03903 ELIOT	04087-04087 WATERBORO	04287-04287 BOWDOIN	04463-04463 MILO
03904-03904 KITTERY	04088-04088 WATERFORD	04288-04288 WEST MINOT	04464-04464 MONSON
03905-03905 KITTERY POINT	04090-04090 WELLS	04289-04289 WEST PARIS	04465-04465 NORTH AMITY
03906-03906 NORTH BERWICK	04091-04091 WEST BALDWIN	04290-04290 PERU	04467-04467 OLAMON
03907-03907 OGUNQUIT	04092-04092 WESTBROOK	04291-04291 WEST POLAND	04468-04468 OLD TOWN
03908-03908 SOUTH BERWICK	04093-04093 WEST BUXTON	04292-04292 SUMNER	04469-04469 ORONO
03909-03909 YORK	04093-04093 BUXTON	04294-04294 WILTON	04471-04471 ORIENT
03910-03910 YORK BEACH	04094-04094 WEST KENNEBUNK	04330-04338 AUGUSTA	04472-04472 ORLAND
03911-03911 YORK HARBOR	04095-04095 WEST NEWFIELD	04341-04341 COOPERS MILLS	04473-04473 ORONO
04001-04001 ACTON	04096-04096 YARMOUTH	04342-04342 DRESDEN	04474-04474 ORRINGTON
04002-04002 ALFRED	04097-04097 NORTH YARMOUTH	04343-04343 EAST WINTHROP	04475-04475 PASSADUMKEAG
04003-04003 BAILEY ISLAND	04098-04098 WESTBROOK	04344-04344 FARMINGDALE	04476-04476 PENOBSCOT
04004-04004 BAR MILLS	04100-04104 PORTLAND	04345-04345 GARDINER	04478-04478 ROCKWOOD
04005-04005 BIDDEFORD	04105-04105 FALMOUTH	04346-04346 RANDOLPH	04479-04479 SANGERVILLE
04006-04006 BIDDEFORD POOL	04106-04106 SOUTH PORTLAND	04347-04347 HALLOWELL	04481-04481 SEBEC
04007-04007 BIDDEFORD	04107-04107 CAPE ELIZABETH	04348-04348 JEFFERSON	04482-04482 GUILFORD
04008-04008 BOWDOINHAM	04108-04108 PEAKS ISLAND	04349-04349 KENTS HILL	04482-04482 SEBEC LAKE
04009-04009 BRIDGTON	04109-04109 PORTLAND	04350-04350 LITCHFIELD	04485-04485 SHIRLEY MILLS
04010-04010 BROWNFIELD	04110-04110 CUMBERLAND FORESIDE	04351-04351 MANCHESTER	04487-04487 SPRINGFIELD
04011-04011 BRUNSWICK	04112-04112 PORTLAND	04352-04352 MOUNT VERNON	04488-04488 STETSON
04013-04013 BUSTINS ISLAND	04116-04116 SOUTH PORTLAND	04353-04353 WHITEFIELD	04489-04489 STILLWATER
04014-04014 CAPE PORPOISE	04122-04124 PORTLAND	04354-04354 PALERMO	04490-04490 TOPSFIELD
04015-04015 CASCO	04210-04212 AUBURN	04355-04355 READFIELD	04491-04491 VANCEBORO
04016-04016 CENTER LOVELL	04216-04216 ANDOVER	04357-04357 RICHMOND	04492-04492 WAITE
04017-04017 CHEBEAGUE ISLAND	04217-04217 BETHEL	04358-04358 SOUTH CHINA	04493-04493 WEST ENFIELD
04019-04019 CLIFF ISLAND	04219-04219 BRYANT POND	04359-04359 SOUTH GARDINER	04495-04495 WINN
04020-04020 CORNISH	04220-04220 BUCKFIELD	04360-04360 VIENNA	04496-04496 WINTERPORT
04021-04021 CUMBERLAND CENTER	04221-04221 CANTON	04361-04361 WEEKS MILLS	04497-04497 WYTOPITLOCK
04022-04022 DENMARK	04222-04222 DURHAM	04362-04362 WHITEFIELD	04530-04530 BATH
04024-04024 EAST BALDWIN	04223-04223 DANVILLE	04363-04363 WINDSOR	04535-04535 ALNA
04027-04027 LEBANON	04224-04224 DIXFIELD	04364-04364 WINTHROP	04536-04536 BAYVILLE
04028-04028 EAST PARSONFIELD	04225-04225 DRYDEN	04401-04402 BANGOR	04537-04537 BOOTHBAY
04029-04029 SEBAGO	04226-04226 EAST ANDOVER	04406-04406 ABBOT VILLAGE	04538-04538 BOOTHBAY HARBOR
04030-04030 EAST WATERBORO	04227-04227 EAST DIXFIELD	04406-04406 ABBOT	04539-04539 BRISTOL
04032-04034 FREEPORT	04228-04228 EAST LIVERMORE	04408-04408 AURORA	04541-04541 CHAMBERLAIN
04037-04037 FRYEBURG	04230-04230 EAST POLAND	04410-04410 BRADFORD	04543-04543 DAMARISCOTTA
04038-04038 GORHAM	04231-04231 EAST STONEHAM	04411-04411 BRADLEY	04544-04544 EAST BOOTHBAY
04039-04039 GRAY	04231-04231 STONEHAM	04412-04412 BREWER	04547-04547 FRIENDSHIP
04040-04040 HARRISON	04233-04233 EAST WATERFORD	04413-04413 BROOKTON	04548-04548 GEORGETOWN
04041-04041 HIRAM	04234-04234 EAST WILTON	04414-04414 BROWNVILLE	04549-04549 ISLE OF SPRINGS
04042-04042 HOLLIS CENTER	04235-04235 FRYE	04415-04415 BROWNVILLE JUNCTION	04551-04551 BREMEN
04043-04043 KENNEBUNK	04236-04236 GREENE	04416-04416 BUCKSPORT	04552-04552 NEWAGEN
04046-04046 KENNEBUNKPORT	04237-04237 HANOVER	04417-04417 BURLINGTON	04553-04553 NEWCASTLE
04047-04047 PARSONSFIELD	04238-04238 HEBRON	04418-04418 CARDVILLE	04554-04554 NEW HARBOR
04048-04048 LIMERICK	04239-04239 JAY	04418-04418 GREENBUSH	04555-04555 NOBLEBORO
04049-04049 LIMINGTON	04240-04243 LEWISTON	04419-04419 CARMEL	04556-04556 EDGECOMB
04050-04050 LONG ISLAND	04250-04250 LISBON	04420-04421 CASTINE	04558-04558 PEMAQUID
04051-04051 LOVELL	04251-04251 LISBON CENTER	04422-04422 CHARLESTON	04562-04562 PHIPPSBURG
04053-04053 MEREPOINT	04252-04252 LISBON FALLS	04423-04423 COSTIGAN	04563-04563 CUSHING
04054-04054 MOODY	04253-04253 LIVERMORE	04424-04424 DANFORTH	04564-04564 ROUND POND
04055-04055 NAPLES	04254-04254 LIVERMORE FALLS	04426-04426 DOVER FOXCROFT	04565-04565 SEBASCO ESTATES
04056-04056 NEWFIELD	04255-04255 LOCKE MILLS	04427-04427 EAST CORINTH	04567-04567 SMALL POINT
04057-04057 NORTH BRIDGTON	04255-04255 GREENWOOD	04427-04427 CORINTH	04568-04568 SOUTH BRISTOL
04058-04058 NORTH FRYEBURG	04256-04256 MECHANIC FALLS	04428-04428 EDDINGTON	04570-04570 SQUIRREL ISLAND
04060-04060 NORTH SHAPLEIGH	04257-04257 MEXICO	04429-04429 HOLDEN	04571-04571 TREVETT
04061-04061 NORTH WATERBORO	04258-04258 MINOT	04430-04430 EAST MILLINOCKET	04572-04572 WALDOBORO
04062-04062 WINDHAM	04259-04259 MONMOUTH	04431-04431 EAST ORLAND	04573-04573 WALPOLE
04063-04063 OCEAN PARK	04260-04260 NEW GLOUCESTER	04433-04433 ENFIELD	04574-04574 WASHINGTON
04064-04064 OLD ORCHARD BEACH	04261-04261 NEWRY	04434-04434 ETNA	04575-04575 WEST BOOTHBAY HARBOR
04066-04066 ORRS ISLAND	04262-04262 NORTH JAY	04435-04435 EXETER	04576-04576 WEST SOUTHPORT
04067-04067 PEJEPSCOT	04263-04263 LEEDS	04438-04438 FRANKFORT	04576-04576 SOUTHPORT
04068-04068 PORTER	04265-04265 NORTH MONMOUTH	04441-04441 GREENVILLE	04578-04578 WISCASSET
04069-04069 POWNAL	04266-04266 NORTH TURNER	04442-04442 GREENVILLE JUNCTION	04579-04579 WOOLWICH
04070-04070 SCARBOROUGH	04267-04267 NORTH WATERFORD	04443-04443 GUILFORD	04605-04605 ELLSWORTH
04071-04071 RAYMOND	04268-04268 NORWAY	04444-04444 HAMPDEN	04606-04606 ADDISON
04072-04072 SACO	04270-04270 OXFORD	04446-04446 HAYNESVILLE	04607-04607 GOULDSBORO
04073-04073 SANFORD	04271-04271 PARIS	04448-04448 HOWLAND	04608-04608 ATLANTIC
04074-04074 SCARBOROUGH	04273-04274 POLAND	04449-04449 HUDSON	04609-04609 BAR HARBOR
04075-04075 SEBAGO LAKE	04275-04275 ROXBURY	04450-04450 KENDUSKEAG	04611-04611 BEALS
04076-04076 SHAPLEIGH	04276-04276 RUMFORD	04451-04451 KINGMAN	04612-04612 BERNARD
04077-04077 SOUTH CASCO	04278-04278 RUMFORD CENTER	04453-04453 LAGRANGE	04613-04613 BIRCH HARBOR
04078-04078 SOUTH FREEPORT	04279-04279 RUMFORD POINT	04454-04454 LAMBERT LAKE	04614-04614 BLUE HILL
04079-04079 HARPSWELL	04280-04280 SABATTUS	04455-04455 LEE	04615-04615 BLUE HILL FALLS
04080-04080 SOUTH HIRAM	04281-04281 SOUTH PARIS	04456-04456 LEVANT	04616-04616 BROOKLIN
04081-04081 SOUTH WATERFORD	04282-04282 TURNER	04457-04457 LINCOLN	04617-04617 BROOKSVILLE
04082-04082 SOUTH WINDHAM	04283-04283 TURNER CENTER	04458-04458 LINCOLN CENTER	04618-04618 BUCKS HARBOR
04083-04083 SPRINGVALE	04284-04284 WAYNE	04459-04459 MATTAWAMKEAG	04619-04619 CALAIS
04084-04084 STANDISH	04285-04285 WELD	04460-04460 MEDWAY	04622-04622 CHERRYFIELD

04623-04623 COLUMBIA FALLS	
04624-04624 COREA	
04625-04625 CRANBERRY ISLES	
04626-04626 CUTLER	
04627-04627 DEER ISLE	
04628-04628 DENNYSVILLE	
04629-04629 EAST BLUE HILL	
04630-04630 EAST MACHIAS	
04631-04631 EASTPORT	
04634-04634 FRANKLIN	
04635-04635 FRENCHBORO	
04637-04637 GRAND LAKE STREAM	
04638-04638 GROVE	
04640-04640 HANCOCK	
04642-04642 HARBORSIDE	
04643-04643 HARRINGTON	
04644-04644 HULLS COVE	
04645-04645 ISLE AU HAUT	
04646-04646 ISLESFORD	
04648-04648 JONESBORO	
04649-04649 JONESPORT	
04650-04650 LITTLE DEER ISLE	
04652-04652 LUBEC	
04653-04653 BASS HARBOR	
04654-04654 MACHIAS	
04655-04655 MACHIASPORT	
04656-04656 MANSET	
04657-04657 MEDDYBEMPS	
04658-04658 MILBRIDGE	
04659-04659 MINTURN	
04660-04660 MOUNT DESERT	
04661-04661 NORTH BROOKLIN	
04662-04662 NORTHEAST HARBOR	
04664-04664 SULLIVAN	
04665-04665 OTTER CREEK	
04666-04666 PEMBROKE	
04667-04667 PERRY	
04668-04668 PRINCETON	
04669-04669 PROSPECT HARBOR	
04671-04671 ROBBINSTON	
04672-04672 SALSBURY COVE	
04673-04673 SARGENTVILLE	
04674-04674 SEAL COVE	
04675-04675 SEAL HARBOR	
04676-04676 SEDGWICK	
04677-04677 SORRENTO	
04678-04678 SOUTH GOULDSBORO	
04679-04679 SOUTHWEST HARBOR	
04680-04680 STEUBEN	
04681-04681 STONINGTON	
04683-04683 SUNSET	
04684-04684 SURRY	
04685-04685 SWANS ISLAND	
04686-04686 WESLEY	
04690-04690 WEST TREMONT	
04691-04691 WHITING	
04692-04692 WHITNEYVILLE	
04693-04693 WINTER HARBOR	
04694-04694 WOODLAND	
04694-04694 BAILEYVILLE	
04730-04730 HOULTON	
04732-04732 ASHLAND	
04733-04733 BENEDICTA	
04734-04734 BLAINE	
04735-04735 BRIDGEWATER	
04736-04736 CARIBOU	
04737-04737 CLAYTON LAKE	
04738-04738 CROUSEVILLE	
04739-04739 EAGLE LAKE	
04740-04740 EASTON	
04741-04741 ESTCOURT STATION	
04742-04742 FORT FAIRFIELD	
04743-04743 FORT KENT	
04744-04744 FORT KENT MILLS	
04745-04745 FRENCHVILLE	
04746-04746 GRAND ISLE	
04747-04747 ISLAND FALLS	
04749-04749 LILLE	
04750-04751 LIMESTONE	
04756-04756 MADAWASKA	
04757-04757 MAPLETON	
04758-04758 MARS HILL	
04759-04759 MASARDIS	

04760-04760 MONTICELLO	
04761-04761 NEW LIMERICK	
04762-04762 NEW SWEDEN	
04763-04763 OAKFIELD	
04764-04764 OXBOW	
04765-04765 PATTEN	
04766-04766 PERHAM	
04767-04767 PLAISTED	
04768-04768 PORTAGE	
04769-04769 PRESQUE ISLE	
04770-04770 QUIMBY	
04772-04772 SAINT AGATHA	
04773-04773 SAINT DAVID	
04774-04774 SAINT FRANCIS	
04775-04775 SHERIDAN	
04776-04776 SHERMAN MILLS	
04776-04776 SHERMAN	
04777-04777 SHERMAN STATION	
04777-04777 STACYVILLE	
04779-04779 SINCLAIR	
04780-04780 SMYRNA MILLS	
04781-04781 SOLDIER POND	
04781-04781 WALLAGRASS	
04782-04782 STACYVILLE	
04783-04783 STOCKHOLM	
04784-04784 UPPER FRENCHVILLE	
04785-04785 VAN BUREN	
04786-04786 WASHBURN	
04787-04787 WESTFIELD	
04788-04788 WINTERVILLE	
04841-04841 ROCKLAND	
04843-04843 CAMDEN	
04846-04846 GLEN COVE	
04847-04847 HOPE	
04848-04848 ISLESBORO	
04849-04849 LINCOLNVILLE	
04850-04850 LINCOLNVILLE CENTER	
04851-04851 MATINICUS	
04852-04852 MONHEGAN	
04853-04853 NORTH HAVEN	
04854-04854 OWLS HEAD	
04855-04855 PORT CLYDE	
04856-04856 ROCKPORT	
04857-04857 SAINT GEORGE	
04857-04857 WILEYS CORNER	
04858-04858 SOUTH THOMASTON	
04859-04859 SPRUCE HEAD	
04860-04860 TENANTS HARBOR	
04861-04861 THOMASTON	
04862-04862 UNION	
04863-04863 VINALHAVEN	
04864-04864 WARREN	
04865-04865 WEST ROCKPORT	
04901-04903 WATERVILLE	
04910-04910 ALBION	
04911-04911 ANSON	
04912-04912 ATHENS	
04915-04915 BELFAST	
04917-04917 BELGRADE	
04918-04918 BELGRADE LAKES	
04920-04920 BINGHAM	
04921-04921 BROOKS	
04922-04922 BURNHAM	
04923-04923 CAMBRIDGE	
04924-04924 CANAAN	
04925-04925 CARATUNK	
04926-04926 CHINA	
04926-04926 CHINA VILLAGE	
04927-04927 CLINTON	
04928-04928 CORINNA	
04929-04929 DETROIT	
04930-04930 DEXTER	
04932-04932 DIXMONT	
04933-04933 EAST NEWPORT	
04935-04935 EAST VASSALBORO	
04936-04936 EUSTIS	
04937-04937 FAIRFIELD	
04938-04938 FARMINGTON	
04939-04939 GARLAND	
04940-04940 FARMINGTON FALLS	
04941-04941 FREEDOM	
04942-04942 HARMONY	
04943-04943 HARTLAND	

04944-04944 HINCKLEY	
04945-04945 JACKMAN	
04947-04947 KINGFIELD	
04949-04949 LIBERTY	
04950-04950 MADISON	
04951-04951 MONROE	
04952-04952 MORRILL	
04953-04953 NEWPORT	
04954-04954 NEW PORTLAND	
04955-04955 NEW SHARON	
04956-04956 NEW VINEYARD	
04957-04957 NORRIDGEWOCK	
04958-04958 NORTH ANSON	
04961-04961 NORTH NEW PORTLAND	
04961-04961 NEW PORTLAND	
04962-04962 NORTH VASSALBORO	
04963-04963 OAKLAND	
04964-04964 OQUOSSOC	
04965-04965 PALMYRA	
04966-04966 PHILLIPS	
04967-04967 PITTSFIELD	
04969-04969 PLYMOUTH	
04970-04970 RANGELEY	
04971-04971 SAINT ALBANS	
04972-04972 SANDY POINT	
04973-04973 SEARSMONT	
04974-04974 SEARSPORT	
04975-04975 SHAWMUT	
04976-04976 SKOWHEGAN	
04978-04978 SMITHFIELD	
04979-04979 SOLON	
04981-04981 STOCKTON SPRINGS	
04982-04982 STRATTON	
04983-04983 STRONG	
04984-04984 TEMPLE	
04985-04985 WEST FORKS	
04986-04986 THORNDIKE	
04987-04987 TROY	
04988-04988 UNITY	
04989-04989 VASSALBORO	
04992-04992 WEST FARMINGTON	

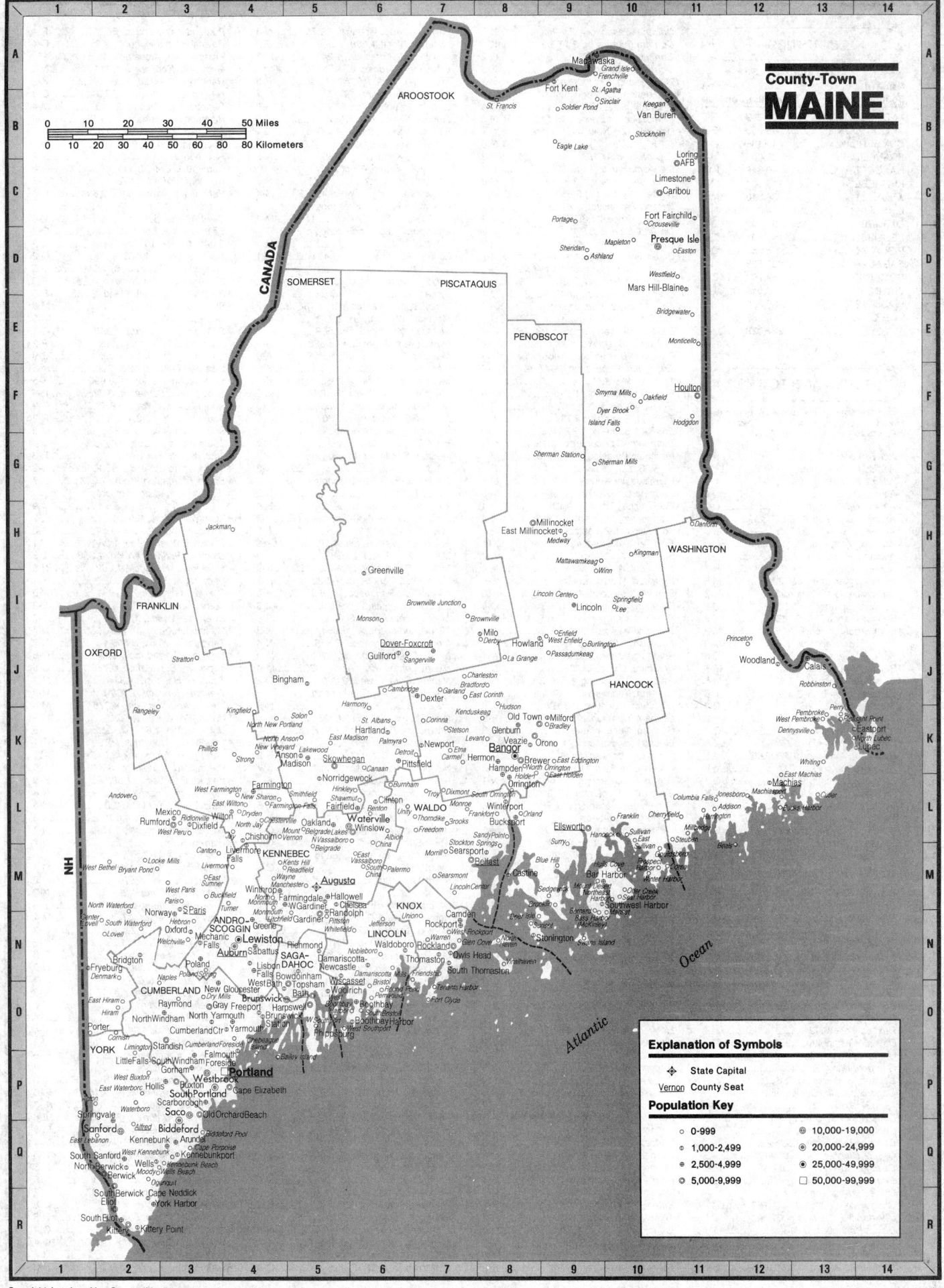

County-Town
MAINE

Explanation of Symbols

◆ State Capital
Vernon County Seat

Population Key

○ 0-999	◉ 10,000-19,000
◉ 1,000-2,499	◉ 20,000-24,999
⊕ 2,500-4,999	◉ 25,000-49,999
◎ 5,000-9,999	☐ 50,000-99,999

COUNTIES

(16 Counties)

Name of County	Population	Location on Map
ANDROSCOGGIN	105,259	N-3
AROOSTOOK	86,936	B-6
CUMBERLAND	243,135	O-2
FRANKLIN	29,008	I-2
HANCOCK	46,948	J-10
KENNEBEC	115,904	M-4
KNOX	36,310	M-6
LINCOLN	30,357	N-6
OXFORD	52,602	J-1
PENOBSCOT	146,601	E-8
PISCATAQUIS	18,653	D-7
SAGADAHOC	33,535	N-4
SOMERSET	49,767	D-5
WALDO	33,018	L-7
WASHINGTON	35,308	H-11
YORK	164,587	O-1
TOTAL	1,227,928	

CITIES AND TOWNS

Note: The first name is that of the city or town, second, that of the county in which it is located, then the population and location on the map.

Acton, York, 1,727	P-2
Addison, Washington, 1,114	L-11
Albion, Kennebec, 1,736	L-6
Alfred, York	Q-2
Alfred, York, 2,238	Q-2
Anson, Somerset, 2,382	K-5
Appleton, Knox, 1,069	M-7
▲ *Arundel, York, 2,669*	Q-3
Ashland, Aroostook, 1,542	D-9
Auburn, Androscoggin, 24,309	N-4
Augusta, Kennebec, 21,325	M-5
Baileyville, Washington, 2,031	J-12
Baldwin, Cumberland, 1,219	O-2
Bangor, Penobscot, 33,181	K-8
• Bar Harbor, Hancock, 2,768	M-9
Bar Harbor, Hancock, 4,443	M-9
Bath, Sagadahoc, 9,799	O-5
Belfast, Waldo, 6,355	M-7
Belgrade, Kennebec, 2,375	M-5
Benton, Kennebec, 2,312	L-6
▲ *Berwick, York, 5,995*	Q-2
Bethel, Oxford, 2,329	M-2
Biddeford, York, 20,710	Q-3
• Bingham, Somerset, 1,071	J-5
Bingham, Somerset, 1,230	J-5
Blue Hill, Hancock, 1,941	M-9
▲ *Boothbay, Lincoln, 2,648*	O-6
• Boothbay Harbor, Lincoln, 1,267	O-6
Boothbay Harbor, Lincoln, 2,347	O-6
Bowdoin, Sagadahoc, 2,207	N-4
Bowdoinham, Sagadahoc, 2,192	N-4
Bradford, Penobscot, 1,103	J-8
Bradley, Penobscot, 1,136	K-9
Brewer, Penobscot, 9,021	K-8
• Bridgton, Cumberland, 2,195	N-2
Bridgton, Cumberland, 4,307	N-2
Bristol, Lincoln, 2,326	O-6
Brownfield, Oxford, 1,034	O-1
Brownville, Piscataquis, 1,506	I-7
• Brunswick, Cumberland, 14,683	O-5
Brunswick, Cumberland, 20,906	O-5
• Brunswick Station, Cumberland, 1,829	O-5
Buckfield, Oxford, 1,566	M-3
• Bucksport, Hancock, 2,989	L-8
Bucksport, Hancock, 4,825	L-8
▲ *Buxton, York, 6,494*	P-3
Calais, Washington, 3,963	J-13
• Camden, Knox, 4,022	N-7
Camden, Knox, 5,060	N-7
Canaan, Somerset, 1,636	K-6
▲ *Cape Elizabeth, Cumberland, 8,854*	P-4
• Cape Neddick, York, 2,193	R-2
Caribou, Aroostook, 9,415	C-10
Carmel, Penobscot, 1,906	K-7
Casco, Cumberland, 3,018	N-3
▲ *Castine, Hancock, 1,161*	M-8
Charleston, Penobscot, 1,187	J-7
▲ *Chelsea, Kennebec, 2,497*	M-5
Cherryfield, Washington, 1,183	L-11
Chesterville, Franklin, 1,012	L-4
China, Kennebec, 3,713	M-6
• Chisholm, Franklin, 1,653	L-4
• Clinton, Kennebec, 1,485	L-6
Clinton, Kennebec, 3,332	L-6
Corinna, Penobscot, 2,196	K-7
Corinth, Penobscot, 2,177	K-8
Cornish, York, 1,178	O-2
Cornville, Somerset, 1,008	K-5
Cumberland, Cumberland, 5,836	O-3
• Cumberland Center, Cumberland, 1,890	O-4
Damariscotta, Lincoln, 1,811	N-6
• Damariscotta-Newcastle, Lincoln, 1,567	N-6
Dayton, York, 1,197	P-3
Dedham, Hancock, 1,229	L-8
Deer Isle, Hancock, 1,829	N-8
• Dexter, Penobscot, 2,650	J-7
Dexter, Penobscot, 4,419	J-7
• Dixfield, Oxford, 1,300	L-3
Dixfield, Oxford, 2,574	L-3
Dixmont, Penobscot, 1,007	L-7
• Dover-Foxcroft, Piscataquis, 3,077	J-7
Dover-Foxcroft, Piscataquis, 4,657	J-7
Dresden, Lincoln, 1,332	N-5
Durham, Androscoggin, 2,842	O-4
East Machias, Washington, 1,218	K-12
• East Millinocket, Penobscot, 2,075	H-9
East Millinocket, Penobscot, 2,166	H-9
Easton, Aroostook, 1,291	D-11
Eastport, Washington, 1,965	K-13
Eddington, Penobscot, 1,947	K-9
▲ *Eliot, York, 5,329*	R-2
Ellsworth, Hancock, 5,975	L-9
Enfield, Penobscot, 1,476	I-9
• Fairfield, Somerset, 2,794	L-6
Fairfield, Somerset, 6,718	L-6
Falmouth, Cumberland, 7,610	P-4
• Falmouth Foreside, Cumberland, 1,708	P-4
• Farmingdale, Kennebec, 2,070	M-5
Farmingdale, Kennebec, 2,918	M-5
• Farmington, Franklin, 4,197	L-4
Farmington, Franklin, 7,436	L-4
• Fort Fairfield, Aroostook, 1,729	C-11
Fort Fairfield, Aroostook, 3,998	C-11
• Fort Kent, Aroostook, 2,123	A-9
Fort Kent, Aroostook, 4,268	A-9
Frankfort, Waldo, 1,020	L-8
Franklin, Hancock, 1,141	L-10
• Freeport, Cumberland, 1,829	O-4
Freeport, Cumberland, 6,905	O-4
Frenchville, Aroostook, 1,338	A-9
Friendship, Knox, 1,099	O-6
• Fryeburg, Oxford, 1,580	N-1
Fryeburg, Oxford, 2,968	N-1
Gardiner, Kennebec, 6,746	N-5
Garland, Penobscot, 1,064	J-7
▲ *Glenburn, Penobscot, 3,198*	K-8
Gorham, Cumberland, 11,856	P-3
• Gorham, Cumberland, 3,618	P-3
Gouldsboro, Hancock, 1,986	M-10
▲ *Gray, Cumberland, 5,904*	O-3
Greenbush, Penobscot, 1,309	J-8
▲ *Greene, Androscoggin, 3,661*	N-4
• Greenville, Piscataquis, 1,601	I-6
Greenville, Piscataquis, 1,884	I-6
• Guilford, Piscataquis, 1,082	J-6
Guilford, Piscataquis, 1,710	J-6
Hallowell, Kennebec, 2,534	M-5
• Hampden, Penobscot, 3,895	L-8
Hampden, Penobscot, 5,974	L-8
Hancock, Hancock, 1,757	L-10
▲ *Harpswell, Cumberland, 5,012*	O-4
Harrison, Cumberland, 1,951	N-2
• Hartland, Somerset, 1,038	K-6
Hartland, Somerset, 1,806	K-6
▲ *Hermon, Penobscot, 3,755*	K-8
Hiram, Oxford, 1,260	O-2
Hodgdon, Aroostook, 1,257	F-11
Holden, Penobscot, 2,952	L-8
▲ *Hollis, York, 3,573*	P-2
Hope, Knox, 1,017	M-7
• Houlton, Aroostook, 5,627	F-11
Houlton, Aroostook, 6,613	F-11
• Howland, Penobscot, 1,304	J-8
Howland, Penobscot, 1,435	J-8
Hudson, Penobscot, 1,048	J-8
Jay, Franklin, 5,080	L-4
Jefferson, Lincoln, 2,111	N-6
Jonesport, Washington, 1,525	L-12
Kenduskeag, Penobscot, 1,234	K-8
• Kennebunkport, York, 1,100	Q-3
Kennebunkport, York, 3,356	Q-3
• Kennebunk, York, 4,206	Q-3
Kennebunk, York, 8,004	Q-3
Kingfield, Franklin, 1,114	K-4
• Kittery, York, 5,151	R-2
Kittery, York, 9,372	R-2
• Kittery Point, York, 1,093	R-2
Lamoine, Hancock, 1,311	L-10
Lebanon, York, 4,263	Q-2
Leeds, Androscoggin, 1,669	M-4
Levant, Penobscot, 1,627	K-8
Lewiston, Androscoggin, 39,757	N-4
Limerick, York, 1,688	P-2
• Limestone, Aroostook, 1,245	C-11
Limestone, Aroostook, 9,922	C-11
Limington, York, 2,796	P-2
Lincolnville, Waldo, 1,809	M-7
• Lincoln, Penobscot, 3,399	I-9
Lincoln, Penobscot, 5,587	I-9
Lisbon, Androscoggin, 9,457	N-4
• Lisbon Falls, Androscoggin, 4,674	N-4
Litchfield, Kennebec, 2,650	N-5
• Little Falls-South Windham, Cumberland, 1,715	P-3
Livermore, Androscoggin, 1,950	M-4
• Livermore Falls, Androscoggin, 1,935	M-4
Livermore Falls, Androscoggin, 3,455	M-4
• Loring AFB, Aroostook, 5,494	C-11
Lubec, Washington	K-13
Lubec, Washington, 1,853	K-13
Lyman, York, 3,390	Q-2
Machiasport, Washington, 1,166	L-12
• Machias, Washington, 1,773	L-12
Machias, Washington, 2,569	L-12
• Madawaska, Aroostook, 3,653	A-9
Madawaska, Aroostook, 4,803	A-9
• Madison, Somerset, 2,956	K-5
Madison, Somerset, 4,725	K-5
Manchester, Kennebec, 2,099	M-5
Mapleton, Aroostook, 1,853	D-10
Mars Hill, Aroostook, 1,760	D-11
• Mars Hill-Blaine, Aroostook, 1,717	D-11
• Mechanic Falls, Androscoggin, 2,388	N-3
Mechanic Falls, Androscoggin, 2,919	N-3
Medway, Penobscot, 1,922	H-9
• Mexico, Oxford, 2,302	L-3
Mexico, Oxford, 3,344	L-3
Milbridge, Washington, 1,305	L-11
• Milford, Penobscot, 2,228	K-9
Milford, Penobscot, 2,884	K-9
• Millinocket, Penobscot, 6,922	H-8
Millinocket, Penobscot, 6,956	H-8
• Milo, Piscataquis, 2,129	I-8
Milo, Piscataquis, 2,600	I-8
Minot, Androscoggin, 1,664	N-3
Monmouth, Kennebec, 3,353	N-4
Mount Desert, Hancock, 1,899	M-9
Mount Vernon, Kennebec, 1,362	M-4
Naples, Cumberland, 2,860	O-2
New Gloucester, Cumberland, 3,916	N-3
New Sharon, Franklin, 1,175	L-4
Newburgh, Penobscot, 1,317	L-7
Newcastle, Lincoln, 1,538	N-6
Newfield, York, 1,042	P-2
• Newport, Penobscot, 1,843	K-7
Newport, Penobscot, 3,036	K-7
Nobleboro, Lincoln, 1,455	N-6
• Norridgewock, Somerset, 1,496	L-5
Norridgewock, Somerset, 3,105	L-5
• North Berwick, York, 1,568	Q-2
North Berwick, York, 3,793	Q-2
• North Windham, Cumberland, 4,077	O-3
▲ *North Yarmouth, Cumberland, 2,429*	O-3
Northport, Waldo, 1,201	M-7
• Norway, Oxford, 3,023	N-3
Norway, Oxford, 4,754	N-3
• Oakland, Kennebec, 3,510	L-5
Oakland, Kennebec, 5,595	L-5
• *Old Orchard Beach, York, 7,789*	P-3
Old Town, Penobscot, 8,317	K-8
Orland, Hancock, 1,805	L-8
Orono, Penobscot, 10,573	K-8
• Orono, Penobscot, 9,789	K-8
▲ *Orrington, Penobscot, 3,309*	L-8
Otisfield, Oxford, 1,136	N-3
▲ *Owls Head, Knox, 1,574*	N-7
• Oxford, Oxford, 1,284	N-3
Oxford, Oxford, 3,705	N-3
Palermo, Waldo, 1,021	M-6
Palmyra, Somerset, 1,867	K-6
Paris, Oxford, 4,492	M-3
Parsonsfield, York, 1,472	P-2
Patten, Penobscot, 1,256	G-9
Penobscot, Hancock, 1,131	M-8
Peru, Oxford, 1,541	L-3
Phillips, Franklin, 1,148	K-3
Phippsburg, Sagadahoc, 1,815	O-5
• Pittsfield, Somerset, 3,222	K-6
Pittsfield, Somerset, 4,190	K-6
Pittston, Kennebec, 2,444	N-5
Plymouth, Penobscot, 1,152	K-7
▲ *Poland, Androscoggin, 4,342*	N-3
Porter, Oxford, 1,301	O-2
Portland, Cumberland, 64,358	P-4
Pownal, Cumberland, 1,262	O-4
Presque Isle, Aroostook, 10,550	D-10
• *Randolph, Kennebec, 1,949*	N-5
Rangeley, Franklin, 1,063	K-2
Raymond, Cumberland, 3,311	O-3
Readfield, Kennebec, 2,033	M-4
• Richmond, Sagadahoc, 1,775	N-5
Richmond, Sagadahoc, 3,072	N-5
Rockland, Knox, 7,972	N-7
▲ *Rockport, Knox, 2,854*	N-7
• Rumford, Oxford, 5,419	L-3
Rumford, Oxford, 7,078	L-3
▲ *Sabattus, Androscoggin, 3,696*	N-4
Saco, York, 15,181	P-3
Saint Albans, Somerset, 1,724	K-6
Saint George, Knox, 2,261	O-7
• Sanford, York, 10,296	Q-2
Sanford, York, 20,463	Q-2
Sangerville, Piscataquis, 1,398	J-7
Scarborough, Cumberland, 12,518	P-3
• Scarborough, Cumberland, 2,586	P-3
• Searsport, Waldo, 1,151	M-8
Searsport, Waldo, 2,603	M-8
Sebago, Cumberland, 1,259	O-2
Shapleigh, York, 1,911	P-2
Sherman, Aroostook, 1,027	G-9
Sidney, Kennebec, 2,593	M-5
• Skowhegan, Somerset, 6,990	K-5
Skowhegan, Somerset, 8,725	K-5
▲ *South Berwick, York, 5,877*	R-2
• South Eliot, York, 3,112	R-2
• South Paris, Oxford, 2,320	M-3
South Portland, Cumberland, 23,163	P-3
• South Sanford, York, 3,929	Q-2
▲ *South Thomaston, Knox, 1,227*	N-7
▲ *Southwest Harbor, Hancock, 1,952*	M-9
• Springvale, York, 3,542	Q-2
▲ *Standish, Cumberland, 7,678*	O-2
Steuben, Washington, 1,084	L-11
Stockton Springs, Waldo, 1,383	L-8
▲ *Stonington, Hancock, 1,252*	N-8
Strong, Franklin, 1,217	K-4
Sullivan, Hancock, 1,118	L-10
Surry, Hancock, 1,004	L-9
Swanville, Waldo, 1,130	L-7
• Thomaston, Knox, 2,445	N-7
Thomaston, Knox, 3,306	N-7
• Topsham, Sagadahoc, 6,147	O-5
Topsham, Sagadahoc, 8,746	O-5
Tremont, Hancock, 1,324	M-9
Trenton, Hancock, 1,060	M-9
Turner, Androscoggin, 4,315	M-4
Union, Knox, 1,989	N-7
Unity, Waldo, 1,817	L-6
• Van Buren, Aroostook, 2,759	B-11
Van Buren, Aroostook, 3,045	B-11
Vassalboro, Kennebec, 3,679	L-6
▲ *Veazie, Penobscot, 1,633*	K-8
Vinalhaven, Knox, 1,072	N-8
• Waldoboro, Lincoln, 1,420	N-6
Waldoboro, Lincoln, 4,601	N-6
Wales, Androscoggin, 1,223	N-4
Warren, Knox, 3,192	N-7
Washburn, Aroostook, 1,880	C-10
Washington, Knox, 1,185	M-6
Waterboro, York, 4,510	P-2
Waterford, Oxford, 1,299	N-2
Waterville, Kennebec, 17,173	L-6
Wayne, Kennebec, 1,029	M-4
Wells, York	Q-2
Wells, York, 7,778	Q-2
▲ *West Bath, Sagadahoc, 1,716*	O-5
▲ *West Gardiner, Kennebec, 2,531*	N-5
West Paris, Oxford, 1,514	M-3
Westbrook, Cumberland, 16,121	P-3
Whitefield, Lincoln, 1,931	N-6
• Wilton, Franklin, 2,453	L-4
Wilton, Franklin, 4,242	L-4
Windham, Cumberland, 13,020	O-3
Windsor, Kennebec, 1,895	M-6
• Winslow, Kennebec, 5,436	L-6
Winslow, Kennebec, 7,997	L-6
Winter Harbor, Hancock, 1,157	M-10
• Winterport, Waldo, 1,274	L-8
Winterport, Waldo, 3,175	L-8
• Winthrop, Kennebec, 2,819	M-4
Winthrop, Kennebec, 5,968	M-4
• Wiscasset, Lincoln, 1,233	N-5
Wiscasset, Lincoln, 3,339	N-5
Woodland, Aroostook, 1,402	D-10
• Woodland, Washington, 1,287	J-12
Woodstock, Oxford, 1,194	M-3
Woolwich, Sagadahoc, 2,570	O-5
• Yarmouth, Cumberland, 3,338	O-4
Yarmouth, Cumberland, 7,862	O-4
York, York, 9,818	R-2
• York Harbor, York, 2,555	R-2

Explanation of symbols: • – Census Designated Place (CDP); ▲ *italics* – Townships (shown on the map); • *italics* – Township shown which is also a CDP; *italics* – Townships (not shown on the map)

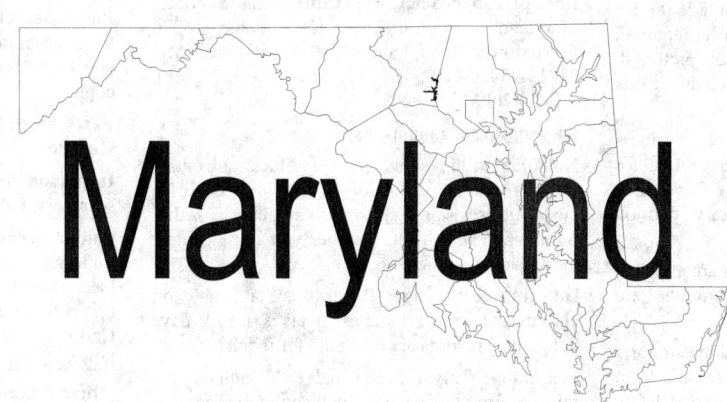

Maryland

General Help Numbers:

Governor's Office

State House, 100 State Circle   410-974-3901
Annapolis, MD 21401   Fax 410-974-3275
www.gov.state.md.us   9AM-5PM

Attorney General's Office

200 St Paul Place   410-576-6300
Baltimore, MD 21202   Fax 410-576-6404
www.oag.state.md.us   8AM-5PM

Legislative Records

Legislative Information Desk, Library & Information Srv
90 State Circle, Basement Level   410-946-5400
Annapolis, MD 21401-1991   Fax 410-946-5405
http://mlis.state.md.us   8AM-5PM

State Archives

Hall of Records   410-260-6400
350 Rowe Blvd   Fax 410-974-2525
Annapolis, MD 21401   8AM-4:30PM TU-FR;
www.mdarchives.state.md.us   8:30-4:30 SA

State Specifics:

Capital:	Annapolis
	Anne Arundel County
Time Zone:	EST
Number of Counties:	23
Population:	5,508,909
Web Site:	www.maryland.gov

State Agencies

Criminal Records

Criminal Justice Information System, Public Safety & Correctional Records, PO Box 5743, Pikeville, MD 21282-5743 (Courier: 6776 Reisterstown Rd, Rm 200, Pikeville, MD 21208); 410-764-4501, 888-795-0011, 410-653-6320 (Fax), 7:30AM-5:00PM.

www.dpscs.state.md.us

Indexing & Storage: Records are available from 1978. It takes a week if not submitted electornically. before new records are available for inquiry. Records are indexed on in-house computer. Records are normally destroyed after person reaches age 100.

Searching: Release of criminal records is restricted. All private parties must first write/fax/phone this office and request a "petition package," then apply for a petition number. Employers are eligible to request a petition number; 3rd parties may not, directly. Include the following in your request-set of fingerprints. A signed release is not necessary but is helpful. When applying for fingerprinting, a photo ID is required. 100% of records are fingerprint-supported. All searches require fingerprints and all require an authorization number including government. Investigators and all 3rd parties are considered as agents of employers and must use employer's authorization.

Access by: mail, in person.

Fee & Payment: The fee is $18.00 per request, add $1.00 for a "gold seal." If a statutorily-required FBI fingerpint check is required, add $24.00. Total fee, including FBI check, is $24.00 with a child care waiver stamp, or $26.00 for volunteers. Fee payee: CJIS. Prepayment required. Money orders and cashier's checks are preferred. Personal checks accepted. No credit cards accepted.

Mail search: Turnaround time: 10-15 business days. You may mail a request for a petition for authorization to the Customer Service Dept.; they can mail or fax you the necessary petition information.

In person search: In person requests are allowed, though signed release and fingerprints are required, and turnaround time is 5 days.

Other access: The State Court Administrator's Office has online access to criminal records from all state district courts, 3 circuit courts, and 1 city court. See that profile for more information.

Expedited service: Will rush expedite your request for no add'l charge, however a written request including a legitimate reason why must be submitted. An FBI check cannot be expedited. Will expedite the return if you provide a prepaid shipper envelope.

Statewide Court Records

Administrative Office of the Courts, 580 Taylor Ave, Annapolis, MD 21401; 410-260-1400, 410-974-2169 (Fax), 8AM-5PM.

www.courts.state.md.us

Access by: online.

Online search: Appellate opinions are available from www.courts.state.md.us/opinions.html. At www.courts.state.md.us/dialup.html, the Judicial Information System (JIS) or (SJIS) provides dial-up access to civil and criminal case information from certain courts. All District Courts provide civil and misdemeanors. All Circuit Courts provide civil records and three Circuit Courts (Anne Arundel, Carroll, and Baltimore City Court) provide criminal records on JIS. Fees are involved. All case information may be searched by party name or case number. For a registration packet, call 410-260-1031 or visit the website.

Sexual Offender Registry

Criminal Justice Information System, PO Box 5743, SOR Unit, Pikeville, MD 21282-5743 (Courier: 6776 Reistertown Rd, Baltimore, MD); 410-585-3649, 866-368-8657, 410-653-5690 (Fax), 7:30AM-5:00PM.

www.dpscs.state.md.us/sor/

Note: Access to the Sexual Offender Registry can be requested by email at sor@dpscs.state.md.us.

Indexing & Storage: Records are available from 10/01/95. It takes a week if not submitted electornically. before new records are available for inquiry. Records are indexed on in-house computer (90+%).

Searching: Copies of registration statements will include the registrant's photograph but will not include fingerprints, SSN, or the victim's date of birth.

Access by: mail, online.

Mail search: Turnaround time: 1 to 2 weeks. Include requester's full name, address, and reason for the request.

Online search: Online access is at www.dpscs.state.md.us/sor/online_view.shtml.

Incarceration Records

Dept of Public Safety and Correctional Services, Maryland Division of Corrections, 6776 Reistertown Road, Suite 310, Baltimore, MD 21215-2342; 410-585-3351, 410-764-4182 (Fax), 8AM-4:30PM.

www.dpscs.state.md.us/doc

Note: For an inmate's DOC # and location contact Data Processing via methods below or email to cwood@dpscs.state.md.us. To obtain any other information than DOC number you must contact individual institutions.

Indexing & Storage: Records are available on current and former inmates. It takes 1 to 2 days before new records are available for inquiry.

Searching: Only location and DOC number are released from this agency. Include the following in your request-inmates race, sex, full name, DOB and the SSN if known. Records computerized since 1980. The following data is not released: medical and certain personal information

Access by: mail, phone, fax, online.

Fee & Payment: No fee for search.

Mail search: Turnaround time: 1-3 days.

Phone search: Name searching available by phone.

Fax search: Can request via the fax.

Online search: Search inmates online at http://www1.dpscs.state.md.us/inmate/. The Locator may not list some short sentenced inmates who, although committed to the Commissioner of Correction, are in fact housed at Division of Pretrial and Detention Services facilities. Also, a private company offers free web access at www.vinelink.com/index.jsp, including state, DOC, and a few county jails.

Corporation, Limited Partnerships, Trade Names, Limited Liability Company, Fictitious Name, Limited Liability Partnerships

Department of Assessments and Taxation, Corporations Division, 301 W Preston St, Room 801, Baltimore, MD 21201; 410-767-1340, 410-767-1330 (Charter Information), 410-767-1184, 410-333-7097 (Fax), 8AM-4:30PM.

www.dat.state.md.us/

Indexing & Storage: Records are available from 1908 on. New records are available for inquiry immediately. Records are indexed on inhouse computer.

Searching: Officers and directors info is not immediately available. Include the following in your request-full name of business, corporation file number. The following is available; the Articles of Incorporation, Annual Reports, Officers, Directors, DBA's, Prior (merged) names, Inactive and Reserved names.

Access by: mail, phone, fax, in person, online.

Fee & Payment: An abstract of corporate records is $20.00, A Good Standing is $20.00. Copies are $1.00 per page plus $20.00 to certify. Fee payee: SDAT. Prepayment required. Personal checks accepted. Credit cards accepted: MasterCard, Visa.

Mail search: Turnaround time: 7 days. Officer and director information takes 2 weeks. Expedite

service will improve turnaround time for mail or fax requests. No SASE is required.

Phone search: Charter information includes date of incorporation, agent, and status. They will let you know how many pages if you wish to order copies.

Fax search: This is considered expedited service, see below.

In person search: The office closes at 5 PM for searchers. Public access terminals are available.

Online search: Search for corporate name and trade name records for free at the main website (see above); also includes real estate statewide (cannot search by name) and UCC records. A Certificate of Good Standing is available online at http://sdatcert1.resiusa.org/certificate/.

Other access: This agency will release information in a bulk output format. Contact 410-561-9600 for details.

Expedited service: Expedited service is available for mail, phone and fax searches. Turnaround time is 3 days. There is an additional $20.00 fee to expedite a copy or expedite a certificate. A credit card must be used if requesting by fax.

Trademarks/Servicemarks

Secretary of State, Trademarks Division, State House, Annapolis, MD 21401; 410-974-5521, 410-974-5479, 410-974-5527 (Fax), 9AM-5PM.

www.sos.state.md.us

Indexing & Storage: Records are available for the past 10 years. New records are available for inquiry immediately. Records are indexed on inhouse computer.

Searching: Include the following in your request-trademark/servicemark name.

Access by: mail, phone, fax, in person, online.

Fee & Payment: There is no search fee. Certification is $5.00, copies are $.30 per page. Fee payee: Secretary of State. Prepayment required. Personal checks accepted. No credit cards accepted.

Mail search: Turnaround time: 1 week. No fee for mail request.

Phone search: No fee for telephone request. Only limited information is available.

Fax search: Will return information by mail in 1 week.

In person search: No fee for request. Call before visiting.

Online search: Online searching is available at the Internet site. Search can be by keyword in the description field, the service or product, the owner, the classification, or the mark name or keyword in the mark name. The site offers application forms to register, renew, or assign trade and service marks, and general information about registration. Click on "Trade & Service Marks."

Other access: A computer printout of all marks registered, renewed or assigned within a 3 month period is available for $.05 per trademark.

Uniform Commercial Code

UCC Division-Taxpayer's Services, Department of Assessments & Taxation, 301 West Preston St, Baltimore, MD 21201; 410-767-1340 x2, 410-333-7097 (Fax), 8AM-4:30PM.

http://sdatcert3.resiusa.org/ucc-charter/

Note: This agency will not do a general name or entity search. A searcher must come in person, hire a retriever, use the Internet, or buy the database.

Indexing & Storage: Records are available for all active files.

Searching: Tax liens are not filed here, but are filed with the clerk of the circuit court of the debtor's jurisdiction. For help, email charterhelp@dat.state.md.us.

Access by: mail, in person, online.

Fee & Payment: There is no search fee. The copy fee is $1.00 per page. Fee payee: Department of Assessments & Taxation Prepayment required. Personal checks accepted. No credit cards accepted.

Mail search: Will not do name searching, but will make copies if exact number of pages paid in advance.

In person search: Records can be viewed at no charge on public access terminals.

Online search: The Internet site above offers free access to UCC index information. Also, there is a related site offering access to real property data for the whole state at www.dat.state.md.us/.

Other access: The agency has available for sale copies of public release master data files including corporation, real estate, and UCC. In addition, they can produce customized files on paper or disk. Visit the website for more information.

Federal Tax Liens, State Tax Liens

Records not maintained by a state level agency.

Note: All tax liens are filed at the county level.

Sales Tax Registrations

Taxpayer Services, Revenue Administration Division, 301 W Preston St #206, Baltimore, MD 21201; 410-767-1313, 410-767-1571 (Fax), 8AM-5PM.

www.comp.state.md.us

Indexing & Storage: Records are available on a computer index for the past 4 years of applicants. It takes 7 days before new records are available for inquiry.

Searching: This agency will only confirm that a business's number is valid and confirm the name and address of the business. They will provide no other information. The business name and federal ID# or SSN of owner is required to search.

Access by: mail, phone, fax, online.

Fee & Payment: There are no fees.

Mail search: Turnaround time: 7 working days. Records are not returned by mail, they will call you. No SASE is required.

Phone search: Call only if you have the permit number.

Fax search: Records are available by fax.

Online search: Using the web, one can determine if a MD sales tax account number is valid.

Birth Certificates

Department of Health, Division of Vital Records, PO Box 68760, Baltimore, MD 21215-0020 (Courier: 6550 Reisterstown Plaza, Baltimore, MD

21215); 410-764-3038, 410-764-3170 (Order), 410-318-6119 (Recording), 410-358-7381 (Fax), 8AM-4PM M-F; 3rd Saturday of each month.

www.dhmh.state.md.us

Indexing & Storage: Records are available from 1898 to present for all counties and 1910 to present for City of Baltimore. For prior records, contact the State Archives or city of Baltimore. It takes 6-8 weeks before new records are available for inquiry. Records are indexed on index cards. Records are maintained indefinitely.

Searching: Must have a notarized signed release from person of record or mother or father, unless requester is parent or guardian. Include the following in your request-full name, names of parents, mother's maiden name, date of birth, place of birth, relationship to person of record.

Access by: mail, phone, fax, in person, online.

Fee & Payment: The search fee is $12.00. Only fax, phone and expedited requesters may use a credit card and there is an additional $7.00 fee. Fee payee: Division of Vital Records. Prepayment required. Cash is accepted for walk in requesters only. Personal checks accepted. Credit cards accepted: MasterCard, Visa, AmEx, Discover.

Mail search: Turnaround time: 2 to 3 weeks. A SASE is requested.

Phone search: Credit card prepayment required. Turnaround time is 3 to 5 days.

Fax search: See expedited service.

In person search: Turnaround time is same day (typically, 15 to 30 minutes). Walk in requesters may pay with cash or check; no credit cards. Presentation of photo ID is required for walk in requesters.

Online search: Records may be ordered over the web at www.vitalchek.com. Use of credit card is required.

Expedited service: Expedited service is available for FedEx return of online, phone and fax searches. Turnaround time: 2 days. Add $13.50 per package plus charge for use of credit card.

Death Records

Department of Health, Division of Vital Records, PO Box 68760, Baltimore, MD 21215-0020 (Courier: 6550 Reisterstown Plaza, Baltimore, MD 21215); 410-764-3038, 410-764-3170 (Order), 410-318-6119 (Recording), 410-358-7381 (Fax), 8AM-4PM M-F; 3rd Saturday of each month.

www.dhmh.state.md.us

Indexing & Storage: Records are available from 1969 to present. For records prior to 1969 contact Maryland State Archives, 410-260-6429. It takes 2-3 weeks (if filed at county) before new records are available for inquiry. Records are indexed on index cards.

Searching: Must have a signed release from immediate family member. A signature is required from the requester. Include the following in your request-full name, date of death, place of death, relationship to person of record, reason for information request. Request must be signed. Include copy of photo ID with request.

Access by: mail, phone, fax, in person, online.

Fee & Payment: The search fee is $12.00. Only phone, fax and expedited requesters may use a credit card for an extra $7.00 fee. Fee payee: Division of Vital Records. Prepayment required.

Personal checks, M.O.s accepted. Credit cards accepted: MasterCard, Visa, AmEx, Discover.

Mail search: Turnaround time: 2 to 4 weeks. A SASE is requested.

Phone search: Credit card pre-payment required. Turnaround time is 2-3 days.

Fax search: See expedited service.

In person search: Turnaround time is same day.

Online search: Records may be ordered over the web at www.vitalchek.com. Use of credit card is required.

Expedited service: Expedited service is available for FedEx return of online, phone and fax searches. Turnaround time: 2 days. Add $13.50 per package for express delivery. Use of credit card and fee is required, also.

Marriage Certificates

Department of Health, Division of Vital Records, PO Box 68760, Baltimore, MD 21215-0020 (Courier: 6550 Reisterstown Plaza, Baltimore, MD 21215); 410-764-3038, 410-764-3170 (Order), 410-318-6119 (Recording), 410-358-7381 (Fax), 8AM-4PM M-F; 3rd Saturday of each month.

www.dhmh.state.md.us

Indexing & Storage: Records are available from June 1951 to present. Prior records must be obtained form the court of record. Also, marriages from 1973, 1974, 1978, and 1979 are unavailable from this location and must be searched at local level. It takes 6 months before new records are available for inquiry. Records are indexed on computer. Records are normally destroyed after (records kept indefinitely).

Searching: Must have a notarized signed release from persons of record or authorized representative. Include the following in your request-names of husband and wife, date of marriage, place or county of marriage, besides permission letter. Include copy of photo ID with request.

Access by: mail, phone, fax, in person, online.

Fee & Payment: The search fee is $12.00. Only phone, fax and expedited requesters may use a credit card for an additional fee of $7.00. Fee payee: Division of Vital Records. Prepayment required. Personal checks & M.O.s accepted. Credit cards accepted: MasterCard, Visa, AmEx, Discover.

Mail search: Turnaround time: 2 to 3 weeks. A SASE is requested.

Phone search: Credit Card prepayment required. Turnaround time is 2-3 days.

Fax search: See expedited service.

In person search: Turnaround time same day.

Online search: Records may be ordered over the web at www.vitalchek.com. Use of credit card is required.

Expedited service: Expedited service is available for FedEx return of online, phone and fax searches. Turnaround time: 2 days. Add $13.50 per package for express delivery. Use of credit card and fee is required, also.

Divorce Records

Department of Health, Division of Vital Records, PO Box 68760, Baltimore, MD 21215-0020 (Courier: 6550 Reisterstown Plaza, Baltimore, MD 21215); 410-764-3038, 410-318-6119

(Recording), 800-832-3277, 410-358-7381 (Fax), 8AM-4PM M-F; 3rd Saturday of each month.

www.dhmh.state.md.us

Note: This office does not issue a certificate of divorce, but can verify those names involved. The divorce decree must be obtained from the circuit court granting the divorce.

Indexing & Storage: Records are available from July 1961 to present. It takes 6 months before new records are available for inquiry. Records are indexed on index cards. 1983-84 indexes are not available for searching.

Searching: Must have a notarized release from persons of record or authorized agent. Include the following in your request-names of husband and wife (maiden name), date of divorce.

Access by: mail, fax, in person, online.

Fee & Payment: There is $12.00 fee to receive a Verification of Report of Divorce and Absolute Annulment. Add $7.00 for use of credit card. The clerk of the court issuing the decree holds the actual hard copy record. Fee payee: Division of Vital Records. Prepayment required. Personal checks accepted.

Mail search: Turnaround time: 2 to 3 weeks. SASE is required.

Fax search: See expedited service.

In person search: Turnaround time same day.

Online search: Records may be ordered over the web at www.vitalchek.com. Use of credit card is required.

Expedited service: Expedited service is available for FedEx return of online, phone and fax searches. Turnaround time: 2 days. Add $13.50 per package for express delivery. Use of credit card and fee is required, also.

Workers' Compensation Records

Workers Compensation Commission, 10 E Baltimore St, Baltimore, MD 21202; 410-864-5100, 410-864-5120 (Information Technology), 8AM-4:30PM.

www.charm.net/~wcc

Indexing & Storage: Records are available for past 10 years are on computer. New records are available for inquiry immediately. Records are indexed on microfilm, inhouse computer.

Searching: Include the following in your request-claimant name, Social Security Number, date of accident, place of employment at time of accident. The claim number helps. The following data is not released: medical records.

Access by: mail, phone, in person, online.

Fee & Payment: Fee for copies is $.50 per page. There is no search fee. Fee payee: Workers Compensation Commission. Prepayment required. Personal checks accepted. No credit cards accepted.

Mail search: Turnaround time: 1 week. For copies of documents, the claimant's authorization is needed for requesters not an involved party. A SASE is requested.

Phone search: Limited verification information is available by phone for three names only per call. You must have the 6 digit claim number or the name and SSN.

In person search: Turnaround time while you wait.

Online search: Request for online hook-up must be in writing on letterhead. There is no search fee, but there is a $7.00 set-up fee, $5.00 monthly fee and a $.01-03 per minute connect fee assessed by Verizon or other provider. The system is open 24 hours a day to only in-state accounts. Write to the Commission at address above, care of Information Technology Division, or call Pat H. at 410-864-5170.

Other access: This agency will sell its entire database depending on the use of the purchaser. Contact the commission for further information.

Driver Records

MVA, Driver Records Unit, 6601 Ritchie Hwy, NE, Glen Burnie, MD 21062; 410-787-7758, 410-424-3678 (Fax), 8:15AM-4:30PM.

www.mva.state.md.us

Note: Copies of tickets can be obtained from the MD District Court/MATS, 1750 Forest Dr, Annapolis, 21401. There is no charge for ticket copies, but a self addressed stamped envelope is advised.

Indexing & Storage: Records are available for 3 years for moving violations, 10 years for DWIs, and 5 years for suspensions. Law requires a request from the driver to have violations purged from the driving record. Accidents are indicated. It takes 5 to 10 days before new records are available for inquiry.

Searching: Casual requesters cannot obtain records with personal information unless consent of subject is given. Records may not be resold or used for direct mail advertising or selling. Include the following in your request-driver's license number or the name and DOB. Permissible use requesters must submit form DR-057 if an account has not been established.

Access by: mail, in person, online.

Fee & Payment: The fee for a driving record is $9.00. There is an additional $3.00 if you wish to have a non-electronic record certified. Fee payee: MVA. Prepayment required. Credit cards are not accepted for mail requests. Personal checks accepted. Credit cards accepted: MasterCard, Visa.

Mail search: Turnaround time: 2 to 3 days. MVA offices statewide will also accept mail-in requests for records. A SASE is requested.

In person search: Up to 5 requests will be processed in-person, additional requests are available the next day. In-person inquires may be processed at over 25 Motor Vehicle offices throughout the state.

Online search: The network is available 6 days a week, twenty-four hours a day to qualified and bonded individuals and businesses. Access is through PC and modem. The communication network is the Public Data Network (Bell Atlantic). Fee is $9.00 per record. Call Ms. Barbara Bentley at 410-768-7234 for account information.

Other access: Drivers may order their own record online via the website. Records are not mailed out-of-state.

Vehicle Ownership, Vehicle Identification

Department of Motor Vehicles, Vehicle Registration Division, Room 204, 6601 Ritchie

Hwy, NE, Glen Burnie, MD 21062; 410-768-7250, 410-768-7653 (Fax), 8:15AM-4:30PM.

www.mva.state.md.us

Indexing & Storage: Records are available from 1920. It takes 3 to 5 days before new records are available for inquiry. Records are normally destroyed after scanning to file.

Searching: All vehicle/ownership records are open to the public; however, personal information is not released to casual requesters without consent of subject. The following data is not released: medical information.

Access by: mail, in person, online.

Fee & Payment: Fees are $9.00 for non-certified records and $12.00 for certified records. Fee payee: MVA. Prepayment required. Credit cards are only accepted for walk-in requesters. Personal checks accepted. Credit cards accepted: MasterCard, Visa.

Mail search: Turnaround time: 3 to 5 days. Requester can provide prepaid express mail package for faster service. No SASE is required.

In person search: Turnaround time is generally in a few minutes.

Online search: The state offers vehicle and ownership data over the same online network utilized for driving record searches. Fee is $9.00 per record and line charges will be incurred. For more information, call 410-768-7234.

Accident Reports

Maryland State Police, Central Records Division, 1711 Belmont Ave, Baltimore, MD 21244; 410-298-3390, 410-298-3198 (Fax), 8AM-5PM.

Note: This agency does not have reports for the City of Baltimore. Call 410-396-2359 for those reports.

Indexing & Storage: Records are available for 5 years. Records are computer indexed from 1996 to present.

Searching: If a fatality was involved, please so state in the request. Copies of accident reports investigated by the state police and other police agencies may be requested by giving the date of incident and driver name(s).

Access by: mail, in person.

Fee & Payment: The search fee is $4.00 which includes all copies and is non-refundable. Fee payee: Maryland State Police. Prepayment required. Personal checks accepted. No credit cards accepted.

Mail search: Turnaround time: 3 to 4 weeks. A SASE is requested.

In person search: Immediate service limited to simple requests.

Vessel Ownership, Vessel Registration

Dept of Natural Resources, Licensing & Registration Service, 580 Taylor Ave C-1, Annapolis, MD 21401; 410-260-3220, 8:30AM-4:30PM.

www.dnr.state.md.us

Note: Boat trailers, (only trailers) are registered through the Maryland Motor Vehicle Administration. They can be reached at 1-800-950-1682.

Indexing & Storage: Records are available from the 1960s to the present. This is a title state: all motorized boats must be titled and registered. Records are on indexed on microfiche or CDs from the 1960s to the present, and on computer for the last 4 years.

Searching: The agency follows the mandates of the DPPA. Only those with a legitimate business can obtain records with personal information. Casual requesters must have a signed release of subject. Include the following in your request-one of the following is required: Maryland boat #, tidal fish license #, or name and address of boat owner/license holder. There are five additional Regional Service Centers in the state that will process record requests.

Access by: mail, in person.

Fee & Payment: Certified true copies are $10.00 each. Microfiche history files are $5.00 each. Current computer file copies are $5.00 each. Fee payee: DNR. Prepayment required. Personal checks accepted. No credit cards accepted.

Mail search: Turnaround time: 2 weeks. No SASE is required.

In person search: Turnaround time is immediate, unless historical records needed.

Voter Registration
Access to Records is Restricted

State Board of Elections, PO Box 6486, Annapolis, MD 21401-0486 (Courier: 151 West Street, #200, Annapolis, MD 21401); 410-269-2840, 800-222-8683, 410-974-2019 (Fax), 8AM-5PM.

www.elections.state.md.us

Note: Agency may sell voter registration lists in bulk media for all twenty-four jurisdictions to MD registered voter only. If voter history is requested, then list must be purchased from each local jurisdiction. Commercial use of list is banned. The website offers free access to the campaign finance database for checking compaign contributions and overall summaries and statistics.

GED Certificates

State Department of Education, GED Office, 200 W Baltimore St, Baltimore, MD 21201; 410-767-0538, 410-333-8435 (Fax), 8:30AM-5PM.

www.research.umbc.edu/~ira/GED1.html

Indexing & Storage: It takes 30 days before new records are available for inquiry.

Searching: Include the following in your request-name, date of birth, Social Security Number, signed release. The signed release is needed for either the verification or transcript copy.

Access by: mail, fax, in person.

Fee & Payment: The fee is $5.00 for a copy of a transcript. There is no fee for a verification. Fee payee: GED Office. Prepayment required. Personal checks accepted. No credit cards accepted.

Mail search: Turnaround time: 3 to 5 days. No SASE is required.

Fax search: Results are returned by mail. You can call for results, if desired.

In person search: Results can be picked up at office (around the corner) at 4 N Liberty, between the hours of 10AM and 1PM.

Hunting and Fishing License Information

Department of Natural Resources, Licensing & Registration Service, 580 Taylor Ave, Annapolis, MD 21401; 410-260-3220, 410-260-8239 (Fax), 8:30AM-4:30PM.

www.dnr.state.md.us

Note: They have a central computer database. Licenses can be issued online at the webpage.

Indexing & Storage: Records are available since 1999. It takes 1-2 days before new records are available for inquiry.

Searching: Requests are subject to DPPA. Requests must be in writing, submit as many identifiers as possible.

Access by: mail, in person.

Fee & Payment: There is a $5.00 fee per name, if by mail. Fee payee: Department of Natural Resources. Personal checks accepted.

Mail search: Turnaround time is as time permits.

In person search: No fee for request.

Maryland State Licensing Agencies

Licenses Searchable Online

Architect #30 .... www.dllr.state.md.us/query/arch.html
Architectural Partnership/Corporation #12 .... www.dllr.state.md.us/license/occprof/
Barber #8 .... www.dllr.state.md.us/query/barber.html
Certification #28 .... www.sos.state.md.us/Certifications/certifications.htm
Charity #28 .... www.sos.state.md.us/charity/charityhome.htm
Condominium/Timeshare #28 .... www.sos.state.md.us/Registrations/condo_TS.htm
Contractor #10 .... www.dllr.state.md.us/query/home_imprv.html
Cosmetologist #8 .... www.dllr.state.md.us/query/cosmet.html
Election #28 .... www.sos.state.md.us/ElectionsInfo.htm
Electrician, Master #12 .... www.dllr.state.md.us/license/occprof/
Engineer, Examining #12 .... www.dllr.state.md.us/license/occprof/
Engineer, Professional #12 .... www.dllr.state.md.us/license/occprof/
Esthetician #8 .... www.dllr.state.md.us/query/cosmet.html
Extradition/Requisition #28 .... www.sos.state.md.us/Services/Extradit.htm
Forester #12 .... www.dllr.state.md.us/license/occprof/
Fund Raising Counsel #28 .... www.sos.state.md.us/charity/RegisterProfSol.htm
Grain Dealer #4 .... www.mda.state.md.us/geninfo/genera6.htm
Home Improvement #12 .... www.dllr.state.md.us/license/occprof/
Home Improvement Salesperson #10 .... www.dllr.state.md.us/query/home_imprv.html
HVACR Contractor #12 .... www.dllr.state.md.us/license/occprof/
Interior Designer #12 .... www.dllr.state.md.us/license/occprof/
Land Surveyor #12 .... www.dllr.state.md.us/license/occprof/
Landscape Architect #12 .... www.dllr.state.md.us/license/occprof/
Limousine Driver #18 .... www.psc.state.md.us/psc/
Lobbyist #14 .... http://ethics.gov.state.md.us/listing.htm
Lobbyist Employer #14 .... http://ethics.gov.state.md.us/listing.htm
Makeup Artist #8 .... www.dllr.state.md.us/query/cosmet.html
MD Flag Protocol #28 .... www.sos.state.md.us/Services/flagprotocol.htm
Medical Doctor #22 .... www.mbp.state.md.us/
Military Monuments Commission #28 .... www.sos.state.md.us/MMMC/MMMChome.htm
Mortgage Broker #13 .... www.dllr.state.md.us/query/real_est.html
Nail Technician #8 .... www.dllr.state.md.us/query/cosmet.html
Notary Public #28 .... www.sos.state.md.us/notary/notary.htm
Nurse-RN/LPN #24 .... www.mbon.org/main.php
Nursery, Plant #4 .... www.mda.state.md.us/plant/nursery.htm
Nursing Assistant #24 .... www.mbon.org/main.php
Optometrist #22 .... www.arbo.org/odfinder/LicSearch.asp
Pardon/Commutation #28 .... www.sos.state.md.us/Services/Pardons.htm
Pawnbroker #12 .... www.dllr.state.md.us/query/sec_hand_deal.html
Pesticide Applicator/Operator #4 .... www.mda.state.md.us/geninfo/genera10.htm
Pesticide Business/Dealer #4 .... www.mda.state.md.us/geninfo/genera10.htm
Pesticide Consultant #4 .... www.mda.state.md.us/geninfo/genera10.htm
Pesticide, Private Applicator #4 .... www.mda.state.md.us/geninfo/genera10.htm
Plant Broker/Dealer #4 .... www.mda.state.md.us/plant/nursery.htm
Plumber #12 .... www.dllr.state.md.us/query/plumb.html
Polygraph Examiner #32 .... www.mpapolygraph.org/
Precious Metals & Gem Dealer/2nd-hand #12 .... www.dllr.state.md.us/query/sec_hand_deal.html
Public Accountant-CPA #12 .... www.dllr.state.md.us/query/cpa.html
Radiation Therapy Technician #22 .... www.mbp.state.md.us/
Real Estate Agent #15 .... www.dllr.state.md.us/query/real_est.html
Real Estate Appraiser #11 .... www.dllr.state.md.us/query/real_est_app.html
Respiratory Care Practitioner #22 .... www.mbp.state.md.us/
Solicitor, Professional #28 .... www.sos.state.md.us/charity/RegisterProfSol.htm#ps
Special Police/Railroad Police #28 .... www.sos.state.md.us/Services/Police.htm
Subcontractor #10 .... www.dllr.state.md.us/query/home_imprv.html
Taxi Driver #18 .... www.psc.state.md.us/psc/
Trademark/Service Mark #28 .... www.sos.state.md.us/Registrations/Trademarks/Trademarks.htm

Maryland Licensing Quick Finder

Acupuncturist #22 410-764-4766

Airport #19 410-859-7064

Airport License, Public/Priv. Regis. #19 410-859-7137

Alarm Technician #27 410-799-0191

Architect #30 410-230-6322

Architectural Partnership/Corp. #12 410-230-6261

Asbestos Abatement Company #6 410-537-3200

Athletic Agent #17 410-230-6223

Attorney #3 410-260-1950

Audiologist #22 410-764-4723

Bail Bondsman #21 410-468-2383

Barber #8 410-230-6320

Boxer/Boxing Professional #17 410-230-6223

Bus Driver #18 410-768-7232

Charity #28 410-974-5534

Chiropractor/Chiropractic Assistant #22 410-764-5902

Collection Agency #13 410-230-6230

Contractor #10 410-230-6231

Cosmetologist #8 410-230-6320

Counselor #22 410-764-4732

Day Care Provider #2 410-321-2216

Dental Assistant #22 410-764-4730

Dental Hygienist #22 410-764-4730

Dentist #22 410-764-4730

Dietitian/Nutritionist #22 410-764-4733

Electrician, Master #12 410-230-6231

Electrologist #7 410-585-1952

Embalmer #22 410-764-4792

Engineer, Examining #12 410-230-6231

Engineer, Professional #12 410-230-6322

Esthetician #8 410-230-6320

Forester #12 410-230-6231

Franchises, Bus. Opportunity, Multi-level Mktng
    Programs #29 410-576-7785

Fund Raising Counsel #28 410-974-5534

Funeral Director #22 410-764-4792

Funeral Establishment #22 410-764-4792

Grain Dealer #4 410-841-5769

Guidance Counselor #5 410-767-0412

Handgun Permittee #27 410-799-0191

Harness Racing #9 410-230-6330

Hazardous Waste #6 410-537-3343

Hearing Aid Dispenser #22 410-764-4792

Home Improvement #12 410-230-6209

Home Improvement Salesperson #10 .. 410-230-6231

Horse Racing #9 410-230-6330

HVACR Contractor #12 410-230-6200

Insurance Agent #21 410-468-2383

Insurance Broker/Advisor #21 410-468-2383

Interior Designer #12 410-230-6322

Investment Adviser/Rep. #29 410-576-7784

Land Surveyor #12 410-230-6322

Landscape Architect #12 410-230-6322

Lead Inspectors/Contractors #6 410-537-3863

Limousine Driver #18
                     410-768-7232, PSC 410-767-8000

Lobbyist #14 410-974-2068

Lobbyist Employer #14 410-974-2068

Makeup Artist #8 410-230-6320

Massage Therapist #22 410-764-2431

Medical Doctor #22 410-764-4777

Mining Foreman/Fire Boss #6 410-537-3557

Mortgage Broker #13 410-230-6230

Mortician #22 410-764-4792

Nail Technician #8 410-230-6320

Notary Public #28 410-974-5520

Notice Filing #29 410-576-7050

Nurse-RN/LPN #24 410-585-1900

Nursery, Plant #4 410-841-5920

Nursing Assistant #24 410-585-1990

Nursing Home Administrator #22 410-764-4750

Occupational Therapist/Assistant #22.. 410-402-8560

Optometrist #22 410-764-4710

Pawnbroker #12 410-230-4640

Pesticide Applicator/Operator #4 410-841-5710

Pesticide Business/Dealer #4 410-841-5710

Pesticide Consultant #4 410-841-5710

Pesticide, Private Applicator #4 410-841-5710

Pharmacist #22 410-764-4755

Physical Therapist #22 410-764-4752

Physical Therapist Assistant #22 410-764-4752

Pilot #12 410-230-6329

Plant Broker/Dealer #4 410-841-5920

Plumber #12 410-230-6231

Podiatrist #22 410-764-4785

Police Officer, Special #27 410-799-0191

Polygraph Examiner #32 .... 301 791-7039 x117

Precious Metals & Gem Dealer/2nd-hand #12
.... 410-230-4640

Private Investigator #27 410-799-0191

Psychologist #22 410-764-4787

Psychometrist (Education) #5 410-767-0412

Public Accountant-CPA #12 410-230-6258

Pump Installer #6 .... 410-537-3557 x3510

Pupil Personnel Worker #5 410-767-0412

Radiation Therapy Technician #22 410-764-4775

Reading Specialist #5 410-767-0412

Reading Teacher #5 410-767-0412

Real Estate Agent #15 410-230-6230

Real Estate Appraiser #11 410-230-6231

Referee #17 410-230-6223

Respiratory Care Practitioner #22........ 410-764-4775

Sanitarian #6 .... 410-537-3557 x3597

School Admin'r/Superintendent #5 410-767-0412

School Library Media Generalist/Specialist #5
.... 410-767-0412

School Psychologist #5 410-767-0412

Securities Broker/Dealer #29 410-576-6494

Securities Sales Agent #29 410-576-6494

Security Guard #27 410-799-0191

Security Registration #29 410-576-7050

Sewage Treatment #6 410-537-3510

Social Worker #22 410-764-4788

Solicitor, Professional #28 410-974-5534

Speech Pathologist #22 410-764-4725

Subcontractor #10 410-230-6231

Taxi Driver #18 .... 410-768-7232, PSC 410-767-8000

Taxicab #31 410-767-8107

Teacher #5 410-767-0412

Truck Driver #18 410-768-7232

Veterinarian #1 410-841-5862

Veterinary Hospital #1 410-841-5862

Waste Water Treatment Plant Superintendent #6
.... 410-537-3167

Water Conditioner Installer #6 410-537-3000

Well Driller #6 410-537-3597

Maryland Licensing Agency Information

1 Board of Veterinary Medical Examiners, 50 Harry S Truman Pky, Annapolis, MD 21401; 410-841-5862, Fax: 410-841-5999. www.michigan.gov/cis

2 Child Care Administration, Region 3, 409 Washington Ave LL8, Towson, MD 21204; 410-321-2216, Fax: 410-321-2240. www.dhr.state.md.us/cca-home.htm Email: rhayes@dhr.state.md.us

3 Client Security Trust Fund, Robert F Sweeney Dist Ct Bldg, 251 Rowe Blvd 3rd Fl, Annapolis, MD 21401; 410-260-1950, Fax: 410-260-1954. Note: The MSBA and the CSTF are separate organizations. The MSBA phone number is 410-685-7878, fax 410-685-1016; 520 W Fayette St, Balt. MD 21201.

4 Department of Agriculture, Pesticide Regulation Section, 50 Harry S Truman Pky, Annapolis, MD 21401; 410-841-5710, Fax: 410-841-2765. www.mda.state.md.us Email: howarddw@mda.state.md.us

5 Department of Education, Division of Certification & Accreditation, 200 W Baltimore St, Baltimore, MD 21201-2595; 410-767-0412, Fax: 410-333-8963. www.msde.state.md.us/certification/certification.html

6 Department of Environment, 1800 Washington Blvd., Baltimore, MD 21230; 410-537-3000, Fax: separate at each unit. www.mde.state.md.us

7 Department of Health & Mental Hygiene, Board of Nursing, Electrology Practice Committee, 4201 Patterson Ave, Baltimore, MD 21215; 410-585-1952, Fax: 410-358-3530. www.bon.org

8 Department of Labor, Licensing & Regulation, Board of Barbers & Cosmetologists, 500 N Calvert St, 3rd Fl, Rm 307, Baltimore, MD 21202; 410-230-6320, Fax: 410-230-6314. www.dllr.state.md.us/license/occprof/barber.html Email: mbrown@dllr.state.md.us Search Database at www.dllr.state.md.us /query/barber.html (or) cosmet.html

9 Department of Labor, Licensing & Regulation, Racing Commission, 500 N Calvert St #201, Baltimore, MD 21202; 410-230-6330, Fax: 410-333-8308. www.dllr.state.md.us/racing/ Email: mhopkins@dllr.state.md.us

10 Department of Licensing & Regulation, Home Improvement Commission, 500 N Calvert St, #306, Baltimore, MD 21202-3651; 410-230-6309. www.dllr.state.md.us/license/occprof/homeim.html Email: krosenthal@dllr.state.md.us Search Database at www.dllr.state.md.us/query/home_imprv.html

11 Department of Labor, Licensing & Regulation, Board of Real Estate Appraisers, 500 N Calvert St, Baltimore, MD 21202; 410-230-6200, Fax: 410-333-1229. www.dllr.state.md.us/license/occprof/reappr.html Email: pschott@dllr.state.md.us Search Database at www.dllr.state.md.us/query/real_est_app.html

12 Department of Licensing & Regulation, Occupational Boards, 500 N Calvert St, Baltimore, MD 21202; 410-230-6200, Fax: 410-333-1229. www.dllr.state.md.us/license/occprof/ Email: twhite@dllr.state.md.us

13 Department of Licensing & Regulation, Office of Financial Regulations, 500 N Calvert St, #402, Baltimore, MD 21202; 1-888-218-5925 (toll free). www.dllr.state.md.us/license/fin_reg/mortlend/mdfinreg.html

14 State Ethics Commission, 9 State Circle #200 (188 Main St), Annapolis, MD 21401; 877-669-6085, 410-974-2068, Fax: 410-974-2418. http://ethics.gov.state.md.us Search Database at http://ethics.gov.state.md.us/listing.htm Note: A paper copy of the lobbyist list can be purchased for $10.00.

15 Department of Licensing & Regulation, Real Estate Commission, 500 N Calvert St, 3rd Fl, Baltimore, MD 21202-3551; 410-230-6230, Fax: 410-230-0023. www.dllr.state.md.us/license/occprof/recomm.html Email: mrec@dllr.state.md.us Search Database at www.dllr.state.md.us/query/real_est.html

17 Department of Licensing & Regulation, Athletic Commission, 500 N Calvert St, 2nd Fl, Baltimore, MD 21202; 410-230-6223, Fax: 410-230-6314. www.dllr.state.md.us/license/occprof/athlet.html

18 Department of Transportation, Motor Vehicle Administration, 6601 Ritchie Hwy NE, Glen Burnie, MD 21062; 410-768-7232, Fax: 410-333-6088. Note: Taxi and Limo drivers also have to have permits from the Public Service Commission.

19 Department of Transportation, Aviation Administration, PO Box 8766, BWI Airport, Baltimore, MD 21240; 410-859-7064, Fax: 410-859-7287. Email: maaadmin@mdot.state.md.us

21 Licensing & Regulation, Insurance Agent/Brokers Licensing & Investigation, 525 St Paul Pl, Baltimore, MD 21202; 410-468-2000, Fax: 410-468-2399. www.mdinsurance.state.md.us

22 Licensing Boards, 4201 Patterson Ave, Baltimore, MD 21215-2299; 410-764-4700, Fax: 410-358-0128. Email: jchull@dhmh.state.md.us

24 Board of Nursing, 4140 Patterson Ave, Baltimore, MD 21215; 888-202-9861, 410-585-1900, Fax: 410-358-3530. www.mbon.org/main.php Email: mbon@dhmh.state.md.us Search Database at www.mbon.org/main.php Note: A telephone voice response system called IVR is available; 410-585-1978.

27 State Police, Licensing Division, 7751 Washington Blvd, Jessup, MD 20794; 410-799-0191, Fax: 410-799-5934. www.inform.u md.edu/UMS+State/MD_Resources/MDSP/

28 Office of Secretary of State, Statehouse, 16 Francis St, Annapolis, MD 21401; 410-974-5521, Fax: 410-974-5190. www.sos.state.md.us Email: mdsos@sos.state.md.us

29 Securities Division, Attorney General's Office, 200 St. Paul Place, 25th Fl, Baltimore, MD 21202; 410-576-6360, Fax: 410-576-6532. www.oag.state.md.us/Securities/index.htm Email: securities@oag.state.md.us

30 Board of Architects, 500 N Calvert St 3rd Fl, Baltimore, MD 21202-2272; 888-218-5925, 410-230-6322, Fax: 410-333-0021. www.dllr.state.md.us Email: architect@dllr.state.md.us Search Database at www.dllr.state.md.us/query/arch.html Note: Lists of currently licensed individual architect & firms can be purchased for a fee. Call 410-230-6352.

31 Public Service Commission, PO Box 2224, Haggerstown, MD 21741; 301-791-7039, Fax: 410-333-6088. www.polygraphexaminer.com/MPA/

32 Polygraph Association, PO Box 2224, Hagerstown, MD 21741; 301 791-7039 ex. 117. www.mpapolygraph.org

Maryland Federal Courts

The following list indicates the district and division name for each county in the state. If the bankruptcy court location is different from the district court, then the location of the bankruptcy court appears in parentheses.

County/Court Cross Reference

Allegany	Baltimore	Harford	Baltimore
Anne Arundel	Baltimore	Howard	Baltimore
Baltimore	Baltimore	Kent	Baltimore
Baltimore City City	Baltimore	Montgomery	Greenbelt
Calvert	Greenbelt	Prince George's	Greenbelt
Caroline	Baltimore	Queen Anne's	Baltimore
Carroll	Baltimore	Somerset	Baltimore
Cecil	Baltimore	St. Mary's	Greenbelt
Charles	Greenbelt	Talbot	Baltimore
Dorchester	Baltimore	Washington	Baltimore
Frederick	Baltimore	Wicomico	Baltimore
Garrett	Baltimore	Worcester	Baltimore

Standards for Federal Courts: See Maine Federal Courts section for information on Federal Courts standards and fees.

US District Court

Northern District of Maryland

Baltimore Division Clerk, 4th Floor, Room 4415, 101 W Lombard St, Baltimore, MD 21201 (courier address: Use mail address for courier delivery) 410-962-2600. www.mdd.uscourts.gov

Counties: Allegany, Anne Arundel, Baltimore, City of Baltimore, Caroline, Carroll, Cecil, Dorchester, Frederick, Garrett, Harford, Howard, Kent, Queen Anne's, Somerset, Talbot, Washington, Wicomico, Worcester.

Indexing & Storage: New cases available in the index 1-2 days after filing date.

Fee & Payment: Payment may be made by money order, cashier check, personal check. Payee: Clerk, USDC.

Phone Search: The court will verify questions over the phone, but will not read long dockets.

In Person Search: Fee charged if court conducts your in person search for you.

PACER: PACER is available online at http://pacer.mdd.uscourts.gov. Records purged every six months. New records online after 1 day.

Electronic Filing: Electronic filing information online at https://ecf.mdd.uscourts.gov

Opinions Online: Court opinions are online at www.mdd.uscourts.gov

U.S. Bankruptcy Court

Northern District of Maryland

Baltimore Division U.S. Courthouse, 101 W Lombard St, Ste 8303, Baltimore, MD 21201 (courier address: Use mail address for courier delivery) 410-962-2688. www.mdb.uscourts.gov

Counties: Anne Arundel, Baltimore, City of Baltimore, Caroline, Carroll, Cecil, Dorchester, Harford, Howard, Kent, Queen Anne's, Somerset, Talbot, Wicomico, Worcester.

Indexing & Storage: Cases indexed by debtor as well as by case number. New cases available in the index 2 days after filing date. The name and/or case number of the debtor(s) as well as specific identification of the pleading involved are required to search for a record. Closed files are retained for the existing year and the previous calendar year.

Fee & Payment: Payment may be made by money order, cashier check. Business checks are not accepted. Personal checks are not accepted. Non-certified copy work is available from an onsite vendor, Document Technology, 410-837-0409 for information. Payee: Clerk, U.S. Bankruptcy Court.

Phone Search: Only docket information available by phone. Automated voice case information service (VCIS) is available. Call VCIS at 800-829-0145 or 410-962-0733.

Mail Search: A SASE not required.

In Person Search: Fee charged if court conducts your in person search for you. Public can search automated records and paper dockets only.

PACER: PACER is available online at http://pacer.mdb.uscourts.gov. Records purged every six months. New civil records are online after 2 days.

Electronic Filing: Electronic filing information online at https://ecf.mdb.uscourts.gov

U.S. District Court

Southern District of Maryland

Greenbelt Division Clerk, Room 240, 6500 Cherrywood Lane, Greenbelt, MD 20770 (courier address: Use mail address for courier delivery) 301-344-0660. www.mdd.uscourts.gov

Counties: Calvert, Charles, Montgomery, Prince George's, St. Mary's.

Indexing & Storage: New cases available in the index 3 days after filing date. Case records indexed on computer since 1990.

Fee & Payment: Make payment by money order, cashier check, personal check. Payee: Clerk, USDC.

Phone Search: The court will verify information over the phone, but will not read long dockets.

Mail Search: An outside copy service, Office Solutions, 301-982-4682, is contracted to do all searching and copies. Include SASE for return.

In Person Search: Fee charged if court conducts your in person search for you. Office Solutions copying service, 301-982-4682, can do searching and copies.

PACER: PACER is available online at http://pacer.mdd.uscourts.gov. Records purged every six months. New records online after 1 day.

Electronic Filing: Electronic filing information online at https://ecf.mdd.uscourts.gov

Opinions Online: Court opinions are online at www.mdd.uscourts.gov

U.S. Bankruptcy Court

Southern District of Maryland

Greenbelt Division 6500 Cherrywood Ln, #300, Greenbelt, MD 20770 (courier address: Use mail address for courier delivery) 301-344-8018. www.mdb.uscourts.gov

Counties: Allegany, Calvert, Charles, Frederick, Garrett, Montgomery, Prince George's, St. Mary's, Washington.

Indexing & Storage: Cases indexed by debtor as well as by case number. New cases available in the index 2-3 days after filing date. The name and/or case number of the debtor(s) as well as specific identification of the pleading involved are required to search for a record.

Fee & Payment: Payee: Clerk, U.S. Bankruptcy Court. Payment may be made by money order, cashier check, personal check. In house copy work (4 pages or less and copies that need to be certified) is done on an "as time permits" basis. Copy work of 5 pages or more is done off premises but the cost is less.

Phone Search: Only docket information available by phone. Automated voice case information service (VCIS) is available. Call VCIS at 800-829-0145 or 410-962-0733.

Mail Search: SASE not required.Open cases are searched by Ikon Office Solutions, 301-982-4682.

In Person Search: Fee charged if court conducts your in person search for you.

PACER: PACER is available online at http://pacer.mdb.uscourts.gov. Records purged every six months. New civil records are online after 2 days.

Electronic Filing: Electronic filing information online at https://ecf.mdb.uscourts.gov

Maryland County Courts

Court	Jurisdiction	No. of Courts	How Organized
Circuit Courts*	General	25	8 Circuits
District Courts*	Limited	26	12 Districts
Orphan's Courts*	Probate	24	Register of Wills

* Profiled in this Sourcebook.

CIVIL								
Court	Tort	Contract	Real Estate	Min. Claim	Max. Claim	Small Claims	Estate	Eviction	Domestic Relations
Circuit Courts*	X	X	X	$25000	No Max				X
District Courts*	X	X	X	$2500	$25000	$2500		X	X
Orphan's Court*							X		

CRIMINAL					
Court	Felony	Misdemeanor	DWI/DUI	Preliminary Hearing	Juvenile
Circuit Courts*	X	X			X
District Courts*		X	X	X	X
Orphan's Court*					

ADMINISTRATION

Court Administrator, Administrative Office of the Courts, 580 Taylor Ave, Annapolis, MD, 21401; 410-260-1400, Fax: 410-974-2169.

www.courts.state.md.us

COURT STRUCTURE

The Circuit Court is the highest court of record. There is a Circuit Court with an elected clerk in each county of Maryland and Baltimore City.

The jurisdiction of the District Court includes all landlord-tenant cases, replevin actions, motor vehicle violations, misdemeanors and certain felonies. In civil cases the District Court has exclusive jurisdiction in claims for amounts up to $5,000, and concurrent jurisdiction with the circuit courts in claims for amounts above $5,000 but less than $25,000. The jurisdiction of the court in criminal cases is concurrent with the Circuit Court for offenses in which the penalty may be confinement for three years or more or a fine of $2,500 or more; or offenses which are felonies.

In most circuit courts, copies are $.50 per page and certification is $5.00. In most district courts, copies are $.25 per page and certification is $5.00.

ONLINE ACCESS

At www.courts.state.md.us/dialup.html see the Judicial Information System (JIS) or (SJIS) for dial-up access to civil and criminal case information from the following:

> All District Courts - All civil and all misdemeanors
>
> All Circuit Courts Civil - All civil records are online through JIS.
>
> Circuit Courts Criminal - Three courts are on JIS - Anne Arundel, Carroll county, and Baltimore City Court

Inquiries may be made to: the District Court traffic system for case information data, calendar information data, court schedule data, or officer schedule data; the District Court criminal system for case information data or calendar caseload data; the District Court civil system for case information data, attorney name and address data; the land records system for land and plat records. There is an annual fee for JIS dial-up access of $50.00, which must be included with the application. For additional information or to receive a registration packet, write or call Judicial Information Systems, Security Administrator, 2661 Riva Rd., Suite 900, Annapolis, MD 21401, 410-260-1031, or visit the web site. Appellate opinions are available from www.courts.state.md.us/opinions.html.

PROBATE COURTS

The Circuit Court handles Probate in Montgomery and Harford counties. In other counties, probate is handled by the Register of Wills and is a county, not a court, function.

Allegany County

4th Judicial Circuit Court 30 Washington St, Cumberland, MD 21502; 301-777-5922; Fax: 301-777-2100. Hours: 8AM-4:30PM (EST). *Felony, Misdemeanor, Civil Actions Over $25,000.*
Civil Records: Access: In person only. Visitors must perform in person searches for themselves. No search fee. Required to search: name, years to search. Civil cases indexed by defendant, plaintiff. Civil records on computer since 11/92, archived and indexed from 1790. Online access is through JIS. See state introduction or visit www.courts.state.md.us.
Criminal Records: Access: In person only. Visitors must perform in person searches for themselves. No search fee. Required to search: name, years to search; also helpful: DOB. Criminal records on computer since 9/99, archived and indexed from 1790.
General Information: Public Access terminal is available. No adoptions, juvenile, sealed, expunged or mental records released. Copy fee: $.50 per page. Certification fee: $5.00 per instrument. Payee: Circuit Court. Personal checks accepted. Prepayment required.

District Court 3 Pershing St, 2nd Floor, Cumberland, MD 21502; 301-777-2105. Hours: 8:30AM-4:30PM (EST). *Misdemeanor, Civil Actions Under $25,000, Eviction, Small Claims.*
Civil Records: Access: Mail, online, in person. Both court and visitors may perform in person searches. No search fee. Required to search: name, years to search. Civil cases indexed by defendant. Civil records on computer from 1990, on index books from 1970. Online access is through JIS. See state introduction or visit www.courts.state.md.us.
Criminal Records: Access: Mail, online, in person. Visitors must perform in person searches for themselves. No search fee. Required to search: name, years to search, signed release; also helpful: SSN. Criminal records on computer from 1980, index books. Online access through JIS. See state introduction or visit www.courts.state.md.us. Court requires a case number for a search.
General Information: No adoptions, juvenile, sealed, expunged or mental records released. Copy fee: $.25 per page. Certification fee: $5.00 per page. Payee: District Court of MD. Personal checks accepted. Prepayment required. Mail requests: SASE required. Mail turnaround time 7 days.

Register of Wills 59 Prospect Sq. 1St. Floor, Cumberland, MD 21502; 301-724-3760, 888-724-0148 in MD; Fax: 301-724-1249. Hours: 8AM-4:30PM (EST). *Probate.*
www.registers.state.md.us/county/al/html/allegany.html

Anne Arundel County

5th Judicial Circuit Court Box 71 (7 Church St), Annapolis, MD 21404-0071; 410-222-1397; Civil phone: 410-222-1431. Hours: 8:30AM-4:30PM (Phone hours-11AM-3:30pm) (EST). *Felony, Misdemeanor, Civil Actions Over $25,000.*
Civil Records: Access: Phone, mail, online, in person. Both court and visitors may perform in person searches. No search fee. Required to search: name, years to search. Civil cases indexed by defendant, plaintiff. Civil records on computer from 1991, on index from 1900. Online access is through JIS. See state introduction or visit www.courts.state.md.us.
Criminal Records: Access: Online, in person. Both court and visitors may perform in person searches. No search fee. Required to search: name, years to search; also helpful: SSN. Criminal records on computer from 1988, indexed from 1960, archived from 1900. Online access through JIS. See state introduction or visit www.courts.state.md.us.

General Information: Public Access terminal is available. No adoptions, juvenile, sealed, expunged or mental records released. Copy fee: $.50 per page. Certification fee: $5.00. Payee: Clerk of Circuit Court. Personal checks accepted. Prepayment required. Mail requests: SASE required. Mail turnaround time 1 week.

District Court 251 Rowe Blvd, #141, Annapolis, MD 21401; 410-260-1370. Hours: 8:30AM-4:30PM (EST). *Misdemeanor, Civil Actions Under $25,000, Eviction, Small Claims.*
Civil Records: Access: Mail, online, in person. Both court and visitors may perform in person searches. No search fee. Required to search: name, years to search. Civil cases indexed by defendant. Civil records on computer from 1982, archived and indexed from 1900s. Online access is through JIS. See state introduction or visit www.courts.state.md.us.
Criminal Records: Access: Mail, online, in person. Both court and visitors may perform in person searches. No search fee. Required to search: name, years to search. Criminal records on computer from 1982, archived and indexed from 1900s. Online access through JIS. See state introduction or visit www.courts.state.md.us.
General Information: Public Access terminal is available. Copy fee: $.25 per page. Certification fee: $5.00. Payee: District Court. Personal checks accepted. Prepayment required. Mail requests: SASE required. Mail turnaround time 5 days.

Register of Wills PO Box 2368, 7 1/2 Circuit Courthouse-Church Circle #403, Annapolis, MD 21404-2368; 410-222-1430, 800-679-6665 in MD; Fax: 410-222-1467. Hours: 8:30AM-4:30PM (EST). *Probate.*
www.registers.state.md.us/county/aa/html/annearundel.html
Note: Wills only; no genealogy searches

Baltimore County

3rd Judicial Circuit Court 401 Bosley Ave, 2nd Floor, Towson, MD 21204; 410-887-2601. Hours: 8:30AM-4:30PM (EST). *Felony, Civil Actions Over $25,000.*
Civil Records: Access: Online, in person. Visitors must perform in person searches for themselves. No search fee. Required to search: name, years to search; also helpful: address. Civil cases indexed by defendant, plaintiff. Civil records in books, file jackets. Online access is through JIS. See state introduction or visit www.courts.state.md.us.
Criminal Records: Access: In person only. Visitors must perform in person searches for themselves. No search fee. Required to search: name, years to search; also helpful: address, DOB, SSN. Criminal records on computer from 1984, prior on books.
General Information: Public Access terminal is available. (Civil only.) No adoptions, juvenile, sealed, expunged or mental records released. Will not fax results. Copy fee: $.50 per page. Certification fee: $5.00 per page. Payee: Suzanne Mensh, Clerk. Personal checks accepted. Out of state checks not accepted. Prepayment required.

District Court 120 E Chesapeake Ave, Towson, MD 21286-5307; 410-512-2000; Criminal phone: 410-512-2101. Hours: 8:30AM-4:30PM (EST). *Misdemeanor, Civil Actions Under $25,000, Eviction, Small Claims.*
Civil Records: Access: Online, in person. Visitors must perform in person searches for themselves. No search fee. Required to search: name, years to search; also helpful: address. Civil cases indexed by defendant. Civil records on computer from 1985, on microfiche from 1971, archived from 1970, on card index from 1971. Online access is through

JIS. See state introduction or visit www.courts.state.md.us.
Criminal Records: Access: Online, in person. Visitors must perform in person searches for themselves. No search fee. Required to search: name, years to search. Criminal records on computer since 1981. Online access through JIS. See state introduction or visit www.courts.state.md.us.
General Information: Public Access terminal is available. No adoptions, juvenile, sealed, expunged or medical records released. Copy fee: $.50 per page. Certification fee: $5.00. Payee: District Court of MD. Personal checks accepted. Prepayment required.

Register of Wills 401 Bosley Ave, Mail Stop 3507, Towson, MD 21204-4403; 410-887-6685, 888-642-5387 in MD; Fax: 410-583-2517. Hours: 8AM-4:30PM (EST). *Probate.*
www.registers.state.md.us/county/ba/html/baltimore.html

Baltimore City

8th Judicial Circuit Court - Civil Division 111 N Calvert, Rm 409, Baltimore, MD 21202; 410-396-5188; Civil phone: 410-369-3045. Hours: 8:30AM-4:30PM (EST). *Civil Actions Over $25,000.*
www.baltocts.state.md.us
Civil Records: Access: Phone, mail, online, in person. Both court and visitors may perform in person searches. No search fee. Required to search: name, years to search; also helpful: address. Civil cases indexed by defendant. Civil records on computer from 1983. Online access is through JIS. See state introduction or visit www.courts.state.md.us. Court conducts searches on a limited basis.
General Information: Public Access terminal is available. No adoptions, juvenile, sealed, expunged or mental records released. Copy fee: $.50 per page. Certification fee: $5.00. Payee: Clerk of the Circuit Court. Business checks accepted. Prepayment required. Mail requests: SASE not required. Mail turnaround time 5 days.

8th Judicial Circuit Court - Criminal Division 110 N Calvert Rm 200, Baltimore, MD 21202; 410-333-3750. Hours: 8:30AM-4:30PM (EST). *Felony, Misdemeanor.*
Criminal Records: Access: Online, in person. Visitors must perform in person searches for themselves. No search fee. Required to search: name, years to search; also helpful: address, DOB. Criminal records on computer from 1994, on microfilm from 1973. Online access through SJIS; see www.courts.state.md.us.
General Information: Public Access terminal is available. No adoptions, juvenile, sealed, expunged or mental records released. Copy fee: $.50 per page. Certification fee: $5.00. Payee: Clerk of Circuit Court. Business checks accepted.

District Court - Civil Division 501 E Fayette St, Baltimore, MD 21202; 410-878-8900. Hours: 8:30AM-4:30PM (EST). *Civil Actions Under $25,000, Eviction, Small Claims.*
Civil Records: Access: Mail, online, in person. Both court and visitors may perform in person searches. No search fee. Required to search: name, years to search. Civil cases indexed by defendant. Civil records on computer from 1986, on card index from 1971. Online access is through JIS. See state introduction or visit www.courts.state.md.us.
General Information: Public Access terminal is available. No medical or sealed records released. Copy fee: $.25 per page. Certification fee: $5.00. Payee: District Court of MD. Personal checks accepted. Prepayment required. Mail requests: SASE required. Mail turnaround time 1-2 days.

District Court - Criminal Division 5800 Wabash Ave, Baltimore, MD 21215; 410-878-8000. Hours: 8;30AM-4:30PM (EST). *Misdemeanor.*

Criminal Records: Access: Mail, online, in person. Only court performs in person searches. No search fee. Required to search: name, years to search; also helpful: SSN. Criminal records on computer from 1983, prior on index cards from 1970. Online access through JIS. See state introduction or visit www.courts.state.md.us.

General Information: No adoptions, juvenile, sealed, expunged, medical or mental records released. Copy fee: $.25 per page. Certification fee: $5.00. Payee: District Court. Personal checks accepted. Prepayment required. Mail requests: SASE required. Mail turnaround time 1 week.

Register of Wills Courthouse East, 111 N Calvert St, Rm 352, Baltimore, MD 21202; 410-752-5131, 888-876-0035 in MD; Fax: 410-752-3494. Hours: 8AM-4:30PM (EST). *Probate.*
www.registers.state.md.us/city/bc/html/baltimorecity.html

Calvert County

7th Judicial Circuit Court 175 Main St Courthouse, Prince Frederick, MD 20678; 410-535-1660. Hours: 8:30AM-4:30PM (EST). *Felony, Misdemeanor, Civil Actions Over $25,000.*
www.courts.state.md.us/clerks/calvert

Civil Records: Access: Online, in person. Visitors must perform in person searches for themselves. No search fee. Required to search: name, years to search. Civil cases indexed by defendant, plaintiff. Civil records on computer back to 10/1997, prior on index books back to 1959. Online access is through JIS. See state introduction or visit www.courts.state.md.us.

Criminal Records: Access: In person only. Visitors must perform in person searches for themselves. No search fee. Required to search: name, years to search; also helpful: SSN. Criminal records on computer from 4/2000; prior in books back to 1967.

General Information: Public Access terminal is available. No adoptions, juvenile, sealed, expunged or mental records released. Copy fee: $.25 per page. Certification fee: $5.00. Payee: Clerk of Circuit Court. Personal checks accepted. Prepayment required.

District Court 200 Duke St Rm 2200, Prince Frederick, MD 20678; 410-535-8800. Hours: 8:30AM-4:30PM (EST). *Misdemeanor, Civil Actions Under $25,000, Eviction, Small Claims.*

Civil Records: Access: Mail, in person, online. Visitors must perform in person searches for themselves. No search fee. Required to search: name; also helpful: address. Civil cases indexed by defendant. Civil records on computer from mid-80s, archived from 1971 to 1981, prior on Cott index. Online access is through JIS. See state introduction or visit www.courts.state.md.us.

Criminal Records: Access: In person, online. Visitors must perform in person searches for themselves. No search fee. Required to search: name; also helpful: address, DOB. Criminal records on computer from 1981, archived from 1971-1981, prior on cott index. Online access through JIS. See state introduction or visit www.courts.state.md.us.

General Information: Public Access terminal is available. No adoptions, juvenile, sealed, expunged or medical records released. Copy fee: $.25 per page. Certification fee: $5.00. Payee: District Court of Maryland. Personal checks accepted. Prepayment required. Mail requests: SASE required. Mail turnaround time 1-3 days.

Register of Wills Courthouse, 175 Main St, Prince Frederick, MD 20678; 410-535-0121, 888-374-0015 in MD; Fax: 410-414-3952. Hours: 8:30AM-4:30PM (EST). *Probate.*

www.registers.state.md.us/county/cv/html/calvert.html

Caroline County

2nd Judicial Circuit Court Box 458, Denton, MD 21629; 410-479-1811; Fax: 410-479-1142. Hours: 8:30AM-4:30PM (EST). *Felony, Misdemeanor, Civil Actions Over $25,000.*
Note: Misdemeanor case records held at District Court until appealed, then stored at Circuit Court.

Civil Records: Access: Online, in person. Visitors must perform in person searches for themselves. No search fee. Required to search: name, years to search; also helpful: address. Civil cases indexed by defendant, plaintiff. Civil records on computer from 10/98, card index from 1774. Online access is through JIS. See state introduction or visit www.courts.state.md.us.

Criminal Records: Access: In person only. Visitors must perform in person searches for themselves. No search fee. Required to search: name, years to search; also helpful: address, DOB, SSN. Criminal records on computer from 2000, card index from 1774.

General Information: Public Access terminal is available. No adoptions, juvenile, sealed, expunged or mental records released. Copy fee: $.50 per page; $.25 self serve. Certification fee: $5.00. Payee: F Dale Minner, Clerk. Personal checks accepted. Prepayment required.

District Court 207 S 3rd St, Denton, MD 21629; 410-819-4600; Fax: 410-479-5808. Hours: 8:30AM-4:30PM (EST). *Misdemeanor, Civil Actions Under $25,000, Eviction, Small Claims.*

Civil Records: Access: Online, in person. Visitors must perform in person searches for themselves. No search fee. Required to search: name, years to search; also helpful: address. Civil cases indexed by defendant. Civil records on cards from 1971, computerized since 1981. Online access is through JIS. See state introduction or visit www.courts.state.md.us.

Criminal Records: Access: Online, in person. Visitors must perform in person searches for themselves. No search fee. Required to search: name, years to search; also helpful: address, DOB. Criminal records on cards from 1971, computerized since 1981. Online access through JIS. See state introduction or visit www.courts.state.md.us.

General Information: No adoptions, juvenile, sealed, expunged or mental records released. Copy fee: $.50. Certification fee: $5.00. Payee: District Court. Personal checks accepted. Prepayment required.

Register of Wills County Courthouse, 109 Market St, Rm 119, PO Box 416, Denton, MD 21629; 410-479-0717, 888-786-0019 in MD; Fax: 410-479-4983. Hours: 8AM-4:30PM (EST). *Probate.*
www.registers.state.md.us/county/ca/html/caroline.html

Carroll County

5th Judicial Circuit Court 55 N Court St., Westminster, MD 21157; 410-386-2026; Civil phone: 410-386-2326; Criminal phone: 410-386-2025; Probate phone: 410-848-2586; Fax: 410-876-0822. Hours: 8:30AM-4:30PM (EST). *Felony, Misdemeanor, Civil Actions Over $25,000.*

Civil Records: Access: Online, in person. Visitors must perform in person searches for themselves. No search fee. Required to search: name; also helpful: years to search. Civil cases indexed by defendant, plaintiff. Civil records on computer from 1990, on card books from 1837 to 1990. Online access is through JIS. See state introduction or visit www.courts.state.md.us.

Criminal Records: Access: Online, in person. Visitors must perform in person searches for

themselves. No search fee. Required to search: name; also helpful: years to search. Criminal records on computer from 1990, on card books from 1837 to 1990. Online access through JIS. See state introduction or visit www.courts.state.md.us.

General Information: Public Access terminal is available. No adoptions, juvenile, sealed, expunged or mental records released. Copy fee: $.50 per page. Certification fee: $5.00 per document. Payee: Clerk of Court. Personal checks accepted. Visa, MC accepted. Prepayment required.

District Court 101 N Court St, Westminster, MD 21157; 410-871-3500. Hours: 8:30AM-4:30PM (EST). *Misdemeanor, Civil Actions Under $25,000, Eviction, Small Claims.*

Civil Records: Access: Online, in person. Visitors must perform in person searches for themselves. No search fee. Required to search: name, years to search. Civil cases indexed by defendant, plaintiff. Civil records on computer back to 1991; on card index from 1971. Online access is through JIS. See state introduction or visit www.courts.state.md.us.

Criminal Records: Access: Online, in person. Visitors must perform in person searches for themselves. No search fee. Required to search: name, years to search; also helpful: DOB. Criminal records on computer back to 1982; on card index from 1971. Online access through JIS. See state introduction or visit www.courts.state.md.us.

General Information: Public Access terminal is available. No adoptions, juvenile, sealed, expunged or mental records released. Copy fee: $.25 per page. Certification fee: $5.00 per document. Payee: District Court. Personal checks accepted. Prepayment required.

Register of Wills 55 N Court St, Rm 104, Westminster, MD 21157; 410-848-2586, 888-876-0034 in MD; Fax: 410-876-0657. Hours: 8:30AM-4:30PM (EST). *Probate.*
www.registers.state.md.us/county/cr/html/carroll.html

Cecil County

2nd Judicial Circuit Court 129 E Main St, Rm 108, Elkton, MD 21921; 410-996-5325; Civil phone: 410-996-5369; Fax: 410-392-6032. Hours: 8:30AM-4:30PM (EST). *Felony, Misdemeanor, Civil Actions Over $25,000.*

Civil Records: Access: Online, in person. Visitors must perform in person searches for themselves. No search fee. Required to search: name, years to search. Civil cases indexed by defendant. Civil records on card index from 1948. Online access is through JIS. See state introduction or visit www.courts.state.md.us.

Criminal Records: Access: in person only. Visitors must perform in person searches for themselves. No search fee. Required to search: name, years to search; also helpful: DOB, SSN. Criminal records on card index from 1948; computerized records since 1993.

General Information: Public Access terminal is available. No adoptions, juvenile, sealed, expunged or mental records released. Certification fee: $5.00 per page. Payee: Clerk of Court. Personal checks accepted. Prepayment required.

District Court 170 E Main St, Elkton, MD 21921; 410-996-2700. Hours: 8:30AM-4:30PM (EST). *Misdemeanor, Civil Actions Under $25,000, Eviction, Small Claims.*

Civil Records: Access: Online, in person. Visitors must perform in person searches for themselves. No search fee. Required to search: name, years to search. Civil cases indexed by defendant. Civil records on computer from 1987, on card index from 1971. Online access is through JIS. See state introduction or visit www.courts.state.md.us.

Criminal Records: Access: Online, in person. Visitors must perform in person searches for themselves. No search fee. Required to search: name, years to search. Criminal records on computer from 1981, on card index from 1971. Online access through JIS. See state introduction or visit www.courts.state.md.us.

General Information: Public Access terminal is available. No adoptions, juvenile, sealed, expunged or mental records released. Copy fee: $.25 per page. Certification fee: $5.00. Payee: District Court. Personal checks accepted. Prepayment required.

Register of Wills County Courthouse, #101, PO Box 468, Elkton, MD 21922-0468; 410-398-2737, 888-398-0301 in MD; Fax: 410-996-1039. Hours: 8:30AM-4:30PM (EST). *Probate.*
www.registers.state.md.us/county/ce/html/cecil.html

Charles County

Circuit Court for Charles County PO Box 970, La Plata, MD 20646; 301-932-3201x223. Hours: 8:30AM-4:30PM (EST). *Felony, Misdemeanor, Civil Actions Over $2,500.*
www.courts.state.md.us/clerks/charles
Civil Records: Access: Online, in person. Visitors must perform in person searches for themselves. No search fee. Required to search: name, years to search. Civil cases indexed by defendant, plaintiff. Civil records on index books from 1950, on computer back to 1996. Online access is through JIS. See state introduction or visit www.courts.state.md.us.
Criminal Records: Access: In person only. Visitors must perform in person searches for themselves. No search fee. Required to search: name, years to search. Criminal records on index books from 1950, on computer back to 1996.
General Information: Public Access terminal is available. No adoptions, juvenile, sealed, expunged or medical records released. Copy fee: $.50 per page. Certification fee: $5.00. Payee: Clerk of the Circuit Court. Personal checks accepted. Prepayment required.

District Court PO Box 3070, La Plata, MD 20646; 301-932-3300; Civil phone: 301-932-3290; Criminal phone: 301-932-3295. Hours: 8:30AM-4:30PM (EST). *Misdemeanor, Civil Actions Under $25,000, Eviction, Small Claims.*
Civil Records: Access: Online, in person. Visitors must perform in person searches for themselves. No search fee. Required to search: name, years to search. Civil cases indexed by defendant, plaintiff. Civil records on computer from 1987, on card index from 1980. Online access is through JIS. See state introduction or visit www.courts.state.md.us.
Criminal Records: Access: Online, in person. Visitors must perform in person searches for themselves. No search fee. Required to search: name, years to search. Criminal records on computer from 1984, on card index from 1980, from 09/98 on public access terminal. Online access through SJIS; see state introduction or visit www.courts.state.md.us.
General Information: Public Access terminal is available. (Civil records only.) No confidential info, unserved warrants, medical records released. Copy fee: $.50 per page. Certification fee: $10.00. Payee: District Court. Personal checks accepted. Prepayment required.

Register of Wills Box 3080 (Courthouse, 200 E Charles St), La Plata, MD 20646; 301-932-3345, 888-256-0054 in MD; Fax: 301-932-3349. Hours: 8:30AM-4:30PM (EST). *Probate.*
www.registers.state.md.us/county/ch/html/charles.html

Dorchester County

1st Judicial Circuit Court Box 150, Cambridge, MD 21613; 410-228-0481. Hours: 8:30AM-4:30PM (EST). *Felony, Misdemeanor, Civil Actions Over $25,000.*
Civil Records: Access: Online, in person. Visitors must perform in person searches for themselves. No search fee. Required to search: name, years to search. Civil cases indexed by defendant, plaintiff. Civil records on computer from 1993. Online access is through JIS. See state introduction or visit www.courts.state.md.us.
Criminal Records: Access: In person only. Visitors must perform in person searches for themselves. No search fee. Required to search: name, years to search. Criminal records on computer from 1993.
General Information: Public Access terminal is available. No adoptions, juvenile, sealed, expunged or mental records released. Copy fee: $.25 per page. Certification fee: $5.00. Payee: Clerk of Circuit Court.

District Court 310 Gay St, Cambridge, MD 21613; 410-901-1420. Hours: 8:30AM-4:30PM (EST). *Misdemeanor, Civil Actions Under $25,000, Eviction, Small Claims.*
Civil Records: Access: Online, in person. Visitors must perform in person searches for themselves. No search fee. Required to search: name, years to search; also helpful: address. Civil cases indexed by defendant. Civil records archived and indexed from 1971; computerized records since 1985. Online access is through JIS. See state introduction or visit www.courts.state.md.us.
Criminal Records: Access: Online, in person. Visitors must perform in person searches for themselves. No search fee. Required to search: name, years to search; also helpful: address, DOB, SSN. Criminal records on card index from 1971; computerized records since 1985. Online access through JIS. See state introduction or visit www.courts.state.md.us.
General Information: Public Access terminal is available. No adoptions, sealed, juvenile, expunged or mental records released. Copy fee: $.25 per page. Certification fee: $5.00 per page. Payee: District Court. Personal checks accepted. Prepayment required.

Register of Wills 206 High St, Cambridge, MD 21613; 410-228-4181, 888-242-6257 in MD; Fax: 410-228-4988. Hours: 8AM-4:30PM; Public hours 8:30AM-4:30PM (EST). *Probate.*
www.registers.state.md.us/county/do/html/dorchester.html

Frederick County

6th Judicial Circuit Court 100 W Patrick St, Frederick, MD 21701; 301-694-1970. Hours: 8:30AM-4:30PM (EST). *Felony, Misdemeanor, Civil Actions Over $25,000.*
Civil Records: Access: Online, in person. Visitors must perform in person searches for themselves. No search fee. Required to search: name, years to search. Civil cases indexed by defendant, plaintiff. Civil records on computer from 08/94, prior on card books. Online access is through JIS. See state introduction or visit www.courts.state.md.us.
Criminal Records: Access: In person only. Visitors must perform in person searches for themselves. No search fee. Required to search: name, years to search. Criminal records on computer from 12/81, prior on index books.
General Information: Public Access terminal is available. No adoptions, juvenile, sealed, expunged or mental records released. Copy fee: $.25 per page. Certification fee: $5.00. Payee: Clerk of Circuit Court. Personal checks accepted. Prepayment required.

District Court 100 W Patrick St, Frederick, MD 21701; 301-694-2000. Hours: 8:30AM-4:30PM (EST). *Misdemeanor, Civil Actions Under $25,000, Eviction, Small Claims.*
Note: If the case number is known, the court will supply a copy of the disposition for $1.00 per page, turnaround time is 30 days.
Civil Records: Access: Online, in person. Visitors must perform in person searches for themselves. No search fee. Required to search: name; also helpful: years to search. Civil cases indexed by defendant, plaintiff. Civil records on computer and microfiche from 1986, archived and on card index from 1971. Online access is through JIS. See state introduction or visit www.courts.state.md.us.
Criminal Records: Access: Online, in person. Visitors must perform in person searches for themselves. No search fee. Required to search: name, DOB; also helpful: years to search. Criminal records on computer and microfiche from 1982, archived and on card index from 1971. Online access through JIS. See state introduction or visit www.courts.state.md.us.
General Information: Public Access terminal is available. No adoptions, juvenile, sealed, expunged or mental records released. Copy fee: $.25 per page. Certification fee: $5.00. Payee: District Court. Personal checks accepted. Visa, MC, AmEx accepted. Prepayment required.

Register of Wills 100 W Patrick St, Frederick, MD 21701; 301-663-3722, 888-258-0526; Fax: 301-846-0744. Hours: 8AM-4:30PM (EST). *Probate.*
www.registers.state.md.us/county/fr/html/frederick.html

Garrett County

4th Judicial Circuit Court PO Box 447, Oakland, MD 21550; 301-334-1937; Civil phone: 301-334-1944; Criminal phone: 301-334-1943; Fax: 301-334-5017. Hours: 8:30AM-4:30PM (EST). *Felony, Misdemeanor, Civil Actions Over $25,000.*
Civil Records: Access: Mail, online, in person. No search fee. Required to search: name, years to search. Civil cases indexed by defendant, plaintiff. Civil records on computer since 11/97. Online access is through JIS. See state introduction or visit www.courts.state.md.us.
Criminal Records: Access: Mail, in person. Both court and visitors may perform in person searches. No search fee. Required to search: name, years to search, DOB. Criminal records on computer since 11/97.
General Information: Public Access terminal is available. No adoptions, juvenile, sealed, expunged or mental records released. Copy fee: $.50 per page. Certification fee: $5.00 per page. Payee: David K Martin, Clerk. Personal checks accepted. Prepayment required. Mail requests: SASE not required. Mail turnaround time 1 day.

District Court 205 S 3rd St, Oakland, MD 21550; 301-334-8020. Hours: 8:30AM-4:30PM (EST). *Misdemeanor, Civil Actions Under $25,000, Eviction, Small Claims.*
www.courts.state.md.us/district/dcgarrett.html
Civil Records: Access: Mail, online, in person. Visitors must perform in person searches for themselves. No search fee. Required to search: name, years to search. Civil cases indexed by defendant. Civil records on computer from 1990, on index books from 1971. Online access is through JIS. See state introduction or visit www.courts.state.md.us.
Criminal Records: Access: Online, in person. Visitors must perform in person searches for themselves. No search fee. Required to search: name, years to search, DOB. Criminal records on computer from 1981. Online access through JIS. See state introduction or visit www.courts.state.md.us.

General Information: No adoptions, juvenile, sealed, expunged or mental records released. Copy fee: $.25 per page. Certification fee: $5.00 per page. Payee: District Court. Personal checks accepted. Prepayment required. Mail requests: SASE required. Mail turnaround time 1 week.

Register of Wills Courthouse, 313 E Alder St, Rm 103, Oakland, MD 21550; 301-334-1999, 888-334-2203 in MD; Fax: 301-334-1984. Hours: 8AM-4:30PM (EST). *Probate.*
www.registers.state.md.us/county/ga/html/garrett.html

Harford County

3rd Judicial Circuit 20 W Courtland St, Bel Air, MD 21014; Civil phone: 410-638-3430; Criminal phone: 410-638-3042; Probate phone: 410-638-3275. Hours: 8:30AM-4:30PM (EST). *Felony, Misdemeanor, Civil Actions Over $25,000.*
www.courts.state.md.us/harford.html
Civil Records: Access: Online, in person. Visitors must perform in person searches for themselves. No search fee. Required to search: name, years to search; also helpful: address. Civil cases indexed by defendant, plaintiff. Civil records on computer since 08/92 and on books prior. Online access is through JIS. See state introduction or visit www.courts.state.md.us.
Criminal Records: Access: In person only. Visitors must perform in person searches for themselves. No search fee. Required to search: name, years to search; also helpful: DOB. Criminal records on computer since 08/92 and on books prior.
General Information: Public Access terminal is available. No adoptions, presentence investigations, juvenile, sealed, expunged or mental records released. Copy fee: $.50 per page, $.25 if searcher does copy. Certification fee: $5.00. Payee: Clerk of the Circuit Court. Only cashiers checks and money orders accepted. Prepayment required.

District Court 2 S Bond St, Bel Air, MD 21014; 410-836-4545. Hours: 8:30AM-4:30PM (EST). *Misdemeanor, Civil Actions Under $25,000, Eviction, Small Claims.*
Civil Records: Access: Mail, online, in person. Visitors must perform in person searches for themselves. No search fee. Required to search: name, years to search. Civil cases indexed by defendant. Civil records on computer from 1989, on microfiche from 1972, archived from 1900. Online access is through JIS. See state introduction or visit www.courts.state.md.us.
Criminal Records: Access: Mail, online, in person. Visitors must perform in person searches for themselves. No search fee. Required to search: name, years to search; also helpful: address, DOB. Criminal records on computer from 1981, on microfiche from 1972, archived from 1900. Online access through JIS. See state introduction or visit www.courts.state.md.us.
General Information: Public Access terminal is available. No motor vehicle, sealed, expunged or mental records released. Copy fee: $.25 per page. Certification fee: $5.00. Payee: District Court of MD. Personal checks accepted. Visa, MC, AmEx accepted. Prepayment required. Mail requests: SASE required. Mail turnaround time 3-4 days.

Register of Wills 20 W Courtland St, Rm 304, Court House, Bel Air, MD 21014; 410-638-3275, 888-258-0525 in MD; Fax: 410-893-3177. Hours: 8:30AM-4:30PM (EST). *Probate.*
www.registers.state.md.us/county/ha/html/harford.html

Howard County

5th Judicial Circuit Court 8360 Court Ave, Ellicott City, MD 21043; 410-313-2111. Hours: 8:30AM-4:30PM (EST). *Felony, Misdemeanor, Civil Actions Over $25,000.*
Civil Records: Access: Online, in person. Visitors must perform in person searches for themselves. No search fee. Required to search: name, years to search; also helpful: address. Civil cases indexed by defendant, plaintiff. Civil records on computer from 1984, archived from 1900, on card index from 1900. Online access is through JIS. See state introduction or visit www.courts.state.md.us.
Criminal Records: Access: In person only. Visitors must perform in person searches for themselves. No search fee. Required to search: name, years to search; also helpful: address, DOB, SSN. Criminal records on card index to 1840, on computer since 1984.
General Information: Public Access terminal is available. No adoptions, juvenile, sealed, expunged or mental records released. Copy fee: $.50 per page. Certification fee: $5.00 per page. Payee: Office of Clerk. Personal checks accepted. Prepayment required.

District Court 3451 Courthouse Dr, Ellicott City, MD 21043; 410-480-7700. Hours: 8:30AM-4:30PM (EST). *Misdemeanor, Civil Actions Under $25,000, Eviction, Small Claims.*
Civil Records: Access: Mail, online, in person. Both court and visitors may perform in person searches. No search fee. Required to search: name, years to search. Civil cases indexed by defendant. Civil records on computer from 1992, on card index prior from 1971. Online access is through JIS. See state introduction or visit www.courts.state.md.us.
Criminal Records: Access: Mail, online, in person. Both court and visitors may perform in person searches. No search fee. Required to search: name, years to search. Criminal records on computer from 1989, on card index prior from 1971. Online access through JIS. See state introduction or visit www.courts.state.md.us.
General Information: Public Access terminal is available. No adoptions, juvenile, sealed, expunged or mental records released. Copy fee: $.25 per page. Certification fee: $5.00. Payee: District Court of MD. Personal checks accepted. Credit cards accepted: Visa. Prepayment required. Mail requests: SASE required if return receipt requested. Turnaround time before 1989 4-6 weeks, 1989-present 7 days.

Register of Wills 8360 Court Ave, Ellicott City, MD 21043; 410-313-2133, 888-848-0136 in MD; Fax: 410-313-3409. Hours: 8:30AM-4:30PM (EST). *Probate.*
www.registers.state.md.us/county/ho/html/howard.html

Kent County

2nd Judicial Circuit Court 103 N Cross St Courthouse, Chestertown, MD 21620; 410-778-7460; Fax: 410-778-7412. Hours: 8:30AM-4:30PM (EST). *Felony, Misdemeanor, Civil Actions Over $25,000.*
www.courts.state.md.us/clerks/kent/records.html
Civil Records: Access: Online, in person. Visitors must perform in person searches for themselves. No search fee. Required to search: name, years to search. Civil cases indexed by defendant, plaintiff. Civil records on computer from 1991, on card index from 1656. Online access is through JIS. See state introduction or visit www.courts.state.md.us.
Criminal Records: Access: In person only. Visitors must perform in person searches for themselves. No search fee. Required to search: name, years to search; also helpful: DOB, SSN. Criminal records on computer from 07/98, on card index from 1949, archived to 1656.

General Information: Public Access terminal is available. No adoptions, juvenile, sealed, expunged or mental records released. Copy fee: $.50 per page. Certification fee: $5.00. Payee: Mark L Mumford, Clerk. Personal checks accepted. Prepayment required.

District Court 103 N Cross St, Chestertown, MD 21620; 410-810-3362; Fax: 410-810-3361. Hours: 8:30AM-4:30PM (EST). *Misdemeanor, Civil Actions Under $25,000, Eviction, Small Claims.*
Civil Records: Access: Online, in person. Visitors must perform in person searches for themselves. No search fee. Required to search: name, years to search. Civil cases indexed by defendant. Civil records on computer from 1989; on card index from 1971. Online access is through JIS. See state introduction or visit www.courts.state.md.us.
Criminal Records: Access: Online, in person. Visitors must perform in person searches for themselves. No search fee. Required to search: name, years to search, DOB. Criminal records on computer from 1988, on card index from 1971. Online access through JIS. See state introduction or visit www.courts.state.md.us.
General Information: No sealed, expunged, mental records or judge's notes released. Copy fee: $.25 per page. Certification fee: $5.00 per page. Payee: District Court of MD. Personal checks accepted. Visa, Discover accepted. Prepayment required.

Register of Wills 103 N Cross St, Chestertown, MD 21620; 410-778-7466, 888-778-0179 in MD; Probate phone: 410-778-7465 & 410-778-7463; Fax: 410-778-2466. Hours: 8AM-4:30PM (EST). *Probate.*
www.registers.state.md.us/county/ke/html/kent.html

Montgomery County

6th Judicial Circuit Court 50 Maryland Ave, Rockville, MD 20850; 240-777-9466. Hours: 8:30AM-4:30PM (EST). *Felony, Misdemeanor, Civil Actions Over $25,000.*
www.montgomerycountymd.gov/mc/judicial
Civil Records: Access: Phone, mail, in person, online. Both court and visitors may perform in person searches. No search fee. Required to search: name, years to search; also helpful: case number. Civil cases indexed by defendant, plaintiff. Civil records on computer from 1977, archived from 1900, on card index from 1977. Online access is through JIS. See state introduction or visit www.courts.state.md.us. The daily calendar is free at www.montgomerycountymd.gov/mc/judicial/circuit/docket.html. This court will not provide name searches, only copies of specific documents.
Criminal Records: Access: Phone, mail, fax, in person. Both court and visitors may perform in person searches. No search fee. Required to search: name, years to search; also helpful: case number. Criminal records on computer from 1973, archived from 1900, on card index from 1977. Will not provide name searches, only copies of specific documents.
General Information: Public Access terminal is available. No adoptions, juvenile, sealed, expunged or mental records released. Copy fee: $.50. Certification fee: $5.00 plus $.50 per page. Payee: Clerk of Circuit Court. Personal checks accepted. Prepayment required. Mail requests: SASE requested. Turnaround time is 5-7 days.

District Court 8665 Georgia Ave, Silver Spring, MD 20910; 301-608-0660. Hours: 8:30AM-4:30PM (EST). *Misdemeanor, Civil Actions Under $25,000, Eviction, Small Claims.*
Note: Address to change in late 2004 to 8552 Second Ave.
Civil Records: Access: Mail, online, in person. Both court and visitors may perform in person searches. No

search fee. Required to search: name, years to search. Civil cases indexed by defendant, plaintiff. Civil records on computer from 1986, in book index and case folder. Online access is through JIS. See state introduction or visit www.courts.state.md.us.
Criminal Records: Access: Mail, online, in person. Both court and visitors may perform in person searches. No search fee. Required to search: name, years to search. Criminal records on computer, index book and case folder. Online access through JIS. See state introduction or visit www.courts.state.md.us.
General Information: Public Access terminal is available. No juvenile, sealed, expunged or mental records or judge's notes released. Copy fee: $.25 per page. Certification fee: $5.00. Payee: District Court. Personal checks accepted. Prepayment required. Mail requests: SASE required. Mail turnaround time 2-4 weeks.

Rockville District Court 27 Courthouse Square, Rockville, MD 20850; Civil phone: 301-279-1500; Criminal phone: 301-279-1565. Hours: 8:30AM-4:30PM (EST). *Misdemeanor, Civil Actions Under $25,000, Eviction, Small Claims.*
Civil Records: Access: Mail, online, in person. Both court and visitors may perform in person searches. No search fee. Required to search: name, years to search. Civil cases indexed by defendant. Civil records go back to 1971; on computer back to 1990, prior in case folder. Online access is through JIS. See state introduction or visit www.courts.state.md.us.
Criminal Records: Access: Mail, online, in person. Both court and visitors may perform in person searches. No search fee. Required to search: name, years to search; also helpful: DOB, SSN. Criminal records go back to 1971; on computer back to 1987. Online access to criminal records is the same as civil.
General Information: Public Access terminal is available. No juvenile, sealed, expunged, mental records or judge's notes released. Copy fee: $.25 per page. Certification fee: $5.00 per page. Payee: District Court. Personal checks accepted. Prepayment required. Mail requests: SASE required. Mail turnaround time 2-4 weeks.

Register of Wills Judicial Center, 50 Maryland Ave, #322, Rockville, MD 20850; 240-777-9600; Fax: 240-777-9602. Hours: 8:30AM-4:30PM (EST). *Probate.*
www.registers.state.md.us/county/mo/html/montgomery.html

Prince George's County

7th Judicial Circuit Court 14735 Main St, Upper Marlboro, MD 20772; Civil phone: 301-952-3240; Criminal phone: 301-952-3344. Hours: 8:30AM-4:30PM (EST). *Felony, Misdemeanor, Civil Actions Over $25,000.*
Civil Records: Access: In person, online. Visitors must perform in person searches for themselves. No search fee. Required to search: name, years to search. Civil cases indexed by defendant, plaintiff. Civil records on computer from 1981, on microfiche from 1979, on card index prior. Online access is through JIS. See state introduction or visit www.courts.state.md.us.
Criminal Records: Access: In person. Visitors must perform in person searches for themselves. No search fee. Required to search: name, years to search, DOB; also helpful: SSN. Criminal records on computer from 1981, on microfiche from 1979, on card index prior.
General Information: No adoptions, juvenile, sealed, expunged or mental records released. Copy fee: $.50 per page. Certification fee: $5.00 per page. Payee: Clerk of Circuit Court. Personal checks accepted. Prepayment required.

District Court 14735 Main St, Rm 173B, Upper Marlboro, MD 20772; 301-952-4080. Hours: 8:30AM-4:30PM (EST). *Misdemeanor, Civil Actions Under $25,000, Eviction, Small Claims.*
Civil Records: Access: Mail, online, in person. Both court and visitors may perform in person searches. No search fee. Required to search: name, years to search. Civil cases indexed by defendant. Civil records on computer from 1988, on card index from 1970. Online access is through JIS. See state introduction or visit www.courts.state.md.us.
Criminal Records: Access: Mail, online, in person. Visitors must perform in person searches for themselves. No search fee. Required to search: name, years to search. Criminal records on computer from 1984, on cards from 1970. Online access through JIS. See state introduction or visit www.courts.state.md.us.
General Information: Public Access terminal is available. No adoptions, juvenile, sealed, expunged or mental records released. Copy fee: $.25 per page. Certification fee: $5.00 per page. Payee: District Court of Maryland. Personal checks accepted. Prepayment required. Mail requests: SASE required. Mail turnaround time 1-2 weeks.

Register of Wills PO Box 1729, Upper Marlboro, MD 20773; 301-952-3250, 888-464-4219 in MD; Fax: 301-952-4489. Hours: 8:30AM-4:30PM (3:30 is paperwork cutoff time) (EST). *Probate.*
www.registers.state.md.us/county/pg/html/princegeorges.html

Queen Anne's County

2nd Judicial Circuit Court Courthouse, 100 Courthouse Sq, Centreville, MD 21617; 410-758-1773. Hours: 8:30AM-4:30PM (EST). *Felony, Misdemeanor, Civil Actions Over $25,000.*
Note: Misdemeanor case records held at District Court until appealed, then stored at Circuit Court.
Civil Records: Access: Online, in person. Visitors must perform in person searches for themselves. No search fee. Required to search: name, years to search. Civil cases indexed by defendant, plaintiff. Civil records on computer from 11/92; on index books from 1978. Online access is through JIS. See state introduction or visit www.courts.state.md.us.
Criminal Records: Access: In person only. Visitors must perform in person searches for themselves. No search fee. Required to search: name, years to search, SSN. Criminal records on computer from 11/92; on index books from 1978.
General Information: Public Access terminal is available. No adoptions, juvenile, sealed, expunged or mental records released. Certification fee: $5.00. Payee: Clerk of Circuit Court. Personal checks accepted. Prepayment required.

District Court 120 Broadway, Centreville, MD 21617; 410-819-4000. Hours: 8:30AM-4:30PM (EST). *Misdemeanor, Civil Actions Under $25,000, Eviction, Small Claims.*
Civil Records: Access: Online, in person. Visitors must perform in person searches for themselves. No search fee. Required to search: name, years to search; also helpful: address. Civil cases indexed by defendant. Civil records on computer from 1988, archived from 1974, prior on index books. Online access is through JIS. See state introduction or visit www.courts.state.md.us.
Criminal Records: Access: Online, in person. Visitors must perform in person searches for themselves. No search fee. Required to search: name, years to search; also helpful: address, DOB, SSN. Criminal records on computer from 1981, prior on index books. Online access through JIS. See state introduction or visit www.courts.state.md.us.

General Information: No adoptions, juvenile, sealed, expunged or mental records released. Copy fee: $.50. Certification fee: $5.00. Payee: District Court of Maryland. Personal checks accepted. Visa, Discover accepted. Prepayment required.

Register of Wills Liberty Bldg, 107 N Liberty St #220, PO Box 59, Centreville, MD 21617; 410-758-0585, 888-758-0010 in MD; Fax: 410-758-4408. Hours: 8AM-4:30PM (EST). *Probate.*
www.registers.state.md.us/county/qa/html/queenannes.html

Somerset County

1st Judicial Circuit Court PO Box 99, Princess Anne, MD 21853; 410-651-1555; Fax: 410-651-1048. Hours: 8:30AM-4:30PM (EST). *Felony, Misdemeanor, Civil Actions Over $25,000.*
Civil Records: Access: Online, in person. Visitors must perform in person searches for themselves. No search fee. Required to search: name, years to search; also helpful: address. Civil cases indexed by defendant, plaintiff. Civil records on computer from 9/93; prior archived and on index books. Online access is through JIS. See state introduction or visit www.courts.state.md.us.
Criminal Records: Access: In person only. Visitors must perform in person searches for themselves. No search fee. Required to search: name, years to search; also helpful: address, DOB, SSN. Criminal records on computer from 9/93; prior archived and on index books.
General Information: Public Access terminal is available. No adoptions, juvenile, sealed, expunged or mental records released. Will not fax results. Copy fee: $.50 per page. Certification fee: $5.00. Payee: Clerk of Circuit Court. Personal checks accepted. Prepayment required.

District Court 12155 Elm St #C, Princess Anne, MD 21853-1358; 410-845-4700. Hours: 8:30AM-4:30PM (EST). *Misdemeanor, Civil Actions Under $25,000, Eviction, Small Claims.*
Note: Misdemeanor cases go to Circuit Court if preliminary hearing waived. Records held at court where trial heard.
Civil Records: Access: Online, in person. Visitors must perform in person searches for themselves. No search fee. Required to search: name, years to search. Civil cases indexed by defendant, plaintiff. Civil records on computer from 1987, archived and on index books from 1971. Online access is through JIS. See state introduction or visit www.courts.state.md.us.
Criminal Records: Access: Online, in person. Visitors must perform in person searches for themselves. No search fee. Required to search: name, years to search; also helpful: SSN. Criminal records on computer from 1987, archived and on index books from 1971. Online access through JIS. See state introduction or visit www.courts.state.md.us.
General Information: No adoptions, juvenile, sealed, expunged or mental records released. Copy fee: $.25 per page. Certification fee: $5.00. Payee: District Court. Personal checks accepted. Prepayment required.

Register of Wills 30512 Prince William St, Princess Anne, MD 21853; 410-651-1696, 888-758-0039 in MD; Fax: 410-651-3873. Hours: 8:30AM-4:30PM (EST). *Probate.*
www.registers.state.md.us/county/so/html/somerset.html

St. Mary's County

7th Judicial Circuit Court PO Box 676, Leonardtown, MD 20650; 301-475-4567. Hours: 8:30AM-4:30PM (EST). *Felony, Misdemeanor, Civil Actions Over $25,000.*
Civil Records: Access: Online, in person. Visitors must perform in person searches for themselves. No

search fee. Required to search: name, years to search. Civil cases indexed by defendant, plaintiff. Civil records on computer from 1987, on card index from 1970. Online access is through JIS. See state introduction or visit www.courts.state.md.us.

Criminal Records: Access: In person only. Visitors must perform in person searches for themselves. No search fee. Required to search: name, years to search; also helpful: SSN. Criminal records on computer from 1987, on card index from 1970.

General Information: Public Access terminal is available. No adoptions, juvenile, sealed, expunged or mental records released. Copy fee: $.50 per page. Certification fee: $5.00. Payee: Clerk of the Circuit Court. Personal checks accepted. Prepayment required.

District Court Carter State Office Bldg, 23110 Leonard Hall Dr, PO Box 653, Leonardtown, MD 20650; 301-475-4530. Hours: 8:30AM-4:30PM (EST). *Misdemeanor, Civil Actions Under $25,000, Eviction, Small Claims.*

Civil Records: Access: Online, in person. Visitors must perform in person searches for themselves. No search fee. Required to search: name, years to search. Civil cases indexed by defendant. Civil records on computer from 1987, archived from 1971. Online access is through JIS. See state introduction or visit www.courts.state.md.us.

Criminal Records: Access: Online, in person. Visitors must perform in person searches for themselves. No search fee. Required to search: name, years to search; also helpful: DOB. Criminal records on computer from 1985, archived from 1971. Online access through JIS. See state introduction or visit www.courts.state.md.us.

General Information: Public Access terminal is available. No adoptions, juvenile, sealed, expunged or mental records released. Copy fee: $.50 per page. Certification fee: $5.00, or triple seal for $10.00. Payee: District Court of Maryland. Personal checks accepted. Prepayment required.

Register of Wills 41605 Court House Drive, Leonardtown, MD 20650; 301-475-5566, 888-475-4821 in MD; Fax: 301-475-4968. Hours: 8:30AM-4:30PM (EST). *Probate.*
www.registers.state.md.us/county/sm/html/stmarys.html

Talbot County

Circuit Court PO Box 723, Easton, MD 21601; 410-822-2611; Fax: 410-820-8168. Hours: 8:30AM-4:30PM (EST). *Felony, Misdemeanor, Civil Actions Over $25,000.*
www.courts.state.md.us/clerks/talbot/index.html

Civil Records: Access: Online, in person. Visitors must perform in person searches for themselves. No search fee. Required to search: name, years to search; also helpful: address. Civil cases indexed by defendant, plaintiff. Civil records on card index from 1993. Online access is through JIS. See state introduction or visit www.courts.state.md.us.

Criminal Records: Access: In person only. Visitors must perform in person searches for themselves. No search fee. Required to search: name, years to search; also helpful: address, DOB, SSN. Criminal records on card index from 1993.

General Information: Public Access terminal is available. No adoptions, juvenile, sealed, expunged or mental records released. Will not fax results. Copy fee: $.50 per page. Certification fee: $5.00. Payee: Mary Ann Shorall, Clerk of Court. Personal checks accepted. Prepayment required.

District Court 108 W Dover St, Easton, MD 21601; 410-819-5850. Hours: 8:30AM-4:30PM (EST). *Misdemeanor, Civil Actions Under $25,000, Eviction, Small Claims.*

Civil Records: Access: Online, in person. Visitors must perform in person searches for themselves. No search fee. Required to search: name, years to search. Civil cases indexed by defendant. Civil records go back to 1971; on computer back to 1988. Online access is through JIS. See state introduction or visit www.courts.state.md.us.

Criminal Records: Access: Online, in person. Visitors must perform in person searches for themselves. No search fee. Required to search: name, years to search. Criminal records go back to 1971; on computer back to 1984. Online access through JIS. See state introduction or visit www.courts.state.md.us.

General Information: Public Access terminal is available. No adoptions, juvenile, sealed, expunged or mental records released. Will not fax results. Copy fee: $.50 per page. Certification fee: $5.00. Payee: District Court of MD. Personal checks accepted. Prepayment required.

Register of Wills Courthouse, 11 N Washington St, Easton, MD 21601; 410-770-6700, 888-822-0039 in MD; Fax: 410-822-5452. Hours: 8AM-4:30PM (EST). *Probate.*
www.registers.state.md.us/county/ta/html/talbot.html

Washington County

Washington County Circuit Court Box 229, Hagerstown, MD 21741; 301-733-8660; Civil phone: 301-790-4972; Criminal phone: 301-790-7941; Fax: 301-791-1151. Hours: 8:30AM-4:30PM (EST). *Felony, Misdemeanor, Civil Actions Over $25,000.*

Civil Records: Access: Online, in person. Visitors must perform in person searches for themselves. Search fee: none. Required to search: name, years to search. Civil cases indexed by defendant. Civil records on case files, docket books to 1900; on computer back to 1985. Online access is through JIS. See state introduction or visit www.courts.state.md.us.

Criminal Records: Access: In person only. Visitors must perform in person searches for themselves. Search fee: none. Required to search: name, years to search; also helpful: DOB. Criminal records on case files, docket books to 1900; on computer back to 1985.

General Information: Public Access terminal is available. No adoptions, juvenile, sealed, expunged or mental records released. Copy fee: $.25 per page. Certification fee: $5.00. Payee: Clerk of Circuit Court. Personal checks accepted. Prepayment required.

District Court 36 W Antietam St, Hagerstown, MD 21740; 240-420-4600. Hours: 8:30AM-4:30PM (EST). *Misdemeanor, Civil Actions Under $25,000, Eviction, Small Claims.*

Civil Records: Access: Phone, mail, online, in person. Both court and visitors may perform in person searches. No search fee. Required to search: name, years to search; also helpful: address. Civil cases indexed by defendant. Civil records on computer from 1986, archived and on index books from 1971. Online access is through JIS. See state introduction or visit www.courts.state.md.us.

Criminal Records: Access: Online, in person. Visitors must perform in person searches for themselves. No search fee. Required to search: name, years to search; also helpful: address, DOB, SSN, case number. Criminal records on computer from 1982, on index books from 1971. Online access through JIS. See state introduction or visit www.courts.state.md.us.

General Information: Public Access terminal is available. No adoptions, juvenile, sealed, expunged or

mental records released. Copy fee: $.25 per page. Certification fee: $5.00. Payee: District Court. Personal checks accepted. Visa, Discover accepted. Prepayment required. Mail requests: SASE required. Mail turnaround time less than 30 days.

Register of Wills 95 W Washington, Hagerstown, MD 21740; 301-739-3612, 888-739-0013 in MD; Fax: 301-733-8636. Hours: 8:00AM-4:30PM (EST). *Probate.*
www.registers.state.md.us/county/wa/html/washington.html

Wicomico County

1st Judicial Circuit Court PO Box 198, Salisbury, MD 21803-0198; 410-543-6551; Fax: 410-546-8590. Hours: 8:30AM-4:30PM (EST). *Felony, Misdemeanor, Civil Actions Over $25,000.*

Civil Records: Access: Phone, mail, online, in person. Both court and visitors may perform in person searches. No search fee. Required to search: name, years to search. Civil cases indexed by defendant, plaintiff. Civil records on books since 1867, cases filed after 05/93 on computer. Online access is through JIS. See state introduction or visit www.courts.state.md.us. All phone requests must include case number.

Criminal Records: Access: Phone, mail, in person. Both court and visitors may perform in person searches. No search fee. Required to search: name, years to search; also helpful: DOB, SSN. Criminal records on books since 1867, cases filed after 05/93 on computer. Phone requests must include case number.

General Information: Public Access terminal is available. No adoptions, juvenile, sealed, expunged or mental records released. Copy fee: $.50 per page. Certification fee: $5.00. Payee: Clerk of Circuit Court. Personal checks accepted. Out of state checks not accepted. Prepayment required. Mail requests: SASE not required. Mail turnaround time 1-2 days.

District Court 201 Baptist St, Salisbury, MD 21801; 410-543-6600. Hours: 8:30AM-4:30PM (EST). *Misdemeanor, Civil Actions Under $25,000, Eviction, Small Claims.*

Civil Records: Access: Online, in person. Visitors must perform in person searches for themselves. No search fee. Required to search: name, years to search; also helpful: address. Civil cases indexed by defendant, plaintiff. Civil records on computer go back to 1985, archived from 1984, on card index from 1971. Online access is through JIS. See state introduction or visit www.courts.state.md.us.

Criminal Records: Access: Online, in person. Visitors must perform in person searches for themselves. No search fee. Required to search: name, years to search; also helpful: address, DOB. Criminal records go back to 1971; on computer back 1983. Online access through JIS. See state introduction or visit www.courts.state.md.us.

General Information: Public Access terminal is available. No adoptions, juvenile, sealed, expunged or mental records released. Copy fee: $.50. Certification fee: $5.00. Payee: District Court. Personal checks accepted. Prepayment required.

Register of Wills 101 N Division St, Rm 102, Salisbury, MD 21801; 410-543-6635, 888-786-0018 in MD; Fax: 410-334-3440. Hours: 8:30AM-4:30PM (EST). *Probate.*
www.registers.state.md.us/county/wi/html/wicomico.html

Worcester County

1st Judicial Circuit Court Box 40, Snow Hill, MD 21863; Civil phone: 410-632-5501; Criminal phone: 410-632-5502. Hours: 8:30AM-4:30PM (EST). *Felony, Misdemeanor, Civil Actions Over $25,000.*

Civil Records: Access: In person only. Visitors must perform in person searches for themselves. No search fee. Required to search: name, years to search. Civil cases indexed by defendant. Civil records on computer since 7/93, on docket books prior.

Criminal Records: Access: In person only. Visitors must perform in person searches for themselves. No search fee. Required to search: name, years to search. Criminal records on computer since 7/93, on docket books prior.

General Information: Public Access terminal is available. No adoptions, juvenile, sealed or expunged records released. Will not fax results. Copy fee: $.50 per page. Certification fee: $5.00. Payee: Clerk of Circuit Court. Personal checks accepted. Prepayment required.

District Court 301 Commerce St, Snow Hill, MD 21863-1007; 410-219-7830; Fax: 410-219-7840. Hours: 8:30AM-4:30PM (EST). *Misdemeanor, Civil Actions Under $25,000, Eviction, Small Claims.*

Civil Records: Access: Online, in person. Visitors must perform in person searches for themselves. No search fee. Required to search: name, years to search; also helpful: address. Civil cases indexed by defendant. Civil records on computer since 1988. Online access is through JIS. See state introduction or visit www.courts.state.md.us. Records can be researched via books in the lobby.

Criminal Records: Access: Online, in person. Visitors must perform in person searches for themselves. No search fee. Required to search: name, years to search; also helpful: address, DOB, SSN. Criminal records on computer since 1982. Online access through JIS. See state introduction or visit www.courts.state.md.us. Records can be researched via books in the lobby.

General Information: No sealed or juvenile records released. Copy fee: $1.00 per page. Certification fee: $5.00 per page. Payee: District Court. Personal checks accepted. Prepayment required.

Register of Wills Courthouse, 1 W Market St, Rm 102, Snow Hill, MD 21863-1074; 410-632-1529, 888-256-0047 in MD; Fax: 410-632-5600. Hours: 8AM-4:30PM (EST). *Probate.*
www.registers.state.md.us/county/wo/html/worcester.html

Maryland Recording Offices

ORGANIZATION: 23 counties and one independent city, 24 recording offices. The recording officer is Clerk of the Circuit Court. Baltimore City has a recording office separate from the county of Baltimore. See the City/County Locator section at the end of this chapter for ZIP Codes that include both the city and the county. The entire state is in the Eastern Time Zone (EST).

REAL ESTATE RECORDS: Counties will not perform real estate searches. Copies usually cost $.50 per page, and certification fees $5.00 per document.

UCC RECORDS: This was a dual filing state until July 1995. As of July 1995, all new UCC filings except for consumer goods, farm related and real estate related filings were submitted only to the central filing office. Starting July 2001, only real estate related filing are submitted to the Clerk of Circuit Court.

TAX LIEN RECORDS: All tax liens are filed with the county Clerk of Circuit Court. Counties will not perform name searches.

OTHER LIENS: Judgment, mechanics, county, hospital, condominium.

ONLINE ACCESS: Search statewide property records data free at http://sdatcert3.resiusa.org/rp_rewrite/. There is no name searching. Also, the Maryland State Dept. of Planning offers MDPropertyview with property maps/parcels and assessments on the web or CD-Rom. Registration required; visit www.mdp.state.md.us or call 410-767-4614 or 410-767-4474. There is no name searching. Also, vendors provide online access in several places. County tax records are at www.taxrecords.com. Land survey, condominium and survey plats is available free by county at www.plats.net. Use username "Plato" and password "plato#". No name searching.

Allegany County

County Clerk of the Circuit Court, 30 Washington St, Cumberland, MD 21502-2948. **Phone**-301-777-5922; fax-301-777-2100; hours 8AM-4:30PM

Will not search records. UCC copy- $1.00 per page. RE record copy- $.50 per page. Cert fee: $5.00 per doc. Payee: Allegany County Clerk of the Circuit Court. **Online Access to Real Property, Land Survey/Plat records:** Search real property data free at http://sdatcert3.resiusa.org/rp_rewrite/. No name searching. Also, see state introduction for add'l land records online. **Other phones:** Assessor-301-777-2108; Treasurer-301-777-5965.

Anne Arundel County

County Clerk of the Circuit Court, PO Box 71, Annapolis, MD 21404. **Phone**-410-222-1425; fax-410-222-1087; hours 8:30AM-4:30PM

Will search UCC records. UCC copy- $1.00 per page. Will not search real estate or tax lien records. Cert fee: $5.00 per cert. Payee: Clerk of the Circuit Court. **Online Access to Real Property, Land Survey/Plat records:** Search real property data free at http://sdatcert3.resiusa.org/rp_rewrite/. No name searching. Also, see state introduction for add'l land records online. **Other phones:** Assessor-410-974-5727.

Baltimore City

City Clerk, 100 N. Calvert St, Rm 610, Baltimore, MD 21202. **Phone**-410-333-3760; hours 8AM-4:30PM

Will not search records. UCC copy- $1.00 per page. Cert fee: $5.00 per cert. Payee: Circuit Court for Baltimore City. **Online Access to Real Property, Land Survey/Plat, Property Tax records:** Search real property data free at http://sdatcert3.resiusa.org/rp_rewrite/. No name searching. Also, search real property tax account information at http://cityservices.baltimorecity.gov/realproperty/default.aspx. Also, see state introduction for add'l land records online. **Other phones:** Assessor-401-512-4900.

Baltimore County

County Clerk of the Circuit Court, PO Box 6754, Baltimore, MD 21285. **Phone**-410-887-2652; fax-410-887-3062; hours 8:30AM-4:30PM. Will not search records. Record copy- $.50 per page. Cert fee: $5.00 per cert + $.50 per page. Payee: Baltimore County Clerk of the Circuit Court. **Online Access to Real Property, Land Survey/Plat records:** Search real property data for free at http://sdatcert3.resiusa.org/rp_rewrite/. No name searching. Also, see state introduction for add'l land records online. **Other phones:** Assessor-410-512-4906; Treasurer-410-887-2416; Elections-410-887-5700; Vital Records-410-764-3038.

Calvert County

County Clerk of the Circuit Court, 175 Main St, Courthouse, Prince Frederick, MD 20678. **Phone**-410-535-1660, R/E Recording- 410-535-1600 x269, UCC Recording- 410-535-1600 x269; hours 8:30AM-4:30PM. Will search UCC records. UCC copy- $1.00 per page. Will not search real estate or tax lien records. RE record copy- $.50 per page. Cert fee: $5.00 per instrument. Payee: Calvert County Clerk of the Circuit Court. **Online Access to Real Property, Land Survey/Plat records:** Search real property data free at http://sdatcert3.resiusa.org/rp_rewrite/. No name searching. Also, see state intro for add'l land records online. **Other phones:** Assessor-410-535-8850; Treasurer-410-535-1600 x272.

Caroline County

County Clerk of the Circuit Court, PO Box 458, Denton, MD 21629. **Phone**-County Clerk of the Circuit Court, R/E & UCC Recording- 410-479-1811; fax-410-479-1142; hours 8:30AM-4:30PM

Will not search records. UCC copy- $1.00 per page. Cert fee: $5.00 per cert. Payee: Caroline County Clerk of the Circuit Court. **Online Access to Real Property, Land Survey/Plat records:** Search real property data free at http://sdatcert3.resiusa.org/rp_rewrite/ no name searching. See state introduction for add'l land records online. **Other phones:** Assessor-410-479-5950; Treasurer-410-479-0410.

Carroll County

County Clerk of the Circuit Court, 55 N. Court St, Rm G8, Westminster, MD 21157. **Phone**-410-386-2022; fax-410-876-0822; hours 8:30AM-4:30PM

Will not search records. Record copy- $.50 per page. Cert fee: $5.00 per cert + $.50 per page. Payee: Carroll County Clerk of the Circuit Court. **Online Access to Real Property, Land Survey/Plat records:** Search real property data free at http://sdatcert3.resiusa.org/rp_rewrite/. No name searching. Also,

see state introduction for add'l land records online. **Other phones:** Assessor-410-857-0600; Treasurer-410-386-2971; Appraiser/ Auditor-410-857-0600.

Cecil County

County Clerk of the Circuit Court, 129 E. Main St., Rm 108, Elkton, MD 21921-5971. **Phone**-410-996-5375; hours 8:30AM-4:30PM

Will not search records. UCC copy- $.50 per page. Cert fee: $5.00. Payee: Cecil County Clerk of the Circuit Court. **Online Access to Real Property, Land Survey/Plat records:** Search real property data free at http://sdatcert3.resiusa.org/rp_rewrite/. No name searching. Also, see state introduction for add'l land records online. **Other phones:** Assessor-410-996-0525; Treasurer-410-996-5394.

Charles County

Clerk of the Circuit Court, PO Box 970, La Plata, MD 20646. **Phone**-301-932-3201; hours 8:30AM-4:30PM www.courts.state.md.us/clerks/charles

Will not search records. Cert fee: $5.00 per cert. Payee: Charles County Clerk of the Circuit Court. **Online Access to Real Property, Land Survey/Plat, Treasurer, Property Tax records:** Search real property data free at http://sdatcert3.resiusa.org/rp_rewrite/. No name searching. Also, see state introduction for add'l land records online. Also, access to property tax data is free at www.charlescounty.org/treas/taxes/acctinquiry/sel ction.jsp. **Other phones:** Assessor-301-932-2440; Treasurer-301-645-0685; Elections-301-934-8962.

Dorchester County

County Clerk of the Circuit Court, PO Box 150, Cambridge, MD 21613. **Phone**-410-228-0481, R/E Recording- 410-228-0480, UCC Recording- 410-228-0480; fax-410-228-1860; hours 8:30AM-4:30PM

Will not search records. Record copy- $.25 per page. Cert fee: $5.00 per cert. Payee: Dorchester County Clerk of the Circuit Court. **Online Access to Real Property, Land Survey/Plat records:** Search real property data free at http://sdatcert3.resiusa.org/rp_rewrite/. No name searching. Also, see state introduction for add'l land records online. **Other phones:** Assessor-410-228-3380; Treasurer-410-228-4343 (County).

Frederick County

County Clerk of the Circuit Court, 100 W. Patrick St, Frederick, MD 21701. **Phone**-301-694-1964; fax-301-846-2245; hours 8:30AM-4:30PM

Will search UCC records. UCC copy- $.50 per page. Will not search real estate or tax lien records. Cert fee: $5.00 per cert. Payee: Frederick County Clerk of the Circuit Court. **Online Access to Real Property, Land Survey/Plat records:** Search real property data free at http://sdatcert3.resiusa.org/rp_rewrite/. No name searching. Also, see state introduction for add'l land records online. **Other phones:** Assessor-301-694-2040; Treasurer-301-694-1111.

Garrett County

County Clerk of the Circuit Court, PO Box 447, Oakland, MD 21550-0447. **Phone**-301-334-1937, R/E Recording- 301-334-1938, UCC Recording- 301-334-5016; fax-301-334-5017; hours 8:30AM-4:30PM

Will not search records. UCC copy- $1.00 per page. RE record copy- $.50 per page. Cert fee: $5.00 per cert. Payee: Garrett County Clerk of the Circuit Court. **Online Access to Real Property, Land Survey/Plat records:** Search real property data free at http://sdatcert3.resiusa.org/rp_rewrite/. No name searching. Also, see state introduction for add'l land records online. **Other phones:** Assessor-301-334-1950; Treasurer-301-334-1965; Elections-301-334-1962.

Harford County

County Clerk of the Circuit Court, 20 W. Courtland St, Bel Air, MD 21014. **Phone**-410-638-3244; hours 8:30AM-4PM

Will not search records. UCC copy- $.50 per page. RE record copy- $.25 per page. Cert fee: $5.00 per cert. Payee: Harford County Clerk of the Circuit Court. **Online Access to Real Property, Land Survey/Plat records:** Search real property data free at http://sdatcert3.resiusa.org/rp_rewrite/. No name searching. Also, see state introduction for add'l land records online. **Other phones:** Assessor-410-838-4800; Treasurer-410-638-3269.

Howard County

County Clerk of the Circuit Court, 9250 Bendix Rd, Columbia, MD 21045. **Phone**-410-313-6117; hours 8:30AM-4:30PM

Will search UCC records. UCC copy- $1.00 per page. Will not search real estate or tax lien records. Cert fee: $5.00 per cert. Payee: Howard County Clerk of the Circuit Court. **Online Access to Real Property, Land Survey/Plat records:** Search real property data free at http://sdatcert3.resiusa.org/rp_rewrite/. No name searching. Also, see state introduction for add'l land records online. **Other phones:** Assessor-410-480-7940.

Kent County

Clerk of the Circuit Court, 103 N. Cross St., Chestertown, MD 21620. **Phone**-410-778-7431, R/E Recording- 410-778-7460; hours 8:30AM-4:30PM

Will not search records. UCC copy- $1.00 per page. Cert fee: $5.00 per cert. Payee: Kent County Clerk of the Circuit Court. **Online Access to Real Property, Land Survey/Plat records:** Search real property data free at http://sdatcert3.resiusa.org/rp_rewrite/. No name searching. Also, see state introduction for add'l land records online. **Other phones:** Assessor-410-778-7447; Treasurer-410-778-7443; Elections-410-778-0038.

Montgomery County

County Clerk of the Circuit Court, 50 Maryland Ave, Rm 122A, County Courthouse, Rockville, MD 20850. **Phone**-240-777-9466, R/E Recording- 240-777-9470; fax-240-777-9486; hours-8:30AM-4:30PM www.montgomerycountymd.gov/mc/judicial/

Will not search records. Record copy- $.50 per page. Cert fee: $5.00 per cert. Payee: Montgomery County Clerk of the Circuit Court. **Online Access to Real Property, Land Survey/Plat, Property Tax, Assessor records:** Access to clerk records is via JIS Dialup Access; contact Mary Hutchins 410-260-1031. Also, search real property data for free at http://sdatcert3.resiusa.org/rp_rewrite. No name searching. Also, see state introduction for add'l land records online. Also, access to the assessor's property tax account database is available free at www.montgomerycountymd.gov/apps/tax/index.asp.

Other phones: Assessor-301-279-1701; Treasurer-240-777-8995; Elections-240-777-8500; Vital Records-240-777-1755.

Prince George's County

County Clerk of the Circuit Court, 14735 Main St, Upper Marlboro, MD 20772. **Phone**-301-952-3352; hours 8:30AM-3PM www.co.pg.md.us

Will search UCC records. UCC copy- $1.00 per page. Will not search real estate or tax lien records. Cert fee: $5.00 per cert. Payee: Prince George's County Clerk of the Circuit Court. **Online Access to Real Property, Land Survey/Plat, Property Tax records:** Search real property data free at http://sdatcert3.resiusa.org/rp_rewrite. No name searching. Also, see state introduction for add'l land records online. Also, search the Treasurer's property tax inquiry system at http://tax-acct-info.co.pg.md.us/index1.html. No name searching. **Other phones:** Assessor-301-952-2500; Treasurer-301-952-3946.

Queen Anne's County

County Clerk of the Circuit Court, 100 Court House Sq, Centreville, MD 21617. **Phone**-410-758-1773; hours 8:30AM-4:30PM

Will not search records. UCC copy- $.50 per page. Cert fee: $5.00 per cert. Payee: Queen Anne's County Clerk of the Circuit Court. **Online Access to Real Property, Land Survey/Plat records:** Search real property data free at http://sdatcert3.resiusa.org/rp_rewrite. No name searching. Also, see state introduction for add'l land records online. **Other phones:** Assessor-410-758-5030; Treasurer-410-758-0414.

Somerset County

County Clerk of the Circuit Court, PO Box 99, Princess Anne, MD 21853. **Phone**-410-651-1555; fax-410-651-1048; hours 8:30AM-4:30PM

Will not search records. UCC copy- $1.00 per page. Cert fee: $5.00. Payee: Somerset County Clerk of the Circuit Court. **Online Access to Real Property, Land Survey/Plat records:** Search real property data free at http://sdatcert3.resiusa.org/rp_rewrite. No name searching. Also, see state introduction for add'l land records online. **Other phones:** Assessor-410-651-0868; Treasurer-410-651-0440; Vital Records-410-651-1555.

St. Mary's County

County Clerk of the Circuit Court, PO Box 676, Leonardtown, MD 20650. **Phone**-301-475-4567, R/E Recording- 301-475-4554; hours 8:30AM-4:30PM

Will search UCC records. Will not search real estate or tax lien records. Record copy- $.50 per page. Cert fee: $5.00 per cert. Payee: St. Mary's County Clerk of the Circuit Court. **Online Access to Real Property, Land Survey/Plat records:** Search real property data free at http://sdatcert3.resiusa.org/rp_rewrite. No name searching. See state introduction for add'l land records online. **Other phones:** Assessor-301-475-4610; Treasurer-301-475-4473.

Talbot County

County Clerk of the Circuit Court, PO Box 723, Easton, MD 21601. **Phone**-410-822-2611; fax-410-820-8168; hours 8:30AM-4:30PM www.courts.state.md.us

Will not search records. Record copy- $.50 per page. Cert fee: $5.00 per cert. Payee: Talbot County Clerk of the Circuit Court. **Online Access to Real Property, Land Survey/Plat records:** Search real property data free at http://sdatcert3.resiusa.org/rp_rewrite. No name searching. Also, see state introduction for add'l land records online. **Other phones:** Assessor-410-819-5920; Treasurer-410-770-8020; Elections-410-770-8099; Vital Records-410-764-3038.

Washington County

Clerk of the Circuit Court, PO Box 229, Hagerstown, MD 21741-0229. **Phone**-Clerk of the Circuit Court, R/E & UCC Recording- 301-733-8660; fax-301-791-1151; hours-8:30AM-4:30PM www.courts.state.md.us/washington.html

Will not search records. Copy fee-$.50 per page. Cert fee: $5.00 per doc. Payee: Washington County Clerk of the Circuit Court. **Online Access to Real Property, Land Survey/Plat records:** Search real property data free at http://sdatcert3.resiusa.org/rp_rewrite. No name searching. Also, see state introduction for add'l land records online. **Other phones:** Assessor-301-791-3050; Treasurer-240-313-2110; Elections-240-313-2050; Vital Records-301-733-8660.

Wicomico County

County Clerk of the Circuit Court, PO Box 198, Salisbury, MD 21803-0198. **Phone**-410-543-6551; hours 8:30AM-4:30PM

Will search UCC records. Copy fee- $.50 per page. Will not search real estate or tax lien records. Cert fee: $5.00 per cert. Payee: Wicomico County Clerk of the Circuit Court. **Online Access to Real Property, Land Survey/Plat records:** Search real property data free at http://sdatcert3.resiusa.org/rp_rewrite. No name searching. Also, see state introduction for add'l land records online. **Other phones:** Assessor-410-543-6623.

Worcester County

County Clerk of the Circuit Court, PO Box 40, Snow Hill, MD 21863-0040. **Phone**-410-632-5500, UCC Recording- 410-632-1196; hours 8:30AM-4:30PM

Will search UCC records. UCC copy- $.50 per page, $5.00 min. Will not search real estate or tax lien records. RE record copy- $.50 per page. Cert fee: $5.00 per cert + $.50 per page. Payee: Worcester County Clerk of the Circuit Court. **Online Access to Real Property, Land Survey/Plat records:** Search real property data free at http://sdatcert3.resiusa.org/rp_rewrite. No name searching. Also, see state introduction for add'l land records online. **Other phones:** Assessor-410-632-1194; Elections-410-632-1320.

Maryland County Locator

You will usually be able to find the city name in the City/County Cross Reference below. In that case, it is a simple matter to determine the county from the cross reference. However, only the official US Postal Service city names are included in this index. There are an additional 40,000 place names that people use in their addresses. Therefore, we have also included a ZIP/City Cross Reference immediately following the City/County Cross Reference.

If you know the ZIP Code but the city name does not appear in the City/County Cross Reference index, look up the ZIP Code in the ZIP/City Cross Reference, find the city name, then look up the city name in the City/County Cross. Reference. For example, you want to know the county for an address of Menands, NY 12204. There is no "Menands" in the City/County Cross Reference. The ZIP/City Cross Reference shows that ZIP Codes 12201-12288 are for the city of Albany. Looking back in the City/County Cross Reference, Albany is in Albany County.

Maryland City/County Cross Reference

ABELL St. Mary's
ABERDEEN Harford
ABERDEEN PROVING GROUND Harford
ABINGDON Harford
ACCIDENT Garrett
ACCOKEEK Prince George's
ADAMSTOWN Frederick
ALESIA (21107) Carroll(59), Baltimore(40)
ALLEN Wicomico
ANDREWS AIR FORCE BASE Prince George's
ANNAPOLIS Anne Arundel
ANNAPOLIS JUNCTION (20701) Howard(77), Anne Arundel(22)
AQUASCO Prince George's
ARNOLD Anne Arundel
ASHTON Montgomery
AVENUE St. Mary's
BALDWIN (21013) Baltimore(70), Harford(29)
BALTIMORE (21209) Baltimore(52), Baltimore City(47)
BALTIMORE (21239) Baltimore City(80), Baltimore(19)
BALTIMORE Anne Arundel
BALTIMORE Baltimore
BALTIMORE Baltimore City
BARCLAY Queen Anne's
BARNESVILLE Montgomery
BARSTOW Calvert
BARTON (21521) Allegany(72), Garrett(27)
BEALLSVILLE Montgomery
BEL AIR Harford
BEL ALTON Charles
BELCAMP Harford
BELTSVILLE Prince George's
BENEDICT Charles
BENSON Harford
BETHESDA Montgomery
BETHLEHEM Caroline
BETTERTON Kent
BIG POOL Washington
BISHOPVILLE Worcester
BITTINGER Garrett
BIVALVE Wicomico
BLADENSBURG Prince George's
BLOOMINGTON Garrett
BOONSBORO Washington
BORING Baltimore
BOWIE Prince George's
BOYDS Montgomery
BOZMAN Talbot
BRADDOCK HEIGHTS Frederick
BRADSHAW Baltimore
BRANDYWINE (20613) Prince George's(88), Charles(11)
BRENTWOOD Prince George's
BRINKLOW Montgomery
BROOKEVILLE (20833) Montgomery(96), Howard(3)
BROOKLANDVILLE Baltimore
BROOKLYN (21225) Baltimore City(54), Anne Arundel(45)
BROOMES ISLAND Calvert

BROWNSVILLE Washington
BRUNSWICK Frederick
BRYANS ROAD Charles
BRYANTOWN Charles
BUCKEYSTOWN Frederick
BURKITTSVILLE Frederick
BURTONSVILLE Montgomery
BUSHWOOD St. Mary's
BUTLER Baltimore
CABIN JOHN Montgomery
CALIFORNIA St. Mary's
CALLAWAY St. Mary's
CAMBRIDGE Dorchester
CAPITOL HEIGHTS Prince George's
CARDIFF Harford
CASCADE (21719) Washington(98), Frederick(1)
CATONSVILLE Baltimore
CAVETOWN Washington
CECILTON Cecil
CENTREVILLE Queen Anne's
CHANCE Somerset
CHAPTICO St. Mary's
CHARLESTOWN Cecil
CHARLOTTE HALL (20622) Charles(64), St. Mary's(35)
CHASE Baltimore
CHELTENHAM Prince George's
CHESAPEAKE BEACH Calvert
CHESAPEAKE CITY Cecil
CHESTER Queen Anne's
CHESTERTOWN (21620) Kent(95), Queen Anne's(4)
CHESTERTOWN Queen Anne's
CHEVY CHASE Montgomery
CHEWSVILLE Washington
CHILDS Cecil
CHURCH CREEK Dorchester
CHURCH HILL Queen Anne's
CHURCHTON Anne Arundel
CHURCHVILLE Harford
CLAIBORNE Talbot
CLARKSBURG (20871) Montgomery(89), Frederick(10)
CLARKSVILLE Howard
CLEAR SPRING Washington
CLEMENTS St. Mary's
CLINTON Prince George's
COBB ISLAND Charles
COCKEYSVILLE Baltimore
COLLEGE PARK Prince George's
COLORA Cecil
COLTONS POINT St. Mary's
COLUMBIA Howard
COMPTON St. Mary's
CONOWINGO Cecil
COOKSVILLE (21723) Howard(85), Carroll(14)
CORDOVA Talbot
CORRIGANVILLE Allegany
CRAPO Dorchester
CRISFIELD Somerset
CROCHERON Dorchester
CROFTON Anne Arundel

CROWNSVILLE Anne Arundel
CRUMPTON Queen Anne's
CUMBERLAND Allegany
CURTIS BAY (21226) Baltimore City(56), Anne Arundel(43)
DAMASCUS Montgomery
DAMERON St. Mary's
DAMES QUARTER Somerset
DARLINGTON Harford
DAVIDSONVILLE Anne Arundel
DAYTON Howard
DEAL ISLAND Somerset
DEALE Anne Arundel
DELMAR Wicomico
DENTON Caroline
DERWOOD Montgomery
DETOUR Carroll
DICKERSON (20842) Montgomery(79), Frederick(20)
DISTRICT HEIGHTS Prince George's
DOWELL Calvert
DRAYDEN St. Mary's
DUNDALK (21222) Baltimore(97), Baltimore City(2)
DUNKIRK (20754) Calvert(90), Anne Arundel(10)
EARLEVILLE Cecil
EAST NEW MARKET Dorchester
EASTON Talbot
ECKHART MINES Allegany
EDEN (21822) Worcester(89), Somerset(10)
EDGEWATER Anne Arundel
EDGEWOOD Harford
ELK MILLS Cecil
ELKRIDGE Howard
ELKTON Cecil
ELLERSLIE Allegany
ELLICOTT CITY (21043) Howard(97), Baltimore(2)
ELLICOTT CITY Howard
EMMITSBURG Frederick
ESSEX Baltimore
EWELL Somerset
FAIRPLAY Washington
FALLSTON Harford
FAULKNER Charles
FEDERALSBURG Caroline
FINKSBURG Carroll
FISHING CREEK Dorchester
FLINTSTONE Allegany
FOREST HILL Harford
FORK Baltimore
FORT GEORGE G MEADE Anne Arundel
FORT HOWARD Baltimore
FORT WASHINGTON Prince George's
FREDERICK Frederick
FREELAND (21107) Carroll(59), Baltimore(40)
FREELAND Baltimore
FRIENDSHIP Anne Arundel
FRIENDSVILLE Garrett
FROSTBURG (21532) Allegany(84), Garrett(15)

FRUITLAND Wicomico
FULTON Howard
FUNKSTOWN Washington
GAITHER Carroll
GAITHERSBURG Montgomery
GALENA Kent
GALESVILLE Anne Arundel
GAMBRILLS Anne Arundel
GAPLAND Washington
GARRETT PARK Montgomery
GARRISON Baltimore
GEORGETOWN Cecil
GERMANTOWN Montgomery
GIBSON ISLAND Anne Arundel
GIRDLETREE Worcester
GLEN ARM Baltimore
GLEN BURNIE Anne Arundel
GLEN ECHO Montgomery
GLENELG Howard
GLENN DALE Prince George's
GLENWOOD Howard
GLYNDON Baltimore
GOLDSBORO Caroline
GRANTSVILLE Garrett
GRASONVILLE Queen Anne's
GREAT MILLS St. Mary's
GREENBELT Prince George's
GREENSBORO Caroline
GUNPOWDER Harford
GWYNN OAK (21207) Baltimore(67), Baltimore City(32)
GWYNN OAK Baltimore
HAGERSTOWN Washington
HALETHORPE (21227) Baltimore(98), Baltimore City(1)
HAMPSTEAD (21074) Carroll(88), Baltimore(11)
HANCOCK Washington
HANOVER (21076) Anne Arundel(91), Howard(8)
HANOVER Anne Arundel
HARMANS Anne Arundel
HARWOOD Anne Arundel
HAVRE DE GRACE Harford
HEBRON Wicomico
HELEN St. Mary's
HENDERSON Caroline
HENRYTON Carroll
HIGHLAND (20777) Howard(95), Montgomery(4)
HILLSBORO Caroline
HOLLYWOOD St. Mary's
HUGHESVILLE Charles
HUNT VALLEY Baltimore
HUNTINGTOWN Calvert
HURLOCK Dorchester
HYATTSVILLE Prince George's
HYDES (21082) Baltimore(96), Harford(3)
IJAMSVILLE Frederick
INDIAN HEAD Charles
INGLESIDE Queen Anne's
IRONSIDES Charles
ISSUE Charles
JARRETTSVILLE Harford

JEFFERSON Frederick
JESSUP (20794) Howard(80), Anne Arundel(19)
JOPPA Harford
KEEDYSVILLE Washington
KENNEDYVILLE Kent
KENSINGTON Montgomery
KEYMAR (21757) Frederick(50), Carroll(49)
KINGSVILLE (21087) Baltimore(79), Harford(20)
KITZMILLER Garrett
KNOXVILLE (21758) Frederick(50), Washington(49)
LA PLATA Charles
LADIESBURG Frederick
LANHAM Prince George's
LAUREL Anne Arundel
LAUREL Howard
LAUREL Prince George's
LEONARDTOWN St. Mary's
LEXINGTON PARK St. Mary's
LIBERTYTOWN Frederick
LINEBORO Carroll
LINEBORO CPO Carroll
LINKWOOD Dorchester
LINTHICUM HEIGHTS Anne Arundel
LINWOOD Carroll
LISBON Howard
LITTLE ORLEANS Allegany
LONACONING (21539) Allegany(67), Garrett(32)
LONG GREEN Baltimore
LOTHIAN Anne Arundel
LOVEVILLE St. Mary's
LUKE Allegany
LUSBY Calvert
LUTHERVILLE TIMONIUM Baltimore
LYNCH Kent
MADISON Dorchester
MAGNOLIA Harford
MANCHESTER (21102) Carroll(98), Baltimore(1)
MANOKIN Somerset
MARBURY Charles
MARDELA SPRINGS Wicomico
MARION STATION Somerset
MARRIOTTSVILLE (21104) Carroll(53), Howard(38), Baltimore(8)
MARYDEL Caroline
MARYLAND LINE Baltimore
MASSEY Kent
MAUGANSVILLE Washington
MAYO Anne Arundel
MC HENRY Garrett
MCDANIEL Talbot
MECHANICSVILLE (20659) St. Mary's(97), Charles(2)
MIDDLE RIVER Baltimore
MIDDLEBURG Carroll
MIDDLETOWN Frederick
MIDLAND Allegany
MIDLOTHIAN Allegany
MILLERS (21107) Carroll(59), Baltimore(40)
MILLERSVILLE Anne Arundel

MILLINGTON (21651) Queen Anne's(59), Kent(40)
MONKTON (21111) Baltimore(87), Harford(12)
MONROVIA Frederick
MONTGOMERY VILLAGE Montgomery
MORGANZA St. Mary's
MOUNT AIRY (21771) Frederick(47), Carroll(39), Howard(11), Montgomery(1)
MOUNT RAINIER Prince George's
MOUNT SAVAGE Allegany
MOUNT VICTORIA Charles
MYERSVILLE Frederick
NANJEMOY Charles
NANTICOKE Wicomico
NEAVITT Talbot
NEW MARKET Frederick
NEW MIDWAY Frederick
NEW WINDSOR (21776) Carroll(82), Frederick(17)
NEWARK Worcester
NEWBURG Charles
NEWCOMB Talbot
NIKEP Allegany
NORTH BEACH (20714) Calvert(87), Anne Arundel(12)
NORTH EAST Cecil
NOTTINGHAM Baltimore
OAKLAND Garrett
OCEAN CITY Worcester
ODENTON Anne Arundel
OLDTOWN Allegany
OLNEY Montgomery
OWINGS Calvert
OWINGS MILLS Baltimore
OXFORD Talbot
OXON HILL Prince George's
PARK HALL St. Mary's
PARKTON Baltimore
PARKVILLE (21234) Baltimore(89), Baltimore City(10)
PARSONSBURG Wicomico
PASADENA Anne Arundel
PATUXENT RIVER St. Mary's
PERRY HALL Baltimore
PERRY POINT Cecil
PERRYMAN Harford
PERRYVILLE Cecil
PHOENIX Baltimore
PIKESVILLE (21208) Baltimore(93), Baltimore City(6)
PINEY POINT St. Mary's
PINTO Allegany
PITTSVILLE Wicomico
POCOMOKE CITY (21851) Worcester(86), Somerset(13)
POINT OF ROCKS Frederick
POMFRET Charles
POOLESVILLE Montgomery
PORT DEPOSIT Cecil
PORT REPUBLIC Calvert
PORT TOBACCO Charles
POTOMAC Montgomery
POWELLVILLE Wicomico
PRESTON Caroline
PRINCE FREDERICK Calvert
PRINCESS ANNE Somerset

PYLESVILLE Harford
QUANTICO Wicomico
QUEEN ANNE Queen Anne's
QUEENSTOWN Queen Anne's
RANDALLSTOWN Baltimore
RAWLINGS Allegany
REHOBETH Somerset
REISTERSTOWN (21136) Baltimore(97), Carroll(2)
RHODES POINT Somerset
RHODESDALE Dorchester
RIDERWOOD Baltimore
RIDGE St. Mary's
RIDGELY Caroline
RISING SUN Cecil
RIVA Anne Arundel
RIVERDALE Prince George's
ROCK HALL Kent
ROCK POINT Charles
ROCKVILLE Montgomery
ROCKY RIDGE Frederick
ROHRERSVILLE Washington
ROSEDALE (21237) Baltimore(96), Baltimore City(3)
ROYAL OAK Talbot
SABILLASVILLE (21780) Frederick(94), Washington(5)
SAINT INIGOES St. Mary's
SAINT JAMES Washington
SAINT LEONARD Calvert
SAINT MARYS CITY St. Mary's
SAINT MICHAELS Talbot
SALISBURY Wicomico
SANDY SPRING Montgomery
SAVAGE Howard
SCOTLAND St. Mary's
SECRETARY Dorchester
SEVERN Anne Arundel
SEVERNA PARK Anne Arundel
SHADY SIDE Anne Arundel
SHARPSBURG Washington
SHARPTOWN Wicomico
SHERWOOD Talbot
SHOWELL Worcester
SILVER SPRING (20903) Montgomery(84), Prince George's(15)
SILVER SPRING Montgomery
SIMPSONVILLE Howard
SMITHSBURG (21783) Washington(79), Frederick(20)
SNOW HILL Worcester
SOLOMONS Calvert
SOUTHERN MD FACILITY Prince George's
SPARKS GLENCOE Baltimore
SPARROWS POINT Baltimore
SPENCERVILLE Montgomery
SPRING GAP Allegany
STEVENSON Baltimore
STEVENSVILLE Queen Anne's
STILL POND Kent
STOCKTON Worcester
STREET Harford
SUBURB MARYLAND FAC Montgomery
SUDLERSVILLE Queen Anne's
SUITLAND Prince George's
SUNDERLAND Calvert

SWANTON Garrett
SYKESVILLE (21784) Carroll(94), Howard(5)
TAKOMA PARK (20912) Montgomery(89), Prince George's(10)
TAKOMA PARK Prince George's
TALL TIMBERS St. Mary's
TANEYTOWN (21787) Carroll(93), Frederick(6)
TAYLORS ISLAND Dorchester
TEMPLE HILLS Prince George's
TEMPLEVILLE Caroline
THURMONT Frederick
TILGHMAN Talbot
TODDVILLE Dorchester
TOWSON Baltimore
TRACYS LANDING Anne Arundel
TRAPPE Talbot
TUSCARORA Frederick
TYASKIN Wicomico
TYLERTON Somerset
UNION BRIDGE (21791) Carroll(52), Frederick(47)
UNIONVILLE Frederick
UPPER FAIRMOUNT Somerset
UPPER FALLS Baltimore
UPPER HILL Somerset
UPPER MARLBORO Prince George's
UPPERCO (21155) Baltimore(90), Carroll(9)
VALLEY LEE St. Mary's
VIENNA Dorchester
WALDORF (20601) Charles(95), Prince George's(4)
WALDORF Charles
WALKERSVILLE Frederick
WARWICK Cecil
WASHINGTON Prince George's
WASHINGTON GROVE Montgomery
WELCOME Charles
WENONA Somerset
WEST FRIENDSHIP Howard
WEST RIVER Anne Arundel
WESTERNPORT Allegany
WESTMINSTER Carroll
WESTOVER Somerset
WHALEYVILLE Worcester
WHITE HALL (21161) Baltimore(57), Harford(42)
WHITE MARSH Baltimore
WHITE PLAINS Charles
WHITEFORD Harford
WILLARDS Wicomico
WILLIAMSPORT Washington
WINDSOR MILL Baltimore
WINGATE Dorchester
WITTMAN Talbot
WOODBINE (21797) Carroll(52), Howard(46)
WOODSBORO Frederick
WOODSTOCK (21163) Baltimore(51), Howard(48)
WOOLFORD Dorchester
WORTON Kent
WYE MILLS Talbot

Maryland ZIP/City Cross Reference

20331-20331 WASHINGTON	20732-20732 CHESAPEAKE BEACH	20892-20894 BETHESDA	21120-21120 PARKTON
20601-20604 WALDORF	20733-20733 CHURCHTON	20895-20895 KENSINGTON	21122-21123 PASADENA
20606-20606 ABELL	20735-20735 CLINTON	20896-20896 GARRETT PARK	21128-21128 PERRY HALL
20607-20607 ACCOKEEK	20736-20736 OWINGS	20897-20897 SUBURB MARYLAND FAC	21130-21130 PERRYMAN
20608-20608 AQUASCO	20737-20738 RIVERDALE	20898-20899 GAITHERSBURG	21131-21131 PHOENIX
20609-20609 AVENUE	20740-20742 COLLEGE PARK	20900-20911 SILVER SPRING	21132-21132 PYLESVILLE
20610-20610 BARSTOW	20743-20743 CAPITOL HEIGHTS	20912-20913 TAKOMA PARK	21133-21133 RANDALLSTOWN
20611-20611 BEL ALTON	20744-20744 FORT WASHINGTON	20914-20997 SILVER SPRING	21136-21136 REISTERSTOWN
20612-20612 BENEDICT	20745-20745 OXON HILL	21001-21001 ABERDEEN	21139-21139 RIDERWOOD
20613-20613 BRANDYWINE	20746-20746 SUITLAND	21005-21005 ABERDEEN PROVING	21140-21140 RIVA
20615-20615 BROOMES ISLAND	20747-20747 DISTRICT HEIGHTS	GROUND	21144-21144 SEVERN
20616-20616 BRYANS ROAD	20748-20748 TEMPLE HILLS	21009-21009 ABINGDON	21146-21146 SEVERNA PARK
20617-20617 BRYANTOWN	20749-20749 FORT WASHINGTON	21010-21010 GUNPOWDER	21150-21150 SIMPSONVILLE
20618-20618 BUSHWOOD	20750-20750 OXON HILL	21012-21012 ARNOLD	21152-21152 SPARKS GLENCOE
20619-20619 CALIFORNIA	20751-20751 DEALE	21013-21013 BALDWIN	21153-21153 STEVENSON
20620-20620 CALLAWAY	20752-20752 SUITLAND	21014-21015 BEL AIR	21154-21154 STREET
20621-20621 CHAPTICO	20753-20753 DISTRICT HEIGHTS	21017-21017 BELCAMP	21155-21155 UPPERCO
20622-20622 CHARLOTTE HALL	20754-20754 DUNKIRK	21018-21018 BENSON	21156-21156 UPPER FALLS
20623-20623 CHELTENHAM	20755-20755 FORT GEORGE G MEADE	21020-21020 BORING	21157-21158 WESTMINSTER
20624-20624 CLEMENTS	20757-20757 TEMPLE HILLS	21021-21021 BRADSHAW	21160-21160 WHITEFORD
20625-20625 COBB ISLAND	20758-20758 FRIENDSHIP	21022-21022 BROOKLANDVILLE	21161-21161 WHITE HALL
20626-20626 COLTONS POINT	20759-20759 FULTON	21023-21023 BUTLER	21162-21162 WHITE MARSH
20627-20627 COMPTON	20762-20762 ANDREWS AIR FORCE	21024-21024 CARDIFF	21163-21163 WOODSTOCK
20628-20628 DAMERON	BASE	21027-21027 CHASE	21200-21203 BALTIMORE
20629-20629 DOWELL	20763-20763 SAVAGE	21028-21028 CHURCHVILLE	21204-21204 TOWSON
20630-20630 DRAYDEN	20764-20764 SHADY SIDE	21029-21029 CLARKSVILLE	21205-21206 BALTIMORE
20632-20632 FAULKNER	20765-20765 GALESVILLE	21030-21030 COCKEYSVILLE	21207-21207 GWYNN OAK
20634-20634 GREAT MILLS	20768-20768 GREENBELT	21031-21031 HUNT VALLEY	21208-21208 PIKESVILLE
20635-20635 HELEN	20769-20769 GLENN DALE	21032-21032 CROWNSVILLE	21209-21218 BALTIMORE
20636-20636 HOLLYWOOD	20770-20771 GREENBELT	21034-21034 DARLINGTON	21219-21219 SPARROWS POINT
20637-20637 HUGHESVILLE	20772-20775 UPPER MARLBORO	21035-21035 DAVIDSONVILLE	21220-21220 MIDDLE RIVER
20639-20639 HUNTINGTOWN	20776-20776 HARWOOD	21036-21036 DAYTON	21221-21221 ESSEX
20640-20640 INDIAN HEAD	20777-20777 HIGHLAND	21037-21037 EDGEWATER	21222-21222 DUNDALK
20643-20643 IRONSIDES	20778-20778 WEST RIVER	21040-21040 EDGEWOOD	21223-21224 BALTIMORE
20645-20645 ISSUE	20779-20779 TRACYS LANDING	21041-21043 ELLICOTT CITY	21225-21225 BROOKLYN
20646-20646 LA PLATA	20780-20789 HYATTSVILLE	21044-21046 COLUMBIA	21226-21226 CURTIS BAY
20650-20650 LEONARDTOWN	20790-20791 CAPITOL HEIGHTS	21047-21047 FALLSTON	21227-21227 HALETHORPE
20653-20653 LEXINGTON PARK	20792-20792 UPPER MARLBORO	21048-21048 FINKSBURG	21228-21228 CATONSVILLE
20656-20656 LOVEVILLE	20794-20794 JESSUP	21050-21050 FOREST HILL	21229-21233 BALTIMORE
20657-20657 LUSBY	20797-20797 SOUTHERN MD FACILITY	21051-21051 FORK	21234-21234 PARKVILLE
20658-20658 MARBURY	20799-20799 CAPITOL HEIGHTS	21052-21052 FORT HOWARD	21235-21235 BALTIMORE
20659-20659 MECHANICSVILLE	20800-20800 SUBURB MARYLAND FAC	21053-21053 FREELAND	21236-21236 NOTTINGHAM
20660-20660 MORGANZA	20810-20811 BETHESDA	21054-21054 GAMBRILLS	21237-21237 ROSEDALE
20661-20661 MOUNT VICTORIA	20812-20812 GLEN ECHO	21055-21055 GARRISON	21239-21241 BALTIMORE
20662-20662 NANJEMOY	20813-20814 BETHESDA	21056-21056 GIBSON ISLAND	21244-21244 GWYNN OAK
20664-20664 NEWBURG	20815-20815 CHEVY CHASE	21057-21057 GLEN ARM	21244-21244 WINDSOR MILL
20667-20667 PARK HALL	20816-20817 BETHESDA	21060-21062 GLEN BURNIE	21250-21285 BALTIMORE
20670-20670 PATUXENT RIVER	20818-20818 CABIN JOHN	21065-21065 COCKEYSVILLE	21286-21286 TOWSON
20674-20674 PINEY POINT	20824-20824 BETHESDA	21065-21065 HUNT VALLEY	21287-21299 BALTIMORE
20675-20675 POMFRET	20825-20825 CHEVY CHASE	21071-21071 GLYNDON	21400-21412 ANNAPOLIS
20676-20676 PORT REPUBLIC	20827-20827 BETHESDA	21074-21074 HAMPSTEAD	21501-21505 CUMBERLAND
20677-20677 PORT TOBACCO	20830-20832 OLNEY	21075-21075 ELKRIDGE	21520-21520 ACCIDENT
20678-20678 PRINCE FREDERICK	20833-20833 BROOKEVILLE	21076-21076 HANOVER	21521-21521 BARTON
20680-20680 RIDGE	20837-20837 POOLESVILLE	21077-21077 HARMANS	21522-21522 BITTINGER
20682-20682 ROCK POINT	20838-20838 BARNESVILLE	21078-21078 HAVRE DE GRACE	21523-21523 BLOOMINGTON
20684-20684 SAINT INIGOES	20839-20839 BEALLSVILLE	21080-21080 HENRYTON	21524-21524 CORRIGANVILLE
20685-20685 SAINT LEONARD	20841-20841 BOYDS	21082-21082 HYDES	21528-21528 ECKHART MINES
20686-20686 SAINT MARYS CITY	20842-20842 DICKERSON	21084-21084 JARRETTSVILLE	21529-21529 ELLERSLIE
20687-20687 SCOTLAND	20847-20853 ROCKVILLE	21085-21085 JOPPA	21530-21530 FLINTSTONE
20688-20688 SOLOMONS	20854-20854 POTOMAC	21087-21087 KINGSVILLE	21531-21531 FRIENDSVILLE
20689-20689 SUNDERLAND	20855-20855 DERWOOD	21088-21088 LINEBORO	21532-21532 FROSTBURG
20690-20690 TALL TIMBERS	20856-20858 ROCKVILLE	21088-21088 LINEBORO CPO	21536-21536 GRANTSVILLE
20692-20692 VALLEY LEE	20858-20858 SILVER SPRING	21090-21090 LINTHICUM HEIGHTS	21538-21538 KITZMILLER
20693-20693 WELCOME	20859-20859 POTOMAC	21092-21092 LONG GREEN	21539-21539 LONACONING
20695-20695 WHITE PLAINS	20860-20860 SANDY SPRING	21093-21094 LUTHERVILLE TIMONIUM	21540-21540 LUKE
20697-20697 SOUTHERN MD FACILITY	20861-20861 ASHTON	21098-21098 HANOVER	21541-21541 MC HENRY
20701-20701 ANNAPOLIS JUNCTION	20862-20862 BRINKLOW	21101-21101 MAGNOLIA	21542-21542 MIDLAND
20703-20703 LANHAM	20866-20866 BURTONSVILLE	21102-21102 MANCHESTER	21543-21543 MIDLOTHIAN
20704-20705 BELTSVILLE	20868-20868 SPENCERVILLE	21104-21104 MARRIOTTSVILLE	21545-21545 MOUNT SAVAGE
20706-20706 LANHAM	20871-20871 CLARKSBURG	21105-21105 MARYLAND LINE	21546-21546 NIKEP
20707-20709 LAUREL	20872-20872 DAMASCUS	21106-21106 MAYO	21550-21550 OAKLAND
20710-20710 BLADENSBURG	20874-20879 GERMANTOWN	21107-21107 ALESIA	21555-21555 OLDTOWN
20711-20711 LOTHIAN	20877-20879 GAITHERSBURG	21107-21107 FREELAND	21556-21556 PINTO
20712-20712 MOUNT RAINIER	20880-20880 WASHINGTON GROVE	21107-21107 MILLERS	21557-21557 RAWLINGS
20714-20714 NORTH BEACH	20882-20885 GAITHERSBURG	21108-21108 MILLERSVILLE	21560-21560 SPRING GAP
20715-20721 BOWIE	20886-20886 MONTGOMERY VILLAGE	21111-21111 MONKTON	21561-21561 SWANTON
20722-20722 BRENTWOOD	20889-20889 BETHESDA	21113-21113 ODENTON	21562-21562 WESTERNPORT
20723-20726 LAUREL	20890-20890 SUBURB MARYLAND FAC	21114-21114 CROFTON	21601-21606 EASTON
20731-20731 CAPITOL HEIGHTS	20891-20891 KENSINGTON	21117-21117 OWINGS MILLS	21607-21607 BARCLAY

21609-21609	BETHLEHEM
21610-21610	BETTERTON
21612-21612	BOZMAN
21613-21613	CAMBRIDGE
21617-21617	CENTREVILLE
21619-21619	CHESTER
21620-21620	CHESTERTOWN
21622-21622	CHURCH CREEK
21623-21623	CHURCH HILL
21624-21624	CLAIBORNE
21625-21625	CORDOVA
21626-21626	CRAPO
21627-21627	CROCHERON
21628-21628	CRUMPTON
21629-21629	DENTON
21631-21631	EAST NEW MARKET
21632-21632	FEDERALSBURG
21634-21634	FISHING CREEK
21635-21635	GALENA
21636-21636	GOLDSBORO
21637-21637	GALENA
21638-21638	GRASONVILLE
21639-21639	GREENSBORO
21640-21640	HENDERSON
21641-21641	HILLSBORO
21643-21643	HURLOCK
21644-21644	INGLESIDE
21645-21645	KENNEDYVILLE
21646-21646	LYNCH
21647-21647	MCDANIEL
21648-21648	MADISON
21649-21649	MARYDEL
21650-21650	MASSEY
21651-21651	MILLINGTON
21652-21652	NEAVITT
21653-21653	NEWCOMB
21654-21654	OXFORD
21655-21655	PRESTON
21656-21656	CHURCH HILL
21657-21657	QUEEN ANNE
21658-21658	QUEENSTOWN
21659-21659	RHODESDALE
21660-21660	RIDGELY
21661-21661	ROCK HALL
21662-21662	ROYAL OAK
21663-21663	SAINT MICHAELS
21664-21664	SECRETARY
21665-21665	SHERWOOD
21666-21666	STEVENSVILLE
21667-21667	STILL POND
21668-21668	SUDLERSVILLE
21669-21669	TAYLORS ISLAND
21670-21670	TEMPLEVILLE
21671-21671	TILGHMAN
21672-21672	TODDVILLE
21673-21673	TRAPPE
21675-21675	WINGATE
21676-21676	WITTMAN
21677-21677	WOOLFORD
21678-21678	WORTON
21679-21679	WYE MILLS
21681-21688	RIDGELY
21690-21690	CHESTERTOWN
21701-21709	FREDERICK
21710-21710	ADAMSTOWN
21711-21711	BIG POOL
21713-21713	BOONSBORO
21714-21714	BRADDOCK HEIGHTS
21715-21715	BROWNSVILLE
21716-21716	BRUNSWICK
21717-21717	BUCKEYSTOWN
21718-21718	BURKITTSVILLE
21719-21719	CASCADE
21720-21720	CAVETOWN
21721-21721	CHEWSVILLE
21722-21722	CLEAR SPRING
21723-21723	COOKSVILLE
21725-21725	DETOUR
21727-21727	EMMITSBURG
21733-21733	FAIRPLAY
21734-21734	FUNKSTOWN
21735-21735	GAITHER
21736-21736	GAPLAND

21737-21737	GLENELG
21738-21738	GLENWOOD
21740-21749	HAGERSTOWN
21750-21750	HANCOCK
21754-21754	IJAMSVILLE
21755-21755	JEFFERSON
21756-21756	KEEDYSVILLE
21757-21757	KEYMAR
21758-21758	KNOXVILLE
21759-21759	LADIESBURG
21762-21762	LIBERTYTOWN
21764-21764	LINWOOD
21765-21765	LISBON
21766-21766	LITTLE ORLEANS
21767-21767	MAUGANSVILLE
21768-21768	MIDDLEBURG
21769-21769	MIDDLETOWN
21770-21770	MONROVIA
21771-21771	MOUNT AIRY
21773-21773	MYERSVILLE
21774-21774	NEW MARKET
21775-21775	NEW MIDWAY
21776-21776	NEW WINDSOR
21777-21777	POINT OF ROCKS
21778-21778	ROCKY RIDGE
21779-21779	ROHRERSVILLE
21780-21780	SABILLASVILLE
21781-21781	SAINT JAMES
21782-21782	SHARPSBURG
21783-21783	SMITHSBURG
21784-21784	SYKESVILLE
21787-21787	TANEYTOWN
21788-21788	THURMONT
21790-21790	TUSCARORA
21791-21791	UNION BRIDGE
21792-21792	UNIONVILLE
21793-21793	WALKERSVILLE
21794-21794	WEST FRIENDSHIP
21795-21795	WILLIAMSPORT
21797-21797	WOODBINE
21798-21798	WOODSBORO
21801-21804	SALISBURY
21810-21810	ALLEN
21811-21811	BERLIN
21813-21813	BISHOPVILLE
21814-21814	BIVALVE
21816-21816	CHANCE
21817-21817	CRISFIELD
21820-21820	DAMES QUARTER
21821-21821	DEAL ISLAND
21822-21822	EDEN
21824-21824	EWELL
21826-21826	FRUITLAND
21829-21829	GIRDLETREE
21830-21830	HEBRON
21835-21835	LINKWOOD
21836-21836	MANOKIN
21837-21837	MARDELA SPRINGS
21838-21838	MARION STATION
21840-21840	NANTICOKE
21841-21841	NEWARK
21842-21843	OCEAN CITY
21849-21849	PARSONSBURG
21850-21850	PITTSVILLE
21851-21851	POCOMOKE CITY
21852-21852	POWELLVILLE
21853-21853	PRINCESS ANNE
21856-21856	QUANTICO
21857-21857	REHOBETH
21858-21858	RHODES POINT
21861-21861	SHARPTOWN
21862-21862	SHOWELL
21863-21863	SNOW HILL
21864-21864	STOCKTON
21865-21865	TYASKIN
21866-21866	TYLERTON
21867-21867	UPPER FAIRMOUNT
21868-21868	UPPER HILL
21869-21869	VIENNA
21870-21870	WENONA
21871-21871	WESTOVER
21872-21872	WHALEYVILLE
21874-21874	WILLARDS

21875-21875	DELMAR
21890-21890	WESTOVER
21901-21901	NORTH EAST
21902-21902	PERRY POINT
21903-21903	PERRYVILLE
21904-21904	PORT DEPOSIT
21911-21911	RISING SUN
21912-21912	WARWICK
21913-21913	CECILTON
21914-21914	CHARLESTOWN
21915-21915	CHESAPEAKE CITY
21916-21916	CHILDS
21917-21917	COLORA
21918-21918	CONOWINGO
21919-21919	EARLEVILLE
21920-21920	ELK MILLS
21921-21922	ELKTON
21930-21930	GEORGETOWN

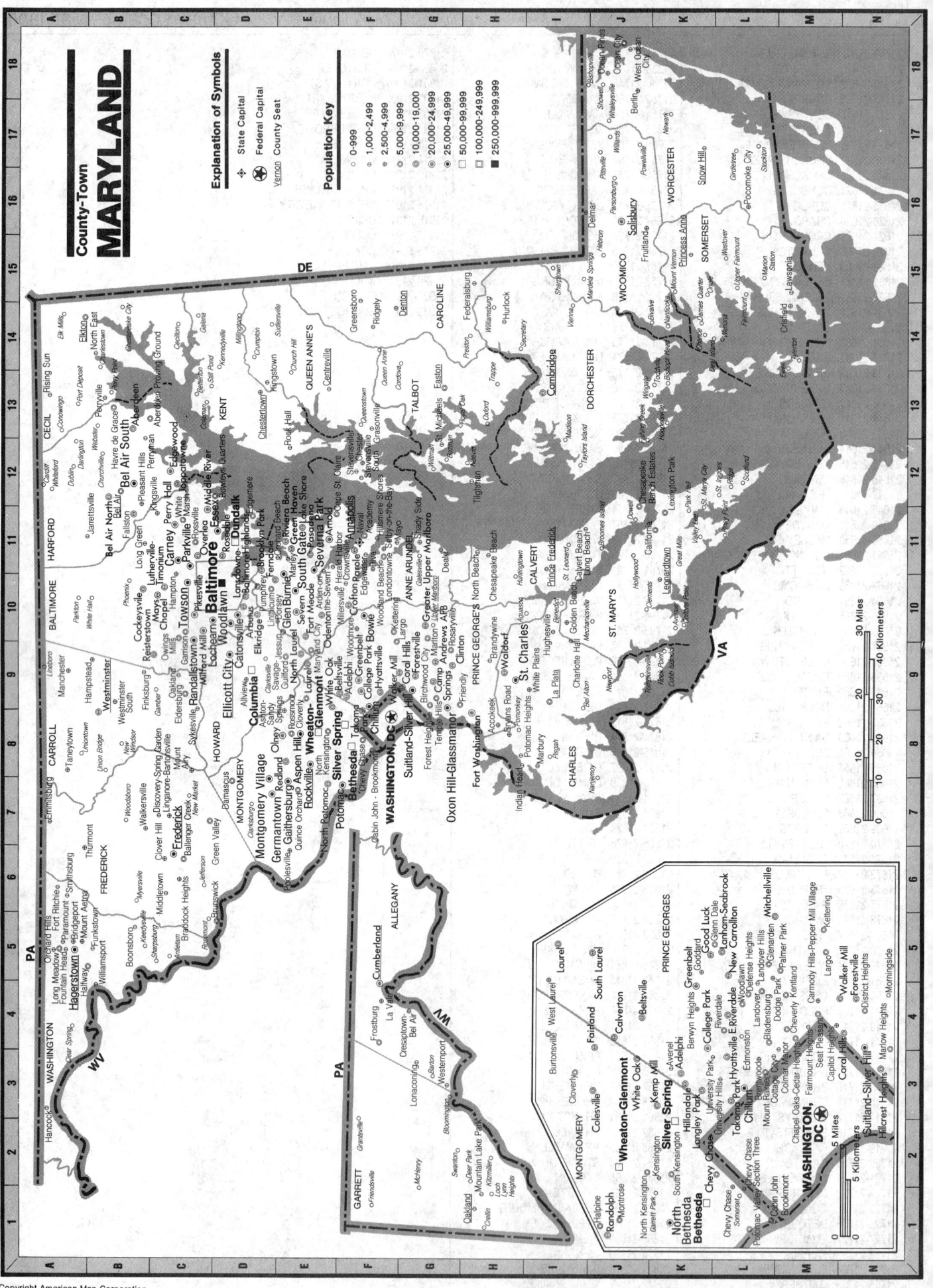

County-Town
MARYLAND

Explanation of Symbols

✛ State Capital
★ Federal Capital
Vernon County Seat

Population Key

○ 0-999
⊙ 1,000-2,499
⊕ 2,500-4,999
⊛ 5,000-9,999
⊗ 10,000-19,000
⊚ 20,000-24,999
⊕ 25,000-49,999
□ 50,000-99,999
□ 100,000-249,999
■ 250,000-999,999

COUNTIES

(24 Counties)

Name of County	Population	Location on Map
ALLEGANY	74,946	F-5
ANNE ARUNDEL	427,239	G-10
BALTIMORE	692,134	A-10
BALTIMORE (Independent City)	736,014	D-10
CALVERT	51,372	I-10
CAROLINE	27,035	G-14
CARROLL	123,372	A-8
CECIL	71,347	A-13
CHARLES	101,154	I-7
DORCHESTER	30,236	J-13
FREDERICK	150,208	B-6
GARRETT	28,138	F-1
HARFORD	182,132	A-11
HOWARD	187,328	D-8
KENT	17,842	D-13
MONTGOMERY	757,927	D-7
PRINCE GEORGE'S	729,268	H-9
QUEEN ANNE'S	33,953	E-13
SOMERSET	23,440	K-15
SAINT MARY'S	75,974	J-10
TALBOT	30,549	G-13
WASHINGTON	121,393	A-3
WICOMICO	74,339	J-15
WORCESTER	35,028	K-16
TOTAL	4,782,368	

CITIES AND TOWNS

Note: The first name is that of the city or town, second, that of the county in which it is located, then the population and location on the map.

Aberdeen, Harford, 13,087 ... B-13
• Aberdeen Proving Ground, Harford, 5,267 ... C-13
• Accokeek, Prince George's, 4,477 ... H-8
• Adelphi, Montgomery/Prince George's, 13,524 ... F-9
Allview, Howard ... D-9
• Andrews AFB, Prince George's, 10,228 ... G-9
Annapolis, Anne Arundel, 33,187 ... F-11
• Arbutus, Baltimore, 19,750 ... D-10
• Arden-on-the-Severn, Anne Arundel, 2,427 ... E-11
• Arnold, Anne Arundel, 20,261 ... E-11
• Ashton-Sandy Springs, Montgomery, 3,092 ... E-8
• Aspen Hill, Montgomery, 45,494 ... E-8
Avenel, Prince George's ... K-3
• Ballenger Creek, Frederick, 5,546 ... C-6
Baltimore, Baltimore (Independent City), 736,014 ... D-10
Bel Air, Harford, 8,860 ... B-12
• Bel Air North, Harford, 14,880 ... B-12
• Bel Air South, Harford, 26,421 ... B-12
• Beltsville, Prince George's, 14,476 ... F-9
Berlin, Worcester, 2,616 ... J-18
Berwyn Heights, Prince George's, 2,952 ... K-4
• Bethesda, Montgomery, 62,936 ... F-8
Birchwood City, Prince George's ... G-9
Bladensburg, Prince George's, 8,064 ... L-4
Boonsboro, Washington, 2,445 ... B-5
Bowie, Prince George's, 37,589 ... F-10
• Bowleys Quarters, Baltimore, 5,595 ... D-12
• Braddock Heights, Frederick, 4,778 ... C-6
• Brandywine, Prince George's, 1,406 ... H-9
Brentwood, Prince George's, 3,005 ... L-3
• Bridgeport, Washington, 2,702 ... A-5
• Brooklyn Park, Anne Arundel, 10,987 ... D-11
Brunswick, Frederick, 5,117 ... D-5
• Bryans Road, Charles, 3,809 ... H-8
• Burtonsville, Montgomery, 5,853 ... E-9
• Cabin John-Brookmont, Montgomery, 5,341 ... F-8
• California, St. Mary's, 7,626 ... K-11
• Calvert Beach-Long Beach, Calvert, 1,728 ... J-11
• Calverton, Montgomery/Prince George's, 12,046 ... J-4
Cambridge, Dorchester, 11,514 ... I-13
• Camp Springs, Prince George's, 16,392 ... G-9
• Cape St. Claire, Anne Arundel, 7,878 ... E-11
Capitol Heights, Prince George's, 3,633 ... M-4
• Carmody Hills-Pepper Mill Village, Prince George's, 4,815 ... M-4
• Carney, Baltimore, 25,578 ... C-11
• Catonsville, Baltimore, 35,233 ... D-10
Centreville, Queen Anne's, 2,097 ... E-13
Chapel Oaks-Cedar Heights, Prince George's ... M-4
• Charlotte Hall, Charles/St. Mary's, 1,992 ... I-10
Chesapeake Beach, Calvert, 2,403 ... H-11
• Chesapeake Ranch Estates, Calvert, 5,423 ... J-12
Chester, Queen Anne's ... F-12
Chestertown, Kent, 4,005 ... D-13
Cheverly, Prince George's, 6,023 ... M-4
• Chevy Chase, Montgomery, 8,559 ... F-8
Chevy Chase, Montgomery, 2,675 ... F-8
Chevy Chase Section Four, Montgomery ... L-1
Chevy Chase Section Three, Montgomery, 2,078 ... L-1
• Chillum, Prince George's, 31,309 ... F-9
• Clinton, Prince George's, 19,987 ... G-9
• Clover Hill, Frederick, 2,823 ... C-6
• Cloverly, Montgomery, 7,904 ... E-9
• Cockeysville, Baltimore, 18,668 ... B-10
• Colesville, Montgomery, 18,819 ... J-3
College Park, Prince George's, 21,927 ... F-9
Colmar Manor, Prince George's, 1,249 ... M-4
• Columbia, Howard, 75,883 ... D-9
• Coral Hills, Prince George's, 11,032 ... G-9
Cottage City, Prince George's, 1,236 ... L-3
• Cresaptown-Bel Air, Allegany, 4,586 ... G-4
Crisfield, Somerset, 2,880 ... M-14
• Crofton, Anne Arundel, 12,781 ... F-10
• Crownsville, Anne Arundel, 1,514 ... F-10
Cumberland, Allegany, 23,706 ... F-4
• Damascus, Montgomery, 9,817 ... D-7
• Deale, Anne Arundel, 4,151 ... G-11
Defense Heights, Prince George's ... L-4
Delmar, Wicomico, 1,430 ... I-16
Denton, Caroline, 2,977 ... F-14
• Discovery-Spring Garden, Frederick, 2,443 ... C-7
District Heights, Prince George's, 6,704 ... N-4
• Dodge Park, Prince George's, 4,842 ... L-5
Dorsey, Anne Arundel/Howard ... E-10
• Dundalk, Baltimore, 65,800 ... D-11
• East Riverdale, Prince George's, 14,187 ... L-4
Easton, Talbot, 9,372 ... G-13
• Edgemere, Baltimore, 9,226 ... D-11
Edgewater, Anne Arundel ... F-11
• Edgewood, Harford, 23,903 ... C-12
• Eldersburg, Carroll, 9,720 ... C-9
• Elkridge, Howard, 12,953 ... D-10
Elkton, Cecil, 9,073 ... A-14
• Ellicott City, Howard, 41,396 ... D-9
Emmitsburg, Frederick, 1,688 ... A-7
• Essex, Baltimore, 40,872 ... D-11
• Fairland, Montgomery, 19,828 ... J-4
Fairmount Heights, Prince George's, 1,238 ... M-4
• Fallston, Harford, 5,730 ... B-11
Federalsburg, Caroline, 2,365 ... H-15
• Ferndale, Anne Arundel, 16,355 ... D-10
Finksburg, Carroll ... B-9
Forest Heights, Prince George's, 2,859 ... G-8
• Forestville, Prince George's, 16,731 ... G-9
• Fort Meade, Anne Arundel, 12,509 ... E-10
• Fort Ritchie, Washington, 1,249 ... A-6
• Fort Washington, Prince George's, 24,032 ... H-8
Fountain Head, Washington ... A-5
Frederick, Frederick, 40,148 ... C-6
• Friendly, Prince George's, 9,028 ... G-9
Frostburg, Allegany, 8,075 ... F-4
Fruitland, Wicomico, 3,511 ... J-16
Funkstown, Washington, 1,136 ... B-5
Gaithersburg, Montgomery, 39,542 ... E-7
• Garrison, Baltimore, 5,045 ... C-10
• Germantown, Montgomery, 41,145 ... D-7
• Glen Burnie, Anne Arundel, 37,305 ... E-10
Glenarden, Prince George's, 5,025 ... L-5
• Glenn Dale, Prince George's, 9,689 ... L-5
• Goddard, Prince George's, 4,576 ... K-5
• Golden Beach, St. Mary's, 2,944 ... I-10
Good Luck, Prince George's ... K-5
• Grasonville, Queen Anne's, 2,439 ... F-13
• Greater Upper Marlboro, Prince George's, 11,528 ... G-10
• Green Haven, Anne Arundel, 14,416 ... E-11
• Green Valley, Frederick, 9,424 ... C-7
Greenbelt, Prince George's, 21,096 ... F-9
Greensboro, Caroline, 1,441 ... F-15
Hagerstown, Washington, 35,445 ... A-5
• Halfway, Washington, 8,873 ... B-5
Halpine, Montgomery ... J-1
• Hampstead, Baltimore/Carroll, 2,608 ... B-9
• Hampton, Baltimore, 4,926 ... C-11
Hancock, Washington, 1,926 ... A-3
Havre de Grace, Harford, 8,952 ... B-13
• Herald Harbor, Anne Arundel, 1,707 ... E-11
• Hillandale, Montgomery/Prince George's, 10,318 ... K-3
• Hillcrest Heights, Prince George's, 17,136 ... N-3
• Hillsmere Shores, Anne Arundel, 3,321 ... F-11
• Hughesville, Charles, 1,319 ... I-10
Hurlock, Dorchester, 1,706 ... H-14
Hyattsville, Prince George's, 13,864 ... F-9
Indian Head, Charles, 3,531 ... H-8
• Jarrettsville, Harford, 2,148 ... A-11
• Jessup, Anne Arundel/Howard, 6,537 ... E-10
• Joppatowne, Harford, 11,084 ... C-12
Kemp Mill, Montgomery ... K-3
Kensington, Montgomery, 1,713 ... K-2
• Kentland, Prince George's, 7,967 ... M-4
• Kettering, Prince George's, 9,901 ... F-10
• Kingstown, Queen Anne's, 1,660 ... D-13
• Kingsville, Baltimore, 3,550 ... C-11
La Plata, Charles, 5,841 ... I-9
• La Vale, Allegany, 4,694 ... F-4
• Lake Shore, Anne Arundel, 13,269 ... E-11
• Landover, Prince George's, 5,052 ... L-4
Landover Hills, Prince George's, 2,074 ... L-5
• Langley Park, Montgomery/Prince George's, 17,474 ... K-3
• Lanham-Seabrook, Prince George's, 16,792 ... L-5
• Lansdowne-Baltimore Highlands, Baltimore, 15,509 ... D-10
• Largo, Prince George's, 9,475 ... F-9
Laurel, Prince George's, 19,438 ... I-5
• Lawsonia, Somerset, 1,326 ... M-15
Leonardtown, St. Mary's, 1,475 ... K-10
• Lexington Park, St. Mary's, 9,943 ... K-11
• Linganore-Bartonsville, Frederick, 4,079 ... C-7
• Linthicum, Anne Arundel, 7,547 ... D-10
• Lochearn, Baltimore, 25,240 ... D-10
Lonaconing, Allegany, 1,122 ... G-3
• Londontowne, Anne Arundel, 6,992 ... F-11
Long Green, Baltimore ... B-11
• Long Meadow, Washington, 5,594 ... A-5
• Lutherville-Timonium, Baltimore, 16,442 ... C-10
Manchester, Carroll, 2,810 ... A-9
• Marbury, Charles, 1,244 ... I-8
Marley, Anne Arundel ... E-11
• Marlow Heights, Prince George's, 5,885 ... N-4
• Marlton, Prince George's, 5,523 ... G-10
• Maryland City, Anne Arundel, 6,813 ... E-9
• Mayo, Anne Arundel, 2,537 ... F-11
• Mays Chapel, Baltimore, 10,132 ... C-10
• Middle River, Baltimore, 24,616 ... C-11
Middletown, Frederick, 1,834 ... C-6
• Milford Mill, Baltimore, 22,547 ... C-10
Millersville, Anne Arundel ... E-10
• Mitchellville, Prince George's, 12,593 ... M-5
• Montgomery Village, Montgomery, 32,315 ... D-7
Montrose, Montgomery ... J-1
• Mount Aetna, Washington, 3,608 ... A-5
Mount Airy, Carroll/Frederick, 3,730 ... C-8
Mount Rainier, Prince George's, 7,954 ... L-3
Mountain Lake Park, Garrett, 1,938 ... H-1
• Naval Academy, Anne Arundel, 5,420 ... F-11
New Carrollton, Prince George's, 12,002 ... L-5
North Beach, Calvert, 1,173 ... H-11
• North Bethesda, Montgomery, 29,656 ... K-1
North East, Cecil, 1,913 ... B-14
• North Kensington, Montgomery, 8,607 ... E-8
• North Laurel, Howard, 15,008 ... E-9
• North Potomac, Montgomery, 18,456 ... E-7
• Oakland, Carroll, 2,078 ... C-9
Oakland, Garrett, 1,741 ... H-1
Ocean City, Worcester, 5,146 ... J-18
• Ocean Pines, Worcester, 4,251 ... J-18
• Odenton, Anne Arundel, 12,833 ... E-10
• Olney, Montgomery, 23,019 ... E-8
Orchard Beach, Anne Arundel ... E-11
• Overlea, Baltimore, 12,137 ... C-11
• Owings Mills, Baltimore, 9,474 ... C-10
• Oxon Hill-Glassmanor, Prince George's, 35,794 ... G-9
• Palmer Park, Prince George's, 7,019 ... M-5
• Parkville, Baltimore, 31,617 ... C-11
• Parole, Anne Arundel, 10,054 ... F-11
• Pasadena, Anne Arundel, 10,012 ... E-11
• Perry Hall, Baltimore, 22,723 ... C-11
• Perryman, Harford, 2,160 ... B-12
Perryville, Cecil, 2,456 ... B-13
• Pikesville, Baltimore, 24,815 ... C-10
• Pleasant Hills, Harford, 2,591 ... B-12
Pocomoke City, Worcester, 3,922 ... L-16
Poolesville, Montgomery, 3,796 ... E-6
• Potomac, Montgomery, 45,634 ... F-7
• Potomac Heights, Charles, 1,524 ... H-8
Potomac Valley, Montgomery ... L-1
• Prince Frederick, Calvert, 1,885 ... I-11
Princess Anne, Somerset, 1,666 ... K-15
• Pumphrey, Anne Arundel, 5,483 ... D-10
• Randallstown, Baltimore, 26,277 ... C-9
Randolph, Montgomery ... J-1
• Redland, Montgomery, 16,145 ... E-8
• Reisterstown, Baltimore, 19,314 ... C-9
Ridgely, Caroline, 1,034 ... F-14
Rising Sun, Cecil, 1,263 ... A-13
• Riva, Anne Arundel, 3,438 ... F-11
Riverdale, Prince George's, 5,185 ... L-4
• Riviera Beach, Anne Arundel, 11,376 ... E-11
Rock Hall, Kent, 1,584 ... E-12
Rockville, Montgomery, 44,835 ... E-8
• Rosaryville, Prince George's, 8,976 ... G-9
• Rosedale, Baltimore, 18,703 ... D-11
• Rossmoor, Montgomery, 6,182 ... E-8
• Rossville, Baltimore, 9,492 ... C-11
• Saint Charles, Charles, 28,717 ... H-9
Saint Michaels, Talbot, 1,301 ... G-12
Salisbury, Wicomico, 20,592 ... J-16
• Savage-Guilford, Howard, 9,669 ... E-9
Seat Pleasant, Prince George's, 5,359 ... M-4
• Selby-on-the-Bay, Anne Arundel, 3,101 ... F-11
• Severn, Anne Arundel, 24,499 ... E-10
• Severna Park, Anne Arundel, 25,879 ... E-11
• Shady Side, Anne Arundel, 4,107 ... G-11
• Silver Spring, Montgomery, 76,046 ... F-8
Smithsburg, Washington, 1,221 ... A-6
Snow Hill, Worcester, 2,217 ... K-17
• South Gate, Anne Arundel, 27,564 ... E-10
• South Kensington, Montgomery, 8,777 ... K-2
• South Laurel, Prince George's, 18,591 ... J-5
• Stevensville, Queen Anne's, 1,862 ... F-12
• Stevensville South, Queen Anne's, 1,751 ... F-12
• Suitland-Silver Hill, Prince George's, 35,111 ... G-9
Sykesville, Carroll, 2,303 ... C-9
Takoma Park, Montgomery/Prince George's, 16,700 ... F-8
Taneytown, Carroll, 3,695 ... A-8
• Temple Hills, Prince George's, 6,865 ... G-9
Thurmont, Frederick, 3,398 ... A-6
Tilghman, Talbot ... H-12
• Towson, Baltimore, 49,445 ... C-10
University Hills, Prince George's ... L-3
University Park, Prince George's, 2,243 ... L-3
Upper Marlboro, Prince George's, 745 ... G-10
• Waldorf, Charles, 15,058 ... H-9
• Walker Mill, Prince George's, 10,920 ... F-9
Walkersville, Frederick, 4,145 ... B-7
• West Laurel, Prince George's, 4,151 ... I-5
• West Ocean City, Worcester, 1,928 ... J-18
Westernport, Allegany, 2,454 ... G-3
Westminster, Carroll, 13,068 ... B-8
• Westminster South, Carroll, 4,284 ... B-9
• Wheaton-Glenmont, Montgomery, 53,720 ... E-8
• White Marsh, Baltimore, 8,183 ... C-11
• White Oak, Montgomery, 18,671 ... E-9
• White Plains, Charles, 3,560 ... I-9
Williamsport, Washington, 2,103 ... B-4
Woodland Beach, Anne Arundel ... F-11
• Woodlawn, Baltimore, 32,907 ... D-10
• Woodlawn, Prince George's, 5,329 ... L-4
• Woodmore, Prince George's, 2,874 ... F-10

Washington, DC, 606,900 ... F-8

Explanation of symbols: • – Census Designated Place (CDP)

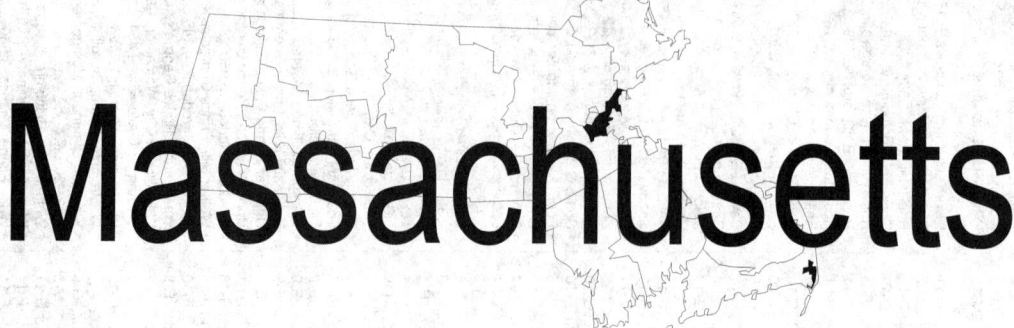

Massachusetts

General Help Numbers:

Governor's Office

State House, Room 360
Boston, MA 02133
www.state.ma.us/gov

617- 727-6250
Fax 617-727-9725
8AM-6PM

Attorney General's Office

One Ashburton Place, Room 2010
Boston, MA 02108-1698
www.ago.state.ma.us

617-727-2200
Fax 617-727-5768
9AM-5PM

Legislative Records

Massachusetts General Court, State House
Beacon St, Room 428 (Document Room)
Boston, MA 02133
www.mass.gov/legis/

617-722-2860

9AM-5PM

State Archives

Archives Division
220 Morrissey Blvd
Boston, MA 02125
www.sec.state.ma.us/arc/

617-727-2816
Fax 617-288-8429
9AM-5PM M-F; 9-3 SA

State Specifics:

Capital:	Boston
	Suffolk County
Time Zone:	EST
Number of Counties:	14
Population:	6,433,422
Web Site:	www.mass.gov/portal/index.jsp

State Agencies

Criminal Records

Criminal History Systems Board, 200 Arlington Street, #2200, Chelsea, MA 02150; 617-660-4600, 617-660-4613 (Fax), 9AM-5PM.

www.mass.gov/chsb/

Note: These searches are offered: 1) Personal, 2) Certified Agency, 3) Publicly Accessible (PUBAC). Certified Agency requests are pre-approved via statute or the Board. PUBAC is open to the public; data is limited.

Indexing & Storage: Records are available for at least 50 years. It takes 1 day before new records are available for inquiry. Records are indexed on inhouse computer, file folders.

Searching: PUBAC requesters are limited to adult records; the crime must include a sentence of 5 years or more OR sentenced and convicted for any term if, at the time of request, the subject is on probation or has been released within 2 years of felony conviction. Include the following in your request-name, date of birth. The Personal request (on one's self) requires a notarized signature. A

"certified agency" search may include youth organizations, child care providers, and others approved by CHSB. This agency does not conduct FBI fingerprint searches.

Access by: mail.

Fee & Payment: The Personal request is $25.00. The Certified Agency request is $30.00. The PUBAC request is $30.00. No fingerprint requests are permitted, thus no fingerprint fees. In fact, 0% of the records are fingerprint-supported. Fee payee: The Commonwealth of Massachusetts.

Prepayment required. Personal checks accepted. No credit cards accepted.

Mail search: Turnaround time: 2 weeks. A SASE is required.

Statewide Court Records

Chief Justice for Administration & Management, 2 Center Plaza, Room 540, Boston, MA 02108; 617-742-8575, 617-742-0968 (Fax), 8:30AM-5PM.

www.mass.gov/courts/admin/index.html

Searching: Opinions to the Mass Supreme and Appellate courts can be found at http://massreports.com.

Access by: online.

Online search: Opinions to the Mass Supreme and Appellate courts can be found at http://massreports.com/. Online access to records on the statewide Trial Courts Information Center website is available to attorneys and law firms at www.ma-trialcourts.org/tcic/welcome.jsp. Contact Peter Nylin by email at nylin_p@jud.state.ma.us. Site is updated daily.

Sexual Offender Registry

Sex Offender Registry Board, PO Box 4547, Salem, MA 01970; 978-740-6400, 978-740-6464 (Fax), 8:45AM-5PM.

www.mass.gov/sorb/

Note: The Sex Offender Registry Board estimates that there are nearly 18,000 sex offenders living and/or working in the Commonwealth of Massachusetts.

Indexing & Storage: Records are available from 08/01/81.

Searching: Information about a sex offender is available to the public only if subject has been classified by the Board as a Level 2 or a Level 3 Offender. In person requests should be conducted at local law enforcement offices. Requests to this office must be in writing or online access is available from the Internet site.

Access by: mail, online.

Fee & Payment: There is no fee.

Mail search: Turnaround time: 1-2 weeks.

Online search: Search free at http://ma-sorb.gis.net/intro.htm.

Incarceration Records

Massachusetts Executive Office of Public Safety, Criminal History Systems Board, 200 Arlington #2200, Chelsea, MA 02150; 617-660-4600, 877-421-8463 (Locator), 617-660-4690 (Criminal Histories Systems Board), 8AM-5PM.

www.mass.gov/doc/

Indexing & Storage: Records are available on current and former inmates by mail, current inmates only online. It takes about 7 days before new records are available for inquiry.

Searching: Include the following in your request-full name; AIS number helpful.

Access by: mail, phone, online.

Fee & Payment: There is no fee.

Mail search: Turnaround time: 2-3 days. Requests in writing must be on letterhead paper

Phone search: Use the Locator phone number: 877-421-8463.

Online search: No searching online is offered by this agency, however a private company offers free web access to DOC offenders at www.vinelink.com/index.jsp. There is also a DOC Most Wanted list at www.mass.gov/doc/wanted/index.html.

Corporation, Trademarks, Servicemarks, Limited Liability Partnerships, Limited Partnerships, Limited Liability Companys

Secretary of the Commonwealth, Corporation Division, One Ashburton Pl, 17th Floor, Boston, MA 02108; 617-727-9640 (Corporations), 617-727-2850 (Records), 617-727-8329 (Trademarks), 617-727-9440 (Forms Requests), 617-742-4538 (Fax), 8:45AM-5PM.

www.sec.state.ma.us/cor/coridx.htm

Indexing & Storage: Records are available for corporations and business entities organized since 1978 on computer. Corporations and business entities organized prior to 1978 may or may not be available. Annual reports are maintained for 10 years. New records are available for inquiry immediately. Records are indexed on microfilm, inhouse computer. Images available August 2001 to present.

Searching: Include the following in your request-full name of business. In addition to the articles of incorporation, corporation records include the following information: Annual Reports, Officers and Directors names and addresses, Prior (merged) names, Inactive and Reserved names and US Tax ID numbers.

Access by: mail, phone, in person, online.

Fee & Payment: Uncertified copies cost $.30 per page. Certified copies cost $7.00 for the first page and $2.00 for each additional page. Certified copies of articles of incorporation are $12.00 per organization. Fee payee: Commonwealth of Massachusetts. Prepayment required. Personal checks accepted. No credit cards accepted.

Mail search: Turnaround time: 3 to 5 days. A SASE is requested.

Phone search: No fee for telephone request. Telephone room hours are 8:45AM-5PM.

In person search: Turnaround time: while you wait.

Online search: There is a free Internet lookup from the website. This site also provides UCC information.

Other access: Bulk sale on CD is available.

Uniform Commercial Code, Federal and State Tax Liens

UCC Division, Secretary of the Commonwealth, One Ashburton Pl, Room 1711, Boston, MA 02108; 617-727-2860, 900-555-4500 (Computer Prints), 900-555-4600 (Copies), 8:45AM-5PM.

http://corp.sec.state.ma.us/portal/UCC/UCCMain.htm

Indexing & Storage: Records are available from 09/01/81 on computer and 01/01/84 on microfiche. It takes 24 hours before new records are available for inquiry. Records are indexed on inhouse computer.

Searching: Use search request form UCC-11. Federal tax liens are filed at the US District Courts, PO & Courthouse Bldg, Boston, MA 02109 (617-233-9152). A list of state tax liens is available here, but must be searched in person separately from UCC filings. Include the following in your request-debtor name. Only active filings are available.

Access by: mail, in person, online.

Fee & Payment: Information listing only is $10.00. Search with copies is $30.00 for first 15 pages, $1.00 per page of copies after 15. State tax liens cost $0.30 per copy made. The state does not certify any state tax lien. Fee payee: Commonwealth of Massachusetts. Prepayment required. Credit cards accepted for fax and online searches. Personal checks accepted.

Mail search: Turnaround time: 2 days. Information requests are available.

In person search: You may request information in person, but turnaround time for certified documents is 24 hours. You may search on an in-house public terminal.

Online search: The UCC Public Browse function gives free access to record index from the website.

Other access: Microfiche may be purchased.

Sales Tax Registrations

Revenue Department - Customer Serv. Bur, Sales Tax Registrations, PO Box 7010, Boston, MA 02204 (Courier: 200 Arlington Street, 4th Floor, Chelsea, MA 02150); 617-887-6367, 8AM-5PM.

www.dor.state.ma.us

Note: There are actually 6 offices in the state that will allow walk-in researchers. The office in Chelsea will not let you in the building.

Searching: This agency will only confirm that a business is registered. They will provide no other information. Include the following in your request-business name. They will also search by tax permit number.

Access by: mail, phone, fax, in person.

Mail search: Turnaround time: 5 to 10 days. A SASE is requested. No fee for mail request.

Phone search: No fee for telephone request.

Fax search: They ask that you call first to get the number, they do not wish to publish their fax number.

In person search: No fee for request. Call to find closest office.

Birth Certificates

Registry of Vital Records and Statistics, 150 Mt Vernon St, 1st FL, Dorchester, MA 02125; 617-740-2600, 617-740-2606, 617-825-7755 (Fax), 8:45AM-4:45PM.

www.mass.gov/dph/bhsre/rvr/vrcopies.htm

Indexing & Storage: Records are available from 1911 to present. Records from 1841 to 1905 are located at the Massachusetts Archives, 220 Morrissey Blvd., Boston, MA 02125. Records prior to 1841 are located at the town/city level. It takes 6 months before new records are available for inquiry.

Searching: Access to out-of-wedlock birth records and health information is strictly limited. A court order is required for adopted children's records. Otherwise, records are open. Include the following in your request-full name, names of parents, mother's maiden name, date of birth, place of birth. Must present a photo ID or provide a copy of a photo ID to search. Phone and fax searchers must give exact place and date of event.

Access by: mail, phone, fax, in person, online.

Fee & Payment: The fee is $18.00 per record. Fee payee: Commonwealth of Massachusetts. Personal checks accepted. Credit cards accepted: MasterCard, Visa, AmEx, Discover.

Mail search: Turnaround time: 3 to 4 weeks. A SASE is requested.

Phone search: See expedited service. Must use a credit card.

Fax search: See expedited service. Must use a credit card.

In person search: Turnaround time is immediate. You can also do your own searching of records. First 20 minutes is free, then there is a $3.00 fee. The research center is open 9AM-12PM and 2PM-4:30PM, M-F.

Online search: You can order online at www.vitalchek.com, a state designated vendor.

Expedited service: Expedited service is available for phone, fax, and online orders. Turnaround time: 2 days. The fax number to use is 617-740-2713. Total fee is $44.00 plus cost of express delivery.

Death Records

Registry of Vital Records and Statistics, 150 Mt Vernon St, 1st FL, Dorchester, MA 02125; 617-740-2600, 617-740-2606, 617-825-7755 (Fax), 8:45AM-4:45PM.

www.mass.gov/dph/bhsre/rvr/vrcopies.htm

Indexing & Storage: Records are available from 1906 to present. Prior records at State Archives to 1841. It takes 4 months before new records are available for inquiry.

Searching: Fetal death records are not available. A court order is required to access the originals of amended records. Include the following in your request-full name, date of death, place of death. Name of spouse and age at time of death will help facilitate the search. Phone and fax requesters must supply exact place and date of event.

Access by: mail, phone, fax, in person, online.

Fee & Payment: The fee is $18.00 per record. Fee payee: Commonwealth of Massachusetts. Personal checks accepted. Credit cards accepted: MasterCard, Visa, AmEx, Discover.

Mail search: Turnaround time: 3 to 4 weeks. A SASE is requested.

Phone search: See expedited service. You must use a credit card.

Fax search: See expedited service.

In person search: There is a research center open 9AM-12PM and 2PM-4:30PM M-F. Searching is free the first 20 minutes, then it is $3.00 per hour.

Online search: You can order online at www.vitalchek.com, a state designated vendor.

Expedited service: Expedited service is available for phone, fax, and online orders. Turnaround time: 2 days. The fax number to use is 617-740-2713. Total fee is $44.00 plus cost of express delivery.

Marriage Certificates

Registry of Vital Records and Statistics, 150 Mt Vernon St, 1st FL, Dorchester, MA 02125; 617-740-2600, 617-740-2606, 617-825-7755 (Fax), 8:45AM-4:45PM.

www.mass.gov/dph/bhsre/rvr/vrcopies.htm

Indexing & Storage: Records are available from 1906 to present. Prior records to 1841 are at State Archives. It takes 5 months before new records are available for inquiry.

Searching: A court order is required for originals of amended records. Include the following in your request-names of husband and wife, date of marriage, place or county of marriage. Phone or fax searchers must submit exact place and date of event. Also helpful are parents' names.

Access by: mail, phone, fax, in person, online.

Fee & Payment: The fee is $18.00 per record. Fee payee: Commonwealth of Massachusetts. Personal checks accepted. Major credit cards accepted.

Mail search: Turnaround time: 3 to 4 weeks. A SASE is requested. See expedited service.

Phone search: See expedited service. You must use a credit card.

Fax search: See expedited service.

In person search: There is a research center open from 9AM-12PM and 2PM-4:30PM, M-F. The first 20 minutes are free, then a $3.00 per hour fee is charged.

Online search: You can order online at www.vitalchek.com, a state designated vendor.

Expedited service: Expedited service is available for phone, fax, and online orders. Turnaround time: 2 days. The fax number to use is 617-740-2713. Total fee is $44.00 plus cost of express delivery.

Divorce Records

Access to Records is Restricted

Registry of Vital Records and Statistics, 150 Mt Vernon St, 1st FL, Dorchester, MA 02125; 617-740-2600, 617-740-2606.

www.mass.gov/dph/bhsre/rvr/vrcopies.htm

Note: Divorce records are found at county of issue. However, this agency maintains an index from 1952 to present. The state will do a search for free by mail only to determine the county.

Workers' Compensation Records

Keeper of Records, Department of Industrial Accidents, 600 Washington St, 7th Floor, Boston, MA 02111; 617-727-4900 x301,209, 617-727-4440 (Fax), 8AM-4PM.

www.mass.gov/dia

Note: Records are under the jurisdiction of Sec of State, per the state public record law.

Indexing & Storage: Records are available from 1995 on, and prior records located at State Archives. The index is computerized since 1981. Earlier records may be researched via microfiche for an index number. It takes 2 weeks before new records are available for inquiry. Records are indexed on inhouse computer. Records are normally destroyed after 40 years.

Searching: You need a signed release from claimant to receive data regarding medical records,

DOB, and SSN. Include the following in your request-claimant name, Social Security Number, date of injury, employer, insurance carrier, and other pertinent information. E-mail address is infodesk@dia.state.ma.us. The following data is not released: medical records, date of birth or Social Security Numbers.

Access by: mail, in person.

Fee & Payment: There is a standard fee of $5.00 prior to release of record(s). Add $.20 per page and $.50 per page if computer generated. They will invoice, but will add postage amount to bill. Fee payee: Commonwealth of Massachusetts. Personal checks accepted. No credit cards accepted.

Mail search: Turnaround time: as much as 6 weeks. No SASE is required.

In person search: All requests must be in writing.

Driver Records-Registry

Registry of Motor Vehicles, Driver Control Unit, Box 199150, Boston, MA 02119-1950; 617-351-9213 (Registry), 617-351-9219 (Fax), 8AM-4:30PM M-T-W-F; 8AM-7PM TH.

www.mass.gov/rmv/

Note: The driving records provided by the Registry are for employment or general business use. The Merit Rating Board oversees records for insurance use. Both the Registry and the Merit Rating Board use the same database of driving record histories.

Indexing & Storage: Records are available for 6 years plus current year for moving violations. It takes 1 week before new records are available for inquiry.

Searching: Casual requesters can only obtain records without personal information. Include the following in your request-full name, driver's license number, date of birth. The address of the requester should also be included. The following data is not released: bulk information or lists for commercial purposes.

Access by: mail, phone, in person.

Fee & Payment: The fee is $15.00 per record via the Registry. Fee payee: Registry of Motor Vehicles. Prepayment required. Personal checks accepted.

Mail search: Turnaround time: 8 working days. No SASE is required.

Phone search: For pre-approved accounts, the Registry offers a phone-in request line at 617-351-9213. Orders can be paid with a credit card, results are mailed.

In person search: Up to 10 requests will be processed immediately; the rest are available the next day. You may request a record from any field office.

Driver Records-Insurance

Merit Rating Board, Attn: Driving Records, PO Box 199100, Boston, MA 02119-9100; 617-351-4400, 617-351-9660 (Fax), 8:45AM-5:00PM.

www.mass.gov/rmv/

Note: The Merit Rating Board processes driving records for the insurance industry in accordance with state statutes.

Indexing & Storage: Records are available for 6 years for moving violations and at fault accidents (process date). The license number and name are validated against the Registry license file.

Searching: These records do not show revocation or suspension action. Include the following in your request-driver's license number, full name, date of birth. All requests must be on the agency form.

Access by: mail, in person, online.

Fee & Payment: The fee is $15.00 per record. Fee payee: Commonwealth of Massachusetts. Prepayment required. Personal checks accepted. No credit cards accepted.

Mail search: Turnaround time: 2 days. No SASE is required.

In person search: Turnaround time while you wait.

Online search: The Merit Rating Board provides both online and tape inquiry to the insurance industry for rating and issuance of new and renewal automobile insurance policies. Per statute, this method of retrieval is not open to the general public.

Vehicle Ownership, Vehicle Identification

Registry of Motor Vehicles, Document Control, PO Box 199100, Boston, MA 02119-9100; 617-351-9458, 617-351-9524 (Fax), 8AM-4:30PM.

www.mass.gov/rmv/

Note: In general, license, ownership, and registration information is available to the public. Personal information is not available to casual requesters without consent.

Indexing & Storage: Records are available from the 1940's for licenses, from 1963 for registrations and names. Records are computerized from 1986.

Searching: Requesters with a DPPA permissible use should use "A Request for Personal Information In RMV Records for Multiple Records." Casual requesters should use "A Request for Personal Information In RMV Records for Individual." The agency does not do VIN look-ups. Lien information is provided as part of the record.

Access by: mail, fax, in person, online.

Fee & Payment: The current fee is $5.00 for per record request if on computer, $10.00 if on microfiche. Fee payee: Commonwealth of Massachusetts. Prepayment required. Personal checks accepted. No credit cards accepted.

Mail search: Turnaround time: 7 to 10 days. A SASE is requested.

Fax search: Records are available by fax.

In person search: In person requesters may get computer records immediately, microfiche records take 3 days.

Online search: Searching is limited to Massachusetts based insurance companies and agents for the purpose of issuing or renewing insurance. This system is not open to the public. There is no fee, but line charges will be incurred.

Other access: This agency offers an extensive array of customized bulk record requests to authorzied users. For further information, contact the Production Control Office.

Accident Reports

Crash Records, Registry of Motor Vehicles, PO Box 199100, Roxbury, MA 02119-9100; 617-351-9434, 617-351-9401 (Fax), 8:45AM-5PM.

www.mass.gov/rmv/forms/21278.htm

Note: Accident reports may also be obtained from the local police department in the investigating jurisdiction.

Indexing & Storage: Records are available for 2 years to present. Records are indexed on computer. It takes 8 weeks before new records are available for inquiry. Records are normally destroyed after 2 years.

Searching: Criminal Offender Record Information (CORI) will not be released. Items required for search include; full name, date of accident, location of accident, and license or registration number.

Access by: mail.

Fee & Payment: The non-refundable charge is $10.00 per report. Fee payee: Registry of Motor Vehicles. Prepayment required. Personal checks accepted. No credit cards accepted.

Mail search: Turnaround time: 4 weeks.

Vessel Ownership, Vessel Registration

Massachusetts Environmental Police, Registration and Titling Bureau, 251 Causeway Street, #101, Boston, MA 02114; 617-626-1610, 617-626-1630 (Fax), 8:45AM-5PM.

www.mass.gov/dfwele/dle/dle_toc.htm

Note: Lien information is kept by this agency and appears on the title record.

Indexing & Storage: Records are available from 1988 to present. All motor powered boats and jet skis must be registered with this agency. All boats over 14ft must be titled. Records are indexed on computer.

Searching: Include the following in your request-name or hull number. The following data is not released: Social Security Numbers or phone numbers.

Access by: mail, phone, fax.

Fee & Payment: There is no search fee.

Mail search: Turnaround time: 1 week. No SASE is required.

Phone search: Records are available by phone.

Fax search: Turnaround time is usually 5 minutes.

Other access: To obtain printed lists or CD, contact the Bureau Chief at 617-626-1611. Generally, the fee is $50.00 for a CD.

Voter Registration

Records not maintained by a state level agency.

Note: Records are maintained at the local city and town level. In general, they are open to the public.

GED Certificates

Massachusetts Dept of Education, GED Processing, 350 Main St, Malden, MA 02148; 781-338-6636, 781-338-3391, 781-338-3391 (Fax), 9AM-5PM.

www.doe.mass.edu/ged

Indexing & Storage: It takes 1 month before new records are available for inquiry. Records are normally destroyed after 60 years.

Searching: Although this agency is able to verify a GED, they will not release copies of transcripts. You must go to one of the 32 test centers. They can tell you which center to request the copy. Include the following in your request-signed release, DOB, SSN. The year and the name of institution are also helpful.

Access by: mail, fax.

Fee & Payment: The fee is $2.00 per for a certifed letter of verification. There is no fee for a simpl eyes or no answer via fax. Fee payee: Commonwealth of Massachusetts. Prepayment required. Only money orders are accepted. No credit cards accepted.

Mail search: Turnaround time: 2 to 5 days. No SASE is required.

Fax search: Fax requesting is available to all requesters.

Hunting and Fishing License Information

Division of Fisheries & Wildlife, 251 Causeway St #400, Boston, MA 02114-2104; 617-626-1590, 617-626-1517 (Fax), 9AM-5PM.

www.mass.gov/dfwele/

Indexing & Storage: Records are available for 1 year back only. Older records are maintained at one of several locations off premises and take longer to research.

Searching: All requests must be in writing and on their form. You may call to request the form. Need to know the store where license was purchased and month it was purchased. They are filed by license number only.

Access by: mail, in person.

Fee & Payment: There is no search fee.

Mail search: Turnaround time: same day if possible. No SASE is required.

In person search: You must complete their form.

Massachusetts State Licensing Agencies
Licenses Searchable Online

Adjuster, Fire Loss #38 .... www.mass.gov/doi/Producer/Producer_list.html
Adoption Center #52 .... www.qualitychildcare.org/adoption_search_a.asp
Aesthetician #7 .... http://license.reg.state.ma.us/pubLic/licque.asp?color=red&Board=HD
Alarm Installer, Burglar/Fire #7 .... http://license.reg.state.ma.us/pubLic/licque.asp?color=red&Board=EL
Amusement Device Inspector #27 .... www.mass.gov/dps/Lic_srch.htm
Appraiser, MVR Damage #38 .... www.mass.gov/doi/Producer/Producer_list.html
Architect #42 .... http://license.reg.state.ma.us/pubLic/licque.asp?color=red&Board=AR
Athletic Trainer #7 .... http://license.reg.state.ma.us/pubLic/licque.asp?color=red&Board=AH
Attorney #2 .... http://massbbo.org/
Auctioneer School #43 .... www.state.ma.us/standards/auc-sch.htm
Auto Repair Shop, Registered #38 .... www.aib.org/BDYSHOP/bdshind.htm
Automobile Dealer #48 .... www.mass.gov/dob/liclist.htm
Automobile Sales Finance Company #48 ..... www.mass.gov/dob/liclist.htm
Bank & Savings Institution #35 .... http://db.state.ma.us/dob/in-choose.asp
Barber/Barber Shop #7 .... http://license.reg.state.ma.us/pubLic/licque.asp?color=red&Board=BR
Boilers/Pressure Vessels Inspector #27 ..... www.mass.gov/dps/Lic_srch.htm
Boxer #50 .... www.state.ma.us/mbc/ranking.htm
Brokerage Firm #49 .... www.nasdr.com
Building Inspector/Local Inspector #3 .... www.mass.gov/bbrs/bocert.PDF
Building Producer #3 .... www.mass.gov/bbrs/mfg98.pdf
Check Casher/Seller #35 .... www.mass.gov/dob/liclist.htm
Chiropractor #7 .... http://license.reg.state.ma.us/pubLic/licque.asp?color=red&Board=CH
Collection Agency #35 .... www.mass.gov/dob/liclist.htm
Concrete Technician #3 .... www.mass.gov/bbrs/programs.htm
Concrete Testing Laboratory #3 .... www.mass.gov/bbrs/programs.htm
Construction Supervisor #18 .... www.mass.gov/bbrs/cslsearch.htm
Contractor, Home Improvement #3 .... www.mass.gov/bbrs/Hicsearch.htm
Cosmetologist/Manicurist/Aesthetician) #7 ..... http://license.reg.state.ma.us/pubLic/licque.asp?color=red&Board=HD
Credit Union #35 .... http://db.state.ma.us/dob/in-choose.asp
Day Care Center #52 .... www.qualitychildcare.org/
Dental Hygienist #7 .... http://license.reg.state.ma.us/pubLic/licque.asp?color=red&Board=DN
Dentist #7 .... http://license.reg.state.ma.us/pubLic/licque.asp?color=red&Board=DN
Electrician #7 .... http://license.reg.state.ma.us/pubLic/licque.asp?color=red&Board=EL
Electrologist #7 .... http://license.reg.state.ma.us/pubLic/licque.asp?color=red&Board=ET
Embalmer #40 .... http://license.reg.state.ma.us/pubLic/licque.asp?color=red&Board=EM
Engineer #7 .... http://license.reg.state.ma.us/pubLic/licque.asp?color=red&Board=EN
Family Child Care Provider #52 .... www.qualitychildcare.org/
Finfishing, Commercial #34 .... www.mass.gov/dfwele/dmf/
Fire Protection Sprinkler Contractor/Fitter #27 .... www.mass.gov/dps/Lic_srch.htm
Firemen / Engineer #27 .... www.mass.gov/dps/Lic_srch.htm
Foreign Transmittal Agency #35 .... www.mass.gov/dob/liclist.htm
Foster Care Provider #52 .... www.qualitychildcare.org/adoption_search_fc.asp
Funeral Director #40 .... http://license.reg.state.ma.us/pubLic/licque.asp?color=red&Board=EM
Fur Buyer #34 .... www.mass.gov/dfwele/dfw/
Gas Fitter #7 .... http://license.reg.state.ma.us/pubLic/licque.asp?color=red&Board=PL
Health Insurer #38 .... www.mass.gov/doi/Companies/companies_lists.html
Health Officer, Certified #12 .... http://license.reg.state.ma.us/pubLic/licque.asp?color=red&Board=HO
Health Profession, Allied #7 .... http://license.reg.state.ma.us/pubLic/licque.asp?color=red&Board=AH
HMO #38 .... www.mass.gov/doi/Consumer/CSS_health_HMO_Licensed.HTML
Hoisting Machinery Operator, Forklift, etc. #27 .... www.mass.gov/dps/Lic_srch.htm
Home Improvement Supervisor #18 .... www.mass.gov/bbrs/Hicsearch.htm
Home Improvement Contractor #3 .... www.mass.gov/bbrs/Hicsearch.htm
Home Inspector #7 .... http://license.reg.state.ma.us/pubLic/v_list_hi.asp
Insurance Advisor/Adjuster #38 .... www.mass.gov/doi/Producer/Producer_list.html
Insurance Agent/Broker #38 .... www.mass.gov/doi/Producer/Producer_list.html
Insurance Premium Financer #35 .... www.mass.gov/dob/liclist.htm

Insurance, Domestic/Foreign Company #38 .... www.mass.gov/doi/Companies/companies_lists.html
Investment Advisor #49 .... www.nasdr.com
Land Surveyor #7 .... http://license.reg.state.ma.us/pubLic/licque.asp?color=red&Board=EN
Landscape Architect #42 .... http://license.reg.state.ma.us/pubLic/licque.asp?color=red&Board=LA
Loan Company, Small #35 .... www.mass.gov/dob/liclist.htm
Lobbyist/Lobbyist Employer #21 .... http://db.state.ma.us/SEC/PRE/search.asp
Lobstering #34 .... www.mass.gov/dfwele/dmf/
Lumber Producer, Native #3 .... www.mass.gov/bbrs/lumber.pdf
Lumber Producer, Native #3 .... www.mass.gov/bbrs/lumber99.PDF
Manufactured Building Producer #3 .... www.mass.gov/bbrs/MFB.htm
Marriage & Family Therapist #7 .... http://license.reg.state.ma.us/pubLic/licque.asp?query=personal&color=red&board=MH
Medical Doctor #53 .... http://profiles.massmedboard.org/Profiles/MA-Physician-Profile-Find-Doctor.asp
Mental Health & Human Svcs Prof., Allied #7 .... http://license.reg.state.ma.us/pubLic/licque.asp?query=personal&color=red&board=MH
Mental Health Counselor #7 .... http://license.reg.state.ma.us/pubLic/licque.asp?query=personal&color=red&board=MH
Mortgage Broker/Lender #48 .... www.mass.gov/dob/liclist.htm
Mortgage Broker/Lender #35 .... www.mass.gov/dob/liclist.htm
Motor Vehicle Sales Financer #35 .... www.mass.gov/dob/liclist.htm
Nuclear Power Plant Engineer/Operator #27 .... www.mass.gov/dps/Lic_srch.htm
Nurse, LPN/RN/Midwife #7 .... http://license.reg.state.ma.us/pubLic/licque.asp?color=red&Board=RN
Nursing Home Administrator #12 .... http://license.reg.state.ma.us/pubLic/licque.asp?color=red&Board=NH
Nursing Home/Rest Home #45 .... www.medicare.gov/NHCompare/Home.asp
Occupational Therapist/Assistant #7 .... http://license.reg.state.ma.us/pubLic/licque.asp?color=red&Board=AH
Oil Burner Technician/Contractor #27 .... www.mass.gov/dps/Lic_srch.htm
Optician #0 .... http://license.reg.state.ma.us/pubLic/licque.asp?query=personal&color=red&board=DO
Optician, Dispensing #7 .... http://license.reg.state.ma.us/pubLic/licque.asp?color=red&Board=DO
Optometrist #7 .... http://license.reg.state.ma.us/pubLic/licque.asp?color=red&Board=OP
P&C Insurance Agency #38 .... www.mass.gov/doi/Producer/Producer_list.html
Perfusionist #7 .... http://license.reg.state.ma.us/pubLic/licque.asp?color=red&Board=PF
Pharmacist #7 .... http://license.reg.state.ma.us/pubLic/licque.asp?color=red&Board=PH
Physical Therapist/Assistant #7 .... http://license.reg.state.ma.us/pubLic/licque.asp?color=red&Board=AH
Physician Assistant #13 .... http://license.reg.state.ma.us/pubLic/licque.asp?color=red&Board=AP
Pipefitter #27 .... www.mass.gov/dps/Lic_srch.htm
Plumber #7 .... http://license.reg.state.ma.us/pubLic/licque.asp?color=red&Board=PL
Podiatrist #7 .... http://license.reg.state.ma.us/pubLic/licque.asp?color=red&Board=PD
Psychologist, Educational #7 .... http://license.reg.state.ma.us/pubLic/licque.asp?query=personal&color=red&board=MH
Psychologist/Provider #12 .... http://license.reg.state.ma.us/pubLic/licque.asp?color=red&Board=PY
Public Accountant-CPA #7 .... http://license.reg.state.ma.us/pubLic/licque.asp?color=red&Board=PA
Radio & TV Repair Technician #7 .... http://license.reg.state.ma.us/pubLic/licque.asp?color=red&Board=TV
Real Estate Agent/Broker/Sales #7 .... http://license.reg.state.ma.us/pubLic/licque.asp?color=red&Board=RE
Real Estate Appraiser #7 .... http://license.reg.state.ma.us/pubLic/licque.asp?color=red&Board=RA
Refrigeration Technician/Contractor #27 .... www.mass.gov/dps/Lic_srch.htm
Rehabilitation Therapist #7 .... http://license.reg.state.ma.us/pubLic/licque.asp?query=personal&color=red&board=MH
Residential Care, Youth #52 .... www.qualitychildcare.org/residential_search.asp
Respiratory Care Therapist #7 .... http://license.reg.state.ma.us/pubLic/licque.asp?color=red&Board=RC
Retail Installment Financer #35 .... www.mass.gov/dob/liclist.htm
Sales Finance Company #48 .... www.mass.gov/dob/liclist.htm
Sanitarian #42 .... http://license.reg.state.ma.us/pubLic/licque.asp?color=red&Board=SA
Seafood Dealer #34 .... www.mass.gov/dfwele/dmf/
Securities Agent #49 .... www.nasdr.com
Securities Broker/Dealer #49 .... www.nasdr.com
Shellfishing, Commercial #34 .... www.mass.gov/dfwele/dmf/
Social Worker #7 .... http://license.reg.state.ma.us/pubLic/licque.asp?color=red&Board=SW
Speech-Language Pathologist/Audiologist #7 .... http://license.reg.state.ma.us/pubLic/licque.asp?color=red&Board=SP
Surplus Lines Broker #38 .... www.mass.gov/doi/Producer/Producer_list.html
Taxidermist #34 .... www.mass.gov/dfwele/dfw/
Third party Inspection Agency (Bldg.) #3 .... www.mass.gov/bbrs/MFB.htm
Trapping #34 .... www.mass.gov/dfwele/dfw/
Veterinarian #7 .... http://license.reg.state.ma.us/pubLic/licque.asp?color=red&Board=VT
Water Supply Facility Operator #7 .... http://license.reg.state.ma.us/pubLic/licque.asp?color=red&Board=DW

Massachusetts Licensing Quick Finder

Acupuncturist #5	617-727-3086
Adjuster, Fire Loss #38	617-521-7794
Adoption Center #52	617-626-2069
Aerial Passenger Cable Car #27	617-727-3200 x662
Aesthetician #7	617-727-9940
Aircraft/Airport Manager #46	617-973-8883
Alarm Installer, Burglar/Fire #7	617-727-9931
Alcoholic Bev/Wine Transporter #1	617-727-3040
Alcoholic Beverage/Wine Sales/Broker/Whlse #1	617-727-3040
Alcoholism/Drug Facility/Program #15	617-624-5111
Ambulance Service #14	617-753-7300
Ambulatory Surgical Center #45	617-753-8000
Amusement Device Inspector #27	617-727-3200 x607
Appraiser (MVD) #47	617-521-7453
Appraiser, MVR Damage #38	617-521-7447
Architect #42	617-727-3072
Asbestos/Lead Abatement #24	617-727-7047
Athletic Trainer #7	617-727-3071
Attorney #2	617-728-8800
Auctioneer /Auctioneer School #43	617-727-3480
Auto Repair Shop, Registered #38	617-727-3480
Automobile Dealer #48	617-956-1500 x501
Automobile Sales Finance Co.#48	617-956-1500 x501
Bank/Savings Institution #35	617-956-1500
Barber/Barber Shop #7	617-727-7367
Birthing Center #45	617-753-8000
Blood Bank #45	617-753-8000
Boiler Engineer #27	617-727-3200
Boilers/Pressure Vessels Inspector #27	617-727-3200 x607
Boxer #50	617-727-3200 x25257
Boxing Judge/Referee/Trainer/2nd #50	617-727-3200 x25257
Boxing Physician #50	617-727-3200 x25257
Boxing Professional #50	617-727-3200 x25257
Boxing Timekeeper/Mgr/Promoter #50	617-727-3200 x25257
Brewery/Pub/Sacramental Wine #1	617-727-3040
Brewery/Winery Storage/Farmer #1	617-727-3040
Brokerage Firm #49	617-727-3548
Building Inspector/Local Inspector #3	617-727-7532
Building Producer #3	617-727-7532
Bus/Motor Coach Driver #31	617-305-3559
Cattle Dealer/Transporter #19	617-626-1700
Chair Lift #27	617-727-3200 x662
Check Casher/Seller #35	617-956-1500
Chiropractor #7	617-727-3093
Cigarette Seller #32	617-887-5090
Clinic #45	617-753-8000
Collection Agency #35	617-956-1500
Concrete Technician #3	617-727-7532
Concrete Testing Laboratory #3	617-727-7532
Construction Supervisor, Resid'l #3	617-727-7532
Construction Supervisor #18	617-727-7532 x25205
Consumer Credit Grantor #35	617-956-1500
Contractor, Home Improvem't #3	508-821-9375 x502
Cosmetologist/Manicurist/Aesthet'n #7	617-727-9940
Credit Union #35	617-956-1500
Day Care Center #52	617-626-2069
Day Care Center Teacher/Director #52	617-626-2069
Dentist/Dental Examiner /Hygienist #7	617-727-9928
Domestics Agency #22	617-727-3696
Electrician #7	617-727-9931
Electrologist #7	617-727-9957
Elevator Construct/n/Maint.#27	617-727-3200 x25238
Elevator Operator #27	617-727-3200 x25238
Embalmer #40	617-727-1718
Emergency Medical Technician #14	617-753-7300
Employment Agency, Placement/Temporary #22	617-727-3696
Engineer #7	617-727-9957
Exterminator #19	617-626-1776
Family Child Care Assistant #52	617-626-2069
Family Child Care Provider #52	617-626-2069
Finfishing, Commercial #34	617-626-1520
Fire Protectionn Sprinkler Contr./Fitter #27	617-727-3200 x607
Firemen / Engineer #27	617-727-3200 x607
Foreign Transmittal Agency #35	617-956-1500
Foster Care Provider #52	617-626-2069
Funeral Director #40	617-727-1718
Fur Buyer #34	617-626-1590
Gas Fitter #7	617-727-9952
Gas Station Owner #43	617-727-3480
Guard Dog/Hearing Dog Business #19	617-626-1786
Hairdresser #7	617-727-9940
Health Care Plan, Managed #38	617-521-7372
Health Insurer #38	617-521-7794
Health Officer, Certified #12	617-727-3074
Health Profession, Allied #7	617-727-3071
HMO #38	617-521-7794
Hoisting Machinery (Forklift, Hydraulic, Crane) Operator #27	617-727-3200 x607
Home Health Care Provider #22	617-727-3696
Home Improvement Supr. #18	617-727-7532 x25207
Home Improvement Contr. #3	508-821-9375 x502
Home Inspector #7	617-727-4459
Horse (Equine) Dealer #19	617-626-1797
Horse/Greyhound #16	617-727-2581
Hospice #45	617-753-8000
Hospital #45	617-753-8000
Insurance Advisor/Adjuster #38	617-521-7794
Insurance Agent/Broker #38	617-521-7794
Insurance Premium Financer #35	617-956-1500
Insurance, Domestic/Foreign Company #38	617-321-7391
Investment Advisor #49	617-727-3548
Jockey #16	617-727-2581
Justice of the Peace #44	617-725-4016 x5
Laboratory, Medical-related #45	617-753-8000
Land Surveyor #7	617-727-9957
Landscape Architect #42	617-727-3072
Lead Inspector #24	617-727-7047
Library Media Specialist #17	781-338-3000 x6600
Loan Company, Small #48	617-956-1500 x501
Lobbyist/Lobbyist Employer #21	617-878-3434
Lobstering #34	617-626-1520
Lumber Producer, Native #3	617-727-3636 x561
Mammography Radiologic Tech. #26	617- 427 2944
Manicurist #7	617-727-9940
Manufactured Building Producer #3	617-727-7532
Marriage & Family Therapist #7	617-727-3071
Medical Doctor #53	617-654-9800
Mental Health & Human Svcs Professional, Allied #7	617-727-3071
Mental Health Counselor #7	617-727-3071
Milk Plant #19	617-626-1811
Modeling Industry/Agency #22	617-727-3696
Mortgage Broker/Lender #48	617-956-1500 x501
Motion Picture Operator #27	617-727-3200 x25223
Motor Vehicle Repair Shop (Auto Body/ Glass/etc.) #43	617-727-3480
Motor Vehicle Sales Financer #35	617-956-1500
Nanny Agency #22	617-727-3696
Notary Public #44	617-725-4016 x1
Nuclear Medicine Technologists (Radiologists) #26	617- 427 2944
Nuclear Power Plant Engineer/Operator #27	617-727-3200 x607
Nurse, LPN/RN/Midwife #7	617-727-9961
Nursery #19	617-626-1801
Nursery Agent #19	617-626-1801
Nurses' Aide in Long Term Care Facility #45	617-753-8143
Nursing Home Administrator #12	617-727-3074
Nursing Home/Rest Home #45	617-753-8000
Occupational Therapist/Assistant #7	617-727-3071
Oil Burner Technician/Contr. #27	617-727-3200 x607
Optician, Dispensing #7	617-727-3093
Optometrist #7	617-727-3093
Out-Patient Rehabilitation Facility #45	617-753-8000
Owner/Trainer, Horse/Greyhound #16	617-727-2581
P&C Insurance Agency #38	617-521-7794
Pasteurization Plant #19	617-626-1811
Peddler/Hawker #43	617-727-3480
Perfusionist #7	617-727-4499
Personal Agent #27	617-727-3200 x637
Pesticide Applicator/Dealer #19	617-626-1776
Pet Shop #19	617-626-1795
Pharmacist #7	617-727-9953
Physical Therapist/Assistant #7	617-727-3071
Physician Assistant #13	617-727-3074
Pipefitter #27	617-727-3200 x607
Plumber #7	617-727-9952
Podiatrist #7	617-727-1747
Private Detective/Investigator #33	978-538-6128
Psychologist, Educational #7	617-727-3071
Psychologist/Provider #12	617-727-3074
Public Accountant-CPA #7	617-727-1806
Racetrack, Horse/Greyhound #16	617-727-2581
Radiation Therapy/Radiologic Technologist #26	617- 427 2944
Radio & TV Repair Technician #7	617-727-3074
Radiographer #26	617- 427 2944
Radiologic Technologist #26	617- 427 2944
Radon Specialist #26	617- 427 2944
Real Estate Agent/Broker/Sales #7	617-727-2373
Real Estate Appraiser #7	617-727-3055
Refrigeration Tech./Contr. #27	617-727-3200 x607
Rehabilitation Therapist #7	617-727-3071
Renal Dialysis (End Stage) #45	617-753-8000
Residential Care, Youth #52	617-626-2069
Respiratory Care Therapist #7	617-727-1747
Retail Installment Financer #35	617-956-1500
Riding Instructor #19	617-626-1797
Riding School #19	617-626-1797
Sales Finance Company #48	617-956-1500 x501
Sanitarian #42	617-727-3072
School Administrator #17	781-338-3000 x6600
School Bus #31	617-305-3559
School Guidance Counselor #17	781-338-3000 x6600
Seafood Dealer #34	617-626-1520
Securities Agent #49	617-727-3548
Securities Broker/Dealer #49	617-727-3548
Security Guard Agency #33	978-538-6128
Shellfishing, Commercial #34	617-626-1520
Simulcast & Inter-Track Wagering #16	617-727-2581
Ski Tow #27	617-727-3200 x662
Skimobile #27	617-727-3200 x662
Social Worker #7	617-727-3073
Speech-Language Pathologist/Audiologist #7	617-727-1747
Stable (Horse & Buggy Operator) #19	617-626-1797
Surplus Lines Broker #38	617-521-7794
Swine Dealer #19	617-626-1700
Taxidermist #34	617-626-1590
Teacher #17	781-338-3000 x6600
Theatrical Booking Agent #27	617-727-3200 x637
Third party Inpection Agency #3	617-727-7532
Ticket Reseller #27	617-727-3200 x637
Tramway Inspector #27	617-727-3200 x662
Trapping #34	617-626-1590
Trust Company #35	617-956-1500
Vending Machine #25	617-983-6712
Vendor, Transient #43	617-727-3480
Veterinarian #7	617-727-3080
Water Supply Facility Operator #7	617-727-3074
Weights & Measures #43	617-727-3480
Wine & Malt Beverage Permit #1	617-727-3040

Massachusetts Licensing Agency Information

1 Alcoholic Beverages Control Commission, 239 Causeway St #200, Boston, MA 02114-2130; 617-727-3040, Fax: 617-727-1258.
www.mstc.state.ms.us/abc/main.htm
Email: errol.flynn@state.ma.us

2 Board of Overseers Registry Dept, Board of Bar Examiners, 99 High Street, Boston, MA 02110; 617-728-8700, Fax: 617-482-8000.
http://massbbo.org/
Search Database at http://massbbo.org

3 Board of Building Regulations & Standards, Construction-related Licensing Programs, 1 Ashburton Place, Rm 1301, Boston, MA 02108; 617-727-7532, Fax: 617-727-1754.
www.mass.gov/bbrs/
Email: david.bratton@eps.state.ma.us Search Database at www.mass.gov/bbrs/programs.htm

5 Committee on Acupuncture, Board of Registration in Medicine, 560 Harrison Ave #G-4, Boston, MA 02118;
617-654-9800, Fax: 617-451-9568.
www.massmedboard.org/acupuncture.htm
Email: nick@docboard.org

7 Division of Registration, Boards of Registration & Exams, 239 Causeway St #400, Boston, MA 02114-2130; 617-727-3074, Fax: 617-727-2197.
www.state.ma.us/reg/home.htm
Email: REG.WebMaster@State.ma.us Search Database at http://license.reg.state.ma.us/pubLic/licque.asp

12 Division of Registration, Boards of Registration of Nursing Home Admin., 239 Causeway St #400, Boston, MA 02114-2130; 617-727-3074, Fax: 617-727-2197.
www.state.ma.us/reg/home.htm Search at: www.state.ma.us/reg/apps/reg15.htm

13 Division of Professional Licensure, Boards of Registration of Physicians Assistants, 239 Causeway Street, Suite 500, Boston, MA 02114; 617-727-3074, Fax: 617-727-2197.
www.state.ma.us/reg/boards/ap/default.htm
Search Database at
http://license.reg.state.ma.us/pubLic/licque.asp

14 Office of Emergency Medical Services, 2 Boylston St 3rd Floor, Boston, MA 02116-4737; 617-753-7300, Fax: 617-753-7320.
www.state.ma.us/dph/oems

15 Department of Public Health, Bureau of Substance Abuse Services, 250 Washington St, 3rd Fl, Boston, MA 02108;
617-624-5111, Fax: 617-624-5185.
www.state.ma.us/dph/bsas/
Email: bsas.questions@state.ma.us

16 Consumer Department, Racing Commission, 1 Ashburton Place, 13th Fl, Rm 1313, Boston, MA 02108; 617-727-2581, Fax: 617-227-6062.
www.state.ma.us/src

17 Division of Educational Personnel, Department of Education & Arts, 350 Main St, Malven, MA 02148; 781-338-3000 x6600, Fax: 781-338-3391.
www.doe.mass.edu/cert

18 Home Improvement Contractor/Construction Supervisor Licensing, Board of Build Regulations and Standards, 1 Ashburton Pl, Rm 1301, Boston, MA 02108; 617-727-7532.
www.state.ma.us/bbrs/programs.htm Search at: www.state.ma.us/bbrs/programs.htm

19 Department of Food & Agriculture, Pesticide Bureau, 251 Causeway St, Ste 500, Boston, MA 02114-2151; 617-626-1776, Fax: 617-626-1850.
www.mass.gov/agr/ Email: lee.corte-real@state.ma.us

21 Secretary of the Commonwealth, Lobbyist & Lobbyist Employer Directory, One Ashburton Place, Room 1719, Boston, MA 02108; 617-878-3434, Fax: 617-727-5914.
www.state.ma.us/sec/pre/prelob/
Email: lob@sec.state.ma.us Search Database at http://db.state.ma.us/SEC/PRE/search.asp

22 Division of Occupational Safety, Employment Agency Prog., 399 Washington St, 5th Fl, Boston, MA 02108; 617-727-3696, Fax: 617-727-7568.
www.state.ma.us/dos/pages/employ.htm

24 Department of Occupational Safety, Licensing Division, Labor & Workforce Development, 399 Washington St, 5th Fl, Boston, MA 02100-5212; 617-727-7047, Fax: 617-727-7568.
www.state.ma.us/dos

25 Department of Public Health, Divison of Food & Drugs, 305 South St, Jamaica Plain, MA 02130; 617-983-6712, Fax: 617-524-8062.
www.state.ma.us/dph mail: mark.leccese@state.ma.us

26 Radiation Control Program, Department of Public Health, 90 Washington Street, Dorchester, MA 02121; 617- 427 2944, Fax: 617-727-2098.
www.state.ma.us/dph

27 Department of Public Safety, 1 Ashburton Pl, 13th Fl, Rm 1301, Boston, MA 02108; 617-727-3200 x623, Fax: 617-727-5732.
www.state.ma.us/dps email: MailBox.DPS@state.ma.us

31 Department of Telecommunications and Energy, Transportation Division, 1 South Sta #2, Boston, MA 02110-2208;
617-305-3559, Fax: 617-478-2598. www.state.ma.us/dpu/transportation/transportation.htm

32 Department of Revenue, Excises Unit, PO Box 7012, Boston, MA 02204;
617-887-5090, Fax: 617-887-5039.
www.dor.state.ma.us/cigarette/cigarette.htm
Email: dortsd@shore.net

33 Department of State Police, Certification Unit, 485 Maple St, Danvers, MA 01923;
978-538-6128, Fax: 978-538-6021.
www.state.ma.us/msp/
Email: webmaster@eps.state.ma.us

34 Department of Fisheries, Wildlife & Environmental Enforcement, Division of Fish & Wildlife, 251 Causeway St #S-400, Boston, MA 02114-2104; 617-626-1500, Fax: 617-626-1505.
www.state.ma.us/dfwele/dpt_toc.htm
Email: steve.mcrae@state.ma.us

35 Division of Banks & Loan Agencies, 1 South Station, 3rd FL, Boston, MA 02110;
617-956-1500, Fax: 617-956-1599.
www.state.ma.us/dob
email: bernard.n.waxman@state.ma.us
Search Database at www.mass.gov/dob/liclist.htm

38 Division of Insurance, Agents & Brokers Licensing, One South Station, 5th Fl, Boston, MA 02110-2208; 617-521-7794, Fax: 617-521-7772.
www.state.ma.us/doi Search Database at www.mass.gov/doi/Consumer/CSS_health.html
Note: For searching, this agency provides lists which you can view or download.

40 Division of Registration, Board of Funeral Directors & Embalmers, 239 Causeway St #500, Boston, MA 02114-2130;
617-727-1718, Fax: 617-727-2197.
www.state.ma.us/reg/boards/em/default.htm
Search Database at http://license.reg.state.ma.us/pubLic/licque.asp?color=red&Board=EM

42 Division of Regulation of Architecture, 239 Causeway St #500, Boston, MA 02114; 617-727-3072, Fax: 617-727-2197.
www.state.ma.us/reg/boards/ar/default.htm
Email: REG.Webmaster@State.ma.us
Search Database at www.mass.gov/dpl/

43 Division of Standards, 1 Ashburton Pl, Boston, MA 02108; 617-727-3480, Fax: 617-727-5705.
www.state.ma.us/standards
Email: charles.carroll@state.ma.us
Search Database at
www.state.ma.us/standards/license.htm

44 Governor's Council, Public Records Division, State House, Rm 184, Boston, MA 02133; 617-725-4016.
www.state.ma.us/sec/pre/preidx.htm

45 Department of Public Health, Health Care Quality, 10 West St, 5th Fl, Boston, MA 02111; 617-753-8000, Fax: 617-753-8095.
www.state.ma.us/dph/dhcq/hcqskel.htm

46 Massachusetts Aeronautics Commission, 10 Park Plaza, Rm 6620, Boston, MA 02116-3966; 617-973-8881, Fax: 617-973-8889.
www.massaeronautics.org/default.htm

47 Division of Insurance, Motor Vehicle Damage Appraisers Licensing Board, 1 South Station, 5th Fl, Boston, MA 02110; 617-521-7447, Fax: 617-521-7576.
www.state.ma.us/doi/mvda/Mvda_home.html

48 Consumer Compliance Unit, Division of Banks, 1 South Station, 3rd Fl, Boston, MA 02110; 617-956-1500 x501, Fax: 617-956-1599.
www.state.ma.us/dob
Search Database at www.mass.gov/dob/liclist.htm

49 Securities Division, Licensing and Registration Section, 1 Ashburton Place, 17th Fl, Boston, MA 02108; 617-727-3548, Fax: 617-248-0177.
www.state.ma.us/sec/sct/sctidx.htm
Email: securities@sec.state.ma.us
Search Database at www.nasdr.com

50 Boxing Commission, 1 Ashburton Pl, Rm 1301, Boston, MA 02108;
617-727-3200 x25257, Fax: 617-727-5732.
www.state.ma.us/dps/Boxing.htm Search at: www.state.ma.us/mbc/ranking.htm

52 Executive Office of Human Svcs, Office for Children, Staff Qualifications, 1 Ashburton Pl Rm 1105, Boston, MA 02108-1518; 617-626-2069, Fax: 617-626-2027. www.qualitychildcare.org
Search Database at
www.qualitychildcare.org/childcare_finding.asp

53 Board of Registration in Medicine, 560 Harrison Ave G4, Boston, MA 02118; 617-654-9800, 800-377-0550, Fax: 617-451-9568.
www.massmedboard.org
Email: webmaster@massmedboard.org Search at: www.docboard.org/ma/df/name.html

Massachusetts Federal Courts

The following list indicates the district and division name for each county in the state. If the bankruptcy court location is different from the district court, then the location of the bankruptcy court appears in parentheses.

County/Court Cross Reference

Barnstable	Boston	Hampshire	Springfield (Worcester)
Berkshire	Springfield (Worcester)	Middlesex	Boston
Bristol	Boston	Nantucket	Boston
Dukes	Boston	Norfolk	Boston
Essex	Boston	Plymouth	Boston
Franklin	Springfield (Worcester)	Suffolk	Boston
Hampden	Springfield (Worcester)	Worcester	Worcester

Standards for Federal Courts: See Maine or Michigan Federal Courts section for information on Federal Courts standards and fees.

US District Court

District of Massachusetts

Boston Division U.S. Courthouse, 1 Courthouse Way Ste 2300, Boston, MA 02210 (courier address: Use mail address for courier delivery) 617-748-9152, Fax: 617-748-9096. www.mad.uscourts.gov

Barnstable, Bristol, Dukes, Essex, Middlesex, Nantucket, Norfolk, Plymouth, Suffolk.

Indexing & Storage: New cases available in the index 1 day to 1 week after filing date. The civil and criminal database dates from the early 1900's until the present. Records available when they are not in the possession of the judge or his/her clerks.

Fee & Payment: Payment may be made by money order, cashier check, personal check. Payee: Clerk, U.S. District Court.

Phone Search: No searching by telephone.

Mail Search: A SASE not required.

In Person Search: Fee charged if court conducts your in person search for you.

PACER: PACER is available online at http://pacer.mad.uscourts.gov. Document images available. Records purged every 12 months. New records are online after 1 day.

Electronic Filing: Electronic filing information online at https://ecf.mad.uscourts.gov

Springfield Division 1550 Main St, Springfield, MA 01103 (courier address: Use mail address for courier delivery) 413-785-0015, Fax: 413-785-0204. www.mad.uscourts.gov

Berkshire, Franklin, Hampden, Hampshire.

Indexing & Storage: New cases available in the index immediately after filing date. There is a microfiche index for pre-1989 cases. The civil and criminal database dates from July 1979. Records are not available when they are in the possession of a judge or a judge's clerk.

Fee & Payment: Payment may be made by money order, cashier check, personal check. Payee: Clerk, U.S. Court. Will fax results at $.50 per page.

Phone Search: Docket information available over the phone if Clerk has time. Will fax results at $.50 per page. **Mail Search:** A SASE not required.

In Person Search: Fee charged if court conducts your in person search for you.

PACER: PACER is available online at http://pacer.mad.uscourts.gov. Document images available. Records purged every 12 months. New records are online after 1 day.

Electronic Filing: Electronic filing information online at https://ecf.mad.uscourts.gov

Worcester Division 595 Main St., Room 502, Worcester, MA 01608 (courier address: Use mail address for courier delivery) 508-929-9900. www.mad.uscourts.gov   **Counties:** Worcester.

Indexing & Storage: New cases available in the index immediately after filing date. Indexes are on computer from 1988 and on microfiche from 1981. Earlier indexes are in storage from the early 1900's. Records are not available when in the possession of a judge or the judge's clerks.

Fee & Payment: Payment may be made by money order, cashier check, personal check. Payee: Clerk, U.S. District Court.

Phone Search: Only docket information available by telephone.

In Person Search: Fee charged if court conducts your in person search for you.

PACER: PACER is available online at http://pacer.mad.uscourts.gov. Document images available. Records purged every 12 months. New records are online after 1 day.

Electronic Filing: Electronic filing information online at https://ecf.mad.uscourts.gov

U.S. Bankruptcy Court

District of Massachusetts

Boston Division Room 1101, 10 Causeway, Boston, MA 02222-1074 (courier address: Use mail address for courier delivery) 617-565-8950, Fax: 617-565-6651. www.mab.uscourts.gov

Counties: Barnstable, Bristol, Dukes, Essex (except towns assigned to Worcester Division), Nantucket, Norfolk (except towns assigned to Worcester Division), Plymouth, Suffolk, and the following towns in Middlesex: Arlington, Belmont, Burlington, Everett, Lexington, Malden, Medford, Melrose, Newton, North Reading, Reading, Stoneham, Wakefield, Waltham, Watertown, Wilmington, Winchester and Woburn.

Indexing & Storage: Cases indexed by debtor as well as by case number. New cases available in the index immediately after filing date.

Fee & Payment: Payment may be made by money order, cashier check, personal check. Copy fees will be billed after the search is completed. Checks are not accepted from debtors. Payee: U.S. Bankruptcy Court.

Phone Search: Only general information will be released over the phone. Automated voice case information service (VCIS) is available. Call VCIS at 888-201-3572 or 617-565-6025.

In Person Search: Fee charged if court conducts your in person search for you.

PACER: PACER is available online at http://pacer.mab.uscourts.gov. Document images available. Records purged every 12 months. New civil records are online after 1 day.

Electronic Filing: Electronic filing information online at https://ecf.mab.uscourts.gov

Worcester Division 595 Main St, Room 211, Worcester, MA 01608 (courier address: Use mail address for courier delivery) 508-770-8900, Fax: 508-793-0189. www.mab.uscourts.gov

Berkshire, Franklin, Hampden, Hampshire, Middlesex (except towns assigned to the Boston Division), Worcester and the following towns: in Essex-Andover, Haverhill, Lawrence, Methuen and North Andover; in Norfolk-Bellingham, Franklin, Medway, Millis and Norfolk.

Indexing & Storage: Cases indexed by debtor as well as by case number. New cases available in the index immediately after filing date.

Fee & Payment: Payment may be made by money order, cashier check, personal check. Checks are not accepted from debtors. Payee: U.S. Bankruptcy Court.

Phone Search: Only docket information available by phone. Automated voice case information service (VCIS) is available. Call VCIS at 888-201-3572 or 617-565-6025.

Mail Search: A SASE not required.

In Person Search: Fee charged if court conducts your in person search for you.

PACER: PACER is available online at http://pacer.mab.uscourts.gov. Document images available. Records purged every 12 months. New civil records are online after 1 day.

Electronic Filing: Electronic filing information online at https://ecf.mab.uscourts.gov

Massachusetts County Courts

Court	Jurisdiction	No. of Courts	How Organized
Superior Courts*	General	19	14 Counties
District Courts*	General	68	62 Geographic Divisions
Boston Municipal Court*	General	1	
Housing Courts*	General	7	
Probate and Family Courts*	Probate	15	14 Counties
Juvenile Courts	Special	7	11 Divisions
Land Court	Special	1	

* Profiled in this Sourcebook.

Court	CIVIL								
	Tort	Contract	Real Estate	Min. Claim	Max. Claim	Small Claims	Estate	Eviction	Domestic Relations
Superior Courts*	X	X	X	$25,000	No Max				
District Courts*	X	X	X	$0	No Max	$2000	X	X	X
Boston Municipal Court*	X	X	X	$0	No Max	$2000			X
Housing Courts*			X	$0	No Max	$2000			
Probate and Family Courts*							X		X
Juvenile Courts									
Land Court			X						

Court	CRIMINAL				
	Felony	Misdemeanor	DWI/DUI	Preliminary Hearing	Juvenile
Superior Courts*	X				
District Courts*	X	X	X	X	X
Boston Municipal Court*		X	X		
Housing Courts*		X		X	
Probate and Family Courts*					
Juvenile Courts					X
Land Court					

ADMINISTRATION   Chief Justice for Administration and Management, 2 Center Plaza, Room 540, Boston, MA, 02108; 617-742-8575, Fax: 617-742-0968. www.mass.gov/courts/admin/index.html

COURT STRUCTURE   The various court sections are called "Departments." While Superior and District Courts have concurrent jurisdiction in civil cases, the practice is to assign cases less than $25,000 to the District Court and those over $25,000 to Superior Court. In addition to misdemeanors, District Courts and Boston Municipal Courts have jurisdiction over certain minor felonies. . In July 2003, the state mandated that the certification fee be $2.50 and the copy fee be $1.00 per page for all Superior and District Courts.

Eviction cases may be filed at a county District Court or at the regional "Housing Court." A case may be moved from a District Court to a Housing Court, but never the reverse. They also hear misdemeanor "Code Violation" cases and prelims for these. There are five Housing Court Regions - Boston (Suffolk County), Worcester (County), Southeast (Plymouth and

Bristol Counties), Northeast (Essex County), and Western (Berkshire, Franklin, Hampden and Hampshire Counties). The Southeast Housing Court has three branches - Brockton, Fall River, and New Bedford

ONLINE ACCESS Opinions to the Mass Supreme and Appellate courts can be found at http://massreports.com/. An online access to records on the statewide Trial Courts Information Center web site is only available to attorneys and law firms. For more information, Contact Peter Nylin by email at nylin_p@jud.state.ma.us. Site updated daily.

PROBATE COURTS There are more than 20 Probate and Family Court locations in MA - one per county plus two each in Bristol, plus a Middlesex satellite in Cambridge and Lawrence.

Barnstable County

Superior Court 3195 Main St, PO Box 425, Barnstable, MA 02630; 508-375-6684. Hours: 8:30AM-4:30PM (EST). *Felony, Civil Actions Over $25,000.*
Note: Their public access terminal is connected to the statewide Superior Court system.
Civil Records: Access: In person only. Visitors must perform in person searches for themselves. No search fee. Required to search: name, years to search; also helpful: address. Civil cases indexed by defendant, plaintiff. Civil records on computer back to 1/2001; on index cards from 1985 and books from 1830s.
Criminal Records: Access: In person only. Visitors must perform in person searches themselves. No search fee. Required to search: name, years to search, DOB; also helpful: address, SSN. Criminal records on computer back to 1/2001; on index cards from 1985 and books from 1830s.
General Information: Public Access terminal is available. No victims names released. Copy fee: $1.00 per page. Certification fee: $2.50. Payee: Barnstable Superior Court. Business checks not accepted. Prepayment required.

Barnstable District Court Route 6A, PO Box 427, Barnstable, MA 02630; 508-375-6600. Hours: 8:30AM-4:30PM (EST). *Felony, Misdemeanor, Civil, Eviction, Small Claims.*
Note: Includes Barnstable, Yarmouth, and Sandwich.
Civil Records: Access: Phone, mail, in person. Only the court performs in person searches; visitors may not. No search fee. Required to search: name, years to search. Civil cases indexed by defendant, plaintiff. Civil records on index cards and docket books.
Criminal Records: Access: Phone, mail, in person. Only the court performs in person searches; visitors may not. No search fee. Required to search: name, years to search; also helpful: DOB. Criminal records on computer since 1996; prior records on index cards and docket books.
General Information: No impounded records released. Copy fee: $1.00 per page. Certification fee: $2.50. Payee: District Court. Only cashiers checks and money orders accepted. Prepayment required. Mail turnaround time 1-2 weeks.

Falmouth District Court 161 Jones Rd, Falmouth, MA 02540; 508-495-1500; Fax: 505-495-0992. Hours: 8:30AM-4:30PM (EST). *Felony, Misdemeanor, Civil, Eviction, Small Claims.*
Note: Includes Falmouth, Mashpee, and Bourne.
Civil Records: Access: Phone, in person. Only the court performs in person searches; visitors may not. No search fee. Required to search: name, years to search. Civil cases indexed by defendant, plaintiff. Civil records computerized since 1996.
Criminal Records: Access: Phone, in person. Only the court performs in person searches; visitors may not. No search fee. Required to search: name, years to search. Criminal records computerized since 1996.
General Information: No impounded records released. Copy fee: $1.00 per page. Certification fee:

$2.50. Payee: Falmouth District Court. Personal checks accepted. Prepayment required.

Orleans District Court 237 Rock Harbor Rd, Orleans, MA 02653; 508-255-4700. Hours: 8:30AM-4:30PM (EST). *Felony, Misdemeanor, Civil, Eviction, Small Claims.*
Note: Includes Brewster, Chatham, Dennis, Eastham, Orleans, Truro, Wellfleet, Harwich, Provincetown.
Civil Records: Access: In person only. Visitors must perform in person searches for themselves. No search fee. Required to search: name, years to search. Civil cases indexed by defendant, plaintiff. Civil records kept in storage from 1978. Some prior records destroyed.
Criminal Records: Access: In person only. Visitors must perform in person searches for themselves. No search fee. Required to search: name, years to search. Criminal records kept in storage from 1978. Some prior records destroyed.
General Information: No impounded records released. Copy fee: $1.00 per page. Certification fee: $2.50. Payee: Orleans District Court. Personal checks accepted. Prepayment required.

Probate & Family Court PO Box 346, Barnstable, MA 02630; 508-375-6600; Fax: 508-362-3662. Hours: 8AM-4PM (EST). *Probate.*

Berkshire County

Superior Court 76 East St, Pittsfield, MA 01201; 413-499-7487; Fax: 413-442-9190. Hours: 8:30AM-4:30PM (EST). *Felony, Civil Actions Over $25,000.*
Civil Records: Access: Mail, in person. Both court and visitors may perform in person searches. No search fee. Required to search: name, years to search. Civil cases indexed by defendant, plaintiff. Civil records on index cards from 1900s, on computer back to 2000.
Criminal Records: Access: Mail, in person. Both court and visitors may perform in person searches. No search fee. Required to search: name, years to search. Criminal records on index cards from 1900s, on computer back to 2000. Because their index does not contain DOBs or SSNs, they cannot verify the subject, thus they recommend you contact the Criminal History Board in Boston, MA.
General Information: Public Access terminal is available. (Records go back to 2000.) No impounded records released. Copy fee: $1.00 per page. Certification fee: $2.50 per document. Payee: Berkshire Superior Court. Personal checks accepted. Prepayment required. Mail turnaround time 3-4 weeks.

North Berkshire District Court #28 City Hall - 10 Main St, North Adams, MA 01247; 413-663-5339; Fax: 413-664-7209. Hours: 8AM-4:30PM (EST). *Felony, Misdemeanor, Civil, Eviction, Small Claims.*
Note: Handles cases for Adams, Chesire, Clarksburg, Florida, Hancock, New Ashford, North Adams, Savoy, Williamstown, and Windsor. Exercises concurrent jurisdiction over Hancock and Windsor with the Pittsfield Division. Includes cases from closed Court #30.

Civil Records: Access: Fax, mail, in person. Only the court performs in person searches; visitors may not. No search fee. Required to search: name, years to search. Civil cases indexed by defendant, plaintiff. Civil records on index cards from 1983, docket books to 1900.
Criminal Records: Access: Fax, mail, in person. Only the court performs in person searches; visitors may not. No search fee. Required to search: name, years to search, DOB, SSN. Criminal records on index cards from 1983, docket books to 1900.
General Information: No impounded records released. Will fax results to local or toll free line. Copy fee: $1.00 per page. Certification fee: $2.50. Payee: District Court. Business checks accepted. Prepayment required. Mail turnaround time 1-2 weeks.

Pittsfield District Court #27 24 Wendell Ave, Pittsfield, MA 01201; 413-442-5468; Fax: 413-499-7327. Hours: 8:30AM-4:30PM (EST). *Felony, Misdemeanor, Civil, Eviction, Small Claims.*
Note: Includes Becket, Dalton, Hancock, Hinsdale, Lanesborough, Lenox, Peru, Pittsfield, Richmond, Washington and Windsor. This court exercises concurrent jurisdiction over Hancock and Windsor with the North Berkshire Divisions.
Civil Records: Access: Phone, mail, in person. No search fee. Required to search: name, years to search. Civil cases indexed by defendant, plaintiff. Civil records on docket books and in recent years in the computer.
Criminal Records: Access: Phone, mail, in person. No search fee. Required to search: name, years to search; DOB. Criminal records on docket books and in recent years in the computer.
General Information: Public Access terminal is available. No juvenile or sealed records released. Will fax results for $1.00 per page. Copy fee: $1.00 per page. Certification fee: $2.50. Payee: Pittsfield District Court. Personal checks accepted. Prepayment required. Mail requests: SASE required. Mail turnaround time 1-2 weeks.

South Berkshire District Court 9 Gilmore Ave, Great Barrington, MA 01230; 413-528-3520; Fax: 413-528-0757. Hours: 8:30AM-4:30PM (EST). *Felony, Misdemeanor, Civil, Eviction, Small Claims.*
Note: Includes Alford, Becket, Egremont, Great Barrington, Lee, Lenox, Monterey, Mt. Washington, New Marlborough, Otis, Sandisfield, Sheffield, Stockbridge, Tyringham, and West Stockbridge. Shares jurisdiction of Becket and Lenox with Pittsfield Dist. Court.
Civil Records: Access: Fax, mail, in person. Both court and visitors may perform in person searches. No search fee. Required to search: name, years to search. Civil cases indexed by defendant, plaintiff. Civil records on index cards from 1984, docket books to 1900. Court will only perform search if given the docket number.
Criminal Records: Access: Fax, mail, in person. Both court and visitors may perform in person searches. No search fee. Required to search: name, years to search, DOB. Criminal records on index

cards from 1984, docket books to 1900. Court will only do search if given docket number.

General Information: No juvenile, impounded records released. Copy fee: $1.00 per page. Certification fee: $2.50. Payee: District Court. Personal checks accepted. Prepayment required. Mail requests: SASE required. Mail turnaround time 1-2 weeks.

Probate & Family Court 44 Bank Row, Pittsfield, MA 01201; 413-442-6941; Fax: 413-443-3430. Hours: 8:30AM-4PM (EST). *Probate.*

Western Housing Court *Eviction, Misdemeanor (Code Violations), Small Claims.*
Note: See Hampden County Western Housing Court for many housing code cases, real estate-related small claims and eviction cases for this county; also see district courts in this county.

Bristol County

Superior Court - Taunton 9 Court St, Taunton, MA 02780; 508-823-6588 X1. Hours: 8AM-4:30PM (EST). *Felony, Civil Actions Over $25,000.*
Civil Records: Access: Mail, in person. Both court and visitors may perform in person searches. No search fee. Required to search: name, years to search. Civil cases indexed by defendant, plaintiff. Civil records on computer link to Boston from 1985, index books from 1935.
Criminal Records: Access: Mail, in person. Both court and visitors may perform in person searches. No search fee. Required to search: name, years to search; also helpful: DOB. Criminal records on computer link to Boston from 1985, index books from 1935.
General Information: Public Access terminal is available. No impounded records released. Copy fee: $1.00 per page. Certification fee: $2.50. Payee: Clerk of Superior Court of Bristol County. Personal checks accepted. Prepayment required. Mail turnaround time 2 weeks.

Attleboro District Court 34 Courthouse, 88 N Main St, Attleboro, MA 02703; 508-222-5900; Fax: 508-223-3916 crim; 508-222-4869 civ. Hours: 8AM-4:30PM (EST). *Felony, Misdemeanor, Civil, Eviction, Small Claims.*
Note: Includes Attleboro, Mansfield, North Attleboro, and Norton.
Civil Records: Access: Phone, mail, in person. Both court and visitors may perform in person searches. No search fee. Required to search: name, years to search. Civil cases indexed by defendant, plaintiff. Civil records on computer since 1995; prior records on index cards from 1983, docket books from 1900.
Criminal Records: Access: Phone, mail, in person. Only the court performs in person searches; visitors may not. No search fee. Required to search: name, years to search, DOB, SSN. Criminal records on computer since 1995; prior records on index cards from 1983, docket books from 1900.
General Information: Public Access terminal is available. (Civil and small claims only; terminal goes back to 2001.) No impounded records released. Copy fee: $1.00 per page. Certification fee: $2.50. Payee: District Court, Attleboro District Court. Business checks accepted. Prepayment required. Mail turnaround time 1-2 weeks.

Fall River District Court 45 Rock St, Fall River, MA 02720; 508-679-8161; Fax: 508-675-5477. Hours: 8AM-4:30PM (EST). *Felony, Misdemeanor, Civil, Eviction, Small Claims.*
Note: Includes Fall River, Freetown, Somerset, Swansea, and Westport.
Civil Records: Access: Mail, in person, fax. Both court and visitors may perform in person searches. No

search fee. Required to search: name, years to search. Civil cases indexed by defendant, plaintiff. Civil records on index on computer from 1989, on docket books in vault from 1985.
Criminal Records: Access: Mail, in person, fax. Both court and visitors may perform in person searches. No search fee. Required to search: name, years to search, DOB or SSN. Criminal records on index on computer from 1991, on docket books in vault from 1985.
General Information: No sealed, minor, confidential address records released. Fee to fax results is $.50 per page. Copy fee: $1.00 per page. Certification fee: $2.50 per page. Payee: District Court. Only cashiers checks and money orders accepted. Prepayment required. Mail requests: SASE requested. Turnaround time 1-2 weeks.

New Bedford District Court 33 75 N 6th St, New Bedford, MA 02740; 508-999-9700. Hours: 8:30AM-4PM (EST). *Felony, Misdemeanor, Civil, Eviction, Small Claims.*
Note: Includes Acushnet, Dartmouth, Fairhaven, Freetown, New Bedford, and Westport.
Civil Records: Access: Mail, in person. Only the court performs in person searches; visitors may not. No search fee. Required to search: name, years to search. Civil cases indexed by defendant, plaintiff. Civil records filed from 1989, prior on docket books; on computer back to 1995.
Criminal Records: Access: Mail, in person, fax. Only the court performs in person searches; visitors may not. No search fee. Required to search: name, years to search, DOB; also helpful: SSN. Criminal records filed from 1989, prior on docket books; on computer back to 1995. Searches are limited to pending charges, this agency recommends searching elsewhere for closed case files.
General Information: No impounded records released. Copy fee: $1.00 per page. Certification fee: $2.50. Payee: District Court. Business checks accepted. Prepayment required. Mail requests: SASE required. Mail turnaround time 1-2 weeks.

Taunton District Court 15 Court St, Taunton, MA 02780; 508-824-4032; Fax: 508-824-2282. 8:30AM-4:30PM (EST). *Felony, Misdemeanor, Civil, Eviction, Small Claims.*
Note: Includes Berkley, Dighton, Easton, Raynham, Rehoboth, Seekonk, and Taunton.
Civil Records: Access: Phone, mail, in person. Visitors must perform in person searches for themselves. No search fee. Required to search: name, years to search. Civil cases indexed by defendant, plaintiff. Civil records on index cards for 6 years; computerized records since 1980s.
Criminal Records: Access: Phone, mail, in person. Visitors must perform in person searches for themselves. No search fee. Required to search: name, years to search, DOB. Criminal records on index cards for 6 years; computerized records since 1980s.
General Information: Copy fee: $1.00 per page. Certification fee: $2.50. Payee: District Court. Personal checks accepted. Prepayment required. Mail turnaround time 1-2 days.

New Bedford Probate & Family Court 505 Pleasant St, New Bedford, MA 02740; 508-999-5249; Fax: 508-999-1269. Hours: 8AM-4:30PM (EST). *Probate.*

Southeast Housing Court - Fall River 289 Rock St., Fall River, MA 02720; 508-677-1505; Fax: 508-672-9621. Hours: 8AM-4PM (EST). *Eviction, Misdemeanor (Code Violations), Small Claims.*
Note: Also known as Fall River Trial Court. Includes housing code cases, real estate-related smalll claims,

and many eviction cases for Bristol County except the New Bedford area; also see district courts.

Southeast Housing Court - New Bedford 139 Hathaway Rd, New Bedford, MA 02740; 508-994-0156. Hours: 8AM-4PM Mon. & Fri. (EST). *Eviction, Misdemeanor (Code Violations), Small Claims.*
Note: Open Mondays and Fridays only. Includes many code, real estate-related small claims, and eviction cases for the New Bedford area only; also see area district court.

Taunton Probate & Family Court 11 Court St, PO Box 567, Taunton, MA 02780; 508-824-4004; Fax: 508-821-4630. 9AM-4PM (EST). *Probate.*

Dukes County

Superior Court PO Box 1267, Edgartown, MA 02539; 508-627-4668. Hours: 8AM-4PM (EST). *Felony, Civil Actions Over $25,000.*
Civil Records: Access: Mail, in person. Both court and visitors may perform in person searches. No search fee. Required to search: name, years to search. Civil cases indexed by defendant, plaintiff. Civil records on index cards from 1976 and books from 1695.
Criminal Records: Access: Mail, in person. Both court and visitors may perform in person searches. No search fee. Required to search: name, years to search. Criminal records on index cards from 1976 and books from 1695.
General Information: Public Access terminal is available. No sealed records released. Copy fee: $1.00 per page. Certification fee: $2.50. Payee: Clerk of Superior Court. Personal checks accepted. Prepayment required. Mail requests: SASE required. Mail turnaround time 1-2 days.

Edgartown District Court PO Box 1284, Courthouse, 81 Main St, Edgartown, MA 02539-1284; 508-627-3751/4622. Hours: 8:30AM-4:30PM (EST). *Felony, Misdemeanor, Civil, Eviction, Small Claims.*
Note: Includes Edgartown, Oak Bluffs, Tisbury, West Tisbury, Aquinnah (formerly Gay Head), Gosnold, and Elizabeth Islands.
Civil Records: Access: In person only. Both court and visitors may perform in person searches. No search fee. Required to search: name, years to search. Civil cases indexed by defendant, plaintiff. Civil records on index cards from 1983, docket books to 1900.
Criminal Records: Access: In person only. Both court and visitors may perform in person searches. No search fee. Required to search: name, years to search, DOB; also helpful: SSN. Criminal records on index cards from 1983, docket books to 1900.
General Information: No sealed records released. Copy fee: $1.00 per page. Certification fee: $2.50. Payee: District Court. Personal checks accepted. Prepayment required.

Probate & Family Court PO Box 237, Rm 104, 1st Fl, Edgartown, MA 02539; 508-627-4703; Fax: 508-627-7664. 10AM-3PM (EST). *Probate.*

Essex County

Superior Court - Lawrence 43 Appleton Way, Lawrence, MA 01840; 978-687-7463. Hours: 8AM-4:30PM (EST). *Civil Actions Over $25,000.*
Note: Index cards are found in the Salem office (records prior to 1985)
Civil Records: Access: In person. Both court and visitors may perform in person searches. No search fee. Required to search: name, years to search. Civil cases indexed by defendant, plaintiff. Civil records on

computer since 1985; prior records on index cards in Salem office.

General Information: Public Access terminal is available. No impounded records released. Copy fee: $1.00 per page. Certification fee: $2.50. Payee: Clerk of Superior Court. Personal checks accepted. Prepayment required.

Superior Court - Newburyport 145 High St,
Newburyport, MA 01950; 978-462-4474. Hours: 8AM-4:30PM (EST). *Felony, Civil Actions Over $25,000.*

Note: All finished criminal record files are in Salem and civil case records Session A in Salem, Session B in Newburyport and Session C & D in Lawrence.

Civil Records: Access: Mail, in person. Both court and visitors may perform in person searches. No search fee. Required to search: name, years to search. Civil cases indexed by defendant, plaintiff. Civil records on computer back to 1988.

Criminal Records: Access: In person. Both court and visitors may perform in person searches. No search fee. Required to search: name, years to search.

General Information: No impounded records released. Copy fee: $1.00 per page. Certification fee: $2.50. Payee: Clerk of Superior Court. Personal checks accepted. Prepayment required. Mail turnaround time 1-2 days.

Superior Court - Salem 34 Federal St, Salem,
MA 01970; 978-744-5500; Civil phone: X223; Criminal phone: X343; Fax: 978-741-0691 (civ); 978-825-9989 (crim). Hours: 8:00AM-4:30PM (EST). *Felony, Civil Actions Over $25,000.*

Civil Records: Access: Mail, in person. Visitors must perform in person searches for themselves. No search fee. Required to search: name, years to search. Civil cases indexed by defendant, plaintiff. Civil records are entered on computer for civil actions from all three Superior courts in this county. Computer records go back to 1985.

Criminal Records: Access: In person only. Visitors must perform in person searches for themselves. No search fee. Required to search: name, years to search. Criminal records are entered on computer for civil actions from all three Superior courts in this county. Computer records go back to 1985.

General Information: Public Access terminal is available. Impounded cases are not released. Fee to fax results is $1.50 per page. Copy fee: $1.00 per page. Certification fee: $2.50. Payee: Clerk of Superior Court. Personal checks accepted. Prepayment required. Mail turnaround time 1-2 days.

Gloucester District Court 197 Main St,
Gloucester, MA 01930; 978-283-2620. Hours: 8:30AM-4:30PM (EST). *Felony, Misdemeanor, Civil, Eviction, Small Claims.*

Note: Includes Essex, Gloucester, and Rockport.

Civil Records: Access: Mail, in person. Visitors must perform in person searches for themselves. No search fee. Required to search: name, years to search; also helpful: DOB. Civil cases indexed by defendant, plaintiff.

Criminal Records: Access: Mail, in person. Visitors must perform in person searches for themselves. No search fee. Required to search: name, years to search; also helpful: DOB.

General Information: Public Access terminal is available. No juvenile records released. Copy fee: $1.00 per page. Certification fee: $2.50 per page. Payee: Gloucester District Court. Personal checks accepted. Prepayment required.

Haverhill District Court PO Box 1389,
Haverhill, MA 01831; 978-373-4151; Fax: 978-521-6886. Hours: 8:30AM-4:30PM (EST). *Felony, Misdemeanor, Civil, Eviction, Small Claims.*

Note: Includes Boxford, Bradford, Georgetown, Groveland, and Haverhill.

Civil Records: Access: Phone, fax, mail, in person. Only the court performs in person searches; visitors may not. No search fee. Required to search: name, years to search. Civil cases indexed by defendant, plaintiff. Civil records on index cards from 1983. Non-active in storage.

Criminal Records: Access: Phone, fax, mail, in person. Only the court performs in person searches; visitors may not. No search fee. Required to search: name, years to search; also helpful: DOB. Criminal records on index cards from 1992, computerized since 2000. Non-active in storage.

General Information: No juvenile, sealed cases, confidential records released. Copy fee: $1.00 per page. Certification fee: $2.50. Payee: District Court. Personal checks accepted. Prepayment required. Mail requests: SASE required. Mail turnaround time 1-2 weeks.

Ipswich District Court 30 South Main St, PO
Box 246, Ipswich, MA 01938; 978-356-2681; Fax: 978-356-4396. Hours: 8:30AM-4:30PM (EST). *Felony, Misdemeanor, Civil, Eviction, Small Claims.*

Note: Includes Hamilton, Ipswich, Topsfield, and Wenham.

Civil Records: Access: In person only. Visitors must perform in person searches for themselves. No search fee. Required to search: name, years to search. Civil cases indexed by defendant, plaintiff. Civil records on index cards, small claims from 1984, civil from 1964. Civil on docket books from 1970.

Criminal Records: Access: In person only. Visitors must perform in person searches for themselves. No search fee. Required to search: name, years to search; also helpful: DOB. Criminal records on index cards from 1979.

General Information: No juvenile records released. Copy fee: $1.00 per page. Certification fee: $2.50 per page. Payee: District Court. Personal checks accepted. Prepayment required.

Lawrence District Court 2 Appleton St.,
Lawrence, MA 01840; 978-687-7184; Civil phone: 978-689-2810. Hours: 8AM-4:30PM (EST). *Felony, Misdemeanor, Civil, Eviction, Small Claims.*

Note: Includes Andover, Lawrence, Methuen, and North Andover.

Civil Records: Access: In person. Visitors must perform in person searches for themselves. No search fee. Required to search: name, years to search. Civil cases indexed by defendant, plaintiff. Civil records on index cards from 1983, docket books from 1900, on computer since 1990.

Criminal Records: Access: Mail, in person. Both court and visitors may perform in person searches. No search fee. Required to search: name, years to search, DOB; also helpful: address, SSN. Criminal records on index cards from 1983, docket books from 1900, on computer since 1990.

General Information: No medical, police reports, impounded, juvenile records released. Copy fee: $1.00 per page. Certification fee: $2.50. Payee: District Court. Personal checks accepted. Prepayment required. Mail requests: SASE requested. Turnaround time 1-2 weeks.

Lynn District Court 580 Essex St, Lynn, MA
01901; 781-598-5200. Hours: 8AM-4:30PM (EST). *Felony, Misdemeanor, Civil, Eviction, Small Claims.*

Note: Includes Lynn, Marblehead, Nahant, Saugus, and Swampscott.

Civil Records: Access: Mail, in person. Visitors must perform in person searches for themselves. No search fee. Required to search: name, years to search. Civil cases indexed by defendant, plaintiff. Civil records on index cards from 1983, docket books from approx 1900. Records older than 15 years are difficult to find and may take longer.

Criminal Records: Access: Mail, in person. Visitors must perform in person searches for themselves. No search fee. Required to search: name, years to search; also helpful: DOB, SSN. Criminal records on index cards from 1983, docket books from approx 1900. Records older than 15 years are difficult to find and may take longer.

General Information: Public Access terminal is available. (The terminal is only for civil case data.) No juvenile, impounded or sealed records released. Copy fee: $1.00 per page. Certification fee: $2.50. Payee: Lynn District Court. Personal checks accepted. Prepayment required.

Newburyport District Court 22 188 State St,
Newburyport, MA 01950; 978-462-2652. Hours: 8:30AM-4:30PM (EST). *Felony, Misdemeanor, Civil, Eviction, Small Claims.*

Note: Includes Amesbury, Merrimac, Newbury, Newburyport, Rowley, Salisbury, and West Newbury.

Civil Records: Access: Mail, in person. Only the court may perform in person searches No search fee. Required to search: name, years to search. Civil cases indexed by defendant, plaintiff. Civil records on index cards from 1983, prior archived in Worcester.

Criminal Records: Access: Mail, in person. Only the court performs in person searches; visitors may not. No search fee. Required to search: name, years to search, DOB. Criminal records on index cards from 1983, prior archived in Worcester.

General Information: No juvenile or impounded records released. Copy fee: $1.00 per page. Certification fee: $2.50. Payee: District Court. Personal checks accepted. Prepayment required. Mail turnaround time 1-2 weeks.

Peabody District Court 86 One Lowell St.,
Peabody, MA 01960; 978-532-3100. Hours: 8:30AM-4:30PM (EST). *Felony, Misdemeanor, Civil, Eviction, Small Claims.*

Note: Includes Lynnfield and Peabody.

Civil Records: Access: In person. Visitors must perform in person searches for themselves. No search fee. Required to search: name, years to search. Civil cases indexed by defendant, plaintiff. Civil records stored in office for 10 years, prior stored in basement and are difficult to find.

Criminal Records: Access: In person. Visitors must perform in person searches for themselves. No search fee. Required to search: name, years to search, DOB. Criminal records stored in office for 10 years, prior stored in basement and are difficult to find. Will do mail search for 1 name only.

General Information: Public access terminal has civil records only. No juvenile or impounded records released. Copy fee: $1.00 per page. Certification fee: $2.50. Payee: District Court. Personal checks accepted. Prepayment required.

Salem District Court 36 65 Washington St,
Salem, MA 01970; 978-744-1167. Hours: 8:30AM-4:30PM (EST). *Felony, Misdemeanor, Civil, Eviction, Small Claims.*

Note: Includes Beverly, Danvers, Manchester by the Sea, Middleton, and Salem.

Civil Records: Access: In person. Visitors must perform in person searches on Thursday or Friday 2Pm-4:30PM No search fee. Required to search: name, years to search. Civil cases indexed by defendant, plaintiff. Civil records on index cards and docket books.

Criminal Records: Access: In person. Visitors must perform in person searches on Thursday or Friday 2PM-4:30PM No search fee. Required to search: name, years to search, DOB, SSN. Criminal records on index cards and docket books.

General Information: Public Access terminal is available. No juvenile or impounded records released. Copy fee: $1.00 per page. Certification fee: $2.50. Payee: District Court. Personal checks accepted. Prepayment required.

Northeast Housing Court 2 Appleton St, Fenton Judicial Center, Lawrence, MA 01840; 978-689-7833. Hours: 8:30AM-4:30PM (EST). *Eviction, Misdemeanor (Code Violations), Small Claims.*
Note: Includes many housing code cases, real estate-related small claims and eviction cases for Essex County and Billerica, Chelmsford, Dracut, Dunstable, Groton, Lowell, Pepperell, Shirley, Tewksbury, Tyngsboro, Westford; also see district courts.

Probate & Family Court 36 Federal St, Salem, MA 01970; 978-744-1020; Fax: 978-741-2957. Hours: 8:00AM-4:30PM (EST). *Probate.*

Franklin County

Superior Court PO Box 1573, Greenfield, MA 01302; 413-774-5535; Fax: 413-774-4770. Hours: 8:30AM-4:30PM (EST). *Felony, Civil Actions Over $25,000.*
Civil Records: Access: Fax, in person. Both court and visitors may perform in person searches. No search fee. Required to search: name, years to search. Civil cases indexed by defendant, plaintiff. Civil records in files; on computer back 25 years.
Criminal Records: Access: Fax, in person. Both court and visitors may perform in person searches. No search fee. Required to search: name, years to search, DOB. Criminal records in files; on computer back 8 years.
General Information: Public Access terminal is available. No impounded or juvenile records released. Copy fee: $1.00 per page. Certification fee: $2.50 per page. Payee: Franklin County Superior Court. Personal checks accepted. Prepayment required.

Greenfield District Court 425 Main St, Greenfield, MA 01301; 413-774-5533; Probate phone: 413-774-7011; Fax: 413-774-5328. Hours: 8:30AM-4:30PM (EST). *Felony, Misdemeanor, Civil, Eviction, Small Claims.*
Note: Includes Ashfield, Bernardston, Buckland, Charlemont, Colrain, Conway, Deerfield, Gill, Greenfield, Hawley, Leath, Leverett, Leyden, Monroe, Montague, Northfield, Rowe, Shelburne, Shutesbury, Sunderland, and Whately.
Civil Records: Access: In person only. Both court and visitors may perform in person searches. No search fee. Required to search: name, years to search. Civil cases indexed by defendant, plaintiff. Civil records on docket books or index cards; on computer back to 1998.
Criminal Records: Access: In person only. Both court and visitors may perform in person searches. No search fee. Required to search: name, years to search, DOB. Criminal records on docket books or index cards; on computer back to 1994.
General Information: No juvenile records released. Copy fee: $1.00 per page. Certification fee: $2.50. Payee: Greenfield District Court. Personal checks accepted. Prepayment required.

Orange District Court #42 One Court Square, Orange, MA 01364; 978-544-8277; Fax: 978-544-5204. Hours: 8:30AM-4:30PM (EST). *Felony, Misdemeanor, Civil, Eviction, Small Claims.*
Note: Includes Athol, Erving, New Salem, Orange, Warwick, and Wendell, Shutesbury, Leverett.

Civil Records: Access: Phone, mail, in person. Both court and visitors may perform in person searches. No search fee. Required to search: name, years to search. Civil cases indexed by defendant, plaintiff. Civil records on docket books from 1975.
Criminal Records: Access: Phone, mail, in person. Only the court performs in person searches; visitors may not. No search fee. Required to search: name, years to search. Criminal records on docket books from 1975.
General Information: No juvenile records released. Copy fee: $1.00 per page. Certification fee: $2.50 per page. Payee: District Court. Personal checks accepted. Prepayment required. Mail turnaround: 1-2 weeks.

Probate & Family Court PO Box 590, Greenfield, MA 01302; 413-774-7011; Fax: 413-774-3829. Hours: 8AM-4:30PM (EST). *Probate.*
www.fcpfc.com

Western Housing Court *Eviction, Misdemeanor (Code Violations), Small Claims.*
Note: See Hampden County Western Housing Court for many housing code cases, real estate-related small claims and eviction cases for this county; also see district courts in this county.

Hampden County

Superior Court 50 State St, PO Box 559, Springfield, MA 01102-0559; 413-735-6016; Fax: 413-737-1611. Hours: 8:30AM-4:30PM (EST). *Felony, Civil Actions Over $25,000.*
Civil Records: Access: Phone, mail, in person. Both court and visitors may perform in person searches. No search fee. Required to search: name, years to search. Civil cases indexed by defendant, plaintiff. Civil records on computer from 1989 to present; prior on index cards from 1930s, books from 1812.
Criminal Records: Access: In person only. Visitors must perform in person searches for themselves. No search fee. Required to search: name, years to search. Criminal records on computer from 1992 to present; prior on index cards from 1930s.
General Information: Public Access terminal is available. No impounded case records released. Copy fee: $1.00 per page. Certification fee: $2.50. Payee: Clerk of Superior Court. Personal checks accepted. Prepayment required. Mail requests: SASE requested. Turnaround time 1 week.

Chicopee District Court #20 30 Church St, Chicopee, MA 01020; 413-598-0099; Fax: 413-598-8176. Hours: 8:30AM-4:30PM (EST). *Felony, Misdemeanor, Civil, Eviction, Small Claims.*
Civil Records: Access: Phone, mail, in person. Visitors must perform in person searches for themselves. No search fee. Required to search: name, years to search. Civil cases indexed by defendant, plaintiff. Civil records on index cards from 1983, docket books to 1960; computerized since 2001.
Criminal Records: Access: In person. Both court and visitors may perform in person searches. No search fee. Required to search: name, years to search, DOB. Criminal records on index cards from 1983, docket books to 1900.
General Information: No juvenile records released. Fee to fax results is $.50 per page. Copy fee: $1.00 per page. Certification fee: $2.50. Payee: District Court. Personal checks accepted. Prepayment required. Mail requests: SASE required. Mail turnaround time 1-2 weeks.

Holyoke District Court 20 Court Sq, Holyoke, MA 01041-5075; 413-538-9710; Fax: 413-533-7165. Hours: 9AM-3:00PM (EST). *Felony, Misdemeanor, Civil, Eviction, Small Claims.*
Civil Records: Access: Phone, mail, fax, in person. Both court and visitors may perform in person

searches. No search fee. Required to search: name, years to search. Civil cases indexed by defendant, plaintiff. Civil records on index cards and docket books back to 1989.
Criminal Records: Access: Fax, mail, in person. Both court and visitors may perform in person searches. No search fee. Required to search: name, years to search, DOB or SSN, signed release. Criminal records on index cards and docket books since 1976; on computer back to 1986.
General Information: No juvenile, sealed records released. Copy fee: $1.00 per page. Certification fee: $2.50. Payee: District Court. Only cashiers checks and money orders accepted. Prepayment required. Mail requests: SASE requested. Turnaround time 1-2 weeks.

Palmer District Court 235 Sykes St, Palmer, MA 01069; 413-283-8916; Fax: 413-283-6775. 8:30AM-4:30PM (EST). *Felony, Misdemeanor, Civil, Eviction, Small Claims.*
Note: Includes Ludlow, Monson, Wilbraham, Palmer, Wales, Brimfield, Holland, and Hampden.
Civil Records: Access: In person only. Visitors must perform in person searches for themselves. No search fee. Required to search: name, years to search. Civil cases indexed by defendant, plaintiff. Civil records on index cards back to 1982.
Criminal Records: Access: In person only. Visitors must perform in person searches for themselves. No search fee. Required to search: name, years to search. Criminal records on index cards for 10 years; on computer back to 1995.
General Information: No sealed or juvenile records released. Copy fee: $1.00 per page. Certification fee: $2.50. Payee: Palmer District Court. Personal checks accepted. Prepayment required.

Springfield District Court 50 State St, Springfield, MA 01103; 413-748-7613; Civil phone: 413-748-8659; Criminal phone: 413-748-7982; Fax: 413-747-4841. Hours: 8:00AM-4:30PM (EST). *Felony, Misdemeanor, Civil, Eviction, Small Claims.*
Note: Includes Agawam, East Longmeadow, Longmeadow, Springfield, and West Springfield.
Civil Records: Access: In person only. Visitors must perform in person searches for themselves. No search fee. Required to search: name, years to search. Civil cases indexed by defendant, plaintiff. Civil records on index cards; computerized records since 1992.
Criminal Records: Access: In person. Visitors must perform in person searches for themselves. No search fee. Required to search: name, years to search. Criminal records on index cards; computerized records since 1992.
General Information: No sealed, expunged, or adoption records released. Copy fee: $1.00 per page. Certification fee: $2.50. Payee: District Court. Business checks accepted. Prepayment required.

Westfield District Court 224 Elm St, Westfield, MA 01085; 413-568-8946; Fax: 413-568-4863. Hours: 8AM-4PM (EST). *Felony, Misdemeanor, Civil, Eviction, Small Claims.*
Includes Blandford, Chester, Granville, Montgomery, Russell, Southwick, Tolland, and Westfield.
Civil Records: Access: Mail, in person. Both court and visitors may perform in person searches. No search fee. Required to search: name, years to search. Civil cases indexed by defendant, plaintiff. Civil records on index cards and in files.
Criminal Records: Access: In person only. Both court and visitors may perform in person searches. No search fee. Required to search: name, years to search. Criminal records on index cards and in files.
General Information: No sealed or juvenile records released. Copy fee: $1.00 per page. Certification fee: $2.50. Payee: District Court. Only cashiers checks and

money orders accepted. Prepayment required. Mail turnaround time 1-2 weeks.

Probate & Family Court 50 State St, Springfield, MA 01103-0559; 413-748-7746; Fax: 413-781-5605. Hours: 8AM-4:25PM (EST). *Probate.*

Western Housing Court PO Box 559 (37 Elm St), Springfield, MA 01102; 413-748-7838; Fax: 413-732-4607. Hours: 8:30AM-4:30PM (EST). *Eviction, Misdemeanor (Code Violations), Small Claims.*
Note: Includes many housing code cases, real estate-related small claims and eviction cases for counties of Berkshire, Franklin, Hampden, and Hampshire; also see district courts.

Hampshire County

Superior Court PO Box 1119, Northampton, MA 01061; 413-584-5810 x331; Probate phone: 413-586-8500; Fax: 413-586-8217. Hours: 9AM-4PM (EST). *Felony, Civil Actions Over $25,000.*
Civil Records: Access: Mail, fax, in person. Both court and visitors may perform in person searches. No search fee. Required to search: name, years to search. Civil cases indexed by defendant, plaintiff. Civil records in files, index cards from 1800s; on computer back to 2000.
Criminal Records: Access: Mail, fax, in person. Both court and visitors may perform in person searches. No search fee. Required to search: name, years to search. Criminal records in files, index cards from 1800s; on computer back to 1983.
General Information: Public Access terminal is available. (Criminal and Civil.) No impounded case records released. Will fax results to local or toll free line. Copy fee: $1.00 per page. Certification fee: $20.00. Payee: Clerk of Superior Court. Personal checks accepted. Prepayment required. Mail turnaround time 1 week.

Northampton District Court Courthouse, 15 Gothic St, Northampton, MA 01060; 413-584-7776; Civil phone: 413-584-7400; Criminal phone: 413-584-7400; Fax: 413-584-9479. Hours: 8:30AM-4:30PM (EST). *Felony, Misdemeanor, Civil, Eviction, Small Claims.*
Note: Includes Chesterfield, Cummington, Easthampton, Goshen, Hatfield, Huntington, Middlefield, Northampton, Plainfield, Southampton, Westhampton, Williamsburg, and Worthington.
Civil Records: Access: Fax, mail, in person. Only the court performs in person searches; visitors may not. No search fee. Required to search: name, years to search, address. Civil cases indexed by defendant, plaintiff. Civil records on index cards and docket books back to 1970, computerized since 05/02.
Criminal Records: Access: Fax, mail, in person. Both court and visitors may perform in person searches. No search fee. Required to search: name, years to search, DOB, SSN. Criminal records on docket books go back to 1970, on computer since 1997.
General Information: No CHINS-care & protection, show cause-mental health records released. No fee to fax results. Copy fee: $1.00 per page. Certification fee: $2.50 per page. Payee: District Court. Personal checks not accepted. Prepayment required. Mail requests: SASE requested. Turnaround time 1-2 weeks.

Ware District Court PO Box 300, Ware, MA 01082; 413-967-3301; Fax: 413-967-7986. Hours: 8AM-4:00PM (EST). *Felony, Misdemeanor, Civil, Eviction, Small Claims.*
Note: Includes Amherst, Belchertown, Granby, Hadley, South Hadley, Pelham, Ware, all the MDC Quabbin Reservoir and Watershed Area.

Civil Records: Access: Fax, mail, in person. Only the court performs in person searches; visitors may not. No search fee. Required to search: name, years to search. Civil cases indexed by defendant, plaintiff. Civil records on index cards or docket books back to 1960. Some records sent to archives in Worcester.
Criminal Records: Access: Fax, mail, in person. Only the court performs in person searches; visitors may not. No search fee. Required to search: name, years to search, DOB, SSN. Criminal records on index cards or docket books back to 1920; on computer back to 1996. Some records sent to archives in Worcester.
General Information: No sealed, impounded, confidential or juvenile records released. Copy fee: $1.00 per page. Certification fee: $2.50. Payee: Ware District Court. Personal checks accepted. Prepayment required. Mail requests: SASE helpful. Turnaround time 1-2 weeks.

Probate & Family Court 33 King St #3, Northampton, MA 01060; 413-586-8500; Fax: 413-584-1132. Hours: 8:30AM-4:30PM (EST). *Probate.*

Western Housing Court, MA. *Eviction, Misdemeanor (Code Violations), Small Claims.*
Note: See Hampden County Western Housing Court for many housing code cases, real estate-related small claims and eviction cases for this county; also see district courts in this county.

Middlesex County

Superior Court - East Cambridge 40 Thorndike St, Edward J Sullivan Courthouse, East Cambridge, MA 02141; 617-494-4010. Hours: 8:30AM-4:30PM (EST). *Felony, Civil Actions Over $25,000.*
Civil Records: Access: Mail, in person. Both court and visitors may perform in person searches. No search fee. Required to search: name, years to search; also helpful: address. Civil cases indexed by defendant, plaintiff. Civil records on computer from 1986, rest on card indexes to 1986. The court is planning to have Internet access.
Criminal Records: Access: Mail, in person. Both court and visitors may perform in person searches. No search fee. Required to search: name, years to search; also helpful: address. Criminal records on computer back to 1991, rest on card indexes to 1986. The court is planning to have Internet access.
General Information: Public Access terminal is available. No impounded or those restricted by statute records released. Copy fee: $1.00 per page. Certification fee: $2.50. Payee: Clerk of Superior Court. Personal checks accepted. Prepayment required. Mail turnaround time 3-5 days for criminal records.

Superior Court - Lowell 360 Gorham St, Lowell, MA 01852; 978-453-0201. Hours: 8:30AM-4:30PM (EST). *Felony, Civil Actions Over $25,000.*
Civil Records: Access: Mail, in person. Both court and visitors may perform in person searches. No search fee. Required to search: name, years to search. Civil cases indexed by defendant, plaintiff. Civil records on computer since 1990; prior records kept at East Cambridge Middlesex Superior Court, 40 Thorndike, Cambridge, MA 02141.
Criminal Records: Access: Mail, in person. Both court and visitors may perform in person searches. No search fee. Required to search: name, years to search. Criminal records on computer since 1990; prior records kept at East Cambridge Middlesex Superior Court, 40 Thorndike, Cambridge, MA 02141.
General Information: Copy fee: $1.00 per page. Certification fee: $2.50. Payee: Clerk of Superior Court. Personal checks accepted. Prepayment required. Mail turnaround time 1-2 days.

Ayer District Court 25 E Main St, Ayer, MA 01432; 978-772-2100; Fax: 978-772-5345. Hours: 8:30AM-4:30PM (EST). *Felony, Misdemeanor, Civil, Eviction, Small Claims.*
Note: Includes Ayer, Ashby, Boxborough, Dunstable, Groton, Littleton, Pepperell, Shirley, Townsend, Westford and Devens Regional Enterprise Zone.

Civil Records: Access: Mail, in person. No search fee. Required to search: name, years to search. Civil cases indexed by defendant, plaintiff. Civil records on index cards from 1977 to present; only required to keep records 20 years. DOB required on subject.
Criminal Records: Access: Mail, in person. Both court and visitors may perform in person searches. No search fee. Required to search: name, years to search, DOB. Criminal records on index cards from 1977 to 1995, computerized 1996 forward; Only required to keep records 10 years.
General Information: Juvenile records not released. Copy fee: $1.00 per page. Certification fee: $1.50 per page in addition to copy charge. Payee: Ayer District Court. Personal checks accepted. Prepayment required. Mail requests: SASE required. Mail turnaround time 1-2 weeks.

Cambridge District Court 52 PO Box 338, East Cambridge, MA 02141; 617-494-4095; Civil phone: 617-494-4095 X502; Criminal phone: 617-494-4095 X501; Probate phone: 617-768-5800. Hours: 8:30AM-4:30PM (EST). *Felony, Misdemeanor, Civil, Eviction, Small Claims.*
Note: Includes Cambridge, Arlington, and Belmont.

Civil Records: Access: In person. Visitors must perform in person searches for themselves. No search fee. Required to search: name, years to search. Civil cases indexed by defendant, plaintiff. Civil records on index cards or docket books. State law requires records be retained for 10 years.
Criminal Records: Access: In person, mail. Visitors must perform in person searches for themselves. No search fee. Required to search: name, years to search, DOB. Criminal records on index cards or docket books; computerized records since 1997. State law requires records be retained for 10 years.
General Information: No sealed or juvenile records released. Will fax results to local or toll free line. Copy fee: $1.00 per page. Certification fee: $2.50. Payee: District Court. Personal checks accepted. Prepayment required. Mail requests: SASE required. Mail turnaround time 1-2 weeks.

Concord District Court 47 305 Walden St, Concord, MA 01742; 978-369-0500. Hours: 8:30AM-4:30PM (EST). *Felony, Misdemeanor, Civil, Eviction, Small Claims.*
Note: Includes Concord, Carlisle, Lincoln, Lexington, Bedford, Acton, Maynard, and Stow.

Civil Records: Access: Mail, in person. Visitors must perform in person searches for themselves. No search fee. Required to search: name, years to search; also helpful: address. Civil cases indexed by defendant, plaintiff. Civil records on computer from 1991, index cards and books from 1950, archived from 1643. In person searches performed from 10AM-4PM only.
Criminal Records: Access: Mail, in person. Visitors must perform in person searches for themselves. No search fee. Required to search: name, years to search; also helpful: address, DOB, SSN. Criminal records index printed from computer from 1998, index cards and books from 1950, archived from 1643. In person searches performed from from 10AM-4PM only.
General Information: No impounded files released. Copy fee: $1.00 per page. Certification fee: $2.50. Payee: Commonwealth of Massachusetts. Personal checks accepted. Prepayment required. Mail requests: SASE requested. Mail turnaround time 1-2 weeks.

Framingham District Court 600 Concord St (PO Box 1669), Framingham, MA 01701; 508-875-7461. Hours: 8:30AM-4:30PM (EST). *Felony, Misdemeanor, Civil, Eviction, Small Claims.*
Note: Includes Ashland, Framingham, Holliston, Hopkinton, Sudbury, and Wayland.

Civil Records: Access: Mail, in person. Both court and visitors may perform in person searches. No search fee. Required to search: name, years to search. Civil cases indexed by defendant, plaintiff. Civil records on index cards or docket books back to 1900; on computer back to 1986. Special form required for mail request.

Criminal Records: Access: Mail, in person, fax. Both court and visitors may perform in person searches. No search fee. Required to search: name, years to search. Criminal records on index cards or docket books back to 1900; on computer back to 1986. Special form required for mail request.

General Information: No sealed, expunged or juvenile records released. Copy fee: $1.00 per page. Certification fee: $2.50 per page. Payee: District Court. Only cashiers checks and money orders accepted. Prepayment required. Mail requests: SASE requested. Turnaround time is 7 days.

Lowell District Court 41 Hurd St, Lowell, MA 01852; 978-459-4101; Civil phone: x235; Criminal phone: X204. Hours: 8:30AM-4:30PM (EST). *Felony, Misdemeanor, Civil, Eviction, Small Claims.*
Note: Includes Billerica, Chelmsford, Dracut, Lowell, Tewksbury, and Tyngsboro.

Civil Records: Access: In person only. Visitors must perform in person searches for themselves. No search fee. Required to search: name, years to search. Civil cases indexed by defendant, plaintiff. Civil records on index cards or docket books. Records retained for 10 years.

Criminal Records: Access: Mail, in person. Visitors must perform in person searches for themselves. No search fee. Required to search: name, years to search, DOB. Criminal records on index cards or docket books. Records retained for 10 years.

General Information: No impounded records released. Copy fee: $1.00 per page. Certification fee: $2.50. Payee: District Court, Lowell Division. Business checks accepted. Prepayment required.

Malden District Court 89 Summer St., Malden, MA 02148; 781-322-7500. Hours: 8:30AM-4:30PM (EST). *Felony, Misdemeanor, Civil, Eviction, Small Claims.*
Note: Includes Malden, Melrose, Everett, and Wakefield.

Civil Records: Access: Phone, mail, in person. Only the court performs in person searches; visitors may not. No search fee. Required to search: name, years to search. Civil cases indexed by defendant, plaintiff. Civil records on index cards or docket books back to 1970; on computer back to 1992.

Criminal Records: Access: In person only. Both court and visitors may perform in person searches. No search fee. Required to search: name, years to search, DOB. Criminal records on index cards or docket books back to 1970; on computer back to 1992.

General Information: No juvenile records released. Copy fee: $1.00 per page. Certification fee: $2.50 per document. Payee: District Court. Personal checks accepted. Prepayment required.

Marlborough District Court 21 45 Williams St, Marlborough, MA 01752; 508-485-3700. Hours: 8AM-4:30PM (EST). *Felony, Misdemeanor, Civil, Eviction, Small Claims.*
Note: Includes Marlborough and Hudson.

Civil Records: Access: Phone, mail, in person. Both court and visitors may perform in person searches. No

search fee. Required to search: name, years to search. Civil cases indexed by defendant, plaintiff. Civil records on index cards or docket books. State law requires records be retained for 10 years.

Criminal Records: Access: Phone, mail, in person. Both court and visitors may perform in person searches. No search fee. Required to search: name, years to search, DOB. Criminal records on index cards or docket books. State law requires records be retained for 10 years.

General Information: No juvenile records released. Copy fee: $1.00 per page. Certification fee: $2.50. Payee: District Court. Personal checks accepted. Prepayment required. Mail turnaround time 1-2 weeks.

Natick District Court 117 E Central, Natick, MA 01760; 508-653-4332. Hours: 8:30AM-4:30PM (EST). *Felony, Misdemeanor, Civil, Eviction, Small Claims.*
Note: Includes Natick and Sherborn.

Civil Records: Access: In person. Visitors must perform in person searches on Friday 3PM-4:30PM. No search fee. Required to search: name, years to search. Civil cases indexed by defendant, plaintiff. Civil records on index cards and docket books, back for 10 years.

Criminal Records: Access: In person only. Visitors must perform in person searches on Friday 3PM-4:30PM. No search fee. Required to search: name, years to search, DOB. Criminal records on index cards and docket books, back for 10 years.

General Information: No juvenile records released. Copy fee: $1.00 per page. Certification fee: $2.50. Payee: District Court. Personal checks accepted. Prepayment required.

Newton District Court 1309 Washington, West Newton, MA 02141; 617-494-0102. Hours: 8:30AM-1PM; 2-4:30PM (EST). *Felony, Misdemeanor, Civil, Eviction, Small Claims.*
www.state.ma.us/courts/courtsandjudges/courts/newtondistrictmain.html
Civil Records: Access: Phone, mail, in person. Both court and visitors may perform in person searches. No search fee. Required to search: name, years to search. Civil cases indexed by defendant, plaintiff. Civil records on index cards back to 1930.

Criminal Records: Access: Phone, mail, in person. Both court and visitors may perform in person searches. No search fee. Required to search: name, years to search. Criminal records on index books back to 1930.

General Information: Public Access terminal is available. No juvenile, (some) 209-A cases or mental health records released. Will not fax results. Copy fee: $1.00 per page. Certification fee: $2.50. Payee: District Court of Newton. Personal checks accepted. Turnaround time 1 week.

Somerville District Court 175 Fellsway, Somerville, MA 02145; 617-666-8000. Hours: 8:30AM-4:30PM (EST). *Felony, Misdemeanor, Civil, Eviction, Small Claims.*
Note: Includes Medford and Somerville.

Civil Records: Access: In person. Visitors must perform in person searches for themselves. No search fee. Required to search: name, years to search. Civil cases indexed by defendant, plaintiff. Civil records on index cards or docket books. State law requires records be retained for 20 years.

Criminal Records: Access: In person. Visitors must perform in person searches for themselves. No search fee. Required to search: name, years to search, DOB. Criminal records on computer since 1997; prior records on index cards or docket books. State law requires records be retained for 20 years.

General Information: No juvenile or impounded records released. Copy fee: $1.00 per page. Certification fee: $2.50. Payee: District Court. Personal checks accepted. Prepayment required.

Waltham District Court 51 38 Linden St, Waltham, MA 02154; 781-894-4500. Hours: 8:30AM-4:30PM (EST). *Felony, Misdemeanor, Civil, Eviction, Small Claims.*
Note: Includes Waltham, Watertown, and Weston.

Civil Records: Access: Mail, in person. Both court and visitors may perform in person searches. No search fee. Required to search: name, years to search. Civil cases indexed by defendant, plaintiff. Civil records on index cards and docket books, back for 10 years.

Criminal Records: Access: Mail, in person. Both court and visitors may perform in person searches. No search fee. Required to search: name, years to search; also helpful: DOB. Criminal records on index cards and docket books, back for 10 years.

General Information: Public Access terminal is available. No juvenile records released. Copy fee: $1.00 per page. Certification fee: $2.50. Payee: District Court. No personal checks. Prepayment required. Mail requests: SASE required. Mail turnaround time 1 week.

Woburn District Court 53 30 Pleasant St, Woburn, MA 01801; 781-935-4000. Hours: 8:30AM-4:30PM (EST). *Felony, Misdemeanor, Civil, Eviction, Small Claims.*
Note: Includes Burlington, North Reading, Reading, Stoneham, Wilmington, Winchester, and Woburn.

Civil Records: Access: Mail, in person. Both court and visitors may perform in person searches. No search fee. Required to search: name, years to search. Civil cases indexed by defendant, plaintiff. Civil records on index cards, computer listing or docket books back 30 years.

Criminal Records: Access: Mail, in person. Both court and visitors may perform in person searches. No search fee. Required to search: name, years to search; also helpful: DOB. Criminal records on index cards, computer listing or docket books back 30 years.

General Information: Public Access terminal is available. (Has records since 1996.) No statutorily non-public records released. Copy fee: $1.00 per page. Certification fee: $2.50. Payee: District Court. Personal checks accepted. Prepayment required. Mail requests: SASE requested. Turnaround time 1-2 weeks.

Probate & Family Court 208 Cambridge St, PO Box 410480, East Cambridge, MA 02141-0005; 617-768-5800; Fax: 617-225-0781. Hours: 8AM-4:30PM (EST). *Probate.*

Nantucket County

Superior Court PO Box 967, Nantucket, MA 02554; 508-228-2559; Fax: 508-228-3725. Hours: 8:30AM-4PM (EST). *Felony, Civil Actions Over $25,000.*
Civil Records: Access: Phone, fax, mail, in person. Both court and visitors may perform in person searches. No search fee. Required to search: name, years to search. Civil cases indexed by defendant, plaintiff. Civil records on index books from 1762.

Criminal Records: Access: Phone, fax, mail, in person. Both court and visitors may perform in person searches. No search fee. Required to search: name, years to search. Criminal records on index books from 1762.

General Information: No impounded records released. No fee to fax results. In-state faxing only. Copy fee: $1.00 per page. Certification fee: $2.50. Payee: Nantucket Superior Court. Personal checks

accepted. Prepayment required. Mail requests: SASE required. Mail turnaround time 1 week.

Nantucket District Court
16 Broad St., PO Box 1800, Nantucket, MA 02554; 508-228-0460. Hours: 8AM-4PM (EST). *Felony, Misdemeanor, Civil, Eviction, Small Claims.*

Civil Records: Access: In person only. Visitors must perform in person searches for themselves. No search fee. Required to search: name, years to search. Civil cases indexed by defendant, plaintiff. Civil records on index cards or docket books. State law requires records be retained for 10 years.

Criminal Records: Access: In person only. Visitors must perform in person searches for themselves. No search fee. Required to search: name, years to search. Criminal records on index cards or docket books back to 1917. State law requires records be retained for 10 years.

General Information: Copy fee: $1.00 per page. Certification fee: $2.50. Payee: Nantucket District Court. Prepayment required.

Probate & Family Court
PO Box 1116, Nantucket, MA 02554; 508-228-2669; Fax: 508-228-3662. Hours: 8:30AM-4PM (EST). *Probate.*

Norfolk County

Superior Court
650 High St, Dedham, MA 02026; 781-326-1600; Civil phone: X1; Criminal phone: X2; Fax: 781-326-3871(Civ); 781-320-9726(Crim). Hours: 8:30AM-4:30PM (EST). *Felony, Civil Actions Over $25,000.*

Civil Records: Access: Phone, mail, in person. Both court and visitors may perform in person searches. No search fee. Required to search: name, years to search. Civil cases indexed by defendant, plaintiff. Civil records on index books from 1900, on computer back to 9/2000.

Criminal Records: Access: Mail, in person. Visitors must perform in person searches for themselves. No search fee. Required to search: name, years to search; also helpful: address, DOB, SSN. Criminal records on index books from 1900; on computer back to 9/2000.

General Information: Public Access terminal is available. No impounded records released. No one may view a file of a sex-related crime without authorization from a judge. Copy fee: $1.00 per page. Certification fee: $2.50. Payee: Clerk of Superior Court. Personal checks accepted for copies only. Prepayment required. Mail requests: SASE not required. Mail turnaround time 1 week; 1-2 days for criminal phone in requests.

Brookline District Court
360 Washington St, Brookline, MA 02445; 617-232-4660; Fax: 617-739-0734. Hours: 8:30AM-4:30PM (EST). *Felony, Misdemeanor, Civil, Eviction, Small Claims.*

Civil Records: Access: Mail, in person. Both court and visitors may perform in person searches. No search fee. Required to search: name, years to search. Civil cases indexed by defendant, plaintiff. Civil records on index cards and docket books back for 10 years.

Criminal Records: Access: Mail, in person. Only the court performs in person searches; visitors may not. No search fee. Required to search: name, years to search; also helpful: DOB. Criminal records on index cards and docket books back for 10 years.

General Information: No sealed case records released. Copy fee: $1.00 per page. Certification fee: $2.50. Payee: Brookline District Court. Personal checks accepted. Prepayment required. Mail turnaround time 1-2 weeks.

Dedham District Court
631 High St, Dedham, MA 02026; 781-329-4777. Hours: 8:15AM-4:30PM (EST). *Felony, Misdemeanor, Civil, Eviction, Small Claims.*

Note: Includes Dedham, Dover, Medfield, Needham, Norwood, Wellesley, and Westwood.

Civil Records: Access: In person only. Visitors must perform in person searches for themselves. No search fee. Required to search: name, years to search. Civil cases indexed by defendant, plaintiff. Civil records on computer since 1997, and on index cards or docket books prior to that. State law requires records be retained for 10 years.

Criminal Records: Access: In person only. Visitors must perform in person searches for themselves. No search fee. Required to search: name, years to search. Criminal records on computer since 1997, and on index cards or docket books prior to that. State law requires records be retained for 10 years. Access is available after 10AM.

General Information: No juvenile records released. Copy fee: $1.00 per page. Certification fee: $2.50. Payee: District Court. Personal checks accepted. Prepayment required.

Quincy District Court
One Dennis Ryan Parkway, Quincy, MA 02169; 617-471-1650. Hours: 8:30AM-4:30PM (EST). *Felony, Misdemeanor, Civil, Eviction, Small Claims.*

Note: Includes Braintree, Cohasset, Holbrook, Quincy, Randolph, and Weymouth, Quincy.

Civil Records: Access: In person only. Visitors must perform in person searches for themselves. No search fee. Required to search: name, years to search. Civil cases indexed by defendant, plaintiff. Civil records on index cards or docket books. State law requires records be retained for 10 years.

Criminal Records: Access: In person only. Visitors must perform in person searches for themselves. No search fee. Required to search: name, years to search; also helpful: DOB. Criminal records on computer since 1996; prior records on index cards or docket books. State law requires records be retained for 10 years.

General Information: Juvenile records current now with Norfolk Juv. Court; no juvenile records released. Copy fee: $1.00 per page. Certification fee: $2.50. Payee: District Court. Only cashiers checks and money orders accepted. Prepayment required.

Stoughton District Court
1288 Central St, Stoughton, MA 02072; 781-344-2131. Hours: 8:30AM-4:30PM (EST). *Felony, Misdemeanor, Civil, Eviction, Small Claims.*

Note: Includes Avon, Canton, Sharon, and Stoughton.

Civil Records: Access: Mail, in person. Both court and visitors may perform in person searches. No search fee. Required to search: name, years to search. Civil cases indexed by defendant, plaintiff. Civil records on index cards or docket books for 10 years or more.

Criminal Records: Access: Mail, in person. Only the court performs in person searches; visitors may not. No search fee. Required to search: name, years to search; also helpful: DOB. Criminal records on computer since 1996; prior records on index cards or docket books for 10 years or more.

General Information: No juvenile records released. Copy fee: $1.00 per page. Certification fee: $2.50. Payee: District Court. Personal checks accepted. Prepayment required. Mail turnaround time 1 week.

Wrentham District Court
60 East St., Wrentham, MA 02093; 508-384-3106; Fax: 508-384-5052. Hours: 8:30AM-4:30PM (EST). *Felony, Misdemeanor, Civil, Eviction, Small Claims.*

Note: Includes Foxborough, Franklin, Medway, Millis, Norfolk, Plainville, Walpole, and Wrentham.

Civil Records: Access: In person. Visitors must perform in person searches for themselves. No search fee. Required to search: name, years to search. Civil cases indexed by defendant, plaintiff. Criminal records retained 20 years. Physical records go back to 1985; pre-1985 on docket books.

Criminal Records: Access: In person. Visitors must perform in person searches for themselves. No search fee. Required to search: name, years to search; also helpful: DOB. Criminal records retained 20 years. Physical records go back to 1985; on computer back to 1999; pre-1985 on docket books.

General Information: No show cause hearing or juvenile records released. Will not fax results. Copy fee: $1.00 per page. Certification fee: $2.50 per page. Payee: District Court. Personal checks accepted. Prepayment required.

Probate & Family Court
35 Shawmut Rd, Canton, MA 02021; 781-830-1200; Fax: 781-830-4310 (Reg) 781-830-4320 (Probation) 781-730-4355 (Trial). Hours: 8:15AM-4:30PM (EST). *Probate.*

Note: Due to health concerns, Probate was moved from the old location on High St in Dedham in 2003. Should remain at this new Canton location for 5 years. However, the Register of Deeds remains in Dedham at old address.

Plymouth County

Superior Court - Brockton
72 Belmont St, Brockton, MA 02401; 508-583-8250. Hours: 8:30AM-4:30PM (EST). *Felony, Civil Actions Over $25,000.*

Civil Records: Access: In person only. Visitors must perform in person searches for themselves. No search fee. Required to search: name, years to search. Civil cases indexed by defendant, plaintiff. Civil records for current civil cases are here, closed case are in Plymouth, some pending; computerized records since 2000.

Criminal Records: Access: In person only. Visitors must perform in person searches for themselves. No search fee. Required to search: name, years to search. Criminal records for current civil cases are here, closed case are in Plymouth, some pending; computerized records since 2000.

General Information: Public Access terminal is available. No impounded records released. Copy fee: $1.00 per page. Certification fee: $2.50. Payee: Clerk of Superior Court. Personal checks accepted. Prepayment required.

Superior Court - Plymouth
Plymouth Superior Court, Court St, Plymouth, MA 02360; 508-747-6911. Hours: 8:30AM-4:30PM (EST). *Felony, Civil Actions Over $25,000.*

Civil Records: Access: Phone, mail, in person. Only the court performs in person searches; visitors may not. No search fee. Required to search: name, years to search. Civil cases indexed by defendant, plaintiff. Civil records for all closed cases are kept here; computerized records since 1977.

Criminal Records: Access: In person only, with exception. No search fee. Required to search: name, years to search. Criminal records 10 years or older are here; for recent cases go to the Brockton Superior Court. This court's criminal records under ten years old can be searched in person only at Brockton Superior Court, 72 Belmont St, Brockton, 508-583-8250.

General Information: Public Access terminal is available. No impounded records released. Copy fee: $1.00 per page. Certification fee: $2.50. Payee: Clerk of Superior Court. Personal checks accepted. Prepayment required. Mail turnaround time 1 week; immediate four phone requests.

Brockton District Court PO Box 7610 (215 Main St.), Brockton, MA 02303-7610; 508-587-8000. Hours: 8:30AM-4:30PM (EST). *Felony, Misdemeanor, Civil, Eviction, Small Claims.*
Note: Includes Abington, Bridgewater, Brockton, East Bridgewater, West Bridgewater, and Whitman.

Civil Records: Access: Mail, in person. Both court and visitors may perform in person searches. No search fee. Required to search: name, years to search. Civil cases indexed by defendant, plaintiff. Civil records on index cards or docket books, retained for 10 years.
Criminal Records: Access: Mail, in person. Both court and visitors may perform in person searches. No search fee. Required to search: name, years to search; also helpful: DOB. Criminal records on index cards or docket books, retained for 10 years.
General Information: Public Access terminal is available. No juvenile or impounded records released. Copy fee: $1.00 per page. Certification fee: $2.50. Payee: District Court. Personal checks accepted. Prepayment required. Mail turnaround time 1-2 weeks.

Hingham District Court 28 George Washington Blvd, Hingham, MA 02043; 781-749-7000; Fax: 781-740-8390. Hours: 8:30AM-4:30PM (EST). *Felony, Misdemeanor, Civil, Eviction, Small Claims.*
Note: Includes Hanover, Hingham, Hull, Norwell, Rockland, and Scituate.

Civil Records: Access: Mail, in person. Only the court performs in person searches; visitors may not. No search fee. Required to search: name, years to search. Civil cases indexed by defendant, plaintiff. Civil records on index cards or docket books, retained for 10 years or more.
Criminal Records: Access: Mail, in person. Only the court performs in person searches; visitors may not. No search fee. Required to search: name, years to search; also helpful: DOB. Criminal records on index cards or docket books, retained for 10 years or more.
General Information: No juvenile records released. Copy fee: $1.00 per page. Certification fee: $2.50. Payee: District Court. Personal checks accepted. Prepayment required. Mail turnaround time 1-2 weeks.

Plymouth 3rd District Court Courthouse, South Russell St, Plymouth, MA 02360; 508-747-0500. Hours: 8:30AM-4:30PM (EST). *Felony, Misdemeanor, Civil, Eviction, Small Claims.*
Note: Includes Duxbury, Halifax, Hanson, Kingston, Marshfield, Pembroke, Plymouth, and Plympton.

Civil Records: Access: Mail, in person. Both court and visitors may perform in person searches. No search fee. Required to search: name, years to search. Civil cases indexed by defendant, plaintiff. Civil records on index cards or docket books. State law requires records be retained for 10 years. Visitors can only access the index cards.
Criminal Records: Access: Mail, in person. Both court and visitors may perform in person searches. No search fee. Required to search: name, years to search; also helpful: DOB. Criminal records on index cards or docket books. State law requires records be retained for 10 years. Visitors can only access the index cards.
General Information: No juvenile or impounded records released. Copy fee: $1.00 per page. Certification fee: $2.50. Payee: Plymouth District

Court. Personal checks accepted. Prepayment required. Mail turnaround time 3-4 days.

Wareham District Court 2200 Cranberry Hwy, Junction Routes 28 & 58, West Wareham, MA 02576; 508-295-8300; Fax: 508-291-6376. Hours: 8AM-4:30PM (EST). *Felony, Misdemeanor, Civil, Eviction, Small Claims.*
Note: Includes Carver, Lakeville, Marion, Mattpoinsett, Middleboro, Rochester, and Wareham.

Civil Records: Access: Phone, mail, in person. Both court and visitors may perform in person searches. No search fee. Required to search: name, years to search. Civil cases indexed by defendant, plaintiff. Criminal records back to 1960. Computerized records back to 1995.
Criminal Records: Access: Phone, mail, in person. Only the court performs in person searches; visitors may not. No search fee. Required to search: name, years to search; also helpful: DOB. Criminal records back to 1960. Computerized records back to 1995.
General Information: No juvenile records released. Copy fee: $1.00 per page. Certification fee: $2.50. Payee: District Court. Personal checks accepted. Prepayment required. Mail requests: SASE requested. Turnaround time 1-2 weeks.

Probate & Family Court 11 Russell, PO Box 3640, Plymouth, MA 02361; 508-747-6204; Fax: 508-746-6846. Hours: 8:30AM-4:30PM (EST). *Probate.*

Southeast Housing Court PO Box 7520 (215 Main St), Brockton, MA 02303; 508-894-4170; Fax: 508-894-4168. Hours: 8AM-4PM (EST). *Eviction, Misdemeanor (Code Violations), Small Claims.*
Note: Includes housing code cases, real estate-related small claims, and many eviction cases for Plymouth County; also see district courts.

Suffolk County

Superior Court - Civil 90 Devonshire St, Rm 807, Copy Dept, Boston, MA 02109; 617-788-7677. Hours: 8:30AM-5PM (EST). *Civil.*
Civil Records: Access: Mail, in person. Both court and visitors may perform in person searches. No search fee. Required to search: name, years to search. Civil cases indexed by defendant, plaintiff. Civil records on computer from 1991, index cards and books from 1860.
General Information: Public Access terminal is available. No impounded records released. Copy fee: $1.00 per page. Certification fee: $2.50. Payee: Clerk of Superior Court. Business checks accepted. Prepayment required. Mail turnaround time 1 week.

Superior Court - Criminal 90 Devonshire St #607, USPO & Courthouse, Boston, MA 02109; 617-788-8160; Fax: 617-788-7798. Hours: 8;30AM-5PM (EST). *Felony.*
Criminal Records: Access: Mail, in person. Both court and visitors may perform in person searches. No search fee. Required to search: name, years to search. Criminal records on computer back to 1991, index cards and books from 1950, archived from 1864.
General Information: Public Access terminal is available. Copy fee: $1.00 per page. Certification fee: $20.00. Payee: Superior Court. Personal checks accepted. Prepayment required. Mail turnaround time 1-2 weeks.

Boston Municipal Court Civil Clerk's Office, 90 Devonshire St, Boston, MA 02109; 617-788-8412. Hours: 8:30AM-4:30PM (EST). *Misdemeanor, Civil, Small Claims.*
Civil Records: Access: Mail, in person. Both court and visitors may perform in person searches. No search fee. Required to search: name, years to

Civil cases indexed by defendant, plaintiff. Civil records on computer from 1995 to present, and only court searches those records. Public can search prior records on index cards and look-up. State law requires records be retained for 10 years.
Criminal Records: Access: Mail, in person. Both court and visitors may perform in person searches. No search fee. Required to search: name, years to search; also helpful: DOB. Criminal records on computer from 1995 to present, and only court searches those records. Public can search prior records on index cards and look-up. State law requires records be retained for 10 years.
General Information: No impounded records released. Copy fee: $1.00 per page. Certification fee: $2.50. Payee: District Court. Personal checks accepted. Prepayment required. Mail turnaround time 1-2 weeks.

Brighton District Court 52 Academy Hill Rd, Brighton, MA 02135; 617-782-6521; Fax: 617-254-2127. Hours: 8:30AM-4:30PM (EST). *Felony, Misdemeanor, Civil, Eviction, Small Claims.*
Note: Includes Allston and Brighton.

Civil Records: Access: In person only. Visitors must perform in person searches for themselves. No search fee. Required to search: name, years to search. Civil cases indexed by defendant, plaintiff. Civil records on index cards or docket books back to 1980. State law requires records be retained for 10 years.
Criminal Records: Access: Phone, mail, in person. Visitors must perform in person searches for themselves. No search fee. Required to search: name, years to search, DOB. Computerized records from 1990, criminal records on index cards or docket books back to 1978. State law requires records be retained for 10 years.
General Information: No sealed or impounded records released. Copy fee: $1.00 per page. Certification fee: $2.50 per page. Payee: District Court. Personal checks accepted. Prepayment required. Mail turnaround time 1-2 weeks.

Charlestown District Court 3 City Square, Charlestown, MA 02129; 617-242-5400; Fax: 617-242-1677. Hours: 8:30AM-4:30PM (EST). *Felony, Misdemeanor, Civil, Eviction, Small Claims.*
Civil Records: Access: Fax, mail, in person. Only the court performs in person searches; visitors may not. No search fee. Required to search: name, years to search. Civil cases indexed by defendant, plaintiff. Civil records on index cards or docket books. State law requires records be retained for 10 years.
Criminal Records: Access: Fax, mail, in person. Only the court performs in person searches; visitors may not. No search fee. Required to search: name, years to search; also helpful: DOB. Criminal records on index cards or docket books. State law requires records be retained for 10 years.
General Information: No juvenile records released. Copy fee: $1.00 per page. Certification fee: $2.50. Payee: District Court. Personal checks accepted. Prepayment required. Mail turnaround time 1-2 weeks.

Chelsea District Court 120 Broadway, Chelsea, MA 02150-2606; 617-660-9200. Hours: 8:30AM-4:30PM (EST). *Felony, Misdemeanor, Civil, Eviction, Small Claims.*
Note: Includes Chelsea and Revere.

Civil Records: Access: Phone, mail, in person. Both court and visitors may perform in person searches. No search fee. Required to search: name, years to search. Civil cases indexed by defendant, plaintiff. Civil records on index cards or docket books back to 1900; on computer back to 1990.
Criminal Records: Access: Phone, mail, in person. Both court and visitors may perform in person

searches. No search fee. Required to search: name, years to search; also helpful: address, DOB. Criminal records on index cards or docket books back to 1900; on computer back to 1990.

General Information: No closed cases, impounded, sealed, mental health commitment, alcoholic or victim of sexual offense records released. Copy fee: $1.00 per page. Certification fee: $2.50. Payee: District Court. Personal checks accepted. Prepayment required. Mail requests: SASE required. Mail turnaround time 1-2 weeks.

Dorchester District Court 510 Washington St, Dorchester, MA 02124; 617-288-9500. Hours: 8:30AM-4:30PM (EST). *Felony, Misdemeanor, Civil, Eviction, Small Claims.*
Civil Records: Access: Mail, in person. Both court and visitors may perform in person searches. No search fee. Required to search: name, years to search. Civil cases indexed by defendant, plaintiff. Civil records on index cards or docket books from 1970. State law requires records be retained for 20 years.
Criminal Records: Access: Mail, in person. Only the court performs in person searches; visitors may not. No search fee. Required to search: name, years to search, DOB. Criminal records on index cards or docket books to 1950s; on computer since 1998. State law requires records be retained for 20 years.
General Information: No juvenile records released. Will fax results to local or toll free line. Copy fee: $1.00 per page. Certification fee: $2.50. Payee: District Court. Personal checks accepted. Prepayment required. Mail turnaround time 1-2 weeks.

East Boston District Court 37 Meridian St, East Boston, MA 02128; 617-569-7550; Fax: 617-561-4988. Hours: 8:30AM-4:30PM (EST). *Misdemeanor, Civil Actions Under $25,000, Eviction, Small Claims.*
Note: Includes East Boston and Winthrop.
Civil Records: Access: In person. Both court and visitors may perform in person searches. No search fee. Required to search: name, years to search. Civil cases indexed by defendant, plaintiff. Civil records on index cards or docket books since 1965, computerized since 1988. State law requires records be retained for 20 years.
Criminal Records: Access: In person. Both court and visitors may perform in person searches. No search fee. Required to search: name, years to search. Criminal records on index cards or docket books, computerized since 1988. State law requires records be retained for 20 years.
General Information: No juvenile records released. Copy fee: $1.00 per page. Certification fee: $2.50. Payee: Boston Municipal Court/ East Boston Division. Personal checks accepted. Prepayment required.

Roxbury District Court 85 Warren St, Roxbury, MA 02119; 617-427-7000; Fax: 617-442-0615. Hours: 8:30AM-4:30PM (EST). *Felony, Misdemeanor, Civil, Eviction, Small Claims.*
Civil Records: Access: Phone, fax, mail, in person. Both court and visitors may perform in person searches. No search fee. Required to search: name, years to search. Civil cases indexed by defendant, plaintiff. Civil records on index cards or docket books since 1981; on computer back to 1999. State law requires records be retained for 10 years.
Criminal Records: Access: Phone, fax, mail, in person. Both court and visitors may perform in person searches. No search fee. Required to search: name, years to search, DOB; also helpful: address. Criminal records on index cards or docket books since 1981; on computer back to 1999. State law requires records be retained for 10 years.

General Information: Public Access terminal is available. No juvenile records released. Fee to fax results is $1.00 per page. Copy fee: $1.00 per page. Certification fee: $2.50. Payee: District Court. Prepayment required. Mail turnaround time 1-2 weeks.

South Boston District Court 535 East Broadway, South Boston, MA 02127; 617-268-9292/9293; Fax: 617-268-7321. Hours: 8:30AM-4:30PM (EST). *Felony, Misdemeanor, Civil, Eviction, Small Claims.*
Civil Records: Access: In person only. Visitors must perform in person searches for themselves. No search fee. Required to search: name, years to search, address. Civil cases indexed by defendant, plaintiff. Civil records on index cards or docket books. Records go back 20 years.
Criminal Records: Access: In person only. Visitors must perform in person searches for themselves. No search fee. Required to search: name, years to search, address, DOB. Criminal records on index cards or docket books. Records go back 20 years; from 2000 on computer.
General Information: No juvenile or medical records released. Copy fee: $1.00 per page. Certification fee: $2.50. Payee: District Court. Personal checks accepted. Prepayment required.

West Roxbury District Court Courthouse, 445 Arborway, Jamaica Plain, MA 02130; 617-971-1200. Hours: 8:30AM-4:30PM (EST). *Felony, Misdemeanor, Civil, Eviction, Small Claims.*
Note: Includes West Roxbury, Jamaica Plain, Hyde Park, Roslindale, Parts of Mission Hill, and Mattapan sections of Boston.
Civil Records: Access: In person. Visitors must perform in person searches for themselves. No search fee. Required to search: name, years to search; also helpful: address. Civil cases indexed by defendant, plaintiff. Civil records on index cards or docket books. State law requires records be retained for 10 years. Include type of civil action to be searched.
Criminal Records: Access: In person. Visitors must perform in person searches for themselves. No search fee. Required to search: name, years to search; also helpful: DOB. Criminal records on index cards or docket books. State law requires records be retained for 10 years.
General Information: No juvenile records released. Copy fee: $1.00 per page. Certification fee: $2.50. Payee: District Court. Personal checks accepted. Prepayment required.

Boston Housing Court 24 New Chardon St - 3rd Fl, Edward W Brooke Courthouse, Boston, MA 02114; 617-788-8485; Fax: 617-788-8981. Hours: 8;30AM-4;30PM (EST). *Eviction, Misdemeanor (Code Violations) for residential, commercial or industrial property.*
www.mass.gov/courts/
Note: Small claims phone is 617-788-8515. Includes many housing code cases, real estate-related small claims and eviction cases for Boston, Brighton, Charlestown, Dorchester, East Boston, Roxbury, S. Boston and West Roxbury; also see district courts.

Probate & Family Court 24 New Chardon St, PO Box 9667, Boston, MA 02114-4703; 617-788-8300; Fax: 617-788-8962. Hours: 8:30AM-4:30PM (EST). *Probate.*

Worcester County

Superior Court 2 Main St Rm 21, Worcester, MA 01608; 508-770-1899. Hours: 8AM-4:30PM (EST). *Felony, Civil Actions Over $25,000.*
Civil Records: Access: Mail, in person. Both court and visitors may perform in person searches. No

search fee. Required to search: name, years to search. Civil cases indexed by defendant, plaintiff. Civil records on computer from 1990, index books from 1900.
Criminal Records: Access: Mail, in person. Both court and visitors may perform in person searches. No search fee. Required to search: name, years to search. Criminal records on computer from 1990, index books from 1900.
General Information: Public Access terminal is available. No impounded or juvenile records released. Copy fee: $1.00 per page. Certification fee: $2.50. Payee: Clerk of Superior Court. Personal checks accepted. Prepayment required. Mail turnaround time 1 week.

Clinton District Court 300 Boylston St, Clinton, MA 01510; 978-368-7811; Fax: 978-368-7827. Hours: 8:30AM-4:30PM (EST). *Felony, Misdemeanor, Civil, Eviction, Small Claims.*
Note: Includes Berlin, Bolton, Boylston, Clinton, Harvard, Lancaster, Sterling, and West Boylston.
Civil Records: Access: Mail, in person. Only the court performs in person searches; visitors may not. No search fee. Required to search: name, years to search; also helpful: DOB, SSN. Civil cases indexed by defendant, plaintiff. Civil records on index cards or docket books back to 1968. State law requires records be retained for 20 years.
Criminal Records: Access: Mail, in person. Only the court performs in person searches; visitors may not. No search fee. Required to search: name, years to search, address, DOB, SSN, signed release. Criminal records on index cards or docket books back to 1978. State law requires records be retained for 20 years.
General Information: No juvenile records released. Copy fee: $1.00 per page. Certification fee: $2.50 per page. Payee: District Court Clerk Magistrate. Prepayment required. Mail requests: SASE required. Mail turnaround time 1-2 weeks.

Dudley District Court 64 PO Box 100, Dudley, MA 01571; 508-943-7123; Fax: 508-949-0015. Hours: 8AM-4:30PM (EST). *Felony, Misdemeanor, Civil, Eviction, Small Claims.*
Note: Includes Charlton, Dudley, Oxford, Southbridge, Sturbridge, and Webster.
Civil Records: Access: Phone, fax, mail, in person. Both court and visitors may perform in person searches. No search fee. Required to search: name, years to search. Civil cases indexed by defendant, plaintiff. Civil records on computer back to 2002; prior on index cards or docket books; records retained for 10 years.
Criminal Records: Access: Phone, fax, mail, in person. Both court and visitors may perform in person searches. No search fee. Required to search: name, years to search, DOB. Criminal records on computer back to 06/96; prior records on index cards or docket books; records retained for 10 years.
General Information: Public Access terminal is available. (Only civil available.) No juvenile records released. Copy fee: $1.00 per page. Certification fee: $2.50. Payee: District Court. Business checks accepted. Prepayment required. Mail requests: SASE not required. Mail turnaround time 1-2 weeks.

East Brookfield District Court 544 E Main St, East Brookfield, MA 01515-1701; 508-885-6305/6306; Fax: 508-885-7623. Hours: 8:30AM-4:30PM (EST). *Felony, Misdemeanor, Civil, Eviction, Small Claims.*
Note: Includes Brookfield, East Brookfield, Hardwick, Leicester, New Braintree, North Brookfield, Spencer, Warren, and West Brookfield.
Civil Records: Access: Mail, in person. Both court and visitors may perform in person searches. No search fee. Required to search: name, years to search.

Civil cases indexed by defendant, plaintiff. Civil records on index cards or docket books. State law requires records be retained for 10 years.

Criminal Records: Access: Mail, in person. Both court and visitors may perform in person searches. No search fee. Required to search: name, years to search; also helpful: DOB. Criminal records on index cards or docket books to 1945, computerized since 1999.

General Information: Public Access terminal is available. No juvenile, mental health records released. Copy fee: $1.00 per page. Certification fee: $2.50. Payee: District Court. Personal checks accepted. Prepayment required. Mail requests: SASE requested. Turnaround time 1-2 weeks; strongly suggest to use a retriever when possible.

Fitchburg District Court 16 100 Elm St, Fitchburg, MA 01420; 978-345-2111; Fax: 978-342-2461. Hours: 8:30AM-4:30PM (EST). *Felony, Misdemeanor, Civil, Eviction, Small Claims.*
Note: Includes Fitchburg and Lunenburg.

Civil Records: Access: In person only. Visitors must perform in person searches for themselves. No search fee. Required to search: name, years to search. Civil cases indexed by defendant, plaintiff. Civil records on index cards or docket books back 10 years.

Criminal Records: Access: In person only. Visitors must perform in person searches for themselves. No search fee. Required to search: name, years to search. Criminal records on index cards or docket books back 10 years; on computer back to 1994.

General Information: Public Access terminal is available. No juvenile or mental health records released. Will not fax results. Copy fee: $1.00 per page. Certification fee: $2.50. Payee: District Court. Personal checks accepted. Prepayment required.

Gardner District Court 108 Matthews St, Gardner, MA 01440-0040; 978-632-2373; Fax: 978-630-3902. Hours: 8:30AM-4:30PM (EST). *Felony, Misdemeanor, Civil, Small Claims.*
Note: Includes Gardner, Hubbardston, Petersham, and Westminster.

Civil Records: Access: mail, in person. Both court and visitors may perform in person searches. No search fee. Required to search: name, years to search, address. Civil cases indexed by defendant, plaintiff. Civil records on index cards or docket books. State law requires records be retained for 10 years.

Criminal Records: Access: Phone, fax, mail, in person. Both court and visitors may perform in person searches. No search fee. Required to search: name, years to search, DOB. Criminal records on index cards or docket books. State law requires records be retained for 10 years.

General Information: No juvenile records released. No fee to fax results. Copy fee: $1.00 per page. Certification fee: $2.50. Payee: District Court. Personal checks accepted. Prepayment required. Mail turnaround time 1-2 weeks; quicker for phone and fax verifications.

Leominster District Court 25 School St, Leominster, MA 01453; 978-537-3722; Fax: 978-537-3970. Hours: 8:30AM-4:30PM (EST). *Felony, Misdemeanor, Civil, Eviction, Small Claims.*
Note: Includes Princeton and Leominster.

Civil Records: Access: Phone, mail, in person. Both court and visitors may perform in person searches. No search fee. Required to search: name, years to search. Civil cases indexed by defendant, plaintiff. Civil records on index cards or docket books. State law requires records be retained for 10 years.

Criminal Records: Access: Phone, mail, in person. Both court and visitors may perform in person searches. No search fee. Required to search: name, years to search; also helpful: DOB. Criminal records on computer since 1987; Prior records on index cards or docket books. State law requires records be retained for 10 years.

General Information: No juvenile or impounded records released. Copy fee: $1.00 per page. Certification fee: $2.50. Payee: District Court. Personal checks accepted. Prepayment required. Mail turnaround time 1-2 weeks.

Milford District Court PO Box 370, Milford, MA 01757; 508-473-1260. Hours: 8:30AM-4:30PM (EST). *Felony, Misdemeanor, Civil, Eviction, Small Claims.*
Note: Includes Mendon, Upton, Hopedale, and Milford in Worcester County; also includes Bellingham in Norfolk County.

Civil Records: Access: In person only. Both court and visitors may perform in person searches. No search fee. Required to search: name, years to search. Civil cases indexed by defendant, plaintiff. Civil records on index cards or docket books.

Criminal Records: Access: In person only. Both court and visitors may perform in person searches. No search fee. Required to search: name, years to search, DOB; also helpful: aliases. Criminal records on computer since 1998; prior records on index cards & docket books; computer indexes only searchable by court.

General Information: No mental health, impounded, alcohol, commitment, sexual abuse victim, waivers of fees or costs for indigents, delinquency, C & P, CHINS, 209A minor or 209A address records released. Copy fee: $1.00 per page. Certification fee: $2.50. Payee: District Court. Business checks accepted. Prepayment required.

Uxbridge District Court 261 S Main St, Uxbridge, MA 01569; 508-278-2454; Fax: 508-278-2929. Hours: 8:30AM-4:30PM (EST). *Felony, Misdemeanor, Civil, Eviction, Small Claims.*
Note: Includes Blackstone, Douglas, Millville, Northbridge, Sutton, and Uxbridge.

Civil Records: Access: Mail, in person. Only the court performs in person searches; visitors may not. No search fee. Required to search: name, years to search. Civil cases indexed by defendant, plaintiff. Civil records on index cards or docket books. State law requires records be retained for 10 years. All requests must be in writing.

Criminal Records: Access: Mail, in person. Only the court performs in person searches; visitors may not. No search fee. Required to search: name, years to search; also helpful: DOB. Criminal records on index cards or docket books. State law requires records be retained for 10 years. All requests must be in writing.

General Information: Copy fee: $1.00 per page. Certification fee: $2.50. Payee: District Court. Personal checks accepted. Prepayment required. Mail turnaround time 1-2 weeks.

Westborough District Court 175 Milk St, Westborough, MA 01581; 508-366-8266; Fax: 508-366-8268. Hours: 8AM-4:30PM (EST). *Felony, Misdemeanor, Civil, Eviction, Small Claims.*
Note: Includes Grafton, Northborough, Shrewsbury, Southborough, and Westborough.

Civil Records: Access: In person. Both court and visitors may perform in person searches. No search fee. Required to search: name, years to search. Civil

cases indexed by defendant, plaintiff. Civil records go back to 1986, on books and cards.

Criminal Records: Access: Mail, in person. Both court and visitors may perform in person searches. No search fee. Required to search: name, years to search; also helpful: DOB. Criminal records go back to 1986, on books and cards.

General Information: No impounded, juvenile records released. Copy fee: $1.00 per page. Certification fee: $2.50. Payee: District Court Westborough Division. Personal checks accepted. Prepayment required. Mail requests: SASE required. Mail turnaround time 5 days.

Winchendon District Court 80 Central St, Winchendon, MA 01475; 978-297-0156; Fax: 978-297-0161. Hours: 8:30AM-4:30PM (EST). *Felony, Misdemeanor, Civil, Eviction, Small Claims.*
Note: Includes Ashburnham, Winchendon, Phillipston, Royalston, and Templeton.

Civil Records: Access: Phone, mail, in person. Both court and visitors may perform in person searches. No search fee. Required to search: name, years to search. Civil cases indexed by defendant, plaintiff. Civil records on index cards or docket books. State law requires records be retained for 10 years.

Criminal Records: Access: Phone, mail, in person. Both court and visitors may perform in person searches. No search fee. Required to search: name, years to search; also helpful: DOB, docket number. Criminal records on index cards or docket books. State law requires records be retained for 10 years.

General Information: Copy fee: $1.00 per page. Certification fee: $2.50 per page. Payee: District Court. Personal checks accepted. Prepayment required. Mail turnaround time 1-2 weeks.

Worcester District Court 50 Harvard St, Worcester, MA 01608; 508-757-8350; Fax: 508-797-0716. Hours: 8AM-4:30PM (EST). *Felony, Misdemeanor, Civil, Eviction, Small Claims.*
Note: Includes Auburn, Millbury, and Worcester.

Civil Records: Access: Mail, in person. Both court and visitors may perform in person searches. No search fee. Required to search: name, years to search. Civil cases indexed by defendant, plaintiff. Civil records on index cards or docket books since 1982. State law requires records be retained for 20 years.

Criminal Records: Access: Mail, in person. Both court and visitors may perform in person searches. No search fee. Required to search: name, years to search. Criminal records on computer since 1999; prior records on docket books since 1982.

General Information: Public Access terminal is available. No sealed, expunged, adoption or sex offense records released. Will not fax results. Copy fee: $1.00 per page. Certification fee: $2.50. Payee: District Court. Personal checks accepted. Prepayment required. Mail turnaround time 1-2 weeks.

Probate & Family Court 2 Main St, Worcester, MA 01608; 508-770-0825 x217; Fax: 508-752-6138. Hours: 8:30AM-4:00PM (EST). *Probate.*

Worcester Housing Court 2 Main St, Rm #101, Worcester, MA 01608; 508-792-0800; Fax: 508-792-1170. 8:30AM-4:30PM (EST). *Eviction, Misdemeanor (Code Violations), Small Claims.*
Note: Includes housing code cases, real estate-related small claims and many eviction cases for Worcester County; also see district courts

Massachusetts Recording Offices

ORGANIZATION: 14 counties, 312 towns, and 39 cities; 21 recording offices and 365 UCC filing offices. Each town/city profile indicates the county in which the town/city is located. Filing locations vary depending upon the type of document, as noted below. Berkshire and Bristol counties each has three recording offices. Essex, Middlesex and Worcester counties each has two recording offices. Cities/towns bearing the same name as a county are Barnstable, Essex, Franklin, Hampden, Nantucket, Norfolk, Plymouth, and Worcester. Some UCC financing statements on personal property collateral are were submitted to cities/towns until June 30, 2001, while real estate recording is handled by the counties. Recording officers are Town/City Clerk (UCC), County Register of Deeds (real estate), and Clerk of US District Court (federal tax liens). The entire state is in the Eastern Time Zone (EST).

REAL ESTATE RECORDS: Real estate records are located at the county level. Each town/city profile indicates the county in which the town/city is located. Counties will not perform searches. Copy fee with certification is usually $.75 per page. Each town also has Assessor/Tax Collector/Treasurer offices from which real estate ownership and tax information is available.

UCC RECORDS: This was a dual filing state. Until July 1, 2001, financing statements were usually filed both with the Town/City clerk and at the state level, except for real estate related collateral, which is recorded at the county Register of Deeds. Now, all filing are at the state except for the real estate related collateral. Most all recording offices perform searches. Use search request form UCC-11. Search fees are usually $10.00 per debtor name. Copy fees vary widely.

TAX LIEN RECORDS: Federal tax liens on personal property were filed with the Town/City Clerks prior to 1970. Since that time, federal tax liens on personal property are filed with the US District Court in Boston as well as with the towns/cities. Following is how to search the central index for federal tax liens - Address:

US District Court (617-748-9152)
1 Courthouse Way.
Boston, MA 02110

The federal tax liens are indexed here on a computer system. Searches are available by mail or in person. Do not use the telephone. The court suggests including the Social Security number and/or address of individual names in your search request in order to narrow the results. A mail search costs $15.00 and will take about two weeks. Copies are included. Make your check payable to Clerk, US District Court. You can do the search yourself at no charge on their public computer terminal.

State tax liens on personal property are filed with the Town/City Clerk or Tax Collector. All tax liens against real estate are filed with the county Register of Deeds. Some towns file state tax liens on personal property with the UCC index and include tax liens on personal property automatically with a UCC search. Others will perform a separate state tax lien search, usually for a fee of $10.00 plus $1.00 per page of copies.

OTHER LIENS: Medical, town/city tax, child support.

ONLINE ACCESS: A large number of towns and several counties offer online access to assessor records via the Internet for no charge. Also, a private vendor has placed on the Internet the assessor records from a number of towns. Visit http://data.visionappraisal.com

Abington Town

Town Clerk, 500 Gliniewicz Way, Abington, MA 02351. **Phone**-781-982-2112, R/E Recording- 781-982-2107; fax-781-982-2138; hours 8:30AM-4:30PM www.abingtonmass.com
UCC record search per debtor- $10.00. Tax lien search fee- $10.00 per debtor. RE records at Plymouth Cty. Payee: Town of Abington. **Other phones:** Assessor-781-982-2107; Treasurer-781-982-2131; Elections-781-982-2112; Vital Records-781-982-2112.

Acton Town

Town Clerk, 472 Main St, Town Hall, Acton, MA 01720. **Phone**-978-264-9615, R/E Recording- 978-264-9618; fax-978-264-9630; hours 8AM-5PM www.town.acton.ma.us
UCC record search per debtor- $10.00. UCC copy fee- $1.00 per page. UCC search includes tax liens. RE records at Middlesex Cty. Cert fee: $5.00 per doc. Payee: Town of Acton. **Other phones:** Assessor-978-264-9622; Treasurer-978-264-9612; Elections-978-264-9615; Vital Records-978-264-9615.

Acushnet Town

Town Clerk, 122 Main St, Town Hall, Acushnet, MA 02743. **Phone**-508-998-0215; fax-508-998-0203; hours 8AM-4PM. Will not search UCC records. Tax lien search- $20.00 per debtor. Copy fee- $.25 per page. RE records at Bristol Cty. Payee: Town of Acushnet. **Other phones:** Assessor-508-998-0205; Treasurer-508-998-0212; Vital Records-508-998-0215.

Adams Town

Town Clerk, 8 Park St, Adams, MA 01220. **Phone**-413-743-8320; fax-413-743-8316; 8:30AM-4PM. UCC record search per debtor- $10.00. UCC copy- $2.00 per page. Tax liens not included in UCC search. RE records at Berkshire Cty. Cert fee: $.25 per page. Payee: Town Clerk of Adams. **Other phones:** Assessor-413-743-8350.

Agawam Town

Town Clerk, 36 Main St., Agawam, MA 01001-1837. **Phone**-413-786-0400 x215; fax-413-786-9927; hours 8:30AM-4:30PM. Will not search records. RE records at Hampden Cty. Payee: Town of Agawam. **Online Access to Property Assessor, Real Estate, Recording, Lien records:** Access to property assessment data is free at www.patriotproperties.com/agawam/Default.asp?br=exp&vr=5. See Hampden Cty. for recording records searching. **Other phones:** Assessor-413-786-0400 x205; Treasurer-413-786-0400 x221; Elections-413-786-0400 x215; Vital recs-413-786-0400 x216.

Alford Town

Town Clerk, 5 Alford Center Rd, Town Hall, Alford, MA 01230-8914. **Phone**-413-528-4536; fax-413-528-4581; hours 4:30-7:30PM Th. Will not search records. RE records at Berkshire Cty. Payee: Town of Alford. **Other phones:** Assessor-413-528-4536 x2.

Amesbury Town

Town Clerk, 62 Friend St, Town Hall, Amesbury, MA 01913. **Phone**-978-388-8100; fax-978-388-8150; hours 8AM-4PM M-Th; 5PM-8PM Th; 8AM-Noon F
Will search UCC records prior to 7/2001 only. Search per debtor- $10.00. UCC copy- $1.00 per page. Will not search tax liens. RE records at Essex Cty. Cert fee: No charge. Payee: Town of Amesbury. **Online Access to Property Assessor records:** town assessor data is at http://data.visionappraisal.com/AmesburyMA/. Free registration for full data. **Other phones:** Assessor-978-388-8102; Treasurer-978-388-8105; Elections-978-388-8100; vital -978-388-8100.

Amherst Town

Town Clerk, 4 Boltwood Ave., Town Hall, Amherst, MA 01002. **Phone**-Town Clerk, R/E & UCC Recording- 413-256-4035; fax-413-256-2504; hours 8AM-4:30PM www.town.amherst.ma.us
UCC record search per debtor- $30.00. UCC copy fee- $2.00 per page. Tax lien searches done by Hampshire Cty Registry of Deeds. RE records at Hampshire Cty. Cert fee: $10.00 per cert. Payee: Town of Amherst. **Online Access to Property Assessor records:** Search the town assessor data at http://data.visionappraisal.com/AmherstMA/. Free registration for full data. **Other phones:** Assessor-413-256-4024; Treasurer-413-256-4020; Elections-413-256-4035; Vital Records-413-256-4035.

Andover Town

Town Clerk, 36 Bartlet St, Andover, MA 01810-3882. **Phone**-978-623-8256, R/E Recording- 978-623-8200, UCC Recording- 978-623-8200; fax-978-623-8221; hours 8:30AM-4:30PM www.town.andover.ma.us
UCC record search per debtor- $10.00. UCC copy fee- $2.00 per copy/filing. Federal/state combined tax lien search- $10.00 per search. RE records at Essex Cty. Cert fee: $2.00 per cert. Payee: Town of Andover. **Online Access to Assessor, Land, Grantor/Grantee, Recording records:** Property tax records on the Assessor's database are free at www.town.andover.ma.us/assess/values.htm. Also, search the county recorder database free at www.lawrencedeeds.com/dsSearch.asp. **Other phones:** Assessor-978-623-8200; Treasurer-978-623-8200; Elections-978-623-8200; Vital Records-978-623-8200.

Arlington Town

Town Clerk, 730 Mass Ave, Town Hall, Arlington, MA 02476-9109. **Phone**-781-316-3073, R/E Recording-781-316-3051, UCC Recording- 781-316-3051; fax-781-316-3079; hours 9AM-5PM (8AM-4PM Summer Hours) www.town.arlington.ma.us
UCC record search per debtor- $10.00. UCC copy fee- $2.00 per page. Tax liens included in UCC search. Separate federal/state combined tax lien search- $10.00 per debtor. RE records at Middlesex Cty. Payee: Town of Arlington. **Online Access to Assessor records:** Search town assessor database free at http://arlserver.town.arlington.ma.us/property.html. There is also a website at http://arlingtonma.virtualtownhall.net/Search for searching for names on town public records. **Other phones:** Assessor-781-316-3051; Treasurer-781-316-3030; Elections-781-316-3070; Vital Records-781-316-3070.

Ashburnham Town

Town Clerk, 54 Willard Rd., Ashburnham, MA 01430. **Phone**-978-827-4102; fax-978-827-4105; hours 9AM-5PM (7-9PM 1st & 3rd Mon of month)
UCC record search per debtor- $5.00. UCC copy fee-$.50 per page. UCC search includes tax liens if requested. Separate federal/state combined tax lien search- $5.00 per debtor. RE records at Worcester Cty. Payee: Town of Ashburnham. **Other phones:** Assessor-978-827-4100; Treasurer-978-827-4102; Elections-978-827-4102; Vital Records-978-827-4102.

Ashby Town

Town Clerk, 895 Main St., Ashby, MA 01431. **Phone**-978-386-2424; fax-978-386-2490; hours 9AM-2PM, 6-8PM W. UCC record search per debtor- $10.00. UCC copy- $2.00 per page. Will not search tax liens. RE records at Middlesex Cty. Payee: Town of Ashby. **Online Access to Property, Assessor records:** Access to property data is free at http://csc-ma.us/PropertyContent/jsp/Home.jsp?Page=1. Click on Ashby Town. **Other phones:** Assessor-978-386-2427; Treasurer-978-386-2424; Elections-978-386-2424; Vital Records-978-386-2424.

Ashfield Town

Town Clerk, PO Box 560, Ashfield, MA 01330-0595. **Phone**-Town Clerk, R/E & UCC Recording- 413-628-4441; fax-413-628-4588; hours 9AM-12:30PM, 1:30-5PM M-W,F; 7-9PM F
Will not search records. UCC copy- $2.00 per page. RE records at Franklin Cty. Payee: Town of Ashfield. **Other phones:** Assessor-413-628-4439; Treasurer-413-628-4441; Elections-413-628-4441; Vital Records-413-628-4441; Town Collector-413-628-4428.

Ashland Town

Town Clerk, 101 Main St, Town Hall, Ashland, MA 01721. **Phone**-508-881-0101; fax-508-881-0102; hours 8:30AM-4:30PM www.ashlandmass.com
Will search UCC records. UCC search per debtor- $10.00 per search. UCC copy- $1.00 per page. Will search tax liens. Federal/state combined tax lien search- $10.00 per debtor. RE records at Middlesex Cty. Cert fee: $5.00 per seal. Payee: Town of Ashland. **Other phones:** Assessor-508-881-0104; Treasurer-508-881-0107; Elections-508-881-0101; Vital Records-508-881-0101.

Athol Town

Town Clerk, 584 Main St, Athol, MA 01331. **Phone**-978-249-4551; fax-978-249-2491; hours 8AM-5PM M,W,Th; 8AM-8PM T; Closed Fri.
UCC record search per debtor- $10.00. UCC copy-$2.00 for 1st 3 pages; $1.00 each add'l. UCC search includes tax liens. RE records at Worcester Cty. Cert fee: $1.00 per page. Payee: Town of Athol. **Other phones:** Assessor-978-249-3880; Treasurer-978-249-3374; Elections-978-249-4551; Vital Records-978-249-4551.

Attleboro City

City Clerk, 77 Park St, City Hall, Attleboro, MA 02703. **Phone**-508-223-2222; fax-508-222-3046; 8:30AM-4:30PM. UCC record search per debtor- $10.00. UCC copy- $2.00 per page. UCC search includes tax liens if requested. RE records at Bristol Cty. Payee: City of Attleboro. **Other phones:** Assessor-508-223-2222 x3135; Treasurer-508-223-2222 x3214; Elections-508-223-2222 x3271; Vital Records-508-223-2222 x3111.

Auburn Town

Town Clerk, 104 Central St, Auburn, MA 01501. **Phone**-508-832-7701; fax-508-832-7702; hours 8AM-4PM; extended hours 2nd & 4th Mon. 8AM-7PM www.auburnguide.com
UCC record search per debtor- $10.00. UCC copy-$2.00 per page. UCC search includes tax liens. RE records at Worcester Cty. Payee: Town of Auburn. **Other phones:** Assessor-508-832-7708; Treasurer-508-832-7700; Elections-508-832-7701; Vital Records-508-832-7701.

Avon Town

Town Clerk, Buckley Ctr, Avon, MA 02322. **Phone**-508-588-0414; fax-508-559-0209; 8:30AM-4:30PM
UCC record search per debtor- $10.00. UCC copy fee- $.25 per page. UCC search includes tax liens. Separate federal/state combined tax lien search-$10.00 per search. RE records at Norfolk County. RE record copy- $.25 per page. Payee: Town of Avon. **Other phones:** Assessor-508-588-0414; Treasurer-508-588-0414.

Ayer Town

Town Clerk, PO Box 308, Ayer, MA 01432. **Phone**-978-772-8215; fax-978-772-8222; 8:30AM-5PM
UCC record search per debtor- $5.00. UCC copy fee-$.25 per page. Tax liens included in UCC search if requested. Separate federal/state combined tax lien search- $5.00 per debtor. RE records at Middlesex Cty. Cert fee: $5.00. Payee: Town of Ayer. **Online Access to Property, Assessor records:** Access to property data is free at http://csc-ma.us/PropertyContent/jsp/Home.jsp?Page=1. Click on Ayer Town. **Other phones:** Assessor-978-772-8211; Treasurer-978-772-8216.

Barnstable County

County Register of Deeds, PO Box 368, Barnstable, MA 02630. **Phone**-508-362-7733; fax-508-362-5065; hours 8AM-4PM www.bcrd.co.barnstable.ma.us
Will not search records. Record copy- $1.00 per page. Cert fee: $10.00 per doc. Payee: Barnstable County Register of Deeds. **Online Access to Real Estate, Lien, Deed records:** Access to County records is free at http://199.232.150.242/ALIS/WW400R.PGM. Search for free, but to print requires a $50 annual fee. Records date back to 1940. Lending agency information is available. **Other phones:** Assessor-508-362-4022; Treasurer-508-362-4653.

Barnstable Town

Town Clerk, 367 Main St., Hyannis, MA 02601. **Phone**-508-862-4044, R/E Recording- 508-362-7733, UCC Recording- 508-862-4094; fax-508-790-6326; hours 8:30AM-4:30PM www.town.barnstable.ma.us
Hyannis, ZIP Code 02601, is located here, as well as the villages of Barnstable, West Barnstable, Centerville, Cotuit, Osterville and Marstons Mills. UCC record search per debtor- $15.00 for up to 15 pages. UCC copy- $1.00 per page. Tax liens included in UCC search if requested. Federal/state combined tax lien search- $3.00 up to 15 pages. RE records at Barnstable Cty. Cert fee: $5.00 per doc. Payee: Town of Barnstable. **Online Access to Assessor records:** Town of Barnstable Assessor records free at www.town.barnstable.ma.us/tob02/DNet/AssessingDNet/Disclaimer.aspx. Email questions or comments to webadm@town.barnstable.ma.us or call the Assessing Dept. at 508-862-4022. **Other phones:** Assessor-508-862-4022; Treasurer-508-862-4653; Elections-508-862-4044; Vital Records-508-862-4095.

Barre Town

Town Clerk, PO Box 418, Barre, MA 01005. **Phone**-978-355-5003, R/E Recording- 978-355-5001; fax-978-355-5032; 7-9PM M,W; 9AM-Noon, 1-4PM T,Th
UCC record search per debtor- $10.00. UCC copy-$1.00 per page. Will not search tax liens. RE records at Worcester County. **Other phones:** Assessor-978-355-5010; Treasurer-978-355-5000; Elections-978-355-5003; Vital Records-978-355-5003.

Becket Town

Town Clerk, 557 Main St., Jeanne W Pryor, Becket, MA 01223. **Phone**-413-623-8934; fax-413-623-6036; 12-4:30PM M; 8:30AM-1PM T,F; Noon-8PM W
Will not search records. UCC copy- $1.00 per page. RE records at Berkshire Cty. Payee: Town of Becket. **Other phones:** Assessor-413-623-8934; Treasurer-413-623-8934; Elections-413-623-8934; Vital Records-413-623-8934.

Bedford Town

Town Clerk, 10 Mudge Way, Town Hall, Bedford, MA 01730-0083. **Phone**-781-275-0083; fax-781-687-6157; hours 8AM-4PM www.town.bedford.ma.us
UCC record search per debtor- $10.00. UCC copy fee- $2.00 1st page; $1.00 each attachment. UCC search includes tax liens if requested. Separate federal/state combined tax lien search-no charge. RE records at Middlesex Cty. Payee: Town of Bedford. **Other phones:** Assessor-781-275-0046; Treasurer-781-275-8996; Elections-781-275-0083; Vital Records-781-275-0083.

Belchertown Town

Town Clerk, PO Box 629, Belchertown, MA 01007-0607. **Phone**-413-323-0281, R/E Recording- 413-584-3637; fax-413-323-0107; hours 8AM-5PM www.belchertown.org
UCC record search per debtor- $5.00 plus copy fee. UCC copy- $2.00 per page. UCC search includes tax liens if requested. Separate federal/state combined tax lien search-no charge. RE records at old county courthouse. Cert fee: $5.00 per page. Payee: Town of Belchertown. **Other phones:** Assessor-413-323-0413; Treasurer-413-323-0400; Elections-413-323-0281; Vital Records-413-323-0281.

Bellingham Town

Town Clerk, PO Box 367, Bellingham, MA 02019-0367. **Phone**-508-966-5827; fax-508-966-5804; hours 8:30AM-4:30PM T,W,Th; 8:30AM-1PM F; 8:30AM-7PM M www.bellinghamma.org
Will search UCC records. UCC search per debtor-$2.00 per page. UCC copy- $2.00 per page. Will search tax liens. Tax lien search fee- $10.00 per search. RE records at Norfolk Cty. Payee: Town of Bellingham. **Other phones:** Assessor-508-966-5825; Treasurer-508-966-5828; Elections-508-966-5827; Vital Records-508-966-5827.

Belmont Town

Town Clerk, 455 Concord Ave, Town Hall, Belmont, MA 02178-2514. **Phone**-617-489-8201, UCC Recording- 617-489-8200; fax-617-489-2185; hours 8AM-4PM www.town.belmont.ma.us
UCC record search per debtor- $5.00. UCC copy- $1.00 per page. Will not search tax liens. RE records at Middlesex Cty. Cert fee: $3.00 per doc. Payee: Town of Belmont. **Online Access to Assessor, Property records:** Access to the town assessor data is available free at www2.town.belmont.ma.us/assessors/assessment.htm.
Other phones: Assessor-617-489-8231; Treasurer-617-489-8234; Elections-617-489-8201; Vital Records-617-489-8200.

Berkley Town

Town Clerk, 1 N. Main St, Berkley, MA 02779. **Phone**-508-822-3348; fax-508-822-3511; hours 9AM-3PM. UCC record search per debtor- $10.00. UCC copy- $3.00 per page. UCC search includes tax liens if requested. RE records at Bristol Cty. Payee: Town of Berkley. **Online Access to Property, Assessor records:** Access to property data is free at http://csc-ma.us/PropertyContent/jsp/Home.jsp?Page=1. Click on Berkley Town. **Other phones:** Assessor-508-822-7955.

Berkshire County (Middle District)

County Register of Deeds, 44 Bank Row, Pittsfield, MA 01201. **Phone**-413-443-7438; fax-413-448-6025; hours 8:30AM-4:30PM (No Recording after 3:59PM) Will not search records. UCC copy- $1.00 per page. Cert fee: $1.00. Payee: Berkshire County Register of Deeds. **Online Access to Real Estate, Lien records:** Online search: see Berkshire County Southern District. **Other phones:** Assessor-413-443-5502.

Berkshire County (Northern Dist.)

Register of Deeds, 65 Park St, #1, Adams, MA 01220. **Phone**-Register of Deeds, R/E & UCC Recording- 413-743-0035; fax-413-743-1003; hours 8:30AM-4:30PM
Will not search UCC records, but only real estate related UCC filed here. UCC copy- $1.00 per page. Will not search real estate or tax lien records. Payee: Commonwealth of Massachusetts. **Online Access to Real Estate, Lien records:** Online search: see Berkshire County Southern District. **Other phones:** Assessor-413-743-8350 (Town of Adams); Treasurer-

413-743-8390 (Town of Adams); Vital Records-413-743-8320 (Town of Adams).

Berkshire County (Southern Dist.)

County Register of Deeds, 334 Main St, Great Barrington, MA 01230. **Phone**-413-528-0146; fax-413-528-6878; hours 8:30AM-4:30PM; Recording hours 8:30AM-4PM. Will not search UCC records; only real estate related UCC filed here. UCC copy- $1.00 per page. Will not search real estate or tax lien records. Payee: Berkshire County Register of Deeds. **Online Access to Real Estate, Lien records:** Searching of Titlesearch records requires a one-time $100 signup and $.50 per minute of use. System provides access to all three District Recorder's records; records date back to 1985. Searchable indices: recorded land, plans, registered land. Lending agency information available. For information, contact Sharon Henault at 413-443-7438.

Berlin Town

Town Clerk, 23 Linden St, Box 8, Berlin, MA 01503. **Phone**-978-838-2931; fax-978-838-0014; hours 12-3PM T,Th; 7-9PM W
UCC record search per debtor- $10.00. UCC copy fee- $.50 per page. Tax liens not included in UCC search. Direct tax lien search requests to town tax collector. Separate federal/state combined tax lien search- $10.00 per debtor. RE records at Worcester Cty. Payee: Town of Berlin. **Other phones:** Assessor-978-838-2256; Treasurer-978-838-0344; Elections-978-838-2931; Vital Records-978-838-2931; Tax Collector-978-838-2765.

Bernardston Town

Town Clerk, PO Box 504, Bernardston, MA 01337-0435. **Phone**-413-648-5400, R/E Recording- 413-648-5407; fax-413-648-5408; hours 9AM-2PM
Will not search records. UCC copy- $1.00 per page. RE records at Franklin Cty. Cert fee: $10.00. Payee: Town of Bernardston. **Online Access to Property Assessor records:** Access to property data is free at http://csc-ma.us/PropertyContent/jsp/Home.jsp?Page=1. Select Bernardston Town. **Other phones:** Assessor-413-648-5407; Treasurer-413-648-5400; Elections-413-648-5400; Vital Records-413-648-5400; Tax Collector-413-648-5401.

Beverly City

City Clerk, 191 Cabot St, Beverly, MA 01915-1031. **Phone**-978-921-6000 x164; fax-978-921-8511; hours 8:30AM-4:30PM M,T,W; 8:30AM-7:30PM Th; 8:30AM-1PM www.beverlyma.gov
UCC record search per debtor- $10.00. Will search state tax liens. Will search real estate records. Record copy- $1.00 per page. Cert fee: $3.00. Payee: City of Beverly. **Other phones:** Assessor-978-921-6003; Treasurer-978-921-6135; Elections-978-921-6000 x163; Vital Records-978-921-6000 x161-165.

Billerica Town

Town Clerk, 365 Boston Rd, Town Hall, Billerica, MA 01821-1885. **Phone**-978-671-0924; fax-978-663-6510; hours 8:30AM-4PM
UCC record search per debtor- $10.00. UCC copy- $2.00 per doc. Will not search tax liens. RE records at Middlesex Cty. Cert fee: $3.00 per doc. Payee: Town of Billerica. **Other phones:** Assessor-978-671-0971; Treasurer-978-671-0928; Elections-978-671-0926; Vital Records-978-671-0924.

Blackstone Town

Town Clerk, 15 St Paul St, Municipal Ctr, Blackstone, MA 01504-2295. **Phone**-508-883-1500 x146; fax-508-883-7043; hours 9AM-4:30PM M-F, 5:30-7:30PM Tues. UCC record search per debtor- $10.00. UCC copy- $5.00 per page. Will not search tax liens. RE records at Worcester Cty. Cert fee: $5.00 per copy.

Payee: Town of Blackstone. **Other phones:** Assessor-508-883-1500 x122; Treasurer-508-883-1500 x117; Elections-508-883-1500 x116; Vital Records-508-883-1500 x116.

Blandford Town

Town Clerk, PO Box 101, Blandford, MA 01008. **Phone**-413-848-2747, UCC Recording- 413-848-0054; fax-413-848-0908; hours 6-8PM Mon Evening
Will not search UCC records. UCC copy- $1.00 per page. RE records at Hampden County. Copy fee payee: Town of Blandford. **Online Access to Real Estate, Recording, Lien records:** See Hampden County for recording records searching. **Other phones:** Assessor-413-848-2791; Treasurer-413-848-2782; Elections-413-848-0054; Vital Records-413-848-0054.

Bolton Town

Town Clerk, PO Box 278, Bolton, MA 01740. **Phone**-978-779-2771; fax-978-779-5461; hours 9AM-1PM W,Th; 7-9PM Tuesday; 9AM-4PM Friday www.townofbolton.com
UCC record search per debtor- $10.00.Tax liens not included in UCC search. Separate state tax lien search- $5.00 per debtor. RE records at Worcester Cty. Cert fee: $2.00 per seal. Payee: Town of Bolton. **Online Access to Real Estate, Deed records:** See Worcester County Southern District for online information. **Other phones:** Assessor-978-779-5556.

Boston City

City Clerk, 1 City Hall Plaza, City Hall, Rm 601, Boston, MA 02201. **Phone**-617-635-4600, R/E Recording- 617-788-8575, UCC Recording- 617-635-2689; fax-617-635-4658; hours 9AM-5PM www.ci.boston.ma.us/assessing
Will not search UCC records. RE records at Suffolk County. Copy fee payee: City of Boston. **Online Access to Assessor records:** Records on the City of Boston Assessor database are free at www.ci.boston.ma.us/assessing/search.asp. Property tax bill and payment is searchable by parcel number for free at www.cityofboston.gov/assessing/paysearch.asp. **Other phones:** Assessor-617-635-4287; Treasurer-617-535-4138; Elections-617-635-4634; Vital Records-617-635-4175.

Bourne Town

Town Clerk, 24 Perry Ave, Town Hall, Buzzards Bay, MA 02532. **Phone**-508-759-0613, UCC Recording-508-759-0600; fax-508-759-8026; hours 8:30AM-4:30PM. UCC record search per debtor- $10.00.UCC search includes tax liens if requested. Separate tax lien search fee- $10.00 per request. RE records at Barnstable Cty. Cert fee: $2.00 per page. Payee: Town of Bourne. **Other phones:** Assessor-508-759-0600; Treasurer-508-759-0600; Elections-508-759-0600; Vital Records-508-759-0600.

Boxborough Town

Town Clerk, 29 Middle Rd, Boxborough, MA 01719-1499. **Phone**-Town Clerk, R/E & UCC Recording-978-263-1116; fax-978-264-3127; hours 10AM-2PM; Closed Tuesday; 7-9PM M; 10AM-1PM Th www.town.boxborough.ma.us
UCC record search per debtor- $10.00. UCC copy- $1.00 per page. Tax liens not included in UCC search. Federal/state tax lien search- $10.00 per debtor RE records at Middlesex Cty. Cert fee: $2.00 per seal. Payee: Town of Boxborough. **Other phones:** Assessor-978-263-1116; Treasurer-978-263-1116; Elections-Vital Records-978-263-1116.

Boxford Town

Town Clerk, 7A Spofford Rd, Boxford, MA 01921. **Phone**-978-887-6000 x501; fax-978-887-3546; hours 8AM-4:30PM M-Th

UCC record search per debtor- $20.00. UCC copy-$1.00 per page. UCC search includes tax liens if requested. RE records at Essex Cty. Payee: Town of Boxford. **Other phones:** Assessor-978-887-6000 x504; Treasurer-978-887-6000 x505; Elections-978-887-6000 x501; Vital Records-978-887-6000 x501.

Boylston Town

Town Clerk, 221 Main St, Boylston, MA 01505. **Phone**-508-869-2234; fax-508-869-6210; hours 8AM-2PM M,T; (til 1PM W,TH); 6-8PM M; 9AM-2PM T-Th
UCC record search per debtor- $10.00. UCC copy-$1.00 per page. Tax liens not included in UCC search. Contact the town tax collector for searches. Separate federal/state combined tax lien search- $10.00 per debtor. RE records at Worcester Cty. Payee: Town of Boylston. **Other phones:** Assessor-508-869-6543; Treasurer-508-869-2972; Elections-508-869-2234; Tax Collector-508-869-2972.

Braintree Town

Town Clerk, 1 JFK Memorial Drive, Braintree, MA 02184-6498. **Phone**-781-794-8000 x8241, UCC Recording- 781-794-8000; fax-781-794-8259; hours 8:30AM-4:30PM
UCC record search per debtor- $10.00. UCC copy-$2.00 1st 3 pages; $1.00 each add'l. UCC search includes tax liens if requested. Separate federal/state combined tax lien search- $10.00 per debtor. RE records at Norfolk Cty. Payee: Town of Braintree. **Other phones:** Assessor-781-794-8050; Treasurer-781-794-8060; Elections-781-794-8241; Vital Records-781-794-8241.

Brewster Town

Town Clerk, 2198 Main St, Brewster, MA 02631. **Phone**-508-896-4506; fax-508-896-8089; hours 8:30AM-4PM
UCC record search per debtor- $10.00. Copy fee is $.20 per copy. UCC search includes tax liens if requested. RE records at Barnstable Cty. Payee: Town of Brewster. **Other phones:** Assessor-508-896-3701 x22; Treasurer-508-896-3701 x112; Elections-508-896-4506; Vital Records-508-896-4506.

Bridgewater Town

Town Clerk, 64 Central Sq, Town Hall, Bridgewater, MA 02324. **Phone**-Town Clerk, R/E & UCC Recording- 508-697-0921; fax-508-697-0941; hours 8AM-4PM M-Th; 8AM-1PM Friday. www.bridgewaterma.org
UCC record search per debtor- $10.00. UCC copy fee- $.20 per copy. Will not search tax liens. RE records at Plymouth Cty. Cert fee: $5.00 per cert. Payee: Town of Bridgewater. **Other phones:** Assessor-508-697-0928; Treasurer-508-697-0923; Elections-508-697-0921; Vital Records-508-697-0921.

Brimfield Town

Town Clerk, PO Box 508, Brimfield, MA 01010. **Phone**-413-245-4101; fax-413-245-4107; hours 6:30PM-8PM T; 9-11AM Sat
UCC record search per debtor- $10.00. UCC copy-$1.00 per page. UCC search includes tax liens if requested. Separate federal/state combined tax lien search- $10.00 per debtor. RE records at Hampden Cty. Payee: Town of Brimfield. **Online Access to Real Estate, Recording, Lien records:** See Hampden County for recording records searching. **Other phones:** Assessor-413-245-4100.

Bristol County (Fall River District)

County Register of Deeds, 441 N. Main St, Fall River, MA 02720. **Phone**-508-673-1651, R/E Recording-508-673-1651 or 2910, UCC Recording- 508-673-1651 or 2910; fax-508-673-7633; hours 8AM-4:30PM www.fr-registry.com
Will not search records. Record copy- $1.00 per page. Cert fee: No charge. Payee: Fall River Registry of Deeds. **Online Access to Real Estate, Lien records:** Online search: see Bristol County Southern District. Indexes are 1982 to present. **Other phones:** Assessor-508-324-2302.

Bristol County (Northern District)

County Register of Deeds, 11 Court St, Taunton, MA 02780-0248. **Phone**-508-822-0502; fax-508-880-4975; hours 8AM-4:30PM. Will not search records. UCC copy- $1.00 per page. Cert fee: No charge. Payee: Bristol County Register of Deeds. **Online Access to Real Estate, Lien records:** Online search: see Bristol County Southern District. **Other phones:** Treasurer-508-824-4028.

Bristol County (Southern District)

County Register of Deeds, 25 N. 6th St, New Bedford, MA 02740. **Phone**-508-993-2603; fax-508-997-4250; hours 8:30AM-4:30PM www.newbedforddeeds.com
Will search UCC records, but only real estate related UCC filed here. UCC copy- $1.00 per page. Will not search real estate or tax lien records. Cert fee: No extra fee. Payee: Bristol County Register of Deeds. **Online Access to Real Estate, Lien records:** Access to County records requires a $100 set up fee and $.50 per minute of use. All three districts are on this system; the record dates vary by district. Lending agency information is available. For information, contact Rosemary at 508-993-2605. Real Estate searches found at www.newbedforddeeds.com/dsSearch.asp.

Brockton City

City Clerk, 45 School St, Brockton, MA 02401. **Phone**-City Clerk, R/E & UCC Recording- 508-580-7114; fax-508-580-7104; hours 8:30AM-4:30PM
Will search UCC records only in reference to Real Estate UCCs. Search per debtor- $10.00. UCC copy-$1.00 per page. Will not search tax liens. RE records at Plymouth Cty. Payee: City of Brockton. **Other phones:** Assessor-508-580-7194; Treasurer-508-580-7159; Elections-508-580-7117; Vital Records-508-580-7114.

Brookfield Town

Town Clerk, 6 Central St., Brookfield, MA 01506. **Phone**-508-867-2930 X12, R/E Recording- 508-867-2930 x15; fax-508-867-5091; hours 9AM-3PM Tu. Th, 7-8PM Tu. www.brookfieldma.us
UCC record search per debtor- $10.00. UCC copy-$1.00 per page. Tax liens included in UCC search if requested. Separate federal/state combined tax lien search- $25.00 per debtor. RE records at Worcester Cty. Payee: Town of Brookfield. **Online Access to Property, Assessor records:** Access to assessor property data is free at www.brookfieldma.us/Assessors.htm. Also, Access to property data is free at http://csc-ma.us/PropertyContent/jsp/Home.jsp?Page=1. Select Brookfield Town. **Other phones:** Assessor-508-867-2930 x15; Treasurer-508-867-2930 x14; Elections-508-867-2930 x12; Vital Records-508-867-2930 x12.

Brookline Town

Town Clerk, 333 Washington St, Town Hall, Brookline, MA 02445. **Phone**-617-730-2010, R/E Recording- 617-730-2020; fax-617-730-2043; hours 8AM-5PM M-W, 8AM-8PM Th, 8AM-12:30PM F www.town.brookline.ma.us/Assessors
Will not search UCC records. UCC copy- $2.00 per page; $1.00 per page after 3rd. State tax lien search is free. RE records at Norfolk Cty. Cert fee: $10.00. Payee: Town of Brookline. **Online Access to Assessor, Property records:** Records on the Town of Brookline Assessors database are free at www.townofbrooklinemass.com/assessors/propertyloo

kup.asp. **Other phones:** Assessor-617-730-2060; Treasurer-617-730-2020; Elections-617-730-2010; Vital Records-617-730-2010.

Buckland Town

Town Clerk, PO Box 159, Buckland, MA 01338. **Phone**-413-625-8572; fax-413-625-8570; hours 10AM-3PM M-Th
Postal designation "Shelburne Falls" is not a town. It refers either to Shelburne or Buckland. UCC record search per debtor- $10.00. UCC copy fee- $.35 per page. Will not search tax liens. RE records at Franklin Cty. Payee: Town of Buckland. **Other phones:** Assessor-413-625-2335; Treasurer-413-625-9474; Elections-413-625-8572; Vital Records-413-625-8572.

Burlington Town

Town Clerk, 29 Center St, Town Hall, Burlington, MA 01803. **Phone**-781-270-1660; fax-781-270-1608; hours 8:30AM-4:30PM www.burlington.org/clerk
UCC record search per debtor- $10.00. UCC copy-$2.00 per page. UCC search includes tax liens if requested. RE records at Middlesex Cty. Cert fee: $2.00 per filing. Payee: Town of Burlington. **Other phones:** Assessor-781-270-1650; Treasurer-781-270-1624; Vital Records-781-270-1660.

Cambridge City

City Clerk, 795 Massachusetts Ave., City Hall, Rm 103, Cambridge, MA 02139. **Phone**-617-349-4260; fax-617-349-4269; hours 8:30AM-8PM M; 8:30AM-5PM T-TH; 8:30-noon F
http://www2.ci.cambridge.ma.us/assessor
UCC record search per debtor- $10.00.Will not search tax liens. RE records at Middlesex Cty. Payee: City of Cambridge. **Online Access to Assessor records:** Records on the City of Cambridge Assessor database are free at www.ci.cambridge.ma.us/fiscalaffairs/. No name searching. **Other phones:** Assessor-617-349-4343; Treasurer-617-349-4220; Elections-617-349-4361; Vital Records-617-349-4260.

Canton Town

Town Clerk, 801 Washington St, Memorial Hall, Canton, MA 02021. **Phone**-781-821-5013; fax-781-821-5016; hours 9AM-5PM
UCC record search per debtor- $10.00. UCC copy fee- $.50 per page. Tax liens included in UCC search if requested. Separate federal/state combined tax lien search- $10.00 per search. RE records at Norfolk Cty. Payee: Town of Canton. **Other phones:** Assessor-781-821-5008; Treasurer-781-821-5006; Elections-781-821-5013; Vital Records-781-821-5013.

Carlisle Town

Town Clerk, 66 Westford St, Carlisle, MA 01741. **Phone**-978-369-6155; fax-978-371-0594; hours 9AM-3PM. UCC record search per debtor- $10.00.Will not search tax liens. RE records at Middlesex Cty. Payee: Town of Carlisle. **Other phones:** Assessor-978-369-0392; Treasurer-978-369-5557; Elections-978-369-6155; Vital Records-978-369-6155.

Carver Town

Town Clerk, 108 Main St, Carver, MA 02330. **Phone**-508-866-3403, UCC Recording- 508-86-3403; fax-508-866-3408; hours 8AM-4PM M-Th; 8AM-Noon F, Tues. 8AM-4PM; 5-8PM. UCC record search per debtor- $10.00. UCC copy- $1.00 per page. Will not do a tax lien search, records kept at Treasurer. RE records at Plymouth Cty. Cert fee: $5.00. Payee: Town of Carver. **Other phones:** Assessor-508-86-3410; Treasurer-508-866-3435; Elections-508-86-3403; Vital Records-508-86-3403.

Charlemont Town

Town Clerk, PO Box 605, Charlemont, MA 01339-0605. **Phone**-413-625-6157; fax-413-339-0320; hours By appointment. Will not search records. UCC copy-$1.00 per page. RE records at Franklin Cty. Payee: Town of Charlemont. **Other phones:** Assessor-413-339-8586; Treasurer-413-625-1097; Elections-413-625-6157; Vital Records-413-625-6157; Tax Lien/Tax Collector-413-339-5707.

Charlton Town

Town Clerk, 37 Main St, Charlton, MA 01507. **Phone**-508-248-2249; fax-508-248-2073; hours 10AM-3PM M-Th; 1st & 3rd Tues of month 6-8PM
UCC record search per debtor- $5.00. UCC copy-$2.00 1st 3 pages; $1.00 each add'l. Tax liens not included in UCC search. Separate federal/state combined tax lien search- $10.00 per debtor. RE records at Worcester Cty. Payee: Town of Charlton. **Other phones:** Assessor-508-248-2203; Treasurer-508-248-2242; Elections-508-248-2249; Vital Records-508-248-2249.

Chatham Town

Town Clerk, 549 Main St, Chatham, MA 02633. **Phone**-508-945-5101; fax-508-945-3550; hours 8AM-4PM www.town.chatham.ma.us
Will search UCC records, phone search requests cannot be honored. Search per debtor- $10.00. UCC copy fee- $.20 per page. Tax liens included in UCC search if requested. Separate federal/state combined tax lien search- $10.00 per debtor. RE records at Barnstable Cty. Cert fee: $5.00 per doc. Payee: Town of Chatham. **Other phones:** Assessor-508-945-5103; Treasurer-508-945-5108; Elections-508-945-5101; Vital Records-508-945-5101.

Chelmsford Town

Town Clerk, 50 Billerica Rd, Chelmsford, MA 01824. **Phone**-978-250-5205; fax-978-840-5208; hours 8:30AM-5PM www.townofchelmsford.us
UCC record search per debtor- $10.00. UCC copy-$2.00 per page. Tax liens not included in UCC search. Separate federal/state combined tax lien search- $10.00 per debtor. RE records at Middlesex Cty. Payee: Town of Chelmsford. **Other phones:** Assessor-978-250-5220; Treasurer-978-250-5210; Elections-978-250-5205; Vital Records-978-250-5205.

Chelsea City

City Clerk, 500 Broadway, City Hall, Rm 209, Chelsea, MA 02150. **Phone**-617-889-8226, R/E Recording-617-889-8213; fax-617-889-8367; hours 8AM-4PM M,W,Th; 8AM-7PM T; 8AM-Noon F
UCC record search per debtor- $10.00. UCC copy fee- $2.00 1st page; $1.00 each add'l. Tax liens included in UCC search if requested. Separate federal/state combined tax lien search- $10.00 per debtor. RE records at Suffolk Cty. Payee: City of Chelsea. **Online Access to Assessor records:** Search the city assessor database at http://data.visionappraisal.com/ChelseaMA/. Free registration for full data. **Other phones:** Assessor-617-889-8213; Treasurer-617-889-8210; Elections-617-889-8226; Vital Records-617-889-8226.

Cheshire Town

Town Clerk, PO Box S, 80 Church St, Cheshire, MA 01225. **Phone**-413-743-1690; fax-413-743-0389; hours 9AM-3PM M,T,W; 9AM-Noon Th
UCC record search per debtor- $10.00.Will not search tax liens. RE records at Berkshire Cty. Payee: Town of Cheshire. **Other phones:** Assessor-413-743-1690.

Chester Town

Town Clerk, Town Hall, Chester, MA 01011. **Phone**-413-354-6603; fax-413-354-2268; hours 7-9PM M
Will not search records. UCC copy- $1.00 per page. RE records at Hampden Cty. Cert fee: $10.00. Payee: Chester Town Clerk. **Online Access to Property, Assessor, Real Estate, Recording, Lien records:** Access to property data is free at http://csc-ma.us/PropertyContent/jsp/Home.jsp?Page=1. Select Chester Town. Also, see Hampden County for recording records searching. **Other phones:** Assessor-413-354-6357; Treasurer-413-354-7761.

Chesterfield Town

Town Clerk, 422 Main St, Davenport Bldg, Chesterfield, MA 01012-0013. **Phone**-413-296-4741, R/E Recording- 413-296-4771; fax-413-296-4394; hours 7-9PM M or by Appointment
UCC record search per debtor- $10.00. UCC copy-$1.00 per page. Tax liens not included in UCC search. RE records at Hampshire Cty. Cert fee: $5.00 per record (Vitals Only). Payee: Town of Chesterfield. **Other phones:** Assessor-413-296-4010; Treasurer-413-296-4771; Elections-413-296-4741; Vital Records-413-296-4741.

Chicopee City

City Clerk, 17 Springfield St, City Hall, Chicopee, MA 01013. **Phone**-413-594-1466; fax-413-594-2057; hours 8AM-5PM. UCC record search per debtor- $10.00. UCC copy fee- $2.00 per copy. UCC search includes tax liens. RE records at Hampden Cty. Payee: City of Chicopee. **Online Access to Real Estate, Recording, Lien records:** See Hampden County for recording records searching. **Other phones:** Assessor-413-594-1430; Treasurer-413-594-1560; Elections-413-594-1550.

Chilmark Town

Town Clerk, PO Box 119, Chilmark, MA 02535-0119. **Phone**-508-645-2107, R/E Recording- 508-645-2102; fax-508-645-2110; hours-9AM-Noon www.ci.chilmark.ma.us
No real estate recordings; real estate records at courthouse in Edgartown, 508-627-3751. UCC record search per debtor- $10.00. UCC copy- $1.00 per page. RE records at Dukes Cty. Cert fee: $3.00 per page. Payee: Town of Chilmark. **Other phones:** Assessor-508-645-2102; Treasurer-508-645-2106; Elections-508-645-2107; Vital Records-508-645-2107; Exec. Secretary - Timothy R Carroll-508-645-2101.

Clarksburg Town

Town Clerk, 111 River Rd, Town Hall, Clarksburg, MA 01247. **Phone**-413-663-8247; fax-413-664-6575; hours 9AM-2PM W-F
Will not search records. UCC copy- $1.00 per page. RE records at Berkshire Cty. Payee: Town of Clarksburg. **Other phones:** Assessor-413-663-8255; Treasurer-413-663-8247; Elections-413-663-7940; Vital Records-413-663-8247.

Clinton Town

Town Clerk, 242 Church St, Clinton, MA 01510. **Phone**-978-365-4119; fax-978-895-4130; hours 8:30AM-4PM
UCC record search per debtor- $10.00. UCC copy-$2.00 per page. Tax liens included in UCC search if requested. Separate federal/state combined tax lien search- $10.00 per debtor. RE records at Worcester Cty. Payee: Town of Clinton. **Other phones:** Assessor-978-365-4117; Treasurer-978-365-4129; Elections-978-365-4119; Vital Records-978-365-4119.

Cohasset Town

Town Clerk, 41 Highland Ave, Cohasset, MA 02025-1814. **Phone**-781-383-4100; fax-781-383-1561; hours 8:30AM-4:30PM M,W,Th; 8:30AM-7PM Tu; 8:30AM-1PM F. UCC record search per debtor-$5.00. UCC copy fee- $.20 per page. Will not search tax liens. RE records at Norfolk Cty. Payee: Town of Cohasset. **Other phones:** Assessor-781-383-4114; Treasurer-781-383-4102; Elections-781-383-4100; Vital Records-781-383-4100.

Colrain Town

Town Clerk, PO Box 31, Colrain, MA 01340-0031. **Phone**-413-624-3454; fax-413-624-8852; hours 9AM-4PM M-Th
UCC record search per debtor- $10.00. UCC copy-$.50 per page. Tax liens included in UCC search. Separate federal/state combined tax lien search-$10.00 per debtor. RE records at Franklin Cty. Payee: Town of Colrain. **Other phones:** Assessor-413-624-3356; Treasurer-413-624-3454; Elections-413-624-3454; Vital Records-413-624-3454.

Concord Town

Town Clerk, PO Box 535, Concord, MA 01742. **Phone**-978-318-3080, R/E Recording- 617-679-6300; fax-978-318-3093; hours 8:30AM-4:30PM www.concordnet.org
Will search UCC records to July 2001 only. Search per debtor- $10.00. UCC copy- $2.00 per page for 1st 3 pages, $1.00 per each add'l. Will search state tax liens. RE records at Middlesex Cty. Cert fee: $2.00 per doc plus doc cost. Payee: Town of Concord. **Online Access to Property Assessor records:** Alpha search residential and commercial assessments at www.concordnet.org/assessor/fy01value_main.htm. **Other phones:** Assessor-978-318-3070; Treasurer-978-318-3050; Elections-978-318-3080; Vital Records-978-318-3080.

Conway Town

Town Clerk, PO Box 240, Conway, MA 01341. **Phone**-413-369-4235; fax-413-369-4237; hours 9AM-Noon T,Th,F
UCC record search per debtor- $10.00. UCC copy-$.20 per page. Will not search tax liens. RE records at Franklin Cty. Cert fee: $2.00 per page. Payee: Town of Conway. **Other phones:** Assessor-413-369-4773; Treasurer-413-369-4235; Elections-413-369-4235; Vital Records-413-369-4235.

Cummington Town

Town Clerk, 585 Berkshire Trail, Cummington, MA 01026. **Phone**-413-634-5458; fax-413-634-5568; hours 6-8PM W
Will not search UCC records. Tax liens not included in UCC search. Separate federal/state combined tax lien search- $10.00 per debtor. RE records at Hampshire Cty. Payee: Cummington Town Clerk. **Other phones:** Assessor-413-634-5354; Elections-413-634-5458; Vital Records-413-634-5457.

Dalton Town

Town Clerk, 462 Main St, Town Hall, Dalton, MA 01226. **Phone**-413-684-6103 x14; fax-413-684-6129; hours 8AM-4PM M-W; 8AM-6PM Th
UCC record search per debtor- $10.00. They reserve the right to charge more for an extended search. UCC copy- $1.00 per page. UCC search includes tax liens. Separate federal/state combined tax lien search- $10.00 per debtor. RE records at Berkshire Cty. Cert fee: $5.00 per page. Payee: Town of Dalton-Town Clerk. **Other phones:** Assessor-413-684-6105; Treasurer-413-684-6111 x18; Elections-413-684-6103 x15; Vital Records-413-684-6103 x15.

Danvers Town

Town Clerk, 1 Sylvan St, Town Hall, Danvers, MA 01923. **Phone-**Town Clerk, R/E & UCC Recording-978-777-0001; fax-978-777-1025; hours 8AM-5PM M-W; 8AM-7:30PM Th; 8AM-1:30PM F www.danvers-ma.org
UCC record search per debtor- $10.00. UCC copy fee- $.25 per page. Will not search tax liens. RE records at Essex Cty. Cert fee: $6.00 per doc. Payee: Town of Danvers. **Other phones:** Assessor-978-777-0001; Treasurer-978-777-0001; Elections-978-777-0001; Vital Records-978-777-0001.

Dartmouth Town

Town Clerk, PO Box 79399, Dartmouth, MA 02747. **Phone-**508-910-1800, R/E Recording- 508-910-1809; fax-508-910-1894; hours-8:30AM-4:30PM www.town.dartmouth.ma.us/town_hall.htm
UCC record search per debtor- $10.00. UCC copy fee- $.20 per page. UCC search includes tax liens. RE records at Bristol Cty. Cert fee: $2.00 up to 3 pages. Payee: Town of Dartmouth. **Online Access to Assessor records:** Search the town assessor data at http://data.visionappraisal.com/DartmouthMA/. Free registration for full data. **Other phones:** Assessor-508-910-1809; Treasurer-508-910-1802; Elections-508-910-1800; Vital Records-508-910-1800.

Dedham Town

Town Clerk, PO Box 306, Dedham, MA 02027. **Phone-**781-751-9200; fax-781-751-9109; hours 8:30AM-4:30PM
UCC record search per debtor- $10.00. UCC copy- $2.00 per page. UCC search includes tax liens if requested. Separate federal & state combined tax lien search- $10.00 per debtor. RE records at Norfolk Cty. Cert fee: No charge. Payee: Town of Dedham. **Online Access to Assessor records:** Property records on the Assessor's database are free at http://data.visionappraisal.com/dedhamma/. Registration is required for full access; registration is free. **Other phones:** Assessor-781-751-9130; Treasurer-781-751-9170; Elections-781-751-9200; Vital Records-781-751-9200.

Deerfield Town

Town Clerk, 8 Conway St., South Deerfield, MA 01373. **Phone-**Town Clerk, R/E & UCC Recording-413-665-2130; fax-413-665-7275; hours 9AM-4PM www.town.deerfield.ma.us
Will search UCC records. UCC search per debtor- $1.00 per page. Separate federal/state combined tax lien search- $10.00 per debtor. RE records at Franklin Cty. Cert fee: $.25 per parcel. Payee: Town of Deerfield. **Other phones:** Assessor-413-665-7184; Treasurer-413-665-2130.

Dennis Town

Town Clerk, PO Box 1419, South Dennis, MA 02660-1419. **Phone-**508-760-6115, R/E Recording- 508-362-2511, UCC Recording- 508-760-6112; fax-508-394-8309; 8:30AM-4:30PM www.town.dennis.ma.us/
UCC record search per debtor- $10.00.Tax liens not included in UCC search. Separate federal/state combined tax lien search- $10.00 per debtor. RE records at Barnstable Cty. Payee: Town of Dennis. **Online Access to Assessor, Property records:** Access to assessor property records is free at http://townofdennis.bonsailogic.com/. **Other phones:** Assessor-508-760-6142; Treasurer-508-760-6117; Elections-508-760-6112; Vital Records-508-760-6112.

Dighton Town

Town Clerk, 979 Somerset Ave, Dighton, MA 02715-0465. **Phone-**508-669-5411; fax-508-669-5932; hours 8:00AM-4PM M,T,Th; 8AM-5PM W; 8AM-N Fri. www.dighton-ma.gov/Home/

UCC record search per debtor- $5.00. UCC copy-$2.00 per page. Will not search tax liens. RE records at Bristol Cty. Payee: Town of Dighton. **Other phones:** Assessor-508-669-5043; Treasurer-508-669-5411; Elections-508-669-5411; Vital Records-508-669-5411.

Douglas Town

Town Clerk, 29 Depot St., Municipal Ctr, Douglas, MA 01516. **Phone-**508-476-4000 x355, R/E Recording-508-476-4000 x353; fax-508-476-4012; hours 9AM-1PM, 1:30-4PM M-Th; 6-8PM T
UCC record search per debtor- $5.00. UCC copy-$2.00 per page. Tax liens not included in UCC search. Separate federal/state combined tax lien search- $5.00 per debtor. RE records at Worcester Cty. Payee: Town of Douglas. **Other phones:** Assessor-508-476-4000 x353; Treasurer-508-476-4000 x356; Elections-508-476-4000 x355; Vital Records-508-476-4000 x355.

Dover Town

Town Clerk, PO Box 250, Dover, MA 02030-0250. **Phone-**508-785-0032, R/E Recording- 508-785-0032 x241, UCC Recording- 508-785-0032 x226; fax-508-785-2341; hours 9AM-1PM M,W,F; 9AM-4PM T,Th http://doverma.org/townclerk.shtml
UCC record search per debtor- $5.00. UCC copy fee-$.20 per page. Tax liens not included in UCC search. Federal/state combined tax lien search-$5.00 per debtor. RE records at Norfolk Cty. Cert fee: $5.00 per item. Payee: Town of Dover. **Online Access to Property, Assessor records:** Access to the assessor's property values data is free at www.doverma.org/assessorsoffice.shtml. You must open individual tables to search by name. **Other phones:** Assessor-508-785-0032 x241; Treasurer-508-785-0032 x228; Elections-508-785-0032 x226; Vital Records-508-785-0032 x226.

Dracut Town

Town Clerk, 62 Arlington St, Rm 4, Dracut, MA 01826. **Phone-**978-453-0951; fax-978-452-7924; hours 8:30AM-4:30PM
Will not search UCC records. UCC copy fee- $2.00 per page. Will do tax lien search. RE records at Middlesex Cty. Cert fee: $2.00. Payee: Town of Dracut. **Online Access to Assessor records:** Search the town assessor database at http://data.visionappraisal.com/DracutMA/. Free registration for full data. **Other phones:** Assessor-978-453-2451.

Dudley Town

Town Clerk, 40 Schofield Ave, Town Hall #17, Dudley, MA 01571. **Phone-**508-949-8004; fax-508-949-7115; hours 8AM-noon, 12:30-4:30 PM M-Th; 6-8PM Th; 8AM-1PM F www.dudleyma.gov
UCC record search per debtor- $10.00. UCC copy-$2.00 per page. UCC search includes tax liens. RE records at Worcester Cty. Payee: Town of Dudley. **Online Access to Assessor records:** Search the town assessor database at http://data.visionappraisal.com/DudleyMA/. Free registration for full data. **Other phones:** Assessor-508-949-8006; Treasurer-508-949-8002; Elections-508-949-8004; Vital Records-508-949-8004.

Dukes County

County Register of Deeds, PO Box 5231, Edgartown, MA 02539. **Phone-**County Register of Deeds, R/E & UCC Recording- 508-627-4025; fax-508-627-7821; hours 8:30AM-4:30PM
This county is comprised of 7 towns; there is no County Assessor, Appraiser, Elections, etc. Will not search records. Record copy- $1.00 per page. Cert fee: $1.00 per doc. Payee: Dukes County Register of Deeds.

Dunstable Town

Town Clerk, 511 Main St., Dunstable, MA 01827. **Phone-**978-649-4514; fax-978-649-2205; hours M 6PM-9PM; TWTH 9AM-2PM; F 9AM-NOON
Will not search UCC records. UCC copy- $1.00 per page. Will not search tax liens. RE records at Middlesex Cty. Payee: Town of Dunstable. **Other phones:** Assessor-978-649-3257; Treasurer-978-649-3257; Elections-978-649-4514; Vital Records-978-649-4514.

Duxbury Town

Town Treasurer, 878 Tremont St, Duxbury, MA 02332-4499. **Phone-**781-934-1100; fax-781-934-9278; hours 8AM-noon,1-4PM. Will not search UCC records. UCC copy- $2.00 per financing statement. Treasurer office processes municipal lien certificates. Line certificates- $25.00 per search. RE records at Plymouth Cty. Payee: Town of Duxbury. **Online Access to Property Assessor records:** Search the town public documents free at http://duxburyma.virtualtownhall.net/Public_Document s/Search. **Other phones:** Assessor-781-934-1109; Treasurer-781-934-1102.

East Bridgewater Town

Town Clerk, PO Box 387, East Bridgewater, MA 02333. **Phone-**508-378-1606, R/E Recording- 325-378-1602 (town collector), UCC Recording- 325-378-1606; fax-508-378-1638; hours 8:30AM-8PM Tu-Th; 8:30AM-4:30PM M; 8:30AM-N F
UCC record search per debtor- $10.00. UCC copy-$1.00 per page. Tax liens not included in UCC search. RE records at Plymouth Cty. Payee: Town of East Bridgewater. **Other phones:** Assessor-508-378-1609; Treasurer-508-378-1604; Elections-508-378-1606; Vital Records-508-378-1606.

East Brookfield Town

Town Clerk, Town Hall, East Brookfield, MA 01515. **Phone-**Town Clerk, R/E & UCC Recording- 508-867-6769, UCC Recording- 508-867-6769 x301; fax-508-867-4190; hours 9AM-12 M; 11AM-1PM F
UCC record search per debtor- $10.00. UCC copy-$1.00 per page. UCC search includes tax liens if requested at no extra fee. If it is a separate search, same fees apply. RE records at Worcester Cty. Cert fee: $10.00 per doc. Payee: Town of East Brookfield. **Online Access to Assessor, Property records:** Access to property data is free at http://csc-ma.us/PropertyContent/jsp/Home.jsp?Page=1. Select East Brookfield Town. **Other phones:** Assessor-508-867-6769 x302; Treasurer-508-867-6769 x304; Elections-508-867-6769 x301; Vital Records-508-867-6769 x301.

East Longmeadow Town

Town Clerk, 60 Center Sq, East Longmeadow, MA 01028-2446. **Phone-**Town Clerk, R/E & UCC Recording- 413-525-5400 x410; fax-413-525-0022; hours 8AM-4PM www.eastlongmeadow.org
UCC record search per debtor- $10.00. UCC copy-$1.00 per page. Tax liens not included in UCC search. Separate state tax lien search- $10.00 per debtor. RE records at Hampden Cty. Cert fee: $5.00 per page. Payee: Town of East Longmeadow. **Online Access to Real Estate, Recording, Lien records:** See Hampden County for recording records searching. **Other phones:** Assessor-413-525-5425 x450; Treasurer-413-525-5400 x410; Elections-413-525-5400 x410; Vital Records-413-525-5400 x410.

Eastham Town

Town Clerk, 2500 State Highway, Eastham, MA 02642. **Phone-**508-240-5900 x223; hours 8AM-4PM
UCC record search per debtor- $10.00.UCC search includes tax liens if requested. Separate

federal/state combined tax lien search- $6.00 per debtor. RE records at Barnstable Cty. Cert fee: $5.00. Payee: Town of Eastham. **Other phones:** Assessor-508-255-0333.

Easthampton City

City Clerk, 50 Payson Ave #100, Easthampton, MA 01027. **Phone**-413-529-1460, R/E Recording- 413-529-1401; fax-413-529-1488; hours 8AM-4PM M-F; 7-8PM W.

UCC record search per debtor- $5.00. UCC copy-$.30 per page. UCC search includes tax liens if requested. RE records at Hampshire Cty. Payee: City of Easthampton. **Online Access to Propety Assessor records:** Search the city assessor data at http://data.visionappraisal.com/EasthamptonMA/. Free registration for full data. **Other phones:** Assessor-413-529-1401; Treasurer-413-529-1416; Elections-413-529-1460; Vital Records-413-529-1460.

Easton Town

Town Clerk, 136 Elm St, North Easton, MA 02356-0129. **Phone**-508-230-0530, R/E Recording- 508-230-0520; fax-508-230-0539; hours 8:30AM-8:30PM M; 7AM-4:30PM T Th; 8:30AM-12:30PM F www.easton.ma.us

UCC record search per debtor- $15.00. UCC copy-$8.00 for 1st 3 pages; $2.00 each add'l. Tax liens included in UCC search if requested. Separate federal/state combined tax lien search- $15.00 per debtor. RE records at Bristol Cty. Payee: Town of Easton. **Other phones:** Assessor-508-230-0520; Treasurer-508-230-0610; Elections-508-230-0530; Vital Records-508-230-0530.

Edgartown Town

Town Clerk, PO Box 35, Edgartown, MA 02539-0035. **Phone**-508-627-6110, R/E Recording- 508-627-4025 (county); fax-508-627-6123; hours 8AM-4PM

UCC record search per debtor- $10.00. UCC copy-$2.00 per page. Tax liens not included in UCC search. RE records at Dukes Cty. Payee: Town of Edgartown. **Online Access to Real Estate, Property Tax records:** Search the Town assessor's database at http://data.visionappraisal.com/EdgartownMA. Free registration for full data. **Other phones:** Assessor-508-627-6140; Treasurer-508-627-6130; Elections-508-627-6110; Vital Records-508-627-6110.

Egremont Town

Town Clerk, PO Box 56, North Egremont/ So. Egremont, MA 01258-0056. **Phone**-413-528-0182, R/E Recording- 413-528-0182 x12; fax-413-528-5465; hours 7-9PM Tues.

UCC record search per debtor- $5.00. UCC copy-$1.00 per page. UCC search includes tax liens if requested. Separate federal/state combined tax lien search- $5.00 per debtor. Payee: Town of Egremont. **Online Access to Property, Assessor records:** Access to property data is free at http://csc-ma.us/PropertyContent/jsp/Home.jsp?Page=1. Select Egremont Town. **Other phones:** Assessor-413-528-0182; Elections-413-528-0182; Vital Records-413-528-0182.

Erving Town

Town Clerk, 12 E Main St, Town Hall, Erving, MA 01344. **Phone**-413-422-2800, R/E Recording- 413-422-2800 x107, UCC Recording- 413-422-2800 x102; fax-413-422-2808; hours 2-5PM, 6-9PM M

UCC record search per debtor- $10.00. UCC copy-$1.00 per page. UCC search includes tax liens if requested. RE records at Franklin Cty. Cert fee: $5.00 per page. Payee: Town of Erving. **Other phones:** Assessor-413-422-2800 x107; Treasurer-413-422-2800 x104; Elections-413-422-2800 x102; Vital Records-413-422-2800 x102.

Essex County (Northern District)

County Register of Deeds, 381 Common St, Lawrence, MA 01840. **Phone**-978-683-2745; fax-978-681-5409; hours 8AM-4:30PM (recording until 4PM) www.lawrencedeeds.com

Will search UCC records, but only real estate related UCC filed here. Will not search real estate or tax lien records. Record copy- $1.00 per page. Cert fee: $1.00 per page. Payee: Essex County Register of Deeds. **Online Access to Real Estate, Lien, Grantor/Grantee, Recording records:** Search the county recorder database for free at www.lawrencedeeds.com/dsSearch.asp. Also see Andover Town and Essex County Southern District. **Other phones:** Assessor-978-683-2745; Treasurer-978-683-2745.

Essex County (Southern District)

County Register of Deeds, 36 Federal St, Salem, MA 01970. **Phone**-978-741-0201; fax-978-744-5865; hours 8AM-4PM www.salemdeeds.com

Will not search records. UCC copy- $.50 per page self-serve; $1.00 if they copy. Cert fee: $1.00 per page. Payee: Essex County Register of Deeds. **Online Access to Real Estate, Lien, Deed records:** Records on the Essex County South Registry of Deeds database are free at www.salemdeeds.com. Click on "Deeds online". Images start 1/1992; records back to 1/1984. Search by grantee/grantor, town & date, street, or book & page. **Other phones:** Assessor-978-741-0200.

Essex Town

Town Clerk, Martin St., Town Hall, Essex, MA 01929. **Phone**-978-768-7111; hours 8:30AM-1PM M,W; 1-4PM T & Th; Closed F

Do not confuse Essex Town with Essex County. UCC records are filed with the Town/City Clerk, real estate records are at the county level with the Register of Deeds. UCC record search per debtor- $10.00.Will not search tax liens. RE records at Essex Cty. Payee: Town of Essex.

Everett City

City Clerk, City Hall, Rm 10, Everett, MA 02149. **Phone**-617-394-2225; fax-617-387-5770; hours M 8AM-7:30PM; 8AM-4PM T-Th; 8-11:30AM Fri. UCC record search per debtor- $10.00. UCC copy fee- $2.00 each for 1st 3; $1.00 each add'l. UCC search includes tax liens. Separate federal/state combined tax lien search- $10.00 per debtor. RE records at Middlesex Cty. Payee: City of Everett. **Other phones:** Assessor-617-394-2205; Treasurer-617-394-2315; Elections-617-394-2229; Vital Records-617-394-2225; Registrar of Voters-617-394-2297.

Fairhaven Town

Town Clerk, 40 Center St, Fairhaven, MA 02719-2999. **Phone**-508-979-4025; fax-508-979-4079; hours 8:30AM-4:30PM

UCC record search per debtor- $10.00. UCC copy fee- $.25 per page. Tax liens not included in UCC search. RE records at Bristol Cty. Cert fee: $5.00 per copy. Payee: Town of Fairhaven. **Other phones:** Assessor-508-979-4018; Treasurer-508-979-4026; Elections-508-979-4025; Vital Records-508-979-4025.

Fall River City

City Clerk, One Government Ctr, Fall River, MA 02722. **Phone**-508-324-2220; fax-508-324-2211; hours 9AM-5PM. UCC record search per debtor- $5.00. UCC copy- $2.00 for 2st 3 pages; $1.00 each add'l. Tax liens not included in UCC search. Tax lien search fee- $5.00 per debtor. RE records at Bristol Cty. Cert fee: $1.00 per page. Payee: City of Fall River. **Other phones:** Assessor-508-324-2300;

Treasurer-508-324-2260; Elections-508-324-2630; Vital Records-508-324-2220.

Falmouth Town

Town Clerk, PO Box 904, Falmouth, MA 02541. **Phone**-508-548-7611, R/E Recording- 508-495-7675, UCC Recording- 508-495-7357; fax-508-457-2511; hours 8AM-4:30PM www.town.falmouth.ma.us

UCC record search per debtor- $10.00.Will not search tax liens. RE records at Barnstable Cty. Cert fee: $5.00 per cert. Payee: Town of Falmouth. **Online Access to Assessor records:** Records on the Town of Falmouth Assessor database are free by experiment on the Internet at www.town.falmouth.ma.us/propinq.html. Provides owner, address, and valuation only. **Other phones:** Assessor-508-495-7377; Treasurer-508-495-7362; Elections-508-495-7358; Vital Records-508-495-7357; Switchboard-508-548-7611.

Fitchburg City

City Clerk, 718 Main St, Fitchburg, MA 01420-3198. **Phone**-978-345-9592; fax-978-345-9595; 8:30AM-4:30PM. UCC record search per debtor- $10.00. UCC copy- $2.00 per page. Will not search tax liens. RE records at Worcester Cty. Cert fee: $7.00 per page. Payee: City of Fitchburg. **Other phones:** Assessor-978-345-9562; Treasurer-978-345-9605; Elections-978-345-9592; Vital Records-978-345-9592.

Florida Town

Town Clerk, 20 South St, Town Hall, Drury, MA 01343. **Phone**-413-664-6685; fax-413-664-8640; hours By Appointment. UCC record search per debtor- $10.00. UCC copy- $1.00 per page. Tax liens not included in UCC search. RE records at Berkshire Cty. Payee: Town of Florida. **Other phones:** Assessor-413-662-2448; Treasurer-413-663-9851.

Foxborough Town

Town Clerk, 40 South St, Foxborough, MA 02035-2397. **Phone**-508-543-1208, R/E Recording- 508-543-1215; fax-508-543-6278; hours 8:30AM-4PM M,W,Th; 8:30AM-4PM, 5-8PM T; 8:30AM-12: UCC record search per debtor- $10.00. UCC copy fee- $2.00 per filing & $1.00 per page over 3. Will search tax liens. Tax lien search fee- $10.00 per debtor. RE records at Norfolk Cty. Cert fee: $2.00 per copy. Payee: Town of Foxborough. **Other phones:** Assessor-508-543-1215; Elections-508-543-1208; Vital Records-508-543-1208; Main Number-508-543-1200.

Framingham Town

Town Clerk, 150 Concord St, Memorial Bldg. - Rm 105, Framingham, MA 01702-8374. **Phone**-508-620-4863, R/E Recording- 508-628-1311; fax-508-628-1358; hours 8:30AM-5PM M; 8:30AM-5PM T-F www.framinghamma.org

UCC record search per debtor- $10.00. UCC copy-$1.00 per page. UCC search includes tax liens if requested. RE records at Middlesex Cty. Cert fee: $6.00 per certified copy. Payee: Framingham Town Clerk. **Other phones:** Assessor-508-620-4858; Treasurer-508-628-1311; Elections-508-620-4863; Vital Records-508-620-4863.

Franklin County

County Register of Deeds, PO Box 1495, Greenfield, MA 01302-1495. **Phone**-413-772-0239; fax-413-774-7150; hours 8:30AM-4:30PM (Recording til 4PM) Will not search records. Record copy- $1.00 per page. Cert fee: No extra fee. Payee: Commonwealth of Massachusetts. **Online Access to Real Property, Recording, Lien, Deed, Judgment records:** Access to Franklin County Real Property database is free at http://216.60.44.25. Select Franklin County.

Franklin Town

Town Clerk, 355 Easr Central St., Municipal Bldg., Franklin, MA 02038. **Phone**-508-520-4900; fax-508-520-4903; hours 8AM-4PM M,T,Th, 8AM-6PM,W,8am -1PM,F
UCC record search per debtor- $5.00. UCC copy-$1.00 per page. Tax liens included in UCC search. Separate state tax lien search- $5.00 per debtor. RE records at Franklin Cty. Cert fee: $3.00. Payee: Town of Franklin. **Other phones:** Assessor-508-520-4920; Treasurer-508-520-4950.

Freetown Town

Town Clerk, PO Box 438, Assonet, MA 02702. **Phone**-508-644-2203, R/E Recording- 508-644-2205; fax-508-644-9826; hours 9AM-7PM M, 9AM-4PM F T-F
http://town.freetown.ma.us/tg/
UCC record search per debtor- $15.00. Includes UCC face copies up to 15 pages. Add'l pages are $1.00 per page. Tax liens not included in UCC search. RE records at Bristol Cty. Cert fee: $2.00 per copy. Payee: Town of Freetown. **Other phones:** Assessor-508-644-2205; Treasurer-508-644-2204; Elections-508-644-2203; Vital Records-508-644-2203; Tax Collector-508-644-2206.

Gardner City

City Clerk, 95 Pleasant St, City Hall, Rm 118, Gardner, MA 01440. **Phone**-978-630-4008; fax-978-630-2520; hours 8AM-4:30PM; F 8AM-4PM
UCC record search per debtor- $10.00. UCC copy-$1.00 per page. Tax liens not included in UCC search. RE records at Worcester Cty. Cert fee: $10.00. Payee: City of Gardner. **Online Access to Property Assessor records:** Search the city assessor data at http://data.visionappraisal.com/GardnerMA/. Free registration for full data. **Other phones:** Assessor-978-630-4004; Treasurer-978-630-4016.

Georgetown Town

Town Clerk, 1 Library St, Georgetown, MA 01833. **Phone**-978-352-5711, R/E Recording- 978-352-5708; fax-978-352-5725; hours M&W 9AM-Noon,T&Th 9AM-4PM; Closed Fri.
UCC record search per debtor- $5.00. UCC copy-$1.00 per page. Will not search tax liens. RE records at Essex Cty. Payee: Town of Georgetown. **Other phones:** Assessor-978-352-5708; Treasurer-978-352-5723; Elections-978-352-5711; Vital Records-978-352-5711.

Gill Town

Town Clerk, 325 Main Rd, Town Clerk's Office, Gill, MA 01376. **Phone**-413-863-8103, R/E Recording-413-863-0138; fax-413-863-7775; hours 10AM-4PM W-F. Will search UCC records. UCC search per debtor- $20.00 per closure. UCC copy- $1.00 per page. Will not search tax liens. See Tax Collector's Office. RE records at Franklin Cty. Cert fee: $5.00 per cert. Payee: Town of Gill. **Other phones:** Assessor-413-863-0138; Treasurer-413-863-0138; Elections-413-863-8103; Vital Records-413-863-8103; Tax Collector-413-863-8103.

Gloucester City

City Clerk, 9 Dale Ave, Gloucester, MA 01930-5998. **Phone**-978-281-9720; fax-978-281-8472; hours 8:30AM-4PM M-W,F Winter; 8:30AM-6:30PM Th www.ci.gloucester.ma.us
UCC record search per debtor- $10.00. UCC copy-$2.00 per page and $.25 per attachment. UCC search includes tax liens if requested. Separate federal/state combined tax lien search- $10.00 per debtor. RE records at Essex Cty. Payee: City of Gloucester. **Other phones:** Assessor-978-281-9715; Treasurer-978-281-9707; Elections-978-281-9720; Vital Records-978-281-9720.

Goshen Town

Town Clerk, PO Box 124, Goshen, MA 01032-0124. **Phone**-413-268-8236; fax-413-268-8237; hours 7-8:30PM Monday. UCC record search per debtor-$10.00. UCC copy- $1.00 per page. Will not search tax liens. Contact tax collector. RE records at Hampshire Cty. Cert fee: $3.00 per item. Payee: Town of Goshen. **Other phones:** Assessor-413-268-7856; Treasurer-413-268-8236; Elections-413-268-8236; Vital Records-413-268-8236; Tax Collector-413-268-8236.

Gosnold Town

Town Clerk, Town Hall, Gosnold, MA 02713. **Phone**-Town Clerk, R/E & UCC Recording- 508-990-7408; fax-508-990-7408; hours By Appointment
UCC record search per debtor- $10.00. UCC copy-$1.00 per page. Will not search tax liens. RE records at Dukes Cty. Payee: Town of Gosnold. **Other phones:** Assessor-508-990-7408; Treasurer-508-990-7408; Elections-508-990-7408; Vital Records-508-990-7408.

Grafton Town

Town Clerk, 30 Providence Rd, Municipal Ctr, Grafton, MA 01519-1186. **Phone**-508-839-4722, UCC Recording- 508-839-5335 x195; fax-508-839-4602; hours 8:30AM-4:30PM (T 8:30AM-7PM)
UCC record search per debtor- $5.00. UCC copy-$1.00 per page. UCC search includes tax liens. Separate federal/state combined tax lien search-$5.00 per debtor. RE records at Worcester Cty. Payee: Town of Grafton. **Online Access to Property, Assessor records:** Access to property data is free at http://csc-ma.us/PropertyContent/jsp/Home.jsp?Page=1. Select Grafton Town. **Other phones:** Assessor-508-839-5335 x165; Treasurer-508-839-5335 x170; Elections-508-839-5335 x195; Vital Records-508-839-5335 x195.

Granby Town

Town Clerk, 250 State St., Kellogg Hall, Granby, MA 01033. **Phone**-413-467-7178, R/E Recording- 413-584-3637; fax-413-467-2080; hours 9AM-3PM M,T,W,Th; 9AM-Noon F; 7-9PM 1st & 3rd M
UCC record search per debtor- $10.00. UCC copy-$1.00 per page. UCC search includes tax liens. Separate federal/state combined tax lien search-$1.00 per copy. RE records at Hampshire Cty. Cert fee: $6.00 per copy. Payee: Town of Granby. **Other phones:** Assessor-413-467-7196; Treasurer-413-467-7176; Elections-413-467-7178; Vital Records-413-467-7178.

Granville Town

Town Clerk, PO Box 247, Granville, MA 01034-0247. **Phone**-Town Clerk, R/E & UCC Recording- 413-357-8585; fax-413-357-6002; hours 9-11AM, 7-9PM M
UCC record search per debtor- $10.00. UCC copy-$1.00 per page. Will search tax liens. Tax lien search fee- $10.00 per item. RE records at Hampden Cty. Payee: Town of Granville. **Online Access to Real Estate, Recording, Lien records:** See Hampden County for recording records searching. **Other phones:** Assessor-413-357-8585; Treasurer-413-357-8585; Elections-413-357-8585; Vital Records-413-357-8585.

Great Barrington Town

Town Clerk, 334 Main St, Great Barrington, MA 01230-1802. **Phone**-413-528-3140, R/E Recording-413-528-0146; fax-413-528-2290; hours 8:30AM-4PM. UCC record search per debtor- $10.00. UCC copy-$2.00 per page. Will not search tax liens. RE records at Southern Berkshire Cty. Payee: Town of Great Barrington. **Other phones:** Assessor-413-528-2220; Treasurer-413-528-1025; Elections-Vital Records-413-528-3140; Selectman-413-528-1619.

Greenfield Town

Town Clerk, 14 Court Sq, Town Hall, Greenfield, MA 01301. **Phone**-413-772-1555 x112; fax-413-772-1542; hours 8:30AM-5PM. UCC record search per debtor-$20.00. UCC copy fee- $2.00 for no more that 3 pages then $1.00 per page thereafter. UCC search includes tax liens if requested. RE records at Franklin Cty. Cert fee: $10.00 per certified copy. Payee: Town of Greenfield. **Other phones:** Assessor-413-772-1506; Treasurer-413-772-1563.

Groton Town

Town Clerk, 173 Main St., Town Hall, Groton, MA 01450. **Phone**-978-448-1100; fax-978-448-2030; hours 8:30AM-7PM M; 8:30AM-4:30PM T-Th; 9-4 F; 9-1 Sat
Will not search UCC records. Tax lien search fee-$5.00 per search. RE records at Middlesex Cty. Payee: Town of Groton. **Other phones:** Assessor-978-448-1127; Treasurer-978-448-1103; Elections-978-448-1100; Vital Records-978-448-1100.

Groveland Town

Town Clerk, Town Hall, Groveland, MA 01830. **Phone**-Town Clerk, R/E & UCC Recording- 978-372-6861, UCC Recording- 978-372-5005; fax-978-469-5006; hours 9AM-1PM M,T,Th,F; 9AM-Noon W
UCC record search per debtor- $10.00. UCC copy-$1.00 per page. Will not search tax liens. RE records at Essex Cty. Payee: Town of Groveland. **Other phones:** Assessor-978-372-8528; Treasurer-978-372-6861; Elections-978-372-5005; Vital Records-978-372-5005.

Hadley Town

Town Clerk, 100 Middle St, Hadley, MA 01035-9517. **Phone**-413-584-1590; fax-413-586-5661; hours 9AM-4PM www.hadleyma.org
Will not search UCC records by name. UCC copy-$2.00 per page. RE records at Hampshire Cty. Payee: Town of Hadley. **Other phones:** Assessor-413-586-6320; Treasurer-413-586-3354; Elections-413-584-1590; Vital Records-413-584-1590.

Halifax Town

Town Clerk, 499 Plymouth St, Halifax, MA 02338-1395. **Phone**-781-293-7970; fax-781-294-7684; hours 7AM-4PM; 6:30-8:30PM Tues (closed Fri)
UCC record search per debtor- $10.00.Tax liens not included in UCC search. RE records at Plymouth Cty. Payee: Town of Halifax. **Other phones:** Assessor-781-293-5960; Treasurer-781-294-8348; Elections-781-293-7970; Vital Records-781-293-7970.

Hamilton Town

Town Clerk, PO Box 429, Hamilton, MA 01936. **Phone**-978-468-5570; fax-978-468-2682; hours 8AM-4:30PM (Fri open until Noon); 4:30-7PM M Eve. www.town.hamilton.ma.us
UCC record search per debtor- $5.00. UCC copy-$1.00 per page. Will not do a tax lien search; see Treasurer. RE records at Essex Cty. Payee: Town of Hamilton. **Other phones:** Assessor-978-468-5574; Treasurer-978-468-5575; Elections-978-468-5570; Vital Records-978-468-5570; Selectmen-978-468-5572.

Hampden County

County Register of Deeds, 50 State St, Hall of Justice, Springfield, MA 01103. **Phone**-413-755-1722; fax-413-731-8190; hours 8:30AM-4:30PM; 9AM-4PM(Recording)
http://registryofdeeds.co.hampden.ma.us
Will search UCC records, but only real estate related UCC filed here. UCC copy- $1.00 per page. Will not search real estate or tax lien records. Payee: Hampden County Register of Deeds. **Online Access**

to Real Estate, Lien, Recording records: county index of land records is free or via subscription at http://204.213.242.147/alis/ww400r.pgm. Images can be viewed free, but cannot be printed unless you subscribe. Access to images via dial-up or web requires a $100 annual fee and $.50 per minute of use. Records go back to 1962. Lending agency info is available. Searchable indexes are bankruptcy (from PACER), unregistered land site and registered land site. For information, contact Mary Caron at 413-755-1722 x121.

Hampden Town

Town Clerk, PO Box 215, Hampden, MA 01036. **Phone**-413-566-3214, R/E Recording- 413-755-1722; fax-413-566-2010; hours 9AM-1PM M-Th; Closed F www.hampden.org
UCC record search per debtor- $10.00. UCC copy-$1.00 per page. Tax liens not included in UCC search. Separate federal/state combined tax lien search- $10.00 per debtor. RE records at Hampden Cty. Cert fee: $25.00 per LMC. Payee: Town of Hampden. **Online Access to Real Estate, Recording, Lien records:** See Hampden County for recording records searching. **Other phones:** Assessor-413-566-3223; Treasurer-413-566-2401; Elections-413-566-3214; Vital Records-413-566-3214.

Hampshire County

County Register of Deeds, 33 King St, Hall of Records, Northampton, MA 01060. **Phone**-County Register of Deeds, R/E & UCC Recording- 413-584-3637; fax-413-584-4136; hours 8:30AM-4:30PM (Recording ends at 4PM)
Will not search records. Record copy- $1.00 per page. Cert fee: No extra fee. Payee: Commonwealth of Massachusetts. **Online Access to Real Estate, Lien records:** Access to property records is available; records date back to 9/2/1986. Lending agency information is available. For information, contact MaryAnn Foster at 413-584-3637. Also, recordings and real estate data is free online at http://216.60.44.25. Select Hampshire County. Land/property records are also searchable at www.masslandrecords.com.

Hancock Town

Town Clerk, 3650 Hancock Rd., Hancock, MA 01237-1097. **Phone**-Town Clerk, R/E & UCC Recording-413-738-5225; fax-413-738-5310; hours 7-9PM T; 9AM-Noon Th; 9-11AM 1st Sat of the month
UCC record search per debtor- $10.00. UCC copy-$1.00 per page. Will not search tax liens. RE records at Berkshire Cty. Cert fee: $1.00 per page. Payee: Town of Hancock. **Other phones:** Assessor-413-738-5225; Treasurer-413-738-5225; Elections-413-738-5225; Vital Records-413-738-5225.

Hanover Town

Town Clerk, 550 Hanover St, Hanover, MA 02339-2217. **Phone**-781-826-2691; fax-781-826-5950; hours 8AM-4PM
UCC record search per debtor- $10.00. UCC copy fee- $.25 per page. UCC search includes tax liens. Tax lien search fee- $5.00. RE records at Plymouth Cty. Cert fee: $5.00 per certification. Payee: Town of Hanover. **Other phones:** Assessor-781-826-6401; Treasurer-781-826-3571; Elections-781-826-8796; Vital Records-781-826-2691.

Hanson Town

Town Clerk, 542 Liberty St., Town Hall, Hanson, MA 02341. **Phone**-781-293-2772; fax-781-294-0884; hours 8AM-5PM M,T,W,Th; 7-9PM Tue
UCC record search per debtor- $10.00. UCC copy-$1.00 per page. Tax liens not included in UCC search. Federal/state combined tax lien search-$15.00 per debtor. RE records at Plymouth Cty. Cert fee: $1.00 per page. Payee: Town of Hanson.

Other phones: Assessor-781-293-5259; Treasurer-781-293-2422; Elections-781-293-2772; Vital Records-781-293-2772.

Hardwick Town

Town Clerk, PO Box 575, Gilbertville, MA 01031-0575. **Phone**-413-477-6197, UCC Recording- 413-477-6700; fax-413-477-6703; hours 6:30-8:30PM M; 9AM-Noon Sat
UCC record search per debtor- $10.00. UCC copy-$1.00 per page. UCC search includes tax liens if requested. RE records at Worcester Cty. Cert fee: $5.00 per page. Payee: Town of Hardwick. **Online Access to Property, Assessor records:** Access to property data is available free at http://csc-ma.us/PropertyContent/jsp/Home.jsp?Page=1. Select Harwick Town. **Other phones:** Assessor-413-477-6197 x102; Treasurer-413-477-6197 x105; Elections-413-477-6700; Vital Records-413-477-6700.

Harvard Town

Town Clerk, 13 Ayer Rd, Town Hall, Harvard, MA 01451-1458. **Phone**-978-456-4100, UCC Recording-978-456-4100 x16; fax-978-456-4113; hours 8:30AM-4PM M-Th www.harvard.ma.us/townclerk.htm
No real estate recordings; real estate records are at the county level with the Register of Deeds. The Village of Still River is in the Town of Harvard. Will search UCC records prior to 7/2001. Search per debtor- $10.00. UCC copy- $1.00 per page. UCC search includes tax liens prior to 7/2001. RE records at Worcester Cty. Cert fee: $1.00 per doc. Payee: Town of Harvard. **Other phones:** Assessor-978-456-4100 x14; Treasurer-978-456-4100 x18; Elections-978-456-4100 x16; Vital Records-978-456-4100 x16.

Harwich Town

Town Clerk, 732 Main St, Harwich, MA 02645-2717. **Phone**-508-430-7516, R/E Recording- 508-430-7503; fax-508-432-5039; hours 8:30AM-4PM
UCC record search per debtor- $10.00. UCC copy-$2.00 per page. Will not search tax liens. RE records at Barnstable Cty. Payee: Town of Harwich. **Other phones:** Assessor-508-430-7503; Treasurer-508-430-7501; Elections-508-430-7516; Vital Records-508-430-7516; Board of Selectmen-508-430-7513.

Hatfield Town

Town Clerk, 59 Main St, Hatfield, MA 01038-9702. **Phone**-413-247-0492; fax-413-347-5029; hours 8:30AM-4PM (F 8:30AM-12). UCC record search per debtor- $10.00. UCC copy- $1.00 per page. UCC search includes tax liens. Tax lien search fee-$10.00 per debtor. RE records at Hampshire Cty. Payee: Town of Hatfield. **Other phones:** Assessor-413-247-0322; Treasurer-413-247-0492.

Haverhill City

City Clerk, 4 Summer St, City Hall, Rm 118, Haverhill, MA 01830-5880. **Phone**-978-374-2312; fax-978-373-8490; hours 8AM-4PM www.ci.haverhill.ma.us
Will not search UCC records. UCC copy fee- $2.00 1st page, $1.00 each add'l. Separate state tax lien search- $10.00 per debtor. RE records at Essex Cty. Cert fee: $10.00 per cert. Payee: City of Haverhill. **Other phones:** Assessor-978-347-2316; Treasurer-978-374-2320; Elections-978-374-2312; Vital Records-978-374-2312.

Hawley Town

Town Clerk, Town Hall, Hawley, MA 01339-9624. **Phone**-413-339-5518; fax-413-339-4959; hours 1-5PM Wed. Will not search records. UCC copy-$1.00 per page. RE records at Franklin Cty. Payee: Town of Hawley. **Other phones:** Assessor-413-339-5518; Treasurer-413-339-4231; Elections-413-339-5818; Vital Records-413-339-5818.

Heath Town

Town Clerk, 1 E Main St, Town Hall, Heath, MA 01346. **Phone**-413-337-4934; fax-413-337-8542; hours 9AM-2PM M-Th
UCC record search per debtor- $10.00. UCC copy-$1.00 per page. Tax liens included in UCC search if requested. Separate federal/state combined tax lien search- $10.00 per debtor. RE records at Franklin Cty. Cert fee: $5.00 per page. Payee: Town of Heath. **Online Access to Property, Assessor records:** Access to property data is free at http://csc-ma.us/PropertyContent/jsp/Home.jsp?Page=1. Select Heath Town. **Other phones:** Assessor-413-337-4934; Treasurer-413-337-4934.

Hingham Town

Town Clerk, 210 Central St, Hingham, MA 02043. **Phone**-781-741-1410, R/E Recording- 781-741-1408; fax-781-740-0239; hours 8:30AM-4:30PM
UCC record search per debtor- $10.00. UCC copy fee- $2.00 per copy. Will not search tax liens. RE records at Plymouth Cty. Cert fee: $1.00 per copy. Payee: Town of Hingham. **Online Access to Propert, Assessor records:** Search the property rolls for free at www.hingham-ma.com/html/assessment_data.html. Click on "Click here to view data." Also, access to property data is free at http://csc-ma.us/PropertyContent/jsp/Home.jsp?Page=1. Select Hingham Town. **Other phones:** Assessor-781-741-1455; Treasurer-781-741-1408; Elections-781-741-1410; Vital Records-781-741-1410.

Hinsdale Town

Town Clerk, PO Box 803, Hinsdale, MA 01235. **Phone**-413-655-2301, R/E Recording- 413-443-7438; fax-413-655-8807; hours 1-3PM, 6:30-8PM W; 12:45-3PM Th
UCC record search per debtor- $10.00. UCC copy-$1.00 per page. Tax liens included in UCC search if requested. Separate state tax lien search- $10.00 per debtor. RE records at Berkshire Cty. Payee: Town of Hinsdale. **Other phones:** Assessor-413-655-2300; Treasurer-413-655-2306; Elections-413-655-2301; Vital Records-413-655-2301.

Holbrook Town

Town Clerk, Town Hall, Holbrook, MA 02343-1502. **Phone**-781-767-4314; fax-781-767-9054; hours 8AM-4PM. UCC record search per debtor- $10.00. UCC copy- $2.00 per page. Federal/state combined tax lien search- $10.00 per search. RE records at Norfolk Cty. Cert fee: $5.00 per doc. Payee: Town of Holbrook. **Other phones:** Assessor-781-767-4315; Treasurer-781-767-4316; Elections-781-767-4314; Vital Records-781-767-4314.

Holden Town

Town Clerk, 1196 Main St, Town Hall, Holden, MA 01520-1092. **Phone**-508-829-0265; fax-508-829-0281; hours 8:30AM-4:30PM; Summer Hr 8AM-4Pm
UCC record search per debtor- $12.00. UCC copy fee- $.25 per page. Tax liens included in UCC search if requested. Separate federal/state combined tax lien search- $10.00 per debtor. RE records at Worcester Cty. Cert fee: $1.00 per page. Payee: Town of Holden. **Online Access to Real Estate, Property Tax records:** Search the Town assessor's database free at http://data.visionappraisal.com/HOLDENMA. Registration is required; sign-up is free. **Other phones:** Assessor-508-829-0223; Treasurer-508-829-0235.

Holland Town

Town Clerk, 27 Sturbridge Rd, Holland, MA 01521-9712. **Phone**-413-245-7108; fax-413-245-7037; hours 9AM-Noon, 1-4PM M,W,Th; 9AM-Noon, 1-5PM, 7-8:30PM

Will not search records. UCC copy- $1.00 per page. RE records at Hampden Cty. Payee: Town of Holland. **Online Access to Real Estate, Recording, Deed, Lien records:** See Hampden County for recording records searching.

Holliston Town

Town Clerk, 703 Washington St, Holliston, MA 01746. **Phone**-508-429-0601; fax-508-429-0684; hours 8:30AM-4:30PM www.townofholliston.us
UCC record search per debtor- $10.00. UCC copy fee- $.25 per page. UCC search includes tax liens. Separate federal/state combined tax lien search- $10.00 per debtor. RE records at Middlesex Cty. Payee: Town of Holliston. **Online Access to Property, Assessor records:** Access to property data is free at http://csc-ma.us/PropertyContent/jsp/Home.jsp?Page=1. Select Holliston Town. **Other phones:** Assessor-508-429-0604; Treasurer-508-429-0602; Vital Records-508-429-0601.

Holyoke City

City Clerk, 536 Dwight St, Holyoke, MA 01040. **Phone**-413-322-5520; fax-413-322-5521; hours 8:30AM-4:30PM www.ci.holyoke.ma.us
UCC record search per debtor- $10.00. UCC copy- $2.00 for 1st page and $1.00 per add'l. UCC search includes tax liens if requested. RE records at Hampden Cty. Payee: Holyoke City Clerk. **Online Access to Assessor, Property, Real Estate, Recording, Lien records:** Access to property valuations on the tax assessor database are free at www.ci.holyoke.ma.us/legend.htm. No name searching, but you can search by property types. Also, see Hampden County for recording records searching. **Other phones:** Assessor-413-322-5550; Treasurer-413-322-5560; Elections-413-332-5520.

Hopedale Town

Town Clerk, PO Box 7, Hopedale, MA 01747. **Phone**-508-634-2203, UCC Recording- 508-634-2203 x15; fax-508-634-2200; hours 9AM-2PM M-Th
All search information should be called in first. UCC record search per debtor- $10.00. UCC copy- $2.00 per page. UCC search includes tax liens if requested. Separate federal/state combined tax lien search- $10.00 per debtor. RE records at Worcester Cty. Cert fee: $5.00 per cert. Payee: Town of Hopedale. **Other phones:** Assessor-508-634-2203 x14; Treasurer-508-634-2203 x18; Elections-508-634-2203 x15.

Hopkinton Town

Town Clerk, 18 Main St, Hopkinton, MA 01748-1260. **Phone**-508-497-9710; fax-508-497-9702; 8:30AM-4PM. UCC record search per debtor- $10.00. UCC copy- $2.00 per page. Will not search tax liens. RE records at Middlesex Cty. Payee: Town of Hopkinton. **Other phones:** Assessor-508-497-9720; Treasurer-508-497-9715; Vital Records-508-497-9710.

Hubbardston Town

Town Clerk, PO Box H, Hubbardston, MA 01452. **Phone**-978-928-5244; fax-978-928-1402; hours 2-8PM M; 8AM-4PM T-Th
UCC record search per debtor- $10.00. UCC copy- $2.00 per page. Tax liens not included in UCC search. Federal/state combined tax lien search- $10.00 per debtor. RE records at Worcester Cty. Cert fee: $5.00 per page. Payee: Town of Hubbardston. **Other phones:** Assessor-978-928-1400; Treasurer-978-928-1401; Elections-978-928-5244; Vital Records-978-928-5244.

Hudson Town

Town Clerk, 78 Main St, Town Hall, Hudson, MA 01749. **Phone**-978-568-9615; hours 8AM-4:30PM www.townofhudson.org

Searches on UCCs are only for filings prior to July 1, 2001. Separate state tax lien search- $10.00 per debtor. RE records at Middlesex Cty. Payee: Town of Hudson. **Online Access to Property, Assessor records:** Access to the Town Assessor reocrds is free at http://beta.whatifnet.com/assess/hudsonma/. **Other phones:** Assessor-978-568-9620; Treasurer-978-568-9605; Elections-978-568-9615; Vital Records-978-568-9615.

Hull Town

Town Clerk, Town Hall, 253 Atlantic Ave, Hull, MA 02045. **Phone**-781-925-2262; fax-781-925-0224; hours 8AM-4PM M,W; 8:30AM-7:30PMT, Th
UCC record search per debtor- $10.00. UCC copy fee- $.20 per page. Tax liens not included in UCC search. Separate federal/state combined tax lien search- $10.00 per debtor. RE records at Plymouth Cty. Cert fee: $5.00. Payee: Town of Hull. **Other phones:** Assessor-781-925-2205.

Huntington Town

Town Clerk, PO Box 523, Office of Town Clerk, Huntington, MA 01050. **Phone**-413-667-3186; fax-413-667-3507; hours Town Hall:9AM-Noon M.; 6-8PM Wed. UCC record search per debtor- $10.00. UCC copy- $1.00 per page. UCC search includes tax liens if requested. RE records at Hampshire Cty. Cert fee: $5.00 per copy. Payee: Town of Huntington. **Other phones:** Assessor-413-667-3501; Treasurer-413-667-3501; Vital Records-413-667-3186.

Ipswich Town

Town Clerk, 25 Green St, Ipswich, MA 01938-2357. **Phone**-978-356-6600; fax-978-356-6616; hours 8AM-7PM M; 8AM-4PM T,W,Th; 8AM-Noon F www.town.ipswich.ma.us/
UCC record search per debtor- $10.00. UCC copy- $2.00 per page. Tax liens not included in UCC search. RE records at Essex Cty. Cert fee: $5.00 per cert. Payee: Town of Ipswich. **Other phones:** Assessor-978-356-6603; Treasurer-978-356-6610; Elections-978-356-6600; Vital Records-978-356-6600.

Kingston Town

Town Clerk, 26 Evergreen St., Kingston, MA 02364. **Phone**-781-585-0502; fax-781-585-0542; hours 8:30AM-Noon, 1-4:30PM www.kingstonmass.org
Will search UCC records filed through 6/30/2001. Search per debtor- $5.00. UCC copy- $2.00 per page. Will search tax liens. Federal/state combined tax lien search- $5.00 per debtor. RE records at Plymouth Cty. Cert fee: $10.00 per doc. Payee: Town of Kingston. **Other phones:** Assessor-781-585-0509; Treasurer-781-585-0508; Elections-781-585-0502; Vital Records-781-585-0502.

Lakeville Town

Town Clerk, 346 Bedford St, Lakeville, MA 02347. **Phone**-508-946-8814; fax-508-946-3970; hours 9AM-4PM. UCC record search per debtor- $2.00. UCC copy- $1.00 per page. Tax liens located in the Treasurer's Office. Separate state tax lien search- $2.00 per debtor. RE records at Plymouth Cty. Cert fee: $5.00 per page. Payee: Town of Lakeville. **Other phones:** Assessor-508-947-4428; Treasurer-508-946-8801; Elections-508-946-8814; Vital Records-508-946-8814.

Lancaster Town

Town Clerk, Box 97, Town Hall, Lancaster, MA 01523-0097. **Phone**-978-365-2542, R/E Recording-978-365-9562; fax-978-368-4005; hours 9AM-6PM M; 9AM-4PM T-TH www.ci.lancaster.ma.us
Will not search records. UCC copy- $2.00 per page. RE records at Worcester Cty. Cert fee: $5.00 per cert. Payee: Town of Lancaster. **Online Access to Property, Assessor records:** Access to property data

is free at http://csc-ma.us/PropertyContent/jsp/Home.jsp?Page=1. Select Lancaster Town. **Other phones:** Assessor-978-365-9562; Treasurer-978-365-6115; Elections-978-365-2542; Vital Records-978-365-2542.

Lanesborough Town

Town Clerk, PO Box 1492, Lanesborough, MA 01237. **Phone**-413-442-1351, R/E Recording- 413-442-0813; fax-413-443-5811; hours 8AM-1PM
UCC record search per debtor- $5.00. UCC copy- $.30 per page. UCC search includes tax liens if requested. RE records at Berkshire Cty. Payee: Town of Lanesborough. **Other phones:** Assessor-413-442-8622; Treasurer-413-442-1167 x23; Elections-413-442-1351; Vital Records-413-442-1351.

Lawrence City

City Clerk, 200 Common St, Lawrence, MA 01840. **Phone**-978-794-5803, R/E Recording- 978-683-2745; fax-978-557-0285; hours-8:30AM-4:30PM www.cityoflawrence.com/Departments.asp
UCC record search per debtor- $10.00. UCC copy- $2.00 per financing statement. Will search tax liens. Tax lien search fee- $10.00. RE records at Essex Cty. Payee: City of Lawrence. **Online Access to Land, Grantor/Grantee, Recording records:** Search the county recorder database for free at www.lawrencedeeds.com/dsSearch.asp. **Other phones:** Assessor-978-794-5790; Treasurer-978-794-5843; Elections-978-794-5807; Vital Records-978-794-5803.

Lee Town

Town Clerk, 32 Main St, Town Hall, Lee, MA 01238. **Phone**-413-243-5505; fax-413-243-5507; 8:30AM-4PM. UCC record search per debtor- $10.00. UCC copy fee- $.10 per page. Tax liens not included in UCC search. Tax lien search fee- $10.00. RE records at Berkshire Cty. Cert fee: $25.00. Payee: tax collectors office. **Other phones:** Assessor-413-243-5512; Treasurer-413-243-5506; Elections-413-243-5505; Vital Records-413-243-5505; Tax Collector-413-243-5515.

Leicester Town

Town Clerk, 3 Washburn Sq, Leicester, MA 01524. **Phone**-508-892-7011; fax-508-892-7070; hours 8:30AM-4PM. UCC record search per debtor- $10.00. UCC copy- $1.00 per page. Will not search tax liens. RE records at Worcester Cty. Cert fee: $5.00 per page. Payee: Town of Leicester. **Other phones:** Assessor-508-892-7001; Treasurer-508-892-7002.

Lenox Town

Town Clerk, 6 Walker St, Town Hall, Lenox, MA 01240-2718. **Phone**-413-637-5506; fax-413-637-5518; hours 9AM-4PM. Will not search records. RE records at Berkshire Cty. Payee: Town of Lenox. **Other phones:** Assessor-413-637-5502; Treasurer-413-637-5506; Elections-413-637-5506; Vital Records-413-637-5506.

Leominster City

City Clerk, 25 West St, Leominster, MA 01453. **Phone**-978-534-7536; fax-978-534-7546; hours 8:30AM-4PM M-W & F; 8:30AM-5:30PM Th www.ci.leominster.us
UCC record search per debtor- $10.00. UCC copy- $2.00 1st 3 copies then $1.00 each add'l. Will search tax liens. Federal/state combined tax lien search- $5.00 per copy. RE records at Worcester Cty. Payee: City of Leominster. **Online Access to Assessor records:** Search the assessor's database at http://data.visionappraisal.com/leominsterma. Free registration for full data. **Other phones:** Assessor-978-

534-7531; Treasurer-978-537-7509; Elections-978-534-7536; Vital Records-978-534-7536.

Leverett Town

Town Clerk, PO Box 178, Leverett, MA 01054. **Phone**-413-548-9150, R/E Recording- 413-548-9699; fax-413-548-9150; hours 7PM-9PM M; 9AM-Noon W,Th. UCC record search per debtor- $10.00. UCC copy- $1.00 per page. Will not search tax liens. RE records at Franklin Cty. Cert fee: $5.00 per copy. Payee: Town of Leverett. **Other phones:** Assessor-413-548-4945.

Lexington Town

Town Clerk, 1625 Massachusetts Ave, Town Office Bldg., Lexington, MA 02420. **Phone**-781-862-0500 x270; fax-781-861-2754; hours 8:30AM-4:30PM http://ci.lexington.ma.us UCC record search per debtor- $5.00. UCC copy- $1.00 per page. Tax liens not included in UCC search. RE records at Middlesex Cty. Cert fee: $2.00 per page. Payee: Town of Lexington. **Online Access to Assessor records:** Assessor information is at http://data.visionappraisal.com/LexingtonMA/. **Other phones:** Assessor-781-862-0500 x203; Treasurer-781-862-0500 x265; Elections-781-862-0500 x270; Vital Records-781-862-0500 x270.

Leyden Town

Town Clerk, Town Hall, Leyden, MA 01337. **Phone**-413-774-7769; fax-413-772-0146; 10AM-1PM W-F Will not search UCC records. UCC copy- $1.00 per page. Separate state tax lien search- $10.00 per debtor. RE records at Franklin Cty. Payee: Town of Leyden. **Other phones:** Assessor-413-774-4111; Treasurer-413-774-4111; Elections-413-774-7769; Vital Records-413-774-7769.

Lincoln Town

Town Clerk, PO Box 6353, Lincoln Center, MA 01773-6353. **Phone**-781-259-2607; fax-781-259-1677; \8:30AM-4:30PM www.state.ma.us/cc/lincoln.html UCC record search per debtor- $10.00. UCC copy- $2.00 per page. Will search tax liens. RE records at Middlesex Cty. Payee: Town of Lincoln. **Other phones:** Assessor-781-259-2611; Treasurer-781-259-2606; Elections-781-259-2607; Vital Records-781-259-2607.

Littleton Town

Town Clerk, PO Box 1305, Littleton, MA 01460. **Phone**-978-952-2314; fax-978-952-2321; hours 9AM-3PM M,T,W,F; 9AM-9PM Th www.littletonma.org UCC record search per debtor- $10.00 per name. UCC copy fee- $.35 per page. UCC search includes tax liens if requested. RE records at Middlesex Cty. Cert fee: $5.00. Payee: Town of Littleton. **Other phones:** Assessor-978-952-2309; Treasurer-978-952-2306; Elections-978-952-2314; Vital Records-978-952-2314; Tax Collector-978-952-2349.

Longmeadow Town

Town Clerk, 20 Williams St, Town Hall, Longmeadow, MA 01106. **Phone**-413-567-1066; fax-413-565-4112; hours 8:15AM-4:30PM www.longmeadow.org Will not search UCC records. UCC copy fee- $.20 per page. Separate state tax lien search- $5.00 per debtor. RE records at Hampden Cty. Payee: Town of Longmeadow. **Online Access to Assessor, Real Estate, Recording, Lien records:** Access to tax records is at http://data.visionappraisal.com/LONGMEADOWMA/. Free registration for full data. Also, see Hampden County for recording records searching. **Other phones:** Assessor-413-565-4115; Treasurer-413-567-1066; Elections-413-567-1066; Vital Records-413-567-1066.

Lowell City

City Clerk, 375 Merrimack St, City Hall, Lowell, MA 01852. **Phone**-978-970-4161, R/E Recording- 978-970-4224, UCC Recording- 978-970-4159; fax-978-970-4162; hours 8AM-5PM www.ci.lowell.ma.us UCC record search per debtor- $10.00. UCC copy- $3.00 1st page, $2.00 each add'l. UCC search includes tax liens if requested. RE records at Middlesex Cty. Cert fee: $5.00 per docoment. Payee: City of Lowell. **Online Access to Assessor records:** Search the Assessor's database at http://data.visionappraisal.com/LowellMA/. Free registration for full data. **Other phones:** Assessor-978-970-4200; Treasurer-978-970-4224; Elections-978-970-4046; Vital Records-978-970-4161.

Ludlow Town

Town Clerk, 488 Chapin St, Ludlow, MA 01056. **Phone**-413-583-5610, R/E Recording- 413-583-5608; fax-413-583-5603; hours 8:30AM-4:30PM www.ludlow.ma.us/clerk/ UCC record search per debtor- $10.00. UCC copy- $2.00 per page. Tax liens included in UCC search if requested. Separate federal/state combined tax lien search- $10.00 per debtor. RE records at Hampden Cty. Cert fee: $1.00 per page. Payee: Town of Ludlow. **Online Access to Real Estate, Recording, Lien records:** See Hampden County for recording records searching. **Other phones:** Assessor-413-583-5608; Treasurer-413-583-5616; Elections-413-583-5610; Vital Records-413-583-5610.

Lunenburg Town

Town Clerk, PO Box 135, Lunenburg, MA 01462. **Phone**-978-582-4131; fax-978-582-4148; hours 8AM-6:30PM M,W,Th; 8AM-4:00 PM Tu.; Closed Fridays UCC record search per debtor- $10.00. UCC copy- $1.00 per page. Tax liens not included in UCC search. RE records at Worcester Cty. Cert fee: $5.00 per page. Payee: Town of Lunenburg. **Other phones:** Assessor-978-582-4145; Treasurer-978-582-4130; Elections-978-582-4132; Vital Records-978-582-4131.

Lynn City

City Clerk, 3 City Hall Sq, Lynn, MA 01901. **Phone**-781-598-4000; fax-781-477-7032; hours 8:30AM-4PM M,W,Th; 8:30AM-8PM T; 8:30AM-12:30PM F. Will search UCC records until 7/2008. Search per debtor- $10.00. UCC copy- $1.00 per page. Tax liens at Tax Collector's Office. RE records at Essex Cty. Payee: City of Lynn. **Other phones:** Assessor-781-598-4000.

Lynnfield Town

Town Clerk, 55 Summer St, Lynnfield, MA 01940-1823. **Phone**-781-334-3128; fax-781-334-0014; hours 8AM-4:30PM (F 8AM-1PM) UCC record search per debtor- $10.00. UCC copy- $1.00 per page. Will search tax liens. Separate federal/state combined tax lien search- $10.00 per debtor. Will search real estate records. Payee: Town of Lynnfield. **Other phones:** Assessor-781-334-2231; Treasurer-781-334-7663; Elections-781-334-3128; Vital Records-781-334-3128.

Malden City

City Clerk, 200 Pleasant St, City Hall, Malden, MA 02148. **Phone**-781-397-7116; fax-781-388-0610; hours 8AM-4PM M,W,Th; 8AM-7PM T; 8AM-Noon F Will not search records. RE records at Middlesex Cty. Payee: City of Malden. **Other phones:** Assessor-781-397-7100.

Manchester-by-the-Sea Town

Town Clerk, 10 Central St, Town Hall, Manchester-by-the-Sea, MA 01944-1399. **Phone**-978-526-2040; fax-978-526-2001; hours 9AM-5PM M-W; 9AM-8PM Th www.manchester.ma.us UCC record search per debtor- $10.00. UCC copy- $1.00 per page. Tax liens not included in UCC search. RE records at Essex Cty. Payee: Town of Manchester-by-the-Sea. **Online Access to Property Assessor records:** Search the property assessment data at www.patriotproperties.com/manchester. **Other phones:** Assessor-978-526-2010; Treasurer-978-526-2030; Elections-978-526-2040; Vital Records-978-526-2040.

Mansfield Town

Town Clerk, 6 Park Row, Town Hall, Mansfield, MA 02048-2433. **Phone**-508-261-7345; fax-508-261-1083; hours 8AM-4PM M, T, Th; 8AM-8PM W; 8AM-Noon F. UCC record search per debtor- $10.00.UCC search includes tax liens. Separate state tax lien search- $10.00 per debtor. RE records at Bristol Cty. Payee: Town of Mansfield. **Other phones:** Assessor-508-261-7350; Treasurer-508-261-7340; Elections-508-261-7345; Vital Records-508-261-7345.

Marblehead Town

Town Clerk, Abbot Hall, Marblehead, MA 01945. **Phone**-781-631-0528; fax-781-631-8571; hours 8AM-5PM, M, T, Th; 7:30AM-7:30PM, W; 8AM-1PM F www.marblehead.org UCC record search per debtor- $10.00.Will not search tax liens. RE records at Essex Cty. Payee: Town of Marblehead. **Online Access to Assessor, Property records:** Access to assessor data is free at www.patriotproperties.com/marblehead/Default.asp?br =exp&vr=6. **Other phones:** Assessor-781-631-0236; Treasurer-781-631-1033; Elections-781-631-0528; Vital Records-781-631-0528.

Marion Town

Town Clerk, 2 Spring St, Marion, MA 02738. **Phone**-508-748-3502; fax-508-748-2845; hours 8AM-4:30PM M-Th; 8AM-3:30PM Friday www.townofmarion.org UCC record search per debtor- $10.00. UCC copy- $1.00 per page. Tax liens included in UCC search if requested. Separate federal/state combined tax lien search- $25.00 per debtor. RE records at Plymouth Cty. Payee: Town of Marion. **Online Access to Property Assessor records:** Search town assessor data at http://data.visionappraisal.com/MarionMA/. Free registration for full data. **Other phones:** Assessor-508-748-3510; Treasurer-508-748-3505.

Marlborough City

City Clerk, 140 Main St, Marlborough, MA 01752-3812. **Phone**-508-460-3775; fax-508-624-6504; hours 8:30AM-5PM UCC record search per debtor- $10.00. UCC copy- $2.00 per page. Will not search tax liens. RE records at Middlesex Cty. Payee: City of Marlborough. **Online Access to Property Assessor records:** Search the city assessor data at http://data.visionappraisal.com/MarlboroughMA/. Free registration for full data. **Other phones:** Assessor-508-460-3779; Treasurer-508-460-3730; Elections-508-460-3775; Vital Records-508-460-3775.

Marshfield Town

Town Clerk, Town Hall, Marshfield, MA 02050. **Phone**-781-834-5540; fax-781-837-7163; hours 8:30AM-4:30PM. UCC record search per debtor- $10.00. UCC copy- $1.00 per copy. UCC search includes tax liens. RE records at Plymouth Cty. Payee: Town of Marshfield. **Other phones:**

Assessor-781-834-5585; Treasurer-781-834-5545; Elections-781-834-5540; Vital Records-781-834-5540.

Mashpee Town

Town Clerk, 16 Great Neck Rd. N., Town Hall, Mashpee, MA 02649. **Phone**-508-539-1400 x561, R/E Recording- 508-539-1400 x537; fax-508-539-1403; hours 9AM-4PM www.ci.mashpee.ma.us
UCC record search per debtor- $5.00. UCC copy fee- $.20 per page. UCC search includes tax liens if requested. RE records at Barnstable Cty. Cert fee: $5.00. Payee: Town of Mashpee. **Online Access to Assessor records:** Records on the Town of Mashpee Assessor database are free at www.capecode.com/mashpee/search.asp. **Other phones:** Assessor-508-539-1400 x529; Treasurer-508-539-1400 x537; Elections-508-539-1400 x561; Vital Records-508-539-1400 x561.

Mattapoisett Town

Town Clerk, PO Box 89, Mattapoisett, MA 02739-0089. **Phone**-508-758-4103, R/E Recording- 508-758-4106; fax-508-758-3030; hours 8AM-4PM www.mattapoisett.net
UCC record search per debtor- $10.00. UCC copy- $1.00 per page. Tax liens included in UCC search if requested. Separate federal/state combined tax lien search-No fee. RE records at Plymouth Cty. Cert fee: $1.00 per page. Payee: Town of Mattapoisett. **Online Access to Property, Assessor records:** Access to property data is free at http://csc-ma.us/PropertyContent/jsp/Home.jsp?Page=1. Select Mattapoisett Town. **Other phones:** Assessor-508-758-4106; Treasurer-508-758-4108; Elections-508-758-4103; Vital Records-508-758-4103.

Maynard Town

Town Clerk, 195 Main St, Town Hall, Maynard, MA 01754-2575. **Phone**-978-897-1000, R/E Recording-978-897-1005; fax-978-897-8457; hours 8AM-4PM
UCC record search per debtor- $5.00. UCC copy- $1.00 per page. Tax liens not included in UCC search. Separate state tax lien search- $5.00 per debtor. RE records at Middlesex Cty. Payee: Town of Maynard. **Other phones:** Assessor-978-897-1004; Treasurer-978-897-1005; Elections-978-897-1000; Vital Records-978-897-1000.

Medfield Town

Town Clerk, 459 Main St, Town Hall, Medfield, MA 02052. **Phone**-508-359-8505, R/E Recording- 508-359-8505 x625, UCC Recording- 508-359-8505x630; fax-508-359-6182; hours 8:30AM-4:30PM M-W; 8:30AM-7:30PM Th; 8:30AM-1PM Friday www.town.medfield.net
UCC record search per debtor- $10.00. UCC copy- $1.00 per page. UCC search includes tax liens if requested. RE records at Norfolk Cty. Payee: Town of Medfield. **Other phones:** Treasurer-508-359-8505 X625.

Medford City

City Clerk, 85 George P. Hassett Drive, City Clerk, Medford, MA 02155. **Phone**-781-393-2425; fax-781-391-1895; hours 8:30AM-4:30PM M,T,Th; 8:30AM-7:30PM W; 8:30AM-12:30PM F. www.medford.org
UCC record search per debtor- $10.00.Will not search tax liens. RE records at Middlesex Cty. Payee: City of Medford. **Online Access to Property Assessor records:** Search the city assessor database at http://data.visionappraisal.com/MedfordMA/. Free registration for full data. **Other phones:** Assessor-781-393-2435; Treasurer-781-393-2550; Elections-781-393-2491; Vital Records-781-393-2425.

Medway Town

Town Clerk, 155 Village St., Medway, MA 02053. **Phone**-508-533-3204; fax-508-533-3287; hours 8AM-7:30PM M; 8AM-4PM Tu-Th; 8AM-1PM F
Will search UCC records. UCC copy- $2.00 per page. Will not search tax liens. RE records at Norfolk Cty. Payee: Town of Medway. **Other phones:** Assessor-508-533-3203; Treasurer-508-533-3205.

Melrose City

City Clerk, 562 Main St, Melrose, MA 02176. **Phone**-781-979-4114; fax-781-665-6877; hours 8AM-4:30PM (July-August:8AM-4:30PM M-Th; 8AM-1PM F www.cityofmelrose.org
UCC record search per debtor- $15.00. UCC copy fee- $.25 per page. Will search tax liens including federal tax liens. RE records at Middlesex Cty. Payee: City of Melrose. **Other phones:** Assessor-781-979-4104; Treasurer-781-979-4160; Elections-781-979-4125; Vital Records-781-979-4114.

Mendon Town

Town Clerk, PO Box 54, Mendon, MA 01756-0054. **Phone**-508-473-1085; fax-508-478-8241; hours 8AM-3:30PM M-Th, 6:30-9PM M; Closed F
UCC record search per debtor- $5.00. UCC copy- $2.00 per page. RE records at Worcester Cty. Payee: Town of Mendon. **Other phones:** Assessor-508-473-2738; Treasurer-508-473-6410; Elections-508-473-1085; Vital Records-508-473-1085.

Merrimac Town

Town Clerk, 2 School St, Merrimac, MA 01860. **Phone**-978-346-8013; fax-978-346-0522; hours 9AM-4PM M-Th. UCC record search per debtor- $5.00. UCC copy- $2.00 per page. Will not search tax liens. RE records at Essex Cty. Payee: Town of Merrimac. **Other phones:** Assessor-978-346-9022; Treasurer-978-346-0524; Elections-978-346-8013; Vital Records-978-346-8013.

Methuen City

City Clerk, 41 Pleasant St, Rm 112, Methuen, MA 01844. **Phone**-978-794-3213, R/E Recording- 978-794-3219; fax-978-794-3215; hours 8:30AM-5:30PM M-TH; 8:30AM-12:00PM F www.ci.methuen.ma.us
UCC record search per debtor- $10.00 min. UCC copy- $2.00 per page. UCC search includes tax liens if requested. RE records at Essex County at Northern Essex Register of Deeds, Lawrence, MA. Payee: City of Methuen. **Online Access to Property Assessor, Land, Grantor/Grantee, Recording records:** Search the property assessment data free at http://host229.ci.methuen.ma.us. Also, search the county recorder database for free at www.lawrencedeeds.com/dsSearch.asp. **Other phones:** Assessor-978-794-3220; Treasurer-978-794-3205; Elections-978-794-3213; Vital Records-978-794-3213.

Middleborough Town

Town Clerk, 20 Centre St, 1st Fl, Middleborough, MA 02346. **Phone**-508-946-2415, R/E Recording- 508-946-2410; fax-508-946-2308; hours 8:45AM-5PM
UCC record search per debtor- $15.00.Will not search tax liens. RE records at Plymouth Cty. Cert fee: $5.00 per doc. Payee: Town of Middleborough. **Other phones:** Assessor-508-946-2410; Treasurer-508-946-2420; Elections-508-946-2415; Vital Records-508-946-2415.

Middlefield Town

Town Clerk, PO Box 265, Middlefield, MA 01243. **Phone**-Town Clerk, R/E & UCC Recording- 413-623-8966; fax-413-623-6108; hours 7PM-9PM; 9AM-Noon Sat

UCC record search per debtor- $10.00. UCC copy- $1.00 per page. Will not search tax liens. RE records at Hampshire Cty. Payee: Town of Middlefield. **Other phones:** Assessor-413-623-8966; Treasurer-413-623-5182; Elections-413-623-8966; Town Clerk-413-623-2079.

Middlesex County Northern Dist.

County Register of Deeds, 360 Gorham St, Lowell, MA 01852. **Phone**-978-322-9000; fax-978-322-9001; hours 8:30AM-4:15PM www.lowelldeeds.com
Will not search records. UCC copy- $1.00 per page. Payee: Commonwealth of Massachusetts. **Other phones:** Assessor-978-970-4200.

Middlesex County Southern Dist.

County Registry of Deeds, 208 Cambridge St, Cambridge, MA 02141. **Phone**-County Registry of Deeds, R/E & UCC Recording- 617-679-6300; hours 8AM-4PM. Will not search records. UCC copy- $1.00 per page. Cert fee: $1.00 per page. Payee: Commonwealth of Massachusetts. **Online Access to Real Estate, Lien records:** Access to the LandTrack online system with Southern District records- no new customers are being accepted and the system will be replaced by free web access late 2003.

Middleton Town

Town Clerk, Memorial Hall, Middleton, MA 01949. **Phone**-978-774-6927; fax-978-774-6167; hours 9AM-4PM M-W-TH; 9AM-1PM Fri.; 6-8PM Tuesday www.townofmiddleton.org
UCC record search per debtor- $5.00. UCC copy fee- $.20 per page. Will not search tax liens. RE records at Essex Cty. Cert fee: $5.00 per page. Payee: Town of Middleton. **Other phones:** Assessor-978-774-2099; Treasurer-978-774-8327; Elections-978-774-6927; Vital Records-978-774-6927.

Milford Town

Town Clerk, 52 Main St, Milford, MA 01757. **Phone**-508-634-2307; fax-508-634-2324; hours 8:30AM-4;30PM. Will not search UCC records. Copy fee- $1.00 per page. Separate state tax lien search- $10.00 per debtor. RE records at Worcester Cty. Cert fee: $6.00,$5.00 in person. Payee: Town of Milford. **Other phones:** Assessor-508-634-2306.

Millbury Town

Town Clerk, 127 Elm St, Municipal Office Bldg., Millbury, MA 01527. **Phone**-508-865-9110, R/E Recording- 508-865-9121; hours 9AM-4PM
UCC record search per debtor- $10.00.UCC search includes tax liens. Separate federal/state combined tax lien search- $10.00 per debtor. RE records at Worcester Cty. Payee: Town of Millbury. **Online Access to Property, Assessor records:** Access to the town tax assessor info is free at http://data.visionappraisal.com/MillburyMA/. **Other phones:** Assessor-508-865-4732; Treasurer-508-865-8040; Elections-508-865-9110; Vital Records-508-865-9110.

Millis Town

Town Clerk, 900 Main St., Millis, MA 02054-1512. **Phone**-508-376-7046; fax-508-376-7053; hours 8:30AM-4:30PM
UCC record search per debtor- $10.00. UCC copy- $1.00 per page. Will not search tax liens. RE records at Norfolk Cty. Payee: Town of Millis. **Online Access to Assessor records:** Assessor information at http://data.visionappraisal.com/MillisMA/. **Other phones:** Assessor-508-376-7049; Tax Collector-508-376-7048.

Millville Town

Town Clerk, PO Box 703, Millville, MA 01529-0703. **Phone**-508-883-5849; fax-508-883-2994; hours M-Th 8:30-1PM; 6-8PM W http://millvillema.org
See Worcester County Register of Deeds searchable website for Town recordings. Will not search records. UCC copy- $1.00 per page. RE records at Worcester Cty. Cert fee: $5.00 per doc. Payee: Town of Millville. **Online Access to Real Estate, Deed, Tax Lien records:** Visit www.worcesterdeeds.com/worcester/dsbppagelist.asp to search the index. **Other phones:** Assessor-508-883-5031; Treasurer-508-883-7449; Elections-508-883-5849; Vital Records-508-883-5849.

Milton Town

Town Clerk, 525 Canton Ave, Town Hall, Milton, MA 02186. **Phone**-617-696-5414; hours 8:30AM-5PM
UCC record search per debtor- $10.00. UCC copy- $2.00 per page. Tax liens included in UCC search if requested. Separate federal/state combined tax lien search- $10.00 per debtor. RE records at Norfolk Cty. Cert fee: $2.00 per page. Payee: Town of Milton. **Other phones:** Assessor-617-696-5703; Treasurer-617-696-5409.

Monroe Town

Town Clerk, PO Box 6, Monroe, MA 01350. **Phone-**Town Clerk, R/E & UCC Recording- 413-424-5272; fax-413-424-7580.
May search UCC records. UCC search per debtor- $10.00. UCC copy- $1.00 per page. Tax liens included in UCC search if requested. Separate federal/state combined tax lien search-No fee. RE records at Franklin Cty. Payee: Town of Monroe. **Other phones:** Assessor-413-424-5272; Treasurer-413-424-5272.

Monson Town

Town Clerk, 110 Main St. #4, Monson, MA 01057-1332. **Phone**-413-267-4115; fax-413-267-3726; hours 9AM-12:30 PM, 1:30-4PM (3:30 on Tu)
UCC record search per debtor- $14.72 per hour. UCC copy fee- $7.00 per filing, regardless of # of pages. UCC search includes tax liens if requested. RE records at Hampden Cty. Cert fee: No additional charge. Payee: Town of Monson. **Online Access to Real Estate, Recording, Lien records:** See Hampden County for recording records searching. **Other phones:** Assessor-413-267-4120; Treasurer-413-267-4125; Elections-413-267-4115; Vital Records-413-267-4115.

Montague Town

Town Clerk, 1 Avenue A, Turners Falls, MA 01376-1128. **Phone**-413-863-3211; fax-413-863-3224; hours 8:30AM-4:30PM
Will not search UCC records. UCC copy- $1.00 per page. Tax lien searches conducted in Treasurer Office. RE records at Franklin Cty. Payee: Town of Montague. **Other phones:** Assessor-413-863-4654; Treasurer-413-863-3207; Elections-413-863-3211; Vital Records-413-863-3211.

Monterey Town

Town Clerk, Town Hall, Monterey, MA 01245. **Phone**-413-528-5175; fax-413-528-9452; hours 9:30AM-12:30PM Sat, or by appointment
UCC record search per debtor- $10.00 for old UCC's only. UCC copy- $1.00 per page. Tax liens included in UCC search if requested. Separate federal/state combined tax lien search- $10.00 per debtor. RE records at Berkshire County Registers Office. Cert fee: $5.00 per page. Payee: Town of Monterey. **Other phones:** Assessor-413-528-6481; Treasurer-413-528-1443; Elections-413-528-5175; Vital Records-413-528-5175.

Montgomery Town

Town Clerk, Town Hall, Montgomery, MA 01085. **Phone**-413-862-4478; fax-413-862-3204; hours By appointment. Will not search records. UCC copy- $1.00 per page. RE records at Hampden Cty. Payee: Town of Montgomery. **Online Access to Real Estate, Recording, Lien records:** See Hampden County for recording records searching. **Other phones:** Assessor-413-862-3386; Treasurer-413-862-3386.

Mt. Washington Town

Town Clerk, 118 East St., Mt. Washington, MA 01258. **Phone**-413-528-2839; fax-413-528-2839; hours 8-9PM M-Town Clerk; 8:30AM-1:30PM M-T for Town Sec
UCC record search per debtor- $10.00. UCC copy- $1.00 per page. Will not search tax liens. RE records at Berkshire Cty. Payee: Town of Mt. Washington. **Other phones:** Assessor-413-528-2839; Treasurer-413-528-2839; Elections-413-528-2839; Vital Records-413-528-2839.

Nahant Town

Town Clerk, Town Hall, Nahant, MA 01908-0075. **Phone**-781-581-0018; fax-781-593-0340; hours 9AM-Noon. Will search UCC records. UCC search includes tax liens. RE records at Essex Cty. Payee: Town of Nahant. **Other phones:** Assessor-781-581-0212; Treasurer-781-581-0018; Elections-781-581-0018; Vital Records-781-581-0018; Town Accountant-781-581-0099; Town Adminstrator-781-581-9927.

Nantucket County

County Register of Deeds, 16 Broad St, Nantucket, MA 02554. **Phone**-508-228-7250; fax-508-325-5331; hours 8AM-4PM; Recording hours- 8AM-Noon, 1-3:45PM www.nantucketdeeds.com
Will not search UCC records, but only real estate related UCC filed here. UCC copy fee- $1.00 per page. Will not search real estate or tax lien records. **Online Access to Real estate, Deed, Recording, Lien records:** Access the county register of deeds database by yearly subscription at www.nantucketdeeds.com/dsLogin.asp. Yearly fee is $100.00 per user; call 508-228-7250 for more information. **Other phones:** Assessor-508-228-7211; Treasurer-508-228-7265; Elections-508-228-7217; Vital Records-508-228-7217.

Nantucket Town

Town Clerk, 16 Broad St, Town & County Bldg., Nantucket, MA 02554. **Phone**-508-228-7217, R/E Recording- 508-228-7250; fax-508-325-5313; hours 8AM-4PM www.town.nantucket.ma.us
UCC record search per debtor- $20.00.Tax liens not included in UCC search. RE records at Nantucket Cty. Payee: Town of Nantucket. **Other phones:** Assessor-508-228-7211; Treasurer-508-325-5314; Elections-508-228-7217; Vital Records-508-228-7717; 508-228-7255.

Natick Town

Town Clerk, 13 E. Central St, Natick, MA 01760. **Phone**-508-647-6430; fax-508-655-6715; hours 8AM-5PM www.natickma.org
UCC record search per debtor- $5.00. UCC copy- $1.00 per page. UCC search includes tax liens. RE records at Middlesex Cty. Payee: Town of Natick. **Online Access to Assessor, Property records:** Search town assessments free at www.natickma.org/assess/assessinfo.asp. Includes name searches. **Other phones:** Assessor-508-647-6420; Treasurer-508-647-6425; Elections-508-647-6430; Vital Records-508-647-6430.

Needham Town

Town Clerk, PO Box 663, Needham, MA 02192. **Phone**-781-455-7510; fax-781-449-4569; hours 8:30AM-5PM www.town.needham.ma.us

UCC record search per debtor- $10.00. UCC copy- $1.00 per page. Will search tax liens. Federal/state combined tax lien search- $10.00 per debtor. RE records at Norfolk Cty. Cert fee: $1.00 per item. Payee: Town of Needham. **Online Access to Property, Assessor records:** property data is free at http://csc-ma.us/PropertyContent/jsp/Home.jsp?Page=1. Select Needham Town. **Other phones:** Assessor-781-455-7507; Treasurer-781-455-7504; Elections-781-455-7501; Vital Records-781-455-7501.

New Ashford Town

Town Clerk, 142 Beach Hill Rd, New Ashford, MA 01237. **Phone**-413-458-5461; fax-413-458-5461; hours by appointment. UCC record search per debtor- $10.00. UCC copy- $2.00 per page. UCC search includes tax liens if requested. RE records at Berkshire Cty. Payee: Town of New Ashford. **Other phones:** Assessor-413-743-9154.

New Bedford City

City Clerk, 133 William St, New Bedford, MA 02740. **Phone**-508-979-1450; fax-508-991-6225; hours 8AM-4PM www.ci.new-bedford.ma.us/Nav3.htm
UCC record search per debtor- $10.00. UCC copy- $2.00 per page. Tax liens not included in UCC search. Federal/state combined tax lien search- $10.00 per debtor RE records at Bristol Cty. Cert fee: $5.00 per page base rate. Payee: City of New Bedford. **Online Access to Property, Assessor records:** Access to the assessor's property database is free at www.ci.new-bedford.ma.us/Assessors/RealPropertyLookup.htm. **Other phones:** Assessor-508-979-1440; Treasurer-508-979-1430; Elections-508-979-1420; Vital Records-508-979-1450.

New Braintree Town

Town Clerk, 20 Memorial Dr Rm 5, New Braintree, MA 01531. **Phone**-508-867-4952; fax-508-867-6316; hours 7AM-9PM Monday; 9AM-1PM Friday www.newbraintree.net
Will not search UCC records. Tax lien (for town only) search fee- $5.00 per debtor. RE records at Worcester Cty. Cert fee: $5.00 per copy. Payee: Town of New Braintree. **Other phones:** Assessor-508-867-4467; Treasurer-508-867-2581; Elections-508-867-4952; Vital Records-508-867-4952.

New Marlborough Town

Town Clerk, PO Box 99, Mill River, MA 01244. **Phone**-413-229-8116; fax-413-229-6674; hours 9AM-2PM www.new-marlborough.ma.us
UCC record search per debtor- $10.00. UCC copy- $1.00 per page. UCC search includes tax liens. RE records at Berkshire Cty. Cert fee: $5.00 per page. Payee: New Marlborough Town CLerk. **Other phones:** Assessor-413-229-8926; Treasurer-413-229-8963; Elections-413-229-8278; Vital Records-413-229-8278.

New Salem Town

Town Clerk, 15 S Main St, Town Hall, New Salem, MA 01355. **Phone**-978-544-2731; fax-978-544-5775; hours 6-8PM M; 9-11AM W
UCC record search per debtor- $10.00. UCC copy- $1.00 per page. Tax liens included in UCC search if requested. Separate federal/state combined tax lien search- $10.00 per debtor. RE records at Franklin Cty. Payee: Town of New Salem.

Newbury Town

Town Clerk, 25 High Rd, Newbury, MA 01951-4799. **Phone**-978-462-2332; fax-978-465-3064; hours 8AM-3:30PM M,T,W,Th; 8AM-1PM Friday www.townofnewbury.org
UCC record search per debtor- $10.00. UCC search includes tax liens if requested. RE records at Essex County. Record copy- $1.00 per page. Cert fee:

$5.00 per page. Payee: Town of Newbury. **Online Access to Assessor, Property Tax records:** Access to yearly property tax information is free at www.townofnewbury.org/assessors/asp2.htm. **Other phones:** Assessor-978-465-0211; Treasurer-978-465-0862; Elections-978-462-2332; Vital Records-978-462-2332.

Newburyport City

City Clerk, 60 Pleasant St, Newburyport, MA 01950. **Phone-**978-465-4407; fax-978-462-79236; hours 8AM-4PM M,T,W; 8AM-8PM Th; 8AM-Noon F UCC record search per debtor- no charge. UCC copy- $1.00 per page. UCC search includes tax liens if requested. RE records at Essex Cty. Cert fee: $7.00. Payee: City of Newburyport. **Online Access to Assessor records:** Search city assessor database at http://data.visionappraisal.com/NewBURYPORTMA/. Free registration for full data. **Other phones:** Assessor-978-465-4403; Treasurer-978-465-4415; Elections-978-465-4407; Vital Records-978-465-4407.

Newton City

City Clerk, 1000 Commonwealth Ave, Newton Center, MA 02159. **Phone-**617-796-1200; fax-617-964-2333; hours 8:30AM-5PM M; 8:30AM-8:00PM T 8:30AM-5PM W www.ci.newton.ma.us UCC record search per debtor- $10.00.Tax liens included in UCC search if requested. Separate federal/state combined tax lien search- $10.00 per debtor. RE records at Middlesex Cty. Payee: City of Newton. **Online Access to Assessor records:** search the City Fiscal 1998 Assessment database free at www.ci.newton.ma.us/assessors2003/Search.asp. Data represents market value as of January of current year. **Other phones:** Assessor-617-552-7065; Treasurer-617-552-7080.

Norfolk County

County Register of Deeds, PO Box 69, Dedham, MA 02027-0069. **Phone-**County Register of Deeds, R/E & UCC Recording- 781-461-6122; fax-781-326-4742; hours 8:30AM-4:45PM www.norfolkdeeds.org Will not search UCC records, but only real estate related UCC filed here. Will not search real estate or tax lien records. Reecord copy- $1.00 per page. Cert fee: no fee. Payee: Norfolk County Register of Deeds. **Online Access to Real Estate, Lien, Deed, Judgment records:** Access to county online records is on two levels, both accessible via www.norfolkdeeds.org/Search/. You may search images and indices free, however, to print requires a subscription; $100 per year + $1.00 per page. Land records go back to 1974; images to 1996. Land court records go back to 9/1984, with images back to 1996. This replaces the old subscription system. **Other phones:** Customer Service-781-461-6101.

Norfolk Town

Town Clerk, 1 Liberty Lane, Norfolk, MA 02056. **Phone-**508-528-1400, R/E Recording- 781-461-6100, UCC Recording- 617-727-9180; fax-508-541-3363; hours 9AM-4PM www.virtualnorfolk.org UCC record search per debtor- $10.00. UCC copy- $2.00 per page. Will not search tax liens. RE records at Norfolk Cty. Payee: Town of Norfolk. **Other phones:** Assessor-508-528-1120; Treasurer-508-528-0058; Vital Records-508-528-1400.

North Adams City

City Clerk, 10 Main St, North Adams, MA 01247. **Phone-**413-662-3015, R/E Recording- 413-743-0035 North; 443-7438 Cent.; 528-0146 South; hours 8AM-4:30PM Will not search UCC records. UCC copy- $2.00 per page. RE records at Berkshire Cty. Payee: City of North Adams. **Other phones:** Assessor-413-662-3012; Treasurer-413-662-3044; Elections-413-662-3015; Vital Records-413-662-3015.

North Andover Town

Town Clerk, 120 Main St, North Andover, MA 01845. **Phone-**978-688-9502; fax-978-688-9556; hours 8:30AM-4:30PM www.townofnorthandover.com UCC record search per debtor- $10.00. UCC copy- $2.00 per page. UCC search includes tax liens if requested. RE records at Essex Cty. Payee: Town of North Andover. **Online Access to Land, Grantor/Grantee, Recording records:** Search the county recorder database for free at www.lawrencedeeds.com/dsSearch.asp. **Other phones:** Assessor-978-688-9566; Treasurer-978-688-9550; Elections-978-688-9501; Vital Records-978-688-9501.

North Attleborough Town

Town Clerk, PO Box 871, North Attleborough, MA 02761-0871. **Phone-**508-699-0108, R/E Recording-508-822-3081; fax-508-699-2354; hours 8AM-4PM (Th 8AM-7PM) UCC record search per debtor- $5.00. UCC copy- $1.00 per page. UCC search includes tax liens if requested. RE records at Bristol Cty. Payee: Town of North Attleborough. **Online Access to Assessor records:** Search the town assessor database at http://data.visionappraisal.com/NorthAttleboroMA/. Free registration for full data. **Other phones:** Assessor-508-699-0117; Treasurer-508-699-0114; Elections-508-699-0106; Vital Records-508-699-0142; Tax Office:-508-699-0108.

North Brookfield Town

Town Clerk, 185 No. Main St., North Brookfield, MA 01535. **Phone-**508-867-0203; fax-508-867-0249; hours Noon-2:30PM 6PM-8PM T; Noon-2:30PM Th; 9AM-Noon F UCC record search per debtor- $10.00. UCC copy- $1.00 per page. UCC search includes tax liens if requested. Separate federal/state combined tax lien search- $10.00 per debtor. RE records at Worcester Cty. Payee: Town of North Brookfield. **Online Access to Property, Assessor records:** Access to property data is free at http://csc-ma.us/PropertyContent/jsp/Home.jsp?Page=1. Select North Brookfield Town. **Other phones:** Assessor-508-867-0209; Treasurer-508-867-0204; Elections-508-867-0203; Vital Records-508-867-0203.

North Reading Town

Town Clerk, 235 N. St, North Reading, MA 01864-1294. **Phone-**978-664-6030, R/E Recording- 978-664-6021; fax-978-664-6048; hours 8AM-4PM M-Th; 8AM-1PM F. Will search UCC records up to 6/30/2001. Search per debtor- $10.00. UCC copy- $1.00 per page. Will not search tax liens. RE records at Middlesex Cty. Cert fee: $10.00 per doc. Payee: Town of North Reading. **Other phones:** Assessor-978-664-6021; Treasurer-978-664-6019; Elections-978-664-6030; Vital Records-978-664-6030.

Northampton City

City Clerk, 210 Main St, Northampton, MA 01060. **Phone-**413-587-1224; fax-413-587-1264; hours 8:30AM-4:30PM UCC record search per debtor- $10.00. UCC copy fee- $1.00 per page. UCC search includes tax liens if requested. RE records at Hampshire Cty. Payee: City of Northampton. **Other phones:** Assessor-413-587-1200; Treasurer-413-587-1297; Elections-413-587-1224; Vital Records-413-587-1224.

Northborough Town

Town Clerk, 63 Main St, Northborough, MA 01532-1994. **Phone-**508-393-5001; fax-508-393-6996; hours 8AM-4PM M,W,Th; 8AM-7PM T; 7AM-Noon F www.town.northborough.ma.us UCC record search per debtor- $10.00. UCC copy fee- $2.00 per page. UCC search includes tax liens

if requested. RE records at Worcester Cty. Cert fee: $5.00 per doc. Payee: Town of Northborough. **Other phones:** Assessor-508-393-5005; Treasurer-508-393-5045; Elections-508-393-5001; Vital Records-508-393-5001; 508-393-5002-.

Northbridge Town

Town Clerk, 7 Main St, Town Hall, Whitinsville, MA 01588. **Phone-**508-234-2001, R/E Recording- 508-234-5432; fax-508-234-2001; hours 8:30AM-7PM M; 8:30AM-4:30PM T-Th; 8:30AM-1PM Friday www.northbridgemass.org UCC record search per debtor- $10.00. UCC copy fee- $10.00 per name. UCC search includes tax liens if requested. RE records at Worcester Cty. Payee: Town of Northbridge. **Other phones:** Assessor-508-234-2740; Treasurer-508-234-5432; Elections-508-234-2001; Vital Records-508-234-2001.

Northfield Town

Town Clerk, Town Hall, Northfield, MA 01360. **Phone-**413-498-2901; fax-413-498-5103; hours 8:30AM-4PM M-Tu; 9-Noon 4-Noon;12-8PM W UCC record search per debtor- $10.00. UCC copy- $.10 per page. Tax liens included in UCC search. Separate federal/state combined tax lien search- $10.00 per debtor. RE records at Franklin Cty. Payee: Town of Northfield. **Other phones:** Assessor-413-498-2901; Treasurer-413-498-2901; Elections-413-498-2901; Vital Records-413-498-2901.

Norton Town

Town Clerk, 70 E. Main St, Town Hall, Norton, MA 02766. **Phone-**508-285-0231, R/E Recording- 508-285-0270, UCC Recording- 508-285-0230; fax-508-285-0297; hours 8:30AM-4:30PM M,T,W,F; 8:30AM-8PM Th. UCC record search per debtor- $10.00. UCC copy- $2.00 per page. Tax liens included in UCC search if requested. Separate federal/state combined tax lien search- $10.00 per debtor. RE records at Bristol Cty. Payee: Town of Norton. **Other phones:** Assessor-508-285-0270; Treasurer-508-285-0223; Elections-508-285-0230; Vital Records-508-285-0230.

Norwell Town

Town Clerk, PO Box 295, Norwell, MA 02061-0295. **Phone-**781-659-8072, R/E Recording- 781-659-8014; fax-781-659-7795; hours-8AM-4PM www.townofnorwell.net Will search UCC records as of 6/30/2001 only. Search per debtor- $10.00. UCC copy- $1.00 per page. Tax liens included in UCC search if requested. Separate federal/state combined tax lien search- $10.00 per debtor. RE records at Plymouth Cty. Payee: Town of Norwell. **Other phones:** Assessor-781-659-8014; Treasurer-781-659-8070; Elections-781-659-8072; Vital Records-781-659-8072.

Norwood Town

Town Clerk, PO Box 40, Norwood, MA 02062. **Phone-**781-762-1240 x193, UCC Recording- 781-762-1240; fax-781-762-0954; hours 8:15AM-4:30PM UCC record search per debtor- $10.00. UCC copy fee- $2.00 per UCC; $1.00 per attachment. Tax liens included in UCC search if requested. Separate federal/state combined tax lien search- $10.00 per debtor. RE records at Norfolk Cty. Payee: Town of Norwood. **Other phones:** Assessor-781-762-1240; Treasurer-781-762-1240; Elections-781-762-1240; Vital Records-781-762-1240.

Oak Bluffs Town

Town Clerk, PO Box 2490, Oak Bluffs, MA 02557-2490. **Phone-**508-693-5515; fax-508-696-7736; hours 8:30AM-4PM UCC record search per debtor- $10.00. UCC copy- $1.00 per page. Tax lien search fee- $5.00 per debtor. RE records at Dukes Cty. Cert fee: $5.00 per copy. Payee: Town of Oak Bluffs. **Online Access to Assessor records:** Search the town assessor database at http://data.visionappraisal.com/OakBluffsMA/. Free registration for full data. **Other phones:** Assessor-508-693-5519; Treasurer-508-693-5514; Elections-508-693-5515; Vital Records-508-693-5515.

Oakham Town

Town Clerk, PO Box 222, Oakham, MA 01068-0222. **Phone**-508-882-5549; fax-508-882-3060; hours 5:30-7PM T; 9AM-11:30AM,Th
Will not search records. UCC copy- $1.00 per page. RE records at Worcester Cty. Payee: Town of Oakham. **Online Access to Property, Assessor records:** Access to property data is free at http://csc-ma.us/PropertyContent/jsp/Home.jsp?Page=1. Select Oakham Town. **Other phones:** Assessor-508-882-5549; Treasurer-508-882-5549.

Orange Town

Town Clerk, 6 Prospect St, Orange, MA 01364. **Phone**-978-544-2254; fax-978-544-1120; hours 8AM-4PM M-Th; 8AM-1PM F. Will not search records. RE records at Franklin Cty. Cert fee: $2.00 per page. Payee: Town of Orange. **Other phones:** Assessor-978-544-1108; Treasurer-978-544-1103; Elections-978-544-2254; Vital Records-978-544-2254.

Orleans Town

Town Clerk, 19 School Rd, Orleans, MA 02653-3699. **Phone**-508-240-3700, UCC Recording- 508-240-3700 x304; fax-508-240-3388; hours 8:30AM-4:30PM
UCC record search per debtor- $5.00. UCC copy-$2.00 per page. UCC search includes tax liens if requested. Tax lien search fee- $25.00 per lien. RE records at Barnstable Cty. Payee: Town of Orleans. **Other phones:** Assessor-508-240-3700 x331; Treasurer-508-240-3700 x323.

Otis Town

Town Clerk, PO Box 237, Otis, MA 01253. **Phone**-413-269-0101; fax-413-269-0111; hours 7:30AM-2:30PM M-F; 9AM-Noon Sat
UCC record search per debtor- $5.00. Copy fee is $2.00 per page. RE records at Berkshire Cty. Payee: Town of Otis. **Other phones:** Assessor-413-269-0102; Treasurer-413-269-0108; Elections-413-269-0101; Vital Records-413-269-0101.

Oxford Town

Town Clerk, 325 Main St, Oxford, MA 01540. **Phone**-508-987-6032; fax-508-987-6048; hours 9AM-4:30PM www.town.oxford.ma.us
UCC record search per debtor- $10.00. UCC copy-$2.00 per page. Will search tax liens. Tax lien search fee- $10.00 per search. RE records at Worcester Cty. Cert fee: $5.00 per page. Payee: Town of Oxford. **Online Access to Property Assessor records:** Search assessment records by street name for free at www.town.oxford.ma.us/Assessor/Assessor.htm. **Other phones:** Assessor-508-987-6036; Treasurer-508-987-6038; Elections-508-987-6032; Vital Records-508-987-6032.

Palmer Town

Town Clerk, 4417 Main St., Palmer Town Bldg., Palmer, MA 01069. **Phone**-413-283-2608, R/E Recording- 413-283-2607; fax-413-283-2637; hours 9AM-4:30PM
UCC record search per debtor- $20.00. UCC copy-$2.00 per page. Separate federal/state combined tax lien search-No fee. RE records at Hampden Cty. Payee: Town of Palmer. **Online Access to Real Estate, Recording, Lien records:** See Hampden County for recorded records searching. **Other phones:** Assessor-413-283-2607; Treasurer-413-283-2600; Elections-413-283-2608; Vital Records-413-283-2608.

Paxton Town

Town Clerk, 697 Pleasant St, Paxton, MA 01612. **Phone**-508-799-7347 x13; fax-508-797-0966; hours 8AM-2PM M-Th
UCC record search per debtor- $10.00. UCC copy-$1.00 per page. UCC search includes tax liens if requested. Separate federal/state combined tax lien search- $1.00 per page. RE records at Worcester Cty. Payee: Town of Paxton. **Online Access to Assessor records:** search assessor data for free at http://data.visionappraisal.com/PaxtonMA/. **Other phones:** Assessor-508-799-7231 x16; Treasurer-508-799-7347 x15; Elections-508-799-7347 x13; Vital Records-508-799-7347 x13.

Peabody City

City Clerk, 24 Lowell St, City Hall, Peabody, MA 01960. **Phone**-978-538-5900, UCC Recording- 978-538-5753; fax-978-538-5985; hours 8:30AM-4PM M-W; 8:30AM-7PM Th; 8:30AM-12:30PM F www.ci.peabody.ma.us
UCC record search per debtor- $10.00. UCC copy fee- $.25 per copy. Will search tax liens. RE records at Essex Cty. Cert fee: $1.00 per page. Payee: City of Peabody. **Other phones:** Assessor-978-538-5729; Treasurer-978-538-5764; Elections-978-538-5750; Vital Records-978-538-5752 or 5751.

Pelham Town

Town Clerk, 351 Amherst Rd., Rhodes Bldg, Pelham, MA 01002-9753. **Phone**-413-253-7129; fax-413-256-1061; hours 8:30AM-4:30PM M-Th www.townofpelham.org
UCC record search per debtor- $10.00. Copy fee is $2.00 per copy. RE records at Hampshire Cty. Cert fee: $5.00 per cert. Payee: Town of Pelham. **Other phones:** Assessor-413-253-0734; Treasurer-413-253-2267; Elections-413-253-7129; Vital Records-413-253-7129.

Pembroke Town

Town Clerk, 100 Center St, Pembroke, MA 02359. **Phone**-781-293-7211; fax-781-293-4650; 8:30AM-4:30PM. UCC record search per debtor- $10.00. UCC copy- $1.00 per page. Will not search tax liens. RE records at Plymouth Cty. Payee: Town of Pembroke. **Other phones:** Assessor-781-293-2393; Treasurer-781-293-3893; Elections-781-293-7211; Vital Records-781-293-7211; Town Administrator-781-293-3844.

Pepperell Town

Town Clerk, 1 Main St, Town Hall, Pepperell, MA 01463-1644. **Phone**-978-433-0339; fax-978-433-0338; hours 8AM-4:30PM www.town.pepperell.ma.us
Will not search UCC records. RE records at Middlesex Cty. Payee: Town of Pepperell. **Other phones:** Assessor-978-433-0322; Treasurer-978-433-0337; Elections-978-433-0339; Vital Records-978-433-0339.

Peru Town

Town Clerk, PO Box 564, Peru, MA 01235. **Phone**-413-655-8326, UCC Recording- 413-655-8312; fax-413-655-8312; hours 6-8PM Mondays. Will not search records. RE records at Berkshire Cty. Cert fee: $25.00 per Municipal Lien Certificate. Payee: Town of Peru. **Other phones:** Assessor-413-655-8312; Treasurer-413-655-8312; Elections-413-655-8326; Vital Records-413-655-8326; Tax Collector-413-655-0072.

Petersham Town

Town Clerk, PO Box 486, Petersham, MA 01366. **Phone**-978-724-6649; fax-978-724-3501; hours 6-8PM Monday
This agency will not search records. Real estate records searches and tax lien searches are performed by the tax collector. UCC copy- $1.00 per page. RE records at Worcester Cty. Payee: Town of Petersham. **Other phones:** Assessor-978-724-6658; Treasurer-978-724-6699; Elections-978-724-6649; Vital Records-978-724-6649; Tax Collector-978-724-6620.

Phillipston Town

Town Clerk, 50 The Common, Phillipston, MA 01331. **Phone**-978-249-1733, R/E Recording- 978-249-1732; fax-978-249-3356; hours 12-2PM, 6-8PM M; 5-7PM W; 8:30AM-10AM SAT
UCC record search per debtor- $10.00. UCC copy-$1.00 per page. Will not search tax liens. Contact Tax Collector. RE records at Worcester Cty. Payee: Town of Phillipston. **Other phones:** Assessor-978-249-1732; Treasurer-978-249-3415; Elections-978-249-1733; Vital Records-978-249-1733; General Town Hall-978-249-6828; Tax Collector-978-249-1731.

Pittsfield City

City Clerk, 70 Allen St, City Hall, Pittsfield, MA 01201. **Phone**-413-499-9361; fax-413-499-9363; hours 8:30AM-4PM www.pittsfield-ma.org
UCC record search per debtor- $2.00. UCC copy-$1.00 per page. UCC search includes tax liens if requested. RE records at Berkshire Cty. Cert fee: $5.00 per copy. Payee: City of Pittsfield. **Other phones:** Assessor-413-395-0102; Treasurer-413-499-9466; Elections-413-499-9460; Vital Records-413-499-9361.

Plainfield Town

Town Clerk, 12 Broom St, Plainfield, MA 01070. **Phone**-413-634-5582; hours 10AM-Noon Sat
Will not search records. UCC copy- $1.00 per page. RE records at Hampshire Cty. Payee: Town of Plainfield. **Other phones:** Assessor-413-634-5420; Treasurer-413-634-5420; Elections-413-634-5417; Vital Records-413-634-5417.

Plainville Town

Town Clerk, PO Box 1717, Plainville, MA 02762. **Phone**-508-695-3142 x20, R/E Recording- 508-695-3142 x14; fax-508-695-1857; hours 8AM-4:00PM
UCC record search per debtor- $10.00. UCC copy-$2.00 per page. Tax liens included in UCC search if requested. Separate federal/state combined tax lien search- $10.00 per debtor. RE records at Norfolk Cty. Cert fee: $5.00 per cert. Payee: Town of Plainville. **Other phones:** Assessor-508-695-3142 x14; Treasurer-508-695-3142 x17,18; Elections-508-695-3142 x19; Vital Records-508-695-3142 x20.

Plymouth County

Registry of Deeds, PO Box 3535, Plymouth, MA 02361. **Phone**-508-830-9200, R/E Recording- 508-830-9261; fax-508-830-9280; hours 8:15AM-4:30PM (Recording 8:30AM-4PM)
www.regdeeds.co.plymouth.ma.us
Will not search records. UCC copy- $1.00 per page. Payee: Plymouth County Register of Deeds. **Online Access to Real Estate, Lien, Judgment records:** Access to Online Titleview for Plymouth County records requires a usage charge of $.60 per minute of use. Records date back to 1971. Lending agency information is available. A fax back service is $3 + $1 per page in county, $5. + $1 per page, outside. For information, call 508-830-9287.

Plymouth Town

Town Clerk, 11 Lincoln St, Plymouth, MA 02360-3386. **Phone**-508-830-4050; fax-508-830-4062; hours 8AM-4:30PM www.townofplymouth.org
UCC record search per debtor- $3.00 per UCC. UCC copy fee- $3.00 per UCC + $.20 per page. Tax liens not included in UCC search. RE records at Plymouth Cty. Cert fee: $2.00 per item. Payee: Town of Plymouth. **Other phones:** Assessor-508-

830-4020; Treasurer-508-830-4051; Elections-508-830-4050; Vital Records-508-830-4052.

Plympton Town

Town Clerk, PO Box 153, Plympton, MA 02367-0153. **Phone**-781-585-3220; fax-781-582-1505; hours 9AM-2PM, 7-9PM M; 9AM-2PM T-Th. http://town.plympton.ma.us
UCC record search per debtor- $10.00. UCC copy-$1.00 per page. Will not search tax liens. RE records at Plymouth Cty. Payee: Town of Plympton. **Other phones:** Assessor-781-585-3227; Treasurer-781-585-0409; Elections-781-585-3220; Vital Records-781-585-3220.

Princeton Town

Town Clerk, 6 Town Hall Drive, Princeton, MA 01541-1137. **Phone**-978-464-2103; fax-978-464-2106; hours 8:30AM-3:30PM http://town.princeton.ma.us
Will not search records. UCC copy- $2.00 per page. RE records at Worcester Cty. Cert fee: $10.00 per record. Payee: Town of Princeton. **Other phones:** Assessor-978-464-2104; Treasurer-978-464-2105; Elections-978-464-2103; Vital Records-978-464-2103; Switchboard-978-464-2100.

Provincetown Town

Town Clerk, 260 Commercial St, Provincetown, MA 02657. **Phone**-508-487-7013; fax-508-487-9560; hours 8AM-5PM www.provincetowngov.org
UCC record search per debtor- $10.00.UCC search includes tax liens if requested. RE records at Barnstable Cty. Payee: Town of Provincetown. **Online Access to Assessor, Property Sale records:** Records on the Provincetown Assessor database are free at www.provincetowngov.org/assessor.html. **Other phones:** Assessor-508-487-7017; Treasurer-508-487-7015; Elections-508-487-7013; Vital Records-508-487-7013.

Quincy City

City Clerk, 1305 Hancock St, City Hall, Quincy, MA 02169. **Phone**-617-376-1136; fax-617-376-1139; hours 8:30AM-4:30PM www.ci.quincy.ma.us
UCC record search per debtor- $10.00. UCC copy-$1.00 per page. UCC search includes tax liens. RE records at Norfolk Cty. Cert fee: $8.00 per page. Payee: City of Quincy. **Other phones:** Assessor-617-376-1178; Elections-617-376-1141; Vital Records-617-376-1135, 1136, 1137.

Randolph Town

Town Clerk, 41 S. Main St., Randolph, MA 02368. **Phone**-781-961-0900; fax-781-961-0919; hours 8:30AM-4:30PM. UCC record search per debtor-$10.00. UCC copy- $2.00 per page. Will not search tax liens. RE records at Norfolk Cty. Payee: Town of Randolph. **Other phones:** Assessor-781-961-0906; Treasurer-781-961-0934.

Raynham Town

Town Clerk, 53 Orchard St, Raynham, MA 02767-1320. **Phone**-508-824-2700; fax-508-823-1812; hours 8:30AM-4:30PM M-Th; 8:30AM-Noon F www.town.raynham.ma.us
UCC record search per debtor- $10.00. UCC copy-$2.00 per page. Will not search tax liens. RE records at Bristol Cty. Payee: Town of Raynham. **Other phones:** Assessor-508-824-2704; Treasurer-508-824-2702; Elections-508-824-2700; Vital Records-508-824-2700; Tax Collector Office-508-824-2709.

Reading Town

Town Clerk, 16 Lowell St, Reading, MA 01867. **Phone**-781-942-9050, UCC Recording- 781-942-9049; fax-781-942-9070; hours-8:30AM-5PM www.ci.reading.ma.us

UCC record search per debtor- $10.00. UCC copy-$2.00 1st page; $1.00 each add'l. Federal/state combined tax lien search- $10.00 per debtor. RE records at Middlesex Cty. Payee: Town of Reading. **Online Access to Assessor records:** Records on the Town of Reading Assessor database are free at www.ziplink.net/~reading1/assessor.htm. **Other phones:** Assessor-781-942-9027; Treasurer-781-942-9032; Elections-781-942-9050; Vital Records-781-942-9048.

Rehoboth Town

Town Clerk, 148 Peck St, Rehoboth, MA 02769-3099. **Phone**-508-252-6502; fax-508-252-5342; hours 9AM-4PM
UCC record search per debtor- $5.00. UCC copy-$2.00 per page. UCC search includes tax liens if requested. Separate federal/state combined tax lien search- $5.00 per debtor. RE records at Bristol Cty. Cert fee: $5.00. Payee: Town of Rehoboth. **Other phones:** Assessor-508-252-3352; Treasurer-508-252-3571; Vital Records-508-252-6502.

Revere City

City Clerk, 281 Broadway, City Hall, Revere, MA 02151-5087. **Phone**-781-286-8160; fax-781-286-8135; hours 8:15AM-5PM M-Th; 8:15AM-Noon F
Will not search records. UCC copy- $1.00 per page. RE records at Suffolk Cty. Cert fee: $10.00. Payee: City of Revere. **Online Access to Assessor records:** Search the town assessor data at http://data.visionappraisal.com/RevereMA/. Free registration for full data. **Other phones:** Assessor-781-286-8169; Treasurer-781-286-8136.

Richmond Town

Town Clerk, PO Box 81, Richmond, MA 01254. **Phone**-413-698-3315; fax-413-698-3272; hours 9AM-Noon T,Th-Sat
Will not search records. UCC copy- $1.00 per page. RE records at Berkshire Cty. Cert fee: $5.00 per unit. Payee: Town of Richmond. **Other phones:** Assessor-413-698-2525; Treasurer-413-698-3315; Elections-413-698-3315.

Rochester Town

Town Clerk, 1 Constitution Way, Town Hall, Rochester, MA 02770. **Phone**-508-763-3871; fax-508-763-4892; hours 7-9PM M
UCC record search per debtor- $10.00.Tax liens not included in UCC search. RE records at Plymouth Cty. Payee: Town of Rochester.

Rockland Town

Town Clerk, 242 Union St, Rockland, MA 02370. **Phone**-781-871-1892, R/E Recording- 781-871-0137; hours 8:30AM-4:30PM
UCC record search per debtor- $10.00. UCC copy-$2.00 per page. Will not search tax liens. Contact the town tax collector office for municipal lien search fee, 781-871-2642. RE records at Plymouth Cty. Payee: Town of Rockland. **Other phones:** Assessor-781-871-0137; Treasurer-781-871-1895; Elections-781-871-1892; Vital Records-781-871-1892.

Rockport Town

Town Clerk, PO Box 429, Rockport, MA 01966. **Phone**-978-546-6894, R/E Recording- 978-546-2011; fax-978-546-3562; hours-8AM-4PM www.town.rockport.ma.us
UCC record search per debtor- $10.00. UCC copy fee- $1.00 per copy. Will not search tax liens. RE records at Essex Cty. Payee: Town of Rockport. **Other phones:** Assessor-978-546-2011; Treasurer-978-546-6648; Elections-978-546-6894; Vital Records-978-546-6894.

Rowe Town

Town Clerk, Town Hall, Rowe, MA 01367. **Phone**-413-339-5520; fax-413-339-5316; hours 8-11AM W
UCC record search per debtor- $10.00. UCC copy-$1.00 per page. Will not search tax liens. RE records at Berkshire Cty. Payee: Town of Rowe. **Other phones:** Assessor-413-339-5520; Treasurer-413-339-5520; Vital Records-413-339-5520.

Rowley Town

Town Clerk, PO Box 351, Rowley, MA 01969-0351. **Phone**-978-948-2081; fax-978-948-2162; hours by appointment
Will not search records. RE records at Essex Cty. Payee: Town of Rowley. **Online Access to Property Assessor records:** Search the town assessor data at http://data.visionappraisal.com/RowleyMA/. Free registration for full data. **Other phones:** Assessor-978-948-2021; Treasurer-978-948-2631; Elections-978-948-2081; Vital Records-978-948-2081.

Royalston Town

Town Clerk, 94 Athol Rd, Royalston, MA 01368-0118. **Phone**-978-249-0493; fax-978-575-0493; hours 9:30AM-2:30PM Tuesdays
UCC record search per debtor- $10.00. UCC copy-$1.00 per page. Will not search tax liens. RE records at Worcester Cty. Payee: Town of Royalston. **Online Access to Assessor, Property records:** Access to property data is free at http://csc-ma.us/PropertyContent/jsp/Home.jsp?Page=1. Select Royalston Town. **Other phones:** Assessor-978-249-0337; Treasurer-978-249-0493; Elections-978-249-0493; Vital Records-978-249-0493; Tax Collector-978-249-2927.

Russell Town

Town Clerk, 65 Main St, Town Hall, Russell, MA 01071. **Phone**-413-862-3265; fax-413-862-3103; hours 4:30-6:30PM T; 4-6PM F
UCC record search per debtor- $10.00. UCC copy-$1.00 per page. Will not search tax liens. RE records at Hampden Cty. Payee: Town of Russell. **Online Access to Real Estate, Recording, Lien records:** See Hampden County for recording records searching. **Other phones:** Assessor-413-862-3103; Treasurer-413-862-3265; Elections-413-862-3265; Vital Records-413-862-3265.

Rutland Town

Town Clerk, 250 Main St, Rutland, MA 01543. **Phone**-508-886-4104; fax-508-886-2929; hours 7:30AM-4PM M,W,Th; 7:30AM-7PM T
Will not search records. UCC copy- $2.00 per page. RE records at Worcester Cty. Cert fee: $5.00. Payee: Town of Rutland. **Online Access to Assessor, Property records:** Access town assessor records free at http://data.visionappraisal.com/RutlandMA/. **Other phones:** Assessor-508-886-4101; Treasurer-508-886-4103.

Salem City

City Clerk, 93 Washington, City Hall, Salem, MA 01970-3593. **Phone**-978-745-9595; fax-978-740-9209; hours 8AM-4PM M-W; 8AM-7PM Th; 8AM-Noon F
UCC record search per debtor- $10.00. UCC copy fee- $.20 per page. Tax liens not included in UCC search. Separate federal tax lien search- $5.00 per debtor. RE records at Essex Cty. Cert fee: $3.00 per doc. Payee: City of Salem. **Other phones:** Assessor-978-745-9595 x261.

Salisbury Town

Town Clerk, 5 Beach Rd, Salisbury, MA 01952. **Phone**-978-462-7591; fax-978-462-4176; hours 8:30AM-4PM, 7-9PM M; 8:30AM-4PM T-Th;

8:30AM-1PM F. Will not search records. UCC copy- $2.00 per page. RE records at Essex Cty. Payee: Town of Salisbury. **Other phones:** Assessor-978-462-7591; Treasurer-978-465-0331; Vital Records-978-462-7591.

Sandisfield Town

Town Clerk, PO Box 163, Sandisfield, MA 01255. **Phone**-413-258-4711, R/E Recording- 413-258-4701, UCC Recording- 413-258-4075; fax-413-258-4225; hours 10AM-2PM, 6-8PM M; 10AM-2PM Th or by Appointment. UCC record search per debtor- $10.00. UCC copy- $1.00 per page. Tax liens not included in UCC search. RE records at Berkshire Cty. Payee: Sandisfield Town Clerk. **Other phones:** Assessor-413-258-4701; Treasurer-413-258-8102; Elections-413-258-4075; Vital Records-413-258-4075; Selectmen-413-258-4711.

Sandwich Town

Town Clerk, 145 Main St, Sandwich, MA 02563. **Phone**-508-888-0340; fax-508-888-2497; hours 8:30AM-4:30PM www.sandwichmass.org
UCC record search per debtor- $10.00. UCC copy fee- $.20 per page. UCC search includes tax liens if requested. RE records at Barnstable Cty. Cert fee: $2.00 per page. Payee: Town of Sandwich. **Other phones:** Assessor-508-888-0157; Treasurer-508-888-6508; Elections-508-888-0340; Vital Records-508-888-0340.

Saugus Town

Town Clerk, 298 Central St, Town Hall, Saugus, MA 01906. **Phone**-781-231-4101; fax-781-231-4109; hours 8:30AM-7PM M; 8:30AM-5PM T,W,Th; 8:30AM-12:30PM F; www.saugus.net
Will not search records. UCC copy- $2.00 per page. RE records at Essex Cty. Payee: Town of Saugus. **Other phones:** Assessor-781-231-4130; Treasurer-781-231-4135; Elections-781-231-4101; Vital Records-781-231-4101.

Savoy Town

Town Clerk, 720 Main Rd., Town Office, Savoy, MA 01256. **Phone**-413-743-3759; fax-413-743-4292; hours 1-5PM Tu, Th; 7-9PM Tu by appointment only
UCC record search per debtor- $10.00. UCC copy- $1.00 per page. Will not search real estate or tax lien records. Payee: Town of Savoy. **Other phones:** Assessor-413-743-4290; Treasurer-413-743-4290; Elections-413-743-3759; Vital Records-413-743-3759; Main Town Office-413-743-4290.

Scituate Town

Town Clerk, 600 C. J. Cushing Way, Town Hall, Scituate, MA 02066. **Phone**-781-545-8744; fax-781-545-8704; hours 8:30AM-4:45PM M,W,Th; 8:30-7:30 Tu, 8:30-11;45AM F www.town.scituate.ma.us
UCC record search per debtor- $10.00. RE records at Plymouth County. Record copy- $2.00 per page. Cert fee: $2.00 per page. Payee: Town of Scituate. **Other phones:** Assessor-781-545-8713; Treasurer-781-545-8719; Elections-781-545-8744; Vital Records-781-545-8744.

Seekonk Town

Town Clerk, 100 Peck St, Seekonk, MA 02771. **Phone**-508-336-2920; fax-508-336-0764; hours 9AM-4:30PM www.ci.seekonk.ma.us
UCC record search per debtor- $10.00. UCC copy- $1.00 per page. Tax liens included in UCC search. Separate state tax lien search- $10.00. RE records at Bristol Cty. Payee: Town of Seekonk. **Other phones:** Assessor-508-336-2980; Treasurer-508-336-2930; Elections-508-336-2920; Vital Records-508-336-2920.

Sharon Town

Town Clerk, 90 S. Main St, Town Hall, Sharon, MA 02067. **Phone**-781-784-1505; fax-781-784-1503; hours 8:30AM-5PM M-W; 8:30AM-8PM Th; 8:30AM-12:30PM F
UCC record search per debtor- $10.00. Copy fee is $.20 per page. UCC search includes tax liens. Separate federal/state combined tax lien search-$10.00 per debtor. RE records at Norfolk Cty. Cert fee: $5.20 per cert. Payee: Town of Sharon. **Other phones:** Assessor-781-784-1507; Treasurer-781-784-1500; Elections-781-784-1505; Vital Records-781-784-1505.

Sheffield Town

Town Clerk, PO Box 175, Sheffield, MA 01257. **Phone**-413-229-8752; fax-413-229-7010; hours 9AM-4PM. Will search UCC records prior to July 1, 2001. Search per debtor- $15.00. UCC copy- $.20 per page. UCC search includes tax liens if requested. RE records at Berkshire Cty. Payee: Town of Sheffield. **Other phones:** Assessor-413-229-7001; Treasurer-413-229-7007; Elections-413-229-8752; Vital Records-413-229-8752.

Shelburne Town

Town Clerk, 51 Bridge St, Town Hall, Shelburne, MA 01370. **Phone**-413-625-0301; fax-413-625-0312; hours 9AM-5PM T 5-8PM Th
UCC record search per debtor- $10.00. UCC copy-$1.00 per page. Tax liens included in UCC search if requested. Separate federal/state combined tax lien search- $10.00 per debtor. RE records at Franklin Cty. Payee: Town of Shelburne. **Other phones:** Assessor-413-625-0302; Treasurer-413-625-0301.

Sherborn Town

Town Clerk, 19 Washignton St, Sherborn, MA 01770. **Phone**-508-651-7853; fax-508-651-7854; hours 9AM-1PM M-Th & Tues eves 6-8PM www.sherbornma.org
Will search older UCC records prior to 7/2001. Search per debtor- $10.00. UCC copy- $3.00 per page. UCC search includes tax liens if requested. RE records at Middlesex Cty. Cert fee: $5.00 per copy. Payee: Town of Sherborn. **Other phones:** Assessor-508-651-7857; Treasurer-508-651-7859; Elections-508-651-7853; Vital Records-508-651-7853.

Shirley Town

Town Clerk, PO Box 782, Shirley, MA 01464. **Phone**-978-425-2610, UCC Recording- 978-425-2600 x205; fax-978-425-2602; hours 8AM-3PM (6-9PM M Evening)
UCC record search per debtor- $10.00. UCC copy-$1.00 per page. Tax liens included in UCC search if requested. Separate federal/state combined tax lien search- $6.00 per debtor. RE records at Middlesex Cty. Payee: Town of Shirley. **Other phones:** Assessor-978-425-2600 x220; Treasurer-978-425-2600 x215; Vital Records-978-425-2610.

Shrewsbury Town

Town Clerk, 100 Maple Ave, Town Hall, Shrewsbury, MA 01545. **Phone**-508-841-8507; fax-508-842-0587; hours 8AM-4:30PM
UCC record search per debtor- $10.00. UCC copy-$2.00 per page. UCC search includes tax liens. RE records at Worcester Cty. Payee: Town of Shrewsbury. **Other phones:** Assessor-508-841-8501; Treasurer-508-841-8509; Elections-508-841-8507; Vital Records-508-841-8507.

Shutesbury Town

Town Clerk, PO Box 264, Shutesbury, MA 01072-0264. **Phone**-413-259-1204, R/E Recording- 413-259-3790; fax-413-259-1107; hours 9AM-1PM M-Th www.shutesbury.org
Will search UCC records; only records prior to 7/1/2001 available. Search per debtor- $10.00. UCC copy- $1.00 per page. UCC search includes tax liens. Separate federal/state combined tax lien search- $10.00 per debtor. RE records at Franklin Cty. Cert fee: $5.00 per page. Payee: Town of Shutesbury. **Other phones:** Assessor-413-259-3790; Treasurer-413-259-1801; Elections-413-259-1204; Vital Records-413-259-1204; Local Tax Collector for local liens-413-259-1615.

Somerset Town

Town Clerk, 140 Wood St, Somerset, MA 02726. **Phone**-508-646-2818; fax-508-646-2802; hours-8:30AM-4PM
UCC record search per debtor- $10.00. UCC copy-$2.00 per page. Will not search tax liens. RE records at Bristol Cty. Payee: Town of Somerset. **Online Access to Property, Assessor records:** Access to property data is free at http://csc-ma.us/PropertyContent/jsp/Home.jsp?Page=1. Select Somerset Town. **Other phones:** Assessor-508-646-2824; Treasurer-508-646-2822; Vital Records-508-646-2818.

Somerville City

City Clerk, 93 Highland Ave, Somerville, MA 02143. **Phone**-617-625-6600 x4100; fax-617-625-4239; hours 8:30AM-4:30PM M-W; 8:30-7:30PM Th; 8:30-12:30PM F www.ci.somerville.ma.us
UCC record search per debtor- $10.00. UCC copy-$1.00 per page. Will search tax liens. Tax lien search fee- $10.00 per search. RE records at Middlesex Cty. Payee: City of Somerville. **Online Access to Assessor records:** Search city assessor data at http://data.visionappraisal.com/SomervilleMA/. Free registration for full data. **Other phones:** Assessor-617-625-6600 x3100; Treasurer-617-625-6600 x3500; Elections-617-625-6600 x4200; Vital Records-617-625-6600 x4100.

South Hadley Town

Town Clerk, 116 Main St, South Hadley, MA 01075-2833. **Phone**-413-538-5023; fax-413-538-7565; hours 8:30AM-4:30PM
UCC record search per debtor- $5.00. UCC copy-$1.00 per page. Will search tax liens. Tax lien search fee- $1.00 per debtor per page. RE records at Hampshire Cty. Cert fee: $5.00 per page. Payee: Town of South Hadley. **Other phones:** Assessor-413-538-5027; Treasurer-413-538-5023; Elections-413-538-5023; Vital Records-413-538-5023.

Southampton Town

Town Clerk, PO Box 276, Southampton, MA 01073. **Phone**-413-527-8392; fax-413-529-1006; hours 8:30AM-4PM M-Th
UCC record search per debtor- $10.00. UCC copy-$1.00 per page. Tax liens not included in UCC search. Separate federal/state combined tax lien search- $5.00 per debtor. RE records at Hampshire Cty. Cert fee: $3.00. Payee: Town of Southampton. **Online Access to Assessor records:** Assessor data at http://data.visionappraisal.com/SouthamptonMA/. **Other phones:** Assessor-413-527-4741; Treasurer-413-527-4920; Elections-413-527-8392; Selectman-413-529-0106.

Southborough Town

Town Clerk, 17 Common St, Town Hall, Southborough, MA 01772-9109. **Phone**-508-485-0710; fax-508-480-0161; hours 9AM-5PM
UCC record search per debtor- $10.00. UCC copy fee- $2.00 per page. Tax liens not included in UCC search. Federal/state combined tax lien search-$10.00 per lien. RE records at Worcester Cty. Cert

fee: $2.00 per page. Payee: Town Clerk. **Other phones:** Assessor-508-485-0710; Treasurer-508-485-0710; Elections-508-485-0710; Vital Records-508-485-0710.

Southbridge Town

Town Clerk, 41 Elm St, Southbridge, MA 01550. **Phone-**508-764-5408; fax-508-764-5425; hours 8AM-4PM M-W; 8AM-8PM Th; 8AM-Noon F www.ci.southbridge.ma.us
UCC record search per debtor- $10.00. UCC copy- $2.00 per page. UCC search includes tax liens if requested. Separate tax lien search fee- $10.00 per search. RE records at Worcester Cty. Payee: Town of Southbridge. **Other phones:** Assessor-508-764-5404; Treasurer-508-764-5401; Elections-508-764-5408; Vital Records-508-764-5408.

Southwick Town

Town Clerk, 454 College Hwy, Southwick, MA 01077. **Phone-**413-569-5504; fax-413-569-0667; hours 8:30AM-4:30PM www.southwickma.org
Will search UCC records prior to 7/2001. Search per debtor- $10.00. UCC copy- $.75 per page. UCC search includes tax liens if requested. RE records at Hampden Cty. Cert fee: $25.00 per doc. Payee: Town of Southwick. **Online Access to Assessor, Real Estate, Recording, Lien records:** Search the town assessor database at http://data.visionappraisal.com/SouthwickMA/. Free registration for full data. Also, see Hampden County for recording records searching. **Other phones:** Assessor-413-569-0565; Treasurer-413-569-5504; Elections-413-569-5504; Vital Records-413-569-5504.

Spencer Town

Town Clerk, 157 Main St, Town Hall, Spencer, MA 01562-2197. **Phone-**508-885-7500; fax-508-885-7528; hours 8AM-4PM, 6-8PM M; 8AM-4PM TTh; 8AM-Noon, 1PM-4PM W. UCC record search per debtor- $10.00. UCC copy- $2.00 per page. Tax liens included in UCC search. Separate federal/state combined tax lien search- $10.00 per debtor. RE records at Worcester Cty. Cert fee: $3.00 per cert. Payee: Town of Spencer. **Other phones:** Assessor-508-885-7520; Treasurer-508-885-7510; Elections-508-885-7500; Vital Records-508-885-7500.

Springfield City

City Clerk, 36 Court St, Springfield, MA 01103. **Phone-**413-787-6094; hours 9AM-4PM (Th open until 6PM)
UCC record search per debtor- $20.00. UCC copy fee- $2.00 for 3 pages; $1.00 each add'l. Will search tax liens. Tax lien search fee- $10.00 per debtor. RE records at Hampden Cty. Payee: City of Springfield. **Online Access to Real Estate, Recording, Lien records:** See Hampden County for recording records searching. **Other phones:** Assessor-413-787-6160; Treasurer-413-787-6130.

Sterling Town

Town Clerk, 1 Park St, Mary Ellen Butterick Muni. Bldg, Sterling, MA 01564. **Phone-**978-422-8111; fax-978-422-0289; hours 8AM-4:30PM
UCC record search per debtor- $10.00. UCC copy- $1.00 per page. Will not search tax liens. RE records at Worcester Cty. Payee: Town of Sterling. SASE required. **Other phones:** Assessor-978-422-8113; Treasurer-978-422-3028; Elections-978-422-8111; Vital Records-978-422-8111.

Stockbridge Town

Town Clerk, PO Box 417, Stockbridge, MA 01262-0417. **Phone-**413-298-4568; fax-413-298-4485; hours 9AM-Noon M, Tu, Th, F; 1-4PM W www.townofstockbridge.com

UCC record search per debtor- $10.00. UCC copy- $1.00 per page. UCC search includes tax liens if requested. Separate tax lien search fee- $10.00 per debtor. RE records at Berkshire Cty. Cert fee: $5.00 per signature. Payee: Town of Stockbridge. **Other phones:** Assessor-413-298-3509; Treasurer-413-298-4534; Elections-413-298-4568; Vital Records-413-298-4568; Central Switchboard-413-298-4714.

Stoneham Town

Town Clerk, 35 Central St, Stoneham, MA 02180. **Phone-**781-279-2650; fax-781-279-2653; hours 8AM-4PM M,W-Th; 8AM-7PM T; 8AM-Noon F
Will search UCC records prior to 7/2001. Search per debtor- $10.00. UCC copy- $2.00 per page. Separate federal/state combined tax lien search- $10.00 per debtor. RE records at Middlesex Cty. Cert fee: $10.00. Payee: Town of Stoneham. **Other phones:** Assessor-781-279-2640.

Stoughton Town

Town Clerk, 10 Pearl St, Town Hall, Stoughton, MA 02072. **Phone-**781-341-1300; fax-781-341-1032; hours 8:30AM-4:30PM M-W; 8:30AM-7PM Th; 8:30AM-1PM F www.stoughton.org
UCC record search per debtor- $10.00. UCC copy- $2.00 per page. Tax liens included in UCC search if requested. Separate federal/state combined tax lien search- $10.00 per debtor. RE records at Norfolk Cty. Payee: Town of Stoughton. **Other phones:** Assessor-781-341-1300; Treasurer-781-341-1300.

Stow Town

Town Clerk, 380 Great Rd, Town Bldg., Stow, MA 01775. **Phone-**978-897-4514; fax-978-897-4534; hours 8AM-7PM M; 8AM-12:30PM T; 8AM-4PM W-F
Will search UCC records prior to July 1, 2001. Search per debtor- $10.00.Will not search tax liens. RE records at Middlesex Cty. Cert fee: $5.00 per doc,. Payee: Town of Stow. **Other phones:** Assessor-978-897-4597; Treasurer-978-897-2834; Elections-978-897-4514 x1; Vital Records-978-897-4514 x1.

Sturbridge Town

Town Clerk, 308 Main, Sturbridge, MA 01566. **Phone-**508-347-2510, R/E Recording- 508-347-2503; fax-508-347-5886; hours 8AM-Noon, 1-4PM, 6-8PM M; 8AM-Noon, 1-4PM T-F www.town.sturbridge.ma.us
UCC record search per debtor- $10.00. UCC copy- $2.00 per page. UCC search includes tax liens if requested. RE records at Worcester Cty. Cert fee: $1.00 per page. Payee: Town of Sturbridge. **Online Access to Real Estate, Deed records:** See Worcester County Southern District for online information. **Other phones:** Assessor-508-347-2503; Treasurer-508-347-2509; Elections-508-347-2510; Vital Records-508-347-2510.

Sudbury Town

Town Clerk, 322 Concord Rd, Sudbury, MA 01776-1800. **Phone-**978-443-8891 x351; fax-978-443-0264; hours 9AM-5PM www.town.sudbury.ma.us/services
UCC record search per debtor- $5.00. UCC copy- $2.00 per page. Federal/state combined tax lien search- $5.00. RE records at Middlesex Cty. Cert fee: $2.00 per cert. Payee: Town of Sudbury. **Online Access to Assessor, Property records:** Access to the property valuations list for current year is free at www.town.sudbury.ma.us/services/department_home.asp?dept=Assessors. No name searching on this address index list. **Other phones:** Assessor-978-443-8891 x393; Treasurer-978-443-8891 x375; Elections-978-443-8891 x351; Vital Records-978-443-8891 x351.

Suffolk County

County Register of Deeds, PO Box 9660, Boston, MA 02114-9660. **Phone-**County Register of Deeds, R/E & UCC Recording- 617-788-8575; fax-617-720-4163; hours 8AM-4:30PM www.suffolkdeeds.com
Will not search records. UCC copy- $1.00 per page. Cert fee: No extra fee. Payee: Suffolk County Register of Deeds. **Online Access to Real Estate, Lien, Deed, Property Assessor records:** Searches on the Registry of Deeds site are free; real estate/liens on the county online system is not. Access to the County online system requires a written request submitted to Register of Deeds, POB 9660, Boston MA 02114. Online charges are $.50 per minute. A fax back service available. Records on the County Registry of Deeds database are free on the Internet at www.suffolkdeeds.com/search/default.asp. Search by name, corporation, and grantor/grantee. Recorded land records begin 1979; Registered land, 1983. Also, search the Boston assessor property records for free at www.cityofboston.gov/assessing/search.asp. City property taxes also available, but no name searching. **Other phones:** Assessor-617-788-8575; Treasurer-617-788-8575; Elections-617-788-8575; Vital Records-617-788-8575.

Sunderland Town

Town Clerk, 12 School St., Sunderland, MA 01375-9503. **Phone-**413-665-1442, R/E Recording- 413-665-1445; fax-413-665-1446; hours 9AM-3PM M-Th
UCC record search per debtor- $10.00. UCC copy- $1.00 per page. UCC search includes tax liens if requested. RE records at Franklin Cty. Payee: Town of Sunderland. **Other phones:** Assessor-413-665-1445; Treasurer-413-665-1444; Elections-413-665-1442; Vital Records-413-665-1442.

Sutton Town

Town Clerk, 4 Uxbridge Rd., Town Hall, Sutton, MA 01590. **Phone-**508-865-8725; fax-508-865-8721; hours 9AM-4PM M,T,W,Th; 7-9PM T; 9AM-Noon F
UCC record search per debtor- $10.00. UCC copy- $1.00 per page. Will search tax liens. RE records at Worcester Cty. Payee: Town of Sutton.

Swampscott Town

Town Clerk, 22 Monument Ave, Town Hall, Swampscott, MA 01907. **Phone-**781-596-8856; fax-781-596-8870; hours 8:30AM-4:30PM M-Th; 8AM-12:30PM F www.town.swampscott.ma.us
UCC record search per debtor- $10.00. UCC copy- $2.00 per page. Tax liens not included in UCC search. Separate federal/state combined tax lien search- $10.00 per debtor. RE records at Essex Cty. Cert fee: $2.00 per doc. Payee: Town of Swampscott. **Online Access to Assessor, Real Estate records:** Access the assessor's Property Valuation data fy-2003 for free at http://swampscott.patriotproperties.com/Default.asp?br=exp&vr=6. **Other phones:** Assessor-781-596-8858; Elections-781-596-8855; Vital Records-781-596-8856.

Swansea Town

Town Clerk, 81 Main St, Town Hall, Swansea, MA 02777. **Phone-**508-678-9389; 9AM-4PM M,T,Th,F; 9AM-5PM W
Will search UCC records. UCC search per debtor- $10.00 per written search only. UCC copy fee- $1.00 per page. RE records at Bristol County, Fall River Registry of Deeds. Cert fee: $10.00 per page. Payee: Town of Swansea. **Online Access to Property, Assessor records:** Access to property data is free at http://csc-ma.us/PropertyContent/jsp/Home.jsp?Page=1. Select Swansea Town. **Other phones:** Assessor-508-324-6702; Treasurer-508-679-6489; Elections-508-678-9389; Vital Records-508-678-9389; Selectman's Office-508-678-2981.

Taunton City

City Clerk, 15 Summer St, City Hall, Taunton, MA 02780. **Phone**-508-821-1024, R/E Recording- 508-822-0502; fax-508-821-1098; hours 9AM-5PM www.ci.taunton.ma.us
UCC record search per debtor- $10.00. UCC copy-$2.00 per copy. UCC search includes tax liens if requested. RE records at Bristol Cty. Payee: City of Taunton. **Online Access to Assessor records:** Access assessor data at http://data.visionappraisal.com /TauntonMA/. **Other phones:** Assessor-508-821-1011; Treasurer-508-821-1057; Elections-508-821-1044; Vital Records-508-821-1024.

Templeton Town

Town Clerk, 9 Main St., Town Office Bldg., Baldwinville, MA 01436. **Phone**-978-939-8466; fax-978-939-8327; hours 8AM-7 PM M; 8AM-4PM T,TH; 8AM-1PM F (Closed W)
Will not search UCC records. UCC copy- $1.00 per page plus postage. RE records at Worcester Cty. Payee: Town of Templeton. **Online Access to Assessor records:** Access assessor data at http://data.visionappraisal.com/TempletonMA/. **Other phones:** Assessor-978-939-2793; Treasurer-978-939-4475; Elections-978-939-8466; Vital Records-978-939-8466; Tax Collector-978-939-2216.

Tewksbury Town

Town Clerk, 1009 Main St, Town Hall, Tewksbury, MA 01876-2796. **Phone**-978-640-4355; fax-978-640-4302; hours 8:30AM-4:30PM www.tewksbury.info
UCC record search per debtor- $10.00. UCC copy fee- $.20 per page. UCC search includes tax liens. Tax lien search fee- $10.00. RE records at Middlesex Cty. Cert fee: $1.00 per page. Payee: Town of Tewksbury. **Other phones:** Assessor-978-640-4330; Treasurer-978-640-4340; Elections-978-640-4355; Vital Records-978-640-4355.

Tisbury Town

Town Clerk, PO Box 606, Tisbury, MA 02568-0606. **Phone**-508-696-4215; fax-508-693-5876; hours 8:30AM-4:30PM www.ci.tisbury.ma.us
UCC record search per debtor- $10.00. UCC copy-$2.00 per page. Will not search tax liens. RE records at Dukes Cty. Payee: Town of Tisbury. **Online Access to Assessor records:** Search assessor data at http://data.visionappraisal.com/TisburyMA/. Free registration for full data. **Other phones:** Assessor-508-696-4206; Treasurer-508-696-4250; Elections-508-696-4215; Vital Records-508-696-4215.

Tolland Town

Town Clerk, 241 W. Granville Rd, Tolland, MA 01034. **Phone**-413-259-4794; fax-413-258-4048; hours 2-7PM Mondays. Will not search records. RE records at Hampden Cty. Payee: Town of Tolland. **Online Access to Real Estate, Recording, Lien records:** See Hampden County for recording records searching. **Other phones:** Assessor-413-259-4794; Treasurer-413-259-4794; Elections-413-259-4794; Vital Records-413-259-4794.

Topsfield Town

Town Clerk, 8 W. Common St, Town Hall, Topsfield, MA 01983. **Phone**-978-887-1505; fax-978-887-1502; hours 8:30AM-4PM M-Th (Summer hours- 8AM-Noon) Will not search UCC records. UCC copy-$1.00 per page. No tax liens filed here. RE records at Essex Cty. Cert fee: $5.00 per sheet. Payee: Town of Topsfield. **Other phones:** Assessor-978-887-1514; Treasurer-978-887-1511; Elections-978-887-1505; Vital Records-978-887-1505.

Town of Aquinnah

Town Clerk, 65 State Rd, Aquinnah, MA 02535. **Phone**-508-645-2306; fax-508-645-2310; hours By Appointment
The Town of Aquinnah was formerly known as Gay Head. Will not search records. UCC copy- $1.00 per page. RE records at Dukes Cty. Payee: Clerk of Aquinnah. **Other phones:** 508-645-2300.

Townsend Town

Town Clerk, 272 Main St, Memorial Hall, Townsend, MA 01469. **Phone**-978-597-1704; fax-978-597-8135; hours 9AM-4PM; 9AM-8PM Tu; 9AM-Noon 1st & 3rd Sat.
Will not search UCC records. UCC copy- $2.00 per page. RE records at Middlesex Cty. Payee: Town of Townsend. **Other phones:** Assessor-978-597-6612; Treasurer-978-597-1708; Elections-978-597-1704; Vital Records-978-597-1704.

Truro Town

Town Clerk, PO Box 2012, Truro, MA 02666-2012. **Phone**-508-349-7004 ext 14; fax-508-349-7720; hours 8AM-4PM. UCC record search per debtor- $10.00. UCC copy- $1.00 per page. Separate federal/state combined tax lien search-10.00 RE records at Barnstable Cty. Cert fee: $1.00. Payee: Town of Truro. **Other phones:** Assessor-508-349-9248; Treasurer-508-349-3860.

Tyngsborough Town

Town Clerk, 25 Bryants Lane, Tyngsborough, MA 01879. **Phone**-978-649-2300 x129; fax-978-649-2301; hours 8AM-7PM M; 8AM-4PM Tu-Th; 8AM-12:30PM F www.tyngsboroughmass.com
UCC record search per debtor- $10.00. UCC copy-$1.00 per page. Will search tax liens. Federal/state tax lien search- $10.00 per debtor. RE records at Middlesex Cty. Cert fee: $4.00 per page. Payee: Town of Tyngsborough. **Online Access to Assessor, Property records:** Access to assessor property records is free at www.cobrai.com/assessors/search1.cgi. **Other phones:** Assessor-978-649-2300 x121; Treasurer-978-649-2300 x125; Elections-978-649-2300 x129; Vital Records-978-649-2300 x129.

Tyringham Town

Town Clerk, Main Rd, Tyringham, MA 01264. **Phone**-413-243-1749, R/E Recording- 413-234-1749, UCC Recording- 413-234-1749; fax-413-243-4942; hours 9AM-1PM or by appointment www.tyngsboroughmass.com/clerk.htm
UCC record search per debtor- $15.00. UCC copy-$4.00 per page. Will not search tax liens. RE records at Berkshire Cty. Cert fee: $5.00 per copy. Payee: Town Clerk. **Other phones:** Assessor-413-234-1749; Treasurer-413-234-1749; Elections-413-234-1749; Vital Records-413-234-1749.

Upton Town

Town Clerk, Box 969, Upton, MA 01568. **Phone**-Town Clerk, R/E & UCC Recording- 508-529-3565; fax-508-529-1010; hours MW9-3; TTh9-1 & 6-8; F 9AM -1PM www.upton.ma.us
UCC record search per debtor- $10.00. UCC copy-$5.00 per page. Will not search tax liens. RE records at Worcester Cty. Payee: Town of Upton. **Other phones:** Assessor-508-529-1002; Treasurer-508-529-3737; Elections-508-529-3565; Vital Records-508-529-3565.

Uxbridge Town

Town Clerk, 21 S. Main St, Uxbridge, MA 01569. **Phone**-508-278-3156; fax-508-278-3154; hours 9AM-4PM. UCC record search per debtor- $5.00, or $2.00 per statement. UCC copy- $1.00 per page. UCC search includes tax liens if requested. Combined

tax lien search- $5.00 per debtor, or $2.00 per statement. RE records at Worcester Cty. Payee: Town of Uxbridge. **Other phones:** Assessor-508-278-8602; Treasurer-508-278-8606; Elections-508-278-3156; Vital Records-508-278-3156; Switchboard-508-278-8600.

Wakefield Town

Town Clerk, 1 Lafayette St, Town Hall, Wakefield, MA 01880-2383. **Phone**-781-246-6383, R/E Recording- 781-246-6380; fax-781-246-4155; hours 8:30AM-5PM
UCC record search per debtor- $10.00. UCC copy-$2.00 per page. Tax liens not included in UCC search. Separate federal/state combined tax lien search- $10.00 per debtor. RE records at Middlesex Cty. Cert fee: $3.00. Payee: Town of Wakefield. **Other phones:** Assessor-781-246-5159; Treasurer-781-246-6340; Elections-781-246-6384; Vital Records-781-246-6383; Town Adm./Selectmen-781-246-6390.

Wales Town

Town Clerk, PO Box 834, Wales, MA 01081-0834. **Phone**-413-245-7571; fax-413-245-3261; hours 9AM-3PM Mon & Tues.
UCC record search per debtor- $25.00. UCC copy-$1.00 per page. UCC search includes tax liens if requested. Separate federal/state combined tax lien search- $25.00 per debtor. RE records at Hampden Cty. Payee: Town of Wales. **Online Access to Real Estate, Recording, Lien records:** See Hampden County for recording records searching. **Other phones:** Assessor-413-245-3260 x103; Treasurer-413-245-3260 x102; Vital Records-413-245-7571 x101.

Walpole Town

Town Clerk, 135 School St, Town Hall, Walpole, MA 02081-2898. **Phone**-508-660-7297, UCC Recording-508-660-7296; fax-508-660-7303; hours 8AM-4PM; M-F; 7-9PM T www.walpole.ma.us
UCC record search per debtor- $10.00. UCC copy-$2.00 per page. UCC search includes tax liens. RE records at Norfolk Cty. Payee: Town of Walpole. **Online Access to Property Assessor records:** Search the town assessor database at http://data.visionappraisal.com/WalpoleMA/. Free registration for full data. **Other phones:** Assessor-508-660-7314; Treasurer-508-660-7311; Elections-508-660-7296; Vital Records-508-660-7296.

Waltham City

City Clerk, 610 Main St, 2nd Fl, Waltham, MA 02452. **Phone**-781-314-3120; fax-781-314-3130; hours 8:30AM-4:30PM www.city.waltham.ma.us
UCC record search per debtor- $5.00 per name. UCC copy- $5.00 for 1st 3 pages; $1.00 each add'l. UCC search includes tax liens. RE records at Middlesex Cty. Payee: City of Waltham. **Online Access to Assessor Property records:** Search addresses at www.patriotproperties.com/waltham/Default.asp?br=exp&vr=6. **Other phones:** Assessor-781-314-3200; Treasurer-781-314-3250; Elections-781-314-3120; Vital Records-781-314-3120.

Ware Town

Town Clerk, 126 Main St, Ware, MA 01082. **Phone**-413-967-4471, UCC Recording- 413-967-4471 x104; fax-413-967-9600; hours 8:30AM-4:30PM
UCC record search per debtor- $10.00. UCC copy-$2.00 per page. Will not search tax liens. RE records at Hampshire Cty. Payee: Town of Ware. **Other phones:** Assessor-413-967-9610; Treasurer-413-967-4471; Vital Records-413-967-4471 x104.

Wareham Town

Town Clerk, 54 Marion Rd, Wareham, MA 02571. **Phone**-508-291-3140, R/E Recording- 508-830-9200; fax-508-291-3116; hours 8:30AM-4:30PM

UCC record search per debtor- $10.00. UCC copy- $1.00 per page. Tax liens included in UCC search if requested. Separate federal/state combined tax lien search- $10.00 per debtor. RE records at Plymouth Cty. Payee: Town of Wareham. **Online Access to Assessor records:** Accessor data at http://data.visionappraisal.com/WarehamMA/. **Other phones:** Assessor-508-291-3160; Treasurer-508-291-3100 x3146; Elections-508-291-3140; Vital Records-508-291-3140.

Warren Town

Town Clerk, PO Box 603, Warren, MA 01083-0603. **Phone**-413-436-5702; fax-413-436-9754; hours 9AM-3:30PM M-W,F; 5-8PM Th
Will search UCC records. UCC copy fee- $2.00 per page. Tax liens- contact the Tax Collector. RE records at Middlesex County. **Other phones:** Assessor-413-436-5703; Treasurer-413-436-5700; Elections-413-436-5702; Vital Records-413-436-5702; Tax Collector-413-436-5709.

Warwick Town

Town Clerk, 12 Athol Rd, Town Hall, Warwick, MA 01378. **Phone**-978-544-8304; fax-978-544-6499; hours 8AM-2PM, M
Will not search records. UCC copy- $1.00 per page. RE records at Franklin Cty. Cert fee: $10.00. Payee: Town Clerk. **Other phones:** Assessor-978-544-8304; Treasurer-978-544-3845; Vital Records-978-544-8304.

Washington Town

Town Clerk, 8 Summit Hill Rd., GA094, Washington, MA 01223. **Phone**-413-623-8878; fax-413-623-2116; hours 7PM-9PM M or by appointment
UCC record search per debtor- $10.00. UCC copy fee- $.50 per page. UCC search includes tax liens if requested. RE records at Berkshire Cty. Payee: Town of Washington. **Other phones:** Assessor-413-623-8878; Treasurer-413-623-8878; Elections-413-623-2185; Vital Records-413-623-2185.

Watertown Town

Town Clerk, 149 Main St, Admin. Bldg., Watertown, MA 02472. **Phone**-617-972-6486; fax-617-972-6595; hours 8:30AM-5PM www.ci.watertown.ma.us
UCC record search per debtor- $10.00. UCC copy fee- $.20 per page. Will search tax liens. RE records at Middlesex Cty. Payee: Town of Watertown. **Online Access to Assessor records:** Records on the Watertown Town Online Assessed Values site free at www.townonline.com/watertown/realestate/assessments/index.html. **Other phones:** Assessor-617-972-6410; Treasurer-617-972-6450; Elections-617-972-6488; Vital Records-617-972-6486.

Wayland Town

Town Clerk, 41 Cochituate Rd, Wayland, MA 01778-2697. **Phone**-508-358-3630 or 3631, UCC Recording-508-358-3630; fax-508-358-3627; hours 8:30AM-4:30PM www.wayland.ma.us
UCC record search per debtor- $5.00. UCC copy- $2.00 per page. Will not search tax liens. RE records at Middlesex Cty. Cert fee: $2.00 per doc. Payee: Town of Wayland. **Online Access to Assessor records:** records on the Assessor's database are free at www.wayland.ma.us/assessors/search.html. No name searching; street name required. **Other phones:** Assessor-508-358-3658; Treasurer-508-358-3635; Elections-508-358-3631; Vital Records-508-358-3630.

Webster Town

Town Clerk, 350 Main St, Webster, MA 01570. **Phone**-508-949-3850, R/E Recording- 508-949-3810; fax-508-949-3888; hours 8AM-4PM, Closed F
UCC record search per debtor- $10.00. UCC copy- $2.00 per page. UCC search includes tax liens if requested. RE records at Worcester Cty. Cert fee: $5.00. Payee: Town of Webster. **Other phones:** Assessor-508-949-3810; Treasurer-508-949-3820; Elections-508-949-3850; Vital Records-508-949-3850.

Wellesley Town

Town Clerk, 525 Washington St, Wellesley, MA 02482. **Phone**-781-431-1019 x250; fax-781-239-1043; 8AM-5PM www.ci.wellesley.ma.us/town/index.html
UCC record search per debtor- $5.00. UCC copy- $2.00 for 1st page 3 pages, $1.00 each add'l. UCC search includes tax liens. Separate federal/state combined tax lien search-no fee. RE records at Norfolk Cty. Cert fee: $10.00 per record. Payee: Town of Wellesley. **Online Access to Assessor, Town By-Law, Zoning By-Law, Election results records:** assessor property tax records are free at www.ci.wellesley.ma.us/asr/index.html. **Other phones:** Assessor-781-431-1019; Elections-781-431-1019 x253; Vital Records-781-431-1019 x252.

Wellfleet Town

Town Clerk, 300 Main St, Wellfleet, MA 02667. **Phone**-508-349-0301, R/E Recording- 508-349-0304; fax-508-349-0317; hours 8AM-4PM
UCC record search per debtor- $10.00. UCC Termination fee $5.00. UCC copy- $1.00 per page. Will not search tax liens. RE records at Barnstable Cty. Payee: Town of Wellfleet. **Other phones:** Assessor-508-349-0304; Treasurer-508-349-0301; Elections-508-349-0301; Vital Records-508-349-0301.

Wendell Town

Town Clerk, 270 Wendell Depot Rd., Wendell Depot, MA 01380. **Phone**-978-544-6682; hours By Appt.
UCC record search per debtor- $10.00. UCC copy- $1.00 per page. Will not search tax liens. RE records at Franklin Cty. Cert fee: $10.00. Payee: Town of Wendell.

Wenham Town

Town Clerk, 138 Main St., Town Hall, Wenham, MA 01984. **Phone**-978-468-5520; fax-978-468-6164; 9AM-4:30PM M,W,Th; 9AM-7PM T; 9AM-1PM Friday. UCC record search per debtor- $10.00. UCC copy fee- $.20 per page. Will not search tax liens. RE records at Essex Cty. Cert fee: $5.00 per copy. Payee: Town of Wenham. **Other phones:** Assessor-978-468-5524; Treasurer-978-468-5525; Elections-978-468-5520; Vital Records-978-468-5520.

West Boylston Town

Town Clerk, 120 Prescott St, West Boylston, MA 01583. **Phone**-508-835-6240, R/E Recording- 508-835-6093; fax-508-835-4102; hours 9AM-3:30PM M,T,Th,F; 5-9PM W www.westboylston.com
UCC record search per debtor- $1.00. UCC copy- $.50 per page. Tax lien search fee- $1.00 per page. RE records at Worcester Cty. Cert fee: $2.00 per page. Payee: Town of West Boylston. **Other phones:** Assessor-508-835-6093; Treasurer-508-835-6092; Elections-508-835-6240; Vital Records-508-835-6240.

West Bridgewater Town

Town Clerk, 65 N. Main St, Town Hall, West Bridgewater, MA 02379-1734. **Phone**-508-894-1200; fax-508-894-1210; hours 8AM-4PM; 1st & 3rd W 7PM-9PM www.town.west-bridgewater.ma.us
Bridgewater, East Bridgewater and West Bridgewater are separate towns. Real estate records are at the county level with the Register of Deeds. UCC record search per debtor- $10.00. Tax lien search fee- $10.00 per search. RE records at Plymouth Cty. Payee: Town of West Bridgewater. **Other phones:** Assessor-508-894-1212; Treasurer-508-894-1203; Elections-508-894-1200; Vital Records-508-894-1200.

West Brookfield Town

Town Clerk, PO Box 766, West Brookfield, MA 01585. **Phone**-508-867-1415; fax-508-867-1401; hours 9AM-Noon. UCC record search per debtor- $20.00. UCC copy- $1.00 per page. UCC search includes tax liens if requested. RE records at Worcester Cty. Payee: Town of West Brookfield. **Other phones:** Assessor-508-867-1402; Treasurer-508-867-1418; Elections-508-867-1415; Vital Records-508-867-1415.

West Newbury Town

Town Clerk, 381 Main St., Town Office Bldg, West Newbury, MA 01985-1499. **Phone**-978-363-1100 x15, UCC Recording- 978-363-1100 x10; fax-978-363-1117; hours 8AM-4:30PM M-Th; 8AM-Noon F www.town.west-newbury.ma.us
UCC record search per debtor- $10.00. UCC copy- $1.00 per page. UCC search includes tax liens if requested. Finance Dept. handles local property tax liens. Finance Dept. tax lien search fee- $5.00 per debtor which includes copy fee. More involved searches may be charged by the hour. Complete tax lien role is $25.00. Will not search real estate records. RE record copy- $1.00 per parcel. Payee: Town of West Newbury. **Other phones:** Assessor-978-363-1100 x17; Treasurer-978-363-1100 x14; Elections-978-363-1100 x10; Vital Records-978-363-1100 x10.

West Springfield Town

Town Clerk, 26 Central St, Town Hall, West Springfield, MA 01089-2779. **Phone**-413-263-3012, R/E Recording- 413-263-3055; fax-413-263-3046; hours 8AM-4:30PM www.west-springfield.ma.us
UCC record search per debtor- $10.00. UCC copy- $3.00 for 1st 3 pages and $1.00 each add'l. Will search tax liens. Tax lien search fee- $5.00 per record. RE records at Hampden Cty. Cert fee: $5.00 per record. Payee: Town of West Springfield. **Online Access to Assessor, Real Estate, Recording, Lien records:** Search the town assessor database at http://data.visionappraisal.com/WestSpringfieldMA/. Free registration for full data. Also, see Hampden County for recording records searching. **Other phones:** Assessor-413-263-3055; Treasurer-413-263-3004; Elections-413-263-3012; Vital Records-413-263-3012.

West Stockbridge Town

Town Clerk, PO Box 163, West Stockbridge, MA 01266. **Phone**-413-232-0300, R/E Recording- 413-528-0146; fax-413-232-0318; hours 1-6PM M; 10AM-3PM T TH www.weststockbridgetown.com
UCC record search per debtor- $10.00. UCC copy- $1.00 per page. Tax liens not included in UCC search. Separate state tax lien search- $25.00 per debtor. RE records at Southern Berkshire Registry of Deeds. Cert fee: $5.00 per sheet. Payee: Town of West Stockbridge. **Other phones:** Assessor-413-232-0303; Treasurer-413-232-0316; Elections-413-232-0300; Vital Records-413-232-0300.

West Tisbury Town

Town Clerk, Box 278, West Tisbury, MA 02575-0278. **Phone**-508-696-0148; fax-508-696-0103; hours 8:30AM-1:30PM
Will search UCC records. UCC copy- $.20 per page. Will not search tax liens. RE records at Dukes Cty. Payee: Town of West Tisbury. **Online Access to Assessor records:** Access assessor data at http://data.visionappraisal.com/WestTisburyMA/. **Other phones:** Assessor-508-693-0101; Treasurer-508-696-0108; Elections-508-696-0148; Vital Records-508-696-0148.

Westborough Town

Town Clerk, 34 W. Main St, Town Hall, Westborough, MA 01581-1998. **Phone**-508-366-3020; fax-508-366-

3099; hours 8AM-5PM M W TH; 8AM-8PM T; 7:30AM-Noon F.   UCC record search per debtor- $10.00.UCC search includes tax liens if requested. RE records at Worcester Cty. Payee: Town of Westborough. **Other phones:** Assessor-508-366-3010; Treasurer-508-366-3025; Elections-508-366-3020; Vital Records-508-366-3020.

Westfield City

City Clerk, 59 Court St, Westfield, MA 01085-3574. **Phone**-413-572-6235; fax-413-564-3114; hours 9AM-5PM www.cityofwestfield.org
UCC record search per debtor- $10.00. UCC copy- $1.00 per page. Will not search tax liens. RE records at Hampden Cty. Cert fee: $5.00 per page. Payee: City of Westfield. **Online Access to Real Estate, Recording, Lien, Assessor records:** Aassessor records can be found online for Westfield City at http://data.visionappraisal.com/WestfieldMA/, also see the Hampden County Register of Deeds for online recorded property data. **Other phones:** Assessor-413-572-6222; Treasurer-413-572-6230; Elections-413-572-6266; Vital Records-413-572-6236.

Westford Town

Town Clerk, 55 Main St, Town Hall, Westford, MA 01886. **Phone**-978-692-5515; fax-978-399-2555; hours 8AM-4PM www.westford.com
UCC record search per debtor- $5.00. UCC copy- $1.00 per page. UCC search includes tax liens. Tax lien search fee- $5.00 per debtor. RE records at Middlesex Cty. Cert fee: $2.00 per page. Payee: Town of Westford. **Other phones:** Assessor-978-692-5504; Treasurer-978-692-5518; Elections-978-692-5515; Vital Records-978-692-5515; Tax Collector-978-692-5506.

Westhampton Town

Town Clerk, Town Hall, Westhampton, MA 01027. **Phone**-413-527-0463; fax-413-527-8655; hours 7PM-8:30PM M. UCC record search per debtor- $10.00. UCC copy- $1.00 per page. Will not search tax liens. RE records at Hampshire Cty. Payee: Town of Westhampton.

Westminster Town

Town Clerk, PO Box 456, Westminster, MA 01473. **Phone**-978-874-7406; fax-978-874-7411; 8AM-1PM, 2-4:30PM M-Th; 8AM-1PM F www.westminster-ma.org
UCC record search per debtor- $10.00. UCC copy- $2.00 per page. Tax liens included in UCC search. Separate federal/state combined tax lien search- $10.00 per debtor. RE records at Worcester Cty. Payee: Town of Westminster. **Other phones:** Assessor-978-874-7401; Treasurer-978-874-7403; Elections-978-874-7406; Vital Records-978-874-7406.

Weston Town

Town Clerk, PO Box 378, Weston, MA 02493. **Phone**-781-893-7320; fax-781-891-3697; hours 8:30AM-5PM www.weston.org
Will not search records. UCC copy- $.20 per page. RE records at Registry of Deeds; Southern Middlesex District located in Cambridge. Cert fee: $1.00 per page. Payee: Town of Weston. **Other phones:** Assessor-781-893-7320 x313; Treasurer-781-893-7320 x316; Elections-781-893-7320 x303; Vital Records-781-893-7320 x303.

Westport Town

Town Clerk, 816 Main Rd., Town Hall, Westport, MA 02790. **Phone**-508-636-1000, R/E Recording- 508-993-2605 (Registry of Deeds in New Bedford); fax-508-636-1147; hours 8:30AM-Noon, 12:30-4PM
UCC record search per debtor- $10.00. UCC copy- $2.00 per page. State tax liens not included in UCC search. Separate state tax lien search-$10.00

per debtor. RE records at Bristol Cty. Cert fee: $2.00 per page. Payee: Town of Westport. **Other phones:** Assessor-508-636-1012; Treasurer-508-636-1007; Elections-508-636-1001; Vital Records-508-636-1000; Selectmen-508-636-1003.

Westwood Town

Town Clerk, 580 High St, Westwood, MA 02090. **Phone**-781-326-3964; fax-781-329-8030; hours 8:30AM-4:30PM M,W,Th; 8:30AM-7PM T; 8:30AM-1PM F
UCC record search per debtor- $10.00.Tax liens not included in UCC search. Separate state tax lien search- $25.00 per debtor. RE records at Norfolk Cty. Payee: Town of Westwood. **Other phones:** Assessor-781-326-6450.

Weymouth Town

Town Clerk, 75 Middle St, Town Hall, East Weymouth, MA 02189. **Phone**-781-335-2000; fax-781-335-3283; hours 8:30AM-4:30PM
UCC record search per debtor- $10.00. UCC copy- $.25 per page. RE records at Norfolk Cty. Cert fee: $2.00. Payee: Town of Weymouth. **Other phones:** Assessor-781-335-2000; Treasurer-781-335-2000.

Whately Town

Town Clerk, 218 Chestnut Plain Rd., Whately, MA 01093-0002. **Phone**-413-665-0054; fax-413-665-9560; hours Noon-7PM M; 9AM-1PM Th
UCC record search per debtor- $10.00 per hour. UCC copy- $.20 per page. UCC search includes tax liens if requested. Separate federal/state combined tax lien search- $10.00 per hour. RE records at Franklin Cty. Cert fee: $3.00 per paper. Payee: Town of Whately. **Other phones:** Assessor-413-665-3470; Treasurer-413-665-2595; Elections-413-665-0054; Vital Records-413-665-0054.

Whitman Town

Town Clerk, PO Box 426, Whitman, MA 02382. **Phone**-781-618-9710; fax-781-618-9791; hours 8AM-4PM M,W,Th-F; 8AM-7:30PM T
Will not search UCC records. UCC copy fee- $2.00 per page. Separate federal/state combined tax lien search- $2.00 per page. RE records at Plymouth Cty. Payee: Town of Whitman. **Other phones:** Assessor-781-618-9760; Treasurer-781-618-9730; Elections-781-618-9710; Vital Records-781-618-9710.

Wilbraham Town

Town Clerk, 240 Springfield St, Wilbraham, MA 01095. **Phone**-413-596-2809; fax-413-596-2830; hours 8:30AM-4:30PM
UCC record search per debtor- $15.00. UCC copy- $1.00 for cover; $.25 each add'l. UCC search includes tax liens if requested. RE records at Hampden Cty. Payee: Town of Wilbraham. **Online Access to Real Estate, Recording, Lien records:** See Hampden County for recording records searching. **Other phones:** Assessor-413-596-2818; Treasurer-413-596-2811; Elections-413-596-2809; Vital Records-413-596-2809; Collector-413-596-2813.

Williamsburg Town

Town Clerk, PO Box 447, Haydenville, MA 01039-0447. **Phone**-413-268-8402; fax-413-268-8409; hours 11-3 M, 9:15-3 & 6:30-8 Tu, 11-1 W, 9:15-3 Th www.burgy.org
UCC record search per debtor- $15.00. UCC copy- $5.00 per page. Will not search tax liens. RE records at Hampshire Cty. Cert fee: $3.00 per page. Payee: Town of Williamsburg. **Other phones:** Assessor-413-268-8403; Treasurer-413-268-8415; Elections-413-268-8402; Vital Records-413-268-8402.

Williamstown Town

Town Clerk, 31 North St, Williamstown, MA 01267. **Phone**-413-458-9341, R/E Recording- 413-743-0035; fax-413-458-4839; hours-8:30AM-5PM www.williamstown.net
UCC record search per debtor- $5.00. UCC copy- $1.00 per page. Will search municipal tax liens only. Tax lien search fee- $25.00 per search. RE records at Berkshire Cty. Payee: Town of Williamstown. **Other phones:** Assessor-413-458-9342; Treasurer-413-458-9342; Elections-413-458-9341; Vital Records-413-458-9341.

Wilmington Town

Town Clerk, 121 Glen Rd, Town Hall, Wilmington, MA 01887. **Phone**-978-658-2030, R/E Recording- 978-658-3531; fax-978-658-3334; hours 8:30AM-4:30PM www.town.wilmington.ma.us
UCC record search per debtor- $10.00. UCC copy- $1.00 per page. Tax liens included in UCC search if requested. Separate federal/state combined tax lien search- $10.00 per debtor. RE records at Middlesex Cty. Cert fee: $1.00 per page. Payee: Town of Wilmington. **Other phones:** Assessor-978-658-3675; Treasurer-978-658-3531; Elections-978-658-2030; Vital Records-978-658-2030.

Winchendon Town

Town Clerk, 109 Front St, Winchendon, MA 01475. **Phone**-978-297-2766; fax-978-297-1616; 8:30AM-6PM M; 8:30AM-4:30PM T-Th; 8:30AM-Noon F
UCC record search per debtor- $10.00. UCC copy- $2.00 per page. Tax liens not included in UCC search. Separate state tax lien search- $10.00 per debtor. RE records at Worcester Cty. Payee: Town of Winchendon. **Other phones:** Assessor-978-297-0155; Treasurer-978-297-0152; Elections-978-297-2766; Vital Records-978-297-2766.

Winchester Town

Town Clerk, 71 Mount Vernon St, Town Hall, Winchester, MA 01890. **Phone**-781-721-7130; fax-781-721-1153; hours 8AM-4PM
UCC record search per debtor- $10.00. UCC copy fee- $.20 per page. Will not search tax liens. RE records at Middlesex Cty. Cert fee: $3.00 per doc. Payee: Town of Winchester. **Other phones:** Assessor-781-721-7111; Treasurer-781-721-7123.

Windsor Town

Town Clerk, 3 Hinsdale Rd., Windsor, MA 01270. **Phone**-413-684-3977; fax-413-684-1585; hours 5-7PM Monday or by appointment
UCC record search per debtor- $10.00. UCC copy- $1.00 per page. Will not search tax liens. RE records at Berkshire Cty. Payee: Town of Windsor-Clerk. **Other phones:** Assessor-413-684-3811; Treasurer-413-684-3811; Elections-413-684-3977; Vital Records-413-684-3977.

Winthrop Town

Town Clerk, Town Hall, Winthrop, MA 02152-3156. **Phone**-617-846-1742; fax-617-539-5814; hours 8AM-7PM M; 8AM-4PM T-Th; 8AM-Noon F
UCC record search per debtor- $10.00. UCC copy- $1.00 per page. Tax liens included in UCC search if requested. Separate federal/state combined tax lien search- $25.00 per debtor. RE records at Suffolk Cty. Payee: Town of Winthrop. **Other phones:** Assessor-617-846-2716; Treasurer-617-846-3226; Elections-617-846-1742; Vital Records-617-846-1742; Municipal Tax Liens-617-846-1750.

Woburn City

City Clerk, 10 Common St, Woburn, MA 01801-4197. **Phone**-781-932-4453, UCC Recording- 781-932-4450;

fax-781-932-4455; hours 9AM-4:30PM M-W; 9AM-7PM Th; 9AM-1PM F www.cityofwoburn.com
Will not search records. UCC copy- $2.00 cover sheet; $1.00 each page. RE records at Middlesex Cty. Cert fee: $3.00 per copy. Payee: City of Woburn. **Online Access to Property Assessor records:** Search the city assessor data at http://data.visionapprai sal.com/WoburnMA/. Free registration for full data. **Other phones:** Assessor-781-932-4430; Treasurer-781-932-4470; Elections-781-932-4450; Vital Records-781-932-4450.

Worcester City

City Clerk, 455 Main St, City Hall, Rm 206, Worcester, MA 01608. **Phone-**508-799-1121; fax-508-799-1194; 8:45AM-4:15PM T,W,Th,F; 8:45AM-5PM M
UCC record search per debtor- $10.00. UCC copy-$.50 per page. UCC search includes tax liens. Separate federal/state combined tax lien search-$10.00 per debtor. RE records at Worcester Cty. Cert fee: $4.00 for 1st 3 pages; $2.00 each add'l. **Online Access to Real Estate, Lien, Assessor records:** Data is online in 2 ways. Online access to the City Assessor Valuation Search database is free at www.ci.worcester.ma.us/aso/value_search.htm. And, access to the "Landtrack System" for Worcester District records requires a $50 annual fee + $.25 per minute of use. Index records date back to 1966. Images are viewable from 1974 onward. Lending agency info is available. Fax back service: $.50 per page. For information, contact Joe Ursoleo at 508-798-7713 X233. **Other phones:** Assessor-508-799-1112; Treasurer-508-799-1077.

Worcester County Northern Dist.

County Register of Deeds, PO Box 983, Fitchburg, MA 01420. **Phone-**978-342-2132; fax-978-345-2865; hours 8:30AM-4:30PM; Recording Hours 8:30AM-4PM www.state.ma.us/nwrod

Will not search records. UCC copy fee- $1.00 per page. Cert fee: $1.00 per page. Payee: Worcester North Register of Deeds. **Online Access to Real Estate, Lien records:** Access to the "Northfield" online service requires a $.25 per minute of use. Records date back to 1983. Viewable images go back to 1995. Lending agency information available, also a fax back service. For information, contact Ruth Piermarini at 978-342-2637.Records will soon be on the web. Also, county recorded land images from 1731 to 1974 are at www.worcesterdeeds.com/worcester/dsbppagelist.asp; book and page number required. **Other phones:** Assessor-508-799-1098.

Worcester County Worcester Dist.

County Register of Deeds, 2 Main St, Courthouse, Worcester, MA 01608. **Phone-**508-798-7717; fax-508-753-1338; hours 8:15AM-4:30PM (Recording hours- 9AM-Noon, 1-4PM)
www.worcesterdeeds.com
Will not search records. UCC copy- $1.00 per page. Cert fee: $1.00 per cert. Payee: Worcester County Register of Deeds. **Online Access to Real Estate, Deed, Lien, Grantor/Grantee, Judgment, Property Tax records:** Access to the Register of Deeds database is free at www.masslandrecords.com. Also, county recorded land images from 1731 to 1974 are free at www.worcesterdeeds.com/worcester/dsbppagelist.asp Also, name search grantor/grantee found at www.masslandrecords.com/malr/controller. **Other phones:** Assessor-508-799-1000; Treasurer-508-798-2441.

Worthington Town

Town Clerk, Town Hall, Worthington, MA 01098-0247. **Phone-**413-238-5578; fax-413-238-5579; hours 10AM-Noon Saturday
UCC record search per debtor- $10.00. UCC copy-$1.00 per page. Will not search tax liens. RE

records at Hampshire Cty. Cert fee: $5.00 per page. Payee: Town of Worthington. **Other phones:** Assessor-413-238-5578; Treasurer-413-238-5577.

Wrentham Town

Town Clerk, 100 Stonewall Blvd, Wrentham, MA 02093. **Phone-**508-384-5415; fax-508-384-5434; hours 8AM-4PM M-Th; 8AM-1:30PM F
UCC record search per debtor- $10.00. UCC copy-$2.00 per page. Will search tax liens including federal tax liens. RE records at Norfolk Cty. Cert fee: $3.00 per page. Payee: Town of Wrentham. **Other phones:** Assessor-508-384-5408; Treasurer-508-384-5413; Elections-508-384-5415; Vital Records-508-384-5415.

Yarmouth Town

Town Clerk, 1146 Route 28, Town Hall, South Yarmouth, MA 02664. **Phone-**508-398-2231, R/E Recording- 508-362-7733 x106, UCC Recording- 508-398-2231 x216; fax-508-398-2365; 8:30AM-4:30PM
UCC record search per debtor- $10.00. UCC copy fee- $.20 per page. Tax liens included in UCC search if requested. Separate federal/state combined tax lien search- $10.00 per debtor. RE records at Barnstable Cty. Cert fee: $1.00 per page. Payee: Town of Yarmouth. **Online Access to Assessor records:** Records on the Assessor's database are free at http://data.visionappraisal.com/yarmouthma. Free registration for full data. Non-registered users can access a limited set of data. **Other phones:** Assessor-508-398-2231 x221; Treasurer-508-398-2231 x219; Elections-508-398-2231 x216; Vital Records-508-398-2231 x216.

Massachusetts County Locator

You will usually be able to find the city name in the City/County Cross Reference below. In that case, it is a simple matter to determine the county from the cross reference. However, only the official US Postal Service city names are included in this index. There are an additional 40,000 place names that people use in their addresses. Therefore, we have also included a ZIP/City Cross Reference immediately following the City/County Cross Reference.

If you know the ZIP Code but the city name does not appear in the City/County Cross Reference index, look up the ZIP Code in the ZIP/City Cross Reference, find the city name, then look up the city name in the City/County Cross Reference. For example, you want to know the county for an address of Menands, NY 12204. There is no "Menands" in the City/County Cross Reference. The ZIP/City Cross Reference shows that ZIP Codes 12201-12288 are for the city of Albany. Looking back in the City/County Cross Reference, Albany is in Albany County.

Massachusetts City/County Cross Reference

ABINGTON Plymouth
ACCORD Plymouth
ACTON Middlesex
ACUSHNET Bristol
ADAMS Berkshire
AGAWAM Hampden
ALLSTON Suffolk
AMESBURY Essex
AMHERST Hampshire
ANDOVER Essex
ARLINGTON Middlesex
ARLINGTON HEIGHTS Middlesex
ASHBURNHAM Worcester
ASHBY Middlesex
ASHFIELD Franklin
ASHLAND Middlesex
ASHLEY FALLS Berkshire
ASSONET Bristol
ATHOL Worcester
ATTLEBORO Bristol
ATTLEBORO FALLS Bristol
AUBURN Worcester
AUBURNDALE Middlesex
AVON Norfolk
AYER Middlesex
BABSON PARK Norfolk
BALDWINVILLE Worcester
BAR CODE MCCORMACK Suffolk
BARNSTABLE Barnstable
BARRE Worcester
BECKET Berkshire
BEDFORD Middlesex
BELCHERTOWN Hampshire
BELLINGHAM Norfolk
BELMONT Middlesex
BERKLEY Bristol
BERKSHIRE Berkshire
BERLIN Worcester
BERNARDSTON Franklin
BEVERLY Essex
BILLERICA Middlesex
BLACKSTONE Worcester
BLANDFORD Hampden
BOLTON Worcester
BONDSVILLE Hampden
BOSTON Middlesex
BOSTON Suffolk
BOXBOROUGH Middlesex
BOXFORD Essex
BOYLSTON Worcester
BRAINTREE Norfolk
BRANT ROCK Plymouth
BREWSTER Barnstable
BRIDGEWATER Plymouth
BRIGHTON Suffolk
BRIMFIELD Hampden
BROCKTON Plymouth
BROOKFIELD Worcester
BROOKLINE Norfolk
BROOKLINE VILLAGE Norfolk
BRYANTVILLE Plymouth
BUCKLAND Franklin
BURLINGTON Middlesex

BUZZARDS BAY (02532) Barnstable(74),
   Plymouth(25)
BUZZARDS BAY Barnstable
BYFIELD Essex
CAMBRIDGE Middlesex
CANTON Norfolk
CARLISLE Middlesex
CARVER Plymouth
CATAUMET Barnstable
CENTERVILLE Barnstable
CHARLEMONT Franklin
CHARLESTOWN Suffolk
CHARLTON Worcester
CHARLTON CITY Worcester
CHARLTON DEPOT Worcester
CHARTLEY Bristol
CHATHAM Barnstable
CHELMSFORD Middlesex
CHELSEA Suffolk
CHERRY VALLEY Worcester
CHESHIRE Berkshire
CHESTER (01011) Hampden(89),
   Hampshire(5), Berkshire(5)
CHESTERFIELD Hampshire
CHESTNUT HILL Middlesex
CHICOPEE Hampden
CHILMARK Dukes
CLINTON Worcester
COHASSET Norfolk
COLRAIN Franklin
CONCORD Middlesex
CONWAY Franklin
COTUIT Barnstable
CUMMAQUID Barnstable
CUMMINGTON Hampshire
CUTTYHUNK Dukes
DALTON Berkshire
DANVERS Essex
DARTMOUTH Bristol
DEDHAM Norfolk
DEERFIELD Franklin
DENNIS Barnstable
DENNIS PORT Barnstable
DEVENS (01434) Worcester(54),
   Middlesex(45)
DIGHTON Bristol
DOUGLAS Worcester
DOVER Norfolk
DRACUT Middlesex
DRURY Berkshire
DUDLEY Worcester
DUNSTABLE Middlesex
DUXBURY Plymouth
EAST BOSTON Suffolk
EAST BRIDGEWATER Plymouth
EAST BROOKFIELD Worcester
EAST DENNIS Barnstable
EAST FALMOUTH Barnstable
EAST FREETOWN Bristol
EAST LONGMEADOW Hampden
EAST MANSFIELD Bristol
EAST ORLEANS Barnstable
EAST OTIS Berkshire

EAST PRINCETON Worcester
EAST SANDWICH Barnstable
EAST TAUNTON Bristol
EAST TEMPLETON Worcester
EAST WALPOLE Norfolk
EAST WAREHAM Plymouth
EASTHAM Barnstable
EASTHAMPTON Hampshire
EASTON Bristol
EDGARTOWN Dukes
ELMWOOD Plymouth
ERVING Franklin
ESSEX Essex
EVERETT Middlesex
FAIRHAVEN Bristol
FALL RIVER Bristol
FALMOUTH Barnstable
FAYVILLE Worcester
FEEDING HILLS Hampden
FISKDALE Worcester
FITCHBURG Worcester
FLORENCE Hampshire
FORESTDALE Barnstable
FORT DEVENS (01433) Worcester(53),
   Middlesex(46)
FOXBORO Norfolk
FRAMINGHAM Middlesex
FRANKLIN Norfolk
GARDNER Worcester
GEORGETOWN Essex
GILBERTVILLE Worcester
GLENDALE Berkshire
GLOUCESTER Essex
GOSHEN Hampshire
GRAFTON Worcester
GRANBY Hampshire
GRANVILLE Hampden
GREAT BARRINGTON Berkshire
GREEN HARBOR Plymouth
GREENBUSH Plymouth
GREENFIELD Franklin
GROTON Middlesex
GROVELAND Essex
HADLEY Hampshire
HALIFAX Plymouth
HAMILTON Essex
HAMPDEN Hampden
HANOVER (02339) Plymouth(98),
   Norfolk(1)
HANOVER Plymouth
HANSCOM AFB Middlesex
HANSON Plymouth
HARDWICK Worcester
HARVARD Worcester
HARWICH Barnstable
HARWICH PORT Barnstable
HATFIELD Hampshire
HATHORNE Essex
HAVERHILL Essex
HAYDENVILLE Hampshire
HEATH Franklin
HINGHAM Plymouth
HINSDALE Berkshire

HOLBROOK Norfolk
HOLDEN Worcester
HOLLAND Hampden
HOLLISTON Middlesex
HOLYOKE Hampden
HOPEDALE Worcester
HOPKINTON Middlesex
HOUSATONIC Berkshire
HUBBARDSTON Worcester
HUDSON Middlesex
HULL Plymouth
HUMAROCK Plymouth
HUNTINGTON (01050) Hampshire(98),
   Hampden(1)
HYANNIS Barnstable
HYANNIS PORT Barnstable
HYDE PARK Suffolk
INDIAN ORCHARD Hampden
IPSWICH Essex
JAMAICA PLAIN Suffolk
JEFFERSON Worcester
KINGSTON Plymouth
LAKE PLEASANT Franklin
LAKEVILLE Plymouth
LANCASTER Worcester
LANESBORO Berkshire
LAWRENCE Essex
LEE Berkshire
LEEDS Hampshire
LEICESTER Worcester
LENOX Berkshire
LENOX DALE Berkshire
LEOMINSTER Worcester
LEVERETT (01054) Franklin(77),
   Hampshire(22)
LEXINGTON Middlesex
LINCOLN Middlesex
LINWOOD Worcester
LITTLETON Middlesex
LONGMEADOW Hampden
LOWELL Middlesex
LUDLOW Hampden
LUNENBURG Worcester
LYNN Essex
LYNNFIELD Essex
MALDEN Middlesex
MANCHAUG Worcester
MANCHESTER Essex
MANOMET Plymouth
MANSFIELD Bristol
MARBLEHEAD Essex
MARION Plymouth
MARLBOROUGH Middlesex
MARSHFIELD Plymouth
MARSHFIELD HILLS Plymouth
MARSTONS MILLS Barnstable
MASHPEE Barnstable
MATTAPAN Suffolk
MATTAPOISETT Plymouth
MAYNARD Middlesex
MEDFIELD Norfolk
MEDFORD Middlesex
MEDWAY Norfolk

MELROSE Middlesex
MENDON Worcester
MENEMSHA Dukes
MERRIMAC Essex
METHUEN Essex
MIDDLEBORO Plymouth
MIDDLEFIELD Hampshire
MIDDLETON Essex
MILFORD Worcester
MILL RIVER Berkshire
MILLBURY Worcester
MILLIS Norfolk
MILLVILLE Worcester
MILTON Norfolk
MILTON VILLAGE Norfolk
MINOT Plymouth
MONPONSETT Plymouth
MONROE BRIDGE Franklin
MONSON Hampden
MONTAGUE Franklin
MONTEREY Berkshire
MONUMENT BEACH Barnstable
NAHANT Essex
NANTUCKET Nantucket
NATICK Middlesex
NEEDHAM Norfolk
NEW BEDFORD Bristol
NEW BRAINTREE Worcester
NEW SALEM Franklin
NEW TOWN Middlesex
NEWBURY Essex
NEWBURYPORT Essex
NEWTON Middlesex
NEWTON CENTER Middlesex
NEWTON HIGHLANDS Middlesex
NEWTON LOWER FALLS Middlesex
NEWTON UPPER FALLS Middlesex
NEWTONVILLE Middlesex
NONANTUM Middlesex
NORFOLK Norfolk
NORTH ADAMS Berkshire
NORTH AMHERST Hampshire
NORTH ANDOVER Essex
NORTH ATTLEBORO Bristol
NORTH BILLERICA Middlesex
NORTH BROOKFIELD Worcester
NORTH CARVER Plymouth
NORTH CHATHAM Barnstable
NORTH CHELMSFORD Middlesex
NORTH DARTMOUTH Bristol
NORTH DIGHTON Bristol
NORTH EASTHAM Barnstable
NORTH EASTON Bristol
NORTH EGREMONT Berkshire
NORTH FALMOUTH Barnstable
NORTH GRAFTON Worcester
NORTH HATFIELD Hampshire
NORTH MARSHFIELD Plymouth
NORTH OXFORD Worcester
NORTH PEMBROKE Plymouth
NORTH READING Middlesex
NORTH SCITUATE Plymouth
NORTH TRURO Barnstable
NORTH UXBRIDGE Worcester
NORTH WALTHAM Middlesex
NORTHAMPTON Hampshire
NORTHBOROUGH Worcester
NORTHBRIDGE Worcester
NORTHFIELD Franklin

NORTON Bristol
NORWELL Plymouth
NORWOOD Norfolk
NUTTING LAKE Middlesex
OAK BLUFFS Dukes
OAKDALE Worcester
OAKHAM Worcester
OCEAN BLUFF Plymouth
ONSET Plymouth
ORANGE Franklin
ORLEANS Barnstable
OSTERVILLE Barnstable
OTIS Berkshire
OXFORD Worcester
PALMER Hampden
PAXTON Worcester
PEABODY Essex
PEMBROKE Plymouth
PEPPERELL Middlesex
PETERSHAM (01366) Franklin(51),
    Worcester(48)
PINEHURST Middlesex
PITTSFIELD Berkshire
PLAINFIELD Hampshire
PLAINVILLE (02762) Norfolk(98), Bristol(1)
PLYMOUTH Plymouth
PLYMPTON Plymouth
POCASSET Barnstable
PRIDES CROSSING Essex
PRINCETON Worcester
PROVINCETOWN Barnstable
QUINCY Norfolk
RANDOLPH Norfolk
RAYNHAM Bristol
RAYNHAM CENTER Bristol
READING Middlesex
READVILLE Suffolk
REHOBOTH Bristol
REVERE Suffolk
RICHMOND Berkshire
ROCHDALE Worcester
ROCHESTER Plymouth
ROCKLAND Plymouth
ROCKPORT Essex
ROSLINDALE Suffolk
ROWE Franklin
ROWLEY Essex
ROYALSTON Worcester
RUSSELL Hampden
RUTLAND Worcester
SAGAMORE Barnstable
SAGAMORE BEACH (02562)
    Barnstable(98), Plymouth(1)
SALEM Essex
SALISBURY Essex
SANDISFIELD Berkshire
SANDWICH Barnstable
SAUGUS Essex
SAVOY Berkshire
SCITUATE Plymouth
SEARS ROEBUCK Suffolk
SEEKONK Bristol
SHARON Norfolk
SHATTUCKVILLE Franklin
SHEFFIELD Berkshire
SHELBURNE FALLS Franklin
SHELDONVILLE Norfolk
SHERBORN Middlesex
SHIRLEY Middlesex

SHREWSBURY Worcester
SHUTESBURY Franklin
SIASCONSET Nantucket
SILVER BEACH Barnstable
SOMERSET Bristol
SOMERVILLE Middlesex
SOUTH BARRE Worcester
SOUTH CARVER Plymouth
SOUTH CHATHAM Barnstable
SOUTH DARTMOUTH Bristol
SOUTH DEERFIELD Franklin
SOUTH DENNIS Barnstable
SOUTH EASTON Bristol
SOUTH EGREMONT Berkshire
SOUTH GRAFTON Worcester
SOUTH HADLEY Hampshire
SOUTH HAMILTON Essex
SOUTH HARWICH Barnstable
SOUTH LANCASTER Worcester
SOUTH LEE Berkshire
SOUTH ORLEANS Barnstable
SOUTH WALPOLE Norfolk
SOUTH WELLFLEET Barnstable
SOUTH YARMOUTH Barnstable
SOUTHAMPTON Hampshire
SOUTHBOROUGH Worcester
SOUTHBRIDGE Worcester
SOUTHFIELD Berkshire
SOUTHWICK Hampden
SPENCER Worcester
SPRINGFIELD Hampden
STERLING Worcester
STILL RIVER Worcester
STOCKBRIDGE Berkshire
STONEHAM Middlesex
STOUGHTON Norfolk
STOW Middlesex
STURBRIDGE Worcester
SUDBURY Middlesex
SUNDERLAND Franklin
SUTTON Worcester
SWAMPSCOTT Essex
SWANSEA Bristol
TAUNTON Bristol
TEMPLETON Worcester
TEWKSBURY Middlesex
THORNDIKE Hampden
THREE RIVERS Hampden
TOPSFIELD Essex
TOWNSEND Middlesex
TRURO Barnstable
TURNERS FALLS Franklin
TYNGSBORO Middlesex
TYRINGHAM Berkshire
UPTON Worcester
UXBRIDGE Worcester
VILLAGE OF NAGOG WOODS Middlesex
VINEYARD HAVEN Dukes
WABAN Middlesex
WAKEFIELD Middlesex
WALES Hampden
WALPOLE Norfolk
WALTHAM Middlesex
WARE Hampshire
WAREHAM Plymouth
WARREN Worcester
WARWICK Franklin
WATERTOWN Middlesex
WAVERLEY Middlesex

WAYLAND Middlesex
WEBSTER Worcester
WELLESLEY Norfolk
WELLESLEY HILLS Norfolk
WELLFLEET Barnstable
WENDELL Franklin
WENDELL DEPOT Franklin
WENHAM Essex
WEST BARNSTABLE Barnstable
WEST BOXFORD Essex
WEST BOYLSTON Worcester
WEST BRIDGEWATER Plymouth
WEST BROOKFIELD Worcester
WEST CHATHAM Barnstable
WEST CHESTERFIELD Hampshire
WEST DENNIS Barnstable
WEST FALMOUTH Barnstable
WEST GROTON Middlesex
WEST HARWICH Barnstable
WEST HATFIELD (01088) Worcester(98),
    Hampshire(1)
WEST HYANNISPORT Barnstable
WEST MEDFORD Middlesex
WEST MILLBURY Worcester
WEST NEWBURY Essex
WEST NEWTON Middlesex
WEST ROXBURY Suffolk
WEST SPRINGFIELD Hampden
WEST STOCKBRIDGE Berkshire
WEST TISBURY Dukes
WEST TOWNSEND Middlesex
WEST WAREHAM Plymouth
WEST WARREN Worcester
WEST YARMOUTH Barnstable
WESTBOROUGH Worcester
WESTFIELD Hampden
WESTFORD Middlesex
WESTMINSTER Worcester
WESTON Middlesex
WESTPORT Bristol
WESTPORT POINT Bristol
WESTWOOD Norfolk
WEYMOUTH Norfolk
WHATELY Franklin
WHEELWRIGHT Worcester
WHITE HORSE BEACH Plymouth
WHITINSVILLE Worcester
WHITMAN Plymouth
WILBRAHAM Hampden
WILLIAMSBURG Hampshire
WILLIAMSTOWN Berkshire
WILMINGTON Middlesex
WINCHENDON Worcester
WINCHENDON SPRINGS Worcester
WINCHESTER Middlesex
WINDSOR (01270) Franklin(95),
    Berkshire(4)
WINTHROP Suffolk
WOBURN Middlesex
WOODS HOLE Barnstable
WOODVILLE Middlesex
WORCESTER Worcester
WORONOCO Hampden
WORTHINGTON Hampshire
WRENTHAM Norfolk
YARMOUTH PORT Barnstable

Massachusetts ZIP/City Cross Reference

ZIP Range	City	ZIP Range	City	ZIP Range	City	ZIP Range	City
01001-01001	AGAWAM	01240-01240	LENOX	01503-01503	BERLIN	01773-01773	LINCOLN
01002-01004	AMHERST	01242-01242	LENOX DALE	01504-01504	BLACKSTONE	01775-01775	STOW
01005-01005	BARRE	01243-01243	MIDDLEFIELD	01505-01505	BOYLSTON	01776-01776	SUDBURY
01007-01007	BELCHERTOWN	01244-01244	MILL RIVER	01506-01506	BROOKFIELD	01778-01778	WAYLAND
01008-01008	BLANDFORD	01245-01245	MONTEREY	01507-01507	CHARLTON	01784-01784	WOODVILLE
01009-01009	BONDSVILLE	01247-01247	NORTH ADAMS	01508-01508	CHARLTON CITY	01801-01801	WOBURN
01010-01010	BRIMFIELD	01252-01252	NORTH EGREMONT	01509-01509	CHARLTON DEPOT	01803-01803	BURLINGTON
01011-01011	CHESTER	01253-01253	OTIS	01510-01510	CLINTON	01806-01808	WOBURN
01012-01012	CHESTERFIELD	01254-01254	RICHMOND	01515-01515	EAST BROOKFIELD	01810-01812	ANDOVER
01013-01022	CHICOPEE	01255-01255	SANDISFIELD	01516-01516	DOUGLAS	01813-01815	WOBURN
01026-01026	CUMMINGTON	01256-01256	SAVOY	01517-01517	EAST PRINCETON	01821-01822	BILLERICA
01027-01027	EASTHAMPTON	01257-01257	SHEFFIELD	01518-01518	FISKDALE	01824-01824	CHELMSFORD
01028-01028	EAST LONGMEADOW	01258-01258	SOUTH EGREMONT	01519-01519	GRAFTON	01826-01826	DRACUT
01029-01029	EAST OTIS	01259-01259	SOUTHFIELD	01520-01520	HOLDEN	01827-01827	DUNSTABLE
01030-01030	FEEDING HILLS	01260-01260	SOUTH LEE	01521-01521	HOLLAND	01830-01832	HAVERHILL
01031-01031	GILBERTVILLE	01262-01263	STOCKBRIDGE	01522-01522	JEFFERSON	01833-01833	GEORGETOWN
01032-01032	GOSHEN	01264-01264	TYRINGHAM	01523-01523	LANCASTER	01834-01834	GROVELAND
01033-01033	GRANBY	01266-01266	WEST STOCKBRIDGE	01524-01524	LEICESTER	01835-01835	HAVERHILL
01034-01034	GRANVILLE	01267-01267	WILLIAMSTOWN	01525-01525	LINWOOD	01840-01843	LAWRENCE
01035-01035	HADLEY	01270-01270	WINDSOR	01526-01526	MANCHAUG	01844-01844	METHUEN
01036-01036	HAMPDEN	01301-01302	GREENFIELD	01527-01527	MILLBURY	01845-01845	NORTH ANDOVER
01037-01037	HARDWICK	01330-01330	ASHFIELD	01529-01529	MILLVILLE	01850-01854	LOWELL
01038-01038	HATFIELD	01331-01331	ATHOL	01531-01531	NEW BRAINTREE	01860-01860	MERRIMAC
01039-01039	HAYDENVILLE	01337-01337	BERNARDSTON	01532-01532	NORTHBOROUGH	01862-01862	NORTH BILLERICA
01040-01041	HOLYOKE	01338-01338	BUCKLAND	01534-01534	NORTHBRIDGE	01863-01863	NORTH CHELMSFORD
01050-01050	HUNTINGTON	01339-01339	CHARLEMONT	01535-01535	NORTH BROOKFIELD	01864-01864	NORTH READING
01053-01053	LEEDS	01340-01340	COLRAIN	01536-01536	NORTH GRAFTON	01865-01865	NUTTING LAKE
01054-01054	LEVERETT	01341-01341	CONWAY	01537-01537	NORTH OXFORD	01866-01866	PINEHURST
01056-01056	LUDLOW	01342-01342	DEERFIELD	01538-01538	NORTH UXBRIDGE	01867-01867	READING
01057-01057	MONSON	01343-01343	DRURY	01539-01539	OAKDALE	01876-01876	TEWKSBURY
01059-01059	NORTH AMHERST	01344-01344	ERVING	01540-01540	OXFORD	01879-01879	TYNGSBORO
01060-01061	NORTHAMPTON	01346-01346	HEATH	01541-01541	PRINCETON	01880-01880	WAKEFIELD
01062-01062	FLORENCE	01347-01347	LAKE PLEASANT	01542-01542	ROCHDALE	01885-01885	WEST BOXFORD
01063-01063	NORTHAMPTON	01349-01349	TURNERS FALLS	01543-01543	RUTLAND	01886-01886	WESTFORD
01066-01066	NORTH HATFIELD	01350-01350	MONROE BRIDGE	01545-01546	SHREWSBURY	01887-01887	WILMINGTON
01068-01068	OAKHAM	01351-01351	MONTAGUE	01549-01549	BERLIN	01888-01888	WOBURN
01069-01069	PALMER	01354-01354	NORTHFIELD	01550-01550	SOUTHBRIDGE	01889-01889	NORTH READING
01070-01070	PLAINFIELD	01355-01355	NEW SALEM	01560-01560	SOUTH GRAFTON	01890-01890	WINCHESTER
01071-01071	RUSSELL	01360-01360	NORTHFIELD	01561-01561	SOUTH LANCASTER	01899-01899	ANDOVER
01072-01072	SHUTESBURY	01364-01364	ORANGE	01562-01562	SPENCER	01901-01905	LYNN
01073-01073	SOUTHAMPTON	01366-01366	PETERSHAM	01564-01564	STERLING	01906-01906	SAUGUS
01074-01074	SOUTH BARRE	01367-01367	ROWE	01566-01566	STURBRIDGE	01907-01907	SWAMPSCOTT
01075-01075	SOUTH HADLEY	01368-01368	ROYALSTON	01568-01568	UPTON	01908-01908	NAHANT
01077-01077	SOUTHWICK	01369-01369	SHATTUCKVILLE	01569-01569	UXBRIDGE	01910-01910	LYNN
01079-01079	THORNDIKE	01370-01370	SHELBURNE FALLS	01570-01570	WEBSTER	01913-01913	AMESBURY
01080-01080	THREE RIVERS	01373-01373	SOUTH DEERFIELD	01571-01571	DUDLEY	01915-01915	BEVERLY
01081-01081	WALES	01375-01375	SUNDERLAND	01580-01582	WESTBOROUGH	01921-01921	BOXFORD
01082-01082	WARE	01376-01376	TURNERS FALLS	01583-01583	WEST BOYLSTON	01922-01922	BYFIELD
01083-01083	WARREN	01378-01378	WARWICK	01585-01585	WEST BROOKFIELD	01923-01923	DANVERS
01084-01084	WEST CHESTERFIELD	01379-01379	WENDELL	01586-01586	WEST MILLBURY	01929-01929	ESSEX
01085-01086	WESTFIELD	01380-01380	WENDELL DEPOT	01587-01587	UPTON	01930-01931	GLOUCESTER
01088-01088	WEST HATFIELD	01420-01420	FITCHBURG	01588-01588	WHITINSVILLE	01936-01936	HAMILTON
01089-01090	WEST SPRINGFIELD	01430-01430	ASHBURNHAM	01590-01590	SUTTON	01937-01937	HATHORNE
01092-01092	WEST WARREN	01431-01431	ASHBY	01600-01610	WORCESTER	01938-01938	IPSWICH
01093-01093	WHATELY	01432-01432	AYER	01611-01611	CHERRY VALLEY	01940-01940	LYNNFIELD
01094-01094	WHEELWRIGHT	01433-01433	FORT DEVENS	01612-01612	PAXTON	01944-01944	MANCHESTER
01095-01095	WILBRAHAM	01434-01434	DEVENS	01613-01655	WORCESTER	01945-01945	MARBLEHEAD
01096-01096	WILLIAMSBURG	01436-01436	BALDWINVILLE	01701-01705	FRAMINGHAM	01947-01947	SALEM
01097-01097	WORONOCO	01438-01438	EAST TEMPLETON	01718-01718	VILLAGE OF NAGOG WOODS	01949-01949	MIDDLETON
01098-01098	WORTHINGTON	01440-01441	GARDNER	01719-01719	BOXBOROUGH	01950-01950	NEWBURYPORT
01101-01105	SPRINGFIELD	01441-01441	WESTMINSTER	01720-01720	ACTON	01951-01951	NEWBURY
01106-01106	LONGMEADOW	01450-01450	GROTON	01721-01721	ASHLAND	01952-01952	SALISBURY
01107-01115	SPRINGFIELD	01451-01451	HARVARD	01730-01730	BEDFORD	01960-01964	PEABODY
01116-01116	LONGMEADOW	01452-01452	HUBBARDSTON	01731-01731	HANSCOM AFB	01965-01965	PRIDES CROSSING
01118-01144	SPRINGFIELD	01453-01453	LEOMINSTER	01740-01740	BOLTON	01966-01966	ROCKPORT
01151-01151	INDIAN ORCHARD	01460-01460	LITTLETON	01741-01741	CARLISLE	01969-01969	ROWLEY
01152-01199	SPRINGFIELD	01462-01462	LUNENBURG	01742-01742	CONCORD	01970-01971	SALEM
01201-01203	PITTSFIELD	01463-01463	PEPPERELL	01745-01745	FAYVILLE	01982-01982	SOUTH HAMILTON
01220-01220	ADAMS	01464-01464	SHIRLEY	01746-01746	HOLLISTON	01983-01983	TOPSFIELD
01222-01222	ASHLEY FALLS	01466-01466	ASHBURNHAM	01747-01747	HOPEDALE	01984-01984	WENHAM
01223-01223	BECKET	01467-01467	STILL RIVER	01748-01748	HOPKINTON	01985-01985	WEST NEWBURY
01224-01224	BERKSHIRE	01468-01468	TEMPLETON	01749-01749	HUDSON	02018-02018	ACCORD
01225-01225	CHESHIRE	01469-01469	TOWNSEND	01752-01752	MARLBOROUGH	02019-02019	BELLINGHAM
01226-01227	DALTON	01470-01471	GROTON	01754-01754	MAYNARD	02020-02020	BRANT ROCK
01229-01229	GLENDALE	01472-01472	WEST GROTON	01756-01756	MENDON	02021-02021	CANTON
01230-01230	GREAT BARRINGTON	01473-01473	WESTMINSTER	01757-01757	MILFORD	02025-02025	COHASSET
01235-01235	HINSDALE	01474-01474	WEST TOWNSEND	01760-01760	NATICK	02026-02027	DEDHAM
01236-01236	HOUSATONIC	01475-01475	WINCHENDON	01770-01770	SHERBORN	02030-02030	DOVER
01237-01237	LANESBORO	01477-01477	WINCHENDON SPRINGS	01772-01772	SOUTHBOROUGH	02031-02031	EAST MANSFIELD
01238-01238	LEE	01501-01501	AUBURN			02032-02032	EAST WALPOLE

02035-02035	FOXBORO
02038-02038	FRANKLIN
02040-02040	GREENBUSH
02041-02041	GREEN HARBOR
02043-02044	HINGHAM
02045-02045	HULL
02047-02047	HUMAROCK
02048-02048	MANSFIELD
02050-02050	MARSHFIELD
02051-02051	MARSHFIELD HILLS
02052-02052	MEDFIELD
02053-02053	MEDWAY
02054-02054	MILLIS
02055-02055	MINOT
02056-02056	NORFOLK
02059-02059	NORTH MARSHFIELD
02060-02060	NORTH SCITUATE
02061-02061	NORWELL
02062-02062	NORWOOD
02065-02065	OCEAN BLUFF
02066-02066	SCITUATE
02067-02067	SHARON
02070-02070	SHELDONVILLE
02071-02071	SOUTH WALPOLE
02072-02072	STOUGHTON
02081-02081	WALPOLE
02090-02090	WESTWOOD
02093-02093	WRENTHAM
02100-02125	BOSTON
02126-02126	MATTAPAN
02127-02128	BOSTON
02129-02129	CHARLESTOWN
02130-02130	JAMAICA PLAIN
02131-02131	ROSLINDALE
02132-02132	WEST ROXBURY
02133-02133	BOSTON
02134-02134	ALLSTON
02135-02135	BRIGHTON
02136-02136	HYDE PARK
02137-02137	READVILLE
02138-02142	CAMBRIDGE
02143-02145	SOMERVILLE
02146-02146	BROOKLINE
02147-02147	BROOKLINE VILLAGE
02148-02148	MALDEN
02149-02149	EVERETT
02150-02150	CHELSEA
02151-02151	REVERE
02152-02152	WINTHROP
02153-02153	MEDFORD
02154-02154	WALTHAM
02155-02155	MEDFORD
02156-02156	WEST MEDFORD
02157-02157	BABSON PARK
02158-02162	NEWTON
02163-02163	BOSTON
02164-02165	NEWTON
02166-02166	AUBURNDALE
02167-02167	CHESTNUT HILL
02168-02168	WABAN
02169-02171	QUINCY
02172-02172	WATERTOWN
02173-02173	LEXINGTON
02174-02174	ARLINGTON
02175-02175	ARLINGTON HEIGHTS
02176-02176	MELROSE
02178-02178	BELMONT
02179-02179	WAVERLEY
02180-02180	STONEHAM
02181-02181	WELLESLEY
02184-02185	BRAINTREE
02186-02186	MILTON
02187-02187	MILTON VILLAGE
02188-02191	WEYMOUTH
02192-02192	NEEDHAM
02193-02193	WESTON
02194-02194	NEEDHAM
02195-02195	NEWTON
02196-02222	BOSTON
02228-02228	EAST BOSTON
02238-02239	CAMBRIDGE
02241-02241	BOSTON
02254-02254	WALTHAM

02258-02258	NEWTON
02266-02266	BOSTON
02269-02269	QUINCY
02272-02277	WATERTOWN
02283-02293	BOSTON
02294-02294	SEARS ROEBUCK
02295-02297	BOSTON
02299-02299	BAR CODE MCCORMACK
02301-02305	BROCKTON
02322-02322	AVON
02324-02325	BRIDGEWATER
02327-02327	BRYANTVILLE
02330-02330	CARVER
02331-02332	DUXBURY
02333-02333	EAST BRIDGEWATER
02334-02334	EASTON
02337-02337	ELMWOOD
02338-02338	HALIFAX
02339-02340	HANOVER
02341-02341	HANSON
02343-02343	HOLBROOK
02344-02344	MIDDLEBORO
02345-02345	MANOMET
02346-02346	MIDDLEBORO
02347-02347	LAKEVILLE
02348-02349	MIDDLEBORO
02350-02350	MONPONSETT
02351-02351	ABINGTON
02355-02355	NORTH CARVER
02356-02357	NORTH EASTON
02358-02358	NORTH PEMBROKE
02359-02359	PEMBROKE
02360-02363	PLYMOUTH
02364-02364	KINGSTON
02366-02366	SOUTH CARVER
02367-02367	PLYMPTON
02368-02368	RANDOLPH
02370-02371	ROCKLAND
02375-02375	SOUTH EASTON
02379-02379	WEST BRIDGEWATER
02381-02381	WHITE HORSE BEACH
02382-02382	WHITMAN
02401-02411	BROCKTON
02420-02421	LEXINGTON
02445-02446	BROOKLINE
02447-02447	BROOKLINE VILLAGE
02451-02454	WALTHAM
02455-02455	NORTH WALTHAM
02456-02456	NEW TOWN
02457-02457	BABSON PARK
02458-02458	NEWTON
02459-02459	NEWTON CENTER
02460-02460	NEWTONVILLE
02461-02461	NEWTON HIGHLANDS
02462-02462	NEWTON LOWER FALLS
02464-02464	NEWTON UPPER FALLS
02465-02465	WEST NEWTON
02466-02466	AUBURNDALE
02467-02467	CHESTNUT HILL
02468-02468	WABAN
02471-02472	WATERTOWN
02474-02474	ARLINGTON
02475-02475	ARLINGTON HEIGHTS
02476-02476	ARLINGTON
02477-02477	WATERTOWN
02478-02478	BELMONT
02479-02479	WAVERLEY
02481-02481	WELLESLEY HILLS
02482-02482	WELLESLEY
02492-02492	NEEDHAM
02493-02493	WESTON
02494-02494	NEEDHAM
02495-02495	NONANTUM
02499-02499	BROCKTON
02532-02532	BUZZARDS BAY
02534-02534	CATAUMET
02535-02535	CHILMARK
02536-02536	EAST FALMOUTH
02537-02537	EAST SANDWICH
02538-02538	EAST WAREHAM
02539-02539	EDGARTOWN
02540-02541	FALMOUTH
02542-02542	BUZZARDS BAY

02543-02543	WOODS HOLE
02552-02552	MENEMSHA
02553-02553	MONUMENT BEACH
02554-02554	NANTUCKET
02556-02556	NORTH FALMOUTH
02557-02557	OAK BLUFFS
02558-02558	ONSET
02559-02559	POCASSET
02561-02561	SAGAMORE
02562-02562	SAGAMORE BEACH
02563-02563	SANDWICH
02564-02564	SIASCONSET
02565-02565	SILVER BEACH
02568-02568	VINEYARD HAVEN
02571-02571	WAREHAM
02573-02573	VINEYARD HAVEN
02574-02574	WEST FALMOUTH
02575-02575	WEST TISBURY
02576-02576	WEST WAREHAM
02584-02584	NANTUCKET
02601-02601	HYANNIS
02630-02630	BARNSTABLE
02631-02631	BREWSTER
02632-02632	CENTERVILLE
02633-02633	CHATHAM
02634-02634	CENTERVILLE
02635-02635	COTUIT
02636-02636	CENTERVILLE
02637-02637	CUMMAQUID
02638-02638	DENNIS
02639-02639	DENNIS PORT
02641-02641	EAST DENNIS
02642-02642	EASTHAM
02643-02643	EAST ORLEANS
02644-02644	FORESTDALE
02645-02645	HARWICH
02646-02646	HARWICH PORT
02647-02647	HYANNIS PORT
02648-02648	MARSTONS MILLS
02649-02649	MASHPEE
02650-02650	NORTH CHATHAM
02651-02651	NORTH EASTHAM
02652-02652	NORTH TRURO
02653-02653	ORLEANS
02655-02655	OSTERVILLE
02657-02657	PROVINCETOWN
02659-02659	SOUTH CHATHAM
02660-02660	SOUTH DENNIS
02661-02661	SOUTH HARWICH
02662-02662	SOUTH ORLEANS
02663-02663	SOUTH WELLFLEET
02664-02664	SOUTH YARMOUTH
02666-02666	TRURO
02667-02667	WELLFLEET
02668-02668	WEST BARNSTABLE
02669-02669	WEST CHATHAM
02670-02670	WEST DENNIS
02671-02671	WEST HARWICH
02672-02672	WEST HYANNISPORT
02673-02673	WEST YARMOUTH
02675-02675	YARMOUTH PORT
02702-02702	ASSONET
02703-02703	ATTLEBORO
02712-02712	CHARTLEY
02713-02713	CUTTYHUNK
02714-02714	DARTMOUTH
02715-02715	DIGHTON
02717-02717	EAST FREETOWN
02718-02718	EAST TAUNTON
02719-02719	FAIRHAVEN
02720-02724	FALL RIVER
02725-02726	SOMERSET
02738-02738	MARION
02739-02739	MATTAPOISETT
02740-02742	NEW BEDFORD
02743-02743	ACUSHNET
02744-02746	NEW BEDFORD
02747-02747	NORTH DARTMOUTH
02748-02748	SOUTH DARTMOUTH
02754-02754	NORTH DIGHTON
02760-02761	NORTH ATTLEBORO
02762-02762	PLAINVILLE
02763-02763	ATTLEBORO FALLS

02764-02764	NORTH DIGHTON
02766-02766	NORTON
02767-02767	RAYNHAM
02768-02768	RAYNHAM CENTER
02769-02769	REHOBOTH
02770-02770	ROCHESTER
02771-02771	SEEKONK
02777-02777	SWANSEA
02779-02779	BERKLEY
02780-02783	TAUNTON
02790-02790	WESTPORT
02791-02791	WESTPORT POINT
05501-05544	ANDOVER

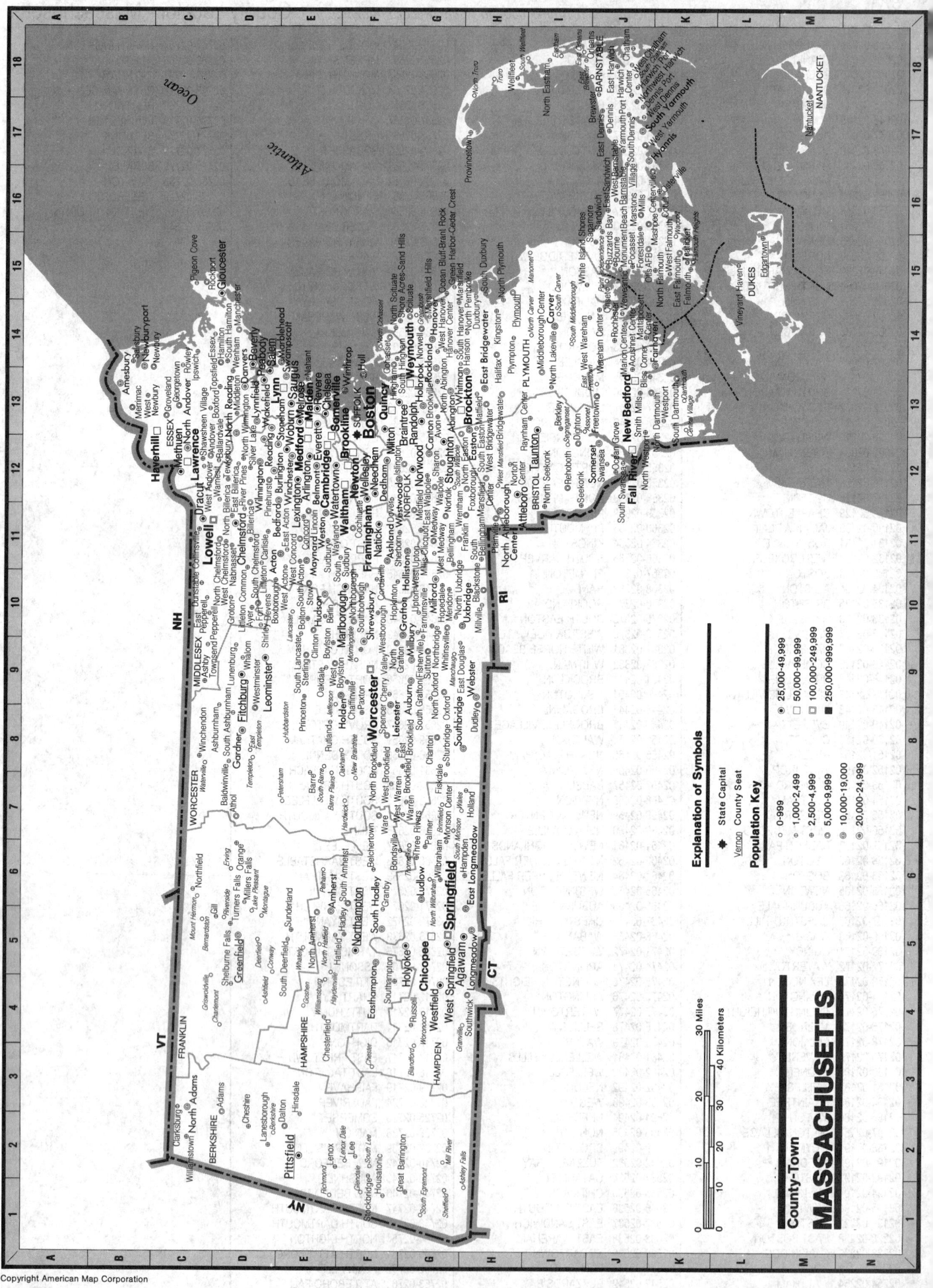

MASSACHUSETTS

County-Town

Explanation of Symbols

✦ State Capital
⬚ _Vernon_ County Seat

Population Key

○ 0-999	⊙ 25,000-49,999
⊙ 1,000-2,499	▢ 50,000-99,999
⊙ 2,500-4,999	▣ 100,000-249,999
◉ 5,000-9,999	■ 250,000-999,999
⊛ 10,000-19,000	
⊛ 20,000-24,999	

30 Miles

40 Kilometers

Explanation of symbols:

● – Census Designated Place (CDP)

▲ italics – Township (shown on the map)

● italics – Township shown which is also a CDP

italics – Township (not shown on the map)

Michigan

General Help Numbers:

Governor's Office
PO Box 30013
Lansing, MI 48909
www.michigan.gov/gov

517-373-7858
Fax 517-335-6863
8AM-5PM

Attorney General's Office
PO Box 30212
Lansing, MI 48909
http://www.michigan.gov/ag/

517-373-1110
Fax 517-373-3042
8AM-5PM

Legislative Records
Michigan Legislature Document Room
State Capitol, PO Box 30036
Lansing, MI 48909
www.michiganlegislature.org

517-373-0169

8:30AM-5PM

State Archives
Michigan Historical Center
717 W Allegan
Lansing, MI 48918-1837
www.sos.state.mi.us/history/archive

517-373-1408
Fax 517-241-1658
10AM-4PM

State Specifics:

Capital:

Lansing
Ingham County

Time Zone:

EST*

* Four north-western Michigan counties are CST:
They are: Dickinson, Gogebic, Iron, Menominee.

Number of Counties:

83

Population:

10,079,985

Web Site:

www.state.mi.us

State Agencies

Criminal Records

Michigan State Police, Criminal History Section, Criminal Justice Information Center, 7150 Harris Dr, Lansing, MI 48913; 517-322-1956, 517-322-0635 (Fax), 8AM-5PM.

www.michigan.gov/msp

Note: Non-profit and charitable organizations may submit a copy of Federal Form 501C3 in lieu of payment for a name search.

Indexing & Storage: Records are available until the subject's DOB indicates 99 years or a death is

reported. It takes up to 30 days before new records are available for inquiry. Records are indexed on inhouse computer. Records are normally destroyed after death.

Searching: Search state police lists of missing persons/children, most wanted, and fugitives at www.michigan.gov/msp/0,1607,7-123-1589_1878---,00.html. Include the following in your request-full name, sex, race, date of birth. A SSN or maiden name/previous name is very helpful. Records can be searched with or without a fingerprint card. The following data is not released: non-conviction information.

Access by: mail, online.

Fee & Payment: The search fee is $10.00 per name without a fingerprint card, $30.00 with a fingerprint card, and $54.00 with state and FBI fingerprint cards. Registered users may be eligible for a fee waiver. Fee payee: State of Michigan. Prepayment required. Payment required in advance unless a prepaid account has been arranged with Division cashier. Personal checks accepted. Credit cards accepted for online access.

Mail search: Turnaround time: 4 to 6 weeks.

Online search: Online access is available at www.michigan.gov/ichat. Results are available in seconds; fee is $10.00 per name. Call 517-322-5546. This is a non-fingerprint search. You are also allowed up to three variations on one name search.

Statewide Court Records

State Court Administrator, PO Box 30048, Lansing, MI 48909 (Courier: 925 W Ottawa St, Lansing, MI 48909); 517-373-2222, 517-373-2112 (Fax), 8:30AM-5PM.

http://courts.michigan.gov

Access by: online. No searching by mail.

Online search: Subscribe to email updates of appellate opinions at http://courtofappeals.mijud.net/resources/subscribe .htm. There is no fee. There is a wide range of online computerization of the judicial system from "none" to "fairly complete," but there is no statewide court records network.

Other access: Zip files are provided for recent Supreme Court and Court of Appeals releases.

Sexual Offender Registry

Michigan State Police, SOR Unit, 7150 Harris Dr, Lansing, MI 48913; 517-322-5098, 517-322-4957 (Fax), 8AM-5PM.

www.mipsor.state.mi.us/

Note: Records may be searched at the local law enforcement level. There are over 33,000 registered sex offenders living in Michigan.

Indexing & Storage: Records are available since 1995. It takes up to 24 hours before new records are available for inquiry.

Searching: Include the following in your request-name and DOB. Only those offenders who have been convicted of a listed offense on or after October 1, 1995 or convicted prior to that date who were still incarcerated, on parole or probation for a listed offense on October 1, 1995 are listed.

Access by: online.

Fee & Payment: There is no search fee. Mail search requests no longer offered.

Online search: One may search the registry at the website, there is no charge.

Incarceration Records

Michigan Department of Corrections, Central Records Office, PO Box 30003, Lansing, MI 48909 (Courier: 206 E. Michigan Ave., Lansing, MI 48909); 517-373-0284, 517-373-2628 (Fax), 8AM-4:30PM.

www.michigan.gov/corrections

Note: For copies, contact Freedom of Information Act Coordinator, FOIA Coordinator: Michigan Department of Corrections, 206 E. Michigan Ave, Grandview Plaza, PO Box 30003, Lansing, MI 48909.

Indexing & Storage: Records are available on current and former inmates. It takes 2-3 weeks before new records are available for inquiry. Records are normally destroyed after 7 years from discharge.

Searching: Almost complete computer records go back to 1981. Computer records prior to that year become less complete the further back you search. Include the following in your request-full name or MDOC number. The DOB and SSN are helpful. Location, MDOC number, conviction and sentencing information, physical identifiers, and release dates are provided.

Access by: mail, phone, fax, online.

Fee & Payment: There is a fee for copies; usually these are FOIA requests.

Mail search: Turnaround time: 5 to 7 days. A mail search can also be directed through the Attorney General's office (phone 510-682-2007).

Phone search: Name searches are available by phone.

Fax search: Requests may be faxed.

Online search: The online access through the main website and at www.state.mi.us/mdoc/asp/otis2.html has many search criteria capabilites. There is also a DOC Most Wanted list at www.state.mi.us/mdoc/MostWanted/MostWanted. asp.

Other access: Bulk sales of database information is available.

Corporation, Limited Liability Company, Limited Partnership, Assumed Name

Department of Consumer & Industry Svcs, bureau of Commercial Services, PO Box 30054, Lansing, MI 48909-7554 (Courier: 7150 Harris Dr, Lansing, MI 48909); 517-241-6470, 517-241-0538 (Fax), 8AM-noon, 1-5PM.

http://michigan.gov/cis/0,1607,7-154-10557_12901---,00.html

Note: The Harris address above represents the delivery address for shipping. The actual physical location is on 2501 Woodlake Circle in Okemos MI.

Indexing & Storage: Records are available from the first corporation in Michigan. Older records were indexed on cards. The index to records for active entities are maintained on computer. It takes 24 hours or less before new records are available for inquiry.

Searching: Forms, policies, and procedures may be viewed at their website. The fax listed above is for record requests. The fax for copies or certificates is 517-241-0537. Include the following in your request-full name of business, corporation file number. The directors are only listed on the annual report.

Access by: mail, phone, fax, in person, online.

Fee & Payment: There is no search fee. The minimum charge for copies is $6.00 per record and $1.00 per page if over 6 pages. The minimum charge for a certificate is $10.00. Fee payee: State of Michigan. Credit cards are accepted for in person requests only. Personal checks accepted. Credit cards accepted: MasterCard, Visa.

Mail search: Turnaround time: 5 to 7 days. There is no fee unless copies or certificates are needed, then there is a minimum $6.00 fee. No SASE is required. Copies cost $1.00 per page.

Phone search: You can order copies or certificates.

Fax search: Same criteria as mail searches.

In person search: The agency has a public access terminal for viewing records.

Online search: A the website, search by company name or file number for records of domestic corporations, limited liability companies, and limited partnerships and of foreign corporations, and limited partnerships qualified to transact business in the state.

Other access: The database is for sale on tape or microfiche.

Expedited service: The fee for expedited service is 25% of the invoice.

Trademarks/Servicemarks

Bureau of Commercial Services, Trademarks & Service Marks, PO Box 30054, Lansing, MI 48909-7554 (Courier: 7150 Harris Dr, Lansing, MI 48909); 517-241-6470, 8AM-5PM (closed at noon for 1 hr).

www.michigan.gov/cis/0,1607,7-154-10557_21107---,00.html

Note: The Harris address above represents the delivery address for shipping. The actual physical location is on 2501 Woodlake Circle in Okemos MI.

Indexing & Storage: Records are available for current records. The index is available since 1990.

Access by: mail, phone, fax, in person, online.

Fee & Payment: The fee is $5.00 if this agency does the search.

Mail search: They suggest to use the web instead.

Phone search: No fee for telephone request. Search is limited, they will let you know if a wording exists.

Fax search: Requests are accepted by fax.

In person search: No fee for request. There is a public access terminal.

Online search: Free searching is available at www.cis.state.mi.us/bcs/corp/pdf/markcom.pdf. This is a search of a PDF file of their system. It is very tricky to get to on the web.

Uniform Commercial Code, Federal and State Tax Liens

MI Department of State, UCC Section, PO Box 30197, Lansing, MI 48909-7697 (Courier: 7064 Crowner Dr, Dimondale, MI 48821); 517-322-1144, 517-322-5434 (Fax), 8AM-5PM.

www.michigan.gov/sos

Note: To find information at the website on UCC, click on the Services to Businesses tab.

Indexing & Storage: Records are available from 1964. Records are computerized since 1990. It takes 7 to 10 days before new records are available for inquiry.

Searching: Use search request form UCC-11. The search includes federal and state tax liens on businesses and individuals except collateral specified per UCC Revised Article 9. Include the following in your request-debtor name.

Access by: mail, phone, fax, in person, online.

Fee & Payment: The search fee is $6.00. The copy fee is $2.00. Certification (official seal) is an additional $6.00. Fee payee: State of Michigan. Prepayment required. Personal checks accepted. Credit cards accepted for online access only.

Mail search: Turnaround time: 1 week.

Phone search: Phone searching is available on a prepaid account basis, results are returned by mail.

Fax search: See expedited services.

In person search: Requests are serviced in person, but the agency would prefer that requesters use the online access. See expedited services.

Online search: From the website, click on Online Services. Conducting a Debtor Name Quick Search is free. No login is needed. Documents may be ordered for a fee. Registration and credit card are required.

Other access: A monthly subscription service is available for the bulk purchase of UCC filings on microfilm. The fee is $50 or actual cost, whichever is greater. Call 517-322-1144 for additional information.

Expedited service: Expedited service is available for an additional $25.00 fee. Expedited searches are provided on a prepaid account basis at $25.00 + $6.00 per debtor name. If request is received by 11 AM, search is mailed that same day.

Sales Tax Registrations
Access to Records is Restricted

Michigan Dept of Treasury, Sales, Use, Withholding Tax Division, Lansing, MI 48922; 517-636-4660, 517-636-4491, 517-335-1135 (Fax), 8AM-4:45PM.

www.michigan.gov/treasury

Note: The agency will only verify or confirm data, no searches provided.

Birth Certificates

Department of Community Health, Vital Records Requests, PO Box 30721, Lansing, MI 48909 (Courier: 3423 N Martin Luther King, Jr Blvd, Lansing, MI 48906); 517-335-8656 (Instructions), 517-335-8666 (Request Unit), 517-321-5884 (Fax), 8AM-5PM.

www.michigan.gov/mdch

Note: Any Michigan vital record can be "verified" for a fee of $5.00. Verification is only for names, date and place of filing. Application for records can be downloaded from the website.

Indexing & Storage: Records are available from 1867 on. Records over 100 yrs old are open to the public. It takes 90 to 120 days after birth before new records are available for inquiry. Records are indexed on microfiche, inhouse computer.

Searching: Certified copies of birth records are only issued to the individual to whom the record pertains, the parent(s) named on the record, an heir, legal guardian or legal rep. of an eligible person, or through court order. Include the following in your request-full name, names of parents, mother's maiden name, date of birth, place of birth, relationship to person of record. The signature and relationship to the subject are required items on the request form. Also include copy of photo ID. The following data is not released: sealed records.

Access by: mail, in person, online.

Fee & Payment: The fee is $15.00 per name for every 3 years searched. The fee is $4.00 for each additional year. Additional copies of the same record are $5.00 each. Use of a credit card is additional $6.00. An "Authenticated Copy" is available for $18.00. Fee payee: State of Michigan. Prepayment required. Personal checks accepted. Credit cards accepted: MasterCard, Visa, AmEx, Discover.

Mail search: Turnaround time: 2 to 3 weeks. No SASE is required.

In person search: Turnaround time up to 3 hours. Counter closes at 3:30 PM.

Online search: Records may be ordered from the web site. Step-by-step instructions given, use of credit card required.

Expedited service: Expedited service is available for mail and online searches. Turnaround time: 1 to 3 days. Add credit card fee and express mail fee. Add $5.00 for same day service.

Death Records

Department of Health, Vital Records Requests, PO Box 30721, Lansing, MI 48909 (Courier: 3423 N Martin Luther King, Jr Blvd, Lansing, MI 48906); 517-335-8656 (Instructions), 517-335-8666 (Request Unit), 517-321-5884 (Fax), 8AM-5PM.

www.michigan.gov/mdch

Note: Application for records can be downloaded from the website.

Indexing & Storage: Records are available from 1867 to present. New records are available for inquiry immediately. Records are indexed on microfiche, inhouse computer.

Searching: Records are open to the public. Include the following in your request-full name, date of death, place of death, relationship to person of record. The following data is not released: sealed records.

Access by: mail, in person, online.

Fee & Payment: The fee for a certified copy is $15.00 which includes 3 years searched. Each additional year searched is another $4.00. Use of credit card is an additional $6.00. An "Authenticated Copy" is available for $18.00. Fee payee: State of Michigan. Prepayment required. Personal checks, money orders accepted. Credit cards accepted: MasterCard, Visa, AmEx, Discover.

Mail search: Turnaround time: 2 to 3 weeks. No SASE is required.

In person search: Turnaround time 2-3 hours. Counter closes at 3:30 PM.

Online search: Records may be ordered from the web. Use of a credit card is required. Records are returned by mail or express delivery. If problems, call 800-255-2414.

Expedited service: Expedited service is available for mail and online searches. Turnaround time: 1 to 3 days. Add credit card fee and express mail fee. Add $5.00 for same day service.

Marriage Certificates

Department of Health, Vital Records Requests, PO Box 30721, Lansing, MI 48909 (Courier: 3423 N Martin Luther King, Jr Blvd, Lansing, MI 48906); 517-335-8656 (Instructions), 517-335-8666 (Requests Unit), 517-321-5884 (Fax), 8AM-5PM.

www.michigan.gov/mdch

Note: Application for records can be downloaded from the website.

Indexing & Storage: Records are available from 1867 to present. New records are available for inquiry immediately. Records are indexed on microfiche, inhouse computer.

Searching: Records are open to the public. There is no bride index for the years 1950 thru 1975. Include the following in your request-names of husband and wife, date of marriage, place or county of marriage.

Access by: mail, in person, online.

Fee & Payment: The fee for a certified copy is $15.00 which includes 3 years searched. Each additional year searched is another $4.00. Use of credit card is an additional $6.00. An "Authenticated Copy" is available for $18.00. Fee payee: State of Michigan. Prepayment required. Personal checks accepted. Credit cards accepted: MasterCard, Visa, AmEx, Discover.

Mail search: Turnaround time: 2 to 3 weeks. No SASE is required.

In person search: Turnaround time up to 3 hours minutes. Counter closes at 3:30 PM.

Online search: Records can be ordered from the web site, credit card is required.

Expedited service: Expedited service is available for mail and online searches. Turnaround time: 1 to 3 business days. Add credit card fee and express mail fee. Add $5.00 for same day service.

Divorce Records

Department of Health, Vital Records Requests, PO Box 30721, Lansing, MI 48909 (Courier: 3423 N Martin Luther King, Jr Blvd, Lansing, MI 48906); 517-335-8656 (Instructions), 517-335-8666 (Requests Unit), 517-321-5884 (Fax), 8AM-5PM.

www.michigan.gov/mdch

Note: Application for records can be downloaded from the website.

Indexing & Storage: Records are available from 1897 to present. It takes 6-10 months before new records are available for inquiry. Records are indexed on microfiche, inhouse computer.

Searching: Records are not restricted. There are no divorce records for Detroit for 1973 and 1974. There is no "wife index" available prior to 1978. Include the following in your request-names of husband and wife, date of divorce, county where divorce granted.

Access by: mail, in person, online.

Fee & Payment: The fee is $15.00 per name for every 3 years searched. The fee is $4.00 for each additional year. Additional copies of the same record are $5.00 each. Use of a credit card is additional $6.00. An "Authenticated Copy" is available for $18.00. Fee payee: State of Michigan. Prepayment required. Personal checks accepted. Credit cards accepted: MasterCard, Visa, AmEx, Discover.

Mail search: Turnaround time: 2 to 3 weeks. No SASE is required.

In person search: Turnaround time 45 minutes. Counter closes at 3:30 PM.

Online search: Records can be ordered from the web site, credit card is required.

Expedited service: Expedited service is available for mail and online searches. Turnaround time: 1 to 3 days. Add credit card fee and express mail fee. Add $5.00 for same day service.

Workers' Compensation Records

Department of Labor & Economic Dev., Workers' Compensation Agency, 7150 Harris Dr, Lansing, MI 48909, 888-396-5041, 517-322-1808 (Fax), 8AM-5PM.

www.michigan.gov/wca

Note: In person requests are discouraged due to confidentiality of records and records may not be on site. Injured employee may review their own records, but should call first and make arrangements.

Indexing & Storage: Records are available from 1981 on computer and from 1976 to 1981 records on microfilm. You can request by fax, but results are mailed. It takes 1 week before new records are available for inquiry. Records are normally destroyed after 20 years from date of file closure.

Searching: Request must be in writing and cannot be for pre-employment screening. Only litigated cases are released. Include the following in your request-claimant name, Social Security Number.

Access by: mail, online.

Fee & Payment: Fee is $.25 per page plus postage and research labor cost if over 30 pages. Fee payee: Labor & Economic Growth Personal checks accepted. No credit cards accepted.

Mail search: Turnaround time: 1 to 2 weeks. Turnaround time may be longer if records must be searched at archives. No SASE is required.

Online search: Go to the website and follow the links to see if an employer has coverage. The site does not allow searching by employee name.

Driver Records

Department of State Police, Record Look-up Unit, 7064 Crowner Dr, Lansing, MI 48918; 517-322-1624 (Look-up Unit), 517-322-1181 (Fax), 8AM-4:45PM.

www.michigan.gov/sos

Note: Copies of court abstracts of convictions may be purchased at the same address for a fee of $7.00 per copy. Copies of tickets must be obtained from the courts involved.

Indexing & Storage: Records are available for 7 years from conviction date; unless there is an alcohol or controlled substance conviction which will remain on record for 10 years. Accidents are reported on the record only if the driver is cited. It takes 14 days before new records are available for inquiry.

Searching: The agency is in compliance with DPPA. Casual requesters must submit form BDVR-154, with written consent of subject, to receive records with personal information. Otherwise, records without personal information are released. Include the following in your request-name and either DOB or DL number.

Access by: mail, phone, fax, in person, online.

Fee & Payment: The fee for obtaining a record is $7.00 per search. If certification is needed, there is an additional $1.00 fee. Fee payee: State of Michigan. The fee may accompany the request for mail-in, or a bill can be sent with the records. There is a full charge for a "no record found." Credit cards are accepted for fax and phone requests only. Personal checks accepted. Credit cards accepted: MasterCard, Visa, Discover.

Mail search: Turnaround time: 18 working days. No SASE is required.

Phone search: Phone requesting is available for pre-approved accounts and government agencies or with a credit card.

Fax search: Established accounts can order by fax, results are returned by mail.

In person search: Turnaround time is 24 hours unless you are the actual driver, then the record is immediately available.

Online search: Online ordering is available on an interactive basis. The system is open 7 days a week. Ordering is by DL or name and DOB. An account must be established and billing is monthly. Access is also available from the Internet. Fee is $7.00 per record. For more information, call 517-322-6281.

Other access: Magnetic tape inquiry is available. Also, the state offers the license file for bulk purchase. Customized runs are $64.00 per thousand records; complete database can be purchased for $16.00 per thousand. A $10,000 surety bond is required. Call 517-322-1042.

Vehicle and Vessel Ownership and Registration

Department of State Police, Record Look-up Unit, 7064 Crowner Dr, Lansing, MI 48918; 517-322-1624, 517-322-1181 (Fax), 8AM-4:45PM.

www.michigan.gov/sos

Indexing & Storage: Records are available for 10 years to present for vehicle information and 3 years to present for registration information. Vessel titles are on computer since 1974. All motorized boats must be registered, if 20 ft or over they must also be titled. It takes 14 days before new records are available for inquiry.

Searching: Requests for vehicle and ownership records must be submitted in writing with a statement of intended use. Large volume users or fax requesters must be pre-approved.

Access by: mail, phone, fax, in person, online.

Fee & Payment: The fee is $7.00 per transaction. Normal searching requires the plate or VIN number. Records to be accessed include mobile homes and boats. Copy fee is $1.00 per record. Add $1.00 for certification Fee payee: State of Michigan. The fee may accompany the request for mail-in, or a bill can be sent with the records. Requests made by fax will be sent a bill with the records. There is a full charge for a "no record found." Personal checks accepted. Credit cards accepted: MasterCard, Visa.

Mail search: Turnaround time: 10 days. A SASE is requested.

Phone search: Call-in requests are for established, approved accounts only. Records may be mailed or faxed back. They will usually also accept a credit card.

Fax search: Established accounts may order by fax and receive results by fax.

In person search: You can make your request in person, but they will mail back the records in 4 or 5 days. Requests must be in writing.

Online search: Online searching is single inquiry and requires a VIN or plate number. (no name searches). A $25,000 surety bond is required. Fee is $7.00 per record. Direct dialup or Internet access is offered. For more information, call 517-322-5784.

Other access: Michigan offers bulk retrieval from the VIN and plate database. A written request letter, stating purpose, must be submitted and approved. A surety bond is required upon approval. Please call 517-322-3452.

Accident Reports

Department of State Police, Criminal Justice Information Center, 7150 Harris Dr, Lansing, MI 48913, 517-322-5509 (FOIA), 517-323-5350 (Fax), 8AM-5PM.

www.michigan.gov/msp/0,1607,7-123--28578--,00.html

Note: All requests coming from non-government agencies are considered FOIA requests.

Indexing & Storage: Records are available from 1983 to present for state police records. UD10's for all law enforcement agencies in Michigan are available for the current year plus 2 years back, first page only. It takes 3 to 4 weeks before new records are available for inquiry.

Searching: Include the following in your request-full name, date of accident, location of accident.

Access by: mail, fax, in person.

Fee & Payment: Accident reports are currently free of charge, unless extensive searching is involved. Fee payee: State of Michigan. Prepayment required. Personal checks accepted. No credit cards accepted.

Mail search: Turnaround time: 10 days. A SASE is requested.

Fax search: Records are available by fax. Turnaround time is 5 days.

In person search: You may request information in person; turnaround time for return is 5 days.

Online search: Records may be requested by email from WhiteL3@michigan.gov.

Voter Registration

Bureau of Elections, Election Liaison Division, 430 W Allegan St, 1st Fl, Lansing, MI 48918; 517-373-2540, 517-373-0941 (Fax), 8AM-5PM.

www.michigan.gov/sos/1,1607,7-127-1633---.00.html

Note: In general, the records are open to the public.

Indexing & Storage: Records are available from 08/98 forward. It takes 1 to 2 days before new records are available for inquiry.

Searching: Include the following in your request-name, DOB. The record includes name, address, and DOB.

Access by: mail, fax.

Fee & Payment: The fee is $6.55 per name. If an identifer (such as a DOB) is not given, each common name is $6.55. Fee payee: State of Michigan

Mail search: Turnaround time: 2 to 3 days. Records are available by mail.

Fax search: Records are available by fax, if request is prepaid.

Other access: The agency will sell district, statewide or customized subsets of the database on CD. Fees are usually $100 to $170, depending on data requested.

GED Certificates

MI Department of Labor & Econ Growth, Adult Education - GED Testing, 201 N Washington Square, 3rd Fl, Lansing, MI 48913; 517-373-1692, 517-335-3461 (Fax), 7AM-5PM.

www.michigan.gov/adulteducation

Indexing & Storage: Records are available 3/1969 to present.

Searching:. To search, include the SSN, DOB and date and location of test. For a copy of a transcript, also include a signed release.

Access by: mail, phone, fax, in person, online.

Fee & Payment: There are no fees.

Mail search: Turnaround time is 1 week; 3 weeks if record is prior to 1979. No SASE is required.

Phone search: You request a verification by leaving a message and fax a signed release. The agency will call back with the information.

Fax search: Same criteria as mail searching.

In person search: The building is also known as the Victor Building.

Online search: Will accept email requests with scanned signature. Call for details.

Hunting and Fishing License Information

Access to Records is Restricted

Dept of Natural Resources, Customer Systems, PO Box 30181, Lansing, MI 48909 (Courier: 530 W Allegan St, Lansing, MI 48933); 517-373-1204, 517-335-6813 (Fax), 8AM-5PM.

Note: Hunting and fishing license information is no longer released. All FOIA requests are now being denied because it is personal information.

Michigan State Licensing Agencies
Licenses Searchable Online

Airport Manager #24 .... www.michigan.gov/documents/MGRLST_17899_7.pdf
Alarm System Service #23 .... www.michigan.gov/commerciallicensing
Ambulance Attendant #10 .... www.michigan.gov/cis/0,1607,7-154-10557---,00.html
Amusement Ride #8 .... http://cis.state.mi.us/verify.htm
Appraiser, Real Estate/General/Residential #8 .. http://cis.state.mi.us/verify.htm
Architect #8 .... http://cis.state.mi.us/verify.htm
Assessor #25 .... www.michigan.gov/documents/CertificationLevel_3022_7.pdf
Attorney, State Bar #27 .... www.michbar.org/memberdirectory/
Auto Dealer/Mechanic/Repair Facility #28 .... www.michigan.gov/sos/0,1607,7-127-1631_8849-51047--,00.html
Bank & Trust Company #14 .... www.michigan.gov/cis/1,1607,7-154--22352--,00.html
Barber #8 .... http://cis.state.mi.us/verify.htm
Barber Shop/School #8 .... http://cis.state.mi.us/verify.htm
Boxing/Wrestling Occupation #8 .... http://cis.state.mi.us/verify.htm
Builder, Residential #8 .... http://cis.state.mi.us/verify.htm
Camp, Children/Adult Foster Care #13 .... www.michigan.gov/cis/0,1607,7-154-10568_17846_17885---,00.html
Carnival #8 .... http://cis.state.mi.us/verify.htm
Casino Interest Personnel/Company #29 .... http://miboecfr.nicusa.com/cgi-bin/cfr/casino_srch.cgi
Cemetery #8 .... http://cis.state.mi.us/verify.htm
Check Seller #3 .... www.michigan.gov/cis/0,1607,7-154-10555_13251_13257---,00.html
Child Care Institution #26 .... www.dleg.state.mi.us/brs_cwl/sr_cwl.asp
Child Day Care #13 .... www.michigan.gov/cis/0,1607,7-154-10568_17949---,00.html
Child Facility, Court Operated #26 .... www.dleg.state.mi.us/brs_cwl/sr_cwl.asp
Child Welfare/Child Placing Agency #26 .... www.dleg.state.mi.us/brs_cwl/sr_cwl.asp
Chiropractor #15 .... www.michigan.gov/healthlicense
Collection Manager #8 .... http://cis.state.mi.us/verify.htm
Community Planner #8 .... http://cis.state.mi.us/verify.htm
Community Planner (Mfg. Home) #16 .... www.cis.state.mi.us/bcs_free/
Consumer Financial Service #3 .... www.michigan.gov/cis/0,1607,7-154-10555_13251_13257---,00.html
Contractor, Residential #8 .... http://cis.state.mi.us/verify.htm
Cosmetologist #8 .... http://cis.state.mi.us/verify.htm
Cosmetology Shop/School #8 .... http://cis.state.mi.us/verify.htm
Counselor #15 .... www.michigan.gov/healthlicense
Credit Card Issuer #3 .... www.michigan.gov/cis/0,1607,7-154-10555_13251_13257---,00.html
Credit Union #14 .... www.michigan.gov/cis/1,1607,7-154--22352--,00.html
Debt Management Firm #12 .... www.michagan.gov/CIS/0,1607,7-154-10555_13251---,00.html
Dental Hygenist #15 .... www.michigan.gov/healthlicense
Dentist/Dental Assistant #15 .... www.michigan.gov/healthlicense
Election Campaign Finance Committee #29 ...... http://miboecfr.nicusa.com/cgi-bin/cfr/mi_com.cgi
Election Candidate Committee #29 .... http://miboecfr.nicusa.com/cgi-bin/cfr/can_search.cgi
Emergency Medical Personnel #15 .... www.michigan.gov/healthlicense
Employment Agency, fee only #8 .... http://cis.state.mi.us/verify.htm
EMT Advanced/Specialist/Instructor #10 .... www.michigan.gov/cis/0,1607,7-154-10557---,00.html
Engineer #9 .... http://cis.state.mi.us/verify.htm
Flight School #24 .... www.michigan.gov/aero/0,1607,7-145-6774_6887---,00.html
Forester #8 .... http://cis.state.mi.us/verify.htm
Foster Care Facility/Adult Camp #13 .... www.michigan.gov/emi/1,1303,7-102-117_401_459---Cl,00.html
Foster Care Program #21 .... www.michigan.gov/cis/0,1607,7-154-10568_17801---,00.html
Foster Care, Child #13 .... www.michigan.gov/cis/0,1607,7-154-10568_17846_17865---,00.html
Foster Family Home #21 .... www.michigan.gov/cis/0,1607,7-154-10568_17801---,00.html
Funeral Home #8 .... http://cis.state.mi.us/verify.htm
Funeral Salesperson #8 .... http://cis.state.mi.us/verify.htm
Funeral, Prepaid Funeral Contract Regis. #8 ..... http://cis.state.mi.us/verify.htm
Grain Dealer #2 .... www.mda.state.mi.us/prodag/GrainDealers/dealers.html
Health Facilities/Laboratory #15 .... www.michigan.gov/healthlicense
Hearing Aid Dealer #8 .... http://cis.state.mi.us/verify.htm
HMO #5 .... www.michigan.gov/cis/0,1607,7-154-10555_13251_13262---,00.html

Insurance Adjuster #5 .... www.michigan.gov/cis/0,1607,7-154-10555_13251_13262---,00.html
Insurance Agent/Counselor/Solicitor/Admin. #5 .. www.michigan.gov/cis/0,1607,7-154-10555_13251_13262---,00.html
Insurance-related Entity #5 .... www.michigan.gov/cis/0,1607,7-154-10555_13251_13262---,00.html
Landscape Architect #8 .... http://cis.state.mi.us/verify.htm
Liquor Dist./Whlse./Mfg. #6 .... http://www2.cis.state.mi.us:7778/llist/
Liquor Finance Division #6 .... http://www2.cis.state.mi.us:7778/llist/
Liquor Hearings & Appeals #6 .... http://www2.cis.state.mi.us:7778/llist/
Liquor License #6 .... http://www2.cis.state.mi.us:7778/llist/
Liquor Licensing Director #6 .... http://www2.cis.state.mi.us:7778/llist/
Living Care Facility #12 .... www.michigan.gov/CIS/0,1607,7-154-10555_13251---,00.html
Lobbyable Public Official #29 .... www.michigan.gov/sos/0,1607,7-127-1633_11945-30499--,00.html
Lobbyist/Lobbyist Agent #29............................. http://miboecfr.nicusa.com/cgi-bin/cfr/lobby_srch.cgi
Long Term Care Company #5 .... www.michigan.gov/cis/0,1607,7-154-10555_13251_13262---,00.html
Mammography Facility #15.................................. www.michigan.gov/healthlicense
Marriage & Family Therapist #15...................... www.michigan.gov/healthlicense
Medical Doctor #15.. www.michigan.gov/healthlicense
Medical First Responder #10 .... www.michigan.gov/cis/0,1607,7-154-10557---,00.html
Mortgage Licensee #3 .... www.michigan.gov/cis/0,1607,7-154-10555_13251_13257---,00.html
Mortuary Science #8.. http://cis.state.mi.us/verify.htm
Motor Vehicle Installment Seller/Financer #3 ..... www.michigan.gov/cis/0,1607,7-154-10555_13251_13257---,00.html
Nurse #15 .... www.michigan.gov/healthlicense
Nursery Dealer/Grower #2.................................. www.mda.state.mi.us/industry/Nursery/license/index.html
Nurses' Aide #15 .... www.michigan.gov/healthlicense
Nursing Home #15 .... www.michigan.gov/healthlicense
Nursing Home Administrator #15........................ www.michigan.gov/healthlicense
Ocularist #8.. http://cis.state.mi.us/verify.htm
Optometrist #15 .... www.michigan.gov/healthlicense
Osteopathic Physician #15 .... www.michigan.gov/healthlicense
Paramedic #10... www.michigan.gov/cis/0,1607,7-154-10557---,00.html
Personnel Agency #17.. http://cis.state.mi.us/verify.htm
Pesticide Applicator Company #2...................... www.michigan.gov/mda/0,1607,7-125-1569_2459-13075--,00.html
Pharmacist #15.. www.michigan.gov/healthlicense
Physical Therapist #15 .... www.michigan.gov/healthlicense
Physician Assistant #15..................................... www.michigan.gov/healthlicense
Podiatrist #15.. www.michigan.gov/healthlicense
Political Action Committee #29 .... http://miboecfr.nicusa.com/cgi-bin/cfr/pac_search.cgi
Political Party Committee #29............................. http://miboecfr.nicusa.com/cgi-bin/cfr/mi_com.cgi?com_type=PPY
Polygraph Examiner #8 .... http://cis.state.mi.us/verify.htm
Potato Dealer #2.. www.michigan.gov/mda/0,1607,7-125-1566_1733_2321-11149--,00.html
Private Detective #23... www.michigan.gov/commerciallicensing
Private Investigator #17 .... http://cis.state.mi.us/verify.htm
Private Security/Security Arrest Authority #23.... www.michigan.gov/commerciallicensing
Psychologist #15.. www.michigan.gov/healthlicense
Public Accountant-CPA #8 .... http://cis.state.mi.us/verify.htm
Pump Installer #20... www.deq.state.mi.us/documents/deq-dwrpd-gws-reg-contractors-by-county.pdf
Real Estate Agent/Broker/Sales #9 .... http://cis.state.mi.us/verify.htm
Regulatory Loan Licensee #3............................. www.michigan.gov/cis/0,1607,7-154-10555_13251_13257---,00.html
Sanitarian #15.. www.michigan.gov/healthlicense
Savings Bank #14.. www.michigan.gov/cis/1,1607,7-154--22352--,00.html
Security Agency #17... http://cis.state.mi.us/verify.htm
Security Alarm Installer #17 .... http://cis.state.mi.us/verify.htm
Security Guard, Private #17............................... http://cis.state.mi.us/verify.htm
Social Worker #15 .... www.michigan.gov/healthlicense
Surety Company #5.. www.michigan.gov/cis/0,1607,7-154-10555_13251_13262---,00.html
Surplus Line Broker #5 .... www.michigan.gov/cis/0,1607,7-154-10555_13251_13262---,00.html
Surveyor, Professional #9.................................. http://cis.state.mi.us/verify.htm
Teacher #19... http://meis.mde.state.mi.us/teachercert/sr_teaCerts.asp
Third-Party Administrator #5.............................. www.michigan.gov/cis/0,1607,7-154-10555_13251_13262---,00.html
Veterinarian/Veterinary Technician #15 .... www.michigan.gov/healthlicense
Well Contractor #20... www.deq.state.mi.us/documents/deq-dwrpd-gws-reg-contractors-by-county.pdf

Michigan Licensing Quick Finder

Adoption Service #13	517-335-0918
Aircraft/Aeronautics #24	517-335-9283
Airport Manager #24	517-335-9283
Airport/ Heliport #24	517-335-9283
Alarm System Service #23	517-241-5645
Ambulance Attendant #10	517-241-3018
Amusement Ride #8	517-241-9265
Animal (Dead) Renderer #2	800-292-3939
Animal Control Officer #2	800-292-3939
Animal Feed (Commercial) #2	800-292-3939
Animal Shelter #2	800-292-3939
Appraiser, Real Estate/General/Residential #8	517-241-9201
Aquaculture Facility #2	800-292-3939
Architect #8	517-241-9253
Asbestos Accreditation, Individual #11	517-322-1320
Asbestos License #11	517-322-1320
Assessor #25	517-373-8320
Athletic-related Event, Boxing, etc. #8	517-241-9246
Attorney, State Bar #27	800-968-1442
Auto Dealer/Mechanic/Repair Facility #28	517-373-9460
Bank & Trust Company #14	517-373-6950
Barber #8	517-241-9201
Barber Shop/School #8	517-241-9258
BIDCO #14	517-373-6930
Bingo Operation, Special/Weekly #1	517-335-5756
Boiler Repairer #7	517-241-9334
Boilermaker, Installer #7	517-241-9334
Boxing/Wrestling Occupation #8	517-241-9246
Builder, Residential #8	517-241-9427
Camp, Children/Adult Foster Care #13	517-335-0918
Carnival #8	517-241-9265
Casino Interest Personnel/Company #29	517-373-2540
Cemetery #8	517-241-9244
Charitable Gaming (Supplier) #1	517-335-5756
Check Seller #3	517-373-0220
Child Care Institution #26	517-373-8383
Child Day Care #13	517-335-0918
Child Facility, Court Operated #26	517-373-8383
Child Welfare/Child Placing Agency #26	517-373-8383
Chiropractor #15	517-241-9427
Collection Manager #8	517-241-9258
Community Planner #8	517-241-9253
Community Planner (Mfg. Home) #16	517-241-6300
Consumer Financial Service #3	517-373-0220
Contractor, Residential #8	517-241-9427
Corrections Officer #18	517-335-1426
Cosmetologist #8	517-241-9201
Cosmetology Shop/School #8	517-241-9258
Counselor #15	517-241-9427
Counselor, School Guidance #19	517-373-6505
Credit Card Issuer #3	517-373-0220
Credit Union #14	517-373-6930
Debt Management Firm #12	877-999-6442
Dental Hygienist #15	517-241-9427

Dentist/Dental Assistant #15	517-241-9427
Election Campaign Finance Committee #29	517-373-2540
Election Candidate Committee #29	517-373-2540
Electrician (various types) #7	517-241-9320
Elevator Service #7	517-241-9337
Emergency Medical Personnel #15	517-241-9427
Employment Agency, fee only #8	517-241-9258
EMT Advanced/Specialist/Instr. #10	900-555-8374
Engineer #9	517-241-9253
Family/Group Day Care #13	517-335-0918
Fieldperson (Dairy/Farm related) #2	800-292-3939
Flight School #24	517-335-9283
Forester #8	517-241-9288
Foster Care Facility/Adult Camp #13	517-335-0918
Foster Care Program #21	517-335-6124
Foster Care, Child #13	517-335-0918
Foster Family Home #21	517-335-6124
Funeral Home #8	517-241-9252
Funeral Salesperson #8	517-241-9252
Funeral, Prepaid Funeral Contract Regis. #8	517-241-9252
Gasoline Seller (Retail) #2	800-292-3939
Grain Dealer #2	800-292-3939
Grain Trucker #2	800-292-3939
Health Facilities/Laboratory #15	517-241-2648
Hearing Aid Dealer #8	517-241-9234
HMO #5	877-999-6442
Insurance Adjuster #5	877-999-6442
Insurance Agent/Counselor/Solicitor/Admin. #5	877-999-6442
Insurance-related Entity #5	877-999-6442
Investment Adviser #12	877-999-6442
Landscape Architect #8	517-241-8364
Liquor Dist./Whlse./Mfg. #6	517-322-1415
Liquor Finance Division #6	517-322-1071
Liquor Hearings & Appeals #6	517-322-1390
Liquor License #6	517-322-1408
Liquor Licensing Director #6	517-322-1408
Livestock Dealer #2	800-292-3939
Living Care Facility #12	877-999-6442
Lobbyable Public Official #29	517-373-2540
Lobbyist/Lobbyist Agent #29	517-373-2540
Long Term Care Company #5	877-999-6442
Lottery Retailer #1	517-335-5756
Mammography Facility #15	517-241-1989
Manufactured Home Community #16	517-241-6300
Manufactured Home Installer/Svcs./Retailer #16	517-241-6300
Marriage & Family Therapist #15	517-241-9427
Mechanical Construction #7	517-241-9325
Medical Doctor #15	517-241-9427
Medical First Responder #10	900-555-8374
Milk Distributor #2	800-292-3939
Milk Facility/Wash Facility #2	800-292-3939
Milk Plant/Hauler/Installer #2	800-292-3939
Millionaire Party/Vegas Nite Gaming #1	517-335-5756

Mortgage Licensee #3	517-373-0220
Mortuary Science #8	517-241-9252
Motor Vehicle Installment Seller/Financer #3	517-373-0220
Notary Public #22	517-373-2531
Nurse #15	517-241-9427
Nursery Dealer/Grower #2	800-292-3939
Nurses' Aide #15	517-241-9427
Nursing Home #15	517-334-8408
Nursing Home Administrator #15	517-241-9427
Ocularist #8	517-241-9258
Optometrist #15	517-241-9427
Osteopathic Physician #15	517-241-9427
Paramedic #10	900-555-8374
Personnel Agency #17	517-241-5645
Pesticide Applicator Company #2	800-292-3939
Pesticide Applicator/Technician #2	800-292-3939
Pet Shop #2	800-292-3939
Pharmacist #15	517-241-9427
Physical Therapist #15	517-241-9427
Physician Assistant #15	517-241-9427
Plumber #7	517-241-9330
Podiatrist #15	517-241-9427
Political Action Committee #29	517-373-2540
Political Party Committee #29	517-373-2540
Polygraph Examiner #8	517-241-9234
Potato Dealer #2	800-292-3939
Private Detective #23	517-241-5645
Private Investigator #17	517-241-5645
Private Security/Security Arrest Authority #23	517-241-5645
Psychologist #15	517-241-9427
Public Accountant-CPA #8	517-241-9427
Pump Installer #20	517-241-1389
Race Track Employee #4	734-462-2400
Racing Professional #4	734-462-2400
Raffle #1	517-335-5756
Railroad Commission #23	517-241-5645
Real Estate Agent/Broker/Sales #9	517-241-9288
Regulatory Loan Licensee #3	517-373-0220
Riding Stable #2	800-292-3939
Sanitarian #15	517-241-9427
Savings Bank #14	517-373-6930
School Librarian #19	517-373-6505
Securities Agent #12	877-999-6442
Securities Broker/Dealer #12	877-999-6442
Security Agency #17	517-241-5645
Security Alarm Installer #17	517-241-5645
Security Guard, Private #17	517-241-5645
Social Worker #15	517-241-9427
Surety Company #5	877-999-6442
Surplus Line Broker #5	877-999-6442
Surveyor, Professional #9	517-241-9253
Teacher #19	517-373-6505
Third-Party Administrator #5	877-999-6442
Veterinarian/Veterinary Technician #15	517-241-9427
Well Contractor #20	517-241-1389

Michigan Licensing Agency Information

1 Bureau of State Lottery, PO Box 3023 (101 E Hillsdale), Lansing, MI 48909; 517-335-5756, Fax: 517-373-5644. www.michigan.gov/lottery

2 Department of Agriculture, Licensing, Certification & Registration, PO Box 30017 (525 W Alegan, 4th Fl), Lansing, MI 48909; 800-292-3939. www.michigan.gov/mda Email: mdainfo@state.mi.us Note: Food establishment licensing is at the local/county level.

3 Department of Consumer & Industry Services, Consumer Finance Division, PO Box 30220 (611 Ottawa, 2nd Fl), Lansing, MI 48909; 517-373-0220. www.michigan.gov/cis Email: ofis-fin-info@michigan.gov Search Database at www.michigan.gov/cis/0,1607,7-154-10555_13251_13257---,00.html

4 Department of Agriculture, Office of Racing Commissioner, 37650 Professional Center Dr, Livonia, MI 48154-1100; 734-462-2400, Fax: 734-462-2429. www.michigan.gov/mda

5 Department of Commerce, Financial and Insurance Services, PO Box 30220 (611 W Ottawa, 2nd Fl), Lansing, MI 48909; 877-999-6442, Fax: 517-335-4978. www.michigan.gov/ofis Email: ofis-ins-info@michigan.gov Search Database at www.michigan.gov/cis/0,1607,7-154-10555_13251_13262---,00.html

6 Department of Labor & Economic Growth, Liquor Control Commission, PO Box 30005 (7150 Harris Dr), Lansing, MI 48909-7505; 517-322-1345, Fax: 517-322-6137. www.michigan.gov/dleg email: lccinfo@cis.state.mi.us Search Database at http://www2.cis.state.mi.us:7778/llist/ Note: They do sell/provide lists or offer other means of verification.

7 Department of Consumer & Industry Services, Bureau of Construction Codes, PO Box 30254, Lansing, MI 48909; 517-241-9313, Fax: 517-241-9308. www.michigan.gov/bccfs

8 Department of Consumer & Industry Services, Commercial Services/Licensing Division, PO Box 30018, Lansing, MI 48909; 517-241-9288, Fax: 517-241-9280. www.michigan.gov/cis Search Database at http://cis.state.mi.us/verify.htm Note: Also, search licensees lists at http://cis.state.mi.us/bcs_free/default.asp.

9 Department of Consumer & Industry Services, Bureau of Commercial Services/Licensing Division, PO Box 30018, Lansing, MI 48909; 517-241-9254, Fax: 517-241-9280. www.michigan.gov/cis Search Database at http://cis.state.mi.us/verify.htm

10 Department of Consumer & Industry Services, Division of Emergency Medical Services, 525 W Ottawa, Lansing, MI 48909; 517-335-0918, Fax: 517-373-2179. www.michigan.gov/cis Search Database at www.michigan.gov/cis/0,1607,7-154-10557---,00.html

11 Department of Consumer & Industry Services, Occupational Health Division, PO Box 30671, Lansing, MI 48909-8171; 517-322-1320, Fax: 517-322-1713. www.cis.state.mi.us/bsr/divisions/occ/asbestos.htm

12 Department of Consumer & Industry Services, Securities Division, OFIS, PO Box 30220 (611 Ottawa, 2nd Fl), Lansing, MI 48909; 517-373-0220, Fax: 517-335-4978. www.michigan.gov/cis/ Email: ofis-sec-info@michigan.gov

13 Department of Consumer & Industry Svcs, Health and Human Svcs, 525 W Ottawa, Lansing, MI 48909; 517-335-0918, Fax: 517-333-6121. www.michigan.gov/cis/

14 Department of Consumer & Industry Services, Office of Financial & Insurance Services, PO Box 30224 (333 S. Capitol Ave, #A) (611 W Ottawa St), Lansing, MI 48933; 517-373-3460, Fax: 517-373-9475. www.michigan.gov/cis/ Email: ofis-fin-info@michigan.gov Search Database at www.cis.state.mi.us/fis/ind_srch/cht_bank/state_charter_bank_criteria.asp

15 Department of Consumer & Industry Services, Health Services Licensing Division, 611 W Ottawa, 1st Fl, Lansing, MI 48909-8170; 517-335-0918, Fax: 517-373-2179. www.michigan.gov/healthlicense Search Database at www.michigan.gov/healthlicense

16 Department of Consumer & Industry Services, Manufactured Home & Land Development Division, PO Box 30703, Lansing, MI 48909; 517-241-6300, Fax: 517-241-6301. www.michigan.gov/cis Search Database at www.cis.state.mi.us/bcs_free/

17 Bureau of Commercial Services, Commercial Services/Licensing Division/Security, P.O. Box 30018, Lansing, MI 48909; 517-241-9288, Fax: 517-241-9280. www.michigan.gov/cis Search Database at http://cis.state.mi.us/verify.htm

18 Department of Corrections, 206 E Michigan Ave, Lansing, MI 48909; 517-335-1426. www.michigan.gov/corrections

19 Department of Education, Office of Professional Preparation & Certification, Hannah Bldg, 2nd Fl, Lansing, MI 48909; 517-373-3310, Fax: 517-373-0542. www.michigan.gov/mde Search Database at http://meis.mde.state.mi.us/teachercert/sr_teaCerts.asp

20 Department of Environmental Quality, Ground Water Supply Sec., Well Construction, PO Box 30273 (525 W Allegan, 2nd Fl N), Lansing, MI 48909-7773; 517-241-1389, Fax: 517-241-1328. www.michigan.gov/deq Email: crigierj@state.mi.us Search Database at www.deq.state.mi.us/documents/deq-dwrpd-gws-reg-contractors-by-county.pdf

21 Department of Consumer & Industry Services, Bureau of Reg. Services-Div of Child Welfare Licensing/Child Foster Home Licensing, 7109 W Saginaw, 2nd Floor, Lansing, MI 48909-8150; 517-335-6108. www.michigan.gov/cis/ Search Database at www.michigan.gov/cis/0,1607,7-154-10568_17801---,00.html

22 Department of State, Office of the Great Seal, 717 W Allegan St, Lansing, MI 48918; 517-373-2531, Fax: 517-373-3706. www.michigan.gov/sos Email: www.sos.state.mi.us/greatse/index.html

23 Department of Consumer and Industry Services, Private Security & Investigator Unit, P.O. Box 30018, Lansing, MI 48909; 517-241-5645, Fax: 517-373-2162. www.michigan.gov/commerciallicensing Email: besinfo@michigan.gov Search Database at www.michigan.gov/commerciallicensing

24 Department of Transportation, Bureau of Aeronautics, 2700 E Airport Service Dr, Lansing, MI 48906; 517-335-9283, Fax: 517-321-6522. www.mdot.state.mi.us/aero Email: krashent@state.mi.us

25 Department of Treasury, Treasury Bldg, Lansing, MI 48922; 517-373-3200, Fax: 517-373-3553. www.michigan.gov/treasury/0,1607,7-121-1751_2220---,00.html Search Database at www.michigan.gov/documents/CertificationLevel_3022_7.pdf

26 Department of labor & Economic Growth, Family Independence Agency, 7109 W Saginaw, 2nd Fl, Lansing, MI 48909-8150; 517-373-8383, Fax: 517-335-6121. www.michigan.gov/cis/ Search Database at www.dleg.state.mi.us/brs_cwl/sr_cwl.asp

27 State Bar, 306 Townsend, Lansing, MI 48933; 800-968-1442, Fax: 517-482-6248. www.michbar.org Search Database at www.michbar.org/memberdirectory/

28 Business Licensing Section, Bureau of Automobile Regulation, 208 N Capitol Ave, Lansing, MI 48918; 517-373-9460, Fax: 517-335-2810. www.michigan.gov/sos

29 Bureau of Elections, Campaign Finance & Elections Reporting, PO Box 20126 (430 W Allegan St, Treasury Bldg, 1st Fl, 48913), Lansing, MI 48901-0726; 517-373-2540. http://miboecfr.nicusa.com Search Database at http://miboecfr.nicusa.com

Michigan Federal Courts

The following list indicates the district and division name for each county in the state. If the bankruptcy court location is different from the district court, then the location of the bankruptcy court appears in parentheses.

County/Court Cross Reference

County	District	Division
Alcona	Eastern	Bay City
Alger	Western	Marquette-Northern (Marquette)
Allegan	Western	Kalamazoo (Grand Rapids)
Alpena	Eastern	Bay City
Antrim	Western	Grand Rapids
Arenac	Eastern	Bay City
Baraga	Western	Marquette-Northern (Marquette)
Barry	Western	Grand Rapids
Bay	Eastern	Bay City
Benzie	Western	Grand Rapids
Berrien	Western	Kalamazoo (Grand Rapids)
Branch	Western	Lansing (Grand Rapids)
Calhoun	Western	Kalamazoo (Grand Rapids)
Cass	Western	Kalamazoo (Grand Rapids)
Charlevoix	Western	Grand Rapids
Cheboygan	Eastern	Bay City
Chippewa	Western	Marquette-Northern (Marquette)
Clare	Eastern	Bay City
Clinton	Western	Lansing (Grand Rapids)
Crawford	Eastern	Bay City
Delta	Western	Marquette-Northern (Marquette)
Dickinson	Western	Marquette-Northern (Marquette)
Eaton	Western	Lansing (Grand Rapids)
Emmet	Western	Grand Rapids
Genesee	Eastern	Flint
Gladwin	Eastern	Bay City
Gogebic	Western	Marquette-Northern (Marquette)
Grand Traverse	Western	Grand Rapids
Gratiot	Eastern	Bay City
Hillsdale	Western	Lansing (Grand Rapids)
Houghton	Western	Marquette-Northern (Marquette)
Huron	Eastern	Bay City
Ingham	Western	Lansing (Grand Rapids)
Ionia	Western	Grand Rapids
Iosco	Eastern	Bay City
Iron	Western	Marquette-Northern (Marquette)
Isabella	Eastern	Bay City
Jackson	Eastern	Ann Arbor (Detroit)
Kalamazoo	Western	Kalamazoo (Grand Rapids)
Kalkaska	Western	Grand Rapids
Kent	Western	Grand Rapids
Keweenaw	Western	Marquette-Northern (Marquette)
Lake	Western	Grand Rapids
Lapeer	Eastern	Flint
Leelanau	Western	Grand Rapids
Lenawee	Eastern	Ann Arbor (Detroit)
Livingston	Eastern	Flint
Luce	Western	Marquette-Northern (Marquette)
Mackinac	Western	Marquette-Northern (Marquette)
Macomb	Eastern	Detroit
Manistee	Western	Grand Rapids
Marquette	Western	Marquette-Northern (Marquette)
Mason	Western	Grand Rapids
Mecosta	Western	Grand Rapids
Menominee	Western	Marquette-Northern (Marquette)
Midland	Eastern	Bay City
Missaukee	Western	Grand Rapids
Monroe	Eastern	Ann Arbor (Detroit)
Montcalm	Western	Grand Rapids
Montmorency	Eastern	Bay City
Muskegon	Western	Grand Rapids
Newaygo	Western	Grand Rapids
Oakland	Eastern	Ann Arbor (Detroit)
Oceana	Western	Grand Rapids
Ogemaw	Eastern	Bay City
Ontonagon	Western	Marquette-Northern (Marquette)
Osceola	Western	Grand Rapids
Oscoda	Eastern	Bay City
Otsego	Eastern	Bay City
Ottawa	Western	Grand Rapids
Presque Isle	Eastern	Bay City
Roscommon	Eastern	Bay City
Saginaw	Eastern	Bay City
Sanilac	Eastern	Detroit
Schoolcraft	Western	Marquette-Northern (Marquette)
Shiawassee	Eastern	Flint
St. Clair	Eastern	Detroit
St. Joseph	Western	Kalamazoo (Grand Rapids)
Tuscola	Eastern	Bay City
Van Buren	Western	Kalamazoo (Grand Rapids)
Washtenaw	Eastern	Ann Arbor (Detroit)
Wayne	Eastern	Detroit
Wexford	Western	Grand Rapids

Standards for Federal Courts: The search fee is $20.00 per item (one party name or case number). Certification fee is $7.00 per document. Copy fee is $.50 per page. All fees standard unless noted in profile. Mail Search: always enclose a stamped self addressed envelope unless otherwise noted.

Most courts accept fax requests or will suggest a copying/search vendor. Before releasing records, courts require prepayment unless noted in profile.

Federal Courts Notes: Open records are located at the court unless otherwise noted. District courts index by defendant and plaintiff as well as by case number. Bankruptcy courts usually index by debtor and case number. While most courts now have their indexes on computer, many still maintain index card files as well.

PACER: The universal PACER sign-up number is 800-676-6856. Find PACER and the Party/Case

Index on the Web at http://pacer.psc.uscourts.gov. PACER dial-up access is $.60 per minute. Also, courts offering internet access via RACER, PACER, Web-PACER or the new CM-ECF charge $.07 per page fee unless noted as free.

US District Court

Eastern District of Michigan

Ann Arbor Division PO Box 8199, Ann Arbor, MI 48107 (courier address: 200 E Liberty St, Room 120, Ann Arbor, MI 48104), 734-741-2380, Fax: 734-741-2065. www.mied.uscourts.gov

Counties: Jackson, Lenawee, Monroe, Oakland, Washtenaw, Wayne. Civil cases in these counties are assigned randomly to the Detroit, Flint or Port Huron Divisions. Case files are maintained where the case is assigned.

Indexing & Storage: New cases available in the index immediately after filing date.

Fee & Payment: Payment may be made by money order, cashier check, personal check. Payee: Clerk, U.S. District Court.

Phone Search: Only docket information available.

In Person Search: Fee charged if court conducts your in person search for you.

PACER: PACER is available online at http://pacer.mied.uscourts.gov. New records are online after 2 days.

Electronic Filing: Electronic filing information online at https://ecf.mied.uscourts.gov

Bay City Division 1000 Washington Ave Rm 304, PO Box 913, Bay City, MI 48707 (Use mail address for courier delivery) 989-894-8800, Fax: 989-894-8804. www.mied.uscourts.gov

Counties: Alcona, Alpena, Arenac, Bay, Cheboygan, Clare, Crawford, Gladwin, Gratiot, Huron, Iosco, Isabella, Midland, Montmorency, Ogemaw, Oscoda, Otsego, Presque Isle, Roscommon, Saginaw, Tuscola.

Indexing & Storage: New cases available in the index 24 hours after filing date. Records are also indexed on microfiche. District wide searches are available for cases from this division.

Fee & Payment: Payment may be made by money order, cashier check, personal check. Payee: Clerk, U.S. District Court.

Phone Search: Only docket information available.

In Person Search: Fee charged if court conducts your in person search for you.

PACER: PACER is available online at http://pacer.mied.uscourts.gov. New records are online after 2 days.

Electronic Filing: Electronic filing information online at https://ecf.mied.uscourts.gov

Detroit Division 231 W Lafayette Blvd, Detroit, MI 48226 (courier address: Use mail address for courier delivery) 313-234-5005, Fax: 313-234-5393. www.mied.uscourts.gov

Counties: Macomb, St. Clair, Sanilac. Civil cases for these counties are assigned randomly among the Flint, Ann Arbor and Detroit divisions. Port Huron cases may also be assigned here. Case files are kept where the case is assigned.

Indexing & Storage: New cases available in the index 2 days after filing date. A card index is maintained for older cases. Court is in process of adding older records to the PACER system.

Fee & Payment: Payment may be made by money order, cashier check, personal check. Prepayment is required for all copying. Make checks for the exact amount. Payee: Clerk, U.S. District Court.

Phone Search: Only docket information on active cases will be released over the phone.

Mail Search: A SASE not required.

In Person Search: Fee charged if court conducts your in person search for you. Visa/MC may be used for payment in person.

PACER: PACER is available online at http://pacer.mied.uscourts.gov. New records are online after 2 days.

Electronic Filing: Electronic filing information online at https://ecf.mied.uscourts.gov

Flint Division Clerk, Federal Bldg, Room 140, 600 Church St, Flint, MI 48502 (courier: Use mail address for courier delivery) 810-341-7840. www.mied.uscourts.gov

Counties: Genesee, Lapeer, Livingston, Shiawassee. This office handles all criminal cases for these counties. Civil cases are assigned randomly among the Detroit, Ann Arbor and Flint divisions.

Indexing & Storage: New cases available in the index 2-5 days after filing date. As of July 3, 1995, cases from these counties may also be assigned to Detroit, Ann Arbor or Port Huron. Case files are maintained where the case is handled. Records are also indexed on microfiche. The only records indexed on index cards are old Flint cases. District wide searches are available from this division. The date the information is available varies.

Fee & Payment: Payment may be made by money order, cashier check, personal check. Payee: Clerk, U.S. District Court.

Phone Search: Only general information and a reasonable number of requests will be released over the phone. All docket data is not released.

Mail Search: A SASE not required.

In Person Search: permitted. A reasonable number of free searches can be requested in person. Searchers can search microfiched cases in person free. Court personnel can also conduct free searches for computer cases.

PACER: PACER is available online at http://pacer.mied.uscourts.gov. New records are online after 2 days.

Electronic Filing: Electronic filing information online at https://ecf.mied.uscourts.gov

U.S. Bankruptcy Court

Eastern District of Michigan

Bay City Division PO Box 911, Bay City, MI 48707 (courier address: 111 1st St, Bay City, MI 48708), 989-894-8840. www.mieb.uscourts.gov

Counties: Alcona, Alpena, Arenac, Bay, Cheboygan, Clare, Crawford, Gladwin, Gratiot, Huron, Iosco, Isabella, Midland, Montmorency, Ogemaw, Oscoda, Otsego, Presque Isle, Roscommon, Saginaw, Tuscola.

Indexing & Storage: Cases indexed by debtor as well as by case number. New cases available in the index immediately after filing date. District wide searches are available from this division for records filed on or after 10/1/92.

Fee & Payment: Payment may be made by money order, cashier check, personal check. Payee: U.S. Bankruptcy Court.

Phone Search: Use VCIS to obtain docket information. Automated voice case information service (VCIS) is available. Call VCIS at 877-422-3066 or 313-961-4940.

In Person Search: Permitted.

PACER: PACER is available online at http://pacer.mieb.uscourts.gov. Toll-free access: 800-498-5061. Local access: 313-961-4934. New civil records are online after 1-2 days.

Electronic Filing: Currently in the process of implementing CM/ECF.

Detroit Division Clerk, 21st Floor, 211 W Fort St, Detroit, MI 48226 (courier address: Use mail address for courier delivery) 313-234-0065. www.mieb.uscourts.gov

Counties: Jackson, Lenawee, Macomb, Monroe, Oakland, Sanilac, St. Clair, Washtenaw, Wayne.

Indexing & Storage: Cases indexed by debtor as well as by case number. New cases available in the index immediately after filing date. District wide searches are available from this division for records filed on or after 10/1/92.

Fee & Payment: Payment may be made by money order, cashier check, business check. Personal checks are not accepted. Payee: U.S. Bankruptcy Court.

Phone Search: Only the case number, case name, filing date, chapter, 341 date, attorney and trustee names will be released. Automated voice case information service (VCIS) is available. Call VCIS at 877-422-3066 or 313-961-4940.

In Person Search: Fee charged if court conducts your in person search for you.

PACER: PACER is available online at http://pacer.mieb.uscourts.gov. Toll-free access: 800-498-5061. Local access: 313-961-4934. New civil records are online after 1-2 days.

Electronic Filing: Currently in the process of implementing CM/ECF.

Flint Division 226 W 2nd St, Flint, MI 48502 (courier address: Use mail address for courier delivery) 810-235-4126. www.mieb.uscourts.gov

Counties: Genesee, Lapeer, Livingston, Shiawassee.

Indexing & Storage: Cases indexed by debtor as well as by case number. New cases available in the index immediately after filing date. District wide searches are available from this division for records filed on or after 10/1/92.

Fee & Payment: Payment may be made by money order, cashier check, business check. Personal checks are not accepted. Payee: Clerk, U.S. Bankruptcy Court.

Phone Search: Only the case number, case name, filing date, chapter, 341 date, attorney and trustee names will be released. Automated voice case information service (VCIS) is available. Call VCIS at 877-422-3066 or 313-961-4940.

In Person Search: Fee charged if court conducts your in person search for you.

PACER: PACER is available online at http://pacer.mieb.uscourts.gov. Toll-free access:

800-498-5061. Local access: 313-961-4934. New civil records are online after 1-2 days.

Electronic Filing: Currently in the process of implementing CM/ECF.

U.S. District Court

Western District of Michigan

Grand Rapids Division PO Box 3310, Grand Rapids, MI 49501 (courier address: Gerald Ford Federal Building, 110 Michigan St NW, Rm 399, Grand Rapids, MI 49503), 616-456-2381. www.miwd.uscourts.gov

Counties: Antrim, Barry, Benzie, Charlevoix, Emmet, Grand Traverse, Ionia, Kalkaska, Kent, Lake, Leelanau, Manistee, Mason, Mecosta, Missaukee, Montcalm, Muskegon, Newaygo, Oceana, Osceola, Ottawa, Wexford. The Lansing and Kalamazoo Divisions also handle cases from these counties.

Indexing & Storage: New cases available in the index 24-48 hours after filing date. Cases in these counties may also be tried in the Kalamazoo or Lansing courts.

Fee & Payment: Payment may be made by money order, cashier check, personal check. Will bill businesses and law firms for search and copy fees only; otherwise, Payee: Clerk, U.S. District Court.

Phone Search: Only docket information available by phone.

In Person Search: Fee charged if court conducts your in person search for you.

PACER: PACER is available online at http://pacer.miwd.uscourts.gov. Case records go back to September 1989. Records never purged. New records are online after 1-2 days.

Electronic Filing: Electronic filing information online at https://ecf.miwd.uscourts.gov

Kalamazoo Division 410 W Michigan, Rm B-35, Kalamazoo, MI 49007 (courier address: Use mail address for courier delivery) 269-337-5706. www.miwd.uscourts.gov

Counties: Allegan, Berrien, Calhoun, Cass, Kalamazoo, St. Joseph, Van Buren. Also handle cases from counties in the Grand Rapids Division.

Indexing & Storage: New cases available in the index 24-48 hours after filing date.

Fee & Payment: Payment may be made by money order, cashier check, personal check, Visa, Mastercard. Prepayment is required, except for law firms. Payee: Clerk, U.S. District Court.

Phone Search: Only docket information available.

In Person Search: Fee charged if court conducts your in person search for you.

PACER: PACER is available online at http://pacer.miwd.uscourts.gov. Case records go back to September 1989. Records never purged. New records are online after 1-2 days.

Electronic Filing: Electronic filing information online at https://ecf.miwd.uscourts.gov

Lansing Division 113 Federal Building, 315 W Allegan, Rm 101, Lansing, MI 48933 (courier address: Use mail address for courier delivery) 517-377-1559. www.miwd.uscourts.gov

Counties: Branch, Clinton, Eaton, Hillsdale, Ingham. Also handle cases from the counties in the Grand Rapids Division.

Indexing & Storage: New cases available in the index 24-48 hours after filing date.

Fee & Payment: Payment may be made by money order, cashier check, personal check, Visa, Mastercard. Prepayment is required except from businesses and law firms. Payee: Clerk, U.S. District Court.

Phone Search: Only docket information available by phone.

In Person Search: Fee charged if court conducts your in person search for you.

PACER: PACER is available online at http://pacer.miwd.uscourts.gov. Case records go back to September 1989. Records never purged. New records are online after 1-2 days.

Electronic Filing: Electronic filing information online at https://ecf.miwd.uscourts.gov

Marquette-Northern Division PO Box 698, Marquette, MI 49855 (courier address: 202 W Washington, Room 229, Marquette, MI 49855), 906-226-2117, Fax: 906-226-6735. www.miwd.uscourts.gov

Counties: Alger, Baraga, Chippewa, Delta, Dickinson, Gogebic, Houghton, Iron, Keweenaw, Luce, Mackinac, Marquette, Menominee, Ontonagon, Schoolcraft.

Indexing & Storage: New cases available in the index 24-48 hours after filing date.

Fee & Payment: Payment may be made by money order, cashier check, personal check, Visa, Mastercard. Prepayment is required, except from businesses and law firms. Payee: Clerk, U.S. District Court.

Phone Search: Use a credit card for telephone searching. Copies will be mailed.

Mail Search: A SASE not required.

In Person Search: Fee charged if court conducts your in person search for you.

PACER: PACER is available online at http://pacer.miwd.uscourts.gov. Case records go back to September 1989. Records never purged. New records are online after 1-2 days.

Electronic Filing: Electronic filing information online at https://ecf.miwd.uscourts.gov

U.S. Bankruptcy Court

Western District of Michigan

Grand Rapids Division PO Box 3310, Grand Rapids, MI 49501 (courier: 110 Michigan NW, Grand Rapids, MI 49503), 616-456-2693, Fax: 616-456-2919. www.miwb.uscourts.gov

Counties: Allegan, Antrim, Barry, Benzie, Berrien, Branch, Calhoun, Cass, Charlevoix, Clinton, Eaton, Emmet, Grand Traverse, Hillsdale, Ingham, Ionia, Kalamazoo, Kalkaska, Kent, Lake, Leelanau, Manistee, Mason, Mecosta, Missaukee, Montcalm, Muskegon, Newaygo, Oceana, Osceola, Ottawa, St. Joseph, Van Buren, Wexford. Marquette cases also available electronically on the Grand Rapids Division public access terminal.

Indexing & Storage: Cases indexed by debtor and creditors as well as by case number. New cases available in the index immediately after filing date. Records are on the computer from 1990.

Fee & Payment: Payment may be made by money order, cashier check, personal check, Visa or Mastercard. \Checks will not be accepted from debtors. Payee: U.S. Bankruptcy Court. Will fax back results.

Phone Search: The court will only verify by phone whether a case was filed. Automated voice case information service (VCIS) is available. Call VCIS at 616-456-2075. Will fax back results.

In Person Search: Fee charged if court conducts your in person search for you.

PACER: PACER is available online at http://pacer.miwb.uscourts.gov. Records purged six months after case closed. New civil records are online after 1 day.

Electronic Filing: Electronic filing information online at https://ecf.miwb.uscourts.gov

Marquette Division PO Box 909, Marquette, MI 49855 (courier address: 202 W Washington, Room 314, Marquette, MI 49855), 906-226-2117, Fax: 906-226-7388. www.miwb.uscourts.gov

Counties: Alger, Baraga, Chippewa, Delta, Dickinson, Gogebic, Houghton, Iron, Keweenaw, Luce, Mackinac, Marquette, Menominee, Ontonagon, SchoolcraftMarquette cases are also available electronically on the Grand Rapids Division public access terminal, but Grand Rapids cases are not available on Marquette's pub access computer as yet.

Indexing & Storage: Cases indexed by debtor as well as by case number. New cases available in the index immediately after filing date. Records are on computer from 1990.

Fee & Payment: Payment may be made by money order, cashier check, personal check, Visa or Mastercard. Checks from debtors not accepted. Payee: U.S. Bankruptcy Court. Will fax results at $.50 per page.

Phone Search: The court will only verify by phone if a case is filed. Automated voice case information service (VCIS) is available. Call VCIS at 616-456-2075. Will fax results at $.50 per page.

Mail Search: For the fee, the following items will be sent: Case number, list of creditors, and when the first meeting of creditors is scheduled. A SASE not required.

In Person Search: Fee charged if court conducts your in person search for you.

PACER: PACER is available online at http://pacer.miwb.uscourts.gov. Records purged six months after case closed. New civil records are online after 1 day.

Electronic Filing: Electronic filing information online at https://ecf.miwb.uscourts.gov

Michigan County Courts

Court	Jurisdiction	No. of Courts	How Organized
Circuit Courts*	General	83	57 Circuits
District Courts*	Limited	104	98 Districts
Municipal Courts	Municipal	5	
Probate Courts*	Probate	78	83 Counties

* Profiled in this Sourcebook.

Court	CIVIL								
	Tort	Contract	Real Estate	Min. Claim	Max. Claim	Small Claims	Estate	Eviction	Domestic Relations
Circuit Courts*	X	X	X	$25,000	No Max				X
District Courts*	X	X	X	$0	$25,000	$3000		X	
Municipal Courts	X	X	X	$0	$3000				
Probate Courts*							X		

Court	CRIMINAL				
	Felony	Misdemeanor	DWI/DUI	Preliminary Hearing	Juvenile
Circuit Courts*	X				X
District Courts*		X	X	X	
Municipal Courts		X	X	X	
Probate Courts*					

ADMINISTRATION

State Court Administrator, 309 N. Washington Sq, PO Box 30048, Lansing, MI, 48909; 517-373-2222, Fax: 517-373-2112. http://courts.michigan.gov/scao/

COURT STRUCTURE

The Circuit Court is the court of general jurisdiction. District Courts and Municipal Courts have jurisdiction over certain minor felonies and handle all preliminary hearings.

There is a Court of Claims in Lansing that is a function of the 30th Circuit Court with jurisdiction over claims against the state of Michigan. A Recorder's Court in Detroit was abolished as of October 1, 1997.

As of January 1, 1998, the Family Division of the Circuit Court was created. Domestic relations actions and juvenile cases, including criminal and abuse/neglect, formerly adjudicated in the Probate Court, were transferred to the Family Division of the Circuit Court. Mental health and estate cases continue to be handled by the Probate Courts.

Several counties (Barry, Berrien, Iron, Isabella, Lake, and Washtenaw) and the 46th Circuit Court are participating in a "Demonstration" pilot project designed to streamline court services and consolidate case management. These courts may refer to themselves as County Trial Courts.

ONLINE ACCESS

There is a wide range of online computerization of the judicial system from "none" to "fairly complete," but there is no statewide court records network. Some Michigan courts provide public access terminals in clerk's offices, and some courts are developing off-site electronic filing and searching capability. A few offer remote online to the public. The Criminal Justice Information Center (CJIC), the repository for MI criminal record info, offers online access. Results are available in seconds; fee is $10.00 per name. Go to www.michigan.gov/ichat or call 517-322-5546. Subscribe to email updates of appellate opinions at http://courtofappeals.mijud.net/resources/subscribe.htm. There is no fee.

ADDITIONAL INFORMATION

Court records are considered public except for specific categories: controlled substances, spousal abuse, Holmes youthful trainee, parental kidnapping, set aside convictions and probation, and sealed records. Courts will, however, affirm that cases exist and provide case numbers. Some courts will not perform criminal searches. Rather, they refer requests to the State Police. Note that costs, search requirements, and procedures vary widely because each jurisdiction may create its own administrative orders.

Alcona County

23rd Circuit Court PO Box 308, Harrisville, MI 48740; 989-724-6807; Fax: 989-724-5838. Hours: 8:30AM-Noon, 1-4:30PM (EST). *Felony, Civil Actions Over $25,000.*
Civil Records: Access: Phone, mail, in person. Only the court performs in person searches; visitors may not. No search fee. Required to search: name, years to search. Civil cases indexed by defendant, plaintiff. Civil records on computer since 1990, pleading headings in books since 1869.
Criminal Records: Access: Phone, mail, in person. Only the court performs in person searches; visitors may not. No search fee. Required to search: name, years to search, DOB. Criminal records on computer since 1990, pleading headings in books since 1869.
General Information: No suppressed, juvenile, sex offenders, mental health, or adoption records released. Copy fee: $1.00 per page. Certification fee: $10.00 plus $1.00 per page after first. Payee: Alcona County Clerk. Personal checks accepted. Prepayment required. Mail requests: SASE required. Mail turnaround time 1-2 days.

81st District Court PO Box 385, Harrisville, MI 48740; 989-724-5313; Fax: 989-724-5397. Hours: 8:30AM-4:30PM (EST). *Misdemeanor, Civil Actions Under $25,000, Eviction, Small Claims.*
Civil Records: Access: Phone, fax, mail, in person. Both court and visitors may perform in person searches. Search fee: $5.00. Required to search: name, years to search. Civil cases indexed by defendant, plaintiff. Civil records on books since 1980; on computer back to 1997.
Criminal Records: Access: Fax, mail, in person. Both court and visitors may perform in person searches. Search fee: $5.00. Required to search: name, years to search, DOB; also helpful: SSN. Criminal records on books since 1980; on computer back to 1997.
General Information: No suppressed, juvenile, sex offenders, mental health, or adoption records released. Fee to fax results is $10.00 1st page, $1.00 each add'l. Copy fee: $1.00 per page. Certification fee: $15.00. Payee: 81st District Court. Personal checks accepted. Prepayment required. Mail requests: SASE required. Mail turnaround time 1 week.

Probate Court PO Box 328, Harrisville, MI 48740; 989-724-6880; Fax: 989-724-6196. Hours: 8:30AM-4:30PM (EST). *Probate.*

Alger County

11th Circuit Court 101 Court St, PO Box 538, Munising, MI 49862; 906-387-2076; Fax: 906-387-2156. Hours: 8AM-4PM (EST). *Felony, Civil Actions Over $25,000.*
Civil Records: Access: Phone, mail, in person. Both court and visitors may perform in person searches. No search fee. Required to search: name, years to search. Civil cases indexed by defendant, plaintiff. Civil records on index books back to 1884; on computer back to 2000.
Criminal Records: Access: Phone, mail, in person. Both court and visitors may perform in person searches. No search fee. Required to search: name, years to search. Criminal records on index books back to 1884; on computer back to 2000.
General Information: No juvenile, sex offenders, mental health, or adoption records released. Will fax results to toll-free number. Copy fee: $1.00 per page. Certification fee: $10.00 plus $1.00 per page after first. Payee: Alger County Clerk. Personal checks accepted. Prepayment required. Mail turnaround time 1 week.

93rd District Court PO Box 186, Munising, MI 49862; 906-387-3879; Fax: 906-387-2688. Hours: 8AM-4PM (EST). *Misdemeanor, Civil Actions Under $25,000, Eviction, Small Claims.*
Civil Records: Access: Mail, in person. Only the court performs in person searches; visitors may not. Search fee: $10.00 per name. Required to search: name, years to search. Civil cases indexed by defendant, plaintiff. Civil records on index books from 1988; on computer back to 2000.
Criminal Records: Access: Fax, mail, in person. Only the court performs in person searches; visitors may not. Search fee: $10.00 per name. Required to search: name, years to search, DOB. Criminal records on index books from 1988; on computer back to 2000.
General Information: No suppressed records released. Will fax results to local or toll free line. Copy fee: $.25 per page. Certification fee: $15.00. Payee: District Court. Business checks accepted. Prepayment required. Mail requests: SASE required. Mail turnaround time 5-7 days.

Probate Court 101 Court St, Munising, MI 49862; 906-387-2080; Fax: 906-387-4134. Hours: 8AM-Noon, 1-4PM (EST). *Probate.*

Allegan County

48th Circuit Court 113 Chestnut St, Allegan, MI 49010; 269-673-0300; Probate phone: 269-673-0250; Fax: 269-673-0298. Hours: 8AM-5PM (EST). *Felony, Civil Actions Over $25,000.*
Civil Records: Access: Mail, in person. Only the court performs in person searches; visitors may not. Search fee: $5.00 per name. Required to search: name, years to search. Civil cases indexed by defendant, plaintiff. Civil records on computer since 1985.
Criminal Records: Access: Mail, in person. Only the court performs in person searches; visitors may not. Search fee: $5.00 per name. Required to search: name, years to search, DOB; also helpful: SSN. Criminal records on computer since 1985.
General Information: No suppressed, juvenile, sex offenders, mental health, or adoption records released. Will fax results to local or toll free line. Copy fee: $1.00 per page. Certification fee: $10.00. Payee: Allegan County Clerk. Personal checks accepted. Visa, MC accepted for fax filings only. Prepayment required. Mail requests: SASE required. Mail turnaround time 1-7 days.

57th District Court 113 Chestnut St, Allegan, MI 49010; 269-673-0400; Civil phone: 269-673-0355; Criminal phone: 269-673-0400. Hours: 8:30AM-4:30PM (EST). *Misdemeanor, Civil Actions Under $25,000, Eviction, Small Claims.*
www.allegancounty.org/districtct/index.htm
Civil Records: Access: Mail, in person. Both court and visitors may perform in person searches. No search fee. Required to search: name, years to search. Civil cases indexed by defendant, plaintiff. Civil records on index books.
Criminal Records: Access: Mail, in person. Both court and visitors may perform in person searches. No search fee. Required to search: name, years to search, DOB. Criminal records on index books.
General Information: Public Access terminal is available. No non-public records released. Will fax results to local or toll free line. Copy fee: $1.00 per page. Certification fee: $10.00. Payee: 57th District Court. Prepayment required. Mail turnaround: 1 week.

Probate Court 2243 33rd St, Allegan, MI 49010; 269-673-0250; Fax: 269-673-5875. Hours: 8AM-5PM (EST). *Probate.*

Alpena County

26th Circuit Court 720 West Chisholm #2, Alpena, MI 49707; 989-354-9520; Fax: 989-356-9644. Hours: 8:30AM-4:30PM (EST). *Felony, Civil Actions Over $25,000.*
Civil Records: Access: Fax, mail, in person. Only the court performs in person searches; visitors may not. Search fee: $5.00 per name. Required to search: name, years to search. Civil cases indexed by defendant, plaintiff. Civil records on computer since 1988, prior on docket books.
Criminal Records: Access: Fax, mail, in person. Only the court performs in person searches; visitors may not. Search fee: $5.00 per name. Required to search: name, years to search. Criminal records on computer since 1988; prior on docket books.
General Information: No suppressed, juvenile, sex offenders, mental health, or adoption records released. Will fax results for $5.00 per document plus $1.00 per page. Copy fee: $2.00 per page. Certification fee: $10.00 plus $1.00 per page after first. Payee: County Clerk. Personal checks accepted. Prepayment required. Mail requests: SASE required. Mail turnaround time 3-4 days.

88th District Court 719 West Chisholm #3, Alpena, MI 49707; 989-354-9678; Fax: 989-354-9678. Hours: 8:30AM-4:30PM (EST). *Misdemeanor, Civil Actions Under $25,000, Eviction, Small Claims.*
Civil Records: Access: Fax, mail, in person. Only the court performs in person searches; visitors may not. No search fee. Required to search: name, years to search. Civil cases indexed by defendant, plaintiff. Civil records on computer back to 1989, prior on cards back to 1970s.
Criminal Records: Access: Fax, mail, in person. Only the court performs in person searches; visitors may not. No search fee. Required to search: name, years to search, DOB; also helpful: SSN. Criminal records on computer back to 1989, prior on cards back to 1970s.
General Information: No suppressed, juvenile, sex offenders, mental health, or adoption records released. Will fax results to local or toll free line. Copy fee: $1.00 per page. No certification fee. Payee: 88th District Court. Only cashiers checks and money orders accepted. Prepayment required. Mail requests: SASE required. Mail turnaround time 1-2 days.

Probate Court 719 West Chisholm St, Alpena, MI 49707; 989-354-9650; Fax: 989-354-9782. Hours: 8:30AM-4:30PM (EST). *Probate.*

Antrim County

13th Circuit Court PO Box 520, Bellaire, MI 49615; 231-533-6353; Probate phone: 231-533-6681; Fax: 231-533-6935. Hours: 8:30AM-5PM (EST). *Felony, Civil Actions Over $25,000.*
Civil Records: Access: Fax, mail, in person. Both court and visitors may perform in person searches. Search fee: $5.00 per name. Required to search: name, years to search. Civil cases indexed by defendant, plaintiff. Civil records on computer since 1977, prior on books. Only court can search on computer, in person searchers may look at old records on docket books.
Criminal Records: Access: Fax, mail, in person. Both court and visitors may perform in person searches. Search fee: $5.00 per name. Required to search: name, years to search; also helpful: SSN, DOB. Criminal records on books from 1800s, on computer since 1997. Only court can search on computer, in person searchers may review old docket books.
General Information: No suppressed, juvenile, sex offenders, or adoption records released.

Will fax results $5.00 per doc. Copy fee: $1.00 per page. Certification fee: $10.00 plus $1.00 per page. Payee: Antrim County Clerk. Prepayment required. Mail requests: SASE required. Mail turnaround time 1 week.

86th District Court PO Box 597, Bellaire, MI 49615; 231-533-6441; Fax: 231-533-6322. Hours: 8AM-4:30PM (EST). *Misdemeanor, Civil Actions Under $25,000, Eviction, Small Claims.*
Civil Records: Access: Fax, mail, in person. Only the court performs in person searches; visitors may not. Search fee: $10.00. Required to search: name, years to search. Civil cases indexed by defendant, plaintiff. Civil records on computer since 1986, prior on cards.
Criminal Records: Access: Fax, mail, in person. Only the court performs in person searches; visitors may not. Search fee: $10.00 per name. Required to search: name, years to search, DOB; also helpful: SSN. Criminal records on computer since 1986, prior on cards.
General Information: No suppressed, sex offenders records released. Will fax results. Copy fee: $1.00 per page. Certification fee: $10.00. Payee: District Court. Business checks accepted. Prepayment required. Mail requests: SASE not required. Mail turnaround time usually same day.

Probate Court 205 Cayuga St, PO Box 130, Bellaire, MI 49615; 231-533-6681; Fax: 231-533-6600. Hours: 8:30AM-12;00, 12;30-4:30PM (EST). *Probate.*

Arenac County

23rd Circuit Court 120 N Grove St, PO Box 747, Standish, MI 48658; 989-846-9186; Fax: 989-846-9199. Hours: 8:30AM-5PM (EST). *Felony, Civil Actions Over $25,000.*
Civil Records: Access: Mail, in person. Both the court and visitors may perform in person searches. Search fee: $5.00 per name. Required to search: name, years to search. Civil cases indexed by defendant, plaintiff. Civil records go back to 1883, civil records on computer back to 1991, prior on index books.
Criminal Records: Access: Mail, in person. Both the court and visitors may perform in person searches. Search fee: $5.00 per name. Required to search: name, years to search, DOB; also helpful: SSN. Criminal records go back to 1883, criminal records on computer back to 1991, prior on index books.
General Information: Public Access terminal is available. No suppressed, juvenile, mental health, or adoption records released. Copy fee: $1.00 per page. Certification fee: $10.00 plus $1.00 per page after first. Payee: Arenac County Clerk. Personal checks accepted. Prepayment required. Mail requests: SASE required. Mail turnaround time 1-5 days.

81st District Court PO Box 129, Standish, MI 48658; 989-846-9538; Fax: 989-846-2008. Hours: 8:30AM-5PM (EST). *Misdemeanor, Civil Actions Under $25,000, Eviction, Small Claims.*
Civil Records: Access: Phone, fax, mail, in person. Only the court performs in person searches; visitors may not. Search fee: $5.00. Required to search: name, years to search. Civil cases indexed by defendant, plaintiff. Civil records on computer since 1990, prior on docket books.
Criminal Records: Access: Phone, fax, mail, in person. Only the court performs in person searches; visitors may not. Search fee: $5.00. Required to search: name, years to search, DOB; also helpful: SSN. Criminal records on computer since 1990, prior on cards by name.
General Information: No suppressed, juvenile, sex offenders, mental health, or adoption records released. Will fax results $2.00 1st page, $.50 each add'l. No

charge for fax cover sheet. Copy fee: $.25 per page. No certification fee. Payee: 81st District Court. Personal checks accepted. Prepayment required. Mail requests: SASE required. Mail turnaround time 5 days.

Probate Court 120 N Grove, PO Box 666, Standish, MI 48658; 989-846-6941; Fax: 989-846-6757. Hours: 8:30AM-5PM (EST). *Probate.*

Baraga County

12th Circuit Court 16 North 3rd St, L'Anse, MI 49946; 906-524-6183; Fax: 906-524-6186. Hours: 8:30AM-4:30PM (EST). *Felony, Civil Actions Over $25,000.*
Civil Records: Access: Phone, mail, in person. Both court and visitors may perform in person searches. Search fee: $5.00. Required to search: name, years to search. Civil cases indexed by defendant, plaintiff. Civil records on docket books, are computerized since 1998.
Criminal Records: Access: Phone, mail, in person. Both court and visitors may perform in person searches. Search fee: $5.00 per name. Required to search: name, years to search, DOB; also helpful: SSN. Criminal records on docket books, are computerized since 1998.
General Information: Public Access terminal is available. No suppressed records released. Will fax back results. Copy fee: $2.00 per page. Certification fee: $10.00 plus $1.00 per page after first. Payee: County Clerk. Personal checks accepted. Prepayment required. Mail requests: SASE required. Mail turnaround time same day.

97th District Court 16 North 3rd St, L'Anse, MI 49946; 906-524-6109; Fax: 906-524-7017. Hours: 8:30AM-Noon,1-4:30PM (EST). *Misdemeanor, Civil Actions Under $25,000, Eviction, Small Claims.*
Civil Records: Access: Mail, in person. Only the court performs in person searches; visitors may not. Search fee: $10.00 per name. Required to search: name, years to search. Civil cases indexed by defendant, plaintiff. Civil records listed on docket books since 1968.
Criminal Records: Access: Mail, in person. Only the court performs in person searches; visitors may not. Search fee: $10.00 per name. Required to search: name, years to search, DOB; also helpful: SSN. Criminal records listed on docket books since 1968.
General Information: No suppressed, sex offenders records released. Copy fee: $1.00 per page. Certification fee: $10.00 plus $1.00 per page after first. Payee: 97th District Court. Personal checks accepted. Prepayment required. Mail requests: SASE requested. Turnaround time 2-3 days.

Probate Court County Courthouse, 16 N 3rd St, L'Anse, MI 49946; 906-524-6390; Fax: 906-524-6186. Hours: 8:30AM-Noon, 1-4:30PM (EST). *Probate.*

Barry County

5th Circuit Court 220 W State St, Hastings, MI 49058; 269-945-1285; Fax: 269-945-0209. Hours: 8AM-5PM (EST). *Felony, Civil Actions Over $25,000.*
www.barrycounty.org
Civil Records: Access: Fax, mail, in person. Only the court performs in person searches; visitors may not. Search fee: $5.00 per name. Required to search: name, years to search. Civil cases indexed by defendant, plaintiff. Civil records on computer since 1992, card index back to 1977, prior on books.
Criminal Records: Access: Fax, mail, in person. Only the court performs in person searches; visitors may not. Search fee: $5.00 per name. Required to search: name, years to search, DOB; also helpful:

SSN. Criminal records on computer since 1992, card index back to 1977, prior on books.
General Information: No suppressed, juvenile, sex offenders, mental health, or adoption records released. Will fax results $1.00 per page. Copy fee: $1.00 per page. Certification fee: $10.00. Payee: County Clerk. Personal checks accepted. Prepayment required. Mail requests: SASE required. Mail turnaround: 2 days.

56B District Court 206 W Court St #202, Hastings, MI 49058; 269-945-1404; Fax: 269-948-3314. Hours: 8AM-5PM (EST). *Misdemeanor, Civil Actions Under $25,000, Eviction, Small Claims.*
Civil Records: Access: Phone, fax, mail, in person. Only the court performs in person searches; visitors may not. Search fee: $5.00 per name. Required to search: name, years to search. Civil cases indexed by defendant, plaintiff. Civil records on computer since 1990, prior on index books.
Criminal Records: Access: Phone, fax, mail, in person. Only the court performs in person searches; visitors may not. Search fee: $5.00 per name. Required to search: name, years to search, DOB; also helpful: SSN. Criminal records on computer since 1990, prior on index books.
General Information: No suppressed, sex offenders, or mental health records released. Will fax results $1.00 per page. Copy fee: $.25 per page. Certification fee: $10.00 plus $1.00 per page after first. Payee: 56B District Court. Personal checks accepted. Prepayment required. Mail requests: SASE required. Mail turnaround time 2 days.

Probate Court 206 West Court St, #302, Hastings, MI 49058; 269-945-1390; Fax: 269-948-3322. Hours: 8AM-5PM (EST). *Probate.*
www.barrycounty.org/Departments/Probate.htm

Bay County

18th Circuit Court 1230 Washington Ave #725, Bay City, MI 48708-5737; 989-895-4265; Fax: 989-895-4099. Hours: 8AM-5PM (EST). *Felony, Civil Actions Over $25,000.*
http://baycountycourt.com
Civil Records: Access: Phone, fax, mail, in person. Both court and visitors may perform in person searches. No search fee. Required to search: name, years to search. Civil cases indexed by defendant, plaintiff. Civil records on computer for the last since 1986. Access the county courts' calendar of scheduled cases for free at www.baycountycourts.com/bcc/home.nsf/public/court_calendar.htm.
Criminal Records: Access: Phone, fax, mail, in person. Both the court and visitors may perform in person searches. No search fee. Required to search: name, years to search, DOB. Criminal records on computer for the last since 1986. Access the county courts' calendar of scheduled cases for free at www.baycountycourts.com/bcc/home.nsf/public/court_calendar.htm.
General Information: Public Access terminal is available. No suppressed records released. Copy fee: $.25 per page. Certification fee: $10.00. Payee: County Clerk. Personal checks accepted. Prepayment required. Mail requests: SASE requested. Turnaround time same day.

74th District Court 1230 Washington Ave, Bay City, MI 48708; 989-895-4232; Civil phone: 989-895-4203; Criminal phone: 989-895-4229; Fax: 989-895-4233. Hours: 8AM-5PM (EST). *Misdemeanor, Civil Actions Under $25,000, Eviction, Small Claims.*
www.baycountycourts.com
Note: Current docket data is on the website; in the future, case information will also be available.
Civil Records: Access: In person only. Visitors must perform in person searches for themselves. No search

fee. Required to search: name, years to search. Civil cases indexed by defendant, plaintiff. Civil records on computer since 1992, listed on index cards prior.

Criminal Records: Access: In person only. Visitors must perform in person searches for themselves. No search fee. Required to search: name, years to search, DOB; also helpful: SSN. Criminal records on computer since 1992, listed on index cards prior.

General Information: Public Access terminal is available. No suppressed, juvenile, sex offenders, mental health, or adoption records released. Copy fee: $1.00 per page. Certification fee: $10.00. Payee: 74th District Court. Personal checks accepted. Prepayment required.

Probate Court 1230 Washington, #715, Bay City, MI 48708; 989-895-4205; Fax: 989-895-4194. Hours: 8AM-5PM (EST). *Probate.*

Note: Access the county courts' calendar of scheduled cases for free at www.baycountycourts.co m/bcc/home.nsf/public/court_calendar.htm.

Benzie County

19th Circuit Court PO Box 377, Beulah, MI 49617; 231-882-9671 & 800-315-3593; Fax: 231-882-5941. Hours: 8AM-5PM (EST). *Felony, Civil Actions Over $25,000.*

Civil Records: Access: Phone, fax, mail, in person. Both court and visitors may perform in person searches. No search fee. Required to search: name, years to search. Civil cases indexed by defendant, plaintiff. Civil records on computer since 1980, records go back to 1869.

Criminal Records: Access: Phone, fax, mail, in person. Both court and visitors may perform in person searches. No search fee. Required to search: name, years to search. Criminal records on computer since 1980, records go back to 1869.

General Information: Public Access terminal is available. No suppressed or home-youthful training case records released. Will fax results $3.00 1st page, $1.00 each add'l. Copy fee: $.50 per page. Certification fee: $10.00 plus $1.00 per page after first. Payee: Benzie County Clerk. Personal checks accepted. Prepayment required. Mail requests: SASE not required. Mail turnaround time 1-2 days.

85th District Court PO Box 377, Beulah, MI 49617; 231-882-0019; Fax: 231-882-0022. Hours: 9AM-5PM (EST). *Misdemeanor, Civil Actions Under $25,000, Eviction, Small Claims.*

Civil Records: Access: Fax, mail, in person. Only the court performs in person name searches; visitors may not. Search fee: $3.00 per name. Required to search: name, years to search. Civil cases indexed by defendant, plaintiff. Civil records on computer back to 1990, prior on cards to 1965. Visitors may use the law library to do their own searches at no charge.

Criminal Records: Access: Fax, mail, in person. Only the court performs in person name searches; visitors may not. Search fee: $3.00 per name. Required to search: name, years to search, DOB; also helpful: SSN. Criminal records on computer back to 1990, prior on cards to 1965.

General Information: Public Access terminal is available. (The public access terminal can be used to look up by case number.) No suppressed, juvenile, sex offenders, mental health, or adoption records released. Will fax results for $3.00 for 1st page, $1.00 each add'l. Copy fee: $.50 per page. Certification fee: $10.00. Payee: 85th District Court. Personal checks accepted. Out of state checks not accepted. Prepayment required. Mail requests: SASE required. Mail turnaround time 1 week.

Probate Court 448 Court Pl, County Gov't Ctr., PO Box 377, Beulah, MI 49617; 231-882-9675; Fax: 231-882-5987. Hours: 8:30AM-Noon, 1-5PM (EST). *Probate.*

Berrien County

2nd Circuit Court 811 Port St, St Joseph, MI 49085; 269-983-7111 X8368; Fax: 269-982-8642. Hours: 8:30AM-5PM (EST). *Felony, Civil Actions Over $25,000.*
www.berriencounty.org
Civil Records: Access: Mail, in person. Only the court performs in person searches; visitors may not. Search fee: $10.00 per name. Required to search: name, years to search. Civil cases indexed by defendant, plaintiff. Civil records on computer since 1981, prior on books (domestic) back to 1835, (civil & criminal) back to 1837.

Criminal Records: Access: Mail, in person. Only the court performs in person searches; visitors may not. Search fee: $10.00 per name. Required to search: name, years to search, DOB; also helpful: SSN. Criminal records on computer since 1981, prior on books (domestic) back to 1835, (civil & criminal) back to 1837.

General Information: No suppressed, juvenile, sex offenders, mental health, or adoption records released. Will fax results to lcoal or toll free line. Copy fee: $1.00 per page. Certification fee: $13.00 plus $1.00 per page after first. Payee: Berrien County Clerk. Personal checks accepted. Prepayment required. Mail requests: SASE required. Mail turnaround: 2-3 days.

5th District Court - Trial Court Criminal Division Attn: Records, 811 Port St, St Joseph, MI 49085; 269-983-7111; Fax: 269-982-8643. Hours: 8:30AM-5PM (EST). *Misdemeanor, Civil Actions Under $25,000, Eviction, Small Claims.*
www.berriencounty.org
Civil Records: Access: Mail, in person. Both court and visitors may perform in person searches. In person requesters must call ahead five days in advance; records held for 3 add'l days. Searching is limited and must be supervised. Search fee: $10.00 per name. Required to search: name, years to search; also helpful: address. Civil cases indexed by defendant, plaintiff. Civil records on computer since 1988, on logs from 1976-87, on index cards from 1969-75. Will do civil record check searches for only seven years.

Criminal Records: Access: Mail, in person. Only the court performs in person searches; visitors may not. In person requesters must call ahead five days in advance; records held for 3 add'l days. Search fee: $10.00 per name. Required to search: name, years to search, DOB or SSN; also helpful: signed release, address. Criminal records on computer back ten years, on microfiche back to 1970.

General Information: No suppressed or mental health records released. Will fax results if prepaid. Copy fee: $1.00 per page; microfilm copies are $2.00 per page. Certification fee: $10.00 plus $1.00 per page after 1st; no charge if search fee is paid. Payee: 5th District Court. Personal checks accepted. Prepayment required. Mail requests: SASE not required. Mail turnaround time 5 days.

Probate Court 811 Port St., St Joseph, MI 49085; 269-983-7111 X8365; Fax: 269-982-8644. Hours: 8:30AM-5PM (EST). *Probate.*

Branch County

15th Circuit Court 31 Division St, Coldwater, MI 49036; 517-279-4306; Fax: 517-278-5627. Hours: 9AM-5PM (EST). *Felony, Civil Actions Over $25,000.*
www.co.branch.mi.us

Civil Records: Access: Mail, in person. Both court and visitors may perform in person searches. Search fee: $10.00 for 10 year search; $1.00 per name per each add'l year. Required to search: name, years to search. Civil cases indexed by defendant, plaintiff. Civil records on computer since 1988, prior in books back to 1830s.

Criminal Records: Access: Mail, in person. Both court and visitors may perform in person searches. Search fee: $10.00 for 10 year search; $1.00 per name per each add'l year. Required to search: name, years to search, DOB. Criminal records on computer since 1988, prior in books back to 1830s.

General Information: Public Access terminal is available. No suppressed records released. Will fax results if all other fees paid. Copy fee: $1.00 per page. Certification fee: $10.00 plus $1.00 per page. Payee: Branch County Clerk. Business checks accepted. Prepayment required. Mail requests: SASE required. Mail turnaround time 1-5 days.

3A District Court 31 Division St., Coldwater, MI 49036; 517-279-4308; Civil phone: 517-279-4331; Criminal phone: 517-279-4329; Fax: 517-279-4333. Hours: 8AM-5PM (EST). *Misdemeanor, Civil Actions Under $25,000, Eviction, Small Claims.*
www.branchcountycourts.com
Note: Small Claims is 279-4330; Traffic is 279-4328.

Civil Records: Access: Mail, in person. Only the court performs in person searches; visitors may not. Search fee: $10.00 per name. Required to search: name, years to search. Civil cases indexed by defendant, plaintiff. Civil records on computer since June 1991, prior on index books.

Criminal Records: Access: Mail, in person. Only the court performs in person searches; visitors may not. Search fee: $10.00 per name. Required to search: name, years to search, DOB; also helpful: SSN. Criminal records on computer since Oct. 1988.

General Information: No suppressed or non-public records released. Will fax results if search fee paid. Copy fee: $1.00 per page. Certification fee: $10.00. Payee: 3A District Court. Personal checks accepted. Credit cards accepted. Prepayment required. Mail turnaround time: immediate if possible, otherwise 2-3 days.

Probate Court 31 Division St., Coldwater, MI 49036; 517-279-4318; Fax: 517-279-0516. Hours: 8AM-Noon, 1-5PM (EST). *Probate.*

Calhoun County

37th Circuit Court 161 E Michigan Ave, Battle Creek, MI 49014-4066; 269-969-6518, 269-969-6530. Hours: 8AM-Noon, 1-5PM (EST). *Felony, Civil Actions Over $25,000.*
www.calhouncountymi.gov/Departments/CircuitCour t/OverviewCircuitCourt.htm
Civil Records: Access: Mail, in person. Both court and visitors may perform in person searches. Search fee: $5.00 per name. Required to search: name, years to search. Civil cases indexed by defendant, plaintiff. Civil records on computer since 1984, prior on microfilm. The court will provide case number, filed date, case title, case status, and date of final judgment for the search fee.

Criminal Records: Access: In person only. Both court and visitors may perform in person searches. Search fee: $5.00 per name. Required to search: name, years to search, DOB; also helpful: SSN. Criminal records on computer since 1984, prior on microfilm. The court refers requests to the State Police (517-322-5531). Searcher may view public court file if case number known.

General Information: No suppressed, juvenile, sex offenders, mental health, or adoption records released. Will fax results for $3.00 plus $1.00 per copy. Copy fee: $1.00 per page. Certification fee: $10.00 plus $1.00 per page. Payee: 37th Circuit Court Clerk. Personal checks accepted. Prepayment required. Mail requests: SASE required. Mail turnaround time 1 week; 2-3 weeks for microfilm records.

10th District Court 161 E Michigan Ave, Battle Creek, MI 49014; 269-969-6666; Civil phone: 269-969-6683; Criminal phone: 269-969-6678; Probate phone: 269-969-6794; Fax: 269-969-6663. Hours: 8:00AM-4PM (EST). *Misdemeanor, Civil Actions Under $25,000, Eviction, Small Claims.*
www.calhouncountymi.gov/Departments/DistrictCourt/OverviewDistrictCourt.htm
Note: The 10th District Court Marshall Branch's records and administration is now housed here.

Civil Records: Access: Mail, fax, in person. Visitors must perform in person searches for themselves. Search fee: $0.00 unless case is in archives, then $10.00. Required to search: name, years to search. Civil cases indexed by defendant, plaintiff. Civil records on computer back to 1986, prior on docket books. Public access terminal searches back to 10/1997. Fax requests must be signed.
Criminal Records: Access: Fax, mail, in person. Visitors must perform in person searches for themselves. Search fee: $0.00 unless case is in archives, then $10.00. Required to search: name, DOB; also helpful-case number. Criminal records on computer back to 1986, prior on docket books. Public access terminal searches back to 10/1997. One to five requests per day are accepted. Fax requests must be signed.
General Information: Public Access terminal is available. No suppressed or non-public records released. Will fax back results to an toll-free number only. Copy fee: $1.00 per page. Certification fee: $10.00 plus $1.00 per page after first. Payee: 10th District Court. Personal checks accepted. Visa, MC credit cards accepted. Prepayment required. Mail requests: SASE required. Mail turnaround time is 5 days.

Probate Court Justice Center, 161 E Michigan Ave, Battle Creek, MI 49014; 269-969-6794; Fax: 269-969-6797. 8AM-5PM (EST). *Probate.*
www.calhouncountymi.gov/Departments/ProbateCourt/OverviewProbateCourt.htm

Cass County

43rd Circuit Court 120 North Broadway, File Rm; 60296 M-62, #10, Cassopolis, MI 49031; 269-445-4416; Civil phone: 269-445-4453; Fax: 269-445-4406. Hours: 8AM-5PM (EST). *Felony, Civil Actions Over $25,000.*
Civil Records: Access: Phone, fax, mail, in person. Both court and visitors may perform in person searches. No search fee. Required to search: name, years to search. Civil cases indexed by defendant, plaintiff. Civil records on computer back to 1988; books since 1963.
Criminal Records: Access: Fax, mail, in person. Only the court performs in person searches; visitors may not. No search fee. Required to search: name, years to search, DOB; also helpful: SSN. Criminal records on computer back to 1988; books since 1963.
General Information: No suppressed, juvenile, sex offenders, mental health, or adoption records released. No fee to fax to a toll-free number. Copy fee: $1.00 per page. Certification fee: $10.00. Payee: Cass County Clerk. Business checks accepted. Prepayment required. Mail requests: SASE required. Mail turnaround time 2 weeks by mail.

4th District Court 60296 M 62 #10, Cassopolis, MI 49031-8716; 269-445-4424; Fax: 269-445-4486. Hours: 8AM-5PM (EST). *Misdemeanor, Civil Actions Under $25,000, Eviction, Small Claims.*
Civil Records: Access: Phone, mail, in person. Court may perform in person searches. No search fee. Required to search: name, years to search; also helpful: address. Civil cases indexed by defendant, plaintiff. Civil records on computer since 1988, indexed on cards prior back to 1969. You can fax requests, but results will not be returned by fax.
Criminal Records: Access: Phone, mail, in person. Court may perform in person searches. No search fee. Required to search: name, years to search, DOB; also helpful: address. Criminal records on computer since 1988, indexed on cards prior back to 1969. You can fax requests, but results will not be returned by fax.
General Information: No suppressed, juvenile, sex offenders, mental health, or adoption records released. Will fax results for $10.00 per name. Copy fee: $1.00 for first page, $.10 each add'l. Certification fee: $10.00 plus $1.00 per page after first. Payee: 4th District Court. Personal checks accepted. Prepayment required. Mail requests: SASE not required. Mail turnaround time 2 weeks.

Probate Court 60296 - M62, Cassopolis, MI 49031; 269-445-4454; Fax: 269-445-4453. Hours: 8AM-Noon, 1-5PM (EST). *Probate.*

Charlevoix County

33rd Circuit Court 203 Antrim St, Charlevoix, MI 49720; 231-547-7200; Fax: 231-547-7217. Hours: 9AM-5PM (EST). *Felony, Civil Actions Over $25,000.*
www.charlevoixcounty.org/clerk.asp
Civil Records: Access: Mail, by fax, in person. Only the court performs in person searches; visitors may not. No search fee. Required to search: name, years to search. Civil cases indexed by defendant, plaintiff. Civil records on computer from 1991, microfiche and archives from 1868.
Criminal Records: Access: Mail, by fax, in person. Only the court performs in person searches; visitors may not. No search fee. Required to search: name, years to search, DOB; also helpful: SSN. Criminal records on computer from 1991, microfiche and archives from 1868.
General Information: No suppressed, juvenile, adoption records released. Will fax results, usually same day. Copy fee: $1.00 per page. Certification fee: $10.00. Payee: Charlevoix County Clerk. Personal checks accepted. Prepayment required. Mail requests: SASE requested. Turnaround time 1 week.

90th District Court 301 State St, Court Bldg, Charlevoix, MI 49720; 231-547-7227; Civil phone: 231-547-7254; Fax: 231-547-7253. Hours: 9AM-5PM (EST). *Misdemeanor, Civil Actions Under $25,000, Eviction, Small Claims.*
Civil Records: Access: Phone, mail, fax, in person. Both court and visitors may perform in person searches. No search fee. Required to search: name, years to search. Civil cases indexed by defendant, plaintiff. Civil records on computer back to 1987, listed on index cards to 1963.
Criminal Records: Access: Mail, fax, in person. Both court and visitors may perform in person searches. No search fee. Required to search: name, years to search, DOB. Criminal records on computer back to 1987, listed on index cards to 1963.
General Information: Public Access terminal is available. No suppressed records released. Copy fee: $1.00 per page. Payee: 90th District Court. Personal checks accepted. Prepayment required. Mail requests: SASE helpful. Turnaround time 1-2 days.

Probate Court 301 State St, County Bldg, Charlevoix, MI 49720; 231-547-7214; 547-7215; Fax: 231-547-7256. 9AM-5PM (EST). *Probate.*
Note: Shares the same judge with Emmet County Probate Court.

Cheboygan County

53rd Circuit Court PO Box 70, Cheboygan, MI 49721; 231-627-8808. Hours: 8:30AM-5PM (EST). *Felony, Civil Actions Over $25,000.*
Civil Records: Access: Phone, mail, in person. Only the court performs in person searches; visitors may not. No search fee. Required to search: name, years to search. Civil cases indexed by defendant, plaintiff. Civil records on computer from 1987, index cards from 1886.
Criminal Records: Access: Phone, mail, in person. Only the court performs in person searches; visitors may not. No search fee. Required to search: name, years to search, DOB. Criminal records on computer from 1987, index cards from 1886.
General Information: Public Access terminal is available. No suppressed records released. Will fax results for $1.00 per page payable in advance. Copy fee: $1.00 per page. Certification fee: $10.00 plus $1.00 each add'l page. Payee: County Clerk. Personal checks accepted. Prepayment required. Mail requests: SASE requested. Turnaround time 3-4 days.

89th District Court PO Box 70, Cheboygan, MI 49721; 231-627-8809; Fax: 231-627-8444. Hours: 8:30AM-4PM (EST). *Misdemeanor, Civil Actions Under $25,000, Eviction, Small Claims.*
www.89thdistrictcourt.org
Civil Records: Access: Phone, fax, mail, in person. Both court and visitors may perform in person searches. No search fee. Required to search: name, years to search. Civil cases indexed by defendant, plaintiff. Civil records on computer back to 1988, microfilmed prior.
Criminal Records: Access: Phone, fax, mail, in person. Both court and visitors may perform in person searches. No search fee. Required to search: name, years to search, DOB. Criminal records on computer back to 1986.
General Information: Public Access terminal is available. No suppressed, juvenile, sex offenders, mental health, or adoption records released. No fee to fax results. Copy fee: $1.00 per page. Certification fee: $10.00 plus $1.00 per page after first. Payee: 89th District Court. Personal checks accepted. Prepayment required. Mail requests: SASE required. Mail turnaround time 3-4 days.

Probate Court 870 S Main St, PO Box 70, Cheboygan, MI 49721; 231-627-8823; Fax: 231-627-8868. Hours: 8:30AM-4:30PM (EST). *Probate.*

Chippewa County

50th Circuit Court 319 Court St, Sault Ste Marie, MI 49783; 906-635-6300; Fax: 906-635-6851. Hours: 8AM-5PM (EST). *Felony, Civil Actions Over $25,000.*
Civil Records: Access: Mail, in person. Only the court performs in person searches; visitors may not. Search fee: $5.00 per name. Fee is for 10 year search. Required to search: name, years to search. Civil cases indexed by defendant, plaintiff. Civil records on computer since 1990, prior on index books to late 1800s.
Criminal Records: Access: Mail, in person. Only the court performs in person searches; visitors may not. Search fee: $5.00 per name. Fee is for 10 year search. Required to search: name, years to search, DOB; also helpful: SSN. Criminal records on computer since 1990, prior on index books to late 1800s.

General Information: No suppressed, juvenile, sex offenders, mental health, or adoption records released. Will fax results to local or toll free line. Copy fee: $1.00 per page. Certification fee: $10.00 plus $1.00 per page after first. Payee: County Clerk. Personal checks accepted. Prepayment required. Mail requests: SASE not required. Mail turnaround time 1-2 days.

91st District Court 325 Court St, Sault Ste Marie, MI 49783; 906-635-6320; Fax: 906-635-7605. Hours: 9AM-4:30PM (EST). *Misdemeanor, Civil Actions Under $25,000, Eviction, Small Claims.*
Note: Call before faxing for instructions.

Civil Records: Access: Mail, fax, in person. Both court and visitors may perform in person searches. Search fee: $5.00 per name. Required to search: name, years to search. Civil cases indexed by defendant, plaintiff. Civil records on computer since 1989, prior on index books to 1968.
Criminal Records: Access: Mail, fax, in person. Both court and visitors may perform in person searches. Search fee: $5.00 per name. Required to search: name, years to search, DOB; also helpful: SSN. Criminal records on computer since 1989, prior on index books to 1968.
General Information: Public Access terminal is available. No suppressed, juvenile, or adoption records released. Will fax results to toll-free number. Copy fee: $1.00 per page. Certification fee: $10.00. Payee: 91st District Court. Only cashiers checks and money orders accepted. Prepayment required. Mail requests: SASE required. Mail turnaround time 10 days.

Probate Court 319 Court St., Sault Ste Marie, MI 49783; 906-635-6314; Fax: 906-635-6852. Hours: 9AM-5PM (EST). *Probate.*

Clare County

55th Circuit Court 225 West Main St, PO Box 438, Harrison, MI 48625; 989-539-7131; Fax: 989-539-6616. Hours: 8AM-4:30PM (EST). *Felony, Civil Actions Over $25,000.*
Civil Records: Access: Mail, in person. Only the court performs in person searches; visitors may not. Search fee: $6.00 per name. Add $1.00 per year if more than five. Required to search: name, years to search DOB. Civil cases indexed by defendant, plaintiff. Civil records on computer since 1992, on books from 1925.
Criminal Records: Access: Mail, in person. Only the court performs in person searches; visitors may not. Search fee: $6.00 per name. Add $1.00 per year if more than five. Required to search: name, years to search, DOB; also helpful: SSN. Criminal records on computer since 1992, on books from 1925.
General Information: No suppressed, juvenile, sex offenders, mental health, or adoption records released. Fax results will be sent to 800 fax numbers only. Copy fee: $1.00 per page. Certification fee: $10.00 per document plus $1.00 per page. Payee: Clare County Clerk. Personal checks accepted. Prepayment required. Mail requests: SASE required. Mail turnaround time 1-5 days.

80th District Court 225 W. Main St, Harrison, MI 48625; 989-539-7173; Fax: 989-539-4036. Hours: 8AM-4:30PM (EST). *Misdemeanor, Civil Actions Under $25,000, Eviction, Small Claims.*
Civil Records: Access: Mail, fax, in person. Only the court performs in person searches. Visitors may not. No search fee. Required to search: name, years to search. Civil cases indexed by defendant, plaintiff. Civil records go back to 1969; on computer back to 1988.
Criminal Records: Access: Mail, fax, in person. Only the court performs in person searches; visitors may not. Search fee: $5.00 per name;and $1.00 per yr

over 5yrs. Required to search: name, years to search, DOB, SSN. Criminal records go back to 1969; on computer back to 1988.
General Information: No suppressed, juvenile, sex offenders, mental health, or adoption records released. Copy fee: $1.00 per page. Certification fee: $10.00. Payee: 80th District Court. Personal checks accepted. Prepayment required. Mail requests: SASE required. Mail turnaround time 5 days.

Probate Court 225 W. Main St., PO Box 96, Harrison, MI 48625; 989-539-7109. Hours: 8AM-4:30PM (EST). *Probate.*
Note: This is combined with Gladwin County Probate Court.

Clinton County

29th Circuit Court PO Box 69, St Johns, MI 48879-0069; 989-224-5140; Fax: 989-227-6421. Hours: 8AM-5PM (EST). *Felony, Civil Actions Over $25,000.*
www.clinton-county.org
Civil Records: Access: Mail, in person. Both court and visitors may perform in person searches. Search fee: $10.00 per name. Fee is for 10 year search. Required to search: name, years to search. Civil cases indexed by defendant, plaintiff. Civil records in calendar books since 1800s, some on microfiche; on computer since 1996.
Criminal Records: Access: Mail, in person. Both court and visitors may perform in person searches. Search fee: $10.00 per name. Fee is for 10 year search. Required to search: name, years to search; also helpful: DOB. Criminal records in calendar books since 1800s, some on microfiche; on computer since 1996.
General Information: No suppressed or non public records released. Will fax results for $3.00 plus normal copy fee up to 20 pages. Copy fee: $1.00 per page. Certification fee: $10.00 plus $1.00 per page. Payee: Clinton County Clerk. Personal checks accepted. Prepayment required. Mail requests: SASE required. Mail turnaround time 24 hrs.

65th District Court 100 E State St, #3400, St Johns, MI 48879-1571; 989-224-5150; Fax: 989-224-5154. Hours: 8AM-5PM (EST). *Misdemeanor, Civil Actions Under $25,000, Eviction, Small Claims.*
Civil Records: Access: In person. Visitors must perform in person searches for themselves. No search fee. Required to search: name, years to search. Civil cases indexed by defendant, plaintiff. Civil records on computer since 1989-90.
Criminal Records: Access: In person. Visitors must perform in person searches for themselves. No search fee. Required to search: name, years to search, DOB, SSN. Criminal records on computer since 1986.
General Information: Public Access terminal is available. No suppressed, juvenile, sex offenders, mental health, or adoption records released. Copy fee: $1.00 per page. No certification fee. Payee: 65th District Court. Personal checks accepted. Prepayment required.

Probate Court 100 E State St #4300, St Johns, MI 48879; 989-224-5190; Fax: 989-224-5102. Hours: 8AM-5PM (EST). *Probate.*
www.clinton-county.org

Crawford County

46th Circuit Court 200 West Michigan Ave, Grayling, MI 49738; 989-348-2841; Fax: 989-344-3223. Hours: 8:30AM-3:30PM (EST). *Felony, Civil Actions Over $25,000.*
www.Circuit46.org
Civil Records: Access: Mail, in person, online. Only the court performs in person searches; visitors may

not. No search fee. Required to search: name, years to search. Civil cases indexed by defendant, plaintiff. Civil records on computer since 1990, prior on books to 1930s. Online access to court case records (closed cases for 90 days only) is free at www.circuit46.org/Cases/cases.html.
Criminal Records: Access: Mail, in person, online, phone,fax. Only the court performs in person searches; visitors may not. Search fee: $5.00 per name. Required to search: name, years to search, DOB. Criminal records on computer since 1990, prior on books to 1960. Online access to criminal records is the same as civil.
General Information: No suppressed records released. Copy fee: $1.00 per page. Certification fee: $10.00 plus $1.00 per page after first. Payee: Crawford County. Personal checks accepted. Prepayment required. Mail requests: SASE required. Mail turnaround time 2-3 days.

46th Circuit Trial Court - District Division 200 West Michigan Ave., Grayling, MI 49738; 989-348-2841 X242; Fax: 989-344-3290. Hours: 8AM-4:30PM (EST). *Misdemeanor, Civil Actions Under $25,000, Eviction, Small Claims.*
www.Circuit46.org
Civil Records: Access: Phone, mail, fax, in person, online. Only the court performs in person searches; visitors may not. No search fee. Required to search: name, years to search. Civil cases indexed by defendant, plaintiff. Civil records on computer since 1990, books from 1969. Online access to court case records (open or closed cases for 90 days only) is free at www.circuit46.org/Cases/cases.html.
Criminal Records: Access: Phone, mail, fax, in person, online. Only the court performs in person searches; visitors may not. No search fee. Required to search: name, years to search, DOB. Criminal records on computer since 1989. Online access to criminal records is the same as civil.
General Information: No suppressed, juvenile, sex offenders, mental health, or adoption records released. Copy fee: $1.00 per page. Certification fee: $10.00 plus $1.00 each add'l page. Payee: District Division Court. Personal checks accepted. Visa, MC accepted. Prepayment required. Mail requests: SASE not required. Mail turnaround time 1-4 days.

Probate Court 200 W Michigan Ave., Grayling, MI 49738; 989-344-3237; Fax: 989-344-3277. Hours: 8:00AM-4:30PM (EST). *Probate.*
www.Circuit46.org
Note: Search cases by name free online at www.circuit46.org/Cases/cases.html.

Delta County

47th Circuit Court 310 Ludington St, Escanaba, MI 49829; 906-789-5105; Fax: 906-789-5196. Hours: 8AM-4PM (EST). *Felony, Civil Actions Over $25,000.*
Civil Records: Access: Mail, in person. Both court and visitors may perform in person searches. Search fee: $5.00 per name. Required to search: name; also helpful: years to search, address. Civil cases indexed by defendant, plaintiff. Civil records on computer from 1986, archived into 1800s.
Criminal Records: Access: Mail, in person. Both court and visitors may perform in person searches. Search fee: $5.00 per name. Required to search: name; also helpful: years to search, DOB, SSN. Criminal records on computer from 1989, archived into 1800s.
General Information: No suppressed, juvenile, sex offenders, mental health, or adoption records released. Copy fee: $.25 per page. Certification fee: $10.00 plus $1.00 per page after first. Payee: Delta County. Personal checks accepted. Prepayment required. Mail

requests: SASE required. Mail turnaround time same day.

94th District Court 310 Ludington St., Escanaba, MI 49829; Civil phone: 906-789-5106; Criminal phone: 906-789-5108; Fax: 906-789-5198. Hours: 8AM-4PM (EST). *Misdemeanor, Civil Actions Under $25,000, Eviction, Small Claims.*
Civil Records: Access: Mail, in person. Only the court performs in person searches; visitors may not. Search fee: $5.00. Required to search: name, years to search; also helpful: address. Civil cases indexed by defendant, plaintiff. Civil records on computer back to 1988, prior on books to 1968.
Criminal Records: Access: Mail, in person. Only the court performs in person searches; visitors may not. Search fee: $5.00 per name. Required to search: name, years to search, DOB; also helpful: address, SSN. Criminal records on computer back to 1988, prior on books to 1968.
General Information: No suppressed, juvenile, sex offenders, mental health, or adoption records released. Will fax results to toll-free number. Copy fee: $.25 per page. Certification fee: $10.00. Payee: 94th District Court. Personal checks accepted. Prepayment required. Mail requests: SASE required. Mail turnaround time 3 days.

Probate Court 310 Ludington St., Escanaba, MI 49829; 906-789-5112; Fax: 906-789-5140. Hours: 8AM-Noon, 1-4PM (EST). *Probate.*

Dickinson County

41st Circuit Court PO Box 609, Iron Mountain, MI 49801; 906-774-0988; Fax: 906-774-4660. Hours: 8AM-4:30PM (CST). *Felony, Civil Actions Over $25,000.*
Civil Records: Access: Mail, in person. Both court and visitors may perform in person searches. Search fee: $15.00 per name. Fee is for 10 year search. Required to search: name, years to search. Civil cases indexed by defendant, plaintiff. Civil records on docket books since 1891; on computer since 05/95.
Criminal Records: Access: Mail, in person. Both court and visitors may perform in person searches. Search fee: $5.00 per name. Fee is for 10 year search. Required to search: name, years to search, DOB; also helpful: SSN. Criminal records on docket books since 1891; on computer since 05/95.
General Information: No suppressed, juvenile, sex offenders, mental health, or adoption records released. Fee to fax results is $1.50 per page. Copy fee: $1.00 per page. Certification fee: $10.00 plus $1.00 per page. Payee: County Clerk. Business checks accepted. Prepayment required. Mail requests: SASE required. Mail turnaround time 1-2 days.

95 B District Court County Courthouse, PO Box 609, Iron Mountain, MI 49801; 906-774-0506; Fax: 906-774-8560. Hours: 8AM-4:30PM (CST). *Misdemeanor, Civil Actions Under $25,000, Eviction, Small Claims.*
Note: May require a signed release for certain records.
Civil Records: Access: Phone, mail, fax. Only the court may perform in person searches. Search fee: $5.00 per name if pre-2/1995. Required to search: name, years to search; also helpful: address. Civil cases indexed by defendant, plaintiff. Civil records on index cards from 1981; on computer back to 2/1995.
Criminal Records: Access: Mail, fax, in person. Only the court may perform in person searches. Search fee: $5.00 per name if pre-2/1995. Required to search: name, years to search, DOB; also helpful: address, SSN. Criminal records on index cards from 1981; on computer back to 2/1995.
General Information: No suppressed, juvenile, sex offenders, mental health, or adoption records released. Copy fee: $1.00 per page. Certification fee: $10.00.

Payee: 95-B District Court. Only cashiers checks and money orders accepted. Prepayment required. Mail turnaround time 1 week.

Probate Court PO Box 609, Iron Mountain, MI 49801; 906-774-1555; Fax: 906-774-1561. Hours: 8AM-4:30PM (CST). *Probate.*

Eaton County

56th Circuit Court 1045 Independence Blvd, Charlotte, MI 48813; 517-543-7500 X396; Fax: 517-543-4475. Hours: 8AM-5PM (EST). *Felony, Civil Actions Over $25,000.*
www.eatoncountycourts.org/courts.html
Civil Records: Access: Phone, fax, mail, in person. Both court and visitors may perform in person searches. No search fee. Required to search: name, years to search. Civil cases indexed by defendant, plaintiff. Civil records on computer back to 1988, microfilm since 1930s, books from 1848.
Criminal Records: Access: Fax, mail, in person. Both court and visitors may perform in person searches. Search fee: $5.00 per name. Required to search: name, years to search, DOB; also helpful: SSN. Criminal records on computer back to 1985, microfilm since 1930s, books from 1860s.
General Information: No suppressed, juvenile, sex offenders, mental health, or adoption records released. Will fax results. Copy fee: $1.00 for first page, $.50 each add'l. Certification fee: $10.00. Payee: Eaton County Circuit Court Clerk. Personal checks accepted. Prepayment required. Mail requests: SASE required. Mail turnaround time 1-3 days.

56A District Court 1045 Independence Blvd, Charlotte, MI 48813; 517-543-7500; Civil phone: x281; Criminal phone: x283; Fax: 517-541-1469. Hours: 8AM-5PM (EST). *Misdemeanor, Civil Actions Under $25,000, Eviction, Small Claims.*
www.eatoncountycourts.org/courts.html
Civil Records: Access: Mail, fax, in person. Visitors must perform in person searches for themselves. Search fee: none. Required to search: name, years to search. Civil records on computer back to 1990; prior in books.
Criminal Records: Access: In person only. Visitors must perform in person searches for themselves. No search fee. Required to search: name, years to search, DOB; also helpful: SSN. Criminal records on computer back to 1990.
General Information: Public Access terminal is available. No suppressed, sex offenders, mental health, or adoption records released. Copy fee: $.30 per page. Certification fee: $10.00. Payee: 56A District Court. Personal checks accepted. Prepayment required. Mail requests: SASE required.

Probate Court 1045 Independence Blvd, Probate Court, Charlotte, MI 48813; 517-543-7500 X234. Hours: 8AM-5PM (EST). *Probate.*
www.eatoncountycourts.org/courts.html

Emmet County

57th Circuit Court 200 Division St, Petoskey, MI 49770; 231-348-1744; Fax: 231-348-0602. Hours: 8AM-5PM (EST). *Felony, Civil Actions Over $25,000.*
www.co.emmet.mi.us
Civil Records: Access: Mail, in person. Only the court performs in person searches; visitors may not. Search fee: $5.00 per name. Required to search: name, years to search. Civil cases indexed by defendant, plaintiff. Civil records on computer from 1867 to present.
Criminal Records: Access: Mail, in person. Only the court performs in person searches; visitors may not. Search fee: $5.00 per name. Required to search:

name, years to search, DOB. Criminal records on computer from 1867 to present.
General Information: No suppressed records released. Copy fee: $.50 per page. Certification fee: $10.00 plus $1.00 per page. Payee: Emmet County Clerk. Personal checks accepted. Visa, MC accepted. Prepayment required. Mail requests: SASE required. Mail turnaround time 5 days.

90th District Court 200 Division St., Petoskey, MI 49770; 231-348-1750; Civil phone: 231-348-1753; Criminal phone: 231-348-1752; Fax: 231-348-0616. Hours: 8AM-5PM (EST). *Misdemeanor, Civil Actions Under $25,000, Eviction, Small Claims.*
Civil Records: Access: Fax, mail, in person. Only the court performs in person searches; visitors may not. No search fee. Required to search: name, years to search. Civil cases indexed by defendant, plaintiff. Civil records on computer since 1981, prior listed in books.
Criminal Records: Access: Fax, mail, in person. Only the court performs in person searches; visitors may not. No search fee. Required to search: name, years to search, DOB; also helpful: SSN. Criminal records on computer since 1981, prior listed on microfiche.
General Information: No suppressed, juvenile, sex offenders, mental health, or adoption records released. Will fax results $6.00 1st page, $1.00 each add'l. Copy fee: $2.00 per page. Fee is for non-parties. Certification fee: $10.00. Payee: 90th District Court. Business checks accepted. Prepayment required. Mail turnaround time on all Division searches is 24 hours.

Probate Court 200 Division St., Petoskey, MI 49770; 231-348-1707; Fax: 231-348-0672. Hours: 8AM-5PM (EST). *Probate.*
Note: Shares the same judge with Charlevoix County Probate Court.

Genesee County

7th Circuit Court 900 South Saginaw, Flint, MI 48502; 810-257-3220; Probate phone: 810-257-3528. Hours: 8AM-5PM (EST). *Felony, Civil Actions Over $25,000, and domestic (i.e. Divorce, Support, Custody).*
www.co.genesee.mi.us
Note: Cases files could be located at one of seven lower courts in the county. The Clerk's index will indicate the exact location. Probate court is located in a separate office at the same address.

Civil Records: Access: Mail, in person, online. Both court and visitors may perform in person searches. Search fee: $5.00 per name. Required to search: name, years to search. Civil cases indexed by defendant, plaintiff. Civil records on computer since 1978, prior on index cards. Online access to court records is free at www.co.genesee.mi.us/clerk/#; click on "Circuit Court Records."
Criminal Records: Access: Mail, in person, online. Both court and visitors may perform in person searches. Search fee: $5.00 per name. Required to search: name, years to search, DOB; also helpful: SSN, sex. Criminal records on computer since 1978, prior on index cards. Online access to criminal records is the same as civil.
General Information: Public Access terminal is available. No suppressed, juvenile, adoption, or mental health records released. Will fax results. Copy fee: $1.00 per page. Certification fee: $10.00 plus $1.00 pe page. Payee: Genesee County Clerk. Business checks accepted. Prepayment required. Mail requests: SASE required. Mail turnaround time 1-2 weeks.

67th District Court 630 South Saginaw, Flint, MI 48502; 810-257-3170. Hours: 8AM-4PM (EST). *Misdemeanor, Civil Actions Under $25,000, Eviction, Small Claims.*
www.co.genesee.mi.us
Note: Cases files can be located at any one of 7 lower courts in the county. The Clerk's index will indicate the exact location.
Civil Records: Access: Mail, in person. Only the court performs in person searches; visitors may not. Search fee: $15.00 per name. Required to search: name, years to search; also helpful: address. Civil cases indexed by defendant, plaintiff. Civil records on computer since 1983, on microfilm since 1969, prior archived.
Criminal Records: Access: Mail, in person. Only the court performs in person searches; visitors may not. Search fee: $15.00 per name. Required to search: name, years to search, DOB, offense; also helpful: address, SSN. Criminal records on computer since 1983, on microfilm since 1969, prior archived.
General Information: No drug related case records released. Copy fee: $1.00 per page. Certification fee: $10.00. Payee: 67th District Court. Only cashiers checks, business checks, and money orders accepted. Prepayment required. Mail requests: SASE helpful. Turnaround time 1 week.

Probate Court 900 S Saginaw St #502, Flint, MI 48502; 810-257-3528; Fax: 810-257-2713. Hours: 8AM-4PM (EST). *Probate.*

Gladwin County

55th Circuit Court 401 West Cedar, Gladwin, MI 48624; 989-426-7351; Fax: 989-426-6917. Hours: 8:30AM-4:30PM (EST). *Felony, Civil Actions Over $25,000.*
Civil Records: Access: Fax, mail, in person. Both court and visitors may perform in person searches. Search fee: None, but if search requirements are not met, fee is $5.00. Required to search: name, years to search. Civil cases indexed by defendant, plaintiff. Civil records on computer since 1994, prior on books.
Criminal Records: Access: Fax, mail, in person. Both court and visitors may perform in person searches. Search fee: None, but if search requirements are not met, fee is $5.00. Required to search: name, years to search, DOB; also helpful: SSN. Criminal records on computer since 1994, prior on books.
General Information: No suppressed, juvenile, sex offenders, mental health, or adoption records released. Will fax results. Copy fee: $1.00 per page. Certification fee: $10.00 plus $1.00 per page after first. Payee: Gladwin County Clerk. Personal checks accepted. Prepayment required. Mail requests: SASE required. Mail turnaround time 2-3 days.

80th District Court 401 West Cedar, Gladwin, MI 48624; 989-426-9207; Fax: 989-246-0894. Hours: 8:30AM-4:30PM (EST). *Misdemeanor, Civil Actions Under $25,000, Eviction, Small Claims.*
Civil Records: Access: Mail, fax, in person. Only the court performs in person searches; visitors may not. No search fee. Required to search: name, years to search. Civil cases indexed by defendant, plaintiff. Civil records on computer since 1988, prior on index cards and docket books, archived to late 1968.
Criminal Records: Access: Mail, fax, in person. Only the court performs in person searches; visitors may not. Search fee: $1.00 per summery; $5.00 per case documents. Required to search: name, years to search, DOB; also helpful: SSN. Criminal records on computer since 1988, prior on index cards and docket books, archived to late 1968.
General Information: No suppressed, juvenile, sex offenders, mental health, or adoption records released. Copy fee: $1.00 per page. Certification fee: $10.00

plus $1.00 per page after first. Payee: 80th District Court. Personal checks accepted. Prepayment required. Mail requests: SASE required. Mail turnaround time same day when possible.

Probate Court 401 West Cedar, Gladwin, MI 48624; 989-426-7451; Fax: 989-426-6936. Hours: 8:30AM-4:30PM (EST). *Probate.*
Note: Combined with Clare County Probate Court.

Gogebic County

32nd Circuit Court 200 North Moore St, Bessemer, MI 49911; 906-663-4518; Probate phone: 906-667-0421; Fax: 906-663-4660. Hours: 8:30AM-4:30PM (CST). *Felony, Civil Actions Over $25,000.*
www.gogebic.org/circuit.htm
Civil Records: Access: Mail, in person. Only the court may perform in person searches. Search fee: $5.00 per name. Required to search: name, years to search. Civil cases indexed by defendant, plaintiff. Civil records in books since 1887, computerized since 1996.
Criminal Records: Access: Mail, in person. Only the court may perform in person searches. Search fee: $5.00 per name. Required to search: name, years to search, DOB; also helpful: SSN. Criminal records in books since 1887, computerized sionce 1996.
General Information: No suppressed, juvenile, sex offenders, mental health, or adoption records released. Will fax results for $1.50 per page. Copy fee: $1.00 per page. Certification fee: $10.00. Payee: Gogebic County Clerk's Office. Personal checks accepted. Prepayment required. Mail requests: SASE requested. Turnaround time 1-2 days.

98th District Court 200 North Moore St, Bessemer, MI 49911; 906-663-4611; Fax: 906-667-1102. Hours: 8:30AM-4:30PM (CST). *Misdemeanor, Civil Actions Under $25,000, Eviction, Small Claims.*
Civil Records: Access: Mail, in person. Only the court performs in person searches; visitors may not. Search fee: $5.00 per name. Required to search: name, years to search. Civil cases indexed by defendant, plaintiff. Civil records on computer since 6/88.
Criminal Records: Access: Mail, in person. Only the court performs in person searches; visitors may not. Search fee: $5.00 per name. Required to search: name, years to search, DOB, SSN. Criminal records on computer since 6/88.
General Information: No suppressed, juvenile, sex offenders, mental health, or adoption records released. Copy fee: $1.00 per page. Certification fee: $10.00 per document. Payee: District Court. Business checks accepted. Prepayment required. Mail requests: SASE not required. Mail turnaround time 10 days.

Probate Court 200 North Moore St., Bessemer, MI 49911; 906-667-0421; Fax: 906-663-4660. Hours: 8:30AM-Noon, 1-4:30PM (CST). *Probate.*

Grand Traverse County

13th Circuit Court 328 Washington St, Traverse City, MI 49684; 231-922-4710. Hours: 8AM-5PM (EST). *Felony, Civil Actions Over $25,000.*
Civil Records: Access: Phone, mail, in person. Only the court performs in person searches; visitors may not. Search fee: $10.00 per name. Required to search: name, years to search. Civil cases indexed by defendant, plaintiff. Civil records on computer since 1971, prior on books since 1859.
Criminal Records: Access: Phone, mail, in person. Only the court performs in person searches; visitors may not. Search fee: $10.00 per name. Required to search: name, years to search; also helpful: DOB, SSN. Criminal records on computer since 1981.

General Information: No suppressed records released. Copy fee: $1.00 for first page, $.25 each add'l. Certification fee: $10.00 plus $1.00 per page after first. Payee: 13th Circuit Court. Personal checks accepted. Prepayment required. Mail requests: SASE required. Mail turnaround time 1 week.

86th District Court 328 Washington St., Traverse City, MI 49684; 231-922-4580; Fax: 231-922-4454. Hours: 8AM-5PM (EST). *Misdemeanor, Civil Actions Under $25,000, Eviction, Small Claims.*
Civil Records: Access: Phone, mail, in person. Only the court performs in person searches; visitors may not. No search fee. Required to search: name, years to search. Civil cases indexed by defendant, plaintiff. Civil records on computer since 1988, prior on books.
Criminal Records: Access: Phone, mail, in person. Only the court performs in person searches; visitors may not. No search fee. Required to search: name, years to search, DOB; also helpful: SSN. Most criminal records on computer.
General Information: No suppressed, juvenile, sex offenders, mental health, or adoption records released. Copy fee: $.25 per page. Certification fee: $10.00. Payee: 86th District Court. Business checks accepted. Prepayment required. Mail requests: SASE required. Mail turnaround time 2-3 days.

Probate Court 400 Boardman Av, Traverse City, MI 49684; 231-922-6862; Fax: 231-922-4458. Hours: 8AM-5PM (EST). *Probate.*

Gratiot County

29th Circuit Court 214 East Center St, Ithaca, MI 48847; 989-875-5215. Hours: 8:00AM-Noon, 1:00PM-4:30PM (EST). *Felony, Civil Actions Over $25,000.*
Civil Records: Access: Mail, in person. Only the court performs in person searches; visitors may not. Search fee: $10.00 per name. Fee is for 5 years, $1.00 each add'l year. Required to search: name, years to search. Civil cases indexed by defendant, plaintiff. Records computerized back 7 years.
Criminal Records: Access: Mail, in person. Only the court performs in person searches; visitors may not. Search fee: $10.00 per name. Fee is for 5 years, $1.00 each add'l year. Required to search: name, years to search. Records computerized back 7 years.
General Information: No suppressed, juvenile, sex offenders, mental health, or adoption records released. Will fax results to local or toll free line. Copy fee: $1.00 per page. Certification fee: $10.00. Payee: Gratiot County Clerk. Personal checks accepted. Prepayment required. Mail requests: SASE required. Mail turnaround time 1-3 days.

65-B District Court 245 East Newark St, Ithaca, MI 48847; 989-875-5240; Fax: 989-875-5290. Hours: 8AM-4:30PM (EST). *Misdemeanor, Civil Actions Under $25,000, Eviction, Small Claims.*
Civil Records: Access: In person only. Visitors must perform in person searches for themselves. No search fee. Required to search: name, years to search. Civil cases indexed by defendant, plaintiff. Civil records on index books from 1969 to present, computerized since 1996.
Criminal Records: Access: In person only. Visitors must perform in person searches for themselves. No search fee. Required to search: name, years to search, DOB; also helpful: SSN. Criminal records on computer since 02/20/96, in books since 1969.
General Information: Public Access terminal is available. No non-public records released. Copy fee: $1.00 per page. Certification fee: $10.00 plus $1.00 per page after first. Payee: 65B District Court. Personal checks accepted. Prepayment required.

Probate Court 214 E Center St, PO Box 217, Ithaca, MI 48847; 989-875-5231; Fax: 989-875-5331. Hours: 8AM-12;00,1PM-4:30PM (EST). *Probate.*

Hillsdale County

1st Circuit Court 29 North Howell, Hillsdale, MI 49242; 517-437-3391; Fax: 517-437-3392. Hours: 8:30AM-5PM (EST). *Felony, Civil Actions Over $25,000.*
Civil Records: Access: Mail, in person. Only the court performs in person searches; visitors may not. Search fee: $1.00 per name per year. Required to search: name, years to search. Civil cases indexed by defendant, plaintiff. Civil records on computer back to 1985, prior on docket books, archived to 1844.
Criminal Records: Access: Mail, in person. Only the court performs in person searches; visitors may not. Search fee: $1.00 per name per year. Required to search: name, years to search, DOB; also helpful: SSN. Criminal records on computer back to 1985, prior on docket books, archived to 1844.
General Information: No suppressed, juvenile, sex offenders, mental health, or adoption records released. Will fax results to local or toll free line. Copy fee: $1.00 per page. Certification fee: $10.00. Payee: Hillsdale County Clerk. Personal checks accepted; out-of-state personal checks not accepted. Prepayment required. Mail requests: SASE required. Mail turnaround time 2-3 days.

2nd District Court 49 North Howell, Hillsdale, MI 49242; 517-437-7329; Fax: 517-437-2908. Hours: 8AM-4:30PM; 8AM-5PM Traffic (EST). *Misdemeanor, Civil Actions Under $25,000, Eviction, Small Claims.*
Civil Records: Access: Phone, mail, in person. Both court and visitors may perform in person searches. Search fee: $10.00. Required to search: name, years to search. Civil cases indexed by defendant, plaintiff. Civil records kept in docket books back to 1969; on computer back to 2001. A request in writing may be required.
Criminal Records: Access: Phone, mail, in person. Only the court performs in person searches; visitors may not. Search fee: $10.00. Required to search: name, years to search, DOB; also helpful: SSN. Criminal records kept in docket books back to 1964; on computer back to 2001.
General Information: No suppressed records released. Will fax results to local or toll free line. Copy fee: $.15 per page. Certification fee: $10.00 plus $1.00 each add'l page. Payee: Hillsdale District Court. Personal checks accepted. Prepayment required. Mail turnaround time 1 week.

Probate Court 29 North Howell, Hillsdale, MI 49242; 517-437-4643; Fax: 517-437-4148. Hours: 8:30AM-Noon, 1-5PM (EST). *Probate.*

Houghton County

12th Circuit Court 401 East Houghton Ave, Houghton, MI 49931; 906-482-5420. Hours: 8AM-4:30PM (EST). *Felony, Civil Actions Over $25,000.*
Civil Records: Access: Mail, in person. Only the court performs in person searches; visitors may not. Search fee: $10.00 per name. Required to search: name, years to search. Civil cases indexed by defendant, plaintiff. Civil records kept on docket books, cards since 6/76; are computerized as of 1997.
Criminal Records: Access: Mail, in person. Only the court performs in person searches; visitors may not. Search fee: $10.00 per name. Required to search: name, years to search, DOB; also helpful: SSN. Criminal records kept on docket books, cards since 11/63; are computerized as of 1997.
General Information: No suppressed, juvenile, sex offenders, mental health, or adoption records released.

Will fax results to local or toll free line. Copy fee: $1.00 per page. Certification fee: $10.00 plus $1.00 per page after first. Payee: Clerk of Circuit Court. Personal checks accepted. Prepayment required. Mail requests: SASE required. Mail turnaround time 1-2 days.

97th District Court 401 East Houghton Ave., Houghton, MI 49931; 906-482-4980; Fax: 906-482-5270. Hours: 8AM-4:30PM (EST). *Misdemeanor, Civil Actions Under $25,000, Eviction, Small Claims.*
Civil Records: Access: Mail, fax, in person. Only the court may perform in person searches. Search fee: $10.00 per name. Required to search: name, years to search; also helpful: address. Civil cases indexed by defendant, plaintiff. Civil records listed in "Registers of Actions." Records on computer back to 1998; others back to 1969.
Criminal Records: Access: Mail, fax, in person. Only the court may perform in person searches. Search fee: $10.00 per name. Required to search: name, years to search, DOB, SSN; also helpful: address, signed release. Criminal records listed in "Registers of Actions." Records on computer back to 1998; others back to 1969.
General Information: Will not fax results. Copy fee: $1.00 for first page, $.25 each add'l. Certification fee: $10.00 plus $1.00 per page after first. Payee: 97th District Court. Business checks accepted. Prepayment required. Mail requests: SASE required. Mail turnaround time up to 1 week.

Probate Court 401 E. Houghton Ave., Houghton, MI 49931; 906-482-3120; Fax: 906-487-5964. Hours: 8AM-4:30PM (EST). *Probate.*

Huron County

52nd Circuit Court 250 East Huron Ave, Bad Axe, MI 48413; 989-269-9942; Probate phone: 989-269-9944; Fax: 989-269-6160. Hours: 8:30AM-5PM (EST). *Felony, Civil Actions Over $25,000.*
Civil Records: Access: Mail, in person. Both court and visitors may perform in person searches. Search fee: $5.00 per name. Required to search: name, years to search. Civil cases indexed by defendant, plaintiff. Civil records on computer since 1992, prior on books to 1867.
Criminal Records: Access: Phone, mail, in person. Both court and visitors may perform in person searches. Search fee: $5.00 per name. Required to search: name, years to search, DOB; also helpful: SSN. Criminal records on computer since 1992, prior on books to 1867.
General Information: No suppressed, juvenile, sex offenders, mental health, or adoption records released. Will fax results to local or toll free line. Copy fee: $1.00 per page. Certification fee: $10.00 plus $1.00 per page after first. Payee: Huron County Clerk. Personal checks accepted. Prepayment required. Mail requests: SASE required. Mail turnaround time 2-3 days.

73B District Court 250 East Huron Ave., Bad Axe, MI 48413; 989-269-9987; Fax: 989-269-6167. Hours: 8:30AM-5PM (EST). *Misdemeanor, Civil Actions Under $25,000, Eviction, Small Claims.*
Civil Records: Access: Phone, fax, mail, in person. Only the court performs in person searches; visitors may not. Search fee: $5.00 per name. Required to search: name, years to search. Civil cases indexed by defendant, plaintiff. Civil records on computer since June 1992, prior on books since 1969.
Criminal Records: Access: Phone, fax, mail, in person. Only the court performs in person searches; visitors may not. Search fee: $5.00 per name. Required to search: name, years to search, DOB; also

helpful: SSN. Criminal records on computer since June 1992, prior on books since 1969.
General Information: No suppressed, juvenile, sex offenders, mental health, or adoption records released. No fee to fax results. Copy fee: $1.00 per page. No certification fee. Payee: 73B District Court. Business checks accepted. Prepayment required. Mail requests: SASE required. Mail turnaround time 1-5 days.

Probate Court 250 E. Huron Ave., Bad Axe, MI 48413; 989-269-9944; Fax: 989-269-0004. Hours: 8:30AM-Noon, 1-5PM (EST). *Probate.*

Ingham County

30th Circuit Court 313 W. Kalamazoo (PO Box 40771), Lansing, MI 48933; 517-483-6500; Fax: 517-483-6501. Hours: 9:00AM-5:00PM M-F (EST). *Felony, Civil Actions Over $25,000.*
www.ingham.org/cc/circuit.htm
Civil Records: Access: Phone, mail, in person. Both court and visitors may perform in person searches. No search fee. Required to search: name, years to search. Civil cases indexed by defendant, plaintiff. Civil records on computer since 1986.
Criminal Records: Access: Mail, in person. Both court and visitors may perform in person searches. Search fee: $8.00 per name. Required to search: name, years to search; also helpful: DOB. Criminal records on computer since 1986.
General Information: Public Access terminal is available. All circuit court files are public record unless specifically suppressed by Judge. Copy fee: $5.00 for 1st 5 pages $.50 thereafter. Certification fee: $10.00 plus $1.00 per page after first. Payee: Ingham County Circuit Court. Personal checks accepted. Prepayment required. Mail requests: SASE required. Mail turnaround time 1-2 days; if file is in storage, then 1 week.

54 A District Court 124 West Michigan Ave, Lansing, MI 48933; 517-483-4433; Civil phone: 517-483-4426; Criminal phone: 517-483-4445; Fax: 517-483-4108. Hours: 8AM-4:30PM (EST). *Misdemeanor, Civil Actions Under $25,000, Eviction, Small Claims.*
Note: This court covers the City of Lansing.

Civil Records: Access: In person only. Visitors must perform in person searches for themselves. No search fee. Required to search: name, years to search. Civil cases indexed by defendant, plaintiff. Civil records on computer since 1990, microfiche from 1985, prior archived.
Criminal Records: Access: In person only. Visitors must perform in person searches for themselves. No search fee. Required to search: name, years to search, DOB, offense, date of offense. Criminal records on computer since 1990, microfiche from 1985, prior not archived; may be on microfiche before 1969.
General Information: Public Access terminal is available. No suppressed, juvenile, sex offenders, mental health, or adoption, non-public records released. Will not fax results. Copy fee: $.50 per page. Certification fee: $10.00 plus $1.00 per page after first. Payee: 54A District Court. No Personal checks accepted. Visa, MC accepted. Prepayment required.

54 B District Court 101 Linden, East Lansing, MI 48823; 517-351-7000; Civil phone: 517-351-1730; Criminal phone: 517-336-8630; Fax: 517-351-3371. 8AM-4:30PM (EST). *Misdemeanor, Civil Actions Under $25,000, Eviction, Small Claims.*
http://cityofeastlansing.com
Note: This court covers the City of East Lansing.

Civil Records: Access: Mail, in person. Both court and visitors may perform in person searches. Older records must be searched by court personnel and can take 1-3 days. No search fee. Required to search:

name, years to search. Civil cases indexed by defendant, plaintiff. Civil records on computer since 1991, ROA's are kept indefinitely.

Criminal Records: Access: Mail, in person. Both court and visitors may perform in person searches. No search fee. Required to search: name, DOB; if prior to 1989 give years needed. Criminal records on computer since 1989, files stored prior, ROAs keep indefinitely.

General Information: Public Access terminal is available. (Criminal cases 1989 forward; for civil 1991 forward.) No suppressed, juvenile, sex offenders, mental health, or adoption records released. Copy fee: $.25 per page. Certification fee: $10.00 plus $1.00 per page after first. Payee: 54-B District Court. Two party or payroll checks not allowed. Visa, MC accepted. Debit card. Prepayment required. Mail turnaround time 1 hour to 1 week; depends on availability.

55th District Court 700 Buhl St., Mason, MI 48854; 517-676-8400. Hours: 8:30AM-5PM (EST). *Misdemeanor, Civil Actions Under $25,000, Eviction, Small Claims.*
Note: This court covers all of Ingham County except for Lansing and East Lansing.

Civil Records: Access: Mail, in person. Both court and visitors may perform in person searches. No search fee. Required to search: name, years to search. Civil records on computer since 11/91, prior listed in index books.

Criminal Records: Access: Mail, in person. Both court and visitors may perform in person searches. No search fee. Required to search: name, years to search, DOB; case number; also helpful: SSN. Criminal records on computer since 1994, prior on books.

General Information: Public Access terminal is available. No suppressed, juvenile, sex offenders, mental health, or adoption records released. Copy fee: $1.00 per page. Certification fee: $10.00 plus $1.00 each add'l. Payee: 55th District Court. Personal checks accepted. Prepayment required. Mail requests: SASE helpful. Turnaround time varies.

Lansing Probate Court 313 West Kalamazoo, Lansing, MI 48933; 517-483-6300; Fax: 517-483-6150. Hours: 8AM-Noon, 1-5PM (EST). *Probate.*
Note: The probate court located in Mason was closed; all of their records reside here.

Ionia County

8th Circuit Court 100 Main, Ionia, MI 48846; 616-527-5322; Probate phone: 616-527-5326; Fax: 616-527-8201. Hours: 8:30AM-5PM (EST). *Felony, Civil Actions Over $25,000.*
www.ioniacounty.org/Circuit/Circuit-Home.asp
Civil Records: Access: Phone, fax, mail, in person. Only the court performs in person searches; visitors may not. No search fee. Required to search: name, years to search. Civil cases indexed by defendant, plaintiff. Civil records on computer since 1990; prior records kept in books and files, archived to 1800s.
Criminal Records: Access: Phone, fax, mail, in person. Only the court performs in person searches; visitors may not. No search fee. Required to search: name, years to search; also helpful: DOB, SSN. Criminal records on computer since 6/84; in books and files prior.
General Information: No suppressed records released. Copy fee: $1.00 per page. Certification fee: $10.00 plus $1.00 per page after first. Payee: Ionia County Clerk. Personal checks accepted. Prepayment required. Mail requests: SASE not required. Mail turnaround time 1 week.

64 A District Court 101 West Main, Ionia, MI 48846; 616-527-5346; Fax: 616-527-5343. Hours: 7:45AM-5:30PM (EST). *Misdemeanor, Civil Actions Under $25,000, Eviction, Small Claims.*
www.ioniacounty.org/district/home1.asp
Civil Records: Access: Fax, mail, in person. Only the court performs in person searches; visitors may not. Search fee: $3.00 per name. Required to search: name, years to search. Civil cases indexed by defendant, plaintiff. Civil records in files and books since 1969. Fax request must be followed up by originals.
Criminal Records: Access: Fax, mail, in person. Only the court performs in person searches; visitors may not. Search fee: $3.00 per name. Required to search: name, years to search, DOB; also helpful: address. Criminal records in files and books since 1969. Fax must be followed up by originals.
General Information: No suppressed, juvenile, sex offenders, mental health, or adoption records released. Copy fee: $.50 per page. Certification fee: $10.00 plus $1.00 per page after first. Payee: 64-A District Court. Personal checks accepted. Prepayment required. Mail requests: SASE requested. Turnaround time 10 days.

Probate Court 100 Main, Ionia, MI 48846; 616-527-5326; Fax: 616-527-5321. Hours: 8:30AM-5PM (EST). *Probate.*
www.ioniacounty.org/Probate/Probate_home.asp

Iosco County

23rd Circuit Court PO Box 838, Tawas City, MI 48764; 989-362-3497; Probate phone: 989-362-3991; Fax: 989-984-1012. Hours: 9AM-5PM (EST). *Felony, Civil Actions Over $25,000.*
www.iosco.net
Civil Records: Access: Phone, mail, in person. Both court and visitors may perform in person searches. Search fee: $15.00 per name. Required to search: name, years to search. Civil records on computer since 1987, prior on books.
Criminal Records: Access: Phone, mail, in person. Both court and visitors may perform in person searches. Search fee: $15.00 per name. Required to search: name, years to search, DOB; also helpful: SSN. Criminal records on computer since 1983.
General Information: No suppressed, parental waivers, mental health, or adoption records released. Copy fee: $1.00 per page. Certification fee: $10.00 plus $1.00 per page after first. Payee: Iosco County Clerk. Cashiers checks, money orders and credit cards accepted. Prepayment required. Mail requests: SASE not required. Mail turnaround time 1 week.

81st District Court PO Box 388, Tawas City, MI 48764; 989-362-4441; Fax: 989-984-1021. Hours: 8:30AM-5PM (EST). *Misdemeanor, Civil Actions Under $25,000, Eviction, Small Claims.*
Civil Records: Access: Mail, in person. Only the court performs in person searches; visitors may not. Search fee: $5.00. Required to search: name, years to search. Civil cases indexed by defendant, plaintiff. Civil records on computer since 1987, prior on books.
Criminal Records: Access: Mail, in person. Only the court performs in person searches; visitors may not. Search fee: $5.00. Required to search: name, years to search, DOB; also helpful: SSN. Criminal records on computer since 1987, prior on books.
General Information: No suppressed, juvenile, sex offenders, mental health, or adoption records released. Will fax results to local or toll free line. Copy fee: $2.00 for first page, $.50 each add'l. Certification fee: $10.00 plus $1.00 per page after first. Payee: 81st District Court. Personal checks accepted. Prepayment required. Mail requests: SASE required. Mail turnaround time 2-3 days.

Probate Court PO Box 421, Tawas City, MI 48764; 989-984-1037; Fax: 989-984-1035. Hours: 8AM-5PM (EST). *Probate.*

Iron County

41st Circuit Court 2 South 6th St #9, Crystal Falls, MI 49920; 906-875-3221; Fax: 906-875-6675. Hours: 8AM- 1200-12;30-4PM (CST). *Felony, Civil Actions Over $25,000.*
Civil Records: Access: Fax, mail, in person. Only the court performs in person searches; visitors may not. Search fee: $6.00 per name. Required to search: name, years to search. Civil cases indexed by defendant, plaintiff. Most records on books, on microfiche 1958-67.
Criminal Records: Access: Fax, mail, in person. Only the court performs in person searches; visitors may not. Search fee: $6.00 per name. Required to search: name, years to search, DOB; also helpful: SSN. Most records on books, on microfiche 1958-67.
General Information: No suppressed, juvenile, sex offenders, mental health, or adoption records released. Will fax results $1.50 per page. Copy fee: $.25 per page. Certification fee: $10.00 plus $4.00 per page after first. Payee: Iron County Clerk. Personal checks accepted. Prepayment required. Mail requests: SASE requested. Turnaround time 2-3 days.

95 B District Court 2 South 6th St., Crystal Falls, MI 49920; 906-875-0619; Fax: 906-875-6775. Hours: 8AM-4PM (CST). *Misdemeanor, Civil Actions Under $25,000, Eviction, Small Claims.*
Civil Records: Access: Mail, in person. Only the court performs in person searches; visitors may not. Search fee: $5.00. Required to search: name, years to search. Civil cases indexed by defendant, plaintiff. Civil records computerized since 1999, earlier records index kept on cards, accessible from 1970.
Criminal Records: Access: Mail, in person. Only the court performs in person searches; visitors may not. Search fee: $5.00. Required to search: name, years to search, DOB; also helpful: SSN. Criminal records computerized since 1999, earlier records index kept on cards, accessible from 1970.
General Information: No suppressed, juvenile, sex offenders, mental health, or adoption records released. Copy fee: $.25 per page. Certification fee: $10.00 plus $1.00 per page after first. Payee: 95-B District Court. Personal checks accepted. Prepayment required. Mail requests: SASE required. Mail turnaround time 1 week.

Probate Court 2 South 6th St, #10, Crystal Falls, MI 49920; 906-875-0659; Fax: 906-875-0656. Hours: 8AM-Noon, 12:30-4PM (CST). *Probate.*
www.iron.org

Isabella County

21st Circuit Court 200 North Main St, Mount Pleasant, MI 48858; 989-772-0911 X259. Hours: 8AM-4:30PM (EST). *Felony, Civil Actions Over $25,000.*
Civil Records: Access: Mail, in person. Both court and visitors may perform in person searches. Search fee: $5.00 from 1980 to present. Prior years $1.00 per year. Required to search: name, years to search. Civil cases indexed by defendant, plaintiff. Civil records on computer since 1980, archived from 1900.
Criminal Records: Access: Mail, in person. Only the court performs in person searches; visitors may not. Search fee: $5.00 from 1980 to present. Prior years $1.00 per year. Required to search: name, years to search, DOB; also helpful: SSN. Criminal records on computer since 1980, archived from 1900.
General Information: No suppressed, juvenile, sex offenders, mental health, or adoption records released. Will fax results to local or toll free line. Copy fee:

$1.00 per page. Certification fee: $10.00 plus $1.00 per page after first. Payee: Isabella County Court. Personal checks accepted. Prepayment required. Mail requests: SASE required. Mail turnaround time 1-2 weeks.

76th District Court 300 North Main St., Mount Pleasant, MI 48858; 989-772-0911 X490; Probate phone: x316; Fax: 989-779-8022. Hours: 8AM-4:30PM (EST). *Misdemeanor, Civil Actions Under $25,000, Eviction, Small Claims.*
www.isabellacounty.org/trial.html
Civil Records: Access: Mail, in person. Both court and visitors may perform in person searches. Search fee: $5.00 per name. Required to search: name, years to search. Civil cases indexed by defendant, plaintiff. Civil records on computer since 1988, on books since 1960s.
Criminal Records: Access: Mail, in person. Both court and visitors may perform in person searches. Search fee: $5.00 per name. Required to search: name, years to search, DOB; also helpful: SSN. Criminal records on computer since 1988, on books since 1960s.
General Information: No suppressed, juvenile, sex offenders, or adoption records released. Will fax results. Copy fee: $1.00 per page. Certification fee: $10.00 1st page; $1.00 each add'l page. Payee: Isabella County Trial Court. Business checks accepted. Prepayment required. Mail requests: SASE required. Mail turnaround time 5-7 days.

Probate Court 300 N Main St, Mount Pleasant, MI 48858; 989-772-0911 x316 (or x276); Fax: 989-779-8022. Hours: 8AM-4:30PM (EST). *Probate.*
www.isabellacounty.org

Jackson County

4th Circuit Court 312 South Jackson St, Jackson, MI 49201; 517-788-4268. Hours: 8AM-5PM (EST). *Felony, Civil Actions Over $25,000.*
www.co.jackson.mi.us
Civil Records: Access: Phone, mail, in person. Only the court performs in person searches; visitors may not. Search fee: $10.50 per hour. Required to search: name, years to search. Civil cases indexed by defendant, plaintiff. Civil records on computer since 1982, prior on index cards and docket books since 1800s.
Criminal Records: Access: Phone, mail, in person. Only the court performs in person searches; visitors may not. Search fee: $10.00 per hour. Required to search: name, years to search; also helpful: DOB, SSN. Criminal records on computer since 1982, prior on index cards and docket books since 1800s.
General Information: No adoption or juvenile records released. Will fax results for $3.00 per page. Copy fee: $.50 per page. Certification fee: $10.00 plus $2.00 per page after first. Payee: Jackson County Clerk. Only cashiers checks and money orders accepted. Visa, MC accepted. Prepayment required. Prepayment of fax and mail service required. Fees billed to Attorneys. Turnaround time 1 week.

12th District Court 312 South Jackson St., Jackson, MI 49201; 517-788-4260; Fax: 517-788-4262. Hours: 7AM-6PM (EST). *Misdemeanor, Civil Actions Under $25,000, Eviction, Small Claims.*
www.d12.com
Civil Records: Access: Fax, mail, in person. Only the court performs in person searches; visitors may not. No search fee. Required to search: name, years to search. Civil cases indexed by defendant, plaintiff. Civil records on computer since 1986; microfilm to 1969.
Criminal Records: Access: Fax, mail, in person. Only the court performs in person searches; visitors may not. No search fee. Required to search: name,

years to search, DOB; also helpful: SSN. Criminal records on computer since 1986; microfilm from 1969.
General Information: No suppressed, juvenile, sex offenders, mental health, or probation records released. Will fax results $5.00 1st page, $1.00 each add'l. Copy fee: $.25 per page. Certification fee: $10.00 plus $1.00 per page after first. Payee: 12th District Court. Personal checks accepted. Prepayment required. Mail requests: SASE helpful. Turnaround time 5 days.

Probate Court 312 S Jackson St, 1st Fl, Jackson, MI 49201; 517-788-4290; Fax: 517-788-4291. Hours: 8AM-5PM (EST). *Probate.*

Kalamazoo County

9th Circuit Court 227 West Michigan Ave, Kalamazoo, MI 49007; 269-383-8837. Hours: 8AM-5PM (EST). *Felony, Civil Actions Over $25,000.*
www.kalcounty.com/courts/index.htm
Civil Records: Access: Mail, in person. Visitors must perform in person searches for themselves. Search fee: $1.00. Required to search: name, years to search. Civil cases indexed by defendant, plaintiff. Civil records stored as hard copies, some records kept off-site; computerized records go back to 1984.
Criminal Records: Access: Mail, in person. Visitors must perform in person searches for themselves. Search fee: $1.00. Required to search: name, years to search, DOB. Criminal records stored as hard copies, some records kept off-site; computerized records go back to 1984.
General Information: Public Access terminal is available. No suppressed or non-public records released. Will not fax results. Copy fee: $1.00 per page. Certification fee: $13.00. Payee: Circuit Court Clerk. Personal checks accepted. Prepayment required. Mail turnaround time 2 days.

8th District Court - South 7810 Shaver Rd., Portage, MI 49002; 269-383-6460; Fax: 269-321-3645. Hours: 8AM-5PM (EST). *Misdemeanor, Civil Actions Under $25,000, Eviction, Small Claims.*
Note: This court covers Kalamazoo County South of N Avenue (Kilgore Rd).
Civil Records: Access: Mail, in person. Both the court and visitors may perform in person searches. Search fee: $20.00 per name if prior to 1992. Required to search: name, years to search. Civil cases indexed by defendant, plaintiff. Civil records on computer back to 1991, prior on index books to 1969. Up to 5 case files may be reviewed in person immediately, otherwise subject to availability of court staff.
Criminal Records: Access: Mail, in person. Both the court and visitors may perform in person searches. Search fee: $20.00 per name if prior to 1992. Required to search: name, years to search, DOB; also helpful: SSN. Criminal records on computer back to 1991, prior on index books to 1969. Up to 5 case files may be reviewed in person immediately, otherwise subject to availability of court staff.
General Information: Public Access terminal is available. No suppressed, juvenile, sex offenders, mental health, or adoption records released. Fee to fax results is $1.00 per page. Copy fee: $1.00 per page. Certification fee: $10.00 plus $1.00 per page after first. Payee: 8th District Court. Personal checks accepted. Prepayment required. Mail requests: SASE required. Mail turnaround time 5 days.

8th District Court - Crosstown 150 E Crosstown Parkway, Kalamazoo, MI 49001; 269-384-8020; Fax: 269-383-8899. Hours: 8AM-5PM (EST). *Civil Actions Under $25,000, Eviction, Small Claims.*
Note: This court covers City of Kalamazoo.

Civil Records: Access: Fax, mail, in person. Both court and visitors may perform in person searches. No search fee. Required to search: name, years to search. Civil cases indexed by defendant, plaintiff. Civil records on computer back to 1998, prior on index books to 1969. Up to 5 case files may be reviewed in person immediately, otherwise subject to availability of court staff.
General Information: Public Access terminal is available. Copy fee: $1.00 per page. Certification fee: $10.00. Payee: 8th District Court. Personal checks accepted. Visa, MC, Discover accepted. Prepayment required. Mail requests: SASE not required. Mail turnaround time 1-3 days.

8th District Court - North 227 West Michigan St., Kalamazoo, MI 49007; 269-384-8171; Fax: 269-384-8047. Hours: 8AM-5PM (EST). *Misdemeanor.*
Note: This court covers Kalamazoo County.

Criminal Records: Access: Fax, mail, in person. Both court and visitors may perform in person searches. No search fee. Required to search: name, years to search, DOB; also helpful: SSN. Some criminal records on computer back to 1991, prior on books to 1969. Up to 5 case files may be reviewed in person immediately, otherwise subject to availability of court staff.
General Information: Public Access terminal is available. No suppressed or non-public records released. No fee to fax results. Copy fee: $1.00 per page. Certification fee: $10.00. Payee: 8th District Court. Personal checks accepted. Visa, MC, Discover accepted. Prepayment required. Mail requests: SASE requested. Turnaround time 2 days, 5 days if files in storage.

Probate Court 150 E Crosstown Parkway, Kalamazoo, MI 49001; 269-383-8666/8933; Fax: 269-383-8685. Hours: 9AM-Noon, 1-5PM T; 8AM-Noon, 1-5PM M,W-F (EST). *Probate.*

Kalkaska County

46th Circuit Court PO Box 10, Kalkaska, MI 49646; 231-258-3300. Hours: 9AM-5PM (EST). *Felony, Civil Actions Over $25,000.*
www.Circuit46.org
Civil Records: Access: Mail, in person, online. Only the court performs in person searches; visitors may not. Search fee: $5.00 per name. Required to search: name, years to search. Civil cases indexed by defendant, plaintiff. Civil records on computer since 1989, prior on books, indexed to 1800s. Online access to court case records (open or closed cases for 90 days only) is free at www.circuit46.org/Cases/cases.html.
Criminal Records: Access: Mail, in person, online. Only the court performs in person searches; visitors may not. Search fee: $5.00 per name. Required to search: name, years to search, DOB; also helpful: SSN. Criminal records on computer since 1989, prior on books, indexed to 1800s. Online access to criminal records is the same as civil.
General Information: No suppressed records released. Will fax results for $3.00 plus $1.00 per page (on certain records some we are unable to fax). Copy fee: $.30 per page. Certification fee: $10.00 plus $1.00 per page. Payee: Kalkaska County Clerk. Personal checks accepted. Prepayment required. Mail requests: SASE required. Mail turnaround time 2-3 days.

46th Circuit Trial Court - District Court 605 N Birch St., Kalkaska, MI 49646; 231-258-9031; Fax: 231-258-2424. Hours: 8AM-4:30PM (EST). *Misdemeanor, Civil Actions Under $25,000, Eviction, Small Claims.*
www.Circuit46.org
Civil Records: Access: Phone, mail, in person, online. Both court and visitors may perform in person

searches (but public access terminal is restricted). No search fee. Required to search: name, years to search. Civil cases indexed by defendant, plaintiff. Civil records on computer since 1989, prior on books. Online access to court case records (open or closed cases for 90 days only) is free at www.circuit46.org/Cases/cases.html.

Criminal Records: Access: Phone, mail, in person, online. Both court and visitors may perform in person searches (but public access terminal is restricted). No search fee. Required to search: name, years to search, DOB. Criminal records on computer since 1989, prior on books. Online access to criminal records is the same as civil.

General Information: Public Access terminal is available. (Terminal is in a secured area, by approved appointment only.) No suppressed records released. Will fax results to local or toll free line. Copy fee: $1.00 per page. Certification fee: $10.00 plus $1.00 per page after first. Payee: 46th Circuit Trial Court. Only cashiers checks and money orders accepted. Prepayment required. Mail requests: SASE required. Mail turnaround time 4 days.

Circuit Trial Court - Probate Division 605 North Birch, Kalkaska, MI 49646; 231-258-3330ext.2; Fax: 231-258-3329. Hours: 8AM-4:30PM (EST). *Probate.*

www.Circuit46.org

Note: Search cases by name free online at www.circuit46.org/Cases/cases.html.

Kent County

17th Circuit Court 180 Ottawa Ave NW, #2400, Grand Rapids, MI 49503; 616-632-5480; Fax: 616-632-5458. Hours: 8AM-5PM (EST). *Felony, Civil Actions Over $25,000.*

www.accesskent.com/government/courts/17cc_index.htm

Civil Records: Access: Mail, in person. Only the court performs in person searches; visitors may not. Search fee: $5.00 per name. Required to search: name, years to search. Civil cases indexed by defendant, plaintiff. Civil records on computer since 1986, prior on books. •

Criminal Records: Access: Mail, in person. Only the court performs in person searches; visitors may not. Search fee: $5.00 per name. Required to search: name, years to search, DOB. Criminal records on computer since 1986, prior on books.

General Information: No suppressed records released. Will fax results to local or toll free line. Copy fee: $1.00 per page. Certification fee: $10.00 plus $1.00 per page after first. Payee: Kent County Clerk. Personal checks accepted. Prepayment required. Mail requests: SASE not required. Mail turnaround time 2-3 days.

59th District Court - Walker 4343 Remembrance Rd NW, Walker, MI 49544; 616-453-5765; Fax: 616-791-6851. Hours: 8AM-5PM (EST). *Misdemeanor, Civil Actions Under $25,000, Eviction, Small Claims.*

Civil Records: Access: Mail, in person. Only the court performs in person searches; visitors may not. Search fee: $1.00 per name. Add $.50 per year requested. Required to search: name, years to search; also helpful: address. Civil cases indexed by defendant, plaintiff. Civil records on computer from 1980, docket books and cards prior.

Criminal Records: Access: Mail, in person. Only the court performs in person searches; visitors may not. Search fee: $1.00 per name. Add $.50 per year requested. Required to search: name, years to search, DOB; also helpful: address, SSN. Criminal records on computer from 1989, docket books and cards prior.

General Information: No suppressed, juvenile, sex offenders, mental health, or adoption records released. Will fax results for $1.00 per name. Copy fee: $1.00 per page. Certification fee: $10.00 plus $1.00 per page after first. Payee: 59th District Court. Personal checks accepted. Prepayment required. Mail requests: SASE required. Mail turnaround time varies.

59th District Court - Grandville 3181 Wilson Ave SW, Grandville, MI 49418; 616-538-9660; Fax: 616-538-5144. Hours: 8:30AM-5PM (EST). *Misdemeanor, Civil Actions Under $25,000, Eviction, Small Claims.*

Civil Records: Access: Mail, in person. Both court and visitors may perform in person searches. Search fee: $1.00 per name. Add $.50 per year requested. Required to search: name, years to search; also helpful: address. Civil cases indexed by defendant, plaintiff. Civil records on computer from 1986, docket books and cards prior.

Criminal Records: Access: Mail, in person. Both court and visitors may perform in person searches. Search fee: $1.00 per name. Add $.50 per year requested. Required to search: name, years to search, DOB; also helpful: address, SSN. Criminal records on computer from 1986, docket books and cards prior.

General Information: Public Access terminal is available. No suppressed, juvenile, sex offenders, mental health, or adoption records released. Copy fee: $1.00 per page. Certification fee: $10.00 plus $1.00 per page after first. Payee: 59th District Court. Personal checks accepted. Prepayment required. Mail requests: SASE required. Mail turnaround time varies.

61st District Court - Grand Rapids 180 Ottawa Ave NW #1400, Kent County Courthouse, Grand Rapids, MI 49503; 616-632-5525; Fax: 616-632-5582. Hours: 7:45AM-4:45PM (EST). *Misdemeanor, Civil Actions Under $25,000, Eviction, Small Claims.*

www.grcourt.org

Civil Records: Access: Mail, in person, online. Both court and visitors may perform in person searches. No search fee. Required to search: name, years to search. Civil cases indexed by defendant, plaintiff. Civil records kept in files and books, computerized since 1999. Search online at www.ci.grand-rapids.mi.us/index.pl?page_id=645.

Criminal Records: Access: Mail, in person, online. Both court and visitors may perform in person searches. Search fee: $1.00 per name per year. Required to search: name, years to search, DOB; also helpful: SSN. Criminal records are automated from 1999, images on microfiche from 1980. Search online at www.ci.grand-rapids.mi.us/index.pl?page_id=645.

General Information: Public Access terminal is available. (Records go back to 10/1999.) No suppressed, juvenile, sex offenders, mental health, or adoption records released. Copy fee: $1.00 for first page, $.50 each add'l. Certification fee: $10.00 plus $1.00 per page after first. Payee: 61st District Court. Personal checks accepted. Prepayment required. Prepayment of mail service required. Mail requests: SASE not required. Mail turnaround time 7-10 days.

62 A District Court - Wyoming 2650 De Hoop Ave SW, Wyoming, MI 49509; 616-530-7385; Civil phone: 616-530-7386; Criminal phone: 616-257-9814; Fax: 616-249-3419. Hours: 8AM-5PM (EST). *Misdemeanor, Civil Actions Under $25,000, Eviction, Small Claims.*

www.ci.wyoming.mi.us/courts.htm

Civil Records: Access: Mail, fax, in person. Both court and visitors may perform in person searches. Search fee: $1.00 per name & $.50 per year. Required to search: name, years to search. Civil cases indexed by defendant, plaintiff. Civil records kept on docket books since 1980; on computer back to 1997. The judge must approve all requests from collection agencies.

Criminal Records: Access: Mail, fax, in person. Both court and visitors may perform in person searches. Search fee: $1.00 per name & $.50 per year. Required to search: name, years to search, DOB; also helpful: Case #. Criminal records kept on docket books since 1980; on computer back to 1997. The court suggests mail requests be sent to the state police.

General Information: Public Access terminal is available. No suppressed, juvenile, sex offenders, mental health, or adoption records released. Copy fee: $1.00 per page. Certification fee: $10.00 plus $1.00 per page after first. Payee: 62 A District Court. Personal checks accepted. Credit cards accepted: Visa. Accepted in person only. Prepayment required. Mail requests: SASE required. Mail turnaround time 2-3 days.

62 B District Court - Kentwood 4740 Walma Ave, Kentwood, MI 49512; 616-698-9310; Fax: 616-698-8199. Hours: 8AM-5PM (EST). *Misdemeanor, Civil Actions Under $25,000, Eviction, Small Claims.*

Civil Records: Access: Mail, in person. Only the court performs in person searches; visitors may not. Search fee: $5.00 per name. Required to search: name, years to search. Civil cases indexed by defendant, plaintiff. Civil records on computer since 11/88, prior on books.

Criminal Records: Access: Mail, in person. Only the court performs in person searches; visitors may not. Search fee: $5.00 per name. Required to search: name, years to search, DOB. Criminal records on computer since 11/88, prior on books.

General Information: Public Access terminal is available. No suppressed, juvenile, sex offenders, mental health, or adoption records released. Copy fee: $2.00 for first page, $.25 each add'l. Certification fee: $10.00. Payee: 62 B District Court. Personal checks accepted. Prepayment required. Mail requests: SASE required. Mail turnaround time 1-2 days.

63rd District Court - 1st Division 105 Maple St, Rockford, MI 49341; 616-866-1576; Fax: 616-866-3080. Hours: 8AM-5PM (EST). *Misdemeanor, Civil Actions Under $25,000, Eviction, Small Claims.*

Civil Records: Access: Mail, in person. Both court and visitors may perform in person searches. No search fee. Required to search: name, years to search. Civil cases indexed by defendant, plaintiff. Civil records on computer since 8/94, prior on books.

Criminal Records: Access: Mail, in person, fax. Both court and visitors may perform in person searches. No search fee. Required to search: name, years to search, DOB; also helpful: SSN. Criminal records on computer since 8/94, prior on books.

General Information: Public Access terminal is available. No suppressed, juvenile, sex offenders, mental health, or adoption records released. Copy fee: $1.00 per page. Certification fee: $10.00. Payee: 63rd District Court. Personal checks accepted. Prepayment required. Mail requests: SASE required. Mail turnaround time 1 week.

Probate Court 180 Ottawa Ave NW #2500, Grand Rapids, MI 49503; 616-632-5440; Fax: 616-632-5430. Hours: 8:30AM-4:30PM (EST). *Probate.*

Keweenaw County .

12th Circuit Court 5095 4th St., Eagle River, MI 49950-9744; 906-337-2229; Fax: 906-337-2795. Hours: 9AM-4PM (EST). *Felony, Civil Actions Over $25,000.*

Civil Records: Access: Mail, in person. Only the court performs in person searches; visitors may not. No search fee. Required to search: name, years to search. Civil cases indexed by defendant, plaintiff. Civil records kept on index books since 1963.

Criminal Records: Access: Mail, in person. Only the court performs in person searches; visitors may not. Search fee: $10.00. Required to search: name, years to search, DOB. Criminal records kept on index books since 1964.

General Information: No suppressed, juvenile, sex offenders, mental health, or adoption records released. Will fax results. Copy fee: $1.00 per page. Certification fee: $10.00. Payee: Keweenaw County. Personal checks accepted. Prepayment required. Mail requests: SASE requested. Turnaround time 1-2 days.

97th District Court 5095 4th St., Eagle River, MI 49950; 906-337-2229; Fax: 906-337-2795. Hours: 9AM-4PM (EST). *Misdemeanor, Civil Actions Under $25,000, Eviction, Small Claims.*

Civil Records: Access: Fax, mail, in person. Only the court performs in person searches; visitors may not. Search fee: $10.00 per name. Required to search: name, years to search. Civil cases indexed by defendant, plaintiff. Civil records kept on books to 1970s. Results cannot be faxed.

Criminal Records: Access: Fax, mail, in person. Only the court performs in person searches; visitors may not. Search fee: $10.00 per name. Required to search: name, years to search, DOB; also helpful: SSN. Criminal records kept on books to 1970s. Results cannot be faxed.

General Information: No suppressed, juvenile, sex offenders, mental health, or adoption records released. Copy fee: $1.00 per page. Certification fee: $10.00. Payee: Keweenaw County. Personal checks accepted. Prepayment required. Mail requests: SASE required. Mail turnaround time 1-2 days.

Probate Court HC1 Box 607, Courthouse, Eagle River, MI 49950; 906-337-1927; Fax: 906-337-2795. Hours: 9AM-4PM (EST). *Probate.*

Lake County

Lake County Trial Court 800 10th St, #300, Baldwin, MI 49304; 231-745-4614. Hours: 8AM-Noon, 1-5PM (EST). *Felony, Misdemeanor, Civil Actions, Eviction, Small Claims, Probate.*

Civil Records: Access: Mail, in person. Only the court performs in person searches; visitors may not. Search fee: $5.00 per name per year. Required to search: name, years to search. Civil cases indexed by defendant, plaintiff. Civil records on computer since 7/89, prior on books to 1876.

Criminal Records: Access: Mail, in person. Only the court performs in person searches; visitors may not. Search fee: $5.00 per name per year. Required to search: name, years to search, DOB; also helpful: SSN. Criminal records on computer since 7/89, prior on books to 1876.

General Information: No suppressed, sex offenders, mental health, or adoption records released. Fee to fax results is $1.00 per document. Copy fee: $1.00 per page. Certification fee: $10.00. Payee: Lake County Trial Court. Personal checks accepted. Prepayment required. Mail requests: SASE not required. Mail turnaround time 1-2 days.

Lake County Trial Court Probate, 800 10th St., #300, Baldwin, MI 49304-7970; 231-745-4614; Fax: 231-745-6232. Hours: 8:30AM-5PM (EST). *Probate.*

Lapeer County

40th Circuit Court 255 Clay St, Lapeer, MI 48446; 810-667-0358. Hours: 8AM-5PM (EST). *Felony, Civil Actions Over $25,000.*
Civil Records: Access: Mail, in person. Visitors must perform in person searches for themselves. Search fee: $5.00 search fee covers 10 year span. Required to search: name, years to search. Civil cases indexed by

defendant, plaintiff. Civil records on computer since 1994, prior on index cards.

Criminal Records: Access: Mail, in person. Visitors must perform in person searches for themselves. Search fee: $5.00 search fee covers 10 year span. Required to search: name, years to search; DOB, sex helpful. Criminal records on computer since 1996, prior on index cards.

General Information: Public Access terminal is available. No suppressed records released. Copy fee: $1.00 per page. Certification fee: $10.00 plus $1.00 per page after first. Payee: 40th Circuit Court. Personal checks accepted. Prepayment required. Mail requests: SASE required. Mail turnaround: 24 hours.

71 A District Court 255 Clay St., Lapeer, MI 48446; 810-667-0314. Hours: 8AM-5PM (EST). *Misdemeanor, Civil Actions Under $25,000, Eviction, Small Claims.*

Civil Records: Access: Mail, in person. Only the court performs in person searches; visitors may not. Search fee: $5.00 per name. Required to search: name, years to search. Civil cases indexed by defendant, plaintiff. Civil records on computer since 1992, cards and dockets from 1969.

Criminal Records: Access: Mail, in person. Only the court performs in person searches; visitors may not. Search fee: $5.00 per name. Required to search: name, years to search, DOB; also helpful: SSN. Criminal records on computer since 1992, cards and dockets from 1969.

General Information: No suppressed, juvenile, sex offenders, mental health, or adoption records released. Copy fee: $1.00 per page. Certification fee: $10.00 plus $1.00 per page after first. Payee: 71 A District Court. Third party checks not accepted. Prepayment required. Mail requests: SASE required. Mail turnaround time 10 days.

Probate Court 255 Clay St., Lapeer, MI 48446; 810-667-0261; Fax: 810-667-0271. Hours: 8AM-5PM (EST). *Probate.*

Leelanau County

13th Circuit Court PO Box 467, Leland, MI 49654; 231-256-9824; Fax: 231-256-8295. Hours: 9AM-5PM (EST). *Felony, Civil Actions Over $25,000.*

Civil Records: Access: Mail, fax, in person. Both court and visitors may perform in person searches. Search fee: $3.00 per name. Required to search: name, years to search. Civil cases indexed by defendant, plaintiff. Civil records on computer since 1/93, prior on docket books.

Criminal Records: Access: Mail, fax, in person. Both court and visitors may perform in person searches. Search fee: $3.00 per name. Required to search: name, years to search. Criminal records on computer since 1/97; prior records on books.

General Information: No suppressed, juvenile, sex offenders, mental health, or adoption records released. Will fax results to local or toll free line. Copy fee: $.50 per page. Certification fee: $10.00 plus $1.00 per page after first. Payee: County Clerk. Personal checks accepted. Prepayment required. Mail requests: SASE required. Mail turnaround time 2-3 days.

86th District Court PO Box 486, Leland, MI 49654; 231-256-8250; Fax: 231-256-8275. Hours: 8AM-4PM (EST). *Misdemeanor, Civil Actions Under $25,000, Eviction, Small Claims.*
www.co.leelanau.mi.us/government0254.asp
Civil Records: Access: Fax, mail, in person. Only the court performs in person searches; visitors may not. No search fee. Required to search: name, years to search. Civil cases indexed by defendant, plaintiff. Civil records on computer since 1991, prior on books to 1969.

Criminal Records: Access: Phone, fax, mail, in person. Only the court performs in person searches; visitors may not. No search fee. Required to search: name, years to search, DOB; also helpful: SSN. Criminal records on computer since 1991, prior on books to 1969.

General Information: No suppressed, sex offenders records released. Fee to fax results is $.25 per page. Copy fee: $.25 per page. Certification fee: $10.00. Payee: 86th District Court. Business checks accepted. Prepayment required. Mail requests: SASE requested. Turnaround time 3 days.

Family Court PO Box 595, Leland, MI 49654; 231-256-9803; Fax: 231-256-9845. Hours: 9AM-5PM (EST). *Probate.*

Lenawee County

39th Circuit Court 425 North Main St, Adrian, MI 49221; 517-264-4597. Hours: 8AM-4:30PM (EST). *Felony, Civil Actions Over $25,000.*

Civil Records: Access: Mail, in person. Both court and visitors may perform in person searches. Search fee: $10.00 per name. Fee is for ten years. Required to search: name, years to search. Civil records on computer back to 1/89, prior on books.

Criminal Records: Access: Mail, in person. Both court and visitors may perform in person searches. Search fee: $10.00 per name. Fee is for 10 years. Required to search: name, years to search. Criminal records on computer back to 1/89, prior on books.

General Information: Public Access terminal is available. No suppressed, juvenile, sex offenders, mental health, or adoption records released. Will fax results. Copy fee: $1.00 per page. Certification fee: $13.00. Payee: Lenawee County Clerk or 39th Circuit Court. Personal checks accepted. Prepayment required. Mail requests: SASE helpful. Turnaround time 1-2 days.

2A District Court 425 North Main St., Adrian, MI 49221; 517-264-4673 & 264-4668; Fax: 517-264-4665 Probation; 264-4681. Hours: 8AM-4:30PM (EST). *Misdemeanor, Civil Actions Under $25,000, Eviction, Small Claims.*

Civil Records: Access: Fax, mail, in person. Both court and visitors may perform in person searches. Search fee: $10.00 per name. Required to search: name, years to search. Civil cases indexed by defendant, plaintiff. Civil records on computer since 1988, prior on index books, cards and microfilm back to 1968.

Criminal Records: Access: In person only. Both court and visitors may perform in person searches. Search fee: $10.00 per name. Required to search: name, years to search, DOB. Criminal records on computer since 1988, prior on index books, cards and microfilm back to 1969.

General Information: No suppressed, juvenile, sex offenders, mental health, or adoption records released. Will fax results to local or toll free line. Copy fee: $.25 per page. Certification fee: $10.00. Payee: 2A District Court. Personal checks accepted. Prepayment required. Mail requests: SASE required. Mail turnaround time 1 week.

Probate Court 425 North Main St., Adrian, MI 49221; 517-264-4614; Fax: 517-264-4616. Hours: 8AM-4:30PM (EST). *Probate.*

Livingston County

44th Circuit Court 204 South Highlander Way #4, Howell, MI 48843; 517-546-9816; Probate phone: 517-346-3750. Hours: 8AM-5PM (EST). *Felony, Civil Actions Over $25,000.*
www.co.livingston.mi.us
Note: Juvenile Unit records are at 517-546-1500.

Civil Records: Access: Mail, in person. Both court and visitors may perform in person searches. No search fee. Required to search: name, years to search. Civil cases indexed by defendant, plaintiff. Civil records computerized from 1987, on microfiche and archived from 1900s.

Criminal Records: Access: Mail, in person. Both court and visitors may perform in person searches. No search fee. Required to search: name, years to search. Criminal records computerized from 1987, microfiche and archived from 1900s.

General Information: Public Access terminal is available. All records released, none are restricted. Will fax results to local or toll free line. Copy fee: $1.00 per page. Certification fee: $10.00 plus $1.00 each add'l page. Payee: Livingston County Clerk. Personal checks accepted. Out of state checks not accepted. Prepayment required. Mail requests: SASE required. Mail turnaround time 5 days.

53 A District Court 204 South Highlander Way #1, Howell, MI 48843; 517-548-1000; Civil phone: 517-548-1000 x369; Criminal phone: 517-548-1000 x279; Fax: 517-548-9445. Hours: 8AM-5PM (EST). *Misdemeanor, Civil Actions Under $25,000, Eviction, Small Claims.*
http://co.livingston.mi.us/DistrictCourt

Civil Records: Access: Mail, in person. Visitors must perform in person searches for themselves. No search fee. Required to search: name, years to search; also helpful: address. Civil cases indexed by defendant, plaintiff. Civil records on computer since 1982.

Criminal Records: Access: In person only. Visitors must perform in person searches for themselves. No search fee. Required to search: name, years to search, DOB; also helpful: address, SSN. Criminal records on computer since 1982.

General Information: Public Access terminal is available. No suppressed, juvenile, sex offenders, mental health, or adoption records released. Copy fee: $1.00 per page. Certification fee: $10.00. Payee: 53 District Court. Personal checks accepted. Prepayment required.

53 B District Court 224 N 1st St., Brighton, MI 48116; 810-229-6615; Fax: 810-229-1770. Hours: 8AM-5PM (EST). *Misdemeanor, Civil Actions Under $25,000, Eviction, Small Claims.*
http://co.livingston.mi.us/DistrictCourt/brighton.htm

Civil Records: Access: Mail, in person. Only the court performs in person searches; visitors may not. No search fee. Required to search: name, years to search. Civil cases indexed by defendant, plaintiff. Civil records on computer since 1985, prior on index books.

Criminal Records: Access: Mail, in person, fax. Only the court performs in person searches; visitors may not. No search fee. Required to search: name, years to search, DOB; also helpful: SSN. Criminal records on computer since 1985, prior on index books.

General Information: No suppressed, juvenile, sex offenders, mental health, or adoption records released. Copy fee: $1.00 per page. Certification fee: $10.00. Payee: 53rd District Court. Personal checks accepted. Prepayment required. Mail requests: SASE required. Mail turnaround time 1 week.

Probate Court 204 Highlander Way #2, Howell, MI 48843; 517-546-3750; Fax: 517-552-2510. Hours: 8AM-5PM (EST). *Probate.*
www.co.livingston.mi.us/probatecourt

Luce County

11th Circuit Court 407 W Harrie, Newberry, MI 49868; 906-293-5521; Probate phone: 906-293-5601; Fax: 906-293-0050. Hours: 8AM-4PM (EST). *Felony, Civil Actions Over $25,000.*

Civil Records: Access: Mail, in person. Only the court performs in person searches; visitors may not. No search fee. Required to search: name, years to search. Civil cases indexed by defendant, plaintiff. Civil records listed on cards since 1876.

Criminal Records: Access: Mail, in person. Only the court performs in person searches; visitors may not. No search fee. Required to search: name, years to search, DOB. Criminal records listed on cards since 1876.

General Information: No suppressed, juvenile, sex offenders, mental health, or adoption records released. Will fax results for $1.00 per page plus $1.00 fax fee. Copy fee: $1.00 per page. Certification fee: $10.00. Payee: 11th Circuit Court. Personal checks accepted. Prepayment required. Mail requests: SASE required. Mail turnaround time 4-5 days.

92nd District Court 407 W Harrie, Newberry, MI 49868; 906-293-5531; Fax: 906-293-3581. Hours: 8AM-4PM (EST). *Misdemeanor, Civil Actions Under $25,000, Eviction, Small Claims.*

Civil Records: Access: Phone, fax, mail, in person. Only the court performs in person searches; visitors may not. No search fee. Required to search: name, years to search. Civil cases indexed by defendant, plaintiff. Civil records to 1969, some on computer.

Criminal Records: Access: Phone, fax, mail, in person. Only the court performs in person searches; visitors may not. No search fee. Required to search: name, years to search, DOB; also helpful: SSN. Criminal records to 1969, some on computer.

General Information: Will fax results $1.00 per page. Copy fee: $1.00 per page. No certification fee. Payee: 92nd District Court. In state personal checks accepted. Prepayment required. Mail requests: SASE preferred. Turnaround time 1 week.

Probate Court 407 W. Harrie, Newberry, MI 49868; 906-293-5601; Fax: 906-293-3581. Hours: 8AM-Noon, 1-4PM (EST). *Probate.*
Note: This is a combined court with Mackinac County Probate Court.

Mackinac County

11th Circuit Court 100 S Marley St, Rm 10, St Ignace, MI 49781; 906-643-7300; Fax: 906-643-7302. Hours: 8:30AM-4:30PM (EST). *Felony, Civil Actions Over $25,000.*

Civil Records: Access: Mail, in person. Both court and visitors may perform in person searches. Search fee: $10.00. Required to search: name, years to search. Civil cases indexed by defendant, plaintiff. Civil records on docket book; on computer back to 1998.

Criminal Records: Access: Mail, in person. Only the court performs in person searches; visitors may not. Search fee: $10.00. Required to search: name, years to search, DOB. Criminal records on docket book; on computer back to 1998.

General Information: No suppressed, juvenile, sex offenders, mental health, or adoption records released. Copy fee: $1.00 per page. Certification fee: $10.00 plus $1.00 per page after first. Payee: County Clerk. Personal checks accepted. Prepayment required. Mail requests: SASE required. Mail turnaround time: 10 days.

92nd District Court 100 South Marley, Rm 55, St Ignace, MI 49781; 906-643-7321; Fax: 906-643-7302. 8:30AM-4:30PM (EST). *Misdemeanor, Civil Actions Under $25,000, Eviction, Small Claims.*

Civil Records: Access: Mail, in person, fax, phone. Both court and visitors may perform in person

searches. Search fee: $10.00 per name. Required to search: name, years to search. Civil cases indexed by defendant. Civil records on computer since 11/92, prior in files to 1980.

Criminal Records: Access: Mail, in person. Both court and visitors may perform in person searches. Search fee: $10.00 per name. Required to search: name, years to search, DOB. Criminal records on computer since 11/92, prior in files to 1970.

General Information: No suppressed, juvenile, sex offenders, mental health, or adoption records released. Will fax results for $10.00 per name. Copy fee: $1.00 per page. No certification fee. Prepayment required. Mail requests: SASE required. Mail turnaround: 1 wk.

Probate Court 100 S Marley St Rm. 15, St Ignace, MI 49781; 906-643-7303; Fax: 906-643-8861. Hours: 8:30AM-Noon, 1-4:30PM (EST). *Probate.* Note: This is a combined court with Luce County Probate Court.

Macomb County

16th Circuit Court 40 N Main St, Mount Clemens, MI 48043; 586-469-5120. Hours: 8AM-4:30PM (EST). *Felony, Civil Actions Over $25,000.*
www.macombcountymi.gov/CIRCUITCOURT/index.htm

Civil Records: Access: Mail, in person. Both court and visitors may perform in person searches. Search fee: $1.00 per name per year. Required to search: name, years to search. Civil cases indexed by defendant, plaintiff. Civil records on computer since 1977, on microfiche to 1969, prior to 1800s archived.

Criminal Records: Access: Mail, in person. Both court and visitors may perform in person searches. Search fee: $1.00 per name. Required to search: name, years to search; also helpful: DOB. Criminal records on computer since 1970, on microfiche to 1969, prior to 1800s archived.

General Information: Public Access terminal is available. No suppressed, juvenile, sex offenders, mental health, or adoption records released. Copy fee: $.40 per page. Certification fee: $10.00 plus $1.00 per page after first. Payee: Macomb County Clerk. Personal checks accepted. Most credit cards accepted. Prepayment required. Mail requests: SASE required. Mail turnaround time 1 week.

37th District Court - Warren & Center Line 8300 Common Rd., Warren, MI 48093; 586-574-4900; Fax: 586-574-4932. Hours: 8:30AM-4:30PM (EST). *Misdemeanor, Civil Actions Under $25,000, Eviction, Small Claims.*

Civil Records: Access: Mail, in person. Only the court performs in person searches; visitors may not. Search fee: $10.00 per name. Required to search: name, years to search. Civil cases indexed by defendant, plaintiff. Civil records on computer since 1992, prior on index cards.

Criminal Records: Access: Mail, in person, fax. Only the court performs in person searches; visitors may not. Search fee: $10.00 per name. Required to search: name, years to search, DOB; also helpful: SSN. Criminal records on computer since 1992, prior on index cards.

General Information: No suppressed, juvenile, sex offenders, mental health, or adoption records released. Copy fee: $.25 per page. Certification fee: $10.00. Payee: 37th District Court. Personal checks accepted. Prepayment required. Mail requests: SASE not required. Mail turnaround time 2 weeks.

39th District Court - Roseville & Fraser 29733 Gratiot Ave, Roseville, MI 48066; 586-773-2010; Fax: 586-445-5070. Hours: 8AM-4:30PM (EST). *Misdemeanor, Civil Actions Under $25,000, Eviction, Small Claims.*

Civil Records: Access: Mail, in person. Only the court performs in person searches; visitors may not.

No search fee. Required to search: name, years to search. Civil cases indexed by defendant, plaintiff. Civil records on computer since 1985, prior on microfilm.

Criminal Records: Access: Mail, in person. Only the court performs in person searches; visitors may not. No search fee. Required to search: name, years to search, DOB; also helpful: SSN. Criminal records on computer since 1985, prior on microfilm.

General Information: No suppressed, juvenile, sex offenders, mental health, or adoption records released. Copy fee: $2.00 per page. No certification fee. Payee: 39th District Court. Personal checks accepted. Prepayment required. Mail requests: SASE not required. Mail turnaround time 1-2 days.

40th District Court - St. Clair Shores

27701 Jefferson, St. Clair Shores, MI 48081; 586-445-5281; Civil phone: 586-445-5282; Criminal phone: 586-445-5281; Fax: 586-445-4003. Hours: 8:30AM-4:30PM (EST). *Misdemeanor, Civil Actions Under $25,000, Eviction, Small Claims.*

Civil Records: Access: Mail, in person. Visitors must perform in person searches for themselves. Search fee: $10.00 per name. Required to search: name, years to search. Civil cases indexed by defendant, plaintiff. Civil records on computer since 1991; prior records on index books. The court has a request form that must be used with all searches.

Criminal Records: Access: Mail, in person, fax. Only the court performs in person searches; visitors may not. Search fee: $10.00 per name. Required to search: name, years to search, DOB; also helpful: SSN. Criminal records on computer since 1991; prior records on index books. Mail requests must have case number. The court has a request form that must be used with all searches.

General Information: No suppressed, juvenile, sex offenders, mental health, or adoption records released. Copy fee: $1.00 per page. Certification fee: $10.00. Payee: 40th District Court. Personal checks accepted. Prepayment of mail search required. Mail requests: SASE required. Mail turnaround time 2 weeks.

41 A District Court - Shelby

51660 Van Dyke, Shelby Township, MI 48316; 586-739-7325; Fax: 586-726-4555; 997-6172 (Civil). Hours: 8AM-12;00-1-4:30PM (EST). *Misdemeanor, Civil Actions Under $25,000, Eviction, Small Claims.*

Civil Records: Access: Mail, in person. Both court and visitors may perform in person searches. No search fee. Required to search: name, years to search. Civil cases indexed by defendant, plaintiff. Civil records on computer since 1992, prior on index cards.

Criminal Records: Access: Mail, in person. Both court and visitors may perform in person searches. No search fee. Required to search: name, years to search, DOB. Criminal records on computer since 1992, prior on index cards.

General Information: Public Access terminal is available. (Available Friday afternoons by appointment only.) No suppressed, sex offenders, mental health records released. Copy fee: $.50 per page. Certification fee: $10.00. Payee: 41A District Court. Personal checks accepted. Credit cards accepted. Prepayment required. Mail requests: SASE required. Mail turnaround time 10 days.

41 A District Court - Sterling Heights

40111 Dodge Park, Sterling Heights, MI 48313; 586-446-2500; Civil phone: 586-446-2535; Criminal phone: 586-446-2550; Probate phone: 586-446-2565. Hours: 8:30AM-4:30PM (EST). *Misdemeanor, Civil Actions Under $25,000, Eviction, Small Claims.*

Civil Records: Access: Mail, in person. Only the court performs in person searches; visitors may not. No search fee. Required to search: name, years to search. Civil cases indexed by defendant, plaintiff.

Civil records on computer since 1986; prior records on books.

Criminal Records: Access: Mail, in person. Only the court performs in person searches; visitors may not. No search fee. Required to search: name, years to search, DOB; also helpful: SSN. Criminal records on computer since 1986; prior records on books.

General Information: No suppressed, juvenile, sex offenders, mental health, or adoption records released. Copy fee: $.50 per page. Certification fee: $10.00. Payee: Clerk of Court. Personal checks accepted. Prepayment required. Mail requests: SASE required. Mail turnaround time 1 week.

41 B District Court - Clinton TWP

40700 Romeo Plank Rd, Clinton Township, MI 48038-2951; 586-286-8010; Fax: 586-228-2555. Hours: 8:30AM-4:30PM (EST). *Misdemeanor, Civil Actions Under $25,000, Eviction, Small Claims.*

Civil Records: Access: Mail, in person. Only the court performs in person searches; visitors may not. No search fee. Required to search: name, years to search. Civil cases indexed by defendant, plaintiff. Civil records on computer back to 1993, prior on microfilm to 1970s.

Criminal Records: Access: Mail, in person. Only the court performs in person searches; visitors may not. No search fee. Required to search: name, years to search, DOB; also helpful: SSN. Criminal records on computer back to 1993, prior on microfilm to 1970s.

General Information: No suppressed, juvenile, sex offenders, mental health, or adoption records released. Copy fee: $.50 per page. Certification fee: $10.00. Payee: 41 B District Court. Personal, cashiers checks and money orders accepted. Credit cards accepted: Visa, MasterCard. Prepayment required. Mail requests: SASE required.

42nd District Court Division 1

14713 Thirty-three Mile Rd., PO Box 6, Romeo, MI 48065; 586-752-9679; Fax: 586-469-5515. Hours: 8:30AM-4:45PM (EST). *Misdemeanor, Civil Actions Under $25,000, Eviction, Small Claims.*
www.macombcountymi.gov

Civil Records: Access: Mail, in person. Only the court performs in person searches; visitors may not. Search fee: $10.00 per name. Required to search: name, years to search. Civil cases indexed by defendant, plaintiff. Civil records on computer since 1990, prior on index books.

Criminal Records: Access: Mail, in person. Only the court performs in person searches; visitors may not. Search fee: $10.00 per name. Required to search: name, years to search, DOB; also helpful: SSN, sex, signed release. Criminal records on computer since 1990, prior on index books.

General Information: Copy fee: $.35 per page. Certification fee: $10.00. Payee: 42-1 District Court. Personal checks accepted. Prepayment required. Mail requests: SASE requested. Turnaround time 2-3 days.

42nd District Court Division 2

43565 Elizabeth St., Mount Clemens, MI 48043; 586-725-9500; Civil phone: 586-493-0567; Criminal phone: 586-469-5046; Fax: 586-469-5516. Hours: 8:30AM-5PM (EST). *Misdemeanor, Civil Actions Under $25,000, Eviction, Small Claims.*
www.macombcountymi.gov/
Note: Includes City of New Baltimore, Village of New Haven, and townships of Lenox and Chesterfield. This court was formerly located in New Baltimore.

Civil Records: Access: Mail, in person. Only the court performs in person searches; visitors may not. No search fee. Required to search: name, years to search. Civil cases indexed by defendant, plaintiff. Civil records on computer back to 1990.

Criminal Records: Access: Mail, in person. Only the court performs in person searches; visitors may not. No search fee. Required to search: name, years to search, DOB; also helpful: SSN. Criminal records on computer back to 1990.

General Information: Will fax case file documents for $.50 per page. Copy fee: $.50 per page. Certification fee: $10.00. Payee: 42nd District Court. Personal checks accepted. Prepayment required. Prepayment of mail search required. Mail requests: SASE required. Mail turnaround time 1 week.

41 B District Court - Mt Clemens

1 Crocker Blvd, Mount Clemens, MI 48043; 586-469-6870; Fax: 586-469-5037. Hours: 8AM-4:30PM (EST). *Civil Actions Under $25,000, Eviction, Small Claims.*

Civil Records: Access: Mail, fax, in person. Only the court performs in person searches; visitors may not. No search fee. Required to search: name, years to search; also helpful-DOB, case number. Civil cases indexed by defendant, plaintiff. Civil records on computer back to 1996; prior on books back to 1930s.

General Information: No suppressed, juvenile, sex offenders, mental health, or adoption records released. Copy fee: $.50 per page. No certification fee. Payee: 41 B District Court. Business checks accepted. Visa, MC accepted. Prepayment required. Mail requests: SASE required. Mail turnaround time 3 days.

Probate Court 21850 Dumham, Mount Clemens, MI 48043-1075; 586-469-5290; Fax: 586-783-0971. Hours: 8:30AM-5PM (EST). *Probate.*
www.macombcountymi.gov

Manistee County

19th Circuit Court 415 3rd St, Manistee, MI 49660; 231-723-3331; Fax: 231-723-1492. Hours: 8:30AM-5PM (EST). *Felony, Civil Actions Over $25,000.*

Civil Records: Access: Mail, in person. Only the court performs in person searches; visitors may not. Search fee: $5.00 per name. Required to search: name, years to search. Civil cases indexed by defendant, plaintiff. Civil records on computer since 7/90, index books from 1867.

Criminal Records: Access: Mail, in person. Only the court performs in person searches; visitors may not. Search fee: $5.00 per name. Required to search: name, years to search, DOB. Criminal records on computer since 7/90, index books from 1867.

General Information: No suppressed, juvenile, sex offenders, mental health, or adoption records released. Will fax results for $2.00 per name. Copy fee: $.50 per page. Certification fee: $13.00 plus $2.00 each add'l page. Payee: Manistee County Clerk. Personal checks accepted. Prepayment required. Mail requests: SASE required. Mail turnaround time 2-3 days.

85th District Court 415 3rd St, Manistee, MI 49660; 231-723-5010; Fax: 231-723-1491. Hours: 8:30AM-5PM (EST). *Misdemeanor, Civil Actions Under $25,000, Eviction, Small Claims.*

Civil Records: Access: Fax, mail, in person. Both court and visitors may perform in person searches. Search fee: $5.00 per name plus $1.00 per page. Required to search: name, years to search. Civil cases indexed by defendant, plaintiff. Civil records on computer since 4/89, prior on index books.

Criminal Records: Access: Fax, mail, in person. Both court and visitors may perform in person searches. Search fee: $5.00 per name plus $1.00 per page. Required to search: name, years to search, DOB. Criminal records on computer since 4/89, prior on index books.

General Information: No suppressed, juvenile, sex offenders, mental health, or adoption records released. Copy fee: $1.00 per page. Certification fee: $10.00.

Payee: 85th District Court. Personal checks accepted. Prepayment required. Mail requests: SASE required. Mail turnaround time 5-7 days.

Probate Court 415 3rd St, Manistee, MI 49660; 231-723-3261; Fax: 231-398-3558. Hours: 8:30AM-Noon, 1-5PM (EST). *Probate.*

Marquette County

25th Circuit Court 234 W Baraga, Marquette, MI 49855; 906-225-8330; Fax: 906-228-1572. Hours: 8AM-5PM (EST). *Felony, Civil Actions Over $25,000.*

Civil Records: Access: Mail, in person. Only the court performs in person searches; visitors may not. Search fee: $5.00 per name. Required to search: name, years to search. Civil cases indexed by defendant, plaintiff. Civil records on books since 1852, on computer from 04/95.

Criminal Records: Access: Mail, in person. Only the court performs in person searches; visitors may not. Search fee: $5.00 per name. Required to search: name, years to search, DOB. Criminal records on books since 1852, on computer from 04/95.

General Information: No suppressed, juvenile, sex offenders, mental health, or adoption records released. Will fax results to local or toll free line. Copy fee: $1.00 per page. Certification fee: $10.00 plus $1.00 per page after first. Payee: County Clerk. Personal checks accepted. Prepayment required. Mail turnaround time 2-3 business days.

96th District Court County Courthouse, Marquette, MI 49855; 906-225-8235; Fax: 906-225-8255. Hours: 8:00AM-5PM (EST). *Misdemeanor, Civil Actions Under $25,000, Eviction, Small Claims.*

Civil Records: Access: Fax, mail, in person. Only the court performs in person searches; visitors may not. Search fee: $5.00 per name. Required to search: name, years to search; also helpful: address. Civil cases indexed by defendant, plaintiff. Civil records on computer since 1995, prior on docket books and microfiche.

Criminal Records: Access: Fax, mail, in person. Only the court performs in person searches; visitors may not. Search fee: $5.00 per name. Required to search: name, years to search, DOB. Criminal records on computer since 1995, prior on docket books and microfiche.

General Information: No suppressed records released. No fee to fax results. Copy fee: $1.00 per page. Certification fee: $10.00 plus $1.00 per page after first. Payee: 96th District Court. Business checks accepted. Prepayment required. Mail requests: SASE required. Mail turnaround time 1-2 weeks.

Probate Court 234 W Baraga, Marquette, MI 49855; 906-225-8300; Fax: 906-225-8293/228-1533. Hours: 8AM-5PM (EST). *Probate.*

Mason County

51st Circuit Court 304 E Ludington Ave, Ludington, MI 49431; 231-845-1445; Fax: 231-843-1972. Hours: 9AM-5PM (EST). *Felony, Civil Actions Over $25,000.*

Civil Records: Access: Phone, mail, in person. Only the court performs in person searches; visitors may not. No search fee. Required to search: name, years to search. Civil cases indexed by defendant, plaintiff. Civil records on file since 1867.

Criminal Records: Access: Phone, mail, in person. Only the court performs in person searches; visitors may not. No search fee. Required to search: name, years to search, DOB; also helpful: SSN. Criminal records on file since 1867.

General Information: No suppressed, juvenile, sex offenders, mental health, or adoption records released.

Copy fee: $1.00 per page. Certification fee: $10.00. Payee: Mason County Clerk. Personal checks accepted. Prepayment required. Prepayment of mail service required. Mail requests: SASE required. Mail turnaround time 1 week.

79th District Court County Court, 304 E.Ludington Ave., Ludington, MI 49431; 231-843-4130; Fax: 231-845-9076. Hours: 9AM-5PM (EST). *Misdemeanor, Civil Actions Under $25,000, Eviction, Small Claims.*

Civil Records: Access: Fax, mail, in person. Only the court performs in person searches; visitors may not. No search fee. Required to search: name, years to search. Civil cases indexed by defendant, plaintiff. Civil records on Register of Action Docket Cards since 1969, computerized since 10/96.

Criminal Records: Access: In person only. Only the court performs in person searches; visitors may not. No search fee. Required to search: name, years to search, DOB. Criminal records on Register of Action Docket Cardssince 1969, computerized since 10/96.

General Information: No suppressed, juvenile, sex offenders, mental health, or adoption records released. No fee to fax results. Local faxing only. Copy fee: $1.00 per page. Certification fee: $10.00 plus $1.00 per page after first. Payee: 79th District Court. Only cashiers checks and money orders accepted. Prepayment required.

Probate Court 304 E Ludington Ave, Ludington, MI 49431; 231-843-8666; Fax: 231-843-1972. Hours: 9AM-Noon, 1-5PM (EST). *Probate.*

Mecosta County

49th Circuit Court 400 Elm, Big Rapids, MI 49307; 231-592-0783; Fax: 231-592-0193. Hours: 8:30AM-5PM (EST). *Felony, Civil Actions Over $25,000.*
www.co.mecosta.mi.us/circuit.asp

Civil Records: Access: Fax, mail, in person. Only the court performs in person searches; visitors may not. Search fee: $5.00 per name. Required to search: name, years to search. Civil cases indexed by defendant, plaintiff. Civil records on computer since 10/70, archived and microfiche since 1900s.

Criminal Records: Access: Fax, mail, in person. Only the court performs in person searches; visitors may not. Search fee: $5.00 per name. Required to search: name, years to search. Criminal records on computer since 10/70, archived and microfiche since 1900s.

General Information: No suppressed, juvenile, mental health, or adoption records released. Will fax results to local or toll free line. Copy fee: $1.00 per page. Certification fee: $10.00. Payee: Mecosta County Clerk. Personal checks not accepted; money orders and cashiers checks preferred. Prepayment required. Mail requests: SASE requested. Turnaround time 1 week.

77th District Court 400 Elm, Big Rapids, MI 49307; 231-592-0799; Civil phone: 231-592-0799; Criminal phone: 231-592-0190; Probate phone: 231-592-0135; Fax: 231-796-2180. Hours: 8:30AM-4:30PM (EST). *Misdemeanor, Civil Actions Under $25,000, Eviction, Small Claims.*

Civil Records: Access: Mail, fax, in person. Only the court performs in person searches; visitors may not. Search fee: $10.00 per name. Required to search: name, years to search. Civil cases indexed by defendant, plaintiff. Civil records on computer to 1992, archived and microfiche prior.

Criminal Records: Access: Mail, in person. Only the court performs in person searches; visitors may not. Search fee: $10.00 per name. Required to search: name, years to search, DOB. Criminal records on

computer for 10 years, archived and microfiche prior. Signed release required for employment screening.

General Information: No suppressed, juvenile, sex offenders, mental health, or adoption records released. Will fax results to local or toll free line. Copy fee: $1.00 per page. Certification fee: $10.00. Payee: 77th District Court. Business checks accepted. Prepayment required. Mail requests: SASE not required. Mail turnaround time 7 days.

Probate Court 400 Elm St, PO Box 820, Big Rapids, MI 49307; 231-592-0135; Fax: 231-592-0191. Hours: 8:30AM-5PM (EST). *Probate.*
Note: Shares the same judge with Osceola County Probate Court.

Menominee County

41st Circuit Court 839 10th Ave, Menominee, MI 49858; 906-863-9968; Fax: 906-863-8839. Hours: 8AM-4:30PM (CST). *Felony, Civil Actions Over $25,000.*

Civil Records: Access: Mail, in person. Only the court performs in person searches; visitors may not. Search fee: $1.00 per name per year. Required to search: name, years to search. Civil cases indexed by defendant, plaintiff. Civil records kept by docket entry in file folders, archived to 1900, computerized since 1998.

Criminal Records: Access: Mail, in person. Only the court performs in person searches; visitors may not. Search fee: $5.00 per name for first 7 years, then $1.00 each add'l year. Required to search: name, years to search, DOB; also helpful: SSN. Criminal records kept by docket entry in file folders to 1900; on computer back to 1998.

General Information: No suppressed, juvenile, sex offenders, mental health, or adoption records released. Fee to fax results is $3.00 1st page, $1.00 each add'l. Copy fee: $1.00 per page. Certification fee: $10.00 plus $1.00 per page after first. Payee: 41st Circuit Court. Personal checks accepted. Prepayment required. Mail turnaround time 2-3 days.

95 A District Court 839 10th Ave, Menominee, MI 49858; 906-863-8532; Fax: 906-863-2023. Hours: 8AM-4:30PM (CST). *Misdemeanor, Civil Actions Under $25,000, Eviction, Small Claims.*

Civil Records: Access: Fax, mail, in person. Only the court performs in person searches; visitors may not. Search fee: $5.00 per name. Required to search: name, years to search. Civil cases indexed by defendant, plaintiff. Civil records on index books since 1969.

Criminal Records: Access: Fax, mail, in person. Only the court performs in person searches; visitors may not. Search fee: $5.00 per name. Required to search: name, years to search, DOB. Criminal records on index books since 1969.

General Information: No suppressed, juvenile, sex offenders, mental health, or adoption records released. Will fax results $.20 per page. Copy fee: $.20 per page. Certification fee: $10.00. Payee: District Court 95A. Personal checks accepted. Prepayment required. Mail requests: SASE required. Mail turnaround time 1 week.

Probate Court 839 10th Ave., Menominee, MI 49858; 906-863-2634; Fax: 906-863-9904. Hours: 8AM-4:30PM (CST). *Probate, Juvenile.*

Midland County

42nd Circuit Court Courthouse, 301 W Main St, Midland, MI 48640; 989-832-6735; Fax: 989-832-6610. Hours: 8AM-5PM (EST). *Felony, Civil Actions Over $25,000.*
www.midlandcounty.org/circuitcourt/index.htm

Civil Records: Access: Phone, mail, in person. Only the court performs in person searches; visitors may not. No search fee. Required to search: name, years to search. Civil cases indexed by defendant, plaintiff. Civil records on computer from 1985, prior on books since 1800s.

Criminal Records: Access: Phone, mail, in person. Only the court performs in person searches; visitors may not. No search fee. Required to search: name, years to search, DOB. Criminal records on computer from 1985, prior on books since 1800s.

General Information: No suppressed records released. Copy fee: $1.00 per page. Certification fee: $15.00 plus $1.00 per page after first. Payee: Clerk of Circuit Court. Personal checks accepted. Prepayment required. Mail requests: SASE required. Mail turnaround time same day.

75th District Court - Civil Division 301 W Main St, Midland, MI 48640; 989-832-6701. Hours: 8:30AM-4:30PM (EST). *Civil Actions Under $25,000, Eviction, Small Claims.*

Note: Small Claims can be reached at 989-832-6717

Civil Records: Access: Mail, in person. Both court and visitors may perform in person searches. Search fee: $1.00 per name per year. Required to search: name, years to search; also helpful: address. Civil cases indexed by defendant, plaintiff. Civil records on computer since 06/89; on index books until 06/89.

General Information: No suppressed, juvenile, sex offenders, mental health, or adoption records released. Copy fee: $1.00 per page. Certification fee: $10.00 for the first page, add'l pages $1.00 each. Payee: 75th District Court. Personal checks accepted. Prepayment required. Mail requests: SASE not required. Mail turnaround time 5-7 days.

75th District Court - Criminal Division 301 W Main St, Midland, MI 48640-5183; 989-832-6702 (6714-traffic). Hours: 8:30AM-5PM (EST). *Misdemeanor.*

Criminal Records: Access: Mail, in person. Only the court performs in person searches; visitors may not. Search fee: $1.00 per name per year. Required to search: name, years to search, DOB. Criminal records on computer since 1991, prior on docket books and paper index.

General Information: No suppressed, sex offenders or mental health records released. Copy fee: $1.00 per page. Certification fee: $1.00 per document. Payee: 75th District Court. Personal checks accepted. Prepayment required. Mail requests: SASE not required. Mail turnaround time 1 week.

Probate Court 301 W Main St, Midland, MI 48640; 989-832-6880; Fax: 989-832-6607. Hours: 8AM-5PM (EST). *Probate.*
www.midlandcounty.org

Missaukee County

28th Circuit Court PO Box 800, Lake City, MI 49651; 231-839-4967; Fax: 231-839-3684. Hours: 9AM-5PM (EST). *Felony, Civil Actions Over $25,000.*
www.missaukee.org/court.htm?
Civil Records: Access: Phone, fax, mail, in person. Both court and visitors may perform in person searches. Search fee: $5.00 per name. Required to search: name, years to search. Civil cases indexed by defendant, plaintiff. Civil records on computer since 1990, prior on books.
Criminal Records: Access: Phone, fax, mail, in person. Both court and visitors may perform in person searches. Search fee: $5.00 per name. Required to search: name, years to search; also helpful: DOB, SSN. Criminal records on computer since 1990, prior on books.

General Information: Public Access terminal is available. No suppressed, juvenile, sex offenders, mental health, or adoption records released. Will fax results $5.00 1st page, $1.00 each add'l. Copy fee: $1.00 per page. Certification fee: $10.00. Payee: Missaukee County Clerk. Personal checks accepted. Prepayment required. Mail requests: SASE not required. Mail turnaround time 2 days.

84th District Court PO Box 800, Lake City, MI 49651; 231-839-4590. Hours: 9AM-5PM (EST). *Misdemeanor, Civil Actions Under $25,000, Eviction, Small Claims.*
Civil Records: Access: Mail, in person. Both court and visitors may perform in person searches. Search fee: $5.00 per name. Required to search: name, years to search. Civil cases indexed by defendant, plaintiff. Civil records on computer since 1989.
Criminal Records: Access: Mail, in person. Both court and visitors may perform in person searches. Search fee: $5.00 per name. Required to search: name, years to search, DOB, SSN. Criminal records on computer since 1988.

General Information: No suppressed, juvenile, sex offenders, mental health, or adoption records released. Will fax results to local or toll free line. Copy fee: $1.00 per page. Certification fee: $10.00 plus $1.00 per page after first. Payee: District Court. Personal checks accepted. Prepayment required. Mail requests: SASE required. Mail turnaround time 1 week.

Probate Court PO Box 800, Lake City, MI 49651; 231-839-2266; Fax: 231-839-5856. Hours: 9AM-Noon, 1-5PM (EST). *Probate.*
Note: Will accept email search requests.

Monroe County

38th Circuit Court 106 E 1st St, Monroe, MI 48161; 734-240-7020; Fax: 734-240-7045. Hours: 8:30AM-5PM (EST). *Felony, Civil Actions Over $25,000.*
www.co.monroe.mi.us/Courts/index.html
Civil Records: Access: Mail, fax, in person. Both court and visitors may perform in person searches. Search fee: $8.00 per name. Fee is per name per 5 years. Required to search: name, years to search. Civil cases indexed by defendant, plaintiff. Civil records on computer back to 1990; prior on docket books.
Criminal Records: Access: Mail, in person. Both court and visitors may perform in person searches. Search fee: $8.00 per name. Fee is per name per 5 years. Required to search: name, years to search, DOB. Criminal records on computer back to 1990; prior on docket books.
General Information: Public Access terminal is available. No suppressed records released. Copy fee: $1.00 per page. Certification fee: $3.00. Payee: 38th Circuit Court. Personal checks accepted. Prepayment required. Mail requests: SASE required. Mail turnaround time same day.

1st District Court 106 E 1st St, Monroe, MI 48161; 734-240-7075; Fax: 734-240-7098. Hours: 8AM-4;45 PM (EST). *Misdemeanor, Civil Actions Under $25,000, Eviction, Small Claims.*
www.co.monroe.mi.us/DistrictCourt/index.html
Civil Records: Access: Mail, in person. Only the court performs in person searches; visitors may not. No search fee. Required to search: name, years to search, address. Civil cases indexed by defendant, plaintiff. Civil records on computer since 1993; prior records to 1969 on microfiche.
Criminal Records: Access: Mail, in person. Both court and visitors may perform in person searches. No search fee. Required to search: name, years to search, DOB; also helpful: address, SSN. Criminal records on computer since 1993; prior records to 1969 on microfiche.

General Information: No suppressed, juvenile, sex offenders, mental health, or adoption records released. Copy fee: $1.00 per page. Certification fee: $10.00 per page. Payee: 1st District Court. Business checks accepted. Prepayment required. Mail turnaround time 1 week.

Probate Court 106 E 1st St, Monroe, MI 48161; 734-240-7346. 8AM-Noon, 1-5PM (EST). *Probate.*
www.co.monroe.mi.us/Courts/index.html

Montcalm County

8th Circuit Court 639 N.State St., Stanton, MI 48888; 989-831-3520; Fax: 989-831-3525. Hours: 8AM-5PM (EST). *Felony, Civil Actions Over $25,000.*
www.montcalm.org/
Note: The office closes for lunch for one hour.

Civil Records: Access: Mail, in person. Only the court performs in person searches; visitors may not. Search fee: $5.00 for 5 years then $1.00 for each add'l year searched. Required to search: name, years to search. Civil cases indexed by defendant, plaintiff. Civil records on docket books to 1867, computerized since 1990.
Criminal Records: Access: Mail, in person, fax. Only the court performs in person searches; visitors may not. Search fee: $10.00 for 1st. yr. $1.00 each yr after. Required to search: name, years to search, DOB. Criminal records on docket books to 1867, computerized since 1990.

General Information: No suppressed, juvenile, sex offenders, mental health, adoption, birth or DD214 records released. Copy fee: $1.00 per page. Certification fee: $10.00 plus $1.00 per page after first. Payee: Montcalm County Clerk. Personal checks accepted. Prepayment required. Mail requests: SASE required. Mail turnaround time 1-3 days.

64 B District Court 617 N State Rd #D, Stanton, MI 48888; 989-831-7450; Fax: 989-831-7452. Hours: 8AM-5PM (EST). *Misdemeanor, Civil Actions Under $25,000, Eviction, Small Claims.*
Civil Records: Access: Mail, in person. Only the court performs in person searches; visitors may not. No search fee. Required to search: name, years to search. Civil cases indexed by defendant, plaintiff. Civil records on computer since 1989, prior on books and microfiche.
Criminal Records: Access: Mail, in person, fax. Only the court performs in person searches; visitors may not. No search fee. Required to search: name, years to search, DOB; also helpful: SSN. Criminal records on computer since 1989, prior on books and microfiche.
General Information: No suppressed records released. Copy fee: $.25 per page. Certification fee: $10.00 plus $1.00 each add'l page. Payee: 64 B District Court. Personal checks accepted. Prepayment required. Mail requests: SASE required. Mail turnaround time 7 days.

Probate Court 625 N State St., PO Box 309, Stanton, MI 48888; 989-831-7316; Fax: 989-831-7314. Hours: 8AM-5PM (EST). *Probate.*

Montmorency County

26th Circuit Court PO Box 789, Atlanta, MI 49709; 989-785-8022; Probate phone: 989-785-8064; Fax: 989-785-8023. Hours: 8:30AM-Noon, 1-4:30PM (EST). *Felony, Civil Actions Over $25,000.*
Civil Records: Access: Mail, in person. Both court and visitors may perform in person searches. Search fee: $5.00 per name. Required to search: name, years to search. Civil cases indexed by defendant, plaintiff. Civil records on computer since 1990, prior on books

since 1940s, microfiche to 1970. For in person searches, call ahead two days in advance.

Criminal Records: Access: Mail, in person. Both court and visitors may perform in person searches. Search fee: $5.00 per name. Required to search: name, years to search; also helpful: DOB. Criminal records on computer since 1990, prior on books since 1940s. For in person searches, call ahead two days in advance.

General Information: No suppressed, birth certificate (except to heir or parent) adoption records released. Fee to fax results is $1.00 per page. Copy fee: $1.00 per page. Certification fee: $10.00 plus $1.00 each add'l page. Payee: County Clerk. Personal checks accepted. Prepayment required. Mail turnaround time 7-10 days.

88th District Court County Courthouse, PO Box 789, Atlanta, MI 49709; 989-785-8035; Fax: 989-785-8036. Hours: 8:30AM-Noon, 1-4:30PM (EST). *Misdemeanor, Civil Actions Under $25,000, Eviction, Small Claims.*

Civil Records: Access: Mail, fax, in person. Only the court performs in person searches; visitors may not. Search fee: $5.00 per name. Required to search: name, years to search; also helpful: address. Civil cases indexed by defendant, plaintiff. Civil records on computer back to 1990, prior on books and card file since 1969.

Criminal Records: Access: Mail, fax, in person. Only the court performs in person searches; visitors may not. Search fee: $5.00 per name. Required to search: name, years to search, DOB; also helpful: address, SSN, signed release. Criminal records on computer back to 1990, prior on books and card file since 1969.

General Information: No suppressed, juvenile, sex offenders, mental health, or adoption records released. Fee to fax results is $1.00 per document. Copy fee: $1.00 per page. Certification fee: $10.00. Payee: 88th District Court-Montmorency County. Personal checks accepted; credit cards accepted. Prepayment required. Mail requests: SASE required. Mail turnaround time 1-3 days.

Probate Court PO Box 789, Atlanta, MI 49709-0789; 989-785-8064; Fax: 989-785-8065. *Probate.*

Muskegon County

14th Circuit Court County Bldg, 6th Floor, 990 Terrace St, Muskegon, MI 49442; 231-724-6251; Fax: 231-724-6695. Hours: 8AM-5PM (EST). *Felony, Civil Actions Over $25,000.*

Civil Records: Access: Phone, mail, fax, in person. Both court and visitors may perform in person searches. Search fee: $10.00 per name. Required to search: name, years to search. Civil cases indexed by defendant, plaintiff. Civil records on computer back to 1984, prior on books since 1853.

Criminal Records: Access: Phone, mail, fax, in person. Both court and visitors may perform in person searches. Search fee: $10.00 per name. Required to search: name, years to search, DOB; also helpful: SSN. Criminal records on computer back to 1984, prior on books since 1853.

General Information: Public Access terminal is available. No suppressed, juvenile, sex offenders, mental health, or adoption records released. Fee to fax results is $1.00 per page. Copy fee: $1.00 per page. Certification fee: $10.00 plus $1.00 per page after first. Payee: Circuit Court Records. Personal checks accepted. Prepayment required. Mail requests: SASE required. Mail turnaround time 2-3 days.

60th District Court 990 Terrace, 1st Floor, Muskegon, MI 49442; 231-724-6250; Fax: 231-724-3489. 8:30AM-4:45PM (EST). *Misdemeanor, Civil Actions Under $25,000, Eviction, Small Claims.* www.co.muskegon.mi.us/60thdistrict

Civil Records: Access: Mail, in person. Both court and visitors may perform in person searches. No search fee. Required to search: name, years to search. Civil cases indexed by defendant, plaintiff. Civil records on computer since 5/93, prior on hard copy. Online access to the court weekly docket is free at www.co.muskegon.mi.us/60thdistrict/docket.htm.

Criminal Records: Access: Mail, in person. Both court and visitors may perform in person searches. No search fee. Required to search: name, years to search, DOB. Criminal records on computer since 5/93, prior on hard copy. Online access to the court weekly docket is free at www.co.muskegon.mi.us/60thdistrict/docket.htm.

General Information: Public Access terminal is available. No suppressed, juvenile, sex offenders, mental health, or adoption records released. Copy fee: $1.00 per page. Certification fee: $10.00. Payee: 60th District Court. Personal checks accepted. Prepayment required. Mail requests: SASE required. Mail turnaround time 3 days.

Probate Court 990 Terrace St, 5th Floor, Muskegon, MI 49442; 231-724-6241; Fax: 231-724-6232. Hours: 8AM-5PM (EST). *Probate.*

Newaygo County

27th Circuit Court PO Box 885, White Cloud, MI 49349-0885; 231-689-7269; Probate phone: 231-689-7270 fax 689-7276; Fax: 231-689-7007. Hours: 8AM-noon; 1-5PM (EST). *Felony, Civil Actions Over $25,000.*

Civil Records: Access: Mail, fax, in person. Only the court performs in person searches; visitors may not. No search fee. Required to search: name, years to search. Civil cases indexed by defendant, plaintiff. Civil records archived since 1880s; on computer since 7/1994.

Criminal Records: Access: Mail, fax, in person. Only the court performs in person searches; visitors may not. No search fee. Required to search: name, years to search; also helpful: DOB. Criminal records archived since 1880s; on computer since 7/1994.

General Information: No suppressed records released. Will fax results to toll-free number only. Copy fee: $1.00 per page. Certification fee: $10.00 plus $1.00 per page after first. Payee: Newaygo County Circuit Court. Personal checks accepted. Prepayment required. Mail requests: SASE requested. Turnaround time 2-5 days.

78th District Court 1092 Newell St, White Cloud, MI 49349; 231-689-7257; Fax: 231-689-7258. Hours: 8AM-noon, 1-5PM (EST). *Misdemeanor, Civil Actions Under $25,000, Eviction, Small Claims.*

Civil Records: Access: Fax, mail, in person. Both court and visitors may perform in person searches. No search fee. Required to search: name, years to search; also helpful: address. Civil cases indexed by defendant, plaintiff. Civil records on computer since 7/27/89, prior in folders.

Criminal Records: Access: Fax, mail, in person. Both court and visitors may perform in person searches. No search fee. Required to search: name, years to search, DOB; also helpful: address, SSN. Criminal records on computer since 7/27/89, prior in folders.

General Information: Public Access terminal is available. No suppressed records released. No fee to fax results. Copy fee: $1.00 per page. Certification fee: $10.00 plus $1.00 per page after first. Payee: 78th

District Court. Personal checks accepted. Prepayment required. Mail requests: SASE required. Mail turnaround time 7-10 days.

Probate Court PO Box 885 (1092 Newell St.), White Cloud, MI 49349; 231-689-7270; Fax: 231-689-7276. 8AM-Noon, 1-5PM (EST). *Probate.*

Oakland County

6th Circuit Court 1200 N Telegraph Rd, Pontiac, MI 48341; 248-858-0581. Hours: 8:30AM-4:30PM (EST). *Felony, Civil Actions Over $25,000.* www.co.oakland.mi.us

Civil Records: Access: Mail, in person. Both court and visitors may perform in person searches. Search fee: $1.00 per name. Required to search: name, years to search. Civil cases indexed by defendant, plaintiff. Civil records on computer since 1963, prior on microfilm & books.

Criminal Records: Access: Mail, in person. Both court and visitors may perform in person searches. Search fee: $1.00 per name. Required to search: name; also helpful: years to search, DOB, SSN. Criminal records on computer since 1963, prior on microfilm & books.

General Information: Public Access terminal is available. No suppressed, non-public, sex offenders or mental health records released. Will fax results to local or toll free line. Copy fee: $1.00 per page. Certification fee: $10.00 plus $1.00 per page after first. Payee: Circuit Court. Personal checks not accepted, but most credit cards are. Prepayment required. Mail requests: SASE required. Mail turnaround time 7 days.

43rd District Court 43 E Nine Mile Rd, Hazel Park, MI 48030; 248-547-3034; Fax: 248-546-4088. Hours: 8:30AM-4:30PM (EST). *Misdemeanor, Civil Actions Under $25,000, Eviction, Small Claims.*

Civil Records: Access: Mail, in person. Both court and visitors may perform in person searches. No search fee. Required to search: name, years to search. Civil cases indexed by defendant, plaintiff. Civil records on computer since 1989, prior on books since 1970.

Criminal Records: Access: Mail, in person. Both court and visitors may perform in person searches. No search fee. Required to search: name, years to search, DOB. Criminal records on computer since 1989, prior on books since 1970.

General Information: Public Access terminal is available. No suppressed, juvenile, sex offenders, mental health, or adoption records released. Copy fee: $.25 per page. Certification fee: $10.00. Payee: 43rd District Court. Only cashiers checks, cash or money orders accepted. Prepayment required. Mail requests: SASE not required. Mail turnaround time 3-7 days.

44th District Court - Royal Oak 400 E Eleven Mile Rd, Box 20, Royal Oak, MI 48068; 248-246-3600; Fax: 248-246-3601. Hours: 8AM-4:30PM (EST). *Misdemeanor, Civil Actions Under $25,000, Eviction, Small Claims.* www.ci.royal-oak.mi.us

Civil Records: Access: Mail, in person. Both court and visitors may perform in person searches. Search fee: $10.00 per name. Required to search: name, years to search. Civil cases indexed by defendant, plaintiff. Civil records on computer since 1983s, prior on docket books and index cards.

Criminal Records: Access: Mail, in person. Both court and visitors may perform in person searches. Search fee: $10.00 per name. Required to search: name, years to search, DOB, signed release, offense; also helpful: address. Criminal records on computer since 1983s, prior on docket books and index cards.

General Information: No suppressed, juvenile, sex offenders, mental health, or adoption records released.

Copy fee: $1.00 per page. Certification fee: $10.00 plus $1.00 per page after first. Payee: 44th District Court. Personal checks accepted. Prepayment required. Mail requests: SASE required. Mail turnaround time 5 days.

45 A District Court - Berkley
3338 Coolidge, Berkley, MI 48072; 248-544-3300; Fax: 248-546-2416. Hours: 8:30AM-4:45PM (EST). *Misdemeanor, Civil Actions Under $25,000, Eviction, Small Claims.*

Civil Records: Access: Mail, in person. Only the court performs in person searches; visitors may not. Search fee: $1.00 per name. Required to search: name, years to search. Civil cases indexed by defendant, plaintiff. Civil records on computer since 1989 prior on books.

Criminal Records: Access: Mail, in person. Only the court performs in person searches; visitors may not. No search fee. Required to search: name, years to search, DOB; also helpful: SSN. Criminal records on computer since 1989, prior on books.

General Information: No suppressed records released. Copy fee: $1.00 per page. Certification fee: $10.00. Payee: 45 A District Court. Personal checks accepted. Prepayment required. Mail requests: SASE required. Mail turnaround time 1 week.

45 B District Court
13600 Oak Park Blvd, Oak Park, MI 48237; 248-691-7440; Fax: 248-691-7158. Hours: 9AM-5PM (EST). *Misdemeanor, Civil Actions Under $25,000, Eviction, Small Claims.*
Note: Court covers Huntington Woods, Oak Park, Pleasant Ridge, and Royal Oak Township.

Civil Records: Access: Mail, in person. Both the court and visitors may perform in person searches. No search fee. Required to search: name, years to search. Civil cases indexed by defendant, plaintiff. Civil records on computer back to 1988. Docket books and index cards back to 1987.

Criminal Records: Access: Mail, in person. Both the court and visitors may perform in person searches. No search fee. Required to search: name, years to search, DOB; also helpful: SSN. Criminal records on computer back to 1993. Docket books and index cards go back to 1988.

General Information: Public Access terminal is available. No suppressed records released. Copy fee: $1.00 per page. Certification fee: $10.00. Payee: 45 B District Court. Business checks accepted. Prepayment required. Mail turnaround time varies.

46th District Court
26000 Evergreen Rd, Southfield, MI 48076; 248-796-5800; Civil phone: 248-796-5870; Criminal phone: 248-796-5880. Hours: 8AM-4:30PM (counter) (EST). *Misdemeanor, Civil Actions Under $25,000, Eviction, Small Claims.*
www.cityofsouthfield.com/46court

Civil Records: Access: Mail, in person. Both court and visitors may perform in person searches. No search fee. Required to search: name, years to search. Civil cases indexed by defendant, plaintiff. Civil records prior to 1992 are on microfilm; most recent records are computerized.

Criminal Records: Access: Mail, in person. Both court and visitors may perform in person searches. Court will search only 1990 to present with case # provided. No search fee. Required to search: name, years to search, DOB. Criminal records on computer since 1992, prior on microfiche.

General Information: No suppressed or "non-public" records released, such as juvenile, sex offenders, mental health, or adoption records. Copy fee: $.50 per page. Certification fee: $10.00 plus $1.00 per page after first. Payee: 46th District Court. Personal checks accepted. Visa, MC accepted.

Prepayment required. Mail requests: SASE not requested. Turnaround time varies.

47th District Court - Farmington, Farmington Hills
31605 W 11 Mile Rd, Farmington Hills, MI 48336; 248-871-2900. Hours: 8:30AM-4:30PM; 'til 6:30PM 3rd Tues each month (EST). *Misdemeanor, Civil Actions Under $25,000, Eviction, Small Claims.*

Civil Records: Access: Mail, fax, in person. No search fee. Required to search: name, years to search, case number. Civil cases indexed by defendant, plaintiff. Civil records on computer since 7/19/93; prior on microfiche since 1975.

Criminal Records: Access: In person only. Visitors must perform in person searches for themselves. No search fee. Required to search: name, years to search, case number DOB; also helpful: offense. Criminal records on computer since 7/19/93; prior on microfiche since 1975.

General Information: Public Access terminal is available. No suppressed, sex offenders or mental health records released. Copy fee: $1.00 per page. Certification fee: $10.00 plus $1.00 per page after first. Payee: 47th District Court. Personal checks accepted. Visa, MC accepted. Prepayment required. Mail requests: SASE required. Mail turnaround time varies.

48th District Court
4280 Telegraph Rd, Bloomfield Hills, MI 48302; 248-647-1141; Fax: 248-647-8955. Hours: 8:30AM-4:30PM (EST). *Misdemeanor, Civil Actions Under $25,000, Eviction, Small Claims.*

Civil Records: Access: Phone, mail, in person. Both court and visitors may perform in person searches. No search fee. Required to search: name, years to search, address. Civil cases indexed by defendant, plaintiff. Civil records on computer since 1980, prior on index cards.

Criminal Records: Access: Phone, mail, in person. Both court and visitors may perform in person searches. No search fee. Required to search: name, years to search, address, DOB; also helpful: SSN. Criminal records on computer since 1980, prior on index cards.

General Information: Public Access terminal is available. No suppressed, juvenile, sex offenders, mental health, victim or adoption records released. Copy fee: $.50 per page. Certification fee: $10.00 plus $1.00 per page after first. Payee: 48th District Court. Personal checks accepted. Visa, MC, AmEx accepted. Debit Card accepted. Prepayment required. Mail turnaround time varies.

51st District Court - Waterford
5100 Civic Center Dr, Waterford, MI 48329; 248-674-4655. Hours: 8:30AM-4:45PM (EST). *Misdemeanor, Civil Actions Under $25,000, Eviction, Small Claims.*

Civil Records: Access: Mail, in person. Only the court performs in person searches; visitors may not. Search fee: None. Will perform in person searches 10-11AM and 2-4PM. Required to search: name, years to search. Civil cases indexed by defendant, plaintiff. Civil records on computer since 1980s, prior on docket books and index cards to 1969.

Criminal Records: Access: Mail, in person. Only the court performs in person searches; visitors may not. Search fee: None. Will perform in person searches 10-11AM and 2-4PM only. Required to search: name, years to search, DOB; also helpful: SSN. Criminal records on computer since 1980s, prior on docket books and index cards to 1969.

General Information: No suppressed, juvenile, sex offenders, mental health, or adoption records released. Copy fee: $.25 per page. Certification fee: $10.00. Payee: 51st District Court. Personal checks accepted.

Visa, MC accepted. Prepayment required. Mail turnaround time 10 days.

52nd District Court - Division 1
48150 Grand River, Novi, MI 48374; Civil phone: 248-305-6080; Criminal phone: 248-305-6460. Hours: 8:30AM-4:30PM (EST). *Misdemeanor, Civil Actions Under $25,000, Eviction, Small Claims.*
www.52-1districtcourt.com

Civil Records: Access: Phone, mail, in person. Only the court performs in person searches; visitors may not. Search fee: None. Prefers to do large name lists on Tuesday & Friday. Required to search: name, years to search. Civil cases indexed by defendant, plaintiff. Civil records on computer since 1984, prior on books.

Criminal Records: Access: Phone, mail, in person. Only the court performs in person searches; visitors may not. Search fee: None. Best to do large name lists on Thursday & Friday. Required to search: name, years to search; also helpful: DOB. Criminal records on computer since 1984, prior on books.

General Information: No suppressed, juvenile, sex offenders or mental health records released. Copy fee: $1.00 per page. Certification fee: $10.00. Payee: 52-1 District Court. Personal checks accepted. Visa, MC accepted. Prepayment required. Mail requests: SASE required. Mail turnaround time 1 month.

52nd District Court - Division 2
5850 Lorac, Clarkston, MI 48346; Civil phone: 248-625-4994; Criminal phone: 248-625-4888; Fax: 248-625-5602. Hours: 8:30AM-4:30PM (EST). *Misdemeanor, Civil Actions Under $25,000, Eviction, Small Claims.*
Note: Court covers Springfield, Holly, Groveland, Brandon, Independence, Clarkston & Ortonville and townships of Whie Lake and Rose.

Civil Records: Access: Phone, fax, mail, in person. Only the court performs in person searches; visitors may not. No search fee. Required to search: name, years to search. Civil cases indexed by defendant, plaintiff. Civil records on computer since 1982, prior on microfiche since 1976.

Criminal Records: Access: Phone, fax, mail, in person. Only the court performs in person searches; visitors may not. No search fee. Required to search: name, years to search, DOB; also helpful: SSN. Criminal records on computer since 1982, prior on microfiche since 1976.

General Information: No suppressed, juvenile or sex offender records released. Fax service and fee is under consideration. Copy fee: $1.00 per page. Certification fee: $10.00. Payee: 52-2 District Court. Personal checks accepted. Visa, MC accepted. Prepayment required. Mail turnaround time 3-5 days.

52nd District Court - Division 3
700 Barclay Circle, Rochester Hills, MI 48307; 248-853-5553; Fax: 248-853-3277. Hours: 8:30AM-4:30PM (EST). *Misdemeanor, Civil Actions Under $25,000, Eviction, Small Claims.*
www.co.oakland.mi.us/courts

Civil Records: Access: Phone, fax, mail, in person. Only the court performs in person searches; visitors may not. No search fee. Required to search: name; also helpful: years to search. Civil cases indexed by defendant, plaintiff. Civil records on computer for 10 years, prior on docket books and index cards.

Criminal Records: Access: Phone, fax, mail, in person. Only the court performs in person searches; visitors may not. No search fee. Required to search: name, DOB; also helpful: years to search. Criminal records on computer for 10 years, prior on docket books and index cards.

General Information: No suppressed records released. Copy fee: $1.00 per page. Certification fee: $10.00. Payee: 52-3 District Court. Personal checks accepted. Visa, MC accepted. In person only. Prepayment required. Mail turnaround time varies.

52nd District Court - Division 4 (Troy, Clawson) 520 W Big Beaver Rd, Troy, MI 48084; 248-528-0400; Fax: 248-528-3588. Hours: 8:15AM-4:15PM (EST). *Misdemeanor, Civil Actions Under $25,000, Eviction, Small Claims.*

Civil Records: Access: Mail, fax, in person. Only the court may perform in person searches. No search fee. Required to search: name, years to search. Civil cases indexed by defendant, plaintiff.

Criminal Records: Access: Fax, mail, in person. Only the court performs in person searches; visitors may not. No search fee. Required to search: name; also helpful: years to search, DOB, SSN. Criminal records.

General Information: No suppressed, juvenile, sex offenders, mental health, or adoption records released. No fee to fax results. Fax for criminal records and local calls only. Copy fee: $1.00 per page. No certification fee. Payee: 52-4 District Court. Personal checks accepted. Visa, MC accepted. Prepayment required. Mail requests: SASE required. Mail turnaround time 1 week.

50th District Court - Pontiac Civil Division 70 N Saganaw, Pontiac, MI 48342; 248-758-3820; Criminal phone: 248-758-3820; Fax: 248-758-3888. Hours: 8:30AM-4:30PM (EST). *Civil Actions Under $25,000, Eviction, Small Claims.*

Civil Records: Access: Mail, in person, best results via Fax. Both court and visitors may perform in person searches. No search fee. Required to search: name, years to search. Civil cases indexed by defendant, plaintiff. Civil records on computer since 1985.

General Information: Public Access terminal is available. No suppressed, juvenile, sex offenders, mental health, or adoption records released. Copy fee: $1.00 1st page, $.10 each add'l page. No certification fee. Payee: 50th District Court. Personal checks accepted. Prepayment required. Mail turnaround time 3-4 days.

50th District Court - Pontiac Criminal Division 70 N Saganaw, Pontiac, MI 48342; 248-758-3820; Fax: 248-758-3888. Hours: 8:30AM-4:30PM (EST). *Misdemeanor.*

Criminal Records: Access: Mail, fax, in person. Both court and visitors may perform in person searches. No search fee. Required to search: name, years to search, DOB; also helpful: SSN. Criminal records on computer since 1984, prior on index cards since 1975.

General Information: Public Access terminal is available. No suppressed, juvenile, sex offenders, mental health, or adoption records released. Will fax results to lcoal or toll free line. Copy fee: $1.00 first page, $.25 thereafter. Certification fee: $10.00. Payee: 50th District Court. Business checks accepted. Prepayment required. Mail turnaround time 2-3 days.

Probate Court 1200 N Telegraph Rd, 1st Fl, Oakland County Complex, East Wing, Pontiac, MI 48341; 248-858-0260; Fax: 248-452-2016. Hours: 8AM-5PM (EST). *Probate.*

Oceana County

27th Circuit Court 100 State St., #M-34, Hart, MI 49420; 231-873-3977. Hours: 9AM-5PM (EST). *Felony, Civil Actions Over $25,000.*

Civil Records: Access: Mail, in person. Only the court performs in person searches; visitors may not. Search fee: $5.00 per name. Required to search: name, years to search. Civil cases indexed by defendant, plaintiff. Civil records on computer since 1994, paper records to 1800s.

Criminal Records: Access: Mail, in person. Only the court performs in person searches; visitors may not. Search fee: $5.00 per name. Required to search: name, years to search; also helpful: DOB. Criminal records on computer since 1994, paper records to 1800s.

General Information: No suppressed, juvenile, sex offenders, mental health, or adoption records released. Copy fee: $1.00 per page. Certification fee: $10.00 plus $1.00 per page after first. Payee: Oceana County Circuit Court. Personal checks accepted. Prepayment required. Mail requests: SASE requested. Turnaround time same day.

79th District Court PO Box 471, Hart, MI 49420; 231-873-4530; Fax: 231-873-1861. Hours: 8AM-5PM (EST). *Misdemeanor, Civil Actions Under $25,000, Eviction, Small Claims.*

Civil Records: Access: Mail, in person. Only the court performs in person searches; visitors may not. Search fee: $5.00 per name. Required to search: name, years to search. Civil cases indexed by plaintiff. Civil records on file cards and in file folders since 1967; on computer back to 1999.

Criminal Records: Access: Mail, in person. Only the court performs in person searches; visitors may not. Search fee: $5.00 per name. Required to search: name, years to search, DOB. Criminal records on file cards and in file folders since 1967; on computer back to 1999.

General Information: No suppressed records released. Copy fee: $1.00 per page. Certification fee: $10.00 plus $1.00 per page after first. Payee: 79th District Court. No personal checks accepted. Prepayment required. Mail requests: SASE not required. Mail turnaround time same day.

Probate Court County Bldg, 100 S State St, #M-10, Hart, MI 49420; 231-873-3666; Fax: 231-873-1943. Hours: 9AM-Noon, 1-5PM (EST). *Probate.*

Ogemaw County

34th Circuit Court 806 W Houghton, West Branch, MI 48661; 989-345-0215; Fax: 989-345-7223. Hours: 8:30AM-4:30PM (EST). *Felony, Civil Actions Over $25,000.*

Civil Records: Access: Phone, fax, mail, in person. Only the court performs in person searches; visitors may not. Search fee: $10.00 per name. Fee is for search prior to 1993. Required to search: name, years to search. Civil cases indexed by defendant, plaintiff. Civil records on index cards since 1970, library books in vault since 1960; on computer back to 1993.

Criminal Records: Access: Phone, fax, mail, in person. Only the court performs in person searches; visitors may not. Search fee: $10.00 per name. Fee is for search prior to 1993. Required to search: name, years to search, DOB; also helpful: SSN. Criminal records on index cards since 1970, library books in vault since 1960; on computer back to 1993.

General Information: No suppressed, juvenile, sex offenders, mental health, or adoption records released. Will fax results $2.00 1st page, $1.00 each add'l. Copy fee: $.50 per page. Certification fee: $10.00 plus $1.00 per page. Payee: 34th Circuit Court. Personal checks accepted. Prepayment required. Mail requests: SASE required. Mail turnaround time 1-3 weeks.

82nd District Court PO Box 365, West Branch, MI 48661; 989-345-5040; Fax: 989-345-5910. Hours: 8:30AM-4:30PM (EST). *Misdemeanor, Civil Actions Under $25,000, Eviction, Small Claims.*

Civil Records: Access: Fax, mail, in person. Only the court performs in person searches; visitors may not. Search fee: $2.00 per name. Required to search: name, years to search. Civil cases indexed by defendant, plaintiff. Civil records on computer since 1990, prior on books since 1969.

Criminal Records: Access: Fax, mail, in person. Only the court performs in person searches; visitors may not. Search fee: $2.00 per name. Required to search: name, years to search, DOB. Criminal records on computer since 1990, prior on books since 1969.

General Information: No suppressed records released. No fee to fax results. Copy fee: $.50 per page. Certification fee: $10.00. Payee: 82nd District Court. Personal checks accepted. Prepayment required. Prepayment of mail search required. Mail requests: SASE requested. Turnaround time 2-3 days.

Probate Court County Courthouse, Rm 203, 806 W Houghton Ave, West Branch, MI 48661; 989-345-0145; Fax: 989-345-5901. Hours: 8:30AM-Noon, 1-4:30PM (EST). *Probate.*

Ontonagon County

32nd Circuit Court 725 Greenland Rd, Ontonagon, MI 49953; 906-884-2806; Fax: 906-884-6796. Hours: 8:30AM-4:30PM (EST). *Felony, Civil Actions Over $25,000.*

Civil Records: Access: Mail, fax, in person. Both court and visitors may perform in person searches. Search fee: $5.00 per name. Required to search: name, years to search. Civil cases indexed by defendant, plaintiff. Civil records on index cards and in folders.

Criminal Records: Access: Mail, fax, in person. Both court and visitors may perform in person searches. Search fee: $5.00 per name. Required to search: name, years to search. Criminal records in folders.

General Information: No suppressed records released. Copy fee: $1.00 per page. Certification fee: $10.00. Payee: County Clerk. Personal checks accepted. Prepayment required. Mail requests: SASE not required. Mail turnaround time 2-3 days.

98th District Court 725 Greenland Rd, Ontonagon, MI 49953; 906-884-2865; Fax: 906-884-2916. Hours: 8:30AM-4:30PM (EST). *Misdemeanor, Civil Actions Under $25,000, Eviction, Small Claims.*

Civil Records: Access: Mail, in person. Only the court performs in person searches; visitors may not. Search fee: $5.00 each name. Required to search: name, years to search. Civil cases indexed by defendant, plaintiff. Civil records kept for 10 years then destroyed.

Criminal Records: Access: Mail, in person. Only the court performs in person searches; visitors may not. Search fee: $5.00 each name. Required to search: name, years to search, DOB. Criminal records kept for 10 years then destroyed.

General Information: No suppressed records released. Copy fee: $1.00 per page. Certification fee: $10.00 plus $1.00 per page. Payee: 98th District Court. Business checks accepted. Prepayment required. Mail requests: SASE required. Mail turnaround time 1 week.

Probate Court 725 Greenland Rd, Ontonagon, MI 49953; 906-884-4117; Fax: 906-884-2916. Hours: 8:30AM-4:30PM (EST). *Probate.*

Osceola County

49th Circuit Court 301 W Upton, Reed City, MI 49677; 231-832-6103; Fax: 231-832-6149. Hours: 9AM-5PM (EST). *Felony, Civil Actions Over $25,000.*

Civil Records: Access: Phone, fax, mail, in person. Both court and visitors may perform in person searches. No search fee. Required to search: name, years to search. Civil cases indexed by defendant, plaintiff. Civil records on computer since 1992, prior on docket books.

Criminal Records: Access: Phone, fax, mail, in person. Both court and visitors may perform in person searches. No search fee. Required to search: name, years to search, DOB. Criminal records on computer since 1992, prior on docket books back to 1967.

General Information: No suppressed or adoption records released. Will fax results for $1.00 1st 5 pages, $.50 each add'l. Copy fee: $1.00 per page. Certification fee: $10.00 plus $1.00 per page after first. Payee: 49th Circuit Court. Personal checks accepted. Prepayment required. Mail requests: SASE required. Mail turnaround time 1-2 days.

77th District Court 410 W Upton, Reed City, MI 49677; 231-832-6155; Fax: 231-832-9190. Hours: 8:30AM-4:30PM (EST). *Misdemeanor, Civil Actions Under $25,000, Eviction, Small Claims.*

Civil Records: Access: Phone, mail, fax, in person. Only the court performs in person searches; visitors may not. No search fee. Required to search: name, years to search. Civil cases indexed by defendant, plaintiff. Civil records on computer since 6/91; on index cards to 1987.

Criminal Records: Access: Phone, mail, fax, in person. Only the court performs in person searches; visitors may not. No search fee. Required to search: name, years to search, DOB. Criminal records on computer since 6/91; on index cards back to 1987.

General Information: No suppressed records released. Copy fee: $1.00 per page. Certification fee: $10.00. Payee: 77th District Court. Only cashiers checks and money orders accepted. Prepayment required. Mail requests: SASE required. Mail turnaround time 2 days.

Probate Court 410 W Upton, Reed City, MI 49677; 231-832-6124; Fax: 231-832-6181. Hours: 8:30AM-Noon, 1-4:30PM (EST). *Probate.*
Note: Shares the same judge with Mecosta County Probate Court.

Oscoda County

23rd Circuit Court PO Box 399, 311 Morenci Ave, Mio, MI 48647; 989-826-1110; Probate phone: 989-826-1107; Fax: 989-826-1136. Hours: 8:30AM-4:30PM (EST). *Felony, Civil Actions Over $25,000.*

Civil Records: Access: Mail, in person. Only the court performs in person searches; visitors may not. Search fee: $15.00 per name per year. Required to search: name, years to search. Civil cases indexed by defendant, plaintiff. Civil records on computer since 1989, prior on docket books to 1880s.

Criminal Records: Access: Mail, in person. Only the court performs in person searches; visitors may not. Search fee: $15.00 per name per year. Required to search: name, years to search, DOB. Criminal records on computer since 1989, prior on docket books to 1880s.

General Information: No suppressed records released. Copy fee: $1.00 per page. Certification fee: $10.00 plus $1.00 per page after first. Payee: Oscoda County Clerk. Personal checks accepted. Prepayment required. Mail requests: SASE required. Mail turnaround time 2-3 weeks.

81st District Court PO Box 625, Mio, MI 48647; 989-826-1106. Hours: 8:30AM-4:30PM (EST). *Misdemeanor, Civil Actions Under $25,000, Eviction, Small Claims.*

Civil Records: Access: Mail, in person. Only the court performs in person searches; visitors may not. Search fee: $2.00 per name. Required to search: name, years to search. Civil cases indexed by defendant, plaintiff. Civil records on computer back to 1990, prior on index cards.

Criminal Records: Access: Mail, in person. Only the court performs in person searches; visitors may not. Search fee: $2.00 per name. Required to search:

name, years to search, DOB; also helpful: SSN. Criminal records on computer back to 1990, prior on index cards.

General Information: No suppressed records released. Will fax results to local or toll free line. Copy fee: $.50 per page. Certification fee: $10.00 plus $1.00 per page after first. Payee: 81st District Court. Personal checks accepted. Prepayment required. Mail requests: SASE required. Mail turnaround: 1-2 days.

Probate Court PO Box 399, Mio, MI 48647; 989-826-1107; Fax: 989-826-1158. Hours: 8:30AM-Noon, 1-4:30PM (EST). *Probate.*

Otsego County

46th Circuit Court 225 Main St, Gaylord, MI 49735; 989-732-7500(Clerk); Fax: 989-731-7519. Hours: 8AM-4:30PM (EST). *Felony, Civil Actions Over $25,000.*
www.Circuit46.org

Civil Records: Access: Phone, mail, in person, online. Both court and visitors may perform in person searches. Search fee: $1.00 per name. Required to search: name, years to search. Civil records on computer since 1988, prior on indexes since 1800s. Online access to court case records (closed cases for 90 days only) is free online at www.circuit46.org/Cases/cases.html.

Criminal Records: Access: Phone, mail, in person, online. Both court and visitors may perform in person searches. Search fee: $1.00 per name. Required to search: name, years to search, DOB. Criminal records on computer since 1988, prior on indexes since 1800s. Online access to criminal records is the same as civil.

General Information: Public Access terminal is available. No suppressed, juvenile, mental health, or adoption records released. Will fax results to local or toll-free number; all others for fee of $5.00 per page. Copy fee: $1.00 per page. Certification fee: $10.00. Payee: Otsego County Clerk. Personal checks accepted. Prepayment required. Mail requests: SASE required. Mail turnaround time varies.

46th Circuit Trial Court - District Court 800 Livingston Blvd, #1C, Gaylord, MI 49735; 989-732-6486; Fax: 989-732-5130. Hours: 8AM-4:30PM (EST). *Misdemeanor, Civil Actions Under $25,000, Eviction, Small Claims.*
www.circuit46.org

Civil Records: Access: Mail, in person, online. Both court and visitors may perform in person searches. No search fee. Required to search: name, years to search. Civil cases indexed by defendant, plaintiff. Civil records on computer since 1985, prior index cards. Online access to court case records (closed cases for 90 days only) is free online at www.circuit46.org/Cases/cases.html.

Criminal Records: Access: Mail, in person, online. Both court and visitors may perform in person searches. No search fee. Required to search: name, years to search, DOB. Criminal records on computer since 1985, prior index cards to 1969. Access to online criminal records is the same as civil, but records go back 6 months.

General Information: Public Access terminal is available. No suppressed records released. Copy fee: $1.00 per page. Certification fee: $10.00 plus $1.00 per page after first. Payee: 87th District Court. Personal checks accepted. Prepayment required. Mail requests: SASE required. Mail turnaround: 4 days.

Probate Court 800 Livingston Blvd, #1C, Gaylord, MI 49735; 989-731-0204, 989-731-0201; Fax: 989-732-5130. Hours: 8AM-4:30PM (EST). *Probate.*
www.Circuit46.org
Note: Search cases by name free online at www.circuit46.org/Cases/cases.html.

Ottawa County

20th Circuit Court 414 Washington Ave, Grand Haven, MI 49417; 616-846-8136; Fax: 616-846-8138. Hours: 8AM-5PM (EST). *Felony, Civil Actions Over $25,000.*
www.co.ottawa.mi.us/Courts/courts.htm

Civil Records: Access: Mail, fax, in person. Visitors must perform in person searches for themselves. No search fee. Required to search: name, years to search. Civil cases indexed by defendant, plaintiff. Civil records on computer since June, 1984.

Criminal Records: Access: Mail, in person. Visitors must perform in person searches themselves. No search fee. Required to search: name, years to search, DOB; also helpful: SSN. Criminal records on computer since 1990.

General Information: Public Access terminal is available. No suppressed, juvenile, sex offenders, mental health, or adoption records released. Copy fee: $.50 per page. Certification fee: $10.00 plus $1.00 per page. Payee: Ottawa County Clerk. Personal checks accepted. Prepayment required. Mail requests: SASE requested. Turnaround time 2-3 days; phone search - 24 hours.

58th District Court - Grand Haven 414 Washington Ave, Grand Haven, MI 49417; 616-846-8280; Civil phone: 616-846-8289; Criminal phone: 616-846-8127; Probate phone: 616-846-8281; Fax: 616-846-8291. Hours: 8AM-5PM (EST). *Misdemeanor, Civil Actions Under $25,000, Eviction, Small Claims.*
www.co.ottawa.mi.us/Courts/courts.htm

Civil Records: Access: Mail, fax, in person. Both the court and visitors may perform in person searches. Search fee: $3.00. Required to search: name, years to search. Civil cases indexed by defendant, plaintiff. Civil records on computer back to 1993, prior on index cards since 1969.

Criminal Records: Access: Mail, fax, in person. Both the court and visitors may perform in person searches. Search fee: $3.00. Required to search: name, years to search, DOB. Criminal records on computer back to 1990, prior on index cards since 1969.

General Information: Public Access terminal is available. No suppressed records released. Will fax results for $3.00 per page. Copy fee: $.1.00 per page. Certification fee: $10.00 plus $1.00 per page after first. Payee: 58th District Court. Personal checks accepted. Out of state checks not accepted. Prepayment required. Mail requests: SASE required. Mail turnaround time 4 days.

58th District Court - Holland 57 W 8th St, Holland, MI 49423; 616-392-6991; Fax: 616-392-5013. Hours: 8AM-5PM (EST). *Misdemeanor, Civil Actions Under $25,000, Eviction, Small Claims.*
www.co.ottawa.mi.us/Courts/courts.htm

Civil Records: Access: Mail, in person. Only the court performs in person searches; visitors may not. No search fee. Required to search: name, years to search. Civil cases indexed by defendant, plaintiff. Civil records on computer since 1988, prior on books since 1969.

Criminal Records: Access: Mail, in person. Only the court performs in person searches; visitors may not. No search fee. Required to search: name, years to search, DOB; also helpful: SSN. Criminal records on computer since 1988, prior on books since 1969.

General Information: No suppressed records released. Copy fee: $1.00 per page. Certification fee: $10.00 per document. Payee: 58th District Court. Personal checks accepted. Out of state checks not accepted. Prepayment required. Mail requests: SASE required. Mail turnaround time varies.

58th District Court - Hudsonville

3100 Port Sheldon, Hudsonville, MI 49426; 616-662-3100 x2; Fax: 616-669-2950. Hours: 8AM-noon; 1-5PM (EST). *Misdemeanor, Civil Actions Under $25,000, Eviction, Small Claims.*

www.co.ottawa.mi.us/Courts/courts.htm

Civil Records: Access: Mail, in person. Only the court performs in person searches; visitors may not. Search fee: $3.00 per name. Required to search: name, years to search; also helpful: address. Civil cases indexed by defendant, plaintiff. Civil records on computer since July, 1993, prior on index file.

Criminal Records: Access: Mail, in person. Only the court performs in person searches; visitors may not. Search fee: $3.00 per name. Required to search: name, years to search, DOB; also helpful: address. Criminal records on computer since 1990.

General Information: No suppressed records released. Will fax results for $3.00 per name; $1.00 per copied page. Copy fee: $1.00 per page. Certification fee: $10.00. Payee: 58th District Court. Personal checks accepted. Prepayment required. Mail requests: SASE not required. Mail turnaround: 2 days.

Probate Court 12120 Fillmore St, West Olive, MI 49460; 616-786-4110; Fax: 616-738-4624. Hours: 8AM-5PM (EST). *Probate.*

www.co.ottawa.mi.us/Courts/Probate/probate.htm

Presque Isle County

53rd Circuit Court PO Box 110, Rogers City, MI 49779; 989-734-3288; Probate phone: 989-734-3268; Fax: 989-734-7635. Hours: 8:30AM-4:30PM (EST). *Felony, Civil Actions Over $25,000.*

Civil Records: Access: Phone, fax, mail, in person. Only the court performs in person searches; visitors may not. No search fee. Required to search: name, years to search. Civil cases indexed by defendant, plaintiff. Civil records on docket books since 1800s.

Criminal Records: Access: Phone, fax, mail, in person. Only the court performs in person searches; visitors may not. No search fee. Required to search: name, years to search, DOB. Criminal records on docket books since 1800s.

General Information: No suppressed, juvenile, sex offenders, mental health, or adoption records released. Copy fee: $1.00 per page. Certification fee: $10.00 plus $1.00 per page after first. Payee: Presque Isle County Clerk. Personal checks accepted. Prepayment required. Mail requests: SASE required. Mail turnaround time 1 week.

89th District Court PO Box 110, Rogers City, MI 49779; 989-734-2411; Fax: 989-734-3400. Hours: 8:30AM-4:30PM (EST). *Misdemeanor, Civil Actions Under $25,000, Eviction, Small Claims.*

Civil Records: Access: Mail, in person. Only the court performs in person searches; visitors may not. No search fee. Required to search: name, years to search. Civil cases indexed by defendant, plaintiff. Civil records on computer since 6/94, prior on index books.

Criminal Records: Access: Mail, in person. Only the court performs in person searches; visitors may not. No search fee. Required to search: name, years to search, DOB. Criminal records on computer since 6/94, prior on index books.

General Information: No suppressed records released. Copy fee: $1.00 for first page, $.25 each add'l. Certification fee: $10.00 plus $1.00 per page after first. Payee: 89th District Court. Personal checks accepted. Prepayment required. Mail requests: SASE required. Mail turnaround time 2 weeks.

Probate Court 151 Huron Ave, PO Box 110, Rogers City, MI 49779; 989-734-3268; Fax: 989-734-4420. Hours: 8:30AM-4:30PM (EST). *Probate.*

Roscommon County

34th Circuit Court 500 Lake St #1, Attn: County Clerk Reg of Deeds, Roscommon, MI 48653; 989-275-1902; Fax: 989-275-0602. Hours: 8:30AM-4:30PM (EST). *Felony, Civil Actions Over $25,000.*

Civil Records: Access: Fax, mail, in person. Both visitors and court may perform searches. Search fee: No fee. Required to search: name, years to search. Civil records on computer since 3/94, prior on docket books and cards.

Criminal Records: Access: Fax, mail, in person. Both visitors and court may perform search. Search fee: No fee. Required to search: name, years to search, DOB. Criminal records on computer since 3/94, prior on docket books and cards.

General Information: Public Access terminal is available. No suppressed, sex offenders or mental health records released. Fee to fax results is $3.00 1st page, $1.00 each add'l. Copy fee: $.50 per page. Certification fee: $10.00 plus $1.00 per page after first. Payee: 34th Circuit Court. Personal checks accepted. Prepayment required. Mail requests: SASE required. Mail turnaround time 24 hours.

83rd District Court, 500 Lake St., Roscommon, MI 48653; 989-275-5312; Fax: 989-275-6033. Hours: 8:30AM-4:30PM (EST). *Misdemeanor, Civil Actions Under $25,000, Eviction, Small Claims.*

Civil Records: Access: Phone, fax, mail, in person. Only the court performs in person searches; visitors may not. No search fee. Required to search: name, years to search. Civil cases indexed by defendant, plaintiff. Civil records on computer since 1988, prior on index cards since 1969.

Criminal Records: Access: Phone, fax, mail, in person. Only the court performs in person searches; visitors may not. No search fee. Required to search: name, years to search, DOB; also helpful: SSN. Criminal records on computer since 1988, prior on index cards since 1969.

General Information: No suppressed, juvenile, sex offenders, mental health, or adoption records released. No fee to fax results. Copy fee: $.50 per page. No certification fee. Payee: 83rd District Court. Personal checks accepted. Prepayment required. Mail turnaround time same day.

Probate Court PO Box 607, 500 Lake St. Rm. 132, Roscommon, MI 48653; 989-275-5221; Fax: 989-275-8537. 8:30AM-4:30PM (EST). *Probate.*

Saginaw County

10th Circuit Court 111 S Michigan Ave, Saginaw, MI 48602; 989-790-5541; Probate phone: 989-790-5233; Fax: 989-790-5248. Hours: 8AM-5:00PM (EST). *Felony, Civil Actions Over $25,000.*

www.saginawcounty.com/clerk/court/index.html

Civil Records: Access: Mail, in person. Both court and visitors may perform in person searches. Search fee: None at this time. Required to search: name, years to search. Civil cases indexed by defendant, plaintiff. Civil records on computer since 1985, prior on index books, microfilm. Search calendars at www.saginawcounty.com/clerk/docket/index.html.

Criminal Records: Access: Mail, in person. Both court and visitors may perform in person searches. Search fee: None at this time. Required to search: name, years to search, DOB; also helpful: SSN. Criminal records on computer since 1986, prior on index books.

General Information: Public Access terminal is available. No suppressed, sex offenders, mental health or guardianship records released. Will fax results. Copy fee: $1.00 per page. Certification fee: $10.00 plus $.25 per docket page. Payee: Saginaw County Clerk. No personal checks accepted. Prepayment

required. Mail requests: SASE required. Mail turnaround time 2 days.

70th District Court - Civil Division

111 S Michigan Ave, Saginaw, MI 48602; 989-790-5380; Fax: 989-790-5562. Hours: 8AM-4:45PM (EST). *Civil Actions Under $25,000, Eviction, Small Claims.*

Civil Records: Access: Mail, in person. Only the court performs in person searches; visitors may not. Search fee: $10.00 per name. Required to search: name, years to search. Civil cases indexed by defendant, plaintiff. Civil records on computer since 1982, prior on docket books.

General Information: No suppressed records released. Will fax results to local or toll free line. Copy fee: $1.00 per page. Certification fee: $10.00. Payee: 70th District court. Personal checks accepted. Prepayment required. Mail requests: SASE required. Mail turnaround time 1 week.

70th District Court - Criminal Division

111 S Michigan Ave, Saginaw, MI 48602; 989-790-5385; Fax: 989-790-5589. Hours: 8AM-4:45PM (EST). *Misdemeanor.*

www.saginawcounty.com/DistrictCourt

Criminal Records: Access: Fax, mail, in person. Only the court performs in person searches; visitors may not. Search fee: $10.00 per name. Required to search: name, years to search, DOB, signed release; also helpful: address. Criminal records on computer back to 1987, prior on microfiche since 1972. Fax information received only if pre-paid. They must receive $5.00 fee before they fax out information.

General Information: No suppressed, juvenile, sex offenders, mental health, or adoption records released. Will fax results to local or toll free line. Copy fee: $1.00 per page. Certification fee: $10.00. Payee: 70th District Court. Business checks accepted. Visa, MC accepted. Prepayment required. Mail requests: SASE required. Mail turnaround time 1 week.

Probate/Family Court 111 S Michigan St, Saginaw, MI 48602; 989-790-5320; Fax: 989-790-5328. Hours: 8AM-5PM (EST). *Probate.*

Sanilac County

24th Circuit Court 60 W Sanilac, Rm 203, Sandusky, MI 48471; 810-648-3212 x8227; Fax: 810-648-5466. Hours: 8AM-4:30PM (EST). *Felony, Civil Actions Over $25,000.*

www.sanilaccounty.net

Civil Records: Access: Mail, in person. Both court and visitors may perform in person searches. Search fee: $10.00 per name. Required to search: name, years to search. Civil cases indexed by defendant, plaintiff. Civil records on computer since 1993.

Criminal Records: Access: Mail, in person. Both court and visitors may perform in person searches. Search fee: $10.00 per name. Required to search: name, years to search. Criminal records on computer since 1993.

General Information: Public Access terminal is available. No suppressed, juvenile, sex offenders, mental health, or adoption records released. Will fax results to local or toll free line. Copy fee: $1.00 per page. Certification fee: $10.00. Payee: Sanilac County Clerk. Personal checks accepted. Prepayment required. Mail requests: SASE required. Mail turnaround time 2-3 days.

73rd District Court 60 W Sanilac, Sandusky, MI 48471; 810-648-3250. Hours: 8AM-4:30PM (EST). *Misdemeanor, Civil Actions Under $25,000, Eviction, Small Claims.*

Civil Records: Access: Mail, in person. Only the court performs in person searches; visitors may not. Search fee: $1.00 per name per year. Required to search: name, years to search; also helpful: address. Civil cases indexed by defendant, plaintiff. Civil records on computer back to 1989, prior on docket books to 1969.

Criminal Records: Access: Mail, in person. Only the court performs in person searches; visitors may not. Search fee: $1.00 per name per year. Required to search: name, years to search, DOB; also helpful: address. Criminal records on computer back to 1989, prior on docket books to 1969.

General Information: No suppressed records released. Will fax results to local or toll free line. Fax fee included in search. Copy fee: $1.00 per page. Certification fee: $10.00 plus $1.00 per page after first. Payee: 73rd District Court. Personal checks accepted. Prepayment required. Mail requests: SASE required. Mail turnaround time 1 week.

Probate Court 60 W Sanilac Ave., Rm 106, Sandusky, MI 48471-1096; 810-648-3221; Fax: 810-648-2900. 8AM-Noon, 1-4:30PM (EST). *Probate.*

Schoolcraft County

11th Circuit Court 300 Walnut St, Rm 164, Manistique, MI 49854; 906-341-3618; Probate phone: 906-341-3644. Hours: 8AM-4PM (EST). *Felony, Civil Actions Over $25,000.*

Civil Records: Access: Phone, fax, mail, in person. Both court and visitors may perform in person searches. No search fee. Required to search: name, years to search. Civil cases indexed by defendant, plaintiff. Civil records on docket books and index since 1881.

Criminal Records: Access: Phone, fax, mail, in person. Only the court may perform in person searches. No search fee. Required to search: name, years to search. Criminal records on docket books and index since 1881.

General Information: No suppressed, juvenile, sex offenders, mental health, or adoption records released. Will fax results to local or toll free line. Copy fee: $1.00 per page. Certification fee: $10.00. Payee: Schoolcraft County Clerk. Personal checks accepted. Prepayment required. Mail requests: SASE requested. Turnaround time 2-3 days.

93rd District Court 300 Walnut St, Rm 135, Manistique, MI 49854; 906-341-3630; Fax: 906-341-8006. Hours: 8AM-4PM (EST). *Misdemeanor, Civil Actions Under $25,000, Eviction, Small Claims.*

Civil Records: Access: Mail, in person. Both court and visitors may perform in person searches. Search fee: $10.00. Required to search: name, years to search. Civil cases indexed by defendant, plaintiff. Civil records kept on index cards.

Criminal Records: Access: Mail, in person. Only the court performs in person searches; visitors may not. Search fee: $10.00. Required to search: name, years to search, DOB; also helpful: SSN. Criminal records kept on index cards.

General Information: No suppressed, sex offenders or mental health records released. Copy fee: $1.00 per page. Certification fee: $10.00 plus $1.00 per page after first. Payee: 93rd District Court. Business checks accepted. Prepayment required. Mail requests: SASE required. Mail turnaround time 2-3 days.

Probate Court 300 Walnut St, Rm 129, Manistique, MI 49854; 906-341-3641; Fax: 906-341-3627. Hours: 8AM-Noon, 1-4PM (EST). *Probate.*

Shiawassee County

35th Circuit Court 208 N Shiawassee St, Corunna, MI 48817; 989-743-2262; Fax: 989-743-2241. Hours: 8AM-5PM (EST). *Felony, Civil Actions Over $25,000.*

Civil Records: Access: Phone, mail, in person. Both court and visitors may perform in person searches.

Search fee: $1.00 per name per year. Required to search: name, years to search. Civil cases indexed by defendant, plaintiff. Civil records on computer since 09/87, prior on docket books and cards.

Criminal Records: Access: Phone, fax, mail, in person. Both court and visitors may perform in person searches. Search fee: $10.00 for up to 10 years. Required to search: name, years to search, DOB. Criminal records on computer since 10/93.

General Information: No suppressed records released. Copy fee: $1.00 per page. Certification fee: $10.00. Payee: 35th Circuit Court. Personal checks accepted. Prepayment required. Mail requests: SASE required. Mail turnaround time 1 week.

66th District Court 110 E Mack St, Corunna, MI 48817; 989-743-2395; Fax: 989-743-2469. Hours: 8AM-5PM (EST). *Misdemeanor, Civil Actions Under $25,000, Eviction, Small Claims.*

Civil Records: Access: Phone, fax, mail, in person. Both court and visitors may perform in person searches. No search fee. Required to search: name, years to search; also helpful: DOB, SSN. Civil cases indexed by defendant, plaintiff. Civil records on computer back to 1995, prior on microfiche.

Criminal Records: Access: Phone, fax, mail, in person. Both court and visitors may perform in person searches. No search fee. Required to search: name, years to search, DOB. Case number required for pre-1995 research. Criminal records on computer back to 1995, prior on microfiche to 1969.

General Information: Public Access terminal is available. No suppressed records released. Friday is their day to fax results. Copy fee: $1.00 per page. Certification fee: $10.00. Payee: 66th District Court. Personal checks accepted. Prepayment required. Mail requests: SASE required. Mail turnaround: 1 week.

Probate Court 110 E Mack St, Corunna, MI 48817; 989-743-2211; Fax: 989-743-2349. Hours: 8AM-5PM (EST). *Probate.*

St. Clair County

31st Circuit Court 201 McMorran Blvd, Port Huron, MI 48060; 810-985-2200; Fax: 810-985-4796. Hours: 8AM-4:30PM (EST). *Felony, Civil Actions Over $25,000.*

www.stclaircounty.org/index.asp

Civil Records: Access: Mail, fax, in person. Both court and visitors may perform in person searches. No search fee. Required to search: name, years to search; also helpful: address. Civil cases indexed by defendant, plaintiff. Civil records on computer back to 1987, non computerzied records back to 1936.

Criminal Records: Access: Mail, fax, in person. Both court and visitors may perform in person searches. No search fee. Required to search: name, years to search, DOB; also helpful: address. Criminal records on computer back to 1987, non computerized records back to 1936.

General Information: Public Access terminal is available. No suppressed, juvenile, mental health, or adoption records released. Copy fee: $1.00 per page. Certification fee: $10.00. Payee: St. Clair Clerk of Court. Will accept In state checks. Prepayment required. Mail requests: SASE required. Mail turnaround time 24 hours.

72nd District Court 201 McMorran Blvd, Rm 2900, Port Huron, MI 48060; Civil phone: 810-985-2077; Criminal phone: 810-985-2072. Hours: 8AM-4:30PM M-Thl; 9AM-4:30PM (EST). *Misdemeanor, Civil Actions Under $25,000, Eviction, Small Claims.*

Civil Records: Access: In person only. Visitors must perform in person searches for themselves. No search fee. Required to search: name, years to search. Civil cases indexed by defendant, plaintiff. Civil records on

computer since 1987, prior on docket books back to 1969.

Criminal Records: Access: in person only. Visitors must perform in person searches for themselves. No search fee. Required to search: name, years to search, DOB; also helpful: SSN. Criminal records on computer since 1987, prior on docket books back to 1969.

General Information: Public Access terminal is available. No suppressed records released. Copy fee: $1.00 per page. Certification fee: $10.00. Payee: 72nd District Court. Personal checks accepted. Prepayment required.

Probate Court 201 McMorran Blvd Rm 2600, Port Huron, MI 48060; 810-985-2066; Fax: 810-985-2179. Hours: 8AM-4:30PM (EST). *Probate.*

St. Joseph County

45th Circuit Court PO Box 189, Centreville, MI 49032; 269-467-5531; Fax: 269-467-5628. Hours: 9AM-5PM (EST). *Felony, Civil Actions Over $25,000.*

www.stjosephcountymi.org/ccircuit.htm

Civil Records: Access: Mail, in person. Both court and visitors may perform in person searches. Search fee: $1.00 per name per year. For records prior to 1988, fee is $1.00 per year searched. Required to search: name, years to search. Civil cases indexed by defendant, plaintiff. Civil records on computer since 1988, prior on books from 1900, earlier in archives.

Criminal Records: Access: Mail, in person. Both court and visitors may perform in person searches. Search fee: $1.00 per name per year. Required to search: name, years to search. Criminal records on computer since 1988, prior on books from 1900, earlier in archives.

General Information: Public Access terminal is available. No suppressed records released. Copy fee: $1.00 per page. Certification fee: $10.00. Payee: St. Joseph County Clerk. Business checks accepted. Prepayment required. Mail requests: SASE not required. Mail turnaround time same day.

3-B District Court PO Box 67, Centreville, MI 49032; 269-467-5627. Hours: 8AM-5PM (EST). *Misdemeanor, Civil Actions Under $25,000, Eviction, Small Claims.*

Civil Records: Access: Phone, mail, in person. Both court and visitors may perform in person computer searches. No search fee. Required to search: name, years to search; also helpful: address. Civil cases indexed by defendant, plaintiff. Civil records on computer since 1987, prior in archives. Phone search access limited.

Criminal Records: Access: Fax, mail, in person. Both court and visitors may perform in person searches. No search fee. Required to search: name, years to search, DOB, date of offense. Criminal records on computer since 1987, prior in archives. Signed release required for some searches.

General Information: Public Access terminal is available. No suppressed records released. Copy fee: $.15 per page. Certification fee: $10.00 plus $1.00 each add'l page. Payee: 3-B District Court. Business checks accepted. Prepayment required. Mail turnaround time 2 weeks.

Probate Court PO Box 190, Centreville, MI 49032; 269-467-5538; Fax: 269-467-5560. Hours: 8AM-5PM (EST). *Probate.*

www.stjosephcountymi.org/cprobate.htm

Tuscola County

54th Circuit Court 440 N State St, Caro, MI 48723; 989-672-3780; Civil phone: 989-672-3775; Criminal phone: 989-672-3776; Probate phone: 989-672-3850; Fax: 989-672-4266. Hours: 8AM-Noon, 1-3:30PM (EST). *Felony, Civil Actions Over $25,000.* www.tuscolacounty.org

Civil Records: Access: Mail, in person. Only the court performs in person searches; visitors may not. Search fee: $5.00 per name. Fee is $1.00 for each year prior to 1989. Required to search: name, years to search. Civil cases indexed by defendant, plaintiff. Civil records on computer since 1989, prior on books since beginning.

Criminal Records: Access: Mail, in person. Only the court performs in person searches; visitors may not. Search fee: $5.00 per name. Fee is $1.00 for each year prior to 1989. Required to search: name, years to search, DOB; also helpful: SSN. Criminal records on computer since 1989, prior on books since beginning.

General Information: No suppressed, juvenile, sex offenders, mental health, or adoption records released. Will not fax results. Copy fee: $1.00 per page. Certification fee: $10.00 plus $1.00 per page after first. Payee: County Clerk. Personal checks not accepted. Prepayment required. Mail requests: SASE required. Mail turnaround time 3-4 days.

71 B District Court 440 N State St., Caro, MI 48723; 989-672-3800; Fax: 989-673-0451. Hours: 8AM-4:30PM (EST). *Misdemeanor, Civil Actions Under $25,000, Eviction, Small Claims.*

Civil Records: Access: Phone, mail, in person. Both court and visitors may perform in person searches. No search fee. Required to search: name, years to search. Civil cases indexed by defendant, plaintiff. Civil records on computer since 1991, prior on cards.

Criminal Records: Access: Phone, mail, in person. Both court and visitors may perform in person searches. No search fee. Required to search: name, years to search, DOB; also helpful: SSN. Criminal records on computer since 1991; others back to 1969.

General Information: No suppressed records released. Copy fee: $.50 per page. Certification fee: $10.00 plus $1.00 per page after first. Payee: 71 B District Court. Personal checks accepted. Prepayment required. Mail requests: SASE not required.

Probate Court 440 N State St, Caro, MI 48723; 989-672-3850; Fax: 989-672-2057. Hours: 8AM-Noon, 1-4:30PM (EST). *Probate.*

Van Buren County

36th Circuit Court 212 Paw Paw St #101, Paw Paw, MI 49079; 269-657-8218. Hours: 8:30AM-5PM (EST). *Felony, Civil Actions Over $25,000.*

Civil Records: Access: Mail, in person. Only the court performs in person searches; visitors may not. Search fee: $1.00 per name per year. Fee includes combined civil and criminal search. Required to search: name, years to search. Civil cases indexed by defendant, plaintiff. Civil records on computer back to 1990, prior on docket books since 1800s.

Criminal Records: Access: Mail, in person. Only the court performs in person searches; visitors may not. Search fee: $1.00 per name per year. Required to search: name, years to search, DOB, signed release. Criminal records on computer back to 1990, prior on docket books since 1800s.

General Information: No suppressed, sex offender records released. Will phone with results if a toll-free number is provided. Copy fee: $1.00 per page. Certification fee: $10.00 plus $1.00 per page after first. Payee: Van Buren County Clerk. Personal checks accepted. Prepayment required. Mail requests: SASE required. Mail turnaround time 1 day.

7th District Court 212 Paw Paw St, Paw Paw, MI 49079; 269-657-8222; Fax: 269-657-8223. Hours: 9AM-4:30PM (EST). *Misdemeanor, Civil Actions Under $25,000, Eviction, Small Claims.*

Civil Records: Access: Mail, fax, in person. Both court and visitors may perform in person searches. No search fee. Required to search: name, years to search. Civil cases indexed by defendant, plaintiff. Civil records kept in file folder; computerized records since 1999.

Criminal Records: Access: Mail, in person. Both court and visitors may perform in person searches. No search fee. Required to search: name, years to search, DOB, SSN. Criminal records kept in file folder; computerized since 1999.

General Information: No suppressed records released. Copy fee: $1.00 per page. Certification fee: $10.00. Payee: 7th District Court. No personal checks accepted. Prepayment required. Mail requests: SASE required. Mail turnaround time 1-2 days.

7th District Court - West Division 1007 E Wells, PO Box 311, South Haven, MI 49090; 269-637-5258; Fax: 269-637-9169. Hours: 8:30AM-4:30PM (EST). *Misdemeanor, Civil Actions Under $25,000, Eviction, Small Claims.*

Civil Records: Access: Mail, in person. Only the court performs in person searches; visitors may not. Search fee: $1.00 per name. Required to search: name, years to search. Civil cases indexed by defendant, plaintiff. Civil records on computer since 1991, prior on index cards since 1982.

Criminal Records: Access: Mail, in person. Only the court performs in person searches; visitors may not. Search fee: $1.00 per name. Required to search: name, years to search, DOB; also helpful: SSN. Criminal records on computer since 1991, prior on index cards since 1982.

General Information: No suppressed, juvenile, sex offenders, mental health, or adoption records released. Copy fee: $.25 per page. Certification fee: $10.00 plus $1.00 per page after first. Payee: 7th District Court. Personal checks accepted. Prepayment required. Mail turnaround time 3 days.

Probate Court 212 Paw Paw St, #220, Paw Paw, MI 49079; 269-657-8225; Fax: 269-657-7573. Hours: 8:30AM-5PM (EST). *Probate.*

Washtenaw County

22nd Circuit Court PO Box 8645, Ann Arbor, MI 48107-8645; 734-222-3001. Hours: 8:30AM-4:30PM (EST). *Felony, Civil Actions Over $25,000.* www.e.washtenaworg/depts/courts/index.htm

Civil Records: Access: Mail, in person. Both court and visitors may perform in person searches. Search fee: $5.00 per name from 1979 to present; $1.00 per name per year prior to 1979. Required to search: name, years to search. Civil cases indexed by defendant, plaintiff. Civil records kept as originals in file folders, records go back to 1900; computerized since 1979.

Criminal Records: Access: Mail, in person. Both court and visitors may perform in person searches. Search fee: Same fees as civil. Required to search: name, years to search, DOB. Criminal records kept as originals in file folders, records go back to 1900; computerized since 1979.

General Information: Public Access terminal is available. No suppressed records released. Copy fee: $1.00 per page. Certification fee: $10.00 plus $1.00 per page. Payee: Washtenaw County Clerk. Personal checks accepted. Prepayment required. Mail requests: SASE required. Mail turnaround time 2-3 days.

14A-1 District Court 4133 Washtenaw, Ann Arbor, MI 48107-8645; 734-973-4545; Fax: 734-973-4693. Hours: 8AM-4:30PM (EST). *Misdemeanor, Civil Actions Under $25,000, Eviction, Small Claims.* www.co.washtenaw.mi.us/depts/courts/index.htm?qlink

Civil Records: Access: Mail, in person. Both court and visitors may perform in person searches. No search fee. Required to search: name, years to search. Civil cases indexed by defendant, plaintiff. Civil records on computer since 1985, prior on index cards.

Criminal Records: Access: Mail, in person. Both court and visitors may perform in person searches. No search fee. Required to search: name, years to search, DOB, SSN. Criminal records on computer since 1985, prior on index cards.

General Information: Public Access terminal is available. No suppressed records released. Copy fee: $.25 per page. Certification fee: $10.00 plus $1.00 per page. Payee: 14 A-1 District Court. Personal checks accepted. Prepayment required. Mail requests: SASE required. Mail turnaround time 1-2 weeks.

14th District Court A-2 415 W Michigan Ave, Ypsilanti, MI 48197; 734-484-6690; Fax: 734-484-6697. Hours: 8AM-4:30PM (EST). *Misdemeanor, Civil Actions Under $25,000, Eviction, Small Claims.*

Civil Records: Access: Mail, in person. Only the court performs in person searches; visitors may not. No search fee. Required to search: name, years to search. Civil cases indexed by defendant, plaintiff. Civil records on computer since 1985, prior on file cards since 1969. Specific docket information must be given, the court will not do name searches.

Criminal Records: Access: Mail, in person. Only the court performs in person searches; visitors may not. No search fee. Required to search: name, years to search, DOB; also helpful: SSN. Criminal records on computer since 1985, prior on file cards since 1969. The court will not do name searches.

General Information: No suppressed, juvenile, sex offenders, mental health, or adoption records released. Copy fee: $.25 per page. Certification fee: $10.00 plus $1.00 per page. Payee: 14 A-2 District Court. Personal checks accepted. Prepayment required. Mail requests: SASE requested. Turnaround time 1 week; phone turnaround is immediate up to 2 days.

14th District Court A-3 122 S Main St, Chelsea, MI 48118; 734-475-8606; Fax: 734-475-0460. 8AM-4:30PM (EST). *Misdemeanor, Civil Actions Under $25,000, Eviction, Small Claims.*

Civil Records: Access: Mail, fax, in person. Only the court performs in person searches, time permitting; visitors may not. No search fee. Required to search: name, years to search. Civil cases indexed by defendant, plaintiff. Civil records on computer since 1986; prior on index cards.

Criminal Records: Access: In person only. Only the court performs in person searches, time permitting; visitors may not. No search fee. Required to search: name, years to search, DOB; also helpful: SSN. Criminal records on computer since 1986; prior on index cards.

General Information: No suppressed records released. Copy fee: $.25 per page. Certification fee: $10.00. Payee: 14th District Court. Personal checks accepted. Prepayment required. Mail requests: SASE required.

14th District Court B - Civil Division 7200 S Huron River Dr, Ypsilanti, MI 48197; 734-483-5300; Fax: 734-483-3630. Hours: 8AM-5PM (EST). *Civil Actions Under $25,000, Eviction, Small Claims.*

Civil Records: Access: Mail, in person. Only the court performs in person searches; visitors may not.

No search fee. Required to search: name, years to search. Civil cases indexed by defendant, plaintiff. Civil records on computer since 1990, prior on card files from 1985-1989.

General Information: No suppressed, juvenile, sex offenders, probation, mental health, or adoption records released. Copy fee: $.50 per page. Certification fee: $10.00. Payee: 14-B District Court. Business checks accepted. Credit cards accepted. Prepayment required. Mail requests: SASE not required. Mail turnaround time 1 week, phone turnaround is 1 day.

14th District Court B - Criminal Division

7200 S Huron River Dr, Ypsilanti, MI 48197; 734-483-1333; Fax: 734-483-3630. Hours: 8AM-5PM (EST). *Misdemeanor.*

Criminal Records: Access: Mail, in person. Only the court performs in person searches; visitors may not. No search fee. Required to search: name, years to search, DOB; also helpful: SSN. Criminal records on computer since 1990, prior records kept by name.

General Information: No suppressed, probation, juvenile, sex offenders, probation, mental health, or adoption records released. Copy fee: $.50 per page. Certification fee: $10.00. Payee: 14-B District Court. Personal checks accepted. Credit cards accepted. Prepayment required. Mail requests: SASE not required. Mail turnaround time 1 week; phone turnaround is 1 day.

15th District Court - Civil Division

101 E Huron, Box 8650, Ann Arbor, MI 48107; 734-222-3389; Criminal phone: 734-222-3380 (crim traffic); Fax: 734-222-3335. 8:30AM-4:30PM (EST). *Civil Actions Under $25,000, Eviction, Small Claims.*
www.co.washtenaw.mi.us/depts/courts/index.htm

Civil Records: Access: Phone, fax, mail, in person. Both court and visitors may perform in person searches. No search fee. Required to search: name, years to search. Civil cases indexed by defendant, plaintiff. Civil records on computer since 1990, prior on docket books.

General Information: No suppressed records released. Will not fax results. Copy fee: $.25 per page. Certification fee: $10.00. Payee: 15th District Court. Personal checks accepted. Visa, MC, Discover accepted. Prepayment required. Mail requests: SASE required. Mail turnaround time 2-3 days.

15th District Court - Criminal Division

101 E Huron, Box 8650, Ann Arbor, MI 48107-8650; 734-222-3380; Civil phone: 734-222-3389; Fax: 734-222-3335. Hours: 8AM-4:30PM (EST). *Misdemeanor, Traffic.*
www.co.washtenaw.mi.us/depts/courts/index.htm

Criminal Records: Access: Mail, fax, in person. Both court and visitors may perform in person searches. No search fee. Required to search: name, years to search, DOB; also helpful: SSN, offense. Criminal records on computer since 1996; prior on docket cards since 1965. The court will not do a name search. Either a case number or charge and incident date is required.

General Information: Public Access terminal is available. (Limited data available.) No suppressed, juvenile, sex offenders, mental health, or adoption records released. Copy fee: $.25 per page. Certification fee: $10.00. Payee: 15th District Court. Check, cashiers checks and money orders accepted. Visa, MC, Discover accepted. Prepayment required. Mail requests: SASE required. Mail turnaround time 2-3 days.

Probate Court

PO Box 8645, Ann Arbor, MI 48107; 734-994-2474 ext 2; Fax: 734-222-3019. Hours: 8:30AM-4:30PM (EST). *Probate.*
www.co.washtenaw.mi.us/depts/courts/index.htm

Wayne County

3rd Circuit Court

201 Coleman A Young Municipal Center, Detroit, MI 48226; 313-224-5530. Hours: 8AM-4:30PM (EST). *Civil Actions Over $25,000.*
www.3rdcc.org

Civil Records: Access: Phone, mail, in person. Both court and visitors may perform in person searches. No search fee. Required to search: name, years to search. Civil cases indexed by defendant, plaintiff. Civil records on computer since 1984, prior on index cards.

General Information: No suppressed records released. Copy fee: $2.25 per page. Certification fee: $10.00 plus $1.00 per page. Payee: 3rd Circuit Court. Business checks accepted. Prepayment required. Mail turnaround time 1 week.

Frank Murphy Hall of Justice

1441 St Antoine, Detroit, MI 48226; 313-224-2500; Fax: 313-224-2786. Hours: 8AM-4:30PM (EST). *Felony.*

Criminal Records: Access: Mail, in person. Both court and visitors may perform in person searches. Search fee: $2.25 per name. Required to search: name, years to search, DOB; also helpful: SSN, city where crime occurred, aliases. Criminal records on computer since mid 1974, prior on microfiche through 1976, archives off-site 1800s to 1997.

General Information: Public Access terminal is available. No suppressed, juvenile, sex offenders, mental health, or adoption records released. Fee to fax results is $2.00 per page. Copy fee: $1.00 per page. Certification fee: $10.00 plus $1.00 per page after 1st. Payee: Wayne County Clerk. Prepayment required. Mail requests: SASE required. Mail turnaround time 3-4 days.

36th District Court

421 Madison, Detroit, MI 48226; Civil phone: 313-965-6098; Criminal phone: 313-965-5029. Hours: 8AM-4:30PM (EST). *Felony, Misdemeanor, Civil Actions Under $25,000, Eviction, Small Claims Under $3000.*
www.36thdistrictcourt.org/criminal-faq.html
Note: Small Claims phone number is 313-965-5972.

Civil Records: Access: In person only. Visitors must perform in person searches for themselves. No search fee. Required to search: name, years to search, address. Civil cases indexed by name, case number. Civil records on computer since 1985, prior kept in file folders. If a case number is provided, then court will retrieve records.

Criminal Records: Access: Phone, in person. Both court and visitors may perform in person searches. No search fee. Required to search: name, DOB; also helpful: SSN. Will do a single name search over the phone to let you know index numbers, if any.

General Information: Public Access terminal is available. (Civil records terminal is on 2nd Fl; Criminal records on 1st Fl.) No suppressed records released. Copy fee: $1.00 per page. Certification fee: $10.00 plus $1.00 per page after first. Payee: 36th District Court. Personal checks accepted. Visa, MC accepted. Prepayment required.

16th District Court

15140 Farmington Rd, Livonia, MI 48154-5498; 734-466-2500; 466-2550 Probation; Civil phone: X3541; Criminal phone: X3452. Hours: 8:30AM-4:30PM (EST). *Misdemeanor, Civil Actions Under $25,000, Eviction, Small Claims.*

Civil Records: Access: Mail, in person. Both court and visitors may perform in person searches. No search fee. Required to search: name, years to search. Civil cases indexed by defendant, plaintiff. Civil records on computer since 1990, prior on microfiche.

Criminal Records: Access: In person only. Visitors must perform in person searches for themselves. No search fee. Required to search: name, years to search,

DOB; also helpful: offense, date of offense, case number. Criminal records on computer since 1991, prior on microfiche. General searches are not performed.

General Information: Public Access terminal is available. (Civil only.) No suppressed records released. Will fax results to local or toll free line. Copy fee: $1.00 per page. Certification fee: $10.00. Payee: 16th District Court. Personal checks accepted. Prepayment required. Mail requests: SASE required. Mail turnaround time 1 week.

17th District Court

15111 Beech-Daly Rd, Redford, MI 48239; 313-387-2790; Fax: 313-538-3468. Hours: 8:30AM-4:15PM (EST). *Misdemeanor, Civil Actions Under $25,000, Eviction, Small Claims.*

Civil Records: Access: Mail, in person. Only the court performs in person searches; visitors may not. No search fee. Required to search: name, years to search. Civil cases indexed by defendant, plaintiff. Civil records on computer since 1990, prior on index cards.

Criminal Records: Access: Mail, in person. Only the court performs in person searches; visitors may not. No search fee. Required to search: name, years to search, DOB, SSN. Criminal records on computer since 1990, prior on index cards.

General Information: No suppressed, child and spousal abuse records released. Copy fee: $1.00 per page. Certification fee: $10.00. Payee: 17th District Court. Personal checks accepted. Visa, MC accepted. ATM cards accepted. Prepayment required. Mail requests: SASE required. Mail turnaround: 2 days.

18th District Court

36675 Ford Rd, Westland, MI 48185; 734-595-8720; Fax: 734-595-0160. Hours: 8:30AM-4PM M,F; 8:30AM-5:30PM T,W; 8:30AM-5:30PM Th (EST). *Misdemeanor, Civil Actions Under $25,000, Eviction, Small Claims.*
www.18thdistrictcourt.com

Civil Records: Access: Phone, mail, fax, in person. Only the court performs in person searches; visitors may not. Search fee: none. Required to search: name, years to search; also helpful: case number or title. Civil cases indexed by defendant, plaintiff. Civil records on computer since 1987, prior on microfilm back to 1969. Will name search free, but cert fee applied to copy.

Criminal Records: Access: Phone, mail, in person. Only the court performs in person searches; visitors may not. Search fee: none. Required to search: name, years to search, DOB; also helpful: case number. Criminal records on computer since 1992, prior on microfilm back to 1969. Will name search free, but cert fee applied to copy.

General Information: No suppressed records released. Will fax results to local or toll free line. Copy fee: $1.00 per page. Certification fee: $10.00. Payee: 18th District Court. Personal checks accepted. Prepayment required. Mail requests: SASE required. Mail turnaround time 1-2 weeks.

19th District Court

16077 Michigan Ave, Dearborn, MI 48126; 313-943-2056; Fax: 313-943-3071. Hours: 8AM-4:30PM (EST). *Misdemeanor, Civil Actions Under $25,000, Eviction, Small Claims.*
www.cityofdearborn.org

Civil Records: Access: Fax, mail, in person. Only the court performs in person searches; visitors may not. No search fee. Required to search: name, years to search. Civil cases indexed by defendant, plaintiff. Civil records on computer since 1986.

Criminal Records: Access: Fax, mail, in person. Only the court performs in person searches; visitors may not. No search fee. Required to search: name, years to search, DOB, offense, date of offense.

Criminal records on computer since 1987, prior on docket books.

General Information: No suppressed records released. Copy fee: $1.00 per page. Certification fee: $10.00. Payee: 19th District Court. Only cashiers checks and money orders accepted. Visa, MC accepted. Prepayment required. Mail requests: SASE helpful.

20th District Court 6045 Fenton, Dearborn Heights, MI 48127; 313-277-7480; Fax: 313-277-7141. Hours: 9AM-5PM (EST). *Misdemeanor, Civil Actions Under $25,000, Eviction, Small Claims.*

Civil Records: Access: Mail, in person. Only the court performs in person searches; visitors may not. No search fee. Required to search: name, years to search; also helpful: address. Civil cases indexed by defendant, plaintiff. Civil records on computer since April 1991, prior records on microfiche or books.

Criminal Records: Access: Mail, in person. Only the court performs in person searches; visitors may not. No search fee. Required to search: name, years to search, DOB; also helpful: SSN. Criminal records on computer since April 1991, prior records on microfiche or books.

General Information: No suppressed, juvenile, sex offenders, mental health, or adoption records released. Copy fee: $1.00 per page. Certification fee: $10.00. Payee: 20th District Court. Business checks accepted. Visa, MC accepted. Prepayment required. Mail requests: SASE required. Mail turnaround time 1 week-10 days.

21st District Court 6000 Middlebelt Rd, Garden City, MI 48135; 734-525-8805; Fax: 734-421-4797. Hours: 8:30AM-4:30PM (EST). *Misdemeanor, Civil Actions Under $25,000, Eviction, Small Claims.*

Civil Records: Access: Mail, in person. Only the court performs in person searches; visitors may not. Visitors can first search the printed case index to locate a case number. No search fee. Required to search: name, years to search. Civil cases indexed by defendant, plaintiff. Civil records on computer back to 1989, prior on books, microfilm, and cards. In person searchers must fill out a "File/copy Request Form."

Criminal Records: Access: Mail, in person. Only the court performs in person searches; visitors may not. Visitors can first search the printed case index to locate a case number. No search fee. Required to search: name, years to search, DOB. Criminal records on computer back to 1989, prior on books, microfilm, and cards. In person searchers must fill out a "File/copy Request Form."

General Information: No suppressed records released. Will not fax results. Copy fee: $1.00 per page. No certification fee. Payee: 21st District Court. Personal checks accepted. Prepayment required. Mail requests: SASE required. Mail turnaround time 1-2 days.

22nd District Court 27331 S River Park Dr, Inkster, MI 48141; 313-277-8200; Fax: 313-277-8221. Hours: 8:30AM-4:30PM (EST). *Misdemeanor, Civil Actions Under $25,000, Eviction, Small Claims.*

Civil Records: Access: Mail, in person. Only the court performs in person searches; visitors may not. No search fee. Required to search: name, years to search. Civil cases indexed by defendant, plaintiff. Civil records on computer since 1985, prior on docket books.

Criminal Records: Access: Mail, in person. Only the court performs in person searches; visitors may not. No search fee. Required to search: name, years to search, DOB; also helpful: SSN. Criminal records on computer since 1985, prior on books.

General Information: Public Access terminal is available. No suppressed records released. Copy fee:

$.25 per page. Certification fee: $10.00 for 1st page; $1.00 each add'l. Payee: 22nd District Court. Personal checks accepted. Prepayment required. Mail requests: SASE required. Mail turnaround time 2 weeks.

23rd District Court 23511 Goddard Rd, Taylor, MI 48180; 734-374-1334; Civil phone: 734-374-1328; Fax: 734-374-1303. Hours: 8:15AM-4:45PM (EST). *Misdemeanor, Civil Actions Under $25,000, Eviction, Small Claims.*

Civil Records: Access: Mail, in person. Only the court performs in person searches; visitors may not. No search fee. Required to search: name, years to search. Civil cases indexed by defendant, plaintiff. Civil records on computer since 1993, prior on books.

Criminal Records: Access: Mail, in person. Only the court performs in person searches; visitors may not. No search fee. Required to search: name, years to search, DOB; also helpful: SSN. Criminal records on computer since 1993, prior on index cards.

General Information: No suppressed, sexual abuse or drug abuse records released. Copy fee: $1.00 per page. Certification fee: $10.00. Payee: 23rd District Court. Personal checks accepted. Prepayment required. Mail requests: SASE not required. Mail turnaround time 1-2 days.

24th District Court - Allen Park & Melvindale 6515 Roosevelt, Allen Park, MI 48101-2524; 313-928-0535; Civil phone: 313-928-1899; Fax: 313-928-1860. Hours: 8:30AM-4:30PM (EST). *Misdemeanor, Civil Actions Under $25,000, Eviction, Small Claims.*
www.24thdiscourt.org

Civil Records: Access: Phone, mail, fax, in person. Only the court performs in person searches; visitors may not. No search fee. Required to search: name, years to search, case number. Civil cases indexed by defendant, plaintiff. Civil records on computer since 1992, prior records stored as hard-copies.

Criminal Records: Access: Fax, mail, in person. Only the court performs in person searches; visitors may not. No search fee. Required to search: name, years to search, DOB; also helpful: SSN. Criminal records on computer since 1993, prior records stored as hard-copies.

General Information: No non-public records, including driving and probation records, released. Will fax results to local or toll free line. Copy fee: $.50 per page. Certification fee: $10.00. Payee: 24th District Court. Personal checks accepted. Prepayment required. Mail requests: SASE required if return mail requested. Turnaround time 1 week.

25th District Court 1475 Cleophus, Lincoln Park, MI 48146; 313-382-8603; Civil phone: 313-382-9317; Criminal phone: 313-382-8600; Fax: 313-382-9361. 9AM-4:30PM (EST). *Misdemeanor, Civil Actions Under $25,000, Eviction, Small Claims.*

Civil Records: Access: Mail, phone, in person. Only the court performs in person searches; visitors may not. No search fee. Required to search: name, years to search. Civil cases indexed by defendant, plaintiff. Civil records on computer since 1988, prior records stored as hard-copies.

Criminal Records: Access: Mail, phone, in person. Only the court performs in person searches; visitors may not. No search fee. Required to search: name, years to search, DOB. Criminal records on computer since 1987, prior on docket books and cards.

General Information: No suppressed or expunged records released. Copy fee: $1.00 per page. Certification fee: $11.00. Payee: 25th District Court. Personal checks accepted. Visa, MC accepted. Prepayment required. Mail requests: SASE required. Mail turnaround time 1 week.

26-1 District Court 10600 W Jefferson, River Rouge, MI 48218; 313-842-7819; Fax: 313-842-5923. 8:30AM-4:30PM (EST). *Misdemeanor, Civil Actions Under $25,000, Eviction, Small Claims.*

Civil Records: Access: Mail, in person. Only the court performs in person searches; visitors may not. No search fee. Required to search: name, years to search. Civil cases indexed by defendant, plaintiff. Civil records on computer since 11/93; prior records on cards.

Criminal Records: Access: Mail, in person. Only the court performs in person searches; visitors may not. No search fee. Required to search: name, years to search, DOB. Criminal records on computer since 1993, prior on index cards.

General Information: No suppressed records released. Will fax results for $2.00. Copy fee: $1.00 per page. No certification fee. Payee: 26-1 District Court. No personal checks accepted. Prepayment required. Mail requests: SASE required. Mail turnaround time 1 week.

26-2 District Court 3869 W Jefferson, Ecorse, MI 48229; 313-386-7900; Fax: 313-928-5956. Hours: 9AM-4PM (EST). *Misdemeanor, Civil Actions Under $25,000, Eviction, Small Claims.*

Civil Records: Access: Mail, fax, in person. Only the court performs in person searches; visitors may not. Search fee: $25.00. Required to search: name, years to search. Civil cases indexed by defendant, plaintiff. Civil records on computer back to 1992, prior on index cards.

Criminal Records: Access: Mail, fax, in person. Only the court performs in person searches; visitors may not. Search fee: $25.00. Required to search: name, years to search, DOB; also helpful: SSN. Criminal records on computer back to 1992, prior on index cards.

General Information: No suppressed records released. Will fax results for a fee of $.25 per name. Copy fee: $.50 per page. Certification fee: $10.00. Payee: 26-2 District Court. Business checks accepted. Prepayment required. Mail requests: SASE not required. Mail turnaround time 1 week.

27th District Court 2015 Biddle Ave, Wyandotte, MI 48192; 734-324-4475; Fax: 734-324-4472. Hours: 8:30AM-4:30PM (EST). *Misdemeanor, Civil Actions Under $25,000, Eviction, Small Claims.* Note: The 27-2 District Court in Riverview was closed as of 12/31/03. All of their records are now at this court.

Civil Records: Access: Mail, in person. Only the court performs in person searches; visitors may not. Search fee: $1.00. Required to search: name, years to search. Civil cases indexed by defendant, plaintiff. Civil records on computer since 1988, prior on index cards.

Criminal Records: Access: Mail, in person. Only the court performs in person searches; visitors may not. Search fee: $1.00. Required to search: name, years to search, DOB. Criminal records on computer since 1988, prior on index cards.

General Information: No suppressed records released. Will fax results to local or toll free line. Copy fee: $1.00 per page. Certification fee: $10.00 plus $1.00 per page after first. Payee: 27th District Court. Money order or in person cash accepted. Prepayment required. Mail requests: SASE required. Mail turnaround time 1 week.

28th District Court 14720 Reaume Parkway, Southgate, MI 48195; 734-258-3068; Civil phone: 734-258-3068; Criminal phone: 734-258-3068; Fax: 734-246-1405. Hours: 8:30AM-4:30PM (EST). *Misdemeanor, Civil Actions Under $25,000, Eviction, Small Claims.*
www.28thdistrictcourt.com

Civil Records: Access: In person only. Both court and visitors may perform in person searches. No search fee. Required to search: name, years to search; also helpful: address. Civil cases indexed by defendant, plaintiff. Civil records on computer back to 1987, prior on card files by party back to 1979.

Criminal Records: Access: In person only. Only the court performs in person searches; visitors may not. No search fee. Required to search: name, years to search, DOB; also helpful: address, SSN, case number. Criminal records go back to 1979; on computer back to 1986.

General Information: No suppressed, probation, sex offenders, or mental health records released. Copy fee: $1.00 per page. Certification fee: $10.00. Payee: 28th District Court. Cash, cashiers checks, money orders, Visa, MC or Discover accepted In person only. Prepayment required.

29th District Court 34808 Sims Ave, Wayne, MI 48184; 734-722-5220; Fax: 734-722-7003. Hours: 8AM-4:30PM (EST). *Misdemeanor, Civil Actions Under $25,000, Eviction, Small Claims.*

Civil Records: Access: Phone, mail, in person. Only the court performs in person searches; visitors may not. No search fee. Required to search: name, years to search. Civil cases indexed by defendant, plaintiff. Civil records on computer since 1990. Will name search free, but there will be a copy fee.

Criminal Records: Access: Phone, mail, in person. Only the court performs in person searches; visitors may not. No search fee. Required to search: name, years to search, DOB; also helpful: address, SSN. Criminal records on computer since 1990. Will name search free, but there will be a copy fee.

General Information: No suppressed, juvenile, sex offenders, mental health, or adoption records released. Will fax results to local or toll free line. Copy fee: $.50 per page. Certification fee: $10.00. Payee: 29th District Court. Personal checks accepted. Visa, MC accepted. Prepayment required. Mail requests: SASE required. Mail turnaround time 1 week, phone turnaround is 1 day.

30th District Court 12050 Wood Ward Ave, Highland Park, MI 48203; 313-252-0300; Fax: 313-865-1115. 8AM-4:30PM (EST). *Misdemeanor, Civil Actions Under $25,000, Eviction, Small Claims.*

Civil Records: Access: Mail, in person. Both court and visitors may perform in person searches. Search fee: $5.00 per name. Required to search: name, years to search. Civil cases indexed by defendant, plaintiff. Civil records on computer since 1989, prior on index cards or docket books.

Criminal Records: Access: Mail, in person. Both court and visitors may perform in person searches. Search fee: $5.00 per name. Required to search: name, years to search, DOB. Records on computer since 1989, prior on index cards or docket books.

General Information: No suppressed records released. Will fax results. Copy fee: $1.00 per page. Certification fee: $5.00. Payee: 30th District Court. Prepayment required. Mail requests: SASE required. Mail turnaround time 1 week.

31st District Court 3401 Evaline Ave, Hamtramck, MI 48212; 313-876-7710; Fax: 313-876-7724. Hours: 8AM-4PM (EST). *Misdemeanor, Civil Actions Under $25,000, Eviction, Small Claims.*

Civil Records: Access: Mail, in person. Only the court performs in person searches; visitors may not. No search fee. Required to search: name, years to search. Cases indexed by defendant, plaintiff. Civil records on computer since 1989, prior on index cards.

Criminal Records: Access: Mail, in person. Only the court performs in person searches; visitors may not. No search fee. Required to search: name, years to

search, DOB. Criminal records on computer since 1989, prior on index cards.

General Information: No suppressed records released. Will fax results for $1.00 per page. Copy fee: $1.00 per page. Certification fee: $10.00 plus $1.00 per page after first. Payee: 31st District Court. Personal checks accepted. Prepayment required. Mail requests: SASE required. Mail turnaround: 1-2 days.

32 A District Court 19617 Harper Ave, Harper Woods, MI 48225; 313-343-2590; Civil phone: 313-343-2592; Fax: 313-343-2594. Hours: 8:30AM-4:30PM (EST). *Misdemeanor, Civil Actions Under $25,000, Small Claims.*

Civil Records: Access: Phone, fax, mail, in person. Only the court performs in person searches; visitors may not. No search fee. Required to search: name, years to search. Civil cases indexed by defendant, plaintiff. Civil records indexed by name and case number on computer, microfiche, and paper.

Criminal Records: Access: Phone, fax, mail, in person. Only the court performs in person searches; visitors may not. No search fee. Required to search: name, years to search. Records indexed by name and case number on computer, microfiche, and paper.

General Information: No suppressed records released. Will fax results, no fee. Copy fee: $.50 per page. Certification fee: $10.00. Payee: 32A District Court. Personal checks accepted. Visa, MC accepted. Prepayment required. Mail requests: SASE requested. Turnaround time same day.

33rd District Court 19000 Van Horn Rd, Woodhaven, MI 48183; 734-671-0201; Civil phone: 734-671-0225; Criminal phone: 734-671-0201; Fax: 734-671-0307. Hours: 8:30AM-4:30PM (EST). *Misdemeanor, Civil Actions Under $25,000, Eviction, Small Claims.*

Civil Records: Access: Mail, fax, in person. Both court and visitors may perform in person searches. No search fee. Required to search: name, years to search; also helpful: address. Civil cases indexed by defendant, plaintiff. Civil records on computer since 1995, prior on microfilm and microfiche.

Criminal Records: Access: Mail, fax, in person. Both court and visitors may perform in person searches. No search fee. Required to search: name, years to search, DOB; also helpful: address. Criminal records on computer since 1995, prior on microfilm and microfiche.

General Information: Public Access terminal is available. No suppressed records released. Copy fee: $.25 per page. Certification fee: $10.00 plus $1.00 per page after first. Payee: 33rd District Court. Business checks accepted. Visa, MC accepted. Prepayment required. Mail requests: SASE required. Mail turnaround time 1-5 days.

34th District Court 11131 S Wayne Rd, Romulus, MI 48174; 734-941-4462; Fax: 734-941-7530. 8:30AM-4PM (EST). *Misdemeanor, Civil Actions Under $25,000, Eviction, Small Claims.*

Civil Records: Access: Mail, in person. Only the court performs in person searches; visitors may not. No search fee. Required to search: name, years to search. Civil cases indexed by defendant, plaintiff. Civil records on computer since 1984, prior on index cards and docket books.

Criminal Records: Access: Mail, in person. Only the court performs in person searches; visitors may not. No search fee. Required to search: name, years to search, DOB; also helpful: SSN. Records on computer since 1984, prior on index cards and docket books.

General Information: No suppressed records released. Copy fee: $1.00 per page. Certification fee: $10.00 per page. Payee: 34th District Court. Personal

checks accepted. Prepayment required. Mail requests: SASE required. Mail turnaround time 1 week.

35th District Court 660 Plymouth Rd, Plymouth, MI 48170; 734-459-4740; Fax: 734-454-9303. Hours: 8:30AM-4:25PM (EST). *Misdemeanor, Civil Infractions, Civil Actions Under $25,000, Landlord Tenant, Small Claims, Juvenile.* www.35thdistrictcourt.org

Civil Records: Access: Mail, in person. Both court and visitors may perform in person searches. No search fee. Required to search: name, years to search. Civil cases indexed by defendant, plaintiff. Civil records on computer since 1990.

Criminal Records: Access: Mail, in person. Both court and visitors may perform in person searches. No search fee. Required to search: name, years to search, DOB; also helpful: SSN, sex, signed release. Criminal records on computer since 1990.

General: Public Access terminal is available. No suppressed, juvenile, sex offenders, mental health, or adoption records released. Fee to fax results is $1.00 per document. Copy fee: $1.00 per page. Certification fee: $10.00. Payee: 35th District Court. Third party checks not accepted. Debit cards accepted. Prepayment required. Mail turnaround time: 1 week.

Wexford County

28th Circuit Court PO Box 490, Cadillac, MI 49601; 231-779-9450. Hours: 8:30AM-5PM (EST). *Felony, Civil Actions Over $25,000.*

Civil Records: Access: Mail, in person. Only the court performs in person searches; visitors may not. Search fee: $1.00 per name. Required to search: name, years to search. Civil cases indexed by defendant, plaintiff. Civil records go back to 1868, civil records on computer since 1977.

Criminal Records: Access: Mail, in person. Only the court performs in person searches; visitors may not. Search fee: $1.00 per name. Required to search: name, years to search. Criminal records go back to 1868, criminal records on computer since 1977.

General Information: No suppressed, YTA files, juvenile, sex offenders, mental health, or adoption records released. Copy fee: $1.00 per page. Certification fee: $10.00, plus $1.00 per each add'l page on multi page documents. Payee: Wexford County Clerk. Only cashiers checks and money orders accepted. Prepayment required. Mail requests: SASE required. Mail turnaround time same day.

84th District Court 437 E Division St, Cadillac, MI 49601; 231-779-9515; Fax: 231-779-5396. Hours: 8:30AM-5PM (EST). *Misdemeanor, Civil Actions Under $25,000, Eviction, Small Claims.*

Civil Records: Access: Phone, fax, mail, in person. Both court and visitors may perform in person searches. Search fee: $1.00 per name. Required to search: name, years to search. Civil cases indexed by defendant, plaintiff. Civil records on computer since 1984; on index from 1969 to 1984.

Criminal Records: Access: Mail, fax, in person. Both court and visitors may perform in person searches. Search fee: $1.00 per name. Required to search: name, years to search, DOB; also helpful: SSN. Criminal records on computer since 1984; prior records on blue cards.

General Information: No suppressed, juvenile, sex offenders, mental health, or adoption records released. Copy fee: $1.00 per page. Certification fee: $10.00. Payee: 84th District Court. Personal checks accepted. Prepayment required. Mail requests: SASE required. Mail turnaround time 1 week.

Probate Court 437 E Division, Cadillac, MI 49601; 231-779-9510; Probate phone: 231-779-9511; Fax: 231-779-9485. 8:30AM-5PM (EST). *Probate.*

Michigan Recording Offices

ORGANIZATION: 83 counties, 83 recording offices. The recording officer is County Register of Deeds. 79 counties are in the Eastern Time Zone (EST) and 4 counties that border on Wisconsin (Gogebic, Iron, Dickinson, and Menominee) are in the Central Time Zone (CST).

REAL ESTATE RECORDS: Some counties will perform real estate searches. Copies usually cost $1.00 per page. and certification fees vary. Ownership records are located at the Equalization Office, designated "Assessor" in this section. Tax records are located at the Treasurer's Office.

UCC RECORDS: Financing statements are filed at the state level, except for real estate related collateral, which are filed with the County Register. However, prior to 07/2001, consumer goods and farm collateral were also filed at the County Register and these older records can be searched there. All counties will perform UCC searches. Use search request form UCC-11. Search fees are usually $3.00 to $6.00 per debtor name if federal tax identification number or Social Security Number are given, or $6.00 to $12.00 without a number. Copies usually cost $1.00 per page.

TAX LIEN RECORDS: Federal and state tax liens on personal property of businesses are filed with the Secretary of State. Other federal and state tax liens are filed with the Register of Deeds. Most counties search each tax lien index separately. Some charge one fee to search both, while others charge a separate fee for each one. When combining a UCC and tax lien search, total fee is usually $9.00 for all three searches. Some counties require tax identification number as well as name to do a search. Copy fees are usually $1.00 per page.

OTHER LIENS: Construction, lis pendens.

ONLINE ACCESS: There is no statewide online access, but a number of counties, including Wayne, offer free access to assessor and register of deeds records.

Alcona County

County Register of Deeds, PO Box 269, Harrisville, MI 48740-0269. **Phone**-County Register of Deeds, R/E & UCC Recording- 989-724-6802; fax-989-724-5684; hours 8:30AM-4:30PM
Will search UCC records prior to 7/2001. Search request with SS/TIN (per name)- $3.00. Search request without SS/TIN (per name)- $6.00. UCC search includes tax liens if requested. Tax lien search fee- $10.00 per debtor. Will not search real estate records. Record copy- $1.00 per page. Cert fee: $2.00 per cert. Payee: Alcona County Register of Deeds. **Other phones:** Assessor-989-724-6223; Treasurer-989-724-5140; Elections-989-724-6807; Vital Records-989-724-6807.

Alger County

County Register of Deeds, PO Box 538, Munising, MI 49862. **Phone**-906-387-2076; fax-906-387-2156; hours 8AM-4PM. Will search UCC records prior to 7/2001 and current fixture (land) files. UCC search per debtor- $6.00. UCC copy- $1.00 per page. Tax liens not included in UCC search. Separate federal/state combined tax lien search- $6.00 per debtor. Will not search real estate records. Cert fee: $1.00 per cert. Payee: Alger County Register of Deeds. **Other phones:** Assessor-906-387-2567; Treasurer-906-387-4535.

Allegan County

County Register of Deeds, 113 Chestnut St, County Court House, Allegan, MI 49010-1360. **Phone**-County Register of Deeds, R/E & UCC Recording- 269-673-0390, UCC Recording- 269-673-0390 x3280; fax-269-673-0289; hours 8AM-5PM www.allegancounty.org/
Will search UCC records. UCC search per debtor- $6.00. UCC copy- $2.00 per page. Tax liens not included in UCC search. Separate federal/state combined tax lien search- $6.00 per debtor. Will search individual real estate records. RE record copy- $1.00 per page. Cert fee: $1.00 per page. Payee: Allegan County Register of Deeds. **Online Access to Real Estate records:** Search by nmae or address at www.allegancounty.org/prdwebeq/. **Other phones:**

Assessor-269-673-0230; Treasurer-269-673-0260; Elections-269-673-0450; Vital Records-269-673-0450.

Alpena County

County Register of Deeds, 720 W. Chisholm St, Courthouse, Alpena, MI 49707-2487. **Phone**-989-354-9547, R/E Recording- 989-356-3887; fax-989-354-9646; hours 8:30AM-4:30PM
Will search UCC records prior to 7/2001 and current fixture (land) files. UCC search per debtor- $6.00. UCC copy- $2.00 per page. Separate federal/state combined tax lien search- $6.00 per debtor. Will not search real estate records. RE record copy- $1.00 per page. Cert fee: $1.00 per cert. Payee: Alpena County Register of Deeds. **Other phones:** Assessor-989-356-2015; Treasurer-989-356-1751.

Antrim County

County Register of Deeds, PO Box 376, Bellaire, MI 49615. **Phone**-County Register of Deeds, R/E & UCC Recording- 231-533-6683; fax-231-533-8317; hours 8:30AM-5PM www.antrimcounty.org
Will search UCC records prior to 7/2001 and current fixture (land) files. UCC search per debtor- $6.00. UCC copy- $2.00 per page. UCC search includes tax liens if requested. Will search real estate records. RE record copy- $1.00 per page. Cert fee: $1.00 per cert. Payee: Antrim County Register of Deeds. **Online Access to Most Wanted records:** Access to the sheriff's most wanted list is free at www.torchlake.com/acsd/. **Other phones:** Assessor-231-533-6320; Treasurer-231-533-6720.

Arenac County

County Register of Deeds, PO Box 296, Standish, MI 48658. **Phone**-989-846-9201, R/E Recording- 517-846-9201; hours 8:30AM-5PM Will search UCC records prior to 7/2001 and current fixture (land) files. UCC search per debtor- $6.00. UCC copy- $1.00 per page. Federal/state combined tax lien search- $12.00 per debtor. Will not search real estate records. Cert fee: $1.00 per cert. Payee: County Register of Deeds. **Other phones:** Assessor-517-846-6246.

Baraga County

County Register of Deeds, 16 N. 3rd St., Courthouse, L'Anse, MI 49946-1085. **Phone**-906-524-6183; fax-906-524-6186; hours 8:30AM-Noon, 1-4:30PM
Will search UCC records prior to 7/2001 and current fixture (land) files. Search request with SS/TIN (per name)- $5.00. UCC copy- $1.00 per page. UCC search includes tax liens if requested. Will not search real estate records. Cert fee: $3.00 per cert. Payee: County Register of Deeds. **Other phones:** Assessor-906-524-7331; Treasurer-906-524-7773; Elections-906-524-6183; Vital Records-906-524-6183.

Barry County

County Register of Deeds, PO Box 7, Hastings, MI 49058-0007. **Phone**-269-948-4824, R/E Recording- 269-945-1289, UCC Recording- 269-945-1289; fax-269-948-4820; 8AM-5PM www.barrycounty.org
Will search UCC records prior to 7/2001 and current fixture (land) files. UCC search per debtor- $6.00. UCC search includes tax liens. Separate federal/state combined tax lien search- $6.00 per debtor. Will not search real estate records. Record copy- $1.00 per page. Cert fee: $1.00 per cert. Payee: Barry County Register of Deeds. **Online Access to Property, Assessor, Delinquent Tax records:** Access to county parcel data is free at www.barrycounty.org/ParcelData.htm. County property Index is from 12/95 to 1/04. **Other phones:** Assessor-269-945-1288; Treasurer-269-945-1287; Elections-269-945-1285; Vital Records-269-945-1285.

Bay County

County Register of Deeds, 515 Center Ave, Bay City, MI 48708-5994. **Phone**-County Register of Deeds, R/E & UCC Recording- 989-895-4228; fax-989-895-4296; hours 8AM-5PM (June-September 7:30AM-4PM) www.co.bay.mi.us
Will search UCC records. UCC search per debtor- $6.00. UCC copy- $2.00 per page. Separate federal/state combined tax lien search- $6.00 per debtor. Will not search real estate records. RE record copy- $1.00 per page. Cert fee: $3.00 per cert. Payee: Bay County Register of Deeds. **Online Access to Property Tax records:** Access county

property tacx data for free at www.co.bay.mi.us/bay/ptq.nsf. **Other phones:** Assessor-989-895-4075; Treasurer-989-895-4285; Vital Records-989-895-4280.

Benzie County

County Register of Deeds, PO Box 377, Beulah, MI 49617. **Phone**-231-882-0016; fax-231-882-0167; hours 8AM-Noon, 1-5PM
Will search UCC records prior to 7/2001 and current fixture (land) files. UCC search per debtor-$6.00. Will expedite for add'l $25.00. UCC copy- $2.00 per page. Tax liens not included in UCC search. Separate federal/state combined tax lien search-$4.00 per debtor. Will not search real estate records unless document specified. RE record copy- $1.00 per page. Cert fee: $1.00 per seal. Payee: Benzie County Register of Deeds. **Other phones:** Assessor-231-882-0015; Treasurer-231-882-0011; Elections-231-882-0001; Vital Records-231-882-0001.

Berrien County

County Register of Deeds, 701 Main St., Berrien County Admin. Ctr, St. Joseph, MI 49085. **Phone**-616-983-7111 x8562, R/E Recording- 269-983-7111 x8562; fax-616-982-8659; hours-8:30AM-5PM www.berriencounty.org/
Will search UCC records prior to 7/2001 and current fixture (land) files. UCC search per debtor- $6.00. UCC copy- $2.00 per page. Tax lien search fee- $3.00 per debtor. Will not search real estate records. RE record copy- $1.00 per page. Cert fee: $1.00 per cert. Payee: Berrien County Register of Deeds. **Other phones:** Assessor-269-983-7111 x8215; Treasurer-269-983-7111 x8208; Vital Records-269-983-7111 x8233.

Branch County

County Register of Deeds, 570 Marshall Rd, #C, Coldwater, MI 49036. **Phone**-County Register of Deeds, R/E & UCC Recording- 517-279-4320; hours 9AM-Noon, 1-5PM www.co.branch.mi.us/
Will search UCC records prior to 7/2001 and current fixture (land) files. UCC search per debtor- $6.00. UCC copy- $2.00 per page. UCC search includes tax liens. Will not search real estate records. RE record copy- $2.00 per doc. Cert fee: $2.00 per cert. Payee: Branch County Register of Deeds. **Online Access to Vital Statistic, Business Name, DBA records:** search the countyvital records free at www.co.branch.mi.us/vital/vital.html#dba. Search business names and DBAs at www.co.branch.mi.us/dbasearch.taf. **Other phones:** Assessor-517-279-4312; Treasurer-517-279-8411.

Calhoun County

County Register of Deeds, 315 W. Green St, Marshall, MI 49068. **Phone**-269-781-0718; fax-269-781-0721; hours 8AM-5PM http://co.calhoun.mi.us
Will search UCC records prior to 7/2001 and current fixture (land) files. Search per debtor- $6.00. UCC copy- $2.00 per page. Tax lien search fee- $6.00 per debtor. Will not search real estate records. RE record copy- $1.00 per page. Cert fee: $1.00 per page. Payee: Calhoun County Register of Deeds. **Other phones:** Assessor-269-781-0745; Treasurer-269-969-6910/616-781-0807; Elections-269-781-0988; Vital Records-269-781-0718.

Cass County

County Register of Deeds, PO Box 355, Cassopolis, MI 49031-0355. **Phone**-County Register of Deeds, R/E & UCC Recording- 269-445-4464; fax-269-445-4406; hours 8AM-5PM www.casscountymi.org
Will search UCC records prior to 7/2001 and current fixture (land) files. UCC search per debtor- $6.00 per year. UCC copy- $2.00 per page. UCC search includes tax liens if requested with extra fee.

Separate federal/state combined tax lien search-$3.00 per year per debtor. Will search real estate records; written request only. RE record copy- $1.00 per page. Cert fee: $1.00 per cert. Payee: Cass County Clerk/Register. **Other phones:** Treasurer-269-445-4468; Elections-269-445-4464; Vital Records-269-445-4464.

Charlevoix County

County Register of Deeds, 301 State St, County Bldg., Charlevoix, MI 49720. **Phone**-231-547-7204; fax-231-547-7246; hours 9AM-5PM
Will search UCC records prior to 7/2001 and current fixture (land) files. Search request with SS/TIN (per name)- $6.00. UCC copy- $1.00 per page. UCC search includes tax liens if requested for add'l fee. Separate federal/state combined tax lien search-$6.00 per debtor Will not search real estate records. Cert fee: $1.00 per cert. Payee: Charlevoix County Register of Deeds. **Online Access to Birth, Marriage, Obituary, Cemetery, Birth records:** Access to these unofficial records is courtesy of genealogical researcher at www.rootsweb.com/~micharle/charlevx.htm. **Other phones:** Assessor-231-547-7230; Treasurer-231-547-7202.

Cheboygan County

County Register of Deeds, PO Box 70, Cheboygan, MI 49721. **Phone**-231-627-8866; fax-231-627-8453; hours 8;30AM-5PM
Will search UCC records prior to 7/2001 and current fixture (land) files. UCC search per debtor- $6.00. UCC copy- $2.00 per page. Federal/state combined tax lien search- $6.00 per debtor. Will not search real estate records. RE record copy- $1.00 per page. Cert fee: $1.00 per cert. Payee: County Register of Deeds. **Other phones:** Assessor-231-627-8845; Treasurer-231-627-8821; Elections-231-627-8808; Vital Records-231-627-8808.

Chippewa County

County Register of Deeds, 319 Court St, Courthouse, Sault Ste. Marie, MI 49783. **Phone**-County Register of Deeds, R/E & UCC Recording- 906-635-6312; fax-906-635-6855; hours-8AM-5PM www.sault.com/~chippewa
Will search UCC records prior to 7/2001 and current fixture (land) files. Search per debtor- $6.00. Tax liens not included in UCC search. Tax lien search fee- $6.00 per debtor. Will not search real estate records but will search for a specific item. Record copy- $1.00 per page. Cert fee: $1.00 per cert. Payee: County Register of Deeds. **Other phones:** Assessor-906-635-6304; Treasurer-906-635-6308; Elections-906-635-6300; Vital Records-906-635-6300.

Clare County

County Register of Deeds, PO Box 586, Harrison, MI 48625. **Phone**-County Register of Deeds, R/E & UCC Recording- 989-539-7131; fax-989-539-6616; hours 8AM-4:30PM www.claremi.com/local_contacts.html
Will search UCC records. UCC search per debtor-$6.00. UCC copy- $2.00 per page. Will search tax liens. Separate federal/state tax lien search- $3.00 per debtor. Only title searches are available. RE record copy- $1.00 per page. Cert fee: $1.00 per cert. Payee: Clare County Register of Deeds. **Other phones:** Assessor-989-539-3867; Treasurer-989-539-7801; Elections-989-539-7131; Vital Records-989-539-7131.

Clinton County

County Register of Deeds, PO Box 435, St. Johns, MI 48879-0435. **Phone**-County Register of Deeds, R/E & UCC Recording- 989-224-5270; fax-989-227-6473; hours 8AM-5PM www.clinton-county.org/
Will search UCC records prior to 7/2001 and current fixture (land) files. UCC search per debtor- $6.00.

UCC copy- $2.00 per page. UCC search includes tax liens if requested with extra fee. Separate federal/state combined tax lien search- $6.00 per debtor. Will not search real estate records. RE record copy- $1.00 per page. Cert fee: $1.00 per cert. Payee: County Register of Deeds. **Other phones:** Assessor-989-224-5170; Treasurer-989-224-5280.

Crawford County

County Register of Deeds, 200 W. Michigan, Grayling, MI 49738. **Phone**-989-348-2841, R/E Recording- 989-344-3203, UCC Recording- 989-344-3203; fax-989-344-3223; hours-8:30AM-4:30PM www.crawfordco.org/deeds/deeds.htm
Will search UCC records prior to 7/2001 and current fixture (land) files. UCC search per debtor- $6.00. UCC copy- $2.00 per page. UCC search includes tax liens if requested. Will not search real estate records. RE record copy- $1.00 per page. Cert fee: $1.00 per doc. Payee: Crawford County Register of Deeds. **Online Access to Most Wanted records:** Access to the sheriff's most wanted list is at www.crawfordsheriff.org/Misc/wanted/wanted.htm. **Other phones:** Assessor-989-344-3235; Treasurer-989-344-3229; Appraiser/ Auditor-989-344-3234; Elections-989-344-3200; Vital Records-989-344-3207.

Delta County

County Register of Deeds, 310 Ludington St, #104, Escanaba, MI 49829-4039. **Phone**-County Register of Deeds, R/E & UCC Recording- 906-789-5116; fax-906-789-5196; hours 8AM-4PM
Will search UCC records. UCC search per debtor-$6.00. UCC copy- $2.00 per page. Tax liens not included in UCC search. Federal/state combined tax lien search- $9.00 per debtor. Will not search real estate records. RE record copy- $.50 per year, $5.00 min. Cert fee: $3.00 per cert. Payee: Register of Deeds. **Other phones:** Assessor-906-789-5109; Treasurer-906-789-5117; Appraiser/ Auditor-906-789-5109; Elections-906-789-5105; Vital Records-906-789-5105.

Dickinson County

County Register of Deeds, PO Box 609, Iron Mountain, MI 49801. **Phone**-906-774-0955; fax-906-774-4660; hours 8AM-4:30PM
Will search UCC records prior to 7/2001 and current fixture (land) files. UCC search per debtor- $6.00. UCC copy- $2.00 per page. UCC search includes tax liens if requested. Separate federal/state combined tax lien search- $3.00 per debtor. Will not search real estate records. RE record copy- $1.00 per page. Cert fee: $1.00 per doc. Payee: County Register of Deeds. **Other phones:** Assessor-906-774-2515; Treasurer-906-774-8130.

Eaton County

County Register of Deeds, 1045 Independence Blvd., Rm 104, Charlotte, MI 48813-1095. **Phone**-County Register of Deeds, R/E & UCC Recording- 517-543-7500 x232, UCC Recording- 517-543-7500 x231; fax-517-543-7377; hours-8AM-5PM www.co.eaton.mi.us/cntsrv/online.htm
Will search UCC records prior to 7/2001 and current fixture (land) files. UCC search per debtor- $6.00. UCC copy- $2.00 per page. Will search tax liens. Federal/state combined tax lien search- $6.00 per debtor. Will search real estate records. RE record copy- $1.00 per page. Cert fee: $1.00 per cert. Payee: Eaton County Register of Deeds. **Online Access to Assessor, Tax, Recorder, Marriage, Divorce records:** Two levels of service are on the County Online Data Service site. For free information, click on the Free Limited Public Information on the main page; then, on the Access System Page, at "User" enter PUBLIC. For "password," enter PUBLIC. The sophisticated, restricted "Enhanced Records Access"

requires registration, a password, and fee. Access fees are billable monthly and can be prepaid to cover usage. Also, Marriages and divorces can be searched at www.co.eaton.mi.us/Cntsrv/COUNTY.HTM. Also, search the Delta Charter Township assessments free at www.township.delta.mi.us/Assessing/BSALink.htm. **Other phones:** Assessor-517-543-7500 x236; Treasurer-517-543-7500 x210; Appraiser/ Auditor-517-543-7500 x219; Elections-517-543-7500 x225; Vital Records-517-543-7500 x225; Information Systems-517-543-7500 x207.

Emmet County

County Register of Deeds, 200 Division, Petoskey, MI 49770. **Phone**-231-348-1761; fax-231-348-0633; hours 8:30AM-5PM
Will search UCC records prior to 7/2001 and current fixture (land) files. UCC search per debtor- $6.00. UCC copy- $2.00 per page. Federal/state combined tax lien search- $6.00 per debtor. Will not search real estate records. RE record copy- $1.00 per apge. Cert fee: $1.00 per cert. Payee: Emmet County Register of Deeds. **Other phones:** Assessor-231-348-1708; Treasurer-231-348-1715.

Genesee County

County Register of Deeds, 1101 Beach St, Admin. Bldg., Flint, MI 48502. **Phone**-County Register of Deeds, R/E & UCC Recording- 810-257-3060; fax-810-768-7965; 8AM-5PM www.co.genesee.mi.us
Will search UCC records prior to 7/2001 and current fixture (land) files. UCC search per debtor- $10.00. UCC copy- $2.00 per page. UCC search includes tax liens if requested. Separate federal/state combined tax lien search- $6.00 per debtor. Will not search real estate records. RE record copy- $1.00 per page. Cert fee: $1.00 per cert. Payee: Genesee County Register of Deeds. **Online Access to Recording, Property, Deed, Marriage, Death records:** Access to Register of Deeds database is free at www.co.genesee.mi.us/rod/. But to view documents back to 10/2000, there is a fee, and user ID and password required. Also, online access to the county clerk's marriage (back to 1963) and death (back to 1930) indexes are free at www.co.genesee.mi.us/vitalrec. Search property index at www.co.genesee.mi.us/cgi-bin/gweb.exe?mode=7800&sessionname=gentax&command=connect. **Other phones:** Assessor-810-257-3017; Treasurer-810-257-3059; Elections-810-257-3283; Vital Records-810-257-3225.

Gladwin County

County Register of Deeds, 401 W. Cedar Ave, #7, Gladwin, MI 48624-2093. **Phone**-989-426-7551; fax-989-426-6902; hours 8:30AM-4:30PM
Will fax back results for add'l $1.00 per page, prepaid. Will search UCC records prior to 7/2001 and current fixture (land) files. UCC search per debtor- $10.00. UCC copy- $2.00 per page. UCC search includes tax liens if requested. Separate federal/state combined tax lien search- $10.00 per debtor. Will only search real estate records on computer since 3/14/1991. RE record copy- $1.00 per page. Cert fee: $1.00 per cert. Payee: Gladwin County Register of Deeds. **Other phones:** Assessor-989-426-9327; Treasurer-989-426-7351; Elections-989-426-7351; Vital Records-989-426-7351.

Gogebic County

County Register of Deeds, 200 N. Moore St., Courthouse, Bessemer, MI 49911. **Phone**-County Register of Deeds, R/E & UCC Recording- 906-667-0381; fax-906-663-4660; hours 8:30AM-4:30PM
Will search UCC records prior to 7/2001 and current fixture (land) files. UCC search per debtor- $6.00. UCC search includes tax liens if requested. Separate federal/state combined tax lien search-

$6.00 per search. Real estate owner, mortgage, and property transfer searches available. Record copy- $1.00 per copy. Cert fee: $3.00 per cert. Payee: Gogebic County Register of Deeds. **Other phones:** Assessor-906-663-4414; Treasurer-906-667-4517; Elections-906-667-4518; Vital Records-906-667-4518.

Grand Traverse County

County Register of Deeds, 400 Boardman Ave, Traverse City, MI 49684-2577. **Phone**-231-922-4750; fax-231-922-2770; hours 8AM-5PM (Vault closes at 4:30PM)
Will search UCC records prior to 7/2001 and current fixture (land) files. UCC search per debtor- $10.00. UCC copy- $1.00 per page. Tax liens not included in UCC search. Federal/state combined tax lien search- $6.00 per debtor Will search grantor/grantee or mortgagor/mortgagee records. Cert fee: $1.00 per cert. Payee: Grand Traverse County Register of Deeds. **Online Access to Marriage, Death records:** Access to the county death and marriage indices are free at www.tcnet.org/gtcounty/index.html. **Other phones:** Assessor-231-922-4772; Treasurer-231-922-4735.

Gratiot County

County Register of Deeds, PO Box 5, Ithaca, MI 48847. **Phone**-989-875-5217; 8AM-Noon-1PM-4:30PM
Will search UCC records. UCC search per debtor- $6.00. $6.00 add'l fee for more than 100 debtor records. $25.00 add'l fee for expedited service. UCC copy- $2.00 per page. Will not search real estate or tax lien records. RE record copy- $1.00 per page. Cert fee: $1.00 per cert. Payee: Gratiot County Register of Deeds. **Other phones:** Assessor-989-875-5203; Treasurer-989-875-5220.

Hillsdale County

County Register of Deeds, 29 N Howell, Rm 3, Courthouse, Hillsdale, MI 49242. **Phone**-517-437-2231; fax-517-437-3139; hours 8:30AM-5PM www.co.hillsdale.mi.us
Will search UCC records prior to 7/2001 and current fixture (land) files. UCC search per debtor- $6.00. UCC copy- $2.00 per page. UCC search includes tax liens if requested. Separate federal/state combined tax lien search- $6.00 per debtor. Will not search real estate records. RE record copy- $1.00 per page. Cert fee: $1.00 per cert. Payee: Hillsdale County Register of Deeds. **Other phones:** Assessor-517-439-9166; Treasurer-517-437-4700; Elections-517-437-3391; Vital Records-517-437-3391.

Houghton County

County Register of Deeds, 401 E. Houghton Ave, Houghton, MI 49931. **Phone**-906-482-1311; fax-906-483-0364; hours 8AM-4:30PM
Will search UCC records prior to 7/2001. UCC search per debtor- $6.00. UCC copy- $2.00 per page side. UCC search includes tax liens if requested with extra fee. Separate federal/state combined tax lien search- $3.00 per debtor. Will search for last owner by property location. RE record copy- $1.00 per page. Cert fee: $6.00 per doc + copy fees. Payee: Houghton County Register of Deeds. **Other phones:** Assessor-906-482-0250; Treasurer-906-482-0560.

Huron County

County Register of Deeds, 250 E Huron Ave, Bad Axe, MI 48413. **Phone**-989-269-9941; fax-989-269-8786; hours 8:30AM-5PM
Will search UCC records prior to 7/2001 and current fixture (land) files. UCC search per debtor- $6.00. UCC copy- $2.00 per page. UCC search includes tax liens if requested. Will not search real estate records. RE record copy- $1.00 per page. Cert fee: $1.00 per cert. Payee: Huron County Register of Deeds. **Other phones:** Assessor-989-269-6497;

Treasurer-989-269-9238; Elections-989-269-9942; Vital Records-989-269-9942.

Ingham County

County Register of Deeds, PO Box 195, Mason, MI 48854-0195. **Phone**-County Register of Deeds, R/E & UCC Recording- 517-676-7216; fax-517-676-7287; hours 8AM-5PM www.ingham.org/rd/rodindex.htm
Will search UCC records prior to 7/2001 and current fixture (land) files. UCC search per debtor- $6.00. UCC copy- $1.00 per page. Tax liens not included in UCC search. Separate federal & state combined tax lien search including MSE-$7.00 per debtor. Will not search real estate records. Cert fee: $1.00 per cert. Payee: Ingham County Register of Deeds. **Online Access to Assumed Business Name, Recording, Deed, Grantor/Grantee, Assessor, Property, Delinquent Tax, Marriage Applicant records:** Access to the Register of Deeds database is free at www.ingham.org/icors/deeds.asp. Also, county DBA and co-partnership listings are free at www.ingham.org/CL/dbalists.htm. Also, marriage applicants can be searched by the week for free at www.ingham.org/CL/marrind.htm. **Other phones:** Assessor-517-676-7212; Treasurer-517-676-7220; Elections-517-676-7205; Vital Records-517-676-7201.

Ionia County

County Register of Deeds, PO Box 35, Ionia, MI 48846. **Phone**-616-527-5320; fax-616-527-5380; hours 8:30AM-Noon, 1-5PM www.ioniacounty.org
Will search UCC records prior to 7/2001 and current fixture (land) files. Search request per name is $6.00. UCC search includes tax liens if requested. Separate federal/state combined tax lien search- $6.00 per debtor. Will not search real estate records. Record copy- $1.00 per page. Cert fee: $1.00 per cert. Payee: Ionia County Register of Deeds. **Other phones:** Assessor-616-527-5376; Treasurer-616-527-5329; Elections-616-527-5322; Vital Records-616-527-5322.

Iosco County

County Register of Deeds, PO Box 367, Tawas City, MI 48764. **Phone**-County Register of Deeds, R/E & UCC Recording- 989-362-2021; fax-989-984-1101; hours 9AM-5PM www.iosco.net
Will search UCC records prior to 7/2001 and current fixture (land) files. Search request with SS/TIN (per name)- $3.00. Search request without SS/TIN (per name)- $6.00. UCC copy- $2.00 per page. UCC search includes tax liens if requested. Separate federal/state combined tax lien search- $6.00 per debtor. Real estate owner, mortgage, and property transfer searches available only over phone or in person RE record copy- $1.25 per page. Cert fee: $1.00 per cert. Payee: Iosco County Register of Deeds. **Other phones:** Assessor-989-362-5801; Treasurer-989-362-4409; Appraiser/ Auditor-989-362-5801; Elections-989-362-3497; Vital Records-989-362-3497.

Iron County

County Register of Deeds, 2 S. Sixth St, #11, Courthouse Annex, #11, Crystal Falls, MI 49920-1413. **Phone**-906-875-3321; fax-906-875-0658; hours 8AM-Noon, 12:30-4PM
Will search UCC records prior to 7/2001 and current fixture (land) files. UCC search per debtor- $6.00. UCC search includes tax liens if requested. Separate federal/state combined tax lien search- $6.00 per debtor. Will do limited searches of real estate records. Record copy- $1.00 per page. Cert fee: $1.00 per cert. Payee: Iron County Register of Deeds. **Other phones:** Assessor-906-875-6502; Treasurer-906-875-3362.

Isabella County

County Register of Deeds, 200 N. Main St, Mt. Pleasant, MI 48858. **Phone**-County Register of Deeds, R/E & UCC Recording- 989-772-0911 x253; fax-989-953-7219; 8AM-4:30PM www.isabellacounty.org
Faxed search request- they will name search for $5.00 for 10 years. Need exact name as you want it searched, approx. date of document & type of document, need name of person requesting search, name of company, and how to return. Add'l $5.00 if faxed. Will search UCC records prior to 7/2001. UCC search per debtor- $6.00. UCC copy- $2.00 per page. UCC search includes tax liens if requested. Separate federal/state combined tax lien search- $6.00 per debtor. Will not search real estate records. RE record copy- $1.00 per page. Cert fee: $1.00 per cert. Payee: Isabella County Register of Deeds. **Other phones:** Assessor-989-772-0911 x242; Treasurer-989-772-0911 x254; Elections-989-772-0911 x259; Vital Records-989-772-0911 x259.

Jackson County

County Register of Deeds, 120 W. Michigan Ave, 11th Fl, Jackson, MI 49201. **Phone**-517-788-4350; fax-517-788-4686; 8AM-5PM www.co.jackson.mi.us/rod/
Will search UCC records prior to 7/2001 and current fixture (land) files. UCC search per debtor- $7.00. UCC copy- $2.00 per page. UCC search includes tax liens if requested. Separate federal/state combined tax lien search- $6.00 per debtor. Will not search real estate records. RE record copy- $1.00 per page. Cert fee: $1.00 per page. Payee: Jackson County Register of Deeds. **Online Access to Real Estate, Lien, Deed, Grantor/Grantee, Foreclosed Property Sale records:** Search recorded documents at http://68.23.73.16/icris/splash.jsp. Search foreclosed property sales lists at www.jacksoncountytaxsale.com/local_units.htm. No name searching. **Other phones:** Assessor-517-788-4378; Treasurer-517-788-4418.

Kalamazoo County

County Register of Deeds, 201 W. Kalamazoo Ave, #102, Kalamazoo, MI 49007. **Phone**-269-383-8970; hours 8AM-4:30PM
Will search UCC records prior to 7/2001 and current fixture (land) files. UCC search per debtor- $6.00. Will not search real estate or tax lien records. Record copy- $1.00 per page. Cert fee: $1.00 per cert. Payee: Kalamazoo County Register of Deeds. **Other phones:** Assessor-269-383-8960; Treasurer-269-383-8124.

Kalkaska County

County Register of Deeds, 605 N. Birch St, Kalkaska, MI 49646. **Phone**-County Register of Deeds, R/E & UCC Recording- 231-258-3315; fax-231-258-3345; hours 9AM-5PM
Will search UCC records prior to 7/2001 and current fixture (land) files. UCC search per debtor- $6.00. UCC copy- $2.00 per page. Separate federal/state combined tax lien search- $3.00 per debtor. Mortgage searches available. RE record copy- $1.00 per page. Cert fee: $1.00 per page. Payee: Kalkaska County Register of Deeds. **Other phones:** Assessor-231-258-3340; Treasurer-231-258-3310; Vital Records-231-258-3300.

Kent County

County Register of Deeds, 300 Monroe Ave NW, Grand Rapids, MI 49503-2286. **Phone**-616-336-3558; fax-616-336-8938; hours-8AM-5PM www.co.kent.mi.us/YourGovernment/RegisterofDeeds/deeds_index.htm
Will search UCC records prior to 7/2001 and current fixture (land) files. Search per debtor- $3.00. UCC copy- $1.00 per page. UCC search includes tax liens. Separate federal/state combined tax lien search- $4.00 per debtor. Will not search real estate records. Cert fee: $1.00 per cert. Payee: Kent County Register of Deeds. **Online Access to Recording, Deed, Lien, Assessor, Property, Accident Report, Vital Statistic, Treasurer records:** Search county parcel data free at www.accesskent.com/PropSearch.jsp. With username, password & credit card you can view records for $1. or subscribe for $75. per year at 616-632-6516. Accident reports are $3.00 at www.accesskent.com/AccidentReports. Records on Walker City assessing database are free at www.ci.walker.mi.us/Services/Assessor/AssessingData/DataIntro.html. Also, search assessments for Ada, Bowne, Caledonia, Grand Rapids, Lowell, Vergennes at www.addorio.com/assessmenttax.htm. Also, Alpine Assessments records are at http://alpine.data-web.net. No name searching. Order vital statistic records for $7 at https://www.accesskent.com/servlet/VitalRec. Search Grand Rapids property at www.ci.grand-rapids.mi.us/22. **Other phones:** Assessor-616-336-3527; Treasurer-616-336-0762.

Keweenaw County

County Register of Deeds, HC 1 Box 607, Eagle River, MI 49950-9744. **Phone**-County Register of Deeds, R/E & UCC Recording- 906-337-2229; fax-906-337-2795; hours 9AM-4PM
Will search UCC records. Search request with SS/TIN (per name)- $3.00. Search request without SS/TIN (per name)- $6.00. UCC search includes tax liens if requested. Separate federal/state combined tax lien search- $3.00 per debtor. Will not search real estate records. Record copy- $1.00 per page. Cert fee: $10.00 per cert. Payee: Keweenaw County Register of Deeds. **Other phones:** Assessor-906-337-3471; Treasurer-906-337-1625.

Lake County

County Register of Deeds, 800 Tenth St. #200, Baldwin, MI 49304. **Phone**-County Register of Deeds, R/E & UCC Recording- 231-745-4641; fax-231-745-2241; 8:30AM-Noon, 1-5PM www.michigan.gov
Will search UCC records prior to 7/2001 and current fixture (land) files. Search request with SS/TIN (per name)- $3.00. Search request without SS/TIN (per name)- $6.00. UCC search includes tax liens if requested. Separate federal/state combined tax lien search- $3.00 per debtor. Will search real estate records prior to 1990, if request is in writing. Record copy- $1.00 per page. Cert fee: $1.00 per cert. Payee: Lake County Register of Deeds. **Other phones:** Assessor-231-745-2723; Treasurer-231-745-4622; Appraiser/ Auditor-231-745-4641; Elections-231-745-4641; Vital Records-231-745-2725.

Lapeer County

County Register of Deeds, 279 N. Court St, Lapeer, MI 48446. **Phone**-810-667-0211; fax-810-667-0293; hours 8AM-5PM www.county.lapeer.org/deeds
Will search UCC records prior to 7/2001 and current fixture (land) files. UCC search per debtor- $6.00. UCC copy- $2.00 per page. Federal/state combined tax lien search- $6.00 per debtor. Will not search real estate records. RE record copy- $1.00 per page. Cert fee: $1.00 per cert. Payee: Lapeer County Register of Deeds. **Other phones:** Assessor-810-667-0228; Treasurer-810-667-0239; Elections-810-667-0356; Vital Records-810-667-0356.

Leelanau County

County Register of Deeds, PO Box 595, Leland, MI 49654. **Phone**-County Register of Deeds, R/E & UCC Recording- 231-256-9682; fax-231-256-8149; hours 9AM-5PM www.leelanaucounty.com
Will search UCC records prior to 7/2001 and current fixture (land) files. UCC search per debtor- $3.00. UCC search includes tax liens if requested. Separate federal/state combined tax lien search- $6.00 per debtor. Will not search real estate records. Record copy- $1.00 per page. Cert fee: $1.00 per cert. Payee: Leelanau County Register of Deeds. **Other phones:** Assessor-231-256-9823; Treasurer-231-256-9838; Appraiser/ Auditor-231-256-9823; Elections-231-256-9824; Vital Records-231-256-9824.

Lenawee County

County Register of Deeds, 301 N. Main St., Adrian, MI 49221. **Phone**-County Register of Deeds, R/E & UCC Recording- 517-264-4538, UCC Recording- 517-264-4540; fax-517-264-4543; hours 8AM-4:30PM
Will search UCC records. UCC search per debtor- $6.00. UCC copy- $2.00 per page. UCC search includes tax liens if requested. Separate federal/state combined tax lien search- $6.00 per debtor. Will not search real estate records. RE record copy- $1.00 per page. Cert fee: $1.00 per cert. Payee: County Register of Deeds. **Other phones:** Assessor-517-264-4522; Treasurer-517-264-4554.

Livingston County

County Register of Deeds, PO Box 197, Howell, MI 48844. **Phone**-517-546-0270; fax-517-546-5966; hours 8AM-5PM
Will search UCC records prior to 7/2001. UCC search per debtor- $6.00. UCC copy- $2.00 per page. UCC search includes tax liens. Separate federal/state combined tax lien search- $6.00 per debtor. Will not search real estate records. RE record copy- $1.00 per page. Cert fee: $1.00 per cert. Payee: Livingston County Register of Deeds. **Online Access to Real Estate, Lien, Tax Assessor, Death records:** Access to county online records is available for occasional users, and a dedicated line is available for $1200 for professional users. Annual fee for occasional use is $400, + $.000043 per second. Records date back to 1984. Lending agency information is available. For info, contact Judy Epley at 517-546-2530. Also, search the county death indices to 1948 at www.livgenmi.com/deathlisting.htm. **Other phones:** Assessor-517-546-4182; Treasurer-517-546-7010; Elections-517-546-0500; Vital Records-517-546-0500.

Luce County

County Register of Deeds, County Gov't Bldg., Newberry, MI 49868. **Phone**-County Register of Deeds, R/E & UCC Recording- 906-293-5521; fax-906-293-0050; hours 8AM-4PM
Will search UCC records. UCC search per debtor- $6.00. UCC copy- $2.00 per page. Will search tax liens. Tax lien search fee- $5.00 per debtor. Real estate record owner and mortgage searches available. RE record copy- $1.00 per page. Cert fee: $10.00 per cert. Payee: Luce County Register of Deeds. **Other phones:** Assessor-906-293-5611; Treasurer-906-293-8171; Elections-906-293-5521; Vital Records-906-293-5521.

Mackinac County

County Register of Deeds, 100 Marley St, Saint Ignace, MI 49781. **Phone**-906-643-7306; fax-906-643-7302; hours 8:30AM-4:30PM
Will search UCC records prior to 7/2001 and current fixture (land) files. Search request with SS/TIN (per name)- $3.00. Search request without SS/TIN (per name)- $6.00. UCC copy- $2.00 per page. UCC search includes tax liens if requested. Will not search real estate records. Cert fee: $1.00 per cert. Payee: Mackinac County Register of Deeds. **Other phones:** Assessor-906-643-7310; Treasurer-906-643-7317; Vital Records-906-643-7300.

Macomb County

County Register of Deeds, 10 N. Main, Mt. Clemens, MI 48043. **Phone**-586-469-5342, R/E Recording- 586-

469-5309; fax-586-469-5130; hours 8:30AM-5PM www.co.macomb.mi.us
Will search UCC records prior to 7/2001 and current fixture (land) files. UCC search per debtor- $12.00. Will search tax liens. Federal/state combined tax lien search- $6.00 per debtor. Real estate record owner and mortgage searches available. Record copy- $2.00 per page. Cert fee: $1.00 per page. Payee: Macomb County Register of Deeds. **Online Access to Recorder, Deed, Business Registration, Death, Campaign Committee/Candidate, Most Wanted, Sex Offender records:** Business registration data is free at http://macomb.mcntv.com/businessnames. Search by full or partial company name. Search campaign committees/candidates at www.macomb.mcntv.com/campaigncomms/. County death records are at http://macomb.mcntv.com/deathrecords. Search by name or apx. date. Also, County Recorder images are from a private source at www.courthousedirect.com/pac-info/Main.asp; Fees/registration required. Search sex offender and most wanted lists at sheriff site at www.macombsheriff.com. Also, Clinton Township Assessor records are free online at www.clintontownship.com/assprd.htm. Enter user name: "clintwp" and password "assessor". **Other phones:** Assessor-586-469-5190; Treasurer-586-469-5190; Elections-586-469-5209; Vital Records-586-469-5120.

Manistee County

County Register of Deeds, 415 Third St, Courthouse, Manistee, MI 49660-1606. **Phone**-231-723-2146; fax-231-398-3544; hours 8:30AM-Noon, 1-5PM
Will search UCC records prior to 7/2001 and current fixture (land) files. UCC search per debtor- $6.00. UCC copy- $2.00 per page. Tax liens not included in UCC search. Separate federal/state combined tax lien search- $6.00 per debtor. Will not search real estate records. RE record copy- $1.00 per page. Cert fee: $2.00 per cert. Payee: Manistee County Register of Deeds. **Other phones:** Assessor-231-723-5957.

Marquette County

County Register of Deeds, 234 W. Baraga Ave, C-105, Marquette, MI 49855. **Phone**-County Register of Deeds, R/E & UCC Recording- 906-225-8415; fax-906-225-8420; 8AM-5PM www.co.marquette.mi.us
Will search UCC records prior to 7/2001 and current fixture (land) files. UCC search per debtor- $6.00. UCC copy- $2.00 per page. UCC search includes tax liens if requested. Separate federal/state combined tax lien search- $6.00 per debtor. Will not search real estate records. RE record copy- $1.00 per page. Cert fee: $1.00 per cert. Payee: Marquette County Register of Deeds. **Online Access to Warrant List records:** Access to the sheriff's warrants list is free at www.co.marquette.mi.us/sheriff/warrant%5Flist.htm. **Other phones:** Assessor-906-225-8405; Treasurer-906-225-8425; Appraiser/ Auditor-906-225-8405; Elections-906-225-8330; Vital Records-906-225-8330.

Mason County

County Register of Deeds, PO Box 57, Ludington, MI 49431-0057. **Phone**-231-843-4466; fax-231-845-7977; hours 9AM-5PM
Will search UCC records prior to 7/2001 and current fixture (land) files. Search per debtor- $3.00. Separate federal/state combined tax lien search- $6.00 per debtor. Will not search real estate records. Record copy- $1.00 per page. Cert fee: $1.00 per cert. Payee: Mason County Register of Deeds. **Other phones:** Assessor-231-845-6288; Treasurer-231-845-8411.

Mecosta County

County Register of Deeds, PO Box 718, Big Rapids, MI 49307. **Phone**-231-592-0148; hours 8:30AM-5PM
Will not search records. UCC copy- $2.00 per page. RE record copy- $1.00 per page. Cert fee: $1.00 per cert. Payee: Mecosta County Register of Deeds. **Online Access to Assessor, Property records:** Search the City of Big Rapids assessing and tax page for free at www.ci.big-rapids.mi.us/Assessing/onlinesearch.htm. **Other phones:** Assessor-231-592-0108; Treasurer-231-592-0169.

Menominee County

Register of Deeds, 839 10th Ave, Courthouse, Menominee, MI 49858. **Phone**-906-863-2822; fax-906-863-8839; hours-8AM-4:30PM www.menomineecounty.com
Will search UCC records prior to 7/2001 and current fixture (land) files. Search request per name- $6.00. UCC copy- $2.00 per page. Tax liens not included in UCC search. Tax lien search fee- $3.00 per debtor. Property transfer searches available. RE record copy- $1.00 per page. Cert fee: $1.00 per page. Payee: Register of Deeds. **Online Access to Land, Deed, Recording records:** Access to land records is free at http://66.84.189.211/landweb.dll/EXEC. First, contact the Register of Deeds, 906-863-2822, for ID and password. Documents may be ordered by Faxing for $1.50 each or mail for $1.00 each. **Other phones:** Treasurer-906-863-5548; Elections-906-863-9968; Vital Records-906-863-9968; Equalization-906-753-4007.

Midland County

County Register of Deeds, 220 W. Ellsworth St, County Services Bldg., Midland, MI 48640-5194. **Phone**-989-832-6820; fax-989-832-6608; hours 8AM-5PM
Will search UCC records prior to 7/2001 and current fixture (land) files. UCC search per debtor- $10.00. Will not search real estate or tax lien records. Record copy- $1.00 per page. Cert fee: $1.00 per page. Payee: Midland County Register of Deeds. **Other phones:** Assessor-989-837-3334; Treasurer-989-832-6850; Elections-989-832-6739; Vital Records-989-832-6739.

Missaukee County

County Register of Deeds, PO Box 800, Lake City, MI 49651. **Phone**-231-839-4967; fax-231-839-3684; hours 9AM-5PM www.missaukee.org
Will search UCC records prior to 7/2001 and current fixture (land) files. Search request with SS/TIN (per name)- $3.00. Search request using non-standard form (per name)- $6.00. UCC copy- $2.00 per page. UCC search includes tax liens if requested. Separate federal/state combined tax lien search- $3.00 per debtor. Will search real estate records 1990 forward on computer. Cert fee: $5.00 per cert. Payee: Missaukee County Register of Deeds. **Other phones:** Assessor-231-839-2702; Treasurer-231-839-2169; Vital Records-231-839-4967.

Monroe County

County Register of Deeds, 51 S Macomb St, Monroe, MI 48161. **Phone**-County Register of Deeds, R/E & UCC Recording-734-240-7390; hours 8:30AM-5PM
Will search UCC records prior to 7/2001 and current fixture (land) files. UCC search per debtor- $6.00. UCC search includes tax liens if requested. Separate federal/state combined tax lien search- $6.00 per debtor. Will not search real estate records. Record copy- $1.00 per page. Cert fee: No charge. Payee: Monroe County Register of Deeds. **Other phones:** Assessor-734-240-7235; Treasurer-734-240-7365.

Montcalm County

County Register of Deeds, PO Box 188, Stanton, MI 48888. **Phone**-989-831-7337; fax-989-831-7320; hours 8AM-Noon, 1-5PM
Will search UCC records prior to 7/2001 and current fixture (land) files. UCC search per debtor- $6.00. UCC copy- $2.00 per page. Separate federal/state combined tax lien search- $6.00 per debtor. Will search for records after 1/88 for last owner from property location. RE record copy- $1.00 per page. Cert fee: $1.00 per doc. Payee: Montcalm County Register of Deeds. **Online Access to Real Estate, Lien records:** Two sources are available. To view the index, the monthly fee is $300. To view both the index and document image, the monthly fee is $700. Records date back to 1/1/1988. Lending agency information is available. For information, call contact the Register of Deeds office. **Other phones:** Assessor-989-831-5226 x203; Treasurer-989-831-5226 x234.

Montmorency County

County Register of Deeds, PO Box 789, Atlanta, MI 49709. **Phone**-County Register of Deeds, R/E & UCC Recording- 989-785-8079; fax-989-785-8080; hours 8:30AM-Noon, 1-4:30PM
Will search UCC records prior to 7/2001 and current fixture (land) files. UCC search per debtor- $6.00. UCC copy- $2.00 per page. UCC search includes tax liens if requested. Separate federal & state combined tax lien search- $5.00 per debtor. Will not search real estate records. RE record copy- $1.00 per page. Cert fee: $3.00 per cert. Payee: Montmorency County Register of Deeds. **Other phones:** Assessor-989-785-8046; Treasurer-989-785-8086; Elections-989-785-8022; Vital Records-989-785-8022.

Muskegon County

County Register of Deeds, 990 Terrace St., 2nd Fl, Muskegon, MI 49442. **Phone**-231-724-6271; fax-231-724-6842; hours 8AM-5PM; Recording hours: 8AM-4:30PM www.co.muskegon.mi.us/deeds/
Will search UCC records prior to 7/2001 and current fixture (land) files. UCC search per debtor- $6.00. UCC copy- $2.00 per page. Tax liens not included in UCC search. Separate federal/state combined tax lien search- $6.00 per debtor. Real estate record owner and mortgage searches available. RE record copy- $1.00 per page. Cert fee: $1.00 per page. Payee: Muskegon County Register of Deeds. **Online Access to Death records:** Access the county genealogical death index system for free at www.co.muskegon.mi.us/clerk/websearch.cfm. Records 1867-1965. **Other phones:** Assessor-231-724-6386; Treasurer-231-724-6261.

Newaygo County

County Register of Deeds, PO Box 885, White Cloud, MI 49349. **Phone**-County Register of Deeds, R/E & UCC Recording- 231-689-7246; fax-231-689-7271; hours 8AM-N, 1-5PM
Will search UCC records prior to 7/2001 and current fixture (land) files. Search request with SS/TIN (per name)- $3.00. Search request without SS/TIN (per name)- $6.00. UCC copy- $2.00 per page. UCC search includes tax liens if requested. Separate federal/state combined tax lien search- $6.00 per debtor. Will not search real estate records. RE record copy- $1.00 per page. Cert fee: $1.00 per page. Payee: Newaygo County Register of Deeds. **Other phones:** Assessor-231-689-7240; Treasurer-231-689-7230; Elections-231-689-7235; Vital Records-231-689-7235; Sheriff-231-689-6623.

Oakland County

County Register of Deeds, 1200 N. Telegraph Rd, Bldg 12 East, Pontiac, MI 48341-0480. **Phone-**248-858-0605, R/E Recording- 248-858-0581; hours 8AM-4:30PM www.co.oakland.mi.us/clerkrod/
Will search UCC records prior to 7/2001 and current fixture (land) files. UCC search per debtor- $9.00. UCC copy- $1.00 per page. Will search tax liens. Federal/state combined tax lien search- $3.00 per debtor. Will not search real estate records. Cert fee: $1.00 per copy. Payee: Oakland County Register of Deeds. **Online Access to Real Estate, Property Tax, Tax Lien, Most Wanted, Foreclosure records:** Access to Access Oakland property information is by subscription. Available monthly or per use. For information or sign-up, visit www.co.oakland.mi.us (click on "Access Oakland") or call Information Services at 248-858-0861. Search foreclosure property lists for free at www.co.oakland.mi.us/fcloser/fmain?cmd=fcvt. Also, search the county sheriff's most wanted list at www.co.oakland.mi.us/sheriff/most_wanted/. Search the tax assessor database at www.rochesterhills.org/. Click on "online tax and assessing inquiry.". **Other phones:** Assessor-248-858-0740; Treasurer-248-858-0599; Elections-248-858-0564; Vital Records-248-858-0571.

Oceana County

County Register of Deeds, PO Box 111, Hart, MI 49420. **Phone-**County Register of Deeds, R/E & UCC Recording- 231-873-4158; fax-231-873-9218; hours 9AM-5PM
Will search UCC records prior to 7/2001 and current fixture (land) files. UCC search per debtor- $6.00. UCC copy- $2.00 per page. UCC search includes tax liens if requested. Will not search real estate records. RE record copy- $1.00 per page. Cert fee: $1.00 per cert. Payee: Oceana County Register of Deeds. **Other phones:** Assessor-231-873-4609; Treasurer-231-873-3980; Elections-231-873-4328; Vital Records-231-873-1748.

Ogemaw County

County Register of Deeds, 806 W. Houghton Ave, Rm 104, West Branch, MI 48661. **Phone-**County Register of Deeds, R/E & UCC Recording- 989-345-0728; fax-989-345-6221; hours 8:30AM-4:30PM
Will search UCC records prior to 7/2001. UCC search per debtor- $6.00. UCC copy- $2.00 per page. Tax liens not included in UCC search. Tax lien search fee- $3.00 per debtor. Federal/state combined tax lien search fee- $6.00 per debtor. Will not search real estate records. RE record copy- $1.00 per page. Cert fee: $1.00 per cert. Payee: Ogemaw County Register of Deeds. **Other phones:** Assessor-989-345-0328; Treasurer-989-345-0084; Elections-989-345-0215; Vital Records-989-345-0215.

Ontonagon County

County Register of Deeds, 725 Greenland Rd, Ontonagon, MI 49953-1492. **Phone-**County Register of Deeds, R/E & UCC Recording- 906-884-4255; fax-906-884-6796; hours 8:30AM-4:30PM
Will search UCC records prior to 6/31/2001only and current fixture (land) files. UCC search per debtor- $6.00. UCC copy- $2.00 per page. Tax liens not included in UCC search. Separate federal/state combined tax lien search- $3.00 per debtor. Will search real estate records. RE record copy- $1.00 per page. Cert fee: $1.00 per cert. Payee: Ontonagon County Register of Deeds. **Other phones:** Assessor-906-884-2765; Treasurer-906-884-4665; Appraiser/Auditor-906-884-2765; Elections-906-884-4255; Vital Records-906-884-2806.

Osceola County

County Register of Deeds, 301 W Upton Ave., Reed City, MI 49677-0208. **Phone-**231-832-6113; hours 9AM-5PM
Will search UCC records prior to 7/2001 and current fixture (land) files. UCC search per debtor- $6.00. UCC copy- $2.00 per page. Federal/state combined tax lien search- $6.00 per debtor. Will not search real estate records. RE record copy- $1.00 per page. Cert fee: $2.00 per page. Payee: Osceola County Register of Deeds. **Other phones:** Assessor-231-832-6119; Treasurer-231-832-6110.

Oscoda County

County Register of Deeds, PO Box 399, Mio, MI 48647. **Phone-**989-826-1116; fax-989-826-1136; hours 8:30AM-12PM, 1PM-4.30PM
Will search UCC records prior to 7/2001 and current fixture (land) files. UCC search per debtor- $6.00. Tax liens not included in UCC search. Separate federal/state combined tax lien search- $3.00 per debtor. Will not search real estate records. Record copy- $1.00 per page. Cert fee: $1.00 per cert. Payee: Oscoda County Register of Deeds. **Other phones:** Assessor-989-826-1113; Treasurer-989-826-3241 x112.

Otsego County

County Register of Deeds, 225 W. Main St, Rm 110, Rm 108, Gaylord, MI 49735. **Phone-**989-731-7550 x301/2, R/E Recording- 989-989-731-7550; fax-989-731-7519; hours 8AM-Noon, 1-4:30PM
Requests must be in writing along with money up front. Will search UCC records. UCC search per debtor- $6.00. UCC copy- $2.00 per page. UCC search includes tax liens. Separate federal/state combined tax lien search- $9.00 per debtor. Will not search real estate records. RE record copy- $1.00 per page. Cert fee: $1.00 per doc. Payee: Otsego County Register of Deeds. **Other phones:** Assessor-989-731-7540; Treasurer-989-731-7560; Elections-989-731-7501; Vital Records-989-731-7500.

Ottawa County

County Register of Deeds, PO Box 265, Grand Haven, MI 49417-0265. **Phone-**County Register of Deeds, R/E & UCC Recording- 616-846-8240; fax-616-846-8131; hours 8AM-5PM www.co.ottawa.mi.us
Will search UCC records prior to 7/2001 and current fixture files. UCC search per debtor- $6.00. UCC copy- $2.00 per page. Tax liens not included in UCC search. Tax lien search fee- $3.00 per debtor. Federal/state combined tax lien search fee- $6.00 per debtor. Will not search real estate records. RE record copy- $1.00 per page. Cert fee: $1.00 per cert. Payee: Ottawa County Register of Deeds. **Online Access to Property, Mapping, Deed, UCC, Judgment records:** The county offers a free online mapping service with parcel identification at www.gis.co.ottawa.mi.us/ottawa/. No name searching. Also, access to recorder records by subscription is at www.landaccess.com/ottawa/sub.jsp?county=miottawa. Yearly sub fee is $200.00 per year + $.50 per search and $.25 per doc. Credit cards searching accepted. **Other phones:** Treasurer-616-846-8230; Elections-616-846-8310; Vital Records-616-846-8310.

Presque Isle County

County Register of Deeds, PO Box 110, Rogers City, MI 49779-0110. **Phone-**989-734-2676; fax-989-734-0506; hours 8:30AM-4:30PM
Will search UCC records prior to 7/2001 and current fixture (land) files. UCC search per debtor- $9.00. UCC search includes tax liens if requested. Separate federal/state combined tax lien search- $3.00 per debtor. Will not search real estate records. Record copy- $1.00 per copy. Cert fee: $1.00 per

cert. Payee: Presque Isle County Register of Deeds. **Other phones:** Assessor-989-734-3810; Treasurer-989-734-4075; Elections-989-734-3288; Vital Records-989-734-3288.

Roscommon County

County Register of Deeds, PO Box 98, Roscommon, MI 48653. **Phone-**989-275-5931, R/E Recording- 517-275-5931, UCC Recording- 517-275-5931; fax-989-275-8640; hours 8:30AM-4:30PM
Will search UCC records. Search request with SS/TIN (per name)- $6.00. Search request without SS/TIN (per name)- $12.00. UCC copy- $2.00 per page. Will search tax liens. Tax lien search fee- $3.00 per debtor. Will not search real estate records. RE record copy- $1.00 per page. Cert fee: $1.00 per cert. Payee: Roscommon County Register of Deeds. **Other phones:** Assessor-989-275-8121 x5754; Treasurer-989-275-5823; Elections-989-275-5923; Vital Records-989-275-5923.

Saginaw County

County Register of Deeds, 111 S. Michigan Ave, Saginaw, MI 48602. **Phone-**989-790-5270; fax-989-790-5278; hours 8AM-5PM www.saginawcounty.com
Will search UCC records prior to 7/2001 and current fixture (land) files. UCC search per debtor- $6.00. UCC copy- $2.00 per page. UCC search includes tax liens if requested. Separate federal/state combined tax lien search- $6.00 per debtor Real estate record owner searches available. RE record copy- $1.00 per page. Cert fee: $1.00 per cert. Payee: Saginaw County Register of Deeds. **Online Access to Assessor, Assumed Business Name, Marriage, Death, Election, Notary, Grantor/Grantee, Recording, Obituary records:** Access to the county clerks database is free at www.saginawcounty.com/clerk/search/index.html. Vital statistic records go back to 1995. Search obituaries at www.tricitynet.com/pls/obit.nsf Also, records on the Saginaw Charter Township Assessor's Property Data Page are free at www.sagtwp.org/pt_scripts/search.cfm. Search by address, tax roll number, or owner name. Also, search Register of Deeds data (except tax liens) back to 1982 for free at www.saginawtownship.org/property/search.cfm. Also, search equalization board tax records at www.saginawcounty.com/equ/prop_info.htm. **Other phones:** Assessor-989-790-5260; Treasurer-989-790-5225.

Sanilac County

County Register of Deeds, Box 168, Sandusky, MI 48471-0168. **Phone-**County Register of Deeds, R/E & UCC Recording- 810-648-2313; fax-810-648-5461; hours 8AM-Noon, 1-4:30PM
Will search UCC records prior to 7/2001. UCC search per debtor- $6.00. UCC copy- $2.00 per copy. UCC search includes tax liens if requested. Separate federal/state combined tax lien search- $12.00 per debtor. Real estate record owner and property searches available. RE record copy- $1.00 per copy. Cert fee: $1.00 per cert. Payee: Sanilac County Register of Deeds. **Other phones:** Assessor-810-648-2955; Treasurer-810-648-2127; Elections-810-648-3212; Vital Records-810-648-3212.

Schoolcraft County

County Register of Deeds, 300 Walnut St, Rm 164, Manistique, MI 49854. **Phone-**906-341-3618; fax-906-341-5680; hours 8AM-4PM
Will not search UCC records. UCC copy- $1.00 per page. Will do tax lien search on computer, but only for only a few years back. Will not search real estate records. Cert fee: $1.00 per cert. Payee: County Register of Deeds. **Other phones:** Assessor-906-341-3677; Treasurer-906-341-3622.

Shiawassee County

County Register of Deeds, PO Box 103, Corunna, MI 48817. **Phone**-989-743-2216, R/E Recording- 517-743-2216; fax-989-743-2459; hours 8AM-5PM
Will search UCC records prior to 7/2001 and current fixture (land) files. UCC search per debtor- $6.00. UCC copy- $2.00 per page. Federal/state combined tax lien search- $6.00 per debtor Will not search real estate records. RE record copy- $1.00 per page. Cert fee: $1.00 per cert. Payee: Shiawassee County Register of Deeds. **Other phones:** Assessor-989-743-2263; Treasurer-989-743-2224.

St. Clair County

County Register of Deeds, 200 Grand River Blvd, Rm 105, Port Huron, MI 48060. **Phone**-810-989-6930, R/E Recording- 810-985-2275; fax-810-985-4297; hours 8AM-4:30PM
Will search UCC records prior to 7/2001 and current fixture (land) files. UCC search per debtor- $6.00. UCC copy- $2.00 per page. UCC search includes tax liens if requested. Separate federal/state combined tax lien search- $6.00 per debtor. Will not search real estate records. RE record copy- $1.00 per page. Cert fee: $1.00 per cert. Payee: St. Clair County Register of Deeds. **Online Access to Marriage, Death records:** Access to unofficial death records up to 1974 are free at www.rootsweb.com/~mistcla2/. 19th century marriages are also available. **Other phones:** Assessor-810-985-6925; Treasurer-810-985-2295.

St. Joseph County

County Register of Deeds, PO Box 388, Centreville, MI 49032-0388. **Phone**-269-467-5552 x552, R/E Recording- 269-467-5552, UCC Recording- 269-467-5552; fax-269-467-5592; hours 9AM-5PM www.stjosephcountymi.org
Will search UCC records prior to 7/2001 and current fixture (land) files. UCC search per debtor- $6.00. UCC copy- $2.00 per page. UCC search includes tax liens if requested. Tax number required. Separate state/federal tax lien search fee- $3.00 per debtor. Will not search real estate records. RE record copy- $1.00 per page. Cert fee: $1.00 per cert. Payee: St. Joseph County Register of Deeds. **Online Access to Assessor records:** Search assessor records at www.stjosephcountymi.org/taxsearch/default.asp. Can do a name search. **Other phones:** Assessor-269-467-5576; Treasurer-269-467-5581; Elections-269-467-5603; Vital Records-269-467-5603.

Tuscola County

Register of Deeds, 440 N. State St, Caro, MI 48723. **Phone**-Register of Deeds, R/E & UCC Recording- 989-672-3840, UCC Recording- 989-672-3780; fax-989-672-4266; hours 8AM-Noon, 1-4:30PM www.tuscolacounty.org
Will search UCC records prior to 7/2001. USS search request per name- $6.00. UCC copy- $2.00 per page. UCC search includes tax liens if requested. Separate federal/state combined tax lien search- $6.00 per debtor. Will not search real estate records. RE record copy- $1.00 per page. Cert fee: $1.00 per cert. Payee: Tuscola County Register of Deeds. **Other phones:** Treasurer-989-672-3890; Elections-989-672-3780.

Van Buren County

County Register of Deeds, 219 Paw Paw St, #102, Paw Paw, MI 49079. **Phone**-County Register of Deeds, R/E & UCC Recording- 269-657-8242; fax-269-657-7573; 8:30AM-5PM www.vbco.org/government0104.asp
Will search UCC records prior to 7/2001 and current fixture (land) files. Search request with SS/TIN (per name)- $3.00. Search request without SS/TIN (per name)- $6.00. UCC search includes tax liens if requested. Separate state/federal tax lien search fee- $6.00 per debtor. Will not search real estate records. Record copy- $1.00 per page. Cert fee: $1.00 per cert. Payee: Van Buren County Register of Deeds. **Online Access to Real Estate records:** Search ownership of real property at www.vbco.org/mapsearch.asp. **Other phones:** Assessor-269-657-8234; Treasurer-269-657-8228; Elections-269-657-8218; Vital Records-269-657-8218.

Washtenaw County

County Register of Deeds, PO Box 8645, Ann Arbor, MI 48107. **Phone**-County Register of Deeds, R/E & UCC Recording- 734-222-6710; fax-734-222-6819; hours 8:30AM-5PM www.ewashtenaw.org/government/clerk_register
Will search UCC records prior to 7/2001 and current fixture (land) files. UCC search per debtor- $3.00. UCC copy- $2.00 per page. UCC search includes tax liens if requested. Separate state/federal tax lien search fee- $6.00 per debtor. Will not search real estate records. RE record copy- $1.00 per page. Cert fee: $1.00 per cert. Payee: Washtenaw County Register of Deeds. **Online Access to Property, Vital Statistic, Business Name, Deed records:** Go to www.ewashtenaw.org/online/ for a menu of searchable databases. **Other phones:** Assessor-734-994-2511; Treasurer-734-222-6600; Elections-734-222-6730; Vital Records-734-222-6700.

Wayne County

County Register of Deeds, 400 Monroe, Rm 620, Detroit, MI 48226. **Phone**-313-224-5860/5860, R/E Recording- 313-224-5854; fax-313-224-5884; hours 8AM-4:30PM www.waynecounty.com/register/
Will search UCC records prior to 7/2001 and current fixture (land) files. UCC search per debtor- $5.00 in person; $15.00 by mail. Tax liens not included in UCC search. Separate federal/state combined tax lien search- $3.00 per debtor. Real estate owner, mortgage, and property transfer searches available. Record copy- $1.00 per page. Plat copies are $5.00 per page. Plat copies and large volume search requests are provided on a special request basis; call 224-5868 for information. Cert fee: $10.00 per cert. Payee: Wayne County Register of Deeds. **Online Access to Assessor, Recording, Deed, Judgment, Lien, Assumed Name,Delinquent Property records:** Search the recorders land records database for free at www.waynecountylandrecords.com/. A full data on-demand or business service is also available; call 313-967-6857 for info or sign-up or visit www.waynecountylandrecords.com/RODC/Default.asp. Search the county assumed names at www.waynecounty.com/clerk/AssumedNames/search.asp. Search the treasurers delinquent tax list free at www.waynecounty.com/pta/Default.asp, Records on the City of Dearborn Residential Property Assessment Database are free online at www.dearbornfordcenter.com/dbnassessor/. No name searching. **Other phones:** Assessor-313-224-2326; Treasurer-313-224-5990.

Wexford County

County Register of Deeds, 437 E. Division St, PO Box 303, Cadillac, MI 49601. **Phone**-231-779-9455; fax-231-779-0292; hours 8:30AM-5PM (Vault hours 8:30AM-4PM)
www.wexfordcounty.org/services_deeds.php
Will search UCC records prior to 7/2001 and current fixture (land) files. UCC search per debtor- $6.00. UCC copy- $2.00 per page. UCC search includes tax liens if requested. Separate federal/state combined tax lien search- $6.00 per debtor. Will not search real estate records. RE record copy- $1.00 per page. Cert fee: $1.00 per cert. Payee: Wexford County Register of Deeds. **Online Access to Real Estate records:** Search treasurer's record at www.wexfordcounty.org/treas/search.htm. **Other phones:** Assessor-231-779-9531; Treasurer-231-779-9475.

Michigan County Locator

You will usually be able to find the city name in the City/County Cross Reference below. In that case, it is a simple matter to determine the county from the cross reference. However, only the official US Postal Service city names are included in this index. There are an additional 40,000 place names that people use in their addresses. Therefore, we have also included a ZIP/City Cross Reference immediately following the City/County Cross Reference.

If you know the ZIP Code but the city name does not appear in the City/County Cross Reference index, look up the ZIP Code in the ZIP/City Cross Reference, find the city name, then look up the city name in the City/County Cross Reference. For example, you want to know the county for an address of Menands, NY 12204. There is no "Menands" in the City/County Cross Reference. The ZIP/City Cross Reference shows that ZIP Codes 12201-12288 are for the city of Albany. Looking back in the City/County Cross Reference, Albany is in Albany County.

Michigan City/County Cross Reference

ACME Grand Traverse
ADA Kent
ADDISON Lenawee
ADRIAN Lenawee
AFTON Cheboygan
AHMEEK Keweenaw
AKRON Tuscola
ALANSON (49706) Emmet(82), Cheboygan(17)
ALBA Antrim
ALBION Calhoun
ALDEN (49612) Antrim(69), Kalkaska(30)
ALGER (48610) Arenac(34), Ogemaw(33), Gladwin(32)
ALGONAC St. Clair
ALLEGAN Allegan
ALLEN Hillsdale
ALLEN PARK Wayne
ALLENDALE Ottawa
ALLENTON St. Clair
ALLOUEZ Keweenaw
ALMA Gratiot
ALMONT Lapeer
ALPENA (49707) Alpena(97), Presque Isle(2)
ALPHA Iron
ALTO Kent
AMASA Iron
ANCHORVILLE St. Clair
ANN ARBOR Washtenaw
APPLEGATE Sanilac
ARCADIA (49613) Manistee(79), Benzie(20)
ARGYLE Sanilac
ARMADA (48005) Macomb(96), St. Clair(3)
ARNOLD Marquette
ASHLEY Gratiot
ATHENS (49011) Calhoun(96), St. Joseph(1), Branch(1)
ATLANTA Montmorency
ATLANTIC MINE Houghton
ATLAS Genesee
ATTICA Lapeer
AU GRES Arenac
AU TRAIN Alger
AUBURN Bay
AUBURN HILLS Oakland
AUGUSTA Kalamazoo
AVOCA St. Clair
AZALIA Monroe
BAD AXE Huron
BAILEY (49303) Muskegon(86), Newaygo(12)
BALDWIN Lake
BANCROFT Shiawassee
BANGOR Van Buren
BANNISTER (48807) Gratiot(63), Saginaw(34), Clinton(1)
BARAGA Baraga
BARBEAU Chippewa
BARK RIVER (49807) Delta(47), Dickinson(33), Menominee(19)
BARODA Berrien
BARRYTON (49305) Mecosta(93), Isabella(6)

BARTON CITY Alcona
BATH Clinton
BATTLE CREEK Calhoun
BAY CITY Bay
BAY PORT Huron
BAY SHORE Charlevoix
BEAR LAKE Manistee
BEAVER ISLAND Charlevoix
BEAVERTON (48612) Gladwin(96), Clare(2), Midland(1)
BEDFORD Calhoun
BELDING (48809) Ionia(90), Kent(9)
BELLAIRE Antrim
BELLEVILLE Wayne
BELLEVUE (49021) Eaton(63), Barry(27), Calhoun(9)
BELMONT Kent
BENTLEY (48613) Bay(88), Gladwin(9), Arenac(2)
BENTON HARBOR (49022) Berrien(98), Van Buren(1)
BENTON HARBOR Berrien
BENZONIA Benzie
BERGLAND Ontonagon
BERKLEY Oakland
BERRIEN CENTER (49102) Berrien(98), Cass(1)
BERRIEN SPRINGS Berrien
BESSEMER Gogebic
BEULAH Benzie
BIG BAY Marquette
BIG RAPIDS (49307) Mecosta(97), Newaygo(2)
BIRCH RUN (48415) Saginaw(97), Tuscola(1), Genesee(1)
BIRMINGHAM Oakland
BITELY (49309) Newaygo(90), Lake(9)
BLACK RIVER Alcona
BLANCHARD (49310) Isabella(63), Mecosta(33), Montcalm(3)
BLISSFIELD Lenawee
BLOOMFIELD HILLS Oakland
BLOOMINGDALE (49026) Van Buren(89), Allegan(10)
BOON Wexford
BOYNE CITY (49712) Charlevoix(97), Antrim(2)
BOYNE FALLS (49713) Charlevoix(92), Emmet(7)
BRADLEY Allegan
BRANCH (49402) Mason(51), Lake(45), Oceana(3)
BRANT Saginaw
BRECKENRIDGE (48615) Gratiot(73), Midland(26)
BREEDSVILLE Van Buren
BRETHREN Manistee
BRIDGEPORT Saginaw
BRIDGEWATER Washtenaw
BRIDGMAN Berrien
BRIGHTON Livingston
BRIMLEY Chippewa
BRITTON (49229) Lenawee(89), Monroe(8), Washtenaw(1)
BROHMAN Newaygo

BRONSON Branch
BROOKLYN Jackson
BROWN CITY (48416) Sanilac(57), Lapeer(36), St. Clair(5)
BRUCE CROSSING Ontonagon
BRUNSWICK (49313) Muskegon(77), Newaygo(22)
BRUTUS (49716) Emmet(56), Cheboygan(43)
BUCHANAN Berrien
BUCKLEY (49620) Wexford(56), Grand Traverse(43)
BURLINGTON Calhoun
BURNIPS Allegan
BURR OAK (49030) St. Joseph(90), Branch(9)
BURT Saginaw
BURT LAKE Cheboygan
BURTON Genesee
BYRON (48418) Shiawassee(67), Genesee(23), Livingston(9)
BYRON CENTER (49315) Kent(94), Ottawa(3), Allegan(1)
CADILLAC (49601) Wexford(98), Missaukee(1)
CADMUS Lenawee
CALEDONIA (49316) Kent(88), Allegan(8), Barry(3)
CALUMET Houghton
CAMDEN Hillsdale
CANNONSBURG Kent
CANTON Wayne
CAPAC (48014) St. Clair(98), Lapeer(1)
CARLETON Monroe
CARNEY Menominee
CARO Tuscola
CARP LAKE (49718) Emmet(70), Cheboygan(29)
CARROLLTON Saginaw
CARSON CITY (48811) Montcalm(75), Gratiot(24)
CARSONVILLE Sanilac
CASCO St. Clair
CASEVILLE Huron
CASNOVIA (49318) Muskegon(66), Newaygo(22), Kent(10)
CASPIAN Iron
CASS CITY (48726) Tuscola(84), Sanilac(12), Huron(3)
CASSOPOLIS Cass
CEDAR Leelanau
CEDAR LAKE Montcalm
CEDAR RIVER Menominee
CEDAR SPRINGS Kent
CEDARVILLE Mackinac
CEMENT CITY (49233) Lenawee(77), Jackson(22)
CENTER LINE Macomb
CENTRAL LAKE Antrim
CENTREVILLE St. Joseph
CERESCO Calhoun
CHAMPION Marquette
CHANNING Dickinson
CHARLEVOIX (49720) Charlevoix(98), Antrim(1)

CHARLOTTE Eaton
CHASE Lake
CHASSELL Houghton
CHATHAM Alger
CHEBOYGAN Cheboygan
CHELSEA Washtenaw
CHESANING Saginaw
CHIPPEWA LAKE Mecosta
CLARE (48617) Clare(79), Isabella(20)
CLARKLAKE Jackson
CLARKSTON Oakland
CLARKSVILLE (48815) Ionia(97), Kent(2)
CLAWSON Oakland
CLAYTON Lenawee
CLIFFORD (48727) Lapeer(50), Tuscola(49)
CLIMAX Kalamazoo
CLINTON (49236) Lenawee(83), Washtenaw(16)
CLINTON TOWNSHIP Macomb
CLIO (48420) Genesee(97), Tuscola(1)
CLOVERDALE Barry
COHOCTAH Livingston
COLDWATER Branch
COLEMAN (48618) Midland(83), Isabella(13), Gladwin(2)
COLOMA (49038) Berrien(94), Van Buren(5)
COLON (49040) St. Joseph(89), Branch(10)
COLUMBIAVILLE (48421) Lapeer(95), Genesee(4)
COLUMBUS St. Clair
COMINS (48619) Oscoda(78), Montmorency(21)
COMMERCE TOWNSHIP Oakland
COMSTOCK Kalamazoo
COMSTOCK PARK Kent
CONCORD Jackson
CONKLIN (49403) Ottawa(91), Muskegon(4), Kent(3)
CONSTANTINE (49042) St. Joseph(98), Cass(1)
CONWAY Emmet
COOKS (49817) Delta(56), Schoolcraft(43)
COOPERSVILLE (49404) Ottawa(96), Muskegon(3)
COPEMISH (49625) Manistee(92), Wexford(7)
COPPER CITY Houghton
COPPER HARBOR Keweenaw
CORAL Montcalm
CORNELL (49818) Delta(86), Marquette(13)
CORUNNA Shiawassee
COVERT Van Buren
COVINGTON Baraga
CROSS VILLAGE Emmet
CROSWELL Sanilac
CRYSTAL Montcalm
CRYSTAL FALLS Iron
CURRAN (48728) Alcona(87), Oscoda(12)
CURTIS Mackinac
CUSTER Mason
DAFTER Chippewa

DAGGETT Menominee
DANSVILLE Ingham
DAVISBURG Oakland
DAVISON Genesee
DE TOUR VILLAGE Chippewa
DEARBORN Wayne
DEARBORN HEIGHTS Wayne
DECATUR (49045) Van Buren(90), Cass(8)
DECKER (48426) Sanilac(91), Tuscola(8)
DECKERVILLE Sanilac
DEERFIELD Lenawee
DEERTON (49822) Alger(96), Marquette(3)
DEFORD (48729) Tuscola(98), Sanilac(1)
DELTON Barry
DETROIT Wayne
DEWITT Clinton
DEXTER Washtenaw
DIMONDALE (48821) Eaton(95),
    Ingham(4)
DODGEVILLE Houghton
DOLLAR BAY Houghton
DORR (49323) Allegan(98), Ottawa(1)
DOUGLAS Allegan
DOWAGIAC (49047) Cass(93), Van
    Buren(6)
DOWLING Barry
DRAYTON PLAINS Oakland
DRUMMOND ISLAND Chippewa
DRYDEN (48428) Lapeer(97), Oakland(2)
DUNDEE Monroe
DURAND (48429) Shiawassee(97),
    Genesee(2)
EAGLE Clinton
EAGLE RIVER Keweenaw
EAST CHINA St. Clair
EAST JORDAN (49727) Charlevoix(68),
    Antrim(31)
EAST LANSING (48823) Ingham(84),
    Clinton(15)
EAST LANSING Ingham
EAST LEROY Calhoun
EAST TAWAS Iosco
EASTLAKE Manistee
EASTPOINTE Macomb
EASTPORT Antrim
EATON RAPIDS (48827) Eaton(93),
    Ingham(6)
EAU CLAIRE (49111) Berrien(90), Cass(9)
EBEN JUNCTION Alger
ECKERMAN Chippewa
ECORSE Wayne
EDENVILLE Midland
EDMORE (48829) Montcalm(98),
    Isabella(1)
EDWARDSBURG Cass
ELBERTA Benzie
ELK RAPIDS Antrim
ELKTON Huron
ELLSWORTH (49729) Antrim(88),
    Charlevoix(11)
ELM HALL Gratiot
ELMIRA (49730) Antrim(70), Otsego(22),
    Charlevoix(6)
ELSIE (48831) Clinton(58),
    Shiawassee(20), Saginaw(17), Gratiot(3)
ELWELL Gratiot
EMMETT St. Clair
EMPIRE (49630) Leelanau(98), Benzie(1)
ENGADINE Mackinac
ERIE Monroe
ESCANABA Delta
ESSEXVILLE Bay
EUREKA Clinton
EVART (49631) Osceola(92), Mecosta(7)
EWEN Ontonagon
FAIR HAVEN St. Clair
FAIRGROVE Tuscola
FAIRVIEW Oscoda
FALMOUTH Missaukee
FARMINGTON Oakland
FARWELL (48622) Clare(82), Isabella(17)
FELCH (49831) Dickinson(82),
    Marquette(17)

FENNVILLE Allegan
FENTON (48430) Genesee(65),
    Livingston(30), Oakland(4)
FENWICK (48834) Montcalm(64), Ionia(35)
FERNDALE Oakland
FERRYSBURG Ottawa
FIFE LAKE (49633) Kalkaska(60), Grand
    Traverse(32), Wexford(4), Missaukee(2)
FILER CITY Manistee
FILION Huron
FLAT ROCK Wayne
FLINT Genesee
FLUSHING Genesee
FORESTVILLE Sanilac
FORT GRATIOT St. Clair
FOSTER CITY Dickinson
FOSTORIA (48435) Tuscola(56),
    Lapeer(43)
FOUNTAIN Mason
FOWLER (48835) Clinton(98), Gratiot(1)
FOWLERVILLE Livingston
FRANKENMUTH (48734) Saginaw(97),
    Tuscola(2)
FRANKENMUTH Saginaw
FRANKFORT Benzie
FRANKLIN Oakland
FRASER Macomb
FREDERIC (49733) Crawford(78),
    Otsego(21)
FREE SOIL (49411) Mason(97),
    Manistee(2)
FREELAND (48623) Saginaw(81),
    Midland(10), Bay(8)
FREEPORT (49325) Barry(77), Ionia(13),
    Kent(9)
FREMONT (49412) Newaygo(96),
    Oceana(2)
FREMONT Newaygo
FRONTIER Hillsdale
FRUITPORT (49415) Muskegon(89),
    Ottawa(10)
FULTON (49052) Kalamazoo(78),
    Calhoun(17), St. Joseph(4)
GAASTRA Iron
GAGETOWN (48735) Tuscola(60),
    Huron(39)
GAINES (48436) Genesee(90),
    Shiawassee(9)
GALESBURG Kalamazoo
GALIEN Berrien
GARDEN Delta
GARDEN CITY Wayne
GAYLORD Otsego
GENESEE Genesee
GERMFASK (49836) Schoolcraft(57),
    Mackinac(42)
GILFORD Tuscola
GLADSTONE Delta
GLADWIN (48624) Gladwin(91), Clare(5),
    Roscommon(1)
GLEN ARBOR Leelanau
GLENN Allegan
GLENNIE (48737) Alcona(91), Iosco(8)
GOBLES (49055) Van Buren(92),
    Allegan(7)
GOETZVILLE Chippewa
GOOD HART Emmet
GOODELLS St. Clair
GOODRICH (48438) Genesee(81),
    Lapeer(18)
GOULD CITY Mackinac
GOWEN (49326) Kent(71), Montcalm(28)
GRAND BLANC (48439) Genesee(98),
    Oakland(1)
GRAND BLANC Genesee
GRAND HAVEN Ottawa
GRAND JUNCTION (49056) Van
    Buren(75), Allegan(24)
GRAND LEDGE (48837) Eaton(89),
    Clinton(9)
GRAND MARAIS Alger
GRAND RAPIDS (49544) Kent(72),
    Ottawa(27)

GRAND RAPIDS Kent
GRANDVILLE (49418) Kent(84),
    Ottawa(15)
GRANDVILLE Kent
GRANT Newaygo
GRASS LAKE (49240) Jackson(91),
    Washtenaw(8)
GRAWN Grand Traverse
GRAYLING (49738) Crawford(95),
    Kalkaska(3)
GRAYLING Crawford
GREENBUSH (48738) Alcona(90), Iosco(9)
GREENLAND Ontonagon
GREENVILLE (48838) Montcalm(89),
    Kent(10)
GREGORY (48137) Livingston(98),
    Washtenaw(1)
GROSSE ILE Wayne
GROSSE POINTE Wayne
GULLIVER Schoolcraft
GWINN Marquette
HADLEY Lapeer
HAGAR SHORES Berrien
HALE (48739) Iosco(75), Ogemaw(24)
HAMBURG Livingston
HAMILTON Allegan
HAMTRAMCK Wayne
HANCOCK Houghton
HANOVER Jackson
HARBERT Berrien
HARBOR BEACH Huron
HARBOR SPRINGS Emmet
HARPER WOODS Wayne
HARRIETTA (49638) Wexford(91),
    Manistee(8)
HARRIS Menominee
HARRISON Clare
HARRISON TOWNSHIP Macomb
HARRISVILLE Alcona
HARSENS ISLAND St. Clair
HART Oceana
HARTFORD Van Buren
HARTLAND Livingston
HASLETT (48840) Ingham(94), Clinton(5)
HASTINGS Barry
HAWKS Presque Isle
HAZEL PARK Oakland
HEMLOCK (48626) Saginaw(95),
    Midland(4)
HENDERSON (48841) Shiawassee(82),
    Saginaw(17)
HERMANSVILLE Menominee
HERRON Alpena
HERSEY (49639) Osceola(78),
    Mecosta(21)
HESPERIA (49421) Oceana(70),
    Newaygo(29)
HESSEL Mackinac
HICKORY CORNERS (49060) Barry(66),
    Kalamazoo(33)
HIGGINS LAKE Roscommon
HIGHLAND Oakland
HIGHLAND PARK Wayne
HILLMAN (49746) Montmorency(88),
    Alpena(11)
HILLSDALE Hillsdale
HOLLAND (49423) Ottawa(66), Allegan(33)
HOLLAND Ottawa
HOLLY (48442) Oakland(93), Genesee(5),
    Livingston(1)
HOLT Ingham
HOLTON (49425) Muskegon(83),
    Oceana(10), Newaygo(6)
HOMER Calhoun
HONOR Benzie
HOPE (48628) Midland(82), Gladwin(17)
HOPKINS Allegan
HORTON (49246) Jackson(96), Hillsdale(3)
HOUGHTON Houghton
HOUGHTON LAKE Roscommon
HOUGHTON LAKE HEIGHTS Roscommon
HOWARD CITY (49329) Montcalm(84),
    Newaygo(15)

HOWELL Livingston
HUBBARD LAKE (49747) Alpena(50),
    Alcona(49)
HUBBARDSTON (48845) Ionia(59),
    Clinton(20), Montcalm(14), Gratiot(6)
HUBBELL Houghton
HUDSON (49247) Lenawee(72),
    Hillsdale(27)
HUDSONVILLE Ottawa
HULBERT Chippewa
HUNTINGTON WOODS Oakland
IDA Monroe
IDLEWILD Lake
IMLAY CITY (48444) Lapeer(97), St.
    Clair(2)
INDIAN RIVER Cheboygan
INGALLS Menominee
INKSTER Wayne
INTERLOCHEN (49643) Grand
    Traverse(67), Benzie(32)
IONIA Ionia
IRON MOUNTAIN Dickinson
IRON RIVER Iron
IRONS (49644) Lake(79), Manistee(19)
IRONWOOD Gogebic
ISHPEMING Marquette
ITHACA Gratiot
JACKSON Jackson
JAMESTOWN Ottawa
JASPER Lenawee
JEDDO (48032) St. Clair(81), Sanilac(18)
JENISON Ottawa
JEROME (49249) Hillsdale(95), Jackson(4)
JOHANNESBURG (49751) Otsego(93),
    Montmorency(6)
JONES Cass
JONESVILLE Hillsdale
KALAMAZOO Kalamazoo
KALEVA Manistee
KALKASKA Kalkaska
KARLIN Grand Traverse
KAWKAWLIN Bay
KEARSARGE Houghton
KEEGO HARBOR Oakland
KENDALL Van Buren
KENT CITY (49330) Kent(91), Newaygo(5),
    Ottawa(1), Muskegon(1)
KENTON Houghton
KEWADIN Antrim
KINCHELOE Chippewa
KINDE Huron
KINGSFORD Dickinson
KINGSLEY (49649) Grand Traverse(96),
    Wexford(3)
KINGSTON (48741) Tuscola(93),
    Sanilac(6)
KINROSS Chippewa
LA SALLE Monroe
LACHINE Alpena
LACOTA Van Buren
LAINGSBURG (48848) Shiawassee(67),
    Clinton(32)
LAKE (48632) Clare(76), Isabella(22),
    Osceola(1)
LAKE ANN Benzie
LAKE CITY Missaukee
LAKE GEORGE Clare
LAKE LEELANAU Leelanau
LAKE LINDEN (49945) Houghton(97),
    Keweenaw(2)
LAKE ODESSA (48849) Ionia(81),
    Barry(14), Eaton(3)
LAKE ORION Oakland
LAKELAND Livingston
LAKESIDE Berrien
LAKEVIEW (48850) Montcalm(81),
    Mecosta(18)
LAKEVILLE Oakland
LAMBERTVILLE Monroe
LAMONT Ottawa
LANSE Baraga
LANSING (48917) Eaton(81), Ingham(18)

LANSING (48906) Ingham(60), Clinton(37), Eaton(2)
LANSING (48911) Ingham(87), Eaton(12)
LANSING Eaton
LANSING Ingham
LAPEER Lapeer
LAWRENCE Van Buren
LAWTON Van Buren
LELAND Leelanau
LENNON (48449) Shiawassee(57), Genesee(42)
LEONARD Oakland
LEONIDAS St. Joseph
LEROY (49655) Osceola(93), Lake(6)
LESLIE Ingham
LEVERING (49755) Emmet(64), Cheboygan(35)
LEWISTON (49756) Montmorency(50), Oscoda(47), Otsego(1)
LEXINGTON Sanilac
LINCOLN Alcona
LINCOLN PARK Wayne
LINDEN (48451) Genesee(90), Livingston(9)
LINWOOD Bay
LITCHFIELD (49252) Hillsdale(91), Jackson(3), Branch(2), Calhoun(2)
LITTLE LAKE Marquette
LIVONIA Wayne
LONG LAKE (48743) Iosco(92), Ogemaw(8)
LORETTO Dickinson
LOWELL (49331) Kent(89), Ionia(10)
LUDINGTON Mason
LUNA PIER Monroe
LUPTON Ogemaw
LUTHER Lake
LUZERNE Oscoda
LYONS Ionia
MACATAWA Ottawa
MACKINAC ISLAND Mackinac
MACKINAW CITY (49701) Emmet(63), Cheboygan(36)
MACOMB Macomb
MADISON HEIGHTS Oakland
MANCELONA (49659) Antrim(78), Kalkaska(21)
MANCHESTER Washtenaw
MANISTEE (49660) Manistee(96), Mason(3)
MANISTIQUE (49854) Schoolcraft(98), Delta(1)
MANITOU BEACH Lenawee
MANTON (49663) Wexford(79), Missaukee(20)
MAPLE CITY Leelanau
MAPLE RAPIDS Clinton
MARCELLUS (49067) Cass(63), St. Joseph(24), Van Buren(11)
MARENISCO (49947) Gogebic(66), Ontonagon(33)
MARINE CITY St. Clair
MARION (49665) Osceola(83), Clare(11), Missaukee(4)
MARLETTE (48453) Sanilac(88), Lapeer(7), Tuscola(4)
MARNE (49435) Ottawa(96), Kent(3)
MARQUETTE Marquette
MARSHALL Calhoun
MARTIN Allegan
MARYSVILLE St. Clair
MASON Ingham
MASS CITY Ontonagon
MATTAWAN (49071) Van Buren(83), Kalamazoo(16)
MAYBEE Monroe
MAYFIELD Grand Traverse
MAYVILLE (48744) Tuscola(89), Lapeer(10)
MC BAIN Missaukee
MC MILLAN Luce
MCBRIDES Montcalm
MEARS Oceana

MECOSTA Mecosta
MELVIN Sanilac
MELVINDALE Wayne
MEMPHIS (48041) St. Clair(74), Macomb(25)
MENDON St. Joseph
MENOMINEE Menominee
MERRILL (48637) Saginaw(73), Midland(14), Gratiot(12)
MERRITT Missaukee
MESICK (49668) Wexford(98), Manistee(1)
METAMORA (48455) Lapeer(98), Oakland(1)
MICHIGAMME (49861) Baraga(59), Marquette(40)
MICHIGAN CENTER Jackson
MIDDLETON Gratiot
MIDDLEVILLE (49333) Barry(97), Kent(1)
MIDLAND (48642) Midland(96), Bay(3)
MIDLAND Midland
MIKADO (48745) Alcona(94), Iosco(5)
MILAN (48160) Washtenaw(70), Monroe(29)
MILFORD (48380) Oakland(73), Livingston(26)
MILFORD Oakland
MILLBROOK Mecosta
MILLERSBURG Presque Isle
MILLINGTON (48746) Tuscola(89), Genesee(10)
MINDEN CITY (48456) Sanilac(79), Huron(20)
MIO Oscoda
MOHAWK Keweenaw
MOLINE Allegan
MONTAGUE (49437) Muskegon(84), Oceana(15)
MONTGOMERY (49255) Branch(96), Hillsdale(3)
MONTROSE (48457) Genesee(78), Saginaw(21)
MORAN Mackinac
MORENCI Lenawee
MORLEY (49336) Mecosta(92), Montcalm(7)
MORRICE Shiawassee
MOSCOW Hillsdale
MOSHERVILLE Hillsdale
MOUNT CLEMENS Macomb
MOUNT MORRIS Genesee
MOUNT PLEASANT Isabella
MUIR Ionia
MULLETT LAKE Cheboygan
MULLIKEN (48861) Eaton(89), Ionia(10)
MUNGER (48747) Bay(96), Saginaw(3)
MUNISING Alger
MUNITH Jackson
MUSKEGON Muskegon
NADEAU Menominee
NAHMA Delta
NAPOLEON Jackson
NASHVILLE (49073) Barry(90), Eaton(9)
NATIONAL CITY Iosco
NATIONAL MINE Marquette
NAUBINWAY Mackinac
NAZARETH Kalamazoo
NEGAUNEE Marquette
NEW BALTIMORE Macomb
NEW BOSTON Wayne
NEW BUFFALO Berrien
NEW ERA Oceana
NEW HAVEN Macomb
NEW HUDSON Oakland
NEW LOTHROP (48460) Shiawassee(60), Saginaw(34), Genesee(5)
NEW RICHMOND Allegan
NEW TROY Berrien
NEWAYGO (49337) Newaygo(96), Montcalm(3), Mecosta(1)
NEWBERRY Luce
NEWPORT Monroe
NILES (49120) Berrien(82), Cass(17)
NILES Berrien

NISULA Houghton
NORTH ADAMS Hillsdale
NORTH BRANCH Lapeer
NORTH STAR Gratiot
NORTH STREET St. Clair
NORTHLAND Marquette
NORTHPORT Leelanau
NORTHVILLE (48167) Wayne(61), Oakland(31), Washtenaw(6)
NORVELL Jackson
NORWAY Dickinson
NOTTAWA St. Joseph
NOVI Oakland
NUNICA (49448) Ottawa(86), Muskegon(13)
OAK GROVE Livingston
OAK PARK Oakland
OAKLAND Oakland
OAKLEY (48649) Saginaw(95), Shiawassee(4)
ODEN Emmet
OKEMOS Ingham
OLD MISSION Grand Traverse
OLIVET (49076) Eaton(71), Calhoun(28)
OMENA Leelanau
OMER Arenac
ONAWAY (49765) Presque Isle(66), Cheboygan(33)
ONEKAMA Manistee
ONONDAGA (49264) Ingham(65), Jackson(30), Eaton(4)
ONSTED Lenawee
ONTONAGON Ontonagon
ORLEANS Ionia
ORTONVILLE (48462) Oakland(95), Lapeer(3)
OSCODA Iosco
OSHTEMO Kalamazoo
OSSEO Hillsdale
OSSINEKE Alpena
OTISVILLE (48463) Genesee(98), Lapeer(1)
OTSEGO (49078) Allegan(92), Kalamazoo(5), Van Buren(2)
OTTAWA LAKE (49267) Monroe(83), Lenawee(16)
OTTER LAKE (48464) Lapeer(82), Genesee(9), Tuscola(8)
OVID (48866) Clinton(64), Shiawassee(35)
OWENDALE Huron
OWOSSO Shiawassee
OXFORD (48371) Oakland(94), Lapeer(5)
OXFORD Oakland
PAINESDALE Houghton
PALMER Marquette
PALMS Sanilac
PALMYRA Lenawee
PALO Ionia
PARADISE Chippewa
PARIS (49338) Mecosta(63), Newaygo(29), Osceola(6)
PARMA Jackson
PAW PAW Van Buren
PECK Sanilac
PELKIE (49958) Houghton(80), Baraga(20)
PELLSTON (49769) Emmet(86), Cheboygan(13)
PENTWATER (49449) Oceana(80), Mason(19)
PERKINS Delta
PERRINTON Gratiot
PERRONVILLE (49873) Menominee(87), Dickinson(12)
PERRY (48872) Shiawassee(92), Ingham(6)
PETERSBURG Monroe
PETOSKEY Emmet
PEWAMO (48873) Ionia(72), Clinton(27)
PICKFORD (49774) Chippewa(91), Mackinac(8)
PIERSON Montcalm
PIGEON Huron
PINCKNEY Livingston

PINCONNING (48650) Bay(95), Arenac(4)
PITTSFORD Hillsdale
PLAINWELL (49080) Allegan(69), Barry(20), Kalamazoo(9)
PLEASANT LAKE Jackson
PLEASANT RIDGE Oakland
PLYMOUTH (48170) Wayne(95), Washtenaw(4)
POINTE AUX PINS Mackinac
POMPEII Gratiot
PONTIAC Oakland
PORT AUSTIN Huron
PORT HOPE Huron
PORT HURON St. Clair
PORT SANILAC Sanilac
PORTAGE Kalamazoo
PORTLAND (48875) Ionia(93), Clinton(6)
POSEN (49776) Presque Isle(74), Alpena(25)
POTTERVILLE Eaton
POWERS Menominee
PRATTVILLE Hillsdale
PRESCOTT Ogemaw
PRESQUE ISLE Presque Isle
PRUDENVILLE Roscommon
PULLMAN Allegan
QUINCY (49082) Branch(91), Hillsdale(8)
QUINNESEC Dickinson
RALPH Dickinson
RAMSAY Gogebic
RAPID CITY (49676) Kalkaska(61), Antrim(38)
RAPID RIVER (49878) Delta(91), Alger(8)
RAVENNA (49451) Muskegon(96), Ottawa(3)
RAY Macomb
READING Hillsdale
REDFORD Wayne
REED CITY (49677) Osceola(82), Lake(14), Newaygo(2)
REESE (48757) Tuscola(68), Saginaw(28), Bay(3)
REMUS (49340) Mecosta(66), Isabella(33)
REPUBLIC Marquette
RHODES (48652) Gladwin(58), Bay(26), Midland(15)
RICHLAND Kalamazoo
RICHMOND Macomb
RICHVILLE Tuscola
RIDGEWAY Lenawee
RIGA (49276) Lenawee(70), Monroe(29)
RIVER ROUGE Wayne
RIVERDALE (48877) Gratiot(57), Montcalm(31), Isabella(11)
RIVERSIDE Berrien
RIVES JUNCTION Jackson
ROCHESTER (48306) Oakland(97), Macomb(2)
ROCHESTER Oakland
ROCK (49880) Delta(68), Marquette(31)
ROCKFORD Kent
ROCKLAND Ontonagon
ROCKWOOD Wayne
RODNEY Mecosta
ROGERS CITY Presque Isle
ROLLIN Lenawee
ROMEO Macomb
ROMULUS Wayne
ROSCOMMON (48653) Roscommon(80), Crawford(19)
ROSE CITY (48654) Ogemaw(81), Oscoda(18)
ROSEBUSH Isabella
ROSEVILLE Macomb
ROTHBURY Oceana
ROYAL OAK Oakland
RUDYARD (49780) Chippewa(95), Mackinac(4)
RUMELY Alger
RUTH (48470) Huron(98), Sanilac(1)
SAGINAW Saginaw
SAGOLA Dickinson
SAINT CHARLES Saginaw

SAINT CLAIR St. Clair
SAINT CLAIR SHORES Macomb
SAINT HELEN Roscommon
SAINT IGNACE Mackinac
SAINT JOHNS Clinton
SAINT JOSEPH Berrien
SAINT LOUIS (48880) Gratiot(91),
    Midland(8)
SALEM Washtenaw
SALINE Washtenaw
SAMARIA Monroe
SAND CREEK Lenawee
SAND LAKE (49343) Kent(60),
    Newaygo(22), Montcalm(16)
SANDUSKY Sanilac
SANFORD Midland
SARANAC Ionia
SAUGATUCK Allegan
SAULT SAINTE MARIE Chippewa
SAWYER Berrien
SCHOOLCRAFT (49087) Kalamazoo(96),
    Van Buren(2)
SCOTTS Kalamazoo
SCOTTVILLE Mason
SEARS Osceola
SEBEWAING (48759) Huron(98),
    Tuscola(1)
SENECA Lenawee
SENEY (49883) Alger(60), Schoolcraft(39)
SHAFTSBURG Shiawassee
SHELBY Oceana
SHELBYVILLE (49344) Barry(51),
    Allegan(48)
SHEPHERD (48883) Isabella(75),
    Midland(23), Gratiot(1)
SHERIDAN Montcalm
SHERWOOD Branch
SHINGLETON (49884) Alger(97),
    Schoolcraft(2)
SIDNAW Houghton
SIDNEY Montcalm
SILVERWOOD (48760) Tuscola(59),
    Lapeer(40)
SIX LAKES (48886) Montcalm(98),
    Mecosta(1)
SKANDIA (49885) Marquette(78), Alger(21)
SKANEE Baraga
SMITHS CREEK St. Clair
SMYRNA Ionia
SNOVER Sanilac
SODUS Berrien

SOMERSET Hillsdale
SOMERSET CENTER Hillsdale
SOUTH BOARDMAN Kalkaska
SOUTH BRANCH (48761) Iosco(41),
    Ogemaw(28), Alcona(27), Oscoda(2)
SOUTH HAVEN (49090) Van Buren(95),
    Allegan(4)
SOUTH LYON (48178) Oakland(65),
    Livingston(23), Washtenaw(10)
SOUTH RANGE Houghton
SOUTH ROCKWOOD Monroe
SOUTHFIELD Oakland
SOUTHGATE Wayne
SPALDING Menominee
SPARTA Kent
SPRING ARBOR Jackson
SPRING LAKE (49456) Ottawa(95),
    Muskegon(4)
SPRINGPORT (49284) Jackson(60),
    Calhoun(30), Eaton(9)
SPRUCE (48762) Alcona(89), Alpena(10)
STALWART Chippewa
STAMBAUGH Iron
STANDISH (48658) Arenac(95), Bay(4)
STANTON Montcalm
STANWOOD Mecosta
STEPHENSON Menominee
STERLING (48659) Arenac(95), Bay(4)
STERLING HEIGHTS Macomb
STEVENSVILLE Berrien
STOCKBRIDGE (49285) Ingham(87),
    Jackson(4), Livingston(4), Washtenaw(3)
STRONGS Chippewa
STURGIS St. Joseph
SUMNER (48889) Gratiot(98), Montcalm(1)
SUNFIELD (48890) Eaton(61), Ionia(38)
SUTTONS BAY Leelanau
SWARTZ CREEK Genesee
TAWAS CITY (48763) Iosco(94), Arenac(5)
TAWAS CITY Iosco
TAYLOR Wayne
TECUMSEH Lenawee
TEKONSHA (49092) Calhoun(83),
    Branch(16)
TEMPERANCE Monroe
THOMPSONVILLE (49683) Benzie(61),
    Manistee(31), Grand Traverse(6)
THREE OAKS Berrien
THREE RIVERS St. Joseph
TIPTON Lenawee

TOIVOLA (49965) Houghton(94),
    Ontonagon(5)
TOPINABEE Cheboygan
TOWER Cheboygan
TRAUNIK Alger
TRAVERSE CITY (49684) Grand
    Traverse(79), Leelanau(20)
TRAVERSE CITY Grand Traverse
TRENARY Alger
TRENTON Wayne
TROUT CREEK (49967) Ontonagon(58),
    Houghton(34), Iron(7)
TROUT LAKE Chippewa
TROY Oakland
TRUFANT (49347) Montcalm(94), Kent(5)
TURNER (48765) Arenac(65), Iosco(34)
TUSCOLA Tuscola
TUSTIN (49688) Osceola(91), Lake(5),
    Wexford(2)
TWIN LAKE Muskegon
TWINING (48766) Arenac(96), Iosco(3)
UBLY (48475) Huron(64), Sanilac(35)
UNION Cass
UNION CITY (49094) Branch(97),
    Calhoun(2)
UNION LAKE Oakland
UNION PIER Berrien
UNIONVILLE (48767) Tuscola(97),
    Huron(2)
UNIVERSITY CENTER Bay
UTICA Macomb
VANDALIA Cass
VANDERBILT (49795) Otsego(81),
    Cheboygan(15), Charlevoix(3)
VASSAR Tuscola
VERMONTVILLE Eaton
VERNON Shiawassee
VESTABURG Montcalm
VICKSBURG (49097) Kalamazoo(97), St.
    Joseph(2)
VULCAN (49892) Dickinson(76),
    Menominee(23)
WABANINGO Muskegon
WAKEFIELD Gogebic
WALDRON Hillsdale
WALHALLA Mason
WALKERVILLE (49459) Oceana(90),
    Newaygo(9)
WALLACE Menominee
WALLED LAKE Oakland
WALLOON LAKE Charlevoix

WARREN Macomb
WASHINGTON Macomb
WATERFORD Oakland
WATERS Otsego
WATERSMEET Gogebic
WATERVLIET (49098) Berrien(91), Van
    Buren(8)
WATTON Baraga
WAYLAND (49348) Allegan(78), Barry(21)
WAYNE Wayne
WEBBERVILLE (48892) Ingham(78),
    Livingston(21)
WEIDMAN Isabella
WELLS Delta
WELLSTON (49689) Manistee(86),
    Wexford(13)
WEST BLOOMFIELD Oakland
WEST BRANCH Ogemaw
WEST OLIVE Ottawa
WESTLAND Wayne
WESTON Lenawee
WESTPHALIA Clinton
WETMORE (49895) Alger(65), Delta(29),
    Schoolcraft(4)
WHEELER (48662) Gratiot(85),
    Midland(14)
WHITE CLOUD Newaygo
WHITE LAKE Oakland
WHITE PIGEON (49099) St. Joseph(87),
    Cass(12)
WHITE PINE Ontonagon
WHITEHALL Muskegon
WHITMORE LAKE (48189)
    Washtenaw(54), Livingston(45)
WHITTAKER Washtenaw
WHITTEMORE (48770) Iosco(96),
    Ogemaw(2), Arenac(1)
WILLIAMSBURG (49690) Grand
    Traverse(87), Antrim(7), Kalkaska(5)
WILLIAMSTON Ingham
WILLIS Washtenaw
WILSON Menominee
WINN Isabella
WIXOM Oakland
WOLVERINE Cheboygan
WOODLAND Barry
WYANDOTTE Wayne
WYOMING Kent
YALE (48097) St. Clair(82), Sanilac(17)
YPSILANTI Washtenaw
ZEELAND Ottawa

Michigan ZIP/City Cross Reference

48001-48001 ALGONAC
48002-48002 ALLENTON
48003-48003 ALMONT
48004-48004 ANCHORVILLE
48005-48005 ARMADA
48006-48006 AVOCA
48007-48007 TROY
48009-48012 BIRMINGHAM
48014-48014 CAPAC
48015-48015 CENTER LINE
48017-48017 CLAWSON
48021-48021 EASTPOINTE
48022-48022 EMMETT
48023-48023 FAIR HAVEN
48025-48025 FRANKLIN
48026-48026 FRASER
48027-48027 GOODELLS
48028-48028 HARSENS ISLAND
48030-48030 HAZEL PARK
48032-48032 JEDDO
48034-48034 SOUTHFIELD
48035-48036 CLINTON TOWNSHIP
48037-48037 SOUTHFIELD
48038-48038 CLINTON TOWNSHIP
48039-48039 MARINE CITY
48040-48040 MARYSVILLE

48041-48041 MEMPHIS
48042-48042 MACOMB
48043-48043 MOUNT CLEMENS
48044-48044 MACOMB
48045-48045 HARRISON TOWNSHIP
48046-48046 MOUNT CLEMENS
48047-48047 NEW BALTIMORE
48048-48048 NEW HAVEN
48049-48049 NORTH STREET
48050-48050 NEW HAVEN
48051-48051 NEW BALTIMORE
48052-48052 ALGONAC
48054-48054 EAST CHINA
48059-48059 FORT GRATIOT
48060-48061 PORT HURON
48062-48062 RICHMOND
48063-48063 COLUMBUS
48064-48064 CASCO
48065-48065 ROMEO
48066-48066 ROSEVILLE
48067-48068 ROYAL OAK
48069-48069 PLEASANT RIDGE
48070-48070 HUNTINGTON WOODS
48071-48071 MADISON HEIGHTS
48072-48072 BERKLEY
48073-48073 ROYAL OAK

48074-48074 SMITHS CREEK
48075-48076 SOUTHFIELD
48079-48079 SAINT CLAIR
48080-48082 SAINT CLAIR SHORES
48083-48085 TROY
48086-48086 SOUTHFIELD
48088-48093 WARREN
48094-48095 WASHINGTON
48096-48096 RAY
48097-48097 YALE
48098-48099 TROY
48101-48102 ALLEN PARK
48103-48109 ANN ARBOR
48110-48110 AZALIA
48111-48112 BELLEVILLE
48113-48113 ANN ARBOR
48114-48114 BRIGHTON
48115-48115 BRIDGEWATER
48116-48116 BRIGHTON
48117-48117 CARLETON
48118-48118 CHELSEA
48120-48121 DEARBORN
48122-48122 MELVINDALE
48123-48124 DEARBORN
48125-48125 DEARBORN HEIGHTS
48126-48126 DEARBORN

48127-48127 DEARBORN HEIGHTS
48128-48128 DEARBORN
48130-48130 DEXTER
48131-48131 DUNDEE
48133-48133 ERIE
48134-48134 FLAT ROCK
48135-48136 GARDEN CITY
48137-48137 GREGORY
48138-48138 GROSSE ILE
48139-48139 HAMBURG
48140-48140 IDA
48141-48141 INKSTER
48143-48143 LAKELAND
48144-48144 LAMBERTVILLE
48145-48145 LA SALLE
48146-48146 LINCOLN PARK
48150-48154 LIVONIA
48157-48157 LUNA PIER
48158-48158 MANCHESTER
48159-48159 MAYBEE
48160-48160 MILAN
48161-48162 MONROE
48164-48164 NEW BOSTON
48165-48165 NEW HUDSON
48166-48166 NEWPORT
48167-48167 NORTHVILLE

ZIP Range	City	ZIP Range	City	ZIP Range	City	ZIP Range	City
48169-48169	PINCKNEY	48422-48422	CROSWELL	48650-48650	PINCONNING	48821-48821	DIMONDALE
48170-48170	PLYMOUTH	48423-48423	DAVISON	48651-48651	PRUDENVILLE	48822-48822	EAGLE
48173-48173	ROCKWOOD	48426-48426	DECKER	48652-48652	RHODES	48823-48826	EAST LANSING
48174-48174	ROMULUS	48427-48427	DECKERVILLE	48653-48653	ROSCOMMON	48827-48827	EATON RAPIDS
48175-48175	SALEM	48428-48428	DRYDEN	48654-48654	ROSE CITY	48829-48829	EDMORE
48176-48176	SALINE	48429-48429	DURAND	48655-48655	SAINT CHARLES	48830-48830	ELM HALL
48177-48177	SAMARIA	48430-48430	FENTON	48656-48656	SAINT HELEN	48831-48831	ELSIE
48178-48178	SOUTH LYON	48432-48432	FILION	48657-48657	SANFORD	48832-48832	ELWELL
48179-48179	SOUTH ROCKWOOD	48433-48433	FLUSHING	48658-48658	STANDISH	48833-48833	EUREKA
48180-48180	TAYLOR	48434-48434	FORESTVILLE	48659-48659	STERLING	48834-48834	FENWICK
48182-48182	TEMPERANCE	48435-48435	FOSTORIA	48661-48661	WEST BRANCH	48835-48835	FOWLER
48183-48183	TRENTON	48436-48436	GAINES	48662-48662	WHEELER	48836-48836	FOWLERVILLE
48184-48184	WAYNE	48437-48437	GENESEE	48663-48663	SAGINAW	48837-48837	GRAND LEDGE
48185-48186	WESTLAND	48438-48438	GOODRICH	48667-48686	MIDLAND	48838-48838	GREENVILLE
48187-48188	CANTON	48439-48439	GRAND BLANC	48701-48701	AKRON	48840-48840	HASLETT
48189-48189	WHITMORE LAKE	48440-48440	HADLEY	48703-48703	AU GRES	48841-48841	HENDERSON
48190-48190	WHITTAKER	48441-48441	HARBOR BEACH	48705-48705	BARTON CITY	48842-48842	HOLT
48191-48191	WILLIS	48442-48442	HOLLY	48706-48708	BAY CITY	48843-48843	HOWELL
48192-48192	WYANDOTTE	48444-48444	IMLAY CITY	48710-48710	UNIVERSITY CENTER	48845-48845	HUBBARDSTON
48195-48195	SOUTHGATE	48445-48445	KINDE	48720-48720	BAY PORT	48846-48846	IONIA
48197-48198	YPSILANTI	48446-48446	LAPEER	48721-48721	BLACK RIVER	48847-48847	ITHACA
48200-48202	DETROIT	48449-48449	LENNON	48722-48722	BRIDGEPORT	48848-48848	LAINGSBURG
48203-48203	HIGHLAND PARK	48450-48450	LEXINGTON	48723-48723	CARO	48849-48849	LAKE ODESSA
48204-48211	DETROIT	48451-48451	LINDEN	48724-48724	CARROLLTON	48850-48850	LAKEVIEW
48212-48212	HAMTRAMCK	48452-48452	ATTICA	48725-48725	CASEVILLE	48851-48851	LYONS
48213-48217	DETROIT	48453-48453	MARLETTE	48726-48726	CASS CITY	48852-48852	MCBRIDES
48218-48218	RIVER ROUGE	48454-48454	MELVIN	48727-48727	CLIFFORD	48853-48853	MAPLE RAPIDS
48219-48219	DETROIT	48455-48455	METAMORA	48728-48728	CURRAN	48854-48854	MASON
48220-48220	FERNDALE	48456-48456	MINDEN CITY	48729-48729	DEFORD	48855-48855	HOWELL
48221-48224	DETROIT	48457-48457	MONTROSE	48730-48730	EAST TAWAS	48856-48856	MIDDLETON
48225-48225	HARPER WOODS	48458-48458	MOUNT MORRIS	48731-48731	ELKTON	48857-48857	MORRICE
48226-48228	DETROIT	48460-48460	NEW LOTHROP	48732-48732	ESSEXVILLE	48858-48859	MOUNT PLEASANT
48229-48229	ECORSE	48461-48461	NORTH BRANCH	48733-48733	FAIRGROVE	48860-48860	MUIR
48230-48230	GROSSE POINTE	48462-48462	ORTONVILLE	48734-48734	FRANKENMUTH	48861-48861	MULLIKEN
48231-48235	DETROIT	48463-48463	OTISVILLE	48735-48735	GAGETOWN	48862-48862	NORTH STAR
48236-48236	GROSSE POINTE	48464-48464	OTTER LAKE	48736-48736	GILFORD	48863-48863	OAK GROVE
48237-48237	OAK PARK	48465-48465	PALMS	48737-48737	GLENNIE	48864-48864	OKEMOS
48238-48238	DETROIT	48466-48466	PECK	48738-48738	GREENBUSH	48865-48865	ORLEANS
48239-48240	REDFORD	48467-48467	PORT AUSTIN	48739-48739	HALE	48866-48866	OVID
48242-48299	DETROIT	48468-48468	PORT HOPE	48740-48740	HARRISVILLE	48867-48867	OWOSSO
48301-48304	BLOOMFIELD HILLS	48469-48469	PORT SANILAC	48741-48741	KINGSTON	48870-48870	PALO
48306-48309	ROCHESTER	48470-48470	RUTH	48742-48742	LINCOLN	48871-48871	PERRINTON
48310-48314	STERLING HEIGHTS	48471-48471	SANDUSKY	48743-48743	LONG LAKE	48872-48872	PERRY
48315-48318	UTICA	48472-48472	SNOVER	48744-48744	MAYVILLE	48873-48873	PEWAMO
48320-48320	KEEGO HARBOR	48473-48473	SWARTZ CREEK	48745-48745	MIKADO	48874-48874	POMPEII
48321-48321	AUBURN HILLS	48475-48475	UBLY	48746-48746	MILLINGTON	48875-48875	PORTLAND
48322-48325	WEST BLOOMFIELD	48476-48476	VERNON	48747-48747	MUNGER	48876-48876	POTTERVILLE
48326-48326	AUBURN HILLS	48480-48480	GRAND BLANC	48748-48748	NATIONAL CITY	48877-48877	RIVERDALE
48327-48329	WATERFORD	48500-48507	FLINT	48749-48749	OMER	48878-48878	ROSEBUSH
48330-48330	DRAYTON PLAINS	48509-48529	BURTON	48750-48753	OSCODA	48879-48879	SAINT JOHNS
48331-48336	FARMINGTON	48531-48559	FLINT	48754-48754	OWENDALE	48880-48880	SAINT LOUIS
48340-48343	PONTIAC	48601-48609	SAGINAW	48755-48755	PIGEON	48881-48881	SARANAC
48346-48348	CLARKSTON	48610-48610	ALGER	48756-48756	PRESCOTT	48882-48882	SHAFTSBURG
48350-48350	DAVISBURG	48611-48611	AUBURN	48757-48757	REESE	48883-48883	SHEPHERD
48353-48353	HARTLAND	48612-48612	BEAVERTON	48758-48758	RICHVILLE	48884-48884	SHERIDAN
48356-48357	HIGHLAND	48613-48613	BENTLEY	48759-48759	SEBEWAING	48885-48885	SIDNEY
48359-48362	LAKE ORION	48614-48614	BRANT	48760-48760	SILVERWOOD	48886-48886	SIX LAKES
48363-48363	OAKLAND	48615-48615	BRECKENRIDGE	48761-48761	SOUTH BRANCH	48887-48887	SMYRNA
48366-48366	LAKEVILLE	48616-48616	CHESANING	48762-48762	SPRUCE	48888-48888	STANTON
48367-48367	LEONARD	48617-48617	CLARE	48763-48764	TAWAS CITY	48889-48889	SUMNER
48370-48371	OXFORD	48618-48618	COLEMAN	48765-48765	TURNER	48890-48890	SUNFIELD
48374-48377	NOVI	48619-48619	COMINS	48766-48766	TWINING	48891-48891	VESTABURG
48380-48381	MILFORD	48620-48620	EDENVILLE	48767-48767	UNIONVILLE	48892-48892	WEBBERVILLE
48382-48382	COMMERCE TOWNSHIP	48621-48621	FAIRVIEW	48768-48768	VASSAR	48893-48893	WEIDMAN
48383-48386	WHITE LAKE	48622-48622	FARWELL	48769-48769	TUSCOLA	48894-48894	WESTPHALIA
48387-48387	UNION LAKE	48623-48623	FREELAND	48770-48770	WHITTEMORE	48895-48895	WILLIAMSTON
48390-48391	WALLED LAKE	48624-48624	GLADWIN	48787-48787	FRANKENMUTH	48896-48896	WINN
48393-48393	WIXOM	48625-48625	HARRISON	48801-48802	ALMA	48897-48897	WOODLAND
48397-48397	WARREN	48626-48626	HEMLOCK	48804-48804	MOUNT PLEASANT	48900-48980	LANSING
48398-48398	CLAWSON	48627-48627	HIGGINS LAKE	48805-48805	OKEMOS	49001-49001	KALAMAZOO
48401-48401	APPLEGATE	48628-48628	HOPE	48806-48806	ASHLEY	49002-49002	PORTAGE
48410-48410	ARGYLE	48629-48629	HOUGHTON LAKE	48807-48807	BANNISTER	49003-49003	KALAMAZOO
48411-48411	ATLAS	48630-48630	HOUGHTON LAKE HEIGHTS	48808-48808	BATH	49010-49010	ALLEGAN
48412-48412	ATTICA	48631-48631	KAWKAWLIN	48809-48809	BELDING	49011-49011	ATHENS
48413-48413	BAD AXE	48632-48632	LAKE	48811-48811	CARSON CITY	49012-49012	AUGUSTA
48414-48414	BANCROFT	48633-48633	LAKE GEORGE	48812-48812	CEDAR LAKE	49013-49013	BANGOR
48415-48415	BIRCH RUN	48634-48634	LINWOOD	48813-48813	CHARLOTTE	49014-49014	BATTLE CREEK
48416-48416	BROWN CITY	48635-48635	LUPTON	48815-48815	CLARKSVILLE	49019-49019	KALAMAZOO
48417-48417	BURT	48636-48636	LUZERNE	48816-48816	COHOCTAH	49020-49020	BEDFORD
48418-48418	BYRON	48637-48637	MERRILL	48817-48817	CORUNNA	49021-49021	BELLEVUE
48419-48419	CARSONVILLE	48640-48642	MIDLAND	48818-48818	CRYSTAL	49022-49023	BENTON HARBOR
48420-48420	CLIO	48647-48647	MIO	48819-48819	DANSVILLE	49024-49024	PORTAGE
48421-48421	COLUMBIAVILLE	48649-48649	OAKLEY	48820-48820	DEWITT	49026-49026	BLOOMINGDALE

49027-49027 BREEDSVILLE	49129-49129 UNION PIER	49319-49319 CEDAR SPRINGS	49523-49599 GRAND RAPIDS
49028-49028 BRONSON	49130-49130 UNION	49320-49320 CHIPPEWA LAKE	49601-49601 CADILLAC
49029-49029 BURLINGTON	49201-49204 JACKSON	49321-49321 COMSTOCK PARK	49610-49610 ACME
49030-49030 BURR OAK	49220-49220 ADDISON	49322-49322 CORAL	49611-49611 ALBA
49031-49031 CASSOPOLIS	49221-49221 ADRIAN	49323-49323 DORR	49612-49612 ALDEN
49032-49032 CENTREVILLE	49224-49224 ALBION	49325-49325 FREEPORT	49613-49613 ARCADIA
49033-49033 CERESCO	49227-49227 ALLEN	49326-49326 GOWEN	49614-49614 BEAR LAKE
49034-49034 CLIMAX	49228-49228 BLISSFIELD	49327-49327 GRANT	49615-49615 BELLAIRE
49035-49035 CLOVERDALE	49229-49229 BRITTON	49328-49328 HOPKINS	49616-49616 BENZONIA
49036-49036 COLDWATER	49230-49230 BROOKLYN	49329-49329 HOWARD CITY	49617-49617 BEULAH
49038-49038 COLOMA	49231-49231 CADMUS	49330-49330 KENT CITY	49618-49618 BOON
49039-49039 HAGAR SHORES	49232-49232 CAMDEN	49331-49331 LOWELL	49619-49619 BRETHREN
49040-49040 COLON	49233-49233 CEMENT CITY	49332-49332 MECOSTA	49620-49620 BUCKLEY
49041-49041 COMSTOCK	49234-49234 CLARKLAKE	49333-49333 MIDDLEVILLE	49621-49621 CEDAR
49042-49042 CONSTANTINE	49235-49235 CLAYTON	49334-49334 MILLBROOK	49622-49622 CENTRAL LAKE
49043-49043 COVERT	49236-49236 CLINTON	49335-49335 MOLINE	49623-49623 CHASE
49045-49045 DECATUR	49237-49237 CONCORD	49336-49336 MORLEY	49625-49625 COPEMISH
49046-49046 DELTON	49238-49238 DEERFIELD	49337-49337 NEWAYGO	49626-49626 EASTLAKE
49047-49047 DOWAGIAC	49239-49239 FRONTIER	49338-49338 PARIS	49627-49627 EASTPORT
49048-49048 KALAMAZOO	49240-49240 GRASS LAKE	49339-49339 PIERSON	49628-49628 ELBERTA
49050-49050 DOWLING	49241-49241 HANOVER	49340-49340 REMUS	49629-49629 ELK RAPIDS
49051-49051 EAST LEROY	49242-49242 HILLSDALE	49341-49341 ROCKFORD	49630-49630 EMPIRE
49052-49052 FULTON	49245-49245 HOMER	49342-49342 RODNEY	49631-49631 EVART
49053-49053 GALESBURG	49246-49246 HORTON	49343-49343 SAND LAKE	49632-49632 FALMOUTH
49055-49055 GOBLES	49247-49247 HUDSON	49344-49344 SHELBYVILLE	49633-49633 FIFE LAKE
49056-49056 GRAND JUNCTION	49248-49248 JASPER	49345-49345 SPARTA	49634-49634 FILER CITY
49057-49057 HARTFORD	49249-49249 JEROME	49346-49346 STANWOOD	49635-49635 FRANKFORT
49058-49058 HASTINGS	49250-49250 JONESVILLE	49347-49347 TRUFANT	49636-49636 GLEN ARBOR
49060-49060 HICKORY CORNERS	49251-49251 LESLIE	49348-49348 WAYLAND	49637-49637 GRAWN
49061-49061 JONES	49252-49252 LITCHFIELD	49349-49349 WHITE CLOUD	49638-49638 HARRIETTA
49062-49062 KENDALL	49253-49253 MANITOU BEACH	49351-49351 ROCKFORD	49639-49639 HERSEY
49063-49063 LACOTA	49254-49254 MICHIGAN CENTER	49355-49357 ADA	49640-49640 HONOR
49064-49064 LAWRENCE	49255-49255 MONTGOMERY	49401-49401 ALLENDALE	49642-49642 IDLEWILD
49065-49065 LAWTON	49256-49256 MORENCI	49402-49402 BRANCH	49643-49643 INTERLOCHEN
49066-49066 LEONIDAS	49257-49257 MOSCOW	49403-49403 CONKLIN	49644-49644 IRONS
49067-49067 MARCELLUS	49258-49258 MOSHERVILLE	49404-49404 COOPERSVILLE	49645-49645 KALEVA
49068-49069 MARSHALL	49259-49259 MUNITH	49405-49405 CUSTER	49646-49646 KALKASKA
49070-49070 MARTIN	49261-49261 NAPOLEON	49406-49406 DOUGLAS	49647-49647 KARLIN
49071-49071 MATTAWAN	49262-49262 NORTH ADAMS	49408-49408 FENNVILLE	49648-49648 KEWADIN
49072-49072 MENDON	49263-49263 NORVELL	49409-49409 FERRYSBURG	49649-49649 KINGSLEY
49073-49073 NASHVILLE	49264-49264 ONONDAGA	49410-49410 FOUNTAIN	49650-49650 LAKE ANN
49074-49074 NAZARETH	49265-49265 ONSTED	49411-49411 FREE SOIL	49651-49651 LAKE CITY
49075-49075 NOTTAWA	49266-49266 OSSEO	49412-49413 FREMONT	49653-49653 LAKE LEELANAU
49076-49076 OLIVET	49267-49267 OTTAWA LAKE	49415-49415 FRUITPORT	49654-49654 LELAND
49077-49077 OSHTEMO	49268-49268 PALMYRA	49416-49416 GLENN	49655-49655 LEROY
49078-49078 OTSEGO	49269-49269 PARMA	49417-49417 GRAND HAVEN	49656-49656 LUTHER
49079-49079 PAW PAW	49270-49270 PETERSBURG	49418-49418 GRANDVILLE	49657-49657 MC BAIN
49080-49080 PLAINWELL	49271-49271 PITTSFORD	49419-49419 HAMILTON	49659-49659 MANCELONA
49081-49081 PORTAGE	49272-49272 PLEASANT LAKE	49420-49420 HART	49660-49660 MANISTEE
49082-49082 QUINCY	49273-49273 PRATTVILLE	49421-49421 HESPERIA	49663-49663 MANTON
49083-49083 RICHLAND	49274-49274 READING	49422-49424 HOLLAND	49664-49664 MAPLE CITY
49084-49084 RIVERSIDE	49275-49275 RIDGEWAY	49425-49425 HOLTON	49665-49665 MARION
49085-49085 SAINT JOSEPH	49276-49276 RIGA	49426-49426 HUDSONVILLE	49666-49666 MAYFIELD
49087-49087 SCHOOLCRAFT	49277-49277 RIVES JUNCTION	49427-49427 JAMESTOWN	49667-49667 MERRITT
49088-49088 SCOTTS	49278-49278 ROLLIN	49428-49429 JENISON	49668-49668 MESICK
49089-49089 SHERWOOD	49279-49279 SAND CREEK	49430-49430 LAMONT	49670-49670 NORTHPORT
49090-49090 SOUTH HAVEN	49280-49280 SENECA	49431-49431 LUDINGTON	49673-49673 OLD MISSION
49091-49091 STURGIS	49281-49281 SOMERSET	49434-49434 MACATAWA	49674-49674 OMENA
49092-49092 TEKONSHA	49282-49282 SOMERSET CENTER	49435-49435 MARNE	49675-49675 ONEKAMA
49093-49093 THREE RIVERS	49283-49283 SPRING ARBOR	49436-49436 MEARS	49676-49676 RAPID CITY
49094-49094 UNION CITY	49284-49284 SPRINGPORT	49437-49437 MONTAGUE	49677-49677 REED CITY
49095-49095 VANDALIA	49285-49285 STOCKBRIDGE	49440-49445 MUSKEGON	49679-49679 SEARS
49096-49096 VERMONTVILLE	49286-49286 TECUMSEH	49446-49446 NEW ERA	49680-49680 SOUTH BOARDMAN
49097-49097 VICKSBURG	49287-49287 TIPTON	49447-49447 NEW RICHMOND	49682-49682 SUTTONS BAY
49098-49098 WATERVLIET	49288-49288 WALDRON	49448-49448 NUNICA	49683-49683 THOMPSONVILLE
49099-49099 WHITE PIGEON	49289-49289 WESTON	49449-49449 PENTWATER	49684-49686 TRAVERSE CITY
49101-49101 BARODA	49301-49301 ADA	49450-49450 PULLMAN	49688-49688 TUSTIN
49102-49102 BERRIEN CENTER	49302-49302 ALTO	49451-49451 RAVENNA	49689-49689 WELLSTON
49103-49104 BERRIEN SPRINGS	49303-49303 BAILEY	49452-49452 ROTHBURY	49690-49690 WILLIAMSBURG
49106-49106 BRIDGMAN	49304-49304 BALDWIN	49453-49453 SAUGATUCK	49696-49696 TRAVERSE CITY
49107-49107 BUCHANAN	49305-49305 BARRYTON	49454-49454 SCOTTVILLE	49701-49701 MACKINAW CITY
49111-49111 EAU CLAIRE	49306-49306 BELMONT	49455-49455 SHELBY	49705-49705 AFTON
49112-49112 EDWARDSBURG	49307-49307 BIG RAPIDS	49456-49456 SPRING LAKE	49706-49706 ALANSON
49113-49113 GALIEN	49309-49309 BITELY	49457-49457 TWIN LAKE	49707-49707 ALPENA
49115-49115 HARBERT	49310-49310 BLANCHARD	49458-49458 WALHALLA	49709-49709 ATLANTA
49116-49116 LAKESIDE	49311-49311 BRADLEY	49459-49459 WALKERVILLE	49710-49710 BARBEAU
49117-49117 NEW BUFFALO	49312-49312 BROHMAN	49460-49460 WEST OLIVE	49711-49711 BAY SHORE
49119-49119 NEW TROY	49313-49313 BRUNSWICK	49461-49461 WHITEHALL	49712-49712 BOYNE CITY
49120-49121 NILES	49314-49314 BURNIPS	49463-49463 WABANINGO	49713-49713 BOYNE FALLS
49125-49125 SAWYER	49315-49315 BYRON CENTER	49464-49464 ZEELAND	49715-49715 BRIMLEY
49126-49126 SODUS	49316-49316 CALEDONIA	49468-49468 GRANDVILLE	49716-49716 BRUTUS
49127-49127 STEVENSVILLE	49317-49317 CANNONSBURG	49500-49518 GRAND RAPIDS	49717-49717
49128-49128 THREE OAKS	49318-49318 CASNOVIA	49519-49519 WYOMING	

BURT LAKE		49777-49777	PRESQUE ISLE	49840-49840	GULLIVER	49908-49908	BARAGA
49718-49718	CARP LAKE	49778-49778	BRIMLEY	49841-49843	GWINN	49909-49909	IRON RIVER
49719-49719	CEDARVILLE	49779-49779	ROGERS CITY	49845-49845	HARRIS	49910-49910	BERGLAND
49720-49720	CHARLEVOIX	49780-49780	RUDYARD	49847-49847	HERMANSVILLE	49911-49911	BESSEMER
49721-49721	CHEBOYGAN	49781-49781	SAINT IGNACE	49848-49848	INGALLS	49912-49912	BRUCE CROSSING
49722-49722	CONWAY	49782-49782	BEAVER ISLAND	49849-49849	ISHPEMING	49913-49913	CALUMET
49723-49723	CROSS VILLAGE	49783-49783	SAULT SAINTE MARIE	49852-49852	LORETTO	49915-49915	CASPIAN
49724-49724	DAFTER	49784-49788	KINCHELOE	49853-49853	MC MILLAN	49916-49916	CHASSELL
49725-49725	DE TOUR VILLAGE	49789-49789	STALWART	49854-49854	MANISTIQUE	49917-49917	COPPER CITY
49726-49726	DRUMMOND ISLAND	49790-49790	STRONGS	49855-49855	MARQUETTE	49918-49918	COPPER HARBOR
49727-49727	EAST JORDAN	49791-49791	TOPINABEE	49858-49858	MENOMINEE	49919-49919	COVINGTON
49728-49728	ECKERMAN	49792-49792	TOWER	49861-49861	MICHIGAMME	49920-49920	CRYSTAL FALLS
49729-49729	ELLSWORTH	49793-49793	TROUT LAKE	49862-49862	MUNISING	49921-49921	DODGEVILLE
49730-49730	ELMIRA	49795-49795	VANDERBILT	49863-49863	NADEAU	49922-49922	DOLLAR BAY
49733-49733	FREDERIC	49796-49796	WALLOON LAKE	49864-49864	NAHMA	49924-49924	EAGLE RIVER
49734-49735	GAYLORD	49797-49797	WATERS	49865-49865	NATIONAL MINE	49925-49925	EWEN
49736-49736	GOETZVILLE	49799-49799	WOLVERINE	49866-49866	NEGAUNEE	49927-49927	GAASTRA
49737-49737	GOOD HART	49801-49801	IRON MOUNTAIN	49868-49868	NEWBERRY	49929-49929	GREENLAND
49738-49739	GRAYLING	49802-49802	KINGSFORD	49869-49869	NORTHLAND	49930-49930	HANCOCK
49740-49740	HARBOR SPRINGS	49805-49805	ALLOUEZ	49870-49870	NORWAY	49931-49931	HOUGHTON
49743-49743	HAWKS	49806-49806	AU TRAIN	49871-49871	PALMER	49934-49934	HUBBELL
49744-49744	HERRON	49807-49807	BARK RIVER	49872-49872	PERKINS	49935-49935	IRON RIVER
49745-49745	HESSEL	49808-49808	BIG BAY	49873-49873	PERRONVILLE	49938-49938	IRONWOOD
49746-49746	HILLMAN	49812-49812	CARNEY	49874-49874	POWERS	49942-49942	KEARSARGE
49747-49747	HUBBARD LAKE	49813-49813	CEDAR RIVER	49876-49876	QUINNESEC	49943-49943	KENTON
49748-49748	HULBERT	49814-49814	CHAMPION	49877-49877	RALPH	49945-49945	LAKE LINDEN
49749-49749	INDIAN RIVER	49815-49815	CHANNING	49878-49878	RAPID RIVER	49946-49946	LANSE
49751-49751	JOHANNESBURG	49816-49816	CHATHAM	49879-49879	REPUBLIC	49947-49947	MARENISCO
49752-49752	KINROSS	49817-49817	COOKS	49880-49880	ROCK	49948-49948	MASS CITY
49753-49753	LACHINE	49818-49818	CORNELL	49881-49881	SAGOLA	49950-49950	MOHAWK
49755-49755	LEVERING	49819-49819	ARNOLD	49883-49883	SENEY	49952-49952	NISULA
49756-49756	LEWISTON	49820-49820	CURTIS	49884-49884	SHINGLETON	49953-49953	ONTONAGON
49757-49757	MACKINAC ISLAND	49821-49821	DAGGETT	49885-49885	SKANDIA	49955-49955	PAINESDALE
49759-49759	MILLERSBURG	49822-49822	DEERTON	49886-49886	SPALDING	49958-49958	PELKIE
49760-49760	MORAN	49825-49825	EBEN JUNCTION	49887-49887	STEPHENSON	49959-49959	RAMSAY
49761-49761	MULLETT LAKE	49826-49826	RUMELY	49890-49890	TRAUNIK	49960-49960	ROCKLAND
49762-49762	NAUBINWAY	49827-49827	ENGADINE	49891-49891	TRENARY	49961-49961	SIDNAW
49764-49764	ODEN	49829-49829	ESCANABA	49892-49892	VULCAN	49962-49962	SKANEE
49765-49765	ONAWAY	49831-49831	FELCH	49893-49893	WALLACE	49963-49963	SOUTH RANGE
49766-49766	OSSINEKE	49833-49833	LITTLE LAKE	49894-49894	WELLS	49964-49964	STAMBAUGH
49768-49768	PARADISE	49834-49834	FOSTER CITY	49895-49895	WETMORE	49965-49965	TOIVOLA
49769-49769	PELLSTON	49835-49835	GARDEN	49896-49896	WILSON	49967-49967	TROUT CREEK
49770-49770	PETOSKEY	49836-49836	GERMFASK	49901-49901	AHMEEK	49968-49968	WAKEFIELD
49774-49774	PICKFORD	49837-49837	GLADSTONE	49902-49902	ALPHA	49969-49969	WATERSMEET
49775-49775	POINTE AUX PINS	49838-49838	GOULD CITY	49903-49903	AMASA	49970-49970	WATTON
49776-49776	POSEN	49839-49839	GRAND MARAIS	49905-49905	ATLANTIC MINE	49971-49971	WHITE PINE

County-Town
MICHIGAN

Explanation of Symbols

State Capital
Vernon County Seat

Population Key

○ 0-999
◔ 1,000-2,499
◑ 2,500-4,999
◕ 5,000-9,999
◉ 10,000-19,000
◉ 20,000-24,999

◉ 25,000-49,999
□ 50,000-99,999
□ 100,000-249,999
■ 250,000-999,999
■ 1,000,000+

COUNTIES

(83 Counties)

Name of County	Population	Location on Map
ALCONA	10,145	H-12
ALGER	8,972	E-6
ALLEGAN	90,509	M-8
ALPENA	30,605	G-12
ANTRIM	18,185	H-9
ARENAC	14,931	J-11
BARAGA	7,954	D-4
BARRY	50,057	M-9
BAY	111,723	K-11
BENZIE	12,200	I-8
BERRIEN	161,378	O-7
BRANCH	41,502	O-9
CALHOUN	135,982	N-10
CASS	49,477	O-8
CHARLEVOIX	21,468	G-9
CHEBOYGAN	21,398	G-10
CHIPPEWA	34,604	E-9
CLARE	24,952	J-10
CLINTON	57,883	L-10
CRAWFORD	12,260	H-10
DELTA	37,780	E-6
DICKINSON	26,831	E-4
EATON	92,879	M-10
EMMET	25,040	F-10
GENESEE	430,459	M-12
GLADWIN	21,896	J-10
GOGEBIC	18,052	D-1
GRAND TRAVERSE	64,273	I-9
GRATIOT	38,982	L-10
HILLSDALE	43,431	O-10
HOUGHTON	35,446	C-3
HURON	34,951	J-13
INGHAM	281,912	N-11
IONIA	57,024	L-10
IOSCO	30,209	I-12
IRON	13,175	E-3
ISABELLA	54,624	K-10
JACKSON	149,756	N-11
KALAMAZOO	223,411	N-9
KALKASKA	13,497	H-9
KENT	500,631	L-8
KEWEENAW	1,701	B-4
LAKE	8,583	J-8
LAPEER	74,768	L-13
LEELANAU	16,527	H-8
LENAWEE	91,476	O-11
LIVINGSTON	115,645	M-11
LUCE	5,763	D-8
MACKINAC	10,674	E-8
MACOMB	717,400	M-13
MANISTEE	21,265	I-8
MARQUETTE	70,887	D-5
MASON	25,537	J-7
MECOSTA	37,308	K-9
MENOMINEE	24,920	G-5
MIDLAND	75,651	K-11
MISSAUKEE	12,147	I-9
MONROE	133,600	O-12
MONTCALM	53,059	K-9
MONTMORENCY	8,936	G-11
MUSKEGON	158,983	L-7
NEWAYGO	38,202	K-8
OAKLAND	1,083,592	M-12
OCEANA	22,454	K-7
OGEMAW	18,681	I-11
ONTONAGON	8,854	D-2
OSCEOLA	20,146	J-9
OSCODA	7,842	H-11
OTSEGO	17,957	H-10
OTTAWA	187,768	M-8
PRESQUE ISLE	13,743	G-11
ROSCOMMON	19,776	I-10
SAGINAW	211,946	L-11
SAINT CLAIR	145,607	M-13
SAINT JOSEPH	58,913	O-8
SANILAC	39,928	K-13
SCHOOLCRAFT	8,302	E-7
SHIAWASSEE	69,770	L-11
TUSCOLA	55,498	K-12
VAN BUREN	70,060	N-8
WASHTENAW	282,937	O-12
WAYNE	2,111,687	N-12
WEXFORD	26,360	I-8
TOTAL	9,295,297	

CITIES AND TOWNS

Note: The first name is that of the city or town, second, that of the county in which it is located, then the population and location on the map.

Adrian, Lenawee, 22,097 ... O-11
Albion, Calhoun, 10,066 ... N-10
Algonac, St. Clair, 4,551 ... M-14
Allegan, Allegan, 4,547 ... N-8
Allen Park, Wayne, 31,092 ... K-3
•Allendale, Ottawa, 6,950 ... M-8
Alma, Gratiot, 9,034 ... K-10
Almont, Lapeer, 2,354 ... F-4
Alpena, Alpena, 11,354 ... H-12
Anchor Bay Gardens, Macomb ... N-5
•Anchorville, St. Clair, 3,202 ... M-14
Ann Arbor, Washtenaw, 109,592 . N-12
•Argentine, Genesee, 1,907 ... M-12
Armada, Macomb, 1,548 ... M-5
•Au Sable, Iosco, 1,542 ... I-12
Auburn, Bay, 1,855 ... K-11
Auburn Hills, Oakland, 17,076 ... G-3
Bad Axe, Huron, 3,484 ... K-13
Baldwin, Lake, 821 ... J-8
Bangor, Van Buren, 1,922 ... N-8
Baraga, Baraga, 1,231 ... D-4
•Barnes Lake-Millers Lake, Lapeer, 1,304 ... L-13
Battle Creek, Calhoun, 53,540 ... N-9
Bay City, Bay, 38,936 ... K-12
Beaverton, Gladwin, 1,150 ... J-11
•Beecher, Genesee, 14,465 ... L-12
•Beechwood, Ottawa, 2,676 ... M-8
Belding, Ionia, 5,969 ... L-9
Bellaire, Antrim, 1,104 ... H-9
Belleville, Wayne, 3,270 ... K-2
Bellevue, Eaton, 1,401 ... N-10
Benton Harbor, Berrien, 12,818 ... Q-5
•Benton Heights, Berrien, 5,465 ... N-7
Benton South, Berrien ... Q-5
Berkley, Oakland, 16,960 ... I-3
Berrien Springs, Berrien, 1,927 ... Q-6
Bertrand, Berrien ... R-6
Bessemer, Gogebic, 2,272 ... D-1
Beulah, Benzie, 421 ... I-8
Beverly Hills, Oakland, 10,610 ... I-3
Big Rapids, Mecosta, 12,603 ... K-9
Bingham Farms, Oakland, 1,001 ... I-2
Birmingham, Oakland, 19,997 ... H-3
Blissfield, Lenawee, 3,172 ... R-14
Bloomfield Hills, Oakland, 4,288 ... H-3
•Bloomfield Township, Oakland, 42,137 ... H-3
Boyne City, Charlevoix, 3,478 ... G-10
Breckenridge, Gratiot, 1,301 ... L-11
•Bridgeport, Saginaw, 8,569 ... L-12
Bridgman, Berrien, 2,140 ... Q-5
Brighton, Livingston, 5,686 ... N-12
Bronson, Branch, 2,342 ... O-9
Brooklyn, Jackson, 1,027 ... Q-12
Brown City, Lapeer/Sanilac, 1,244 ... L-13
•Brownlee Park, Calhoun, 2,536 ... Q-2
Buchanan, Berrien, 4,992 ... O-7
•Buena Vista, Saginaw, 8,196 ... A-2
•Burt, Saginaw, 1,169 ... B-3
Burton, Genesee, 27,617 ... L-12
Cadillac, Wexford, 10,104 ... J-9
•Canton, Wayne, 57,047 ... J-2
Capac, St. Clair, 1,583 ... L-13
Carleton, Monroe, 2,770 ... L-2
Caro, Tuscola, 4,054 ... K-12
•Carrollton, Saginaw, 6,521 ... L-12
Carson City, Montcalm, 1,158 ... L-10
Caspian, Iron, 1,031 ... E-4
Cass City, Tuscola, 2,276 ... K-13
Cassopolis, Cass, 1,822 ... O-8
Cedar Springs, Kent, 2,600 ... L-9
Center Line, Macomb, 9,026 ... O-4
Centreville, St. Joseph, 1,516 ... O-9
Charlevoix, Charlevoix, 3,116 ... G-9
Charlotte, Eaton, 8,083 ... M-10
Cheboygan, Cheboygan, 4,999 ... F-10
Chelsea, Washtenaw, 3,772 ... N-11
Chesaning, Saginaw, 2,567 ... L-11
Clair Haven, Macomb ... O-5
Clair Haven West, Macomb ... O-5
Clare, Clare/Isabella, 3,021 ... K-10
Clarenceville, Oakland ... I-2
Clarkston, Oakland, 1,005 ... G-2
Clawson, Oakland, 13,874 ... I-3
Clinton, Lenawee, 2,475 ... Q-13
•Clinton, Macomb, 85,866 ... O-4
Clio, Genesee, 2,629 ... L-12
Coldwater, Branch, 9,607 ... O-10
Coleman, Midland, 1,237 ... K-10
Coloma, Berrien, 1,679 ... P-6
Colon, St. Joseph, 1,224 ... O-9
Commerce, Oakland ... H-2
•Comstock Northwest, Kalamazoo, 3,402 ... N-9
•Comstock Park, Kent, 6,530 ... N-1
Constantine, St. Joseph, 2,032 ... O-8
Coopersville, Ottawa, 3,421 ... L-8
Corunna, Shiawassee, 3,091 ... M-11
Croswell, Sanilac, 2,174 ... L-14
Crystal Falls, Iron, 1,922 ... E-4
•Cutlerville, Kent, 11,228 ... O-2
Davison, Genesee, 5,693 ... L-12
De Witt, Clinton, 3,964 ... M-10
Dearborn, Wayne, 89,286 ... N-13
Dearborn Heights, Wayne, 60,838 .. J-3
Decatur, Van Buren, 1,760 ... Q-7
Deckerville, Sanilac, 1,015 ... K-14
Detroit, Wayne, 1,027,974 ... N-13
•Detroit Beach, Monroe, 2,113 ... O-13
Dexter, Washtenaw, 1,497 ... R-11
Dimondale, Eaton, 1,247 ... Q-8
Douglas, Allegan, 1,040 ... M-8
Dowagiac, Cass, 6,409 ... Q-7
Dundee, Monroe, 2,664 ... O-12
Durand, Shiawassee, 4,283 ... M-11
Eagle River, Keweenaw ... B-4
East Detroit, Macomb, 35,283 ... O-4
East Grand Rapids, Kent, 10,807 .. O-2
East Jordan, Charlevoix, 2,240 ... G-9
East Kingsford, Dickinson ... F-4
East Lansing, Ingham, 50,677 ... M-11
East Tawas, Iosco, 2,887 ... I-12
•Eastwood, Kalamazoo, 6,340 ... N-9
Eaton Rapids, Eaton, 4,695 ... Q-8
Ecorse, Wayne, 12,180 ... K-4
•Edgemont Park, Ingham, 2,532 ... P-8
Edmore, Montcalm, 1,126 ... L-10
Edwardsburg, Cass, 1,142 ... R-7
Elk Rapids, Antrim, 1,626 ... H-9
Escanaba, Delta, 13,659 ... F-6
Essexville, Bay, 4,088 ... K-12
Evart, Osceola, 1,744 ... J-9
•Fair Haven, St. Clair, 1,505 ... M-14
•Fair Plain, Berrien, 8,051 ... Q-5
Farmington, Oakland, 10,132 ... I-2
Farmington Hills, Oakland, 74,652 ... I-2
Fennville, Allegan, 1,023 ... N-8
Fenton, Genesee, 8,444 ... G-1
Ferndale, Oakland, 25,084 ... I-4
Ferrysburg, Ottawa, 2,919 ... L-7
Flat Rock, Wayne, 7,290 ... L-3
Flint, Genesee, 140,761 ... L-12
Flushing, Genesee, 8,542 ... L-12
•Forest Hills, Kent, 16,690 ... O-2
Fowlerville, Livingston, 2,648 ... P-10
Frankenmuth, Saginaw, 4,408 ... L-12
Frankfort, Benzie, 1,546 ... I-8
Franklin, Oakland, 2,626 ... I-3
Fraser, Macomb, 13,899 ... O-4
•Freeland, Saginaw, 1,421 ... K-11
Fremont, Newaygo, 3,875 ... K-8
Fruitport, Muskegon, 1,090 ... L-8
Galesburg, Kalamazoo, 1,863 ... N-9
Garden City, Wayne, 31,846 ... J-2
Gaylord, Otsego, 3,256 ... H-10
Gibraltar, Wayne, 4,297 ... L-3
Gladstone, Delta, 4,565 ... F-6
Gladwin, Gladwin, 2,682 ... J-11
Grand Blanc, Genesee, 7,760 ... F-1
Grand Haven, Ottawa, 11,951 ... L-7
Grand Ledge, Eaton, 7,579 ... P-8
Grand Rapids, Kent, 189,126 ... L-8
Grandville, Kent, 15,624 ... O-1
Grayling, Crawford, 1,944 ... I-10
•Greater Galesburg, Kalamazoo, 1,260 ... N-9
Greenville, Montcalm, 8,101 ... L-9
•Greilickville, Leelanau, 1,165 ... H-8
•Grosse Ile, Wayne, 9,781 ... L-4
Grosse Pointe, Wayne, 5,681 ... J-5
Grosse Pointe Farms, Wayne, 10,092 ... J-5
Grosse Pointe Park, Wayne, 12,857 ... J-5
Grosse Pointe Shores, Macomb/Wayne, 2,955 ... O-5
Grosse Pointe Woods, Wayne, 17,715 ... I-5
•Gwinn, Marquette, 2,370 ... E-5
Hamburg, Livingston ... N-12
Hamtramck, Wayne, 18,372 ... J-4
Hancock, Houghton, 4,547 ... C-4
Harbor Beach, Huron, 2,089 ... J-14
Harbor Springs, Emmet, 1,540 ... G-10
Harper Woods, Wayne, 14,903 ... J-5
Harrison, Clare, 1,835 ... J-10
•Harrison, Macomb, 24,685 ... O-5
Harrisville, Alcona, 470 ... I-13
Hart, Oceana, 1,942 ... K-7
Hartford, Van Buren, 2,341 ... N-8
•Harvey, Marquette, 1,377 ... D-6
•Haslett, Ingham, 10,230 ... P-9
Hastings, Barry, 6,549 ... M-9
Hazel Park, Oakland, 20,051 ... I-4
•Hemlock, Saginaw, 1,601 ... K-11
Highland, Oakland ... H-1
Highland Park, Wayne, 20,121 ... J-4
Hillsdale, Hillsdale, 8,170 ... O-10
Holland, Allegan/Ottawa, 30,745 ... M-8
Holly, Oakland, 5,595 ... G-1
•Holt, Ingham, 11,744 ... M-10
Homer, Calhoun, 1,758 ... R-3
Houghton, Houghton, 7,498 ... C-4
•Houghton Lake, Roscommon, 3,353 ... I-10
Houghton Lake Heights, Roscommon ... I-10
Howard City, Montcalm, 1,351 ... L-9
Howell, Livingston, 8,184 ... M-12
•Hubbell, Houghton, 1,174 ... C-4
Hudson, Lenawee, 2,580 ... O-11
Hudsonville, Ottawa, 6,170 ... M-8
Huntington Woods, Oakland, 6,419 . I-3
Huron Heights, Oakland ... H-3
Imlay City, Lapeer, 2,921 ... L-13
Inkster, Wayne, 30,772 ... K-3
Ionia, Ionia, 5,935 ... L-9
Iron Mountain, Dickinson, 8,525 ... F-5
Iron River, Iron, 2,095 ... E-3
Ironwood, Gogebic, 6,849 ... D-1
Ishpeming, Marquette, 7,200 ... D-5
Ithaca, Gratiot, 3,009 ... L-10
Jackson, Jackson, 37,446 ... N-11
•Jenison, Ottawa, 17,882 ... M-8
Jonesville, Hillsdale, 2,283 ... Q-11
•K.I. Sawyer AFB, Marquette, 6,577 ... E-6
Kalamazoo, Kalamazoo, 80,277 ... N-9
Kalkaska, Kalkaska, 1,952 ... H-9
Keego Harbor, Oakland, 2,932 ... H-3
Kentwood, Kent, 37,826 ... O-2
Kingsford, Dickinson, 5,480 ... F-4
Laingsburg, Shiawassee, 1,148 .. M-11
Lake City, Missaukee, 858 ... I-9
•Lake Fenton, Genesee, 4,091 ... M-12
Lake Linden, Houghton, 1,203 ... C-4
•Lake Michigan Beach, Berrien, 1,694 ... P-6
Lake Odessa, Ionia, 2,256 ... M-9
Lake Orion, Oakland, 3,057 ... G-3
Lakeview, Montcalm, 1,108 ... K-9
•Lambertville, Monroe, 7,860 ... O-12
L'Anse, Baraga, 2,151 ... D-4
Lansing, Eaton/Ingham, 127,321 . M-10
Lapeer, Lapeer, 7,759 ... L-13
Lapeer Heights, Genesee ... L-12
Lathrup Village, Oakland, 4,329 ... I-3
Laurium, Houghton, 2,268 ... C-4
Lawton, Van Buren, 1,685 ... N-8
Leland, Leelanau ... H-8
Leslie, Ingham, 1,872 ... Q-9
•Level Park-Oak Park, Calhoun, 3,502 ... P-1
Lincoln Park, Wayne, 41,832 ... K-3
Linden, Genesee, 2,415 ... M-12
Litchfield, Hillsdale, 1,317 ... O-10
Livonia, Wayne, 100,850 ... J-2
Lowell, Kent, 3,983 ... O-3
Ludington, Mason, 8,507 ... J-7
Luna Pier, Monroe, 1,507 ... O-12
Madison Heights, Oakland, 32,196 ... I-4
Mancelona, Antrim, 1,370 ... H-10
Manchester, Washtenaw, 1,753 ... P-13
Manistee, Manistee, 6,734 ... J-7
Manistique, Schoolcraft, 3,456 ... F-7
•Manitou Beach-Devils Lake, Lenawee, 2,061 ... Q-12
Manton, Wexford, 1,161 ... I-9
Marcellus, Cass, 1,193 ... O-8
Marine City, St. Clair, 4,556 ... M-14
Marlette, Sanilac, 1,924 ... L-13
Marquette, Marquette, 21,977 ... D-6
Marshall, Calhoun, 6,891 ... N-10
Marysville, St. Clair, 8,515 ... M-14
Mason, Ingham, 6,768 ... M-11
Mattawan, Van Buren, 2,456 ... N-8
Mayville, Tuscola, 1,010 ... L-12
Melvindale, Wayne, 11,216 ... J-4
Memphis, Macomb/St. Clair, 1,221 ... M-5
Menominee, Menominee, 9,398 ... G-5
•Michigan Center, Jackson, 4,863 . N-11
Middletown, Shiawassee, 1,010 ... L-11
Middleville, Barry, 1,966 ... M-9
Midland, Bay/Midland, 38,053 ... K-11
Milan, Monroe/Washtenaw, 4,040 ... Q-14
Milford, Oakland, 5,511 ... H-1
Millington, Tuscola, 1,114 ... L-12
•Mio, Oscoda, 1,886 ... I-11
Monroe, Monroe, 22,902 ... O-13
Montague, Muskegon, 2,276 ... K-7
Montrose, Genesee, 1,811 ... L-12
Morenci, Lenawee, 2,342 ... R-13
Mount Clemens, Macomb, 18,405 ... M-13
Mount Morris, Genesee, 3,292 ... L-12
Mount Pleasant, Isabella, 23,285 . K-10
Munising, Alger, 2,783 ... E-7
Muskegon, Muskegon, 40,283 ... L-7
Muskegon Heights, Muskegon, 13,176 ... L-7
•Napoleon, Jackson, 1,332 ... P-12
Nashville, Barry, 1,654 ... M-9
Negaunee, Marquette, 4,741 ... D-5
New Baltimore, Macomb, 5,798 ... N-5
New Buffalo, Berrien, 2,317 ... O-7
New Haven, Macomb, 2,331 ... N-5
New Hudson, Oakland ... I-1
Newaygo, Newaygo, 1,336 ... K-8
Newberry, Luce, 1,873 ... E-9
Niles, Berrien/Cass, 12,458 ... O-7
North Branch, Lapeer, 1,023 ... L-13
North Muskegon, Muskegon, 3,919 ... L-7
•Northview, Kent, 13,712 ... N-2
Northville, Oakland/Wayne, 6,226 ... I-2
Norton Shores, Muskegon, 21,755 ... L-7
Norway, Dickinson, 2,910 ... F-5
Novi, Oakland, 32,998 ... I-2
Oak Park, Oakland, 30,462 ... I-3
•Okemos, Ingham, 20,216 ... M-11
Olivet, Eaton, 1,604 ... N-10
Onaway, Presque Isle, 1,039 ... G-11
Ontonagon, Ontonagon, 2,040 ... C-3
Orchard Lake Village, Oakland, 2,286 ... H-3
Ortonville, Oakland, 1,252 ... G-2
•Oscoda, Iosco, 1,061 ... I-13
•Ossineke, Alpena, 1,091 ... H-12
Otsego, Allegan, 3,937 ... N-8
Ovid, Clinton/Shiawassee, 1,442 .. L-11
Owosso, Shiawassee, 16,322 ... L-11
Oxbow, Oakland ... H-2
Oxford, Oakland, 2,929 ... G-3
Parchment, Kalamazoo, 1,958 ... N-9
Paw Paw, Van Buren, 3,169 ... N-8
•Paw Paw Lake, Berrien, 3,782 ... P-6
•Pearl Beach, St. Clair, 3,394 ... M-14
Pentwater, Oceana, 1,050 ... K-7
Perry, Shiawassee, 2,163 ... M-11
Petersburg, Monroe, 1,201 ... O-12
Petoskey, Emmet, 6,056 ... G-10
Pigeon, Huron, 1,207 ... K-13
Pinckney, Livingston, 1,603 ... N-11
Pinconning, Bay, 1,291 ... J-11
Plainfield Heights, Kent ... N-2
Plainwell, Allegan, 4,057 ... N-9
Pleasant Ridge, Oakland, 2,775 ... I-3
Plymouth, Wayne, 9,560 ... J-2
•Plymouth Township, Wayne, 23,646 ... J-2
Pontiac, Oakland, 71,166 ... M-13
Port Huron, St. Clair, 33,694 ... L-14
Portage, Kalamazoo, 41,042 ... N-9
Portland, Ionia, 3,889 ... M-10
Potterville, Eaton, 1,523 ... Q-8
•Prudenville, Roscommon, 1,513 ... I-10
Quincy, Branch, 1,680 ... O-10
•Quinnesec, Dickinson, 1,254 ... F-4
Reading, Hillsdale, 1,127 ... O-10
•Redford, Wayne, 54,387 ... J-3
Reed City, Osceola, 2,379 ... J-9
Reese, Tuscola, 1,414 ... K-12
Richmond, Macomb, 4,141 ... N-5
River Rouge, Wayne, 11,314 ... K-3
Riverview, Wayne, 13,894 ... K-3
Robin Glen-Indiantown, Saginaw, 1,395 ... A-3
Rochester, Oakland, 7,130 ... H-4
Rochester Hills, Oakland, 61,766 ... H-3
Rockford, Kent, 3,750 ... L-9
Rockwood, Wayne, 3,141 ... L-3
Rogers City, Presque Isle, 3,642 . G-12
Romeo, Macomb, 3,520 ... N-4
Romulus, Wayne, 22,897 ... K-2
Roosevelt Park, Muskegon, 3,885 .. L-8
Roscommon, Roscommon, 858 ... I-10
Roseville, Macomb, 51,412 ... N-13
Royal Oak, Oakland, 65,410 ... I-4
Saginaw, Saginaw, 69,512 ... K-11
•Saginaw Township North, Saginaw, 23,018 ... A-2
•Saginaw Township South, Saginaw, 13,987 ... A-2
Saint Charles, Saginaw, 2,144 ... L-11
Saint Clair, St. Clair, 5,116 ... M-14
Saint Clair Shores, Macomb, 68,107 ... O-5
•Saint Helen, Roscommon, 2,390 ... I-11
Saint Ignace, Mackinac, 2,568 ... F-10
Saint Johns, Clinton, 7,284 ... L-10
Saint Joseph, Berrien, 9,214 ... Q-5
Saint Louis, Gratiot, 3,828 ... K-10
Saline, Washtenaw, 6,660 ... N-12
Sandusky, Sanilac, 2,403 ... K-13
Saranac, Ionia, 1,461 ... M-9
Sault Ste. Marie, Chippewa, 14,689 ... E-11
Schoolcraft, Kalamazoo, 1,517 ... N-8
Scottville, Mason, 1,287 ... J-7
Sebewaing, Huron, 1,923 ... K-12
Selfridge Base, Macomb ... O-5
Selfridge-Capehart, Macomb ... N-5
•Shelby, Macomb, 48,655 ... N-4
Shelby, Oceana, 1,871 ... K-7
Shepherd, Isabella, 1,413 ... K-10
•Shields, Saginaw, 6,634 ... L-11
•Shorewood-Tower Hills-Harbert, Berrien, 1,636 ... R-5
•Skidway Lake, Ogemaw, 2,569 ... J-12
•South Gull Lake, Kalamazoo, 1,453 ... N-9
South Haven, Allegan/Van Buren, 5,563 ... N-7
South Lyon, Oakland, 5,857 ... I-1
•South Monroe, Monroe, 5,266 ... O-12
South Rockwood, Monroe, 1,221 ... L-3
Southfield, Oakland, 75,728 ... I-3
Southgate, Wayne, 30,771 ... K-3
Southland, Jackson ... P-12
•Sparlingville, St. Clair, 1,974 ... M-14
Sparta, Kent, 3,968 ... N-1
•Spring Arbor, Jackson, 2,010 ... P-11
Spring Lake, Ottawa, 2,537 ... L-8
Springfield, Calhoun, 5,582 ... Q-1
Stambaugh, Iron, 1,281 ... E-3
Standish, Arenac, 1,377 ... J-11
Stanton, Montcalm, 1,504 ... L-9
Sterling Heights, Macomb, 117,810 ... O-4
Stevensville, Berrien, 1,230 ... Q-5
Stockbridge, Ingham, 1,202 ... N-11
•Stony Point, Monroe, 1,598 ... O-13
Sturgis, St. Joseph, 10,130 ... O-9
Swartz Creek, Genesee, 4,851 ... M-12
Sylvan Lake, Oakland, 1,884 ... H-3
Tawas City, Iosco, 2,009 ... J-12
Taylor, Wayne, 70,811 ... K-2
Tecumseh, Lenawee, 7,462 ... O-12
•Temperance, Monroe, 6,542 ... O-12
Three Oaks, Berrien, 1,786 ... R-5
Three Rivers, St. Joseph, 7,413 ... O-9
Traverse City, Grand Traverse/Leelanau, 15,155 ... H-9
Trenton, Wayne, 20,586 ... L-3
•Trowbridge Park, Marquette, 1,831 ... D-6
Troy, Oakland, 72,884 ... M-13
•Twin Lake, Muskegon, 1,328 ... L-7
Union City, Branch/Calhoun, 1,767 ... R-1
Union Lake, Oakland ... H-2
Utica, Macomb, 5,081 ... M-13
•Vandercook Lake, Jackson, 4,642 ... P-12
Vassar, Tuscola, 2,559 ... L-12
Vicksburg, Kalamazoo, 2,216 ... O-9
Wakefield, Gogebic, 2,318 ... D-1
Walker, Kent, 17,279 ... O-1
Walled Lake, Oakland, 6,278 ... I-2
Warren, Macomb, 144,864 ... O-4
Washington, Macomb ... N-4
•Waterford, Oakland, 66,692 ... H-2
Watervliet, Berrien, 1,867 ... P-6
•Waverly, Eaton, 15,614 ... M-10
Wayland, Allegan, 2,751 ... M-8
Wayne, Wayne, 19,899 ... K-2
Webberville, Ingham, 1,698 ... Q-10
Wells, Delta ... F-6
•West Bloomfield Township, Oakland, 54,843 ... I-2
West Branch, Ogemaw, 1,914 ... I-11
•West Monroe, Monroe, 3,919 ... O-12
Westland, Wayne, 84,724 ... J-2
•Westwood, Kalamazoo, 8,957 ... N-8
White Cloud, Newaygo, 1,147 ... K-8
White Pigeon, St. Joseph, 1,458 ... O-8
Whitehall, Muskegon, 3,027 ... K-7
•Whitmore Lake, Livingston/Washtenaw, 3,251 ... N-12
Williamston, Ingham, 2,922 ... P-9
Wixom, Oakland, 8,550 ... I-2
•Wolf Lake, Muskegon, 4,110 ... L-8
Wolverine Lake, Oakland, 4,727 ... H-2
Woodhaven, Wayne, 11,631 ... L-3
•Woodland Beach, Monroe, 2,309 ... L-3
Woodville, Jackson ... R-9
•Wurtsmith AFB, Iosco, 5,080 ... I-12
Wyandotte, Wayne, 30,938 ... N-13
Wyoming, Kent, 63,891 ... O-1
Yale, St. Clair, 1,977 ... L-14
Ypsilanti, Washtenaw, 24,846 ... N-12
Zeeland, Ottawa, 5,417 ... M-8
Zilwaukee, Saginaw, 1,850 ... K-12

Explanation of symbols: •– Census Designated Place (CDP)

Minnesota

General Help Numbers:

Governor's Office
130 State Capitol Bldg, 75 Constitution Ave 651-296-3391
St Paul, MN 55155   Fax 651-296-2089
www.governor.state.mn.us   7:30AM-5PM

Attorney General's Office
1400 NCL Tower   651-296-3353
445 Minnesota St   Fax 651-297-4193
St Paul, MN 55101   8AM-5PM
www.ag.state.mn.us

Legislative Records
Minnesota Legislature, State Capitol
House-Room 211, Senate-Room 231   651-296-2887
St Paul, MN 55155   Fax 651-651-296-1563
www.leg.state.mn.us   8AM-5PM

State Archives
Division of Library & Archives   651-296-6126
345 Kellogg Blvd West   Fax 651-297-7436
St Paul, MN 55102-1906   9AM-5PM M-SA;
www.mnhs.org   till 9PM TU

State Specifics:

Capital:	St. Paul
	Ramsey County
Time Zone:	CST
Number of Counties:	87
Population:	5,059,375
Web Site:	www.state.mn.us

State Agencies

Criminal Records

Bureau of Criminal Apprehension, Criminal Justice Information Systems, 1430 Maryland Ave E, St Paul, MN 55106; 651-793-2400, 651-793-2401 (Fax), 8:15AM-4PM.

www.bca.state.mn.us/

Indexing & Storage: Records are available from 1924. It takes 1 day before new records are available for inquiry. Records are indexed on inhouse computer, microfilm and digital disc.

Records are normally destroyed after subject reaches 100 years of age or death.

Searching: For most requesters, to obtain the entire adult history, including all arrests, you must have a notarized release form signed by person of record. To get a 15-year record of convictions only, a consent form is not required. Include the following in your request-name, date of birth, and sex. Fingerprint searches are not permitted. However, 100% of records are fingerprint-

supported. The following data is not released: juvenile records.

Access by: mail, in person.

Fee & Payment: The fee for the full adult history is $15.00, for non-profits the fee is $8.00. The fee for the 15-year public record is $4.00. Non-profits have a reduced fee, call first. Fee payee: BCA. Prepayment required. Business checks, personal checks, money orders and certified funds are accepted. No credit cards accepted.

Mail search: Turnaround time: 1 to 2 weeks. A SASE is requested.

In person search: You use the public access terminal for $4.00. For the full adult history the turnaround time is 2 days, unless you are the person of record, then it is immediate.

Other access: A public database is available on CD-ROM. Monthly updates can be purchased. Data is in ASCII format and is raw data. Fee is $80.00

Statewide Court Records

State Court Administrator, 135 Minnesota Judicial Center, 2 Rev ML King Blvd, St Paul, MN 55155; 651-296-2474, 651-297-5636 (Fax), 8AM-4:30PM.

www.courts.state.mn.us/home/

Note: Except for certain online research capabilities, all court record access must be done at the local level.

Access by: online. No searching by mail.

Online search: Appellate and Supreme Court opinions are available from the website. There is an online system in place that allows internal and external access for government personnel only.

Sexual Offender Registry

Bureau of Criminal Apprehension, Minnesota Predatory Offender Program, 1430 Maryland Ave E, St Paul, MN 55106; 651-793-7070, 888-234-1248, 651-793-7071 (Fax), 8AM-4:30PM.

www.dps.state.mn.us/bca/

Note: This is not a notification state. The state does not permit public access to this information beyond the Level 3 names found on the web page. This means local law enforcement offices cannot give the public access to all names.

Indexing & Storage: It takes 48 hours before new records are available for inquiry.

Access by: online.

Fee & Payment: There is no fee. No mail searching.

Online search: Level 3 offenders may be searched at www.doc.state.mn.us/level3/Search.asp. Also, you can bring up lists by city, county, or ZIP Code.

Incarceration Records

Minnesota Department of Corrections, Records Management Unit, 450 Energy Park Drive, Suite 200, St. Paul, MN 55108; 651-642-0200, 651-643-3588 (Fax), 8AM-5PM.

www.corr.state.mn.us

Indexing & Storage: Records are available on current and former inmates; however, the online search is limited to those either still in prison or under probation. It takes about 7 days before new records are available for inquiry. Records are normally destroyed after ninety-nine years.

Searching: Records are computerized since 1978. Include the following in your request-name and DOB. Location, OID number, physical identifiers, conviction and sentencing information, and release dates are provided.

Access by: mail, phone, fax, online.

Fee & Payment: There is a $10.00 retrieval fee and a copy fee of $.25 per page. Personal checks accepted.

Mail search: Turnaround time: 2-4 days.

Phone search: Searching is available via telephone.

Fax search: Fax requires full name and DOB.

Online search: Search at the web to retrieve public information about adult offenders who have been committed to the Commissioner of Corrections, and who are still under our jurisdiction (i.e. in prison, or released from prison and still under supervision). Also, a private company offers free web access at www.vinelink.com/index.jsp, including state, DOC, and most county jail systems.

Corporation, Limited Liability Company, Assumed Name, Trademarks, Servicemarks, Limited Partnerships

Business Records Services, Secretary of State, 180 State Office Bldg, 100 Martin Luther King Blvd, St Paul, MN 55155-1299; 651-296-2803 (Information), 651-297-7067 (Fax), 8AM-4:30PM.

www.sos.state.mn.us

Note: Records are also held for non-profits.

Indexing & Storage: Records are available from 1850's on. All records are indexed together. It takes one day before new records are available for inquiry. Records are indexed on computer and microfilm.

Searching: Part II of foreign corporation annual reports are not released. Include the following in your request-full name of business, corporation file number. In addition to articles of incorporation, corporation records include the following information: Annual Reports, Prior (merged) names, Inactive and Reserved names.

Access by: mail, phone, fax, in person, online.

Fee & Payment: Copies of most documents are $3.00 per page, $6.00 if original document plus amendments requested. Add $5.00 for certification. Fee payee: Secretary of State. Prepayment required. Personal checks accepted. No credit cards accepted.

Mail search: Turnaround time: 10 business days. No SASE is required.

Phone search: Phone hours are 9AM to 4PM. Limited verification information is given over the phone.

Fax search: Call the number above to receive information via the "fax library."

In person search: The counter closes at 3PM. There is no fee to view the database or microfilm. However, if you walk-in and wish copies immediately, there is an additional $20.00 fee.

Online search: The Internet site permits free look-ups of "business" names. Also, a commercial program called Direct Access is available 24 hours. There is an annual subscription fee of $75.00. Record copies or certificates may be ordered for an additional fee. Visit http://da.sos.state.mn.us/minnesota/home/dahome.asp for more information.

Other access: Information can be purchased in bulk format. Call for more information.

Expedited service: Add $20.00 per transaction. Turnaround time: immediate.

Uniform Commercial Code, Federal Tax Liens, State Tax Liens

UCC Division, Secretary of State, 180 State Office Bldg, St Paul, MN 55155-1299; 651-296-2803, 651-215-1009 (Fax), 8AM-4:30PM.

www.sos.state.mn.us

Indexing & Storage: Records are available from 1966 on computer. Tax liens are on microfilm. Records are indexed on inhouse computer. Records are normally destroyed after imaging completed.

Searching: Use search request form UCC-11 for UCC filings. Use a separate UCC-12 request form to obtain federal and state tax liens on businesses. All tax liens on individuals are filed at the county level. Include the following in your request-debtor name.

Access by: mail, fax, in person, online.

Fee & Payment: Search fee is $20.00 per name. The search fee includes all copies. Fee payee: Secretary of State. Prepayment required. Personal checks accepted.

Mail search: Turnaround time: 2 days.

Fax search: Same criteria as mail searches.

In person search: A free public access terminal is available.

Online search: There is a free look-up by filing number available from the website. A comprehensive commercial program called Direct Access is available 24 hours. There is an annual subscription fee of $75.00 per year, plus $5.00 per debtor name. Call 651-296-2803 for more information.

Other access: This agency will provide information in bulk form on paper, CD or disk. Call 651-296-2803 or 877-551-6767 for more information.

Sales Tax Registrations

Minnesota Revenue Dept, Tax OPS Division, 600 N Robert Street MS:4410, St Paul, MN 55146-4410, 651-282-5225, 651-556-3124 (Fax), 9AM-4PM.

www.taxes.state.mn.us

Indexing & Storage: Records are available from 1967 on computer. It takes 3 days before new records are available for inquiry.

Searching: This agency will only confirm that a business is registered, business name, tax number, and date permit was issued. They can't provide any other information. Include the following in your request-business name and MN business identification number.

Access by: mail, phone, fax, in person, online.

Fee & Payment: There is no fee. No credit cards accepted.

Mail search: Turnaround time: 7 days. No SASE is required.

Phone search: Record information will be given over the phone within 3 minutes.

Fax search: Fax searching available.

In person search: In many instances, walk-in requesters must come back the next day for results.

Online search: Email requests are accepted at don.harens@state.mn.us.

Birth Certificates

Minnesota Department of Health, Vital Records, PO Box 9441, Minneapolis, MN 55440-9441 (Courier: 717 Delaware St SE, Minneapolis, MN 55414); 612-676-5120, 612-331-5776 (Fax), 8AM-4:30PM.

www.health.state.mn.us

Note: For information pertaining to adoption records, call 612-676-5129,

Indexing & Storage: Records are available from 1900 on. Prior records must be obtained from the county level. It takes 3 months before new records are available for inquiry. Records are indexed on microfiche, inhouse computer, depending on years.

Searching: Only those with a "tangible interest" may request a certified record. Anyone may order a non-certified record. Births to unmarried parents require a notarized from parent or child if 16 years or older. Include the following in your request-full name, date of birth, place of birth, names of parents, mother's maiden name. Also, requester's signature must be notarized.

Access by: mail, fax, in person.

Fee & Payment: Fees are $10.00 for a non-certified copy, $13.00 for a certified copy and $7.00 for an additional certified copy of the same name. Fee payee: Minnesota Department of Health. Prepayment required. Credit cards may be used for fax requesters. Personal checks accepted. Credit cards accepted: MasterCard, Visa, AmEx, Discover.

Mail search: Turnaround time: 2 to 3 weeks. No SASE is required.

Fax search: See expedited services.

In person search: Records may only be searched by appointment. Records are not issued in person.

Other access: Bulk lists and files of information, if public record, are avaiilable on paper and in electronic format. Call Linda Salkowicz at 612-676-5120 for details.

Expedited service: Fax search reqeusts are considered expedited. Turnaround time: 4 weeks. Use of credit card required. Add $6.00 for use of credit card and $16.00 for overnight delivery.

Death Records

Minnesota Department of Health, Section of Vital Records, PO Box 9441, Minneapolis, MN 55440-9441 (Courier: 717 Delaware St SE, Minneapolis, MN 55414); 612-676-5120, 612-331-5776 (Fax), 8AM-4:30PM.

www.health.state.mn.us

Indexing & Storage: Records are available from 1908 on. Prior records must be obtained at the county level. It takes 3 months before new records are available for inquiry.

Searching: Only those with a "tangible interest" may request a certified record. Those without such interest made receive non-certified. Include the following in your request-full name, date of death, place of death. Also, requester's signature must be notarized. If date or place not known, include last year known to be alive.

Access by: mail, fax, in person.

Fee & Payment: The search fees are $13.00 for a certified record or $1.00 for a non-certified, and

$5.00 for additional identical copy of same name. Fee payee: Minnesota Department of Health. Prepayment required. Credit cards may be used for ordering by fax only. Personal checks accepted. Credit cards accepted: MasterCard, Visa, AmEx, Discover.

Mail search: Turnaround time: 2 to 3 weeks. No SASE is required.

Fax search: See expedited services.

In person search: Records may only be searched by appointment. Records are not issued in person.

Other access: Bulk lists and files of information, if public record, are avaiilable on paper and in electronic format. Call Linda Salkowicz at 612-676-5120 for details.

Expedited service: Expedited service is available for fax searches. Turnaround time: 4 weeks. Use of credit card is required. Add $6.00 for credit card and $16.00 for overnight express.

Marriage Certificates, Divorce Records

Records not maintained by a state level agency.

Note: Marriage and divorce records are found at the county level. The Section of Vital Records has an index and they will direct you to the proper county (Marriage since 1958, Divorce since 1970). Call the Section of Vital Records at 612-676-5120.

Workers' Compensation Records

Labor & Industry Department, Workers Compensation Division - File Review, 443 Lafayette Rd, St Paul, MN 55155; 651-284-5435, 651-284-5731 (Fax), 8AM-4:30PM.

www.doli.state.mn.us/workcomp.html

Indexing & Storage: Records are available on microfilm or image and paper for 18 years after file closure. New records are available for inquiry immediately. Records are indexed on microfilm, microfiche, inhouse computer. Records are normally destroyed after 18 years old or more.

Searching: Must have a signed release from claimant to obtain all files. Include the following in your request-claimant name, Social Security Number. Include any and all dates of injury in your authorized request.

Access by: mail, phone, fax, in person.

Fee & Payment: There is no search fee. Copies are $.65 each. Add 6.5% tax and postage. Fee payee: Department of Labor & Industry. Prepayment required. Personal checks accepted. No credit cards accepted.

Mail search: Turnaround time: 2 to 4 weeks. No SASE is required.

Phone search: Phone searching is limited to employees involved within a case.

Fax search: This office will accept fax search requests.

In person search: If you request in person, they will mail requested copies.

Driver Records

Driver & Vehicle Services, Records Section, 445 Minnesota St, #180, St Paul, MN 55101; 651-296-6911, 8AM-4:30PM.

www.dps.state.mn.us/dvs/index.html

Note: Copies of tickets can be requested from the same address. The fee is $4.00 per record, $5.00 if certified.

Indexing & Storage: Records are available for 5 years minimum for moving violations and suspensions; 10 years for open revocation; retained indefinitely for DWIs for 2 or more convictions. Accidents and up to 10 mph over in a 55 zone on interstate roads are not shown. It takes no more than 15 days before new records are available for inquiry.

Searching: A casual requester can receive a record, but can only receive the driver's address with consent of driver. The driver's license number or full name and DOB is required for a search. Surrendered licenses will be purged after one year if clear; after five years if the record has convictions. The following data is not released: medical information.

Access by: mail, in person, online.

Fee & Payment: The fee is $4.50 per non-certified record or $4.00 if requester is obtaining own record. Add $1.00 for certification. Fee payee: Department of Public Safety. Prepayment required. Personal checks accepted. No credit cards accepted.

Mail search: Turnaround time: 1 week or more. No SASE is required.

In person search: Up to 3 requests will be processed for walk-in requesters, the rest are available the next day.

Online search: Online access costs $2.50 per record. Online inquiries can be processed either as interactive or as batch files (overnight) 24 hours a day, 7 days a week. Requesters operate from a "bank." Records are accessed by either DL number or full name and DOB. Call 651-297-1714 for more information.

Other access: Minnesota will sell its entire database of driving record information with monthly updates. Customized request sorts are available. Fees vary by type with programming and computer time and are quite reasonable.

Vehicle Ownership, Vehicle Identification

Driver & Vehicle Services, Vehicle Record Requests, 445 Minnesota St, #180, St Paul, MN 55101; 651-296-6911 (General Information), 8AM-4:30PM.

www.dps.state.mn.us/dvs/index.html

Note: Their "Record Request Form" can be downloaded from the website.

Indexing & Storage: Records are available for past 7 years. It takes 5 days before new records are available for inquiry.

Searching: The agency adopted the 14 permissible uses of DPPA. Casual requesters can obtain records without personal information. If consent is given, then personal information is released.

Access by: mail, in person, online.

Fee & Payment: The fee is $4.50 per "display record" (print screen), and for a copy of a $1.50 for a vehicle title document or vehicle registration document. Certification is an additional $1.00. Fee payee: Department of Public Safety. Prepayment required. Personal checks accepted. No credit cards accepted.

Mail search: Turnaround time: 1 week. A SASE is requested.

In person search: Turnaround time is immediate for walk-in requesters.

Online search: Online access costs $2.50 per record. There is an additional monthly charge for dial-in access. The system is the same as described for driving record requests. It is open 24 hours a day, 7 days a week. Lien holder information is included. Users, who must qualify per DPPA, will receive address information Call 651-297-1714 for more information.

Accident Reports

Driver & Vehicle Services, Accident Records, 445 Minnesota St, Suite 181, St Paul, MN 55101-5181; 651-296-2060, 651-282-2360 (Fax), 8AM-4:30PM.

www.mndriveinfo.org

Indexing & Storage: Records are available from 1994 to 1997 on microfilm, and from 1998 to present records are electronically imaged. It takes 3 weeks from date of accident before new records are available for inquiry. Records are normally destroyed after 10 years.

Searching: Police reports may be obtained with the written and signed authorization from the person involved in the accident. Include the following in your request-date of accident, full name, date of birth, driver's license number. Records are indexed by driver names.

Access by: mail, fax, in person.

Fee & Payment: The fee is $4.00 per police report. Fee payee: DVS. Prepayment required. Personal checks accepted. No credit cards accepted.

Mail search: Turnaround time: 1 week. A SASE is requested.

Fax search: Fax requests require an account with the agency. Turnaround time 3 days if the request is received after the file has become available.

In person search: Walk-in requesters may obtain copies of accident reports with the authorization of the individual(s) involved in the accident. Turnaround time: while you wait (typically, 5 to 10 minutes).

Vessel Ownership, Vessel Registration

Department of Natural Resources, License Bureau, 500 Lafayette Rd, St Paul, MN 55155-4026; 651-296-2316, 800-285-2000, 651-297-8851 (Fax), 8AM-4:30PM.

www.dnr.state.mn.us

Note: Lien information shows on title records obtained at this agency.

Indexing & Storage: Records are available for the last 15 yrs. Records maintained for watercraft, snowmobiles, off-highway vehicles (all terrain) and off-highway motorcycles. A watercraft must be titled if over 16 ft and 1980 model or newer; registered if over 9 ft. It takes 1 month before new records are available for inquiry. Records are normally destroyed after 1 year.

Searching: The name and hull number or registration number is required to complete a search.

Access by: mail, phone, fax, in person.

Fee & Payment: There is no search fee.

Mail search: Turnaround time: 2 weeks.

Phone search: Up to 2 names may be searched over the phone.

Fax search: Same criteria as mail searching.

In person search: Turnaround time is usually immediate.

Other access: Bulk requests are offered in several media types. Call 651-297-8023 for more information.

Voter Registration
Access to Records is Restricted

Secretary of State-Election Division, 180 State Office Bldg, 100 Dr Martin L King Blvd, St Paul, MN 55155; 651-215-1440, 877-600-8683, 651-296-9073 (Fax), 8AM-4:30PM.

www.sos.state.mn.us/election/

Note: Records are sold by the state only for political, election, or law enforcement purposes and only to MN registered voters. Some counties will honor record requests.

GED Certificates

Department of Children, Families & Learning, GED Testing, 1500 Highway 36 West, Roseville, MN 55113-4266; 651-582-8446, 651-582-8445 (Instructions), 651-582-8458 (Fax), 7AM-3:30PM.

http://education.state.mn.us/html/intro_adult_ged.htm

Searching: Include the following in your request-name, DOB, last four digits of SSN, and signed release. The year of the test is helpful. A signed release is needed for a either a copy of a transcript or a verification.

Access by: mail, phone, fax.

Fee & Payment: There is no fee.

Mail search: Turnaround time: 1 to 2 days. No SASE is required.

Phone search: Telephone request. For verification only.

Fax search: Same criteria as mail searching.

Hunting and Fishing License Information

ELS Licensing, DNR License Bureau, 500 Lafayette Rd, St Paul, MN 55155-4026; 651-297-1230, 888-646-6367, 651-297-8851 (Fax), 8AM-4:30PM.

www.dnr.state.mn.us

Indexing & Storage: Records are available on computer for 4 years for doe, turkey; Spring permits for moose; for bear and turkey Fall permits, as well as other hunting and fishing licenses. It takes 30 days before new records are available for inquiry.

Searching: Records are open to public; all information is released. Include the following in your request-full name, date of birth. The driver's license is also helpful.

Access by: mail, phone, fax, in person.

Fee & Payment: There is no search fee. Fee payee: DNR. Prepayment required. Personal checks accepted. No credit cards accepted.

Mail search: Turnaround time: 1 to 3 days. No SASE is required.

Phone search: They will confirm information over the phone.

Fax search: They will confirm information, turnaround time is 1 week.

In person search: Simple requests are processed, time permitting.

Other access: They have mailing lists available for purchase. Call 651-296-0930 for details.

Minnesota State Licensing Agencies

Licenses Searchable Online

Abstractor #23	https://www.egov.state.mn.us/Commerce/license_lookup.do?action=lookupForm
Acupuncturist #9	www.docboard.org/mn/df/mndf.htm
Adjuster #23	https://www.egov.state.mn.us/Commerce/license_lookup.do?action=lookupForm
Alarm & Com. System Contr./Installer #6	www.electricity.state.mn.us/Elec_lic/index.html
Alcohol/Drug Counselor #29	www.health.state.mn.us/divs/hpsc/hop/adc/index.html
Ambulance Service/Personnel #28	www.emsrb.state.mn.us/cert.asp?p=s
Appraiser #23	https://www.egov.state.mn.us/Commerce/license_lookup.do?action=lookupForm
Architect #37	www.aelslagid.state.mn.us/roster.html
Athletic Trainer #9	www.docboard.org/mn/df/mndf.htm
Attorney #40	www.courts.state.mn.us/mars/default.aspx
Attorney Specialist #31	http://mail.statebar.gen.mn.us/search/search.asp
Auditor #39	www.boa.state.mn.us/Contact/contact_us.html
Bingo Operation #35	www.gcb.state.mn.us/
Campground Membership Agent #23	https://www.egov.state.mn.us/Commerce/license_lookup.do?action=lookupForm
Chiropractor #4	https://www.hlb.state.mn.us/chi/publicaccess/search.asp
Collection Agency #23	https://www.egov.state.mn.us/Commerce/license_lookup.do?action=lookupForm
Consumer Credit/Payday Lender #24	www.commerce.state.mn.us/pages/FinService/FSLicensees/SL.HTM
Contractor/Remodeler, Residential #23	https://www.egov.state.mn.us/Commerce/license_lookup.do?action=lookupForm
Cosmetologist #23	https://www.egov.state.mn.us/Commerce/license_lookup.do?action=lookupForm
Cosmetology School/Shop #23	https://www.egov.state.mn.us/Commerce/license_lookup.do?action=lookupForm
Credit Union #24	www.commerce.state.mn.us/pages/FinService/FSLicensees/CU.HTM
Crematory #27	www.health.state.mn.us/divs/hpsc/mortsci/mortsciselect.cfm
Currency Exchange #23	https://www.egov.state.mn.us/Commerce/license_lookup.do?action=lookupForm
Debt Collector #23	https://www.egov.state.mn.us/Commerce/license_lookup.do?action=lookupForm
Debt Prorate Company #24	www.commerce.state.mn.us/pages/FinService/FSLicensees/DP.HTM
Dentist /Dental Assistant /Hygienist #5	https://www.hlb.state.mn.us/mnbod/glsweb/homeframe.aspx
Electrician #6	www.electricity.state.mn.us/Elec_lic/index.html
Emergency Medical Technician #28	www.emsrb.state.mn.us/cert.asp?p=s
EMS Examiner #28	www.emsrb.state.mn.us/examiner.asp?p=s
Engineer #37	www.aelslagid.state.mn.us/roster.html
Esthetician #23	https://www.egov.state.mn.us/Commerce/license_lookup.do?action=lookupForm
Funeral Director #27	www.health.state.mn.us/divs/hpsc/mortsci/mortsciselect.cfm
Funeral Establishment #27	www.health.state.mn.us/divs/hpsc/mortsci/mortsciselect.cfm
Gambling Equipment Dist./Mfg. #35	www.gcb.state.mn.us/
Gambling, Lawful Organization #35	www.gcb.state.mn.us/
Geologist #37	www.aelslagid.state.mn.us/roster.html
Grain Licensing #21	http://www2.mda.state.mn.us/webapp/lis/default.jsp
Insurance Agency/Agent/Salesman #23	https://www.egov.state.mn.us/Commerce/license_lookup.do?action=lookupForm
Interior Designer #37	www.aelslagid.state.mn.us/roster.html
Landscape Architect #37	www.aelslagid.state.mn.us/roster.html
Lender, Small #24	www.commerce.state.mn.us/pages/FinService/FSLicensees/SL.HTM
Liquor Onsale Store #34	www.dps.state.mn.us/alcgamb/alcenf/liquorlic/liquorlic.html
Livestock Dealer/Market/Weigher #21	http://www2.mda.state.mn.us/webapp/lis/default.jsp
Loan Company #24	www.commerce.state.mn.us/pages/FinService/FSLicensees/RL.HTM
Lobbyist #19	www.cfboard.state.mn.us/Lobby.htm
Lottery Retailer #42	www.lottery.state.mn.us/retailer/lookup.html
LPA #39	www.boa.state.mn.us/Contact/contact_us.html
Managing General Agent #23	https://www.egov.state.mn.us/Commerce/license_lookup.do?action=lookupForm
Manicurist #23	https://www.egov.state.mn.us/Commerce/license_lookup.do?action=lookupForm
Medical Doctor #9	www.docboard.org/mn/df/mndf.htm
Midwife #9	www.docboard.org/mn/df/mndf.htm
Money Transmitter #24	www.commerce.state.mn.us/pages/FinService/FSLicensees/MoneyTransmitList.pdf
Mortgage Originator/Servicer, Residential #24	https://www.egov.state.mn.us/Commerce/license_lookup.do?action=lookupForm
Mortician #27	www.health.state.mn.us/divs/hpsc/mortsci/mortsciselect.cfm
Motor Vehicle Financer #24	www.commerce.state.mn.us/pages/FinService/FSLicensees/MV.HTM
Notary Public #23	https://www.egov.state.mn.us/Commerce/license_lookup.do?action=lookupForm
Nurse, LPN-RN #10	www.nursingboard.state.mn.us
Occupational Therapist/Assistant #29	www.health.state.mn.us/divs/hpsc/hop/otp/licprac.html
Optometrist #11	www.arbo.org/odfinder/LicSearch.asp
Pesticide Applicator Company #22	http://www2.mda.state.mn.us/webapp/lis/pestappdefault.jsp

Pesticide Applicator, Private #22	http://www2.mda.state.mn.us/webapp/PrivApp/default.jsp
Physical Therapist #9	www.docboard.org/mn/df/mndf.htm
Physician Assistant #9	www.docboard.org/mn/df/mndf.htm
Political Candidate #19	www.cfboard.state.mn.us/legcand.html
Professional Firm #9	www.docboard.org/mn/df/mndf.htm
Public Accountant-CPA #39	www.boa.state.mn.us/Contact/contact_us.html
Real Estate Agent/Broker/Dealer #23	https://www.egov.state.mn.us/Commerce/license_lookup.do?action=lookupForm
Re-Insurance Intermediary #23	https://www.egov.state.mn.us/Commerce/license_lookup.do?action=lookupForm
Respiratory Care Practitioner #9	www.docboard.org/mn/df/mndf.htm
Soil Scientist #37	www.aelslagid.state.mn.us/roster.html
Surgeon #9	www.docboard.org/mn/df/mndf.htm
Surveyor, Land #37	www.aelslagid.state.mn.us/roster.html
Teacher #17	(search site being reconstructed)
Telemedicine #9	www.docboard.org/mn/df/mndf.htm
Thrift/Industrial Loan Company #24	www.commerce.state.mn.us/pages/FinService/FSLicensees/IL.HTM
Underground Storage Tank Contr./Spvr. #43	www.pca.state.mn.us/cleanup/ust.html#certification
Weather Modifier #21	http://www2.mda.state.mn.us/webapp/lis/default.jsp

Minnesota Licensing Quick Finder

Abstractor #23	651-296-6319
Abstractor/Abstractor Company #25	800-657-3978
Acupuncturist #9	612-617-2130
Adjuster #23	651-296-6319
Adoption/Guardianship Agency #30	651-296-0584
Alarm & Com. System Contr./Instal. #6	651-642-0800
Alcohol/Drug Counselor #29	651-282-5619
All-Terrain Vehicle Registration #32	651-296-2316
Ambulance Service/Personnel #28	612-627-6000
Applicant Background Study & Inv #30	651-296-3971
Appraiser #23	651-296-6319
Architect #37	651-297-2208
Asbestos Abatem't Contr./Worker #26	651-215-0900
Assessor, Accredited/Specialist #1	651-296-0209
Athletic Trainer #9	612-617-2130
Attorney #40	651-296-2254
Attorney Specialist #31	651-297-1857
Audiologist #29	651-282-5629
Auditor #39	651-296-7938
Bank #24	651-297-3779
Barber #2	651-642-0489
Bingo Operation #35	651-639-4000
Boat & Canoe Registration #32	651-296-2316
Boat Title #32	651-296-2316
Boats for Hire #36	651-284-5080
Boiler Inspector #36	651-284-5080
Bondsman (Insurance) #23	651-296-6319
Building Contractor, Residential #23	651-296-6319
Campground Membership Agent #23	651-296-6319
Chemical Dependency Profession'l #30	651-582-1832
Child Care Facility #30	651-296-3971
Children's Service #30	651-297-3840
Chiropractor #4	612-617-2223
Collection Agency #23	651-296-6319
Consumer Credit/Payday Lender #24	651-296-2297
Contractor/Remodeler, Resd'l #23	651-296-6319
Controlled substance #13	612-617-2201
Cosmetologist #23	651-296-6319
Cosmetology School/Shop #23	651-296-6319
County Fair #41	952-496-7950
Credit Union #24	651-296-2297
Crematory #27	651-282-3829
Currency Exchange #23	651-296-6319
Debt Collector #23	651-296-6319
Debt Prorate Company #24	651-296-2297
Dental Assistant #5	888-240-4762, 612-617-2250
Dental Hygienist #5	888-240-4762, 612-617-2250
Dentist #5	888-240-4762, 612-617-2250
Developmental Disabilities License #30	651-582-1998
Dietitian #46	612-617-2175
Electrician #6	651-642-0800
Emergency Medical Technician #28	612-627-6000

EMS Examiner #28	612-627-6000
Engineer #37	651-296-2388
Esthetician #23	651-296-6319
Food Manager #26	651-215-0870
Foster Care Program #30	651-296-3971
Funeral Director #27	651-282-3829
Funeral Establishment #27	651-282-3829
Gambling Equipment Dist./Mfg. #35	651-639-4000
Gambling, Lawful Organization #35	651-639-4000
Geologist #37	651-296-2388
Grain Licensing #21	651-296-2980
Hearing Aid Dispenser #29	651-282-5620
High Pressure Inspector #36	651-284-5080
Insurance Agency #23	651-296-6319
Insurance Agent/Salesman #23	651-296-6319
Interior Designer #37	651-296-2388
Landscape Architect #37	651-296-2388
Lender, Small #24	651-296-2297
Liquor and Wine Offsale Retail #34	651-296-9519
Liquor Consumption & Display Info #34	651-296-6439
Liquor On-sale Retail #34	651-296-6939
Liquor Store, On-sale Retail/Muni'l #34	651-215-6209
Liquor Whlse/Mfg./Labeler/Importer #34	651-296-6939
Livestock Dealer/Market #21	651-297-5509
Livestock Weigher #21	651-296-2980
Loan Company #24	651-296-2297
Lobbyist #19	651-296-5148
Lottery Retailer #42	651-635-8119
LPA #39	651-296-7938
Managing General Agent #23	651-296-6319
Manicurist #23	800-657-3978
Manufactured Home Installer #38	651-296-8458
Manufactured Home Mfg./Dealer #38	651-296-4628
Manufactured Structures Section #38	651-296-4628
Marriage & Family Therapist #8	612-617-2220
Med Gas Dist #13	612-617-2201
Medical Doctor #9	612-617-2130
Mental Health Practitioner, Unlicensed #29	651-282-5621
Mental Health, Chemical Dependency Professional #30	651-582-1990
Midwife #9	612-617-2130
Money Transmitter #24	651-296-2297
Mortgage Originator/Servicer, Resid'l #24	651-282-9855
Mortician #27	651-282-3829
Motor Vehicle Financer #24	651-296-2297
Notary Public #23	651-296-6319
Nurse-LPN #10	612-617-2270
Nurse-RN #10	612-617-2270
Nursing Home Administrator #7	612-617-2117
Nutritionist #46	612-617-2175

Occupational Therapist/Assistant #29	651-282-5624
Off-Highway Motorcycle #32	651-296-2316
Off-Road Vehicle #32	651-296-2316
Optometrist #11	612-617-2173
Pesticide Applicator Company #22	651-297-2200
Pharmaceutical Mfg./Whlse #13	612-617-2201
Pharmaceutical Technician #13	612-617-2201
Pharmacist #13	612-617-2201
Pharmacy #13	612-617-2201
Physical Therapist #9	612-627-5406
Physician Assistant #9	612-617-2130
Plumber #26	651-215-0836
Podiatrist #14	612-617-2200
Police (Peace) Officer #12	651-643-3060
Political Candidate #19	651-296-5148
Private Detective / Investigator #44	651-793-2666
Professional Firm #9	612-617-2130
Psychological Practitioner #15	651-617-2230
Psychologist #15	651-617-2230
Public Accountant-CPA #39	651-296-7938
Racetrack/Card Club Operator #41	952-496-7950
Racing (Racing Class "A"- Owners of Track) #41	952-496-7950
Racing/Card Club Occupation #41	952-496-7950
Real Estate Agent/Broker/Dealer #23	651-296-6319
Re-Insurance Intermediary #23	651-296-6319
Respiratory Care Practitioner #9	612-617-2130
Sanitarian #26	651-215-0870
Securities Sales/Investm'tAdvisor #23	651-296-2283
Security Agent/Protective Agent #44	651-793-2666
Snowmobile Registration #32	651-296-2316
Social Worker #16	612-617-2100
Soil Scientist #37	651-296-2388
Speech-Language Pathologist #29	651-282-5629
Surgeon #9	612-617-2130
Surveyor, Land #37	651-296-2388
Teacher #17	651-582-8691
Telemedicine #9	612-617-2130
Thrift/Industrial Loan Company #24	651-296-2297
Underground Storage Tank Contr./Supervisor #43	651-297-8616
Veterinarian #18	612-617-2170
Waste Disposal Facility Inspector #43	651-296-7162
Waste Water Disposal Facility Operator #43	651-296-7162
Water Conditioning Installer/Contr. #26	651-215-0836
Water Supply Operator #26	651-215-0770
Water Well Contractor #26	651-215-0811
Watercraft #32	651-296-2316
Weather Modifier #21	651-296-0591
X-ray Operator #20	651-643-2151

Minnesota Licensing Agency Information

1 Board of Assessors, Mail Station 3340, St Paul, MN 55146-3340; 651-556-6086, Fax: 651-556-3128.   www.taxes.state.mn.us Email: pam.e.lundgrn@state.mn.us

2 Board of Barber Examiners, 1885 University Ave W, #335, St Paul, MN 55104-3403; 651-642-0489, Fax: 651-649-5997.

3 Department of Commerce, Board of Boxing (Abolished in 2001), St Paul, MN 55101.

4 Board of Chiropractic Examiners, 2829 University Ave SE, ste 300, Minneapolis, MN 55414-3220; 612-617-2222, Fax: 612-617-2224. www.mn-chiroboard.state.mn.us Email: chiropractic.board@state.mn.us Search Database at https://www.hlb.state.mn.us/chi/publicaccess/search.asp

5 Board of Dentistry, 2829 University Ave SE, #450, Minneapolis, MN 55414; 888-240-4762, 612-617-2250, Fax: 612-617-2260. www.dentalboard.state.mn.us Email: julie.jeppesen@state.mn.us Search Database at https://www.hlb.state.mn.us/mnbod/glsweb/homeframe.aspx

6 Board of Electricity, 1821 University - RM S-128, St Paul, MN 55104; 651-642-0800, Fax: 651-642-0441. www.electricity.state.mn.us   Search Database at www.electricity.state.mn.us/Elec_lic/index.html

7 Board of Examiners for Nursing Home Administrators, 2829 University Ave SE #440, Minneapolis, MN 55414; 612-617-2117, Fax: 612-617-2119. www.benha.state.mn.us   Email: benha@state.mn.us

8 Board of Marriage & Family Therapy, 2829 University Ave SE #330, Minneapolis, MN 55414-3222; 612-617-2220, Fax: 612-617-2221. www.bmft.state.mn.us email:robert.butler@state.mn.us

9 Board of Medical Practice, 2829 University Ave SE, #400, Minneapolis, MN 55414-3246; 612-617-2130, Fax: 612-617-2166. www.bmp.state.mn.us Email: medical.board@state.mn.us Search Database at www.docboard.org/mn/df/mndf.htm

10 Board of Nursing, 2829 University Ave SE, #500, Minneapolis, MN 55414; 612-617-2181, Fax: 612-617-2190. www.nursingboard.state.mn.us Email: nursing.board@state.mn.us Search Database at www.nursingboard.state.mn.us

11 Board of Optometry, 2829 University Av SE #550, Minneapolis, MN 55414; 612-617-2173, Fax: 612-617-2174. www.odfinder.org/LicSearch.asp Email: optometry.board@state.mn.us   Search Database at www.arbo.org/odfinder/LicSearch.asp

12 Board of Peace Officers Standards & Training, 1600 University Av #200, St Paul, MN 55104-3825; 651-643-3060, Fax: 651-643-3072. www.dps.state.mn.us/newpost/ Email: neil.melton@state.mn.us

13 Board of Pharmacy, 2829 University Ave SE, #530, Minneapolis, MN 55414-3251; 612-617-2201, Fax: 651-617-2212. www.phcybrd.state.mn.us Email: pharmacy.board@state.mn.us

14 Board of Podiatric Medicine, 2829 University Av SE #430, Minneapolis, MN 55414; 612-617-2200, Fax: 612-617-2698. www.podiatry.state.mn.us Email: benesh.pod@state.mn.us

15 Board of Psychology, 2829 University Ave. SE, #320, Minneapolis, MN 55414-3237; 612-612-2230, Fax: 612-617-2240. www.psychologyboard.state.mn.us Email: psychology.board@state.mn.us Note: Written requests only. There may be a $20 per name verification fee.

16 Board of Social Work, 2829 University Ave SE, #340, Minneapolis, MN 55414-3239; 612-617-2100, Fax: 612-617-2103. www.socialwork.state.mn.us Email: social.work@state.mn.us

17 Licensing Unit, Department of Education, Board of Teaching, 1500 Highway 36 W, Roseville, MN 55113-4266; 651-582-8691, Fax: 651-582-8809. http://education.state.mn.us/stellent/groups/public/documents/translatedcontent/pub_intro_licensure.jsp Email: personnellicensing@state.mn.us

18 Board of Veterinary Medicine, 2829 University Ave SE, Minneapolis, MN 55414; 612-617-2170, Fax: 612-617-2172. www.vetmed.state.mn.us Email: vet.med@state.mn.us

19 Division of Plant Health, Campaign Finance Board, 658 Cedar St, Centennial Bld, 1st Fl, St Paul, MN 55155; 651-296-5148, Fax: 651-296-1722.   www.cfboard.state.mn.us Email: cf.board@state.mn.us Search Database at www.cfboard.state.mn.us/

20 Department of Health, Radiation Control, 1645 Energy Park Dr #300, St Paul, MN 55108; 651-643-2151, Fax: 651-613-2152. www.health.state.mn.us/divs/eh/radiation/

21 Department of Agriculture, Livestock Weighing & Licensing, 90 W Plato Blvd, St Paul, MN 55107; 651-297-2980, Fax: 651-297-2504. www.mda.state.mn.us   Search database at http://www2.mda.state.mn.us/webapp/lis/default.jsp

22 Department of Agriculture, Pesticide Registration, 90 W Plato Blvd, St Paul, MN 55107; 651-297-2200, Fax: 651-297-2271. www.mda.state.mn.us   Search Database at www.mda.state.mn.us/lis/default.htm

23 Department of Commerce, Licenses, Registration, Certification Division, 85 7th Pl E #500, St Paul, MN 55101-2198; 800-657-3978, Fax: 651-284-4107.   www.commerce.state.mn.us Email: licensing.commerce@state.mn.us Note: For securities registration requests, you may email securities.commerce@state.mn.us.

24 Department of Commerce, Division of Financial Exams, 85 7th Place E #500, St Paul, MN 55101; 651-298-4026, Fax: 651-296-8591. www.commerce.state.mn.us Email: commerce@state.mn.us Search at www.commerce.state.mn.us/pages/FinService/FSLicensees/

25 Department of Commerce, Licensing Unit for Abstractors, 85 7th Pl E #600, St Paul, MN 55101-2198; 800-657-3978.   www.state.mn.us/cgi-bin/portal/mn/jsp/home.do?agency=Commerce

26 Department of Health, Environmental Health Division, 121 E 7th Pl #230, St Paul, MN 55164-0975; 651-215-0700, Fax: 651-215-0979. www.health.state.mn.us/divs/eh/

27 Department of Health, Mortuary Science Section, PO Box 64975, St Paul, MN 55164-0975; 651-282-3829, Fax: 651-282-3839.   www.health.state.mn.us/divs/hpsc/mortsci/mortsci.htm Email: mortsci@health.state.mn.us Search at www.health.state.mn.us/divs/hpsc/mortsci/finda.htm

28 Emergency Medical Services, Regulatory Board, 2829 University Av SE #310, Minneapolis, MN 55414-3222; 612-627-6000, Fax: 612-627-5442.   www.emsrb.state.mn.us Search Database at www.emsrb.state.mn.us

29 Health Occupation Programs, Health Policy & Systems Compliance, 121 E 7th Pl #450, Metro Square Bldg, St Paul, MN 55164-0975; 651-282-6366, Fax: 651-282-5628. www.health.state.mn.us/divs/hpsc/hop/home/homepg.html Note: Online searching is under construction, check the website.

30 Department of Human Services, 444 Lafayette Rd, St Paul, MN 55155; 651-296-6117, Fax: 651-297-1490.   www.dhs.state.mn.us

31 State Board of Law Examiners, Board of Legal Certification, St. Galtier Plaza, #201, St Paul, MN 55101; 651-297-1857, Fax: 651-296-5866. www.blc.state.mn.us/Specialty_Fields/specialty_fields.html   Search Database at http://mail.statebar.gen.mn.us/search/search.asp Note: The web search features only Bar Association members.

32 Department of Natural Resources, License Bureau, 500 Lafayette Rd, St Paul, MN 55155; 651-296-2316, Fax: 651-297-8851. www.dnr.state.mn.us   Email: info@dnr.state.mn.us

34 Department of Public Safety, Alcohol & Gambling Enforcement, 444 Cedar St #133, St Paul, MN 55101-5133; 651-296-6159, Fax: 651-297-5259. www.dps.state.mn.us/alcgamb/alcenf/alcenf.html Email: dps.webmaster@state.mn.us Search Database at www.dps.state.mn.us/alcgamb/alcenf/liquorlic/liquorlic.html Note: Also, search the liquor license database at www.dps.state.mn.us/alcgamb/New_Folder/search1.asp.

35 Gambling Control Board, 1711 W County B, #300 South, Roseville, MN 55113; 651-639-4000. www.gcb.state.mn.us Search Database at www.gcb.state.mn.us

36 Labor & Industry, Code Administration & Inspection Services, 443 Lafayette Rd, St Paul, MN 55155-4304; 651-284-5080, Fax: 651-284-5737. www.doli.state.mn.us/code.html Email: dli.code@state.mn.us

37 Board of AELSLAGID, Licensing Boards, 85 E 7th Pl #160, St Paul, MN 55101; 651-296-2388, Fax: 651-297-5310.   Search Database at www.aelslagid.state.mn.us/roster.html

38 Building Codes & Standards Division, Manufactured Structures Section, 408 Metro Square Bldg, 121 7th Pl E, St Paul, MN 55101-2181; 800-657-3944, 651-297-7081, Fax: 651-297-1973. www.admin.state.mn.us/buildingcodes

39 Board of Accountancy, 85 E. 7th Pl #125, St Paul, MN 55101;
651-296-7938, Fax: 651-282-2644.
www.boa.state.mn.us/Contact/contact_us.html

40 Supreme Court, Attorney Registration, 25 Rev. Martin Luther King Jr. Blvd. #305, St Paul, MN 55155; 651-296-2254, Fax: 651-297-4149.
www.courts.state.mn.us
Email: attorneyregistration@courts.state.mn.us
Search Database at www.courts.state.mn.us/mars/default.aspx Note: Lists are also available to download for free at the search page.

41 Racing Commission, PO Box 630, Shakopee, MN 55379; 952-496-7950, Fax: 952-496-7954.
www.mnrace.commission.state.mn.us/
Email: colleen.hurlbert@state.mn.us

42 State Lottery, 2645 Long Lake Rd, Roseville, MN 55113; 651-635-8100, Fax: 651-297-7498.
www.lottery.state.mn.us
Email: drewv@msl.state.mn.us   Search Database at www.lottery.state.mn.us/retailer/lookup.html

43 Pollution Control Agency, 520 Lafayette Rd N, St Paul, MN 55155-4194;
651-297-8367, Fax: 651-282-6247.

www.pca.state.mn.us/index.cfm
Email: webmaster@pca.state.mn.us

44 Private Detective & Protective Agent Services Board, 1430 E Maryland Ave, St Paul, MN 55106; 651-793-2666, Fax: 651-793-7065.
www.dps.state.mn.us/pdb/
Email: mn.pdb@state.mn.us

46 Board of Dietetics & Nutrition Practice, 2829 University Ave SE #555, Minneapolis, MN 55414-3250; 612-617-2175, Fax: 612- 617-2174.
www.dieteticsnutritionboard.state.mn.us/
Email: board.dietetics-nutrition@state.mn.us

Minnesota Federal Courts

The following list indicates the district and division name for each county in the state. If the bankruptcy court location is different from the district court, then the location of the bankruptcy court appears in parentheses.

County/Court Cross Reference

County	Court	County	Court
Aitkin	Duluth	Martin	Minneapolis (St Paul)
Anoka	Minneapolis	McLeod	Minneapolis
Becker	Minneapolis (Fergus Falls)	Meeker	Minneapolis
Beltrami	Minneapolis (Fergus Falls)	Mille Lacs	Duluth
Benton	Duluth	Morrison	Duluth
Big Stone	Minneapolis (Fergus Falls)	Mower	Minneapolis (St Paul)
Blue Earth	Minneapolis (St Paul)	Murray	Minneapolis (St Paul)
Brown	Minneapolis (St Paul)	Nicollet	Minneapolis (St Paul)
Carlton	Duluth	Nobles	Minneapolis (St Paul)
Carver	Minneapolis	Norman	Minneapolis (Fergus Falls)
Cass	Duluth	Olmsted	Minneapolis (St Paul)
Chippewa	Minneapolis	Otter Tail	Minneapolis (Fergus Falls)
Chisago	Minneapolis (St Paul)	Pennington	Minneapolis (Fergus Falls)
Clay	Minneapolis (Fergus Falls)	Pine	Duluth
Clearwater	Minneapolis (Fergus Falls)	Pipestone	Minneapolis (St Paul)
Cook	Duluth	Polk	Minneapolis (Fergus Falls)
Cottonwood	Minneapolis (St Paul)	Pope	Minneapolis (Fergus Falls)
Crow Wing	Duluth	Ramsey	St Paul
Dakota	Minneapolis (St Paul)	Red Lake	Minneapolis (Fergus Falls)
Dodge	Minneapolis (St Paul)	Redwood	Minneapolis (St Paul)
Douglas	Minneapolis (Fergus Falls)	Renville	Minneapolis
Faribault	Minneapolis (St Paul)	Rice	Minneapolis (St Paul)
Fillmore	Minneapolis (St Paul)	Rock	Minneapolis (St Paul)
Freeborn	Minneapolis (St Paul)	Roseau	Minneapolis (Fergus Falls)
Goodhue	Minneapolis (St Paul)	Scott	Minneapolis (St Paul)
Grant	Minneapolis (Fergus Falls)	Sherburne	Minneapolis
Hennepin	Minneapolis	Sibley	Minneapolis (St Paul)
Houston	Minneapolis (St Paul)	St. Louis	Duluth
Hubbard	Minneapolis (Fergus Falls)	Stearns	Minneapolis (Fergus Falls)
Isanti	Minneapolis	Steele	Minneapolis (St Paul)
Itasca	Duluth	Stevens	Minneapolis (Fergus Falls)
Jackson	Minneapolis (St Paul)	Swift	Minneapolis
Kanabec	Duluth	Todd	Minneapolis (Fergus Falls)
Kandiyohi	Minneapolis	Traverse	Minneapolis (Fergus Falls)
Kittson	Minneapolis (Fergus Falls)	Wabasha	Minneapolis (St Paul)
Koochiching	Duluth	Wadena	Minneapolis (Fergus Falls)
Lac qui Parle	Minneapolis (St Paul)	Waseca	Minneapolis (St Paul)
Lake	Duluth	Washington	Minneapolis (St Paul)
Lake of the Woods	Minneapolis (Fergus Falls)	Watonwan	Minneapolis (St Paul)
Le Sueur	Minneapolis (St Paul)	Wilkin	Minneapolis (Fergus Falls)
Lincoln	Minneapolis (St Paul)	Winona	Minneapolis (St Paul)
Lyon	Minneapolis (St Paul)	Wright	Minneapolis
Mahnomen	Minneapolis (Fergus Falls)	Yellow Medicine	Minneapolis (St Paul)
Marshall	Minneapolis (Fergus Falls)		

Standards for Federal Courts: The search fee is $20.00 per item (one party name or case number). Certification fee is $7.00 per document. Copy fee is $.50 per page. All fees standard unless noted in profile. Mail Search: always enclose a stamped self addressed envelope unless otherwise noted. Most courts accept fax requests or will suggest a copying/search vendor. Before releasing records, all courts require prepayment unless noted in profile.

Open records are located at the court unless otherwise noted. District courts index by defendant and plaintiff as well as by case number. Bankruptcy courts usually index by debtor and case number. While most courts now have their indexes on computer, many still maintain index card files as well.

The universal PACER sign-up number is 800-676-6856. Find PACER and the Party/Case Index on the Web at http://pacer.psc.uscourts.gov. PACER dial-up access is $.60 per minute. Also, courts offering internet access via RACER, PACER, Web-PACER or the new CM-ECF charge $.07 per page fee unless noted as free.

US District Court

District of Minnesota

Duluth Division Clerk's Office, 417 Federal Bldg, 515 W. 1st St., Duluth, MN 55802-1397 (courier address: Use mail address for courier delivery) 218-529-3500, Fax: 218-529-3505. www.mnd.uscourts.gov

Counties: Aitkin, Becker*, Beltrami*, Benton, Big Stone*, Carlton, Cass, Clay*, Clearwater*, Cook, Crow Wing, Douglas*, Grant*, Hubbard*, Itasca, Kanabec, Kittson*, Koochiching, Lake, Lake of the Woods*, Mahnomen*, Marshall*, Mille Lacs, Morrison, Norman*, OtterTail,* Pennington*, Pine, Polk*, Pope*, Red Lake*, Roseau*, Stearns*, Stevens*, St. Louis, Todd*, Traverse*, Wadena*, Wilkin*. From March 1, 1995, to 1998, cases from the counties marked with an asterisk (*) were heard here.Before and after that period, cases were and are allocated between St. Paul and Minneapolis.

Indexing & Storage: New cases available in the index immediately after filing date.

Fee & Payment: Payment may be made by money order, cashier check, personal check. Payee: Clerk, U.S. District Court.

Phone Search: Only docket information available by phone.

Mail Search: A SASE not required.

In Person Search: Fee charged if court conducts your in person search for you.

PACER: PACER is available online at http://pacer.mnd.uscourts.gov. New records are online after 1 day.

Electronic Filing: Electronic filing information at https://ecf.mnd.uscourts.gov/cgi-bin/login.pl

Minneapolis Division Court Clerk, Room 202, 300 S 4th St, Minneapolis, MN 55415 (courier address: Use mail address for courier delivery) 612-664-5000, Fax: 612-664-5033. www.mnd.uscourts.gov

Counties: All counties not covered by the Duluth Division. Cases are allocated between Minneapolis and St Paul.

Indexing & Storage: New cases available in the index immediately after filing date. Records are also indexed on microfiche.

Fee & Payment: Payment may be made by money order, cashier check, personal check. Payee: Clerk, U.S. District Court.

Phone Search: The case number and parties involved will be released over the phone.

Mail Search: A SASE not required.

In Person Search: Fee charged if court conducts your in person search for you.

PACER: PACER is available online at http://pacer.mnd.uscourts.gov. New records are online after 1 day.

Electronic Filing: Electronic filing information at https://ecf.mnd.uscourts.gov/cgi-bin/login.pl

St Paul Division 700 Federal Bldg, 316 N Robert, St Paul, MN 55101 (courier address: Use mail address for courier delivery) 651-848-1100, Fax: 651-848-1109. www.mnd.uscourts.gov

Counties: All counties not covered by the Duluth Division. Cases are allocated between Minneapolis and St Paul.

Indexing & Storage: New cases available in the index immediately after filing date. Records are also indexed on microfiche.

Fee & Payment: Payment may be made by money order, cashier check, personal check. Payee: Clerk, U.S. District Court.

Phone Search: Only the case number and parties involved will be released over the phone.

Mail Search: A SASE not required.

In Person Search: Fee charged if court conducts your in person search for you.

PACER: PACER is available online at http://pacer.mnd.uscourts.gov. New records are online after 1 day.

Electronic Filing: Electronic filing information at https://ecf.mnd.uscourts.gov/cgi-bin/login.pl

U.S. Bankruptcy Court

District of Minnesota

Duluth Division 416 U.S. Courthouse, 515 W 1st St, Duluth, MN 55802 (courier address: Use mail address for courier delivery) 218-529-3600. www.mnb.uscourts.gov

Counties: Aitkin, Benton, Carlton, Cass, Cook, Crow Wing, Itasca, Kanabec, Koochiching, Lake, Mille Lacs, Morrison, Pine, St. Louis. A petition commencing Chapter 11 or 12 proceedings may initially be filed in any of the four divisons, but may be assigned toanother division.

Indexing & Storage: Cases indexed by debtor as well as by case number. New cases available in the index 1-2 days after filing date. Chapter 7 and 13 cases in Benton, Kanabec, Mille Lacs, Morrison and Pine may also be filed in St.Paul.

Fee & Payment: Payment may be made by money order, personal check. Payee: Clerk, U.S. Bankruptcy Court.

Phone Search: Only basic information is released over the phone. Automated voice case information service (VCIS) is available. Call VCIS at 800-959-9002 or 612-664-5302.

Mail Search: A SASE not required.

In Person Search: Fee charged if court conducts your in person search for you.

PACER: PACER online is not available. Local access: 651-848-1096. Records purged up to April 1996. New civil records are online after 1 day.

Electronic Filing: Currently in the process of implementing CM/ECF.

Other Online Access: Search records using the Web at www.mnb.uscourts.gov/ers-bin/mnb-651-main.pl. Searching is currently free. Images go back to 1997.

Fergus Falls Division 204 U.S. Courthouse, 118 S Mill St, Fergus Falls, MN 56537 (courier address: Use mail address for courier delivery) 218-739-4671. www.mnb.uscourts.gov

Counties: Becker, Beltrami, Big Stone, Clay, Clearwater, Douglas, Grant, Hubbard, Kittson, Lake of the Woods, Mahnomen, Marshall, Norman, Otter Tail, Pennington, Polk, Pope, Red Lake, Roseau, Stearns, Stevens, Todd, Traverse, Wadena, Wilkin. A petition commencingChapter 11 or 12 proceedings may be filed initially in any of the four divisions, but may then be assigned to another division.

Indexing & Storage: Cases indexed by debtor as well as by case number. New cases available in the index immediately after filing date.

Fee & Payment: Payment may be made by money order, cashier check, personal check. Payee: U.S. Bankruptcy Court.

Phone Search: Only docket information available by phone. Automated voice case information service (VCIS) is available. Call VCIS at 800-959-9002 or 612-664-5302.

Mail Search: A SASE not required.

In Person Search: Fee charged if court conducts your in person search for you.

PACER: PACER online is not available. Local access: 651-848-1096. Records purged up to April 1996. New civil records are online after 1 day.

Electronic Filing: Currently in the process of implementing CM/ECF.

Other Online Access: Search records using the Web at www.mnb.uscourts.gov/ers-bin/mnb-651-main.pl. Searching is currently free. Images go back to 1997.

Minneapolis Division 301 U.S. Courthouse, 300 S 4th St, Minneapolis, MN 55415 (courier address: Use mail address for courier delivery) 612-664-5200. www.mnb.uscourts.gov

Counties: Anoka, Carver, Chippewa, Hennepin, Isanti, Kandiyohi, McLeod, Meeker, Renville, Sherburne, Swift, Wright. Initial petitions for Chapter 11 or 12 may be filed initially at any of the four divisions, but may then be assigned to a judge in another division.

Indexing & Storage: Cases indexed by as well as by case number. New cases available in the index immediately after filing date. Records are also indexed on microfiche. District wide searches are available for information from 1994 from this court. This division holds closed cases from St. Paul for 4 years (no indexing available at this office).

Fee & Payment: Payment may be made by money order, cashier check, personal check. Payee: Clerk, U.S. Bankruptcy Court.

Phone Search: Only basic information is released over the phone. Automated voice case information service (VCIS) is available. Call VCIS at 800-959-9002 or 612-664-5302.

Mail Search: A SASE not required.

In Person Search: Fee charged if court conducts your in person search for you.

PACER: PACER online is not available. Local access: 651-848-1096. Records purged up to April 1996. New civil records are online after 1 day.

Electronic Filing: Currently in the process of implementing CM/ECF.

Other Online Access: Search records using the Web at www.mnb.uscourts.gov/ers-bin/mnb-651-main.pl. Searching is currently free. Images go back to 1997.

St Paul Division 200 U.S. Courthouse, 316 N Robert St, St Paul, MN 55101 (courier address: Use mail address for courier delivery) 651-848-1000. www.mnb.uscourts.gov

Counties: Blue Earth, Brown, Chisago, Cottonwood, Dakota, Dodge, Faribault, Fillmore, Freeborn, Goodhue, Houston, Jackson, Lac qui Parle, Le Sueur, Lincoln, Lyon, Martin, Mower, Murray, Nicollet, Nobles, Olmsted, Pipestone, Ramsey, Redwood, Rice, Rock, Scott,Sibley, Steele, Wabasha, Waseca, Washington, Watonwan, Winona, Yellow Medicine. Cases from Benton, Kanabec, Mille Lacs, Morrison and Pine may also be heard here. A petition commencing Chapter 11 or 12 proceedings may be filed initially with any of thefour divisions, but may then be assigned to another division.

Indexing & Storage: Cases indexed by debtor as well as by case number. New cases available in the index 1 day after filing date.

Fee & Payment: Payment may be made by money order, cashier check, personal check. Payee: Clerk, U.S. Bankruptcy Court.

Phone Search: Only docket information available by phone. Automated voice case information service (VCIS) is available. Call VCIS at 800-959-9002 or 612-664-5302.

Mail Search: A SASE not required.

In Person Search: Fee charged if court conducts your in person search for you.

PACER: PACER online is not available. Local access: 651-848-1096. Records purged up to April 1996. New civil records are online after 1 day.

Electronic Filing: Currently in the process of implementing CM/ECF.

Other Online Access: Search records using the Web at www.mnb.uscourts.gov/ers-bin/mnb-651-main.pl. Searching is currently free. Images go back to 1997.

Minnesota County Courts

Court	Jurisdiction	No. of Courts	How Organized
District Courts*	General	97	10 Districts

* Profiled in this Sourcebook.

Court	CIVIL								
	Tort	Contract	Real Estate	Min. Claim	Max. Claim	Small Claims	Estate	Eviction	Domestic Relations
District Courts*	X	X	X	$0	No Max	$7500	X	X	X

Court	CRIMINAL				
	Felony	Misdemeanor	DWI/DUI	Preliminary Hearing	Juvenile
District Courts*	X	X	X		X

ADMINISTRATION

State Court Adminstrator, 135 Minn. Judicial Center, 25 Constitution Ave, St Paul, MN, 55155; 651-296-2474, Fax: 651-297-5636. www.courts.state.mn.us

COURT STRUCTURE

There are 97 District Courts (some counties gave divisional courts) comprising 10 judicial districts. Effective July 1, 1994, the limit for small claims was raised from $5000 to $7500. The limit is $4,000 if it involves a consumer credit transaction.

ONLINE ACCESS

Appellate and Supreme Court opinions are available from the web site. There is an online system in place that allows internal and external access for government personnel only.

ADDITIONAL INFORMATION

Statewide certification and copy fees are as follows: Certification: $10.00 per document, Copy Fee: $5.00 per document (not per page).

An exact name is required to search, e.g., a request for "Robert Smith" will not result in finding "Bob Smith." The requester must request both names and pay two search and copy fees.

When a search is permitted by "plaintiff or defendant," most jurisdictions stated that a case is indexed by only the 1st plaintiff or defendant, and a 2nd or 3rd party would not be sufficient to search.

The 3rd, 5th, 8th and 10th Judicial Districts no longer will perform criminal record searches for the public.

Most courts take personal checks. Exceptions are noted.

📖 📖 📖 📖 📖 📖 📖

Aitkin County

9th Judicial District Court 209 Second St NW, Aitkin, MN 56431; 218-927-7350; Fax: 218-927-4535. Hours: 8AM-4:30PM (CST). *Felony, Misdemeanor, Civil, Eviction, Small Claims, Probate.*

Civil Records: Access: Mail, in person. Both court and visitors may perform in person searches. Search fee: $5.00 per name. Required to search: name, years to search. Civil cases indexed by defendant, plaintiff. Civil records on computer from 2/90, cards to 1982, index books prior.

Criminal Records: Access: Mail, in person. Both court and visitors may perform in person searches. Search fee: $5.00 per name. Required to search: name, years to search, DOB. Criminal records on computer from 2/90, cards to 1982, index books prior.

General Information: Public Access terminal is available. No adoption, juvenile, sex offender or sealed records released. Copy fee: $5.00 per document. Certification fee: $10.00. Payee: Aitkin District Court. Personal checks accepted. Prepayment required. Mail requests: SASE required. Mail turnaround time 1 week.

Anoka County

10th Judicial District Court 325 E Main St, Anoka, MN 55303; 763-323-5966; Criminal phone: 763-422-7385; Fax: 763-323-6013. Hours: 8AM-4:30PM (CST). *Felony, Misdemeanor, Civil, Eviction, Small Claims, Probate.*

Civil Records: Access: In person only. Visitors must perform in person searches for themselves. Search fee: none. Required to search: name, years to search. Civil cases indexed by defendant, plaintiff. Civil records on computer from 1985, prior on microfiche.

Criminal Records: Access: In person only. Visitors must perform in person searches for themselves. Search fee: none. Required to search: name, years to search, DOB; also helpful: SSN. Criminal records on computer from 1985, prior on microfiche.

General Information: Public Access terminal is available. No adoption, juvenile, sex offender or sealed records released. Copy fee: $5.00 per document. Certification fee: $10.00. Payee: Court Administrator. Personal checks accepted. Visa, MC accepted. Prepayment required.

Becker County

7th Judicial District Court PO Box 787, Detroit Lakes, MN 56502; 218-846-7305; Fax: 218-847-7620. Hours: 8AM-4:30PM (CST). *Felony, Misdemeanor, Civil, Eviction, Small Claims, Probate.*

Civil Records: Access: Phone, fax, mail, in person. Both court and visitors may perform in person searches. No search fee. Required to search: name; also helpful: years to search. Civil cases indexed by defendant, plaintiff. Civil records on computer from 8/86, prior on books from 1891.

Criminal Records: Access: In person only. Visitors must perform in person searches for themselves. No search fee. Required to search: name, years to search. Criminal records on computer from 8/86, prior on books from 1891.

General Information: Public Access terminal is available. No adoption, juvenile, sex offender or sealed records released. Will fax results $5.00 per doc. Copy fee: $5.00 per document. Certification fee: $10.00. Payee: Becker County. Personal checks accepted. Prepayment required. Mail requests: SASE required. Mail turnaround time same day.

Beltrami County

District Court 619 Beltrami Ave NW, #10, Bemidji, MN 56601-3068; 218-759-4531; Civil phone: 218-759-4128; Criminal phone: 281-759-4125; Fax: 218-759-4209. Hours: 8AM-4:30PM (CST). *Felony, Misdemeanor, Civil, Eviction, Small Claims, Probate.*

Civil Records: Access: Mail, in person. Both court and visitors may perform in person searches. Search fee: $5.00 per name. Required to search: name, years to search. Civil cases indexed by defendant, plaintiff. Civil records on computer back to 1983.

Criminal Records: Access: In person only. Visitors must perform in person searches for themselves. No search fee. Required to search: name, years to search, DOB. Criminal records on computer back to 1983.

General Information: Public Access terminal is available. No adoption, juvenile, sex offender or sealed records released. Will fax results to local or toll free line. Copy fee: $5.00 per document. Certification fee: $10.00. Payee: Court Administrator. Personal checks accepted. Prepayment required. Mail requests: SASE not required. Mail turnaround time 1-5 days.

Benton County

7th Judicial District Court 615 Highway 23, PO Box 189, Foley, MN 56329-0189; 320-968-5205; Fax: 320-968-5353. Hours: 8AM-4:30PM (CST). *Felony, Misdemeanor, Civil, Eviction, Small Claims, Probate, Family.*

Civil Records: Access: In person only. Visitors must perform in person searches for themselves. Search fee: $ 5.00. Required to search: name, years to search. Civil cases indexed by defendant, plaintiff. Civil records on computer from 1986.

Criminal Records: Access: In person only. Visitors must perform in person searches for themselves. No search fee. Required to search: name, years to search, DOB. Criminal records on computer from 1986.

General Information: Public Access terminal is available. No adoption, juvenile records released. Will not fax results. Copy fee: $5.00 per document. Certification fee: $10.00. Payee: Court Administrator. Personal checks accepted. Prepayment required.

Big Stone County

Big Stone District Court 20 SE 2nd St, Ortonville, MN 56278; 320-839-2536; Fax: 320-839-2537. 8AM-4:30PM (CST). *Felony, Misdemeanor, Civil, Eviction, Small Claims, Probate.*

Civil Records: Access: Mail, in person. Both court and visitors may perform in person searches. Search fee: $5.00. Required to search: name, years to search. Civil cases indexed by defendant, plaintiff. Civil records on computer from 1989, prior on cards and in books.

Criminal Records: Access: In person only. Visitors must perform in person searches for themselves. No search fee. Required to search: name, years to search, DOB; also helpful: SSN. Criminal records on computer from 1989, prior on cards and in books.

General Information: No adoption, juvenile, sex offender or sealed records released. Will not fax results. Copy fee: $5.00 per document. Certification fee: $10.00. Payee: Court Administrator. Personal checks accepted. Prepayment required. Mail requests: SASE required. Mail turnaround time 3 days.

Blue Earth County

5th Judicial District Court 204 S 5th St, Mankato, MN 56001; 507-389-8841; Fax: 507-389-8437. 8AM-4:30PM (CST). *Felony, Misdemeanor, Civil, Eviction, Small Claims, Probate.*
www.co.blue-earth.mn.us/dept/courts.php3

Civil Records: Access: Mail, in person. Both court and visitors may perform in person searches. Search fee: $10.00 per hour. Required to search: name, years to search. Civil cases indexed by defendant, plaintiff. Civil records on computer from 8/85, prior in books and cards.

Criminal Records: Access: In person only. Visitors must perform in person searches for themselves. No search fee. Required to search: name, years to search; also helpful: DOB. Criminal records on computer from 8/85, prior in books and cards. The county forwards mail requests to the state Bureau of Criminal Apprehension.

General Information: Public Access terminal is available. No juvenile, adoption, sealed records released. Will fax results for $5.00 per doc. Copy fee: $5.00 per document. Certification fee: $10.00. Payee: Court Administrator. Personal checks accepted. MC/Visa accepted. Prepayment required. Mail requests: SASE not required. Mail turnaround time is time permitting.

Brown County

5th Judicial District Court PO Box 248, New Ulm, MN 56073-0248; 507-233-6670; Fax: 507-359-9562. 8AM-5PM (CST). *Felony, Misdemeanor, Civil, Eviction, Small Claims, Probate.*

Civil Records: Access: Mail, in person. Both court and visitors may perform in person searches. Search fee: $5.00. Required to search: name, years to search. Civil cases indexed by defendant, plaintiff. Civil records on computer from 1988, microfiche 1981-1988, prior on books.

Criminal Records: Access: In person only. Visitors must perform in person searches for themselves. No search fee. Required to search: name, years to search. Criminal records on computer from 1988, microfiche 1981-1988, prior on books. Requests must be made to the state Bureau of Criminal Apprehension.

General Information: Public Access terminal is available. No adoption, juvenile, sex offender or sealed records released. Fee to fax results is $5.00. Copy fee: $5.00 per document. Certification fee: $10.00. Payee: Court Administrator. Personal checks accepted. Visa, MC accepted. Prepayment required. Mail requests: SASE required. Mail turnaround time 3 days.

Carlton County

6th Judicial District Court PO Box 190 (301 Walnut St), Carlton, MN 55718; 218-384-4281; Civil phone: 218-384-9139; Criminal phone: 218-384-9109; Probate phone: 218-384-9113; Fax: 218-384-9182. 8AM-4PM (CST). *Felony, Misdemeanor, Civil, Eviction, Small Claims, Probate.*
www.courts.state.mn.us/districts/sixth/index.html

Civil Records: Access: Mail, fax, in person. Both court and visitors may perform in person searches. Search fee: $5.00 per name. Required to search: name, years to search; also helpful: address. Civil cases indexed by defendant, plaintiff. Civil records on computer from 1985, in books from 1982.

Criminal Records: Access: In person only. Visitors must perform in person searches for themselves. No search fee. Required to search: name, years to search; also helpful: address, DOB. Criminal records on computer from 1985, in books from 1972. If you cannot come to the courthouse, the court recommends using a retriever or contact the state Bureau of Criminal Apprehension.

General Information: Public Access terminal is available. No adoption, juvenile, sex offender or sealed records released. Will fax results for $5.00. Copy fee: $5.00 per document. Certification fee: $10.00. Payee: Court Administrator. Personal checks

accepted. Prepayment required. Mail requests: SASE required. Mail turnaround time 1 day.

Carver County

1st Judicial District Court 604 E 4th St, Box 4, Chaska, MN 55318-2183; 952-361-1420; Fax: 952-361-1491. Hours: 8AM-4:30PM (CST). *Felony, Misdemeanor, Civil, Eviction, Small Claims, Probate.*
www.co.carver.mn.us/depts.htm

Civil Records: Access: Mail, in person. Both court and visitors may perform in person searches. Search fee: $5.00 per name. Required to search: name, years to search. Civil cases indexed by defendant, plaintiff. Civil records on computer from 2/92, prior on books.

Criminal Records: Access: Mail, in person. Both court and visitors may perform in person searches. Search fee: $5.00 per name. Required to search: name, years to search, DOB. Criminal records on computer from 2/92, prior on books.

General Information: Public Access terminal is available. No adoption, juvenile, sex offender or sealed records released. Copy fee: $5.00 per document. Certification fee: $10.00 per document. Payee: Court Administrator. Personal checks accepted. Prepayment required. Mail requests: SASE not required. Mail turnaround time 7 days.

Cass County

9th Judicial District Court 300 Minnesota Ave, PO Box 3000, Walker, MN 56484; 218-547-7200; Fax: 218-547-1904. Hours: 8AM-4:30PM (CST). *Felony, Misdemeanor, Civil, Eviction, Small Claims, Probate.*

Civil Records: Access: Mail, in person. Both court and visitors may perform in person searches. Search fee: $5.00 per name. Required to search: name, years to search; also helpful: address. Civil cases indexed by defendant, plaintiff. Civil records on computer from mid-1990, on index cards from 1983-1990, on books to 1983, cards to 1900.

Criminal Records: Access: In person only. Visitors must perform in person searches for themselves. No search fee. Required to search: name, years to search, DOB; also helpful: address. Criminal records on computer from mid-1990, on index cards from 1983-1990, on books to 1983; cards to 1900.

General Information: Public Access terminal is available. No adoption, juvenile or sealed records released. Fee to fax results is $5.00 per document. Copy fee: $5.00 per document. Certification fee: $10.00. Payee: District Court. Personal checks accepted. Prepayment required. Mail requests: SASE required. Mail turnaround time up to 2 weeks.

Chippewa County

8th Judicial District Court Chippewa County Court Administor, 629 N 11th St, Montevideo, MN 56265; 320-269-7774; Fax: 320-269-7733. Hours: 8AM-4:30PM (CST). *Felony, Misdemeanor, Civil, Eviction, Small Claims, Probate.*

Civil Records: Access: Mail, in person. Visitors must perform in person searches for themselves. No search fee. Required to search: name, years to search. Civil cases indexed by defendant, plaintiff. Civil records on computer from 1988, in books from 1870.

Criminal Records: Access: In person only. Visitors must perform in person searches for themselves. No search fee. Required to search: name, years to search, DOB. Criminal records on computer from 1988, in books from 1870.

General Information: Public Access terminal is available. No adoption, juvenile, sex offender or sealed records released. Copy fee: $5.00 document. Certification fee: $10.00 per document. Payee: Court Administrator. Personal checks accepted. Prepayment required. Mail requests: SASE required. Mail turnaround time same day.

Chisago County

10th Judicial District Court 313 N Main St, Rm 358, Center City, MN 55012; 651-213-0485; Fax: 651-213-0359. Hours: 8AM-4:30PM (CST). *Felony, Misdemeanor, Civil, Eviction, Small Claims, Probate.*
Civil Records: Access: Mail, in person. Both court and visitors may perform in person searches. No search fee. Required to search: name, years to search. Civil cases indexed by defendant, plaintiff. Civil records on computer from 1984, prior on index cards.
Criminal Records: Access: In person only. Visitors must perform in person searches for themselves. No search fee. Required to search: name, years to search; also helpful: DOB. Criminal records on computer from 1984, prior on index cards.
General Information: Public Access terminal is available. No adoption, juvenile, sex offender or sealed records released. Copy fee: $.25 per page. Certification fee: $10.00. Payee: Court Administrator. Personal checks accepted. Prepayment required. Mail requests: SASE required. Mail turnaround time 1-2 days.

Clay County

7th Judicial District Court PO Box 280, c/o County Court Administration, Moorhead, MN 56561; 218-299-5065; Fax: 218-299-7307. Hours: 8AM-4:30PM (CST). *Felony, Misdemeanor, Civil, Eviction, Small Claims, Probate.*
www.co.clay.mn.us/Depts/CourtAdm/CourtAdm.htm
Civil Records: Access: Fax, mail, in person. Both court and visitors may perform in person searches. Search fee: $5.00. Required to search: name; also helpful: years to search. Civil cases indexed by defendant, plaintiff. Civil records on computer back to 1982; prior on microfiche and microfilm.
Criminal Records: Access: In person only. Visitors must perform in person searches for themselves. Search fee: none. Required to search: name, years to seach, DOB. Criminal records on computer back to 1982; prior on microfiche and microfilm. Court no longer performs searches as of July 1, 1997.
General Information: Public Access terminal is available. No adoption or sealed records released. Will fax results for $5.00. Copy fee: $5.00 per document. Certification fee: $10.00. Payee: Court Administrator. Personal checks accepted. Prepayment required. Mail requests: SASE required. Mail turnaround time 3 days.

Clearwater County

9th Judicial District Court 213 Main Ave North, Bagley, MN 56621; 218-694-6177; Fax: 218-694-6213. Hours: 8AM-4:30PM (CST). *Felony, Misdemeanor, Civil, Eviction, Small Claims, Probate.*
Civil Records: Access: Mail, in person. Both court and visitors may perform in person searches. Search fee: $5.00 per name, by court. Required to search: name, years to search. Civil cases indexed by defendant, plaintiff. Civil records on computer from 1990, on cards and books prior back to 1903.
Criminal Records: Access: In person only. Visitors must perform in person searches for themselves. No search fee. Required to search: name, years to search; also helpful: DOB. Criminal records on computer from 1990, on cards and books prior back to 1903. Court personnel will not perform name searches. Requests are referred to the state criminal agency.
General Information: Public Access terminal is available. No adoption, juvenile or sealed records released. Copy fee: $5.00 per document. Certification

fee: $10.00. Payee: Court Administrator. Personal checks accepted. Prepayment required. Mail requests: SASE not required. Mail turnaround time 3-5 days.

Cook County

6th Judicial District Court 411 W 2nd St., Grand Marais, MN 55604-2307; 218-387-3610; Fax: 218-387-3007. Hours: 8AM-4PM (CST). *Felony, Misdemeanor, Civil, Eviction, Small Claims, Probate, Juvenile, Traffic.*
www.6courts.com
Civil Records: Access: In person only. Visitors must perform in person searches for themselves. No search fee. Required to search: name, years to search. Civil cases indexed by defendant, plaintiff. Civil records on computer back to 2/91, prior on card files.
Criminal Records: Access: In person only. Visitors must perform in person searches for themselves. No search fee. Required to search: name, years to search, DOB. Criminal records on computer back to 2/91, prior on card files.
General Information: Public Access terminal is available. No adoption, juvenile, sex offender or sealed records released. Copy fee: $5.00 per document. Certification fee: $10.00. Payee: Court Administrator. Business checks accepted. Prepayment required.

Cottonwood County

5th Judicial District Court PO Box 97, Windom, MN 56101; 507-831-4551; Fax: 507-831-1425. Hours: 8AM-4:30PM (CST). *Felony, Misdemeanor, Civil, Eviction, Small Claims, Probate.*
Civil Records: Access: Mail, fax, in person. Only the court performs in person searches; visitors may not. Search fee: $10.00 per name. Required to search: name; also helpful: years to search. Civil cases indexed by defendant, plaintiff. Civil records on computer back to 1989; probate on microfilm. There is a $5.00 fee to certify a judgment search done on computer.
Criminal Records: Access: Mail, fax, in person. Both court and visitors may perform in person searches. Search fee: $10.00 per name. Required to search: name, years to search, DOB. Criminal records on computer back to 1989; prior records on card file. Court will only do searches if caseload permits.
General Information: Public Access terminal is available. No adoption, juvenile, sex offender or sealed records released. Will fax results to local or toll free line. Copy fee: $5.00 per document. Certification fee: $10.00. Payee: Court Administrator. Personal checks accepted. Prepayment required. Mail requests: SASE required. Mail turnaround time 2-3 days.

Crow Wing County

District Court 326 Laurel St, Brainerd, MN 56401; 218-824-1310; Fax: 218-824-1311. Hours: 8AM-5PM (CST). *Felony, Misdemeanor, Civil, Eviction, Small Claims, Probate.*
Civil Records: Access: Mail, in person. Both court and visitors may perform in person searches. Search fee: $5.00 per name. Required to search: name, years to search. Civil cases indexed by defendant, plaintiff. Civil records on computer from 1989, prior in books from 1873.
Criminal Records: Access: In person only. Both court and visitors may perform in person searches. Search fee: $5.00 per name. Required to search: name, years to search; also helpful: DOB. Criminal records on computer from 1989, prior in books from 1873.
General Information: Public Access terminal is available. No adoption, juvenile, sex offender or sealed records released. Copy fee: $5.00 per

document. Certification fee: $10.00. Payee: Court Administrator. Personal checks accepted. Prepayment required. Mail requests: SASE required. Mail turnaround time 7-14 days.

Dakota County

1st Judicial District Court - Apple Valley 14955 Galaxie Ave, Apple Valley, MN 55124; 952-891-7256; Civil phone: 952-891-7244; Criminal phone: 952-891-7239; Fax: 952-891-7285. Hours: 8AM-4:30PM (CST). *Misdemeanor, Civil, Eviction, Small Claims, Traffic.*
www.co.dakota.mn.us/courts
Civil Records: Access: In person only. Visitors must perform in person searches for themselves. Search fee: none. Required to search: name, years to search. Civil cases indexed by defendant, plaintiff. Civil records on computer back to 1988, prior in files in index books back to 1969.
Criminal Records: Access: In person only. Visitors must perform in person searches for themselves. Search fee: none. Required to search: name, years to search, DOB. Criminal records on computer back to 1988, prior in files to 1987 if not destroyed.
General Information: Public Access terminal is available. No adoption, juvenile, sex offender or sealed records released. Copy fee: $5.00 per document. Certification fee: $10.00 per document. Payee: District Court. Personal checks accepted. Prepayment required.

1st Judicial District Court - Division 3 1 Mendota Rd West, #140, West St Paul, MN 55118-4767; 651-554-6200; Fax: 651-554-6226. Hours: 8AM-4:30PM (CST). *Felony, Misdemeanor, Civil, Eviction, Small Claims, Probate.*
www.co.dakota.mn.us/courts Note: Formerly located at 125 3rd Ave North, S. St. Paul.
Civil Records: Access: In person only. Visitors must perform in person searches for themselves. No search fee. Required to search: name, years to search. Civil records on computer from 12/87, prior on ledgers.
Criminal Records: Access: In person only. Visitors must perform in person searches for themselves. No search fee. Required to search: name, years to search. Criminal records on computer from 12/87, prior on ledgers.
General Information: Public Access terminal is available. No adoption, juvenile, sex offender or sealed records released. Copy fee: $5.00 per document. Certification fee: $10.00. Payee: Court Administrator. Personal checks accepted. Prepayment required.

District Court Judicial Center, 1560 Hwy 55, Hastings, MN 55033; 651-438-8100; Fax: 651-438-8162. 8AM-4:30PM (CST). *Felony, Misdemeanor, Civil, Eviction, Small Claims, Probate.*
www.co.dakota.mn.us/courts
Civil Records: Access: In person only. Visitors must perform in person searches for themselves. No search fee. Required to search: name, years to search. Civil cases indexed by defendant, plaintiff. Civil records on computer from 1/88, on ledgers prior.
Criminal Records: Access: In person only. Visitors must perform in person searches for themselves. No search fee. Required to search: name, years to search. Criminal records on computer from 1/88, on ledgers prior.
General Information: Public Access terminal is available. No adoption, juvenile, sealed records released. Copy fee: $5.00 per document. Certification fee: $10.00. Payee: District Court. Personal checks accepted. Prepayment required.

Dodge County

3rd Judicial District Court 22 Sixth St E, Dept. 12, Mantorville, MN 55955; 507-635-6260; Fax: 507-635-6271. Hours: 8AM-4:30PM (CST). *Felony, Misdemeanor, Civil, Eviction, Small Claims, Probate.*
www.courts.state.mn.us/districts/third/counties/dodge.htm
Civil Records: Access: Fax, mail, in person. Both court and visitors may perform in person searches. No search fee. Required to search: name, years to search. Civil cases indexed by defendant, plaintiff. Civil records on computer back to 1984, on cards from 1984, on books from 1972. Daily Court calendar is posted at www.courts.state.mn.us/districts/third/counties/dodge.htm.
Criminal Records: Access: In person only. Visitors must perform in person searches for themselves. Search fee: none. Required to search: name, years to search, DOB. Criminal records on computer back to 1984, on cards from 1984, on books from 1972. Daily court calendar is posted at the website.
General Information: Public Access terminal is available. No adoption, juvenile, sex offender or sealed records released. Fee to fax results is $5.00 per document. Copy fee: $5.00 per document. Certification fee: $10.00. Payee: Court Administrator. Personal checks accepted. Prepayment required. Mail requests: SASE required. Mail turnaround time 1-2 days.

Douglas County

7th Judicial District Court 305 8th Ave West, Alexandria, MN 56308; 320-762-3882; Fax: 320-762-8863. 8AM-4:30PM (CST). *Felony, Misdemeanor, Civil, Eviction, Small Claims, Probate.*
Civil Records: Access: Mail, in person. Both court and visitors may perform in person searches. Search fee: $5.00 per name. Required to search: name, years to search. Civil cases indexed by defendant, plaintiff. Civil records on computer from 1987, on microfiche from 1951, books prior. The books are grouped by letter, but not alphabetized.
Criminal Records: Access: In person only. Visitors must perform in person criminal searches for themselves. Search fee: none. Required to search: name. Criminal records on computer from 1987, on microfiche from 1951, books prior. The books are grouped by letter, but not alphabetized.
General Information: Public Access terminal is available. No adoption, juvenile or sealed records released. Will not fax results. Copy fee: $5.00 per document. Certification fee: $10.00. Payee: Court Administrator. Personal checks accepted. Prepayment required. Mail requests: SASE required. Mail turnaround time 1-7 days.

Faribault County

5th Judicial District Court PO Box 130, Blue Earth, MN 56013; 507-526-6273; Fax: 507-526-3054. Hours: 8AM-4:30PM (CST). *Felony, Misdemeanor, Civil, Eviction, Small Claims, Probate.*
Civil Records: Access: Mail, in person. Visitors must perform in person searches for themselves. No search fee. Required to search: name, years to search. Civil cases indexed by defendant, plaintiff. Civil records on computer from 1989, in books from 1870.
Criminal Records: Access: In person only. Visitors must perform in person searches for themselves. No search fee. Required to search: name, years to search; also helpful: DOB. Criminal records on computer from 1989, in books from 1870. The county suggests sending requests to the state Bureau of Criminal Apprehension.
General Information: Public Access terminal is available. No adoption, juvenile, sex offender or sealed records released. Will fax results for $5.00.

Copy fee: $5.00 per document. Certification fee: $10.00. Payee: Court Administrator. Personal checks accepted. Prepayment required. Mail requests: SASE required. Mail turnaround time 7 days or less.

Fillmore County

3rd Judicial District Court 101 Fillmore St, PO Box 436, Preston, MN 55965; 507-765-4483; Fax: 507-765-4571. Hours: 8AM-4:30PM (CST). *Felony, Misdemeanor, Civil, Eviction, Small Claims, Probate.*
www.courts.state.mn.us/districts/third
Civil Records: Access: Mail, in person. Both court and visitors may perform in person searches. Search fee: none. Required to search: name, years to search. Civil cases indexed by defendant, plaintiff. Civil records on computer from 1990, books from 1860s.
Criminal Records: Access: In person only. Visitors must perform in person searches for themselves. Search fee: none. Required to search: name, years to search, DOB. Criminal records on computer from 1990, books from 1860s.
General Information: Public Access terminal is available. No adoption, juvenile or sealed records released. Copy fee: $5.00 per document. Certification fee: $10.00. Payee: Court Administrator. Personal checks accepted. Prepayment required. Mail requests: SASE not required. Mail turnaround time 1-2 days.

Freeborn County

3rd Judicial District Court 411 S Broadway, Albert Lea, MN 56007; 507-377-5153; Fax: 507-377-5260. 8AM-5PM (CST). *Felony, Misdemeanor, Civil, Eviction, Small Claims, Probate.*
www.courts.state.mn.us/districts/third
Civil Records: Access: Mail, in person. Both court and visitors may perform in person searches. Search fee: $5.00. Required to search: name, years to search. Civil cases indexed by defendant, plaintiff. Civil records on computer from 11/89.
Criminal Records: Access: In person only. Visitors must perform in person searches for themselves. No search fee. Required to search: name, years to search, DOB. Criminal records on computer from 11/89.
General Information: Public Access terminal is available. No adoption, juvenile, sex offender or sealed records released. Copy fee: $5.00 per document. Certification fee: $10.00. Payee: Court Administrator. Personal checks accepted. Prepayment required. Mail requests: SASE required. Mail turnaround time 3-5 days.

Goodhue County

1st Judicial District Court 454 W 6th St, Red Wing, MN 55066; 651-267-4800; Fax: 651-267-4989. 8AM-4:30PM (CST). *Felony, Misdemeanor, Civil, Eviction, Small Claims, Probate.*
Civil Records: Access: Mail, in person. Both court and visitors may perform in person searches. No search fee. Required to search: name, years to search. Civil cases indexed by defendant, plaintiff. Civil records on computer from 3/92, prior records on docket books.
Criminal Records: Access: In person only. Visitors must perform in person searches for themselves. No search fee. Required to search: name. Criminal records on computer from 3/92, prior records on docket books.
General Information: Public Access terminal is available. No adoption, juvenile, sex offender or sealed records released. Will fax results if prepaid and not-certified. Copy fee: $5.00 per document. Certification fee: $10.00. Payee: Court Administrator. Personal checks accepted. Prepayment required. Mail requests: SASE required. Mail turnaround time same day.

Grant County

8th Judicial District Court PO Box 1007 (10 2nd St NE), Elbow Lake, MN 56531; 218-685-4825. Hours: 8AM-4PM (CST). *Felony, Misdemeanor, Civil, Eviction, Small Claims, Probate.*
Civil Records: Access: Mail, in person. Visitors must perform in person searches for themselves. No search fee. Required to search: name, years to search. Civil cases indexed by defendant, plaintiff. Civil records on computer from 6/89, on cards from 1930, prior at Historical Society.
Criminal Records: Access: In person only. Visitors must perform in person searches for themselves. No search fee. Required to search: name, years to search; also helpful: DOB. Criminal records on computer from 6/89, on cards from 1930, prior at Historical Society.
General Information: Public Access terminal is available. No adoption, juvenile, sex offender or sealed records released. Fee to fax results is $5.00 per document. Copy fee: $5.00 per document. Certification fee: $10.00. Payee: Court Administrator. Personal checks accepted. Prepayment required. Mail requests: SASE required. Mail turnaround: 1-2 days.

Hennepin County

4th Judicial District Court - Division 1 Civil 1251 C Government Center, 300 S 6th St, Minneapolis, MN 55487; 612-348-3164; Civil phone: 612-348-3170; Fax: 612-348-2131. Hours: 8AM-4:30PM (CST). *Civil.*
www.courts.state.mn.us/districts/fourth
Civil Records: Access: Fax, mail, in person. Both court and visitors may perform in person searches. No search fee. Required to search: name, years to search. Civil cases indexed by defendant, plaintiff. Civil records on computer from 1978, prior on microfilm.
General Information: Public Access terminal is available. No sex offender or sealed records released, domestic abuse and paternity cases are limited. Copy fee: $.50 per document. Certification fee: $10.00. Payee: Court Administrator. Personal checks accepted. Prepayment required. Mail requests: SASE required. Mail turnaround time 7-10 days.

4th Judicial District Court - Division 1 Criminal 300 S 6th St, Minneapolis, MN 55487; 612-348-2612; Fax: 612-348-6099. Hours: 8AM-4:30PM (CST). *Felony, Misdemeanor.*
www.courts.state.mn.us/districts/fourth/
Note: Online access to court records is under development.
Criminal Records: Access: Fax, mail, in person. Both court and visitors may perform in person searches. Search fee: $5.00 per name if no record found; certified is $10.00 per name. Required to search: name, years to search, DOB. Felony records go back to 1886. Computerized records back to 1978.
General Information: Public Access terminal is available. No adoption, juvenile, sex offender or sealed records released. Will fax results. Copy fee: $5.00 per document. Certification fee: $10.00. Payee: Court Administrator. Personal checks accepted. Prepayment required. Mail requests: SASE required. Mail turnaround time 14-21 days.

4th Judicial District Court - Division 3 Ridgedale 12601 Ridgedale Dr, Minnetonka, MN 55305; 952-541-7000; Fax: 952-541-6297. Hours: 8AM-4:30PM (CST). *Misdemeanor, Eviction, Small Claims.*
www.courts.state.mn.us/districts/fourth
Civil Records: Access: Mail, in person, online. Both court and visitors may perform in person searches. Search fee: $5.00 per name. Required to search: name, years to search. Civil cases indexed by

defendant and plaintiff. Civil records on computer. A plaintiff, defendant search of small claims is free at www2.co.hennepin.mn.us/ccourt/ccsrch.jsp.

Criminal Records: Access: Mail, in person. Both court and visitors may perform in person searches. Search fee: $5.00 per name. Required to search: name, years to search; also helpful: DOB. Criminal records on computer since 1989; prior records on microfiche.

General Information: Public Access terminal is available. (Limited data available.) No police reports, juvenile or sealed records released. Copy fee: $5.00 per document. Certification fee: $10.00. Payee: Hennepin County District Court. Personal checks accepted. Prepayment required. Mail requests: SASE required. Mail turnaround time 3-4 weeks.

4th Judicial District Court - Division 4 Southdale 7009 York Ave South, Edina, MN 55435; 952-830-4877; Fax: 952-830-4993. Hours: 8AM-4:30PM (CST). *Misdemeanor.*
www.courts.state.mn.us/districts/fourth

Criminal Records: Access: Mail, in person. Visitors must perform in person searches for themselves. Search fee: $5.00. Required to search: name, years to search, DOB; also helpful: offense, date of offense. Criminal records on computer since late 1970s, felonies on computer earlier. In person search with court assistance $10.00.

General Information: Public Access terminal is available. (Criminal and traffic only.) No juvenile or sealed records released. Copy fee: $5.00 per document. Certification fee: $10.00. Payee: Hennepin County District Court. Personal checks accepted. Prepayment required. Mail requests: SASE required. Mail turnaround time is 1 week.

4th Judicial District Court - Division 2 Brookdale 6125 Shingle Creek Parkway, Brooklyn Center, MN 55430; 763-569-2799; Fax: 763-569-3697. Hours: 8AM-4:30PM (CST). *Misdemeanor.*
www.courts.state.mn.us/districts/fourth

Criminal Records: Access: Mail, in person. Both court and visitors may perform in person searches. Search fee: $5.00 per name. Required to search: name, years to search, DOB. Criminal records on computer since 1987.

General Information: Public Access terminal is available. No juvenile court, conciliation court, unlawful detainers or sealed records released. Copy fee: $5.00 per document. Certification fee: $10.00. Payee: Hennepin County District Court. Personal checks accepted. Prepayment required. Mail requests: SASE required. Mail turnaround time 1-7 days.

4th Judicial District Court - Division 1 C400 Government Center, 300 S 6th St, Minneapolis, MN 55487; 612-348-3244; Fax: 612-348-2130. Hours: 7AM-5PM (CST). *Probate.*
www.courts.state.mn.us/districts/fourth

Houston County

3rd Judicial District Court 304 S Marshall, Rm 204, Caledonia, MN 55921; 507-725-5806; Criminal phone: 507-725-5828; Fax: 507-725-5550. Hours: 8AM-4:30PM (CST). *Felony, Misdemeanor, Civil, Eviction, Small Claims, Probate.*
www.courts.state.mn.us/districts/third

Civil Records: Access: Mail, in person. Visitors must perform in person searches for themselves. No search fee. Required to search: name, years to search, DOB. Civil cases indexed by defendant, plaintiff. Civil records on computer back to 8/89, prior on cards and books. Probate on microfilm to 1990.

Criminal Records: Access: In person only. Visitors must perform in person searches for themselves. No search fee. Required to search: name, years to search;

also helpful: DOB. Criminal records on computer back to 8/89, prior on cards and books.

General Information: Public Access terminal is available. No adoption, juvenile, sex offender or sealed records released. Fee to fax results is $5.00 per document. Copy fee: $5.00 per document. Certification fee: $10.00. Payee: Court Administrator. Personal checks accepted. Prepayment required. Mail requests: SASE required. Mail turnaround: 2 days.

Hubbard County

9th Judicial District Court 301 Court St, Park Rapids, MN 56470; 218-732-3573; Fax: 218-732-0137. 8AM-4:30PM (CST). *Felony, Misdemeanor, Civil, Eviction, Small Claims, Probate.*

Civil Records: Access: Mail, in person. Visitors must perform in person searches for themselves. Search fee: $5.00 per name. Required to search: name, years to search. Civil cases indexed by defendant, plaintiff. Civil records on computer since 1990, prior on index cards.

Criminal Records: Access: Mail, in person. Visitors must perform in person searches for themselves. Search fee: $5.00 per name. Required to search: name, DOB. Criminal records on computer since 1990, prior on index cards.

General Information: Public Access terminal is available. No adoption, juvenile, sex offender or sealed records released. Copy fee: $5.00 per document. Certification fee: $10.00. Payee: Court Administrator. Personal checks accepted. Prepayment required. Mail requests: SASE required. Mail turnaround time 1 week.

Isanti County

10th Judicial District Court 555 18th Ave SW, Cambridge, MN 55008-9386; 763-689-2292; Fax: 763-689-8340. Hours: 8AM-4:30PM (CST). *Felony, Misdemeanor, Civil, Eviction, Small Claims, Probate.*

Civil Records: Access: Mail, in person. Visitors must perform in person searches for themselves. Search fee: none. Required to search: name, years to search. Civil cases indexed by defendant, plaintiff. Civil records on computer from 12/84, prior on microfiche.

Criminal Records: Access: In person only. Visitors must perform in person searches for themselves. Search fee: none. Required to search: name, years to search. Criminal records on computer from 12/84, prior on microfiche.

General Information: Public Access terminal is available. No adoption, juvenile, sex offender or sealed records released. Will fax free to local or toll-free numbers. Copy fee: $5.00 per document. Certification fee: $10.00. Payee: Court Administrator. Personal checks accepted. Prepayment required. Mail requests: SASE required. Mail turnaround time up to 10 days.

Itasca County

9th Judicial District Court 123 4th St NE, Grand Rapids, MN 55744-2600; 218-327-2870; Fax: 218-327-2897. Hours: 8AM-4PM (CST). *Felony, Misdemeanor, Civil, Eviction, Small Claims, Probate.*
www.co.itasca.mn.us/Court/Gov_cou.htm

Civil Records: Access: Mail, in person. Both court and visitors may perform in person searches. Search fee: $5.00 per name. Required to search: name, years to search, DOB. Civil cases indexed by defendant, plaintiff. Civil records on computer from 4-87, on microfiche to 1982, on books prior.

Criminal Records: Access: Mail, in person. Visitors must perform in person searches for themselves. No search fee. Required to search: name, years to search, DOB. Criminal records on computer from 4-87, on

microfiche to 1982, on books prior. Record checks are made through the Bureau of Criminal Apprehension; see state section on criminal records.

General Information: Public Access terminal is available. No adoption, juvenile or sealed records released. Fee to fax results is add'l $5.00 per document. Copy fee: $5.00 per document. Certification fee: $10.00. Payee: Court Administrator. Personal checks accepted. Prepayment required. Mail requests: SASE not required. Mail turnaround time 7-14 days, 24 hours required to pull from off-site storage.

Jackson County

5th Judicial District Court PO Box 177, Jackson, MN 56143; 507-847-4400; Fax: 507-847-5433. Hours: 8:30AM-4:30PM (CST). *Felony, Misdemeanor, Civil, Eviction, Small Claims, Probate.*

Civil Records: Access: Fax, mail, in person. Both court and visitors may perform in person searches. Search fee: $10.00 per name. Required to search: name, years to search, address. Civil cases indexed by defendant, plaintiff. Civil records on computer from 5/89. Probate on microfiche from 1870.

Criminal Records: Access: Fax, mail, in person. Visitors must perform in person searches for themselves. Search fee: $10.00 per name if referred to state agency. Required to search: name, years to search, DOB. Criminal records on computer from 5/89. Probate on microfiche from 1870.

General Information: Public Access terminal is available. No adoption, juvenile, sex offender or sealed records released. Will fax results for $5.00 up to 5 pages, each add'l page $1.00. Copy fee: $5.00 per document. Certification fee: $10.00. Payee: Court Administrator. Personal checks accepted. Prepayment required. Mail requests: SASE required. Mail turnaround time 2-3 days.

Kanabec County

10th Judicial District Court 18 North Vine, #318, Mora, MN 55051-1385; 320-679-6400; Fax: 320-679-6411. Hours: 8AM-4:30PM (CST). *Felony, Misdemeanor, Civil, Eviction, Small Claims, Probate.*

Civil Records: Access: In person only. Visitors must perform in person searches for themselves. No search fee. Required to search: name, years to search. Civil cases indexed by defendant, plaintiff. Civil records on computer from 1986, prior on books and microfiche.

Criminal Records: Access: In person only. Visitors must perform in person searches for themselves. No search fee. Required to search: name, years to search; also helpful: DOB. Criminal records on computer from 1986, prior on books and microfiche.

General Information: Public Access terminal is available. No adoption, juvenile or sealed records released. Copy fee: $5.00 per document. Certification fee: $10.00. Payee: Court Administrator. Personal checks accepted. Prepayment required.

Kandiyohi County

8th Judicial District Court 505 Becker Ave SW, Willmar, MN 56201; 320-231-6206; Fax: 320-231-6276. Hours: 8:30AM-4:30PM (CST). *Felony, Misdemeanor, Civil, Eviction, Small Claims, Probate.*

Civil Records: Access: In person only. Both court and visitors may perform in person searches. Search fee: $5.00. Required to search: name, years to search. Civil cases indexed by defendant, plaintiff. Civil records on computer from 1986, prior on microfilm.

Criminal Records: Access: In person only. Visitors must perform in person searches for themselves. Search fee: $5.00. Required to search: name, years to search, DOB; also helpful: SSN. Criminal records on computer from 1986, prior on microfilm.

General Information: Public Access terminal is available. No adoption, juvenile, sex offender or sealed records released. Will fax specific document for $10.00; emergency requests only. Copy fee: $5.00 per document. Certification fee: $10.00. Payee: Court Administrator. Personal checks accepted. Prepayment required.

Kittson County

9th Judicial District Court 410 Fifth St S, #204, Hallock, MN 56728; 218-843-3632; Fax: 218-843-3634. Hours: 8:00AM-4:30PM (CST). *Felony, Misdemeanor, Civil, Eviction, Small Claims, Probate.*

Civil Records: Access: In person. Both court and visitors may perform in person searches. Search fee: $5.00 per name. Will charge $20.00 per hour for extensive searches. Required to search: name, years to search. Civil cases indexed by defendant, plaintiff. Civil records on computer from 9/90, prior on books and index cards. Visitors may look at judgment docket.

Criminal Records: Access: In person. Both court and visitors may perform in person searches. Search fee: $5.00 per name. Will charge $20.00 per hour for extensive searches. Required to search: name, years to search, DOB, offense. Criminal records on computer from 9/90, prior on books and index cards.

General Information: Public Access terminal is available. No adoption, juvenile, sex offender or sealed records released. No fee to fax results. Copy fee: $5.00 per document. Certification fee: $10.00. Payee: Court Administrator. Personal checks accepted. Prepayment required.

Koochiching County

9th Judicial District Court Court House, 715 4th St, International Falls, MN 56649; 218-283-1160; Fax: 218-283-1162. Hours: 8AM-4PM (CST). *Felony, Misdemeanor, Civil, Eviction, Small Claims, Probate.*
www.courts.state.mn.us/districts/ninth
Civil Records: Access: Mail, in person. Both court and visitors may perform in person searches. Search fee: $5.00 per name. Required to search: name, years to search. Civil cases indexed by defendant, plaintiff. Civil records on computer from 5/90, on TCIS cards from 1984, on books from 1906. The weekly court calendar is at the website.

Criminal Records: Access: In person only. Visitors must perform in person searches for themselves. No search fee. Required to search: name, years to search, DOB. Criminal records on computer from 5/90, on TCIS cards from 1984, on books from 1906. The weekly court calendar is at the website. Criminal record checks can be done from BCA.

General Information: Public Access terminal is available. No adoption, juvenile, sex offender or sealed records released. Fee to fax results is $5.00 per document. Copy fee: $5.00 per document. Certification fee: $10.00. Payee: Court Administrator. Personal checks accepted. Prepayment required. Mail requests: SASE required. Mail turnaround time 1 week.

Lac qui Parle County

8th Judicial District Court PO Box 36 (600 6th St), Madison, MN 56256; 320-598-3536; Fax: 320-598-3915. Hours: 8:30AM-4:30PM (CST). *Felony, Misdemeanor, Civil, Eviction, Small Claims, Probate.*
www.courts.state.mn.us/districts/eighth/dist08.htm
Civil Records: Access: Fax, phone, mail, in person. Only the court performs in person searches; visitors

may not. Search fee: $5.00 per name. Required to search: name, years to search. Civil cases indexed by defendant, plaintiff. Civil records on computer from 1988, prior on index cards.

Criminal Records: Access: In person only. Mail, in person. No search fee. Required to search: name, years to search, DOB; also helpful: SSN. Criminal records on computer from 1988, prior on index cards. Court may refer criminal searches requests to the sheriff's office, 320-598-3720. Sheriff address is 600 6th St.

General Information: Public Access terminal is available. No adoption, juvenile, sex offender or sealed records released. Will fax results $5.00 per doc. Copy fee: $5.00 per document. Certification fee: $10.00. Payee: Court Administrator. Personal checks accepted. Prepayment required. Mail requests: SASE required. Mail turnaround time 1-3 days.

Lake County

6th Judicial District Court 601 3rd Ave, Two Harbors, MN 55616; 218-834-8330; Fax: 218-834-8397. Hours: 8AM-4:30PM (CST). *Felony, Misdemeanor, Civil, Eviction, Small Claims, Probate.*
www.6courts.com
Civil Records: Access: Fax, mail, in person. Both court and visitors may perform in person searches. Search fee: $5.00 per name. Required to search: name, years to search. Civil cases indexed by defendant, plaintiff. Civil records on computer back to 1991, prior on index cards.

Criminal Records: Access: In person only. Visitors must perform in person searches for themselves. No search fee. Required to search: name, years to search, DOB. Criminal records on computer back to 1991, prior on index cards.

General Information: Public Access terminal is available. No adoption, juvenile, sex offender or sealed records released. Fee to fax results is $5.00 per document. Copy fee: $5.00 per document. Certification fee: $10.00. Payee: Court Administrator. Personal checks accepted. Visa, MC accepted. Prepayment required. Mail requests: SASE required. Mail turnaround time 1 day.

Lake of the Woods County

9th Judicial District Court PO Box 808, Baudette, MN 56623; 218-634-1451/1388; Fax: 218-634-9444. Hours: 7:30AM-4PM (CST). *Felony, Misdemeanor, Civil, Eviction, Small Claims, Probate.*
Civil Records: Access: Fax, mail, in person. Both court and visitors may perform in person searches. Search fee: $10.00 per name. Required to search: name, years to search. Civil records on computer back to 1990; on microfilm to 1923.

Criminal Records: Access: Fax, mail, in person. Both court and visitors may perform in person searches. Search fee: $10.00 per name. Required to search: name, years to search, DOB. Criminal records on computer back to 1990; on microfilm back to 1923.

General Information: Public Access terminal is available. No adoption, juvenile, sex offender or sealed records released. No fee to fax results. Copy fee: $5.00 per document. Certification fee: $10.00. Payee: Court Administrator. Personal checks accepted. Prepayment required. Mail requests: SASE not required. Mail turnaround time 2 days; no phone searches.

Le Sueur County

1st Judicial District Court 88 S Park Ave, Le Center, MN 56057; 507-357-2251; Fax: 507-357-6433. Hours: 8AM-4:30PM (CST). *Felony, Misdemeanor, Civil, Eviction, Small Claims, Probate.*
Civil Records: Access: In person only. Visitors must perform in person searches for themselves. No search fee. Required to search: name, years to search. Civil cases indexed by defendant, plaintiff. Civil records on computer from 1992, prior on books.

Criminal Records: Access: In person only. Visitors must perform in person searches for themselves. No search fee. Required to search: name, years to search, DOB, signed release. Criminal records on computer from 1992, prior on books.

General Information: Public Access terminal is available. No adoption, juvenile, sex offender or sealed records released. Copy fee: $5.00 per document. Certification fee: $10.00. Payee: Court Administrator. Personal checks accepted. Prepayment required.

Lincoln County

5th Judicial District Court PO Box 15, Ivanhoe, MN 56142-0015; 507-694-1355 or 507-694-1505; Fax: 507-694-1717. Hours: 8AM-Noon,12:30-4:30PM (CST). *Felony, Misdemeanor, Civil, Eviction, Small Claims, Probate.*
Civil Records: Access: Mail, in person. Only the court performs in person searches; visitors may not. No search fee. Required to search: name, years to search. Civil cases indexed by defendant(s), plaintiff(s). The TCIS public terminal is available to access cases from January 1989, on TCIS manual index cards from 12/82, on books from late 1800.

Criminal Records: Access: In person only. Visitors must perform in person searches for themselves. Search fee: $15.00 per name - statewide criminal history search. Required to search: name, years to search, DOB. Criminal records on computer from 1989, on TCIS from 12/82, on books from late 1800. All written requests for criminal record information are referred to Bureau of Criminal Apprehension (state agency). Call first for form, 650-642-0670.

General Information: Public Access terminal is available. (Records go back to 1989.) No adoption, juvenile, sex offender or sealed records released. Will fax court files for fee of $5.00 per transmission. Copy fee: $5.00 per document. Certification fee: $5.00 plus copy fee. Payee: Court Administrator. Personal checks accepted. Prepayment required. Mail requests: SASE required. Mail turnaround time 1 week.

Lyon County

5th Judicial District Court 607 W Main, Marshall, MN 56258; 507-537-6734; Fax: 507-537-6150. Hours: 8:30AM-4:30PM (CST). *Felony, Misdemeanor, Civil, Eviction, Small Claims, Probate.*
Civil Records: Access: Mail, in person. Both court and visitors may perform in person searches. Search fee: $5.00. Required to search: name, years to search. Civil cases indexed by defendant, plaintiff. Civil records on computer from 1987, prior on index cards.

Criminal Records: Access: In person only. Visitors must perform in person searches for themselves. No search fee. The court requires sending requests to the state Bureau of Criminal Apprehension.

General Information: Public Access terminal is available. No adoption, juvenile, sex offender or sealed records released. Copy fee: $5.00 per document. Certification fee: $10.00. Payee: Court Administrator. Personal checks accepted. Visa, MC accepted. Prepayment required. Mail requests: SASE required.

Mahnomen County

9th Judicial District Court PO Box 459, Mahnomen, MN 56557; 218-935-2251; Fax: 218-935-2851. Hours: 8AM-4:30PM (CST). *Felony, Misdemeanor, Civil, Eviction, Small Claims, Probate.*

Civil Records: Access: In person. Both the court and visitors may perform in person searches. Search fee: $5.00 per name. Required to search: name, years to search. Civil cases indexed by defendant, plaintiff. Civil records on computer from 8/90, prior on books from 1907.

Criminal Records: Access: In person. Both the court and visitors may perform in person searches. Search fee: $5.00 per name. Required to search: name, years to search. Criminal records on computer from 8/90, prior on books from 1907.

General Information: Public Access terminal is available. No adoption, juvenile, sex offender or sealed records released. Copy fee: $5.00 per document. Certification fee: $10.00. Payee: Court Administrator. Personal checks accepted. Prepayment required.

Marshall County

9th Judicial District Court 208 E Colvin, Warren, MN 56762; 218-745-4921; Fax: 218-745-4343. Hours: 8AM-4:30PM (CST). *Felony, Misdemeanor, Civil, Eviction, Small Claims, Probate.*

Civil Records: Access: Mail, in person. Both the court and visitors may perform in person searches. Search fee: $5.00 per name. Required to search: name, years to search; also helpful: address. Civil cases indexed by defendant, plaintiff. Civil records on computer from 5/90, on cards from 1982, on books from 1885.

Criminal Records: Access: Mail, in person. Visitors must perform in person searches for themselves. Search fee: $5.00 per name. Required to search: name, years to search; also helpful: address, DOB. Criminal records on computer from 5/90, on cards from 1982, on books from 1885.

General Information: Public Access terminal is available. No adoption, juvenile, sex offender or sealed records released. Copy fee: $5.00 per document. Certification fee: $10.00. Payee: Court Administrator. Personal checks accepted. Prepayment required. Mail requests: SASE required. Mail turnaround time same day.

Martin County

5th Judicial District Court 201 Lake Ave, Rm 304, Martin County Court Administration, Fairmont, MN 56031; 507-238-3205; Fax: 507-238-1913. Hours: 8AM-5PM (CST). *Felony, Misdemeanor, Civil, Eviction, Small Claims, Probate.*

Civil Records: Access: Mail, in person. Both court and visitors may perform in person searches. Search fee: $10.00. Required to search: name, years to search; also helpful: address. Civil cases indexed by defendant, plaintiff. Civil records on computer from 7/89, on cards from 1986, on books from 1800s.

Criminal Records: Access: In person only. Visitors must perform in person searches for themselves. No search fee. Required to search: name, years to search, DOB; also helpful: address, SSN. Criminal records on computer from 7/89, on cards from 1986, on books from 1800s. The court suggests sending requests to the state Bureau of Criminal Apprehension.

General Information: Public Access terminal is available. No adoption, most juvenile, or sealed records released. Will fax civil search results or

specific case files for $5.00 per fax; must be prepaid. Copy fee: $5.00 per document. Certification fee: $5.00 per document plus copy fee. Payee: Court Administrator. Personal checks accepted. Visa, MC accepted. Prepayment required. Mail requests: SASE required. Mail turnaround time 1-2 weeks.

McLeod County

1st Judicial District Court 830 E 11th, Glencoe, MN 55336; 320-864-5551; Fax: 320-864-5905. Hours: 8AM-4:30PM (CST). *Felony, Misdemeanor, Civil, Eviction, Small Claims, Probate.*

www.co.mcleod.mn.us/mcleodco.cfm?pageID=14&sub=yes

Civil Records: Access: Mail, in person. Both court and visitors may perform in person searches. Search fee: $5.00. Required to search: name, years to search. Civil records on computer from 4/92, prior on books.

Criminal Records: Access: In person only. Visitors must perform in person searches for themselves. No search fee. Required to search: name, years to search. Criminal records on computer from 4/92, prior on books.

General Information: Public Access terminal is available. No adoption, juvenile, sex offender or sealed records released. Copy fee: $5.00 per document. Certification fee: $10.00. Payee: Court Administrator. Personal checks accepted. Prepayment required. Mail requests: SASE required. Mail turnaround time 3-4 weeks.

Meeker County

8th Judicial District Court 325 N Sibley, Litchfield, MN 55355; 320-693-5230; Fax: 320-693-5254. Hours: 8AM-4:30PM (CST). *Felony, Misdemeanor, Civil, Eviction, Small Claims, Probate.*

Civil Records: Access: Fax, mail, in person. Both court and visitors may perform in person searches. Search fee: $5.00 per name. Required to search: name; also helpful: years to search, address. Civil cases indexed by defendant, plaintiff. Civil records on computer from 11/88, prior on index cards.

Criminal Records: Access: In person only. Visitors must perform in person searches for themselves. No search fee. Required to search: name; also helpful: years to search, DOB. Criminal records on computer from 11/88, prior on index cards back to 1880s.

General Information: Public Access terminal is available. No adoption, juvenile, sex offender or sealed records released. Will fax results $5.00 per doc. Copy fee: $5.00 per document. Certification fee: $10.00. Payee: Court Administrator. Personal checks accepted. Prepayment required. Mail requests: SASE required. Mail turnaround time 3 days.

Mille Lacs County

7th Judicial District Court Courthouse, 635 2nd St SE, Milaca, MN 56353; 320-983-8313; Fax: 320-983-8384. Hours: 8AM-4:30PM (CST). *Felony, Misdemeanor, Civil, Eviction, Small Claims, Probate.*

Civil Records: Access: Fax, mail, in person. Both court and visitors may perform in person searches. Search fee: $5.00. Required to search: name, years to search. Civil records on computer from 4/86, cards from 1981, books prior.

Criminal Records: Access: Fax, in person. Visitors must perform in person searches for themselves. No search fee. Required to search: name, years to search. Criminal records on computer from 4/86, cards from 1981, books prior.

General Information: Public Access terminal is available. No adoption, juvenile, sex offender or sealed records released. Will fax results $5.00 per doc. Copy fee: $5.00 per document. Certification fee:

$10.00. Payee: District Court. Personal checks accepted. Prepayment required. Mail requests: SASE required. Mail turnaround time 1 week.

Morrison County

7th Judicial District Court 213 SE 1st Ave, Little Falls, MN 56345; 320-632-0325; Probate phone: 320-632-0327; Fax: 320-632-0340. Hours: 8AM-4:30PM (CST). *Felony, Misdemeanor, Civil, Eviction, Small Claims, Probate.*

Civil Records: Access: Fax, mail, in person. Both court and visitors may perform in person searches. Search fee: $5.00. Required to search: name, years to search. Civil cases indexed by defendant, plaintiff. Civil records on computer from 5/86, prior on cards and books.

Criminal Records: Access: In person only. Visitors must perform in person searches for themselves. No search fee. Required to search: name, years to search, DOB. Criminal records on computer from 5/86, prior on cards and books.

General Information: Public Access terminal is available. No adoption, juvenile, sex offender or sealed records released. Will fax results $5.00 per doc. Copy fee: $5.00 per document. Certification fee: $10.00. Payee: Court Administrator. Personal checks accepted. Prepayment required. Mail requests: SASE required. Mail turnaround time 2-3 days.

Mower County

Mower County District Court 201 1st St NE, Austin, MN 55912; 507-437-9465; Fax: 507-434-2702. 8AM-5PM (CST). *Felony, Misdemeanor, Civil, Eviction, Small Claims, Probate.*

www.co.mower.mn.us/administrator.html

Civil Records: Access: Mail, in person. Both court and visitors may perform in person searches. Search fee: $5.00. Required to search: name, years to search. Civil cases indexed by defendant, plaintiff. Civil records on computer from 1989.

Criminal Records: Access: In person only. Visitors must perform in person searches for themselves. No search fee. Required to search: name, years to search, DOB. Criminal records on computer from 1989. Effective July 1, 1997, this court will no longer conduct criminal record searches.

General Information: Public Access terminal is available. No adoption, juvenile, paternity or sealed records released. Copy fee: $5.00 per document. Certification fee: $10.00. Payee: Court Administrator. Personal checks accepted. Prepayment required. Mail requests: SASE required. Mail turnaround time 2-3 weeks for civil, 3-4 days for criminal.

Murray County

5th Judicial District Court PO Box 57, Slayton, MN 56172-0057; 507-836-6163; Fax: 507-836-6019. 8AM-5PM (CST). *Felony, Misdemeanor, Civil, Eviction, Small Claims, Probate.*

Civil Records: Access: Fax, mail, in person. Both court and visitors may perform in person searches. Search fee: $5.00 per name. Required to search: name, years to search. Civil cases indexed by defendant, plaintiff. Civil records on computer from 7/88.

Criminal Records: Access: In person only. Visitors must perform in person searches for themselves. No search fee. Required to search: name, years to search; also helpful: SSN. Criminal records on computer from 7/88. The court suggests sending requests to the state Bureau of Criminal Apprehension.

General Information: No adoption, juvenile, or sealed records released. Will fax results $5.00 per doc. Copy fee: $5.00 per document. Certification fee: $10.00. Payee: Court Administrator. Personal checks accepted. Prepayment required.

Nicollet County

5th Judicial District Court PO Box 496, St Peter, MN 56082; 507-931-6800; Civil phone: 507-934-0386; Criminal phone: 507-934-0388; Probate phone: 507-934-0380; Fax: 507-931-4278. Hours: 8AM-5PM (CST). *Felony, Misdemeanor, Civil, Eviction, Small Claims, Probate.*
Note: Fine Inquiry telephone is 507-934-7503.

Civil Records: Access: Mail, in person. Both court and visitors may perform in person searches. Search fee: $10.00. Required to search: name, years to search. Civil cases indexed by defendant, plaintiff. Civil records on computer from 9/25/88, on books from 1890. The civil records prior to 9/25/88 for the entire county are located here. The court in North Mankato is closed. All records from that District Court branch are located here.
Criminal Records: Access: In person only. Both court and visitors may perform in person searches. Search fee: $10.00. Required to search: name, years to search, DOB. Criminal records on computer since 9/25/88. Prior records for this court only are located here on books and cards.
General Information: Public Access terminal is available. No adoption, juvenile, sex offender or sealed records released. Will not fax results. Copy fee: $5.00 per document. Certification fee: $10.00. Payee: Court Administrator. Personal checks accepted. Prepayment required. Mail requests: SASE required. Mail turnaround time 2 days.

Nobles County

5th Judicial District Court PO Box 547, Worthington, MN 56187; 507-372-8263; Fax: 507-372-4994. Hours: 8AM-4:30PM (CST). *Felony, Misdemeanor, Civil, Eviction, Small Claims, Probate.*
Civil Records: Access: Mail, in person. Both court and visitors may perform in person searches. Search fee: $5.00 per name. Required to search: name, years to search. Civil cases indexed by defendant, plaintiff. Civil records on computer from 7/88, on books and index cards prior.
Criminal Records: Access: In person only. Visitors must perform in person searches for themselves. No search fee. Required to search: name, years to search; also helpful: SSN. Criminal records on computer from 7/88, on books and index cards prior. The court suggests sending requests to the state Bureau of Criminal Apprehension.
General Information: Public Access terminal is available. No adoption, juvenile, sex offender or sealed records released. Copy fee: $5.00 per document. Certification fee: $10.00. Payee: Court Administrator. Personal checks accepted. Visa, MC accepted. In person only. Prepayment required. Mail requests: SASE required. Mail turnaround time 1 week.

Norman County

9th Judicial District Court 16 3rd Ave E, Ada, MN 56510-0146; 218-784-5458; Fax: 218-784-3110. Hours: 8AM-4:30PM (CST). *Felony, Misdemeanor, Civil, Eviction, Small Claims, Probate.*
Civil Records: Access: Mail, in person. Both court and visitors may perform in person searches. Search fee: $5.00 per name. Required to search: name, years to search. Civil records on computer since 5/90, prior on index cards.
Criminal Records: Access: In person only. Visitors must perform in person searches for themselves. No search fee. Required to search: name, years to search, DOB. Criminal records on computer since 5/90, prior

on index cards. Criminal searches directed to BCA- 1-800-832-6446, Fax 218-935-9999
General Information: No adoption, juvenile, sex offender or sealed records released. Copy fee: $5.00 per document. Certification fee: $10.00. Payee: Court Administrator. Business checks accepted. Prepayment required.

Olmsted County

Olmsted County District Court 151 4th St SE, Rochester, MN 55904; Civil phone: 507-285-8108; Criminal phone: 507-285-8201; Fax: 507-285-8996. Hours: 8AM-5PM (CST). *Felony, Misdemeanor, Civil, Eviction, Small Claims, Probate, Juvenile.*
www.courts.state.mn.us/districts/third/counties/olmsted.htm
Civil Records: Access: Mail, in person, online. Both court and visitors may perform in person searches. Search fee: $5.00 for each name found. Required to search: name, years to search. Civil cases indexed by defendant, plaintiff. Civil records on computer from mid-1989, prior to 1856 on index cards. Online access is to probate records only, and these are from a private library source at www.selco.lib.mn.us/apps/ochs/probate.cfm. Files vary greatly, but most contain date and place of death, list of heirs, copy of will (if one was written), inventory of personal property, and final disposition of the estate.
Criminal Records: Access: In person only. Visitors must perform in person searches for themselves. No search fee. Required to search: name, DOB. Criminal records on computer from mid-1989, prior to 1856 on index cards. Access the daily court calendar at the website.
General Information: Public Access terminal is available. No adoption, juvenile, sex offender or sealed records released. Copy fee: $5.00 per document. Certification fee: $10.00. Payee: Court Administrator. Personal checks accepted. Visa, MC, Discover accepted. Prepayment required. Mail requests: SASE required. Mail turnaround time 2-7 days.

Otter Tail County

Otter Tail County District Court PO Box 417, Fergus Falls, MN 56538-0417; 218-998-8420; Fax: 218-998-8438. Hours: 8AM-5PM (CST). *Felony, Misdemeanor, Civil, Eviction, Small Claims, Probate.*
Civil Records: Access: Mail, in person. Both court and visitors may perform in person searches. No search fee. Required to search: name; also helpful: years to search. Civil cases indexed by defendant, plaintiff. Civil records on computer from 1987, prior on index books.
Criminal Records: Access: In person only. Visitors must perform in person searches for themselves. No search fee. Required to search: name, years to search, DOB; also helpful: address. Criminal records on computer from 1987, prior on index books.
General Information: Public Access terminal is available. No adoption, juvenile or sealed records released. Copy fee: $5.00 per document. Certification fee: $10.00. Payee: Court Administrator. Personal checks accepted. Prepayment required. Mail requests: SASE required. Mail turnaround time 2-3 days.

Pennington County

9th Judicial District Court PO Box 619, Thief River Falls, MN 56701; 218-681-7023; Fax: 218-681-0907. 8AM-4:30PM (CST). *Felony, Misdemeanor, Civil, Eviction, Small Claims, Probate.*
Civil Records: Access: In person only. Both court and visitors may perform in person searches. Search fee: $5.00 per name. Required to search: name, years

to search. Civil cases indexed by defendant, plaintiff. Civil records on computer back to 1990, prior on TCIS cards and books to 1911.
Criminal Records: Access: Mail, in person. Both court and visitors may perform in person searches. Search fee: $5.00 per name. Required to search: name, years to search, DOB. Criminal records on computer back to 1990, prior on TCIS cards and books to 1911.
General Information: Public Access terminal is available. No adoption, juvenile, sex offender or sealed records released. Copy fee: $5.00 per document. Certification fee: $10.00. Payee: Court Administrator. Personal checks accepted. Prepayment required. Mail requests: SASE required. Mail turnaround time 1 day.

Pine County

10th Judicial District Court 315 Main St S., Pine City, MN 55063; 320-629-5634. Hours: 8AM-4:30PM (CST). *Felony, Misdemeanor, Civil, Eviction, Small Claims, Probate.*
Civil Records: Access: In person. Visitors must perform in person searches for themselves. No search fee. Required to search: name, years to search. Civil records on computer from 2/85.
Criminal Records: Access: In person only. Visitors must perform in person searches for themselves. No search fee. Required to search: name, years to search. Criminal records on computer from 2/85.
General Information: Public Access terminal is available. No adoption, juvenile, or sealed records released. Copy fee: $5.00 per document. Certification fee: $10.00. Payee: Court Administrator. Personal checks accepted. Prepayment required.

Pipestone County

5th Judicial District Court 416 S Hiawatha Ave (PO Box 337), Pipestone, MN 56164; 507-825-6730; Fax: 507-825-6733. Hours: 8:30AM-4:30PM (CST). *Felony, Misdemeanor, Civil, Eviction, Small Claims, Probate.*
Civil Records: Access: Mail, in person. Both court and visitors may perform in person searches. No search fee. Required to search: name, years to search. Civil cases indexed by defendant, plaintiff. Civil records on computer from 1989, prior on books.
Criminal Records: Access: In person only. Visitors must perform in person searches for themselves. No search fee. Required to search: name, years to search. Criminal records on computer from 1989, prior on books. The court suggests sending requests to the state Bureau of Criminal Apprehension.
General Information: Public Access terminal is available. No adoption, juvenile, sex offender victims or sealed records released. Copy fee: $5.00 per document. Certification fee: $10.00. Payee: Court Administrator. Personal checks accepted. Prepayment required. Mail requests: SASE required. Mail turnaround time 1 week.

Polk County

9th Judicial District Court Court Administrator, 612 N Broadway #301, Crookston, MN 56716; 218-281-2332; Fax: 218-281-2204. Hours: 8AM-4:30PM (CST). *Felony, Misdemeanor, Civil, Eviction, Small Claims, Probate.*
Note: Child protection and child service cases are available as of 7/1/2002.

Civil Records: Access: Mail, in person. Visitors must perform in person searches for themselves. Search fee: $5.00 per name. Required to search: name, years to search. Civil cases indexed by defendant, plaintiff. Civil records on computer from 1990, prior on index cards or books.

Criminal Records: Access: Mail, in person. Visitors must perform in person searches for themselves. Search fee: $5.00 per name. Required to search: name, years to search, DOB. Criminal records on computer from 1990, prior on index cards or books.

General Information: Public Access terminal is available. No adoption, non-felony under age 16 juvenile or sealed records released. Will fax results for $5.00. Copy fee: $5.00 per document. Certification fee: $10.00. Payee: Court Administrator. Personal checks accepted. Credit cards accepted. Prepayment required. Mail requests: SASE required. Mail turnaround time 3-5 days.

Pope County

8th Judicial District Court 130 E Minnesota Ave, Glenwood, MN 56334; 320-634-5222; Fax: 320-634-5527. Hours: 8AM-4:30PM (CST). *Felony, Misdemeanor, Civil, Eviction, Small Claims, Probate.*
www.courts.state.mn.us/districts/eighth/default.htm
Civil Records: Access: Mail, in person. No search fee. Required to search: name, years to search. Civil cases indexed by defendant, plaintiff. Civil records on computer from 2/89, prior on TCIS cards ad books.
Criminal Records: Access: In person only. Visitors must perform in person searches for themselves. No search fee. Required to search: name, years to search. Criminal records on computer from 2/89, prior on TCIS cards ad books.
General Information: Public Access terminal is available. No adoption, juvenile, sex offender or sealed records released. Copy fee: $5.00 per document. Certification fee: $10.00. Payee: Court Administrator. Personal checks accepted. Prepayment required. Mail requests: SASE required. Mail turnaround time 1-2 days.

Ramsey County

2nd Judicial District Court 15 W Kellogg, Rm 1700, St Paul, MN 55102; Civil phone: 651-266-8253; Criminal phone: 651-266-8180; Fax: 651-266-8263 civil; 266-8172 crim. Hours: 8AM-4:30PM (CST). *Felony, Misdemeanor, Civil, Probate.*
www.ramsey.courts.state.mn.us
Civil Records: Access: Mail, in person. Both court and visitors may perform in person searches. Search fee: $10.00 per name. Required to search: name, years to search. Civil cases indexed by defendant or plaintiff. Civil records on computer from 5/88, prior on books.
Criminal Records: Access: In person only. Visitors must perform in person searches for themselves. No search fee. Required to search: name, years to search, DOB. Felony records on computer go back to 1987; misdemeanors go back to 1985, prior on books to 1932, felonies only.
General Information: Public Access terminal is available. No adoption, juvenile, sex offender or sealed records released. Copy fee: $5.00 per document. Certification fee: $10.00. Payee: Court Administrator. Personal checks accepted. Prepayment required. Mail requests: SASE required. Mail turnaround time 3-5 days.

2nd Judicial District Court - Maplewood Area 2785 White Bear Ave, Maplewood, MN 55109; 651-777-9111; Fax: 651-777-3970. Hours: 8AM-4:30PM (CST). *Misdemeanor.*
www.ramsey.courts.state.mn.us Note: This court holds the records for the closed New Brighton Court.
Criminal Records: Access: In person only. Visitors must perform in person searches for themselves. No search fee. Required to search: name; also helpful: address, DOB, offense, date of offense. Criminal records on computer from 11/90, prior on books or index cards.

General Information: Public Access terminal is available. No adoption, juvenile, sex offender victim, sealed or medical records released. Copy fee: $5.00 per document. Certification fee: $10.00. Payee: Ramsey County District Court. Personal checks accepted. Visa, MC, Discover accepted. Not accepted over the phone. Prepayment required.

Red Lake County

9th Judicial District Court PO Box 339, Red Lake Falls, MN 56750; 218-253-4281; Fax: 218-253-4287. Hours: 8AM-4:30PM (CST). *Felony, Misdemeanor, Civil, Eviction, Small Claims, Probate.*
Civil Records: Access: Mail, in person. Both court and visitors may perform in person searches. Search fee: $5.00 per name. Required to search: name, years to search. Civil cases indexed by defendant, plaintiff. Civil records on computer and microfiche from 1990, on books from 1897.
Criminal Records: Access: In person only. Visitors must perform in person searches for themselves, or contact BCA. Search fee: $15.00. Required to search: name, years to search, DOB. Criminal records on computer and microfiche from 1990, on books from 1897.
General Information: Public Access terminal is available. (Only civil available.) No adoption, juvenile, sex offender or sealed records released. Will not fax results. Copy fee: $5.00 per document. Certification fee: $10.00. Payee: Court Administrator. Personal checks accepted. Prepayment required. Mail requests: SASE required. Mail turnaround time 1 week.

Redwood County

5th Judicial District Court PO Box 130, Redwood Falls, MN 56283; 507-637-4020; Fax: 507-637-4021. Hours: 8AM-4:30PM (CST). *Felony, Misdemeanor, Civil, Eviction, Small Claims, Probate.*
Civil Records: Access: Mail, in person. Both court and visitors may perform in person searches. Search fee: $5.00 per name. Required to search: name, years to search. Civil cases indexed by defendant, plaintiff. Civil records on computer from 11/88, prior on card and books.
Criminal Records: Access: In person only. Visitors must perform in person searches for themselves. No search fee. Required to search: name, years to search. Criminal records on computer from 11/88, prior on card and books. No felony or gross misdemeanor searches will be performed.
General Information: Public Access terminal is available. No adoption, juvenile, sex offender or sealed records released. Copy fee: $5.00 per document. Certification fee: $10.00. Payee: Court Administrator. Personal checks accepted. Prepayment required. Mail requests: SASE required. Mail turnaround time 2-3 days.

Renville County

8th Judicial District Court 500 E DePue Ave, 3rd level, Olivia, MN 56277; 320-523-3680; Fax: 320-523-3689. Hours: 8AM-4:30PM (CST). *Felony, Misdemeanor, Civil, Eviction, Small Claims, Probate.*
Civil Records: Access: Mail, in person. Visitors must perform in person searches for themselves. No search fee. Required to search: name, years to search. Civil cases indexed by defendant, plaintiff. Civil records on computer from 1988, prior on index cards.
Criminal Records: Access: In person only. Visitors must perform in person searches for themselves. No search fee. Required to search: name. Criminal records on computer from 1988, prior on index cards.

General Information: Public Access terminal is available. No adoption, juvenile, sex offender, criminal or sealed records released. Copy fee: $5.00 per document. Certification fee: $10.00. Payee: Court Administrator. Personal checks accepted. Prepayment required. Mail requests: SASE required. Mail turnaround time 1-5 days.

Rice County

3rd Judicial District Court 218 NW 3rd St, Faribault, MN 55021; 507-332-6107; Fax: 507-332-6199. 8AM-4:30PM (CST). *Felony, Misdemeanor, Civil, Eviction, Small Claims, Probate.*
www.courts.state.mn.us/districts/third
Civil Records: Access: Mail, in person. Both court and visitors may perform in person searches. Search fee: $5.00. Required to search: name, years to search. Civil cases indexed by defendant, plaintiff. Civil records on computer from 1990, prior on index cards.
Criminal Records: Access: In person only. Visitors must perform in person searches for themselves. No search fee. Required to search: name, years to search; also helpful: SSN. Criminal records on computer from 1990, prior on index cards.
General Information: Public Access terminal is available. No adoption, juvenile, sex offender or sealed records released. Copy fee: $5.00 per document. Certification fee: $10.00. Payee: Court Administrator. Personal checks accepted. Prepayment required. Mail requests: SASE required. Mail turnaround time 1-2 days.

Rock County

5th Judicial District Court PO Box 745, Luverne, MN 56156; 507-283-5020; Fax: 507-283-5017. 8AM-5PM (CST). *Felony, Misdemeanor, Civil, Eviction, Small Claims, Probate.*
Civil Records: Access: Mail, in person. Only the court performs in person searches on computer; visitors may not. Visitors may search in books for records prior to 1985. Search fee: $10.00 per name. Required to search: name, years to search. Civil cases indexed by defendant, plaintiff. Civil records on computer from 1989, prior on books.
Criminal Records: Access: Mail, in person. Only the court performs in person searches on computer; visitors may not. Visitors may search in books for records prior to 1985. Search fee: $10.00 per name. Required to search: name, years to search; also helpful: SSN. Criminal records on computer from 1989, prior on books. The court will provide address for the state Bureau of Criminal Apprehension for complete record searches.
General Information: No adoption, juvenile, sex offender or sealed records released. Will fax results for $5.00 if search fee has been received. Copy fee: $5.00 per document. Certification fee: $10.00. Payee: Court Administrator. Personal checks accepted. Prepayment required. Mail requests: SASE required. Mail turnaround time same day if possible.

Roseau County

9th Judicial District Court 606 5th Ave SW Rm 20, Roseau, MN 56751; 218-463-2541; Fax: 218-463-1889. Hours: 8AM-4:30PM (CST). *Felony, Misdemeanor, Civil, Eviction, Small Claims, Probate.*
Civil Records: Access: Mail, in person. Both court and visitors may perform in person searches. Search fee: $5.00 per name. Required to search: name, years to search. Civil cases indexed by defendant, plaintiff. Civil records on computer back to 1990, prior on index cards to 1895.
Criminal Records: Access: Mail, in person. Both court and visitors may perform in person searches; however, the court will perform only statutorily

required searches. Search fee: $5.00 per name. Required to search: name, years to search; also helpful: DOB. Criminal records on computer back to 1990, prior on index cards to 1895.

General Information: Public Access terminal is available. No adoption, juvenile, paternity or sealed records released. Will fax results to toll-free number only. Copy fee: $5.00 per document. Certification fee: $10.00. Payee: Court Administrator. Personal checks accepted. Prepayment required. Mail requests: SASE required. Mail turnaround time same day if possible.

Scott County

1st Judicial District Court Scott County Justice Center, 200 Fourth Ave W, Shakopee, MN 55379; 952-496-8200; Fax: 952-496-8211. Hours: 8AM-4:30PM (CST). *Felony, Misdemeanor, Civil, Eviction, Small Claims, Probate.*

Civil Records: Access: Mail, in person. Both court and visitors may perform in person searches. No search fee. Required to search: name, years to search. Civil cases indexed by defendant, plaintiff. Civil records on computer from 1981, prior on books.

Criminal Records: Access: In person only. Visitors must perform in person searches for themselves. No search fee. Required to search: name, years to search, DOB. Criminal records on computer from 1981, prior on books.

General Information: Public Access terminal is available. No adoption, juvenile or sealed records released. Will fax results $5.00. Copy fee: $.35 per document. Certification fee: $10.00. Payee: Scott County. Personal checks accepted. Prepayment required. Mail requests: SASE required. Mail turnaround time 3 days.

Sherburne County

10th Judicial District Court Sherburne County Government Center, 13880 Hwy #10, Elk River, MN 55330-4608; 763-241-2800; Fax: 763-241-2816. Hours: 8AM-5PM (CST). *Felony, Misdemeanor, Civil, Eviction, Small Claims, Probate.*

Civil Records: Access: Mail, in person. Both court and visitors may perform in person searches. Search fee: $10.00. Required to search: name, years to search. Civil cases indexed by defendant, plaintiff. Civil records on computer from 02/85, prior on books.

Criminal Records: Access: In person only. Both court and visitors may perform in person searches. Search fee: $10.00. Required to search: name, years to search, DOB. Criminal records on computer from 02/85, prior on books back to 1930s.

General Information: Public Access terminal is available. No adoption, juvenile, confidential or sealed records released. Copy fee: $5.00 per document. Certification fee: $10.00. Payee: Court Administrator. Personal checks accepted. Prepayment required. Mail requests: SASE required. Mail turnaround: 5 days.

Sibley County

1st Judicial District Court PO Box 867, Gaylord, MN 55334; 507-237-4051; Fax: 507-237-4062. 8AM-4:30PM (CST). *Felony, Misdemeanor, Civil, Eviction, Small Claims, Probate.*

Civil Records: Access: Mail, in person. Both court and visitors may perform in person searches. Search fee: $5.00 per name. Required to search: name, years to search. Civil cases indexed by defendant, plaintiff. Civil records on computer from 5/92, prior on books to 1800s.

Criminal Records: Access: Mail, in person. Both court and visitors may perform in person searches. Search fee: $5.00 per name. Required to search: name, years to search, DOB. Criminal records on computer from 5/92, prior on books to 1800s.

General Information: Public Access terminal is available. No adoption, juvenile or sealed records released. Fee to fax results is $5.00 per document. Copy fee: $5.00 per document. Certification fee: $10.00 per document. Payee: Court Administrator. Personal checks accepted. Prepayment required. Mail requests: SASE required. Mail turnaround time 2-3 weeks.

St. Louis County

6th Judicial District Court 100 N 5th Ave W, Rm 320, Duluth, MN 55802-1294; 218-726-2460; Civil phone: 218-726-2430; Criminal phone: 218-726-2460; Probate phone: 218-726-2521; Fax: 218-726-2473. Hours: 8AM-4:30PM (CST). *Felony, Misdemeanor, Civil, Eviction, Small Claims, Probate.*

www.6courts.com

Note: All three St Louis County courts can access computer records for the county and direct you to the appropriate court to get the physical file.

Civil Records: Access: Mail, in person. Both court and visitors may perform in person searches. Search fee: $5.00 per name. Required to search: name, years to search. Civil records on computer from 1976.

Criminal Records: Access: In person only. Visitors must perform in person searches for themselves. No search fee. Required to search: name. Criminal records on computer from 1976.

General Information: Public Access terminal is available. No adoption, juvenile, juvenile victim of sex offense, sealed records released. Will not fax results. Copy fee: $5.00 per document. Certification fee: $10.00. Payee: Court Administrator. Personal checks accepted. Prepayment required. Mail requests: SASE not required. Mail turnaround time 5 days.

6th Judicial District Court - Hibbing Branch 1810 12th Ave East, Hibbing, MN 55746; 218-262-0105; Fax: 218-262-0219. Hours: 8AM-4:30PM (CST). *Felony, Misdemeanor, Civil, Eviction, Small Claims, Probate.*

www.courts.state.mn.us/districts/sixth/index.html

Note: All three St Louis County courts can access county computer records and direct you to the appropriate court for the physical file.

Civil Records: Access: Mail, in person. Both court and visitors may perform in person searches. Search fee: $5.00 per name/per judgment. Required to search: name, years to search. Civil cases indexed by defendant, plaintiff. Civil records on computer from 1985, prior on card or books.

Criminal Records: Access: Mail, in person. Visitors must perform in person searches for themselves. No search fee. Required to search: name, years to search. Criminal records on computer from 1985, prior on card or books. Mail requests are forwarded to MN BCA for processing.

General Information: Public Access terminal is available. No adoption, juvenile, sex offender or sealed records released. Will fax results for a $10.00 fee. Copy fee: $5.00 per document. Certification fee: $10.00. Payee: Court Administrator. Personal checks accepted. Prepayment required. Mail requests: SASE required. Mail turnaround time 2 days.

6th Judicial District Court - Virginia Branch 300 S 5th Ave, Virginia, MN 55792; 218-749-7106; Fax: 218-749-7109. Hours: 8AM-4:30PM (CST). *Felony, Misdemeanor, Civil, Eviction, Small Claims, Probate.*

www.6courts.com

Note: All three St Louis County courts can access computer records for the county and direct you to the appropriate court for the physical files.

Civil Records: Access: Mail, in person. Both court and visitors may perform in person searches. No search fee. Required to search: name, years to search. Civil cases indexed by defendant, plaintiff. Civil records on computer back to 1991, prior on books.

Criminal Records: Access: In person only. Visitors must perform in person searches for themselves. No search fee. Required to search: name, years to search, DOB. Criminal records on computer back to 1991, prior on books.

General Information: Public Access terminal is available. No adoption, juvenile, sex offender or sealed records released. Copy fee: $5.00 per document. Certification fee: $10.00. Payee: Court Administrator. Personal checks accepted. Prepayment required. Mail requests: SASE required. Mail turnaround time 2-3 days.

Stearns County

Stearns County District Court 725 Courthouse Square, St Cloud, MN 56303; 320-656-3620; Fax: 320-656-6335. Hours: 8AM-4:30PM (CST). *Felony, Misdemeanor, Civil, Small Claims, Eviction, Probate, Traffic.*

www.co.stearns.mn.us/departments/other/court/index.htm

Civil Records: Access: Mail, in person. Both court and visitors may perform in person searches. Search fee: $5.00 per name. Required to search: name, years to search. Civil cases indexed by defendant, plaintiff. Civil records on computer back to 1984, on books from the 1920s.

Criminal Records: Access: In person only. Both court and visitors may perform in person searches. Search fee: $5.00 but the fee may vary. Required to search: name. Criminal records on computer back to 1984, on books from the 1920s.

General Information: Public Access terminal is available. No adoption or other sealed records released without court petition. Will fax results for $5.00 fee. Copy fee: $5.00 per document. Certification fee: $10.00. Payee: District Court. Personal checks accepted. Visa, MC, Discover accepted. Prepayment required. Mail requests: SASE not required. Mail turnaround time 1-2 days.

Steele County

3rd Judicial District Court PO Box 487 (111 E Main St), Owatonna, MN 55060; 507-444-7700; Fax: 507-444-7491. Hours: 8AM-4:30PM (CST). *Felony, Misdemeanor, Civil, Eviction, Small Claims, Probate.*

www.courts.state.mn.us/districts/third

Civil Records: Access: Mail, in person. Both court and visitors may perform in person searches. Search fee: $5.00. Required to search: name, years to search. Civil cases indexed by defendant, plaintiff. Civil records on computer from 1990, on books from 1870.

Criminal Records: Access: In person only. Visitors must perform in person searches for themselves. No search fee. Required to search: name, years to search; also helpful: SSN. Criminal records on computer from 1990, on books from 1870.

General Information: Public Access terminal is available. No adoption, juvenile, sex offender or sealed records released. Copy fee: $5.00 per document. Certification fee: $10.00. Payee: Court Administrator. Personal checks accepted. Prepayment required. Mail requests: SASE required. Mail turnaround time 1-3 days.

Stevens County

8th Judicial District Court PO Box 530, Morris, MN 56267; 320-589-7287; Fax: 320-589-7288. Hours: 8AM-4:30PM (8AM-4PM Summer hours) (CST). *Felony, Misdemeanor, Civil, Eviction, Small Claims, Probate.*

Civil Records: Access: Mail, in person. Both court and visitors may perform in person searches. Search fee: $5.00 per name. Required to search: name, years to search. Civil cases indexed by defendant, plaintiff. Civil records on computer from 2/89, on cards from 5/86, on books from 1900.

Criminal Records: Access: In person only. Only the court performs in person searches; visitors may not. No search fee. Required to search: name, years to search. Criminal records on computer from 2/89, on cards from 5/86, on books from 1900. For access to criminal history information, the court recommends the BCA at 651-642-0610.

General Information: Public Access terminal is available. No adoption, juvenile, sex offender or sealed records released. Will fax results to local or toll free line. Copy fee: $5.00 per document. Certification fee: $10.00. Payee: Court Administrator. Personal checks accepted. Prepayment required. Mail requests: SASE required. Mail turnaround time 1-2 days.

Swift County

8th Judicial District Court PO Box 110, Benson, MN 56215; 320-843-2744; Fax: 320-843-4124. 8AM-4:30PM (CST). *Felony, Misdemeanor, Civil, Eviction, Small Claims, Probate.*

Civil Records: Access: Phone, fax, mail, in person. Both court and visitors may perform in person searches. No search fee. Required to search: name, years to search. Civil cases indexed by defendant, plaintiff. Civil records on computer back to 8/1988, prior in files and books from 1800s.

Criminal Records: Access: In person only. Visitors must perform in person searches for themselves. No search fee. Required to search: name, years to search; also helpful: DOB. Criminal records on computer back to 1988, prior in files and books from 1800s.

General Information: Public Access terminal is available. No adoption, juvenile, minor victim of sex offense, sealed records released. Copy fee: $5.00 per document. Certification fee: $10.00 per document. Payee: Court Administrator. Personal checks accepted. Prepayment required. Mail requests: SASE required. Mail turnaround time 1 week.

Todd County

7th Judicial District Court 221 1st Ave South, Long Prairie, MN 56347; 320-732-7800; Fax: 320-732-2506. Hours: 8AM-4:30PM (CST). *Felony, Misdemeanor, Civil, Eviction, Small Claims, Probate.*

Civil Records: Access: Mail, in person. Both court and visitors may perform in person searches. Search fee: $5.00. Required to search: name, years to search, address. Civil cases indexed by defendant, plaintiff. Civil records on computer 7/86, prior on index cards and books.

Criminal Records: Access: In person, mail. Both the court and visitors may perform in person searches. Search fee: $5.00. Required to search: name, years to search, address, DOB; also helpful: SSN. Criminal records on computer 7/86, prior on index cards and books.

General Information: Public Access terminal is available. No adoption, juvenile or sealed records released. Fee to fax results is $5.00 per document. Copy fee: $5.00 per document. Certification fee: $10.00. Payee: Court Administrator. Personal checks

accepted. Prepayment required. Mail requests: SASE required. Mail turnaround time 3-4 days.

Traverse County

8th Judicial District Court 702 2nd Ave N, PO Box 867, Wheaton, MN 56296; 320-563-4343; Fax: 320-563-4311. Hours: 8AM-Noon, 12:30-4:30PM (CST). *Felony, Misdemeanor, Civil, Eviction, Small Claims, Probate.*

Civil Records: Access: Mail, in person. Both court and visitors may perform in person searches. No search fee. Required to search: name, years to search. Civil cases indexed by defendant, plaintiff. Civil records on computer from 6/89, prior on index cards and books. Only judgment searches accepted by mail.

Criminal Records: Access: In person only. Visitors must perform in person searches for themselves. No search fee. Required to search: name, years to search. Criminal records on computer from 6/89, prior on index cards and books.

General Information: No adoption, juvenile, sex offender or sealed records released. Copy fee: $5.00 per document. Certification fee: $10.00. Payee: Court Administrator. Personal checks accepted. Prepayment required. Mail requests: SASE required. Mail turnaround time 1 day.

Wabasha County

3rd Judicial District Court 625 Jefferson Ave, Wabasha, MN 55981; 651-565-3012; Civil phone: 651-565-3012/3087/3051; Criminal phone: 651-565-3010/3524/3070; Fax: 651-565-3160. Hours: 8AM-4PM (CST). *Felony, Misdemeanor, Civil, Eviction, Small Claims, Probate.*

www.courts.state.mn.us/districts/third/counties/wabasha.htm

Civil Records: Access: Phone, fax, mail, in person. Both court and visitors may perform in person searches. No search fee. Required to search: name, years to search. Civil cases indexed by defendant, plaintiff. Civil records on computer from 6/89, prior on index cards and books. Search daily court calendar at the website.

Criminal Records: Access: In person only. Visitors must perform in person searches for themselves. No search fee. Required to search: name, years to search; also helpful: DOB. Criminal records on computer from 6/89, prior on index cards and books. Daily court calendar is at the website.

General Information: Public Access terminal is available. No adoption, juvenile, sex offender or sealed records released. Fee to fax results is $5.00 1st page; $1.00 each add'l. Copy fee: $5.00 per document. Certification fee: $10.00. Payee: Wabasha District Court. Personal checks accepted. Prepayment required. Mail requests: SASE required. Mail turnaround time 2 days.

Wadena County

7th Judicial District Court County Courthouse, 415 South Jefferson St, Wadena, MN 56482; 218-631-7634; Fax: 218-631-7635. Hours: 8AM-4:30PM (CST). *Felony, Misdemeanor, Civil, Eviction, Small Claims, Probate.*

Civil Records: Access: In person only. Both court and visitors may perform in person searches. No search fee. Required to search: name, years to search. Civil cases indexed by defendant, plaintiff. Civil records on computer from 7/86; prior on books, cards and microfiche.

Criminal Records: Access: In person only. Both court and visitors may perform in person searches. Search fee: $5.00 per name. Required to search: name, years to search, DOB; also helpful: address. Criminal records on computer from 7/86; prior on books, cards and microfiche.

General Information: Public Access terminal is available. No adoption, juvenile, or sealed records released. Copy fee: $5.00 per document. Certification fee: $10.00. Payee: Court Administrator. Personal checks accepted. Prepayment required.

Waseca County

3rd Judicial District Court 307 N State St, Waseca, MN 56093; 507-835-0540; Fax: 507-835-0633. Hours: 8AM-4:30PM (CST). *Felony, Misdemeanor, Civil, Eviction, Small Claims, Probate.*

www.courts.state.mn.us/districts/third

Civil Records: Access: Mail, in person. Both court and visitors may perform in person searches. No search fee. Required to search: name, years to search. Civil cases indexed by defendant, plaintiff. Civil records on computer from 1990, prior on TCIS cards and books.

Criminal Records: Access: In person only. Visitors must perform in person searches for themselves. No search fee. Required to search: name, years to search, DOB. Criminal records on computer from 1990, prior on TCIS cards and books.

General Information: Public Access terminal is available. No adoption, juvenile, sex offender victim or sealed records released. Copy fee: $5.00 per document. Certification fee: $10.00. Payee: Court Administrator. Personal checks accepted. Prepayment required. Mail requests: SASE required. Mail turnaround time 2 days.

Washington County

10th Judicial District Court 14949 62nd St North, PO Box 3802, Stillwater, MN 55082-3802; 651-430-6263; Fax: 651-430-6300. Hours: 7:30AM-5PM (CST). *Felony, Misdemeanor, Civil, Eviction, Small Claims, Probate.*

www.co.washington.mn.us/crtadmn.htm

Civil Records: Access: Mail, in person. Both court and visitors may perform in person searches. Search fee: $5.00 per name. Required to search: name, years to search. Civil cases indexed by defendant, plaintiff. Civil records on computer back to 12/83, prior on books.

Criminal Records: Access: In person only. Visitors must perform in person searches for themselves. No search fee. Required to search: name, years to search, DOB. Criminal records on computer back to 12/83, prior on books. Fax & mail access limited to statute requirements.

General Information: Public Access terminal is available. No adoption, juvenile, sex offender or sealed records released. Will not fax results. Copy fee: $5.00 per document. Certification fee: $10.00. Payee: Court Administrator. Personal checks accepted. Visa, MC accepted. Prepayment required. Mail requests: SASE required. Mail turnaround time 1 week.

Watonwan County

5th Judicial District Court PO Box 518, 710 2nd Ave.South, St James, MN 56081; 507-375-1236; Civil phone: 507-375-1235; Criminal phone: 507-375-1237; Probate phone: 507-375-1234; Fax: 507-375-5010. Hours: 8AM-5PM (CST). *Felony, Misdemeanor, Civil, Eviction, Small Claims, Probate.* Note: The Jury Office can be reached at 507-375-1230.

Civil Records: Access: Mail, in person. Both court and visitors may perform in person searches. Search fee: $10.00 per name. Required to search: name, years to search. Civil cases indexed by defendant, plaintiff. Civil records on computer from 5/89, prior on index cards.

Criminal Records: Access: In person,mail. Visitors must perform in person searches for themselves.

Search fee: $10.00 per name. Required to search: name, years to search; also helpful: DOB. Criminal records on computer from 5/89, prior on index cards. A signed release is necessary if court does search.

General Information: Public Access terminal is available. No adoption, juvenile, sex offender or sealed records released. Fee to fax results is $5.00 per page. Copy fee: $5.00 per document. Certification fee: $10.00. Payee: Court Administrator. Personal checks accepted. Prepayment required. Mail requests: SASE required. Mail turnaround time 5 business days.

Wilkin County

8th Judicial District Court PO Box 219, Breckenridge, MN 56520; 218-643-7172; Fax: 218-643-7167. Hours: 8AM-4:30PM (CST). *Felony, Misdemeanor, Civil, Eviction, Small Claims, Probate.*

Civil Records: Access: Mail, in person. Both court and visitors may perform in person searches. No search fee. Required to search: name; also helpful: years to search. Civil cases indexed by defendant, plaintiff. Civil records on computer from 1989, prior on books.

Criminal Records: Access: In person only. Only the court may perform in person searches. No search fee. Required to search: name; also helpful: years to search. Criminal records on computer from 1989, prior on books.

General Information: No adoption, juvenile, sex offender or sealed records released. Copy fee: $5.00 per document. Certification fee: $10.00. Payee: Court Administrator. Personal checks accepted. Prepayment required. Mail requests: SASE required. Mail turnaround time 3-5 days.

Winona County

3rd Judicial District Court 171 West 3rd St, Winona, MN 55987; 507-457-6386; Fax: 507-457-6392. 8AM-4:30PM (CST). *Felony, Misdemeanor, Civil, Eviction, Small Claims, Probate.*
www.courts.state.mn.us/districts/third/counties/winona.htm

Civil Records: Access: Mail, in person. Both court and visitors may perform in person searches. Search fee: $10.00 per hour. Required to search: name, years to search. Civil cases indexed by defendant, plaintiff. Civil records on computer from 1986, on books from 1888.

Criminal Records: Access: In person only. Visitors must perform in person searches for themselves. No search fee. Required to search: name, years to search, DOB. Criminal records on computer from 1986, on books from 1888. Criminal searchers are usually referred to the MN State BCA.

General Information: Public Access terminal is available. No adoption, juvenile, sex offender or sealed records released. Copy fee: $10.00 per document. Certification fee: $10.00. Payee: Court Administrator. Personal checks accepted. Prepayment required. Mail requests: SASE not required. Mail turnaround time 5-10 working days.

Wright County

10th Judicial District Court 10 NW 2nd St, Rm 201, Buffalo, MN 55313-1192; 763-682-7549; Fax: 763-682-7300. Hours: 8AM-4:30PM (CST). *Felony, Misdemeanor, Civil, Eviction, Small Claims, Probate.*
www.courts.state.mn.us/home

Civil Records: Access: In person only. Visitors must perform in person searches for themselves. No search fee. Required to search: name, years to search, approx. date. Civil cases indexed by defendant, plaintiff. Civil records on computer from 8/84, prior on books, cards & microfiche. Certificates for outstanding docketed money judgments may be requested by mail. Each name variation requires $5.00 fee.

Criminal Records: Access: In person only. Visitors must perform in person searches for themselves. No search fee. Required to search: name, years to search; also helpful: DOB, approx. date. Criminal records on computer from 8/84, prior on books, cards & microfiche.

General Information: Public Access terminal is available. No adoption, juvenile, confidential or sealed records released. Copy fee: $5.00 per document. Certification fee: $10.00. Payee: Court Administrator. Personal checks accepted. Visa, MC accepted. Prepayment required.

Yellow Medicine County

8th Judicial District Court 415 9th Ave, Granite Falls, MN 56241; 320-564-3325; Fax: 320-564-4435. Hours: 8AM-4PM (CST). *Felony, Misdemeanor, Civil, Eviction, Small Claims, Probate.*

Civil Records: Access: Mail, in person. Both court and visitors may perform in person searches. Search fee: $10.00 for certified search. Required to search: name, years to search; also helpful: address. Civil cases indexed by defendant, plaintiff. Civil records on computer from 1988.

Criminal Records: Access: In person only. Visitors must perform in person searches for themselves. No search fee. Required to search: name, years to search. Criminal records on computer from 1988.

General Information: Public Access terminal is available. No adoption, juvenile or sealed records released. Will not fax results. Copy fee: $5.00 per document. Certification fee: $10.00. Payee: Court Administrator. Personal checks accepted. Prepayment required. Mail requests: SASE required. Mail turnaround time 2-3 days.

Minnesota Recording Offices

ORGANIZATION:	87 counties, 87 recording offices. The recording officer is County Recorder. The entire state is in the Central Time Zone (CST).
REAL ESTATE RECORDS:	Many Minnesota counties will perform real estate searches, especially short questions over the telephone. Copy fees vary, but do not apply to certified copies. Certification fees are usually $1.00 per page with a minimum of $5.00.
UCC RECORDS:	Until July 2001, Minnesota maintained a centralized database of financing statements filed at the state level and all counties entered all non-real estate filings into the central statewide database which was accessible from any county office. Now, the only filings recorded by the County Recorder are real estate related collateral. All counties will perform UCC searches. Use search request form UCC-11. Search fees are usually $20.00 per debtor name. A UCC search can include tax liens. Copies usually cost $1.00 per page.
TAX LIEN RECORDS:	Federal and state tax liens on personal property of businesses are filed with the Secretary of State. Other federal and state tax liens are filed with the County Recorder. A special search form UCC-12 is used for separate tax lien searches. Some counties search each tax lien index separately. Some charge one $15.00 or $20.00 fee to search both indexes, but others charge a separate fee for each index searched. Search and copy fees vary widely.
OTHER LIENS:	Mechanics, hospital, judgment, attorneys.
ONLINE ACCESS:	There is no statewide system, but a number of counties offer web access to assessor data and recorded deeds.

Aitkin County

County Recorder, 209 Second St NW, Rm 205, Aitkin, MN 56431. **Phone**-County Recorder, R/E & UCC Recording- 218-927-7336; fax-218-927-7324; hours 8AM-4:30PM
Will search UCC records. Search per debtor, including 10 copies/listings- $20.00. UCC copy- $1.00 per page after 10 pages. Will not search real estate or tax lien records. RE record copy- $.25 per page uncertified. Cert fee: $1.00 per page, $5.00 min. Payee: Aitkin County Recorder. **Other phones:** Assessor-218-927-7327; Treasurer-218-927-7325; Auditor-218-927-7327; Elections-218-927-7354; Vital Records-218-927-7336; Marriage Records-218-927-7325.

Anoka County

County Recorder, 2100 3rd Ave., Anoka, MN 55303-2265. **Phone**-763-323-5416, R/E Recording- 763-323-5413; fax-763-323-5421; hours 8AM-4:30PM www.co.anoka.mn.us
Will search UCC records. Search per debtor, including 10 copies/listings- $20.00. UCC copy- $1.00 per page after 10 pages. UCC search includes tax liens if requested. Separate state/federal tax lien search fee- $15.00. Will not search real estate records. RE record copy- $.55 per page uncertified. Cert fee: $1.00 per page, $5.00 min. Payee: Anoka County Recorder. **Online Access to Real Estate, Tax Assessor records:** Access to the County online records requires an annual fee of $35 and a $25 monthly fee and $.25 per transaction. Records date back to 1995. Lending agency information is available. For information, contact Pam LeBlanc at 763-323-5424. Also, you may access property information at https://anoka.mn.ezgov.com/ezproperty/review_search.jsp. No name searching. There is also a dial-up property information system at 763-323-5400. **Other phones:** Assessor-763-323-5400; Treasurer-763-323-5400.

Becker County

County Recorder, PO Box 787, Detroit Lakes, MN 56502. **Phone**-County Recorder, R/E & UCC Recording- 218-846-7304; fax-218-846-7323; hours 8AM-4:30PM www.beckercounty.com
Will search UCC records. Search per debtor- $20.00. UCC copy- $1.00 per page after 5 pages. UCC search includes tax liens if requested. Separate state/federal tax lien search fee- $10.00. Real estate owner, mortgage, and property searches available by phone; very restricted. RE record copy- $1.00 per page. (Fax back -$5.00 + $1.00 per page). Cert fee: $5.00 up to 10 pages. Payee: Becker County Recorder. **Online Access to Property Tax, Assessor records:** Access to the assessor property data is free at www.co.becker.mn.us/taxation/. **Other phones:** Assessor-218-846-7300; Treasurer-218-846-7311; Auditor-218-846-7301; Elections-218-846-7301; Vital Records-218-846-7304.

Beltrami County

County Recorder, 619 Beltrami Ave NW, Courthouse, Bemidji, MN 56601. **Phone**-218-333-4170, R/E Recording- 218-759-4170; fax-218-333-4527; hours 8AM-4:30PM. Will search UCC records. Search per debtor- $20.00. UCC copy fee- $1.00. UCC search includes tax liens if requested. Separate state/federal tax lien search fee- $20.00. Will not search real estate records. Cert fee: $5.00. Payee: Beltrami County Recorder. **Other phones:** Assessor-218-759-4114; Treasurer-218-759-4175.

Benton County

County Recorder, PO Box 129, Foley, MN 56329. **Phone**-County Recorder, R/E & UCC Recording- 320-968-5037; fax-320-968-5329; hours 8AM-4:30PM www.co.benton.mn.us/departments/recorder/
Will search UCC records. Search per debtor- $20.00. UCC copy- $1.00 per page. UCC search includes tax liens if requested. Separate state/federal tax lien search fee- $20.00. Will not search real estate records. Cert fee: $1.00 per page, $5.00 min. Payee: Benton County Recorder. **Other phones:** Assessor-320-968-5019; Treasurer-320-968-5006; Elections-320-968-5027; Vital Records-320-968-5037.

Big Stone County

County Recorder, PO Box 218, Ortonville, MN 56278. **Phone**-County Recorder, R/E & UCC Recording- 320-839-2308; fax-320-839-2308; hours 8AM-4:30PM
Will search UCC records. Search per debtor- $20.00. Must use Federal form. UCC tax liens searches will be done on UCC 12 form. Separate federal/state combined tax lien search- $15.00 per debtor. Will not search real estate records. Record copy- $1.00 per page. ($2.00 min. per doc plus fax fee if faxed). Cert fee: $1.00 per page, $5.00 min. Payee: Big Stone County Recorder. **Other phones:** Assessor-320-839-3272; Treasurer-320-839-3445; Vital Records-320-839-2308.

Blue Earth County

County Recorder, PO Box 3567, Mankato, MN 56002-3567. **Phone**-507-389-8251; fax-507-389-8808; hours 8AM-5PM www.co.blue-earth.mn.us
Will search UCC records. Search per debtor- $20.00. UCC copy- $1.00 per page. Tax liens not included in UCC search. Separate federal/state combined tax lien search- $15.00 per debtor. Real estate owner, mortgage, and property transfer searches available. Legal description required. RE record copy- $3.00 per page uncertified. Cert fee: $1.00 per page, $5.00 min. Payee: Blue Earth County Recorder. **Online Access to Property records:** Access to the property information search database is free at www.co.blue-earth.mn.us/tax/. No name searching. **Other phones:** Assessor-507-389-8251; Treasurer-507-389-8251; Elections-507-389-8341; Vital Records-507-389-8343.

Brown County

County Recorder, PO Box 248, New Ulm, MN 56073-0248. **Phone**-County Recorder, R/E & UCC Recording- 507-233-6653, UCC Recording- 507-233-6657; fax-507-233-6668; hours 8AM-5PM www.co.brown.mn.us
Will search UCC records. Search per debtor, including 10 copies/listings- $20.00. UCC copy- $1.00 per page after 10 pages. Tax liens not included in UCC search. Federal/state combined tax lien search- $4.00 per debtor. Real estate owner,

mortgage, and property transfer searches available. RE record copy- $1.00 per page; $5.00 min. Cert fee: $5.00 per doc. Payee: Brown County Recorder. **Other phones:** Assessor-507-233-6609; Treasurer-507-233-6617; Auditor-507-233-6609; Elections-507-233-6617; Vital Records-507-233-6657.

Carlton County

County Recorder, Box 70, Carlton, MN 55718. **Phone-**County Recorder, R/E & UCC Recording- 218-384-9122, UCC Recording- 218-384-9156; fax-218-384-9157; hours 8AM-4PM

Will search UCC records. Search per debtor, including 10 copies/listings- $20.00. UCC copy- $1.00 per page after 1st 10 pages free. Will not search tax liens. Real estate owner, mortgage, and property transfer searches available. Legal description required. RE record copy- $1.00 per page. Cert fee: $1.00 per page, $5.00 min. Payee: Carlton County Treasurer. **Other phones:** Assessor-218-384-9144; Treasurer-218-384-9594; Vital Records-218-384-9156.

Carver County

County Recorder, 600 E Fourth St, Carver County Govt Ctr, Admin Bldg, Chaska, MN 55318-2158. **Phone-**952-361-1930; fax-952-361-1931; hours 8AM-4:30PM www.co.carver.mn.us

Will search UCC records. Search per debtor, including 10 copies/listings- $20.00. UCC copy- $1.00 per page after 10 pages. Tax liens not included in UCC search. Separate federal/state combined tax lien search- $15.00 per debtor. Will not search real estate records. Cert fee: $1.00 per page, $5.00 min. Payee: Carver County Treasurer. **Online Access to Real Estate, Grantor/Grantee, Lien, Property Tax records:** Access to county recorder land records and porprty tax records is free at www.co.carver.mn.us/egov.asp. Select Land Title Information or Property Tax Information. **Other phones:** Assessor-952-361-1960; Treasurer-952-361-1980; Vital Records-952-361-1930.

Cass County

County Recorder, PO Box 3000, Walker, MN 56484. **Phone-**218-547-7381, R/E Recording- 218-547-7381/7249, UCC Recording- 218-547-7233; fax-218-547-7292; hours 8AM-4:30PM www.co.cass.mn.us
Will search UCC records; requests must be on approved forms. Search per debtor- $20.00. Tax liens not included in UCC search. Federal/state combined tax lien search- $20.00 per debtor. Will search real estate records. Will go back 2 years only. Results are verbal only. Record copy- $1.00 per page. Cert fee: $1.00 per page, $5.00 min. Payee: Cass County Recorder. **Online Access to Property, GIS, Warrant, Most Wanted records:** Access to parcel, tax, and limited real estate data is free at the GID-mapping site at www.co.cass.mn.us/maps/map_parcel_info.html. No name searching. Also, search sheriff's warrant list for free at www.co.cass.mn.us/sheriff/sheriff_warrants.html; most wanted list is at www.co.cass.mn.us/sheriff/sheriff_most_wanted.html. Also, Real Estate records from 4-1-87 to present at www.fidlar.com. **Other phones:** Assessor-218-547-7298; Treasurer-218-547-7247; Elections-218-547-7281; Vital Records-218-547-7293; Auditor-218-547-7260.

Chippewa County

County Recorder, 629 No. 11th St., Montevideo, MN 56265. **Phone-**320-269-9431, R/E Recording- 320-269-7447; fax-320-269-7168; hours 8AM-4:30PM
Will search UCC records. UCC search fee- $20.00 per hour. Tax liens not included in UCC search. Tax lien search fee- $20.00 per debtor. Will search real estate records. Record copy- $.50 per page. Cert fee: $1.00 per page, $5.00 min. Payee: Chippewa County Recorder. **Other phones:** Assessor-320-269-

7696; Treasurer-320-269-7347; Elections-320-269-7447; Vital Records-320-269-9431.

Chisago County

County Recorder, 313 N Main St., Government Ctr, Rm/Box 277, Center City, MN 55012-9663. **Phone-**651-213-0438, R/E Recording- 651-257-1300; fax-651-213-0454; hours 8AM-4:30PM
Will not search records. UCC copy- $1.00 per page after 10 pages. Cert fee: $5.00 per doc. Payee: Chisago County Recorder. **Other phones:** Assessor-651-213-0401.

Clay County

County Recorder, PO Box 280, Moorhead, MN 56561-0280. **Phone-**County Recorder, R/E & UCC Recording- 218-299-5031; fax-218-299-7500; hours 8AM-4:30PM www.co.clay.mn.us
Will search UCC records; requests must be on approved forms. Search per debtor, including copies/listings- $20.00. Tax liens not included in UCC search. Separate federal/state combined tax lien search- $20.00 per debtor. Will not search real estate records. Record copy- $1.00 per page. Cert fee: $1.00 per page, $5.00 min. Payee: Clay County Recorder. **Online Access to Real Estate records:** The county online GIS mapping service at www.gis.co.clay.mn.us/map/Clay/disclaimer.htm provides property record searching, but by parcel number only. County Recorder records may be searched at the website in the near future. Plats and corner certificates online free at www.co.clay.mn.us/depts/recorder/laredo/rerrol.htm. **Other phones:** Assessor-218-299-5017; Treasurer-218-299-5011; Elections-218-299-5006; Vital Records-218-299-5031.

Clearwater County

County Recorder, 213 Main Ave North, Dept. 207, Bagley, MN 56621. **Phone-**County Recorder, R/E & UCC Recording- 218-694-6129; fax-218-694-6179; hours 8AM-4:30PM
Will search UCC records. Search per debtor, including 10 copies/listings- $20.00. UCC copy- $1.00 per page after 10 pages. UCC search includes tax liens if requested. Separate state/federal tax lien search fee- $15.00 per debtor. Real estate record owner searches available. RE record copy- $1.00 per page. Cert fee: $5.00 per doc. Payee: Clearwater County Recorder. **Other phones:** Assessor-218-694-6260; Treasurer-218-694-6130; Vital Records-218-694-6129.

Cook County

County Recorder, 411 W. 2nd St., Grand Marais, MN 55604-2307. **Phone-**218-387-3660, R/E Recording- 218-387-2282, UCC Recording- 218-387-3000 x160/161; fax-218-387-3043; hours 8AM-4PM
Will search UCC records. Search per debtor, including 10 copies/listings- $20.00. UCC copy- $1.00 per page after 10 pages. Separate federal & state combined tax lien search- $5.00 Real estate owner, mortgage, and property transfer searches available. Cert fee: $5.00 min. Payee: Cook County Recorder. **Other phones:** Assessor-218-387-3000 x150-153; Treasurer-218-387-3000; Vital Records-218-387-3000 x160/161.

Cottonwood County

County Recorder, PO Box 326, Windom, MN 56101. **Phone-**County Recorder, R/E & UCC Recording- 507-831-1458; fax-507-831-3675; hours 8AM-4:30PM
Will search UCC records. Search per debtor- $20.00. Record copy fee- $1.00 per page. Tax liens not included in UCC search. Federal/state combined tax lien search- $15.00 per debtor. Real estate owner, mortgage, and property transfer searches available. Cert fee: $1.00 per page, $5.00 min.

Payee: County Recorder. **Other phones:** Assessor-507-831-2458; Treasurer-507-831-1342; Elections-507-831-1905; Vital Records-507-831-1458.

Crow Wing County

County Recorder, PO Box 383, Brainerd, MN 56401. **Phone-**218-824-1280; fax-218-824-1281; hours 8AM-5PM
Will search UCC records. Search per debtor- $20.00. UCC copy- $.25 per page. Tax liens not included in UCC search. Separate federal/state combined tax lien search- $20.00 per debtor. Will not search real estate records. Cert fee: $1.00 per page, $5.00 min. Payee: Crow Wing County Recorder. **Other phones:** Assessor-218-824-1010.

Dakota County

County Recorder, 1590 Highway 55, Hastings, MN 55033. **Phone-**651-438-4355; fax-651-438-8176; hours 8AM-4:30PM www.co.dakota.mn.us
Will search UCC records. Search per debtor, including 10 copies/listings- $20.00. UCC copy- $1.00 per page after 10 pages. Tax liens not included in UCC search. No charge for verbal search. Separate federal/state combined tax lien search- $15.00 per debtor. Will not search real estate records. Cert fee: $1.00 per page, $5.00 min. Payee: Dakota County Recorder. **Online Access to Real Estate, Assessor records:** Records on the County Real Estate Inquiry database are free at www.co.dakota.mn.us/assessor/real_estate_inquiry.htm. Information includes items such as address, estimated value, taxes, last sale price, building details. **Other phones:** Assessor-651-438-4200; Treasurer-651-438-4576.

Dodge County

County Recorder, PO Box 128, Mantorville, MN 55955-0128. **Phone-**County Recorder, R/E & UCC Recording- 507-635-6250; fax-507-635-6265; hours 8AM-4:30PM www.co.dodge.mn.us
Will search UCC records. Search per debtor, including 10 copies/listings- $20.00. UCC copy- $1.00 per page after 10 pages. UCC search includes tax liens if requested. Real estate record owner and mortgage searches available. RE record copy- $1.00 per page. Cert fee: $5.00 per doc. Payee: Dodge County Recorder. **Other phones:** Assessor-507-635-6245; Treasurer-507-635-6240; Elections-507-635-6239; Vital Records-507-635-6250.

Douglas County

County Recorder, 305 8th Ave West, Courthouse, Alexandria, MN 56308. **Phone-**County Recorder, R/E & UCC Recording- 320-762-3877; fax-320-762-2389; hours 8AM-4:30PM www.co.douglas.mn.us
Will search UCC records. Search per debtor, including 10 copies/listings- $20.00. UCC copy- $1.00 per page after 10 pages. UCC search includes tax liens. Separate federal/state combined tax lien search- $20.00 per debtor. Verbal tax lien search is $3.00 per debtor. Property transfer searches available. Legal description required. RE record copy- $1.00 per page. Mailing and faxing fee extra. Cert fee: $5.00 per cert up to 5 pages; $1.00 each add'l. Payee: Douglas County Recorder. **Online Access to Assessor records:** Look-up assessor property tax data free at http://morris.state.mn.us/tax/. **Other phones:** Assessor-320-762-3854; Treasurer-320-762-3077; Vital Records-320-762-3877.

Faribault County

County Recorder, PO Box 130, Blue Earth, MN 56013. **Phone-**County Recorder, R/E & UCC Recording- 507-526-6252; fax-507-526-6227; hours 8AM-4:30PM
Will search UCC records. UCC search per debtor- $20.00 per name. Will search tax liens including federal tax liens. Federal/state combined tax lien

search- $20.00 per debtor. Will give last document of record. Record copy- $1.00 per page. Cert fee: $1.00 per page, $5.00 min. Payee: Faribault County Recorder. **Online Access to Property records:** Access to property information is from a private company at https://www.landrecords.net.You may subscribe or search using credit card payment per search. Index goes back to 1995; images back to 9/15/2003. **Other phones:** Assessor-507-526-6201; Treasurer-507-526-6260; Auditor-507-526-6201; Elections-507-526-6212; Vital Records-507-526-6252.

Fillmore County

County Recorder, Box 465, Preston, MN 55965-0465. **Phone-**County Recorder, R/E & UCC Recording- 507-765-3852; fax-507-765-4571; hours 8AM-4:30PM
Will search UCC records. Search per debtor, including 10 copies/listings- $20.00. UCC copy-$1.00 per page after 10 pages. Will search tax liens. Search fee- $5.00 per debtor. Real estate owner, mortgage, and property transfer searches available. RE record copy- $1.00 per page. Cert fee: $1.00 per page, $5.00 min. Payee: Fillmore County Recorder. **Other phones:** Assessor-507-765-3868; Treasurer-507-765-3811; Elections-507-765-4701; Vital Records-507-765-5339.

Freeborn County

County Recorder, 411 S. Broadway, Court House, Albert Lea, MN 56007-4506. **Phone-**County Recorder, R/E & UCC Recording- 507-377-5130; fax-507-377-5265; hours-8AM-5PM www.co.freeborn.mn.us/recorder.html
Will search UCC records. UCC search per debtor-$20.00. UCC copy fee included in search fee. Will not search real estate or tax lien records. RE record copy- $.50 per page uncertified. Cert fee: $1.00 per page, $5.00 min. Payee: Freeborn County Recorder. **Other phones:** Assessor-507-377-5176; Treasurer-507-377-5117; Elections-507-377-5116; Vital Records-507-377-5130.

Goodhue County

County Recorder, Box 408, Red Wing, MN 55066. **Phone-**651-385-3149; fax-651-385-3119; hours 8AM-4:30PM
Will accept faxed search requests for add'l $5.00 fee. Will search UCC records. Search per debtor- $20.00. Tax liens not included in UCC search. Separate federal/state combined tax lien search- $20.00 per debtor. Will not search real estate records. Record copy- $1.00 per page. Cert fee: $1.00 per page, $6.00 min. Payee: Goodhue County Recorder. **Other phones:** Assessor-651-385-3006; Treasurer-651-385-3032.

Grant County

County Recorder, PO Box 1007, Elbow Lake, MN 56531-4300. **Phone-**County Recorder, R/E & UCC Recording- 218-685-4133; fax-218-685-4521; hours 8AM-4PM
Will search UCC records. Search per debtor- $20.00. UCC copy- included in search fee. Tax liens not included in UCC search. Tax lien search fee- $2.00 per debtor. Real estate owner, mortgage, and property transfer searches available. Legal description required. Cert fee: $5.00 per cert. Payee: Grant County Recorder. **Other phones:** Assessor-218-685-4644.

Hennepin County

County Recorder, 300 S. 6th St, 8-A Gov't Ctr, Minneapolis, MN 55487. **Phone-**612-348-3049, R/E Recording- 612-348-3050; hours 8AM-4:30PM www.co.hennepin.mn.us
Will not search records. RE record copy- $1.00 per page. Cert fee: $1.00 per page, $5.00 min. Payee: Hennepin County Recorder. **Online Access to Real Estate, Lien, Most Wanted records:** Three sources

available. Access to Hennepin County online records requires a $35 annual fee with a charge of $5 per hour from 7AM-7PM, or $4.15 per hour at other times. Records date back to 1988. Only UCC & lending agency information is available. Property tax info is at the Treasurer office. For information, contact Jerry Erickson at 612-348-3856. Also, records on the County Property Information Search database are free on the Internet at www2.co.hennepin.mn.us/pins. Search by Property ID #, address, or addition name. An Automated phone system is also available; 612-348-3011. **Other phones:** Assessor-612-348-3046.

Houston County

County Recorder, PO Box 29, Caledonia, MN 55921-0029. **Phone-**County Recorder, R/E & UCC Recording- 507-725-5813; fax-507-725-2647; hours 8AM-4:30PM
Will search UCC records. Search per debtor, including 10 copies/listings- $20.00 per name. UCC copy- $1.00 per number. UCC search includes tax liens if requested. Separate federal/state combined tax lien search- $15.00 per debtor. Real estate owner, mortgage, and property transfer searches available. RE record copy- $1.00 per page. Cert fee: $1.00 per page, $5.00 min. Payee: Houston County Recorder. **Other phones:** Assessor-507-725-5801; Treasurer-507-725-5815; Auditor-507-725-5801; Elections-507-725-5803; Vital Records-507-725-5813.

Hubbard County

County Recorder, 301 Court Ave, Park Rapids, MN 56470. **Phone-**218-732-3552; fax-218-732-3645; hours 8AM-4:30PM www.co.hubbard.mn.us/Recorder.htm
Will not search UCC records. UCC copy- $1.00 per page after 10 pages. Will search real estate records. RE record copy- $1.00 per page. Cert fee: $1.00 per page, $5.00 min. Payee: Hubbard County Recorder. **Online Access to Property, GIS records:** Access to parcel data is free at www.co.hubbard.mn.us/website/hubbard/disclaimer.htm. **Other phones:** Assessor-218-732-3452; Treasurer-218-732-4348; Vital Records-218-732-3552; Auditor-218-732-3196.

Isanti County

County Recorder, 555 18th Ave SW, Courthouse, Cambridge, MN 55008. **Phone-**763-689-1191, R/E Recording- 612-689-1191; fax-none; hours 8AM-4:30PM www.co.isanti.mn.us
Will search UCC records. Search per debtor- $20.00. UCC copy fee included in search fee. Tax liens not included in UCC search. Federal/state combined tax lien search- $20.00 per debtor. Will not search real estate records. RE record copy- $1.00 per page. Cert fee: $5.00 per doc + $1.00 per page over 5. Payee: Isanti County Recorder. **Other phones:** Assessor-763-689-2752; Treasurer-763-689-1781; Auditor-763-689-2752; Elections-763-689-1644; Vital Records-763-689-1191.

Itasca County

County Recorder, 123 NE 4th St, Grand Rapids, MN 55744-2600. **Phone-**County Recorder, R/E & UCC Recording- 218-327-2856; fax-218-327-0689; hours 8AM-4:30PM www.co.itasca.mn.us
Will search UCC records. Search per debtor, including 10 copies/listings- $20.00. UCC copy-$1.00 per page after 10 pages. Tax liens not included in UCC search. Separate federal/state combined tax lien search- $20.00 per debtor. Real estate record owner and mortgage searches available. Cert fee: $1.00 per page, $5.00 min. Payee: Itasca County Recorder. **Online Access to Property, Auditor records:** Access to property and parcel data is from a private company at www.parcelinfo.com. Subscriptions are as low as $15 per month - $50 if you

require weekly updates. A limited free guest account is available. **Other phones:** Assessor-218-327-2861; Treasurer-218-327-2859; Auditor-218-327-2860; Elections-218-327-2849; Vital Records-218-327-7327.

Jackson County

County Recorder, PO Box 209, Jackson County Recorder, Jackson, MN 56143. **Phone-**County Recorder, R/E & UCC Recording- 507-847-2580; fax-507-847-6824; hours 8AM-4:30PM
Will search UCC records. Search per debtor, including copies $20.00. UCC search includes tax liens if requested. Separate federal/state combined tax lien search- $15.00 per debtor. Real estate owner, mortgage, and property transfer searches available. Legal description required. RE record copy- $.50 per page. Cert fee: $5.00 per doc. Payee: Jackson County Recorder. **Other phones:** Assessor-507-847-4033; Treasurer-507-847-2763; Elections-507-847-2763; Vital Records-507-847-2580.

Kanabec County

County Recorder, 18 N. Vine St, Mora, MN 55051. **Phone-**320-679-6466, R/E Recording- 320-679-1441; fax-320-679-6431; hours 8AM-4:30PM
Will not search UCC records. Real estate owner, mortgage, and property transfer searches available. Legal description required. RE record copy- $1.00 per page. Cert fee: $5.00 per cert. Payee: Kanabec County Recorder. **Other phones:** Assessor-320-679-3381; Treasurer-320-679-1951.

Kandiyohi County

County Recorder, PO Box 736, Willmar, MN 56201-0736. **Phone-**County Recorder, R/E & UCC Recording- 320-231-6223; fax-320-231-6284; hours 8AM-4:30PM www.co.kandiyohi.mn.us
Will search UCC records. Search per debtor, including 10 copies/listings- $20.00. UCC copy-$1.00 per page after 10 pages. Tax liens not included in UCC search. Tax lien search fee-$20.00 per debtor. Will search real estate records. RE record copy- $1.00 per page uncertified. Cert fee: $5.00 per cert, + $1.00 per page over 5 pages. Payee: Kandiyohi County Recorder. **Online Access to Property, Assessor records:** Access to county property tax data is free at http://morris.state.mn.us/tax/. Also, access to property information is from a private company at https://www.landrecords.net.You may subscribe or search using credit card payment per search. Index goes back to 3/1987; images to 3/1988. **Other phones:** Assessor-320-231-6200; Treasurer-320-231-6202; Auditor-320-231-6202; Elections-320-231-6202 x6338; Vital Records-320-231-6532.

Kittson County

County Recorder, 410 Fifth St #202, Hallock, MN 56728. **Phone-**218-843-2842; fax-218-843-2538; hours 8:30AM-4:30PM
Will search UCC records. Search per debtor, including 10 copies/listings- $20.00. UCC copy-$1.00 per page after 10 pages. Tax liens not included in UCC search. Tax lien search fee-$20.00 per debtor. Real estate owner, mortgage, and property transfer searches available. Legal description required. Cert fee: $5.00 per cert. Payee: Kittson County Recorder. **Other phones:** Assessor-218-843-3615; Treasurer-218-843-3432.

Koochiching County

County Recorder, 715 4th St., Courthouse, International Falls, MN 56649. **Phone-**218-283-1193; fax-218-283-1194; hours 8AM-5PM www.co.koochiching.mn.us
Will search UCC records. Search per debtor, including 10 copies/listings- $20.00. UCC copy-$1.00 per page after 10 pages. Tax liens not included in UCC search. Separate federal/state combined tax lien search- $4.00 per debtor. Will

search real estate records. Cert fee: $5.00 per doc. Payee: Koochiching County Treasurer. **Online Access to Property, Auditor records:** Access to property and parcel data is from a private company at www.parcelinfo.com. Subscriptions are as low as $15 per month - $50 if you require weekly updates. A limited free guest account is available. **Other phones:** Assessor-218-283-1121; Treasurer-218-283-1112; Elections-218-283-1101; Vital Records-218-283-1193.

Lac qui Parle County

County Recorder, PO Box 132, Madison, MN 56256-0132. **Phone**-320-598-3724; hours 8:30AM-4:30PM Will search UCC records. Search per debtor, including 10 copies/listings- $20.00. UCC copy- $1.00 per page after 10 pages. Tax liens included in UCC search if requested. Real estate owner, mortgage, and property transfer searches available. RE record copy- $1.00 per page. Cert fee: $5.00 per cert. Payee: County Recorder. **Other phones:** Assessor-320-598-3187; Treasurer-320-598-3648.

Lake County

County Recorder, 601 Third Ave, Two Harbors, MN 55616. **Phone**-County Recorder, R/E & UCC Recording- 218-834-8347; fax-218-834-8493; hours 8AM-4:30PM www.co.lake.mn.us Will search UCC records. Search per debtor, including 10 copies/listings- $20.00. Will search tax liens. Tax lien search fee- $20.00 per search name. Will not search real estate records. Record copy- $1.00 per page. Cert fee: $1.00 per page, $5.00 min. Payee: Lake County Recorder. **Online Access to Assessor, Property, Warrant records:** Access to county auditor property data is free at www.parcelinfo.com/parcels/. Also, access to the sheriff's warrant list is free at www.lakecosheriff.com/warrants.htm. **Other phones:** Assessor-218-834-8313; Treasurer-218-834-8344; Elections-218-834-8318; Vital Records-218-834-8301.

Lake of the Woods County

County Recorder, PO Box 808, Baudette, MN 56623. **Phone**-218-634-1902; fax-218-634-2509; hours 7:30AM-4PM Will search UCC records. Search per debtor, including 10 copies/listings- $20.00. UCC copy- $1.00 per page after 10 pages. Tax liens not included in UCC search. Separate federal/state combined tax lien search- $15.00 per debtor. Will not search real estate records. Cert fee: $5.00 per doc. Payee: County Recorder. **Other phones:** Assessor-218-634-2536; Treasurer-218-634-2361.

Le Sueur County

County Recorder, 88 S. Park Ave, Courthouse, Le Center, MN 56057-1620. **Phone**-507-357-2251; fax-507-357-6375; hours 8AM-4:30PM Will search UCC records. Search per debtor, including 10 copies/listings- $20.00. UCC copy- $1.00 per page after 10 pages. Tax liens not included in UCC search. Tax lien search fee- $6.00 per debtor. Real estate record owner and mortgage searches available. Cert fee: $5.00. Payee: County Recorder. **Other phones:** Assessor-507-357-2257.

Lincoln County

County Recorder, PO Box 119, Ivanhoe, MN 56142. **Phone**-County Recorder, R/E & UCC Recording- 507-694-1360; fax-507-694-1198; hours 8:30AM-4:30PM Will search UCC records. Search per debtor- $20.00. UCC copy fee included in search fee. UCC search includes tax liens if requested. Separate federal/state combined tax lien search- $15.00 per debtor. Real estate owner, mortgage, and property transfer searches available. Cert fee: $5.00 per doc. Payee: Lincoln County Recorder. **Other phones:** Assessor-507-694-1522; Treasurer-507-694-1550.

Lyon County

County Recorder, 607 W. Main St, Marshall, MN 56258. **Phone**-County Recorder, R/E & UCC Recording- 507-537-6722; fax-507-537-7988; hours 8:30AM-4:30PM Will search UCC records. Search per debtor- $20.00. UCC copy fee included in search fee. UCC search includes tax liens if requested. Separate federal/state combined tax lien search- $15.00 per debtor. Only telephone searches performed for real estate records. Cert fee: $1.00 per page, $5.00 min. Payee: Lyon County Recorder. **Online Access to Property records:** Access to real estate records is via a private company at https://www.landrecords.net/. Subscription or pay-per search service available. Index goes back to 1987; images back to 1988. **Other phones:** Assessor-507-537-6731.

Mahnomen County

County Recorder, PO Box 380, Mahnomen, MN 56557. **Phone**-County Recorder, R/E & UCC Recording- 218-935-5528; fax-218-935-5946; hours 8AM-4:30PM M-T Will search UCC records. Search per debtor- $20.00. UCC copy- $1.00 per page after 10 pages. Tax liens not included in UCC search. Tax lien search fee- $15.00 per debtor. Real estate owner, mortgage, and property transfer searches available. RE record copy- $2.00 per page. Cert fee: $5.00 per doc. Payee: Mahnomen County Recorder. **Other phones:** Assessor-218-935-2417.

Marshall County

County Recorder, 208 E Colvin, Warren, MN 56762. **Phone**-218-745-4801, R/E Recording- 218-745-4851; fax-218-745-5013; hours 8AM-4:30PM Will search UCC records. Search per debtor, including 10 copies/listings- $20.00. UCC copy- $1.00 per page after 10 pages. Tax liens not included in UCC search. Separate federal/state combined tax lien search- $20.00 per debtor. Will search real estate records. Cert fee: $5.00 per doc. Payee: Marshall County Recorder. **Other phones:** Assessor-218-745-5331; Treasurer-218-745-4831.

Martin County

County Recorder, PO Box 785, Fairmont, MN 56031-0785. **Phone**-County Recorder, R/E & UCC Recording- 507-238-3213; fax-507-235-8537; hours 8AM-5PM www.co.martin.mn.us Will search UCC records. Search per debtor- $20.00. Tax liens not included in UCC search. Tax lien search fee- $15.00 per debtor. Real estate owner, mortgage, and property transfer searches available. Legal description required. Record copy- $1.00 per page. Cert fee: $5.00 without copy fee. Payee: Martin County Recorder. **Online Access to Property records:** Access to property information is from a private company at https://www.landrecords.net.You may subscribe or search using credit card payment per search. Index goes back to 1987; images back to 1992. **Other phones:** Assessor-507-238-3210; Treasurer-507-238-3211; Elections-507-238-3211; Vital Records-507-238-3213.

McLeod County

County Recorder, 2389 Hennepin Ave N, Glencoe, MN 55336. **Phone**-320-864-1327; fax-320-864-1295; hours 8AM-4:30PM Will not search UCC records. Federal/state separate or combined tax lien search- $6.00 per debtor. Will not search real estate records. Record copy- $1.00 per page. Cert fee: $5.00 per name. Payee: McLeod County Recorder. **Online Access to Property records:** County recorder indicates that they intend to have records online in May, 2004. **Other phones:**

Assessor-320-864-1254; Treasurer-320-864-1203; Vital Records-320-864-1234.

Meeker County

County Recorder, 325 N. Sibley Ave, Courthouse, Litchfield, MN 55355. **Phone**-320-693-5440; fax-320-693-5444; hours 8AM-4:30PM Will search UCC records. Search per debtor- $20.00. UCC copy- $1.00 per page. Tax liens not included in UCC search. Separate federal/state combined tax lien search- $15.00 per debtor. Real estate owner, mortgage, and property transfer searches available. RE record copy- $.50 per page. Cert fee: $5.00 per cert. Payee: Meeker County Recorder. **Other phones:** Assessor-320-693-5205; Treasurer-320-693-5345; Elections-320-693-5212; Vital Records-320-693-5345.

Mille Lacs County

County Recorder, 635 2nd St S.E., Milaca, MN 56353. **Phone**-County Recorder, R/E & UCC Recording- 320-983-8308, UCC Recording- 320-983-8309; fax-320-983-8388; hours 8AM-4:30PM Will search UCC records with written UCCII request. UCC search per debtor- $20.00. UCC copy- $1.00 per page after 10 pages. Tax liens not included in UCC search. Separate federal/state combined tax lien search- $20.00 per debtor. Will not search real estate records. RE record copy- $1.00 per page. Cert fee: $1.00 per page, $5.00 min. Payee: Mille Lacs County Recorder. **Other phones:** Assessor-320-983-8311; Treasurer-320-983-8310; Auditor-320-983-8281; Elections-320-983-8301; Vital Records-320-983-8236.

Morrison County

County Recorder, 213 SE 1st Ave., Admin. Bldg., Little Falls, MN 56345. **Phone**-320-632-0145, R/E Recording- 320-632-0145, 0146, 0143, 0144 or 0147, UCC Recording- 320-632-0142; fax-320-632-0141; hours-8AM-4:30PM www.co.morrison.mn.us/wsite/index.htm Files UCC's in their office. Will search UCC records. Search per debtor, including 10 copies/listings- $20.00. Tax liens not included in UCC search. Separate federal/state combined tax lien search- $15.00 per debtor. Real estate owner, mortgage, and property transfer searches available. Record copy- $1.00 per page. Cert fee: $1.00 par page, $5.00 min. Payee: Morrison County Recorder. **Other phones:** Assessor-320-632-0100; Treasurer-320-632-0151; Auditor-320-632-0101; Elections-320-632-0132; Vital Records-320-632-0146.

Mower County

County Recorder, 201 1st St NE, Austin, MN 55912-3475. **Phone**-County Recorder, R/E & UCC Recording- 507-437-9446; fax-507-437-9471; hours 8AM-5PM www.co.mower.mn.us Payments must be paid in advance or an account set up with a security deposit for copies mailed or faxed. Will search UCC records. Search per debtor, including copies/listings- $20.00. UCC copy- $1.00 per page. Tax liens not included in UCC search. Search fee- $15.00 per debtor, with copies included. Will not search real estate records. RE record copy- $1.00 per page + $3.00 mailing fee. Cert fee: $5.00 per cert. Payee: Mower County Recorder. **Other phones:** Assessor-507-437-9440; Treasurer-507-437-9456; Elections-507-437-9536; Vital Records-507-437-9456; Information-507-437-9493; Auditor-507-437-9535.

Murray County

County Recorder, PO Box 57, Slayton, MN 56172-0057. **Phone**-507-836-6148 x144; fax-507-836-8904; hours 8:30AM-Noon, 1-5PM Will search UCC records. UCC filing is also done in each county. Search per debtor- $20.00. UCC copy-

$1.00 per page after 10 pages. Tax liens not included in UCC search. Federal/state combined tax lien search- $20.00 per debtor. Will not search real estate records. RE record copy- $1.00 per page. Cert fee: $5.00 per cert. Payee: Murray County Recorder. **Other phones:** Assessor-507-836-6148 x151; Treasurer-507-836-6148 x150; Elections-507-836-6148 x147; Vital Records-507-836-6148 x150.

Nicollet County

County Recorder, PO Box 493, St. Peter, MN 56082-0493. **Phone**-County Recorder, R/E & UCC Recording- 507-934-0320; fax-507-934-4487; hours 8AM-5PM www.co.nicollet.mn.us/dept.php3?id=16 Will search UCC records. Search per debtor $20.00. UCC copy- $1.00 per page. Tax liens not included in UCC search. Separate federal/state combined tax lien search- $2.00 per debtor. Will search real estate records but only tract information for one year. RE record copy- $3.00 per page. Cert fee: $1.00 per page, $5.00 min. Payee: Nicollet County Recorder. **Other phones:** Assessor-507-931-6800; Treasurer-507-931-6800; Elections-507-931-6800; Vital Records-507-934-0325.

Nobles County

County Recorder, PO Box 757, Worthington, MN 56187. **Phone**-507-372-8236; hours 8AM-4:30PM Will search UCC records. Search per debtor, including copies $20.00.Tax liens not included in UCC search. Separate federal/state combined tax lien search- $20.00 per debtor. Will not search real estate records. Cert fee: $5.00 per doc. Payee: Nobles County Recorder. **Other phones:** Assessor-507-372-8234; Treasurer-507-372-8231.

Norman County

County Recorder, PO Box 146, Ada, MN 56510. **Phone**-County Recorder, R/E & UCC Recording- 218-784-5481; fax-218-784-2399; hours 8:30AM-4:30PM Will not search UCC records. Separate federal/state combined tax lien search- $20.00 per debtor. Real estate owner, mortgage, and property transfer searches available. RE record copy- $2.00 per doc. Cert fee: $5.00 per cert. Payee: Norman County Recorder. **Online Access to Assessor records:** Look-up assessor property tax data free at http://morris.state.mn.us/tax/. **Other phones:** Assessor-218-784-5487; Treasurer-218-784-5473; Elections-218-784-5471; Vital Records-218-784-5481.

Olmsted County

Property Records & Licensing, 151 4th St. SE, Rochester, MN 55904. **Phone**-507-285-8194, R/E Recording- 507-285-8195, UCC Recording- 507-285-8204; fax-507-287-7186; hours 8AM-5PM www.olmstedcounty.com Will search UCC records. Search per debtor, including 10 copies/listings $20.00. Real estate owner, mortgage, and property transfer searches available. RE record copy- $1.00 per page. Cert fee: $10.00 per cert. Payee: Olmsted County Property Records & Licensing. **Online Access to Probate records:** Access to county probate records is free at www.selco.lib.mn.us/apps/ochs/probate.cfm. Files vary greatly, but most contain date and place of death, list of heirs, copy of will (if one was written), inventory of personal property, and final disposition of the estate. Tract Index of recorded documents is available from a contract vendor-call for details. **Other phones:** Assessor-507-285-8124; Treasurer-507-285-8197; Auditor-507-285-8124; Elections-507-287-2118; Vital Records-507-287-1444.

Otter Tail County

County Recorder, PO Box 867, Fergus Falls, MN 56538. **Phone**-County Recorder, R/E & UCC Recording- 218-739-2271; hours 8AM-5PM

Will search UCC records. Search per debtor- $20.00. UCC copy fee- $1.00 per page. Tax liens not included in UCC search. Tax lien search fee- $20.00 per debtor. Real estate owner, mortgage, and property transfer searches available. RE record copy- $2.00 per page up to six. Cert fee: $1.00 per page, $5.00 min. Payee: Otter Tail County Recorder. **Online Access to Property Tax records:** Search property tax data at www.co.otter-tail.mn.us/taxes/default.htm. Parcel searching or map searching only. **Other phones:** Assessor-218-739-2271.

Pennington County

County Recorder, PO Box 616, Thief River Falls, MN 56701. **Phone**-218-683-7027; fax-218-683-7026; hours 8AM-4:30PM Will search UCC records. Search per debtor- $20.00. UCC copy- $1.00 per page after 10 pages. Tax liens not included in UCC search. Separate federal/state combined tax lien search- $20.00 per debtor. Will give recent real estate documents related to a property location. RE record copy- $.50 per page. Cert fee: $1.00 per page, $5.00 min. Payee: Pennington County Recorder. **Other phones:** Assessor-218-683-7029; Treasurer-218-683-7022; Vital Records-218-683-7027.

Pine County

County Recorder, 315 Main St S. #3, Courthouse, Pine City, MN 55063. **Phone**-320-629-5665, R/E Recording- 320-629-6781; fax-320-629-5765; hours 8AM-4:30PM Will search UCC records. Search per debtor, including 10 copies/listings- $20.00. UCC copy- $1.00 per page after 10 pages. Tax liens not included in UCC search. Tax lien search fee- $5.00 per debtor. Will not search real estate records. Cert fee: $5.00 per doc. Payee: Pine County Recorder. **Other phones:** Assessor-320-629-6781 x150; Treasurer-320-629-6781 x138.

Pipestone County

County Recorder, 416 Hiawatha Ave. S., Pipestone, MN 56164. **Phone**-County Recorder, R/E & UCC Recording- 507-825-6755; fax-507-825-6767; hours 8AM-4:30PM Will search UCC records. Search per debtor- $20.00. Tax liens not included in UCC search. Separate federal/state combined tax lien search- $15.00 per debtor. Will search real estate records with specific legal description. Record copy- $1.00 per page. Cert fee: $5.00 for 1st 5 pages, $1.00 per add'l. Payee: Pipestone County Recorder. **Other phones:** Assessor-507-825-6750; Treasurer-507-825-6745; Elections-507-825-6740; Vital Records-507-825-6755.

Polk County

County Recorder, PO Box 397, Crookston, MN 56716. **Phone**-218-281-3464; fax-218-281-1636; hours 8AM-4:30PM Will search UCC records. Search per debtor, including 10 copies/listings- $20.00. UCC copy- $1.00 per page after 10 pages. Tax liens not included in UCC search. Separate federal/state combined tax lien search- $20.00 per debtor. Will not search real estate records. Cert fee: $5.00 per page. Payee: Polk County Recorder. **Other phones:** Assessor-218-281-4186.

Pope County

County Recorder, 130 E. Minnesota Ave., Glenwood, MN 56334. **Phone**-320-634-5723; fax-320-634-5717; hours 8AM-4:30PM www.mncounties.org/pope/ Will Search UCC records. Search per debtor- $20.00. UCC copy- $.50 per page. Tax liens not included in UCC search. Separate federal/state combined tax lien search- $15.00 per debtor. Real estate

owner, mortgage, and property transfer searches available. Cert fee: $5.00 per page. Payee: Pope County Recorder. **Online Access to Property records:** Access to real estate records is via a private company at https://www.landrecords.net/. Subscription or pay-per search service available. Index and images goes back to 11/1996. Also, for records search go to www.mncounties3.org/pope/. Look-up assessor property tax data free at http://morris.state.mn.us/tax/. **Other phones:** Assessor-320-634-5728; Treasurer-320-634-5705; Auditor-320-634-5728; Elections-320-634-5705; Vital Records-320-634-5723.

Ramsey County

County Recorder, 50 W. Kellogg Blvd., #812 RCGC-W, St. Paul, MN 55102-1693. **Phone**-651-266-2060, R/E Recording- 612-266-2060; hours 8AM-4:30PM Will not search UCC or tax lien records. RE search-will give owner for a property location. Record copy- $1.00 per page. Cert fee: $5.00 per cert min.; add $1 per pg over 5. Payee: Ramsey County Recorder. **Online Access to Property Assessor records:** Search the property assessment rolls free at www.co.ramsey.mn.us/prr/propertytax/index.asp. No name searching. **Other phones:** Assessor-612-266-2000.

Red Lake County

County Recorder, Box 3, Red Lake Falls, MN 56750-0003. **Phone**-County Recorder, R/E & UCC Recording- 218-253-2997; fax-218-253-2052; hours 9AM-5PM Will search UCC records. Search per debtor- $20.00. UCC copy fee- $1.00 per doc. Tax liens not included in UCC search. Tax lien search fee- $15.00 per debtor. Real estate owner, mortgage, and property transfer searches available. RE record copy- $1.00 per page. Cert fee: $5.00 per cert. Payee: Red Lake County Recorder. **Other phones:** Assessor-218-253-2596; Treasurer-218-253-2997; Vital Records-218-253-2997.

Redwood County

County Recorder, PO Box 130, Redwood Falls, MN 56283. **Phone**-507-637-4032, R/E Recording- 507-637-8325; fax-507-637-4064; hours 8AM-4:30PM Will search UCC records. Search per debtor, including 10 copies/listings- $20.00. UCC copy- $1.00 per page after 10 pages. UCC search includes tax liens if requested. Separate federal/state combined tax lien search- $15.00 per debtor. Will not search real estate records. Cert fee: $1.00 per page, $5.00 min. Payee: Redwood County Recorder. **Other phones:** Assessor-507-637-5345.

Renville County

County Recorder, 500 E. DePue, 2nd Fl, Olivia, MN 56277. **Phone**-County Recorder, R/E & UCC Recording- 320-523-3669; fax-320-523-3679; hours 8AM-4:30PM www.co.renville.mn.us/dept.html Will search UCC records. Search per debtor- $20.00. UCC copy- $1.00 per page. Tax liens not included in UCC search. Tax lien search fee- $15.00 per debtor. Will not search real estate records. RE record copy- $.50 per page, min. $1.00. Cert fee: $7.00 per doc, $1.00 each add'l. Payee: Renville County Recorder. **Online Access to Assessor records:** Look-up assessor property tax data free at http://morris.state.mn.us/tax/. **Other phones:** Assessor-320-523-3645; Treasurer-320-523-3676; Auditor-320-523-3645; Elections-320-523-2071; Vital Records-320-523-3669.

Rice County

County Recorder, 320 NW 3rd St, #10, Faribault, MN 55021-6146. **Phone**-County Recorder, R/E & UCC

Recording- 507-332-6114; fax-507-332-5999; hours 8AM-4:30PM www.co.rice.mn.us

Will search UCC records. Search per debtor, including 10 copies/listings- $20.00. UCC copy- $1.00 per page. Will do verbal searches over the phone. Real estate owner, mortgage, and property transfer searches available. RE record copy- $.50 per page. Cert fee: $1.00 per cert. Payee: Rice County Recorder. **Online Access to Property Assessor, Property Sale records:** Search parcel information and residential/commercial sales data free at www.minnesotaassessors.com/rice/. No name searching. **Other phones:** Assessor-507-332-6102; Treasurer-507-332-6104; Auditor-507-332-6102; Elections-507-332-6104; Vital Records-507-332-6114.

Rock County

County Recorder, PO Box 509, Luverne, MN 56156. **Phone-**County Recorder, R/E & UCC Recording- 507-283-5014; fax-507-283-1343; hours 8AM-5PM

Will search UCC records. Search per debtor, including 10 copies/listings- $20.00. UCC copy- $1.00 per page after 10 pages. UCC search includes tax liens if requested. Separate federal/state combined tax lien search- $20.00 per debtor. Real estate record owner and mortgage searches available. RE record copy- $1.00 per page. Cert fee: $5.00 min. or $1.00 per page. Payee: Rock County Recorder. **Online Access to Assessor records:** Look-up assessor property tax data free at http://morris.state.mn.us/tax/. **Other phones:** Assessor-507-283-5022; Treasurer-507-283-5055; Elections-507-283-5060; Vital Records-507-283-5060.

Roseau County

County Recorder, 606 5th Ave. SW, Rm 170, Roseau, MN 56751-1477. **Phone-**County Recorder, R/E & UCC Recording- 218-463-2061; fax-218-463-4294; hours 8AM-4:30PM

Will search UCC records. Search per debtor, including 10 copies/listings- $20.00. UCC copy- $1.00 per page after 10 pages. Tax liens not included in UCC search. Separate federal/state combined tax lien search- $15.00 per debtor. Will not search real estate records. Cert fee: $1.00 per page, $5.00 min. Payee: Roseau County Recorder. **Other phones:** Assessor-218-463-1861; Treasurer-218-463-1215; Elections-218-463-1282; Vital Records-218-463-1215.

Scott County

County Recorder, 200 Fourth Ave West, Shakopee, MN 55379. **Phone-**County Recorder, R/E & UCC Recording- 952-496-8150; fax-952-496-8138; hours 8AM-4:30PM www.co.scott.mn.us

Will not search records. Record copy- $1.00 per page. Cert fee: $1.00 per page, $5.00 min. Payee: Scott County Recorder. **Online Access to Real Estate, Recorder, Property Tax, Assessor, GIS records:** Search the county property databases free at www.co.scott.mn.us/xpedio/groups/public/documents/ web_files/scottcountywebframe.hcsp. There is also a free online document subscription service and GIS mapping. At left hand side, click on land records for recordings, or property tax for assessor records. **Other phones:** Assessor-952-496-8150; Treasurer-952-496-8150; Auditor-952-496-8150; Elections-952-496-8161; Vital Records-952-496-8150.

Sherburne County

County Recorder, 13880 Highway 10, Elk River, MN 55330. **Phone-**763-241-2915, R/E Recording- 800-719-2826, UCC Recording- 800-719-2826; fax-763-241-2995; hours 8AM-4:30PM www.co.sherburne.mn.us

Will search UCC records. Search per debtor, including 10 copies/listings- $20.00. UCC copy- $1.00 per page after 10 pages. UCC search includes tax liens if requested. Separate

federal/state combined tax lien search- $20.00 per debtor. Real estate owner, mortgage, and property transfer searches available. RE record copy- $2.00 1st page, $.50 each add'l. Cert fee: $1.00 per page, min. $5.00. Payee: Sherburne County Recorder. **Online Access to Real Estate, Tax Assessor, Most Wanted records:** Property records from the county tax assessor database are free at www.sherburne.mn.promap.com. However, to perform a name search, you must subscribe; fee is $25.00 setup and $300.00 per year. A free 30-day trial is offered. Call 763-241-2880 for information on how to subscribe, or visit website. Also, search the sheriff's most wanted list at www.co.sherburne.mn.us/sheriff/mostwanted.htm. **Other phones:** Assessor-800-438-0577; Treasurer-800-438-0575; Vital Records-800-719-2826.

Sibley County

County Recorder, PO Box 44, Gaylord, MN 55334-0044. **Phone-**507-237-4306, R/E Recording- 507-237-4080, UCC Recording- 507-237-4080; fax-507-237-4062; hours 8AM-5PM http://co.sibley.mn.us

Will search UCC records. Search per debtor, including 10 copies/listings- $20.00. Will search tax liens. Tax lien search fee- $5.00 per debtor. Real estate record owner searches available. Record copy- $1.00 per page. Cert fee: $1.00 per page, $5.00 min. Payee: Sibley County Recorder. **Other phones:** Assessor-507-237-4078; Treasurer-507-237-4084; Elections-507-237-4070; Vital Records-507-237-4080.

St. Louis County

County Recorder, PO Box 157, Duluth, MN 55801-0157. **Phone-**County Recorder, R/E & UCC Recording- 218-726-2677; fax-218-725-5052; hours 8AM-4:30PM

www.stlouiscounty.org/recordersoffice/recordersoffice.htm Will not search UCC records. Separate federal/state combined tax lien search- $20.00 per debtor. Will not search real estate records. Record copy- $1.00 per page, $3.00 min. Cert fee: $1.00 per page, $5.00 min. Payee: St. Louis County Recorder. **Online Access to Real Estate, Property Tax, Auditor records:** Access to the auditor and recorder's tax records for tax professionals database is by subscription. Fee is $100 monthly; password provided. For info or sign-up, contact Pam Palen at 218-726-2380 or email to palenp@co.st-louis.mn.us or visit www.co.st-louis.mn.us/auditorsoffice/subscription.pdf. Also, search auditor info for free at www.co.st-louis.mn.us/parcelinfo/st-louis/start.asp. Also, search the City of Duluth property assessor data free at www.ci.duluth.mn.us/city/assessor/index.htm. **Other phones:** Assessor-218-726-2304; Treasurer-218-726-2380; Auditor-218-726-2304; Elections-218-726-2385; Vital Records-218-726-2559; Torrens Division-218-726-2680.

Stearns County

County Recorder, 705 Courthouse Sq, Admin. Ctr, Rm 131, St. Cloud, MN 56303. **Phone-**320-656-3855, R/E Recording- 320-259-3855; fax-320-656-3916; hours 8AM-4:30PM www.co.stearns.mn.us

Will search UCC records. Search per debtor- $20.00. Tax liens not included in UCC search. Separate federal/state combined tax lien search- $15.00 per debtor. Will not search real estate records. Record copy- $1.00 per page. Cert fee: $1.00 per page, $5.00 min. Payee: Stearns County Recorder. **Online Access to Real Estate, Tax Assessor records:** Records from the county tax assessor database are free at http://secure.co.stearns.mn.us/. No name searching. **Other phones:** Assessor-320-656-3680; Treasurer-320-656-3870; Elections-320-656-3920.

Steele County

County Recorder, PO Box 890, Owatonna, MN 55060. **Phone-**County Recorder, R/E & UCC Recording- 507-444-7450; fax-507-444-7470; hours 8AM-5PM

Will search UCC records. UCC search per debtor- $20.00. UCC copy- $1.00 per page after 10 pages. Tax liens not included in UCC search. Separate federal/state combined tax lien search- $15.00 per debtor. Will not search real estate records. There is a $5.00 document handling fee on mortgages and transfer documents. A SASE is required. Cert fee: $1.00 per page, $5.00 min. Payee: Steele County Recorder. **Online Access to Property Tax records:** Search using parcel data at www.co.steele.mn.us/auditor/auditor.html. **Other phones:** Assessor-507-444-7435; Treasurer-507-444-7420; Elections-507-444-7410; Vital Records-507-444-7490.

Stevens County

County Recorder, PO Box 530, Morris, MN 56267. **Phone-**320-589-7414; fax-320-589-7112; hours 8:30AM-4:30PM (Summer hours 8AM-4PM)

Will not search UCC records. Copy fee- $1.00 per page. Separate federal/state combined tax lien search- $30.00 per debtor. Real estate owner, mortgage, and property transfer searches available. Cert fee: $10.00 per doc. Payee: Stevens County Recorder. **Online Access to Assessor records:** Look-up assessor property tax data free at http://morris.state.mn.us/tax/. **Other phones:** Assessor-320-589-7407; Treasurer-320-589-7418.

Swift County

County Recorder, PO Box 246, Benson, MN 56215. **Phone-**County Recorder, R/E & UCC Recording- 320-843-3377; fax-320-843-2275; hours 8AM-4:30PM

Will search UCC records. Search per debtor, including 10 copies/listings- $20.00. UCC copy- $1.00 per page after 10 pages. Tax liens not included in UCC search. Separate federal/state combined tax lien search- $20.00 per debtor. Will search real estate records. RE record copy- $2.00 per doc. Cert fee: $5.00 up to 15 pages. Payee: Swift County Recorder. **Other phones:** Assessor-320-842-5891; Treasurer-320-843-3544; Vital Records-320-843-3544.

Todd County

County Recorder, 221 1st Ave South, #300, Long Prairie, MN 56347-1391. **Phone-**County Recorder, R/E & UCC Recording- 320-732-4428; fax-320-732-4001; hours-8AM-4:30PM

www.co.todd.mn.us/Recorder/recorder.htm Will search UCC records. Search per debtor- $20.00. Tax liens not included in UCC search. Separate federal/state combined tax lien search- $15.00 per debtor. Will not search real estate records. Record copy- $1.00 per page. Cert fee: $5.00 per doc. Payee: Todd County Recorder. **Online Access to Property, GIS-Mapping records:** Access to property information on the GIS-mapping site is free at www.co.todd.mn.us/toddcounty/propertyinfo0009.asp, although search options are limited; no name or address searching. **Other phones:** Assessor-320-732-4430; Treasurer-320-732-4471; Auditor-320-732-4430; Elections-320-732-4471; Vital Records-320-732-4428.

Traverse County

County Recorder, PO Box 487, Wheaton, MN 56296-0487. **Phone-**320-563-4622, R/E Recording- 320-563-4242; fax-320-563-4424; hours 8AM-4:30PM

Will search UCC records. Search per debtor, including 10 copies/listings- $20.00. UCC copy- $1.00 per page after 10 pages. Tax liens not included in UCC search. Tax lien search fee- $20.00 per debtor. Real estate owner, mortgage, and property transfer searches available. Cert fee: $10.00 per doc. Payee: County Recorder. **Other phones:** Assessor-320-563-4113; Treasurer-320-563-4616.

Wabasha County

County Recorder, 625 Jefferson Ave, Wabasha, MN 55981. **Phone-**651-565-3623, R/E Recording- 612-565-3623; fax-651-565-2774; hours 8AM-4PM
Will search UCC records. Search per debtor,copies included $20.00. UCC search includes tax liens if requested. Separate federal/state combined tax lien search- $2.00 per debtor. Real estate record owner and mortgage searches available. RE record copy-$1.00 per page. Cert fee: $5.00 per doc for 1st 5 pages; $1.00 each add'l. Payee: Wabasha County Recorder. **Other phones:** Assessor-651-565-3669; Treasurer-651-565-3669.

Wadena County

County Recorder, 415 Jefferson St S, Wadena, MN 56482. **Phone-**County Recorder, R/E & UCC Recording- 218-631-7622; fax-218-631-5709; hours 8AM-4:30PM www.co.wadena.mn.us
Will search UCC records. Search per debtor, including 10 copies/listings- $20.00. UCC copy-$1.00 per page after 10 pages. Tax liens not included in UCC search. Tax lien search fee-$20.00 per debtor. Will not search real estate records. RE record copy- $1.00 per page. Cert fee: $5.00 per doc. Payee: Wadena County Recorder. **Other phones:** Assessor-218-631-7628; Treasurer-218-631-7621; Auditor-218-631-7628; Elections-218-631-7650; Vital Records-218-631-7788; Auditor-218-631-7785.

Waseca County

County Recorder, 307 N. State St, Waseca, MN 56093. **Phone-**507-835-0670, R/E Recording- 5-7-835-0670; fax-507-835-0633; hours 8AM-4:30PM
Will search UCC records. Search per debtor, including 10 copies/listings- $20.00. UCC copy-$1.00 per page after 10 pages. Tax liens not included in UCC search. Separate federal/state combined tax lien search- $15.00 per debtor. Will not search real estate records. RE record copy- $1-3.00 per page. Cert fee: $1.00 per page, $5.00 min. Payee: Waseca County Recorder. **Other phones:** Assessor-507-835-0640.

Washington County

County Recorder, 14900 N. 61st St, PO Box 6, Stillwater, MN 55082. **Phone-**County Recorder, R/E & UCC Recording- 651-430-6755, UCC Recording- 651-275-7061; fax-651-275-7060; hours 7:30AM-5PM www.co.washington.mn.us
Will search UCC records. Search per debtor- $20.00. Tax liens not included in UCC search. Tax lien search fee- $20.00 per debtor. Real estate owner, mortgage, and property transfer searches available. Record copy- $1.00 per page. Cert fee: $1.00 per page, $5.00 min. Payee: Washington County Recorder. **Online Access to Real Estate Tract records:** Access to county online records requires a monthly set up fee; UCC information is on a state system. Online access to property tax records is free at www2.co.washington.mn.us/opip/; no name searching - property ID or address required, also www.co.washington.mn.us/recorder/index.ntml. **Other phones:** Assessor-651-430-6175; Treasurer-651-430-6175; Vital Records-651-275-7062; Torren Division-651-430-6756.

Watonwan County

County Recorder, PO Box 518, St. James, MN 56081. **Phone-**County Recorder, R/E & UCC Recording- 507-375-1216; hours 8:30AM-Noon, 1-5PM
Will search UCC records. Search per debtor, including 10 copies/listings- $20.00. UCC copy-$1.00 per page after 10 pages. Tax liens not included in UCC search. Tax lien search fee-$15.00 per debtor. Real estate owner, mortgage, and property transfer searches available. RE record copy-$1.00 per page. Cert fee: $5.00 per doc. Payee: Watonwan County Recorder. **Other phones:** Assessor-507-375-1205; Treasurer-507-375-1213; Vital Records-507-375-1216.

Wilkin County

County Recorder, PO Box 29, Breckenridge, MN 56520. **Phone-**County Recorder, R/E & UCC Recording- 218-643-7164; fax-218-643-7170; hours 8AM-4:30PM www.co.wilkin.mn.us/recorder.asp
Will search UCC records. Search per debtor, including 10 copies/listings- $20.00. UCC copy fee- $1.00. Tax liens not included in UCC search. Tax lien search fee- $15.00 per debtor. Real estate owner, mortgage, and property transfer searches available. RE record copy- $3.00 1st 2 pages; $.50 each add'l. Cert fee: $1.00 per page, $5.00 min. Payee: Wilkin County Recorder. **Other phones:** Assessor-218-643-7162; Treasurer-218-643-7112; Vital Records-218-643-7112.

Winona County

County Recorder, 177 Main St, Winona, MN 55987. **Phone-**507-457-6340; fax-507-454-9371; hours 8AM-4:30PM
Will search UCC records. Search per debtor- $20.00. UCC copy- $2.00 per page. Tax liens not included in UCC search. Separate federal/state combined tax lien search- $20.00 per debtor. Real estate owner, mortgage, and property transfer searches available. RE record copy- $2.00 per record. Cert fee: $5.00 per doc. Payee: Winona County Recorder. **Other phones:** Treasurer-507-457-6450.

Wright County

County Recorder, 10 2nd St NW, Rm 210, Buffalo, MN 55313-1196. **Phone-**County Recorder, R/E & UCC Recording- 763-682-7357, UCC Recording- 763-684-4551; fax-763-684-4558; hours 8AM-4:30PM www.co.wright.mn.us
Will search UCC records. Search per debtor, including 10 copies/listings- $20.00. UCC copy-$1.00 per page after 10 pages. Tax liens not included in UCC search. Tax lien search fee-$15.00 per debtor. Real estate owner, mortgage, and property transfer searches available. RE record copy-$1.00 per page. Cert fee: $1.00 per page, $5.00 min. Payee: Wright County Recorder. **Online Access to Recorder, Land, Lien, Grantor/Grantee, Property Tax records:** Access to Land Title database is free at www.co.wright.mn.us/department/recorder/landtitle/index.htm. Also, search the property tax database for free at www.co.wright.mn.us/department/audtreas/proptax/default.asp. **Other phones:** Assessor-763-682-7367; Treasurer-763-682-7578; Elections-763-682-7578; Vital Records-763-682-7594.

Yellow Medicine County

County Recorder, 415 9th Ave, Courthouse, Granite Falls, MN 56241. **Phone-**320-564-2529, R/E Recording- 320-564-3132; fax-320-564-3670; hours 8AM-4PM http://yellowmedicine.govoffice.com
Will search UCC records. Search per debtor, including 10 copies/listings- $20.00. UCC copy-$1.00 per page after 10 pages. Tax liens not included in UCC search. Separate federal/state combined tax lien search- $2.00 per debtor. Will not search real estate records. Cert fee: $1.00 per page. Payee: Yellow Medicine County Recorder. **Other phones:** Assessor-320-564-3678; Treasurer-320-564-3231.

Minnesota County Locator

You will usually be able to find the city name in the City/County Cross Reference below. In that case, it is a simple matter to determine the county from the cross reference. However, only the official US Postal Service city names are included in this index. There are an additional 40,000 place names that people use in their addresses. Therefore, we have also included a ZIP/City Cross Reference immediately following the City/County Cross Reference.

If you know the ZIP Code but the city name does not appear in the City/County Cross Reference index, look up the ZIP Code in the ZIP/City Cross Reference, find the city name, then look up the city name in the City/County Cross Reference. For example, you want to know the county for an address of Menands, NY 12204. There is no "Menands" in the City/County Cross Reference. The ZIP/City Cross Reference shows that ZIP Codes 12201-12288 are for the city of Albany. Looking back in the City/County Cross Reference, Albany is in Albany County.

Minnesota City/County Cross Reference

ADA Norman
ADAMS Mower
ADOLPH St. Louis
ADRIAN Nobles
AFTON Washington
AH GWAH CHING Cass
AITKIN (56431) Aitkin(69), Crow Wing(30)
AKELEY (56433) Hubbard(84), Cass(15)
ALBANY Stearns
ALBERT LEA Freeborn
ALBERTA (56207) Stevens(98), Swift(1)
ALBERTVILLE Wright
ALBORN St. Louis
ALDEN Freeborn
ALDRICH (56434) Todd(67), Wadena(32)
ALEXANDRIA Douglas
ALMELUND Chisago
ALPHA (56111) Martin(60), Jackson(39)
ALTURA (55910) Winona(86), Wabasha(14)
ALVARADO (56710) Marshall(85), Polk(14)
AMBOY (56010) Blue Earth(97), Faribault(1)
AMIRET Lyon
ANGLE INLET Lake of the Woods
ANGORA St. Louis
ANGUS Polk
ANNANDALE Wright
ANOKA Anoka
APPLETON (56208) Swift(91), Lac qui Parle(5), Big Stone(2)
ARCO (56113) Lincoln(81), Lyon(18)
ARGYLE Marshall
ARLINGTON Sibley
ASHBY (56309) Grant(64), Otter Tail(29), Douglas(6)
ASKOV Pine
ATWATER (56209) Kandiyohi(83), Meeker(16)
AUDUBON Becker
AURORA St. Louis
AUSTIN (55912) Mower(94), Freeborn(5)
AVOCA Murray
AVON Stearns
BABBITT St. Louis
BACKUS (56435) Cass(96), Crow Wing(3)
BADGER Roseau
BAGLEY (56621) Clearwater(94), Polk(5)
BAKER Clay
BALATON (56115) Lyon(56), Murray(43)
BANGOR Pope
BARNESVILLE (56514) Clay(90), Wilkin(8)
BARNUM Carlton
BARRETT Grant
BARRY Big Stone
BATTLE LAKE Otter Tail
BAUDETTE (56623) Lake of the Woods(84), Koochiching(15)
BAXTER Crow Wing
BAYPORT Washington
BEARDSLEY (56211) Big Stone(72), Traverse(27)
BEAVER BAY Lake

BEAVER CREEK Rock
BECIDA Hubbard
BECKER Sherburne
BEJOU (56516) Mahnomen(77), Norman(22)
BELGRADE (56312) Stearns(67), Kandiyohi(32)
BELLE PLAINE (56011) Scott(78), Sibley(13), Le Sueur(4), Carver(2)
BELLINGHAM Lac qui Parle
BELTRAMI (56517) Polk(98), Norman(1)
BELVIEW (56214) Redwood(90), Yellow Medicine(9)
BEMIDJI (56601) Beltrami(93), Hubbard(6)
BEMIDJI Beltrami
BENA Cass
BENEDICT Hubbard
BENSON (56215) Swift(95), Pope(4)
BEROUN Pine
BERTHA (56437) Todd(85), Otter Tail(14)
BETHEL (55005) Anoka(97), Isanti(2)
BIG FALLS Koochiching
BIG LAKE Sherburne
BIGELOW Nobles
BIGFORK Itasca
BINGHAM LAKE (56118) Cottonwood(92), Jackson(7)
BIRCHDALE Koochiching
BIRD ISLAND Renville
BIWABIK St. Louis
BLACKDUCK (56630) Itasca(42), Aitkin(41), Beltrami(16)
BLOMKEST Kandiyohi
BLOOMING PRAIRIE (55917) Steele(65), Dodge(19), Mower(8), Freeborn(6)
BLUE EARTH (56013) Faribault(97), Martin(2)
BLUFFTON Otter Tail
BOCK Mille Lacs
BORUP (56519) Norman(58), Clay(42)
BOVEY Itasca
BOWLUS (56314) Morrison(95), Stearns(4)
BOWSTRING Itasca
BOY RIVER Cass
BOYD (56218) Lac qui Parle(61), Yellow Medicine(38)
BRAHAM (55006) Isanti(35), Washington(31), Pine(13), Kanabec(11)
BRAINERD (56401) Crow Wing(94), Cass(5)
BRANDON (56315) Douglas(96), Otter Tail(3)
BRECKENRIDGE Wilkin
BREWSTER (56119) Nobles(68), Jackson(31)
BRICELYN Faribault
BRIMSON (55602) St. Louis(93), Lake(6)
BRITT St. Louis
BROOK PARK (55007) Pine(98), Kanabec(1)
BROOKS (56715) Red Lake(97), Polk(2)
BROOKSTON St. Louis

BROOTEN (56316) Stearns(88), Kandiyohi(10)
BROWERVILLE Todd
BROWNS VALLEY (56219) Traverse(95), Big Stone(4)
BROWNSDALE Mower
BROWNSVILLE Houston
BROWNTON McLeod
BRUNO Pine
BUCKMAN Morrison
BUFFALO Wright
BUFFALO LAKE (55314) Renville(81), Sibley(18)
BUHL St. Louis
BURNSVILLE Dakota
BURTRUM (56318) Todd(71), Morrison(28)
BUTTERFIELD (56120) Watonwan(59), Cottonwood(40)
BYRON (55920) Olmsted(98), Dodge(1)
CALEDONIA Houston
CALLAWAY Becker
CALUMET Itasca
CAMBRIDGE Isanti
CAMPBELL (56522) Wilkin(88), Otter Tail(9), Grant(2)
CANBY (56220) Yellow Medicine(80), Lac qui Parle(11), Lincoln(7)
CANNON FALLS (55009) Goodhue(92), Dakota(7)
CANTON Fillmore
CANYON St. Louis
CARLOS Douglas
CARLTON Carlton
CARVER Carver
CASS LAKE (56633) Cass(69), Beltrami(26), Hubbard(3)
CASTLE ROCK Dakota
CEDAR Anoka
CENTER CITY Chisago
CEYLON Martin
CHAMPLIN Hennepin
CHANDLER Murray
CHANHASSEN Carver
CHASKA Carver
CHATFIELD (55923) Fillmore(53), Olmsted(46)
CHISAGO CITY Chisago
CHISHOLM St. Louis
CHOKIO (56221) Stevens(90), Big Stone(8), Traverse(1)
CIRCLE PINES Anoka
CLARA CITY Chippewa
CLAREMONT (55924) Dodge(72), Steele(27)
CLARISSA Todd
CLARKFIELD (56223) Yellow Medicine(98), Lac qui Parle(1)
CLARKS GROVE Freeborn
CLEAR LAKE Sherburne
CLEARBROOK (56634) Clearwater(55), Polk(44)
CLEARWATER (55320) Wright(61), Stearns(38)

CLEMENTS Redwood
CLEVELAND Le Sueur
CLIMAX Polk
CLINTON Big Stone
CLITHERALL Otter Tail
CLONTARF (56226) Swift(85), Pope(14)
CLOQUET (55720) Carlton(90), St. Louis(9)
COHASSET Itasca
COKATO Wright
COLD SPRING Stearns
COLERAINE Itasca
COLLEGEVILLE Stearns
COLOGNE Carver
COMFREY (56019) Brown(64), Cottonwood(27), Watonwan(7)
COMSTOCK Clay
CONGER Freeborn
COOK (55788) Itasca(77), St. Louis(22)
COOK (55723) St. Louis(78), Itasca(21)
CORRELL Big Stone
COSMOS (56228) Meeker(94), Renville(5)
COTTAGE GROVE Washington
COTTON St. Louis
COTTONWOOD (56229) Lyon(78), Yellow Medicine(20)
COURTLAND Nicollet
CRANE LAKE St. Louis
CROMWELL Carlton
CROOKSTON Polk
CROSBY Crow Wing
CROSSLAKE Crow Wing
CRYSTAL BAY Hennepin
CULVER St. Louis
CURRIE Murray
CUSHING (56443) Morrison(77), Todd(22)
CYRUS (56323) Pope(86), Stevens(13)
DAKOTA Winona
DALBO Isanti
DALTON (56324) Otter Tail(97), Grant(2)
DANUBE Renville
DANVERS Swift
DARFUR Watonwan
DARWIN Meeker
DASSEL Meeker
DAWSON Lac qui Parle
DAYTON Hennepin
DE GRAFF (56233) Swift(82), Chippewa(17)
DEBS Beltrami
DEER CREEK Otter Tail
DEER RIVER (56636) Itasca(92), Cass(7)
DEERWOOD Crow Wing
DELANO (55328) Wright(97), Carver(2)
DELAVAN Faribault
DELFT Cottonwood
DENHAM Pine
DENHAM St. Louis
DENNISON (55018) Goodhue(86), Rice(12)
DENT Otter Tail
DETROIT LAKES (56501) Becker(97), Otter Tail(2)

DETROIT LAKES Becker
DEXTER Mower
DILWORTH Clay
DODGE CENTER Dodge
DONALDSON Kittson
DONNELLY (56235) Grant(53),
    Stevens(46)
DOVER Olmsted
DOVRAY Murray
DULUTH (55810) St. Louis(97), Carlton(2)
DULUTH St. Louis
DUMONT (56236) Traverse(70), Big
    Stone(29)
DUNDAS Rice
DUNDEE (56126) Nobles(65),
    Cottonwood(18), Murray(12), Jackson(3)
DUNNELL Martin
DUQUETTE Pine
EAGLE BEND (56446) Todd(93),
    Douglas(6)
EAGLE LAKE Blue Earth
EAST GRAND FORKS Polk
EASTON Faribault
ECHO Yellow Medicine
EDEN PRAIRIE Hennepin
EDEN VALLEY (55329) Stearns(50),
    Meeker(49)
EDGERTON (56128) Pipestone(76),
    Nobles(16), Rock(6)
EFFIE (56639) Itasca(93), Koochiching(6)
EITZEN Houston
ELBOW LAKE Grant
ELGIN (55932) Wabasha(55), Olmsted(44)
ELIZABETH Otter Tail
ELK RIVER (55330) Sherburne(76),
    Wright(17), Anoka(5)
ELKO Scott
ELKTON Mower
ELLENDALE (56026) Steele(57),
    Freeborn(41), Waseca(1)
ELLSWORTH (56129) Nobles(84),
    Rock(14), Lyon(1)
ELMORE (56027) Faribault(96), Martin(3)
ELROSA Stearns
ELY (55731) St. Louis(88), Lake(11)
ELYSIAN (56028) Le Sueur(92),
    Waseca(7)
EMBARRASS St. Louis
EMILY Crow Wing
EMMONS Freeborn
ERHARD Otter Tail
ERSKINE (56535) Polk(96), Red Lake(3)
ESKO (55733) Carlton(96), St. Louis(3)
ESSIG Brown
EUCLID Polk
EVAN (56238) Redwood(75), Brown(25)
EVANSVILLE (56326) Douglas(85), Otter
    Tail(11), Grant(3)
EVELETH St. Louis
EXCELSIOR (55331) Hennepin(98),
    Carver(1)
EYOTA Olmsted
FAIRFAX (55332) Renville(85),
    Nicollet(13), Sibley(1)
FAIRMONT Martin
FARIBAULT Rice
FARMINGTON Dakota
FARWELL (56327) Douglas(56), Pope(43)
FEDERAL DAM Cass
FELTON Clay
FERGUS FALLS Otter Tail
FERTILE (56540) Polk(93), Norman(6)
FIFTY LAKES Crow Wing
FINLAND Lake
FINLAYSON (55735) Pine(75), Aitkin(24)
FISHER Polk
FLENSBURG Morrison
FLOM Norman
FLOODWOOD (55736) St. Louis(93),
    Itasca(6)
FOLEY (56329) Benton(94), Morrison(5)
FORBES St. Louis

FOREST LAKE (55025) Washington(78),
    Anoka(12), Chisago(9)
FORESTON (56330) Mille Lacs(77),
    Benton(22)
FORT RIPLEY (56449) Crow Wing(84),
    Morrison(15)
FOSSTON (56542) Polk(95), Mahnomen(4)
FOUNTAIN Fillmore
FOXHOME Wilkin
FRANKLIN (55333) Renville(92),
    Redwood(4), Brown(3)
FRAZEE (56544) Becker(83), Otter Tail(16)
FREEBORN Freeborn
FREEPORT (56331) Stearns(98), Todd(1)
FRONTENAC Goodhue
FROST Faribault
FULDA (56131) Murray(84), Nobles(10),
    Cottonwood(5)
GARDEN CITY Blue Earth
GARFIELD Douglas
GARRISON (56450) Crow Wing(60), Mille
    Lacs(39)
GARVIN Lyon
GARY Norman
GATZKE (56724) Marshall(98), Roseau(1)
GAYLORD (55334) Sibley(93), Nicollet(6)
GENEVA Freeborn
GEORGETOWN Clay
GHENT Lyon
GIBBON (55335) Sibley(78), Nicollet(21)
GILBERT St. Louis
GILMAN Benton
GLENCOE (55336) McLeod(93), Sibley(6)
GLENVILLE Freeborn
GLENWOOD Pope
GLYNDON Clay
GONVICK (56644) Clearwater(84),
    Polk(15)
GOOD THUNDER Blue Earth
GOODHUE (55027) Goodhue(97),
    Wabasha(2)
GOODLAND Itasca
GOODRIDGE (56725) Pennington(71),
    Marshall(27)
GRACEVILLE (56240) Big Stone(75),
    Traverse(24)
GRANADA (56039) Martin(97), Faribault(2)
GRAND MARAIS Cook
GRAND MEADOW Mower
GRAND PORTAGE Cook
GRAND RAPIDS Itasca
GRANDY Isanti
GRANGER Fillmore
GRANITE FALLS (56241) Yellow
    Medicine(83), Chippewa(11), Renville(4)
GRASSTON (55030) Pine(91), Kanabec(8)
GREEN ISLE (55338) Sibley(96), Carver(3)
GREENBUSH Roseau
GREENWALD Stearns
GREY EAGLE Todd
GROVE CITY Meeker
GRYGLA (56727) Beltrami(59),
    Marshall(40)
GULLY (56646) Polk(95), Clearwater(4)
HACKENSACK Cass
HADLEY Murray
HALLOCK Kittson
HALMA Kittson
HALSTAD Norman
HAMBURG (55339) Carver(69), Sibley(26),
    McLeod(4)
HAMEL Hennepin
HAMMOND Wabasha
HAMPTON Dakota
HANCOCK (56244) Stevens(68), Pope(29),
    Swift(2)
HANLEY FALLS Yellow Medicine
HANOVER (55341) Wright(76),
    Hennepin(23)
HANSKA (56041) Brown(98), Watonwan(1)
HARDWICK Rock
HARMONY Fillmore
HARRIS Chisago

HARTLAND (56042) Freeborn(95),
    Waseca(4)
HASTINGS (55033) Dakota(91),
    Washington(8)
HAWICK Kandiyohi
HAWLEY Clay
HAYFIELD (55940) Dodge(81),
    Olmsted(17), Mower(1)
HAYWARD Freeborn
HAZEL RUN Yellow Medicine
HECTOR (55342) Renville(95), Sibley(3)
HENDERSON (56044) Sibley(88), Le
    Sueur(10)
HENDRICKS (56136) Lincoln(97),
    Dodge(2)
HENDRUM Norman
HENNING Otter Tail
HENRIETTE Pine
HERMAN (56248) Grant(87), Traverse(6),
    Stevens(5)
HERON LAKE (56137) Jackson(74),
    Cottonwood(19), Nobles(5)
HEWITT (56453) Todd(79), Otter Tail(20)
HIBBING (55746) St. Louis(98), Itasca(1)
HIBBING St. Louis
HILL CITY (55748) Aitkin(68), Itasca(31)
HILLMAN (56338) Morrison(95), Crow
    Wing(4)
HILLS Rock
HINCKLEY (55037) Pine(97), Kanabec(2)
HINES Beltrami
HITTERDAL (56552) Clay(79), Becker(20)
HOFFMAN (56339) Grant(88), Douglas(11)
HOKAH Houston
HOLDINGFORD Stearns
HOLLAND Pipestone
HOLLANDALE Freeborn
HOLLOWAY Swift
HOLMES CITY Douglas
HOLYOKE (55749) Carlton(71), Pine(28)
HOMER Winona
HOPE Steele
HOPKINS Hennepin
HOUSTON (55943) Houston(84),
    Winona(15)
HOVLAND Cook
HOWARD LAKE Hennepin
HOWARD LAKE Wright
HOYT LAKES St. Louis
HUGO (55038) Washington(67), Anoka(32)
HUMBOLDT Kittson
HUNTLEY Faribault
HUTCHINSON (55350) McLeod(91),
    Renville(5), Meeker(3)
IHLEN Pipestone
INTERNATIONAL FALLS Koochiching
INVER GROVE HEIGHTS Dakota
IONA (56141) Murray(90), Nobles(10)
IRON St. Louis
IRONTON Crow Wing
ISABELLA Lake
ISANTI Isanti
ISLE (56342) Mille Lacs(74), Kanabec(18),
    Aitkin(6)
IVANHOE Lincoln
JACOBSON (55752) Itasca(82), Aitkin(17)
JANESVILLE (56048) Waseca(98), Blue
    Earth(1)
JASPER (56144) Rock(77), Pipestone(18),
    Murray(3), Mower(1)
JEFFERS Cottonwood
JENKINS Crow Wing
JOHNSON (56250) Big Stone(70),
    Traverse(29)
JORDAN Scott
KABETOGAMA (56669) Koochiching(60),
    St. Louis(39)
KANARANZI (56146) Nobles(96), Rock(3)
KANDIYOHI Kandiyohi
KARLSTAD (56732) Kittson(89),
    Marshall(6), Roseau(4)
KASOTA (56050) Le Sueur(97), Blue
    Earth(2)

KASSON (55944) Dodge(94), Olmsted(5)
KEEWATIN Itasca
KELLIHER Beltrami
KELLOGG Wabasha
KELSEY St. Louis
KENNEDY Kittson
KENNETH (56147) Rock(72), Nobles(27)
KENSINGTON (56343) Douglas(69),
    Pope(15), Stevens(7), Grant(6)
KENT Wilkin
KENYON (55946) Goodhue(83), Rice(12),
    Dodge(3), Steele(1)
KERKHOVEN (56252) Kandiyohi(58),
    Swift(32), Chippewa(9)
KERRICK (55756) Pine(92), Carlton(7)
KETTLE RIVER Carlton
KIESTER (56051) Faribault(97),
    Freeborn(2)
KILKENNY (56052) Rice(66), Le Sueur(33)
KIMBALL (55353) Stearns(76), Meeker(23)
KINNEY St. Louis
KLOSSNER Nicollet
KNIFE RIVER Lake
LA CRESCENT (55947) Houston(88),
    Winona(11)
LA SALLE Watonwan
LAFAYETTE (56054) Nicollet(90), Sibley(9)
LAKE BENTON (56149) Lincoln(97),
    Pipestone(2)
LAKE BRONSON Kittson
LAKE CITY (55041) Wabasha(84),
    Goodhue(15)
LAKE CRYSTAL Blue Earth
LAKE ELMO Washington
LAKE GEORGE Hubbard
LAKE HUBERT Crow Wing
LAKE ITASCA Clearwater
LAKE LILLIAN Kandiyohi
LAKE PARK (56554) Becker(95), Clay(4)
LAKE WILSON Murray
LAKEFIELD Jackson
LAKELAND Washington
LAKEVILLE (55044) Dakota(86), Scott(13)
LAMBERTON (56152) Redwood(81),
    Cottonwood(18)
LANCASTER (56735) Kittson(97),
    Roseau(2)
LANESBORO Fillmore
LANSING Mower
LAPORTE (56461) Hubbard(94), Cass(5)
LASTRUP Morrison
LE CENTER Le Sueur
LE ROY (55951) Rice(60), Fillmore(40)
LE SUEUR (56058) Le Sueur(84),
    Sibley(11), Nicollet(3)
LENGBY (56651) Mahnomen(61), Polk(38)
LEONARD (56652) Clearwater(97),
    Beltrami(2)
LEOTA Nobles
LESTER PRAIRIE McLeod
LEWISTON Winona
LEWISVILLE (56060) Watonwan(87), Blue
    Earth(12)
LINDSTROM Chisago
LISMORE Nobles
LITCHFIELD Meeker
LITTLE FALLS Morrison
LITTLEFORK Koochiching
LOMAN Koochiching
LONDON Freeborn
LONG LAKE Hennepin
LONG PRAIRIE (56347) Todd(98),
    Morrison(1)
LONG PRAIRIE Todd
LONGVILLE Cass
LONSDALE Rice
LORETTO Hennepin
LOUISBURG Lac qui Parle
LOWRY (56349) Pope(84), Douglas(15)
LUCAN Redwood
LUTSEN Cook
LUVERNE Rock

LYLE (55953) Mower(80), Rice(14), Freeborn(4)
LYND Lyon
MABEL (55954) Fillmore(89), Houston(10)
MADELIA (56062) Watonwan(91), Brown(8)
MADISON Lac qui Parle
MADISON LAKE (56063) Blue Earth(59), Waseca(28), Le Sueur(11)
MAGNOLIA (56158) Rock(75), Nobles(25)
MAHNOMEN (56557) Mahnomen(95), Clearwater(2), Norman(2)
MAHTOWA Carlton
MAKINEN St. Louis
MANCHESTER Freeborn
MANHATTAN BEACH Crow Wing
MANKATO Blue Earth
MANKATO Nicollet
MANTORVILLE Dodge
MAPLE LAKE Wright
MAPLE PLAIN Hennepin
MAPLE PLAIN Wright
MAPLETON (56065) Blue Earth(56), Faribault(32), Waseca(11)
MARBLE Itasca
MARCELL Itasca
MARGIE Koochiching
MARIETTA (56257) Lac qui Parle(98), Grant(1)
MARINE ON SAINT CROIX Washington
MARSHALL Lyon
MAX Itasca
MAYER Carver
MAYNARD (56260) Chippewa(70), Renville(29)
MAZEPPA (55956) Wabasha(74), Goodhue(24), Olmsted(1)
MC GRATH Aitkin
MC KINLEY St. Louis
MCGREGOR Aitkin
MCINTOSH Polk
MEADOWLANDS St. Louis
MEDFORD (55049) Steele(89), Rice(10)
MELROSE Stearns
MELRUDE St. Louis
MENAHGA (56464) Wadena(52), Becker(29), Hubbard(15), Otter Tail(2)
MENDOTA Dakota
MENTOR (56736) Polk(88), Red Lake(11)
MERIDEN (56067) Waseca(69), Steele(30)
MERRIFIELD Crow Wing
MIDDLE RIVER Marshall
MILACA (56353) Mille Lacs(97), Isanti(2)
MILAN (56262) Chippewa(83), Swift(16)
MILLVILLE Wabasha
MILROY (56263) Redwood(83), Lyon(16)
MILTONA Douglas
MINNEAPOLIS Anoka
MINNEAPOLIS Carver
MINNEAPOLIS Hennepin
MINNEOTA (56264) Lyon(87), Yellow Medicine(11), Lincoln(1)
MINNESOTA CITY Winona
MINNESOTA LAKE (56068) Waseca(44), Faribault(43), Blue Earth(11)
MINNETONKA Hennepin
MINNETONKA BEACH Hennepin
MIZPAH Koochiching
MONTEVIDEO (56265) Chippewa(88), Lac qui Parle(8), Yellow Medicine(3)
MONTGOMERY (56069) Le Sueur(61), Rice(38)
MONTICELLO Carver
MONTICELLO Wright
MONTROSE (55363) Wright(98), Carver(1)
MOORHEAD Clay
MOOSE LAKE (55767) Carlton(80), Pine(19)
MORA Kanabec
MORGAN (56266) Redwood(75), Brown(24)
MORRIS Stevens

MORRISTOWN (55052) Rice(94), Waseca(5)
MORTON (56270) Renville(52), Redwood(47)
MOTLEY (56466) Morrison(48), Cass(40), Todd(11)
MOUND Hennepin
MOUNTAIN IRON St. Louis
MOUNTAIN LAKE (56159) Cottonwood(95), Jackson(3)
MURDOCK (56271) Swift(84), Chippewa(15)
MYRTLE Freeborn
NASHUA (56565) Wilkin(80), Grant(19)
NASHWAUK Itasca
NASSAU Lac qui Parle
NAVARRE Hennepin
NAYTAHWAUSH Mahnomen
NELSON Douglas
NERSTRAND (55053) Rice(80), Goodhue(19)
NETT LAKE St. Louis
NEVIS Hubbard
NEW AUBURN Sibley
NEW GERMANY Carver
NEW LONDON Kandiyohi
NEW MARKET Scott
NEW MUNICH Stearns
NEW PRAGUE (56071) Scott(55), Le Sueur(41), Rice(3)
NEW RICHLAND (56072) Waseca(90), Freeborn(9)
NEW ULM (56073) Brown(86), Nicollet(12), Blue Earth(1)
NEW YORK MILLS Otter Tail
NEWFOLDEN Marshall
NEWPORT Washington
NICOLLET Nicollet
NIELSVILLE (56568) Polk(92), Norman(7)
NIMROD Wadena
NISSWA (56468) Crow Wing(69), Cass(30)
NORCROSS (56274) Grant(68), Traverse(31)
NORTH BRANCH (55056) Chisago(79), Isanti(20)
NORTHFIELD (55057) Rice(81), Dakota(18)
NORTHHOME (56661) Itasca(51), Koochiching(36), Beltrami(12)
NORTHROP Martin
NORWOOD (55368) Carver(97), McLeod(2)
NORWOOD Carver
NOYES Kittson
OAK ISLAND Lake of the Woods
OAK PARK Benton
OAKLAND Freeborn
ODESSA (56276) Big Stone(74), Lac qui Parle(25)
ODIN (56160) Watonwan(41), Martin(36), Jackson(21)
OGEMA Becker
OGILVIE (56358) Kanabec(88), Mille Lacs(11)
OKABENA Jackson
OKLEE (56742) Red Lake(79), Pennington(16), Polk(3)
OLIVIA Renville
ONAMIA Mille Lacs
ORMSBY (56162) Martin(55), Watonwan(44)
ORONOCO Olmsted
ORR (55771) St. Louis(91), Koochiching(8)
ORTONVILLE (56278) Big Stone(98), Lac qui Parle(1)
OSAGE Becker
OSAKIS (56360) Todd(57), Douglas(42)
OSLO (56744) Marshall(57), Polk(24), Mower(15), Crow Wing(3)
OSSEO Hennepin
OSTRANDER (55961) Mower(66), Fillmore(33)
OTISCO Waseca

OTTERTAIL Otter Tail
OUTING Cass
OWATONNA Steele
PALISADE Aitkin
PARK RAPIDS (56470) Hubbard(88), Becker(11)
PARKERS PRAIRIE (56361) Otter Tail(63), Douglas(36)
PARKVILLE St. Louis
PAYNESVILLE (56362) Stearns(89), Meeker(6), Kandiyohi(3)
PEASE Mille Lacs
PELICAN RAPIDS (56572) Otter Tail(95), Becker(2), Clay(1)
PEMBERTON (56078) Waseca(73), Blue Earth(26)
PENGILLY Itasca
PENNINGTON Beltrami
PENNOCK Kandiyohi
PEQUOT LAKES (56472) Crow Wing(76), Cass(23)
PERHAM Otter Tail
PERLEY (56574) Norman(95), Clay(4)
PETERSON (55962) Fillmore(94), Winona(5)
PIERZ (56364) Morrison(97), Crow Wing(2)
PILLAGER Cass
PINE CITY Pine
PINE ISLAND (55963) Goodhue(51), Olmsted(31), Dodge(17)
PINE RIVER (56474) Cass(95), Crow Wing(4)
PIPESTONE (56164) Pipestone(97), Lincoln(2)
PITT Lake of the Woods
PLAINVIEW (55964) Wabasha(96), Olmsted(2), Winona(1)
PLATO McLeod
PLUMMER (56748) Red Lake(90), Pennington(9)
PONEMAH Beltrami
PONSFORD Becker
PORTER (56280) Yellow Medicine(63), Lincoln(36)
PRESTON Fillmore
PRINCETON (55371) Mille Lacs(59), Sherburne(23), Isanti(15), Benton(1)
PRINSBURG Kandiyohi
PRIOR LAKE Scott
PUPOSKY Beltrami
RACINE Mower
RANDALL Morrison
RANDOLPH Dakota
RANIER Koochiching
RAY (56669) Koochiching(60), St. Louis(39)
RAYMOND (56282) Kandiyohi(81), Chippewa(18)
READING Nobles
READS LANDING Wabasha
RED LAKE FALLS (56750) Red Lake(94), Polk(3), Pennington(2)
RED WING Goodhue
REDBY Beltrami
REDLAKE Beltrami
REDWOOD FALLS (56283) Redwood(95), Renville(4)
REMER Cass
RENVILLE (56284) Renville(86), Kandiyohi(10), Redwood(2)
REVERE (56166) Redwood(74), Cottonwood(25)
RICE (56367) Benton(82), Stearns(16)
RICHMOND Stearns
RICHVILLE Otter Tail
RICHWOOD Becker
ROCHERT Becker
ROCHESTER Olmsted
ROCK CREEK Pine
ROCKFORD (55373) Wright(65), Hennepin(34)
ROCKFORD Hennepin
ROCKVILLE Stearns

ROGERS (55374) Hennepin(94), Wright(5)
ROLLINGSTONE Winona
ROOSEVELT (56673) Roseau(83), Lake of the Woods(16)
ROSCOE Stearns
ROSE CREEK Mower
ROSEAU Roseau
ROSEMOUNT Dakota
ROTHSAY (56579) Wilkin(63), Otter Tail(36)
ROUND LAKE (56167) Nobles(54), Jackson(45)
ROYALTON (56373) Morrison(89), Benton(10)
RUSH CITY (55069) Chisago(95), Pine(4)
RUSHFORD (55971) Fillmore(82), Houston(10), Winona(6)
RUSHMORE Nobles
RUSSELL Lyon
RUTHTON (56170) Pipestone(73), Lyon(13), Murray(10), Lincoln(2)
RUTLEDGE Pine
SABIN Clay
SACRED HEART Renville
SAGINAW St. Louis
SAINT BONIFACIUS (55375) Hennepin(98), Carver(1)
SAINT CHARLES (55972) Winona(85), Olmsted(14)
SAINT CLAIR Blue Earth
SAINT CLOUD (56304) Sherburne(50), Benton(49)
SAINT CLOUD Stearns
SAINT FRANCIS (55070) Anoka(90), Isanti(9)
SAINT HILAIRE (56754) Pennington(87), Red Lake(12)
SAINT JAMES (56081) Watonwan(98), Brown(1)
SAINT JOSEPH Stearns
SAINT LEO Yellow Medicine
SAINT MARTIN Stearns
SAINT MICHAEL Wright
SAINT PAUL (55118) Dakota(98), Ramsey(1)
SAINT PAUL (55110) Ramsey(85), Washington(13), Anoka(1)
SAINT PAUL (55126) Ramsey(98), Anoka(1)
SAINT PAUL Dakota
SAINT PAUL Hennepin
SAINT PAUL Ramsey
SAINT PAUL Washington
SAINT PAUL PARK Washington
SAINT PETER (56082) Nicollet(89), Le Sueur(10)
SAINT STEPHEN Stearns
SAINT VINCENT Kittson
SALOL Roseau
SANBORN (56083) Redwood(54), Cottonwood(29), Brown(15)
SANDSTONE (55072) Pine(83), Kanabec(15)
SANTIAGO Sherburne
SARGEANT (55973) Mower(96), Dodge(3)
SARTELL (56377) Stearns(79), Benton(20)
SAUK CENTRE (56378) Stearns(80), Todd(19)
SAUK RAPIDS (56379) Benton(98), Stearns(1)
SAUM Beltrami
SAVAGE Scott
SAWYER Carlton
SCANDIA (55073) Washington(62), Chisago(37)
SCHROEDER Cook
SEAFORTH Redwood
SEARLES Brown
SEBEKA (56477) Wadena(80), Otter Tail(19)
SEDAN Pope
SHAFER Chisago
SHAKOPEE Scott

SHELLY Norman
SHERBURN Martin
SHEVLIN (56676) Beltrami(54), Clearwater(45)
SIDE LAKE St. Louis
SILVER BAY Lake
SILVER CREEK Wright
SILVER LAKE McLeod
SLAYTON Murray
SLEEPY EYE (56085) Brown(97), Redwood(2)
SOLWAY (56678) Hubbard(74), Beltrami(24)
SOUDAN St. Louis
SOUTH HAVEN (55382) Stearns(46), Wright(45), Meeker(7)
SOUTH INTERNATIONAL FALLS Koochiching
SOUTH SAINT PAUL Dakota
SPICER Kandiyohi
SPRING GROVE (55974) Houston(98), Fillmore(1)
SPRING LAKE Itasca
SPRING PARK Hennepin
SPRING VALLEY (55975) Fillmore(87), Mower(12)
SPRINGFIELD (56087) Brown(90), Redwood(9)
SQUAW LAKE Itasca
STACY (55079) Chisago(48), Anoka(31), Isanti(20)
STACY (55078) Washington(80), Chisago(20)
STANCHFIELD (55080) Isanti(63), Chisago(36)
STAPLES (56479) Todd(67), Wadena(32)
STARBUCK Pope
STEEN (56173) Rock(71), Polk(28)
STEPHEN (56757) Marshall(98), Kittson(1)
STEWART (55385) McLeod(53), Renville(33), Sibley(12)
STEWARTVILLE (55976) Olmsted(96), Mower(2), Fillmore(1)
STILLWATER Washington
STOCKTON Winona
STORDEN Cottonwood
STRANDQUIST Marshall
STRATHCONA (56759) Roseau(73), Marshall(26)

STURGEON LAKE (55783) Pine(97), Carlton(2)
SUNBURG (56289) Kandiyohi(75), Swift(22), Pope(1)
SWAN RIVER Itasca
SWANVILLE (56382) Morrison(58), Todd(41)
SWATARA (55785) Cass(53), Aitkin(46)
SWIFT Roseau
TACONITE Itasca
TALMOON Itasca
TAMARACK (55787) Aitkin(79), Carlton(20)
TAOPI Mower
TAUNTON (56291) Lyon(46), Yellow Medicine(34), Lincoln(18)
TAYLORS FALLS Chisago
TENSTRIKE Beltrami
THEILMAN Wabasha
THIEF RIVER FALLS (56701) Pennington(95), Marshall(4)
TINTAH (56583) Wilkin(86), Traverse(13)
TOFTE Cook
TOWER St. Louis
TRACY (56175) Lyon(92), Redwood(7)
TRAIL (56684) Pennington(57), Polk(28), Red Lake(13)
TRIMONT Martin
TROSKY Pipestone
TRUMAN (56088) Martin(71), Watonwan(24), Blue Earth(4)
TWIG St. Louis
TWIN LAKES Freeborn
TWIN VALLEY Norman
TWO HARBORS Lake
TYLER (56178) Lincoln(89), Lyon(10)
ULEN (56585) Clay(76), Becker(21), Norman(1)
UNDERWOOD Otter Tail
UPSALA Morrison
UTICA (55979) Winona(98), Fillmore(1)
VERDI (56179) Lincoln(92), Pipestone(7)
VERGAS Otter Tail
VERMILLION Dakota
VERNDALE (56481) Wadena(78), Todd(18), Cass(2)
VERNON CENTER Blue Earth
VESTA (56292) Redwood(97), Yellow Medicine(2)
VICTORIA Carver

VIKING (56760) Marshall(98), Pennington(1)
VILLARD (56385) Pope(57), Stearns(37), Douglas(5)
VINING Otter Tail
VIRGINIA St. Louis
WABASHA Wabasha
WABASSO Redwood
WACONIA (55387) Carver(98), Hennepin(1)
WADENA (56482) Wadena(81), Otter Tail(17)
WAHKON Mille Lacs
WAITE PARK Stearns
WALDORF Waseca
WALKER Cass
WALNUT GROVE (56180) Redwood(81), Cottonwood(12), Murray(6)
WALTERS (56092) Faribault(92), Freeborn(7)
WALTHAM (55982) Mower(98), Dodge(1)
WANAMINGO Goodhue
WANDA Redwood
WANNASKA (56761) Roseau(95), Marshall(3)
WARBA Itasca
WARREN (56762) Marshall(70), Polk(29)
WARROAD Roseau
WARSAW Rice
WASECA (56093) Waseca(96), Steele(3)
WASKISH Beltrami
WATERTOWN (55388) Carver(85), Wright(12), Hennepin(2)
WATERVILLE (56096) Le Sueur(84), Rice(7), Waseca(7)
WATKINS (55389) Meeker(80), Stearns(20)
WATSON Chippewa
WAUBUN (56589) Becker(98), Mahnomen(1)
WAVERLY Wright
WAWINA Itasca
WAYZATA Hennepin
WEBSTER (55088) Rice(68), Scott(30)
WELCH (55089) Goodhue(88), Dakota(11)
WELCOME Martin
WELLS (56097) Faribault(86), Freeborn(11), Waseca(2)
WENDELL (56590) Grant(98), Otter Tail(1)

WEST CONCORD Dodge
WEST UNION Todd
WESTBROOK (56183) Cottonwood(92), Murray(7)
WHALAN Fillmore
WHEATON Traverse
WHIPHOLT Cass
WHITE EARTH Becker
WILLERNIE Washington
WILLIAMS Lake of the Woods
WILLMAR Kandiyohi
WILLOW RIVER Pine
WILMONT Nobles
WILTON Beltrami
WINDOM (56101) Cottonwood(84), Jackson(15)
WINGER (56592) Polk(97), Mahnomen(2)
WINNEBAGO (56098) Faribault(89), Martin(10)
WINONA Winona
WINSTED (55395) McLeod(91), Carver(8)
WINTON St. Louis
WIRT Itasca
WOLF LAKE Becker
WOLVERTON Wilkin
WOOD LAKE (56297) Yellow Medicine(94), Redwood(3), Lyon(1)
WOODSTOCK (56186) Murray(79), Pipestone(20)
WORTHINGTON (56187) Nobles(98), Jackson(1)
WRENSHALL (55797) Carlton(94), Pine(5)
WRIGHT Carlton
WYKOFF Fillmore
WYOMING (55092) Chisago(60), Anoka(40)
YOUNG AMERICA Carver
YOUNG AMERICA Hennepin
ZIM St. Louis
ZIMMERMAN (55398) Sherburne(90), Isanti(9)
ZUMBRO FALLS (55991) Wabasha(90), Olmsted(9)
ZUMBROTA Goodhue

Minnesota ZIP/City Cross Reference

55001-55001 AFTON	55033-55033 HASTINGS	55071-55071 SAINT PAUL PARK	55311-55311 OSSEO
55002-55002 ALMELUND	55036-55036 HENRIETTE	55072-55072 SANDSTONE	55312-55312 BROWNTON
55003-55003 BAYPORT	55037-55037 HINCKLEY	55073-55073 SCANDIA	55313-55313 BUFFALO
55004-55004 BEROUN	55038-55038 HUGO	55074-55074 SHAFER	55314-55314 BUFFALO LAKE
55005-55005 BETHEL	55040-55040 ISANTI	55075-55075 SOUTH SAINT PAUL	55315-55315 CARVER
55006-55006 BRAHAM	55041-55041 LAKE CITY	55076-55077 INVER GROVE HEIGHTS	55316-55316 CHAMPLIN
55007-55007 BROOK PARK	55042-55042 LAKE ELMO	55078-55079 STACY	55317-55317 CHANHASSEN
55008-55008 CAMBRIDGE	55043-55043 LAKELAND	55080-55080 STANCHFIELD	55318-55318 CHASKA
55009-55009 CANNON FALLS	55044-55044 LAKEVILLE	55082-55083 STILLWATER	55319-55319 CLEAR LAKE
55010-55010 CASTLE ROCK	55045-55045 LINDSTROM	55084-55084 TAYLORS FALLS	55320-55320 CLEARWATER
55011-55011 CEDAR	55046-55046 LONSDALE	55085-55085 VERMILLION	55321-55321 COKATO
55012-55012 CENTER CITY	55047-55047 MARINE ON SAINT CROIX	55087-55087 WARSAW	55322-55322 COLOGNE
55013-55013 CHISAGO CITY	55049-55049 MEDFORD	55088-55088 WEBSTER	55323-55323 CRYSTAL BAY
55014-55014 CIRCLE PINES	55051-55051 MORA	55089-55089 WELCH	55324-55324 DARWIN
55016-55016 COTTAGE GROVE	55052-55052 MORRISTOWN	55090-55090 WILLERNIE	55325-55325 DASSEL
55017-55017 DALBO	55053-55053 NERSTRAND	55092-55092 WYOMING	55327-55327 DAYTON
55018-55018 DENNISON	55054-55054 NEW MARKET	55100-55146 SAINT PAUL	55328-55328 DELANO
55019-55019 DUNDAS	55055-55055 NEWPORT	55150-55150 MENDOTA	55329-55329 EDEN VALLEY
55020-55020 ELKO	55056-55056 NORTH BRANCH	55155-55199 SAINT PAUL	55330-55330 ELK RIVER
55021-55021 FARIBAULT	55057-55057 NORTHFIELD	55301-55301 ALBERTVILLE	55331-55331 EXCELSIOR
55024-55024 FARMINGTON	55060-55060 OWATONNA	55302-55302 ANNANDALE	55332-55332 FAIRFAX
55025-55025 FOREST LAKE	55063-55063 PINE CITY	55303-55304 ANOKA	55333-55333 FRANKLIN
55026-55026 FRONTENAC	55065-55065 RANDOLPH	55305-55305 HOPKINS	55334-55334 GAYLORD
55027-55027 GOODHUE	55066-55066 RED WING	55306-55306 BURNSVILLE	55335-55335 GIBBON
55029-55029 GRANDY	55067-55067 ROCK CREEK	55307-55307 ARLINGTON	55336-55336 GLENCOE
55030-55030 GRASSTON	55068-55068 ROSEMOUNT	55308-55308 BECKER	55337-55337 BURNSVILLE
55031-55031 HAMPTON	55069-55069 RUSH CITY	55309-55309 BIG LAKE	55338-55338 GREEN ISLE
55032-55032 HARRIS	55070-55070 SAINT FRANCIS	55310-55310 BIRD ISLAND	55339-55339 HAMBURG

55340-55340 HAMEL	55595-55599 LORETTO	55781-55781 SIDE LAKE	55982-55982 WALTHAM
55341-55341 HANOVER	55601-55601 BEAVER BAY	55782-55782 SOUDAN	55983-55983 WANAMINGO
55342-55342 HECTOR	55602-55602 BRIMSON	55783-55783 STURGEON LAKE	55985-55985 WEST CONCORD
55343-55343 HOPKINS	55603-55603 FINLAND	55784-55784 SWAN RIVER	55986-55986 WHALAN
55344-55344 EDEN PRAIRIE	55604-55604 GRAND MARAIS	55785-55785 SWATARA	55987-55987 WINONA
55345-55345 MINNETONKA	55605-55605 GRAND PORTAGE	55786-55786 TACONITE	55988-55988 STOCKTON
55346-55347 EDEN PRAIRIE	55606-55606 HOVLAND	55787-55787 TAMARACK	55990-55990 WYKOFF
55348-55348 MAPLE PLAIN	55607-55607 ISABELLA	55788-55788 COOK	55991-55991 ZUMBRO FALLS
55349-55349 HOWARD LAKE	55609-55609 KNIFE RIVER	55789-55789 MEADOWLANDS	55992-55992 ZUMBROTA
55350-55350 HUTCHINSON	55612-55612 LUTSEN	55790-55790 TOWER	56001-56006 MANKATO
55351-55351 YOUNG AMERICA	55613-55613 SCHROEDER	55791-55791 TWIG	56007-56007 ALBERT LEA
55352-55352 JORDAN	55614-55614 SILVER BAY	55792-55792 VIRGINIA	56009-56009 ALDEN
55353-55353 KIMBALL	55615-55615 TOFTE	55793-55793 WARBA	56010-56010 AMBOY
55354-55354 LESTER PRAIRIE	55616-55616 TWO HARBORS	55794-55794 WAWINA	56011-56011 BELLE PLAINE
55355-55355 LITCHFIELD	55701-55701 ADOLPH	55795-55795 WILLOW RIVER	56013-56013 BLUE EARTH
55356-55356 LONG LAKE	55702-55702 ALBORN	55796-55796 WINTON	56014-56014 BRICELYN
55357-55357 LORETTO	55703-55703 ANGORA	55797-55797 WRENSHALL	56016-56016 CLARKS GROVE
55358-55358 MAPLE LAKE	55704-55704 ASKOV	55798-55798 WRIGHT	56017-56017 CLEVELAND
55359-55359 MAPLE PLAIN	55705-55705 AURORA	55799-55799 ZIM	56019-56019 COMFREY
55360-55360 MAYER	55706-55706 BABBITT	55800-55816 DULUTH	56020-56020 CONGER
55361-55361 MINNETONKA BEACH	55707-55707 BARNUM	55901-55906 ROCHESTER	56021-56021 COURTLAND
55362-55362 MONTICELLO	55708-55708 BIWABIK	55909-55909 ADAMS	56022-56022 DARFUR
55363-55363 MONTROSE	55709-55709 BOVEY	55910-55910 ALTURA	56023-56023 DELAVAN
55364-55364 MOUND	55710-55710 BRITT	55912-55912 AUSTIN	56024-56024 EAGLE LAKE
55365-55365 MONTICELLO	55711-55711 BROOKSTON	55917-55917 BLOOMING PRAIRIE	56025-56025 EASTON
55366-55366 NEW AUBURN	55712-55712 BRUNO	55918-55918 BROWNSDALE	56026-56026 ELLENDALE
55367-55367 NEW GERMANY	55713-55713 BUHL	55919-55919 BROWNSVILLE	56027-56027 ELMORE
55368-55368 NORWOOD	55716-55716 CALUMET	55920-55920 BYRON	56028-56028 ELYSIAN
55369-55369 OSSEO	55717-55717 CANYON	55921-55921 CALEDONIA	56029-56029 EMMONS
55370-55370 PLATO	55718-55718 CARLTON	55922-55922 CANTON	56030-56030 ESSIG
55371-55371 PRINCETON	55719-55719 CHISHOLM	55923-55923 CHATFIELD	56031-56031 FAIRMONT
55372-55372 PRIOR LAKE	55720-55720 CLOQUET	55924-55924 CLAREMONT	56032-56032 FREEBORN
55373-55373 ROCKFORD	55721-55721 COHASSET	55925-55925 DAKOTA	56033-56033 FROST
55374-55374 ROGERS	55722-55722 COLERAINE	55926-55926 DEXTER	56034-56034 GARDEN CITY
55375-55375 SAINT BONIFACIUS	55723-55723 COOK	55927-55927 DODGE CENTER	56035-56035 GENEVA
55376-55376 SAINT MICHAEL	55724-55724 COTTON	55929-55929 DOVER	56036-56036 GLENVILLE
55377-55377 SANTIAGO	55725-55725 CRANE LAKE	55931-55931 EITZEN	56037-56037 GOOD THUNDER
55378-55378 SAVAGE	55726-55726 CROMWELL	55932-55932 ELGIN	56039-56039 GRANADA
55379-55379 SHAKOPEE	55727-55727 CULVER	55933-55933 ELKTON	56041-56041 HANSKA
55380-55380 SILVER CREEK	55728-55728 DENHAM	55934-55934 EYOTA	56042-56042 HARTLAND
55381-55381 SILVER LAKE	55729-55729 DUQUETTE	55935-55935 FOUNTAIN	56043-56043 HAYWARD
55382-55382 SOUTH HAVEN	55730-55730 GRAND RAPIDS	55936-55936 GRAND MEADOW	56044-56044 HENDERSON
55383-55383 NORWOOD	55731-55731 ELY	55937-55937 GRANGER	56045-56045 HOLLANDALE
55384-55384 SPRING PARK	55732-55732 EMBARRASS	55938-55938 HAMMOND	56046-56046 HOPE
55385-55385 STEWART	55733-55733 ESKO	55939-55939 HARMONY	56047-56047 HUNTLEY
55386-55386 VICTORIA	55734-55734 EVELETH	55940-55940 HAYFIELD	56048-56048 JANESVILLE
55387-55387 WACONIA	55735-55735 FINLAYSON	55941-55941 HOKAH	56050-56050 KASOTA
55388-55388 WATERTOWN	55736-55736 FLOODWOOD	55942-55942 HOMER	56051-56051 KIESTER
55389-55389 WATKINS	55738-55738 FORBES	55943-55943 HOUSTON	56052-56052 KILKENNY
55390-55390 WAVERLY	55740-55740 DENHAM	55944-55944 KASSON	56053-56053 KLOSSNER
55391-55391 WAYZATA	55741-55741 GILBERT	55945-55945 KELLOGG	56054-56054 LAFAYETTE
55392-55392 NAVARRE	55742-55742 GOODLAND	55946-55946 KENYON	56055-56055 LAKE CRYSTAL
55393-55393 MAPLE PLAIN	55744-55745 GRAND RAPIDS	55947-55947 LA CRESCENT	56056-56056 LA SALLE
55394-55394 YOUNG AMERICA	55746-55747 HIBBING	55949-55949 LANESBORO	56057-56057 LE CENTER
55395-55395 WINSTED	55748-55748 HILL CITY	55950-55950 LANSING	56058-56058 LE SUEUR
55396-55396 WINTHROP	55749-55749 HOLYOKE	55951-55951 LE ROY	56060-56060 LEWISVILLE
55397-55397 YOUNG AMERICA	55750-55750 HOYT LAKES	55952-55952 LEWISTON	56061-56061 LONDON
55398-55398 ZIMMERMAN	55751-55751 IRON	55953-55953 LYLE	56062-56062 MADELIA
55399-55399 YOUNG AMERICA	55752-55752 JACOBSON	55954-55954 MABEL	56063-56063 MADISON LAKE
55400-55488 MINNEAPOLIS	55753-55753 KEEWATIN	55955-55955 MANTORVILLE	56064-56064 MANCHESTER
55550-55554 YOUNG AMERICA	55754-55754 HIBBING	55956-55956 MAZEPPA	56065-56065 MAPLETON
55554-55554 NORWOOD	55755-55755 KELSEY	55957-55957 MILLVILLE	56067-56067 MERIDEN
55555-55560 YOUNG AMERICA	55756-55756 KERRICK	55959-55959 MINNESOTA CITY	56068-56068 MINNESOTA LAKE
55561-55561 MONTICELLO	55757-55757 KETTLE RIVER	55960-55960 ORONOCO	56069-56069 MONTGOMERY
55562-55562 YOUNG AMERICA	55758-55758 KINNEY	55961-55961 OSTRANDER	56070-56070 MYRTLE
55563-55563 MONTICELLO	55760-55760 MCGREGOR	55962-55962 PETERSON	56071-56071 NEW PRAGUE
55564-55564 YOUNG AMERICA	55761-55761 MC KINLEY	55963-55963 PINE ISLAND	56072-56072 NEW RICHLAND
55565-55565 MONTICELLO	55762-55762 MAHTOWA	55964-55964 PLAINVIEW	56073-56073 NEW ULM
55566-55568 YOUNG AMERICA	55763-55763 MAKINEN	55965-55965 PRESTON	56074-56074 NICOLLET
55569-55569 OSSEO	55764-55764 MARBLE	55967-55967 RACINE	56075-56075 NORTHROP
55570-55572 MAPLE PLAIN	55765-55765 MEADOWLANDS	55968-55968 READS LANDING	56076-56076 OAKLAND
55572-55572 ROCKFORD	55766-55766 MELRUDE	55969-55969 ROLLINGSTONE	56077-56077 OTISCO
55573-55573 YOUNG AMERICA	55767-55767 MOOSE LAKE	55970-55970 ROSE CREEK	56078-56078 PEMBERTON
55574-55574 MAPLE PLAIN	55768-55768 MOUNTAIN IRON	55971-55971 RUSHFORD	56080-56080 SAINT CLAIR
55575-55575 HOWARD LAKE	55769-55769 NASHWAUK	55972-55972 SAINT CHARLES	56081-56081 SAINT JAMES
55576-55577 MAPLE PLAIN	55771-55771 ORR	55973-55973 SARGEANT	56082-56082 SAINT PETER
55577-55577 ROCKFORD	55772-55772 NETT LAKE	55974-55974 SPRING GROVE	56083-56083 SANBORN
55578-55579 MAPLE PLAIN	55773-55773 PARKVILLE	55975-55975 SPRING VALLEY	56084-56084 SEARLES
55580-55582 MONTICELLO	55775-55775 PENGILLY	55976-55976 STEWARTVILLE	56085-56085 SLEEPY EYE
55583-55583 NORWOOD	55777-55777 VIRGINIA	55977-55977 TAOPI	56087-56087 SPRINGFIELD
55584-55591 MONTICELLO	55778-55778 RUTLEDGE	55978-55978 THEILMAN	56088-56088 TRUMAN
55592-55593 MAPLE PLAIN	55779-55779 SAGINAW	55979-55979 UTICA	56089-56089 TWIN LAKES
55594-55594 YOUNG AMERICA	55780-55780 SAWYER	55981-55981 WABASHA	56090-56090 VERNON CENTER

56091-56091 WALDORF	56211-56211 BEARDSLEY	56312-56312 BELGRADE	56443-56443 CUSHING
56092-56092 WALTERS	56212-56212 BELLINGHAM	56313-56313 BOCK	56444-56444 DEERWOOD
56093-56093 WASECA	56214-56214 BELVIEW	56314-56314 BOWLUS	56446-56446 EAGLE BEND
56096-56096 WATERVILLE	56215-56215 BENSON	56315-56315 BRANDON	56447-56447 EMILY
56097-56097 WELLS	56216-56216 BLOMKEST	56316-56316 BROOTEN	56448-56448 FIFTY LAKES
56098-56098 WINNEBAGO	56218-56218 BOYD	56317-56317 BUCKMAN	56449-56449 FORT RIPLEY
56101-56101 WINDOM	56219-56219 BROWNS VALLEY	56318-56318 BURTRUM	56450-56450 GARRISON
56110-56110 ADRIAN	56220-56220 CANBY	56319-56319 CARLOS	56452-56452 HACKENSACK
56111-56111 ALPHA	56221-56221 CHOKIO	56320-56320 COLD SPRING	56453-56453 HEWITT
56112-56112 AMIRET	56222-56222 CLARA CITY	56321-56321 COLLEGEVILLE	56455-56455 IRONTON
56113-56113 ARCO	56223-56223 CLARKFIELD	56323-56323 CYRUS	56456-56456 JENKINS
56114-56114 AVOCA	56224-56224 CLEMENTS	56324-56324 DALTON	56458-56458 LAKE GEORGE
56115-56115 BALATON	56225-56225 CLINTON	56325-56325 ELROSA	56459-56459 LAKE HUBERT
56116-56116 BEAVER CREEK	56226-56226 CLONTARF	56326-56326 EVANSVILLE	56460-56460 LAKE ITASCA
56117-56117 BIGELOW	56227-56227 CORRELL	56327-56327 FARWELL	56461-56461 LAPORTE
56118-56118 BINGHAM LAKE	56228-56228 COSMOS	56328-56328 FLENSBURG	56463-56463 MANHATTAN BEACH
56119-56119 BREWSTER	56229-56229 COTTONWOOD	56329-56329 FOLEY	56464-56464 MENAHGA
56120-56120 BUTTERFIELD	56230-56230 DANUBE	56330-56330 FORESTON	56465-56465 MERRIFIELD
56121-56121 CEYLON	56231-56231 DANVERS	56331-56331 FREEPORT	56466-56466 MOTLEY
56122-56122 CHANDLER	56232-56232 DAWSON	56332-56332 GARFIELD	56467-56467 NEVIS
56123-56123 CURRIE	56233-56233 DE GRAFF	56333-56333 GILMAN	56468-56468 NISSWA
56124-56124 DELFT	56235-56235 DONNELLY	56334-56334 GLENWOOD	56469-56469 PALISADE
56125-56125 DOVRAY	56236-56236 DUMONT	56335-56335 GREENWALD	56470-56470 PARK RAPIDS
56126-56126 DUNDEE	56237-56237 ECHO	56336-56336 GREY EAGLE	56472-56472 PEQUOT LAKES
56127-56127 DUNNELL	56238-56238 EVAN	56338-56338 HILLMAN	56473-56473 PILLAGER
56128-56128 EDGERTON	56239-56239 GHENT	56339-56339 HOFFMAN	56474-56474 PINE RIVER
56129-56129 ELLSWORTH	56240-56240 GRACEVILLE	56340-56340 HOLDINGFORD	56475-56475 RANDALL
56131-56131 FULDA	56241-56241 GRANITE FALLS	56341-56341 HOLMES CITY	56477-56477 SEBEKA
56132-56132 GARVIN	56243-56243 GROVE CITY	56342-56342 ISLE	56478-56478 NIMROD
56133-56133 HADLEY	56244-56244 HANCOCK	56343-56343 KENSINGTON	56479-56479 STAPLES
56134-56134 HARDWICK	56245-56245 HANLEY FALLS	56344-56344 LASTRUP	56481-56481 VERNDALE
56136-56136 HENDRICKS	56246-56246 HAWICK	56345-56345 LITTLE FALLS	56482-56482 WADENA
56137-56137 HERON LAKE	56247-56247 HAZEL RUN	56346-56347 LONG PRAIRIE	56484-56484 WALKER
56138-56138 HILLS	56248-56248 HERMAN	56349-56349 LOWRY	56485-56485 WHIPHOLT
56139-56139 HOLLAND	56249-56249 HOLLOWAY	56350-56350 MC GRATH	56501-56502 DETROIT LAKES
56140-56140 IHLEN	56250-56250 JOHNSON	56352-56352 MELROSE	56510-56510 ADA
56141-56141 IONA	56251-56251 KANDIYOHI	56353-56353 MILACA	56511-56511 AUDUBON
56142-56142 IVANHOE	56252-56252 KERKHOVEN	56354-56354 MILTONA	56513-56513 BAKER
56143-56143 JACKSON	56253-56253 LAKE LILLIAN	56355-56355 NELSON	56514-56514 BARNESVILLE
56144-56144 JASPER	56254-56254 LOUISBURG	56356-56356 NEW MUNICH	56515-56515 BATTLE LAKE
56145-56145 JEFFERS	56255-56255 LUCAN	56357-56357 OAK PARK	56516-56516 BEJOU
56146-56146 KANARANZI	56256-56256 MADISON	56358-56358 OGILVIE	56517-56517 BELTRAMI
56147-56147 KENNETH	56257-56257 MARIETTA	56359-56359 ONAMIA	56518-56518 BLUFFTON
56149-56149 LAKE BENTON	56258-56258 MARSHALL	56360-56360 OSAKIS	56519-56519 BORUP
56150-56150 LAKEFIELD	56260-56260 MAYNARD	56361-56361 PARKERS PRAIRIE	56520-56520 BRECKENRIDGE
56151-56151 LAKE WILSON	56262-56262 MILAN	56362-56362 PAYNESVILLE	56521-56521 CALLAWAY
56152-56152 LAMBERTON	56263-56263 MILROY	56363-56363 PEASE	56522-56522 CAMPBELL
56153-56153 LEOTA	56264-56264 MINNEOTA	56364-56364 PIERZ	56523-56523 CLIMAX
56155-56155 LISMORE	56265-56265 MONTEVIDEO	56367-56367 RICE	56524-56524 CLITHERALL
56156-56156 LUVERNE	56266-56266 MORGAN	56368-56368 RICHMOND	56525-56525 COMSTOCK
56157-56157 LYND	56267-56267 MORRIS	56369-56369 ROCKVILLE	56527-56527 DEER CREEK
56158-56158 MAGNOLIA	56270-56270 MORTON	56371-56371 ROSCOE	56528-56528 DENT
56159-56159 MOUNTAIN LAKE	56271-56271 MURDOCK	56372-56372 SAINT CLOUD	56529-56529 DILWORTH
56160-56160 ODIN	56272-56272 NASSAU	56373-56373 ROYALTON	56531-56531 ELBOW LAKE
56161-56161 OKABENA	56273-56273 NEW LONDON	56374-56374 SAINT JOSEPH	56533-56533 ELIZABETH
56162-56162 ORMSBY	56274-56274 NORCROSS	56375-56375 SAINT STEPHEN	56534-56534 ERHARD
56164-56164 PIPESTONE	56276-56276 ODESSA	56376-56376 SAINT MARTIN	56535-56535 ERSKINE
56165-56165 READING	56277-56277 OLIVIA	56377-56377 SARTELL	56536-56536 FELTON
56166-56166 REVERE	56278-56278 ORTONVILLE	56378-56378 SAUK CENTRE	56537-56538 FERGUS FALLS
56167-56167 ROUND LAKE	56279-56279 PENNOCK	56379-56379 SAUK RAPIDS	56540-56540 FERTILE
56168-56168 RUSHMORE	56280-56280 PORTER	56380-56380 BANGOR	56541-56541 FLOM
56169-56169 RUSSELL	56281-56281 PRINSBURG	56380-56380 SEDAN	56542-56542 FOSSTON
56170-56170 RUTHTON	56282-56282 RAYMOND	56381-56381 STARBUCK	56543-56543 FOXHOME
56171-56171 SHERBURN	56283-56283 REDWOOD FALLS	56382-56382 SWANVILLE	56544-56544 FRAZEE
56172-56172 SLAYTON	56284-56284 RENVILLE	56384-56384 UPSALA	56545-56545 GARY
56173-56173 STEEN	56285-56285 SACRED HEART	56385-56385 VILLARD	56546-56546 GEORGETOWN
56174-56174 STORDEN	56286-56286 SAINT LEO	56386-56386 WAHKON	56547-56547 GLYNDON
56175-56175 TRACY	56287-56287 SEAFORTH	56387-56388 WAITE PARK	56548-56548 HALSTAD
56176-56176 TRIMONT	56288-56288 SPICER	56389-56389 WEST UNION	56549-56549 HAWLEY
56177-56177 TROSKY	56289-56289 SUNBURG	56393-56399 SAINT CLOUD	56550-56550 HENDRUM
56178-56178 TYLER	56291-56291 TAUNTON	56401-56401 BRAINERD	56551-56551 HENNING
56179-56179 VERDI	56292-56292 VESTA	56425-56425 BAXTER	56552-56552 HITTERDAL
56180-56180 WALNUT GROVE	56293-56293 WABASSO	56430-56430 AH GWAH CHING	56553-56553 KENT
56181-56181 WELCOME	56294-56294 WANDA	56431-56431 AITKIN	56554-56554 LAKE PARK
56183-56183 WESTBROOK	56295-56295 WATSON	56433-56433 AKELEY	56556-56556 MCINTOSH
56185-56185 WILMONT	56296-56296 WHEATON	56434-56434 ALDRICH	56557-56557 MAHNOMEN
56186-56186 WOODSTOCK	56297-56297 WOOD LAKE	56435-56435 BACKUS	56560-56563 MOORHEAD
56187-56187 WORTHINGTON	56301-56304 SAINT CLOUD	56436-56436 BENEDICT	56565-56565 NASHUA
56201-56201 WILLMAR	56307-56307 ALBANY	56437-56437 BERTHA	56566-56566 NAYTAHWAUSH
56207-56207 ALBERTA	56308-56308 ALEXANDRIA	56438-56438 BROWERVILLE	56567-56567 NEW YORK MILLS
56208-56208 APPLETON	56309-56309 ASHBY	56440-56440 CLARISSA	56568-56568 NIELSVILLE
56209-56209 ATWATER	56310-56310 AVON	56441-56441 CROSBY	56569-56569 OGEMA
56210-56210 BARRY	56311-56311 BARRETT	56442-56442 CROSSLAKE	56570-56570 OSAGE

56571-56571 OTTERTAIL	56575-56575 PONSFORD	56579-56579 ROTHSAY	56584-56584 TWIN VALLEY
56572-56572 PELICAN RAPIDS	56576-56576 RICHVILLE	56580-56580 SABIN	56585-56585 ULEN
56573-56573 PERHAM	56577-56577 RICHWOOD	56581-56581 SHELLY	56586-56586 UNDERWOOD
56574-56574 PERLEY	56578-56578 ROCHERT	56583-56583 TINTAH	56587-56587 VERGAS
56588-56588 VINING	56650-56650 KELLIHER	56679-56679 SOUTH INTERNATIONAL	56729-56729 HALMA
56589-56589 WAUBUN	56651-56651 LENGBY	FALLS	56731-56731 HUMBOLDT
56590-56590 WENDELL	56652-56652 LEONARD	56680-56680 SPRING LAKE	56732-56732 KARLSTAD
56591-56591 WHITE EARTH	56653-56653 LITTLEFORK	56681-56681 SQUAW LAKE	56733-56733 KENNEDY
56592-56592 WINGER	56654-56654 LOMAN	56682-56682 SWIFT	56734-56734 LAKE BRONSON
56593-56593 WOLF LAKE	56655-56655 LONGVILLE	56683-56683 TENSTRIKE	56735-56735 LANCASTER
56594-56594 WOLVERTON	56657-56657 MARCELL	56684-56684 TRAIL	56736-56736 MENTOR
56601-56619 BEMIDJI	56658-56658 MARGIE	56685-56685 WASKISH	56737-56737 MIDDLE RIVER
56621-56621 BAGLEY	56659-56659 MAX	56686-56686 WILLIAMS	56738-56738 NEWFOLDEN
56623-56623 BAUDETTE	56660-56660 MIZPAH	56687-56687 WILTON	56740-56740 NOYES
56625-56625 BECIDA	56661-56661 NORTHOME	56688-56688 WIRT	56741-56741 OAK ISLAND
56626-56626 BENA	56662-56662 OUTING	56701-56701 THIEF RIVER FALLS	56742-56742 OKLEE
56627-56627 BIG FALLS	56663-56663 PENNINGTON	56710-56710 ALVARADO	56744-56744 OSLO
56628-56628 BIGFORK	56664-56664 DEBS	56711-56711 ANGLE INLET	56748-56748 PLUMMER
56629-56629 BIRCHDALE	56665-56665 PITT	56712-56712 ANGUS	56750-56750 RED LAKE FALLS
56630-56630 BLACKDUCK	56666-56666 PONEMAH	56713-56713 ARGYLE	56751-56751 ROSEAU
56631-56631 BOWSTRING	56667-56667 PUPOSKY	56714-56714 BADGER	56754-56754 SAINT HILAIRE
56632-56632 BOY RIVER	56668-56668 RANIER	56715-56715 BROOKS	56755-56755 SAINT VINCENT
56633-56633 CASS LAKE	56669-56669 RAY	56716-56716 CROOKSTON	56756-56756 SALOL
56634-56634 CLEARBROOK	56669-56669 KABETOGAMA	56720-56720 DONALDSON	56757-56757 STEPHEN
56636-56636 DEER RIVER	56670-56670 REDBY	56721-56721 EAST GRAND FORKS	56758-56758 STRANDQUIST
56637-56637 TALMOON	56671-56671 REDLAKE	56722-56722 EUCLID	56759-56759 STRATHCONA
56639-56639 EFFIE	56672-56672 REMER	56723-56723 FISHER	56760-56760 VIKING
56641-56641 FEDERAL DAM	56673-56673 ROOSEVELT	56724-56724 GATZKE	56761-56761 WANNASKA
56644-56644 GONVICK	56674-56674 SAUM	56725-56725 GOODRIDGE	56762-56762 WARREN
56646-56646 GULLY	56676-56676 SHEVLIN	56726-56726 GREENBUSH	56763-56763 WARROAD
56647-56647 HINES	56678-56678 SOLWAY	56727-56727 GRYGLA	
56649-56649 INTERNATIONAL FALLS		56728-56728 HALLOCK	

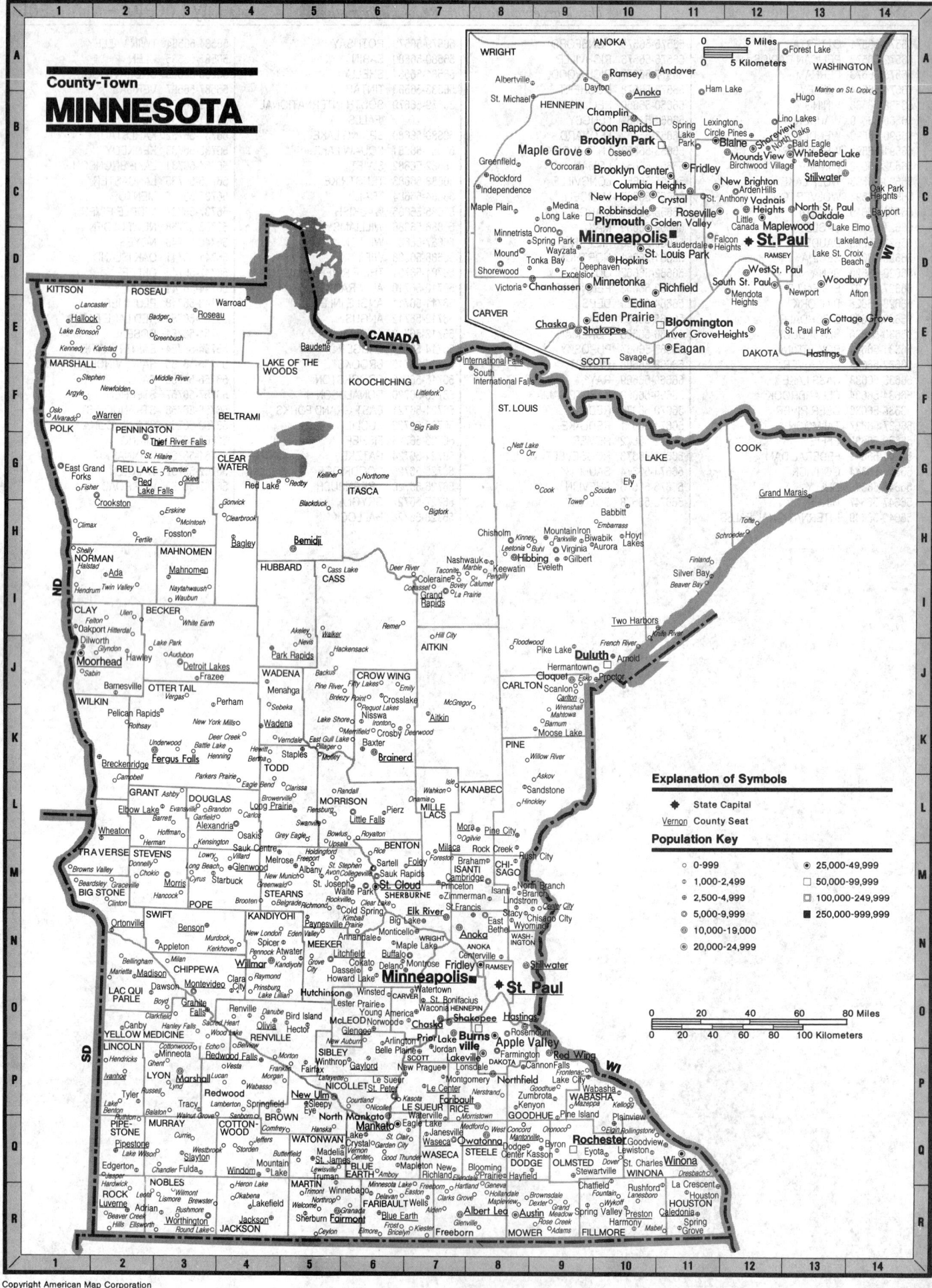

County-Town
MINNESOTA

COUNTIES

(87 Counties)

CITIES AND TOWNS

Note: The first name is that of the city or town, second, that of the county in which it is located, then the population and location on the map.

Explanation of symbols: ●– Census Designated Place (CDP)

Mississippi

General Help Numbers:

Governor's Office

PO Box 139
Jackson, MS 39201
www.governor.state.ms.us

601-359-3100
Fax 601-359-3741
8AM-5PM

Attorney General's Office

PO Box 220
Jackson, MS 39205
www.ago.state.ms.us

601-359-3680
Fax 601-359-3796
8AM-5PM

Legislative Records

PO Box 1018
Jackson, MS 39215
www.ls.state.ms.us

359-3229 (Senate)
601-359-3358 (House
8:30AM-5PM

State Archives

Archives & Library Division
PO Box 571
Jackson, MS 39205-0571
www.mdah.state.ms.us

601-359-6850
Fax 601-359-6975

8AM-5PM TU-F;
8AM-1PM SA

State Specifics:

Capital:

Jackson
Hinds County

Time Zone:

CST

Number of Counties:

82

Population:

2,881,281

Web Site:

www.ms.gov

State Agencies

Criminal Records
Access to Records is Restricted

Criminal Information Center, Dept. of Public Safety, PO Box 958, Jackson, MS 39205; 601-933-2600.

Note: Mississippi does not permit the public to access their central state repository of criminal records, except for pre-approved entities with purposes provided for by state statute such as health care, banking/finance, military, childcare and schools. They suggest that you obtain information at the county level. The records on file are 100% fingerprint supported. 40% of the records contain dispositions.

Statewide Court Records

Administrative Office of Courts, PO Box 117, Jackson, MS 39205 (Courier: 450 High St, Jackson, MS 39205); 601-354-7406, 601-354-7459 (Fax), 8AM-5PM.

www.mssc.state.ms.us

Access by: fax, online.

Fee & Payment: For fax requests, there is a $25.00 start-up fee and a $5.00 per name search fee. No searching by mail.

Fax search: The Administrative Office of Courts offers a statewide search via fax requesting with a

24 hour turnaround time. Call 601-354-7449 or fax 601-354-7459 for details.

Online search: The website offers searching of the MS Supreme Court and Court of Appeals Decisions, and dockets of the trial courts. It is difficult to do a name search in the trial courts because the sequance number of the docket must be included in request.

Sexual Offender Registry

Dept. of Public Safety, Sexual Offender Registry, PO Box 958, Jackson, MS 39205; 601-368-1740.

www.sor.mdps.state.ms.us/

Note: Also, it is suggested to search at the local sheriff's office.

Indexing & Storage: Records are available from 07/01/95.

Access by: mail, phone, online.

Mail search: Turnaround time: 1 to 2 weeks.

Phone search: Time permitting.

Online search: The state Sex Offender Registry can be accessed at the website. Search by last name, city, county, or ZIP Code.

Incarceration Records

Mississippi Department of Corrections, Records Department, PO Box 880, Parchman, MS 38738; 601-359-5608, 8AM-5PM.

www.mdoc.state.ms.us

Indexing & Storage: Records are available on current and former inmates. It takes less than 72 hours before new records are available for inquiry.

Searching: Computer records go back to 1978. Include the following in your request-provide full name. The inmate #, county of crime and DOB are helpful.

Access by: mail, phone, online.

Fee & Payment: There is no fee.

Mail search: Turnaround time: 1-2 weeks. No SASE is required.

Phone search: Name searching available via phone.

Online search: Search online by name only from the website. Click on Inmate Search. Also, search the Parole Board at www.mpb.state.ms.us/inmatesearch.asp.

Corporation, Limited Partnership, Limited Liability Company Records, Trademarks/Servicemarks

Corporation Commission, Business Services, PO Box 136, Jackson, MS 39205-0136; 601-359-1633, 800-256-3494, 601-359-1607 (Fax), 8AM-5PM.

www.sos.state.ms.us

Indexing & Storage: Records are available from the 1800's, computerized since 1995. New records are available for inquiry immediately. Records are indexed on microfilm, inhouse computer.

Searching: Include the following in your request-full name of business. In addition to the articles of incorporation, corporation records include the following information: Annual Reports, Officers, Directors, Prior (merged) names, Inactive and

Reserved names. The following data is not released: federal ID numbers or phone numbers.

Access by: mail, phone, fax, in person, online.

Fee & Payment: There is no search fee. The certification fee is $10.00 per package. Copies are $1.00 per page. Fee payee: Secretary of State. Prepayment required. You must prepay if the invoice amount is over $50.00. If under $50.00 they will invoice. Personal checks accepted. Credit cards accepted: MasterCard, Visa.

Mail search: Turnaround time: 1 to 2 days.

Phone search: Will only verify if record exists.

Fax search: Requests only are accepted, will return to toll-free fax numbers.

In person search: Computer screen prints are free.

Online search: A variety of online search services are available at www.sos.state.ms.us/busserv/corp/soskb/csearch.asp. There is no fee to view records, including officers and registered agents. You can download images for no charge.

Other access: The Data Division offers bulk release of information on paper or disk.

Uniform Commercial Code, Federal and State Tax Liens

Secretary of State, Business Services - UCC, PO Box 136, Jackson, MS 39205-0136 (Courier: 700 N Jackson St, Jackson, MS 39202); 601-359-1633, 800-256-3494, 601-359-1607 (Fax), 8AM-5PM.

www.sos.state.ms.us

Indexing & Storage: Records are available from 1968. Records are computerized since 1987. It takes 24-48 hours before new records are available for inquiry. Records are indexed on inhouse computer. Records are normally destroyed after lapsing, per a retention schedule (not disclosed).

Searching: Use search request form UCC-11. The search includes tax liens. Include the following in your request-debtor name.

Access by: mail, phone, in person, online.

Fee & Payment: The search fee is $5.00, copies are $2.00 each, financing statements are $2.00 each. Fee payee: Secretary of State. Prepayment required. The state offers ACH accounts for regular requesters. Personal checks accepted. Credit cards accepted: MasterCard, Visa.

Mail search: Turnaround time: 1 to 2 days. No SASE is required.

Phone search: Limited information is released over the phone.

In person search: Simple requests are processed, time permitting.

Online search: Two systems available. Free searching for UCC debtors is at www.sos.state.ms.us/busserv/ucc/soskb/SearchStandardRA9.asp.

Other access: A monthly list of farm liens is available for purchase.

Sales Tax Registrations

Office of Revenue, Sales and Use Tax Bureau, PO Box 1033, Jackson, MS 39215-1033 (Courier: 1577 Springridge Rd, Raymond, MS 39154); 601-923-7000, 8AM-5PM.

www.mstc.state.ms.us

Indexing & Storage: Records are available for the most current 3 years and are computerized.

Searching: The agency will only verify if a business is registered and will not release ownership data. Include the following in your request-business name. They will also search by tax permit number.

Access by: mail, phone, fax, in person.

Fee & Payment: Prepayment required. Fee payee: Revenue Bureau. Personal checks accepted. No credit cards accepted.

Mail search: Turnaround time: 5 to 10 working days. No SASE is required. No fee for mail request. Copies cost $2.00 per page.

Phone search: No fee for telephone request.

Fax search: Same criteria as phone or mail searches.

In person search: No fee for request. Copies cost $2.00 per page.

Online search: Requests may be emailed to sales@mstc.state.ms.us.

Birth Certificates

State Department of Health, Vital Statistics & Records, PO Box 1700, Jackson, MS 39215-1700 (Courier: 571 Stadium Dr, Jackson, MS 39216); 601-576-7960, 601-576-7988, 601-576-7505 (Fax), 7:30AM-5PM.

www.msdh.state.ms.us/phs/index.htm

Indexing & Storage: Records are available from November 1, 1912 to present. New records are available for inquiry immediately. Records are indexed on microfiche, inhouse computer.

Searching: Employers need written release from person of record. Records are not public access documents, they are only available to persons with legitimate and tangible interest. Include the following in your request-full name, names of parents, mother's maiden name, date of birth, place of birth, relationship to person of record, reason for information request. Records may be ordered online via a vendor at www.vitalcheck.com. The following data is not released: original records of adoption.

Access by: mail, phone, fax, in person.

Fee & Payment: The $7.00 fee is for the short form. The fee for the long form certified is $12.00, plus is a $3.00 per for each additional copy. There is a $7.00 charge for no record found. Fee payee: Mississippi Vital Records Prepayment required. Use credit card for phone and/or expedited service only. Personal checks accepted only if in-state. Credit cards accepted: MasterCard, Visa, AmEx, Discover.

Mail search: Turnaround time: 7 to 10 days. No SASE is required.

Phone search: Must use a credit card for an additional $5.50 fee. Turnaround time is 2 to 3 days.

Fax search: Same criteria as phone searches.

In person search: Turnaround time for Short Form-while you wait, Long Form-next day mail.

Expedited service: Expedited service is available for mail, phone and fax searches, via www.vitalcheck.com. Turnaround time: overnight delivery. Add a $5.50 credit card fee and $$ for overnight shipping if desired.

Death Records

State Department of Health, Vital Statistics & Records, PO Box 1700, Jackson, MS 39215-1700 (Courier: 571 Stadium Dr, Jackson, MS 39216); 601-576-7960, 601-576-7988, 601-576-7505 (Fax), 7:30AM-5PM.

www.msdh.state.ms.us/phs/index.htm

Indexing & Storage: Records are available from November 1, 1912 to present. New records are available for inquiry immediately. Records are indexed on microfiche, inhouse computer.

Searching: Employers need written release from immediate family member. Records are not considered public access documents. They are only available to persons with legitimate and tangible interest. Include the following in your request-full name, date of death, place of death, Social Security Number, relationship to person of record, reason for information request. Records may be ordered online via a vendor at www.vitalcheck.com.

Access by: mail, phone, fax, in person.

Fee & Payment: Fee is $10.00 if you want a certified copy, and an additional $2.00 for each additional copy ordered at same time. If no record is found, the fee is $6.00. Fee payee: Mississippi Vital Records Prepayment required. Use credit cards for phone, fax and/or expedited service only. Credit cards accepted: MasterCard, Visa, AmEx, Discover.

Mail search: Turnaround time: 7 to 10 days. No SASE is required.

Phone search: Must use a credit card for an additional $5.50 fee. Turnaround time is 2 to 3 days.

Fax search: Same criteria as phone searching.

In person search: Turnaround time next day mail.

Expedited service: Expedited service is available for mail, phone and fax searches, via www.vitalcheck.com. Turnaround time: 1 day. Add a $5.50 credit card fee and $$ for overnight shipping if desired.

Marriage Certificates

State Department of Health, Vital Statistics & Records, PO Box 1700, Jackson, MS 39215-1700 (Courier: 571 Stadium Dr, Jackson, MS 39216); 601-576-7960, 601-576-7988, 601-576-7505 (Fax), 7:30AM-5PM.

www.msdh.state.ms.us/phs/index.htm

Note: Records are also available at the county level, including those records from 1938 to 1942.

Indexing & Storage: Records are available from January 1926 to June 1938 and January 1942 to present. New records are available for inquiry immediately. Records are indexed on microfiche, inhouse computer.

Searching: Employers need written release from persons of record. Records are not considered public access documents. They are only available to persons with legitimate and tangible interest. Include the following in your request-names of husband and wife, date of marriage, place or county of marriage, relationship to person of record, reason for information request, wife's maiden name. Records may be ordered online via a vendor at www.vitalcheck.com.

Access by: mail, phone, fax, in person.

Fee & Payment: The fee is $10.00 and $2.00 for each additional copy ordered at same time. If

record not found fee is $6.00. Fee payee: Mississippi Vital Records Prepayment required. Use credit cards for phone, fax and/or expedited service only. Personal checks accepted only if in-state. Credit cards accepted: MasterCard, Visa, AmEx, Discover.

Mail search: Turnaround time: 4 to 7 days. No SASE is required.

Phone search: Must use a credit card for an additional $5.50 fee. Turnaround time is 2 to 3 days.

Fax search: Same criteria as phone searching.

In person search: Search costs $10.00 per request. Turnaround time next day mail.

Expedited service: Expedited service is available for mail, phone and fax searches, via www.vitalchek.com. Turnaround time: 1 day. Add a $5.50 credit card fee and $$ for overnight shipping if desired.

Divorce Records

State Department of Health, Vital Statistics & Records, PO Box 1700, Jackson, MS 39215-1700 (Courier: 571 Stadium Dr, Jackson, MS 39216); 601-576-7960, 601-576-7988, 601-576-7505 (Fax), 7:30AM-5PM.

www.msdh.state.ms.us/phs/index.htm

Note: The state maintains a state-wide index and can refer to book and page number in county records. Requests for copies must be made to the county of record.

Indexing & Storage: Records are available from 1930 to present in county of record. This office will only confirm that a record exists and where. New records are available for inquiry immediately. Records are indexed on microfiche, inhouse computer.

Searching: Employers need written release from person of record. Records are not public access documents and are available only to persons with legitimate and tangible interest. Include the following in your request-names of husband and wife, date of divorce, year divorce case began, case number (if known), relationship to person of record, reason for information request. Records may be ordered online via a vendor at www.vitalcheck.com.

Access by: mail, phone, fax, in person.

Fee & Payment: The fee to do an index search is $6.00. Copies are not released from this agency. Fee payee: Mississippi Vital Records Prepayment required. Personal checks accepted if in-state. Credit cards accepted: MasterCard, Visa, AmEx, Discover.

Mail search: Turnaround time: 1 to 3 days. No SASE is required.

Phone search: Must use a credit card for an additional $5.50 fee. Turnaround time is 2 to 3 days.

Fax search: Same criteria as phone searching.

In person search: Turnaround time next day mail.

Expedited service: Expedited service is available for mail, phone and fax searches, via www.vitalcheck.com. Turnaround time: 1 day. Add a $5.50 credit card fee and $$ for overnight shipping if desired.

Workers' Compensation Records

Workers Compensation Commission, PO Box 5300, Jackson, MS 39296-5300 (Courier: 1428 Lakeland Dr, Jackson, MS 39216); 601-987-4200, 8AM-5PM.

www.mwcc.state.ms.us

Indexing & Storage: Records are available for 10 years back to present. New records are available for inquiry immediately. Records are indexed on inhouse computer.

Searching: All requests must be in writing. Claimant's attorney must have contract or medical authorization. Employer/carrier must be party to action to obtain records. They do not conduct searches for pre-employment screening. Include the following in your request-claimant name, SSN, docket number, place of employment at time of accident.

Access by: mail, in person, online.

Fee & Payment: Copy fee is $.50 with a $5.00 minimum, there is no search fee. Fee payee: Mississippi Workers' Compensation Commission. They will invoice. Personal checks accepted. No credit cards accepted.

Mail search: Turnaround time: 3 to 4 working days. No SASE is required.

In person search: Anyone can come in to view. Medical information is not made available and copies cannot be made unless there is written authorization by party of record.

Online search: The First Report of Injury and other documents are available via the web. There is no fee, but users must register.

Other access: A first report of injury database is available on CD-ROM for $500.00.

Driver Records

Department of Public Safety, Driver Records, PO Box 958, Jackson, MS 39205 (Courier: 1900 E Woodrow Wilson, Jackson, MS 39216); 601-987-1274, 8AM-5PM.

www.dps.state.ms.us

Note: Copies of tickets may be obtained from the same address for a fee of $5.00 per record and notorized signature. A pre-addressed, stamped envelope is advised.

Indexing & Storage: Records are available for 3 years for moving violations, DUIs and suspensions. Accidents appear on driving records. The driver's address is provided on the record. It takes 45 days or more before new records are available for inquiry.

Searching: Casual requesters can obtain personal information only with notorized consent of subject. The state adopted the provisions of the DPPA. The driver's full name, license number, and/or DOB are needed when ordering. The magnetic tape system requires only the driver's last name and number (first name and DOB are optional). Surrendered license records can only be obtained by a manual search.

Access by: mail, in person, online.

Fee & Payment: The fee is $9.00 per request. Fee payee: Department of Public Safety. Prepayment required. Personal checks accepted. No credit cards accepted.

Mail search: Turnaround time: 2 days. A SASE is requested.

In person search: Walk-in requesters may submit up to 10 requests for immediate delivery; the rest are available the next day.

Online search: Both interactive and batch delivery is offer for high volume users only. Billing is monthly. Hook-up is through the Advantis System, fees apply. Lookup is by name only; not by driver license number. Fee is $9.00 per record. For more information, call the Director's office.

Other access: Overnight batch delivery by tape is available.

Vehicle Ownership, Vehicle Identification

Mississippi State Tax Commission, Registration Department, PO Box 1140, Jackson, MS 39215 (Courier: 1577 Springridge Rd, Raymond, MS 39154); 601-923-7100 (Registration), 601-923-7200 (Titles), 601-923-7134 (Fax), 8AM-5PM.

www.mstc.state.ms.us/mvl/main.htm

Note: Please note that title information (liens, histories) requests are processed by a different section than registration information. For mail requests, use PO Box 1033 for the Title Department.

Indexing & Storage: Records are available from July 1, 1969 to present. Title records are computer indexed from July 1, 1969 to present, and on microfiche from July 1, 1969 to present. It takes 6 to 8 weeks before new records are available for inquiry.

Searching: Personal information is not released to casual requesters without consent from the subject. State suggests to use their disclosure form. The turnaround time will be one week longer if the request requires a search farther back than 5 years.

Access by: mail, in person.

Fee & Payment: Fees are $4.50 per search for title, $1.00 per search for VIN or registration, and $2.00 for lien history. Fee payee: Mississippi State Tax Commission. Prepayment required. No cash will be accepted for mail requests. Personal checks accepted. No credit cards accepted.

Mail search: Turnaround time: 2 days. A SASE is requested.

In person search: Turnaround time is immediate.

Other access: Mississippi offers some standardized files as well as some customization for bulk requesters of VIN and registration information. For more information, contact MLVB at the address listed above.

Accident Reports

Safety Responsibility, Accident Records, PO Box 958, Jackson, MS 39205 (Courier: 1900 E Woodrow Wilson, Jackson, MS 39216); 601-987-1254, 601-987-1261 (Fax), 8AM-5PM.

www.dps.state.ms.us

Note: The above address is for Highway Patrol accident investigations only. Reports require authorization from person involved. You must go to the agency that did the investigation for reports not found with the Highway Patrol.

Indexing & Storage: Records are available for 3 years to present on computer. Records are on microfiche from 1990 to present. Records are normally destroyed after 5 years.

Searching: Must have authorization from individuals involved in the accident. Accident reports are only available to persons involved, their legal counsel and their insurance representative. Include the following in your request-date of accident, location of accident, full name, written authorization. SSN is helpful. Requests must be in writing. In person requests are returned by mail.

Access by: mail.

Fee & Payment: The fee is $10.00 per record. Fee payee: Department of Public Safety. Prepayment required. Personal checks accepted. No credit cards accepted.

Mail search: Turnaround time: 5 days. A SASE is requested.

Vessel Ownership, Vessel Registration

Dept of Wildlife, Fisheries, & Parks, Boating Registration, PO Box 451, Jackson, MS 39205; 601-432-2067, 601-432-2066, 601-432-2071 (Fax), 8AM-5PM.

www.mdwfp.com

Note: All motorized vessels and all sailboats have to be registered. Liens are recorded if the vessel has been titled. Starting July 1998, boats are titled at the option of the owner/lender.

Indexing & Storage: Records are available from 1981 to present. Records are indexed on computer from 1985 to present. It takes 2 weeks or so before new records are available for inquiry.

Searching: This agency follows the mandates of the DPPA, allowing access to record information for those with a legitimate buisness interest. Casual requesters must present a signed release before information is released. Include the following in your request-the name or DL number or MS number or hull number.

Access by: mail, phone, fax, in person.

Fee & Payment: There is no search fee.

Mail search: Turnaround time is the same day, except during the summer, which can take 3-4 weeks. A SASE is requested.

Phone search: Records are available by phone.

Fax search: Results will be mailed back usually the same day.

In person search: Turnaround time is usually immediate.

Other access: This agency makes records available on printed lists and magnetic tapes. Fees vary.

Voter Registration

Secretary of State, Elections Division, PO Box 136, Jackson, MS 39205-0136; 800-829-6786, 601-359-1350, 601-359-5019 (Fax), 8AM-5PM.

www.sos.state.ms.us/elections/elections.asp

Note: Records are open to the public, but currently name searches must be done at the county level. Also lists may be purchsed at the county level (see below).

Searching: This agency is in the processs of implementing a statewide database. This should be accomplished prior to 2006.

Access by: mail.

Mail search: Records are available by mail.

GED Certificates

State Board for Community & Jr Colleges, GED Office, 3825 Ridgewood Rd, Jackson, MS 39211; 601-432-6338, 601-432-6890 (Fax), 8AM-5PM.

www.sbcjc.cc.ms.us

Searching: Transcripts are only available by written request. To search, all of the following is required: a signed release, name, date of birth, and SSN. If known, the diploma number is helpful.

Access by: mail, in person.

Fee & Payment: The fee is $5.00 for either a verification or a transcript.

Mail search: Turnaround time: 3 days. Turnaround time is 3 days. No SASE is required.

In person search: In person searchers must have a picture ID. Turnaround time: 2-3 minutes for a verification.

Hunting and Fishing License Information

Department of Wildlife, Fisheries & Parks, PO Box 451, Jackson, MS 39205; 601-432-2055 (License Division), 601-432-2041 (Data Processing Div), 601-432-2071 (Fax), 8AM-5PM.

www.mdwfp.com

Indexing & Storage: Records are available for present data only.

Searching: Records are open to the public. They hold records on "sportsman" license holders which is a combination of hunting and fishing. Temporary license information is not maintained. You can search using the name or driver's license number.

Access by: mail, phone, fax, in person.

Fee & Payment: There is no search fee.

Mail search: Turnaround time: 10 days. No SASE is required.

Phone search: Records are available by phone.

Fax search: Same criteria as mail searches.

In person search: You can make the request in person but they will mail back your response.

Other access: They offer bulk sale of various license groups in a variety of media methods. Visit the website for more information, or call 601-432-2025.

Mississippi State Licensing Agencies

Licenses Searchable Online

Architect #3	www.archbd.state.ms.us/roster.html
Attorney/Attorney Firm #27	www.msbar.org/lawyerdirectory.htm
Camp, Youth #40	www.health.ms.gov/msdhsite/index.cfm/13,333,81,html
Charity #32	www.sos.state.ms.us/regenf/charities/charannrpt/index.asp
Child Care Facility #40	www.health.ms.gov/msdhsite/index.cfm/13,333,81,html
Contractor, General #6	www.msboc.state.ms.us/Search.cfm
CPA-Certified Public Accountant #19	www.msbpa.state.ms.us/licsearch.html
Dental Hygienist #8	www.msbde.state.ms.us
Dental Radiologist #8	www.msbde.state.ms.us
Dentist #8	www.msbde.state.ms.us
Engineer #9	http://dsitspe01.its.state.ms.us/pepls/EngSurveyors.nsf
Fund Raiser #32	www.sos.state.ms.us/regenf/charities/charannrpt/index.asp
Funeral Preneed Contractor #32	www.sos.state.ms.us
Geologist #23	www.msbrpg.state.ms.us/rpg.htm
HMO #25	www.doi.state.ms.us/hmolist.pdf
Home Inspector #34	www.mrec.state.ms.us/asp/findrealtor.asp
Insurance Company #25	www.doi.state.ms.us/compdir.html
Investment Advisor #32	www.sos.state.ms.us
Landscape Architect #3	www.archbd.state.ms.us/roster.html
Lobbyist #31	www.sos.state.ms.us/elections/Lobbying/Lobbyist_Dir.asp
Long Term Care Insurance Company #25	www.doi.state.ms.us/ltclist.html
Medical Doctor #12	www.msbml.state.ms.us
Notary Public #31	www.sos.state.ms.us/regenf/notaries/notaries.asp
Optometrist #15	www.arbo.org/odfinder/LicSearch.asp
Osteopathic Physician #12	www.msbml.state.ms.us
Podiatrist #12	www.msbml.state.ms.us
Psychologist #18	www.psychologyboard.state.ms.us/msbp/msbp.nsf/Search?OpenForm
Real Estate Agent/Broker/Sales #34	www.mrec.state.ms.us/asp/findrealtor.asp
Real Estate Appraiser #30	www.mrec.state.ms.us/asp/findappraiser.asp
Securities Agent #32	www.sos.state.ms.us
Securities Broker/Dealer #32	www.sos.state.ms.us
Security Offering #32	www.sos.state.ms.us
Surveyor, Land #9	http://dsitspe01.its.state.ms.us/pepls/EngSurveyors.nsf
Youth Home, Residential #40	www.health.ms.gov/msdhsite/index.cfm/13,333,81,html

Mississippi Licensing Quick Finder

Air Monitor #22	601-961-5100
Alcohol Beverage Employee #26	601-856-1330
Alcoholic Beverage Retailer #2	601-856-1320
Animal/Veterinary Technician #29	662-324-9380
Architect #3	601-899-9071
Asbestos Contractor/Inspector/Supervisor #22	601-961-5100
Asbestos Project Designer/Mgmt. Planner #22	601-961-5100
Asbestos Worker #22	601-961-5100
Athletic Trainer #37	601-576-7260
Attorney/Attorney Firm #27	601-948-4471
Bank #4	601-359-1031
Barber Instructor/School #5	601-359-1015
Barber/Barber Shop #5	601-359-1015
Beauty Shop/Salon #7	601-987-6837
Boiler & Pressure Vessel Inspector #37	601-576-7917
Camp, Youth #40	601-576-7613
Charity #32	601-359-1371
Child Care Facility #40	601-576-7613
Chiropractor #35	662-773-4433
Contractor, General #6	601-354-6161
Cosmetologist #7	601-987-6837
Cosmetology Instructor #7	601-987-6837
Counselor, Licensed Professional #10	662-716-3932
CPA-Certified Public Accountant #19	601-354-7320
Dental Hygienist #8	601-944-9622

Dental Radiologist #8	601-944-9622
Dentist #8	601-944-9622
Dietitian #37	601-576-7260
Educator, Citizen/Emergency/Non-Licensed #36	601-359-3483
Emergency Medical Technician #37	601-576-7681
Engineer #9	601-359-6160
Esthetician #7	601-987-6837
Eye Enucleator #37	601-576-7260
Finance Company #4	601-359-1031
Fishing, Commercial #24	601-432-2400
Fund Raiser #32	601-359-6371
Funeral Director #11	601-932-1973
Funeral Preneed Contractor #32	601-359-6371
Funeral Service Practitioner #11	601-932-1973
Gaming #26	601-351-2800
Geologist #23	601-54-6370
Health Facility #1	601-576-7400
Hearing Aid Dealer (Specialist) #37	601-576-7260
HMO #25	601-359-3582
Home Inspector #34	601-932-9191
Insurance Agent/Solicitor/Advisor #25	601-359-3582
Insurance Company #25	601-359-3582
Investment Advisor #32	601-359-6363
Landscape Architect #3	601-899-9071
Liquor Control #2	601-856-1310
Lobbyist #31	601-359-6353

Long Term Care Insurance Co. #25	601-359-3582
Manicurist #7	601-987-6837
Marriage & Family Therapist #28	601-987-6806
Medical Doctor #12	601-987-3079
Mortgage Lender/Company #4	601-359-1031
Notary Public #31	601-359-1633
Nurse, Nurse-LPN #13	601-987-6858
Nursing Home Administrator #14	601-932-1442
Occupational Therapist/Assistant #33	601-576-7260
Optometrist #15	601-853-4338
Osteopathic Physician #12	601-987-3079
Pawn Shop #4	601-359-1031
Pharmacist #16	601-354-6750
Pharmacy #16	601-354-6750
Pharmacy Intern/Technician #16	601-354-6750
Physical Therapist/Assistant #33	601-576-7260
Podiatrist #12	601-987-3079
Polygraph Examiner #17	601-987-1596
Psychologist #18	662-716-3934
Radiation Technician #37	601-576-7260
Real Estate Agent/Broker Sales #34	601-932-9191
Real Estate Appraiser #30	601-932-6770
Savings Institution #4	601-359-1031
School Administrator #36	601-359-3483
Securities Agent /Broker/Dealer #32	601-359-6363
Security Offering #32	601-359-6369
Septic Tank Installer #37	601-576-7260

Shorthand Reporter #20 601-354-6056
Social Worker #28 601-987-6806
Speech-Language Pathologist/Audiologist #21
.... 601-576-7260

Surveyor, Land #9 601-359-6160
Tattoo Artist #37 601-576-7260
Teacher #36 601-359-3483
Title & Loan Company #4 601-359-1031

Veterinarian #29 662-324-9380
Veterinary Facility #29 662-324-9380
Youth Home, Residential #40 601-576-7613

Mississippi Licensing Agency Information

1 Department of Health, Health Facilities Licensure & Certification, PO Box 1700 (570 E Woodrow Wilson Blvd), Jackson, MS 39216; 601-576-7400, Fax: 601-576-7350. www.msdh.state.ms.us

2 Office of Alcoholic Beverage Control, PO Box 540, Madison, MS 39110-0540; 601-856-1330, Fax: 601-856-1390. www.mstc.state.ms.us Email: bsmith@mstc.state.ms.us

3 Board of Architecture, 400 Legacy Park Dr #B, Ridgeland, MS 39157; 601-899-9071, Fax: 601-899-9171. www.archbd.state.ms.us Email: msboa@archbd.state.ms.us Search at www.archbd.state.ms.us/roster.html Note: Includes the Landscape Architecture Advisory Committee.

4 Department of Banking & Consumer Finance, Board of Banking Review, 501 NW St, 901 Woolfolk Bldg, Ste. A, Jackson, MS 39202; 601-359-1031, Fax: 601-359-3557. www.dbcf.state.ms.us/review.htm

5 Board of Barber Examiners, 510 George St, Rm 240, Jackson, MS 39205; 601-359-1015, Fax: 601-359-1050. Email: msbbe@bellsouth.net

6 Board of Contractors, 2001 Airport Rd. #101, Jackson, MS 39208; 601-354-6161, Fax: 601-354-6715. www.msboc.state.ms.us/index.cfm Search at www.msboc.state.ms.us/Search.cfm

7 Board of Cosmetology, PO Box 55689, Jackson, MS 39296-5689; 601-987-6837, Fax: 601-987-6840. www.msbc.state.ms.us/msbc/Cosmetology.nsf

8 Mississppi State Board of Dental Examiners, 600 E Amite #100, Jackson, MS 39201-2801; 601-944-9622, Fax: 601-924- 9624. www.msbde.state.ms.us Email: dental@msbde.state.ms.us Search Database at www.msbde.state.ms.us Note: There is a $125.00 fee for list or labels; $150.00 fee for diskette.

9 Board of Engineers & Land Surveyors, PO Box 3 (239 N. Lamar St #501), Jackson, MS 39205-0003; 601-359-6160, Fax: 601-359-6159. www.pepls.state.ms.us Email: information@pepls.state.ms.us Search at http://ds itspe01.its.state.ms.us/pepls/EngSurveyors.nsf

10 Board of Examiners for Licensed Professional Counselors, 419 E Broadway St, Yazoo City, MS 39194-4530; 662-716-3932, Fax: 662-751-4628. www.lpc.state.ms.us Email: acox@maminc.net

11 Board of Funeral Service, 3010 Lakeland Cove, Suite W, Flowood, MS 39232; 601-932-1973, Fax: 601-932-1901. www.msfuneralboard.com Email: msfuneralboard@msfuneralboard.com Note: The website will soon list funeral homes.

12 Board of Medical Licensure, 1867 Crane Ridge Drive, Ste 200-B, Jackson, MS 39216; 601-987-3079, Fax: 601-987-4159. www.msbml.state.ms.us Email: mboard@msbml.state.ms.us Note: A fee based online verification system is available.

13 Board of Nursing, 1935 Lakeland Dr #B, Jackson, MS 39216; 601-987-4188, Fax: 601-364-2352. www.msbn.state.ms.us/index.html

14 Board of Nursing Home Administrators, 644 Lakeland East Dr. Ste C, Flowood, MS 39232; 601-932-1442, Fax: 601-932-1544. www.bnha.state.ms.us/

15 Board of Optometry, PO Box 12370, Jackson, MS 39236; 601-853-4338, Fax: 601-853-0336. www.msoptometry.org email: office@msoptometry.org Search at www.arbo.org/odfinder/LicSearch.asp

16 Board of Pharmacy, 204 Key Dr #D, Madison, MS 39110-7361; 601-605-5388, Fax: 601-605-9546. www.mbp.state.ms.us Email: sstovall@mbp.state.ms.us

17 Board of Polygraph Examiners, PO Box 958, Jackson, MS 39205; 601-987-1596.

18 Board of Psychology, 419 E Broadway St, Yazoo City, MS 39194-4530; 662-716-3934, Fax: 662-751-4628. www.psychologyboard.state.ms.us/msbp/msbp.nsf Search Database at www.psychologyboard.st ate.ms.us/msbp/msbp.nsf/Search?OpenForm

19 Board of Public Accountancy, 5 Old River Place Ste 104, Jackson, MS 39202; 601-354-7320, Fax: 601-354-7290. www.msbpa.state.ms.us Search at www.msbpa.state.ms.us/licsearch.html

20 Board of Certified Court Reporters, PO Box 369 (656 N State St, Jackson, MS 39205; 601-354-6056, Fax: 601-354-6058. www.mssc.state.ms.us Email: tgraves@mssc.state.ms.us

21 Department of Health, Council of Advisors in Speech Pathology/Audiology, PO Box 1700 (570 Woodrow Wilson, 39216), Jackson, MS 39215-1700; 601-576-7260, Fax: 601-576-7267. www.msdh.state.ms.us Email: stephanie.boyette@ohr.ms.gov

22 Department of Environmental Quality, Pollution Control, PO Box 10385, Jackson, MS 39289-0385; 601-961-5171, Fax: 601-354-6612. www.deq.state.ms.us/MDEQ.nsf

23 Board of Registered Professional Geologists, PO Box 22742 (931 Hwy. 80 West), Jackson, MS 39225-2742; 601-54-6370, Fax: 601-354-6032. www.msbrpg.state.ms.us Email: geology@msbrpg.state.ms.us Search at www.msbrpg.state.ms.us/rpg.htm

24 Department of Wildlife, Fisheries & Parks, 1505 Eastover Dr, Jackson, MS 39211-6322; 601-432-2400, Fax: 601-432-2024. www.mdwfp.com

25 Insurance Department, Licensing Division, PO Box 79, Jackson, MS 39205; 601-359-3582, Fax: 601-359-1951. www.doi.state.ms.us/agents.html Email: licensing@mid.state.ms.us

26 Gaming Commission, 200 E Pearl St, Jackson, MS 39205; 601-351-2800, Fax: 601-351-2817. www.mgc.state.ms.us

27 Board of Bar Admissions, PO Box 2168, Jackson, MS 39225; 601-948-4471, Fax: 601-355-8635. www.msbar.org Search at www.msbar.org/lawyerdirectory.htm

28 Marriage & Family Therapists, Board of Examiners for Social Workers, PO Box 4508, Jackson, MS 39296-4508; 601-987-6806, Fax: 601-987-6808. www.msboeswmft.com Email: mboe@swmft.state.ms.us

29 Board of Veterinary Medicine, 209 S Lafayette, Starkville, MS 39759; 662-324-9380, Fax: 662-324-9380. Note: Lists of Veterinarians are available in paper form only. Resuests must be approved, and they are charged by the minute.

30 Real Estate Appraiser, Licensing & Certification Board, 2506 Lakeland Dr. Ste 300 PO Box 12685, Jackson, MS 39236-2685; 601-932-9191, Fax: 601-932-3880. www.mrec.state.ms.us/default.asp Search at www.mrec.state.ms.us/asp/findappraiser.asp

31 Office of Secretary of State, Regulation & Enforcement, PO Box 136, Jackson, MS 39205-0136; 601-359-1350, Fax: 601-359-1499. www.sos.state.ms.us Search Database at www.sos.state.ms.us

32 Office of Secretary of State, Business Regulation & Enforcement Division, PO Box 136 (700 North St, 39202), Jackson, MS 39205-0136; 601-359-1350, Fax: 601-359-1499. www.sos.state.ms.us Email: administrator@sos.state.ms.us Note: They provid lists. Contact for price.

33 Professional Licensure Division, MSDH, PO Box 1700, Jackson, MS 39215-1700; 601-576-7260, Fax: 601-576-7267. www.msdh.state.ms.us Email: stephanie.boyette@ohr.doh.ms.gov

34 Real Estate Commission, Licensing & Certification Board, PO Box 12685 (2506 Lakeland Dr, #300), Jackson, MS 39236; 601-932-9191, Fax: 601-932-2990. www.mrec.state.ms.us Search database at www.mrec.state.ms.us/asp/findrealtor.asp

35 Board of Chiropractic Examiners, PO Box 775, Louisville, MS 39339; 662-773-4478, Fax: 662-773-4433. Email: msbce@bellsouth.net

36 Department of Education, Teacher Licensure/Certification, PO Box 771 (359 N West Street), Jackson, MS 39205; 601-359-3483, Fax: 601-359-2778. www.mde.k12.ms.us Email: cchester@mde.k12.ms.us

37 Department of Health, Licensing Division, 570 E Woodrow Wilson, Jackson, MS 39215; 601-576-7917, Fax: 601-576-7923. www.msdh.state.ms.us

40 Department of Health, Childcare Facilities Licensure, 570 E Woodrow Wilson, Jackson, MS 39215; 601-576-7613. www.msdh.state.ms.us Search at www.health.ms.gov/msdhsite/in dex.cfm/13,333,81,html

Mississippi Federal Courts

The following list indicates the district and division name for each county in the state. If the bankruptcy court location is different from the district court, then the location of the bankruptcy court appears in parentheses.

County/Court Cross Reference

County	District	Division
Adams	Southern	Vicksburg (Jackson)
Alcorn	Northern	Aberdeen-Eastern (Aberdeen)
Amite	Southern	Jackson
Attala	Northern	Aberdeen-Eastern (Aberdeen)
Benton	Northern	Oxford-Northern (Aberdeen)
Bolivar	Northern	Clarksdale/Delta (Aberdeen)
Calhoun	Northern	Oxford-Northern (Aberdeen)
Carroll	Northern	Greenville (Aberdeen)
Chickasaw	Northern	Aberdeen-Eastern (Aberdeen)
Choctaw	Northern	Aberdeen-Eastern (Aberdeen)
Claiborne	Southern	Vicksburg (Jackson)
Clarke	Southern	Meridian (Biloxi)
Clay	Northern	Aberdeen-Eastern (Aberdeen)
Coahoma	Northern	Clarksdale/Delta (Aberdeen)
Copiah	Southern	Jackson
Covington	Southern	Hattiesburg (Biloxi)
De Soto	Northern	Clarksdale/Delta (Aberdeen)
Forrest	Southern	Hattiesburg (Biloxi)
Franklin	Southern	Jackson
George	Southern	Biloxi-Southern (Biloxi)
Greene	Southern	Hattiesburg (Biloxi)
Grenada	Northern	Oxford-Northern (Aberdeen)
Hancock	Southern	Biloxi-Southern (Biloxi)
Harrison	Southern	Biloxi-Southern (Biloxi)
Hinds	Southern	Jackson
Holmes	Southern	Jackson
Humphreys	Northern	Greenville (Aberdeen)
Issaquena	Southern	Vicksburg (Jackson)
Itawamba	Northern	Aberdeen-Eastern (Aberdeen)
Jackson	Southern	Biloxi-Southern (Biloxi)
Jasper	Southern	Meridian (Biloxi)
Jefferson	Southern	Vicksburg (Jackson)
Jefferson Davis	Southern	Hattiesburg (Biloxi)
Jones	Southern	Hattiesburg (Biloxi)
Kemper	Southern	Meridian (Biloxi)
Lafayette	Northern	Oxford-Northern (Aberdeen)
Lamar	Southern	Hattiesburg (Biloxi)
Lauderdale	Southern	Meridian (Biloxi)
Lawrence	Southern	Hattiesburg (Biloxi)
Leake	Southern	Jackson
Lee	Northern	Aberdeen-Eastern (Aberdeen)
Leflore	Northern	Greenville (Aberdeen)
Lincoln	Southern	Jackson
Lowndes	Northern	Aberdeen-Eastern (Aberdeen)
Madison	Southern	Jackson
Marion	Southern	Hattiesburg (Jackson)
Marshall	Northern	Oxford-Northern (Aberdeen)
Monroe	Northern	Aberdeen-Eastern (Aberdeen)
Montgomery	Northern	Oxford-Northern (Aberdeen)
Neshoba	Southern	Meridian (Biloxi)
Newton	Southern	Meridian (Biloxi)
Noxubee	Southern	Meridian (Biloxi)
Oktibbeha	Northern	Aberdeen-Eastern (Aberdeen)
Panola	Northern	Clarksdale/Delta (Aberdeen)
Pearl River	Southern	Biloxi-Southern (Biloxi)
Perry	Southern	Hattiesburg (Biloxi)
Pike	Southern	Jackson
Pontotoc	Northern	Oxford-Northern (Aberdeen)
Prentiss	Northern	Aberdeen-Eastern (Aberdeen)
Quitman	Northern	Clarksdale/Delta (Aberdeen)
Rankin	Southern	Jackson
Scott	Southern	Jackson
Sharkey	Southern	Vicksburg (Jackson)
Simpson	Southern	Jackson
Smith	Southern	Jackson
Stone	Southern	Biloxi-Southern (Biloxi)
Sunflower	Northern	Greenville (Aberdeen)
Tallahatchie	Northern	Clarksdale/Delta (Aberdeen)
Tate	Northern	Clarksdale/Delta (Aberdeen)
Tippah	Northern	Oxford-Northern (Aberdeen)
Tishomingo	Northern	Aberdeen-Eastern (Aberdeen)
Tunica	Northern	Clarksdale/Delta (Aberdeen)
Union	Northern	Oxford-Northern (Aberdeen)
Walthall	Southern	Hattiesburg (Biloxi)
Warren	Southern	Vicksburg (Jackson)
Washington	Northern	Greenville (Aberdeen)
Wayne	Southern	Meridian (Biloxi)
Webster	Northern	Oxford-Northern (Aberdeen)
Wilkinson	Southern	Vicksburg (Jackson)
Winston	Northern	Aberdeen-Eastern (Aberdeen)
Yalobusha	Northern	Oxford-Northern (Aberdeen)
Yazoo	Southern	Vicksburg (Jackson)

Standards for Federal Courts: The search fee is $20.00 per item (one party name or case number). Certification fee is $7.00 per document. Copy fee is $.50 per page. All fees standard unless noted in profile. Mail Search: always enclose a stamped self addressed envelope unless otherwise noted. Most courts accept fax requests or will suggest a copying/search vendor. Before releasing records, all courts require prepayment unless noted in profile.

Open records are located at the court unless otherwise noted. District courts index by defendant and plaintiff as well as by case number. Bankruptcy courts usually index by debtor and case number. While most courts now have their indexes on computer, many still maintain index card files as well.

The universal PACER sign-up number is 800-676-6856. Find PACER and the Party/Case Index on the Web at http://pacer.psc.uscourts.gov. PACER dial-up access is $.60 per minute. Also, courts offering internet access via RACER, PACER, Web-PACER or the new CM-ECF charge $.07 per page fee unless noted as free.

US District Court

Northern District of Mississippi

Aberdeen-Eastern Division PO Box 704, Aberdeen, MS 39730 (courier address: 301 W Commerce, Room 310, Aberdeen, MS 39730), 662-369-4952. www.msnd.uscourts.gov

Counties: Alcorn, Attala, Chickasaw, Choctaw, Clay, Itawamba, Lee, Lowndes, Monroe, Oktibbeha, Prentiss, Tishomingo, Winston.

Indexing & Storage: New cases available in the index 48 hours after filing date.

Fee & Payment: Payment may be made by money order, cashier check, personal check. Payee: Clerk, U.S. District Court.

Phone Search: No searching by telephone. If a case number is provided over the phone, the court will verify that the case number is correct.

In Person Search: Fee charged if court conducts your in person search for you.

PACER: PACER is available online at http://pacer.msnd.uscourts.gov. Records purged every six months. New records are online after 1 day.

Opinions Online: Court opinions are online at http://sunset.backbone.olemiss.edu/~llibcoll/ndms

Clarksdale/Delta Division c/o Oxford-Northern Division, PO Box 727, Oxford, MS 38655 (courier address: Suite 369, 911 Jackson Ave, Oxford, MS 38655), 662-234-1971. www.msnd.uscourts.gov

Counties: Bolivar, Coahoma, De Soto, Panola, Quitman, Tallahatchie, Tate, Tunica.

Indexing & Storage: Cases indexed by as well as by case number. New cases available in the index after filing date. Open records are located at the Oxford-Northern Division.

Fee & Payment: Payment may be made by money order, cashier check. Business checks are not accepted. Personal checks are not accepted.

Phone Search: No searching by telephone.

In Person Search: Permitted.

PACER: PACER is available online at http://pacer.msnd.uscourts.gov. Records purged every six months. New records are online after 1 day.

Opinions Online: Court opinions are online at http://sunset.backbone.olemiss.edu/~llibcoll/ndms

Greenville Division PO Box 190, Greenville, MS 38702-0190 (courier address: U.S. Post Office & Federal Bldg, 305 Main, Greenville, MS 38701), 662-335-1651, Fax: 662-332-4292. www.msnd.uscourts.gov

Counties: Carroll, Humphreys, Leflore, Sunflower, Washington.

Indexing & Storage: New cases available in the index immediately after filing date.

Fee & Payment: Payment may be made by money order, cashier check, personal check. Payee: Clerk, U.S. District Court.

Phone Search: Only docket information based on case number is available by phone.

In Person Search: Fee charged if court conducts your in person search for you.

PACER: PACER is available online at http://pacer.msnd.uscourts.gov. Records purged every six months. New records are online after 1 day.

Opinions Online: Court opinions are online at http://sunset.backbone.olemiss.edu/~llibcoll/ndms

Oxford-Northern Division PO Box 727, Oxford, MS 38655 (courier address: Suite 369, 911 Jackson Ave, Oxford, MS 38655), 662-234-1971. www.msnd.uscourts.gov

Counties: Benton, Calhoun, Grenada, Lafayette, Marshall, Montgomery, Pontotoc, Tippah, Union, Webster, Yalobusha.

Indexing & Storage: New cases available in the index 48 hours after filing date. Records are also indexed on microfiche. Civil records are sent to the Atlanta Federal Records Center 5 years after closing. Criminal records are sent to the Atlanta Federal Records Ce10 years after closing. All criminal records for the Delta Division (Clarksdale) are maintained in this office.

Fee & Payment: Payment may be made by money order, cashier check, personal check. Payee: Clerk, U.S. District Court.

Phone Search: No searching by telephone. If a case number is provided over the phone, the court will verify that the case number is correct.

In Person Search: Fee charged if court conducts your in person search for you.

PACER: PACER is available online at http://pacer.msnd.uscourts.gov. Records purged every six months. New records are online after 1 day.

Opinions Online: Court opinions are online at http://sunset.backbone.olemiss.edu/~llibcoll/ndms

U.S. Bankruptcy Court

Northern District of Mississippi

Aberdeen Division PO Drawer 867, Aberdeen, MS 39730-0867 (courier: 205 Federal Bldg, 301 W. Commerce St, Aberdeen, MS 39730), 662-369-2596. www.msnb.uscourts.gov

Counties: Alcorn, Attala, Benton, Bolivar, Calhoun, Carroll, Chickasaw, Choctaw, Clay, Coahoma, De Soto, Grenada, Humphreys, Itawamba, Lafayette, Lee, Leflore, Lowndes, Marshall, Monroe, Montgomery, Oktibbeha, Panola, Pontotoc, Prentiss, Quitman, Sunflower, Tallahatchie, Tate, Tippah, Tishomingo, Tunica, Union, Washington, Webster, Winston, Yalobusha.

Indexing & Storage: Cases indexed by debtor as well as by case number. New cases available in the index 1-2 days after filing date.

Fee & Payment: Payment may be made by money order, cashier check, personal check. Payee: Clerk, U.S. Bankruptcy Court, Northern District.

Phone Search: Only docket information available by phone. Automated voice case information service (VCIS) is available. Call VCIS at 800-392-8653 or 662-369-8147.

In Person Search: Fee charged if court conducts your in person search for you. The $20.00 charge is per name or item. You may not take case files from the court for copies.

PACER: PACER is available online at http://pacer.msnb.uscourts.gov. Records purged every 6 months. New civil records are online after 2 days.

Electronic Filing: Electronic filing information online at https://ecf.msnb.uscourts.gov

U.S. District Court

Southern District of Mississippi

Biloxi-Southern Division Room 243, 725 Dr. Martin Luther King Jr. Blvd, Biloxi, MS 39530 (courier address: Use mail address for courier delivery) 228-432-8623, Fax: 601-436-9632. www.mssd.uscourts.gov

Counties: George, Hancock, Harrison, Jackson, Pearl River, Stone.

Indexing & Storage: New cases available in the index 48 hours after filing date.

Fee & Payment: Payment may be made by money order, cashier check, personal check. Payee: Clerk, U.S. District Court.

Phone Search: No searching by telephone. Only docket information available by phone.

In Person Search: Fee charged if court conducts your in person search for you.

PACER: PACER is available online at http://pacer.mssd.uscourts.gov. New records are online after 2 days.

Eastern Division c/o Jackson Division, Suite 316, 245 E Capitol St, Jackson, MS 39201 (courier address: Use mail address for courier delivery) 601-965-4439. www.mssd.uscourts.gov

Counties: Clarke, Jasper, Kemper, Lauderdale, Neshoba, Newton, Noxubee, Wayne.

Indexing & Storage: New cases available in the index after filing date. Open records are located at the Jackson Division.

Fee & Payment: Payment may be made by money order, cashier check. Business checks are not accepted. Personal checks are not accepted.

Phone Search: No searching by telephone.

In Person Search: Permitted.

PACER: PACER is available online at http://pacer.mssd.uscourts.gov. New records are online after 2 days.

Hattiesburg Division Suite 200, 701 Main St, Hattiesburg, MS 39401 (courier address: Use mail address for courier delivery) 601-583-2433. www.mssd.uscourts.gov

Counties: Covington, Forrest, Greene, Jefferson Davis, Jones, Lamar, Lawrence, Marion, Perry, Walthall.

Indexing & Storage: New cases available in the index 48 hours after filing date.

Fee & Payment: Payment may be made by money order, cashier check, personal check. Payee: Clerk, U.S. District Court.

Phone Search: Only docket information is available by case number over the phone.

In Person Search: Fee charged if court conducts your in person search for you.

PACER: PACER is available online at http://pacer.mssd.uscourts.gov. New records are online after 2 days.

Jackson Division Suite 316, 245 E Capitol St, Jackson, MS 39201 (courier address: Use mail address for courier delivery) 601-965-4439. www.mssd.uscourts.gov

Counties: Amite, Copiah, Franklin, Hinds, Holmes, Leake, Lincoln, Madison, Pike, Rankin, Scott, Simpson, Smith.

Indexing & Storage: New cases available in the index 48 hours after filing date. Microfiche index also maintained.

Fee & Payment: Payment may be made by money order, cashier check, personal check. Payee: Clerk, U.S. District Court. Documents will be faxed only with special permission of clerk; fee is $1.00 per page.

Phone Search: No searching by telephone. Documents will be faxed only with special permission of clerk; fee is $1.00 per page.

In Person Search: Fee charged if court conducts your in person search for you.

PACER: PACER is available online at http://pacer.mssd.uscourts.gov. New records are online after 2 days.

Weatern Division c/o Jackson Division, Suite 316, 245 E Capitol St, Jackson, MS 39201 (courier address: Use mail address for courier delivery) 601-965-4439. www.mssd.uscourts.gov

Counties: Adams, Claiborne, Issaquena, Jefferson, Sharkey, Warren, Wilkinson, Yazoo.

Indexing & Storage: Cases indexed by as well as by case number. New cases available in the index after filing date. Open records are located at the Jackson Division.

Fee & Payment: Payment may be made by money order, cashier check. Business checks are not accepted. Personal checks are not accepted.

Phone Search: No searching by telephone.

In Person Search: Permitted.

PACER: PACER is available online at http://pacer.mssd.uscourts.gov. New records are online after 2 days.

U.S. Bankruptcy Court
Southern District of Mississippi

Biloxi Division Room 117, 725 Dr. Martin Luther King Jr. Blvd, Biloxi, MS 39530 (courier address: Use mail address for courier delivery) 228-432-5542. www.mssb.uscourts.gov

Counties: Clarke, Covington, Forrest, George, Greene, Hancock, Harrison, Jackson, Jasper, Jefferson Davis, Jones, Kemper, Lamar, Lauderdale, Lawrence, Marion, Neshoba, Newton, Noxubee, Pearl River, Perry, Stone, Walthall, Wayne.

Indexing & Storage: Cases indexed by debtor as well as by case number. New cases available in the index a few hours after filing date.

Fee & Payment: Payment may be made by money order, cashier check, personal check. Payee: Clerk, U.S. Bankruptcy Court.

Phone Search: Automated voice case information service (VCIS) is available. Call VCIS at 800-293-2723 or 601-435-2905.

In Person Search: Fee charged if court conducts your in person search for you.

PACER: PACER is available online at https://pacer.login.uscourts.gov/cgi-bin/login.pl?court_id=mssbk. New civil records are online after 1 day.

Electronic Filing: Currently in the process of implementing CM/ECF.

Jackson Division PO Box 2448, Jackson, MS 39225-2448 (courier address: 200 E Capitol St, Jackson, MS 39201), 601-965-5301. www.mssb.uscourts.gov

Counties: Adams, Amite, Claiborne, Copiah, Franklin, Hinds, Holmes, Issaquena, Jefferson, Leake, Lincoln, Madison, Pike, Rankin, Scott, Sharkey, Simpson, Smith, Warren, Wilkinson, Yazoo.

Indexing & Storage: Cases indexed by debtor as well as by case number. New cases available in the index a few hours after filing date.

Fee & Payment: Payment may be made by money order, cashier check, personal check. Payee: Clerk, U.S. Bankruptcy Court.

Phone Search: Automated voice case information service (VCIS) is available. Call VCIS at 800-601-8859 or 601-965-6106.

In Person Search: Fee charged if court conducts your in person search for you.

PACER: PACER is available online at https://pacer.login.uscourts.gov/cgi-bin/login.pl?court_id=mssbk.

Electronic Filing: Currently in the process of implementing CM/ECF.

Mississippi County Courts

Court	Jurisdiction	No. of Courts	How Organized
Circuit Courts*	General	70	22 Districts
County Courts*	Limited	3	19 Counties
Combined Courts*		20	
Chancery Courts*	General	91	20 Districts
Justice Courts	Limited	88	
Municipal Courts	Municipal	154	
Family Court	Special	1	

* Profiled in this Sourcebook.

Court	CIVIL								
	Tort	Contract	Real Estate	Min. Claim	Max. Claim	Small Claims	Estate	Eviction	Domestic Relations
Circuit Courts*	X	X	X	$2500	No Max			X	X
County Courts*	X	X	X	$0	$75,000			X	X
Combined Courts*									
Chancery Court*	X	X	X	$0	No Max		X		X
Justice Courts*	X	X	X	$0	$2500	$2500		X	
Municipal Courts								X	
Family Court									X

Court	CRIMINAL				
	Felony	Misdemeanor	DWI/DUI	Preliminary Hearing	Juvenile
Circuit Courts*	X				
County Courts*		X	X	X	X
Combined Courts*					
Chancery Court*					X
Justice Courts*		X	X	X	
Municipal Courts		X	X	X	
Family Court					X

ADMINISTRATION　　Court Administrator, Supreme Court, Box 117, Jackson, MS, 39205; 601-359-3697, Fax: 601-359-2443. www.mssc.state.ms.us

COURT STRUCTURE　　The court of general jurisdiction is the Circuit Court with 70 courts in 22 districts. Justice Courts were first created in 1984, replacing the Justice of the Peace. Prior to 1984, records were kept separately by each Justice of the Peace, so the location of such records today is often unknown. Probate is handled by the Chancery Courts, as are property matters.

ONLINE ACCESS　　A statewide online computer system is in use internally for court personnel. There are plans underway to make this system available to the public, however this has been put on hold. The web site offers searching of the MS Supreme Court and Court of Appeals Decisions, including dockets of the trial courts. It is difficult to do a name search in the trial courts because the sequence number of the docket must be included in request.

ADDITIONAL INFORMATION　　A number of Mississippi counties have two Circuit Court Districts. A search of either court in such a county will include the index from the other court.

Full Name is a search requirement for all courts. DOB and SSN are very helpful for differentiating between like-named individuals.

CRIMINAL RECORDS

The Administrative Office of Courts offers a statewide search via fax requesting with a 24 hour turnaround time. There is a $25.00 start-up fee and a $5.00 per name search fee. Call 601-354-7449 or fax 601-354-7459 for details.

Adams County

Circuit & County Court PO Box 1224, 115 S Wall, Natchez, MS 39121; 601-446-6326; Fax: 601-445-7955. Hours: 8AM-5PM (CST). *Felony, Misdemeanor, Civil Actions Over $2,500.*
Civil Records: Access: Fax, mail, in person. Both court and visitors may perform in person searches. Search fee: $10.00 per name. Required to search: name, years to search. Civil cases indexed by defendant, plaintiff. Civil records on computer; docket books to 1950s; records stored in basement to 1799.
Criminal Records: Access: Mail, fax, in person. Both court and visitors may perform in person searches. Search fee: $10.00 per name. Required to search: name, years to search; also helpful: SSN. Criminal records on computer; docket books to 1950s; records stored in basement to 1799.
General Information: Public Access terminal is available. No sealed, adoptions, mental health, juvenile, sex, or expunged records released. Copy fee: $1.00 per page. Certification fee: $2.00. Payee: Circuit Clerk. Personal checks accepted. Prepayment required. Mail turnaround time 1-2 days if on computer.

Justice Court 115 S Wall, Natchez, MS 39121; 601-446-6326; Fax: 601-445-7955. Hours: 8AM-5PM (CST). *Misdemeanor, Civil Actions Under $2,500, Eviction, Small Claims.*

Chancery Court PO Box 1006, Natchez, MS 39121; 601-446-6684; Fax: 601-445-7913. Hours: 8AM-5PM (CST). *Probate.*

Alcorn County

Circuit Court PO Box 430 Attn: Circuit Clerk, Corinth, MS 38835; 662-286-7740; Fax: 662-286-7767. Hours: 8AM-5PM (CST). *Felony, Civil Actions Over $2,500.*
Civil Records: Access: Mail, fax, in person. Both court and visitors may perform in person searches. Search fee: $10.00 per name. Required to search: name, years to search. Civil cases indexed by defendant, plaintiff. Civil records on docket books from the 1930s.
Criminal Records: Access: Mail, fax, in person. Both court and visitors may perform in person searches. Search fee: $10.00 per name. Required to search: name, years to search, DOB; also helpful: SSN, sex. Criminal records on docket books from the 1930s.
General Information: Public Access terminal is available. No sealed, adoptions, mental health, juvenile, sex, or expunged records released. Fee to fax results is $10.00 per document. Copy fee: $.50 per page. No certification fee. Payee: Circuit Clerk. Personal checks accepted. Prepayment required. Mail requests: SASE required. Mail turnaround time varies.

Justice Court PO Box 226, Corinth, MS 38834; 662-286-7776; Fax: 662-286-2157. Hours: 8AM-5PM (CST). *Misdemeanor, Civil Actions Under $2,500, Eviction, Small Claims.*

Chancery Court PO Box 69, Corinth, MS 38835-0069; 662-286-7702; Fax: 662-286-7706. Hours: 8AM-5PM (CST). *Probate.*

Amite County

Circuit Court PO Box 312, Liberty, MS 39645; 601-657-8932; Fax: 601-657-1082. Hours: 8AM-5PM (CST). *Felony, Civil Actions Over $2,500.*
Civil Records: Access: Phone, fax, mail, in person. Both court and visitors may perform in person searches. Search fee: $10.00 per name. Required to search: name, years to search. Civil cases indexed by defendant, plaintiff. Civil records on docket books since 1976; judgements on computer back to 1990.
Criminal Records: Access: Fax, mail, in person. Both court and visitors may perform in person searches. Search fee: $10.00 per name. Required to search: name, years to search, DOB; also helpful: SSN. Criminal records on docket books since 1976.
General Information: Marriage records from 1809 - present. Will fax results for $3.00. Copy fee: $.50 per page. Certification fee: $10.00. Payee: Circuit Clerk. Personal checks accepted. Turnaround time same day.

Justice Court PO Box 362, Liberty, MS 39645; 601-657-4527; Fax: 601-657-8604. Hours: 8AM-5PM (CST). *Misdemeanor, Civil Actions Under $2,500, Eviction, Small Claims.*

Chancery Court PO Box 680, Liberty, MS 39645; 601-657-8022; Fax: 601-657-8288. Hours: 8AM-5PM (CST). *Probate.*

Attala County

Circuit Court Courthouse, Kosciusko, MS 39090; 662-289-1471; Fax: 662-289-7666. Hours: 8AM-5PM (CST). *Felony, Civil Actions Over $2,500.*
Civil Records: Access: Fax, mail, in person. Both court and visitors may perform in person searches. Search fee: $10.00 per name. Required to search: name, years to search. Civil cases indexed by defendant, plaintiff. Civil records kept on docket books since 1915.
Criminal Records: Access: Fax, mail, in person. Both court and visitors may perform in person searches. Search fee: $10.00 per name. Required to search: name, years to search, DOB; also helpful: SSN. Criminal records kept on docket books since 1915.
General Information: Will fax results. Copy fee: $.50 per page. Certification fee: $1.00. Payee: Circuit Clerk. Business checks accepted. Prepayment required. Mail requests: SASE required. Mail turnaround time same day.

Justice Court 100 Courthouse, #4, Kosciusko, MS 39090; 662-289-7272; Fax: 662-289-0105. Hours: 8AM-5PM (CST). *Misdemeanor, Civil Actions Under $2,500, Eviction, Small Claims.*

Chancery Court 230 W. Washington, Kosciusko, MS 39090; 662-289-2921; Fax: 662-289-7662. Hours: 8AM-5PM (CST). *Probate.*

Benton County

Circuit Court PO Box 262, Ashland, MS 38603; 662-224-6310; Fax: 662-224-6312. Hours: 8AM-5PM (CST). *Felony, Civil Actions Over $2,500.*
Civil Records: Access: Mail, in person. Both court and visitors may perform in person searches. Search fee: $10.00 per name. Required to search: name, years to search, address. Civil cases indexed by defendant, plaintiff. Civil records kept on index books since 1871.
Criminal Records: Access: Mail, in person. Both court and visitors may perform in person searches.
Search fee: $10.00 per name. Required to search: name, years to search, DOB; also helpful: SSN. Criminal records kept on index books since 1871.
General Information: No sealed, adoptions, mental health, juvenile, sex, or expunged records released. Will fax results for fee. Copy fee: $.50 per page. Certification fee: $1.00. Payee: Circuit Court. Only cashiers checks and money orders accepted. Prepayment required. Mail turnaround time same day.

Justice Court PO Box 152, Ashland, MS 38603; 662-224-6320; Fax: 662-224-6313. Hours: 8AM-5PM (CST). *Misdemeanor, Civil Actions Under $2,500, Eviction, Small Claims.*

Chancery Court PO Box 218, Ashland, MS 38603; 662-224-6300; Fax: 662-224-6303. Hours: 8AM-5PM (CST). *Probate.*

Bolivar County

Circuit & County Court - 1st District PO Box 205, Rosedale, MS 38769; 662-759-6521. Hours: 8AM-5PM (CST). *Felony, Misdemeanor, Civil.*
Civil Records: Access: In person only. Visitors must perform in person searches for themselves. No search fee. Required to search: name, years to search. Civil cases indexed by defendant, plaintiff. Civil records on docket books since 1900s.
Criminal Records: Access: Mail, in person. Both court and visitors may perform in person searches. Search fee: $10.00 per name. Fee is for 7 year search. Required to search: name, years to search. Criminal records on docket books since 1900s.
General Information: Public Access terminal is available. No sealed, juvenile, sex, or expunged records released. Copy fee: $.50 per page. Certification fee: $1.50. Payee: Circuit Clerk. Personal checks accepted. Prepayment required. Mail requests: SASE required. Mail turnaround time 2-3 days.

Circuit & County Court - 2nd District PO Box 670, Cleveland, MS 38732; 662-843-2061; Fax: 662-846-2943. Hours: 8AM-5PM (CST). *Felony, Misdemeanor, Civil.*
Civil Records: Access: In person only. Visitors must perform in person searches for themselves. No search fee. Required to search: name, years to search. Civil cases indexed by defendant, plaintiff. Civil records on docket books since 1940.
Criminal Records: Access: Mail, in person. Both court and visitors may perform in person searches. Search fee: $10.00 per name. Fee is for 7 year search. Required to search: name, years to search. Criminal records on docket books since 1940.
General Information: No sealed, juvenile or expunged records released. Copy fee: $.50 per page. Certification fee: $1.50. Payee: Circuit Clerk. Personal checks accepted. Prepayment required. Mail requests: SASE required. Mail turnaround time 2-3 days.

Justice Court PO Box 1507, Cleveland, MS 38732; 662-843-4008; Fax: 662-846-6783. Hours: 8:00AM-5:00PM (CST). *Misdemeanor, Civil Actions Under $2,500, Eviction, Small Claims.*

Cleveland Chancery Court PO Box 789, Cleveland, MS 38732; 662-843-2071; Fax: 662-846-2940. Hours: 8AM-5PM (CST). *Probate.*

Rosedale Chancery Court PO Box 238, Rosedale, MS 38769; 662-759-3762; Fax: 662-759-3467. Hours: 8AM-Noon, 1-5PM (CST). *Probate.*

Calhoun County

Circuit Court PO Box 25, Pittsboro, MS 38951; 662-412-3101; Fax: 662-412-3103. Hours: 8AM-5PM (CST). *Felony, Civil Actions Over $2,500.*

Civil Records: Access: Mail, in person. Both court and visitors may perform in person searches. Search fee: $10.00 per name. Required to search: name, years to search, DOB or SSN. Civil cases indexed by defendant, plaintiff. Civil records on docket books since 1922; computerized records go back to 1922.

Criminal Records: Access: Mail, in person. Both court and visitors may perform in person searches. Search fee: $10.00 per name. Required to search: name, years to search, DOB; also helpful: SSN. Criminal records on docket books since 1922; computerized records go back to 1922.

General Information: Public Access terminal is available. No sealed, mental health, juvenile, sex, or expunged records released. Fee to fax results is $2.00 per page. Copy fee: $1.00 per page. Certification fee: $1.50. Payee: Circuit Clerk. Personal checks accepted. Prepayment required. Mail requests: SASE required. Mail turnaround time same day; phone search info released when payment is received.

Justice Court PO Box 7, Pittsboro, MS 38951; 662-412-3134; Fax: 662-412-3136. Hours: 8AM-5PM (CST). *Misdemeanor, Civil Actions Under $2,500, Eviction, Small Claims.*

Chancery Court PO Box 8, Pittsboro, MS 38951; 662-412-3117; Fax: 662-412-3128. Hours: 8AM-5PM (CST). *Probate.*

Carroll County

Circuit Court PO Box 6, Vaiden, MS 39176; 662-464-5476; Fax: 662-464-5407. Hours: 8AM-5PM (CST). *Felony, Civil Actions Over $2,500.*

Civil Records: Access: Mail, in person. Both court and visitors may perform in person searches. Search fee: $10.00 per name. Required to search: name, years to search. Civil cases indexed by defendant, plaintiff. Civil records on books since 1900s.

Criminal Records: Access: Mail, in person. Both court and visitors may perform in person searches. Search fee: $10.00 per name. Required to search: name, years to search; also helpful: SSN. Criminal records on books since 1900s.

General Information: No adoptions, mental health or juvenile records released. Will fax results to local or toll free line. Copy fee: $.50 per page. Certification fee: $2.00. Payee: Circuit Court. Personal checks accepted. Prepayment required. Mail turnaround time 2 days.

Justice Court PO Box 10, Carrollton, MS 38917; 662-237-9285; Fax: 662-237-6833. Hours: 8AM-5PM (CST). *Misdemeanor, Civil Actions Under $2,500, Eviction, Small Claims.*

Chancery Court PO Box 60, Carrollton, MS 38917; 662-237-9274; Fax: 662-237-9642. Hours: 8AM-12; 1-5PM (CST). *Probate.*

Chickasaw County

Circuit Court - 1st District 1 Pinson Sq, Rm 2, Houston, MS 38851; 662-456-2331; Fax: 662-456-4831. Hours: 8AM-5PM (CST). *Felony, Civil Actions Over $2,500.*

Civil Records: Access: Fax, mail, in person. Both court and visitors may perform in person searches. Search fee: $10.00 per name. There is no fee if the visitor performs the search. Required to search: name, years to search; also helpful: address. Civil cases indexed by defendant, plaintiff. Civil records on docket books since mid-1800s.

Criminal Records: Access: Fax, mail, in person. Both court and visitors may perform in person searches. Search fee: $10.00 per name. Required to search: name, years to search, DOB; also helpful: address, SSN. Criminal records on docket books since mid-1800s.

General Information: Public Access terminal is available. (Civil records only.) No sealed, adoptions, mental health, juvenile, sex, or expunged records released. Will fax results $1.00 per page. Copy fee: $.25 if visitor does; $1.00 if court does. Certification fee: $1.00 plus $.50 per page after first. Payee: Circuit Clerk. Business checks accepted. Prepayment required. Mail requests: SASE required. Mail turnaround time 2-3 days.

Circuit Court - 2nd District Courthouse, 234 W Main St Rm #203, Okolona, MS 38860; 662-447-2838; Fax: 662-447-5024. Hours: 8AM-5PM (CST). *Felony, Civil Actions Over $2,500.*

Civil Records: Access: Fax, mail, in person. Both court and visitors may perform in person searches. Search fee: $10.00 per name. Required to search: name, years to search; also helpful: address. Civil cases indexed by defendant, plaintiff. Civil records on docket books.

Criminal Records: Access: Fax, mail, in person. Both court and visitors may perform in person searches. Search fee: $10.00 per name. Required to search: name, years to search, DOB; also helpful: SSN. Criminal records on docket books.

General Information: Public Access terminal is available. No sealed, adoptions, mental health, juvenile, sex, or expunged records released. Will fax results to local or toll free line. Copy fee: $.50 per page self; $1.00 if by court. Certification fee: $1.00 plus $.50 per page after first. Payee: Circuit Clerk. Business checks accepted. Prepayment required. Mail requests: SASE required. Mail turnaround time 2-3 days.

Justice Court Courthouse, 1 Pinson Sq, Houston, MS 38851; 662-456-3941; Fax: 662-448-8122. Hours: 8AM-5PM (CST). *Misdemeanor, Civil Actions Under $2,500, Eviction, Small Claims.*

Justice Court District 2 236 W Main, Okolona, MS 38860; 662-447-3402; Fax: 662-447-5020. Hours: 8AM-Noon; 1-5PM (CST). *Misdemeanor, Civil Actions Under $2,500, Eviction, Small Claims.*

Chancery Court Courthouse Bldg, 1 Pinson Square, Houston, MS 38851; 662-456-2513; Fax: 662-456-5295. Hours: 8AM-5PM (CST). *Probate.*

Chancery Court 234 W Main, Rm 201, Okolona, MS 38860-1438; 662-447-2092; Fax: 662-447-5024. Hours: 8AM-Noon;1-5PM (CST). *Probate.*

Choctaw County

Circuit Court PO Box 34, Ackerman, MS 39735; 662-285-6245; Fax: 662-285-2196. Hours: 8AM-5PM (CST). *Felony, Civil Actions Over $2,500.*

Civil Records: Access: Mail, in person. Both court and visitors may perform in person searches. Search fee: $10.00 per name. Required to search: name, years to search. Civil cases indexed by defendant, plaintiff. Civil records in books back to 1926.

Criminal Records: Access: Mail, in person. Both court and visitors may perform in person searches. Search fee: $10.00 per name. Same fee for in person search. Required to search: name, years to search; also helpful: DOB, SSN. Criminal records in books back to 1926.

General Information: No sealed, adoptions, mental health, juvenile, sex, or expunged records released. Will fax results to local or toll free line. Copy fee: $1.00 per page. Certification fee: $1.00. Payee: Choctaw County Circuit Clerk. Personal checks accepted. Prepayment required. Mail requests: SASE required. Mail turnaround time 14 days legal maximum.

Justice Court PO Box 357, Ackerman, MS 39735; 662-285-3599; Fax: 662-285-9039. Hours: 8AM-5PM (CST). *Misdemeanor, Civil Actions Under $2,500, Eviction, Small Claims.*

Chancery Court PO Box 250, Ackerman, MS 39735; 662-285-6329; Fax: 662-285-3444. Hours: 8AM-5PM (CST). *Probate.*

Claiborne County

Circuit Court PO Box 549, Port Gibson, MS 39150; 601-437-5841; Fax: 601-437-4543. Hours: 8AM-5PM (CST). *Felony, Civil Actions Over $2,500.*

Civil Records: Access: Mail, in person. Both court and visitors may perform in person searches. Search fee: $10.00 per name. Required to search: name, years to search, address. Civil cases indexed by defendant, plaintiff. Civil records on docket books since 1820.

Criminal Records: Access: Mail, in person. Both court and visitors may perform in person searches. Search fee: $10.00 per name. Required to search: name, years to search, address, DOB, signed release. Criminal records on docket books since 1820.

General Information: No sealed, adoptions, mental health, juvenile, sex, or expunged records released. Will fax results for $2.00 per page, if not extensive. Copy fee: $2.00 per page. Certification fee: $1.50. Payee: Sammie L Good, Circuit Clerk. Personal checks accepted. Prepayment required. Mail turnaround time varies.

Justice Court PO Box 497, Port Gibson, MS 39150; 601-437-4478; Fax: 601-437-3833. Hours: 8AM-5PM (CST). *Misdemeanor, Civil Actions Under $2,500, Eviction, Small Claims.*

Chancery Court PO Box 449, Port Gibson, MS 39150; 601-437-4992; Fax: 601-437-3137. Hours: 8AM-5PM (CST). *Probate, Small Claims.*

Clarke County

Circuit Court PO Box 216, Quitman, MS 39355; 601-776-3111; Fax: 601-776-1001. Hours: 8AM-5PM (CST). *Felony, Civil Actions.*

Civil Records: Access: Fax, mail, in person. Both court and visitors may perform in person searches. Search fee: $10.00 per name. Required to search: name, years to search; also helpful: address. Civil cases indexed by defendant, plaintiff. Civil records kept on docket books since 1950s.

Criminal Records: Access: Fax, mail, in person. Both court and visitors may perform in person searches. Search fee: $10.00 per name. Required to search: name, years to search; also helpful: address, DOB, SSN, sex. Criminal records kept on docket books since 1950s.

General Information: Public Access terminal is available. (Judgments only.) No sealed, adoptions, mental health, juvenile, sex, or expunged records released. No fee to fax results. Copy fee: $.50 per page. Certification fee: $1.50. Payee: Circuit Clerk. Personal checks accepted. Prepayment required. Mail turnaround time 1 day.

Justice Court PO Box 4, Quitman, MS 39355; 601-776-5371; Fax: 601-776-1014. Hours: 8AM-5PM (CST). *Misdemeanor, Civil Actions Under $2,500, Eviction, Small Claims.*

Chancery Court PO Box 689, Quitman, MS 39355; 601-776-2126; Fax: 601-776-2756. Hours: 8AM-5PM (CST). *Probate.*

Clay County

Circuit Court PO Box 364, West Point, MS 39773; 662-494-3384; Fax: 662-495-2057. Hours: 8AM-5PM (CST). *Felony, Civil Actions Over $2,500.*

Civil Records: Access: Phone, mail, in person. Both court and visitors may perform in person searches. Search fee: $10.00 per name. Required to search: name, years to search. Civil cases indexed by defendant, plaintiff. Civil records on docket books back to 1962; archived since mid-1800s.

Criminal Records: Access: Mail, in person. Both court and visitors may perform in person searches. Search fee: $10.00 per name. Required to search: name, years to search, address, DOB; also helpful: SSN. Criminal records on docket books back to 1962; archived since mid-1800s.

General Information: No sealed, adoptions, mental health, juvenile, sex, or expunged records released. Will fax results. Copy fee: $1.00 per page. Certification fee: $10.00. Payee: Clay County Circuit Clerk. Personal checks accepted. Prepayment required. Mail requests: SASE required. Mail turnaround time same day.

Justice Court PO Box 674, West Point, MS 39773; 662-494-6141; Fax: 662-494-6141. Hours: 8AM-5PM (CST). *Misdemeanor, Civil Actions Under $2,500, Eviction, Small Claims.*

Chancery Court PO Box 815, West Point, MS 39773; 662-494-3124; Fax: 662-492-4059. Hours: 8AM-5PM (CST). *Probate.*

Coahoma County

Circuit & County Court PO Box 849, Clarksdale, MS 38614-0849; 662-624-3014; Fax: 662-624-3075. Hours: 8AM-5PM (CST). *Felony, Civil.*

Civil Records: Access: Fax, mail, in person. Both court and visitors may perform in person searches. Search fee: $10.00 per name. Required to search: name, years to search, address. Civil cases indexed by defendant, plaintiff. Civil records on dockets since 1950, archived since 1836.

Criminal Records: Access: Fax, mail, in person. Both court and visitors may perform in person searches. Search fee: $10.00 per name. Required to search: name, years to search, DOB, signed release; also helpful: address, SSN. Criminal records on dockets since 1910, archived since 1836.

General Information: No sealed, adoptions, mental health, juvenile, sex, or expunged records released. No fee to fax results. Copy fee: $1.00 per page. Certification fee: $1.00. Payee: Circuit Clerk. Personal checks accepted. Prepayment required. Mail requests: SASE not required. Mail turnaround time 2 days.

Justice Court 144 Ritch, Clarksdale, MS 38614; 662-624-3060; Fax: 662-625-5528. Hours: 8AM-5PM (CST). *Misdemeanor, Civil Actions Under $2,500, Eviction, Small Claims.*

Chancery Court PO Box 98, Clarksdale, MS 38614; 662-624-3000; Fax: 662-624-3040. Hours: 8AM-5PM (CST). *Probate.*

Copiah County

Circuit Court PO Box 467, Hazlehurst, MS 39083; 601-894-1241; Fax: 601-894-3026. Hours: 8AM-5PM (CST). *Felony, Civil Actions Over $2,500.*

Note: Also, use 601-894-3301 for the 22nd Circuit Court District.

Civil Records: Access: Fax, mail, in person. Both court and visitors may perform in person searches. No search fee. Required to search: name, years to search.

Civil cases indexed by defendant. Civil records on docket books since late 1800s.

Criminal Records: Access: Fax, mail, in person. Both court and visitors may perform in person searches. Search fee: $10.00 per name. Required to search: name, years to search; also helpful: DOB, SSN. Criminal records on docket books since late 1800s.

General Information: No sealed, adoptions, mental health, juvenile, sex, or expunged records released. No fee to fax results. Copy fee: $.25 per page. Certification fee: $1.50. Payee: Circuit Clerk. Business checks accepted. Prepayment required. Mail turnaround time 1-2 days.

Justice Court PO Box 798, Hazlehurst, MS 39083; 601-894-3218; Fax: 601-894-6038. Hours: 8:00AM-5:00PM (CST). *Misdemeanor, Civil Actions Under $2,500, Eviction, Small Claims.*

Chancery Court 122 S Lowe St, Hazlehurst, MS 39083; 601-894-3021; Fax: 601-894-4081. Hours: 8AM-5PM (CST). *Probate.*

Covington County

Circuit Court PO Box 667, Collins, MS 39428; 601-765-6506; Fax: 601-765-5012. Hours: 8AM-5PM (CST). *Felony, Civil Actions Over $2,500.*

Civil Records: Access: Fax, mail, in person. Both court and visitors may perform in person searches. Search fee: $10.00 per name. Required to search: name, years to search. Civil cases indexed by defendant, plaintiff. Civil records on docket books since 1915.

Criminal Records: Access: Fax, mail, in person. Both court and visitors may perform in person searches. Search fee: $10.00 per name. Required to search: name, years to search, DOB; also helpful: SSN. Criminal records on docket books since 1915.

General Information: No sealed, adoptions, mental health, juvenile, sex, or expunged records released. No fee to fax results. Copy fee: $.50 per page. Certification fee: $3.00. Payee: Circuit Clerk. Personal checks accepted. Prepayment required. Mail turnaround time 2-3 days.

Justice Court PO Box 665, Collins, MS 39428; 601-765-6581; Fax: 601-765-5014. Hours: 8AM-5PM (CST). *Misdemeanor, Civil Actions Under $2,500, Eviction, Small Claims.*

Chancery Court PO Box 1679, Collins, MS 39428; 601-765-4242; Fax: 601-765-5016. Hours: 8AM-5PM (CST). *Probate.*

De Soto County

Circuit & County Court 2535 Hwy 51 South, Hernando, MS 38632; 662-429-1325. Hours: 8AM-5PM (CST). *Felony, Misdemeanor, Civil.*

www.desotoms.com

Civil Records: Access: Mail, in person. Both court and visitors may perform in person searches. Search fee: $10.00 per name. Required to search: name, years to search; also helpful: address. Civil cases indexed by defendant, plaintiff. Civil records on docket books since 1972.

Criminal Records: Access: Mail, in person. Both court and visitors may perform in person searches. Search fee: $10.00 per name. Required to search: name, years to search, DOB; also helpful: SSN. Criminal records on docket books since 1972.

General Information: Public Access terminal is available. No sealed, juvenile, sex, or expunged records released. Copy fee: $.50 per page. Certification fee: $2.50. Payee: Circuit Clerk. Personal checks accepted. Prepayment required. Mail requests: SASE not required. Mail turnaround time 3 days.

Justice Court 8525 Highway 51 North, Southaven, MS 38671; 662-393-5810; Fax: 662-393-5859. Hours: 8AM-5PM (CST). *Misdemeanor, Civil Actions Under $2,500, Eviction, Small Claims.*

Note: Records maintained since 1984, search fee is $5.00.

Chancery Court, Rm 100 2535 Hwy 51 South, (PO Box 949), Hernando, MS 38632; 662-429-1320; Fax: 662-449-1420. Hours: 8AM-5PM (CST). *Probate.*

Forrest County

Circuit & County Court PO Box 992, Hattiesburg, MS 39403; 601-582-3213; Fax: 601-545-6065. Hours: 8AM-5PM (CST). *Felony, Misdemeanor, Civil.*

Civil Records: Access: Phone, mail, in person. Both court and visitors may perform in person searches. Search fee: $10.00 per name. Required to search: name, years to search; also helpful: address. Civil cases indexed by defendant, plaintiff. Civil records on docket books since 1900s. Limited phone access.

Criminal Records: Access: Mail, in person. Both court and visitors may perform in person searches. Search fee: $10.00 per name. Required to search: name, years to search, DOB, SSN; also helpful: address. Criminal records on docket books since 1900s; on computer since 1995.

General Information: Public Access terminal is available. No juvenile or expunged records released. Will fax results. Copy fee: $.50 per page. Certification fee: $1.50. Payee: Circuit Clerk. Business checks accepted. Attorney checks accepted. Prepayment required. Mail turnaround time 10 days.

Justice Court 316 Forrest St, Hattiesburg, MS 39401; 601-544-3136 x500; Fax: 601-545-6114. Hours: 8AM-5PM (CST). *Misdemeanor, Civil Actions Under $2,500, Eviction, Small Claims.*

Note: Searches performed by the court only on Thursdays, or after 2PM rest of week.

Chancery Court PO Box 951, Hattiesburg, MS 39403; 601-545-6040; Fax: 601-545-6043. Hours: 8AM-5PM (CST). *Probate.*

Franklin County

Circuit Court PO Box 267, Meadville, MS 39653; 601-384-2320; Fax: 601-384-8244. Hours: 8AM-5PM (CST). *Felony, Civil Actions Over $2,500.*

Civil Records: Access: Phone, fax, mail, in person. Both court and visitors may perform in person searches. Search fee: $10.00 per name. Required to search: name, years to search. Civil cases indexed by defendant, plaintiff. Civil records on books since 1944.

Criminal Records: Access: Fax, mail, in person. Both court and visitors may perform in person searches. Search fee: $10.00 per name. Required to search: name, years to search, DOB or SSN; also helpful: address. Criminal records on books since 1944.

General Information: Public Access terminal is available. No sealed, adoptions, mental health, juvenile, sex, or expunged records released. Will fax results to a local or toll free line. Copy fee: $1.00 per page. Certification fee: $.50. Payee: Circuit Clerk. Personal checks accepted. Prepayment required. Mail turnaround time 2-3 days.

Justice Court PO Box 365, Meadville, MS 39653; 601-384-2002; Fax: 601-384-2001. Hours: 8AM-5PM (CST). *Misdemeanor, Civil Actions Under $2,500, Eviction, Small Claims.*

Chancery Court PO Box 297, Meadville, MS 39653; 601-384-2330; Fax: 601-384-5864. Hours: 8AM-5PM (CST). *Probate.*

George County

Circuit Court 355 Cox St, #C, Lucedale, MS 39452; 601-947-4881; Fax: 601-947-8804. Hours: 8AM-5PM M-F, 9AM-12PM Sat (CST). *Felony, Civil Actions Over $2,500.*
Civil Records: Access: Fax, mail, in person. Both court and visitors may perform in person searches. Search fee: $10.00 per name. Required to search: name, years to search. Civil cases indexed by defendant, plaintiff. Civil records on docket books since 1910.
Criminal Records: Access: Fax, mail, in person. Both court and visitors may perform in person searches. Search fee: $10.00 per name. Required to search: name, years to search; also helpful: SSN. Criminal records on docket books since 1910.
General Information: No sealed, adoptions, mental health, juvenile, sex, or expunged records released. Will fax results for no add'l fee. Copy fee: $.50 per page. Certification fee: $2.00. Payee: Circuit Clerk. Personal checks accepted. Prepayment required. Mail requests: SASE requested. Turnaround time 1-2 days.

Justice Court 356 A Cox St, Lucedale, MS 39452; 601-947-4834; Fax: 601-947-1911. Hours: 8AM-5PM (CST). *Misdemeanor, Civil Actions Under $2,500, Eviction, Small Claims.*
Note: Records on computer (5/92 forward) are $4.00 per name. Prior to 5/92, searches are $20 for first 1/2 hour then $5.00 each 1/4 hour.

Chancery Court 355 Cox St, #A, Lucedale, MS 39452; 601-947-4801; Fax: 601-947-1300. Hours: 8AM-5PM (CST). *Probate.*

Greene County

Circuit Court PO Box 310, Leakesville, MS 39451; 601-394-2379; Fax: 601-394-2334. Hours: 8AM-5PM M-F (CST). *Felony, Civil Actions Over $2,500.*
Civil Records: Access: Phone, fax, mail, in person. Both court and visitors may perform in person searches. Search fee: $10.00 per name. Required to search: name, years to search; also helpful: address. Civil cases indexed by defendant, plaintiff. Civil records on docket books since early 1900s.
Criminal Records: Access: Phone, fax, mail, in person. Both court and visitors may perform in person searches. Search fee: $10.00 per name. Required to search: name, years to search; also helpful: SSN. Criminal records on docket books since early 1900s. Misdemeanor records are kept in Greene County Justice Court, 601-394-2347.
General Information: No sealed, adoptions, mental health, juvenile, sex, or expunged records released. No fee to fax results. Copy fee: $.50 per page. Certification fee: $1.00. Payee: Circuit Clerk. Personal checks accepted. Prepayment required. Mail requests: SASE requested. Turnaround time 1-2 days.

Justice Court PO Box 547, Leakesville, MS 39451; 601-394-2347; Fax: 601-394-2114. Hours: 8AM-5PM (CST). *Misdemeanor, Civil Actions Under $2,500, Eviction, Small Claims.*

Chancery Court PO Box 610, Leakesville, MS 39451; 601-394-2377; Fax: 601-394-4445. Hours: 8AM-5PM (CST). *Probate.*

Grenada County

Circuit Court PO Box 1517, Grenada, MS 38902-1517; 662-226-1941; Fax: 662-227-2865. Hours: 8AM-5PM (CST). *Felony, Civil Actions Over $2,500.*
Civil Records: Access: In person only. Visitors must perform in person searches for themselves. No search fee. Required to search: name, years to search. Civil cases indexed by defendant, plaintiff. Civil records on docket books since mid-1970s.
Criminal Records: Access: In person only. Visitors must perform in person searches for themselves. No search fee. Required to search: name, years to search. Criminal records on docket books since mid-1970s.
General Information: Public Access terminal is available. (Judgment roll on terminal from 1996.) No sealed, juvenile, or expunged records released. Copy fee: $.50 per page. Certification fee: $1.50. Payee: Circuit Clerk. No personal checks accepted. Prepayment required.

Justice Court 16 First St, Grenada, MS 38901; 662-226-3331; Fax: 662-227-5513. Hours: 8AM-5PM (CST). *Misdemeanor, Civil Actions Under $2,500, Eviction, Small Claims.*

Chancery Court PO Box 1208, Grenada, MS 38902; 662-226-1821; Fax: 662-227-2860. Hours: 8AM-5PM (CST). *Probate.*

Hancock County

Circuit Court PO Box 249, 152 Main St., Bay St. Louis, MS 39520; 228-467-5265; Probate phone: 228-467-5404; Fax: 228-467-2779. Hours: 8AM-5PM (CST). *Felony, Civil Actions Over $2,500.*
Civil Records: Access: Mail, in person. Both court and visitors may perform in person searches. Search fee: $10.00 per name. Required to search: name, years to search. Civil cases indexed by defendant, plaintiff. Civil records on docket books since 1975.
Criminal Records: Access: Mail, in person. Both court and visitors may perform in person searches. Search fee: $10.00 per name. Required to search: name, years to search, DOB; also helpful: SSN. Criminal records on docket books since 1970.
General Information: Public Access terminal is available. No sealed, adoptions, mental health, juvenile, sex, or expunged records released. Copy fee: $.50 per page. Certification fee: $1.50 per page. Payee: Circuit Clerk. Personal checks accepted. Prepayment required. Mail turnaround time 1 week.

Justice Court 306 Hwy 90, Bay St. Louis, MS 39520; 228-467-5573; Fax: 228-467-3126. Hours: 8AM-5PM (CST). *Misdemeanor, Civil Actions Under $2,500, Eviction, Small Claims.*

Chancery Court PO Box 550, Bay St. Louis, MS 39520; 228-467-5404; Fax: 228-467-3159. Hours: 8AM-5PM (CST). *Probate.*

Harrison County

Circuit Court - 1st District PO Box 998, Gulfport, MS 39502; 228-865-4147; Fax: 228-865-4009. Hours: 8AM-5PM (CST). *Felony, Civil Actions Over $75,000.*
Civil Records: Access: Mail, in person, online. Both court and visitors may perform in person searches. Search fee: $10.00 per name. Required to search: name, years to search. Civil cases indexed by defendant, plaintiff. Civil records on computer back to 7/1991, prior on docket books, older records are archived. Access to Judicial District judgments are free at http://co.harrison.ms.us/departments/circlerk/rolls/.
Criminal Records: Access: Mail, in person. Both court and visitors may perform in person searches.

Search fee: $10.00 per name. Required to search: name, years to search, DOB; also helpful: SSN. Criminal records on computer back to 7/1991, prior on docket books, older records are archived.
General Information: Public Access terminal is available. No sealed, adoptions, mental health, juvenile, sex, or expunged records released. Copy fee: $.50 per page. Certification fee: $1.00. Payee: Circuit Clerk. Business checks accepted. Prepayment required. Mail requests: SASE requested. Turnaround time 1-2 days.

Circuit Court - 2nd District PO Box 235, Biloxi, MS 39533; 228-435-8258; Fax: 228-435-8277. Hours: 8AM-5PM (CST). *Felony, Civil Actions Over $75,000.*
Civil Records: Access: Fax, mail, in person, online. Both court and visitors may perform in person searches. Search fee: $10.00 per name. Required to search: name, years to search. Civil cases indexed by defendant, plaintiff. Civil records on computer since July 1991. Access to Judicial District judgments are free at http://co.harrison.ms.us/departments/circlerk/rolls/.
Criminal Records: Access: Fax, mail, in person. Both court and visitors may perform in person searches. Search fee: $10.00 per name. Required to search: name, years to search, DOB; also helpful: SSN. Criminal records on computer since July 1991.
General Information: Public Access terminal is available. No sealed or expunged records released. Will fax results $.50 per page. Copy fee: $.50 per page. Certification fee: $1.00. Payee: Circuit Clerk. Business checks accepted. Attorney checks accepted. Prepayment required. Mail requests: SASE required. Mail turnaround time 3 days.

County Court - 1st District PO Box 998, Gulfport, MS 39502; 228-865-4097; Criminal phone: 228-865-4145; Fax: 228-865-4099. Hours: 8AM-5PM (CST). *Misdemeanor, Civil Actions Under $75,000.*
Civil Records: Access: Mail, in person, online. Both court and visitors may perform in person searches. Search fee: $10.00 per name. Required to search: name, years to search. Civil cases indexed by defendant, plaintiff. Civil records on computer since 1991, prior on docket books since early 1900s. Access Judicial District judgments free at http://co.harrison.ms.us/departments/circlerk/rolls/.
Criminal Records: Access: Mail, in person. Both court and visitors may perform in person searches. Search fee: $10.00 per name. Required to search: name, years to search; also helpful: DOB. Criminal records on computer since 1991, prior on docket books since early 1900s.
General Information: Public Access terminal is available. No sealed, adoptions, mental health, juvenile, sex, or expunged records released. Copy fee: $.50 per page. Certification fee: $1.00. Payee: County Clerk. Business checks accepted. Prepayment required. Mail requests: SASE helpful. Turnaround time 1-2 days.

County Court - 1st District PO Box 998, Gulfport, MS 39502; 228-435-8294/8232; Fax: 228-435-8277. Hours: 8AM-5PM (CST). *Misdemeanor, Civil Actions Under $200,000.*
Civil Records: Access: Fax, mail, in person, online. Both court and visitors may perform in person searches. Search fee: $10.00 per name. Required to search: name, years to search. Civil cases indexed by defendant, plaintiff. Civil records on computer since July 1991, prior on books. Access to Judicial District judgments are free at http://co.harrison.ms.us/departments/circlerk/rolls/.
Criminal Records: Access: Fax, mail, in person. Both court and visitors may perform in person

searches. Search fee: $10.00 per name. Required to search: name, years to search, DOB; also helpful: SSN, aliases. Criminal records on computer since July 1991, prior on books.

General Information: Public Access terminal is available. No sealed or expunged records released. No fee to fax results. Copy fee: $.50 per page. Certification fee: $1.00. Payee: Circuit Clerk. Business checks accepted. Attorney checks accepted. Prepayment required. Mail requests: SASE required. Mail turnaround time 3 days.

Justice Court District 1 PO Box 1754, 1620 23rd Ave., Gulfport, MS 39502; Civil phone: 228-865-4193; Criminal phone: 228-865-4214; Fax: 228-865-4216. Hours: 8AM-5PM (CST). *Misdemeanor, Civil Actions Under $2,500, Eviction, Small Claims.* http://co.harrison.ms.us/departments/justice/cntdst1.asp

Justice Court District 2 PO Box 1141, 190 Lameuse St, Biloxi, MS 39533; Civil phone: 228-435-8250; Criminal phone: 228-435-8251; Fax: 228-435-8279. Hours: 8AM-5PM (CST). *Misdemeanor, Civil Actions Under $2,500, Eviction, Small Claims.* http://co.harrison.ms.us/departments/justice/cntdst2.asp

Biloxi Chancery Court PO Box 544, Biloxi, MS 39533; 228-435-8228; Fax: 228-435-8281. Hours: 8AM-5PM (CST). *Probate.* http://co.harrison.ms.us/departments/chanclerk/court.asp

Note: Search Chancery Court dockets for free at http://co.harrison.ms.us/dockets/.

Gulfport Chancery Court PO Drawer CC, Gulfport, MS 39502; 228-865-4092, 865-4095; Fax: 228-865-1646/865-4054. Hours: 8AM-Noon, 1-5PM (CST). *Probate.* http://co.harrison.ms.us/departments/chanclerk/court.asp

Note: Search Chancery Court dockets for free at http://co.harrison.ms.us/dockets/.

Hinds County

Circuit & County Court - 1st District PO Box 327, Jackson, MS 39205; 601-968-6628. Hours: 8AM-5PM (CST). *Felony, Misdemeanor, Civil.* www.co.hinds.ms.us/pgs/index.asp

Civil Records: Access: Mail, in person. Both court and visitors may perform in person searches. Search fee: $9.00 per name. Required to search: name, years to search. Civil cases indexed by defendant, plaintiff. Civil records on docket books back to 1900s.

Criminal Records: Access: Mail, in person. Both court and visitors may perform in person searches. Search fee: $9.00 per name. Required to search: name, years to search, DOB; also helpful: SSN. Criminal records on docket books back to 1900s.

General Information: Public Access terminal is available. No sealed, adoptions, mental health, juvenile, sex, or expunged records released. Copy fee: $1.00 per page. Certification fee: $1.00. Payee: Circuit Clerk. Personal checks accepted. Prepayment required. Mail turnaround time 14 days.

Circuit & County Court - 2nd District PO Box 999, Raymond, MS 39154; 601-857-8038. Hours: 8AM-Noon, 1-5PM (CST). *Felony, Misdemeanor, Civil.*

Civil Records: Access: Mail, in person. Both court and visitors may perform in person searches. Search fee: $9.00 per name. Required to search: name, years to search. Civil cases indexed by defendant, plaintiff. Civil records on computer since 1994, prior on docket books since late 1800s.

Criminal Records: Access: Mail, in person. Both court and visitors may perform in person searches. Search fee: $9.00 per name. Required to search: name, years to search; also helpful: DOB, SSN. Criminal records on computer since 1994, prior on docket books since late 1800s.

General Information: Public Access terminal is available. (Raymond 2nd Dist. and Jackson 1st Dist. records are on the terminal.) No sealed, adoptions, mental health, juvenile, sex, expunged or some preliminary criminal records released. Copy fee: $.50 per page if searcher makes copy, $1.00 if court does. Certification fee: $1.50. Payee: Circuit Clerk. Personal checks accepted. Prepayment required. Mail requests: SASE requested. Turnaround time 1 week.

Justice Court 407 E Pascagoula, 3rd floor, PO Box 3490, Jackson, MS 39207; 601-965-8800; Fax: 601-973-5532. Hours: 8AM-Noon, 1-5PM (CST). *Misdemeanor, Civil Actions Under $2,500, Eviction, Small Claims.*

Jackson Chancery Court PO Box 686, Jackson, MS 39205; 601-968-6540; Fax: 601-973-5554. Hours: 8AM-5PM (CST). *Probate.*

Raymond Chancery Court PO Box 88, Raymond, MS 39154; 601-857-8055; Fax: 601-857-4953. Hours: 8AM-5PM (CST). *Probate.*

Holmes County

Circuit Court PO Box 718, Lexington, MS 39095; 662-834-2476; Fax: 662-834-3870. Hours: 8AM-5PM (CST). *Felony, Civil Actions Over $2,500.*

Civil Records: Access: Fax, mail, in person. Both court and visitors may perform in person searches. Search fee: $10.00 per name. Required to search: name, years to search. Civil cases indexed by defendant, plaintiff. Civil records on docket books since 1940s.

Criminal Records: Access: Fax, mail, in person. Both court and visitors may perform in person searches. Search fee: $10.00 per name. Required to search: name, years to search; also helpful: DOB, SSN. Criminal records on docket books since 1940s.

General Information: No sealed or expunged records released. No fee to fax results. Copy fee: $1.00 per page. Certification fee: $1.50. Payee: Holmes County Circuit Clerk. Business checks accepted. Prepayment required. Mail turnaround time 1-2 days.

Justice Court PO Box 99, Lexington, MS 39095; 662-834-4565; Fax: 662-834-1402. Hours: 8AM-5PM (CST). *Misdemeanor, Civil Actions Under $2,500, Eviction, Small Claims.*

Chancery Court PO Box 239, Lexington, MS 39095; 662-834-2508; Fax: 662-834-3020. Hours: 8AM-5PM (CST). *Probate.*

Humphreys County

Circuit Court PO Box 696, Belzoni, MS 39038; 662-247-3065; Fax: 662-247-3906. Hours: 8AM-5PM (CST). *Felony, Civil Actions Over $2,500.*

Civil Records: Access: Fax, mail, in person. Both court and visitors may perform in person searches. Search fee: $10.00 per name. Required to search: name, years to search. Civil cases indexed by defendant, plaintiff. Civil records on books since 1918.

Criminal Records: Access: Fax, mail, in person. Both court and visitors may perform in person searches. Search fee: $10.00 per name. Required to search: name, years to search; also helpful: DOB, SSN. Criminal records on books since 1918.

General Information: No sealed, adoptions, mental health, juvenile, sex, or expunged records released.

Will fax results for $1.00. Copy fee: $1.00 per page. Certification fee: included in search fee, unless you do search yourself then $1.00. Payee: Circuit Clerk. Personal checks accepted. Prepayment required. Mail requests: SASE not required. Mail turnaround time 1 day; phone turnaround 30 minutes.

Justice Court 102 Castleman St, Belzoni, MS 39038; 662-247-4337; Fax: 662-247-1095. Hours: 8AM-5PM (CST). *Misdemeanor, Civil Actions Under $2,500, Eviction, Small Claims.*

Chancery Court PO Box 547, Belzoni, MS 39038; 662-247-1740; Fax: 662-247-0101. Hours: 8AM-Noon, 1-5PM (CST). *Probate.*

Issaquena County

Circuit Court PO Box 27, Mayersville, MS 39113; 662-873-2761; Fax: 662-873-2061. Hours: 8AM-12;00-1-5PM (CST). *Felony, Civil Actions Over $2,500.*

Civil Records: Access: Mail, in person. Both court and visitors may perform in person searches. Search fee: $20.00 per name. Required to search: name, years to search. Civil cases indexed by defendant, plaintiff. Civil records on docket books since 1846.

Criminal Records: Access: Mail, in person. Both court and visitors may perform in person searches. Search fee: $20.00 per name. Required to search: name, years to search; also helpful: DOB, SSN. Criminal records on docket books since 1846.

General Information: No sealed, adoptions, mental health, juvenile, sex, or expunged records released. Will fax results to local or toll free line. Copy fee: $.50 per page. Certification fee: $1.00. Payee: Circuit Clerk. Personal checks accepted. Prepayment required. Mail requests: SASE requested. Turnaround time 1 week.

Justice Court PO Box 58, Mayersville, MS 39113; 662-873-6287; Fax: 662-873-2061. Hours: 8AM-Noon, 1-5PM (CST). *Misdemeanor, Civil Actions Under $2,500, Eviction, Small Claims.*

Chancery Court PO Box 27, Mayersville, MS 39113; 662-873-2761; Fax: 662-873-2061. Hours: 8AM-12;00,1-5PM (CST). *Probate.*

Itawamba County

Circuit Court 201 W Main, Fulton, MS 38843; 662-862-3511; Fax: 662-862-4006. Hours: 8AM-5PM (CST). *Felony, Civil Actions Over $2,500.*

Civil Records: Access: Phone, fax, mail, in person. Both court and visitors may perform in person searches. Search fee: $10.00 for a written request. Required to search: name, years to search. Civil cases indexed by defendant, plaintiff. Civil records on books since 1940s.

Criminal Records: Access: Phone, fax, mail, in person. Both court and visitors may perform in person searches. Search fee: $10.00 for a written request. Required to search: name, years to search, DOB; also helpful: SSN. Criminal records on books since 1940s.

General Information: Public Access terminal is available. Will fax results to local or toll free line. No copy fee. No certification fee. Mail requests: SASE required. Mail turnaround time 1 week.

Justice Court 304 D West Wiygul St., Fulton, MS 38843; 662-862-4315; Fax: 662-862-5805. Hours: 8am-5PM (CST). *Misdemeanor, Civil Actions Under $2,500, Eviction, Small Claims.*

Chancery Court 201 W Main, Fulton, MS 38843; 662-862-3421; Fax: 662-862-3421. Hours: 8AM-5PM M-F; 8AM-Noon Sat (CST). *Probate.*

Jackson County

Circuit Court PO Box 998, Pascagoula, MS 39568-0998; 228-769-3025; Fax: 228-769-3180. Hours: 8AM-5PM (CST). *Felony, Civil.*
www.co.jackson.ms.us
Civil Records: Access: Mail, in person, online. Both court and visitors may perform in person searches. Search fee: $10.00 per name per 10 years searched. Required to search: name, years to search. Civil cases indexed by defendant, plaintiff. Civil records on computer back to 1993, prior on docket books since 1920s. Access to Court monthly dockets is free at www.co.jackson.ms.us/DS/CircuitDockets.html.
Criminal Records: Access: Mail, in person, online. Both court and visitors may perform in person searches. Search fee: $10.00 per name, per 10 years searched. Required to search: name, years to search, DOB; also helpful: SSN. Criminal records on computer back to 1992, prior on docket books since 1920s. Online access to criminal dockets is the same as civil.
General Information: Public Access terminal is available. No sealed or expunged records released. Fee to fax results is $2.00 per page. Copy fee: $1.00 per page. Certification fee: $2.50. Payee: Circuit Clerk. Business checks accepted. Prepayment required. Mail requests: SASE required. Mail turnaround time varies.

County Court PO Box 998 (3104 Magnolia St), Pascagoula, MS 39568; 228-769-3181. Hours: 8AM-5PM (CST). *Misdemeanor, Civil Actions over $25,000.*
www.co.jackson.ms.us
Civil Records: Access: Mail, in person. Both court and visitors may perform in person searches. Search fee: $10.00 per name. Required to search: name, years to search. Civil cases indexed by defendant, plaintiff. Civil records files go back 20 years; on computer back to 1992.
Criminal Records: Access: Mail, in person. Both court and visitors may perform in person searches. Search fee: $10.00 per name. Required to search: name, years to search, DOB. Criminal records go back 12 years; on computer back to 1992.
General Information: Public Access terminal is available. No sealed, adoptions, mental health, juvenile, sex, or expunged records released. Will fax results. Copy fee: $1.00 per page. Certification fee: $2.50. Payee: Clerk of County Court. Only cashiers checks and money orders accepted. Prepayment required. Mail turnaround time 1 week.

Justice Court 5343 Jefferson St, Moss Point, MS 39563; 228-769-3096; Civil phone: 228-769-3087; Criminal phone: 228-769-3080; Fax: 228-769-3364. Hours: 8AM-5PM (CST). *Misdemeanor, Civil Actions Under $2,500, Eviction, Small Claims.*
www.co.jackson.ms.us

Chancery Court PO Box 998, Pascagoula, MS 39568; 228-769-3124, 769-3124; Fax: 228-769-3397. Hours: 8AM-5PM (CST). *Probate.*
www.co.jackson.ms.us/
Note: Access Chancery Court monthly dockets free at www.co.jackson.ms.us/DS/ChanceryDockets.html.

Jasper County

Circuit Court - 1st District PO Box 58, Paulding, MS 39348; 601-727-4941; Fax: 601-727-4475. Hours: 8AM-5PM (CST). *Felony, Civil Actions Over $2,500.*
Civil Records: Access: Fax, mail, in person. Both court and visitors may perform in person searches. Search fee: $10.00 per name. Fee includes a search of both districts in the county. Required to search: name,

years to search. Civil cases indexed by defendant, plaintiff. Civil records on docket books since 1932.
Criminal Records: Access: Fax, mail, in person. Both court and visitors may perform in person searches. Search fee: $10.00 per name. Fee includes a search of both districts in the county. Required to search: name, years to search; also helpful: DOB, SSN. Criminal records on docket books since 1932.
General Information: No sealed or expunged records released. Will fax results $5.00 per doc. Copy fee: $.50 per page. Certification fee: $1.50. Payee: Circuit Clerk. Personal checks accepted. Prepayment required. Mail turnaround time 1 week.

Circuit Court - 2nd District PO Box 447, Bay Springs, MS 39422; 601-764-2245; Fax: 601-764-3078. Hours: 8AM-5PM (CST). *Felony, Civil Actions Over $2,500.*
Civil Records: Access: Mail, in person. Both court and visitors may perform in person searches. Search fee: $10.00 per name. Fee includes a search of both districts in the county. Required to search: name, years to search. Civil cases indexed by defendant, plaintiff. Civil records on docket books since 1932.
Criminal Records: Access: Mail, in person, fax. Both court and visitors may perform in person searches. Search fee: $10.00 per name. Fee includes a search of both districts in the county. Required to search: name, years to search; also helpful: SSN. Criminal records on docket books since 1932.
General Information: No sealed, adoptions, mental health, juvenile, sex, or expunged records released. Will fax results to local or toll free line. Copy fee: $.50 per page. Certification fee: $1.50. Payee: Circuit Clerk. Personal checks accepted. Prepayment required. Mail requests: SASE requested. Turnaround time 1-2 days.

Justice Court PO Box 1054, Bay Springs, MS 39422; 601-764-2065; Fax: 601-764-3402. Hours: 8AM-5PM (CST). *Misdemeanor, Civil Actions Under $2,500, Eviction, Small Claims.*
Note: This Justice Court houses all the Justices for Jasper County.

Bay Springs Chancery Court PO Box 1047, Bay Springs, MS 39422; 601-764-3368; Fax: 601-764-3999. Hours: 8AM-5PM (CST). *Probate.*

Paulding Chancery Court PO Box 38, Paulding, MS 39348; 601-727-4941; Fax: 601-727-4475. Hours: 8AM-5PM (CST). *Probate.*

Jefferson County

Circuit Court PO Box 305, Fayette, MS 39069; 601-786-3422; Fax: 601-786-9676. Hours: 8AM-5PM (CST). *Felony, Civil Actions Over $2,500.*
Civil Records: Access: Phone, mail, in person. Both court and visitors may perform in person searches. Search fee: $10.00 per name. Required to search: name, years to search, DOB; also helpful: SSN, sex, signed release. Civil cases indexed by defendant, plaintiff. Civil records on docket books since 1966, prior archived.
Criminal Records: Access: Phone, mail, in person. Both court and visitors may perform in person searches. Search fee: $10.00 per name. Required to search: name, years to search, DOB; also helpful: SSN. Criminal records on docket books since 1971, prior archived.
General Information: No sealed, adoptions, mental health, juvenile, sex, or expunged records released. Will fax results to local or toll free line. Copy fee: $.50 per page. Certification fee: $1.50. Payee: Jefferson County Circuit Court. Business checks accepted. Prepayment required. Mail requests: SASE required. Mail turnaround time same day.

Justice Court PO Box 1047, Fayette, MS 39069; 601-786-8594; Fax: 601-786-6017. Hours: 8AM-5PM (CST). *Misdemeanor, Civil Actions Under $2,500, Eviction, Small Claims.*

Chancery Court PO Box 145, Fayette, MS 39069; 601-786-3021; Fax: 601-786-6009. Hours: 8AM-5PM (CST). *Probate.*

Jefferson Davis County

Circuit Court PO Box 1082, Prentiss, MS 39474; 601-792-4231; Fax: 601-792-4957. Hours: 8AM-5PM (CST). *Felony, Civil Actions Over $2,500.*
Civil Records: Access: Phone, fax, mail, in person. Both court and visitors may perform in person searches. Search fee: $10.00 per name. Required to search: name, years to search. Civil cases indexed by defendant, plaintiff. Civil records on docket books since 1906.
Criminal Records: Access: Phone, fax, mail, in person. Both court and visitors may perform in person searches. Search fee: $10.00 per name. Required to search: name, years to search; also helpful: SSN. Criminal records on docket books since 1906.
General Information: No sealed, adoptions, mental health, juvenile, sex, or expunged records released. Fee to fax results is $1.00 per page. Copy fee: $1.00 per page. Certification fee: $2.00. Payee: Circuit Clerk. Personal checks accepted. Prepayment required. Mail turnaround time 1-2 days.

Justice Court PO Box 1407, Prentiss, MS 39474; 601-792-5129; Fax: 601-792-5128. Hours: 8AM-Noon, 1-5PM (CST). *Misdemeanor, Civil Actions Under $2,500, Eviction, Small Claims.*

Chancery Court PO Box 1137, Prentiss, MS 39474; 601-792-4204; Fax: 601-792-2894. Hours: 8AM-5PM (CST). *Probate.*

Jones County

Circuit & County Court - 1st District 101 N. Court St., #B, Ellisville, MS 39437; 601-477-8538. Hours: 8AM-5PM (CST). *Felony, Misdemeanor, Civil.*
Civil Records: Access: Mail, fax, in person. Visitors must perform in person searches for themselves. Search fee: $10.00. Required to search: name, years to search. Civil cases indexed by defendant, plaintiff. Civil records on docket books since 1960s.
Criminal Records: Access: Mail, fax, in person. Both court and visitors may perform in person searches. Search fee: $10.00 per name. Required to search: name, years to search. Criminal records on docket books since 1960s.
General Information: No sealed, adoptions, mental health, juvenile, sex, or expunged records released. Will fax results to local or toll free line. Copy fee: $.50 per page. Certification fee: $1.50. Payee: Circuit Clerk. Personal checks accepted. Prepayment required. Mail turnaround time 1-2 days.

Circuit & County Court - 2nd District PO Box 1336, Laurel, MS 39441; 601-425-2556. Hours: 8AM-5PM (CST). *Felony, Misdemeanor, Civil.*
Civil Records: Access: In person only. Visitors must perform in person searches for themselves. No search fee. Required to search: name, years to search. Civil cases indexed by defendant, plaintiff. Civil records on docket books since 1960s.
Criminal Records: Access: Mail, in person. Both court and visitors may perform in person searches. Search fee: $10.00 per name. Fee is per district. Required to search: name, years to search; also helpful: SSN. Criminal records on docket books since 1960s.
General Information: No sealed or Juvenile Youth Court records released. Will fax results to local or toll

free line. Copy fee: $.50 per page. Certification fee: $1.50. Payee: Jones County Circuit Clerk. Personal checks accepted. Prepayment required. Mail requests: SASE required. Mail turnaround time 2 days.

Justice Court PO Box 1997, Laurel, MS 39441; 601-428-3137; Fax: 601-428-0526. Hours: 8AM--5PM M-F (CST). *Misdemeanor, Civil Actions Under $2,500, Eviction, Small Claims.*

Note: This Justice Court houses all the Justices for Jones County.

Ellisville Chancery Court 101 N Court St. #D, PO Box 248, Ellisville, MS 39437; 601-477-3307; Fax: 601-477-1240. Hours: 8AM-Noon, 1-5PM (CST). *Probate.*

Laurel Chancery Court PO Box 1468, Laurel, MS 39441; 601-428-0527; Probate phone: 602-428-3182; Fax: 601-428-3610. Hours: 8AM-5PM (CST). *Probate.*
www.chancery19thms.com

Kemper County

Circuit Court PO Box 130, De Kalb, MS 39328; 601-743-2224; Fax: 601-743-4173. Hours: 8AM-5PM (CST). *Felony, Civil Actions Over $2,500.*
Civil Records: Access: Phone, fax, mail, in person. Both court and visitors may perform in person searches. Search fee: $10.00 per name. Required to search: name, years to search, address. Civil cases indexed by defendant, plaintiff. Civil records on docket books since 1960s, archived since 1912.
Criminal Records: Access: Fax, mail, in person. Both court and visitors may perform in person searches. Search fee: $10.00 per name. Required to search: name, years to search, address, DOB; also helpful: SSN. Criminal records on docket books since 1960s, archived since 1912.
General Information: No sealed, adoptions, mental health, juvenile, sex, or expunged records released. Will fax results $.25 per page. Copy fee: $.50 per page $.25 self serve. Certification fee: $1.00 per page. Payee: Circuit Clerk. Business checks accepted. Prepayment required. Mail requests: SASE requested. Turnaround time 1 week.

Justice Court PO Box 661, De Kalb, MS 39328; 601-743-2793; Civil phone: 601-743-9933; Fax: 601-743-4893. Hours: 8AM-5PM (CST). *Misdemeanor, Civil Actions Under $2,500, Eviction, Small Claims.*

Chancery Court PO Box 188, De Kalb, MS 39328; 601-743-2460; Fax: 601-743-2789. Hours: 8AM-5PM (CST). *Probate.*

Lafayette County

Circuit Court LaFayette County Courthouse, One Couerthouse Sq, #201, Oxford, MS 38655; 662-234-4951; Fax: 662-236-0238. Hours: 8AM-5PM (CST). *Felony, Civil Actions Over $2,500.*
Civil Records: Access: Mail, in person. Both court and visitors may perform in person searches. Search fee: $10.00 per name. Fee is per 10 years searched. Required to search: name, years to search; also helpful: address. Civil cases indexed by defendant, plaintiff. Civil records on docket books from 1900; on computer back to 1995.
Criminal Records: Access: Mail, in person. Both court and visitors may perform in person searches. Search fee: $10.00 per name. Fee is per 10 years searched. Required to search: name, years to search, DOB; also helpful: address, SSN. Criminal records on docket books from 1900, on computer back to 1995.
General Information: Public Access terminal is available. No sealed, adoptions, mental health, juvenile, sex, or expunged records released. Will fax results to local or toll free line. Copy fee: $1.00 per

page. Certification fee: $1.50. Payee: Circuit Clerk. Business checks accepted. Prepayment required. Mail turnaround time 1-2 days.

Justice Court 713 Jackson Ave E, Oxford, MS 38655; 662-234-1545; Fax: 662-238-7990. Hours: 8AM-5PM (CST). *Misdemeanor, Civil Actions Under $2,500, Eviction, Small Claims.*

Chancery Court PO Box 1240, Oxford, MS 38655; 662-234-2131; Fax: 662-234-5038. Hours: 8AM-5PM (CST). *Probate.*

Lamar County

Circuit Court PO Box 369, Purvis, MS 39475; 601-794-8504; Fax: 601-794-3905. Hours: 8AM-5PM (CST). *Felony, Civil Actions Over $2,500.*
Civil Records: Access: Mail, in person. Both court and visitors may perform in person searches. Search fee: $10.00 per name. Required to search: name, years to search. Civil cases indexed by defendant, plaintiff. Civil records on docket books since 1904.
Criminal Records: Access: Mail, in person. Both court and visitors may perform in person searches. Search fee: $10.00 per name. Required to search: name, years to search; also helpful: SSN. Criminal records on docket books since 1904.
General Information: No sealed, adoptions, mental health, juvenile, sex, or expunged records released. Will not fax results. Copy fee: $1.00 per page. No certification fee. Payee: Circuit Clerk. Business checks accepted. Prepayment required. Mail requests: SASE requested. Turnaround time 1-2 days.

Justice Court PO Box 1010, Purvis, MS 39475; 601-794-2950; Fax: 601-794-1076. Hours: 8AM-5PM (CST). *Misdemeanor, Civil Actions Under $2,500, Eviction, Small Claims.*

Chancery Court PO Box 247, Purvis, MS 39475; 601-794-8504; Fax: 601-794-3903. Hours: 8AM-5PM (CST). *Probate.*

Lauderdale County

Circuit & County Court PO Box 1005, Meridian, MS 39302-1005; 601-482-9738; Fax: 601-484-3970. Hours: 8AM-5PM (CST). *Felony, Civil Actions Over $2,500.*
Note: County Court can be reached at 601-482-9715.
Civil Records: Access: Phone, mail, fax, in person. Both court and visitors may perform in person searches. Search fee: $10.00 per name. Required to search: name, years to search, SSN. Civil cases indexed by defendant, plaintiff. Civil records on docket books back to 1950s, on computer back to 1992. Court will only search computer records.
Criminal Records: Access: Mail, fax, in person. Both court and visitors may perform in person searches. Search fee: $10.00 per name. Required to search: name, years to search, DOB; also helpful: SSN. Criminal records on computer (Felony) back to 1965.
General Information: Public Access terminal is available. No sealed, adoptions, mental health, juvenile, sex, or expunged records released. Copy fee: $.50 per page. No certification fee. Payee: Circuit Clerk. Business checks accepted. Prepayment required. Will bill complete files to attorneys. Mail requests: SASE requested. Turnaround time 1 week, phone turnaround is 1 week.

Justice Court PO Box 5126, Meridian, MS 39302; 601-482-9879; Fax: 601-482-9813. Hours: 8AM-5PM (CST). *Misdemeanor, Civil Actions Under $2,500, Eviction, Small Claims.*

Chancery Court PO Box 1587, Meridian, MS 39302; 601-482-9701; Fax: 601-486-4921. Hours: 8AM-5PM (CST). *Probate.*

Lawrence County

Circuit Court PO Box 1249, Monticello, MS 39654; 601-587-4791; Fax: 601-587-0750. Hours: 8AM-5PM (CST). *Felony, Civil Actions Over $2,500.*
Civil Records: Access: Phone, fax, mail, in person. Both court and visitors may perform in person searches. Search fee: $10.00 per name. Required to search: name, years to search; also helpful: address. Civil cases indexed by defendant, plaintiff. Civil records on docket books since 1977. For fax request send copy of check for fee.
Criminal Records: Access: Phone, fax, mail, in person. Both court and visitors may perform in person searches. Search fee: $10.00 per name. Required to search: name, years to search, DOB; also helpful: address, SSN. Criminal records on docket books since 1977. For fax request send copy of check for fee.
General Information: No sealed, adoptions, mental health, juvenile, sex, or expunged records released. Will fax results $10.00 per doc. No copy fee. Certification fee: $1.50. Payee: Circuit Clerk. Personal checks accepted. Prepayment required. Mail requests: SASE requested. Turnaround time 1 week, phone turnaround is 1-2 days.

Justice Court PO Box 903, Monticello, MS 39654; 601-587-7183 & 587-4854; Civil phone: 601-587-4854; Fax: 601-587-0755. Hours: 8AM-5PM (CST). *Misdemeanor, Civil Actions Under $2,500, Eviction, Small Claims.*

Chancery Court 517 Broad St, Courthouse Sq, PO Box 821, Monticello, MS 39654; 601-587-7162; Fax: 601-587-0767. Hours: 8AM-5PM (CST). *Probate.*

Leake County

Circuit Court PO Box 67, Carthage, MS 39051; 601-267-8357; Fax: 601-267-8889. Hours: 8AM-5PM (CST). *Felony, Civil Actions Over $2,500.*
Civil Records: Access: In person only. Visitors must perform in person searches for themselves. No search fee. Required to search: name, years to search. Civil cases indexed by defendant, plaintiff. Civil records on docket books since 1970s.
Criminal Records: Access: Mail, in person. Both court and visitors may perform in person searches. Search fee: $10.00 per name. Required to search: name, years to search, DOB; also helpful: SSN. Criminal records on docket books since 1977.
General Information: Public Access terminal is available. (Voting and Judgments only.) No sealed, adoptions, mental health, juvenile, sex, or expunged records released. Copy fee: $.50 per page. Certification fee: $1.50. Payee: Circuit Clerk. Prepayment required. Mail requests: SASE required. Mail turnaround time 1-2 days.

Justice Court PO Box 69, Carthage, MS 39051; 601-267-5677; Fax: 601-267-6134. Hours: 8:00AM-5:00PM (CST). *Misdemeanor, Civil Actions Under $2,500, Eviction, Small Claims.*

Chancery Court PO Box 72, Carthage, MS 39051; 601-267-7371/72; Fax: 601-267-6137. Hours: 8AM-5PM (CST). *Probate.*
www.co.leake.ms.us

Lee County

Circuit & County Court Circuit Court - PO Box 762, County Court - PO Box 736, Tupelo, MS 38802; 662-841-9022/9023(Circuit) 9730 (County); Fax: 662-680-6079. Hours: 8AM-5PM (CST). *Felony, Civil Actions Over $2,500.*
Civil Records: Access: Mail, in person. Both court and visitors may perform in person searches. Search

fee: $10.00 per name. Required to search: name, years to search. Civil cases indexed by defendant, plaintiff. Circuit records on computer since 1990, others on docket books since 1987. County records not on computer.

Criminal Records: Access: Mail, in person. Both court and visitors may perform in person searches. Search fee: $10.00 per name. Required to search: name, years to search; also helpful: DOB, SSN. Circuit records on computer since 1990, others on docket books since 1987. County records not on computer.

General Information: No sealed or expunged records released. Copy fee: $.25 per page. Certification fee: $1.50. Payee: Lee County & Circuit Court. Business checks accepted. Prepayment required. Mail requests: SASE required. Mail turnaround time 1-2 days.

Justice Court PO Box 108, Tupelo, MS 38802; 662-841-9014; Fax: 662-680-6021. Hours: 8AM-5PM (CST). *Misdemeanor, Civil Actions Under $2,500, Eviction, Small Claims.*

Chancery Court PO Box 7127, Tupelo, MS 38802; 662-841-9100; Fax: 662-680-6091. Hours: 8AM-5PM (CST). *Probate.*

Leflore County

Circuit & County Court PO Box 1953, Greenwood, MS 38935-1953; 662-453-1435; Fax: 662-455-1278. Hours: 8AM-5PM (CST). *Felony, Civil Actions Over $2,500.*

Civil Records: Access: Phone, fax, mail, in person. Both court and visitors may perform in person searches. Search fee: $10.00 per name. Required to search: name, years to search. Civil cases indexed by defendant, plaintiff. Civil records on computer index goes back 10 years; prior records on docket books since mid-1800s. There is a private company that permits online access to civil records. Go to www.recordsusa.com. User ID and password are both demo.

Criminal Records: Access: Fax, mail, in person. Both court and visitors may perform in person searches. Search fee: $10.00 per name. Required to search: name, years to search; also helpful: DOB, SSN. Criminal records on computer index goes back 10 years; prior records on docket books since mid-1800s.

General Information: Public Access terminal is available. No sealed or expunged records released. Call for fax back fee. Copy fee: $1.00 per page. Certification fee: $1.50. Payee: Circuit Clerk. Personal checks accepted. Prepayment required. Mail turnaround time 1-2 days.

Justice Court PO Box 8056, Greenwood, MS 38935; 662-453-1605; Fax: 662-455-8759. Hours: 8AM-5PM (CST). *Misdemeanor, Civil Actions Under $2,500, Eviction, Small Claims.*

Chancery Court PO Box 250, Greenwood, MS 38935-0250; 662-453-1041; 453-1432 (court admin); Fax: 662-455-7959/7965. Hours: 8AM-5PM (CST). *Probate.*

Lincoln County

Circuit Court PO Box 357, Brookhaven, MS 39602; 601-835-3435; Fax: 601-835-3482. Hours: 8AM-5PM (CST). *Felony, Civil Actions Over $2,500.*

Civil Records: Access: Fax, mail, in person. Both court and visitors may perform in person searches. Search fee: $10.00 per name. Required to search: name, years to search. Civil cases indexed by defendant, plaintiff. Civil records on computer since 1986, prior on docket books.

Criminal Records: Access: Fax, mail, in person. Both court and visitors may perform in person searches. Search fee: $10.00 per name. Required to search: name, years to search; also helpful: DOB, SSN. Criminal records on computer since 1982, prior on docket books.

General Information: Public Access terminal is available. No sealed or expunged records released. Will fax results $10.00 per doc. Copy fee: $1.00 per page. Certification fee: $1.00. Payee: Circuit Clerk. Personal checks accepted. Out of state checks not accepted. Prepayment required. Mail turnaround time 1-2 days.

Justice Court PO Box 767, Brookhaven, MS 39602; 601-835-3474; Fax: 601-835-3494. Hours: 8:00AM-5:00PM (CST). *Misdemeanor, Civil Actions Under $2,500, Eviction, Small Claims.*

Chancery Court PO Box 555, Brookhaven, MS 39602; 601-835-3412; Fax: 601-835-3423. Hours: 8AM-5PM (CST). *Probate.*
www.15thchancerydistrictms.org

Lowndes County

Circuit & County Court PO Box 31, Columbus, MS 39703; 662-329-5900. Hours: 8AM-5PM (CST). *Felony, Civil.*

Civil Records: Access: Mail, in person. Both court and visitors may perform in person searches. Search fee: $10.00 per name. Required to search: name, years to search. Civil cases indexed by defendant, plaintiff. Civil records on computer from 2/94, on docket books from 1900s.

Criminal Records: Access: Mail, in person. Both court and visitors may perform in person searches. Search fee: $10.00 per name per year. Required to search: name, years to search, DOB; also helpful: SSN. Criminal records on computer since 11/93; prior on docket books.

General Information: Public Access terminal is available. No sealed, adoption, mental health, juvenile, sex or expunged cases released. Will fax results to local or toll free line. Copy fee: $1.00 per page. Certification fee: $1.50. Payee: Clerk of Court. Personal checks accepted. Prepayment required. Mail turnaround time is 14 days.

Justice Court 11 Airline Rd, Columbus, MS 39702; 662-329-5929; Fax: 662-245-4619. Hours: 8AM-5PM (CST). *Misdemeanor, Civil Actions Under $2,500, Eviction, Small Claims.*

Chancery Court PO Box 684, Columbus, MS 39703; 662-329-5800. Hours: 8AM-5PM (CST). *Probate.*

Madison County

Circuit & County Court PO Box 1626, Canton, MS 39046; 601-859-4365; Fax: 601-859-8555. Hours: 8AM-5PM (CST). *Felony, Civil.*

Civil Records: Access: Phone, fax, mail, in person. Both court and visitors may perform in person searches. No search fee. Required to search: name, years to search. Civil cases indexed by defendant, plaintiff. Civil records on computer since 1987, prior on docket books since 1950.

Criminal Records: Access: Mail, in person. Both court and visitors may perform in person searches. Search fee: $10.00 per name. Required to search: name, years to search. Criminal records on computer since 1992, prior on docket books since 1945.

General Information: Public Access terminal is available. No sealed, adoptions, mental health, juvenile, sex, or expunged records released. Will fax results to local or toll free line. Copy fee: $.25 per page. Certification fee: $1.50. Payee: Circuit Clerk.

Personal checks accepted. Prepayment required. Mail requests: SASE requested. Turnaround time 1 week.

Justice Court 175 N Union, Canton, MS 39046; 601-859-6337; Fax: 601-859-5878. Hours: 8AM-5PM (CST). *Misdemeanor, Civil Actions Under $2,500, Eviction, Small Claims.*
Note: Request for history must be in writing with a $6.00 fee made out to Madison County Justice Court.

Chancery Court PO Box 404, Canton, MS 39046; 601-859-1177; Fax: 601-859-0795. Hours: 8AM-5PM (CST). *Probate.*

Marion County

Circuit Court 250 Broad St, #1, Columbia, MS 39429; 601-736-8246. Hours: 8AM-5PM (CST). *Felony, Civil Actions Over $2,500.*

Civil Records: Access: Mail, in person. Both court and visitors may perform in person searches. Search fee: $10.00 per name. Required to search: name, years to search. Civil cases indexed by defendant, plaintiff. Civil records on docket books since 1800s.

Criminal Records: Access: Mail, in person, fax. Both court and visitors may perform in person searches. Search fee: $10.00 per name. Required to search: name, years to search; also helpful: SSN. Criminal records on docket books since 1800s.

General Information: Public Access terminal is available. No sealed, adoptions, mental health, juvenile, sex, or expunged records released. Will fax results to local or toll free line. No copy fee. No certification fee. Payee: Circuit Clerk. Personal checks accepted. Prepayment required. Mail requests: SASE required. Mail turnaround time 1-2 days.

Justice Court 500 Courthouse Square, Columbia, MS 39429; 601-736-2572; Fax: 601-731-3781. Hours: 8AM-5PM (CST). *Misdemeanor, Civil Actions Under $2,500, Eviction, Small Claims.*

Chancery Court 250 Broad St, #2, Columbia, MS 39429; 601-444-0205; Civil phone: 601-736-2691; Fax: 601-444-0206. Hours: 8AM-5PM (CST). *Probate.*

Marshall County

Circuit Court PO Box 459, Holly Springs, MS 38635; 662-252-3434; Fax: 662-252-5951. Hours: 8AM-5PM (CST). *Felony, Civil Actions Over $2,500.*

Civil Records: Access: Fax, mail, in person. Both court and visitors may perform in person searches. Search fee: $10.00 per name. Required to search: name, years to search. Civil cases indexed by defendant, plaintiff. Civil records on docket books since 1960s; computerized records go back to 1999.

Criminal Records: Access: Mail, in person, fax. Both court and visitors may perform in person searches. Search fee: $10.00 per name. Required to search: name, years to search; also helpful: DOB, SSN. Criminal records on docket books since 1960s; computerized records go back to 1999.

General Information: Public Access terminal is available. No sealed or expunged records released. No fee to fax results. Fax copy of your search fee check. Copy fee: $.50 per page. Certification fee: $3.50. Payee: Circuit Court Clerk. Personal checks accepted. Prepayment required. Mail requests: SASE requested. Turnaround time 1-2 days.

Justice Court - North & South Districts
PO Box 729, Holly Springs, MS 38635; 662-252-3585; Fax: 662-252-0028. Hours: 8AM-5PM (CST). *Misdemeanor, Civil Actions Under $2,500, Eviction, Small Claims.*

Chancery Court PO Box 219, Holly Springs, MS 38635; 662-252-4431; Fax: 662-252-0004. Hours: 8AM-5PM (CST). *Probate.*

Monroe County

Circuit Court PO Box 843, Aberdeen, MS 39730; 662-369-8695; Fax: 662-369-3684. Hours: 8AM-5PM (CST). *Felony, Civil Actions Over $2,500.*
Civil Records: Access: In person only. Visitors must perform in person searches for themselves. No search fee. Required to search: name, years to search; also helpful: address. Civil cases indexed by defendant, plaintiff. Civil records on docket books since 1821.
Criminal Records: Access: In person only. Visitors must perform in person searches for themselves. No search fee. Required to search: name, years to search, DOB; also helpful: address, SSN. Criminal records on docket books since 1821.
General Information: No sealed, adoptions, mental health, juvenile, sex, or expunged records released. Copy fee: $1.00 per page. Certification fee: $3.00. Payee: Monroe County Circuit Clerk. Only cashiers checks and money orders accepted. Prepayment required.

Justice Court - District 1, 2, 3 PO Box 518, Amory, MS 38821; 662-256-8493; Fax: 662-256-7876. Hours: 8AM-5PM. *Misdemeanor, Civil Actions Under $2,500, Eviction, Small Claims.*
Note: Aberdeen Justice Court is closed.; records now at Amory Justice Court 1 & 2.

Chancery Court PO Box 578, Aberdeen, MS 39730; 662-369-8143; Fax: 662-369-7928. Hours: 8AM-5PM (CST). *Probate.*

Montgomery County

Circuit Court PO Box 765, Winona, MS 38967; 662-283-4161; Fax: 662-283-3363. Hours: 8AM-5PM (CST). *Felony, Civil Actions Over $2,500.*
Civil Records: Access: Mail, in person. Both court and visitors may perform in person searches. Search fee: $10.00 per name. Required to search: name, years to search. Civil cases indexed by defendant, plaintiff. Civil records on docket books since early 1900s.
Criminal Records: Access: Mail, in person. Both court and visitors may perform in person searches. Search fee: $10.00 per name. Required to search: name, years to search. Criminal records on docket books since early 1900s.
General Information: No sealed or expunged records released. Will fax results to local or toll free line. Copy fee: $1.00 per page. Certification fee: $2.00. Payee: Circuit Clerk. Personal checks accepted. Prepayment required. Mail requests: SASE required. Mail turnaround time 1-2 days.

Justice Court PO Box 229, Winona, MS 38967; 662-283-2290; Fax: 662-283-2233. Hours: 8AM-5PM (CST). *Misdemeanor, Civil Actions Under $2,500, Eviction, Small Claims.*

Chancery Court PO Box 71, Winona, MS 38967; 662-283-2333; Fax: 662-283-2233. Hours: 8AM-5PM (CST). *Probate.*

Neshoba County

Circuit Court 401 E Beacon St #110, Philadelphia, MS 39350; 601-656-4781; Fax: 601-650-3997. Hours: 8AM-5PM (CST). *Felony, Civil Actions Over $2,500.*
Civil Records: Access: Mail, in person. Both court and visitors may perform in person searches. Search fee: $10.00 per name. Required to search: name, years to search. Civil cases indexed by defendant. Civil records in-house back 10 years; indexed back 50 years.

Criminal Records: Access: Mail, in person. Both court and visitors may perform in person searches. Search fee: $10.00 per name. Required to search: name, years to search, DOB; also helpful: SSN. Criminal records in-house back 20 years; on docket books back 50 years.
General Information: No sealed, adoptions, mental health, juvenile, sex, or expunged records released. Will fax results. Copy fee: $.50 per page. Certification fee: $2.00. Payee: Circuit Clerk. Business checks accepted. Prepayment required. Mail requests: SASE requested. Turnaround time 1-2 days.

Justice Court 200 Byrd Ave., Philadelphia, MS 39350; 601-656-5361/1101; Fax: 601-656-6482. Hours: 8AM-5PM (CST). *Misdemeanor, Civil Actions Under $2,500, Eviction, Small Claims.*

Chancery Court 401 Beacon St #107, Philadelphia, MS 39350; 601-656-3581; Fax: 601-656-5915. Hours: 8AM-5PM (CST). *Probate.*

Newton County

Circuit Court PO Box 447, Decatur, MS 39327; 601-635-2368; Fax: 601-635-3210. Hours: 8AM-5PM (CST). *Felony, Civil Actions Over $2,500.*
Civil Records: Access: Mail, in person. Both court and visitors may perform in person searches. Search fee: $10.00 per name. Required to search: name, years to search. Civil cases indexed by defendant, plaintiff. Civil records on docket books since 1968.
Criminal Records: Access: Mail, in person. Both court and visitors may perform in person searches. Search fee: $10.00 per name. Required to search: name, years to search, DOB; also helpful: SSN. Criminal records on docket books since 1968.
General Information: Public Access terminal is available. No sealed, adoptions, mental health, juvenile, sex, or expunged records released. Will fax results to local or toll free line. Copy fee: $.50 per page. Certification fee: $1.50. Payee: Circuit Court. Personal checks accepted. Prepayment required. Mail requests: SASE required. Mail turnaround time same day.

Justice Court PO Box 69, Decatur, MS 39327; 601-635-2740; Fax: 601-635-4047. Hours: 8AM-5PM (CST). *Misdemeanor, Civil Actions Under $2,500, Eviction, Small Claims.*

Chancery Clerk Office PO Box 68, Decatur, MS 39327; 601-635-2367; Civil phone: 601-635-3370; Fax: 601-635-3479. Hours: 8AM-5PM (CST). *Probate.*

Noxubee County

Circuit Court PO Box 431, Macon, MS 39341; 662-726-5737; Fax: 662-726-6041. Hours: 8AM-5PM (CST). *Felony, Civil Actions Over $2,500.*
Civil Records: Access: Mail, fax, in person. Both court and visitors may perform in person searches. Search fee: $10.00 per name. Required to search: name, years to search. Civil cases indexed by defendant. Civil records on docket books since 1800s.
Criminal Records: Access: Mail, fax, in person. Both court and visitors may perform in person searches. Search fee: $10.00 per name. Required to search: name, years to search; also helpful: SSN. Criminal records on docket books since 1800s.
General Information: No sealed, adoptions, mental health, juvenile, sex, or expunged records released. Copy fee: $.50 per page. Certification fee: $5.00. Payee: Circuit Clerk. Business checks accepted. Prepayment required. Mail requests: SASE required. Mail turnaround time 1 week.

Justice Court - North & South Districts 507 S Jefferson, PO Box 550, Macon, MS 39341; 662-726-5834; Fax: 662-726-2944. Hours: 8AM-5PM (CST). *Misdemeanor, Civil Actions Under $2,500, Eviction, Small Claims.*

Chancery Court PO Box 147, Macon, MS 39341; 662-726-4243; Fax: 662-726-2272. Hours: 8AM-5PM (CST). *Probate.*

Oktibbeha County

Circuit Court Courthouse, 101 E Main, Starkville, MS 39759; 662-323-1356. Hours: 8AM-5PM (CST). *Felony, Civil Actions Over $2,500.*
Civil Records: Access: Mail, fax, in person. Both court and visitors may perform in person searches. Search fee: $10.00 per name. Required to search: name, years to search; also helpful: address. Civil cases indexed by defendant, plaintiff. Civil records on docket books since 1938.
Criminal Records: Access: Mail, fax, in person. Both court and visitors may perform in person searches. Search fee: $10.00 per name. Required to search: name, years to search; also helpful: DOB, SSN. Criminal records on docket since 1950.
General Information: Public Access terminal is available. No sealed, adoptions, mental health, juvenile, sex, or expunged records released. Copy fee: $1.00 per page. Certification fee: $1.50. Payee: Circuit Clerk. Personal checks accepted. Prepayment required. Mail requests: SASE required. Mail turnaround time 1 week.

Justice Court - Districts 1-3 104 Felix Long Dr, Starkville, MS 39759; 662-324-3032; Fax: 662-338-1078. Hours: 8AM-5PM (CST). *Misdemeanor, Civil Actions Under $2,500, Eviction, Small Claims.*

Chancery Court Courthouse, 101 E Main, Starkville, MS 39759; 662-323-5834; Fax: 662-338-1064. Hours: 8AM-5PM (CST). *Probate.*

Panola County

Circuit Court - 1st District PO Box 130, Sardis, MS 38666; 662-487-2073; Fax: 662-487-3595. Hours: 8AM-5PM (CST). *Felony, Civil Actions Over $2,500.*
Civil Records: Access: Fax, mail, in person. Both court and visitors may perform in person searches. Search fee: $10.00 per name. Fee is for dual district search. Required to search: name, years to search. Civil cases indexed by defendant, plaintiff. Civil records on docket books since 1970s, archived since 1925.
Criminal Records: Access: Fax, mail, in person. Both court and visitors may perform in person searches. Search fee: $10.00 per name. Fee is for dual district search. Required to search: name, years to search, DOB; also helpful: SSN. Criminal records on docket books since 1970, archived since 1925, records are not computerized.
General Information: No sealed, adoptions, mental health, juvenile, sex, or expunged records released. No fee to fax results. Fax copy of your search fee check. Copy fee: $.50 per page. Certification fee: $1.50. Payee: Circuit Clerk. Business checks accepted. Prepayment required. Mail requests: SASE required. Mail turnaround time 1-2 days.

Circuit Court - 2nd District PO Box 346, Batesville, MS 38606; 662-563-6210; Fax: 662-563-8233. Hours: 8AM-5PM (CST). *Felony, Civil Actions Over $2,500.*
Civil Records: Access: Phone, fax, mail, in person. Both court and visitors may perform in person searches. Search fee: $10.00 per name. Fee is per district. Required to search: name, years to search.

Civil cases indexed by defendant, plaintiff. Civil records on docket books since 1900.

Criminal Records: Access: Fax, mail, in person. Both court and visitors may perform in person searches. Search fee: $10.00 per name. Fee is per district. Required to search: name, years to search, address, DOB; also helpful: SSN. Criminal records on docket books since 1900.

General Information: No sealed, adoptions, mental health, juvenile, sex, or expunged records released. Will fax results $1.00 per page. Copy fee: $.50 per page. Certification fee: $10.00. Payee: Circuit Clerk's Office. Personal checks accepted. Prepayment required. Mail requests: SASE required. Mail turnaround time same day.

Justice Court PO Box 249, Sardis, MS 38666; 662-487-2080; Fax: 662-487-2008. Hours: 8AM-5PM (CST). *Misdemeanor, Civil Actions Under $2,500, Eviction, Small Claims.*
Note: This Justice Court houses all the Justices for Panola County.

Panola County Chancery Clerk 151 Public Square, Batesville, MS 38606; 662-563-6205; Fax: 662-563-6277. Hours: 8AM-5PM (CST). *Probate.*

Sardis Chancery Court PO Box 130, Sardis, MS 38666; 662-487-2070; Fax: 662-487-3595. Hours: 8AM-Noon, 1-5PM (CST). *Probate.*

Pearl River County

Circuit Court Courthouse, Poplarville, MS 39470; 601-403-2300; Civil phone: ext 324; Criminal phone: ext 323; Fax: 601-403-2327. Hours: 8AM-5PM (CST). *Felony, All Civil Actions.*

Civil Records: Access: Mail, fax, in person. Both court and visitors may perform in person searches. Search fee: $10.00 per name. Required to search: name, years to search, DOB, SSN. Civil cases indexed by defendant, plaintiff. Civil records on docket books since 1890.

Criminal Records: Access: Mail, fax, in person. Both court and visitors may perform in person searches. Search fee: $10.00 per name. Required to search: name, years to search. Criminal records on computer since late 1960s, prior on docket books since 1890.

General Information: Public Access terminal is available. (For cases 2003 to present.) No sealed, adoptions, mental health, juvenile, sex, or expunged records released. Will fax results to local or toll free line. Copy fee: $.50 per page. Certification fee: $2.50. Payee: Circuit Clerk. Personal checks accepted. Prepayment required. Mail turnaround time 1-2 days.

Justice Court - Northern, Southeastern & Southwestern Districts 204 Julia St, Poplarville, MS 39470; 601-403-2300; Fax: 601-403-2364. Hours: 8AM-5PM (CST). *Misdemeanor, Civil Actions Under $2,500, Eviction, Small Claims, Felony.*

Chancery Court PO Box 431, Poplarville, MS 39470; 601-403-2300; Fax: 601-403-2317. Hours: 8AM-5PM (CST). *Probate.*

Perry County

Circuit Court PO Box 198, New Augusta, MS 39462; 601-964-8663; Fax: 601-964-8740. Hours: 8AM-5PM (CST). *Felony, Civil Actions Over $2,500.*

Civil Records: Access: Mail, fax, in person. Both court and visitors may perform in person searches. Search fee: $10.00 per name. Fee is per 10 years searched. Required to search: name, years to search. Civil cases indexed by defendant, plaintiff. Civil records on docket books since 1980.

Criminal Records: Access: Mail, fax, in person. Both court and visitors may perform in person searches. Search fee: $10.00 per name. Fee is per 10 years searched. Required to search: name, years to search, DOB; also helpful: SSN, sex, signed release. Criminal records on docket books since 1971; on computer since.

General Information: Public Access terminal is available. No sealed, adoptions, mental health, juvenile, sex, or expunged records released. Will fax results to local or toll free line. Copy fee: $.50 per page. Certification fee: $2.50. Payee: Circuit Clerk. Personal checks accepted. Prepayment required. Mail turnaround time 1-2 days.

Justice Court PO Box 455, New Augusta, MS 39462; 601-964-8366; Fax: 601-964-8368. Hours: 8AM-5PM (CST). *Misdemeanor, Civil Actions Under $2,500, Eviction, Small Claims.*

Chancery Court PO Box 198, New Augusta, MS 39462; 601-964-8398; Fax: 601-964-8746. Hours: 8AM-5PM (CST). *Probate.*

Pike County

Circuit & County Court PO Drawer 31, Magnolia, MS 39652; 601-783-2581; Fax: 601-783-6322. Hours: 8AM-5PM (CST). *Felony, Civil.*

Civil Records: Access: Fax, mail, in person. Both court and visitors may perform in person searches. Search fee: $6.00 per name. Required to search: name, years to search. Civil cases indexed by defendant, plaintiff. Civil records on docket books since 1950s; on computer from 2000 to present.

Criminal Records: Access: Fax, mail, in person. Both court and visitors may perform in person searches. Search fee: $6.00 per name. Required to search: name, years to search, DOB; also helpful: SSN. Criminal records on docket books and computerized since 1960s.

General Information: Public Access terminal is available. No sealed, adoptions, mental health, juvenile, sex, or expunged records released. Copy fee: $1.00 per page. Certification fee: $1.50. Payee: Circuit Clerk. Personal checks accepted. Prepayment required. Mail requests: SASE required. Mail turnaround time 1-2 days.

Justice Court - Divisions 1-3 PO Box 509, Magnolia, MS 39652; 601-783-5333; Fax: 601-783-4181. Hours: 8AM-5PM (CST). *Misdemeanor, Civil Actions Under $2,500, Eviction, Small Claims.*

Chancery Court PO Box 309, Magnolia, MS 39652; 601-783-3362; Fax: 601-783-5982. Hours: 8AM-5PM (CST). *Probate, Civil.*

Pontotoc County

Circuit Court PO Box 428, Pontotoc, MS 38863; 662-489-3908. Hours: 8AM-5PM (CST). *Felony, Civil Actions Over $2,500.*

Civil Records: Access: Mail, in person. Both court and visitors may perform in person searches. Search fee: $5.00 per name. Required to search: name, years to search. Civil cases indexed by defendant, plaintiff. Civil records on books from 1849.

Criminal Records: Access: Mail, in person. Both court and visitors may perform in person searches. Search fee: $5.00 per name. Required to search: name, years to search, DOB; also helpful: SSN. Criminal records on books from 1849. Records are not computerized.

General Information: Public Access terminal is available. No sealed, adoptions, mental health, juvenile, sex, or expunged records released. Will fax results to local or toll free line. Copy fee: $.50 per page. No certification fee. Payee: Circuit Clerk.

Prepayment required. Mail requests: SASE required. Mail turnaround time 1 week.

Justice Court - East & West Districts 29 E Washington St, Pontotoc, MS 38863-2923; 662-489-3920; Fax: 662-488-2986. Hours: 8AM-5PM (CST). *Misdemeanor, Civil Actions Under $2,500, Eviction, Small Claims.*

Chancery Court 11East Washington, PO Box 209, Pontotoc, MS 38863; 662-489-3900; Fax: 662-489-3940. Hours: 8AM-5PM (CST). *Probate.*

Prentiss County

Circuit Court PO Box 727, 101 N Main St, Booneville, MS 38829; 662-728-4611; Fax: 662-728-2006. Hours: 8AM-5PM (CST). *Felony, Civil Actions Over $2,500.*

Civil Records: Access: Mail, in person. Both court and visitors may perform in person searches. Search fee: $10.00 per name. Required to search: name, years to search. Civil cases indexed by defendant, plaintiff. Civil records on docket books from 1880, only judgments are on computer since 1985.

Criminal Records: Access: Fax, mail, in person. Both court and visitors may perform in person searches. Search fee: $10.00 per name. Required to search: name, years to search; also helpful: DOB, SSN. Criminal records on docket books from 1880, computerized since 1985. Prepaid account is required for fax access.

General Information: No sealed, adoptions, mental health, juvenile, sex, or expunged records released. Copy fee: $.50 per page. Certification fee: $2.00. Payee: Circuit Clerk. Personal checks accepted. Prepayment required. Billing accounts available. Mail requests: SASE required. Mail turnaround time varies.

Justice Court 1901C East Chambers Dr, Booneville, MS 38829; 662-728-8696; Civil phone: 662-728-2011; Fax: 662-728-2009. Hours: 8AM-5PM (CST). *Misdemeanor, Civil Actions Under $2,500, Eviction, Small Claims.*

Chancery Court PO Box 477, Booneville, MS 38829; 662-728-8151; Fax: 662-728-2007. Hours: 8AM-5PM (CST). *Probate.*

Quitman County

Circuit Court Courthouse, 230 Chestnut St, Marks, MS 38646; 662-326-8003; Fax: 662-326-8004. Hours: 8AM-5PM (CST). *Felony, Civil Actions Over $2,500.*

Civil Records: Access: Fax, mail, in person. Both court and visitors may perform in person searches. Search fee: $10.00 per name. Required to search: name, years to search. Civil cases indexed by defendant, plaintiff. Civil records on books and files since 1890.

Criminal Records: Access: Fax, mail, in person. Both court and visitors may perform in person searches. Search fee: $10.00 per name. Required to search: name, years to search, DOB; also helpful: SSN. Criminal records on books and files since 1890.

General Information: No sealed, adoptions, mental health, juvenile, sex, or expunged records released. No fax fee when $10.00 has been paid. Copy fee: $.50 per page. Certification fee: $1.50. Payee: Circuit Clerk. Business checks accepted. Prepayment required. Mail requests: SASE not required. Mail turnaround time 2 days; phone results 10 minutes.

Justice Court - Districts 1 & 2 PO Box 100, Marks, MS 38646; 662-326-2104/7906; Fax: 662-326-2330. Hours: 8AM-5PM (CST). *Misdemeanor, Civil Actions Under $2,500, Eviction, Small Claims.*

Chancery Court 230 Chestnut St, Marks, MS 38646; 662-326-2661; Fax: 662-326-8004. Hours: 8AM-Noon, 1-5PM (CST). *Probate.*

Rankin County

Circuit & County Court PO Drawer 1599, Brandon, MS 39043; 601-825-1466. Hours: 8AM-5PM (CST). *Felony, Misdemeanor, Civil.*
www.rankincounty.org
Civil Records: Access: Mail, in person. Both court and visitors may perform in person searches. Search fee: $10.00 per name. Required to search: name, years to search. Civil cases indexed by defendant, plaintiff. Civil records on computer since 1990, prior on docket books.
Criminal Records: Access: Mail, in person. Both court and visitors may perform in person searches. Search fee: $10.00 per name. Required to search: name, years to search; also helpful: DOB, SSN. Criminal records on computer since 1990, prior on docket books.
General Information: Public Access terminal is available. No sealed or expunged records released. Will fax results to local or toll free line. Copy fee: $.50 per page. Certification fee: $1.50. Payee: Circuit Clerk. Personal checks accepted. Prepayment required. Mail turnaround time 1-2 days.

Justice Court - Districts 1-4 117 N. Timber, Brandon, MS 39042; 601-824-2665; Fax: 601-824-2668. Hours: 8AM-5PM (CST). *Misdemeanor, Civil Actions Under $2,500, Eviction, Small Claims.*

Chancery Court 203 Town Sq, PO Box 700, Brandon, MS 39042; 601-825-1649; Fax: 601-824-2450. Hours: 8AM-5PM (CST). *Probate, Civil.*
www.rankincounty.org

Scott County

Circuit Court PO Box 371, Forest, MS 39074; 601-469-3601. Hours: 8AM-5PM (CST). *Felony, Civil Actions Over $2,500.*
Note: The court began computerization of records in 2002.
Civil Records: Access: Mail, in person. Both court and visitors may perform in person searches. Search fee: $10.00 per name. Fee is for 7 year search. Required to search: name, years to search. Civil cases indexed by defendant, plaintiff. Civil records on docket books since 1865.
Criminal Records: Access: Mail, in person. Both court and visitors may perform in person searches. Search fee: $10.00 per name. Fee is for 7 year search. Required to search: name, years to search, DOB; also helpful: SSN. Criminal records on docket books since 1865.
General Information: No sealed, adoptions, mental health, juvenile, sex, or expunged records released. Will fax results to local or toll free line. Copy fee: $.50 per page. Certification fee: $1.50. Payee: Circuit Clerk. Personal checks accepted. Prepayment required. Mail requests: SASE required. Mail turnaround time 1 week.

Justice Court PO Box 371, Forest, MS 39074; 601-469-4555; Fax: 601-469-5193. Hours: 8AM-5PM (CST). *Misdemeanor, Civil Actions Under $2,500, Eviction, Small Claims.*

Chancery Court 100 Main St, PO Box 630, Forest, MS 39074; 601-469-1922, 601-469-1927; Fax: 601-469-5180. Hours: 8AM-5PM (CST). *Probate.*

Sharkey County

Circuit Court PO Box 218 (400 Locust St), Rolling Fork, MS 39159; 662-873-2766; Fax: 662-873-6045. Hours: 8AM-Noon, 1-5PM (CST). *Felony, Civil Actions Over $2,500.*
Civil Records: Access: Fax, mail, in person. Both court and visitors may perform in person searches. Search fee: $10.00 per name. Required to search: name, years to search. Civil cases indexed by defendant, plaintiff. Civil records on docket books since 1893.
Criminal Records: Access: Fax, mail, in person. Both court and visitors may perform in person searches. Search fee: $10.00 per name. Required to search: name, years to search, DOB; also helpful: SSN. Criminal records on docket books since 1893.
General Information: No sealed, adoptions, mental health, juvenile, sex, or expunged records released. Fee to fax results is $1.00 per page. Copy fee: $.50 per page; $.25 if self-serve. Certification fee: $2.00 per page. Payee: Circuit Clerk. Business checks accepted. Prepayment required. Mail turnaround time 1 week.

Justice Court PO Box 235, Rolling Fork, MS 39159; 662-873-6140; Fax: 662-873-0154. Hours: 8AM-5PM (CST). *Misdemeanor, Civil Actions Under $2,500, Eviction, Small Claims.*

Chancery Court 120 Locust St, PO Box 218, Rolling Fork, MS 39159; 662-873-2755; Fax: 662-873-6045. Hours: 8AM-Noon,1-5PM (CST). *Probate.*

Simpson County

Circuit Court PO Box 307, Mendenhall, MS 39114; 601-847-2474; Fax: 601-847-4011. Hours: 8AM-5PM (CST). *Felony, Civil Actions Over $2,500.*
Civil Records: Access: Fax, mail, in person. Both court and visitors may perform in person searches. Search fee: $10.00 per name. Required to search: name, years to search. Civil cases indexed by defendant, plaintiff. Civil records on docket books since 1978.
Criminal Records: Access: Fax, mail, in person. Both court and visitors may perform in person searches. Search fee: $10.00 per name. Required to search: name, years to search; also helpful: DOB, SSN. Criminal records on docket books since 1978.
General Information: No sealed or expunged records released. No fee to fax results. Copy fee: $.50 per page. Certification fee: $1.50. Payee: Circuit Clerk. Business checks accepted. Prepayment required. Mail turnaround time 1-2 days.

Justice Court 1498 Simpson Highway, 149, Mendenhall, MS 39114; 601-847-5848; Fax: 601-847-5856. Hours: 8AM-5PM (CST). *Misdemeanor, Civil Actions Under $2,500, Eviction, Small Claims.*

Chancery Court Chancery Building, PO Box 367, Mendenhall, MS 39114; 601-847-2626; Fax: 601-847-7016. Hours: 8AM-5PM (CST). *Probate.*

Smith County

Circuit Court PO Box 517, Raleigh, MS 39153; 601-782-4751; Fax: 601-782-4007. Hours: 8AM-5PM (CST). *Felony, Civil Actions Over $2,500.*
Civil Records: Access: Mail, in person. Both court and visitors may perform in person searches. Search fee: $10.00 per name. Required to search: name, years to search. Civil cases indexed by defendant, plaintiff. Civil records on docket books since 1912.
Criminal Records: Access: Mail, in person. Both court and visitors may perform in person searches. Search fee: $10.00 per name. Required to search:

name, years to search, DOB; also helpful: SSN. Criminal records on docket books since 1912.
General Information: No sealed or expunged records released. Fee to fax results is $3.00 1st page, $.50 each add'l. Copy fee: $.50 per page. Certification fee: $5.00. Payee: Circuit Clerk. Personal checks accepted. Prepayment required. Mail requests: SASE required. Mail turnaround time 2 days.

Justice Court PO Box 171, Raleigh, MS 39153; 601-782-4334; Fax: 601-782-4005. Hours: 8AM-5PM (CST). *Misdemeanor, Civil Actions Under $2,500, Eviction, Small Claims.*

Chancery Court 123 Main St, PO Box 39, Raleigh, MS 39153; 601-782-9811; Fax: 601-782-4690. Hours: 8AM-5PM (CST). *Probate.*

Stone County

Circuit Court Courthouse, 323 Cavers Ave, Wiggins, MS 39577; 601-928-5246; Fax: 601-928-5248. Hours: 8AM-5PM (CST). *Felony, Civil Actions Over $2,500.*
Civil Records: Access: Fax, mail, in person. Both court and visitors may perform in person searches. Search fee: $10.00 per name. Required to search: name, years to search. Civil cases indexed by defendant, plaintiff. Civil records on docket books since 1945.
Criminal Records: Access: Fax, mail, in person. Both court and visitors may perform in person searches. Search fee: $10.00 per name. Required to search: name, years to search, DOB, notarized release; also helpful: SSN. Criminal records on docket books since 1945.
General Information: No sealed, adoptions, mental health, juvenile, sex, or expunged records released. Will fax results $3.00 1st page, $.50 each add'l. Copy fee: $.50 per page. Certification fee: $1.50. Payee: Circuit Clerk. Business checks accepted. Prepayment required. Mail turnaround time same day.

Justice Court - West District 231 3rd St South, Wiggins, MS 39577-2808; 601-928-4415; Fax: 610-928-2114. Hours: 8AM-5PM (CST). *Misdemeanor, Civil Actions Under $2,500, Eviction, Small Claims.*

Chancery Court 323 E Cavers, PO Drawer 7, Wiggins, MS 39577; 601-928-5266; Fax: 601-928-6464. Hours: 8AM-5PM (CST). *Probate.*

Sunflower County

Circuit Court PO Box 569, Indianola, MS 38751; 662-887-1252; Fax: 662-887-7077. Hours: 8AM-5PM (CST). *Felony, Civil Actions Over $2,500.*
Civil Records: Access: Mail, in person. Both court and visitors may perform in person searches. Search fee: $10.00 per name. Fee is for 7 year search. Required to search: name, years to search. Civil cases indexed by defendant, plaintiff. Civil records on docket books since 1881; on computer since 2000.
Criminal Records: Access: Mail, in person. Both court and visitors may perform in person searches. Search fee: $10.00 per name. Fee is for 7 year search. Required to search: name, years to search, DOB; also helpful: SSN. Criminal records on docket books since 1913; on computer since 2000.
General Information: Public Access terminal is available. No sealed, adoptions, mental health, juvenile, sex, or expunged records released. Fee to fax results is $1.00 per page. Copy fee: $.50 per page. Certification fee: $1.50. Payee: Circuit Clerk. Personal checks accepted. Prepayment required. Mail turnaround time 1-3 days.

Justice Court - Northern District PO Box 52, Ruleville, MS 38771; 662-756-2835; Fax: 662-756-4175. Hours: 8AM-Noon, 1-5PM (CST). *Misdemeanor, Civil Actions Under $2,500, Eviction, Small Claims.*

Justice Court - Southern District PO Box 487, Indianola, MS 38751; 662-887-6921; Fax: 662-887-2798. Hours: 8AM-5PM (CST). *Misdemeanor, Civil Actions Under $2,500, Eviction, Small Claims.*

Chancery Court 200 Main St, PO Box 988, Indianola, MS 38751; 662-887-4703; Fax: 662-887-7054. Hours: 8AM-5PM (CST). *Probate.*

Tallahatchie County

Charleston Circuit Court PO Box 86, Charleston, MS 38921; 662-647-8758; Probate phone: 662-647-5551; Fax: 662-647-8490. Hours: 8AM-5PM (CST). *Felony, Civil Actions Over $2,500.*
Civil Records: Access: Mail, in person. Both court and visitors may perform in person searches. Search fee: $10.00 per name. Required to search: name, years to search. Civil cases indexed by defendant, plaintiff. Civil records on books since 1920s.
Criminal Records: Access: Mail, in person. Both court and visitors may perform in person searches. Search fee: $10.00 per name. Required to search: name, years to search, DOB; also helpful: SSN. Criminal records on books since 1920s.
General Information: Public Access terminal is available. No sealed, adoptions, mental health, juvenile, sex, or expunged records released. Will fax results for fee. Copy fee: $2.00 per page. Certification fee: $3.00. Payee: Circuit Clerk. Personal checks accepted. Prepayment required. Mail requests: SASE requested. Turnaround time 3 days.

Charleston Justice Court PO Box 440, Charleston, MS 38921; 662-647-3477; Fax: 662-647-3478. Hours: 8AM-5PM (CST). *Misdemeanor, Civil Actions Under $2,500, Eviction, Small Claims.*
Note: Court is located upstairs of the Charleston Circuit Court; records are not comingled.

Sumner Justice Court PO Box 155, Sumner, MS 38957; 662-375-9452; Fax: 662-375-8200. Hours: 8AM-Noon; 1PM-5PM (CST). *Misdemeanor, Civil Actions Under $2,500, Eviction, Small Claims.*

Chancery Court #1 Main St, PO Box 350, Charleston, MS 38921; 662-647-5551; Fax: 662-647-8490. Hours: 8AM-5PM (CST). *Probate.*

Chancery Court PO Box 180, Sumner, MS 38957; 662-375-8731; Fax: 662-375-7252. Hours: 8AM-Noon, 1-5PM (CST). *Probate.*

Tate County

Circuit Court 201 Ward St, Senatobia, MS 38668; 662-562-5211; Fax: 662-562-7486. Hours: 8AM-5PM (CST). *Felony, Civil Actions Over $2,500.*
Civil Records: Access: Mail, in person. Both court and visitors may perform in person searches. Search fee: $10.00 per name. Required to search: name, years to search. Civil cases indexed by defendant, plaintiff. Civil records on books since 1872.
Criminal Records: Access: Mail, in person. Both court and visitors may perform in person searches. Search fee: $10.00 per name. Required to search: name, years to search; also helpful: SSN. Criminal records on books since 1872.
General Information: Public Access terminal is available. No sealed, adoptions, mental health, juvenile, sex, or expunged records released. Copy fee: $.50 for first page, $.25 each add'l. Certification fee: $1.50. Payee: Circuit Clerk. Personal checks accepted.

Prepayment required. Mail requests: SASE requested. Turnaround time same day.

Justice Court 103 Preston Mccay Dr, Senatobia, MS 38668; 662-562-7626; Fax: 662-562-7663. Hours: 8AM-12;00,1-5PM (CST). *Misdemeanor, Civil Actions Under $2,500, Eviction, Small Claims.*

Chancery Court 201 Ward St, Senatobia, MS 38668; 662-562-5661; Fax: 662-560-6205. Hours: 8AM-5PM (CST). *Probate.*

Tippah County

Circuit Court Courthouse, Ripley, MS 38663; 662-837-7370; Fax: 662-837-1030. Hours: 8AM-5PM (CST). *Felony, Civil Actions Over $2,500.*
Civil Records: Access: Phone, fax, mail, in person. Both court and visitors may perform in person searches. Search fee: $5.00 per name. Required to search: name, years to search. Civil cases indexed by defendant. Civil records on docket books since 1800s.
Criminal Records: Access: Phone, fax, mail, in person. Both court and visitors may perform in person searches. Search fee: $5.00 per name. Required to search: name, years to search, DOB; also helpful: SSN. Criminal records on docket books since 1800s.
General Information: No sealed, adoptions, mental health, juvenile, sex or expunged records released. Will fax results $1.00 per page. Copy fee: $.50 per page. No certification fee. Payee: Circuit Clerk. Personal checks accepted. Prepayment required. Mail requests: SASE not required. Mail turnaround time 1 week; phone turnaround is 30 minutes.

Justice Court Justice Court, 205-B Spring Ave, Ripley, MS 38663; 662-837-8842; Fax: 662-837-1398. Hours: 8AM-5PM (CST). *Misdemeanor, Civil Actions Under $2,500, Eviction, Small Claims.*

Chancery Court PO Box 99, Ripley, MS 38663; 662-837-7374; Probate phone: 662-837-3607; Fax: 662-837-7148. Hours: 8AM-5PM (CST). *Probate.*

Tishomingo County

Circuit Court 1008 Battleground Dr, Iuka, MS 38852; 662-423-7026; Fax: 662-423-1667. Hours: 8AM-5PM (CST). *Felony, Civil Actions Over $2,500.*
Civil Records: Access: Mail, in person. Both court and visitors may perform in person searches. Search fee: $10.00 per name. Required to search: name, years to search. Civil cases indexed by defendant, plaintiff. Civil records on computer back to 2000, in docket books since 1950s, others in storage.
Criminal Records: Access: Mail, in person. Both court and visitors may perform in person searches. Search fee: $10.00 per name. Required to search: name, years to search, DOB; also helpful: SSN, signed release. Criminal records on computer back to 2000, in docket books since 1950s, others in storage.
General Information: Public Access terminal is available. No sealed, adoptions, mental health, juvenile, sex, or expunged records released. Will fax results for $10.00 per name. Copy fee: $.50 per page. Certification fee: $1.00. Payee: Circuit Clerk. Business checks accepted. Prepayment required. Mail requests: SASE requested. Turnaround time 1-2 days.

Justice Court - Northern & Southern Districts 1008 Battleground Drive, Rm 212, Iuka, MS 38852; 662-423-7033; Fax: 662-423-7094. Hours: 8AM-5PM (CST). *Misdemeanor, Civil Actions Under $2,500, Eviction, Small Claims.*

Chancery Court 1008 Battleground Dr, Iuka, MS 38852; 662-423-7010; Fax: 662-423-7005. Hours: 8AM-5PM (CST). *Probate.*

Tunica County

Circuit Court PO Box 184, Tunica, MS 38676; 662-363-2842. Hours: 8AM-5PM (CST). *Felony, Civil Actions Over $2,500.*
Civil Records: Access: Mail, in person. Both court and visitors may perform in person searches. Search fee: $10.00 per name. Required to search: name, years to search. Civil cases indexed by defendant, plaintiff. Civil records on docket books for 10 years; archived prior.
Criminal Records: Access: Mail, in person. Both court and visitors may perform in person searches. Search fee: $10.00 per name. Required to search: name, years to search, DOB; also helpful: SSN. Criminal records on docket books for 10 years.
General Information: No sealed, adoptions, mental health, juvenile, sex, or expunged records released. Will fax results to local or toll free line. Copy fee: $.50 per page. Add postage. Certification fee: $1.50. Payee: Circuit Clerk. Personal checks accepted. Prepayment required. Mail requests: SASE requested. Turnaround time 1 week.

Justice Court 5130 Old Moon Landing Rd., Tunica, MS 38676; 662-363-2178; Fax: 662-363-4234. Hours: 8AM-5PM (CST). *Misdemeanor, Civil Actions Under $2,500, Eviction, Small Claims.*

Chancery Court PO Box 217, Tunica, MS 38676; 662-363-2451; Fax: 662-357-5934. Hours: 8AM-Noon, 1-5PM (CST). *Probate.*

Union County

Circuit Court PO Box 298, New Albany, MS 38652; 662-534-1910; Fax: 662-534-2059. Hours: 8AM-5PM (CST). *Felony, Civil Actions Over $2,500.*
Civil Records: Access: Fax, mail, in person. Both court and visitors may perform in person searches. Search fee: $10.00 per name. Includes certification fee. Required to search: name, years to search, address. Civil cases indexed by defendant, plaintiff. Civil records on docket books since early 1900s.
Criminal Records: Access: Fax, mail, in person. Both court and visitors may perform in person searches. Search fee: $10.00 per name. Fee includes certification. Required to search: name, years to search, DOB; also helpful: SSN. Criminal records on docket books since early 1900s.
General Information: No adoptions, mental health or juvenile records released. No fee to fax results. Copy fee: $.50 per page. Certification fee: $5.00. Payee: Union County Circuit Clerk. Personal checks accepted. Prepayment required. Mail requests: SASE requested. Turnaround time 1 week.

Justice Court - East & West Posts PO Box 27, New Albany, MS 38652; 662-534-1951; Fax: 662-534-1935. Hours: 8AM-5PM (CST). *Misdemeanor, Civil Actions Under $2,500, Eviction, Small Claims.*

Chancery Court PO Box 847, New Albany, MS 38652; 662-534-1900; Fax: 662-534-1907. Hours: 8AM-5PM (CST). *Probate.*

Walthall County

Circuit Court 200 Ball Ave, Tylertown, MS 39667; 601-876-5677; Fax: 601-876-4077. Hours: 8AM-Noon; 1-5PM (CST). *Felony, Civil Actions Over $2,500.*
Civil Records: Access: Mail, in person. Both court and visitors may perform in person searches. Search fee: $10.00 per name. Required to search: name, years to search. Civil cases indexed by defendant, plaintiff. Civil records on docket books since 1914.

Criminal Records: Access: Mail, in person. Both court and visitors may perform in person searches. Search fee: $10.00 per name. Required to search: name, years to search; also helpful: SSN. Criminal records on docket books since 1914.

General Information: No sealed, adoptions, mental health, juvenile, sex, or expunged records released. Will fax results. Copy fee: $.50 per page. Certification fee: $1.50 plus $.50 per page. Payee: Circuit Clerk. Personal checks accepted. Prepayment required. Mail turnaround time 1-2 days.

Justice Court - Districts 1 & 2 PO Box 507, Tylertown, MS 39667; 601-876-2311; Fax: 601-876-6866. Hours: 8AM-5PM (CST). *Misdemeanor, Civil Actions Under $2,500, Eviction, Small Claims.*

Chancery Court PO Box 351, Tylertown, MS 39667; 601-876-3553; Fax: 601-876-6026. Hours: 8AM-5PM (CST). *Probate.*

Warren County

Circuit & County Court PO Box 351, Vicksburg, MS 39181; 601-636-3961. Hours: 8AM-5PM (CST). *Felony, Misdemeanor, Civil.*

Civil Records: Access: Mail, in person. Both court and visitors may perform in person searches. Search fee: $10.00 per name. Required to search: name, years to search. Civil cases indexed by defendant, plaintiff. Civil records on books since 1970s.

Criminal Records: Access: Mail, in person. Both court and visitors may perform in person searches. Search fee: $10.00 per name. Required to search: name, years to search; also helpful: DOB, SSN. Criminal records on books since 1970s.

General Information: Public Access terminal is available. No sealed or expunged records released. Copy fee: $1.00 per page. Certification fee: $5.00 per page. Payee: Circuit Clerk. Personal checks accepted. Prepayment required. Mail requests: SASE required. Mail turnaround time 1 day.

Justice Court - Northern, Central & Southern Districts PO Box 1598, Vicksburg, MS 39181; 601-634-6402; Fax: 601-630-8015. Hours: 8AM-5PM (CST). *Misdemeanor, Civil Actions Under $2,500, Eviction, Small Claims.*

Chancery Court PO Box 351, Vicksburg, MS 39181; 601-636-4415; Fax: 601-630-8016. Hours: 8AM-5PM (CST). *Probate.*

Washington County

Circuit & County Court PO Box 1276, Greenville, MS 38702; 662-378-2747; Fax: 662-334-2698. Hours: 8AM-5PM (CST). *Felony, Misdemeanor, Civil.*

Civil Records: Access: Fax, mail, in person. Both court and visitors may perform in person searches. Search fee: $10.00 per name. Required to search: name, years to search. Civil cases indexed by defendant, plaintiff. Civil records on books since 1964.

Criminal Records: Access: Fax, mail, in person. Both court and visitors may perform in person searches. Search fee: $10.00 per name for 7 years, $1.00 each add'l year. Required to search: name, years to search; also helpful: DOB, SSN. Criminal records on books since 1964.

General Information: No sealed or expunged records released. No fee to fax results. Copy fee: $1.00 per page. Certification fee: $1.50. Payee: Circuit Clerk. Business checks accepted. Prepayment required. Mail requests: SASE required. Mail turnaround time 5-10 days.

Justice Court - Districts 1-3 905 W Alexander, Greenville, MS 38701; 662-332-0633.

Hours: 8AM-5PM (CST). *Misdemeanor, Civil Actions Under $2,500, Eviction, Small Claims.*

Chancery Court PO Box 309, Greenville, MS 38702-0309; 662-332-1595; Fax: 662-334-2725. Hours: 8AM-5PM (CST). *Probate.*

Wayne County

Circuit Court PO Box 428, Waynesboro, MS 39367; 601-735-1171; Fax: 601-735-6261. Hours: 8AM-5PM (CST). *Felony, Civil Actions Over $2,500.*

Note: This court is in process of computerizing their records.

Civil Records: Access: Phone, fax, mail, in person. Both court and visitors may perform in person searches. Search fee: $10.00 per name. Required to search: name, years to search. Civil cases indexed by defendant, plaintiff. Civil records on docket books since 1980, others in storage.

Criminal Records: Access: Fax, mail, in person. Both court and visitors may perform in person searches. Search fee: $10.00 per name. Required to search: name, years to search; also helpful: DOB, SSN, signed release. Criminal records on docket books since 1980, others in storage.

General Information: Public Access terminal is available. No sealed or expunged records released. Fee to fax results is $1.00 per page. Copy fee: $.50 per page. Certification fee: $1.50. Payee: Circuit Clerk. Business checks accepted. Prepayment required. Mail turnaround time 1-2 days.

Justice Court - Posts 1 & 2 810 Chickasawhay St, #C, Waynesboro, MS 39367; 601-735-3118; Fax: 601-735-6266. Hours: 8AM-5PM (CST). *Misdemeanor, Civil Actions Under $2,500, Eviction, Small Claims.*

Chancery Court Courthouse, 609 Azalea Dr, Waynesboro, MS 39367; 601-735-2873; Fax: 601-735-6224. Hours: 8AM-5PM (CST). *Probate.*

Webster County

Circuit Court PO Box 308, Walthall, MS 39771; 662-258-6287; Fax: 662-258-7686. Hours: 8AM-5PM (CST). *Felony, Civil Actions Over $2,500.*

Civil Records: Access: Phone, fax, mail, in person. Both court and visitors may perform in person searches. Search fee: $10.00 per name. Required to search: name, years to search. Civil cases indexed by defendant, plaintiff. Civil records on docket books since 1874.

Criminal Records: Access: Fax, mail, in person. Both court and visitors may perform in person searches. Search fee: $10.00 per name. Required to search: name, years to search, DOB; also helpful: SSN. Criminal records on docket books since 1874.

General Information: Public Access terminal is available. No sealed, adoptions, mental health, juvenile, sex, or expunged records released. No fee to fax results. Copy fee: $.50 per page. Certification fee: $1.00. Payee: Circuit Clerk. Business checks accepted. Prepayment required. Mail turnaround time 1-2 days.

Justice Court - Districts 1 & 2 114 Hwy 9 N, Eupora, MS 39744; 662-258-2590; Fax: 662-258-3093. Hours: 8AM-5PM (CST). *Misdemeanor, Civil Actions Under $2,500, Eviction, Small Claims.*

Chancery Court PO Box 398, Walthall, MS 39771; 662-258-4131; Fax: 662-258-6657. Hours: 8AM-5PM (CST). *Probate.*

Wilkinson County

Circuit Court PO Box 327, Woodville, MS 39669; 601-888-6697; Fax: 601-888-6984. Hours: 8:00AM-5:00PM (CST). *Felony, Civil Actions Over $2,500.*

Civil Records: Access: Mail, in person. Both court and visitors may perform in person searches. Search fee: $10.00 per name. Required to search: name, years to search. Civil cases indexed by defendant, plaintiff. Civil records on docket books since 1940s.

Criminal Records: Access: Mail, in person. Both court and visitors may perform in person searches. Search fee: $10.00 per name. Required to search: name, years to search; also helpful: DOB, SSN. Criminal records on docket books since 1940s.

General Information: No sealed or expunged records released. Copy fee: $.50 per page. Certification fee: $5.00. Payee: Circuit Clerk. Personal checks accepted. Prepayment required. Mail turnaround time 1-2 days.

Justice Court - East & West Districts PO Box 40, Woodville, MS 39669; 601-888-3538, 601-888-3972; Fax: 601-888-7591. Hours: 8AM-5PM (CST). *Misdemeanor, Civil Actions Under $2,500, Eviction, Small Claims.*

Chancery Court PO Box 516, Woodville, MS 39669; 601-888-4381; Fax: 601-888-6776. Hours: 8AM-5PM (CST). *Probate.*

Winston County

Circuit Court PO Drawer 785, Louisville, MS 39339; 662-773-3581; Fax: 662-773-7192. Hours: 8AM-5PM (CST). *Felony, Civil Actions Over $2,500.*

Note: You may email requests to kim@winstoncounty.org.

Civil Records: Access: Phone, fax, mail, in person. Both court and visitors may perform in person searches. Search fee: $10.00 per name. Required to search: name, years to search. Civil cases indexed by defendant, plaintiff. Civil records on docket books since early 1950s; some on computer back to 1994; all since 2000.

Criminal Records: Access: Fax, mail, in person. Both court and visitors may perform in person searches. Search fee: $10.00 per name. Required to search: name, years to search, DOB; also helpful: SSN. Criminal records on docket books since early 1800s; on computer back to 2000.

General Information: Public Access terminal is available. No sealed, adoptions, mental health, juvenile or expunged records released. Will fax results $5.00 1st page, $1.00 each add'l. Copy fee: $1.00 per page. Certification fee: $2.00. Payee: Circuit Clerk. Personal checks accepted. Prepayment required. Mail requests: SASE requested. Turnaround time 14 days.

Justice Court PO Box 327, Louisville, MS 39339; 662-773-6016; Fax: 662-773-8817. Hours: 8AM-5PM (CST). *Misdemeanor, Civil Actions Under $2,500, Eviction, Small Claims.*

Chancery Court PO Drawer 69, Louisville, MS 39339; 662-773-3631; Fax: 662-773-8814. Hours: 8AM-5PM (CST). *Probate.*

Yalobusha County

Coffeeville Circuit Court PO Box 260, Coffeeville, MS 38922; 662-675-8187; Fax: 662-675-8004. Hours: 8AM-5PM (CST). *Felony, Civil Actions Over $2,500.*

Civil Records: Access: Phone, fax, mail, in person. Both court and visitors may perform in person searches. Search fee: $10.00 per name. May mail request with check or fax request with copy of check to be mailed. Required to search: name, years to search. Civil cases indexed by defendant, plaintiff. Civil records on docket books since 1930s.

Criminal Records: Access: Phone, fax, mail, in person. Both court and visitors may perform in person searches. Search fee: $10.00 per name. May mail request with check or fax request with copy of check to be mailed. Required to search: name, years to search; also helpful: DOB. Criminal records on docket books since 1930s.

General Information: No sealed, adoptions, mental health, juvenile, sex, or expunged records released. Will fax results to local or toll free line. Copy fee: $.25 per page. Certification fee: $10.00. Payee: Circuit Clerk. Personal checks accepted. Prepayment required. Mail requests: SASE requested. Turnaround time 1-2 days.

Water Valley Circuit Court PO Box 1431, Water Valley, MS 38965; 662-473-1341; Fax: 662-473-5020. Hours: 8AM-5PM (CST). *Felony, Civil Actions Over $2,500.*

Civil Records: Access: Fax, mail, in person. Both court and visitors may perform in person searches. Search fee: $10.00 per name. Includes certification fee. Required to search: name, years to search. Civil cases indexed by defendant, plaintiff. Civil records on docket books since 1930s.

Criminal Records: Access: Fax, mail, in person. Both court and visitors may perform in person searches. Search fee: $10.00 per name. Fee includes certification. Required to search: name, years to

search, DOB; also helpful: SSN. Criminal records on docket books since 1930s.

General Information: No sealed, adoptions, mental health, juvenile, sex, or expunged records released. No fee to fax results. Copy fee: $.50 per page. Certification fee: $10.00 per docket. Payee: Circuit Clerk. Personal checks accepted. Prepayment required. Mail turnaround time 1 week.

Justice Court - District 1 PO Box 218, Coffeeville, MS 38922; 662-675-8115; Fax: 662-675-8452. Hours: 8AM-5PM (CST). *Misdemeanor, Civil Actions Under $2,500, Eviction, Small Claims.*

Justice Court - Division 2 PO Box 918, Water Valley, MS 38965; 662-473-4502. Hours: 8AM-5PM only open Tu & We (CST). *Misdemeanor, Civil Actions Under $2,500, Eviction, Small Claims.*

Chancery Court PO Box 664, Water Valley, MS 38965; 662-473-2091; Fax: 662-473-3622. Hours: 8AM-5PM (CST). *Probate.*

Chancery Court PO Box 260, Coffeeville, MS 38922; 662-675-2716; Fax: 662-675-8004/473-3622. Hours: 8AM-Noon, 1-5PM (CST). *Probate.*

Yazoo County

Circuit & County Court PO Box 108, Yazoo City, MS 39194; 662-746-1872. Hours: 8AM-5PM (CST). *Felony, Misdemeanor, Civil.*

Civil Records: Access: Mail, in person. Both court and visitors may perform in person searches. Search

fee: $10.00 per name. Required to search: name, years to search. Civil cases indexed by defendant, plaintiff. Civil records for Civil Circuit on docket books since 1973; for Civil County on docket books since 1977.

Criminal Records: Access: Mail, in person. Both court and visitors may perform in person searches. Search fee: $10.00 per name. Required to search: name, years to search, DOB; also helpful: SSN. Criminal records for Criminal Circuit from 1975; Criminal County on docket books since 1975.

General Information: No sealed, adoptions, mental health, juvenile, sex, or expunged records released. Will fax back results. Copy fee: $.50 per page. Certification fee: $1.00. Payee: Circuit Clerk. Business checks accepted. Prepayment required. Mail requests: SASE required. Mail turnaround time 1 day.

Justice Court - Northern & Southern Districts PO Box 798, Yazoo City, MS 39194; 662-746-8181; Fax: 662-746-2186. Hours: 8AM-5PM (CST). *Misdemeanor, Civil Actions Under $2,500, Eviction, Small Claims.*

Chancery Court PO Box 68, Yazoo City, MS 39194; 662-746-2661; Fax: 662-746-3893. Hours: 8AM-5PM (CST). *Probate*

Mississippi Recording Offices

ORGANIZATION: 82 counties, 92 recording offices. The recording officers are Chancery Clerk and Clerk of Circuit Court (state tax liens). Ten counties have two separate recording offices - Bolivar, Carroll, Chickasaw, Craighead, Harrison, Hinds, Jasper, Jones, Panola, Tallahatchie, and Yalobusha. See the notes under each county for how to determine which office is appropriate to search. The entire state is in the Central Time Zone (CST).

REAL ESTATE RECORDS: A few counties will perform real estate searches. Copies usually cost $.50 per page and certification fees $1.00 per document. The Assessor maintains tax records.

UCC RECORDS: This was a dual filing state. Until 07/2001, financing statements were filed both at the state level and with the Chancery Clerk, except for consumer goods, farm related and real estate related filings, which were filed only with the Chancery Clerk. Now, only real estate related filings are filed at the county level. Nearly all counties will perform UCC searches. Use search request form UCC-11. Search fees are usually $5.00 per debtor name. Copy fees vary from $.25 to $2.00 per page.

TAX LIEN RECORDS: Federal tax liens on personal property of businesses are filed with the Secretary of State. Federal tax liens on personal property of individuals are filed with the county Chancery Clerk. State tax liens on personal property are filed with the county Clerk of Circuit Court. Refer to the County Court section for information about Mississippi Circuit Courts. State tax liens on real property are filed with the Chancery Clerk. Most Chancery Clerk offices will perform a federal tax lien search for a fee of $5.00 per name. Copy fees vary.

OTHER LIENS: Mechanics, lis pendens, judgment (Circuit Court), construction.

ONLINE ACCESS: A limited number of counties offer online access to records, there is no statewide system except for the Secretary of State's UCC access – see State Agencies section. A vendor provides access to thirteen counties at http://deltacomputersystems.com.

Adams County

Chancery Clerk, PO Box 1006, Natchez, MS 39121. **Phone-**Chancery Clerk, R/E & UCC Recording- 601-446-6684; fax-601-445-7913; hours 8AM-5PM
Will search UCC records. Search per debtor- $5.00. UCC copy fee- $2.00 per page. Will search tax liens including federal tax liens. Tax lien search fee- $10.00 per debtor. Will not search real estate records. RE record copy- $.50 per page. Cert fee: $1.00 per cert. Payee: Chancery Clerk. **Other phones:** Assessor-601-442-6732; Elections-601-446-6326.

Alcorn County

Chancery Clerk, PO Box 69, Corinth, MS 38835-0069. **Phone-**Chancery Clerk, R/E & UCC Recording- 662-286-7700; fax-662-286-7706; hours 8AM-5PM
Will search UCC records. Search per debtor- $5.00. Copy fee is $2.00 per page. Will not search real estate records. Cert fee: $1.00 per name. Payee: Chancery Clerk. **Online Access to Property Tax, Appraisal records:** Access is free at www.delta computersystems.com/MS/MS02/index.html. **Other phones:** Assessor-662-286-7733; Elections-662-286-7740.

Amite County

Chancery Clerk, PO Box 680, Liberty, MS 39645-0680. **Phone-**601-657-8022; fax-601-657-8288; hours 8AM-5PM
Will search UCC records. Search per debtor- $10.00. UCC copy fee- $.50 per page. Separate federal & state combined tax lien search- $10.00 Will not search real estate records. Cert fee: $3.00. Payee: Amite County Chancery Clerk. **Other phones:** Assessor-601-657-8973; Treasurer-601-657-8932; Elections-601-657-8932.

Attala County

Chancery Clerk, 230 W. Washington St., Chancery Court Bldg., Kosciusko, MS 39090. **Phone-**662-289-2921; fax-662-289-7662; hours 8AM-5PM

Will search UCC records. Search per debtor- $5.00. UCC copy fee- $1.00 per page. Will not search real estate records. Cert fee: $1.00 per cert. Payee: Attala County Chancery Clerk. **Other phones:** Assessor-662-289-5731; Elections-662-289-1471.

Benton County

Chancery Clerk, PO Box 218, Ashland, MS 38603. **Phone-**662-224-6300; fax-662-224-6303; 8AM-5PM
Will search UCC records. Search per debtor- $5.00. UCC copy fee- $2.00 per page. Will not search real estate or tax lien records. Cert fee: $1.50. Payee: County Chancery Clerk. **Other phones:** Assessor-662-224-6315; Elections-662-224-6310.

Bolivar County (1st District)

Chancery Clerk, PO Box 238, Rosedale, MS 38769-0238. **Phone-**662-759-3762; fax-662-759-3467; hours 8AM-12;00-1-5PM. Will search UCC records. Search per debtor- $5.00. UCC copy fee- $2.00 per page. Will not search real estate records. Cert fee: $1.00 per cert. Payee: Bolivar County Chancery Clerk. **Other phones:** Assessor-662-843-3826; Treasurer-662-843-2531; Elections-662-843-2061.

Bolivar County (2nd District)

Chancery Clerk, PO Box 789, Cleveland, MS 38732. **Phone-**Chancery Clerk, R/E & UCC Recording- 662-843-2071; fax-662-846-2940; hours 8-5. Will search UCC records prior to 1/2002. Search per debtor- $5.00. Copy fee- $2.00. per copy if office makes copy. UCC copy fee- $.50 per page self serve. Will search federal tax liens. Will not search real estate records. RE record copy- $.50 per page. Cert fee: $1.00 per record. Payee: Jeanne Walker-Chancery Clerk. **Other phones:** Assessor-662-843-3926; Treasurer-662-843-2071; Elections-662-843-2061.

Calhoun County

Chancery Clerk, PO Box 8, Pittsboro, MS 38951. **Phone-**Chancery Clerk, R/E & UCC Recording- 662-412-3117, UCC Recording- 662-412-3121; fax-662-412-3128; hours 8AM-5PM

Will search UCC records. Search per debtor- $5.00. UCC copy- $2.00 per page. Will not do federal tax lien search. Will not search real estate records. RE record copy- $.50 per page. Cert fee: $5.00 per page. Payee: County Clerk of the Chancery Court. **Other phones:** Assessor-662-412-3140; Treasurer-662-412-3117; Appraiser-662-412-3146; Elections-662-412-3101; Vital Records-662-412-3101.

Carroll County (1st District)

Chancery Clerk, PO Box 60, Carrollton, MS 38917. **Phone-**662-237-9274; fax-662-237-9642; 8AM-N, 1-5PM. Will search UCC records. Search per debtor- $10.00. Will not search real estate records. Payee: Carroll County Chancery Clerk. **Other phones:** Assessor-662-237-9217; Elections-662-464-5476.

Carroll County (2nd District)

Chancery Clerk, PO Box 6, Vaiden, MS 39176. **Phone-**662-464-5476; fax-662-464-5407; hours 8AM-5PM
The 2nd district is split by section, township and range. Will not search records. UCC copy- $2.00 per page. RE record copy- $1.00 per page. Cert fee: $2.00 per doc. Payee: Carroll County Clerk of the Chancery Court. **Other phones:** Assessor-662-464-8852; Elections-662-464-5476.

Chickasaw County (1st District)

Chancery Clerk, Courthouse, 1 Pinson Sq, Houston, MS 38851. **Phone-**662-456-2513; fax-662-456-5295; hours 8AM-12;00-1-5PM
Will search UCC records. Search per debtor- $5.00. UCC copy fee- $.50 per page. Will not search real estate records. Cert fee: $6.00. Payee: Chancery Clerk. **Other phones:** Assessor-662-456-3327; Treasurer-662-456-3941; Elections-662-456-2331.

Chickasaw County (2nd District)

Chancery Clerk, 234 Main St, Rm 201, Okolona, MS 38860-1438. **Phone-**662-447-2092; fax-662-447-5024. Will search UCC records. Search per debtor- $5.00. Will not search real estate records. **Other phones:**

Assessor-662-447-2242; Treasurer-662-456-2513; Elections-662-456-2331.

Choctaw County

Chancery Clerk, PO Box 250, Ackerman, MS 39735-0250. **Phone**-662-285-6329; fax-662-285-3444; hours 8AM-5PM. Will search UCC records. Search per debtor- $10.00. Searches must be pre-paid. UCC copy fee- $1.00 per page. Will not search real estate records. Cert fee: $2.00. Payee: Choctaw County Chancery Clerk. **Other phones:** Assessor-662-285-6320; Elections-662-285-6245.

Claiborne County

Chancery Clerk, PO Box 449, Port Gibson, MS 39150. **Phone**-Chancery Clerk, R/E & UCC Recording- 601-437-4992; fax-601-437-3731; hours 8AM-5PM
Will search UCC records. Search per debtor- $5.00. Tax liens not included in UCC search. Tax lien search fee- $5.00 per debtor. Will not search real estate records. Record copy- $.50 per page. Cert fee: $1.00 per cert. Payee: Claiborne County Clerk of the Chancery Court. **Other phones:** Assessor-601-437-5591; Treasurer-601-437-4992; Appraiser-601-437-5591; Elections-601-437-5841.

Clarke County

Chancery Clerk, PO Box 689, Quitman, MS 39355. **Phone**-Chancery Clerk, R/E & UCC Recording- 601-776-2126; fax-601-776-2756; hours 8AM-5PM
Will search UCC records. Search per debtor- $5.00. UCC copy- $2.00 per page. Will not do federal tax lien search. Will not search real estate records. RE record copy- $.50 per page. Cert fee: $1.00 per cert. Payee: Clarke County Clerk of the Chancery Court. **Other phones:** Assessor-601-776-6931; Treasurer-601-776-2126; Appraiser-601-776-1021; Elections-601-776-3111.

Clay County

Chancery Clerk, PO Box 815, West Point, MS 39773. **Phone**-Chancery Clerk, R/E & UCC Recording- 662-494-3124; hours 8AM-5PM
Will search UCC records prior to 1/2002. Search per debtor- $5.00. UCC copy- $2.00 per page. UCC search does not include federal tax liens. Will not search real estate records. RE record copy- $.50 per page. Cert fee: $1.00 per page. Payee: Clay County Clerk of the Chancery Court. **Other phones:** Assessor-662-494-3432; Appraiser-662-494-3432; Elections-662-494-3384.

Coahoma County

Chancery Clerk, PO Box 98, Clarksdale, MS 38614. **Phone**-Chancery Clerk, R/E & UCC Recording- 662-624-3000; fax-662-624-3040; hours 8AM-5PM
Will search UCC records. Search per debtor- $5.00. Will search tax liens. Tax lien search fee- $5.00 per debtor. Will not search real estate records. Record copy- $.50 per page. Cert fee: $1.00 per instrument. Payee: Coahoma County Chancery Clerk. **Other phones:** Assessor-662-624-3006; Treasurer-662-624-3020; Elections-662-624-3014; Vital Records-662-624-3014.

Copiah County

Chancery Clerk, PO Box 507, Hazlehurst, MS 39083-0507. **Phone**-Chancery Clerk, R/E & UCC Recording-601-894-3021; fax-601-894-3026. Will search UCC records. Search per debtor- $5.00. UCC copy fee- $2.00 per page. Will not search real estate records. RE record copy- $.50 per page. Cert fee: $1.00 per cert. Payee: Chancery Clerk. **Other phones:** Assessor-601-894-2721; Elections-601-894-1241.

Covington County

Chancery Clerk, PO Box 1679, Collins, MS 39428. **Phone**-601-765-4242; fax-601-765-5016; 8AM-5PM

Will not search records. RE record copy- $1.00 per page. Cert fee: $1.00 per cert. Payee: County Clerk of the Chancery Court. **Other phones:** Assessor-601-756-6402; Elections-601-765-6506.

De Soto County

Chancery Clerk, PO Box 949, Hernando, MS 38632. **Phone**-Chancery Clerk, R/E & UCC Recording- 662-429-1318; fax-662-449-1420; hours 8AM-5PM www.desotoms.info
Will search UCC records. Search per debtor- $5.00. UCC copy- $2.00 per page. UCC search does not include federal tax liens. Will not search real estate records. Cert fee: $1.00 per cert + $.50 per copy. Payee: De Soto County Clerk of the Chancery Court. **Online Access to Property Tax, Assessor, Grantor/Grantee, Deed, Recording, Voter Registration records:** Access to assessor property data is free at www.desotoms.info. Click on "Tax Assessor." GIS-mapping site is also available. Also, access to Chancery Clerk grantor/grantee index is also available; click on "Chancery Clerk." For voter registration data, click on Circuit Clerk and then Voter Registration tab. GIS mapping site is also available, also board and planning com. minutes. **Other phones:** Assessor-662-429-1335; Elections-662-429-1325.

Forrest County

Chancery Clerk, PO Box 951, Hattiesburg, MS 39403. **Phone**-Chancery Clerk, R/E & UCC Recording- 601-545-6014; fax-601-545-6095; hours 8AM-5PM
Will search UCC records. Search per debtor- $5.00. Copy fee is $2.00 per page. Will not search real estate records. RE record copy- $.50 per page. Cert fee: $1.00 per instrument. Payee: Chancery Clerk. **Other phones:** Assessor-601-545-6130; Treasurer-601-582-8228; Elections-601-582-3213; Vital Records-601-576-7960.

Franklin County

Chancery Clerk, PO Box 297, Meadville, MS 39653-0297. **Phone**-601-384-2330; fax-601-384-5864; hours 8AM-5PM
Will search UCC records. Search per debtor- $5.00. Search must be pre-paid. UCC copy- $2.00 per page. Will not search real estate or tax lien records. Cert fee: $1.00. Payee: Franklin County Chancery Clerk. **Other phones:** Assessor-601-384-2359; Elections-601-384-2320; Tax Collector-601-384-2359.

George County

Chancery Clerk, 355 Cox St, Lucedale, MS 39452. **Phone**-Chancery Clerk, R/E & UCC Recording- 601-947-4801; fax-601-947-1300; hours 8AM-5PM; 9AM-Noon Sat
Will search UCC records. Search per debtor- $5.00. UCC copy- $2.00 per page. UCC search includes federal tax liens if requested. Will not search real estate records. RE record copy- $.50 per copy. Cert fee: $1.00 per cert. Payee: George County Clerk of the Chancery Court. **Online Access to Assessor, Property records:** property tax records are free at www.deltacomputersystems.com/MS/MS20/plinkquerym.html. **Other phones:** Assessor-601-947-7541; Treasurer-601-947-3766; Appraiser-601-947-7541; Elections-601-947-4881.

Greene County

Chancery Clerk, PO Box 610, Leakesville, MS 39451. **Phone**-601-394-2377; hours 8AM-5PM
Will search UCC records. UCC search per debtor-$5.00. Search request using non-standard form (per name)- $10.00. UCC copy- $1.00 per page. UCC search includes federal tax liens if requested. Real estate owner, mortgage, and property transfer searches available. RE record copy- $.50 per copy. Cert fee: $1.00 per cert. Payee: County Chancery

Clerk. **Other phones:** Assessor-601-394-2377; Treasurer-601-394-2377; Elections-601-394-2379.

Grenada County

Chancery Clerk, PO Drawer 1208, Grenada, MS 38902-1208. **Phone**-662-226-1821; fax-662-227-2860; hours 8AM-5PM
Will search UCC records. UCC search per debtor-$5.00, $2.00 per add'l. UCC copy- $2.00 per page. Will search tax liens including federal tax liens. Will not search real estate records. RE record copy-$.50 per page. Cert fee: $1.00 per cert. Payee: Grenada County Clerk of the Chancery Court. **Other phones:** Treasurer-662-226-1821; Elections-662-226-1941; Tax Collector-662-226-1741.

Hancock County

Chancery Clerk, PO Box 429, Bay Saint Louis, MS 39520. **Phone**-228-467-5404, R/E Recording- 228-467-0455, UCC Recording- 228-467-0455; fax-228-467-3159; hours 8AM-5PM
Will search UCC records. Search per debtor- $5.00. Copy fee is $.50 per page. Will search tax liens including federal tax liens. Tax lien search fee-$5.00. Will not search real estate records. Cert fee: $1.00 per cert. Payee: Chancery Clerk. **Other phones:** Assessor-228-467-5727; Treasurer-228-467-4425; Appraiser-228-467-0130; Elections-228-467-5265; Tax Collector-228-467-4425; Delinquent Taxes-228-467-2252.

Harrison County (1st District)

Chancery Clerk, PO Drawer CC, Gulfport, MS 39502. **Phone**-228-865-4195, R/E Recording- 228-865-4036, UCC Recording- 228-865-4235; fax-228-868-1480; hours 8AM-5PM http://co.harrison.ms.us
Will search UCC records. Search per debtor- $5.00. UCC copy fee- $2.00 per page. Will search federal tax liens. Will not search real estate records. RE record copy- $1.00 per doc. Cert fee: $1.00 per doc. Payee: Chnacery Clerk. **Online Access to Property, Deed, Recording, UCC, Voter Registration, Deed, Grantor/Grantee, Marriage, Inmate, Court records:** Access to property tax data is free at www.deltacomputersystems.com/MS/MS24DELTA/DATALINK.html or http://co.harrison.ms.us. You may also choose to search chancery clerk Deed & Record index back 15 years. Also search voter registration and marriage licenses. Also, the delinquent tax sales list no longer appears online. Access the jail docket at www.harrisoncountysheriff.com/docket/. Also, search circuit court judgment rolls at http://co.harrison.ms.us/departments/circlerk/rolls/ and court dockets at http://co.harrison.ms.us/dockets/. **Other phones:** Assessor-228-865-4043; Treasurer-228-865-4040; Appraiser-228-865-4044; Elections-228-865-4049; Vital Records-228-960-7400.

Harrison County (2nd District)

Chancery Clerk, PO Box 544, Biloxi, MS 39533. **Phone**-228-435-8220; fax-228-435-8292; hours 8AM-5PM http://co.harrison.ms.us
Will search UCC records. Search per debtor- $5.00. UCC copy- $2.00 per page. Will not search real estate or tax lien records. **Online Access to Property, Deed, Recording, UCC, Voter Registration, Deed, Grantor/Grantee, Marriage, Inmate, Court records:** Access to property tax data is free at www.deltacomputersystems.com/MS/MS24DELTA/DATALINK.html or http://co.harrison.ms.us. You may also choose to search chancery clerk Deed & Record index back 15 years. Also search voter registration and marriage licenses. Also, the delinquent tax sales list no longer appears on the web. Access the jail docket at www.harrisoncountysheriff.com/docket/. Also, search circuit court judgment rolls at http://co.harrison.ms.us/departments/circlerk/rolls/ and court dockets at http://co.harrison.ms.us/dockets/.

Other phones: Assessor-228-435-8265; Elections-228-865-4167.

Hinds County (1st District)

Chancery Clerk, PO Box 686, Jackson, MS 39205-0686. **Phone-**Chancery Clerk, R/E & UCC Recording-601-968-6508, UCC Recording- 601-968-6516; fax-601-973-5535; hours-8AM-5PM www.co.hinds.ms.us/pgs/elected/chanceryclerk.asp Will search UCC records. Search per debtor- $5.00. UCC copy fee- $.50 per page. Will search federal tax liens. Tax lien search fee- $5.00 per debtor. Will not search real estate records. Cert fee: $1.00 per doc. Payee: Hinds County Chancery. **Online Access to Real Estate, Grantor/Grantee, Judgment, Lien, Assessor, Condominium, Acreage records:** Access to the county records databases are free at www.co.hinds.ms.us/pgs/apps/gindex.asp. Also, search the assessor landrolls for free at www.co.hinds.ms.us/pgs/apps/landroll_query.asp. **Other phones:** Assessor-601-968-6616; Treasurer-601-968-6588; Elections-601-968-6628; Tax Collector-601-968-6588.

Hinds County (2nd District)

Chancery Clerk, PO Box 88, Raymond, MS 39154. **Phone-**601-857-8055; hours-8AM-5PM www.co.hinds.ms.us The 2nd District consists of all towns/cities outside the limits of Jackson, including Bolton, part of Clinton, Edwards, Learned, Raymond, part of Terry, and Utica. Will search UCC records. Search per debtor- $5.00. UCC copy- $2.00 per page. UCC search does not include federal tax liens. Will not search real estate records. RE record copy- $.50 per page. Cert fee: $1.00 per cert. Payee: Hinds County Clerk of the Chancery Court. **Online Access to Real Estate, Assessor, Grantor/Grantee, Judgment records:** Access to the county clerk database is free at www.co.hinds.ms.us/pgs/apps/gindex.asp. Chose to search general index, landroll, judgments, acreage, subdivision, condominiums. **Other phones:** Assessor-601-857-8787; Treasurer-601-857-5574; Elections-601-968-6628; Tax Collector-601-857-5574.

Holmes County

Chancery Clerk, PO Box 239, Lexington, MS 39095. **Phone-**662-834-2508, R/E Recording- 662-834-0005, UCC Recording- 662-834-0005; fax-662-834-3020. Will search UCC records. Search per name- $5.00. Tax lien search fee- $5.00 per debtor. Will not search real estate records. Record copy- $.50 per page. Cert fee: $1.00 per copy. **Other phones:** Assessor-662-834-2865; Treasurer-662-834-0005; Appraiser-662-834-3737; Elections-662-834-2476; Vital Records-662-834-2476.

Humphreys County

Chancery Clerk, PO Box 547, Belzoni, MS 39038. **Phone-**662-247-1740; fax-662-247-0101; hours 8AM-Noon, 1-5PM Will search UCC records. Search per debtor- $5.00. UCC copy- $2.00 per page. UCC search includes federal tax liens if requested. Mortgage and property transfer searches available. RE record copy- $.50 per page. Cert fee: $1.00 per cert. Payee: Humphreys County Clerk of the Chancery Court. **Other phones:** Assessor-662-247-3174; Treasurer-662-247-2552; Appraiser-662-247-0106; Elections-662-247-3065; Tax Collector-662-247-2552.

Issaquena County

Chancery Clerk, PO Box 27, Mayersville, MS 39113-0027. **Phone-**Chancery Clerk, R/E & UCC Recording-662-873-2761; fax-662-873-2061; hours 8AM-Noon; 1-5PM. Will search UCC records. Search per debtor- $5.00. Record copy- $.50 per page. Cert fee: $1.00 per instrument. Payee: Chancery Clerk.

Other phones: Assessor-662-873-4665; Treasurer-662-873-2761; Elections-662-873-2761; Marriages/Divorces-662-873-2761.

Itawamba County

Chancery Clerk, PO Box 776, Fulton, MS 38843. **Phone-**Chancery Clerk, R/E & UCC Recording- 662-862-3421; fax-662-862-3421. Will search UCC records. Search per debtor- $5.00. UCC copy fee- $2.00 per page. Will not search real estate records. **Other phones:** Assessor-662-862-7598; Appraiser-662-862-7598; Elections-662-862-3511; Vital Records-662-862-3511.

Jackson County

Chancery Clerk, PO Box 998, Pascagoula, MS 39568. **Phone-**228-769-3131; fax-228-769-3135; 8-5PM Will search UCC records. Search per debtor- $5.00. UCC copy fee- $2.00 per page. Will not search real estate records. Cert fee: $1.00. Payee: Jackson County Chancery Clerk. **Other phones:** Assessor-228-769-3070; Treasurer-228-769-3131; Elections-228-769-3040.

Jasper County (1st District)

Chancery Clerk, PO Box 38, Paulding, MS 39348-0038. **Phone-**601-727-4941, R/E Recording- 601-764-3368, UCC Recording- 601-764-3368; fax-601-727-4475; hours 8AM-5PM Will search UCC records. Search per debtor- $5.00. UCC copy- $2.00 per page. Tax liens not included in UCC search. Separate federal tax lien search- $2.00 for each 10 minutes. Will not search real estate records. RE record copy- $.50 per page. Cert fee: $1.00 per page. Payee: Jasper County Clerk of the Chancery Court. **Other phones:** Assessor-601-764-2813; Elections-601-764-2245.

Jasper County (2nd District)

Chancery Clerk, PO Box 1047, Bay Springs, MS 39422. **Phone-**601-764-3026; fax-601-764-3999; hours 8AM-5PM. Will search UCC records. Search per debtor- $5.00. Copy fee is $2.00 per copy. Will not search real estate or tax lien records. **Other phones:** Assessor-601764-2813; Treasurer-601-764-3469; Elections-601-764-2245.

Jefferson County

Chancery Clerk, PO Box 145, Fayette, MS 39069. **Phone-**Chancery Clerk, R/E & UCC Recording- 601-786-3021, UCC Recording- 601-359-1350; fax-601-786-6009; hours 8AM-5PM. Will search UCC records. Search per debtor- $10.00. Copy fee is $2.00 per each. Will not search real estate records. RE record copy- $.50 per page. Cert fee: $1.00 per doc. Payee: Chancery Clerk. **Other phones:** Assessor-601-786-3781; Appraiser-601-786-3781; Elections-601-786-3422; Tax Collector-601-786-3781.

Jefferson Davis County

Chancery Clerk, PO Box 1137, Prentiss, MS 39474. **Phone-**601-792-4204; fax-601-792-2894. Will search UCC records. Search per debtor- $5.00. Will not search real estate records. RE record copy- $.50 per page. Cert fee: $1.00 per page. Payee: Chancery Clerk. **Other phones:** Assessor-601-792-4291; Treasurer-601-792-4204; Elections-601-792-4231.

Jones County (1st District)

Chancery Clerk, 101 N. Court St, Jones County Courthouse, Ellisville, MS 39437. **Phone-**601-477-3307; fax-601-477-1240; hours 8-12;00-1-5PM Will search UCC records. Search per debtor- $5.00. UCC copy- $2.00 per page. Will not do federal tax lien search. Will not search real estate records. RE record copy- $.50 per page. Cert fee: $1.00 per page. Payee: Jones County Chancery Clerk. **Other**

phones: Assessor-601-477-3250; Elections-601-425-2556.

Jones County (2nd District)

Chancery Clerk, PO Box 1468, Laurel, MS 39441. **Phone-**Chancery Clerk, R/E & UCC Recording- 601-428-0527, UCC Recording- 601-428-3131; fax-601-428-3602; hours 8AM-5PM Will search UCC records. Search per debtor- $5.00. Search per debtor (non-standard form)- $8.00., $2.00 extra with add'l debtor. Copy fee is $2.00 per page. Tax lien search fee- $5.00 per debtor. Will not search real estate records. RE record copy- $5.00 per request. Cert fee: $1.00. Payee: Chancery Clerk. **Other phones:** Assessor-601-428-3248; Treasurer-501-428-3128; Appraiser-601-649-1896; Elections-601-425-2556; Vital Records-601-576-7981.

Kemper County

Chancery Clerk, PO Box 188, De Kalb, MS 39328. **Phone-**Chancery Clerk, R/E & UCC Recording- 601-743-2460; fax-601-743-2789; hours 8AM-5PM Will search UCC records. Search per debtor- $5.00. Will not search real estate or tax lien records. Record copy- $.50 per page. Cert fee: $1.00 per page. Payee: Chancery Clerk. **Other phones:** Assessor-601-743-2693; Treasurer-601-743-4290; Appraiser-601-743-2693; Elections-601-743-2224; Vital Records-601-743-2224.

Lafayette County

Chancery Clerk, PO Box 1240, Oxford, MS 38655. **Phone-**Chancery Clerk, R/E & UCC Recording- 662-234-2131; fax-662-234-5038; hours 8AM-5PM Will search UCC records. Search per debtor- $10.00. UCC copy- $2.00 per page. Will not do federal tax lien search. Will not search real estate records. Cert fee: $3.50. Payee: Lafayette County Clerk of the Chancery Court. **Online Access to Property Tax, Appraisal records:** Access to property data is free at www.deltacomputersystems.com/ms/ms36/plinkquery m.html. **Other phones:** Assessor-662-234-6006; Appraiser-662-234-5562; Elections-662-234-4951.

Lamar County

Chancery Clerk, PO Box 247, Purvis, MS 39475. **Phone-**601-794-8504; fax-601-794-3903; 8AM-5PM Will search UCC records. Search per debtor- $5.00. Copy fee is $2.00 per page. Will not search real estate records. Cert fee: $1.00. Payee: Lamar County Chancery Clerk. **Online Access to Property Tax, Appraisal records:** Access to property data is free at www.deltacomputersystems.com/MS/MS37/INDEX.html. **Other phones:** Elections-601-794-8504.

Lauderdale County

Chancery Clerk, PO Box 1587, Meridian, MS 39302-1587. **Phone-**Chancery Clerk, R/E & UCC Recording-601-482-9701, UCC Recording- 601-482-9710; hours 8AM-5PM www.lauderdalecounty.org Will search UCC records. Search per debtor- $10.00. UCC copy- $2.00 per page. Tax liens not included in UCC search. Separate federal tax lien search- $5.00 per debtor. Will not search real estate records. RE record copy- $1.00 per page. Cert fee: $7.00 per cert. Payee: Lauderdale County Clerk of the Chancery Court. **Online Access to Property Tax, Appraisal records:** Access to property data is free at www.deltacomputersystems.com/MS/MS38/INDEX.html. **Other phones:** Assessor-601-482-9779; Treasurer-601-482-4701; Elections-601-482-9731.

Lawrence County

Chancery Clerk, PO Box 821, Monticello, MS 39654. **Phone-**Chancery Clerk, R/E & UCC Recording- 601-587-7162; fax-601-587-0767; hours 8AM-5PM

Will search UCC records. Search per debtor- $10.00. Will not search real estate records. Record copy- $.50 per copy. Cert fee: $2.00 per copy. Payee: Lawrence County Chancery Clerk. **Other phones:** Treasurer-601-587-2211; Elections-601-587-4791; Tax Collector-601-587-2211.

Leake County

Leake County, PO Box 72, Carthage, MS 39051. **Phone**-601-267-7371; fax-601-267-6137; 8AM-5PM Will search UCC records. Search per debtor- $10.00. UCC copy fee- $1.00 per page. Will not search real estate records. Cert fee: $1.00. Payee: County Leake County. **Other phones:** Assessor-601-267-3021; Treasurer-601-267-7371; Elections-601-267-8357.

Lee County

Chancery Clerk, PO Box 7127, Tupelo, MS 38802. **Phone**-662-841-9100; fax-662-680-6091.
Will search UCC records. Search per debtor- $5.00. UCC copy fee- 2.00 per page. Will not search real estate records. Cert fee: $1.00 per doc. **Online Access to Property Tax, Appraisal records:** Access is to property records is free at www.deltacomputersystems.com/MS/MS41/INDEX.html. **Other phones:** Assessor-662-841-9030; Treasurer-662-841-9100; Elections-662-841-9024.

Leflore County

Chancery Clerk, PO Box 250, Greenwood, MS 38935-0250. **Phone**-662-455-7913; fax-662-455-7965.
Will search UCC records. Search per debtor- $10.00. UCC copy fee- $2.00 per page. Will not search real estate records. Cert fee: $1.50 per page. **Other phones:** Assessor-662-453-1041; Elections-662-453-1435.

Lincoln County

Chancery Clerk, PO Box 555, Brookhaven, MS 39602. **Phone**-601-835-3411; hours 8AM-5PM
Will search UCC records. Search per debtor- $5.00. UCC copy- $2.00 per page. UCC search includes federal tax liens if requested. Will not search real estate records. RE record copy- $.50 per page. Cert fee: $1.00 per page. Payee: Lincoln County Clerk of the Chancery Court. **Online Access to Real Estate, Grantor/Grantee, Deed records:** Access to county deed records is free at www.deltacomputersystems.com/MS/MS43/drlinkquerym.html. **Other phones:** Assessor-601-835-3428; Treasurer-601-835-3412; Elections-601-835-3435.

Lowndes County

Chancery Clerk, PO Box 684, Columbus, MS 39703. **Phone**-Chancery Clerk, R/E & UCC Recording- 662-329-5800, UCC Recording- 662-329-5807; hours 8AM-5PM
Will search UCC records. Search per debtor- $10.00. UCC copy- $2.00 per page, and $2.00 per file found. UCC search does not include federal tax liens. Will not search real estate records. RE record copy- $.50 per page. Cert fee: $1.00 per cert. Payee: Lowndes County Chancery Clerk. **Other phones:** Assessor-662-329-5700; Treasurer-662-329-5700; Appraiser-662-329-5701; Elections-662-329-5900; Vital Records-601-576-7960.

Madison County

Chancery Clerk, PO Box 404, Canton, MS 39046. **Phone**-601-859-1177; 8AM-5PM http://mcatax.com
Will search UCC records. Search per debtor- $5.00. UCC copy- $2.00 per page. UCC search does not include federal tax liens. Will not search real estate records. RE record copy- $.50 per page. Cert fee: $1.00 per cert. Payee: Madison County Clerk. **Online Access to Property Tax, Appraisal records:** Records from the county Assessor office are free at www.mcatax.com/mcasearch.asp. Click on "Search

The Database." Records include parcel number, address, legal description, value information, and tax district. **Other phones:** Assessor-601-859-1921; Elections-601-352-2049.

Marion County

Chancery Clerk, 250 Broad St, #2, Columbia, MS 39429. **Phone**-Chancery Clerk, R/E & UCC Recording- 601-736-2691; fax-601-441-0538; hours 8AM-5PM. Will search UCC records. Search per debtor- $5.00. UCC copy fee-$2.00 per page if staff copies. UCC copy fee- $.50 self serve per page. Will not search tax liens. RE record copy- $.50 per page. Cert fee: $1.00 per instrument. Payee: Chancery Clerk. **Other phones:** Assessor-601-736-8256; Elections-601-736-8246; Vital Records-601-736-2691.

Marshall County

Chancery Clerk, PO Box 219, Holly Springs, MS 38635. **Phone**-662-252-4431; fax-662-252-0004.
Will search UCC records. Search per debtor- $5.00. Will not search real estate records. Copy fee for any records is $.25 per page. **Online Access to Property Tax, Appraisal records:** property tax records are free at www.deltacomputersystems.com/MS/MS47/INDEX.html. **Other phones:** Assessor-662-252-3661; Elections-662-252-3434.

Monroe County

Chancery Clerk, PO Box 578, Aberdeen, MS 39730. **Phone**-Chancery Clerk, R/E & UCC Recording- 662-369-8143; fax-662-369-7928; hours 8AM-5PM
Will search UCC records. Search per debtor- $5.00. Copy fee is $2.00 per copy. Will not search real estate or tax lien records. RE record copy- $.50 per page. Cert fee: $1.00 per cert. Payee: Chancery Clerk. **Other phones:** Assessor-662-369-2033; Treasurer-662-369-8143; Elections-662-369-8695.

Montgomery County

Chancery Clerk, PO Box 71, Winona, MS 38967. **Phone**-662-283-2333; fax-662-283-2233; 8AM-5PM
Will search UCC records. Search per debtor- $5.00. UCC copy fee- $2.00 per page. Will not search real estate or tax lien records. Cert fee: $1.00. Payee: County Chancery Clerk. **Other phones:** Assessor-662-283-2112; Elections-662-283-4161.

Neshoba County

Chancery Clerk, 401 Beacon St, #107, Philadelphia, MS 39350. **Phone**-601-656-3581; hours 8AM-5PM
Will search UCC records. Search per debtor- $5.00. Will not do federal tax lien search. Will not search real estate records. Record copy- $2.00 per page. Cert fee: $1.00 per page. Payee: Neshoba County Clerk of the Chancery Court. **Online Access to Property Tax, Appraisal records:** Access to property data is free at http://deltacomputersystems.com/MS/MS50/plinkquerym.html. **Other phones:** Elections-601-656-4781.

Newton County

Chancery Clerk, PO Box 68, Decatur, MS 39327. **Phone**-601-635-2367; fax-601-635-3210.
Will search UCC records. Search per debtor- $5.00. UCC copy fee- $2.00 per sheet. Will not search real estate or tax lien records. RE record copy- $.50 per sheet. Cert fee: $1.00 per cert. Payee: Newton County Chancery Clerk. **Other phones:** Assessor-601-635-2367; Elections-601-635-2368.

Noxubee County

Chancery Clerk, PO Box 147, Macon, MS 39341. **Phone**-Chancery Clerk, R/E & UCC Recording- 662-726-4243; fax-662-726-2272; hours 8AM-5PM
Will search UCC records. Search per debtor- $5.00. Separate federal tax lien search- $5.00 per debtor.

Will not search real estate records. UCC copy- $2.00 per page. Cert fee: $.50 per page. Payee: Noxubee County Clerk of the Chancery Court. **Other phones:** Assessor-662-726-4744; Treasurer-662-726-4243; Appraiser-662-726-2772; Elections-662-726-5737; Vital Records-601-576-7981.

Oktibbeha County

Chancery Clerk, 101 E. Main, Courthouse, Starkville, MS 39759. **Phone**-Chancery Clerk, R/E & UCC Recording- 662-323-5834; fax-662-338-1064; hours 8AM-5PM
Will search UCC records. Search per debtor- $5.00. Will not search real estate or tax lien records. RE record copy- $.25 per page. UCC copy- $1.00 per page. Cert fee: $1.00 per cert. Payee: Oktibbeha County Clerk of the Chancery Court. **Other phones:** Assessor-662-323-1273; Appraiser-662-323-1273; Elections-662-323-1356.

Panola County (1st District)

Chancery Clerk, PO Box 130, Sardis, MS 38666. **Phone**-662-487-2070; fax-662-487-3595; hours 8AM-12;00-1-5PM
Will search UCC records. Search per debtor- $10.00. Search request using non-standard form (per name)- $13.00. Will not search real estate records. UCC copy- $0.0 per page. Cert fee: $1.00 per cert. Payee: Panola County Clerk. **Other phones:** Assessor-662-487-2093; Treasurer-662-487-6215; Elections-662-563-6210; Tax Collector-662-487-6215.

Panola County (2nd District)

Chancery Clerk, 151 Public Sq, Batesville, MS 38606. **Phone**-662-563-6205; fax-662-563-8233; hours 8AM-5PM. Will search UCC records. Search per debtor- $10.00. Will not search real estate records. UCC copy- $2.00 per page. Cert fee: $1.50. Payee: Panola County Chancery Clerk. **Other phones:** Assessor-662-563-6270; Treasurer-662-563-6215; Elections-662-563-6210.

Pearl River County

Chancery Clerk, PO Box 431, Poplarville, MS 39470. **Phone**-601-403-2317; fax-601-403-2318; hours 8AM-5PM. Will search UCC records. Will not search real estate or tax lien records. RE record copy- $.50 per page. UCC copy- $2.00 per page. Cert fee: $1.00 per cert. Payee: Pearl River County Clerk of the Chancery Court. **Online Access to Property Tax, Appraisal records:** Access to property data is free at www.deltacomputersystems.com/MS/MS55/INDEX.html. **Other phones:** Assessor-601-403-2215; Elections-601-795-4911.

Perry County

Chancery Clerk, PO Box 198, New Augusta, MS 39462. **Phone**-Chancery Clerk, R/E & UCC Recording- 601-964-8398; fax-601-964-8265.
Will search UCC records. Search per debtor- $5.00. Will not search real estate or tax lien records. Record copy- $.50 per page. Cert fee: $1.00 per doc. Payee: Vickie Walters-Clerk. **Other phones:** Assessor-601-964-3398; Appraiser-601-964-3400; Elections-601-964-8663.

Pike County

Chancery Clerk, PO Box 309, Magnolia, MS 39652. **Phone**-601-783-3362; fax-601-783-2001. www.co.pike.ms.us
Will search UCC records. Search per debtor- $5.00. Will not search real estate records. **Online Access to Real Estate, Grantor/Grantee, Deed records:** Access to the county Deeds & Records link is free at www.co.pike.ms.us/drlinkquery.html. Also property assessor records may soon be at www.co.pike.ms.us/tax.html. **Other phones:** Assessor-601-783-5511; Elections-601-783-2581.

Pontotoc County

Chancery Clerk, PO Box 209, Pontotoc, MS 38863. **Phone**-662-489-3900; fax-662-489-3940; hours 8AM-5PM. Will search UCC records. Search per debtor-$5.00. UCC search does not include federal tax liens. Will not search real estate records. UCC copy-$2.00 per page. Cert fee: $1.00 per page. Payee: Pontotoc County Clerk of the Chancery Court. **Other phones:** Assessor-662-489-3903; Treasurer-662-489-3904; Appraiser-662-489-3903; Elections-662-489-3908; Tax Collector-662-489-3904.

Prentiss County

Chancery Clerk, PO Box 477, Booneville, MS 38829. **Phone**-Chancery Clerk, R/E & UCC Recording- 662-728-8151; fax-662-728-2007; hours 8:00AM-5:00PM Will search UCC records. Search per debtor- $5.00. Will search federal tax liens. Will not search real estate records. RE record copy- $1.00 per page. Cert fee: $1.00 per doc. Payee: Chancery Clerk. **Other phones:** Assessor-662-728-5044; Treasurer-662-728-8151; Appraiser-662-728-4349; Elections-662-728-4611.

Quitman County

Chancery Clerk, Chestnut St, Courthouse, Marks, MS 38646. **Phone**-Chancery Clerk, R/E & UCC Recording- 662-326-2661; fax-662-326-8004.
Will search UCC records. Search per debtor- $5.00. Federal/state combined tax lien search- $5.00 per debtor. Will not search real estate records. UCC copy-$5.00 per page. Cert fee: $1.00 per cert. Payee: Chancery Clerk. **Other phones:** Assessor-662-326-8928; Treasurer-662-326-2661; Appraiser-662-326-8928; Elections-662-326-8003.

Rankin County

Chancery Clerk, PO Box 700, Brandon, MS 39043. **Phone**-601-825-1469;   fax-601-824-7116. www.rankincounty.org
Will search UCC records. Search per debtor- $5.00. Will not search real estate records. **Online Access to Real Estate, Tax Assessor, Voter Registration records:** Records on the county Land Roll database are free at www.rankincounty.org/ta/interact.html. Also, voter registration files can be downloaded at www.rankincounty.org/ci. **Other phones:** Assessor-601-825-1470; Treasurer-601-825-1366; Elections-601-825-1466.

Scott County

Chancery Clerk, PO Box 630, Forest, MS 39074. **Phone**-601-469-1922; fax-601-469-5180; hours 8AM-5PM. Will search UCC records. Search per debtor-$10.00. Will not search real estate records. RE record copy- $.50 per page. UCC copy- $2.00 per page. Cert fee: $1.00 per doc. **Other phones:** Elections-601-469-3601; Tax Collector-601-469-4051.

Sharkey County

Chancery Clerk, PO Box 218, Rolling Fork, MS 39159. **Phone**-662-873-2755; fax-662-873-6045; hours 8AM-5PM. Will search UCC records. Search per debtor-$10.00. Tax lien search- $10.00 per debtor. Will not search real estate records. Record copy- $.50 per page. Cert fee: $2.00 per doc. Payee: Sharkey County Clerk. **Other phones:** Elections-662-873-2755; Tax Collector-662-873-4317.

Simpson County

Chancery Clerk, PO Box 367, Mendenhall, MS 39114. **Phone**-601-847-2626, R/E Recording-601-847-2624; fax-601-847-7016; hours 8AM-5PM
Will search UCC records. Search per debtor- $10.00. Will not search real estate or tax lien records. UCC copy- $2.00 per page. Cert fee: $1.00. Payee:

Simpson County Chancery Clerk. **Other phones:** Assessor-601-847-1744; Elections-601-847-2474.

Smith County

Chancery Clerk, PO Box 39, Raleigh, MS 39153. **Phone**-601-782-9811; fax-601-782-4690; hours 8AM-5PM. Will search UCC records. Search per debtor-$5.00, then after search $2.00 per listing on search & $2.00 per copy for return. Will not search real estate or tax lien records. UCC copy- $2.00 pe listing. Cert fee: $1.00 per instrument. Payee: Chancery Clerk. **Other phones:** Assessor-601-782-9803; Treasurer-601-782-9811; Elections-601-782-4751.

Stone County

Chancery Clerk, PO Drawer 7, Wiggins, MS 39577. **Phone**-601-928-5266; hours 8-5PM
Will not search records. Cert fee: $1.00. Payee: Stone County Chancery Clerk. **Other phones:** Assessor-601-928-3121; Treasurer-601-928-5266; Elections-601-928-5246.

Sunflower County

Chancery Clerk, PO Box 988, Indianola, MS 38751-0988. **Phone**-Chancery Clerk, R/E & UCC Recording-662-887-4703; fax-662-887-7054.
Will search UCC records. Search per debtor- $5.00. Will not search real estate records. **Other phones:** Assessor-662-887-1454; Treasurer-662-887-4703; Appraiser-662-887-1454; Elections-662-887-1252; Vital Records-662-887-1252.

Tallahatchie County (1st District)

Chancery Clerk, PO Box 350, Charleston, MS 38921. **Phone**-Chancery Clerk, R/E & UCC Recording- 662-647-5551; fax-662-647-8490; hours 8AM-Noon,1-5PM. Will search UCC records. Search per debtor-$5.00. Will not do federal tax lien search. Will not search real estate records. UCC copy- $2.00 per page. Cert fee: None. Payee: Tallahatchie County Clerk of the Chancery Court. **Other phones:** Assessor-662-647-8922; Elections-662-647-8758.

Tallahatchie County (2nd District)

Chancery Clerk, PO Box 180, Sumner, MS 38957. **Phone**-Chancery Clerk, R/E & UCC Recording- 662-375-8731; fax-662-375-7252; hours 8AM-5PM
Will search UCC records. Search per debtor- $5.00. UCC search does not include federal tax liens. Will not search real estate records. RE record copy- $.50 per page. UCC copy- $2.00 per page. Cert fee: $1.00 per cert. Payee: Tallahatchie County Clerk of the Chancery Court. **Other phones:** Assessor-662-375-8386; Elections-662-375-8515.

Tate County

Chancery Clerk, 201 Ward St, PO Box 309, Senatobia, MS 38668. **Phone**-Chancery Clerk, R/E & UCC Recording- 662-562-5661; fax-662-560-6205; hours 8AM-5PM
Will search UCC records. Search per debtor- $5.00. Will search federal tax liens only. Will not search real estate records. RE record copy- $1.00 per page. UCC copy- $2.00 per page. Cert fee: $1.00 per doc. Payee: Tate-Co Chancery Clerk. **Other phones:** Assessor-662-562-6011; Elections-662-562-5211; Tax Collector-662-562-4404; Vital Records (Jackson, MS)-601-576-7960.

Tippah County

Chancery Clerk, PO Box 99, Ripley, MS 38663. **Phone**-662-837-7374; fax-662-837-7148.
Will search UCC records. Search per debtor- $5.00. Separate federal & state combined tax lien search-$7.00 Will not search real estate records. UCC copy-$2.00 per page. Cert fee: $1.00. Payee: Tippah

Chancery Clerk. **Other phones:** Assessor-662-837-9410; Elections-662-837-7370.

Tishomingo County

Chancery Clerk, 1008 Battleground Dr., Courthouse, Iuka, MS 38852. **Phone**-662-423-7010; fax-662-423-7005; hours 8-5PM
Will search UCC records. Search per debtor- $5.00. Will not search real estate records. UCC copy- $.25 per page. Cert fee: $1.00. Payee: Chancery Clerk. **Other phones:** Assessor-662-423-7048; Treasurer-662-423-7032; Elections-662-423-7026.

Tunica County

Chancery Clerk, PO Box 217, Tunica, MS 38676. **Phone**-662-363-2451; fax-662-357-5934; hours 8AM-Noon, 1-5PM
Will search UCC records. Search per debtor- $5.00. UCC search includes federal tax liens if requested. Real estate owner, mortgage, and property transfer searches available. RE record copy- $.50 per page. UCC copy- $2.00 per page. Cert fee: $1.00 per page. Payee: Tunica County Clerk of the Chancery Court. **Other phones:** Assessor-662-363-1266; Treasurer-662-363-1465; Elections-662-363-2842.

Union County

Chancery Clerk, PO Box 847, New Albany, MS 38652. **Phone**-Chancery Clerk, R/E & UCC Recording- 662-534-1900; fax-662-534-1907; hours 8AM-5PM
Will search UCC records. Search per debtor- $10.00. Tax lien search- $10.00 per debtor. Will not search real estate records. Record copy- $.50 per copy. **Other phones:** Assessor-662-534-1972; Treasurer-662-534-1973; Elections-662-534-1910; Tax Collector-662-534-1973.

Walthall County

Chancery Clerk, PO Box 351, Tylertown, MS 39667. **Phone**-Chancery Clerk, R/E & UCC Recording- 601-876-3553;   fax-601-876-6026. www.walthallcountychamber.org/
Will search UCC records. Search per debtor- $10.00. Separate federal & state combined tax lien search-$10.00 per debtor. Will not search real estate records. Copy fee is $2.00 per page. Cert fee: $1.00 per instrument. Payee: Chancery Clerk. **Other phones:** Assessor-601-876-4349; Appraiser-601-876-4349; Elections-601-876-5677.

Warren County

Chancery Clerk, PO Box 351, Vicksburg, MS 39181. **Phone**-Chancery Clerk, R/E & UCC Recording- 601-636-4415; fax-601-634-4815. www.co.warren.ms.us
Will search UCC records. Search per debtor- $5.00. Search request using non-standard form (per name)- $10.00. Will not search real estate records. **Online Access to Property Tax, Appraisal records:** Access is free at www.deltacomputersystems.com/MS/MS75/INDEX.html. **Other phones:** Assessor-601-638-6161; Treasurer-601-638-6181; Appraiser-601-638-6161; Elections-601-636-3961; Tax Collector-601-638-6181.

Washington County

Chancery Clerk, PO Box 309, Greenville, MS 38702-0309. **Phone**-Chancery Clerk, R/E & UCC Recording-662-332-1595; fax-662-334-2725; hours 8AM-5PM
Will search UCC records. Search per debtor- $5.00. UCC search includes federal tax liens if requested. Will not search real estate records. RE record copy-$.50 per page. UCC copy- $2.00 per page. Cert fee: $1.00 per page. Payee: Washington County Clerk of the Chancery Court. **Online Access to Property Tax, Appraisal records:** Access is free at www.deltacomputersystems.com/MS/MS76/INDEX.html. **Other phones:** Assessor-662-332-2651; Treasurer-

662-332-2922; Appraiser-662-332-2651; Elections-662-378-2747.

Wayne County

Chancery Clerk, 609 Azalea Dr., Wayne County Courthouse, Waynesboro, MS 39367. **Phone**-Chancery Clerk, R/E & UCC Recording- 601-735-2873; fax-601-735-6224; hours 8AM-5PM

Will search UCC records. Search per debtor- $10.00. Federal/state combined tax lien search- $10.00 Will not search real estate records. Copy fee is $2.00 per copy. Cert fee: $1.00. Payee: Wayne County Chancery Clerk. **Other phones:** Assessor-601-735-3381; Treasurer-601-735-2588; Appraiser-601-735-3381; Elections-662-258-1171.

Webster County

Chancery Clerk, PO Box 398, Walthall, MS 39771. **Phone**-662-258-4131; fax-662-258-6657; 8-5PM Will search UCC records. Search per debtor- $5.00. Will not search real estate records. UCC copy- $.50 per page. Cert fee: $1.00. Payee: Webster County Clerk. **Other phones:** Assessor-662-258-6446; Elections-662-258-6287.

Wilkinson County

Chancery Clerk, PO Box 516, Woodville, MS 39669. **Phone**-Chancery Clerk, R/E & UCC Recording- 601-888-4381; fax-601-888-6776; hours 8AM-5PM

Will search UCC records. Search per debtor- $5.00. Will not search real estate records. Copy fee is $2.00 per page. **Other phones:** Assessor-601-888-4562; Treasurer-601-888-4381; Appraiser-601-888-6146; Elections-601-888-6697; Vital Records-601-960-7960.

Winston County

Chancery Clerk, PO Drawer 69, Louisville, MS 39339. **Phone**-662-773-3631; fax-662-773-8814; 8AM-5PM Will search UCC records. Search per debtor- $5.00. Will not search real estate or tax lien records. UCC copy- $1.00 per page. Cert fee: None. Payee: Winston County Chancery Clerk. **Other phones:** Assessor-662-773-3694; Treasurer-662-773-3631; Elections-662-773-3581.

Yalobusha County (1st District)

Chancery Clerk, PO Box 260, Coffeeville, MS 38922. **Phone**-662-675-2716, R/E Recording-662-675-2091, UCC Recording-662-675-2091; fax-662-675-8004. Will search UCC records. Search per debtor- $5.00. Tax lien search- $15.00 per debtor. Will not search real estate records. UCC copy- $.50 per page. Cert fee: $1.00 per cert + $.50 per page. Payee: Amy F McMinn, Chancery Clerk. **Other phones:** Assessor-662-473-1235; Treasurer-662-675-2091; Appraiser-662-675-1235; Elections-662-675-1341.

Yalobusha County (2nd District)

Chancery Clerk, PO Box 664, Water Valley, MS 38965. **Phone**-Chancery Clerk, R/E & UCC Recording- 662-473-2091; fax-662-473-3622; hours 8AM-5PM. Will search UCC records. Search per debtor- $5.00. Tax lien search- $10.00 per debtor. Will not search real estate records. RE record copy- $.50 per copy. Copy fee is $2.00 per page. Cert fee: $1.00 per doc. Payee: Chancery Clerk. **Other phones:** Assessor-662-473-1235; Treasurer-662-473-2092; Appraiser-662-473-1235; Elections-662-473-1341; Vital Records-601-576-7960.

Yazoo County

Chancery Clerk, PO Box 68, Yazoo City, MS 39194. **Phone**-Chancery Clerk, R/E & UCC Recording- 662-746-2661; fax-662-746-3893; hours 8AM-5PM Will search UCC records. Search per debtor- $5.00 +$2.00 per copy. Will not search real estate records. RE record copy- $.50 per page. UCC copy- $2.00 per page. Cert fee: $1.00 per cert. Payee: Yazoo County Clerk of the Chancery Court. **Other phones:** Assessor-662-746-1583; Treasurer-662-746-2661; Appraiser-662-746-1583; Elections-662-746-1872.

Mississippi County Locator

You will usually be able to find the city name in the City/County Cross Reference below. In that case, it is a simple matter to determine the county from the cross reference. However, only the official US Postal Service city names are included in this index. We have also included a ZIP/City Cross Reference immediately following the City/County Cross Reference. If you know the ZIP Code but the city name does not appear in the City/County Cross Reference index, look up the ZIP Code in the ZIP/City Cross Reference, find the city name, then look up the city name in the City/County Cross Reference.

Mississippi City/County Cross Reference

ABBEVILLE Lafayette
ABERDEEN Monroe
ACKERMAN Choctaw
ALGOMA Pontotoc
ALLIGATOR (38720) Bolivar(67), Coahoma(32)
AMORY Monroe
ANGUILLA Sharkey
ARCOLA Washington
ARKABUTLA Tate
ARTESIA Lowndes
ASHLAND (38603) Benton(97), Tippah(2)
AVALON Carroll
AVON Washington
BAILEY (39320) Lauderdale(81), Kemper(18)
BALDWYN (38824) Prentiss(47), Lee(31), Itawamba(14), Union(4)
BANNER (38913) Calhoun(91), Lafayette(8)
BASSFIELD (39421) Jefferson Davis(77), Marion(22)
BATESVILLE Panola
BAY SAINT LOUIS Hancock
BAY SPRINGS (39422) Jasper(72), Smith(27)
BEAUMONT Perry
BECKER Monroe
BELDEN (38826) Lee(55), Pontotoc(44)
BELEN Quitman
BELLEFONTAINE Webster
BELMONT Tishomingo
BELZONI (39038) Humphreys(90), Holmes(7), Leflore(1)
BENOIT Bolivar
BENTON Yazoo
BENTONIA Yazoo
BEULAH Bolivar
BIG CREEK Calhoun
BIGBEE VALLEY Noxubee
BILOXI (39532) Harrison(71), Jackson(28)
BILOXI Harrison
BLUE MOUNTAIN (38610) Tippah(85), Benton(7), Union(6)
BLUE SPRINGS Union
BOGUE CHITTO Lincoln
BOLTON Hinds
BOONEVILLE (38829) Prentiss(94), Tippah(5)
BOYLE Bolivar
BRANDON Rankin
BRAXTON (39044) Simpson(77), Rankin(22)
BROOKHAVEN (39601) Lincoln(97), Franklin(2)
BROOKHAVEN Lincoln
BROOKLYN (39425) Forrest(55), Perry(44)
BROOKSVILLE Noxubee
BRUCE Calhoun
BUCKATUNNA Wayne
BUDE Franklin
BURNSVILLE (38833) Tishomingo(89), Prentiss(5), Alcorn(4)
BYHALIA (38611) Marshall(81), De Soto(18)
BYRAM Hinds
CALEDONIA (39740) Lowndes(90), Monroe(9)
CALHOUN CITY (38916) Calhoun(97), Webster(2)

CAMDEN Madison
CANTON Madison
CARLISLE Claiborne
CARRIERE Pearl River
CARSON Jefferson Davis
CARTHAGE (39051) Leake(94), Neshoba(3), Attala(1)
CARY Sharkey
CASCILLA (38920) Grenada(82), Tallahatchie(17)
CEDARBLUFF Clay
CENTREVILLE (39631) Wilkinson(77), Amite(22)
CHARLESTON Tallahatchie
CHATAWA Pike
CHATHAM Washington
CHUNKY (39323) Newton(79), Lauderdale(20)
CHURCH HILL Jefferson
CLARA Wayne
CLARKSDALE Coahoma
CLEVELAND (38732) Bolivar(96), Sunflower(3)
CLEVELAND Bolivar
CLINTON Hinds
COAHOMA (38617) Coahoma(91), Quitman(8)
COFFEEVILLE (38922) Yalobusha(86), Grenada(13)
COILA Carroll
COLDWATER Tate
COLLINS Covington
COLLINSVILLE (39325) Lauderdale(68), Neshoba(13), Kemper(9), Newton(8)
COLUMBUS Lowndes
COMO (38619) Panola(81), Lafayette(12), Tate(6)
CONEHATTA (39057) Newton(87), Scott(12)
CORINTH Alcorn
COURTLAND Panola
CRAWFORD (39743) Lowndes(74), Oktibbeha(21), Noxubee(4)
CRENSHAW (38621) Panola(75), Quitman(24)
CROSBY (39633) Wilkinson(75), Amite(24)
CROWDER Quitman
CRUGER (38924) Holmes(81), Leflore(11), Carroll(7)
CRYSTAL SPRINGS (39059) Copiah(96), Hinds(3)
D LO Simpson
DALEVILLE (39326) Lauderdale(71), Kemper(28)
DARLING Quitman
DE KALB (39328) Kemper(52), Neshoba(31), Noxubee(15)
DECATUR Newton
DELTA CITY Sharkey
DENNIS Tishomingo
DERMA Calhoun
DIAMONDHEAD Hancock
DIBERVILLE Harrison
DODDSVILLE (38736) Sunflower(57), Leflore(42)
DREW (38737) Sunflower(98), Tallahatchie(1)
DUBLIN Coahoma
DUCK HILL (38925) Montgomery(69), Grenada(30)

DUMAS (38625) Tippah(83), Union(16)
DUNCAN Bolivar
DUNDEE (38626) Tunica(73), Coahoma(26)
DURANT Holmes
EASTABUCHIE Jones
EBENEZER Holmes
ECRU (38841) Pontotoc(97), Union(2)
EDWARDS Hinds
ELLIOTT Grenada
ELLISVILLE Jones
ENID (38927) Tallahatchie(82), Panola(16)
ENTERPRISE (39330) Clarke(85), Lauderdale(8), Jasper(3), Newton(2)
ESCATAWPA Jackson
ETHEL Attala
ETTA Union
EUPORA (39744) Webster(91), Choctaw(6), Calhoun(2)
FALCON Quitman
FALKNER (38629) Tippah(77), Benton(22)
FARRELL Coahoma
FAYETTE Jefferson
FERNWOOD Pike
FITLER Issaquena
FLORA (39071) Madison(96), Hinds(3)
FLORENCE Rankin
FLOWOOD Rankin
FOREST (39074) Scott(90), Smith(9)
FORKVILLE Scott
FOXWORTH (39483) Marion(97), Walthall(2)
FRENCH CAMP (39745) Choctaw(46), Montgomery(38), Attala(15)
FRIARS POINT Coahoma
FULTON Itawamba
GALLMAN Copiah
GATTMAN Monroe
GAUTIER Jackson
GEORGETOWN Copiah
GLEN (38846) Alcorn(84), Tishomingo(15)
GLEN ALLAN Washington
GLENDORA Tallahatchie
GLOSTER Amite
GOLDEN (38847) Itawamba(88), Tishomingo(11)
GOODMAN (39079) Holmes(92), Attala(4), Madison(3)
GORE SPRINGS (38929) Grenada(89), Webster(5), Calhoun(5)
GRACE Issaquena
GREENVILLE Bolivar
GREENVILLE Washington
GREENWOOD Leflore
GREENWOOD SPRINGS (38848) Monroe(98), Itawamba(1)
GRENADA Grenada
GULFPORT Harrison
GUNNISON Bolivar
GUNTOWN (38849) Lee(89), Union(8), Itawamba(1)
HAMILTON Monroe
HARPERVILLE Scott
HARRISTON Jefferson
HARRISVILLE Simpson
HATTIESBURG (39402) Lamar(66), Forrest(33)
HATTIESBURG Forrest
HAZLEHURST Copiah

HEIDELBERG (39439) Jasper(66), Jones(21), Clarke(9), Wayne(3)
HERMANVILLE (39086) Claiborne(78), Copiah(21)
HERNANDO De Soto
HICKORY (39332) Newton(89), Jasper(10)
HICKORY FLAT (38633) Benton(90), Union(9)
HILLSBORO Scott
HOLCOMB (38940) Grenada(93), Carroll(3), Tallahatchie(2)
HOLLANDALE (38748) Washington(90), Sharkey(9)
HOLLY BLUFF Yazoo
HOLLY RIDGE Sunflower
HOLLY SPRINGS (38635) Marshall(89), Benton(6), Tate(3)
HOLLY SPRINGS Marshall
HORN LAKE De Soto
HOULKA (38850) Chickasaw(56), Pontotoc(29), Calhoun(13)
HOUSTON Chickasaw
HURLEY Jackson
INDEPENDENCE Tate
INDIANOLA Sunflower
INVERNESS (38753) Sunflower(93), Humphreys(6)
ISOLA (38754) Humphreys(85), Sunflower(14)
ITTA BENA Leflore
IUKA Tishomingo
JACKSON (39213) Hinds(98), Madison(1)
JACKSON Hinds
JACKSON Rankin
JAYESS (39641) Lawrence(52), Walthall(37), Pike(7), Lincoln(1)
JONESTOWN Coahoma
KILMICHAEL (39747) Montgomery(97), Attala(2)
KILN Hancock
KOKOMO (39643) Marion(85), Walthall(14)
KOSCIUSKO (39090) Attala(84), Leake(15)
LAKE (39092) Scott(71), Newton(25), Smith(3)
LAKE CORMORANT De Soto
LAKESHORE Hancock
LAMAR (38642) Benton(58), Marshall(41)
LAMBERT (38643) Quitman(97), Tallahatchie(2)
LAUDERDALE (39335) Lauderdale(93), Kemper(6)
LAUREL (39443) Jones(86), Jasper(8), Wayne(4)
LAUREL Jones
LAWRENCE Newton
LEAKESVILLE Greene
LELAND Washington
LENA (39094) Leake(53), Scott(38), Rankin(7)
LEXINGTON (39095) Holmes(98), Yazoo(1)
LIBERTY Amite
LITTLE ROCK (39337) Newton(95), Neshoba(3)
LONG BEACH Harrison
LORMAN (39096) Jefferson(64), Claiborne(35)
LOUIN (39338) Jasper(51), Smith(48)
LOUISE Humphreys
LOUISVILLE Winston

LUCEDALE (39452) George(83), Jackson(16)
LUDLOW Scott
LULA Coahoma
LUMBERTON (39455) Lamar(44), Pearl River(42), Stone(11)
LYON Coahoma
MABEN (39750) Webster(77), Oktibbeha(15), Clay(6)
MACON (39341) Noxubee(88), Winston(11)
MADDEN Leake
MAGEE Simpson
MAGNOLIA (39652) Pike(87), Amite(12)
MANTACHIE (38855) Itawamba(98), Lee(1)
MANTEE (39751) Clay(63), Webster(25), Chickasaw(9), Calhoun(2)
MARIETTA (38856) Itawamba(70), Prentiss(29)
MARION Lauderdale
MARKS (38646) Quitman(98), Panola(1)
MATHISTON (39752) Webster(95), Choctaw(4)
MATTSON Coahoma
MAYERSVILLE Issaquena
MAYHEW Lowndes
MC ADAMS Attala
MC CALL CREEK (39647) Franklin(96), Lincoln(2), Wilkinson(1)
MC CARLEY Carroll
MC COMB Pike
MC CONDY Chickasaw
MC COOL (39108) Winston(40), Attala(37), Choctaw(21)
MC HENRY Stone
MC LAIN (39456) Greene(68), Perry(30)
MC NEILL Pearl River
MEADVILLE (39653) Franklin(97), Jefferson(1)
MENDENHALL (39114) Simpson(93), Rankin(6)
MERIDIAN (39301) Lauderdale(89), Clarke(10)
MERIDIAN Lauderdale
MERIGOLD (38759) Sunflower(85), Bolivar(14)
METCALFE Washington
MICHIGAN CITY Benton
MIDNIGHT Humphreys
MINERAL WELLS De Soto
MINTER CITY Leflore
MISSISSIPPI STATE Oktibbeha
MIZE Smith
MONEY Leflore
MONTICELLO (39654) Lawrence(98), Lincoln(1)
MONTPELIER Clay
MOOREVILLE Lee
MOORHEAD Sunflower
MORGAN CITY Leflore
MORGANTOWN Marion
MORTON (39117) Scott(77), Smith(19), Rankin(2)
MOSELLE Jones
MOSS Jasper
MOSS POINT Jackson
MOUND BAYOU Bolivar
MOUNT OLIVE (39119) Covington(50), Simpson(25), Smith(14), Jefferson Davis(8)
MOUNT PLEASANT Marshall
MYRTLE (38650) Union(91), Benton(7)
NATCHEZ (39120) Adams(90), Jefferson(9)
NATCHEZ Adams
NEELY Greene
NESBIT De Soto
NETTLETON (38858) Itawamba(42), Monroe(31), Lee(26)
NEW ALBANY Union
NEW AUGUSTA Perry

NEW SITE Prentiss
NEWHEBRON (39140) Lawrence(91), Jefferson Davis(8)
NEWTON Newton
NICHOLSON Pearl River
NITTA YUMA Sharkey
NORTH CARROLLTON Carroll
NOXAPATER Winston
OAK VALE (39656) Jefferson Davis(80), Lawrence(19)
OAKLAND (38948) Yalobusha(89), Tallahatchie(10)
OCEAN SPRINGS Jackson
OKOLONA (38860) Chickasaw(82), Monroe(8), Lee(7), Pontotoc(1)
OLIVE BRANCH De Soto
OSYKA (39657) Pike(70), Amite(26), Walthall(3)
OVETT (39464) Jones(91), Perry(8)
OXFORD Lafayette
PACE Bolivar
PACHUTA (39347) Jasper(68), Clarke(31)
PANTHER BURN Sharkey
PARCHMAN Sunflower
PARIS Lafayette
PASCAGOULA Jackson
PASS CHRISTIAN (39571) Harrison(97), Hancock(2)
PATTISON (39144) Claiborne(80), Jefferson(14), Copiah(5)
PAULDING Jasper
PEARL Rankin
PEARLINGTON Hancock
PELAHATCHIE (39145) Rankin(95), Scott(4)
PERKINSTON (39573) Stone(59), Hancock(28), George(5), Pearl River(3)
PETAL (39465) Forrest(89), Perry(10)
PHEBA (39755) Clay(91), Oktibbeha(8)
PHILADELPHIA Neshoba
PHILIPP (38950) Tallahatchie(71), Leflore(28)
PICAYUNE Pearl River
PICKENS (39146) Yazoo(66), Madison(31), Holmes(2)
PINEY WOODS Rankin
PINOLA Simpson
PITTSBORO Calhoun
PLANTERSVILLE Lee
PLEASANT GROVE Panola
POCAHONTAS Hinds
PONTOTOC Pontotoc
POPE Panola
POPLARVILLE (39470) Pearl River(98), Hancock(1)
PORT GIBSON Claiborne
PORTERVILLE Kemper
POTTS CAMP (38659) Marshall(82), Benton(17)
PRAIRIE (39756) Clay(75), Monroe(20), Chickasaw(4)
PRAIRIE POINT Noxubee
PRENTISS Jefferson Davis
PRESTON (39354) Kemper(61), Winston(32), Neshoba(4), Noxubee(1)
PUCKETT Rankin
PULASKI (39152) Smith(66), Scott(33)
PURVIS Lamar
QUITMAN Clarke
RALEIGH Smith
RANDOLPH (38864) Pontotoc(95), Calhoun(4)
RAYMOND Hinds
RED BANKS Marshall
REDWOOD Warren
REFORM Choctaw
RENA LARA Coahoma
RICH Coahoma
RICHTON (39476) Perry(94), Wayne(5)
RIDGELAND Madison
RIENZI Alcorn
RIPLEY Tippah

ROBINSONVILLE Tunica
ROLLING FORK Sharkey
ROME Sunflower
ROSE HILL Jasper
ROSEDALE Bolivar
ROXIE (39661) Franklin(89), Adams(8), Jefferson(1)
RULEVILLE Sunflower
RUTH (39662) Lincoln(63), Pike(29), Lawrence(7)
SALLIS Attala
SALTILLO Lee
SANATORIUM Simpson
SANDERSVILLE Jones
SANDHILL Rankin
SANDY HOOK (39478) Marion(56), Walthall(43)
SARAH (38665) Tate(79), Panola(19), Tunica(1)
SARDIS Panola
SATARTIA (39162) Warren(95), Yazoo(4)
SAUCIER Harrison
SCHLATER Leflore
SCOBEY (38953) Yalobusha(52), Grenada(32), Tallahatchie(14)
SCOOBA Kemper
SCOTT Bolivar
SEBASTOPOL Scott
SEMINARY Covington
SENATOBIA Tate
SHANNON (38868) Lee(84), Pontotoc(10), Monroe(3), Chickasaw(1)
SHARON Madison
SHAW (38773) Bolivar(75), Sunflower(24)
SHELBY Bolivar
SHERARD Coahoma
SHERMAN Pontotoc
SHUBUTA (39360) Clarke(78), Wayne(21)
SHUQUALAK Noxubee
SIBLEY Adams
SIDON (38954) Leflore(93), Carroll(5), Holmes(1)
SILVER CITY Humphreys
SILVER CREEK (39663) Lawrence(97), Jefferson Davis(2)
SKENE Bolivar
SLATE SPRING Calhoun
SLEDGE (38670) Quitman(79), Tunica(19)
SMITHDALE (39664) Franklin(59), Amite(33), Lincoln(7)
SMITHVILLE (38870) Monroe(90), Itawamba(9)
SONTAG (39665) Lawrence(80), Lincoln(19)
SOSO (39480) Jones(97), Smith(2)
SOUTHAVEN De Soto
STAR Rankin
STARKVILLE Oktibbeha
STATE LINE (39362) Greene(64), Wayne(35)
STEENS Lowndes
STENNIS SPACE CENTER Hancock
STEWART (39767) Montgomery(41), Webster(37), Choctaw(21)
STONEVILLE Washington
STONEWALL Clarke
STRINGER Jasper
STURGIS (39769) Oktibbeha(79), Winston(19), Choctaw(1)
SUMMIT (39666) Pike(72), Amite(17), Lincoln(9)
SUMNER Tallahatchie
SUMRALL (39482) Lamar(94), Jefferson Davis(3), Marion(2)
SUNFLOWER Sunflower
SWAN LAKE Tallahatchie
SWIFTTOWN Leflore
TAYLOR Lafayette
TAYLORSVILLE (39168) Smith(83), Jones(14), Covington(2)
TCHULA Holmes
TERRY Hinds

THAXTON (38871) Pontotoc(87), Lafayette(10), Union(1)
THOMASTOWN Leake
THORNTON Holmes
TIE PLANT Grenada
TILLATOBA (38961) Yalobusha(83), Tallahatchie(15), Grenada(1)
TINSLEY Yazoo
TIPLERSVILLE Tippah
TIPPO Tallahatchie
TISHOMINGO (38873) Tishomingo(91), Prentiss(8)
TOCCOPOLA Lafayette
TOOMSUBA Lauderdale
TOUGALOO (39174) Hinds(91), Madison(8)
TREBLOC Chickasaw
TREMONT Itawamba
TRIBBETT Washington
TULA Lafayette
TUNICA Tunica
TUPELO (38801) Lee(93), Pontotoc(6)
TUPELO (38804) Lee(98), Itawamba(1)
TUPELO Lee
TUTWILER (38963) Coahoma(79), Tallahatchie(18), Sunflower(2)
TYLERTOWN (39667) Walthall(91), Pike(5), Marion(2)
UNION (39365) Neshoba(70), Newton(28), Leake(1)
UNION CHURCH (39668) Jefferson(81), Lincoln(10), Copiah(4), Franklin(3)
UNIVERSITY Lafayette
UTICA (39175) Hinds(82), Copiah(8), Claiborne(8)
VAIDEN (39176) Carroll(65), Attala(29), Montgomery(4)
VALLEY PARK Issaquena
VAN VLEET Chickasaw
VANCE (38964) Quitman(87), Tallahatchie(12)
VARDAMAN (38878) Calhoun(95), Chickasaw(4)
VAUGHAN Yazoo
VERONA Lee
VICKSBURG Warren
VICTORIA Marshall
VOSSBURG (39366) Clarke(63), Jasper(36)
WALLS De Soto
WALNUT (38683) Tippah(79), Alcorn(15), Benton(5)
WALNUT GROVE (39189) Leake(76), Scott(23)
WALTHALL Webster
WASHINGTON Adams
WATER VALLEY (38965) Yalobusha(92), Panola(4), Lafayette(2)
WATERFORD (38685) Marshall(92), Lafayette(7)
WAVELAND Hancock
WAYNESBORO (39367) Wayne(97), Clarke(2)
WAYSIDE Washington
WEBB Tallahatchie
WEIR Choctaw
WESSON (39191) Copiah(58), Lincoln(40)
WEST (39192) Holmes(81), Attala(17), Carroll(1)
WEST POINT (39773) Clay(97), Monroe(2)
WHEELER Prentiss
WHITFIELD Rankin
WIGGINS (39577) Stone(84), Forrest(8), Perry(6)
WINONA (38967) Montgomery(95), Carroll(4)
WINSTONVILLE Bolivar
WINTERVILLE Washington
WOODLAND (39776) Chickasaw(77), Clay(22)
WOODVILLE Wilkinson
YAZOO CITY Yazoo

Mississippi ZIP/City Cross Reference

38601-38601 ABBEVILLE	38740-38740 DUNCAN	38880-38880 WHEELER	39080-39080 HARPERVILLE
38602-38602 ARKABUTLA	38744-38744 GLEN ALLAN	38901-38902 GRENADA	39081-39081 HARRISTON
38603-38603 ASHLAND	38745-38745 GRACE	38912-38912 AVALON	39082-39082 HARRISVILLE
38606-38606 BATESVILLE	38746-38746 GUNNISON	38913-38913 BANNER	39083-39083 HAZLEHURST
38609-38609 BELEN	38748-38748 HOLLANDALE	38914-38914 BIG CREEK	39086-39086 HERMANVILLE
38610-38610 BLUE MOUNTAIN	38749-38749 HOLLY RIDGE	38915-38915 BRUCE	39087-39087 HILLSBORO
38611-38611 BYHALIA	38751-38751 INDIANOLA	38916-38916 CALHOUN CITY	39088-39088 HOLLY BLUFF
38614-38614 CLARKSDALE	38753-38753 INVERNESS	38917-38917 CARROLLTON	39090-39090 KOSCIUSKO
38617-38617 COAHOMA	38754-38754 ISOLA	38920-38920 CASCILLA	39092-39092 LAKE
38618-38618 COLDWATER	38755-38755 GREENVILLE	38921-38921 CHARLESTON	39094-39094 LENA
38619-38619 COMO	38756-38756 LELAND	38922-38922 COFFEEVILLE	39095-39095 LEXINGTON
38620-38620 COURTLAND	38758-38758 MATTSON	38923-38923 COILA	39096-39096 LORMAN
38621-38621 CRENSHAW	38759-38759 MERIGOLD	38924-38924 CRUGER	39097-39097 LOUISE
38622-38622 CROWDER	38760-38760 METCALFE	38925-38925 DUCK HILL	39098-39098 LUDLOW
38623-38623 DARLING	38761-38761 MOORHEAD	38926-38926 ELLIOTT	39107-39107 MC ADAMS
38625-38625 DUMAS	38762-38762 MOUND BAYOU	38927-38927 ENID	39108-39108 MC COOL
38626-38626 DUNDEE	38763-38763 NITTA YUMA	38928-38928 GLENDORA	39109-39109 MADDEN
38627-38627 ETTA	38764-38764 PACE	38929-38929 GORE SPRINGS	39110-39110 MADISON
38628-38628 FALCON	38765-38765 PANTHER BURN	38930-38935 GREENWOOD	39111-39111 MAGEE
38629-38629 FALKNER	38767-38767 RENA LARA	38940-38940 HOLCOMB	39112-39112 SANATORIUM
38630-38630 FARRELL	38768-38768 ROME	38941-38941 ITTA BENA	39113-39113 MAYERSVILLE
38631-38631 FRIARS POINT	38769-38769 ROSEDALE	38943-38943 MC CARLEY	39114-39114 MENDENHALL
38632-38632 HERNANDO	38771-38771 RULEVILLE	38944-38944 MINTER CITY	39115-39115 MIDNIGHT
38633-38633 HICKORY FLAT	38772-38772 SCOTT	38945-38945 MONEY	39116-39116 MIZE
38634-38635 HOLLY SPRINGS	38773-38773 SHAW	38946-38946 MORGAN CITY	39117-39117 MORTON
38637-38637 HORN LAKE	38774-38774 SHELBY	38947-38947 NORTH CARROLLTON	39119-39119 MOUNT OLIVE
38638-38638 INDEPENDENCE	38775-38775 SKENE	38948-38948 OAKLAND	39120-39122 NATCHEZ
38639-38639 JONESTOWN	38776-38776 STONEVILLE	38949-38949 PARIS	39130-39130 MADISON
38641-38641 LAKE CORMORANT	38778-38778 SUNFLOWER	38950-38950 PHILIPP	39140-39140 NEWHEBRON
38642-38642 LAMAR	38779-38779 TRIBBETT	38951-38951 PITTSBORO	39144-39144 PATTISON
38643-38643 LAMBERT	38780-38780 WAYSIDE	38952-38952 SCHLATER	39145-39145 PELAHATCHIE
38644-38644 LULA	38781-38781 WINSTONVILLE	38953-38953 SCOBEY	39146-39146 PICKENS
38645-38645 LYON	38782-38782 WINTERVILLE	38954-38954 SIDON	39148-39148 PINEY WOODS
38646-38646 MARKS	38801-38804 TUPELO	38955-38955 SLATE SPRING	39149-39149 PINOLA
38647-38647 MICHIGAN CITY	38820-38820 ALGOMA	38957-38957 SUMNER	39150-39150 PORT GIBSON
38648-38648 MINERAL WELLS	38821-38821 AMORY	38958-38958 SWAN LAKE	39151-39151 PUCKETT
38649-38649 MOUNT PLEASANT	38824-38824 BALDWYN	38959-38959 SWIFTOWN	39152-39152 PULASKI
38650-38650 MYRTLE	38825-38825 BECKER	38960-38960 TIE PLANT	39153-39153 RALEIGH
38651-38651 NESBIT	38826-38826 BELDEN	38961-38961 TILLATOBA	39154-39154 RAYMOND
38652-38652 NEW ALBANY	38827-38827 BELMONT	38962-38962 TIPPO	39156-39156 REDWOOD
38654-38654 OLIVE BRANCH	38828-38828 BLUE SPRINGS	38963-38963 TUTWILER	39157-39158 RIDGELAND
38655-38655 OXFORD	38829-38829 BOONEVILLE	38964-38964 VANCE	39159-39159 ROLLING FORK
38657-38657 PLEASANT GROVE	38833-38833 BURNSVILLE	38965-38965 WATER VALLEY	39160-39160 SALLIS
38658-38658 POPE	38834-38835 CORINTH	38966-38966 WEBB	39161-39161 SANDHILL
38659-38659 POTTS CAMP	38838-38838 DENNIS	38967-38967 WINONA	39162-39162 SATARTIA
38661-38661 RED BANKS	38839-38839 DERMA	39038-39038 BELZONI	39163-39163 SHARON
38662-38662 RICH	38841-38841 ECRU	39039-39039 BENTON	39165-39165 SIBLEY
38663-38663 RIPLEY	38843-38843 FULTON	39040-39040 BENTONIA	39166-39166 SILVER CITY
38664-38664 ROBINSONVILLE	38844-38844 GATTMAN	39041-39041 BOLTON	39167-39167 STAR
38665-38665 SARAH	38846-38846 GLEN	39042-39043 BRANDON	39168-39168 TAYLORSVILLE
38666-38666 SARDIS	38847-38847 GOLDEN	39044-39044 BRAXTON	39169-39169 TCHULA
38668-38668 SENATOBIA	38848-38848 GREENWOOD SPRINGS	39045-39045 CAMDEN	39170-39170 TERRY
38669-38669 SHERARD	38849-38849 GUNTOWN	39046-39046 CANTON	39171-39171 THOMASTOWN
38670-38670 SLEDGE	38850-38850 HOULKA	39047-39047 BRANDON	39172-39172 THORNTON
38671-38672 SOUTHAVEN	38851-38851 HOUSTON	39049-39049 CARLISLE	39173-39173 TINSLEY
38673-38673 TAYLOR	38852-38852 IUKA	39051-39051 CARTHAGE	39174-39174 TOUGALOO
38674-38674 TIPLERSVILLE	38854-38854 MC CONDY	39054-39054 CARY	39175-39175 UTICA
38675-38675 TULA	38855-38855 MANTACHIE	39055-39055 CHURCH HILL	39176-39176 VAIDEN
38676-38676 TUNICA	38856-38856 MARIETTA	39056-39056 CLINTON	39177-39177 VALLEY PARK
38677-38677 UNIVERSITY	38857-38857 MOOREVILLE	39057-39057 CONEHATTA	39179-39179 VAUGHAN
38679-38679 VICTORIA	38858-38858 NETTLETON	39058-39058 CLINTON	39180-39183 VICKSBURG
38680-38680 WALLS	38859-38859 NEW SITE	39059-39059 CRYSTAL SPRINGS	39189-39189 WALNUT GROVE
38683-38683 WALNUT	38860-38860 OKOLONA	39060-39060 CLINTON	39190-39190 WASHINGTON
38685-38685 WATERFORD	38862-38862 PLANTERSVILLE	39061-39061 DELTA CITY	39191-39191 WESSON
38686-38686 WALLS	38863-38863 PONTOTOC	39062-39062 D LO	39192-39192 WEST
38701-38704 GREENVILLE	38864-38864 RANDOLPH	39063-39063 DURANT	39193-39193 WHITFIELD
38720-38720 ALLIGATOR	38865-38865 RIENZI	39064-39064 EBENEZER	39194-39194 YAZOO CITY
38721-38721 ANGUILLA	38866-38866 SALTILLO	39066-39066 EDWARDS	39200-39208 JACKSON
38722-38722 ARCOLA	38868-38868 SHANNON	39067-39067 ETHEL	39208-39208 PEARL
38723-38723 AVON	38869-38869 SHERMAN	39069-39069 FAYETTE	39209-39232 JACKSON
38725-38725 BENOIT	38870-38870 SMITHVILLE	39070-39070 FITLER	39232-39232 FLOWOOD
38726-38726 BEULAH	38871-38871 THAXTON	39071-39071 FLORA	39235-39272 JACKSON
38730-38730 BOYLE	38873-38873 TISHOMINGO	39072-39072 POCAHONTAS	39272-39272 BYRAM
38731-38731 CHATHAM	38874-38874 TOCCOPOLA	39073-39073 FLORENCE	39282-39298 JACKSON
38732-38733 CLEVELAND	38875-38875 TREBLOC	39074-39074 FOREST	39301-39309 MERIDIAN
38736-38736 DODDSVILLE	38876-38876 TREMONT	39076-39076 FORKVILLE	39320-39320 BAILEY
38737-38737 DREW	38877-38877 VAN VLEET	39077-39077 GALLMAN	39322-39322 BUCKATUNNA
38738-38738 PARCHMAN	38878-38878 VARDAMAN	39078-39078 GEORGETOWN	39323-39323 CHUNKY
38739-38739 DUBLIN	38879-38879 VERONA	39079-39079 GOODMAN	39324-39324 CLARA

39325-39325 COLLINSVILLE	39427-39427 CARSON	39552-39552 ESCATAWPA	39665-39665 SONTAG
39326-39326 DALEVILLE	39428-39428 COLLINS	39553-39553 GAUTIER	39666-39666 SUMMIT
39327-39327 DECATUR	39429-39429 COLUMBIA	39555-39555 HURLEY	39667-39667 TYLERTOWN
39328-39328 DE KALB	39436-39436 EASTABUCHIE	39556-39556 KILN	39668-39668 UNION CHURCH
39330-39330 ENTERPRISE	39437-39437 ELLISVILLE	39558-39558 LAKESHORE	39669-39669 WOODVILLE
39332-39332 HICKORY	39439-39439 HEIDELBERG	39560-39560 LONG BEACH	39701-39710 COLUMBUS
39335-39335 LAUDERDALE	39440-39443 LAUREL	39561-39561 MC HENRY	39730-39730 ABERDEEN
39336-39336 LAWRENCE	39451-39451 LEAKESVILLE	39562-39563 MOSS POINT	39735-39735 ACKERMAN
39337-39337 LITTLE ROCK	39452-39452 LUCEDALE	39564-39566 OCEAN SPRINGS	39736-39736 ARTESIA
39338-39338 LOUIN	39455-39455 LUMBERTON	39567-39569 PASCAGOULA	39737-39737 BELLEFONTAINE
39339-39339 LOUISVILLE	39456-39456 MC LAIN	39571-39571 PASS CHRISTIAN	39738-39738 BIGBEE VALLEY
39341-39341 MACON	39457-39457 MC NEILL	39572-39572 PEARLINGTON	39739-39739 BROOKSVILLE
39342-39342 MARION	39459-39459 MOSELLE	39573-39573 PERKINSTON	39740-39740 CALEDONIA
39345-39345 NEWTON	39460-39460 MOSS	39574-39574 SAUCIER	39741-39741 CEDARBLUFF
39346-39346 NOXAPATER	39461-39461 NEELY	39576-39576 WAVELAND	39743-39743 CRAWFORD
39347-39347 PACHUTA	39462-39462 NEW AUGUSTA	39577-39577 WIGGINS	39744-39744 EUPORA
39348-39348 PAULDING	39463-39463 NICHOLSON	39581-39595 PASCAGOULA	39745-39745 FRENCH CAMP
39350-39350 PHILADELPHIA	39464-39464 OVETT	39601-39603 BROOKHAVEN	39746-39746 HAMILTON
39352-39352 PORTERVILLE	39465-39465 PETAL	39629-39629 BOGUE CHITTO	39747-39747 KILMICHAEL
39353-39353 PRAIRIE POINT	39466-39466 PICAYUNE	39630-39630 BUDE	39750-39750 MABEN
39354-39354 PRESTON	39470-39470 POPLARVILLE	39631-39631 CENTREVILLE	39751-39751 MANTEE
39355-39355 QUITMAN	39474-39474 PRENTISS	39632-39632 CHATAWA	39752-39752 MATHISTON
39356-39356 ROSE HILL	39475-39475 PURVIS	39633-39633 CROSBY	39753-39753 MAYHEW
39358-39358 SCOOBA	39476-39476 RICHTON	39635-39635 FERNWOOD	39754-39754 MONTPELIER
39359-39359 SEBASTOPOL	39477-39477 SANDERSVILLE	39638-39638 GLOSTER	39755-39755 PHEBA
39360-39360 SHUBUTA	39478-39478 SANDY HOOK	39641-39641 JAYESS	39756-39756 PRAIRIE
39361-39361 SHUQUALAK	39479-39479 SEMINARY	39643-39643 KOKOMO	39757-39757 REFORM
39362-39362 STATE LINE	39480-39480 SOSO	39645-39645 LIBERTY	39759-39760 STARKVILLE
39363-39363 STONEWALL	39481-39481 STRINGER	39647-39647 MC CALL CREEK	39762-39762 MISSISSIPPI STATE
39364-39364 TOOMSUBA	39482-39482 SUMRALL	39648-39649 MC COMB	39766-39766 STEENS
39365-39365 UNION	39483-39483 FOXWORTH	39652-39652 MAGNOLIA	39767-39767 STEWART
39366-39366 VOSSBURG	39484-39484 MORGANTOWN	39653-39653 MEADVILLE	39769-39769 STURGIS
39367-39367 WAYNESBORO	39500-39507 GULFPORT	39654-39654 MONTICELLO	39771-39771 WALTHALL
39400-39407 HATTIESBURG	39520-39522 BAY SAINT LOUIS	39656-39656 OAK VALE	39772-39772 WEIR
39421-39421 BASSFIELD	39522-39522 STENNIS SPACE CENTER	39657-39657 OSYKA	39773-39773 WEST POINT
39422-39422 BAY SPRINGS	39525-39525 DIAMONDHEAD	39661-39661 ROXIE	39776-39776 WOODLAND
39423-39423 BEAUMONT	39529-39529 BAY SAINT LOUIS	39662-39662 RUTH	
39425-39425 BROOKLYN	39530-39535 BILOXI	39663-39663 SILVER CREEK	
39426-39426 CARRIERE	39540-39540 DIBERVILLE	39664-39664 SMITHDALE	

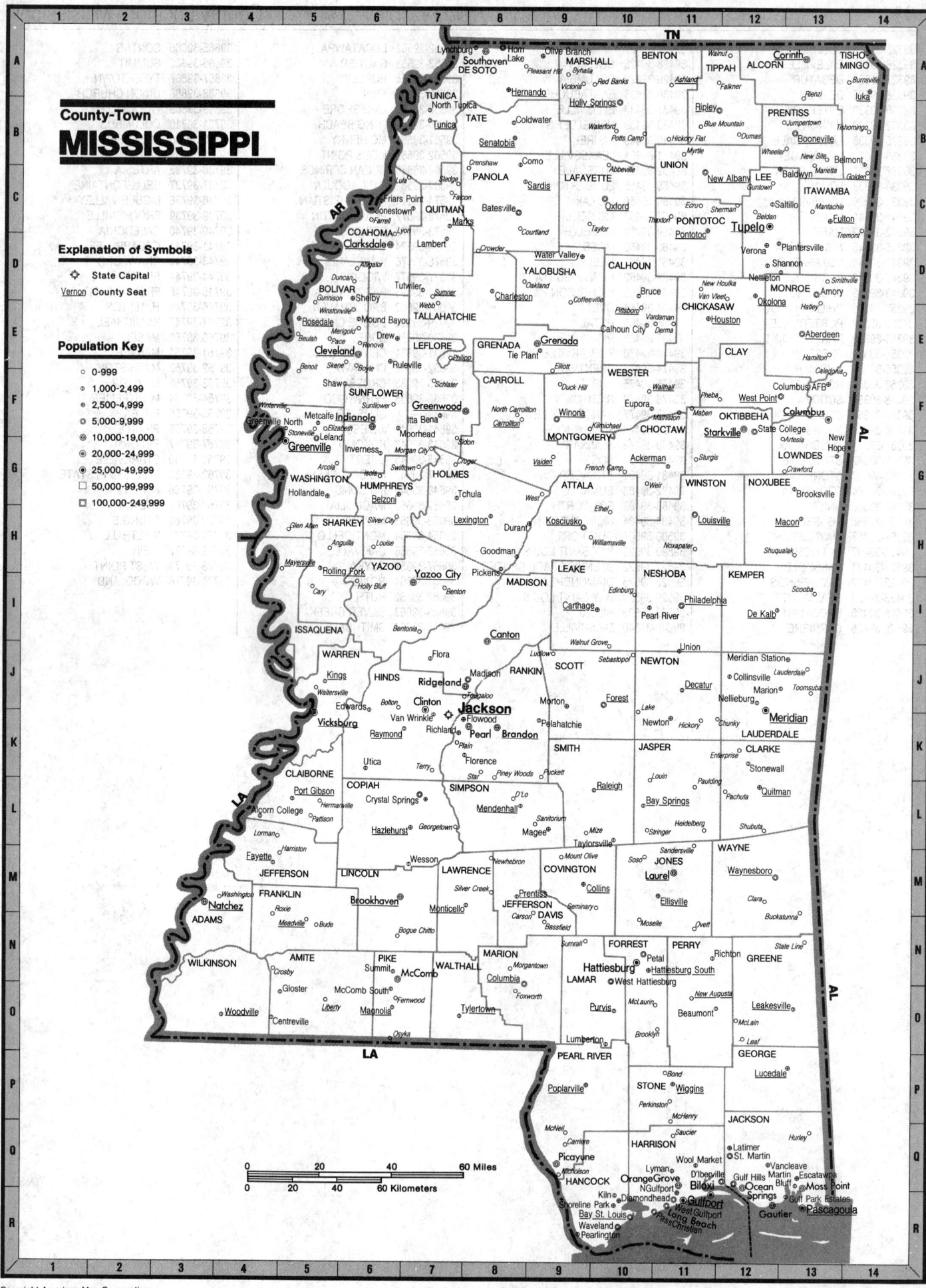

County-Town
MISSISSIPPI

Explanation of Symbols

◇ State Capital

Vernon County Seat

Population Key

- ∘ 0-999
- ⊕ 1,000-2,499
- ⊕ 2,500-4,999
- ⊚ 5,000-9,999
- ⊛ 10,000-19,000
- ⊛ 20,000-24,999
- ● 25,000-49,999
- □ 50,000-99,999
- ▢ 100,000-249,999

COUNTIES

(82 Counties)

Name of County	Population	Location on Map
ADAMS	35,356	N-3
ALCORN	31,722	A-12
AMITE	13,328	N-5
ATTALA	18,481	G-9
BENTON	8,046	A-10
BOLIVAR	41,875	D-5
CALHOUN	14,908	D-10
CARROLL	9,237	F-8
CHICKASAW	18,085	E-11
CHOCTAW	9,071	F-10
CLAIBORNE	11,370	K-5
CLARKE	17,313	K-12
CLAY	21,120	E-12
COAHOMA	31,665	C-6
COPIAH	27,592	L-6
COVINGTON	16,527	M-9
DESOTO	67,910	A-7
FORREST	68,314	N-10
FRANKLIN	8,377	M-4
GEORGE	16,673	O-12
GREENE	10,220	N-12
GRENADA	21,555	E-8
HANCOCK	31,760	Q-9
HARRISON	165,365	Q-10
HINDS	254,441	J-6
HOLMES	21,604	G-7
HUMPHREYS	12,134	G-6
ISSAQUENA	1,909	I-5
ITAWAMBA	20,017	C-13
JACKSON	115,243	P-12
JASPER	17,114	K-10
JEFFERSON	8,653	M-4
JEFFERSON DAVIS	14,051	M-8
JONES	62,031	M-11
KEMPER	10,356	H-12
LAFAYETTE	31,826	C-9
LAMAR	30,424	N-9
LAUDERDALE	75,555	K-12
LAWRENCE	12,458	M-7
LEAKE	18,436	H-9
LEE	65,581	C-12
LEFLORE	37,341	E-7
LINCOLN	30,278	M-6
LOWNDES	59,308	G-12
MADISON	53,794	I-8
MARION	25,544	N-8
MARSHALL	30,361	A-9
MONROE	36,582	D-12
MONTGOMERY	12,388	F-9
NESHOBA	24,800	H-10
NEWTON	20,291	J-10
NOXUBEE	12,604	G-12
OKTIBBEHA	38,375	F-12
PANOLA	29,996	C-8
PEARL RIVER	38,714	P-9
PERRY	10,865	N-11
PIKE	36,882	N-6
PONTOTOC	22,237	C-11
PRENTISS	23,278	B-12
QUITMAN	10,490	C-7
RANKIN	87,161	J-8
SCOTT	24,137	J-9
SHARKEY	7,066	H-5
SIMPSON	23,953	L-7
SMITH	14,798	K-9
STONE	10,750	P-10
SUNFLOWER	32,867	F-6
TALLAHATCHIE	15,210	E-7
TATE	21,432	B-8
TIPPAH	19,523	A-11
TISHOMINGO	17,683	A-13
TUNICA	8,164	A-7
UNION	22,085	B-11
WALTHALL	14,352	N-7
WARREN	47,880	J-5
WASHINGTON	67,935	G-5
WAYNE	19,517	L-12
WEBSTER	10,222	E-10
WILKINSON	9,678	N-3
WINSTON	19,433	G-11
YALOBUSHA	12,033	D-8
YAZOO	25,506	H-6
TOTAL	**2,573,216**	

CITIES AND TOWNS

Note: The first name is that of the city or town, second, that of the county in which it is located, then the population and location on the map.

Aberdeen, Monroe, 6,837		E-13
Ackerman, Choctaw, 1,573		G-11
Alcorn College, Claiborne		L-4
Amory, Monroe, 7,093		D-13
Ashland, Benton, 490		A-11
Baldwyn, Lee/Prentiss, 3,204		C-12
Batesville, Panola, 6,403		C-8
Bay Springs, Jasper, 1,729		L-10
Bay St. Louis, Hancock, 8,063		R-10
Beaumont, Perry, 1,054		O-11
Belmont, Tishomingo, 1,554		B-14
Belzoni, Humphreys, 2,536		G-6
Biloxi, Harrison, 46,391		R-11
Booneville, Prentiss, 7,955		B-13
Brandon, Rankin, 11,077		K-8
Brookhaven, Lincoln, 10,243		M-6
Brooksville, Noxubee, 1,098		G-13
Bruce, Calhoun, 2,127		D-10
Calhoun City, Calhoun, 1,838		E-10
Canton, Madison, 10,062		I-8
Carrollton, Carroll, 221		F-8
Carthage, Leake, 3,819		I-10
Centreville, Amite/Wilkinson, 1,771		O-4
Charleston, Tallahatchie, 2,328		D-8
Clarksdale, Coahoma, 19,717		D-6
Cleveland, Bolivar, 15,384		E-6
Clinton, Hinds, 21,847		J-7
Coldwater, Tate, 1,502		B-8
Collins, Covington, 2,541		M-9
• Collinsville, Lauderdale, 1,364		J-10
Columbia, Marion, 6,815		N-8
Columbus, Lowndes, 23,799		F-13
• Columbus AFB, Lowndes, 2,890		F-13
Como, Panola, 1,387		B-8
Corinth, Alcorn, 11,820		A-13
Crystal Springs, Copiah, 5,643		L-7
De Kalb, Kemper, 1,073		I-12
Decatur, Newton, 1,248		J-11
• Diamondhead, Hancock, 2,661		R-10
D'Iberville, Harrison, 6,566		Q-12
Drew, Sunflower, 2,349		E-6
Durant, Holmes, 2,838		H-8
Edwards, Hinds, 1,279		J-6
Ellisville, Jones, 3,634		M-11
• Escatawpa, Jackson, 3,902		Q-13
Eupora, Webster, 2,145		F-10
Fayette, Jefferson, 1,853		M-4
Flora, Madison, 1,482		J-7
Florence, Rankin, 1,831		K-8
Flowood, Rankin, 2,860		K-6
Forest, Scott, 5,060		J-10
Friars Point, Coahoma, 1,334		C-6
Fulton, Itawamba, 3,387		C-13
Gautier, Jackson, 10,088		R-11
Gloster, Amite, 1,323		O-5
Goodman, Holmes, 1,256		H-8
Greenville, Washington, 45,226		G-5
Greenville North, Washington		F-5
Greenwood, Leflore, 18,906		F-7
Grenada, Grenada, 10,864		E-8
• Gulf Hills, Jackson, 5,004		Q-12
• Gulf Park Estates, Jackson, 2,314		R-11
Gulfport, Harrison, 40,775		R-11
Hattiesburg, Forrest/Lamar, 41,882		N-10
Hattiesburg South, Forrest		N-10
Hazlehurst, Copiah, 4,221		L-7
Hernando, DeSoto, 3,125		A-8
Hollandale, Washington, 3,576		G-5
Holly Springs, Marshall, 7,261		A-8
Horn Lake, DeSoto, 9,069		A-7

Houston, Chickasaw, 3,903		E-11
Indianola, Sunflower, 11,809		F-6
Inverness, Sunflower, 1,174		G-6
Itta Bena, Leflore, 2,377		F-6
Iuka, Tishomingo, 3,122		A-14
Jackson, Hinds/Madison/Rankin, 196,637		J-7
Jonestown, Coahoma, 1,467		C-7
• Kiln, Hancock, 1,262		R-8
Kings, Warren		J-5
Kosciusko, Attala, 6,986		H-9
Lambert, Quitman, 1,131		D-7
• Latimer, Jackson, 3,222		Q-10
Laurel, Jones, 18,827		M-11
Leakesville, Greene, 1,129		O-13
Leland, Washington, 6,366		F-5
Lexington, Holmes, 2,227		H-8
Liberty, Amite, 624		O-5
Long Beach, Harrison, 15,804		R-9
Louisville, Winston, 7,169		H-11
Lucedale, George, 2,592		P-13
Lumberton, Lamar/Pearl River, 2,121		O-10
• Lyman, Harrison, 1,117		Q-9
• Lynchburg, DeSoto, 2,071		A-6
Macon, Noxubee, 2,256		H-13
Madison, Madison, 7,471		J-8
Magee, Simpson, 3,607		L-9
Magnolia, Pike, 2,245		O-6
Marion, Lauderdale, 1,359		J-11
Marks, Quitman, 1,758		C-7
• Martin Bluff, Jackson, 1,928		R-11
Mayersville, Issaquena, 329		H-5
McComb, Pike, 11,591		N-6
McComb South, Pike		O-6
Meadville, Franklin, 453		N-5
Mendenhall, Simpson, 2,463		L-8
Meridian, Lauderdale, 41,036		J-12
• Meridian Station, Lauderdale, 2,503		J-13
Metcalfe, Washington, 1,092		F-3
Monticello, Lawrence, 1,755		M-8
Moorhead, Sunflower, 2,417		F-6
Morton, Scott, 3,212		J-9
Moss Point, Jackson, 17,837		Q-13
Mound Bayou, Bolivar, 2,222		E-6
Natchez, Adams, 19,460		M-3
• Nellieburg, Lauderdale, 1,208		J-12
Nettleton, Lee/Monroe, 2,462		D-12
New Albany, Union, 6,775		C-11
New Augusta, Perry, 668		O-11
• New Hope, Lowndes, 1,663		G-12
Newton, Newton, 3,701		K-11
North Gulfport, Harrison, 4,966		Q-11
• North Tunica, Tunica, 1,314		B-7
Ocean Springs, Jackson, 14,658		Q-12
Okolona, Chickasaw, 3,267		D-12
Olive Branch, DeSoto, 3,567		A-9
• Orange Grove, Harrison, 15,676		Q-11
Oxford, Lafayette, 9,984		C-10
Pascagoula, Jackson, 25,899		R-13
Pass Christian, Harrison, 5,557		R-11
Pearl, Rankin, 19,588		K-8
• Pearl River, Neshoba, 2,136		I-9
• Pearlington, Hancock, 1,603		R-8
Pelahatchie, Rankin, 1,553		K-9
Petal, Forrest, 7,883		N-10
Philadelphia, Neshoba, 6,758		I-11
Picayune, Pearl River, 10,633		Q-9
Pickens, Holmes, 1,285		H-8
Pittsboro, Calhoun, 277		E-10
Plantersville, Lee, 1,046		D-11
Pontotoc, Pontotoc, 4,570		C-11
Poplarville, Pearl River, 2,561		P-9
Port Gibson, Claiborne, 1,810		L-5
Prentiss, Jefferson Davis, 1,487		M-8
Purvis, Lamar, 2,140		O-10
Quitman, Clarke, 2,736		L-12

Raleigh, Smith, 1,291		L-8
Raymond, Hinds, 2,275		K-7
Richland, Rankin, 4,014		K-7
Richton, Perry, 1,034		N-11
Ridgeland, Madison, 11,714		J-6
Ripley, Tippah, 5,371		B-11
Rolling Fork, Sharkey, 2,444		H-5
Rosedale, Bolivar, 2,595		E-5
Ruleville, Sunflower, 3,245		E-6
• Saint Martin, Jackson, 6,349		Q-10
Saltillo, Lee, 1,782		C-12
Sardis, Panola, 2,128		C-8
Senatobia, Tate, 4,772		B-8
Shannon, Lee, 1,419		D-11
Shaw, Bolivar/Sunflower, 2,349		F-6
Shelby, Bolivar, 2,806		D-6
• Shoreline Park, Hancock, 2,775		R-8
Southaven, DeSoto, 17,949		A-8
Starkville, Oktibbeha, 18,458		F-12
State College, Oktibbeha		F-12
Stonewall, Clarke, 1,148		K-12
Summit, Pike, 1,566		N-6
Taylorsville, Smith, 1,412		L-10
Tchula, Holmes, 2,186		G-7
Tie Plant, Grenada		E-9
Tunica, Tunica, 1,175		B-7
Tupelo, Lee, 30,685		C-12
Tutwiler, Tallahatchie, 1,391		D-7
Tylertown, Walthall, 1,938		O-7
Union, Neshoba/Newton, 1,875		J-11
Utica, Hinds, 1,033		K-4
Van Wrinkle, Hinds		K-7
• Vancleave, Jackson, 3,214		Q-12
Verona, Lee, 2,893		D-12
Vicksburg, Warren, 20,908		K-4
Walthall, Webster, 167		F-10
Water Valley, Yalobusha, 3,610		D-9
Waveland, Hancock, 5,369		R-10
Waynesboro, Wayne, 5,143		M-12
Wesson, Copiah, 1,510		M-7
West Gulfport, Harrison		R-11
• West Hattiesburg, Lamar, 5,450		O-8
West Point, Clay, 8,489		F-12
Wiggins, Stone, 3,185		P-11
Winona, Montgomery, 5,705		F-9
Woodville, Wilkinson, 1,393		O-4
• Wool Market, Harrison, 1,166		Q-10
Yazoo City, Yazoo, 12,427		I-7

Explanation of symbols: • – Census Designated Place (CDP)

Missouri

General Help Numbers:

Governor's Office
PO Box 720
Jefferson City, MO 65102-0720
www.gov.state.mo.us

573-751-3222
Fax 573-751-1495
8AM-5PM

Attorney General's Office
PO Box 899
Jefferson City, MO 65102
www.ago.state.mo.us

573-751-3321
Fax 573-751-0774
8AM-5PM

Legislative Records
Legislative Library
117A State Capitol
Jefferson City, MO 65101
www.moga.state.mo.us

573-751-4633

8:30AM-4:30PM

State Archives
Archives Division
PO Box 1747
Jefferson City, MO 65101
www.sos.state.mo.us/archives/

573-751-3280
Fax 573-526-7333
8-5 M-F
(till 9PM on Th);
8:30-3:30 SA

State Specifics:

Capital:	Jefferson City
	Cole County
Time Zone:	CST
Number of Counties:	114
Population:	5,704,484
Web Site:	www.state.mo.us

State Agencies

Criminal Records

Missouri State Highway Patrol, Criminal Record & Identification Division, 1510 E Elm St, Jefferson City, MO 65102; 573-526-6153, 573-751-9382 (Fax), 8AM-5PM.

www.mshp.dps.missouri.gov

Indexing & Storage: Records are available from 1970 on. It takes 5 weeks before new records are available for inquiry. Records are indexed on inhouse computer (84%) including images. Records maintained indefinitely.

Searching: Youth service providers must have signature of the subject. Include the following in your request-full name, date of birth, sex, race, Social Security Number. Fingerprints are an option. A request form can be downloaded from the website. Records are 100% fingerprint-supported.

Access by: mail, in person.

Fee & Payment: The search fee is $5.00 per individual for a name search. Searches by fingerprint cost $14.00 each. Add $24.00 if the fingerprint search to include an FBI fingerprint check. Fee payee: State of Missouri Criminal Record System Fund Prepayment required. Personal checks accepted. No credit cards accepted.

Mail search: Turnaround time: 3-4 weeks. No SASE is required.

In person search: Turnaround time is while you wait for one search only.

Other access: Bulk/multiple requests can be submitted on diskette; prior arrangement and agency approval required. Responses are printed out, checked for accuracy and returned; however they cannot be returned on diskette. Alias or maiden names require separate search.

Statewide Court Records

Court Administrator, 2112 Industrial Drive - PO Box 104480, Jefferson City, MO 65110; 573-751-4377, 573-751-5540 (Fax), 8AM-5PM.

www.osca.state.mo.us

Access by: online.

Online search: Casenet, a limited but growing online system, is available at http://casenet.osca.state.mo.us/casenet. You are able to inquire on case records including docket entries, parties, judgments, and charges in public court. The system includes 75 counties (with more projected) as well as the Eastern, Western, and Southern Appellate Courts, the Supreme Court, and Fine Collection Center. Cases can be searched by case number, filing date, or litigant name.

Sexual Offender Registry

Missouri State Highway Patrol, Sexual Offender Registry, PO Box 9500, Jefferson City, MO 65102-0568 (Courier: 1510 E Elm St, Jefferson City, MO 65102); 573-526-6153, 573-751-9382 (Fax), 8AM-5PM.

www.mshp.dps.missouri.gov/

Note: The Revised Statutes of Missouri, Sections 589.400 to 589.425 and 43.650, RSMo., mandate that the Missouri State Highway Patrol shall maintain a sex offender database and a web site on the Internet that is accessible to the public.

Registry information is available from the sheriff in the county where the offender resides. The county list may be released to any person upon request.

Access by: online.

Online search: The name index can be searched at the website, by name, county or ZIP Code. The web page also gives links lists to the county sheriffs that have online access.

Incarceration Records

Missouri Department of Corrections, Probation and Parole, 1511 Christy Dr., Jefferson City, MO 65101; 573-751-8488, 573-751-8501 (Fax), 8AM-5PM.

www.corrections.state.mo.us/

Indexing & Storage: Records are available on current and former inmates. Will release limited information on former inmates. It takes about 30 days before new records are available for inquiry.

Searching: Include the following in your request-full name, DOB; SSN helpful. Location, conviction and sentencing information are released.

Access by: mail, phone, fax, online.

Fee & Payment: There is no fee.

Mail search: Turnaround time: 4-6 days. Record requests must include reason for request.

Phone search: Searching available by phone.

Fax search: Same criteria as mail search.

Online search: No internet searching is available from this agency. However, you may email a single request to mocorxns@doc.mo.gov. Spell the full name correctly. An email response will be provided to you, usually within 24 hours of receipt during regular business hours. This only provides general search information and policy information. Department does not provide search information to companies conducting employee background checks. Although this agency provides no direct internet access, a private company offers free web access at www.vinelink.com/index.jsp.

Corporation Fictitious Name, Limited Partnership, Limited Liability Company Assumed Name, Trademarks, Servicemarks

Secretary of State, Corporation Services, PO Box 778, Jefferson City, MO 65102 (Courier: 600 W Main, Jefferson City, MO 65101); 573-751-4153, 866-223-6535, 573-751-5841 (Fax), 8AM-5PM.

www.sos.mo.gov

Note: Trademarks and servicemarks are handled by the Commissions Division within Sec. of State and can be reached at 573-751-4756.

Indexing & Storage: Records are available from the 1800s. New records are available for inquiry immediately. Records are indexed on microfilm, inhouse computer, hard copy.

Searching: Include the following in your request-full name of business, specific records that you need copies of. In addition to the articles of incorporation, corporation records include the following information: Annual Reports, Officers, Directors, DBAs, Prior (merged) names, Inactive and Reserved names.

Access by: mail, phone, fax, in person, online.

Fee & Payment: The fee for an abstract is $10.00, including a Good Standing. An uncertified copy of a record is $.50 per page, a certified copy of a record is $10.00 certification fee plus $.50 per page. A trademark or servicemark search is $5.00. Fee payee: Secretary of State. Prepayment required. They will invoice. Personal checks accepted. Credit cards accepted: MasterCard, Visa.

Mail search: Turnaround time: 2 to 3 days. No SASE is required.

Phone search: Status, registered agent, type of entity, and historical information is given over the phone at no charge.

Fax search: Same criteria as mail searching. Records are returned by mail.

In person search: Results are returned by mail.

Online search: Search free online at www.sos.state.mo.us/BusinessEntity/soskb/csearch.asp. The corporate name, the agent name or the charter number is required to search. The site will indicate the currency of the data. Many business entity type searches are available.

Uniform Commercial Code

UCC Division, Attn: Records, PO Box 1159, Jefferson City, MO 65102 (Courier: 600 W Main St, Rm 302, Jefferson City, MO 65101); 866-223-6565, 8AM-5PM.

www.sos.state.mo.us/ucc/

Indexing & Storage: Records are available from 1965. Records are on microfiche from 7-1-80 to present.

Searching: Use search request form UCC-11. Please note that all tax liens are filed at the county level. Include the following in your request-debtor name.

Access by: mail, phone, in person, online.

Fee & Payment: A UCC-11 search is $27.00 plus $1.00 per page for copies. UCC-3's are not listed on the summary; order copies to review them. Fee payee: Secretary of State. Prepayment required. Personal checks accepted. Credit cards accepted: MasterCard, Visa.

Mail search: Turnaround time: 2 weeks.

Phone search: General information is available without charge.

In person search: You may request information in person.

Online search: Free searching for debtor names is available on the Internet at www.sos.state.mo.us/ucc/soskb/SearchStandardRA9.asp. Images are available for a fee.

Other access: The agency will release information for bulk purchase, call for procedures and pricing.

Federal Tax Liens, State Tax Liens
Records not maintained by a state level agency.

Note: All tax liens are filed at the county level.

Sales Tax Registrations
Access to Records is Restricted

Department of Revenue, Business Tax, PO Box 3300, Jefferson City, MO 65105-3300; 573-751-5860, 573-751-2836, 573-522-1722 (Fax), 7:45AM-4:45PM.

www.dor.mo.gov/tax/

Note: This agency will neither confirm nor supply any information. Confidential information is only released to owners or corporate officers registered with the Department. They suggest requesters to check at the city level.

Birth Certificates

Department of Health, Bureau of Vital Records, PO Box 570, Jefferson City, MO 65102-0570 (Courier: 930 Wildwood, Jefferson City, MO 65109); 573-751-6387, 573-751-6400 (Message Number), 866-550-1851 (Orders), 573-526-3846 (Fax), 8AM-5PM.

www.health.state.mo.us

Indexing & Storage: Records are available from 1910 on. Older records archived or see online below. New records are available for inquiry immediately. Records are indexed on microfiche, inhouse computer.

Searching: Records are only released to person of record or legal representative of immediate family member. Must have a signed release from person of record or immediate family member for investigative purposes. Include the following in your request-full name, names of parents, mother's maiden name, date of birth, place of birth, relationship to person of record, reason for information request.

Access by: mail, phone, fax, in person, online.

Fee & Payment: Search fee is $10.00 per 5 years searched. Fee is charged regardless if record is found. Emergency requests using a credit card pay an additional $9.95 fee. Fee payee: Missouri Department of Health. Prepayment required. Personal checks accepted. Credit cards accepted: MasterCard, Visa, AmEx, Discover.

Mail search: Turnaround time: 2 to 3 weeks. A SASE is required.

Phone search: See expedited service.

Fax search: See expedited service.

In person search: Turnaround time is usually 10 minutes.

Online search: Orders may be placed online at www.vitalchek.com. Records prior to 1910 are available by county at www.sos.mo.gov/archives/resources/birthdeath/.

Expedited service: Expedited service is available for online, fax and phone searches via www.vitalchek.com. Turnaround time: 1-3 days. Add $9.95 fee for use of credit and additional fee for express delivery.

Death Records

Department of Health, Bureau of Vital Records, PO Box 570, Jefferson City, MO 65102-0570 (Courier: 930 Wildwood, Jefferson City, MO 65109); 573-751-6370, 573-751-6400 (Message Number), 866-550-1851 (Orders), 573-526-3846 (Fax), 8AM-5PM.

www.health.state.mo.us

Indexing & Storage: Records are available from 1910 on. Older records archived or see online below. New records are available for inquiry immediately. Records are indexed on microfiche, inhouse computer.

Searching: Records are only released to legal representative of person of record or immediate family member. Must have a signed release from immediate family member for investigative purposes. Include the following in your request-full name, date of death, place of death, relationship to person of record, reason for information request.

Access by: mail, phone, in person, online.

Fee & Payment: The $10.00 search fee is for 5 years searched. Use of credit card is additional $9.95. Fee payee: Missouri Department of Health. Prepayment required. Personal checks accepted.

Mail search: Turnaround time: 2 to 3 weeks. A SASE is required.

Phone search: See expedited service.

In person search: Turnaround time is usually 10 minutes.

Online search: Orders accepted online only at www.vitalchek.com. Records prior to 1910 can be searched at www.sos.mo.gov/archives/resources/birthdeath/.

Expedited service: Expedited service is available for online, fax and phone searches via www.vitalchek.com. Turnaround time: 1-3 days. Add $9.95 fee for use of credit and additional fee for express delivery.

Marriage Certificates, Divorce Records

Records not maintained by a state level agency.

Note: Actual marriage and divorce records are found at county of issue. For marriage, contact the Record of Deeds in the county where license was issued. For divorce decrees, visit the Clerk of the county where issued.

Workers' Compensation Records

Labor & Industrial Relations Department, Workers Compensation Division, PO Box 58, Jefferson City, MO 65102-0058 (Courier: 3315 W Truman Blvd, Jefferson City, MO 65101); 573-751-4231 x5, 573-751-2012 (Fax), 8AM-4:30PM.

www.dolir.mo.gov/

Indexing & Storage: Records are available from 1945. Records are computerized since 1994. It takes 1 day before new records are available for inquiry. Records are indexed on inhouse computer.

Searching: Report of injury and medical records released only with a release form. All other records are open. Include the following in your request-claimant name, Social Security Number, date of accident.

Access by: mail, fax, in person.

Fee & Payment: The search fee is $5.00. Fee payee: Workers Compensation Division. Personal checks accepted. No credit cards accepted.

Mail search: Turnaround time: 1 to 2 days. No SASE is required.

Fax search: The initial fax must include a written request for the search. Turnaround time is 1 to 2 days.

In person search: To search in person, you must be party to the case in question or possess written authorization.

Driver Records

Department of Revenue, Driver and Vehicle Services Bureau, PO Box 200, Jefferson City, MO 65105-0200 (Courier: Harry S Truman Bldg, 301 W High St, Room 470, Jefferson City, MO 65105); 573-751-4300, 573-526-7367 (Fax), 7:45AM-4:45PM.

www.dor.state.mo.us/mvdl/drivers

Note: Copies of tickets are available from the same address. Requests must be in writing, include the name, DOB, license number, and specific violation information. The cost is $3.75 per ticket.

Indexing & Storage: Records are available for 3 yrs for moving violations, 5 yrs for suspensions, permanent for alcohol-related, disq's and mand. ins. 0-point violations are not shown on non-CDL record. Accidents are not shown on driving record unless suspension/revocation action taken.

Searching: The agency complies with DPPA. Frequent requesters should establish an account for electronic access. Casual requesters can receive records without personal information, unless written consent of subject is provided. Include the following in your request-fullname, DOB and DL or SSN.

Access by: mail, phone, fax, in person, online.

Fee & Payment: The fee is $1.25 per record for walk-in or mail-in requests, $4.00 if certified. The fee for online retrieval is $1.25 per record plus network line charges. Fee payee: Department of Revenue. Prepayment required. Cashier's check and money orders preferred. Personal checks accepted. No credit cards accepted.

Mail search: Turnaround time: 2 days. A SASE is requested.

Phone search: Pre-approved accounts may request records for 24 hour mail or fax return. To establish an account, call 573-751-4300.

Fax search: Pre-approved accounts may order records by phone and receive by fax for an additional $.50 per record.

In person search: You may request information in person.

Online search: Online access costs $1.25 per record. Online inquiries can be put in Missouri's "mailbox" any time of the day. These inquiries are then picked up at 2 AM the following morning, and the resulting MVR's are sent back to each customer's "mailbox" approx. 2 hours later.

Other access: The tape-to-tape process has been replaced by the online system. The entire license file can be purchased, with updates. Call 573-751-5579 for more information.

Vehicle Ownership, Vehicle Identification, Vessel Ownership, Vessel Registration

Department of Revenue, Driver and Vehicle Services Bureau, PO Box 100, Jefferson City, MO 65105-0100 (Courier: Harry S Truman Bldg, 301 W High St, Jefferson City, MO 65105); 573-526-3669, 573-751-4509, 573-751-7060 (Fax), 7:45AM-4:45PM.

www.dor.state.mo.us/mvdl/default.htm

Note: Lien information shows on the title records.

Indexing & Storage: Records are available from 1968 to present. Records are indexed on microfiche from 1968 to present, and microfilm from 1981 to present. Records include boats and mobile homes. All motorized boats 12 ft or longer must be titled and registered. It takes minutes before new records are available for inquiry. Records are normally destroyed after microfilmed.

Searching: Ownership and vehicle information is available with no restrictions to access, if request is of a legal nature. Casual requesters must have consent of subject to obtain records with personal information, other this data is blocked. Include the following in your request-year, make, VIN. Current registration/title records are on computer. Records are purged from the computer files after 2 years of no activity. However, the records will remain on microfiche.

Access by: mail, phone, fax, in person.

Fee & Payment: The fee for a record search is $4.50 and a complete title history is $8.00. There is an additional $3.00 for certification. Fee payee: Department of Revenue. Prepayment required. Pre-approved accounts may be billed. Personal checks accepted. No credit cards accepted.

Mail search: Turnaround time: 2 to 4 weeks.

Phone search: This agency offers a phone-in service for title verification and lien holder information ONLY for dealers and lienholders.

The fee is $1.50 per record. For more information, call 573-526-3669 or 751-4509.

Fax search: To have results returned by fax costs an additional $.50 per page.

In person search: You may request records in person.

Other access: Missouri has an extensive range of records and information available on magnetic tape, labels or paper. Besides offering license, vehicle, title, dealer, and marine records, specific public report data is also available.

Expedited service: The cost is the same as stated above. Depending on the type of request, turnaround time could be the same or next day.

Accident Reports

Missouri Highway Patrol, Traffic Division, PO Box 568, Jefferson City, MO 65102-0568 (Courier: 1510 E Elm St, Jefferson City, MO 65101); 573-526-6113, 573-751-9921 (Fax), 8AM-5PM.

www.mshp.dps.mo.gov

Indexing & Storage: Records are available from 1997 to present on computer. Records are indexed on an in-house computer. Records are on a document imaging system or microfilm from 1941. It takes 14 to 30 days before new records are available for inquiry. Records are normally destroyed after being microfilmed.

Searching: Record requests must be in writing. Generally, these records are open to the public. Include the following in your request-full name, date of accident, location of accident, relationship of requester to the subject. There is no telephone searching, but you can call to determine if an accident is on file.

Access by: mail, in person.

Fee & Payment: There is a $10.00 fee for a standard 4-page report on record dated 1997 or later. The fee is $37.00 for mircofilmed archived records 1996 and prior. Personal checks are accepted.

Mail search: Turnaround time: 3 to 4 working days. A SASE is requested.

In person search: Turnaround time is immediate.

Voter Registration

Access to Records is Restricted

Secretary of State, Division of Elections, PO Box 1767, Jefferson City, MO 65102; 573-751-2301, 573-526-3242 (Fax), 8AM-5PM.

www.sos.mo.gov/section4.asp

Note: For individual look-ups, the agency recommends searching at the county level by the County Clerks.

GED Certificates

GED Office, PO Box 480, Jefferson City, MO 65102; 573-751-3504, 8AM-4:30PM.

http://dese.mo.gov/divcareered/

Indexing & Storage: Records are available from 1960 to present. It takes 2 to 3 weeks before new records are available for inquiry.

Searching: Include the following in your request-signed release, date of birth, Social Security Number. The year and location of the test are very helpful and should also be included in the request.

Access by: mail, in person.

Fee & Payment: The fee is $2.00 for either a verification or a transcript. Fee payee: Treasurer, State of Missouri. Prepayment required. Personal checks accepted.

Mail search: Turnaround time: same day. No SASE is required.

In person search: $2.00 fee per request.

Hunting and Fishing License Information

Conservation Department, Business & Support Services, PO Box 180, Jefferson City, MO 65102-0180 (Courier: 2901 W Truman Blvd, Jefferson City, MO 65109); 573-751-4115, 573-751-4467 (Fax), 8AM-5PM.

www.mdc.missouri.gov/

Indexing & Storage: Records are available for since 1/1/99. It takes hours before new records are available for inquiry. Records are indexed on inhouse computer, hard copy. Records are normally destroyed after 5 years.

Searching: Records are only released to the permitee. Otherwise, they are not released until the reason for the request is reviewed by the Department's General Counsel. Names and addresses may be released, if request is approved. Include the following in your request-full name. For older records, you will need the permittee's name, date of birth, and type of permit.

Access by: mail, fax.

Fee & Payment: Prepayment required. Fee payee: Conservation Department. Price is based upon type of service provided. Personal checks accepted.

Mail search: Turnaround time: 10 days. No SASE is required.

Fax search: Records are available by fax.

Other access: Mailing lists of the hunting and fishing permit vendors are available. The cost is about $100.

Missouri State Licensing Agencies

Licenses Searchable Online

Acupuncturist #45 ....http://pr.mo.gov/licensee-search.asp
Anesthesia Permit, Dental #17 ....http://pr.mo.gov/licensee-search.asp
Animal Technician #31..http://pr.mo.gov/licensee-search.asp
Ankle Specialist #10...http://pr.mo.gov/licensee-search.asp
Announcer, Ring #44 ....http://pr.mo.gov/licensee-search.asp
Architect #2 ....http://pr.mo.gov/licensee-search.asp
Athletic Trainer #11...http://pr.mo.gov/licensee-search.asp
Attorney #40...www.mobar.org/directory/index.htm
Audiologist #11 ....http://pr.mo.gov/licensee-search.asp
Audiologist, Clinical #16.......................................http://pr.mo.gov/licensee-search.asp
Audiologist/Speech Pathologist, Clinical #16........http://pr.mo.gov/licensee-search.asp
Barber Instructor/School #3 ....http://pr.mo.gov/licensee-search.asp
Barber/Barber Shop #3 ....http://pr.mo.gov/licensee-search.asp
Beauty Shop #5 ....http://pr.mo.gov/licensee-search.asp
Body Piercer/Branding Establishment #13 ....http://pr.mo.gov/licensee-search.asp
Boxer/Boxing Professional #44 ....http://pr.mo.gov/licensee-search.asp
Brander, Cosmetic #13 ....http://pr.mo.gov/licensee-search.asp
Cemetery #25 ....http://pr.mo.gov/licensee-search.asp
Chiropractor #4 ....http://pr.mo.gov/licensee-search.asp
Cosmetologist/Cosmetology school/Instr./Shop #5http://pr.mo.gov/licensee-search.asp
Counselor, Professional/Trainee #23...................http://pr.mo.gov/licensee-search.asp
Dentist/Dental Hygienist /Dental Specialist #17....http://pr.mo.gov/licensee-search.asp
Drug Distributor #9...http://pr.mo.gov/licensee-search.asp
Embalmer #6..http://pr.mo.gov/licensee-search.asp
Engineer #2..http://pr.mo.gov/licensee-search.asp
Esthetician #5 ....http://pr.mo.gov/licensee-search.asp
Funeral Director/Establishment #6........................http://pr.mo.gov/licensee-search.asp
Funeral Preneed Provider/Seller #6.....................http://pr.mo.gov/licensee-search.asp
Geologist/Geologist Registrant #47 ....http://pr.mo.gov/licensee-search.asp
Hairdresser #5 ....http://pr.mo.gov/licensee-search.asp
Hearing Instrument Specialist #27 ....http://pr.mo.gov/licensee-search.asp
Insurance Agent/Broker #20 ....www.insurance.mo.gov/industry/producer/agtstatus.htm
Insurance Consultant, Chiropractic #4.................http://pr.mo.gov/licensee-search.asp
Interior Designer #22 ....http://pr.mo.gov/licensee-search.asp
Interpreter for the Deaf #46..................................http://pr.mo.gov/licensee-search.asp
Landfill/Landfill Operator #37 ....www.dnr.state.mo.us/alpd/swmp/forms/form_permit.htm
Landscape Architect #2 ....http://pr.mo.gov/licensee-search.asp
Manicurist #5...http://pr.mo.gov/licensee-search.asp
Marital & Family Therapist #43 ....http://pr.mo.gov/licensee-search.asp
Martial Artist/Martial Arts Occupation #44...........http://pr.mo.gov/licensee-search.asp
Massage Therapist /Therapy Business #28..........http://pr.mo.gov/licensee-search.asp
Medical Doctor #11..http://pr.mo.gov/licensee-search.asp
Nurse Midwife #7 ....http://pr.mo.gov/licensee-search.asp
Nurse, Advanced Practical, Regist., Specialist #7 http://pr.mo.gov/licensee-search.asp
Nurse-LPN #7 ....http://pr.mo.gov/licensee-search.asp
Nursing School #7..http://pr.mo.gov/licensee-search.asp
Occupational Therapist/Therapist Assistant #41 ..http://pr.mo.gov/licensee-search.asp
Optometrist #8 ....http://pr.mo.gov/licensee-search.asp
Osteopathic Physician #11 ....http://pr.mo.gov/licensee-search.asp
Perfusionist #11 ....http://pr.mo.gov/licensee-search.asp
Pesticide Applicator/Tech./Dealer #18.................www.kellysolutions.com/MO/
Pharmacist/Pharmacy Intern/Tech/Pharmacy #9 ..http://pr.mo.gov/licensee-search.asp
Physical Therapist /Therapist Assistant #11 ....http://pr.mo.gov/licensee-search.asp
Physician Assistant #11 ....http://pr.mo.gov/licensee-search.asp
Physician, Athletic Event #44................................http://pr.mo.gov/licensee-search.asp
Podiatrist #10 ....http://pr.mo.gov/licensee-search.asp

Preneed Provider/Seller, Funeral #6......................http://pr.mo.gov/licensee-search.asp
Psychologist #36..http://pr.mo.gov/licensee-search.asp
Public Accountant Partnership #1.........................http://pr.mo.gov/licensee-search.asp
Public Accountant-CPA #1...................................http://pr.mo.gov/licensee-search.asp
Real Estate Agent/Seller #35...............................http://pr.mo.gov/licensee-search.asp
Real Estate Appraiser #14...................................http://pr.mo.gov/licensee-search.asp
Real Estate Broker/Partner/Assoc. #35 ....http://pr.mo.gov/licensee-search.asp
Real Estate Instructor/School #35.........................http://pr.mo.gov/licensee-search.asp
Real Estate Officer/Corp/Association #35...............http://pr.mo.gov/licensee-search.asp
Respiratory Care Practitioner #42.........................http://pr.mo.gov/licensee-search.asp
School Nurse #7...http://pr.mo.gov/licensee-search.asp
Social Worker, Clinical #15..................................http://pr.mo.gov/licensee-search.asp
Speech Language Pathologist #11.........................http://pr.mo.gov/licensee-search.asp
Speech-Language Pathologist/Audiologist #16 ....http://pr.mo.gov/licensee-search.asp
Surveyor, Land #2..http://pr.mo.gov/licensee-search.asp
Tattoo Artist #13..http://pr.mo.gov/licensee-search.asp
Teacher #24......................................http://k12apps.dese.mo.gov/webapps/tcertsearch/tc_search1.asp
Timekeeper, Athletic Event #44 ....http://pr.mo.gov/licensee-search.asp
Transfer Station #37 ....www.dnr.state.mo.us/alpd/swmp/facilities/tranlist.htm
Veterinarian/Veterinary Tech/Vet Facility #31.......http://pr.mo.gov/licensee-search.asp
Waste Tire Processor/Hauler #37 ....www.dnr.state.mo.us/alpd/swmp/tires/tirehaul.htm
Wrestler/Wrestling Professional #44 ....http://pr.mo.gov/licensee-search.asp

Missouri Licensing Quick Finder

Acupuncturist #45...................................573-526-1555
Alcohol & Tobacco Control #21.............573-751-2333
Anesthesia Permit, Dental #17..............573-751-0040
Animal Technician #31..........................573-751-0031
Ankle Specialist #10.............................573-751-0873
Announcer, Ring #44.............................573-751-0243
Architect #2..573-751-0047
Athletic Trainer #11...............................573-751-0098
Attorney #40...573-635-4128
Audiologist #11.....................................573-751-0171
Audiologist, Clinical #16........................573-751-0171
Audiologist/Speech Pathologist, Clinical #16
....573-751-0171
Barber Instructor/School #3...................573-751-0805
Barber/Barber Shop #3..........................573-751-0805
Beauty Shop #5.....................................573-751-1052
Bingo Worker/Officer/Operation #30 573-526-5370
Body Piercer #13...................................573-526-8288
Branding Establishm't #13......................573-526-8288
Boxer/Boxing Professional #44 573-751-0243
Brander, Cosmetic #13..........................573-526-8288
Cemetery #25..573-751-0849
Child Care Facility #29 573-751-2450
Chiropractor #4.....................................573-751-2104
Cosmetologist #5..................................573-751-1052
Cosmetology School/Instr./Shop #5.....573-751-1052
Counselor, Professional/Trainee #23...573-751-0018
Counselor, Substance Abuse #39........573-751-9211
Court Reporter #12................................573-751-4144
Dental Hygienist #17.............................573-751-0040
Dental Specialist #17.............................573-751-0040
Dentist #17..573-751-0040
Drug Distributor #9................................573-751-0091
Embalmer #6...573-751-0813
Emergency Medical Tech., Basic #19..573-751-6356
Engineer #2...573-751-0047
Esthetician #5..573-751-1052
Funeral Director #6...............................573-751-0813
Funeral Establishment #6......................573-751-0813
Funeral Preneed Provider/Seller #6.....573-751-0813
Gaming Occupational License #30 573-526-4092

Gaming Property, Boat #30.................573-526-4092
Gaming Supply #30.............................573-526-4092
Geologist #47......................................573-526-7625
Geologist Registrant in Training #47....573-526-7625
Hairdresser #5....................................573-751-1052
Hearing Instrument Specialist #27.......573-751-0240
Horse Racing Occupation #30............573-526-4083
Insurance Agent/Broker #20...............573-751-3518
Insurance Consultant, Chiropractic #4.573-751-2104
Interior Designer #22...........................573-522-4683
Interpreter for the Deaf #46................573-526-7787
Investment Advisor #34.......................573-751-2061
Landfill #37..573-751-5401
Landfill Operator #37...........................573-751-5401
Landscape Architect #2.......................573-751-0047
Manicurist #5.......................................573-751-1052
Marital & Family Therapist #43 573-751-0870
Martial Artist/Martial Arts Occupation #44
....573-751-0243
Massage Therapist #28.......................573-522-6277
Massage Therapy Business #28..........573-522-6277
Medical Doctor #11.............................573-751-0108
Notary Public #33................................573-751-2783
Nurse Midwife #7................................573-751-0681
Nurse, Advanced Practical #7.............573-751-0681
Nurse, Registered #7 573-751-0681
Nurse, Specialist #7............................573-751-0681
Nurse-LPN #7......................................573-751-0681
Nursing Home Administrator #32.........573-751-3511
Nursing School #7...............................573-751-0681
Occupational Therapist/Therapist Assistant #41
....573-751-0877
Optometrist #8.....................................573-751-0814
Osteopathic Physician #11..................573-751-0108
Perfusionist #11...................................573-751-0108
Pesticide Applicator/Technician #18....573-751-5504
Pesticide Dealer #18 573-751-5504
Pesticide Technician #18.....................573-751-5504
Pharmacist/Pharmacy Intern/Tech. #9.573-751-0091
Pharmacy #9.......................................573-751-0091
Physical Therapist #11.........................573-751-0171

Physical Therapist Assistant #11.........573-751-0171
Physician Assistant #11.......................573-751-0171
Physician, Athletic Event #44...............573-751-0243
Podiatrist #10.......................................573-751-0873
Preneed Provider/Seller, Funeral #6....573-751-0813
Prevention Specialist, Social Work #39 573-751-9211
Psychologist #36..................................573-751-0099
Public Accountant Partnership #1........573-751-0012
Public Accountant-CPA #1...................573-751-0012
Real Estate Agent/Seller #35...............573-751-2628
Real Estate Appraiser #14...................573-751-0038
Real Estate Broker/Partner/Assoc. #35 573-751-2628
Real Estate Instructor/School #35 573-751-2628
Real Estate Officer/Business/Association #35
....573-751-2628
Respiratory Care Practitioner #42.........573-522-2864
School Commissioner Assistant #24 ...573-751-4369
School Librarian #24 573-751-4369
School Nurse #7...................................573-751-0681
Securities Agent #34............................573-751-2061
Securities Broker/Dealer #34...............573-751-2061
Social Worker, Clinical #15.................573-751-0885
Speech Language Pathologist #11......573-751-0171
Speech-Language Pathologist/Audiologist #16
....573-751-0171
Substance Abuse Assoc-in-Training #39
....573-751-9211
Substance Abuse Counselor #39........573-751-9211
Surveyor, Land #2................................573-751-0047
Tattoo Artist #13..................................573-526-8288
Teacher #24......................573-751-0051, 751-4369
Timekeeper, Athletic Event #44...........573-751-0243
Transfer Station #37............................573-751-5401
Veterinarian/Veterinary Tech. #31.......573-751-0031
Veterinary Facility #31.........................573-751-0031
Waste Tire End User/Site #37.............573-751-5401
Waste Tire Processor/Hauler #37........573-751-5401
Waste Water System Operator #38.....573-751-3443
Water Supply Operator #38.................573-751-3443
Wrestler/Wrestling Professional #44....573-751-0243

Missouri Licensing Agency Information

1 Board of Accountancy, 3605 Missouri Blvd, Jefferson City, MO 65102-0613; 573-751-1052, Fax: 573-751-0890.
www.ecodev.state.mo.us/pr/account
Email: boa@mail.state.mo.us
Search Database at http://pr.mo.gov/licensee-search.asp Note: Lists are available at www.ecodev.state.mo.us/pr/ftp4.htm.

2 Engineers, Land Survey & Landscape Architects, Board of Architects, 3605 Missouri Blvd, #380, Jefferson City, MO 65102; 573-751-0047, Fax: 573-751-8046.
http://pr.mo.gov/apelsla.asp
Email: moapels@pr.mo.gov
Search Database at http://pr.mo.gov/licensee-search.asp Note: Lists are available at www.ecodev.state.mo.us/pr/ftp4.htm.

3 Board of Barber Examiners, 3605 Missouri Blvd, Jefferson City, MO 65102-1335; 573-751-0805, Fax: 573-751-8167.
www.pr.mo.gov/
Email: barber.board@pr.mo.gov
Search Database at http://pr.mo.gov/licensee-search.asp Note: Lists are available at www.ecodev.state.mo.us/pr/ftp4.htm.

4 Board of Chiropractic Examiners, 3605 Missouri Blvd, Jefferson City, MO 65102-0672; 573-751-2104, Fax: 573-751-0735.
http://pr.mo.gov
Email: chiropractic@pr.mo.gov
Search Database at http://pr.mo.gov/licensee-search.asp Note: Lists are available at http://pr.mo.gov.

5 Board of Cosmetology, 3605 Missouri Blvd, Jefferson City, MO 65102; 573-751-1052, Fax: 573-751-8167.
www.pr.mo.gov
Email: cosmo@pr.mo.gov
Search Database at http://pr.mo.gov/licensee-search.asp Note: Lists are available through cosmo@pr.mo.gov.

6 Board of Embalmers & Funeral Directors, 3605 Missouri Blvd, Jefferson City, MO 65102-0625; 573-751-0813, Fax: 573-751-1155.
www.ecodev.state.mo.us/pr/embalm
Email: emblamer@mail.state.mo.us
Search Database at http://pr.mo.gov/licensee-search.asp Note: Lists are available at www.ecodev.state.mo.us/pr/ftp4.htm.

7 Board of Nursing, PO Box 656, Jefferson City, MO 65102; 573-751-0681, Fax: 573-751-6745.
www.pr.mo.gov/nursing.asp
Email: nursing@mail.state.mo.us
Search Database at http://pr.mo.gov/licensee-search.asp Note: Nursing lists are available at www.ecodev.state.mo.us/pr/nursingdown.html.

8 Board of Optometry, PO Box 1335 (3605 Missouri Blvd), Jefferson City, MO 65102-0423; 573-751-0814, Fax: 573-751-8216.
http://pr.mo.gov/regulated-professions.asp
Email: optom@mail.state.mo.us
Search Database at http://pr.mo.gov/licensee-search.asp Note: Lists are available at www.ecodev.state.mo.us/pr/ftp4.htm.

9 Board of Pharmacy, 3605 Missouri Blvd, Jefferson City, MO 65102; 573-751-0091, Fax: 573-526-3464.
www.pr.mo.gov/pharmacists.asp
Email: pharmacy@mail.state.mo.us
Search Database at http://pr.mo.gov/licensee-search.asp Note: Lists are available at www.ecodev.state.mo.us/pr/ftp4.htm.

10 Board of Podiatric Medicine, 3605 Missouri Blvd, Jefferson City, MO 65102; 573-751-0873, Fax: 573-751-1155.
www.ecodev.state.mo.us/pr/podiatry
Email: podiatry@mail.state.mo.us
Search Database at http://pr.mo.gov/licensee-search.asp Note: Lists are available at www.ecodev.state.mo.us/pr/ftp4.htm.

11 Board of Registration for Healing Arts, 3605 Missouri Blvd, Jefferson City, MO 65102; 573-751-0098, Fax: 573-751-3166.
www.pr.mo.gov/healingarts.asp
Email: healarts@mail.state.mo.us
Search Database at http://pr.mo.gov/licensee-search.asp Note: Lists are available at www.ecodev.state.mo.us/pr/healingdown.html.

13 Office of Tattooing, Body Piercing and Branding, PO Box 1335, Jefferson City, MO 65102-1335; 573-526-8288, Fax: 573.526.3489.
http://pr.mo.gov/tattooing.asp Search Database at http://pr.mo.gov/licensee-search.asp

14 Commission of Real Estate Appraisers, 3605 Missouri Blvd, Jefferson City, MO 65109; 573-751-0038, Fax: 573-526-3489.
www.ecodev.state.mo.us/pr/rea
Email: reacom@mail.state.mo.us
Search Database at http://pr.mo.gov/licensee-search.asp Note: Lists are available at www.ecodev.state.mo.us/pr/ftp4.htm.

15 Division of Professional Registration, Committee for Licensed Clinical Social Workers, 3605 Missouri Blvd, Jefferson City, MO 65102; 573-751-0885, Fax: 573-526-3489.
http://pr.mo.gov/socialworkers.asp
Email: lcsw@pr.mo.gov
Search Database at http://pr.mo.gov/licensee-search.asp Note: Lists are available at www.ecodev.state.mo.us/pr/ftp4.htm.

16 Committee of Speech Pathology & Audiology, 3605 Missouri Blvd, PO Box 4, Jefferson City, MO 65102; 573-751-0098, Fax: 573-751-3166.
http://pr.mo.gov/speech.asp
Email: healarts@mail.state.mo.us
Search Database at http://pr.mo.gov/licensee-search.asp Note: Lists are available at www.ecodev.state.mo.us/pr/healingdown.html.

17 Dental Board, 3605 Missouri Blvd, PO Box 1367, Jefferson City, MO 65102; 573-751-0040, Fax: 573-751-8216.
http://pr.mo.gov/dental.asp
Email: dental@pr.mo.gov
Search Database at http://pr.mo.gov/licensee-search.asp Note: Lists are available at www.ecodev.state.mo.us/pr/ftp4.htm.

18 Department of Agriculture, Division of Plant Industries, Bureau of Pesticide, 1616 Missouri Blvd, Jefferson City, MO 65102; 573-751-5504, Fax: 573-751-0005. www.mda.mo.gov
Email: paul_bailey@mda.mo.gov
Search Database at www.kellysolutions.com/MO/

19 Department of Health, Emergency Medical Services, PO Box 570 (912 Wildwood Dr), Jefferson City, MO 65102-0570; 573-751-6356, Fax: 573-751-6348.
www.health.state.mo.us/EMS/

20 Department of Insurance, Licensing Section, PO Box 690 (301 W High St), Jefferson City, MO 65102-0690; 573-751-4126, Fax: 573-526-3416.
www.insurance.mo.gov
Email: mdimedia@mail.state.mo.us
Search Database at www.insurance.mo.gov/industry/producer/agtstatus.htm

21 Department of Public Safety, Division of Alcohol & Tobacco Control, Truman Bldg, Rm 860 (PO Box 837), Jefferson City, MO 65102-0837; 573-751-2333, Fax: 573-526-4540.
www.mdlc.state.mo.us
Email: liquor@mail.state.mo.us

22 Interior Design Council, PO Box 1335 (3605 Missouri Blvd), Jefferson City, MO 65109; 573-522-4683, Fax: 573-526-3489.
http://pr.mo.gov/interior.asp
Email: intdesn@pr.mo.gov
Search Database at http://pr.mo.gov/licensee-search.asp

23 Division of Professional Regulation, Committee for Professional Counselors, PO Box 1335 (3605 Missouri Blvd), Jefferson City, MO 65102-1335; 573-751-0018, Fax: 573-526-3489.
www.ecodev.state.mo.us/pr/counselr/
Email: couns@mail.state.ma.us
Search Database at http://pr.mo.gov/licensee-search.asp Note: Lists are available at www.ecodev.state.mo.us/pr/ftp4.htm.

24 Department of Elementary & Secondary Education, Division of Teacher Quality & Urban Education, PO Box 480 (205 Jefferson St), Jefferson City, MO 65102-0480; 573-751-0051, 751-4212, Fax: 573-751-8613.
www.dese.state.mo.us

25 Endowed Care Cemeteries Registration, Missouri Division of Professional Registration, 3605 Missouri Blvd (PO Box 1335, 65102), Jefferson City, MO 65102-1335; 573-751-0849, Fax: 573-751-0878.
www.ecodev.state.mo.us/pr/endowed/
Email: endocare@mail.state.mo.us
Search Database at http://pr.mo.gov/licensee-search.asp

27 Board of Hearing Instrument Specialists, PO Box 1335 (3605 Missouri Blvd), Jefferson City, MO 65102-1335; 573-751-0240, Fax: 573-526-3856.
www.pr.mo.gov/hearing.asp
Email: behis@mail.state.mo.us Search Database at http://pr.mo.gov/licensee-search.asp

28 State Board of Therapeutic Massage, PO Box 1335 (3605 Missouri Blvd), Jefferson City, MO 65102-1335; 573-522-6277, Fax: 573-751-0735.
http://pr.mo.gov Email: massagether@pr.mo.gov
Search Database at http://pr.mo.gov/licensee-search.asp

29 Department of Health, Bureau of Child Care Safety & Licensure, 1715 South Ridge, Jefferson City, MO 65109; 573-751-2450, Fax: 573-526-5345.
www.health.state.mo.us/AbouttheDepartment/BofCC.html

30 Gaming Commission, 3417 Knipp Dr, Jefferson City, MO 65102; 573-526-4080, Fax: 573-526-1999.
www.mgc.state.mo.us
Email: hbailey@mail.state.mo.us

31 Veterinary Medical Board, 3605 Missouri Blvd, Jefferson City, MO 65102-0633; 573-751-0031, Fax: 573-751-3856.
www.ecodev.state.mo.us/pr/vet
Email: vets@mail.state.mo.us
Search Database at http://pr.mo.gov/licensee-search.asp Note: Lists are available at www.ecodev.state.mo.us/pr/ftp4.htm.

32 Board of Nursing Home Administrators, 2033 St Mary's Blvd (PO Box 570), Jefferson City, MO 65102; 573-751-3511, Fax: 573-573-4314.
Email: loved2@dhhs.mo.gov

33 Office of Secretary of State, State Capitol Rm 208, Jefferson City, MO 65101; 573-751-4936, Fax: 573-526-3489.
www.sos.mo.gov   Email: trish.vincent@sos.mo.gov

34 Secretary of State, Securities Division, 600 W Main St #229, Jefferson City, MO 65101; 573-751-4136, Fax: 573-526-3124.
www.sos.mo.gov/securities/

35 Real Estate Commission, PO Box 1339 (3605 Missouri Blvd), Jefferson City, MO 65102-1339; 573-751-2628, Fax: 573-751-2777.
www.ecodev.state.mo.us/pr/restate
Email: realesta@mail.state.mo.us
Search Database at http://pr.mo.gov/licensee-search.asp Note: Lists are available at www.ded.state.mo.us/regulatorylicensing/professionalregistration/.

36 Committee of Psychology, 3605 Missouri Blvd, Jefferson City, MO 65102-1335; 573-751-0099, Fax: 573-526-3489.
www.ecodev.state.mo.us/pr/psych/
Email: scop@mail.state.mo.us
Search Database at http://pr.mo.gov/licensee-search.asp Note: Lists are available at www.ecodev.state.mo.us/pr/ftp4.htm.

37 Department of Natural Resources, Div of Environmental Quality, Solid Waste Mgmt, 1738 E Elm, PO Box 176, Jefferson City, MO 65102-0176; 573-751-5401, Fax: 573-526-3902.
www.dnr.mo.gov
Email: beth.marsala@dnr.mo.gov
Search Database at www.dnr.state.mo.us/alpd/swmp/forms/form_permit.htm

38 Department of Natural Resources, Environmental Assistance Program, PO Box 176 (1659 Elm St), Jefferson City, MO 65102; 573-751-3443, Fax: 573-526-5808.
www.dnr.state.mo.us/oac/oprtrain.htm

39 Substance Abuse Counselors Certification Board, PO Box 1250, Jefferson City, MO 65102; 573-751-9211, Fax: 573-522-2073.
www.modmh.state.mo.us/msaccb
Email: msaccb@mail.dmh.state.mo.us

40 The Missouri Bar, PO Box 119 (326 Monroe St), Jefferson City, MO 65102-0119; 573-635-4128, Fax: 573-635-2811.
www.mobar.org
Search Database at www.mobar.org/directory/index.htm

41 Division of Professional Registration, Board of Occupational Therapy, PO Box 1335 (3605 Missouri Blvd, 65109), Jefferson City, MO 65102-1335; 573-751-0877, Fax: 573-526-3489.
www.ecodev.state.mo.us/pr/octherap
Email: ot@mail.state.mo.us
Search Database at http://pr.mo.gov/licensee-search.asp Note: Lists are available at www.ecodev.state.mo.us/pr/ftp4.htm.

42 Board for Respiratory Care, 3605 Missouri Blvd, Jefferson City, MO 65102-1335; 573-522-5864, Fax: 573-526-3464.
www.pr.mo.gov/respiratorycare.asp
Email: rcp@mail.state.mo.us
Search Database at http://pr.mo.gov/licensee-search.asp Note: Lists are available at www.ecodev.state.mo.us/pr/ftp4.htm.

43 Committee of Marital & Family Therapists, 3605 Missouri Blvd, Jefferson City, MO 65102-1335; 573-751-0870, Fax: 573-526-3489.
http://pr.mo.gov
Email: maritalfam@pr.mo.gov
Search Database at http://pr.mo.gov/licensee-search.asp Note: Lists are available at http://pr.mo.gov.

44 Office of Athletics, 3605 Missouri Blvd, Jefferson City, MO 65102-1335; 573-751-0243, Fax: 573-751-5649.
www.ecodev.state.mo.us/pr/athletic
Email: athletic@mail.state.mo.us
Search Database at http://pr.mo.gov/licensee-search.asp

45 Acupuncturist Advisory Committee, P.O. Box 1335 (3605 Missouri Blvd), Jefferson City, MO 65102-0672; 573-526-1555, Fax: 573-751-0735.
http://pr.mo.gov/
Email: acupuncture@pr.mo.gov
Search Database at http://pr.mo.gov/licensee-search.asp

46 Committee of Interpreters, PO Box 1335 (3605 Missouri Blvd), Jefferson City, MO 65102-1335; 573-526-7787, Fax: 573-526-3489.
www.ecodev.state.mo.us/pr/inter/
Email: interp@mail.state.mo.us
Search Database at http://pr.mo.gov/licensee-search.asp Note: Lists are available at www.ecodev.state.mo.us/pr/ftp4.htm.

47 Board of Geologist Registration, 3605 Missouri Blvd, PO Box 1335, Jefferson City, MO 65102; 573-526-7625, Fax: 573-526-3489.
www.ecodev.state.mo.us/pr/geo
Email: geo@mail.state.mo.us
Search Database at http://pr.mo.gov/licensee-search.asp Note: Lists are available at www.ecodev.state.mo.us/pr/ftp4.htm

Missouri Federal Courts

The following list indicates the district and division name for each county in the state. If the bankruptcy court location is different from the district court, then the location of the bankruptcy court appears in parentheses.

County/Court Cross Reference

County	District	Division
Adair	Eastern	Hannibal (St Louis)
Andrew	Western	St Joseph (Kansas City - Western)
Atchison	Western	St Joseph (Kansas City - Western)
Audrain	Eastern	Hannibal (St Louis)
Barry	Western	Joplin-Southwestern (Kansas City)
Barton	Western	Joplin-Southwestern (Kansas City)
Bates	Western	Kansas City - Western
Benton	Western	Jefferson City-Central (Kansas City)
Bollinger	Eastern	Cape Girardeau (St Louis)
Boone	Western	Jefferson City-Central (Kansas City)
Buchanan	Western	St Joseph (Kansas City - Western)
Butler	Eastern	Cape Girardeau (St Louis)
Caldwell	Western	St Joseph (Kansas City - Western)
Callaway	Western	Jefferson City-Central (Kansas City)
Camden	Western	Jefferson City-Central (Kansas City)
Cape Girardeau	Eastern	Cape Girardeau (St Louis)
Carroll	Western	Kansas City - Western
Carter	Eastern	Cape Girardeau (St Louis)
Cass	Western	Kansas City - Western
Cedar	Western	Springfield-Southern (Kansas City)
Chariton	Eastern	Hannibal (St Louis)
Christian	Western	Springfield-Southern (Kansas City)
Clark	Eastern	Hannibal (St Louis)
Clay	Western	Kansas City - Western
Clinton	Western	St Joseph (Kansas City - Western)
Cole	Western	Jefferson City-Central (Kansas City)
Cooper	Western	Jefferson City-Central (Kansas City)
Crawford	Eastern	St Louis
Dade	Western	Springfield-Southern (Kansas City)
Dallas	Western	Springfield-Southern (Kansas City)
Daviess	Western	St Joseph (Kansas City - Western)
De Kalb	Western	St Joseph (Kansas City - Western)
Dent	Eastern	St Louis
Douglas	Western	Springfield-Southern ((Kansas City)
Dunklin	Eastern	Cape Girardeau (St Louis)
Franklin	Eastern	St Louis
Gasconade	Eastern	St Louis
Gentry	Western	St Joseph (Kansas City - Western)
Greene	Western	Springfield-Southern (Kansas City)
Grundy	Western	St Joseph (Kansas City - Western)
Harrison	Western	St Joseph (Kansas City - Western)
Henry	Western	Kansas City - Western
Hickory	Western	Jefferson City-Central (Kansas City)
Holt	Western	St Joseph (Kansas City - Western)
Howard	Western	Jefferson City-Central (Kansas City)
Howell	Western	Springfield-Southern (Kansas City)
Iron	Eastern	St Louis
Jackson	Western	Kansas City – Western
Jasper	Western	Joplin-Southwestern (Kansas City)
Jefferson	Eastern	St Louis
Johnson	Western	Kansas City - Western
Knox	Eastern	Hannibal (St Louis)
Laclede	Western	Springfield-Southern (Kansas City
Lafayette	Western	Kansas City - Western
Lawrence	Western	Joplin-Southwestern (Kansas City)
Lewis	Eastern	Hannibal (St Louis)
Lincoln	Eastern	St Louis
Linn	Eastern	Hannibal (St Louis)
Livingston	Western	St Joseph (Kansas City - Western)
Macon	Eastern	Hannibal (St Louis)
Madison	Eastern	Cape Girardeau (St Louis)
Maries	Eastern	St Louis
Marion	Eastern	Hannibal (St Louis)
McDonald	Western	Joplin-Southwestern (Kansas City)
Mercer	Western	St Joseph (Kansas City - Western)
Miller	Western	Jefferson City-Central (Kansas City)
Mississippi	Eastern	Cape Girardeau (St Louis)
Moniteau	Western	Jefferson City-Central (Kansas City)
Monroe	Eastern	Hannibal (St Louis)
Montgomery	Eastern	Hannibal (St Louis)
Morgan	Western	Jefferson City-Central (Kansas City)
New Madrid	Eastern	Cape Girardeau (St Louis)
Newton	Western	Joplin-Southwestern (Kansas City)
Nodaway	Western	St Joseph (Kansas City - Western)
Oregon	Western	Springfield-Southern (Kansas City)
Osage	Western	Jefferson City-Central (Kansas City)
Ozark	Western	Springfield-Southern (Kansas City)
Pemiscot	Eastern	Cape Girardeau (St Louis)
Perry	Eastern	Cape Girardeau (St Louis)
Pettis	Western	Jefferson City-Central (Kansas City)
Phelps	Eastern	St Louis
Pike	Eastern	Hannibal (St Louis)
Platte	Western	St Joseph (Kansas City - Western)
Polk	Western	Springfield-Southern (Kansas City)
Pulaski	Western	Springfield-Southern (Kansas City)
Putnam	Western	St Joseph (Kansas City - Western)
Ralls	Eastern	Hannibal (St Louis)
Randolph	Eastern	Hannibal (St Louis)
Ray	Western	Kansas City - Western
Reynolds	Eastern	Cape Girardeau (St Louis)
Ripley	Eastern	Cape Girardeau (St Louis)
Saline	Western	Kansas City - Western
Schuyler	Eastern	Hannibal (St Louis)
Scotland	Eastern	Hannibal (St Louis)
Scott	Eastern	Cape Girardeau (St Louis)
Shannon	Eastern	Cape Girardeau (St Louis)
Shelby	Eastern	Hannibal (St Louis)
St. Charles	Eastern	St Louis
St. Clair	Western	Kansas City - Western
St. Francois	Eastern	St Louis

St. Louis	Eastern	St Louis	
St. Louis City City	Eastern	St Louis	
Ste. Genevieve	Eastern	St Louis	
Stoddard	Eastern	Cape Girardeau (St Louis)	
Stone	Western	Joplin-Southwestern (Kansas City)	
Sullivan	Western	St Joseph (Kansas City - Western)	
Taney	Western	Springfield-Southern (Kansas City)	
Texas	Western	Springfield-Southern (Kansas City)	
Vernon	Western	Joplin-Southwestern (Kansas City)	
Warren	Eastern	St Louis	
Washington	Eastern	St Louis	
Wayne	Eastern	Cape Girardeau (St Louis)	
Webster	Western	Springfield-Southern (Kansas City)	
Worth	Western	St Joseph (Kansas City - Western)	
Wright	Western	Springfield-Southern (Kansas City)	

Standards for Federal Courts: The search fee is $20.00 per item (one party name or case number). Certification fee is $7.00 per document. Copy fee is $.50 per page. All fees standard unless noted in profile. Mail Search: always enclose a stamped self addressed envelope unless otherwise noted. Most courts accept fax requests or will suggest a copying/search vendor. Before releasing records, all courts require prepayment unless noted in profile.

Open records are located at the court unless otherwise noted. District courts index by defendant and plaintiff as well as by case number. Bankruptcy courts usually index by debtor and case number. While most courts now have their indexes on computer, many still maintain index card files as well.

The universal PACER sign-up number is 800-676-6856. Find PACER and the Party/Case Index on the Web at http://pacer.psc.uscourts.gov. PACER dial-up access is $.60 per minute. Also, courts offering internet access via RACER, PACER, Web-PACER or the new CM-ECF charge $.07 per page fee unless noted as free.

US District Court

Eastern District of Missouri

Cape Girardeau Division 339 Broadway, Room 240, Cape Girardeau, MO 63701 (courier address: Use mail address for courier delivery) 573-335-8538, Fax: 573-335-0379. www.moed.uscourts.gov

Counties: Bollinger, Butler, Cape Girardeau, Carter, Dunklin, Madison, Mississippi, New Madrid, Pemiscot, Perry, Reynolds, Ripley, Scott, Shannon, Stoddard, Wayne.

Indexing & Storage: New cases available in the index 1-2 days after filing date. Computerized records are available from 1994.

Fee & Payment: Payment may be made by money order, cashier check, personal check. Payee: Clerk, U.S. District Court.

Phone Search: Only docket information available.

Mail Search: A SASE not required.

In Person Search: Fee charged if court conducts your in person search for you.

PACER: PACER is available online at http://pacer.moed.uscourts.gov. Case records go back to 1994. Records never purged. New records are online after 4-5 days.

Electronic Filing: Electronic filing information online at https://ecf.moed.uscourts.gov

St Louis Division 111 S. 10th St, Ste 3.300, St Louis, MO 63102 (courier address: Use mail address for courier delivery) 314-244-7900, Fax: 314-244-7909. www.moed.uscourts.gov

Counties: Adair, Audrain, Chariton, Clark, Crawford, Dent, Franklin, Gasconade, Iron, Jefferson, Knox, Lewis, Lincoln, Linn, Macon, Maries, Marion, Monroe, Montgomery, Phelps,Pike, Ralls, Randolph, Schuyler, Scotland, Shelby, St. Charles, St. Francois, St. Louis, St. Louis City, Ste. Genevieve, Warren, Washington,This court also holds records for the Hannibal Division.

Indexing & Storage: New cases available in the index immediately after filing date.

Fee & Payment: Payment may be made by money order, cashier check, personal check. Payee: Clerk, U.S. District Court.

Phone Search: Only docket information available.

Mail Search: A SASE not required.

In Person Search: Fee charged if court conducts your in person search for you.

PACER: PACER is available online at http://pacer.moed.uscourts.gov. Case records go back to 1994. Records never purged. New records are online after 4-5 days.

Electronic Filing: Electronic filing information online at https://ecf.moed.uscourts.gov

U.S. Bankruptcy Court

Eastern District of Missouri

St Louis Division 4th Floor, 111 S. 10th St, St Louis, MO 63102-2734 (courier address: Use mail address for courier delivery) 314-244-4500, Fax: 314-244-4990. www.moeb.uscourts.gov

Counties: Adair, Audrain, Bollinger, Butler, Cape Girardeau, Carter, Chariton, Clark, Crawford, Dent, Dunklin, Franklin, Gasconade, Iron, Jefferson, Knox, Lewis, Lincoln, Linn, Macon, Madison, Maries, Marion, Mississippi, Monroe, Montgomery, New Madrid, Pemiscot,Perry, Phelps, Pike, Ralls, Randolph, Reynolds, Ripley, Schuyler, Scotland, Scott, Shannon, Shelby, St. Charles, St. Francois, St. Louis, St.Louis City, Ste. Genevieve, Stoddard, Warren, Washington, Wayne.

Indexing & Storage: Cases indexed by debtor as well as by case number. New cases available in the index 24 hours after filing date.

Fee & Payment: Payment may be made by money order, cashier check, personal check. Payee: Clerk, U.S. Bankruptcy Court.

Phone Search: Docket information is available by phone. Automated voice case information service (VCIS) is available. Call VCIS at 888-223-6431 or 314-425-4054.

Mail Search: A SASE not required.

In Person Search: Fee charged if court conducts your in person search for you.

PACER: PACER is available online at http://pacer.moeb.uscourts.gov. Document images available. Records purged every six months. New civil records are online after 1 day.

Electronic Filing: Electronic filing information online at https://ecf.moeb.uscourts.gov

Other Online Access: Search records on the Internet using RACER at http://racer.moeb.uscourts.gov/perl/bkplog.html. Access fee is $.07 per page.

U.S. District Court

Western District of Missouri

Jefferson City-Central Division 131 W High St, Jefferson City, MO 65101 (courier address: Use mail address for courier delivery) 573-636-4015, Fax: 573-636-3456. www.mow.uscourts.gov

Counties: Benton, Boone, Callaway, Camden, Cole, Cooper, Hickory, Howard, Miller, Moniteau, Morgan, Osage, Pettis.

Indexing & Storage: New cases available in the index 1-2 days after filing date.

Fee & Payment: Payment may be made by money order, cashier check, personal check. Payee: Clerk, U.S. District Court.

Phone Search: Only docket information available by phone.

In Person Search: Fee charged if court conducts your in person search for you.

PACER: PACER is available online at http://pacer.mowd.uscourts.gov. Records purged as deemed necessary. New records are online after 1 day.

Electronic Filing: Electronic filing information online at https://ecf.mowd.uscourts.gov

Joplin-Southwestern Division c/o Kansas City Division, Charles Evans Whitttaker Courthouse, 400 E 9th St, Kansas City, MO 64106 (courier address: Use mail address for courier delivery) 816-512-5000, Fax: 816-512-5078. www.mow.uscourts.gov

Counties: Barry, Barton, Jasper, Lawrence, McDonald, Newton, Stone, Vernon.

Indexing & Storage: New cases available in the index after filing date. Open records are located at the Kansas City Division.

Fee & Payment: Payment may be made by money order, cashier check. Business checks are not accepted. Personal checks are not accepted.

Phone Search: No searching by telephone. Searching is not available by phone.

Mail Search: A SASE not required.

In Person Search: Permitted.

PACER: PACER is available online at http://pacer.mowd.uscourts.gov. Records purged as deemed necessary. New records are online after 1 day.

Electronic Filing: Electronic filing information online at https://ecf.mowd.uscourts.gov

Kansas City-Western Division

Clerk of Court, 201 U.S. Courthouse, Rm 1056, 400 E 9th St, Kansas City, MO 64106 (courier address: Use mail address for courier delivery) 816-512-5000, Fax: 816-512-5078. www.mow.uscourts.gov

Counties: Bates, Carroll, Cass, Clay, Henry, Jackson, Johnson, Lafayette, Ray, St. Clair, Saline.

Indexing & Storage: New cases available in the index 1-2 days after filing date. Records are indexed on computer and microfiche.

Fee & Payment: Payment may be made by money order, cashier check, personal check. Payee: U.S. District Court Clerk.

Phone Search: Only docket information available.

Mail Search: A SASE not required.

In Person Search: Fee charged if court conducts your in person search for you.

PACER: PACER is available online at http://pacer.mowd.uscourts.gov. Records purged as deemed necessary. New records are online after 1 day.

Electronic Filing: Electronic filing information online at https://ecf.mowd.uscourts.gov

Springfield-Southern Division

222 N John Q Hammons Pkwy, Suite 1400, Springfield, MO 65806 (courier address: Use mail address for courier delivery) 417-865-3869, Fax: 417-865-7719. www.mow.uscourts.gov

Counties: Cedar, Christian, Dade, Dallas, Douglas, Greene, Howell, Laclede, Oregon, Ozark, Polk, Pulaski, Taney, Texas, Webster, Wright.

Indexing & Storage: New cases available in the index immediately after filing date.

Fee & Payment: Payment may be made by money order, cashier check, personal check. Payee: Clerk, U.S. District Court.

Phone Search: Only docket information available by phone.

In Person Search: Fee charged if court conducts your in person search for you.

PACER: PACER is available online at http://pacer.mowd.uscourts.gov. Records purged as deemed necessary. New records are online after 1 day.

Electronic Filing: Electronic filing information online at https://ecf.mowb.uscourts.gov

St Joseph Division

PO Box 387, 201 S 8th St, St Joseph, MO 64501 (courier address: Use mail address for courier delivery) Fax: 816-279-0177. www.mow.uscourts.gov

Counties: Andrew, Atchison, Buchanan, Caldwell, Clinton, Daviess, De Kalb, Gentry, Grundy, Harrison, Holt, Livingston, Mercer, Nodaway, Platte, Putnam, Sullivan, Worth.

Indexing & Storage: New cases available in the index immediately after filing date.

Fee & Payment: Payment may be made by money order, cashier check, personal check. Payee: Clerk, U.S. District Court. Will fax copies at $.50 per page, prepaid.

Phone Search: Only docket information available by phone. Will fax copies at $.50 per page, prepaid.

Mail Search: A SASE not required.

In Person Search: Fee charged if court conducts your in person search for you.

PACER: PACER is available online at http://pacer.mowd.uscourts.gov. Records purged as deemed necessary. New records are online after 1 day.

Electronic Filing: Electronic filing information online at https://ecf.mowd.uscourts.gov

U.S. Bankruptcy Court
Western District of Missouri

Kansas City-Western Division Room 1510, 400 E 9th st, Kansas City, MO 64106 (courier address: Use mail address for courier delivery) 816-512-1800. www.mow.uscourt.gov

Counties: Andrew, Atchison, Barry, Barton, Bates, Benton, Boone, Buchanan, Caldwell, Callaway, Camden, Carroll, Cass, Cedar, Christian, Clay, Clinton, Cole, Cooper, Dade, Dallas, Daviess, De Kalb, Douglas, Gentry, Greene, Grundy, Harrison, Henry, Hickory, Holt,Howard, Howell, Jackson, Jasper, Johnson, Laclede, Lafayette, Lawrence, Livingston, McDonald, Mercer, Miller, Moniteau, Morgan, Newton, Nodaway, Oregon, Osage, Ozark, Pettis, Platte, Polk, Pulaski, Putnam, Ray, Saline, St. Clair, Stone, Sullivan, Taney,Texas, Vernon, Webster, Worth, Wright.

Indexing & Storage: Cases indexed by debtor and creditors as well as by case number. New cases available in the index 24 hours after filing date. Older records are indexed on microfiche. District wide searches are available from June 1989 from this division.

Fee & Payment: Payment may be made by money order, cashier check, personal check. Payee: Clerk, U.S. Bankruptcy Court.

Phone Search: Use VCIS for docket information. In addition to numbers given, call 816-426-2913 for information on cases closed prior to October 1995. Automated voice case information service (VCIS) is available. Call VCIS at 888-205-2527 or 816-426-5822.

In Person Search: Permitted. There is no search fee for in person searches.

PACER: PACER is available online at http://pacer.mowb.uscourts.gov/bc/index.html.

Electronic Filing: Electronic filing information online at https://ecf.mowb.uscourts.gov

Missouri County Courts

Court	Jurisdiction	No. of Courts	How Organized
Circuit Courts*	General	115	45 Circuits
Associate Circuit Courts*	Limited	114	45 Circuits
Combined Courts*		23	
Probate Courts*	Probate	5	
Municipal Courts	Municipal	406	
Family Courts	Special	8	

* Profiled in this Sourcebook.

CIVIL									
Court	Tort	Contract	Real Estate	Min. Claim	Max. Claim	Small Claims	Estate	Eviction	Domestic Relations
Circuit Courts*	X	X	X	$25,000	No Max				X
Associate Circuit Courts*	X	X	X	$0	$25,000	$3000		X	
Municipal Courts									
Probate Courts*							X		
Family Courts									X

CRIMINAL					
Court	Felony	Misdemeanor	DWI/DUI	Preliminary Hearing	Juvenile
Circuit Courts*	X				X
Associate Circuit Courts*		X	X	X	
Probate Courts*					
Family Courts					X

ADMINISTRATION

State Court Administrator, 2112 Industrial Dr., PO Box 104480, Jefferson City, MO, 65109; 573-751-4377, Fax: 573-751-5540. www.osca.state.mo.us

COURT STRUCTURE

The Circuit Court is the court of general jurisdiction. There are 45 circuits comprised of 114 county circuit courts and one independent city court. There are also Associate Circuit Courts with limited jurisdiction and some counties have Combined Courts, a growing trend. Municipal Courts only have jurisdiction over traffic and ordinance violations.

ONLINE ACCESS

Available at www.courts.mo.gov/casenet is Casenet, a limited but growing online system. The system includes 69 counties (with more projected) as well as the Eastern, Western, and Southern Appellate Courts, the Supreme Court, and Fine Collection Center. Cases can be searched case number, filing date, or litigant name. One may search supreme and appellate court opinions at the home page.

ADDITIONAL INFORMATION

Starting in 2004, many circuit and associate courts no longer accept mail or fax requests to perform criminal record searches. Instead, the court instructs you to forward your mail criminal search request to the MO State Highway Patrol Criminal Records Division, PO Box 563, Jefferson City, MO 65102. 573-526-6288 (instructions) or 573-526-6153 (voice); Fax 573-751-9382. $5.00 check or money order required for search. Note that most courts participate in the MO CaseNet online system where record searches can be perfomed for free on the Internet.

While the Missouri State Statutes set the Civil Case limit at $25,000 for the Associate Courts, and over $25,000 for the Circuit Courts, a great many Missouri County Courts have adopted their own Local Court Rules regarding civil cases and the monetary limits. Presumably, Local Court's Rules are setup to allow the county to choose which court - Circuit or Associate - to send a case. This may depend on the court's case load, but generally, the cases are assigned more by "the nature of the case" and less by the monetary amount involved. Often, Local Court Rules are found where both the Circuit and the Associate Court are located in the same building, or share the same offices and perhaps the same phones. A solution for court record searches is to use this source to find a telephone number of a County's Court Clerk, and call to determine the court location of the case.

Adair County

Circuit Court PO Box 690, Kirksville, MO 63501; 660-665-2552; Fax: 660-665-3420. Hours: 8AM-5PM (CST). *Felony, Misdemeanor, Civil Actions Over $25,000.*
Civil Records: Access: In person only. Only the court performs in person searches; visitors may not. No search fee. Required to search: name, years to search. Civil cases indexed by defendant, plaintiff. Prior on index cards.
Criminal Records: Access: In person only. Visitors must perform in person searches for themselves. No search fee. Required to search: name, years to search. Criminal records on computer since 1991, prior on index cards. Court recommends criminal searches at MO State Highway Patrol, 573-526-6288.
General Information: No juvenile, mental, expunged, sealed, dismissed or suspended records released. Copy fee: $.10 per page. Certification fee: $1.00. Payee: Circuit Clerk. Personal checks accepted. Prepayment required.

Associate Circuit Court Courthouse, Kirksville, MO 63501; 660-665-3877; Fax: 660-785-3222. Hours: 8AM-5PM (CST). *Misdemeanor, Civil Actions Under $25,000, Eviction, Small Claims, Probate.*
Civil Records: Access: Phone, fax, mail, in person. Only the court performs in person searches; visitors may not. No search fee. Required to search: name, years to search. Civil cases indexed by defendant, plaintiff. Civil records on computer back to 1990; probate records on microfilm since 1840.
Criminal Records: Access: None. No search fee. Criminal records on computer back to 1990; prior records in files. Court personnel will not perform a name search. They refer requesters to the state criminal record agency. However, they will look up a case if docket number given.
General Information: No juvenile, mental, expunged, sealed, dismissed or suspended imposition of case records released. Copy fee: $.25 per page. No certification fee. Payee: Associate Circuit Court. Personal checks accepted. Prepayment required. Mail requests: SASE required. Mail turnaround time 1 day.

Andrew County

Circuit Court PO Box 208 Division I, Savannah, MO 64485; 816-324-4221; Fax: 816-324-5667. Hours: 8AM-5PM (CST). *Felony, Civil Actions Over $45,000.*
Civil Records: Access: Phone, fax, mail, in person, online. Both court and visitors may perform in person searches. No search fee. Required to search: name, years to search. Civil cases indexed by defendant, plaintiff. Civil records on index cards since 1976, archived since 1850, computerized since 06/00. Participates in the free state online court record system at www.courts.mo.gov/casenet. Online records go back to 1993.
Criminal Records: Access: In person, online. Visitors must perform in person searches for themselves. No search fee. Required to search: name, years to search; also helpful: DOB. Criminal records on computer since 06/00, archived from 1841. Online access to criminal records is the same as civil. Court recommends criminal searches at MO State Highway Patrol, 573-526-6288.
General Information: Public Access terminal is available. No juvenile, mental, expunged, sealed, dismissed or suspended imposition of sentence records released. Copy fee: $.25 per page. Certification fee: $2.50. Payee: Andrew County Circuit Clerk. Personal checks accepted. Prepayment required. Mail turnaround time 1-2 days.

Associate Circuit Court PO Box 49, Savannah, MO 64485; 816-324-3921; Fax: 816-324-3191. Hours: 8AM-5PM (CST). *Misdemeanor, Civil Actions Under $45,000, Eviction, Small Claims, Probate.*
Civil Records: Access: Mail, in person, online. Both court and visitors may perform in person searches. No search fee. Required to search: name, years to search. Civil cases indexed by defendant, plaintiff. Civil records on card file, archived from 1950. Participates in the free state online court record system at www.courts.mo.gov/casenet. Online records go back to 1993.
Criminal Records: Access: Mail, in person, online. Both court and visitors may perform in person searches. No search fee. Required to search: name, years to search. Criminal records on computer since mid-1993. Online access to criminal records is the same as civil.
General Information: No juvenile, mental, expunged, sealed, dismissed or suspended imposition of sentence records released. Copy fee: $.25 per page. Certification fee: $1.50 plus $.25 each add'l page. Payee: Associate Circuit Court. Personal checks accepted. Prepayment required. Mail requests: SASE required. Mail turnaround time varies.

Atchison County

Circuit Court PO Box 280, Rock Port, MO 64482; 660-744-2707; Fax: 660-744-5705. Hours: 8:30AM-4:30PM (CST). *Felony, Misdemeanor, Civil Actions Over $25,000.*
Civil Records: Access: Mail, in person. Visitors must perform in person searches for themselves. No search fee. Required to search: name, years to search. Civil cases indexed by defendant, plaintiff. Civil records on index books, and archived from 1845.
Criminal Records: Access: In person only. Visitors must perform in person searches for themselves. Search fee: $4.00 per name. Required to search: name, years to search. Criminal records on index books, and archived from 1845. Court recommends criminal searches at MO State Highway Patrol, 573-526-6288.
General Information: No juvenile, mental, expunged, sealed, dismissed or suspended imposition of sentence records released. Will fax results to local or toll free line. Copy fee: $1.00 per page. Certification fee: $1.00. Payee: Circuit Clerk. Personal checks accepted. Prepayment required. Mail turnaround time 1 day.

Associate Division PO Box 187, Rock Port, MO 64482; 660-744-2700; Fax: 660-744-6100. Hours: 8AM-4:30PM (CST). *Misdemeanor, Civil Actions Under $25,000, Eviction, Small Claims, Probate, Traffic.*
Civil Records: Access: In person only. Only court does search. Search fee: None. Required to search: name, years to search; also helpful: address. Civil cases indexed by defendant, plaintiff. Civil records on books and cardex system, archived since 1845.
Criminal Records: Access: In person only. Court does not do name searches. No search fee. Required to search: name, years to search; also helpful: address, DOB, SSN, offense. Criminal records on computer since mid 1980s; prior on books and cardex system. Traffic cases disposed through the Fine Collection Center may appear free on the state online court record system at www.courts.mo.gov/casenet. Court recommends criminal searches at MO State Highway Patrol, 573-526-6288.
General Information: No juvenile, mental, expunged, sealed, dismissed or suspended imposition of sentence records released. Copy fee: $1.00 per page. Certification fee: $1.50. Payee: Circuit Court

Division II. Personal checks not accepted. Prepayment required.

Audrain County

Circuit Court Courthouse, 101 N Jefferson, Mexico, MO 65265; Civil phone: 573-473-5842; Criminal phone: 573-473-5840; Fax: 573-581-3237. Hours: 8AM-5PM (CST). *Felony, Misdemeanor, Civil Actions Over $25,000.*
www.audrain-county.org
Civil Records: Access: In person, online. Visitors must perform in person searches for themselves. No search fee. Required to search: name, years to search. Civil cases indexed by defendant, plaintiff. Civil records on computer since 8/92, prior on index cards, older records archived at Genealogy Club in Mexico, MO. Participates in the free state online court record system at www.courts.mo.gov/casenet.
Criminal Records: Access: In person, online. Visitors must perform in person searches for themselves. No search fee. Required to search: name, years to search; also SSN, case number. Criminal records on computer since 8/92, stored for 25 years on site then archived (back to 1800s). Participates in the free state online court record system at www.courts.mo.gov/casenet. Court recommends criminal searches at MO State Highway Patrol, 573-526-6288.
General Information: Public Access terminal is available. No juvenile, mental, expunged, sealed, dismissed or suspended imposition of sentence records released. Copy fee: $.25 per page. Certification fee: $1.50 for first 2 pages; $.25 each add'l. Payee: Circuit Clerk. Prepayment required.

Associate Circuit Court Div II Courthouse, 101 N Jefferson, Rm 205, Mexico, MO 65265; 573-473-5850; Probate phone: 573-473-5854; Fax: 573-581-3364. Hours: 8AM-5PM (CST). *Misdemeanor, Civil Actions Under $25,000, Eviction, Small Claims, Probate.*
Civil Records: Access: Mail, in person, online. Both court and visitors may perform in person searches. No search fee. Required to search: name, years to search. Civil cases indexed by defendant, plaintiff. Civil records on computer since 9/93, prior on cards, archived to 1800s. Participates in the free state online court record system at www.courts.mo.gov/casenet.
Criminal Records: Access: Mail, in person, online. Both court and visitors may perform in person searches. No search fee. Required to search: name, years to search, DOB, SSN, signed release. Criminal records on computer since 9/93, prior on cards, archived to 1800s. Participates in the free state online court record system at www.courts.mo.gov/casenet.
General Information: Public Access terminal is available. No juvenile, mental, expunged, sealed, dismissed or suspended imposition of sentence records released. Will fax results to "800" numbers. Copy fee: $.15 per page. Certification fee: $1.50 first page, $1.00 each add'l. Payee: Circuit Court Division II. Only cashiers checks and money orders accepted. Prepayment required. Mail turnaround time 1 week.

Barry County

Circuit Court 102 West St #1, Barry County Courthouse, Cassville, MO 65625; 417-847-2361. Hours: 8AM-4PM (CST). *Felony, Misdemeanor, Civil Actions Over $25,000.*
Civil Records: Access: Mail, in person. Both court and visitors may perform in person searches. Search fee: $4.00 per name. Required to search: name, years to search. Civil cases indexed by defendant, plaintiff. Civil records on index cards, archived since mid-1800s.
Criminal Records: Access: In person only. Visitors must perform in person searches for themselves. No

search fee. Required to search: name, years to search. Criminal records on index cards, archived since mid-1800s. Court recommends criminal searches at MO State Highway Patrol, 573-526-6288.

General Information: No juvenile, mental expunged, sealed, dismissed or suspended imposition of sentence records released. Copy fee: $.25 per page. Certification fee: $1.00. Payee: Circuit Clerk. Personal checks accepted. Prepayment required. Mail requests: SASE required. Mail turnaround time 1-3 days.

Associate Circuit Court 102 West St #2, Judicial Center, Cassville, MO 65625; Civil phone: 417-847-2127; Criminal phone: 417-847-6557. Hours: 7:30AM-4PM (CST). *Misdemeanor, Civil Actions Under $25,000, Eviction, Small Claims, Probate.*

Civil Records: Access: Mail, in person. Both court and visitors may perform in person searches. No search fee. Required to search: name, years to search. Civil cases indexed by defendant, plaintiff. Civil records on index cards since 1982; prior records on index books to mid 1800s.

Criminal Records: Access: Mail, in person. Both court and visitors may perform in person searches. No search fee. Required to search: name, years to search. Criminal records on computer since 1996; prior records on index books to mid 1800s.

General Information: No juvenile, mental, expunged, sealed, dismissed or suspended imposition of sentence records released. Copy fee: $1.00 per page. No certification fee. Payee: Barry County. Personal checks accepted. Prepayment required. Mail turnaround time 1-3 days.

Barton County

Circuit & Associate Court Courthouse, 1007 Broadway, Lamar, MO 64759; 417-682-2444; Fax: 417-682-2960. Hours: 8AM-4:30PM (CST). *Felony, Misdemeanor, Civil, Eviction, Small Claims, Probate.*

Civil Records: Access: Mail, online, in person. Both court and visitors may perform in person searches. No search fee. Required to search: name, years to search; also helpful: address. Civil cases indexed by defendant, plaintiff. Civil records on computer since 1999; prior from 1880 on books or archived. Participates in the free state online court record system at www.courts.mo.gov/casenet. Online records go back to 4/1/1999.

Criminal Records: Access: Mail, online, in person. Both court and visitors may perform in person searches. No search fee. Required to search: name, years to search; also helpful: address, DOB, SSN. Criminal records on computer since 1993; prior from 1880on books or archived. Online access to criminal records is the same as civil.

General Information: Public Access terminal is available. No juvenile, mental, expunged, dismissed, or suspended imposition of sentence records released. Fee to fax results is $2.00 per document. Copy fee: $1.00 per page. Certification fee: $1.50. Payee: Circuit Court. Personal checks accepted. Prepayment required. Mail requests: SASE required. Mail turnaround time 3 weeks.

Bates County

Circuit Court Bates County Courthouse, Butler, MO 64730; 660-679-5171; Fax: 660-679-4446. Hours: 8AM-4:30PM (CST). *Felony, Misdemeanor, Civil Actions Over $25,000.*

http://tacnet.missouri.org/~court27

Civil Records: Access: Fax, mail, in person, online. Both court and visitors may perform in person searches. No search fee. Required to search: name, years to search. Civil cases indexed by defendant, plaintiff. Civil records on computer since 9/1/92, prior

on books since 1858. Participates in the free state online court record system at www.courts.mo.gov/casenet.

Criminal Records: Access: Fax, mail, in person, online. Both court and visitors may perform in person searches. No search fee. Required to search: name, years to search. Criminal records on computer since 9/1/92, prior on books since 1858. Participates in the free state online court record system at www.courts.mo.gov/casenet.

General Information: Public Access terminal is available. No juvenile, mental, expunged, dismissed, or suspended imposition of sentence records released. No fee to fax results. Copy fee: $.25 per page. Certification fee: $1.50. Payee: Circuit Court. Only cashiers checks and money orders accepted. Prepayment required. Mail requests: SASE required. Mail turnaround time varies.

Associate Circuit Court Courthouse, Butler, MO 64730; 660-679-3311. Hours: 8:30AM-4PM (CST). *Misdemeanor, Civil Actions Under $25,000, Eviction, Small Claims, Probate.*

Civil Records: Access: Mail, in person, online. Both court and visitors may perform in person searches, though visitors are limited. No search fee. Required to search: name, years to search. Civil cases indexed by defendant, plaintiff. Civil records on index cards (unsure of starting date). Participates in the free state online court record system at www.courts.mo.gov/casenet.

Criminal Records: Access: Mail, in person, online. Only the court performs in person searches; visitors may not. No search fee. Required to search: name, years to search, DOB; also helpful: SSN. Criminal records on computer since 1992, prior on index cards. Participates in the free state online court record system at www.courts.mo.gov/casenet.

General Information: Public Access terminal is available. No juvenile, mental, expunged, dismissed, or suspended imposition of sentence records released. Copy fee: $.50 per page. Certification fee: $1.50. Payee: Associate Circuit Court. Only cashiers checks and money orders accepted. Prepayment required. Mail requests: SASE required. Mail turnaround: 1 wk.

Benton County

Circuit & Associate Court PO Box 37, Warsaw, MO 65355; 660-438-7712; Fax: 660-438-5755. 8AM-4:30PM (CST). *Felony, Misdemeanor, Civil Actions, Eviction, Small Claims, Probate.*

www.positech.net/~dcourt

Note: Associate court clerk phone is 660-438-6231.

Civil Records: Access: Mail, in person, online. Visitors must perform in person searches for themselves. Search fee: none. Required to search: name, years to search. Civil cases indexed by defendant, plaintiff. Civil records on computer since 1993, prior on index cards since 1800. Participates in the statewide Casenet system at www.courts.mo.gov/casenet/.

Criminal Records: Access: In person, online. Visitors must perform in person searches for themselves, however, court may conduct search if time permits. Search fee: none. Required to search: name, years to search, DOB; also helpful: SSN. Criminal records on computer since 1993, prior on index cards since 1800. Participates in the statewide Casenet system at www.courts.mo.gov/casenet/. The court will only indicate if subject is on probation or has open case. Court recommends criminal searches at MO State Highway Patrol, 573-526-6288.

General Information: Public Access terminal is available. No juvenile, mental, expunged, dismissed, or suspended imposition of sentence records released. Copy fee: $1.00 for first page, $.25 each add'l. Certification fee: $2.50. Payee: Clerk of Circuit Court.

Cashier check or money orders accepted. Prepayment required.

Bollinger County

Circuit Court PO Box 949, Marble Hill, MO 63764; 573-238-1900 Ext 6; Fax: 573-238-2773. Hours: 8AM-4PM (CST). *Felony, Misdemeanor, Civil Actions Over $25,000.*

Civil Records: Access: Mail, in person, online. Only the court performs in person searches; visitors may not. No search fee. Required to search: name, years to search. Civil cases indexed by defendant, plaintiff. Civil records on computer since 1990, prior on index cards 1976-1990. Access to civil records is free at www.courts.mo.gov/casenet/. At the website, select the judicial district, then search by name, case # or date. Online records go back to 7/1/2001.

Criminal Records: Access: In person, online. Only the court performs in person searches; visitors may not. No search fee. Required to search: name, years to search. Criminal records on computer since 1990, prior on index cards 1976-1990. Online access to criminal records is the same as civil. Online public case records go back to 7/1/2001; judgments to 8/23/1993.

General Information: Public Access terminal is available. No juvenile, mental, expunged, dismissed, or suspended imposition of sentence records released. Copy fee: $1.00 for first page, $1.00 each add'l. Certification fee: $1.00. Payee: Circuit Clerk. Personal checks accepted. Prepayment required. Mail requests: SASE required. Mail turnaround: 1 day to 1 week.

Associate Circuit Court PO Box 1040, Marble Hill, MO 63764-1040; 573-238-1900 ext 4; Fax: 573-238-4511. Hours: 8AM-4PM (CST). *Misdemeanor, Civil Actions Under $25,000, Eviction, Small Claims, Probate.*

Civil Records: Access: In person, online. Visitors must perform in person searches for themselves. No search fee. Required to search: name, years to search. Civil cases indexed by defendant, plaintiff. Civil records on computer back to 1995, prior on books, archived to 1890. Participates in the free state online Banner court record system at www.courts.mo.gov/casenet. Online records go back to 7/1/2001.

Criminal Records: Access: In person, online. Visitors must perform in person searches for themselves. No search fee. Required to search: name, years to search. Criminal records on computer back to 1995, prior on books, archived to 1890. Online access to criminal records is the same as civil. Online public case records go back to 7/1/2001; judgments to 8/23/1993. Court recommends criminal searches at MO State Highway Patrol, 573-526-6288.

General Information: Public Access terminal is available. No juvenile, mental, expunged, dismissed, or suspended imposition of sentence records released. Copy fee: $1.00 per page. Certification fee: $1.50. Payee: Circuit Court Division V. Personal checks accepted. Prepayment required.

Boone County

Circuit and Associate Court 705 E Walnut, Columbia, MO 65201; 573-886-4000; Probate phone: 573-886-4090; Fax: 573-886-4044. Hours: 8AM-5PM (CST). *Felony, Misdemeanor, Civil, Eviction, Small Claims, Probate.*

Civil Records: Access: Phone, mail, online, in person. Visitors must perform in person searches for themselves. No search fee. Required to search: name, years to search. Civil cases indexed by defendant, plaintiff. Civil records on computer for recent cases, others on books. Participates in the free state online court record system at www.courts.mo.gov/casenet. Online civil records go back to 1986. Probate records back to 1986 are also online.

Criminal Records: Access: Online, in person. Visitors must perform in person searches for themselves. Search fee: None. Required to search: name, years to search, DOB. Criminal records on computer for recent cases, others on books. Online access to criminal records is the same as civil. Online criminal records go back to 1983. Court recommends criminal searches at MO State Highway Patrol, 573-526-6288.

General Information: Public Access terminal is available. No juvenile, mental, paternity, expunged, dismissed, or suspended imposition of sentence records released. Will not fax results. Copy fee: $.25 per page. Certification fee: $1.00. Payee: Boone County Circuit Clerk. Business checks accepted. Prepayment required. Mail requests: SASE required. Mail turnaround time varies.

Buchanan County

Circuit & Associate Court 411 Jules St, Rm 331, St Joseph, MO 64501; 816-271-1462; Fax: 816-271-1538. Hours: 8AM-5PM (CST). *Felony, Misdemeanor, Civil, Eviction, Small Claims.*

Civil Records: Access: In person, online. Visitors must perform in person searches for themselves. No search fee. Required to search: name, years to search. Civil cases indexed by defendant, plaintiff. Civil records on computer since 2/92, on index cards since 1976, prior archived. Participates in the free state online court record system at www.courts.mo.gov/casenet. Online records go back to 1992.

Criminal Records: Access: In person, online. Visitors must perform in person searches for themselves. No search fee. Required to search: name, years to search. Criminal records on computer since 2/92, on index cards since 1976, prior archived. Online access to criminal records is the same as civil. County Case.net records go back to 1992. Court recommends criminal searches at MO State Highway Patrol, 573-526-6288.

General Information: Public Access terminal is available. No juvenile, mental, expunged, dismissed, or suspended imposition of sentence records released. Copy fee: $.25 per page. Certification fee: $2.50. Payee: Buchanan Circuit Clerk. Personal checks accepted. Prepayment required.

Probate Court Buchanan County Courthouse, 411 Jules St, Rm 333, St Joseph, MO 64501; 816-271-1477; Fax: 816-271-1538. Hours: 8AM-5PM (CST). *Probate.*

Butler County

Circuit Court Courthouse, Poplar Bluff, MO 63901; 573-686-8082; Fax: 573-686-8094. Hours: 7:30AM-4PM (CST). *Felony, Misdemeanor, Civil Actions Over $25,000.*

Civil Records: Access: Fax, mail, in person. Visitors must perform in person searches for themselves. Search fee: $1.00 per name per year. Required to search: name, years to search. Civil cases indexed by defendant, plaintiff. Civil records on computer since 9/91, prior on cards and books since 1865.

Criminal Records: Access: In person only. Visitors must perform in person searches for themselves. Search fee: $1.00 per name per year. Required to search: name, years to search. Criminal records on computer since 9/91, prior on cards and books since 1865. Court personnel will not do name searches. Court recommends criminal searches at MO State Highway Patrol, 573-526-6288.

General Information: Public Access terminal is available. No juvenile, mental, expunged, dismissed, or suspended imposition of sentence records released. Will fax results $1.00 per page. Copy fee: $.25 per page. Certification fee: $2.50. Payee: Clerk of Circuit Court. Business checks accepted. Prepayment

required. Mail requests: SASE not required. Mail turnaround time 1-2 days.

Associate Circuit Court Courthouse, Poplar Bluff, MO 63901; 573-686-8087; Probate phone: 573-686-8073; Fax: 573-686-8093. Hours: 7:30AM-4PM (CST). *Misdemeanor, Civil Actions Under $25,000, Eviction, Small Claims, Probate.*

Note: Probate records are in a separate office at the courthouse.

Civil Records: Access: Phone, fax, mail, in person. Both court and visitors may perform in person searches. No search fee. Required to search: name, years to search. Civil cases indexed by defendant, plaintiff. Civil records on cards since 1976, and index books since 1900s.

Criminal Records: Access: Fax, mail, in person. Only the court performs in person searches; visitors may not. No search fee. Required to search: name, years to search, signed release. Criminal records on cards since 1976, and index books since early 1990s, computer back to 1991.

General Information: No juvenile, mental, expunged, dismissed, or suspended imposition of sentence records released. Fee to fax results is $.25 per page. Copy fee: $.25 per page. Certification fee: $2.50. Payee: Circuit Court Division II. Business checks accepted. Prepayment required. Mail requests: SASE required. Mail turnaround time varies.

Caldwell County

Circuit and Associate Court PO Box 68, Kingston, MO 64650; 816-586-2581; Fax: 816-586-2333. Hours: 7:30AM-4:30PM (CST). *Felony, Misdemeanor, Civil, Eviction, Small Claims, Probate.*

Civil Records: Access: Phone, mail, in person. Both court and visitors may perform in person searches. No search fee. Required to search: name, years to search. Civil cases indexed by defendant, plaintiff. Civil records archived since 1860; on computer back to 1995.

Criminal Records: Access: Phone, mail, in person. Both court and visitors may perform in person searches. No search fee. Required to search: name, years to search. Criminal records archived since 1860; on computer back to 1995.

General Information: Public Access terminal is available. No juvenile, mental, expunged, dismissed, or suspended imposition of sentence records released. Copy fee: $.25 per page. Certification fee: $1.50 per page. Payee: Circuit Clerk. Personal checks accepted. Prepayment required. Mail requests: SASE required. Mail turnaround: 3 days; phone turnaround: 1 day.

Callaway County

Circuit & Associate Court 10 E 5th St, Fulton, MO 65251; 573-642-0780; Fax: 573-642-0700. 8AM-5PM (CST). *Felony, Misdemeanor, Civil Actions, Eviction, Small Claims, Probate.*

Civil Records: Access: Fax, mail, in person, online. Both court and visitors may perform in person searches. Court will only perform searches as time permits No search fee. Required to search: name, years to search. Civil cases indexed by defendant, plaintiff. Civil records on index books and cards since 1821. Participates in the free state online court record system at www.courts.mo.gov/casenet. Online public cases go back to 2000; online probate to 1977.

Criminal Records: Access: In person, online. Visitors must perform in person searches for themselves. No search fee. Required to search: name, years to search; also helpful: DOB, SSN. Criminal records on computer since 1993, prior on index books and cards since 1821. Online access to criminal records is the same as civil.

General Information: Public Access terminal is available. No juvenile, mental, expunged, dismissed, or suspended imposition of sentence records released. Will fax results $.25 per page. Copy fee: $.25 per page. Certification fee: $1.00. Payee: Circuit Clerk. Business checks accepted. Attorney/law firm checks accepted. Prepayment required. Mail requests: SASE not required. Mail turnaround time 3 days.

Camden County

Circuit Court 1 Court Circle, #8, Camdenton, MO 65020; 573-346-4440; Fax: 573-346-5422. Hours: 8:30AM-4:30PM (CST). *Felony, Misdemeanor, Civil Actions Over $25,000.*

www.camdenmo.org

Civil Records: Access: Mail, in person. Both court and visitors may perform in person searches. No search fee. Required to search: name, years to search. Civil cases indexed by defendant, plaintiff. Civil records on computer since 1989, on index cards from 1965 to 1989, prior on index books since 1903.

Criminal Records: Access: In person only. Both court and visitors may perform in person searches. No search fee. Required to search: name, years to search; also helpful: DOB, SSN. Criminal records on computer since 1989, on index cards from 1965 to 1989, prior on index books since 1903. Court recommends criminal searches at MO State Highway Patrol, 573-526-6288.

General Information: No juvenile, mental, expunged, dismissed, or suspended imposition of sentence records released. Copy fee: $.25 per page. Certification fee: $1.50. Payee: Circuit Clerk. Only cashiers checks and money orders accepted.

Associate Circuit Court 1 Court Circle #8, Camdenton, MO 65020; 573-346-4440; Civil phone: X261; Criminal phone: X305; Fax: 573-346-5422. Hours: 8:00AM-5:00PM (CST). *Misdemeanor, Civil Actions Under $25,000, Eviction, Small Claims, Probate.*

www.camdenmo.org

Civil Records: Access: In person only. Visitors must perform in person searches for themselves. No search fee. Required to search: name, years to search. Civil cases indexed by defendant, plaintiff. Civil records on index cards since 1976; on computer back to 1989.

Criminal Records: Access: In person only. Both court and visitors may perform in person searches. No search fee. Required to search: name, years to search, DOB; also helpful: SSN. Criminal records on computer back to 1989, prior on index cards since 1980. Court recommends criminal searches at MO State Highway Patrol, 573-526-6288.

General Information: Public Access terminal is available. No juvenile, mental, expunged, dismissed, or suspended imposition of sentence records released. Will fax results for $1.00 per page. Copy fee: $.25 per page. Certification fee: $1.50. Payee: Circuit Clerk. Personal checks accepted.

Cape Girardeau County

Circuit & Associate Circuit Court - Civil Division 44 N Lorimier, PO Box 2047, Cape Girardeau, MO 63702; 573-335-8253; Fax: 573-331-2565. Hours: 8AM-4:30PM (CST). *Civil.*

Civil Records: Access: Mail, in person, online. Both court and visitors may perform in person searches. No search fee. Required to search: name, years to search. Civil cases indexed by defendant, plaintiff. Civil records on computer since 1994, prior on index cards since 10/75. Access to civil records is free at www.courts.mo.gov/casenet/. At the website, select the judicial district, then search by name, case # or date. Online records go back to 7/1/2001.

General Information: Public Access terminal is available. No juvenile, mental, expunged, dismissed, or suspended imposition of sentence, paternity, cases where one party on AFDC records released. Will fax results to local or toll free line. Copy fee: $1.00 for first page, $1.00 each add'l. Certification fee: $1.00. Payee: Circuit Clerk. Personal checks accepted. Prepayment required. Mail requests: SASE required. Mail turnaround time 1 week.

Circuit Court - Criminal Division I & II 100
Court St, Jackson, MO 63755; 573-243-8446 (misdemeanors); Criminal phone: 573-243-1755 (felo.); Fax: 573-204-2405. Hours: 8AM-4:30PM (CST). *Felony, Misdemeanor.*
Criminal Records: Access: Mail, in person, online. Both court and visitors may perform in person searches. Search fee: $10.00 per name. Required to search: name, years to search. Criminal records on computer since 1991, prior on books. Access to criminal records is free at www.courts.mo.gov/casenet/. Online public case records go back to 7/1/01; Circuit court judgments to 8/23/1993.
General Information: Public Access terminal is available. No juvenile, mental, expunged, dismissed, or suspended imposition of sentence records released. Will fax results to local or toll free line. Copy fee: $1.00 for first page, $.50 each add'l. Certification fee: $1.00. Payee: Circuit Clerk. Personal checks accepted. Prepayment required. Mail requests: SASE required. Mail turnaround time 1 week.

Carroll County

Circuit Court PO Box 245, Carrollton, MO 64633; 660-542-1466; Fax: 660-542-1444. Hours: 8:30AM-4:30PM (CST). *Felony, Misdemeanor, Civil Actions Over $25,000.*
Civil Records: Access: Fax, mail, in person, online. Both court and visitors may perform in person searches. No search fee. Required to search: name, years to search. Civil cases indexed by defendant, plaintiff. Civil records on books since 1833. Participates in the free state online court record system at www.courts.mo.gov/casenet. Records from 09/19/01 forward.
Criminal Records: Access: Fax, mail, in person, online. Both court and visitors may perform in person searches. No search fee. Required to search: name, years to search. Criminal records on books since 1833. Participates in the free state online court record system at www.courts.mo.gov/casenet. Records go back to 9/19/01 forward.
General Information: No juvenile, mental, expunged, dismissed, or suspended imposition of sentence records released. No fee to fax results. No copy fee. Certification fee: $2.00. Payee: Circuit Clerk. Personal checks accepted. Prepayment required. Mail requests: SASE not required. Mail turnaround time varies.

Associate Circuit Court Courthouse, 8 S
Main, #1, Carrollton, MO 64633; 660-542-1818; Fax: 660-542-1877. Hours: 8:30AM-4:30PM (CST). *Misdemeanor, Civil Actions Under $25,000, Eviction, Small Claims, Probate.*
Civil Records: Access: Mail, in person, online. Visitors must perform in person searches for themselves. No search fee. Required to search: name, years to search, address. Civil cases indexed by defendant, plaintiff. Civil records go back to 1990; on computer back to 12/2001. Participates in the free statewide Casenet court record system at www.courts.mo.gov/casenet. Online records go back to 09/19/01.
Criminal Records: Access: In person, online. Visitors must perform in person searches for themselves. No search fee. Required to search: name, years to search, address, DOB. Criminal records go back to 1990; on computer back to 12/2001.

Participates in the free statewide Casenet court record system at www.courts.mo.gov/casenet. Online records go back to 09/19/01. Court recommends criminal searches at MO State Highway Patrol, 573-526-6288.
General Information: Public Access terminal is available. No juvenile, mental, expunged, dismissed, or suspended imposition of sentence records released. Copy fee: $.35 per page. Certification fee: $2.50. Payee: Associate Circuit Court. Only cashiers checks and money orders accepted. Prepayment required.

Carter County

Circuit Court PO Box 578, Van Buren, MO 63965; 573-323-4513; Fax: 573-323-4885. Hours: 8AM-4PM (CST). *Felony, Misdemeanor, Civil Actions Over $20,000.*
Civil Records: Access: Fax, mail, in person, online. Both the court and visitors may perform in person searches. No search fee. Required to search: name, years to search. Civil cases indexed by defendant, plaintiff. Civil records on computer since 1979, on index cards since 1988, archived since late-1800s. Participates in the free state online court record system at www.courts.mo.gov/casenet. Online records go back to 4/17/2000.
Criminal Records: Access: In person, online. Visitors must perform in person searches. No search fee. Required to search: name, years to search. Criminal records on computer since 1979, on index cards since 1988, archived since late-1800s. Online access to criminal records is the same as civil. Court recommends criminal searches at MO State Highway Patrol, 573-526-6288.
General Information: No juvenile, mental, paternity, expunged, dismissed, or suspended imposition of sentence records released. Will fax results for fee. Copy fee: $.25 per page. Certification fee: $1.00. Payee: Circuit Clerk. Personal checks accepted. Prepayment required.

Associate Circuit Court PO Box 328, Van
Buren, MO 63965; 573-323-4344; Fax: 573-323-8914. Hours: 8AM-4PM (CST). *Misdemeanor, Civil Actions Under $20,000, Eviction, Small Claims, Probate.*
Civil Records: Access: Phone, fax, mail, in person, online. Only the court performs in person searches; visitors may not. Search fee: $5.00 per name. Required to search: name, years to search. Civil cases indexed by defendant, plaintiff. Civil records on index since 1994, prior on docket sheets. Participates in the free state online court record system at www.courts.mo.gov/casenet. Online records go back to 4/17/2000.
Criminal Records: Access: Phone, fax, mail, in person, online. Only the court performs in person searches; visitors may not. Search fee: $5.00 per name. Required to search: name, years to search. Criminal records on index since 1999, prior on docket sheets. Online access to criminal records is the same as civil.
General Information: No juvenile, mental, expunged, dismissed, or suspended imposition of sentence records released. Copy fee: $.25 per page. No certification fee. Payee: Circuit Court Division II. Personal checks accepted. Prepayment required. Mail requests: SASE required. Mail turnaround time varies.

Cass County

Circuit Court 102 E Wall, Harrisonville, MO 64701; 816-380-8230; Civil phone: 816-380-8235/8240; Probate phone: 816-380-8218; Fax: 816-380-8225. Hours: 8AM-5:00PM (CST). *Felony, Misdemeanor, Civil Actions Over $25,000.*
Note: Felony court can be reached at 816-380-8229. Misdemeanor Court can be reached at 816-380-8226.

Civil Records: Access: Phone, mail, in person. Both court and visitors must perform in person searches. No search fee. Required to search: name, years to search. Civil cases indexed by defendant, plaintiff. Civil records on computer since 1992, on index cards since 1976, prior on judgment books since 1800s.
Criminal Records: Access: Phone, mail, in person. Both court and visitors may perform in person searches. No search fee. Required to search: name, years to search. Criminal records on computer since 1992, on index cards since 1976, prior on judgment books since 1800s.
General Information: Public Access terminal is available. No juvenile, mental, expunged, dismissed, or suspended imposition of sentence records released. Copy fee: $.25 per page. Certification fee: $1.50. Payee: Cass County Circuit Clerk. Personal checks not accepted. Prepayment required. Mail requests: SASE required. Mail turnaround time 2-3 weeks.

Associate Circuit Court 2501 W Well St,
Harrisonville, MO 64701; 816-380-8200; Fax: 816-380-8195. Hours: 8AM-4:30PM (CST). *Misdemeanor, Civil Actions Under $25,000, Eviction, Small Claims, Felony.*
Civil Records: Access: Mail, in person. Visitors must perform in person searches for themselves. No search fee. Required to search: name, years to search. Civil cases indexed by defendant, plaintiff. Civil records go back to 1960s; on index cards since 1983.
Criminal Records: Access: Mail, in person. Visitors must perform in person searches for themselves. No search fee. Required to search: name, years to search, signed release. Criminal records go back to 1960s; on index cards since 1983; on computer back to 1995.
General Information: Public Access terminal is available. No juvenile, mental, expunged, dismissed, or suspended imposition of sentence records released. Copy fee: $.35 per page. No certification fee. Payee: Division III. Business checks accepted. Prepayment required. Mail requests: SASE required. Mail turnaround time varies.

Probate Court 2501 W. Wall St, Harrisonville,
MO 64701; 816-380-8217; Fax: 816-380-8215. Hours: 8AM-4:30PM (CST). *Probate.*

Cedar County

Circuit & Associate Court PO Box 665, Stockton, MO 65785; 417-276-6700; Fax: 417-276-5001. Hours: 8AM-4:30PM (CST). *Felony, Misdemeanor, Civil Actions, Eviction, Small Claims, Probate.*
Civil Records: Access: Fax, mail, in person, online. Both court and visitors may perform in person searches. No search fee. Required to search: name, years to search. Civil cases indexed by defendant, plaintiff. Civil records on index cards since 1979, prior on docket books to 1830. Participates in the free state online court record system at www.courts.mo.gov/casenet. online records go back to 9/11/2000. Online records include Probate Court.
Criminal Records: Access: Fax, mail, in person, online. Both court and visitors may perform in person searches. No search fee. Required to search: name, years to search. Criminal records on index cards since 1979, prior on docket books. Online access to criminal records is the same as civil.
General Information: Public Access terminal is available. No juvenile, mental, expunged, dismissed, or suspended imposition of sentence records released. Fee to fax results is $1.00 per page. Copy fee: $.25 per page. Certification fee: $1.50, includes copy fee. Payee: Cedar County Circuit Court. Personal checks accepted. Prepayment required. Mail turnaround time varies.

Chariton County

Circuit Court PO Box 112, Keytesville, MO 65261; 660-288-3602; Fax: 660-288-3763. Hours: 8:30AM-4:30PM (CST). *Felony, Misdemeanor, Civil Actions Over $25,000.*

Civil Records: Access: Fax, mail, in person, online. Both court and visitors may perform in person searches. Search fee: $4.00 per name. Required to search: name, years to search. Civil cases indexed by defendant, plaintiff. Civil records on index books since 1975, prior on docket books to 1827. Record access fee at www.courts.mo.gov/casenet/.

Criminal Records: Access: Fax, mail, in person, online. Both court and visitors may perform in person searches. Search fee: $4.00 per name. Required to search: name, years to search; also helpful: DOB, SSN. Criminal records on index books since 1975, prior on docket books to 1827. Participates in the free state online court record system at www.courts.mo.gov/casenet.

General Information: Public Access terminal is available. No juvenile, mental, expunged, dismissed, or suspended imposition of sentence records released. Fee to fax results is $1.00 per page. Copy fee: $1.00 per page. Certification fee: $1.50. Payee: Chariton County Circuit Clerk. Personal checks accepted. Prepayment required. Mail requests: SASE required. Mail turnaround time same day.

Associate Circuit Court 306 South Cherry, Keytesville, MO 65261; 660-288-3271; Fax: 660-288-1511. Hours: 8AM-4:30PM (CST). *Misdemeanor, Civil Actions Under $25,000, Eviction, Small Claims, Probate.*

Civil Records: Access: Phone, fax, mail, in person, online. Both court and visitors may perform in person searches. No search fee. Required to search: name, years to search. Civil cases indexed by defendant, plaintiff. Civil from records indexed on cards by year 1977 thru 2002, and on computer from 5/13/2002. Participates in the free state online court record system at www.courts.mo.gov/casenet/.

Criminal Records: Access: Phone, fax, mail, in person. Both court and visitors may perform in person searches. No search fee. Required to search: name, years to search; also helpful: DOB, SSN. Criminal from records indexed on cards by year 1977 thru 2002, and on computer from 5/13/2002. Participates in the free state online court record system at www.courts.mo.gov/casenet/.

General Information: Public Access terminal is available. No juvenile, mental, expunged, dismissed, or suspended imposition of sentence records released. Copy fee: $1.00 per page. Certification fee: $1.50. Payee: Associate Circuit Court or Probate Court (depending on search). Personal checks accepted. Prepayment required. Mail requests: SASE required. Mail turnaround: 1 week; phone turnaround is 2 days.

Christian County

Circuit Court PO Box 278, Ozark, MO 65721; 417-581-6372; Probate phone: 417-581-4523; Fax: 417-581-0391. Hours: 8AM-4:30PM (CST). *Felony, Misdemeanor, Civil Actions Over $45,000.*
www.geocities.com/circuit38

Civil Records: Access: Mail, in person, online. Both court and visitors may perform in person searches. Search fee: $6.00 per name. Required to search: name, years to search. Civil cases indexed by defendant, plaintiff. Civil records on computer since 9/97, pending cases indexed in card files. Old case card files back to 1979. Participates in the free state online court record system at www.courts.mo.gov/casenet. Online records are from 6/13/03 forward only.

Criminal Records: Access: Mail, in person, online. Both court and visitors may perform in person searches. Search fee: $6.00 per name. Required to search: name, years to search. Criminal records on computer since 9/97, pending cases indexed in card files. Old case card files back to 1979. Participates in the free state online court record system at www.courts.mo.gov/casenet. Online records are from 6/13/03 forward only.

General Information: Public Access terminal is available. No juvenile, mental, expunged, dismissed, or suspended imposition or execution of sentence records released. Will fax results for $.50 per page. Copy fee: $.50 per page. Certification fee: $1.00. Payee: Christian County Circuit Clerk. Personal checks accepted. Prepayment required. Mail requests: SASE required. Mail turnaround time 1 week.

Associate Circuit Court - Civil Division 1 110 W Elm St, Rm 203, Ozark, MO 65721; 417-581-2425. Hours: 8AM-4:30PM (CST). *Civil Actions Under $45,000, Eviction, Small Claims.*

Civil Records: Access: Phone, mail, in person, online. Both court and visitors may perform in person searches. No search fee. Required to search: name, years to search. Civil cases indexed by defendant. Civil records on computer since 07/91. Participates in the free state online court record system at www.courts.mo.gov/casenet.

General Information: No juvenile, mental, expunged or dismissed records released. Copy fee: If court makes copy $.50, otherwise no charge. No certification fee. Payee: Associate Division I. Personal checks accepted. Prepayment required. Mail requests: SASE required. Mail turnaround time 5 days, phone turnaround is immediate.

Associate Circuit Court - Criminal Division 2 110 W Elm St, Rm 105, Ozark, MO 65721; 417-581-4523; Fax: 417-581-1443. Hours: 8AM-4:30PM (CST). *Misdemeanor, Probate.*

Note: This court will not perform name searches and asks searcheres to contact the MSHP at 573-526-6288.

Criminal Records: Access: In person, online. Visitors must perform in person searches for themselves. No search fee. Required to search: name, years to search. Criminal records on computer since 1989; some prior on index cards. Participates in the free state online court record system at www.courts.mo.gov/casenet. Will accept phone requests from attorneys and law enforcement officials. Court recommends criminal searches at MO State Highway Patrol, 573-526-6288.

General Information: Public Access terminal is available. (The terminal is in the Circuit Clerk's office, but does include records from this court.) No juvenile, mental, expunged or dismissed records released. Copy fee: $.30 per page. Certification fee: $1.50. Payee: Associate Division 2. Prepayment required.

Clark County

Circuit Court 111 E Court, #2, Kahoka, MO 63445; 660-727-3292; Fax: 660-727-1051. Hours: 8AM-4PM (CST). *Felony, Misdemeanor, Civil Actions Over $45,000.*

Civil Records: Access: Phone, fax, mail, in person, online. Both court and visitors may perform in person searches. No search fee. Required to search: name, years to search. Civil cases indexed by defendant, plaintiff. Civil records on books since 1991, prior archived since 1836. Participates in the free statewide Casenet court record system at www.courts.mo.gov/casenet. Online records go back to 09/19/01.

Criminal Records: Access: Phone, fax, mail, in person, online. Both court and visitors may perform in person searches. No search fee. Required to search: name, years to search. Criminal records on books since 1991, prior archived since 1836. Participates in the free statewide Casenet court record system at www.courts.mo.gov/casenet. Online records go back to 09/19/01.

General Information: Public Access terminal is available. No juvenile, mental, expunged, dismissed, or suspended imposition of sentence records released. Fee to fax results is $1.00 per page. Copy fee: $.50 per page. Certification fee: $3.00. Payee: Clerk of Circuit Court. Personal checks accepted. Prepayment required. Mail requests: SASE required. Mail turnaround time 4 days.

Associate Circuit Court 113 W Court, Kahoka, MO 63445; 660-727-3628; Fax: 660-727-2544. Hours: 8AM-4PM (CST). *Misdemeanor, Civil Actions Under $45,000, Eviction, Small Claims, Probate.*

Civil Records: Access: Mail, fax, in person, online. Both the court and visitors may perform in person searches. No search fee. Required to search: name, years to search. Civil cases indexed by defendant, plaintiff. Civil records on index cards, archived since 1836. Participates in the free statewide Casenet court record system at www.courts.mo.gov/casenet. Online records go back to 09/19/01.

Criminal Records: Access: Mail, fax, in person, online. Both the court and visitors may perform in person searches. No search fee. Required to search: name, years to search. Criminal records on computer since 1988, prior archived since 1836. Participates in the free statewide Casenet court record system at www.courts.mo.gov/casenet. Online records go back to 09/19/01.

General Information: Public Access terminal is available. No juvenile, mental, expunged, dismissed, or suspended imposition of sentence records released. Copy fee: $.25 per page. Certification fee: $1.50 plus $1.00 per add'l page. Payee: Associate Circuit Court. Personal checks accepted. Prepayment required. Mail requests: SASE required. Mail turnaround time 1-10 days.

Clay County

Circuit Court PO Box 218, Liberty, MO 64069-0218; 816-792-7706; Fax: 816-792-7778. Hours: 8AM-5PM (CST). *Felony, Misdemeanor, Civil Actions Over $25,000.*
www.circuit7.net

Civil Records: Access: Fax, mail, in person, online. Both court and visitors may perform in person searches. No search fee. Required to search: name, years to search. Civil cases indexed by defendant, plaintiff. Civil records on computer since 1988; prior records on index. Online access to civil records on the circuit database is free at www.circuit7.net/pages/publicaccess/publicaccess.htm. Includes traffic.

Criminal Records: Access: In person, online. Visitors must perform in person searches for themselves. No search fee. Required to search: name, years to search, DOB. Criminal records on computer since 1994, prior on index cards. Online access to Circuit criminal records is free at www.circuit7.net/pages/publicaccess/publicaccess.htm. Court recommends criminal searches at MO State Highway Patrol, 573-526-6288.

General Information: Public Access terminal is available. No juvenile, mental, expunged, dismissed, or suspended imposition of sentence records released. Copy fee: $.25 per page. Certification fee: $5.00. Payee: Clay County Circuit Clerk. Personal checks accepted. Prepayment required. Mail requests: SASE required. Mail turnaround time 1-2 days.

Associate Circuit Court PO Box 218, Liberty, MO 64069-0218; 816-792-7706; Fax: 816-792-7778. 8AM-5PM (CST). *Misdemeanor, Civil Actions Under $25,000, Eviction, Small Claims, Probate.* www.circuit7.net

Civil Records: Access: Mail, in person, online. Both court and visitors may perform in person searches. No search fee. Required to search: name, years to search. Civil cases indexed by defendant, plaintiff. Civil records on computer since 6/86, prior on microfilm. Access to Circuit records is free at www.circuit7.net/pages/publicaccess/publicaccess.htm.

Criminal Records: Access: Mail, in person, online. Both court and visitors may perform in person searches. No search fee. Required to search: name, years to search. Criminal records on computer since 01/99, prior on microfilm. Online access to Circuit 7 records is free at www.circuit7.net/pages/publicaccess/publicaccess.htm.

General Information: Public Access terminal is available. No juvenile, mental, expunged, dismissed, or suspended imposition of sentence records if record closed released. Copy fee: $.25 per page. Certification fee: $5.00. Payee: Clay County Circuit Court. Personal checks accepted. Prepayment required. Mail requests: SASE required. Mail turnaround: 7-10 days.

Clinton County

Circuit Court PO Box 275, Plattsburg, MO 64477; 816-539-3731; Fax: 816-539-3893. Hours: 8AM-5PM (CST). *Felony, Misdemeanor, Civil Actions Over $25,000.*

Civil Records: Access: In person only. Visitors must perform in person searches for themselves. No search fee. Required to search: name, years to search. Civil cases indexed by defendant, plaintiff. Civil records (Judgments) on computer from 1976, archived since 1833.

Criminal Records: Access: In person only. Visitors must perform in person searches for themselves. No search fee. Required to search: name, years to search. Criminal records (Judgments) on computer from 1976, archived since 1833. Court recommends criminal searches at MO State Highway Patrol, 573-526-6288.

General Information: Public Access terminal is available. No juvenile, mental, expunged, dismissed, or suspended imposition of sentence records released. Copy fee: $1.00 per page. Certification fee: $1.50. Payee: Circuit Clerk. Personal checks not accepted. Prepayment required.

Associate Circuit Court PO Box 383, Plattsburg, MO 64477; 816-539-3755; Probate phone: 816-539-3298; Fax: 816-539-3439. Hours: 8AM-4:30PM (CST). *Misdemeanor, Civil Actions Under $45,000, Eviction, Small Claims, Probate.*

Civil Records: Access: Fax, mail, in person. Only the court performs in person searches; visitors may not. No search fee. Required to search: name, years to search. Civil cases indexed by defendant, plaintiff. Civil records on computer since 1992, prior on index cards since 1940s. Letterhead required for mail searches.

Criminal Records: Access: Fax, mail, in person. Only the court performs in person searches; visitors may not. No search fee. Required to search: name, years to search, DOB; also helpful - SSN. Criminal records on computer since 1992, prior on index cards since 1940s. Letterhead required for mail searches.

General Information: No juvenile, mental, expunged, dismissed, or suspended imposition of sentence records released. No copy fee. No certification fee. Mail requests: SASE required. Mail turnaround time 1 week.

Cole County

Circuit & Associate Court PO Box 1870, Jefferson City, MO 65102-1870; Civil phone: 573-634-9151; Criminal phone: 573-634-9171; Fax: 573-635-0796. Hours: 7:30AM-4:30PM (CST). *Felony, Misdemeanor, Civil Actions, Eviction, Small Claims, Probate.*

Note: The Circuit and Associate Courts consolidated on 01/01.

Civil Records: Access: Fax, mail, in person, online. Both court and visitors may perform in person searches. No search fee. Required to search: name, years to search. Civil cases indexed by defendant, plaintiff. Civil records (pending) on computer, on books since 1820. Participates in the free state online court record system at www.courts.mo.gov/casenet. Online records go back to 1/1980; probate to 6/2/72.

Criminal Records: Access: In person, online, fax, mail. Both court and visitors may perform in person searches. No search fee. Required to search: name, years to search; also helpful: DOB, SSN. Criminal records on computer since 1989, prior on book since 1820. Participates in the free state online court record system at www.courts.mo.gov/casenet. Online records go back to 1/1980. Court recommends criminal searches at MO State Highway Patrol, 573-526-6288.

General Information: Public Access terminal is available. No juvenile, mental, expunged, dismissed, or suspended imposition of sentence records released. Other access to criminal records: the court prefers that requesters go to the state highway patrol. Copy fee: $.25 per page. Certification fee: $1.00. Payee: Cole County Circuit Clerk. Personal checks accepted. Prepayment required. Mail requests: SASE requested. Turnaround time 2-5 days.

Cooper County

Circuit Court 200 Main St, Rm 26, Boonville, MO 65233; 660-882-2232; Fax: 660-882-2043. Hours: 8:30AM-5:00PM (CST). *Felony, Misdemeanor, Civil Actions Over $25,000.*

Civil Records: Access: Phone, fax, mail, in person, online. Both court and visitors may perform in person searches. No search fee. Required to search: name, years to search. Civil cases indexed by defendant, plaintiff. Civil records on cards since 1975, case files from 1819 forward; on computer back to 2001. Access to civil records is free at www.courts.mo.gov/casenet/. At the website, select the judicial district, then search by name, case # or date. Online records go back to 4/2001.

Criminal Records: Access: Mail, in person, online. Both court and visitors may perform in person searches. No search fee. Required to search: name, years to search, DOB; also helpful: SSN. Criminal records on cards since 1975, case files from 1819 forward; on computer back to 2001. Online access to criminal records is the same as civil.

General Information: Public Access terminal is available. No juvenile, mental, expunged, dismissed, or suspended imposition of sentence records released. Copy fee: $1.00 per page. Certification fee: $1.50. Payee: Circuit Clerk or Recorder of Deeds. Personal checks accepted. Prepayment required. Mail requests: SASE required. Mail turnaround time 1-2 days. Can tell you if record is available and cost over phone.

Associate Circuit Court 200 Main, Rm 31, Boonville, MO 65233; 660-882-5604; Fax: 660-882-8747. Hours: 8:30AM-5PM (CST). *Misdemeanor, Civil Actions Under $25,000, Eviction, Small Claims, Probate.*

Civil Records: Access: Mail, in person, online. No search fee. Required to search: name, years to search. Civil cases indexed by defendant, plaintiff. Civil

records on index cards since 1990, computerized since 2000. Access to civil records is free at www.courts.mo.gov/casenet/. At the website, select the judicial district, then search by name, case # or date. Online records go back to 4/2001.

Criminal Records: Access: Mail, in person, online. Both court and visitors may perform in person searches. No search fee. Required to search: name, years to search, DOB; also helpful: SSN. Criminal records on computer since mid-1990s, on index cards from 1980-1990. Online access to criminal records is the same as civil. Online criminal records go back 1/1990.

General Information: Public Access terminal is available. No juvenile, mental, expunged, dismissed, or suspended imposition of sentence records released. Copy fee: $1.00 per page. Certification fee: $1.50. Payee: Cooper County Associate Circuit Court. Prepayment required. Mail requests: SASE required. Mail turnaround time 10 days.

Crawford County

Circuit Court PO Box 177, Steelville, MO 65565; 573-775-2866; Probate phone: 573-775-214; Fax: 573-775-2452. Hours: 8AM-4:30PM (CST). *Felony, Misdemeanor, Civil Actions Over $25,000.*

Civil Records: Access: Mail, in person, online. Both court and visitors may perform in person searches. Search fee: $4.00 per name. Required to search: name, years to search. Civil cases indexed by defendant, plaintiff. Civil records on computer from 03/02/92 for judgments only, archived from 1800s, some records on index cards and books. Participates in the free state online JIS Banner court record system at www.courts.mo.gov/casenet.

Criminal Records: Access: Mail, in person, online. Both court and visitors may perform in person searches. Search fee: $4.00 per name. Required to search: name, years to search, offense, date of offense. Criminal records on computer since 03/02/92, prior on cards. Online access to criminal court records is the same as civil.

General Information: Public Access terminal is available. No juvenile, mental, expunged, dismissed, or suspended imposition of sentence records released. Copy fee: $.50 per page. Certification fee: $1.00. Payee: Crawford County Circuit Clerk. Personal checks not accepted. Prepayment required. Mail requests: SASE required. Mail turnaround time as time permits.

Associate Circuit Court PO Box B.C., Steelville, MO 65565; 573-775-2149; Fax: 573-775-4010. Hours: 8AM-5PM (CST). *Misdemeanor, Civil Actions Under $25,000, Eviction, Small Claims, Probate.*

Note: The court will not do record searches, however the court will look up specific case file is case number given.

Civil Records: Access: In person, online. Visitors must perform in person searches for themselves. No search fee. Required to search: name, years to search. Civil cases indexed by defendant, plaintiff. Civil records kept since 1989 on paper, prior destroyed. Access to records is free at www.courts.mo.gov/casenet/.

Criminal Records: Access: Online only. Per judge's orders, court will not accept search requests or perform criminal record searches. No search fee. Criminal records kept since 1996, prior destroyed. Access to records is free at www.courts.mo.gov/casenet/. Court recommends criminal searches at MO State Highway Patrol, 573-526-6288.

General Information: No sealed records released. No fee to fax results. Copy fee: $.30 per page. Certification fee: $2.50. Payee: Associate Circuit

Court. Personal checks accepted. Prepayment required.

Dade County

Circuit & Associate Court Courthouse, Greenfield, MO 65661; 417-637-2271; Fax: 417-637-5055. 8AM-4PM (CST). *Felony, Misdemeanor, Civil Actions, Eviction, Small Claims, Probate.*

Civil Records: Access: Mail, in person, online. Both court and visitors may perform in person searches. Search fee: $5.00. Required to search: name, years to search. Civil cases indexed by defendant, plaintiff. Civil records in index cards since 1982, prior on books to 1800s; on computer back to 2000. Participates in the free state online court record system at www.courts.mo.gov/casenet. Online records go back to 9/20/1999. Online records include Probate Court.

Criminal Records: Access: Mail, in person, online. Both court and visitors may perform in person searches. Search fee: $5.00. Required to search: name, years to search; also helpful-DOB, SSN, signed release. Criminal records in index cards since 1982, prior on book to 1800s; on computer back to 2000. Online access to criminal records is the same as civil.

General Information: Public Access terminal is available. No juvenile, mental, expunged, dismissed, or suspended imposition of sentence records released. Will fax results. Copy fee: $1.00 per page. Certification fee: $2.50. Payee: Dade County Circuit Clerk. Personal checks accepted. Prepayment required. Mail requests: SASE required. Mail turnaround time 2-3 days.

Dallas County

Circuit Court PO Box 373, 108 S Maple St, Buffalo, MO 65622; 417-345-2243; Fax: 417-345-5539. Hours: 7:30AM-4PM (CST). *Felony, Misdemeanor, Civil Actions Over $25,000.* www.positech.net/~dcourt

Civil Records: Access: Phone, fax, mail, in person, online. Both court and visitors may perform in person searches. No search fee. Required to search: name, years to search. Civil cases indexed by defendant, plaintiff. Civil records on computer since 1991, prior on book since 1951. Participates in the free state online court record system at www.courts.mo.gov/casenet.

Criminal Records: Access: In person, online. Visitors must perform in person searches for themselves. No search fee. Required to search: name, years to search; also helpful: DOB. Criminal records on computer since 1992, prior on book since 1951. Online access to criminal records is the same as civil. Court recommends criminal searches at MO State Highway Patrol, 573-526-6288.

General Information: Public Access terminal is available. No juvenile, mental, expunged, dismissed, or suspended imposition of sentence records released. Fee to fax results is $1.00 per page. Copy fee: $.25 per page. Certification fee: $1.00 per doc. Payee: Circuit Clerk. Personal checks accepted. Prepayment required. Mail requests: SASE required. Mail turnaround time 1-2 days.

Associate Circuit Court PO Box 1150, Buffalo, MO 65622; 417-345-7641; Fax: 417-345-5358. Hours: 8AM-Noon, 1-4PM (CST). *Misdemeanor, Civil Actions Under $45,000, Eviction, Small Claims, Probate.*

Civil Records: Access: Phone, mail, in person, online. Both court and visitors may perform in person searches. No search fee. Required to search: name, years to search. Civil cases indexed by defendant, plaintiff. Civil records on index cards since 1800s; computerized since 1990. Participates in the free statewide Casenet court record system at www.courts.mo.gov/casenet. Records go back to 1992.

Criminal Records: Access: Phone, in person, online. Visitors must perform in person searches for themselves. No search fee. Required to search: name, years to search. Criminal records on computer since 1990, on index cards since 1800s. Participates in the free statewide Casenet court record system at www.courts.mo.gov/casenet. Records go back to 1992. Court recommends criminal searches at MO State Highway Patrol, 573-526-6288. Court will do a single name search only, maybe.

General Information: Public Access terminal is available. (Public terminal located in main Circuit Court Clerk office.) No juvenile, mental, expunged, dismissed, or suspended imposition of sentence records released. Copy fee: $.25 per page. Certification fee: $1.00 per page. Payee: Associate Circuit Court. Only cashiers checks and money orders accepted. Prepayment required. Mail requests: SASE required. Mail turnaround time 1 day.

Daviess County

Circuit Court PO Box 337, Gallatin, MO 64640; 660-663-2932; Probate phone: 660-663-2532; Fax: 660-663-3876. Hours: 8AM-4:30PM (CST). *Felony, Misdemeanor, Civil Actions Over $45,000.*

Civil Records: Access: Phone, fax, mail, in person. Both court and visitors may perform in person searches. Search fee: $10.00 per name. Required to search: name, years to search. Civil cases indexed by defendant, plaintiff. Civil records on records books since 1839.

Criminal Records: Access: Phone, fax, mail, in person. Both court and visitors may perform in person searches. Search fee: $10.00 per name. Required to search: name, years to search, DOB. Criminal records on records books since 1839.

General Information: No juvenile, mental, expunged, dismissed, or suspended imposition of sentence records released. Will fax results $2.00 per page. Copy fee: $1.00 per page. Certification fee: $2.00. Payee: Daviess County Circuit Clerk. Business checks accepted. Prepayment required. Mail requests: SASE required. Mail turnaround time 1 day; phone turnaround is immediate.

Associate Division Circuit Court Courthouse, PO Box 233, 102 N Main St #6, Gallatin, MO 64640; 660-663-2532. Hours: 8AM-4:30PM (CST). *Misdemeanor, Civil Actions Under $45,000, Eviction, Small Claims, Probate.*

Note: Probate records are unavailable before 1890 due to Courthouse fire.

Civil Records: Access: Fax, mail, in person. Only the court may perform in person searches. No search fee. Required to search: name, years to search. Civil cases indexed by defendant, plaintiff. Civil records index cards since 9/84, prior on judgment books.

Criminal Records: Access: Mail, in person. Only the court may perform in person searches. No search fee. Required to search: name, years to search. Criminal records on index cards since 1979, prior on judgment books.

General Information: No juvenile, mental, expunged, dismissed, or suspended imposition of sentence records released. Will fax results for $2.00. Copy fee: $1.00 per page. Certification fee: $1.50. Payee: Associate Division Court. Only cashiers checks and money orders accepted. Prepayment required. Mail requests: SASE required. Mail turnaround time 1-2 days.

De Kalb County

Circuit Court PO Box 248, Maysville, MO 64469; 816-449-2602; Probate phone: 816-449-5400; Fax: 816-449-2440. Hours: 8:30AM-4:30PM (CST). *Felony, Civil Actions Over $45,000.*

Civil Records: Access: In person only. Visitors must perform in person searches for themselves. Search fee: none. Required to search: name, years to search. Civil cases indexed by defendant, plaintiff. Civil records on index cards since 1970, computerized since 2003.

Criminal Records: Access: In person only. Visitors must perform in person searches for themselves. No search fee. Required to search: name, years to search. Criminal records on index cards since 1970, computerized since 2003. Court recommends criminal searches at MO State Highway Patrol, 573-526-6288.

General Information: No juvenile or suspended imposition of sentence records released. Copy fee: $1.00 per page. Certification fee: $1.00. Payee: Clifton DeShon, Circuit Clerk. Personal checks accepted. Prepayment required. Mail turnaround time 2 days if specific case number given.

Associate Circuit Court PO Box 248, Maysville, MO 64469; 816-449-5400; Fax: 816-449-2440. Hours: 8:30AM-4:30PM (CST). *Misdemeanor, Civil Actions Under $45,000, Eviction, Small Claims, Probate.*

Note: Court personbel will not do name searches.

Civil Records: Access: In person only. Visitors must perform in person searches for themselves. No search fee. Required to search: name, years to search. Civil cases indexed by defendant, plaintiff. Civil records on index cards since 1960s.

Criminal Records: Access: In person only. Visitors must perform in person searches for themselves. No search fee. Required to search: name, years to search; DOB; also helpful-SSN, case number. Criminal records on index cards since 1980s. Court recommends criminal searches at MO State Highway Patrol, 573-526-6288.

General Information: No juvenile, mental, expunged, dismissed, or suspended imposition of sentence records released. Copy fee: $1.00 per page. Certification fee: $2.50. Payee: Associate Circuit Court. Only cashiers checks and money orders accepted. Prepayment required.

Dent County

Circuit Court 112 E 5th St, Salem, MO 65560; 573-729-3931; Probate phone: 573-729-3134; Fax: 573-729-9414. Hours: 8AM-4:30PM (CST). *Felony, Misdemeanor, Civil Actions Over $25,000.*

Note: Small Claims and Probate fax is 573-729-5172.

Civil Records: Access: Mail, fax, in person, online. Both court and visitors may perform in person searches. No search fee. Required to search: name, years to search. Civil cases indexed by defendant, plaintiff. Civil records on computer since 1993, on index cards since 1978. Participates in the free statewide Casenet court record system at www.courts.mo.gov/casenet.

Criminal Records: Access: In person, online. Visitors must perform in person searches for themselves. No search fee. Required to search: name, years to search. Criminal records on computer since 1993, on index cards since 1978. Participates in the free statewide Casenet court record system at www.courts.mo.gov/casenet.

General Information: Public Access terminal is available. No juvenile, mental, expunged, dismissed, or suspended imposition of sentence records released. Copy fee: $.25 per page. Certification fee: $2.00. Payee: Dent County Circuit Clerk. Only cashiers checks and money orders accepted. Prepayment required. Mail requests: SASE required. Mail turnaround time 3-4 days.

Associate Circuit Court

Associate Circuit Court 112 E 5th St, Salem, MO 65560; 573-729-3134; Fax: 573-729-5172. 8AM-4:30PM (CST). *Misdemeanor, Civil Actions Under $25,000, Eviction, Small Claims, Probate.*
Civil Records: Access: Mail, fax, in person, online. Both court and visitors may perform in person searches. No search fee. Required to search: name, years to search. Civil cases indexed by defendant, plaintiff. Civil records on computer since 1985, prior on index cards. Participates in the free statewide Casenet court record system at www.courts.mo.gov/casenet.
Criminal Records: Access: Mail, fax, in person, online. Both court and visitors may perform in person searches. No search fee. Required to search: name, years to search, DOB, signed release. Criminal records on computer since 1985, prior on index cards. Participates in the free statewide Casenet court record system at www.courts.mo.gov/casenet.
General Information: Public Access terminal is available. No juvenile, mental, expunged, dismissed, or suspended imposition of sentence records released. Will not fax results. Copy fee: $.25 per page. Certification fee: $2.00. Payee: Associate Circuit Court or Probate Court. Business checks accepted. Prepayment required. Mail requests: SASE required. Mail turnaround time 2-3 days.

Douglas County

Circuit Court PO Box 249, Ava, MO 65608; 417-683-4713; Fax: 417-683-2794. 8AM-4:30PM (CST). *Felony, Misdemeanor, Civil Actions Over $25,000.*
Civil Records: Access: Phone, mail, in person. Visitors must perform in person searches for themselves. Search fee: $10.00 per hour. Required to search: name, years to search. Civil cases indexed by defendant, plaintiff. Civil records on alpha cards since 1977.
Criminal Records: Access: Phone, mail, in person. Visitors must perform in person searches for themselves. Search fee: $10.00 per hour. Required to search: name, years to search; also helpful: DOB, SSN. Criminal records on alpha cards since 1977.
General Information: Public Access terminal is available. No juvenile, mental, expunged, dismissed, or suspended imposition of sentence records released. Will fax results to local or toll free line. Copy fee: $.25 per page. Certification fee: $2.50. Payee: Circuit Clerk. Personal checks accepted. Prepayment required. Mail requests: SASE required. Mail turnaround time 1 week.

Associate Circuit Court PO Box 276, 203 SE 2nd St, Ava, MO 65608; 417-683-2114; Fax: 417-683-3121. 8AM-4:30PM (CST). *Misdemeanor, Civil Actions Under $25,000, Eviction, Small Claims, Probate.*
Civil Records: Access: Mail, in person. Only the court performs in person searches; visitors may not. No search fee. Required to search: name, years to search. Civil cases indexed by defendant, plaintiff. Civil records on index cards and computer.
Criminal Records: Access: In person only. Only the court performs in person searches; visitors may not. Court rarely allows for mail requests. No search fee. Required to search: name, years to search; also helpful: SSN. Criminal records on computer back to 1991.
General Information: No juvenile, mental, expunged, dismissed, or suspended imposition of sentence records released. Copy fee: $.25 per page. Certification fee: $1.50. Payee: Associate Circuit Court. Personal checks accepted. Prepayment

required. Mail requests: SASE required. Mail turnaround time 2-3 days.

Dunklin County

Circuit Court Division I PO Box 567, Kennett, MO 63857; 573-888-2456; Fax: 573-888-0319. 8:30AM-4:30PM (CST). *Felony, Misdemeanor, Civil Actions Over $25,000.*
www.osca.state.mo.us
Civil Records: Access: In person, online. Visitors must perform in person searches for themselves. No search fee. Required to search: name, years to search. Civil cases indexed by defendant, plaintiff. Civil records on index cards back to 1900; on computer back to 1990. Access to civil records is free at www.courts.mo.gov/casenet/. At the website, select the judicial district, then search by name, case number or date. Online records go back to 7/1/2001.
Criminal Records: Access: In person, online. Visitors must perform in person searches for themselves. No search fee. Required to search: name, years to search, DOB, SSN. Criminal records on computer back to 8/94. Online access to criminal records is the same as civil. Court recommends criminal searches at MO State Highway Patrol, 573-526-6288.
General Information: Public Access terminal is available. No juvenile, mental, expunged or dismissed records released. Copy fee: $.50 per page. Certification fee: $2.00. Payee: Circuit Clerk. Personal checks accepted. Prepayment required. Will bill attorneys, courts and abstract companies.

Associate Circuit Court Courthouse Rm 103, Kennett, MO 63857; 573-888-3378; Probate phone: 573-888-3272; Fax: 573-888-0754. Hours: 8AM-4:30PM (CST). *Felony, Misdemeanor, Civil Actions Under $25,000, Eviction, Small Claims, Probate.*
Note: Probate address is Rm #202.
Civil Records: Access: In person, online. Visitors must perform in person searches for themselves. No search fee. Required to search: name, years to search. Civil cases indexed by defendant, plaintiff. Civil records on index cards; on computer back to 2001. Access to civil records is free at www.courts.mo.gov/casenet/. At the website, select the judicial district, then search by name, case number or date. Online records go back to 7/1/2001.
Criminal Records: Access: In person, online. Visitors must perform in person searches for themselves. No search fee. Required to search: name, years to search, DOB. Criminal records on index cards back to 1979; on computer back to 1990. Online access to criminal records is the same as civil. Court recommends criminal searches at MO State Highway Patrol, 573-526-6288.
General Information: Public Access terminal is available. No juvenile, mental, expunged, dismissed, or suspended imposition of sentence records released. Copy fee: $.50 per page. Certification fee: $2.50. Payee: Circuit Court Div 2. Business checks accepted. Prepayment required.

Franklin County

Circuit Court 300 E Main St, Rm 301, Union, MO 63084; 636-583-6303. Hours: 8AM-4:30PM (CST). *Felony, Civil Actions Over $25,000.*
Civil Records: Access: Mail, online, in person. Both court and visitors may perform in person searches. Search fee: $2.00 per name. Required to search: name, years to search. Civil cases indexed by defendant, plaintiff. Civil records on computer back to 1995; others filed as originals to 1821. Participates in the free state online court record system at www.courts.mo.gov/casenet. Online records go back to 1/1995.

Criminal Records: Access: Mail, online, in person. Both court and visitors may perform in person searches. Search fee: $2.00 per name. Required to search: name, years to search, DOB. Criminal records on computer back to 1995; others filed as originals to 1940. Participates in the free state online court record system at www.courts.mo.gov/casenet. Online records go back to 1/1995.
General Information: Public Access terminal is available. No juvenile, mental, expunged, dismissed, or suspended imposition of sentence records released. Copy fee: $1.00 per page or $.25 do-it-yourself. Certification fee: $1.00. Payee: Circuit Clerk. Personal checks accepted. Prepayment required. Mail requests: SASE required. Mail turnaround time 1-5 days.

Associate Circuit Court 120 S hurch Sreet, #B, Union, MO 63084; 636-583-6326. Hours: 8AM-4:30PM (CST). *Misdemeanor, Civil Actions Under $25,000, Eviction, Small Claims, Probate.*
Civil Records: Access: Online, in person. Both court and visitors may perform in person searches. No search fee. Required to search: name, years to search. Civil cases indexed by defendant, plaintiff. Civil records on computer (limited), on index cards since 1983. Participates in the free state online court record system at www.courts.mo.gov/casenet. Online records go back to 1/1995. Online probate court records go back to 10/14/1967.
Criminal Records: Access: Online, in person. Both court and visitors may perform in person searches. No search fee. Required to search: name, years to search. Criminal records on index cards since 1979. Participates in the free state online court record system at www.courts.mo.gov/casenet. Online records go back to 1/1995. Court recommends criminal searches at MO State Highway Patrol, 573-526-6288.
General Information: No juvenile, mental, expunged, dismissed, or suspended imposition of sentence records released. Will not fax results. Copy fee: $.25. No certification fee. Prepayment required.

Gasconade County

Circuit Court 119 E 1st St, Rm 6, Hermann, MO 65041-1182; 573-486-2632; Fax: 573-486-5812. Hours: 8AM-4:30PM (CST). *Felony, Misdemeanor, Civil Actions Over $25,000.*
Civil Records: Access: Mail, in person, online. Both court and visitors may perform in person searches. No search fee. Required to search: name, years to search. Civil cases indexed by defendant, plaintiff. Civil records on index cards since 1976, prior on books stored in vault; online since 9/2001. Participates in the free state online court record system at www.courts.mo.gov/casenet.
Criminal Records: Access: In person, online. Visitors must perform in person searches for themselves. No search fee. Required to search: name, years to search; also helpful: DOB, SSN. Criminal records on index cards since 1976, prior on books stored in vault; online since 9/2001. Participates in the free state online court record system at www.courts.mo.gov/casenet. Court recommends criminal searches at MO State Highway Patrol, 573-526-6288.
General Information: Public Access terminal is available. No juvenile, mental, expunged, dismissed, or suspended imposition of sentence records released. Will fax results for $2.00 1st page, $1.00 each add'l. Copy fee: $1.00 per page. Certification fee: $1.00. Payee: Gasconade Circuit Court. Prepayment required. Mail turnaround time is 2 days.

Associate Circuit Court 119 E. 1st St. Rm 3, Hermann, MO 65041; 573-486-2321; Fax: 573-486-5812. Hours: 8AM-4:30PM (CST). *Misdemeanor, Civil Actions Under $25,000, Eviction, Small Claims, Probate.*

Civil Records: Access: Fax, mail, in person, online. Only the court performs in person searches for records prior to 09/00. No search fee. Required to search: name, years to search. Civil cases indexed by defendant, plaintiff. Civil records on computer since 09/00, prior on index cards since 1979. Participates in the free state online court record system at www.courts.mo.gov/casenet. Online records go back to 7/31/2000.

Criminal Records: Access: Online, in person. Only the court performs in person searches for records prior to 09/00. No search fee. Required to search: name, years to search. Criminal records on computer since 1988, prior on index cards since 1979. Participates in the free state online court record system at www.courts.mo.gov/casenet. Online records go back to 7/31/2000. Court recommends criminal searches at MO State Highway Patrol, 573-526-6288.

General Information: Public Access terminal is available. The terminal is in the Circuit Court office and goes back to 09/00. No juvenile, mental, expunged, dismissed, or suspended imposition of sentence records released. Copy fee: $1.00 per page. Certification fee: $2.50. Payee: Associate Circuit Court. Personal checks accepted. Prepayment required. Will bill probate fees. Mail requests: SASE required. Mail turnaround time varies.

Gentry County

Circuit Court PO Box 27, Albany, MO 64402; 660-726-3618; Fax: 660-726-4102. Hours: 8AM-4:30PM (CST). *Felony, Misdemeanor, Civil Actions Over $25,000.*

Civil Records: Access: Mail, fax, in person. Both court and visitors may perform in person searches. No search fee. Required to search: name, years to search. Civil cases indexed by defendant, plaintiff. Civil records archived since 1885.

Criminal Records: Access: Mail, in person. Both court and visitors may perform in person searches. Search fee: $5.00 per search. Required to search: name, years to search; also helpful: DOB, SSN. Criminal records archived since 1885.

General Information: No juvenile, mental, expunged, dismissed, or suspended imposition of sentence records released. Fee to fax results is $1.00 per page. Copy fee: $1.00 per page. Certification fee: $1.00. Payee: Circuit Clerk. Personal checks accepted. Prepayment required. Mail requests: SASE required. Mail turnaround time 5 working days.

Associate Circuit Court 200 W Clay St, Albany, MO 64402; 660-726-3411; Fax: 660-726-4102. Hours: 8AM-4:30PM (CST). *Misdemeanor, Civil Actions Under $25,000, Eviction, Small Claims, Probate.*

Civil Records: Access: In person only. Visitors must perform in person searches for themselves. No search fee. Required to search: name, years to search. Civil cases indexed by defendant, plaintiff. Civil records on index cards.

Criminal Records: Access: In person, mail, fax. Visitors must perform in person searches for themselves. Search fee: $5.00 per name. Required to search: name, years to search. Criminal records on index cards. Court recommends criminal searches at MO State Highway Patrol, 573-526-6288.

General Information: No juvenile, mental, expunged, dismissed, or suspended imposition of sentence records released. Copy fee: $1.00 per page. Certification fee: $1.50. Payee: Associate Circuit Court. Personal checks accepted. Prepayment

required. Mail requests: SASE required. Mail turnaround time is 7 days.

Greene County

Circuit Court 1010 Booneville, Springfield, MO 65802; 417-868-4074; Fax: 417-868-4168. Hours: 8AM-5AM (CST). *Felony, Civil Actions Over $25,000.*

www.greenecountymo.org

Civil Records: Access: Mail, in person, online. Both court and visitors may perform in person searches. Search fee: $5.00 per name. Required to search: name, years to search. Civil cases indexed by defendant, plaintiff. Civil records on computer back to 7/89, prior on index cards. Access to records at the court's website is free at www.greenecountymo.org/ccourt31/search.htm.

Criminal Records: Access: Mail, in person, online. Both court and visitors may perform in person searches. Search fee: $5.00 per name. Required to search: name, years to search; also helpful: address, DOB, SSN. Criminal records on computer back to 7/89, prior on index cards. Access to records at the court's website is free at www.greenecountymo.org/ccourt31/search.htm.

General Information: Public Access terminal is available. No juvenile, mental, expunged, sealed, dismissed or suspended imposition of sentence records released. Copy fee: $.20 per page. Certification fee: $5.00. Payee: Circuit Clerk. Personal checks accepted. Prepayment required. Mail requests: SASE required. Mail turnaround time 1 week.

Associate Circuit Court 1010 N Boonville, Springfield, MO 65802; 417-868-4110; Probate phone: 417-868-4027. Hours: 8AM-5PM (CST). *Misdemeanor, Civil Actions Under $25,000, Eviction, Small Claims, Probate.*

www.greenecountymo.org

Note: Probate is a separate court at the same address.

Civil Records: Access: Phone, mail, in person, online. Both court and visitors may perform in person searches. Search fee: $5.00 per name. Required to search: name, years to search. Civil cases indexed by defendant, plaintiff. Civil records on computer since mid-1989, prior on index cards. Access to records at the court's website is free at www.greenecountymo.org/ccourt31/search.htm.

Criminal Records: Access: Mail, in person, online. Both court and visitors may perform in person searches. Search fee: $5.00. Required to search: name, years to search; also helpful: SSN. Criminal records on computer since mid-1989, prior on index cards. Access to records at the court's website is free at www.greenecountymo.org/ccourt31/search.htm.

General Information: Public Access terminal is available. (Very limited records available.) No juvenile, mental, expunged, sealed, dismissed or suspended imposition of sentence records released. Copy fee: $.10 per page. No certification fee. Payee: Associate Circuit Clerk. Business checks accepted. Prepayment required. Mail requests: SASE required. Mail turnaround time 2 days; if certified, 1 week.

Grundy County

Circuit Court Courthouse, 700 Main St, PO Box 196, Trenton, MO 64683; 660-359-6605; Fax: 660-359-6604. Hours: 8:30AM-4:30PM (CST). *Felony, Misdemeanor, Civil Actions Over $25,000.*

Civil Records: Access: In person, online. Visitors must perform in person searches for themselves. No search fee. Required to search: name, years to search. Civil cases indexed by defendant, plaintiff. Civil records archived since 1841; on computer back to 2000. Participates in the free state online court record

system at www.courts.mo.gov/casenet. Online records go back to 3/2000.

Criminal Records: Access: In person, online. Visitors must perform in person searches for themselves. No search fee. Required to search: name, years to search. Criminal records archived since 1841; on computer back to 2000. Online access to criminal records is the same as civil. Online records go back to 3/2000. Court recommends criminal searches at MO State Highway Patrol, 573-526-6288.

General Information: Public Access terminal is available. No juvenile, Title 4D, child support, mental, expunged, dismissed, or suspended imposition of sentence cases. Will fax specifc case file for $2.00 fee per document. Copy fee: $.25 per page. Certification fee: $2.00. Payee: Circuit Clerk. Personal checks accepted. Prepayment required.

Associate Circuit Court PO Box 26, 7th and Main Sts., Trenton, MO 64683; 660-359-6606/6909. Hours: 8AM-4:30PM (CST). *Misdemeanor, Civil Actions Under $25,000, Eviction, Small Claims, Probate.*

Civil Records: Access: Mail, in person, online. Visitors must perform in person searches for themselves. No search fee. Required to search: name, years to search. Civil cases indexed by defendant, plaintiff. Civil records on index cards, probate records archived. Participates in the free state online court record system at www.courts.mo.gov/casenet. Online records go back to 3/29/2000.

Criminal Records: Access: In person, online. Visitors must perform in person searches for themselves. No search fee. Required to search: name, years to search. Criminal records on index cards, probate records archived. Online access to criminal records is the same as civil.

General Information: Public Access terminal is available. No juvenile, mental, expunged, dismissed, or suspended imposition of sentence records released. Copy fee: $1.00 per page. Certification fee: $2.50 per document. Payee: Grundy County Circuit Court Division II. Business checks accepted. Prepayment required. Mail requests: SASE required. Mail turnaround time 1-2 days.

Harrison County

Circuit & Associate Court PO Box 189, Bethany, MO 64424; 660-425-6425/6432; Fax: 660-425-6390. Hours: 8AM-4:30PM (CST). *Felony, Misdemeanor, Civil Actions, Eviction, Small Claims, Probate.*

Civil Records: Access: Mail, in person, online. Visitors must perform in person searches for themselves. No search fee. Required to search: name, years to search. Civil cases indexed by defendant, plaintiff. Civil records on index cards since 1979, prior on index books. Participates in the free state online court record system at www.courts.mo.gov/casenet. Online records go back to 3/29/2000.

Criminal Records: Access: In person, online. Visitors must perform in person searches for themselves. No search fee. Required to search: name, years to search. Criminal records on index cards since 1979, prior on index books. Online access to criminal records is the same as civil. Court recommends criminal searches at MO State Highway Patrol, 573-526-6288.

General Information: Public Access terminal is available. No juvenile, mental, expunged, dismissed, or suspended imposition of sentence records released. Copy fee: $.25 per page. Certification fee: $1.00 per page. Payee: Harrison County Circuit Court. Personal checks accepted. Prepayment required. Mail requests: SASE required. Mail turnaround time varies.

Henry County

Circuit& Associate Court PO Box 487, Clinton, MO 64735; 660-885-7232; Fax: 660-885-8247. Hours: 8AM-4:30PM (CST). *Felony, Misdemeanor, Civil, Small Claims.*
http://tacnet.missouri.org/~court27
Note: The Circuit and Associate Courts merged into a consolidated court as of 01/03.

Civil Records: Access: Mail, in person, online. Both court and visitors may perform in person searches. No search fee. Required to search: name, years to search. Civil cases indexed by defendant, plaintiff. Civil records on computer since 8/92, on index cards since 1979, archived since 1877. Participates in the free state online court record system at www.courts.mo.gov/casenet.

Criminal Records: Access: In person, online. Only the court may perform in person searches. No search fee. Required to search: name, years to search. Criminal records on computer since 8/92, on index cards since 1979, archived since 1877. Participates in the free state online court record system at www.courts.mo.gov/casenet. Court recommends criminal searches at MO State Highway Patrol, 573-526-6288.

General Information: Public Access terminal is available. (Judgments only.) No juvenile, mental, expunged, dismissed, or suspended imposition of sentence records released. Will not fax results. Copy fee: $.25 per page. There is a $2.50 fee for records copied from big books. Certification fee: $1.50. Payee: Henry County Circuit Clerk. Personal checks accepted. Prepayment required. Copy fees may be billed. Mail requests: SASE required. Mail turnaround time 2 days.

Hickory County

Circuit Court PO Box 101, Hermitage, MO 65668; 417-745-6421; Fax: 417-745-6670. Hours: 8AM-4:30PM (CST). *Felony, Misdemeanor, Civil Actions Over $45,000.*
www.positech.net/~dcourt
Civil Records: Access: Mail, in person, online. Both court and visitors may perform in person searches. No search fee. Required to search: name, years to search. Civil cases indexed by defendant, plaintiff. Civil records on computer since 1992, prior on index books since 1976. Participates in the free state online court record system at www.courts.mo.gov/casenet.
Criminal Records: Access: Mail, in person, online. Both court and visitors may perform in person searches. No search fee. Required to search: name, years to search, signed release. Criminal records on computer since 1992, prior on index books since 1976. Online access to criminal records is the same as civil.

General Information: Public Access terminal is available. No juvenile, mental, expunged, dismissed, or suspended imposition of sentence records released. Fee to fax results is $1.00 per page. Copy fee: $1.00 per page. Certification fee: $1.00. Payee: Hickory County Circuit Clerk. Personal checks accepted. Prepayment required. Mail requests: SASE required. Mail turnaround time 1 week-10 days.

Associate Circuit Court PO Box 75, Courthouse Square, Hermitage, MO 65668; 417-745-6822; Fax: 417-745-6670. Hours: 8AM-Noon; 12:30PM-4:30PM (CST). *Misdemeanor, Civil Actions Under $45,000, Eviction, Small Claims, Probate.*
www.positech.net/~dcourt
Civil Records: Access: Mail, in person, online. Both court and visitors may perform in person searches. No search fee. Required to search: name, years to search. Civil cases indexed by defendant, plaintiff. Civil

records on index cards since 1980. Participates in the free statewide Casenet court record system at www.courts.mo.gov/casenet.
Criminal Records: Access: Mail, in person, online. Both court and visitors may perform in person searches. No search fee. Required to search: name, years to search, DOB. Criminal records on index cards since 1980. Participates in the free statewide Casenet court record system at www.courts.mo.gov/casenet.
General Information: Public Access terminal is available. No juvenile, mental, expunged, dismissed, or suspended imposition of sentence records released. Will fax results no fee. Copy fee: $.25. No certification fee. Mail requests: SASE required. Mail turnaround time 2-3 days.

Holt County

Circuit Court PO Box 318, Oregon, MO 64473; 660-446-3301; Fax: 660-446-3328. Hours: 8AM-4:30PM (CST). *Felony, Misdemeanor, Civil Actions Over $25,000.*
Civil Records: Access: Fax, mail, in person. Only the court performs in person searches; visitors may not. Search fee: $4.00. Required to search: name, years to search. Civil cases indexed by defendant, plaintiff. Civil records on books.
Criminal Records: Access: Fax, mail, in person. Only the court performs in person searches; visitors may not. Search fee: $4.00. Required to search: name, years to search. Criminal records on books.
General Information: No juvenile, mental, expunged, dismissed, or suspended imposition of sentence records released. Will fax results $2.00 per doc. Copy fee: $1.00 per page. Certification fee: $1.00. Payee: Recorder. Personal checks accepted. Prepayment required. Mail requests: SASE required. Mail turnaround time varies.

Associate Circuit Court PO Box 173, Oregon, MO 64473; 660-446-3380. Hours: 8:30AM-4:30PM (CST). *Misdemeanor, Civil Actions Under $25,000, Eviction, Small Claims, Probate.*
Civil Records: Access: Mail, fax, in person. Both the court and visitors may perform in person searches. No search fee. Required to search: name, years to search. Civil cases indexed by defendant, plaintiff. Civil records on index cards since 1979.
Criminal Records: Access: In person only. Visitors must perform in person searches for themselves. No search fee. Required to search: name, years to search. Criminal records on computer since 1991, prior on index cards since 1979. Court recommends criminal searches at MO State Highway Patrol, 573-526-6288.
General Information: No juvenile, mental, expunged, dismissed, or suspended imposition of sentence records released. Copy fee: $.25 per page. Certification fee: $1.50. Payee: Associate Circuit Court. Personal checks accepted. Prepayment required. Mail requests: SASE required. Mail turnaround time varies.

Howard County

Circuit Court 1 Courthouse Square, Fayette, MO 65248; 660-248-2194; Probate phone: 660-248-3326; Fax: 660-248-1075. Hours: 8:30AM-4:30PM (CST). *Felony, Civil Actions Over $30,000.*
Civil Records: Access: In person, online. Visitors must perform in person searches for themselves. No search fee. Required to search: name, years to search. Civil cases indexed by defendant, plaintiff. Civil records on index cards; computer records go back to the 1970s. Participates in the free state online court record system at www.courts.mo.gov/casenet.
Criminal Records: Access: In person, online. Visitors must perform in person searches for themselves. No search fee. Required to search: name,

years to search. Criminal records on index cards; computer records go back to the 1970s. Online access to criminal records is the same as civil. Court recommends criminal searches at MO State Highway Patrol, 573-526-6288.
General Information: Public Access terminal is available. No juvenile, mental, expunged, dismissed, or suspended imposition of sentence records released. Will fax specific case file requests for $2.00 per document. Copy fee: $.25 per page. Certification fee: $2.00. Payee: Circuit Clerk. Personal checks accepted. Prepayment required.

Associate Circuit Court PO Box 370, Fayette, MO 65248; 660-248-3326; Fax: 660-248-1075. Hours: 8:30AM-4:30PM (CST). *Misdemeanor, Civil Actions Under $45,000, Eviction, Small Claims, Probate.*
Civil Records: Access: In person, online. Visitors must perform in person searches for themselves. No search fee. Required to search: name, years to search. Civil cases indexed by defendant, plaintiff. Civil records go back to 1975. Participates in the free state online court record system at www.courts.mo.gov/casenet. Includes Probate and Traffic records.
Criminal Records: Access: In person, online. Visitors must perform in person searches for themselves. No search fee. Required to search: name, years to search, DOB. Criminal records go back to 1975. Online access to criminal records is the same as civil, see above. Court recommends criminal searches at MO State Highway Patrol, 573-526-6288.
General Information: Public Access terminal is available. No juvenile, mental, expunged, dismissed, or suspended imposition of sentence records released. Copy fee: $.25 per page. Certification fee: $1.50. Payee: Associate Circuit Court. Personal checks accepted. Prepayment required.

Howell County

Circuit Court PO Box 967, West Plains, MO 65775; 417-256-3741; Fax: 417-256-4650. Hours: 8AM-4:30PM (CST). *Felony, Misdemeanor, Civil Actions Over $25,000.*
Civil Records: Access: Phone, fax, mail, in person, online. Both court and visitors may perform in person searches. No search fee. Required to search: name, years to search. Civil cases indexed by defendant, plaintiff. Civil records on index cards since 1977. Participates in the free state online court record system at www.courts.mo.gov/casenet. Online records go back to 8/2000; pending cases back to 1990.
Criminal Records: Access: In person, online. Visitors must perform in person searches for themselves. No search fee. Required to search: name, years to search. Criminal records on index cards since 1977. Online access to criminal records is the same as civil. Court recommends criminal searches at MO State Highway Patrol, 573-526-6288.
General Information: No juvenile, mental, expunged, dismissed, or suspended imposition of sentence records released. Will fax results $1.00 per page. Copy fee: $.10 per page. Certification fee: $1.50. Payee: Howell County Circuit Clerk. Personal checks accepted. Prepayment required. Will bill to attorneys. Mail requests: SASE required. Mail turnaround time varies.

Associate Circuit Court 222 Courthouse, West Plains, MO 65775; 417-256-4050; Fax: 417-256-5826. Hours: 8AM-4:30PM (CST). *Misdemeanor, Civil Actions Under $45,000, Eviction, Small Claims, Probate.*
Civil Records: Access: Mail, in person, online. Both court and visitors may perform in person searches. No search fee. Required to search: name, years to search. Civil cases indexed by defendant, plaintiff. Civil records on index cards since 1/1/79, computerized

since 2000. Participates in the free state online court record system at www.courts.mo.gov/casenet. Online records go back to 1990.

Criminal Records: Access: Mail, in person, online. Both court and visitors may perform in person searches. No search fee. Required to search: name, years to search, DOB; also helpful: SSN. Criminal records on computer since early 1991, on index cards since 1/1/79, prior on books. Online access to criminal records is the same as civil.

General Information: No juvenile, mental, expunged, dismissed, or suspended imposition of sentence records released. Copy fee: none reported. Certification fee: $2.50 for 1st page, $1.00 each add'l. Payee: Associate/Probate Court. Only cashiers checks and money orders accepted. Prepayment required. Mail requests: SASE required. Mail turnaround time ASAP.

Iron County

Circuit Court PO Box 24, Ironton, MO 63650; 573-546-2811; Fax: 573-546-2166. Hours: 8AM-4PM (CST). *Felony, Civil Actions Over $25,000.*

Civil Records: Access: In person, online. Visitors must perform in person searches for themselves. No search fee. Required to search: name, years to search. Civil cases indexed by defendant, plaintiff. Civil records on index cards since 1976, prior on books. Participates in the free statewide Casenet court record system at www.courts.mo.gov/casenet. Files requested by case number take 10 days.

Criminal Records: Access: In person, online. Visitors must perform in person searches for themselves. No search fee. Required to search: name, years to search. Criminal records on index cards since 1976, prior on books to 1856. Participates in the free statewide Casenet court record system at www.courts.mo.gov/casenet. Files requested by case number take 10 days. Court recommends criminal searches at MO State Highway Patrol, 573-526-6288.

General Information: Public Access terminal is available. No juvenile, mental, expunged, dismissed, or suspended imposition of sentence records released. Copy fee: $1.00 per page. Certification fee: $2.00. Payee: Iron County Circuit Clerk. Personal checks not accepted. Prepayment required.

Associate Circuit Court PO Box 325, Ironton, MO 63650; 573-546-2511; Fax: 573-546-6006. Hours: 8:30AM-4PM (CST). *Misdemeanor, Civil Actions Under $25,000, Eviction, Small Claims, Probate.*

Civil Records: Access: Mail, in person, online. Both court and visitors may perform in person searches. No search fee. Required to search: name, years to search; also helpful: address. Civil cases indexed by defendant, plaintiff. Civil records on index cards since 1979, computerized from 04/01. Participates in the free statewide Casenet court record system at www.courts.mo.gov/casenet.

Criminal Records: Access: Fax, mail, in person, online. Only court amay perform in person searches. No search fee. Required to search: name, years to search, DOB; also helpful: address, signed release. Criminal records computerized from 04/01. Participates in the free statewide Casenet court record system at www.courts.mo.gov/casenet.

General Information: Public Access terminal is available. No juvenile, mental, expunged, dismissed, or suspended imposition of sentence records released. Copy fee: $.25 per page. Certification fee: $1.50 plus $1.00 per page. Payee: Associate Circuit Court. Personal checks accepted. Prepayment required. Mail requests: SASE required. Mail turnaround time 5 days.

Jackson County

Circuit Court - Civil Division 415 E 12th, 3rd Fl, Kansas City, MO 64106; 816-881-3926; 881-3522; Probate phone: 816-881-3755; Fax: 816-881-4327. Hours: 8AM-5PM (CST). *Civil, Eviction, Small Claims, Probate.*

www.16thcircuit.org

Note: There is a combined computer system with the Independence civil court.

Civil Records: Access: Online, in person. Visitors must perform in person searches for themselves. No search fee. Required to search: name, years to search. Civil cases indexed by defendant, plaintiff. Civil records on computer since 1973, some records on microfiche and books, older records archived off-site. Participates in the free state online court record system at www.courts.mo.gov/casenet. Jackson Casenet records go back to 1/89. The Probate Court also participates in the Casenet system; also, probate records are at www.16thcircuit.org/publicaccess.asp.

General Information: Public Access terminal is available. No juvenile, mental, expunged, dismissed, or suspended imposition of sentence records released. Copy fee: $.50 per page. Certification fee: $2.50. Payee: Court Administrator's Office. Business checks accepted. Prepayment required.

Independence Circuit Court - Civil Annex 308 W Kansas #310, Independence, MO 64050; 816-881-3943; Probate phone: 816-881-4552; Fax: 816-881-3681. Hours: 8AM-5PM (CST). *Civil, Eviction, Small Claims, Probate.*

Note: Direct mail criminal record searches to #310; civil to #204. This court is on the same computer system as Kansas City for civil cases, but files maintained separately.

Civil Records: Access: Mail, online, in person. Both court and visitors may perform in person searches. No search fee. Required to search: name, years to search. Civil cases indexed by defendant, plaintiff. Civil records on computer since 1989. Participates in the free state online court record system at www.courts.mo.gov/casenet. Online records go back to 1/89. Online access to probate records is free at www.16thcircuit.org/publicaccess.asp. This includes private process servers, jury verdicts, criminal traffic, and criminal sureties. The court will not do background checks, except for attorneys. You must have case number if the court is to pull a record.

Criminal Records: Access: In person, mail. Both court and visitors may perform in person searches. No search fee. Required to search: name. The court will not do background checks, except for attorneys and government offices. Otherwise, requestor must have the case number to request file copies. Court recommends criminal searches at MO State Highway Patrol, 573-526-6288.

General Information: Public Access terminal is available. No sealed records released. Copy fee: $.50 per page. Certification fee: $2.50. Payee: District Court Clerk. Only cashiers checks and money orders accepted. Prepayment required. Mail turnaround time 1 day.

Circuit Court - Criminal Division 1315 Locust, 2nd Fl, Kansas City, MO 64106; 816-881-4350; Fax: 816-881-3420. Hours: 8AM-5PM (CST). *Felony, Misdemeanor.*

www.16thcircuit.org

Note: All background checks are sent to the Missouri Highway Patrol in Jefferson City. Court will only pull file copies if a case number is given.

Criminal Records: Access: Online, in person. Visitors must perform in person searches for themselves. No search fee. Required to search: name, years to search, DOB, signed release; also helpful:

SSN. Criminal records on computer since 1968 for felonies, 1980 for misdemeanors. Participates in the free state online court record system at www.courts.mo.gov/casenet. Jackson Casenet records go back to 1/89. Also, online access to criminal traffic dockets is at www.16thcircuit.org/trafficdockets.asp. Also, search surety bonding agents at www.16thcircuit.org/suretyqualifications.asp. Court recommends criminal searches at MO State Highway Patrol, 573-526-6288.

General Information: No juvenile, mental, expunged, dismissed, or suspended imposition of sentence records released. Copy fee: $.50 per page. Certification fee: $1.50. Payee: Dept. of Civil or Criminal Records. Only cashiers checks and money orders accepted. Prepayment required.

Jasper County

Circuit Court Courthouse, Rm 303, 302 S. Main St, Carthage, MO 64836; 417-358-0441; Fax: 417-358-0461. Hours: 8:00AM-5:00PM (CST). *Felony, Misdemeanor, Civil Actions, Eviction, Small Claims, Probate.*

www.osca.state.mo.us/circuits/index.nsf

Note: Although the Carthage Circuit and Associate Circuit courts merged, the records are only comingled from 07/00 forward. Each of the 4 courts in the county must be searched for an accurate overall search.

Civil Records: Access: Mail, in person, online. No search fee. Required to search: name, years to search. Civil cases indexed by defendant, plaintiff. Civil records on computer since 7/1/91, prior on cards since 1975. Participates in the free statewide Casenet court record system at www.courts.mo.gov/casenet. Online records go back to 6/26/2000.

Criminal Records: Access: Mail, in person, online. Both court and visitors may perform in person searches. No search fee. Required to search: name, years to search. Criminal records on computer since 7/1/91, prior on cards since 1975. Online access to criminal records is the same as civil.

General Information: Public Access terminal is available. No juvenile, mental, expunged, dismissed, or suspended imposition of sentence records released. Will fax results to local number only. Copy fee: $.25 per page. Certification fee: $1.50. Payee: Jasper County Circuit Clerk. Business checks accepted. Prepayment required. Mail requests: SASE required. Mail turnaround time 1 week.

Joplin Circuit Court Courthouse, 3rd Fl, 601 S Pearl, Joplin, MO 64801; 417-625-4310. Hours: 8:00AM-Noon, 1-5:00PM (CST). *Felony, Misdemeanor, Civil Actions Over $45,000.*

Note: Although the Joplin Circuit and Associate Circuit courts merged, the records are only comingled from 07/00 forward. Each of the 4 courts in the county must be searched for an accurate overall search.

Civil Records: Access: In person, online. Visitors must perform in person searches for themselves. No search fee. Required to search: name, years to search. Civil cases indexed by defendant, plaintiff. Civil records on computer since 7/1/91, prior on cards since 1975. Participates in the free statewide Casenet court record system at www.courts.mo.gov/casenet. Online records go back to 6/26/2000.

Criminal Records: Access: In person, online. Visitors must perform in person searches for themselves. No search fee. Required to search: name, years to search. Criminal records on computer back to 1993, prior on cards back to 1975. Online access to criminal records is the same as civil. Court recommends criminal searches at MO State Highway Patrol, 573-526-6288.

General Information: Public Access terminal is available. No juvenile, mental, expunged, dismissed, or suspended imposition of sentence records released.

Copy fee: $.25 per page. Certification fee: $1.50. Payee: Jasper County Circuit Clerk. No personal checks accepted. Prepayment required.

Carthage Associate Circuit Court
Courthouse, Rm 304, 302 S. Main St, Carthage, MO 64836; 417-358-0450; Fax: 417-358-0460. Hours: 8:30AM-Noon, 1-4:30PM (CST). *Misdemeanor, Civil Actions Under $45,000, Eviction, Small Claims, Probate.*

Note: Although the Carthage Circuit and Associate Circuit courts merged, the records are only co-mingled from 07/00 forward. Each of the 4 courts in the county must be searched for an accurate overall search.

Civil Records: Access: Fax, in person, online. Visitors must perform in person searches for themselves. Search fee: Court does not perform civil searches. Required to search: name, years to search. Civil cases indexed by defendant, plaintiff. Civil records on computer back to 2000, prior on cards back to 1979. Participates in the free statewide Casenet record system at www.courts.mo.gov/casenet. Online records go back to 6/26/2000. For mail or fax searches, court recommends Amer. Research at 417-358-6494.

Criminal Records: Access: In person, online. Visitors must perform in person searches for themselves. Search fee: Court does not perform criminal searches. Required to search: name, years to search. Criminal records on computer back to 2000, prior on cards back to 1979. Online access to criminal records is the same as civil. For mail or fax searches, court recommends Amer. Research at 417-358-6494. Court recommends criminal searches at MO State Highway Patrol, 573-526-6288.

General Information: Public Access terminal is available. No juvenile, mental, expunged, dismissed, or suspended imposition of sentence records released. Copy fee: $.25 per page. Certification fee: $1.50.

Joplin Associate Circuit Court
Courthouse, 2nd Fl, 601 S Pearl, Joplin, MO 64801; 417-625-4316; Fax: 417-625-4340. Hours: 8AM-noon, 1-5PM (CST). *Misdemeanor, Civil Actions Under $45,000, Eviction, Small Claims, Probate.*

Note: Although the Joplin Circuit and Associate Circuit courts merged, the records are only comingled from 07/00 forward. Each of the 4 courts in the county must be searched for an accurate overall search.

Civil Records: Access: Mail, fax, in person, online. Both court and visitors may perform in person searches. No search fee. Required to search: name, years to search. Civil cases indexed by defendant, plaintiff. Civil records on computer back to 1993, prior on cards back to mid-1970s. Participates in the free statewide Casenet court record system at www.courts.mo.gov/casenet. Online records go back to 6/26/2000.

Criminal Records: Access: Mail, fax, in person, online. Both court and visitors may perform in person searches. No search fee. Required to search: name, years to search. Criminal records on computer back to 1993, prior on cards back to mid-1970s. Online access to criminal records is the same as civil. Online records only go back to 6/26/2000.

General Information: Public Access terminal is available. No juvenile, mental, expunged, dismissed, or suspended imposition of sentence records released. Will fax results, no fee. Copy fee: $.25 per page. Certification fee: $1.50. Personal checks accepted. Prepayment required. Mail requests: SASE required. Mail turnaround time is 1-3 days.

Jefferson County

Circuit & Associate Court - Civil Division
PO Box 100, Hillsboro, MO 63050; 636-797-5443; Fax: 636-797-5073. Hours: 8AM-5PM (CST). *Civil Actions, Eviction, Small Claims, Probate.*

Civil Records: Access: Phone, fax, mail, in person. Both court and visitors may perform in person searches. No search fee. Required to search: name, years to search. Civil cases indexed by defendant, plaintiff. Civil records on computer since 10/90, prior on books since 1966.

General Information: Public Access terminal is available. No juvenile, mental, expunged, dismissed, or suspended imposition of sentence records released. Copy fee: $1.00 per page. Certification fee: $.50. Payee: Circuit Clerk. Business checks accepted. Prepayment required. Mail requests: SASE required.

Circuit & Associate Court - Criminal Division
PO Box 100, Hillsboro, MO 63050; 636-797-5370; Fax: 636-797-5073. Hours: 8AM-4:30PM (CST). *Felony, Misdemeanor.*

Criminal Records: Access: Mail, fax, in person. Only the court performs in person searches; visitors may not. Search fee: $10.00 per name. Required to search: name, years to search, signed release, DOB or SSN. Criminal records on computer since 1989, on index cards 1976 to 1988, prior on books or microfilm.

General Information: No juvenile, mental, expunged, dismissed, or suspended imposition of sentence records released. Copy fee: $1.00 per page. No certification fee. Payee: Circuit Clerk. Business checks accepted. Prepayment required. Mail requests: SASE required. Mail turnaround time 1 week.

Johnson County

Circuit Court
Johnson County Justice Center, 101 W Market, Warrensburg, MO 64093; 660-422-7413; Fax: 660-422-7417. Hours: 8AM-4:30PM (CST). *Felony, Civil Actions Over $25,000.*

Civil Records: Access: In person, mail. Visitors must perform in person searches for themselves, except prior to 1976. Search fee: $10.00. Required to search: name, years to search. Civil cases indexed by defendant, plaintiff. Civil records on file since 1800s, microfilmed from 1950s to 1988.

Criminal Records: Access: In person, mail. Visitors must perform in person searches for themselves, except prior to 1976. Search fee: $10.00. Required to search: name, years to search, DOB, SSN. Criminal records on file since 1800s, microfilmed through 1988.

General Information: Public Access terminal is available. No juvenile, adoptions, mental, expunged, dismissed, or suspended imposition of sentence records released. Will fax results for $3.00 1st.page + $1.00 add'l pages. Copy fee: $.25 per page. Certification fee: $1.50. Payee: Circuit Clerk. Personal checks accepted. Prepayment required. Mail turnaround time is 1 week.

Associate Circuit Court
Johnson County Courthouse, 300 N Holden #304, Warrensburg, MO 64093; 660-422-7410. Hours: 8AM-4:30PM (CST). *Misdemeanor, Civil Actions Under $45,000, Eviction, Small Claims.*

Civil Records: Access: Mail, in person. Visitors must perform in person searches for themselves. No search fee. Required to search: name, years to search. Civil cases indexed by defendant, plaintiff. Civil records on computer since 1994, prior on index since 1979.

Criminal Records: Access: Mail, in person. Visitors must perform in person searches for themselves. No search fee. Required to search: name, years to search.

Criminal records on computer since 1994, prior on index since 1979.

General Information: No juvenile, mental, expunged, dismissed, or suspended imposition of sentence records released. Copy fee: 1st 10 pages free, $.25 per page thereafter. No certification fee. Payee: Associate Circuit Court. Personal checks accepted. Prepayment required. Mail requests: SASE required. Mail turnaround time varies.

Knox County

Circuit Court
PO Box 116, Edina, MO 63537; 660-397-2305; Fax: 660-397-3331. Hours: 8:30AM-Noon, 1-4PM (CST). *Felony, Misdemeanor, Civil Actions Over $25,000.*

Civil Records: Access: Mail, in person. Both court and visitors may perform in person searches. No search fee. Required to search: name, years to search. Civil cases indexed by defendant, plaintiff. Civil records on microfiche since 3/83, archived since 1845, no computerization.

Criminal Records: Access: Mail, in person. Both court and visitors may perform in person searches. No search fee. Required to search: name, years to search. Criminal records archived since 1845, no computerization.

General Information: No juvenile, mental, expunged, dismissed, or suspended imposition of sentence records released. Will fax results; fee varies but usually $3.50 per doc. Copy fee: $.25 per page. Certification fee: $2.00. Payee: Circuit Court. Personal checks accepted. Prepayment required. Mail requests: SASE not required. Mail turnaround time same day.

Associate Circuit Court
PO Box 126, Edina, MO 63537; 660-397-3146; Fax: 660-397-3331. Hours: 8:30AM-4PM (CST). *Misdemeanor, Civil Actions Under $25,000, Eviction, Small Claims, Probate.*

Civil Records: Access: Mail, in person. Both court and visitors may perform in person searches. No search fee. Required to search: name, years to search. Civil cases indexed by defendant, plaintiff. Civil records on computer since 1993, prior on index cards to 1850.

Criminal Records: Access: Mail, in person. Only the court performs in person searches; visitors may not. No search fee. Required to search: name, years to search; also helpful: DOB, SSN. Criminal records on computer since 1993, prior on index cards.

General Information: No juvenile, mental, expunged, dismissed, or suspended imposition of sentence records released. Copy fee: $.25 per page. Certification fee: $2.00. Payee: Associate Circuit Court. Personal checks accepted. Prepayment required. Mail requests: SASE required. Mail turnaround time 2-3 days.

Laclede County

Circuit & Associate Court
200 N Adams St, Lebanon, MO 65536; 417-532-2471, 532-9196; Fax: 417-532-3683. Hours: 8AM-4PM (CST). *Felony, Misdemeanor, Civil. Eviction, Small Claims, Probate.*

Note: Now a consolidated court.

Civil Records: Access: Phone, fax, mail, in person. Both court and visitors may perform in person searches. No search fee. Required to search: name, years to search. Civil cases indexed by defendant, plaintiff. Civil records on cards since 1976, prior on books.

Criminal Records: Access: Phone, fax, mail, in person. Both court and visitors may perform in person searches. No search fee. Required to search: name, years to search; also helpful: SSN. Criminal records on cards since 1976, prior on books.

General Information: Public Access terminal is available. No juvenile, mental, expunged, dismissed, or suspended imposition of sentence records released. Will fax results $3.00 1st page, $1.00 each add'l. Copy fee: $.25 per page. Certification fee: $1.50. Payee: Laclede County Circuit Clerk. Personal checks accepted. Prepayment required. Copy fees may be billed. Mail requests: SASE required. Mail turnaround time 1-2 days.

Lafayette County

Circuit & Associate Court PO Box 10, Lexington, MO 64067; 660-259-6101; Probate phone: 660-259-2324; Fax: 660-259-6148. Hours: 8AM-4:30PM (CST). *Felony, Misdemeanor, Civil Actions, Eviction, Small Claims, Probate.*
Note: Circuit and Associate courts are combined as of 9/2004; telephone numbers may be changed!

Civil Records: Access: Mail, fax, in person, online. Visitors must perform in person searches for themselves. No search fee. Required to search: name, years to search. Civil cases indexed by defendant, plaintiff, case number. Civil records on books, archived since 1821; on computer back to 1987. Participates in the free statewide Casenet court record system at www.courts.mo.gov/casenet. Online records go back to 04/01/02. All search requests to clerk must be in writing.
Criminal Records: Access: In person, online. Visitors must perform in person searches for themselves. No search fee. Required to search: name, years to search; also helpful-case number. Criminal records on books, archived since 1823; on computer back to 1987. Participates in the free statewide Casenet court record system at www.courts.mo.gov/casenet. Online records go back to 04/01/02.
General Information: Public Access terminal is available. No juvenile, mental, expunged, dismissed, or suspended imposition of sentence records released. Fee to fax results is $1.00 per page. Copy fee: $.25 per page. Certification fee: $2.50. Payee: Circuit Clerk. No personal checks accepted; money orders only. Attorney of record and copy fees may be billed. Mail requests: SASE required. Mail turnaround time up to 5 days.

Lawrence County

Circuit Court One Courthouse Square #201, Mt Vernon, MO 65712; 417-466-2471. Hours: 8AM-4:30PM (CST). *Felony, Civil Actions Over $25,000.*
Civil Records: Access: Mail, in person. Both court and visitors may perform in person searches. Search fee: $5.00 per name. Required to search: name, years to search. Civil cases indexed by defendant, plaintiff. Civil records on computer back to 1991, prior archived since 1890.
Criminal Records: Access: Mail, in person. Both court and visitors may perform in person searches. Search fee: $5.00 per name. Required to search: name, years to search, DOB; also helpful: SSN. Criminal records on computer back to 1991, prior archived since 1890.
General Information: Public Access terminal is available. No juvenile, mental, expunged, dismissed, or suspended imposition of sentence records released. Copy fee: $.25 per page. Certification fee: $2.00. Payee: Circuit Court. Business checks accepted. Prepayment required. Mail requests: SASE required. Mail turnaround time 1 week.

Associate Circuit Court 1 Courthouse Square, # 102, Mt Vernon, MO 65712; 417-466-2463; Probate phone: 417-466-2105. Hours: 8:30AM-5PM (CST). *Misdemeanor, Civil Actions Under $45,000, Eviction, Small Claims, Probate.*
Civil Records: Access: Mail, in person. Both court and visitors may perform in person searches. No search fee. Required to search: name, years to search. Civil cases indexed by defendant, plaintiff. Civil records on index cards since 1979, prior on books.
Criminal Records: Access: Mail, in person. Both court and visitors may perform in person searches. No search fee. Required to search: name, years to search; also helpful: DOB, SSN. Criminal records on index cards since 1979, prior on books.
General Information: No juvenile, mental, expunged, dismissed, or suspended imposition of sentence records released. Copy fee: $.35 per page. No certification fee. Payee: Associate Circuit Court. Personal checks accepted. Prepayment required. Mail requests: SASE required. Mail turnaround time 2-3 days.

Lewis County

Circuit & Associate Court PO Box 97, Monticello, MO 63457; 573-767-5232; Fax: 573-767-5342. Hours: 8AM-Noon,1-4:30PM (CST). *Felony, Misdemeanor, Civil Actions, Eviction, Small Claims, Probate.*
Note: Consolidated court on 4-1-03.
Civil Records: Access: Mail, in person. Visitors must perform in person searches for themselves. Search fee: $1.00. Required to search: name, years to search. Civil cases indexed by defendant, plaintiff. Civil records on computer back to 1976 (judgments) and index books, archived since 1830s.
Criminal Records: Access: In person only. Visitors must perform in person searches for themselves. No search fee. Required to search: name, years to search. Criminal records on computer and index books, archived since 1830s. Court recommends criminal searches at MO State Highway Patrol, 573-526-6288.
General Information: No juvenile, mental, expunged, dismissed, or suspended imposition of sentence records released. Copy fee: $1.00. Certification fee: $2.50. Prepayment required. Mail turnaround time is 1 day.

Lincoln County

Circuit & Associate Court Lincoln County Justice Center, 45 Business park Dr, Troy, MO 63379; 636-528-6300. Hours: 8:00AM-4:30PM (CST). *Felony, Misdemeanor, Civil Actions, Eviction, Small Claims, Probate.*
Note: The official name of the court is the Consolidated Circuit Court.
Civil Records: Access: In person, online. Visitors must perform in person searches for themselves. No search fee. Required to search: name, years to search. Civil cases indexed by defendant, plaintiff. Civil records on computer since 8/92, prior on index cards since 1978. Record access fee at www.courts.mo.gov/casenet/. Records from 04/03/02 forward.
Criminal Records: Access: In person, online. Visitors must perform in person searches for themselves. No search fee. Required to search: name, years to search. Criminal records on computer since 8/92, prior on index cards since 1978. Participates in the free state online court record system at www.courts.mo.gov/casenet. Records go back to 4/03/02 forward. Court recommends criminal searches at MO State Highway Patrol, 573-526-6288.
General Information: Public Access terminal is available. No juvenile, mental, expunged, dismissed, or suspended imposition of sentence records released.

Will fax specific case file information only, not search results. Copy fee: $.25 per page. Certification fee: $1.75 (includes copy fee). Payee: Lincoln County Circuit Clerk. Personal checks accepted. Prepayment required.

Linn County

Circuit & Associate Court PO Box 84, 108 S High St, Linneus, MO 64653-0084; 660-895-5212; Fax: 660-895-5277. Hours: 8AM-noon, 1-4:30PM (CST). *Felony, Misdemeanor, Civil Actions, Eviction, Small Claims, Probate.*
Civil Records: Access: Fax, mail, in person, online. Only the court performs in person searches; visitors may not. No search fee. Required to search: name, years to search. Civil cases indexed by defendant, plaintiff. Civil records on books. Participates in the free statewide Casenet court record system at www.courts.mo.gov/casenet.
Criminal Records: Access: Fax, mail, in person, online. Only the court performs in person searches; visitors may not. No search fee. Required to search: name, years to search. Criminal records on books. Participates in the free statewide Casenet court record system at www.courts.mo.gov/casenet.
General Information: Public Access terminal is available. No juvenile, mental, expunged, dismissed, or suspended imposition of sentence records released. No fee to fax results. Copy fee: $.25 per page. Certification fee: $2.00. Payee: Linn County Circuit Court. Only cashiers checks and money orders accepted. Prepayment required. Mail requests: SASE required. Mail turnaround time 1 week, phone turnaround is 1-2 days.

Consolidated Circuit Court Box 84, Linneus, MO 64653; 660-895-5212; Fax: 660-895-5277. Hours: 8AM-4:30PM (CST). *Misdemeanor, Civil Actions Under $25,000, Eviction, Small Claims, Probate.*
Civil Records: Access: Phone, mail, in person, online. Only the court performs in person searches; visitors may not. No search fee. Required to search: name, years to search. Civil cases indexed by defendant, plaintiff. Civil records on index cards since 1979. Participates in the free statewide Casenet court record system at www.courts.mo.gov/casenet.
Criminal Records: Access: Phone, mail, in person, online. Only the court performs in person searches; visitors may not. No search fee. Required to search: name, years to search. Criminal records on index cards since 1979. Participates in the free statewide Casenet court record system at www.courts.mo.gov/casenet.
General Information: No juvenile, mental, expunged, dismissed, or suspended imposition of sentence records released. Copy fee: $1.00 per page. Certification fee: $1.50. Payee: Associate Circuit Court. Personal checks accepted. Prepayment required. Mail requests: SASE required.

Livingston County

Circuit Court 700 Webster St, Chillicothe, MO 64601; 660-646-1718; Fax: 660-646-2734. Hours: 8:00AM-5:00PM (CST). *Felony, Civil Actions Over $25,000.*
Civil Records: Access: Mail, fax, in person. Visitors must perform in person searches for themselves. No search fee. Required to search: name, years to search. Civil cases indexed by defendant, plaintiff. Civil records on index cards since 1974, prior on record books.
Criminal Records: Access: In person only. Visitors must perform in person searches for themselves. No search fee. Required to search: name, years to search. Criminal records on index cards since 1974, prior on record books.

General Information: No juvenile, mental, expunged, dismissed, or suspended imposition of sentence records released. Will fax results to local or toll free line. Copy fee: $.25 per page. No certification fee. Payee: Livingston County Circuit Clerk. Personal checks accepted. Prepayment required. Attorneys may be billed for copy fees.

Associate Circuit Court Livingston County Courthouse, #8, Chillicothe, MO 64601; 660-646-3103; Fax: 660-646-8014. Hours: Public hours: 8:30AM-4:30PM; Office hours: 8AM-5PM (CST). *Misdemeanor, Civil Actions Under $25,000, Eviction, Small Claims, Probate.*
Civil Records: Access: Phone, fax, mail, in person. Both court and visitors may perform in person searches. No search fee. Required to search: name, years to search; also helpful: address; Signed release required for closed records. Civil cases indexed by defendant, plaintiff. Civil records on index cards and record books since 1975, prior on record books.
Criminal Records: Access: Phone, fax, mail, in person. Both court and visitors may perform in person searches. No search fee. Required to search: name, years to search, DOB; Signed release required for closed records. Criminal records on index cards and record books since 1975, prior on record books.
General Information: No juvenile, mental, expunged, dismissed, or suspended imposition of sentence records released. Call for fax back fee. Copy fee: $1.00 per page. Certification fee: $1.50. Payee: Associate Circuit Court. Personal checks accepted. Prepayment required. Mail requests: SASE required. Mail turnaround time 5 days.

Macon County

Circuit Court PO Box 382, Macon, MO 63552; 660-385-4631; Civil phone: 660-385-4631; Criminal phone: 660-385-4631; Probate phone: 660-385-3531; Fax: 660-385-4235. Hours: 8:AM-5PM (CST). *Felony, Misdemeanor, Civil Actions Over $25,000.*
Civil Records: Access: Fax, mail, in person, online. Both court and visitors may perform in person searches. No search fee. Required to search: name, years to search. Civil cases indexed by defendant, plaintiff. Civil records on computer since 1/1/91, on index cards from 1976-1990, prior on books. Participates in the free state online court record system at www.courts.mo.gov/casenet. Online records go back to 11/13/03.
Criminal Records: Access: Fax, mail, in person, online. Both court and visitors may perform in person searches. Search fee: $1.00 per name. Required to search: name, years to search. Criminal records on computer since 1/1/91, on index cards from 1976-1990, prior on books. Online access same as civil.
General Information: No juvenile, mental, expunged, dismissed, or suspended imposition of sentence records released. Will fax results $2.50 1st page, $.50 each add'l. Copy fee: $.25 per page. Certification fee: $3.00. Payee: Clerk of Circuit Court. Personal checks accepted. Prepayment required. Mail requests: SASE required. Mail turnaround time 2-5 days.

Associate Circuit Court PO Box 491, Macon, MO 63552; 660-385-3531; Fax: 660-385-3132. Hours: 8AM-4:30PM (CST). *Misdemeanor, Civil Actions Under $25,000, Eviction, Small Claims, Probate.*
Civil Records: Access: Fax, mail, in person, online. Both court and visitors may perform in person searches. No search fee. Required to search: name, years to search. Civil cases indexed by defendant, plaintiff. Civil records on index cards and books; on computer back to 1992. Participates in the free state online court record system at www.courts.mo.gov/casenet.

Criminal Records: Access: In person, online. Visitors must perform in person searches for themselves. No search fee. Required to search: name, years to search, DOB. Criminal records on computer since 1992, prior on index cards back to 1989. Online access is the same as civil. Court recommends criminal searches at MO State Highway Patrol, 573-526-6288.
General Information: Public Access terminal is available. No juvenile, mental, expunged, dismissed, or suspended imposition of sentence records released. Will fax results for fee. Copy fee: $1.00 per page. Certification fee: $1.50. Payee: Circuit Court Division II or Probate Court. Prepayment required. Mail requests: SASE required. Mail turnaround time 2 weeks.

Madison County

Circuit Court PO Box 470, Fredericktown, MO 63645-0470; 573-783-2102; Fax: 573-783-2715. Hours: 8AM-5PM (CST). *Felony, Misdemeanor, Civil Actions Over $25,000.*
Civil Records: Access: Mail, in person, online. Visitors must perform in person searches for themselves. No search fee. Required to search: name, years to search. Civil cases indexed by defendant, plaintiff. Civil records on computer back to 1993, prior on index cards from 1979-1992. Participates in the free state online court record system at www.courts.mo.gov/casenet. Records from 11/01/00 forward. Limit one name per mail request.
Criminal Records: Access: In person, online. Visitors must perform in person searches for themselves. No search fee. Required to search: name, years to search. Criminal records on computer back to 1993, prior on index cards from 1979-1993. Participates in the free state online court record system at www.courts.mo.gov/casenet. Records go back to 11/01/00 forward. Court recommends criminal searches at MO State Highway Patrol, 573-526-6288.
General Information: Public Access terminal is available. No juvenile, mental, expunged, dismissed, or suspended imposition of sentence records released. Will not fax results. Copy fee: $1.00 per page. Certification fee: $2.00. Payee: Madison County Circuit Clerk. Personal checks accepted. Prepayment required. Mail turnaround time 2 days.

Associate Circuit Court PO Box 521, Fredericktown, MO 63645; 573-783-3105; Fax: 573-783-5920. Hours: 8AM-5PM (CST). *Misdemeanor, Civil Actions Under $25,000, Small Claims, Probate, Traffic.*
Civil Records: Access: Phone, fax, mail, in person, online. Both court and visitors may perform in person searches. No search fee. Required to search: name, years to search. Civil cases indexed by defendant, plaintiff. Civil records on index cards since 1979, prior on judgment books to 1960s; on computer back to 11/2000. Participates in the free statewide Casenet court record system at www.courts.mo.gov/casenet. Online records go back to 11/00.
Criminal Records: Access: Phone, fax, mail, in person, online. Both court and visitors may perform in person searches. No search fee. Required to search: name, years to search; also helpful: DOB, SSN. Criminal records on index cards since 1979, prior on judgment books; on computer back to 11/2000. Participates in the free statewide Casenet court record system at www.courts.mo.gov/casenet. Online records go back to 11/00.
General Information: Public Access terminal is available. No juvenile, mental, expunged, dismissed, or suspended imposition of sentence records released. Copy fee: $.50 per page. Certification fee: $2.50. Payee: Associate Circuit Court. Only cashiers checks and money orders accepted. Prepayment required.

Mail requests: SASE required. Mail turnaround time 1 week.

Maries County

Circuit Court PO Box 213, Vienna, MO 65582; 573-422-3338; Fax: 573-422-3976. Hours: 8AM-4PM (CST). *Felony, Misdemeanor, Civil Actions Over $25,000.*
Civil Records: Access: Fax, mail, in person. Both court and visitors may perform in person searches. No search fee. Required to search: name, years to search. Civil cases indexed by defendant, plaintiff. Civil records go back to 1940.
Criminal Records: Access: Fax, mail, in person. Both court and visitors may perform in person searches. No search fee. Required to search: name, years to search. Criminal records go back 10 1940.
General Information: No juvenile, mental, expunged, dismissed, or suspended imposition of sentence records released. Will fax results $.25 per page. Copy fee: $.25 per page. Certification fee: $1.50. Payee: Maries County Circuit Clerk. Personal checks accepted. Prepayment required. Mail turnaround time 1-3 days.

Associate Circuit Court PO Box 490, Vienna, MO 65582; 573-422-3303; Fax: 573-422-3976. 8AM-4PM (CST). *Misdemeanor, Civil Actions Under $25,000, Eviction, Small Claims, Probate.*
Note: Most civil cases are directed to the Circuit Court regardless of limit.
Civil Records: Access: Mail, fax, in person. Both court and visitors may perform in person searches. No search fee. Required to search: name, years to search. Civil cases indexed by defendant, plaintiff. Civil records on index cards since 1985, archived since 1868.
Criminal Records: Access: in person only. Only the court performs in person searches; visitors may not. No search fee. Required to search: name, years to search, DOB, signed release; also helpful-SSN. Criminal records on index cards since 1985, archived since 1868. Court recommends criminal searches at MO State Highway Patrol, 573-526-6288.
General Information: No juvenile, mental, expunged, dismissed, or suspended imposition of sentence records released. Will not fax results. Copy fee: $.25 per page. Certification fee: $1.50. Payee: Sheriff of Maries County. Only cashiers checks and money orders accepted. Prepayment required. Mail requests: SASE required. Mail turnaround: 5 days.

Marion County

Circuit Court Division 1 PO Box 392, 100 S Main St, Palmyra, MO 63461; 573-769-2550; Fax: 573-769-6012. Hours: 8:30AM-noon, 1-5PM (CST). *Felony, Civil Actions Over $25,000.*
Civil Records: Access: In person only. Visitors must perform in person searches for themselves. No search fee. Required to search: name, years to search. Civil cases indexed by defendant, plaintiff. Civil records on index cards since 1977, prior on judgment books.
Criminal Records: Access: In person only. Visitors must perform in person searches for themselves. No search fee. Required to search: name, years to search, DOB. Criminal records on index cards since 1977, prior on judgment books. Court recommends criminal searches at MO State Highway Patrol, 573-526-6288.
General Information: No juvenile, mental, expunged, dismissed, or suspended imposition of sentence records released. Copy fee: $.25 per page. Certification fee: $2.00. Payee: Marion County Circuit Clerk of Division I. Business checks accepted.

Circuit Court Division 2 906 Broadway, Rm 105, Hannibal, MO 63401; 573-221-0198; Fax: 573-221-9328. Hours: 8:30AM-noon, 1-5PM (CST). *Felony, Misdemeanor, Civil Actions Over $45,000.*
Note: Jurisdiction is Twps of Miller and Mason only.

Civil Records: Access: Fax, mail, in person. Both court and visitors may perform in person searches. No search fee. Required to search: name, years to search. Civil cases indexed by defendant, plaintiff. Civil records on computer since 1991, prior on index cards.
Criminal Records: Access: In person only. Visitors must perform in person searches for themselves. No search fee. Required to search: name, years to search. Criminal records on computer. Court recommends criminal searches at MO State Highway Patrol, 573-526-6288.
General Information: Public Access terminal is available. No juvenile, mental, expunged, dismissed, or suspended imposition of sentence records released. Copy fee: $.50 per page. Certification fee: $5.00. Payee: Circuit Clerk District II. Personal checks accepted.

Hannibal Associate Circuit Court 906 Broadway, Hannibal, MO 63401; 573-221-0288; Fax: 573-221-0945. Hours: 8AM-5PM (CST). *Misdemeanor, Civil Actions Under $45,000, Eviction, Small Claims, Probate.*
Civil Records: Access: Mail, in person. Visitors must perform in person searches for themselves. No search fee. Required to search: name, years to search. Civil cases indexed by defendant, plaintiff. Civil records on index cards since 1979, prior on judgment books.
Criminal Records: Access: in person only. Visitors must perform in person searches for themselves. No search fee. Required to search: name, years to search. Criminal records on computer since 3/93, on index cards since 1979, prior on judgment books. Court recommends criminal searches at MO State Highway Patrol, 573-526-6288.
General Information: Public Access terminal is available. No juvenile, mental, expunged, dismissed, or suspended imposition of sentence records released. No copy fee. No certification fee.

Palmyra Associate Circuit Court PO Box 449, 100 S. Main St, Palmyra, MO 63461; 573-769-2318; Fax: 573-769-4558. Hours: 8AM-Noon, 1-5PM (CST). *Misdemeanor, Civil Actions Under $45,000, Eviction, Small Claims, Probate.*
Civil Records: Access: Mail, in person. Only the court performs in person searches; visitors may not. No search fee. Required to search: name, years to search. Civil cases indexed by defendant, plaintiff. Civil records on index cards since 1979, prior on judgment books.
Criminal Records: Access: In person only. Only the court performs in person searches; visitors may not. No search fee. Required to search: name, years to search; also helpful: DOB. Criminal records on computer since 1994, on index cards from 1979-1994, prior on judgment books. Court recommends criminal searches at MO State Highway Patrol, 573-526-6288.
General Information: Public Access terminal is available. (Public terminal offers civil cases only.) No juvenile, mental, expunged, dismissed, or suspended imposition of sentence records released. Will fax results. Copy fee: $.50 per page. No certification fee. Payee: Circuit Court. Personal checks accepted. Prepayment required. Mail requests: SASE required. Mail turnaround time varies.

McDonald County

Circuit & Associate Court PO Box 157, Pineville, MO 64856; 417-223-7515; Fax: 417-223-4125. Hours: 8AM-4:30PM (CST). *Felony, Misdemeanor, Civil, Small Claims, Probate.*
Civil Records: Access: Fax, mail, in person, online. Visitors must perform in person searches for themselves. No search fee. Required to search: name, years to search. Civil cases indexed by defendant, plaintiff. Civil records on computer since 1991, on index cards since 1979, prior on index cards. Participates in the free state online court record system at www.courts.mo.gov/casenet.
Criminal Records: Access: Fax, mail, in person, online. Visitors must perform in person searches themselves. No search fee. Required to search: name, years to search; also helpful-charge. Criminal records on computer since 1991, on index cards since 1979, prior on index cards. Participates in the free state online court record system at www.courts.mo.gov/casenet. Court recommends criminal searches at MO State Highway Patrol, 573-526-6288.
General Information: Public Access terminal is available. No juvenile, mental, expunged, dismissed, paternity or suspended imposition of sentence records released. Fee to fax results is $.25 per page, $1.00 if for probate. Copy fee: $.25 per page. Certification fee: $2.00; Probate $1.00 per page. Payee: McDonald County Circuit Clerk. Business checks accepted. Prepayment required. Mail requests: SASE required. Mail turnaround time is less than 10 days.

Mercer County

Circuit Court Courthouse, 802 E Main, Princeton, MO 64673; 660-748-4335; Fax: 660-748-4339. Hours: 8:30AM-noon, 1-4:30PM (CST). *Felony, Misdemeanor, Civil Actions Over $45,000.*
Civil Records: Access: In person, online. Visitors must perform in person searches for themselves. No search fee. Required to search: name, years to search. Civil cases indexed by defendant, plaintiff. Civil records on computer since 1991, on index cards since 1977, prior on books. Participates in the free state online court record system at www.courts.mo.gov/casenet. Online records go back to 3/29/2000.
Criminal Records: Access: In person, online. Visitors must perform in person searches for themselves. No search fee. Required to search: name, years to search, DOB. Criminal records on computer since 1991, on index cards since 1977, prior on books. Online access to criminal records is the same as civil. Court recommends criminal searches at MO State Highway Patrol, 573-526-6288.
General Information: Public Access terminal is available. No juvenile, mental, expunged, dismissed, or suspended imposition of sentence records released. Copy fee: $.25 per page. Certification fee: $1.00 per page. Payee: Mercer County Circuit Clerk. Personal checks not accepted if out of state; money orders preferred. Prepayment required.

Associate Circuit Court Courthouse Rm 304, 302 S Main St, Carthage, MO 64836; 417-358-0450; Fax: 417-358-0460. Hours: 8:30AM-4:30PM (CST). *Misdemeanor, Civil Actions Under $45,000, Eviction, Small Claims, Probate.*
Civil Records: Access: In person, online. Visitors must perform in person searches for themselves. No search fee. Required to search: name, years to search. Civil cases indexed by defendant, plaintiff. Civil records on computer since 2000, prior on index cards since 1979. Participates in the free state online court record system at www.courts.mo.gov/casenet. Online records go back to 3/29/2000.

Criminal Records: Access: In person, online. Visitors must perform in person searches for themselves. No search fee. Required to search: name, years to search. Criminal records on computer since 2000, prior on index cards since 1979. Online access to criminal records is the same as civil. Court recommends criminal searches at MO State Highway Patrol, 573-526-6288.
General Information: Public Access terminal is available. No juvenile, mental, expunged, dismissed, or suspended imposition of sentence records released. Copy fee: $.25 per page. No certification fee.

Associate Circuit Court Mercer County Courthouse, 802 E Main St., Princeton, MO 64673; 660-748-4232; Fax: 660-748-4292. Hours: 8:30AM-4:30PM (CST). *Misdemeanor, Civil Actions Under $45,000, Eviction, Small Claims, Probate.*
Civil Records: Access: In person, online. Visitors must perform in person searches for themselves. No search fee. Required to search: name, years to search. Civil cases indexed by defendant. Civil records on index. Participates in the free state online court record system at www.courts.mo.gov/casenet. Online records go back to 3/2000.
Criminal Records: Access: In person, online. Visitors must perform in person searches for themselves. No search fee. Required to search: name, years to search; also helpful: DOB, SSN. Criminal records on index. Online access to criminal records is the same as civil. Court recommends criminal searches at MO State Highway Patrol, 573-526-6288.
General Information: Public Access terminal is available. No juvenile, mental, expunged, dismissed, or suspended imposition of sentence records released. Copy fee: $.25 per page. Certification fee: $1.50 plus $1.00 per page. Payee: Circuit Court Division II. Personal checks accepted. Prepayment required.

Miller County

Circuit Court PO Box 11, Tuscumbia, MO 65082; 573-369-1980. Hours: 8AM-4:30PM (CST). *Felony, Misdemeanor, Civil Actions Over $25,000.*
Civil Records: Access: Phone, fax, mail, in person. Both court and visitors may perform in person searches. Search fee: $4.00 per name. Required to search: name, years to search. Civil cases indexed by defendant, plaintiff. Civil records on index cards since 1976, prior on books.
Criminal Records: Access: Phone, fax, mail, in person. Both court and visitors may perform in person searches. Search fee: $4.00 per name. Required to search: name, years to search. Criminal records on index cards since 1976, prior on books.
General Information: Public Access terminal is available. No juvenile, mental, expunged, dismissed, or suspended imposition of sentence records released. No fee to fax results; other fees must be prepaid. Will fax to local and toll-free numbers only. Copy fee: $.50 per page. Certification fee: $2.00. Payee: Miller County Circuit Court. Personal checks accepted. Prepayment required. Mail requests: SASE required. Mail turnaround time 1 week.

Associate Circuit Court Miller County Courthouse Annex, Tuscumbia, MO 65082; 573-369-1970. Hours: 8AM-4PM (CST). *Misdemeanor, Civil Actions Under $25,000, Eviction, Small Claims, Probate.*
Civil Records: Access: Mail, in person. Only the court performs in person searches; visitors may not. No search fee. Required to search: name, years to search. Civil cases indexed by defendant, plaintiff. Civil records on computer since 1/92, on microfiche since 1980, on cards since 1979, prior archived.
Criminal Records: Access: Mail, in person. Only the court performs in person searches; visitors may not.

No search fee. Required to search: name, years to search. Criminal records on computer since 1979, on microfiche since 1980, prior archived.

General Information: No juvenile, mental, expunged, dismissed, or suspended imposition of sentence records released. Copy fee: $1.00 per page. Certification fee: $1.50. Payee: Associate Circuit Court. Only cashiers checks and money orders accepted. Prepayment required. Mail requests: SASE required. Mail turnaround time 1 week.

Mississippi County

Circuit & Associate Court PO Box 369, Charleston, MO 63834; 573-683-2146 x1; Fax: 573-683-7696. Hours: 8AM-5PM (CST). *Felony, Misdemeanor, Civil, Small Claims, Eviction, Probate.*

Civil Records: Access: In person, online. Visitors must perform in person searches for themselves. No search fee. Required to search: name, years to search. Civil cases indexed by defendant, plaintiff. Civil records in case files since 1976. Access to civil records is free at www.courts.mo.gov/casenet/. At the website, select the judicial district, then search by name, case # or date. Online records go back to 6/15/2001.

Criminal Records: Access: in person, online. Visitors must perform in person searches for themselves. No search fee. Required to search: name, years to search, DOB. Criminal records in case files since 1951. Online access to criminal records is the same as civil.

General Information: Public Access terminal is available. No juvenile, mental, expunged, dismissed, or suspended imposition of sentence records released. No fee to fax results. Copy fee: $.25 per page. Certification fee: $.50. Payee: Circuit Clerk. Personal checks accepted. Prepayment required.

Moniteau County

Circuit Court 200 E Main, California, MO 65018; 573-796-2071. Hours: 8AM-4:30PM (CST). *Felony, Misdemeanor, Civil Actions Over $25,000, Small Claims.*

Civil Records: Access: In person. Both court and visitors may perform in person searches. No search fee. Required to search: name, years to search; also helpful: case number. Civil records indexed by defendant, plaintiff. Civil records on computer since 1992, prior on index cards and books.

Criminal Records: Access: In person only. Both court and visitors may perform in person searches. No search fee. Required to search: name, years to search; also helpful: case number. Criminal records on computer since 1980, prior on index cards and books to 1845. Court recommends criminal searches at MO State Highway Patrol, 573-526-6288.

General Information: No juvenile, mental, expunged, dismissed, or suspended imposition of sentence records released. Copy fee: $.30 per page. Certification fee: $1.00. Payee: Moniteau County Circuit Court. Personal checks accepted. Prepayment required.

Associate Circuit Court 200 E Main, California, MO 65018; 573-796-4671. Hours: 8AM-4:30PM (CST). *Misdemeanor, Civil Actions Under $45,000, Eviction, Small Claims, Probate.*
Note: The court will not do probate record searches.

Civil Records: Access: Phone, in person. Visitors must perform in person searches for themselves. No search fee. Required to search: name, years to search. Civil cases indexed by defendant, plaintiff. Civil records on index cards since 1979, prior on index books from 1948 to 1979, archived before.

Criminal Records: Access: In person only. Visitors must perform in person searches for themselves. No search fee. Required to search: name, years to search. Criminal records on index cards since 1979, prior on index books from 1948 to 1979, archived before. Court recommends criminal searches at MO State Highway Patrol, 573-526-6288.

General Information: No juvenile, mental, expunged, dismissed, or suspended imposition of sentence records released. Copy fee: $.25 per page. Certification fee: $2.50 first page, $1.00 each add'l. Personal checks accepted. Prepayment required.

Monroe County

Circuit Court PO Box 227, Paris, MO 65275; 660-327-5204; Fax: 660-327-5781. Hours: 8AM-4:30PM (CST). *Felony, Misdemeanor, Civil Actions Over $45,000.*

Civil Records: Access: Mail, in person. Both court and visitors may perform in person searches. Search fee: $14.00 per name. Required to search: name, years to search. Civil cases indexed by defendant, plaintiff. Civil records on computer since 1996; index cards since 1979, prior on index books.

Criminal Records: Access: Mail, in person. Both court and visitors may perform in person searches. Search fee: $14.00 per name. Required to search: name, years to search, SSN, signed release. Criminal records on computer since 1996, on index cards from 1979 to 1990.

General Information: No juvenile, mental, expunged, dismissed, or suspended imposition of sentence records released. Fee to fax results is $1.00 per page. Copy fee: $1.00 per page. Certification fee: $2.00. Payee: Monroe County Circuit Court. Personal checks accepted. Prepayment required. Mail requests: SASE required. Mail turnaround time 1 week.

Associate Circuit Court 300 N Main, Courthouse, Paris, MO 65275; 660-327-5220; Fax: 660-327-5651. Hours: 8AM-Noon, 1-4:30PM (CST). *Misdemeanor, Civil Actions Under $45,000, Eviction, Small Claims, Probate.*

Civil Records: Access: Mail, in person. Both court and visitors may perform in person searches. No search fee. Required to search: name, years to search. Civil cases indexed by defendant, plaintiff. Civil records on index cards since 1979, prior on books.

Criminal Records: Access: Mail, in person. Both court and visitors may perform in person searches. No search fee. Required to search: name, years to search. Criminal records on index cards since 1979, prior on books.

General Information: No juvenile, mental, expunged, dismissed, or suspended imposition of sentence records released. Copy fee: $.25 per page. Certification fee: $1.50 first page, $1.00 each add'l. Payee: Associate Circuit Court. Personal checks accepted. Prepayment required. Mail requests: SASE required. Mail turnaround time 2 weeks.

Montgomery County

Circuit Court 211 E 3rd, Montgomery City, MO 63361; 573-564-3341; Fax: 573-564-3914. Hours: 8AM-4:30PM (CST). *Felony, Misdemeanor, Civil Actions Over $25,000.*

Civil Records: Access: Online, in person. Visitors must perform in person searches for themselves. No search fee. Required to search: name, years to search. Civil cases indexed by defendant, plaintiff. Civil records on computer since 1987 for judgments, on index cards since 1979, prior on books to 1864. Participates in the free state online court record system at www.courts.mo.gov/casenet. Online records go back to 6/25/1997.

Criminal Records: Access: Online, in person. Visitors must perform in person searches for

themselves. No search fee. Required to search: name, years to search. Criminal records on computer since 1987 for judgments, on index cards since 1979, prior on books. Online access to criminal records is the same as civil. Online criminal records go back to 12/10/1996. Court recommends criminal searches at MO State Highway Patrol, 573-526-6288.

General Information: Public Access terminal is available. (Judgments only.) No juvenile, mental, expunged, dismissed, or suspended imposition of sentence records released. Copy fee: $.25 per page. Certification fee: $1.50 plus $.25 per page. Payee: Montgomery County Circuit Court. Personal checks accepted. Prepayment required.

Associate Circuit Court 211 E 3rd St, Montgomery City, MO 63361; 573-564-3348. Hours: 8:00AM-4:30PM (CST). *Misdemeanor, Civil Actions Under $25,000, Eviction, Small Claims, Probate.*

Civil Records: Access: Online, in person. Visitors must perform in person searches for themselves. No search fee. Required to search: name, years to search. Civil cases indexed by defendant, plaintiff. Civil records on computer back to 1976, prior on index cards. Participates in the free state online court record system at www.courts.mo.gov/casenet. Online civil records go back to 6/25/1997.

Criminal Records: Access: Online, in person. Visitors must perform in person searches for themselves. No search fee. Required to search: name, years to search, DOB. Criminal records on computer back to 1976, prior on index cards. Online access to criminal records is the same as civil. Online criminal records go back to 8/29/1950. Court recommends criminal searches at MO State Highway Patrol, 573-526-6288.

General Information: Public Access terminal is available. (Public terminal limited to judgments.) No juvenile, mental, expunged, dismissed, or suspended imposition of sentence records released. Copy fee: $.25 per page. Certification fee: $1.50 per page. Payee: Montgomery Circuit Clerk's Office. Personal checks accepted. Prepayment required.

Morgan County

Circuit Court 211 E Newton, Versailles, MO 65084; 573-378-4413; Fax: 573-378-5356. Hours: 8AM-5PM (CST). *Felony, Civil Actions Over $25,000.*

Civil Records: Access: Phone, mail, in person. Both court and visitors may perform in person searches. No search fee. Required to search: name, years to search. Civil cases indexed by defendant, plaintiff. Civil records on computer since 1992, on index cards since 1979, prior archived since mid-1800s.

Criminal Records: Access: Phone, mail, in person. Both court and visitors may perform in person searches. No search fee. Required to search: name, years to search. Criminal records on computer since 1992, on index cards since 1979, prior archived since mid-1800s.

General Information: Public Access terminal is available. No juvenile, mental, expunged, dismissed, or suspended imposition of sentence records released. Copy fee: $.50 per page. Certification fee: $1.50. Payee: Circuit Court. Personal checks accepted. Prepayment required. Copy fees may be billed. Mail requests: SASE required. Mail turnaround time 1 week; phone turnaround is immediate.

Associate Circuit Court 211 E Newton St, Versailles, MO 65084; 573-378-4235; Criminal phone: 573-378-4060; Fax: 573-378-6847. Hours: 8:30AM-5PM (CST). *Misdemeanor, Civil Actions Under $25,000, Eviction, Small Claims, Probate.*

Civil Records: Access: Phone, mail, in person. Both court and visitors may perform in person searches. No search fee. Required to search: name, years to search.

Civil cases indexed by defendant, plaintiff. Civil records on computer since 1991, prior on index to 1970.

Criminal Records: Access: Phone, mail, in person. Only the court performs in person searches; visitors may not. No search fee. Required to search: name, years to search; also helpful: address, DOB, SSN, singed release. Criminal records on computer since 1989, prior on index to 1970. Signed release required for some searches.

General Information: No juvenile, mental, expunged, dismissed, or suspended imposition of sentence records released. Copy fee: $1.00 per page. Certification fee: $1.50. Payee: Associate Circuit Court or Probate Court. Only cashiers checks and money orders accepted. Prepayment required. Mail requests: SASE required. Mail turnaround: 2-3 days.

New Madrid County

Circuit Court County Courthouse, 450 Main St, New Madrid, MO 63869; 573-748-2228. Hours: 8AM-4:30PM (CST). *Felony, Misdemeanor, Civil Actions Over $25,000.*
www.osca.state.mo.us
Civil Records: Access: In person, online. Visitors must perform in person searches for themselves. No search fee. Required to search: name, years to search. Civil cases indexed by defendant, plaintiff. Civil records on Cott index since 1979, prior on books. Access to civil records is free at www.courts.mo.gov/casenet/. At the website, select the judicial district, then search by name, case # or date. Online records go back to 2/7/2001.
Criminal Records: Access: In person, online. Visitors must perform in person searches for themselves. No search fee. Required to search: name, years to search. Criminal records on Cott index since 1979, prior on books. Online access to criminal records is the same as civil.
General Information: Public Access terminal is available. No juvenile, mental, expunged, dismissed, or suspended imposition of sentence records released. Will fax results. Copy fee: $1.00 per page. Certification fee: $5.00 per doc. Payee: Circuit Clerk. Personal checks not accepted. Prepayment required.

Associate Circuit Court County Courthouse, New Madrid, MO 63869; 573-748-5556; Fax: 573-748-5409. Hours: 8AM-5PM (CST). *Misdemeanor, Civil Actions Under $25,000, Eviction, Small Claims, Probate.*
Civil Records: Access: Mail, in person, online. Both court and visitors may perform in person searches. No search fee. Required to search: name, years to search. Civil cases indexed by defendant, plaintiff. Probate records archived since 1803, records go back to 1980; computerized back to 1992. Access to civil records is free at www.courts.mo.gov/casenet/. At the website, select the judicial district, then search by name, case # or date. Online records go back to 2/7/2001.
Criminal Records: Access: Mail, in person, online. Only the court performs in person searches; visitors may not. No search fee. Required to search: name, years to search. Criminal records archived since 1947; records go back to 1980; computerized records back to 1992. Online access to criminal records is the same as civil.
General Information: Public Access terminal is available. (Only Division 1 records on public terminal.) No juvenile, mental, expunged, dismissed, or suspended imposition of sentence records released. No copy fee. No certification fee. Turnaround time 1-2 weeks.

Newton County

Circuit and Associate Court PO Box 130, Neosho, MO 64850; 417-451-8257; Civil phone: 417-451-8257; Criminal phone: 417-451-8214; Probate phone: 417-451-8232; Fax: 417-451-8298 Civ. Hours: 8AM-5PM (CST). *Felony, Misdemeanor, Civil Actions, Eviction, Small Claims, Probate.*
Note: Probate is a separate division; Probate mailing address is 101 S Wood #204, same ZIP Code.
Civil Records: Access: Phone, mail, in person, online. Visitors must perform in person searches for themselves. No search fee. Required to search: name, years to search. Civil cases indexed by defendant, plaintiff. Civil records on computer since 1991, prior on index cards and books. Participates in the free state online court record system at www.courts.mo.gov/casenet.
Criminal Records: Access: In person, online. Visitors must perform in person searches for themselves. No search fee. Required to search: name, years to search; also helpful: DOB, SSN. Criminal records on computer since 1991, prior on index cards and books. Online access to criminal records is the same as civil.
General Information: Public Access terminal is available. No juvenile, mental, expunged, dismissed, or suspended imposition of sentence records released. Will fax results for $2.00 per page. Copy fee: $.25 per page. Certification fee: $1.00. Payee: Newton County Circuit Clerk. Business checks accepted. Prepayment required. Copy fees may be billed. Mail requests: SASE required.

Nodaway County

Circuit Court 305 N Main St #206, Maryville, MO 64468; 660-582-5431; Probate phone: 660-582-4221; Fax: 660-582-5499. 8AM-4:30PM (CST). *Felony, Misdemeanor, Civil Actions Over $25,000.*
Civil Records: Access: Phone, mail, in person. Visitors must perform in person searches for themselves. No search fee. Required to search: name, years to search. Civil cases indexed by defendant, plaintiff. Civil records on computer back to 5/91, archived since 1845.
Criminal Records: Access: In person only. Visitors must perform in person searches for themselves. Search fee: $5.00 per name. Required to search: name, years to search, DOB. Criminal records on computer back to 5/91, archived since 1845. Court recommends criminal searches at MO State Highway Patrol, 573-526-6288.
General Information: Public Access terminal is available. No juvenile, mental, expunged, dismissed, or suspended imposition of sentence records released. Fee to fax results is $1.00 per page. Copy fee: $1.00 per page. Certification fee: $1.00. Payee: Circuit Clerk. Personal checks accepted. Prepayment required.

Associate Circuit Court 303 N Market, Courthouse Annex, Maryville, MO 64468; 660-582-2531; Fax: 660-582-2047. Hours: 8AM-Noon; 1-4:30PM (CST). *Misdemeanor, Civil Actions Under $45,000, Eviction, Small Claims, Probate.*
Civil Records: Access: In person only. Only the court performs in person searches; visitors may not. Court will look up name for you. No search fee. Required to search: name, years to search. Civil cases indexed by defendant, plaintiff. Civil records on computer since 1981, archived since 1845.
Criminal Records: Access: In person only. Only the court performs in person searches; visitors may not. Court will look up name for you. No search fee. Required to search: name, years to search. Criminal records on computer since 1981, archived since 1845.

Court recommends criminal searches at MO State Highway Patrol, 573-526-6288.
General Information: No juvenile, mental, expunged, dismissed, or suspended imposition of sentence records released. Copy fee: $.50 per page. Certification fee: $1.50. Payee: Circuit Court Associate Division. Business checks accepted. Prepayment required.

Oregon County

Circuit Court PO Box 406, Alton, MO 65606; 417-778-7460; Fax: 417-778-7206. Hours: 8AM-4PM (CST). *Felony, Misdemeanor, Civil Actions Over $45,000.*
Civil Records: Access: Phone, fax, mail, in person, online. Both court and visitors may perform in person searches. No search fee. Required to search: name, years to search; also helpful: address. Civil cases indexed by defendant, plaintiff. Civil records on books. Participates in the free state online court record system at www.courts.mo.gov/casenet. Online records go back to 1991.
Criminal Records: Access: Phone, fax, mail, in person, online. Both court and visitors may perform in person searches. Court will only search if not busy, and may refer you to MO State Hiway Patrol. No search fee. Required to search: name, years to search; also helpful: DOB, SSN. Criminal records on books. Online access to criminal records is the same as civil.
General Information: Public Access terminal is available. (Public terminal is in the recorder's office.) No juvenile, mental, expunged, dismissed, or suspended imposition of sentence records released. Will fax results $1.00 1st page, $.50 each add'l. Copy fee: $.50 per page. Certification fee: $2.00. Payee: Circuit Court. Personal checks accepted. Prepayment required. Mail requests: SASE required. Mail turnaround time 1-2 days.

Associate Circuit Court PO Box 211, Alton, MO 65606; 417-778-7461; Fax: 417-778-6209. Hours: 8:00AM-4:00PM (CST). *Misdemeanor, Civil Actions Under $45,000, Eviction, Small Claims, Probate.*
Civil Records: Access: Mail, in person, online. Both court and visitors may perform in person searches. No search fee. Required to search: name, years to search. Civil cases indexed by defendant, plaintiff. Civil records on index cards, archived since 1850. Participates in the free state online court record system at www.courts.mo.gov/casenet. Online records go back to 1991.
Criminal Records: Access: Mail, in person, online. Only court may perform in person searches. No search fee. Required to search: name, years to search. Criminal records on computer since 3/11/92, prior on files. Online access to criminal records is the same as civil.
General Information: Public Access terminal is available. No juvenile, mental, expunged, or dismissed records released. (Suspended Imposition of Sentence only available during probationary period.). Copy fee: $1.00 per page. Certification fee: $2.00. Payee: Associate Circuit Court. Business checks accepted. Prepayment required. Mail requests: SASE required. Mail turnaround time varies.

Osage County

Circuit Court PO Box 825, Linn, MO 65051; 573-897-3114 573-897-2136 (Assoc Div). Hours: 8AM-4:30PM (CST). *Felony, Misdemeanor, Civil Actions Over $25,000.*
Civil Records: Access: Phone, mail, in person, online. Both court and visitors may perform in person searches. No search fee. Required to search: name, years to search. Civil cases indexed by defendant, plaintiff. Civil records on index cards and books.

Participates in the free state online court record system at www.courts.mo.gov/casenet. Online civil records go back to 9/01/2000.

Criminal Records: Access: Phone, mail, fax, in person, online. Both court and visitors may perform in person searches. No search fee. Required to search: name, years to search, DOB; also helpful: SSN. Criminal records on index cards and books, computerized since 1992. Participates in the free state online court record system at www.courts.mo.gov/casenet. Online criminal records go back to 8/28/1992.

General Information: Public Access terminal is available. No juvenile, mental, expunged, dismissed, or suspended imposition of sentence records released. Fee to fax results is $1.00 per page. Copy fee: $.50 per page. $1.00 minimum. Certification fee: $2.00. Payee: Circuit Clerk. Personal checks accepted. Prepayment required. Mail requests: SASE required. Mail turnaround time ASAP.

Associate Circuit Court PO Box 470, Linn, MO 65051; 573-897-2136; Fax: 573-897-4741. 8AM-4:30PM (CST). *Misdemeanor, Civil Actions Under $25,000, Eviction, Small Claims, Probate.*

Civil Records: Access: Phone, mail, in person, online. Both the court and visitors may perform in person searches. No search fee. Required to search: name, years to search. Civil cases indexed by defendant, plaintiff. Civil records on computer back to 2000, prior on index cards. Participates in the free state online court record system at www.courts.mo.gov/casenet. Online civil records go back to 09/05/00. Online probate records go back to 9/05/2000.

Criminal Records: Access: Phone, mail, in person, online. Both the court and visitors may perform in person searches. No search fee. Required to search: name, years to search; also helpful: DOB, SSN. Criminal records on computer back to 1995, prior on index cards. Participates in the free state online court record system at www.courts.mo.gov/casenet. Online criminal records go back to 1995. Also, traffic records go back to 9/05/00.

General Information: Public Access terminal is available. No juvenile, mental, expunged, dismissed, or suspended imposition of sentence records released. Copy fee: $.25 per page. Certification fee: $2.00. Payee: Osage County Circuit Court-Associate Division. Personal checks accepted. Prepayment required. Mail requests: SASE not required. Mail turnaround time 2 weeks.

Ozark County

Circuit Court PO Box 36, Gainesville, MO 65655; 417-679-4232; Fax: 417-679-4554. Hours: 8AM-Noon, 12:30-4:30PM (CST). *Felony, Misdemeanor, Civil Actions Over $25,000.*

Civil Records: Access: Mail, in person. Only the court performs in person searches: visitors may not. No search fee. Required to search: name, years to search. Civil cases indexed by defendant, plaintiff. Civil records on index cards since 1979, archived since 1933.

Criminal Records: Access: In person only. Only the court performs in person searches; visitors may not. No search fee. Required to search: name, years to search, DOB. Criminal records on index cards since 1979, archived since 1933. Court recommends criminal searches at MO State Highway Patrol, 573-526-6288.

General Information: No juvenile, mental, expunged, dismissed, or suspended imposition of sentence records released. Copy fee: $.25 per page. Certification fee: $1.50. Payee: Ozark County Circuit Court. Personal checks accepted. Prepayment required.

Associate Circuit Court PO Box 278, Gainesville, MO 65655; 417-679-4611; Fax: 417-679-2099. Hours: 8AM-4:30PM (CST). *Misdemeanor, Civil Actions Under $25,000, Eviction, Small Claims, Probate.*

Civil Records: Access: Fax, mail, in person. Only the court performs in person searches; visitors may not. No search fee. Required to search: name, years to search. Civil cases indexed by defendant, plaintiff. Civil records on case files.

Criminal Records: Access: In person only. Only the court performs in person searches; visitors may not. No search fee. Required to search: name, years to search, DOB, signed release; also helpful: SSN. Criminal records on computer since 1990. Court recommends criminal searches at MO State Highway Patrol, 573-526-6288.

General Information: No juvenile, mental, expunged, dismissed, or suspended imposition of sentence records released. Will fax results for $1.00 per page. Copy fee: $1.00 per page. Certification fee: $1.50. Payee: Associate Circuit Court. Personal checks accepted. Prepayment required. Mail requests: SASE required. Mail turnaround time 2 weeks.

Pemiscot County

Circuit Court, Division I County Courthouse, PO Box 34, Caruthersville, MO 63830; 573-333-0182. Hours: 7:30AM-4:30PM (CST). *Felony, Misdemeanor, Civil Actions Over $45,000.*

Civil Records: Access: In person, online. Visitors must perform in person searches for themselves. No search fee. Required to search: name, years to search. Civil cases indexed by defendant, plaintiff. Civil records on index cards since 1979, prior on books. Participates in the free state online court record system at www.courts.mo.gov/casenet. Online records go back to 2/7/2001.

Criminal Records: Access: In person, online. Visitors must perform in person searches for themselves. No search fee. Required to search: name, years to search. Criminal records on index cards since 1979, prior on books. Online access to criminal records is the same as civil. Court recommends criminal searches at MO State Highway Patrol, 573-526-6288.

General Information: Public Access terminal is available. No juvenile, mental, expunged, dismissed, or suspended imposition of sentence records released. Copy fee: $.50 per page. No certification fee. Payee: Pemiscot County Treasurer. No personal checks accepted.

Associate Circuit Court County Courthouse, PO Drawer 228, Caruthersville, MO 63830; 573-333-2784. Hours: 7:30AM-4:30PM (CST). *Misdemeanor, Civil Actions Under $45,000, Eviction, Small Claims, Probate.*

Civil Records: Access: Mail, in person, online. Only the court performs in person searches; visitors may not. No search fee. Required to search: name, years to search. Civil cases indexed by defendant, plaintiff. Civil records on computer back to 2001, index cards since 1979, prior on books. Participates in the free state online court record system at www.courts.mo.gov/casenet. Online records go back to 2/14/2001.

Criminal Records: Access: Mail, in person. Only the court performs in person searches; visitors may not. No search fee. Required to search: name, years to search. Criminal records on computer back to 5/90, on index cards from 1979-1990, prior on books. Online access to criminal records is the same as civil.

General Information: No juvenile, mental, expunged, dismissed, or suspended imposition of sentence records released. Copy fee: $1.00 per page. No certification fee. Payee: Pemiscot County Clerk.

Only cashiers checks and money orders accepted. Prepayment required. Mail requests: SASE required. Mail turnaround time varies.

Perry County

Circuit Court 15 W Saint Maries St #2, Perryville, MO 63775-1399; 573-547-6581; Fax: 573-547-9323. Hours: 8AM-5PM (CST). *Felony, Misdemeanor, Civil Actions Over $25,000.*

Civil Records: Access: Fax, mail, in person, online. Visitors must perform in person searches for themselves. No search fee. Required to search: name, years to search. Civil cases indexed by defendant, plaintiff. Civil records on computer since 1994, prior on index cards. Access to civil records is free at www.courts.mo.gov/casenet/. At the website, select the judicial district, then search by name, case # or date. Online records go back to 7/1/2001.

Criminal Records: Access: Fax, mail, in person, online. Both court and visitors may perform in person searches. No search fee. Required to search: name, years to search. Criminal records on computer since 1993, prior on index cards. Online access to criminal records is the same as civil. Online public case records go back to 7/1/2001; judgments to 8/23/1993.

General Information: Public Access terminal is available. No juvenile, mental, paternity (except final judgment), expunged, dismissed, or suspended imposition of sentence records released. Will fax results for $1.00 per page. Copy fee: $1.00 per page. Certification fee: $1.00. Payee: Perry County Circuit Clerk. Personal checks accepted. Prepayment required. Mail requests: SASE required. Mail turnaround time: time permitting.

Associate Circuit Court 15 W Ste. Marie, #2, Perryville, MO 63775-1399; 573-547-7861; Fax: 573-547-9323. Hours: 8AM-5PM (CST). *Misdemeanor, Civil Actions Under $25,000, Eviction, Small Claims, Probate.*

Civil Records: Access: Mail, in person, online. Visitors must perform in person searches for themselves. No search fee. Required to search: name, years to search; also helpful: address. Civil cases indexed by defendant, plaintiff. Civil records on computer since 1994, prior on index cards. Access to civil records is free at www.courts.mo.gov/casenet/. At the website, select the judicial district, then search by name, case # or date. Online records go back to 7/1/2001.

Criminal Records: Access: Mail, in person, online. Visitors must perform in person searches for themselves. No search fee. Required to search: name, years to search, DOB; also helpful: address, SSN. Criminal records on computer since 1994, prior on index cards. Online access to criminal records is the same as civil. Online public case records go back to 7/1/2001.

General Information: Public Access terminal is available. No juvenile, mental, expunged, dismissed, or suspended imposition of sentence records released. Will fax results for $1.00 per page. Copy fee: $1.00 per page. Certification fee: $1.00 per page. Payee: Circuit Court Division 6. Only cashiers checks and money orders accepted. Prepayment required. Mail requests: SASE required. Mail turnaround time varies.

Pettis County

Circuit Court PO Box 804, Sedalia, MO 65302-0804; 660-826-0617; Fax: 660-826-4520. Hours: 8AM-5PM (CST). *Felony, Misdemeanor, Civil Actions Over $45,000.*

Note: Also see Associate Circuit Court for add'l civil actions over $45,000.

Civil Records: Access: Phone, fax, mail, in person, online. Both court and visitors may perform in person searches. No search fee. Required to search: name, years to search. Civil cases indexed by defendant, plaintiff. Civil records on index books since 9/75, prior on judgment books. Access to civil records is free at www.courts.mo.gov/casenet/. At the website, select the judicial district, then search by name, case # or date. Online records go back to 4/2001.

Criminal Records: Access: Phone, fax, mail, in person, online. Both court and visitors may perform in person searches. No search fee. Required to search: name, years to search, DOB. Criminal records on computer since 1993, prior on index cards since 9/75. Online access to criminal records is the same as civil. Online criminal records go back to 1/1992.

General Information: Public Access terminal is available. No juvenile, mental, expunged, dismissed, or suspended imposition of sentence records released. Will fax results $2.50 1st page, $1.50 each add'l. Copy fee: $.15 per page. Certification fee: $1.50. Payee: Pettis County Circuit Clerk. Personal checks accepted. Prepayment required. Mail requests: SASE required. Mail turnaround time 1-2 days.

Associate Circuit Court 415 S Ohio, Sedalia, MO 65301; 660-826-4699; Probate phone: 660-826-0368; Fax: 660-827-8613. Hours: 8:30AM-5PM (CST). *Misdemeanor, Civil Actions Under $45,000, Eviction, Small Claims, Probate.*

Note: Civil actions over $45,000 may also be filed here.

Civil Records: Access: Phone, fax, mail, in person, online. Both court and visitors may perform in person searches. No search fee. Required to search: name, years to search. Civil cases indexed by defendant, plaintiff. Civil records on index cards since 1975, prior on judgment books; on computer back to 4/2001. Access to civil records is free at www.courts.mo.gov/casenet/. At the website, select the judicial district, then search by name, case # or date. Online records go back to 4/2001.

Criminal Records: Access: Phone, fax, mail, in person, online. Both court and visitors may perform in person searches. No search fee. Required to search: name, years to search, DOB, SSN; on some cases: signed release. Criminal records on computer back to 1993, on index cards from 1975-1993, prior on judgment books. Online access to criminal records is the same as civil. Online criminal records go back to 1/1993.

General Information: Public Access terminal is available. No juvenile, mental, expunged, dismissed, or suspended imposition of sentence records released. Will fax results for free. Copy fee: $.15 per page. Certification fee: $1.50 per page. Payee: Circuit Court Division 6. Only cashiers checks and money orders accepted. Prepayment required. Mail requests: SASE required. Mail turnaround time 1-2 weeks.

Probate Court 415 S. Ohio, Sedalia, MO 65301; 660-826-0368; Fax: 660-827-8637. Hours: 8:30AM-5PM (CST). *Probate.*

Note: Access to probate records is free at http://casenet.osca.state.mo.us/casenet/. At the website, select the judicial district, then search by name, case # or date.

Phelps County

Circuit & Associate Court 200 N Main St, Rolla, MO 65401; 573-364-1891 X200; Civil phone: 573-364-1891 X214; Criminal phone: 573-364-1891 X202; Probate phone: 573-364-1891 X251; Fax: 573-364-1419. Hours: 8AM-5PM (CST). *Felony, Misdemeanor, Civil, Small Claims, Eviction, Probate.*

Civil Records: Access: Fax, mail, in person. Visitors must perform in person searches for themselves. No search fee. Required to search: name, years to search.

Civil cases indexed by defendant, plaintiff. Civil records on computer since 1991; prior on books to 1957.

Criminal Records: Access: In person only. No search fee. Required to search: names, years to search. Criminal records computerized since 1991, prior indexed on books to 1957. Court recommends criminal searches at MO State Highway Patrol, 573-526-6288.

General Information: Public Access terminal is available. No juvenile, mental, expunged or dismissed records released. Will fax results for $1.00 per page. Copy fee: $.20 per page. Certification fee: $1.00. Payee: Circuit Clerk. No out-of-state checks accepted. Prepayment required. Copy fees may be billed. Mail requests: SASE required. Mail turnaround: 1 week.

Pike County

Circuit Court 115 W Main, Bowling Green, MO 63334; 573-324-3112. Hours: 8AM-4:30PM (CST). *Felony, Misdemeanor, Civil Actions Over $25,000.*

Civil Records: Access: Mail, in person, online. Both court and visitors may perform in person searches. No search fee. Required to search: name, years to search; also helpful: address. Civil cases indexed by defendant, plaintiff. Civil records on index cards since 1977, prior on books. Participates in the free state online court record system at www.courts.mo.gov/casenet. Online records go back 4/2002.

Criminal Records: Access: In person, online. Visitors must perform in person searches for themselves. No search fee. Required to search: name, years to search; also helpful: DOB. Criminal records on index cards since 1977, prior on books. Participates in the free state online court record system at www.courts.mo.gov/casenet. Online records go back 4/2002. Court recommends criminal searches at MO State Highway Patrol, 573-526-6288.

General Information: Public Access terminal is available. No juvenile, mental, expunged, dismissed, or suspended imposition of sentence records released. Copy fee: $.50 per page. Certification fee: $1.00 per page and $1.00 per doc. Payee: Pike County Circuit Clerk. Personal checks accepted. Prepayment required. Mail requests: SASE required. Mail turnaround time 1-2 days.

Associate Circuit Court 115 W Main, Bowling Green, MO 63334; 573-324-5582; Fax: 573-324-6297. Hours: 8AM-4:30PM (CST). *Misdemeanor, Civil Actions Under $25,000, Eviction, Small Claims, Probate.*

Civil Records: Access: Phone, mail, fax, in person, online. Both court and visitors may perform in person searches. No search fee. Required to search: name, years to search. Civil cases indexed by defendant, plaintiff. Civil records on index cards since 1979, archived since 1819. Record access fee at www.courts.mo.gov/casenet/. Records go back to 04/03/02.

Criminal Records: Access: In person, online. Visitors must perform in person searches for themselves. No search fee. Required to search: name, years to search; also helpful: DOB. Criminal records on index cards since 1979, archived since 1819. Participates in the free statewide Casenet court record system at www.courts.mo.gov/casenet. Online records go back to 04/03/02. Court recommends criminal searches at MO State Highway Patrol, 573-526-6288.

General Information: No juvenile, mental, expunged, dismissed records released. Copy fee: $.25 per page. Certification fee: $1.50. Payee: Associate Circuit or Probate Court. Business checks accepted. Prepayment required. Mail requests: SASE required. Mail turnaround time 3-7 days.

Platte County

Circuit Court 415 Third St. #5, Platte City, MO 64079; 816-858-2232; Fax: 816-858-3392. Hours: 8AM-5PM (CST). *Felony, Misdemeanor, Civil Actions Over $25,000.*

Civil Records: Access: Mail, online, in person. Both court and visitors may perform in person searches. No search fee. Required to search: name, years to search. Civil cases indexed by defendant, plaintiff. Civil records on computer since 10/91. Participates in the free state online court record system at www.courts.mo.gov/casenet.

Criminal Records: Access: Mail, online, in person. Both court and visitors may perform in person searches. No search fee. Required to search: name, years to search, DOB; also helpful: SSN. Criminal records on computer since 10/91. Online access to criminal records is the same as civil.

General Information: Public Access terminal is available. No juvenile, mental, expunged, dismissed, or suspended imposition of sentence records released. Copy fee: $.25 per page. Certification fee: $1.00. Payee: Platte County Circuit Clerk. Only cashiers checks and money orders accepted. Prepayment required. Mail requests: SASE required. Mail turnaround time 2-3 days.

Associate Circuit Court 415 Third St. #5, Platte City, MO 64079; 816-858-2232; Fax: 816-858-3392. Hours: 8AM-5PM (CST). *Misdemeanor, Civil Actions Under $25,000, Eviction, Small Claims.*

Civil Records: Access: Mail, online, in person. Both court and visitors may perform in person searches. No search fee. Required to search: name, years to search. Civil cases indexed by defendant, plaintiff. Civil records on computer since 11/91, prior on index cards. Participates in the free state online court record system at www.courts.mo.gov/casenet.

Criminal Records: Access: Mail, online, in person. Both court and visitors may perform in person searches. No search fee. Required to search: name, years to search, DOB; also helpful: SSN. Criminal records on computer since 11/91, prior on index cards. Online access to criminal records is the same as civil.

General Information: Public Access terminal is available. No juvenile, mental, expunged, dismissed, or suspended imposition of sentence records released. Copy fee: $.25 per page. Certification fee: $1.00. Payee: Circuit Clerk. Only cashiers checks and money orders accepted. Prepayment required. Mail requests: SASE required. Mail turnaround time 1-3 days.

Probate Court 415 Third St, #95, Platte City, MO 64079; 816-858-3438; Probate phone: 816-858-3440; Fax: 816-858-3392. 8AM-5PM (CST). *Probate.*

Note: Can search by name or case number at http://casenet.osca.state.mo.us/casenet/.

Polk County

Circuit & Associate Court 102 E Broadway, Rm 14, Bolivar, MO 65613; 417-326-4912; Fax: 417-326-4194. 8AM-5PM (CST). *Felony, Misdemeanor, Civil Actions, Eviction, Small Claims, Probate.* www.positech.net/~dcourt

Note: The Circuit and Associate courts consolidated as of 01/03.

Civil Records: Access: In person, online. Visitors must perform in person searches for themselves. No search fee. Required to search: name, years to search. Civil cases indexed by defendant, plaintiff. Civil records on computer since 1991, prior on card index since 1979. Participates in the free state online court record system at www.courts.mo.gov/casenet.

Criminal Records: Access: In person, online. Vsitors must perform in person searches for themselves. No search fee. Required to search: name, years to search.

Criminal records on computer since 1991, prior on card index since 1979. Online access to criminal records is the same as civil. Court recommends criminal searches at MO State Highway Patrol, 573-526-6288.

General Information: Public Access terminal is available. No juvenile, mental, expunged, dismissed, or suspended imposition of sentence records released. Copy fee: $.25 per page. Certification fee: $2.00. Payee: Circuit Clerk. Personal checks accepted. Prepayment required.

Pulaski County

Circuit & Associate Circuit Courts 301 Historic Rt 66 E, #202, Waynesville, MO 65583; 573-774-4755; Probate phone: 573-774-4784; Fax: 573-774-6967. Hours: 8AM-4:30PM (CST). *Felony, Misdemeanor, Civil, Eviction, Small Claims.*

Civil Records: Access: In person only. Visitors must perform in person searches for themselves. No search fee. Required to search: name, years to search; also helpful: address. Civil cases indexed by defendant, plaintiff. Civil records on computer since 1990, prior on books since 1903.

Criminal Records: Access: In person only. Visitors must perform in person searches for themselves. No search fee. Required to search: name, years to search; also helpful: DOB, SSN. Criminal records on computer since 1990, prior on books since 1903. Court recommends criminal searches at MO State Highway Patrol, 573-526-6288.

General Information: Public Access terminal is available. No juvenile, mental, paternity, expunged, dismissed, or suspended imposition of sentence records released. Will fax specific case files for $2.00 per 5 pages. Copy fee: $.25 per page. Certification fee: $2.00. Payee: Circuit Clerk. Business checks accepted. Prepayment required.

Probate Court 301 Historic 66 East, #316, Waynesville, MO 65583; 573-774-4784; Fax: 573-774-6673. *Probate.*

Putnam County

Circuit Court Courthouse Rm 202, Unionville, MO 63565; 660-947-2071; Fax: 660-947-2320. Hours: 8AM-12; 1PM-5PM (CST). *Felony, Misdemeanor, Civil Actions Over $45,000.*

Civil Records: Access: Mail, in person, online. Both court and visitors may perform in person searches. No search fee. Required to search: name, years to search. Civil cases indexed by defendant, plaintiff. Civil records on index cards since 1848; on computer since 03/00. Participates in the free state online court record system at www.courts.mo.gov/casenet. Online records go back to 3/29/2000.

Criminal Records: Access: Mail, in person, online. Both court and visitors may perform in person searches. No search fee. Required to search: name, years to search. Criminal records on index cards since 1848; on computer since 03/00. Online access to criminal records is the same as civil.

General Information: Public Access terminal is available. No juvenile, mental, expunged, dismissed, or suspended imposition of sentence records released. Will fax results for $1.00 for 1st page; $50 each add'l; plus copy fee of $.25 per page. Copy fee: $.25 per page. Certification fee: $1.00. Payee: Circuit Clerk. Business checks accepted. Prepayment required. Mail requests: SASE required. Mail turnaround time same day.

Associate Circuit Court Courthouse Rm 101, Unionville, MO 63565; 660-947-2117; Fax: 660-947-7348. Hours: 9AM-5PM (CST). *Misdemeanor, Civil Actions Under $45,000, Eviction, Small Claims, Probate.*

Civil Records: Access: Mail, in person, online. Both court and visitors may perform in person searches. No search fee. Required to search: name, years to search. Civil cases indexed by defendant, plaintiff. Civil records on computer since 1994, prior on books. Participates in the free state online court record system at www.courts.mo.gov/casenet. Online records go back to 3/29/2000.

Criminal Records: Access: Mail, in person, online. Both court and visitors may perform in person searches. No search fee. Required to search: name, years to search, DOB, SSN. Criminal records on computer since 1994, prior on books. Online access to criminal records is the same as civil.

General Information: Public Access terminal is available. No mental, expunged, dismissed, or suspended imposition of sentence records released. Will fax results. Copy fee: $1.00 per page. Certification fee: $1.50. Payee: Associate Circuit Court. Only cashiers checks and money orders accepted. Prepayment required. Mail requests: SASE required. Mail turnaround time 30-60 days.

Ralls County

Circuit Court PO Box 444, New London, MO 63459; 573-985-5633. Hours: 8:30AM-4:30PM (CST). *Felony, Misdemeanor, Civil Actions Over $25,000.*

Civil Records: Access: Mail, in person. Both court and visitors may perform in person searches. No search fee. Required to search: name, years to search, DOB, SSN and signed release. Civil cases indexed by defendant, plaintiff. Civil records on index cards since 1976, prior on books.

Criminal Records: Access: Mail, in person. Only the court performs in person searches; visitors may not. No search fee. Required to search: name, years to search, signed release and SSN. Criminal records on index cards since 1976, prior on books.

General Information: Public Access terminal is available. (Public terminal for judgements only.) No juvenile, mental, expunged, dismissed, or suspended imposition of sentence records released. Copy fee: $.25 per page. Certification fee: $1.00. Payee: Ralls County Circuit Clerk. Personal checks accepted. Prepayment required. Mail requests: SASE required. Mail turnaround time varies.

Associate Circuit Court PO Box 466, 311 S Main, New London, MO 63459; 573-985-5641; Fax: 573-985-3446. Hours: 8:00AM-4:30PM (CST). *Misdemeanor, Civil Actions Under $25,000, Eviction, Small Claims, Probate.*

Civil Records: Access: Phone, mail, fax, in person. Both court and visitors may perform in person searches. No search fee. Required to search: name, years to search. Civil cases indexed by defendant, plaintiff. Civil records on index cards since 1979, prior on record books.

Criminal Records: Access: Phone, mail, fax, in person. Both court and visitors may perform in person searches. Court will search only if not busy. No search fee. Required to search: name, years to search, signed release. Criminal records on index cards since 1979, prior on record books. Court will only search back 7 years for criminal records.

General Information: No juvenile, mental, expunged, dismissed, or suspended imposition of sentence records released. Copy fee: $.25 per page (subject to change). Certification fee: $1.50. Payee: Associate Circuit Court. Personal checks accepted. Prepayment required. Mail requests: SASE required.

Mail turnaround time 1-2 weeks; genealogy turnaround time varies.

Randolph County

Circuit & Associate Court 223 N Williams, Moberly, MO 65270; 660-263-4474; Fax: 660-263-5966 Crim; 263-1007 civil. Hours: 8AM-4:30PM (CST). *Felony, Misdemeanor, Civil Actions, Eviction, Small Claims, Probate.*

Civil Records: Access: Fax, mail, in person, online. Both court and visitors may perform in person searches. No search fee. Required to search: name, years to search, address. Civil cases indexed by defendant, plaintiff. Civil records on index cards since 1975, prior on record books. Participates in the free state online court record system at www.courts.mo.gov/casenet.

Criminal Records: Access: Fax, mail, in person, online. Both court and visitors may perform in person searches. No search fee. Required to search: name, years to search, address, DOB; also helpful: SSN. Criminal records on computer since 1994, prior on index books. Online access to criminal records is the same as civil.

General Information: Public Access terminal is available. No juvenile, mental, expunged, dismissed, or suspended imposition of sentence records released. Will fax results for $4.00 per page. Advanced payment required. Copy fee: $.25 per page. Certification fee: $1.50. Payee: Randolph County Circuit Clerk. No personal checks accepted. Prepayment required. Mail requests: SASE required. Mail turnaround time 1 week.

Ray County

Circuit Court PO Box 594, Richmond, MO 64085; 816-776-3377; Fax: 816-776-6016. Hours: 8AM-4PM (CST). *Felony, Misdemeanor, Civil Actions Over $25,000.*

www.osca.state.mo.us/circuits/index.nsf/County+/+Ray

Civil Records: Access: Phone, fax, mail, in person, online. Only the court performs in person searches; visitors may not. No search fee. Required to search: name, years to search. Civil cases indexed by defendant, plaintiff. Civil records on index cards since 1977, prior on judgment books. Participates in the free state online court record system at www.courts.mo.gov/casenet. Online records only go back to 2001.

Criminal Records: Access: In person, online. Only the court performs in person searches; visitors may not. No search fee. Required to search: name, years to search; also helpful: DOB, SSN. Criminal records on index cards since 1977, prior on judgment books. Online access to criminal records is the same as civil. Court recommends criminal searches at MO State Highway Patrol, 573-526-6288.

General Information: No juvenile, mental, expunged, dismissed, or suspended imposition of sentence records released. Fee to fax results is $1.00 per page. Copy fee: $.25 per page. Certification fee: $1.50. Payee: Ray County Circuit Clerk. Business checks accepted. Prepayment required. Mail requests: SASE required. Mail turnaround time varies.

Associate Circuit Court Ray County Courthouse, 100 W Main St, Richmond, MO 64085-1710; 816-776-2335; Fax: 816-776-2185. Hours: 8AM-4PM (CST). *Misdemeanor, Civil Actions Under $25,000, Eviction, Small Claims, Probate.*

Civil Records: Access: Fax, mail, in person, online. Both court and visitors may perform in person searches. No search fee. Required to search: name; also helpful: years to search. Civil cases indexed by defendant, plaintiff. Civil records on index cards since 1979, prior on books. Participates in the free state online court record system at www.courts.mo.gov/casenet.

Criminal Records: Access: Fax, mail, in person, online. Both court and visitors may perform in person searches. No search fee. Required to search: name, DOB; also helpful: years to search. Criminal records on index cards since 1979, prior on books. Online access to criminal records is the same as civil.

General Information: Public Access terminal is available. (Public terminal is located in main Circuit Court Clerk office.) No juvenile, mental, expunged, dismissed, or suspended imposition of sentence records released. No fee to fax results. Copy fee: $.20 per page. Certification fee: $1.50 to certify and $1.00 per page. Payee: Associate Circuit Court. Business checks accepted. Prepayment required.

Reynolds County

Circuit Court PO Box 76, Centerville, MO 63633; 573-648-2494 X34; Fax: 573-648-2503. Hours: 8AM-4PM (CST). *Felony, Civil Actions Over $45,000.*

Civil Records: Access: Phone, mail, in person, online. Both court and visitors may perform in person searches. No search fee. Required to search: name, years to search. Civil cases indexed by defendant, plaintiff. Civil records on cards and books, archived since 1872. Access to civil records is free at www.courts.mo.gov/casenet/. At the website, select the judicial district, then search by name, case # or date.

Criminal Records: Access: Phone, mail, in person, online. Both court and visitors may perform in person searches. No search fee. Required to search: name, years to search, DOB; also helpful: SSN, sex, signed release. Criminal records on cards and books, archived since 1872. Online access to criminal records is the same as civil.

General Information: Public Access terminal is available. No juvenile, mental, expunged, dismissed, or suspended imposition of sentence records released. Fee to fax results is $2.00 per document plus $1.00 per page. Copy fee: $1.00 per page. Certification fee: $2.00. Payee: Randy L Cowin. Personal checks accepted. Prepayment required. Mail requests: SASE required. Mail turnaround time 2 days.

Associate Circuit Court PO Box 39, Centerville, MO 63633; 573-648-2494 X31; Probate phone: x35; Fax: 573-648-2503. Hours: 8AM-4PM (CST). *Misdemeanor, Civil Actions Under $45,000, Eviction, Small Claims, Probate.*

Civil Records: Access: Phone, mail, in person, online. Both court and visitors may perform in person searches. No search fee. Required to search: name, years to search. Civil cases indexed by defendant, plaintiff. Civil records on index cards and files (probate in books); on computer back to 2000. Participates in the free state online court record system at www.courts.mo.gov/casenet.

Criminal Records: Access: In person, online. Both court and visitors may perform in person searches. No search fee. Required to search: name, years to search. Criminal records on index cards and files back to early 1970s; on computer back to 2000. Online access to criminal records is the same as civil. Court recommends criminal searches at MO State Highway Patrol, 573-526-6288.

General Information: Public Access terminal is available. No juvenile, mental, expunged, dismissed, or suspended imposition of sentence records released. Copy fee: $1.00 per page. Certification fee: $2.00. Payee: Associate Circuit Court. Personal checks accepted. Prepayment required. Mail requests: SASE not required. Mail turnaround time 1 day; phone turnaround is same day.

Ripley County

Circuit Court Courthouse, Doniphan, MO 63935; 573-996-2818; Fax: 573-996-7826. Hours: 8AM-4PM (CST). *Felony, Misdemeanor, Civil Actions Over $25,000.*

Civil Records: Access: Phone, fax, mail, in person. Both court and visitors may perform in person searches. Search fee: $5.00 per name. Required to search: name, years to search. Civil cases indexed by defendant, plaintiff. Civil records on cards and books since 1976, archived since 1850s.

Criminal Records: Access: Fax, mail, in person. Both court and visitors may perform in person searches. Search fee: $5.00 per name. Required to search: name, years to search, DOB. Criminal records on cards and books since 1976, archived since 1850s.

General Information: No juvenile, mental, expunged, dismissed, or suspended imposition of sentence records released. Will fax results for $5.00 per name. Copy fee: $3.00 per page. Certification fee: $2.00 if done by in-person searcher, otherwise certification is included in the search fee. Payee: Circuit Clerk. Personal checks accepted. Prepayment required. Mail requests: SASE required. Mail turnaround time same day.

Associate Circuit Court 100 Court Sq, Courthouse, Doniphan, MO 63935; 573-996-2013; Fax: 573-996-5014. Hours: 8AM-4PM (CST). *Misdemeanor, Civil Actions Under $25,000, Eviction, Small Claims, Probate.*

Civil Records: Access: Phone, fax, mail, in person. Both court and visitors may perform in person searches. No search fee. Required to search: name, years to search. Civil cases indexed by defendant, plaintiff. Civil records on index cards since 1984, prior on books.

Criminal Records: Access: In person only. Visitors must perform in person searches for themselves. No search fee. Required to search: name, years to search; also helpful: DOB, SSN. Criminal records on index cards since 1984, prior on books. Court recommends criminal searches at MO State Highway Patrol, 573-526-6288.

General Information: No juvenile, mental, expunged, dismissed, or suspended imposition of sentence records released. Will not fax results. Copy fee: $.25 per page. Certification fee: $1.00. Payee: Circuit Court Division II. Only cashiers checks and money orders accepted. Prepayment required. Mail requests: SASE required. Mail turnaround: 1 week.

Saline County

Circuit Court PO Box 597, 101 E Main St #205, Marshall, MO 65340; 660-886-2300; Probate phone: 660-886-8808. Hours: 8:00AM-4:30PM (CST). *Felony, Misdemeanor, Civil Actions Over $25,000.*

Civil Records: Access: In person, online. Visitors must perform in person searches for themselves. No search fee. Required to search: name, years to search. Civil cases indexed by defendant, plaintiff. Civil records on index cards since 1974, prior on books since 1820. Records free on state online court record system at www.courts.mo.gov/casenet. Records only go back to 4/2002.

Criminal Records: Access: In person, online. Visitors must perform in person searches for themselves. No search fee. Required to search: name, years to search. Criminal records on index cards since 1974, prior on books since 1820. Records free on state online court record system at www.courts.mo.gov/casenet. Records only go back to 4/2002. Court recommends criminal searches at MO State Highway Patrol, 573-526-6288.

General Information: Public Access terminal is available. No juvenile, mental, expunged, dismissed,

or suspended imposition of sentence records released. Copy fee: $.25 per page. Certification fee: $1.50. Payee: Saline County Circuit Court. Personal checks accepted. Prepayment required.

Associate Circuit Court PO Box 751, Marshall, MO 65340; 660-886-6988; Fax: 660-886-2919. Hours: 8AM-4:30PM (CST). *Misdemeanor, Civil Actions Under $25,000, Eviction, Small Claims.*

Civil Records: Access: Phone, mail, in person, online. Only the court performs in person searches; visitors may not. No search fee. Required to search: name, years to search. Civil cases indexed by defendant, plaintiff. Civil records on index cards since 1979, prior on books. Participates in the free statewide Casenet court record system at www.courts.mo.gov/casenet.

Criminal Records: Access: Phone, mail, in person, online. Only the court performs in person searches; visitors may not. No search fee. Required to search: name, years to search. Criminal records on computer since 1993, prior on cards and books. Participates in the free statewide Casenet court record system at www.courts.mo.gov/casenet.

General Information: No juvenile, mental, expunged, dismissed, or suspended imposition of sentence records released. No copy fee. No certification fee. Mail requests: SASE required. Mail turnaround time 1-2 days.

Schuyler County

Circuit Court PO Box 186, Lancaster, MO 63548; 660-457-3784; Fax: 660-457-3016. Hours: 8AM-4PM (CST). *Felony, Misdemeanor, Civil Actions Over $45,000.*

Note: Misdemeanor and probate phone is 660-457-3755.

Civil Records: Access: Mail, in person, online. Both court and visitors may perform in person searches. Search fee: $14.00 per name. Required to search: name, years to search. Civil cases indexed by defendant, plaintiff. Civil records on index cards & books. Participates in the free state online court record system at www.courts.mo.gov/casenet. Records from 9/19/01 forward.

Criminal Records: Access: Mail, in person, online. Both court and visitors may perform in person searches. Search fee: $14.00 per name. Required to search: name, years to search. Criminal records on index cards & books. Participates in the free state online court record system at www.courts.mo.gov/casenet. Records go back to 9/19/01 forward.

General Information: Public Access terminal is available. No juvenile, mental, expunged, dismissed, or suspended imposition of sentence records released. Will fax results for $2.00 plus $1.00 each page. Copy fee: $1.00 per page. Certification fee: $1.00. Payee: Schuyler County Circuit Clerk. Personal checks accepted. Prepayment required. Mail requests: SASE required. Mail turnaround time 1-2 days.

Associate Circuit Court Box 158, Lancaster, MO 63548; 660-457-3755; Fax: 660-457-3016. Hours: 8:00AM-4PM (CST). *Misdemeanor, Civil Actions Under $45,000, Eviction, Small Claims, Probate.*

Civil Records: Access: Mail, fax, in person, online. Both court and visitors may perform in person searches. Search fee: $5.00 per name. Required to search: name, years to search. Civil cases indexed by defendant, plaintiff. Civil records on index cards since 1976; computerized records go back to 1992. Participates in the free statewide Casenet court record system at www.courts.mo.gov/casenet. Online records go back to 09/19/01.

Criminal Records: Access: Mail, fax, in person, online. Both court and visitors may perform in person searches. Search fee: $5.00 per name. Required to search: name, years to search, SSN, DOB. Criminal records on computer since 5/92, prior on index cards. Participates in the free statewide Casenet court record system at www.courts.mo.gov/casenet. Online records go back to 09/19/01.

General Information: Public Access terminal is available. No juvenile, mental, expunged, dismissed, or suspended imposition of sentence records released. Copy fee: $1.00 per page. Certification fee: $1.50. Payee: Associate Circuit Court. Business checks accepted. Prepayment required. Mail requests: SASE required. Mail turnaround time 4 days.

Scotland County

Circuit Court 117 S Market St #106, Memphis, MO 63555; 660-465-8605; Fax: 660-465-8673. Hours: 8AM-4PM (CST). *Felony, Civil Actions Over $25,000.*

Civil Records: Access: Mail, in person, online. Both court and visitors may perform in person searches. No search fee. Required to search: name, years to search. Civil cases indexed by defendant, plaintiff. Civil records on index cards since 1979, prior on books. Computerized records go back to 2001. Participates in the free state online court record system at www.courts.mo.gov/casenet. Records from 9/19/01 forward.

Criminal Records: Access: Mail, in person, online. Both court and visitors may perform in person searches. No search fee. Required to search: name, years to search, DOB, signed release; also helpful: address. Criminal records on index cards since 1979, prior on books. Computerized records go back to 9/2001. Participates in the free state online court record system at www.courts.mo.gov/casenet. Records go back to 9/19/01 forward.

General Information: Public Access terminal is available. No juvenile, mental, expunged, dismissed, or suspended imposition of sentence records released. Will fax results for $1.00 per page. Copy fee: $.10 per page. Certification fee: $1.50. Payee: Scotland County Circuit Clerk. Personal checks accepted. Prepayment required. Mail requests: SASE required. Mail turnaround time same day.

Associate Circuit Court Courthouse, Rm 102, 117 S Market, Memphis, MO 63555; 660-465-2404; Fax: 660-465-8673. Hours: 8AM-4:30PM (CST). *Misdemeanor, Civil Actions Under $25,000, Eviction, Small Claims, Probate.*

Civil Records: Access: Phone, mail, fax, in person, online. Both court and visitors may perform in person searches. No search fee. Required to search: name, years to search. Civil cases indexed by defendant, plaintiff. Civil records on computer since 1986, prior on cards and books to 1841. Participates in the free statewide Casenet court record system at www.courts.mo.gov/casenet. Online records go back to 09/19/01.

Criminal Records: Access: Phone, mail, in person, online. Both court and visitors may perform in person searches. No search fee. Required to search: name, years to search. Criminal records on computer since 1986, prior on cards and books to 1841. Participates in the free statewide Casenet court record system at www.courts.mo.gov/casenet. Online records go back to 09/19/01.

General Information: Public Access terminal is available. (Public terminal is located in main Circuit Court Clerk office.) No juvenile, mental, expunged, dismissed, or suspended imposition of sentence records released. Fee to fax results is 1.00 per page. Copy fee: $.10 per page. Certification fee: $1.50 plus $1.00 per page. Payee: Info provided on bill. Personal

checks accepted. Prepayment required. Mail requests: SASE required. Mail turnaround time ASAP.

Scott County

Circuit Court PO Box 277, Benton, MO 63736; 573-545-3596; Fax: 573-545-3597. Hours: 8:00AM-5PM (CST). *Felony, Misdemeanor, Civil Actions Over $25,000.*

Civil Records: Access: In person, online. Visitors must perform in person searches for themselves. No search fee. Required to search: name, years to search. Civil cases indexed by defendant, plaintiff. Civil records on computer since 1991, prior on index cards and books. Access to civil records is free at www.courts.mo.gov/casenet/. At the website, select the judicial district, then search by name, case # or date. Online records go back to 6/15/2001.

Criminal Records: Access: In person, online. Visitors must perform in person searches for themselves. No search fee. Required to search: name, years to search, DOB. Criminal records on computer since 1991, prior on index cards and books. Online access to criminal records is the same as civil. Court recommends criminal searches at MO State Highway Patrol, 573-526-6288.

General Information: Public Access terminal is available. No juvenile, mental, expunged, dismissed, or suspended imposition of sentence records released. Copy fee: $1.00 for first page, $.25 each add'l. Certification fee: $3.00. Payee: Pam Glastetter, Circuit Clerk. Personal checks accepted. Prepayment required.

Associate Circuit Court PO Box 249, Benton, MO 63736; 573-545-3576; Fax: 573-545-4231. Hours: 8AM-Noon, 1-5PM (CST). *Misdemeanor, Civil Actions Under $45,000, Eviction, Small Claims, Probate.*

Civil Records: Access: Phone, mail, in person, online. Visitors must perform in person searches for themselves. No search fee. Required to search: name, years to search. Civil cases indexed by defendant, plaintiff. Civil records on index cards and books. Access to civil records is free at www.courts.mo.gov/casenet/. At the website, select the judicial district, then search by name, case # or date. Online records go back to 6/15/2001.

Criminal Records: Access: Mail, in person, online. Visitors must perform in person searches for themselves. No search fee. Required to search: name, years to search. Criminal records on index cards and books. Online access to criminal records is the same as civil.

General Information: No juvenile, mental, expunged, dismissed, or suspended imposition of sentence records released. No copy fee. No certification fee. Mail requests: SASE required. Mail turnaround time varies.

Shannon County

Circuit Court PO Box 148, Eminence, MO 65466; 573-226-3315; Fax: 573-226-5321. Hours: 8AM-4:30PM (CST). *Felony, Misdemeanor, Civil Actions Over $45,000.*

Civil Records: Access: Mail, in person, online. Both the court and visitors may perform in person searches. No search fee. Required to search: name, years to search. Civil cases indexed by defendant, plaintiff. Civil records on index cards and books. Record index searchable on computer back to 1980. Participates in the free state online court record system at www.courts.mo.gov/casenet. Online records go back to 1992.

Criminal Records: Access: Mail, in person, online. Both the court and visitors may perform in person searches. No search fee. Required to search: name, years to search, offense. Criminal records on index

cards and books. Record index searchable on computer back to 1980. Online access to criminal records is the same as civil.

General Information: Public Access terminal is available. No juvenile, mental, expunged, dismissed, or suspended imposition of sentence records released. Fee to fax results is $2.00 per page. Copy fee: $.25 per page. Certification fee: $2.00. Payee: Shannon County Circuit Clerk. Personal checks accepted. Prepayment required. Mail requests: SASE required. Mail turnaround time 1 week.

Associate Circuit Court PO Box 845, Eminence, MO 65466-0845; 573-226-5515; Fax: 573-226-3239. Hours: 8AM-4:30PM (CST). *Misdemeanor, Civil Actions Under $45,000, Eviction, Small Claims, Probate.*

Civil Records: Access: Mail, fax, in person, online. Only the court performs in person searches; visitors may not. Search fee: $10.00 per name. Required to search: name, years to search. Civil cases indexed by defendant, plaintiff. Civil records on index cards since 1979, archived since 1881. Participates in the free state online court record system at www.courts.mo.gov/casenet. Online records go back to 1992.

Criminal Records: Access: Mail, fax, in person, online. Only the court performs in person searches; visitors may not. Search fee: $10.00 per name. Required to search: name, years to search, DOB; also helpful: SSN. Criminal records on computer since 1992; prior on index cards to 1979. Online access to criminal records is the same as civil.

General Information: No juvenile, mental, expunged, dismissed, or suspended imposition of sentence records released. Fee to fax results is $3.00 per page. Copy fee: $.25 per page. Certification fee: $3.00. Payee: Associate Circuit Court. Personal checks accepted. Prepayment required. Mail requests: SASE required. Mail turnaround time 1 week.

Shelby County

Circuit Court PO Box 176, Shelbyville, MO 63469; 573-633-2151; Fax: 573-633-1004. Hours: 8AM-4:30PM (CST). *Felony, Misdemeanor, Civil Actions Over $45,000.*

Civil Records: Access: Mail, fax, in person. Only the court may perform in person searches. No search fee. Required to search: name, years to search. Civil cases indexed by defendant, plaintiff. Civil records on index cards since 1975, prior on books since 1835.

Criminal Records: Access: Mail, fax, in person. Only the court may perform in person searches. No search fee. Required to search: name, years to search. Criminal records on index cards since 1975, prior on books since 1835.

General Information: No juvenile, mental, expunged, dismissed, or suspended imposition of sentence records released. Fee to fax results is $3.00 per document. Copy fee: $.25 per page. Certification fee: $2.00. Payee: Shelby County Circuit Clerk. Personal checks accepted. Prepayment required. Mail requests: SASE required. Mail turnaround time 1 day.

Associate Circuit Court PO Box 206, Shelbyville, MO 63469; 573-633-2251; Fax: 573-633-2142. Hours: 8AM-4:30PM (CST). *Misdemeanor, Civil Actions Under $25,000, Eviction, Small Claims, Probate.*

Civil Records: Access: Phone, fax, mail, in person. Both court and visitors may perform in person searches. No search fee. Required to search: name, years to search. Civil cases indexed by defendant, plaintiff. Civil records on index cards to 1990, archived from 1845.

Criminal Records: Access: Phone, fax, mail, in person. Only the court may perform in person searches. No search fee. Required to search: name, years to search, DOB. Criminal records on index cards to 1980, archived from 1845.

General Information: No juvenile, mental, expunged, dismissed, or suspended imposition of sentence records released. No fee to fax results. Copy fee: $.50 per page. Certification fee: $1.50. Payee: Probate Court or Associate Circuit Court. Personal checks accepted. Prepayment required. Mail requests: SASE not required. Mail turnaround time 2 weeks.

St. Charles County

Circuit & Associate Court 300 N 2nd St, St. Charles, MO 63301; 636-949-7900 x3098; Criminal phone: 636-949-7380; Probate phone: 636-949-7900 x3086; Fax: 636-949-7390. Hours: 8:30AM-5PM (CST). *Felony, Misdemeanor, Civil Actions, Eviction, Small Claims, Probate.*
Note: The Circuit and Associate courts consolidated as of 01/03. Traffic Court is reached at 636-949-7385.

Civil Records: Access: Mail, online, in person. Both court and visitors may perform in person searches. No search fee. Required to search: name, years to search. Civil cases indexed by defendant, plaintiff. Civil records on index cards since 1971, prior on books; judgment records (A-M) on computer since 1987. Participates in the free state online court record system at www.courts.mo.gov/casenet. Online civil records go back to 1982.

Criminal Records: Access: Online, in person. Visitors must perform in person searches for themselves. No search fee. Required to search: name, years to search; also helpful: DOB. Criminal records on index cards since 1971, prior on books; judgment records (A-M) on computer since 1987. Online access to criminal records is the same as civil. Online criminal records go back to 10/1992. Court recommends criminal searches at MO State Highway Patrol, 573-526-6288.

General Information: Public Access terminal is available. No juvenile, mental, expunged, dismissed, or suspended imposition of sentence records released. Copy fee: $.25 per page. Certification fee: $1.00. Payee: St. Charles Circuit Clerk. Personal checks accepted. Prepayment required. Mail requests: SASE required. Mail turnaround time varies.

St. Clair County

Circuit & Associate Circuit Courts PO Box 493, Osceola, MO 64776; 417-646-2226; Fax: 417-646-2401. Hours: 8AM-4:30PM (CST). *Felony, Misdemeanor, Civil, Eviction, Small Claims, Probate.*

Civil Records: Access: Mail, in person, online. Both court and visitors may perform in person searches. Search fee: $2.00 per name. Required to search: name, years to search. Civil cases indexed by defendant, plaintiff. Civil judgment records on computer since 1991, on index cards since 1980, prior records on index books. Participates in the free state online court record system at www.courts.mo.gov/casenet.

Criminal Records: Access: Mail, in person, online. Both court and visitors may perform in person searches. Search fee: $2.00 per name. Required to search: name, years to search, DOB. Criminal records on computer since 1991, on index cards since 1980, prior records on index books. Participates in the free state online court record system at www.courts.mo.gov/casenet.

General Information: Public Access terminal is available. (Terminal has judgments only.) No juvenile, mental, expunged, dismissed, or suspended imposition of sentence records released. Will fax results. Copy fee: $1.00 per page. Certification fee: $.50 per document. Payee: St Clair County Circuit

Clerk. Personal checks accepted. Prepayment required. Mail requests: SASE required. Mail turnaround time 1-2 days.

St. Francois County

Circuit Court - Division I & II 1 N Washington, Rm 303, Farmington, MO 63640; 573-756-4551; Fax: 573-756-3733. Hours: 8AM-5PM (CST). *Felony, Civil Actions Over $25,000.*
www.sfcgov.org
Civil Records: Access: Fax, mail, in person, online. Both court and visitors may perform in person searches. No search fee. Required to search: name, years to search. Civil cases indexed by defendant, plaintiff. Civil records on computer since 6/90, on microfiche since 1970, archived since 1821. Participates in the free state online court record system at www.courts.mo.gov/casenet. Records from 11/01/00 forward.
Criminal Records: Access: In person, online. Both court and visitors may perform in person searches. No search fee. Required to search: name, years to search; also helpful: DOB, SSN. Criminal records on computer since 3/1/93. Participates in the free state online court record system at www.courts.mo.gov/casenet. Records go back to 11/01/00 forward. Court recommends criminal searches at MO State Highway Patrol, 573-526-6288.
General Information: Public Access terminal is available. No juvenile, mental, expunged, dismissed, or suspended imposition of sentence records released. Copy fee: $.25 per page. Certification fee: $1.50. Payee: Clerk of Circuit Court. Business checks accepted. Prepayment required. Mail requests: SASE required. Mail turnaround time 1-2 weeks.

Associate Circuit Court County Courthouse, 2nd Fl, 1 N Washington, Rm 202, Farmington, MO 63640; 573-756-5755; Fax: 573-756-8173. Hours: 8AM-5PM (CST). *Misdemeanor, Civil Actions Under $25,000, Eviction, Small Claims, Probate.*
Civil Records: Access: Phone, in person, online. Only the court performs in person searches; visitors may not. No search fee. Required to search: name, years to search. Civil cases indexed by defendant, plaintiff. Civil records on index cards since 1979; on computer back to 1990. Participates in the free statewide Casenet court record system at www.courts.mo.gov/casenet. Online records go back to 1992, probate records to 11/06/00.
Criminal Records: Access: In person, online. Visitors must perform in person searches for themselves. No search fee. Required to search: name, years to search. Criminal records on computer back to 1990; other records go back to 1980. Participates in the free statewide Casenet court record system at www.courts.mo.gov/casenet. Online records go back to 1992. Court recommends criminal searches at MO State Highway Patrol, 573-526-6288.
General Information: No juvenile, mental, expunged, dismissed, or suspended imposition of sentence records released. Copy fee: $.25 per page. No certification fee. Business checks accepted.

St. Louis County

Circuit Court of St. Louis County 7900 Carondelet, Clayton, MO 63105-1766; 314-615-8029; Fax: 314-615-8739. Hours: 8AM-5PM (CST). *Felony, Misdemeanor, Civil.*
www.stlouisco.com/circuitcourt
Civil Records: Access: Phone, fax, mail, in person. Both court and visitors may perform in person searches. No search fee. Required to search: name, years to search; also helpful: address. Civil cases indexed by defendant, plaintiff. Civil records on computer back to 1978, prior on index cards. Case files archived for 25 years.

Criminal Records: Access: Phone, fax, mail, in person. Both court and visitors may perform in person searches. No search fee. Required to search: name, years to search, DOB; also helpful: SSN. Criminal records on computer back to 1990; prior on index cards. Case files archived for 25 years.
General Information: Public Access terminal is available. No juvenile, paternity, mental, expunged, dismissed, or suspended imposition of sentence records released. Will not fax results. Copy fee: $.30 per page. Certification fee: $1.50 plus $.30 per page after first. Payee: Circuit Clerk. Personal checks accepted. Prepayment required. Mail requests: SASE not required. Mail turnaround time up to 3 days.

Associate Circuit - Civil Division 7900 Carondolet, Clayton, MO 63105; 314-615-8090; Probate phone: 314-615-2629; Fax: 314-615-2689. Hours: 8AM-5PM (CST). *Civil Actions Under $25,000, Eviction, Small Claims, Probate.*
Note: The small claims court can be reached at 314-615-8091.
Civil Records: Access: Phone, mail, in person. Both court and visitors may perform in person searches. No search fee. Required to search: name, years to search. Civil cases indexed by defendant, plaintiff. Civil records on computer since 1986, prior on cards. Probate records are free on the state online court record system at www.courts.mo.gov/casenet.
General Information: Public Access terminal is available. No juvenile, mental, expunged, dismissed, paternity, suspended imposition of sentence records released. Copy fee: $.30 per page. Certification fee: $1.50. Payee: Circuit Clerk-Civil Division. Personal checks accepted. Prepayment required. Mail requests: SASE required. Mail turnaround time 1 week.

Associate Circuit Court - Criminal Division 7900 Carondolet Av, Clayton, MO 63105; 314-615-2675; Fax: 314-615-2689. Hours: 8AM-5PM (CST). *Misdemeanor.*
www.stlouisco.com/circuitcourt
Criminal Records: Access: Phone, mail, fax, in person. Both court and visitors may perform in person searches. No search fee. Required to search: name, years to search, DOB, offense, date of offense. Criminal records on computer back to 1990, prior on index cards. Permanent records on microfiche since 1978, earlier in books. Case files archived for 25 years.
General Information: Public Access terminal is available. No juvenile, mental, expunged, dismissed, or suspended imposition of sentence records released. Will not fax results. Copy fee: $.30 per page. Certification fee: $1.50. Payee: Circuit Clerk. Personal checks accepted. Prepayment required. Mail requests: SASE required. Mail turnaround time varies.

St. Louis City

Circuit & Associate Circuit Courts - Civil 10 N Tucker, Civil Courts Bldg, St Louis, MO 63101; 314-622-4405; Probate phone: 314-622-4300; Fax: 314-622-4537. Hours: 8:00AM-5:00PM (CST). *Civil, Eviction, Small Claims, Probate.*
www.stlcitycircuitcourt.com
Note: Small Claims telephone number is 314-622-3788. Probate is located on the 10th Fl.
Civil Records: Access: Mail, online, in person. Both court and visitors can perform in person searches. No search fee. Required to search: name, years to search. Civil cases indexed by defendant, plaintiff. Civil records on computer since 1/80, on index cards since early 1800s. Online access to civil records is free at https://www.stlcitycircuitcourt.com/SSL/getCivil.cfm. Remote access is also through MoBar Net and is open only to attorneys. Call 314-535-1950 for information. Also, probate records are free online at

www.courts.mo.gov/casenet. Online probate records go back to 5/31/2000.

General Information: Public Access terminal is available. No sealed or confidential records released. Will not fax results. Copy fee: $.30 per page. Certification fee: $3.50 for 1st page; $.50 each add'l page. Payee: City of St. Louis Circuit Clerk. Only cashiers checks and money orders accepted. Mail requests: SASE required. Mail turnaround time usually 1 week.

City of St Louis Circuit Court - Criminal

1114 Market St, 2nd Fl, Carnahan Courthouse, Attention: Case Records/File Section, St Louis, MO 63101; 314-622-4773 (gen info); Criminal phone: 314-622-4485 or 4486 (felony), 314-622-4548 (misd.); Fax: 314-613-7486 (crim). Hours: 9AM-4PM (CST). *Felony, Misdemeanor.*
www.stlcitycircuitcourt.com/PDF/TelephoneList/Tele Directory.pdf Note: The Court clerk's admin. office is located 10 N Tucker.

Criminal Records: Access: In person, mail, fax, online. Both court and visitors may perform in person searches. No search fee. Required to search: name, years to search, DOB, signed release; also helpful: address, SSN. Criminal records on computer since 1990 for misdemeanor; since 1992 for felony. Access to criminal records is free at https://www.stlcitycircuitcourt.com/SSL/getCriminal. cfm Courts criminal case records/copy section telephone is 714-613-4156 or 4408 (fax given above). Criminal searches may also be conducted through MO State Highway Patrol, 573-526-6288.

General Information: Public Access terminal is available. (There is a public access terminal on the 3rd fl with limited case information.) No juvenile, mental, expunged, dismissed, or suspended imposition of sentence records released. Copy fee: $.50 per page. Certification fee: $3.50. Payee: City of St. Louis Circuit Clerk. Business checks accepted. Prepayment required. Mail requests: SASE required.

Ste. Genevieve County

Circuit Court 55 S 3rd, Rm 23, Ste Genevieve, MO 63670; 573-883-2705; Fax: 573-883-9351. Hours: 8AM-5PM (CST). *Felony, Misdemeanor, Civil Actions Over $25,000.*

Civil Records: Access: In person, online. Visitors must perform in person searches for themselves. No search fee. Required to search: name, years to search. Civil cases indexed by defendant, plaintiff. Civil records on books since early 1800s, recent civil records (1995) computerized. Participates in the free state online court record system at www.courts.mo.gov/casenet. Records from 11/06/00 forward.

Criminal Records: Access: In person, online. Visitors must perform in person searches for themselves. No search fee. Required to search: name, years to search. Criminal Record indexes on books, not computerized. Participates in the free state online court record system at www.courts.mo.gov/casenet. Records go back to 11/06/00 forward. Court recommends criminal searches at MO State Highway Patrol, 573-526-6288.

General Information: Public Access terminal is available. No juvenile, mental, expunged, paternity, dismissed, or suspended imposition of sentence records released. Copy fee: $1.00 per page. Certification fee: $1.50. Payee: St Genevieve County Circuit Clerk. Business checks accepted. Prepayment required.

Associate Circuit Court 55 S 3rd St, Ste Genevieve, MO 63670; 573-883-2265; Fax: 573-883-9351. Hours: 8AM-5PM (CST). *Misdemeanor, Civil Actions Under $45,000, Eviction, Small Claims, Probate.*

Civil Records: Access: In person, online. Visitors must perform in person searches for themselves. No search fee. Required to search: name, years to search. Civil cases indexed by defendant, plaintiff. Civil records on books. Participates in the free statewide Casenet court record system at www.courts.m o.gov/casenet. Online records go back to 11/06/00.

Criminal Records: Access: In person, online. Visitors must perform in person searches for themselves. No search fee. Required to search: name, years to search. Criminal records on books. Participates in the free statewide Casenet court record system at www.courts.mo.gov/casenet. Online records go back to 11/06/00. Court recommends criminal searches at MO State Highway Patrol, 573-526-6288.

General Information: Public Access terminal is available. No juvenile, mental, expunged, dismissed, or suspended imposition of sentence records released. Copy fee: $1.00 per page. Certification fee: $2.50. Only cashiers checks and money orders accepted.

Stoddard County

Circuit Court PO Box 30, Bloomfield, MO 63825; 573-568-4640; Fax: 573-568-2271. Hours: 8:30AM-4:30PM (CST). *Felony, Misdemeanor, Civil Actions Over $25,000.*

Civil Records: Access: Fax, mail, in person, online. Both court and visitors may perform in person searches. No search fee. Required to search: name, years to search. Civil cases indexed by defendant, plaintiff. Civil records on computer since 1991, prior on cards and books. Access to civil records is free at www.courts.mo.gov/casenet/. At the website, select the judicial district, then search by name, case # or date. Online records go back to 7/1/2001.

Criminal Records: Access: Mail, in person, online. Both court and visitors may perform in person searches. No search fee. Required to search: name, years to search; also helpful: DOB, SSN. Criminal records on computer since 1991, prior on cards and books. Online access to criminal records is the same as civil.

General Information: Public Access terminal is available. No juvenile, mental, expunged, dismissed, or suspended imposition of sentence records released. Copy fee: $.10 per page. Certification fee: $1.50. Payee: Stoddard County Circuit Clerk. Personal checks accepted. Prepayment required. Mail requests: SASE required. Mail turnaround time 1-3 days.

Associate Division III & Probate PO Box 518, Bloomfield, MO 63825; 573-568-4640 x3; Fax: 573-568-3229. 7:30AM-4PM (CST). *Civil Actions Under $25,000, Eviction, Small Claims, Probate.*

Civil Records: Access: Fax, mail, in person, online. Both court and visitors may perform in person searches. No search fee. Required to search: name, years to search. Civil cases indexed by defendant, plaintiff. Civil records on computer since 1993, prior on index cards. Access to civil records is free at www.courts.mo.gov/casenet/. At the website, select the judicial district, then search by name, case # or date. Online records go back to 7/1/2001.

General Information: Public Access terminal is available. No juvenile, mental, expunged, dismissed, or suspended imposition of sentence records released. Copy fee: $.50 per page. Certification fee: $1.50. Prepayment required. Mail requests: SASE required. Mail turnaround time 2-3 days.

Associate Circuit Court - Criminal Division II PO Box 218, Bloomfield, MO 63825; 573-568-4640 x2; Fax: 573-568-2299. Hours: 8:30AM-4:30PM (CST). *Misdemeanor.*

Criminal Records: Access: In person, online. Visitors must perform in person searches for themselves. No search fee. Required to search: name, years to search, DOB, SSN, signed release. Criminal records on index cards, traffic on computer since 1996. Access to records is free at www.courts.mo.gov/casenet/. At the website, select the judicial district, then search by name, case # or date. Online records go back to 7/1/2001. Court recommends criminal searches at MO State Highway Patrol, 573-526-6288.

General Information: Public Access terminal is available. No juvenile, mental, expunged, dismissed, or suspended imposition of sentence records released. No copy fee. No certification fee. Payee: Stoddard County. Personal checks accepted. Prepayment required.

Stone County

Circuit Court PO Box 18, Galena, MO 65656; 417-357-6114; 417-357-6115 child support; Fax: 417-357-6163. 7:30AM-Noon; 12:30PM-4:00PM (CST). *Felony, Misdemeanor, Civil Actions Over $25,000.*

Civil Records: Access: Phone, fax, mail, in person. Both court and visitors may perform in person searches. No search fee. Required to search: name, years to search. Civil cases indexed by defendant, plaintiff. Civil records on cards and books, archived since 1852; computerized records since 1992.

Criminal Records: Access: Phone, fax, mail, in person. Both court and visitors may perform in person searches. No search fee. Required to search: name, years to search; also helpful: DOB, SSN. Criminal records on cards and books, archived since 1852; computerized records since 1992.

General Information: No juvenile, mental, expunged, dismissed, or suspended imposition of sentence records released. Will fax results for $3.00 per page. Copy fee: $.25 per page. Certification fee: $1.50. Payee: Circuit Court. Personal checks accepted. Prepayment required. Mail requests: SASE required. Mail turnaround time 1 week.

Circuit Court - Division II & III PO Box 186, Galena, MO 65656; 417-357-6511; Fax: 417-357-6163. Hours: 7:30AM-4PM (CST). *Misdemeanor, Civil Actions, Eviction, Small Claims, Probate.*
www.stoneco-mo.us
Note: No collar limit on civil actions; prior to 2001, the civil action maximum limit was $25,000.

Civil Records: Access: Phone, fax, mail, in person. Both court and visitors may perform in person searches. No search fee. Required to search: name, years to search; also helpful: address. Civil cases indexed by defendant, plaintiff. Civil records go back to 1970.

Criminal Records: Access: Phone, fax, mail, in person. Both court and visitors may perform in person searches. No search fee. Required to search: name, years to search, DOB, SSN, signed release. Criminal records on computer back to 1990 and on microfiche.

General Information: No juvenile, mental, expunged, dismissed, or suspended imposition of sentence records released. Will fax results $3.00 per page. Copy fee: $.25 per page. Certification fee: $2.50. Payee: Circuit Court Division II. Only cashiers checks and money orders accepted. Prepayment required. Mail requests: SASE required. Mail turnaround time 2-3 weeks.

Sullivan County

Circuit & Associate Court Courthouse, 109 N Main, Milan, MO 63556-1358; 660-265-4717 (Circ.); 660-265-3303 (Assoc. Circ); Fax: 660-265-5071. 9:00AM-4:30PM (CST). *Felony, Misdemeanor, Civil Actions, Eviction, Small Claims, Probate.*
Civil Records: Access: In person, online. Visitors must perform in person searches for themselves. No search fee. Required to search: name, years to search. Civil cases indexed by defendant, plaintiff. Civil records on index cards since 1979, prior on books. Participates in the free statewide Casenet court record system at www.courts.mo.gov/casenet.
Criminal Records: Access: In person, online. Visitors must perform in person searches for themselves. No search fee. Required to search: name, years to search; also helpful: DOB, SSN. Criminal records on index cards since 1979, prior on books. Participates in the free statewide Casenet court record system at www.courts.mo.gov/casenet. Court recommends criminal searches at MO State Highway Patrol, 573-526-6288.
General Information: Public Access terminal is available. No juvenile, mental, expunged, dismissed, or suspended imposition of sentence records released. Copy fee: $.25 per page. Certification fee: $1.50. Payee: Consolidated Circuit Court of Sullivan County. Personal checks accepted. Prepayment required.

Taney County

Circuit Court PO Box 335, Forsyth, MO 65653; 417-546-7230; Fax: 417-546-6133. Hours: 8AM-5PM (CST). *Felony, Civil Actions Over $25,000.*
Civil Records: Access: Mail, in person, online. Both court and visitors may perform in person searches. Search fee: $4.00 per name. Required to search: name, years to search. Civil cases indexed by defendant, plaintiff. Civil records on computer since 1/95, prior on index cards and books since 1885. Participates in the free state online court record system at www.courts.mo.gov/casenet. Online records include probate court.
Criminal Records: Access: Mail, in person, online. Both court and visitors may perform in person searches. Search fee: $4.00 per name. Required to search: name, years to search, DOB; also helpful: SSN. Criminal records on computer since 1/95, prior on index cards and books since 1885. Online access to criminal records is the same as civil.
General Information: Public Access terminal is available. No juvenile, mental, expunged, dismissed, or suspended imposition of sentence records released. Will fax results. Copy fee: $.25 per page. Certification fee: $1.50. Payee: Circuit Clerk. Personal checks accepted. Prepayment required. Mail requests: SASE helpful. Turnaround time 2 days.

Associate Circuit Court - Division I PO Box 129, Forsyth, MO 65653; 417-546-7212; Fax: 417-546-4513. Hours: 8AM-5PM (CST). *Felony, Misdemeanor, Probate.*
Criminal Records: Access: Mail, in person, online. Only the court performs in person searches; visitors may not. Search fee: $4.00 per name. Required to search: name, years to search, DOB, SSN. Criminal records on computer since 1984, prior on cards and books. Participates in the free statewide Casenet court record system at www.courts.mo.gov/casenet.
General Information: No juvenile, mental, expunged, dismissed, or suspended imposition of sentence records released. Copy fee: $.25 per page. Certification fee: $1.50; Probate is $1.00 per page. Payee: Associate Circuit Court. Personal checks not accepted. Prepayment required. Mail requests: SASE required. Mail turnaround time 10 days, more if busy.

Associate Circuit Court - Division II PO Box 1030, Forsyth, MO 65653; 417-546-7206; Fax: 417-546-5821. Hours: 8AM-5PM (CST). *Civil Actions Under $25,000, Eviction, Small Claims.*
Civil Records: Access: Mail, in person, online. Only the court performs in person searches; visitors may not. Search fee: $4.00 per name. Required to search: name, years to search. Civil cases indexed by defendant, plaintiff. Civil records on computer since 1984, prior on cards and books. Beginning in October, 2003, this court participates in the free statewide Casenet court record system at www.courts.mo.gov/casenet.
General Information: No juvenile, mental, expunged, dismissed, or suspended imposition of sentence records released. Copy fee: $.25 per page. Certification fee: $1.50. Payee: Associate Circuit Court. Personal checks accepted. Prepayment required. Mail requests: SASE required. Mail turnaround time 2 days, more if busy.

Texas County

Circuit Court 210 N Grand, Houston, MO 65483; 417-967-3742; Fax: 417-967-4220. Hours: 8:30-Noon; 12:30PM-4:30PM (CST). *Felony, Misdemeanor, Civil Actions Over $25,000.*
Civil Records: Access: In person only. Visitors must perform in person searches for themselves. No search fee. Required to search: name, years to search. Civil cases indexed by defendant, plaintiff. Civil records on index books since 1900s.
Criminal Records: Access: In person only. Visitors must perform in person searches for themselves. No search fee. Required to search: name, years to search. Criminal records on index books since 1900s. Court recommends criminal searches at MO State Highway Patrol, 573-526-6288.
General Information: No juvenile, mental, expunged, dismissed, or suspended imposition of sentence records released. Copy fee: $1.00 per page. Certification fee: $2.00. Payee: Texas County Circuit Clerk. Personal checks accepted. Prepayment required.

Associate Circuit Court County Courthouse, 210 N Grand, #302, Houston, MO 65483; 417-967-3663; Fax: 417-967-4128. Hours: 8AM-noon; 1-5PM (CST). *Misdemeanor, Civil Actions Under $25,000, Eviction, Small Claims, Probate.*
Civil Records: Access: Phone, fax, mail, in person. Only the court performs in person searches; visitors may not. No search fee. Required to search: name, years to search. Civil cases indexed by defendant, plaintiff. Civil records on index cards since 1979, prior on cards and books.
Criminal Records: Access: Phone, fax, mail, in person. Only the court performs in person searches; visitors may not. No search fee. Required to search: name, years to search, SSN. Criminal records on index cards since 1979, prior on cards and books.
General Information: No juvenile, mental, expunged, dismissed, or suspended imposition of sentence records released. Will fax results $2.00 1st page, $.50 each add'l. Copy fee: $1.00 per page. Certification fee: $2.00. Payee: Associate Circuit Court. Business checks accepted. Prepayment required. Mail requests: SASE required. Mail turnaround time 7-10 days; phone turnaround is immediate.

Vernon County

Circuit & Associate Court Courthouse, 3rd Fl, 100 W Cherry St, Nevada, MO 64772; 417-448-2525/2550; Fax: 417-448-2512. Hours: 8AM-4:30PM (CST). *Felony, Misdemeanor, Civil Actions, Eviction, Small Claims, Probate.*
Civil Records: Access: In person, online, email. Visitors must perform in person searches for themselves. No search fee. Required to search: name, years to search. Civil cases indexed by defendant, plaintiff. Civil records go back to 1863; on computer back to 2000. Judgments on index cards up until 1992. Participates in the free state online court record system at www.courts.mo.gov/casenet. Online records go back to 9/11/2001. Online records include probate court.
Criminal Records: Access: In person, online. Visitors must perform in person searches for themselves. Search fee: $5.00 per name. Required to search: name, years to search, DOB. Criminal records go back to 1863; on computer back to 1990 for Assoc. Court records, back to 2001 for Circuit Court records. Online access to criminal records is the same as civil. Court recommends criminal searches at MO State Highway Patrol, 573-526-6288.
General Information: Public Access terminal is available. No juvenile, mental, expunged, dismissed, or suspended imposition of sentence records released. Copy fee: $.20 per page; microfilmed records copies are $1.00 per page. Certification fee: $1.50. Payee: Vernon County Circuit Clerk. Personal checks accepted. Prepayment required.

Warren County

Circuit Court 104 W Main, Warrenton, MO 63383; 636-456-3363; Fax: 636-456-8573. Hours: 8AM-4:30PM (CST). *Felony, Misdemeanor, Civil Actions Over $25,000.*
Civil Records: Access: Online, in person. Visitors must perform in person searches for themselves. No search fee. Required to search: name, years to search. Civil cases indexed by defendant, plaintiff. Civil records on index cards since 1976, prior on books. Participates in the free state online court record system at www.courts.mo.gov/casenet. Online records go back to 9/20/1999.
Criminal Records: Access: Online, in person. Visitors must perform in person searches for themselves. No search fee. Required to search: name, years to search. Criminal records on index cards since 1976, prior on books. Online access to criminal records is the same as civil. Court recommends criminal searches at MO State Highway Patrol, 573-526-6288.
General Information: Public Access terminal is available. No juvenile, mental, expunged, dismissed, or suspended imposition of sentence records released. Copy fee: $.25 per page. Certification fee: $1.00. Payee: Warren County Circuit Clerk. Business checks accepted. Prepayment required.

Associate Circuit Court Warren County Courthouse, 104 W Main, Warrenton, MO 63383; 636-456-3375; Fax: 636-456-2422. Hours: 8:30AM-4:30PM (CST). *Misdemeanor, Civil Actions Under $25,000, Eviction, Small Claims, Probate.*
Civil Records: Access: Phone, fax, online, mail, in person. Both court and visitors may perform in person searches. No search fee. Required to search: name, years to search. Civil cases indexed by defendant, plaintiff. Civil records on index cards since 1979, prior on books. Records may be free on state online court record system at www.courts.mo.gov/casenet.
Criminal Records: Access: Phone, fax, mail, online, in person. Only the court performs in person searches; visitors may not. No search fee. Required to search:

name, years to search; also helpful: DOB, SSN. Criminal records on computer since 2/92, on cards since 1979, prior on books. Online access to criminal records is the same as civil.

General Information: Public Access terminal is available. No juvenile, mental, expunged, dismissed, or suspended imposition of sentence records released. Will fax results for $1.00 per page; limit on number of pages. Copy fee: $.25 per page. Certification fee: $1.50 plus $1.00 per page. Payee: Associate Circuit Clerk. No personal checks accepted. Prepayment required. Mail requests: SASE not required. Mail turnaround time 1 week.

Washington County

Circuit Court PO Box 216, Potosi, MO 63664; 573-438-4171; Fax: 573-438-7900. Hours: 8AM-5PM (CST). *Felony, Misdemeanor, Civil Actions Over $45,000.*

Civil Records: Access: Mail, online, in person. Both court and visitors may perform in person searches. No search fee. Required to search: name, years to search. Civil cases indexed by defendant, plaintiff. Civil records on index cards since 1976, prior on books. Participates in the free state online court record system at www.courts.mo.gov/casenet. Records from 11/09/00 forward.

Criminal Records: Access: Mail, in person, online. Both court and visitors may perform in person searches. No search fee. Required to search: name, years to search. Criminal records on index cards since 1976, prior on books. Participates in the free state online court record system at www.courts.mo.gov/casenet. Records go back to 11/09/00 forward.

General Information: Public Access terminal is available. (Criminal records go back to 11/00, civil to 1988. A card file open to the public to view older criminal records.) No juvenile, mental, expunged, dismissed, or suspended imposition of sentence records released. Copy fee: $.50 per page. Certification fee: $2.00. Payee: Washington County Circuit Clerk. Personal checks accepted. Prepayment required. Mail requests: SASE required. Mail turnaround time 5-10 days.

Associate Circuit Court 102 N Missouri St, Potosi, MO 63664; 573-438-3691; Fax: 573-438-7900. Hours: 8AM-5PM (CST). *Misdemeanor, Civil Actions Under $45,000, Eviction, Small Claims, Probate.*

Civil Records: Access: Phone, fax, mail, in person, online. Only the court performs in person searches; visitors may not. No search fee. Required to search: name, years to search. Civil cases indexed by defendant, plaintiff. Civil records on index cards for 12 years, computerized since 1996, older records archived. Participates in the free statewide Casenet court record system at www.courts.mo.gov/casenet. Online records go back to 11/00.

Criminal Records: Access: Phone, fax, mail, in person, online. Only the court performs in person searches; visitors may not. No search fee. Required to search: name, years to search; also helpful: DOB, SSN. Criminal records on index cards for 12 years, computerized since 1996, older records archived. Participates in the free statewide Casenet court record system at www.courts.mo.gov/casenet. Online records go back to 11/00.

General Information: No juvenile, mental, expunged, dismissed, or suspended imposition of sentence records released. Copy fee: $.50 per page. No certification fee. Payee: Associate Circuit Clerk. Personal checks accepted. Prepayment required. Mail requests: SASE required. Mail turnaround time 1 week.

Wayne County

Circuit Court PO Box 78, Greenville, MO 63944; 573-224-3014; Fax: 573-224-3015. Hours: 8:30AM-4:30PM (CST). *Felony, Misdemeanor, Civil Actions Over $45,000.*

Civil Records: Access: Mail, in person, online. Both court and visitors may perform in person searches. Search fee: $14.00 per name. Required to search: name, years to search. Civil cases indexed by defendant, plaintiff. Civil records on index cards since 1978, prior on books. Participates in the free statewide Casenet court record system at www.courts.mo.gov/casenet.

Criminal Records: Access: Mail, in person, online. Both court and visitors may perform in person searches. Search fee: $14.00 per name. Required to search: name, years to search; also helpful: DOB. Criminal records on index cards since 1978, prior on books. Participates in the free statewide Casenet court record system at www.courts.mo.gov/casenet. Online records go back to 09/19/01.

General Information: No juvenile, mental, expunged, dismissed, or suspended imposition of sentence records released. Copy fee: $.25 per page. Certification fee: $2.00. Payee: Wayne County Circuit Clerk. Personal checks accepted. Prepayment required. Mail requests: SASE required. Mail turnaround time 1 week.

Div. III Circuit Court PO Box 47, Greenville, MO 63944; 573-224-3052; Fax: 573-224-3225. 8:30AM-4:30PM (CST). *Misdemeanor, Civil Actions Under $45,000, Eviction, Small Claims, Probate.*

Civil Records: Access: Phone, fax, mail, in person, online. Both court and visitors may perform in person searches. No search fee. Required to search: name, years to search. Civil cases indexed by defendant, plaintiff. Civil records on index cards since 1979; on computer back to 4/2001. Participates in the free statewide Casenet court record system at www.courts.mo.gov/casenet.

Criminal Records: Access: Phone, fax, mail, in person, online. Both court and visitors may perform in person searches. No search fee. Required to search: name, years to search, DOB; also helpful: SSN. Criminal records on computer since 1992, prior on index cards. Participates in the free statewide Casenet court record system at www.courts.mo.gov/casenet.

General Information: Public Access terminal is available. (Access terminal is in Circuit Court office.) No juvenile, mental, expunged, dismissed, or suspended imposition of sentence records released. Will fax results $.50 per page. Copy fee: $.25 per page. Certification fee: $1.50 per page. Payee: Div. III Circuit Court. Personal checks accepted. Prepayment required. Mail requests: SASE required. Mail turnaround time 1 day.

Webster County

Circuit Court PO Box 529, Marshfield, MO 65706; 417-859-2006; Probate phone: 417-859-2041; Fax: 417-468-3786 (Circuit). Hours: 8AM-5PM (CST). *Felony, Civil Actions Over $25,000.*

Civil Records: Access: Fax, mail, in person, online. Both court and visitors may perform in person searches. No search fee. Required to search: name, years to search. Civil cases indexed by defendant, plaintiff. Civil records on computer since 1976 (judgment index). Participates in the free state online court record system at www.courts.mo.gov/casenet.

Criminal Records: Access: In person, online. Only the court performs in person searches; visitors may not. No search fee. Required to search: name, years to search, DOB. Criminal records on computer since 1976 (judgment index). Online access to criminal records is the same as civil. Court recommends

criminal searches at MO State Highway Patrol, 573-526-6288.

General Information: Public Access terminal is available. (Judgments only.) No juvenile, mental, expunged, dismissed, or suspended imposition of sentence records released. Will fax results $2.00 per page. Copy fee: $.15 per page. Certification fee: $2.00. Payee: Webster County Circuit Clerk. Personal checks accepted. Prepayment required. Mail requests: SASE required. Mail turnaround time 1 day.

Associate Circuit Court Courthouse, Marshfield, MO 65706; 417-859-2041; Fax: 417-859-6265. Hours: 8AM-5PM (CST). *Misdemeanor, Civil Actions Under $25,000, Eviction, Small Claims, Probate.*

www.osca.state.mo.us

Civil Records: Access: Phone, fax, mail, in person, online. Only the court performs in person searches; visitors may not. No search fee. Required to search: name, years to search. Civil cases indexed by defendant, plaintiff. Civil records on computer since 1992; prior records on index cards since 1980 & on books. Access to civil records is free at www.courts.mo.gov/casenet/. At the website, select the judicial district, then search by name, case # or date.

Criminal Records: Access: Mail, in person, online. Only the court performs in person searches; visitors may not. No search fee. Required to search: name, years to search; also helpful: DOB, SSN. Criminal records on computer since 1992. Online access to criminal records is the same as civil.

General Information: No juvenile, mental, expunged, dismissed, or suspended imposition of sentence records released. Copy fee: $1.00 per page. Certification fee: $1.50. Payee: Associate Circuit Court. Only cashiers checks and money orders accepted. Prepayment required. Mail requests: SASE required. Mail turnaround time varies.

Worth County

Circuit Court PO Box 340, Grant City, MO 64456; 660-564-2210; Fax: 660-564-2432. Hours: 8:30AM-4:30PM (CST). *Felony, Misdemeanor, Civil Actions Over $45,000.*

Civil Records: Access: Mail, in person. Both court and visitors may perform in person searches. No search fee. Required to search: name, years to search. Civil cases indexed by defendant, plaintiff. Civil records on computer since 1990, prior on index cards.

Criminal Records: Access: Mail, in person. Both court and visitors may perform in person searches. No search fee. Required to search: name, years to search. Criminal records on computer since 1990, prior on index cards.

General Information: Public Access terminal is available. No juvenile, mental, expunged, dismissed, or suspended imposition of sentence records released. Copy fee: $.20 per page. Certification fee: $2.50. Payee: Worth County Circuit Clerk. Personal checks accepted. Prepayment required. Mail requests: SASE required. Mail turnaround time same day.

Associate Circuit Court PO Box 428, Grant City, MO 64456; 660-564-2152; Fax: 660-564-2432. Hours: 9AM-4:30PM (CST). *Misdemeanor, Civil Actions Under $45,000, Eviction, Small Claims, Probate.*

Civil Records: Access: In person only. Visitors must perform in person searches for themselves. No search fee. Required to search: name, years to search. Civil cases indexed by defendant, plaintiff. Civil records on index cards since 1979, prior on index books.

Criminal Records: Access: Mail, in person. Both court and visitors may perform in person searches. No search fee. Required to search: name, years to search.

Criminal records on index cards since 1979, prior on index books.

General Information: No juvenile, mental, expunged, dismissed, or suspended imposition of sentence records released. Copy fee: $1.00 per page. Certification fee: $2.50. Payee: Associate Circuit Court. Personal checks accepted. Prepayment required. Mail requests: SASE required. Mail turnaround time varies.

Wright County

Circuit Court PO Box 39, Hartville, MO 65667; 417-741-7121; Fax: 417-741-7504. Hours: 8AM-4:30PM (CST). *Felony, Misdemeanor, Civil Actions Over $25,000.*

Civil Records: Access: Mail, in person. Both court and visitors may perform in person searches. No search fee. Required to search: name, years to search. Civil cases indexed by defendant, plaintiff. Civil records on index cards since 1979, prior on books to 1900s.

Criminal Records: Access: Mail, in person. Both court and visitors may perform in person searches. No search fee. Required to search: name, years to search. Criminal records on index cards since 1979, prior on books to 1900s.

General Information: No juvenile, mental, expunged, dismissed, or suspended imposition of sentence records released. Will fax results for $3.00. Copy fee: $.25 per page. Certification fee: $2.00. Payee: Wright County Circuit Clerk. Personal checks accepted. Prepayment required. Mail requests: SASE not required. Mail turnaround time 1 day.

Associate Circuit Court PO Box 58, Hartville, MO 65667; 417-741-6450; Fax: 417-741-7120. Hours: 8AM-4:30PM (CST). *Misdemeanor, Civil Actions Under $25,000, Eviction, Small Claims, Probate.*

Civil Records: Access: Phone, fax, mail, in person. Only the court performs in person searches; visitors may not. No search fee. Required to search: name, years to search. Civil cases indexed by defendant, plaintiff. Civil records on index cards since 1979, prior on books; on computer back to 1990.

Criminal Records: Access: Phone, fax, mail, in person. Only the court performs in person searches; visitors may not. No search fee. Required to search: name, years to search; also helpful: DOB, SSN. Criminal records on computer since 1989, prior on cards and books; on computer back to 1990.

General Information: No juvenile, mental, expunged, or dismissed records released. Fee to fax results is $1.00 per page. Copy fee: $.25 per page. Certification fee: $1.00. Payee: Associate Circuit Court. Only cashiers checks and money orders accepted. Prepayment required. Mail requests: SASE required. Mail turnaround time 1 week

Missouri Recording Offices

ORGANIZATION: 114 counties and one independent city, 115 recording offices. The recording officer is. Recorder of Deeds. The City of St. Louis has its own recording office. See the City/County Locator section at the end of this chapter for ZIP Codes that cover both the city and county of St. Louis. The entire state is in the Central Time Zone (CST).

REAL ESTATE RECORDS: A few counties will perform real estate searches. Copy and certification fees vary.

UCC RECORDS: Missouri was a dual filing state. Until 07/2001, financing statements were filed both at the state level and with the Recorder of Deeds, except for consumer goods, farm related and real estate related filings, which were filed only with the Recorder. Now only real estate relating filings are filed at the county level. Most all counties will perform UCC searches. Use search request form UCC-11. Search fees are usually $14.00 per debtor name without copies and $28.00 with copies. Copies usually cost $.50 per page.

TAX LIEN RECORDS: All federal and state tax liens are filed with the county Recorder of Deeds. They are usually indexed together. Some counties will perform tax lien searches. Search and copy fees vary widely.

OTHER LIENS: Mechanics, judgment, child support.

ONLINE ACCESS: A handful of counties offer online access. UCCs are available from the Secretary of State.

Adair County

Recorder of Deeds, 106 W. Washington St., Courthouse, Kirksville, MO 63501. **Phone-**Recorder of Deeds, R/E & UCC Recording- 660-665-3890; fax-660-785-3212; hours 8:30AM-Noon, 1-4:30PM
UCC search per debtor- $14.00. Search + copy request (w/10 pages of copies)- $28.00. UCC search includes tax liens if requested. Tax lien search- $14.00 per debtor. Will not search real estate records. UCC copy- $1.00 per page after 10 pages. Cert fee: $2.00 per cert. Payee: Adair County Recorder of Deeds. **Other phones:** Assessor-660-665-4423; Treasurer-660-665-6755; Appraiser/ Auditor-660-665-4423; Elections-660-665-3350; Vital Records-660-665-8491.

Andrew County

Recorder of Deeds, PO Box 208, Savannah, MO 64485. **Phone-**Recorder of Deeds, R/E & UCC Recording- 816-324-4221; fax-816-324-5667; hours 8AM-5PM. UCC search per debtor (including 10 pages of copies)- $14.00. Will not search real estate or tax lien records. Record copy fee- $1.00 per page after 10 pages. Payee: Andrew County Recorder of Deeds. **Other phones:** Assessor-816-324-3023; Treasurer-816-324-3614; Elections-816-324-3624.

Atchison County

Recorder of Deeds, Box 280, Rock Port, MO 64482. **Phone-**660-744-2707, R/E Recording-660-744-2707/2705, UCC Recording-660-744-2707/2705; fax-660-744-5705; hours 8:30AM-Noon, 1-4:30PM www.morecorders.com
UCC search per debtor- $14.00. Search + copy request (w/10 pages of copies)- $14.00. Will not search real estate or tax lien records. RE record copy- $1.00 per page. UCC copy- $.50 per page after 10 pages. Cert fee: $1.00 per cert. Payee: Atchison County Recorder of Deeds. **Other phones:** Assessor-660-744-2948; Treasurer-660-744-2800; Elections-660-744-6214.

Audrain County

Recorder of Deeds, 101 N Jefferson, Rm 105, Audrain County Courthouse, Mexico, MO 65265. **Phone-**573-473-5830; fax-573-581-8087; hours 8AM-5PM
UCC search per debtor- $14.00. Search + copy request (w/10 pages of copies)- $28.00. Will not search real estate or tax lien records. UCC copy-$1.00 per page after 10 pages $.50. Cert fee: $1.00 per cert. Payee: Audrain County Recorder of Deeds. **Other phones:** Assessor-573-473-5827.

Barry County

Recorder of Deeds, PO Box 340, Cassville, MO 65625. **Phone-**Recorder of Deeds, R/E & UCC Recording-417-847-2914; fax-417-847-2914; hours 8AM-4PM
UCC search per debtor- $14.00. Search + copy request (w/10 pages of copies)- $28.00. Tax lien search- $4.00 per debtor. Will not search real estate records. RE record copy- $2.00 per doc. UCC copy-$.50 per page after 10 pages. Cert fee: $1.00 per doc. Payee: Barry County Recorder of Deeds. **Other phones:** Assessor-417-847-4589.

Barton County

Recorder of Deeds, 1004 Gulf, Courthouse, Rm 107, Lamar, MO 64759. **Phone-**Recorder of Deeds, R/E & UCC Recording- 417-682-2110; fax-417-682-4102; hours 8:30AM-Noon, 12:30-4:30PM
UCC search per debtor- $14.00. Search + copy request (w/10 pages of copies)- $28.00. Will not search real estate or tax lien records. Record copy-$1.00 per page after 10 pages. Cert fee: $1.00 per cert. Payee: Barton County Recorder of Deeds. **Other phones:** Assessor-417-682-3553; Treasurer-417-682-5881; Elections-417-682-3529; Circuit Court-417-682-2444.

Bates County

Recorder of Deeds, Box 186, Butler, MO 64730. **Phone-**Recorder of Deeds, R/E & UCC Recording-660-679-3611; hours 8:30AM-4:30PM
UCC search per debtor- $14.00. Search + copy request (w/10 pages of copies)- $28.00. Will not search tax liens. Real estate record owner and mortgage searches available. RE record copy- $2.00 per page. UCC copy- $1.00 per page. Cert fee: $1.00. Payee: Bates County Recorder of Deeds. **Other phones:** Assessor-660-679-3157; Treasurer-660-679-3341; Elections-660-679-3371.

Benton County

Recorder of Deeds, PO Box 37, Warsaw, MO 65355. **Phone-**Recorder of Deeds, R/E & UCC Recording-660-438-5732; fax-660-438-3652; hours 8AM-Noon, 1-4:30PM. UCC search per debtor- $14.00. Search + copy request (w/10 pages of copies)- $28.00. Will not search real estate or tax lien records. Record copy- $1.00 per page after 10 pages. Cert fee: $2.00 per cert. Payee: Benton County Recorder of Deeds. **Other phones:** Assessor-660-438-5323; Treasurer-660-438-6313; Elections-660-438-7326.

Bollinger County

Recorder of Deeds, Box 49, Marble Hill, MO 63764. **Phone-**573-238-1900 ext 301, R/E Recording-573-238-1900 x7, UCC Recording-573-238-1900 x7; fax-573-238-4511; hours 8AM-4PM. Will not search records. UCC copy- $14.00 per doc. Cert fee: $2.00. Payee: Bollinger County Recorder of Deeds.

Boone County

Recorder of Deeds, 801 E. Walnut, Rm 132, Boone County Gov't Ctr, Columbia, MO 65201-7728. **Phone-**Recorder of Deeds, R/E & UCC Recording- 573-886-4345, UCC Recording-573-886-4355; fax-573-886-4359;   hours-8AM-5PM www.showmeboone.com/RECORDER/
UCC search per debtor- $14.00. Search + copy request (w/10 pages of copies)- $28.00. Will not search real estate or tax lien records. Record copy-$1.00 per page after 10 pages. Cert fee: $1.00 per cert. Payee: Boone County Recorder of Deeds. **Online Access to Real Estate, Lien, Marriage, UCC, Real Property, Personal Property records:** Access to the County Recorder database is free at www.showmeboone.com/recorder. Also, the assessor data is free at www.showmeboone.com/assessor/. Free registration and password are required for access. **Other phones:** Assessor-573-886-4270; Treasurer-573-886-4365; Appraiser/ Auditor-573-886-4270; Elections-573-886-4295; Marriage License-573-886-4350.

Buchanan County

Recorder of Deeds, 411 Jules Sts, Courthouse, St. Joseph, MO 64501-1789. **Phone-**Recorder of Deeds, R/E & UCC Recording- 816-271-1437; fax-816-271-1582; hours 8AM-4:30PM www.co.buchanan.mo.us
UCC search per debtor- $14.00. Search + copy request (w/10 pages of copies)- $28.00. Will not search real estate or tax lien records. RE record copy- $2.00 1st page, $1.00 per page thereafter. UCC copy- $.50 per page. Cert fee: $1.00 per doc. Payee: Buchanan County Recorder of Deeds. **Other phones:** Assessor-816-271-1469; Treasurer-816-271-1432.

Butler County

Recorder of Deeds, 100 N. Main St, Courthouse, Poplar Bluff, MO 63901. **Phone**-Recorder of Deeds, R/E & UCC Recording- 573-686-8086; hours 8AM-4PM Will not search records. RE record copy- $2.00 1st page, $1.00 per page thereafter. UCC copy- $.50 per page after 10 pages. Cert fee: $1.00 per cert. Payee: Butler County Recorder of Deeds. **Online Access to Death Index records:** Search the county death index at www.rootsweb.com/~mobutle2/dndx/bc-death.htm?. **Other phones:** Assessor-573-686-8084; Treasurer-573-686-8083; Appraiser/ Auditor-573-686-8084; Elections-573-686-8050; Vital Records-573-686-8086.

Caldwell County

Recorder of Deeds, PO Box 65, Kingston, MO 64650. **Phone**-Recorder of Deeds, R/E & UCC Recording- 816-586-3080; hours 8AM-4:30PM. UCC search per debtor- $14.00. Will not search real estate or tax lien records. RE record copy- $2.00 1st page; $1.00 each add'l. UCC copy- $.50 per page after 10 pages. Payee: Caldwell County Recorder of Deeds. **Other phones:** Assessor-816-586-5261; Treasurer-816-586-2781; Elections-816-586-2571.

Callaway County

Recorder of Deeds, PO Box 406, Fulton, MO 65251. **Phone**-573-642-0787; fax-573-642-7929; 8AM-5PM UCC search per debtor- $14.00. Search + copy request (w/10 pages of copies)- $28.00. UCC search includes tax liens if requested. Will search real estate records. Record copy- $1.00 per page after 10 pages. Cert fee: $1.00 per cert. Payee: Callaway County Recorder of Deeds. **Online Access to Death records:** Access to unofficial death records up to 1926 are free from a private company at www.ancestry.com/ancestry/search/3074.htm. **Other phones:** Assessor-573-642-0766.

Camden County

Recorder of Deeds, 1 Court Circle, Camdenton, MO 65020. **Phone**-573-346-4440, R/E Recording-573-346-4440 x234, UCC Recording-573-346-4440 x235; fax-573-346-8367; hours 8:30AM-4:30PM UCC search per debtor- $14.00. Search + copy request (w/10 pages of copies)- $28.00. Will not search real estate or tax lien records. Record copy- $1.00 per page after 10 pages. Cert fee: $1.00 per copy. Payee: Camden County Recorder of Deeds. **Other phones:** Assessor-573-346-4440 x224-6; Treasurer-573-346-4440 x215-6.

Cape Girardeau County

Recorder of Deeds, PO Box 248, Jackson, MO 63755. **Phone**-573-243-8123; fax-573-204-2477; hours 8AM-4:30PM. UCC search per debtor- $14.00. Search + copy request (w/10 pages of copies)- $28.00. Will not search real estate or tax lien records. RE record copy- $2.00 for 1st page; $1.00 each add'l. UCC copy- $1.00 per page after 10 pages. Cert fee: $1.00 per cert. Payee: Cape Girardeau County Recorder of Deeds. **Other phones:** Assessor-573-243-2468; Treasurer-573-243-3720.

Carroll County

Recorder of Deeds, PO Box 245, Carrollton, MO 64633. **Phone**-660-542-1466; fax-660-542-1444; hours 8:30AM-4:30PM UCC search per debtor- $14.00. Search + copy request (w/10 pages of copies)- $28.00. UCC search includes tax liens if requested. Will not search real estate records. UCC copy- $1.00 per page after 10 pages. Cert fee: 2.00 per page. Payee: Carroll County Recorder of Deeds. **Other phones:** Assessor-660-542-2184; Treasurer-660-542-1977.

Carter County

Recorder of Deeds, PO Box 1107, Van Buren, MO 63965. **Phone**-Recorder of Deeds, R/E & UCC Recording- 573-323-9656; fax-573-323-4885; hours 8AM-N, 1-4PM UCC search per debtor- $14.00. Search + copy request (w/10 pages of copies)- $28.00. Tax liens not included in UCC search. Will not search real estate records. Record copy- $1.00 per page after 10 pages. Cert fee: $1.00 per page. Payee: Carter County Recorder of Deeds. **Other phones:** Assessor-573-323-4709; Treasurer-573-323-8271; Elections-573-323-4527.

Cass County

Recorder of Deeds, 102 E. Wall St, Cass County Court House, Harrisonville, MO 64701. **Phone**-Recorder of Deeds, R/E & UCC Recording- 816-380-8117, UCC Recording-816-380-8119; fax-816-380-8165; hours 8AM-4:30PM www.casscounty.com/cassfr.htm Computer records date back to 1991. Prepaid fax accounts available. For information, contact Sandy Gregory at 816-380-8117. Will search UCC records. Computer screen printout only. Search per debtor- $14.00. Search + copy request (w/10 pages of copies)- $28.00. Tax liens not included in UCC search. Tax lien search- $10.00 per search. Will not search real estate records. Record copy- $1.00 per page. Cert fee: $1.00 per seal + $1 per page. Payee: Cass County Recorder of Deeds. **Other phones:** Assessor-816-380-8165 (FAX).

Cedar County

Recorder of Deeds, PO Box 607, Stockton, MO 65785. **Phone**-Recorder of Deeds, R/E & UCC Recording- 417-276-6700 x246; fax-417-276-5001; hours 8AM-Noon, 1-4PM UCC search per debtor- $14.00. Search + copy request (w/10 pages of copies)- $28.00. Will not search real estate or tax lien records. UCC copy- $1.00 per page after 10 pages. Cert fee: $1.00. Payee: Cedar County Recorder of Deeds. **Other phones:** Assessor-417-276-6700 X248; Treasurer-417-276-6700 X245; Elections-417-276-6700 X221.

Chariton County

Recorder of Deeds, PO Box 112, Keytesville, MO 65261. **Phone**-660-288-3602; fax-660-288-3763; hours 8:30AM-Noon, 1-4:30PM. UCC search per debtor- $14.00. Search + copy request (w/10 pages of copies)- $28.00. Will not search real estate or tax lien records. Record copy- $1.00 per page after 10 pages. Cert fee: $1.50 per cert. Payee: Chariton County Recorder of Deeds. **Other phones:** Assessor-660-288-3873; Treasurer-660-288-3789.

Christian County

Recorder of Deeds, PO Box 358, Ozark, MO 65721. **Phone**-417-581-9941; fax-417-581-9943; hours 8AM-4:30PM. UCC search per debtor- $14.00. Search + copy request (w/10 pages of copies)- $28.00. Will not search real estate or tax lien records. Record copy- $1.00 per page after 10 pages. Cert fee: $1.00 per doc. Payee: Christian County Recorder of Deeds. **Other phones:** Assessor-417-581-2440.

Clark County

Recorder of Deeds, 111 E. Court #2, Courthouse, Kahoka, MO 63445. **Phone**-Recorder of Deeds, R/E & UCC Recording- 660-727-3292; fax-660-727-1051; hours 8AM-Noon,1-4PM UCC search per debtor- $14.00. Search + copy request (w/10 pages of copies)- $28.00. UCC search includes tax liens. Separate Tax lien search-usually done over phone for no charge, but is $14.00 if mail request. Will not search real estate records. Record copy- $1.00 per page after 10

pages. Cert fee: $3.00 per cert. Payee: Clark County Recorder of Deeds. **Other phones:** Assessor-660-727-3023; Treasurer-660-727-3272; Elections-660-727-3283.

Clay County

Recorder of Deeds, PO Box 238, Liberty, MO 64069. **Phone**-Recorder of Deeds, R/E & UCC Recording- 816-792-7641; fax-816-792-7777; hours 8AM-4PM http://recorder.co.clay.mo.us Database from July 1, 1986 is on website. UCC search per debtor- $14.00. Search + copy request (w/10 pages of copies)- $28.00. Federal tax lien search- $9.00; state tax lien-$3.00. Will not search real estate records. Copy fee-$2.00 for 1st page, $1.00 add'l. UCC copy- $.50 per page. Cert fee: $1.00 per cert. Payee: Clay County Recorder of Deeds. **Online Access to Real Estate, Marriage, Military Discharge, UCC, Recording records:** Access to recorder's data is free at http://recorder.co.clay.mo.us/pages/online_access.asp. Overall index goes back to 1986; images back to 1998. UCCs are 1986-91 real estate only. **Other phones:** Assessor-816-792-7664; Treasurer-816-792-7649 x284.

Clinton County

Recorder of Deeds, PO Box 275, Plattsburg, MO 64477. **Phone**-816-539-3719; fax-816-539-3893; hours 8AM-Noon, 1-5PM UCC search per debtor- $14.00. Search + copy request (w/10 pages of copies)- $28.00. Will not search real estate or tax lien records. RE record copy- $1.00 per page. UCC copy- $2.00 per page after 10 pages. Cert fee: $3.00 per cert. Payee: Clinton County Recorder of Deeds. **Other phones:** Assessor-816-539-3716; Treasurer-816-539-3724; Elections-816-539-3713.

Cole County

Recorder of Deeds, PO Box 353, Jefferson City, MO 65102. **Phone**-573-634-9115; hours 8AM-4:30PM UCC search per debtor (including 10 pages of copies)- $14.00. Tax liens not included in UCC search. Federal/state combined tax lien search-$28.00 per debtor. Real estate owner, mortgage, and property transfer searches available. Record copy-$1.00 per page after 1st 10 pages. Cert fee: $1.00 per cert. Payee: Cole County Recorder of Deeds. **Online Access to Death records:** unofficial death records up to 1907 are free from a private company at www.ancestry.com/ancestry/search/3074.htm. **Other phones:** Assessor-573-634-9135; Treasurer-573-634-9121.

Cooper County

Recorder of Deeds, 200 Main St, Courthouse - Rm 26, Boonville, MO 65233-1276. **Phone**-660-882-2232; fax-660-882-2043; hours 8:30AM-5PM UCC search per debtor- $14.00. Will not search real estate or tax lien records. Record copy- $1.00 per page after 10 pages. Cert fee: $1.50 per cert. Payee: Cooper County Recorder of Deeds. **Other phones:** Assessor-660-882-2646.

Crawford County

Recorder of Deeds, PO Box 177, Steelville, MO 65565. **Phone**-Recorder of Deeds, R/E & UCC Recording- 573-775-5048; fax-573-775-3365; hours 8AM-4:30PM. UCC search per debtor- $14.00. Search + copy request (w/10 pages of copies)- $28.00. Will not search tax liens. Real estate record owner searches available for genealogical purposes only RE record copy- $.30 per page. UCC copy- $.50 per page after 10 pages. Cert fee: $2.00 per cert. Payee: Crawford County Recorder of Deeds. **Other phones:** Assessor-573-775-2065; Treasurer-573-775-2897.

Dade County

Recorder of Deeds, Courthouse, Greenfield, MO 65661. **Phone**-Recorder of Deeds, R/E & UCC Recording- 417-637-5373; fax-417-637-5055; hours 8AM-4PM

UCC search per debtor- $14.00. Search + copy request (w/10 pages of copies)- $14.00. UCC search includes tax liens. Will not search real estate records. Record copy- $1.00 per page after 10 pages. Cert fee: $1.00 per doc. Payee: Dade County Recorder of Deeds. **Other phones:** Assessor-417-637-2224; Treasurer-417-637-2732.

Dallas County

Recorder of Deeds, PO Box 373, Buffalo, MO 65622. **Phone**-Recorder of Deeds, R/E & UCC Recording- 417-345-2242; fax-417-345-5539; hours 8AM-Noon,1-4PM

UCC search per debtor- $14.00. Search + copy request (w/10 pages of copies)- $28.00. Will not search real estate or tax lien records. Record copy- $1.00 per page after 10 pages. Cert fee: $1.00 per cert. Payee: Dallas County Recorder of Deeds. **Other phones:** Assessor-417-345-8774; Treasurer-417-345-2020; Elections-417-345-2632.

Daviess County

Recorder of Deeds, PO Box 132, Gallatin, MO 64640. **Phone**-660-663-3183; fax-660-663-3376; hours 8AM-Noon, 1-4:30PM

UCC search per debtor- $14.00. Search + copy request (w/10 pages of copies)- $28.00. UCC search includes tax liens if requested. Will not search real estate records. RE record copy- $1.00 per doc. UCC copy- $1.00 per page after 10 pages. Cert fee: $2.00 per cert. Payee: Daviess County Recorder of Deeds. **Other phones:** Assessor-660-663-3300; Treasurer-660-663-2432.

De Kalb County

Recorder of Deeds, PO Box 248, Maysville, MO 64469-0248. **Phone**-Recorder of Deeds, R/E & UCC Recording- 816-449-2602; fax-816-449-2440; hours 8:30AM-Noon, 1-4:30PM. UCC search per debtor- $14.00. Search + copy request (w/10 pages of copies)- $28.00. Will not search tax liens. Real estate record owner and mortgage searches available. RE record copy- $1.00 per page. UCC opy fee is $1.00 per page and $.50 per page after 10 pages. Cert fee: $1.00 per cert. Payee: De Kalb County Recorder of Deeds. **Other phones:** Assessor-816-449-2212; Treasurer-816-449-5810.

Dent County

Recorder of Deeds, 112 E. 5th St, Salem, MO 65560-1444. **Phone**-Recorder of Deeds, R/E & UCC Recording- 573-729-3931; fax-573-729-9414; hours 8AM-4:30PM

UCC search per debtor- $14.00. Search + copy request (w/10 pages of copies)- $14.00. UCC search includes tax liens if requested. Separate federal/state combined tax lien search- $8.00 per debtor. Will not search real estate records. RE record copy- $.25 per page. UCC copy- $1.00 per page. Cert fee: $1.00 per cert. Payee: Dent County Recorder of Deeds. **Other phones:** Assessor-573-729-6010; Treasurer-573-729-8260.

Douglas County

Recorder of Deeds, PO Box 249, Ava, MO 65608. **Phone**-Recorder of Deeds, R/E & UCC Recording- 417-683-4713; fax-417-683-2794; hours 8AM-4:30PM

UCC search per debtor- $14.00. Search + copy request (w/10 pages of copies)- $28.00. Tax liens not included in UCC search. Separate federal/state combined tax lien search- $15.00 per debtor. Real estate owner, mortgage, and property transfer searches available. Record copy- $1.00 per page after 10 pages. Cert fee: $2.50 per page. Payee: Douglas County Recorder of Deeds. **Other phones:** Assessor-417-683-2829; Treasurer-417-683-2183; Elections-417-683-4714.

Dunklin County

Recorder of Deeds, PO Box 389, Kennett, MO 63857. **Phone**-Recorder of Deeds, R/E & UCC Recording- 573-888-3468; hours 8:30AM-Noon, 1-4:30PM

UCC search per debtor- $14.00. Search + copy request (w/10 pages of copies)- $28.00. Will not search real estate or tax lien records. UCC copy- $.50 per page after 10 pages. Cert fee: $1.00. Payee: Dunklin County Recorder of Deeds. **Other phones:** Assessor-573-888-1409.

Franklin County

Recorder of Deeds, 300 E Main St #101, Union, MO 63084. **Phone**-Recorder of Deeds, R/E & UCC Recording- 636-583-6367; fax-636-583-7330; hours 8AM-4:30PM www.franklinmo.org.

Will search UCC records. UCC search per debtor- $14.00. Will not search real estate or tax lien records. RE record copy- $2.00 1st page, $1.00 each add'l. UCC copy- $1.00 per page after 10 pages. Cert fee: $1.00 per cert. Payee: Franklin County Recorder of Deeds. **Other phones:** Assessor-636-583-6346; Treasurer-636-583-6392.

Gasconade County

Recorder of Deeds, 119 E.1st St, Rm 6, Hermann, MO 65041-1182. **Phone**-Recorder of Deeds, R/E & UCC Recording- 573-486-2632; fax-573-486-5812; hours 8AM-4:30PM

UCC search per debtor- $14.00. Search + copy request (w/10 pages of copies)- $28.00. Will not search real estate or tax lien records. Copy fee- $2.00 1st page, $1.00 each add'l. UCC copy- $1.00 per page after 10 pages. Cert fee: $1.00 per page. Payee: Gasconade County Recorder of Deeds. **Other phones:** Assessor-573-486-3100; Treasurer-573-486-2411; Appraiser/ Auditor-573-486-3100; Elections-573-486-5427.

Gentry County

Recorder of Deeds, PO Box 27, Albany, MO 64402. **Phone**-660-726-3618; fax-660-726-4102; hours 8AM-4:30PM. UCC search per debtor- $14.00. Search + copy request (w/10 pages of copies)- $28.00. Will not search real estate or tax lien records. RE record copy- $1.00 per page; only if Book/Page of document is provided. UCC copy- $1.00 per page after 10 pages. Cert fee: $1.00 per doc. Payee: Gentry County Recorder of Deeds. **Other phones:** Assessor-660-726-5289.

Greene County

Recorder of Deeds, 940 Boonville, Rm 100, Springfield, MO 65802. **Phone**-Recorder of Deeds, R/E & UCC Recording- 417-868-4068; fax-417-868-4807; hours 8AM-4:30PM www.greenecountymo.org

Will search UCC records. Information request only (per debtor) - $14.00. Search + copy request (w/10 pages of copies) - $28.00. Federal/state combined tax lien search- $1.00 per page. Will not search real estate records. UCC copy- $1.00 per page after 10 pages. Cert fee: $1.00 per cert. Payee: Greene County Recorder of Deeds. **Online Access to Assessor, Property, Deed, Lien, UCC, Recording, Death, Divorce records:** Search the assessor database for free at www.greenecountyassessor.org. Also, search the recorder database for free at www.greenecountymo.org/Recorder/search.php.

Search UCCs & tax liens at www.greenecountymo.org/Recorder/ucctaxsearch.php. Records for divorces that occurred 1837 to 1920 in County are free at http://userdb.rootsweb.com/divorces. **Other phones:** Assessor-417-868-4101; Treasurer-417-868-4051; Elections-417-868-4055.

Grundy County

Recorder of Deeds, PO Box 196, Trenton, MO 64683. **Phone**-Recorder of Deeds, R/E & UCC Recording- 660-359-5409; fax-660-359-6604; hours 8:30AM-4:30PM. UCC search per debtor- $14.00. Search + copy request (w/10 pages of copies)- $28.00. Will not search real estate or tax lien records. RE record copy- $.25 per page. UCC copy- $1.00 per page after 10 pages. Cert fee: $2.00 per cert. Payee: Grundy County Recorder of Deeds. **Other phones:** Assessor-660-359-2413; Treasurer-660-359-2171; Elections-660-359-6305.

Harrison County

Recorder of Deeds, PO Box 189, Bethany, MO 64424. **Phone**-Recorder of Deeds, R/E & UCC Recording- 660-425-6425; fax-660-425-3772; hours 8AM-Noon, 1-4:30PM

Current records are filed at the state office in Jefferson City www.sos.mo.gov/. Will not search records. UCC copy- $1.00 per page after 10 pages. Cert fee: $1.00 per cert. Payee: Harrison County Recorder of Deeds. **Other phones:** Assessor-660-425-2313; Treasurer-660-425-6442.

Henry County

Recorder of Deeds, 100 W. Franklin #4, Courthouse, Clinton, MO 64735. **Phone**-Recorder of Deeds, R/E & UCC Recording- 660-885-6963 x7209; fax-660-885-2264; hours 8:30AM-4:30PM

UCC search per debtor- $14.00. Search + copy request (w/10 pages of copies)- $28.00. Will not search real estate or tax lien records. Record copy- $1.00 per page after 10 pages. Cert fee: $.50 per page. Payee: Henry County Recorder of Deeds. **Other phones:** Assessor-660-885-6963 x7213; Treasurer-660-885-6963 x7208; Elections-660-885-6963 x7206.

Hickory County

Recorder of Deeds, PO Box 101, Hermitage, MO 65668. **Phone**-417-745-6421; fax-417-745-6670; hours 8AM-Noon, 12:30-4:30PM

UCC search per debtor- $14.00. Search + copy request (w/10 pages of copies)- $28.00. Will not search real estate or tax lien records. UCC copy- $1.00 per page after 10 pages. Cert fee: $1.00 per page. Payee: Hickory County Recorder of Deeds. **Other phones:** Assessor-417-745-6346; Treasurer-417-745-6310; Appraiser/ Auditor-417-745-6957; Elections-417-745-6450.

Holt County

Recorder of Deeds, PO Box 318, Oregon, MO 64473. **Phone**-Recorder of Deeds, R/E & UCC Recording- 660-446-3301; hours 8:30AM-Noon, 1-4:30PM

UCC search per debtor- $14.00. Search + copy request (w/10 pages of copies)- $28.00. UCC search includes tax liens if requested. Separate federal/state combined tax lien search- $4.00 per debtor. Will not search real estate records. Record copy- $1.00 per page after 10 pages. Cert fee: $1.00 per cert. Payee: Holt County Recorder of Deeds. **Other phones:** Assessor-660-446-3329; Treasurer-660-446-3397; Elections-660-446-3303.

Howard County

Recorder of Deeds, 1 Courthouse Sq, Fayette, MO 65248. **Phone**-Recorder of Deeds, R/E & UCC Recording- 660-248-2194; fax-660-248-1075; hours 8:30AM-4:30PM

UCC search per debtor- $15.00. Will not search tax liens. Real estate owner, mortgage, and property transfer searches available. RE record copy- $.25 per page. UCC copy- $1.00 per page after 10 pages. Cert fee: $3.00 per cert. Payee: Howard County Recorder of Deeds. **Other phones:** Assessor-660-248-3400; Treasurer-660-248-2196.

Howell County

Recorder of Deeds, PO Box 967, West Plains, MO 65775. **Phone**-417-256-3750; hours 8AM-4:30PM UCC search per debtor- $14.00. Search + copy request (w/10 pages of copies)- $28.00. Tax liens not included in UCC search. Tax lien search- $14.00 per debtor. Will not search real estate records. Record copy- $1.00 per page after 10 copies. Cert fee: $1.50 per cert. Payee: Howell County Recorder of Deeds. **Other phones:** Assessor-417-256-8284; Treasurer-417-256-4261.

Iron County

Recorder of Deeds, PO Box 24, Ironton, MO 63650. **Phone**-Recorder of Deeds, R/E & UCC Recording-573-546-2811; fax-573-546-2166; hours 8AM-4:30PM. UCC search per debtor- $14.00. Search + copy request (w/10 pages of copies)- $28.00. Will not search real estate or tax lien records. Record copy- $1.00 per page after 10 pages. Cert fee: $2.00 per cert. Payee: Iron County Recorder of Deeds. **Other phones:** Assessor-573-546-7319; Treasurer-573-546-7611; Elections-573-546-2912; Vital Records-573-546-2811.

Jackson County (Kansas City)

Recorder of Deeds, 415 E. 12th St, Rm 104, Kansas City, MO 64106. **Phone**-816-881-3192, R/E Recording-816-881-3048, UCC Recording-816-881-3048; fax-816-881-3719; hours 8AM-5PM www.co.jackson.mo.us
There is another office in Independence, which covers the eastern part of the county. However, it is not necessary to file there as the Kansas City office can search and record any UCC filings for the entire county. UCC search per debtor- $8.00. Search + copy request (w/10 pages of copies)- $16.00. Will not search tax liens. Real estate record owner searches available. RE record copy- $2.00 per page. UCC copy- $1.00 per page after 10 pages. Cert fee: $1.00 per cert. Payee: Jackson County Recorder of Deeds. **Online Access to Property, Tax Assessor, Recording, Marriages, Grantor/Grantee, Deed, Lien, Judgment, UCC records:** Records from the county tax assessor database are free at www.jacksongov.org/Tax/Choice.asp. Search the recorder Grantor/Grantee database for free at http://records.co.jackson.mo.us/search.asp?cabinet=opr. Search Kansas City land information for free at http://kivaweb.kcmo.org/kivanet/2/land/lookup/index.cfm?fa=dslladdr. Search the marriage records for free at http://records.co.jackson.mo.us/search.asp?cabinet=marriage. Search the UCC database at http://records.co.jackson.mo.us/search.asp?cabinet=ucc. **Other phones:** Assessor-816-881-3530; Treasurer-816-881-3232; Appraiser/ Auditor-816-881-3091; Elections-816-881-4820.

Jasper County

Recorder of Deeds, PO Box 387, Carthage, MO 64836-0387. **Phone**-417-358-0432, UCC Recording-417-358-0431; fax-417-359-12--; hours 8:30AM-4:30PM www.jaspercounty.org/recorder/
UCC search per debtor- $14.00. Search + copy request (w/10 pages of copies)- $28.00. Will not search real estate or tax lien records. RE record copy- $1.00 per page. UCC copy- $.50 per page after 10 pages. Cert fee: $1.00 per cert. Payee: Jasper County Recorder of Deeds. **Other phones:** Assessor-417-358-0437; Treasurer-417-358-0448.

Jefferson County

Recorder of Deeds, PO Box 100, Hillsboro, MO 63050. **Phone**-Recorder of Deeds, R/E & UCC Recording-636-797-5414, UCC Recording-636-797-5499; hours 8:00AM-5:00PM www.jeffcomo.org
UCC search per debtor- $14.00. Will not search real estate or tax lien records. UCC copy- $.50 per page. Payee: Jefferson County Recorder of Deeds. **Online Access to Real Estate, Recording, Judgment, Assessor, Property Tax records:** Land and judgment records are on subscription service, call 870-856-3055 for info. Also, search the assessor property data for free at www.jcao.org/myinfo.htm. **Other phones:** Assessor-636-797-5466; Treasurer-636-797-5368; Appraiser/ Auditor-636-797-5474; Elections-636-797-5486; Birth & Death Records-636-789-3372.

Johnson County

Recorder of Deeds, PO Box 32, Warrensburg, MO 64093. **Phone**-660-747-6811; hours 8:30AM-4:30PM UCC search per debtor- $14.00. Search + copy request (w/10 pages of copies)- $28.00. Will not search real estate or tax lien records. UCC copy- $1.00 per page after 10 pages. Cert fee: $2.25. Payee: County Recorder of Deeds. **Other phones:** Assessor-660-747-9822; Treasurer-660-747-7411.

Knox County

Recorder of Deeds, PO Box 116, Edina, MO 63537. **Phone**-660-397-2305; fax-660-397-3331; hours 8:30AM-12;00-1-4PM. UCC search per debtor- $14.00. Search + copy request (w/10 pages of copies)- $28.00. Will not search real estate or tax lien records. UCC copy- $1.00 per page after 10 pages. Cert fee: $1.50. Payee: Knox County Recorder of Deeds. **Other phones:** Assessor-660-397-2423; Treasurer-660-397-3364.

Laclede County

Recorder of Deeds, 200 N Adams, Lebanon, MO 65536-3046. **Phone**-Recorder of Deeds, R/E & UCC Recording- 417-532-4011; fax-417-532-3852; hours 8AM-4PM http://laclede.county.missouri.org/recorder/
Will search UCC records. UCC search per debtor- $14.00. Search + copy request (w/10 pages of copies)- $28.00. UCC search includes tax liens if requested. Separate federal/state combined tax lien search-no charge. Will not search real estate records. Record copy- $1.00 per page after 10 pages. Cert fee: $.50 per cert. Payee: Laclede County Recorder of Deeds. **Other phones:** Assessor-417-532-7163; Treasurer-417-532-4741; Appraiser/ Auditor-417-532-7163; Elections-417-532-5471; Vital Records-417-532-2134 (birth); 4011 (marriage); Collector-417-532-4301.

Lafayette County

Recorder of Deeds, PO Box 416, Lexington, MO 64067. **Phone**-660-259-6178; fax-660-259-2918; hours 8:30AM-4:30PM. UCC search per debtor- $14.00. Search + copy request (w/10 pages of copies)- $28.00. Will not search real estate or tax lien records. Record copy- $1.00 per page after 10 pages. Cert fee: $1.00 per cert. Payee: Lafayette County Recorder of Deeds. **Other phones:** Assessor-660-259-6158; Treasurer-660-259-3711.

Lawrence County

Recorder of Deeds, PO Box 449, Mount Vernon, MO 65712. **Phone**-Recorder of Deeds, R/E & UCC Recording- 417-466-2670; fax-417-466-4995; hours 9AM-Noon, 1-5PM
UCC search per debtor- $14.00. Search + copy request (w/10 pages of copies)- $28.00. Will not search tax liens. Will search real estate records if book and page number is provided. Record copy- $1.00 per page after 10 pages. Cert fee: $2.00 per doc. Payee: Lawrence County Recorder of Deeds.

Other phones: Assessor-417-466-2831; Treasurer-417-466-2662.

Lewis County

Recorder of Deeds, PO Box 97, Monticello, MO 63457-0097. **Phone**-573-767-5440; fax-573-767-5378; hours 8AM-Noon,1-4PM. UCC search per debtor- $14.00. Will not search real estate or tax lien records. UCC copy- $1.00 per page after 10 pages. Payee: Lewis County Recorder of Deeds. **Other phones:** Assessor-573-767-5209; Treasurer-573-767-5446; Elections-573-767-5205.

Lincoln County

Recorder of Deeds, 201 Main St, Troy, MO 63379. **Phone**-636-528-6300, R/E Recording-636-528-6300 or 528-0325; fax-636-528-2665; hours 8AM-4:30PM Will search UCC records. UCC search per debtor- $15.00 per name. Will not search real estate or tax lien records. Record copy- $.50 per page. Cert fee: $1.00 per cert. Payee: Lincoln County Recorder of Deeds. **Other phones:** Assessor-636-528-0320.

Linn County

Recorder of Deeds, PO Box 151, Linneus, MO 64653. **Phone**-660-895-5216, R/E Recording-660-895-5216/ Real Estate Records; fax-660-895-5379; hours 9AM-Noon, 1-4:30PM
UCC search per debtor- $14.00. Search + copy request (w/10 pages of copies)- $28.00. UCC search includes tax liens if requested. Separate federal/state combined tax lien search- no fee to search. Will not search real estate records. Record copy- $1.00 per page after 10 pages. Cert fee: $1.00 per doc. Payee: Linn County Recorder of Deeds. **Other phones:** Assessor-660-895-5387; Treasurer-660-895-5410; County Clerk-660-895-5417; Circuit Clerk-660-895-5215.

Livingston County

Recorder of Deeds, 700 Webster St, Courthouse, #6, Chillicothe, MO 64601. **Phone**-Recorder of Deeds, R/E & UCC Recording- 660-646-0166; hours 8:30AM-Noon, 1-4:30PM
UCC search per debtor- $14.00. Search + copy request (w/10 pages of copies)- $28.00. Will not search real estate or tax lien records. RE record copy- $1.00 per instrument. UCC copy- $1.00 per page after 10 pages. Cert fee: $2.00 per cert. Payee: Livingston County Recorder of Deeds. **Other phones:** Assessor-660-646-2027; Treasurer-660-646-3076; Elections-660-646-2293.

Macon County

Recorder of Deeds, PO Box 382, Macon, MO 63552. **Phone**-Recorder of Deeds, R/E & UCC Recording-660-385-2732; fax-660-385-4235; 8:30AM-4PM UCC search per debtor- $14.00. Will not search real estate or tax lien records. RE record copy- $.25 per page. UCC copy- $.50 per page after 10 pages. Cert fee: $2.00 per cert. Payee: Macon County Recorder of Deeds. **Other phones:** Assessor-660-385-2416; Treasurer-660-385-2713.

Madison County

Recorder of Deeds, PO Box 470, Fredericktown, MO 63645-0470. **Phone**-573-783-2102; fax-573-783-2715; hours 8AM-5PM. UCC search per debtor- $14.00. Will not search real estate or tax lien records. UCC copy- $.50 per page after 10 pages. Cert fee: $2.00 per cert. Payee: Madison County Recorder of Deeds. **Other phones:** Assessor-573-783-3325; Treasurer-573-783-3325.

Maries County

Recorder of Deeds, PO Box 213, Vienna, MO 65582. **Phone**-Recorder of Deeds, R/E & UCC Recording-573-422-3338; fax-573-422-3976; hours 8AM-4PM

UCC search per debtor- $14.00. Search + copy request (w/10 pages of copies)- $28.00. Tax liens not included in UCC search. Separate federal/state combined tax lien search- $14.00 per debtor. Will not search real estate records. UCC copy- $1.00 per page after 10 pages. Cert fee: $2.50 per cert. Payee: Maries County Recorder of Deeds. **Other phones:** Assessor-573-422-3540; Treasurer-573-422-3311; Elections-573-422-3388; Vital Records-573-422-3338; Collector-573-422-3343; Sheriff-573-422-3381.

Marion County

Recorder of Deeds, PO Box 392, Palmyra, MO 63461. **Phone**-573-769-2550; fax-573-769-6012; hours 8:30AM-5PM. UCC search per debtor- $14.00. Search + copy request (w/10 pages of copies)- $28.00. Will not search real estate or tax lien records. UCC copy- $.50 per page after 10 pages. Cert fee: $2.00 per cert. Payee: County Recorder of Deeds. **Other phones:** Assessor-573-248-1514; Treasurer-573-769-2552; Elections-573-729-2549.

McDonald County

Recorder of Deeds, PO Box 157, Pineville, MO 64856. **Phone**-Recorder of Deeds, R/E & UCC Recording-417-223-7523; fax-417-223-4125; hours 8AM-4PM Will not search records. UCC copy- $1.00 per page. Cert fee: $2.00 per doc. Payee: McDonald County Recorder of Deeds. **Other phones:** Assessor-417-223-4361; Treasurer-417-223-4462.

Mercer County

Recorder of Deeds, 802 E Main St, Princeton, MO 64673. **Phone**-660-748-4335; fax-660-748-4339; hours 8:30AM-Noon, 1-4:30PM UCC search per debtor- $14.00. Search + copy request (w/10 pages of copies)- $28.00. Tax liens not included in UCC search. Separate federal/state combined tax lien search- $14.00 per debtor. Will not search real estate records. UCC copy- $1.00 per page after 10 pages. Cert fee: $1.50. Payee: Mercer County Recorder of Deeds. **Other phones:** Assessor-660-748-3511; Treasurer-660-748-3435.

Miller County

Recorder of Deeds, PO Box 11, Tuscumbia, MO 65082. **Phone**-Recorder of Deeds, R/E & UCC Recording- 573-369-1935; fax-573-369-1939; hours 8:30AM-4:30PM
UCC search per debtor- $14.00. Search + copy request (w/10 pages of copies)- $28.00. Will not search real estate or tax lien records. Record copy- $.50 per page. Cert fee: $2.00 per cert; $.50 per page. **Other phones:** Assessor-573-369-1960; Treasurer-573-369-1920; Vital Records-573-751-6387.

Mississippi County

County Recorder, PO Box 369, Charleston, MO 63834. **Phone**-573-683-2146, R/E Recording-573-683-2146 x226; fax-573-683-7696; hours 8AM-5PM
UCC search per debtor- $14.00. Search + copy request (w/10 pages of copies)- $28.00. Will not search real estate or tax lien records. **Online Access to Real Estate Recording records:** Land records are at https://www.etitlesearch.com/services.asp. You can do a name search; choose from $200.00 monthly subscription or per click account. **Other phones:** Assessor-573-683-2146 x238; Treasurer-573-683-2146 x235; Elections-573-683-2146 x222.

Moniteau County

Circuit Clerk and Recorder, 200 E. Main St, California, MO 65018. **Phone**-573-796-2071, R/E Recording-573-796-4822, UCC Recording-573-796-4822; fax-573-796-2591; hours 8AM-4:30PM. UCC search per debtor- $14.00. Search + copy request (w/10 pages of copies)- $28.00. Will not search real estate or tax lien records. Cert fee: $1.00 per doc. Payee:

Recorder of Deeds. **Other phones:** Assessor-573-796-4637; Treasurer-573-796-4608; Elections-573-796-4661; Vital Records-573-796-4671.

Monroe County

Recorder of Deeds, PO Box 246, Paris, MO 65275. **Phone**-660-327-1131; fax-660-327-1130; hours 8AM-4:30PM
UCC search per debtor- $14.00. Search + copy request (w/10 pages of copies)- $28.00. UCC search includes tax liens. Tax lien search- $14.00 per search. Will not search real estate records. Copy fee is $.50 per page after 10 pages. Cert fee: $2.00 per doc. Payee: Monroe County Recorder. **Other phones:** Assessor-660-327-5607; Treasurer-660-327-4711; Elections-660-327-5106.

Montgomery County

Recorder of Deeds, 211 E. 3rd St, Montgomery City, MO 63361. **Phone**-Recorder of Deeds, R/E & UCC Recording- 573-564-3157; hours 8AM-4:30PM
UCC search per debtor- $14.00. Search + copy request (w/10 pages of copies)- $28.00. Will not search real estate or tax lien records. Record copy- $1.00 per page. Payee: Montgomery County Recorder. **Online Access to Death records:** Access to unofficial death records up to 1994 are free from a private company at www.ancestry.com/ancestry/search/3074.htm. **Other phones:** Assessor-573-564-2445; Treasurer-573-564-2319; Elections-573-564-3357.

Morgan County

County Recorder, 100 E. Newton St, Courthouse, Versailles, MO 65084. **Phone**-County Recorder, R/E & UCC Recording- 573-378-4029; fax-573-378-6431; hours 8AM-4:30PM. UCC search per debtor- $14.00. Search + copy request (w/10 pages of copies)- $28.00. Will not search real estate or tax lien records. RE record copy- $.50 per page. UCC copy fee is $.50 per page after 10 pages. Cert fee: $.50 per page. Payee: Morgan County Recorder. **Other phones:** Assessor-573-378-5459; Treasurer-573-378-4404; Elections-573-378-5436.

New Madrid County

Recorder of Deeds, PO Box 217, New Madrid, MO 63869. **Phone**-573-748-5146; hours 8:30AM-Noon, 1-4:30PM. UCC search per debtor- $14.00. Search + copy request (w/10 pages of copies)- $28.00. Tax liens not included in UCC search. Separate federal/state combined tax lien search- $14.00 per debtor. Will not search real estate records. RE record copy- $2.00 1st page, $1.00 each add'l. UCC copy- $.50 per page after 10 pages. Cert fee: $1.00. Payee: New Madrid County Recorder of Deeds. **Online Access to Real Estate Recording records:** Land records are at https://www.etitlesearch.com/services.asp. You can do a name search; choose from $200.00 monthly subscription or per click account. **Other phones:** Assessor-573-748-2387.

Newton County

Recorder of Deeds, PO Box 604, Neosho, MO 64850-0130. **Phone**-417-451-8224, R/E Recording-417-451-8224 or 8225, UCC Recording-417-451-8225; fax-417-451-8273; hours 8:30AM-5PM www.ncrecorder.org
UCC search per debtor- $14.00. Search + copy request (w/10 pages of copies)- $28.00. Will not search real estate or tax lien records. RE record copy- $1.00 per page. UCC copy- included in search fee up to 10 pages. Cert fee: $2.00 1st page. Payee: Recorder of Deeds. **Online Access to Deed, Mortgage, UCC, Lien, Vital Statistic records:** Access to the Recorder's database requires a $200 sign-up fee; images go back to 1999; index to 1994. **Other phones:** Assessor-417-451-8228 or 8218; Treasurer-417-451-8226; Elections-417-451-8220; Vital Records-

573-751-6387; Health Dept (Birth & Death)-417-451-3743; Mapping-417-451-8229.

Nodaway County

Recorder of Deeds, 305 N. Main, Rm 104, Maryville, MO 64468. **Phone**-660-582-5711; fax-660-582-5282; hours 8;30AM-4;30PM
UCC search per debtor- $15.00. Search + copy request (w/10 pages of copies)- $29.00. Tax liens not included in UCC search. Federal/state combined tax lien search- $15.00 Will not search real estate records. UCC copy- $1.00 per page. Cert fee: $5.00. Payee: Recorder of Deeds. **Other phones:** Assessor-660-582-3372.

Oregon County

Recorder of Deeds, PO Box 406, Alton, MO 65606. **Phone**-Recorder of Deeds, R/E & UCC Recording-417-778-7460; fax-417-778-7206; 8:00AM-4:00PM
UCC search per debtor- $14.00. Search + copy request (w/10 pages of copies)- $28.00. Will not search real estate or tax lien records. RE record copy- $.25 per page. Cert fee: $1.00 per instrument. Payee: Recorder of deeds. **Other phones:** Assessor-417-778-7471; Treasurer-417-778-6303; Elections-417-778-7475.

Osage County

Recorder of Deeds, PO Box 825, Linn, MO 65051-0825. **Phone**-Recorder of Deeds, R/E & UCC Recording- 573-897-3114; fax-573-897-4075; hours 8AM-4:30PM
UCC search per debtor- $14.00. Search + copy request (w/10 pages of copies)- $28.00. UCC search includes tax liens if requested. Will not search real estate records. Record copy- $.50 per page. Cert fee: $2.00 per cert. Payee: Osage County Recorder of Deeds. **Other phones:** Assessor-573-897-2217; Treasurer-573-897-3095; Elections-573-897-2139; Vital Records-573-751-6001.

Ozark County

Circuit Clerk & Recorder, PO Box 36, Gainesville, MO 65655. **Phone**-Circuit Clerk & Recorder, R/E & UCC Recording- 417-679-4232; fax-417-679-4554; hours 8AM-Noon 12:30PM-4:30PM
UCC search per debtor- $14.00. Search + copy request (w/10 pages of copies)- $28.00. Tax liens not included in UCC search. Will not search real estate records. Copy fee is $.50 per page after 10 pages. **Other phones:** Assessor-417-679-4705; Treasurer-417-679-3553; Elections-417-679-3516.

Pemiscot County

Recorder of Deeds, 610 Ward Ave, #1A, Pemiscot County Courthouse, Caruthersville, MO 63830. **Phone**-Recorder of Deeds, R/E & UCC Recording- 573-333-2204; hours 8:30AM-4:30PM
UCC search per debtor- $14.00. Search + copy request (w/10 pages of copies)- $28.00. UCC search includes tax liens if requested. Separate federal/state combined tax lien search- $14.00 per debtor. Will not search real estate records. RE record copy- $1.00 per page. Search includes 1st 10 pages, then copy fee- $.50 per page. Payee: County Recorder of Deeds. **Online Access to Real Estate Recording records:** Land records are at https://www.etitlesearch.com/services.asp. You can do a name search; choose from $200.00 monthly subscription or per click account. **Other phones:** Assessor-573-333-1390; Treasurer-573-333-4171.

Perry County

Recorder of Deeds, 15 W. Ste. Marie St, #1, Perryville, MO 63775. **Phone**-Recorder of Deeds, R/E & UCC Recording- 573-547-1611; fax-573-547-3879; hours 8AM-5PM. UCC search per debtor- $14.00. Search + copy request (w/10 pages of copies)- $28.00.

Will not search real estate records. RE record copy-$2.00 1st page; $1.00 each add'l. UCC copy fee after 1st 10 pages is $.50 per page. Cert fee: $1.00 per doc. Payee: Perry County recorder. **Other phones:** Assessor-573-547-5211; Treasurer-573-547-4502; Elections-573-547-4242.

Pettis County

Recorder of Deeds, 415 S. Ohio, Sedalia, MO 65301. **Phone-**Recorder of Deeds, R/E & UCC Recording-660-826-1136; fax-660-829-4479; 8:00AM-5:00PM UCC search per debtor- $14.00. Tax liens not included in UCC search. Will not search real estate records. UCC copy- $1.00 per page. Cert fee: $1.00 per doc. Payee: Recorder of Deeds. **Other phones:** Assessor-660-827-0023; Treasurer-660-827-0486; Elections-660-826-5395; Vital Records-660-826-1136.

Phelps County

Recorder of Deeds, 200 N Main, Courthouse, Rolla, MO 65401. **Phone-**573-364-1891, R/E Recording-573-364-1891 x210/206, UCC Recording-573-364-1891 x210/206; fax-573-364-1419; hours 8AM-5PM www.phelpscounty.org/cthouse.html UCC search per debtor- $14.00. Search + copy request (w/10 pages of copies)- $28.00. UCC search includes tax liens if requested. Will not search real estate records. RE record copy- $1.00 per page. Cert fee: $2.00 per page. Payee: County Recorder. **Other phones:** Assessor-573-364-1891 x140; Treasurer-573-364-1891 x130; Elections-573-364-1891 x100; Vital Records-573-364-1891 x490.

Pike County

Recorder of Deeds, 115 W. Main St, Bowling Green, MO 63334. **Phone-**573-324-5567; hours 8AM-4:30PM. UCC search per debtor- $14.00. Search + copy request (w/10 pages of copies)- $28.00. Tax liens not included in UCC search. Will search tax liens. Will not search real estate records. Record copy- $1.00 per page after 10 pages. Cert fee: $1.00 per cert. Payee: Pike County Recorder of Deeds. **Other phones:** Assessor-573-324-3261; Treasurer-573-324-3281; Appraiser/ Auditor-636-528-5180; Elections-573-324-2412.

Platte County

Chief Deputy, 415 3rd St, #70, Platte City, MO 64079. **Phone-**816-858-3323, R/E Recording-816-858-3326, UCC Recording-816-858-3320; fax-816-858-2379; hours 8AM-5PM www.co.platte.mo.us/recorder.html UCC search per debtor- $14.00. Search + copy request (w/10 pages of copies)- $28.00. Will not search real estate or tax lien records. RE record - $1.00 per page. UCC copy- $1.00 per page after 10 pages. Cert fee: $1.00 per doc. Payee: Recorder of Deeds. **Other phones:** Assessor-816-858-3301; Treasurer-816-858-3318; Elections-816-858-4400.

Polk County

Recorder of Deeds, 102 E. Broadway, Courthouse, Bolivar, MO 65613-1502. **Phone-**Recorder of Deeds, R/E & UCC Recording- 417-326-4924; fax-417-326-6898; hours 8AM-5PM. UCC search per debtor- $14.00 per search. Tax liens not included in UCC search. Separate federal & state combined tax lien search- $1.00 per page. Will not search real estate records. RE record copy- $1.00 per page. Cert fee: $2.00 per doc. Payee: Recorder. **Other phones:** Assessor-417-326-4643; Treasurer-417-326-4913; Appraiser/ Auditor-417-326-4346; Elections-417-326-4031; Vital Records-417-326-4031.

Pulaski County

Recorder of Deeds, 301 Historic Route 66 E., Courthouse #202, Waynesville, MO 65583. **Phone-**573-774-4760; fax-573-774-6967; 8AM-4:30PM

UCC search per debtor- $14.00. Search + copy request (w/10 pages of copies)- $28.00. Will not search real estate or tax lien records. UCC copy-$1.00 per page after 10 pages. Cert fee: $5.00. Payee: Pulaski County Recorder of Deeds. **Other phones:** Assessor-573-774-6609 x117; Treasurer-573-774-6609 x124.

Putnam County

Recorder of Deeds, Courthouse, Rm 202, Unionville, MO 63565-1659. **Phone-**660-947-2071; fax-660-947-2320; hours 8AM-N, 1-5PM

If you contact them with a book and page they can make a copy of that doc for $1.00 per page. Must be prepaid. Will not search records. UCC copy- $14.00 for copy request/info filed. Cert fee: $1.00 per doc. Payee: Rutnam County Recorder. **Other phones:** Assessor-660-947-3900; Treasurer-660-947-2095; Elections-660-947-2674.

Ralls County

Recorder of Deeds, PO Box 444, New London, MO 63459-0444. **Phone-**Recorder of Deeds, R/E & UCC Recording- 573-985-5631; hours 8:30AM-Noon, 1-4:30PM. UCC search per debtor- $14.00. Search + copy request (w/10 pages of copies)- $28.00. Will not search tax liens. Separate federal/state combined tax lien search- $1.00 per debtor. Will not search real estate records. Record copy- $1.00 per page after 10 pages. Cert fee: $1.00 per cert. Payee: Ralls County Recorder of Deeds. **Other phones:** Assessor-573-985-5671; Treasurer-573-985-7151.

Randolph County

Recorder of Deeds, 110 S. Main St., Courthouse, Huntsville, MO 65259. **Phone-**Recorder of Deeds, R/E & UCC Recording- 660-277-4718; fax-660-277-3246; hours 8AM-4PM

UCC search per debtor- $14.00. Search + copy request (w/10 pages of copies)- $28.00. Will not search real estate or tax lien records. Record copy fee- $2.00 1st page; $1 each add'l. UCC copy-$2.00 1st page; $1 each add'l. Cert fee: $1.00 per page. Payee: Recorder of Deeds. **Other phones:** Assessor-660-277-4716; Treasurer-660-277-4714; Elections-660-277-4717.

Ray County

Recorder of Deeds, PO Box 167, Richmond, MO 64085. **Phone-**816-776-4500; 8AM-Noon, 1-4PM UCC search per debtor- $14.00. Search + copy request (w/10 pages of copies)- $28.00. Will not search real estate or tax lien records. UCC copy-$1.00 per page after 10 pages. Cert fee: $1.00 per page. Payee: Ray County Recorder of Deeds. **Other phones:** Assessor-660-776-2676; Treasurer-660-776-6140.

Reynolds County

Recorder of Deeds, PO Box 76, Centerville, MO 63633-0076. **Phone-**573-648-2494; fax-573-648-2503; hours 8AM-4PM

UCC search per debtor- $14.00. Search + copy request (w/10 pages of copies)- $28.00. Will not search real estate or tax lien records. RE record copy- $2.00 per doc. UCC copy- $1.00 per doc. Cert fee: $4.00 per doc. Payee: Reynolds County Recorder. **Other phones:** Assessor-573-648-2494 x18; Treasurer-573-648-2494 x37; Elections-573-648-2494 x12; Vital Records-573-648-2494 x12.

Ripley County

Recorder of Deeds, 100 Courthouse Sq, #3, Doniphan, MO 63935. **Phone-**573-996-2818; fax-573-966-5014. UCC search per debtor- $14.00. Search + copy request (w/10 pages of copies)- $28.00. Will not

search real estate records. **Other phones:** Assessor-573-996-7113.

Saline County

Recorder of Deeds, Courthouse, Rm 206, Marshall, MO 65340. **Phone-**Recorder of Deeds, R/E & UCC Recording- 660-886-2677; fax-660-886-2603; hours 8AM-4:30PM. UCC search per debtor- $14.00. Search + copy request (w/10 pages of copies)- $28.00. Will not search real estate or tax lien records. UCC copy- $,50 per page after 10 pages. **Other phones:** Assessor-660-335-3111; Treasurer-660-886-3636; Elections-660-886-3331; Vital Records-660-886-3434.

Schuyler County

Recorder of Deeds, PO Box 186, Lancaster, MO 63548. **Phone-**660-457-3784; fax-660-457-3016; hours 8AM-4PM

UCC search per debtor- $15.00. Search + copy request (w/10 pages of copies)- $30.00. Will search tax liens. Will not search real estate records. Record copy- $1.00 per page. Cert fee: $1.00 per doc. Payee: Recorder of Deeds. **Other phones:** Assessor-660-457-3211; Treasurer-660-457-3825.

Scotland County

Recorder of Deeds, 117 S. Market St, #106, Memphis, MO 63555-1449. **Phone-**Recorder of Deeds, R/E & UCC Recording- 660-465-8605; fax-660-465-8673; hours 8AM-4PM. UCC search per debtor- $14.00. Search + copy request (w/10 pages of copies)-$14.00. UCC search includes tax liens if requested. Separate federal/state combined tax lien search-$14.00 per debtor. Will not search real estate records. RE record copy- $1.00 per page. UCC copy- $.50 per page after 10 pages. Cert fee: $1.50 per cert. Payee: Scotland County Recorder of Deeds. **Other phones:** Assessor-660-465-2269; Treasurer-660-465-2529.

Scott County

Recorder of Deeds, PO Box 78, Benton, MO 63736. **Phone-**573-545-3551; hours 8:30AM-5PM UCC search per debtor- $14.00. Search + copy request (w/10 pages of copies)- $28.00. Will not search real estate or tax lien records. RE record copy- $2.00 1st page, $1.00 each add'l. UCC copy- $1.00 per page after 10 pages. Cert fee: $2.00 per cert 1st. Page $1.00 add'l. Payee: Scott County Recorder of Deeds. **Online Access to Real Estate Recording records:**. **Other phones:** Assessor-573-545-3535; Treasurer-573-545-3543.

Shannon County

Recorder of Deeds, PO Box 148, Eminence, MO 65466. **Phone-**573-226-3315; fax-573-226-5321; hours 8AM-12;00-12;30-4;30PM

UCC search per debtor- $14.00. Search + copy request (w/10 pages of copies)- $28.00. Federal/state combined tax lien search- $varies Will not search real estate records. UCC copy- $.25 per page. Cert fee: $2.25. Payee: Shannon County Recorder of Deeds. **Other phones:** Assessor-573-226-5539; Treasurer-573-226-3614.

Shelby County

Recorder of Deeds, PO Box 176, Shelbyville, MO 63469. **Phone-**Recorder of Deeds, R/E & UCC Recording- 573-633-2151; fax-573-633-1004; hours 8AM-4:30PM

UCC search per debtor- $14.00. Search + copy request (w/10 pages of copies)- $28.00. Will not search real estate or tax lien records. RE record copy- $1.00 per page. UCC copy- $1.00 Per UCC. Cert fee: $3.00 per page. Payee: Shelby Co. Recorder. **Other phones:** Assessor-573-633-2521; Treasurer-573-633-2574; Elections-573-633-2187.

St. Charles County

Recorder of Deeds, PO Box 99, St. Charles, MO 63302-0099. **Phone**-Recorder of Deeds, R/E & UCC Recording- 636-949-7505, UCC Recording-636-949-7508; fax-636-949-7512; hours 8AM-5PM www.saintcharlescounty.org
UCC search per debtor- $8.00. Search + copy request (w/10 pages of copies)- $16.00. Will not search real estate or tax lien records. Plain paper record copy fee- $2.00 1st page, $1.00 each add'l. UCC copy- $.50 per page after 1st 10. Cert fee: $1.00 per cert. Payee: St. Charles County Recorder of Deeds. **Online Access to Assessor, Property records:** county Property Assessment data is free at www.win.org/library/library_office/assessment. No name searching; search by address, street or map ID. **Other phones:** Assessor-636-949-7425; Appraiser/Auditor-636-949-7431; Elections-636-949-7550; Vital Records-636-949-7558.

St. Clair County

Recorder of Deeds, PO Box 323, Osceola, MO 64776-0493. **Phone**-417-646-2950; hours 8AM-4:30PM
Will search UCC records back 5 years. Search per doc- $14.00. Tax liens not included in UCC search. Tax lien search- $5.00 per doc. Will search real estate records. Record copy- $1.00 per page. Cert fee: $1.00 per certification. Payee: St. Clair Recorder. **Other phones:** Assessor-417-646-2449; Treasurer-417-646-8068.

St. Francois County

Recorder of Deeds, Courthouse, Farmington, MO 63640. **Phone**-573-756-2323; hours 8AM-4PM
UCC search per debtor- $14.00. Search + copy request (w/10 pages of copies)- $28.00. Will not search tax liens. Real estate record owner searches available. RE record copy- $1.00 per page. UCC copy- $.50 per page after 10 pages. Cert fee: $1.00 per cert. Payee: St. Francois County Recorder of Deeds. **Other phones:** Assessor-573-756-2509; Treasurer-573-756-3349.

St. Genevieve County

Recorder of Deeds, 55 S.3rd St. RM 3, Court House, Ste. Genevieve, MO 63670. **Phone**-573-883-2706; fax-573-883-5312; hours 8AM-4;30PM
UCC search per debtor- $14.00. Search + copy request (w/10 pages of copies)- $28.00. Will not search real estate or tax lien records. UCC copy- $.50 per page. Cert fee: $2.00. Payee: Recorder of Deeds. **Other phones:** Assessor-573-883-2333.

St. Louis City

Recorder of Deeds, Tucker & Market Sts, City Hall, Rm 127, St. Louis, MO 63103. **Phone**-314-622-4328; fax-314-622-4175. UCC search per debtor- $8.00. Search + copy request (w/10 pages of copies)- $16.00. Will not search real estate records. UCC copy- $3.00 1st page; $2.00 each add'l. Cert fee: $2.00 per cert. **Online Access to Property records:** Access to real estate records is via a private company at https://www.landrecords.net/. Subscription or pay-per search service available. **Other phones:** Assessor-314-615-5124; Treasurer-314-622-2062.

St. Louis County

Recorder of Deeds, 41 S. Central Ave, 4th Fl, Clayton, MO 63105. **Phone**-Recorder of Deeds, R/E & UCC Recording- 314-615-2500; fax-314-615-4964; hours 8AM-5PM. UCC search per debtor- $8.00. Search + copy request (w/10 pages of copies)- $16.00. Will not search real estate records. UCC copy- $.50 per page after 10 pages. Cert fee: $1.00 per cert.

Payee: St. Louis County Recorder of Deeds. **Other phones:** Assessor-314-615-4225; Vital Records-314-615-1684.

Stoddard County

Recorder of Deeds, PO Box 217, Bloomfield, MO 63825-0217. **Phone**-Recorder of Deeds, R/E & UCC Recording- 573-568-3444; fax-573-568-2545.
UCC search per debtor- $14.00. Search + copy request (w/10 pages of copies)- $28.00. Tax lien search- $14.00 per debtor. Will not search real estate records. RE record copy- $.50 per page. UCC copy- $.50 per page after 10 pages. Cert fee: $1.00 per doc. Payee: Recorder of Deeds. **Other phones:** Assessor-573-568-3163; Treasurer-573-568-3327.

Stone County

Recorder of Deeds, PO Box 18, Galena, MO 65656. **Phone**-Recorder of Deeds, R/E & UCC Recording- 417-357-6362; fax-417-357-8131; 8:00AM-4:00PM
UCC search per debtor- $14.00. Search + copy request (w/10 pages of copies)- $28.00. Will not search real estate or tax lien records. RE record copy- $2.00 per page. UCC copy- $.25 per page. Cert fee: $1.00 per doc. Payee: Stone County Recorder. **Other phones:** Assessor-417-357-6141; Treasurer-417-357-6131; Elections-417-357-6127.

Sullivan County

Recorder of Deeds, Courthouse, Milan, MO 63556. **Phone**-660-265-3630; fax-660-265-5071; hours 9AM-Noon; 1PM-4:30PM. UCC search per debtor-$14.00. Will not search real estate records. Copy fee- $1.00 per page. Cert fee: $1.00 per doc. Payee: Recorder of Deeds. **Other phones:** Assessor-660-265-4474; Treasurer-660-265-4514.

Taney County

Recorder of Deeds, PO Box 428, Forsyth, MO 65653. **Phone**-Recorder of Deeds, R/E & UCC Recording-417-546-7234, UCC Recording-417-546-7235; hours 8AM-5PM www.co.taney.mo.us
UCC search per debtor- $14.00. Search + copy request (w/10 pages of copies)- $28.00. UCC searches do not include tax lien searches. Separate federal/state combined tax lien search- $4.00 per debtor. Will not search real estate records. RE record copy- $1.00 per page. UCC copy- $.50 per page after 10 pages. Cert fee: $1.50 per cert. Payee: Taney County Recorder of Deeds. **Online Access to Property records:** Access to property information is from a private company at https://www.landrecords.net. You may subscribe or search using credit card payment per search. Index goes back to 6/1994; images back to 1/2003. **Other phones:** Assessor-417-546-7240; Treasurer-417-546-7207.

Texas County

Recorder of Deeds, PO Box 287, Houston, MO 65483. **Phone**-417-967-3742; fax-417-967-4220. Will not search UCC or real estate records. UCC copy- $1.00 per page. Cert fee: $3.00. Payee: Recorder of Deeds. **Other phones:** Assessor-417-967-4709; Treasurer-417-967-2589.

Vernon County

Recorder of Deeds, 100 W. Cherry, Courthouse, Nevada, MO 64772. **Phone**-Recorder of Deeds, R/E & UCC Recording- 417-448-2520; fax-417-448-2524; hours 8:30AM-Noon, 1-4:30PM
UCC search per debtor- $14.00. Search + copy request (w/10 pages of copies)- $28.00. Will not search real estate or tax lien records. Record copy- $1.00 per page after 10 pages. Cert fee: $1.00 per cert. Payee: Vernon County Recorder of Deeds.

Other phones: Assessor-417-448-2530; Treasurer-417-448-2510; Elections-417-448-2500.

Warren County

Recorder of Deeds, 104 W Boone's Lick Rd., Warrenton, MO 63383. **Phone**-636-456-9800; hours 8AM-4:30PM
UCC search per debtor- $14.00. Search + copy request (w/10 pages of copies)- $28.00. Will not search real estate or tax lien records. RE record copy- $1.00 per page. UCC copy- $.50 per page after 10 pages. Cert fee: $1.00 per page + $1.00 per cert. Payee: Warren County Recorder of Deeds. **Other phones:** Assessor-636-456-8885; Treasurer-636-456-3389.

Washington County

Recorder of Deeds, 102 N. Missouri St., Potosi, MO 63664. **Phone**-Recorder of Deeds, R/E & UCC Recording- 573-438-5023; fax-573-438-7900; hours 8AM-4:30PM
UCC search per debtor- $14.00. Search + copy request (w/10 pages of copies)- $28.00. Federal/state combined tax lien search- $1.00 per page. Will not search real estate records. RE record copy- $.50 per page. UCC copy- $1.00 per page. Cert fee: $2.00 for cert. & $.50 per page. Payee: Recorder of Deeds. **Other phones:** Assessor-573-438-4992; Treasurer-573-438-2031; Elections-573-438-4901; Real Estate-573-438-2237.

Wayne County

Recorder of Deeds, PO Box 78, Greenville, MO 63944. **Phone**-573-224-3041; fax-573-224-3015; hours 8:30AM-Noon; 1:00PM-4:30PM
UCC search per debtor- $14.00. Search + copy request (w/10 pages of copies)- $28.00. Will not search real estate or tax lien records. Copy fee- $.50 per page. Cert fee: $2.00 per page. Payee: Recorder of Deeds. **Other phones:** Assessor-573-224-3006; Treasurer-573-224-3011.

Webster County

Recorder of Deeds, PO Box 546, Marshfield, MO 65706. **Phone**-Recorder of Deeds, R/E & UCC Recording- 417-859-5882; fax-417-468-3843; hours 8AM-5PM. UCC search per debtor- $14.00. Search + copy request (w/10 pages of copies)- $28.00. Will not search real estate or tax lien records. Cert fee: $1.00 per doc. **Other phones:** Assessor-417-859-2169; Treasurer-417-468-2108; Elections-417-859-8683.

Worth County

Recorder of Deeds, PO Box 14, Grant City, MO 64456. **Phone**-660-564-2484; fax-660-564-2432; 8AM-4PM
UCC search per debtor- $14.00. Search + copy request (w/10 pages of copies)- $28.00. UCC copy- $1.00 per page. Cert fee: None. Payee: Worth County Recorder of Deeds. **Other phones:** Assessor-660-564-2153; Treasurer-660-564-2154.

Wright County

County Recorder, PO Box 39, Hartville, MO 65667. **Phone**-County Recorder, R/E & UCC Recording- 417-741-7322; fax-417-741-7504; hours 8AM-4:30PM
UCC search per debtor- $14.00. Search + copy request (w/10 pages of copies)- $28.00. Will not search real estate or tax lien records. Cert fee: $2.00 per doc. Payee: Wright County Recorder. **Other phones:** Assessor-417-741-6400; Treasurer-417-741-7225; Elections-417-741-6661; Vital Records-573-751-6400.

Missouri County Locator

You will usually be able to find the city name in the City/County Cross Reference below. In that case, it is a simple matter to determine the county from the cross reference. However, only the official US Postal Service city names are included in this index. There are an additional 40,000 place names that people use in their addresses. Therefore, we have also included a ZIP/City Cross Reference immediately following the City/County Cross Reference.

If you know the ZIP Code but the city name does not appear in the City/County Cross Reference index, look up the ZIP Code in the ZIP/City Cross Reference, find the city name, then look up the city name in the City/County Cross Reference. For example, you want to know the county for an address of Menands, NY 12204. There is no "Menands" in the City/County Cross Reference. The ZIP/City Cross Reference shows that ZIP Codes 12201-12288 are for the city of Albany. Looking back in the City/County Cross Reference, Albany is in Albany County.

Missouri City/County Cross Reference

ADRIAN Bates
ADVANCE (63730) Stoddard(78), Cape Girardeau(16), Bollinger(5)
AGENCY Buchanan
ALBA Jasper
ALBANY Gentry
ALDRICH (65601) Polk(70), Dade(28), Cedar(1)
ALEXANDRIA Clark
ALLENDALE Worth
ALLENTON St. Louis
ALMA Lafayette
ALTAMONT Daviess
ALTENBURG (63732) Cape Girardeau(95), Perry(4)
ALTON Oregon
AMAZONIA Andrew
AMITY De Kalb
AMORET Bates
AMSTERDAM Bates
ANABEL Macon
ANDERSON McDonald
ANNADA Pike
ANNAPOLIS (63620) Iron(56), Madison(32), Reynolds(10)
ANNISTON Mississippi
APPLETON CITY (64724) St. Clair(93), Bates(6)
ARBELA (63432) Scotland(88), Clark(11)
ARBYRD Dunklin
ARCADIA (63621) Iron(79), Madison(20)
ARCHIE Cass
ARCOLA (65603) Dade(97), Cedar(2)
ARGYLE (65001) Osage(61), Maries(38)
ARMSTRONG (65230) Howard(86), Randolph(13)
ARNOLD Jefferson
ARROW ROCK Saline
ASBURY (64832) Barton(83), Jasper(16)
ASH GROVE (65604) Greene(65), Lawrence(32), Dade(1)
ASHBURN Pike
ASHLAND Boone
ATLANTA Macon
AUGUSTA St. Charles
AURORA (65605) Lawrence(90), Barry(9)
AUXVASSE (65231) Callaway(98), Audrain(1)
AVA (65608) Douglas(90), Taney(9)
AVALON Livingston
AVILLA Jasper
BAKERSFIELD (65609) Ozark(77), Howell(22)
BALLWIN St. Louis
BARING (63531) Knox(59), Scotland(40)
BARNARD Nodaway
BARNETT (65011) Morgan(94), Moniteau(5)
BARNHART Jefferson
BATES CITY (64011) Lafayette(92), Johnson(7)
BEAUFORT Franklin
BELGRADE Washington
BELL CITY (63735) Stoddard(91), Scott(8)
BELLE (65013) Maries(68), Osage(31)

BELLEVIEW (63623) Iron(97), Reynolds(2)
BELLFLOWER (63333) Montgomery(96), Lincoln(3)
BELTON Cass
BENDAVIS Texas
BENTON Scott
BENTON CITY Audrain
BERGER Franklin
BERNIE (63822) Stoddard(95), Dunklin(4)
BERTRAND (63823) Mississippi(90), Scott(9)
BETHANY Harrison
BETHEL Shelby
BEULAH (65436) Phelps(87), Texas(8), Pulaski(3)
BEVIER Macon
BILLINGS (65610) Christian(95), Lawrence(3)
BIRCH TREE (65438) Shannon(74), Oregon(25)
BISMARCK (63624) St. Francois(70), Washington(25), Iron(4)
BIXBY Iron
BLACK (63625) Reynolds(89), Iron(10)
BLACKBURN (65321) Saline(61), Lafayette(38)
BLACKWATER Cooper
BLACKWELL (63626) Washington(80), St. Francois(19)
BLAIRSTOWN Henry
BLAND (65014) Gasconade(68), Osage(25), Maries(6)
BLODGETT Scott
BLOOMFIELD Stoddard
BLOOMSDALE (63627) Ste. Genevieve(90), Jefferson(9)
BLUE EYE (65611) Stone(95), Taney(4)
BLUE SPRINGS Jackson
BLYTHEDALE Harrison
BOGARD Carroll
BOIS D ARC (65612) Greene(93), Lawrence(6)
BOLCKOW (64427) Andrew(83), Nodaway(16)
BOLIVAR Polk
BONNE TERRE (63628) St. Francois(94), Ste. Genevieve(2), Washington(2)
BONNOTS MILL Osage
BOONVILLE Cooper
BOSS (65440) Dent(59), Reynolds(31), Iron(9)
BOSWORTH Carroll
BOURBON (65441) Crawford(95), Washington(3)
BOWLING GREEN (63334) Pike(98), Lincoln(1)
BRADLEYVILLE (65614) Taney(90), Christian(9)
BRAGG CITY Pemiscot
BRAGGADOCIO Pemiscot
BRANDSVILLE Howell
BRANSON (65616) Taney(93), Stone(6)
BRANSON Taney
BRASHEAR Adair

BRAYMER (64624) Caldwell(69), Carroll(14), Ray(12), Livingston(3)
BRAZEAU Perry
BRECKENRIDGE (64625) Caldwell(82), Livingston(9), Daviess(8)
BRIAR Ripley
BRIDGETON St. Louis
BRIGHTON Polk
BRINKTOWN Maries
BRIXEY Ozark
BRONAUGH (64728) Vernon(73), Barton(26)
BROOKFIELD (64628) Linn(96), Chariton(3)
BROOKLINE STATION Greene
BROSELEY Butler
BROWNING (64630) Linn(64), Sullivan(35)
BROWNWOOD Stoddard
BRUMLEY Miller
BRUNER (65620) Christian(98), Douglas(1)
BRUNSWICK Chariton
BUCKLIN (64631) Linn(79), Macon(20)
BUCKNER Jackson
BUCYRUS Texas
BUFFALO (65622) Dallas(97), Polk(2)
BUNCETON Cooper
BUNKER (63629) Reynolds(66), Dent(25), Shannon(7)
BURFORDVILLE Cape Girardeau
BURLINGTON JUNCTION Nodaway
BUTLER Bates
BUTTERFIELD Barry
CABOOL (65689) Howell(72), Texas(25), Douglas(2)
CADET Washington
CAINSVILLE (64632) Harrison(70), Mercer(29)
CAIRO Randolph
CALEDONIA Washington
CALHOUN Henry
CALIFORNIA (65018) Moniteau(96), Cooper(3)
CALLAO Macon
CAMDEN Ray
CAMDEN POINT Platte
CAMDENTON Camden
CAMERON (64429) Clinton(68), De Kalb(29), Daviess(1)
CAMPBELL Dunklin
CANALOU New Madrid
CANTON (63435) Lewis(94), Clark(5)
CAPE FAIR (65624) Stone(95), Barry(3)
CAPE GIRARDEAU Cape Girardeau
CAPLINGER MILLS Cedar
CARDWELL Dunklin
CARL JUNCTION Jasper
CARTERVILLE Jasper
CARTHAGE Jasper
CARUTHERSVILLE Pemiscot
CASCADE Wayne
CASSVILLE Barry
CATAWISSA (63015) Franklin(75), Jefferson(24)
CATRON New Madrid
CAULFIELD (65626) Howell(66), Ozark(33)

CEDAR CITY Callaway
CEDAR HILL Jefferson
CEDARCREEK Taney
CENSUS BUREAU Boone
CENTER Ralls
CENTERTOWN (65023) Cole(83), Moniteau(16)
CENTERVIEW Johnson
CENTERVILLE Reynolds
CENTRALIA (65240) Boone(72), Audrain(25), Callaway(1)
CHADWICK (65629) Christian(98), Douglas(1)
CHAFFEE Scott
CHAMOIS Osage
CHARLESTON (63834) Mississippi(94), Scott(5)
CHERRYVILLE Crawford
CHESTERFIELD St. Louis
CHESTNUTRIDGE Christian
CHILHOWEE (64733) Johnson(70), Henry(24), Jackson(4)
CHILLICOTHE (64601) Livingston(98), Sullivan(1)
CHULA (64635) Livingston(79), Linn(11), Grundy(9)
CLARENCE (63437) Shelby(88), Macon(6), Monroe(4)
CLARK (65243) Randolph(40), Boone(29), Audrain(22), Howard(5)
CLARKSBURG (65025) Moniteau(57), Cooper(42)
CLARKSDALE De Kalb
CLARKSVILLE Pike
CLARKTON Dunklin
CLEARMONT Nodaway
CLEVELAND Cass
CLEVER Christian
CLIFTON HILL (65244) Randolph(96), Chariton(3)
CLIMAX SPRINGS Camden
CLINTON (64735) Henry(95), Benton(4)
CLUBB Wayne
CLYDE Nodaway
COATSVILLE (63535) Schuyler(56), Putnam(43)
COFFEY (64636) Daviess(93), Harrison(6)
COLE CAMP (65325) Benton(90), Morgan(6), Pettis(3)
COLLINS St. Clair
COLUMBIA Boone
COMMERCE Scott
CONCEPTION Nodaway
CONCEPTION JUNCTION Nodaway
CONCORDIA (64020) Lafayette(90), Johnson(8), Saline(1)
CONRAN New Madrid
CONTEL CORPORATION St. Charles
CONWAY (65632) Laclede(54), Webster(27), Dallas(18)
COOK STATION (65449) Crawford(97), Phelps(2)
COOTER Pemiscot
CORDER Lafayette
CORNING Holt

COSBY Andrew
COTTLEVILLE St. Charles
COUCH Oregon
COWGILL (64637) Caldwell(78), Ray(21)
CRAIG Holt
CRANE (65633) Stone(93), Barry(6)
CREIGHTON (64739) Henry(77), Cass(22)
CROCKER (65452) Pulaski(95), Miller(4)
CROSS TIMBERS (65634) Hickory(89),
    Benton(9), Camden(1)
CRYSTAL CITY Jefferson
CUBA Crawford
CURRYVILLE Pike
DADEVILLE Dade
DAISY Cape Girardeau
DALTON Chariton
DARLINGTON Gentry
DAVISVILLE (65456) Crawford(98), Iron(2)
DAWN (64638) Livingston(72), Carroll(27)
DE KALB Buchanan
DE SOTO Jefferson
DE WITT Carroll
DEARBORN Platte
DEEPWATER (64740) Henry(71), St.
    Clair(28)
DEERFIELD Vernon
DEERING Pemiscot
DEFIANCE St. Charles
DELTA Cape Girardeau
DENVER (64441) Worth(50), Gentry(49)
DES ARC (63636) Iron(66), Madison(29),
    Wayne(3)
DEVILS ELBOW (65457) Pulaski(95),
    Phelps(4)
DEXTER Stoddard
DIAMOND (64840) Newton(98), Jasper(1)
DIGGINS Webster
DITTMER Jefferson
DIXON (65459) Pulaski(74), Maries(23),
    Miller(2)
DOE RUN St. Francois
DONIPHAN (63935) Ripley(96), Carter(1),
    Oregon(1)
DORA (65637) Ozark(63), Howell(22),
    Douglas(14)
DOVER Lafayette
DOWNING (63536) Schuyler(73),
    Scotland(26)
DREXEL (64742) Cass(87), Bates(12)
DRURY (65638) Douglas(89), Ozark(10)
DUDLEY Stoddard
DUENWEG Jasper
DUKE (65461) Phelps(95), Pulaski(4)
DUNNEGAN (65640) Polk(92), Cedar(7)
DURHAM (63438) Lewis(66), Marion(33)
DUTCHTOWN Cape Girardeau
DUTZOW Warren
EAGLE ROCK Barry
EAGLEVILLE Harrison
EARTH CITY St. Louis
EAST LYNNE Cass
EAST PRAIRIE Mississippi
EASTON Buchanan
EDGAR SPRINGS (65462) Phelps(97),
    Dent(2)
EDGERTON (64444) Platte(93),
    Buchanan(6)
EDINA Knox
EDWARDS (65326) Benton(58),
    Camden(40)
EL DORADO SPRINGS (64744)
    Cedar(90), Vernon(5), St. Clair(3)
ELDON (65026) Miller(95), Morgan(4)
ELDRIDGE Laclede
ELK CREEK Texas
ELKLAND (65644) Webster(56), Dallas(43)
ELLINGTON (63638) Reynolds(94),
    Shannon(3), Carter(1)
ELLSINORE (63937) Carter(84), Butler(15)
ELMER Macon
ELMO Nodaway
ELSBERRY (63343) Lincoln(96), Pike(3)
EMDEN (63439) Shelby(65), Marion(34)

EMINENCE Shannon
EMMA Lafayette
EOLIA (63344) Pike(62), Lincoln(37)
ESSEX Stoddard
ETHEL Macon
ETTERVILLE Miller
EUDORA Polk
EUGENE (65032) Cole(66), Miller(33)
EUNICE Texas
EUREKA (63025) St. Louis(66),
    Jefferson(33)
EVERTON (65646) Dade(61),
    Lawrence(38)
EWING (63440) Lewis(70), Marion(25),
    Shelby(4)
EXCELLO Macon
EXCELSIOR SPRINGS (64024) Clay(73),
    Ray(26)
EXETER (65647) Barry(78), Newton(19),
    McDonald(1)
FAGUS Butler
FAIR GROVE (65648) Greene(77),
    Dallas(12), Webster(9)
FAIR PLAY (65649) Polk(95), Cedar(4)
FAIRDEALING Ripley
FAIRFAX (64446) Atchison(94), Holt(5)
FAIRPORT De Kalb
FAIRVIEW (64842) Newton(97), Barry(1)
FALCON (65470) Laclede(82), Wright(16)
FARBER Audrain
FARLEY Platte
FARMINGTON (63640) St. Francois(98),
    Ste. Genevieve(1)
FARRAR Perry
FAUCETT Buchanan
FAYETTE Howard
FENTON (63026) St. Louis(51),
    Jefferson(48)
FENTON St. Louis
FESTUS (63028) Jefferson(93), Ste.
    Genevieve(6)
FILLMORE Andrew
FISK Butler
FLEMINGTON (65650) Polk(51),
    Hickory(48)
FLETCHER (63030) Washington(57),
    Jefferson(42)
FLINTHILL St. Charles
FLORENCE Morgan
FLORISSANT St. Louis
FOLEY Lincoln
FORDLAND (65652) Webster(91),
    Christian(7), Douglas(1)
FOREST CITY Holt
FORISTELL (63348) St. Charles(66),
    Warren(30), Lincoln(3)
FORSYTH (65653) Taney(98), Christian(2)
FORT LEONARD WOOD Pulaski
FORTESCUE Holt
FORTUNA (65034) Morgan(63),
    Moniteau(36)
FOSTER Bates
FRANKFORD (63441) Pike(97), Ralls(2)
FRANKLIN Howard
FREDERICKTOWN (63645) Madison(97),
    Ste. Genevieve(1)
FREEBURG Osage
FREEMAN Cass
FREISTATT Lawrence
FREMONT (63941) Carter(62),
    Oregon(25), Ripley(11)
FRENCH VILLAGE (63036) St.
    Francois(74), Ste. Genevieve(25)
FRIEDHEIM Cape Girardeau
FROHNA Perry
FULTON Callaway
GAINESVILLE Ozark
GALENA (65656) Stone(77), Christian(22)
GALLATIN Daviess
GALT (64641) Grundy(79), Sullivan(20)
GARDEN CITY Cass
GARRISON (65657) Christian(98),
    Taney(1)

GASCONADE Gasconade
GATEWOOD Ripley
GENTRY Gentry
GERALD Franklin
GIBBS Adair
GIBSON Dunklin
GIDEON (63848) New Madrid(62),
    Pemiscot(37)
GILLIAM Saline
GILMAN CITY (64642) Harrison(76),
    Daviess(15), Grundy(8)
GIPSY Bollinger
GLASGOW (65254) Howard(95),
    Chariton(4)
GLENALLEN Bollinger
GLENCOE St. Louis
GLENWOOD Schuyler
GLOVER Iron
GOBLER (63849) Dunklin(63),
    Pemiscot(36)
GOLDEN Barry
GOLDEN CITY (64748) Barton(63),
    Jasper(21), Dade(15)
GOODMAN (64843) McDonald(73),
    Newton(26)
GOODSON Polk
GORDONVILLE Cape Girardeau
GORIN (63543) Scotland(96), Knox(2)
GOWER (64454) Buchanan(53),
    Clinton(46)
GRAFF Wright
GRAHAM (64455) Nodaway(95),
    Andrew(4)
GRAIN VALLEY Jackson
GRANBY Newton
GRANDIN (63943) Carter(79), Ripley(20)
GRANDVIEW Jackson
GRANGER Scotland
GRANT CITY (64456) Worth(98),
    Harrison(1)
GRASSY Bollinger
GRAVOIS MILLS (65037) Morgan(78),
    Camden(21)
GRAY SUMMIT Franklin
GRAYRIDGE Stoddard
GREEN CASTLE (63544) Sullivan(48),
    Adair(44), Putnam(6)
GREEN CITY Sullivan
GREEN RIDGE Pettis
GREENFIELD Dade
GREENTOP (63546) Adair(83),
    Schuyler(14), Scotland(1)
GREENVILLE Wayne
GREENWOOD (64034) Jackson(91),
    Cass(8)
GROVER St. Louis
GROVESPRING (65662) Wright(79),
    Laclede(19)
GRUBVILLE (63041) Franklin(85),
    Jefferson(14)
GUILFORD Nodaway
HALE (64643) Carroll(56), Livingston(43)
HALF WAY Polk
HALLSVILLE Boone
HALLTOWN Lawrence
HAMILTON (64644) Caldwell(84),
    Daviess(15)
HANNIBAL (63401) Marion(83), Ralls(16)
HARDENVILLE Ozark
HARDIN (64035) Ray(95), Carroll(4)
HARRIS (64645) Sullivan(85), Mercer(14)
HARRISBURG (65256) Boone(87),
    Howard(12)
HARRISONVILLE Cass
HARTSBURG (65039) Boone(93),
    Callaway(6)
HARTSHORN (65479) Texas(92),
    Shannon(7)
HARTVILLE Wright
HARVIELL (63945) Butler(97), Ripley(2)
HARWOOD Vernon
HATFIELD (64458) Harrison(96), Worth(3)

HAWK POINT (63349) Lincoln(98),
    Warren(1)
HAYTI Pemiscot
HAZELWOOD St. Louis
HELENA Andrew
HEMATITE Jefferson
HENLEY (65040) Cole(91), Miller(8)
HENRIETTA Ray
HERCULANEUM Jefferson
HERMANN (65041) Gasconade(84),
    Montgomery(13), Warren(1)
HERMANN Montgomery
HERMITAGE Hickory
HIGBEE (65257) Randolph(72),
    Howard(27)
HIGGINSVILLE Lafayette
HIGH HILL Montgomery
HIGH POINT Moniteau
HIGH RIDGE (63049) Jefferson(96), St.
    Louis(3)
HIGHLANDVILLE (65669) Christian(87),
    Stone(12)
HILLSBORO Jefferson
HIRAM Wayne
HOLCOMB (63852) Dunklin(98),
    Pemiscot(1)
HOLDEN Johnson
HOLLAND (63853) Pemiscot(92),
    Dunklin(7)
HOLLIDAY Monroe
HOLLISTER Taney
HOLT Clay
HOLTS SUMMIT Callaway
HOPKINS Nodaway
HORNERSVILLE Dunklin
HORTON Vernon
HOUSE SPRINGS Jefferson
HOUSTON Texas
HOUSTONIA (65333) Pettis(97), Saline(2)
HUGGINS Texas
HUGHESVILLE Pettis
HUMANSVILLE (65674) Polk(81),
    Cedar(13), Hickory(2), St. Clair(2)
HUME (64752) Bates(72), Vernon(27)
HUMPHREYS (64646) Sullivan(88),
    Linn(11)
HUNNEWELL (63443) Shelby(38),
    Monroe(31), Marion(29)
HUNTSVILLE Randolph
HURDLAND (63547) Knox(95), Adair(4)
HURLEY Stone
IBERIA Miller
IMPERIAL Jefferson
INDEPENDENCE Jackson
IONIA (65335) Pettis(66), Benton(33)
IRONDALE (63648) St. Francois(60),
    Washington(39)
IRONTON (63650) Iron(82), St.
    Francois(15), Madison(2)
ISABELLA Ozark
JACKSON Cape Girardeau
JACKSONVILLE (65260) Macon(62),
    Randolph(27), Monroe(9)
JADWIN Dent
JAMESON Daviess
JAMESPORT (64648) Daviess(97),
    Livingston(2)
JAMESTOWN (65046) Moniteau(92),
    Cooper(7)
JASPER (64755) Jasper(91), Barton(8)
JEFFERSON CITY Cole
JERICO SPRINGS (64756) Cedar(91),
    Dade(8)
JEROME Phelps
JONESBURG (63351) Montgomery(56),
    Warren(43)
JOPLIN Jasper
KAHOKA Clark
KAISER (65047) Miller(97), Camden(2)
KANSAS CITY (64188) Clay(92),
    Jackson(7)
KANSAS CITY (64147) Jackson(74),
    Cass(25)

KANSAS CITY (64164) Platte(98), Clay(1)
KANSAS CITY Clay
KANSAS CITY Jackson
KANSAS CITY Platte
KEARNEY Clay
KELSO Scott
KENNETT Dunklin
KEWANEE New Madrid
KEYTESVILLE Chariton
KIDDER (64649) Caldwell(73), Daviess(26)
KIMBERLING CITY Stone
KIMMSWICK Jefferson
KING CITY (64463) Gentry(94), De Kalb(3),
   Andrew(1)
KINGDOM CITY Callaway
KINGSTON Caldwell
KINGSVILLE (64061) Johnson(98),
   Jackson(1)
KIRBYVILLE Taney
KIRKSVILLE Adair
KISSEE MILLS Taney
KNOB LICK St. Francois
KNOB NOSTER (65336) Johnson(91),
   Pettis(8)
KNOX CITY (63446) Knox(90), Lewis(9)
KOELTZTOWN Osage
KOSHKONONG (65692) Oregon(53),
   Howell(46)
LA BELLE (63447) Lewis(97), Knox(2)
LA GRANGE Lewis
LA MONTE Pettis
LA PLATA (63549) Macon(95), Adair(3)
LA RUSSELL (64848) Lawrence(93),
   Jasper(6)
LABADIE Franklin
LACLEDE Linn
LADDONIA (63352) Audrain(93), Ralls(6)
LAKE OZARK (65049) Camden(72),
   Miller(27)
LAKE SAINT LOUIS St. Charles
LAKE SPRING Dent
LAMAR Barton
LAMPE Stone
LANAGAN McDonald
LANCASTER Schuyler
LAQUEY (65534) Pulaski(84), Laclede(15)
LAREDO (64652) Grundy(97), Sullivan(1)
LATHAM Moniteau
LATHROP (64465) Clinton(90), Caldwell(9)
LATOUR (64760) Johnson(50), Cass(49)
LAURIE Morgan
LAWSON (64062) Ray(66), Clay(17),
   Clinton(16)
LEADWOOD St. Francois
LEASBURG Crawford
LEBANON (65536) Laclede(98), Dallas(1)
LECOMA (65540) Dent(70), Phelps(29)
LEES SUMMIT (64082) Jackson(89),
   Cass(10)
LEES SUMMIT Jackson
LEETON (64761) Johnson(92), Henry(7)
LENOX Dent
LENTNER (63450) Shelby(70), Monroe(29)
LEONARD (63451) Shelby(95), Knox(2),
   Macon(2)
LEOPOLD Bollinger
LESLIE Franklin
LESTERVILLE (63654) Reynolds(89),
   Iron(10)
LEVASY Jackson
LEWISTOWN Lewis
LEXINGTON Lafayette
LIBERAL Barton
LIBERTY Clay
LICKING Texas
LIGUORI Jefferson
LILBOURN (63862) Bollinger(77), New
   Madrid(22)
LINCOLN Benton
LINN Osage
LINN CREEK Camden
LINNEUS Linn
LIVONIA Putnam

LOCK SPRINGS Daviess
LOCKWOOD (65682) Dade(83),
   Lawrence(10), Barton(5)
LODI Wayne
LOHMAN Cole
LONE JACK (64070) Jackson(96),
   Johnson(3)
LONEDELL Franklin
LONG LANE Dallas
LOOSE CREEK Osage
LOUISBURG (65685) Dallas(97), Polk(2)
LOUISIANA Pike
LOWNDES Wayne
LOWRY CITY St. Clair
LUCERNE (64655) Putnam(98), Sullivan(1)
LUDLOW Livingston
LUEBBERING Franklin
LURAY Clark
LYNCHBURG Laclede
MACKS CREEK (65786) Camden(98),
   Dallas(1)
MACOMB (65702) Wright(72), Douglas(27)
MADISON (65263) Monroe(95),
   Randolph(3)
MAITLAND Holt
MALDEN (63863) Dunklin(98), New
   Madrid(1)
MALTA BEND Saline
MANSFIELD (65704) Wright(95),
   Douglas(4)
MAPAVILLE Jefferson
MARBLE HILL (63764) Bollinger(91), Cape
   Girardeau(8)
MARCELINE (64658) Linn(68),
   Chariton(31)
MARIONVILLE (65705) Lawrence(81),
   Stone(18)
MARQUAND (63655) Madison(74),
   Bollinger(24), Wayne(1)
MARSHALL (65340) Saline(96), Pettis(3)
MARSHFIELD Webster
MARSTON New Madrid
MARTHASVILLE (63357) Warren(93), St.
   Charles(6)
MARTINSBURG (65264) Audrain(75),
   Callaway(21), Montgomery(3)
MARTINSVILLE Harrison
MARYLAND HEIGHTS St. Louis
MARYVILLE Nodaway
MATTHEWS New Madrid
MAYSVILLE De Kalb
MAYVIEW Lafayette
MAYWOOD (63454) Marion(68), Lewis(31)
MC BRIDE Perry
MC CLURG (65701) Taney(71),
   Douglas(28)
MC FALL (64657) Gentry(65), Harrison(25),
   Daviess(8)
MC GEE Wayne
MC GIRK Moniteau
MEADVILLE Linn
MEMPHIS Scotland
MENDON Chariton
MENFRO Perry
MERCER Mercer
META (65058) Maries(51), Osage(29),
   Miller(12), Cole(5)
METZ Vernon
MEXICO (65265) Audrain(98), Monroe(1)
MIAMI Saline
MID MISSOURI Boone
MIDDLE BROOK (63656) Iron(85),
   Reynolds(14)
MIDDLETOWN (63359) Pike(57),
   Montgomery(31), Lincoln(6), Audrain(4)
MILAN Sullivan
MILFORD Barton
MILL SPRING Wayne
MILLER Lawrence
MILLERSVILLE (63766) Cape
   Girardeau(88), Bollinger(11)
MILO Vernon
MINDENMINES Barton

MINERAL POINT Washington
MISSOURI CITY Clay
MISSOURI STATE LOTTERY COMM Cole
MOBERLY Randolph
MOKANE Callaway
MONETT (65708) Barry(58), Lawrence(41)
MONROE CITY (63456) Monroe(46),
   Marion(33), Ralls(19)
MONTGOMERY CITY (63361)
   Montgomery(82), Callaway(17)
MONTICELLO Lewis
MONTIER Shannon
MONTREAL Camden
MONTROSE (64770) Henry(90), Bates(8)
MOODY Howell
MOORESVILLE (64664) Livingston(98),
   Sullivan(1)
MORA (65345) Pettis(64), Benton(23),
   Morgan(11)
MOREHOUSE New Madrid
MORLEY Scott
MORRISON (65061) Gasconade(86),
   Osage(13)
MORRISVILLE Polk
MORSE MILL Jefferson
MOSBY Clay
MOSCOW MILLS Lincoln
MOUND CITY Holt
MOUNDVILLE Vernon
MOUNT MORIAH Harrison
MOUNT STERLING (65062)
   Gasconade(69), Ozark(21), Osage(9)
MOUNT VERNON Lawrence
MOUNTAIN GROVE (65711) Wright(94),
   Douglas(4)
MOUNTAIN VIEW (65548) Howell(95),
   Shannon(3)
MYRTLE Oregon
NAPOLEON Lafayette
NAYLOR (63953) Ripley(96), Butler(3)
NECK CITY Jasper
NEELYVILLE (63954) Butler(96), Ripley(3)
NELSON (65347) Pettis(46), Saline(31),
   Cooper(22)
NEOSHO Newton
NEVADA Vernon
NEW BLOOMFIELD Callaway
NEW BOSTON (63557) Linn(67),
   Macon(29), Sullivan(1)
NEW CAMBRIA (63558) Macon(83),
   Chariton(16)
NEW FLORENCE (63363)
   Montgomery(88), Warren(11)
NEW FRANKLIN Howard
NEW HAMPTON (64471) Harrison(93),
   Gentry(6)
NEW HARTFORD Pike
NEW HAVEN (63068) Franklin(98),
   Gasconade(1)
NEW LONDON (63459) Ralls(93), Pike(6)
NEW MADRID New Madrid
NEW MELLE St. Charles
NEW OFFENBURG Ste. Genevieve
NEWARK Knox
NEWBURG Phelps
NEWTONIA Newton
NEWTOWN (64667) Sullivan(77),
   Mercer(15), Putnam(7)
NIANGUA (65713) Webster(89), Wright(10)
NIXA (65714) Christian(94), Stone(5)
NOBLE Ozark
NOEL McDonald
NORBORNE (64668) Carroll(78), Ray(21)
NORWOOD (65717) Wright(86),
   Douglas(13)
NOVELTY Knox
NOVINGER (63559) Adair(51), Putnam(48)
O FALLON St. Charles
OAK GROVE (64075) Jackson(89),
   Lafayette(10)
OAK RIDGE Cape Girardeau
ODESSA (64076) Lafayette(98),
   Johnson(1)

OLD APPLETON (63770) Cape
   Girardeau(63), Perry(36)
OLD MONROE Lincoln
OLDFIELD (65720) Christian(78),
   Douglas(21)
OLEAN Miller
OLNEY Lincoln
ORAN (63771) Scott(82), Stoddard(16)
OREGON Holt
ORONOGO (64855) Jasper(95), Barton(4)
ORRICK (64077) Ray(74), Clay(25)
OSAGE BEACH Camden
OSBORN (64474) De Kalb(97), Clinton(2)
OSCEOLA (64776) St. Clair(97), Benton(2)
OTTERVILLE (65348) Cooper(85),
   Morgan(11), Pettis(3)
OWENSVILLE (65066) Gasconade(92),
   Crawford(7)
OXLY Ripley
OZARK (65721) Christian(98), Greene(1)
PACIFIC (63069) Franklin(67),
   Jefferson(16), St. Louis(15)
PAINTON Stoddard
PALMYRA Marion
PARIS Monroe
PARK HILLS St. Francois
PARMA (63870) Stoddard(83), New
   Madrid(16)
PARNELL (64475) Nodaway(88), Worth(9),
   Gentry(2)
PASCOLA Pemiscot
PASSAIC Bates
PATTERSON Wayne
PATTON Bollinger
PATTONSBURG (64670) Daviess(79), De
   Kalb(13), Harrison(4), Gentry(2)
PAYNESVILLE Pike
PEACE VALLEY (65788) Howell(95),
   Oregon(4)
PECULIAR Cass
PERKINS Scott
PERRY (63462) Ralls(79), Monroe(20)
PERRYVILLE Perry
PEVELY Jefferson
PHILADELPHIA (63463) Marion(97),
   Shelby(2)
PHILLIPSBURG (65722) Laclede(87),
   Dallas(12)
PICKERING Nodaway
PIEDMONT Wayne
PIERCE CITY (65723) Lawrence(90),
   Newton(6), Barry(3)
PILOT GROVE Cooper
PILOT KNOB Iron
PINEVILLE McDonald
PITTSBURG Hickory
PLATO (65552) Texas(98), Laclede(1)
PLATTE CITY Platte
PLATTSBURG Clinton
PLEASANT HILL (64080) Cass(96),
   Jackson(3)
PLEASANT HOPE (65725) Greene(89),
   Polk(10)
PLEVNA (63464) Knox(76), Marion(23)
POCAHONTAS Cape Girardeau
POINT LOOKOUT Taney
POLK (65727) Polk(87), Hickory(12)
POLLOCK (63560) Sullivan(92), Putnam(7)
POLO (64671) Caldwell(70), Ray(29)
POMONA Howell
PONCE DE LEON (65728) Christian(75),
   Stone(24)
PONTIAC Ozark
POPLAR BLUFF Butler
PORTAGE DES SIOUX St. Charles
PORTAGEVILLE (63873) New Madrid(84),
   Pemiscot(15)
PORTLAND Callaway
POTOSI Washington
POTTERSVILLE (65790) Howell(88),
   Ozark(11)
POWELL McDonald
POWERSITE Taney

POWERSVILLE (64672) Putnam(97), Mercer(2)
PRAIRIE HOME Cooper
PRESTON (65732) Hickory(94), Dallas(5)
PRINCETON Mercer
PROTEM Taney
PURCELL Jasper
PURDIN Linn
PURDY Barry
PUXICO (63960) Stoddard(96), Bollinger(3)
QUEEN CITY Schuyler
QUINCY (65735) Hickory(68), Benton(24), St. Clair(6)
QUITMAN Nodaway
QULIN Butler
RACINE Newton
RAVENWOOD (64479) Nodaway(95), Gentry(4)
RAYMONDVILLE Texas
RAYMORE Cass
RAYVILLE Ray
REA Andrew
REDFORD Reynolds
REEDS Jasper
REEDS SPRING (65737) Stone(98), Taney(1)
RENICK Randolph
REPUBLIC (65738) Greene(85), Christian(14)
REVERE Clark
REYNOLDS Reynolds
RHINELAND (65069) Montgomery(86), Callaway(13)
RICH HILL (64779) Bates(93), Vernon(6)
RICHARDS Vernon
RICHLAND (65556) Pulaski(61), Laclede(20), Camden(18)
RICHMOND Ray
RICHWOODS (63071) Washington(88), Jefferson(11)
RIDGEDALE Taney
RIDGEWAY Harrison
RISCO New Madrid
RIVES Dunklin
ROACH Camden
ROBERTSVILLE (63072) Franklin(96), Jefferson(3)
ROBY Texas
ROCHEPORT (65279) Boone(86), Howard(13)
ROCK PORT Atchison
ROCKAWAY BEACH Taney
ROCKBRIDGE Ozark
ROCKVILLE (64780) St. Clair(62), Bates(37)
ROCKY COMFORT (64861) McDonald(92), Newton(5), Barry(1)
ROCKY MOUNT (65072) Morgan(85), Miller(14)
ROGERSVILLE (65742) Webster(53), Greene(46)
ROLLA Phelps
ROMBAUER Butler
ROSCOE St. Clair
ROSEBUD (63091) Gasconade(73), Franklin(26)
ROSENDALE Andrew
ROTHVILLE Chariton
RUETER Taney
RUSH HILL Audrain
RUSHVILLE (64484) Buchanan(74), Platte(25)
RUSSELLVILLE (65074) Cole(68), Moniteau(29), Miller(1)
RUTLEDGE (63563) Scotland(56), Knox(43)
SAGINAW Newton
SAINT ALBANS Franklin
SAINT ANN St. Louis
SAINT CATHARINE Linn
SAINT CATHERINE Linn
SAINT CHARLES St. Charles
SAINT CLAIR Franklin

SAINT ELIZABETH Miller
SAINT JAMES (65559) Phelps(98), Maries(1)
SAINT JOSEPH (64506) Buchanan(97), Andrew(2)
SAINT JOSEPH Buchanan
SAINT LOUIS (63143) St. Louis(88), St. Louis City(11)
SAINT LOUIS (63120) St. Louis City(89), St. Louis(10)
SAINT LOUIS St. Louis
SAINT LOUIS St. Louis City
SAINT MARY Ste. Genevieve
SAINT PATRICK Clark
SAINT PETERS St. Charles
SAINT ROBERT Pulaski
SAINT THOMAS (65076) Cole(83), Osage(16)
SAINTE GENEVIEVE Ste. Genevieve
SALEM (65560) Dent(98), Shannon(1)
SALISBURY (65281) Chariton(98), Howard(1)
SANTA FE Monroe
SARCOXIE (64862) Jasper(87), Lawrence(8), Newton(4)
SAVANNAH Andrew
SAVERTON Ralls
SCHELL CITY (64783) Vernon(58), St. Clair(41)
SCOTT CITY Scott
SEDALIA Pettis
SEDGEWICKVILLE (63781) Bollinger(77), Perry(20), Cape Girardeau(2)
SELIGMAN Barry
SENATH Dunklin
SENECA (64865) Newton(89), McDonald(10)
SEYMOUR (65746) Webster(98), Douglas(1)
SHELBINA (63468) Shelby(80), Monroe(19)
SHELBYVILLE (63469) Shelby(98), Knox(1)
SHELDON (64784) Vernon(74), Barton(16), Cedar(7)
SHELL KNOB (65747) Stone(56), Barry(43)
SHERIDAN (64486) Worth(54), Nodaway(45)
SHOOK Wayne
SIBLEY Jackson
SIKESTON (63801) Scott(94), New Madrid(4)
SILEX Lincoln
SILVA (63964) Wayne(88), Madison(11)
SKIDMORE (64487) Nodaway(93), Holt(6)
SLATER Saline
SMITHTON (65350) Pettis(93), Morgan(5)
SMITHVILLE (64089) Clay(98), Platte(1)
SOLO Texas
SOUTH FORK Howell
SOUTH GREENFIELD (65752) Dade(67), Lawrence(32)
SOUTH WEST CITY McDonald
SPARTA (65753) Christian(98), Douglas(1)
SPICKARD (64679) Grundy(89), Mercer(10)
SPOKANE (65754) Christian(84), Stone(15)
SPRINGFIELD Greene
SQUIRES (65755) Douglas(53), Ozark(46)
ST CATHARINE Linn
ST JOSEPH Buchanan
STANBERRY (64489) Gentry(98), Nodaway(1)
STANTON Franklin
STARK CITY Newton
STEEDMAN Callaway
STEELE (63877) Pemiscot(97), Dunklin(2)
STEELVILLE (65565) Crawford(96), Washington(2)
STEFFENVILLE (63470) Lewis(93), Shelby(6)
STELLA (64867) Newton(90), McDonald(9)

STET Carroll
STEWARTSVILLE (64490) De Kalb(56), Clinton(38), Buchanan(4)
STOCKTON (65785) Cedar(98), St. Clair(1)
STOTTS CITY Lawrence
STOUTLAND (65567) Laclede(62), Camden(37)
STOUTSVILLE Monroe
STOVER (65078) Morgan(98), Benton(1)
STRAFFORD (65757) Greene(77), Webster(22)
STRASBURG Cass
STURDIVANT Bollinger
STURGEON (65284) Boone(95), Audrain(4)
SUCCESS Texas
SULLIVAN (63080) Franklin(82), Crawford(12), Washington(4)
SULPHUR SPRINGS Jefferson
SUMMERSVILLE (65571) Texas(83), Shannon(16)
SUMNER (64681) Linn(51), Chariton(48)
SUNRISE BEACH (65079) Camden(87), Morgan(12)
SWEDEBORG Pulaski
SWEET SPRINGS (65351) Saline(76), Pettis(22), Johnson(1)
SYRACUSE (65354) Morgan(89), Cooper(10)
TALLAPOOSA New Madrid
TANEYVILLE Taney
TARKIO Atchison
TAYLOR (63471) Marion(93), Lewis(6)
TEBBETTS Callaway
TECUMSEH Ozark
TERESITA Shannon
THAYER Oregon
THEODOSIA (65761) Ozark(75), Taney(25)
THOMPSON (65285) Audrain(98), Monroe(1)
THORNFIELD Ozark
TIFF Washington
TIFF CITY McDonald
TINA Carroll
TIPTON (65081) Moniteau(89), Cooper(9), Morgan(1)
TRELOAR Warren
TRENTON Grundy
TRIMBLE Clinton
TRIPLETT Chariton
TROY Lincoln
TRUXTON (63381) Lincoln(45), Warren(40), Montgomery(13)
TUNAS Dallas
TURNERS Greene
TURNEY Clinton
TUSCUMBIA Miller
UDALL Ozark
ULMAN Miller
UNION Franklin
UNION STAR De Kalb
UNIONTOWN Perry
UNIONVILLE (63565) Putnam(89), Sullivan(10)
URBANA (65767) Dallas(83), Hickory(15)
URICH (64788) Henry(82), Bates(17)
UTICA Livingston
VALLES MINES (63087) St. Francois(90), Jefferson(9)
VALLEY PARK St. Louis
VAN BUREN (63965) Carter(93), Reynolds(6)
VANDALIA (63382) Audrain(80), Ralls(10), Pike(8)
VANDUSER Scott
VANZANT Douglas
VERONA (65769) Lawrence(78), Barry(21)
VERSAILLES Morgan
VIBURNUM Iron
VICHY Maries
VIENNA Maries
VILLA RIDGE Franklin

VISTA St. Clair
VULCAN (63675) Iron(92), Washington(4), Reynolds(2)
WACO Jasper
WAKENDA Carroll
WALDRON Platte
WALKER Vernon
WALNUT GROVE Greene
WALNUT SHADE Taney
WAPPAPELLO (63966) Butler(67), Wayne(32)
WARDELL (63879) Pemiscot(98), New Madrid(1)
WARRENSBURG Johnson
WARRENTON (63383) Warren(97), Lincoln(2)
WARSAW Benton
WASHBURN (65772) Barry(93), McDonald(6)
WASHINGTON Franklin
WASOLA Ozark
WATSON Atchison
WAVERLY (64096) Lafayette(98), Saline(1)
WAYLAND Clark
WAYNESVILLE Pulaski
WEATHERBY (64497) De Kalb(69), Daviess(30)
WEAUBLEAU (65774) Hickory(90), St. Clair(9)
WEBB CITY Jasper
WELLINGTON Lafayette
WELLSVILLE (63384) Montgomery(88), Audrain(9), Callaway(1)
WENTWORTH (64873) Lawrence(66), Newton(33)
WENTZVILLE St. Charles
WESCO Crawford
WEST ALTON St. Charles
WEST PLAINS Howell
WESTBORO Atchison
WESTON Platte
WESTPHALIA Osage
WHEATLAND (65779) Hickory(85), Benton(14)
WHEATON Barry
WHEELING (64688) Livingston(77), Linn(22)
WHITEMAN AIR FORCE BASE Johnson
WHITEOAK Dunklin
WHITESIDE Lincoln
WHITEWATER Cape Girardeau
WILLARD Greene
WILLIAMSBURG Callaway
WILLIAMSTOWN (63473) Lewis(76), Clark(23)
WILLIAMSVILLE (63967) Butler(58), Wayne(41)
WILLOW SPRINGS (65793) Howell(95), Texas(4)
WINDSOR (65360) Henry(51), Pettis(25), Benton(12), Johnson(9)
WINDYVILLE Dallas
WINFIELD Lincoln
WINIGAN (63566) Linn(80), Sullivan(19)
WINONA (65588) Shannon(93), Oregon(6)
WINSTON Daviess
WITTENBERG Perry
WOLF ISLAND Mississippi
WOOLDRIDGE (65287) Cooper(79), Moniteau(20)
WORTH (64499) Worth(75), Gentry(24)
WORTHINGTON Putnam
WRIGHT CITY (63390) Warren(90), Lincoln(9)
WYACONDA (63474) Clark(91), Scotland(5), Lewis(3)
WYATT Mississippi
YUKON Texas
ZALMA (63787) Bollinger(94), Wayne(5)
ZALMA Bollinger
ZANONI Ozark

Missouri ZIP/City Cross Reference

63001-63001 ALLENTON	63361-63361 MONTGOMERY CITY	63547-63547 HURDLAND	63770-63770 OLD APPLETON
63005-63006 CHESTERFIELD	63362-63362 MOSCOW MILLS	63548-63548 LANCASTER	63771-63771 ORAN
63010-63010 ARNOLD	63363-63363 NEW FLORENCE	63549-63549 LA PLATA	63772-63772 PAINTON
63011-63011 BALLWIN	63364-63364 NEW HARTFORD	63551-63551 LIVONIA	63774-63774 PERKINS
63012-63012 BARNHART	63365-63365 NEW MELLE	63552-63552 MACON	63775-63775 PERRYVILLE
63013-63013 BEAUFORT	63366-63366 O FALLON	63555-63555 MEMPHIS	63776-63776 MC BRIDE
63014-63014 BERGER	63367-63367 LAKE SAINT LOUIS	63556-63556 MILAN	63779-63779 POCAHONTAS
63015-63015 CATAWISSA	63369-63369 OLD MONROE	63557-63557 NEW BOSTON	63780-63780 SCOTT CITY
63016-63016 CEDAR HILL	63370-63370 OLNEY	63558-63558 NEW CAMBRIA	63781-63781 SEDGEWICKVILLE
63017-63017 CHESTERFIELD	63371-63371 PAYNESVILLE	63559-63559 NOVINGER	63782-63782 STURDIVANT
63019-63019 CRYSTAL CITY	63373-63373 PORTAGE DES SIOUX	63560-63560 POLLOCK	63783-63783 UNIONTOWN
63020-63020 DE SOTO	63376-63376 SAINT PETERS	63561-63561 QUEEN CITY	63784-63784 VANDUSER
63021-63022 BALLWIN	63377-63377 SILEX	63563-63563 RUTLEDGE	63785-63785 WHITEWATER
63023-63023 DITTMER	63378-63378 TRELOAR	63565-63565 UNIONVILLE	63786-63786 WITTENBERG
63024-63024 BALLWIN	63379-63379 TROY	63566-63566 WINIGAN	63787-63787 ZALMA
63025-63025 EUREKA	63381-63381 TRUXTON	63567-63567 WORTHINGTON	63801-63801 SIKESTON
63026-63026 FENTON	63382-63382 VANDALIA	63601-63601 PARK HILLS	63820-63820 ANNISTON
63028-63028 FESTUS	63383-63383 WARRENTON	63620-63620 ANNAPOLIS	63821-63821 ARBYRD
63030-63030 FLETCHER	63384-63384 WELLSVILLE	63621-63621 ARCADIA	63822-63822 BERNIE
63031-63034 FLORISSANT	63385-63385 WENTZVILLE	63622-63622 BELGRADE	63823-63823 BERTRAND
63036-63036 FRENCH VILLAGE	63386-63386 WEST ALTON	63623-63623 BELLEVIEW	63824-63824 BLODGETT
63037-63037 GERALD	63387-63387 WHITESIDE	63624-63624 BISMARCK	63825-63825 BLOOMFIELD
63038-63038 GLENCOE	63388-63388 WILLIAMSBURG	63625-63625 BLACK	63826-63826 BRAGGADOCIO
63039-63039 GRAY SUMMIT	63389-63389 WINFIELD	63626-63626 BLACKWELL	63827-63827 BRAGG CITY
63040-63040 GROVER	63390-63390 WRIGHT CITY	63627-63627 BLOOMSDALE	63828-63828 CANALOU
63041-63041 GRUBVILLE	63394-63394 CONTEL CORPORATION	63628-63628 BONNE TERRE	63829-63829 CARDWELL
63042-63042 HAZELWOOD	63401-63401 HANNIBAL	63629-63629 BUNKER	63830-63830 CARUTHERSVILLE
63043-63043 MARYLAND HEIGHTS	63430-63430 ALEXANDRIA	63630-63630 CADET	63833-63833 CATRON
63044-63044 BRIDGETON	63431-63431 ANABEL	63631-63631 CALEDONIA	63834-63834 CHARLESTON
63045-63045 EARTH CITY	63432-63432 ARBELA	63632-63632 CASCADE	63837-63837 CLARKTON
63047-63047 HEMATITE	63433-63433 ASHBURN	63633-63633 CENTERVILLE	63838-63838 CONRAN
63048-63048 HERCULANEUM	63434-63434 BETHEL	63636-63636 DES ARC	63839-63839 COOTER
63049-63049 HIGH RIDGE	63435-63435 CANTON	63637-63637 DOE RUN	63840-63840 DEERING
63050-63050 HILLSBORO	63436-63436 CENTER	63638-63638 ELLINGTON	63841-63841 DEXTER
63051-63051 HOUSE SPRINGS	63437-63437 CLARENCE	63640-63640 FARMINGTON	63845-63845 EAST PRAIRIE
63052-63052 IMPERIAL	63438-63438 DURHAM	63644-63644 PARK HILLS	63846-63846 ESSEX
63053-63053 KIMMSWICK	63439-63439 EMDEN	63645-63645 FREDERICKTOWN	63847-63847 GIBSON
63055-63055 LABADIE	63440-63440 EWING	63646-63646 GLOVER	63848-63848 GIDEON
63056-63056 LESLIE	63441-63441 FRANKFORD	63648-63648 IRONDALE	63849-63849 GOBLER
63057-63057 LIGUORI	63442-63442 GRANGER	63650-63650 IRONTON	63850-63850 GRAYRIDGE
63060-63060 LONEDELL	63443-63443 HUNNEWELL	63651-63651 KNOB LICK	63851-63851 HAYTI
63061-63061 LUEBBERING	63445-63445 KAHOKA	63653-63653 LEADWOOD	63852-63852 HOLCOMB
63065-63065 MAPAVILLE	63446-63446 KNOX CITY	63654-63654 LESTERVILLE	63853-63853 HOLLAND
63066-63066 MORSE MILL	63447-63447 LA BELLE	63655-63655 MARQUAND	63855-63855 HORNERSVILLE
63068-63068 NEW HAVEN	63448-63448 LA GRANGE	63656-63656 MIDDLE BROOK	63857-63857 KENNETT
63069-63069 PACIFIC	63450-63450 LENTNER	63660-63660 MINERAL POINT	63860-63860 KEWANEE
63070-63070 PEVELY	63451-63451 LEONARD	63661-63661 NEW OFFENBURG	63862-63862 LILBOURN
63071-63071 RICHWOODS	63452-63452 LEWISTOWN	63662-63662 PATTON	63863-63863 MALDEN
63072-63072 ROBERTSVILLE	63453-63453 LURAY	63663-63663 PILOT KNOB	63866-63866 MARSTON
63073-63073 SAINT ALBANS	63454-63454 MAYWOOD	63664-63664 POTOSI	63867-63867 MATTHEWS
63074-63074 SAINT ANN	63456-63456 MONROE CITY	63665-63665 REDFORD	63868-63868 MOREHOUSE
63077-63077 SAINT CLAIR	63457-63457 MONTICELLO	63666-63666 REYNOLDS	63869-63869 NEW MADRID
63079-63079 STANTON	63458-63458 NEWARK	63670-63670 SAINTE GENEVIEVE	63870-63870 PARMA
63080-63080 SULLIVAN	63459-63459 NEW LONDON	63673-63673 SAINT MARY	63871-63871 PASCOLA
63083-63083 SULPHUR SPRINGS	63460-63460 NOVELTY	63674-63674 TIFF	63873-63873 PORTAGEVILLE
63084-63084 UNION	63461-63461 PALMYRA	63675-63675 VULCAN	63874-63874 RISCO
63087-63087 VALLES MINES	63462-63462 PERRY	63701-63705 CAPE GIRARDEAU	63875-63875 RIVES
63088-63088 VALLEY PARK	63463-63463 PHILADELPHIA	63730-63730 ADVANCE	63876-63876 SENATH
63089-63089 VILLA RIDGE	63464-63464 PLEVNA	63732-63732 ALTENBURG	63877-63877 STEELE
63090-63090 WASHINGTON	63465-63465 REVERE	63733-63733 ZALMA	63878-63878 TALLAPOOSA
63091-63091 ROSEBUD	63466-63466 SAINT PATRICK	63735-63735 BELL CITY	63879-63879 WARDELL
63099-63099 FENTON	63467-63467 SAVERTON	63736-63736 BENTON	63880-63880 WHITEOAK
63100-63199 SAINT LOUIS	63468-63468 SHELBINA	63737-63737 BRAZEAU	63881-63881 WOLF ISLAND
63301-63304 SAINT CHARLES	63469-63469 SHELBYVILLE	63738-63738 BROWNWOOD	63882-63882 WYATT
63330-63330 ANNADA	63470-63470 STEFFENVILLE	63739-63739 BURFORDVILLE	63901-63902 POPLAR BLUFF
63332-63332 AUGUSTA	63471-63471 TAYLOR	63740-63740 CHAFFEE	63931-63931 BRIAR
63333-63333 BELLFLOWER	63472-63472 WAYLAND	63742-63742 COMMERCE	63932-63932 BROSELEY
63334-63334 BOWLING GREEN	63473-63473 WILLIAMSTOWN	63743-63743 DAISY	63933-63933 CAMPBELL
63336-63336 CLARKSVILLE	63474-63474 WYACONDA	63744-63744 DELTA	63934-63934 CLUBB
63338-63338 COTTLEVILLE	63501-63501 KIRKSVILLE	63745-63745 DUTCHTOWN	63935-63935 DONIPHAN
63339-63339 CURRYVILLE	63530-63530 ATLANTA	63746-63746 FARRAR	63936-63936 DUDLEY
63341-63341 DEFIANCE	63531-63531 BARING	63747-63747 FRIEDHEIM	63937-63937 ELLSINORE
63342-63342 DUTZOW	63532-63532 BEVIER	63748-63748 FROHNA	63938-63938 FAGUS
63343-63343 ELSBERRY	63533-63533 BRASHEAR	63750-63750 GIPSY	63939-63939 FAIRDEALING
63344-63344 EOLIA	63534-63534 CALLAO	63751-63751 GLENALLEN	63940-63940 FISK
63345-63345 FARBER	63535-63535 COATSVILLE	63752-63752 GORDONVILLE	63941-63941 FREMONT
63346-63346 FLINTHILL	63536-63536 DOWNING	63753-63753 GRASSY	63942-63942 GATEWOOD
63347-63347 FOLEY	63537-63537 EDINA	63755-63755 JACKSON	63943-63943 GRANDIN
63348-63348 FORISTELL	63538-63538 ELMER	63758-63758 KELSO	63944-63944 GREENVILLE
63349-63349 HAWK POINT	63539-63539 ETHEL	63760-63760 LEOPOLD	63945-63945 HARVIELL
63350-63350 HIGH HILL	63540-63540 GIBBS	63763-63763 MC GEE	63947-63947 HIRAM
63351-63351 JONESBURG	63541-63541 GLENWOOD	63764-63764 MARBLE HILL	63950-63950 LODI
63352-63352 LADDONIA	63543-63543 GORIN	63765-63765 MENFRO	63951-63951 LOWNDES
63353-63353 LOUISIANA	63544-63544 GREEN CASTLE	63766-63766 MILLERSVILLE	63952-63952 MILL SPRING
63357-63357 MARTHASVILLE	63545-63545 GREEN CITY	63767-63767 MORLEY	63953-63953 NAYLOR
63359-63359 MIDDLETOWN	63546-63546 GREENTOP	63769-63769 OAK RIDGE	63954-63954 NEELYVILLE

63955-63955 OXLY	64442-64442 EAGLEVILLE	64658-64658 MARCELINE	64844-64844 GRANBY
63956-63956 PATTERSON	64443-64443 EASTON	64659-64659 MEADVILLE	64847-64847 LANAGAN
63957-63957 PIEDMONT	64444-64444 EDGERTON	64660-64660 MENDON	64848-64848 LA RUSSELL
63960-63960 PUXICO	64445-64445 ELMO	64661-64661 MERCER	64849-64849 NECK CITY
63961-63961 QULIN	64446-64446 FAIRFAX	64664-64664 MOORESVILLE	64850-64850 NEOSHO
63962-63962 ROMBAUER	64447-64447 FAIRPORT	64665-64665 MOUNT MORIAH	64853-64853 NEWTONIA
63963-63963 SHOOK	64448-64448 FAUCETT	64667-64667 NEWTOWN	64854-64854 NOEL
63964-63964 SILVA	64449-64449 FILLMORE	64668-64668 NORBORNE	64855-64855 ORONOGO
63965-63965 VAN BUREN	64451-64451 FOREST CITY	64670-64670 PATTONSBURG	64856-64856 PINEVILLE
63966-63966 WAPPAPELLO	64452-64452 FORTESCUE	64671-64671 POLO	64857-64857 PURCELL
63967-63967 WILLIAMSVILLE	64453-64453 GENTRY	64672-64672 POWERSVILLE	64858-64858 RACINE
64001-64001 ALMA	64454-64454 GOWER	64673-64673 PRINCETON	64859-64859 REEDS
64011-64011 BATES CITY	64455-64455 GRAHAM	64674-64674 PURDIN	64861-64861 ROCKY COMFORT
64012-64012 BELTON	64456-64456 GRANT CITY	64676-64676 ROTHVILLE	64862-64862 SARCOXIE
64013-64015 BLUE SPRINGS	64457-64457 GUILFORD	64677-64677 SAINT CATHERINE	64863-64863 SOUTH WEST CITY
64016-64016 BUCKNER	64458-64458 HATFIELD	64677-64677 SAINT CATHARINE	64864-64864 SAGINAW
64017-64017 CAMDEN	64459-64459 HELENA	64677-64677 ST CATHARINE	64865-64865 SENECA
64018-64018 CAMDEN POINT	64461-64461 HOPKINS	64679-64679 SPICKARD	64866-64866 STARK CITY
64019-64019 CENTERVIEW	64463-64463 KING CITY	64680-64680 STET	64867-64867 STELLA
64020-64020 CONCORDIA	64465-64465 LATHROP	64681-64681 SUMNER	64868-64868 TIFF CITY
64021-64021 CORDER	64466-64466 MAITLAND	64682-64682 TINA	64869-64869 WACO
64022-64022 DOVER	64467-64467 MARTINSVILLE	64683-64683 TRENTON	64870-64870 WEBB CITY
64024-64024 EXCELSIOR SPRINGS	64468-64468 MARYVILLE	64686-64686 UTICA	64873-64873 WENTWORTH
64028-64028 FARLEY	64469-64469 MAYSVILLE	64687-64687 WAKENDA	64874-64874 WHEATON
64029-64029 GRAIN VALLEY	64470-64470 MOUND CITY	64688-64688 WHEELING	64944-64999 KANSAS CITY
64030-64030 GRANDVIEW	64471-64471 NEW HAMPTON	64689-64689 WINSTON	65001-65001 ARGYLE
64034-64034 GREENWOOD	64473-64473 OREGON	64701-64701 HARRISONVILLE	65010-65010 ASHLAND
64035-64035 HARDIN	64474-64474 OSBORN	64720-64720 ADRIAN	65011-65011 BARNETT
64036-64036 HENRIETTA	64475-64475 PARNELL	64722-64722 AMORET	65013-65013 BELLE
64037-64037 HIGGINSVILLE	64476-64476 PICKERING	64723-64723 AMSTERDAM	65014-65014 BLAND
64040-64040 HOLDEN	64477-64477 PLATTSBURG	64724-64724 APPLETON CITY	65016-65016 BONNOTS MILL
64048-64048 HOLT	64478-64478 QUITMAN	64725-64725 ARCHIE	65017-65017 BRUMLEY
64050-64058 INDEPENDENCE	64479-64479 RAVENWOOD	64726-64726 BLAIRSTOWN	65018-65018 CALIFORNIA
64060-64060 KEARNEY	64480-64480 REA	64728-64728 BRONAUGH	65020-65020 CAMDENTON
64061-64061 KINGSVILLE	64481-64481 RIDGEWAY	64730-64730 BUTLER	65022-65022 CEDAR CITY
64062-64062 LAWSON	64482-64482 ROCK PORT	64733-64733 CHILHOWEE	65023-65023 CENTERTOWN
64063-64065 LEES SUMMIT	64483-64483 ROSENDALE	64734-64734 CLEVELAND	65024-65024 CHAMOIS
64066-64066 LEVASY	64484-64484 RUSHVILLE	64735-64735 CLINTON	65025-65025 CLARKSBURG
64067-64067 LEXINGTON	64485-64485 SAVANNAH	64738-64738 COLLINS	65026-65026 ELDON
64068-64069 LIBERTY	64486-64486 SHERIDAN	64739-64739 CREIGHTON	65031-65031 ETTERVILLE
64070-64070 LONE JACK	64487-64487 SKIDMORE	64740-64740 DEEPWATER	65032-65032 EUGENE
64071-64071 MAYVIEW	64489-64489 STANBERRY	64741-64741 DEERFIELD	65034-65034 FORTUNA
64072-64072 MISSOURI CITY	64490-64490 STEWARTSVILLE	64742-64742 DREXEL	65035-65035 FREEBURG
64073-64073 MOSBY	64491-64491 TARKIO	64743-64743 EAST LYNNE	65036-65036 GASCONADE
64074-64074 NAPOLEON	64492-64492 TRIMBLE	64744-64744 EL DORADO SPRINGS	65037-65037 GRAVOIS MILLS
64075-64075 OAK GROVE	64493-64493 TURNEY	64745-64745 FOSTER	65038-65038 LAURIE
64076-64076 ODESSA	64494-64494 UNION STAR	64746-64746 FREEMAN	65039-65039 HARTSBURG
64077-64077 ORRICK	64496-64496 WATSON	64747-64747 GARDEN CITY	65040-65040 HENLEY
64078-64078 PECULIAR	64497-64497 WEATHERBY	64748-64748 GOLDEN CITY	65041-65041 HERMANN
64079-64079 PLATTE CITY	64498-64498 WESTBORO	64750-64750 HARWOOD	65042-65042 HIGH POINT
64080-64080 PLEASANT HILL	64499-64499 WORTH	64751-64751 HORTON	65043-65043 HOLTS SUMMIT
64081-64082 LEES SUMMIT	64500-64500 SAINT JOSEPH	64752-64752 HUME	65046-65046 JAMESTOWN
64083-64083 RAYMORE	64500-64500 ST JOSEPH	64755-64755 JASPER	65047-65047 KAISER
64084-64084 RAYVILLE	64501-64508 SAINT JOSEPH	64756-64756 JERICO SPRINGS	65048-65048 KOELTZTOWN
64085-64085 RICHMOND	64601-64601 CHILLICOTHE	64759-64759 LAMAR	65049-65049 LAKE OZARK
64086-64086 LEES SUMMIT	64620-64620 ALTAMONT	64760-64760 LATOUR	65050-65050 LATHAM
64087-64087 LIBERTY	64621-64621 AVALON	64761-64761 LEETON	65051-65051 LINN
64088-64088 SIBLEY	64622-64622 BOGARD	64762-64762 LIBERAL	65052-65052 LINN CREEK
64089-64089 SMITHVILLE	64623-64623 BOSWORTH	64763-64763 LOWRY CITY	65053-65053 LOHMAN
64090-64090 STRASBURG	64624-64624 BRAYMER	64765-64765 METZ	65054-65054 LOOSE CREEK
64092-64092 WALDRON	64625-64625 BRECKENRIDGE	64766-64766 MILFORD	65055-65055 MC GIRK
64093-64093 WARRENSBURG	64628-64628 BROOKFIELD	64767-64767 MILO	65056-65056 HERMANN
64096-64096 WAVERLY	64630-64630 BROWNING	64769-64769 MINDENMINES	65058-65058 META
64097-64097 WELLINGTON	64631-64631 BUCKLIN	64770-64770 MONTROSE	65059-65059 MOKANE
64098-64098 WESTON	64632-64632 CAINSVILLE	64771-64771 MOUNDVILLE	65061-65061 MORRISON
64100-64199 KANSAS CITY	64633-64633 CARROLLTON	64772-64772 NEVADA	65062-65062 MOUNT STERLING
64401-64401 AGENCY	64635-64635 CHULA	64776-64776 OSCEOLA	65063-65063 NEW BLOOMFIELD
64402-64402 ALBANY	64636-64636 COFFEY	64777-64777 PASSAIC	65064-65064 OLEAN
64420-64420 ALLENDALE	64637-64637 COWGILL	64778-64778 RICHARDS	65065-65065 OSAGE BEACH
64421-64421 AMAZONIA	64638-64638 DAWN	64779-64779 RICH HILL	65066-65066 OWENSVILLE
64422-64422 AMITY	64639-64639 DE WITT	64780-64780 ROCKVILLE	65067-65067 PORTLAND
64423-64423 BARNARD	64640-64640 GALLATIN	64781-64781 ROSCOE	65068-65068 PRAIRIE HOME
64424-64424 BETHANY	64641-64641 GALT	64783-64783 SCHELL CITY	65069-65069 RHINELAND
64426-64426 BLYTHEDALE	64642-64642 GILMAN CITY	64784-64784 SHELDON	65072-65072 ROCKY MOUNT
64427-64427 BOLCKOW	64643-64643 HALE	64788-64788 URICH	65074-65074 RUSSELLVILLE
64428-64428 BURLINGTON JUNCTION	64644-64644 HAMILTON	64789-64789 VISTA	65075-65075 SAINT ELIZABETH
64429-64429 CAMERON	64645-64645 HARRIS	64790-64790 WALKER	65076-65076 SAINT THOMAS
64430-64430 CLARKSDALE	64646-64646 HUMPHREYS	64801-64804 JOPLIN	65077-65077 STEEDMAN
64431-64431 CLEARMONT	64647-64647 JAMESON	64830-64830 ALBA	65078-65078 STOVER
64432-64432 CLYDE	64648-64648 JAMESPORT	64831-64831 ANDERSON	65079-65079 SUNRISE BEACH
64433-64433 CONCEPTION	64649-64649 KIDDER	64832-64832 ASBURY	65080-65080 TEBBETTS
64434-64434 CONCEPTION JUNCTION	64650-64650 KINGSTON	64833-64833 AVILLA	65081-65081 TIPTON
64435-64435 CORNING	64651-64651 LACLEDE	64834-64834 CARL JUNCTION	65082-65082 TUSCUMBIA
64436-64436 COSBY	64652-64652 LAREDO	64835-64835 CARTERVILLE	65083-65083 ULMAN
64437-64437 CRAIG	64653-64653 LINNEUS	64836-64836 CARTHAGE	65084-65084 VERSAILLES
64438-64438 DARLINGTON	64654-64654 LOCK SPRINGS	64840-64840 DIAMOND	65085-65085 WESTPHALIA
64439-64439 DEARBORN	64655-64655 LUCERNE	64841-64841 DUENWEG	65101-65111 JEFFERSON CITY
64440-64440 DE KALB	64656-64656 LUDLOW	64842-64842 FAIRVIEW	65199-65199 MISSOURI STATE LOTTERY
64441-64441 DENVER	64657-64657 MC FALL	64843-64843 GOODMAN	COMM

65201-65218 COLUMBIA	65354-65354 SYRACUSE	65609-65609 BAKERSFIELD	65710-65710 MORRISVILLE
65230-65230 ARMSTRONG	65355-65355 WARSAW	65610-65610 BILLINGS	65711-65711 MOUNTAIN GROVE
65231-65231 AUXVASSE	65360-65360 WINDSOR	65611-65611 BLUE EYE	65712-65712 MOUNT VERNON
65232-65232 BENTON CITY	65401-65409 ROLLA	65612-65612 BOIS D ARC	65713-65713 NIANGUA
65233-65233 BOONVILLE	65433-65433 BENDAVIS	65613-65613 BOLIVAR	65714-65714 NIXA
65236-65236 BRUNSWICK	65436-65436 BEULAH	65614-65614 BRADLEYVILLE	65715-65715 NOBLE
65237-65237 BUNCETON	65438-65438 BIRCH TREE	65615-65616 BRANSON	65717-65717 NORWOOD
65239-65239 CAIRO	65439-65439 BIXBY	65617-65617 BRIGHTON	65720-65720 OLDFIELD
65240-65240 CENTRALIA	65440-65440 BOSS	65618-65618 BRIXEY	65721-65721 OZARK
65243-65243 CLARK	65441-65441 BOURBON	65619-65619 BROOKLINE STATION	65722-65722 PHILLIPSBURG
65244-65244 CLIFTON HILL	65443-65443 BRINKTOWN	65620-65620 BRUNER	65723-65723 PIERCE CITY
65246-65246 DALTON	65444-65444 BUCYRUS	65622-65622 BUFFALO	65724-65724 PITTSBURG
65247-65247 EXCELLO	65446-65446 CHERRYVILLE	65623-65623 BUTTERFIELD	65725-65725 PLEASANT HOPE
65248-65248 FAYETTE	65449-65449 COOK STATION	65624-65624 CAPE FAIR	65726-65726 POINT LOOKOUT
65250-65250 FRANKLIN	65452-65452 CROCKER	65625-65625 CASSVILLE	65727-65727 POLK
65251-65251 FULTON	65453-65453 CUBA	65626-65626 CAULFIELD	65728-65728 PONCE DE LEON
65254-65254 GLASGOW	65456-65456 DAVISVILLE	65627-65627 CEDARCREEK	65729-65729 PONTIAC
65255-65255 HALLSVILLE	65457-65457 DEVILS ELBOW	65629-65629 CHADWICK	65730-65730 POWELL
65256-65256 HARRISBURG	65459-65459 DIXON	65630-65630 CHESTNUTRIDGE	65731-65731 POWERSITE
65257-65257 HIGBEE	65461-65461 DUKE	65631-65631 CLEVER	65732-65732 PRESTON
65258-65258 HOLLIDAY	65462-65462 EDGAR SPRINGS	65632-65632 CONWAY	65733-65733 PROTEM
65259-65259 HUNTSVILLE	65463-65463 ELDRIDGE	65633-65633 CRANE	65734-65734 PURDY
65260-65260 JACKSONVILLE	65464-65464 ELK CREEK	65634-65634 CROSS TIMBERS	65735-65735 QUINCY
65261-65261 KEYTESVILLE	65466-65466 EMINENCE	65635-65635 DADEVILLE	65737-65737 REEDS SPRING
65262-65262 KINGDOM CITY	65468-65468 EUNICE	65636-65636 DIGGINS	65738-65738 REPUBLIC
65263-65263 MADISON	65470-65470 FALCON	65637-65637 DORA	65739-65739 RIDGEDALE
65264-65264 MARTINSBURG	65473-65473 FORT LEONARD WOOD	65638-65638 DRURY	65740-65740 ROCKAWAY BEACH
65265-65265 MEXICO	65479-65479 HARTSHORN	65640-65640 DUNNEGAN	65741-65741 ROCKBRIDGE
65270-65270 MOBERLY	65483-65483 HOUSTON	65641-65641 EAGLE ROCK	65742-65742 ROGERSVILLE
65274-65274 NEW FRANKLIN	65484-65484 HUGGINS	65644-65644 ELKLAND	65744-65744 RUETER
65275-65275 PARIS	65486-65486 IBERIA	65645-65645 EUDORA	65745-65745 SELIGMAN
65276-65276 PILOT GROVE	65501-65501 JADWIN	65646-65646 EVERTON	65746-65746 SEYMOUR
65278-65278 RENICK	65529-65529 JEROME	65647-65647 EXETER	65747-65747 SHELL KNOB
65279-65279 ROCHEPORT	65532-65532 LAKE SPRING	65648-65648 FAIR GROVE	65752-65752 SOUTH GREENFIELD
65280-65280 RUSH HILL	65534-65534 LAQUEY	65649-65649 FAIR PLAY	65753-65753 SPARTA
65281-65281 SALISBURY	65535-65535 LEASBURG	65650-65650 FLEMINGTON	65754-65754 SPOKANE
65282-65282 SANTA FE	65536-65536 LEBANON	65652-65652 FORDLAND	65755-65755 SQUIRES
65283-65283 STOUTSVILLE	65540-65540 LECOMA	65653-65653 FORSYTH	65756-65756 STOTTS CITY
65284-65284 STURGEON	65541-65541 LENOX	65654-65654 FREISTATT	65757-65757 STRAFFORD
65285-65285 THOMPSON	65542-65542 LICKING	65655-65655 GAINESVILLE	65758-65758 GAINESVILLE
65286-65286 TRIPLETT	65543-65543 LYNCHBURG	65656-65656 GALENA	65759-65759 TANEYVILLE
65287-65287 WOOLDRIDGE	65546-65546 MONTIER	65657-65657 GARRISON	65760-65760 TECUMSEH
65291-65291 CENSUS BUREAU	65548-65548 MOUNTAIN VIEW	65658-65658 GOLDEN	65761-65761 THEODOSIA
65299-65299 MID MISSOURI	65550-65550 NEWBURG	65659-65659 GOODSON	65762-65762 THORNFIELD
65299-65299 COLUMBIA	65552-65552 PLATO	65660-65660 GRAFF	65764-65764 TUNAS
65301-65302 SEDALIA	65555-65555 RAYMONDVILLE	65661-65661 GREENFIELD	65765-65765 TURNERS
65305-65305 WHITEMAN AIR FORCE	65556-65556 RICHLAND	65662-65662 GROVESPRING	65766-65766 UDALL
BASE	65557-65557 ROBY	65663-65663 HALF WAY	65767-65767 URBANA
65320-65320 ARROW ROCK	65559-65559 SAINT JAMES	65664-65664 HALLTOWN	65768-65768 VANZANT
65321-65321 BLACKBURN	65560-65560 SALEM	65666-65666 HARDENVILLE	65769-65769 VERONA
65322-65322 BLACKWATER	65564-65564 SOLO	65667-65667 HARTVILLE	65770-65770 WALNUT GROVE
65323-65323 CALHOUN	65565-65565 STEELVILLE	65668-65668 HERMITAGE	65771-65771 WALNUT SHADE
65324-65324 CLIMAX SPRINGS	65566-65566 VIBURNUM	65669-65669 HIGHLANDVILLE	65772-65772 WASHBURN
65325-65325 COLE CAMP	65567-65567 STOUTLAND	65672-65673 HOLLISTER	65773-65773 WASOLA
65326-65326 EDWARDS	65570-65570 SUCCESS	65674-65674 HUMANSVILLE	65774-65774 WEAUBLEAU
65327-65327 EMMA	65571-65571 SUMMERSVILLE	65675-65675 HURLEY	65775-65775 WEST PLAINS
65329-65329 FLORENCE	65572-65572 SWEDEBORG	65676-65676 ISABELLA	65776-65776 SOUTH FORK
65330-65330 GILLIAM	65573-65573 TERESITA	65679-65679 KIRBYVILLE	65777-65777 MOODY
65332-65332 GREEN RIDGE	65580-65580 VICHY	65680-65680 KISSEE MILLS	65778-65778 MYRTLE
65333-65333 HOUSTONIA	65582-65582 VIENNA	65681-65681 LAMPE	65779-65779 WHEATLAND
65334-65334 HUGHESVILLE	65583-65583 WAYNESVILLE	65682-65682 LOCKWOOD	65781-65781 WILLARD
65335-65335 IONIA	65584-65584 SAINT ROBERT	65685-65685 LOUISBURG	65783-65783 WINDYVILLE
65336-65336 KNOB NOSTER	65586-65586 WESCO	65686-65686 KIMBERLING CITY	65784-65784 ZANONI
65337-65337 LA MONTE	65588-65588 WINONA	65688-65688 BRANDSVILLE	65785-65785 STOCKTON
65338-65338 LINCOLN	65589-65589 YUKON	65689-65689 CABOOL	65786-65786 MACKS CREEK
65339-65339 MALTA BEND	65590-65590 LONG LANE	65690-65690 COUCH	65787-65787 ROACH
65340-65340 MARSHALL	65591-65591 MONTREAL	65692-65692 KOSHKONONG	65788-65788 PEACE VALLEY
65344-65344 MIAMI	65601-65601 ALDRICH	65701-65701 MC CLURG	65789-65789 POMONA
65345-65345 MORA	65603-65603 ARCOLA	65702-65702 MACOMB	65790-65790 POTTERSVILLE
65347-65347 NELSON	65604-65604 ASH GROVE	65704-65704 MANSFIELD	65791-65791 THAYER
65348-65348 OTTERVILLE	65605-65605 AURORA	65705-65705 MARIONVILLE	65793-65793 WILLOW SPRINGS
65349-65349 SLATER	65606-65606 ALTON	65706-65706 MARSHFIELD	65800-65899 SPRINGFIELD
65350-65350 SMITHTON	65607-65607 CAPLINGER MILLS	65707-65707 MILLER	
65351-65351 SWEET SPRINGS	65608-65608 AVA	65708-65708 MONETT	

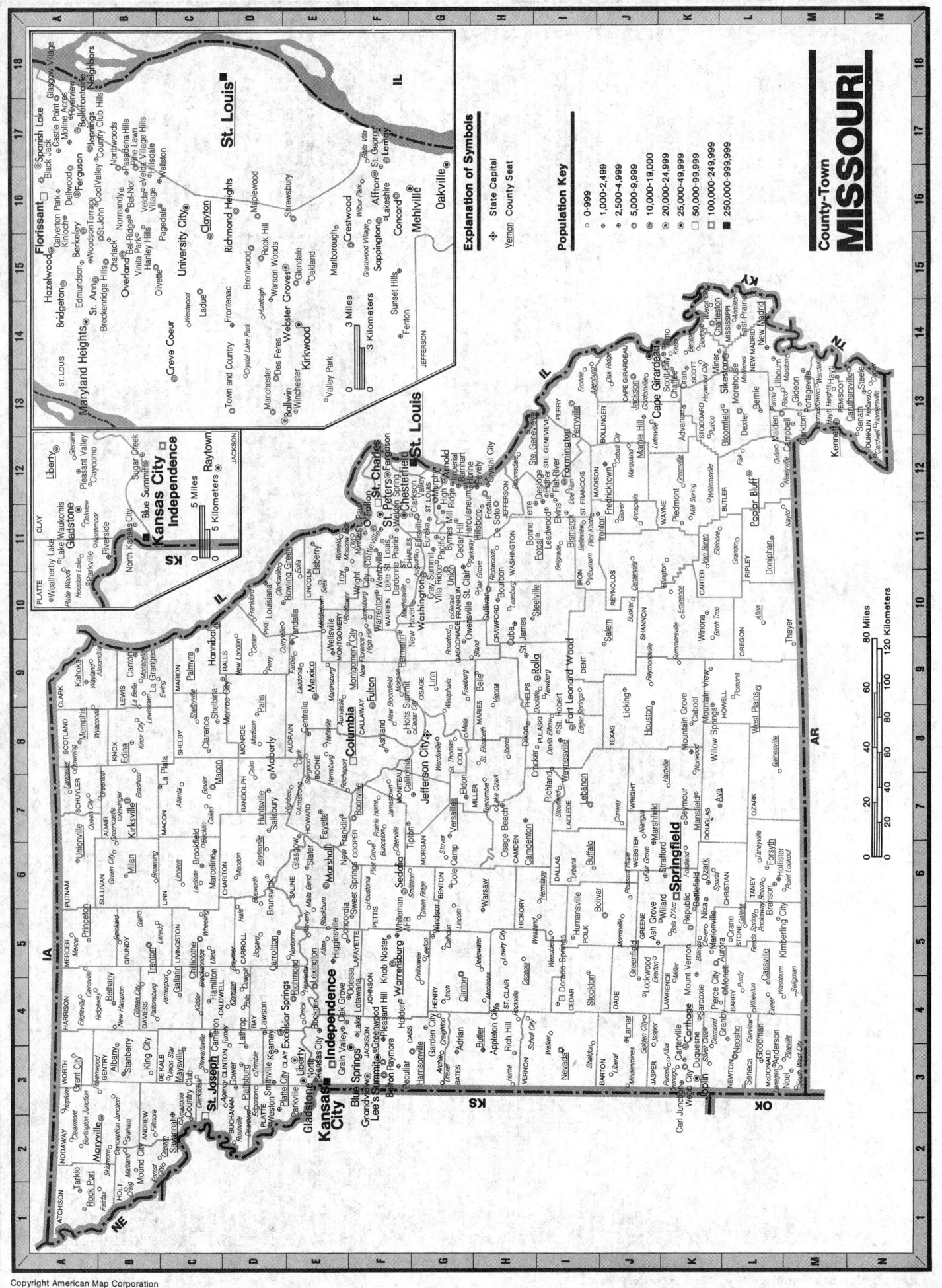

County-Town
MISSOURI

Explanation of Symbols

✪ State Capital
◈ Vernon County Seat

Population Key

○ 0-999
⊙ 1,000-2,499
◉ 2,500-4,999
● 5,000-9,999
● 10,000-19,000
● 20,000-24,999
● 25,000-49,999
□ 50,000-99,999
■ 100,000-249,999
■ 250,000-999,999

CITIES AND TOWNS

Note: The first name is that of the city or town, second, that of the county in which it is located, then the population and location on the map.

Explanation of symbols: •— Census Designated Place (CDP)

Montana

General Help Numbers:

Governor's Office
PO Box 200801, State Capitol   406-444-3111
Helena, MT 59620-0801   Fax 406-444-5529
www.discoveringmontana.com/   8AM-5PM
gov2/css/default.asp

Attorney General's Office
PO Box 201401   406-444-2026
Helena, MT 59620   Fax 406-444-3549
http://www.doj.state.mt.us/   8AM-5PM

Legislative Records
State Capitol, Rm 110   406-444-3064
PO Box 201706   406-444-3660 (Research)
Helena, MT 59620-1706   Fax 406-444-3036
www.leg.state.mt.us   8AM-5PM

State Archives
Library/Archives Division   406-444-2694
PO Box 201201, 225 N Roberts St   Fax 406-444-2696
Helena, MT 59620-1201   8AM-5PM M-F;
www.his.state.mt.us   9AM-4:30PM
1st SA of each month

State Specifics:

Capital:	Helena
	Lewis and Clark County
Time Zone:	MST
Number of Counties:	56
Population:	917,621

Web Site: www.discoveringmontana.com/default.asp

State Agencies

Criminal Records

Department of Justice, Criminal Records, PO Box 201403, Helena, MT 59620-1403 (Courier: 303 N Roberts, 4th Floor, Helena, MT 59620); 406-444-3625, 406-444-0689 (Fax), 8AM-5PM.

www.doj.state.mt.us

Indexing & Storage: Records are available from 1950's on and are 100% computerized. It takes 1 week to 1 month before new records are available for inquiry. Records are normally destroyed after court order.

Searching: Include the following in your request-name, date of birth. The Social Security Number and any aliases are helpful. Place written requests on letterhead. Fingerprint searches are optional. 100% of records are fingerprint-supported. The following data is not released: traffic offenses, unless felony driving under the influence of alcohol.

Access by: mail, in person.

Fee & Payment: The fee is $8.00 per individual for a name check or $8.00 per individual for a fingerprint check; $32.00 for a fingerprint check plus FBI fingerprint check, when required by statute for child care or schools. Account status to approved screening firms. Fee payee: Montana Criminal Records Prepayment required. Personal checks accepted. No credit cards accepted.

Mail search: Turnaround time: 5-10 days. A SASE is requested.

In person search: Turnaround time is usually immediate, unless there is a record or "hit."

Statewide Court Records

Court Administrator, PO Box 203002, Helena, MT 59620-3002 (Courier: 215 N Sanders, Justice Bldg Rm 315, Helena, MT 59620); 406-444-2621, 406-444-0834 (Fax), 8AM-5PM.

www.lawlibrary.state.mt.us

Note: Except for certain online research capabilities, all court record access must be done at the local level.

Access by: online.

Online search: Montana Supreme Court opinions and orders are found at the website.

Sexual Offender Registry

Department of Justice, Sexual and Violent Offender Registry, PO Box 201417, Helena, MT 59620; 406-444-9479, 406-444-2759 (Fax), 8AM-5PM.

http://svor2.doj.state.mt.us:8010/index.htm

Note: There are over 2,500 registered offenders in the database. There are three Tier Levels of offenders, 1 being the lowest and 3 being the highest. Level 3 also indicates the offender is a sexually violent predator.

Indexing & Storage: Records are available from 1989 forward. Tier Levels were instituted in 1997. It takes 1 week to 1 month before new records are available for inquiry.

Access by: mail, phone, fax, in person, online.

Fee & Payment: There is no fee to search.

Mail search: Turnaround time: 2 to 3 days. A SASE is requested.

Phone search: Single name inquiry is available by phone.

Fax search: Search requests are accpted by fax.

In person search: Searching in person permitted.

Online search: The state sexual offender list is available at the website. You can search for this information by name, by city or county, or by the type of offense committed.

Incarceration Records

Montana Department of Corrections, Directors Office, PO Box 201301, Helena, MT 59620-1301 (Courier: 1539 11th Ave, Helena, MT 59620); 406-444-3930, 406-444-7461 (Information Officer), 406-444-4920 (Fax), 8:30AM-4:30PM.

www.cor.state.mt.us/

Indexing & Storage: Records are available on current and former inmates, except for the website which is current only. Computerized records go back to 1980. Older records sent to Historical Society. It takes about 30 days before new records are available for inquiry.

Searching: Location, physical identifiers, conviction and sentencing information, and release dates are provided. Include the following in your request-name; and DOB. Computer records go back to 1978. The following data is not released: SSN and medical information.

Access by: mail, phone, online.

Fee & Payment: There is no fee.

Mail search: Turnaround time: 10 to 40 days.

Phone search: Name searching is permitted by phone.

Online search: Search current or former inmates on the ConWeb system at http://app.discoveringmontana.com/conweb/index.html. Search by ID# or name. Also, a private company offers free web access to DOC records at www.vinelink.com/index.jsp.

Other access: Entire offender database is available for purchase for $100.00; call Discovering Montana, 406-449-3468. Academic or social researchers can acquire the same database for no charge.

Corporation, Limited Liability Company Records, Fictitious Name, Limited Partnerships, Assumed Name, Trademarks, Servicemarks

Business Services Bureau, Secretary of State, PO Box 202801, Helena, MT 59620-2801 (Courier: 1236 East 6th Ave, Helena, MT 59620); 406-444-3665, 406-444-3976 (Fax), 8AM-5PM.

http://sos.state.mt.us/css/index.asp

Indexing & Storage: Records are available from the 1860s. New records are available for inquiry immediately. Records are indexed on inhouse computer.

Searching: Include the following in your request-full name of business, specific records that you need copies of. In addition to the articles of incorporation, corporation records include the following information: Annual Reports, Officers, Directors, DBAs, Prior (merged) names, Inactive and Reserved names.

Access by: mail, phone, fax, in person, online.

Fee & Payment: There is no search fee, but there is a flat fee of $10.00 for all copies of file, records are certified for this price. Fee payee: Secretary of State. Prepayment required. Prepaid accounts may be established. Personal checks accepted. No credit cards accepted.

Mail search: Turnaround time: 2 weeks. A SASE is requested.

Phone search: Limit of three requests per call.

Fax search: Fax requests are accepted for prepaid accounts at a cost of $3.00 for up to 10 pages and $.25 per additional page to fax back. Turnaround time is up to 10 business days.

In person search: Counter service is available.

Online search: Visit http://app.discoveringmontana.com/bes/ for free searches of MT business entities. There is a commercial service for finding finding registered principles, the fee is $4.00 per search. Go to http://app.discoveringmontana.com/walkthrough/rps/.

Other access: Lists of the new corporations per month are available.

Expedited service: Expedited service is available for mail, phone and in person searches. Turnaround time: 1 day. Add $20.00 per search.

Uniform Commercial Code, Federal Tax Liens

Business Services Bureau, Secretary of State, Rm 260, PO Box 202801, Helena, MT 59620-2801 (Courier: 1236 East 6th Ave, Helena, MT 59620); 406-444-1212, 406-444-3976 (Fax), 8AM-5PM.

http://sos.state.mt.us/css/index.asp

Indexing & Storage: Records are available from 1965, indexed on computer and on microfiche. Terminated or expired financing statements are not available prior to 6/30/01, with the exception of notices of federal tax liens. It takes one day before new records are available for inquiry.

Searching: Use search request form UCC-11. The search includes notice of federal tax liens on businesses and individuals. All state tax liens are filed at the county level. Include the following in your request-debtor exact name and any fictitious names.

Access by: mail, fax, in person, online.

Fee & Payment: The search fee is $7.00 per debtor name, copies are $.50 per page. Fee payee: Secretary of State. The state will accept prepaid accounts. Personal checks accepted. No credit cards accepted.

Mail search: Turnaround time: 2 to 5 days. A SASE is requested.

Fax search: Same fees and turnaround time apply.

In person search: Counter service is 2 to 5 days unless expedite fee is paid.

Online search: This web-based subscription service provides information about all active liens filed with the office. To use the service, you need to establish a prepaid account with the Discovering Montana for a fee of $25 per month. Contact Discovering Montana at 101 N Rodney #3, Helena MT 59601, or call 406-449-3468, or visit their web site at discoveringmontana.com.

Other access: The agency offers farm bill filings lists on a monthly basis for $5.00 per category. A CD-Rom for all Farm Products is available for $20.00.

Expedited service: Expedited service is available for fax and in-person searches. Turnaround time: 1 to 2 days. Add $20.00 per document.

State Tax Liens

Records not maintained by a state level agency.

Note: Records are at the county level.

Sales Tax Registrations

State does not impose sales tax.

Birth Certificates

Montana Department of Health, Vital Records, PO Box 4210, Helena, MT 59604 (Courier: 111 N Sanders, Rm 209, Helena, MT 59601); 406-444-4228 (Recording), 406-444-2685, 406-444-1803 (Fax), 8AM-5PM.

http://vhsp.dphhs.state.mt.us/dph_12.htm

Indexing & Storage: Records are available from 1907 on. It takes 3 months before new records are available for inquiry.

Searching: Must be able to show direct and tangible interest of records. The decision if you can get copies of records will be up to the staff of the Vital Records department. Include the following in your request-full name, names of parents, mother's maiden name, date of birth, place of birth, relationship to person of record, reason for information request. Must include copy of guardianship papers, if you are guardian. All requesters must include photo ID and phone number.

Access by: mail, fax, in person, online.

Fee & Payment: A certified copy is $12.00. If you don't know the year add a search fee of $10.00 for first 5 years search, and $1.00 each add'l year. Add $6.00 for using a credit card. The search fee is per 5 years searched. Fee payee: Montana Vital Records. Prepayment required. Personal checks accepted. Credit cards accepted: MasterCard, Visa, AmEx, Discover.

Mail search: Turnaround time: 10 days. No SASE is required. Search costs $10.00 for each name in request.

Fax search: Must use credit card for additional $6.00

In person search: Turnaround time same day.

Online search: Order records via state designated vendor at www.vitalchek.com.

Expedited service: Expedited service is available for fax and online orders. Turnaround time: overnight delivery. Add $16.00 per package for FedEx return plus the $6.00 credit card fee, and the $10.00 search fee.

Death Records

Montana Department of Health, Vital Records, PO Box 4210, Helena, MT 59604 (Courier: 111 N Sanders, Rm 209, Helena, MT 59601); 406-444-4228 (Recording), 406-444-2685, 406-444-1803 (Fax), 8AM-5PM.

http://vhsp.dphhs.state.mt.us/dph_l2.htm

Indexing & Storage: Records are available from 1907 on. It takes 3 months before new records are available for inquiry.

Searching: Records are open. Include the following in your request-full name, date of death, place of death, relationship to person of record, reason for information request. Requesters should include a copy of picture ID and phone number.

Access by: mail, fax, in person, online.

Fee & Payment: A certified copy is $12.00. If year not known, then add a search fee of $10.00 for 5 years searched and $1.00 each add'l year. Add $6.00for using a credit card. Fee payee: Montana Vital Records. Prepayment required. Personal checks accepted. Credit cards accepted: MasterCard, Visa, AmEx, Discover.

Mail search: Turnaround time: 10 days.

Fax search: Must use credit card.

In person search: Turnaround time same day.

Online search: Order records via state designated vendor at www.vitalchek.com.

Expedited service: Expedited service is available for fax and online orders. Turnaround time: overnight delivery. Add $16.00 per package for FedEx return plus the $6.00 credit card fee, and the $10.00 search fee.

Marriage Certificates, Divorce Records

Records not maintained by a state level agency.

Note: Marriage and divorce records are found at county of issue. This agency is required by law to maintain an index of these records. The index is from 1943 to present. The State can direct you to the correct county for a fee of $10.00 per 5 years searched.

Workers' Compensation Records

Montana State Fund, PO Box 4759, Helena, MT 59604-4759 (Courier: 5 S. Last Chance Gulch, Helena, MT 59601); 406-444-6500, 406-444-7796 (Fax), 8AM-5PM.

www.montanastatefund.com

Indexing & Storage: Records are available from mid 1980's to 1995 on microfiche. Records 1996 forward are computerized. It takes 30 days before new records are available for inquiry.

Searching: Put request in writing, including reason for the request. They will determine whether the request is legitimate, unless you include a signed release form. Include the following in your request-claimant name, Social Security Number, date of accident, employer.

Access by: mail, fax.

Fee & Payment: Copy fees are $.35 per page if from computer, $.50 per page if from microfiche. There is no search fee. Fee payee: Montana State Fund. Prepayment required. Personal checks accepted. No credit cards accepted.

Mail search: Turnaround time: 7 days. No SASE is required.

Fax search: Same criteria as mail searches.

Driver Records

Motor Vehicle Division, Driver's Services, PO Box 201430, Helena, MT 59620-1430 (Courier: Records Unit, 303 N Roberts, Room 260, Helena, MT 59620); 406-444-3292, 406-444-7623 (Fax), 8AM-5PM.

www.doj.state.mt.us/driving/default.asp

Indexing & Storage: Records are available for lifetime. It takes up to 45 days before new records are available for inquiry. Records are normally destroyed after scanned and indexed.

Searching: Anyone may order a driving record; however, personal information including address, SSN, photo, and medical information is not released. Opt out is not necessary. Use of the State Form is required. The form can be downloaded at the website. Include the following in your request-driver's full name, DOB, and/or license number. Requester must present copy of state issued ID or have request notarized.

Access by: mail, in person, online.

Fee & Payment: The fee is $4.00 per three year record history and $10.00 for a certified history. Fee payee: Motor Vehicle Division. Prepayment required. Billing or draw accounts available. Personal checks accepted. No credit cards accepted.

Mail search: Turnaround time: 3 days. Requests must be in writing, stating purpose and on letterhead.A SASE is requested.

In person search: Simple requests processed immediately. Up to 5 records may be requested in person for immediate delivery at this location. Use of forms are required.

Online search: Both interactive and batch delivery is offered ($6.50 per record) to users who sign up in advance and pay a $50.00 annual fee. Online services also include a license status conviction activity search available at a reduced rate through batched electronic exchange. For more information, visit http://app.discoveringmontana.com/dojdrs/.

Expedited service: Fax return service is available for an additional $3.00 per page.

Vehicle Ownership, Vehicle Identification, Vessel Ownership, Vessel Registration

Department of Justice, Title and Registration Bureau, 1032 Buckskin Drive, Deer Lodge, MT 59722; 406-846-6000, 406-846-6039 (Fax), 8AM-5PM.

www.doj.state.mt.us/driving/vehicletitleregistration.asp

Note: Lien information appears on the title record.

Indexing & Storage: Records are available from 1976 to present on microfiche. Watercraft data is available from 1988. It takes 5 to 10 days before new records are available for inquiry. Records are normally destroyed after 4 years.

Searching: Casual requesters may not obtain records without written consent of the subject. DPPA requirements enforced. MV210 Form - Release of Motor Vehicle Records - can be downloaded from the website. Requires notarization of the requester or copy of DL. Items required for search could include full name, VIN, plate number, or title number.

Access by: mail, in person, online.

Fee & Payment: The fee is $6.00 per vehicle/vessel or name search; $25.00 for title or odometer history. Fee payee: Title and Registration Bureau. Prepayment required. Personal checks accepted. No credit cards accepted.

Mail search: Turnaround time: 5 to 7 days. Requests must be in writing, signed and notarized. Use of the state form is required. No SASE is required.

In person search: Simple requests may be processed while you wait, if staffing available.

Online search: Online access to vehicle records is available at https://app.discoveringmontana.com/dojvs/. Requesters must pay an annual $50.00 registration fee, and the purpose of the requests must pass DPPA muster. Depending on level of authority granted, the following is available: Vehicle Information, License Plate Information, Vehicle Owner Information, Lien History, Title History and Registration Information. Call 866-449-3468 for more information.

Other access: Bulk or batch ordering of registration information is available on tape, disk, or paper. The user must fill out a specific form, which gives the user the capability of customization. For further information, contact the Registrar at address above.

Accident Reports

Montana Highway Patrol, Crash Records, 2550 Prospect Ave, Helena, MT 59620-1419; 406-444-3278, 406-444-4169 (Fax), 8AM-5PM.

www.doj.state.mt.us/department/highwaypatroldivision.asp

Note: Digital images are available with previous year's data.

Indexing & Storage: Records are available for 10 years to present. Computer indexing since 1996. Digital images are available starting with the year 1995. It takes 10 to 14 days after the accident before new records are available for inquiry. Records are normally destroyed after 10 years.

Searching: Records are only released to persons involved in crash, owner, attorney or insurance representing someone involved in the case. Witness statements are released. An Accident Release Form available on web. Include the following in your request-location of accident, date of accident, full name(s) of drivers.

Access by: mail, phone, in person.

Fee & Payment: The search fee is $2.00 per report, non-fundable. Fee payee: Montana Highway Patrol. Prepayment required. Personal checks accepted. No credit cards accepted.

Mail search: Turnaround time: 3 to 4 working days. Requests must be submitted in writing following guidelines mentioned above. No SASE is required.

Phone search: The agency will only release names over the phone of people involved in crash.

In person search: Records will be released if proper authorization is shown.

Other access: Statistics, but not reports, are available.

Voter Registration

Secretary of State, Elections Bureau, PO Box 202801, Helena, MT 59620-2801; 406-444-5376, 406-444-2023 (Fax), 8AM-5PM.

http://sos.state.mt.us

Note: Searching by state personnel depends on the voter file system workload.

Indexing & Storage: Records are available from 2002 (new centralized system). Counties will update the state database periodically. Therefore, it is suggested to also search at the county level. Records are normally destroyed after 2 years (archived).

Searching: The following data is not released: Social Security Numbers.

Access by: mail, phone, fax, in person, online.

Fee & Payment: There are no fees for searches unless large lists or bulk records needed.

Mail search: Turnaround time: 2 to 4 days. No SASE is required.

Phone search: Records are available by phone.

Fax search: Fax searching available.

In person search: Simple requests may be processed immediately.

Online search: Access records at http://app.discoveringmontana.com/voterfile/index.html. Customized lists are available for $.04 per record. Records can be purchased for non-commercial use only.

Other access: This agency database can be purchased on disk or CD-ROM. Fee of $.012 per record will be assessed. For more information, contact Elaine Graveley.

GED Certificates

Office of Public Instruction, GED Program, PO Box 202501, Helena, MT 59620-2501; 406-444-4438, 406-444-1373 (Fax), 7AM-4PM.

www.opi.state.mt.us/GED/Index.html

Indexing & Storage: It takes three weeks before new records are available for inquiry.

Searching: The agency will not issue duplicate diplomas. Include the following in your request-name, SSN, DOB, approximate year of test, SASE. If the information is going to a third party (employer or screening company) include a signed release from the subject and indicate where to send the documentation.

Access by: mail, in person.

Fee & Payment: There is no search fee for either a verification or transcript. The fee is the cost of the stamped envelope.

Mail search: Turnaround time 1 week. A SASE is required.

In person search: No fee for request. Turnaround time same day.

Hunting and Fishing License Information

Fish, Wildlife & Parks Department, Licensing, PO Box 200701, Helena, MT 59620-0701 (Courier: 1420 E 6th Ave, Helena, MT 59620); 406-444-2950, 406-444-8403 (Fax), 8AM-5PM.

http://fwp.state.mt.us

Indexing & Storage: Records are available from 1976 for the special resident and non-resident permits and the general permits go back for 5 years. Records are computerized for the current year, prior on microfiche. Records are indexed on inhouse computer, microfiche.

Searching: The agency will verify if a person has purchased a license. Include the following in your request-full name, date of birth, Social Security Number. The following data is not released: phone number and SSN.

Access by: mail, phone, in person.

Fee & Payment: There is no search fee.

Mail search: Turnaround time: 1 week. A SASE is requested.

Phone search: Records are available by phone.

In person search: Simple requests may be processed immediately.

Other access: A master list showing names, address, and types of licenses purchased can be ordered from this agency. The cost is $100.00.

Montana State Licensing Agencies

Licenses Searchable Online

Acupuncturist #33 .... http://app.discoveringmontana.com/bsdinq/index.html
Architect #41 .... http://app.discoveringmontana.com/bsdinq/index.html
Athletic Event/Event Timekeeper #3 .... http://app.discoveringmontana.com/bsdinq/index.html
Audiologist #21 .... http://app.discoveringmontana.com/bsdinq/index.html
Barber/Barber Instructor #2 .... http://app.discoveringmontana.com/bsdinq/index.html
Boxer/Boxing Professional #3 .... http://app.discoveringmontana.com/bsdinq/index.html
Cemetery, Privately Owned #3 .... http://app.discoveringmontana.com/bsdinq/index.html
Chemical Dependency Counselor #19 .... http://app.discoveringmontana.com/bsdinq/index.html
Child Care Provider #26 .... http://vhsp.dphhs.state.mt.us/dph_r2.htm
Chiropractor #3 .... http://app.discoveringmontana.com/bsdinq/index.html
Clinical Nurse Specialist #32 .... www.discoveringmontana.com/dli/nur
Clinical Social Worker #17 .... http://app.discoveringmontana.com/bsdinq/index.html
Construction Blaster #18 .... http://app.discoveringmontana.com/bsdinq/index.html
Contractor, Public #36 .... http://erd.dli.state.mt.us/wcregs/mtcontractor.asp
Cosmetologist/Cosmetology Instructor/School #2 .... http://app.discoveringmontana.com/bsdinq/index.html
Crematory/Crematory Operator/Technician #3 .... http://app.discoveringmontana.com/bsdinq/index.html
Day Care Center #26 .... http://vhsp.dphhs.state.mt.us/dph_r2.htm
Dental Hygienist #5 .... http://discoveringmontana.com/dli/bsd/index.asp
Dentist/Dental Assistant/Denturist #5 .... http://discoveringmontana.com/dli/bsd/index.asp
Drug Registration, Dangerous #7 .... http://app.discoveringmontana.com/bsdinq/index.html
Drug Wholesaler #7 .... http://app.discoveringmontana.com/bsdinq/index.html
Electrician #8 .... http://app.discoveringmontana.com/bsdinq/index.html
Electrologist #2 .... http://app.discoveringmontana.com/bsdinq/index.html
Emergency Medical Technician #33 .... http://app.discoveringmontana.com/bsdinq/index.html
Engineer #10 .... http://app.discoveringmontana.com/bsdinq/index.html
Esthetician #2 .... http://app.discoveringmontana.com/bsdinq/index.html
Firearms Instructor #9 .... http://app.discoveringmontana.com/bsdinq/index.html
Funeral Director #3 .... http://app.discoveringmontana.com/bsdinq/index.html
Hairstylist #21 .... http://app.discoveringmontana.com/bsdinq/index.html
Hearing Aid Dispenser #3 .... http://app.discoveringmontana.com/bsdinq/index.html
Insurance Adjuster/Producer #37 .... www.sao.state.mt.us/sao/insurance/findagent.html
Land Surveyor #10 .... http://app.discoveringmontana.com/bsdinq/index.html
Landscape Architect #3 .... http://app.discoveringmontana.com/bsdinq/index.html
Manicurist #2 .... http://app.discoveringmontana.com/bsdinq/index.html
Medical Doctor #33 .... http://app.discoveringmontana.com/bsdinq/index.html
Midwife Nurse #32 .... www.discoveringmontana.com/dli/nur
Midwife, Direct Entry/Apprentice #1 .... http://app.discoveringmontana.com/bsdinq/index.html
Mortuary/Mortician #3 .... http://app.discoveringmontana.com/bsdinq/index.html
Naturopathic Physician #1 .... http://app.discoveringmontana.com/bsdinq/index.html
Nurse Anesthetist #32 .... www.discoveringmontana.com/dli/nur
Nurse-RN/LPN / Nurse Practitioner #32 .... www.discoveringmontana.com/dli/nur
Nutritionist #33 .... http://app.discoveringmontana.com/bsdinq/index.html
Occupational Therapist #21 .... http://app.discoveringmontana.com/bsdinq/index.html
Optometrist #7 .... http://discoveringmontana.com/dli/opt
Osteopathic Physician #33 .... http://app.discoveringmontana.com/bsdinq/index.html
Outfitter, Hunting/Fishing #6 .... http://app.discoveringmontana.com/bsdinq/index.html
Pharmacist #7 .... http://app.discoveringmontana.com/bsdinq/index.html
Physical Therapist #17 .... http://app.discoveringmontana.com/bsdinq/index.html
Physician Assistant #33 .... http://app.discoveringmontana.com/bsdinq/index.html
Plumber #8 .... http://app.discoveringmontana.com/bsdinq/index.html
Podiatrist #33 .... http://app.discoveringmontana.com/bsdinq/index.html
Private Investigator/Private Security Guard #9 .... http://app.discoveringmontana.com/bsdinq/index.html
Process Server #9 .... http://app.discoveringmontana.com/bsdinq/index.html
Property Manager #15 .... http://app.discoveringmontana.com/bsdinq/index.html
Psychologist #11 .... http://app.discoveringmontana.com/bsdinq/index.html
Public Accountant #12 .... http://app.discoveringmontana.com/bsdinq/
Radiologic Technologist #21 .... http://app.discoveringmontana.com/bsdinq/index.html
Real Estate Agent/Broker/Sales #15 .... http://app.discoveringmontana.com/bsdinq/index.html
Real Estate Appraiser #14 .... http://app.discoveringmontana.com/bsdinq/index.html

Referee #3	http://app.discoveringmontana.com/bsdinq/index.html
Respiratory Care Practitioner #21	http://app.discoveringmontana.com/bsdinq/index.html
Sanitarian #21	http://app.discoveringmontana.com/bsdinq/index.html
Security Alarm Installer/Security Company/Organization #9	http://app.discoveringmontana.com/bsdinq/index.html
Security Guard #21	http://app.discoveringmontana.com/bsdinq/index.html
Social Worker, LSW #17	http://app.discoveringmontana.com/bsdinq/index.html
Speech Pathologist #21	http://app.discoveringmontana.com/bsdinq/index.html
Surveyor, Land #10	http://app.discoveringmontana.com/bsdinq/index.html
Teacher #35	http://data.opi.state.mt.us/certification/
Timeshare Broker/Salesperson #15	http://app.discoveringmontana.com/bsdinq/index.html
Veterinarian #11	http://app.discoveringmontana.com/bsdinq/index.html
Wrestler #3	http://app.discoveringmontana.com/bsdinq/index.html
X-ray Technician #21	http://app.discoveringmontana.com/bsdinq/index.html

Montana Licensing Quick Finder

Acupuncturist #33 406-841-2364
Adoption Agency #4 406-444-5916
Apiary #20 406-444-5400
Architect #41 406-841-2367
Asbestos Abatement Contractor/Spvr./Supplier #25
.... 406-444-3490
Asbestos Abatement Occupation #25 ... 406-444-3490
Athletic Event/Event Timekeeper #3 406-841-2393
Attorney #16 406-442-7660
Audiologist #21 406-444-3091
Barber/Barber Instructor #2 406-841-2300
Boxer/Boxing Professional #3 406-841-2393
Boxing Manager/Promoter/Judge #3.... 406-841-2393
Brand (Livestock) #29 406-444-2045
Brand Inspector #29 406-444-2045
Card Contractor/Card Tournament #28. 406-444-1971
Card Dealer/Card Table, Live #28 406-444-1971
Casino Night #28 406-444-1971
Cemetery, Privately Owned #3 406-841-2393
Chemical Dependency Counselor #19.. 406-444-2827
Child Care Agency #4 406-444-1675
Child Care Provider #26 406-444-2012
Chiropractor #3 406-841-2393
Clinical Nurse Specialist #32 406-841-2340
Clinical Social Worker #17 406-841-2369
Commodity Dealer #20 406-444-5400
Construction Blaster #18 406-841-2351
Contractor, Public #36 406-444-7734
Cosmetologist/Cosmetology Instructor/School #2
.... 406-841-2300
Crematory/Crematory Operator/Tech #3406-841-2393
Dam Safety Operation Permit #40 406-444-6601
Day Care Center #26 406-444-2012
Dental Hygienist #5 406-841-2390
Dentist/Dental Assistant/Denturist #5.. 406-841-2390
Dietitian #33 406-841-2364
Drug Registration, Dangerous #7 406-841-2356
Drug Wholesaler #7 406-841-2356
Electrician #8 406-841-2328
Electrologist #2 406-841-2300
Emergency Medical Technician #33 406-841-2380
Engineer #10 406-841-2367
Esthetician #2 406-841-2300
Fertilizer Dealer #20 406-444-5400

Firearms Instructor #9 406-841-2387
Foster Care Home/Program #4 406-444-1675
Funeral Director #3 406-841-2393
Fur/Hide Dealer #27 406-444-4558
Gambling Machine/Operator #28 406-444-1971
Gaming Device Mfg./Dist. #28 406-444-1971
Grain Elevator #20 406-444-5400
Group Home, Youth #30 406-444-6587
Hairstylist #21 406-444-4288
Hearing Aid Dispenser #3 406-841-2395
Horse Racing Occupation #22 406-444-4287
Insurance Adjuster/Producer #37 406-444-2040
Jockey #22 406-444-4287
Land Surveyor #10 406-841-2367
Landscape Architect #3 406-841-2395
Livestock Dealer #29 406-444-2045
Living Trust Seller #38 406-444-2040
Lobbyist #43 406-444-2942
Lottery Retailer #23 406-444-5825
Manicurist #2 406-841-2300
Meat and Poultry #29 406-444-5202
Medical Doctor #33 406-841-2364
Midwife Nurse #32 406-841-2340
Midwife, Direct Entry/Apprentice #1 ... 406-841-2394
Milk/Cream Weigher/Grader/Sampler/Tester #29
.... 406-444-2875
Mint Oil Producer #20 406-444-5400
Mortuary/Mortician #3 406-841-2393
Multi-level Marketing Company #38 406-444-2040
Naturopathic Physician #1 406-841-2394
Notary Public #13 406-444-5379
Nurse Anesthetist #32 406-841-2340
Nurse-RN/LPN/ Nurse Practitioner #32 406-841-2340
Nurseryman #20 406-444-5400
Nutritionist #33 406-841-2364
Occupational Therapist #21 406-444-3091
Optometrist #7 406-841-2390
Osteopathic Physician #33 406-841-2364
Outfitter, Hunting/Fishing #6 406-444-3738
Pesticide Applicator/Dealer #20 406-444-5400
Pharmacist #7 406-841-2356
Physical Therapist #17 406-841-2369
Physician Assistant #33 406-841-2361
Plumber #8 406-841-2328

Podiatrist #33 406-841-2364
Private Investigator #9 406-841-2387
Private Placement Offering #38 406-444-2040
Private Security Guard #9 406-841-2387
Process Server #9 406-841-2387
Property Manager #15 406-444-2961
Psychologist #11 406-841-2394
Public Accountant #12 406-841-2388
Radiologic Technologist #21 406-444-3091
Real Estate Agent/Broker/Sales #15 .. 406-444-2961
Real Estate Appraiser #14 406-841-2386
Referee #3 406-841-2393
Respiratory Care Practitioner #21 406-444-3091
Sanitarian #21 406-444-3091
School Guidance Counselor/ School Pschologist #35
.... 406-444-3150
School Principal #35 406-444-3150
School Superintendent #35 406-444-3150
Securities Broker/Salesperson #38 406-444-2040
Security Alarm Installer #9 406-841-2387
Security Company/Organization #9 406-841-2387
Security Guard #21 406-444-4288
Seed Dealer #20 406-444-5400
Septic Tank Cleaner #25 406-444-5294
Social Worker, LSW #17 406-841-2369
Speech Pathologist #21 406-444-3091
Surveyor, Land #10 406-841-2367
Taxidermist #27 406-444-4558
Teacher #35 406-444-3150
Telephone, Customer-Owned, Coin-Operated #38
.... 406-444-2040
Timeshare Broker/Salesperson #15 406-444-2961
Underground Storage Tank Insp. #42.. 406-444-5300
Underground Storage Tank Installer/Remover #42
.... 406-444-5300
Variable Annuities Seller #38 406-444-2040
Veterinarian #11 406-841-2394
Water & Sewage Plant Operator #25... 406-444-5294
Weather Modifier #40 406-444-6601
Well Driller #40 406-444-6601
Wrestler #3 406-841-2393
X-ray Technician #21 406-444-3091

Montana Licensing Agency Information

1 Board of Alternative Health Care, Health Care License Bureau, PO Box 200513 (301 S Park, 4th Fl), Helena, MT 59620-0513; 406-841-2365, Fax: 406-841-2305. www.discoveringmontana.com/dli/ahc Email: dlibsdahc@state.mt.us Search Database at http://app.discoveringmontana.com/bsdinq/index.html

2 Board of Barbers & Cosmetologists, Division of Professional & Occupational Licensing, PO Box

200513 (301 S Park, 4th Fl), Helena, MT 59620-0513; 406-444-2961, Fax: 406-841-2325. www.discoveringmontana.com/dli/cos Email: dlibsdcos@state.mt.us Search Database at http://app.discovering montana.com/bsdinq/index.html

3 Boards: Chiropractor, Funerary, Hearing, Landscape Architect, Athletic Events, Division of Professional & Occupational Licensing, PO Box 200513 (301 S Park, 4th Fl, #428), Helena, MT 59620-0513; 406-841-2393, Fax: 406-841-2305.

www.discoveringmontana.com/dli/bsd/ Email: cheryls@state.mt.us Search Database at http://app.discovering montana.com/bsdinq/index.html

4 Department of Public Health Human Services, Child & Family Services Division, PO Box 8005 (1400 Boadway), Helena, MT 59604; 406-444-5900, Fax: 406-444-5956. www.dphhs.state.mt.us

5 Board of Dentistry, Division of Health Care Licensing, PO Box 200513 (301 S Park), 4th Floor, Helena, MT 59620-0513; 406-841-2390, Fax: 406-841-2305.
www.discoveringmontana.com/dli/den
Email: compolden@state.mt.us   Search Database at http://discoveringmontana.com/dli/bsd/index.asp
Note: Records availabe online from July 1996.

6 Board of Outfitters, Division of Professional & Occupational Licensing, PO Box 200513 (301 S Park, 4th Fl), Helena, MT 59620-0513; 406-444-5983, Fax: 406-444-1667.
Email: compolout@state.mt.us   Search at http://app.discoveringmontana.com/bsdinq/index.html

7 Board of Optometry, Division of Professional & Occupational Licensing, PO Box 200513 (301 S Park, 4th Fl), Helena, MT 59620-0513; 406-841-2390, Fax: 406-841-2305.
http://discoveringmontana.com/dli/opt
Email: dlibsdopt@state.mt.us Search Database at http://discoveringmontana.com/dli/bsd/index.asp

8 Plumbing and Electrical Board, Division of Professional & Occupational Licensing, PO Box 200513 (301 S Park, 4th Fl), Helena, MT 59620-0513; 406-841-2328, Fax: 406-841-2309.
Email: dlibsdele@state.mt.us   Search at http://app.discovering montana.com/bsdinq/index.html

9 Board of Private Security Patrol Officers & Invest., Division of Professional & Occupational Licensing, PO Box 200513 (301 S Park, 4th Fl), Helena, MT 59620-0513; 406-841-2387, 841-2304, Fax: 406-841-2305. email: tersmith@state.mt.us
Search Database at http://app.discoveringmontana.com/bsdinq/index.html Note: Physical Therapy Board (406-841-2369) is separate, but at the same address. Physical Therapy Board email is dlibsdptp@state.mt.us.

10 Board of Professional Engineers & Land Surveyors, Division of Professional & Occupational Licensing, PO Box 200513 (301 S Park, 4th Fl), Helena, MT 59620-0513; 406-841-2367, Fax: 406-841-2309.
http://discoveringmontana.com/dli/bsd/license/contact_us.html   Email: compolpel@state.mt.us
Search Database at http://app.discoveringmontana.com/bsdinq/index.html

11 Veterinary Board, Board of Psychologists, PO Box 200513 (301 S Park, 4th Fl), Helena, MT 59620-0513; 406-841-2394, Fax: 406-841-2305.
www.discoveringmontana.com/dli/bsd/license/license.htm   Email: compolpsy@state.mt.us
Search Database at http://app.discovering montana.com/bsdinq/index.html

12 Board of Public Accountants, PO Box 200513 (301 South Park), Helena, MT 59620-0513; 406-841-2389, Fax: 406-841-2323.
www.discoveringmontana.com/dli/pac
Email: dlibsdpac@state.mt.us   Search Database at http://app.discoveringmontana.com/bsdinq/

13 Notary Division, Secretary of State, PO Box 202801 (Rm 260), Helena, MT 59620; 406-444-5379, Fax: 406-444-3976.
www.sos.state.mt.us/css/Notary/Contents.asp
Email: sosnotary@state.mt.us

14 Board of Real Estate Appraisers, PO Box 200513 (301 S Park Ave), Helena, MT 59620-0513; 406-841-2386, Fax: 406-841-2305.
www.discoveringmontana.com/dli/bsd/license/bsd_boards/rea_board/board_page.htm
Email: dlibsdrea@state.mt.us   Search at http://app.discoveringmontana.com/bsdinq/index.html

15 Board of Realty Regulation, Division of Professional & Occupational Licensing, PO Box 200513 (301 S. Park, 4th Fl), Helena, MT 59620-0513; 406-444-2961, Fax: 406-841-2323.
www.discoveringmontana.com/dli/bsd/license/bsd_boards/rre_board/board_page.htm
Email: compolrre@state.mt.us   Search at http://app.discoveringmontana.com/bsdinq/index.html

16 State Bar of Montana, PO Box 577 (7 W 6th Ave, #2B), Helena, MT 59624; 406-442-7660, Fax: 406-442-7763.   www.montanabar.org
Email: cwood@montanabar.org   Note: Use email cwood@montanabar.org to request to confirm an attorney's membership.

17 Physical Therapy Board, Division of Professional & Occupational Licensing, PO Box 200513 (301 S Park), Helena, MT 59620-0513; 406-841-2369, Fax: 406-841-2305.
Search Database at http://app.discovering montana.com/bsdinq/index.html

18 Construction Blasters, Division of Professional & Occupational Licensing, PO Box 200513 (301 S Park), Helena, MT 59620-0513; 406-841-2351, Fax: 406-841-2305.   Email: dlibsdbbc@state.mt.us
Search Database at http://app.discoveringmontana.com/bsdinq/index.html

19 Chemical Dependency Counselors Board, Division of Professional & Occupational Licensing, PO Box 200513 (301 S Park), Helena, MT 59620-0513; 406-841-2391, Fax: 406-841-2305.   Search Database at http://app.discoveringmontana.com/bsdinq/index.html

20 Department of Agriculture, Licensing and Registration, PO Box 200201, Helena, MT 59620; 406-444-5400, Fax: 406-444-7336.
http://agr.state.mt.us/license/first.htm

21 Department of Commerce, Licensing Boards, PO Box 200513 (301 S Park, 4th Fl), Helena, MT 59620-0513; 406-841-2300, Fax: 406-841-2305.
www.discoveringmontana.com/dli/bsd/license/license.htm   Email: jokershisnik@state.mt.us
Search Database at http://app.discoveringmontana.com/bsdinq/index.html

22 Department of Livestock, Board of Horse Racing, PO Box 200512 (301 S.Park Rm 468), Helena, MT 59620-0512; 406-444-4287, Fax: 406-444-4305. Email: mstark@state.mt.us
www.discoveringmontana.com/liv/

23 Department of Commerce, Montana Lottery, 2525 N Montana Ave, Helena, MT 59601; 406-444-5825, Fax: 406-444-5830.
www.montanalottery.com
Email: montanalottery@mail.com

25 Department of Environmental Quality, Permitting & Compliance Division, 5210 E 6th Ave, PO Box 200901, Helena, MT 59620-0901; 406-444-2544, Fax: 406-444-1374.
www.deq.state.mt.us   Email: ebenedict@state.mt.us

26 Department of Health & Human Services, Quality Assurance Division, PO Box 202953 (1400 Broadway, Helena), Helena, MT 59620; 406-444-2012, Fax: 406-444-1742.
www.dphhs.state.mt.us/about_us/divisions/quality_assurance/quality_assurance.htm
Email: bfleming@state.mt.us   Search Database at http://vhsp.dphhs.state.mt.us/dph_r2.htm

27 Dept. of Fish, Wildlife & Parks, Licensing/Data Bureau, 1420 E 6th Ave, Helena, MT 59620-0701; 406-444-2535, Fax: 406-444-4952.
www.fwp.state.mt.us/insidefwp/regoffice.asp
Email: bbeukelman@state.mt.us

28 Dept. of Justice, Gambling Control Division, 2550 Prospect Ave, Helena, MT 59620-1424; 406-444-1971, Fax: 406-444-9157.   www.doj.state.mt.us/department/gamblingcontroldivision.asp

29 Department of Livestock, Brand Enforcement, Milk Control, PO Box 202001, Helena, MT 59620; 406-444-2045.   www.liv.state.mt.us

30 Department of Public Health Human Services, Research & Planning Bureau, 48 N Last Chance Gulch, Helena, MT 59620-4001; 406-444-6587, Fax: 406-444-5956.

32 Board of Nursing, Division of Professional & Occupational Licensing, PO Box 200513 (301 S Park), Helena, MT 59620-0513; 406-841-2340, Fax: 406-841-2343.
www.discoveringmontana.com/dli/bsd/license/bsd_boards/nur_board/board_page.htm
Email: dlibsdnur@state.mt.us   Search Database at www.discoveringmontana.com/dli/nur

33 Board of Medical Examiners, PO Box 200513, Helena, MT 59620-0513; 406-841-2364, Fax: 406-841-2343.   www.discoveringmontana.com/dli/med
Email: dlibsdmed@state.mt.us   Search Database at http://app.discoveringmontana.com/bsdinq/index.html   Note: Lists are provided for a fee if offering continuing educational credits.

35 Certification Division, Office of Public Instruction, PO Box 202501, Helena, MT 59620; 406-444-3150, Fax: 406-444-3924.
www.opi.state.mt.us   Search Database at http://data.opi.state.mt.us/certification/

36 Public Contractors Licensing, Department of Labor, PO Box 8011, Helena, MT 59604; 406-444-7734, Fax: 406-444-3465.
http://erd.dli.state.mt.us/wcregs/mtcontractor.asp
Search Database at http://erd.dli.state.mt.us/wcregs/mtcontractor.asp

37 Insurance Division, State Auditor's Office, 840 Helena Ave, Helena, MT 59601; 406-444-2040.
www.sao.state.mt.us   Search Database at www.sao.state.mt.us/sao/insurance/findagent.html

38 Securities Division, State Auditor's Office, 840 Helena Ave, Helena, MT 59601; 406-444-2040, Fax: 406-444-5558.   www.sao.state.mt.us

40 Department of Natural Resources & Conservation, Water Resources Division, PO Box 201601 (1424 N. 0th Ave.), Helena, MT 59620-1601; 406-444-6601, Fax: 406-444-0533.
www.dnrc.state.mt.us They do not provide lists.

41 Board of Architects, Division of Professional & Occupational Licensing, PO Box 200513 (301 S Park), Helena, MT 59620-0513; 406-841-2367, Fax: 406-841-2301.
www.discoveringmontana.com/dli/arc   Search at http://app.discoveringmontana.com/bsdinq/index.html

42 Department of Environmental Quality, Remediation Division, PO Box 200901, Helena, MT 59620-0901; 406-444-5300, Fax: 406-444-1374.   www.deq.state.mt.us/ust/index.asp
Email: ustprogram@state.mt.us

43 Commissioner of Political Practices, Lobbyist Licensing, PO Box 202401 (1205 8th Ave), Helena, MT 59620; 406-444-2942, Fax: 406-444-1643.
http://www2.state.mt.us/cpp/css/default.asp
Email: lvaughey@state.mt.us.

Montana Federal Courts

The following list indicates the district and division name for each county in the state. If the bankruptcy court location is different from the district court, then the location of the bankruptcy court appears in parentheses.

County/Court Cross Reference

County	Court	County	Court
Beaverhead	Butte	Meagher	Helena (Butte)
Big Horn	Billings (Butte)	Mineral	Missoula (Butte)
Blaine	Great Falls (Butte)	Missoula	Missoula (Butte)
Broadwater	Helena (Butte)	Musselshell	Billings (Butte)
Carbon	Billings (Butte)	Park	Billings (Butte)
Carter	Billings (Butte)	Petroleum	Billings (Butte)
Cascade	Great Falls (Butte)	Phillips	Billings (Butte)
Chouteau	Great Falls (Butte)	Pondera	Great Falls (Butte)
Custer	Billings (Butte)	Powder River	Billings (Butte)
Daniels	Billings (Butte)	Powell	Helena (Butte)
Dawson	Billings (Butte)	Prairie	Billings (Butte)
Deer Lodge	Butte	Ravalli	Missoula (Butte)
Fallon	Billings (Butte)	Richland	Billings (Butte)
Fergus	Great Falls (Butte)	Roosevelt	Billings (Butte)
Flathead	Missoula (Butte)	Rosebud	Billings (Butte)
Gallatin	Butte	Sanders	Missoula (Butte)
Garfield	Billings (Butte)	Sheridan	Billings (Butte)
Glacier	Great Falls (Butte)	Silver Bow	Butte
Golden Valley	Billings (Butte)	Stillwater	Billings (Butte)
Granite	Missoula (Butte)	Sweet Grass	Billings (Butte)
Hill	Great Falls (Butte)	Teton	Great Falls (Butte)
Jefferson	Helena (Butte)	Toole	Great Falls (Butte)
Judith Basin	Great Falls (Butte)	Treasure	Billings (Butte)
Lake	Missoula (Butte)	Valley	Billings (Butte)
Lewis and Clark	Helena (Butte)	Wheatland	Billings (Butte)
Liberty	Great Falls (Butte)	Wibaux	Billings (Butte)
Lincoln	Missoula (Butte)	Yellowstone	Billings (Butte)
Madison	Butte	Yellowstone Nat. Park (part)	Billings (Butte)
McCone	Billings (Butte)		

Standards for Federal Courts: The search fee is $20.00 per item (one party name or case number). Certification fee is $7.00 per document. Copy fee is $.50 per page. All fees standard unless noted in profile. Mail Search: always enclose a stamped self addressed envelope unless otherwise noted. Most courts accept fax requests or will suggest a copying/search vendor. Before releasing records,

all courts require prepayment unless noted in profile.

Open records are located at the court unless otherwise noted. District courts index by defendant and plaintiff as well as by case number. Bankruptcy courts usually index by debtor and case number. While most courts now have their indexes on computer, many still maintain index card files as well.

The universal PACER sign-up number is 800-676-6856. Find PACER and the Party/Case Index on the Web at http://pacer.psc.uscourts.gov. PACER dial-up access is $.60 per minute. Also, courts offering internet access via RACER, PACER, Web-PACER or the new CM-ECF charge $.07 per page fee unless noted as free.

US District Court

District of Montana

Billings Division Clerk, Room 5405, Federal Bldg, 316 N 26th St, Billings, MT 59101 (Use mail address for courier delivery) 406-247-7000, Fax: 406-247-7008. www.mtd.uscourts.gov

Counties: Big Horn, Carbon, Carter, Custer, Daniels, Dawson, Fallon, Garfield, Golden Valley, McCone, Musselshell, Park, Petroleum, Powder River, Prairie, Richland, Rosebud, Sheridan, Stillwater, Sweet Grass, Treasure, Wheatland,Wibaux, Yellowstone, Yellowstone National Park.

Indexing & Storage: New cases available in the index 1 week after filing date.

Fee & Payment: Payment may be made by money order, cashier check, personal check. Payee: Clerk, U.S. District Court.

Phone Search: Only docket information available by phone.

Mail Search: A SASE not required.

In Person Search: Fee charged if court conducts your in person search for you.

PACER: PACER is available online at http://pacer.mtd.uscourts.gov. Case records go back to 1994. Records never purged. New records are online after 5 days.

Butte Division U.S. District Court, 400 North Main, Butte, MT 59701 (courier address: Use mail address for courier delivery) 406-782-0432, Fax: 406-782-0537. www.mtd.uscourts.gov

Counties: Beaverhead, Deer Lodge, Gallatin, Madison, Silver Bow.

Indexing & Storage: New cases available in the index 1 week after filing date.

Fee & Payment: Payment may be made by money order, cashier check, personal check. Payee: Clerk, U.S. District Court.

Phone Search: No searching by telephone.

Mail Search: A SASE not required.

In Person Search: Fee charged if court conducts your in person search for you.

PACER: PACER is available online at http://pacer.mtd.uscourts.gov. Case records go back to 1994. Records never purged. New records are online after 5 days.

Great Falls Division Clerk, PO Box 2186, Great Falls, MT 59403 (courier address: 215 1st Ave N, Great Falls, MT 59401), 406-727-1922, Fax: 406-727-7648. www.mtd.uscourts.gov

Counties: Blaine, Cascade, Chouteau, Daniels, Fergus, Glacier, Hill, Judith Basin, Liberty, Phillips, Pondera, Roosevelt, Sheridan, Teton, Toole, Valley.

Indexing & Storage: New cases available in the index immediately after filing date. District wide searches are available for all information from this division.

Fee & Payment: Payment may be made by money order, cashier check, personal check. Payee: Clerk, U.S. District Court.

Phone Search: Only docket information available by case number.

In Person Search: Fee charged if court conducts your in person search for you.

PACER: PACER is available online at http://pacer.mtd.uscourts.gov. Case records go back to 1994. Records never purged. New records are online after 5 days.

Helena Division Paul G. Hatfield Courthouse, 901 Front Street, Helena, MT 59626 (courier address:), 406-441-1355, Fax: 406-441-1357. www.mtd.uscourts.gov

Counties: Broadwater, Jefferson, Lewis and Clark, Meagher, Powell.

Indexing & Storage: New cases available in the index same day if possible after filing date. Cases filed in the Missoula division prior to January 1997 are held here.

Fee & Payment: Payment may be made by money order, cashier check, personal check. Payee: Clerk, U.S. District Court. Will fax results for add'l $5.00 fee, prepaid.

Phone Search: Information by phone is limited. Will fax results for add'l $5.00 fee, prepaid.

In Person Search: Fee charged if court conducts your in person search for you.

PACER: PACER is available online at http://pacer.mtd.uscourts.gov. Case records go back to 1994. Records never purged. New records are online after 5 days.

Missoula Division Russell Smith Courthouse, 201 E Broadway, Missoula, MT 59801 (courier address:), 406-542-7260, Fax: 406-542-7272. www.mtd.uscourts.gov

Counties: Flathead, Granite, Lake, Lincoln, Mineral, Missoula, Ravalli, Sanders.

Indexing & Storage: New cases available in the index 1-2 days after filing date. Cases in this district originate here; after closing they are held here rather than being sent to a Federal Records Center.

Fee & Payment: Payment may be made by money order, cashier check, personal check. Prepayment required except for attorneys. Court will fax results for a $5.00 fee. Payee: Clerk, U.S. District Court. Will fax results $5.00 plus $.50 per page.

Phone Search: Docket information is available by phone. Will fax results $5.00 plus $.50 per page.

Mail Search: A SASE not required.

In Person Search: Fee charged if court conducts your in person search for you.

PACER: PACER is available online at http://pacer.mtd.uscourts.gov. Case records go back to 1994. Records never purged. New records are online after 5 days.

U.S. Bankruptcy Court

District of Montana

Butte Division PO Box 689, Butte, MT 59703 (courier address: 303 Federal Bldg, 400 N Main St, Butte, MT 59703), 406-782-3354, Fax: 406-782-0537. www.mtb.uscourts.gov

Counties: All counties in Montana.

Indexing & Storage: Cases indexed by debtor as well as by case number. New cases available in the index immediately after filing date.

Fee & Payment: Payment may be made by money order, cashier check, personal check. Debtor's checks are not accepted. Payee: Clerk, U.S. Bankruptcy Court. Will fax results for fee of $1.00 per page.

Phone Search: Only docket information available by phone. Automated voice case information service (VCIS) is available. Call VCIS at 888-879-0071 or 406-782-1060. Will fax results at $1.00 per page.

Mail Search: A SASE not required.

In Person Search: Fee charged if court conducts your in person search for you.

PACER: PACER is available online at http://pacer.mtb.uscourts.gov. New civil records are online after 1 day.

Electronic Filing: Electronic filing information online at https://ecf.mtb.uscourts.gov

Other Online Access: Court now participates in the U.S. party case index.

Montana County Courts

Court	Jurisdiction	No. of Courts	How Organized
District Courts*	General	56	22 Districts
Limited Jurisdiction Courts*	Limited	70	56 Counties
City Courts	Limited	83	
Municipal Court	Municipal	5	
Water Courts	Special		4 Divisions
Workers' Compensation Court	Special	1	

* Profiled in this Sourcebook.

Court	CIVIL								
	Tort	Contract	Real Estate	Min. Claim	Max. Claim	Small Claims	Estate	Eviction	Domestic Relations
District Courts*	X	X	X	$5000-7000	No Max		X		X
Limited Jurisdiction Courts*	X	X	X	$0	$5000-7000	$3000		X	
City Courts	X	X	X	$0	$5000				
Municipal Court	X	X	X	$0	$5000	$3000			
Water Courts			X						
Workers' Comp. Court									

Court	CRIMINAL				
	Felony	Misdemeanor	DWI/DUI	Preliminary Hearing	Juvenile
District Courts*	X			X	X
Limited Jurisdiction Courts*		X	X	X	
City Courts		X	X	X	
Municipal Court		X	X	X	
Water Courts					
Workers' Comp. Court					

ADMINISTRATION   Court Administrator, Justice Building, 215 N Sanders, Room 315 (PO Box 203002), Helena, MT, 59620; 406-444-2621, Fax: 406-444-0834. http://www.lawlibrary.state.mt.us

COURT STRUCTURE   The District Courts have no maximum amount for civil judgment cases. Most District Courts handle civil over $7,000; there are exceptions that handle a civil minimum as low as $5,000. Limited Jurisdiction Courts, which are also known as Justice Courts, may handle civil actions up to $7,000. The Small Claims limit is $3000.

Many Montana Justices of the Peace maintain case record indexes on their personal PCs, which does speed the retrieval process.

ONLINE ACCESS   Supreme Courts Opinions, Orders, and recently Filed Briefs may be found at www.lawlibrary.state.mt.us/dscgi/ds.py/View/Collection-36. Federal District court records are also available here. A few individual county courts offer online access.

Beaverhead County

District Court Beaverhead County Courthouse, 2 S Pacific St, Dillon, MT 59725; 406-683-3725; Fax: 406-683-3728. Hours: 8AM-5PM (MST). *Felony, Civil Actions Over $7,000, Eviction, Probate.*

Civil Records: Access: Fax, mail, in person. Both court and visitors may perform in person searches. Search fee: $2.00 per name per year, first 7 years, then $1.00 per year. Required to search: name, years to search. Civil cases indexed by defendant, plaintiff. Civil records in books back to 1870s; on computer since 1997. For fax, send fax copy of check for fee.

Criminal Records: Access: Fax, mail, in person. Both court and visitors may perform in person searches. Search fee: $2.00 per name per year, first 7 years, then $1.00 per year. Required to search: name, years to search. Criminal records in books back to 1870s; on computer since 1997. For fax, send fax copy of check for fee.

General Information: Public Access terminal is available. No adoption, juvenile, sanity, paternity or dismissed criminal records released. Will fax results $1.00 per page. Copy fee: $1.00 per page first 10 pages, then $.50 per page after. Certification fee: $2.00. Payee: Clerk of Court. Personal checks not accepted. Prepayment required. Mail requests: SASE required. Mail turnaround time 1-2 days.

Beaverhead County Justice Court 2 S Pacific St, #16, Dillon, MT 59725; 406-683-3755; Fax: 406-683-3736. Hours: 8AM-5PM (MST). *Misdemeanor, Civil Actions Under $7,000, Eviction, Small Claims.* Note: This court also includeds cases from closed court located in Lima, MT.

Big Horn County

District Court 121 West 3rd St, Rm 221, PO Box 908, Hardin, MT 59034; 406-665-9750; Fax: 406-665-9755. Hours: 8AM-5PM (MST). *Felony, Civil Actions Over $7,000, Probate.*

Civil Records: Access: Fax, mail, in person. Both court and visitors may perform in person searches. Search fee: $2.00 per name per year, first 7 years, then $1.00 per year. Required to search: name, years to search. Civil cases indexed by defendant, plaintiff. Civil records in books, microfilm, and computer back to 1913.

Criminal Records: Access: Fax, mail, in person. Both court and visitors may perform in person searches. Search fee: $2.00 per name per year, first 7 years, then $1.00 per year. Required to search: name, years to search, DOB; also helpful, SSN. Criminal records in books and on microfilm back to 1913; on computer back to 1913. Court order required for confidential information.

General Information: Public Access terminal is available. No adoption, sanity, pre-sentence, psychiatric evaluation, dependent & neglected, or confidential criminal justice records released. Fee to fax results is $1.00 per page. Copy fee: $1.00 per page first 10 pages, then $.50 per page after. Certification fee: $2.00. Payee: Clerk of Court. No personal checks accepted. Prepayment required. Will bill government agencies. Mail requests: SASE required. Mail turnaround time same day.

Limited Jurisdiction Court PO Box 908, Hardin, MT 59034; 406-665-9760; Fax: 406-665-9764. Hours: 8AM-5PM (MST). *Misdemeanor, Civil Actions Under $7,000, Eviction, Small Claims.*

Blaine County

District Court PO Box 969, Chinook, MT 59523; 406-357-3230; Fax: 406-357-3109. Hours: 8AM-5PM (MST). *Felony, Civil Actions Over $5,000, Eviction, Probate.*

Civil Records: Access: Fax, mail, in person. Both court and visitors may perform in person searches. Search fee: $2.00 per name per year, first 7 years, then $1.00 per year. Required to search: name, years to search. Civil cases indexed by defendant, plaintiff. Civil records in books from 1912; on computer back to 1995.

Criminal Records: Access: Fax, mail, in person. Both court and visitors may perform in person searches. Search fee: $2.00 per name per year, first 7 years, then $1.00 per year. Required to search: name, years to search, signed release. Criminal records in books from 1912; on computer back to 1995.

General Information: Public Access terminal is available. No adoption, juvenile or sanity records released. Fee to fax results is $1.00 per page. Copy fee: $1.00 per page first 10 pages, then $.50 per page after. Certification fee: $2.00. Payee: Clerk of Court. Personal checks accepted. Prepayment required. Mail requests: SASE required. Mail turnaround: same day.

Chinook Justice Court PO Box 1266, Chinook, MT 59523; 406-357-2335; Fax: 406-357-2361. Hours: 8AM-5PM M-F (MST). *Misdemeanor, Civil Actions Under $7,000, Eviction, Small Claims.*

Broadwater County

District Court 515 Broadway, Townsend, MT 59644; 406-266-9236; Fax: 406-266-4720. Hours: 8AM-Noon, 1-5PM (MST). *Felony, Civil Actions Over $7,000, Probate.*

Civil Records: Access: Fax, mail, in person. Both court and visitors may perform in person searches. Search fee: $2.00 per name per year, first 7 years, then $1.00 per year. Required to search: name, years to search, DOB. Civil records on microfiche and archives back to 1897; on computer back to 1997.

Criminal Records: Access: Fax, mail, in person. Both court and visitors may perform in person searches. Search fee: $5.00 per name per year, first 7 years, then $1.00 per year. Required to search: name, years to search, DOB. Criminal records on microfiche and archives back to 1897; on computer back to 1997.

General Information: Public Access terminal is available. No adoption, juvenile or sanity records released. Will fax results. Copy fee: $1.00 per page first 10 pages, then $.50 per page after. Certification fee: $2.00. Payee: Clerk of Court. Personal checks accepted. Prepayment required. Mail requests: SASE required. Mail turnaround time same day.

Limited Jurisdiction Court 515 Broadway, Townsend, MT 59644; 406-266-9231; Fax: 406-266-4720. Hours: 8AM-5PM (MST). *Misdemeanor, Civil Actions Under $7,000, Eviction, Small Claims.*

Carbon County

District Court PO Box 948, Red Lodge, MT 59068; 406-446-1225; Fax: 406-446-1911. Hours: 8AM-5PM (MST). *Felony, Civil Actions, Probate.* Note: Also, this court holds youth, adoption and sanity records.

Civil Records: Access: Phone, fax, mail, in person. Both court and visitors may perform in person searches. Search fee: $2.00 per name per year, first 7 years, then $1.00 per year. Required to search: name, years to search. Civil cases indexed by defendant, plaintiff. Civil records on docket books from 1895; on computer back to 1997.

Criminal Records: Access: Fax, mail, in person. Only the court performs in person searches; visitors may not. Search fee: $2.00 per name per year, first 7 years, then $1.00 per year. Required to search: name, years to search. Criminal records on docket books from 1895; on computer back to 1997.

General Information: No adoption, juvenile or sanity records released. Will fax results $1.00 per page; no charge to toll free number. Copy fee: $1.00 per page first 10 pages, then $.50 per page after. Certification fee: $2.00. Payee: Clerk of Court. Personal checks accepted. Prepayment required. Mail requests: SASE required. Mail turnaround: 1-2 days.

Carbon County Justice Court PO Box 2, Red Lodge, MT 59068; 406-446-1440; Fax: 406-446-9175. Hours: 8AM-5PM (MST). *Misdemeanor, Civil Actions Under $7,000, Eviction, Small Claims.*

Joliet City Court PO Box 210, Joliet, MT 59041; 406-962-3567. Hours: 8AM-1PM on 1st, 2nd & 3rd Wed of month (MST). *Misdemeanor, Civil Actions Under $7,000.*

Carter County

District Court PO Box 322, Ekalaka, MT 59324; 406-775-8714; Fax: 406-775-8730. Hours: 8AM-5PM (MST). *Felony, Civil Actions Over $5,000, Eviction, Probate.*

Civil Records: Access: Phone, fax, mail, in person. Both court and visitors may perform in person searches. Search fee: $2.00 per name per year, first 7 years, then $1.00 per year. Required to search: name, years to search. Civil cases indexed by defendant, plaintiff. Civil records in books from 1917; computerized back to 1996.

Criminal Records: Access: Phone, fax, mail, in person. Only the court performs in person searches; visitors may not. Search fee: $2.00 per name per year, first 7 years, then $1.00 per year. Required to search: name, years to search, signed release; also helpful: SSN. Criminal records in books from 1917; computerized back to 1996.

General Information: No adoption, juvenile or sanity records released. Will fax results $1.00 per page. Copy fee: $1.00 per page first 10 pages, then $.50 per page after. Certification fee: $2.00. Payee: Clerk of Court. Personal checks accepted. Prepayment required. Mail requests: SASE required. Mail turnaround time 1-2 days; same to next day for phone requests.

Limited Jurisdiction Court PO Box 72, Ekalaka, MT 59324-0072; 406-775-8730; Fax: 406-775-8714. Hours: 8AM-5PM 1st,2nd,3rd Wed. of the month; 10AM-3:PM every 4th Wed. of the month (MST). *Misdemeanor, Civil Actions Under $7,000, Eviction, Small Claims.*

Cascade County

District Court County Courthouse, 415 2nd Ave North, Great Falls, MT 59401; 406-454-6780. Hours: 8AM-5PM (MST). *Felony, Civil Actions Over $7,000, Probate.*

Civil Records: Access: Mail, in person. Both court and visitors may perform in person searches. Search fee: $2.00 per name per year, first 7 years, then $1.00 per year. Required to search: name, years to search. Civil cases indexed by defendant, plaintiff. Civil records on computer from 1987; on docket books to 1889.

Criminal Records: Access: Mail, in person. Both court and visitors may perform in person searches. Search fee: $2.00 per name per year, first 7 years, then $1.00 per year. Required to search: name, years to search. Criminal records on computer from 1987; on docket books to 1889.

General Information: Public Access terminal is available. No adoption or sanity records released. Will not fax results. Copy fee: $1.00 per page, then $.50 per page after first 10. Certification fee: $2.00. Payee: Clerk of Court. Business checks accepted. Prepayment required. Mail requests: SASE required. Mail turnaround time 1-2 days.

Cascade Justice Court Cascade County Courthouse, 415 2nd Ave N, Great Falls, MT 59401; 406-454-6870; Fax: 406-454-6877. Hours: 8AM-5PM (MST). *Misdemeanor, Civil Actions Under $7,000, Eviction, Small Claims.*

Chouteau County

District Court PO Box 459, Ft Benton, MT 59442; 406-622-5024; Fax: 406-622-3028. Hours: 8AM-5PM (MST). *Felony, Civil Actions Over $5,000, Eviction, Probate.*
Civil Records: Access: Fax, mail, in person. Both court and visitors may perform in person searches. Search fee: $2.00 per name per year, first 7 years, then $1.00 per year. Required to search: name, years to search. Civil cases indexed by defendant, plaintiff. Civil records on books from 1886; on computer back for 10 years.
Criminal Records: Access: Fax, mail, in person. Both court and visitors may perform in person searches. Search fee: $2.00 per name per year, first 7 years, then $1.00 per year. Required to search: name, years to search. Criminal records on books from 1886; on computer back for 10 years.
General Information: Public Access terminal is available. No adoption, paternity, juvenile or sanity records released. Will fax results $2.00 1st page, $1.00 each add'l. Copy fee: $1.00 per page first 10 pages, then $.50 per page after. Certification fee: $2.00. Payee: Clerk of Court. Business checks accepted. Prepayment required. Mail requests: SASE required. Mail turnaround time 1 day.

Chouteau County Justice Court PO Box 459, Ft Benton, MT 59442; 406-622-5502; Fax: 406-622-3815. Hours: 9AM-4PM M-F (MST). *Misdemeanor, Civil Actions Under $7,000, Eviction, Small Claims.*
Note: As of 12/02, the records from the former Justice Court in Big Sandy are housed at this location.

Custer County

District Court 1010 Main, Miles City, MT 59301-3419; 406-874-3326; Fax: 406-874-3451. Hours: 8AM-5PM (MST). *Felony, Civil Actions Over $5,000, Eviction, Probate.*
Civil Records: Access: Phone, fax, mail, in person. Both court and visitors may perform in person searches. Search fee: $2.00 per name per year, first 7 years, then $1.00 per year. Required to search: name, years to search. Civil cases indexed by defendant, plaintiff. Civil records on computer back to 1990; also in books.
Criminal Records: Access: Mail, in person. Both court and visitors may perform in person searches. Search fee: $2.00 per name per year, first 7 years, then $1.00 per year. Required to search: name, years to search. Criminal records on computer back to 1990; also in books.
General Information: Public Access terminal is available. No dependent & neglected, juvenile or sanity records released. Will fax results for $1.00 per page. Copy fee: $1.00 per page first 10 pages, then $.50 per page after. Certification fee: $2.00. Payee: Clerk of District Court. Personal checks accepted. Prepayment required. Mail requests: SASE required. Mail turnaround time 1-2 days.

Limited Jurisdiction Court 1010 Main St, Miles City, MT 59301; 406-874-3408; Fax: 406-874-3452. Hours: 8AM-5PM (MST). *Misdemeanor, Civil Actions Under $7,000, Eviction, Small Claims.*
www.co.custer.mt.us　Note: Record search request must be in writing, fee is $25.00 per search.

Daniels County

District Court PO Box 67, Scobey, MT 59263; 406-487-2651; Fax: 406-487-5432. Hours: 8AM-5PM (MST). *Felony, Civil Actions Over $5,000, Probate.*
Civil Records: Access: Phone, mail, in person. Only the court may perform in person searches, visitors my not. Search fee: $2.00 per name per year, first 7 years, then $1.00 per year. Required to search: name, years to search. Civil cases indexed by defendant, plaintiff. Civil records on books since 1920; on computer back to 1997.
Criminal Records: Access: Mail, in person, fax. Only the court may perform in person searches, visitors may not. Search fee: $2.00 per name per year, first 7 years, then $1.00 per year. Required to search: name, years to search. Criminal records on books since 1920; on computer back to 1986.
General Information: No adoption, juvenile or sanity records released. Fee to fax results is $.50 per page. Copy fee: $1.00 per page first 10 pages, then $.50 per page after first 5. Certification fee: $2.00. Payee: Clerk of Court. Personal checks accepted. Prepayment required. Mail requests: SASE required. Mail turnaround time 1-2 days.

Limited Jurisdiction Court Daniels County Courthouse, Upstairs, Scobey, MT 59263; 406-487-5432; Fax: 406-487-5432. Hours: 8AM-5PM (MST). *Misdemeanor, Civil Actions Under $7,000, Eviction, Small Claims.*

Dawson County

District Court 207 W Bell, Glendive, MT 59330; 406-377-3967; Fax: 406-377-7280. Hours: 8AM-5PM (MST). *Felony, Civil Actions Over $5,000, Eviction, Probate.*
www.dawsoncountymontana.com/clerk_of_court.htm
Civil Records: Access: Mail, in person. Both court and visitors may perform in person searches. Search fee: $2.00 per name per year, first 7 years, then $1.00 per year. Required to search: name, years to search. Civil cases indexed by defendant, plaintiff. Civil records on computer from 1997, on card index prior.
Criminal Records: Access: Mail, in person. Both court and visitors may perform in person searches. Search fee: $2.00 per name per year, first 7 years, then $1.00 per year. Required to search: name, years to search, DOB, SSN. Criminal records on computer from 1997, on card index prior.
General Information: Public Access terminal is available. No adoption, juvenile, sanity or expunged records released. Will fax results to local or toll free line. Copy fee: $1.00 per page first 10 pages, then $.50 per page after. Certification fee: $2.00. Payee: Clerk of District Court. Only cashiers checks and money orders accepted. Prepayment required. Mail requests: SASE required. Mail turnaround: same day.

Limited Jurisdiction Court 207 W Bell, Glendive, MT 59330; 406-377-5425; Fax: 406-377-1869. Hours: 8AM-5PM (MST). *Misdemeanor, Civil Actions Under $7,000, Eviction, Small Claims.*

Deer Lodge County

District Court 800 S Main, Anaconda, MT 59711; 406-563-4041; Fax: 406-563-4077. Hours: 8AM-5PM (MST). *Felony, Civil Actions Over $5,000, Eviction, Probate.*
Civil Records: Access: Phone, mail, in person. Both court and visitors may perform in person searches. Search fee: $2.00 per name per year, first 7 years, then $1.00 per year. Required to search: name, years to search. Civil cases indexed by defendant, plaintiff. Civil records in archives and index books; on computer back to 1996.

Criminal Records: Access: Mail, in person. Both court and visitors may perform in person searches. Search fee: $2.00 per name per year, first 7 years, then $1.00 per year. Required to search: name, years to search. Criminal records in archives and index books; on computer back to 1996.
General Information: Public Access terminal is available. No adoption, juvenile or sanity records released. Fee to fax results is $4.00 per document. Copy fee: $1.00 per page first 10 pages, then $.50 per page after. Certification fee: $2.00. Payee: Clerk of Court. Personal checks accepted. Prepayment required. Mail requests: SASE required. Mail turnaround time 2-3 days.

Limited Jurisdiction Court 800 S Main, Anaconda, MT 59711; 406-563-4025; Fax: 406-563-4028. Hours: 8AM-5PM (MST). *Misdemeanor, Civil Actions Under $7,000, Eviction, Small Claims.*

Fallon County

District Court PO Box 1521, Baker, MT 59313; 406-778-7114; Fax: 406-778-2815. Hours: 8AM-5PM (MST). *Felony, Civil Actions Over $5,000, Eviction, Probate.*
Civil Records: Access: Mail, in person. Both court and visitors may perform in person searches. Search fee: $2.00 per name per year, first 7 years, then $1.00 per year. Required to search: name, years to search, address. Civil cases indexed by defendant, plaintiff. Civil records in books.
Criminal Records: Access: Mail, in person. Both court and visitors may perform in person searches. Search fee: $2.00 per name per year, first 7 years, then $1.00 per year. Required to search: name, years to search. Criminal records in books.
General Information: Public Access terminal is available. No confidential records released. Fee to fax results is $1.00 per page. Copy fee: $1.00 per page first 10 pages, then $.50 per page after. Certification fee: $2.00. Payee: Clerk of Court. Personal checks accepted. Prepayment required. Mail requests: SASE required. Mail turnaround time same day.

Justice Court Box 846, Baker, MT 59313; 406-778-7128; Fax: 406-778-2815. Hours: 11:00AM-4:00PM T,W,Th (MST). *Misdemeanor, Civil Actions Under $7,000, Eviction, Small Claims.*

Fergus County

District Court PO Box 1074 (712 W Main), Lewistown, MT 59457; 406-538-5026; Fax: 406-538-6076. Hours: 8AM-5PM (MST). *Felony, Civil Actions Over $7,000, Eviction, Probate.*
www.co.fergus.mt.us
Civil Records: Access: Phone, fax, mail, in person. Both court and visitors may perform in person searches. Search fee: $2.00 per name per year, first 7 years, then $1.00 per year. Required to search: name, years to search. Civil cases indexed by defendant, plaintiff. Civil records on computer back to 1997; prior on docket books, microfiche.
Criminal Records: Access: Phone, fax, mail, in person. Both court and visitors may perform in person searches. Search fee: $2.00 per name per year, first 7 years, then $1.00 per year. Required to search: name, years to search. Criminal records on computer back to 1997; prior on docket books, microfiche.
General Information: Public Access terminal is available. No adoption, juvenile, sanity or expunged records released. Fee to fax results is $1.00 per page. Copy fee: $1.00 per page first 10 pages, then $.50 per page after. Certification fee: $2.00. Payee: Clerk of Court. Personal checks accepted. Prepayment required. Mail requests: SASE required. Mail turnaround time 1 day.

Limited Jurisdiction Court 121 8th Ave South, Lewistown, MT 59457; 406-538-5418; Fax: 406-538-3860. Hours: 9AM-4PM (MST). *Misdemeanor, Civil Actions Under $7,000, Eviction, Small Claims.* Note: You may email requests to jpcourt@co.fergus.mt.us

Flathead County

District Court 800 S Main (920 S. Main, 3rd Fl), Kalispell, MT 59901; 406-758-5660. 8AM-5PM (MST). *Felony, Civil Actions Over $5,000, Probate.* www.co.flathead.mt.us/clkcrt/index.html
Civil Records: Access: Mail, in person. Both court and visitors may perform in person searches. Search fee: $2.00 per name per year, first 7 years, then $1.00 per year. Required to search: name, years to search. Civil cases indexed by defendant, plaintiff. Civil records on computer to 1990; records go back to 1893.
Criminal Records: Access: Mail, in person. Only the court performs in person searches; visitors may not. Search fee: $2.00 per name per year, first 7 years, then $1.00 per year. Required to search: name, years to search. Criminal records on computer since 1990; records go back to 1893.
General Information: Public Access terminal is available. No adoption, dependent/neglected children or sanity records released. Fee to fax results is $1.00 per page. Copy fee: $1.00. Certification fee: $2.00. Payee: Clerk of Court. Personal checks accepted. Prepayment required. Mail requests: SASE required. Mail turnaround time 3 days.

Limited Jurisdiction Court 800 S Main St, Kalispell, MT 59901; 406-758-5643; Fax: 406-758-5842. Hours: 8AM-5PM (MST). *Misdemeanor, Civil Actions Under $7,000, Eviction, Small Claims.* www.co.flathead.mt.us/justice/index.html

Gallatin County

Clerk of District Court 615 S 16th, Rm 302, Bozeman, MT 59715; 406-582-2165; Fax: 406-582-2176. Hours: 8AM-5PM (MST). *Felony, Civil Actions Over $7,000, Probate.*
Civil Records: Access: Phone, mail, fax, in person. Both court and visitors may perform in person searches. Search fee: $2.00 per name per year, first 7 years, then $1.00 per year. Required to search: name, years to search. Civil cases indexed by defendant, plaintiff. Civil records on computer back to 1985; docket books back to 1860.
Criminal Records: Access: Mail, in person. Both court and visitors may perform in person searches. Search fee: $2.00 per name per year, first 7 years, then $1.00 per year. Required to search: name, years to search. Criminal records on computer back to 1985; docket books back to 1860.
General Information: Public Access terminal is available. No adoption or sanity records released. Fee to fax results is $2.00 per page for the 1st page, $1.00 per page thereafter. Copy fee: $1.00 per page. $.50 per page after first 10 pages. Certification fee: $2.00. Payee: Clerk of Court. Personal checks accepted. Prepayment required. Mail requests: SASE required. Mail turnaround time is 2 days.

Belgrade Justice & City Court 91 E Central, Belgrade, MT 59714; 406-388-3774; Fax: 406-388-3779. Hours: 8AM-Noon; 1PM-5PM M-F (MST). *Misdemeanor, Civil Actions Under $7,000, Eviction.*

Bozeman Justice Court 615 S 16th St, Bozeman, MT 59715; 406-582-2163; Fax: 406-582-2041. Hours: 8AM-5PM (MST). *Misdemeanor, Civil Actions Under $7,000, Eviction, Small Claims.*

Garfield County

District Court PO Box 8, Jordan, MT 59337; 406-557-6254; Fax: 406-557-2625. 8AM-5PM. *Felony, Civil Actions Over $5,000, Eviction, Probate.*
Civil Records: Access: Phone, mail, in person. Both court and visitors may perform in person searches. Search fee: $2.00 per name per year, first 7 years, then $1.00 per year. Required to search: name, years to search. Civil cases indexed by plaintiff. Civil records in books from early 1900s; computerized records go back to 1998. Some records lost due to fire in December, 1997.
Criminal Records: Access: Phone, mail, in person. Both court and visitors may perform in person searches. Search fee: $2.00 per name per year, first 7 years, then $1.00 per year. Required to search: name, years to search; also helpful: DOB. Criminal records in books from early 1900s, computerized records go back to 1998. Some records lost due to fire in December, 1997.
General Information: No adoption, juvenile or sanity records released. Will fax results to local or toll free line. Copy fee: $1.00 per page first 10 pages, then $.50 per page after. Certification fee: $2.00. Payee: Clerk of Court. Personal checks accepted. Prepayment required. Mail requests: SASE required. Mail turnaround time 1 week.

Limited Jurisdiction Court PO Box 482, Jordan, MT 59337; 406-557-2733; Fax: 406-557-2735. Hours: 8AM-5PM Wed (MST). *Misdemeanor, Civil Actions Under $7,000, Eviction, Small Claims.*

Glacier County

District Court 512 E Main St, Cut Bank, MT 59427; 406-873-5063 X36; Fax: 406-873-5627. Hours: 8AM-5PM (MST). *Civil Actions, Probate.*
Civil Records: Access: Phone, fax, mail, in person, email. Both court and visitors may perform in person searches. Search fee: $2.00 per name per year, first 7 years, then $1.00 per year. Required to search: name, years to search. Civil cases indexed by defendant, plaintiff. Civil records in books from 1919; on computer since 1992. Email requests to dianderson@state.mt.us.
Criminal Records: Access: Fax, mail, in person. Both court and visitors may perform in person searches. Search fee: $2.00 per name per year, first 7 years, then $1.00 per year. Required to search: name, years to search, DOB, SSN. Criminal records in books from 1919; computer since 1992. Written request required.
General Information: No adoption, juvenile, sanity or paternity records released without court order. Fee to fax results is $1.00 per page. Copy fee: $1.00 per page first 10 pages, then $.50 per page after. Certification fee: $2.00. Payee: Clerk of District Court. Personal checks accepted. Prepayment required. Mail requests: SASE required. Mail turnaround time usually same day, 2-3 hours for phone requests depending on workload.

Limited Jurisdiction Court 512 E Main St, Cut Bank, MT 59427; 406-873-5063 X39; Fax: 406-873-4218. AM-Noon, 1-5PM (MST). *Misdemeanor, Civil Actions Under $7,000, Eviction, Small Claims.*

Golden Valley County

District Court PO Box 10, Ryegate, MT 59074; 406-568-2231; Fax: 406-568-2231. Hours: 8AM-5PM (MST). *Felony, Civil Actions Over $5,000, Eviction, Probate.*
Civil Records: Access: Fax, mail, in person. Only the court performs in person searches; visitors may not. Search fee: $2.00 per name per year, first 7 years, then $1.00 per year. Required to search: name, years to

search, signed release. Civil cases indexed by defendant, plaintiff. Civil records on books back to 1923. Computerized records back to 1997.
Criminal Records: Access: Fax, mail, in person. Only the court performs in person searches; visitors may not. Search fee: $2.00 per name per year, first 7 years, then $1.00 per year. Required to search: name, years to search, signed release. Criminal records on books to 1923. Computerized records go back to 1997.
General Information: No adoption, juvenile or sanity records released. Will fax results for $1.00 per page. Same fee applies to send them a fax. Copy fee: $1.00 per page first 10 pages, then $.50 per page after. Certification fee: $2.00. Payee: Clerk of Court. Personal checks accepted. Prepayment required. Mail requests: SASE required. Mail turnaround time 2-3 days.

Limited Jurisdiction Court PO Box 10, Ryegate, MT 59074; 406-568-2272; Fax: 406-568-2231. 10AM-2PM Tues (MST). *Misdemeanor, Civil Actions Under $7,000, Eviction, Small Claims.*

Granite County

District Court PO Box 399, Philipsburg, MT 59858-0399; 406-859-3712; Fax: 406-859-3817. Hours: 8AM-Noon, 1-5PM (MST). *Felony, Civil Actions Over $7,000, Eviction, Probate.*
Civil Records: Access: Phone, fax, mail, in person. Both court and visitors may perform in person searches. Search fee: $2.00 per name per year, first 7 years, then $1.00 per year. Required to search: name, years to search. Civil cases indexed by defendant, plaintiff. Civil records on docket books since 1893.
Criminal Records: Access: Phone, fax, mail, in person. Both court and visitors may perform in person searches. Search fee: $2.00 per name per year, first 7 years, then $1.00 per year. Required to search: name, years to search. Criminal records on docket books since 1893.
General Information: Public Access terminal is available. No adoption, juvenile or sanity records released. Copy fee: $1.00 per page first 10 pages, then $.50 per page after. Certification fee: $2.00. Payee: Clerk of Court. Personal checks accepted. Prepayment required. Mail requests: SASE required. Mail turnaround time 1-4 days.

Drummond Justice Court #2 PO Box 159, Drummond, MT 59832; 406-288-3446; Fax: 406-288-3050. Hours: 9AM-4PM M,W,F (MST). *Misdemeanor, Civil Actions Under $7,000, Eviction, Small Claims.*

Philipsburg Justice Court PO Box 356, Philipsburg, MT 59858; 406-859-3006; Fax: 406-859-3817. Hours: 11AM-Noon, 1-5PM M,W,F (MST). *Misdemeanor, Civil Actions Under $7,000, Eviction, Small Claims.*

Hill County

District Court Hill County Courthouse, Havre, MT 59501; 406-265-5481 X224; Fax: 406-265-3693. Hours: 8AM-5PM (MST). *Felony, Civil Actions Over $5,000, Eviction, Probate.* http://co.hill.mt.us
Civil Records: Access: Phone, fax, mail, in person. Both court and visitors may perform in person searches. Search fee: $2.00 per name per year, first 7 years, then $1.00 per year. Required to search: name, years to search. Civil cases indexed by defendant, plaintiff. Civil records on computer since 1985; prior records on docket books to 1912. Maiden name helpful in searching.
Criminal Records: Access: Fax, mail, in person. Both court and visitors may perform in person searches. Search fee: $2.00 per name per year, first 7 years, then $1.00 per year. Required to search: name,

years to search; also helpful: maiden name. Criminal records on computer since 1988; prior records on docket books to 1912. Absolutely no criminal record checks by phone.

General Information: Public Access terminal is available. No adoption, juvenile, paternity, sanity records released. Will fax results $1.00 per page. Copy fee: $1.00 per page first 10 pages, then $.50 per page after. Certification fee: $2.00. Payee: Clerk of Court. Business checks accepted. Prepayment required. Mail requests: SASE required. Mail turnaround time 2-3 days.

Limited Jurisdiction Court Hill County Courthouse, Havre, MT 59501; 406-265-5481 X240; Fax: 406-262-9441. Hours: 8AM-5PM (MST). *Misdemeanor, Civil Actions Under $7,000, Eviction, Small Claims.* http://co.hill.mt.us

Jefferson County

District Court PO Box H, Boulder, MT 59632; 406-225-4041 & 4042; Fax: 406-225-4044. Hours: 8AM-Noon, 1-5PM (MST). *Felony, Civil Actions Over $7,000, Eviction, Probate.*

Civil Records: Access: Mail, fax, in person. Both court and visitors may perform in person searches. Search fee: $2.00 per name per year, first 7 years, then $1.00 per year. Required to search: name, years to search. Civil cases indexed by defendant, plaintiff. Civil records on computer since 1993, on microfilm since 1925.

Criminal Records: Access: Mail, fax, in person. Both court and visitors may perform in person searches. Search fee: $2.00 per name per year, first 7 years, then $1.00 per year. Required to search: name, years to search. Criminal records on computer since 1992, on microfilm since 1925.

General Information: Public Access terminal is available. Juvenile, sanity or adoption records not released. Fee to fax results is $1.00 per page. Copy fee: $1.00 per page first 10 pages, then $.50 per page after. Certification fee: $2.00. Payee: Clerk of Court. Personal checks accepted. Prepayment required. Mail requests: SASE required. Mail turnaround: same day.

Limited Jurisdiction Court PO Box H, Boulder, MT 59632; 406-225-4055; Fax: 406-225-4088. Hours: 8AM-5PM (MST). *Misdemeanor, Civil Actions Under $7,000, Eviction, Small Claims.*

Judith Basin County

District Court PO Box 307, Stanford, MT 59479; 406-566-2277 X113; Fax: 406-566-2211. Hours: 8AM-5PM (MST). *Felony, Civil Actions Over $5,000, Probate.*

Civil Records: Access: Phone, fax, mail, in person. Both court and visitors may perform in person searches. Search fee: $2.00 per name per year, first 7 years, then $1.00 per year. Required to search: name, years to search. Civil cases indexed by defendant, plaintiff. Civil records on books back to 1920; on computer back to 1996.

Criminal Records: Access: Phone, mail, in person. Both court and visitors may perform in person searches. Search fee: $2.00 per name per year, first 7 years, then $1.00 per year. Required to search: name, years to search, signed release. Criminal records on books back to 1920; on computer back to 1996.

General Information: No adoption, sanity records released. Will fax results. Copy fee: $1.00 per page first 10 pages, then $.50 per page after. Certification fee: $2.00. Payee: Clerk of Court. Business checks accepted. Prepayment required. Mail requests: SASE required. Mail turnaround time 10 days.

Stanford Justice Court PO Box 427, Stanford, MT 59479; 406-566-2277 X117; Fax: 406-566-2211.

Hours: 8:00AM-5:00PM M-F (MST). *Misdemeanor, Civil Actions Under $7,000, Eviction, Small Claims.*

Lake County

District Court Clerk of District Court Office, 106 4th Ave E, Polson, MT 59860; 406-883-7254; Fax: 406-883-7343. Hours: 8AM-5PM (MST). *Felony, Civil Actions Over $7,000, Probate.*

Civil Records: Access: Phone, fax, mail, in person. Both court and visitors may perform in person searches. Search fee: $2.00 per name per year, first 7 years, then $1.00 per year. Required to search: name, years to search. Civil cases indexed by defendant, plaintiff. Civil records on books since 1923; on computer since 1990.

Criminal Records: Access: Phone, fax, mail, in person. Both court and visitors may perform in person searches. Search fee: $2.00 per name per year, first 7 years, then $1.00 per year. Required to search: name, years to search, DOB, SSN. Criminal records on books since 1923; on computer since 1990.

General Information: Public Access terminal is available. No adoption, juvenile, sanity or expunged records released. Will fax results $1.00 per page. Copy fee: $1.00 per page first 10 pages, then $.50 per page after. Certification fee: $2.00. Payee: Clerk of Court. Business checks accepted. No credit cards. Prepayment required. Mail requests: SASE required. Mail turnaround: 3 days; 2 hours for phone requests.

Limited Jurisdiction Court 106 4th Ave E, Polson, MT 59860; 406-883-7258; Fax: 406-883-7343. Hours: 8AM-5PM (MST). *Misdemeanor, Civil Actions Under $7,000, Eviction, Small Claims.*

Lewis and Clark County

District Court 228 Broadway, PO Box 158, Helena, MT 59624; 406-447-8216; Fax: 406-447-8275. 8AM-5PM (MST). *Felony, Civil Actions Over $5,000, Eviction, Probate, Small Claims.* www.co.lewis-clark.mt.us

Civil Records: Access: Fax, mail, online, in person. Both court and visitors may perform in person searches. Search fee: $2.00 per name per year, first 7 years, then $1.00 per year. Required to search: name, years to search. Civil cases indexed by defendant, plaintiff. Civil records on computer since 1990, microfilm prior to 01/90. Will accept email record requests to kallio@co.lewis-clark.mt.us.

Criminal Records: Access: Fax, mail, online, in person. Both court and visitors may perform in person searches. Search fee: $2.00 per name per year, first 7 years, then $1.00 per year. Required to search: name, years to search. Criminal records on computer since 1990, microfilm prior to 1/90. Will accept email record requests to ikallio@co.lewis-clark.mt.us.

General Information: Public Access terminal is available. No adoption or sanity records released. Fee to fax results is $1.00 per page. Copy fee: $1.00 per page first 10 pages, then $.50 per page after. Certification fee: $2.00. Payee: Clerk of Court. Personal checks accepted. Prepayment required. Mail requests: SASE required. Mail turnaround: 2 days.

Limited Jurisdiction Court 228 Broadway, Helena, MT 59623; 406-447-8202; Fax: 406-447-8269. 8AM-Noon; 1PM-4PM (MST). *Misdemeanor, Civil Actions Under $7,000, Eviction, Small Claims.*

Liberty County

District Court PO Box 549, Chester, MT 59522; 406-759-5615; Fax: 406-759-5996. Hours: 8AM-5PM (MST). *Felony, Civil Actions Over $5,000, Eviction, Probate.*

Civil Records: Access: Phone, mail, in person. Only the court performs in person searches; visitors may not. Search fee: $2.00 per name per year, first 7 years,

then $1.00 per year. Required to search: name, years to search, address. Civil cases indexed by defendant, plaintiff. Civil records on books since 1920.

Criminal Records: Access: Phone, mail, in person, fax. Both court and visitors may perform in person searches. Search fee: $2.00 per name per year, first 7 years, then $1.00 per year. Required to search: name, years to search, signed release. Criminal records on books since 1920.

General Information: No adoption, juvenile or sanity records released. Will fax results to local or toll free line. Copy fee: $1.00 per page first 10 pages, then $.50 per page after. Certification fee: $2.00. Payee: Clerk of Court. Personal checks accepted. Prepayment required. Mail requests: SASE required. Mail turnaround time 2-3 days.

Limited Jurisdiction Court PO Box 170, Chester, MT 59522; 406-759-5172; Fax: 406-759-5395. Hours: 9AM-5PM Tues (MST). *Misdemeanor, Civil Actions Under $7,000, Eviction, Small Claims.*

Lincoln County

District Court 512 California Ave, Libby, MT 59923; 406-293-7781; Fax: 406-293-9816. Hours: 8AM-5PM (MST). *Felony, Civil Actions Over $7,000, Probate.*

Civil Records: Access: Mail, in person. Both court and visitors may perform in person searches. Search fee: $2.00 per name per year, first 7 years, then $1.00 per year. Required to search: name, years to search. Civil cases indexed by defendant, plaintiff. Civil records on computer from 1991, prior on docket books.

Criminal Records: Access: Mail, in person. Both court and visitors may perform in person searches. Search fee: $2.00 per name per year, first 7 years, then $1.00 per year. Required to search: name, years to search, DOB. Criminal records on computer from 1991, prior on docket books.

General Information: Public Access terminal is available. No adoption, juvenile or sanity records released. Will fax results, no extra fee. Copy fee: $1.00 per page first 10 pages, then $.50 per page after. Certification fee: $2.00. Payee: Clerk of Court. Personal checks accepted. Prepayment required. Mail requests: SASE required. Mail turnaround: 1 week.

Eureka Justice Court #2 PO Box 403, Eureka, MT 59917; 406-297-2622; Fax: 406-297-3829. Hours: 8AM-5M M-W (MST). *Misdemeanor, Civil Actions Under $7,000, Eviction, Small Claims.*

Libby Justice Court #1 418 Mineral Ave, Libby, MT 59923; 406-293-7781 X236, X259, X235; Fax: 406-293-5948.: 8AM-4PM *Misdemeanor, Civil Actions Under $7,000, Eviction, Small Claims.*

Madison County

District Court PO Box 185, Virginia City, MT 59755; 406-843-4230; Fax: 406-843-5207. Hours: 8AM-5PM (MST). *Felony, Civil Actions Over $5,000, Eviction, Probate.*

Civil Records: Access: Phone, fax, mail, in person. Both court and visitors may perform in person searches. Search fee: $2.00 per name per year, first 7 years, then $1.00 per year. Required to search: name, years to search. Civil cases indexed by defendant, plaintiff. Civil records on books since 1864; on computer back to 1990.

Criminal Records: Access: Fax, mail, in person. Both court and visitors may perform in person searches. Search fee: $2.00 per name per year, first 7 years, then $1.00 per year. Required to search: name, years to search. Criminal records on books since 1864; on computer back to 1990.

General Information: Public Access terminal is available. No adoption, juvenile or sanity records released. Fee to fax results is $4.00 1st page, $1.00 each add'l. Copy fee: $1.00 per page first 10 pages, then $.50 per page after. Certification fee: $2.00. Payee: Clerk of Court. Personal checks accepted. Prepayment required. Mail requests: SASE required. Mail turnaround time 1 week.

Madison Couny Justice Court PO Box 277, Virginia City, MT 59755; 406-843-4237; Fax: 406-843-4219. Hours: 8AM-5PM (MST). *Misdemeanor, Civil Actions Under $7,000, Eviction, Small Claims.*

McCone County

District Court PO Box 199, Circle, MT 59215; 406-485-3410; Fax: 406-485-3410. Hours: 8AM-5PM (MST). *Felony, Civil Actions Over $5,000, Eviction, Probate.*
Civil Records: Access: Mail, in person. Only the court performs in person searches; visitors may not. Search fee: $2.00 per name per year, first 7 years, then $1.00 per year. Required to search: name, years to search. Civil cases indexed by defendant, plaintiff. Records in books from 1919, computer since 1996.
Criminal Records: Access: Mail, in person. Only the court performs in person searches; visitors may not. Search fee: $2.00 per name per year, first 7 years, then $1.00 per year. Required to search: name, years to search. Criminal records in books and microfilm since 1919, computerized since 1996.
General Information: No adoption, juvenile, sanity or mental health records released. Will fax results to local or toll free line. Copy fee: $1.00 per page first 10 pages, then $.50 per page after. Certification fee: $2.00. Payee: Clerk of Court. Personal checks accepted. Prepayment required. Mail requests: SASE required. Mail turnaround time 1-2 days.

Limited Jurisdiction Court PO Box 192, Circle, MT 59215; 406-485-3548; Fax: 406-485-2689. 9AM-noon Tu & W (MST). *Misdemeanor, Civil Actions Under $7,000, Eviction, Small Claims.*

Meagher County

District Court PO Box 443, White Sulphur Springs, MT 59645; 406-547-3612 Ext110; Fax: 406-547-3836. Hours: 8AM-5PM (MST). *Felony, Civil Actions Over $5,000, Eviction, Probate.*
Civil Records: Access: Phone, mail, fax, in person. Both court and visitors may perform in person searches. Search fee: $2.00 per name per year, first 7 years, then $1.00 per year. Required to search: name, years to search. Civil cases indexed by defendant, plaintiff. Civil records on docket books or microfiche to 1900; on computer back to 1996.
Criminal Records: Access: Phone, mail, fax, in person. Both court and visitors may perform in person searches. Search fee: $2.00 per name per year, first 7 years, then $1.00 per year. Required to search: name, years to search, DOB. Criminal records on docket books or microfiche to 1900; computer back to 1996.
General Information: No adoption, juvenile or sanity records released. Copy fee: $1.00 per page first 10 pages, then $.50 per page after. Certification fee: $2.00. Payee: Clerk of Court. Personal checks accepted. Prepayment required. Mail requests: SASE required. Mail turnaround time 3 days.

Limited Jurisdiction Court Justice Court, 15 W. Main St. (PO Box 698), White Sulphur Springs, MT 59645; 406-547-3954 X115; Fax: 406-547-3388, 547-3836. 8AM-5PM T-Th (MST). *Misdemeanor, Civil Actions Under $7,000, Eviction, Small Claims.*

Mineral County

District Court PO Box 129, Superior, MT 59872; 406-822-3538; Fax: 406-822-3579. Hours: 8AM-Noon,1-5PM (MST). *Felony, Civil Actions Over $5,000, Probate.*
Civil Records: Access: Fax, mail, in person. Both court and visitors may perform in person searches. Search fee: $2.00 per name per year, first 7 years, then $1.00 per year. Required to search: name, years to search. Civil cases indexed by defendant, plaintiff. Civil records on docket books from 1914, on computer back to 1990.
Criminal Records: Access: Fax, mail, in person. Both court and visitors may perform in person searches. Search fee: $2.00 per name per year, first 7 years, then $1.00 per year. Required to search: name, years to search. Criminal records on docket books from 1914, on computer back to 1990.
General Information: No adoption, sanity records released. Fee to fax results is $5.00 per document. You must fax request with copy of payment (check). Copy fee: $1.00 per page first 10 pages, then $.50 per page after. Certification fee: $2.00. Payee: Clerk of Court. Personal checks accepted. Prepayment required. Mail requests: SASE required. Mail turnaround time same day after payment received.

Limited Jurisdiction Court PO Box 658, Superior, MT 59872; 406-822-3550; Fax: 406-822-3579. Hours: 8AM-5PM (MST). *Misdemeanor, Civil Actions Under $7,000, Eviction, Small Claims.*

Missoula County

District Court 200 W Broadway, Missoula, MT 59802; 406-258-4780; Fax: 406-258-4899. Hours: 8AM-5PM (MST). *Felony, Civil Actions Over $7,000, Probate.*
Civil Records: Access: Fax, mail, in person. Both court and visitors may perform in person searches. Search fee: $2.00 per name per year, first 7 years, then $1.00 per year. Required to search: name, years to search. Civil cases indexed by defendant, plaintiff. Civil records on computer from 10/89, microfilm from 1970s, archived to late 1800s.
Criminal Records: Access: Fax, mail, in person. Both court and visitors may perform in person searches. Search fee: $2.00 per name per year, first 7 years, then $1.00 per year. Required to search: name, years to search. Criminal records on computer from 10/89, microfilm from 1970s, archived to late 1800s.
General Information: Public Access terminal is available. No adoption, juvenile, sealed, expunged or pre-sentence psychiatric records released. Will fax results $2.00 per doc. No fee if returning on toll free line. Copy fee: $1.00 per page first 10 pages, then $.50 per page after. Certification fee: $2.00. Payee: Clerk of Court. Personal checks accepted. Visa, MC accepted. Prepayment required. Mail requests: SASE not required. Mail turnaround time up to 2 weeks.

Limited Jurisdiction Court - Dept 1 200 W Broadway, Missoula County Courthouse, Missoula, MT 59802; 406-523-4871; Fax: 406-258-3935. Hours: 8AM-5PM (MST). *Misdemeanor, Civil Actions Under $7,000, Eviction, Small Claims.* www.co.missoula.mt.us/jp1

Musselshell County

District Court 506 Main St, Roundup, MT 59072; 406-323-1413; Fax: 406-323-1710. Hours: 8AM-5PM (MST). *Felony, Civil Actions Over $5,000, Eviction, Probate.*
Civil Records: Access: Mail, in person. Both court and visitors may perform in person searches. Search fee: $2.00 per name per year, first 7 years, then $1.00 per year. Required to search: name, years to search.

Civil cases indexed by defendant, plaintiff. Computerized records from 7/96, civil records on docket books from 1911.
Criminal Records: Access: Mail, in person. Both court and visitors may perform in person searches. Search fee: $2.00 per name per year, first 7 years, then $1.00 per year. Required to search: name, years to search. Criminal records on docket books from 1911.
General Information: No adoption, (some) juvenile or sanity records released. Will fax results to local or toll free line. Copy fee: $1.00 per page first 10 pages, then $.50 per page after. Certification fee: $2.00. Payee: Clerk of Court. Personal checks accepted. Prepayment required. Mail requests: SASE required. Mail turnaround time 2-3 days.

Limited Jurisdiction Court PO Box 660, Roundup, MT 59072; 406-323-1078; Fax: 406-323-3452. Hours: 9AM-4PM (MST). *Misdemeanor, Civil Actions Under $7,000, Eviction, Small Claims.*

Park County

District Court PO Box 437, Livingston, MT 59047; 406-222-4125; Fax: 406-222-4128. Hours: 8AM-5PM (MST). *Felony, Civil Actions Over $7,000, Eviction, Probate.*
Civil Records: Access: Fax, mail, in person. Both court and visitors may perform in person searches. Search fee: $2.00 per name per year, first 7 years, then $1.00 per year. Required to search: name, years to search. Civil cases indexed by defendant, plaintiff. Civil records on computer, microfiche, and docket books from 1889 to present.
Criminal Records: Access: Fax, mail, in person. Both court and visitors may perform in person searches. Search fee: $2.00 per name per year, first 7 years, then $1.00 per year. Required to search: name, years to search. Criminal records on computer, microfiche, and docket books from 1889 to present.
General Information: Public Access terminal is available. No adoption, juvenile or sanity records released. Copy fee: $1.00 per page first 10 pages, then $.50 per page after. Certification fee: $2.00. Payee: Clerk of Court. Personal checks accepted. Prepayment required. Mail requests: SASE not required. Mail turnaround time 1-2 days for all requests.

Limited Jurisdiction Court 414 E Callender, Livingston, MT 59047; 406-222-4169/4170; Civil phone: 406-222-4171; Fax: 406-222-4103. Hours: 8AM-5:00PM (MST). *Misdemeanor, Civil Actions Under $7,000, Eviction, Small Claims.*

Petroleum County

District Court PO Box 226, Winnett, MT 59087; 406-429-5311; Fax: 406-429-6328. Hours: 8AM-5PM (MST). *Felony, Civil Actions Over $5,000, Eviction, Probate.*
Civil Records: Access: Phone, mail, in person. Both court and visitors may perform in person searches. Search fee: $2.00 per name per year, first 7 years, then $1.00 per year. Required to search: name, years to search. Civil cases indexed by defendant, plaintiff. Civil records on docket books from 1924.
Criminal Records: Access: Phone, mail, in person. Only the court performs in person searches; visitors may not. Search fee: $2.00 per name per year, first 7 years, then $1.00 per year. Required to search: name, years to search. Criminal records on docket books from 1924.
General Information: No adoption, juvenile or sanity records released. Will fax results to local or toll free line. Copy fee: $1.00 per page first 10 pages, then $.50 per page after. Certification fee: $2.00. Payee: Clerk of Court. Personal checks accepted. Prepayment required. Mail requests: SASE required. Mail turnaround time 1 day.

Limited Jurisdiction Court PO Box 226, Winnett, MT 59087; 406-429-5311; Fax: 406-429-6328. Hours: 9AM-Noon M-F (MST). *Misdemeanor, Civil Actions Under $7,000, Eviction, Small Claims.*

Phillips County

District Court PO Box 530, Malta, MT 59538; 406-654-1023; Fax: 406-654-1023. Hours: 8AM-5PM (MST). *Felony, Civil Actions Over $5,000, Eviction, Probate.*

Civil Records: Access: Mail, in person. Only the court performs in person searches; visitors may not. Search fee: $2.00 per name per year, first 7 years, then $1.00 per year. Required to search: name, years to search; also helpful: address. Civil cases indexed by defendant, plaintiff. Civil records on computer back to 1997; books, microfilm back to 1915.

Criminal Records: Access: Mail, in person. Only the court performs in person searches; visitors may not. Search fee: $2.00 per name per year, first 7 years, then $1.00 per year. Required to search: name, years to search, signed release, DOB or SSN; also helpful: address. Criminal records on computer back to 1997; books, microfilm back to 1915.

General Information: No adoption, juvenile or sanity records released. Will fax results for $5.00; no charge to toll free number. Copy fee: $1.00 per page first 10 pages, then $.50 per page after. Certification fee: $2.00. Payee: Clerk of Court. Personal checks accepted. Prepayment required. Mail requests: SASE required. Mail turnaround time 1-2 days.

Limited Jurisdiction Court PO Box 1396, Malta, MT 59538; 406-654-1118; Fax: 406-654-1213. 10AM-4PM M-Th (MST). *Misdemeanor, Civil Actions Under $7,000, Eviction, Small Claims.*

Pondera County

District Court 20 Fourth Ave SW, Conrad, MT 59425; 406-271-4026; Fax: 406-271-4081. Hours: 8AM-5PM (MST). *Felony, Civil Actions Over $5,000, Eviction, Probate.*

Civil Records: Access: Fax, mail, in person. Both court and visitors may perform in person searches. Search fee: $2.00 per name per year, first 7 years, then $1.00 per year. Required to search: name, years to search. Civil cases indexed by defendant, plaintiff. Civil records on docket books from 1919; on computer back to 1995.

Criminal Records: Access: Fax, mail, in person. Both court and visitors may perform in person searches. Search fee: $2.00 per name per year, first 7 years, then $1.00 per year. Required to search: name, years to search. Criminal records on docket books from 1919; on computer back to 1995.

General Information: No adoption or sanity records released. Will fax results $.50 1st 5 pages, $.25 each add'l page; $1.00 for cover page. Copy fee: $1.00 per page first 10 pages, then $.50 per page after. Certification fee: $2.00. Payee: Clerk of Court. Personal checks accepted. Prepayment required. Mail requests: SASE required. Mail turnaround: 2-3 days.

Limited Jurisdiction Court 20 Fourth Ave SW, Conrad, MT 59425; 406-271-4030; Fax: 406-271-4031. Hours: 9AM-4PM (MST). *Misdemeanor, Civil Actions Under $7,000, Eviction, Small Claims.*

Powder River County

District Court PO Box 239, Broadus, MT 59317; 406-436-2320; Fax: 406-436-2325. Hours: 8AM-Noon, 1-5PM (MST). *Felony, Civil Actions Over $5,000, Probate.*

Civil Records: Access: Fax, mail, in person. Both court and visitors may perform in person searches. Search fee: $2.00 per name per year, first 7 years, then $1.00 per year. Required to search: name, years to

search. Civil cases indexed by defendant, plaintiff. Civil records on computer since 1993, microfiche since 1974, and books since 1919.

Criminal Records: Access: Fax, mail, in person. Both court and visitors may perform in person searches. Search fee: $2.00 per name per year, first 7 years, then $1.00 per year. Required to search: name, years to search. Criminal records on computer since 1993, microfiche since 1974, and books since 1919.

General Information: Public Access terminal is available. No adoption, juvenile, sanity, dismissed criminal records released. Fee to fax results is $1.00 per page. Copy fee: $1.00 per page first 10 pages, then $.50 per page after. Certification fee: $2.00. Payee: Clerk of Court. Only cashiers checks and money orders accepted. Prepayment required. Mail requests: SASE required. Mail turnaround: same day if prepaid.

Justice Court PO Box 488, Broadus, MT 59317; 406-436-2503; Fax: 406-436-2866. Hours: 9AM-3:30PM M-Th (MST). *Misdemeanor, Civil Actions Under $7,000, Eviction, Small Claims.*

Powell County

District Court 409 Missouri Ave, Deer Lodge, MT 59722; 406-846-3680 X234/235; Fax: 406-846-2784. Hours: 8AM-5PM (MST). *Felony, Civil Actions Over $5,000, Eviction, Probate.*

Civil Records: Access: Mail, in person. Both court and visitors may perform in person searches. Search fee: $2.00 per name per year, first 7 years, then $1.00 per year. Required to search: name, years to search. Civil cases indexed by defendant, plaintiff. Civil records on docket books since turn of century, on computer since 1996.

Criminal Records: Access: Mail, in person. Both court and visitors may perform in person searches. Search fee: $2.00 per name per year, first 7 years, then $1.00 per year. Required to search: name, years to search, DOB, SSN. Criminal records on docket books since turn of century, on computer since 1996.

General Information: Public Access terminal is available. No adoption, juvenile or sanity records released. Will fax results for $1.00 per page. Copy fee: $1.00 per page first 10 pages, then $.50 per page after. Certification fee: $2.00. Payee: Clerk of Court. Personal checks accepted. Prepayment required. Mail requests: SASE required. Mail turnaround: 2-3 days.

Limited Jurisdiction Court 409 Missouri, Powell County Courthouse, Deer Lodge, MT 59722; 406-846-3680; Fax: 406-846-2784. Hours: 8AM-5PM (MST). *Misdemeanor, Civil Actions Under $7,000, Eviction, Small Claims.*

Prairie County

District Court PO Box 125, Terry, MT 59349; 406-635-5575. 8AM-Noon; 1PM-5PM *Felony, Civil Actions Over $5,000, Eviction, Probate.*

Civil Records: Access: Mail, in person. Both court and visitors may perform in person searches. Search fee: $2.00 per name per year, first 7 years, then $1.00 per year. Required to search: name, years to search. Civil cases indexed by defendant, plaintiff. Civil records on books since 1915; computerized records go back to 1997.

Criminal Records: Access: Mail, in person. Both court and visitors may perform in person searches. Search fee: $2.00 per name per year, first 7 years, then $1.00 per year. Required to search: name, years to search, DOB, SSN. Criminal records on books since 1915; computerized records go back to 1997.

General Information: No adoption, juvenile or sanity records released. Will fax results to local or toll free line. Copy fee: $.25 per page. Certification fee: $2.00. Payee: Clerk of Court. Personal checks

accepted. Prepayment required. Mail requests: SASE required. Mail turnaround time 5 days.

Limited Jurisdiction Court PO Box 40, Terry, MT 59349; 406-635-4126 or 635-2100; Fax: 406-635-5580. 12:30-3PM (MST). *Misdemeanor, Civil Actions Under $7,000, Eviction, Small Claims.*

Ravalli County

District Court Ravalli County Courthouse, 205 Bedford #D, Hamilton, MT 59840; 406-375-6214; Fax: 406-375-6327. Hours: 8AM-5PM (MST). *Felony, Civil Actions Over $7,000, Probate.* http://co.ravalli.mt.us

Civil Records: Access: Mail, in person. Both court and visitors may perform in person searches. Search fee: $2.00 per name per year, first 7 years, then $1.00 per year. Required to search: name, years to search. Civil cases indexed by defendant, plaintiff. Civil records on microfiche (1989), docket books (1914).

Criminal Records: Access: Mail, in person. Both court and visitors may perform in person searches. Search fee: $2.00 per name per year, first 7 years, then $1.00 per year. Required to search: name, years to search. Criminal records on microfiche (1989), docket books (1914).

General Information: Public Access terminal is available. No adoption, juvenile, psychological, medical or expunged records released. Will fax results $1.00 per page. Copy fee: $1.00 per page first 10 pages, then $.50 per page after. Certification fee: $2.00. Payee: Clerk of Court. Personal checks accepted. Prepayment required. Mail requests: SASE required. Mail turnaround time 4-5 days.

Justice Court 205 Bedford St. #F, Hamilton, MT 59840; 406-375-6252; Fax: 406-375-6383. Hours: 9AM-5PM (MST). *Misdemeanor, Civil Actions Under $7,000, Eviction, Small Claims.* Note: Dept #2, Judge Jim Bailey; Dept #1, Judge Rubin Clue

Richland County

District Court 201 W Main, Sidney, MT 59270; 406-433-1709; Fax: 406-433-6945. Hours: 8AM-5PM (MST). *Felony, Civil Actions Over $5,000, Eviction, Probate.*

Civil Records: Access: Phone, fax, mail, in person. Both court and visitors may perform in person searches. Search fee: $2.00 per name per year, first 7 years, then $1.00 per year. Required to search: name, years to search. Civil cases indexed by defendant, plaintiff. Civil records in books since 1914; on computer back to 1997.

Criminal Records: Access: Phone, fax, mail, in person. Both court and visitors may perform in person searches. Search fee: $2.00 per name per year, first 7 years, then $1.00 per year. Required to search: name, years to search. Criminal records in books since 1914; on computer back to 1997.

General Information: No adoption, juvenile, paternity, sanity, dismissed or expunged records released. Will fax results $1.00 per page. Copy fee: $1.00 per page first 10 pages, then $.50 per page after. Certification fee: $2.00. Payee: Clerk of Court. Personal checks accepted. Prepayment required. Mail requests: SASE required. Mail turnaround: 1-3 days.

Limited Jurisdiction Court 123 W Main, Sidney, MT 59270; 406-433-2815; Fax: 406-433-6885. Hours: 8AM-5PM (MST). *Misdemeanor, Civil Actions Under $7,000, Eviction, Small Claims.*

Roosevelt County

District Court County Courthouse, 400 2nd Ave S, Wolf Point, MT 59201; 406-653-6266; Fax: 406-653-6203. Hours: 8AM-5PM (MST). *Felony, Civil Actions Over $5,000, Eviction, Probate.*

Civil Records: Access: Phone, fax, mail, in person. Only the court performs in person searches; visitors may not. Search fee: $2.00 per name per year, first 7 years, then $1.00 per year. Required to search: name, years to search. Civil cases indexed by defendant, plaintiff. Civil records on books and microfiche back to 1919, computerized back to 1996.

Criminal Records: Access: Fax, mail, in person. Only the court performs in person searches; visitors may not. Search fee: $2.00 per name per year, first 7 years, then $1.00 per year. Required to search: name, years to search; also helpful: DOB. Criminal records on books and microfiche back to 1919, computerized back to 1996.

General Information: No adoption, juvenile or sanity records released. Will fax results for $3.00 per document. Copy fee: $1.00 per page first 10 pages, then $.50 per page after. Certification fee: $2.00. Payee: Clerk of Court. Personal checks accepted. Prepayment required. Mail requests: SASE required. Mail turnaround time 2-3 days after payment receipt.

Culbertson Justice Court Post #2 PO Box 421, Culbertson, MT 59218; 406-787-6607; Fax: 406-787-6608. 9AM-3PM M-Th (MST). *Misdemeanor, Civil Actions Under $7,000, Eviction, Small Claims.*

Wolf Point Justice Court Post #1 County Courthouse, 400 Second Ave. S., Wolf Point, MT 59201; 406-653-6261, 406-653-6258; Fax: 406-653-6203. Hours: 8AM-Noon M-F (MST). *Misdemeanor, Civil Actions Under $7,000, Eviction, Small Claims.*

Rosebud County

District Court PO Box 48, Forsyth, MT 59327; 406-356-7322; Fax: 406-356-7551. Hours: 8AM-5PM (MST). *Felony, Civil Actions Over $5,000, Eviction, Probate.*

Civil Records: Access: Fax, mail, in person. Only the court performs in person searches; visitors may not. Search fee: $2.00 per name per year, first 7 years, then $1.00 per year. Written requests only. Required to search: name, years to search. Civil cases indexed by defendant, plaintiff. Civil records in books, on microfiche back to 1901; on computer back to 1996.

Criminal Records: Access: Mail, in person. Both court and visitors may perform in person searches. Search fee: $2.00 per name per year, first 7 years, then $1.00 per year. Written requests only. Required to search: name, years to search, signed release. Criminal records in books, on microfiche back to 1901; on computer back to 1996.

General Information: Public Access terminal is available. No adoption, juvenile, sanity or sealed records released. Copy fee: $1.00 per page first 10 pages, then $.50 per page after. Certification fee: $2.00. Payee: Clerk of Court. Personal checks accepted. Prepayment required. Mail requests: SASE required. Mail turnaround time 2 days.

Limited Jurisdiction Court #1 Rosebud County Courthouse, PO Box 504, Forsyth, MT 59327; 406-346-2638; Fax: 406-346-7551. Hours: 8AM-5PM (MST). *Misdemeanor, Civil Actions Under $7,000, Eviction, Small Claims.*

Limited Jurisdiction Court #2 PO Box 575, Colstrip, MT 59323; 406-748-2934; Fax: 406-748-4832. Hours: 8AM-5PM; Ashland 2nd & 4th Wed 1PM (MST). *Misdemeanor, Civil Actions Under $7,000, Eviction, Small Claims.*

Sanders County

District Court PO Box 519, Thompson Falls, MT 59873; 406-827-6962; Fax: 406-827-0094. Hours: 8AM-5PM (MST). *Felony, Civil Actions Over $7,000, Eviction, Probate.*

Civil Records: Access: Mail, in person. Both court and visitors may perform in person searches. Search fee: $2.00 per name per year, first 7 years, then $1.00 per year. Required to search: name, years to search. Civil cases indexed by defendant, plaintiff. Civil records on docket books since 1906, on computer since 1999.

Criminal Records: Access: Mail, in person. Both court and visitors may perform in person searches. Search fee: $2.00 per name per year, first 7 years, then $1.00 per year. Required to search: name, years to search, DOB, SSN, signed release. Criminal records on docket books since 1906, on computer since 1999.

General Information: Public Access terminal is available. No adoption, juvenile, sanity or pre-sentence investigation records released. Will fax results to local or toll free line. Copy fee: $1.00 per page first 10 pages, then $.50 per page after. Certification fee: $2.00. Payee: Clerk of Court. Personal checks accepted. Prepayment required. Mail requests: SASE required. Mail turnaround: 1-4 days.

Limited Jurisdiction Court PO Box 519, Thompson Falls, MT 59873; 406-827-6941; Fax: 406-827-0094. Hours: 8AM-12;00, 1-5PM (MST). *Misdemeanor, Civil Actions Under $7,000, Eviction, Small Claims.*

Sheridan County

District Court 100 W Laurel, Plentywood, MT 59254; 406-765-3404; Fax: 406-765-2602. Hours: 8AM-Noon, 1-5PM (MST). *Felony, Civil Actions Over $5,000, Eviction, Probate.*
www.co.sheridan.mt.us

Civil Records: Access: Phone, mail, in person. Both court and visitors may perform in person searches. Search fee: $2.00 per name per year, first 7 years, then $1.00 per year. Required to search: name, years to search. Civil cases indexed by defendant, plaintiff. Civil records on docket books since 1913.

Criminal Records: Access: Phone, mail, in person. Both court and visitors may perform in person searches. Search fee: $2.00 per name per year, first 7 years, then $1.00 per year. Required to search: name, years to search. Criminal records on docket books since 1913.

General Information: No adoption, juvenile or sanity records released. Will fax results to toll free line, must be prepaid. Copy fee: $1.00 per page first 10 pages, then $.50 per page after. Certification fee: $2.00. Payee: Clerk of District Court. Personal checks accepted. Prepayment required. Mail requests: SASE required. Mail turnaround time 1-2 days.

Justice Court 100 W Laurel, Plentywood, MT 59254; 406-765-2310; Fax: 406-765-3489. Hours: 8AM-5PM (MST). *Misdemeanor, Civil Actions Under $7,000, Eviction, Small Claims.*

Silver Bow County

District Court 155 W Granite St, Butte, MT 59701; 406-497-6350; Fax: 406-497-6358. Hours: 8AM-5PM (MST). *Felony, Civil Actions Over $5,000, Probate.*

Civil Records: Access: Fax, mail, in person. Both court and visitors may perform in person searches. Search fee: $2.00 per name per year, first 7 years, then $1.00 per year. Required to search: name, years to search. Civil cases indexed by defendant, plaintiff. Civil records in original files since 1970, on microfilm back to 1887; on computer back to 1996.

Criminal Records: Access: Fax, mail, in person. Both court and visitors may perform in person searches. Search fee: $2.00 per name per year, first 7 years, then $1.00 per year. Required to search: name, years to search. Criminal records in original files since 1970, on microfilm back to 1887; on computer back to 1995.

General Information: Public Access terminal is available. No adoption, juvenile or sanity records released. Fee to fax results is $1.00 per page. Copy fee: $1.00 per page first 10 pages, then $.50 per page after. Certification fee: $2.00. Payee: Clerk of Court. Personal checks accepted. Prepayment required. Mail requests: SASE required. Mail turnaround time 1-3 days; will not do phone searches.

Limited Jurisdiction Court #1 & #2 155 W Granite St, Silver Bow County Courthouse, Butte, MT 59701; 406-497-6391/6392; Fax: 406-497-6468. Hours: 8AM-5PM (MST). *Misdemeanor, Civil Actions Under $7,000, Eviction, Small Claims.*
Note: There are two Justice Courts at this location. Both courts must be searched for records

Stillwater County

District Court PO Box 367, Columbus, MT 59019; 406-322-8030; Fax: 406-322-8048. Hours: 8AM-5PM (MST). *Felony, Civil Actions Over $5,000, Eviction, Probate.*

Civil Records: Access: Phone, mail, in person. Both court and visitors may perform in person searches. Search fee: $2.00 per name per year, first 7 years, then $1.00 per year. Required to search: name, years to search. Civil cases indexed by defendant, plaintiff. Civil records on docket books since 1913; on computer back to 1994.

Criminal Records: Access: Phone, mail, in person. Both court and visitors may perform in person searches. Search fee: $2.00 per name per year, first 7 years, then $1.00 per year. Required to search: name, years to search. Criminal records on docket books since 1913; on computer back to 1994.

General Information: No adoption, juvenile or sanity records released. Will fax results for $1.00 per page. Copy fee: $1.00 per page first 10 pages, then $.50 per page after. Certification fee: $2.00. Payee: Clerk of Court. Personal checks accepted. Prepayment required. Mail requests: SASE required. Mail turnaround time 1-2 days.

Limited Jurisdiction Court PO Box 77, Columbus, MT 59019; 406-322-8040; Fax: 406-322-8048. 9AM-5PM M-Th (MST). *Misdemeanor, Civil Actions Under $7,000, Eviction, Small Claims.*

Sweet Grass County

District Court PO Box 698, Big Timber, MT 59011; 406-932-5154; Fax: 406-932-5433. Hours: 8AM-Noon, 1-5PM (MST). *Felony, Civil Actions Over $5,000, Eviction, Probate.*

Civil Records: Access: Phone, mail, in person. Only the court performs in person searches; visitors may not. Search fee: $2.00 per name per year, first 7 years, then $1.00 per year. Required to search: name, years to search. Civil cases indexed by defendant, plaintiff. Civil records in books since 1895, on microfiche since 1972, computerized since 1996.

Criminal Records: Access: Phone, mail, in person. Only the court performs in person searches; visitors may not. Search fee: $2.00 per name per year, first 7 years, then $1.00 per year. Required to search: name, years to search. Criminal records in books since 1895, on microfiche since 1972, computerized since 1996.

General Information: No adoption, juvenile or sanity records released. Will fax results for $1.50 if not a toll free fax return. Copy fee: $1.00 per page first 10 pages, then $.50 per page after. Certification fee:

$2.00. Payee: Clerk of Court. Personal checks accepted. Prepayment required. Mail requests: SASE required. Mail turnaround time 1 day.

Limited Jurisdiction Court PO Box 1432, Big Timber, MT 59011; 406-932-5150; Civil phone: 406-932-5153; Fax: 406-932-5433. Hours: 8AM-5PM (MST). *Misdemeanor, Civil Actions Under $7,000, Eviction, Small Claims.*

Teton County

District Court PO Box 487, Choteau, MT 59422; 406-466-2909; Fax: 406-466-2910. Hours: 8AM-5PM (MST). *Felony, Civil Actions Over $5,000, Eviction, Probate.*

Civil Records: Access: Phone, fax, mail, in person. Only the court performs in person searches; visitors may not. Search fee: $2.00 per name per year, first 7 years, then $1.00 per year. Required to search: name, years to search. Civil cases indexed by defendant, plaintiff. Civil records on books from 1893; on computer back to 1995.

Criminal Records: Access: Phone, mail, in person. Only the court performs in person searches; visitors may not. Search fee: $2.00 per name per year, first 7 years, then $1.00 per year. Required to search: name, years to search. Criminal records on books from 1893; on computer back to 1995.

General Information: No adoption, juvenile or sanity records released. Fee to fax results is $1.00 per page. Copy fee: $1.00 per page 1st 10 pages, then $.50 per page after. Certification fee: $2.00. Payee: Clerk of Court. Personal checks accepted. Prepayment required. Mail requests: SASE required. Mail turnaround time 1 day.

Limited Jurisdiction Court PO Box 337, Choteau, MT 59422; 406-466-5611; Fax: 406-466-2138. Hours: 8AM-Noon (MST). *Misdemeanor, Civil Actions Under $7,000, Eviction, Small Claims.*

Toole County

District Court PO Box 850, Shelby, MT 59474; 406-424-8330; Fax: 406-424-8331. Hours: 8AM-5PM (MST). *Felony, Civil Actions Over $5,000, Eviction, Probate.*

Civil Records: Access: Phone, fax, mail, in person. Both court and visitors may perform in person searches. Search fee: $2.00 per name per year, first 7 years, then $1.00 per year. Required to search: name, years to search. Civil cases indexed by defendant, plaintiff. Civil records in books from 1914; on computer since 1997.

Criminal Records: Access: Phone, fax, mail, in person. Both court and visitors may perform in person searches. Search fee: $2.00 per name per year, first 7 years, then $1.00 per year. Required to search: name, years to search, DOB, SSN. Criminal records in books from 1914; on computer since 1997.

General Information: No adoption, juvenile or sanity records released. Will fax results $.50 per page. Copy fee: $1.00 per page first 10 pages, then $.50 per page after. Certification fee: $2.00 per document. Payee: Clerk of Court. Personal checks accepted. Prepayment required. Mail requests: SASE required. Mail turnaround time same day as request received.

Limited Jurisdiction Court PO Box 738, Shelby, MT 59474; 406-924-8315; Fax: 406-424-8316. Hours: 9AM-5PM M-F (MST). *Misdemeanor, Civil Actions Under $7,000, Eviction, Small Claims.*

Treasure County

District Court PO Box 392, Hysham, MT 59038; 406-342-5547; Fax: 406-342-5445. Hours: 8AM-5PM (MST). *Felony, Civil Actions Over $5,000, Eviction, Probate.*

Civil Records: Access: Fax, mail, in person. Both court and visitors may perform in person searches. Search fee: $2.00 per name per year, first 7 years, then $1.00 per year. Required to search: name, years to search; also helpful: address. Civil cases indexed by defendant, plaintiff. Civil records on books since 1919, on microfilm from 1985 to present; on computer back to 1996.

Criminal Records: Access: Fax, mail, in person. Both court and visitors may perform in person searches. Search fee: $2.00 per name per year, first 7 years, then $1.00 per year. Required to search: name, years to search, DOB; also helpful: address. Criminal records on books since 1919, on microfilm from 1985 to present; on computer back to 1996.

General Information: No adoption or sanity records released. Fee to fax results to $1.50 per page. Copy fee: $1.00 per page first 10 pages, then $.50 per page after. Certification fee: $2.00. Payee: Clerk of Court. Personal checks accepted. Prepayment required. Mail requests: SASE required. Mail turnaround: 1 week.

Limited Jurisdiction Court PO Box 267, Hysham, MT 59038; 406-342-5532; Fax: 406-342-5532. Hours: 9AM-Noon (MST). *Misdemeanor, Civil Actions Under $7,000, Eviction, Small Claims.*

Valley County

Clerk of District Court 501 Court Sq #6, Glasgow, MT 59230; 406-228-6268; Fax: 406-228-6212. Hours: 8AM-5PM (MST). *Felony, Civil Actions Over $5,000, Eviction, Probate.*

Civil Records: Access: Phone, fax, mail, in person. Only the court performs in person searches; visitors may not. Search fee: $2.00 per name per year, first 7 years, then $1.00 per year. Required to search: name, years to search. Civil cases indexed by defendant, plaintiff. Civil records in books since 1893; on computer back to 1996.

Criminal Records: Access: Fax, mail, in person. Only the court performs in person searches; visitors may not. Search fee: $2.00 per name per year, first 7 years, then $1.00 per year. Required to search: name, years to search, signed release. Criminal records in books since 1893; on computer back to 1996.

General Information: No adoption, juvenile or sanity records released. Fee to fax results is $1.00 per page. Copy fee: $1.00 per page first 10 pages, then $.50 per page after. Certification fee: $2.00. Payee: Clerk of Court. Business checks accepted. Prepayment required. Mail requests: SASE required. Mail turnaround time same day.

Limited Jurisdiction Court 501 Court Sq #10, Glasgow, MT 59230; 406-228-6271; Fax: 406-228-4601. Hours: 8AM-Noon (MST). *Misdemeanor, Civil Actions Under $7,000, Eviction, Small Claims.*

Wheatland County

District Court Box 227, Harlowton, MT 59036; 406-632-4893; Fax: 406-632-4873. Hours: 8AM-5PM (MST). *Felony, Civil Actions Over $5,000, Eviction, Probate.*

Civil Records: Access: Fax, mail, in person. Both court and visitors may perform in person searches. Search fee: $2.00 per name per year, first 7 years, then $1.00 per year. Required to search: name, years to search. Civil cases indexed by defendant, plaintiff. Computerized records back to 1996, civil records on docket books to 1917, probate on microfiche to 1984.

Criminal Records: Access: Mail, in person. Both court and visitors may perform in person searches. Search fee: $2.00 per name per year, first 7 years, then $1.00 per year. Required to search: name, years to search. Computerized records back to 1996, criminal records on docket books since 1917, probate on microfiche from 1984.

General Information: No adoption, juvenile or sanity records released. Will fax results to local or toll free line. Copy fee: $1.00 per page first 10 pages, then $.50 per page after. Certification fee: $2.00. Payee: Clerk of Court. Personal checks accepted. Prepayment required. Mail requests: SASE required. Mail turnaround time 2-3 days.

Limited Jurisdiction Court PO Box 524, Harlowton, MT 59036; 406-632-4821; Fax: 406-632-5654. 10AM-1PM T,Th (MST). *Misdemeanor, Civil Actions Under $7,000, Eviction, Small Claims.*

Wibaux County

District Court PO Box 292, Wibaux, MT 59353; 406-796-2484; Fax: 406-796-2484. Hours: 8AM-5PM, Closed 12-1 (MST). *Felony, Civil Actions Over $5,000, Eviction, Probate.*

Civil Records: Access: Phone, fax, mail, in person. Both court and visitors may perform in person searches. Search fee: $2.00 per name per year, first 7 years, then $1.00 per year. Required to search: name, years to search. Civil records on docket books since 1914, on computer since 01/97.

Criminal Records: Access: Phone, fax, mail, in person. Only the court performs in person searches; visitors may not. Search fee: $2.00 per name per year, first 7 years, then $1.00 per year. Required to search: name, years to search. Criminal records on docket books since 1914, on computer since 01/97.

General Information: No adoption, juvenile or sanity records released. Will fax results $2.00 1st page, $.50 each add'l. Copy fee: $1.00 per page first 10 pages, then $.50 per page after. Certification fee: $2.00. Payee: Clerk of Court. Personal checks accepted. Prepayment required. Mail requests: SASE required. Mail turnaround time 1 week.

Limited Jurisdiction Court PO Box 445, Wibaux, MT 59353; 406-796-2484. Hours: 1-5PM M&W, 8AM-Noon F (MST). *Misdemeanor, Civil Actions Under $7,000, Eviction, Small Claims.*

Yellowstone County

District Court PO Box 35030 (217 N 27 St), Billings, MT 59107; 406-256-2862; Civil phone: 406-256-2851; Criminal phone: 406-256-2860; Probate phone: 406-256-2865; Fax: 406-256-2995. 8AM-5PM *Felony, Civil Actions Over $7,000, Probate.* www.co.yellowstone.mt.us/clerk_court

Civil Records: Access: Mail, in person. Both court and visitors may perform in person searches. Search fee: $2.00 per name per year, first 7 years, then $1.00 per year. Required to search: name, years to search. Civil cases indexed by defendant, plaintiff. Civil records in books, on microfilm back to 1800s; on computer back to 1992.

Criminal Records: Access: Mail, in person. Both court and visitors may perform in person searches. Search fee: $2.00 per name per year, first 7 years, then $1.00 per year. Required to search: name, years to search. Criminal records in books, on microfilm back to 1800s; on comptuer back to 1990.

General Information: Public Access terminal is available. No adoption, juvenile or sanity records released. Copy fee: $1.00 per page first 10 pages, then $.50 per page after. Certification fee: $2.00. Payee: Clerk of Court. Personal checks not accepted. Prepayment required. Mail requests: SASE required. Mail turnaround time 1 day if record less than 10 years old.

Limited Jurisdiction Court PO Box 35032, Billings, MT 59107; 406-256-2895; Fax: 406-256-2898. Hours: 9AM-5PM (MST). *Misdemeanor, Civil Actions Under $7,000, Eviction, Small Claims.*

Montana Recording Offices

ORGANIZATION: 57 counties, 56 recording offices. The recording officer is County Clerk and Recorder (Clerk of District Court for state tax liens). Yellowstone National Park is considered a county, but is not included as a filing location. The entire state is in the Mountain Time Zone (MST).

REAL ESTATE RECORDS: Many Montana counties will perform real estate searches. Search and copy fees vary. Certification usually costs $2.00 per document.

UCC RECORDS: Financing statements are filed at the state level, except for real estate related collateral, which are filed with the Clerk and Recorder. However, prior to 07/2001, consumer goods collateral were also filed at the county and these older records can be searched there. All counties will perform UCC searches. Use search request form UCC-11. Search fees are usually $7.00 per debtor name. Copy fees vary.

TAX LIEN RECORDS: Federal tax liens on personal property of businesses are filed with the Secretary of State. Other federal tax liens are filed with the county Clerk and Recorder. State tax liens are filed with the Clerk of District Court. Usually tax liens on personal property filed with the Clerk and Recorder are in the same index with UCC financing statements. Most counties will perform tax lien searches, some as part of a UCC search and others for a separate fee, usually $7.00 per name. Copy fees vary.

OTHER LIENS: Mechanics, thresherman, judgment, lis pendens, construction, logger.

ONLINE ACCESS: Search for a for a Montana property owner by name and county on the Montana Cadastral Mapping Project GIS mapping database at http://gis.doa.state.mt.us

Beaverhead County

Clerk and Recorder, 2 South Pacific, Dillon, MT 59725-2799. **Phone**-406-683-2642, R/E Recording-406-683-3720, UCC Recording-406-683-3720; fax-406-683-5776; hours 8AM-5PM

UCC search per debtor- $7.00. Will not search real estate or tax lien records. RE record copy- $.50 per page. UCC copy- $1.00 per page. Cert fee: $2.00 per cert. Payee: Beaverhead County Clerk and Recorder. Name search for property data free at http://gis.doa.state.mt.us/searchOwner.htm. **Other phones:** Treasurer-406-683-5821; Appraiser/ Auditor-406-683-4000; Elections-406-683-3720; Vital Records-406-683-3720.

Big Horn County

Clerk and Recorder, PO Box 908, Hardin, MT 59034. **Phone**-Clerk and Recorder, R/E & UCC Recording-406-665-9730, UCC Recording-406-665-9732; fax-406-665-9738; hours 8:00AM-5:00PM

UCC search per debtor- $7.00. Will search real estate records. RE copy fee- $.50 1st page, $.25 per subsequent page. UCC copy- $.50 1st page, $.25 per subsequent page. Cert fee: $2.00 per doc. Payee: Clerk - Recorder. Name search for property data free at http://gis.doa.state.mt.us/searchOwner.htm. **Other phones:** Assessor-406-665-9710; Treasurer-406-665-9830; Appraiser/ Auditor-406-665-9710; Elections-406-665-9730; Vital Records-406-665-9730.

Blaine County

Clerk and Recorder, PO Box 278, Chinook, MT 59523-0278. **Phone**-Clerk and Recorder, R/E & UCC Recording- 406-357-3240; fax-406-357-2199; hours 8AM-5PM

UCC search per debtor- $7.00. Tax liens not included in UCC search. Tax lien search- $7.00 per debtor. Will not search real estate records. RE record copy- $.25 per copy, ONLY if book and page given. UCC copy- $.25 per copy. Cert fee: $2.00 per doc. Payee: Blaine County Clerk. Name search for property data free at http://gis.doa.state.mt.us/searchOwner.htm. **Other phones:** Assessor-406-357-3210; Treasurer-406-357-3280; Appraiser/ Auditor-406-357-3210; Elections-406-357-3240; Vital Records-406-357-3240.

Broadwater County

Clerk and Recorder, 515 Broadway, Townsend, MT 59644. **Phone**-Clerk and Recorder, R/E & UCC Recording- 406-266-3443; fax-406-266-3674; hours 8AM-5PM. UCC search per debtor- $7.00. Copy fee is $.50 per copy. Cert fee: $2.00 per doc. Payee: Broadwater County Clerk. Name search for property data free at http://gis.doa.state.mt.us/searchOwner.htm. **Other phones:** Assessor-406-266-3430; Treasurer-406-266-3445; Appraiser/ Auditor-406-266-3430; Elections-406-266-3443; Vital Records-406-266-3443.

Carbon County

Clerk and Recorder, PO Box 887, Red Lodge, MT 59068. **Phone**-Clerk and Recorder, R/E & UCC Recording- 406-446-1220; fax-406-446-2640; hours 7AM-5:30PM. UCC search per debtor- $7.00. Will not search real estate records. RE record copy- $.25 per page; $1.00 min. UCC copy- $.25 per page. Cert fee: $2.00 per doc. Payee: Clerk and Recorder. Name search for property data free at http://gis.doa.state.mt.us/searchOwner.htm. **Other phones:** Assessor-406-466-1223; Treasurer-406-446-1221; Appraiser/ Auditor-406-446-1224; Elections-406-446-1595; Vital Records-406-446-1220.

Carter County

Clerk and Recorder, PO Box 315, Ekalaka, MT 59324-0315. **Phone**-406-775-8749; fax-406-775-8750; hours 8AM-Noon, 1-5PM

UCC search per debtor- $7.00. Separate federal/state combined tax lien search- $7.00 per debtor. Will search real estate records. Copy fee-$.50 per page. Cert fee: $2.00 per doc. Payee: Carter County Clerk. Name search for property data free at http://gis.doa.state.mt.us/searchOwner.htm. **Other phones:** Assessor-406-775-8717; Treasurer-406-775-8735.

Cascade County

Clerk and Recorder, PO Box 2867, Great Falls, MT 59403-2867. **Phone**-406-454-6800, R/E Recording-406-454-6801, UCC Recording-406-454-6801; fax-406-454-6802; 8AM-5PM www.co.cascade.mt.us

UCC search per debtor- $7.00. Federal/state combined tax lien search- $7.00 per debtor. Will not search real estate records. RE record copy- $.50

1st page, $.25 each add'l. UCC copy fee-$.50 per page. Cert fee: $2.00 per doc. Payee: Clerk & Recorder. Name search for property data free at http://gis.doa.state.mt.us/searchOwner.htm. **Other phones:** Assessor-406-454-6744; Treasurer-406-454-6850; Appraiser/ Auditor-406-454-7460; Elections-406-454-6803; Vital Records-406-454-6718.

Chouteau County

Clerk and Recorder, PO Box 459, Fort Benton, MT 59442-0459. **Phone**-406-622-5151; fax-406-622-3012; hours 8AM-5PM

UCC search per debtor- $7.00. UCC search includes federal tax liens if requested. Separate federal/state combined tax lien search- $7.00 per debtor. Real estate owner, mortgage, and property transfer searches available. Real estate copy fee- $.50 per page. UCC copy- $.50 per page. Cert fee: $2.00 per cert; $.50 per page. Payee: Chouteau County Clerk and Recorder. Name search for property data free at http://gis.doa.state.mt.us/searchOwner.htm. **Other phones:** Assessor-406-622-5261; Treasurer-406-622-5032; Elections-406-622-5151; Vital Records-406-622-5151.

Custer County

Clerk and Recorder, 1010 Main St, Miles City, MT 59301-1010. **Phone**-Clerk and Recorder, R/E & UCC Recording- 406-874-3343; fax-406-874-3452; hours 8AM-5PM. UCC search per debtor- $7.00 to search 10 year block per book & $.50 per year for each add'l year. Will search tax liens including federal tax liens. Real estate record owner searches available. RE record copy- $7.00 per 10 years per book. UCC copy- $.50 per page. Cert fee: $2.00 per cert. Payee: Custer County Clerk and Recorder. Name search for property data free at http://gis.doa.state.mt.us/searchOwner.htm. **Other phones:** Assessor-406-232-1295; Treasurer-406-874-3427; Appraiser/ Auditor-406-232-6437; Elections-406-874-3343; Vital Records-406-444-4228.

Daniels County

Clerk and Recorder, PO Box 247, Scobey, MT 59263. **Phone**-Clerk and Recorder, R/E & UCC Recording-406-487-5561; hours 8AM-5PM

UCC search per debtor- $7.00. Real estate record owner and mortgage searches available. Record copy- $.50 1st page, $.25 each add'l. Cert fee: $2.00 per cert. Payee: Daniels County Clerk and Recorder. Name search for property data free at http://gis.doa.state.mt.us/searchOwner.htm. **Other phones:** Assessor-406-487-2791; Treasurer-406-487-2671; Appraiser/ Auditor-406-487-2791; Elections-406-487-5561; Vital Records-406-487-5561.

Dawson County

Clerk and Recorder, 207 W. Bell, Glendive, MT 59330. **Phone-**Clerk and Recorder, R/E & UCC Recording-406-377-3058; fax-406-377-1717; hours 8AM-5PM www.dawsoncountymontana.org
UCC search per debtor- $7.00. Will not search real estate or tax lien records. Copy fee-$.50 1st page; $.25 each add'l. UCC copy- $.50 1st page; $.25 each add'l. Cert fee: $2.00 per doc + $.50 1st page, $.25 each add'l. Payee: Clerk and Recorder. Name search for property data free at http://gis.doa.state.mt.us/searchOwner.htm. **Other phones:** Assessor-406-377-4256; Treasurer-406-377-3026; Appraiser/ Auditor-406-377-4500; Elections-406-377-3058; Vital Records-406-377-3058.

Deer Lodge County

Clerk and Recorder, 800 Main St., Courthouse, Anaconda, MT 59711-2999. **Phone-**406-563-4060, R/E Recording-406-563-4061, UCC Recording-406-563-4001; fax-406-563-4001.
UCC search per debtor- $7.00. Will do limited real estate searches. Copy fee-$.50 per page. Cert fee: $2.00 per doc. Name search for property data free at http://gis.doa.state.mt.us/searchOwner.htm. **Other phones:** Assessor-406-563-4045; Treasurer-406-563-4051; Appraiser/ Auditor-406-563-4045; Elections-406-563-4060; Vital Records-406-563-4062.

Fallon County

Clerk and Recorder, PO Box 846, Baker, MT 59313-0846. **Phone-**Clerk and Recorder, R/E & UCC Recording- 406-778-7106; fax-406-778-2048; hours 8:00AM-5:00PM
UCC search per debtor- $7.00. Will search tax liens including federal tax liens. Tax lien search- $7.00 per debtor. Will search real estate records. RE record copy- $.50 for 1st pg., $.25 each add'l pg. UCC copy- $.50 per page. Cert fee: $2.00 per doc. Payee: Clerk and Recorder. Name search for property data free at http://gis.doa.state.mt.us/searchOwner.htm. **Other phones:** Assessor-406-778-7109; Treasurer-406-778-7109; Appraiser/ Auditor-406-778-7172; Elections-406-778-7105; Vital Records-406-778-7106.

Fergus County

Clerk and Recorder, 712 W. Main, Lewistown, MT 59457. **Phone-**406-538-5242; fax-406-538-9023; hours 8AM-5PM. UCC search per debtor- $7.00. UCC search includes tax liens if requested. Will not search real estate records. UCC copy- $.50 per page. Cert fee: $2.00 per doc. Payee: Clerk and Recorder. Name search for property data free at http://gis.doa.state.mt.us/searchOwner.htm. **Other phones:** Assessor-406-538-5723; Treasurer-406-538-9220; Appraiser/ Auditor-406-538-5723; Elections-406-538-5242; Vital Records-406-538-5242.

Flathead County

Clerk and Recorder, 800 S. Main, 2nd Fl, Courthouse, Kalispell, MT 59901-5400. **Phone-**Clerk and Recorder, R/E & UCC Recording- 406-758-5526; fax-406-758-5865; hours 8AM-5PM www.co.flathead.mt.us
UCC search per debtor- $7.00. UCC search includes federal tax liens if requested. Separate federal/state combined tax lien search- $7.00 per debtor. Will not search real estate records. RE record copy- $.50

1st copy, $.25 each add'l. UCC copy- $1.00 per page. Cert fee: $2.00 per doc. Payee: Flathead County Clerk and Recorder. Name search for property data free at http://gis.doa.state.mt.us/searchOwner.htm. **Other phones:** Assessor-406-758-5700; Treasurer-406-758-5684; Elections-406-758-5535; Vital Records-406-758-5526.

Gallatin County

Clerk and Recorder, 311 W. Main, Rm 204, Rm 204, Bozeman, MT 59715. **Phone-**Clerk and Recorder, R/E & UCC Recording- 406-582-3050; fax-406-582-3037; hours 8AM-5PM
www.co.gallatin.mt.us/webtax/default.asp
UCC search per debtor- $7.00. Will not search tax liens. Real estate record owner and mortgage searches available. RE record copy- $.50 1st page; $.25 each add'l. UCC copy- $1.00 per page. Cert fee: $2.00 per doc, $.50 per page to copy. Payee: Gallatin County Clerk and Recorder. **Online Access to Property, Tax, Treasurer records:** Name search for property data free at http://gis.doa.state.mt.us/searchOwner.htm. Also, access to the treasur'er property tax data is free at www.co.gallatin.mt.us/webtax/default.asp. **Other phones:** Assessor-406-582-3400; Treasurer-406-582-3030; Appraiser/ Auditor-406-582 3400; Elections-406-582-3060; Vital Records-406-582-3050; State tax liens/district court-406-582-2165.

Garfield County

Clerk and Recorder, PO Box 7, Jordan, MT 59337-0007. **Phone-**Clerk and Recorder, R/E & UCC Recording- 406-557-2760; fax-406-557-2625; hours 8AM-5PM. UCC search per debtor- $7.00. UCC search includes tax liens. UCC copy- $.50 1st page, $.25 each add'l. Cert fee: $2.00 per doc. Name search for property data free at http://gis.doa.state.mt.us/searchOwner.htm. **Other phones:** Assessor-406-557-6164; Treasurer-406-557-2233; Appraiser/ Auditor-406-557-2772; Elections-406-557-2760; Vital Records-406-557-2760.

Glacier County

County Clerk and Recorder, 512 E. Main, Cut Bank, MT 59427. **Phone-**County Clerk and Recorder, R/E & UCC Recording- 406-873-5063 x22; fax-406-873-2125; hours 8AM-5PM
UCC search per debtor- $7.00. UCC search includes tax liens if requested. Will not search real estate records. Record copy fee- $.50 per page. Cert fee: $2.00 per doc. Name search for property data free at http://gis.doa.state.mt.us/searchOwner.htm. **Other phones:** Assessor-406-873-5063 x43; Treasurer-406-873-5063 x31; Appraiser/ Auditor-406-873-5063 x45; Elections-406-873-5063 x19; Vital Records-406-873-5063 x22.

Golden Valley County

Clerk and Recorder, PO Box 10, Ryegate, MT 59074. **Phone-**Clerk and Recorder, R/E & UCC Recording-406-568-2231; fax-406-568-2598; hours 8AM-5PM
UCC search per debtor- $7.00 per year. Will not search real estate or tax lien records. Copy fee-$.50 per page. Cert fee: $2.00 per doc. Payee: Clerk/ Recorder/ Clerk of Court. Name search for property data free at http://gis.doa.state.mt.us/searchOwner.htm. **Other phones:** Assessor-406-586-2371; Treasurer-406-586-2342; Elections-406-568-2231; Vital Records-406-568-2231.

Granite County

Clerk and Recorder, PO Box 925, Philipsburg, MT 59858. **Phone-**Clerk and Recorder, R/E & UCC Recording- 406-859-3771; fax-406-859-3817; hours 8AM-5PM
UCC search per debtor- $7.00. UCC search includes tax liens. Tax lien search- $7.00 per debtor. Will

not search real estate records. Copy fee-$.50 1st page; $.25 each add'l. Cert fee: $2.00 per doc. Payee: Clerk & Recorder. Name search for property data free at http://gis.doa.state.mt.us/searchOwner.htm. **Other phones:** Assessor-406-859-3521; Treasurer-406-859-3831; Elections-406-859-3771; Vital Records-406-859-3771.

Hill County

Clerk and Recorder, 315 4th St, Courthouse, Havre, MT 59501. **Phone-**406-265-5481; fax-406-265-2445; hours 8AM-5PM http://co.hill.mt.us
UCC search per debtor- $7.00. UCC search includes tax liens. Tax lien search- $7.00 per debtor. Will not search real estate records. Record copy- $.50 1st page, $.25 each add'l. Cert fee: $2.00 per doc. Payee: Hill County Clerk and Recorder. Name search for property data free at http://gis.doa.state.mt.us/searchOwner.htm. **Other phones:** Assessor-406-265-5481 x210; Treasurer-406-265-5481 x257; Elections-406-265-5481 x221, 222, 223; Vital Records-406-265-5481 x221, 222, 223.

Jefferson County

Clerk and Recorder, PO Box H, Boulder, MT 59632. **Phone-**Clerk and Recorder, R/E & UCC Recording-406-225-4020; fax-406-225-4149; hours 8AM-Noon, 1-5PM http://co.jefferson.mt.us
Will not search UCC records. Copy fee-$.50 1st page, $.25 per each add'l. Cert fee: $2.00 per doc. Name search for property data free at http://gis.doa.state.mt.us/searchOwner.htm. **Other phones:** Assessor-406-225-4001; Treasurer-406-225-4103; Appraiser/ Auditor-406-225-4001; Elections-406-225-4018; Vital Records-406-225-4020.

Judith Basin County

Clerk and Recorder, PO Box 427, Stanford, MT 59479. **Phone-**Clerk and Recorder, R/E & UCC Recording-406-566-2277; fax-406-566-2211; hours 8AM-5PM
UCC search per debtor- $7.00. Will search real estate records but not certify. Record copy- $.50 1st page, $.25 add'ls. Cert fee: varies. Payee: Clerk & Recorder. Name search for property data free at http://gis.doa.state.mt.us/searchOwner.htm. **Other phones:** Assessor-406-566-2291; Treasurer-406-566-2277; Appraiser/ Auditor-406-566-2291; Elections-406-566-2277; Vital Records-406-566-2277.

Lake County

Clerk and Recorder, 106 4th Ave East, Polson, MT 59860. **Phone-**406-883-7210, R/E Recording-406-883-7208; fax-406-883-7283; hours 8AM-5PM www.lakecounty-mt.org
UCC search per debtor- $7.00. Will search limited tax liens. Tax lien search- $7.00 per debtor. Limited Real Estate searches available. Mortgage searches available. RE record copy- $.50 1st page; $.25 each add'l. UCC copy- $.50 per page. Cert fee: $2.00 per cert. Payee: Lake County Clerk and Recorder. Name search for property data free at http://gis.doa.state.mt.us/searchOwner.htm. **Other phones:** Assessor-406-883-7232; Treasurer-406-883-7224; Appraiser/ Auditor-406-883-7232; Elections-406-883-7268; Vital Records-406-883-7208; Clerk of Court (tax liens)-406-883-7254; Commissioners-406-883-7204.

Lewis and Clark County

Clerk and Recorder, PO Box 1721, Helena, MT 59624. **Phone-**Clerk and Recorder, R/E & UCC Recording-406-447-8337; fax-406-457-8598; hours 8AM-5PM www.co.lewis-clark.mt.us
UCC search per debtor- $7.00. UCC search includes federal tax liens if requested. Mortgage and property transfer searches available. RE record copy- $.50 1st page, $.25 each add'l. UCC copy- $1.00 per page. Cert fee: $2.00 per cert. Payee: Lewis and Clark

County Clerk and Recorder. **Online Access to Grantor/Grantee, Real Estate, Lien, Recording, Property records:** The Grantor/Grantee index and recorder records are free at http://records.co.lewis-clark.mt.us/splash.jsp. Registration, logon and password required. This new automation includes document imaging via subscription online service. Records go back to 4/2001. Also, search the GIS map and parcel search at www.co.lewis-clark.mt.us/gis/atlas/index.html. Also, Name search for property data free at http://gis.doa.state.mt.us/searchOwner.htm. **Other phones:** Assessor-406-444-4000; Treasurer-406-447-8329; Elections-406-447-8338; Vital Records-406-447-8335.

Liberty County

Clerk and Recorder, PO Box 459, Chester, MT 59522-0459. **Phone-**Clerk and Recorder, R/E & UCC Recording- 406-759-5365; fax-406-759-5395; hours 8AM-5PM. UCC search per debtor- $7.00. Tax lien search- $7.00 per debtor. Will search real estate records. RE record copy- $.25 per page. UCC copy- $.50 per page. Cert fee: $2.00 per doc, + $.50 per page. Payee: Clerk & Recorder. Name search for property data free at http://gis.doa.state.mt.us/searchOwner.htm. **Other phones:** Treasurer-406-759-5455; Appraiser/ Auditor-406-759-5126; Elections-406-759-5365; Vital Records-406-759-5365.

Lincoln County

Recorder, 512 California Ave, Libby, MT 59923. **Phone-**406-293-7781, R/E Recording-406-293-7781 x205, UCC Recording-406-293-7781 x205; fax-406-293-8577; hours 8AM-5PM

UCC search per debtor- $7.00. Tax liens not included in UCC search. Separate federal tax lien search- $7.00 per debtor. Will not search real estate records. Record copy- $.50 per page. Cert fee: $2.00 per page. Payee: Clerk/Recorder. Name search for property data free at http://gis.doa.state.mt.us/searchOwner.htm. **Other phones:** Assessor-406-293-7781 x213; Treasurer-406-293-7781 x253; Appraiser/ Auditor-406-293-7781 x219; Elections-406-293-7781 x283; Vital Records-406-293-7781 x205; Clerk of Court-406-293-7781 x243.

Madison County

Clerk and Recorder, PO Box 366, Virginia City, MT 59755. **Phone-**406-843-4270; hours 8AM-Noon,1-5PM

UCC search per debtor- $7.00. UCC search includes federal tax liens. Real estate record owner and property searches available. RE record copy- $.50 per page. UCC copy- $1.00 per page. Cert fee: $2.00 per doc + $.50 per copy. Payee: Madison County Clerk and Recorder. Name search for property data free at http://gis.doa.state.mt.us/searchOwner.htm. **Other phones:** Assessor-406-843-5392; Treasurer-406-843-4212.

McCone County

Clerk and Recorder, PO Box 199, Circle, MT 59215-0199. **Phone-**Clerk and Recorder, R/E & UCC Recording- 406-485-3505; fax-406-485-2689; hours 8AM-5PM

UCC search per debtor- $7.00. UCC search includes federal tax liens if requested. Separate federal/state combined tax lien search- $7.00, $.25 per page. Real estate owner, mortgage, and property transfer searches available. RE record copy- $7.00, $.25 per page. UCC copy- $.25 per page. Cert fee: $2.00 per cert. Payee: McCone County Clerk and Recorder. Name search for property data free at http://gis.doa.state.mt.us/searchOwner.htm. **Other phones:** Assessor-406-485-3565; Treasurer-406-485-3590; Appraiser/ Auditor-406-485-3432; Elections-406-485-3505; Vital Records-406-485-3505.

Meagher County

Deputy Clerk & Recording, PO Box 309, White Sulphur Springs, MT 59645. **Phone-**Deputy Clerk & Recording, R/E & UCC Recording- 406-547-3612; fax-406-547-3388; hours 9AM-4PM

UCC search per debtor- $7.00. Will do a separate federal & state combined tax lien search. Will not search real estate records. RE record copy- $.50 per page, with book and page info given. Copy fee- $.50 1st page; $.25 each add'l. Cert fee: $2.00 per cert. Payee: Meagher County Clerk & Recorder. Name search for property data free at http://gis.doa.state.mt.us/searchOwner.htm. **Other phones:** Assessor-406-547-3653; Treasurer-406-547-3641; Appraiser/ Auditor-406-547-3653; Elections-406-547-3612; Vital Records-406-547-3612.

Mineral County

Clerk and Recorder, PO Box 550, Superior, MT 59872-0550. **Phone-**406-822-3520; fax-406-822-3579; hours 8AM-5PM

UCC search per debtor- $7.00. Copy fee-$.50 1st page; $.25 each add'l. Cert fee: $2.00 per doc. Payee: Clerk & Recorder. Name search for property data free at http://gis.doa.state.mt.us/searchOwner.htm. **Other phones:** Assessor-406-822-3540; Treasurer-406-822-3530; Appraiser/ Auditor-406-822-3540; Elections-406-822-3520; Vital Records-406-822-3520.

Missoula County

Clerk and Recorder, 200 W. Broadway, Missoula, MT 59802-4292. **Phone-**Clerk and Recorder, R/E & UCC Recording- 406-528-4752; fax-406-523-2812; hours 8AM-5PM www.co.missoula.mt.us

UCC search per debtor- $7.00. Tax lien search-$7.00 per debtor. Will not search real estate records. Copy fee is $.50 per page. Cert fee: $2.00 per doc. Payee: Missoula Clerk & Recorder. **Online Access to Property, Assessor records:** Access to the county property information system is free at www.co.missoula.mt.us/owner/. No name searching at this time. Also, Name search for property data free at http://gis.doa.state.mt.us/searchOwner.htm. **Other phones:** Assessor-406-329-1400; Treasurer-406-528-4847; Appraiser/ Auditor-406-329-1400; Elections-406-528-4751; Vital Records-406-528-4752.

Musselshell County

Clerk and Recorder, 506 Main St, Courthouse, Roundup, MT 59072. **Phone-**Clerk and Recorder, R/E & UCC Recording- 406-323-1104; fax-406-323-3303; hours 8AM-5PM

UCC search per debtor- $7.00. Will search tax liens including federal tax liens. Will not search real estate records. Record copy- $.50 per page. Cert fee: $2.00 per doc. Payee: Musselshell County. Name search for property data free at http://gis.doa.state.mt.us/searchOwner.htm. **Other phones:** Assessor-406-323-1513; Treasurer-406-323-2504; Appraiser/ Auditor-406-323-1513; Elections-406-323-1104; Vital Records-406-323-1104.

Park County

Clerk and Recorder, 414 E. Callendar, Livingston, MT 59047. **Phone-**406-222-4110; fax-406-222-4199; hours 8AM-5PM

UCC search per debtor- $7.00. UCC search does not include federal tax liens. Will not search real estate records. RE record copy- $.50 1st page, $.25 each add'l. UCC copy- $1.00 per page. Cert fee: $2.00 per cert. Payee: Park County Clerk and Recorder. Name search for property data free at http://gis.doa.state.mt.us/searchOwner.htm.

Petroleum County

Clerk and Recorder, PO Box 226, Winnett, MT 59087. **Phone-**406-429-5311; fax-406-429-6328; 8AM-5PM

UCC search per debtor- $7.00. UCC search does not include federal tax liens. Separate federal/state combined tax lien search- $7.00 per debtor. Mortgage searches available. Record copy- $.50 per page. Cert fee: $2.00 per doc. Payee: Petroleum County Clerk and Recorder. Name search for property data free at http://gis.doa.state.mt.us/searchOwner.htm. **Other phones:** Assessor-406-429-5531; Treasurer-406-429-5551; Appraiser/ Auditor-406-429-5231; Elections-406-429-5311.

Phillips County

Recorder, PO Box 360, Malta, MT 59538. **Phone-**406-654-2423; fax-406-654-2429; hours 8AM-5PM

UCC search per debtor- $7.00. UCC search includes tax liens if requested. Tax lien search- $7.00 per debtor. Will search real estate records. UCC copy- $.50 per page. Cert fee: $2.00 per doc. Name search for property data free at http://gis.doa.state.mt.us/searchOwner.htm. **Other phones:** Assessor-406-654-2123; Treasurer-406-654-1742.

Pondera County

Clerk and Recorder, 20 4th Ave S.W., Conrad, MT 59425. **Phone-**406-271-4000, R/E Recording-406-271-4001; fax-406-271-4070; hours 8AM-5PM http://ponderacountymontana.org

UCC search per debtor- $7.00. Will search tax liens including federal tax liens. Tax lien search- $7.00 per debtor. RE record copy- $.25 per page plus postage. UCC copy fee-$.50 per page. Cert fee: $2.00 per doc. Payee: Clerk & Recorder. **Other phones:** Assessor-406-271-4015; Treasurer-406-271-4015; Appraiser/ Auditor-406-271-4012; Elections-406-271-4000; Vital Records-406-271-4000.

Powder River County

Clerk and Recorder, PO Box 270, Broadus, MT 59317-0270. **Phone-**406-436-2361; fax-406-436-2151; hours 8AM-5PM. UCC search per debtor- $7.00. UCC search does not include federal tax liens. Mortgage and property transfer searches available. RE record copy- $.50 1st page, $.25 each add'l. UCC copy- $1.00 per page. Cert fee: $2.00 per cert. Payee: Powder River County Clerk and Recorder. Name search for property data free at http://gis.doa.state.mt.us/searchOwner.htm. **Other phones:** Assessor-406-436-2407; Treasurer-406-436-2444.

Powell County

Clerk and Recorder, 409 Missouri Ave, Deer Lodge, MT 59722. **Phone-**406-846-3680, R/E Recording-406-846-3680 x222, UCC Recording-406-846-3680 x222; fax-406-846-2784; hours 8AM-5PM

UCC search per debtor- $7.00. Will not search real estate or tax lien records. RE record copy- $.50 1st page, $.25 each add'l. UCC copy- $.50 per page. Cert fee: $2.00 per cert. Payee: Powell County Clerk and Recorder. Name search for property data free at http://gis.doa.state.mt.us/searchOwner.htm. **Other phones:** Assessor-406-846-3680 x230; Treasurer-406-846-3680 x226; Appraiser/ Auditor-406-846-3680 x211; Elections-406-846-3680 x223; Vital Records-406-846-3680 x222.

Prairie County

Clerk and Recorder, PO Box 125, Terry, MT 59349. **Phone-**406-635-5575; fax-406-635-5576.

UCC search per debtor- $7.00. Copy fee-$.50 per page. Cert fee: $2.00 per doc. Name search for property data free at http://gis.doa.state.mt.us/searchOwner.htm.

Ravalli County

Clerk and Recorder, 215 S Fourth St #C, Hamilton, MT 59840. **Phone-**Clerk and Recorder, R/E & UCC

Recording- 406-375-6212; fax-406-375-6326; hours 9AM-5PM www.co.ravalli.mt.us
UCC search per debtor- $7.00. Tax lien search-$7.00 per debtor. Will search real estate records. Record copy- .50 per page. Cert fee: $2.00 per doc + copy fees. Name search for property data free at http://gis.doa.state.mt.us/searchOwner.htm. **Other phones:** Assessor-406-375-6311; Treasurer-406-375-6300; Appraiser/ Auditor-406-375-6312; Elections-406-375-6213; Vital Records-406-375-6212.

Richland County

Clerk and Recorder, 201 W. Main St, Sidney, MT 59270. **Phone-**Clerk and Recorder, R/E & UCC Recording- 406-433-1708; fax-406-433-3731; hours 8AM-5PM www.richland.org
UCC search per debtor- $7.00. Will not search tax liens. Will search real estate records. RE record copy-$1.00 per page. Cert fee: $2.00 per doc. Payee: Richland County Clerk and Recorder. Name search for property data free at http://gis.doa.state.mt.us/searchOwner.htm. **Other phones:** Assessor-406-433-1203; Treasurer-406-433-1707; Appraiser/ Auditor-406-433-2850; Elections-406-433-1708; Vital Records-406-433-1708.

Roosevelt County

Clerk and Recorder, 400 Second Ave South, Wolf Point, MT 59201. **Phone-**406-653-6250, R/E Recording-406-653-6229, UCC Recording-406-653-6229; fax-406-653-6289; hours 8AM-5PM
UCC search per debtor- $7.00. Federal/state combined tax lien search- $7.00 per debtor. Will not search real estate records. Copy fee-$.50 per page. Cert fee: $2.00 per doc. Payee: Clerk & Recorder. Name search for property data free at http://gis.doa.state.mt.us/searchOwner.htm. **Other phones:** Assessor-406-653-6256; Treasurer-406-653-6239; Appraiser/ Auditor-406-653-6255; Elections-406-653-6229; Vital Records-406-653-6252 - 6250; 406-653-6233.

Rosebud County

Clerk and Recorder, PO Box 47, Forsyth, MT 59327. **Phone-**406-346-2251; fax-406-346-7551.
UCC search per debtor- $7.00. Copy fee-$.50 per page. Cert fee: $2.00 per doc. Name search for property data free at http://gis.doa.state.mt.us/searchOwner.htm. **Other phones:** Assessor-406-346-2516; Vital Records-406-444-4228.

Sanders County

Clerk and Recorder, PO Box 519, Thompson Falls, MT 59873. **Phone-**Clerk and Recorder, R/E & UCC Recording- 406-827-6922; fax-406-827-4388.
UCC search per debtor- $7.00. Will not search real estate records. Copy fee-$.50 per page. Cert fee: $2.00 per doc. Payee: Sanders County Clerk. Name search for property data free at http://gis.doa.state.mt.us/searchOwner.htm. **Other phones:** Assessor-406-827-6922; Treasurer-406-827-6924; Appraiser/ Auditor-406-827-6932; Elections-406-827-6922; Vital Records-406-827-6922.

Sheridan County

Clerk and Recorder, 100 W. Laurel Ave, Plentywood, MT 59254. **Phone-**Clerk and Recorder, R/E & UCC Recording- 406-765-3403; fax-406-765-2609; hours 8AM-5PM www.co.sheridan.mt.us
UCC search per debtor- $7.00. Will not search real estate records. Copy fee-$.50 1st page, $.25 each add'l. Cert fee: $2.00 per doc. Name search for property data free at http://gis.doa.state.mt.us/searchOwner.htm. Also, the sexual & violent offender registry is found at

http://svor.doj.state.mt.us./. **Other phones:** Assessor-406-765-2291; Treasurer-406-765-3414; Appraiser/ Auditor-406-765-2291; Elections-406-765-3403; Vital Records-406-765-3403.

Silver Bow County

Clerk and Recorder, 155 W Granite St #208, Butte, MT 59701. **Phone-**406-497-6335, R/E Recording-406-497-6336; fax-406-497-6328. www.co.silverbow.mt.us/clerk_and_recorder.htm
UCC search per debtor- $7.00. Will not search real estate records. Copy fee-$.50 per page. Cert fee: $2.00 per doc. Name search for property data free at http://gis.doa.state.mt.us/searchOwner.htm. **Other phones:** Assessor-406-497-6290; Treasurer-406-497-6300; Elections-406-497-6345.

Stillwater County

Clerk and Recorder, PO Box 149, Columbus, MT 59019. **Phone-**Clerk and Recorder, R/E & UCC Recording- 406-322-8000; fax-406-322-8007; hours 8AM-5PM
Will not search records. RE record copy- $.25 per page. UCC copy-$.50 per page. Cert fee: $2.00 per cert. Payee: Stillwater County Clerk and Recorder. Name search for property data free at http://gis.doa.state.mt.us/searchOwner.htm. **Other phones:** Assessor-406-322-8015; Treasurer-406-322-8020; Appraiser/ Auditor-406-322-8015; Elections-406-322-8000; Vital Records-406-322-8000.

Sweet Grass County

Clerk and Recorder, PO Box 888, Big Timber, MT 59011. **Phone-**Clerk and Recorder, R/E & UCC Recording- 406-932-5152; fax-406-932-5177; hours 8AM-5PM
Will not search records. Copy fee is $.25 per page. Cert fee: $2.50 1st page; $.25 each add'l. Payee: Sweet Grass County. Name search for property data free at http://gis.doa.state.mt.us/searchOwner.htm. **Other phones:** Assessor-406-932-5149; Treasurer-406-932-5151; Appraiser/ Auditor-406-932-5149; Elections-406-932-5152; Vital Records-406-932-5152.

Teton County

Clerk and Recorder, PO Box 610, Choteau, MT 59422. **Phone-**Clerk and Recorder, R/E & UCC Recording-406-466-2693; fax-406-466-2138. www.tetoncomt.org
UCC search per debtor- $7.00. Will search real estate records. UCC copy- $.50 for 1st page; $.25 each add'l. This copy fee applies to all document types. Cert fee: $2.00 per doc. Name search for property data free at http://gis.doa.state.mt.us/searchOwner.htm. **Other phones:** Assessor-406-466-2908; Treasurer-406-466-2694; Appraiser/ Auditor-406-466-2908; Elections-406-466-2907; Vital Records-406-466-2693.

Toole County

Clerk and Recorder, 226 1st St South, Shelby, MT 59474. **Phone-**Clerk and Recorder, R/E & UCC Recording- 406-424-8300; fax-406-424-8301; hours 8AM-5PM
UCC search per debtor- $7.00. Tax lien search-$7.00 per debtor. Copy fee-$.50 per page. Cert fee: $2.00 per doc. Name search for property data free at http://gis.doa.state.mt.us/searchOwner.htm. **Other phones:** Assessor-406-424-8370; Treasurer-406-424-8320; Appraiser/ Auditor-406-424-8370; Elections-406-424-8300; Vital Records-406-424-8300.

Treasure County

Clerk and Recorder, PO Box 392, Hysham, MT 59038. **Phone-**406-342-5547; fax-406-342-5445; hours 8AM-Noon,1-5PM

UCC search per debtor- $7.00. Tax lien search-$7.00 per debtor. Real estate owner, mortgage, and property transfer searches available. RE record copy-$.50 1st page, $.25 each add'l. UCC copy- $.50 per page. Cert fee: $2.00 per doc. Payee: Treasure County Clerk and Recorder. Name search for property data free at http://gis.doa.state.mt.us/searchOwner.htm. **Other phones:** Assessor-406-342-5540; Treasurer-406-342-5545; Appraiser/ Auditor-406-342-5540; Elections-406-342-5547; Vital Records-406-342-5547.

Valley County

Clerk and Recorder, Box 2, 501 Court Sq, Glasgow, MT 59230. **Phone-**Clerk and Recorder, R/E & UCC Recording- 406-228-6220; fax-406-228-9027; hours 8AM-5PM
UCC search per debtor- $7.00. UCC search includes tax liens. Separate federal/state combined tax lien search- $7.00 per debtor. Will not search real estate records. Record copy- $.50 per page. Cert fee: $2.00 per doc. Name search for property data free at http://gis.doa.state.mt.us/searchOwner.htm. **Other phones:** Treasurer-406-228-6231; Appraiser/ Auditor-406-228-6234; Elections-406-228-6220; Vital Records-406-228-6268.

Wheatland County

Clerk and Recorder, PO Box 1903, Harlowton, MT 59036. **Phone-**406-632-4891; fax-406-632-4880; hours 8-12; 1-5. UCC search per debtor- $7.00. Will not search tax liens. Copy fee-$.50 per page. Cert fee: $2.00 per doc. Name search for property data free at http://gis.doa.state.mt.us/searchOwner.htm. **Other phones:** Assessor-406-632-4894; Treasurer-406-632-4892; Elections-406-632-4891; Vital Records-406-632-4891.

Wibaux County

Clerk and Recorder, PO Box 199, Wibaux, MT 59353-0199. **Phone-**Clerk and Recorder, R/E & UCC Recording- 406-796-2481; fax-406-796-2625; hours 8AM-5PM
UCC search per debtor- $7.00. UCC search includes tax liens if requested. Will search real estate records on Grantor/Grantee only. Record copy- $.10 per pae. Cert fee: $2.00 per doc + $.25 each add'l page. Payee: Clerk & Recorder. Name search for property data free at http://gis.doa.state.mt.us/searchOwner.htm. **Other phones:** Assessor-406-795-2483; Treasurer-406-795-2482; Elections-406-796-2481; Vital Records-406-796-2481.

Yellowstone County

Clerk and Recorder, PO Box 35001, Billings, MT 59107. **Phone-**Clerk and Recorder, R/E & UCC Recording- 406-256-2785; fax-406-256-2736; hours 8AM-5PM www.co.yellowstone.mt.us/clerk
UCC search per debtor- $7.00. UCC search does not include federal tax liens. Property transfer searches available. RE record copy- $.50 1st page, $.25 each add'l. UCC copy- $.50 per page. Cert fee: $2.00 per cert. Payee: Yellowstone County Clerk and Recorder. **Online Access to Assessor, Tax, Grantor/Grantee, Property records:** Access to the county clerk & recorder document searches are free at https://secure.co.yellowstone.mt.us/clerk/secure_search.asp. Also, access to the tax assessor records is free at www.co.yellowstone.mt.us/gis. Also, Name search for property data free at http://gis.doa.state.mt.us/searchOwner.htm. **Other phones:** Assessor-406-896-4000; Treasurer-406-256-2785; Elections-406-256-2743; Vital Records-406-256-2788.

Montana County Locator

You will usually be able to find the city name in the City/County Cross Reference below. In that case, it is a simple matter to determine the county from the cross reference. However, only the official US Postal Service city names are included in this index. There are an additional 40,000 place names that people use in their addresses. Therefore, we have also included a ZIP/City Cross Reference immediately following the City/County Cross Reference.

If you know the ZIP Code but the city name does not appear in the City/County Cross Reference index, look up the ZIP Code in the ZIP/City Cross Reference, find the city name, then look up the city name in the City/County Cross Reference. For example, you want to know the county for an address of Menands, NY 12204. There is no "Menands" in the City/County Cross Reference. The ZIP/City Cross Reference shows that ZIP Codes 12201-12288 are for the city of Albany. Looking back in the City/County Cross Reference, Albany is in Albany County.

Montana City/County Cross Reference

ABSAROKEE Stillwater
ACTON Yellowstone
ALBERTON (59820) Missoula(58), Mineral(41)
ALDER Madison
ALZADA Carter
ANACONDA (59711) Deer Lodge(87), Granite(9), Silver Bow(2)
ANGELA (59312) Garfield(66), Rosebud(33)
ANTELOPE Sheridan
ARLEE (59821) Lake(69), Missoula(28), Sanders(2)
ASHLAND Rosebud
AUGUSTA Lewis and Clark
AVON Powell
BABB Glacier
BAINVILLE Roosevelt
BAKER Fallon
BALLANTINE Yellowstone
BASIN Jefferson
BEARCREEK Carbon
BELFRY Carbon
BELGRADE Gallatin
BELT Cascade
BIDDLE Powder River
BIG ARM Lake
BIG SANDY Chouteau
BIG SKY Gallatin
BIG TIMBER Sweet Grass
BIGFORK (59911) Flathead(57), Lake(42)
BIGHORN Treasure
BILLINGS Yellowstone
BIRNEY Rosebud
BLACK EAGLE Cascade
BLOOMFIELD Dawson
BONNER Missoula
BOULDER Jefferson
BOX ELDER Hill
BOYD Carbon
BOYES Carter
BOZEMAN Gallatin
BRADY (59416) Pondera(55), Chouteau(39), Teton(4), Liberty(1)
BRIDGER Carbon
BROADUS Powder River
BROADVIEW (59015) Yellowstone(67), Musselshell(20), Stillwater(11)
BROCKTON Roosevelt
BROCKWAY (59214) McCone(86), Prairie(13)
BROWNING Glacier
BRUSETT Garfield
BUFFALO Fergus
BUSBY Big Horn
BUTTE Silver Bow
BYNUM Teton
CAMERON Madison
CANYON CREEK Lewis and Clark
CAPITOL Carter
CARDWELL (59721) Madison(53), Jefferson(46)
CARTER Chouteau

CASCADE Cascade
CAT CREEK Petroleum
CHARLO Lake
CHESTER Liberty
CHINOOK (59523) Blaine(91), Hill(8)
CHOTEAU Teton
CIRCLE (59215) McCone(93), Dawson(6)
CLANCY Jefferson
CLINTON (59825) Missoula(84), Granite(15)
CLYDE PARK Park
COFFEE CREEK Fergus
COHAGEN Garfield
COLSTRIP Rosebud
COLUMBIA FALLS Flathead
COLUMBUS Stillwater
CONDON Missoula
CONNER Ravalli
CONRAD (59425) Pondera(98), Teton(1)
COOKE CITY Park
CORAM Flathead
CORVALLIS Ravalli
CORWIN SPRINGS Park
CRANE Richland
CROW AGENCY Big Horn
CULBERTSON Roosevelt
CUSTER Yellowstone
CUT BANK Glacier
DAGMAR Sheridan
DARBY Ravalli
DAYTON (59914) Flathead(69), Lake(30)
DE BORGIA Mineral
DECKER Big Horn
DEER LODGE (59722) Powell(92), Deer Lodge(7)
DELL Beaverhead
DENTON Fergus
DILLON Beaverhead
DIVIDE Silver Bow
DIXON Sanders
DODSON (59524) Phillips(88), Blaine(11)
DRUMMOND Granite
DUPUYER Pondera
DUTTON Teton
EAST GLACIER PARK Glacier
EAST HELENA (59635) Lewis and Clark(93), Jefferson(3), Broadwater(3)
EDGAR Carbon
EKALAKA Carter
ELLISTON Powell
ELMO Lake
EMIGRANT Park
ENNIS Madison
ESSEX Flathead
ETHRIDGE Toole
EUREKA Lincoln
FAIRFIELD Teton
FAIRVIEW Richland
FALLON Prairie
FISHTAIL Stillwater
FLAXVILLE Daniels
FLORENCE (59833) Ravalli(64), Missoula(35)

FLOWEREE (59440) Chouteau(73), Cascade(26)
FORESTGROVE Fergus
FORSYTH Rosebud
FORT BENTON Chouteau
FORT HARRISON Lewis and Clark
FORT PECK Valley
FORT SHAW (59443) Cascade(92), Teton(7)
FORTINE Lincoln
FOUR BUTTES Daniels
FRAZER Valley
FRENCHTOWN Missoula
FROID (59226) Roosevelt(78), Sheridan(21)
FROMBERG Carbon
GALATA (59444) Toole(76), Liberty(23)
GALLATIN GATEWAY Gallatin
GARDINER Park
GARNEILL Fergus
GARRISON Powell
GARRYOWEN Big Horn
GERALDINE Chouteau
GEYSER (59447) Judith Basin(96), Chouteau(4)
GILDFORD Hill
GLASGOW Valley
GLEN Beaverhead
GLENDIVE Dawson
GLENTANA Valley
GOLD CREEK Powell
GRANTSDALE Ravalli
GRASS RANGE Fergus
GREAT FALLS Cascade
GREENOUGH Missoula
GREYCLIFF Sweet Grass
HALL Granite
HAMILTON Ravalli
HAMMOND Carter
HARDIN Big Horn
HARLEM Blaine
HARLOWTON Wheatland
HARRISON Madison
HATHAWAY Rosebud
HAUGAN Mineral
HAVRE Hill
HAYS Blaine
HEART BUTTE Pondera
HELENA Lewis and Clark
HELMVILLE Powell
HERON Sanders
HIGHWOOD Chouteau
HILGER Fergus
HINGHAM Hill
HINSDALE Valley
HOBSON Judith Basin
HOGELAND Blaine
HOMESTEAD (59242) Sheridan(83), Roosevelt(16)
HOT SPRINGS (59845) Sanders(86), Lake(9), Flathead(4)
HUNGRY HORSE Flathead

HUNTLEY (59037) Yellowstone(98), Big Horn(1)
HUSON Missoula
HYSHAM Treasure
INGOMAR Rosebud
INVERNESS (59530) Hill(97), Liberty(2)
ISMAY (59336) Custer(42), Fallon(40), Prairie(11), Carter(5)
JACKSON Beaverhead
JEFFERSON CITY Jefferson
JOLIET Carbon
JOPLIN (59531) Liberty(84), Hill(15)
JORDAN Garfield
JUDITH GAP (59453) Fergus(55), Wheatland(44)
KALISPELL Flathead
KEVIN Toole
KILA Flathead
KINSEY Custer
KREMLIN Hill
LAKE MC DONALD Flathead
LAKESIDE (59922) Flathead(73), Lake(26)
LAMBERT Richland
LAME DEER Rosebud
LARSLAN Valley
LAUREL (59044) Yellowstone(97), Carbon(2)
LAVINA Golden Valley
LEDGER (59456) Pondera(52), Liberty(31), Toole(15)
LEWISTOWN Fergus
LIBBY Lincoln
LIMA Beaverhead
LINCOLN (59639) Powell(73), Lewis and Clark(26)
LINDSAY (59339) Dawson(92), Prairie(7)
LIVINGSTON Park
LLOYD Blaine
LODGE GRASS Big Horn
LOLO Missoula
LOMA Chouteau
LONEPINE Sanders
LORING Phillips
LOTHAIR Liberty
LUTHER Carbon
MALMSTROM A F B Cascade
MALTA Phillips
MANHATTAN Gallatin
MARION Flathead
MARTIN CITY Flathead
MARTINSDALE Meagher
MARYSVILLE Lewis and Clark
MC ALLISTER Madison
MC CABE Roosevelt
MC LEOD (59052) Sweet Grass(80), Park(19)
MEDICINE LAKE Sheridan
MELROSE Silver Bow
MELSTONE Musselshell
MELVILLE Sweet Grass
MILDRED Prairie
MILES CITY Custer
MILL IRON Carter

MILLTOWN Missoula
MISSOULA Missoula
MOCCASIN Judith Basin
MOLT (59057) Yellowstone(72), Stillwater(27)
MONARCH Cascade
MOORE Fergus
MOSBY Garfield
MUSSELSHELL Musselshell
NASHUA Valley
NEIHART Cascade
NIARADA (59852) Sanders(85), Flathead(14)
NORRIS Madison
NOXON Sanders
NYE Stillwater
OILMONT Toole
OLIVE Powder River
OLNEY Flathead
OPHEIM Valley
OTTER (59062) Powder River(86), Rosebud(13)
OUTLOOK Sheridan
OVANDO Powell
PABLO Lake
PARADISE Sanders
PARK CITY Stillwater
PEERLESS Daniels
PENDROY Teton
PHILIPSBURG Granite
PINESDALE Ravalli
PLAINS Sanders
PLENTYWOOD Sheridan
PLEVNA Fallon
POLARIS Beaverhead
POLEBRIDGE Flathead
POLSON Lake
POMPEYS PILLAR Yellowstone
PONY Madison
POPLAR Roosevelt
POWDERVILLE Powder River

POWER (59468) Teton(83), Cascade(15)
PRAY Park
PROCTOR Lake
PRYOR Big Horn
RADERSBURG Broadwater
RAMSAY Silver Bow
RAPELJE Stillwater
RAVALLI Lake
RAYMOND Sheridan
RAYNESFORD Judith Basin
RED LODGE Carbon
REDSTONE Sheridan
REED POINT (59069) Stillwater(71), Sweet Grass(28)
REEDPOINT (59069) Stillwater(71), Sweet Grass(28)
RESERVE (59258) Sheridan(88), Roosevelt(11)
REXFORD Lincoln
RICHEY Dawson
RICHLAND Valley
RINGLING Meagher
ROBERTS Carbon
ROLLINS (59931) Flathead(89), Lake(10)
RONAN Lake
ROSCOE Carbon
ROSEBUD (59347) Rosebud(97), Custer(2)
ROUNDUP Musselshell
ROY Fergus
RUDYARD (59540) Hill(86), Chouteau(13)
RYEGATE (59074) Golden Valley(96), Stillwater(3)
SACO Phillips
SAINT IGNATIUS Lake
SAINT MARIE Valley
SAINT REGIS Mineral
SAINT XAVIER Big Horn
SALTESE Mineral
SAND COULEE Cascade
SAND SPRINGS Garfield

SANDERS Treasure
SANTA RITA Glacier
SAVAGE (59262) Richland(60), Dawson(39)
SCOBEY Daniels
SEELEY LAKE Missoula
SHAWMUT Wheatland
SHELBY Toole
SHEPHERD Yellowstone
SHERIDAN Madison
SIDNEY Richland
SILVER GATE Park
SILVER STAR Madison
SIMMS Cascade
SOMERS Flathead
SONNETTE Powder River
SPRINGDALE Park
STANFORD Judith Basin
STEVENSVILLE Ravalli
STOCKETT Cascade
STRYKER Lincoln
SULA Ravalli
SUMATRA Rosebud
SUN RIVER Cascade
SUNBURST Toole
SUPERIOR Mineral
SWEET GRASS Toole
SWEETGRASS Toole
TEIGEN (59084) Petroleum(80), Fergus(20)
TERRY (59349) Prairie(86), Custer(13)
THOMPSON FALLS Sanders
THREE FORKS (59752) Gallatin(88), Broadwater(10)
TOSTON Broadwater
TOWNSEND Broadwater
TREGO Lincoln
TROUT CREEK Sanders
TURNER Blaine
TWIN BRIDGES Madison
TWO DOT Wheatland

TWODOT Wheatland
ULM Cascade
VALIER Pondera
VANDALIA Valley
VAUGHN (59487) Cascade(93), Teton(6)
VICTOR Ravalli
VIDA McCone
VIRGINIA CITY Madison
VOLBORG Custer
WARM SPRINGS Deer Lodge
WARMSPRINGS Deer Lodge
WEST GLACIER Flathead
WEST YELLOWSTONE Gallatin
WESTBY Sheridan
WHITE SULPHUR SPRINGS Meagher
WHITEFISH Flathead
WHITEHALL (59759) Jefferson(84), Madison(15)
WHITETAIL Daniels
WHITEWATER Phillips
WHITLASH Liberty
WIBAUX Wibaux
WILLARD Fallon
WILLOW CREEK Gallatin
WILSALL (59086) Park(79), Gallatin(19), Meagher(1)
WINIFRED Fergus
WINNETT Petroleum
WINSTON Broadwater
WISDOM Beaverhead
WISE RIVER (59762) Beaverhead(53), Deer Lodge(46)
WOLF CREEK Lewis and Clark
WOLF POINT Roosevelt
WORDEN Yellowstone
WYOLA Big Horn
YELLOWTAIL Big Horn
ZORTMAN Phillips
ZURICH Blaine

Montana ZIP/City Cross Reference

59001-59001 ABSAROKEE	59043-59043 LAME DEER	59084-59084 TEIGEN
59002-59002 ACTON	59044-59044 LAUREL	59085-59085 TWODOT
59003-59004 ASHLAND	59046-59046 LAVINA	59085-59085 TWO DOT
59006-59006 BALLANTINE	59047-59047 LIVINGSTON	59086-59086 WILSALL
59007-59007 BEARCREEK	59050-59050 LODGE GRASS	59087-59087 WINNETT
59008-59008 BELFRY	59051-59051 LUTHER	59088-59088 WORDEN
59010-59010 BIGHORN	59052-59052 MC LEOD	59089-59089 WYOLA
59011-59011 BIG TIMBER	59053-59053 MARTINSDALE	59100-59117 BILLINGS
59012-59012 BIRNEY	59054-59054 MELSTONE	59201-59201 WOLF POINT
59013-59013 BOYD	59055-59055 MELVILLE	59211-59211 ANTELOPE
59014-59014 BRIDGER	59057-59057 MOLT	59212-59212 BAINVILLE
59015-59015 BROADVIEW	59058-59058 MOSBY	59213-59213 BROCKTON
59016-59016 BUSBY	59059-59059 MUSSELSHELL	59214-59214 BROCKWAY
59017-59017 CAT CREEK	59061-59061 NYE	59215-59215 CIRCLE
59018-59018 CLYDE PARK	59062-59062 OTTER	59217-59217 CRANE
59019-59019 COLUMBUS	59063-59063 PARK CITY	59218-59218 CULBERTSON
59020-59020 COOKE CITY	59064-59064 POMPEYS PILLAR	59219-59219 DAGMAR
59021-59021 CORWIN SPRINGS	59065-59065 PRAY	59221-59221 FAIRVIEW
59022-59022 CROW AGENCY	59066-59066 PRYOR	59222-59222 FLAXVILLE
59024-59024 CUSTER	59067-59067 RAPELJE	59223-59223 FORT PECK
59025-59025 DECKER	59068-59068 RED LODGE	59224-59224 FOUR BUTTES
59026-59026 EDGAR	59069-59069 REEDPOINT	59225-59225 FRAZER
59027-59027 EMIGRANT	59069-59069 REED POINT	59226-59226 FROID
59028-59028 FISHTAIL	59070-59070 ROBERTS	59230-59230 GLASGOW
59029-59029 FROMBERG	59071-59071 ROSCOE	59231-59231 SAINT MARIE
59030-59030 GARDINER	59072-59073 ROUNDUP	59240-59240 GLENTANA
59031-59031 GARRYOWEN	59074-59074 RYEGATE	59241-59241 HINSDALE
59032-59032 GRASS RANGE	59075-59075 SAINT XAVIER	59242-59242 HOMESTEAD
59033-59033 GREYCLIFF	59076-59076 SANDERS	59243-59243 LAMBERT
59034-59034 HARDIN	59077-59077 SAND SPRINGS	59244-59244 LARSLAN
59035-59035 YELLOWTAIL	59078-59078 SHAWMUT	59245-59245 MC CABE
59036-59036 HARLOWTON	59079-59079 SHEPHERD	59247-59247 MEDICINE LAKE
59037-59037 HUNTLEY	59080-59080 JOLIET	59248-59248 NASHUA
59038-59038 HYSHAM	59081-59081 SILVER GATE	59250-59250 OPHEIM
59039-59039 INGOMAR	59082-59082 SPRINGDALE	59252-59252 OUTLOOK
59041-59041 JOLIET	59083-59083 SUMATRA	59253-59253 PEERLESS

59254-59254 PLENTYWOOD
59255-59255 POPLAR
59256-59256 RAYMOND
59257-59257 REDSTONE
59258-59258 RESERVE
59259-59259 RICHEY
59260-59260 RICHLAND
59261-59261 SACO
59262-59262 SAVAGE
59263-59263 SCOBEY
59270-59270 SIDNEY
59273-59273 VANDALIA
59274-59274 VIDA
59275-59275 WESTBY
59276-59276 WHITETAIL
59301-59301 MILES CITY
59311-59311 ALZADA
59312-59312 ANGELA
59313-59313 BAKER
59314-59314 BIDDLE
59315-59315 BLOOMFIELD
59316-59316 BOYES
59317-59317 BROADUS
59318-59318 BRUSETT
59319-59319 CAPITOL
59322-59322 COHAGEN
59323-59323 COLSTRIP
59324-59324 EKALAKA
59326-59326 FALLON
59327-59327 FORSYTH
59330-59330 GLENDIVE
59332-59332 HAMMOND
59333-59333 HATHAWAY
59336-59336 ISMAY
59337-59337 JORDAN
59338-59338 KINSEY

59339-59339 LINDSAY	59342-59342 MILL IRON	59344-59344 PLEVNA	59347-59347 ROSEBUD
59341-59341 MILDRED	59343-59343 OLIVE	59345-59345 POWDERVILLE	59348-59348 SONNETTE
59349-59349 TERRY	59477-59477 SIMMS	59716-59716 BIG SKY	59841-59841 PINESDALE
59351-59351 VOLBORG	59479-59479 STANFORD	59717-59719 BOZEMAN	59842-59842 HAUGAN
59353-59353 WIBAUX	59480-59480 STOCKETT	59720-59720 CAMERON	59843-59843 HELMVILLE
59354-59354 WILLARD	59482-59482 SUNBURST	59721-59721 CARDWELL	59844-59844 HERON
59401-59401 GREAT FALLS	59483-59483 SUN RIVER	59722-59722 DEER LODGE	59845-59845 HOT SPRINGS
59402-59402 MALMSTROM A F B	59484-59484 SWEETGRASS	59724-59724 DELL	59846-59846 HUSON
59403-59406 GREAT FALLS	59484-59484 SWEET GRASS	59725-59725 DILLON	59847-59847 LOLO
59410-59410 AUGUSTA	59485-59485 ULM	59727-59727 DIVIDE	59848-59848 LONEPINE
59411-59411 BABB	59486-59486 VALIER	59728-59728 ELLISTON	59851-59851 MILLTOWN
59412-59412 BELT	59487-59487 VAUGHN	59729-59729 ENNIS	59852-59852 NIARADA
59414-59414 BLACK EAGLE	59489-59489 WINIFRED	59730-59730 GALLATIN GATEWAY	59853-59853 NOXON
59416-59416 BRADY	59501-59501 HAVRE	59731-59731 GARRISON	59854-59854 OVANDO
59417-59417 BROWNING	59520-59520 BIG SANDY	59732-59732 GLEN	59855-59855 PABLO
59418-59418 BUFFALO	59521-59521 BOX ELDER	59733-59733 GOLD CREEK	59856-59856 PARADISE
59419-59419 BYNUM	59522-59522 CHESTER	59735-59735 HARRISON	59858-59858 PHILIPSBURG
59420-59420 CARTER	59523-59523 CHINOOK	59736-59736 JACKSON	59859-59859 PLAINS
59421-59421 CASCADE	59524-59524 DODSON	59739-59739 LIMA	59860-59860 POLSON
59422-59422 CHOTEAU	59525-59525 GILDFORD	59740-59740 MC ALLISTER	59863-59863 RAVALLI
59424-59424 COFFEE CREEK	59526-59526 HARLEM	59741-59741 MANHATTAN	59864-59864 RONAN
59425-59425 CONRAD	59527-59527 HAYS	59743-59743 MELROSE	59865-59865 SAINT IGNATIUS
59427-59427 CUT BANK	59528-59528 HINGHAM	59745-59745 NORRIS	59866-59866 SAINT REGIS
59430-59430 DENTON	59529-59529 HOGELAND	59746-59746 POLARIS	59867-59867 SALTESE
59432-59432 DUPUYER	59530-59530 INVERNESS	59747-59747 PONY	59868-59868 SEELEY LAKE
59433-59433 DUTTON	59531-59531 JOPLIN	59748-59748 RAMSAY	59870-59870 STEVENSVILLE
59434-59434 EAST GLACIER PARK	59532-59532 KREMLIN	59749-59749 SHERIDAN	59871-59871 SULA
59435-59435 ETHRIDGE	59535-59535 LLOYD	59750-59750 BUTTE	59872-59872 SUPERIOR
59436-59436 FAIRFIELD	59537-59537 LORING	59751-59751 SILVER STAR	59873-59873 THOMPSON FALLS
59440-59440 FLOWEREE	59538-59538 MALTA	59752-59752 THREE FORKS	59874-59874 TROUT CREEK
59441-59441 FORESTGROVE	59540-59540 RUDYARD	59754-59754 TWIN BRIDGES	59875-59875 VICTOR
59442-59442 FORT BENTON	59542-59542 TURNER	59755-59755 VIRGINIA CITY	59901-59904 KALISPELL
59443-59443 FORT SHAW	59544-59544 WHITEWATER	59756-59756 WARMSPRINGS	59910-59910 BIG ARM
59444-59444 GALATA	59545-59545 WHITLASH	59756-59756 WARM SPRINGS	59911-59911 BIGFORK
59445-59445 GARNEILL	59546-59546 ZORTMAN	59758-59758 WEST YELLOWSTONE	59912-59912 COLUMBIA FALLS
59446-59446 GERALDINE	59547-59547 ZURICH	59759-59759 WHITEHALL	59913-59913 CORAM
59447-59447 GEYSER	59601-59626 HELENA	59760-59760 WILLOW CREEK	59914-59914 DAYTON
59448-59448 HEART BUTTE	59631-59631 BASIN	59761-59761 WISDOM	59915-59915 ELMO
59450-59450 HIGHWOOD	59632-59632 BOULDER	59762-59762 WISE RIVER	59916-59916 ESSEX
59451-59451 HILGER	59633-59633 CANYON CREEK	59771-59773 BOZEMAN	59917-59917 EUREKA
59452-59452 HOBSON	59634-59634 CLANCY	59801-59812 MISSOULA	59918-59918 FORTINE
59453-59453 JUDITH GAP	59635-59635 EAST HELENA	59820-59820 ALBERTON	59919-59919 HUNGRY HORSE
59454-59454 KEVIN	59636-59636 FORT HARRISON	59821-59821 ARLEE	59920-59920 KILA
59456-59456 LEDGER	59638-59638 JEFFERSON CITY	59823-59823 BONNER	59921-59921 LAKE MC DONALD
59457-59457 LEWISTOWN	59639-59639 LINCOLN	59824-59824 CHARLO	59922-59922 LAKESIDE
59460-59460 LOMA	59640-59640 MARYSVILLE	59825-59825 CLINTON	59923-59923 LIBBY
59461-59461 LOTHAIR	59641-59641 RADERSBURG	59826-59826 CONDON	59925-59925 MARION
59462-59462 MOCCASIN	59642-59642 RINGLING	59827-59827 CONNER	59926-59926 MARTIN CITY
59463-59463 MONARCH	59643-59643 TOSTON	59828-59828 CORVALLIS	59927-59927 OLNEY
59464-59464 MOORE	59644-59644 TOWNSEND	59829-59829 DARBY	59928-59928 POLEBRIDGE
59465-59465 NEIHART	59645-59645 WHITE SULPHUR SPRINGS	59830-59830 DE BORGIA	59929-59929 PROCTOR
59466-59466 OILMONT	59647-59647 WINSTON	59831-59831 DIXON	59930-59930 REXFORD
59467-59467 PENDROY	59648-59648 WOLF CREEK	59832-59832 DRUMMOND	59931-59931 ROLLINS
59468-59468 POWER	59701-59707 BUTTE	59833-59833 FLORENCE	59932-59932 SOMERS
59469-59469 RAYNESFORD	59710-59710 ALDER	59834-59834 FRENCHTOWN	59933-59933 STRYKER
59471-59471 ROY	59711-59711 ANACONDA	59835-59835 GRANTSDALE	59934-59934 TREGO
59472-59472 SAND COULEE	59713-59713 AVON	59836-59836 GREENOUGH	59935-59935 TROY
59473-59473 SANTA RITA	59714-59714 BELGRADE	59837-59837 HALL	59936-59936 WEST GLACIER
59474-59474 SHELBY	59715-59715 BOZEMAN	59840-59840 HAMILTON	59937-59937 WHITEFISH

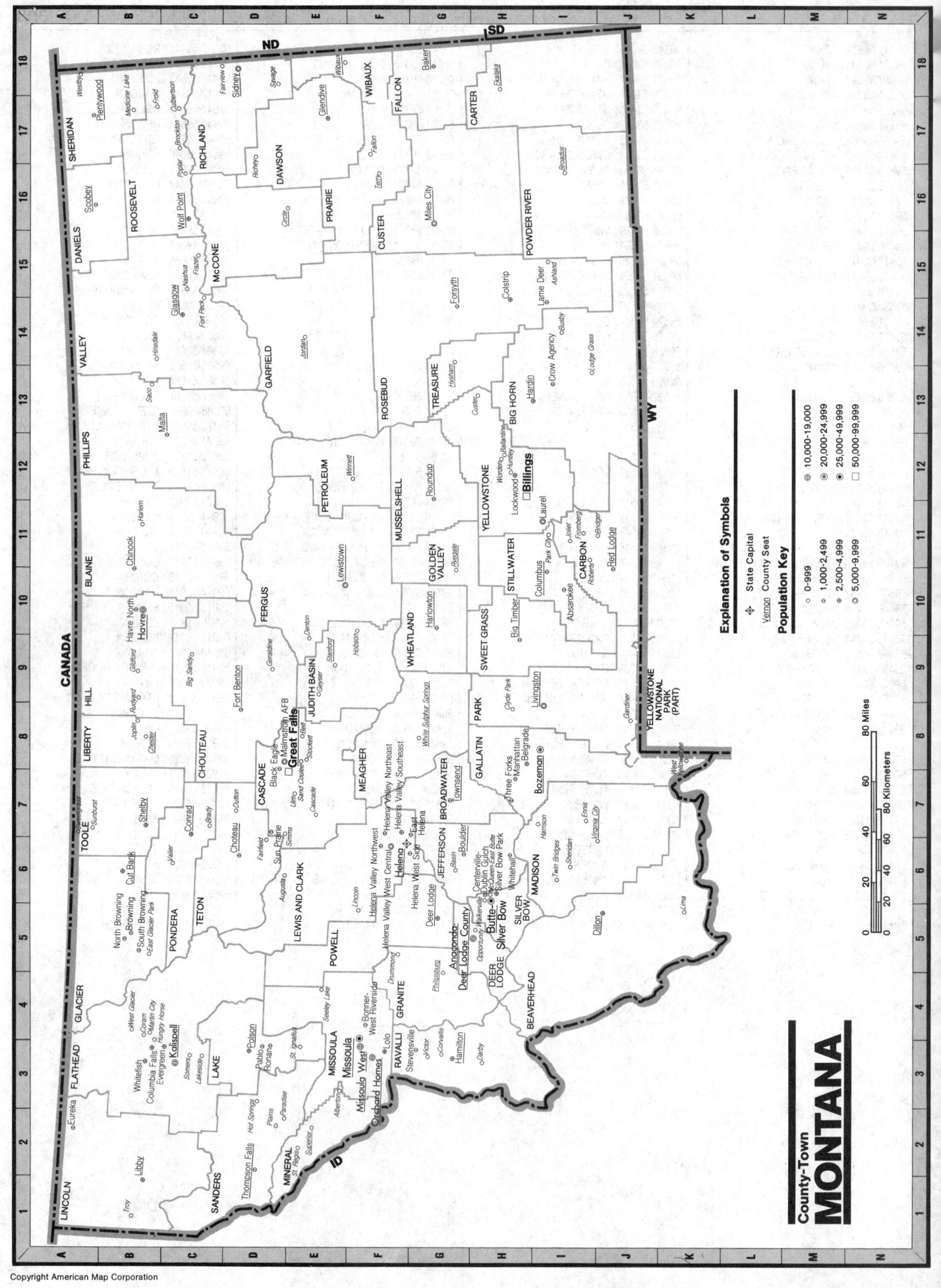

County-Town
MONTANA

Explanation of Symbols

◈ State Capital

Vernon □ County Seat

Population Key

○ 0-999

⊕ 1,000-2,499

⊕ 2,500-4,999

⊚ 5,000-9,999

⊛ 10,000-19,000

⊛ 20,000-24,999

◉ 25,000-49,999

□ 50,000-99,999

ND — SD — WY — CANADA — ID

80 Miles

80 Kilometers

COUNTIES

(56 Counties)

Name of County	Population	Location on Map
BEAVERHEAD	8,424	H-4
BIG HORN	11,337	H-13
BLAINE	6,728	A-10
BROADWATER	3,318	G-7
CARBON	8,080	I-10
CARTER	1,503	H-17
CASCADE	77,691	D-7
CHOUTEAU	5,452	C-7
CUSTER	11,697	F-15
DANIELS	2,266	A-15
DAWSON	9,505	D-16
DEER LODGE	10,278	F-5
FALLON	3,103	E-17
FERGUS	12,083	D-10
FLATHEAD	59,218	A-3
GALLATIN	50,463	H-7
GARFIELD	1,589	D-13
GLACIER	12,121	A-4
GOLDEN VALLEY	912	G-10
GRANITE	2,548	F-4
HILL	17,654	A-8
JEFFERSON	7,939	G-6
JUDITH BASIN	2,282	E-8
LAKE	21,041	C-3
LEWIS AND CLARK	47,495	E-5
LIBERTY	2,295	B-8
LINCOLN	17,481	B-1
MADISON	5,989	H-6
MCCONE	2,276	C-15
MEAGHER	1,819	F-7
MINERAL	3,315	E-1
MISSOULA	78,687	E-3
MUSSELSHELL	4,106	F-11
PARK	14,562	H-8
PETROLEUM	519	E-11
PHILLIPS	5,163	A-12
PONDERA	6,433	C-5
POWDER RIVER	2,090	H-15
POWELL	6,620	E-5
PRAIRIE	1,383	E-16
RAVALLI	25,010	F-3
RICHLAND	10,716	C-16
ROOSEVELT	10,999	B-16
ROSEBUD	10,505	F-13
SANDERS	8,669	C-1
SHERIDAN	4,732	A-17
SILVER BOW	33,941	H-5
STILLWATER	6,536	H-10
SWEET GRASS	3,154	H-9
TETON	6,271	C-5
TOOLE	5,056	A-6
TREASURE	874	G-13
VALLEY	8,239	A-14
WHEATLAND	2,246	G-9
WIBAUX	1,191	F-18
YELLOWSTONE	113,419	H-11
TOTAL	799,023	

CITIES AND TOWNS

Note: The first name is that of the city or town, second, that of the county in which it is located, then the population and location on the map.

- Absarokee, Stillwater, 1,067 ..... I-10
- Anaconda-Deer Lodge County, Deer Lodge, 10,278 ..... H-5
- Baker, Fallon, 1,818 ..... G-18
- Belgrade, Gallatin, 3,411 ..... H-8
- Big Timber, Sweet Grass, 1,557 ..... H-9
- Billings, Yellowstone, 81,151 ..... H-12
- Black Eagle, Cascade D-8
- • Bonner-West Riverside, Missoula, 1,669 ..... F-4
- Boulder, Jefferson, 1,316 ..... G-6
- Bozeman, Gallatin, 22,660 ..... I-8
- Broadus, Powder River, 572 ..... I-16
- Browning, Glacier, 1,170 ..... B-5
- Butte-Silver Bow, Silver Bow, 33,336 ..... H-6
- Centerville-Dublin Gulch, Silver Bow B-8
- Chester, Liberty, 942 ..... B-10
- Chinook, Blaine, 1,512 ..... B-10
- Choteau, Teton, 1,741 ..... D-6
- Circle, McCone, 805 ..... E-16
- • Colstrip, Rosebud, 3,035 ..... H-14
- Columbia Falls, Flathead, 2,942 ..... B-3
- Columbus, Stillwater, 1,573 ..... I-10
- Conrad, Pondera, 2,891 ..... C-7
- • Crow Agency, Big Horn, 1,446 ..... I-13
- Cut Bank, Glacier, 3,329 ..... B-6
- Deer Lodge, Powell, 3,378 ..... G-5
- Dillon, Beaverhead, 3,991 ..... J-5
- East Helena, Lewis and Clark, 1,538 ..... G-7
- Ekalaka, Carter, 439 ..... H-18
- Eureka, Lincoln, 1,043 ..... A-2
- • Evergreen, Flathead, 4,109 ..... B-3
- Forsyth, Rosebud, 2,178 ..... G-14
- Fort Benton, Chouteau, 1,660 ..... D-8
- Glasgow, Valley, 3,572 ..... C-14
- Glendive, Dawson, 4,802 ..... E-17
- Great Falls, Cascade, 55,097 ..... E-7
- Hamilton, Ravalli, 2,737 ..... G-3
- Hardin, Big Horn, 2,940 ..... I-13
- Harlowton, Wheatland, 1,049 ..... G-10
- Havre, Hill, 10,201 ..... B-10
- • Havre North, Hill, 1,110 ..... B-10
- Helena, Lewis and Clark, 24,569 ..... F-6
- • Helena Valley Northeast, Lewis and Clark, 1,585 ..... F-6
- • Helena Valley Northwest, Lewis and Clark, 1,215 ..... F-6
- • Helena Valley Southeast, Lewis and Clark, 4,601 ..... F-6
- • Helena Valley West Central, Lewis and Clark, 6,327 ..... F-6
- • Helena West Side, Lewis and Clark, 1,847 ..... F-6
- Hysham, Treasure, 361 ..... G-14
- Jordan, Garfield, 494 ..... E-14
- Kalispell, Flathead, 11,917 ..... C-3
- Lame Deer, Rosebud, 1,918 ..... I-14
- Laurel, Yellowstone, 5,686 ..... I-11
- Lewistown, Fergus, 6,051 ..... E-10
- Libby, Lincoln, 2,532 ..... B-1
- Livingston, Park, 6,701 ..... I-8
- Lockwood, Yellowstone, 3,967 ..... H-12
- Lolo, Missoula, 2,746 ..... F-3
- Malmstrom AFB, Cascade, 5,938 ..... D-8
- Malta, Phillips, 2,340 ..... C-12
- Manhattan, Gallatin, 1,034 ..... H-7
- Miles City, Custer, 8,461 ..... G-16
- Missoula, Missoula, 42,918 ..... F-3
- Missoula West, Missoula F-3
- • North Browning, Glacier, 1,630 ..... B-5
- • Orchard Homes, Missoula, 10,317 ..... F-3
- Pablo, Lake, 1,298 ..... D-3
- Philipsburg, Granite, 925 ..... G-4
- Plentywood, Sheridan, 2,136 ..... A-17
- Polson, Lake, 3,283 ..... D-3
- Red Lodge, Carbon, 1,958 ..... J-10
- Ronan, Lake, 1,547 ..... D-3
- Roundup, Musselshell, 1,808 ..... G-12
- Ryegate, Golden Valley, 260 ..... G-11
- Scobey, Daniels, 1,154 ..... A-16
- Shelby, Toole, 2,763 ..... B-7
- Sidney, Richland, 5,217 ..... D-18
- Silver Bow Park, Silver Bow H-6
- • South Browning, Glacier, 1,748 ..... B-5
- Stanford, Judith Basin, 529 ..... E-9
- Stevensville, Ravalli, 1,221 ..... G-3
- Sun Prairie, Cascade, 1,424 ..... D-7
- Superior, Mineral, 881 ..... E-2
- Terry, Prairie, 659 ..... F-16
- Thompson Falls, Sanders, 1,319 ..... D-2
- Three Forks, Gallatin, 1,203 ..... H-7
- Townsend, Broadwater, 1,635 ..... G-7
- Virginia City, Madison, 142 ..... J-6
- White Sulphur Springs, Meagher, 963 ..... G-8
- Whitefish, Flathead, 4,368 ..... B-3
- Whitehall, Jefferson, 1,067 ..... H-6
- Wibaux, Wibaux, 628 ..... E-18
- Winnett, Petroleum, 188 ..... F-12
- Wolf Point, Roosevelt, 2,880 ..... C-16

Explanation of symbols: • – Census Designated Place (CDP)

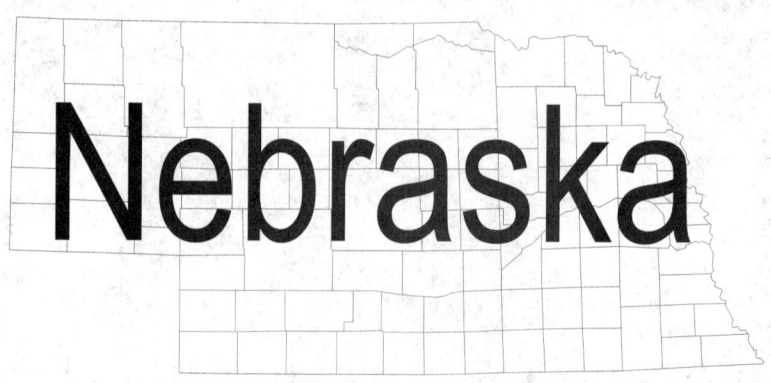

General Help Numbers:

Governor's Office
PO Box 94848　　　　　　　　　402-471-2244
Lincoln, NE 68509-4848　　　　Fax 402-471-6031
http://gov.nol.org　　　　　　　　8AM-5PM

Attorney General's Office
2115 State Capitol　　　　　　　402-471-2682
Lincoln, NE 68509　　　　　　　Fax 402-471-3297
www.ago.state.ne.us/　　　　　　8AM-5PM

Legislative Records
Clerk of Legislature Office
PO Box 94604　　　　　　　　　402-471-2271
Lincoln, NE 68509-4604　　　　Fax 402-471-2126
http://court.nol.org/AOC　　　　8AM-5PM

State Archives
Archives　　　　　　　　　　　402-471-4771
PO Box 82554　　　　　　　　　Fax 402-471-8922
Lincoln, NE 68501-2554　　　9:30AM-4:30PM M-F;
　　　　　　　　　　　　　8-5 SA; 1:30PM-5PM SU

www.nebraskahistory.org

State Specifics:

Capital:
Lincoln
Lancaster County

Time Zone:
CST*

* Nebraska's nineteen western-most counties are MST:

They are: Arthur, Banner, Box Butte, Chase, Cherry, Cheyenne, Dawes, Deuel, Dundy, Garden, Grant, Hooker, Keith, Kimball, Morrill, Perkins, Scotts. Bluff, Sheridan, Sioux.

Number of Counties:
93

Population:
1,739,291

Web Site:
www.state.ne.us

State Agencies

Criminal Records

Nebraska State Patrol, CID, PO Box 94907, Lincoln, NE 68509-4907 (Courier: 1500 Nebraska Highway 2, Lincoln, NE 68502); 402-479-4924, 402-471-4545, 402-479-4002 (Fax), 8AM-4PM.

www.nsp.state.ne.us/

Indexing & Storage: Records are available from 1937 to present. It takes 15 to 60 days before new records are available for inquiry. Records are indexed on inhouse computer, fingerprint cards.

Searching: Include the following in your request-full name, disposition, date of birth, Social Security Number, sex, race. Fingerprints required for certain state occupation checks; this includes an FBI fingerprint search. State keeps record of requesters and will inform the person of record if asked. 100% of records are fingerprint-supported. Felonies are required to be submitted this agency, though not all misdemeanors are. Agency will refer you to the proper county. The following data is not released: juvenile records.

Access by: mail, in person.

Fee & Payment: The search fee is $10.00 per name. A fingerprint search including FBI fingerprint check is $33.00. Fee payee: Nebraska State Patrol. Prepayment required. Personal checks accepted. No credit cards accepted.

Mail search: Turnaround time: 15 days. No SASE is required.

In person search: They accept requests in person and turnaround is 15 minutes, but they will mail back the report if it is lengthy or incomplete (unless it is the requester's own report).

Statewide Court Records

Court Administrator, PO Box 98910, Lincoln, NE 68509-8910; 402-471-3730, 402-471-2197 (Fax), 8AM-4:30PM.

http://court.nol.org/AOC/index.html

Note: Appellate and Supreme Court opinions are available from the website.

Indexing & Storage: Records are available available as courts enter data. It takes 24 hours before new records are available for inquiry.

Access by: online. No searching by mail.

Online search: An online access subscription service is available for NE District and County courts, except Douglas County District Court. Case details, all party listings, payments and actions taken for criminal, civil, probate, juvenile, and traffic is available. Users must be registered with Nebrask@ Online, there is a start-up fee. The fee is $.60 per record or a flat rate of $300.00 per month. Go to www.nebraska.gov/faqs/justice for more info and how far back records go per county. Supreme Court opinions are available from http://court.nol.org/opinions/.

Sexual Offender Registry

Nebraska State Patrol, Sexual Offender Registry, PO Box 94907, Lincoln, NE 68509-4907 (Courier: 1500 Nebraska Highway 2, Lincoln, NE 68502); 402-471-8647, 402-471-8496 (Fax), 8AM-4PM.

www.nsp.state.ne.us/sor/

Note: The public is only granted access to sex offenders who are classified as high risk/Level 3 sex offenders. As of January 2004, there were over 1800 active registered sex offenders in the state of Nebraska.

Indexing & Storage: Records are available from 1997 to present.

Access by: mail, phone, online.

Mail search: Turnaround time: 15 days. No SASE is requested

Phone search: Limited searching by telephone.

Online search: A Level 3 sexual offender registry search is available at the website. The records may be searched by either ZIP Code, last name, city, or county. Search or review the entire list of names.

Incarceration Records

Nebraska Department of Correctional Services, Central Records Office, PO Box 94661, Lincoln, NE 68509-4661; 402-479-5765, 402-479-5913 (Fax), 8AM-5PM.

www.corrections.state.ne.us

Indexing & Storage: Records are available on current and former inmates back to 1977. It takes 1 day before new records are available for inquiry. Records are indexed on microfilm and books. Records are normally destroyed after 3 years.

Searching: Include the following in your request-full name or DOC inmate #. The DOB and SSN number are helpful. To search online, only the name is needed. Location, DOC number, physical identifiers, conviction and sentencing information, and release dates are provided.

Access by: mail, phone, fax, online.

Mail search: Turnaround time: 2 to 4 weeks.

Phone search: Name searching permitted by phone.

Fax search: Records may be requested by fax.

Online search: Click on Inmate Records at the website for a search of current inmates. Also, a private company offers free web access at www.vinelink.com/index.jsp; includes state, DOC, and county jails.

Corporation, Limited Liability Company, Limited Partnerships, Trade Names, Trademarks, Servicemarks

Secretary of State, Corporation Commission, 1301 State Capitol Bldg, Lincoln, NE 68509; 402-471-4079, 402-471-3666 (Fax), 8AM-5PM.

www.sos.state.ne.us/htm/corpmenu.htm

Indexing & Storage: Records are available from the beginning of state corporation filings. It takes less than a day before new records are available for inquiry. Records are indexed on microfilm, index cards. Records are normally destroyed after 5 years if biennial report, otherwise not destroyed.

Searching: Include the following in your request-full name of business. In addition to the articles of incorporation, corporation records include the following information: Reports, Officers, Directors, Prior (merged) names, Inactive and Reserved names and Occupation Tax records for the last 5 years.

Access by: mail, phone, fax, in person, online.

Fee & Payment: No search fee, copies are $1.00 per page, $.45 for copies ordered online. Fee payee: Secretary of State. They will send an invoice. Personal checks accepted. No credit cards accepted.

Mail search: Turnaround time: 2 days. No SASE is required.

Phone search: Records are available by phone.

Fax search: Fax searching available.

In person search: Simple requests may be processed immediately.

Online search: There are two levels of service. The free lookups at https://www.nol.org/sos/corp/corpsearch.cgi?nav=search provide only general information to obtain information on the status of corporations and other business entities registered in this state. At the same site, the state has designated Nebrask@ Online (800-747-8177) to facilitate online retrieval of records. This access to records requires fees.

Other access: Nebrask@ Online has the capability of offering database purchases.

Uniform Commercial Code, Federal and State Tax Liens

UCC Division, Secretary of State, Rm 1301, PO Box 95104, Lincoln, NE 68509-5104 (Courier: 1301 State Capitol Bldg, Lincoln, NE 68509); 402-471-4080, 402-471-4429 (Fax), 7:30AM-5PM.

www.sos.state.ne.us/htm/UCCmenu.htm

Note: Effective July 1, 1999, all federal and state tax liens are filed at this agency. Previously filed tax liens were filed at the county level. But, this agency has index of all tax liens. Actual hard copies must be secured at local level.

Indexing & Storage: Records are available from 1981 to present, on both computer and microfiche.

Searching: Use search request Nebraska version of the UCC-11 form. Include the following in your request-debtor name.

Access by: mail, fax, in person, online.

Fee & Payment: The search fee is $4.50 per debtor name. Copies are $.50 per page. Certification is an additional $10.00. (Note, fees reflect July 16, 2004 price increase from the $3.50 search fee and $4.00 certification fee.) Fee payee: Secretary of State. They will invoice established accounts. Personal checks accepted. No credit cards accepted.

Mail search: Turnaround time: 1 day. A SASE is requested.

Fax search: The fee is $4.50 per debtor. Use the Nebraska Search Form (UCC-11). Turnaround time is 4 hours or less.

In person search: Records are generally available with a short wait.

Online search: Access is outsourced to Nebrask@ Online To set an account, go to www.nol.org. The system is available 24 hours daily. There is an annual $50.00 fee but no further charges to view records. Call 800-747-8177 for more information.

Other access: Check with Nebrask@ Online for bulk purchase programs.

Sales Tax Registrations

Revenue Department, Taxpayer Assistance, PO Box 94818, Lincoln, NE 68509-4818 (Courier: 301 Centennial Mall South, Lincoln, NE 68509); 402-471-5729, 402-471-5990 (Fax), 8AM-5PM.

www.revenue.state.ne.us/salestax.htm

Indexing & Storage: Records are available from 1967. Records are indexed on computer.

Searching: This office will confirm that a business is registered and supply requester with name, address and date of license. Include the following in your request-business name or tax permit number or by federal tax ID.

Access by: mail, phone, in person, online.

Mail search: A SASE is requested. No fee for mail request.

Phone search: No fee for telephone request.

In person search: Simple requests may be processed immediately.

Online search: Information is available through Nebrask@ Online (402-471-7810). This is a commercial service with annual fee and monthly download fees.

Birth Certificates

NE Health & Human Services System, Vital Statistics Section, PO Box 95065, Lincoln, NE 68509-5065 (Courier: 301 Centennial Mall S, 3rd Floor, Lincoln, NE 68509); 402-471-2871, 402-471-6440, 8AM-5PM.

www.hhs.state.ne.us/ced/nevrinfo.htm

Note: Records may also be ordered at regional offices in Omaha, Kearney, North Platte, Norfolk, and Gering.

Indexing & Storage: Records are available from 1904 to present. Records are indexed by Soundex code, year and county. Records are indexed by computer since 1912, and can be found on microfiche from 1912 to 1977. It takes 30 days before new records are available for inquiry.

Searching: Non-family members must have a notarized, signed release from person of record or immediate family member for investigative purposes. If the birth certificate is more than 50 years old, a release form is not required. Closed records are not released. Include the following in your request-full name, date of birth, place of birth, names of parents, mother's maiden name, relationship to person of record, reason for information request. If adopted, indicate so. Also, all requesters must include copy of photo ID. The following data is not released: original records of adoption or sealed records.

Access by: mail, phone, in person, online.

Fee & Payment: The fee is $8.00 per record. Fee payee: Vital Records. Prepayment required. Credit cards may only be used for expedited searches by walk in or calling in. The file search fee is non-refundable if no records are found. Personal checks accepted. Major credit cards accepted.

Mail search: Turnaround time: 2 to 3 weeks. If the agency receives the request by overnight mail, they will mail it back within 2 to 3 days. A SASE is requested.

Phone search: See expedited service.

In person search: Turnaround time is 20 to 30 minutes.

Online search: Records may be ordered online from the Internet site.

Expedited service: Requests sent by Priority Mail, etc. will be processed in 2-3 working days at no additional cost. Expedited phone requests by Fed Ex are available using a credit card for a $31.00 fee ($8.00 for document+$5.50 processing fee+$17.50 FedEx fee). Turnaround time: overnight delivery. Expedited service is available between 9AM and 3PM Central Time.

Death Records

Health and Human Services System, Vital Statistics Section, PO Box 95065, Lincoln, NE 68509-5065 (Courier: 301 Centennial Mall S, 3rd Floor, Lincoln, NE 68509); 402-471-2871, 402-471-6440, 8AM-5PM.

www.hhs.state.ne.us/ced/nevrinfo.htm

Note: If a certificate is more than 50 years in the past, release form is not required.

Indexing & Storage: Records are available from 1904 to present. It takes 30 days before new records are available for inquiry.

Searching: Must have a notarized, signed release from immediate family member for investigative purposes. Include the following in your request-full name, date of death, place of death, relationship to person of record, reason for information request. Also, all requesters must include copy of photo ID.

Access by: mail, phone, in person.

Fee & Payment: The fee is $7.00 per record. Fee payee: Vital Records. Prepayment required. Credit cards may only be used for phone or walk-in expedited service. The file search fee is non-refundable if no records are found. Personal checks accepted. Major credit cards accepted.

Mail search: Turnaround time: 2 to 3 weeks. If the agency receives a search request by overnight mail, they will mail the response within 2 to 3 days. A SASE is requested.

Phone search: See expedited service.

In person search: Turnaround time is 20 to 30 minutes.

Expedited service: Expedited service for phone requests via Fed Ex is available, using a credit card, for a $30.00 fee ($7.00 for the document+$5.50 processing fee+$17.50 FedEx fee). Turnaround time: overnight delivery. Expedited service is available between 9AM and 3PM Central Time.

Marriage Certificates

Health and Human Services System, Vital Statistics Section, PO Box 95065, Lincoln, NE 68509-5065 (Courier: 301 Centennial Mall S, 3rd Floor, Lincoln, NE 68509); 402-471-2871, 402-471-6440, 8AM-5PM.

www.hhs.state.ne.us/ced/nevrinfo.htm

Note: If a certificate is more than 50 years old, a release is not required.

Indexing & Storage: Records are available from 1909 to present. Records are indexed by Soundex code, year and county and are on microfilm from 1956 to present. It takes 30 days before new records are available for inquiry. Records are indexed on microfiche.

Searching: Must have a notarized, signed release from persons of record or immediate family member for investigative purposes. Include the following in your request-names of husband and wife, date of marriage, place or county of marriage, relationship to person of record, reason for information request, wife's maiden name. Also, all requesters must include copy of photo ID.

Access by: mail, phone, in person.

Fee & Payment: The fee is $7.00 per record. Fee payee: Vital Records. Prepayment required. Credit cards may only be used for phone expedited service. The file search fee is non-refundable if no records are found. Personal checks accepted. Major credit cards accepted.

Mail search: Turnaround time: 2 to 3 weeks. If this agency receives a search request by overnight mail, they will mail a response within 2 to 3 days. A SASE is requested.

Phone search: See expedited service.

In person search: Turnaround time is 30 minutes.

Expedited service: Expedited service via Fed Ex is available for phone or walk-in requests using a credit card for a $30.00 fee ($7.00 for the document+$5.50 processing fee+$17.50 FedEx fee). Turnaround time: overnight delivery. Expedited service is available between 9AM and 3PM Central Time.

Divorce Records

Health and Human Services System, Vital Statistics Section, PO Box 95065, Lincoln, NE 68509-5065 (Courier: 301 Centennial Mall S, 3rd Floor, Lincoln, NE 68509); 402-471-2871, 402-471-6440, 8AM-5PM.

www.hhs.state.ne.us/ced/nevrinfo.htm

Note: If a certificate is more than 50 years, a release is not required.

Indexing & Storage: Records are available from 1909 to present. Records are indexed by Soundex code, year and county and are on microfilm from 1956.

Searching: Must have a signed release from person of record or immediate family member for investigative purposes. Include the following in your request-names of husband and wife, date of divorce, relationship to person of record, reason for information request, county where divorce was granted. Also, all requesters must include copy of photo ID.

Access by: mail, phone, in person.

Fee & Payment: Fee is $7.00 per record. Fee payee: Vital Records. Prepayment required. Credit cards may only be used for phone expedited service. The file search fee is non-refundable if no records are found. Personal checks accepted. Major credit cards accepted.

Mail search: Turnaround time: 2 to 3 weeks. If this agency receives a request by overnight mail, they will mail a response within 2-3 days. A SASE is requested.

Phone search: See expedited service.

In person search: Turnaround time is 20-30 minutes.

Expedited service: Expedited service is available using Fed Ex for phone or walk-in requests using a credit card for a $30.00 fee ($7.00 for the document+$5.50 processing fee+$17.50 FedEx fee). Turnaround time: overnight delivery. Expedited service is available between 9AM and 3PM Central Time.

Workers' Compensation Records

Workers' Compensation Court, PO Box 98908, Lincoln, NE 68509-8908 (Courier: State Capitol, 13th Floor, Lincoln, NE 68509); 402-471-6468, 800-599-5155 (In-state), 402-471-2700 (Fax), 8AM-5PM.

www.nol.org/workcomp

Indexing & Storage: Records are available from 1972 on. It takes 5 days before new records are available for inquiry. Records are indexed on microfilm, printout sheets (SS# & name only), computer. Records are normally destroyed after 50 years.

Searching: Must have a release form for medical records. All other records are public record. Include the following in your request-claimant name, Social Security Number, date of birth, date of accident, and docket number if available. A date of injury is required for searches going back more than 10 years. **Access by:** mail, fax, in person.

Fee & Payment: The agency will charge fees if retrieval and copying fees exceed $20.00 This is at the discretion of rthe Court, If costs will exceed $50.00 a deposit is required. Fee payee: Workers' Compensation Court. Personal checks accepted. No credit cards accepted.

Mail search: Turnaround time: 4 days. No SASE is required.

Fax search: Records may be requested by fax.

In person search: Agency will mail results.

Online search: Email requests accepted at newcc@wcc.state.ne.us. Access to this Court's orders and decisions is available from the website. Note this is not access to records.

Driver Records

Department of Motor Vehicles, Driver & Vehicle Records Division, PO Box 94789, Lincoln, NE 68509-4789 (Courier: 301 Centennial Mall, S,

Lincoln, NE 68509); 402-471-3918, 402-471-8694 (Fax), 8AM-5PM.

www.dmv.state.ne.us

Note: It is suggested you obtain copies of tickets at the local courts.

Indexing & Storage: Records are available for 5 years for moving violations and suspensions; lifetime for DWIs. Accidents are reported on the record, but fault is not indicated. Surrendered licenses are purged one year after expiration date. It takes 30 days before new records are available for inquiry. Records are normally destroyed after 5 years.

Searching: SSNs will not be released. Only exempt, approved requesters receive the driver's address. The general public cannot get personal data unless notarized authorization from subject and requester presented. The driver's full name and DOB or license number are needed for ordering. Occasional requesters with a permissible use should use the Application for Copy of Driving Record form.

Access by: mail, in person, online.

Fee & Payment: The fee is $3.00 per record. Fee payee: Department of Motor Vehicles. Prepayment required. Personal checks accepted. No credit cards accepted.

Mail search: Turnaround time: 24 hours. A SASE is requested.

In person search: Walk-in requesters must produce photo ID, are not charged for a no record found.

Online search: Nebraska outsources all online and tape record requests through Nebrask@ Online at www.nol.org/business/ or call 800-747-8177. The system is interactive and open 24 hours a day, 7 days a week. Fee is $3.00 per record. There is an annual fee of $50.00 and a $.12 per minute connect fee or no connect fee if through the Internet.

Vehicle Ownership, Vehicle Identification, Vessel Ownership

Department of Motor Vehicles, Driver & Vehicle Records Division, PO Box 94789, Lincoln, NE 68509-4789 (Courier: 301 Centennial Mall, S, Lincoln, NE 68509); 402-471-3918, 402-471-8694 (Fax), 8AM-5PM.

www.dmv.state.ne.us

Indexing & Storage: Records are available from 1939. Boat ownership information is available from 1997. All motorized boats manufactured after 11/1/72 must be titled. It takes less than 1 day before new records are available for inquiry.

Searching: Only permissible use requesters receive full record data. The general public cannot obtain records, with or without obtain personal data, unless written notarized consent of the subject is provided. Typical items required for search include; full name, VIN or plate number, and year and make.

Access by: mail, in person, online.

Fee & Payment: The fee is $1.00 per record. Lien information appears on the record. Fee payee: Department of Motor Vehicles. Prepayment required. Personal checks accepted. No credit cards accepted.

Mail search: Turnaround time: 7 to 10 days. A SASE is requested.

In person search: Turnaround time is while you wait. "No record founds" are charged the full amount. Requesters must show photo ID.

Online search: Electronic access is through Nebrask@ Online at www.nol.org/business/. There is a start-up fee in addition to the $1.00 per record fee. The system is open 24 hours a day, 7 days a week. Call 800-747-8177 for more information.

Other access: Bulk requesters must be authorized by state officials. Purpose of the request and subsequent usage are reviewed. For more information, call 402-471-3885

Accident Reports

Department of Roads, Accident Records Bureau, Box 94669, Lincoln, NE 68509 (Courier: 1500 Nebraska Highway 2, Lincoln, NE 68502); 402-479-4645, 402-479-3637 (Fax), 7AM-5PM.

www.dor.state.ne.us

Note: Accident reports are required for incidents with property damage in excess of $1,000 or if death or injury.

Indexing & Storage: Records are available from 1978 to 1994 on microfilm; however, fatal accidents are on microfilm since 1956. Records are computerized since 1988. It takes 10 days or more before new records are available for inquiry.

Searching: Individual driver's own reports are not released. Include the following in your request-full name, date of accident, county.

Access by: mail, phone, fax, in person.

Fee & Payment: The fee is $6.00 per record. Fee payee: Accident Records Bureau. Prepayment required. Personal checks accepted. No credit cards accepted.

Mail search: Turnaround time: 1 week to 10 days. No SASE is required.

Phone search: They will schedule requests by phone.

Fax search: Records may be requested by fax.

In person search: Simple requests may be processed immediately.

Other access: Records can be purchased in bulk from the computer database (1988 to present).

Vessel Registration

Records not maintained by a state level agency.

Note: All boats must be registered. Records are found at the county recorder offices. There is no state agency that handles this information.

Voter Registration

Secretary of State, Elections Division-Records, PO Box 94608, Lincoln, NE 68509-4608; 402-471-2554 x2, 402-471-3237 (Fax), 8AM-5PM.

www.sos.state.ne.us/Elections/election.htm

Note: Individual look-ups must be done at the county level.

Indexing & Storage: It takes 3 days before new records are available for inquiry. Records are indexed on computer.

Access by: mail

Mail search: Turnaround time: 2 to 5 days. You must give SSN and DOB.

Other access: Current law dictates that the database can only be sold for political purposes, and not for commercial purposes. A statewide CD can be purchased for $500.

GED Certificates

NE Dept of Education, Adult Education, PO Box 94987, Lincoln, NE 68509 (Courier: 301 Centennial Mall S, Lincoln, NE 68509); 402-471-2475, 402-471-8127 (Fax), 8AM-5PM.

www.nde.state.ne.us/ADED/home.htm

Indexing & Storage: It takes 1 month before new records are available for inquiry. Records are normally destroyed after records are not destroyed.

Searching: To search, all of the following is required: a signed release, date of birth, all last names used, and SSN. If known, the year and city of test are helpful.

Access by: mail, fax, in person.

Fee & Payment: There is no fee for verification. Copies of transcripts are $2.00. Fee payee: NE Dept of Education. Prepayment required. Money orders are accepted. Personal checks accepted. No credit cards accepted.

Mail search: Turnaround time: 1 to 2 days. No SASE is required.

Fax search: Same criteria as mail searching.

In person search: Turnaround time is immediate in most instances.

Expedited service: Will expedite delivery if prepaid overnight envelope is provided.

Hunting and Fishing License Information

Game & Parks Commission, PO Box 30370, Lincoln, NE 68503 (Courier: 2200 N 33rd St, Lincoln, NE 68503); 402-471-5455, 402-471-6586 (Fax), 8AM-5PM.

www.ngpc.state.ne.us/homepage.html

Indexing & Storage: Records are available from 1988 to 2000 on microfiche for Big Game, and 1999 to current year for other hunting and fishing. It takes weeks before new records are available for inquiry. Records are normally destroyed after 5 years (hard copies).

Searching: All information on the face of the license is public information, except for release of SSNs. Include the following in your request-date of birth, name. Date of application helpful.

Access by: mail, phone, in person.

Fee & Payment: There is no search fee.

Mail search: Turnaround time: 1 to 2 days. A SASE is required.

Phone search: Records are available by phone, when personnel available.

In person search: Turnaround immediate.

Other access: Database purchase of information is available.

.

Nebraska State Licensing Agencies

Licenses Searchable Online

Abstracting Company #4 .... www.abe.state.ne.us/local/company_search.phtml
Abstractor #4 .... www.abe.state.ne.us/local/license_search.phtml
Adult Day Care #30 .... www.hhs.state.ne.us/crl/rosters.htm
Alcohol/Drug Testing #30 .... www.hhs.state.ne.us/lis/lis.asp
Animal Technician #30 .... www.hhs.state.ne.us/lis/lis.asp
Architect #2 .... www.ea.state.ne.us/search/arch.htm
Asbestos Worker/Professional #17 .... www.hhs.state.ne.us/lis/lis.asp
Asbestos-related Occupation #30 .... www.hhs.state.ne.us/lis/lis.asp
Assisted Living Facility #30 .... www.hhs.state.ne.us/crl/rosters.htm
Athletic Trainer #30 .... www.hhs.state.ne.us/lis/lis.asp
Attorney #32 .... www.nebar.com/index.htm
Bank #31 .... www.ndbf.org/finsearch.htm#
Barber School #1 .... www.barbers.state.ne.us/
Check Sales #31 .... www.ndbf.org/checklic.htm
Child Care Center/Placing Agency #30 .... www.hhs.state.ne.us/crl/rosters.htm
Chiropractor #30 .... www.hhs.state.ne.us/lis/lis.asp
Collection Agency #26 .... www.sos.state.ne.us/Collections/col-agn.htm
Cosmetologist/Cosmetology Salon/School #30 .... www.hhs.state.ne.us/lis/lis.asp
Credit Union #31 .... www.ndbf.org/finsearch.htm#
Debt Management Agency #26 .... www.sos.state.ne.us/Collections/debtlist.htm
Delayed Deposit Service #31 .... www.ndbf.org/finsearch.htm#
Dental Anesthesia Permit #30 .... www.hhs.state.ne.us/lis/lis.asp
Dentist/Dental Hygienist #30 .... www.hhs.state.ne.us/lis/lis.asp
Developmentally Disabled Center #30 .... www.hhs.state.ne.us/crl/rosters.htm
Drug Distributor, Wholesale #30 .... www.hhs.state.ne.us/crl/rosters.htm
Electrician #29 .... www.nebraska.gov/business/html/342/index.phtml
Electrologist / Electrology Facility #30 .... www.hhs.state.ne.us/lis/lis.asp
Embalmer #30 .... www.hhs.state.ne.us/lis/lis.asp
Emergency Medical Care Facility #30 .... www.hhs.state.ne.us/lis/lis.asp
Engineer #2 .... www.ea.state.ne.us/search/
Environmental Health Specialists #17 .... www.hhs.state.ne.us/lis/lis.asp
Esthetician #30 .... www.hhs.state.ne.us/lis/lis.asp
Esthetician Establishment #30 .... www.hhs.state.ne.us/lis/lis.asp
Fund Transmission #31 .... www.ndbf.org/checklic.htm
Funeral Director/Funeral Establishment #30 .... www.hhs.state.ne.us/lis/lis.asp
Geologist #7 .... www.geology.state.ne.us/board/roster.pdf
Health Clinic #30 .... www.hhs.state.ne.us/lis/lis.asp
Hearing Aid Dispenser/Fitter #30 .... www.hhs.state.ne.us/lis/lis.asp
Hearing Quality Assurance Screening Test #9 .... www.nol.org/home/ncdhh
Home Health Agency #30 .... www.hhs.state.ne.us/crl/rosters.htm
Hospice #30 .... www.hhs.state.ne.us/crl/rosters.htm
Hospital #30 .... www.nlc.state.ne.us/docs/pilot/pubs/h.html
Insurance Company #14 .... www.nol.org/home/NDOI/company_search/index.html
Intermediate Care Facility (Mentally Retarded #30 .... www.hhs.state.ne.us/crl/rosters.htm
Interpreter for the Hearing Impaired (Registry) #9 .... www.nol.org/home/ncdhh
Investigator, Plainclothes #26 .... www.sos.state.ne.us/Privatedetectives/pilist.htm
Investment Advisor/Advisor Rep. #11 .... www.nasdr.com/2001.asp
Labor/Delivery Service/Clinic #30 .... www.hhs.state.ne.us/crl/rosters.htm
Laboratory #30 .... www.hhs.state.ne.us/crl/rosters.htm
Landscape Architect #23 .... www.landarch.state.ne.us/registrants.pdf
Lead Abatement Worker, etc. #17 .... www.hhs.state.ne.us/lis/lis.asp
Liquor Retailers/ Wholesalers/ Shippers #19 .... www.nol.org/home/NLCC/nlccsearch.html
Lobbyist #8 .... www.unicam.state.ne.us
Local Anesthesia Certification #30 .... www.hhs.state.ne.us/lis/lis.asp

Long Term Care Center #30...www.hhs.state.ne.us/crl/rosters.htm
Marriage & Family Therapist #30.......................................www.hhs.state.ne.us/lis/lis.asp
Massage Establishment/Massage Therapy School #30..www.hhs.state.ne.us/lis/lis.asp
Medical Doctor #30...www.hhs.state.ne.us/lis/lis.asp
Mental Health Center #30...www.hhs.state.ne.us/lis/lis.asp
Mentally Retarded Care Service #30................................www.hhs.state.ne.us/crl/rosters.htm
Nail Technologist #30 ....www.hhs.state.ne.us/lis/lis.asp
Notary Public #27 ....www.sos.state.ne.us
Nurse #30 ....www.hhs.state.ne.us/lis/lis.asp
Nursing Home #30 ....www.hhs.state.ne.us/lis/lis.asp
Nursing Home Administrator #30......................................www.hhs.state.ne.us/lis/lis.asp
Nutrition Therapy, Medical #30..www.hhs.state.ne.us/lis/lis.asp
Occupational Therapist #30..www.hhs.state.ne.us/lis/lis.asp
Optometrist #30 ....www.hhs.state.ne.us/lis/lis.asp
Osteopathic Physician #30 ....www.hhs.state.ne.us/lis/lis.asp
Pesticide Applicator/Dealer #18......................................www.kellysolutions.com/ne/
Pharmacist #30..www.hhs.state.ne.us/lis/lis.asp
Pharmacy / Pharmacy, Mail Order #30...........................www.hhs.state.ne.us/lis/lis.asp
Physical Therapist #30...www.hhs.state.ne.us/lis/lis.asp
Physician #30 ....www.hhs.state.ne.us/lis/lis.asp
Physician Assistant #30...www.hhs.state.ne.us/lis/lis.asp
Podiatrist #30...www.hhs.state.ne.us/lis/lis.asp
Polygraph Examiner, Private #26 ....www.sos.state.ne.us/Polygraph/polypri.htm
Polygraph Examiner, Public #26......................................www.sos.state.ne.us/Polygraph/polypub.htm
Polygraph/Voice Stress Examiner #26 ....www.sos.state.ne.us/Polygraph/voice.htm
Preschool #30 ....www.hhs.state.ne.us/crl/rosters.htm
Private Detective/Agency #26..www.sos.state.ne.us/Privatedetectives/pdlist.htm
Psychologist #30..www.hhs.state.ne.us/lis/lis.asp
Public Accountant-CPA #5 ....www.nol.org/home/BPA/license/
Radiographer #30...www.hhs.state.ne.us/lis/lis.asp
Radon Nitigation Specialist/Technician #17 ....www.hhs.state.ne.us/lis/lis.asp
Real Estate Agent/Sales #25...http://nrec.nol.org/licinfodb/
Real Estate Appraiser #22...http://appraiser.dnr.state.ne.us/index.asp
Real Estate Broker #25..http://nrec.nol.org/licinfodb/
Rehabilitation Agency #30 ....www.hhs.state.ne.us/crl/rosters.htm
Respiratory Care Practitioner #30 ....www.hhs.state.ne.us/lis/lis.asp
Respite Care Service #30...www.hhs.state.ne.us/crl/rosters.htm
Sales Finance Company #31..www.ndbf.org/finsearch.htm#
Saving & Loan #31 ....www.ndbf.org/finsearch.htm#
Securities Agent #11..www.nasdr.com/2001.asp
Securities Broker/Dealer #11...www.nasdr.com/2001.asp
Social Worker #30 ....www.hhs.state.ne.us/lis/lis.asp
Speech-Language Pathologist/Audiologist #30 ....www.hhs.state.ne.us/lis/lis.asp
Substance Abuse Treatment Center #30 ....www.nlc.state.ne.us/docs/pilot/pubs/h.html
Surveyor, Land #3 ....www.sso.state.ne.us/bels/
Swimming Pool Operator #30...www.hhs.state.ne.us/lis/lis.asp
Trust Company #31 ....www.ndbf.org/finsearch.htm#
Veterinarian #30 ....www.hhs.state.ne.us/lis/lis.asp
Veterinary Technician #30 ....www.hhs.state.ne.us/lis/lis.asp
Voice Stress Examiner/Analyzer #27 ....www.sos.state.ne.us/Polygraph/voice.htm
Water Operator #30..www.hhs.state.ne.us/lis/lis.asp
Water Treatment Plant Operator #17 ....www.hhs.state.ne.us/lis/lis.asp
Well Driller/Pump Installer #17 ....www.hhs.state.ne.us/lis/lis.asp
X-ray Unit Portable #30 ....www.hhs.state.ne.us/lis/lis.asp

Nebraska Licensing Quick Finder

Abstracting Company #4 402-471-2383
Abstractor #4 402-471-2383
Address Confidentiability Program #27 . 402-471-4094
Adult Day Care #30 402-471-2115
Aerial Applicator #10 402-471-2371
Air Conditioning/Heating Contract'r #12 402-441-7508
Alcohol/Drug Testing #30 402-471-2118
Amusement Ride Inspector #21 402-471-2239
Animal Technician #30 402-471-2118
Architect #2 402-471-2021
Asbestor Worker, etc. #17 402-471-2299
Asbestos-related Occupation #30 402-471-2299
Assisted Living Facility #30 402-471-4970
Athletic Trainer #30 402-471-2299
Attorney #32 402-471-7091
Auctioneer #6 402-441-7437
Bank #31 402-471-2171
Barber #1 402-471-2051
Barber School #1 402-471-2051
Boiler & Pressure Vessel Inspector #16 402-471-4721
Boiler Inspection #21 402-471-2230
Boxer #28 402-471-2009
Boxing Promoter #28 402-471-2009
Chauffeur #6 402-441-7437
Check Sales #31 402-471-2171
Child Care Center #30 402-471-2115
Child Caring/Placing Agency #30 402-471-2115
Child Labor #21 402-471-2230
Chiropractor #30 402-471-2299
Collection Agency #26 .... 402-471-8606, 471-2555
Contractor Registration #21 402-595-3095
Contractor, Building #12 402-441-6456
Cosmetologist #30 402-471-2115
Cosmetology Salon/School #30 402-471-2115
Credit Union #31 402-471-2171
Debt Management Agency #26
.... 402-471-8606, 471-2555
Delayed Deposit Service #31 402-471-2171
Dental Anesthesia Permit #30 402-471-2118
Dental Hygienist #30 402-471-2118
Dentist #30 402-471-2118
Developmentally Disabled Center #30 . 402-471-2115
Drug Distributor, Wholesale #30 402-471-2118
Drug Wholesale Facility #30 402-471-2115
Educational Media Specialist/Librarian #13
.... 402-471-0739
Electrician #29 402-471-3550
Electrologist/Electrology Facility #30 402-471-2115
Elevator Inspector/Inspection Mgr. #21 . 402-595-2523
Embalmer #30 402-471-2115
Emergency Medical Care Facility #30 . 402-471-2115
Employment Agency #21 402-595-3095
Engineer #2 402-471-2021
Environmental Health Specialist #30 . 402-471-2299
Environmental Health Specialists #17 . 402-471-2299

Esthetician #30 402-471-2115
Esthetician Establishment #30 402-471-2115
Farm Labor Contractor #21 402-595-3095
Fertilizer Professional/Business #18 402-471-2394
Fire Protection Sprinkler Contract'r #12 402-441-6456
Fund Transmission #31 402-471-2171
Funeral Director #30 402-471-2115
Funeral Establishment #30 402-471-2115
Geologist #7 402-471-8383
Health Clinic #30 402-471-2115
Hearing Aid Dispenser/Fitter #30 402-471-2299
Hearing Quality Assurance Screening Test #9
.... 402-471-3593
Home Health Agency #30 402-471-2115
Hospice #30 402-471-2115
Hospital #30 402-471-2115
Insurance Agency/Agent/Broker/Producer #14
.... 402-471-2201
Insurance Company #14 402-471-2201
Insurance Consultant #14 402-471-2201
Insurance Utilization Review Agent #14 402-471-2201
Intermediate Care Facility (Mentally Retarded) #30
.... 402-471-2115
Interpreter for the Hearing Impaired (Nebraska
   Registry of Interpreters) #9 402-471-3593
Investigator, Plainclothes #26
.... 402-471-8606, 471-2384
Investment Advisor/Advisor Rep. #11 .. 402-471-3445
Jewelry Dealer, Secondhand #6 402-441-7437
Labor/Delivery Service/Clinic #30 402-471-2115
Laboratory #30 402-471-2115
Landscape Architect #23 402-471-2021
Law Enforcement Officer #20 308-385-6030
Lead Abatement Worker, etc. #17 402-471-2299
Liquor Retailer/ Whlse/ Shipper #19 402-471-2571
Lobbyist #8 402-471-2271
Local Anesthesia Certification #30 402-471-2118
Long Term Care Center #30 402-471-2115
Marriage & Family Therapist #30 402-471-2115
Massage Establishment #30 402-471-2115
Massage Therapy School #30 402-471-2115
Medical Doctor #30 402-471-2118
Mental Health Center #30 402-471-2115
Mentally Retarded Care Service #30 ... 402-471-2115
Nail Technologist #30 402-471-2115
Notary Public #27 402-471-2558
Nurse #30 402-471-2115
Nursing Education Program #30 402-471-2115
Nursing Home #30 402-471-2115
Nursing Home Administrator #30 402-471-2115
Nutrition Therapy, Medical #30 402-471-2115
Occupational Therapist #30 402-471-2299
Optometrist #30 402-471-2118
Osteopathic Physician #30 402-471-2118
Pawnbroker #6 402-441-7437

Pesticide Applicator/Dealer #18 402-471-2394
Pharmacist #30 402-471-2118
Pharmacy #30 402-471-2115
Pharmacy, Mail Order #30 402-471-2115
Physical Therapist #30 402-471-2299
Physician #30 402-471-2118
Physician Assistant #30 402-471-2118
Plant Nursery/Nursery Profession'l #18 402-471-2394
Plumber #12 402-441-6456
Podiatrist #30 402-471-2118
Polygraph Examiner, Private #26 402-471-4070
Polygraph Examiner, Public #26 402-471-4070
Preneed Seller #14 402-471-2201
Preschool #30 402-471-2115
Private Detective/Agency #26
.... 402-471-8606, 471-2384
Psychologist #30 402-471-4905
Public Accountant-CPA #5 402-471-3595
Racing Event/Professional #24 402-471-4155
Radiographer #30 402-471-2118
Radon Nitigation Specialist/Tech. #17 . 402-471-2299
Real Estate Agent/Sales/Broker #25 ... 402-471-2004
Real Estate Appraiser #22 402-471-9015
Rehabilitation Agency #30 402-471-2115
Respiratory Care Practitioner #30 402-471-2299
Respite Care Service #30 402-471-2115
Sales Finance Company #31 402-471-2171
Saving & Loan #31 402-471-2171
School Administrator/Supervisor #13 ... 402-471-0739
School Nurse #13 402-471-0739
Securities Agent #11 402-471-3445
Securities Broker/Dealer #11 402-471-3445
Skin Care Salon #30 402-471-2115
Social Worker #30 402-471-2115
Speech-Language Pathologist/Audiologist #30
.... 402-471-2115
Substance Abuse Treatment Ctr #30 ... 402-471-2115
Surplus Lines Seller #14 402-471-2201
Surveyor, Land #3 402-471-2566
Swimming Pool Operator #30 402-471-2299
Taxi Driver #6 402-441-7437
Teacher #13 402-471-0739
Trust Company #31 402-471-2171
Veterinarian #30 402-471-2118
Veterinary Technician #30 402-471-2115
Voice Stress Examiner/Analyzer #26
.... 402-471-8606; 471-4070
Water Operator #30 402-471-2299
Water Treatment Plant Operator #17 . 402-471-2299
Well Driller/Pump Installer #17 402-471-2299
Wrestler #28 402-471-2009
Wrestling/Boxing Matches #28 402-471-2009
X-ray Unit Portable #30 402-471-2115

Nebraska Licensing Agency Information

1 Board of Barber Examiners, 301 Centennial Mall S, 6th Fl, Lincoln, NE 68509-4723; 402-471-2051, Fax: 402-471-2052. www.barbers.state.ne.us

2 Board of Examiners for Engineers & Architects, PO Box 95165, 301 Centennial Mall S 6th Fl, Lincoln, NE 68509-4751; 402-471-2021, Fax: 402-471-0787. www.ea.state.ne.us Email: board@nol.org Search Database at www.ea.state.ne.us

3 Board of Examiners for Land Surveyors, 555 N Cotner Blvd, Lincoln, NE 68505; 402-471-2566, Fax: 402-471-3057. www.sso.state.ne.us/bels/ Search Database at www.sso.state.ne.us/bels/

4 Abstractors Board of Examiners, PO Box 94944 (1200 N St), Lincoln, NE 68509; 402-471-2383, Fax: 402-471-6575. www.abe.state.ne.us Email: mmccull@abe.state.ne.us Search Database at www.abe.state.ne.us

5 Board of Public Accountancy, PO Box 94725, Lincoln, NE 68509-4725; 402-471-3595, Fax: 402-471-4484. www.nol.org/home/BPA/ Email: nbpa01@nol.org   Search Database at www.nol.org/home/BPA/license/

6 Applications & Permits, City Clerk's Office, 555 S 10th St, Lincoln, NE 68508; 402-441-7437, Fax: 402-441-8325. http://interlinc.ci.lincoln.ne.us

7 Board of Geologists, PO Box 94844, Lincoln, NE 68509; 402-471-8383, Fax: 402-471-0787. www.geology.state.ne.us/board/nbg.htm Email: geology@nol.org Search Database at www.geology.state.ne.us/board/roster.pdf

8 Clerk of the Legislature, PO Box 94604, Lincoln, NE 68509-4604; 402-471-2271, Fax: 402-471-2126. www.unicam.state.ne.us Email: uio@unicam.state.ne.us Search Database at www.unicam.state.ne.us

9 Commission for the Deaf & Hard of Hearing, 4600 Valley Rd #420, Lincoln, NE 68510-4844; 402-471-3593, Fax: 402-471-3067. www.nol.org/home/NCDHH Email: lstaff@ncdhh.state.ne.us

10 Department of Aeronautics, 3431 Aviation Rd #150 (68524), Lincoln, NE 68501; 402-471-2371, Fax: 402-471-2906. www.aero.state.ne.us Email: sonis@mail.state.ne.us

11 Department of Banking & Finance, Bureau of Securities, PO Box 95006 (1200 "N" Street, #311), Lincoln, NE 68509-5006; 402-471-3445. www.ndbf.org/sec.htm Search Database at www.ndbf.org/actions.htm Note: The Orders and Actions search page includes state orders and cancelled or denied licenses. The NASD web search site is national.

12 Department of Building & Safety, 555 S 10th St, Lincoln, NE 68508; 402-441-7791, Fax: 402-471-8214. www.ci.lincoln.ne.us

13 Department of Education, Teacher Accreditation/Certification Division, 301 Centennial Mall S 6th Fl, Lincoln, NE 68509-4987; 402-471-0739, Fax: 402-471-9735. www.nde.state.ne.us

14 Department of Insurance, 941 O St #400, Lincoln, NE 68508-3639; 402-471-2201, Fax: 402-471-6559. www.nol.org/home/NDOI/ Email: consumer_affairs@doi.state.ne.us

16 Division of Safety & Labor Standards, Boiler Inspectors Section, PO Box 95024, Lincoln, NE 68509; 402-471-4721, Fax: 402-471-5039. www.dol.state.ne.us/nwd/center.cfm?PRICAT=2&SUBCAT=2C Email: dburns@dol.state.ne.us

17 Drinking Water & Environmental Sanitation, Credentialing Division, PO Box 95007 (301 Centennial Mall S), Lincoln, NE 68509; 402-471-2299, Fax: 402-471-3577. www.hhs.state.ne.us Search Database at www.hhs.state.ne.us/lis/lis.asp Note: They sell lists, labels and disketts.

18 Department of Agriculture, Bureau of Plant Industry, PO Box 94756 (301 Centennial Mall South), Lincoln, NE 68509; 402-471-2394, Fax: 402-471-6892. www.kellysolutions.com/ne/ Search Database at www.agr.state.ne.us/division/bpi/bpi.htm

19 Liquor Control Commission, 301 Centennial Mall S, 5th Fl, Lincoln, NE 68509-5046; 402-471-2571, Fax: 402-471-2814. www.nol.org/home/NLCC Email: nlcc01@nol.org Search Database at www.nol.org/home/NLCC/nlccsearch.html

20 Crime Commission, 3600 N Academy Rd, Grand Island, NE 68801; 308-385-6030, Fax: 308-385-6032. www.nol.org/home/crimecom Email: slamken@crimecom.state.ne.us

21 Department of Labor, Office of Safety & Labor Standards, 301 Centennial Mall S, Lower Level, Lincoln, NE 68509-5024; 402-471-2230, Fax: 402-471-5039. www.dol.state.ne.us Email: ghirsh@dol.state.ne.us

22 Real Estate Appraiser Board, PO Box 94963, Lincoln, NE 68509-4963; 402-471-9015, Fax: 402-471-9017. http://appraiser.dnr.state.ne.us Email: mjhass_appraiser.dnr.state.ne.us Search Database at http://appraiser.dnr.state.ne.us/index.asp

23 Board of Landscape Architects, PO Box 95165, Lincoln, NE 68509-5165; 402-471-2021, Fax: 402-471-0787. www.landarch.state.ne.us/ Email: landarch@nol.org Search Database at www.landarch.state.ne.us/registrants.pdf

24 Racing Commission, 301 Centennial Mall S 6th Fl, Lincoln, NE 68509-5014; 402-471-4155. www.horseracing.state.ne.us/

25 Real Estate Commission, 1200 N St, Ste 402, Lincoln, NE 68509-4667; 402-471-2004, Fax: 402-471-4492. www.nrec.state.ne.us email: infotech@nrec.state.ne.us Search Database at http://nrec.nol.org/licinfodb/

26 Secretary of State, Business Services, Licensing Division, PO Box 94608 (State Capitol Rm 2300), Lincoln, NE 68509-4608; 402-471-8606, Fax: 402-471-2530. www.sos.state.ne.us Email: sos04@nol.org Search Database at www.sos.state.ne.us/htm/businessmenu.htm

27 Secretary of State, Notary Division, Rm 1301 State Capitol Bldg, Lincoln, NE 68509-5104; 402-471-2558, Fax: 402-471-4429. www.sos.state.ne.us/Notary/notary.htm Email: dpester@nol.org

28 Athletic Commission, 301 Centennial Mall S, 1st Fl, Lincoln, NE 68509-4743; 402-471-2009, Fax: 402-471-3396. www.athcomm.state.ne.us/ Email: contact@athcomm.ne.gov

29 Electrical Division, 800 S 13th St #109, Lincoln, NE 68509; 402-471-3550, Fax: 402-471-4297. Search Database at www.nebraska.gov/business/html/342/index.phtml

30 Health & Human Svcs Regulation & Licensure, Credentialing Division, PO Box 94986, Lincoln, NE 68509-4986; 402-471-2115, Fax: 402-471-3577. www.hhs.state.ne.us/crl/crlindex.htm Email: marie.mcclatchey@hhss.state.ne.us Search Database at www.hhs.state.ne.us/lis/lis.asp Note: Boarding Homes do not need a license as of 1/1/2001. Domiciliary Facility and Residential Care Facility are now combined into Assisted Living Facility.

31 Department of Banking & Finance, Financial Institutions Divison, PO Box 95006 (1200 "N" Street, #311), Lincoln, NE 68509-5006; 402-471-2171. www.ndbf.org/fin.htm Search Database at www.ndbf.org/finsearch.htm#

32 Supreme Court, 635 S 14th PO Box 81809, Lincoln, NE 68501-1809; 402-471-3731, Fax: 402-475-7098. www.nebar.com/index.htm

Nebraska Federal Courts

The following list indicates the district and division name for each county in the state.

County/Court Cross Reference

County	Court	County	Court
Adams	Lincoln	Jefferson	Lincoln
Antelope	Lincoln	Johnson	Lincoln
Arthur	North Platte	Kearney	Lincoln
Banner	North Platte	Keith	North Platte
Blaine	North Platte	Keya Paha	North Platte
Boone	Lincoln	Kimball	North Platte
Box Butte	North Platte	Knox	Omaha
Boyd	Lincoln	Lancaster	Lincoln
Brown	North Platte	Lincoln	North Platte
Buffalo	Lincoln	Logan	North Platte
Burt	Omaha	Loup	North Platte
Butler	Lincoln	Madison	Lincoln
Cass	Lincoln	McPherson	North Platte
Cedar	Omaha	Merrick	Lincoln
Chase	North Platte	Morrill	North Platte
Cherry	North Platte	Nance	Lincoln
Cheyenne	North Platte	Nemaha	Lincoln
Clay	Lincoln	Nuckolls	Lincoln
Colfax	Lincoln	Otoe	Lincoln
Cuming	Omaha	Pawnee	Lincoln
Custer	North Platte	Perkins	North Platte
Dakota	Omaha	Phelps	Lincoln
Dawes	North Platte	Pierce	Omaha
Dawson	North Platte	Platte	Lincoln
Deuel	North Platte	Polk	Lincoln
Dixon	Omaha	Red Willow	North Platte
Dodge	Omaha	Richardson	Lincoln
Douglas	Omaha	Rock	North Platte
Dundy	North Platte	Saline	Lincoln
Fillmore	Lincoln	Sarpy	Omaha
Franklin	Lincoln	Saunders	Lincoln
Frontier	North Platte	Scotts. Bluff	North Platte
Furnas	North Platte	Seward	Lincoln
Gage	Lincoln	Sheridan	North Platte
Garden	North Platte	Sherman	Lincoln
Garfield	North Platte	Sioux	North Platte
Gosper	North Platte	Stanton	Omaha
Grant	North Platte	Thayer	Lincoln
Greeley	Lincoln	Thomas	North Platte
Hall	Lincoln	Thurston	Omaha
Hamilton	Lincoln	Valley	North Platte
Harlan	Lincoln	Washington	Omaha
Hayes	North Platte	Wayne	Omaha
Hitchcock	North Platte	Webster	Lincoln
Holt	Lincoln	Wheeler	Lincoln
Hooker	North Platte	York	Lincoln
Howard	Lincoln		

Standards for Federal Courts: The search fee is $20.00 per item (one party name or case number). Certification fee is $7.00 per document. Copy fee is $.50 per page. All fees standard unless noted in profile. Mail Search: always enclose a stamped self addressed envelope unless otherwise noted. Most courts accept fax requests or will suggest a copying/search vendor. Before releasing records, all courts require prepayment unless noted in profile.

Open records are located at the court unless otherwise noted. District courts index by defendant and plaintiff as well as by case number. Bankruptcy courts usually index by debtor and case number. While most courts now have their indexes on computer, many still maintain index card files as well.

PACER: The universal PACER sign-up number is 800-676-6856. Find PACER and the Party/Case Index on the Web at http://pacer.psc.uscourts.gov. PACER dial-up access is $.60 per minute. Also, courts offering internet access via RACER, PACER, Web-PACER or the new CM-ECF charge $.07 per page fee unless noted as free.

US District Court

District of Nebraska

Lincoln Division PO Box 83468, Lincoln, NE 68501 (courier address: 593 Federal Bldg, 100 Centennial Mall N, Lincoln, NE 68508), 402-437-5225, Fax: 402-437-5651. www.ned.uscourts.gov

Counties: Nebraska cases may be filed in any of the three courts at the option of the attorney, except that filings in the North Platte Division must be during trial session.

Indexing & Storage: New cases available in the index 1-2 days after filing date.

Fee & Payment: Payment may be made by money order, cashier check, personal check. Payee: Clerk, U.S. District Court.

Phone Search: Only docket information available.

In Person Search: Fee charged if court conducts your in person search for you.

PACER: PACER is available online at http://pacer.ned.uscourts.gov. Records purged every year. New records are online after 2 days.

Electronic Filing: Electronic filing information online at https://ecf.ned.uscourts.gov

North Platte Division c/o Lincoln Division, PO Box 83468, Lincoln, NE 68501 (courier address: 593 Federal Bldg, 100 Centennial Mall N, Lincoln, NE 68508), 402-437-5225, Fax: 402-437-5651. www.ned.uscourts.gov

Counties: Nebraska cases may be filed in any of the three courts at the option of the attorney, except that filings in the North Platte Division must be during trial session. Some case records may be in the Omaha Division as well as the Lincoln Division.

Indexing & Storage: New cases available in the index 1-2 days after filing date. Records can also be located at Omaha or Lincoln, depending on the judge assigned. Open records are located at Lincoln Division.

Fee & Payment: Payment may be made by money order, cashier check, personal check. Payee: Clerk, U.S. District Court.

Phone Search: No searching by telephone.

In Person Search: Permitted.

PACER: PACER is available online at http://pacer.ned.uscourts.gov. Records purged every year. New records are online after 2 days.

Electronic Filing: Electronic filing information online at https://ecf.ned.uscourts.gov

Omaha Division 111 S 18th Plaza, Ste 1152, Omaha, NE 68102 (courier address: Use mail address for courier delivery) 402-661-7350, Fax: 402-661-7387. www.ned.uscourts.gov

Counties: Nebraska cases may be filed in any of the three courts at the option of the attorney,

except that filings in the North Platte Division must be during trial session.

Indexing & Storage: New cases available in the index 1-2 days after filing date.

Fee & Payment: Payment may be made by money order, cashier check, personal check. Payee: Clerk, U.S. District Court.

Phone Search: No searching by telephone.

In Person Search: Fee charged if court conducts your in person search for you.

PACER: PACER is available online at http://pacer.ned.uscourts.gov. Records purged every year. New records are online after 2 days.

Electronic Filing: Electronic filing information online at https://ecf.ned.uscourts.gov

U.S. Bankruptcy Court

District of Nebraska

Lincoln Division 460 Federal Bldg, 100 Centennial Mall N, Lincoln, NE 68508 (courier address: Use mail address for courier delivery) 402-437-5100, Fax: 402-437-5454. www.neb.uscourts.gov

Counties: Adams, Antelope, Boone, Boyd, Buffalo, Butler, Cass, Clay, Colfax, Fillmore, Franklin, Gage, Greeley, Hall, Hamilton, Harlan, Holt, Howard, Jefferson, Johnson, Kearney, Lancaster, Madison, Merrick, Nance, Nemaha, Nuckolls, Otoe, Pawnee, Phelps, Platte, Polk, Richardson, Saline, Saunders, Seward, Sherman, Thayer, Webster, Wheeler, York. Cases from the North Platte Division may also be assigned here.

Indexing & Storage: Cases indexed by as well as by case number. New cases available in the index 1 day after filing date. All debtor names are indexed for files from 9/89 to the present. District wide searches are available from this division. This court maintains records for the main bankruptcy office in Omaha.

Fee & Payment: Payment may be made by money order, cashier check, personal check. Debtor's checks are not accepted. Payee: Clerk, U.S. Bankrutpcy Court.

Phone Search: Only the debtor's name, case number, date filed, 341 information and date discharged and closed will be released. Automated voice case information service (VCIS) is available. Call VCIS at 800-829-0112 or 402-221-3757.

Mail Search: A SASE not required.

In Person Search: Fee charged if court conducts your in person search for you.

PACER: PACER is available online at http://pacer.neb.uscourts.gov. Records purged every six months. New civil records are online after 3 days.

Electronic Filing: Electronic filing information online at https://ecf.neb.uscourts.gov

North Platte Division c/o Omaha Division, 111 S 18th Plaza, Ste 1125, Omaha, NE 68102 (courier address: Use mail address for courier delivery) 402-661-7444, Fax: 402-661-7492. www.neb.uscourts.gov

Counties: Arthur, Banner, Blaine, Box Butte, Brown, Chase, Cherry, Cheyenne, Custer, Dawes, Dawson, Deuel, Dundy, Frontier, Furnas, Garden, Garfield, Gosper, Grant, Hayes, Hitchcock, Hooker, Keith, Keya Paha, Kimball, Lincoln, Logan, Loup, McPherson, Morrill, Perkins, Red Willow, Rock, Scotts Bluff, Sheridan, Sioux, Thomas, Valley. Cases may be randomly allocated to Omaha or Lincoln.

Indexing & Storage: Cases indexed by as well as by case number. New cases available in the index 1 day after filing date. Open records are located at the Omaha Division. Case records may also be in the Lincoln Division (Lancaster County).

Fee & Payment: Payment may be made by money order, cashier check. Business checks are not accepted. Personal checks are not accepted.

Phone Search: Automated voice case information service (VCIS) is available. Call VCIS at 800-829-0112 or 402-221-3757.

Mail Search: A SASE not required.

In Person Search: Permitted.

PACER: PACER is available online at http://pacer.neb.uscourts.gov. Records purged every six months. New civil records are online after 3 days.

Electronic Filing: Electronic filing information online at https://ecf.neb.uscourts.gov

Omaha Division 111 S. 18th Plaza, Ste 1125, Omaha, NE 68102 (courier address: Use mail address for courier delivery) 402-661-7444, Fax: 402-661-7441. www.neb.uscourts.gov

Counties: Burt, Cedar, Cuming, Dakota, Dixon, Dodge, Douglas, Knox, Pierce, Sarpy, Stanton, Thurston, Washington, Wayne.

Indexing & Storage: Cases indexed by debtor and creditors as well as by case number. New cases available in the index 24 hours after filing date.

Fee & Payment: Payment may be made by money order, cashier check, personal check. Payee: Clerk, U.S. Bankruptcy Court.

Phone Search: Only docket information available by phone. Automated voice case information service (VCIS) is available. Call VCIS at 800-829-0112 or 402-221-3757.

In Person Search: Permitted.

PACER: PACER is available online at http://pacer.neb.uscourts.gov. Records purged every six months. New civil records are online after 3 days.

Electronic Filing: Electronic filing information online at https://ecf.neb.uscourts.gov

Nebraska County Courts

Court	Jurisdiction	No. of Courts	How Organized
District Courts*	General	93	12 Districts
County Courts*	Limited	93	11 Districts
Juvenile Courts	Special	3	3 Counties
Workers' Compensation Court	Special	1	

* Profiled in this Sourcebook.

Court	CIVIL								
	Tort	Contract	Real Estate	Min. Claim	Max. Claim	Small Claims	Estate	Eviction	Domestic Relations
District Courts*	X	X	X	$15,000	No Max				X
County Courts*	X	X	X	$0	$15,000	$1800	X	X	X
Juvenile Courts									
Workers' Compensation Court									

Court	CRIMINAL				
	Felony	Misdemeanor	DWI/DUI	Preliminary Hearing	Juvenile
District Courts*	X				
County Courts*		X	X	X	X
Juvenile Courts					X
Workers' Compensation Court					

ADMINISTRATION   Court Administrator, PO Box 98910, Lincoln, NE, 68509-8910; 402-471-2643, Fax: 402-471-2197. http://court.nol.org/AOC

COURT STRUCTURE   The District Court is the court of general jurisdiction. The minimum on civil judgment matters for District Courts is $15,000, however, the State raised the County Court limit on civil matters from $15,000 to $45,000 as of Sept. 1, 2001. As it is less expensive to file civil cases in County Court than in District Court, civil cases in the $15,000 to $45,000 range are more likely to be found in County Court, if after Sept. 1, 2001.

The number of judicial districts went from 21 to the current 12 in July 1992. County Courts have juvenile jurisdiction in all but 3 counties. Douglas, Lancaster, and Sarpy counties have separate Juvenile Courts.

ONLINE ACCESS   An online access subscription service is available for NE District and County courts, except Douglas County District Court. Case details, all party listings, payments and actions taken for criminal, civil, probate, juvenile, and traffic is available. Users must be registered with Nebrask@ Online, there is a start-up fee. The fee is $.60 per record or a flat rate of $300.00 per month. Go to www.nebraska.gov/faqs/justice for more info and how far back records go per county. Supreme Court opinions are available from http://court.nol.org/opinions/.

Currently, Douglas, Lancaster, and Sarpy county courts offer internet access with registration and password required.

ADDITIONAL INFORMATION   Most Nebraska courts require the public to do their own in-person searches and will not respond to written search requests. The State Attorney General has recommended that courts not perform searches because of the time involved and concerns over possible legal liability.

Adams County

County Court PO Box 95, Hastings, NE 68902-0095; 402-461-7143; Fax: 402-461-7144. Hours: 8AM-5PM (CST). *Misdemeanor, Civil Actions Under $45,000, Eviction, Small Claims, Probate.*
Civil Records: Access: In person, online. Visitors must perform in person searches for themselves. No search fee. Required to search: name, years to search; also helpful: address. Civil cases indexed by defendant. Civil records on index cards and files from 1970s. An online subscription service is available; same as criminal access. Online civil records date from 10/99 forward, probate from 05/98.
Criminal Records: Access: In person, online. Visitors must perform in person searches for themselves. No search fee. Required to search: name, years to search; also helpful: DOB, SSN. Criminal records on index cards and files from 1970s. A subscription service is available at www.nebraska.gov/faqs/justice/. Fee is $.60 a record or $300 per month flat rate, also there is a start-up fee. Online criminal and traffic records date from 07/97.
General Information: Public Access terminal is available. No adoption or juvenile records released. Copy fee: $.25 per page. Certification fee: $1.00. Payee: Adams County Court. Business checks accepted. Prepayment required.

District Court PO Box 9, Hastings, NE 68902; 402-461-7264; Fax: 402-461-7269. Hours: 8:30AM-5PM (CST). *Felony, Civil Actions Over $15,000.*
http://adamscounty.org/courts/district
Civil Records: Access: In person, online. Visitors must perform in person searches for themselves. No search fee. Required to search: name, years to search. Civil cases indexed by defendant, plaintiff. Civil records on microfiche from 1800s, 5 yrs on index cards, on docket books from 1800s. An online subscription service is available; same as criminal access. Online records date from 07/97.
Criminal Records: Access: In person, online. Visitors must perform in person searches for themselves. No search fee. Required to search: name, years to search. Criminal records on microfiche from 1800s, 5 yrs on index cards, on docket books from 1800s. A subscription service is available at www.nebraska.gov/faqs/justice/. Fee is $.60 a record or $300 per month flat rate, also there is a start-up fee. Online records date from 07/97.
General Information: Public Access terminal is available. No juvenile, search warrants or mental health records released. Copy fee: $.25 per page. Certification fee: $1.00. Prepayment required.

Antelope County

District Court PO Box 45, Neligh, NE 68756; 402-887-4508; Fax: 402-887-4870. Hours: 8:30AM-5PM (CST). *Felony, Civil Actions Over $15,000.*
Civil Records: Access: In person, online. Visitors must perform in person searches for themselves. No search fee. Required to search: name, years to search. Civil cases indexed by defendant, plaintiff. Civil records on index books from 1872, computerized since 1999. An online subscription service is available; same as criminal access. Online records records date from 03/99.
Criminal Records: Access: In person, online. Visitors must perform in person searches for themselves. No search fee. Required to search: name, years to search. Criminal records on index books from 1872, computerized since 1999. A subscription service is at www.nebraska.gov/faqs/justice/. Fee is $.60 a record or $300 per month flat rate, also there is a start-up fee. Online records date from 03/99.
General Information: Public Access terminal is available. No juvenile, sealed, search warrants, or mental health record released. Will fax return specific case file documents for $1.00 per page. Copy fee: $.25 per page. Certification fee: $1.00. Payee: Clerk of District Court. Personal checks accepted. Prepayment required.

Antelope County Court 501 Main, Neligh, NE 68756; 402-887-4650; Fax: 402-887-4160. Hours: 8:30AM-5PM (CST). *Misdemeanor, Civil Actions Under $45,000, Eviction, Small Claims, Probate.*
Civil Records: Access: In person, online. Visitors must perform in person searches for themselves. No search fee. Required to search: name, years to search. Civil cases indexed by defendant, plaintiff. Civil records on computer from 1994, probate on microfiche from 1800s, civil and small claims indexed from 1983. An online subscription service is available; same as criminal access. Online civil and probate records date from 12/99 forward.
Criminal Records: Access: In person, online. Visitors must perform in person searches for themselves. No search fee. Required to search: name, years to search, DOB, signed release; also helpful: SSN. Criminal index on computer from 1994, indexed from 1800s. A subscription service is at www.nebraska.gov/faqs/justice/. Fee is $.60 a record or $300 per month flat rate, also there is a start-up fee. Online criminal and traffic records date from 12/99.
General Information: Public Access terminal is available. No adoption, or sealed records released. Copy fee: $.25 per page. Certification fee: $1.00 plus $.25 per page. Payee: Antelope County Court. Personal checks accepted. Prepayment required.

Arthur County

District & County Court PO Box 126, 205 Fir St., Arthur, NE 69121; 308-764-2203; Fax: 308-764-2216. 8AM-4PM (MST). *Felony, Misdemeanor, Civil, Eviction, Small Claims, Probate.*
Civil Records: Access: Phone, fax, mail, in person. Both court and visitors may perform in person searches. No search fee. Required to search: name, years to search. Civil cases indexed by defendant, plaintiff. Civil records on index books from 1987, on docket books from 1913. An online subscription service is available; same as criminal access. County court online records date from 09/99 forward; District Court records from 06/00.
Criminal Records: Access: Phone, fax, mail, In person. Both court and visitors may perform in person searches. No search fee. Required to search: name, years to search. Criminal records on index books from 1987, on docket books from 1913. A subscription service is at www.nebraska.gov/faqs/justice/. Fee is $.60 a record or $300 per month flat rate, also there is a start-up fee. Online criminal and traffic records date from 09/99 forward; District Court records from 06/00.
General Information: Public Access terminal is available. No search warrants, juvenile, adoption, mental health, or sealed records released. Will fax results $1.00 per page. Incoming fax fee $.25. Copy fee: $.20 per page. Certification fee: $1.50 first page; $.50 each add'l. Payee: Arthur County Clerk. Personal checks accepted. Prepayment required. Mail requests: SASE required. Mail turnaround time 1-2 days.

Banner County

District Court PO Box 67, Harrisburg, NE 69345; 308-436-5265; Probate phone: 308-436-5268; Fax: 308-436-4180. Hours: 8AM-5PM (MST). *Felony, Civil Actions Over $15,000.*
Civil Records: Access: Fax, mail, in person, online. Both court and visitors may perform in person searches. Search fee: $3.00 per name. Required to search: name, years to search; also helpful: address. Civil cases indexed by defendant, plaintiff. Civil records on docket books from 1800s. An online subscription service is available; same as criminal access. Online civil records records date from 06/00 forward.
Criminal Records: Access: Fax, mail, In person, online. Both court and visitors may perform in person searches. Search fee: $3.00 per name. Required to search: name, years to search, DOB; also helpful: address. Criminal records on docket books from 1800s. A subscription service is available at www.nebraska.gov/faqs/justice/. Fee is $.60 a record or $300 per month flat rate, also there is a start-up fee. Online records date from 06/00 forward.
General Information: No search warrants, mental health, or sealed records released. Will fax results $1.00 per page. Copy fee: $.25 per page. Certification fee: $1.50. Payee: Banner County Clerk. Personal checks accepted. Prepayment required. Mail requests: SASE required. Mail turnaround time 5-7 days.

Banner County Court PO Box 67, Harrisburg, NE 69345; 308-436-5268. Hours: 1-5PM (MST). *Misdemeanor, Civil Actions Under $45,000, Eviction, Small Claims, Probate.*
Civil Records: Access: Mail, in person, online. Both court and visitors may perform in person searches. No search fee. Required to search: name, years to search. Civil cases indexed by defendant, plaintiff. Civil records on register of action cards from 1992, prior on docket books, on computer from 12/2000. An online subscription service is available; same as criminal access. Online civil and probate records date from 01/01 forward.
Criminal Records: Access: In person, online, mail. Both court and visitors may perform in person searches. No search fee. Required to search: name, years to search, signed release; also helpful: address, DOB. Criminal records on register of action cards from 1992, prior on docket books, on computer from 6/2000. A subscription service is available at www.nebraska.gov/faqs/justice/. Fee is $.60 a record or $300 per month flat rate, also there is a start-up fee. Online criminal and traffic records date from 04/00 forward.
General Information: No adoption, sealed records released. Copy fee: $.25 per page. Certification fee: $1.00. Payee: Banner County Court. Personal checks accepted. Prepayment required. Mail requests: SASE required. Mail turnaround time 4 days from receipt.

Blaine County

District Court Lincoln Ave, Box 136, Brewster, NE 68821; 308-547-2222 Ext 201; Probate phone: Ext 202; Fax: 308-547-2228. Hours: 8AM-4PM (CST). *Felony, Civil Actions Over $15,000.*
www.nol.org/home/DC8
Civil Records: Access: Fax, mail, in person, online. Only the court performs in person searches; visitors may not. Search fee: $1.00 per name. Required to search: name, years to search. Civil cases indexed by defendant, plaintiff. Civil records on index books from late 1800s. An online subscription service is available; same as criminal access. Online records date from 06/00 forward.
Criminal Records: Access: Fax, mail, In person, online. Only the court performs in person searches; visitors may not. Search fee: $1.00 per name. Required to search: name, years to search, DOB. Criminal records on index books from late 1800s. A subscription service is available at www.nebraska.gov/faqs/justice/. Fee is $.60 a record or $300 per month flat rate, also there is a start-up fee. Online records date from 06/00 forward.
General Information: Public Access terminal is available. No search warrants, mental health, or sealed records released. Will fax results $1.00 per page. Copy fee: $.25 per page. Certification fee: $1.50.

Payee: Blaine County Clerk. Personal checks accepted. Prepayment required. Mail requests: SASE required. Mail turnaround time 1-2 days.

Blaine County Court Lincoln Ave, Box 123, Brewster, NE 68821; 308-547-2222 ext 202; Fax: 308-547-2228. Hours: 8AM-4PM (CST). *Misdemeanor, Civil Actions Under $45,000, Eviction, Small Claims, Probate.*
Civil Records: Access: Phone, fax, mail, in person, online. Only the court performs in person searches; visitors may not. No search fee. Required to search: name, years to search; also helpful: address. Civil cases indexed by defendant, plaintiff. Civil records on index books from 1960. on microfiche prior to 1960. An online subscription service is available; same as criminal access. Online civil and probate records date from 01/01 forward.
Criminal Records: Access: Phone, fax, mail, In person, online. Only the court performs in person searches; visitors may not. No search fee. Required to search: name, years to search; also helpful: address, DOB, SSN. Criminal records on index books from 1960. on microfiche prior to 1960. A subscription service is at www.nebraska.gov/faqs/justice/. Fee is $.60 a record or $300 per month flat rate, also there is a start-up fee. Online criminal and traffic records date from 08/00 forward.
General Information: No juvenile, adoption, or sealed records released. Will fax results $1.00 per page. Copy fee: $.25 per page. Certification fee: $1.25. Payee: Blaine County Court. Personal checks accepted. Prepayment required. Mail requests: SASE required. Mail turnaround time 2 days.

Boone County

District Court 222 Fourth St, Albion, NE 68620; 402-395-2057; Fax: 402-395-6592. Hours: 8:30AM-5PM (CST). *Felony, Civil Actions Over $45,000.*
Civil Records: Access: Phone, fax, mail, in person, online. Both court and visitors may perform in person searches. No search fee. Required to search: name, years to search. Civil cases indexed by defendant, plaintiff. Civil records in general index and dockets from 1800s, computerized records since 2001. An online subscription service is available; same as criminal access. Online records date from 12/99 forward.
Criminal Records: Access: Phone, fax, mail, In person, online. Both court and visitors may perform in person searches. No search fee. Required to search: name, years to search; also helpful: DOB. Criminal records in general index and dockets from 1800s, computerized records since 2001. A subscription service is at www.nebraska.gov/faqs/justice/. Fee is $.60 a record or $300 per month flat rate, also there is a start-up fee. Online records date from 12/99 forward.
General Information: No search warrants, mental health, or sealed records released. Will fax results $3.00 1st page, $1.00 each add'l. Copy fee: $.25 per page. Certification fee: $1.00. Payee: Clerk of District Court. Personal checks accepted. Prepayment required. Mail requests: SASE required. Mail turnaround time 2-3 days.

Boone County Court 222 S 4th St, Albion, NE 68620; 402-395-6184; Fax: 402-395-6592. Hours: 8AM-5PM (CST). *Misdemeanor, Civil Actions Under $45,000, Eviction, Small Claims, Probate.*
Civil Records: Access: Fax, mail, in person, online. Both court and visitors may perform in person searches. No search fee. Required to search: name, years to search. Civil cases indexed by defendant, plaintiff. Civil records on general index and docket books from late 1800s; computerized back to 2000; probate on microfiche from 1970. An online subscription service is available; same as criminal

access. Online civil records date from 10/00 forward, probate from 01/01.
Criminal Records: Access: Fax, mail, In person, online. Both court and visitors may perform in person searches. No search fee. Required to search: name, years to search; also helpful: DOB. Criminal records on general index and docket books from late 1800s; computerized back to 2000; probate on microfiche from 1970. A subscription service is available at www.nebraska.gov/faqs/justice/. Fee is $.60 a record or $300 per month flat rate, also there is a start-up fee. Online criminal and traffic records date from 06/00 forward.
General Information: Public Access terminal is available. No adoption, or sealed records released. No fee to fax results. Copy fee: $.25 per page. Certification fee: $1.00 plus copy fee. Payee: Clerk of County Court. Personal checks accepted. Prepayment required. Mail requests: SASE required. Mail turnaround time 1-2 days. SASE required for large requests.

Box Butte County

District Court 515 Box Butte #300, Alliance, NE 69301; 308-762-6293; Fax: 308-762-5700. 9AM-4PM (MST). *Felony, Civil Actions Over $15,000.*
Civil Records: Access: In person, online. Visitors must perform in person searches for themselves. No search fee. Required to search: name, years to search. Civil cases indexed by defendant, plaintiff. Civil records on general index and docket books from late 1800s. An online subscription service is available; same as criminal access. Online records date from 10/97.
Criminal Records: Access: In person, online. Visitors must perform in person searches for themselves. No search fee. Required to search: name, years to search. Criminal records on general index and docket books from late 1800s. A subscription online service is at www.nebraska.gov/faqs/justice/. Fee is $.60 a record or $300 per month flat rate, also there is a start-up fee. Online records date from 10/97.
General Information: No mental health, or sealed records released. Copy fee: $.25 per page. Certification fee: $1.00.

Box Butte County Court PO Box 613, Alliance, NE 69301; 308-762-6800; Fax: 308-762-2650. Hours: 8:30AM-5PM (MST). *Misdemeanor, Civil Actions Under $45,000, Eviction, Small Claims, Probate.*
Civil Records: Access: in person, online. Visitors must perform in person searches for themselves. No search fee. Required to search: name, years to search. Civil cases indexed by defendant, plaintiff. Civil records on microfiche for 10 years, on index cards to docket books from late 1800s; computerized records since 2000. An online subscription service is available; same as criminal access. Online records date from 11/00 forward.
Criminal Records: Access: In person, online. Visitors must perform in person searches for themselves. No search fee. Required to search: name, years to search, DOB. Criminal records on microfiche for 10 years, on index cards to docket books from late 1800s; computerized records since 2000. A subscription service is available at www.nebraska.gov/faqs/justice/. Fee is $.60 a record or $300 per month flat rate, also there is a start-up fee. Online criminal and traffic records date from 04/00 forward.
General Information: Public Access terminal is available. No adoption or sealed records released. Copy fee: $.25 per page. Certification fee: $1.00. Payee: Box Butte County Court. Personal checks accepted. Prepayment required.

Boyd County

District Court PO Box 26, Butte, NE 68722; 402-775-2391; Probate phone: 402-775-2211; Fax: 402-775-2146. Hours: 8:15AM-4PM (CST). *Felony, Civil Actions Over $15,000.*
Civil Records: Access: Mail, fax, in person, online. Both court and visitors may perform in person searches. Search fee: $3.00 per name. Required to search: name, years to search, address. Civil cases indexed by defendant, plaintiff. Civil records on general index and docket books from late 1800s. An online subscription service is available; same as criminal access. Online records date from 07/00.
Criminal Records: Access: Mail, fax, In person, online. Both court and visitors may perform in person searches. Search fee: $3.00 per name. Required to search: name, years to search, address. Criminal records on general index and docket books from late 1800s. A subscription service is available at www.nebraska.gov/faqs/justice/. Fee is $.60 a record or $300 per month flat rate, also there is a start-up fee. Online records date from 07/00 forward.
General Information: Public Access terminal is available. No search warrants, mental health, or sealed records released. Copy fee: $.25 per page. Certification fee: $1.50. Payee: Boyd County Clerk. Personal checks accepted. Prepayment required. Mail requests: SASE required. Mail turnaround time 3-4 days.

Boyd County Court PO Box 396, Butte, NE 68722; 402-775-2211; Fax: 402-775-2146. Hours: 8AM-5PM W,Th (CST). *Misdemeanor, Civil Actions Under $45,000, Eviction, Small Claims, Probate.*
Civil Records: Access: In person, online. Visitors must perform in person searches for themselves. No search fee. Required to search: name, years to search; also helpful: address. Civil cases indexed by defendant, plaintiff. Civil records on general index and docket books from late 1800s. An online subscription service is available; same as criminal access. Online civil records date from 11/00 forward, probate from 10/00.
Criminal Records: Access: In person, online. Visitors must perform in person searches for themselves. No search fee. Required to search: name, years to search; also helpful: address, DOB, SSN. Criminal records on general index and docket books from late 1800s. A subscription service is at www.nebraska.gov/faqs/justice/. Fee is $.60 a record or $300 per month flat rate, also there is a start-up fee. Online criminal and traffic records date from 08/00.
General Information: No adoption, juvenile, or sealed records released. Copy fee: $.25 per page. Certification fee: $1.00. Payee: Boyd County Court. Personal checks accepted. Prepayment required.

Brown County

District Court 148 W Fourth St, Ainsworth, NE 69210; 402-387-2705; Fax: 402-387-0918. Hours: 8AM-5PM (CST). *Felony, Civil Actions Over $15,000.*
Civil Records: Access: Phone, fax, mail, in person, online. Both court and visitors may perform in person searches. No search fee. Required to search: name, years to search; also helpful: address. Civil cases indexed by defendant, plaintiff. Civil records on general index and docket books from late 1886s; on computer back to 2000. An online subscription service is available; same as criminal access. Online records date from 02/00.
Criminal Records: Access: Fax, mail, In person, online. Both court and visitors may perform in person searches. No search fee. Required to search: name, years to search, signed release; also helpful: address, DOB, SSN. Criminal records on general index and

docket books from late 1886; on computer back to 2000. A subscription service is available at www.nebraska.gov/faqs/justice/. Fee is $.60 a record or $300 per month flat rate, also there is a start-up fee. Online records date from 02/00.

General Information: Public Access terminal is available. No search warrants, mental health, or sealed records released. Fee to fax results is $3.00 per page. Copy fee: $.10 per page. Certification fee: $2.00. Payee: Clerk of District Court, Brown County. Personal checks accepted. Prepayment required. Mail requests: SASE required. Mail turnaround time 3-4 days.

Brown County Court 148 W Fourth St, Ainsworth, NE 69210; 402-387-2864; Fax: 402-387-0918. Hours: 8AM-5PM (CST). *Misdemeanor, Civil Actions Under $45,000, Eviction, Small Claims, Probate.*

Civil Records: Access: Phone, fax, mail, in person, online. Both court and visitors may perform in person searches. No search fee. Required to search: name, years to search. Civil cases indexed by defendant, plaintiff. Civil records in boxes in office since 1980; on computer since 2001. An online subscription service is available; same as criminal access. Online civil records date from 04/01 forward, probate from 03/01.

Criminal Records: Access: Phone, fax, mail, In person, online. Both court and visitors may perform in person searches. No search fee. Required to search: name, years to search, DOB. Criminal records in boxes in office since 1979; on computer since 2000. A subscription service is available at www.nebraska.gov/faqs/justice/. Fee is $.60 a record or $300 per month flat rate, also there is a start-up fee. Online criminal and traffic records date from 08/00.

General Information: Public Access terminal is available. No adoption, juvenile, or sealed records released. Copy fee: $.25 per page. Certification fee: $1.00. Payee: Brown County Court. Personal checks accepted. Prepayment required. Mail requests: SASE required.

Buffalo County

District Court PO Box 520, Kearney, NE 68848; 308-236-1246; Fax: 308-233-3693. Hours: 8AM-5PM (CST). *Felony, Civil Actions Over $15,000.*
Civil Records: Access: Mail, in person, online. Both court and visitors may perform in person searches. No search fee. Required to search: name, years to search; also helpful: address. Civil cases indexed by defendant, plaintiff. Civil records on computer from 1993, on microfiche through 1991, on books from 1800s. An online subscription service is available; same as criminal access. Online records date from 05/97.

Criminal Records: Access: In person, online. Visitors must perform in person searches for themselves. No search fee. Required to search: name, years to search; also helpful: DOB, SSN. Criminal records on computer from 1993, on microfiche through 1991, on books from 1800s. A subscription online service is at www.nebraska.gov/faqs/justice/. Fee is $.60 a record or $300 per month flat rate, also there is a start-up fee. Online records date from 05/97.

General Information: Public Access terminal is available. No juvenile, mental health, search warrants or sealed records released. Copy fee: $.50 per page. Certification fee: $1.50 1st page, $.50 ea add'l. Payee: Clerk of District Court. Business checks accepted. Prepayment required. Mail requests: SASE required. Mail turnaround time 1 week.

Buffalo County Court PO Box 520, Kearney, NE 68848; 308-236-1228; Fax: 308-236-1243. Hours: 8AM-5PM (CST). *Misdemeanor, Civil Actions Under $45,000, Eviction, Small Claims, Probate.*
Civil Records: Access: In person, online. Visitors must perform in person searches for themselves. No search fee. Required to search: name, years to search. Civil cases indexed by defendant, plaintiff. Civil records on computer from 4/94, on microfiche, general index, and docket books from late 1800s. An online subscription service is available; same as criminal access. Online civil and probate records date from 04/94.

Criminal Records: Access: In person, online. Visitors must perform in person searches for themselves. No search fee. Required to search: name, years to search. Criminal records on computer from 4/94, on microfiche, general index, and docket books from late 1800s. A subscription service is at www.nebraska.gov/faqs/justice/. Fee is $.60 a record or $300 per month flat rate, also there is a start-up fee. Online criminal and traffic records date from 04/94.

General Information: Public Access terminal is available. No adoption, or sealed records released. Copy fee: $.25 per page. Certification fee: $1.00. Payee: County Court. Personal checks accepted. Prepayment required.

Burt County

District Court 111 N 13th St, Tekamah, NE 68061; 402-374-2905; Fax: 402-374-2906. Hours: 8AM-4:30PM (CST). *Felony, Civil Actions Over $15,000.*
Civil Records: Access: Mail, in person, online. Both court and visitors may perform in person searches. No search fee. Required to search: name, years to search. Civil cases indexed by defendant, plaintiff. Civil records on books from 1800s. An online subscription service is available; same as criminal access. Online records date from 03/99.

Criminal Records: Access: Mail, In person, online. Both court and visitors may perform in person searches. No search fee. Required to search: name, years to search; also helpful: DOB, SSN. Criminal records on books from 1800s. A subscription service is at www.nebraska.gov/faqs/justice/. Fee is $.60 a record or $300 per month flat rate, also there is a start-up fee. Online records date from 03/99.

General Information: Public Access terminal is available. No mental health records released. Will fax results to local or toll free line. Copy fee: $.50 per page. Certification fee: $2.00. Payee: Clerk of District Court. Personal checks accepted. Prepayment required. Mail requests: SASE required. Mail turnaround time 1 day.

Burt County Court 111 N 13th St, PO Box 87, Tekamah, NE 68061; 402-374-2950; Fax: 402-374-2951. Hours: 8AM-4:30PM (CST). *Misdemeanor, Civil Actions Under $45,000, Eviction, Small Claims, Probate.*
Civil Records: Access: In person, online. Visitors must perform in person searches for themselves. No search fee. Required to search: name, years to search, address. Civil cases indexed by defendant, plaintiff. Civil records on index cards back to 1867, computerized back to 1998. An online subscription service is available; same as criminal access. Online civil records date from 03/00 forward, probate from 05/98.

Criminal Records: Access: In person, online. Visitors must perform in person searches for themselves. No search fee. Required to search: name, years to search, address, DOB, SSN, signed release. Criminal records on index cards back to 1867, computerized back to 1998. A subscription service is at www.nebraska.gov/faqs/justice/. Fee is $.60 a

record or $300 per month flat rate, also there is a start-up fee. Online criminal and traffic records date from 02/98.

General Information: Public Access terminal is available. No adoption records released. Copy fee: $.25 per page. Certification fee: $1.25. Payee: County Court. Personal checks accepted. Prepayment required.

Butler County

District Court 451 5th St, David City, NE 68632-1666; 402-367-7460; Fax: 402-367-3249. Hours: 8:30AM-5PM (CST). *Felony, Civil Actions Over $15,000.*
Civil Records: Access: Mail, in person, online. Both court and visitors may perform in person searches. Search fee: $2.00 per name. Required to search: name, years to search. Civil cases indexed by defendant, plaintiff. Civil records on books. An online subscription service is available; same as criminal access. Online records date from 03/99.

Criminal Records: Access: Mail, In person, online. Both court and visitors may perform in person searches. Search fee: $2.00 per name. Required to search: name, years to search; also helpful: DOB, SSN. Criminal records on books. A subscription service is at www.nebraska.gov/faqs/justice/. Fee is $.60 a record or $300 per month flat rate, also there is a start-up fee. Online records date from 03/99.

General Information: No juvenile, mental health or protection order records released. No fee to fax results. Copy fee: $.10 per page. Certification fee: $1.50. Payee: District Court. Personal checks accepted. Prepayment required. Mail requests: SASE required. Mail turnaround time 1-2 days.

Butler County Court 451 5th St, David City, NE 68632-1666; 402-367-7480; Fax: 402-367-3249. Hours: 8AM-Noon, 1-5PM (CST). *Misdemeanor, Civil Actions Under $45,000, Eviction, Small Claims, Probate.*
Civil Records: Access: In person, online. Visitors must perform in person searches for themselves. No search fee. Required to search: name, years to search. Civil cases indexed by defendant, plaintiff. Civil records on computer since 1998, docket books from late 1800s, probate on microfiche. An online subscription service is available; same as criminal access. Online civil records date from 10/99 forward, probate from 03/98. They can refer requestors to parties who perform searches at the court.

Criminal Records: Access: In person, online. Visitors must perform in person searches for themselves. No search fee. Required to search: name, years to search; also helpful: DOB, SSN. Criminal records on computer since 1998, docket books from late 1800s, probate on microfiche. A subscription service is at www.nebraska.gov/faqs/justice/. Fee is $.60 a record or $300 per month flat rate, also there is a start-up fee. Online criminal and traffic records date from 03/98. They can refer requestors to parties who perform searches at the court.

General Information: Public Access terminal is available. No adoption records released. Some juvenile requires signed release. Copy fee: $.25 per page. Certification fee: $1.00. Payee: Butler County Court. Personal checks accepted. Prepayment required.

Cass County

District Court Cass County Courthouse, 346 Main St., Plattsmouth, NE 68048; 402-296-9339; Probate phone: 402-296-9334; Fax: 402-296-9345. Hours: 8AM-5PM (CST). *Felony, Civil Actions Over $45,000.*
Civil Records: Access: In person, online. Visitors must perform in person searches for themselves. No

search fee. Required to search: name, years to search. Civil cases indexed by defendant, plaintiff. Civil records on index books from 1860s, index on computer since 09/97. An online subscription service is available; same as criminal access. Online records date from 08/97.

Criminal Records: Access: In person, online. Visitors must perform in person searches for themselves. No search fee. Required to search: name, years to search. Criminal records on index books from 1860s, index on computer since 09/97. A subscription service is at www.nebraska.gov/faqs/justice/. Fee is $.60 a record or $300 per month flat rate, also there is a start-up fee. Online records date from 08/97.

General Information: Public Access terminal is available. Copy fee: $.25 per page. Certification fee: $1.25. Payee: Clerk of District Court. Prepayment required.

Cass County Court Cass County Courthouse, 346 Main St Rm 301, Plattsmouth, NE 68048; 402-296-9339; Fax: 402-296-9345. Hours: 8AM-5PM (CST). *Misdemeanor, Civil Actions Under $45,000, Eviction, Small Claims, Probate.*

Civil Records: Access: In person, online. Visitors must perform in person searches for themselves. No search fee. Required to search: name, years to search. Civil cases indexed by defendant, plaintiff. Civil records on index cards for 5 years then sent to Capital for storage; computerized records since 2000. An online subscription service is available; same as criminal access. Online civil records date from 01/00 forward, probate from 05/98.

Criminal Records: Access: In person, online. Visitors must perform in person searches for themselves. No search fee. Required to search: name, years to search. Criminal records on computer since 1/97. A subscription service is at www.nebraska.gov/faqs/justice/. Fee is $.60 a record or $300 per month flat rate, also there is a start-up fee. Online criminal and traffic records date from 01/97.

General Information: Public Access terminal is available. Copy fee: $.25 per page. Certification fee: $1.25. Payee: Cass County Court. No personal checks accepted. Prepayment required.

Cedar County

District Court PO Box 796, Hartington, NE 68739-0796; 402-254-6957; Fax: 402-254-6954. Hours: 8AM-5PM (CST). *Felony, Civil Actions Over $45,000.*

Civil Records: Access: In person, online. Visitors must perform in person searches for themselves. Search fee: none. Required to search: name, years to search. Civil cases indexed by defendant, plaintiff. Civil records in books from 1890. An online subscription service is available; same as criminal access. Online records date from 11/99.

Criminal Records: Access: In person, online. Visitors must perform in person searches for themselves. Search fee: none. Required to search: name, years to search; also helpful: SSN. Criminal records in books from 1890. A subscription service is at www.nebraska.gov/faqs/justice/. Fee is $.60 a record or $300 per month flat rate, also there is a start-up fee. Online records date from 11/99.

General Information: Public Access terminal is available. No mental health records released. Copy fee: $.25 per page. Certification fee: $1.00. Payee: District Court. Prepayment required.

Cedar County Court P O Box 695, Hartington, NE 68739; 402-254-7441; Fax: 402-254-6954. Hours: 8AM-5PM (CST). *Misdemeanor, Civil Actions Under $45,000, Eviction, Small Claims, Probate.*

Civil Records: Access: In person, online. Visitors must perform in person searches for themselves. No

search fee. Required to search: name, years to search. Civil cases indexed by defendant. Civil records on general index, docket books 15 years; some on microfiche to 1983. An online subscription service is available; same as criminal access. Online civil and probate records from 11/00 forward.

Criminal Records: Access: In person, online. Visitors must perform in person searches for themselves. Search fee: none. Required to search: name, years to search, offense; also helpful: DOB. Criminal records on general index, docket books since 1983, some on microfiche. Computerized records go back to 2000. A subscription service is at www.nebraska.gov/faqs/justice/. Fee is $.60 a record or $300 per month flat rate, also there is a start-up fee. Online criminal and traffic records date from 06/00.

General Information: Public Access terminal is available. No juvenile or judge sealed records released. Copy fee: $.25 per page. Certification fee: $1.00. Payee: Cedar County Court. Personal checks accepted. Prepayment required.

Chase County

District Court PO Box 1299, Imperial, NE 69033; 308-882-5266; Fax: 308-882-5390. Hours: 8AM-4PM (MST). *Felony, Civil Actions Over $15,000.*

Civil Records: Access: Phone, fax, mail, in person, online. Both court and visitors may perform in person searches. Search fee: $5.00 per name. Required to search: name, years to search. Civil cases indexed by defendant, plaintiff. Civil records general index, docket books from early 1900s. An online subscription service is available; same as criminal access. Online records date from 05/00.

Criminal Records: Access: Phone, fax, mail, In person, online. Both court and visitors may perform in person searches. Search fee: $5.00 per name. Required to search: name, years to search; also helpful: DOB, SSN. Criminal records general index, docket books from early 1900s, computerized since 2000. A subscription service is at www.nebraska.gov/faqs/justice/. Fee is $.60 a record or $300 per month flat rate, also there is a start-up fee. Online records date from 05/00.

General Information: Public Access terminal is available. No restrictions. Will fax results $1.00 per page. Copy fee: $.25 per page. Certification fee: $1.50. Payee: Chase County Clerk. Personal checks accepted. Prepayment required. Mail requests: SASE required. Mail turnaround time 5 days.

Chase County Court PO Box 1299, Imperial, NE 69033; 308-882-4690; Fax: 308-882-5679. Hours: 8:00AM-4:00PM (MST). *Misdemeanor, Civil Actions Under $45,000, Eviction, Small Claims, Probate.*

Civil Records: Access: Mail, in person, online. Both court and visitors may perform in person searches. No search fee. Required to search: name, years to search. Civil records on general index, docket books from 1910; prior incomplete. Some probate on microfiche. An online subscription service is available; same as criminal access. Online civil records date from 11/00 forward, probate from 12/00.

Criminal Records: Access: Mail, In person, online. Both court and visitors may perform in person searches. No search fee. Required to search: name, years to search, DOB. Criminal records on general index, docket books from 1910; prior incomplete. Some probate on microfiche. A subscription service is at www.nebraska.gov/faqs/justice/. Fee is $.60 a record or $300 per month flat rate, also there is a start-up fee. Online criminal and traffic records date from 09/00.

General Information: Public Access terminal is available. No adoption, juvenile. Will fax results to local or toll free line. Copy fee: $.25 per page.

Certification fee: $1.00. Payee: Chase County Court. Personal checks accepted. Prepayment required. Mail requests: SASE required. Mail turnaround time 1 day.

Cherry County

District Court 365 N Main St, Valentine, NE 69201; 402-376-1840; Fax: 402-376-3830. Hours: 8:30AM-4:30PM (MST). *Felony, Civil Actions Over $45,000.*

Civil Records: Access: In person, online. Visitors must perform in person searches for themselves. No search fee. Required to search: name, years to search; also helpful: address. Civil cases indexed by petitioner, respondent. Civil records on index books from late 1800s. An online subscription service is available; same as criminal access. Justice records date from 03/99.

Criminal Records: Access: In person, online. Visitors must perform in person searches for themselves. No search fee. Required to search: name, years to search. Criminal records on index books from late 1800s; computerized records since 1999. A subscription service is at www.nebraska.gov/faqs/justice/. Fee is $.60 a record or $300 per month flat rate, also there is a start-up fee. Online records date from 03/99.

General Information: Public Access terminal is available. No juvenile records. Will not fax results. Copy fee: $.25 per page. Certification fee: $1.00. Payee: Clerk of District Court. Personal checks accepted. Prepayment required.

Cherry County Court 365 N Main St, Valentine, NE 69201; 402-376-2590; Fax: 402-376-5942. Hours: 8AM-5PM (CST). *Misdemeanor, Civil Actions Under $45,000, Eviction, Small Claims, Probate.*

Civil Records: Access: In person, online. Visitors must perform in person searches for themselves. No search fee. Required to search: name, years to search. Civil cases indexed by defendant. Civil records on docket card file from 1986, general index prior from late 1800s. An online subscription service is available; same as criminal access. Online civil and probate records from 11/00 forward.

Criminal Records: Access: In person, online. Visitors must perform in person searches for themselves. No search fee. Required to search: name, years to search, DOB. Criminal records on docket card file from 1986, general index prior from late 1800s; on computer since 8/2000. A subscription service is at www.nebraska.gov/faqs/justice/. Fee is $.60 a record or $300 per month flat rate, also there is a start-up fee. Online criminal and traffic records date from 08/20.

General Information: Public Access terminal is available. No adoption records released. Juvenile released only to parties involved. Will fax specifc case file requests for $3.00 1st page and $1.00 ea add'l. Copy fee: $.25 per page. Certification fee: $1.25. Payee: Cherry County Court. Personal checks accepted. Prepayment required.

Cheyenne County

District Court PO Box 217, Sidney, NE 69162; 308-254-2814; Fax: 308-254-7832. Hours: 8AM-Noon,1-5PM (MST). *Felony, Civil Actions Over $15,000.*

Civil Records: Access: In person, online. Visitors must perform in person searches for themselves. No search fee. Required to search: name, years to search. Civil cases indexed by defendant, plaintiff. Civil records on general index, docket books going back to late 1800s, on computer since 09/98. An online subscription service is available; same as criminal access. Online records date from 08/98.

Criminal Records: Access: In person, online. Visitors must perform in person searches for themselves. No search fee. Required to search: name, years to search; also helpful: DOB, SSN. Criminal records on general index, docket books going back to late 1800s, on computer since 09/98. A subscription service is at www.nebraska.gov/faqs/justice/. Fee is $.60 a record or $300 per month flat rate, also there is a start-up fee. Online records date from 08/98.

General Information: Public Access terminal is available. No mental health or search warrants released. Will fax results to local or toll free line. Copy fee: $.50 per page. Certification fee: $2.00. Payee: Clerk of District Court. Personal checks not accepted. Prepayment required. Attorneys may be billed.

Cheyenne County Court 1000 10th Ave, Sidney, NE 69162; 308-254-2929; Fax: 308-254-4641 permission to use required. Hours: 8AM-5PM (MST). *Misdemeanor, Civil Actions Under $45,000, Eviction, Small Claims, Probate.*

Civil Records: Access: Mail, in person, online. Both court and visitors may perform in person searches. No search fee. Required to search: name, years to search. Civil cases indexed by defendant, plaintiff. Civil records on index books from late 1800s. Fax access requires special permission. A subscription service is at www.nebraska.gov/business/egov.phtml. Fee is $.60 a record or $300 per month flat rate, also there is a start-up fee.

Criminal Records: Access: Mail, In person, online. Both court and visitors may perform in person searches. No search fee. Required to search: name, years to search; also helpful: DOB. Criminal records on index books from late 1800s; computerized records since 2000. A subscription service is at www.nebraska.gov/faqs/justice/. Fee is $.60 a record or $300 per month flat rate, also there is a start-up fee. Online criminal and traffic records date from 06/00.

General Information: Public Access terminal is available. No adoption, juvenile, confidential records released. Copy fee: $.25 per page. Certification fee: $1.00. Payee: Cheyenne County Court. Personal checks accepted. Prepayment required. Mail requests: SASE required. Mail turnaround time within 1 week.

Clay County

District Court Clerk of The District Court, 111 W Fairfield St, Clay Center, NE 68933; 402-762-3595; Fax: 402-762-3604. Hours: 8:30AM-5PM (CST). *Felony, Civil Actions Over $15,000.*

Civil Records: Access: In person, online. Visitors must perform in person searches for themselves. No search fee. Required to search: name; also helpful: years to search. Civil cases indexed by defendant, plaintiff. Civil records on index books from late 1800s, on microfiche from 1986, computerized since 1997. An online subscription service is available; same as criminal access. Online records date from 09/98.

Criminal Records: Access: In person, online. Visitors must perform in person searches for themselves. No search fee. Required to search: name, DOB; also helpful: years to search, SSN. Criminal records on index books from late 1800s, on microfiche from 1986, computerized since 1997. A subscription service is at www.nebraska.gov/faqs/justice/. Fee is $.60 a record or $300 per month flat rate, also there is a start-up fee. Online records date from 09/98.

General Information: Public Access terminal is available. No mental health records released. Copy fee: $.25 per page. Certification fee: $1.00. Payee: Clerk of District Court. Personal checks accepted.

Clay County Court 111 W Fairfield St, Clay Center, NE 68933; 402-762-3651; Fax: 402-762-3250. Hours: 8:30AM-5PM (CST). *Misdemeanor, Civil Actions Under $45,000, Eviction, Small Claims, Probate, Traffic, Juvenile.*

Civil Records: Access: In person, online. Visitors must perform in person searches for themselves. No search fee. Required to search: name, years to search. Civil cases indexed by defendant. Civil records in index books from late 1800s, on computer from 04/00. An online subscription service is available; same as criminal access. Online records date from 04/00, including probate.

Criminal Records: Access: In person, online. Visitors must perform in person searches for themselves. No search fee. Required to search: name, years to search; also helpful: DOB, SSN. Criminal records in index books from late 1800s. A subscription service is available at www.nebraska.gov/faqs/justice/. Fee is $.60 a record or $300 per month flat rate, also there is a start-up fee. Online criminal and traffic records date from 04/00.

General Information: Public Access terminal is available. No adoption or juvenile records released. Copy fee: $.25 per page. Certification fee: $1.00. Payee: Clay County. Personal checks accepted. Prepayment required.

Colfax County

District Court 411 E 11th St, Schuyler, NE 68661; 402-352-8506; Fax: 402-352-8550. 8:30AM-4:30PM (CST). *Felony, Civil Actions Over $15,000.* www.colfaxcounty.ne.gov

Civil Records: Access: In person, online. Visitors must perform in person searches for themselves. No search fee. Required to search: name, years to search; also helpful: address. Civil cases indexed by defendant, plaintiff. Civil records on index books and general index from 1880. An online subscription service is available; same as criminal access. Online records date from 04/97.

Criminal Records: Access: In person, online. Visitors must perform in person searches for themselves. No search fee. Required to search: name, years to search; also helpful: address, DOB, SSN. Criminal records on index books and general index from 1880. A subscription service is at www.nebraska.gov/faqs/justice/. Fee is $.60 a record or $300 per month flat rate, also there is a start-up fee. Online records date from 04/97.

General Information: Public Access terminal is available. No juvenile or mental health records released. Will fax results for $1.00 per page. Copy fee: $.30 per page. Certification fee: $1.50. Payee: Clerk of District Court. Business checks accepted. Will take local personal check. Prepayment required.

Colfax County Court 411 E 11th St, Box 191, Schuyler, NE 68661; 402-352-8511; Fax: 402-352-8535. Hours: 8AM-4;30PM (CST). *Misdemeanor, Civil Actions Under $45,000, Eviction, Small Claims, Probate.*

Civil Records: Access: In person, online. Visitors must perform in person searches for themselves. No search fee. Required to search: name, years to search. Civil cases indexed by defendant, plaintiff. Civil records on index books from 1880s; computerized records since 1996. An online subscription service is available; same as criminal access. Online civil records date from 10/99 forward, probate from 05/98.

Criminal Records: Access: In person, online. Visitors must perform in person searches for themselves. No search fee. Required to search: name, years to search; also helpful: DOB, SSN. Criminal records on index books from 1880s; computerized records since 1996. A subscription service is at www.nebraska.gov/faqs/justice/. Fee is $.60 a record

or $300 per month flat rate, also there is a start-up fee. Online criminal and traffic records date from 10/96.

General Information: Public Access terminal is available. No juvenile records released. Copy fee: $.25 per page. Certification fee: $1.00. Payee: Colfax County Court. Personal checks accepted. Prepayment required.

Cuming County

District Court 200 S Lincoln, Rm 200, West Point, NE 68788; 402-372-6004; Probate phone: 402-372-6003; Fax: 402-372-6017. Hours: 8:30AM-4:30PM (CST). *Felony, Civil Actions Over $15,000.*

Civil Records: Access: Mail, fax, in person. Both court and visitors may perform in person searches. Search fee: $10.00 (fax only). Required to search: name, years to search. Civil cases indexed by defendant, plaintiff. Civil records in books from 1939; on computer back to 2000. An online subscription service is available; same as criminal access. Online records date from 11/99.

Criminal Records: Access: Fax, in person, online. Both court and visitors may perform in person searches. Search fee: $10.00 (fax only). Required to search: name, years to search. Criminal records in books from 1939; on computer back to 2000. A subscription service is at www.nebraska.gov/faqs/justice/. Fee is $.60 a record or $300 per month flat rate, also there is a start-up fee. Online records date from 11/99.

General Information: Public Access terminal is available. No mental health records released. Will fax results if you provide copy of your check for services. Copy fee: $.25 per page. Certification fee: $1.00. No personal checks accepted. Prepayment required.

Cuming County Court 200 S Lincoln, Rm 103, West Point, NE 68788; 402-372-6003; Fax: 402-372-6030. Hours: 8:30AM-4:30PM (CST). *Misdemeanor, Civil Actions Under $45,000, Eviction, Small Claims, Probate.*

Civil Records: Access: In person, online. Visitors must perform in person searches for themselves. No search fee. Required to search: name, years to search. Civil cases indexed by defendant, plaintiff. Civil records on index cards, also on computer since April 2000. An online subscription service is available; same as criminal access. Online records date from 04/00, including probate.

Criminal Records: Access: In person, online. Visitors must perform in person searches for themselves. No search fee. Required to search: name, years to search; also helpful: DOB, SSN. Criminal records on index cards, also on computer since April 2000. A subscription service is at www.nebraska.gov/faqs/justice/. Fee is $.60 a record or $300 per month flat rate, also there is a start-up fee. Online criminal and traffic records date from 03/00.

General Information: Public Access terminal is available. (Public terminal is located in the District Court office.) No mental health records released. Copy fee: $.25 per page. Certification fee: $1.00. Personal checks accepted; ID required. Prepayment required.

Custer County

District Court 431 S 10th Ave, Broken Bow, NE 68822; 308-872-2121; Fax: 308-872-5826. Hours: 9AM-5PM (CST). *Felony, Civil Actions Over $15,000.*

Civil Records: Access: Phone, fax, mail, in person, online. Both court and visitors may perform in person searches. No search fee. Required to search: name, years to search; also helpful: address. Civil cases indexed by defendant, plaintiff. Civil records on index books and docket books from late 1800s; on computer back to 4/1998. An online subscription service is available; same as criminal access. Online records date from 03/98.

Criminal Records: Access: Phone, fax, mail, In person, online. Both court and visitors may perform in person searches. No search fee. Required to search: name, years to search; also helpful: address, DOB, SSN. Criminal records on index books and docket books from late 1800s; on computer back to 4/1998. A subscription service is available at www.nebraska.gov/faqs/justice/. Fee is $.60 a record or $300 per month flat rate, also there is a start-up fee. Online records date from 03/98.

General Information: Public Access terminal is available. No search warrants, mental health, or sealed records released. Fee to fax results is $3.00 per page. Copy fee: $.25 per page. Certification fee: $1.25. Payee: Clerk of District Court. Business checks accepted. Prepayment required. Mail requests: SASE required. Mail turnaround time 3-4 days.

Custer County Court 431 South 10th Ave, Broken Bow, NE 68822; 308-872-5761; Fax: 308-872-6052. Hours: 8AM-12 1-5PM (CST). *Misdemeanor, Civil Actions Under $45,000, Eviction, Small Claims, Probate.*

Civil Records: Access: In person, online. Visitors must perform in person searches for themselves. No search fee. Required to search: name, years to search. Civil cases indexed by defendant, plaintiff. Civil records on computer back to 2000, on index books from 1988, probate from 1986, balance are archived. An online subscription service is available; same as criminal access. Online records date from 01/01, including probate.

Criminal Records: Access: In person, online. Visitors must perform in person searches for themselves. No search fee. Required to search: name, years to search. Criminal records on computer back to 2000, index books from 1988, probate from 1986, balance are archived. A subscription service is at www.nebraska.gov/faqs/justice/. Fee is $.60 a record or $300 per month flat rate, also there is a start-up fee. Online criminal and traffic records date from 07/17/00.

General Information: No adoption records released. Copy fee: $.25 per page. Certification fee: $1.25. Payee: Custer County Court. Personal checks accepted. Prepayment required.

Dakota County

District Court PO Box 66, Dakota City, NE 68731; 402-987-2115; Fax: 402-987-2117. Hours: 8AM-4:30PM (CST). *Felony, Civil Actions Over $15,000.*

Civil Records: Access: In person, online. Visitors must perform in person searches for themselves. No search fee. Required to search: name, years to search. Civil cases indexed by defendant, plaintiff. Civil records on index books from 1985, prior records archived at NE State Historical Society, Lincoln, NE; computerized records since 1998. An online subscription service is available; same as criminal access. Online records date from 03/98.

Criminal Records: Access: In person, online mail,fax. Both court and visitors may perform in person searches. No search fee. Required to search: name, years to search. Criminal records on index books from 1985, prior records archived at NE State Historical Society, Lincoln, NE; computerized records since 1998. A subscription service is at www.nebraska.gov/faqs/justice/. Fee is $.60 a record or $300 per month flat rate, also there is a start-up fee. Online records date from 03/98.

General Information: Public Access terminal is available. No juvenile or mental health records released. Copy fee: $.25 per page. Certification fee: $1.00. Payee: Clerk of District Court. Personal checks

accepted. Prepayment required. Mail requests: SASE required.

Dakota County Court PO Box 385, Dakota City, NE 68731; 402-987-2145; Fax: 402-987-2185. Hours: 8AM-4:30PM (CST). *Misdemeanor, Civil Actions Under $45,000, Eviction, Small Claims, Probate.*

Civil Records: Access: In person, online mail,fax. Visitors must perform in person searches for themselves. No search fee. Required to search: name, years to search. Civil cases indexed by defendant, plaintiff. Civil records on index books from late 1800s. An online subscription service is available; same as criminal access. Online civil records date from 10/99 forward, probate from 05/98.

Criminal Records: Access: In person, online mail,fax. Visitors must perform in person searches for themselves. No search fee. Required to search: name, years to search. Criminal records on index books from late 1800s. A subscription service is at www.nebraska.gov/faqs/justice/. Fee is $.60 a record or $300 per month flat rate, also there is a start-up fee. Online criminal and traffic records date from 10/97.

General Information: Public Access terminal is available. No adoption or juvenile records released. Copy fee: $.25 per page. Certification fee: $1.00. Payee: Dakota County Court. Business checks accepted. Prepayment required. Mail requests: SASE not required. Mail turnaround time is 1 days.

Dawes County

District Court PO Box 630, Chadron, NE 69337; 308-432-0109; Fax: 308-432-0110. Hours: 8:30AM-4:30PM (MST). *Felony, Civil Actions Over $15,000.*

Civil Records: Access: In person, online. Visitors must perform in person searches for themselves. No search fee. Required to search: name, years to search. Civil cases indexed by defendant, plaintiff. Civil records on general index, docket books from 1886. An online subscription service is available; same as criminal access. Online records date from 08/98.

Criminal Records: Access: In person, online. Visitors must perform in person searches for themselves. No search fee. Required to search: name, years to search. Criminal records on general index, docket books from 1886. A subscription service is at www.nebraska.gov/faqs/justice/. Fee is $.60 a record or $300 per month flat rate, also there is a start-up fee. Online records date from 08/98.

General Information: Public Access terminal is available. No mental health records released. Copy fee: $.25 per page. Certification fee: $1.00. Payee: Clerk of District Court. Personal checks accepted.

Dawes County Court PO Box 806, Chadron, NE 69337; 308-432-0116; Fax: 308-432-0118. Hours: 7:30AM-4:30PM (MST). *Misdemeanor, Civil Actions Under $45,000, Eviction, Small Claims, Probate.*

Civil Records: Access: In person, online. Visitors must perform in person searches for themselves. No search fee. Required to search: name, years to search. Civil cases indexed by defendant, plaintiff. Civil records on case cards, case files kept since 1892; on computer back to 2001. An online subscription service is available; same as criminal access. Online civil and probate records from 11/00 forward.

Criminal Records: Access: In person, online. Visitors must perform in person searches for themselves. No search fee. Required to search: name, years to search, DOB; also helpful: address. Criminal records on case cards, case files kept since 1892; on computer back to 2000. A subscription service is at www.nebraska.gov/faqs/justice/. Fee is $.60 a record or $300 per month flat rate, also there is a start-up fee. Online criminal and traffic records date from 04/00.

General Information: Public Access terminal is available. No confidential records released. No copy fee. Certification fee: $1.00. Payee: Dawes County Court. Personal checks accepted. Prepayment required.

Dawson County

District Court PO Box 429, Lexington, NE 68850; 308-324-4261; Fax: 308-324-3374. Hours: 8AM-5PM (CST). *Felony, Civil Actions Over $15,000.*

www.dawsoncountyne.net

Civil Records: Access: In person, online. Visitors must perform in person searches for themselves. No search fee. Required to search: name, years to search. Civil cases indexed by defendant, plaintiff. Recent civil records on microfiche, some older records on microfilm, index books date to late 1800s. An online subscription service is available; same as criminal access. Online records date from 06/97.

Criminal Records: Access: In person, online. Visitors must perform in person searches for themselves. No search fee. Required to search: name, years to search. Recent records on microfiche, some older records on microfilm, index books date to late 1800s. A subscription service is available at www.nebraska.gov/faqs/justice/. Fee is $.60 a record or $300 per month flat rate, also there is a start-up fee. Online records date from 06/97.

General Information: Public Access terminal is available. No juvenile or mental health records released. Copy fee: $.25 per page. Certification fee: $1.00. Payee: Clerk of District Court. Personal checks accepted. Prepayment required.

Dawson County Court 700 N Washington St, Lexington, NE 68850; 308-324-5606; Fax: 308-324-5607. Hours: 8AM-5PM (CST). *Misdemeanor, Civil Actions Under $45,000, Eviction, Small Claims, Probate.*

Note: Court personnel will only search records if specific case # given, turnaround time is 3-5 days.

Civil Records: Access: In person, online. Visitors must perform in person searches for themselves. No search fee. Required to search: name, years to search; also helpful: address. Civil cases indexed by defendant, plaintiff. Civil records on books from late 1800s, docket books 15 years back; on computer since 1998. An online subscription service is available; same as criminal access. Online civil records date from 10/99 forward, probate from 05/98.

Criminal Records: Access: In person, online. Visitors must perform in person searches for themselves. No search fee. Required to search: name, years to search, offense, DOB; also helpful: address, SSN. Criminal records on books from late 1800s, docket books 15 years back; on computer since 1998. A subscription service is available at www.nebraska.gov/faqs/justice/. Fee is $.60 a record or $300 per month flat rate, also there is a start-up fee. Online criminal and traffic records date from 05/00.

General Information: Public Access terminal is available. No adoption or juvenile records released. Will fax specific documents for $3.00 1st page, $1.00 ea add'l. Copy fee: $.25 per page. Certification fee: $1.00. Payee: Dawson County Court. Personal checks accepted. Visa, MC accepted. Prepayment required.

Deuel County

District Court PO Box 327, Chappell, NE 69129; 308-874-3308/2818; Fax: 308-874-3472. Hours: 8AM-4PM (MST). *Felony, Civil Actions Over $15,000.*

Civil Records: Access: Phone, fax, mail, in person, online. Both court and visitors may perform in person searches. No search fee. Required to search: name;

also helpful: years to search. Civil cases indexed by defendant, plaintiff. Civil records on general index and docket books form late 1800s. An online subscription service is available; same as criminal access. Online records date from 05/00.

Criminal Records: Access: Phone, fax, mail, In person, online. Both court and visitors may perform in person searches. No search fee. Required to search: name; also helpful: years to search, DOB, SSN. Criminal records on general index and docket books form late 1800s. A subscription service is at www.nebraska.gov/faqs/justice/. Fee is $.60 a record or $300 per month flat rate, also there is a start-up fee. Online records date from 05/00.

General Information: No mental health or service discharge records released. No fee to fax results. Copy fee: $.25. Certification fee: $1.00 for 1st page, $.25 each add'l page. Payee: Clerk of District Court. Personal checks accepted. Prepayment required. Mail requests: SASE required. Mail turnaround time 1 week.

Deuel County Court PO Box 514, Chappell, NE 69129; 308-874-2909; Fax: 308-874-3472. Hours: 8AM-4PM (MST). *Misdemeanor, Civil Actions Under $45,000, Eviction, Small Claims, Probate.*
Civil Records: Access: Mail, in person, online. Both court and visitors may perform in person searches. No search fee. Required to search: name, years to search. Civil cases indexed by defendant, plaintiff. Civil records on index cards from 1989, computerized since 2001. An online subscription service is available; same as criminal access. Online civil and probate records from 12/00 forward.
Criminal Records: Access: Mail, In person, online. Both court and visitors may perform in person searches. No search fee. Required to search: name, years to search, DOB, signed release. Criminal records on index cards from 1989, computerized since 2001. A subscription service is at www.nebraska.gov/faqs/justice/. Fee is $.60 a record or $300 per month flat rate, also there is a start-up fee. Online criminal and traffic records date from 12/00.
General Information: Public Access terminal is available. No juvenile records released. Will fax results. Copy fee: $.25 per page. Certification fee: $1.00 per page. Payee: Deuel County Court. No personal checks accepted. Prepayment required. Mail requests: SASE required. Mail turnaround time 3-4 days.

Dixon County

District Court PO Box 395, Ponca, NE 68770; 402-755-2881; Fax: 402-755-2632. 8AM-Noon, 1-5PM (CST). *Felony, Civil Actions Over $15,000.*
Civil Records: Access: In person, online. Visitors must perform in person searches for themselves. No search fee. Required to search: name, years to search. Civil cases indexed by defendant, plaintiff. Civil records on books from 1876; computerized records go back to 1999. An online subscription service is available; same as criminal access. Online records date from 11/99.
Criminal Records: Access: In person, online. Visitors must perform in person searches for themselves. No search fee. Required to search: name, years to search, DOB. Criminal records on books from 1876; computerized records go back to 1999. A subscription service is at www.nebraska.gov/faqs/justice/. Fee is $.60 a record or $300 per month flat rate, also there is a start-up fee. Online records date from 11/99.
General Information: Public Access terminal is available. No mental health records released. Will not fax results. Copy fee: $.25 per page. Certification fee: $1.00. Payee: Clerk of District Court. Personal checks accepted. Will bill copy fees.

Dixon County Court PO Box 497, Ponca, NE 68770; 402-755-2355; Fax: 402-755-2632. Hours: 8AM-4:30PM (CST). *Misdemeanor, Civil Actions Under $45,000, Eviction, Small Claims, Probate.*
Civil Records: Access: In person, online. Visitors must perform in person searches for themselves. No search fee. Required to search: name, years to search. Civil cases indexed by defendant, plaintiff. Civil records in files, cards from 1987, prior in dockets from 1876, computerized since 2000. An online subscription service is available; same as criminal access. Online civil records date from 11/01 forward, probate from 01/01.
Criminal Records: Access: In person, online. Visitors must perform in person searches for themselves. No search fee. Required to search: name, years to search, DOB. Criminal records in files, cards from 1987, prior in dockets from 1876, computerized since 2000. A subscription service is at www.nebraska.gov/faqs/justice/. Fee is $.60 a record or $300 per month flat rate, also there is a start-up fee. Online criminal and traffic records date from 07/00.
General Information: Public Access terminal is available. No adoption or juvenile records released. Copy fee: $.25 per page. Certification fee: $1.00. Payee: Dixon County Court. Personal checks accepted. Prepayment required.

Dodge County

District Court PO Box 1237, Fremont, NE 68026; 402-727-2780; Fax: 402-727-2773. Hours: 8:30AM-4:30PM (CST). *Felony, Civil Actions Over $15,000.*
Civil Records: Access: In person, online. Visitors must perform in person searches for themselves. No search fee. Required to search: name, years to search. Civil cases indexed by defendant, plaintiff. Civil records on general index, docket books from late 1800s; computerized records since 1997. An online subscription service is available; same as criminal access. Online records date from 09/97.
Criminal Records: Access: In person, online. Visitors must perform in person searches for themselves. No search fee. Required to search: name, years to search. Criminal records on general index, docket books from late 1800s; computerized records since 1997. A subscription service is at www.nebraska.gov/faqs/justice/. Fee is $.60 a record or $300 per month flat rate, also there is a start-up fee. Online records date from 09/97.
General Information: Public Access terminal is available. No mental health records released. Copy fee: $.25 per page. Certification fee: $1.50. Payee: District Court. Personal checks accepted. Prepayment required.

Dodge County Court 428 N Broad St, Fremont, NE 68025; 402-727-2755; Fax: 402-727-2762. Hours: 8AM-5PM (CST). *Misdemeanor, Civil Actions Under $45,000, Eviction, Small Claims, Probate.*
Civil Records: Access: In person, online. Visitors must perform in person searches for themselves. No search fee. Required to search: name, years to search. Civil cases indexed by defendant. Civil records on general index, docket books from early 1900s; on computer back to 1998. Probate on microfilm from early 1900s. An online subscription service is available; same as criminal access. Online civil records date from 01/00 forward, probate from 05/98.
Criminal Records: Access: In person, online. Visitors must perform in person searches for themselves. No search fee. Required to search: name, years to search; also helpful: DOB. Criminal records on general index, docket books from early 1900s; on computer back to 1998. A subscription service is at www.nebraska.gov/faqs/justice/. Fee is $.60 a record or $300 per month flat rate, also there is a start-up fee.

Online criminal and traffic records date from 01/20/97.
General Information: Public Access terminal is available. No adoption or juvenile records released. Copy fee: $.25 per page. Certification fee: $1.00 per document plus $.25 per page. Payee: Dodge County Court. Prepayment required.

Douglas County

District Court 1701 Farnam, Hall of Justice, Rm 300, Omaha, NE 68183; 402-444-7018; Fax: 402-444-1757. Hours: 8AM-4:30PM (CST). *Felony, Civil Actions Over $15,000.*

www.co.douglas.ne.us
Civil Records: Access: Mail, in person, online. Both court and visitors may perform in person searches. Search fee: $5.00 per name. Required to search: name, years to search; also helpful: address. Civil cases indexed by defendant, plaintiff. Civil records on computer from 1980, on books back to late 1800s. Access to the Internet system at www.co.douglas.ne.us/cpan/index.htm requires registration and password. Call CPAN at 402-444-7117 for more information. System can be searched by name or case number.
Criminal Records: Access: Mail, In person, online. Visitors must perform in person searches for themselves. Search fee: $5.00 per name. Required to search: name, years to search; also helpful: address, DOB, SSN. Criminal records on computer from 1980, on books back to late 1800s. Access to the Internet system at www.co.douglas.ne.us/cpan/index.htm requires registration and password. Call CPAN at 402-444-7117 for more information. System can be searched by name or case number.
General Information: Public Access terminal is available. No juvenile records released. Copy fee: $.50 per page. $1.00 minimum. Add $.50 postage fee. Certification fee: $3.50 for 1-5 pages, then $.50 per page. Payee: Clerk of District Court. Personal checks accepted. Prepayment required. Mail requests: SASE required. Mail turnaround time 1-2 days.

Douglas County Court 1819 Farnam, #F03, Omaha, NE 68183; Civil phone: 402-444-5424; Criminal phone: 402-444-5387; Fax: 402-444-2325. 8AM-4:30PM (CST). *Misdemeanor, Civil Actions Under $45,000, Eviction, Small Claims, Probate.*
www.co.douglas.ne.us
Civil Records: Access: Mail, online, in person. Visitors must perform in person searches for themselves. No search fee. Required to search: name, years to search. Civil cases indexed by defendant, plaintiff. Civil records on computer from 1987 (small claims), from 1983 (civil). Civil records are purged after about 20 years. Access to the Internet system at www.co.douglas.ne.us/cpan/index.htm requires registration and password. Call CPAN at 402-444-7117 for more information. System can be searched by name or case number. A subscription service is at www.nebraska.gov/business/egov.phtml. Fee is $.60 a record or $300 per month flat rate, also there is a start-up fee. Online civil records date from 10/18/99 forward, probate from 03/00.
Criminal Records: Access: In person, online. Visitors must perform in person searches for themselves. No search fee. Required to search: name, years to search; also helpful: DOB. Criminal records on computer from 1987 (small claims), from 1983 (civil). Civil records are purged after about 20 years. Online access to criminal records is the same as civil. Online criminal and traffic records date from 04/96.
General Information: Public Access terminal is available. Copy fee: $.25 per page. Certification fee: $1.00. Payee: Douglas County Court. Personal checks accepted. Prepayment required.

Dundy County

District Court PO Box 506, Benkelman, NE 69021; 308-423-2058. Hours: 8AM-4PM (MST). *Felony, Civil Actions Over $15,000.*

Civil Records: Access: Phone, mail, in person, online. Both court and visitors may perform in person searches. No search fee. Required to search: name, years to search; also helpful: address. Civil cases indexed by defendant, plaintiff. Civil records on index books from late 1800s. An online subscription service is available; same as criminal access. Online records date from 08/00.

Criminal Records: Access: In person, online. Only the court performs in person searches; visitors may not. No search fee. Required to search: name, years to search; also helpful: address, DOB, SSN. Criminal records on index books from late 1800s. A subscription service is available at www.nebraska.gov/faqs/justice/. Fee is $.60 a record or $300 per month flat rate, also there is a start-up fee. Online records date from 08/00.

General Information: Public Access terminal is available. No juvenile records released. Copy fee: $1.00 per page. Certification fee: $1.50. Payee: Clerk of District Court. Personal checks accepted. Prepayment required.

Dundy County Court PO Box 378, Benkelman, NE 69021; 308-423-2374. Hours: 8AM-4PM (MST). *Misdemeanor, Civil Actions Under $45,000, Eviction, Small Claims, Probate.*

Civil Records: Access: In person, online. Visitors must perform in person searches for themselves. No search fee. Required to search: name, years to search. Civil cases indexed by defendant, plaintiff. Civil records on general index, docket books from late 1800s; some probate, civil on microfiche. An online subscription service is available; same as criminal access. Online civil records date from 11/00 forward, probate from 12/00.

Criminal Records: Access: In person, online. Visitors must perform in person searches themselves. No search fee. Required to search: name, years to search, DOB, signed release; also helpful: address. Criminal records on general index, docket books from late 1800s, computerized since 2001; some probate, civil on microfiche. A subscription service is at www.nebraska.gov/faqs/justice/. Fee is $.60 a record or $300 per month flat rate, also there is a start-up fee. Online criminal and traffic records date from 08/00.

General Information: Public Access terminal is available. No adoption or juvenile records released. Will fax specifc case file requests for $3.00 charge for 1st page, $1.00 each add'l page. Copy fee: $.25 per page. Certification fee: $1.00 per document. Payee: Dundy County Court. Business checks accepted. Prepayment required.

Fillmore County

District Court PO Box 147, Geneva, NE 68361-0147; 402-759-3811; Fax: 402-759-4440. Hours: 8AM-Noon, 1-5PM (CST). *Felony, Civil Actions Over $15,000.*
www.fillmorecounty.org

Civil Records: Access: Phone, fax, mail, in person, online. Both court and visitors may perform in person searches. No search fee. Required to search: name, years to search. Civil cases indexed by defendant, plaintiff. Civil records on index books to late 1800s, last 8 years on computer. An online subscription service is available; same as criminal access. Online records date from 06/98.

Criminal Records: Access: Phone, fax, mail, In person, online. Both court and visitors may perform in person searches. No search fee. Required to search: name, years to search, DOB. Criminal records on index books to late 1800s, last 8 years on computer. A subscription service is at www.nebraska.gov/faqs/justice/. Fee is $.60 a record or $300 per month flat rate, also there is a start-up fee. Online records date from 06/98.

General Information: Public Access terminal is available. No juvenile or mental health records released. Will fax results $2.00 1st page, $1.00 each add'l. Copy fee: $.35 per page. Certification fee: $1.00. Payee: Clerk of District Court. Personal checks accepted. Prepayment required. Will bill fax and copy fees. Mail requests: SASE required. Mail turnaround time 1-5 days.

Fillmore County Court PO Box 66, Geneva, NE 68361; 402-759-3514; Fax: 402-759-4440. Hours: 8AM-5PM (CST). *Misdemeanor, Civil Actions Under $45,000, Eviction, Small Claims, Probate.*

Civil Records: Access: Fax, mail, in person, online. Both court and visitors may perform in person searches. No search fee. Required to search: name, years to search. Civil cases indexed by defendant, plaintiff. Civil records on general index, docket books from late 1800s; probate on microfiche. An online subscription service is available; same as criminal access. Online civil and probate records from 02/00 forward.

Criminal Records: Access: Fax, mail, In person, online. Both court and visitors may perform in person searches. No search fee. Required to search: name, years to search. Criminal records on general index, docket books from late 1800s; probate on microfiche. A subscription service is available at www.nebraska.gov/faqs/justice/. Fee is $.60 a record or $300 per month flat rate, also there is a start-up fee. Online criminal and traffic records date from 02/00.

General Information: Public Access terminal is available. No adoption or juvenile records released. Will fax results $2.00 1st page, $1.00 each add'l. Copy fee: $.25 per page. Certification fee: $1.25. Payee: County Court. Personal checks accepted. Prepayment required. Mail requests: SASE required. Mail turnaround time 7-8 days.

Franklin County

District Court PO Box 146, Franklin, NE 68939; 308-425-6202; Fax: 308-425-6093. Hours: 8:30AM-4:30PM (CST). *Felony, Civil Actions Over $15,000.*

Civil Records: Access: In person, online. Visitors must perform in person searches for themselves. No search fee. Required to search: name, years to search. Civil cases indexed by defendant, plaintiff. Civil records on index books back to turn of century; on computer back to 2/2000. An online subscription service is available; same as criminal access. Online records date from 02/00.

Criminal Records: Access: In person, online. Visitors must perform in person searches for themselves. No search fee. Required to search: name, years to search. Criminal records on index books back to turn of century; on computer back to 2/2000. A subscription service is available at www.nebraska.gov/faqs/justice/. Fee is $.60 a record or $300 per month flat rate, also there is a start-up fee. Online records date from 02/00.

General Information: Public Access terminal is available. No adoption or juvenile records released. Copy fee: $.25 per page. Certification fee: $1.00. Payee: Clerk of District Court or County Clerk. Personal checks accepted. Prepayment required.

Franklin County Court PO Box 174, Franklin, NE 68939; 308-425-6288; Fax: 308-425-6289. Hours: 8:30AM-4:30PM M-F (CST). *Misdemeanor, Civil Actions Under $45,000, Eviction, Small Claims, Probate.*

Note: Court personnel not permitted to do record searches.

Civil Records: Access: In person, online. Visitors must perform in person searches for themselves. No search fee. Required to search: name, years to search. Civil cases indexed by defendant, plaintiff. Civil records on docket cards since 1988, prior on docket books. An online subscription service is available; same as criminal access. Online civil and probate records from 05/00 forward.

Criminal Records: Access: In person, online. Visitors must perform in person searches for themselves. No search fee. Required to search: name, years to search. Criminal records on docket cards since 1988, prior on docket books. A subscription service is at www.nebraska.gov/faqs/justice/. Fee is $.60 a record or $300 per month flat rate, also there is a start-up fee. Online criminal and traffic records date from 05/00.

General Information: Public Access terminal is available. No juvenile, adoption records released. Copy fee: $.25 per page. Certification fee: $1.25. Payee: Franklin County Court. Personal checks accepted. Prepayment required.

Frontier County

District Court PO Box 40, Stockville, NE 69042; 308-367-8641; Fax: 308-367-8730. Hours: 9AM-4:30PM (CST). *Felony, Civil Actions Over $15,000.*

Civil Records: Access: Mail, in person, online. Both court and visitors may perform in person searches. No search fee. Required to search: name, years to search. Civil cases indexed by defendant, plaintiff. Civil records on general index, docket books from late 1800s; computerized records since 6/00. An online subscription service is available; same as criminal access. Online records date from 06/00.

Criminal Records: Access: Mail, In person, online. Both court and visitors may perform in person searches. No search fee. Required to search: name, years to search, DOB, signed release. Criminal records on general index, docket books from late 1800s; computerized records since 6/00. A subscription service is available at www.nebraska.gov/faqs/justice/. Fee is $.60 a record or $300 per month flat rate, also there is a start-up fee. Online records date from 06/00.

General Information: Public Access terminal is available. Will fax results for $3.00 per page. Copy fee: $.25 per page. Certification fee: $1.00. Payee: Clerk of District Court. Only cashiers checks and money orders accepted. Prepayment required. Mail requests: SASE required. Mail turnaround time 5 days.

Frontier County Court PO Box 38, Stockville, NE 69042; 308-367-8629; Fax: 308-367-8730. Hours: 9AM-4:30PM (CST). *Misdemeanor, Civil Actions Under $45,000, Eviction, Small Claims, Probate.*

Civil Records: Access: Fax, mail, in person, online. Both the court and visitors may perform in person searches. No search fee. Required to search: name, years to search. Civil cases indexed by plaintiff. Civil records on general index, docket books from late 1800s; on computer back to 10/2000. An online subscription service is available; same as criminal access. Online civil and probate records from 09/00 forward.

Criminal Records: Access: Fax, mail, In person, online. Both the court and visitors may perform in person searches. No search fee. Required to search: name, years to search, DOB; also helpful-signed release. Criminal records on general index, docket books from late 1800s; on computer back to 10/2000. A subscription service is available at www.nebraska.gov/faqs/justice/. Fee is $.60 a record or $300 per month flat rate, also there is a start-up fee. Online criminal and traffic records date from 09/00.

General Information: Public Access terminal is available. No adoption or juvenile records released. Fee to fax results is $3.00 per page. Copy fee: $.25 per page. Certification fee: $1.00. Payee: County Court. Only cashiers checks and money orders accepted. Prepayment required. Mail requests: SASE required. Mail turnaround time 5 days.

Furnas County

District Court PO Box 413, Beaver City, NE 68926; 308-268-4015; Fax: 308-268-3205. Hours: 10AM-Noon, 1-3PM (CST). *Felony, Civil Actions Over $15,000.*
Civil Records: Access: Mail, in person, online. Both court and visitors may perform in person searches. No search fee. Required to search: name, years to search. Civil cases indexed by defendant, plaintiff. Civil records in general index books and files from late 1800s. An online subscription service is available; same as criminal access. Online records date from 04/00.
Criminal Records: Access: Mail, In person, online. Both court and visitors may perform in person searches. No search fee. Required to search: name, years to search. Criminal records in general index books and files from late 1800s. A subscription service is at www.nebraska.gov/faqs/justice/. Fee is $.60 a record or $300 per month flat rate, also there is a start-up fee. Online records date from 04/00.
General Information: Public Access terminal is available. No mental health records released. Will fax results. Copy fee: $.25 per page. Certification fee: $1.00. Payee: Clerk of District Court. Personal checks accepted. Prepayment required. Mail requests: SASE required. Mail turnaround time 3-4 days.

Furnas County Court 912 R St (PO Box 373), Beaver City, NE 68926; 308-268-4025. Hours: 8AM-4PM (CST). *Misdemeanor, Civil Actions Under $45,000, Eviction, Small Claims, Probate.*
Civil Records: Access: In person, online. Visitors must perform in person searches for themselves. No search fee. Required to search: name, years to search. Civil cases indexed by defendant, plaintiff. Civil records on card system from 1984, docket books back to late 1800s. An online subscription service is available; same as criminal access. Online civil and probate records from 01/01 forward.
Criminal Records: Access: In person, online. Visitors must perform in person searches for themselves. No search fee. Required to search: name, years to search; also helpful: DOB. Criminal records on card system from 1984, docket books back to late 1800s. A subscription service is at www.nebraska.gov/faqs/justice/. Fee is $.60 a record or $300 per month flat rate, also there is a start-up fee. Online criminal and traffic records date from 09/00.
General Information: Public Access terminal is available. No adoption, juvenile or sealed records released. Copy fee: $.25 per page. Certification fee: $1.00 plus $.25 per page. Payee: County Court. Personal checks accepted. Prepayment required.

Gage County

District Court 612 Grant St, #11, Beatrice, NE 68310-2946; 402-223-1332; Fax: 402-223-1313. Hours: 8AM-5PM (CST). *Felony, Civil Actions Over $45,000.*
Civil Records: Access: Mail, fax, in person, online. Both court and visitors may perform in person searches. No search fee. Required to search: name, years to search. Civil cases indexed by defendant, plaintiff. Civil records on index books from late 1800s; on computer back to 1997. An online subscription service is available; same as criminal access. Online records date from 11/96.

Criminal Records: Access: Mail, fax, In person, online. Both court and visitors may perform in person searches. No search fee. Required to search: name, years to search, DOB. Criminal records on index books from late 1800s; on computer back to 1997. A subscription service is available at www.nebraska.gov/faqs/justice/. Fee is $.60 a record or $300 per month flat rate, also there is a start-up fee. Online records date from 11/96.
General Information: Public Access terminal is available. No juvenile or mental health records released. Will fax results to local or toll free line. Copy fee: $.25 per page. Certification fee: $1.00. Payee: Clerk of District Court. Personal checks accepted. Prepayment required. Mail requests: SASE required. Mail turnaround time up to 7-10 days.

Gage County Court 612 Grant St, #17, Beatrice, NE 68310-2946; Civil phone: 402-223-1328; Criminal phone: 402-223-1325; Probate phone: 402-223-1327. Hours: 8AM-5PM (CST). *Misdemeanor, Civil Actions Under $45,000, Eviction, Small Claims, Probate.*
Civil Records: Access: In person, online. Visitors must perform in person searches for themselves. No search fee. Required to search: name, years to search. Civil cases indexed by defendant, plaintiff. Civil records go back to 1987; on computer back to 1999. Probate records from 1860, probate on microfiche. Court personnel will not perform name searches. A subscription service is available at www.nebraska.gov/business/egov.phtml. Fee is $.60 a record or $300 per month flat rate, also there is a start-up fee. Online civil records date from 11/16/98 forward, probate from 05/98.
Criminal Records: Access: Mail, In person, online. Visitors must perform in person searches for themselves. No search fee. Required to search: name, years to search, DOB. Civil records go back to 1976; on computer back to 1996. A subscription service is at www.nebraska.gov/faqs/justice/. Fee is $.60 a record or $300 per month flat rate, also there is a start-up fee. Online criminal and traffic records date from 09/09/96. Court personnel will not perform name searches.
General Information: Public Access terminal is available. No adoption or juvenile records released. Copy fee: $.25 per page. Certification fee: $1.00. Payee: Gage County Court. Personal checks accepted. Prepayment required. Mail requests: SASE required. Mail turnaround time 1-3 weeks.

Garden County

District Court PO Box 486, Oshkosh, NE 69154; 308-772-3924; Fax: 308-772-0124. Hours: 8AM-4PM (MST). *Felony, Civil Actions Over $15,000.*
Civil Records: Access: Fax, mail, in person, online. Both court and visitors may perform in person searches. No search fee. Required to search: name, years to search. Civil cases indexed by defendant, plaintiff. Civil records in files, docket books back to 1910; on computer back to 1998. An online subscription service is available; same as criminal access. Online records date from 08/98.
Criminal Records: Access: Fax, mail, In person, online. Both court and visitors may perform in person searches. No search fee. Required to search: name, years to search. Criminal records in files, docket books back to 1910; on computer back to 1998. A subscription service is available at www.nebraska.gov/faqs/justice/. Fee is $.60 a record or $300 per month flat rate, also there is a start-up fee. Online records date from 08/98.
General Information: Public Access terminal is available. No confidential records released. Will fax results $2.00 1st page, $1.00 each add'l. Copy fee: $.50 per page. Certification fee: $5.00. Payee: Clerk

of District Court. Personal checks accepted. Prepayment required. Mail requests: SASE required. Mail turnaround time same day.

Garden County Court PO Box 465, Oshkosh, NE 69154; 308-772-3696. Hours: 8AM-4PM (MST). *Misdemeanor, Civil Actions Under $45,000, Eviction, Small Claims, Probate.*
Civil Records: Access: In person, online. Visitors must perform in person searches for themselves. No search fee. Required to search: name, years to search. Civil cases indexed by defendant, plaintiff. Civil records on general index, docket books from 1993, computerized since 1998. Phone access limited to short searches. A subscription service is at www.nebraska.gov/business/egov.phtml. Fee is $.60 a record or $300 per month flat rate, also there is a start-up fee. Online civil and probate records from 01/01 forward.
Criminal Records: Access: In person, online. Visitors must perform in person searches for themselves. No search fee. Required to search: name, years to search. Criminal records on general index, docket books from 1992, computerized since 1998. A subscription service is available at www.nebraska.gov/faqs/justice/. Fee is $.60 a record or $300 per month flat rate, also there is a start-up fee. Online criminal and traffic records date from 06/00.
General Information: No adoption or juvenile records released. Certification fee: $1.00. Payee: Garden County Court. Personal checks accepted. Prepayment required.

Garfield County

District Court PO Box 218, Burwell, NE 68823; 308-346-4161. Hours: 9AM-5PM (CST). *Felony, Civil Actions Over $15,000.*
Civil Records: Access: Mail, in person, online. Only the court performs in person searches; visitors may not. Search fee: $5.00. Required to search: name, years to search; also helpful: address. Civil cases indexed by defendant, plaintiff. Civil records on index books from 1885. An online subscription service is available; same as criminal access. Online records date from 07/00.
Criminal Records: Access: Mail, In person. Only the court performs in person searches; visitors may not. Search fee: $5.00 per name. Required to search: name, years to search; also helpful: address, DOB, SSN. Criminal records on index books from 1885. A subscription service is available at www.nebraska.gov/faqs/justice/. Fee is $.60 a record or $300 per month flat rate, also there is a start-up fee. Online records date from 07/00.
General Information: Copy fee: $.25 per page. Certification fee: $1.50. Payee: Clerk of District Court. Personal checks accepted. Prepayment required. Mail requests: SASE required. Mail turnaround time 3-4 days.

Garfield County Court PO Box 431, Burwell, NE 68823; 308-346-4123; Fax: 308-346-5064. Hours: 9AM-4PM (CST). *Misdemeanor, Civil Actions Under $45,000, Eviction, Small Claims, Probate.*
Civil Records: Access: Mail, in person, online. Both court and visitors may perform in person searches. No search fee. Required to search: name, years to search. Civil cases indexed by defendant. Civil records on index books, from 1885 (probate), 25 years for civil; on computer back to 2000. An online subscription service is available; same as criminal access. Online civil and probate records from 10/00 forward.
Criminal Records: Access: Mail, In person, online. Both court and visitors may perform in person searches. No search fee. Required to search: name, years to search. Criminal record keeping back for 25 years; on computer back to 2000. A subscription service is at www.nebraska.gov/faqs/justice/. Fee is

$.60 a record or $300 per month flat rate, also there is a start-up fee. Online criminal and traffic records date from 07/00.

General Information: No juvenile records released. Will fax results $3.00 1st page, $1.00 each add'l. Copy fee: $.25 per page. Certification fee: $1.00. Payee: County Court. Personal checks accepted. Prepayment required. Mail requests: SASE required. Mail turnaround time within 5 days.

Gosper County

District Court PO Box 136, Elwood, NE 68937; 308-785-2611. Hours: 8:30AM-4:30PM (CST). *Felony, Civil Actions Over $15,000.*
www.co.gosper.ne.us/court.html
Civil Records: Access: In person, online. Visitors must perform in person searches for themselves. No search fee. Required to search: name, years to search. Civil cases indexed by defendant, plaintiff. Civil records in general index books since late 1800s. An online subscription service is available; same as criminal access. Online records date from 07/00.
Criminal Records: Access: In person, online. Visitors must perform in person searches for themselves. No search fee. Required to search: name, years to search; also helpful: DOB. Criminal records in general index books since late 1800s. A subscription service is available at www.nebraska.gov/faqs/justice/. Fee is $.60 a record or $300 per month flat rate, also there is a start-up fee. Online records date from 07/00.
General Information: Public Access terminal is available. No juvenile records or search warrants released. Copy fee: $.25 per page. Certification fee: $1.00. Payee: Clerk of District Court. Personal checks accepted. Prepayment required.

Gosper County Court PO Box 55, Elwood, NE 68937; 308-785-2531; Fax: 308-785-2300 (call before faxing). Hours: 8:30AM-4:30PM (CST). *Misdemeanor, Civil Actions Under $45,000, Eviction, Small Claims, Probate.*
Civil Records: Access: In person, online. Visitors must perform in person searches for themselves. No search fee. Required to search: name, years to search. Civil cases indexed by defendant, plaintiff. Civil records on index cards, docket books kept for 10 years (civil), to late 1800s (probate). Mail access limited to short searches. A subscription service is at www.nebraska.gov/business/egov.phtml. Fee is $.60 a record or $300 per month flat rate, also there is a start-up fee. Online civil and probate records from 11/00 forward.
Criminal Records: Access: In person, online. Visitors must perform in person searches for themselves. No search fee. Required to search: name, years to search, DOB. Criminal record keeping back for 15 years, 3 years are computerized. A subscription service is at www.nebraska.gov/faqs/justice/. Fee is $.60 a record or $300 per month flat rate, also there is a start-up fee. Online criminal and traffic records date from 02/00.
General Information: Public Access terminal is available. No adoption or juvenile records released. Copy fee: $.25 per page. Certification fee: $1.00. Payee: Gosper County Court. Personal checks accepted. Out of state checks not accepted. Prepayment required.

Grant County

District Court PO Box 139, Hyannis, NE 69350; 308-458-2488; Fax: 308-458-2780. Hours: 8AM-4PM (MST). *Felony, Civil Actions Over $15,000.*
Civil Records: Access: Fax, mail, in person, online. Both court and visitors may perform in person searches. No search fee. Required to search: name, years to search. Civil cases indexed by defendant,

plaintiff. Civil records on index books from 1888. An online subscription service is available; same as criminal access. Online records date from 06/00.
Criminal Records: Access: Fax, mail, In person, online. Both court and visitors may perform in person searches. No search fee. Required to search: name, years to search. Criminal records on index books from 1888. A subscription service is available at www.nebraska.gov/faqs/justice/. Fee is $.60 a record or $300 per month flat rate, also there is a start-up fee. Online records date from 06/00.
General Information: No mental health records released. Will fax results $.20 per page. Copy fee: $.20 per page. Certification fee: $1.50. Payee: Grant County Clerk. Personal checks accepted. Prepayment required. Mail requests: SASE required. Mail turnaround time 3-4 days.

Grant County Court PO Box 97, Hyannis, NE 69350; 308-458-2433; Civil phone: 308-327-2692; Fax: 308-327-5623. Hours: 11AM-4PM only on 2nd Tues of month (MST). *Misdemeanor, Civil Actions Under $45,000, Eviction, Small Claims, Probate.*
Note: This court will not do record searches by name, etc. but will send and certify copies of specific records.
Civil Records: Access: in person, online. Visitors must perform in person searches for themselves. No search fee. Required to search: name, years to search; also helpful: address. Civil cases indexed by defendant, plaintiff. Civil records in files, docket books from 1888, computerized since 07/00. An online subscription service is available; same as criminal access. Online civil records date from 11/00 forward, probate from 01/01. Limited phone searching for specific records.
Criminal Records: Access: In person, online. Visitors must perform in person searches for themselves. No search fee. Required to search: name, years to search, DOB; also helpful: address, SSN. Criminal records in files, docket books from 1888, computerized since 07/00. A subscription service is at www.nebraska.gov/faqs/justice/. Fee is $.60 a record or $300 per month flat rate, also there is a start-up fee. Online criminal and traffic records date from 07/00. Limited phone searching for specific records.
General Information: No adoption records released. Copy fee: $.20 per page. Certification fee: $1.00. Payee: Grant County Court. Personal checks accepted. Prepayment required.

Greeley County

District Court PO Box 287, Greeley, NE 68842; 308-428-3625; Fax: 308-428-3022. Hours: 8AM-Noon; 1PM-4PM (CST). *Felony, Civil Actions Over $15,000.*
Civil Records: Access: Mail, in person, online. Visitors must perform in person searches for themselves. No search fee. Required to search: name, years to search, address. Civil cases indexed by defendant, plaintiff. Civil records on general index books from late 1800s. An online subscription service is available; same as criminal access. Online records date from 07/00.
Criminal Records: Access: Mail, In person, online. Visitors must perform in person searches for themselves. No search fee. Required to search: name, years to search, DOB, signed release. Criminal records on general index books from late 1800s. A subscription service is available at www.nebraska.gov/faqs/justice/. Fee is $.60 a record or $300 per month flat rate, also there is a start-up fee. Online records date from 07/00.
General Information: Public Access terminal is available. No mental health records released. Will fax results. Copy fee: $.25 per page. Certification fee: $1.50 plus $.25 per page. Payee: Clerk of District

Court. Only cashiers checks and money orders accepted. Prepayment required. Mail requests: SASE required. Mail turnaround time 1 day.

Greeley County Court PO Box 302, Greeley, NE 68842; 308-428-2705; Fax: 308-428-6500. Hours: 8AM-5PM (CST). *Misdemeanor, Civil Actions Under $45,000, Eviction, Small Claims, Probate.*
Civil Records: Access: In person, online. Visitors must perform in person searches for themselves. No search fee. Required to search: name, years to search. Civil cases indexed by defendant, plaintiff. Civil records on index cards, kept from late 1800s, computerized since 5/00. An online subscription service is available; same as criminal access. Online civil and probate records from 05/00 forward.
Criminal Records: Access: In person, online. Visitors must perform in person searches for themselves. No search fee. Required to search: name, years to search. Criminal records on index cards, kept from late 1800s, computerized since 5/00. A subscription service is available at www.nebraska.gov/faqs/justice/. Fee is $.60 a record or $300 per month flat rate, also there is a start-up fee. Online criminal and traffic records date from 05/00.
General Information: Public Access terminal is available. No adoption records released. Copy fee: $.25 per page. Certification fee: $1.00. Payee: County Court. Only cashiers checks and money orders accepted. Prepayment required.

Hall County

District Court 111 W First St, Box 1926, Grand Island, NE 68802; 308-385-5144; Fax: 308-385-5110. Hours: 8AM-5PM (CST). *Felony, Civil Actions Over $15,000.*
Civil Records: Access: Mail, in person, online. Court performs searches for government/law enforcement only. Visitors may perform in person searches. No search fee. Required to search: name, years to search. Civil cases indexed by defendant, plaintiff. Many records on computer since 1985, some on microfilm, original index books back to late 1800s. An online subscription service is available; same as criminal access. Online records date from 10/97.
Criminal Records: Access: Mail, In person, online. Court performs searches for government/law enforcement only. Visitors may perform in person searches. No search fee. Required to search: name, years to search. Many records on computer since 1985, some on microfilm, original index books back to late 1800s. A subscription service is at www.nebraska.gov/faqs/justice/. Fee is $.60 a record or $300 per month flat rate, also there is a start-up fee. Online records date from 10/97.
General Information: Public Access terminal is available. No mental health records released. Fee to fax results is $3.00 1st page, $1.00 each add'l. Copy fee: $.25 per page. Certification fee: $1.00. Payee: Clerk of District Court. Personal checks accepted. Prepayment required. Mail requests: SASE required. Mail turnaround time 3-4 days.

Hall County Court 111 W 1st #1, Grand Island, NE 68801; 308-385-5135. Hours: 8AM-5PM (CST). *Misdemeanor, Civil Actions Under $45,000, Eviction, Small Claims, Probate.*
Civil Records: Access: In person, online. Visitors must perform in person searches for themselves. No search fee. Required to search: name, years to search. Civil cases indexed by defendant. Civil records on index books, on computer after 1/24/00. An online subscription service is available; same as criminal access. Online civil records date from 01/00 forward, probate from 08/98.
Criminal Records: Access: In person, online. Visitors must perform in person searches for themselves. No search fee. Required to search: name,

years to search, DOB. Criminal records on index books; on computer after 5/19/97. A subscription service is at www.nebraska.gov/faqs/justice/. Fee is $.60 a record or $300 per month flat rate, also there is a start-up fee. Online criminal and traffic records date from 05/97.

General Information: Public Access terminal is available. No confidential records released. Copy fee: $.25 per page. Certification fee: $1.00. Payee: County Court. Personal checks accepted. Prepayment required.

Hamilton County

District Court PO Box 201, Aurora, NE 68818-0201; 402-694-3533; Fax: 402-694-2250. 8AM-5PM (CST). *Felony, Civil Actions Over $15,000.*

Civil Records: Access: In person, online. Visitors must perform in person searches for themselves. No search fee. Required to search: name, years to search. Civil cases indexed by defendant, plaintiff. Civil records on index books and files from late 1800s. An online subscription service is available; same as criminal access. Online records date from 03/98.

Criminal Records: Access: In person, online. Visitors must perform in person searches for themselves. No search fee. Required to search: name, years to search. Criminal records on index books and files from late 1800s. A subscription service is at www.nebraska.gov/faqs/justice/. Fee is $.60 a record or $300 per month flat rate, also there is a start-up fee. Online records date from 03/98.

General Information: Public Access terminal is available. No mental health board hearing records released. Copy fee: $.25 per page. Certification fee: $1.00. Payee: Clerk of District Court. Personal checks accepted. Prepayment required.

Hamilton County Court PO Box 323, Aurora, NE 68818; 402-694-6188; Fax: 402-694-2250. Hours: 8AM-5PM (CST). *Misdemeanor, Civil Actions Under $45,000, Eviction, Small Claims, Probate.* Note: Will not do name searches, but will provide specific documents.

Civil Records: Access: In person, online. Visitors must perform in person searches for themselves. No search fee. Required to search: name, years to search. Civil cases indexed by defendant, plaintiff. Civil records computerized since 1998, older on docket cards, probate on microfiche from late 1800s. An online subscription service is available; same as criminal access. Online civil records date from 10/99 forward, probate from 05/98.

Criminal Records: Access: In person, online. Visitors must perform in person searches for themselves. No search fee. Required to search: name, years to search. Computerized since 1997. A subscription service is at www.nebraska.gov/faqs/justice/. Fee is $.60 a record or $300 per month flat rate, also there is a start-up fee. Online criminal and traffic records date from 07/97.

General Information: Public Access terminal is available. No adoption records released. Copy fee: $.25 per page. Certification fee: $1.00. Payee: Hamilton County Court. Personal checks accepted. Prepayment required.

Harlan County

District Court PO Box 698, Alma, NE 68920; 308-928-2173; Fax: 308-928-2079. Hours: 8:30AM-4:30PM (CST). *Felony, Civil Actions Over $15,000.*

Civil Records: Access: Phone, mail, in person, online. Both court and visitors may perform in person searches. Search fee: $5.00 per name. Required to search: name, years to search. Civil cases indexed by defendant, plaintiff. Civil records on books and in files from late 1800s, on computer back to 3/2000. An

online subscription service is available; same as criminal access. Online records date from 04/00.

Criminal Records: Access: Phone, mail, In person, online. Both court and visitors may perform in person searches. Search fee: $5.00 per name. Required to search: name, years to search. Criminal records on books and in files from late 1800s; on computer back to 3/2000. A subscription service is at www.nebraska.gov/faqs/justice/. Fee is $.60 a record or $300 per month flat rate, also there is a start-up fee. Online records date from 04/00.

General Information: Public Access terminal is available. No juvenile records released. Copy fee: $.25 per page. Certification fee: $1.00. Payee: Clerk of District Court. Personal checks accepted. Prepayment required. Mail requests: SASE not required. Mail turnaround time 1 day.

Harlan County Court PO Box 379, Alma, NE 68920; 308-928-2179; Fax: 308-928-2170. Hours: 8:30AM-4:30PM (CST). *Misdemeanor, Civil Actions Under $45,000, Eviction, Small Claims, Probate.*

Civil Records: Access: In person, online. Visitors must perform in person searches for themselves. No search fee. Required to search: name, years to search; also helpful: address. Civil cases indexed by defendant. Civil records on index cards from 1900; computerized since 2000. An online subscription service is available; same as criminal access. Online civil and probate records from 11/00 forward.

Criminal Records: Access: In person, online. Visitors must perform in person searches for themselves. No search fee. Required to search: name, years to search; also helpful: address, DOB. Criminal records on index cards from 1900, computerized since 2000. A subscription service is available at www.nebraska.gov/faqs/justice/. Fee is $.60 a record or $300 per month flat rate, also there is a start-up fee. Online criminal and traffic records date from 03/00.

General Information: Public Access terminal is available. No adoption records released. Limited access to juvenile records. Copy fee: $.25 per page. Certification fee: $1.00. Payee: Harlan County Court. Business checks accepted. Prepayment required. Payment is required at time of search.

Hayes County

District Court PO Box 370, Hayes Center, NE 69032; 308-286-3413; Fax: 308-286-3208. Hours: 8AM-4PM (CST). *Felony, Civil Actions Over $15,000.*

Civil Records: Access: Fax, mail, in person, online. Both court and visitors may perform in person searches. No search fee. Required to search: name; also helpful: years to search, address. Civil cases indexed by defendant, plaintiff. Civil records on index books back to late 1800s. An online subscription service is available; same as criminal access. Online records date from 06/00.

Criminal Records: Access: Fax, mail, In person, online. Both court and visitors may perform in person searches. No search fee. Required to search: name; also helpful: years to search, address, DOB, SSN. Criminal records on index books back to late 1800s. A subscription service is at www.nebraska.gov/faqs/justice/. Fee is $.60 a record or $300 per month flat rate, also there is a start-up fee. Online records date from 06/00.

General Information: No sealed records released. Will fax results to local or toll free line. Copy fee: $.25 per page. Certification fee: $4.00. Payee: Clerk of District Court. Personal checks accepted. Prepayment required. Mail requests: SASE required. Mail turnaround time 2 days.

Hayes County Court PO Box 370, Hayes Center, NE 69032; 308-286-3315. Hours: 9AM-Noon, 1-4PM Tuesday (Clerk's hours) (CST). *Misdemeanor, Civil Actions Under $45,000, Eviction, Small Claims, Probate.*

Civil Records: Access: Phone, mail, in person, online. Both court and visitors may perform in person searches. No search fee. Required to search: name, years to search. Civil cases indexed by defendant, plaintiff. Civil records on general index books and files back to late 1800s; on computer back to mid-2000. An online subscription service is available; same as criminal access. Online civil records date from 11/00 forward, probate from 12/00.

Criminal Records: Access: Phone, mail, In person, online. Both court and visitors may perform in person searches. No search fee. Required to search: name, years to search, DOB. Criminal records on general index books and files back to late 1800s; on computer back to mid-2000. A subscription service is at www.nebraska.gov/faqs/justice/. Fee is $.60 a record or $300 per month flat rate, also there is a start-up fee. Online criminal and traffic records date from 08/00.

General Information: No juvenile or adoption records released. Copy fee: $.25 per page. Certification fee: $1.00. Payee: County Court. Personal checks accepted. Prepayment required. Mail requests: SASE required. Mail turnaround time 1 week.

Hitchcock County

District Court PO Box 248, Trenton, NE 69044; 308-334-5646; Fax: 308-334-5398. Hours: 8:30AM-4PM (CST). *Felony, Civil Actions Over $15,000.* www.co.hitchcock.ne.us/court.html

Civil Records: Access: Phone, fax, mail, in person, online. Both court and visitors may perform in person searches. No search fee. Required to search: name, years to search. Civil cases indexed by defendant, plaintiff. Civil records on books from late 1800s; on computer back to 1999. An online subscription service is available; same as criminal access. Online records date from 06/00.

Criminal Records: Access: Phone, fax, mail, In person, online. Both court and visitors may perform in person searches. No search fee. Required to search: name, years to search. Criminal records on books from late 1800s; on computer back to 1999. A subscription service is available at www.nebraska.gov/faqs/justice/. Fee is $.60 a record or $300 per month flat rate, also there is a start-up fee. Online records date from 06/00.

General Information: Public Access terminal is available. No sealed records released. Will fax results $3.00 1st page, $1.50 each add'l. Copy fee: $.25 per page. Certification fee: $1.00. Payee: Clerk of District Court. Personal checks accepted. Prepayment required. Mail requests: SASE required. Mail turnaround time 2 days.

Hitchcock County Court PO Box 248, Trenton, NE 69044; 308-334-5383. Hours: 8:30AM-4PM (CST). *Misdemeanor, Civil Actions Under $45,000, Eviction, Small Claims, Probate.*

Civil Records: Access: Phone, mail, in person, online. Both court and visitors may perform in person searches. No search fee. Required to search: name, years to search. Civil cases indexed by defendant, plaintiff. Civil records on docket books, cards go back to 1960s; on computer back to 2000. Probate records go back to late 1800s. An online subscription service is available; same as criminal access. Online civil and probate records from 01/01 forward.

Criminal Records: Access: Phone, mail, In person, online. Both court and visitors may perform in person searches. No search fee. Required to search: name, years to search, DOB. Criminal records go back to

1978 apx. on docket books, cards; on computer back to 2000. A subscription service is at www.nebraska.gov/faqs/justice/. Fee is $.60 a record or $300 per month flat rate, also there is a start-up fee. Online criminal and traffic records date from 09/00.

General Information: Public Access terminal is available. (Terminal is across the hall.) No adoption or juvenile records released. Copy fee: $.25 per page. Certification fee: $1.00. Payee: County Court. Personal checks accepted. Prepayment required. Mail requests: SASE required. Mail turnaround time 2 weeks, limited phone searching same day.

Holt County

District Court PO Box 755, O'Neill, NE 68763; 402-336-2840; Fax: 402-336-3601. Hours: 8AM-4:30PM (CST). *Felony, Civil Actions Over $15,000.*
Civil Records: Access: Phone, fax, mail, in person, online. Both court and visitors may perform in person searches. No search fee. Required to search: name, years to search; also helpful: address. Civil cases indexed by defendant, plaintiff. Civil records on docket books and general index books since late 1800, search last 15 years only. An online subscription service is available; same as criminal access. Online records date from 06/98.
Criminal Records: Access: Phone, fax, mail, In person, online. Both court and visitors may perform in person searches. No search fee. Required to search: name, years to search, DOB. Criminal records on docket books and general index books archived since late 1800s, search last 15 years only. A subscription service is at www.nebraska.gov/faqs/justice/. Fee is $.60 a record or $300 per month flat rate, also there is a start-up fee. Online records date from 06/98.
General Information: Public Access terminal is available. No juvenile or mental health records released. Will fax results $3.00 1st page, $1.00 each add'l. Copy fee: $.25 per page. Certification fee: $1.00. Payee: Clerk of District Court. Personal checks accepted. Prepayment required. Mail requests: SASE required. Mail turnaround time 1 week or less.

Holt County Court 204 N 4th St, O'Neill, NE 68763; 402-336-1662; Fax: 402-336-1663. Hours: 8AM-4:30PM (CST). *Misdemeanor, Civil Actions Under $45,000, Eviction, Small Claims, Probate.*
Civil Records: Access: In person, online. Visitors must perform in person searches for themselves. No search fee. Required to search: name, years to search. Civil cases indexed by defendant. Civil records go back to 1980; on comptuer back to 2000; probate kept longer. An online subscription service is available; same as criminal access. Online civil records date from 10/00 forward, probate from 11/00.
Criminal Records: Access: In person, online. Visitors must perform in person searches for themselves. No search fee. Required to search: name, years to search, DOB. Criminal records go back to 1920, on computer back to 2000. A subscription service is at www.nebraska.gov/faqs/justice/. Fee is $.60 a record or $300 per month flat rate, also there is a start-up fee. Online criminal and traffic records date from 07/00.
General Information: Public Access terminal is available. No adoption records released. Copy fee: $.25 per page. Certification fee: $1.25. Payee: Holt County Court. Personal checks accepted. Prepayment required.

Hooker County

District Court PO Box 184, Mullen, NE 69152; 308-546-2244; Fax: 308-546-2490. Hours: 8:30AM-Noon, 1-4:30PM (MST). *Felony, Civil Actions Over $15,000.*
Civil Records: Access: In person, online. Visitors must perform in person searches for themselves. No

search fee. Required to search: name, years to search. Civil cases indexed by defendant, plaintiff. Civil records on index books since late 1800s. An online subscription service is available; same as criminal access. Online records date from 06/00.
Criminal Records: Access: In person, online. Visitors must perform in person searches for themselves. No search fee. Required to search: name, years to search. Criminal records on index books since late 1800s. A subscription service is available at www.nebraska.gov/faqs/justice/. Fee is $.60 a record or $300 per month flat rate, also there is a start-up fee. Online records date from 06/00.
General Information: Public Access terminal is available. No mental health records released. Copy fee: $1.00 per page. Certification fee: $1.50. Payee: Clerk of District Court. Personal checks accepted. Prepayment required.

Hooker County Court PO Box 184, Mullen, NE 69152; 308-546-2249; Fax: 308-546-2490 (Sheriff). Hours: 8:30AM-4:30PM (MST). *Misdemeanor, Civil Actions Under $45,000, Eviction, Small Claims, Probate.*
Civil Records: Access: Fax, mail, in person, online. Only the court performs in person searches; visitors may not. No search fee. Required to search: name, years to search. Civil cases indexed by defendant, plaintiff. Civil records on index cards and books from late 1800s. An online subscription service is available; same as criminal access. Online civil records date from 11/99 forward, probate from 08/98.
Criminal Records: Access: Fax, mail, In person, online. Both court and visitors may perform in person searches. No search fee. Required to search: name, years to search; also helpful: DOB, SSN. Criminal records on index cards and books from late 1800s, computerized 1998. A subscription service is at www.nebraska.gov/faqs/justice/. Fee is $.60 a record or $300 per month flat rate, also there is a start-up fee. Online criminal and traffic records date from 08/98.
General Information: No adoption or juvenile records released. No fee to fax results. Copy fee: $.25 per page. Certification fee: $1.00. Payee: County Court. Business checks accepted. Prepayment required. Mail requests: SASE required. Mail turnaround time 3-4 days.

Howard County

District Court PO Box 25, St Paul, NE 68873; 308-754-4343; Fax: 308-754-4125. Hours: 8AM-5PM (CST). *Felony, Civil Actions Over $15,000.*
Civil Records: Access: In person, online. Both court and visitors may perform in person searches. No search fee. Required to search: name, years to search. Civil cases indexed by defendant, plaintiff. Civil records on microfiche from 1986, books prior. An online subscription service is available; same as criminal access. Online records date from 06/98.
Criminal Records: Access: In person, online. Both court and visitors may perform in person searches. No search fee. Required to search: name, years to search, DOB. Criminal records on microfiche from 1986, books prior; on comptuer back to 9/1998. A subscription service is available at www.nebraska.gov/faqs/justice/. Fee is $.60 a record or $300 per month flat rate, also there is a start-up fee. Online records date from 06/98.
General Information: Public Access terminal is available. No pending case records released. Copy fee: $.25 per page. Certification fee: $5.00. Payee: Clerk of District Court. Personal checks accepted. Prepayment required.

Howard County Court 612 Indian St #6, St Paul, NE 68873; 308-754-4192. Hours: 8AM-Noon; 1PM-4PM (CST). *Misdemeanor, Civil Actions Under $45,000, Eviction, Small Claims, Probate.*
Civil Records: Access: In person, online. Visitors must perform in person searches for themselves. No search fee. Required to search: name, years to search. Civil cases indexed by defendant. Civil records on docket cards since 1982; computerized records since 2000. An online subscription service is available; same as criminal access. Online civil records date from 05/01 forward, probate from 08/00.
Criminal Records: Access: In person, online. Visitors must perform in person searches for themselves. No search fee. Required to search: name, years to search; also helpful: DOB. Criminal records on docket cards since 1982; computerized records since 2000. A subscription service is at www.nebraska.gov/faqs/justice/. Fee is $.60 a record or $300 per month flat rate, also there is a start-up fee. Online criminal and traffic records date from 08/00.
General Information: Public Access terminal is available. Copy fee: $.25 per page. Certification fee: $1.00. Payee: Howard County Court. Business checks accepted. Prepayment required.

Jefferson County

District Court Jefferson County Courthouse, 411 Fourth St., Fairbury, NE 68352; 402-729-2019; Fax: 402-729-6596. Hours: 9AM-5PM (CST). *Felony, Civil Actions Over $15,000.*
Civil Records: Access: Fax, mail, in person, online. Both court and visitors may perform in person searches. Search fee: none. Required to search: name, years to search. Civil cases indexed by defendant, plaintiff. Civil records on index books from 1870s; on computer back to 1996. An online subscription service is available; same as criminal access. Online records date from 11/96.
Criminal Records: Access: In person, online. Visitors must perform in person searches for themselves. Search fee: none. Required to search: name, years to search, DOB. Criminal records on index books from 1870s; on computer back to 1996. A subscription service is available at www.nebraska.gov/faqs/justice/. Fee is $.60 a record or $300 per month flat rate, also there is a start-up fee. Online records date from 11/96.
General Information: Public Access terminal is available. No mental health records released. Fee to fax results is $2.00 per document. Copy fee: $.50 per page. Certification fee: $1.00. Payee: Clerk of District Court. Personal checks accepted. Prepayment required. Mail requests: SASE required. Mail turnaround time 1-2 days.

Jefferson County Court 411 Fourth St, Fairbury, NE 68352; 402-729-2312. Hours: 8AM-Noon, 1-5PM (CST). *Misdemeanor, Civil Actions Under $45,000, Eviction, Small Claims, Probate.*
Note: This court will not longer perform name searches for the public.

Civil Records: Access: In person, online. Visitors must perform in person searches for themselves. No search fee. Required to search: name, years to search. Civil cases indexed by defendant, plaintiff. Civil records on cards from 1988, prior on docket books; computerized records from 10/1999. An online subscription service is available; same as criminal access. Online civil records date from 10/99 forward, probate from 05/98.
Criminal Records: Access: In person, online. Visitors must perform in person searches for themselves. No search fee. Required to search: name, years to search, DOB, signed release. Criminal records on cards from 1988, prior on docket books; computerized records from 9/1996. A subscription

service is at www.nebraska.gov/faqs/justice/. Fee is $.60 a record or $300 per month flat rate, also there is a start-up fee. Online criminal and traffic records date from 09/96.

General Information: Public Access terminal is available. No adoption or sealed records released. Copy fee: $.25 per page. Certification fee: $1.00. Payee: County Court. Personal checks accepted. Prepayment required.

Johnson County

District Court PO Box 416, Tecumseh, NE 68450; 402-335-6301; Fax: 402-335-6311. Hours: 8AM-Noon, 1-4:30PM (CST). *Felony, Civil Actions Over $15,000.*

Civil Records: Access: Mail, in person, online. Both court and visitors may perform in person searches. No search fee. Required to search: name, years to search. Civil cases indexed by defendant, plaintiff. Civil records on index and docket books from late 1800s, microfiche back 7 years. An online subscription service is available; same as criminal access. Online civil and probate records from 04/01 forward.

Criminal Records: Access: In person, online. Both court and visitors may perform in person searches. No search fee. Required to search: name, years to search. Criminal records on index and docket books from late 1800s, microfiche back 7 years. A subscription service is at www.nebraska.gov/faqs/justice/. Fee is $.60 a record or $300 per month flat rate, also there is a start-up fee. Online records date from 04/00.

General Information: Public Access terminal is available. No juvenile records released. Fee to fax results is $2.00 per document. Copy fee: $.50 per page. Certification fee: $1.50. Payee: Clerk of District Court. Personal checks accepted. Prepayment required. Mail turnaround time is 3 days.

Johnson County Court PO Box 285, Tecumseh, NE 68450; 402-335-6313; Fax: 402-335-6314. Hours: 8AM-4:30PM (CST). *Misdemeanor, Civil Actions Under $45,000, Eviction, Small Claims, Probate.*

Note: The court is in the process of computerizing their records.

Civil Records: Access: Mail, in person, online. Both court and visitors may perform in person searches. Search fee: cost of copies. Required to search: name, years to search; also helpful: address. Civil cases indexed by defendant, plaintiff. Civil records on index cards back 15 years, microfiche back to late 1800s for probate. An online subscription service is available; same as criminal access. Online records date from 02/98.

Criminal Records: Access: In person only. Both court and visitors may perform in person searches. Search fee: cost of copies. Required to search: name, years to search, DOB, signed release; also helpful: address, SSN. Criminal records on index cards back 15 years. A subscription service is at www.nebraska.gov/faqs/justice/. Fee is $.60 a record or $300 per month flat rate, also there is a start-up fee. Online criminal and traffic records date from 02/98.

General Information: Public Access terminal is available. No adoption or juvenile records released. Will not fax results. Copy fee: $.25 per page. Certification fee: $1.00. Payee: County Court. Personal checks accepted. Prepayment required.

Kearney County

District Court PO Box 208, Minden, NE 68959; 308-832-1742; Fax: 308-832-0636. Hours: 8:30AM-5PM (CST). *Felony, Civil Actions Over $15,000.*

Civil Records: Access: In person, online. Visitors must perform in person searches for themselves. No search fee. Required to search: name, years to search.

Civil cases indexed by defendant, plaintiff. All records on microfilm since 1800s; on computer back to 9/1998. An online subscription service is available; same as criminal access. Online records date from 08/98. Mail access to attorneys only.

Criminal Records: Access: In person, online. Visitors must perform in person searches for themselves. No search fee. Required to search: name, years to search. Criminal records on microfilm since 1800s; on computer back to 9/1998. A subscription service is at www.nebraska.gov/faqs/justice/. Fee is $.60 a record or $300 per month flat rate, also there is a start-up fee. Online records date from 08/98.

General Information: Public Access terminal is available. (Has records since 9/98.) No mental health records released. Copy fee: $.25 per page. Certification fee: $1.50. Payee: Clerk of District Court. Personal checks accepted. Prepayment required.

Kearney County Court PO Box 377, Minden, NE 68959; 308-832-2719; Fax: 308-832-0636. Hours: 8AM-5PM (CST). *Misdemeanor, Civil Actions Under $45,000, Eviction, Small Claims, Probate.*

Civil Records: Access: In person, online. Visitors must perform in person searches for themselves. No search fee. Required to search: name, years to search. Civil cases indexed by defendant. Civil records computerized since 10/99, rest on index cards, some probate on microfiche. An online subscription service is available; same as criminal access. Online civil records date from 10/99 forward, probate from 05/98.

Criminal Records: Access: In person, online, mail. Visitors must perform in person searches for themselves. No search fee. Required to search: name, years to search. Criminal records computerized since 03/97, indexes availabel since 1988. A subscription service is at www.nebraska.gov/faqs/justice/. Fee is $.60 a record or $300 per month flat rate, also there is a start-up fee. Online criminal and traffic records date from 03/97.

General Information: Public Access terminal is available. Copy fee: $.25 per page. Certification fee: $1.00. Payee: Kearney County Court. Personal checks accepted. Prepayment required. Mail requests: SASE requested. Turnaround time is 1 week.

Keith County

District Court PO Box 686, Ogallala, NE 69153; 308-284-3849; Fax: 308-284-3978. Hours: 8AM-4PM (MST). *Felony, Civil Actions Over $15,000.*

Civil Records: Access: Fax, mail, in person, online. Both court and visitors may perform in person searches. No search fee. Required to search: name, years to search, DOB. Civil cases indexed by defendant, plaintiff. Civil records on index books from late 1800s; on computer back to 1975. An online subscription service is available; same as criminal access. Online records date from 06/97.

Criminal Records: Access: Fax, mail, In person, online. Both court and visitors may perform in person searches. No search fee. Required to search: name, years to search, DOB. Criminal records on index books from late 1800s; on computer back to 1975. A subscription service is available at www.nebraska.gov/faqs/justice/. Fee is $.60 a record or $300 per month flat rate, also there is a start-up fee. Online records date from 06/97.

General Information: Public Access terminal is available. No juvenile or mental health records released. No fee to fax results. Fee is charged if long distance. Copy fee: $.25 per page. Certification fee: $1.00. Payee: Clerk of District Court. Personal checks accepted. Prepayment required. Mail requests: SASE not required. Mail turnaround time 2-3 days.

Keith County Court PO Box 358, Ogallala, NE 69153; 308-284-3693; Fax: 308-284-6825. Hours: 8AM-5PM (MST). *Misdemeanor, Civil Actions Under $45,000, Eviction, Small Claims, Probate.*

Civil Records: Access: In person, online. Visitors must perform in person searches for themselves. No search fee. Required to search: name, years to search. Civil cases indexed by defendant, plaintiff. Civil records on index cards, files; computerized records since 1997. An online subscription service is available; same as criminal access. Online civil records date from 10/99 forward, probate from 05/98.

Criminal Records: Access: In person, online. Visitors must perform in person searches for themselves. No search fee. Required to search: name, years to search. Criminal records on index cards, files; computerized records since 1997. A subscription service is at www.nebraska.gov/faqs/justice/. Fee is $.60 a record or $300 per month flat rate, also there is a start-up fee. Online criminal and traffic records date from 06/97.

General Information: Public Access terminal is available. No adoption records released. Copy fee: $.25 per page. Certification fee: $1.25. Payee: County Court. Local checks only. Prepayment required.

Keya Paha County

District Court PO Box 349, Springview, NE 68778; 402-497-3791; Fax: 402-497-3799. 8AM-5PM (CST). *Felony, Civil Actions Over $15,000.*
www.co.keya-paha.ne.us

Civil Records: Access: Fax, mail, in person, online. Both court and visitors may perform in person searches. No search fee. Required to search: name, years to search. Civil cases indexed by defendant, plaintiff. Civil records on microfiche 7-9 years, on docket books since late 1800s. An online subscription service is available; same as criminal access. Online records date from 07/00.

Criminal Records: Access: Fax, mail, In person, online. Both court and visitors may perform in person searches. No search fee. Required to search: name, years to search. Computerized back to 2000, criminal records on microfiche 7-9 years, on docket books since late 1800s. A subscription service is at www.nebraska.gov/faqs/justice/. Fee is $.60 a record or $300 per month flat rate, also there is a start-up fee. Online records date from 0700.

General Information: Public Access terminal is available. No confidential records released. Will fax results for $2.00 1st page, $1.00 each add'l. Copy fee: $.25 per page. Legal Size Copy Fee: $.30 per page. Certification fee: $4.00. Payee: Clerk of District Court. Personal checks accepted. Prepayment required. Mail requests: SASE required. Mail turnaround time 3-4 days.

Keya Paha County Court PO Box 275, Springview, NE 68778; 402-497-3021; Probate phone: 402-684-3601. Hours: 8AM-4PM every 2nd Friday of each month. (CST). *Misdemeanor, Civil Actions Under $45,000, Eviction, Small Claims, Probate.*

Civil Records: Access: In person, online. Visitors must perform in person searches for themselves. No search fee. Required to search: name, years to search; also helpful: address. Civil cases indexed by defendant, plaintiff. Civil records in index books and files, many records on microfiche, back to late 1800s. An online subscription service is available; same as criminal access. Online civil and probate records from 01/01 forward.

Criminal Records: Access: In person, online. Visitors must perform in person searches for themselves. No search fee. Required to search: name, years to search; also helpful: address, DOB, SSN. Criminal records in index books and files, many records on microfiche, back to late 1800s. A subscription service is available at www.nebraska.gov/faqs/justice/. Fee is $.60 a record or $300 per month flat rate, also there is a start-up fee. Online criminal and traffic records date from 08/00.

General Information: No juvenile records released. Copy fee: $.25 per page. Certification fee: $1.25. Payee: County Clerk. Personal checks accepted. Prepayment required.

Kimball County

District Court 114 E 3rd St, Kimball, NE 69145; 308-235-3591; Fax: 308-235-3654. Hours: 8AM-5PM M-Th, 8AM-4PM F (MST). *Felony, Civil Actions Over $15,000.*

Civil Records: Access: In person, online. Visitors must perform in person searches for themselves. No search fee. Required to search: name, years to search. Civil cases indexed by defendant, plaintiff. Civil records on microfiche from 1960 forward, prior in books from early 1900s, computerized since 11/97. An online subscription service is available; same as criminal access. Online records date from 10/97.

Criminal Records: Access: In person, online. Visitors must perform in person searches for themselves. No search fee. Required to search: name, years to search; also helpful: DOB. Criminal records on microfiche from 1960 forward, prior in books from early 1900s, computerized since 11/97. A subscription service is at www.nebraska.gov/faqs/justice/. Fee is $.60 a record or $300 per month flat rate, also there is a start-up fee. Online records date from 10/97.

General Information: Public Access terminal is available. No mental health records released. Copy fee: $1.00 per page. Certification fee: $1.50. Payee: Clerk of District Court. Personal checks accepted. Prepayment required.

Kimball County Court 114 E 3rd St, Kimball, NE 69145; 308-235-2831. Hours: 8AM-5PM (MST). *Misdemeanor, Civil Actions Under $45,000, Small Claims, Probate.*

Civil Records: Access: In person, online. Visitors must perform in person searches for themselves. No search fee. Required to search: name, years to search. Civil cases indexed by defendant, plaintiff. Civil records on index cards and original files, also state computer. An online subscription service is available; same as criminal access. Online civil and probate records from 11/00 forward.

Criminal Records: Access: In person, online. Visitors must perform in person searches for themselves. No search fee. Required to search: name, years to search. Criminal records on index cards and original files. A subscription service is at www.nebraska.gov/faqs/justice/. Fee is $.60 a record or $300 per month flat rate, also there is a start-up fee. Online criminal and traffic records date from 04/00.

General Information: Public Access terminal is available. Copy fee: $.25 per page. Certification fee: $1.25. Payee: County Court. Only cashiers checks and money orders accepted. Prepayment required.

Knox County

District Court PO Box 126, Center, NE 68724; 402-288-5606; Fax: 402-288-5609. Hours: 8:30AM-4:30PM (CST). *Felony, Civil Actions Over $45,000.*

Civil Records: Access: In person, online. Visitors must perform in person searches for themselves. No search fee. Required to search: name, years to search. Civil cases indexed by defendant, plaintiff. Civil records on index books from 1874; on computer back to 9/1998. An online subscription service is available; same as criminal access. Online records date from 09/98.

Criminal Records: Access: In person, online. Visitors must perform in person searches for

themselves. No search fee. Required to search: name, years to search; also helpful: DOB. Criminal records on index books from 1874; on computer back to 09/98. A subscription service is at www.nebraska.gov/faqs/justice/. Fee is $.60 a record or $300 per month flat rate, also there is a start-up fee. Online records date from 09/98.

General Information: Public Access terminal is available. No mental health records released. Copy fee: $.25 per page. Certification fee: $1.00. Payee: Clerk of District Court. Personal checks accepted. Prepayment required.

Knox County Court PO Box 125, Center, NE 68724; 402-288-5607; Fax: 402-288-5609. Hours: 8:30AM-4:30PM (CST). *Misdemeanor, Civil Actions Under $45,000, Eviction, Small Claims, Probate.*

Civil Records: Access: In person, online. Visitors must perform in person searches for themselves. No search fee. Required to search: name, years to search. Civil cases indexed by defendant, plaintiff. Civil records on index cards and general docket books from late 1800s; on computer from 8/2000. An online subscription service is available; same as criminal access. Online civil records date from 11/00 forward, probate from 09/00.

Criminal Records: Access: In person, online. Visitors must perform in person searches for themselves. No search fee. Required to search: name, years to search; also helpful: DOB. Criminal records on index cards and general docket books from late 1800s; on computer from 8/2000. A subscription service is at www.nebraska.gov/faqs/justice/. Fee is $.60 a record or $300 per month flat rate, also there is a start-up fee. Online criminal and traffic records date from 08/00.

General Information: Public Access terminal is available. No adoption records released. Copy fee: $.25 per page. Certification fee: $1.00. Payee: County Court. Personal checks accepted. Prepayment required.

Lancaster County

District Court 575 S Tenth St, Lincoln, NE 68508-2810; 402-441-7328; Fax: 402-441-6190. Hours: 8AM-4:30PM (CST). *Felony, Civil Actions Over $15,000.*

www.ci.lincoln.ne.us/cnty/discrt/index.htm

Civil Records: Access: Mail, in person, online. Visitors must perform in person searches for themselves. No search fee. Required to search: name, years to search. Civil cases indexed by defendant, plaintiff. Civil records on computer from 1984, microfiche from 1900s, docket books from 1800s. An online subscription service is available; same as criminal access. Online records date from 06/99.

Criminal Records: Access: mail, In person, online. Visitors must perform in person searches themselves. No search fee. Required to search: name, years to search, DOB. Criminal records on computer from 1984, microfiche from 1900s, docket books from 1800s. A subscription service is available at www.nebraska.gov/faqs/justice/. Fee is $.60 a record or $300 per month flat rate, also there is a start-up fee. Online records date from 06/99.

General Information: Public Access terminal is available. No juvenile, mental health or grand jury records released. Will fax results. Copy fee: $.50 per page. Certification fee: $1.50. Payee: Clerk of District Court. Personal checks accepted. Prepayment required. Mail requests: SASE requested. Turnaround time 5 days.

Lancaster County Court 575 S 10th, Lincoln, NE 68508; 402-441-7291. Hours: 8AM-4:30PM (CST). *Misdemeanor, Civil Actions Under $45,000, Eviction, Small Claims, Probate.*

Civil Records: Access: In person, online. Visitors must perform in person searches for themselves. No search fee. Required to search: name, years to search. Civil cases indexed by defendant, plaintiff. Civil records on index books back to 1968, computerized since 11/98. Access to the Internet system requires registration and password. Call John at 402-471-3049 for more information. System can be searched by name or case number. A subscription service is at www.nebraska.gov/business/egov.phtml. Fee is $.60 a record or $300 per month flat rate, also there is a start-up fee. Online civil records date from 11/16/98 forward, probate from 05/98.

Criminal Records: Access: In person, online. Visitors must perform in person searches for themselves. No search fee. Required to search: name, years to search; also helpful: DOB. Criminal records on computer since 2/95; prior records are available if the case number is known. Online access to criminal records is the same as civil. Online criminal and traffic records date from 02/28/95.

General Information: Public Access terminal is available. (Criminal only.) No adoption records released. Copy fee: $.25 per page. Certification fee: $1.00. Payee: County Court. Personal checks accepted. Visa, MC accepted with $3.00 service charge. Prepayment required.

Lincoln County

District Court (301 N Jeffers Third Floor), PO Box 1616, North Platte, NE 69103-1616; 308-534-4350 X301 & X303. Hours: 8AM-5PM (CST). *Felony, Civil Actions Over $15,000.*

www.seda-cog.org/snyder/ical/calendar.asp

Civil Records: Access: In person, online. Visitors must perform in person searches for themselves. No search fee. Required to search: name, years to search. Civil cases indexed by defendant, plaintiff. Civil records on computer back to 5/1997; books from 1866. An online subscription service is available; same as criminal access. Online records date from 04/97.

Criminal Records: Access: In person, online. Visitors must perform in person searches for themselves. No search fee. Required to search: name, years to search. Criminal records on computer back to 5/1997; books from 1866. A subscription service is at www.nebraska.gov/faqs/justice/. Fee is $.60 a record or $300 per month flat rate, also there is a start-up fee. Online records date from 04/97.

General Information: Public Access terminal is available. No sealed, court ordered or mental health records released. Copy fee: $.25 per page. Certification fee: $1.00. Payee: Clerk of District Court. Personal checks accepted. Prepayment required.

Lincoln County Court PO Box 519, North Platte, NE 69103; 308-534-4350; Fax: 308-534-3525. Hours: 8AM-5PM (CST). *Misdemeanor, Civil Actions Under $45,000, Eviction, Small Claims, Probate.*

Civil Records: Access: In person, online. Visitors must perform in person searches for themselves. No search fee. Required to search: name, years to search. Civil cases indexed by defendant, plaintiff. Civil records kept on index books back 20-25 years. An online subscription service is available; same as criminal access. Online civil records date from 10/99 forward, probate from 05/98.

Criminal Records: Access: In person, online. Visitors must perform in person searches for themselves. No search fee. Required to search: name, years to search, DOB. Criminal records on computer since 04/97; prior on books back 20 years. A subscription service is available at www.nebraska.gov/faqs/justice/. Fee is $.60 a record or $300 per month flat rate, also there is a start-up fee. Online criminal and traffic records date from 04/97.

General Information: Public Access terminal is available. No adoption records released. Copy fee: $.25 per page. Certification fee: $1.00. Payee: County Court. Personal checks accepted. Visa, MC, Discover accepted with $3.00 service charge. Prepayment required.

Logan County

District Court PO Box 8, Stapleton, NE 69163; 308-636-2311. Hours: 8:30AM-Noon; 1PM-4:30PM M-TH; 8:30AM-Noon; 1PM-4PM F (CST). *Felony, Civil Actions Over $15,000.*

Civil Records: Access: Mail, in person, online. Both court and visitors may perform in person searches. No search fee. Required to search: name, years to search. Civil cases indexed by defendant, plaintiff. Civil records on docket books; computerized records since 2000. An online subscription service is available; same as criminal access. Online records date from 04/97.

Criminal Records: Access: Mail, In person, online. Both court and visitors may perform in person searches. No search fee. Required to search: name, years to search. Criminal records on docket books; computerized records since 2000. A subscription service is at www.nebraska.gov/faqs/justice/. Fee is $.60 a record or $300 per month flat rate, also there is a start-up fee. Online records date from 04/97.

General Information: Public Access terminal is available. Copy fee: $.50 per page. Certification fee: $1.00. Payee: Clerk of the District Court. Personal checks accepted. Prepayment required. Mail requests: SASE helpful. Turnaround time same day.

Logan County Court PO Box 8, Stapleton, NE 69163; 308-636-2677. Hours: 8AM-Noon, 1-4PM Wed (CST). *Misdemeanor, Civil Actions Under $45,000, Eviction, Small Claims, Probate.*

Civil Records: Access: Fax, mail, in person, online. Both court and visitors may perform in person searches. No search fee. Required to search: name, years to search; also helpful: address. Civil cases indexed by defendant, plaintiff. Civil records on docket books since 1837. An online subscription service is available; same as criminal access. Online civil records date from 01/00 forward, probate from 09/98.

Criminal Records: Access: Fax, mail, In person, online. Both court and visitors may perform in person searches. No search fee. Required to search: name, years to search, signed release; also helpful: DOB. Criminal records on docket books since 1837. A subscription service is available at www.nebraska.gov/faqs/justice/. Fee is $.60 a record or $300 per month flat rate, also there is a start-up fee. Online criminal and traffic records date from 09/98.

General Information: Adoption and juvenile records are not released. Fee to fax results is $3.00 1st page, $1.00 each add'l. Copy fee: $.25 per page. Certification fee: $1.00. Payee: County Court. Personal checks accepted. Prepayment required. Mail requests: SASE required. Mail turnaround time 3-4 days.

Loup County

District Court PO Box 146, Taylor, NE 68879; 308-942-6035; Fax: 308-942-6015. Hours: 8:30AM-4:30PM M-Th, 8:30AM-Noon F (CST). *Felony, Civil Actions Over $15,000.*

Civil Records: Access: In person, online. Visitors must perform in person searches for themselves. No search fee. Required to search: name, years to search. Civil cases indexed by defendant, plaintiff. Civil records in index books from late 1800s. An online

subscription service is available; same as criminal access. Online records date from 06/00.

Criminal Records: Access: In person, online. Visitors must perform in person searches for themselves. No search fee. Required to search: name, years to search; also helpful: address, DOB, SSN. Criminal records in index books from late 1800s. A subscription service is at www.nebraska.gov/faqs/justice/. Fee is $.60 a record or $300 per month flat rate, also there is a start-up fee. Online records date from 06/00.

General Information: Public Access terminal is available. No juvenile or adoption records released. Copy fee: $.25 per page. Certification fee: $1.00. Payee: Clerk of District Court. Personal checks accepted. Prepayment required.

Loup County Court PO Box 146, Taylor, NE 68879; 308-942-6035; Fax: 308-942-3103. Hours: 8:30AM-4:30PM M-Th, 8:30AM-Noon F (CST). *Misdemeanor, Civil Actions Under $45,000, Eviction, Small Claims, Probate.*

Civil Records: Access: In person, online. Visitors must perform in person searches for themselves. No search fee. Required to search: name, years to search. Civil cases indexed by defendant, plaintiff. Civil records on index books since late 1800s. Some records have been filmed and forwarded to state archives. An online subscription service is available; same as criminal access. Online civil records date from 10/00 forward, probate from 11/00.

Criminal Records: Access: In person, online. Visitors must perform in person searches for themselves. No search fee. Required to search: name, years to search. Criminal records on index books since late 1800s. Some records have been filmed and forwarded to state archives. A subscription service is at www.nebraska.gov/faqs/justice/. Fee is $.60 a record or $300 per month flat rate, also there is a start-up fee. Online criminal and traffic records date from 08/00.

General Information: Public Access terminal is available. Copy fee: $.25 per page. Certification fee: $1.00. Payee: County Court. Personal checks accepted. Prepayment required.

Madison County

District Court PO Box 249, Madison, NE 68748; 402-454-3311 X140; Fax: 402-454-6528. Hours: 8AM-5PM (CST). *Felony, Civil Actions Over $45,000.*

Civil Records: Access: In person, online. Visitors must perform in person searches for themselves. No search fee. Required to search: name, years to search. Civil cases indexed by defendant, plaintiff. Civil records on microfiche from late 1970s, prior on docket books from 1800s; computerized records go back to 1987. An online subscription service is available; same as criminal access. Online records date from 09/97.

Criminal Records: Access: In person, online. Visitors must perform in person searches for themselves. No search fee. Required to search: name, years to search. Criminal records on microfiche from late 1970s, prior on docket books from 1800s; computerized records go back to 1987. A subscription service is at www.nebraska.gov/faqs/justice/. Fee is $.60 a record or $300 per month flat rate, also there is a start-up fee. Online records date from 09/97.

General Information: Public Access terminal is available. No mental health records released. Will fax specifc case file requests for $1.00 per page if prepaid. Copy fee: $.25 per page. Certification fee: $1.50. Payee: Clerk of District Court. Personal checks accepted. Prepayment required.

Madison County Court PO Box 230, Madison, NE 68748; 402-454-3311; Civil phone: ext 142; Criminal phone: ext 181; Probate phone: ext 165; Fax: 402-454-3438. Hours: 8:30AM-5PM (CST). *Misdemeanor, Civil Actions Under $45,000, Eviction, Small Claims, Probate.*

Civil Records: Access: Mail, in person, online. Visitors must perform in person searches for themselves. No search fee. Required to search: name, years to search. Civil cases indexed by defendant, plaintiff. Civil records on computer since 1986, prior on docket book, cards. An online subscription service is available; same as criminal access. Online civil records date from 01/99 forward, probate from 05/98.

Criminal Records: Access: Mail, In person, online. Visitors must perform in person searches for themselves. No search fee. Required to search: name, years to search, DOB. Criminal records on computer from 1986. A subscription service is at www.nebraska.gov/faqs/justice/. Fee is $.60 a record or $300 per month flat rate, also there is a start-up fee. Online criminal and traffic records date from 10/96.

General Information: Public Access terminal is available. No adoption records released. Will fax results to local or toll free line. Copy fee: $.25 per page. Certification fee: $1.00. Payee: Madison County Court. Personal checks accepted. Prepayment required. Mail turnaround time is 5 days.

McPherson County

District Court PO Box 122, Tryon, NE 69167; 308-587-2363; Fax: 308-587-2363 (Call first). Hours: 8:30AM-4:30PM (CST). *Felony, Civil Actions Over $15,000.*

Civil Records: Access: Fax, mail, in person, online. Both court and visitors may perform in person searches. No search fee. Required to search: name, years to search; also helpful: address. Civil cases indexed by defendant, plaintiff. Civil records on index books since late 1800s. An online subscription service is available; same as criminal access. Online records date from 06/00.

Criminal Records: Access: Fax, mail, In person, online. Both court and visitors may perform in person searches. No search fee. Required to search: name, years to search; also helpful: address, DOB, SSN. Criminal records on index books since late 1800s. A subscription service is available at www.nebraska.gov/faqs/justice/. Fee is $.60 a record or $300 per month flat rate, also there is a start-up fee. Online records date from 06/00.

General Information: No adoption records released. Will fax results $2.00 1st page, $1.00 each add'l. Copy fee: $.50 per page. Certification fee: $1.50. Payee: Clerk of District Court. Business checks accepted. Prepayment required. Mail requests: SASE required. Mail turnaround time 3-4 days.

McPherson County Court PO Box 122, Tryon, NE 69167; 308-587-2363; Fax: 308-587-2363 (Call first). Hours: 8:30AM-Noon, 1-4:30PM Tu; 8:30AM-Noon, Th (CST). *Misdemeanor, Civil Actions Under $45,000, Eviction, Small Claims, Probate.*

Civil Records: Access: Fax, mail, in person, online. Both court and visitors may perform in person searches. No search fee. Required to search: name, years to search; also helpful: address. Civil cases indexed by defendant, plaintiff. Civil records computerized since 06/99, rest on index cards, are not computerized. An online subscription service is available; same as criminal access. Online civil records date from 01/00 forward, probate from 08/98.

Criminal Records: Access: Fax, mail, In person, online. Both court and visitors may perform in person searches. No search fee. Required to search: name, years to search, signed release; also helpful: address,

DOB. Criminal records computerized since 08/98. A subscription service is available at www.nebraska.gov/faqs/justice/. Fee is $.60 a record or $300 per month flat rate, also there is a start-up fee. Online criminal and traffic records date from 08/98.

General Information: Adoption and juvenile records are not released. Fee to fax results is $3.00 1st page, $1.00 each add'l. Copy fee: $.25 per page. Certification fee: $1.00. Payee: County Court. Personal checks accepted. Prepayment required. Mail requests: SASE required. Mail turnaround: 3-4 days.

Merrick County

District Court PO Box 27, Central City, NE 68826; 308-946-2461; Fax: 308-946-3692. 8AM-5PM (CST). *Felony, Civil Actions Over $15,000.*

Civil Records: Access: In person, online. Visitors must perform in person searches for themselves. No search fee. Required to search: name, years to search. Civil cases indexed by defendant, plaintiff. Civil records on index books from 1860; on computer back to 1994. An online subscription service is available; same as criminal access. Online records date from 07/94.

Criminal Records: Access: In person, online. Visitors must perform in person searches for themselves. No search fee. Required to search: name, years to search, signed release. Criminal records on index books from 1860; on computer back to 1994. A subscription service is available at www.nebraska.gov/faqs/justice/. Fee is $.60 a record or $300 per month flat rate, also there is a start-up fee. Online records date from 07/94.

General Information: Public Access terminal is available. No probation or mental health records released. Will fax specifc case file requests. Copy fee: $.25 per page. Certification fee: $1.00. Payee: Clerk of District Court. Personal checks accepted. Prepayment required.

Merrick County Court County Courthouse, PO Box 27, Central City, NE 68826; 308-946-2812. Hours: 8AM-5PM (CST). *Misdemeanor, Civil Actions Under $45,000, Eviction, Small Claims, Probate.*

Civil Records: Access: In person, online. Visitors must perform in person searches for themselves. No search fee. Required to search: name, years to search. Civil cases indexed by defendant, plaintiff. Civil records on index books from 1860; on computer back to 1994. An online subscription service is available; same as criminal access. Online civil and probate records from 03/94 forward.

Criminal Records: Access: In person, online. Visitors must perform in person searches for themselves. No search fee. Required to search: name, years to search, DOB. Criminal records on index books from 1860; on computer back to 1994. A subscription service is available at www.nebraska.gov/faqs/justice/. Fee is $.60 a record or $300 per month flat rate, also there is a start-up fee. Online criminal and traffic records date from 03/94.

General Information: Public Access terminal is available. No financial affidavits or sealed records released. Copy fee: $.25 per page. Certification fee: $1.00. Payee: County Court. Personal checks accepted. Prepayment required.

Morrill County

District Court PO Box 824, Bridgeport, NE 69336; 308-262-1261; Fax: 308-262-1799. Hours: 8AM-Noon, 1-4:30PM (MST). *Felony, Civil Actions Over $15,000.*

Civil Records: Access: In person, online. Visitors must perform in person searches for themselves. Search fee: none. Required to search: name, years to search. Civil cases indexed by defendant, plaintiff.

Computerized records back to 11/97; civil records on microfilm, books dating back to early 1900. An online subscription service is available; same as criminal access. Online records date from 10/97.

Criminal Records: Access: In person, online. Visitors must perform in person searches for themselves. No search fee. Required to search: name, years to search. Criminal records on microfilm, books dating back to learly 1900. A subscription service is at www.nebraska.gov/faqs/justice/. Fee is $.60 a record or $300 per month flat rate, also there is a start-up fee. Online records date from 10/97.

General Information: Public Access terminal is available. No mental health records released. Copy fee: $.25 a page. Certification fee: $1.00. Payee: Clerk of District Court. Prepayment required.

Morrill County Court PO Box 418, Bridgeport, NE 69336; 308-262-0812. Hours: 8AM-4:30PM (MST). *Misdemeanor, Civil Actions Under $45,000, Eviction, Small Claims, Probate.*

Civil Records: Access: In person, online. Visitors must perform in person searches for themselves. No search fee. Required to search: name, years to search. Civil cases indexed by defendant, plaintiff. Civil records on index books to 1908; probate on microfiche. An online subscription service is available; same as criminal access. Online civil and probate records from 01/01 forward.

Criminal Records: Access: In person, online. Visitors must perform in person searches for themselves. No search fee. Required to search: name, years to search. Criminal records on index books to 1908; probate on microfiche. A subscription service is at www.nebraska.gov/faqs/justice/. Fee is $.60 a record or $300 per month flat rate, also there is a start-up fee. Online criminal and traffic records date from 04/00.

General Information: No adoption records released. No copy fee. Certification fee: $1.00. Payee: County Court. Personal checks accepted. Prepayment required.

Nance County

District Court PO Box 338, Fullerton, NE 68638; 308-536-2365; Fax: 308-536-2742. Hours: 8AM-5PM (CST). *Felony, Civil Actions Over $15,000.*

Civil Records: Access: Phone, fax, mail, in person, online. Both court and visitors may perform in person searches. No search fee. Required to search: name, years to search; also helpful: address. Civil cases indexed by defendant, plaintiff. Civil records on index books from late 1800s. An online subscription service is available; same as criminal access. Online records date from 12/99.

Criminal Records: Access: In person only. Both court and visitors may perform in person searches. No search fee. Required to search: name, years to search; also helpful: address, DOB, SSN. Criminal records on index books from late 1800s. A subscription service is at www.nebraska.gov/faqs/justice/. Fee is $.60 a record or $300 per month flat rate, also there is a start-up fee. Online records date from 12/99.

General Information: Public Access terminal is available. (Public terminal in County Court Office-County will perform searches) No mental health records released. Will fax results $1.00 per page plus copy fees. Copy fee: $.25 per page. Certification fee: $1.00. Payee: Clerk of District Court. Personal checks accepted. Prepayment required. Mail requests: SASE required. Mail turnaround time is 4-5 days.

Nance County Court PO Box 837, Fullerton, NE 68638; 308-536-2675; Fax: 308-536-2742. Hours: 8AM-5PM (CST). *Misdemeanor, Civil Actions Under $45,000, Eviction, Small Claims, Probate.*

Civil Records: Access: Mail, in person, online. Both court and visitors may perform in person searches. No search fee. Required to search: name, years to search; also helpful: address. Civil cases indexed by defendant, plaintiff. Civil records on index cards since late 1800s, computerized since 01/01, probate on microfilm. An online subscription service is available; same as criminal access. Online civil and probate records from 08/00 forward.

Criminal Records: Access: Mail, In person, online. Both court and visitors may perform in person searches. No search fee. Required to search: name, years to search; also helpful: address, DOB. Criminal records go back to 1985, computerized since 2002, probate on microfilm. A subscription service is at www.nebraska.gov/faqs/justice/. Fee is $.60 a record or $300 per month flat rate, also there is a start-up fee. Online criminal and traffic records date from 08/00.

General Information: Public Access terminal is available. No juvenile, psychological reports or adoption records released. Copy fee: $.25 per page. Certification fee: $1.00. Payee: County Court. Personal checks accepted. Prepayment required. Mail requests: SASE required. Mail turnaround: 4-5 days.

Nemaha County

District Court 1824 N St, Auburn, NE 68305; 402-274-3616; Fax: 402-274-4478. Hours: 8AM-5PM (CST). *Felony, Civil Actions Over $15,000.*

Civil Records: Access: In person, mail. Both court and visitors may perform in person searches. Court will search on a time available basis No search fee. Required to search: name, years to search; also helpful: address. Civil cases indexed by defendant, plaintiff. Civil records on general index and docket books since the late 1800s; computerized records go back to 1998. An online subscription service is available; same as criminal access. Online records date from 06/98.

Criminal Records: Access: In person, mail. Both court and visitors may perform in person searches. Court will search on a time available basis. No search fee. Required to search: name, years to search; also helpful: address, DOB, SSN. Criminal records on general index and docket books since1950; computerized records go back to 1998. A subscription service is at www.nebraska.gov/faqs/justice/. Fee is $.60 a record or $300 per month flat rate, also there is a start-up fee. Online records date from 06/98.

General Information: Public Access terminal is available. No mental, juvenile records released. Will fax results to local or toll free line. Copy fee: $.25 per page. Certification fee: $1.00. Payee: Clerk of District Court. Personal checks accepted. Prepayment required. Mail turnaround time is 1 to 3 days.

Nemaha County Court 1824 N St, Auburn, NE 68305; 402-274-3008; Fax: 402-274-4605. 8AM-Noon, 1-5PM (CST). *Misdemeanor, Civil Actions Under $45,000, Eviction, Small Claims, Probate.* Note: This court also handles adoption, juvenile, and preliminary felony hearings.

Civil Records: Access: In person, online. Visitors must perform in person searches for themselves. No search fee. Required to search: name, years to search. Civil cases indexed by defendant, plaintiff. Civil records on index books since late 1800s, computerized records go back to 4/2000. An online subscription service is available; same as criminal access. Online civil and probate records from 04/00 forward.

Criminal Records: Access: In person, online. Visitors must perform in person searches for themselves. No search fee. Required to search: name, years to search; also helpful: DOB, SSN. Criminal records on index books since late 1800s, computerized records go back to 4/2000. A subscription service is available at www.nebraska.gov/faqs/justice/. Fee is $.60 a record or $300 per month flat rate, also there is a start-up fee. Online criminal and traffic records date from 04/00.

General Information: No adoption records released. Copy fee: $.25 per page. Certification fee: $1.00. Payee: Clerk of County Court. Personal checks accepted. Prepayment required.

Nuckolls County

District Court PO Box 362, Nelson, NE 68961; 402-225-4341; Fax: 402-225-2373. Hours: 8:30AM-4:30PM (CST). *Felony, Civil Actions Over $15,000.*
Note: The Court's search services not available to employers using employment agencies.

Civil Records: Access: In person, online. Visitors must perform in person searches for themselves. No search fee. Required to search: name, years to search. Civil cases indexed by defendant, plaintiff. Civil records on index books since late 1800s, computerized since 2000. An online subscription service is available; same as criminal access. Online records date from 03/00.

Criminal Records: Access: In person, online. Visitors must perform in person searches for themselves. No search fee. Required to search: name, years to search. Criminal records on index books since late 1800s, computerized since 2000. A subscription service is at www.nebraska.gov/faqs/justice/. Fee is $.60 a record or $300 per month flat rate, also there is a start-up fee. Online records date from 03/00.

General Information: Public Access terminal is available. Copy fee: $.25 per page. Certification fee: $1.00. Payee: Clerk of District Court. Personal checks accepted. Prepayment required.

Nuckolls County Court PO Box 372, Nelson, NE 68961; 402-225-2371; Fax: 402-225-2373. Hours: 8AM-4:30PM (CST). *Misdemeanor, Civil Actions Under $45,000, Eviction, Small Claims, Probate.*
Note: Mail access limited to short searches.

Civil Records: Access: In person, online. Visitors must perform in person searches for themselves. No search fee. Required to search: name, years to search. Civil cases indexed by defendant, plaintiff. Civil records on index cards, probate on microfilm. An online subscription service is available; same as criminal access. Online civil records date from 12/00 forward, probate from 01/01.

Criminal Records: Access: In person, online. Visitors must perform in person searches for themselves. No search fee. Required to search: name, years to search. Criminal records on index cards, probate on microfilm. A subscription service is at www.nebraska.gov/faqs/justice/. Fee is $.60 a record or $300 per month flat rate, also there is a start-up fee. Online criminal and traffic records date from 08/00.

General Information: No adoption or juvenile records released. Copy fee: $.25 per page. Certification fee: $1.00. Payee: County Court. Personal checks accepted. Prepayment required.

Otoe County

District Court 1021 Central Ave, Rm 209, PO Box 726, Nebraska City, NE 68410; 402-873-9550. Hours: 8AM-5PM Courthouse doors close at 4:30PM. (CST). *Felony, Dissolutions, Civil Actions Over $15,000.*

Civil Records: Access: In person, online. Visitors must perform in person searches for themselves. No search fee. Required to search: name, years to search, address. Civil cases indexed by defendant, plaintiff. Civil records on index books from late 1800s, computerized from 08/97. An online subscription service is available; same as criminal access. Online records date from 08/97.

Criminal Records: Access: In person, online. Visitors must perform in person searches for themselves. No search fee. Required to search: name, years to search. Criminal records on index books from late 1800s, computerized from 08/97. A subscription service is at www.nebraska.gov/faqs/justice/. Fee is $.60 a record or $300 per month flat rate, also there is a start-up fee. Online records date from 08/97.

General Information: Public Access terminal is available. Copy fee: $.50 per page. Certification fee: $1.00. Payee: Clerk of District Court. Personal checks accepted. Prepayment required.

Otoe County Court 1021 Central Ave, Rm 109, PO Box 487, Nebraska City, NE 68410-0487; 402-873-9575; Fax: 402-873-9030. Hours: 8AM-5PM (CST). *Misdemeanor, Civil Actions Under $45,000, Eviction, Small Claims, Probate.*

Civil Records: Access: Phone, fax, mail, in person, online. Only the court performs in person searches; visitors may not. No search fee. Required to search: name, years to search. Civil cases indexed by defendant, plaintiff. Civil records go back to 1986; computerized records go to 1999. An online subscription service is available; same as criminal access. Online civil records date from 10/99 forward, probate from 05/98.

Criminal Records: Access: Fax, mail, In person, online. Both the court and visitors may perform in person searches No search fee. Required to search: name, offense; also helpful: years to search, address, DOB. Criminal records go back to 1981; computerized since 1997. A subscription service is at www.nebraska.gov/faqs/justice/. Fee is $.60 a record or $300 per month flat rate, also there is a start-up fee. Online criminal and traffic records date from 02/97.

General Information: Public Access terminal is available. (Public access is at the District Court terminal.) No adoption records released without court order; juvenile records only released with signed release statement. Will fax results $1.00 per page. Copy fee: $.25 per page. Certification fee: $1.00. Payee: County Court. Personal checks accepted. Prepayment required. Mail requests: SASE required. Mail turnaround time 2-3 days.

Pawnee County

District Court PO Box 431, Pawnee City, NE 68420; 402-852-2963. Hours: 8AM-4PM (CST). *Felony, Civil Actions Over $15,000.*

Civil Records: Access: Phone, mail, in person, online. Both court and visitors may perform in person searches. Search fee: $3.00 per name. Required to search: name, years to search. Civil cases indexed by defendant, plaintiff. Civil records on index books since late 1800s. An online subscription service is available; same as criminal access. Online records date from 03/98.

Criminal Records: Access: Phone, mail, In person, online. Both court and visitors may perform in person searches. Search fee: $3.00 per name. Required to search: name, years to search. Criminal records on index books since late 1800s. A subscription service is at www.nebraska.gov/faqs/justice/. Fee is $.60 a record or $300 per month flat rate, also there is a start-up fee. Online records date from 03/98.

General Information: Public Access terminal is available. No mental health records released. Copy fee: $.50 per page. Certification fee: $1.00. Payee: Clerk of District Court. Personal checks accepted. Prepayment required. Mail requests: SASE required. Mail turnaround time 2 weeks, limited phone searches immediate.

Pawnee County Court PO Box 471, Pawnee City, NE 68420; 402-852-2388; Fax: 402-852-2388. 8AM-4:30PM (CST). *Misdemeanor, Civil Actions Under $45,000, Eviction, Small Claims, Probate.*
Note: Probate requests are accepted by mail.

Civil Records: Access: In person, online. Visitors must perform in person searches for themselves. No search fee. Required to search: name, years to search; also helpful: address. Civil cases indexed by defendant, plaintiff. Civil records indexed on computer since late 1980s and books back to late 1800s. An online subscription service is available; same as criminal access. Online civil and probate records from 06/00 forward.

Criminal Records: Access: In person, online. Visitors must perform in person searches for themselves. No search fee. Required to search: name, years to search, DOB; also helpful: SSN. Criminal records indexed on computer since late 1980s and books back to late 1800s. A subscription service is at www.nebraska.gov/faqs/justice/. Fee is $.60 a record or $300 per month flat rate, also there is a start-up fee. Online criminal and traffic records date from 06/00.

General Information: Public Access terminal is available. No adoption records released. Copy fee: $.25 per page. Certification fee: $1.00. Payee: Pawnee County Court. Personal checks accepted. Prepayment required.

Perkins County

District Court PO Box 156, Grant, NE 69140; 308-352-4643; Fax: 308-352-2455. Hours: 8AM-4PM (MST). *Felony, Civil Actions Over $15,000.*

Civil Records: Access: Fax, mail, in person, online. Both court and visitors may perform in person searches. Search fee: Prepay Fax fee $3.00. Required to search: name, years to search. Civil cases indexed by defendant, plaintiff. Civil records on index books since late 1800s. An online subscription service is available; same as criminal access. Online records date from 06/00.

Criminal Records: Access: Fax, mail, In person, online. Both court and visitors may perform in person searches. Search fee: Prepay Fax fee $3.00. Required to search: name, years to search. Criminal records on index books since late 1800s. A subscription service is at www.nebraska.gov/faqs/justice/. Fee is $.60 a record or $300 per month flat rate, also there is a start-up fee. Online records date from 06/00.

General Information: Public Access terminal is available. All records public. Will fax results for $3.00 prepaid. Copy fee: $.50 per page. Certification fee: $1.50. Payee: Clerk of District Court. Personal checks accepted. Prepayment required. Mail requests: SASE required. Mail turnaround time is 2-4 days.

Perkins County Court PO Box 222, Grant, NE 69140; 308-352-4415; Fax: 308-352-4700. Hours: 8AM-4PM (MST). *Misdemeanor, Civil Actions Under $45,000, Eviction, Small Claims, Probate.*

Civil Records: Access: Phone, fax, mail, in person, online. Both court and visitors may perform in person searches. No search fee. Required to search: name, years to search. Civil cases indexed by defendant, plaintiff. Civil records on index cards from 1987, prior on books; probate on microfilm & hard copy. An online subscription service is available; same as criminal access. Online civil and probate records from 11/00 forward.

Criminal Records: Access: Phone, fax, mail, In person, online. Both court and visitors may perform in person searches. No search fee. Required to search: name, years to search; also helpful: DOB. Criminal records on index cards from 1987, prior on books; probate on microfilm & hard copy. A subscription service is at www.nebraska.gov/faqs/justice/. Fee is $.60 a record or $300 per month flat rate, also there is a start-up fee. Online criminal and traffic records date from 06/00.

General Information: No sealed records released. Copy fee: $.25 per page. Certification fee: $1.00. Payee: Perkins County Court. Personal checks accepted. Prepayment required. Mail requests: SASE required. Mail turnaround time 3-4 days.

Phelps County

District Court PO Box 462, Holdrege, NE 68949; 308-995-2281. Hours: 9AM-5PM (CST). *Felony, Civil Actions Over $45,000.*

Civil Records: Access: In person, online. Visitors must perform in person searches for themselves. Search fee: none. Required to search: name, years to search. Civil cases indexed by defendant, plaintiff. Civil records on computer from 3/1998, on books back to 1885. An online subscription service is available; same as criminal access. Online records date from 03/98.

Criminal Records: Access: In person, online. Visitors must perform in person searches for themselves. No search fee. Required to search: name, years to search; also helpful: DOB. Criminal records on computer from 3/1998, on books prior back to 1885. A subscription service is available at www.nebraska.gov/faqs/justice/. Fee is $.60 a record or $300 per month flat rate, also there is a start-up fee. Online records date from 03/98.

General Information: Public Access terminal is available. No mental health, sealed records released. Will fax specific case files to local or toll-free number. Copy fee: $.25 per page. Certification fee: $1.00. Payee: Clerk of District Court. Personal checks accepted. Prepayment required.

Phelps County Court PO Box 255, Holdrege, NE 68949; 308-995-6561; Fax: 308-995-6562. Hours: 8AM-12;00-1-5PM (CST). *Misdemeanor, Civil Actions Under $45,000, Eviction, Small Claims, Probate.*

Civil Records: Access: In person, online. Visitors must perform in person searches for themselves. No search fee. Required to search: name, years to search. Civil cases indexed by defendant, plaintiff. Civil records computerized since 1999, on index cards going back to late 1970s; probate on microfiche to late 1800s. An online subscription service is available; same as criminal access. Online civil records date from 10/99 forward, probate from 06/98.

Criminal Records: Access: In person, online. Visitors must perform in person searches for themselves. No search fee. Required to search: name, years to search, DOB, signed release. Criminal records computerized since 1998, in files to 1987. A subscription service is at www.nebraska.gov/faqs/justice/. Fee is $.60 a record or $300 per month flat rate, also there is a start-up fee. Online criminal and traffic records date from 06/98.

General Information: Public Access terminal is available. No adoption records released. Copy fee: $.25 per page. Certification fee: $1.25. Payee: County Court. Personal checks accepted. Prepayment required.

Pierce County

District Court 111 W Court St, Rm 12, Pierce, NE 68767; 402-329-4335; Fax: 402-329-6412. Hours: 8:30 AM-4:30PM (CST). *Felony, Civil Actions Over $15,000.*

Civil Records: Access: In person, online. Visitors must perform in person searches for themselves. No search fee. Required to search: name, years to search. Civil cases indexed by defendant, plaintiff. Civil records on index books from 1870s; on computer back to 3/1999. An online subscription service is

available; same as criminal access. Online records date from 03/99.

Criminal Records: Access: In person, online. Visitors must perform in person searches for themselves. No search fee. Required to search: name, years to search; also helpful: address, DOB, SSN. Criminal records on index books from 1870s; on computer back to 3/1999. A subscription service is at www.nebraska.gov/faqs/justice/. Fee is $.60 a record or $300 per month flat rate, also there is a start-up fee. Online records date from 03/99.

General Information: Public Access terminal is available. No mental health records released. Copy fee: $.25 per page. Certification fee: $1.00. Payee: Clerk of District Court. Personal checks accepted. Prepayment required.

Pierce County Court 111 W Court St, Rm 11, Pierce, NE 68767; 402-329-6245; Fax: 402-329-6412. Hours: 8:30AM-4:30PM (CST). *Misdemeanor, Civil Actions Under $45,000, Eviction, Small Claims, Probate.*

Civil Records: Access: In person, online. Visitors must perform in person searches for themselves. No search fee. Required to search: name, years to search. Civil cases indexed by defendant, plaintiff. Civil records on index books back about 15 years, computerized since 05/00. An online subscription service is available; same as criminal access. Online civil and probate records from 05/00 forward.

Criminal Records: Access: In person, online. Visitors must perform in person searches for themselves. No search fee. Required to search: name, years to search. Criminal records on index books back about 15 years, computerized since 05/00. A subscription service is available at www.nebraska.gov/faqs/justice/. Fee is $.60 a record or $300 per month flat rate, also there is a start-up fee. Online criminal and traffic records date from 05/00.

General Information: Public Access terminal is available. No adoption records released. Copy fee: $.25 per page. Certification fee: $1.00. Payee: County Court. Personal checks accepted. Prepayment required.

Platte County

District Court PO Box 1188, Columbus, NE 68602-1188; 402-563-4906; Fax: 402-562-6718. Hours: 8:30AM-5PM (CST). *Felony, Civil Actions Over $15,000.*

Civil Records: Access: In person, online. Visitors must perform in person searches for themselves. No search fee. Required to search: name, years to search. Civil cases indexed by defendant, plaintiff. Civil records go back to 1800, civil records filed as hard copies; also on computer after 8/1/97. An online subscription service is available; same as criminal access. Online records date from 09/97.

Criminal Records: Access: In person, online. Visitors must perform in person searches for themselves. No search fee. Required to search: name, years to search, DOB. Criminal records go back to 1880s, criminal records filed as hard copies; also on computer after 8/1/97. A subscription service is at www.nebraska.gov/faqs/justice/. Fee is $.60 a record or $300 per month flat rate, also there is a start-up fee. Online records date from 09/97.

General Information: Public Access terminal is available. No juvenile or sealed records released. Copy fee: $.25 per page. Certification fee: $1.00. Payee: District Court. Only cashiers checks and money orders accepted. Prepayment required.

Platte County Court PO Box 538, Columbus, NE 68602-0538; 402-563-4905; Fax: 402-562-8158. Hours: 8AM-5PM (CST). *Misdemeanor, Civil Actions Under $45,000, Eviction, Small Claims, Probate.*

Civil Records: Access: In person, online. Visitors must perform in person searches for themselves. No search fee. Required to search: name, years to search. Civil cases indexed by defendant, plaintiff. Civil records on index books from 1980; on computer back to 1996. An online subscription service is available; same as criminal access. Online civil records date from 10/99 forward, probate from 05/98.

Criminal Records: Access: In person, online. Visitors must perform in person searches for themselves. No search fee. Required to search: name, years to search, DOB. Criminal records on index books from 1980; on computer back to 1996. A subscription service is available at www.nebraska.gov/faqs/justice/. Fee is $.60 a record or $300 per month flat rate, also there is a start-up fee. Online criminal and traffic records date from 10/96.

General Information: Public Access terminal is available. No adoption records released. Copy fee: $.25 per page. Certification fee: $1.00 for seal. Payee: Platte County Court. Personal checks accepted. Prepayment required.

Polk County

District Court PO Box 447, Osceola, NE 68651; 402-747-3487; Fax: 402-747-8299. Hours: 8AM-Noon,1-5PM (CST). *Felony, Civil Actions Over $15,000.*

Civil Records: Access: In person, online. Visitors must perform in person searches for themselves. No search fee. Required to search: name, years to search. Civil cases indexed by defendant, plaintiff. Civil records on index books from 1871. An online subscription service is available; same as criminal access. Online records date from 04/98.

Criminal Records: Access: In person, online. Visitors must perform in person searches for themselves. No search fee. Required to search: name, years to search, DOB, signed release. Criminal records on index books from 1871. A subscription service is at www.nebraska.gov/faqs/justice/. Fee is $.60 a record or $300 per month flat rate, also there is a start-up fee. Online records date from 04/98.

General Information: Public Access terminal is available. Copy fee: $.25 per page. Certification fee: $1.00. Payee: Clerk of District Court. Personal checks accepted. Prepayment required.

Polk County Court PO Box 506, Osceola, NE 68651; 402-747-5371; Fax: 402-747-2656. Hours: 8AM-5PM (CST). *Misdemeanor, Civil Actions Under $45,000, Eviction, Small Claims, Probate.*

Civil Records: Access: In person, online. Visitors must perform in person searches for themselves. No search fee. Required to search: name, years to search. Civil cases indexed by defendant, plaintiff. Civil records on index cards back to late 1970s; probate records back to late 1800s. An online subscription service is available; same as criminal access. Online civil and probate records from 01/01 forward.

Criminal Records: Access: In person, online. Visitors must perform in person searches for themselves. No search fee. Required to search: name, years to search, DOB. Criminal records on index cards back to late 1970s; on computer back to 8/2000. A subscription service is available at www.nebraska.gov/faqs/justice/. Fee is $.60 a record or $300 per month flat rate, also there is a start-up fee. Online criminal and traffic records date from 08/00.

General Information: Public Access terminal is available. No adoption, juvenile records released. Copy fee: $.25 per page. Certification fee: $1.00 each.

Payee: County Court. Personal checks accepted. Prepayment required.

Red Willow County

District Court 520 Norris Ave (PO Box 847), McCook, NE 69001; 308-345-4583; Fax: 308-345-7907. Hours: 8AM-4PM (CST). *Felony, Civil Actions Over $15,000.*
Civil Records: Access: Mail, in person, online. Both court and visitors may perform in person searches. No search fee. Required to search: name, years to search. Civil cases indexed by defendant, plaintiff. Civil records on index books since 1871, on microfiche since mid 1980s, computerized since 1998. An online subscription service is available; same as criminal access. Online records date from 06/98.
Criminal Records: Access: Mail, In person, online. Both court and visitors may perform in person searches. No search fee. Required to search: name, years to search. Criminal records on index books since 1871, on microfiche since mid 1980s, computerized since 1998. A subscription service is at www.nebraska.gov/faqs/justice/. Fee is $.60 a record or $300 per month flat rate, also there is a start-up fee. Online records date from 06/98.
General Information: Public Access terminal is available. Will fax results $3.00 1st page, $1.00 each add'l. Copy fee: $.50 per page. Certification fee: $1.00. Payee: Clerk of District Court. Personal checks accepted. Prepayment required. Mail requests: SASE required. Mail turnaround time 2-4 days.

Red Willow County Court 502 Norris Ave (PO Box 199), McCook, NE 69001; 308-345-1904; Fax: 308-345-1904. Hours: 8AM-4PM (CST). *Misdemeanor, Civil Actions Under $45,000, Eviction, Small Claims, Probate.*
Civil Records: Access: Mail, fax, in person, online. Both court and visitors may perform in person searches. No search fee. Required to search: name, years to search. Civil cases indexed by defendant, plaintiff. Civil records on case files and docket cards since 1984, probate on microfilm since 1977; on computer back to 1998. An online subscription service is available; same as criminal access. Online civil records date from 01/00 forward, probate from 08/98.
Criminal Records: Access: Mail, fax, In person, online. Both court and visitors may perform in person searches. No search fee. Required to search: name, years to search, DOB. Criminal records on books since 1984; on computer back to 1998. A subscription service is at www.nebraska.gov/faqs/justice/. Fee is $.60 a record or $300 per month flat rate, also there is a start-up fee. Online criminal and traffic records date from 06/98.
General Information: Public Access terminal is available. No adoption, juvenile, convictions set aside on misdemeanor offense, sealed records released. Copy fee: $.25 per page. Certification fee: $1.00. Payee: County Court. Personal checks accepted. Prepayment required. Mail requests: SASE required. Mail turnaround time 2 days.

Richardson County

District Court 1700 Stone St, Falls City, NE 68355; 402-245-2023; Fax: 402-245-3725. Hours: 8:30AM-5PM (CST). *Felony, Civil Actions Over $15,000.*
Civil Records: Access: In person, online. Visitors must perform in person searches for themselves. No search fee. Required to search: name, years to search. Civil cases indexed by defendant, plaintiff. Civil records on microfiche and at state archives to 1930; on computer back to 1998. An online subscription service is available; same as criminal access. Online records date from 02/98.

Criminal Records: Access: In person, online. Visitors must perform in person searches for themselves. No search fee. Required to search: name, years to search, DOB, signed release. Criminal records on microfiche and at state archives to 1930; on computer back to 1998. A subscription service is at www.nebraska.gov/faqs/justice/. Fee is $.60 a record or $300 per month flat rate, also there is a start-up fee. Online records date from 02/98.
General Information: Public Access terminal is available. No sealed records released. Copy fee: $.25 per page. Certification fee: $1.00. Payee: Clerk of District Court. Personal checks accepted. Prepayment required.

Richardson County Court 1700 Stone St Rm 205, Falls City, NE 68355; 402-245-2812; Fax: 402-245-3352. Hours: 8AM-5PM (CST). *Misdemeanor, Civil Actions Under $45,000, Eviction, Small Claims, Probate.*
Civil Records: Access: In person, online. Visitors must perform in person searches for themselves. No search fee. Required to search: name, years to search. Civil cases indexed by defendant, plaintiff. Civil records on index cards back to 1970s. An online subscription service is available; same as criminal access. Online civil and probate records from 11/00 forward.
Criminal Records: Access: In person, online. Visitors must perform in person searches for themselves. No search fee. Required to search: name, years to search; also helpful: DOB. Criminal records on index cards back to 1970s. A subscription service is at www.nebraska.gov/faqs/justice/. Fee is $.60 a record or $300 per month flat rate, also there is a start-up fee. Online criminal and traffic records date from 06/00.
General Information: Public Access terminal is available. No adoption records released. Copy fee: $.25 per page. Certification fee: $1.00. Payee: County Court. Only cashiers checks and money orders accepted. Prepayment required.

Rock County

District Court PO Box 367, Bassett, NE 68714; 402-684-3933; Fax: 402-684-2741. Hours: 9AM-5PM (CST). *Felony, Civil Actions Over $15,000.*
Civil Records: Access: Phone, fax, mail, in person, online. Both court and visitors may perform in person searches. No search fee. Required to search: name, years to search. Civil cases indexed by defendant, plaintiff. Civil records on index books since 1800s. An online subscription service is available; same as criminal access. Online records date from 08/00.
Criminal Records: Access: Phone, fax, mail, In person, online. Both court and visitors may perform in person searches. No search fee. Required to search: name, years to search, DOB. Criminal records on index books since 1800s. A subscription service is at www.nebraska.gov/faqs/justice/. Fee is $.60 a record or $300 per month flat rate, also there is a start-up fee. Online records date from 08/00.
General Information: No juvenile or sealed records released. Will fax results for $2.00 1st page and $1.00 each add'l. Copy fee: $.25 per page. Certification fee: $1.50. Payee: Clerk of District Court. Personal checks accepted. Prepayment required. Mail requests: SASE required. Mail turnaround time 1-2 days.

Rock County Court PO Box 249, Bassett, NE 68714; 402-684-3601; Fax: 402-684-2741. Hours: 8AM-5PM (CST). *Misdemeanor, Civil Actions Under $45,000, Eviction, Small Claims, Probate.*
Civil Records: Access: In person, online. Visitors must perform in person searches for themselves. No search fee. Required to search: name, years to search. Civil cases indexed by defendant, plaintiff. Civil records on index books from 1800s, index cards from

1985; on computer back to 8/2000. An online subscription service is available; same as criminal access. Online civil and probate records from 10/00 forward.
Criminal Records: Access: In person, online. Visitors must perform in person searches for themselves. No search fee. Required to search: name, years to search, DOB. Criminal records on index books from 1800s, index cards from 1985; on computer back to 8/2000. A subscription service is at www.nebraska.gov/faqs/justice/. Fee is $.60 a record or $300 per month flat rate, also there is a start-up fee. Online criminal and traffic records date from 08/00.
General Information: Public Access terminal is available. Copy fee: $.25 per page. Certification fee: $1.00. Payee: County Court. Personal checks accepted. Prepayment required.

Saline County

District Court PO Box 865, Wilber, NE 68465; 402-821-3179; Fax: 402-821-2132. Hours: 8AM-Noon, 1-5PM (CST). *Felony, Civil Actions Over $15,000.*
Civil Records: Access: Mail, in person, online. Visitors must perform in person searches for themselves. No search fee. Required to search: name, years to search. Civil cases indexed by defendant, plaintiff. Civil records being entered on computer beginning 8/94, index in dockets books from 1800s. An online subscription service is available; same as criminal access. Online records date from 07/94.
Criminal Records: Access: Mail, In person, online. Visitors must perform in person searches for themselves. No search fee. Required to search: name, years to search; also helpful: DOB. Criminal records being entered on computer beginning 8/94, index in dockets books from 1800s. A subscription service is at www.nebraska.gov/faqs/justice/. Fee is $.60 a record or $300 per month flat rate, also there is a start-up fee. Online records date from 07/94.
General Information: Public Access terminal is available. No sealed or mental health records released. Will fax specifc documents, but not name search results. Copy fee: $.25 per page. Certification fee: $1.00. Payee: Clerk of District Court. Personal checks accepted. Prepayment required.

Saline County Court PO Box 865, Wilber, NE 68465; 402-821-2131; Fax: 402-821-2132. Hours: 8AM-Noon; 1PM-5PM (CST). *Misdemeanor, Civil Actions Under $45,000, Eviction, Small Claims, Probate.*
Civil Records: Access: Fax, mail, in person, online. Both court and visitors may perform in person searches. Search fee: $3.00. Required to search: name, years to search. Civil cases indexed by defendant, plaintiff. Civil records on index books from 1860s; computerized records since 1994. An online subscription service is available; same as criminal access. Online civil and probate records from 06/94 forward.
Criminal Records: Access: Fax, mail, In person, online. Both court and visitors may perform in person searches. Search fee: $3.00. Required to search: name, years to search. Criminal records on index books from 1860s; computerized records since 1994. A subscription service is available at www.nebraska.gov/faqs/justice/. Fee is $.60 a record or $300 per month flat rate, also there is a start-up fee. Online criminal and traffic records date from 07/94.
General Information: Public Access terminal is available in District Court. No juvenile or sealed records released. No fee to fax results. Copy fee: $.25 per page. Certification fee: $1.25. Payee: County Court. Personal checks accepted. Prepayment required. Mail requests: SASE required. Mail turnaround time 2-3 days.

Sarpy County

District Court 1210 Golden Gate Dr, #3141, Papillion, NE 68046; 402-593-2267; Fax: 402-593-4403. Hours: 8AM-4:45PM (CST). *Felony, Civil Actions Over $50,000.*

Civil Records: Access: Phone, mail, in person, online. Both court and visitors may perform in person searches. No search fee. Required to search: name, years to search. Civil cases indexed by defendant, plaintiff. Civil records on computer from 1979 forward, on books prior. An online subscription service is available; same as criminal access. Online records date from 12/98.

Criminal Records: Access: Phone, mail, In person, online. Both court and visitors may perform in person searches. No search fee. Required to search: name, years to search. Criminal records on computer from 1979 forward, on books prior. A subscription service is at www.nebraska.gov/faqs/justice/. Fee is $.60 a record or $300 per month flat rate, also there is a start-up fee. Online records date from 12/98. For phone requests, will only verify from computer index.

General Information: Public Access terminal is available. No mental health or search warrant records released. Copy fee: $.75 for first page, $.25 each add'l. Certification fee: $1.00. Payee: Clerk of District Court. Only cashiers checks and money orders accepted. Prepayment required. Mail requests: SASE required. Mail turnaround time 1-2 days.

Sarpy County Court 1210 Golden Gate Dr, #3142, Papillion, NE 68046; 402-593-5775. Hours: 8AM-4:45PM (CST). *Misdemeanor, Civil Actions Under $50,000, Eviction, Small Claims, Probate.* www.sarpy.com

Civil Records: Access: In person, online. Visitors must perform in person searches for themselves. No search fee. Required to search: name, years to search. Civil cases indexed by defendant, plaintiff. Civil records on computer since 08/97; prior records on docket books and cards from 1800s. Access to the Internet system requires registration and password. Call John at 402-471-3049 for more information. System can be searched by name or case number. A subscription service is at www.nebraska.gov/business/egov.phtml. Fee is $.60 a record or $300 per month flat rate, also there is a start-up fee. Online civil records date from 10/00 forward, probate from 04/99.

Criminal Records: Access: In person, online. Visitors must perform in person searches for themselves. No search fee. Required to search: name, years to search, DOB. Criminal records on computer since 08/97; prior records on docket books and cards from 1800s. Online access to criminal records is the same as civil. Online criminal and traffic records date from 08/97.

General Information: Public Access terminal is available. No adoption records released. Copy fee: $.25 per page. Certification fee: $1.00. Payee: County Court. Personal checks accepted. Prepayment required.

Saunders County

District Court County Courthouse, 433 N Chestnut, Wahoo, NE 68066; 402-443-8113; Fax: 402-443-8170. Hours: 8AM-5PM (CST). *Felony, Civil Actions Over $15,000.*

Civil Records: Access: In person, online. Visitors must perform in person searches for themselves. No search fee. Required to search: name, years to search. Civil cases indexed by defendant, plaintiff. Civil records on index books to late 1800s; on computer back to 1998. An online subscription service is available; same as criminal access. Online records date from 06/98.

Criminal Records: Access: In person, online. Visitors must perform in person searches for themselves. No search fee. Required to search: name, years to search; also helpful: DOB, SSN. Criminal records on index books to late 1800s; on computer back to 1998. A subscription service is at www.nebraska.gov/faqs/justice/. Fee is $.60 a record or $300 per month flat rate, also there is a start-up fee. Online records date from 06/98.

General Information: Public Access terminal is available. No mental health records released. Copy fee: $.25 per page. Certification fee: $1.00. Payee: Clerk of District Court. Personal checks accepted. Prepayment required.

Saunders County Court 433 N Chestnut, Wahoo, NE 68066; 402-443-8119; Fax: 402-443-8121. Hours: 8AM-5PM (CST). *Misdemeanor, Civil Actions Under $45,000, Eviction, Small Claims, Probate.*

Civil Records: Access: In person, online. Visitors must perform in person searches for themselves. No search fee. Required to search: name, years to search. Civil cases indexed by defendant, plaintiff. Civil records on index books. An online subscription service is available; same as criminal access. Online civil and probate records from 11/00 forward.

Criminal Records: Access: In person, online. Visitors must perform in person searches for themselves. No search fee. Required to search: name, years to search. Criminal records on index books. A subscription service is available at www.nebraska.gov/faqs/justice/. Fee is $.60 a record or $300 per month flat rate, also there is a start-up fee. Online criminal and traffic records date from 06/26/00.

General Information: Public Access terminal is available. No adoption or sealed records released. Copy fee: $.25 per page. Certification fee: $1.00. Payee: County Court. Personal checks accepted. Prepayment required.

Scotts Bluff County

District Court 1725 10th St, PO Box 47, Gering, NE 69341-0047; 308-436-6641; Fax: 308-436-6759. Hours: 8AM-4:30PM (MST). *Felony, Civil Actions Over $15,000.*

Civil Records: Access: In person, online. Visitors must perform in person searches for themselves. No search fee. Required to search: name, years to search. Civil cases indexed by defendant, plaintiff. Civil records on index books to 1800s; on computer back to 1997. An online subscription service is available; same as criminal access.

Criminal Records: Access: In person, online. Visitors must perform in person searches for themselves. No search fee. Criminal records on index books to 1800s; on computer back to 1997. A subscription service is available at www.nebraska.gov/faqs/justice/. Fee is $.60 a record or $300 per month flat rate, also there is a start-up fee.

General Information: Public Access terminal is available. No juvenile or mental health records released. Will fax results for $3.50 plus copy cost. Copy fee: $.50 per page. Certification fee: $1.00. Payee: Clerk of District Court. Business checks accepted. Prepayment required.

Scotts Bluff County Court 1725 10th St, Gering, NE 69341; 308-436-6648. Hours: 8AM-5PM (MST). *Misdemeanor, Civil Actions Under $45,000, Eviction, Small Claims, Probate.*

Civil Records: Access: In person, online. Visitors must perform in person searches for themselves. No search fee. Required to search: name, years to search. Civil cases indexed by defendant, plaintiff. Civil records computerized since 2000. An online subscription service is available; same as criminal

access. Online civil and probate records from 03/01 forward.

Criminal Records: Access: In person, online. Visitors must perform in person searches for themselves. No search fee. Required to search: name, years to search, DOB. Criminal records computerized since 2000. A subscription service is at www.nebraska.gov/faqs/justice/. Fee is $.60 a record or $300 per month flat rate, also there is a start-up fee. Online criminal and traffic records date from 05/00.

General Information: Public Access terminal is available. No adoption records released. Copy fee: $.25 per page. Certification fee: $1.00. Payee: County Court. Personal checks accepted. Prepayment required.

Seward County

District Court PO Box 36, Seward, NE 68434; 402-643-4895. Hours: 8AM-5PM (CST). *Felony, Civil Actions Over $15,000.*

Civil Records: Access: In person, online. Visitors must perform in person searches for themselves. No search fee. Required to search: name, years to search. Civil cases indexed by defendant, plaintiff. Civil records on index books since late 1800s; computerized since 6/98. An online subscription service is available; same as criminal access. Online records date from 06/98.

Criminal Records: Access: In person, online. Visitors must perform in person searches for themselves. No search fee. Required to search: name, years to search. Criminal records on index books since late 1800s; computerized since 6/98. A subscription service is at www.nebraska.gov/faqs/justice/. Fee is $.60 a record or $300 per month flat rate, also there is a start-up fee. Online records date from 06/98.

General Information: Public Access terminal is available. Copy fee: $.30 per page. Certification fee: $1.00. Personal checks not accepted. Prepayment required.

Seward County Court PO Box 37, Seward, NE 68434; 402-643-3341; Fax: 402-643-2950. Hours: 8AM-5PM (CST). *Misdemeanor, Civil Actions Under $45,000, Eviction, Small Claims, Probate.*

Civil Records: Access: In person, online. Both court and visitors may perform in person searches. No search fee. Required to search: name, years to search. Civil cases indexed by defendant, plaintiff. Civil records on index books, cards back to 1975, computerized back to 1997. An online subscription service is available; same as criminal access. Online civil records date from 10/99 forward, probate from 05/98.

Criminal Records: Access: In person, online. Both court and visitors may perform in person searches. No search fee. Required to search: name, years to search. Criminal records on index books, cards back to 1950. A subscription service is available at www.nebraska.gov/faqs/justice/. Fee is $.60 a record or $300 per month flat rate, also there is a start-up fee. Online criminal and traffic records date from 03/97.

General Information: Public Access terminal is available. No adoption, juvenile or sealed records released. Copy fee: $.25 per page. Certification fee: $1.00. Payee: County Court. Personal checks accepted. Prepayment required.

Sheridan County

District Court PO Box 581, Rushville, NE 69360; 308-327-5654; Fax: 308-327-5618. Hours: 8:30AM-4:30PM (MST). *Felony, Civil Actions Over $10,000.*

Civil Records: Access: Mail, fax, in person, online. Both court and visitors may perform in person searches. Search fee: $5.00 per name. Required to search: name, years to search. Civil cases indexed by defendant, plaintiff. Civil records on index and docket books since 1800s, computerized since 1998. An online subscription service is available; same as criminal access. Online records date from 08/98.

Criminal Records: Access: Mail, fax, In person, online. Both court and visitors may perform in person searches. Search fee: $5.00 per name. Required to search: name, years to search, signed release; also helpful: DOB. Criminal records on index and docket books since 1800s, computerized since 1998. A subscription service is available at www.nebraska.gov/faqs/justice/. Fee is $.60 a record or $300 per month flat rate, also there is a start-up fee. Online records date from 08/98.

General Information: Public Access terminal is available. No mental health, grand jury records released. Will fax results to local and toll free lines. Copy fee: $.25 per page. Certification fee: $1.00. Payee: Clerk of District Court. Personal checks accepted. Mail requests: SASE required. Mail turnaround time 1-2 days.

Sheridan County Court PO Box 430, Rushville, NE 69360; 308-327-2692; Fax: 308-327-5623. Hours: 8AM-4:30PM (MST). *Misdemeanor, Civil Actions Under $45,000, Eviction, Small Claims, Probate.*

Civil Records: Access: In person, online. Visitors must perform in person searches for themselves. No search fee. Required to search: name, years to search. Civil cases indexed by defendant, plaintiff. Civil records on index books, on microfiche from 1920 forward; on computer back to 6/2000. An online subscription service is available; same as criminal access. Online civil and probate records from 11/00 forward.

Criminal Records: Access: Fax, mail, In person, online. Visitors must perform in person searches for themselves. No search fee. Required to search: name, years to search. Criminal records on index books, on microfiche from 1920 forward; on computer back to 6/2000. A subscription service is available at www.nebraska.gov/faqs/justice/. Fee is $.60 a record or $300 per month flat rate, also there is a start-up fee. Online criminal and traffic records date from 06/00.

General Information: Public Access terminal is available. No adoption or confidential records released. No fee to fax results. Faxing available to 800 numbers only. No copy fee. Certification fee: $1.00. Payee: Sheridan County Court. Personal checks accepted. Prepayment required. Mail requests: SASE required. Mail turnaround time 1-2 days.

Sherman County

District Court 630 O St, PO Box 456, Loup City, NE 68853; 308-745-1513 x103; Fax: 308-745-0297. Hours: 8:30AM-4:30PM (CST). *Felony, Civil Actions Over $15,000.*

Civil Records: Access: Mail, in person, online. Visitors must perform in person searches for themselves. No search fee. Required to search: name, years to search. Civil cases indexed by defendant, plaintiff. Civil records on index and docket books since late 1800s; on computer back to 4/2000. An online subscription service is available; same as criminal access. Online records date from 04/00.

Criminal Records: Access: Mail, In person, online. Visitors must perform in person searches for themselves. No search fee. Required to search: name, years to search. Criminal records on index and docket books since late 1800s; on computer back to 4/2000. A subscription service is available at www.nebraska.gov/faqs/justice/. Fee is $.60 a record or $300 per month flat rate, also there is a start-up fee. Online records date from 04/00.

General Information: Public Access terminal is available. No mental health records released. Will not fax results. Copy fee: $.50 per page. Certification fee:

$1.50. Payee: Clerk of District Court. Personal checks accepted. Prepayment required. Mail requests: SASE required. Mail turnaround time 1-2 days.

Sherman County Court 630 O St, PO Box 55, Loup City, NE 68853; 308-745-1513 x102; Fax: 308-745-1510. Hours: 8:30AM-4:30PM (CST). *Misdemeanor, Civil Actions Under $45,000, Eviction, Small Claims, Probate.*

Civil Records: Access: Fax, mail, in person, online Visitors must perform in person searches for themselves. No search fee. Required to search: name, years to search. Civil cases indexed by defendant only. Civil records on index books from late 1800s; on computer back to 5/2000 in DC office. Newer names indexed by defendant only. An online subscription service is available; same as criminal access. Online civil and probate records from 05/00 forward.

Criminal Records: Access: Fax, mail, In person, online. Visitors must perform in person searches for themselves. No search fee. Required to search: name, years to search, DOB. Criminal records on index books from late 1800s; on computer back to 5/2000. Newer names indexed by defendant only. A subscription service is available at www.nebraska.gov/faqs/justice/. Fee is $.60 a record or $300 per month flat rate, also there is a start-up fee. Online criminal and traffic records date from 05/00.

General Information: Public Access terminal is available. (Terminal located in District Court Office, records back to 05/00.) No adoption records released. Fee to fax results is $3.00 1st page; $1.00 each add'l. Copy fee: $.25 per page. Certification fee: $1.00. Payee: Sherman County Court. Business checks accepted. Prepayment required. Mail requests: SASE required. Mail turnaround time 1-2 weeks.

Sioux County

District Court PO Box 158, Harrison, NE 69346; 308-668-2443; Fax: 308-668-2443. Hours: 8AM-4:30PM (MST). *Felony, Civil Actions Over $15,000.*

Civil Records: Access: Mail, in person, online. Both the court and visitors may perform in person searches. No search fee. Required to search: name, years to search. Civil cases indexed by defendant, plaintiff. Civil records in index and docket books since 1800s; computerized records since 1992. An online subscription service is available; same as criminal access. Online records date from 06/00.

Criminal Records: Access: Mail, In person, online. Both the court and visitors may perform in person searches. No search fee. Required to search: name, years to search; also helpful: DOB, SSN. Criminal records in index and docket books since 1800s; computerized records since 1992. A subscription service is at www.nebraska.gov/faqs/justice/. Fee is $.60 a record or $300 per month flat rate, also there is a start-up fee. Online records date from 06/00.

General Information: Public Access terminal is available. No adoption or sealed records released. Will fax results for $1.00 per page. Copy fee: $.25 per page. Certification fee: $1.00 per page. Payee: Clerk of District Court. Personal checks accepted. Prepayment required. Mail requests: SASE required. Mail turnaround time 3-4 days.

Sioux County Court PO Box 158, Harrison, NE 69346; 308-668-2443; Fax: same. Hours: 8AM-4:30 (MST). *Misdemeanor, Civil Actions Under $45,000, Eviction, Small Claims, Probate.*

Civil Records: Access: Phone, fax, mail, in person, online. Both the court and visitors may perform in person searches. No search fee. Required to search: name, years to search. Civil cases indexed by defendant, plaintiff. Civil records on index books from late 1800s. Prefer to take phone requests. Very few civil cases handled each year. A subscription

service is at www.nebraska.gov/business/egov.phtml. Fee is $.60 a record or $300 per month flat rate, also there is a start-up fee. Online civil and probate records from 01/01 forward.

Criminal Records: Access: Phone, fax, mail, In person, online. Both the court and visitors may perform in person searches. No search fee. Required to search: name, years to search. Criminal records on index books from late 1800s. A subscription service is at www.nebraska.gov/faqs/justice/. Fee is $.60 a record or $300 per month flat rate, also there is a start-up fee. Online criminal and traffic records date from 08/00.

General Information: Public Access terminal is available. No sealed, expunged, or adoption records released. Will fax results for $1.00 per page. Copy fee: $.25 per page. Certification fee: $1.00. Payee: County Court. Personal checks accepted. Prepayment required. Mail requests: SASE required. Mail turnaround time 3-4 days.

Stanton County

District Court PO Box 347, Stanton, NE 68779; 402-439-2222; Probate phone: 402-439-2221; Fax: 402-439-2200. Hours: 8:30AM-4:30PM (CST). *Felony, Civil Actions Over $15,000.*

Civil Records: Access: Fax, mail, in person, online. Both court and visitors may perform in person searches. No search fee. Required to search: name, years to search. Civil cases indexed by defendant, plaintiff. Civil records on books from 1867, on computer from December 1999. An online subscription service is available; same as criminal access. Online records date from 12/99.

Criminal Records: Access: Fax, mail, In person, online. Both court and visitors may perform in person searches. No search fee. Required to search: name, years to search; also helpful: address, DOB, SSN. Criminal records on books from 1867, on computer from December 1999. A subscription service is at www.nebraska.gov/faqs/justice/. Fee is $.60 a record or $300 per month flat rate, also there is a start-up fee. Online records date from 12/99.

General Information: Public Access terminal is available. No juvenile records released. Will fax results $2.50 1st page, $1.00 each add'l. Copy fee: $.50 per page. Certification fee: $1.50 per page. Payee: Clerk of District Court. Personal checks accepted. Prepayment required. Mail requests: SASE required. Mail turnaround time 1-2 days, limited phone seraching is immediate.

Stanton County Court 804 Ivy St, PO Box 536, Stanton, NE 68779; 402-439-2221; Fax: 402-439-2229. Hours: 8:30AM-4:30PM (CST). *Misdemeanor, Civil Actions Under $45,000, Eviction, Small Claims, Probate.*

Civil Records: Access: In person, online. Visitors must perform in person searches for themselves. No search fee. Required to search: name, years to search. Civil cases indexed by defendant, plaintiff. Civil records on docket cards and books back to 1950s; criminal records go back to 1999, probate on microfilm. An online subscription service is available; same as criminal access. Online civil and probate records from 10/00 forward.

Criminal Records: Access: In person, online. Visitors must perform in person searches for themselves. No search fee. Required to search: name, years to search, DOB. Criminal records on docket cards and books back to 1900s; criminal records computerized back to 1999, probate on microfilm. A subscription service is available at www.nebraska.gov/faqs/justice/. Fee is $.60 a record or $300 per month flat rate, also there is a start-up fee. Online criminal and traffic records date from 06/00.

General Information: Public Access terminal is available. No adoption records released. Copy fee: $.25 per page. Certification fee: $1.00. Payee: Stanton County. Personal checks accepted. Prepayment required.

Thayer County

District Court PO Box 297, Hebron, NE 68370; 402-768-6116; Fax: 402-768-6128. Hours: 8AM-Noon, 1:00PM-4:30PM (CST). *Felony, Civil Actions Over $15,000.*

Civil Records: Access: In person, online. Visitors must perform in person searches for themselves. No search fee. Required to search: name, years to search. Civil cases indexed by defendant, plaintiff. Civil records on books from 1900s; computerized records go back 6/2000. An online subscription service is available; same as criminal access. Online records date from 03/00.

Criminal Records: Access: Fax, mail, In person, online. Visitors must perform in person searches for themselves. No search fee. Required to search: name, years to search. Criminal records on books from 1900; computerized records go back 6/2000. A subscription service is at www.nebraska.gov/faqs/justice/. Fee is $.60 a record or $300 per month flat rate, also there is a start-up fee. Online records date from 03/00.

General Information: Public Access terminal is available. No mental health or sealed records released. Will not fax results. Copy fee: $.25 per page. Certification fee: $1.00. Payee: Thayer Co. Treasurer. Personal checks accepted. Mail requests: SASE required. Mail turnaround time 5 days.

Thayer County Court PO Box 94, Hebron, NE 68370; 402-768-6325; Fax: 402-768-7232. Hours: 8AM-4:30PM (CST). *Misdemeanor, Civil Actions Under $45,000, Eviction, Small Claims, Probate.*

Civil Records: Access: Mail, in person, online. Both court and visitors may perform in person searches. No search fee. Required to search: name, years to search, address. Civil cases indexed by defendant, plaintiff. Civil records on docket cards from 1871; probate on microfiche. An online subscription service is available; same as criminal access. Online civil and probate records from 02/00 forward.

Criminal Records: Access: Mail, In person, online. Both court and visitors may perform in person searches. No search fee. Required to search: name, years to search, DOB. Criminal records on docket cards from 1871; probate on microfiche. A subscription service is available at www.nebraska.gov/faqs/justice/. Fee is $.60 a record or $300 per month flat rate, also there is a start-up fee. Online criminal and traffic records date from 02/00.

General Information: Public Access terminal is available. No adoption or juvenile records released. Will not fax results. Copy fee: $.25 per page. Certification fee: $1.00. Payee: County Court. Prepayment required. Mail requests: SASE required. Mail turnaround time within 2 weeks.

Thomas County

District Court PO Box 226, Thedford, NE 69166; 308-645-2261; Fax: 308-645-2623. 8AM-Noon, 1-4PM (CST). *Felony, Civil Actions Over $15,000.*

Civil Records: Access: Mail, fax, in person, online. Both court and visitors may perform in person searches. Search fee: $3.00 per name. Required to search: name, years to search. Civil cases indexed by defendant, plaintiff. Civil records indexed in books and in case files since 1800s; on computer back to 6/2000. An online subscription service is available; same as criminal access. Online records date from 06/00.

Criminal Records: Access: Fax, mail, In person, online. Both court and visitors may perform in person searches. Search fee: $3.00 per name. Required to search: name, years to search, DOB; also helpful-SSN, signed release. Criminal records indexed in books and in case files since 1800s; on computer back to 6/2000. A subscription service is available at www.nebraska.gov/faqs/justice/. Fee is $.60 a record or $300 per month flat rate, also there is a start-up fee. Online records date from 06/00.

General Information: Public Access terminal is available. No sealed or juvenile records released. Fee to fax results is $1.00 per document and $.25 per page. Copy fee: $.25 per page. Certification fee: $4.00. Payee: Clerk of District Court. Personal checks accepted. Prepayment required. Mail requests: SASE required. Mail turnaround time 2 days.

Thomas County Court PO Box 233, Thedford, NE 69166; 308-645-2266; Fax: 308-645-2623. Hours: 8AM-Noon, 1-4PM (CST). *Misdemeanor, Civil Actions Under $45,000, Eviction, Small Claims, Probate.*

Civil Records: Access: Phone, fax, mail, in person, online. Both court and visitors may perform in person searches. No search fee. Required to search: name, years to search. Civil cases indexed by defendant, plaintiff. Civil records on index cards and books from late 1800s. An online subscription service is available; same as criminal access. Online civil records date from 10/99 forward, probate from 07/98.

Criminal Records: Access: Fax, mail, In person, online. Both court and visitors may perform in person searches. No search fee. Required to search: name, years to search, DOB, signed release. Criminal records on index cards and books from late 1800s. A subscription service is available at www.nebraska.gov/faqs/justice/. Fee is $.60 a record or $300 per month flat rate, also there is a start-up fee. Online criminal and traffic records date from 07/98.

General Information: Public Access terminal is available. (Civil only.) No adoption or juvenile records released. Copy fee: $.25 per page. Certification fee: $1.00. Payee: County Court. Personal checks accepted. Prepayment required. Mail requests: SASE required. Mail turnaround: 2 days.

Thurston County

District Court PO Box 216, Pender, NE 68047; 402-385-3318; Fax: 402-385-2762. Hours: 8:30AM-5PM (CST). *Felony, Civil Actions Over $15,000.*

Civil Records: Access: In person, online. Visitors must perform in person searches for themselves. No search fee. Required to search: name, years to search. Civil cases indexed by defendant, plaintiff. Civil records on index books from late 1800s; on computer back to 1998. An online subscription service is available; same as criminal access. Online records date from 03/98.

Criminal Records: Access: In person, online. Visitors must perform in person searches for themselves. No search fee. Required to search: name, years to search. Criminal records on index books from late 1800s; on computer back to 1998. A subscription service is at www.nebraska.gov/faqs/justice/. Fee is $.60 a record or $300 per month flat rate, also there is a start-up fee. Online records date from 03/98.

General Information: Public Access terminal is available. No mental health records released. Will not fax results. Copy fee: $.25 per page. Certification fee: $1.00. Payee: Clerk of District Court. No personal checks accepted. Prepayment required.

Thurston County Court County Courthouse, PO Box 129, Pender, NE 68047; 402-385-3136; Fax: 402-385-3143. Hours: 8:30AM-Noon,1-5PM (CST). *Misdemeanor, Civil Actions Under $45,000, Eviction, Small Claims, Probate.*

Civil Records: Access: In person, online. Visitors must perform in person searches for themselves. No

search fee. Required to search: name, years to search. Civil cases indexed by defendant, plaintiff. Civil records on books; probate on microfiche since 1800s; on computer back to 1/2000. An online subscription service is available; same as criminal access. Online civil and probate records from 01/00 forward.

Criminal Records: Access: In person, online. Visitors must perform in person searches for themselves. No search fee. Required to search: name, years to search. Criminal records on books per state requirement; on computer back to 1/2000. A subscription service is available at www.nebraska.gov/faqs/justice/. Fee is $.60 a record or $300 per month flat rate, also there is a start-up fee. Online criminal and traffic records date from 01/00.

General Information: Public Access terminal is available. No adoption or juvenile records released. Copy fee: $.25 per page. Certification fee: $1.00. Payee: County Court. Personal checks accepted. Out of state personal checks not accepted. Prepayment required.

Valley County

District Court 125 S 15th St, Ord, NE 68862; 308-728-3700; Fax: 308-728-7725. Hours: 8AM-5PM (CST). *Felony, Civil Actions Over $15,000.*

Civil Records: Access: Phone, fax, mail, in person, online. Both court and visitors may perform in person searches. Search fee: $5.00 per name. Required to search: name, years to search. Civil cases indexed by defendant, plaintiff. Civil records in general index books since late 1800s. An online subscription service is available; same as criminal access. Online records date from 03/00.

Criminal Records: Access: Fax, mail, In person, online. Both court and visitors may perform in person searches. Search fee: $5.00 per name. Required to search: name, years to search; also helpful: DOB, SSN. Criminal records in general index books since late 1800s; on computer back to 3/2000. A subscription service is available at www.nebraska.gov/faqs/justice/. Fee is $.60 a record or $300 per month flat rate, also there is a start-up fee. Online records date from 03/00. All requests must be in writing.

General Information: Public Access terminal is available. Will fax to a toll-free number. Copy fee: $.10 per page. $.15 per page for legal size copy. Certification fee: $1.00. Payee: Valley County Clerk. Personal checks accepted. Prepayment required. Mail requests: SASE required. Mail turnaround: 3-5 days.

Valley County Court 125 S 15th St, Ord, NE 68862; 308-728-3831; Fax: 308-728-7725. Hours: 8AM-5PM (CST). *Misdemeanor, Civil Actions Under $45,000, Eviction, Small Claims, Probate.*

Civil Records: Access: Phone, fax, mail, in person, online. Both court and visitors may perform in person searches. No search fee. Required to search: name, years to search. Civil cases indexed by defendant, plaintiff. Civil records on books and in files since 1890s; probate on microfiche. An online subscription service is available; same as criminal access. Online civil and probate records from 05/00 forward.

Criminal Records: Access: Phone, fax, mail, In person, online. Both court and visitors may perform in person searches. No search fee. Required to search: name, years to search. Criminal records on books and in files since 1890s; probate on microfiche. A subscription service is available at www.nebraska.gov/faqs/justice/. Fee is $.60 a record or $300 per month flat rate, also there is a start-up fee. Online criminal and traffic records date from 05/00.

General Information: No adoption records released. Will fax results $3.00 1st page, $1.00 each add'l. Copy fee: $.25 per page. Certification fee: $1.25. Payee: Valley County Court. Personal checks

accepted. Prepayment required. Mail requests: SASE required. Mail turnaround time 1 week.

Washington County

District Court PO Box 431, Blair, NE 68008; 402-426-6899; Fax: 402-426-6898. Hours: 8AM-Noon; 1PM-4:30PM (CST). *Felony, Civil Actions Over $15,000.*
Civil Records: Access: In person, online. Visitors must perform in person searches for themselves. No search fee. Required to search: name, years to search. Civil cases indexed by defendant, plaintiff. Civil records on index books and in files since 1930s; computerized records since 1997, prior sent to capitol. An online subscription service is available; same as criminal access. Online records date from 06/97.
Criminal Records: Access: In person, online. Visitors must perform in person searches for themselves. No search fee. Required to search: name, years to search, DOB. Criminal records on index books and in files since 1930s; computerized records since 1997, prior sent to capitol. A subscription service is at www.nebraska.gov/faqs/justice/. Fee is $.60 a record or $300 per month flat rate, also there is a start-up fee. Online records date from 06/97.
General Information: Public Access terminal is available. No juvenile, mental health records released. Copy fee: $.25 per page. Certification fee: $1.00. Payee: Clerk of District Court. Personal checks accepted. Prepayment required.

Washington County Court 1555 Colfax St, Blair, NE 68008; 402-426-6833; Fax: 402-426-6840. Hours: 8AM-4:30PM (CST). *Misdemeanor, Civil Actions Under $45,000, Eviction, Small Claims, Probate.*
Civil Records: Access: In person, online. Visitors must perform in person searches for themselves. No search fee. Required to search: name, years to search. Civil cases indexed by defendant, plaintiff. Civil records on index books, cards; probate on microfilm since 1867; on computer back to 1997. An online subscription service is available; same as criminal access. Online civil records date from 12/99 forward, probate from 05/98.
Criminal Records: Access: In person, online. Visitors must perform in person searches for themselves. No search fee. Required to search: name, years to search, DOB, SSN. Criminal records on index books, cards; probate on microfilm since 1867; on computer back to 1997. A subscription service is at www.nebraska.gov/faqs/justice/. Fee is $.60 a record or $300 per month flat rate, also there is a start-up fee. Online criminal and traffic records date from 02/97.
General Information: Public Access terminal is available. No adoption records released. Copy fee: $.25 per page. Certification fee: $1.25. Payee: Washington County Court. Personal checks not accepted. Prepayment required.

Wayne County

District Court 510 Pearl St, Wayne, NE 68787; 402-375-2260. Hours: 8:30AM-5PM (CST). *Felony, Civil Actions Over $15,000.*
http://county.waynene.org/court_system
Civil Records: Access: In person, online. Visitors must perform in person searches for themselves. No search fee. Required to search: name, years to search. Civil cases indexed by defendant, plaintiff. Civil records on index books from late 1800s, computerized since 03/99. An online subscription service is available; same as criminal access. Online records date from 03/99.
Criminal Records: Access: In person, online. Visitors must perform in person searches for themselves. No search fee. Required to search: name, years to search. Criminal records on index books from

late 1800s, computerized since 03/99. A subscription service is at www.nebraska.gov/faqs/justice/. Fee is $.60 a record or $300 per month flat rate, also there is a start-up fee. Online records date from 03/99.
General Information: Public Access terminal is available. No mental health records released. Copy fee: $.25 per page. $1.00 minimum. Certification fee: $1.00. Payee: Clerk of District Court. Only cashiers checks and money orders accepted. Prepayment required.

Wayne County Court 510 Pearl St, Wayne, NE 68787; 402-375-1622; Fax: 402-375-1622. Hours: 8AM-5PM (CST). *Misdemeanor, Civil Actions Under $45,000, Eviction, Small Claims, Probate.*
Civil Records: Access: In person, online. Visitors must perform in person searches for themselves. No search fee. Required to search: name, years to search. Civil cases indexed by defendant, plaintiff. Civil records on index books, cards from late 1800s. An online subscription service is available; same as criminal access. Online civil and probate records from 02/00 forward.
Criminal Records: Access: In person, online. Visitors must perform in person searches for themselves. No search fee. Required to search: name, years to search. Criminal records on index books, cards from late 1800s. A subscription service is at www.nebraska.gov/faqs/justice/. Fee is $.60 a record or $300 per month flat rate, also there is a start-up fee. Online criminal and traffic records date from 02/00.
General Information: Public Access terminal is available. No adoption records released. Copy fee: $.25 per page. Certification fee: $1.00. Payee: County Court. Personal checks accepted. Prepayment required.

Webster County

District Court 621 N Cedar, Red Cloud, NE 68970; 402-746-2716; Fax: 402-746-2710. Hours: 8:30AM-4:30PM (CST). *Felony, Civil Actions Over $15,000.*
Civil Records: Access: In person, online. Visitors must perform in person searches for themselves. No search fee. Required to search: name, years to search. Civil cases indexed by defendant, plaintiff. Civil records indexed on microfiche; in files back to 1800s. An online subscription service is available; same as criminal access. Online records date from 10/00.
Criminal Records: Access: In person, online. Visitors must perform in person searches for themselves. No search fee. Required to search: name, years to search; also helpful: address, DOB, SSN. Criminal records indexed on microfiche; in files back to 1800s. A subscription service is available at www.nebraska.gov/faqs/justice/. Fee is $.60 a record or $300 per month flat rate, also there is a start-up fee. Online records date from 10/00.
General Information: Public Access terminal is available. No mental health records released. Copy fee: $1.00 per page if by court. Certification fee: $1.50. Payee: Clerk of District Court. Personal checks accepted. Prepayment required.

Webster County Court 621 N Cedar, Red Cloud, NE 68970; 402-746-2777; Fax: 402-746-2771. Hours: 8:30AM-4:30PM (CST). *Misdemeanor, Civil Actions Under $45,000, Eviction, Small Claims, Probate.*
Civil Records: Access: In person, online. Visitors must perform in person searches for themselves. No search fee. Required to search: name, years to search; also helpful: address. Civil cases indexed by defendant. Civil records on index cards and books; probate on microfiche since late 1930, indexed on computer since 07/00. An online subscription service is available; same as criminal access. Online civil records date from 01/00 forward, probate from 02/00.

Criminal Records: Access: In person, online. Visitors must perform in person searches for themselves. No search fee. Required to search: name, years to search, DOB, SSN. Criminal records on index cards and books; probate on microfiche since late 1930, indexed on computer since 07/00. A subscription service is available at www.nebraska.gov/faqs/justice/. Fee is $.60 a record or $300 per month flat rate, also there is a start-up fee. Online criminal and traffic records date from 07/00.
General Information: Public Access terminal is available. No adoption or juvenile records released. Copy fee: $.25 per page. Certification fee: $1.00. Payee: County Court. Business checks accepted. Prepayment required.

Wheeler County

District Court PO Box 127, Bartlett, NE 68622; 308-654-3235; Fax: 308-654-3470. 9AM-Noon, 1-5PM (CST). *Felony, Civil Actions Over $15,000.*
Civil Records: Access: In person, online. Visitors must perform in person searches for themselves. Search fee: $3.00. Required to search: name, years to search. Civil cases indexed by defendant, plaintiff. Civil records on index books from late 1800s. An online subscription service is available; same as criminal access. Mail access limited to short searches.
Criminal Records: Access: In person, online. Visitors must perform in person searches for themselves. Search fee: $3.00. Required to search: name, years to search. Criminal records on index books from late 1800s. A subscription service is at www.nebraska.gov/faqs/justice/. Fee is $.60 a record or $300 per month flat rate, also there is a start-up fee. Online records date from 07/00.
General Information: Public Access terminal is available. No juvenile or adoption records released. Will fax results for $3.00 per document. Copy fee: $.15 per page. Certification fee: $7.00. Payee: Clerk of District Court. Personal checks accepted. Prepayment required.

Wheeler County Court PO Box 127, Bartlett, NE 68622; 308-654-3376; Fax: 308-654-3442. Hours: 10AM-3PM 1st & 2nd Mon & every Th (CST). *Misdemeanor, Civil Actions Under $45,000, Eviction, Small Claims, Probate.*
Civil Records: Access: Mail, in person, online. Only the court performs in person searches; visitors may not. No search fee. Required to search: name, years to search. Civil cases indexed by defendant, plaintiff. Civil records on index books from late 1800s. An online subscription service is available; same as criminal access. Online civil records date from 01/01 forward, probate from 01/02.
Criminal Records: Access: Mail, In person, online. Visitors must perform in person searches for themselves. No search fee. Required to search: name, years to search. Criminal records on index books from late 1800s. A subscription service is available at www.nebraska.gov/faqs/justice/. Fee is $.60 a record or $300 per month flat rate, also there is a start-up fee. Online criminal and traffic records date from 07/00.
General Information: No adoption records released. Will fax results for $3.00 1st page, and $1.00 each add'l page. Copy fee: $.25 per page. Certification fee: $1.00. Payee: County Court. Personal checks accepted. Prepayment required. Mail requests: SASE required. Mail turnaround time 1-2 weeks.

York County

District Court 510 Lincoln Ave, York, NE 68467; 402-362-4038; Fax: 402-362-2577. Hours: 8:30AM-5PM (CST). *Felony, Civil Actions Over $15,000.*
Note: The SSN does not show up in the computer index, but will show in the case files.

Civil Records: Access: In person, online. Visitors must perform in person searches for themselves. No search fee. Required to search: name, years to search. Civil cases indexed by defendant, plaintiff. Civil records on index books and in files from 1875, computerized go back to 1998. An online subscription service is available; same as criminal access. Online records date from 06/98.

Criminal Records: Access: In person, online. Visitors must perform in person searches for themselves. No search fee. Required to search: name, years to search. Criminal records on index books and in files from 1875, computerized records go back to 1998. A subscription service is at www.nebraska.gov/faqs/justice/. Fee is $.60 a record

or $300 per month flat rate, also there is a start-up fee. Online records date from 06/98.

General Information: Public Access terminal is available. Copy fee: $.25 per page. Certification fee: $1.00. Payee: Clerk of District Court. Personal checks accepted. Prepayment required.

York County Court 510 Lincoln Ave, York, NE 68467; 402-362-4925; Fax: 402-362-2577. Hours: 8AM-5PM (CST). *Misdemeanor, Civil Actions Under $45,000, Eviction, Small Claims, Probate.*

Civil Records: Access: In person, online. Visitors must perform in person searches for themselves. No search fee. Required to search: name, years to search. Civil cases indexed by defendant, plaintiff. Civil records on docket cards, files from 1875. An online subscription service is available; same as criminal

access. Online civil records date from 10/99 forward, probate from 05/98.

Criminal Records: Access: In person, online. Visitors must perform in person searches for themselves. No search fee. Required to search: name, years to search. Criminal records on docket cards, files from 1875. A subscription service is at www.nebraska.gov/faqs/justice/. Fee is $.60 a record or $300 per month flat rate, also there is a start-up fee. Online criminal and traffic records date from 03/97.

General Information: Public Access terminal is available. No adoption or sealed records released. Copy fee: $.25 per page. Certification fee: $1.00. Payee: York County Court. Personal checks accepted. Visa, MC accepted. $3.00 service charge. Prepayment required.

Nebraska Recording Offices

ORGANIZATION: 93 counties, 109 recording offices. The recording officers are County Clerk (UCC and some state tax liens) and Register of Deeds (real estate and most tax liens). Most counties have a combined Clerk/Register office, which are designated "County Clerk" in this section. Sixteen counties have separate offices for County Clerk and for Register of Deeds - Adams, Cass, Dakota, Dawson, Dodge, Douglas, Gage, Hall, Lancaster, Lincoln, Madison, Otoe, Platte, Sarpy, Saunders, and Scotts Bluff. In combined offices, the Register of Deeds is frequently a different person from the County Clerk. 74 counties are in the Central Time Zone (CST) and 19 are in the Mountain Time Zone (MST).

REAL ESTATE RECORDS: Some Nebraska counties will perform real estate searches, including owner of record from the legal description of the property. Address search requests and make checks payable to the Register of Deeds, not the County Clerk. Fees vary.

UCC RECORDS: Financing statements are filed at the state level, and real estate related collateral are filed with the County Clerk. Previously, financing statements could be filed at any county. All non-real estate UCC filings are entered into a statewide database that is accessible from any county office. All but a few counties will perform UCC searches. Use search request form UCC-11. The UCC statute allows for telephone searching. Search fees are usually $4.50 per debtor name. Copy fees vary.

TAX LIEN RECORDS: All federal and some state tax liens are filed with the County Register of Deeds. Some state tax liens on personal property are filed with the County Clerk. Most counties will perform tax lien searches, some as part of a UCC search, and others for a separate fee, usually $4.50 per name in each index. Copy fees vary.

OTHER LIENS: Mechanics, artisans, judgment, motor vehicle, agricultural.

ONLINE ACCESS: Nebrask@online offers online access to Secretary of State's UCC database; registration and a usage fee is required. For information, visit http://www.nebraska.gov/business/egov.phtml. The state treasuer's unclaimed proeprty database is searchable free at www.treasurer.state.ne.us/ie/uphome.asp

Adams County Clerk

County Clerk, PO Box 2067, Hastings, NE 68902. **Phone-**402-461-7107, R/E Recording-402-461-7148, UCC Recording-402-461-7148; fax-402-461-7185; hours 9AM-5PM. Will not search UCC or tax liens records. See Register of Deeds for real estate records. UCC copy- $.50 per page. Cert fee: $1.50 per cert. Payee: Adams County Clerk. **Other phones:** Assessor-402-461-7116; Treasurer-402-461-7120; Appraiser-402-461-7116; Elections-402-461-7107.

Adams County Register of Deeds

Register of Deeds, PO Box 203, Hastings, NE 68902. **Phone-**Register of Deeds, R/E & UCC Recording- 402-461-7148; fax-402-461-7154; hours 9AM-5PM www.adamscounty.org
Will search UCC records. UCC search per debtor- $1.00 per name per search. Federal/state combined tax lien search- $1.00 per debtor per search. Will not search real estate records. RE record copy- $.50 per page. UCC copy- $1.00 per page. Cert fee: $1.50 per page. Payee: Adams County Register of Deeds. **Other phones:** Assessor-402-461-7116; Treasurer-402-461-7120; Appraiser-402-461-7116; Elections-402-461-7165; Vital Records-402-471-2871.

Antelope County

County Clerk, PO Box 26, Neligh, NE 68756-0026. **Phone-**402-887-4410; fax-402-887-4719; hours 8:30AM-5PM. Will not search UCC or tax liens records. Will search real estate records. Record copy- $.50 per page. Cert fee: $5.00 per doc. Payee: Antelope County Clerk. **Other phones:** Assessor-402-887-4515; Treasurer-402-887-4247.

Arthur County

County Clerk, Box 126, Arthur, NE 69121-0126. **Phone-**308-764-2203; fax-308-764-2216; hours 8-12;00-1-4PM. UCC records search per debtor- $4.50. UCC search includes tax liens if requested.

Separate federal & state combined tax lien search- $5.00 Will not search real estate records. UCC copy- $.20 per page. Cert fee: $5.00. Payee: Arthur County Clerk. **Other phones:** Assessor-308-764-2203.

Banner County

County Clerk, PO Box 67, Harrisburg, NE 69345-0067. **Phone-**308-436-5265; fax-308-436-4180; hours 8AM-Noon, 1-5PM. UCC records search per debtor- $3.00. UCC search includes tax liens if requested. Separate federal/state combined tax lien search- $2.00 per debtor. Will not search real estate records. UCC copy- $1.00 per page. Payee: Banner County Clerk. **Other phones:** Assessor-308-436-5265; Treasurer-308-436-5260.

Blaine County

County Clerk, PO Box 136, Brewster, NE 68821. **Phone-**308-547-2222, R/E Recording-308-547-2222 ext 201; fax-308-547-2228; hours 8AM-4PM
Will not search UCC records. Tax lien search- $4.00 per debtor. Will search real estate records. Record copy- $1.00 per page. Cert fee: $1.50 per page. Payee: Blaine County Clerk. **Other phones:** Assessor-308-541-2222 ext 201; Treasurer-308-547-2223 ext 202; Elections-308-547-2222.

Boone County

County Clerk, 222 S. 4th St, Albion, NE 68620-1247. **Phone-**County Clerk, R/E & UCC Recording- 402-395-2055, UCC Recording-402-471-4080; fax-402-395-6592; 8:30AM-5PM www.co.boone.ne.us
Will search real estate-related UCC records only. Search per debtor- $4.50. Will not search real estate or tax lien records. Record copy- $.25 per page. Cert fee: $5.00. Payee: Boone County Clerk. **Other phones:** Assessor-402-395-2045; Treasurer-402-395-2513; Elections-402-395-2055; Vital Records-402-395-2055 or 402-471-2871.

Box Butte County

Box Butte County Clerk, Box 678, Alliance, NE 69301-0678. **Phone-**Box Butte County Clerk, R/E & UCC Recording- 308-762-6565, UCC Recording-402-471-4080 (Sec of State); fax-308-762-2867; hours 8AM-4:30PM www.co.box-butte.ne.us/
The recording officers are County Clerk (state tax liens) Register of Deeds (real estate and most tax liens). UCC records search per debtor- $4.50. Tax lien search- $3.50. Will not search real estate records. Cert fee: $1.50 per page. Payee: Box Butte County Clerk. **Other phones:** Assessor-308-762-6101; Treasurer-308-762-6975; Elections-308-762-6565; Vital Records-402-471-2871.

Boyd County

County Clerk, PO Box 26, Butte, NE 68722. **Phone-**402-775-2391; fax-402-775-2146; 8:15AM-4PM
UCC records search per debtor- $4.50. Will not search tax liens. Will search real estate records. Record copy- $.25 per copy. Cert fee: $5.00 per page. Payee: County Clerk. **Other phones:** Assessor-402-775-2311; Treasurer-402-775-2581; Elections-402-775-2391; Vital Records-402-775-2391.

Brown County

Brown County Clerk, 148 W. 4th St., Courthouse, Ainsworth, NE 69210. **Phone-**402-387-2705; fax-402-387-0918; hours 8AM-5PM
UCC records search per debtor- $4.50. UCC search includes tax liens. Separate Tax lien search- $3.50 per debtor. Will not search real estate records. RE record copy- $.10 per page. UCC copy- $.50 per page. Cert fee: $2.00 per page. Payee: Brown County Clerk. **Other phones:** Assessor-402-387-1621; Treasurer-402-387-2650; Elections-402-387-2705; Secretary of State (UCC)-402-471-2554.

Buffalo County

Register of Deeds, PO Box 1270, Kearney, NE 68848-1270. **Phone**-Register of Deeds, R/E & UCC Recording- 308-236-1239, UCC Recording-402-471-2558; fax-308-236-1291; hours 8AM-5PM

Will not search records. UCC copy- $.50 per page. Cert fee: $1.50. Payee: Buffalo County Register of Deeds. **Other phones:** Assessor-308-236-1205; Treasurer-308-236-1250; Elections-308-236-1233; Vital Records-402-471-2871.

Burt County

County Clerk, PO Box 87, Tekamah, NE 68061. **Phone**-402-374-2955; fax-402-374-2956; hours 8AM-4:30PM

UCC records search per debtor- $4.50. UCC search includes tax liens if requested. Separate federal & state combined tax lien search- $4.50 Will not search real estate records. UCC copy- $.50 per page. Cert fee: $3.50 per page. Payee: Burt County Clerk. **Other phones:** Assessor-402-374-2926; Treasurer-402-374-2911; Elections-402-374-2955.

Butler County

Deputy Clerk, PO Box 289, David City, NE 68632-0289. **Phone**-402-367-7430, R/E Recording-402-367-7431, UCC Recording-402-471-4080; fax-402-367-3329; hours 8:30AM-5PM www.nol.org/butler

Will not search UCC or real estate records. Record copy- $1.00 per filing. **Other phones:** Assessor-402-367-7420; Treasurer-402-367-7450; Elections-402-367-7430; Vital Records-402-471-2871.

Cass County Clerk

County Clerk, 346 Main St., Courthouse, Rm 202, Plattsmouth, NE 68048-1964. **Phone**-402-296-9300; fax-402-296-9332; hours 8AM-5PM

Will not search UCC or tax liens records. See Register of Deeds for real estate records. RE record copy- $1.50 per page. UCC copy- $1.00 per page. Cert fee: $5.00 per cert. Payee: Cass County Clerk. **Other phones:** Assessor-402-296-9310.

Cass County Register of Deeds

Register of Deeds, 346 Main St., County Courthouse, Plattsmouth, NE 68048-1964. **Phone**-402-296-9330; fax-402-296-9331; 8AM-5PM www.cassne.org

They will look at their records when asked if request is not too involved or they have the time. Will not search records. Record copy- $.50 per page. Cert fee: $1.50 per page. Payee: Register of Deeds. **Other phones:** Assessor-appraiser-402-296-9310; Treasurer-402-296-9320; Elections-402-296-9306.

Cedar County

County Clerk, PO Box 47, Hartington, NE 68739. **Phone**-County Clerk, R/E & UCC Recording- 402-254-7411, UCC Recording-402-471-2554; fax-402-254-7410; hours 8AM-5PM www.co.cedar.ne.us

UCC records search per debtor- $4.50. Will not search real estate or tax lien records. UCC copy- $.50 per UCC. Cert fee: $1.50 per doc. Payee: County Clerk. **Other phones:** Assessor-402-254-7431; Treasurer-402-254-7421; Elections-402-254-7411; Vital Records-402-254-7411.

Chase County

County Clerk, Box 1299, Imperial, NE 69033-1299. **Phone**-County Clerk, R/E & UCC Recording- 308-882-5266; fax-308-882-5390; hours 8AM-4PM

Will search UCC records. UCC search per debtor- $4.50. Will not search real estate or tax lien records. Cert fee: $5.00 per page. Payee: Chase County. **Other phones:** Assessor-308-882-5207; Treasurer-308-882-4756; Elections-308-882-5266.

Cherry County

County Clerk, Box 120, Valentine, NE 69201-0120. **Phone**-County Clerk, R/E & UCC Recording- 402-376-2771; fax-402-376-3095; hours 8:30AM-Noon, 1-4:30PM. Will search older UCC records. UCC search per debtor- $4.50. Will not search real estate or tax lien records. RE record copy- $.25 per page. **Other phones:** Assessor-402-376-1630; Treasurer-402-376-1580; Elections-402-376-2771; Vital Records-402-471-2871.

Cheyenne County

County Clerk, PO Box 217, Sidney, NE 69162-0217. **Phone**-308-254-2141; fax-308-254-5049; hours 8AM-5PM www.co.cheyenne.ne.us

UCC records search per debtor- $4.50. Will not search real estate or tax lien records. Record copy- $1.00 per page mailed; $2.00 per page faxed-prepaid. Cert fee: $1.50 per page. Payee: Cheyenne County Clerk. **Other phones:** Assessor-308-254-2633; Treasurer-308-254-2733.

Clay County

County Clerk, 111 W. Fairfield St, Clay Center, NE 68933-1499. **Phone**-County Clerk, R/E & UCC Recording- 402-762-3463; fax-402-762-3250; hours 8:30AM-5PM. UCC records search per debtor- $4.50. Will not search real estate or tax lien records. RE record copy- $1.00 per page. Cert fee: $4.00 per doc. Payee: County Clerk. **Other phones:** Assessor-402-762-3792; Treasurer-402-762-3505; Elections-402-762-3463.

Colfax County

County Clerk, 411 E. 11th St, Schuyler, NE 68661. **Phone**-County Clerk, R/E & UCC Recording- 402-352-8504; fax-402-352-8515; hours 8:30AM-5PM www.state.ne.us/colfax/

UCC records search per debtor- $4.50. Will search tax liens including federal tax liens. Will not search real estate records. RE record copy- $.25 per page in office; $1.00 per page by mail. UCC copy- $.50 per page. Cert fee: $1.50 per page. Payee: Colfax County Clerk. **Other phones:** Assessor-402-352-8500; Treasurer-402-352-8519; Appraiser-402-352-8500; Elections-402-352-8504; Vital Records-402-471-2871.

Cuming County

County Clerk, Box 290, West Point, NE 68788. **Phone**-County Clerk, R/E & UCC Recording- 402-372-6002; fax-402-372-6013. www.co.cuming.ne.us

UCC records search per debtor- $4.50. Will not search real estate or tax lien records. RE record copy- $.25 per page. UCC copy fee is $.50 per copy. **Other phones:** Assessor-402-372-6000; Treasurer-402-372-6011; Elections-402-372-6002.

Custer County

County Clerk, 431 S. 10th, Broken Bow, NE 68822. **Phone**-308-872-5701; hours 9AM-5PM. UCC records search per debtor- $3.50. Tax liens not included in UCC search. Tax lien search- $3.00 per debtor. Real estate record owner searches available. UCC copy- $.25 per page. Cert fee: $1.00 per page. Payee: Custer County Clerk. **Other phones:** Assessor-308-872-2981; Treasurer-308-872-2921.

Dakota County

County Register of Deeds, PO Box 511, Dakota City, NE 68731. **Phone**-402-987-2166; 8AM-4:30PM

Will not search records. UCC copy- $1.00 per page. Cert fee: $2.50 per cert. Payee: Dakota County Register of Deeds. **Other phones:** Assessor-402-987-0264; Treasurer-402-987-2131; Elections-402-987-2126; Vital Records-402-471-2871.

Dawes County

County Clerk, 451 Main St, Courthouse, Chadron, NE 69337-2698. **Phone**-County Clerk, R/E & UCC Recording- 308-432-0100; fax-308-432-5179; hours 8:30AM-4:30PM. Will not search UCC or real estate records. Separate federal/state combined tax lien search- $3.00 per debtor. RE record copy- $.50 per page. UCC copy- $1.00 per page. Cert fee: $.50 & $1.50 cert fee. Payee: Dawes County Clerk. **Other phones:** Assessor-308-432-0103; Treasurer-308-432-0105; Elections-308-432-0100.

Dawson County Clerk

County Clerk, PO Box 370, Lexington, NE 68850-0370. **Phone**-308-324-2127, R/E Recording-308-324-4271; fax-308-324-6106.

Will search older UCC records. UCC search per debtor- $4.50. Will not search tax liens. See Register of Deeds for real estate records. UCC copy- $.50 per page. Cert fee: $5.00 per form. Payee: Dawson County Clerk. **Other phones:** Assessor-308-324-3471; Treasurer-308-324-3241; Appraiser-308-324-3471; Elections-308-324-6106; Vital Records-308-324-2127.

Dawson County Register of Deeds

County Register of Deeds, 700 N. Washington, County Courthouse, Lexington, NE 68850. **Phone**-308-324-4271; hours 8AM-Noon, 1-5PM

Will not search records. Record copy- $1.00 per page. Cert fee: $1.50 per cert. Payee: Dawson County Register of Deeds. **Other phones:** Assessor-308-324-3471; Treasurer-308-324-3241.

Deuel County

County Clerk, PO Box 327, Chappell, NE 69129. **Phone**-308-874-3308; fax-308-874-3472; 8AM-4PM

UCC records search per debtor- $4.50. Federal/state combined tax lien search- $4.50 Will not search real estate records. UCC copy- $.50 per page. Cert fee: $2.00. Payee: Deuel County Clerk. **Other phones:** Assessor-308-874-2608; Treasurer-308-874-3307.

Dixon County

County Clerk, Box 546, Ponca, NE 68770-0546. **Phone**-402-755-2208; fax-402-755-4276; hours 8AM-4:30PM. UCC records search per debtor- $4.50. Will not search real estate or tax lien records. RE record copy- $.50 per page. UCC copy- $1.00 per page. Cert fee: $1.50 per cert, + $.50 per page. Payee: Dixon County Clerk. **Other phones:** Assessor-402-755-2626; Treasurer-402-755-2701; Vital Records-402-471-2871.

Dodge County Clerk

County Clerk, 435 North Park, Courthouse - Rm 102, Fremont, NE 68025-4967. **Phone**-402-727-2767, R/E Recording-402-727-2735, UCC Recording-402-471-4080; fax-402-727-2764; hours 8:30AM-4:30PM

UCC records search per debtor- $4.50. Will not search tax liens. See Register of Deeds for real estate records. Copy fee is $1.00 per page. **Other phones:** Assessor-402-727-3911; Treasurer-402-727-2750; Appraiser-402-727-3911; Elections-402-727-2767; Vital Records-402-471-2871; UCC Searches-County Level-402-727-2767.

Dodge County Register of Deeds

County Register of Deeds, 435 North Park, Rm 201, Fremont, NE 68025. **Phone**-402-727-2735; fax-402-727-2734; hours 8:30AM-4:30PM www.registerofdeeds.com

Will not search UCC or real estate records. Will not do a tax lien name search but will look up specific information for no fee. Record copy- $1.00 per page. Cert fee: $1.50 per cert. Payee: Dodge County Register of Deeds. **Online Access to Real**

Estate records: Access to Register of Deeds mortgages database is at the website. Registration is required. The site is under development. **Other phones:** Assessor-402-727-3911; Treasurer-402-727-2750.

Douglas County Clerk

County Clerk, 1819 Farnam St., Rm H09, Omaha, NE 68183-0008. **Phone**-402-444-7159; fax-402-444-6456. http://co.douglas.ne.us/explorer.shtml
UCC records search per debtor- $4.50. See Register of Deeds for real estate records. **Other phones:** Assessor-402-444-7060; Treasurer-402-444-7103; Elections-402-444-8683.

Douglas County Register of Deeds

Register of Deeds, 1819 Farnam, Rm H09, Omaha, NE 68183. **Phone**-402-444-7194; fax-402-444-6693; hours 8AM-4:30PM www.co.douglas.ne.us
Will not search records. Record copy- $.75; copy fee is in-person. Cert fee: $1.50 per page. Payee: Register of Deeds. **Online Access to Property, Assessor, Marriage records:** Assessor to the county assessor property valuation lookup is free at www.dcassessor.org/valuation.html. Search the clerk/comptroller marriage database free at www.co.douglas.ne.us/dept/Clerk/marriagelicense. htm. **Other phones:** Assessor-402-444-7060; Treasurer-402-444-7272; Elections-402-444-7200.

Dundy County

County Clerk, PO Box 506, Benkelman, NE 69021-0506. **Phone**-308-423-2058, R/E Recording-402-471-4429 Fax# 402-471-4429; hours 8AM-5PM
Will not search UCC or real estate records. Record copy- $1.00 per page. Cert fee: $1.50 per cert. Payee: Dundy County Clerk. **Other phones:** Assessor-308-423-2821; Treasurer-308-423-2346; Vital Records-402-471-2871.

Fillmore County

Register of Deeds, PO Box 307, Geneva, NE 68361-0307. **Phone**-402-759-4931; fax-402-759-4307; hours 8AM-5PM
www.fillmorecounty.org/government/gov1.html
The recording officers are County Clerk (Federal and state tax liens) and Register of Deeds (real estate and most tax liens). Will search UCC records. UCC search per debtor- $4.50. UCC search includes tax liens. Separate federal/state combined tax lien search- $3.50 per debtor. Will search real estate records. UCC copy- $.50 per page. Cert fee: $1.50 per page. Payee: Fillmore County Clerk. **Other phones:** Assessor-402-759-3613; Treasurer-402-759-3812; Elections-402-759-4931.

Franklin County

County Clerk, PO Box 146, Franklin, NE 68939. **Phone**-308-425-6202; fax-308-425-6093; hours 8:30AM-4:30PM
Will not search UCC or real estate records. RE record copy- $1.00 per page. Cert fee: $1.50 per page (Real Estate Records). Payee: Franklin County Clerk. **Other phones:** Assessor-308-425-6229; Treasurer-308-425-6265; Elections-308-425-6202.

Frontier County

County Clerk, PO Box 40, Stockville, NE 69042-004. **Phone**-308-367-8641; fax-308-367-8730; hours 8:30AM-Noon, 1-5PM www.co.frontier.ne.us
UCC records search per debtor- $4.50. Tax liens not included in UCC search. Separate federal/state combined tax lien search- $3.00 per debtor. Real estate owner, mortgage, and property transfer searches available. Record copy- $1.00 per page. Cert fee: $1.50 per cert. Payee: Frontier County Register of Deeds. **Other phones:** Assessor-308-367-8637;

Treasurer-308-367-8631; Appraiser-308-367-8637; Elections-308-367-8641.

Furnas County

County Clerk, PO Box 387, Beaver City, NE 68926. **Phone**-308-268-4145; hours 8AM-4PM
Will not search records. UCC copy- $.25 per page. Cert fee: $1.50 per cert. Payee: Furnas County Clerk. **Other phones:** Assessor-308-268-3145; Treasurer-308-268-2195.

Gage County Clerk

County Clerk, PO Box 429, Beatrice, NE 68310-0429. **Phone**-402-223-1300, R/E Recording-402-223-1361; fax-402-223-1371; 8AM-5PM www.nol.org/gage/
UCC records search per debtor- $4.50. See Register of Deeds for real estate records. **Online Access to Property, Assessor records:** Access to property information via the county CIS service is free at http://gage.gisworkshop.com. **Other phones:** Assessor-402-223-1308; Treasurer-402-223-1315; Appraiser-402-223-1308; Elections-402-223-1300; Vital Records-402-223-1300.

Gage County Register of Deeds

County Register of Deeds, PO Box 337, Beatrice, NE 68310. **Phone**-402-223-1361; hours 8AM-4:30PM
Will search UCC records, but only real estate related UCC filed here. Search per debtor- $4.50. Will not search real estate or tax lien records. UCC copy- $.50 per page. Cert fee: $10.50. Payee: Gage County Register of Deeds. **Other phones:** Assessor-402-223-1308; Treasurer-402-223-1315.

Garden County

County Clerk, PO Box 486, Oshkosh, NE 69154. **Phone**-County Clerk, R/E & UCC Recording- 308-772-3924; fax-308-772-4143; hours 8AM-4PM
UCC records search per debtor- $4.50. UCC search includes tax liens. Separate federal & state combined tax lien search-no fee. Will not search real estate records. Record copy- $.50 per page. Cert fee: $1.50 per page. Payee: County Clerk. **Other phones:** Assessor-308-772-4464; Treasurer-308-772-3622.

Garfield County

County Clerk, Box 218, Burwell, NE 68823. **Phone**-308-346-4161; 9AM-Noon, 1-5PM. UCC records search per debtor- $4.50. Tax liens not included in UCC search. Will not search real estate records. UCC copy- $1.00 per page. Cert fee: $1.50. Payee: Garfield County Clerk. **Other phones:** Assessor-308-346-4045; Treasurer-308-346-4125.

Gosper County

County Clerk, PO Box 136, Elwood, NE 68937-0136. **Phone**-County Clerk, R/E & UCC Recording- 308-785-2611; fax-308-785-2300; hours 8:30AM-4:30PM www.co.gosper.ne.us
UCC records search per debtor- $4.50. UCC search includes tax liens if requested. Tax lien search- $.50 per page. Will not search real estate records. UCC copy- $1.00 per page. Payee: Gosper County Clerk. **Other phones:** Assessor-308-785-2250; Treasurer-308-785-2450; Appraiser-308-785-2250; Elections-308-785-2611; Vital Records-308-785-2611.

Grant County

County Clerk, PO Box 139, Hyannis, NE 69350-0139. **Phone**-County Clerk, R/E & UCC Recording- 308-458-2488; fax-308-458-2485; hours 8AM-4PM
UCC records search per debtor- $4.50. Tax lien search- $1.00 per debtor. Will search real estate records. Record copy- $.50 per page. Cert fee: $1.50 per instrument. Payee: Grant County Clerk. **Other phones:** Assessor-308-458-2488; Treasurer-

308-458-2422; Appraiser-308-762-2474; Elections-308-458-2488; Marriages-308-458-2488.

Greeley County

County Clerk, PO Box 287, Greeley, NE 68842. **Phone**-308-428-3625; fax-308-428-3022.
UCC records search per debtor- $4.50. Will not search real estate records. **Other phones:** Assessor-308-428-5310; Treasurer-308-428-3535.

Hall County Clerk

County Clerk, 121 S. Pine, Grand Island, NE 68801. **Phone**-308-385-5080, R/E Recording-308-385-5040, UCC Recording-Sec of State; fax-308-385-5084; hours 8:30AM-5PM. UCC records search per debtor- $4.50. Will not search real estate or tax lien records. UCC copy- $3.50 per name. **Other phones:** Assessor-308-385-5050; Treasurer-308-385-5025; Appraiser-308-385-5050; Elections-308-385-5085; Vital Records-402-471-2871.

Hall County Register of Deeds

County Register of Deeds, PO Box 1692, Grand Island, NE 68802-1692. **Phone**-County Register of Deeds, R/E & UCC Recording- 308-385-5040; hours 8:30AM-5PM www.grand-island.com
Will search UCC records, but only real estate related UCC filed here. Search per debtor- $4.50. Will not search real estate or tax lien records. UCC copy- $1.00 per page. Payee: Hall County Register of Deeds. **Online Access to Real Estate, Grantor/Grantee, Deed, Lien, Judgment records:** Access to the county Register of Deeds Document Search is free at http://mapsifter.ci.grand-island.ne.us/mapsifter/advancedlookupform.asp. **Other phones:** Assessor-308-385-5050; Treasurer-308-385-5025.

Hamilton County

County Clerk, Register of Deeds, 1111 13th St, #1, Courthouse, Aurora, NE 68818-2017. **Phone**-County Clerk, Register of Deeds, R/E & UCC Recording- 402-694-3443, UCC Recording-402-471-2554; fax-402-694-2396; hours 8AM-5PM www.co.hamilton.ne.us
UCC records search per debtor- $4.50. Will not search real estate or tax lien records. Record copy- $.25 per page. Cert fee: $1.50 per page + $1.50 per doc. Payee: Hamilton Co. Clerk. **Other phones:** Assessor-402-694-2757; Treasurer-402-694-2291; Elections-402-694-3443; Vital Records-402-471-2871.

Harlan County

County Clerk, PO Box 698, Alma, NE 68920-0698. **Phone**-308-928-2173; fax-308-928-2079; hours 8:30AM-4:30PM
Will not search records. RE record copy- $.25 per page. UCC copy- $.50 per page. Cert fee: $1.00 1st pg; $.25 each add'l. Payee: Harlan County Clerk. **Other phones:** Assessor-308-928-2177; Treasurer-308-928-2171.

Hayes County

County Clerk, PO Box 370, Hayes Center, NE 69032-0370. **Phone**-308-286-3413; fax-308-286-3208; hours 8AM-4PM. UCC records search per debtor- $4.50. Will not search real estate or tax lien records. RE record copy- $1.00 per page. Cert fee: $4.00 per cert. Payee: Hayes County Clerk. **Other phones:** Assessor-308-286-3399; Treasurer-308-286-3214.

Hitchcock County

County Clerk, PO Box 248, Trenton, NE 69044. **Phone**-County Clerk, R/E & UCC Recording- 308-334-5646; fax-308-334-5398; hours 8:30AM-4PM www.co.hitchcock.ne.us
UCC records search per debtor- $4.50. Tax lien search- $4.00 per debtor. Will search real estate records. Copy fee-$.50 per page. UCC copy- $.50

per page. Cert fee: $1.50 per page. Payee: Hitchcock County Clerk. **Other phones:** Assessor-308-334-5219; Treasurer-308-334-5544; Appraiser-308-334-5219; Elections-308-334-5646; Vital Records-308-334-5646- Marriage Only.

Holt County

County Clerk, PO Box 329, O'Neill, NE 68763-0329. **Phone-**402-336-2250; fax-402-336-1762; 8-4:30PM Will not search UCC or real estate records. Will search tax liens including federal tax liens. Tax lien search- $5.00 per debtor. Cert fee: $1.50 per doc. Payee: Register of Deeds. **Other phones:** Assessor-402-336-1624; Treasurer-402-336-1291.

Hooker County

County Clerk, PO Box 184, Mullen, NE 69152. **Phone-**County Clerk, R/E & UCC Recording- 308-546-2244; fax-308-546-2490; hours 8:30AM-Noon, 1-4:30PM UCC records search per debtor- $4.50. UCC search includes tax liens if requested. Separate federal/state combined tax lien search- $3.00 per debtor. Real estate owner, mortgage, and property transfer searches available. Record copy- $1.00 per page. Cert fee: $10.00 per cert plus cost of copies. Payee: Hooker County Clerk. **Other phones:** Assessor-308-546-2244; Treasurer-308-546-2245; Elections-308-546-2244.

Howard County

County Clerk, PO Box 25, St. Paul, NE 68873. **Phone-**308-754-4343; fax-308-754-4125; hours 8AM-5PM Will search UCC records. UCC search per debtor- $4.50. Will not search real estate or tax lien records. UCC copy- $.50 per page. Cert fee: $5.00 per cert. Payee: Howard County Clerk. **Other phones:** Assessor-308-754-4261; Treasurer-308-754-4852; Elections-308-754-4343.

Jefferson County

County Clerk, 411 4th, Courthouse, Fairbury, NE 68352-1619. **Phone-**County Clerk, R/E & UCC Recording- 402-729-5201, UCC Recording-402-471-2554; fax-402-729-2016.
The recording officers are County Clerk (some state tax liens) and Register of Deeds (real estate and most tax liens). UCC records search per debtor- $4.50. Will not search real estate records. RE record copy- $.50 per page. **Other phones:** Assessor-402-729-3103; Treasurer-402-729-2411; Elections-402-729-2323; Vital Records-402-471-2872.

Johnson County

County Clerk, PO Box 416, Tecumseh, NE 68450. **Phone-**County Clerk, R/E & UCC Recording- 402-335-6300; fax-402-335-6311; hours 8AM-12:30PM, 1-4:30PM
Will not search UCC or real estate records. Separate federal/state combined tax lien search- $3.00 per debtor. UCC copy- $1.00 per page. Cert fee: $1.50. Payee: Johnson County Clerk. **Other phones:** Assessor-402-335-6303; Treasurer-402-335-6310; Elections-402-335-6300.

Kearney County

County Clerk, PO Box 339, Minden, NE 68959-0339. **Phone-**308-832-2723; fax-308-832-2729; 8:30AM-5PM. Will not search records. Cert fee: $3.00. Payee: Kearney County Clerk. **Other phones:** Assessor-308-832-2625; Treasurer-308-832-2730.

Keith County

County Clerk, PO Box 149, Ogallala, NE 69153. **Phone-**308-284-4726; fax-308-284-6277.
Will not search UCC or real estate records. Cert fee: $1.50 per page. Payee: Keith County Clerk. **Other phones:** Assessor-308-284-8040; Treasurer-308-284-3231.

Keya Paha County

County Clerk, PO Box 349, Springview, NE 68778. **Phone-**County Clerk, R/E & UCC Recording- 402-497-3791; fax-402-497-3799; hours 8AM-Noon,1-5PM www.co.keya-paha.ne.us/
UCC records search per debtor- $4.50. UCC search includes tax liens. Separate federal/state combined tax lien search- $4.00 per debtor. Will search real estate records. RE record copy- $.25 per page. UCC copy- $4.00. Cert fee: $4.00 per cert. Payee: Keya Paha County Clerk. **Other phones:** Assessor-402-497-3791; Treasurer-402-497-3891; Elections-402-497-3791.

Kimball County

County Clerk, 114 E. Third St, Kimball, NE 69145-1296. **Phone-**County Clerk, R/E & UCC Recording-308-235-2241; fax-308-235-3654; hours 8AM-5PM M-Th, 8AM-4PM F www.co.kimball.ne.us
UCC records search per debtor- $4.50 per debtor. Tax liens not included in UCC search. Tax lien search- $3.50 per debtor. Searches must be spelled out exactly. Will not search real estate records. Record copy- $1.00 per page. Cert fee: $1.50. **Other phones:** Assessor-308-235-2362; Treasurer-308-235-2242; Elections-308-235-2241.

Knox County Clerk

County Clerk, PO Box 166, Center, NE 68724-0166. **Phone-**402-288-5604, R/E Recording-402-288-5613; fax-402-288-5605; hours-8:30AM-4:30PM www.co.knox.ne.us
UCC records search per debtor- $4.50. Will not search real estate or tax lien records. RE record copy- $1.00 per page if legal description is given. UCC copy- $.50 per page. Cert fee: $1.50 per page. Payee: Knox County Register of Deeds. **Other phones:** Assessor-402-288-5601; Treasurer-402-288-5615; Appraiser-402-288-5601; Elections-402-288-5604.

Lancaster County Clerk

County Clerk, 555 S. 10th St, County-City Bldg., Lincoln, NE 68508-2867. **Phone-**402-441-7482, R/E Recording-402-441-7577; fax-402-441-8728; hours 7:30AM-4:30PM http://interlinc.ci.lincoln.ne.us
Will not search UCC records. Will do a state tax lien search only. See Register of Deeds for real estate records. Cert fee: $1.50 per cert. Payee: Lancaster County Clerk. **Online Access to Assessor, Recording, Grantor/Grantee, Deed, Judgment, Dog Tag, Treasurer, Marriage, Accident, Parking Ticket, Building Permit records:** Records on the county Assessor Property Information Search database are free at www.dcassessor.org/valuation.html. Search parking tickets at www.ci.lincoln.ne.us/city/finance/treas/tickets.htm . Also, search register of deeds Grantor/Grantee index free at www.ci.lincoln.ne.us/cnty/deeds/deeds.htm. Search City of Lincoln accident reports at www.ci.lincoln.ne.us/city/police/stats/acc.htm. Also, search treasurer' property info at www.ci.lincoln.ne.us/cnty/treas/property.htm. Search dog tag registrations at www.ci.lincoln.ne.us/city/health/animal/acttag.htm Search marriages at www.ci.lincoln.ne.us/cnty/clerk/marrsrch.htm. **Other phones:** Assessor-402-441-7463; Treasurer-402-441-7425; Appraiser-402-441-7463; Elections-402-441-7311; Vital Records-402-471-2872.

Lancaster County Register of Deeds

Register of Deeds, 555 S. 10th St, Lincoln, NE 68508. **Phone-**402-441-7577; fax-402-441-7012; hours 7:30AM-4:30PM www.ci.lincoln.ne.us/cnty/co_agenc.htm

Will search UCC records. Will search real estate records. **Online Access to Real Estate, Lien, Grantor/Grantee, Assessor, Treasurer records:** Access to the county online deeds search is free at www.ci.lincoln.ne.us/cnty/deeds/deeds.htm. Also, access to the assessor database is at www.ci.lincoln.ne.us/cnty/assess/property.htm. Treasurer information is also here. Also, search property information free on the map server site at http://ims.ci.lincoln.ne.us/isa/parcel. **Other phones:** Assessor-402-441-7643; Treasurer-402-441-7425; Vital Records-402-441-2871.

Lincoln County Clerk

County Clerk, 301 N. Jeffers, Rm 101, North Platte, NE 69101. **Phone-**308-534-4350; fax-308-535-3522; hours 9AM-5PM www.co.lincoln.ne.us
UCC records search per debtor- $4.50 (access via state computer). UCC search includes state tax liens. Separate federal/state combined tax lien search- $3.50 per debtor (access via state computer) See Register of Deeds for real estate records. UCC copy- $.50 per page. Cert fee: $5.00 per page. Payee: Lincoln County Clerk. **Other phones:** Assessor-308-534-4350; Treasurer-308-534-4350; Elections-308-534-4350.

Lincoln County Register of Deeds

County Clerk, 301 N. Jeffers, Rm 103, North Platte, NE 69101-3931. **Phone-**308-534-4350, R/E Recording-308-534-4350 X 192, UCC Recording-308-534-4350 X 192; fax-308-534-5287; hours 9:00AM-5:00PM Will not search records. UCC copy- $.50 per page. Cert fee: $1.50 per page. Payee: Lincoln County Register of Deeds. **Other phones:** Assessor-308-534-4350; Treasurer-308-534-4350.

Logan County

County Clerk, PO Box 8, Stapleton, NE 69163. **Phone-**308-636-2311; hours 8:30AM-4:30PM M,T,W,Th; 8:30AM-4PM F
UCC records search per debtor- $4.50. UCC search includes tax liens if requested. Separate federal/state combined tax lien search- $3.00 per debtor. Will not search real estate records. UCC copy- $1.00 per page. Cert fee: $1.50 per cert. Payee: Logan County Clerk. **Other phones:** Assessor-308-636-2311; Treasurer-308-636-2441.

Loup County

County Clerk, PO Box 187, Taylor, NE 68879-0187. **Phone-**308-942-3135; fax-308-942-6015; 8:30AM-Noon, 1-5PM M,T,W,Th; 8:30AM-N Fri. UCC records search per debtor- $4.50. UCC search includes tax liens if requested. Will not search real estate records. UCC copy- $.50 per page. Cert fee: $1.00 per page. Payee: Loup County Clerk. **Other phones:** Assessor-308-942-3135; Treasurer-308-942-3115.

Madison County Clerk

County Clerk, PO Box 290, Madison, NE 68748-0290. **Phone-**402-454-3311 x137, R/E Recording-402-454-3311 x124, UCC Recording-402-454-3311 x136; fax-402-454-6682; hours 8:30AM-5PM
UCC records search per debtor- $4.50. Tax liens at Register of Deeds Office. See Register of Deeds for real estate records. Copy fee-$.25 per page. **Other phones:** Assessor-402-454-3311 x178; Treasurer-402-454-3311 x133; Appraiser-402-454-3311; Elections-402-454-3311 x136; Vital Records-402-471-2871.

Madison County Register of Deeds

County Register of Deeds, PO Box 229, Madison, NE 68748. **Phone-**402-454-3311, R/E Recording-402-454-

3311 x124, UCC Recording-402-454-3311 x124; fax-402-454-6682; hours 8:30AM-5PM
Will search UCC records, but only real estate related UCC filed here. Search per debtor- $4.50. UCC search includes tax liens. Separate Tax lien search-$4.00 per debtor. Will not search real estate records. RE record copy- $.50 per page. UCC copy- $1.00 per page. Cert fee: $1.50 per page. Payee: Madison County Register of Deeds. **Other phones:** Assessor-402-454-3311 x178; Treasurer-402-454-3311 x133; Elections-402-454-3311 x136; Vital Records-402-471-2871.

McPherson County

County Clerk, PO Box 122, Tryon, NE 69167-0122. **Phone**-308-587-2363, R/E Recording-308-587-2242; fax-308-587-2363; hours 8:30AM-4:30PM
UCC search per debtor- $4.50. Will not search real estate or tax lien records. Record copy-$.50 per page. Cert fee: $1.50 pe page. Payee: McPherson County Clerk. **Other phones:** Assessor-308-587-2363; Treasurer-308-587-2442.

Merrick County

County Clerk, PO Box 27, Central City, NE 68826. **Phone**-County Clerk, R/E & UCC Recording- 308-946-2881, UCC Recording-The Secretary of State; fax-308-946-2332; hours 8AM-5PM
Will search pre-1999 UCC records. Search per debtor- $4.50 per page (includes copy fee). UCC search does not include tax liens Separate federal/state combined tax lien search- $3.00 per debtor. Will not search real estate records. UCC copy-$1.00 per page. Cert fee: $4.00 per cert. Payee: Merrick County Clerk. **Other phones:** Assessor-308-946-2443; Treasurer-308-946-2171; Appraiser-Do not have on staff; call Assessor's Office; Elections-308-946-2881; Vital Records-402-471-2871.

Morrill County

County Clerk, PO Box 610, Bridgeport, NE 69336. **Phone**-County Clerk, R/E & UCC Recording- 308-262-0860; fax-308-262-1469; hours 8AM-4:30PM
Will not search records. UCC copy- $.50 per page. Cert fee: $1.50per page. Payee: Morrill County Clerk. **Other phones:** Assessor-308-262-1534; Treasurer-308-262-1177; Elections-308-262-0860.

Nance County

County Clerk, PO Box 338, Fullerton, NE 68638. **Phone**-308-536-2331; fax-308-536-2742.
UCC records search per debtor- $4.50. Will search tax liens including federal tax liens. Tax lien search- $5.00 per debtor. Will not search real estate records. Record copy- $1.00 per page. Cert fee: $1.50 per page. Payee: County Clerk. **Other phones:** Assessor-308-536-2653; Treasurer-308-536-2165; Elections-308-536-2331.

Nemaha County

County Clerk, 1824 N St, Courthouse, Auburn, NE 68305-2399. **Phone**-County Clerk, R/E & UCC Recording- 402-274-4213; fax-402-274-4389; hours 8AM-5PM
UCC records search per debtor- $4.50. UCC search includes tax liens. Tax lien search- $3.50 per debtor. Will not search real estate records. RE record copy- $.25 per page. UCC copy- $1.00 per page. Cert fee: $1.50 per cert. Payee: Nemaha County Clerk. **Other phones:** Assessor-402-274-3820; Treasurer-402-274-3319.

Nuckolls County

County Clerk, PO Box 366, Nelson, NE 68961-0366. **Phone**-County Clerk, R/E & UCC Recording- 402-225-4361; fax-402-225-4301; hours 8:30AM-4:30PM
UCC records search per debtor- $4.50 per written request. Will search tax liens. Will search real estate

records if uncomplicated search. RE record copy-$.25 per page. If mailed $.50 for 1st page & $.25 each add'l. UCC copy- $1.00 per page. Cert fee: Varies depending on document. Payee: Nuckolls County Clerk. **Other phones:** Assessor-402-225-2401; Treasurer-402-225-4351; Elections-402-225-4361; Vital Records-402-225-4361.

Otoe County Clerk

Register of Deeds, PO Box 249, Nebraska City, NE 68410-0249. **Phone**-402-873-9505, R/E Recording-402-873-9530; fax-402-873-9506; hours 8AM-4:30PM www.co.otoe.ne.us/deeds.html
Will not search UCC or tax liens records. See Register of Deeds for real estate records. Record copy- $.50 per page. Cert fee: $1.50 per page. Payee: Register of Deeds. **Other phones:** Assessor-402-873-9520; Treasurer-402-873-9510; Appraiser-402-873-9522; Elections-402-873-9505; Vital Records-402-471-2872.

Otoe County Register of Deeds

County Register of Deeds, 1021 Central Ave., Rm 203, Nebraska City, NE 68410. **Phone**-402-873-9530; fax-402-873-9507; hours 8AM-4:30PM
Will not search records. UCC copy- $.50 per page. Cert fee: $1.50. Payee: Otoe County Register of Deeds. **Other phones:** Assessor-402-873-9520; Treasurer-402-873-3589.

Pawnee County

County Clerk, PO Box 431, Pawnee City, NE 68420. **Phone**-402-852-2962; fax-402-852-2963; 8AM-4PM
UCC records search per debtor- $4.50. UCC search includes tax liens if requested. Separate federal/state combined tax lien search- $3.00 per debtor. Real estate record owner and mortgage searches available. UCC copy- $1.00 per page. Cert fee: $5.00 per cert. Payee: Pawnee County Clerk. **Other phones:** Assessor-402-852-2292; Treasurer-402-852-2380.

Perkins County

County Clerk, PO Box 156, Grant, NE 69140-0156. **Phone**-County Clerk, R/E & UCC Recording- 308-352-4643; fax-308-352-2455; hours 8AM-4PM
Will not search records. UCC copy- $.50 per page. Cert fee: $5.00. Payee: Perkins County Clerk. **Other phones:** Assessor-308-352-4938; Treasurer-308-352-4542; Elections-308-352-4643.

Phelps County

County Clerk, PO Box 404, Holdrege, NE 68949-0404. **Phone**-County Clerk, R/E & UCC Recording- 308-995-4469; fax-308-995-4368; hours 9AM-5PM
UCC records search per debtor- $4.50. Will not search tax liens. Will search real estate records only from legal description. Copy fee is $.50 per page. Cert fee: $1.50 per page. Payee: Phelps County Clerk. **Other phones:** Assessor-308-995-4061; Treasurer-308-995-6115; Elections-308-995-4469.

Pierce County

County Clerk, 111 W. Court, Courthouse - Rm 1, Pierce, NE 68767-1224. **Phone**-County Clerk, R/E & UCC Recording- 402-329-4225; fax-402-329-6439; hours 8:30AM-4:30PM www.co.pierce.ne.us
UCC records search per debtor- $4.50. UCC search includes tax liens. Separate federal/state combined tax lien search- $5.00 per debtor. Will not search real estate records. Record copy- $1.00 per page. Cert fee: $1.50 per cert. Payee: Pierce County Clerk. **Other phones:** Assessor-402-329-4215; Treasurer-402-329-6335; Elections-402-329-4225.

Platte County Clerk

County Clerk, 2610 14th St, Columbus, NE 68601. **Phone**-402-563-4904, R/E Recording-402-563-4911;

fax-402-564-4614;   hours-8AM-5PM
www.plattecounty.net
Will not search UCC or tax liens records. See Register of Deeds for real estate records. **Online Access to Warrant records:** Access to the sheriff's warrant list is free at www.megavision.net/pcsher/Warran t%20List.htm. **Other phones:** Assessor-402-563-4902; Treasurer-402-563-4913; Elections-402-563-4908.

Platte County Register of Deeds

County Register of Deeds, 2610 14th St, Columbus, NE 68601. **Phone**-402-563-4911; hours 8AM-5PM
Will not search records. Record copy- $1.00 per page. Cert fee: $1.50 per page. Payee: Platte County Register of Deeds. **Other phones:** Assessor-402-563-4902; Treasurer-402-563-4913.

Polk County

County Clerk, PO Box 276, Osceola, NE 68651-0276. **Phone**-County Clerk, R/E & UCC Recording- 402-747-5431; fax-402-747-2656; hours 8AM-5PM
UCC records search per debtor- $4.50. Computer search only. UCC search includes tax liens if requested. Separate federal/state combined tax lien search- $3.00 per debtor. Will not search real estate records. Record copy- $.50 per page. Cert fee: $1.50 per page. Payee: Polk County Clerk. **Other phones:** Assessor-402-747-4491; Treasurer-402-747-5441; Elections-402-747-5431; Vital Records-402-471-2871.

Red Willow County

County Clerk, 502 Norris Ave, McCook, NE 69001. **Phone**-County Clerk, R/E & UCC Recording- 308-345-1552, UCC Recording-(State Office 402-471-4080); fax-308-345-4460; hours 8AM-4PM www.nol.org/red_willow
UCC records search per debtor- $4.50. UCC search includes tax liens if requested. Separate federal/state combined tax lien search- $3.00 per debtor. Will not search real estate records. Record copy- $1.00 per page. Cert fee: $1.50 per page. Payee: Red Willow County Clerk. **Other phones:** Assessor-308-345-4388; Treasurer-308-345-6515; Appraiser-785-475-2072; Elections-308-345-1552; Vital Records-State Office 402-471-2306).

Richardson County

County Clerk, 1700 Stone St., Courthouse, Falls City, NE 68355. **Phone**-402-245-2911; fax-402-245-2946; hours 8:30-5PM www.nol.org/richardson
UCC records search per debtor- $4.50. No tax liens filed here. Will not search real estate records. UCC copy- $.50 per page. Cert fee: $5.00. Payee: Richardson County Clerk. **Other phones:** Assessor-402-245-4012; Treasurer-402-245-3511.

Rock County

County Clerk, PO Box 367, Bassett, NE 68714. **Phone**-402-684-3933; hours 9AM-Noon, 1-5PM
UCC records search per debtor- $4.50. UCC search includes tax liens. Separate federal/state combined tax lien search- $3.00 per debtor. Will not search real estate records. UCC copy- $1.00 per page. Cert fee: $4.50 per cert. Payee: Rock County Clerk. **Other phones:** Assessor-402-684-3831; Treasurer-402-684-3515.

Saline County

Real Estate-County Clerek, PO Box 865, Wilber, NE 68465. **Phone**-Real Estate-County Clerek, R/E & UCC Recording- 402-821-2374, UCC Recording-402-471-4080 (filed at State level); fax-402-821-3381; hours 8AM-5PM
UCC records search per debtor- $4.50. Will not search real estate or tax lien records. UCC copy-$1.00 per page. Cert fee: $2.00. Payee: Saline

County Clerk. **Other phones:** Assessor-402-821-2588; Treasurer-402-821-2375; Elections-402-821-2374; Vital Records-402-471-2872 (State Bureau of Vital Statistics).

Sarpy County Clerk

County Clerk, 1210 Golden Gate Drive, #1118, Papillion, NE 68046-2895. **Phone-**402-593-2114; fax-402-593-4360; hours 8AM-4:45PM M,T,Th,F; 8AM-6PM W www.sarpy.com

Will not search UCC or tax liens records. See Register of Deeds for real estate records. **Online Access to Real Estate records:** Records on the county Property Lookup database are free at www.sarpy.com/assessor/property-search.htm. **Other phones:** Assessor-402-593-2121.

Sarpy County Register of Deeds

County Clerk, 1210 Golden Gate Drive #1109, Papillion, NE 68046. **Phone-**402-593-2186; fax-402-593-2338; hours 8AM-5PM

UCC records search per debtor- $4.50. UCC search includes tax liens if requested. Will not search real estate records. UCC copy- $1.00 per page. Cert fee: $1.50. Payee: Sarpy County Clerk. **Other phones:** Assessor-402-593-2121; Treasurer-402-436-6621.

Saunders County Clerk

County Clerk, PO Box 61, Wahoo, NE 68066-0187. **Phone-**402-443-8101; fax-402-443-5010; hours 8AM-5PM

UCC records search per debtor- $4.50. See Register of Deeds for records. Federal/state combined tax lien search- $2.00 per debtor See Register of Deeds for real estate records. UCC copy- $1.00 per page. Cert fee: $5.00. Payee: Saunders County Clerk. **Other phones:** Assessor-402-443-5700.

Saunders County Register of Deeds

Register of Deeds, PO Box 184, Wahoo, NE 68066. **Phone-**Register of Deeds, R/E & UCC Recording- 402-443-8111; fax-402-443-5010; hours 8AM-5PM

Will not search records. Cert fee: $1.50 per page. Payee: Register of Deeds. **Other phones:** Assessor-402-443-5700; Treasurer-402-443-8129; Appraiser-402-443-5702; Elections-402-443-8100.

Scotts Bluff County Clerk

County Clerk, 1825 10th St, Admin. Office Bldg., Gering, NE 69341. **Phone-**308-436-6601; fax-308-436-3178; hours 8AM-4:30PM

UCC records search per debtor- $4.50. UCC search includes state tax liens. See Register of Deeds for real estate records. Copy fee is $.50 per page. Cert fee: $5.00 per doc. Payee: Scotts Bluff County Clerk. **Other phones:** Assessor-308-436-6627.

Scotts Bluff County Register of Deeds

County Register of Deeds, 1825 10th St, Admin. Office Bldg., Gering, NE 69341. **Phone-**County Register of Deeds, R/E & UCC Recording- 308-436-6607; fax-308-436-6609; hours 8AM-4:30PM

Will not search records. RE record copy- $.50 per page. UCC copy- $1.00 per page. Cert fee: $1.50 per page. Payee: Scotts Bluff County Register of Deeds. **Other phones:** Assessor-308-436-6627; Treasurer-308-436-6621.

Seward County

County Clerk, PO Box 190, Seward, NE 68434-0190. **Phone-**402-643-2883; fax-402-643-9243; hours 8AM-5PM http://connectseward.org/cs/

UCC records search per debtor- $4.50. Will not search real estate or tax lien records. Record copy- $.50 per page. Cert fee: $1.50 per page. Payee: Seward County Clerk. **Other phones:** Assessor-402-643-3311; Treasurer-402-643-4574; Elections-402-643-2883; Land or Marriage records-402-643-2883.

Sheridan County

County Clerk, PO Box 39, Rushville, NE 69360. **Phone-**308-327-5650, R/E Recording-308-327-2633, UCC Recording-308-327-2633; hours 8:30AM-4:30PM

UCC records search per debtor- $4.50. UCC search includes tax liens if requested. Separate federal/state combined tax lien search- $3.00 per debtor. Will not search real estate records. UCC copy- $1.00 per page. Cert fee: $1.50 per cert. Payee: Sheridan County Clerk. **Other phones:** Assessor-308-327-2113; Treasurer-308-327-2362.

Sherman County

County Clerk, PO Box 456, Loup City, NE 68853-0456. **Phone-**308-745-1513; fax-308-745-1820.

UCC records search per debtor- $4.50. Will not search tax liens. Will search real estate records. Record copy- $.50 per page. **Other phones:** Assessor-308-745-0113; Treasurer-308-745-1513.

Sioux County

County Clerk, PO Box 158, Harrison, NE 69346. **Phone-**308-668-2443; fax-308-668-2443; hours 8AM-4:30PM

UCC records search per debtor- $4.50. Will not search real estate or tax lien records. Copy fee-$.25 per page. Cert fee: $1.00 per page. Payee: Sioux County Clerk. **Other phones:** Assessor-308-668-2443; Treasurer-308-668-2422.

Stanton County

Register of Deeds, PO Box 347, Stanton, NE 68779-0347. **Phone-**Register of Deeds, R/E & UCC Recording- 402-439-2222; fax-402-439-2200; hours 8:30AM-4:30PM

UCC records search per debtor- $4.50 per name. Will not search real estate or tax lien records. UCC copy- $.50 per page. Cert fee: $1.50 per instrument. Payee: County Clerk. **Other phones:** Assessor-402-439-2210; Treasurer-402-439-2223; Elections-402-439-2222.

Thayer County

County Clerk, PO Box 208, Hebron, NE 68370. **Phone-**County Clerk, R/E & UCC Recording- 402-768-6126; hours 8AM-4:30PM

UCC records search per debtor- $4.50. UCC search includes tax liens if requested. Separate federal/state combined tax lien search- $4.00 per debtor. Real estate owner, mortgage, and property transfer searches available. RE record copy- $.25 per copy. UCC copy- $1.00 per page. Cert fee: $5.00 per cert. Payee: County Clerk. **Other phones:** Assessor-402-768-6417; Treasurer-402-768-6227; Appraiser-402-768-6417; Elections-402-768-6126.

Thomas County

County Clerk, PO Box 226, Thedford, NE 69166-0226. **Phone-**308-645-2261; fax-308-645-2623; hours 8AM-Noon, 1-4PM M-Th; 8AM-Noon, 1-3PM F

UCC records search per debtor- $4.50. UCC search includes tax liens if requested. Separate federal/state combined tax lien search- $3.00 per debtor. Will not search real estate records. RE record copy- $.25 per copy. UCC copy- $1.00 per page. Cert fee: $5.00 per record. Payee: Thomas County

Clerk. **Other phones:** Assessor-308-645-2261; Treasurer-308-645-2262.

Thurston County

County Clerk, PO Box G, Pender, NE 68047. **Phone-**402-385-2343; fax-402-385-3544; 8:30AM-5PM

UCC records search per debtor- $4.50. Will not search real estate or tax lien records. UCC copy- $3.00 per search. Cert fee: $5.00 per request. Payee: County Clerk. **Other phones:** Assessor-402-385-2251; Treasurer-402-385-3058; Elections-402-385-2343.

Valley County

County Clerk, 125 S. 15th, Ord, NE 68862-1499. **Phone-**308-728-3700; hours 8AM-5PM

UCC records search per debtor- $4.50. UCC search includes tax liens. Separate federal/state combined tax lien search- $3.00 per debtor. Will search real estate records. RE record copy- $.15 per page. UCC copy- $1.00 per page. Cert fee: $1.00 per cert. Payee: Valley County Clerk. **Other phones:** Assessor-308-728-5081; Treasurer-308-728-5606.

Washington County

County Clerk, PO Box 466, Blair, NE 68008. **Phone-**402-426-6822; fax-402-426-6825; 8AM-4:30PM

UCC records search per debtor- $4.50. Will not search real estate or tax lien records. UCC copy- $.50 per page. Cert fee: $1.50. Payee: Washington County Clerk. **Other phones:** Assessor-402-426-6800; Treasurer-402-426-6888.

Wayne County

County Clerk, PO Box 248, Wayne, NE 68787-0248. **Phone-**402-375-2288; fax-402-375-2288; hours 8:30AM-5PM http://county.waynene.org

UCC records search per debtor- $4.50. Will do tax lien search. Will search real estate records. UCC copy- $1.00 per page. Payee: Wayne County Clerk. **Online Access to Sheriff Sale, Warrant List records:** Search the sheriff's sales list and warrant list for free at http://county.waynene.org/County_Offices/Sheriff/. **Other phones:** Assessor-402-375-1979; Treasurer-402-375-3885; Elections-402-375-2288.

Webster County

County Clerk, PO Box 250, County Clerk Office, Red Cloud, NE 68970. **Phone-**402-746-2716; fax-402-746-2710; hours 8:30AM-4:30PM. Will not search UCC or real estate records. UCC copy- $1.00 per page. Cert fee: $1.50. Payee: Webster County Clerk. **Other phones:** Assessor-402-746-2717; Treasurer-402-746-2877; Elections-402-746-2716.

Wheeler County

County Clerk, PO Box 127, Bartlett, NE 68622. **Phone-**308-654-3235; fax-308-654-3470; hours 9AM-noon, 1-5PM. UCC records search per debtor- $4.50. Will not search real estate or tax lien records. Copy fee- $.50 per page. Cert fee: $7.00 per doc. Payee: Wheeler County Clerk. **Other phones:** Assessor-308-654-3235; Treasurer-308-654-3236.

York County

County Clerk, 510 Lincoln Ave., Courthouse, York, NE 68467. **Phone-**402-362-7759; fax-402-362-2651.

Will not search UCC or real estate records. Will perform a tax lien phone search to determine if document exists. UCC copy- $1.00 per page. Cert fee: $1.50 per page. **Other phones:** Assessor-402-362-4926; Treasurer-402-362-4949.

Nebraska County Locator

You will usually be able to find the city name in the City/County Cross Reference below. In that case, it is a simple matter to determine the county from the cross reference. However, only the official US Postal Service city names are included in this index. There are an additional 40,000 place names that people use in their addresses. Therefore, we have also included a ZIP/City Cross Reference immediately following the City/County Cross Reference.

If you know the ZIP Code but the city name does not appear in the City/County Cross Reference index, look up the ZIP Code in the ZIP/City Cross Reference, find the city name, then look up the city name in the City/County Cross Reference. For example, you want to know the county for an address of Menands, NY 12204. There is no "Menands" in the City/County Cross Reference. The ZIP/City Cross Reference shows that ZIP Codes 12201-12288 are for the city of Albany. Looking back in the City/County Cross Reference, Albany is in Albany County.

Nebraska City/County Cross Reference

ABIE Butler
ADAMS (68301) Gage(71), Lancaster(22), Otoe(5)
AINSWORTH Brown
ALBION Boone
ALDA Hall
ALEXANDRIA (68303) Thayer(97), Jefferson(2)
ALLEN Dixon
ALLIANCE (69301) Box Butte(97), Sioux(1)
ALMA Harlan
ALVO Cass
AMELIA Holt
AMES Dodge
AMHERST Buffalo
ANGORA Morrill
ANSELMO (68813) Custer(83), Blaine(10), Loup(6)
ANSLEY Custer
ARAPAHOE (68922) Furnas(80), Gosper(19)
ARCADIA (68815) Valley(63), Custer(18), Sherman(17)
ARCHER Merrick
ARLINGTON Washington
ARNOLD (69120) Custer(73), Lincoln(16), Logan(9)
ARTHUR Arthur
ASHBY (69333) Grant(89), Garden(10)
ASHLAND (68003) Saunders(74), Cass(24)
ASHTON (68817) Sherman(91), Howard(8)
ATKINSON Holt
ATLANTA Phelps
AUBURN Nemaha
AURORA (68818) Hamilton(98), Clay(1)
AVOCA (68307) Cass(85), Otoe(15)
AXTELL (68924) Kearney(94), Phelps(5)
AYR Adams
BANCROFT (68004) Cuming(98), Burt(1)
BARNESTON Gage
BARTLETT Wheeler
BARTLEY Red Willow
BASSETT (68714) Rock(71), Holt(25), Brown(1)
BATTLE CREEK Madison
BAYARD (69334) Morrill(63), Scotts Bluff(34), Banner(2)
BEATRICE Gage
BEAVER CITY Furnas
BEAVER CROSSING (68313) Seward(98), York(1)
BEE (68314) Seward(88), Butler(11)
BEEMER Cuming
BELDEN Cedar
BELGRADE (68623) Nance(90), Boone(9)
BELLEVUE (68147) Sarpy(97), Douglas(2)
BELLEVUE Sarpy
BELLWOOD Butler
BELVIDERE Thayer
BENEDICT (68316) York(91), Polk(8)
BENKELMAN Dundy
BENNET (68317) Lancaster(95), Otoe(4)
BENNINGTON (68007) Douglas(92), Washington(7)

BERTRAND (68927) Phelps(78), Gosper(21)
BERWYN Custer
BIG SPRINGS (69122) Deuel(85), Keith(6), Perkins(4), Garden(2)
BINGHAM (69335) Garden(73), Sheridan(26)
BLADEN (68928) Webster(79), Adams(20)
BLAIR Washington
BLOOMFIELD Knox
BLOOMINGTON Franklin
BLUE HILL (68930) Webster(80), Adams(19)
BLUE SPRINGS Gage
BOELUS Howard
BOYS TOWN Douglas
BRADSHAW (68319) York(95), Hamilton(4)
BRADY Lincoln
BRAINARD (68626) Butler(98), Saunders(1)
BREWSTER Blaine
BRIDGEPORT (69336) Morrill(97), Banner(2)
BRISTOW Boyd
BROADWATER Morrill
BROCK Nemaha
BROKEN BOW Custer
BROWNVILLE Nemaha
BRULE (69127) Keith(97), Perkins(2)
BRUNING (68322) Thayer(71), Fillmore(28)
BRUNO (68014) Butler(74), Saunders(25)
BRUNSWICK Antelope
BURCHARD (68323) Pawnee(98), Gage(1)
BURR (68324) Otoe(98), Johnson(1)
BURWELL (68823) Garfield(66), Loup(17), Valley(10), Rock(3)
BUSHNELL Kimball
BUTTE Boyd
BYRON Thayer
CAIRO (68824) Hall(96), Howard(3)
CALLAWAY Custer
CAMBRIDGE (69022) Furnas(73), Frontier(13), Red Willow(10), Gosper(2)
CAMPBELL (68932) Franklin(56), Adams(18), Kearney(15), Webster(9)
CARLETON Thayer
CARROLL Wayne
CEDAR BLUFFS Saunders
CEDAR CREEK Cass
CEDAR RAPIDS (68627) Boone(95), Nance(4)
CENTER Knox
CENTRAL CITY Merrick
CERESCO (68017) Saunders(53), Lancaster(46)
CHADRON Dawes
CHAMBERS (68725) Holt(96), Wheeler(2), Garfield(1)
CHAMPION Chase
CHAPMAN Merrick
CHAPPELL (69129) Deuel(87), Garden(12)
CHESTER Thayer
CLARKS (68628) Merrick(78), Polk(12), Hamilton(9)

CLARKSON (68629) Colfax(73), Stanton(26)
CLATONIA Gage
CLAY CENTER Clay
CLEARWATER (68726) Antelope(94), Holt(5)
CODY Cherry
COLERIDGE Cedar
COLON Saunders
COLUMBUS (68601) Platte(94), Polk(2), Butler(1), Colfax(1)
COLUMBUS Platte
COMSTOCK (68828) Custer(68), Valley(31)
CONCORD Dixon
COOK (68329) Otoe(51), Johnson(47), Nemaha(1)
CORDOVA Seward
CORNLEA Platte
CORTLAND Gage
COTESFIELD (68829) Howard(89), Greeley(10)
COZAD Dawson
CRAB ORCHARD (68332) Johnson(92), Gage(7)
CRAIG (68019) Burt(95), Washington(3), Dodge(1)
CRAWFORD Dawes
CREIGHTON (68729) Knox(89), Antelope(9)
CRESTON (68631) Platte(90), Stanton(10)
CRETE (68333) Saline(90), Lancaster(9)
CROFTON (68730) Knox(76), Cedar(23)
CROOKSTON Cherry
CULBERTSON (69024) Hitchcock(82), Hayes(11), Red Willow(6)
CURTIS (69025) Frontier(83), Lincoln(14), Hitchcock(1)
DAKOTA CITY Dakota
DALTON Cheyenne
DANBURY Red Willow
DANNEBROG (68831) Howard(98), Hall(1)
DAVENPORT (68335) Thayer(68), Nuckolls(24), Fillmore(6)
DAVEY Lancaster
DAVID CITY Butler
DAWSON Richardson
DAYKIN (68338) Jefferson(96), Saline(3)
DE WITT (68341) Saline(58), Gage(41)
DECATUR (68020) Burt(92), Thurston(7)
DENTON (68339) Lancaster(59), Seward(39), Saline(1)
DESHLER Thayer
DEWEESE (68934) Clay(72), Nuckolls(27)
DICKENS Lincoln
DILLER (68342) Jefferson(77), Gage(22)
DIX (69133) Kimball(98), Cheyenne(1)
DIXON (68732) Dixon(98), Cedar(1)
DODGE (68633) Dodge(66), Cuming(20), Colfax(12)
DONIPHAN (68832) Hall(66), Hamilton(33)
DORCHESTER (68343) Saline(78), Seward(21)
DOUGLAS Otoe

DU BOIS (68345) Pawnee(75), Richardson(24)
DUNBAR Otoe
DUNCAN Platte
DUNNING (68833) Blaine(79), Logan(13), Custer(6)
DWIGHT Butler
EAGLE (68347) Cass(71), Otoe(27)
EDDYVILLE (68834) Dawson(83), Custer(16)
EDGAR (68935) Clay(82), Nuckolls(17)
EDISON (68936) Furnas(74), Gosper(14), Greeley(11)
ELBA (68835) Howard(96), Greeley(3)
ELGIN (68636) Antelope(97), Wheeler(1), Boone(1)
ELK CREEK (68348) Johnson(71), Nemaha(19), Pawnee(8)
ELKHORN Douglas
ELLSWORTH (69340) Sheridan(91), Garden(8)
ELM CREEK (68836) Buffalo(79), Phelps(14), Dawson(6)
ELMWOOD Cass
ELSIE (69134) Perkins(92), Chase(6)
ELSMERE (69135) Cherry(52), Brown(47)
ELWOOD (68937) Gosper(83), Dawson(16)
ELYRIA Valley
EMERSON (68733) Dakota(44), Dixon(34), Thurston(20)
EMMET Holt
ENDERS (69027) Chase(96), Dundy(3)
ENDICOTT Jefferson
ERICSON (68637) Wheeler(78), Garfield(22)
EUSTIS (69028) Frontier(63), Dawson(27), Gosper(8)
EWING (68735) Holt(75), Antelope(15), Wheeler(9)
EXETER (68351) Fillmore(81), York(18)
FAIRBURY Jefferson
FAIRFIELD Clay
FAIRMONT (68354) Fillmore(91), York(8)
FALLS CITY Richardson
FARNAM (69029) Dawson(82), Lincoln(17)
FARWELL Howard
FILLEY (68357) Gage(98), Johnson(1)
FIRTH (68358) Lancaster(68), Gage(31)
FORDYCE Cedar
FORT CALHOUN Washington
FOSTER Pierce
FREMONT (68025) Dodge(95), Saunders(4)
FREMONT Dodge
FRIEND (68359) Saline(95), Seward(4)
FULLERTON (68638) Nance(97), Merrick(1)
FUNK Phelps
GARLAND Seward
GENEVA Fillmore
GENOA (68640) Nance(63), Platte(33), Merrick(3)
GERING Scotts Bluff
GIBBON (68840) Buffalo(94), Kearney(5)

GILEAD Thayer
GILTNER Hamilton
GLENVIL (68941) Clay(55), Adams(44)
GOEHNER Seward
GORDON (69343) Sheridan(93), Cherry(6)
GOTHENBURG (69138) Dawson(93),
    Lincoln(4), Custer(2)
GRAFTON (68365) Fillmore(95), York(4)
GRAND ISLAND (68801) Hall(97),
    Merrick(2)
GRAND ISLAND Hall
GRANT Perkins
GREELEY Greeley
GREENWOOD (68366) Cass(94),
    Lancaster(3), Saunders(1)
GRESHAM (68367) York(45), Polk(32),
    Seward(20), Butler(1)
GRETNA (68028) Sarpy(98), Douglas(1)
GUIDE ROCK (68942) Webster(80),
    Nuckolls(19)
GURLEY Cheyenne
HADAR Pierce
HAIGLER (69030) Dundy(92), Chase(7)
HALLAM (68368) Lancaster(93), Gage(6)
HALSEY Thomas
HAMLET Hayes
HAMPTON (68843) Hamilton(97), York(2)
HARDY (68943) Nuckolls(99), Thayer(1)
HARRISBURG Banner
HARRISON Sioux
HARTINGTON Cedar
HARVARD (68944) Hamilton(53), Clay(46)
HASTINGS Adams
HAY SPRINGS (69347) Sheridan(65),
    Dawes(34)
HAYES CENTER Hayes
HAZARD Sherman
HEARTWELL Kearney
HEBRON Thayer
HEMINGFORD (69348) Box Butte(67),
    Dawes(32)
HENDERSON (68371) York(73),
    Hamilton(26)
HENDLEY Furnas
HENRY (69349) Scotts Bluff(84), Sioux(15)
HERMAN (68029) Washington(90), Burt(9)
HERSHEY Lincoln
HICKMAN Lancaster
HILDRETH (68947) Franklin(78),
    Kearney(21)
HOLBROOK (68948) Furnas(71),
    Gosper(24), Frontier(3)
HOLDREGE (68949) Phelps(98), Harlan(1)
HOLMESVILLE Gage
HOLSTEIN Adams
HOMER Dakota
HOOPER (68031) Dodge(91),
    Washington(6), Cuming(1)
HORDVILLE Hamilton
HOSKINS (68740) Wayne(89), Stanton(10)
HOWELLS (68641) Colfax(47),
    Cuming(32), Stanton(20)
HUBBARD Dakota
HUBBELL Thayer
HUMBOLDT (68376) Richardson(86),
    Nemaha(11), Pawnee(1)
HUMPHREY (68642) Platte(89),
    Madison(10)
HUNTLEY Harlan
HYANNIS Grant
IMPERIAL (69033) Chase(97), Perkins(2)
INAVALE Webster
INDIANOLA (69034) Red Willow(93),
    Frontier(6)
INLAND Clay
INMAN Holt
ITHACA Saunders
JACKSON Dakota
JANSEN Jefferson
JOHNSON (68378) Nemaha(92),
    Johnson(4), Otoe(3)
JOHNSTOWN (69214) Brown(98),
    Cherry(1)

JULIAN Nemaha
JUNIATA Adams
KEARNEY Buffalo
KENESAW (68956) Adams(80),
    Buffalo(11), Hall(7)
KENNARD Washington
KEYSTONE (69144) Keith(97), Arthur(2)
KILGORE Cherry
KIMBALL (69145) Kimball(96), Banner(3)
LAKESIDE Sheridan
LAMAR Chase
LAUREL (68745) Cedar(95), Wayne(2),
    Dixon(1)
LAVISTA (68128) Sarpy(98), Douglas(1)
LAWRENCE (68957) Nuckolls(57),
    Webster(33), Adams(7), Clay(2)
LEBANON Red Willow
LEIGH (68643) Colfax(47), Platte(35),
    Stanton(16)
LEMOYNE (69146) Keith(95), Arthur(4)
LESHARA Saunders
LEWELLEN (69147) Keith(61), Garden(37)
LEWISTON Pawnee
LEXINGTON Dawson
LIBERTY (68381) Gage(88), Pawnee(11)
LINCOLN Lancaster
LINDSAY (68644) Platte(83), Madison(16)
LINWOOD (68036) Butler(80),
    Saunders(19)
LISCO (69148) Garden(85), Morrill(14)
LITCHFIELD (68852) Sherman(90),
    Custer(9)
LODGEPOLE (69149) Cheyenne(82),
    Garden(14), Deuel(2)
LONG PINE Brown
LOOMIS Phelps
LORTON Otoe
LOUISVILLE Cass
LOUP CITY Sherman
LYMAN Scotts Bluff
LYNCH (68746) Boyd(84), Holt(15)
LYONS (68038) Burt(93), Cuming(6)
MACY Thurston
MADISON (68748) Madison(93),
    Stanton(6)
MADRID Perkins
MAGNET Cedar
MALCOLM Lancaster
MALMO Saunders
MANLEY Cass
MARQUETTE Hamilton
MARSLAND Dawes
MARTELL Lancaster
MASKELL Dixon
MASON CITY Custer
MAX Dundy
MAXWELL Lincoln
MAYWOOD (69038) Frontier(85),
    Lincoln(14)
MC COOK (69001) Red Willow(97),
    Frontier(1)
MC COOL JUNCTION (68401) York(98),
    Fillmore(1)
MCGREW Scotts Bluff
MCLEAN Pierce
MEAD Saunders
MEADOW GROVE (68752) Madison(92),
    Pierce(7)
MELBETA Scotts Bluff
MEMPHIS Saunders
MERNA Custer
MERRIMAN Cherry
MILFORD Seward
MILLER (68858) Buffalo(97), Custer(2)
MILLIGAN Fillmore
MILLS Keya Paha
MINATARE Scotts Bluff
MINDEN Kearney
MITCHELL (69357) Scotts Bluff(95),
    Sioux(4)
MONROE Platte
MOOREFIELD (69039) Frontier(63),
    Lincoln(36)

MORRILL (69358) Scotts Bluff(80),
    Sioux(19)
MORSE BLUFF Saunders
MULLEN Hooker
MURDOCK Cass
MURRAY Cass
NAPER Boyd
NAPONEE (68960) Franklin(78),
    Harlan(21)
NEBRASKA CITY Otoe
NEHAWKA (68413) Cass(97), Otoe(2)
NELIGH Antelope
NELSON Nuckolls
NEMAHA Nemaha
NENZEL Cherry
NEWCASTLE (68757) Dixon(88),
    Cedar(11)
NEWMAN GROVE (68758) Madison(64),
    Platte(21), Boone(13)
NEWPORT (68759) Rock(68), Keya
    Paha(31)
NICKERSON (68044) Washington(57),
    Dodge(42)
NIOBRARA Knox
NORFOLK (68701) Madison(95),
    Stanton(4)
NORFOLK Madison
NORMAN Kearney
NORTH BEND Dodge
NORTH LOUP (68859) Valley(94),
    Greeley(3), Sherman(1)
NORTH PLATTE Lincoln
OAK (68964) Nuckolls(94), Thayer(5)
OAKDALE Antelope
OAKLAND (68045) Burt(94), Cuming(4)
OBERT Cedar
OCONTO (68860) Custer(94), Dawson(5)
OCTAVIA Butler
ODELL Gage
ODESSA Buffalo
OFFUTT A F B Sarpy
OGALLALA (69153) Keith(97), Perkins(2)
OHIOWA (68416) Fillmore(94), Thayer(5)
OMAHA (68152) Douglas(84),
    Washington(15)
OMAHA (68157) Sarpy(97), Douglas(2)
OMAHA Douglas
OMAHA Sarpy
ONEILL Holt
ONG (68452) Clay(76), Fillmore(24)
ORCHARD (68764) Antelope(65),
    Knox(27), Holt(7)
ORD Valley
ORLEANS Harlan
OSCEOLA Polk
OSHKOSH Garden
OSMOND Pierce
OTOE Otoe
OVERTON (68863) Dawson(89),
    Phelps(10)
OXFORD (68967) Furnas(62), Harlan(37)
PAGE Holt
PALISADE (69040) Hayes(63),
    Hitchcock(36)
PALMER (68864) Merrick(77), Nance(21)
PALMYRA (68418) Otoe(96), Cass(3)
PANAMA Lancaster
PAPILLION Sarpy
PARKS Dundy
PAWNEE CITY Pawnee
PAXTON (69155) Keith(96), Perkins(2)
PENDER (68047) Thurston(72),
    Cuming(18), Wayne(9)
PERU (68421) Nemaha(92), Otoe(7)
PETERSBURG (68652) Boone(69),
    Antelope(30)
PHILLIPS (68865) Hamilton(98), Hall(1)
PICKRELL Gage
PIERCE Pierce
PILGER (68768) Stanton(91), Cuming(4),
    Wayne(3)
PLAINVIEW (68769) Pierce(79),
    Antelope(19), Knox(1)

PLATTE CENTER Platte
PLATTSMOUTH Cass
PLEASANT DALE (68423) Seward(82),
    Lancaster(17)
PLEASANTON (68866) Buffalo(98),
    Custer(1)
PLYMOUTH (68424) Jefferson(98),
    Gage(1)
POLK (68654) Polk(66), York(20),
    Hamilton(12)
PONCA (68770) Dixon(55), Dakota(44)
POTTER (69156) Cheyenne(82),
    Banner(12), Kimball(4)
PRAGUE Saunders
PRIMROSE (68655) Boone(96), Greeley(3)
PROSSER Adams
PURDUM (69157) Blaine(47), Cherry(34),
    Thomas(13), Brown(4)
RAGAN Harlan
RANDOLPH (68771) Cedar(57),
    Pierce(25), Wayne(16)
RAVENNA (68869) Buffalo(94),
    Sherman(5)
RAYMOND (68428) Lancaster(97),
    Seward(2)
RED CLOUD Webster
REPUBLICAN CITY Harlan
REYNOLDS Thayer
RICHFIELD Sarpy
RISING CITY Butler
RIVERDALE Buffalo
RIVERTON Franklin
ROCA Lancaster
ROCKVILLE Sherman
ROGERS Colfax
ROSALIE (68055) Thurston(74),
    Cuming(25)
ROSE (68772) Rock(90), Loup(9)
ROSELAND Adams
ROYAL (68773) Antelope(97), Brown(2)
RULO Richardson
RUSHVILLE Sheridan
RUSKIN (68974) Nuckolls(90), Thayer(9)
SAINT EDWARD (68660) Boone(72),
    Platte(23), Nance(3)
SAINT HELENA Cedar
SAINT LIBORY (68872) Howard(82),
    Merrick(17)
SAINT MARY Johnson
SAINT PAUL Howard
SALEM Richardson
SARGENT (68874) Custer(95), Loup(2),
    Hall(1)
SARONVILLE (68975) Fillmore(55),
    Clay(44)
SCHUYLER Colfax
SCOTIA (68875) Greeley(95), Howard(4)
SCOTTSBLUFF Scotts Bluff
SCRIBNER Dodge
SENECA (69161) Thomas(63), Cherry(36)
SEWARD Seward
SHELBY (68662) Polk(96), Butler(3)
SHELTON (68876) Buffalo(86), Hall(13)
SHICKLEY (68436) Fillmore(98), Clay(1)
SHUBERT (68437) Richardson(80),
    Nemaha(19)
SIDNEY Cheyenne
SILVER CREEK (68663) Merrick(41),
    Polk(39), Nance(17), Platte(1)
SMITHFIELD Gosper
SNYDER Dodge
SOUTH BEND Cass
SOUTH SIOUX CITY Dakota
SPALDING (68665) Greeley(78),
    Wheeler(21)
SPARKS Cherry
SPENCER (68777) Boyd(86), Holt(13)
SPRAGUE Lancaster
SPRINGFIELD Sarpy
SPRINGVIEW Keya Paha
ST COLUMBANS Sarpy
ST MARY Johnson

STAMFORD (68977) Harlan(68), Furnas(31)
STANTON Stanton
STAPLEHURST Seward
STAPLETON (69163) Logan(72), Lincoln(27)
STEELE CITY Jefferson
STEINAUER (68441) Pawnee(98), Johnson(1)
STELLA (68442) Richardson(83), Nemaha(16)
STERLING (68443) Johnson(92), Otoe(7)
STOCKVILLE Frontier
STRANG Fillmore
STRATTON (69043) Hitchcock(96), Dundy(3)
STROMSBURG (68666) Polk(98), York(1)
STUART Holt
SUMNER (68878) Dawson(94), Custer(5)
SUPERIOR Nuckolls
SURPRISE Butler
SUTHERLAND (69165) Lincoln(84), McPherson(7), Keith(4), Arthur(3)
SUTTON (68979) Clay(87), Fillmore(7), Hamilton(3)
SWANTON Saline
SYRACUSE Otoe

TABLE ROCK (68447) Pawnee(93), Nemaha(4), Johnson(2)
TALMAGE (68448) Otoe(82), Nemaha(10), Johnson(6)
TAYLOR Loup
TECUMSEH Johnson
TEKAMAH Burt
THEDFORD Thomas
THURSTON Thurston
TILDEN (68781) Madison(66), Antelope(26), Pierce(3), Boone(2)
TOBIAS (68453) Saline(88), Jefferson(7), Thayer(3), Fillmore(1)
TRENTON Hitchcock
TRUMBULL (68980) Clay(53), Adams(28), Hamilton(13), Hall(4)
TRYON McPherson
UEHLING Dodge
ULYSSES (68669) Butler(85), Seward(14)
UNADILLA (68454) Otoe(98), Cass(1)
UNION (68455) Cass(98), Otoe(1)
UPLAND (68981) Franklin(85), Kearney(14)
UTICA Seward
VALENTINE (69201) Cherry(98), Merrick(1)
VALLEY (68064) Douglas(93), Saunders(5), Dodge(1)

VALPARAISO (68065) Saunders(53), Lancaster(39), Seward(4), Butler(2)
VENANGO (69168) Perkins(75), Chase(25)
VERDIGRE Knox
VERDON Richardson
VIRGINIA (68458) Gage(89), Pawnee(6), Johnson(3)
WACO (68460) York(98), Seward(1)
WAHOO Saunders
WAKEFIELD (68784) Dixon(60), Wayne(38)
WALLACE (69169) Lincoln(73), Perkins(21), Hayes(4)
WALTHILL Thurston
WALTON (68461) Lancaster(97), Cass(1)
WATERBURY (68785) Dixon(77), Dakota(22)
WATERLOO (68069) Douglas(96), Sarpy(3)
WAUNETA (69045) Chase(47), Dundy(25), Hayes(24), Hitchcock(2)
WAUSA (68786) Knox(92), Cedar(4), Pierce(2)
WAVERLY (68462) Lancaster(98), Cass(1)
WAYNE (68787) Wayne(98), Dixon(1)
WEEPING WATER Cass
WEISSERT Custer
WELLFLEET Lincoln

WEST POINT Cuming
WESTERN (68464) Saline(95), Jefferson(4)
WESTERVILLE Custer
WESTON Saunders
WHITECLAY Sheridan
WHITMAN Grant
WHITNEY Dawes
WILBER (68465) Saline(93), Gage(4), Lancaster(1)
WILCOX (68982) Harlan(31), Kearney(31), Franklin(22), Phelps(14)
WILLOW ISLAND Dawson
WILSONVILLE (69046) Furnas(93), Red Willow(6)
WINNEBAGO Thurston
WINNETOON Knox
WINSIDE Wayne
WINSLOW Dodge
WISNER (68791) Cuming(94), Wayne(4)
WOLBACH (68882) Greeley(50), Howard(39), Nance(8), Boone(2)
WOOD LAKE Cherry
WOOD RIVER Hall
WYMORE Gage
WYNOT (68792) Cedar(97), Dixon(2)
YUTAN Saunders

Nebraska ZIP/City Cross Reference

68001-68001 ABIE	68071-68071 WINNEBAGO	68347-68347 EAGLE	68430-68430 ROCA
68002-68002 ARLINGTON	68072-68072 WINSLOW	68348-68348 ELK CREEK	68431-68431 RULO
68003-68003 ASHLAND	68073-68073 YUTAN	68349-68349 ELMWOOD	68432-68432 SAINT MARY
68004-68004 BANCROFT	68100-68112 OMAHA	68350-68350 ENDICOTT	68432-68432 ST MARY
68005-68005 BELLEVUE	68113-68113 OFFUTT A F B	68351-68351 EXETER	68433-68433 SALEM
68007-68007 BENNINGTON	68114-68122 OMAHA	68352-68352 FAIRBURY	68434-68434 SEWARD
68008-68009 BLAIR	68123-68123 BELLEVUE	68354-68354 FAIRMONT	68436-68436 SHICKLEY
68010-68010 BOYS TOWN	68124-68127 OMAHA	68355-68355 FALLS CITY	68437-68437 SHUBERT
68014-68014 BRUNO	68128-68128 LAVISTA	68357-68357 FILLEY	68438-68438 SPRAGUE
68015-68015 CEDAR BLUFFS	68130-68132 OMAHA	68358-68358 FIRTH	68439-68439 STAPLEHURST
68016-68016 CEDAR CREEK	68133-68133 PAPILLION	68359-68359 FRIEND	68440-68440 STEELE CITY
68017-68017 CERESCO	68134-68145 OMAHA	68360-68360 GARLAND	68441-68441 STEINAUER
68018-68018 COLON	68147-68147 BELLEVUE	68361-68361 GENEVA	68442-68442 STELLA
68019-68019 CRAIG	68152-68198 OMAHA	68362-68362 GILEAD	68443-68443 STERLING
68020-68020 DECATUR	68301-68301 ADAMS	68364-68364 GOEHNER	68444-68444 STRANG
68022-68022 ELKHORN	68303-68303 ALEXANDRIA	68365-68365 GRAFTON	68445-68445 SWANTON
68023-68023 FORT CALHOUN	68304-68304 ALVO	68366-68366 GREENWOOD	68446-68446 SYRACUSE
68025-68026 FREMONT	68305-68305 AUBURN	68367-68367 GRESHAM	68447-68447 TABLE ROCK
68028-68028 GRETNA	68307-68307 AVOCA	68368-68368 HALLAM	68448-68448 TALMAGE
68029-68029 HERMAN	68309-68309 BARNESTON	68370-68370 HEBRON	68450-68450 TECUMSEH
68030-68030 HOMER	68310-68310 BEATRICE	68371-68371 HENDERSON	68452-68452 ONG
68031-68031 HOOPER	68313-68313 BEAVER CROSSING	68372-68372 HICKMAN	68453-68453 TOBIAS
68033-68033 ITHACA	68314-68314 BEE	68374-68374 HOLMESVILLE	68454-68454 UNADILLA
68034-68034 KENNARD	68315-68315 BELVIDERE	68375-68375 HUBBELL	68455-68455 UNION
68035-68035 LESHARA	68316-68316 BENEDICT	68376-68376 HUMBOLDT	68456-68456 UTICA
68036-68036 LINWOOD	68317-68317 BENNET	68377-68377 JANSEN	68457-68457 VERDON
68037-68037 LOUISVILLE	68318-68318 BLUE SPRINGS	68378-68378 JOHNSON	68458-68458 VIRGINIA
68038-68038 LYONS	68319-68319 BRADSHAW	68379-68379 JULIAN	68460-68460 WACO
68039-68039 MACY	68320-68320 BROCK	68380-68380 LEWISTON	68461-68461 WALTON
68040-68040 MALMO	68321-68321 BROWNVILLE	68381-68381 LIBERTY	68462-68462 WAVERLY
68041-68041 MEAD	68322-68322 BRUNING	68382-68382 LORTON	68463-68463 WEEPING WATER
68042-68042 MEMPHIS	68323-68323 BURCHARD	68401-68401 MC COOL JUNCTION	68464-68464 WESTERN
68044-68044 NICKERSON	68324-68324 BURR	68402-68402 MALCOLM	68465-68465 WILBER
68045-68045 OAKLAND	68325-68325 BYRON	68403-68403 MANLEY	68466-68466 WYMORE
68046-68046 PAPILLION	68326-68326 CARLETON	68404-68404 MARTELL	68467-68467 YORK
68047-68047 PENDER	68327-68327 CHESTER	68405-68405 MILFORD	68500-68588 LINCOLN
68048-68048 PLATTSMOUTH	68328-68328 CLATONIA	68406-68406 MILLIGAN	68601-68602 COLUMBUS
68050-68050 PRAGUE	68329-68329 COOK	68407-68407 MURDOCK	68620-68620 ALBION
68054-68054 RICHFIELD	68330-68330 CORDOVA	68409-68409 MURRAY	68621-68621 AMES
68055-68055 ROSALIE	68331-68331 CORTLAND	68410-68410 NEBRASKA CITY	68622-68622 BARTLETT
68056-68056 ST COLUMBANS	68332-68332 CRAB ORCHARD	68413-68413 NEHAWKA	68623-68623 BELGRADE
68057-68057 SCRIBNER	68333-68333 CRETE	68414-68414 NEMAHA	68624-68624 BELLWOOD
68058-68058 SOUTH BEND	68335-68335 DAVENPORT	68415-68415 ODELL	68625-68625 BOONE
68059-68059 SPRINGFIELD	68336-68336 DAVEY	68416-68416 OHIOWA	68626-68626 BRAINARD
68061-68061 TEKAMAH	68337-68337 DAWSON	68417-68417 OTOE	68627-68627 CEDAR RAPIDS
68062-68062 THURSTON	68338-68338 DAYKIN	68418-68418 PALMYRA	68628-68628 CLARKS
68063-68063 UEHLING	68339-68339 DENTON	68419-68419 PANAMA	68629-68629 CLARKSON
68064-68064 VALLEY	68340-68340 DESHLER	68420-68420 PAWNEE CITY	68630-68630 CORNLEA
68065-68065 VALPARAISO	68341-68341 DE WITT	68421-68421 PERU	68631-68631 CRESTON
68066-68066 WAHOO	68342-68342 DILLER	68422-68422 PICKRELL	68632-68632 DAVID CITY
68067-68067 WALTHILL	68343-68343 DORCHESTER	68423-68423 PLEASANT DALE	68633-68633 DODGE
68068-68068 WASHINGTON	68344-68344 DOUGLAS	68424-68424 PLYMOUTH	68634-68634 DUNCAN
68069-68069 WATERLOO	68345-68345 DU BOIS	68428-68428 RAYMOND	68635-68635 DWIGHT
68070-68070 WESTON	68346-68346 DUNBAR	68429-68429 REYNOLDS	68636-68636 ELGIN

68637-68637 ERICSON	68773-68773 ROYAL	68922-68922 ARAPAHOE	69121-69121 ARTHUR
68638-68638 FULLERTON	68774-68774 SAINT HELENA	68923-68923 ATLANTA	69122-69122 BIG SPRINGS
68640-68640 GENOA	68776-68776 SOUTH SIOUX CITY	68924-68924 AXTELL	69123-69123 BRADY
68641-68641 HOWELLS	68777-68777 SPENCER	68925-68925 AYR	69125-69125 BROADWATER
68642-68642 HUMPHREY	68778-68778 SPRINGVIEW	68926-68926 BEAVER CITY	69127-69127 BRULE
68643-68643 LEIGH	68779-68779 STANTON	68927-68927 BERTRAND	69128-69128 BUSHNELL
68644-68644 LINDSAY	68780-68780 STUART	68928-68928 BLADEN	69129-69129 CHAPPELL
68647-68647 MONROE	68781-68781 TILDEN	68929-68929 BLOOMINGTON	69130-69130 COZAD
68648-68648 MORSE BLUFF	68783-68783 VERDIGRE	68930-68930 BLUE HILL	69131-69131 DALTON
68649-68649 NORTH BEND	68784-68784 WAKEFIELD	68932-68932 CAMPBELL	69132-69132 DICKENS
68650-68650 OCTAVIA	68785-68785 WATERBURY	68933-68933 CLAY CENTER	69133-69133 DIX
68651-68651 OSCEOLA	68786-68786 WAUSA	68934-68934 DEWEESE	69134-69134 ELSIE
68652-68652 PETERSBURG	68787-68787 WAYNE	68935-68935 EDGAR	69135-69135 ELSMERE
68653-68653 PLATTE CENTER	68788-68788 WEST POINT	68936-68936 EDISON	69138-69138 GOTHENBURG
68654-68654 POLK	68789-68789 WINNETOON	68937-68937 ELWOOD	69140-69140 GRANT
68655-68655 PRIMROSE	68790-68790 WINSIDE	68938-68938 FAIRFIELD	69141-69141 GURLEY
68658-68658 RISING CITY	68791-68791 WISNER	68939-68939 FRANKLIN	69142-69142 HALSEY
68659-68659 ROGERS	68792-68792 WYNOT	68940-68940 FUNK	69143-69143 HERSHEY
68660-68660 SAINT EDWARD	68801-68803 GRAND ISLAND	68941-68941 GLENVIL	69144-69144 KEYSTONE
68661-68661 SCHUYLER	68810-68810 ALDA	68942-68942 GUIDE ROCK	69145-69145 KIMBALL
68662-68662 SHELBY	68812-68812 AMHERST	68943-68943 HARDY	69146-69146 LEMOYNE
68663-68663 SILVER CREEK	68813-68813 ANSELMO	68944-68944 HARVARD	69147-69147 LEWELLEN
68664-68664 SNYDER	68814-68814 ANSLEY	68945-68945 HEARTWELL	69148-69148 LISCO
68665-68665 SPALDING	68815-68815 ARCADIA	68946-68946 HENDLEY	69149-69149 LODGEPOLE
68666-68666 STROMSBURG	68816-68816 ARCHER	68947-68947 HILDRETH	69150-69150 MADRID
68667-68667 SURPRISE	68817-68817 ASHTON	68948-68948 HOLBROOK	69151-69151 MAXWELL
68669-68669 ULYSSES	68818-68818 AURORA	68949-68949 HOLDREGE	69152-69152 MULLEN
68701-68702 NORFOLK	68819-68819 BERWYN	68950-68950 HOLSTEIN	69153-69153 OGALLALA
68710-68710 ALLEN	68820-68820 BOELUS	68951-68951 HUNTLEY	69154-69154 OSHKOSH
68711-68711 AMELIA	68821-68821 BREWSTER	68952-68952 INAVALE	69155-69155 PAXTON
68713-68713 ATKINSON	68822-68822 BROKEN BOW	68954-68954 INLAND	69156-69156 POTTER
68714-68714 BASSETT	68823-68823 BURWELL	68955-68955 JUNIATA	69157-69157 PURDUM
68715-68715 BATTLE CREEK	68824-68824 CAIRO	68956-68956 KENESAW	69160-69160 SIDNEY
68716-68716 BEEMER	68825-68825 CALLAWAY	68957-68957 LAWRENCE	69161-69161 SENECA
68717-68717 BELDEN	68826-68826 CENTRAL CITY	68958-68958 LOOMIS	69162-69162 SIDNEY
68718-68718 BLOOMFIELD	68827-68827 CHAPMAN	68959-68959 MINDEN	69163-69163 STAPLETON
68719-68719 BRISTOW	68828-68828 COMSTOCK	68960-68960 NAPONEE	69165-69165 SUTHERLAND
68720-68720 BRUNSWICK	68829-68829 COTESFIELD	68961-68961 NELSON	69166-69166 THEDFORD
68722-68722 BUTTE	68831-68831 DANNEBROG	68963-68963 NORMAN	69167-69167 TRYON
68723-68723 CARROLL	68832-68832 DONIPHAN	68964-68964 OAK	69168-69168 VENANGO
68724-68724 CENTER	68833-68833 DUNNING	68966-68966 ORLEANS	69169-69169 WALLACE
68725-68725 CHAMBERS	68834-68834 EDDYVILLE	68967-68967 OXFORD	69170-69170 WELLFLEET
68726-68726 CLEARWATER	68835-68835 ELBA	68969-68969 RAGAN	69171-69171 WILLOW ISLAND
68727-68727 COLERIDGE	68836-68836 ELM CREEK	68970-68970 RED CLOUD	69190-69190 OSHKOSH
68728-68728 CONCORD	68837-68837 ELYRIA	68971-68971 REPUBLICAN CITY	69201-69201 VALENTINE
68729-68729 CREIGHTON	68838-68838 FARWELL	68972-68972 RIVERTON	69210-69210 AINSWORTH
68730-68730 CROFTON	68840-68840 GIBBON	68973-68973 ROSELAND	69211-69211 CODY
68731-68731 DAKOTA CITY	68841-68841 GILTNER	68974-68974 RUSKIN	69212-69212 CROOKSTON
68732-68732 DIXON	68842-68842 GREELEY	68975-68975 SARONVILLE	69214-69214 JOHNSTOWN
68733-68733 EMERSON	68843-68843 HAMPTON	68976-68976 SMITHFIELD	69216-69216 KILGORE
68734-68734 EMMET	68844-68844 HAZARD	68977-68977 STAMFORD	69217-69217 LONG PINE
68735-68735 EWING	68845-68845 KEARNEY	68978-68978 SUPERIOR	69218-69218 MERRIMAN
68736-68736 FORDYCE	68846-68846 HORDVILLE	68979-68979 SUTTON	69219-69219 NENZEL
68737-68737 FOSTER	68847-68849 KEARNEY	68980-68980 TRUMBULL	69220-69220 SPARKS
68738-68738 HADAR	68850-68850 LEXINGTON	68981-68981 UPLAND	69221-69221 WOOD LAKE
68739-68739 HARTINGTON	68852-68852 LITCHFIELD	68982-68982 WILCOX	69301-69301 ALLIANCE
68740-68740 HOSKINS	68853-68853 LOUP CITY	69001-69001 MC COOK	69331-69331 ANGORA
68741-68741 HUBBARD	68854-68854 MARQUETTE	69020-69020 BARTLEY	69333-69333 ASHBY
68742-68742 INMAN	68855-68855 MASON CITY	69021-69021 BENKELMAN	69334-69334 BAYARD
68743-68743 JACKSON	68856-68856 MERNA	69022-69022 CAMBRIDGE	69335-69335 BINGHAM
68745-68745 LAUREL	68858-68858 MILLER	69023-69023 CHAMPION	69336-69336 BRIDGEPORT
68746-68746 LYNCH	68859-68859 NORTH LOUP	69024-69024 CULBERTSON	69337-69337 CHADRON
68747-68747 MCLEAN	68860-68860 OCONTO	69025-69025 CURTIS	69339-69339 CRAWFORD
68748-68748 MADISON	68861-68861 ODESSA	69026-69026 DANBURY	69340-69340 ELLSWORTH
68749-68749 MAGNET	68862-68862 ORD	69027-69027 ENDERS	69341-69341 GERING
68751-68751 MASKELL	68863-68863 OVERTON	69028-69028 EUSTIS	69343-69343 GORDON
68752-68752 MEADOW GROVE	68864-68864 PALMER	69029-69029 FARNAM	69345-69345 HARRISBURG
68753-68753 MILLS	68865-68865 PHILLIPS	69030-69030 HAIGLER	69346-69346 HARRISON
68755-68755 NAPER	68866-68866 PLEASANTON	69031-69031 HAMLET	69347-69347 HAY SPRINGS
68756-68756 NELIGH	68868-68868 PROSSER	69032-69032 HAYES CENTER	69348-69348 HEMINGFORD
68757-68757 NEWCASTLE	68869-68869 RAVENNA	69033-69033 IMPERIAL	69349-69349 HENRY
68758-68758 NEWMAN GROVE	68870-68870 RIVERDALE	69034-69034 INDIANOLA	69350-69350 HYANNIS
68759-68759 NEWPORT	68871-68871 ROCKVILLE	69035-69035 LAMAR	69351-69351 LAKESIDE
68760-68760 NIOBRARA	68872-68872 SAINT LIBORY	69036-69036 LEBANON	69352-69352 LYMAN
68761-68761 OAKDALE	68873-68873 SAINT PAUL	69037-69037 MAX	69353-69353 MCGREW
68762-68762 OBERT	68874-68874 SARGENT	69038-69038 MAYWOOD	69354-69354 MARSLAND
68763-68763 ONEILL	68875-68875 SCOTIA	69039-69039 MOOREFIELD	69355-69355 MELBETA
68764-68764 ORCHARD	68876-68876 SHELTON	69040-69040 PALISADE	69356-69356 MINATARE
68765-68765 OSMOND	68878-68878 SUMNER	69041-69041 PARKS	69357-69357 MITCHELL
68766-68766 PAGE	68879-68879 TAYLOR	69042-69042 STOCKVILLE	69358-69358 MORRILL
68767-68767 PIERCE	68880-68880 WEISSERT	69043-69043 STRATTON	69360-69360 RUSHVILLE
68768-68768 PILGER	68881-68881 WESTERVILLE	69044-69044 TRENTON	69361-69363 SCOTTSBLUFF
68769-68769 PLAINVIEW	68882-68882 WOLBACH	69045-69045 WAUNETA	69365-69365 WHITECLAY
68770-68770 PONCA	68883-68883 WOOD RIVER	69046-69046 WILSONVILLE	69366-69366 WHITMAN
68771-68771 RANDOLPH	68901-68902 HASTINGS	69101-69103 NORTH PLATTE	69367-69367 WHITNEY
68772-68772 ROSE	68920-68920 ALMA	69120-69120 ARNOLD	

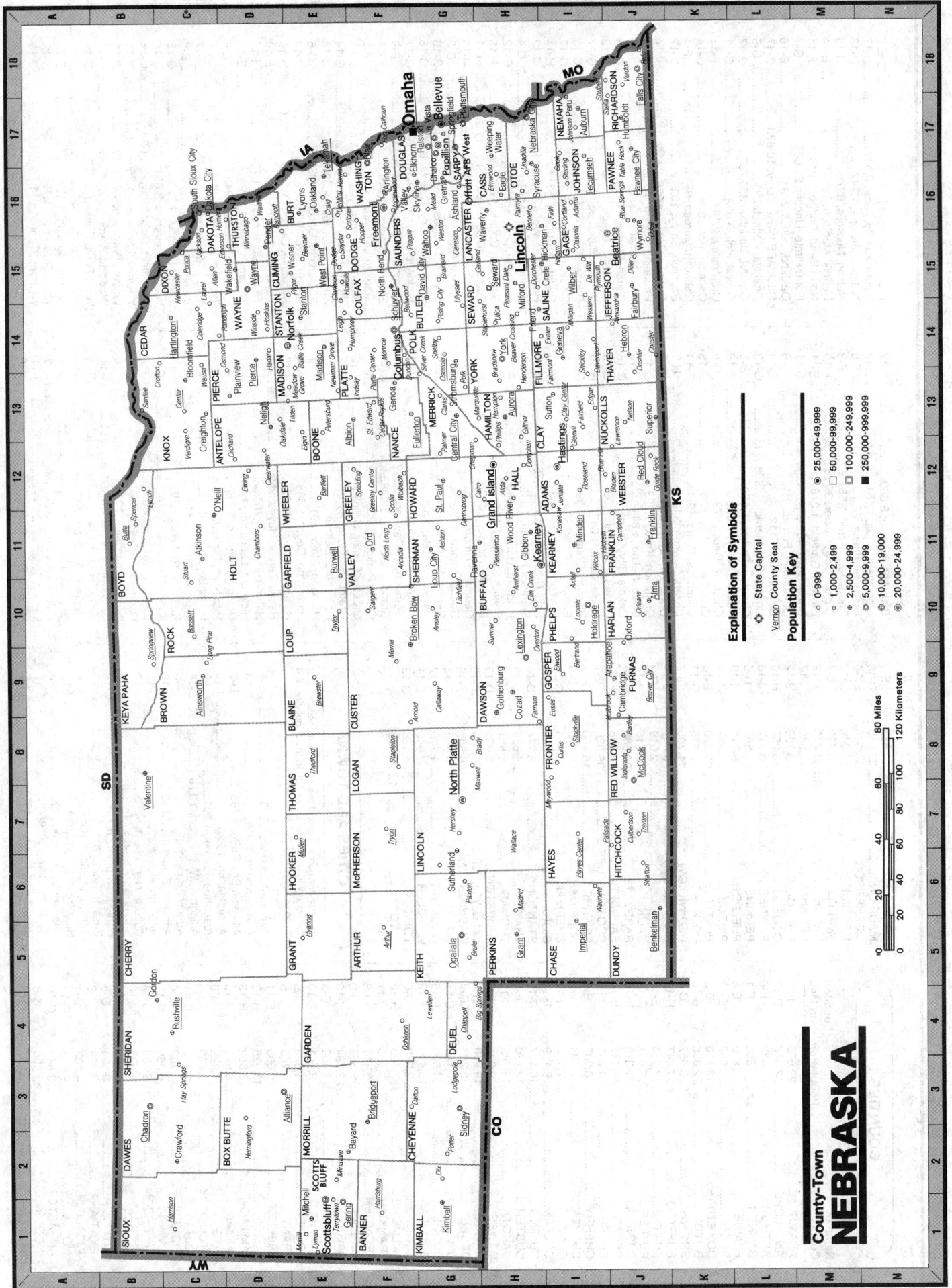

County-Town
NEBRASKA

Copyright American Map Corporation

Explanation of Symbols

◇ State Capital

Vernon County Seat

Population Key

● 0-999
● 1,000-2,499
● 2,500-4,999
● 5,000-9,999
● 10,000-19,000
● 20,000-24,999

◉ 25,000-49,999
☐ 50,000-99,999
☐ 100,000-249,999
■ 250,000-999,999

COUNTIES

CITIES AND TOWNS

Note: The first name is that of the city or town, second, that of the county in which it is located, then the population and location on the map.

Explanation of symbols: ● – Census Designated Place (CDP)

Nevada

General Help Numbers:

Governor's Office
Capitol Building
Carson City, NV 89701
http://gov.state.nv.us

775-684-5670
Fax 775-684-5683
8AM-5PM

Attorney General's Office
100 N Carson St
Carson City, NV 89701
http://ag.state.nv.us

775-684-1100
Fax 775-684-1108
8AM-5PM

Legislative Records
Nevada Legislature
401 S Carson St
Carson City, NV 89701-4747
www.leg.state.nv.us

775-684-6827 (Bill Status)
775-684-6800
Fax 775-684-6600
8AM-5PM

State Archives
100 N Stewart St
Carson City, NV 89701-4285
http://dmla.clan.lib.nv.us/docs/nsla

775-684-3360
Fax 775-684-3330
8AM-5PM M-F

State Specifics:

Capital:	Carson City
	Carson City County
Time Zone:	PST
Number of Counties:	17
Number of Filing Locations:	17
Population:	2,241,154
Web Site:	http://www.nv.gov

State Agencies

Criminal Records

DPS, Nevada Highway Patrol, Record & ID Services, 808 W Nye Lane, Carson City, NV 89703; 775-687-1600, 775-687-1843 (Fax), 8AM-5PM.

www.nvrepository.state.nv.us

Note: Records are available if you provide fingerprints and consent of subject. Otherwise, this agency suggests a court record search instead.

Indexing & Storage: Records are available from 1987 and are on computer. Records are maintained indefinitely, unless purged due to court order. It takes 6 hours before new records are available for inquiry. Records are indexed on computer. Records are normally destroyed after subject reaches 80 years old.

Searching: This repository maintains all "fingerprintable charges," meaning, essentially, all felony records and misdemeanor offenses including DUI and domestic violence. Include the following in your request-set of fingerprints, signed release, full name. DOB, SSN, sex and race are helpful. The following data is not released: sealed records or juvenile records.

Access by: mail, in person.

Fee & Payment: The fingerprint search fee is $21.00 per individual. If the search requires an FBI fingerprint check (for record checks on occupations concerning children or the elderly, per state stutute), the fee is $45.00. Fee payee: Nevada Highway Patrol. Prepayment required. Cash, money order or cashier's check required. No credit cards or personal checks accepted.

Mail search: Turnaround time: 15 working days. No SASE is required.

In person search: Records are still returned by mail.

Statewide Court Records

Supreme Court of Nevada, Administrative Office of the Courts, 201 S Carson St, #250, Carson City, NV 89701-4702; 775-684-1700, 775-684-1723 (Fax), 8AM-5PM.

www.nvsupremecourt.us/aoc/aoc.html

Note: Except for certain online research capabilities, all court record access must be done at the local level.

Access by: online. No searching by mail.

Online search: The Supreme Court website gives access to opinions and decisions. Some Nevada Courts have internal online computer systems, but only Clark County has online access available to the public. A statewide court automation system is being implemented.

Sexual Offender Registry

Records and Identification Bureau, Sex Offender Registry, 808 W Nye Lane, Carson City, NV 89703; 775-687-1600 x253, 775-687-1844 (Fax), 8AM-5PM.

www.nvsexoffenders.gov/

Note: In 1997, the Community Notification of Sex Offenders law was passed (NRS Chapter 179D). There are over 8,700 offenders registered in the state.

Indexing & Storage: Records are available from 1997 forward on computer.

Searching: Based upon NRS 179B.250, the Repository is permitted to share only ZIP Code information. Specific home address information on any convicted sex offender is strictly prohibited. There are less restrictions when requesting data at the local level. Include the following in your request-name, DOB, DL or SSN.

Access by: mail, phone, fax, in person, online.

Fee & Payment: There is no fee. Fee payee: Nevada Highway Patrol. Prepayment required. Money order or cashier's check required. No credit cards or personal checks accepted.

Mail search: Turnaround time: 1 day. No SASE is required.

Phone search: Requests can be made by telephone.

Fax search: Searching by fax permitted.

In person search: Records are still returned by mail.

Online search: Information on the website will include the name, aliases, photograph (where available), conviction information and ZIP Code based on the latest registered address. The website does not contain information on all convicted sex offenders. Information is only provided for sex offenders with a risk assessment score of a TIER Level 3 and certain information regarding a TIER Level 2. Search by name, ZIP Code, or even license plate number.

Incarceration Records

Nevada Department of Corrections, Attn: Records, PO Box 7011, Carson City, NV 89702 (Courier: 5500 Snyder Ave, Bldg 89, Carson City, NV 89701); 775-887-3285, 775-687-6715 (Fax), 8AM-5PM.

www.doc.nv.gov

Indexing & Storage: Records are available on current and former inmates. It takes 1 to 3 days before new records are available for inquiry.

Searching: Records are not destroyed, but are archived after one year. Include the following in your request-full name; DOC number helpful. Location, conviction and sentencing information, case number, and release dates are released. Searches can be done back to 1864, with varing results. The following data is not released: medical and mental health data, disciplinaries, correspondence, chronos.

Access by: mail, phone, online.

Fee & Payment: There is a $.25 fee per page.

Mail search: Turnaround time: 30 days. No SASE is required.

Phone search: Limited name searching available by phone.

Online search: There are two ways to access information at the web page. The first is by clicking on Online Inmate Search or www.doc.nv.gov/ncis/search.php. This will allow you to look up information about a particular individual. If you prefer, you may click on Download Information to obtain text files of all the information available via the Inmate Search. This system contains information about current inmates and those discharged in the past 18 months.

Corporation, Limited Partnerships, Limited Liability Company Records

Secretary of State, Records, 202 N Carson City, Carson City, NV 89701-4707; 775-684-5708 (Expedite), 775-684-5645 (Fax Expedite), 702-486-2880 (Las Vegas Ofc.:), 702-486-2888 (Las Vegas Ofc fax:), 775-684-5725 (Fax), 8AM-5PM.

www.sos.state.nv.us

Note: File are here, but records can also be looked up on computer at the Las Vegas office (555 E Washington Ave., #4000, Las Vegas, NV 89101). To get forms, use their Document-on-Demand System 800-583-9486.

Indexing & Storage: Records are available since inception of laws. Old, inactive records are purged from computer and archived. New records are available for inquiry immediately. Records are indexed on microfiche, inhouse computer.

Searching: Fax searching is available only for state government agencies. Include the following in your request-full name of business, corporation file number. In addition to the articles of incorporation, corporation records include the following information: Annual Lists of Officers & Directors, Prior (merged) names, Inactive and Reserved names, and Resident Agent names.

Access by: mail, phone, in person, online.

Fee & Payment: The search fee is $50.00. The certification fee is $30.00. Copy fees are $2.00 per page. There are set fees for certain specific documents that range from $10.00 to $25.00. Fee payee: Secretary of State. Prepayment required. Personal checks accepted. Credit cards accepted: MasterCard, Visa.

Mail search: Turnaround time: 1 to 2 weeks. No SASE is required.

Phone search: Staff will give status for corporations and partnerships, corporate officer names, and trademark information.

In person search: Information requests are available.

Online search: Online access is offered on the Internet site for no charge. You can search by corporate name, resident agent, corporate officers, or by file number.

Expedited service: Expedited service is available for mail, phone and in person searches. The expedite search fee is $25.00 There is an additional $75.00 fee for overnight service of copies if 1 to 10 pages, and $125.00 if over 10 pages.

Assumed Name, Fictitious Name

Records not maintained by a state level agency.

Note: Records are at the county level.

Trademarks/Servicemarks

Secretary of State, Corporate Expedite Office, 555 E. Washington Ave., #4000, Las Vegas, NV 89101, 702-486-2880, 702-486-2888 (Fax), 8AM-5PM.

http://secretaryofstate.biz/comm_rec/trademk/index.htm

Note: Trademark files are kept here; however, they are on the same computer system as the Carson City office. They can do all of the same searches on corporate records as Carson City, except for making copies of actual documents in files.

Indexing & Storage: Records are available since inception.

Searching: The same search requirements apply here as in Carson City.

Access by: mail, phone, in person.

Fee & Payment: The search fee is $50.00. Copies are $2.00 per page and $30.00 for certification. Fee payee: NV Secretary of State. Prepayment required. Personal checks accepted. No credit cards accepted.

Mail search: Turnaround time: 1 to 2 weeks.

Phone search: Limited information is offered over the phone.

In person search: Turnaround immediate, time permitting.

Uniform Commercial Code, Federal and State Tax Liens

UCC Division, Secretary of State, 200 N Carson St, Carson City, NV 89701-4069; 775-684-7708, 775-684-5630 (Fax), 8AM-5PM.

www.sos.state.nv.us

Note: Federal tax lien search must be requested separately and only contain data on businesses. Tax liens on individuals are filed at the county level. There is no state income tax, thus no recorded state tax liens.

Indexing & Storage: Records are available from 1967 on both computer and microfilm. It takes 1-2 days before new records are available for inquiry. Records are normally destroyed after 6 years.

Searching: Use search request form UCC-11. Include the following in your request-debtor name.

Access by: mail, fax, in person, online.

Fee & Payment: The fee for written request to search a debtor name is $40.00, via the Internet is $20.00. Copies cost $2.00 per page. Fee payee: Secretary of State. Prepayment required. Personal checks accepted. Credit cards accepted: MasterCard, Visa.

Mail search: Turnaround time: 1 to 3 days. A SASE is requested.

Fax search: See expedited service.

In person search: You may request information in person.

Online search: Searching is available from the web, fee is $20.00, an order form may be downloaded. A commercial system is also available. The PC dial-up system fee is based on hourly rate - $6.50 peak time, $4.50 non-peak time. Includes unlimited access. There is a $50.00 minimum deposit. The system is up from 7 AM to 5 PM.

Expedited service: Expedited service is available for mail and fax request searches. Searches will not be returned by fax. Turnaround time: 2 to 24 hours. Add $75.00 for 1 to 10 copies, $125.00 if 11 or more copies.

Sales Tax Registrations
State does not impose sales tax.

Birth Certificates
Nevada Department of Health, Office of Vital Statistics, 505 E King St, Rm 102, Carson City, NV 89701-4749; 775-684-4242, 775-684-4280 (Message Phone), 775-684-4156 (Fax), 8AM-4PM.

http://health2k.state.nv.us/

Indexing & Storage: Records are available from 1911 to present. It takes 30 days of filing before new records are available for inquiry. Records are indexed on microfiche, index cards, inhouse computer, hard copy.

Searching: Birth and death records are considered confidential and not open to the general public. Include the following in your request-full name, names of parents, mother's maiden name, date of birth, place of birth, relationship to person of record, reason for information request. Parents' names are a must to get record.

Access by: mail, phone, fax, in person, online.

Fee & Payment: For a certified copy the fee is $13.00. The fee for a verification only or for a no record found the fee is $8.00. If you wish to purchase using a credit card, there is an additional $5.50 fee. Fee payee: Office of Vital Statistics. Prepayment required. Personal checks accepted. Credit cards accepted: MasterCard, Visa, AmEx, Discover.

Mail search: Turnaround time: 2 to 3 days. No SASE is required.

Phone search: See expedited service.

Fax search: See expedited service.

In person search: Turnaround time 20 minutes.

Online search: Expedited service is available from state designated vendor at www.vitalchek.com.

Expedited service: Expedited service is available for online, phone and fax requests. Add $10.95 for 5 to 7 day service, or $28.45 for 2-5 day service. A credit card is required with fee of additional $5.50.

Death Records
Nevada Department of Health, Office of Vital Statistics, 505 E King St, Rm 102, Carson City, NV 89701-4749; 775-684-4242, 775-684-4280 (Message Phone), 877-456-5410, 775-684-4156 (Fax), 8AM-4PM.

http://health2k.state.nv.us/

Indexing & Storage: Records are available from 1911 on. It takes 30 days of filing before new records are available for inquiry. Records are indexed on microfiche, index cards, inhouse computer, hard copy.

Searching: Records are considered confidential, need to state relationship. However, a verification printout with name, date, and location is available to the public. Include the following in your request-full name, date of death, place of death, relationship to person of record, reason for information request.

Access by: mail, phone, fax, in person, online.

Fee & Payment: A certified copy is $8.00. The fee for a verification only or if no record found is $8.00. Fee payee: Office of Vital Statistics. Prepayment required. Personal checks accepted. Credit cards accepted: MasterCard, Visa, AmEx, Discover.

Mail search: Turnaround time: 5 to 10 working days. No SASE is required.

Phone search: See expedited service.

Fax search: See expedited service.

In person search: Turnaround time is 20 minutes.

Online search: Expedited service is available from state designated vendor at www.vitalchek.com.

Expedited service: Expedited service is available for online, phone and fax requests. Add $10.95 for 5 to 7 day service, or $28.45 for 2-5 day service. A credit card is required with fee of additional $5.50.

Marriage Certificates, Divorce Records
Access to Records is At County Level
Nevada Department of Health, Office of Vital Statistics, 505 E King St, Rm 102, Carson City, NV 89701-4749; 775-684-4481.

http://health2k.state.nv.us/

Note: Marriage and Divorce records are found at county of issue. However, the agency has an index and will relate the county and date of the event. The fee is $8.00. Call 775-684-4242. Request form is available at the webpage.

Workers' Compensation Records
Employers Insurance Co of NV, Workers Compensation Insurance, 2550 Paseo Verde Parkway, Henderson, NV 89074-7117; 888-682-6671, 702-671-7175 (Fax), 8AM-5PM.

www.eicn.com

Note: Effective 1/1/00, Nevada privatized the business of workers' compensation insurance. The state agency formally named State Industrial Insurance System became a private company. This company holds the records from the state agency.

Indexing & Storage: Records are available from 1940's on. It takes 1 week before new records are

available for inquiry. Records are indexed on microfilm, inhouse computer, file folders.

Searching: Must have a signed release from claimant and you must specify what you want from the file. Employers, after a hire, may check records. Older records are kept on microfilm, the records on the in-house computer are for general information only. Include the following in your request-claimant name, Social Security Number. Claim number, date of accident are helpful if known. This office is the phone service center. There are also hard copy records at the Reno office. 9790 Gateway Dr #100, Reno NV 89521. Their fax # is 775-886-1797.

Access by: mail, fax, in person.

Fee & Payment: The fee for a record search is $5.00. Fee is $.50 per page, unless only several copies are required. Fee payee: Employers Insurance Co of NV. Personal checks accepted. No credit cards accepted.

Mail search: Turnaround time: 30 days. A SASE is requested.

Fax search: Fax requests are accepted.

In person search: By going in person, you will only reduce the mail time.

Driver Records
Department of Motor Vehicles, Records Section, 555 Wright Way, Carson City, NV 89711-0250; 775-684-4590, 800-992-7945 (In-state), 775-684-4899 (Fax), 8AM-5PM.

www.dmvstat.com

Note: Copies of citations may be obtained at the same address. There is no fee when requesting your own citation, otherwise the fee is $8.00.

Indexing & Storage: Records are available for 3 yrs. Non-moving violations not listed on the driving record for non-CDL drivers. Nevada complies with the Driver's Privacy Protection Act, so personal data is available only to specific users. Records are computer indexed since 1980.

Searching: Authorized users may establish an account by completing the appropriate application. Call 775-684-4590 to request an application. Casual requesters without written consent of subject receive records without personal information. The driver's license number, or name and DOB are needed for a request. The SSN is helpful for searching, but is only released on the record to governmnet agencies. Accidents do not appear on the record.

Access by: mail, phone, online.

Fee & Payment: The fee is $7.00 per record. Fee payee: Nevada Department of Motor Vehicles. Prepayment required. Personal checks accepted. No credit cards accepted.

Mail search: Turnaround time: 10 days. Your request must be on department approved forms. No SASE is required.

Phone search: Phone-in requesters must be pre-approved, are assigned a 5-digit account number and can request up to 5 records at one time over the phone. Call 775-684-4590 for information. There is an in-state toll free line at 800-992-7945.

Online search: The state has an FTP type online system available for high volume users. All files received by 5:30 PM are processed and returned at 6:30 PM. Fee is $7.00 per record. Call 775-684-4702 for details.

Vehicle Ownership, Vehicle Identification

Department of Motor Vehicles, Motor Vehicle Record Section, 555 Wright Way, Carson City, NV 89711-0250; 775-684-4590, 775-684-4740 (Fax), 8AM-5PM.

www.dmvnv.com

Indexing & Storage: Records are available for the present on computer and on microfilm back to 1980.

Searching: SSNs, withdrawal action, accidents, and information connected to a license plate are not released to the general public. Nevada complies with DPPA and restricts access of records with personal information to permissible users. Requesters must show a legal right to the information or provide written consent or records are released with no personal data.

Access by: mail, phone.

Fee & Payment: The cost is $5.00 per record for current vehicle title or registration information. A vehicle history is $7.00, a title verification letter is also $7.00. Certification is an additional $4.00. Fee payee: Nevada Department of Motor Vehicles. Prepayment required. Personal checks accepted. No credit cards accepted.

Mail search: Turnaround time: 10 days. Be sure to give as much specific information as possible. Your request must be on department-approved forms. No SASE is required.

Phone search: Phone-in requesters must be pre-approved, are assigned a five-digit account number and can request up to five records at one time over the phone. Call 775-684-4590 for more information. There is an in-state toll free line at 800-992-7945.

Other access: Database is available for sale to permissible users under DPPA at costs varying from $500 to $2,500.

Accident Reports

Department of Public Safety, Nevada Highway Patrol, 555 Wright Way, Carson City, NV 89711; 775-684-4488, 775-684-4879 (Fax), 8AM-5PM.

http://nhp.nv.gov/index.htm

Indexing & Storage: Records are available only for those records at least three years old. It takes 7-10 working days before new records are available for inquiry. Records are indexed on inhouse computer. Records are normally destroyed after 6 years.

Searching: Requests must be in writing. Include the following in your request-full name, date of accident, location of accident, report number. For accidents 3 years old or less, the reports will be found at a regional office (Las Vegas 702-486-4100; Reno 775-688-2500; or Elko 775-753-1111)

associated with where the accidents occurred. Same fees apply.

Access by: mail, fax, in person.

Fee & Payment: The fee is $3.50 per report, and report(s) will not be mailed until payment has been received. Fee payee: Nevada Highway Patrol. Prepayment required. Personal checks accepted. No credit cards accepted.

Mail search: Turnaround time: 1 week. The turnaround time for the Las Vegas office is often 4 to 6 weeks. A SASE is requested.

Fax search: Fax searching available, but only of pre-paid.

In person search: Turnaround time is immediate if the record is on file.

Vessel Ownership, Vessel Registration

Department of Wildlife Headquarters, Boat Registration, 1100 Valley Rd, Reno, NV 89512-2815; 775-688-1983, 775-688-1509 (Fax), 8AM-5PM M-F.

www.ndow.org

Indexing & Storage: Records are available from 1972 to the present and are indexed on computer. All boats must be registered. It takes less than 1 day before new records are available for inquiry.

Searching: To search, one of the following is required: hull ID #, boat #, or name, plus name and address of requester. The following data is not released: Social Security Numbers.

Access by: mail, in person.

Fee & Payment: The fee is $5.00 per boat, which includes 1 computer print-out. Photocopies cost $.50 per page. Fee payee: NDOW. Prepayment required. Cash is accepted from in person searchers only. Out-of-state personal checks not accepted. No credit cards accepted.

Mail search: Turnaround time: 4 days. No SASE is required.

In person search: Turnaround time can be immediate if search is not lengthy.

Other access: Information is available on magnetic tape, labels, and printed lists. Fees depend on media type, can be $750 or more.

Voter Registration

Records not maintained by a state level agency.

Note: Records are open to the public at the county level. All data is released except for SSNs. The agency has plans in the near future to create a statewide database.

GED Certificates

Department of Education, State GED Administrator, 700 E 5th Street, Carson City, NV 89701; 775-687-9104, 775-687-9114 (Fax), 8AM-5PM.

www.literacynet.org/nvadulted/

Indexing & Storage: Records are available from 1948 to present, for GED. This agency holds many limited GED records on individuals tested in the military, federal prison, etc. It takes 4 to 6 weeks before new records are available for inquiry.

Searching: Only "passing scores" were kept from 1948 through 2001. Include the following in your request-name used when tested, signed release, date of birth, Social Security Number, information about and signature of requester. It is important to also submit the city location and approximate year of the test. They will fax back.

Access by: mail, fax, in person.

Fee & Payment: There is no fee.

Mail search: Turnaround time: 7 to 10 days.

Fax search: Same criteria as mail searching.

In person search: Turnaround immediate, if request not lengthy.

Hunting and Fishing License Information

Department of Wildlife, Licensing Office, 4600 Kietzke LN, D135, Reno, NV 89502; 775-688-1507, 775-688-1509 (Fax), 8AM-5PM.

www.ndow.org

Indexing & Storage: Records are available from 1976 to present on microfiche. It takes 3-6 months before new records are available for inquiry. Records are normally destroyed after 50 years.

Searching: Include the following in your request-full name, date of birth, Social Security Number. The following data is not released: Social Security Numbers or telephone numbers.

Access by: mail.

Fee & Payment: The fee is $5.00 per name per year searched. Fee payee: NDOW Prepayment required with guaranteed funds. No personal checks accepted. No credit cards accepted.

Mail search: Turnaround time: 1 to 3 working days. It will help to use their record request form, which you can request by phone. No SASE is required.

Other access: The Dapartment offers mailing lists, labels, magnetic tapes of hunting and fishing license holders for fees ranging from $350 to $1900.

Nevada State Licensing Agencies

Licenses Searchable Online

Ambulatory Surgery Ctr. (Pharmacy) #16........... https://nvbop.glsuite.us/renewal/glsweb/homeframe.aspx
Architect #2... http://nsbaidrd.state.nv.us/directory.htm
Athletic Promoter, Professional/Amateur) #35 ... www.boxing.nv.gov/teledir.htm
Attorney #44 .... www.nvbar.org/find_a_lawyer.asp
Bank #29... http://fid.state.nv.us/banks.htm
Boxing Gym #35 .... www.boxing.nv.gov/gyms.htm
Boxing Organization #35 .... www.boxing.nv.gov/teledir.htm
Building Mover #46.. http://nscb.tecxprs.com
Carpentry Contractor #46 .... http://nscb.tecxprs.com
Check Casher #29 .... http://fid.state.nv.us/check-cashing.htm
Chiropractor #3 .... http://chirobd.nv.gov/
Collection Agency #29 .... http://fid.state.nv.us/collection%20agency.htm
Collection Manager #29................................. http://fid.state.nv.us/collection%20manager.htm
Concrete Contractor #46 .... http://nscb.tecxprs.com
Contractor, General #46 .... http://nscb.tecxprs.com
Court Reporter, Certified #23......................... http://crptr.state.nv.us/contact.htm
Credit Union #29... http://fid.state.nv.us/credit%20union.htm
Debt Adjuster #29 .... http://fid.state.nv.us/debt-adjuster.htm
Deferred Deposit Company #29 .... http://fid.state.nv.us/check-cashing.htm
Dental Hygienist #4....................................... www.nvdentalboard.org/databaseRDH.html
Dentist #4.. www.nvdentalboard.org/databaseDDS.html
Doctor #11... http://medboard.nv.gov/default.asp
Doctor, Disciplinary Action #11...................... http://medboard.nv.gov/Disciplinary%20Actions/disciplinary_list.htm
Drug Wholesaler/Dist./Mfg. #16..................... https://nvbop.glsuite.us/renewal/glsweb/homeframe.aspx
Electrical Contractor #46 .... http://nscb.tecxprs.com
Elevator/Conveyor #46 .... http://nscb.tecxprs.com
Engineer #19 .... http://boe.state.nv.us/ROST_HOME.HTM
Engineering, General #46............................... http://nscb.tecxprs.com
Euthanasia Technician (Animal) #16 .... https://nvbop.glsuite.us/renewal/glsweb/homeframe.aspx
Fencing #46.. http://nscb.tecxprs.com
Financial Development Company #29............... http://fid.state.nv.us/development%20co.htm
Fire Protection Contractor #46....................... http://nscb.tecxprs.com
Fishing Guide #26... www.ndow.org/about/contacts/
Floor/Tile/Carpet Layer #46 .... http://nscb.tecxprs.com
Fur Dealer #26.. www.ndow.org/about/contacts/
Gas Fitter #46... http://nscb.tecxprs.com
GCB Most-Wanted & Banned List #36 .... http://gaming.state.nv.us/wanted_main.htm
Glazier Contractor #46.................................. http://nscb.tecxprs.com
Heating & Air Conditioning Mechanic #46 .... http://nscb.tecxprs.com
Hospital Pharmacy, Institutional #16 .... https://nvbop.glsuite.us/renewal/glsweb/homeframe.aspx
Installment Loan Company #29 .... http://fid.state.nv.us/installment%20loan.htm
Insulation Installer Contractor #46 .... http://nscb.tecxprs.com
Insurance Agent #24..................................... www.doi.state.nv.us/PL-ContactUs.htm
Interior Designer #2 .... http://nsbaidrd.state.nv.us/directory.htm
Landscape Contractor #46 .... http://nscb.tecxprs.com
Lobbyist #27 .... www.leg.state.nv.us/lobbyistdb/index.cfm
Marriage & Family Therapist #32.................... http://marriage.state.nv.us/
Mason #46.. http://nscb.tecxprs.com
Medical Device, Equipment or Gas #16 .... https://nvbop.glsuite.us/renewal/glsweb/homeframe.aspx
Medical Doctor #11....................................... http://medboard.nv.gov/default.asp
Money Transmitter Agent #29 .... http://fid.state.nv.us/money_transmitter_agents.htm
Money Transmitter Company #29 .... http://fid.state.nv.us/money%20transmitter.htm
Narcotic Treatment Center #16 .... https://nvbop.glsuite.us/renewal/glsweb/homeframe.aspx
Nurse Anesthetist #13 .... www.nursingboard.state.nv.us/Verification/formLicense.html
Nurse Assistant #13...................................... www.nursingboard.state.nv.us/Verification/formLicense.html
Nurse, Advanced Practitioner (Pharm) #16........ https://nvbop.glsuite.us/renewal/glsweb/homeframe.aspx
Nurse, Adverse Action Report #13 .... www.nursingboard.state.nv.us/dactions/
Nurse, RN/LPN/Advanced Practice #13............. www.nursingboard.state.nv.us/Verification/formLicense.html
Optometrist #0 .... www.arbo.org/odfinder/LicSearch.asp

Osteopathic Physician #15 .... https://nvboo.glsuite.us/renewal/glsweb/homeframe.aspx
Painter #46 .... http://nscb.tecxprs.com
Painter/Paper Hanger #46 .... http://nscb.tecxprs.com
Pharmacist/Pharmaceutical Technician #16 ...... https://nvbop.glsuite.us/renewal/glsweb/homeframe.aspx
Pharmacy #16 .... https://nvbop.glsuite.us/renewal/glsweb/homeframe.aspx
Pharmacy Practitioner #16 .... https://nvbop.glsuite.us/renewal/glsweb/homeframe.aspx
Physician Assistant #11 .... http://medboard.nv.gov/default.asp
Physician Assistant (Pharmacological) #16 .... https://nvbop.glsuite.us/renewal/glsweb/homeframe.aspx
Plaster/Lather #46 .... http://nscb.tecxprs.com
Plasterer/Drywall Installer #46 .... http://nscb.tecxprs.com
Playground Builder #46 .... http://nscb.tecxprs.com
Plumber #46 .... http://nscb.tecxprs.com
Podiatrist #18 .... http://podiatry.state.nv.us/
Prison (correctional - Pharmacy) #16 .... https://nvbop.glsuite.us/renewal/glsweb/homeframe.aspx
Pump Installer #46 .... http://nscb.tecxprs.com
Refractory/Firebrick Contractor #46 .... http://nscb.tecxprs.com
Residential Designer #2 .... http://nsbaidrd.state.nv.us/directory.htm
Respiratory Care Practitioner #11 .... http://medboard.nv.gov/default.asp
Roofer #46 .... http://nscb.tecxprs.com
Savings & Loan #29 .... http://fid.state.nv.us/savings%20and%20loan.htm
Scientific Collection Permit #26 .... www.ndow.org/about/contacts/
Sewerage Contractor #46 .... http://nscb.tecxprs.com
Sheet Metal Fabricator #46 .... http://nscb.tecxprs.com
Siding Installer #46 .... http://nscb.tecxprs.com
Sign Erector #46 .... http://nscb.tecxprs.com
Solar Contractor #46 .... http://nscb.tecxprs.com
Steel Contractor #46 .... http://nscb.tecxprs.com
Surveyor, Land #19 .... http://boe.state.nv.us/ROST_HOME.HTM
Tank Installer, Pressure/Storage #46 .... http://nscb.tecxprs.com
Thift Company #29 .... http://fid.state.nv.us/thrift%20company.htm
Trust Company #29 .... http://fid.state.nv.us/trust%20company.htm
Water Well Driller/Monitor #30 .... http://water.nv.gov/Engineering/welldrill.htm
Well Driller #46 .... http://nscb.tecxprs.com
Wrecker/Demolisher #46 .... http://nscb.tecxprs.com

Nevada Licensing Quick Finder

Acupuncturist #14	702-786-3302
Adult Day Care #22	775-687-4475
Adult Group Care #22	775-687-4475
Aesthetician #38	702-486-6542
Alcohol & Drug Abuse Center #22	775-687-4475
Alcohol & Drug Abuse Counselor #22	775-687-4475
Ambulance Attendant #22	775-687-4475
Ambulance Permit #22	775-687-4475
Ambulatory Surgery Ctr. (Pharm) #16	775-850-1440
Animal Technician #21	775-688-1788
Announcer, Athletic Event (Ring) #35	702-486-2575
Appraiser (MVD) #24	702-486-4009
Architect #2	702-486-7300
Athletic Promoter, Prof'l/Amateur) #35	702-486-2575
Attorney #44	702-382-2200
Audiologist #31	775-857-3500
Auditor #1	775-786-0231
Bank #29	775-684-1830
Barber #45	702-456-4769
Blood Gas Tech./Technologist #22	775-687-4475
Boxer #35	702-486-2575
Boxing Gym #35	702-486-2575
Boxing Organization #35	702-486-2575
Building Mover #46	702-486-1100
Bus Driver #25	775-684-4590
Carpentry Contractor #46	702-486-1100
Casino General Manager #36	775-684-7770
Cemetery #7	702-290-5366
Check Casher #29	775-684-1830
Chiropractor #3	775-688-1921
Claims Adjuster #24	702-486-4009
Clinical Laboratory Technologist #22	775-687-4475
Coach Dealer, Commercial #34	702-486-4590
Collection Agency #29	775-684-1830
Collection Manager #29	775-684-1830
Concrete Contractor #46	702-486-1100
Contractor, General #46	702-486-1100
Cosmetologist #38	702-486-6542
Court Reporter, Certified #23	702-384-1663
Credit Union #29	775-684-1830
Crematorium #7	702-290-5366
Debt Adjuster #29	775-684-1830
Deferred Deposit Company #29	775-684-1830
Dental Hygienist #4	702-486-7044
Dentist #4	702-486-7044
Director (Medical Laboratory) #22	775-687-4475
Doctor #11	775-688-2559
Doctor, Disciplinary Action #11	775-688-2559
Drug Wholesaler/Dist./Mfg. #16	775-850-1440
Electrical Contractor #46	702-486-1100
Electrologist #38	702-486-6542
Elevator/Conveyor #46	702-486-1100
Embalmer #7	702-290-5366
Emergency Care Ctr., Independent #22	775-687-4475
Emergency Medical Technician #22	775-687-4475
Engineer #19	775-688-1231
Engineering, General #46	702-486-1100
Environmental Health Specialist #42	775-328-2422
ESRD #22	775-687-4475
Euthanasia Technician #21	775-688-1788
Euthanasia Technician (Animal) #16	775-850-1440
Exempt Laboratory #22	775-687-4475
Fencing #46	702-486-1100
Financial Advisor (Investments) #40	702-486-2440
Financial Development Company #29	775-684-1830
Fire Protection Contractor #46	702-486-1100
First Responder EMT #22	775-687-4475
Fishing Guide #26	775-688-1512
Floor/Tile/Carpet Layer #46	702-486-1100
Funeral Director #7	702-290-5366
Fur Dealer #26	775-688-1512
Gaming #36	775-684-7770
Gaming Device Mfg./Dist. #36	775-684-7770
Gaming License Company #36	775-684-7770
Gas Fitter #46	702-486-1100
GCB Most-Wanted & Banned List #36	775-684-7770
Glazier Contractor #46	702-486-1100
Groundskeeper/Gardener #28	775-688-1182x243
Guard Dog Handler #39	775-687-3223
Hair Stylist (Designer) #38	702-486-6542
Health Clinic, Rural #22	775-687-4475

Hearing Aid Specialist #8 702-571-9000
Heating & A/C Mechanic #46 702-486-1100
Histotechnologist #22 775-687-4475
Histologic Technician #22 775-687-4475
Home Health Agency #22......................775-687-4475
Homeopathic Physician/Assistant #9 ...702-451-3332
Homeopathic Practitioner, Adv'd #9 702-451-3332
Hospice #22 775-687-4475
Hospital #22 775-687-4475
Hospital Pharmacy, Institutional #16....775-850-1440
IC Emergency Center #22 775-687-4475
Installment Loan Company #29............775-684-1830
Insulation Installer Contr. #46..............702-486-1100
Insurance Agent #24 702-486-4009
Interior Designer #2 702-486-7300
Intermediate Care Facility for the Mentally
    Retarded #22..............................775-687-4475
Intermedical Care Facility #22 775-687-4475
Investment Advisor #40 702-486-2440
Kickboxer #35....................................702-486-2575
Lab Assistant/Blood Gas Assist. #22 775-687-4475
Laboratory Certification #22 775-687-4475
Laboratory Office Assistant #22 775-687-4475
Laboratory, Medical #22 775-687-4475
Landscape Architect #10 775-688-1316
Landscape Contractor #46 702-486-1100
Lobbyist #27 775-684-6800
LPG Gas Distributor/Technician #33....775-687-4890
Manicurist #38 702-486-6542
Marriage & Family Therapist #32 702-486-7388
Mason #46...702-486-1100
Medical Device, Equipment or Gas #16 775-850-1440
Medical Doctor #11.............................775-688-2559
Medical Technician #22 775-687-4475
Mixed Martial Arts #35........................702-486-2575
Mobile Home Dealer #34 702-486-4590
Mobile Home Installer/Mfg. #34............702-486-4590
Mobile Home Salesman #34 702-486-4590
Mobile Home Serviceman #34...............702-486-4590
Mobile/Manufact'd Home Rebuilder #34 702-486-4590
Mobile/Manufactured Home RME #34 . 702-486-4590
Money Transmitter Agent #29 775-684-1830
Money Transmitter Company #29 775-684-1830
Narcotic Treatment Center #16 775-850-1440

Notary Public #41 775-684-5749
Nurse Anesthetist #13 ....888-590-NSBN
Nurse Assistant #13 ....888-590-NSBN
Nurse, Advanced Practitioner (Pharmacological) #16
....775-850-1440
Nurse, Adverse Action Report #13.......800-746-3980
Nurse, RN/LPN/Adv'd Practice #13 ...888-590-NSBN
Nursing Care (Skilled) Facility #22.......775-687-4475
Nursing Facility #22 775-687-4475
Nursing Home Administrator #49 702-486-5445
Nursing Pool Operator #22 775-687-4475
Occupational Therapist/Assistant #12..775-857-1700
Optician #5 775-853-1421
Optician Apprentice #5........................775-853-1421
Optometrist #0 775-883-8367
Osteopathic Physician #15...................702-732-2147
Osteopathic Physician Assistant #15 ... 702-732-2147
Painter #46 702-486-1100
Painter/Paper Hanger #46...................702-486-1100
Pathologist Assistant #22 775-687-4475
Patrol Company/Man, Private #39 775-687-3223
Pest Control Applicator/Company #28
....775-688-1182x252
Pesticide, Restricted Use #28 ......775-688-1182x251
Pharmacist/Pharmaceutical Tech. #16 775-850-1440
Pharmacy #16 775-850-1440
Pharmacy Practitioner #16 775-850-1440
Physical Therapist #17 702-876-5535
Physical Therapist Assistant #17 702-876-5535
Physician Assistant #11 775-688-2559
Physician Assistant (Pharm) #16 775-850-1440
Plaster/Lather #46 702-486-1100
Plasterer/Drywall Installer #46.............702-486-1100
Playground Builder #46 702-486-1100
Plumber #46 702-486-1100
Podiatrist #18....................................775-789-2605
Polygraph Examiner #39 775-687-3223
Prison (correctional - Pharm) #16 775-850-1440
Private Investigator #39......................775-687-3223
Process Server #39 775-687-3223
Psychologist #20 775-688-1268
Public Accountant-CPA #1 775-786-0231
Pump Installer #46.............................702-486-1100
Racing #37 775-684-7900

Real Estate Agent/Sales #50 702-486-4033
Real Estate Broker #50 702-486-4033
Referee/Judge/Timekeeper #35 702-486-2575
Refractory/Firebrick Contr. #46 702-486-1100
Rehabilitation Service #22 775-687-4475
Repossessor #39 775-687-3223
Residential Designer #2 702-486-7300
Respiratory Care Practitioner #11.......775-688-2559
Roofer #46..702-486-1100
Sanitarian, Public #42 775-328-2418
Savings & Loan #29 775-684-1830
School Administrator #47 702-486-6458
School Counselor #47 702-486-6458
School Librarian #47 702-486-6458
School Program Administrator #47 702-486-6458
Scientific Collection Permit #26 775-688-1512
Securities Branch Office #40................702-486-2440
Securities Broker/Dealer #40 702-486-2440
Securities Registration #40 702-486-2440
Securities Sales Rep. #40 702-486-2440
Sewerage Contractor #46 702-486-1100
Sheet Metal Fabricator #46 702-486-1100
Siding Installer #46.............................702-486-1100
Sign Erector #46................................702-486-1100
Slot Route Operator #36 775-684-7770
Social Worker #6 702-688-2555
Solar Contractor #46 702-486-1100
Speech Pathologist/Audiologist #31 775-857-3500
Steel Contractor #46 702-486-1100
Supervisory Medical Technology #22 .. 775-687-4475
Surgical Center, Ambulatory #22 775-687-4475
Surveyor, Land #19............................775-688-1231
Tank Installer, Pressure/Storage #46 .. 702-486-1100
Taxi Cab Company, Clark County #48 . 702-486-6532
Taxi Driver #48..................................702-486-6532
Teacher #47 702-486-6458
Thift Company #29.............................775-684-1830
Trust Company #29............................775-684-1830
Veterinarian / Veterinary Facility #21 ... 775-688-1788
Water Well Driller #30.........................775-687-3861
Well Driller #46..................................702-486-1100
Well Driller/Monitor #30......................775-687-3861
Wrecker/Demolisher #46.....................702-486-1100
Wrestler #35......................................702-486-2575

Nevada Licensing Agency Information

1 Board of Accountancy, 1325 Airmotive Way #220, Reno, NV 89502-3240; 775-786-0231, Fax: 775-786-0234. www.nvaccountancy.com/ Email: cpa@nvaccountancy.com

2 Interior & Residential Design, Board of Interior & Residential Design, 2080 E Flamingo Rd, #225, Las Vegas, NV 89119; 702-486-7300, Fax: 702-486-7304. http://nsbaidrd.state.nv.us/ Email: nsbaidrd@govmail.state.nv.us Search Database at http://nsbaidrd.state.nv.us/directory.htm Note: Phone 702-486-7300 for information about disciplinary actions.

3 Board of Chiropractic Examiners, 4600 Kietzke Ln, M, #245, Reno, NV 89502; 775-688-1921, Fax: 775-688-1920. http://chirobd.nv.gov Email: chirobd@chirobd.nv.gov

Search Database at http://chirobd.nv.gov Note: Data is presented in a PDF format; click on "Licensed Chiropractic Physicians".

4 Board of Dental Examiners, 2295 Renaissance Dr, #B, Las Vegas, NV 89119-6171; 800-337-3926 or 702-486-7044, Fax: 702-486-7046. www.nvdentalboard.org Email: nsbde@nsbdc.nv.gov Search Database at www.nvdentalboard.org/DatabaseIndex.html

5 Board of Dispensing Opticians, PO Box 19625, Reno, NV 89511-0868; 775-853-1421, Fax: 775-853-1408. http://nvbdo.state.nv.us Email: nvbdo@govmail.state.nv.us Note: Complete list available by mail from the board for a minimal fee.

6 Board of Examiners for Social Workers, 4600 Kietzke Ln, Bldg C, Rm 121, Reno, NV 89502; 775-688-2555, Fax: 775-688-2557. http://socwork.state.nv.us

7 Board of Funeral Directors & Embalmers, 4894 Lone Mt Rd PMB186, Las Vegas, NV 89130; 702-290-5366, Fax: 702-648-5858. http://funeral.state.nv.us

8 Board of Hearing Aid Specialists, PO Box 190, Carson City, NV 89702; 702-571-9000, Fax: 775-267-9374. www.state.nv.us/boards/hearing/

9 Board of Homeopathic Medical Examiners, 3663 Pecos McLeod Int., Las Vegas, NV 89121; 702-451-3332, Fax: 702-451-3332. www.nvbhme.com/contact.html Email: homboard@nevadaclinic.com

10 Board of Landscape Architecture, PO Box 51780, Sparks, NV 89435; 775-688-1316, Fax: 775-688-1317. http://nsbla.state.nv.us Email: nsbla@govmail.state.nv.u Note: Complete list is available for $5.00 from the Board.

11 Board of Medical Examiners, 1105 Terminal Way, #301, Reno, NV 89510; 775-688-2559, Fax: 775-688-2321. http://medboard.nv.gov Email: nsbme@medboard.nv.gov   Search Database at http://medboard.nv.gov/default.asp

12 Board of Occupational Therapy, PO Box 70220, Reno, NV 89570-0220; 775-857-1700, Fax: 775-857-2121. www.nvot.org   Email: occtherapy@qbis.com

13 Nevada State Board of Nursing, 2500 W. Sahara Ave #207, Las Vegas, NV 89102-4392; 888-590-6726, 702-486-5800, Consumer hotline-800-746-3980, Lisensure info-888-590-NSBN., Fax: 702-486-5803. www.nursingboard.state.nv.us Email: lasvegas@nsbn.state.nv.us   Search Database at www.nursingboard.state.nv.us/Verification/formLicense.html   Note: Disciplinary actions and investigations are handled by the Reno office, 5011 Meadowood Mall Way #201, 89502, 800-746-3980.

14 Board of Oriental Medicine, 120 Continental Dr., Reno, NV 89509; 702-786-3302, Fax: 702-786-1239. www.oriental_medicine.state.nv.us Email: sbpark@uissbpark@uisreno.com

15 Board of Osteopathic Medicine, 2860 E Flamingo, #G, Las Vegas, NV 89121; 702-732-2147, Fax: 702-732-2079. www.osteo.state.nv.us Email: osteo@govmail.state.nv.us   Search at https://nvboo.glsuite.us/renewal/glsweb/homeframe.aspx

16 Board of Pharmacy, 555 Double Eagle Ct #1100, Reno, NV 89511-8991; 775-850-1440, 800-364-2081, Fax: 775-850-1444. https://nvbop.glsuite.us/renewal/glsweb/homeframe.aspx   Search Database at https://nvbop.glsuite.us/renewal/glsweb/homeframe.aspx

17 Physical Therapy Examiners Board, 810 S. Durango Dr #109, Las Vegas, NV 89145; 702-876-5535, Fax: 702-876-2097. http://ptboard.nv.gov Email: atresca@govmail.state.nv.us

18 Board of Podiatry, PO Box 12215, Reno, NV 89510-2215; 775-789-2605. http://podiatry.state.nv.us Email: nvpodiatry@bop.nv.gov Search Database at http://podiatry.state.nv.us/

19 Board of Professional Engineers & Land Surveyors, 1755 E Plumb Ln, #135, Reno, NV 89502; 775-688-1231, Fax: 775-688-2991. http://boe.state.nv.us Email: jrobins@natinfo.net   Search Database at http://boe.state.nv.us/ROST_HOME.HTM

20 Board of Psychological Examiners, PO Box 2286 (275 Hill St, #246), Reno, NV 89505-2286; 775-688-1268, Fax: 775-688-1272. http://psyexam.state.nv.us/ Email: nbop@govmail.state.nv.us

21 Board of Veterinary Medical Examiners, 4600 Kietzke Lane, Bldg O, #265, Reno, NV 89502; 775-688-1788, Fax: 775-688-1808. Email: vetbbdinfo@govmail.state.nv.us

22 Bureau of Licensure & Certification, Medical Laboratory Services, 1550 College Parkway #158, Carson City, NV 89710; 775-687-4475, Fax: 775-687-6588. www.nursingboard.state.nv.us/

23 Certified Court Reporters Board, 3355 Spring Mountain Rd #2, Las Vegas, NV 89102-8631; 702-384-1663, Fax: 702-876-9249. http://crptr.state.nv.us/contact.htm Email: ccrbnv@juno.com

24 Department of Business & Industry, Insurance Division, 2501 E Sahara Ave, #302, Las Vegas, NV 89104; 702-486-4009, Fax: 702-486-4007. www.doi.state.nv.us

25 Department of Motor Vehicles & Public Safety, Records Section, 555 Wright Way, Carson City, NV 89711-0250; 775-684-4590, Fax: 775-684-4740.   http://nevadadmv.state.nv.us Email: jfogliani@dmv.state.nv.us

26 Department of Wildlife, Licensed Wildlife Services, 1100 Valley Rd, Reno, NV 89520; 775-688-1500, Fax: 775-688-1551. www.ndow.org   Email: tatkinson@ndow.org

27 Director of Legislative Counsel Bureau, 401 S Carson, Carson City, NV 89701-4747; 775-684-6800, Fax: 775-684-6600. www.leg.state.nv.us/lcb/admin/lobbyist.htm Email: wiese@icb.state.nv.us   Search Database at www.leg.state.nv.us/lobbyistdb/index.cfm

28 Department of Agriculture, Pest Control Licensing Division, 350 Capitol Hill, Reno, NV 89502-2923; 775-688-1180, Fax: 775-688-1178. http://agri.state.nv.us

29 Department of Business & Industry, Divison of Financial Institutions, 406 E 2nd St #3, Carson City, NV 89701; 775-684-1830-Reno; 702-486-4120-Las Vegas; Fax: 775-684-1845-Reno; 702-486-4563-Las Vegas. http://fid.state.nv.us Search Database at http://fid.state.nv.us/index.htm Note: Las Vegas office is located at 2501 E. Sahara Ave #300, 89104; phone 702-486-4120.

30 Division of Water Resources, Well Drillers' Advisory Board, 123 W Nye Ln, Capitol Complex Rm 246, Carson City, NV 89706-0818; 775-687-3861, Fax: 775-687-1393. http://ndwr.state.nv.us   Search Database at http://ndwr.state.nv.us/Engineering/welldrill.htm

31 Board of Examiners for Audiology & Speech Pathology, PO Box 70550, Reno, NV 89570; 775-857-3500, Fax: 775-857-2121. http://speech_pathology.state.nv.us

32 Board of Examiners of Marriage & Family Therapists, PO Box 72758, Las Vegas, NV 89170; 702-486-7388, Fax: 702-486-7258. http://marriage.state.nv.us/

33 Liquefied Petroleum Gas Regulation Board, PO Box 338 (106 E Adams, Rm 216), Carson City, NV 89702; 775-687-4890, Fax: 775-687-3956. http://lpg.nv.gov Note: You may email verification requests to lpgasbd@lpg.nv.gov.

34 Attn: Gisele Jordan, Licensing Officer, Manufactured Housing Division, 2501 E Sahara Ave, #205, Las Vegas, NV 89104; 702-486-4590, Fax: 702-486-4309. www.mhd.state.nv.us email: mhlicens@mnd.state.nv.us

35 Athletic Commission, 555 E Washington St #3200, Las Vegas, NV 89101; 702-486-2575, Fax: 702-486-2577. www.boxing.nv.gov   Email: boxing@boxing.nv.gov

36 Tax & License Division, Gaming Control Board, 1919 E College Pky (PO Box 8003, 89702-8003), Carson City, NV 89706; 775-684-7770. http://gaming.nv.gov

37 Gaming Control Board, Enforcement Division, 1919 E College Pky, Carson City, NV 89706; 775-684-7900.   http://gaming.state.nv.us

38 Board of Cosmetology, 1785 E Sahara Ave, #255, Las Vegas, NV 89104; 702-486-6542, Fax: 702-369-8064. Email: nvcosmbd@govmail.state.nv.us

39 Office of the Attorney General, Private Investigators Licensing Board, 3476 Executive Pointe Way #14, Carson City, NV 89706; 775-687-3223, Fax: 775-687-3226. http://ag.state.nv.us/faqs/workingaspi.htm Email: pilbinfo@ag.state.nv.us   Note: Lists only those who want to be listed.

40 Office of the Secretary of State, Securities Division, 555 E Washington Av #5200, Las Vegas, NV 89101; 702-486-2440, Fax: 702-486-2452.   www.sos.state.nv.us/securities

41 Office of the Secretary of State, Notary Division, 101 N Carson St, Carson City, NV 89710-4786; 775-684-5708, Fax: 775-684-5725. http://sos.state.nv.us/notary/ Email: nvnotary@govmail.state.nv.us

42 Environmental Health Services, Washoe County District Health Department, PO Box 1130 (1001 E 9th St), Reno, NV 89520; 775-328-2434, Fax: 775-328-6176. www.co.washoe.nv.us/health/ehs/

44 State Bar of Nevada, 600 E Charleston Blvd, Las Vegas, NV 89104; 702-382-2200, Fax: 702-385-2878. www.nvbar.org   Email: pamik@nvbar.org Search Database at www.nvbar.org/find_a_lawyer.asp

45 Barbers' Health & Sanitation Board, 4710 E Flamingo Rd, Las Vegas, NV 89121; 702-456-4769 LV (775-688-1988 Reno), Fax: 702-456-1948.   http://barber.state.nv.us

46 Contractors' Board, 9670 Gateway Dr #100, Reno, NV 89521; 775-688-1141-Reno, Fax: 775-688-1271-Reno.   http://nscb.state.nv.us Email: cntractr@govmail.state.nv.us Search Database at http://nscb.tecxprs.com Note: The phone number for the Henderson office is 702-486-1100; fax is 702-486-1190; address is 2310 Corporate Circle #200.

47 Department of Education, Teacher Licensure, 1820 E Sahara, #205, Las Vegas, NV 89104; 702-486-6458, Fax: 702-486-6450. www.doe.nv.gov Email: license@nsn.k12.nv.us

48 Taxicab Authority, 1785 E Sahara Ave #200, Las Vegas, NV 89104; 702-486-6532, Fax: 702-486-7350.   http://taxi.state.nv.us Email: ymoore@taxi.state.nv.us

49 Board of Examiners for Long Term Care Administrators, 3157 N Rainbow Blvd, PMB 313, Las Vegas, NV 89108; 702-486-5445.

50 Department of Business & Industry, Real Estate Division, 2501 E Sahara Ave, Las Vegas, NV 89158; 702-486-4033, Fax: 702-486-4275. www.red.state.nv.us Email: realest@govmail.state.nv.us

Nevada Federal Courts

The following list indicates the district and division name for each county in the state. If the bankruptcy court location is different from the district court, then the location of the bankruptcy court appears in parentheses.

County/Court Cross Reference

Carson City	Reno	Lincoln	Las Vegas
Churchill	Reno	Lyon	Reno
Clark	Las Vegas	Mineral	Reno
Douglas	Reno	Nye	Las Vegas
Elko	Reno	Pershing	Reno
Esmeralda	Las Vegas	Storey	Reno
Eureka	Reno	Washoe	Reno
Humboldt	Reno	White Pine	Reno
Lander	Reno		

Standards for Federal Courts: The search fee is $20.00 per item (one party name or case number). Certification fee is $7.00 per document. Copy fee is $.50 per page. All fees standard unless noted in profile. Mail Search: always enclose a stamped self addressed envelope unless otherwise noted. Most courts accept fax requests or will suggest a copying/search vendor. Before releasing records, all courts require prepayment unless noted in profile. Open records are located at the court unless otherwise noted. District courts index by defendant and plaintiff as well as by case number. Bankruptcy courts usually index by debtor and case number. While most courts now have their indexes on computer, many still maintain index card files as well. The universal PACER sign-up number is 800-676-6856. Find PACER and the Party/Case Index on the Web at http://pacer.psc.uscourts.gov. PACER dial-up access is $.60 per minute. Also, courts offering internet access via RACER, PACER, Web-PACER or the new CM-ECF charge $.07 per page fee unless noted as free.

US District Court

District of Nevada

Las Vegas Division Room 4425, 300 Las Vegas Blvd S, Las Vegas, NV 89101 (courier address: Use mail address for courier delivery) 702-464-5400. www.nvd.uscourts.gov

Counties: Clark, Esmeralda, Lincoln, Nye.

Indexing & Storage: New cases available in the index 2 weeks after filing date.

Fee & Payment: Payment may be made by money order, cashier check, personal check. Payee: Clerk, U.S. District Court.

Phone Search: Only docket information available by phone.

Mail Search: A SASE not required.

In Person Search: Fee charged if court conducts your in person search for you.

PACER: PACER is available online at https://pacer.psc.uscourts.gov/cgi-bin/login/login.pl?court_id=nvdc. Document images available.

Reno Division Room 301, 400 S Virginia St, Reno, NV 89501 (courier address: Use mail address for courier delivery) 775-686-5800, Fax: 702-686-5851. www.nvd.uscourts.gov

Counties: Carson City, Churchill, Douglas, Elko, Eureka, Humboldt, Lander, Lyon, Mineral, Pershing, Storey, Washoe, White Pine.

Indexing & Storage: New cases available in the index 1-2 days after filing date. Records are also indexed on microfiche.

Fee & Payment: Payment may be made by money order, cashier check, personal check. Payee: Clerk, U.S. District Court. Will fax results for $.50 per page prepaid.

Phone Search: Only docket information available by phone. Will fax results for $.50 per page prepaid.

Mail Search: A SASE not required.

In Person Search: Fee charged if court conducts your in person search for you.

PACER: PACER is available online at https://pacer.psc.uscourts.gov/cgi-bin/login/login.pl?court_id=nvdc. Document images available.

U.S. Bankruptcy Court

District of Nevada

Las Vegas Division 8th Floor, Suite 8112, Lloyd D. George Federal Bldg, 333 Las Vegas Boulevard South, Las Vegas, NV 89101 (courier address: Clerk's Office, 1st Fl, Lloyd D. George Federal Bldg, 333 Las Vegas Boulevard South, Las Vegas, NV 89101), 702-388-6257. www.nvb.uscourts.gov

Counties: Clark, Esmeralda, Lincoln, Nye.

Indexing & Storage: Cases indexed by debtor as well as by case number. New cases available in the index 24 hours after filing date.

Fee & Payment: Payment may be made by money order, cashier check, personal check. Debtor's checks are not accepted. Payee: Clerk, U.S. Bankruptcy Court.

Phone Search: Automated voice case information service (VCIS) is available. Call VCIS at 800-314-3436 or 702-388-6708.

In Person Search: Fee charged if court conducts your in person search for you.

PACER: PACER is available online at http://pacer.nvb.uscourts.gov. This also contains all the former RACER records. Records purged every 16 months. New civil records are online after 1 day.

Electronic Filing: Electronic filing information online at https://ecf.nvb.uscourts.gov

Other Online Access: Searching records online using RACER has been phased out; a PACER account is now required.

Reno Division Room 1109, 300 Booth St, Reno, NV 89509 (courier address: Use mail address for courier delivery) 775-784-5559. www.nvb.uscourts.gov

Counties: Carson City, Churchill, Douglas, Elko, Eureka, Humboldt, Lander, Lyon, Mineral, Pershing, Storey, Washoe, White Pine.

Indexing & Storage: Cases indexed by debtor as well as by case number. New cases available in the index 24 hours after filing date.

Fee & Payment: Payment may be made by money order, cashier check, personal check. Debtor's checks are not accepted. Payee: Clerk, U.S. Bankruptcy Court.

Phone Search: Automated voice case information service (VCIS) is available. Call VCIS at 800-314-3436 or 702-388-6708.

In Person Search: Fee charged if court conducts your in person search for you. A copy service is available.

PACER: PACER is available online at http://pacer.nvb.uscourts.gov. This also contains all the former RACER records. Records purged every 16 months. New civil records are online after 1 day.

Electronic Filing: Electronic filing information online at https://ecf.nvb.uscourts.gov

Other Online Access: Searching records online using RACER has been phased out; a PACER account is now required.

Nevada County Courts

Court	Jurisdiction	No. of Courts	How Organized
District Courts*	General	17	9 Districts
Justice Courts*	Limited	41	Townships
Municipal Courts	Municipal	17	19 Incorporated Cities/Towns

* Profiled in this Sourcebook.

Court	CIVIL								
	Tort	Contract	Real Estate	Min. Claim	Max. Claim	Small Claims	Estate	Eviction	Domestic Relations
District Courts*	X	X	X	$7,500 $10,000	No Max		X		X
Justice Courts*	X	X	X	$0	$7,500 $10,000	$3500		X	
Municipal Courts	X	X	X	$0	$3500	$3500			

Court	CRIMINAL				
	Felony	Misdemeanor	DWI/DUI	Preliminary Hearing	Juvenile
District Courts*	X	X	X		X
Justice Courts*		X	X	X	
Municipal Courts					

ADMINISTRATION

Supreme Court of Nevada, Administrative Office of the Courts, Capitol Complex, 201 S Carson Street, Carson City, Nevada, 89701; 775-684-1700, Fax: 775-684-1723. www.nvsupremecourt.us/aoc/aoc.html

COURT STRUCTURE

There are 17 District Courts are the courts of general jurisdiction and are within 9 judicial districts. **Their minimum civil limit raises from $7,500 to $10,000 on Jan 1, 2005.** The Justice Courts are named for the township of jurisdiction. Note that, due to their small populations, some townships no longer have Justice Courts. The Justice Courts handle misdemeanor crime and traffic matters, small claims disputes, evictions, and other civil matters less than $7,500(increases to $10,000 on Jan 1, 2005). The justices of the peace also preside over felony and gross misdemeanor arraignments and conduct preliminary hearings to determine if sufficient evidence exists to hold criminals for trial at District Court.

Probate is handled by the District Courts.

ONLINE ACCESS

Some Nevada Courts have internal online computer systems, but only Clark and Washoe counties offer online access to the public. A statewide court automation system is being implemented. The Supreme Court web site gives access to opinions. A growing number of Nevada justice and municipal courts offer current court calendars are at http://sandgate.co.clark.nv.us/JusticeCourt/jcCalendarSearch.html.

ADDITIONAL INFORMATION

Many Nevada Justice Courts are small and have very few records. Their hours of operation vary widely and contact is difficult. It is recommended that requesters call ahead for information prior to submitting a written request or attempting an in-person retrieval.

Carson City

1st Judicial District Court 885 E Musser St #3031, Carson City, NV 89701-4775; 775-887-2082; Fax: 775-887-2177. Hours: 9AM-5PM (PST). *Felony, Gross Misdemeanor, Civil Actions Over $7,500, Probate.* Note: The Justice Courts retain records for minor misdemeanors.
Civil Records: Access: Mail, in person. Only the court performs in person searches; visitors may not. Search fee: $1.00 per name per year. Required to search: name, years to search. Civil cases indexed by

defendant, plaintiff. Civil records on computer from 1987, on microfiche and archives from 1861.
Criminal Records: Access: Mail, in person. Only the court performs in person searches; visitors may not. Search fee: $1.00 per name per year. Required to search: name, years to search. Criminal records on computer from 1987, microfiche and archives prior.
General Information: No sealed or juvenile records released. Will fax results to local or toll free line. Copy fee: $1.00 per page. Cert fee: $5.00. Payee: Carson City. Personal check accepted with check

guarantee card only. Prepayment required. Mail requests: SASE required. Mail turnaround: 2-7 days.

Justice & Municipal Court 885 E Musser St #2007, Carson City, NV 89701-4775; 775-887-2121; Fax: 775-887-2297. Hours: 8:30AM-5PM (PST). *Misdemeanor, Civil Actions Under $7,500, Eviction, Small Claims.*
Civil Records: Access: Mail, in person. Only the court performs in person searches; visitors may not. Search fee: $1.00 per name per year. Required to

search: name, years to search. Criminal records on computer alpha index from 1991.

Criminal Records: Access: Mail, in person. Only the court performs in person searches; visitors may not. Search fee: $1.00 per name per year. Required to search: name, years to search. Criminal records on computer alpha index from 1991.

General Information: No sealed, sexual victims, juvenile records released. Will fax results to local or toll free line. Copy fee: $1.00 per page. Cert fee: $3.00. Payee: Carson City. Personal checks accepted. Prepayment required. Mail requests: SASE required. Mail turnaround time 1 week.

Churchill County

3rd Judicial District Court 73 N Maine St, #B, Fallon, NV 89406; 775-423-6080; Fax: 775-423-8578. 8AM-Noon, 1-5PM (PST). *Felony, Gross Misdemeanor, Civil Actions Over $7,500, Probate.* www.churchillcounty.org/dcourt

Civil Records: Access: Fax, mail, in person. Only the court performs in person searches; visitors may not. Search fee: $1.00 per name per year. Required to search: name, years to search. Civil cases indexed by defendant, plaintiff. Civil records on computer from 1990, prior on books, microfiche.

Criminal Records: Access: Fax, mail, in person. Only the court performs in person searches; visitors may not. Search fee: $1.00 per name per year. Required to search: name, years to search, DOB; also helpful: SSN. Criminal records on computer from 1990, prior on books, microfiche to 1910.

General Information: No juvenile, adoption or sealed records released. No fee to fax results, local or toll free numbers only. Copy fee: $1.00 per page. Cert fee: $5.00. Payee: Office of Court Clerk. Personal checks accepted. Prepayment required. Mail requests: SASE required. Mail turnaround time 1-2 days.

New River Justice Court 71 N Maine St, Fallon, NV 89406; 775-423-2845; Fax: 775-423-0472. Hours: 8AM-5PM (PST). *Misdemeanor, Civil Actions Under $7,500, Eviction, Small Claims.* www.churchillcounty.org/jcourt

Civil Records: Access: Mail, fax, in person. Both court and visitors may perform in person searches. Search fee: $1.00 per name per year. Required to search: name, years to search. Civil cases indexed by defendant, plaintiff. Civil records on computer from 1987, prior on microfiche back to 1980.

Criminal Records: Access: Mail, fax, in person. Both court and visitors may perform in person searches. Search fee: $1.00 per name per year. Required to search: name, years to search, DOB. Criminal records on computer from 1987, prior on microfiche back to 1980.

General Information: No sealed records released. Will fax search results to toll-free line. Copy fee: $.30 per page. Cert fee: $3.00. Payee: Justice Court. Personal checks accepted. Visa, MC accepted. Prepayment required. Mail requests: SASE not required. Mail turnaround time 1 day.

Clark County

8th Judicial District Court 200 S 3rd (PO Box 551601), Las Vegas, NV 89155; 702-455-3156; Fax: 702-455-4929. Hours: 8AM-5PM (PST). *Felony, Gross Misdemeanor, Civil Actions Over $7,500, Probate.* www.co.clark.nv.us/district_court/courthome.htm

Civil Records: Access: Mail, in person. Both court and visitors may perform in person searches. Search fee: $1.00 per name per year, plus copy fees. Fee is per case type. Required to search: name, years to search. Civil cases indexed by defendant, plaintiff. Civil records on computer back to 11/90, prior records on microfilm to 1909. Records from the court are free

online at http://courtgate.coca.co.clark.nv.us:8490. Search by case number or party name. Probate also available. Clerks will do 1 or 2 names, but if a list is presented, expect to wait 24-48 hours for results. The index does not have personal identifiers, so files must be pulled when doing name searches to insure correct subject.

Criminal Records: Access: Mail, in person. Both court and visitors may perform in person searches. Search fee: $1.00 per name per year plus copy fees. Fee is per case type. Required to search: name, years to search. Criminal records on computer back to 11/90, prior records on microfilm to 1909. Online access to criminal records is the same as civil. Clerks will do 1 or 2 names, but if a list is presented, expect to wait 24-48 hours for results. The index does not have personal identifiers, so files must be pulled when doing name searches to insure correct subject.

General Information: Public Access terminal is available. No sealed records released. Copy fee: $1.00 per page. Cert fee: $3.00. Payee: County Clerk's Office. Personal checks accepted. Prepayment required. Mail requests: SASE required. Mail turnaround time 10 working days.

Boulder Township Justice Court 505 Ave. G, Boulder City, NV 89005; 702-455-8000; Fax: 702-455-8003. Hours: 7:30AM-4:30PM M-TH (PST). *Misdemeanor, Civil Actions Under $7,500, Eviction, Small Claims.*

Civil Records: Access: Fax, mail, in person. Both court and visitors may perform in person searches. Search fee: $1.00 per name per year. Required to search: name, years to search; also helpful: address. Civil cases indexed by defendant. Civil records on microfiche varies depending on subject. See section intro for court calendars online.

Criminal Records: Access: Fax, mail, in person. Only the court performs in person searches; visitors may not. Search fee: $1.00 per name per year. Required to search: name, years to search, DOB, date of offense; also helpful: SSN. Criminal records on microfiche varies depending on subject. See section intro for court calendars online.

General Information: No financial records released. Copy fee: $.30 per page. Cert fee: $3.00. Payee: Justice Court. Personal checks accepted. Prepayment required. Mail requests: SASE required. Mail turnaround time 1 week.

Bunkerville Justice Court 190 W Virgin St, Bunkerville, NV 89007; 702-346-5711; Fax: 702-346-7212. Hours: 7AM-4:30PM M-Th (PST). *Misdemeanor, Civil Actions Under $7,500, Eviction, Small Claims.*

Civil Records: Access: Mail, in person. Only the court performs in person searches; visitors may not. Search fee: $1.00 per name per year. Required to search: name, years to search. Civil cases indexed by case number. Civil records (citations) on computer from 1991, on docket books. See section intro for court calendars online.

Criminal Records: Access: Mail, in person. Only the court performs in person searches; visitors may not. Search fee: $1.00 per name per year. Required to search: name, years to search, DOB; also helpful: SSN. Criminal records (citations) on computer from 1991, on docket books. See section intro for court calendars online.

General Information: No sealed or confidential records released. Will fax back results. Copy fee: $.30 per page. Cert fee: $3.00. Payee: Bunkerville Justice Court. Only cashiers checks and money orders accepted. Prepayment required. Mail requests: SASE required. Mail turnaround time 2 weeks.

Goodsprings Township Jean Justice Court 1 Main St (PO Box 19155), Jean, NV 89019; 702-874-1405; Fax: 702-874-1612. Hours: 7AM-4PM M-Th (PST). *Misdemeanor, Civil Actions Under $7,500, Eviction, Small Claims.*

Civil Records: Access: Phone, fax, mail, in person. Only the court performs in person searches; visitors may not. Search fee: $1.00 per name per year. Required to search: name, years to search. Civil cases indexed by defendant, plaintiff. Civil records on computer for 6 months, file reports from 1990. See section intro for court calendars online.

Criminal Records: Access: Phone, fax, mail, in person. Only the court performs in person searches; visitors may not. Search fee: $1.00 per name per year. Required to search: name, years to search, DOB; also helpful: SSN. Criminal records on computer for 6 months, file reports from 1990. See section intro for court calendars online.

General Information: No sealed records released. Copy fee: $.25 per page. Cert fee: $2.00. Payee: Jean Justice Court. Business checks accepted. Prepayment required. Mail requests: SASE required. Mail turnaround time within 2 weeks.

Henderson Township Justice 243 Water St, Henderson, NV 89015; Civil phone: 702-455-7978; Criminal phone: 702-455-7929; Fax: 702-455-7935. Hours: 7AM-5:30PM M-Th (PST). *Misdemeanor, Civil Actions Under $7,500, Eviction, Small Claims.* www.co.clark.nv.us/justicecourt_hd/general_information.htm

Note: Traffic can be reached at 702-455-7980.

Civil Records: Access: Mail, in person. Only the court performs in person searches; visitors may not. Search fee: $1.00 per name per year. Required to search: name, years to search. Civil cases indexed by defendant. Civil records on index cards and docket books. Evictions kept for 2-6 years; civil and small claims for 6 years. See section intro for court calendars online.

Criminal Records: Access: Mail, in person. Only the court performs in person searches; visitors may not. Search fee: $1.00 per name per year. Required to search: name, years to search, DOB; also helpful: SSN. Criminal records on index cards and docket books. See section intro for court calendars online.

General Information: Copy fee: $.30 per page. Cert fee: $3.00. Payee: Henderson Justice Court. Personal checks accepted. Prepayment required. Mail requests: SASE required. Mail turnaround time 2 weeks.

Las Vegas Township Justice PO Box 552511 (200 S 3rd, 2nd Fl), Las Vegas, NV 89155-2511; 702-455-4435; Fax: 702-455-4529. Hours: 8AM-5PM (PST). *Misdemeanor, Civil Actions Under $7,500, Eviction, Small Claims.* www.co.clark.nv.us/justicecourt_lv/welcome.htm

Civil Records: Access: Phone, fax, mail, in person. Both court and visitors may perform in person searches. Search fee: $1.00 per name per year. Required to search: name, years to search. Civil cases indexed by defendant, plaintiff. Civil records go back 8 years. See section intro for court calendars online.

Criminal Records: Access: Phone, fax, mail, in person. Only the court performs in person searches; visitors may not. Search fee: $1.00 per name per year. Required to search: name, years to search, DOB; also helpful: SSN. Criminal records go back 10 years. See section intro for court calendars online.

General Information: No sealed, confidential or judge's notes records released. Will fax results to local or toll free line. Copy fee: $.30 per page. Cert fee: $3.00. Payee: Justice Court, Las Vegas Township. Personal checks accepted. Prepayment required. Mail requests: SASE required. Mail turnaround time 3 weeks.

Laughlin Township Justice Court 101 Civic Way #2, Laughlin, NV 89029; 702-298-4622; Fax: 702-298-7508. Hours: 8AM-4:30PM (T-Fri) (PST). *Misdemeanor, Civil Actions Under $7,000, Eviction, Small Claims.*

Civil Records: Access: Fax, mail, in person. Search fee: $1.00 per name per year. Required to search: name, years to search. Civil cases indexed by defendant, plaintiff. Civil records on docket book by name and case number. See section intro for court calendars online.

Criminal Records: Access: Fax, mail, in person. Only the court performs in person searches; visitors may not. Search fee: $1.00 per name per year. Required to search: name, years to search, DOB. Criminal records on computer from 1990, prior in files and must be cross referenced. See section intro for court calendars online.

General Information: No sealed records released. Will fax results to local or toll free line. Copy fee: $.30 per page. Cert fee: $3.00. Payee: Laughlin Justice Court. Personal checks accepted. Prepayment required. Mail requests: SASE required. Mail turnaround time 2 weeks.

Mesquite Township Justice Court 500 Hillside Dr, Mesquite, NV 89027-3116; 702-346-5298; Fax: 702-346-7319. Hours: 7AM-4PM (PST). *Felony, Misdemeanor, Civil Actions Under $7,500, Eviction, Small Claims.*

Civil Records: Access: Fax, mail, in person. Only the court performs in person searches; visitors may not. Search fee: $1.00 per name per year. Required to search: name, years to search. Civil cases indexed by defendant. Criminal records go back to 1989; on computer back to 1996. See section intro for court calendars online.

Criminal Records: Access: Phone, fax, mail, in person. Only the court performs in person searches; visitors may not. Search fee: $1.00 per name per year. Required to search: name, years to search, DOB; also helpful: SSN. Criminal records go back to 1989; on computer back to 1996. See section intro for court calendars online.

General Information: No sealed records released. Will fax results for $1.00 per year. Copy fee: $.30 per page. Cert fee: $3.00. Payee: Mesquite Justice Court. Only cashiers checks and money orders accepted. Prepayment required. Mail requests: SASE required. Mail turnaround time approx. 1-2 weeks.

Moapa Township Justice Court 1340 E Com Hwy, PO Box 280, Moapa, NV 89025; 702-864-2333; Fax: 702-864-2585. Hours: 8AM-5PM M-Th (PST). *Misdemeanor, Civil Actions Under $7,500, Eviction, Small Claims.* www.co.clark.nv.us

Civil Records: Access: Fax, mail, in person. Only the court performs in person searches; visitors may not. Search fee: $1.00 per name per year. Required to search: name, years to search. Civil cases indexed by defendant, plaintiff. Civil records on computer from 10/90, prior records on index cards and docket books. Archives flooded in 1980s. See section intro for court calendars online.

Criminal Records: Access: Fax, mail, in person. Only the court performs in person searches; visitors may not. Search fee: $1.00 per name per year. Required to search: name, years to search; also helpful: DOB, SSN. Criminal records on computer from 10/90, prior records on index cards and docket books. Archives flooded in 1980s. See section intro for court calendars online.

General Information: No sealed records released. No fee to fax results. Copy fee: $.35 per page. Cert fee: $3.00. Payee: Moapa Township Justice Court. Personal checks accepted. Prepayment required. Mail

requests: SASE required. Mail turnaround time 1-5 days.

Moapa Valley Township Justice Court 320 N Moapa Valley Blvd, PO Box 337, Overton, NV 89040; 702-397-2840; Fax: 702-397-2842. Hours: 6:30AM-4:30PM M-Th (PST). *Misdemeanor, Civil Actions Under $7,500, Eviction, Small Claims.*

Civil Records: Access: Mail, in person. Only the court performs in person searches; visitors may not. Search fee: $1.00 per name per year. Required to search: name, years to search. Civil cases indexed by defendant, plaintiff. Civil records on computer from 1991, prior on docket books. See section intro for court calendars online.

Criminal Records: Access: Mail, in person. Only the court performs in person searches; visitors may not. Search fee: $1.00 per name per year. Required to search: name, years to search, DOB; also helpful: SSN. Criminal records on computer from 1991, prior on docket books. See section intro for court calendars online.

General Information: No sealed records released. Will fax results for $1.00 per page. Copy fee: $.30 per page. Cert fee: $3.00. Payee: Moapa Valley Justice Court. Personal checks accepted. Prepayment required. Mail requests: SASE required. Mail turnaround time approx. 1-2 weeks.

North Las Vegas Township Justice 2428 N Martin L King Blvd, N Las Vegas, NV 89032-3700; 702-455-7802; Civil phone: 702-455-7801; Fax: 702-455-7831. Hours: 7:15AM-5:45PM (PST). *Misdemeanor, Civil Actions Under $7,500, Eviction, Small Claims.*

Note: Judge must approve all search requests.

Civil Records: Access: Phone, in person. Visitors must perform in person searches for themselves. No search fee. Required to search: name, years to search. Civil cases indexed by defendant, plaintiff. Civil records on docket books, microfilm. See section intro for court calendars online.

Criminal Records: Access: Phone, mail, in person. Only the court performs in person searches; visitors may not. Search fee: $1.00 per name per year. Required to search: name, years to search, DOB, SSN. Criminal records on docket books, microfilm. See section intro for court calendars online.

General Information: Copy fee: $.30 per page. Cert fee: $3.00. Payee: N Las Vegas Justice Court. Personal check accepted with bankcard. Prepayment required. Mail requests: SASE required. Mail turnaround time 1-10 days.

Searchlight Township Justice PO Box 815, Searchlight, NV 89046; 702-297-1252; Fax: 702-297-1022. Hours: 7AM-5:30PM M-Th (PST). *Misdemeanor, Civil Actions Under $7,500, Eviction, Small Claims.*

Civil Records: Access: Fax, mail, in person. Only the court performs in person searches; visitors may not. Search fee: $1.00 per name per year. Required to search: name, years to search. Civil cases indexed by defendant, plaintiff. Civil records on computer from 1988, prior to 1988 filed by case number. See section intro for court calendars online.

Criminal Records: Access: Fax, mail, in person. Only the court performs in person searches; visitors may not. Search fee: $1.00 per name per year. Required to search: name, years to search, DOB; also helpful: SSN. Criminal records on computer from 1988, prior to 1988 filed by case number. See section intro for court calendars online.

General Information: No sealed records released. Copy fee: $1.00 per page. Cert fee: $2.00. Payee: Searchlight Justice Court. Personal checks accepted. Prepayment required. Mail requests: SASE required. Mail turnaround time 1-2 weeks.

Douglas County

9th Judicial District Court Box 218, Minden, NV 89423; 775-782-9820; Fax: 775-782-9954. Hours: 8AM-5PM (PST). *Felony, Gross Misdemeanors, Civil Actions Over $7,500, Probate.* http://cltr.co.douglas.nv.us/CourtClerk/courtideas/courtclerkhome.htm

Note: Misdemeanors are handled by the East Fork Justice Court and Tahoe Township Justice Court.

Civil Records: Access: Mail, in person. Only the court performs in person searches; visitors may not. Search fee: $1.00 per name per year. Required to search: name, years to search. Civil cases indexed by defendant, plaintiff. Civil records on index cards from 1962, docket books prior to 1962, archived from mid-1850s. On computer back to 1996.

Criminal Records: Access: Mail, in person. Only the court performs in person searches; visitors may not. Search fee: $1.00 per name per year. Required to search: name, years to search, DOB. Criminal records on index cards from 1962, docket books prior to 1962, archived from mid-1850s. On computer back to 1996.

General Information: No sealed records released. Copy fee: $1.00 per page. Cert fee: $3.00. Payee: Douglas County Court Clerk. Business checks accepted. Prepayment required. Mail requests: SASE required. Mail turnaround time 1 week.

East Fork Justice Court PO Box 218, Minden, NV 89423; 775-782-9955; Fax: 775-782-9947. Hours: 8AM-5PM (PST). *Misdemeanor, Civil Actions Under $7,500, Eviction, Small Claims.*

Civil Records: Access: Mail, in person. Only the court performs in person searches; visitors may not. Search fee: $1.00 per name per year. Required to search: name, years to search, DOB or SSN. Civil cases indexed by defendant, plaintiff. Computerized records from 1996.

Criminal Records: Access: Mail, in person. Only the court performs in person searches; visitors may not. Search fee: $1.00 per name per year. Required to search: name, years to search, DOB or SSN. Computerized records from 1996.

General Information: No sealed records released. Will fax if pre-paid. Copy fee: $.30 per page. Cert fee: $3.00. Payee: East Fork Justice Court. Only local personal or business checks accepted. Prepayment required. Mail requests: SASE required. Mail turnaround time 2-4 days.

Tahoe Justice Court PO Box 7169, Stateline, NV 89449; 775-586-7200; Fax: 775-586-7203. Hours: 9AM-5PM (PST). *Misdemeanor, Civil Actions Under $7,500, Eviction, Small Claims.*

Civil Records: Access: Phone, mail, in person. Only the court performs in person searches; visitors may not. Search fee: $1.00 per name per year. Required to search: name or case #, years to search. Civil cases indexed by defendant, plaintiff. Civil records on index cards from 1985-1995; 1995-present on computer. Prior to 1985 some records in docket books, some on microfilm.

Criminal Records: Access: Phone, mail, in person. Only the court performs in person searches; visitors may not. Search fee: $1.00 per name per year. Required to search: name or case #, years to search, DOB. Criminal records on docket cards 1985-1995; 1995 to present on computer. Pre-1985 records on books and mircofilm.

General Information: No sealed records released. Copy fee: $.30 per page. Cert fee: $3.00 per page. Payee: Tahoe Justice Court. Visa, MC accepted. Prepayment required. Mail requests: SASE required. Mail turnaround time 2 weeks.

Elko County

4th Judicial District Court 571 Idaho St, 3rd Flr, Elko, NV 89801; 775-753-4600; Fax: 775-753-4610. Hours: 9AM-5PM (PST). *Felony, Gross Misdemeanor, Civil Actions Over $7,500, Probate.*
Civil Records: Access: Phone, mail, in person, email. Both court and visitors may perform in person searches. Search fee: $1.00 per name per year. Fee is for years prior to 10/01/91. Required to search: name, years to search. Civil cases indexed by defendant, plaintiff. Civil records on computer back to 1970; prior on microfilm.
Criminal Records: Access: Phone, mail, in person. Both court and visitors may perform in person searches. Search fee: $1.00 per name per year. Fee is for years prior to 1980. Required to search: name, years to search. Criminal records on computer back to 1970; prior primarily on microfilm (including probate).
General Information: Public Access terminal is available. No sealed records released. Fee to fax results is $1.00 per page. Copy fee: $1.00 per page. Cert fee: $3.00 if court prepares copies, $5.00 if you prepare copies. Payee: Elko County Clerk. Personal checks accepted. Visa/MC accepted. Prepayment required. Mail requests: SASE required. Mail turnaround time 1 day.

Carlin Justice Court PO Box 789, Carlin, NV 89822; 775-754-6321; Fax: 775-754-6893. Hours: 8AM-5PM (PST). *Misdemeanor, Civil Actions Under $7,500, Eviction, Small Claims.*
Civil Records: Access: Mail, in person. Both court and visitors may perform in person searches. Search fee: $1.00 per name per year. Required to search: name, years to search. Civil cases indexed by defendant, plaintiff. Civil records on computer starting in 1994, prior are in books.
Criminal Records: Access: Mail, in person. Only the court performs in person searches; visitors may not. Search fee: $1.00 per name per year. Required to search: name, years to search, DOB, SSN. Criminal records on computer starting in 1994, prior are in books.
General Information: Will fax results if toll free number. Copy fee: $.30 per page. Cert fee: $3.00. Payee: Carlin Court. Personal checks accepted. Prepayment required. Mail requests: SASE required. Mail turnaround time 1 week.

Eastline Justice Court PO Box 2300, West Wendover, NV 89883; 775-664-2305; Fax: 775-664-2979. Hours: 9AM-5PM (PST). *Misdemeanor, Civil Actions Under $7,500, Eviction, Small Claims.*
Civil Records: Access: Mail, in person. Only the court performs in person searches; visitors may not. Search fee: $7.00 per name per year. Required to search: name, years to search. Civil cases indexed by defendant. Civil records on computer from 1992, prior on index, docket book.
Criminal Records: Access: Mail, in person. Only the court performs in person searches; visitors may not. Search fee: $1.00 per name per year. Required to search: name, years to search; also helpful: DOB. Criminal records on computer from 1992, prior on index, docket book.
General Information: No open case records released. Copy fee: $.30 per page. Cert fee: $3.00. Payee: Eastline Justice Court. Only cashiers checks and money orders accepted. Prepayment required. Mail requests: SASE required. Mail turnaround time 1 week.

Elko Justice Court PO Box 176, Elko, NV 89803; 775-738-8403; Fax: 775-738-8416. Hours: 9AM-Noon, 1-5PM (PST). *Misdemeanor, Civil Actions Under $7,500, Eviction, Small Claims.*

Civil Records: Access: Fax, mail, in person. Both court and visitors may perform in person searches. Search fee: $1.00 per name per year. Fee is per court. Required to search: name, years to search. Civil cases indexed by defendant, plaintiff. Civil records on computer after 1994, on docket books after 1980s, prior in county archives.
Criminal Records: Access: Mail, in person. Both court and visitors may perform in person searches. Search fee: $1.00 per name per year. Fee is per court. Required to search: name, years to search; DOB or SSN also required. Criminal records on computer after 1994, on docket books after 1980s, prior in county archives.
General Information: No confidential evaluations or sealed records released. Copy fee: $.30 per page. Cert fee: $3.00. Payee: Elko Justice Court. Personal checks accepted. Prepayment required. Mail requests: SASE required. Mail turnaround time 7-10 days.

Jackpot Justice Court PO Box 229, Jackpot, NV 89825; 775-755-2456; Fax: 775-755-9455. Hours: 9AM-Noon, 1-5PM (PST). *Misdemeanor, Civil Actions Under $7,500, Eviction, Small Claims.*
Civil Records: Access: Mail, in person. Only the court performs in person searches; visitors may not. Search fee: $7.00 per name per year. Required to search: name, years to search. Civil cases indexed by defendant. Civil records on docket books per year since 1978; on computer back to 1995.
Criminal Records: Access: Fax, mail, in person. Only the court performs in person searches; visitors may not. Search fee: $7.00 per name per year. Required to search: name, years to search, DOB. Criminal records on docket books per year since 1978; on computer back to 1995.
General Information: No fee to fax results. Copy fee: $.25 per page. Cert fee: $3.00. Payee: Jackpot Justice Court. Business checks accepted. Prepayment required. Mail requests: SASE required. Mail turnaround time 1 week.

Wells Justice Municipal Court PO Box 297, Wells, NV 89835; 775-752-3726; Fax: 775-752-3363. Hours: 9AM-Noon, 1-5PM (PST). *Misdemeanor, Civil Actions Under $7,500, Eviction, Small Claims.*
Civil Records: Access: Mail, in person. Only the court performs in person searches; visitors may not. Search fee: $1.00 per name per year. Required to search: name, years to search. Civil cases indexed by defendant, plaintiff. Civil records on computer from 1989, prior on docket books. In person access may require fee for clerical assistance.
Criminal Records: Access: Mail, in person. Only the court performs in person searches; visitors may not. Search fee: $1.00 per name per year. Required to search: name, years to search; also DOB or SSN. Criminal records on computer from 1989, prior on docket books. Same as civil.
General Information: No pending, confidential records released. Copy fee: $.30 per page. Cert fee: $3.00. Payee: Wells Justice Court. Personal checks accepted. Prepayment required. Mail requests: SASE required. Mail turnaround time 2 weeks.

Jarbidge Justice Court, NV.

Note: This is an "unincorporated ghost town." No criminal or civil cases in more than 20 years. Mostly marriages, fish and game violations. Only 40 year round residents. All records at the Elko Justice Court.

Mountain City Justice Court

Note: Closed. Records held in Elko Justice Court, 775-738-8403.

Esmeralda County

5th Judicial District Court PO Box 547, Goldfield, NV 89013; 775-485-6309; Fax: 775-485-6376. Hours: 8AM-5PM; Closed 12-1PM (PST). *Felony, Gross Misdemeanor, Civil Actions Over $7,500, Probate.*
Civil Records: Access: Fax, mail, in person. Both court and visitors may perform in person searches. Search fee: $1.00 per name per year. Required to search: name, years to search. Civil cases indexed by defendant, plaintiff. Civil records on docket books from 1800s.
Criminal Records: Access: Fax, mail, in person. Both court and visitors may perform in person searches. No search fee. Required to search: name, years to search. Criminal records on docket books from 1800s.
General Information: No juvenile or pre-sentence records released. Fee to fax results is $1.00 per page. Copy fee: $1.00 per page. Cert fee: $3.00. Payee: Esmeralda County Clerk. Personal checks accepted. Visa, MC accepted. Prepayment required. Mail requests: SASE required. Mail turnaround time 2 weeks.

Esmeralda Justice Court PO Box 370, Goldfield, NV 89013; 775-485-6359; Fax: 775-485-3462. Hours: 8AM-5PM (PST). *Misdemeanor, Civil Actions Under $7,500, Eviction, Small Claims.*
Civil Records: Access: Phone, fax, mail, in person. Only the court performs in person searches; visitors may not. Search fee: $1.00 per name per year. Required to search: name, years to search. Civil cases indexed by plaintiff. Civil records on docket books since 1987.
Criminal Records: Access: Phone, fax, mail, in person. Only the court performs in person searches; visitors may not. Search fee: $1.00 per name per year. Required to search: name, years to search. Criminal records on docket books since 1987.
General Information: No sealed records released. Will fax results $1.00 per page. Copy fee: $.30 per page. Cert fee: $3.00. Payee: Justice Court. Only cashiers checks and money orders accepted. Prepayment required. Mail requests: SASE required. Mail turnaround time 1 day.

Eureka County

7th Judicial District Court PO Box 677, Eureka, NV 89316; 775-237-5262; Fax: 775-237-6015. Hours: 8AM-Noon, 1-5PM (PST). *Felony, Gross Misdemeanor, Civil Actions Over $7,500, Probate.*
Civil Records: Access: Phone, fax, mail, in person. Both court and visitors may perform in person searches. Search fee: $1.00 per name per year. Required to search: name, years to search. Civil cases indexed by defendant, plaintiff. Civil records archived from 1873. Public can search docket books.
Criminal Records: Access: Phone, fax, mail, in person. Both court and visitors may perform in person searches. Search fee: $1.00 per name per year. Required to search: name, years to search. Criminal records archived from 1873. Public can search docket books.
General Information: No juvenile, sealed records released. Will fax to toll-free number. Copy fee: $1.00 per page. Cert fee: $3.00. Payee: Eureka County Clerk. Personal checks accepted. Prepayment required. Mail requests: SASE required. Mail turnaround time 1 day.

Beowawe Justice Court PO Box 211338, Crescent Valley, NV 89821; 775-468-0244; Fax: 775-468-0323. Hours: 8AM-Noon, 1-5PM (PST). *Misdemeanor, Civil Actions Under $7,500, Eviction, Small Claims.*

Civil Records: Access: Mail, in person. Only the court performs in person searches; visitors may not. Search fee: $1.00 per name per year. Required to search: name, years to search. Civil cases indexed by plaintiff. Civil records go back to 2/1994; computerized records go back to 1997.

Criminal Records: Access: Mail, in person. Only the court performs in person searches; visitors may not. Search fee: $1.00 per name per year. Required to search: name, years to search. Criminal records go back to 11/1993; computerized records go back to 1997.

General Information: Copy fee: $.30 per page. Cert fee: $3.00. Payee: Beowawe Justice Court. Only cashiers checks and money orders accepted. Prepayment required. Mail requests: SASE required. Mail turnaround time is 5 days.

Eureka Justice Court PO Box 496, Eureka, NV 89316; 775-237-5540; Fax: 775-237-6016. Hours: 8AM-Noon,1-5PM (PST). *Misdemeanor, Civil Actions Under $7,500, Eviction, Small Claims.*
Civil Records: Access: Phone, mail, in person. Only the court performs in person searches; visitors may not. No search fee. Required to search: name, years to search. Civil cases indexed by defendant, plaintiff. Civil records on computer since 1995; on docket books, archived from 1940.
Criminal Records: Access: Phone, mail, in person. Only the court performs in person searches; visitors may not. No search fee. Required to search: name, years to search. Criminal records on computer since 1995; on docket books, archived from 1940.
General Information: Copy fee: $.50 per page. Cert fee: $3.00. Payee: Eureka Justice Court. Only cashiers checks and money orders accepted. Prepayment required. Mail requests: SASE required. Mail turnaround time 2 days.

Humboldt County

6th Judicial District Court 50 W Fifth St, Winnemucca, NV 89445; 775-623-6343; Fax: 775-623-6309. Hours: 8AM-5PM (PST). *Felony, Gross Misdemeanor, Civil Actions Over $7,500, Probate.*
Civil Records: Access: Phone, fax, mail, in person. Both court and visitors may perform in person searches. Search fee: $1.00 per name per year. Required to search: name, years to search. Civil cases indexed by defendant, plaintiff. Civil records on computer from 1984, on microfiche from 1900.
Criminal Records: Access: Phone, fax, mail, in person. Both court and visitors may perform in person searches. Search fee: $1.00 per name per year. Required to search: name, years to search. Criminal records on computer from 1984, on microfiche from 1900.
General Information: No adoption, sealed records released. Copy fee: $1.00 per page. Cert fee: $3.00. Payee: Humboldt County Clerk. Personal checks accepted. Prepayment required. Mail requests: SASE required. Mail turnaround time 1 day, immediate if on computer and requested by phone.

Union Justice Court PO Box 1218, Winnemucca, NV 89446; 775-623-6377; Fax: 775-623-6439. Hours: 8AM-5PM (PST). *Misdemeanor, Civil Actions Under $7,500, Eviction, Small Claims.*
www.humboldt-county-nv.net/justice
Civil Records: Access: Fax, mail, in person. Only the court performs in person searches; visitors may not. Search fee: $1.00 per name per year; minimum of $7.00. Required to search: name, years to search; also helpful: address. Civil cases indexed by defendant,

plaintiff. Civil records on computer from 1988, prior on docket books.
Criminal Records: Access: Fax, mail, in person. Only the court performs in person searches; visitors may not. Search fee: $1.00 per name per year; minimum of $7.00. Required to search: name, years to search, DOB; also helpful: address, SSN. Criminal records on computer from 1988.
General Information: No fee to fax results. Cert fee: $3.00. Payee: Justice Court. Personal checks accepted. Prepayment required. Mail requests: SASE required. Mail turnaround time 1-2 days.

McDermitt Justice Court, NV. *Misdemeanor, Civil Actions Under $7,500, Eviction, Small Claims.*
www.humboldt-county-nv.net/justice/
Note: Closed case records are at the Union Justice Court.

Paradise Valley Justice Court, NV. *Misdemeanor, Civil Actions Under $7,500, Eviction, Small Claims.*
www.humboldt-county-nv.net/justice/
Note: Closed case records are at the Union Justice Court.

Lander County

6th Judicial District Court 315 S Humboldt, Battle Mountain, NV 89820; 775-635-5738; Fax: 775-635-5761. Hours: 8AM-5PM (PST). *Felony, Gross Misdemeanor, Civil Actions Over $7,500, Probate.*
Civil Records: Access: Phone, fax, mail, in person. Only the court performs in person searches; visitors may not. No search fee. Required to search: name, years to search. Civil cases indexed by defendant, plaintiff. Civil records on computer from 1990, on index from 1986-1990, on microfiche until 1985, prior records on docket books.
Criminal Records: Access: Phone, fax, mail, in person. Only the court performs in person searches; visitors may not. No search fee. Required to search: name, years to search. Criminal records on computer from 1990, on index from 1986-1990, on microfiche until 1985, prior records on docket books.
General Information: No juvenile, sealed records released. Fee to fax results is $1.00 per page. Copy fee: $1.00 per page. Cert fee: $5.00. Payee: Lander County Clerk. Personal checks accepted. Prepayment required. Mail requests: SASE required. Mail turnaround time 7 days.

Argenta Justice Court 315 S Humboldt, Battle Mountain, NV 89820; 775-635-5151; Fax: 775-635-0604. Hours: 7:30AM-6PM (PST). *Misdemeanor, Civil Actions Under $10,000, Eviction, Small Claims.*
Civil Records: Access: Phone, fax, mail, in person. Only the court performs in person searches; visitors may not. Search fee: $1.00 per name per year. Required to search: name, years to search. Civil cases indexed by defendant, plaintiff. Civil records on computer from 1988, prior on docket books.
Criminal Records: Access: Phone, fax, mail, in person. Only the court performs in person searches; visitors may not. Search fee: $1.00 per name per year. Required to search: name, years to search; also helpful: DOB, SSN. Criminal records on computer from 1988, prior on docket books.
General Information: No unserved search warrant records released. Fee to fax results is $1.00 per page. Copy fee: $.50 per page. Cert fee: $3.00 per page. Payee: Argenta Justice Court. Only cashiers checks and money orders accepted. Prepayment required. Mail requests: SASE required. Mail turnaround time 1 day.

Austin Justice Court PO Box 100, Austin, NV 89310; 775-964-2380; Fax: 775-964-2327. Hours: 8AM-4PM M, 8AM-Noon T-Th (PST). *Misdemeanor, Civil Actions Under $7,500, Eviction, Small Claims.*
Note: No fees for requests from government agencies.
Civil Records: Access: Phone, mail, fax, in person. Only the court performs in person searches; visitors may not. No search fee. Required to search: name, years to search. Civil cases indexed by plaintiff and defendant. Civil records on docket books, computerized since 1982.
Criminal Records: Access: Phone, mail, fax, in person. Only the court performs in person searches; visitors may not. No search fee. Required to search: name, years to search. Criminal records on computer from 1988, easily available since 1976.
General Information: Will fax results to local or toll free line. Copy fee: $.25 per page. Payee: Austin Justice Court. Mail requests: SASE required. Mail turnaround time 1 week.

Lincoln County

7th Judicial District Court PO Box 90, Pioche, NV 89043; 775-962-5390; Fax: 702-962-5180. Hours: 9AM-5PM (PST). *Felony, Gross Misdemeanor, Civil Actions Over $7,500, Probate.*
Civil Records: Access: Mail, in person. Both court and visitors may perform in person searches. Search fee: $1.00 per name per year. Required to search: name, years to search. Civil cases indexed by defendant, plaintiff. Civil records on docket books from 1876. Records are computerized since 2001.
Criminal Records: Access: Mail, in person. Both court and visitors may perform in person searches. Search fee: $1.00 per name per year. Required to search: name, years to search. Criminal records on docket books from 1876. Records are computerized since 2001.
General Information: No juvenile, sealed records released. Fee to fax results is $1.00 per page. Copy fee: $1.00 per page. Cert fee: $5.00. Payee: Lincoln County Clerk. Personal checks accepted. Prepayment required. Mail requests: SASE required. Mail turnaround time 2-3 days.

Meadow Valley Justice Court PO Box 36, Pioche, NV 89043; 775-962-5140; Fax: 775-962-5559. Hours: 9AM-5PM (PST). *Misdemeanor, Civil Actions Under $7,500, Eviction, Small Claims.*
Civil Records: Access: Phone, fax, mail, in person. Only the court performs in person searches; visitors may not. No search fee. Required to search: name, years to search. Civil cases indexed by defendant, plaintiff. Civil records archived from 1982 on docket books; on computer back to 2000.
Criminal Records: Access: Phone, fax, mail, in person. Only the court performs in person searches; visitors may not. No search fee. Required to search: name, years to search. Criminal records are all originals; they go back to 1982; on computer back to 2000.
General Information: Juvenile records are not released. Will fax results $3.00 1st page, $1.00 each add'l. No copy fee. No cert fee. Prepayment required. Mail requests: SASE required. Mail turnaround time 1-5 days.

Pahranagat Valley Justice Court PO Box 449, Alamo, NV 89001; 775-725-3357; Fax: 775-725-3566. Hours: 9AM-5PM (PST). *Misdemeanor, Civil Actions Under $7,500, Eviction, Small Claims.*
Civil Records: Access: Fax, mail, in person. Only the court performs in person searches; visitors may not. No search fee. Required to search: name, years to search. Civil cases indexed by defendant. Civil

records on docket books to 1980; on computer back to 1997.

Criminal Records: Access: Fax, mail, in person. Only the court performs in person searches; visitors may not. No search fee. Required to search: name, years to search, DOB; also helpful: SSN, signed release. Criminal records on docket books to 1980; on computer back to 1997.

General Information: No personal notes released. No fee to fax results. Copy fee: $.25 per page. Cert fee: $2.00 per page. Payee: Pahranagat Valley Justice Court. Personal checks accepted. Prepayment required. Mail requests: SASE required. Mail turnaround time 1-3 days.

Lyon County

3rd Judicial District Court 27 S Main St (PO box 816), Yerington, NV 89447; 775-463-6503; Fax: 775-463-6575. Hours: 8AM-5PM (PST). *Felony, Gross Misdemeanor, Civil Actions Over $7,500, Probate.*

Civil Records: Access: Phone, mail, in person. Only the court performs in person searches; visitors may not. Search fee: $1.00 per name per year. Required to search: name, years to search. Civil cases indexed by defendant, plaintiff. Civil records on computer back to 1989.

Criminal Records: Access: Phone, mail, in person. Only the court performs in person searches; visitors may not. Search fee: $1.00 per name per year. Required to search: name, years to search. Criminal records on computer back to 1985.

General Information: No adoption, juvenile or sealed records released. Will fax results for $3.00 per page. Copy fee: $.25 per page. Cert fee: $3.00. Payee: Lyon County Clerk. Personal checks accepted. Prepayment required. Mail requests: SASE required. Mail turnaround time 1 week for mail requests, immediate for phone requests.

Dayton Township Justice Court 235 Main St, Dayton, NV 89403; 775-246-6233; Fax: 775-246-6203. Hours: 8AM-5PM (PST). *Misdemeanor, Civil Actions Under $7,500, Eviction, Small Claims.*

Civil Records: Access: Phone, fax, mail, in person. Only the court performs in person searches; visitors may not. Search fee: $1.00 per name per year. Required to search: name, years to search. Civil cases indexed by defendant, plaintiff. Civil records on computer from 1991, prior on docket books by year.

Criminal Records: Access: Phone, fax, mail, in person. Only the court performs in person searches; visitors may not. Search fee: $1.00 per name per year. Required to search: name, years to search. Criminal records on computer from 1991, prior on docket books by year.

General Information: No sealed records released. Copy fee: $.30 per page. Cert fee: $3.00. Payee: Dayton Township Justice Court. Personal checks accepted. Prepayment required. Mail requests: SASE required. Mail turnaround time within 1 week.

Fernley Justice Court 565 E Main St, Fernley, NV 89408; 775-575-3355; Fax: 775-575-3359. Hours: 8AM-5PM (PST). *Misdemeanor, Civil Actions Under $7,500, Eviction, Small Claims.*

Civil Records: Access: Phone, mail, in person. Only the court performs in person searches; visitors may not. Search fee: $1.00 per name per year. Required to search: name, years to search. Civil cases indexed by defendant. Civil records on computer from 1992, prior on docket books.

Criminal Records: Access: Phone, mail, in person. Only the court performs in person searches; visitors may not. Search fee: $1.00 per name per year. Required to search: name, years to search; also helpful: SSN. Criminal records on computer from 1992, prior on docket books.

General Information: No police reports or sealed records released. Copy fee: $.30 per page. Cert fee: $2.00. Payee: Fernley Justice Court. Personal checks accepted. Out of state checks not accepted. Prepayment required. Mail requests: SASE required. Mail turnaround time 1 week.

Mason Valley Justice Court 30 Nevin Way, Yerington, NV 89447; 775-463-6639; Fax: 775-463-6638. Hours: 8AM-5PM (PST). *Misdemeanor, Civil Actions Under $7,500, Eviction, Small Claims.*

Civil Records: Access: Phone, mail, in person. Only the court performs in person searches; visitors may not. Search fee: $1.00 per name per year. Required to search: name, years to search. Civil cases indexed by defendant, plaintiff. Civil records on computer from 1992, archives from 1900s.

Criminal Records: Access: Phone, mail, in person. Only the court performs in person searches; visitors may not. Search fee: $1.00 per name per year. Required to search: name, years to search; also helpful: DOB, SSN. Criminal records on computer from 1992, archives from 1900s.

General Information: No police, sheriff reports released. Copy fee: $.25 per page. Cert fee: $3.00. Payee: Mason Valley Justice Court. Personal checks not accepted. Prepayment required. Mail requests: SASE required. Mail turnaround time 3 days, immediate for phone requests.

Smith Valley Justice Court PO Box 141, Smith, NV 89430; 775-465-2313; Fax: 775-465-2153. Hours: 8AM-Noon Tues & Fri or by appointment (PST). *Misdemeanor, Civil Actions Under $7500.00, Eviction, Small Claims.*

Civil Records: Access: Phone, fax, mail, in person. Only the court performs in person searches; visitors may not. No search fee. Required to search: name, years to search; also helpful: address. Civil cases indexed by defendant, plaintiff. Criminal records on computer from 1994. Overall records go back to 1992.

Criminal Records: Access: Phone, mail, in person. Only the court performs in person searches; visitors may not. No search fee. Required to search: name, years to search; also helpful: address, DOB, SSN. Criminal records on computer from 1994. Overall records go back to 1992.

General Information: Will fax results for $3.00 per page. Copy fee: $.30 per page. Cert fee: $5.00. Payee: Smith Valley Justice Court. Personal checks accepted. Prepayment required. Mail requests: SASE required. Mail turnaround time 1-2 weeks.

Mineral County

5th Judicial District Court PO Box 1450, Hawthorne, NV 89415; 775-945-2446; Fax: 775-945-0706. Hours: 8AM-5PM (PST). *Felony, Gross Misdemeanor, Civil Actions Over $7,500, Probate.*

Civil Records: Access: Phone, fax, mail, in person. Both court and visitors may perform in person searches. Search fee: $1.00 per name per year. Required to search: name, years to search. Civil cases indexed by defendant, plaintiff. Civil records go back to 1911; computerized records since 1993.

Criminal Records: Access: Phone, fax, mail, in person. Both court and visitors may perform in person searches. Search fee: $1.00 per name per year. Required to search: name, years to search. Criminal records go back to 1911; computerized records since 1993.

General Information: No juvenile records released. Will fax results $1.50 per page. Copy fee: $1.00 per page. Cert fee: $3.00. Payee: Mineral County Clerk. Personal checks accepted. Prepayment required. Mail requests: SASE required. Mail turnaround time 1 day.

Hawthorne Justice Court PO Box 1660, Hawthorne, NV 89415; 775-945-3859; Fax: 775-945-0700. Hours: 8AM-5PM (PST). *Misdemeanor, Civil Actions Under $7,500, Eviction, Small Claims.*

Note: This court holds records from Schurz Justice Court.

Civil Records: Access: Phone, mail, in person. Both court and visitors may perform in person searches. No search fee. Required to search: name, years to search. Civil cases indexed by defendant. Civil records on computer from 1994, prior on docket books.

Criminal Records: Access: Phone, mail, in person,fax. Both court and visitors may perform in person searches. No search fee. Required to search: name, years to search. Criminal records on computer from 1992.

General Information: No pending case or sealed records released. Copy fee: $.25 per page. Legal Size Copy Fee: $1.00 per page. No cert fee. Payee: Hawthorne Justice Court. Personal checks accepted. Prepayment required. Mail requests: SASE required. Mail turnaround time 1-5 days.

Mina Justice Court, NV.

Note: Court has been closed. All records at the hawthorne Justice Court

Schurz Justice Court c/o Hawthorne Justice Ct, PO Box 1660, Hawthorne, NV 89415.

Note: Schurz court closed 1/1/2001; records now housed at Hawthorne Justice Court (see above.)

Nye County

5th Judicial District Court PO Box 1031, Tonopah, NV 89049; 775-482-8131; Fax: 775-482-8133. Hours: 8AM-5PM (PST). *Felony, Gross Misdemeanor, Civil Actions Over $7,500, Probate.*

Civil Records: Access: Phone, fax, mail, in person. Search fee: $1.00 per name per year. Required to search: name, years to search. Civil records on computer from 1991, on docket books from 1800s, many are microfilmed.

Criminal Records: Access: Phone, fax, mail, in person. Only the court performs in person searches; visitors may not. Search fee: $1.00 per name per year. Required to search: name, years to search. Criminal records on computer from 1991, on docket books from 1800s, many are microfilmed.

General Information: No adoptions or juvenile records released. Will fax results $2.00 1st page, $1.00 each add'l. Copy fee: $1.00 per page. Cert fee: $3.00. Payee: Nye County Clerk. Business checks accepted. In state personal checks accepted. Prepayment required. Payment required if more than $15.00. Mail requests: SASE required. Mail turnaround time 1 day.

Beatty Justice Court PO Box 805, Beatty, NV 89003; 775-553-2951; Fax: 775-553-2136. Hours: 8AM-5PM (PST). *Misdemeanor, Civil Actions Up to $7,500, Eviction, Small Claims.*

Civil Records: Access: Phone, mail, in person. Only the court performs in person searches; visitors may not. Search fee: $1.00 per name per year. Computer printouts on all civil actions (no way to segregate small claims or evictions) is $0.16 per page. Required to search: name, years to search. Civil cases indexed by defendant, plaintiff. Civil records on computer from 1989, archived from 1950s, some on docket books.

Criminal Records: Access: Phone, mail, in person. Only the court performs in person searches; visitors may not. Search fee: $1.00 per name per year. Required to search: name, years to search, DOB. Criminal records on computer from 1989.

General Information: No sealed, confidential records released. Will fax results if all fees paid; fax copies are $0.16 per page. If project involves more than 15 minutes time, add'l fees may apply. Copy fee: $.30 per page. Cert fee: $3.00. Payee: Beatty Justice Court. Personal checks accepted. Prepayment required. Mail requests: SASE required. Mail turnaround time 1 week for mail requests, same day for phone requests when possible.

Tonopah Justice Court PO Box 1151, Tonopah, NV 89049; 775-482-8155. Hours: 8AM-Noon, 1-5PM (PST). *Misdemeanor, Civil Actions Under $7,500, Eviction, Small Claims.*
Civil Records: Access: Phone, mail, in person. Only the court performs in person searches; visitors may not. Search fee: $1.00 per name per year. Required to search: name, years to search. Civil cases indexed by plaintiff. Civil records on computer from 1992, on archives from 1950s, some on docket books.
Criminal Records: Access: Phone, mail, in person. Only the court performs in person searches; visitors may not. Search fee: $1.00 per name per year. Required to search: name, years to search, offense, date of offense; also helpful: DOB, SSN. Criminal records on computer from 1992, on docket books from 1943.
General Information: Will fax results to local or toll free line. Copy fee: $.30 per page. Cert fee: $3.00 each. Payee: Tonopah Justice Court. Business checks accepted. Prepayment required. Mail requests: SASE required. Mail turnaround time 1-2 weeks.

Gabbs Justice Court, NV.
Note: This court is closed; any records are now at Tonopah 775-482-8155.

Pershing County

6th Judicial District Court PO Box 820, Lovelock, NV 89419; 775-273-2410; Fax: 775-273-2434. Hours: 9AM-5PM (PST). *Felony, Civil Actions Over $7,500, Probate.*
Note: Misdemeanors are handled by the Lake Township Justice Court.
Civil Records: Access: Phone, fax (3 names or less), mail, in person. Only the court performs in person searches; visitors may not. Search fee: $1.00 per year per name. Required to search: name, years to search. Civil cases indexed by defendant, plaintiff. Civil records on computer from 1992, microfilmed from 1919-1938, books from 1919. Court will do up to 3 or more searches by phone.
Criminal Records: Access: Phone, fax (3 names or less), mail, in person. Only the court performs in person searches; visitors may not. Search fee: $1.00 per year per name. Required to search: name, years to search. Criminal records on computer from 1992, microfilmed from 1919-1938, books from 1919. Court will do up to 3 or more searches by phone.
General Information: No adoption, juvenile or sealed records released. No fee to fax results. Copy fee: $1.00 per page. Cert fee: $3.00. Payee: Pershing County Clerk. Personal checks accepted. Prepayment required. Mail requests: SASE required. Mail turnaround time 1-3 days.

Lake Township Justice Court PO Box 8, Lovelock, NV 89419; 775-273-2753; Fax: 775-273-0416. Hours: 8AM-5PM (PST). *Misdemeanor, Civil Actions Under $7,500, Eviction, Small Claims.*
Civil Records: Access: Phone, mail, in person. Visitors must perform in person searches for themselves. Search fee: $1.00 per name per year. Required to search: name, years to search; also helpful: address. Civil cases indexed by defendant, plaintiff. Civil records on computer from 1988, on docket books prior.
Criminal Records: Access: Phone, mail, in person. Visitors must perform in person searches for themselves. Search fee: $1.00 per name per year.

Required to search: name, years to search; also helpful: DOB. Criminal records on computer from 1988, on docket books prior.
General Information: Public Access terminal is available. No sealed, driver's history or highway patrol records released. Copy fee: $.30 per page. Cert fee: $3.00. Payee: Lake Township Justice Court. Personal checks accepted; ID required. Prepayment required. Mail requests: SASE required. Mail turnaround time 2 days, 30 minutes for phone requests for records prior to 1988.

Storey County

1st Judicial District Court PO Drawer D, Virginia City, NV 89440; 775-847-0969; Fax: 775-847-0921. Hours: 9AM-5PM (PST). *Felony, Gross Misdemeanor, Civil Actions Over $7,500, Probate.*
Civil Records: Access: Phone, mail, fax, in person. Both court and visitors may perform in person searches. Search fee: $1.00 per name per year. Required to search: name, years to search. Civil cases indexed by defendant, plaintiff. Civil records on computer since 1992; prior years on books. Search by phone only if paid in advance.
Criminal Records: Access: Phone, mail, fax, in person. Both court and visitors may perform in person searches. Search fee: $1.00 per name per year. Required to search: name, years to search, signed release; also helpful: DOB, SSN. Criminal records on computer since 1992; prior years on books. Search by phone only if pre-paid.
General Information: No juvenile or sealed records released. Will fax results to local or toll free line. Copy fee: $1.00 per page. Cert fee: $6.00. Payee: Storey County Clerk. Personal checks accepted. Prepayment required. Mail requests: SASE required. Mail turnaround time 1 week; 5 minutes for phone requests when possible.

Virginia City Justice Court PO Box 674, Virginia City, NV 89440; 775-847-0962; Fax: 775-847-0915. Hours: 9AM-5PM (PST). *Misdemeanor, Civil Actions Under $7,500, Eviction, Small Claims.*
Civil Records: Access: Phone, mail, in person. Only the court performs in person searches; visitors may not. Search fee: $1.00 per name per year. Required to search: name, years to search. Civil cases indexed by defendant, plaintiff. Civil records retained for 7 years, some on docket books.
Criminal Records: Access: Phone, mail, in person. Both court and visitors may perform in person searches. Search fee: $1.00 per name per year. Required to search: name, years to search, DOB; also helpful: SSN. Criminal records on computer since 1988.
General Information: Will fax results to local or toll free line. Copy fee: $.25 per page. Cert fee: $3.00. Payee: Justice Court. Personal checks accepted. Prepayment required. Mail requests: SASE required. Mail turnaround time 1 week.

Washoe County

2nd Judicial District Court PO Box 30083, Reno, NV 89520; 775-328-3110; Fax: 775-328-3515. Hours: 8AM-5PM (PST). *Felony, Gross Misdemeanor, Civil Actions Over $7,500, Probate.*
www.washoecourts.com/
Note: This court also handles Divorce Actions and Guardianship.
Civil Records: Access: Phone, online, mail, in person. Both court and visitors may perform in person searches. Search fee: $1.00 per name per year. Required to search: name, years to search. Civil cases indexed by defendant, plaintiff. Civil records on computer back to 1984, microfiche from 1983, archives from 1920. Online access is known as CourtConnect and is at the website. Case data in

CourtConnect is only limited to cases filed after January 1st, 2000. However, active cases prior to January 1st, 2000 are also available. Phone access limited to computer records.
Criminal Records: Access: Phone, online, mail, in person. Both court and visitors may perform in person searches. Search fee: $1.00 per name per year. Required to search: name, years to search. Criminal records on computer back to 1984, microfiche from 1983, archives from 1920. Online access is known as CourtConnect and is at the website. Case data in CourtConnect is only limited to cases filed after January 1st, 2000. However, active cases prior to January 1st, 2000 are also available. Phone access limited to computer records.
General Information: Public Access terminal is available. No sealed or juvenile records released. Copy fee: $1.00 per page. Cert fee: $6.00. Payee: Washoe County District Court (WCDC). Business checks accepted. Prepayment required. Mail requests: SASE required. Mail turnaround time 2-4 weeks.

Incline Village Justice Court 865 Tahoe Blvd, #301, Incline Village, NV 89451; 775-832-4100; Fax: 775-832-4162. Hours: 9AM-5PM (PST). *Misdemeanor, Civil Actions Under $7,500, Eviction, Small Claims.*
Civil Records: Access: Mail, in person. Both court and visitors may perform in person searches. Search fee: $1.00 per name per year. Required to search: name, years to search. Civil cases indexed by defendant, plaintiff. Civil records on dockets to 1980s.
Criminal Records: Access: Mail, in person. Both court and visitors may perform in person searches. Search fee: $1.00 per name per year. Required to search: name, years to search; also helpful: DOB, SSN. Full dockets of criminal records searchable for 7 years.
General Information: Will fax results if prepayment received. Copy fee: $.30 per page. Cert fee: $3.00. Payee: Justice Court. Personal checks accepted; check guarantee card required. Prepayment required. Mail turnaround time 1-3 days.

Reno Justice Court PO Box 30083, Reno, NV 89520; 775-325-6501; Criminal phone: 775-325-6500; Fax: 775-325-6510. Hours: 8AM-5PM (PST). *Misdemeanor, Civil Actions Under $7,500, Eviction, Small Claims.*
http://207.228.25.162/rjc/
Note: 775-325-6510 is fax for criminal: 775-325-6715 is fax for civil.

Civil Records: Access: Mail, in person. Both court and visitors may perform in person searches. Search fee: $1.00 per name per year. If search requires offsite to storage, additional fees apply. Required to search: name, years to search. Civil cases indexed by defendant. Civil records archived from 1982, on docket book; computerized records since 1980. For mail access call first. Court will send form to be filled out & returned with payment.
Criminal Records: Access: Mail, in person. Only the court performs in person searches; visitors may not. Search fee: $1.00 per name per year. Required to search: name, years to search; also helpful: DOB, SSN, aliases. Criminal records archived from 1982, on docket books; computerized records since 1980. Same as civil.
General Information: Public Access terminal is available. No sealed records released. Copy fee: $.30 per page. Cert fee: $3.00 per page. Payee: Reno Justice Court. Only cashiers checks and money orders accepted. Prepayment required. Mail requests: SASE required. Mail turnaround time 2-5 days.

Sparks Justice Court 630 Greenbrae Dr, Sparks, NV 89431; 775-352-3003. Hours: 8AM-5PM (PST). *Misdemeanor, Civil Actions Under $7,500, Eviction, Small Claims.*
http://207.228.25.168/sjc/
Note: Traffic record search fees are same as below.

Civil Records: Access: Phone, mail, in person. Both court and visitors may perform in person searches. Search fee: $1.00 per name per year. Required to search: name, years to search. Civil cases indexed by defendant, plaintiff. Civil records on computer 1990 to present, prior in books and on cards. Case number required to search pre-1990 records.

Criminal Records: Access: Phone, mail, in person. Both court and visitors may perform in person searches. Search fee: $1.00 per name per year. Required to search: name, years to search; also helpful: DOB, SSN. Full dockets of criminal records on computer last 6 years, 1990-1996 partially on computer, prior in books and on cards. Case number required to search pre-1990 records.

General Information: Public Access terminal is available. Will fax results if prepayment received. Copy fee: $.30 per page. Cert fee: $3.00. Payee: Justice Court. Personal checks accepted; check guarantee card required. Prepayment required. Mail turnaround time 1-3 days.

Verdi Justice Court PO Box 740, Verdi, NV 89439; 775-345-0173; Fax: 775-345-0633. Hours: 8AM-4PM (PST). *Misdemeanor, Civil Actions Under $7,500, Eviction, Small Claims.*
Note: All record requests must be in writing.

Civil Records: Access: Mail, in person. Both court and visitors may perform in person searches. Search fee: none. Required to search: name, years to search. Civil cases indexed by defendant, plaintiff. Civil records held for at least 20 years.

Criminal Records: Access: Mail, in person. Both court and visitors may perform in person searches. Search fee: none. Required to search: name, years to search; also helpful: DOB, SSN. Full dockets of criminal records held 20 years.

General Information: No copy fee. Cert fee: $3.00. Payee: Justice Court. Turnaround time 1-3 days.

Wadsworth Justice Court PO Box 68, Wadsworth, NV 89442; 775-575-4585; Fax: 775-575-0253. Hours: 8AM-5PM T,W,TH only (PST). *Misdemeanor, Civil Actions Under $7,500, Eviction, Small Claims.*

Civil Records: Access: Mail, in person. Both court and visitors may perform in person searches. Search fee: $1.00 per name. Required to search: name, years to search. Civil cases indexed by defendant, plaintiff.

Criminal Records: Access: Mail, in person. Both court and visitors may perform in person searches. Search fee: $1.00 per name. Required to search: name, years to search; also helpful: DOB, SSN.

General Information: Will fax results if prepayment received. Copy fee: $.30 per page. Cert fee: $3.00. Payee: Justice Court. Personal checks accepted; check guarantee card required. Prepayment required. Mail turnaround time 1-3 days.

White Pine County

Ely Justice Court 801 Clark St #6, Ely, NV 89301; 775-289-2678; Fax: 775-289-3392. Hours: 9AM-5PM (PST). *Misdemeanor, Civil Actions Under $7,500, Eviction, Small Claims.*

Civil Records: Access: Phone, fax, mail, in person. Only the court performs in person searches; visitors may not. Search fee: $1.00 per name per year. Required to search: name, years to search. Civil cases indexed by defendant, plaintiff. Civil records on computer from 1988, archived from 1899.

Criminal Records: Access: Phone, fax, mail, in person. Only the court performs in person searches; visitors may not. Search fee: $1.00 per name per year. Required to search: name, years to search; also helpful: DOB, SSN. Criminal records on computer from 1988, archived from 1899.

General Information: No sealed records released. Copy fee: $.30 per page. Cert fee: $3.00. Payee: Ely Justice Court. Only cashiers checks and money orders accepted. Prepayment required. Mail requests: SASE required. Mail turnaround time 1-5 days.

Lund Justice Court PO Box 87, Lund, NV 89317; 775-238-5400; Fax: 775-238-5400. Hours: 10AM-2:30PM M,W,F (PST). *Misdemeanor, Civil Actions Under $7,500, Eviction, Small Claims.*

Civil Records: Access: Mail, in person. Only the court performs in person searches; visitors may not. Search fee: $1.00 per name per year. Required to search: name, years to search. Civil records only kept in files, archives from 1899.

Criminal Records: Access: Mail, in person. Only the court performs in person searches; visitors may not. Search fee: $1.00 per name per year. Required to search: name, years to search, DOB; also helpful: SSN. Criminal records only kept in files, archives from 1899.

General Information: Will not fax results. Copy fee: $.25 per page. Cert fee: $2.00. Payee: Lund Justice Court. Personal checks accepted. Prepayment required. Mail requests: SASE required. Mail turnaround time 1 day.

Baker Justice Court PO Box 2, Baker, NV 89311; 775-234-7100. *Misdemeanor, Civil Actions Under $7,500, Eviction, Small Claims.*
Note: This court holds very little records and is rarely open.

Nevada Recording Offices

ORGANIZATION: 16 counties and one independent city, 17 recording offices. The recording officer is County Recorder. Carson City has a separate filing office. The entire state is in the Pacific Time Zone (PST).

REAL ESTATE RECORDS: Most counties will not provide real estate searches. Copies cost $1.00 per page and certification fees are usually $4.00 per document.

UCC RECORDS: Financing statements are filed at the state level, except for real estate related collateral, which are filed with the County Recorder. However, prior to 07/2001, consumer goods and farm collateral were also filed at the County Recorder and these older records can be searched there. All recording offices will perform UCC searches. Search fees are $15.00 per debtor name using the approved UCC-3 request form and $20.00 using a non-standard form. Copies cost $1.00 per page.

TAX LIEN RECORDS: Federal tax liens on personal property of businesses are filed with the Secretary of State. Federal tax liens on personal property of individuals are filed with the County Recorder. Although not called state tax liens, employment withholding judgments have the same effect and are filed with the County Recorder. Most counties will provide tax lien searches for a fee of $15.00 per name - $20.00 if the standard UCC request form is not used.

OTHER LIENS: Mechanics

ONLINE ACCESS: Clark County has many searchable databases online. A private company, GoverNet, offers online access to Assessor, Treasurer, Recorder and other county databases. Registration is required, sliding monthly and per-hit fees apply. Counties online are Churchill, Clark, Elko, Esmeralda, Eureka, Humboldt, Lander, Lyon, Mineral, Nye, Pershing, Storey, Washoe, and White Pine. System includes access to Secretary of State's Corporation, Partnership, UCC, Fictitious Name, and Federal Tax Lien records. For more information, visit www.governet.net/SurfNV/ or call 208-522-1225.

Carson City

City Recorder, 885 E. Musser St, #1028, Carson City, NV 89701-4775. **Phone**-City Recorder, R/E & UCC Recording- 775-887-2260, UCC Recording-775-887-2260 city level or 775-687-4280 St level; fax-775-887-2146; hours 8AM-5PM www.carson-city.nv.us/clerk Will search UCC records. Search per debtor- $40.00. Will search federal tax liens. Will not search real estate records. RE record copy- $1.00 per page. UCC copy- $2.00 per page. Cert fee: $4.00 per seal. Payee: Carson City Recorder. **Online Access to Assessor, Recorder, Treasurer, Real Estate, Marriage, Vital Statistic records:** Access is on goverNet (www.governet.net/surfnv) 208-522-1225; requires registration and fees; see beginning of this section. Also, you may search the city clerk-recorder documents for free at http://207.228.41.46/jwalk/docindex.html. Marriage records are free at http://207.228.41.46/jwalk/marriage.html. **Other phones:** Assessor-775-887-2130; Treasurer-775-887-2092; Elections-775-887-2087; Vital Records-775-684-4242.

Churchill County

County Recorder, 155 N. Taylor, #131, Fallon, NV 89406-2748. **Phone**-County Recorder, R/E & UCC Recording- 775-423-6001; fax-775-423-8933; hours 8AM-5PM www.churchillcounty.org Will search UCC records. Search per debtor- $40.00. UCC search includes federal tax liens if requested. Will not search real estate records. RE record copy- $1.00 per page. UCC copy- $2.00 per page. Cert fee: $4.00 per cert. Payee: Churchill County Recorder. **Online Access to Assessor, Treasurer, Recording, Grantor/Grantee, Deed, Real Estate, Property Tax records:** To access the records go to www.churchcillcounty.org. Click on Recorder, Assessor, Planning or Clerk Treasurer. Go to www.vitalchek.com for Vital records. **Other phones:** Assessor-775-423-6584; Treasurer-775-423-6028; Appraiser/ Auditor-775-423-6584; Elections-775-423-6028; Vital Records-775-684-4280 (Birth/Death).

Clark County

County Recorder, PO Box 551510, Las Vegas, NV 89155-1510. **Phone**-702-455-4336, R/E Recording-702-455-6566; fax-702-455-5644. www.co.clark.nv.us/recorder/recindex.htm Will not search records. Record copy- $1.00 per page. Cert fee: $4.00 per cert. **Online Access to Real Estate, Lien, Deed, UCC, Vital Statistic, Marriage, Property Assessor, Fictitious Name, Business License, Inmate records:** Property records, assessor maps, manufactured housing and road documents on the county Assessor database are free at www.co.clark.nv.us/assessor/Disclaim.htm. Search inmates at www.vinelink.com/index.asp. Marriage records are at www.co.clark.nv.us/recorder/mar_srch.htm. Search property owners at GIS site at http://gisgate.co.clark.nv.us. Search business licenses at http://sandgate.co.clark.nv.us/businessLicense/businessSearch/blindex.asp. Recorder's real estate, UCC and vital records are at www.co.clark.nv.us/recorder/recindex.htm. UCCs go back to 1986; liens to '84. Search county fictitious names at http://sandgate.co.clark.nv.us:8498/clarkcounty/clerk/clerkSearch.html. **Other phones:** Assessor-702-455-3891; Treasurer-702-455-4323.

Douglas County

County Recorder, PO Box 218, Minden, NV 89423. **Phone**-County Recorder, R/E & UCC Recording- 775-782-9025; fax-775-783-6413; hours 9AM-5PM http://recorder.co.douglas.nv.us Will search UCC records. Search per debtor- $15.00. Search request using non-standard form (per name)- $20.00. Tax liens not included in UCC search. Tax lien search- $20.00 per debtor. Will not search real estate records. Record copy- $1.00 per page. Cert fee: $4.00 per doc. Payee: Douglas County Recorder. **Online Access to Assessor, Real Estate, Property Tax, Recorder, Deed records:** Property records on the Assessor's database are free at www.co.douglas.nv.us/databases/assessors. Also, the clerk/treasurer property tax database is free at www.co.douglas.nv.us/databases/treasurers/. Also, searth the recorder's document files for free at www.co.douglas.nv.us/databases/recorders/ Records go back to 1/1/1983. **Other phones:** Assessor-775-782-9830; Treasurer-775-782-9017; Vital Records-775-782-9028.

Elko County

County Recorder, 571 Idaho St., Rm 103, Elko, NV 89801-3770. **Phone**-County Recorder, R/E & UCC Recording- 775-738-6526; fax-775-738-3299; hours 9AM-5PM Will search UCC records. Search per debtor- $20.00. Tax liens not included in UCC search. Separate federal tax lien search- $20.00 per debtor. Will not search real estate records. Record copy- $1.00 per page. **Online Access to Assessor, Treasurer, Recording, Marriage, Personal Property, Property Tax records:** Access to the recorder database including marriages is free at www.elkocountynv.net/recorder.html. Recording records go back to 1984. Access to the assessors database including personal property is free at www.elkocountynv.net/assessor.htmll. Also, access to the treasurers property tax data is free at http://170.215.77.129/jwalk/treasurer.html. Also, access no longer via the goverNet system. **Other phones:** Assessor-775-738-5217; Treasurer-775-738-5694; Appraiser/ Auditor-775-738-5217; Elections-775-753-4600; Vital Records-775-684-4242; Marriages-775-738-6526.

Esmeralda County

County Recorder, PO Box 458, Goldfield, NV 89013. **Phone**-County Recorder, R/E & UCC Recording- 775-485-6337; fax-775-485-3524; hours 8AM-5PM

Will search UCC records. Search per debtor- $40.00. Separate federal Tax lien search- $15.00 per debtor. Will search real estate records. Copy fee is $2.00 per page. Cert fee: $4.00 per seal. Payee: Esmeralda County Recorder. **Online Access to Assessor, Treasurer, Recording records:** Access is on goverNet (www.governet.net/surfnv) 208-522-1225; requires registration and fees; see beginning of this section. **Other phones:** Assessor-775-485-6380; Treasurer-775-485-6367; Appraiser/ Auditor-775-485-6380; Elections-775-485-6367.

Eureka County

County Recorder, PO Box 556, Eureka, NV 89316. **Phone**-County Recorder, R/E & UCC Recording- 775-237-5263; fax-775-237-5614; hours 8AM-N, 1-5PM www.co.eureka.nv.us

Will search UCC records. Search per debtor- $40.00. Will not search real estate or tax lien records. ecord copy- $1.00 per page. Cert fee: $4.00 per doc. Payee: Eureka County Recorder. **Online Access to Assessor, Treasurer, Recorder, Deed, Lien, Judgment, Vital Statistic records:** Assess to the recorders index is free at http://207.212.113.130/docindex.html. Search the treasurer's secured property tax roll at http://207.212.113.130/taxcoll.html. Search the assessor property data at http://207.212.113.130/assessor.html. Also, access is on goverNet (www.governet.net/surfnv) 208-522-1225; requires registration and fees; see beginning of this section. May not be updated regularly. **Other phones:** Assessor-775-237-5270; Treasurer-775-237-5262; Appraiser/ Auditor-775-237-5270; Elections-775-237-5262.

Humboldt County

County Recorder, 25 W. 4th St, Winnemucca, NV 89445. **Phone**-County Recorder, R/E & UCC Recording- 775-623-6414, UCC Recording-775-623-6412; fax-775-623-6337; hours 8AM-5PM www.hcnv.us

Will search UCC records. Search per debtor- $40.00. Will not search real estate or tax lien records. Record copy- $1.00 per page. Cert fee: $4.00 per cert. Payee: Humboldt County Recorder. **Online Access to Inmate records:** The Sheriff's inmake list is free at www.hcsonv.com. **Other phones:** Assessor-775-623-6310; Treasurer-775-623-6444; Appraiser/ Auditor-775-623-6310; Elections-775-623-6343; Vital Records-775-623-6412; 775-623-6414.

Lander County

County Recorder, 315 S. Humboldt, Battle Mountain, NV 89820. **Phone**-County Recorder, R/E & UCC Recording- 775-635-5173; fax-775-635-8272; hours 8AM-5PM

Will search UCC records. Search per debtor- $40.00. Search request using non-standard form (per name)- $40.00. Federal tax liens not included in UCC search. Separate federal tax lien search- $40.00 per debtor. Will not search real estate records. Record copy- $1.00 per page. Cert fee: $4.00 per cert. Payee: Lander County Recorder. **Online Access to Assessor, Recorder records:** Access is on

goverNet (www.governet.net/surfnv) 208-522-1225; requires registration and fees; see beginning of this section. **Other phones:** Assessor-775-635-2610; Treasurer-775-635-5127.

Lincoln County

County Recorder, PO Box 218, Pioche, NV 89043. **Phone**-775-962-5495; fax-775-962-5180.

Will search UCC records. Search per debtor- $40.00. Will not search real estate records. Copy fee-$1.00 per page. Cert fee: $4.00 per doc. Payee: Lincon County Recorder. **Other phones:** Assessor-775-962-5890; Treasurer-775-962-5805.

Lyon County

County Recorder, 27 S Main St, Yerington, NV 89447-0927. **Phone**-County Recorder, R/E & UCC Recording- 775-463-6581; fax-775-463-6585; hours 8AM-5PM www.lyon-county.org

Will search UCC records. Search per debtor- $40.00. Federal/state combined tax lien search- $20.00 per debtor. Will not search real estate records. RE record copy- $1.00 per page. UCC copy- $2.00 per page. Cert fee: $4.00 per page + copy fees. Payee: Lyon County Recorder. **Online Access to Assessor, Recorder, Treasurer records:** Access is on goverNet (www.governet.net/surfnv) 208-522-1225; requires registration and fees; see beginning of this section. **Other phones:** Assessor-775-463-6524; Treasurer-775-463-6502; Appraiser/ Auditor-775-463-6524; Elections-775-463-6502; Vital Records-775-463-6581.

Mineral County

County Recorder, PO Box 1447, Hawthorne, NV 89415-1447. **Phone**-775-945-3676; fax-775-945-1749; hours 8AM-5PM

Will not search records. UCC copy- $1.00 per page. Cert fee: $4.00. Payee: Mineral County Clerk. **Online Access to Assessor, Treasurer, Recording records:** Access is on goverNet (www.governet.net/surfnv) 208-522-1225; requires registration and fees; see beginning of this section. **Other phones:** Assessor-775-945-3684; Treasurer-775-945-2446.

Nye County

County Recorder, PO Box 1111, Tonopah, NV 89049-1111. **Phone**-775-482-8116; fax-775-482-8111.

Will search UCC records. Search per debtor- $40.00. Will search tax liens including federal tax liens. Federal/state combined tax lien search- $20.00 per debtor. Will not search real estate records. RE record copy- $1.00 per page. UCC copy- $2.00 per page. Cert fee: $4.00 cert + $1.00 per page. Payee: Nye County Recorder. **Online Access to Assessor, Treasurer, Recording, Deed, Pahrump Business records:** Access is on goverNet at www.governet.net/surfnv, phone 208-522-1225; requires registration and fees; see beginning of this section. Also, search for property assessor data for free at www.nyecounty.net/assess/ver2/. Also, search Pahrump business registrations for free at www.pahrumpnv.org/searchbus.php. **Other phones:** Assessor-775-482-8174; Treasurer-775-482-8194.

Pershing County

County Recorder, PO Box 736, Lovelock, NV 89419-0736. **Phone**-County Recorder, R/E & UCC

Recording- 775-273-2408; fax-775-273-1039; hours 8AM-5PM

Will search UCC records. Search per debtor- $40.00. Will search tax liens. Will not search real estate records. Record copy- $1.00 per page. Cert fee: $4.00 per cert +$1.00 per page copy. Payee: Pershing County Recorder. **Online Access to Assessor, Treasurer, Recording records:** Access is on goverNet (www.governet.net/surfnv) 208-522-1225; requires registration and fees; see beginning of this section. **Other phones:** Assessor-775-273-2369; Treasurer-775-273-2208; Appraiser/ Auditor-775-273-2369; Elections-775-273-2208; Vital Records-775-273-2408 (marriage only).

Storey County

County Recorder, PO Box 493, Virginia City, NV 89440. **Phone**-775-847-0967; fax-775-847-1009; hours 9AM-5PM

Will search UCC records. Search per debtor- $20.00. Will not search real estate or tax lien records. Record copy- $1.00 per page. Cert fee: $4.00 per cert. Payee: Storey County Recorder. **Online Access to Assessor, Treasurer, Recording records:** Access is on goverNet (www.governet.net/surfnv) 208-522-1225; requires registration and fees; see beginning of this section. **Other phones:** Assessor-775-847-0961; Treasurer-775-847-0969; Elections-775-847-0969; Vital Records-775-847-0969.

Washoe County

County Recorder, PO Box 11130, Reno, NV 89520-0027. **Phone**-775-328-3661, R/E Recording-775-328-2230; fax-775-325-8010; hours 8AM-5PM www.co.washoe.nv.us/recorder

Will not search UCC or real estate records. RE record copy- $1.00 per page. UCC copy- $2.00 per page. Cert fee: $4.00 per cert. Payee: Washoe County Recorder. **Online Access to Assessor, Treasurer, Recording, Grantor/Grantee, Real Estate, Inmate records:** Access is on goverNet (www.governet.net/surfnv) 208-522-1225; requires registration and fees, copies can be made for free; see beginning of this section. Also, access to the grantor/grantee index is free at http://207.228.25.173/icris/splash.jsp, however, there is a $1.00 per page fee for documents. Free registration required. Also, search inmate info on private company website at www.vinelink.com/index.jsp. **Other phones:** Assessor-775-328-2277; Treasurer-775-328-2510.

White Pine County

County Recorder, 801 Clark St, #1, Ely, NV 89301. **Phone**-County Recorder, R/E & UCC Recording- 775-289-4567; fax-775-289-9686; hours 9AM-5PM

Will search UCC records. Search per debtor- $40.00. Will not search real estate records. RE record copy- $1.00 per page. UCC copy- $2.00 per page. Cert fee: $4.00. Payee: White Pine County Recorder. **Online Access to Assessor, Recorder records:** Access is on goverNet (www.governet.net/surfnv) 208-522-1225; requires registration and fees; see beginning of this section. **Other phones:** Assessor-775-289-3016; Treasurer-775-289-4783.

Nevada County Locator

You will usually be able to find the city name in the City/County Cross Reference below. In that case, it is a simple matter to determine the county from the cross reference. However, only the official US Postal Service city names are included in this index. There are an additional 40,000 place names that people use in their addresses. Therefore, we have also included a ZIP/City Cross Reference immediately following the City/County Cross Reference.

If you know the ZIP Code but the city name does not appear in the City/County Cross Reference index, look up the ZIP Code in the ZIP/City Cross Reference, find the city name, then look up the city name in the City/County Cross Reference. For example, you want to know the county for an address of Menands, NY 12204. There is no "Menands" in the City/County Cross Reference. The ZIP/City Cross Reference shows that ZIP Codes 12201-12288 are for the city of Albany. Looking back in the City/County Cross Reference, Albany is in Albany County.

Nevada City/County Cross Reference

ALAMO Lincoln
AMARGOSA VALLEY Nye
AUSTIN Lander
BAKER White Pine
BATTLE MOUNTAIN Lander
BEATTY Nye
BLUE DIAMOND Clark
BOULDER CITY Clark
BUNKERVILLE Clark
CAL NEV ARI Clark
CALIENTE Lincoln
CARLIN Elko
CARSON CITY (89706) Carson City(87), Lyon(12)
CARSON CITY Carson City
CARSON CITY Douglas
CRESCENT VALLEY Eureka
CRYSTAL BAY Washoe
DAYTON (89403) Lyon(93), Storey(6)
DEETH Elko
DENIO Humboldt
DUCKWATER White Pine
DYER Esmeralda
EAST ELY White Pine
ELKO Elko
ELY White Pine
EMPIRE Washoe

EUREKA Eureka
FALLON Churchill
FERNLEY (89408) Lyon(97), Churchill(2)
GABBS Nye
GARDNERVILLE Douglas
GENOA Douglas
GERLACH Washoe
GLENBROOK Douglas
GOLCONDA Humboldt
GOLDFIELD Esmeralda
HALLECK Elko
HAWTHORNE Mineral
HENDERSON Clark
HIKO Lincoln
IMLAY Pershing
INCLINE VILLAGE Washoe
INDIAN SPRINGS Clark
JACKPOT Elko
JARBIDGE Elko
JEAN Clark
LAMOILLE Elko
LAS VEGAS Clark
LAUGHLIN Clark
LOGANDALE Clark
LOVELOCK Pershing
LUND White Pine
LUNING Mineral

MANHATTAN Nye
MC DERMITT Humboldt
MC GILL White Pine
MERCURY Nye
MESQUITE Clark
MINA Mineral
MINDEN Douglas
MOAPA Clark
MONTELLO Elko
MOUNTAIN CITY Elko
NELLIS AFB Clark
NIXON Washoe
NORTH LAS VEGAS Clark
OROVADA Humboldt
OVERTON Clark
OWYHEE Elko
PAHRUMP Nye
PANACA Lincoln
PARADISE VALLEY Humboldt
PIOCHE Lincoln
RENO (89521) Washoe(84), Storey(15)
RENO Washoe
ROUND MOUNTAIN Nye
RUBY VALLEY Elko
RUTH White Pine
SCHURZ Mineral
SEARCHLIGHT Clark

SILVER CITY Lyon
SILVER SPRINGS Lyon
SILVERPEAK Esmeralda
SMITH Lyon
SPARKS (89434) Washoe(94), Storey(5)
SPARKS Washoe
SPRING CREEK Elko
STATELINE Douglas
SUN VALLEY Washoe
THE LAKES Clark
TONOPAH Nye
TUSCARORA Elko
VALMY Humboldt
VERDI Washoe
VIRGINIA CITY Storey
WADSWORTH Washoe
WASHOE VALLEY Washoe
WELLINGTON (89444) Lyon(52), Douglas(47)
WELLS Elko
WEST WENDOVER Elko
WINNEMUCCA (89445) Humboldt(91), Pershing(8)
WINNEMUCCA Humboldt
YERINGTON Lyon
ZEPHYR COVE Douglas

Nevada ZIP/City Cross Reference

88901-88901 THE LAKES
88902-88904 LAS VEGAS
88905-88905 THE LAKES
89001-89001 ALAMO
89003-89003 BEATTY
89004-89004 BLUE DIAMOND
89005-89006 BOULDER CITY
89007-89007 BUNKERVILLE
89008-89008 CALIENTE
89009-89009 HENDERSON
89010-89010 DYER
89011-89012 HENDERSON
89013-89013 GOLDFIELD
89014-89016 HENDERSON
89017-89017 HIKO
89018-89018 INDIAN SPRINGS
89019-89019 JEAN
89020-89020 AMARGOSA VALLEY
89021-89021 LOGANDALE
89022-89022 MANHATTAN
89023-89023 MERCURY
89024-89024 MESQUITE
89025-89025 MOAPA
89026-89026 JEAN
89027-89027 MESQUITE
89028-89029 LAUGHLIN
89030-89036 NORTH LAS VEGAS
89039-89039 CAL NEV ARI
89040-89040 OVERTON
89041-89041 PAHRUMP

89042-89042 PANACA
89043-89043 PIOCHE
89044-89044 HENDERSON
89045-89045 ROUND MOUNTAIN
89046-89046 SEARCHLIGHT
89047-89047 SILVERPEAK
89048-89048 PAHRUMP
89049-89049 TONOPAH
89052-89053 HENDERSON
89060-89061 PAHRUMP
89070-89070 INDIAN SPRINGS
89074-89077 HENDERSON
89081-89087 NORTH LAS VEGAS
89101-89162 LAS VEGAS
89163-89163 THE LAKES
89164-89185 LAS VEGAS
89191-89191 NELLIS AFB
89193-89199 LAS VEGAS
89301-89301 ELY
89310-89310 AUSTIN
89311-89311 BAKER
89314-89314 DUCKWATER
89315-89315 EAST ELY
89315-89315 ELY
89316-89316 EUREKA
89317-89317 LUND
89318-89318 MC GILL
89319-89319 RUTH
89402-89402 CRYSTAL BAY
89403-89403 DAYTON

89404-89404 DENIO
89405-89405 EMPIRE
89406-89407 FALLON
89408-89408 FERNLEY
89409-89409 GABBS
89410-89410 GARDNERVILLE
89411-89411 GENOA
89412-89412 GERLACH
89413-89413 GLENBROOK
89414-89414 GOLCONDA
89415-89416 HAWTHORNE
89418-89418 IMLAY
89419-89419 LOVELOCK
89420-89420 LUNING
89421-89421 MC DERMITT
89422-89422 MINA
89423-89423 MINDEN
89424-89424 NIXON
89425-89425 OROVADA
89426-89426 PARADISE VALLEY
89427-89427 SCHURZ
89428-89428 SILVER CITY
89429-89429 SILVER SPRINGS
89430-89430 SMITH
89431-89432 SPARKS
89433-89433 SUN VALLEY
89434-89436 SPARKS
89438-89438 VALMY
89439-89439 VERDI
89440-89440 VIRGINIA CITY

89442-89442 WADSWORTH
89444-89444 WELLINGTON
89445-89446 WINNEMUCCA
89447-89447 YERINGTON
89448-89448 ZEPHYR COVE
89449-89449 STATELINE
89450-89452 INCLINE VILLAGE
89460-89460 GARDNERVILLE
89496-89496 FALLON
89500-89599 RENO
89701-89703 CARSON CITY
89704-89704 WASHOE VALLEY
89705-89721 CARSON CITY
89801-89803 ELKO
89815-89815 SPRING CREEK
89820-89820 BATTLE MOUNTAIN
89821-89821 CRESCENT VALLEY
89822-89822 CARLIN
89823-89823 DEETH
89824-89824 HALLECK
89825-89825 JACKPOT
89826-89826 JARBIDGE
89828-89828 LAMOILLE
89830-89830 MONTELLO
89831-89831 MOUNTAIN CITY
89832-89832 OWYHEE
89833-89833 RUBY VALLEY
89834-89834 TUSCARORA
89835-89835 WELLS
89883-89883 WEST WENDOVER

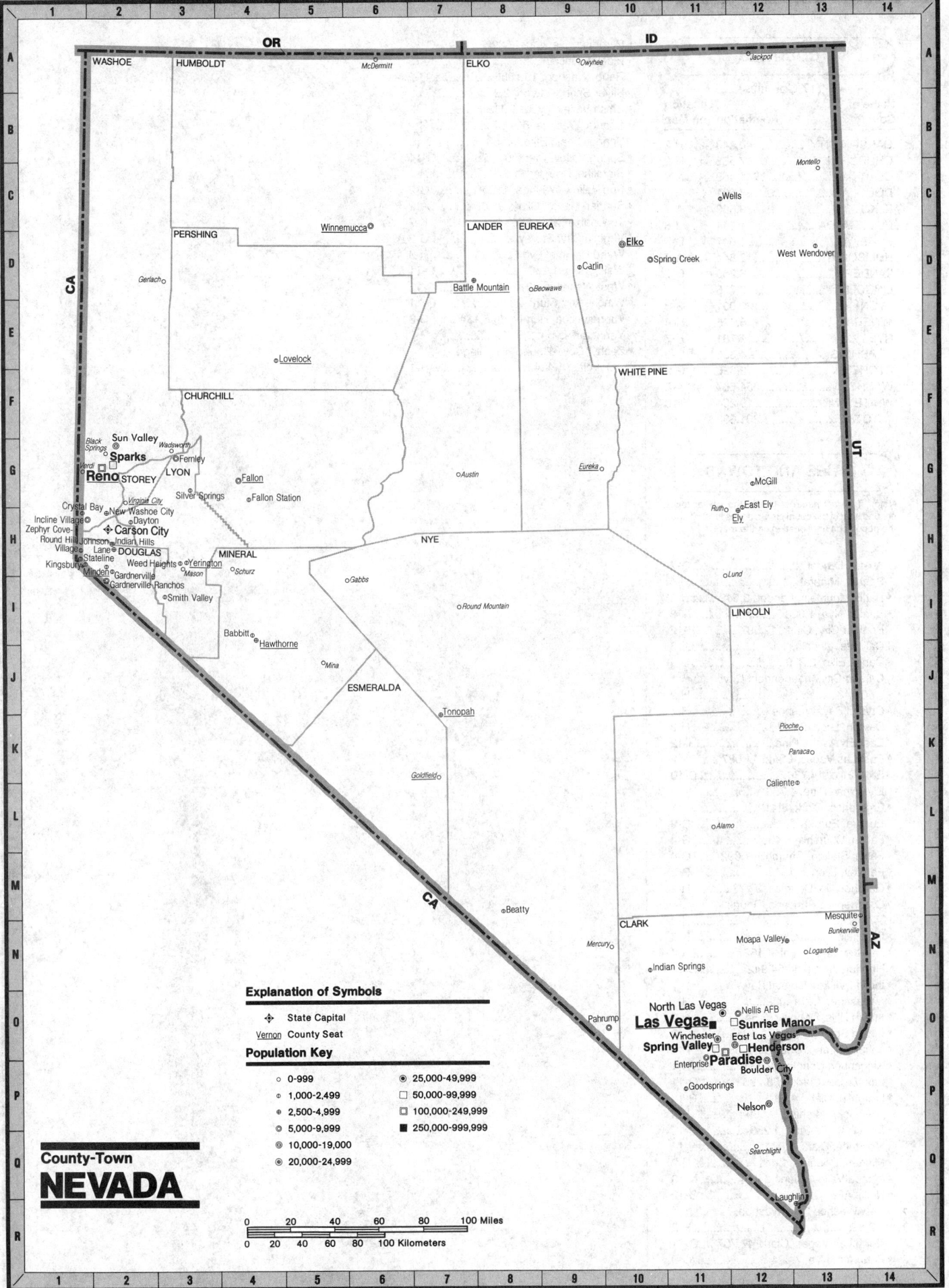

NEVADA
County-Town

Explanation of Symbols

⚬ State Capital
Vernon County Seat

Population Key

○	0-999	◉	25,000-49,999
◔	1,000-2,499	▢	50,000-99,999
⊕	2,500-4,999	▢	100,000-249,999
◍	5,000-9,999	◼	250,000-999,999
◉	10,000-19,000		
◉	20,000-24,999		

0 20 40 60 80 100 Miles
0 20 40 60 80 100 Kilometers

COUNTIES

(17 Counties)

Name of County	Population	Location on Map
CARSON CITY	40,443	H-2
CHURCHILL	17,938	H-2
CLARK	741,459	N-9
DOUGLAS	27,637	H-2
ELKO	33,530	A-7
ESMERALDA	1,344	J-6
EUREKA	1,547	D-8
HUMBOLDT	12,844	A-3
LANDER	6,266	D-7
LINCOLN	3,775	I-12
LYON	20,001	G-3
MINERAL	6,475	H-4
NYE	17,781	H-7
PERSHING	4,336	D-3
STOREY	2,526	G-2
WASHOE	254,667	A-Z
WHITE PINE	9,264	F-10
TOTAL	**1,201,833**	

CITIES AND TOWNS

Note: The first name is that of the city or town, second, that of the county in which it is located, then the population and location on the map.

Austin, Lander G-7
Babbitt, Mineral I-4
● Battle Mountain, Lander, 3,542 .... D-8
● Beatty, Nye, 1,623 .... M-8
Boulder City, Clark, 12,567 .... P-12
Caliente, Lincoln, 1,111 .... L-13
Carlin, Elko, 2,220 .... D-9
Carson City, Independent City,
 40,443 .... H-2
Crystal Bay, Washoe H-1
● Dayton, Lyon, 2,217 .... H-2
East Ely, White Pine H-12
● East Las Vegas, Clark, 11,087 ...... O-12
Elko, Elko, 14,736 .... D-10
Ely, White Pine, 4,756 .... H-12
● Enterprise, Clark, 6,412 .... P-11
Eureka, Eureka G-9
Fallon, Churchill, 6,438 .... G-4
● Fallon Station, Churchill, 1,092 .... G-4
● Fernley, Lyon, 5,164 .... G-3
● Gardnerville, Douglas, 2,177 .... H-2
● Gardnerville Ranchos, Douglas,
 7,455 .... H-2
Goldfield, Esmeralda K-7
● Hawthorne, Mineral, 4,162 .... I-4
Henderson, Clark, 64,942 .... O-12
● Incline Village-Crystal Bay,
 Washoe, 7,119 .... H-1
● Indian Hills, Douglas, 2,544 .... H-2
● Indian Springs, Clark, 1,164 .... N-10
● Johnson Lane, Douglas, 2,551 .... H-2
● Kingsbury, Douglas, 2,238 .... H-1
Las Vegas, Clark, 258,295 .... O-11
● Laughlin, Clark, 4,791 .... R-13
Lovelock, Pershing, 2,069 .... E-4
● McGill, White Pine, 1,258 .... G-12
Mesquite, Clark, 1,871 .... N-14
● Minden, Douglas, 1,441 .... H-2
● Moapa Valley, Clark, 3,444 .... N-13
● Nellis AFB, Clark, 8,377 .... O-12
● New Washoe City, Washoe,
 2,875 .... H-2
North Las Vegas, Clark, 47,707 .... O-11
● Pahrump, Nye, 7,424 .... O-9

● Paradise, Clark, 124,682 .... O-11
Pioche, Lincoln K-13
Reno, Washoe, 133,850 .... G-2
● Silver Springs, Lyon, 2,253 .... G-3
● Smith Valley, Lyon, 1,033 .... I-3
Sparks, Washoe, 53,367 .... G-2
● Spring Creek, Elko, 5,866 .... D-10
● Spring Valley, Clark, 51,726 .... O-11
● Stateline, Douglas, 1,379 .... H-1
● Sun Valley, Washoe, 11,391 .... G-2
● Sunrise Manor, Clark, 95,362 .... O-12
● Tonopah, Nye, 3,616 .... K-7
Virginia City, Storey G-2
Weed Heights, Lyon H-3
Wells, Elko, 1,256 .... C-11
● West Wendover, Elko, 2,007 .... D-13
● Winchester, Clark, 23,365 .... O-11
Winnemucca, Humboldt, 6,134 .... C-6
Yerington, Lyon, 2,367 .... H-3
● Zephyr Cove-Round Hill Village,
 Douglas, 1,434 .... H-1

Explanation of symbols: ● – Census Designated Place (CDP)

New Hampshire

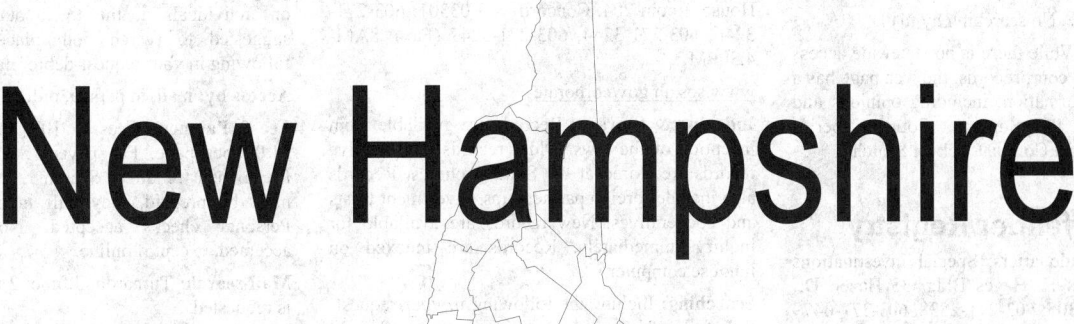

General Help Numbers:

Governor's Office
State House
107 N Main St, Rm 204
Concord, NH 03301-4990
www.state.nh.us/governor/index.html

603-271-2121
Fax 603-271-5686
8AM-5PM

Attorney General's Office
33 Capitol St
Concord, NH 03301-6397
http://webster.state.nh.us/nhdoj

603-271-3658
Fax 603-271-2110
8AM-5PM

Legislative Records
New Hampshire State Library
20 Part St
Concord, NH 03301
http://gencourt.state.nh.us/ie

603-271-2239
Fax 603-271-2205
8AM-4:30PM

State Archives
Division of Records Management & Archives
71 S Fruit St
Concord, NH 03301
http://www.sos.nh.gov/archives/

603-271-2236
Fax 603-271-2272
8AM-4:30PM

State Specifics:

Capital:	Concord Merrimack County
Time Zone:	EST
Number of Counties:	10
Population:	1,287,687
Web Site:	www.state.nh.us

State Agencies

Criminal Records

State Police Headquarters, Criminal Records, James H. Hayes Bldg, 33 Hazen Dr, Concord, NH 03305; 603-271-2538, 603-271-2339 (Fax), 8:15AM-4:15PM.

www.state.nh.us/safety/nhsp/cr.html

Indexing & Storage: Records are available from circa 1900. It takes 1 day before new records are available for inquiry.

Searching: Requester must have "authorization in writing, duly signed and notarized, explicitly allowing the requester to receive such information." Also specify exactly what information is needed. Statutorily-required fingerprint searches include FBI check. Include the following in your request-notarized release, full name, date of birth, any aliases, sex, race. Fingerprint searches are required for certain occupations (i.e. teachers) per state statute. 75% of the records are fingerprint supported.

Access by: mail, in person.

Fee & Payment: The search fee is $10.00 per name. When required, FBI fingerprint searches are an additional $24.00 Fee payee: NH State Police. Prepayment required. Personal checks accepted. No credit cards accepted.

Mail search: Turnaround time: 1 week. A self addressed envelope is requested.

In person search: In person requests are processed immediately.

Statewide Court Records

Administrative Office of Courts, 2 Noble Dr, Supreme Ct Bldg, Concord, NH 03301-6160; 603-271-2521, 603-271-3977 (Fax), 8AM-5PM.

www.courts.state.nh.us/

Note: Except for certain online research capabilities, all court record access must be done at the local level.

Access by: online. No searching by mail.

Online search: While there is no statewide access available for trial court records, the web page has a lot of useful information, including opinions and directives from the Supreme Court, Superior Courts, and District Courts. Click on Search.

Sexual Offender Registry

State Police Headquarters, Special Investigations Unit-SOR, James H. Hayes Bldg, 33 Hazen Dr, Concord, NH 03305; 603-271-2538, 603-271-6479 (Fax), 8:15AM-4:15PM.

www.state.nh.us/safety/nhsp/cr.html

Note: A list of all entries in the database can be accessed through local sheriffs' offices.

Indexing & Storage: It takes 1 day before new records are available for inquiry.

Searching: The agency prefers requesters go to the local police departments if the requester does not have Internet access.

Access by: mail, in person, online.

Fee & Payment: There is no search fee.

Mail search: Limited information is available.

In person search: In person requests are processed immediately.

Online search: For web access, click on the Offenders Against Children link. This list only contains certain information about registered offenders who have committed certain criminal offenses against children. The list also contains outstanding arrest warrants for any sexual offender or offender against children who did not register.

Incarceration Records

New Hampshire Department of Corrections, Offender Records Office, PO Box 14, Concord, NH 03302; 603-271-1825, 603-271-1867 (Fax), 8AM-4PM.

http://www.nh.gov/doc/

Indexing & Storage: Records are available on current and former inmates. It takes up to 3 days before new records are available for inquiry. Records are normally destroyed after 12 years.

Searching: Include the following in your request- full name, DOB helpful. Computerized records go back to 1995. Record requests may also be emailed.

Access by: mail, phone, fax, in person.

Mail search: Turnaround time: 1-2 weeks.

Phone search: Call the number above for a phone name search.

Fax search: Requests may be faxed.

In person search: Searchers must present ID and release info.

Corporation, Limited Partnership, Limited Liability Company, Limited Liability Partnerships, Not For Profit Entities

Trademarks Servicemarks, Trade Names,

Secretary of State, Corporation Division, State House, Room 204, Concord, NH 03301; 603-271-3246, 603-271-3244, 603-271-3247 (Fax), 8AM-4:30PM.

www.sos.nh.gov/corporate

Indexing & Storage: Records are available from inception of the laws. Older records and inactive records are stored at the State Archives. Records also include foreign partnerships, investment trusts and cooperatives. New records are available for inquiry immediately. Records are indexed on inhouse computer.

Searching: Include the following in your request- full name of business, specific records needed. In addition to the articles of incorporation, corporation records include the following information: Annual Reports, Officers, Directors, Prior (merged) names, Inactive and Reserved names.

Access by: mail, phone, fax, in person, online.

Fee & Payment: There is no charge for 20 pages or less. If more than 20 pages, the charge is $.50 per page for every page. Certification is $5.00 plus $1.00 per page. Note that they do not print computer screens, but take copies straight from files. Fee payee: Secretary of State. They will invoice for copy fees, but you must pay in advance for certificates of good standing. Fax accounts may be billed monthly. Personal checks accepted. No credit cards accepted.

Mail search: Turnaround time: 1 to 2 days. A SASE is requested.

Phone search: No fee for telephone request. An information line, 603-271-3246, is open from 9AM-3:30PM. You can obtain name, address, incorporation date, and registered agent, check name availability, and request document copies.

Fax search: Fax requests are considered expedited service. Requests received by 2PM will be completed same business day. Fee is $10.00 per request, two may be faxed per call.

In person search: You may request information in person, the agency does the copying.

Online search: A free business name lookup is available at the website. The agency is converting to a new system that will allow purchase of copies and certificates online.

Other access: Corporation, LLC, or trade name monthly Excel files are $50.00 each or $500.00 for a 1 year subscription. A list of all non-profits on file is available for $250.00.

Expedited service: You may fax requests for same day service (if received by 2 PM) for information on company status, details, annual reports (current and past 2 years only), and name availability. You may request 2 names or items per fax. Add $10.00 per package.

Uniform Commercial Code, Federal and State Tax Liens

UCC Division, Secretary of State, 25 Capitol St, State House Annex, 3rd Floor, Concord, NH 03301; 603-271-3276, 9AM-3:30PM (searches).

www.sos.nh.gov/ucc//index.htm

Indexing & Storage: Records are available for active filings only. It takes three months or less before new records are available for inquiry.

Records are normally destroyed after one year after termination.

Searching: Use search request form UCC-11. In general, tax liens on businesses are filed here and on individuals at the town/county level. It is suggested to search both places. Include the following in your request-debtor name.

Access by: mail, in person, online.

Fee & Payment: Fees is $10.00 per name, copies $1.00 per page. Fee payee: Secretary of State. Prepayment required. Search requests and filings must be prepaid, they will invoice for copies. Personal checks accepted. No credit cards accepted, except if online.

Mail search: Turnaround time: 2 weeks. A SASE is requested.

In person search: See expedited service.

Online search: Visit www.sos.nh.gov/ucconline for commercial online access to records. Accounts may be established using either automated clearing house (ACH) debit account or credit card. The fee is $25.00 per debtor name, or for $5,000.00 subscription fee unlimited online searches for available for one full year.

Expedited service: For in person requests. One hour service is $50.00, 24 hour service is $25.00.

Sales Tax Registrations
State does not impose sales tax.

Birth Certificates

Office of Community and Public Health, Bureau of Vital Records, 6 Hazen Dr, Concord, NH 03301-6527; 603-271-4650, 603-271-4654 (Recording), 800-852-3345 x4651 (In-state), 603-223-6614 (Fax), 8:30AM-4PM.

www.sos.nh.gov/vitalrecords/index.html

Note: For genealogical purposes, birth records prior to 1903 may be released without restriction.

Indexing & Storage: Records are available from 1640 to present. Records are on computer since 1990, indexed since 1948. Records are indexed on microfiche, index cards, computer.

Searching: Must have a signed release from person of record or immediate family member or show proof of "tangible interest." Order forms are available at the website. Include the following in your request-full name, names of parents, mother's maiden name, date of birth, place of birth, relationship to person of record, reason for information request.

Access by: mail, phone, fax, in person, online.

Fee & Payment: The search fee is $12.00 per record and $8.00 for each additional copy of the same record. Fee payee: Treasurer of State of New Hampshire. Prepayment required. Credit cards accepted for expedited service only. Personal checks accepted. Credit cards accepted: MasterCard, Visa, AmEx, Discover.

Mail search: Turnaround time: 4 weeks. A SASE is requested.

Phone search: Must use credit card for additional $6.00 fee.

Fax search: See expedited service.

In person search: Turnaround time while you wait.

Online search: Available via state designated vendor at www.vitalchek.com. Use of credit card ($6.00 fee) is required.

Expedited service: Expedited service is available for fax, phone and online orders. Turnaround time: 3 to 4 days. Add $14.50 per package for overnight delivery. Add regular fees and credit card fee.

Death Records

Office of Community and Public Health, Bureau of Vital Records, 6 Hazen Dr, Concord, NH 03301-6527; 603-271-4650, 603-271-4654 (Recording), 800-852-3345 x4651 (In-state), 603-223-6614 (Fax), 8:30AM-4PM.

www.sos.nh.gov/vitalrecords/index.html

Note: For genealogical purposes, death records prior to 1948 may be released without restriction.

Indexing & Storage: Records are available from 1640 to present. Records are computerized since 1990, indexed on computer since 1948. Records are indexed on microfiche, index cards, computer.

Searching: Must have a signed release from immediate family member. Include the following in your request-full name, date of death, place of death, parents' names, relationship to person of record, reason for information request. The following data is not released: cause of death.

Access by: mail, phone, in person, online.

Fee & Payment: The search fee is $12.00 per record, additional copies are $8.00 each. Fee payee: Treasurer of State of New Hampshire. Prepayment required. Credit cards accepted for expedited service only. Personal checks accepted. Credit cards accepted: MasterCard, Visa, AmEx, Discover.

Mail search: Turnaround time: up to 4 weeks. A SASE is requested.

Phone search: Must use a credit card for an additional $6.00 fee.

In person search: Turnaround time while you wait.

Online search: Available via state designated vendor at www.vitalchek.com. Use of credit card ($6.00 fee) is required.

Expedited service: Expedited service is available for fax, phone and online orders. Turnaround time: 3 to 4 days. Add $14.50 per package for overnight delivery. Add regular fees and credit card fee.

Marriage Certificates

Office of Community and Public Health, Bureau of Vital Records & Health Statistics, 6 Hazen Dr, Concord, NH 03301-6527; 603-271-4650, 603-271-4654 (Recording), 800-852-3345 x4651 (In-state), 603-223-6614 (Fax), 8:30AM-4PM.

www.sos.nh.gov/vitalrecords/index.html

Note: For genealogical purposes, marriage records prior to 1948 may be released without restriction.

Indexing & Storage: Records are available from 1640 to present. Records are computerized from 1990, indexed on computer since 1948. Records are indexed on microfiche, index cards.

Searching: Must have a signed release from persons of record or immediate family member. Include the following in your request-names of husband and wife, date of marriage, place or county of marriage, relationship to person of record, reason for information request, wife's maiden name.

Access by: mail, phone, in person, online.

Fee & Payment: The search fee is $12.00 per record, each additional copy is $8.00. Fee payee: Treasurer of State of New Hampshire. Prepayment required. Credit cards accepted for expedited service only, with $6.00 addional fee. Credit cards accepted: MasterCard, Visa, AmEx, Discover.

Mail search: Turnaround time: up to 4 weeks. A SASE is requested.

Phone search: Must use a credit card for an additional $6.00 fee.

In person search: Turnaround time while you wait.

Online search: Available via state designated vendor at www.vitalchek.com. Use of credit card ($6.00 fee) is required.

Expedited service: Expedited service is available for fax, phone and online orders. Turnaround time: 3 to 5 days. Add $14.50 per package for overnight service. Add regular search fee and credit card fee.

Divorce Records

Office of Community and Public Health, Bureau of Vital Records, 6 Hazen Dr, Concord, NH 03301-6527; 603-271-4650, 603-271-4654 (Recording), 800-852-3345 x4651 (In-state), 603-271-3447 (Fax), 8:30AM-4PM.

www.sos.nh.gov/vitalrecords/index.html

Note: For genealogical purposes, divorce records prior to 1948 may be released without restriction.

Indexing & Storage: Records are available from 1640 to present. Records are computerized since 1990, indexed on computer since 1948. Records are indexed on microfiche, index cards.

Searching: Must have a signed release from person of record or immediate family member. Include the following in your request-names of husband and wife, date of divorce, year divorce case began, city or town, case number (if known), relationship to person of record, reason for information request.

Access by: mail, phone, fax, in person, online.

Fee & Payment: The search fee is $12.00 per record, additional copies are $8.00 each. Fee payee: Treasurer of State of New Hampshire. Prepayment required. Credit cards accepted for expedited service only. Personal checks accepted. Credit cards accepted: MasterCard, Visa, AmEx, Discover.

Mail search: Turnaround time: up to 4 weeks. A SASE is requested.

Phone search: Must use a credit card for an additional $6.00 fee.

Fax search: No searching by fax.

In person search: Turnaround time while you wait.

Online search: Available via state designated vendor at www.vitalchek.com. Use of credit card ($6.00 fee) is required.

Expedited service: Expedited service is available for fax, phone and online orders. Turnaround time: 3 to 5 days. Add $14.50 per package for overnight service. Add search fee and credit card fee.

Workers' Compensation Records

Labor Department, Workers Compensation Division, 95 Pleasant St, Concord, NH 03301;

603-271-3174, 603-271-6149 (Fax), 8AM-4:30PM.

Indexing & Storage: Records are available from 1996 to present. Records prior to 1996 are kept at the State Archives. However, one must go through this office for records. It takes 1-2 weeks before new records are available for inquiry. Records are indexed on microfilm. Records are normally destroyed after 10 years.

Searching: Must have an authorized release from claimant. Include the following in your request-claimant name, Social Security Number, date of accident, place of employment at time of accident.

Access by: mail, fax.

Fee & Payment: There is no search fee, copy fee is $.35 per page. Fee payee: State of NH Prepayment required. Personal checks accepted. No credit cards accepted.

Mail search: Turnaround time: 2 to 3 weeks. A SASE is requested.

Fax search: Same as mail request.

Driver Records

Department of Motor Vehicles, Driving Records, 33 Hazen Dr, Concord, NH 03305; 603-271-2322, 8:15AM-4:15PM.

www.nh.gov/safety/dmv/

Note: New Hampshire recommends going to the local courts for copies of tickets or to state Financial Responsibility agency.

Indexing & Storage: Records are available for 5 years for moving violations and 10 for DWIs. Surrendered license information remains on the system at least 5 years after the expiration date. The driver's address is on manually processed records, but not on electronic records. It takes 2 to 3 weeks normally before new records are available for inquiry.

Searching: Use of DSMV Form 505 is recommended. Frequent requesters should establish an account with the state. Include the following in your request-full name, date of birth. Casual (non-permissible use) requesters are required to submit the subject's notarized signature on the Form 505. The license number is not required for a search, but is suggested.

Access by: mail, in person, online.

Fee & Payment: Records are $8.00. If you wish the record certified the fee is $10.00. Fee payee: Department of Safety. Prepayment required. Personal checks accepted. No credit cards accepted.

Mail search: Turnaround time: 5 days. Mail-in requests must include requester's name and address. A SASE is requested.

In person search: Five requests can be processed while you wait.

Online search: Online access is offered for approved commercial accounts. The system is open 22 hours a day. Searches are by license number or by name and DOB. Fee is $8.00 per record. For more information, call the Director's Office.

Other access: Overnight magnetic tape access is available for higher volume users. Minimum order is 50 requests.

Vehicle Identification

Department of Safety, Bureau of Titles, 33 Hazen Dr, Concord, NH 03305; 603-271-3111 (Bureau of Title), 603-271-0369 (Fax), 8:15AM-4:15PM.

http://nh.gov/safety/dmv/registration/index.html

Indexing & Storage: Records are available 11 years to present. It takes 2 weeks before new records are available for inquiry. Records are normally destroyed after microfilming.

Searching: The agency will only release to requesters authorized by statute or to casual requesters with a signed release from subject. Include the following in your request-Form DSMV 505. Form requires notarized signature of the requester.

Access by: mail, in person.

Fee & Payment: The fee is $20.00 for a title and lien history and $5.00 for a registration listing. Fee payee: Department of Safety. Prepayment required. Personal checks and major credit cards accepted.

Mail search: Turnaround time: 4 to 5 days.

In person search: Turnaround time while you wait, depending on workload of personnel.

Other access: Bulk information is available to approved venders per DPPA. Call 603-271-2314 for information.

Vessel Registration

Department of Safety, Bureau of Registration, Boat Desk, 33 Hazen Dr, Concord, NH 03305; 603-271-2333, 603-271-3242 (Liens), 603-271-1061 (Fax), 8:15AM-4:15PM.

Indexing & Storage: Records are available for current and expired registration records. All motorized boats and all sailboats over 12 ft must be registered. Boats are not titled and liens on boats are found at the Secretary of State - 603-271-3242.

Searching: Records are restricted to those authorized by statute. Authorization is stricter than the DPPA requirements. Include the following in your request-owner's name, plate number or VIN is required to search.

Access by: mail, in person.

Fee & Payment: The fee is $10.00 per record. Fee payee: State of New Hampshire. Prepayment required. Personal checks accepted. Visa. MC, AmEx accepted.

Mail search: Turnaround time: timely manner.

In person search: Turnaround time is immediate.

Accident Reports

Department of Safety, Crash Section, 23 Hazen Dr, Concord, NH 03305; 603-271-2128, 8:15AM-4:15PM.

Indexing & Storage: Records are available for 5 years. Records are indexed on computer. It takes 3 to 4 weeks before new records are available for inquiry. Records are normally destroyed after 10 years.

Searching: Access is not open to the public due to Privacy Act, Chapter 295:260:14. This law requires a notarized DSMV 505 Form to be filled out by the subject involved or by an insurance representative licensed to write auto policies in this state. Include the following in your request-full name, date of birth, date of accident, location of accident. It is suggested to include both operators' names in the request.

Access by: mail, in person.

Fee & Payment: The fee is $1.00 per page. With a $5.00 minimum. There is no charge for a "no record found." Requesters are notified of the fee for reports after the report has become available. Fee payee: Department of Safety. Prepayment required. Personal checks and credit cards accepted.

Mail search: Turnaround time: 3 to 4 weeks. A SASE is requested.

In person search: Over the counter requests are available.

Voter Registration

Records not maintained by a state level agency.

Note: All records are kept by Town Clerks. Records are open.

GED Certificates

Adult Education - Dept of Education, GED Testing, 21 S Fruit Street #20, Concord, NH 03301; 603-271-6699, 603-271-3454 (Fax), 8AM-4:30PM.

www.ed.state.nh.us/GEDhome.htm

Indexing & Storage: Records are indexed on microfiche.

Searching: Include the following in your request-Social Security Number, date of birth, year of issue, name at the time, and a signed release. The date is needed since records are filed by year. The signed release is needed for either a verification or transcript.

Access by: mail, fax.

Fee & Payment: The fee is $5.00 for a transcript, there is no fee for a verification. Fee payee: State of New Hampshire. Prepayment required. No credit cards accepted.

Mail search: Turnaround time: 2 days. No SASE is required.

Fax search: You may request verifications by fax.

Hunting and Fishing License Information

Fish & Game Department, Licensing Department, Eleven Hazen Dr, Concord, NH 03301; 603-271-3421, 603-271-5829 (Fax), 8AM-4:30PM.

www.wildlife.state.nh.us

Indexing & Storage: Records are available for 3 years back to present. Records are indexed on computer. It takes 2 to 4 months before new records are available for inquiry. Records are indexed on inhouse computer. Records are normally destroyed after 3 years.

Searching: Requests must be in writing using their form. Include the following in your request-full name, date of birth. The following data is not released: financial information.

Access by: mail, in person.

Fee & Payment: There may be a charge of $.10 per page. Fee payee: NH Fish & Game. Prepayment required. Personal checks, Visa, M/C accepted.

Mail search: Turnaround time: 3-5 days. Request must be in writing with payment in advance.A SASE is required.

In person search: Written request is require with payment in advance.

Other access: Mailing labels are available at a cost of $25.00 plus $.10 per label.

New Hampshire State Licensing Agencies

Licenses Searchable Online

Architect #34 .... www.state.nh.us/jtboard/arlist.htm
Bank #1 .... http://webster.state.nh.us/banking/banking.html
Credit Union #1 .... http://webster.state.nh.us/banking/banking.html
Drug Wholesaler/Manufacturer #27 . www.state.nh.us/pharmacy/NH%20Wholesaler%20List.html
Engineer #34 .... http://nh.neinetwork.com/cgi-bin/professional/nhprof/search.pl
Forester #34 .... www.state.nh.us/jtboard/forlist.htm
Geologist #34 .... http://nh.neinetwork.com/cgi-bin/professional/nhprof/search.pl
Liquor License #35 .... www.state.nh.us/liquor/index.html
Lobbyist #42 .... www.sos.nh.gov/lobbyist%20information.htm
Marital Mediator #36 .... www.nh.gov/marital/mediators.htm
Nurse, LPN/Practical/Advanced #18 www.nhlicenses.nh.gov/WebLookUp/
Nursing Assistant #18 .... www.nhlicenses.nh.gov/WebLookUp/
Optometrist #23 .... www.arbo.org/odfinder/LicSearch.asp
Pharmacist #27 .... www.state.nh.us/pharmacy/NH%20Pharmacist%20List.html
Pharmacy #27 .... www.state.nh.us/pharmacy/NH%20Pharmacy%20List.html
Pharmacy Technician #27 .... www.state.nh.us/pharmacy/NH%20Tech%20List.html
Pharmacy, Mail Order #27 .... www.state.nh.us/pharmacy/NH%20Mail-Order%20List.html
Physician #19 .... www.state.nh.us/medicine
Physician Assistant #19 .... www.state.nh.us/medicine
Public Health Clinic #27 .... www.state.nh.us/pharmacy/NH%20Clinic%20List.html
Real Estate Agent/Sales #32 .... www.nhlicenses.nh.gov/WebLookUp/
Real Estate Appraiser #31 .... www.asc.gov
Real Estate Broker #32 .... www.nhlicenses.nh.gov/WebLookUp/
Real Estate Firm #32 .... www.nhlicenses.nh.gov/WebLookUp/
Scientist, Natural #34 .... http://nh.neinetwork.com/cgi-bin/professional/nhprof/search.pl
Scientist, Wetlands #34 .... http://nh.neinetwork.com/cgi-bin/professional/nhprof/search.pl
Surveyor, Land #34 .... www.state.nh.us/jtboard/lsis.htm
Tobacco Law Enforcement #35 ...... www.state.nh.us/liquor/index.html

New Hampshire Licensing Quick Finder

Accessibility Lift Mechanic #28 603-271-2585
Acupuncturist #10 603-335-1425
Alcohol/Drug Counselor #41 603-271-6100
Ambulance Attendant #22 603-271-7048
Ambulance Service #22 603-271-7048
Architect #34 603-271-2219
Asbestos Abatement Worker #46 603-271-4609
Athletic Trainer #45 603-271-8389
Attorney #43 603-271-2646
Auctioneer #3 603-271-3242
Audiologist #47 603-271-4501
Bail Bondsman #50 603-271-1463
Bail Recovery Agent #50 603-271-1463
Bank #1 603-271-3561
Bank Holding Company #1 603-271-3561
Bank, Cooperative #1 603-271-3561
Barber #4 603-271-3608
Betting Location #48 603-271-2158
Bingo/Lottery Operation #44 603-271-3391
Boiler Inspector #28 603-271-2585
Boxing/Wrestling Contestant #30 603-627-2071
Boxing/Wrestling Mgr./Promoter #30 ... 603-627-2071
Boxing/Wrestling Referee/Second/Timekeeper #30
.... 603-627-2071

Canadian Broker/Dealer #50 603-271-1463
Cash dispensing machine, non-bank #1 603-271-3561
Child Care Facility #21 603-271-4624
Child Placing Agency #10 800-852-3345
Chiropractor #14 603-271-4560
Concealed Weapons License, Non-Resident #39
.... 603-271-3575
Corrections Officer #49 603-271-2133
Cosmetologist #4 603-271-3608
Court Reporter #37 603-271-2030
Credit Union #1 603-271-3561
Debt Adjuster #1 603-271-3561
Dental Hygienist #15 603-271-4561
Dentist #15 603-271-4561
Dog Trainer #48 603-271-2158
Drug Wholesaler/Manufacturer #27 603-271-2350
Electrician, Master/Journeyman/Apprentice #29
.... 603-271-3748
Electrologist #12 603-271-4814
Elevator Inspector/ Mechanic #28 603-271-2585
Embalmer #17 603-271-4648
Energy Facility Construction #8 603-271-3503
Energy Facility Site #8 603-271-3503
Engineer #34 603-271-2219

Esthetician #4 603-271-3608
Explosive Storage License #39 603-271-3575
Explosives Competency License #39 ... 603-271-3575
Fire Inspector #38 603-271-2661
Firefighter #38 603-271-2661
Fireworks Competency License #39 603-271-3575
Forester #34 603-271-2219
Foster Family Home #10 800-852-3345
Funeral Director #17 603-271-4648
Geologist #34 603-271-2219
Hearing Aid Dispenser/Fitter #25 603-433-7512
High/Medium Voltage Electrician/Trainee #29
.... 603-271-3748
Horse Trainer #48 603-271-2158
Insurance Adjuster #33 603-271-2261
Insurance Advisor/Consultant #33 603-271-2261
Insurance Agent/Broker #33 603-271-2261
Insurance Company #33 603-271-2261
Investment Advisor #50 603-271-1463
Jockey #48 603-271-2158
Leadworker #46 603-271-4609
Liquor License #35 603-271-3523
Loan Company, Small #1 603-271-3561
Loan Production Office #1 603-271-3561

Lobbyist #42 603-271-3242	Pesticide Disposal/Labeling #6 603-271-3550	Respiratory Care Practitioner #45........603-271-8389
Manicurist #4 603-271-3608	Pesticide User #6 603-271-3550	Savings Bank #1 603-271-3561
Marital Mediator #36............................603-271-6593	Pharmacist #27 603-271-2350	School Administrator #7 603-271-3871
Marriage & Family Therapist #26 603-271-6762	Pharmacy #27 603-271-2350	Scientist, Natural #34 603-271-2219
Mental Health Counselor, Clinical #26 ..603-271-6762	Pharmacy Technician #27....................603-271-2350	Scientist, Wetlands #34.......................603-271-2219
Midwife #24................................603-224-0049	Physical Therapist #45 603-271-8389	Securities Broker/Dealer/Agent #50.....603-271-1463
Mortgage (1st) Banker, Non-Depository #1	Physical Therapist Assistant #45 603-271-8389	Securities Salesperson #50 603-271-1463
....603-271-3561	Physician #19 603-271-6936	Security Guard #39 603-271-3575
Mortgage (1st) Broker #1......................603-271-3561	Physician Assistant #19 603-271-6936	Shorthand Reporter #37......................603-271-2030
Mortgage (2nd) Home Loan Lender #1.603-271-3561	Plumber #9 603-271-3267	Social Worker #25...............................603-433-7512
Mortgage Servicer #1 603-271-3561	Podiatrist #19......................................603-271-6936	Social Worker, Clinical #26 603-271-6762
Motor Vehicle Retail Seller #1 603-271-3561	Police Officer/Detective #49.................603-271-2133	Speech-Language Pathologist #45......603-273-8389
Motor Vehicle Sales Finance Co. #1 603-271-3561	Private Detective #39 603-271-3575	Surveyor, Land #34..............................603-271-2219
Naturopath #10...............................603-271-4814	Psychologist #26 603-271-6762	Tattoo Establishm't/Practitioner #13 603-271-4592
Notary Public #42 603-271-3242	Public Accountant-CPA #2 603-271-3286	Teacher #7 603-271-3871
Nurse, LPN/Practical/Advanced #18....603-271-6599	Public Health Clinic #27......................603-271-2350	Tobacco Law Enforcement #35 603-271-8531
Nursing Assistant #18..........................603-271-6599	Pump Installer #40..............................603-271-3503	Trust Company #1................................603-271-3561
Nursing Home Administrator #16 603-271-6936	Racing Owner #48...............................603-271-2158	Vendor, Itinerant #30...........................603-627-2071
Occupational Therapist #45...................603-271-8389	Racing Professional #48 603-271-2158	Veterinary Medicine #5 603-271-3706
Occupational Therapy Assistant #45....603-271-8389	Real Estate Agent/Sales #32 603-271-6658	Vocational Rehabilitation Provider #28.603-271-3328
Ophthalmic Dispenser #10 603-271-5127	Real Estate Appraiser #31 603-271-6186	Waste Water Treatment Plant Operator #40
Optometrist #23................................603-271-6936	Real Estate Broker #32 603-271-2702	603-271-3503
Pastoral Psychotherapist #26..............603-271-6762	Real Estate Firm #32...........................603-271-2702	Water Distrib'n System Operator #40 ...603-271-3503
Pesticide Dealer/Seller #6 603-271-3550	Residential Care Facility, Children #21.603-271-4624	Water Well Contractor #40...................603-271-3503

New Hampshire Licensing Agency Information

1 Banking Department, 64B Old Suncook Road, Concord, NH 03301; 603-271-3561, Fax: 603-271-1090. http://webster.state.nh.us/banking/

2 Department of State, Board of Accountancy, 6 Chenell Dr #220, Concord, NH 03301; 603-271-3286, Fax: 603-271-8702. www.state.nh.us/accountancy/index.html Email: lcollier@boa.state.nh.us

3 Secretary of State, Board of Auctioneers, 107 N Main St., State House Rm 204, Concord, NH 03301; 603-271-3242, Fax: 603-271-6316. www.state.nh.us/sos/administration.htm

4 Board of Barbering, Cosmetology & Esthetics, 2 Industrial Park Dr, Concord, NH 03301; 603-271-3608, Fax: 603-271-8889. http://webster.state.nh.us/cosmet/

5 Board of Veterinary Medicine, PO Box 2042 (25 Capitol St), Concord, NH 03302-2042; 603-271-3706, Fax: 604-271-1109. www.nh.gov/veterinary Email: pduncklee@agr.state.nh.us Note: Lists of currently licensed veterinarians are available for $4.00 on diskette or by e-mail. Lists on paper are $.25 per page plus postage.

6 Department of Agriculture, 25 Capitol St 2nd Fl, Concord, NH 03301-2042; 603-271-3551, Fax: 603-271-1109. http://agriculture.nh.gov/constants/contact.htm

7 Department of Education, Division of Educational Improvement, 101 Pleansant St, State Office Park S, Concord, NH 03301-3860; 603-271-3494, Fax: 603-271-1953. www.ed.state.nh.us   Email: kcafiero@ed.state.nh.us

8 Department of Environmental Services, Energy Services Division, 6 Hazen Dr. POB 95, Concord, NH 03301; 603-271-3503, Fax: 603-271-8013. www.des.state.nh.us

9 Plumbing Licensing Board, PO Box 1386, Concord, NH 03302-1386; 603-271-3267, Fax: 603-271-6656. http://webster.state.nh.us/plumbing/ Email: info@plumbing.state.nh

10 Department of Health & Human Svcs, Licensing & Regulative Services, 129 Pleasant, Concord, NH 03301; 800-852-3345, Fax: 603-271-4729. www.dhhs.state.nh.us/DHHS/Programs+Services/default.htmf   Email: lmeffert@dhhs.state.nh.us

12 Department of Health & Human Svcs, Advisory Board of Electrologists, 129 Pleasant, Concord, NH 03301; 603-271-4814, Fax: 603-271-5590. www.dhhs.state.nh.us/DHHS/LRS/CONTACT+INFO/default.htm

13 Department of Health & Human Svcs, Advisory Board of Massage Practitioners, 129 Pleasant, Concord, NH 03301; 603-271-4592, Fax: 603-271-4968. www.dhhs.state.nh.us/DHHS/LRS/CONTACT+INFO/default.htm

14 Department of Health & Human Svcs, Board of Chiropractic Examiners, 6 Hazen Dr, Concord, NH 03301-6527; 603-271-4560, Fax: 603-271-5199.

15 Department of Health & Human Svcs, Board of Dental Examiners, 2 Industrial Park Dr, Concord, NH 03301-8520; 603-271-4561, Fax: 603-271-6702. http://webster.state.nh.us/dental/ Email: pthomson@nhsa.state.nh.us

16 Board of Examiners of Nursing Home Administrators, 2 Industrial Park Dr #8, Concord, NH 03301; 603-271-4728, Fax: 603-271-6702.

17 Department of Health & Human Svcs, Board of Funeral Directors & Embalmers, 29 Hazen Dr, Concord, NH 03301-6507; 603-271-4648, Fax: 603-271-3447. http://webster.state.nh.us/funeral/ Email: funeralbd@dhhs.state.nh.us

18 Department of Health & Human Svcs, Board of Nursing, PO Box 3898, 78 Regional Dr, Bldg B, Concord, NH 03302-3898; 603-271-2323, Fax: 603-271-6605. www.state.nh.us/nursing/ Email: sgoodness@nursing.state.nh.us Search Database at www.nhlicenses.nh.gov/WebLookUp/ Note: They will sell/provide lists. Contact Kathy Crumb at 603-271-2323.

19 NH Board of Medicine, Board of Podiatry, 2 Industrial Park Dr #8, Concord, NH 03301; 603-271-1203, Fax: 603-271-6702. www.state.nh.us/podiatry/index.html

21 Department of Health & Human Svcs, Bureau of Child Care Licensing, 129 Pleasant St, Brown Bldg, Concord, NH 03301-3857; 603-271-4624, Fax: 603-271-4782. www.dhhs.state.nh.us/DHHS/BCCL/default.htm Note: For a $50.00 fee you can receive our area list on disk.

22 Department of Safety, Division of Emergency Medical Services, 10 Hazen Dr, Concord, NH 03305-0003; 603-271-4568, Fax: 603-271-4567. http://webster.state.nh.us/safety/ems/ Email: tfortier@nhems.mv.com

23 Board of Registration in Optometry, 2 Industrial Park Dr. # 8, Concord, NH 03301; 603-271-2428, Fax: 603-271-6702. http://webster.state.nh.us/optometry/ Search Database at www.arbo.org/odfinder/LicSearch.asp

24 Department of Health & Human Svcs, New Hampshire Midwifery Council, 585 Hopkinton Road, Hopkinton, NH 03229; 603-224-0049, Fax: 603-224-0049.

25 New Hampshire Board of Hearing Care Providers, 8 Fillmore Rd., Portsmouth, NH 03801; 603-433-7512.

26 Board of Mental Health Practices, 49 Donovan St, Concord, NH 03301; 603-271-6762, Fax: 603-271-3950. www.nh.gov/mhpb/ Note: Will do phone verifications.

27 State of New Hampshire, Board of Pharmacy, 57 Regional Dr, Concord, NH 03301-8518; 603-271-2350, Fax: 603-271-2856. www.state.nh.us/pharmacy Email: nhpharmacy@nhsa.state.nh.us Search Database at www.state.nh.us/pharmacy/database2.html

28 Department of Labor, 95 Pleasant St, State Office Park S, Concord, NH 03301-3836; 603-271-3176, Fax: 603-271-2668. www.state.nh.us/dol/index.htm

29 Electricians' Licensing Board, 2 Industrial Park Dr (PO Box 646, 03302-0646), Concord, NH 03302-0646; 603-271-3748, Fax: 603-271-2257. http://webster.state.nh.us/electrician/ Email: inspectors@elecboard.state.nh.us

30 Department of State, Boxing & Wrestling Commission, 1791 Bodwell Rd., Manchester, NH 03109; 603-627-2071.

31 Real Estate Appraiser Board, 25 Capitol St, Rm 426, Concord, NH 03301-6312; 603-271-6186, Fax: 603-271-6513. http://nh.gov/nhreab/ Email: maureen.tully@nhreab.stste.nh.us Search at www.asc.gov Note: Complete lists - $50.00. Individual towns - free, call 603-371-6186.

32 Department of State, Real Estate Commission, 25 Capitol St Rm 434, Concord, NH 03301; 603-271-2701, Fax: 603-271-1039. www.nh.gov/nhrec Email: nhrec@nhrec.state.nh.us Search Database at www.nhlicenses.nh.gov/WebLookUp/ Note: Lists of salespersons,

brokers,and or firms can be purchased by contacting the commission at 603-271-2701.

33 Insurance Department, Division of Licensing, 56 Old Suncook Rd, Concord, NH 03301-7131; 603-271-2261, Fax: 603-271-1406. http://webster.state.nh.us/insurance/ Email: Requests@ins.state.nh.us

34 Joint Board of Licensure & Certification, 57 Regional Dr, Concord, NH 03301; 603-271-2219, Fax: 603-271-6990. www.state.nh.us/jtboard/home.htm Email: llavertu@nhsa.state.nh.us Search Database at http://nh.neinetwork.com/cgi-bin/professional/nhprof/search.pl Note: All the professions under this Joint Board can be searched at http://nh.neinetwork.com/cgi-bin/professional/nhprof/search.pl.

35 Licensing & Enforcement, Liquor Commission, 10 Commercial St, Concord, NH 03301; 603-271-3523, Fax: 603-271-3758. www.state.nh.us/liquor/index.html

36 c/o Judicial Council, Marital Mediator Certification Board, 25 Capitol St Rm 424, Concord, NH 03301; 603-271-6593, Fax: 603-271-1112. www.nh.gov/marital/index.htm Search Database at www.nh.gov/marital/mediators.htm

37 Superior Court Center, 17 Chenell Dr #1, Concord, NH 03301; 603-271-2030, Fax: 603-271-2080.

38 Department of Safety, Division of Fire Standards & Training, 33 Hazen Dr, Concord, NH 03305-0001; 603-271-2661, Fax: 603-271-1091. www.state.nh.us/safety/fst/index.html Email: fireacademy@safety.state.nh.us

39 State Police, Permits and License Unit, 10 Hazen Dr, Concord, NH 03305; 603-271-3575. www.state.nh.us/safety/nhsp/

40 Department of Environmental Services, Water Division, 6 Hazen Dr PO Box 95, Concord, NH 03302-0095; 603-271-3503, Fax: 603-271-2867. www.des.state.nh.us Email: pip@des.state.nh.us

41 Bureau of Substance Abuse Services, 105 Pleasant St, Concord, NH 03301; 603-271-6100, Fax: 603-271-6116.

42 Office of Secretary of State, 107 N Main St, State House Rm 204, Concord, NH 03301-4989; 603-271-3242, Fax: 603-271-6316. http://webster.state.nh.us/sos

43 Supreme Court, Attn: Attorney Registration, 1 Noble Dr, Concord, NH 03301; 603-271-2646, Fax: 603-271-6630. www.courts.state.nh.us

44 New Hampshire Lottery, Bingo/Lucky 7 Division, Sweepstakes Commission, 14 Integra Dr, Concord, NH 03301-1208; 603-271-3391, Fax: 603-271-1160. www.state.nh.us/lottery/nhlotto.htm

45 Department of Health & Human Svcs, Office of Allied Health Professions, 2 Industrial Park Dr, Concord, NH 03301-8520; 603-271-8389, Fax: 603-271-6702. www.dhhs.state.nh.us

46 Dept. of Health & Human Svcs, Bureau of Health Risk Assessment, 6 Hazen Dr, Concord, NH 03301-6527; 603-271-4609, Fax: 603-271-2667.

47 Board of Hearing Care Providers, Division of Public Health Services, 6 Hazen Dr, Concord, NH 03301; 603-271-4501.

48 Pari-Mutuel Commission, 244 N Main St 3rd Fl, Concord, NH 03301; 603-271-2158, Fax: 603-271-3381. http://webster.state.nh.us/nhpmc/

49 Police Standards & Training Council, 17 Institution Dr, Concord, NH 03301-7413; 603-271-2133.

50 Department of State, Bureau of Securities Regulation, State House Rm 204, Concord, NH 03301; 603-271-1463, Fax: 603-271-7933. www.sos.nh.gov/securities

New Hampshire Federal Courts

The following list indicates the district and division name for each county in the state. If the bankruptcy court location is different from the district court, then the location of the bankruptcy court appears in parentheses.

County/Court Cross Reference

Belknap	Concord (Manchester)	Hillsborough	Concord (Manchester)
Carroll	Concord (Manchester)	Merrimack	Concord (Manchester)
Cheshire	Concord (Manchester)	Rockingham	Concord (Manchester)
Coos	Concord (Manchester)	Strafford	Concord (Manchester)
Grafton	Concord (Manchester)	Sullivan	Concord (Manchester)

US District Court

District of New Hampshire

Concord Division Warren B Rudman Courthouse, 55 Pleasant St, #110, Concord, NH 03301 (Use mail address for courier delivery) 603-225-1423. www.nhd.uscourts.gov

Counties: Belknap, Carroll, Cheshire, Coos, Grafton, Hillsborough, Merrimack, Rockingham, Strafford, Sullivan.

Indexing & Storage: New cases available in the index 24 hours after filing date.

Fee & Payment: Payment may be made by money order, cashier check, business check. Personal checks are not accepted. Payee: Clerk, U.S. District Court.

Phone Search: Only docket information available by phone.

Mail Search: A SASE not required.

In Person Search: Fee charged if court conducts your in person search for you. Public copiers available.

PACER: PACER is available online at http://pacer.nhd.uscourts.gov. Records purged every two years. New records are online after 1 day.

Electronic Filing: Electronic filing information online at https://ecf.nhd.uscourts.gov

U.S. Bankruptcy Court

District of New Hampshire

Manchester Division Room 404, 275 Chestnut St, Manchester, NH 03101 (courier address: Use mail address for courier delivery) 603-222-2600, Fax: 603-666-7408. www.nhb.uscourts.gov

Counties: Belknap, Carroll, Cheshire, Coos, Grafton, Hillsborough, Merrimack, Rockingham, Strafford, Sullivan.

Indexing & Storage: Cases indexed by debtor as well as by case number. New cases available in the index 24 hours after filing date.

Fee & Payment: Payment may be made by money order, cashier check, personal check, Visa or Mastercard. Debtor checks are not accepted. Payee: Clerk, U.S. Bankruptcy Court. Will fax docket listings up to 5 pages.

Phone Search: Only the case number, name, trustee, attorney for the debtor and deadlines will be released. Automated voice case information service (VCIS) is available. Call VCIS at 800-851-8954 or 603-666-7424. Will fax docket listings up to 5 pages.

Mail Search: A SASE not required.

In Person Search: Fee charged if court conducts your in person search for you.

PACER: PACER is available online at http://pacer.nhb.uscourts.gov. Records purged every six months. New civil records are online after 2 days.

Electronic Filing: Electronic filing information online at https://ecf.nhb.uscourts.gov

Standards for Federal Courts: The search fee is $20.00 per item (one party name or case number). Certification fee is $7.00 per document. Copy fee is $.50 per page. All fees standard unless noted in profile. Mail Search: always enclose a stamped self addressed envelope unless otherwise noted. Most courts accept fax requests or will suggest a copying/search vendor. Before releasing records, all courts require prepayment unless noted in profile.

Open records are located at the court unless otherwise noted. District courts index by defendant and plaintiff as well as by case number. Bankruptcy courts usually index by debtor and case number. While most courts now have their indexes on computer, many still maintain index card files as well.

The universal PACER sign-up number is 800-676-6856. Find PACER and the Party/Case Index on the Web at http://pacer.psc.uscourts.gov. PACER dial-up access is $.60 per minute. Also, courts offering internet access via RACER, PACER, Web-PACER or the new CM-ECF charge $.07 per page fee unless noted as free.

New Hampshire County Courts

Court	Jurisdiction	No. of Courts	How Organized
Superior Courts*	General	11	10 Counties
District Courts*	Limited	37	40 Districts
Probate Courts*	Probate	10	10 Counties
Family Court	Special	8	

* Profiled in this Sourcebook.

Court	CIVIL								
	Tort	Contract	Real Estate	Min. Claim	Max. Claim	Small Claims	Estate	Eviction	Domestic Relations
Circuit Courts*	X	X	X	$1500	No Max				X
District Courts*	X	X	X	$0	$25,000	$5000		X	X
Probate Courts*							X		X
Family Courts									X

Court	CRIMINAL				
	Felony	Misdemeanor	DWI/DUI	Preliminary Hearing	Juvenile
Circuit Courts*	X				
District Courts*		X	X	X	X
Probate Courts*					
Family Courts					X

ADMINISTRATION

Administrative Office of the Courts, Supreme Court Bldg, 2 Noble Dr, Concord, NH, 03301; 603-271-2521, Fax: 603-271-3977. www.courts.state.nh.us/

COURT STRUCTURE

The Superior Court is the court of General Jurisdiction. Felony cases include Class A misdemeanors.

The District Court upper civil limit was increased to $25,000 from $10,000 on 1/1/93. Filing a civil case in the monetary "overlap" area between the Superior Court minimum and the District Court maximum is at the discretion of the filer.

The municipal courts have been closed as the judges retire. The caseload and records are absorbed by the nearest District Court.

ONLINE ACCESS

While there is no statewide access available for trial court records, the web page has a lot of useful information, including opinions and directives form the Supreme Court, Superior Courts, and District Courts. Click on Search..

ADDITIONAL INFORMATION

Important Notice – Fee Changes Pending

Fees for searching, copies, and certification are set by the New Hampshire Supreme Court. Effective September 10, 2004, the New Hampshire Supreme Court directed all New Hampshire District Courts to immediately enact a most dramatic fee increase (as much as 2500%) for a record search.

The new fee structure is as follows: Record research fee: $25.00 per name; Certificate of Judgment $10.00; certification fee $5.00; copy fee $.50 per page; computer screen printout $.50 per page.

Previously, the fee structure was as follows: Computer search - $10.00 for up to 10 names in one request; $25.00 for 10 or more names in one request; $25.00 per hour for search time beyond one hour.

As we go to press, only one court has made the switchover (Keene District Court in Chesire County). It is uncertain if and when the other District Court Clerks will institute this fee increase. As a result, we are leaving the current fee sturcture in place in the text of this book, and advising readers of possible increase. We also advise to call the District Court before mailing search requests.

Belknap County

Superior Court 64 Court St, Laconia, NH 03246; 603-524-3570. Hours: 8AM-4:30PM (EST). *Felony, Civil Actions Over $1,500.*
Civil Records: Access: Phone, mail, in person. Only the court performs in person searches; visitors may not. No search fee. Required to search: name, years to search. Civil cases indexed by defendant, plaintiff. Civil records on computer from 1/80, index cards from 1900, docket books from 1840.
Criminal Records: Access: Phone, mail, in person. Only the court performs in person searches; visitors may not. No search fee. Required to search: name, years to search; also helpful: DOB, SSN. Criminal records on computer from 1/80, index cards from 1900, docket books from 1840.
General Information: No adoptions, sealed, juvenile, mental health, expunged, or dismissed records released. Copy fee: $.50 per page. Certification fee: $5.00. Payee: Belknap County Superior Court. Business checks accepted. Prepayment required. Mail requests: SASE not required. Mail turnaround time 1 week.

Laconia District Court 26 Academy St, PO Box 1010, Laconia, NH 03247; 603-524-4128. Hours: 8AM-4PM (EST). *Misdemeanor, Civil Actions Under $25,000, Eviction, Small Claims.*
Note: Adoptions handled by probate court. Includes City of Laconia and the towns of Meredith, New Hampton, Gilford, Belmont, Alton, Gilmanton, Center Harbor, and Barnstead.
Civil Records: Access: Mail, in person. Only the court performs in person searches; visitors may not. Search fee: $25.00 for records before 5/2/92; $10.00 (up to 10 names) after 5/92. Fee may increase to $25.00 per name. Required to search: name, years to search. Civil cases indexed by defendant, plaintiff. Civil records on computer from 5/92, index cards from 7/64.
Criminal Records: Access: Mail, in person. Only the court performs in person searches; visitors may not. Search fee: $25.00 for records before 5/2/92; $10.00 (up to 10 names) after 5/92. Fee may increase to $25.00 per name. Required to search: name, years to search, DOB. Criminal records on computer from 1992, index cards from 7/64.
General Information: No sealed, juvenile, mental health, expunged or dismissed records released. Copy fee: $.50 per page. Certification fee: $5.00. Payee: Laconia District Court. Personal checks accepted. Prepayment required. Mail requests: SASE required. Mail turnaround time 2 weeks.

Probate Court 64 Court St, PO Box 1343, Laconia, NH 03247-1343; 603-524-0903. Hours: 8AM-4PM (EST). *Probate.*

Carroll County

Superior Court 96 Water Village Rd, Box 3, Ossipee, NH 03864-7267; 603-539-2201. Hours: 8AM-4PM (EST). *Felony, Civil Actions Over $1,500.*
Civil Records: Access: Mail, in person. Only the court performs in person searches; visitors may not. No search fee. Required to search: name, years to search. Civil cases indexed by defendant, plaintiff. Civil records on index cards from 1960, index books from 1840.
Criminal Records: Access: Mail, in person. Only the court performs in person searches; visitors may not. No search fee. Required to search: name, years to search; also helpful: DOB, SSN. Criminal records on index cards from 1960, index books from 1840.

General Information: No adoptions, sealed, juvenile, mental health, expunged or dismissed records released. Copy fee: $.50 per page. Certification fee: $5.00. Payee: Carroll County. Personal checks accepted. Prepayment required. Mail requests: SASE required. Mail turnaround time same day.

Northern Carroll County District Court PO Box 940, Conway, NH 03818; 603-356-7710. Hours: 8AM-4PM (EST). *Misdemeanor, Civil Actions Under $25,000, Eviction, Small Claims.*
Note: Includes Towns of Conway, Bartlett, Jackson, Eaton, Chatham, Hart's Location, Albany, Madison and the unincorporated places of Hale's Location, Cutt's Grant, Hadley's Purchase, and portions of Livermore and Waterville.
Civil Records: Access: Mail, in person. Both court and visitors may perform in person searches. Search fee: $25.00 before 10/01/92; $10.00 (up to 10 names) after 10/01/92. Fee may increase to $25.00 per name. Required to search: name, years to search. Civil cases indexed by defendant, plaintiff. Civil records on computer from 1993, on index cards from 1980, on index books from 1954.
Criminal Records: Access: Mail, in person. Only the court performs in person searches; visitors may not. Search fee: $10.00 (up to 10 names). Fee may increase to $25.00 per name. Required to search: name, years to search; also helpful: DOB, SSN. Criminal records on computer from 1993, on index cards from 1980, on index books from 1954.
General Information: No adoptions, sealed, juvenile, mental health, expunged or dismissed records released. Copy fee: $.50 per page. Certification fee: $5.00 per page. Payee: District Court for Northern Carroll County. Personal checks accepted. Prepayment required. Mail requests: SASE required. Mail turnaround time 1 week.

Southern Carroll County District Court 96 Water Village Rd #2, Ossipee, NH 03864; 603-539-4561. Hours: 8AM-4PM (EST). *Misdemeanor, Civil Actions Under $25,000, Eviction, Small Claims.*
Note: The former Wolfeboro District Court has been combined with this court. Includes Towns of Ossipee, Tamworth, Freedom, Effingham, Wakefield, Wolfeboro, Brookfield, Tuftonboro, Moultonborough, and Sandwich.
Civil Records: Access: Mail, in person. Only the court performs in person searches; visitors may not. Search fee: $10.00 (up to 10 names). Fee may increase to $25.00 per name. Required to search: name, years to search. Civil cases indexed by defendant, plaintiff. Civil records on computer from 1992, on index cards from 1989.
Criminal Records: Access: Mail, in person. Only the court performs in person searches; visitors may not. Search fee: $10.00 (up to 10 names). Fee may increase to $25.00 per name. Required to search: name, years to search; also helpful: DOB, SSN. Criminal records on computer from 1992, on index cards from 1989.
General Information: No sealed, juvenile, mental health, expunged or dismissed records released. Copy fee: $.50 per page. Certification fee: $5.00. Payee: South Carroll County District Court. Only cashiers checks and money orders accepted. Prepayment required. Mail requests: SASE required. Mail turnaround time 2-3 days.

Probate Court 96 Water Village Rd., Ossipee, NH 03864; 603-539-4123; Fax: 603-539-4761. Hours: 8:AM-4:00PM (EST). *Probate.*

Cheshire County

Superior Court 12 Court St, Keene, NH 03431; 603-352-6902. Hours: 8AM-4PM (EST). *Felony, Civil Actions Over $1,500, Family law.*
Civil Records: Access: Mail, in person. Only the court performs in person searches; visitors may not. No search fee. Required to search: name, years to search. Civil cases indexed by defendant, plaintiff. Civil records on computer from 1992, on index cards from 1920; records prior to 1918 difficult to access; organized 1769.
Criminal Records: Access: Mail, in person. Only the court performs in person searches; visitors may not. No search fee. Required to search: name, years to search, DOB. Criminal records on computer from 1992, criminal records go back to 1900.
General Information: No adoptions, sealed, juvenile, mental health, expunged or dismissed records released. Copy fee: $.50 per page. Certification fee: $5.00. Payee: Clerk of Superior Court. Personal checks accepted. Prepayment required. Mail requests: SASE required. Mail turnaround time 2 weeks.

Jaffrey-Peterborough District Court 84 Peterborough St, PO Box 39, Jaffrey, NH 03452-0039; 603-532-8698. Hours: 8AM-4PM (EST). *Misdemeanor, Civil Actions Under $25,000, Eviction, Small Claims.*
Note: Includes towns of Peterborough, Hancock, Greenville, Greenfield, New Ipswich, Temple, Sharon, Jaffrey, Dublin, Fitzwilliam, and Rindge.
Civil Records: Access: Mail, in person. Only the court performs in person searches; visitors may not. Search fee: $10.00 (up to 10 names); $25.00 for manual (11+). Fee may increase to $25.00 per name. Required to search: name, years to search. Civil cases indexed by defendant, plaintiff. Civil records on computer back to 1993, on index cards from 1980, index books in backroom.
Criminal Records: Access: Mail, in person. Only the court performs in person searches; visitors may not. Search fee: Same as civil. Required to search: name, years to search, DOB; also helpful: SSN. Criminal records on computer back to 4/1993, on index cards from 1980, index books istored.
General Information: No sealed, juvenile, mental health records released. Copy fee: $.50 per page. Certification fee: $5.00. Payee: Jaffrey-Peterborough District Court. Personal checks accepted. Prepayment required. Mail requests: SASE required. Mail turnaround time 3-4 weeks.

Keene District Court PO Box 364, Keene, NH 03431; 603-352-2559. Hours: 8AM-4PM (EST). *Misdemeanor, Civil Actions Under $25,000, Eviction, Small Claims.*
Note: Includes city of Keene and the towns of Stoddard, Westmoreland, Surry, Gilsum, Sullivan, Nelson, Roxbury, Marlow, Swanzey, Marlborough, Winchester, Richmond, Hinsdale, Harrisville, Walpole, Alstead, Troy, and Chesterfield.
Civil Records: Access: Mail, in person. Only the court performs in person searches; visitors may not. Search fee is $25.00 per name. Required to search: name, years to search. Civil cases indexed by defendant, plaintiff. Civil records on computer from 7/92, on index cards from 1980, docket books from 1968 to 1979.
Criminal Records: Access: Mail, in person. Only the court performs in person searches; visitors may not. Search fee is $25.00 per name. Required to search:

name, DOB, years to search; also helpful: SSN. Criminal records on computer from 7/92, on index cards from 1980, docket books from 1968 to 1979. **General Information:** No sealed, juvenile, mental health or expunged records released. Will not fax results. Copy fee: $.50 per page. There is no copy fee is document is certified. Certification fee: $5.00. Payee: Keene District Court. Personal checks accepted. Prepayment required. Mail requests: SASE required. Mail turnaround time 5-10 days.

Probate Court 12 Court St, Keene, NH 03431; 603-357-7786. Hours: 8AM-4:30PM (EST). *Probate.*

Coos County

Superior Court 55 School St #301, Lancaster, NH 03584; 603-788-4900. Hours: 8AM-4PM (EST). *Felony, Civil Actions Over $1,500.*
Civil Records: Access: Mail, in person. Only the court performs in person searches; visitors may not. No search fee. Required to search: name, years to search. Civil cases indexed by defendant, plaintiff. Civil records on computer from 1960; index books from 1887; courthouse burned in 1887, prior records lost (organized 1803).
Criminal Records: Access: Mail, in person. Only the court performs in person searches; visitors may not. No search fee. Required to search: name, years to search, DOB. Criminal records on computer from 1960; index books from 1887.
General Information: No adoptions, sealed, juvenile, mental health, expunged or dismissed records released. Copy fee: $.50 per page. Certification fee: $5.00. Payee: Coos Superior Court. Personal checks accepted. Prepayment required. Mail requests: SASE required. Mail turnaround time 2-3 days.

Berlin District Court 220 Main St, Berlin, NH 03570; 603-752-3160. Hours: 8AM-4PM (EST). *Misdemeanor, Civil Actions Under $25,000, Eviction, Small Claims.*
Note: Includes towns of Berlin, Dummer, and Milan and the unincorporated places of Cambridge and Success.
Civil Records: Access: Mail, in person. Only the court performs in person searches; visitors may not. Search fee: $25.00 per name before 1993; $10.00 (up to 10 names) after 1993. Fee may increase to $25.00 per name. Required to search: name, years to search. Civil cases indexed by defendant, plaintiff. Computerized records from 1993, civil records on index cards from 1980, index books from 1970, prior to 1970 archived in basement.
Criminal Records: Access: Mail, in person. Only the court performs in person searches; visitors may not. Search fee: $25.00 per name before 1993; $10.00 (up to 10 names) after 1993. Fee may increase to $25.00 per name. Required to search: name, years to search, DOB, SSN. Criminal records computerized since 1993, on index cards from 1980, index books from 1970, prior to 1970 archived in basement.
General Information: No sealed, juvenile, mental health, expunged or dismissed records released. Copy fee: $.50 per page. Certification fee: $5.00. Payee: Berlin District Court. Personal checks accepted. Credit cards accepted. Prepayment required. Mail requests: SASE required. Mail turnaround time 1-2 weeks.

Colebrook District Court PO Box 5 - 10 Bridge St, Colebrook, NH 03576; 603-237-4229. Hours: 8AM-Noon,1-4PM (EST). *Misdemeanor, Civil Actions Under $25,000, Eviction, Small Claims.*
Note: Includes towns of Colebrook, Pittsburg, Clarksville, Wentworth's Location, Errol, Millsfield,

Columbia, Stewartstown, Stratford, and unincorp. Dix's Grant, Atkinson & Gilmanton Academy Grant, Second College, Grant, Dixville, Erving's Location, and Odell.
Civil Records: Access: Mail, in person. Only the court performs in person searches; visitors may not. Search fee: $10.00 (up to 10 names) for computer search 93 to present. $25.00 for manual search, prior to 93. Fee may increase to $25.00 per name. Required to search: name, years to search. Civil cases indexed by defendant, plaintiff. Civil records on index cards from 1979, index books from 1964.
Criminal Records: Access: Mail, in person. Only the court performs in person searches; visitors may not. Search fee: $10.00 (up to 10 names) for computer search. $25.00 for manual search. Fee may increase to $25.00 per name. Required to search: name, years to search, DOB. Criminal records on index cards from 1979, index books from 1964.
General Information: No sealed, juvenile, mental health or expunged records released. Copy fee: $.50 per page. Certification fee: $5.00 per page. Payee: Colebrook District Court. Personal checks accepted. Prepayment required. Mail requests: SASE required. Mail turnaround time same day.

Gorham District Court PO Box 176, Gorham, NH 03581; 603-466-2454. Hours: 8AM-4PM (EST). *Misdemeanor, Civil Actions Under $25,000, Eviction, Small Claims.*
Note: Includes towns of Gorham, Shelburne, and Randolph and the unincorporated places of Bean's Purchase, Martin's Location, Green's Grant, Pinkham's Grant, Sargent's Purchase, Thompson & Meserve's Purchase and Low & Burbank's Grant.
Civil Records: Access: Mail, in person. Only the court performs in person searches; visitors may not. Search fee: $25.00 per hour. Electronic searches are $10.00 for less than 10 names, $25.00 for 10-25 names, then the hourly kicks in. Fee may increase to $25.00 per name. Required to search: name, years to search. Civil cases indexed by defendant, plaintiff. Civil records on computer from 1993, on index cards from 1980, index books from 1964.
Criminal Records: Access: Mail, in person. Only the court performs in person searches; visitors may not. Search fee: Same fees as civil. Required to search: name, years to search, DOB. Criminal records on computer from 1993, on index cards from 1980, index books from 1964.
General Information: No adoptions, sealed, juvenile, mental health, expunged or dismissed records released. Copy fee: $.50 per page. Certification fee: $10.00. Payee: Gorham District Court. Personal checks accepted. Prepayment required. Mail requests: SASE required. Mail turnaround time 3-4 days.

Lancaster District Court 55 School St, #201, Lancaster, NH 03584; 603-788-4485. Hours: 8:30AM-4PM (EST). *Misdemeanor, Civil Actions Under $25,000, Eviction, Small Claims.*
Note: Includes Lancaster, Whitefield, Northumberland, Stark, Jefferson, Carroll, Kilkenny, Bean's Grant, Chandler's Purchase and Crawford's Purchase.
Civil Records: Access: Mail, in person. Only the court performs in person searches; visitors may not. Search fee: $25.00 for manual research. Electronic search is $10.00 (up to 10 names). Fee may increase to $25.00 per name. Required to search: name, years to search; also helpful: address. Civil cases indexed by defendant, plaintiff. Civil records on index cards from 1981, index books for public review only, computerized since 1993.
Criminal Records: Access: Mail, in person. Only the court performs in person searches; visitors may not.

Search fee: Same as Civil. Required to search: name, years to search, DOB; also helpful: address. Criminal records on index cards from 1980, index books for public review only, computerized since 1993.
General Information: No adoptions, sealed, juvenile, mental health, expunged or dismissed records released. Copy fee: $.50 per page. Certification fee: $5.00 per page. Payee: Lancaster District Court. Personal checks accepted. Prepayment required. Mail requests: SASE required. Mail turnaround time 1 week.

Probate Court 55 School St #104, Lancaster, NH 03584; 603-788-2001. Hours: 8AM-4PM (EST). *Probate.*

Grafton County

Superior Court 3785 Dartmouth College Hwy, North Haverhill, NH 03774; 603-787-6961. Hours: 8AM-4:30PM (EST). *Felony, Civil Actions Over $1,500.*
Civil Records: Access: Mail, in person. Only the court performs in person searches; visitors may not. No search fee. Required to search: name, years to search. Civil cases indexed by defendant, plaintiff. Civil records on index cards from 1900, index books from 1950. All prior records are found at the Archives in Concord.
Criminal Records: Access: Mail, in person. Only the court performs in person searches; visitors may not. No search fee. Required to search: name, years to search; also helpful: DOB, SSN. Criminal records on index cards from 1900. All prior records are found at the Archives in Concord.
General Information: No sealed records released. Copy fee: $.50 per page. Certification fee: $5.00 plus $.50 per add'l page. Payee: Grafton County Superior Court. Personal checks accepted. Prepayment required. Mail requests: SASE required. Mail turnaround time 10 days.

Haverhill District Court Grafton County Courthouse, 3785 Dartmouth College Highway - Box 10, North Haverhill, NH 03774; 603-787-6626. Hours: 8:00AM-4:30PM (EST). *Misdemeanor, Civil Actions Under $25,000, Eviction, Small Claims.*
Note: Includes towns of Haverhill, Bath, Landaff, Benton, Piermont, and Warren.
Civil Records: Access: Mail, in person. Only the court performs in person searches; visitors may not. Search fee: Electronic records search fee is $10.00 per name (less than 10 names); 10 or more names are $25.00 each search. Manual search fee is $25.00 per hour. Fee may increase to $25.00 per name. Required to search: name, years to search. Civil cases indexed by defendant, plaintiff. Civil records on computer from 1993, on index cards from 1980, index books from 1950s.
Criminal Records: Access: Mail, in person. Only the court performs in person searches; visitors may not. Search fee: Same fees as civil. Required to search: name, years to search, DOB. Criminal records on computer from 1993, on index cards from 1980, index books from 1950s.
General Information: No adoptions, sealed, juvenile, mental health, expunged or dismissed records released. Will fax results if toll-free number provided. Copy fee: $.50 per page. Certification fee: $5.00. Payee: Haverhill District Court. Personal checks accepted. Prepayment required. Mail requests: SASE required. Mail turnaround time 1-2 days.

Lebanon District Court 38 Centerra Parkway, Lebanon, NH 03766; 603-643-3555. Hours: 8AM-4PM (EST). *Misdemeanor, Civil Actions Under $25,000, Eviction, Small Claims.*

Note: Includes towns of Lebanon, Enfield, Canaan, Grafton, Orange, Hanover, Orford, and Lyme.

Civil Records: Access: Mail, in person. Only the court performs in person searches; visitors may not. Search fee: $10.00 (up to 10 names) for computer search (1993-present); $25 for index search (prior to 1993). Fee may increase to $25.00 per name. Required to search: name, years to search. Civil cases indexed by defendant, plaintiff. Civil records on computer from 1993, on index cards from 1986, index books from 1960s.

Criminal Records: Access: Mail, in person. Only the court performs in person searches; visitors may not. Search fee same as Civil. Required to search: name, years to search, DOB. Criminal records on computer from 1993, on index cards from 1986, index books from 1960s.

General Information: No sealed, juvenile, mental health or expunged records released. Copy fee: $.50 per page. Certification fee: $5.00. Payee: Lebanon District Court. Personal checks accepted. Prepayment required. Mail requests: SASE required. Mail turnaround time 5 business days.

Littleton District Court 134 Main St, Littleton, NH 03561; 603-444-7750. Hours: 8AM-4PM (EST). *Misdemeanor, Civil Actions Under $25,000, Eviction, Small Claims.*

Note: Includes towns of Littleton, Monroe, Lyman, Lisbon, Franconia, Bethlehem, Sugar Hill, and Easton.

Civil Records: Access: Mail, in person. Only the court performs in person searches; visitors may not. Search fee: $10.00 (up to 10 names). Fee may increase to $25.00 per name. Required to search: name, years to search. Civil cases indexed by defendant, plaintiff. Civil records on computer from 1993, index cards from 1985, index books from 1950.

Criminal Records: Access: Mail, in person. Only the court performs in person searches; visitors may not. Search fee is same as Civil DOB, SSN. Criminal records on computer from 1993, index cards from 1985, index books from 1950.

General Information: No adoptions, sealed, juvenile, mental health, domestic violence, expunged or dismissed records released. Copy fee: $.50 per page. Certification fee: $5.00. Payee: Littleton District Court. Personal checks accepted. Prepayment required. Mail requests: SASE required. Mail turnaround time 3 weeks.

Plymouth District Court 26 Green St, Plymouth, NH 03264; 603-536-3326. Hours: 8AM-4PM (EST). *Misdemeanor, Civil Actions Under $25,000, Eviction, Small Claims.*

Note: Includes towns of Plymouth, Bristol, Dorchester, Groton, Wentworth, Rumney, Ellsworth, Thornton, Campton, Ashland, Hebron, Holderness, Bridgewater, Alexandria, Lincoln, Woodstock, and portions of Livermore and Waterville.

Civil Records: Access: Mail, in person. Only the court performs in person searches; visitors may not. Search fee: $10.00 (up to 10 names). If a complete search (from 1981) is required, fee is $25.00. Fee may increase to $25.00 per name. Required to search: name, years to search. Civil cases indexed by defendant, plaintiff. Civil records on computer from 1991, index cards from 1981.

Criminal Records: Access: Mail, in person. Only the court performs in person searches; visitors may not. Search fee is same as Civil. Required to search: name, years to search; also helpful: DOB, SSN. Criminal records on computer from 1991, index cards from

1981. Request for an appointment must be made two weeks prior to in person searching.

General Information: No sealed, mental health, expunged or dismissed records released. Copy fee: $.50 per page. Certification fee: $5.00. Payee: Plymouth District Court. Personal checks accepted. Prepayment required. Mail requests: SASE required. Mail turnaround time one week.

Probate Court 3785 Dartmouth College Hwy, Box 3, North Haverhill, NH 03774-4936; 603-787-6931. Hours: 8AM-4PM (EST). *Probate.*

Hillsborough County

Superior Court - North District 300 Chestnut St Rm 127, Manchester, NH 03101; 603-669-7410. Hours: 8;30AM-4PM (EST). *Felony, Civil Actions Over $1,500.*

Civil Records: Access: Mail, in person. Only the court performs in person searches; visitors may not. No search fee. Required to search: name, years to search. Civil cases indexed by defendant, plaintiff. Civil records on computer from 5/85, index cards from 1980s, index books from 1900s; organized 1769.

Criminal Records: Access: Mail, in person. Only the court performs in person searches; visitors may not. No search fee. Required to search: name, years to search, DOB. Criminal records on computer from 5/85, index cards from 1980s, index books from 1900s; organized 1769.

General Information: No sealed, juvenile, mental health records released. Copy fee: $.50 per page. Certification fee: $5.00. Payee: Hillsborough Superior Court-Northern District. Personal checks accepted. Prepayment required. Mail requests: SASE required. Mail turnaround time 3 days.

Superior Court - Southern District 30 Spring St, Nashua, NH 03061; 603-883-6461. Hours: 8AM-4PM (EST). *Felony, Civil Actions Over $1,500.*

Civil Records: Access: Mail, in person. Only the court performs in person searches; visitors may not. No search fee. Required to search: name, years to search. Civil cases indexed by defendant, plaintiff. Civil records on computer back to 3/92; overall records go back to 1992.

Criminal Records: Access: Mail, in person. Only the court performs in person searches; visitors may not. No search fee. Required to search: name, years to search; also helpful: DOB. Criminal records on computer back to 3/92; overall records go back to 1992.

General Information: No sealed, juvenile or annulled records released. Copy fee: $.50 per page. Certification fee: $5.00. Payee: Superior Court. Personal checks accepted. Prepayment required. Mail turnaround time 2-3 days.

Goffstown District Court PO Box 129, Goffstown, NH 03045; 603-497-2597. Hours: 8AM-4PM (EST). *Misdemeanor, Civil Actions Under $25,000, Eviction, Small Claims.*

Note: Includes towns of Goffstown, Weare, New Boston, and Francestown.

Civil Records: Access: Mail, in person. Only the court performs in person searches; visitors may not. Search fee: $10.00 fee for electronic search up to 10 names, $25.00 for 10+ names. Manual search is $25.00 per name. Fee may increase to $25.00 per name. Required to search: name, years to search. Civil cases indexed by defendant, plaintiff. Civil records on computer from 3/92, kept in files prior.

Criminal Records: Access: Mail, in person. Only the court performs in person searches; visitors may not. Search fee: Same fees as civil. Required to search: name, years to search, DOB; also helpful: SSN.

Criminal records on computer from 3/92, kept in files prior.

General Information: No sealed, juvenile, mental health, expunged or dismissed records released. Copy fee: $.50 per page. Certification fee: $5.00. Payee: Goffstown District Court. Personal checks accepted. Prepayment required. Mail requests: SASE helpful. Turnaround time 2 weeks.

Hillsborough District Court PO Box 763, Hillsborough, NH 03244; 603-464-5811. Hours: 8AM-4PM (EST). *Misdemeanor, Civil Actions Under $25,000, Eviction, Small Claims.*

Note: Includes towns of Hillsborough, Deering, Windsor, Antrim, and Bennington.

Civil Records: Access: Mail, in person. Both court and visitors may perform in person searches. Search fee: $10.00 (up to 10 names) for computer; $25.00 for manual (older records). Fee may increase to $25.00 per name. Required to search: name, years to search. Civil cases indexed by defendant, plaintiff. Civil records on computer from 1992, on index cards from 1980, index books from 1960. Appointment required for in person searching.

Criminal Records: Access: Mail, in person. Both court and visitors may perform in person searches. Search fee: Same as Civil. Required to search: name, years to search, DOB; also helpful: SSN. Criminal records on computer from 1992, on index cards from 1980, index books from 1960.

General Information: Public access terminal has civil records only. No adoptions, sealed, juvenile, mental health, expunged or dismissed records released. Copy fee: $.50 per page. Certification fee: $5.00. Payee: Hillsborough District Court. Personal checks accepted. Prepayment required. Mail requests: SASE required. Mail turnaround time 1 week.

Manchester District Court PO Box 456, Manchester, NH 03105; 603-624-6510. Hours: 8AM-4PM (EST). *Misdemeanor, Civil Actions Under $25,000, Eviction, Small Claims.*

Note: Includes city of Manchester.

Civil Records: Access: Mail. Only the court performs in person searches; visitors may not. Search fee: $10.00 per request up to 10 names or $25.00 per request over 10. Manual searches $25.00 per hour. Fee may increase to $25.00 per name. Required to search: name, years to search, DOB; also helpful: address. Civil cases indexed by defendant, plaintiff. Civil records on computer from 6/92, on index cards from 1960. All requests must be in writing.

Criminal Records: Access: Mail. Only the court performs in person searches; visitors may not. Search fee same as Civil. Required to search: name, years to search, DOB; also helpful: address. Criminal records on computer from 6/92, on index cards from 1960. All requests must be in writing.

General Information: No adoptions, sealed, juvenile, mental health, expunged or dismissed records released. Copy fee: $.50 per page. Certification fee: $1.00. Payee: Manchester District Court. Personal checks accepted. Prepayment required. Mail requests: SASE required. Mail turnaround time 2 weeks.

Merrimack District Court PO Box 324, Merrimack, NH 03054-0324; 603-424-9916. Hours: 8AM-4PM (EST). *Misdemeanor, Civil Actions Under $25,000, Eviction, Small Claims.*

Note: Includes towns of Merrimack, Litchfield, and Bedford.

Civil Records: Access: Mail, in person. Only the court performs in person searches; visitors may not. Search fee: $25 per hour for manual searches. For electronic, $10 for up to first 9 names or $25 for first 25 names, then hour rate. Fee may increase to $25.00 per name. Required to search: name, years to search. Civil cases indexed by defendant, plaintiff. Civil records on computer from 7/92, on index cards from 1972, index books in archives at Concord. All requests must be in writing.

Criminal Records: Access: Mail, in person. Both court and visitors may perform in person searches. Search fee: Same fees as civil. Required to search: name, years to search; also helpful: DOB. Criminal records on computer from 7/92, on index cards from 1972, index books in archives at Concord. All requests must be in writing.

General Information: No adoptions, sealed, juvenile, mental health, expunged or dismissed records released. Copy fee: $.50 per page. Certification fee: $5.00. Payee: Merrimack District Court. Personal checks accepted. Prepayment required. Mail requests: SASE required. Mail turnaround time 1-2 days.

Milford District Court 180 Elm St, Milford, NH 03055-4735; 603-673-2900. Hours: 8AM-4PM (EST). *Misdemeanor, Civil Actions Under $25,000, Eviction, Small Claims.*
Note: Includes towns of Milford, Brookline, Amherst, Mason, Wilton, Lyndeborough, and Mont Vernon.

Civil Records: Access: Mail, in person. Only the court performs in person searches; visitors may not. Search fee: Searching via computer is $10.00 (up to 10 names); lengthy manual searching is $25.00 per hour. Fee may increase to $25.00 per name. Required to search: name, years to search. Civil cases indexed by defendant, plaintiff. Civil records on computer from 08/92, on index cards from 1950s, prior records may or may not be at old courthouse.

Criminal Records: Access: Mail, in person. Only the court performs in person searches; visitors may not. Search fee: Same as Civil. Required to search: name, years to search; also helpful: DOB, SSN. Criminal records on computer from 08/92, on index cards from 1950s, prior records may or may not be at old courthouse.

General Information: No adoptions, sealed, juvenile, mental health, expunged or dismissed records released. Copy fee: $.50 per page. Certification fee: $5.00. Payee: Milford District Court. Personal checks accepted. Prepayment required. Mail requests: SASE required. Mail turnaround time 10 days.

Nashua District Court PO Box 310, Nashua, NH 03061-0310; 603-880-3333. Hours: 8AM-4PM (EST). *Misdemeanor, Civil Actions Under $25,000, Eviction, Small Claims.*
Note: Includes city of Nashua and the towns of Hudson and Hollis.

Civil Records: Access: Mail, in person. Only the court performs in person searches; visitors may not. Search fee: $25.00 for records prior to 08/92; after are $10.00 (up to 10 names). Fee may increase to $25.00 per name. Required to search: name, years to search. Civil cases indexed by defendant, plaintiff. Civil records on computer from 1993, index cards from 1982. All requests must be in writing.

Criminal Records: Access: Mail, in person. Only the court performs in person searches; visitors may not. Search fee: Same fees as civil. Required to search: name, years to search; also helpful: DOB, SSN. Criminal records on computer from August 1992, index cards from 1982. All requests must be in writing.

General Information: No adoptions, sealed, juvenile, mental health, expunged records released. Copy fee: $.50 per page. Certification fee: $5.00. Payee: Nashua District Court. Personal checks accepted. Prepayment required. Mail requests: SASE required. Mail turnaround time 5 days.

Probate Court PO Box P, Nashua, NH 03061-6015; 603-882-1231; Fax: 603-882-1620. Hours: 8AM-4PM (EST). *Probate.*

Merrimack County

Superior Court PO Box 2880, Concord, NH 03302-2880; 603-225-5501. Hours: 8AM-4PM (EST). *Felony, Civil Actions Over $1,500.*

Civil Records: Access: Mail, in person. Only the court performs in person searches; visitors may not. No search fee. Required to search: name, years to search. Civil cases indexed by defendant, plaintiff. Civil records on computer from 1983, index cards from 1950, index books from 1800s; organized 1823.

Criminal Records: Access: Phone, mail, in person. Only the court performs in person searches; visitors may not. No search fee. Required to search: name, years to search, DOB; also helpful: SSN. Criminal records on computer since 1984.

General Information: No adoptions, sealed, juvenile, mental health, expunged or dismissed records released. Copy fee: $.50 per page. Certification fee: $5.00. Payee: Merrimack Superior Court. Personal checks accepted. Prepayment required. Mail requests: SASE required. Mail turnaround time 2-3 weeks.

Concord District Court 32 Clinton St, PO Box 3420, Concord, NH 03302-3420; 603-271-6400. Hours: 8AM-4PM (EST). *Misdemeanor, Civil Actions Under $25,000, Eviction, Small Claims.*
Note: The former Pittsfield District Court has been combined with this court. Includes city of Concord, and the towns of Loudon, Canterbury, Dunbarton, Bow, Hopkinton, Pittsfield, Chichester, and Epsom.

Civil Records: Access: Mail, in person. Only the court performs in person searches; visitors may not. Search fee: $10.00 for less than 10 electronic searches or $25 per hour. Fee may increase to $25.00 per name. Required to search: name, years to search. Civil cases indexed by defendant, plaintiff. Civil records on computer from 1989, index cards from 1978, docket books from 1800.

Criminal Records: Access: Mail, in person. Only the court performs in person searches; visitors may not. Search fee: $10.00 for less than 10 electronic searches or $25 per hour. Fee may increase to $25.00 per name. Required to search: name, years to search, DOB. Criminal records on computer from 1989, index cards from 1978, docket books from 1800.

General Information: No sealed, juvenile, mental health, expunged or dismissed records released. Copy fee: $.50 per page. Certification fee: $5.00. Payee: Concord District Court. Personal checks accepted. Prepayment required. Mail requests: SASE required. Mail turnaround time 10 days.

Franklin District Court 7 Hancock Terrace, Franklin, NH 03235; 603-934-3290. Hours: 8AM-4PM (EST). *Misdemeanor, Civil Actions Under $25,000, Eviction, Small Claims.*
Note: Includes city of Franklin and the towns of Northfield, Danbury, Andover, Boscawen, Salisbury, Hill, Webster, Sanbornton, and Tilton.

Civil Records: Access: Mail, in person. Only the court performs in person searches; visitors may not. Search fee: $10.00 (up to 10 names). Fee may increase to $25.00 per name. Required to search: name, years to search. Civil cases indexed by plaintiff. Civil records on computer from 1/91, index cards from 1/80, index books from 1960s.

Criminal Records: Access: Mail, in person. Only the court performs in person searches; visitors may not. Search fee: $10.00 (up to 10 names). Fee may increase to $25.00 per name. Required to search: name, years to search; also helpful: DOB, SSN.

Criminal records on computer from 1/91, index cards from 1/80, index books from 1960s.

General Information: No adoptions, sealed, juvenile, mental health, expunged or dismissed records released. Copy fee: $.50 per page. Certification fee: $5.00 per document. Payee: Franklin District Court. Personal checks accepted. Prepayment required. Mail requests: SASE required. Mail turnaround time 2-3 days.

Henniker District Court 2 Depot St, Henniker, NH 03242; 603-428-3214. Hours: 8AM-4PM (EST). *Misdemeanor, Civil Actions Under $25,000, Eviction, Small Claims.*
Includes towns of Henniker, Warner, and Bradford.

Civil Records: Access: Mail, in person. Only the court performs in person searches; visitors may not. Search fee: Searching via computer is $10.00 (up to 10 names) lengthy manual searching is $25.00 per hour. Fee may increase to $25.00 per name. Required to search: name, years to search. Civil cases indexed by defendant, plaintiff. Civil records on index cards from 1988, index books from 1960s; on computer back to 1989.

Criminal Records: Access: Mail, in person. Only the court performs in person searches; visitors may not. Search fee: Same as Civil. Required to search: name, years to search, DOB; also helpful: SSN. Criminal records on index cards from 1988, index books from 1960s; on computer back to 1989.

General Information: No adoptions, sealed, juvenile, mental health, expunged or dismissed records released. Copy fee: $.50 per page. Certification fee: $5.00. Payee: Henniker District Court. Personal checks accepted. Prepayment required. Mail requests: SASE required. Mail turnaround time can take as long as 6 weeks.

Hooksett District Court 101 Merrimack, Hooksett, NH 03106; 603-485-9901. Hours: 8AM-4PM (EST). *Misdemeanor, Civil Actions Under $25,000, Eviction, Small Claims.*
Note: Includes towns of Allenstown, Pembroke, and Hooksett.

Civil Records: Access: Mail, in person. Only the court performs in person searches; visitors may not. Search fee: Fee for electronic searching is $10.00 per name if less than 10 names submitted; 10 or more names are $25.00 each. Manual research is charged at $25.00 per hour. Browse screens are $.50 per page (bulk case info). Required to search: name, years to search. Civil cases indexed by defendant, plaintiff. Civil records on computer from 1993, on index cards from 1980, index books from 1975. All requests must be in writing.

Criminal Records: Access: Mail, in person. Only the court performs in person searches; visitors may not. Search fee: Same fees as civil. Required to search: name, years to search; also helpful: DOB, SSN. Criminal records on computer from 1993, on index cards from 1980, index books from 1975.

General Information: No sealed, juvenile, mental health, expunged or dismissed records released. Copy fee: $.50 per page. Certification fee: $5.00. Payee: Hooksett District Court. Personal checks accepted. Prepayment required. Mail requests: SASE required. Mail turnaround time 1-2 months.

New London District Court PO Box 1966, New London, NH 03257; 603-526-6519. Hours: 8:30AM-4PM (EST). *Misdemeanor, Civil Actions Under $25,000, Eviction, Small Claims.*
Note: Includes towns of New London, Wilmot, Newbury, and Sutton.

Civil Records: Access: Mail, in person. Only the court performs in person searches; visitors may not. Search fee: $10.00 for 1-3 names; $25.00 each add'l name. Fee may increase to $25.00 per name.

Required to search: name, years to search. Civil cases indexed by defendant, plaintiff. Civil records on computer from 1993, on index cards from 1980, index books from 1970. An appointment is necessary before performing an in person search.

Criminal Records: Access: Mail, in person. Both court and visitors may perform in person searches. Search fee: Same fees as civil. Required to search: name, years to search; also helpful: DOB, SSN. Criminal records on computer from 1993, on index cards from 1980, index books from 1970. An appointment is necessary before performing an in person search.

General Information: Public Access terminal is available. (Criminal only.) No adoptions, sealed, juvenile, mental health, expunged or dismissed records released. Copy fee: $.50 per page. Certification fee: $1.00. Payee: New London District Court. Personal checks accepted. Prepayment required. Mail requests: SASE required. Mail turnaround time 1-2 days.

Probate Court 163 N Main St, Concord, NH 03301; 603-224-9589; Fax: 603-225-0179. Hours: 8AM-4:30PM July-Aug: 8-4PM (EST). *Probate.*

Rockingham County

Superior Court PO Box 1258, Kingston, NH 03848-1258; 603-642-5256. Hours: 8AM-4PM (EST). *Felony, Civil Actions Over $1,500.*
Civil Records: Access: In person only. Only the court performs in person searches; visitors may not. No search fee. Required to search: name, years to search. Civil cases indexed by defendant, plaintiff. Civil records on computer from 1988, index cards from 1920, organized 1769.
Criminal Records: Access: In person only. Only the court performs in person searches; visitors may not. No search fee. Required to search: name, years to search; also helpful: DOB. Criminal records on computer from 1988, index cards from 1920, organized 1769.
General Information: No sealed, juvenile, mental health, expunged, annulled records released. Copy fee: $.50 if court makes the copy, $.25 if visitor makes the copy. Certification fee: $5.00. Payee: Clerk Superior Court. Personal checks accepted. Prepayment required.

Salem District Court 35 Geremonty Dr, Salem, NH 03079; 603-893-4483. Hours: 8AM-4PM (EST). *Misdemeanor, Civil Actions Under $25,000, Eviction, Small Claims.*
Includes towns of Salem, Windham, and Pelham.
Civil Records: Access: Mail, in person. Search fee: $10.00 (up to 10 names), $25.00 per hour for manual searching. Fee may increase to $25.00 per name. Required to search: name, years to search. Civil cases indexed by defendant, plaintiff. Civil records on computer from 4/92, docket cards from 1980, docket books from 1950. An appointment is necessary before performing an in person search.
Criminal Records: Access: Mail, in person. Only the court performs in person searches; visitors may not. Search fee: Same as Civil. Required to search: name, years to search, DOB. Criminal records on computer from 4/92, docket cards from 1980, docket books from 1950.
General Information: No adoptions, sealed, juvenile, mental health, expunged or dismissed records released. Copy fee: $.50 per page. Certification fee: $5.00. Payee: Salem District Court. Personal checks accepted. Prepayment required. Mail requests: SASE required. Mail turnaround: 2-3 weeks.

Auburn District Court 5 Priscilla Lane, Auburn, NH 03032; Civil phone: 603-624-2265; Criminal phone: 603-624-2084. Hours: 8AM-4PM (EST). *Misdemeanor, Civil Actions Under $25,000, Eviction, Small Claims.*
Note: Includes towns of Auburn, Candia, Deerfield, Northwood, Nottingham, and Raymond.
Civil Records: Access: Mail, in person. Only the court performs in person searches; visitors may not. Search fee: $25.00 per hour if manual, $10.00 (up to 10 names) for computer printout. Fee may increase to $25.00 per name. Required to search: name, years to search; also helpful: address. Civil cases indexed by defendant, plaintiff. Civil records on computer from 5/92, index cards from 1980, index books from 1968.
Criminal Records: Access: Mail, in person. Only the court performs in person searches; visitors may not. Search fee: Same as Civil. Required to search: name, years to search, DOB, signed release. Criminal records on computer from 5/92, index cards from 1980, index books from 1968.
General Information: No adoptions, sealed, juvenile, mental health, expunged or dismissed records released. Copy fee: $.50 per page. Certification fee: $5.00. Payee: Auburn District Court. Personal checks accepted. Prepayment required. Mail requests: SASE required. Mail turnaround: 10 days.

Derry District Court 10 Manning St, Derry, NH 03038; 603-434-4676. Hours: 8AM-4PM (EST). *Misdemeanor, Civil Actions Under $25,000, Eviction, Small Claims.*
Note: Includes towns of Derry, Londonderry, Chester, and Sandown.
Civil Records: Access: Phone, mail, in person. Only the court performs in person searches; visitors may not. Search fee: $10.00 fee applies for all computer searches for up to 10 names; over 10 computer names or for index book searches, fee is $25.00. Required to search: name, years to search. Civil cases indexed by defendant, plaintiff. Civil records on computer from 10/92, on index cards prior.
Criminal Records: Access: Phone, mail, in person. Only the court performs in person searches; visitors may not. Search fee: Same fees as civil. Required to search: name, years to search; also helpful: DOB, SSN. Criminal records on computer from 10/92, on index cards prior.
General Information: No adoptions, sealed, juvenile, mental health, expunged, dismissed or annulment records released. Copy fee: $.50 per page. Certification fee: $5.00. Payee: Derry District Court. Personal checks accepted. Prepayment required. Mail requests: SASE required. Mail turnaround: 1 week.

Exeter District Court PO Box 394, Exeter, NH 03833; 603-772-2931. Hours: 8AM-4PM (EST). *Misdemeanor, Civil Actions Under $25,000, Eviction, Small Claims.*
Note: Includes towns of Exeter, Newmarket, Stratham, Newfields, Fremont, East Kingston, Kensington, Epping, and Brentwood.
Civil Records: Access: Mail, in person. Only the court performs in person searches; visitors may not. Search fee: $10.00 (up to 10 names). Fee may increase to $25.00 per name. Required to search: name, years to search; also helpful: address. Civil cases indexed by defendant, plaintiff. Civil records on computer back to 1991.
Criminal Records: Access: Mail, in person. Both court and visitors may perform in person searches. Search fee: $10.00 (up to 10 names). Fee may increase to $25.00 per name. Required to search: name, years to search, DOB. Criminal records on computer back to 1991.
General Information: No adoptions, sealed, juvenile, mental health, expunged or dismissed

records released. Will fax results to local or toll-free number, must be prepaid. Copy fee: $.50 per page. Certification fee: $5.00. Payee: Exeter District Court. Personal checks accepted. Prepayment required. Mail requests: SASE required. Mail turnaround: 3 days.

Hampton District Court PO Box 10, Hampton, NH 03843-0010; 603-926-8117. Hours: 8AM-4PM (EST). *Misdemeanor, Civil Actions Under $25,000, Eviction, Small Claims.*
Note: Includes towns of Hampton, Hampton Falls, North Hampton, South Hampton, and Seabrook.
Civil Records: Access: Mail, in person. Only the court performs in person searches; visitors may not. Search fee: $10.00 fee applies for all computer searches for up to 10 names; over 10 computer names or for index book searches, fee is $25.00. Fee may increase to $25.00 per name. Required to search: name, years to search. Civil cases indexed by defendant. Civil records on computer from 4/91, index cards from 1979, index books from 1900s.
Criminal Records: Access: Mail, in person. Only the court performs in person searches; visitors may not. Search fee: Same fees as civil. Required to search: name, years to search; also helpful: DOB, SSN. Criminal records on computer from 4/91, index cards from 1979, index books from 1900s.
General Information: No adoptions, sealed, juvenile, mental health, expunged or dismissed records released. No copy fee. Certification fee: $5.00. Payee: Hampton District Court. Personal checks accepted. Prepayment required. Mail requests: SASE required. Mail turnaround time 1 week.

Plaistow District Court 14 Elm St. (PO Box 129), Plaistow, NH 03865; 603-382-4651; Fax: 603-382-4952. 8AM-4PM (EST). *Misdemeanor, Civil Actions Under $25,000, Eviction, Small Claims.*
Note: Includes towns of Plaistow, Hampstead, Kingston, Newton, Atkinson, and Danville.
Civil Records: Access: Mail, in person. Only the court performs in person searches; visitors may not. Search fee: $10.00 1-9 names; $25.00 10 or more names. $25.00 per hour manual search fee. Fee may increase to $25.00 per name. Required to search: name, years to search. Civil cases indexed by defendant, plaintiff. Civil records on computer from 7/91, index cards from 1980, index books from 1960s.
Criminal Records: Access: Mail, in person. Only the court performs in person searches; visitors may not. Search fee: $10.00 1-9 names; $25.00 10 or more names. $25.00 per hour manual search fee. Fee may increase to $25.00 per name. Required to search: name, years to search, DOB. Criminal records on computer from 7/91, index cards from 1980, index books from 1960s.
General Information: No adoptions, sealed, juvenile, mental health, expunged or dismissed records released. Copy fee: $.50 per page. Certification fee: $5.00. Payee: Plaistow District Court. Personal checks accepted. Prepayment required. Mail requests: SASE required. Mail turnaround time 2-3 days.

Portsmouth District Court 111 Parrott Ave, Portsmouth, NH 03801; 603-431-2192. Hours: 8AM-4PM (EST). *Misdemeanor, Civil Actions Under $25,000, Eviction, Small Claims.*
Note: Includes city of Portsmouth and the towns of Newington, Greenland, Rye, and New Castle.
Civil Records: Access: Mail, in person. Only the court performs in person searches; visitors may not. Search fee: $10.00 (up to 10 names) if computerized search (after 1992), otherwise $35.00. Fee may increase to $25.00 per name. Required to search: name, years to search. Civil cases indexed by defendant, plaintiff. Civil records on computer from

04/92, docket cards from 1980, index books from 1960s.

Criminal Records: Access: Mail, in person. Only the court performs in person searches; visitors may not. Search fee: Same fees as civil. Required to search: name, years to search; also helpful: DOB, SSN. Criminal records on computer from 04/92, docket cards from 1980, index books from 1960s.

General Information: No adoptions, sealed, juvenile, mental health, expunged or dismissed records released. Copy fee: $.50 per page. Certification fee: $1.00 per page (included in search fee). Payee: Portsmouth District Court. Personal checks accepted. Prepayment required. Mail requests: SASE required. Mail turnaround time 2-3 days.

Probate Court PO Box 789, Kingston, NH 03848; 603-642-7117. 8AM-4PM (EST). *Probate.*

Strafford County

Superior Court PO Box 799, Dover, NH 03821-0799; 603-742-3065. Hours: 8:30AM-4PM (EST). *Felony, Civil Actions Over $1,500.*

Civil Records: Access: Mail, in person. Only the court performs in person searches; visitors may not. No search fee. Required to search: name, years to search. Civil cases indexed by defendant, plaintiff. Civil records on computer from 3/89, index cards from 1970, index books from 1900s, organized 1769.

Criminal Records: Access: Mail, in person. Only the court performs in person searches; visitors may not. No search fee. Required to search: name, years to search; also helpful: DOB, SSN. Criminal records on computer from 3/89, index cards from 1970, index books from 1900s, organized 1769.

General Information: No sealed, juvenile, mental health, expunged or dismissed records released. Copy fee: $.50 per page. Certification fee: $5.00. Payee: Strafford Superior Court. Personal checks accepted. Prepayment required. Mail requests: SASE required. Mail turnaround time 1 week.

Dover District Court 25 St Thomas St, Dover, NH 03820; 603-742-7202; Fax: 603-742-5956. Hours: 8AM-4PM (EST). *Misdemeanor, Civil Actions Under $20,000, Eviction, Small Claims.*

Note: Note: Includes City of Dover, Somersworth, and Rollinsford.

Civil Records: Access: Mail, in person. Only the court performs in person searches; visitors may not. Search fee: $10.00 (up to 10 names). Fee may increase to $25.00 per name. Required to search: name, years to search. Civil cases indexed by defendant, plaintiff. Civil records on computer from 1993, on index cards from 1980, index books from 1970.

Criminal Records: Access: Mail, in person. Only the court performs in person searches; visitors may not. Search fee: $10.00 (up to 10 names). Fee may increase to $25.00 per name. Required to search: name, years to search, DOB. Criminal records on computer from 1993, on index cards from 1980, index books from 1970.

General Information: No adoptions, sealed, juvenile, mental health, expunged or dismissed records released. May fax results. Copy fee: $.50 per page. Certification fee: $5.00. Payee: Dover District Court. Personal checks accepted. Prepayment required. Mail requests: SASE required. Mail turnaround time 1-2 days.

Durham District Court 1 Main St., Durham, NH 03824; 603-868-2323. Hours: 8:30AM-4PM (EST). *Misdemeanor, Civil Actions Under $25,000, Eviction, Small Claims.*

Note: Includes towns of Durham, Lee, and Madbury.

Civil Records: Access: Mail, in person. Only the court performs in person searches; visitors may not. Search fee: Searching via computer is $10.00 per name; lengthy manual searching is $25.00 per hour. Fee may increase to $25.00 per name. Required to search: name, years to search. Civil cases indexed by defendant, plaintiff. Civil records on computer back to 1990; index cards from 1980, index books from 1945.

Criminal Records: Access: Mail, in person. Only the court performs in person searches; visitors may not. Search fee: Same as Civil. Required to search: name, years to search, DOB; also helpful: SSN. Criminal records on computer back to 1990; index cards from 1980, index books from 1948.

General Information: No adoptions, sealed, juvenile, mental health, expunged or dismissed records released. Copy fee: $.50 per page. Certification fee: $5.00. Payee: Durham District Court. Personal checks accepted. Prepayment required. Mail requests: SASE required. Mail turnaround time 4 days.

Rochester District Court 76 N Main St, Rochester, NH 03867; 603-332-3516. Hours: 8AM-4PM (EST). *Misdemeanor, Civil Actions Under $25,000, Eviction, Small Claims.*

Note: Includes city of Rochester and the towns of Barrington, Milton, New Durham, Farmington, Strafford, and Middleton.

Civil Records: Access: Mail, in person. Only the court performs in person searches; visitors may not. Search fee: If on computer, $10 for up to 10 names, $25.00 if over 10 names. If manual, then 25.00. Fee may increase to $25.00 per name. Required to search: name, years to search; also helpful DOB. Civil cases indexed by defendant, plaintiff. Civil records on computer from 1989, index cards from 7/80, index books from 1960s. Requests must be in writing.

Criminal Records: Access: Mail, in person. Only the court performs in person searches; visitors may not. Search fee: Same fees as civil. Required to search: name, years to search; also helpful: DOB. Criminal records on computer from 1989, index cards from 7/80, index books from 1960s. Requests must be in writing.

General Information: No sealed, juvenile, mental health, expunged records released. Copy fee: $.50 per page. Certification fee: $5.00 per page. Payee: Rochester District Court. Personal checks accepted. Prepayment required. Mail requests: SASE required. Mail turnaround time 1 week.

Somersworth District Court *Misdemeanor, Civil Actions Under $25,000, Eviction, Small Claims.*

Note: This court is combined with the Dover District Court as of 11/1/02.

Probate Court PO Box 799, Dover, NH 03821-0799; 603-742-2550. Hours: 8AM-4:30PM (EST). *Probate.* www.state.nh.us/courts/probate.htm

Sullivan County

Superior Court 22 Main St, Newport, NH 03773; 603-863-3450. Hours: 8AM-4:00PM (EST). *Felony, Civil Actions Over $1,500.*

Civil Records: Access: Mail, in person. Only the court performs in person searches; visitors may not. No search fee. Required to search: name, years to search. Civil cases indexed by defendant, plaintiff. Civil records on computer from 1992, on index cards from 1980s, index books from 1800s.

Criminal Records: Access: Mail, in person. Only the court performs in person searches; visitors may not. No search fee. Required to search: name, years to search, DOB. Criminal records on computer from 1992, on index cards from 1980s, index books from 1800s.

General Information: No adoptions, sealed, juvenile, mental health, expunged or dismissed records released. Will not fax results. Copy fee: $.50 per page. Certification fee: $5.00. Payee: Sullivan County Superior Court. Personal checks accepted. Prepayment required. Mail requests: SASE required. Mail turnaround time 1 week.

Claremont District Court PO Box 313, Claremont, NH 03743; 603-542-6064. Hours: 8AM-4PM (EST). *Misdemeanor, Civil Actions Under $25,000, Eviction, Small Claims.*

Note: Includes city of Claremont and the towns of Cornish, Unity, Charlestown, Acworth, Langdon, and Plainfield.

Civil Records: Access: Phone, mail, in person. Only the court performs in person searches; visitors may not. Search fee: $10.00 (up to 10 names) 1992 to present. $35.00 prior to 1992. Fee may increase to $25.00 per name. Required to search: name, years to search, DOB. Civil cases indexed by defendant, plaintiff. Civil records on computer from 10/92, on index cards from 1980, index books from 1960.

Criminal Records: Access: Phone, mail, in person. Only the court performs in person searches; visitors may not. Search fee: $10.00 (up to 10 names) 1992 to present. $35.00 prior to 1992. Fee may increase to $25.00 per name. Required to search: name, years to search, DOB. Criminal records on computer from 10/92, on index cards from 1980, index books from 1960.

General Information: No adoptions, sealed, juvenile, mental health, expunged or dismissed records released. Copy fee: $.50 per page. Certification fee: $5.00. Payee: Claremont District Court. Personal checks accepted. Prepayment required. Mail requests: SASE required. Mail turnaround time 1 week.

Newport District Court 55 Main St, Newport, NH 03773; 603-863-1832. Hours: 8AM-4PM (EST). *Misdemeanor, Civil Actions Under $25,000, Eviction, Small Claims.*

Note: Includes towns of Newport, Grantham, Croydon, Springfield, Sunapee, Goshen, Lempster, and Washington.

Civil Records: Access: Mail, in person. Only the court performs in person searches; visitors may not. Search fee: $25.00 per hour, or $10.00 for electronic search (up to 10 names). Fee may increase to $25.00 per name. Required to search: name, years to search. Civil cases indexed by defendant, plaintiff. Civil records on computer from 1993, on index cards from 1980, index books from 1960s. All requests must be in writing.

Criminal Records: Access: Mail, in person. Only the court performs in person searches; visitors may not. Search fee: Same as Civil. Required to search: name, years to search, DOB. Criminal records on computer from 1993, on index cards from 1980, index books from 1960s. All requests must be in writing.

General Information: No adoptions, sealed, juvenile, mental health, expunged or dismissed records released. Copy fee: $.50 per page. Certification fee: $1.00. Payee: Newport District Court. Personal checks accepted. Prepayment required. Mail requests: SASE required. Mail turnaround time 2-3 days.

Probate Court PO Box 417, Newport, NH 03773; 603-863-3150. Hours: 8AM-4PM (EST). *Probate.*

New Hampshire Recording Offices

ORGANIZATION: 238 cities/towns and 10 counties, 10 recording offices and 242 UCC filing offices. The recording officers are Town/City Clerk (UCC) and Register of Deeds (real estate only). Each town/city profile indicates the county in which the town/city is located. Be careful to distinguish the following names that are identical for both a town/city and a county - Grafton, Hillsborough, Merrimack, Strafford, and Sullivan. Many towns are so small that their mailing addresses are within another town. The following unincorporated towns do not have a Town Clerk, so all liens are located at the corresponding county: Cambridge (Coos), Dicksville (Coos), Green's Grant (Coos), Hale's Location (Carroll), Millsfield (Coos), and Wentworth's Location (Coos). The entire state is in the Eastern Time Zone (EST).

REAL ESTATE RECORDS: Real estate transactions are recorded at the county level, and property taxes are handled at the town/city level. Local town real estate ownership and assessment records are usually located at the Selectman's Office. Each town/city profile indicates the county in which the town/city is located. Most counties will not perform real estate searches. Copy fees vary. Certification fees generally are $2.00 per document.

UCC RECORDS: This was a dual filing state until Revised Article 9. Previously, financing statements were filed at the state level and with the Town/City Clerk, except for consumer goods and farm related collateral, which were filed only with the Town/City Clerk, and real estate related collateral, which was and still is filed with the county Register of Deeds. Most recording offices will perform UCC searches. Use search request form UCC-11. Search fees are usually $5.00 per debtor name using the standard UCC-11 request form and $7.00 using a non-standard form. Copy fees are usually $.75 per page.

TAX LIEN RECORDS: Federal and state tax liens on personal property of businesses are filed with the Secretary of State. Other federal and state tax liens on personal property are filed with the Town/City Clerk. Federal and state tax liens on real property are filed with the county Register of Deeds. There is wide variation in indexing and searching practices among the recording offices. Where a search fee of $7.00 is indicated, it refers to a non-standard request form such as a letter.

OTHER LIENS: Condominium, town tax, mechanics, welfare.

ONLINE ACCESS: The New Hampshire Counties Registry of Deeds web site allows free searching of real estate related records for Belknap, Cheshire, Hillsborough, Rockingham, Strafford and Sullivan counties at www.nhdeeds.com. Also, a private vendor has placed on the Internet the assessor records from a number of towns. Visit http://data.visionappraisal.com

Acworth Town

Town Clerk, PO Box 37, Town Clerk, Acworth, NH 03601. **Phone**-603-835-6879; hours 6:30-8PM M-W; 9-11AM Sat
Will not search UCC or tax liens records. RE records at Sullivan County. UCC copy- $1.00 per page. Cert fee: $10.00. Payee: Town of Acworth.

Albany Town

Town Clerk, 19728 NH Route 16, Conway, NH 03818. **Phone**-603-447-2877; fax-603-447-2877; hours 8AM-Noon M; 4PM-7PM W; 9AM-Noon Sat
Will not search UCC or tax liens records. RE records at Carroll County. UCC copy- $1.00 per page. **Other phones:** Assessor-603-586-4402.

Alexandria Town

Town Clerk, 45 A Washburn Rd, Alexandria, NH 03222. **Phone**-603-744-3288, R/E Recording-603-787-6921; fax-603-744-8577; hours 8AM-5:30PM M T F, Noon-7PM Th, Closed Wed
Will search UCC records. Search per debtor- $10.00. Tax liens not included in UCC search. Separate federal tax lien search- $10.00 RE records at Grafton County. UCC copy- $1.00 per page. Payee: Town of Alexandria. **Other phones:** Assessor-603-744-3220; Treasurer-603-744-3220; Elections-603-744-3288; Vital Records-602-744-3288.

Allenstown Town

Town Clerk, 16 School St, Allenstown, NH 03275. **Phone**-Town Clerk, R/E & UCC Recording- 603-485-4276; fax-603-485-8669; hours M 8:30-1 & 3-7; T/W 8:30-1 & 3-5; Th 8:30-3; No F. www.allenstown.org

Will search UCC records prior to 7/2001. Search per debtor- $10.00. Will not search tax liens. RE records at Merrimack County. UCC copy- $1.00 per page. **Other phones:** Assessor-603-485-4276; Treasurer-603-485-4276; Elections-603-485-4276; Vital Records-603-485-4276.

Alstead Town

Town Clerk, Box 65, Alstead, NH 03602. **Phone**-603-835-2242; fax-603-835-2986; hours 8AM-4PM,Closed F
Will search UCC records prior to 7/2001 and current liens only. Search per debtor- $10.00. Will not search tax liens. RE records at Cheshire County. UCC copy- $1.00 per page. Cert fee: $3.00. Payee: Alstead Town Clerk.

Alton Town

Town Clerk, Box 637, Alton, NH 03809. **Phone**-603-875-2101, R/E Recording-603-875-5095; fax-603-875-3894; hours 8:30AM-4:30PM
Deeds and tax liens from the county are online at www.nhdeeds.com. Will search UCC records prior to 7/2001 and current liens only. Search per debtor-$10.00. Tax liens not included in UCC search. Federal/state combined tax lien search- $10.00 per search. RE records at Belknap County. UCC copy-$1.00 per page. **Other phones:** Assessor-603-875-0205; Treasurer-603-875-2161; Appraiser/ Auditor-603-875-5095; Elections-603-875-2101; Vital Records-603-875-2101; Tax Collector-603-875-2171.

Amherst Town

Town Clerk, PO Box 960, Amherst, NH 03031. **Phone**-603-673-6041, UCC Recording-603-673-6041

x207; fax-603-673-6794; hours 9AM-3PM M-F; 5:30-8PM Mon
Will search UCC records prior to 7/2001 only. Search per debtor- $10.00. Will not search tax liens. RE records at Hillsborough County. UCC copy- $1.00 per page. Payee: Town of Amherst. **Online Access to Property Assessor records:** Records on the town assessor database are free at http://data.visiona ppraisal.com/AmherstNH/. Registration is required to view full data. **Other phones:** Assessor-603-673-6041; Treasurer-603-673-6041.

Andover Town

Town Clerk, PO Box 61, Andover, NH 03216. **Phone**-603-735-5332; fax-603-735-6975; hours 10AM-1PM T Th, 6:30PM-8:30PM W, 9AM-Noon Sat
Will search UCC records. Search per debtor- $10.00. RE records at Merrimack County. UCC copy- $1.00 per page. **Other phones:** Assessor-603-735-5332; Treasurer-603-735-5516; Vital Records-603-735-5332.

Antrim Town

Town Clerk, PO Box 517, Antrim, NH 03440. **Phone**-603-588-6785; fax-603-588-2969; hours 8AM-4PM M-Th
Will search UCC records prior to 7/2001 and current liens only. Search per debtor- $10.00. RE records at Hillsborough County. UCC copy- $1.00 per page. Cert fee: None. Payee: Antrim Town Clerk.

Ashland Town

Town Clerk, PO Box 517, Ashland, NH 03217. **Phone**-603-968-4432; fax-603-968-3776; hours 8AM-4PM
Will search UCC records prior to 7/2001 and current liens only. Search per debtor- $10.00. RE records at

Grafton County. UCC copy- $1.00 per page. **Online Access to Assessor records:** Online access to assessor data at http://data.visionappraisal.com/AshlandNH/.

Atkinson Town

Town Clerk, 21 Academy Ave, Town Hall, Atkinson, NH 03811-2204. **Phone**-603-362-4920, R/E Recording-603-642-5526, UCC Recording-603-271-3242; fax-603-362-5305; hours 8:30AM-6:30PM M; 8:30AM-4PM T-F www.town-atkinsonnh.com
Will search UCC records prior to 7/2001 only. Search per debtor- $15.00. Will not search tax liens. RE records at Rockingham County. UCC copy- $1.00 per page. Payee: Town of Atkinson. **Online Access to Property, Real Estate Transfer records:** Access the town property values for free at www.town-atkinsonnh.com/values.htm. Also, search the last three months of real estate transfers and four months of building permits via the main website. **Other phones:** Assessor-603-362-5266.

Auburn Town

Town Clerk, PO Box 309, Auburn, NH 03032-0309. **Phone**-603-483-2281, UCC Recording-603-483-2281 x1; fax-603-483-0518; hours 8AM-2PM, M,W,TH; 8AM-12PM, F; 6PM-8PM, M Evening
Will search UCC records prior to 7/2001 and current liens only. Search per debtor- $10.00. RE records at Rockingham County. UCC copy- $1.00 per page. **Other phones:** Assessor-603-483-5052.

Barnstead Town

Town Clerk, PO Box 11, Center Barnstead, NH 03225. **Phone**-603-269-4631; fax-603-269-4072. Will search UCC records prior to 7/2001 and current liens only. Search per debtor- $10.00. RE records at Belknap County. UCC copy- $1.00 per page. **Other phones:** Assessor-603-269-4071; Treasurer-603-269-4071; Elections-603-269-4631; Vital Records-603-269-4631.

Barrington Town

Town Clerk, 41 Province Lane, Barrington, NH 03825. **Phone**-603-664-5476; fax-603-664-5179; hours 8AM-4:15PM M T TH; 4-6PM W; 8AM-Noom F
Will search UCC records prior to 7/2001 and current liens only. Search per debtor- $10.00. UCC search includes tax liens. Separate federal & state combined tax lien search- $10.00 per debtor. RE records at Strafford County. UCC copy- $1.00 per page. **Online Access to Property, Deed, Grantor/Grantee records:** Records are free on the Stafford county-wide system at www.nhdeeds.com/stfd/web/agree3.htm. Use the subscription service for full data. **Other phones:** Assessor-603-664-9007; Elections-603-664-5476; Vital Records-603-664-5476; Tax Collector-603-664-2230.

Bartlett Town

Town Clerk, RFD 1 Box 50, Intervale, NH 03845. **Phone**-603-356-2300, R/E Recording-603-356-2950; fax-603-356-2300; hours 8AM-4PM M-W & F; 8-11AM Sat. Will not search UCC or tax liens records. RE records at Carroll County. UCC copy- $1.00 per page. Cert fee: No charge. Payee: Town of Bartlett. **Other phones:** Assessor-603-356-2950; Treasurer-603-356-2950; Elections-603-356-2300; Vital Records-603-356-2300.

Bath Town

Town Clerk, PO Box 165, Bath, NH 03740. **Phone**-603-747-2454; fax-603-747-0497; hours 8AM-12, 1PM-4PM M,W,Th; 8AM-12, 5:30-8:30PM T
Will search UCC records. Will not search tax liens. RE records at Grafton County. UCC copy- $1.00 per page. Payee: Town of Bath. **Other phones:** Treasurer-603-747-2454; Elections-603-747-2454; Vital Records-603-747-2454.

Bedford Town

Town Clerk, 24 N. Amherst Rd, Bedford, NH 03110. **Phone**-603-472-3550; fax-603-472-4573; hours 8AM-4:30PM M,W,Th,F; 7:00AM-4:30PM Tu. www.ci.bedford.nh.us
Will search UCC records prior to 7/2001 and current liens only. Search per debtor- $10.00. RE records at Hillsborough County. UCC copy- $1.00 per page. **Online Access to Assessor records:** Access assessor data at http://data.visionappraisal.com/BedfordNH/. **Other phones:** Assessor-603-472-8104; Elections-603-472-3550; Vital Records-603-472-3550.

Belknap County

Register of Deeds, PO Box 1343, Laconia, NH 03247-1343. **Phone**-Register of Deeds, R/E & UCC Recording- 603-527-5420; fax-603-527-5429; hours 8AM-4PM www.nhdeeds.com
Will not search records. UCC copy- $1.00 per page. Cert fee: $2.00 per doc + $1.00 per page for copy. **Online Access to Real Estate, Deed, Mortgage, Lien records:** Access to county register of deeds data is free at www.nhdeeds.com/belk/web/agree5.htm. Online records go back to 1960. To establish an account for copies of documents on line go to www.nhdeeds.com/belk/web/start.htm.

Belmont Town

Town Clerk, PO Box 310, Belmont, NH 03220. **Phone**-603-267-8302; fax-603-267-8305; hours 7:30AM-4PM
Will search UCC records prior to 7/2001 and current liens only. Search per debtor- $10.00. RE records at Belknap County. UCC copy- $1.00 per page. **Online Access to Assessor, Property records:** Access to property assessor data is at http://data.visionappraisal.com/BelmontNH/. **Other phones:** Assessor-603-267-8300; Treasurer-603-267-8300; Elections-603-267-8302; Vital Records-603-267-8302.

Bennington Town

Town Clerk, 7 School St, #101, Bennington, NH 03442. **Phone**-603-588-2189; fax-603-588-8005; hours 9AM-Noon M & S.;8:30AM-12:30PM Tu.;4:30-8:30PM Th. http://townofbennington.com/
Will search UCC records prior to 7/2001 and current liens only. Search per debtor- $10.00. RE records at Hillsborough County. UCC copy- $1.00 per page. **Other phones:** Assessor-603-588-2189.

Benton Town

Town Clerk, 110 Flanders Rd, Benton, NH 03785-6402. **Phone**-603-787-6541, R/E Recording-603-787-6053; fax-603-787-6646; hours 6:30-8:30PM Monday night. Will search UCC records prior to 7/2001 and current liens only. Search per debtor-$10.00. RE records at Grafton County. UCC copy-$1.00 per page. **Other phones:** Assessor-603-787-6053; Treasurer-603-787-6004; Elections-603-787-2129; Vital Records-603-787-6541.

Berlin City

City Clerk, 168 Main St, City Hall, Berlin, NH 03570. **Phone**-603-752-2340; fax-603-752-1654; hours 8:30-12;00, 1-4:30
Will search UCC records prior to 7/2001 and current liens only. Search per debtor- $10.00. RE records at Coos County. UCC copy- $1.00 per page. Cert fee: $12.00. Payee: City of Berlin. **Other phones:** Assessor-603-752-5245; Treasurer-603-752-1610.

Bethlehem Town

Town Clerk, PO Box 189, Bethlehem, NH 03574. **Phone**-603-869-2293, R/E Recording-603-869-3133; fax-603-869-2280; hours 4:30-7PM M,W; 9AM-1PM T,Th

Will search UCC records prior to 7/2001 and current liens only. Search per debtor- $5.00. UCC search includes federal tax liens if requested. RE records at Grafton County. UCC copy- $.75 per page. Payee: Town of Bethlehem. **Other phones:** Assessor-603-869-3351; Treasurer-603-869-3351; Elections-603-869-2293; Vital Records-603-869-2293.

Boscawen Town

Town Clerk, 116 N. Main St., Boscawen, NH 03303. **Phone**-603-753-9188; fax-603-753-9183; hours M, Th 8am-11am; 12-4:30; T & W 8-11am; 12-6:30pm
Will search UCC records prior to 7/2001 and current liens only. Search per debtor- $10.00. Will not search tax liens. RE records at Merrimack County. UCC copy- $1.00 per page. **Other phones:** Assessor-603-753-9188; Treasurer-603-796-2343.

Bow Town

Town Clerk, 10 Grandview Rd, Bow, NH 03304-3410. **Phone**-603-225-2683; fax-603-225-5428; hours 7:30AM-4:10PM
Will not search UCC or tax liens records. RE records at Merrimack County. UCC copy- $1.00 per page. Payee: Town of Bow. **Online Access to Property Assessor records:** Records on the town assessor database are free at http://data.visionappraisal.com/BowNH/. Registration is required to view full data. **Other phones:** Assessor-603-228-1187x15.

Bradford Town

Town Clerk/Tax Collector, PO Box 607, Bradford, NH 03221-0607. **Phone**-603-938-2288; fax-603-938-2094; hours Noo-7PM Mon.; 7AM-5PM Tues; 8AM-5PM Fri.
Will search UCC records prior to 7/2001 and current liens only. Search per debtor- $10.00. Tax lien search- $10.00 per debtor. RE records at Merrimack County. UCC copy- $1.00 per page. Cert fee: $5.00 per copy. Payee: Town Clerk. **Other phones:** Assessor-603-938-5900.

Brentwood Town

Town Clerk, 1 Dalton Rd, Brentwood, NH 03833. **Phone**-603-642-6400 x14; fax-603-642-6310; hours 9AM-4:30PM M-F; 7-9PM T; 9AM-Noon Sat Sept-May
Will search UCC records prior to 7/2001 only. Search per debtor- $10.00. Tax liens not included in UCC search. Separate federal tax lien search- $10.00. RE records at Rockingham County. UCC copy- $1.00 per page. Payee: Town of Brentwood. **Other phones:** Assessor-603-642-6400 x10; Treasurer-603-642-6400 x19; Elections-603-642-6400 x14; Vital Records-603-642-6400 x14.

Bridgewater Town

Town Clerk, PO Box 419, Plymouth, NH 03264. **Phone**-603-968-7911; fax-603-968-3506; hours 6PM-8:30PM T- W; 8:30-10AM 3rd Sat
Will search UCC records prior to 7/2001 and current liens only. Search per debtor- $10.00. Tax liens not included in UCC search. Tax lien search- $15.00 per copy. RE records at Grafton County. UCC copy-$1.00 per page. Cert fee: $15.00 per page. Payee: Town of Bridgewater.

Bristol Town

Town Clerk, 230 Lake St, #A, Bristol, NH 03222-1120. **Phone**-603-744-8478; fax-603-744-2521; hours 8:30AM-4:00PM
Will search UCC records prior to 7/2001. Search per debtor- $10.00. Will not search tax liens. RE records at Grafton County. UCC copy- $4.00 per page. **Other phones:** Assessor-603-744-3354; Elections-603-744-8478; Vital Records-603-744-8478.

Brookfield Town

Town Clerk, PO Box 756, Sanbornville, NH 03872. **Phone**-603-522-3231; fax-603-522-6245; 1-8PM M
Will search UCC records prior to 7/2001 and current liens only. Search per debtor- $10.00. UCC search includes tax liens if requested. RE records at Carroll County. UCC copy- $1.00 per page. Payee: Town of Brookfield. **Other phones:** Assessor-603-522-0031; Treasurer-603-522-6756; Elections-603-522-3688.

Brookline Town

Town Clerk, PO Box 336, Brookline, NH 03033. **Phone**-603-673-8855 x218; fax-603-673-8136; hours 8AM-2PM M-F, 6PM-9PM W, 9AM-Noon Last SAT of month www.brookline.nh.us
Will search UCC records prior to 7/2001 and current liens only. Search per debtor- $10.00. RE records at Hillsborough County. UCC copy- $1.00 per page. Payee: Town of Brookline. **Other phones:** Assessor-603-673-8855 X216; Elections-603-673-8855 X218; Vital Records-603-673-8855 X218.

Campton Town

Town Clerk, 1307 NH RT 175, Campton, NH 03223. **Phone**-603-726-3223, UCC Recording-603-726-3223 x102 or x103; fax-603-726-9817; hours 9AM-3:30PM
Will not search UCC or tax liens records. RE records at Grafton County. UCC copy- $1.00 per page. **Other phones:** Assessor-603-726-3223 x101; Elections-603-726-3223 X102 or 103.

Canaan Town

Town Clerk, PO Box 38, Canaan, NH 03741-0038. **Phone**-603-523-7106; fax-603-523-4526; hours 9AM-12 1PM-4PM M,W,F; 9AM-12 T TH http://town.canaan.nh.us
Will search UCC records prior to 7/2001. Search per debtor- $15.00. Search request using non-standard form (per name)- $10.00. Will not search tax liens. RE records at Grafton County. UCC copy- $1.00 per page. **Other phones:** Appraiser/ Auditor-603-523-4501; Vital Records-603-523-7106.

Candia Town

Town Clerk, 74 High St, Candia, NH 03034-2713. **Phone**-603-483-5573, R/E Recording-603-483-8101; fax-603-483-0252; hours 8:30-11 M, 5PM-8PM T TH, 9AM-1PM W F
Will search UCC records prior to 7/2001 and current liens only. Search per debtor- $10.00. Tax liens searches included with UCC searches if requested. Federal/state combined tax lien search- $10.00 per debtor. RE records at Rockingham County. UCC copy- $1.00 per page. Cert fee: $5.00. Payee: Pay fees to Town of Canada. **Online Access to Assessor records:** Access asessor data at http://data.visionappraisal.com/CandiaNH/. **Other phones:** Assessor-603-483-8101; Treasurer-603-483-5140; Elections-603-483-5573; Vital Records-603-483-5573.

Canterbury Town

Town Clerk, PO Box 500, Canterbury, NH 03224. **Phone**-603-783-9955; fax-603-783-0501; hours 10AM-2PM M; 11AM-6PM T; 5-8:30PM Th
Will search UCC records prior to 7/2001 and current liens only. Search per debtor- $10.00. UCC search includes tax liens. RE records at Merrimack County. UCC copy- $1.00 per page. Payee: Town of Canterbury.

Carroll County

Register of Deeds, PO Box 163, Ossipee, NH 03864-0163. **Phone**-603-539-4872; fax-603-539-5239; hours 9AM-5PM. Will not search UCC or real estate records. Copy fee- $1.00 per page. Cert fee: $1.00 per doc. Payee: Carroll County Register of Deeds.

Carroll Town

Town Clerk, PO Box 88, Twin Mountain, NH 03595-0088. **Phone**-603-846-5494; fax-603-846-5713; hours 9AM-Noon M; 9AM-3PM T,W,Th
Will search UCC records prior to 7/2001 and current liens only. Search per debtor- $10.00. Will not search tax liens. RE records at Carroll County. UCC copy- $1.00 per page. **Other phones:** Assessor-603-846-5754; Treasurer-603-846-5754.

Center Harbor Town

Town Clerk, PO Box 140, Center Harbor, NH 03226. **Phone**-603-253-4561; fax-603-253-8420; hours 9AM-3PM. Will search UCC records prior to 7/2001 and current liens only. Search per debtor- $10.00. Federal/state combined tax lien search- $20.00 per search RE records at Belknap County. UCC copy- $2.00 per page.

Charlestown Town

Town Clerk, PO Box 834, Charlestown, NH 03603. **Phone**-603-826-5821; fax-603-826-5181; hours 8AM-1PM, 1:30-6PM M; 8AM-1PM, 1:30-4PM T-F
Will search UCC records prior to 7/2001 and current liens only. Search per debtor- $10.00. UCC search includes tax liens if requested. RE records at Sullivan County. UCC copy- $1.00 per page. Payee: Town of Charlestown. **Other phones:** Assessor-603-826-4400; Elections-603-826-5821; Vital Records-603-826-5821.

Chatham Town

Town Clerk, 1681 Main Rd, Chatham, NH 03813. **Phone**-603-694-2043; fax-603-694-2043; hours 5-7PM T
Will search UCC records prior to 7/2001 only. Search per debtor- $10.00. Will search tax liens including federal tax liens. RE records at Carroll County. UCC copy- $1.00 per page. Payee: Town of Chatham. **Other phones:** Treasurer-603-694-2321; Elections-603-694-2043; Vital Records-603-694-2043.

Cheshire County

Register of Deeds, PO Box 584, Keene, NH 03431. **Phone**-603-352-0403; fax-603-352-7678; hours 8:30AM-4:30PM www.nhdeeds.com
Will not search records. Record copy- $1.00 per page. Cert fee: $2.00 per doc. Payee: Registry of deeds. **Online Access to Real Estate, Deed, Mortgage, Lien records:** Access to county register of deeds data is free at www.nhdeeds.com/chsr/web/agree2.htm. Online records go back to 1980.

Chester Town

Town Clerk, PO Box 275, Chester, NH 03036. **Phone**-603-887-3636; hours 8AM-12:30PM M,T,Th,F; 8AM-4PM W
Will search UCC records prior to 7/2001 and current liens only. Search per debtor- $5.00. UCC search includes tax liens if requested. RE records at Rockingham County. UCC copy- $.50 per page. Payee: Town of Chester. **Other phones:** Assessor-603-887-4045; Elections-603-887-4344.

Chesterfield Town

Town Clerk, PO Box 64, Chesterfield, NH 03443-0064. **Phone**-603-363-8071, R/E Recording-603-363-4624; fax-603-363-8047; hours 9AM-5:30PM M,W; 5-8PM Th www.nhchesterfield.com
Will search UCC records prior to 7/2001 only. Search per debtor- $10.00. Will search tax liens including federal tax liens. RE records at Cheshire County. UCC copy- $1.00 per page. Cert fee: $4.00 per doc. Payee: Town of Chesterfield. **Other phones:** Assessor-603-363-4624; Treasurer-603-363-4624; Elections-603-363-8071; Vital Records-603-363-8071.

Chichester Town

Town Clerk, 54 Main St., Chichester, NH 03258. **Phone**-603-798-5808, R/E Recording-603-798-5350; fax-603-798-3170.
Will search UCC records prior to 7/2001 and current liens only. Search per debtor- $10.00. UCC search includes tax liens. RE records at Merrimack County. UCC copy- $1.00 per page. **Other phones:** Assessor-603-798-5350; Elections-603-798-5808; Vital Records-603-798-5808.

Claremont City

City Clerk, 58 Tremont Sq, City Hall, Finance Office, Claremont, NH 03743. **Phone**-603-542-7001, UCC Recording-603-542-7003; fax-603-542-7014; hours 9AM-12:30PM, 1:30-5PM www.claremontnh.com
Will search UCC records prior to 7/2001 and current liens only. Search per debtor- $10.00. Will not search tax liens. RE records at Sullivan County. UCC copy- $1.00 per page. **Other phones:** Assessor-603-542-7008; Treasurer-603-542-7000; Elections-603-542-7003; Vital Records-603-542-7003.

Clarksville Town

Town Clerk, 408 NH Route 145, Clarksville, NH 03592. **Phone**-Town Clerk, R/E & UCC Recording-603-246-7751; fax-603-246-3480; hours 1-6:30PM M; 9AM-4PM T, Th; 12:30-6:30PM W; 9AM-N F
The County Register of Deeds records real estate transactions, and the City Clerk records UCC filings. Will search UCC records prior to 7/2001 and current liens only. Search per debtor- $10.00. UCC search includes tax liens if requested. RE records at Coos County. UCC copy- $1.00 per page. Payee: Town of Clarksville. **Other phones:** Assessor-800-417-2297; Treasurer-603-246-8896; Elections-603-246-7751; Vital Records-603-246-7751.

Colebrook Town

Assessor, 10 Bridge St, Colebrook, NH 03576. **Phone**-603-237-9173, R/E Recording-603-237-4070, UCC Recording-603-237-5200; fax-603-237-5086; hours 8AM-4PM www.colebrook-nh.com
Will search UCC records prior to 7/2001 only. Search per debtor- $10.00. Will not search tax liens. RE records at Coos County. UCC copy- $1.00 per page. **Other phones:** Assessor-603-237-4070; Treasurer-603-237-4142; Elections-603-237-5200; Vital Records-603-237-5200.

Columbia Town

Town Clerk, PO Box 157, Colebrook, NH 03576. **Phone**-603-237-5255; fax-603-237-8270; hours 10AM-5PM, M,W; 8AM-3PM, T, F
Will search UCC records prior to 7/2001 and current liens only. Search per debtor- $10.00. RE records at Coos County. UCC copy- $1.00 per page.

Concord City

City Clerk, 41 Green St, Rm 2, Concord, NH 03301-4255. **Phone**-603-225-8500, R/E Recording-603-228-0101, UCC Recording-603-271-3242; fax-603-225-8592; hours 8AM-4:30PM www.onconcord.com
Will search UCC records prior to 7/2001 and current liens only. Search per debtor- $10.00. Tax lien search- $10.00 per debtor. RE records at Merrimack County. UCC copy- $1.00 per page. Cert fee: $5.00 per doc. **Online Access to Property Assessor records:** Records on the city assessor database are free at http://data.visionappraisal.com/ConcordNH/. Registration is required to view full data. **Other phones:** Assessor-603-225-8550; Treasurer-603-225-8540; Elections-603-225-8550; Vital Records-603-225-8550 (Concord); State Vital Records-603-271-4650.

Conway Town

Town Clerk, 1634 E. Main St., Center Conway, NH 03813. **Phone**-603-447-3822; fax-603-447-1348; hours 9AM-5PM http://conwaynh.org

Will search UCC records prior to 7/2001. Search per debtor- $10.00. Will not search tax liens. RE records at Carroll County. UCC copy- $1.00 per page. **Other phones:** Assessor-603-447-3811; Elections-603-447-3822; Vital Records-603-447-3822.

Coos County

Register of Deeds, 55 School St, #103, Coos County Courthouse, Lancaster, NH 03584. **Phone**-Register of Deeds, R/E & UCC Recording- 603-788-2392; fax-603-788-4291; hours 8AM-4PM

The County Register of Deeds records real estate and Real Estate/UCC transactions, and the Town/City Clerk records UCC filings. Will not search records. RE record copy- $2.00 per page. UCC copy- $1.00 per page. Cert fee: $1.00 per doc. Payee: County Registry of Deeds.

Cornish Town

Town Clerk, PO Box 183, Cornish Flat, NH 03746. **Phone**-603-675-5207; fax-603-675-5605; hours 9MA-Noon M Th F; 4PM-7PM M TH.

Will search UCC records prior to 7/2001 and current liens only. Search per debtor- $10.00. Tax lien search- $20.00 per debtor. RE records at Sullivan County. UCC copy- $1.00 per page.

Croydon Town

Town Clerk, 879 NHRT10, Newport, NH 03773. **Phone**-603-863-7830; fax-603-863-2601; hours 9AM-1PM M-Th; 6PM-8PM W & Th

Will search UCC records prior to 7/2001 only. Search per debtor- $10.00. Will not search tax liens. RE records at Sullivan County. UCC copy- $1.00 per page. Payee: Town of Croydon. **Other phones:** Assessor-603-863-7830.

Dalton Town

Town Clerk, 741 Dalton Rd, Dalton, NH 03598. **Phone**-603-837-2096; fax-603-837-9642; hours 11AM-5:45PM M; 7AM-5PM T,W,Th

Will search UCC records prior to 7/2001 and current liens only. Search per debtor- $10.00. RE records at Coos County. UCC copy- $1.00 per page. **Other phones:** Treasurer-603-837-9802.

Danbury Town

Town Clerk, 23 High St., Danbury, NH 03230. **Phone**-603-768-5448; fax-603-768-3313; hours 8AM-4PM M&W; 1-7PM T

Will search UCC records prior to 7/2001 only. Search per debtor- $10.00. Will not search tax liens. RE records at Merrimack County. UCC copy- $1.00 per page. Payee: Town of Danbury. **Other phones:** Assessor-603-768-3313; Vital Records-603-768-5448.

Danville Town

Town Clerk, PO Box 11, Danville, NH 03819. **Phone**-603-382-8253; fax-603-382-3363; hours 9AM-1PM M; 4-8PM T & Th; 8:30AM-2:30PM W

Will search UCC records prior to 7/2001 and current liens only. Search per debtor- $10.00. RE records at Rockingham County. UCC copy- $1.00 per page.

Deerfield Town

Town Clerk, PO Box 159, Deerfield, NH 03037. **Phone**-603-463-8811; fax-603-463-2820; hours 8AM-2:30PM T-F; 8AM-7PM M www.ci.deerfield-nh.us

Will search UCC records prior to 7/2001. Search per debtor- $10.00. Will not search tax liens. RE records at Rockingham County. UCC copy- $1.00 per page. **Other phones:** Assessor-603-463-8811;

Treasurer-603-463-8811; Elections-603-463-8811; Vital Records-603-463-8811.

Deering Town

Town Clerk, 762 Deering Ctr Rd., Deering, NH 03244. **Phone**-603-464-3224; fax-603-464-3804. www.deering.nh.us

Will search UCC records prior to 7/2001 and current liens only. Search per debtor- $10.00. RE records at Hillsborough County. UCC copy- $1.00 per page. Cert fee: $10.00 per doc. Payee: Derring Town Clerk/Tax Collector.

Derry Town

Town Clerk, 14 Manning St, Derry, NH 03038. **Phone**-603-432-6105, R/E Recording-603-432-6106; fax-603-432-6131; hours 7AM-4PM M-F; 7AM-7PM W www.derry.nh.us

Will search UCC records prior to 7/2001 and current liens only. Search per debtor- $10.00. Federal/state combined tax lien search- $10.00 per tax. RE records at Rockingham County. UCC copy- $1.00 per page. **Online Access to Assessor, Property, Sale records:** Records of Derry assessed values are free at www.derry.nh.us/assessor/default.htm. Lists are by address; names are provided. **Other phones:** Assessor-603-432-6104; Treasurer-603-432-6100; Elections-603-432-6105; Vital Records-603-432-6106.

Dorchester Town

Town Clerk, 368 N Dorchester Rd, Dorecester, NH 03266. **Phone**-603-786-9076, UCC Recording-603-786-9476; hours 9-11AM M; 3-6PM W; 9-11AM last Sat.

Will search UCC records prior to 7/2001 and current liens only. Search per debtor- $10.00. UCC search includes tax liens. RE records at Grafton County. UCC copy- $1.00 per page. Payee: Town of Dorchester. **Other phones:** Assessor-603-523-7658; Treasurer-603-786-9076; Elections-603-786-9076; Vital Records-603-786-9076.

Dover City

City Clerk, 288 Central Ave, City Hall, Dover, NH 03820. **Phone**-603-743-6021; fax-603-516-6666; hours 8AM-4PM www.ci.dover.nh.us

Will search UCC records prior to 7/2001 and current liens only. Search per debtor- $10.00. Federal/state combined tax lien search- $10.00 per search. RE records at Strafford County. UCC copy- $1.00 per page. **Online Access to Property, Deed, Grantor/Grantee records:** Records are free on the Stafford county-wide system at www.nhdeeds.com/stfd/web/agree3.htm. Use the subscription service for full data. **Other phones:** Assessor-603-743-6014; Treasurer-603-743-6030; Elections-603-743-6021; Vital Records-603-743-6021.

Dublin Town

Town Clerk, Box 62, Dublin, NH 03444. **Phone**-603-563-8859; fax-603-563-9221; 8:30AM-4PM M-Th

Will search UCC records. UCC search per debtor- $5.00. Separate federal tax lien search available. Tax lien search- $5.00 per debtor. RE records at Cheshire County. UCC copy- $1.00 per page. **Other phones:** Assessor-603-563-8544; Treasurer-603-563-8544; Elections-603-563-8859; Vital Records-603-563-8859.

Dummer Town

Town Clerk, 1420 East Side River Rd., Dummer, NH 03588. **Phone**-603-449-3408; fax-603-449-3349; hours By appointment

Will search UCC records prior to 7/2001. Search per debtor- $10.00. Will not search tax liens. RE records at Coos County. UCC copy- $1.00 per page. Payee: Town of Dummer. **Other phones:** Treasurer-

603-449-3417; Elections-603-449-3442; Vital Records-603-449-3408.

Dunbarton Town

Town Clerk, 1011 School St., Dunbarton, NH 03045. **Phone**-603-774-3547; fax-603-774-5541; hours 8:30AM-4PM

Will search UCC records prior to 7/2001 and current liens only. Search per debtor- $10.00. RE records at Merrimack County. UCC copy- $1.00 per page. **Other phones:** Assessor-603-774-3547.

Durham Town

Town Clerk/Tax Collector, 15 Newmarket Rd, Town Hall, Durham, NH 03824-2898. **Phone**-603-868-5577; fax-603-868-8033; hours-8AM-5PM www.ci.durham.nh.us/DEPARTMENTS/town_clerk/clerk.html

Will search UCC records prior to 7/2001 and current liens only. Search per debtor- $10.00. Federal/state combined tax lien search- $10.00 per debtor. RE records at Strafford County. UCC copy- $1.00 per page. **Online Access to Property, Deed, Grantor/Grantee, Assessor records:** Records are free on the Stafford county-wide system at www.nhdeeds.com/stfd/web/agree3.htm. Use the subscription service for full data. Also, Assessor data is free at http://data.visionappraisal.com/DurhamNH/. **Other phones:** Assessor-603-868-8065; Treasurer-603-868-8043; Vital Records-603-868-5577.

East Kingston Town

Town Clerk, PO Box 249, East Kingston, NH 03827-0249. **Phone**-Town Clerk, R/E & UCC Recording-603-642-8794; fax-603-642-8406; hours M 6-8PM; T-F 8AM-2PM; Thur eve. 6-8PM

Will search UCC records prior to 7/2001 and current liens only. Search per debtor- $10.00. Will search tax liens including federal tax liens. RE records at Rockingham County. UCC copy- $1.00 per page. **Other phones:** Assessor-603-642-8406; Treasurer-603-642-8406; Elections-603-642-8794; Vital Records-603-642-8794.

Easton Town

Town Clerk, PO Box 741, Franconia, NH 03580. **Phone**-603-823-8017; fax-603-823-7780; hours 10AM-Noon M; 4PM-6PM Th

Will not search UCC or tax liens records. RE records at Grafton County. UCC copy- $1.00 per page. Payee: Town Clerk of Easton.

Eaton Town

Town Clerk, Box 118, Eaton Center, NH 03832. **Phone**-603-447-2840; fax-603-447-2560; hours 9AM-11AM, M; 7PM-9PM T or by appointment

Will search UCC records prior to 7/2001 and current liens only. Search per debtor- $10.00. Tax lien search- $10.00 per debtor or year. RE records at Carroll County. UCC copy- $1.00 per page.

Effingham Town

Town Clerk, PO Box 117, Effingham, NH 03882. **Phone**-603-539-7551; fax-603-539-7799; 8AM-Noon, 3PM-7PM T; 8AM-5PM TH; 8AM-Noon Sat

Will search UCC records prior to 7/2001 and current liens only. Search per debtor- $10.00. Will search tax liens including federal tax liens. Federal/state combined tax lien search- $10.00 per search. RE records at Carroll County. UCC copy- $.75 per page. Cert fee: $10.00 per cert. Payee: Town of Effingham. **Other phones:** Assessor-603-539-7770; Treasurer-603-539-7770; Elections-603-539-7551; Vital Records-603-539-7551.

Ellsworth Town

Town Clerk, 12 Ellsworth Pond Rd, c/o Donna O'Brien, Plymouth, NH 03223. **Phone**-603-726-3551; fax-603-726-8994; hours by appointment only Irregular office hours; call and leave message to request appointment. Town Clerk works out of her house. No real estate recordings on record here. Will search UCC records prior to 7/2001 only. Search per debtor- $10.00. Will not search tax liens. RE records at Grafton County. UCC copy- $1.00 per page. Payee: Town of Ellsworth. **Other phones:** Treasurer-603-726-8668.

Enfield Town

Town Clerk, PO Box 373, Enfield, NH 03748-0373. **Phone**-603-632-5001; fax-603-632-5182; hours 8:30AM-3:30PM M-W & F; 9:30AM-4:30PM T www.enfield.nh.us
Will search UCC records prior to 7/2001 only. Search per debtor- $10.00. Will not search tax liens. RE records at Grafton County. UCC copy- $1.00 per page. Payee: Town of Enfield. **Other phones:** Assessor-603-632-4201; Elections-603-632-5001; Vital Records-603-632-5001.

Epping Town

Town Clerk, 157 Main St, Epping, NH 03042. **Phone**-603-679-8288; fax-603-679-3002.
Will search UCC records prior to 7/2001. Search per debtor- $10.00. Will not search tax liens. RE records at Rockingham County. UCC copy- $1.00 per page. Cert fee: $3.00 per page. Payee: Town of Epping. **Other phones:** Assessor-603-679-5441; Elections-603-679-8288; Vital Records-603-679-8288.

Epsom Town

Town Clerk, PO Box 10, Epsom, NH 03234. **Phone**-603-736-4825; fax-603-736-8539; hours 8-1PM;4:30-6:30PM, M;10-3PM T; 8-3PM TH;8-3PM F
Will search UCC records prior to 7/2001 and current liens only. Search per debtor- $10.00. Tax lien search- $10.00 per debtor. RE records at Merrimack County. UCC copy- $1.00 per page. **Other phones:** Appraiser/ Auditor-603-736-9002.

Errol Town

Town Clerk, PO Box 100, Errol, NH 03579. **Phone**-603-482-3351; fax-603-482-3804; hours 9AM-11AM, M;5PM-7:30PM, T; 8:30AM-11AM, TH
Will search UCC records prior to 7/2001 and current liens only. Search per debtor- $5.00. Will search tax liens including federal tax liens. Tax lien search- $15.00 per debtor. RE records at Coos County. UCC copy- $.75 per page. **Other phones:** Assessor-603-482-3351; Treasurer-603-482-3351; Elections-603-482-3351; Vital Records-603-482-3351.

Exeter Town

Town Clerk, 10 Front St, Exeter, NH 03833-2792. **Phone**-603-778-0591; fax-603-772-4709; hours 8:30AM-3:30PM www.exeternh.org/tnclk/index.html
Will search UCC records prior to 7/2001 and current liens only. Search per debtor- $10.00. RE records at Rockingham County. UCC copy- $1.00 per page. Cert fee: $4.00 per page. Payee: Exeter Clerk. **Other phones:** Assessor-603-778-0591; Vital Records-603-778-0591.

Farmington Town

Town Clerk, 41 S Main St, Town Hall, Farmington, NH 03835. **Phone**-603-755-3657; fax-603-755-9128; hours 8:30AM-5PM M-W, 8:30AM-7PM Th, 8:30AM-12:30 PM F
Will search UCC records prior to 7/2001 and current liens only. Search per debtor- $10.00. Tax lien search- $7.00 per debtor. RE records at Strafford County. UCC copy- $1.00 per page. **Online Access to Property, Deed, Grantor/Grantee records:** Records are free on the Stafford county-wide system at www.nhdeeds.com/stfd/web/agree3.htm. Use the subscription service for full data. **Other phones:** Assessor-603-755-2774; Treasurer-603-755-2731; Elections-603-755-3657; Vital Records-603-755-3657.

Fitzwilliam Town

Town Clerk, PO Box 504, Fitzwilliam, NH 03447-0504. **Phone**-603-585-7791; fax-603-585-7744.
Will search UCC records prior to 7/2001 and current liens only. Search per debtor- $10.00. Will search tax liens. RE records at Cheshire County. UCC copy- $1.00 per page.

Francestown Town

Town Clerk, PO Box 67, Francestown, NH 03043-0067. **Phone**-603-547-6251; fax-603-547-2622; hours 8AM-Noon M-Th; 6-8PM M
Will search UCC records prior to 7/2001 and current liens only. Search per debtor- $10.00. Tax lien search- $10.00 per debtor. RE records at Hillsborough County. UCC copy- $1.00 per page.

Franconia Town

Town Clerk, PO Box 900, Franconia, NH 03580. **Phone**-603-823-5237; fax-603-823-5581; hours 8AM-2PM Tues.; 1-7PM Th
Will search UCC records prior to 7/2001 and current liens only. Search per debtor- $10.00. UCC search includes tax liens if requested. RE records at Grafton County. UCC copy- $1.00 per page. Payee: Town of Franconia.

Franklin City

City Clerk, 316 Central St, Franklin, NH 03235. **Phone**-603-934-3109; fax-603-934-7413; 8AM-5PM
Will search UCC records prior to 7/2001 and current liens only. Search per debtor- $15.00. Tax lien search- $15.00 per debtor. RE records at Merrimack County. UCC copy- $1.00 per page. Payee: City of Franklin. **Other phones:** Assessor-603-934-5449; Treasurer-603-934-3900; Elections-603-934-3109; Vital Records-603-934-3109.

Freedom Town

Town Clerk, PO Box 457, Freedom, NH 03836. **Phone**-603-539-6323, R/E Recording-603-539-4872; fax-603-539-8270; hours 6:30-8PM Mon & Wed; 9AM-Noon Sat.
Will search UCC records prior to 7/2001 and current liens only. Search per debtor- $10.00. Will not search tax liens. RE records at Carroll County. UCC copy- $1.00 per page. **Other phones:** Assessor-603-539-6323; Treasurer-603-539-6323.

Fremont Town

Town Clerk, PO Box 120, Fremont, NH 03044. **Phone**-603-895-8693, R/E Recording-603-895-2226; fax-603-895-3149; hours 9:30AM-N, 1-4PM T,W,F; 3-8PM Th; 3rd Sat 9:30AM-N http://fremont.nh.gov
Will search UCC records prior to 7/2001 and current liens only. Search per debtor- $10.00. Tax liens not included in UCC search. Separate federal & state combined tax lien search- $10.00 per search. RE records at Rockingham County. UCC copy- $1.00 per page. **Other phones:** Assessor-603-895-2226; Treasurer-603-895-2226; Elections-603-895-8693; Vital Records-603-895-8693.

Gilford Town

Town Clerk, 47 Cherry Valley Rd, Town Hall, Gilford, NH 03246. **Phone**-603-527-4713; fax-603-527-4719.
Will search UCC records prior to 7/2001 and current liens only. Search per debtor- $10.00. Search request using non-standard form (per name)- $12.00. No tax liens filed here. RE records at Belknap County. UCC copy- $1.00 per page. Cert fee: None. Payee: Gilford Town Clerk. **Other phones:** Assessor-603-524-3293.

Gilmanton Town

Town Clerk/Tax Collector, PO Box 550, Gilmanton, NH 03237-0550. **Phone**-603-267-6726; fax-603-267-6701; hours 9AM-Noon 7-8:30PM M; 9AM-4PM W F; 9AM-Noon TH
Will search UCC records prior to 7/2001. Search per debtor- $15.00. Tax liens not included in UCC search. Tax lien search- $50.00 per hour (min 1 hour). Will search real estate records. Record copy- $1.00 per page.

Gilsum Town

Town Clerk, PO Box 36, Gilsum, NH 03448. **Phone**-603-357-0320; fax-603-352-0845; hours 6PM-8PM Tu; 8AM-Noon Sat.
No real estate recordings; see tax collector. Will search UCC records. UCC search per debtor-$15.00 per search. Federal/state combined tax lien search- $15.00 per debtor. RE records at Cheshire County. UCC copy- $5.00 per page. Cert fee: $5.00 per page. Payee: Town Clerk. **Other phones:** Assessor-603-357-0320.

Goffstown Town

Town Clerk, 16 Main St, Goffstown, NH 03045. **Phone**-603-497-3613, R/E Recording-603-497-3611; fax-603-497-8993; hours 8:30AM-4:30PM M,T,F; 8:30AM-N W; 8:30AM-6PM Th www.ci.goffstown.nh.us
Will search UCC records prior to 7/2001 and current liens only. Search per debtor- $10.00. Tax lien search- $10.00 per debtor. RE records at Hillsborough County. UCC copy- $1.00 per page. **Other phones:** Assessor-603-497-3611; Treasurer-603-497-3615; Elections-603-497-3613; Vital Records-603-497-3613.

Gorham Town

Town Clerk, 20 Park St, Gorham, NH 03581-1694. **Phone**-603-466-2744; fax-603-466-3100; hours 8:30AM-N, 1-5PM M,W,F; 8:30AM-1PM, 2-5PM T,Th www.gorhamnh.org
Will search UCC records prior to 7/2001 and current liens only. Search per debtor- $10.00. UCC search includes tax liens. Separate federal/state Tax lien search- $10.00 per debtor. RE records at Coos County. UCC copy- $1.00 per page. **Other phones:** Assessor-603-466-3322; Treasurer-603-466-3100; Elections-603-466-2744; Vital Records-603-466-2744.

Goshen Town

Town Clerk, PO Box 58, Goshen, NH 03752. **Phone**-603-863-5655; fax-603-863-6139; hours 8:30AM-Noon, 1-5PM M,W,F
Will search UCC records prior to 7/2001 only. Search per debtor- $10.00. RE records at Sullivan County. UCC copy- $1.00 per page. Payee: Town of Goshen. **Other phones:** Assessor-603-863-5080.

Grafton County

Registry of Deeds, 3785 Dartmouth College Hwy, Box 2, North Haverhill, NH 03774-9700. **Phone**-Registry of Deeds, R/E & UCC Recording- 603-787-6921; fax-603-787-2363; hours 7:30AM-4:30PM
Will not search records. Record copy- $1.00 per page. Cert fee: $2.00. Payee: Grafton County Registry of Deeds. **Online Access to Real Estate, Lien records:** Access to the County dial-up service requires a $100 set up fee and $40 per month access fee. Two years of data are kept on system; prior years on CD. Lending agency information available. A fax-back service is in-state only. For further information, call 603-787-6921. **Other phones:** Treasurer-603-787-6941; Elections-603-787-6941.

Grafton Town

Town Clerk, PO Box 297, Grafton, NH 03240. **Phone-**603-523-7270, R/E Recording-603-523-7700; fax-603-523-4397.

Will search UCC records prior to 7/2001 and current liens only. Search per debtor- $10.00. Federal/state combined tax lien search- $10.00 per debtor RE records at Grafton County. UCC copy- $1.00 per page. Cert fee: $12.00 for 1st copy; $8 2nd. Payee: Town of Grafton. **Other phones:** Treasurer-603-523-7700; Elections-603-523-7270; Vital Records-603-523-7270.

Grantham Town

Town Clerk, PO Box 135, Grantham, NH 03753-0135. **Phone-**603-863-5608; fax-603-863-4499; hours 7:30AM-4:30PM M-Th; 7-9PM Tu-W http://granthamnh.net/

Will search UCC records prior to 7/2001 and current liens only. Search per debtor- $10.00. Tax liens included in UCC search. Federal tax lien search- $10.00. RE records at Sullivan County. UCC copy- $1.00 per page. Payee: Town of Grantham. **Other phones:** Assessor-603-863-6021; Treasurer-603-863-6021; Elections-603-863-5608; Vital Records-603-863-5608.

Greenfield Town

Town Clerk, PO Box 256, Greenfield, NH 03047. **Phone-**603-547-2782; fax-603-547-3004; hours 6AM-7:30PM M-Th; 2nd & 4th Sat. 9AM-Noon http://greenfieldnh.org

Will search UCC records prior to 7/2001 and current liens only. Search per debtor- $10.00. RE records at Hillsborough County. UCC copy- $1.00 per page.

Greenland Town

Town Clerk, PO Box 100, Greenland, NH 03840-0100. **Phone-**Town Clerk, R/E & UCC Recording- 603-431-7111; fax-603-430-3761; hours 12;00-8PM,M; 9AM-4:30PM T-F

Will search UCC records prior to 7/2001 and current liens only. Search per debtor- $10.00. RE records at Rockingham County. UCC copy- $1.00 per page. Cert fee: $1.00. Payee: Greenland Town Clerk. **Online Access to Property Assessor records:** Access is via a private company at http://data.visionappraisal.com/GreenlandNH/. Free registration is required to view full data. **Other phones:** Assessor-603-431-7111; Treasurer-603-431-7111; Elections-603-431-7111; Vital Records-603-431-7111.

Greenville Town

Town Clerk, PO Box 354, Greenville, NH 03048-0354. **Phone-**603-878-4155; fax-603-878-4951; 10AM-12;00-1-4PM,T,TH; 10AM-12;00,1-3PM W Will search UCC records prior to 7/2001 and current liens only. Search per debtor- $10.00. RE records at Hillsborough County. UCC copy- $1.00 per page. **Other phones:** Assessor-603-878-2084.

Groton Town

Town Clerk, 63-1 N. Groton Rd, Groton, NH 03241. **Phone-**603-744-8849; hours 10AM-6PM M,F; 10AM-2PM 1st & last Sat

Will search UCC records prior to 7/2001 only. Search per debtor- $10.00. Will search tax liens including federal tax liens. RE records at Grafton County. UCC copy- $1.00 per page. Payee: Town of Groton.

Hampstead Town

Town Clerk, PO Box 298, Hampstead, NH 03841. **Phone-**603-329-4100; fax-603-329-7174; hours 8AM-7PM, M; 8AM-4PM, T,W,TH; 8AM-12PM, F Will search UCC records prior to 7/2001 and current liens only. Search per debtor- $10.00. RE records at Rockingham County. UCC copy- $1.00 per page.

Hampton Falls Town

Town Clerk, 1 Drinkwater Rd, Town Hall, Hampton Falls, NH 03844. **Phone-**603-926-4618, R/E Recording-603-929-0828; fax-603-926-1848; hours 9AM-N, 1-4PM M,T,Th. Will search UCC records prior to 7/2001 and current liens only. Search per debtor- $10.00. UCC search includes tax liens if requested. Separate federal & state combined tax lien search- $10.00 per debtor. RE records at Rockingham County. UCC copy- $1.00 per page. **Other phones:** Assessor-603-929-0828; Treasurer-603-929-3613; Elections-603-926-4618; Vital Records-603-926-4618; Town Hall-603-926-7101.

Hampton Town

Town Clerk, 100 Winnacunnet Rd, Hampton, NH 03842. **Phone-**603-926-0406; fax-603-929-5917; hours 9AM-4PM

Will search UCC records prior to 7/2001 and current liens only. Search per debtor- $10.00 per doc, $1.00 per page for copies. Federal/state combined tax lien search- $10.00 per debtor. RE records at Rockingham County. UCC copy- $1.00 per page. Cert fee: $4.00 per doc. Payee: Town Clerk. **Online Access to Assessor, Property records:** Access to property assessor data is at http://data.visionappraisal.com/HamptonNH/. Free registration required. **Other phones:** Assessor-603-929-5923; Elections-603-926-0406; Vital Records-603-926-0406.

Hancock Town

Town Clerk, PO Box 6, Hancock, NH 03449. **Phone-**603-525-4441; fax-603-525-4427; hours 9AM-4PM Will search UCC records prior to 7/2001 and current liens only. Search per debtor- $10.00. Will not search tax liens. RE records at Hillsborough County. UCC copy- $1.00 per page. **Other phones:** Assessor-603-525-4441; Treasurer-603-525-4441.

Hanover Town

Town Clerk, PO Box 483, Hanover, NH 03755-0483. **Phone-**603-643-4123; fax-603-643-1720; 8:30AM-4:30PM. Will search UCC records prior to 7/2001 and current liens only. Search per debtor- $10.00. UCC search includes tax liens. RE records at Grafton County. UCC copy- $1.00 per page. Cert fee: no fee. **Other phones:** Assessor-603-643-0703; Treasurer-603-643-4123.

Harrisville Town

Town Clerk, PO Box 284, Harrisville, NH 03450. **Phone-**603-827-5546; fax-603-827-2917; hours 2-7PM, T; 4-6:30PM, W; 9-11:30AM Th.

Will search UCC records prior to 7/2001 and current liens only. Search per debtor- $10.00. Tax lien search- $10.00. RE records at Cheshire County. UCC copy- $2.00 per page. Cert fee: $2.00 per record. Payee: Town Clerk-Harrisville. **Other phones:** Treasurer-603-827-3431; Elections-603-827-5546; Vital Records-603-827-5546.

Hart's Location Town

Town Clerk, 5 Forest Rd, Hart's Location, NH 03812. **Phone-**603-374-2436; hours By Appointment Will search UCC records prior to 7/2001 and current liens only. Search per debtor- $10.00. Federal/state combined tax lien search- $15.00 per lien. RE records at Carroll County. UCC copy- $1.00 per page. Payee: Town Clerk of Hart's Location. **Other phones:** Assessor-603-586-7153; Treasurer-603-383-3605.

Haverhill Town

Town Clerk, 2975 Dartmouth College Hwy, N. Haverhill, NH 03774. **Phone-**603-787-6200, R/E

Recording-603-787-6444, UCC Recording-603-717-6200; fax-603-787-2226; hours 9AM-4:30PM Will search UCC records prior to 7/2001 and current liens only. Search per debtor- $10.00. RE records at Grafton County. UCC copy- $1.00 per page. Payee: Town of Haverhill. **Other phones:** Assessor-603-787-6444; Treasurer-603-747-2735; Elections-603-787-6200; Vital Records-603-787-6200.

Hebron Town

Town Clerk, HC 58 Box 286, East Hebron, NH 03242. **Phone-**603-744-7999; fax-603-744-7999; hours 6-8PM Tu; 9:30-11:30AM Sat.

Will not search UCC or tax liens records. RE records at Grafton County. UCC copy- $1.00 per page. Payee: Town of Hebron.

Henniker Town

Town Clerk, 2 Depot Hill Rd, Henniker, NH 03242. **Phone-**Town Clerk, R/E & UCC Recording- 603-428-3240; fax-603-428-4366; hours 8AM-5:30PM, M; 8AM-Noon, T; 8AM-4:30PM, W, F

Will search UCC records prior to 7/2001 and current liens only. Search per debtor- $10.00. Tax liens not included in UCC search. Separate federal tax lien search- 10.00. RE records at Merrimack County. UCC copy- $1.00 per page. Cert fee: $12.00. Payee: Henniker Town Clerk. **Other phones:** Assessor-603-428-3221; Elections-603-428-3240; Vital Records-603-428-3240.

Hill Town

Town Clerk, PO Box 251, Hill, NH 03243. **Phone-**603-934-3951; fax-603-934-3951; hours Mon/Wed 9AM-12; Tues. 9AM-12 & 6-9PM; Th. 9AM-3PM

Will search UCC records prior to 7/2001 and current liens only. Search per debtor- $10.00. Federal/state combined tax lien search- $10.00 per debtor RE records at Merrimack County. UCC copy- $1.00 per page. Cert fee: $4.00 per doc. Payee: Town of Hill. **Other phones:** Assessor-603-934-1094; Treasurer-603-934-1094; Elections-603-934-3951; Vital Records-603-934-3951.

Hillsborough County

Registrar of Deeds, PO Box 370, Nashua, NH 03061-0370. **Phone-**603-882-6933, R/E Recording-603-882-6933 x115; fax-603-594-4137; hours 8AM-3:45PM www.nhdeeds.com

Will not search records. Copy fee- $1.00 per page. Cert fee: $2.00 per doc. Payee: Hillsborough County Treasurer. **Online Access to Real Estate, Deed, Mortgage, Lien, Grantor/Grantee records:** Access to county register of deeds data is free at www.nhdeeds.com/hils/web/argthc.htm. Online records go back to 1966.

Hillsborough Town

Town Clerk, PO Box 1699, Hillsborough, NH 03244. **Phone-**603-464-5571; fax-603-464-4270; 9AM-5PM Will search UCC records prior to 7/2001 and current liens only. Search per debtor- $10.00. Will not search tax liens. RE records at Hillsborough County. UCC copy- $5.00 per page. Cert fee: $15.00. Payee: Hillsborough Town Clerk. **Other phones:** Assessor-603-464-3877.

Hinsdale Town

Town Clerk, PO Box 31, Hinsdale, NH 03451. **Phone-**603-336-5719; fax-603-366-5711-; hours 11-4 M-W, 1:30-6:30 1st 2nd TH, other TH 11-4

Will search UCC records prior to 7/2001 only. Search per debtor- $10.00. Will not search tax liens. RE records at Cheshire County. UCC copy- $1.00 per page. Payee: Town of Hinsdale. **Online Access to Assessor, Property records:** Access to property assessor data is at http://data.visionappraisal.com/HinsdaleNH/.

Holderness Town

Town Clerk, PO Box 203, Holderness, NH 03245. **Phone**-603-968-7536; fax-603-968-9954; hours 8:30AM-4:30PM www.holderness-nh.gov/
Will search UCC records prior to 7/2001. Search per debtor- $10.00. Will not search tax liens. RE records at Grafton County. RE record copy- $.50 per page. UCC copy- $1.00 per page. **Other phones:** Assessor-603-968-3297; Treasurer-603-968-3297; Elections-603-968-7536; Vital Records-603-968-7536.

Hollis Town

Town Clerk, 7 Monument Sq, Hollis, NH 03049-6568. **Phone**-603-465-2064, R/E Recording-603-465-7987; fax-603-465-2964; hours M-W-F 8AM-1PM; Mon Eve. 7-9PM; 1st Sat. 8-11AM
Will search UCC records prior to 7/2001 and current liens only. Search per debtor- $10.00. Tax lien search- $10.00 per debtor. RE records at Hillsborough County. UCC copy- $1.00 per page. Cert fee: $10.00 per doc. Payee: Town of Hollis. **Online Access to Assessor records:** Access assessor data at http://data.visionappraisal.com/HollisNH/. **Other phones:** Assessor-603-465-9860; Treasurer-603-465-6936; Elections-603-465-2064; Vital Records-603-465-2064.

Hooksett Town

Town Clerk, 16 N. Main St, Hooksett, NH 03106. **Phone**-603-485-9534; fax-603-485-4423; hours 8AM-4:30PM; 8AM-6:30PM W www.hooksett.org
Will search UCC records prior to 7/2001 and current liens only. Search per debtor- $15.00. RE records at Merrimack County. UCC copy- $1.00 per page. **Other phones:** Assessor-603-268-0003.

Hopkinton Town

Town Clerk, PO Box 446, Contoocook, NH 03229-0446. **Phone**-603-746-3180; fax-603-746-4011; hours 8AM-4:30PM www.hopkintonnh.us
Will search UCC records prior to 7/2001 and current liens only. Search per debtor- $10.00. Will not search tax liens. RE records at Merrimack County. UCC copy- $1.00 per page. **Other phones:** Assessor-603-746-3170; Treasurer-603-746-3180.

Hudson Town

Town Clerk, 12 School St, Hudson, NH 03051-4294. **Phone**-603-886-6003; hours 8:30AM-4:30PM
Will search UCC records. Search per debtor- $10.00. Will not search tax liens. RE records at Hillsborough County. UCC copy- $1.00 per page. Payee: Town of Hudson. **Other phones:** Assessor-603-886-6024; Treasurer-603-886-6000.

Jackson Town

Town Clerk, PO Box 336, Jackson, NH 03846-0336. **Phone**-603-383-6248; 8:30AM-12:30PM T,W,F
Will search UCC records prior to 7/2001 and current liens only. Search per debtor- $15.00. Will not search tax liens. RE records at Carroll County. UCC copy- $5.75 per page. Cert fee: $6.25. Payee: Jackson Town Clerk. **Other phones:** Assessor-603-383-4223.

Jaffrey Town

Town Clerk, 10 Goodnow St., Jaffrey, NH 03452. **Phone**-603-532-7861; fax-603-532-7862.
Will search UCC records prior to 7/2001 and current liens only. Search per debtor- $10.00. UCC search includes tax liens if requested. Separate Tax lien search- $10.00 per page. RE records at Cheshire County. UCC copy- $1.00 per page. **Other phones:** Assessor-603-532-7445; Treasurer-603-532-7445.

Jefferson Town

Town Clerk, 84 Stag Hollow Rd, Jefferson, NH 03583. **Phone**-603-586-4553; fax-603-586-4553.
Will search UCC records prior to 7/2001 and current liens only. Search per debtor- $10.00. Federal/state combined tax lien search- $10.00 per debtor RE records at Coos County. UCC copy- $1.00 per page. **Other phones:** Assessor-603-586-4553; Treasurer-603-586-4400; Elections-603-586-4553; Vital Records-603-586-4553.

Keene City

City Clerk, 3 Washington St, Keene, NH 03431. **Phone**-603-352-0133, R/E Recording-603-352-0403; fax-603-357-9884; 8AM-5PM www.keenenh.com
Will search UCC records prior to 7/2001 only. Search per debtor- $10.00. Tax liens not included in UCC search. Separate federal tax lien search- $7.00 per debtor. RE records at Cheshire County. UCC copy- $1.00 per page. **Other phones:** Assessor-603-352-2125; Treasurer-603-357-9801; Elections-603-352-0133; Vital Records-603-352-0133.

Kensington Town

Town Clerk, 95 Amesbury Rd, Rte 150, Town Hall, Kensington, NH 03833. **Phone**-Town Clerk, R/E & UCC Recording- 603-772-5423; fax-603-772-6841. http://town.kensington.nh.us
Will search UCC records prior to 7/2001 and current liens only. Search per debtor- $10.00. UCC search includes tax liens. Tax lien search- $5.00 per debtor. RE records at Rockingham County. UCC copy- $1.00 per page. **Other phones:** Assessor-603-436-5916; Treasurer-603-772-5423; Elections-603-772-5423; Vital Records-603-772-5423.

Kingston Town

Town Clerk, PO Box 657, Kingston, NH 03848-0657. **Phone**-603-642-3112; fax-603-642-3204; hours 8:30AM-noon, 1-4PM M-F; 7-9PM M, T
Will search UCC records. UCC search per debtor- $15.00 per search. Will not search tax liens. RE records at Rockingham County. UCC copy- $1.00 per page. **Other phones:** Assessor-603-642-3342.

Laconia City

City Clerk, PO Box 489, Laconia, NH 03247. **Phone**-603-527-1265, R/E Recording-603-527-5420; fax-603-524-1766; hours 8:30AM-4:30PM
Will search UCC records prior to 7/2001 and current liens only. Search per debtor- $10.00. Federal/state combined tax lien search- $10.00 per debtor. RE records at Belknap County. UCC copy- $1.00 per page. **Online Access to Property Assessor records:** Records on the town assessor database are online at http://data.visionappraisal.com/LaconiaNH. Free registration is required for full access. **Other phones:** Assessor-603-527-1268; Treasurer-603-524-3877; Elections-603-527-1265; Vital Records-603-527-1265; Tax Office-603-527-1269.

Lancaster Town

Town Clerk, 25 Main St, Lancaster, NH 03584. **Phone**-603-788-2306, R/E Recording-603-788-2392; fax-603-788-2114; hours 8:30AM-5PM M-TH; 8:30AM-4:30PM F
Will search UCC records prior to 7/2001 and current liens only. Search per debtor- $10.00. Will search federal tax liens. Separate federal & state combined tax lien search- $10.00 per debtor. RE records at Coos County. UCC copy- $1.00 per page. **Other phones:** Assessor-603-788-3391; Treasurer-603-788-3391; Elections-603-788-2306; Vital Records-603-788-2306.

Landaff Town

Town Clerk, PO Box 125, Landaff, NH 03585. **Phone**-603-838-6220; fax-603-838-6220; hours 9AM-11AM & 5PM-7PM T
Will search UCC records prior to 7/2001 and current liens only. Search per debtor- $10.00. UCC search includes tax liens. Tax lien search- $5.00 per page. RE records at Grafton County. UCC copy- $1.00 per page. Payee: Town of Landaff. **Other phones:** Assessor-207-778-3881; Treasurer-603-838-6116; Elections-603-838-6220; Vital Records-603-838-6220.

Langdon Town

Town Clerk, 5 Walker Hill Rd, Langdon Town Hall, Langdon, NH 03602. **Phone**-603-835-2389; fax-603-835-2389; hours 10AM-Noon, 3-6PM T
Will search UCC records prior to 7/2001 and current liens only. Search per debtor- $10.00. UCC search includes tax liens. RE records at Sullivan County. UCC copy- $1.00 per page. Payee: Town of Langdon.

Lebanon City

City Clerk, 51 N. Park St, Lebanon, NH 03766. **Phone**-603-448-3054; fax-603-448-4891; hours 8AM-5PM www.lebcity.com
Will search UCC records prior to 7/2001 and current liens only. Search per debtor- $10.00. Federal/state combined tax lien search- $10.00 per debtor. RE records at Grafton County. UCC copy- $1.00 per page. **Online Access to Property Assessor records:** Records from the city assessor database are free at http://data.visionappraisal.com/LEBANONNH/. Free registration is required to view full data. **Other phones:** Assessor-603-448-1499; Elections-603-448-3054; Vital Records-603-448-3054.

Lee Town

Town Clerk, 7 Mast Rd, Town Hall, Lee, NH 03824. **Phone**-603-659-2964; fax-603-659-7202; hours 8AM-4PM M, W, F
Will search UCC records prior to 7/2001 and current liens only. Search per debtor- $10.00. UCC search includes tax liens if requested. Separate state/federal Tax lien search- $10.00. RE records at Strafford County. UCC copy- $1.00 per page. Cert fee: $1.00. Payee: Lee Town Clerk. **Online Access to Property, Deed, Grantor/Grantee records:** Records are free on the Stafford county-wide system at www.nhdeeds.com/stfd/web/agree3.htm. Use the subscription service for full data. **Other phones:** Assessor-603-659-5414; Treasurer-603-659-5414; Elections-603-659-2964; Vital Records-603-659-2964.

Lempster Town

Town Clerk, PO Box 33, East Lempster, NH 03605-0033. **Phone**-603-863-3213; fax-603-863-8105; hours 9AM-Noon M-F; 5-7PM W
Will search UCC records prior to 7/2001 and current liens only. Search per debtor- $10.00. RE records at Sullivan County. UCC copy- $1.00 per page. **Other phones:** Treasurer-603-863-3213.

Lincoln Town

Town Clerk, PO Box 39, Lincoln, NH 03251. **Phone**-603-745-8971; fax-603-745-6743; hours 8AM-4PM
Will search UCC records prior to 7/2001 and current liens only. Search per debtor- $10.00. UCC search includes tax liens if requested. Separate state/federal Tax lien search- $10.00. RE records at Grafton County. UCC copy- $1.00 per page. Cert fee: None. Payee: Town of Lincoln. **Other phones:** Assessor-603-745-2757; Treasurer-603-745-8971.

Lisbon Town

Town Clerk, 46 School St, Lisbon, NH 03585. **Phone-**603-838-2862; fax-603-838-6790; hours 9AM-12,1-4:30PM
Will search UCC records prior to 7/2001 and current liens only. Search per debtor- $10.00. RE records at Grafton County. UCC copy- $1.00 per page. Cert fee: $10.00. Payee: Lisbon Town Clerk. **Other phones:** Assessor-603-838-6377.

Litchfield Town

Town Clerk, 2 Liberty Way, #3, Litchfield, NH 03052. **Phone-**603-424-4045, R/E Recording-603-882-6933; hours 10AM-6PM, M; 9AM-4PM, T; 8AM-3PM, W TH F
Will search UCC records prior to 7/2001 only. Search per debtor- $10.00. Will search tax liens including federal tax liens. RE records at Hillsborough County. UCC copy- $1.00 per page. Payee: Town of Litchfield. **Other phones:** Assessor-603-424-4046; Vital Records-603-424-4045.

Littleton Town

Town Clerk, 125 Main St, 2nd Fl, Littleton, NH 03561. **Phone-**603-444-3995 x20; fax-603-444-1715; hours 8:30AM-12:30PM, 1-4PM www.townoflittleton.org
Will search UCC records prior to 7/2001 and current liens only. Search per debtor- $10.00. Federal/state combined tax lien search- $10.00 per debtor RE records at Grafton County. UCC copy- $1.00 per page. **Online Access to Property, Map records:** Access town property data free on the GIS mapping site www.mapsherpa.com/mapsonline/littleton/htdocs/index .html. **Other phones:** Assessor-603-444-3995 x16; Treasurer-603-444-3995 x11; Elections-603-444-3995 x20; Vital Records-603-444-3995 x20.

Londonderry Town

Town Clerk, 50 Nashua Rd, #100, Londonderry, NH 03053. **Phone-**603-432-1100 x195, R/E Recording-603-432-1100 x135; fax-603-432-1142; hours 8:30AM-5PM www.londonderry.org
Will search UCC records prior to 7/2001 and current liens only. Search per debtor- $10.00. Federal/state combined tax lien search- $10.00 per search RE records at Rockingham County. UCC copy- $1.00 per page. **Other phones:** Assessor-603-432-1100 x135; Treasurer-603-432-1126; Appraiser/ Auditor-603-432-1100 x109; Elections-603-432-1100 x114; Vital Records-603-432-1100 x195.

Loudon Town

Town Clerk, PO Box 7837, Loudon, NH 03301. **Phone-**603-798-4542, R/E Recording-603-798-4541; fax-603-798-4546.
Will search UCC records prior to 7/2001 and current liens only. Search per debtor- $10.00. RE records at Merrimack County. UCC copy- $1.00 per page. **Other phones:** Assessor-603-798-4541; Treasurer-603-798-4541; Elections-603-798-4542; Vital Records-603-798-4542.

Lyman Town

Town Clerk, 65 Parker Hill Rd, Lyman, NH 03585. **Phone-**603-838-6113; fax-603-838-6818. Will not search UCC or tax liens records. RE records at Grafton County. UCC copy- $1.00 per page. **Other phones:** Assessor-603-838-5900; Treasurer-603-838-6689.

Lyme Town

Town Clerk, PO Box 342, Lyme, NH 03768. **Phone-**603-795-2535, R/E Recording-603-795-4639 (Selectmen's office); fax-603-795-4637; hours 9AM-12;00PM,M,T,F,
Will search UCC records. Search per debtor- $10.00. Will not search tax liens. RE records at Grafton County. UCC copy- $1.00 per page. Payee: Town

CLerk-Lyme. **Other phones:** Assessor-603-795-4639 (Selectmen's office); Treasurer-603-795-4639 (Selectmen's office); Elections-603-795-2535; Vital Records-603-795-2535.

Lyndeborough Town

Town Clerk, PO Box 164, Lyndeborough, NH 03082. **Phone-**603-654-9653; fax-603-654-5777; hours 8AM-1PM, 2-7PM M; 8AM-1PM, 2-3PM W
Will search UCC records prior to 7/2001 and current liens only. Search per debtor- $10.00. UCC search includes tax liens if requested. RE records at Hillsborough County. UCC copy- $1.00 per page. Payee: Town of Lyndeborough. **Other phones:** Assessor-603-654-5955.

Madbury Town

Town Clerk, 13 Town Hall Rd, Madbury, NH 03820-9510. **Phone-**603-742-5131; fax-603-742-2505.
Will search UCC records prior to 7/2001 and current liens only. Search per debtor- $10.00. RE records at Strafford County. UCC copy- $1.00 per page. **Online Access to Property, Deed, Grantor/Grantee records:** Records are free on the Stafford county-wide system at www.nhdeeds.com/stfd/web/agree3.htm. Use the subscription service for full data. **Other phones:** Assessor-603-742-5131.

Madison Town

Town Clerk, PO Box 248, Madison, NH 03849. **Phone-**603-367-9931, R/E Recording-603-539-4872; fax-603-367-4547; hours 8AM-4PM M,T,W,F
Will search UCC records prior to 7/2001 only. Search per debtor- $10.00. Will not search tax liens. RE records at Carroll County. UCC copy- $1.00 per page. **Other phones:** Assessor-603-367-4332; Treasurer-603-367-4332; Elections-603-367-9931; Vital Records-603-367-9931.

Manchester City

City Clerk, One City Hall Plaza, Manchester, NH 03101. **Phone-**603-624-6455, R/E Recording-603-624-6520; fax-603-624-6481; hours 9AM-5PM www.manchesternh.gov
Will search UCC records prior to 7/2001 and current liens only. Search per debtor- $10.00. UCC search includes tax liens. Separate federal/state combined tax lien search- $10.00 per debtor. RE records at Hillsborough County. UCC copy- $1.00 per page. Payee: City of Manchester. **Other phones:** Assessor-603-624-6520; Treasurer-603-624-6460; Elections-603-624-6455; Vital Records-603-624-6455.

Marlborough Town

Town Clerk, PO Box 487, Marlborough, NH 03455-0487. **Phone-**603-876-4529, R/E Recording-603-876-3751; fax-603-876-4703; 9AM-4:30 M T TH; 9AM-Noon W, 9AM-2PM F www.marlboroughnh.org
Will search UCC records prior to 7/2001 and current liens only. Search per debtor- $10.00. Will search tax liens. RE records at Cheshire County. UCC copy- $1.00 per page. **Other phones:** Assessor-603-876-3751; Treasurer-603-876-3842; Elections-603-876-4529; Vital Records-603-876-4703.

Marlow Town

Tax Collector, PO Box 184, Marlow, NH 03456. **Phone-**603-446-2245; fax-603-446-3806; hours Tues. evening 5-7PM
Will search UCC records prior to 7/2001 and current liens only. Search per debtor- $10.00. RE records at Cheshire County. UCC copy- $1.00 per page. **Other phones:** Treasurer-603-446-2245; Elections-603-446-2245; Vital Records-603-446-2245.

Mason Town

Town Clerk, 16 Darling Hill Rd., Mason, NH 03048-4717. **Phone-**Town Clerk, R/E & UCC Recording-

603-878-2070; fax-603-878-4892; hours 1-4PM T; 9AM-Noon, 7-9PM TH
Will search UCC records prior to 7/2001. Search per debtor- $10.00. Will not search tax liens. RE records at Hillsborough County. UCC copy- $1.00 per page. **Other phones:** Assessor-603-878-2070; Treasurer-603-878-2070; Elections-603-878-3801; Vital Records-603-878-2070.

Meredith Town

Town Clerk, 41 Main St, Meredith, NH 03253-9704. **Phone-**603-279-4538; fax-603-279-1042; hours 8AM-5PM http://meredithnh.org/
Will search UCC records prior to 7/2001 and current liens only. Search per debtor- $10.00. Federal/state combined tax lien search- $10.00 per debtor. RE records at Belknap County. UCC copy- $1.00 per page. Cert fee: $5.00 per doc. Payee: Town of Meredith.

Merrimack County

Register of Deeds, PO Box 248, Concord, NH 03302-0248. **Phone-**603-228-0101; fax-603-226-0868; hours 8AM-4:30PM
www.merrimackcounty.nh.us.landata.com
Will search UCC records. Will not search real estate or tax lien records. Record copy- $1.00 per page. Cert fee: $2.00 per doc. Payee: Register of Deeds. **Online Access to Real Estate, Grantor/Grantee, Deed, Real Estate records:** Access records on the county Registry of Deeds database for a fee at www.merrimackcounty.nh.us.landata.com. Indexes are 1920-present, document images, 1945-present. **Other phones:** Vital Records-603-271-4650 (State).

Merrimack Town

Town Clerk, PO Box 27, Merrimack, NH 03054. **Phone-**603-424-3651; fax-603-424-0461; hours 8:30AM-4:30PM M-F; 2nd & 4th M 8:30AM-7PM www.ci.merrimack.nh.us
Will search UCC records prior to 7/2001 and current liens only. Search per debtor- $10.00. UCC search includes tax liens if requested. Tax lien search- $10.00 per debtor. RE records at Hillsborough County. UCC copy- $1.00 per page. Payee: Town of Merrimack. **Other phones:** Assessor-603-424-5136; Treasurer-603-424-3531.

Middleton Town

Town Clerk, 182 Kings Highway, Middleton Town Offices, Middleton, NH 03887. **Phone-**603-473-2576; fax-603-473-2577.
Will search UCC records prior to 7/2001 and current liens only. Search per debtor- $10.00. Search fee for separate tax lien is $2.00 per debtor. RE records at Strafford County. UCC copy- $1.00 per page. **Online Access to Property, Deed, Grantor/Grantee records:** Records are free on the Stafford county-wide system at www.nhdeeds.com/stfd/web/agree3.htm. Use the subscription service for full data. **Other phones:** Assessor-603-473-2261; Treasurer-603-473-2134; Elections-603-473-2134; Vital Records-603-473-2134.

Milan Town

Town Clerk, PO Box 158, Milan, NH 03588. **Phone-**603-449-3461; fax-603-449-2624; hours 9AM-Noon;1-4PM M/evenings6-8PM;9AM-Noon;1-5PM T-Th. Will search UCC records prior to 7/2001 and current liens only. Search per debtor- $10.00. Will search tax liens including federal tax liens. Tax lien search- $10.00 per debtor. RE records at Coos County. UCC copy- $1.00 per page.

Milford Town

Town Clerk, 1 Union Sq, Milford, NH 03055. **Phone-**603-673-3514, 673-3403, UCC Recording-603-673-3403; fax-603-673-2273; hours 8AM-4PM www.milfordnh.com/town/towninfo.htm

Will search UCC records. Search per debtor- $10.00. Will not search tax liens. RE records at Hillsborough County. UCC copy- $1.00 per page. **Other phones:** Assessor-603-672-0525; Treasurer-603-672-1061; Elections-603-673-3403; Vital Records-603-673-3403.

Milton Town

Town Clerk, PO Box 180, Milton, NH 03851-0180. **Phone-**603-652-9414; fax-603-652-4120. www.miltonnh-us.com
Will search UCC records prior to 7/2001 and current liens only. Search per debtor- $10.00. Tax lien search- $5.00 per debtor. RE records at Strafford County. UCC copy- $1.00 per page. **Online Access to Property, Deed, Grantor/Grantee records:** Records are free on the Stafford county-wide system at www.nhdeeds.com/stfd/web/agree3.htm. Use the subscription service for full data. **Other phones:** Assessor-603-652-4501; Treasurer-603-652-4501; Elections-603-652-9414; Vital Records-603-652-9414.

Monroe Town

Treasurer, PO Box 63, Monroe, NH 03771-0063. **Phone-**603-638-2644; fax-603-638-2021.
Will search UCC records. Search per debtor- $10.00. RE records at Grafton County. UCC copy- $1.00 per page. **Other phones:** Assessor-603-638-2644; Treasurer-603-638-2644; Vital Records-603-638-2644.

Mont Vernon Town

Town Clerk, PO Box 417, Mont Vernon, NH 03057. **Phone-**603-673-9126; fax-603-672-9021; hours 5-8PM M & W; 9AM-Noon T & W
Will search UCC records prior to 7/2001 only. Search per debtor- $10.00. Will only search Federal tax liens. RE records at Hillsborough County. UCC copy- $1.00 per page. **Other phones:** Assessor-603-673-6080; Treasurer-603-673-6080; Elections-603-673-9126; Vital Records-603-673-9126; Tax Collector-603-673-6083; Town Hall fax-603-673-5995.

Moultonborough Town

Town Clerk, PO Box 15, Moultonborough, NH 03254. **Phone-**Town Clerk, R/E & UCC Recording- 603-476-2347; fax-603-476-5835; hours 9AM-Noon 1-4PM M W F; 9AM-1PM T. Will search UCC records. Search per debtor- $10.00. UCC search includes tax liens. Will not search real estate records. UCC copy- $1.00 per page. **Other phones:** Assessor-603-476-2347; Treasurer-603-476-2347; Elections-603-476-2347; Vital Records-603-476-2347.

Nashua City

City Clerk, 229 Main St, Nashua, NH 03061-2019. **Phone-**603-589-3010.
Will search UCC records prior to 7/2001 and current liens only. Search per debtor- $10.00. RE records at Hillsborough County. UCC copy- $1.00 per page. Payee: Nashua City Clerk. **Online Access to Property Assessor records:** Search the City Assessor database for free at www.ci.nashua.nh.us/defaulto.asp?url=/welcome.asp. **Other phones:** Assessor-603-594-3040.

Nelson Town

Town Clerk, 7 Nelson Common Rd., Nelson, NH 03457. **Phone-**603-847-9043, R/E Recording-603-847-0047; fax-603-847-9043; hours 9AM-N Tu.; 5-8PM W; 9AM-1PM Th
Will search UCC records prior to 7/2001 and current liens only. Search per debtor- $10.00. UCC search includes tax liens. RE records at Cheshire County. UCC copy- $1.00 per page. **Other phones:** Assessor-603-847-0047; Treasurer-603-847-0047; Elections-603-847-9043; Vital Records-603-847-9043.

New Boston Town

Town Clerk, PO Box 250, New Boston, NH 03070-0250. **Phone-**603-487-5504 x106; fax-603-487-2975; hours 9AM-7PM M, 9AM-4PM W F, 4PM-8PM TH www.new-boston.nh.us
Will search UCC records prior to 7/2001 only. Search per debtor- $10.00. Will not search tax liens. RE records at Hillsborough County. UCC copy- $1.00 per page. Payee: Town of New Boston. **Other phones:** Assessor-603-487-5504 x 101/102; Treasurer-603-487-5504 x104; Elections-603-487-5504 x106; Vital Records-603-487-5504 x106.

New Castle Town

Town Clerk, PO Box 367, New Castle, NH 03854-0367. **Phone-**Town Clerk, R/E & UCC Recording-603-431-6710; fax-603-433-6198; hours 9AM-1PM M W; 12PM-5PM Th
Will search UCC records prior to 7/2001 and current liens only. Search per debtor- $10.00. Tax lien search- $10.00 per debtor. RE records at Rockingham County. UCC copy- $1.00 per page. Cert fee: $12.00. Payee: Town of New Castle. **Other phones:** Assessor-603-431-6710; Treasurer-603-431-6710; Elections-603-431-6710; Vital Records-603-431-6710.

New Durham Town

Town Clerk, PO Box 207, New Durham, NH 03855. **Phone-**603-859-2091; fax-603-859-6644; hours 9AM-4PM, M-F
Will search UCC records prior to 7/2001 and current liens only. Search per debtor- $10.00. Will search tax liens including federal tax liens. RE records at Strafford County. UCC copy- $1.00 per page. Cert fee: $4.00 per page. Payee: Town of New Durham. **Online Access to Property, Deed, Grantor/Grantee records:** Records are free on the Stafford county-wide system at www.nhdeeds.com/stfd/web/agree3.htm. Use the subscription service for full data. Assessor data is at http://data.visionappraisal.com/NewDurhamNH/. **Other phones:** Assessor-603-859-2091.

New Hampton Town

Town Clerk/Tax Collector, PO Box 538, New Hampton, NH 03256. **Phone-**603-744-8454; fax-603-744-5106; hours 7:30AM-11:45PM/12:45PM-4:15PM M T W F;1-7:30PM Th www.new-hampton.nh.us
Will search UCC records prior to 7/2001 and current liens only. Search per debtor- $10.00. Will not search tax liens. RE records at Belknap County. UCC copy- $1.00 per page. **Other phones:** Elections-603-744-8454; Vital Records-603-744-8454.

New Ipswich Town

Town Clerk, 661 Turnpike Rd., New Ipswich, NH 03071. **Phone-**603-878-3567; fax-603-878-3855; hours 9AM-4PM M,W,Th; 1-7PM T
Will search UCC records prior to 7/2001 only. Search per debtor- $10.00. Will not search tax liens. RE records at Hillsborough County. UCC copy- $1.00 per page. Payee: Town of New Ipswich. **Other phones:** Assessor-603-878-2772; Treasurer-603-878-2772; Elections-603-878-3567; Vital Records-603-878-3567; Tax Colletor-603-878-5068.

New London Town

Town Clerk, PO Box 314, New London, NH 03257-0314. **Phone-**603-526-4046; fax-603-526-9494; hours 8:30AM-4PM
Will not search UCC or tax liens records. RE records at Merrimack County. UCC copy- $1.00 per page. **Online Access to Property Appraiser records:** Search the town assessor database at http://data.visionappraisal.com/NEWLONDONNH/. **Other phones:** Assessor-603-526-4821; Treasurer-603-526-4821; Elections-603-526-4046; Vital Records-603-526-4046.

Newbury Town

Town Clerk, PO Box 253, Newbury, NH 03255. **Phone-**603-763-5326; hours 6PM-9PM M; 8:30AM-3:30PM T-F
Will search UCC records prior to 7/2001 only. Search per debtor- $10.00. Will not search tax liens. RE records at Merrimack County. UCC copy- $1.00 per page. Payee: Town of Newbury. **Online Access to Assessor, Property records:** Access to property assessor data is at http://data.visionappraisal.com/NorthHamptonNH/. Free registration required. **Other phones:** Assessor-603-763-4940; Treasurer-603-763-4940.

Newfields Town

Town Clerk, PO Box 300, Newfields, NH 03856-0300. **Phone-**Town Clerk, R/E & UCC Recording- 603-772-5070; fax-603-772-9004; hours 8:30AM-2:30PM
Will search UCC records prior to 7/2001 and current liens only. Search per debtor- $10.00. Tax lien search- $10.00 per debtor. RE records at Rockingham County. UCC copy- $1.00 per page. **Other phones:** Assessor-603-772-7047; Treasurer-603-772-7199; Elections-603-772-5070; Vital Records-603-772-5070.

Newington Town

Town Clerk, 205 Nimble Hill Rd, Town Offices, Newington, NH 03801. **Phone-**603-436-7640; fax-603-436-7188; hours 9AM-4:30PM T,W,Th
Will search UCC records prior to 7/2001 and current liens only. Search per debtor- $10.00. RE records at Rockingham County. UCC copy- $1.00 per page. **Other phones:** Assessor-603-436-7640.

Newmarket Town

Town Clerk, 186 Main St, Town Hall, Newmarket, NH 03857. **Phone-**603-659-3073; fax-603-659-3441; hours 8AM-4:30PM, till 6PM 1st & last Thursdays www.visionappraisal.com
Will search UCC records prior to 7/2001 and current liens only. Search per debtor- $10.00. Will search tax liens. RE records at Rockingham County. UCC copy- $1.00 per page. **Online Access to Assessor, Property records:** Access is via a private company at http://data.visionappraisal.com/NewMarketNH/. Apply for a free registered user ID (more data) or search anonymously (less data, no name searching). **Other phones:** Assessor-603-659-3073; Elections-603-659-3073; Vital Records-603-659-3073.

Newport Town

Town Clerk, 15 Sunapee St, Newport, NH 03773. **Phone-**603-863-2224, R/E Recording-603-863-6407; fax-603-863-8008; hours 8AM-4:30PM
Will search UCC records prior to 7/2001 and current liens only. Search per debtor- $10.00. Will not search tax liens. RE records at Sullivan County. UCC copy- $1.00 per page. **Other phones:** Assessor-603-863-6407; Treasurer-603-863-3000; Elections-603-863-2224; Vital Records-603-863-2224.

Newton Town

Tax Collector, Box 375, Newton, NH 03858-0375. **Phone-**Tax Collector, R/E & UCC Recording- 603-382-4096; fax-603-382-9140; hours 8AM-4PM M-W
Will search UCC records prior to 7/2001 and current liens only. Search per debtor- $15.00. Tax liens not included in UCC search. Tax lien search- $20.00 per parcel. RE records at Rockingham County. UCC copy- $1.00 per page. Cert fee: $2.00 per parcel. Payee: Town of Newton. **Other phones:** Assessor-603-382-4405; Treasurer-603-382-4405; Elections-603-382-4096; Vital Records-603-382-4096.

North Hampton Town

Town Clerk, PO Box 141, North Hampton, NH 03862-0141. **Phone**-603-964-6029, R/E Recording-603-964-8087; fax-603-964-1514; hours 8:30AM-2:00PM www.northhampton-nh.gov

Will not search UCC or tax liens records. RE records at Rockingham County. UCC copy- $1.00 per page. **Online Access to Assessor, Property records:** Access to property assessor data is at http://data.visionappraisal.com/NorthHamptonNH/. **Other phones:** Assessor-603-964-8087; Treasurer-603-964-8087; Elections-603-964-6029; Vital Records-603-964-6029.

Northfield Town

Town Clerk, 21 Summer St, Northfield, NH 03276. **Phone**-603-286-4482; fax-603-286-3328; hours 8:30AM-5PM, Closed T

Will not search UCC records. RE records at Merrimack County. UCC copy- $1.00 per page. Payee: Northfield Town Clerk. **Other phones:** Assessor-603-286-7039; Elections-603-286-4482; Vital Records-603-286-4482.

Northumberland Town

Town Clerk, 2 State St, Groveton, NH 03582. **Phone**-603-636-1451, UCC Recording-603-636-1450; fax-603-636-1450; hours 8:30AM-Noon, 1-4PM; open to 6PM Th

Will search UCC records prior to 7/2001 and current liens only. Search per debtor- $10.00. Tax lien search- $13.00 per hour, min. 1 hour. Will search real estate records. Record copy- $1.00 per page. **Other phones:** Assessor-603-636-1450; Elections-603-636-1450.

Northwood Town

Town Clerk, 818 1st NH Turnpike, Northwood, NH 03261-0314. **Phone**-Town Clerk, R/E & UCC Recording- 603-942-5586 X201; fax-603-942-9107.

Will search UCC records. Search per debtor- $10.00. Separate federal & state combined tax lien search-$10.00. Will search real estate records. Record copy- $1.00 per page. Cert fee: $12.00 1st copy. Payee: Town of Northwood. **Other phones:** Assessor-603-942-5586 x201; Treasurer-603-942-5586 x201; Elections-603-942-5586 x201; Vital Records-603-942-5586 x201.

Nottingham Town

Town Clerk, PO Box 114, Nottingham, NH 03290. **Phone**-603-679-9598, R/E Recording-603-679-1630; fax-603-679-9598; hours 4-8PM M,W; 1-5PM T; 9AM-1PM Th,Sat

Will search UCC records prior to 7/2001 and current liens only. Search per debtor- $10.00. UCC search includes tax liens. RE records at Rockingham County. UCC copy- $1.00 per page. Payee: Nottingham Town Clerk. **Other phones:** Assessor-603-679-5022; Elections-603-679-9598; Vital Records-603-679-9598; Tax Collector-603-679-1630.

Orford Town

Town Clerk, 59 Archer Town Rd., Clerk's Office, Orford, NH 03777. **Phone**-603-353-4404; hours 2-7PM T; 6-8PM W; 8-11AM Th

Will not search UCC records. Will do tax lien search. RE records at Grafton County. UCC copy- $1.00 per page. Payee: Town of Orford. **Other phones:** Assessor-603-353-4889; Treasurer-603-353-4889; Elections-603-353-4404; Vital Records-603-353-4404.

Ossipee Town

Town Clerk, PO Box 67, Center Ossipee, NH 03814. **Phone**-603-539-2008, R/E Recording-603-539-4872; fax-603-539-4183; hours 8:30AM-4:30PM

Will search UCC records prior to 7/2001 only. Search per debtor- $10.00. RE records at Carroll County. UCC copy- $1.00 per page. **Other phones:** Assessor-603-539-4181; Treasurer-603-539-4181; Elections-603-539-2008; Vital Records-603-539-2008.

Pelham Town

Town Clerk, 6 Village Green, Pelham, NH 03076. **Phone**-603-635-2040; fax-603-508-3096; hours 8:00AM-4PM M,W,Th.,F; 8:00AM-7:00PM Tu. Will search UCC records. UCC search per debtor- $10.00 per search. Federal/state combined tax lien search- $10.00 per search. RE records at Hillsborough County UCC copy- $1.00 per page. **Other phones:** Assessor-603-635-3317; Treasurer-603-635-8233; Elections-603-635-2040; Vital Records-603-635-2040.

Pembroke Town

Town Clerk, 311 Pembroke St, Pembroke, NH 03275. **Phone**-603-485-4747; fax-603-485-3967; hours 8-4PM, Th 5PM-8PM

Will search UCC records prior to 7/2001 and current liens only. Search per debtor- $10.00. Separate federal/state combined tax lien fee is $10.00 per debtor. RE records at Merrimack County. UCC copy-$1.00 per page. Payee: Pembroke Town Clerk. **Online Access to Assessor records:** Access assessor data at http://data.visionappraisal.com/PembrokeNH/. **Other phones:** Assessor-603-485-4747.

Peterborough Town

Tax Collector, 1 Grove St, Peterborough, NH 03458. **Phone**-603-924-8010, R/E Recording-603-924-8000 x103, UCC Recording-603-924-8000 x105; fax-603-924-8001; hours 8AM-4:30 M-F; 5-7PM Th. www.townofpeterborough.com

Countywide records can be searched at www.nhdeeds.com. Will not search UCC or tax liens records. RE records at Hillsborough County. UCC copy- $1.00 per page. **Other phones:** Assessor-603-924-8000 x101; Treasurer-603-924-8000 x103; Elections-603-924-8000 x105; Vital Records-603-924-8000 x105.

Piermont Town

Town Clerk, PO Box 27, Piermont, NH 03779. **Phone**-603-272-4840; fax-603-272-4947; hours 1-7PM Tu,W Will search UCC records prior to 7/2001 only. Search per debtor- $10.00. Will not search tax liens. RE records at Grafton County. UCC copy- $1.00 per page. Cert fee: $5.00 per name. Payee: Town Clerk.

Pittsburg Town

Town Clerk, 1526 Main St, Pittsburg, NH 03592. **Phone**-603-538-6699, R/E Recording-603-538-6697; fax-603-538-6697; hours 8:30AM-5:30PM

Will search UCC records prior to 7/2001 and current liens only. Search per debtor- $10.00. Tax liens not included in UCC search. Separate federal tax lien or state tax lien search- $10.00 per debtor. RE records at Coos County. UCC copy- $1.00 per page. Cert fee: $10.00 per doc. Payee: Town of Pittsburg. **Other phones:** Assessor-603-538-6697; Treasurer-603-538-6697; Elections-603-538-6699; Vital Records-603-538-6674; Tax Collector-603-538-6694.

Pittsfield Town

Town Clerk, Box 98, Pittsfield, NH 03263-0098. **Phone**-603-435-6773; fax-603-435-7922; hours 8AM-6PM M; 8AM-2:30PM T; 8AM-1PM W TH; 2PM-5PM F www.pittsfield-nh.com

Will search UCC records prior to 7/2001 and current liens only. Search per debtor- $10.00. Will do tax lien search. Federal/state combined tax lien search-$10.00 per debtor. RE records at Merrimack County.

UCC copy- $1.00 per page. **Other phones:** Assessor-603-435-6773 or 6774; Treasurer-603-435-6773 or 6774; Elections-603-435-6773 or 6774; Vital Records-603-435-6773 or 6774.

Plainfield Town

Town Clerk, Box 380 Town Clerk's Office, Meriden, NH 03770. **Phone**-Town Clerk, R/E & UCC Recording- 603-469-3201; fax-603-469-3642; hours 8AM-4PM M-Th, closed F

Will search UCC records prior to 7/2001 and current liens only. Search per debtor- $10.00. Tax liens not included in UCC search. Tax lien search- $5.00 per parcel. RE records at Sullivan County. UCC copy- $1.00 per filing. **Other phones:** Assessor-603-469-3201; Elections-603-469-3201; Vital Records-603-469-3201.

Plaistow Town

Town Clerk, 145 Main St, Town Hall, #2, Plaistow, NH 03865. **Phone**-603-382-8129, UCC Recording-603-382-8129 x16; fax-603-382-7183; hours 8:30AM-7PM M, 8:30AM-4:30PM T-F www.plaistow.com Will search UCC records prior to 7/2001 and current liens only. Search per debtor- $10.00. UCC search includes tax liens if requested. Separate federal/state combined tax lien search- $10.00 per search. RE records at Rockingham County. UCC copy- $1.00 per page. **Other phones:** Assessor-603-382-8469; Treasurer-603-382-8469; Vital Records-603-382-8129 x16.

Plymouth Town

Town Clerk, 6 PO Sq, Town Hall, Plymouth, NH 03264. **Phone**-603-536-1732; fax-603-536-0036; hours 8:30AM-4PM

Will search UCC records prior to 7/2001 and current liens only. Search per debtor- $10.00. Federal/state combined tax lien search- $10.00 RE records at Grafton County. UCC copy- $.50 per page. Cert fee: None. Payee: Plymouth Town Clerk. **Other phones:** Assessor-603-536-1731.

Portsmouth City

City Clerk, 1 Junkins Ave, Portsmouth, NH 03802-0628. **Phone**-City Clerk, R/E & UCC Recording- 603-431-2000; fax-603-427-1526; hours 8AM-4:30PM www.cityofportsmouth.com/cityclerk/index.htm

Will search UCC records prior to 7/2001 and current liens only. Search per debtor- $10.00. UCC search includes tax liens. RE records at Rockingham County. UCC copy- $1.00 per page. Cert fee: $3.00 per seal. **Online Access to Property Assessor records:** Records on the Portsmouth Assessed Property Values database are free at www.portsmouthnh.com/realestate/index.cfm. **Other phones:** Assessor-603-431-2000 x212; Treasurer-603-431-2000 x221; Elections-603-431-2000; Vital Records-603-431-2000; Tax Collector-603-431-2006 x244.

Randolph Town

Town Hall, 130 Durand Rd., Randolph, NH 03593. **Phone**-603-466-5771; fax-603-466-9856; hours 9-11AM M; 7-9PM W

Will search UCC records prior to 7/2001 only. Search per debtor- $5.00. Will not search tax liens. RE records at Coos County. UCC copy- $.75 per page. Cert fee: $4.00 per page. Payee: Town of Randolph-Town Clerk. **Other phones:** Treasurer-603-466-5771; Elections-603-466-5771; Vital Records-603-466-5771.

Raymond Town

Town Clerk, Epping St, Town Office Bldg., Raymond, NH 03077. **Phone**-603-895-4735 X110, R/E Recording-603-895-4735, UCC Recording-603-895-

4735; fax-603-895-0903; hours 8:00AM-7:00PM M; 8:00AM-4:30PM T-F
Will search UCC records prior to 7/2001 and current liens only. Search per debtor- $10.00. Federal/state combined tax lien search- $5.00 per search. RE records at Rockingham County. UCC copy- $1.00 per page. **Online Access to Property Assessor records:** Search the town assessor database at http://data.visionappraisal.com/RaymondNH. Free registration is required to view full data. **Other phones:** Assessor-603-895-4735; Treasurer-603-895-4735; Elections-603-895-4735; Vital Records-603-895-4735.

Richmond Town

Town Clerk, 105 Old Homestead Hwy, Richmond, NH 03470. **Phone-**603-239-6202; hours 9AM-Noon, 1-4PM, 6-8PM M; 9AM-N T,Th; 9AM-N, 1-4 W
Will search UCC records prior to 7/2001 and current liens only. Search per debtor- $10.00. UCC search includes tax liens. RE records at Cheshire County. UCC copy- $1.00 per page. Payee: Town of Richmond. **Other phones:** Assessor-603-239-4232; Elections-603-239-6202; Vital Records-603-239-6202.

Rindge Town

Town Clerk, PO Box 11, Rindge, NH 03461. **Phone-**603-899-5181 x107, R/E Recording-603-899-5181 x108; fax-603-899-2101; hours 9AM-1PM M-Th; 6-8PM Th Eve; 9AM-1PM F www.town.rindge.nh.us
See Town Tax Collector for property tax liens. Will search UCC records prior to 7/2001 and current liens only. Search per debtor- $10.00. UCC search includes tax liens if requested. Separate federal/state tax lien search costs same as UCC search. Real estate records and property tax liens are found at the town tax collector. Record copy- $1.00 per page. Cert fee: $10.00 per cert. Payee: Town of Rindge. **Other phones:** Assessor-603-899-5181 x102; Treasurer-603-899-5181 x103; Elections-603-899-5539; Vital Records-603-899-5181 x107.

Rochester City

City Clerk, 31 Wakefield St, City Hall, Rochester, NH 03867-1917. **Phone-**603-332-2130; fax-603-335-7565; hours 8AM-5PM www.rochesternh.net
Will search UCC records. Search per debtor- $10.00. UCC search includes tax liens. Separate federal/state combined tax lien search- $10.00. RE records at Strafford County. UCC copy- $1.00 per page. Cert fee: $4.00 per cert. Payee: City of Rochester. **Online Access to Property, Deed, Grantor/Grantee records:** Records are free on the Stafford county-wide system at www.nhdeeds.com/stfd/web/agree3.htm. Use the subscription service for full data. **Other phones:** Assessor-603-332-5109; Treasurer-603-335-7502; Elections-603-332-2130; Vital Records-603-332-2130.

Rockingham County

Register of Deeds, PO Box 896, Kingston, NH 03848. **Phone-**603-642-5526; fax-603-642-8548/5930; hours 8AM-4PM www.nhdeeds.com
For Assessor data, you must contact the Tax Assessor for each town within the county. Will not search records. Record copy- $1.00 per page. Cert fee: $1.00 per page, + $1.00 to certify. Payee: Rockingham County Recorder of Deeds. **Online Access to Real Estate, Most Wanted, Inmate records:** Access to the register of deeds database is free at www.nhdeeds.com/rock/web/start.htm. Index goes back to 1980. Also, search inmate info on private company website at www.vinelink.com/index.jsp.

Rollinsford Town

Town Clerk, PO Box 309, Rollinsford, NH 03869. **Phone-**603-742-2510; fax-603-740-0254; hours 9AM-1PM M,T,W,F; 3-7PM Th

Will search UCC records prior to 7/2001 and current liens only. Search per debtor- $10.00. Tax liens not included in UCC search. Separate federal tax lien search- $10.00 per debtor. RE records at Strafford County. UCC copy- $1.00 per page. **Online Access to Property, Deed, Grantor/Grantee records:** Records are free on the Stafford county-wide system at www.nhdeeds.com/stfd/web/agree3.htm. Use the subscription service for full data.

Roxbury Town

Town Clerk, 404 Branch Rd., Roxbury, NH 03431. **Phone-**603-352-4903; hours 7PM-8PM M
Will search UCC records prior to 7/2001 only. Search per debtor- $10.00. Will not search tax liens. RE records at Cheshire County. UCC copy- $1.00 per page. Payee: Town of Roxbury.

Rumney Town

Town Clerk, PO Box 275, Rumney, NH 03266. **Phone-**603-786-2237; fax-603-786-2237; hours 4PM-8PM, M; 9AM-2PM, T, W, TH, F
Will search UCC records prior to 7/2001 and current liens only. Search per debtor- $5.00. Search request using non-standard form (per name)- $10.00. Tax liens not included in UCC search. Separate federal & state combined tax lien search- $5.00 per debtor. RE records at Grafton County. UCC copy- $.75 per page. Cert fee: $12.00 per name. Payee: Town of Rumney. **Other phones:** Assessor-603-786-9511; Treasurer-603-786-9511; Elections-603-786-2237; Vital Records-603-786-2237.

Rye Town

Town Clerk, 10 Central Rd, Rye, NH 03870. **Phone-**603-964-8562; fax-603-964-4132.
Will search UCC records prior to 7/2001 and current liens only. Search per debtor- $10.00. RE records at Rockingham County. UCC copy- $1.00 per page. **Online Access to Property Assessor records:** Access is via a private company at http://data.visionappraisal.com/RyeNH. Free registration is required to view full data. **Other phones:** Assessor-603-964-5523.

Salem Town

Town Clerk, 33 Geremonty Drive, Municipal Bldg., Salem, NH 03079-3390. **Phone-**603-890-2110, UCC Recording-603-890-2116; fax-603-898-1223; hours 8:30AM-5PM www.ci.salem.nh.us
Will search UCC records prior to 7/2001 and current tax liens only. Search per debtor- $10.00. UCC search includes tax liens. Separate federal/state combined tax lien search- $10.00 per debtor. RE records at Rockingham County. UCC copy- $2.00 per page. Cert fee: $4.00 per cert. Payee: Town of Salem. **Online Access to Property Assessor records:** Records from the town database are free at http://data.visionappraisal.com/SalemNH/. Registration is required, no charge. **Other phones:** Assessor-603-890-2018.

Salisbury Town

Town Clerk, Box 180, Salisbury, NH 03268-0180. **Phone-**Town Clerk, R/E & UCC Recording- 603-648-2473; fax-603-648-6658; hours 8:30AM-Noon, 5:30-8:30PM T; 2PM-6PM W
Will search UCC records prior to 7/2001 only. Search per debtor- $10.00. Will not search tax liens. RE records at Merrimack County. UCC copy- $1.00 per page. Cert fee: $1.00 per page. Payee: Town Clerk. **Other phones:** All town officers-603-648-2473.

Sanbornton Town

Town Clerk, PO Box 124, Sanbornton, NH 03269. **Phone-**603-286-4034; fax-603-286-9544.
Will search UCC records prior to 7/2001 and current liens only. Search per debtor- $10.00. RE records at

Belknap County. UCC copy- $1.00 per page. **Online Access to Assessor, Property records:** Access to assessor property data is at http://data.visionappraisal.com/SanborntonNH/. Free registration required. **Other phones:** Assessor-603-286-8303.

Sandown Town

Town Clerk, 320 Main St, Town Hall, PO Box 583, Sandown, NH 03873-2627. **Phone-**603-887-4870, R/E Recording-603-887-3646; fax-603-887-5163; hours M 8-12PM/2-8PM; T-Th 8-12PM/12:30-3PM; F 8-12PM www.sandown.us
Will search UCC records prior to 7/2001 and current liens only. Search per debtor- $10.00. Tax lien search- $15.00 per debtor. RE records at Rockingham County. UCC copy- $1.00 per page. Cert fee: no fee. **Other phones:** Assessor-603-887-3646; Treasurer-603-887-3646; Elections-603-887-4870; Vital Records-603-887-4870.

Sandwich Town

Town Clerk, PO Box 194, Center Sandwich, NH 03227. **Phone-**603-284-7113; fax-603-284-6819; hours Mon. evenings 7-9PM
Will search UCC records prior to 7/2001 and current liens only. Search per debtor- $10.00. Tax lien search- $10.00 per debtor. RE records at Carroll County. UCC copy- $1.00 per page.

Seabrook Town

Town Clerk, PO Box 476, Seabrook, NH 03874. **Phone-**603-474-3152; fax-603-474-8007; hours 9AM-4PM
Property records are online at the county website. Will search UCC records prior to 7/2001 and current liens only. Search per debtor- $15.00. UCC search includes tax liens if requested. Separate federal/state combined tax lien search- $10.00 per debtor. RE records at Rockingham County. UCC copy- $1.00 per page. Cert fee: $1.00 per page. Payee: Town of Seabrook. **Other phones:** Assessor-603-474-2966; Elections-603-474-3152; Vital Records-603-474-3152.

Sharon Town

Town Clerk, 432 Route 123, Sharon, NH 03458. **Phone-**603-924-9250; fax-603-924-9250; hours 6-8PM T
Will search UCC records prior to 7/2001 only. Search per debtor- $10.00. Will not search tax liens. RE records at Hillsborough County. UCC copy- $1.00 per page. Payee: Town of Sharon. **Other phones:** Assessor-603-924-9250.

Shelburne Town

Town Clerk, 881 N. Rd, Philbrook Farm Inn, Shelburne, NH 03581. **Phone-**603-466-3831; hours By appointment
Will search UCC records prior to 7/2001 only. Search per debtor- $10.00. Will not search tax liens. RE records at Coos County. UCC copy- $1.00 per page. Payee: Town of Shelburne. **Other phones:** Assessor-603-466-3926.

Somersworth City

City Clerk, 1 Government Way, Somersworth, NH 03878-9574. **Phone-**603-692-4262, UCC Recording-603-692-9511/9512; fax-603-692-9574; hours 9AM-5PM M,W,F; 8AM-5PM T,Th
Will search UCC records prior to 7/2001 and current liens only. Search per debtor- $10.00. Tax lien search- $10.00 per debtor. RE records at Strafford County. UCC copy- $1.00 per page. **Online Access to Property, Deed, Grantor/Grantee records:** Records are free on the Stafford county-wide system at www.nhdeeds.com/stfd/web/agree3.htm. Use the

subscription service for full data. **Other phones:** Assessor-603-692-9520/9518.

South Hampton Town

Town Clerk, 3 Hilldale Ave., South Hampton, NH 03827. **Phone**-603-394-7696; hours 7-8:30PM M,T; 12:30-2PM W; 9:30-11:30AM F
Will search UCC records prior to 7/2001 only. Search per debtor- $10.00. Will not search tax liens. RE records at Rockingham County. UCC copy- $1.00 per page. Payee: Town of South Hampton.

Springfield Town

Town Clerk, PO Box 22, Springfield, NH 03284. **Phone**-603-763-4805; fax-603-763-3336; hours 9AM-Noon, 1-4PM M-F; 6-8PM W; 4-8PM Th
Will search UCC records prior to 7/2001 and current liens only. Search per debtor- $10.00. RE records at Sullivan County. UCC copy- $1.00 per page. Cert fee: $10.00. Payee: Springfield Town Clerk. **Other phones:** Assessor-603-763-4805.

Stark Town

Town Clerk, 1189 Stark Hwy., Stark, NH 03582. **Phone**-Town Clerk, R/E & UCC Recording- 603-636-2118; fax-603-636-6199; hours 10AM-4PM T,Th
Will search UCC records. Will not search tax liens. RE records at Coos County. UCC copy- $1.00 per page. Payee: Town of Stark. **Other phones:** Assessor-603-636-2118; Treasurer-603-636-2118; Elections-603-636-2118; Vital Records-603-636-2118.

Stewartstown Town

Town Clerk, PO Box 35, West Stewartstown, NH 03597-0035. **Phone**-603-246-3329; fax-603-246-3329; hours 9:30AM-2PM Tu.; 9AM-4PM W-F
Will search UCC records prior to 7/2001 and current liens only. Search per debtor- $10.00. UCC search includes tax liens if requested. Separate federal/state combined tax lien search- $15.00 per debtor. RE records at Coos County. UCC copy- $1.00 per page. Cert fee: $12.00 per page. Payee: Town of Stewartstown. **Other phones:** Assessor-603-246-3329.

Stoddard Town

Town Clerk, 2175 Route 9, Stoddard, NH 03464. **Phone**-603-446-2203, R/E Recording-603-446-3487; fax-603-446-2203; hours 9AM-2PM 4PM-6PM T TH
Will search UCC records prior to 7/2001 only. Search per debtor- $10.00. Will not search tax liens. RE records at Cheshire County. UCC copy- $1.00 per page. Cert fee: $15.00 per filing. Payee: Town of Stoddard. **Other phones:** Assessor-603-446-3326; Treasurer-603-446-3442; Elections-603-446-3326; Vital Records-603-446-2203.

Strafford County

Register of Deeds, PO Box 799, Dover, NH 03820. **Phone**-603-742-1741;   fax-603-749-5130. www.nhdeeds.com/stfd/web/start.htm
Will search UCC records prior to 7/2001 and current liens only. Search per debtor- $10.00. Will not search real estate records. UCC copy- $1.00 per page. **Online Access to Real Estate, Deed, Mortgage, Lien, Grantor/Grantee records:** Access to county register of deeds data is free at www.nhdeeds.com/stfd/web/agree3.htm. Online records go back to 1970. **Other phones:** Assessor-603-743-6014; Treasurer-603-742-1458.

Strafford Town

Town Clerk, PO Box 169, Strafford, NH 03884-0169. **Phone**-603-664-2192; fax-603-664-7276; hours 9AM-1PM Mon.;9AM-2:30 Tu.,Wed.;9AM-Noon Th. Will search UCC records prior to 7/2001 and current liens only. Search per debtor- $10.00. Will search

tax liens including federal tax liens. Federal/state combined tax lien search- $10.00 per search. RE records at Strafford County. UCC copy- $1.00 per page. **Online Access to Property, Deed, Grantor/Grantee records:** Records are free on the Stafford county-wide system at www.nhdeeds.com/stfd/web/agree3.htm. Use the subscription service for full data.

Stratford Town

Town Clerk, PO Box 366, North Stratford, NH 03590. **Phone**-603-922-5598; fax-603-922-3317; hours 9AM-Noon 5PM-8PM, M; 9AM-Noon, 4PM-7PM, W
Will not search UCC or tax liens records. RE records at Coos County. UCC copy- $1.00 per page.

Stratham Town

Town Clerk, 10 Bunker Hill Ave, Stratham, NH 03885. **Phone**-603-772-4741;   fax-603-775-0517;   hours 8:30AM-4PM www.strathamnh.org
Will search UCC records prior to 7/2001 only. Search per debtor- $10.00. Will not search tax liens. RE records at Rockingham County. UCC copy- $1.00 per page. **Other phones:** Assessor-603-772-4741.

Sugar Hill Town

Town Clerk, Box 574, Sugar Hill, NH 03585. **Phone**-603-823-8516; fax-603-823-8446; hours 4PM-6PM M; 9AM-1PM T TH
Will not search UCC or tax liens records. RE records at Grafton County. UCC copy- $1.00 per page.

Sullivan County

Register of Deeds, PO Box 448, Newport, NH 03773. **Phone**-Register of Deeds, R/E & UCC Recording- 603-863-2110;   fax-603-863-0013;   hours   8AM-4PM www.nhdeeds.com/
This office will not research records for any reason. Records go back to 1827. Will not search records. UCC copy- $1.00 per page. Cert fee: $2.00 per doc. Payee: Register of Deeds. **Online Access to Real Estate, Grantor/Grantee, Deed records:** Access to the county Register of Deeds database is free at www.nhdeeds.com/slvn/web/agree7.htm.

Sullivan Town

Town Clerk, 522 South Rd, Sullivan, NH 03445. **Phone**-603-352-1495, R/E Recording-603-352-0403; hours 8AM-9AM
Will search UCC records prior to 7/2001 only. Search per debtor- $10.00. Will not search tax liens. RE records at Cheshire County. UCC copy- $1.00 per page. Payee: Lois Woodbury, Town Clerk. **Other phones:** Assessor-603-847-9720; Treasurer-603-847-2340.

Sunapee Town

Town Clerk, PO Box 303, Sunapee, NH 03782-0303. **Phone**-603-763-2449; fax-603-763-4608; hours 9AM-5PM M,T,Th,F; 9AM-1PM W
Will search UCC records prior to 7/2001 only. Search per debtor- $25.00. Will not search tax liens. RE records at Sullivan County. UCC copy- $1.00 per page. Payee: Town of Sunapee. **Other phones:** Assessor-603-763-2212; Vital Records-603-763-2212.

Surry Town

Tax Collector, 1 Village Rd., Surry, NH 03431. **Phone**-603-352-3075; fax-603-357-4890.
Will search UCC records prior to 7/2001 and current liens only. Search per debtor- $10.00. RE records at Cheshire County. UCC copy- $1.00 per page.

Sutton Town

Town Clerk, PO Box 487, North Sutton, NH 03260-0487. **Phone**-603-927-4575; fax-603-927-4631; hours 8AM-4PM T-Th; Noon-7PM M; 9AM-Noon last Sat.

Will not search UCC records. Will search tax liens. RE records at Merrimack County. UCC copy- $1.00 per page. **Other phones:** Assessor-603-927-4416.

Swanzey Town

Town Clerk, PO Box 10009, Swanzey, NH 03446. **Phone**-603-352-7411; fax-603-352-6250; 9AM-5PM
Will search UCC records prior to 7/2001 and current liens only. Search per debtor- $10.00. Federal/state combined tax lien search- $10.00 per debtor. RE records at Cheshire County. UCC copy- $1.00 per page. **Online Access to Assessor records:** Access assessor data at http://data.visionappraisal.com/SwanzeyNH/. **Other phones:** Assessor-603-352-7411.

Tamworth Town

Town Clerk, PO Box 279, Tamworth, NH 03886. **Phone**-603-323-7971; fax-603-323-2347; hours 8AM-Noon 1PM-4:30PM T-F. Will search UCC records prior to 7/2001 and current liens only. Search per debtor- $10.00. UCC search includes tax liens if requested. RE records at Carroll County. UCC copy- $1.00 per page. Payee: Town of Tamworth. **Other phones:** Assessor-603-323-7525.

Temple Town

Town Clerk, Box 69, Temple, NH 03084. **Phone**-603-878-3873;   fax-603-878-5067;   hours   9AM-2PM-T,W,Th.
Will not search UCC or tax liens records. RE records at Hillsborough County. UCC copy- $1.00 per page. **Other phones:** Assessor-603-878-2536; Treasurer-603-878-3873; Elections-603-878-3873; Vital Records-603-878-3873.

Thornton Town

Town Clerk, 16 Merrill Access Rd, Thornton, NH 03223. **Phone**-603-726-4232; fax-603-726-2078.
Will not search UCC or tax liens records. RE records at Grafton County. UCC copy- $1.00 per page. **Other phones:** Assessor-603-726-3223; Treasurer-603-764-9450.

Tilton Town

Town Clerk, 257 Main St, Tilton, NH 03276-1207. **Phone**-603-286-4425;   fax-603-286-3519;   hours 8:30AM-4:15PM www.tiltonnh.org
Will search UCC records prior to 7/2001 and current liens only. Search per debtor- $10.00. Tax lien search- $10.00 per debtor. RE records at Belknap County. UCC copy- $1.00 per page. **Other phones:** Assessor-603-286-4521;   Treasurer-603-286-4521; Elections-603-286-4425; Vital Records-603-286-4425; Land Use-603-286-7817.

Troy Town

Town Clerk, PO Box 249, Troy, NH 03465-0249. **Phone**-603-242-3845; fax-603-242-3430; hours 9AM-4:30PM M-W; 1-7PM Th; 9AM-1:30PM F www.town.troy.nh.us
Will search UCC records prior to 7/2001 only. Search per debtor- $10.00. Will not search tax liens. RE records at Cheshire County. UCC copy- $1.00 per page. Payee: Town of Troy. **Other phones:** Assessor-603-242-7722; Vital Records-603-242-3845.

Tuftonboro Town

Town Clerk, PO Box 98, Center Tuftonboro, NH 03816. **Phone**-603-569-4539; fax-603-569-4328; hours 9AM-4PM,M,T,W,F; 9AM-12;00PM Th
Will search UCC records prior to 7/2001 and current liens only. Search per debtor- $10.00. RE records at Carroll County. UCC copy- $1.00 per page. Cert fee: $5.00. Payee: Tuftonboro Town Clerk. **Other phones:** Assessor-603-569-4539.

Unity Town

Town Clerk, 13 Center Rd., Unity, NH 03603. **Phone-** 603-542-9665; fax-603-542-9736; hours M & T 9AM-5PM; Wed 9AM-6PM; Th 8AM-Noon
Will search UCC records prior to 7/2001 and current liens only. Search per debtor- $10.00. RE records at Sullivan County. UCC copy- $1.00 per page. **Other phones:** Assessor-603-542-9665.

Wakefield Town

Town Clerk, 2 High St., Sanbornville, NH 03872. **Phone-**603-522-6205 x306, R/E Recording-603-539-4872; fax-603-522-6794; hours 8:30-4-T TH F,8:30-12-W,8:30-1:30-SAT www.wakefieldnh.com
Will search UCC records prior to 7/2001 and current liens only. Search per debtor- $10.00. Federal/state combined tax lien search- $10.00 per lien. RE records at Carroll County. UCC copy- $1.00 per page. **Other phones:** Assessor-603-522-6205 x300; Treasurer-603-522-6205; Elections-603-522-6205 x306; Vital Records-603-522-6205 x306.

Walpole Town

Town Clerk, PO Box 756, Walpole, NH 03608. **Phone-**603-756-3514; fax-603-756-4153; hours 7AM-4PM T,W,F; 6-7PM W. Drewsville and North Walpole are in the Town of Walpole. Will search UCC records prior to 7/2001 only. Search per debtor- $15.00 as time permits. Will not search tax liens. RE records at Cheshire County. UCC copy- $.75 per page. Cert fee: $5.00. Payee: Town of Walpole. **Other phones:** Assessor-603-756-3672.

Warner

Town Clerk, PO Box 265, Warner, NH 03278-0265. **Phone-**603-456-3362, R/E Recording-603-228-0101; fax-603-456-3576; hours 8AM-3PM M-TH; 5-7PM T; Closed F www.warner.nh.us/departments.htm
Will search UCC records prior to 7/2001 and current liens only. Search per debtor- $15.00. Search request using non-standard form (per name)- $20.00. UCC search includes tax liens. Tax lien search- $10.00 per search. RE records at Merrimack County. UCC copy- $1.00 per page. **Other phones:** Assessor-603-456-2298; Treasurer-603-456-2298; Elections-603-456-3362; Vital Records-603-456-3362.

Warren Town

Town Clerk, PO Box 66, Warren, NH 03279. **Phone-**603-764-9463, R/E Recording-603-764-5780, UCC Recording-603-764-5780; fax-603-764-9315; hours 4PM-8PM M; 6PM-8PM W
Will search UCC records prior to 7/2001 and current liens only. Search per debtor- $15.00. Tax lien search-Contact Tax Collector for fees. RE records at Grafton County. UCC copy- $1.00 per page. **Other phones:** Assessor-603-764-5780; Treasurer-603-764-5780; Elections-603-764-5780; Vital Records-603-764-5780; Tax Collector-603-764-5780.

Washington Town

Town Clerk, PO Box 109, Washington, NH 03280-0109. **Phone-**603-495-3667; fax-603-495-3299; hours 9AM-3PM F
Will not search UCC or tax liens records. RE records at Sullivan County. UCC copy- $1.00 per page. **Other phones:** Assessor-603-495-3074; Treasurer-603-495-3667.

Waterville Valley Town

Town Clerk, Box 500, Waterville Valley, NH 03215. **Phone-**Town Clerk, R/E & UCC Recording- 603-236-4730; fax-603-236-2056; hours 8AM-4PM
Will search UCC records prior to 7/2001 only. Search per debtor- $10.00. Will not search tax liens. RE records at Grafton County. UCC copy- $1.00 per page. Cert fee: $15.00 per debator. Payee: Town of Waterville Valley. **Other phones:** Assessor-603-236-4730; Treasurer-603-236-4730; Elections-603-236-4730; Vital Records-603-236-4730.

Weare Town

Town Clerk, PO Box 190, Weare, NH 03281-0190. **Phone-**603-529-7575; fax-603-529-7571; hours 8AM-4PM M, T, Th, F; 8AM-7PM W www.town.weare.nh.us
Will search UCC records prior to 7/2001 and current liens only. Search per debtor- $10.00. RE records at Hillsborough County. UCC copy- $1.00 per page. **Other phones:** Assessor-603-629-1515; Elections-603-529-7575; Vital Records-603-529-7575.

Webster Town

Town Clerk, 945 Battle St, Rte 127, Webster, NH 03303. **Phone-**603-648-2538; fax-603-648-6055; hours 9AM-Noon, 1-4PM M, W; 7-9PM Mon
Will search UCC records. Search per debtor- $10.00. Will search tax liens. RE records at Merrimack County. UCC copy- $1.00 per page. Payee: Town Clerk of Webster.

Wentworth Town

Town Clerk, PO Box 2, Wentworth, NH 03282. **Phone-**603-764-5244; fax-603-764-9362; hours 12-7PM Tu; 8:30AM-3PM W,Th.
Will search UCC records prior to 7/2001 and current liens only. Search per debtor- $10.00. RE records at Grafton County. UCC copy- $1.00 per page.

Westmoreland Town

Town Clerk, 108 Pierce Lane, Westmoreland, NH 03467. **Phone-**603-399-7211; hours 7-8:30PM M ; 10AM-1PM F; 1-3PM Tu & Wed. . Will search UCC records prior to 7/2001 only. Search per debtor- $10.00. Will not search tax liens. RE records at Cheshire County. UCC copy- $1.00 per page. Payee: Town of Westmoreland. **Other phones:** Assessor-603-399-4471; Treasurer-603-399-4471; Elections-603-399-7211; Vital Records-603-399-7211.

Whitefield Town

Town Clerk, 7 Jefferson Rd, Whitefield, NH 03598. **Phone-**603-837-9871; fax-603-837-3148. Will search UCC records prior to 7/2001 and current liens only. Search per debtor- $10.00. RE records at Grafton County. UCC copy- $1.00 per page. **Other phones:** Assessor-603-837-2551; Treasurer-603-837-2551.

Wilmot Town

Town Clerk, PO Box 94, Wilmot, NH 03287. **Phone-**603-526-9639; fax-603-526-2523; hours 8:30AM-1:30PM T,Th; 4-7PM W, 8AM-N 1st & last Sat.
Will search UCC records prior to 7/2001 and current liens only. Search per debtor- $15.00. Will not search tax liens. RE records at Merrimack County. UCC copy- $.25 per page. Cert fee: None. Payee:

Wilmot Town Clerk. **Other phones:** Assessor-603-526-4802.

Wilton Town

Town Clerk, PO Box 83, Wilton, NH 03086. **Phone-**603-654-9451; fax-603-654-6663; 9AM-4PM,M,T,F, closed W,9-7PM Th www.ci.wilton.nh.us
Will search UCC records prior to 7/2001 and current liens only. Search per debtor- $10.00. Separate federal & state combined tax lien search- $7.00 RE records at Hillsborough County. UCC copy- $1.00 per page. Cert fee: None. Payee: Town of Wilton. **Other phones:** Assessor-603-654-9451.

Winchester Town

Town Clerk, 1 Richmond Rd, Winchester, NH 03470. **Phone-**603-239-6233; fax-603-239-4146; 8AM-5PM
Clerk will only give book and page number over the phone. UCC search per debtor- $10.00. Will not search tax liens. Federal/state combined tax lien search- $10.00 RE records at Cheshire County UCC copy- $1.00 per page. Cert fee: $2.00 per doc + $1.00 per page. Payee: Town of Winchester. **Other phones:** Assessor-603-239-4951.

Windham Town

Town Clerk, PO Box 120, Windham, NH 03087. **Phone-**603-434-5075, R/E Recording-603-432-7731; fax-603-425-6582; hours 8AM-7PM M, 8AM-4PM T W Th F www.windhamnewhampshire.com
Will search UCC records prior to 7/2001 and current liens only. Search per debtor- $10.00. Tax lien search- $10.00 per debtor. RE records at Rockingham County. UCC copy- $1.00 per page. Cert fee: $1.00 per page. Payee: Windham Town Clerk. **Other phones:** Assessor-603-434-7530; Treasurer-603-432-7732; Elections-603-434-5075; Vital Records-603-434-5057.

Windsor Town

Town Clerk, 14 White Pond Rd, Windsor, NH 03244. **Phone-**603-478-3292; fax-603-478-3213; hours 7PM-9PM W. Will not search UCC or tax liens records. RE records at Hillsborough County. UCC copy- $1.00 per page. Payee: Town of Windsor.

Wolfeboro Town

Town Clerk, Box 1207, Wolfeboro, NH 03894. **Phone-**603-569-5328; fax-603-569-8167; hours 8AM-1;00-2;00-4;00PM
Will not search UCC or tax liens records. RE records at Carroll County. UCC copy- $1.00 per page. Payee: Wolfeboro Town Clerk. **Online Access to Assessor, Property records:** Access to assessor property data is at http://data.visionappraisal.com/wolfeboroNH/. Free registration required. **Other phones:** Assessor-603-569-8152; Elections-603-569-5328; Vital Records-603-569-5328.

Woodstock Town

Tax Collector, PO Box 146, North Woodstock, NH 03262. **Phone-**603-745-9233; fax-603-745-2393; hours 8AM-4PM T-Th
Will not search UCC records. RE records at Grafton County. UCC copy- $1.00 per page. **Other phones:** Assessor-603-745-8752; Treasurer-603-745-9085; Elections-603-745-8752; Vital Records-603-745-8752.

New Hampshire County Locator

You will usually be able to find the city name in the City/County Cross Reference below. In that case, it is a simple matter to determine the county from the cross reference. However, only the official US Postal Service city names are included in this index. There are an additional 40,000 place names that people use in their addresses. Therefore, we have also included a ZIP/City Cross Reference immediately following the City/County Cross Reference.

If you know the ZIP Code but the city name does not appear in the City/County Cross Reference index, look up the ZIP Code in the ZIP/City Cross Reference, find the city name, then look up the city name in the City/County Cross Reference.

New Hampshire City/County Cross Reference

ACWORTH Sullivan
ALSTEAD Cheshire
ALTON Belknap
ALTON BAY Belknap
AMHERST Hillsborough
ANDOVER Merrimack
ANTRIM Hillsborough
ASHLAND Grafton
ASHUELOT Cheshire
ATKINSON Rockingham
AUBURN Rockingham
BARNSTEAD (03218) Belknap(97),
    Strafford(2)
BARRINGTON Strafford
BARTLETT Carroll
BATH Grafton
BEDFORD Hillsborough
BELMONT (03220) Belknap(98),
    Merrimack(1)
BENNINGTON Hillsborough
BERLIN Coos
BETHLEHEM (03574) Grafton(98), Coos(1)
BOW Merrimack
BRADFORD Merrimack
BRETTON WOODS Coos
BRISTOL Grafton
BROOKLINE Hillsborough
CAMPTON Grafton
CANAAN Grafton
CANDIA Rockingham
CANTERBURY Merrimack
CENTER BARNSTEAD (03225)
    Belknap(97), Strafford(2)
CENTER CONWAY Carroll
CENTER HARBOR (03226) Belknap(76),
    Carroll(22)
CENTER OSSIPEE Carroll
CENTER SANDWICH Carroll
CENTER STRAFFORD Strafford
CENTER TUFTONBORO Carroll
CHARLESTOWN Sullivan
CHESTER Rockingham
CHESTERFIELD Cheshire
CHICHESTER Merrimack
CHOCORUA Carroll
CLAREMONT Sullivan
COLEBROOK Coos
CONCORD Merrimack
CONTOOCOOK Merrimack
CONWAY Carroll
CORNISH Sullivan
CORNISH FLAT Sullivan
DANBURY Merrimack
DANVILLE Rockingham
DEERFIELD Rockingham
DERRY Rockingham
DOVER Strafford
DREWSVILLE Cheshire
DUBLIN Cheshire
DUNBARTON Merrimack
DURHAM Strafford
EAST ANDOVER Merrimack
EAST CANDIA Rockingham
EAST DERRY Rockingham
EAST HAMPSTEAD Rockingham
EAST HEBRON Grafton
EAST KINGSTON Rockingham

EAST WAKEFIELD Carroll
EATON CENTER Carroll
ELKINS Merrimack
ENFIELD (03748) Grafton(95), Sullivan(4)
ENFIELD CENTER Grafton
EPPING Rockingham
EPSOM Merrimack
ERROL Coos
ETNA Grafton
EXETER Rockingham
FARMINGTON Strafford
FITZWILLIAM Cheshire
FRANCESTOWN Hillsborough
FRANCONIA Grafton
FRANKLIN Merrimack
FREEDOM Carroll
FREMONT Rockingham
GEORGES MILLS Sullivan
GILFORD Belknap
GILMANTON Belknap
GILMANTON IRON WORKS Belknap
GILSUM Cheshire
GLEN Carroll
GLENCLIFF Grafton
GOFFSTOWN Hillsborough
GORHAM Coos
GOSHEN Sullivan
GRAFTON Grafton
GRANTHAM Sullivan
GREENFIELD Hillsborough
GREENLAND Rockingham
GREENVILLE Hillsborough
GROVETON Coos
GUILD Sullivan
HAMPSTEAD Rockingham
HAMPTON Rockingham
HAMPTON FALLS Rockingham
HANCOCK Hillsborough
HANOVER Grafton
HARRISVILLE Cheshire
HAVERHILL Grafton
HEBRON Grafton
HENNIKER Merrimack
HILL Merrimack
HILLSBORO (03244) Hillsborough(98),
    Sullivan(1)
HINSDALE Cheshire
HOLDERNESS Grafton
HOLLIS Hillsborough
HOOKSETT Merrimack
HUDSON Hillsborough
INTERVALE Carroll
JACKSON Carroll
JAFFREY Cheshire
JEFFERSON Coos
KEARSARGE Carroll
KEENE Cheshire
KINGSTON Rockingham
LACONIA Belknap
LANCASTER Coos
LEBANON Grafton
LEMPSTER Sullivan
LINCOLN Grafton
LISBON Grafton
LITCHFIELD Hillsborough
LITTLETON Grafton
LOCHMERE Belknap

LONDONDERRY Rockingham
LOUDON Merrimack
LYME Grafton
LYME CENTER Grafton
LYNDEBOROUGH Hillsborough
MADBURY Strafford
MADISON Carroll
MANCHESTER Hillsborough
MARLBOROUGH Cheshire
MARLOW Cheshire
MEADOWS Coos
MELVIN VILLAGE Carroll
MEREDITH Belknap
MERIDEN Sullivan
MERRIMACK Hillsborough
MILAN Coos
MILFORD Hillsborough
MILTON Strafford
MILTON MILLS Strafford
MIRROR LAKE Carroll
MONROE Grafton
MONT VERNON Hillsborough
MOULTONBOROUGH Carroll
MOUNT SUNAPEE Merrimack
MOUNT WASHINGTON Coos
MUNSONVILLE Cheshire
NASHUA Hillsborough
NEW BOSTON Hillsborough
NEW CASTLE Rockingham
NEW DURHAM Strafford
NEW HAMPTON Belknap
NEW IPSWICH Hillsborough
NEW LONDON (03257) Merrimack(98),
    Sullivan(1)
NEWBURY Merrimack
NEWFIELDS Rockingham
NEWMARKET Rockingham
NEWPORT Sullivan
NEWTON Rockingham
NEWTON JUNCTION Rockingham
NORTH CONWAY Carroll
NORTH HAMPTON Rockingham
NORTH HAVERHILL Grafton
NORTH SALEM Rockingham
NORTH SANDWICH Carroll
NORTH STRATFORD Coos
NORTH SUTTON Merrimack
NORTH WALPOLE Cheshire
NORTH WOODSTOCK Grafton
NORTHWOOD Rockingham
NOTTINGHAM Rockingham
ORFORD Grafton
OSSIPEE Carroll
PELHAM Hillsborough
PETERBOROUGH (03458)
    Hillsborough(96), Cheshire(3)
PETERBOROUGH Hillsborough
PIERMONT Grafton
PIKE Grafton
PITTSBURG Coos
PITTSFIELD Merrimack
PLAINFIELD Sullivan
PLAISTOW Rockingham
PLYMOUTH Grafton
PORTSMOUTH Rockingham
RANDOLPH Coos
RAYMOND Rockingham

RINDGE Cheshire
ROCHESTER Strafford
ROLLINSFORD Strafford
RUMNEY Grafton
RYE Rockingham
RYE BEACH Rockingham
SALEM Rockingham
SALISBURY Merrimack
SANBORNTON Belknap
SANBORNVILLE Carroll
SANDOWN Rockingham
SEABROOK Rockingham
SILVER LAKE Carroll
SOMERSWORTH Strafford
SOUTH ACWORTH Sullivan
SOUTH EFFINGHAM Carroll
SOUTH NEWBURY Merrimack
SOUTH SUTTON Merrimack
SOUTH TAMWORTH Carroll
SPOFFORD Cheshire
SPRINGFIELD Sullivan
STINSON LAKE Grafton
STODDARD Cheshire
STRAFFORD Strafford
STRATHAM Rockingham
SUGAR HILL Grafton
SULLIVAN Cheshire
SUNAPEE Sullivan
SUNCOOK Merrimack
SWANZEY Cheshire
TAMWORTH Carroll
TEMPLE Hillsborough
TILTON (03276) Belknap(55),
    Merrimack(44)
TILTON Belknap
TROY Cheshire
TWIN MOUNTAIN Coos
UNION (03887) Strafford(70), Carroll(29)
WALPOLE Cheshire
WARNER Merrimack
WARREN Grafton
WASHINGTON Sullivan
WATERVILLE VALLEY Grafton
WEARE Hillsborough
WENTWORTH Grafton
WEST CHESTERFIELD Cheshire
WEST LEBANON Grafton
WEST NOTTINGHAM Rockingham
WEST OSSIPEE Carroll
WEST PETERBOROUGH Hillsborough
WEST STEWARTSTOWN Coos
WEST SWANZEY Cheshire
WESTMORELAND Cheshire
WHITEFIELD Coos
WILMOT Merrimack
WILTON Hillsborough
WINCHESTER Cheshire
WINDHAM Rockingham
WINNISQUAM Belknap
WOLFEBORO Carroll
WOLFEBORO FALLS Carroll
WONALANCET Carroll
WOODSTOCK Grafton
WOODSVILLE Grafton

New Hampshire ZIP/City Cross Reference

00210-00215 PORTSMOUTH	03261-03261 NORTHWOOD	03601-03601 ACWORTH	03855-03855 NEW DURHAM
03031-03031 AMHERST	03262-03262 NORTH WOODSTOCK	03602-03602 ALSTEAD	03856-03856 NEWFIELDS
03032-03032 AUBURN	03263-03263 PITTSFIELD	03603-03603 CHARLESTOWN	03857-03857 NEWMARKET
03033-03033 BROOKLINE	03264-03264 PLYMOUTH	03604-03604 DREWSVILLE	03858-03858 NEWTON
03034-03034 CANDIA	03265-03265 ANDOVER	03605-03606 LEMPSTER	03859-03859 NEWTON JUNCTION
03036-03036 CHESTER	03266-03266 RUMNEY	03607-03607 SOUTH ACWORTH	03860-03860 NORTH CONWAY
03037-03037 DEERFIELD	03268-03268 SALISBURY	03608-03608 WALPOLE	03862-03862 NORTH HAMPTON
03038-03038 DERRY	03269-03269 SANBORNTON	03609-03609 NORTH WALPOLE	03864-03864 OSSIPEE
03040-03040 EAST CANDIA	03272-03272 SOUTH NEWBURY	03740-03740 BATH	03865-03865 PLAISTOW
03041-03041 EAST DERRY	03273-03273 SOUTH SUTTON	03741-03741 CANAAN	03866-03868 ROCHESTER
03042-03042 EPPING	03274-03274 STINSON LAKE	03743-03743 CLAREMONT	03869-03869 ROLLINSFORD
03043-03043 FRANCESTOWN	03275-03275 SUNCOOK	03745-03745 CORNISH	03870-03870 RYE
03044-03044 FREMONT	03276-03276 TILTON	03746-03746 CORNISH FLAT	03871-03871 RYE BEACH
03045-03045 GOFFSTOWN	03278-03278 WARNER	03748-03748 ENFIELD	03872-03872 SANBORNVILLE
03046-03046 DUNBARTON	03279-03279 WARREN	03749-03749 ENFIELD CENTER	03873-03873 SANDOWN
03047-03047 GREENFIELD	03280-03280 WASHINGTON	03750-03750 ETNA	03874-03874 SEABROOK
03048-03048 GREENVILLE	03281-03281 WEARE	03751-03751 GEORGES MILLS	03875-03875 SILVER LAKE
03049-03049 HOLLIS	03282-03282 WENTWORTH	03752-03752 GOSHEN	03878-03878 SOMERSWORTH
03051-03051 HUDSON	03284-03284 SPRINGFIELD	03753-03753 GRANTHAM	03882-03882 SOUTH EFFINGHAM
03052-03052 LITCHFIELD	03285-03285 CAMPTON	03754-03754 GUILD	03883-03883 SOUTH TAMWORTH
03053-03053 LONDONDERRY	03287-03287 WILMOT	03755-03755 HANOVER	03884-03884 STRAFFORD
03054-03054 MERRIMACK	03289-03289 WINNISQUAM	03756-03756 LEBANON	03885-03885 STRATHAM
03055-03055 MILFORD	03290-03290 NOTTINGHAM	03765-03765 HAVERHILL	03886-03886 TAMWORTH
03057-03057 MONT VERNON	03291-03291 WEST NOTTINGHAM	03766-03766 LEBANON	03887-03887 UNION
03060-03064 NASHUA	03293-03293 WOODSTOCK	03768-03768 LYME	03890-03890 WEST OSSIPEE
03070-03070 NEW BOSTON	03298-03299 TILTON	03769-03769 LYME CENTER	03894-03894 WOLFEBORO
03071-03071 NEW IPSWICH	03300-03303 CONCORD	03770-03770 MERIDEN	03896-03896 WOLFEBORO FALLS
03073-03073 NORTH SALEM	03304-03304 BOW	03771-03771 MONROE	03897-03897 WONALANCET
03076-03076 PELHAM	03305-03306 CONCORD	03772-03772 MOUNT SUNAPEE	
03077-03077 RAYMOND	03307-03307 LOUDON	03773-03773 NEWPORT	
03079-03079 SALEM	03431-03435 KEENE	03774-03774 NORTH HAVERHILL	
03082-03082 LYNDEBOROUGH	03440-03440 ANTRIM	03777-03777 ORFORD	
03084-03084 TEMPLE	03441-03441 ASHUELOT	03779-03779 PIERMONT	
03086-03086 WILTON	03442-03442 BENNINGTON	03780-03780 PIKE	
03087-03087 WINDHAM	03443-03443 CHESTERFIELD	03781-03781 PLAINFIELD	
03100-03105 MANCHESTER	03444-03444 DUBLIN	03782-03782 SUNAPEE	
03106-03106 HOOKSETT	03445-03445 SULLIVAN	03784-03784 WEST LEBANON	
03107-03109 MANCHESTER	03446-03446 SWANZEY	03785-03785 WOODSVILLE	
03110-03110 BEDFORD	03447-03447 FITZWILLIAM	03801-03804 PORTSMOUTH	
03111-03111 MANCHESTER	03448-03448 GILSUM	03805-03805 ROLLINSFORD	
03215-03215 WATERVILLE VALLEY	03449-03449 HANCOCK	03809-03809 ALTON	
03216-03216 ANDOVER	03450-03450 HARRISVILLE	03810-03810 ALTON BAY	
03217-03217 ASHLAND	03451-03451 HINSDALE	03811-03811 ATKINSON	
03218-03218 BARNSTEAD	03452-03452 JAFFREY	03812-03812 BARTLETT	
03220-03220 BELMONT	03455-03455 MARLBOROUGH	03813-03813 CENTER CONWAY	
03221-03221 BRADFORD	03456-03456 MARLOW	03814-03814 CENTER OSSIPEE	
03222-03222 BRISTOL	03457-03457 MUNSONVILLE	03815-03815 CENTER STRAFFORD	
03223-03223 CAMPTON	03458-03460 PETERBOROUGH	03816-03816 CENTER TUFTONBORO	
03224-03224 CANTERBURY	03461-03461 RINDGE	03817-03817 CHOCORUA	
03225-03225 CENTER BARNSTEAD	03462-03462 SPOFFORD	03818-03818 CONWAY	
03226-03226 CENTER HARBOR	03464-03464 STODDARD	03819-03819 DANVILLE	
03227-03227 CENTER SANDWICH	03465-03465 TROY	03820-03822 DOVER	
03229-03229 CONTOOCOOK	03466-03466 WEST CHESTERFIELD	03823-03823 MADBURY	
03230-03230 DANBURY	03467-03467 WESTMORELAND	03824-03824 DURHAM	
03231-03231 EAST ANDOVER	03468-03468 WEST PETERBOROUGH	03825-03825 BARRINGTON	
03232-03232 EAST HEBRON	03469-03469 WEST SWANZEY	03826-03826 EAST HAMPSTEAD	
03233-03233 ELKINS	03470-03470 WINCHESTER	03827-03827 EAST KINGSTON	
03234-03234 EPSOM	03561-03561 LITTLETON	03830-03830 EAST WAKEFIELD	
03235-03235 FRANKLIN	03570-03570 BERLIN	03832-03832 EATON CENTER	
03237-03237 GILMANTON	03574-03574 BETHLEHEM	03833-03833 EXETER	
03238-03238 GLENCLIFF	03575-03575 BRETTON WOODS	03835-03835 FARMINGTON	
03240-03240 GRAFTON	03576-03576 COLEBROOK	03836-03836 FREEDOM	
03241-03241 HEBRON	03579-03579 ERROL	03837-03837 GILMANTON IRON WORKS	
03242-03242 HENNIKER	03580-03580 FRANCONIA	03838-03838 GLEN	
03243-03243 HILL	03581-03581 GORHAM	03839-03839 ROCHESTER	
03244-03244 HILLSBORO	03582-03582 GROVETON	03840-03840 GREENLAND	
03245-03245 HOLDERNESS	03583-03583 JEFFERSON	03841-03841 HAMPSTEAD	
03246-03247 LACONIA	03584-03584 LANCASTER	03842-03843 HAMPTON	
03249-03249 GILFORD	03585-03585 LISBON	03844-03844 HAMPTON FALLS	
03251-03251 LINCOLN	03586-03586 SUGAR HILL	03845-03845 INTERVALE	
03252-03252 LOCHMERE	03587-03587 MEADOWS	03846-03846 JACKSON	
03253-03253 MEREDITH	03588-03588 MILAN	03847-03847 KEARSARGE	
03254-03254 MOULTONBOROUGH	03589-03589 MOUNT WASHINGTON	03848-03848 KINGSTON	
03255-03255 NEWBURY	03590-03590 NORTH STRATFORD	03849-03849 MADISON	
03256-03256 NEW HAMPTON	03592-03592 PITTSBURG	03850-03850 MELVIN VILLAGE	
03257-03257 NEW LONDON	03593-03593 RANDOLPH	03851-03851 MILTON	
03258-03258 CHICHESTER	03595-03595 TWIN MOUNTAIN	03852-03852 MILTON MILLS	
03259-03259 NORTH SANDWICH	03597-03597 WEST STEWARTSTOWN	03853-03853 MIRROR LAKE	
03260-03260 NORTH SUTTON	03598-03598 WHITEFIELD	03854-03854 NEW CASTLE	

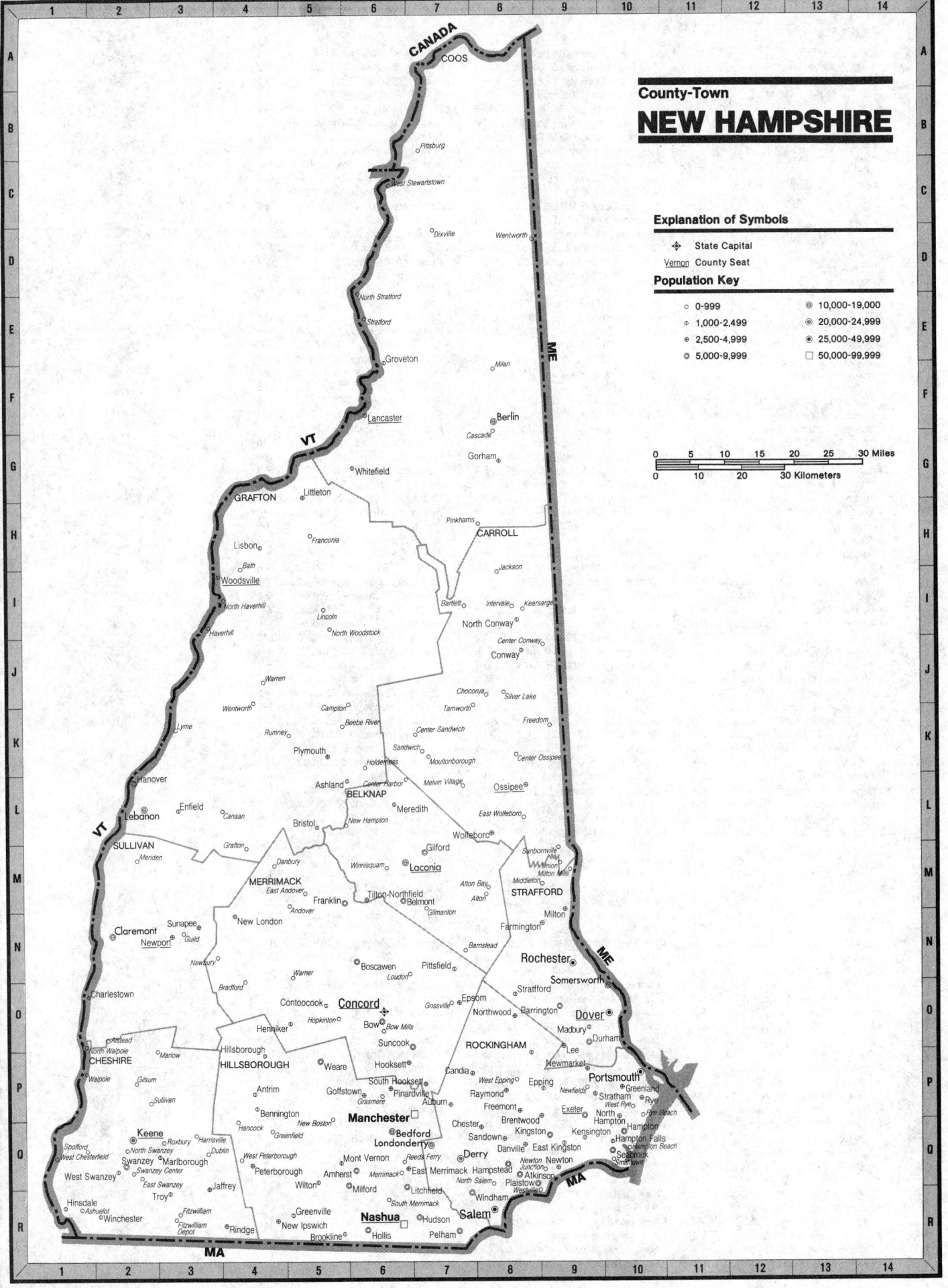

County-Town
NEW HAMPSHIRE

Explanation of Symbols

⊹ State Capital

Vernon County Seat

Population Key

∘ 0-999		⊛ 10,000-19,000
⊙ 1,000-2,499		⊛ 20,000-24,999
⊕ 2,500-4,999		⊛ 25,000-49,999
⊜ 5,000-9,999		☐ 50,000-99,999

0 5 10 15 20 25 30 Miles
0 10 20 30 Kilometers

CANADA

COOS

Pittsburg

West Stewartstown

Dixville

Wentworth

North Stratford

Stratford

Groveton

Milan

VT

Lancaster

Berlin

Cascade

Gorham

Whitefield

GRAFTON

Littleton

Pinkhams

CARROLL

Franconia

Jackson

Lisbon

Bath

Woodsville

Bartlett

Intervale

Kearsarge

North Haverhill

Lincoln

North Woodstock

North Conway

Haverhill

Center Conway

Conway

Warren

Chocorua

Silver Lake

Wentworth

Tamworth

Freedom

Lyme

Rumney

Campton

Beebe River

Center Sandwich

Plymouth

Holderness

Sandwich

Moultonborough

Center Ossipee

Ashland

Center Harbor

Melvin Village

Ossipee

Hanover

BELKNAP

Enfield

Canaan

Bristol

New Hampton

Meredith

East Wolfeboro

Lebanon

Grafton

Gilford

Wolfeboro

Sanbornville

SULLIVAN

Danbury

Winnisquam

Laconia

Meriden

MERRIMACK

Middleton

Milton Mills

STRAFFORD

East Andover

Franklin

Tilton-Northfield

Alton Bay

Claremont

Sunapee

Andover

Belmont

Alton

Milton

Newport

Guild

New London

Gilmanton

Farmington

Newbury

Warner

Barnstead

Bradford

Boscawen

Pittsfield

Rochester

Charlestown

Loudon

Stratford

Somersworth

Contoocook

Concord

Gossville

Epsom

Northwood

Barrington

Dover

Hopkinton

Bow

Bow Mills

Madbury

Durham

Henniker

Northwood

Alstead

Hillsborough

Suncook

ROCKINGHAM

Lee

Marlow

HILLSBOROUGH

Weare

Hooksett

Newmarket

CHESHIRE

Candia

West Epping

Epping

Portsmouth

Walpole

Gilsum

Antrim

South Hooksett

Goffstown

Pinardville

Auburn

Raymond

Newfields

Greenland

Rye

Sullivan

Bennington

Grasmere

Freemont

Stratham

West Rye

Hancock

New Boston

Manchester

Chester

Brentwood

Exeter

North

Rye Beach

Keene

Roxbury

Harrisville

Greenfield

Bedford

Danville

Kingston

Hampton

Spofford

North Swanzey

Dublin

West Peterborough

Londonderry

Sandown

East Kingston

Kensington

West Chesterfield

Swanzey

Marlborough

Peterborough

Derry

Hampton Falls

Swanzey Center

Mont Vernon

Reeds Ferry

Newton Newton

Hampton Beach

West Swanzey

East Swanzey

Amherst

Merrimack

East Merrimack

Hampstead

Atkinson

Seabrook

Jaffrey

Wilton

Milford

Litchfield

North Salem

Plaistow

Smithtown

Troy

Fitzwilliam

South Merrimack

Windham

Westville

MA

Hinsdale

Ashuelot

Greenville

Winchester

New Ipswich

Nashua

Hudson

Salem

MA

Fitzwilliam Depot

Rindge

Brookline

Hollis

Pelham

VT

ME

MA

Copyright American Map Corporation

COUNTIES

(10 Counties)

Name of County	Population	Location on Map
BELKNAP	49,216	L-6
CARROLL	35,410	H-8
CHESHIRE	70,121	P-2
COOS	34,828	A-7
GRAFTON	74,929	G-4
HILLSBOROUGH	336,073	P-4
MERRIMACK	120,005	M-4
ROCKINGHAM	245,845	O-8
STRAFFORD	104,233	M-8
SULLIVAN	38,592	L-2
TOTAL	1,109,252	

CITIES AND TOWNS

Note: The first name is that of the city or town, second, that of the county in which it is located, then the population and location on the map.

Alexandria, Grafton, 1,190 .... L-5
● Allenstown, Merrimack, 4,649 .... P-7
Alstead, Cheshire, 1,721 .... O-2
Alton, Belknap, 3,286 .... M-8
▲ Amherst, Hillsborough, 9,068 .... Q-6
Andover, Merrimack, 1,883 .... M-5
● Antrim, Hillsborough, 1,325 .... R-4
Antrim, Hillsborough, 2,360 .... P-4
▲ Ashland, Grafton, 1,915 .... L-5
▲ Atkinson, Rockingham, 5,188 .... Q-8
▲ Auburn, Rockingham, 4,085 .... P-7
Barnstead, Belknap, 3,100 .... N-7
▲ Barrington, Strafford, 6,164 .... O-9
Bartlett, Carroll, 2,290 .... I-7
▲ Bedford, Hillsborough, 12,563 .... Q-6
▲ Belmont, Belknap, 5,796 .... M-6
▲ Bennington, Hillsborough, 1,236 ...... P-4
Berlin, Coos, 11,824 .... F-8
Bethlehem, Grafton, 2,033 .... H-5
▲ Boscawen, Merrimack, 3,586 .... N-6
▲ Bow, Merrimack, 5,500 .... O-6
Bradford, Merrimack, 1,405 .... O-4
▲ Brentwood, Rockingham, 2,590 ...... P-8
● Bristol, Grafton, 1,483 .... L-5
Bristol, Grafton, 2,537 .... L-5
▲ Brookline, Hillsborough, 2,410 .... R-5
Campton, Grafton, 2,377 .... J-6
Canaan, Grafton, 3,045 .... L-4
▲ Candia, Rockingham, 3,557 .... P-7
Canterbury, Merrimack, 1,687 .... N-6
● Charlestown, Sullivan, 1,173 .... O-1
Charlestown, Sullivan, 4,630 .... O-1
▲ Chester, Rockingham, 2,691 .... Q-8
Chesterfield, Cheshire, 3,112 .... Q-1
Chichester, Merrimack, 1,942 .... O-7
Claremont, Sullivan, 13,902 .... N-2
Colebrook, Coos, 2,444 .... C-6
Concord, Merrimack, 36,006 .... O-6
● Contoocook, Merrimack, 1,334 .... O-5
● Conway, Carroll, 1,604 .... J-8
Conway, Carroll, 7,940 .... J-8
Cornish, Sullivan, 1,659 .... M-2
▲ Danville, Rockingham, 2,534 .... Q-8
Deerfield, Rockingham, 3,124 .... O-8
Deering, Hillsborough, 1,707 .... P-4
● Derry, Rockingham, 20,446 .... Q-7
Derry, Rockingham, 29,603 .... Q-7
▲ Dover, Strafford, 25,042 .... O-10
Dublin, Cheshire, 1,474 .... Q-3
Dunbarton, Merrimack, 1,759 .... P-6
Durham, Strafford, 11,818 .... O-9
● Durham, Strafford, 9,236 .... O-9
▲ East Kingston, Rockingham,
      1,352 .... Q-9
● East Merrimack, Hillsborough,
      3,656 .... Q-6
● Enfield, Grafton, 1,560 .... L-3
Enfield, Grafton, 3,979 .... L-3
● Epping, Rockingham, 1,384 .... P-8
Epping, Rockingham, 5,162 .... P-8
● Epsom, Merrimack, 3,591 .... O-7
Exeter, Rockingham, 12,481 .... P-9
● Exeter, Rockingham, 9,556 .... P-9

● Farmington, Strafford, 3,567 .... N-9
Farmington, Strafford, 5,739 .... N-9
Fitzwilliam, Cheshire, 2,011 .... R-3
Francestown, Hillsborough, 1,217 ... P-4
Franklin, Merrimack, 8,304 .... M-5
▲ Freemont, Rockingham, 2,576 .... P-8
▲ Gilford, Belknap, 5,867 .... M-7
Gilmanton, Belknap, 2,609 .... M-7
Goffstown, Hillsborough P-6
Goffstown, Hillsborough, 14,621 ..... P-6
● Gorham, Coos, 1,910 .... G-8
Gorham, Coos, 3,173 .... G-8
Grantham, Sullivan, 1,247 .... M-3
Greenfield, Hillsborough, 1,519 ...... Q-4
▲ Greenland, Rockingham, 2,768 ...... P-10
● Greenville, Hillsborough, 1,135 ...... R-5
Greenville, Hillsborough, 2,231 ...... R-5
▲ Groveton, Coos, 1,255 .... F-6
▲ Hampstead, Rockingham, 6,732 .... Q-8
● Hampton, Rockingham, 7,989 .... Q-10
Hampton, Rockingham, 12,278 .. Q-10
▲ Hampton Falls, Rockingham,
      1,503 .... Q-10
Hancock, Hillsborough, 1,604 .... Q-4
● Hanover, Grafton, 6,538 .... L-2
Hanover, Grafton, 9,212 .... L-2
Haverhill, Grafton, 4,164 .... I-3
● Henniker, Merrimack, 1,693 .... O-5
Henniker, Merrimack, 4,151 .... O-5
● Hillsborough, Hillsborough, 1,826 ... P-4
Hillsborough, Hillsborough, 4,498 .. P-4
● Hinsdale, Cheshire, 1,718 .... R-1
Hinsdale, Cheshire, 3,936 .... R-1
Holderness, Grafton, 1,694 .... K-6
▲ Hollis, Hillsborough, 5,705 .... R-6
● Hooksett, Merrimack, 2,573 .... P-6
Hooksett, Merrimack, 8,767 .... P-6
Hopkinton, Merrimack, 4,806 .... O-6
Hudson, Hillsborough, 19,530 .... R-7
● Hudson, Hillsborough, 7,626 .... R-7
● Jaffrey, Cheshire, 2,558 .... Q-3
Jaffrey, Cheshire, 5,361 .... Q-3
Keene, Cheshire, 22,430 .... Q-2
▲ Kensington, Rockingham, 1,631 .... Q-9
▲ Kingston, Rockingham, 5,591 .... Q-9
Laconia, Belknap, 15,743 .... M-6
● Lancaster, Coos, 1,859 .... F-6
Lancaster, Coos, 3,522 .... F-6
Lebanon, Grafton, 12,183 .... L-2
▲ Lee, Strafford, 3,729 .... O-9
Lincoln, Grafton, 1,229 .... J-6
● Lisbon, Grafton, 1,246 .... H-4
Lisbon, Grafton, 1,664 .... H-4
▲ Litchfield, Hillsborough, 5,516 ...... Q-6
● Littleton, Grafton, 4,633 .... G-5
Littleton, Grafton, 5,827 .... G-5
● Londonderry, Rockingham,
      10,114 .... Q-7
Londonderry, Rockingham,
      19,781 .... Q-7
Loudon, Merrimack, 4,114 .... N-6
Lyme, Grafton, 1,496 .... H-4
Lyndeborough, Hillsborough,
      1,294 .... Q-5
▲ Madbury, Strafford, 1,404 .... O-9
Madison, Carroll, 1,704 .... J-8
Manchester, Hillsborough, 99,567 ... P-7
● Marlborough, Cheshire, 1,211 .... Q-3
Marlborough, Cheshire, 1,927 .... Q-3
Mason, Hillsborough, 1,212 .... R-5
● Meredith, Belknap, 1,654 .... L-6
Meredith, Belknap, 4,837 .... L-6
Merrimack, Hillsborough, 22,156 ... Q-6
Middleton, Strafford, 1,183 .... M-8
Milan, Coos, 1,295 .... F-8
Milford, Hillsborough, 11,795 .... Q-5
● Milford, Hillsborough, 8,015 .... Q-5
● Milton, Strafford, 3,691 .... N-9
▲ Mont Vernon, Hillsborough, 1,812 .. Q-5
Moultonborough, Carroll, 2,956 .... K-J
Nashua, Hillsborough, 79,662 .... R-6
New Boston, Hillsborough, 3,214 .. Q-5
New Durham, Strafford, 1,974 .... M-8
New Hampton, Belknap, 1,606 ...... L-6
▲ New Ipswich, Hillsborough, 4,014 .. R-4
▲ New London, Merrimack, 3,180 ...... N-4
Newbury, Merrimack, 1,347 .... N-3
● Newmarket, Rockingham, 4,917 ... P-9

Newmarket, Rockingham, 7,157 ..... P-9
● Newport, Sullivan, 3,772 .... N-3
Newport, Sullivan, 6,110 .... N-3
▲ Newton, Rockingham, 3,473 .... Q-9
● North Conway, Carroll, 2,032 .... I-8
▲ North Hampton, Rockingham,
      3,637 .... P-10
Northfield, Merrimack, 4,263 .... N-6
Northumberland, Coos, 2,492 .... F-6
▲ Northwood, Rockingham, 3,124 ..... O-8
Nottingham, Rockingham, 2,939 ... P-8
Orford, Grafton, 1,008 .... J-3
▲ Ossipee, Carroll L-8
Ossipee, Carroll, 3,309 .... L-8
▲ Pelham, Hillsborough, 9,408 .... R-7
Pembroke, Merrimack, 6,561 .... O-7
● Peterborough, Hillsborough,
      2,685 .... Q-4
Peterborough, Hillsborough,
      5,239 .... Q-4
● Pinardville, Hillsborough, 4,654 ..... P-6
● Pittsfield, Merrimack, 1,717 .... N-7
Pittsfield, Merrimack, 3,701 .... N-7
Plainfield, Sullivan, 2,056 .... M-2
▲ Plaistow, Rockingham, 7,316 .... Q-8
● Plymouth, Grafton, 3,967 .... K-5
Plymouth, Grafton, 5,811 .... K-5
Portsmouth, Rockingham,
      25,925 .... P-10
● Raymond, Rockingham, 2,516 .... P-8
Raymond, Rockingham, 8,713 .... P-8
▲ Rindge, Cheshire, 4,941 .... R-4
Rochester, Strafford, 26,630 .... N-9
▲ Rollinsford, Strafford, 2,645 .... O-10
Rumney, Grafton, 1,446 .... K-5
▲ Rye, Rockingham, 4,612 .... P-10
▲ Salem, Rockingham, 25,746 .... R-8
Salisbury, Merrimack, 1,061 .... N-5
Sanbornton, Belknap, 2,136 .... M-6
▲ Sandown, Rockingham, 4,060 ...... Q-8
Sandwich, Carroll, 1,066 .... K-7
▲ Seabrook, Rockingham, 6,503 ..... Q-10
Somersworth, Strafford, 11,249 .. O-10
● South Hooksett, Merrimack,
      3,638 .... P-7
Stewartstown, Coos, 1,048 .... C-7
Strafford, Strafford, 2,965 .... O-8
▲ Stratham, Rockingham, 4,955 ...... P-9
▲ Sunapee, Sullivan, 2,559 .... N-3
● Suncook, Merrimack, 5,214 .... O-6
Sutton, Merrimack, 1,457 .... N-4
Swanzey, Cheshire, 6,236 .... Q-2
Tamworth, Carroll, 2,165 .... K-7
Temple, Hillsborough, 1,194 .... R-4
Thornton, Grafton, 1,505 .... J-5
Tilton, Belknap, 3,240 .... M-6
● Tilton-Northfield, Belknap/
      Merrimack, 3,081 .... M-6
▲ Troy, Cheshire, 2,097 .... R-3
Tuftonboro, Carroll, 1,842 .... L-7
Unity, Sullivan, 1,341 .... N-2
Wakefield, Carroll, 3,057 .... L-9
Walpole, Cheshire, 3,210 .... P-1
Warner, Merrimack, 2,250 .... N-5
▲ Weare, Hillsborough, 6,193 .... P-5
Webster, Merrimack, 1,405 .... N-6
● West Swanzey, Cheshire, 1,055 .... Q-2
Westmoreland, Cheshire, 1,596 .... Q-1
● Whitefield, Coos, 1,041 .... G-6
Whitefield, Coos, 1,909 .... G-6
● Wilton, Hillsborough, 1,165 .... Q-5
Wilton, Hillsborough, 3,122 .... Q-5
● Winchester, Cheshire, 1,735 .... R-2
Winchester, Cheshire, 4,038 .... R-2
▲ Windham, Rockingham, 9,000 ...... R-7
● Wolfeboro, Carroll, 2,783 .... L-8
Wolfeboro, Carroll, 4,807 .... L-8
Woodstock, Grafton, 1,167 .... J-5
● Woodsville, Grafton, 1,122 .... I-4

Explanation of symbols: ● – Census Designated Place (CDP)   ▲ *italics* – Townships (shown on the map)   *italics* – Townships (not shown on the map)

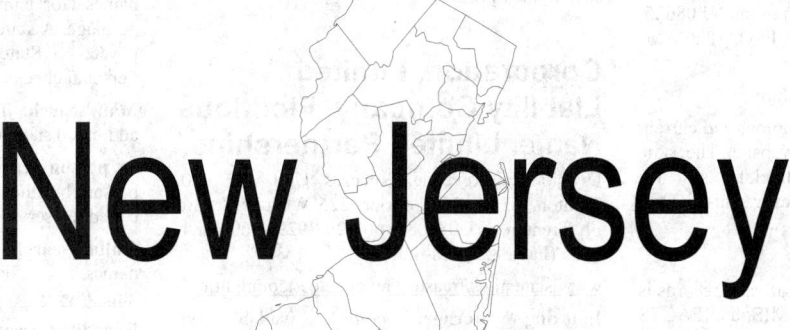

New Jersey

General Help Numbers:

Governor's Office
PO Box 001, 125 W State St   609-292-6000
Trenton, NJ 08625-0001   Fax 609-292-3454
www.state.nj.us/governor   8:30AM-4:30PM

Attorney General's Office
Law & Public Safety Department   609-292-8740
PO Box 080, 25 Market St   Fax 609-292-3508
Trenton, NJ 08625-0080   8:30AM-5PM
www.state.nj.us/lps

Legislative Records
State House Annex, Room B01   609-292-4840
PO Box 068   Fax 609-777-2440
Trenton, NJ 08625-0068   8:30AM-5PM
www.njleg.state.nj.us

State Archives
PO Box 307, 225 W. State Street, L2   609-292-6260
Trenton, NJ 08625-0307   Fax 609-396-2454
www.state.nj.us/state/darm/index.html
8:30AM-4:30PM TU-F

State Specifics:

Capital:	Trenton
	Mercer County
Time Zone:	EST
Number of Counties:	21
Population:	8,638,396
Web Site:	www.state.nj.us

State Agencies

Criminal Records

Division of State Police, Records and Identification Section, PO Box 7068, West Trenton, NJ 08628-0068; 609-882-2000 x2878, 609-530-5780 (Fax), 9AM-5PM.

www.njsp.org

Indexing & Storage: Records are available from 1921 forward. It takes 1 to 5 days before new records are available for inquiry. Records are indexed on computer. Records are normally destroyed after verification that subject is no longer alive.

Searching: Criminal records are not open to the public but can be obtained by employers, private investigators, screening firms, attorney firms, and the subject. Include the following in your request- date of birth, Social Security Number. A set of fingerprints is optional. The name must match exactly. All requesters, except attorney firms, must submit Form 212 B which must be signed by the subject. Attorney firms require a subpoena. 100% of the records are fingerprint supported. The following data is not released: Juvenile records, dismissals, acquittals, and not-guilty verdicts.

Access by: mail, in person.

Fee & Payment: The fee is $18.00 for a name check and $30.00 for a full check with fingerprints. Will not do FBI fingerprint checks. Fee payee: Division of State Police-SBI. Prepayment required. No personal checks or credit cards accepted.

Mail search: Turnaround time: 5 to 10 days.

In person search: Walk-in requests are treated as mail requests. Results are mailed.

Statewide Court Records

Administrative Office of Courts, RJH Justice Complex, 7th Fl, PO Box 037, Trenton, NJ 08625; 609-984-0275, 609-984-6968 (Fax), 8:30AM-4:30PM.

www.judiciary.state.nj.us/admin.htm

Note: Supreme and Appellete opinions and current calendars are available at the website. The state has several automated case tracking systems, including case histories. However, this is not accessible directly by the public.

Access by: online.

Online search: Online access to all civil records is available through the ACMS, AMIS, and FACTS systems. The fee is $1.00 per minute of use. For more information, contact the Superior Court Clerk's Office, Electronic Access Program. Write to 25 Market St, CN971, Trenton NJ 08625, or fax 609-292-6564, or call 609-292-4987. Ask for the Inquiry System Guidebook containing hardware and software requirements and an enrollment form. A Superior Court Civil Motion Calendar is at http://lawlibrary.rutgers.edu/search.shtml and www.judiciary.state.nj.us/acms/MOTN/CV0390W0E.ASP.

Sexual Offender Registry

Division of State Police, Sexual Offender Registry, PO Box 7068, West Trenton, NJ 08628-0068; 609-882-2000 x2886, 609-538-0544 (Fax), 9AM-5PM.

www.njsp.org/

Note: Local law enforcement will assist with localized searches.

Indexing & Storage: It takes 1 to 5 days before new records are available for inquiry. Records are indexed on inhouse computer. Records are normally destroyed after court order.

Searching: Include the following in your request-name, date of birth.

Access by: online. No searching by mail.

Online search: Data can be searched online at the website. Click on NJ Sex Offender Registry. Search can be done by name, by county or by physical characteristics.

Incarceration Records

New Jersey Department of Corrections, Central Administrative Offices, PO Box 863, Trenton, NJ 08625-0863; 609-777-5753, 609-777-8367 (Fax), 8AM-5PM.

www.state.nj.us/corrections/index.html

Indexing & Storage: Records are available on current and former inmates. It takes 1 day before new records are available for inquiry. Records are normally destroyed after 10 years after release.

Searching: Location, DOC number, physical identifiers, conviction information, and release dates are released. Include the following in your request-full name, DOB and SSN helpful.

Access by: mail, phone, fax, online.

Mail search: Turnaround time: 5 working days.

Phone search: Limited telephone searching available; less than three names per request.

Fax search: Fax requests can be used in place of phone requests if four or more names needed to search.

Online search: Extensive search capabilities are offered from the website; click on "Offender Search." Offenders on Work Release, Furlough, or in a Halfway House are not necessarily reflected as such in their profile.

Corporation, Limited Liability Company, Fictitious Name, Limited Partnerships

Division of Revenue, Records Unit, PO 450, Trenton, NJ 08625 (Courier: 225 W State St, 3rd Fl, Trenton, NJ 08608); 609-292-9292, 609-984-6855 (Fax), 8:30AM-4:30PM.

www.state.nj.us/treasury/revenue/certcomm.htm

Indexing & Storage: Records are available from inception of laws. New records are available for inquiry immediately. Records are indexed on inhouse computer.

Searching: Include the following in your request-full name of business. In addition to the articles of incorporation, corporation records include the following information: Annual Reports, Amendments, Alternative names, Officers, Directors, Prior (merged) names, and Inactive names. Tradenames are filed at the county level.

Access by: mail, phone, fax, in person, online.

Fee & Payment: A status report is $5.00. Copies are $1.00 per page (except LLC, then $10.00 first and $2.00 each additional). There is a $25.00 ($15.00 if non-profit) fee to certify a document. A Good Standing is $25.00. Fee payee: Treasurer, State of NJ. Prepayment required. Ongoing requesters may set up a pre-paid account. Call 609-633-8255 for more information. Personal checks accepted. Credit cards accepted: MasterCard, Visa, Discover, AMEX

Mail search: Turnaround time: 2 to 3 weeks.

Phone search: This is considered expedited service.

Fax search: This is considered expedited service.

In person search: You can look at 3 records per day for no fee. Otherwise the turnaround time is over 1 week.

Online search: Records are available from the New Jersey Business Gateway Service (NJBGS) website at www.state.nj.us/njbgs. There is no fee to browse the site to locate a name; however fees are involved for copies or status reports. There is also a business list search function at www.state.nj.us/treasury/revenue/searchfile.htm.

Expedited service: Expedited service is available for phone, fax, and in person searches. Turnaround time: 8.5 business hours. Add $15.00 per transaction for corporations, non-profits and LPs and $25.00 per filing for LLCs and LLP. Records may be picked up the next day.

Trademarks/Servicemarks

Department of Treasury, Trademark Division, PO Box 453, Trenton, NJ 08625-0453 (Courier: 225 W State St, 3rd Floor, Trenton, NJ 08608); 609-292-9292, 609-984-6681 (Fax), 8:30AM-5PM.

www.state.nj.us/treasury/revenue/

Indexing & Storage: Records are available from the inception of the Division. It takes less than 1 day before new records are available for inquiry. Records are indexed on computer.

Searching: Include the following in your request-trademark/servicemark name, name of owner, date of application. Information returned includes name and address of owner and date of filing.

Access by: mail, in person, online.

Fee & Payment: Search fee is $25.00 for up to 3 names (for name availability). Copies are $1.00 per page. A status is $5.00 per name searched. Fee payee: NJ State Treasurer. Prepayment required. Personal checks and major credit cards accepted.

Mail search: Turnaround time: 1 week. A self addressed stamped envelope is appreciated.

In person search: You can take the request in person, but they return the records by mail unless expedited service is requested.

Online search: Search the trademarks and trade names list for free at https://www.accessnet.state.nj.us/home.asp.

Expedited service: Add $15.00 per document. Turnaround time: next day service.

Uniform Commercial Code

UCC Section, Certification and Status Unit, PO 303, Trenton, NJ 08625 (Courier: 225 West State St, Trenton, NJ 08618); 609-292-9292, 8AM-5PM.

www.state.nj.us/njbgs

Indexing & Storage: Records are indexed on inhouse computer.

Searching: Use search request form UCC-11. Federal tax liens are filed at the county level. State tax liens follow two rules: certificates of debt are filed in Superior Court at Trenton; a warrant of execution is filed at the county level. Include the following in your request-debtor name, address.

Access by: mail, fax, in person, online.

Fee & Payment: The fee is $25.00 for a search certificate per debtor name, $5.00 for non-certified computer printout of any document, copies are $1.00 per page. Fee payee: Treasurer, State of NJ Prepayment required. Regular requesters can set up a pre-paid account. Personal checks accepted. Credit cards accepted: MasterCard, Visa.

Mail search: Turnaround time: 2 weeks. A SASE is requested.

Fax search: You can order using a credit card; however, results will be mailed or available for pickup by a courier.

In person search: Information is mailed, unless you pay the $15.00 expedite fee for quicker service, or pickup later by courier.

Online search: Go to https://accessnet.state.nj.us/home.asp to find a business entity, UCC debtor, or other business name without accruing a service charge with the Division of Revenue. However, if you wish to receive status reports or other information services, you will need to pay the applicable statutory fee. Also, you may search for debtors at https://www.state.nj.us/treasury/revenue/dcr/filing/ucc_lead.htm.

Expedited service: Expedited services is available, when requested, by mail, fax or in person. Turnaround time: 8 1/2 hours. The fee is $15.00 per transaction and is in addition to other charges.

Federal and State Tax Liens

Records not maintained by a state level agency.

Note: Federal tax liens are filed with the county clerk or register of deeds. All state "docket judgment" liens are filed at the Superior Court in

Trenton. "Certificates of Debt" are filed at the respective county superior court.

Sales Tax Registrations

Access to Records is Restricted

Department of Revenue, Sales tax Licensing, PO Box 252, Trenton, NJ 08646-0252; 609-292-1730, 609-292-4291 (Fax), 8:30AM-4:30PM.

www.state.nj.us/treasury/taxation

Note: Sales tax information is considered confidential.

Birth Certificates

Department of Health, Bureau of Vital Statistics, PO Box 370, Trenton, NJ 08625-0370 (Courier: S Warren St, Room 504, Health & Agriculture Building, Trenton, NJ 08625); 609-292-4087, 877-622-7549 (Credit Card Requests), 609-392-4292 (Fax), 9AM-5PM.

www.state.nj.us/health/vital/vital.htm

Indexing & Storage: Records are available from 1878 to present. It takes 30 days before new records are available for inquiry. Records are indexed on microfiche.

Searching: The general public is denied access to records unless birth occured over 80 years ago. You must include the county in your request if it is regarding events before 1903. Include the following in your request-full name, names of parents, mother's maiden name, date of birth, place of birth.

Access by: mail, phone, fax, in person, online.

Fee & Payment: The fee is $4.00 per record. Add $2.00 per copy for additional copies. Add $1.00 per year for each additional year searched. The fee for using a credit card is $10.95. Fee payee: New Jersey Department of Health & Senior Services. Prepayment required. Personal checks accepted. Major credit cards accepted.

Mail search: Turnaround time: 6 to 8 weeks. No SASE is required.

Phone search: Must use a credit card.

Fax search: Same criteria as phone searching.

In person search: Turnaround time 2 hours.

Online search: Online ordering is available via www.vitalchek.com, a state approved vendor.

Expedited service: Expedited service is available for fax searches. Turnaround time: 2 to 3 days. Add fee of overnight carrier and credit card fee.

Death Records

Department of Health, Bureau of Vital Statistics, PO Box 370, Trenton, NJ 08625-0370 (Courier: S Warren St, Room 504, Health & Agriculture Building, Trenton, NJ 08625); 609-292-4087, 877-622-7549 (Credit Card Requests), 609-392-4292 (Fax), 8:30AM-4PM.

www.state.nj.us/health/vital/vital.htm

Indexing & Storage: Records are available from 1878 to present. It takes t30 days before new records are available for inquiry. Records are indexed on microfiche.

Searching: Cause of death, unless immediate family, is not released. Only those with a legal interest may obtain a record, unless death occurred over 40 years ago (then considered a genealogical search). Include the following in your request-full name, date of death, place of death, parents names. Submit photo ID and relationship to deceased.

Access by: mail, phone, fax, in person, online.

Fee & Payment: The fee is $4.00 per record. Add $2.00 per copy for additional copies. Add $1.00 per year for each additional year searched. Add $10.95 if credit card is used. Fee payee: NJ Department of Health and Senior Services. Prepayment required. Personal checks accepted. Major credit cards accepted.

Mail search: Turnaround time: 6 to 8 months. No SASE is required.

Phone search: Must use a credit card, open 24 hours.

Fax search: Same criteria as phone, turnaround time is 5-12 days.

In person search: Turnaround time 1-2 hours.

Online search: Records can be ordered online from www.vitalcheck.com, a state approved vendor partner.

Expedited service: Expedited service is available for mail, phone and fax searches. Turnaround time: 2 to 3 days. Add carrier fee plus the $10.95 credit card fee.

Marriage Certificates

Department of Health, Bureau of Vital Statistics, PO Box 370, Trenton, NJ 08625-0370 (Courier: S Warren St, Room 504, Health & Agriculture Building, Trenton, NJ 08625); 609-292-4087, 877-622-7549 (Credit Card Requests), 609-392-4292 (Fax), 8:45AM-5PM.

www.state.nj.us/health/vital/vital.htm

Indexing & Storage: Records are available from 1878 to present. It takes 30 days before new records are available for inquiry. Records are indexed on microfiche.

Searching: The general public is denied access to the records unless marriage occurred over 50 years ago. You must include the county in your request if it is regarding events before 1903. Include the following in your request-names of husband and wife, date of marriage, place or county of marriage. Also sumbit photo ID and state the relationship to the subject.

Access by: mail, phone, fax, in person, online.

Fee & Payment: The fee is $4.00 per record. Add $2.00 per copy for additional copies. Add $1.00 per year for each additional year searched. The fee to use a credit card is $10.95. Fee payee: New Jersey Department of Health. Prepayment required. Personal checks accepted. Credit cards accepted: MasterCard, Visa, AmEx, Discover.

Mail search: Turnaround time: 6 to 8 weeks. No SASE is required.

Phone search: Must use a credit card. Open 24 hours.

Fax search: Same criteria as phone searches.

In person search: Turnaround time 2 hours.

Online search: Records can be ordered online from www.vitalcheck.com, a state approved vendor partner.

Expedited service: Expedited service is available for fax searches. Turnaround time: 2 to 3 days. Add $14.75 carrier fees for overnight shipping and the $10.95 credit card fee. Federal Express 5-7 day service available.

Divorce Records

Clerk of Superior Court, Records Center, PO Box 967, Trenton, NJ 08625-0967 (Courier: Corner of Jerser & Tremont Streets, Building #2, Trenton, NJ 08625); 609-777-0092, 609-777-0094 (Fax), 8:30AM-4PM.

www.judiciary.state.nj.us

Indexing & Storage: Records are available until 9/89. Records after 1989 must be obtained from the Family Division Court in county of occurrence.

Searching: Also provide married name, unless maiden name was used during the marriage. Information on cases that are impounded is not released. Include the following in your request-names of husband and wife, date of divorce, year divorce case began, docket number (if known). No copies are made and no records are retrieved after 3:30PM. The following data is not released: adoption, impound cases.

Access by: mail, fax, in person, online.

Fee & Payment: There is no search fee, but there is a $10.00 certification fee. Fee payee: Clerk of Superior Court. Prepayment required. If you are not sure how many pages the results or your request will be, you may send a blank check with "Not to exceed $25.00" written in the memo. Personal checks accepted. No credit cards accepted.

Mail search: Turnaround time: 2 to 3 weeks. Mail is the preferred request method.A SASE is requested.

Fax search: Requesters must be pre-approved to fax, and only written information is faxed back. Attorneys with charge accounts with the Superior Court can receive copies, without the seal of the court, via fax.

In person search: Turnaround time: while you wait. The Clerk's Office recommends not come to the office in person except for emergency requests.

Online search: Records can be ordered online from www.vitalcheck.com, a state approved vendor partner.

Workers' Compensation Records

Labor Department, Division of Workers Compensation, PO Box 381, Trenton, NJ 08625-0381 (Courier: Labor Building, 6th Floor, John Fitch Plaza, Trenton, NJ 08625); 609-292-6026, 609-292-2515 (General Hotline), 609-984-2515 (Fax), 8:30AM-4:30PM.

www.nj.gov/labor/wc/wcindex.html

Indexing & Storage: Records are available for 45 years, then are purged. New records are available for inquiry immediately. Records are indexed on inhouse computer.

Searching: First report of injury-accident is not available to the public. All other records are subject to NJSA 34:15-128 which prohibits the copying of records for resale. Use WC-147 if you want copies of a case. Include the following in your request-claimant name, Social Security Number, date of accident. Use the agency's record request form found at www.nj.gov/labor/wc/forms/wc-147(r7-04).pdf.

Access by: mail, in person, online.

Fee & Payment: There is no search fee. The certified copy fee is $.75 each for first 10 pages; $.50 each for next 10; and $.25 per page over 20. A processing fee of $15.0 is billed, plus any postage costs. Fee payee: Division of Workers' Compensation. Copies can be billed Personal checks accepted. No credit cards accepted.

Mail search: Turnaround time: 4 to 6 weeks. If request is just to know if the person has a claim, the turnaround time is same day. A SASE is requested. Otherwise postage is added to copy fees.

In person search: Turnaround time is same day.

Online search: COURTS on-line is a secure Internet website that provides authorized subscribers access to the Division's database. Possible subscribers include: Insurance Carrier/Law Firms; Court Reporting Firms; and WC Forensic Experts (Physicians).

Driver Records

Motor Vehicle Services, Driver History Abstract Unit, PO Box 142, Trenton, NJ 08666; 609-292-6500 (Forms request), 609-292-7500 (Suspensions), 8AM-4:30PM.

www.state.nj.us/mvc/

Note: Copies of tickets are not kept on file and must be obtained from the municipal courts.

Indexing & Storage: Records are available for 5 yrs for the public (complete history for attorneys). Non-moving violations are not reported on the record. Accidents in excess of $500 are reported, but fault is not shown. Driver's address is provided on the record. It takes 3 days to 2 weeks normally before new records are available for inquiry.

Searching: Access of driving records is strict, release to casual requesters is prohibited unless Form DO-21A contains notarized authority from subject. Permissible use requesters should use Form ISM-21. Include the following in your request-full name, DOB and DL. Sex, and eye color are also helpful for manual requests. The driver's license number should be submitted with all requests. The full name, DOB, The following data is not released: Social Security Numbers or medical records.

Access by: mail, in person, online.

Fee & Payment: The current fee is $10.00 for certified mail-in or walk-in requests, and $8.00 for other media including magnetic tape, control cards (100 minimum purchase), and online access. Fee payee: Motor Vehicle Services. Prepayment required. Personal checks accepted. No credit cards accepted.

Mail search: Turnaround time: 2 weeks. A SASE is requested.

In person search: Driving records can obtained at any one of the four Regional Service Centers - Deptford, Wayne, Eatontown, and Trenton.

Online search: Fee is $10.00 per record. Access is limited to insurance, bus and trucking companies, parking authorities, and approved vendors. For more information, call 609-292-4572 NJ drivers may order their own record online at www.state.nj.us/mvc/d_driver_history.html. A user ID number must be obtained first.

Vehicle and Vessel Ownership and Registration

Motor Vehicle Commission, Certified Information Unit, PO Box 146, Trenton, NJ 08666; 609-292-6500, 888-486-3339 (In-state), 8AM-5PM.

www.state.nj.us/mvc/cit_title/v_title.html

Note: Lien records must be ordered from Special Titles at Motor Vehicle Commission, PO Box 017 (Zip is 08666-0017). Lien searches are on current record or particular requests, also can be purchased at $5.00 for each lien history search.

Indexing & Storage: Records are available for 3 years (registration) and 8 years (title). All boats over 12 feet must be titled and registered. Also, this agency maintains records on mobile homes. It takes 3 to 4 months before new records are available for inquiry. Records are normally destroyed after 3 years after expiration.

Searching: SSNs and medical information are not currently released and more restrictions are forthcoming. Casual requesters cannot obtain records. A special request form is required for most searches as follows: DO-22A for title search, /DO-22 for lien search, ISM/DO-11A for vehicle registration application search.

Access by: mail, online.

Fee & Payment: The fee is $8.00 per record non-certified and $10.00 certified and take 6-8 weeks to process. A lien history search is $5.00 for each lien. A complete title history costs $10.50 and can take as long as 12 weeks to obtain. Fee payee: Motor Vehicle Commission Prepayment required. Personal checks and money orders accepted. No credit cards accepted.

Mail search: Turnaround time: 6 to 8 weeks. Requests must be submitted on Form ISM/DO-11A for registration requests, Form DO-22A for title record requests, Form ISM/DO-22 for lien search requests.

Online search: Limited online access is available for insurance companies, bus and trucking companies, highway/parking authorities, and approved vendors for these businesses. Fees are $4.00 per request for registration record and $8.00 for ownership history. Call 609-292-4572 for more information.

Other access: There is no program for massive/customized bulk look-ups. Each request is looked at on an individual basis. Records are not sold for commercial or political reasons.

Accident Reports

New Jersey State Police, Criminal Justice Records Section, PO Box 7068, West Trenton, NJ 08628-0068; 609-882-2000 x2234, 8AM-5PM.

www.njsp.org

Indexing & Storage: Records are available for 6 years. Records are computer indexed by driver name and case number. It takes 3 to 4 weeks before new records are available for inquiry. Records are normally destroyed after 6 years.

Searching: Only the basics of fatal accident reports are available until the full report has been released from the County Prosecutor. While the report is pending, no statements, evidence or photogrpahs can be released without the written consent of the prosecutor. Include the following in your request-location of accident, date of accident, driver's full name.

Access by: mail, online.

Fee & Payment: Fees: $10.00 for first 3 pages and $2.00 for each additional page with a maximum fee of $16.00. Fee payee: New Jersey State Police Department. Prepayment required.

Personal checks or money orders accepted. No credit cards accepted.

Mail search: Turnaround time: 3 to 4 weeks. A SASE is requested.

Online search: No online access to accidents reports is available, however, you may access the Insurance Company name codes online for free at www.state.nj.us/mvc/cit_insurance/v_insurance_codes.html. By reading the code on the accident report, you can then use this website to determine the insurance company involved.

Expedited service: If the report is available in the agency office, then they can return it via overnight delivery if you provide a prepaid shipping envelope.

Voter Registration
Access to Records is Restricted

Dept of Law and Public Safety, Division of Elections, PO Box 304, Trenton, NJ 08625; 609-292-3760, 609-777-1280 (Fax), 8:30AM-5PM.

www.njelections.org

Note: The Commissioner of Registration maintains these records, but they can only be accessed at the county level. While these county agencies may permit individual look-ups, records in mass may only be purchased for political purposes.

GED Certificates

GED Testing Program, Dept. of Education - Bureau Adult Ed. & Literacy, PO Box 500, Trenton, NJ 08625-0500; 609-777-0577, 609-777-1050 (Forms), 609-984-0573 (Fax), 9AM-4PM.

www.state.nj.us/njded/students/ged

Indexing & Storage: It takes 2 to 4 weeks before new records are available for inquiry.

Searching: GED Information Request Form is required and can be obtained by calling 609-777-1050 or at www.state.nj.us/njded/students/ged/inforeq.pdf. Include the following in your request-a signed release, name, date/year of test, Social Security Number, and city of test. Records are not maintained for persons tested at federal correctional institutions.

Access by: mail.

Fee & Payment: The fee is $5.00 for a verification or a copy of the transcript. Fee payee: Commissioner of Education. Prepayment required. Money orders and business checks are accepted. No personal checks accepted. No credit cards accepted.

Mail search: Turnaround time: up to 4 weeks.

Hunting and Fishing License Information
Records not maintained by a state level agency.

Note: They do not have a central database. You must contact the vendor where the license was purchased. Plans are underway to implement a computerized database by the end of 2006.

New Jersey State Licensing Agencies

Licenses Searchable Online

Acupuncturist #1 .... www.state.nj.us/cgi-bin/consumeraffairs/search/searchentry.pl?searchprofession=3251
Alcohol/Drug Counselor #13 .... www.state.nj.us/cgi-bin/consumeraffairs/search/searchentry.pl?searchprofession=3703
Appraiser, General/Residential #23 .... www.state.nj.us/cgi-bin/consumeraffairs/search/searchentry.pl?searchprofession=4202
Architect #6 .... www.state.nj.us/cgi-bin/consumeraffairs/search/searchentry.pl
Athletic Trainer #4 .... www.state.nj.us/cgi-bin/consumeraffairs/search/searchentry.pl
Audiologist #7 .... www.state.nj.us/cgi-bin/consumeraffairs/search/search.pl
Barber / Barber Shop #9 .... www.state.nj.us/cgi-bin/consumeraffairs/search/searchentry.pl
Beautician #9 .... www.state.nj.us/cgi-bin/consumeraffairs/search/searchentry.pl
Candidate report #43 .... www.elec.state.nj.us/eleconline/default.asp?main_frame=reports_main.asp
Cemetery / Cemetery Salesperson #46 .... www.state.nj.us/cgi-bin/consumeraffairs/search/searchentry.pl?searchprofession=4701
Certificate of Authorization #6 .... www.state.nj.us/cgi-bin/consumeraffairs/search/searchentry.pl
Charities #61 .... www.state.nj.us/lps/ca/charfrm.htm
Chiropractor #8 .... www.state.nj.us/cgi-bin/consumeraffairs/search/searchentry.pl
Contributor, Political #43 .... www.elec.state.nj.us/eleconline/default.asp?main_frame=contrib_main.asp
Cosmetologist/Hairstylist #9 .... www.state.nj.us/cgi-bin/consumeraffairs/search/searchentry.pl
Cosmetology/Manicurist Shop #9 .... www.state.nj.us/cgi-bin/consumeraffairs/search/searchentry.pl
Counselor, Professional #13 .... www.state.nj.us/cgi-bin/consumeraffairs/search/searchentry.pl
Court Reporter #24 .... www.state.nj.us/cgi-bin/consumeraffairs/search/searchentry.pl?searchprofession=3000
CPA/Public Accountant #5 .... www.state.nj.us/cgi-bin/consumeraffairs/search/searchentry.pl?searchprofession=2000
Dental Assistant, Ltd/Registered #10 .... www.state.nj.us/cgi-bin/consumeraffairs/search/searchentry.pl
Dentist / Dental Hygienist #10 .... www.state.nj.us/cgi-bin/consumeraffairs/search/searchentry.pl
Electrical Contractor #11 .... www.state.nj.us/cgi-bin/consumeraffairs/search/searchentry.pl?searchprofession=3400
Embalmer #15 .... www.state.nj.us/cgi-bin/consumeraffairs/search/searchentry.pl?searchprofession=2
Engineer #20 .... www.njconsumeraffairs.com/nonmedical/pels.htm
Funeral Home #15 .... www.state.nj.us/cgi-bin/consumeraffairs/search/searchentry.pl
Funeral Practitioner #15 .... www.state.nj.us/cgi-bin/consumeraffairs/search/searchentry.pl?searchprofession=2
Hearing Aid Dispenser/Fitter #44 .... www.state.nj.us/cgi-bin/consumeraffairs/search/searchentry.pl?searchprofession=2253
Home Health Aide #16 .... www.state.nj.us/cgi-bin/consumeraffairs/search/searchentry.pl
Home Inspection #20 .... www.njconsumeraffairs.com/nonmedical/pels.htm
Insurance Agent /Public Adjuster #41 .... www.nj.gov/dobi/licenseesearch/insurancelicensee.htm
Lab Director, Bio-Analytical #14 .... www.state.nj.us/cgi-bin/consumeraffairs/search/searchentry.pl?searchprofession=2505
Landscape Architect #6 .... www.state.nj.us/cgi-bin/consumeraffairs/search/searchentry.pl
Lobbyist #43 .... www.elec.state.nj.us/eleconline/default.asp?main_frame=reports_main.asp
Manicurist/Manicurist Shop #9 .... www.state.nj.us/cgi-bin/consumeraffairs/search/searchentry.pl
Marriage & Family Counselor #13 .... www.state.nj.us/cgi-bin/consumeraffairs/search/searchentry.pl?searchprofession=3703
Midwife #14 .... www.state.nj.us/cgi-bin/consumeraffairs/search/searchentry.pl?searchprofession=2510
Mortician #15 .... www.state.nj.us/cgi-bin/consumeraffairs/search/searchentry.pl?searchprofession=2
Nurse, Advance Practice #16 .... www.state.nj.us/cgi-bin/consumeraffairs/search/searchentry.pl
Nurse-LPN #16 .... www.state.nj.us/cgi-bin/consumeraffairs/search/searchentry.pl
Nurse-RN #16 .... www.state.nj.us/cgi-bin/consumeraffairs/search/searchentry.pl
Occupational Therapist #60 .... www.state.nj.us/cgi-bin/consumeraffairs/search/searchentry.pl?searchprofession=4601
Occupational Therapy Asst. #60 .... www.state.nj.us/cgi-bin/consumeraffairs/search/searchentry.pl
Opthalmic Dispenser #51 .... www.state.nj.us/cgi-bin/consumeraffairs/search/searchentry.pl
Optician/Opthalmic Technician #51 .... www.state.nj.us/cgi-bin/consumeraffairs/search/searchentry.pl?searchprofession=3102
Optometrist #17 .... www.state.nj.us/cgi-bin/consumeraffairs/search/searchentry.pl?searchprofession=2701
Pharmacist #18 .... www.state.nj.us/cgi-bin/consumeraffairs/search/searchentry.pl?searchprofession=2801
Physical Therapist/Assistant #19 .... www.state.nj.us/cgi-bin/consumeraffairs/search/searchentry.pl?searchprofession=4001
Physician #14 .... www.state.nj.us/cgi-bin/consumeraffairs/search/searchentry.pl?searchprofession=2501
Physician Assistant #14 .... www.state.nj.us/cgi-bin/consumeraffairs/search/searchentry.pl
Planner, Professional #21 .... www.state.nj.us/cgi-bin/consumeraffairs/search/searchentry.pl?searchprofession=3300
Plumber/Master Plumber #12 .... www.state.nj.us/cgi-bin/consumeraffairs/search/searchentry.pl?searchprofession=3601
Podiatrist #14 .... www.state.nj.us/cgi-bin/consumeraffairs/search/searchentry.pl?searchprofession=2507
Psychologist #22 .... www.state.nj.us/cgi-bin/consumeraffairs/search/searchentry.pl?searchprofession=3
Real Estate Agent/Broker/Sales #48 .... www.state.nj.us/dobi/licenseesearch/realestatelicensee.htm
Real Estate Appraiser/Apprentice #23 .... www.state.nj.us/cgi-bin/consumeraffairs/search/searchentry.pl?searchprofession=4202
Real Estate School/ Instructor #48 .... www.state.nj.us/dobi/recskool.htm
Respiratory Therapist #54 .... www.state.nj.us/cgi-bin/consumeraffairs/search/searchentry.pl?searchprofession=4301
Shorthand Reporter #24 .... www.state.nj.us/cgi-bin/consumeraffairs/search/searchentry.pl?searchprofession=3000
Skin Care Specialist/Shop #9 .... www.state.nj.us/cgi-bin/consumeraffairs/search/searchentry.pl
Social Worker #25 .... www.state.nj.us/cgi-bin/consumeraffairs/search/searchentry.pl?searchprofession=4401

Speech-Language Pathologist #7 .... www.state.nj.us/cgi-bin/consumeraffairs/search/search.pl
Surveyor, Land #20 .... www.njconsumeraffairs.com/nonmedical/pels.htm
Tree Expert #55 .... www.state.nj.us/dep/parksandforests/forest/community/cte.html
Veterinarian #26 .... www.state.nj.us/cgi-bin/consumeraffairs/search/searchentry.pl?searchprofession=2901
Viatical Settlement Broker #41 .... www.nj.gov/dobi/licenseesearch/insurancelicensee.htm

New Jersey Licensing Quick Finder

Accountant, Municipal #5 973-504-6380	Emergency Medical Technician #32 609-633-7777	Optometrist #17 973-504-6440
Acupuncturist #1 609-826-7100	Employment Agency #40 973-504-6261	Orthodontic Assistant, Ltd/ Registered #10
Alcohol/Drug Counselor #13 973-504-6582	Engineer #20 973-504-6460	 973-504-6405
Amusement Ride Inspector #45 609-984-7834	Fire Protection Inspector #45 609-984-7834	Orthopedist #14 609-292-4843
Animal Control Officer #59 609-588-3121	Firefighter #58 609-633-6117	Orthotist/Prosthetist #52 973-504-6445
Appraiser, General/Residential #23 973-504-6480	Firm #5 973-504-6380	Paramedic #32 609-633-7777
Architect #6 973-504-6385	Funeral Home #15 973-504-6425	Pesticide Applicator/Operator #31 609-530-4070
Asbestos Employee/Employer #33 609-633-3760	Funeral Practitioner #15 973-504-6425	Pesticide Dealer #31 609-530-4070
Asbestos Permit #33 609-633-3760	Health Care Service Agency #40 973-504-6261	Pharmacist #18 973-504-6450
Athletic Booking Agency #40 973-504-6261	Health Spa #40 973-504-6261	Pharmacy #18 973-504-6450
Athletic Trainer #4 609-292-4843	Hearing Aid Dispenser/Fitter #44 973-504-6331	Physical Therapist/Assistant #19 973-504-6455
Attorney #49 609-292-8079	Home Health Aide #16 973-504-6504	Physician #14 609-292-4843
Audiologist #7 973-504-6390	Home Inspection #20 973-504-6460	Physician Assistant #14 609-292-4843
Automobile Dealer #42 609-292-4517	Home Repair Contractor/Seller #39 609-292-3420	Planner, Professional #21 973-504-6465
Barber #9 973-504-6400	Hotel/Motel #37 609-984-3231	Plumber/Master Plumber #12 973-504-6420
Barber Shop #9 973-504-6400	Housing Code Official #45 609-984-7834	Plumbing Inspector #45 609-984-7834
Beautician #9 973-504-6400	Inplant Inspector #45 609-984-7834	Podiatrist #14 609-292-4843
Boiler Operator #34 609-984-3001	Inspector of Hotels & Multiple Dwellings Inspector #45	Private Detective #56 .... 609-882-2000 X2680
Boiler Pressure Vessel & Refrigeration Inspector #45	 609-984-7834	Psychologist #22 973-504-6470
.... 609-984-7834	Insurance Agent #41 609-292-4337	Pump Installer #30 609-984-6831
Boxer #53 609-292-0317	Insurance Public Adjuster #41 609-292-4337	Race Horse Owner/Trainer #47 609-292-0613
Boxing Manager #28 609-292-0317	Investment Advisor/Rep. #27 973-504-3600	Real Estate Agent/Broker #48 609-292-8280
Building Inspector #45 609-984-7834	Job Listing Service #40 973-504-6261	Real Estate Agent/Sales #48 609-292-8280
Candidate report #43 609-292-8700	Lab Director, Bio-Analytical #14 609-292-4843	Real Estate Appraiser/Apprentice #23.. 973-504-6480
Career Counselor #40 973-504-6221	Landscape Architect #6 973-504-6385	Real Estate School/ Instructor #48 609-292-8280
Casino #28 609-441-3555	Lender, Consumer #39 609-292-5340	Refrigeration Technician #34 609-984-3001
Casino Employee #28 609-441-3015	Librarian #29 609-292-2070	Respiratory Therapist #54 973-504-6485
Cemetery #46 973-504-6553	Liquor Control #37 609-984-3231	Resume Service #40 973-504-6261
Cemetery Salesperson #46 973-504-6553	Liquor Distribution, Plenary Retail/Limited Retail #37	School Accountant #5 973-504-6380
Certificate of Authorization #6 973-504-6385	 609-984-3231	School Counselor #29 609-292-0739
Charities #61 973-504-6215	Liquor Rectifier/Blender #37 609-984-3231	School Principal/Admin./Supv'r #29 609-292-0739
Check Casher/Seller #38 609-292-5340	Liquor Retail, Plenary/Seasonal #37 ... 609-984-3231	School, Accredited #29 609-292-0739
Chiropractor #8 973-504-6395	Liquor Sales, Retail/Ltd/Plenary #37 ... 609-984-3231	Securities Agent #27 973-504-3600
Club/Cabaret #37 609-984-3231	Liquor Transit, Plenary Retail #37 609-984-3231	Securities Broker/Dealer #27 973-504-3600
Collection Agency Bond #36 609-292-9292	Liquor Wholesale, Limited/Plenary #37. 609-984-3231	Securities Issuer #27 973-504-3600
Computer Job-Matching Service #40 ... 973-504-6261	Lobbyist #43 609-292-8700	Shorthand Reporter #24 973-504-6490
Construction Code Official #45 609-984-7834	Manicurist/Manicurist Shop #9 973-504-6400	Skin Care Specialist/Shop #9 973-504-6400
Contributor, Political #43 609-292-8700	Marriage & Family Counselor #13 973-504-6582	Social Worker #25 973-504-6495
Cosmetologist/Hairstylist #9 973-504-6400	Marriage Counselor #13 973-504-6582	Speech-Language Pathologist #7 973-504-6390
Cosmetology/Manicurist Shop #9 973-504-6400	Mechanical Inspector 1 & 2 Family #45 609-984-7834	Stable Mate #47 609-292-0613
Counselor, Professional #13 973-504-6582	Midwife #14 609-292-4843	Student Personnel Svc Director #29 609-292-0739
Court Reporter #24 973-504-6490	Modeling & Talent Agency #40 973-504-6261	Surveyor, Land #20 973-504-6460
CPA/Public Accountant #5 973-504-6380	Mortgage (2nd) Lender #39 609-292-5340	Teacher #29 609-292-0739
CPE Sponsor #5 973-504-6380	Mortician #15 973-504-6425	Temporary Help Agency #40 973-504-6261
Crane Operator #34 609-984-3001	Mover/Warehouseman #2 973-504-6512	Theater #37 609-984-3231
Dental Assistant, Ltd/Registered #10 ... 973-504-6405	Notary Public #36 609-292-9292	Ticket Reseller #40 973-504-6261
Dental Hygienist #10 973-504-6405	Nurse, Advance Practice #16 973-504-6504	Trademark #36 609-292-9292
Dentist #10 973-504-6405	Nurse-LPN #16 973-504-6504	Tree Expert #55 609-292-2532
Educational Media Specialist/Librarian #29	Nurse-RN #16 973-504-6504	Veterinarian #26 973-504-6500
.... 609-292-0739	Nursing Home Administrator #50 609-633-9706	Viatical Settlement Broker #41 609-292-4337
Electrical Contractor #11 973-504-6410	Nursing Registry Svc #40 973-504-6261	Waste Water System Operator #30 609-984-6831
Electrical Inspector #45 609-984-7834	Occupational Therapist #60 973-504-6570	Weighmaster #35 732-815-4840
Elevator Inspector #45 609-984-7834	Occupational Therapy Asst. #60 973-504-6570	Weights & Measures Mechanic #35 732-815-4840
Embalmer #15 973-504-6425	Opthalmic Dispenser #51 973-504-6435	Well Driller #30 609-984-6831
Emergency Medical Svc Provider #32 . 609-633-7777	Optician/Opthalmic Technician #51 973-504-6435	Wine Wholesaler/Winery #37 609-984-3231

New Jersey Licensing Agency Information

1 Board of Medical Examiners, Acupuncture Examining Board, PO Box 183, Trenton, NJ 08625-0183; 609-826-7100. Search Database at www.state.nj.us/lps/ca/bme/acupdir.htm

2 Office of Consumer Protection, Regulated Business Section, 124 Halsey St, Newark, NJ 07101; 973-504-6442, Fax: 973-648-2807. www.state.nj.us/lps/ca
Email: askconsumeraffairs@smtp.lps.state.nj.us

4 Board of Medical Examiners, Athletic Training Advisory Commission, 140 E Front St, 2nd Fl, Trenton, NJ 08625-0183; 609-292-4843, Fax: 609-826-7117. www.state.nj.us/lps/ca/medical.htm

5 Board of Accountancy, PO Box 45000, Newark, NJ 07101; 973-504-6380, Fax: 973-648-2855. www.state.nj.us/lps/ca/nonmed.htm#acc1
Search Database at
www.state.nj.us/lps/ca/accountancy/accdir.htm

6 Board of Architects, Division of Consumer Affairs, PO Box 45001, Newark, NJ 07101; 973-504-6385, Fax: 973-504-6458.
www.state.nj.us/lps/ca/arch/arch.htm
Search Database at www.state.nj.us/cgi-bin/consumeraffairs/search/searchentry.pl

7 Board of Audiology & Speech Language Pathology, Division of Consumer Affairs, P.O. Pox 45002, 124 Halsey St, Newark, NJ 07101; 973-504-6390, Fax: 973-648-3355.
www.state.nj.us/lps/ca/medical.htm
Search Database at www.state.nj.us/cgi-bin/consumeraffairs/search/search.pl

8 Board of Chiropractic Examiners, Division of Consumer Affairs, PO Box 45004, Newark, NJ 07101; 973-504-6395, Fax: 973-648-3538.
www.state.nj.us/lps/ca/medical.htm
Email: lpygidr@oag.lps.state.nj.us
Search Database at www.state.nj.us/cgi-bin/consumeraffairs/search/search.pl

9 Board of Cosmetology & Hairstyling, PO Box 45003, Newark, NJ 07101; 973-504-6400, Fax: 973-648-3536.
www.state.nj.us/lps/ca/nonmed.htm#cos4
Search Database at
www.state.nj.us/lps/ca/director.htm

10 Board of Dentistry, PO Box 45005, 124 Halsey St, Newark, NJ 07101; 973-504-6405, Fax: 973-273-8075.
www.state.nj.us/lps/ca/medical.htm#den3
Search Database at
www.state.nj.us/lps/ca/medical.htm#den3
Note: There is an automated license verification line (need license number) 973-273-8090 with fax back capability for written verifications.

11 Board of Examiners of Electrical Contractors, Division of Consumer Affairs, 124 Halsey St (07102), Newark, NJ 07101; 973-504-6410, Fax: 973-648-3355.
www.state.nj.us/lps/ca/boards/list1.htm
Email: AskConsumerAffairs@oag.lps.state.nj.us
Search Database at
www.state.nj.us/lps/ca/electric/elecdir.htm

12 Board of Examiners of Master Plumbers, PO Box 45008 (124 Halsey St, 07102), Newark, NJ 07101; 973-504-6420.
www.state.nj.us/lps/ca/home.htm
Search Database at
www.state.nj.us/lps/ca/plumber/plumdir.htm

13 Board of Marriage & Family Therapy Examiners, 124 Halsey St, 6th Fl, Newark, NJ 07101; 973-504-6582.
www.state.nj.us/lps/ca/boards.htm
Search Database at
www.state.nj.us/lps/ca/marriage/pcdir.htm

14 Board of Medical Examiners, PO Box 183, Trenton, NJ 08625-0183; 609-292-4843, Fax: 609-984-3950.
www.state.nj.us./lps/ca/medical.htm Search Database at www.state.nj.us/lps/ca/director.htm

15 Board of Mortuary Science, Division of Consumer Affairs, 124 Halsey St, Newark, NJ 07102; 973-504-6425, Fax: 973-648-2855.
www.state.nj.us/lps/ca/nonmedical/mortuary.htm
Email: lpywidr@oag.lps.state.nj.us Search Database at www.state.nj.us/lps/ca/mort/mortdir.htm

16 Board of Nursing, 124 Halsey St (07102), Newark, NJ 07101; 973-504-6430, Fax: 973-648-3481. www.state.nj.us/lps/ca/home.htm
Email: AskConsumerAffairs@oag.lps.state.nj.us
Search Database at
www.state.nj.us/lps/ca/medical.htm#nur6

17 Board of Optometrists, Division of Consumer Affairs, 124 Halsey St (07102), Newark, NJ 07101; 973-504-6440, Fax: 973-648-3536.
www.state.nj.us/lps/ca/optometry/optdir.htm
Search Database at
www.state.nj.us/lps/ca/optometry/optdir.htm

18 Board of Pharmacy, PO Box 45013 (124 Halsey St, 07102), Newark, NJ 07101; 973-504-6450, Fax: 973-648-3355.
www.state.nj.us/lps/ca/medical.htm#pharm11
Search Database at
www.state.nj.us/lps/ca/pharm/pharmdir.htm

19 Board of Physical Therapists, 124 Halsey St, Newark, NJ 07101; 973-504-6455, Fax: 973-648-3536. Search Database at
www.state.nj.us/lps/ca/pt/ptdir.htm

20 Board of Professional Engineers & Land Surveyors, 124 Halsey St, 3rd Fl, Newark, NJ 07102; 973-504-6460, Fax: 973-273-8020.
www.njconsumeraffairs.com/nonmedical/pels.htm
Search Database at
www.njconsumeraffairs.com/nonmedical/pels.htm

21 Board of Professional Planners, PO Box 45016 (124 Halsey St, 07102), Newark, NJ 07101; 973-504-6465, Fax: 973-648-3536.
www.state.nj.us/lps/ca/plan/planner.htm
Search Database at
www.state.nj.us/lps/ca/plan/plandir.htm

22 Board of Psychological Examiners, Division of Consumer Affairs, 124 Halsey St, Newark, NJ 07102; 973-504-6470.
www.state.nj.us/lps/ca Search Database at www.state.nj.us/lps/ca/psy/psydir.htm

23 Board of Real Estate Appraisers, Division of Consumer Affairs, PO Box 45032 (124 Halsey St, 07102), Newark, NJ 07101; 973-504-6480, Fax: 973-648-3536. www.state.nj.us/lps/ca
Search Database at
www.state.nj.us/lps/ca/real/realdir.htm

24 Board of Shorthand Reporting, Po Box 45019, Newark, NJ 07101; 973-504-6490.
www.state.nj.us/lps/ca/nonmed.htm#short12
Search Database at
www.state.nj.us/lps/ca/short/shortdir.htm

25 Board of Social Work Examiners, PO Box 45033, Newark, NJ 07101; 973-504-6495, Fax: 973-273-8067.
www.state.nj.us/lps/ca/medical.htm#sw15
Search Database at
www.state.nj.us/lps/ca/social/socdir.htm License verification telephone number is 973-273-8090.

26 Board of Veterinary Medical Examiners, PO Box 45033, Newark, NJ 07101; 973-504-6500, Fax: 973-648-3355.
www.state.nj.us/lps/ca/medical.htm
Email: ROMANOD@smtd.lps.state.nj.us
Search Database at
www.state.nj.us/lps/ca/vetmed/vetdir.htm

27 Bureau of Securities, PO Box 47029, 153 Halsey St 6th Fl, Newark, NJ 07101; 973-504-3600, Fax: 973-504-3601.
www.state.nj.us/lps/ca/bos.htm

28 Casino Control Commission, Tennessee Ave & Boardwalk, Arcade Bldg, Atlantic City, NJ 08401; 609-441-3000, Fax: 609-441-3752.
www.state.nj.us/casinos

29 Department of Education, Licensing and Credentials, PO Box 500, 100 Riverview Plaza, Trenton, NJ 08625-0500; 609-292-2045, Fax: 609-292-3768.

30 Department of Environmental Protection, Bureau of Water Allocations, PO Box 402 (401 E State St, CN-402), Trenton, NJ 08625; 609-984-6831, Fax: 609-633-1231.
www.state.nj.us/dep/watersupply/well.htm

31 Department of Environmental Protection, Pesticide Control Program, PO Box 411, Trenton, NJ 08625-0411; 609-530-4070, Fax: 609-984-6555.
www.state.nj.us/dep/enforcement/pcp
Email: askDEP@dep.state.nj.us

32 Office of Emergency Medical Svcs, Department of Health, 50 E State St 6th Fl (PO Box 360), Trenton, NJ 08625; 609-633-7777, Fax: 609-633-7954.
www.state.nj.us/health/ems/index.html
Email: ems@doh.state.ny.us Note: Only disciplinary actions, fines, and enforcement actions are online.

33 Asbestos Control and Licensing, Dept. of Workforce Dev.; Occupational Safety & Health, PO Box 949 (1 John Fitch Plaza, 3rd Fl), Trenton, NJ 08625-0949; 609-633-3760, Fax: 609-633-0664.

34 Bureau of Boiler & Pressure Vessel Compliance, Department of Community Affairs, PO Box 814 (101 South Broad St), Trenton, NJ 08625-0814; 609-984-3001, Fax: 609-984-1577.

35 Department of Law & Public Safety, Office of Weights & Measures, P.O. Box 490, Avanel, NJ 07001; 732-815-4840, Fax: 732-382-5298.
www.state.nj.us/lps/ca/weights/wmreg.htm

36 Department of Treasury, Division of Revenue, Notary Section, PO Box 452, West Trenton, NJ 08625; 609-292-9292, Fax: 609-984-6681.
www.state.nj.us/treasury/revenue/dcr/programs/notary.html

37 Division of Alcoholic Beverage Control, 140 E Front St, CN087, Trenton, NJ 08625-0087; 609-984-3230, Fax: 609-633-6078.
www.state.nj.us/lps/abc/licensing.html

38 Division of Banking, Consumer Credit Bureau, 20 W State St CN-040, Trenton, NJ 08625; 609-292-5340, Fax: 609-292-5461.
www.state.nj.us/dobi/bankmnu.shtml

39 Division of Banking, Office of Consumer Finance, 20 W State St CN-040, Trenton, NJ 08625; 609-292-7659, Fax: 609-292-5461.
www.state.nj.us/dobi/index.shtml
Email: lhughes@cobi.state.nj.us

40 Regulated Business Section, Division of Consumer Affairs, PO Box 45028 (124 Halsey St), Newark, NJ 07101; 973-504-6261, Fax: 973-648-2807. www.state.nj.us/lps/ca

41 Division of Insurance, License Processing, PO Box 327 (20 W. State St), Trenton, NJ 08625-0327; 609-292-4337, Fax: 609-984-0092.
www.njdobi.org/insmnu.shtml
Email: inslic@dobi.state.nj.us
Search Database at www.nj.gov/dobi/licensee search/insurancelicensee.htm

42 Division of Motor Vehicles, Dealer Licensing Section, 225 E State St, Trenton, NJ 08666; 609-292-4517, Fax: 609-292-5153.
www.state.nj.us/mvc/bc_licensing/bc_motor_vehi cle_dealership_license.html

43 Election Law Enforcement Commission, PO Box 185, CN-185 (28 W State St), Trenton, NJ 08625-0185; 609-292-8700, Fax: 609-633-9854.
www.elec.state.nj.us

44 Hearing Aid Dispensers Examining Committee, PO Box 45002, Newark, NJ 07101; 973-504-6331, Fax: 973-648-3355.
www.state.nj.us/lps/ca/medical.htm
Search Database at
www.state.nj.us/lps/ca/hear/heardir.htm

45 Department of Community Affairs, Bureau of Code Services, Attn: Licensing Unit, PO Box 816, Trenton, NJ 08625-0816; 609-984-7834, Fax: 609-984-7952. www.state.nj.us/dca/codes/

Email: codeslicensing@dca.state.nj.us Search Database at www.nj.gov/dca/codes/licensingunit/index.html

46 Cemetery Board, PO Box 45036, Newark, NJ 07101; 973-504-6553, Fax: 973-648-3536.
www.state.nj.us/lps/ca/nonmed.htm
Search Database at
www.state.nj.us/lps/ca/director.htm

47 Racing Commission, POB 088 (140 Front St), Trenton, NJ 08625-0080;
609-292-0613, Fax: 609-599-1785.

48 Department of Banking & Insurance, Real Estate Commission, 240 W State St, (PO Box 328), Trenton, NJ 08625-0328; 609-292-8280, Fax: 609-292-0944.
www.state.nj.us/dobi/remnu.htm
Email: realestate@dobi.state.nj.us
Search Database at www.state.nj.us/dobi/licens eesearch/realestatelicensee.htm

49 Supreme Court, New Jersey Lawyers Fund, PO Box 961, Trenton, NJ 08625;
609-292-8079, Fax: 609-394-3637.
www.judiciary.state.nj.us/cpf/index.htm

50 Nursing Home Administrators Licensing Board, PO Box 367, Trenton, NJ 08625-0367; 609-633-9706, Fax: 609-633-9087.
www.state.nj.us/health/

51 Ophthalmic Dispensers & Ophthalmic Technicians Board, Division of Consumer Affairs, 124 Halsey St, Newark, NJ 07102; 973-504-6435. Search Database at
www.state.nj.us/lps/ca/director.htm

52 Orthotics & Prosthetics Board of Examiners, Division of Consumer Affairs, PO Box 45034 (124 Halsey St., Newark, NJ 07112; 973-504-6445, Fax: 973-648-3536. www.state.nj.us/lps/ca

53 Athletic Control Board, 140 E Front St, CN-180, Trenton, NJ 08625-0180;
609-292-0317, Fax: 609-292-3756.

54 Board of Respiratory Care, 122 Halsey St, Newark, NJ 07101;
973-504-6485, Fax: 973-648-3355.
www.state.nj.us/lps/ca/home.htm
Search Database at
www.state.nj.us/lps/ca/respcare/respdir.htm

55 Forestry Service, 501 E State St CN-404, Trenton, NJ 08625-0404; 609-292-2532, Fax: 609-984-0378.
www.state.nj.us/dep/forestry/community/home.htm
Search Database at www.state.nj.us/dep/par ksandforests/forest/community/cte.html

56 State Police Department, Private Detective Division, River Rd, Trenton, NJ 08628; 609-882-2000 x2680, Fax: 609-637-9583.
www.njsp.org/about/srb.html

58 Department of Community Affairs, Division of Fire Safety, PO Box 809, Trenton, NJ 08625-0809; 609-633-6117, Fax: 609-633-6744.

59 Department of Health & Senior Svcs, Infectious & Zoonotic Program, PO Box 369, Trenton, NJ 08625-0369; 609-588-3121, Fax: 609-588-3894. www.state.nj.us

60 Occupational Therapy Advisory Council, Division of Consumer Affairs, PO Box 45027 (124 Halsey St), Newark, NJ 07101; 973-504-6570.
www.state.nj.us/lps/ca/home.htm
Email: lpygidr@oag.lps.state.nj.us Search Database at www.state.nj.us/lps/ca/director.htm

61 Charities Registration Section, Division of Consumer Affairs, PO Box 45021 (124 Halsey St), Newark, NJ 07101;
973-504-6215, Fax: 973-273-8035.
www.state.nj.us/lps/ca
Search Database at
www.state.nj.us/lps/ca/charfrm.htm

New Jersey Federal Courts

The following list indicates the district and division name for each county in the state. If the bankruptcy court location is different from the district court, then the location of the bankruptcy court appears in parentheses.

County/Court Cross Reference

Atlantic	Camden	Middlesex	Newark (Trenton)
Bergen	Newark	Monmouth	Newark (Trenton)
Burlington	Camden	Morris	Newark
Camden	Camden	Ocean	Trenton
Cape May	Camden	Passaic	Newark
Cumberland	Camden	Salem	Camden
Essex	Newark	Somerset	Trenton
Gloucester	Camden	Sussex	Newark
Hudson	Newark	Union	Newark
Hunterdon	Trenton	Warren	Trenton
Mercer	Trenton		

Standards for Federal Courts: The search fee is $20.00 per item (one party name or case number). Certification fee is $7.00 per document. Copy fee is $.50 per page. All fees standard unless noted in profile. Mail Search: always enclose a stamped self addressed envelope unless otherwise noted. Most courts accept fax requests or will suggest a copying/search vendor. Before releasing records, all courts require prepayment unless noted in profile.

Open records are located at the court unless otherwise noted. District courts index by defendant and plaintiff as well as by case number. Bankruptcy courts usually index by debtor and case number. While most courts now have their indexes on computer, many still maintain index card files as well.

The universal PACER sign-up number is 800-676-6856. Find PACER and the Party/Case Index on the Web at http://pacer.psc.uscourts.gov. PACER dial-up access is $.60 per minute. Also, courts offering internet access via RACER, PACER, Web-PACER or the new CM-ECF charge $.07 per page fee unless noted as free.

US District Court

District of New Jersey

Camden Division Clerk, PO Box 2797, Camden, NJ 08101 (courier: Room 1050, 4th & Cooper Sts, Camden, NJ 08101), 856-757-5021, Fax: 856-757-5370. http://pacer.njd.uscourts.gov

Counties: Atlantic, Burlington, Camden, Cape May, Cumberland, Gloucester, Salem.

Indexing & Storage: New cases available in the index 1-2 days after filing date. Records are also indexed on microfiche. District wide searches are available for all information from this court.

Fee & Payment: Payment may be made by money order, cashier check, personal check. Payee: Clerk, U.S. District Court.

Phone Search: Only docket information available by phone.

In Person Search: Fee charged if court conducts your in person search for you. Searchers can print dockets from the computer.

PACER: PACER is available online at http://pacer.njd.uscourts.gov. Case records go back to May 1991. Records never purged. New records are online after 1 day.

Electronic Filing: Electronic filing information online at https://ecf.njd.uscourts.gov

Opinions Online: Court opinions are online at http://lawlibrary.rutgers.edu/fed/search.html

Newark Division ML King, Jr Federal Bldg. & U.S. Courthouse, 50 Walnut St, Room 4015, Newark, NJ 07101 (courier address: Use mail address for courier delivery) 973-645-3730. http://pacer.njd.uscourts.gov

Counties: Bergen, Essex, Hudson, Middlesex, Monmouth, Morris, Passaic, Sussex, Union. Monmouth County was transferred from Trenton Division in late 1997; closed cases remain in Trenton.

Indexing & Storage: New cases available in the index 1-3 days after filing date.

Fee & Payment: Payment may be made by money order, cashier check, business check. Personal checks are not accepted. Payee: Clerk, U.S. District Court.

Phone Search: Only docket information available by telephone.

In Person Search: Fee charged if court conducts your in person search for you.

PACER: PACER is available online at http://pacer.njd.uscourts.gov. Case records go back to May 1991. Records never purged. New records are online after 1 day.

Electronic Filing: Electronic filing information online at https://ecf.njd.uscourts.gov

Opinions Online: Court opinions are online at http://lawlibrary.rutgers.edu/fed/search.html

Trenton Division Clerk, U.S. District Court, Room 2020, 402 E State St, Trenton, NJ 08608 (courier address: Use mail address for courier delivery) 609-989-2065. http://pacer.njd.uscourts.gov

Counties: Hunterdon, Mercer, Ocean, Somerset, Warren. Monmouth County was transferred to Newark and Camden Division in late 1997; closed Monmouth cases remain in Trenton.

Indexing & Storage: New cases available in the index several days after filing date. Records are also indexed on microfiche. District wide searches are available for information from 1920 from this district. This court also maintained closed files for the Newark division until 1997.

Fee & Payment: Payment may be made by money order, cashier check, personal check. Payee: Clerk, U.S. District Court.

Phone Search: Only docket information available by phone.

Mail Search: A SASE not required.

In Person Search: Fee charged if court conducts your in person search for you.

PACER: PACER is available online at http://pacer.njd.uscourts.gov. Case records go back to May 1991. Records never purged. New records are online after 1 day.

Electronic Filing: Electronic filing information online at https://ecf.njd.uscourts.gov

Opinions Online: Court opinions are online at http://lawlibrary.rutgers.edu/fed/search.html

U.S. Bankruptcy Court

District of New Jersey

Camden Division PO Box 2067, Camden, NJ 08101 (courier address: 401 Market St, 2nd Floor, Camden, NJ 08101), 856-757-5485. www.njb.uscourts.gov

Counties: Atlantic, Burlington (partial), Camden, Cape May, Cumberland, Gloucester, Salem.

Indexing & Storage: Cases indexed by debtor as well as by case number. New cases available in the index immediately after filing date.

Fee & Payment: Payment may be made by money order, cashier check, business check. Personal checks are not accepted. Payee: Clerk, U.S. Bankruptcy Court.

Phone Search: Only docket information available by phone. Automated voice case information service (VCIS) is available. Call VCIS at 877-239-2547 or 973-645-6044.

In Person Search: Fee charged if court conducts your in person search for you.

PACER: PACER is available online at http://pacer.njb.uscourts.gov. Document images available. Records purged every 6 months. New civil records are online after 1 day.

Electronic Filing: Electronic filing information online at https://ecf.njb.uscourts.gov

Newark Division PO Box 1352, Newark, NJ 07101-1352 (courier address: ML King Jr Federal Bldg, 50 Walnut St, 3rd Fl, Newark, NJ 07102), 973-645-4764. www.njb.uscourts.gov

Counties: Bergen, Essex, Hudson, Morris, Passaic, Sussex. Also Elizabeth, Springfield and Hillside townships in Union County.

Indexing & Storage: Cases indexed by debtor as well as by case number. New cases available in the index immediately after filing date.

Fee & Payment: Payment may be made by money order, cashier check, business check. Personal checks are not accepted. Payee: Clerk, U.S. Bankruptcy Court.

Phone Search: Automated voice case information service (VCIS) is available. Call VCIS at 877-239-2547 or 973-645-6044.

In Person Search: Fee charged if court conducts your in person search for you.

PACER: PACER is available online at http://pacer.njb.uscourts.gov. Document images available. Records purged every 6 months. New civil records are online after 1 day.

Electronic Filing: Electronic filing information online at https://ecf.njb.uscourts.gov

Trenton Division Clerk of Court, 402 E State St, 1st Fl, Trenton, NJ 08608 (courier address: Use mail address for courier delivery) 609-989-2129. www.njb.uscourts.gov

Counties: Burlington (partial), Hunterdon, Mercer, Middlesex, Monmouth, Ocean, Somerset, Warren, Union except the townships of Elizabeth, Hillside and Springfield.

Indexing & Storage: Cases indexed by debtor as well as by case number. New cases available in the index immediately after filing date.

Fee & Payment: Payment may be made by money order, cashier check, business check. Personal checks are not accepted. Payee: Clerk, U.S. Bankruptcy Court.

Phone Search: Automated voice case information service (VCIS) is available. Call VCIS at 877-239-2547 or 973-645-6044.

In Person Search: Fee charged if court conducts your in person search for you.

PACER: PACER is available online at http://pacer.njb.uscourts.gov. Document images available. Records purged every 6 months. New civil records are online after 1 day.

Electronic Filing: Electronic filing information online at https://ecf.njb.uscourts.gov

New Jersey County Courts

Court	Jurisdiction	No. of Courts	How Organized
Superior Courts*	General	21	21 Counties/15 Vicinages
Special Civil Part*	Limited	21	21 Counties
Municipal Courts	Municipal	535	
Tax Court	Special	1	

* Profiled in this Sourcebook.

Court	CIVIL								
	Tort	Contract	Real Estate	Min. Claim	Max. Claim	Small Claims	Estate	Eviction	Domestic Relations
Superior Courts*	X	X	X	$15,000	No Max		X		X
Special Civil Part*	X	X	X	$3000	$10,000	$3000		X	
Municipal Courts									
Tax Court									

Court	CRIMINAL				
	Felony	Misdemeanor	DWI/DUI	Preliminary Hearing	Juvenile
Superior Courts*	X				X
Special Civil Part*					
Municipal Courts		X	X		
Tax Court					

ADMINISTRATION   Administrative Office of the Courts, RJH Justice Complex, Courts Bldg 7th Fl, PO Box 037, Trenton, NJ, 08625; 609-984-0275, Fax: 609-984-6968. `www.judiciary.state.nj.us`

COURT STRUCTURE   Each Superior Court has 2 divisions; one for the Civil Division and another for the Criminal Division. Search requests should be addressed separately to each division.

The Civil cases in which the amounts in controversy exceeds $15,000 are heard in the Civil Division of Superior Court. Cases in which the amounts in controversy are between $3,000 and $15,000 are heard in the Special Civil Part of the Civil Division. Those in which the amounts in controversy are less than $3,000 also are heard in the Special Civil Part and are known as small claims cases. Probate is handled by Surrogates.

ONLINE ACCESS   The Judiciary's civil motion calendar is searchable at http://www.judiciary. state.nj.us/calendars.htm. The database includes all Superior Court Motion Calendars for the Civil Division (Law-Civil Part, Special CivilPart and Chancery-General Equity), and proceeding information for a six-week period (2 weeks prior to the current date and 4 weeks following the current date). Another useful site giving decisions is maintained by the Rutgers law School, go to http://lawlibrary.rutgers.edu/search.shtml.

Also, the state has three computerized case management systems - ACMS, AMIS, and FACTS - which are not open to the general public:

- ACMS (Automated Case Management System) contains data on all active civil cases statewide from the Law Division-Civil Part, Chancery Division-Equity Part, the Special Civil Part statewide, and the Appellate Division.

- AMIS (Archival Management Information System) contains closed civil case information. Records go back to the late 1980s.

- FACTS (Family Automated Case Tracking System) contains information on dissolutions from all counties.

The fee is $1.00 per minute of use, and a $500 collateral account is required. For info or a guidebook containing requirements and an enrollment form, write to: Superior Court Clerk's Office, Electronic Access Program, 25 Market St, CN971, Trenton NJ 08625, FAX 609-292-6564, or call 609-292-4987.

ADDITIONAL INFORMATION   Starting in 2004, Superior Courts have the option of directing civil case inquiries to the main NJ Superior Court, PO Box 971, Trenton, NJ 08625, Attn: Judgment Unit; telephone 609-

292-4804. The Judgment Unit will not accept fax requests, but will do a phone search; there is also a public access terminal for case lookups at their office at the Justice Complex, 25 Market St, Trenton.

Criminal searches may be done in person at the court on their public access terminal, but the Superior court now directs non-in person searches to the New Jersey State Police Records and ID Section at 609-882-2000, x2991 or x2918, which are fingerprint-based searches. For information on purchase of the statewide public access criminal records databases, call 609-292-4681.

Note that Cape May County offices are located in City of Cape May Court House, and not in City of Cape May.

Atlantic County

Superior Court - Criminal Division
Criminal Courthouse, 5909 Main St, Mays Landing, NJ 08330; 609-625-7000; Criminal phone: 609-909-8140; Fax: 609-645-5875. Hours: 8:30AM-4:30PM (EST). *Felony.*
www.judiciary.state.nj.us/atlantic/index.htm
Criminal Records: Access: In person only. Visitors must perform in person searches. No search fee. Required to search: name, years to search, DOB; also helpful: SSN. Criminal records on computer to 1985, prior on docket books and index cards back to 1940.
General Information: Public Access terminal is available. No sealed, expunged, judges notes, PSI's, or mental illness records released. Copy fee: $.75 per page. Certification fee: $5.00. Payee: Treasurer-State of New Jersey. No personal checks accepted. Prepayment required.

Superior Court - Civil Division
5905 Main St, Mays Landing, NJ 08330; 609-625-7000 X3370; Fax: 609-645-5875. Hours: 8:30AM-4:30PM (EST). *Civil Actions Over $15,000, Probate.*
www.judiciary.state.nj.us/atlantic/index.htm
Note: Records location is 1201 Bacharach Blvd. Mays Landing, N.J. 08330
Civil Records: Access: Mail, in person. No search fee. Required to search: name, years to search. Civil cases indexed by defendant, plaintiff. Civil records on computer from 9/84, on dockets from 1960, prior to 1960 archived. Prior to 1960 records are for public review only (in large books, difficult to find records). Participates in the court records statewide Electronic Access Program; for signup, information and booklet call 609-292-4987.
General Information: Public Access terminal is available. No sealed, expunged, judges notes, PSI's, or mental illness records released. Copy fee: $.75 per page 1st 1-10 pages; $.50 per page 11-20 pages; $.25 per page 20 plus pages. No certification fee. Payee: Treasurer-State of New Jersey. No personal checks accepted. Prepayment required. Mail requests: SASE required. Mail turnaround time 1 day.

Superior Court Special Civil Part
1201 Bacharach Blvd., Atlantic City, NJ 08401; 609-345-6700 X3347; Fax: 609-343-2326. Hours: 8:30AM-4:30PM (EST). *Civil Actions Under $15,000, Eviction, Small Claims.*
www.judiciary.state.nj.us/atlantic/index.htm
Civil Records: Access: Mail, online, in person fax. Both court and visitors may perform in person searches. No search fee. Required to search: name, years to search. Civil cases indexed by defendant, plaintiff. Civil records on computer from 1985 (some from 1987), prior on index books. In order to review index books, call in advance for an appointment. Participates in the court records statewide Electronic

Access Program; for signup, information and booklet call 609-292-4987.
General Information: Public Access terminal is available. No adoption, sealed, juvenile, expunged, dismissed, or mental health records released. Copy fee: $.75 per page. Certification fee: $5.00. Payee: Clerk, Special Civil Part. Personal checks accepted. Prepayment required. Mail requests: SASE required. Mail turnaround time 1 week.

Bergen County

Superior Court - Criminal Division
10 Main St, Rm 134, Justice Center, Hackensack, NJ 07601; 201-527-2445; Fax: 201-342-9083. Hours: 8:30AM-4:30PM (EST). *Felony.*
www.judiciary.state.nj.us/bergen/index.htm
Criminal Records: Access: In person only. Both court and visitors may perform in person searches. No search fee. Required to search: name, years to search, SSN, DOB, signed release; also helpful: address, DOB. Criminal records on computer from 1973.
General Information: No sealed, expunged, dismissed, judges notes, PSI's, or discovery packets records released. Copy fee: $.25. No charge for single copy of criminal record. Certification fee: $5.00. Payee: Bergen County Clerk. Personal checks accepted. Prepayment required.

Superior Court - Civil Division
10 Main St. Rm 119, Justice Center, Hackensack, NJ 07601; 201-527-2700 ext 2; Fax: 201-752-4031. Hours: 8:30AM-4:30PM (EST). *Civil Actions Over $15,000, Probate.*
www.judiciary.state.nj.us/bergen/index.htm
Civil Records: Access: Mail, online, in person. Only the court performs in person searches; visitors may not. No search fee. Required to search: name, years to search. Civil cases indexed by defendant, plaintiff. Civil records on computer for 2-5 years, on dockets from 1900s. Participates in the court records statewide Electronic Access Program; for signup, information and booklet call 609-292-4987.
General Information: No sealed, expunged, dismissed, judges notes, PSI's, or discovery packets records released. Copy fee: $.50 per page. Certification fee: $5.00. Payee: Bergen County Clerk. Personal checks accepted. Prepayment required. Mail requests: SASE required. Mail turnaround: 1 week.

Superior Court Special Civil Part
10 Main St. Rm 430, Justice Center, Hackensack, NJ 07601; 201-527-2700 ext 2. Hours: 8:30AM-4:30PM (EST). *Civil Actions Under $15,000, Eviction, Small Claims.*
www.judiciary.state.nj.us/bergen/index.htm
Civil Records: Access: Mail, online, in person, phone. Both court and visitors may perform in person searches. No search fee. Required to search: name, years to search. Civil cases indexed by defendant, plaintiff. Civil records on computer from 1990, prior on index cards. Participates in the court records

statewide Electronic Access Program; for signup, information and booklet call 609-292-4987.
General Information: Public Access terminal is available. (Terminal is located in the law library.) No adoption, sealed, juvenile, expunged, dismissed, or mental illness records released. Will not fax results. Copy fee: $.75 per page 1st 10 pgs; $.50 each add'l. Certification fee: $5.00. Payee: Bergen County Special Civil Part. Personal checks accepted. Prepayment required. Mail requests: SASE required. Mail turnaround time varies from 2 days to 3 weeks.

Burlington County

Superior Court - Criminal Division
49 Rancocas Rd, Mount Holly, NJ 08060; 609-518-2568. Hours: 8AM-5PM (EST). *Felony.*
www.judiciary.state.nj.us/burlington/index.htm
Criminal Records: Access: In person only. Visitors must perform in person searches for themselves. No search fee. Required to search: name, years to search; also helpful: DOB, SSN. Criminal records on computer from 11/93, on docket books from 1954, archived from early 1900s.
General Information: Public Access terminal is available. No sealed, expunged, judges notes, PSI's, or discovery packets released. Copy fee: $.75 per page for first ten pages; $.50 per page next ten; each add'l page $.25. Certification fee: $5.00. Payee: State of New Jersey. Personal checks accepted. Prepayment required.

Superior Court - Civil Division
49 Rancocas Rd, Mount Holly, NJ 08060; 609-518-2622; Criminal phone: 609-518-2566. Hours: 8AM-5PM (EST). *Civil Actions Over $15,000, Probate.*
www.judiciary.state.nj.us/burlington/index.htm
Civil Records: Access: Mail, online, in person. Both court and visitors may perform in person searches. No search fee. Required to search: name, years to search. Civil cases indexed by defendant, plaintiff. Local judgment records on computer since 1989, all others from 1954 to present. Participates in the court records statewide Electronic Access Program; for signup, information and booklet call 609-292-4987.
General Information: Public Access terminal is available. No sealed, expunged, judges notes, PSI's, or discovery packets released. Copy fee: $.75 per page for first ten, $.50 per page for next ten pages, and $.25 per page thereafter. Certification fee: $5.00. Payee: State of New Jersey. Personal checks accepted. Prepayment required. Mail requests: SASE required. Mail turnaround time 10 days.

Superior Court Special Civil Part
49 Rancocas Rd., Mount Holly, NJ 08060; 609-518-2865; Fax: 609-518-2872. Hours: 8AM-5PM (EST). *Civil Actions Under $15,000, Eviction, Small Claims.*
www.judiciary.state.nj.us/burlington/index.htm

Civil Records: Access: Phone, fax, mail, in person. Both court and visitors may perform in person searches. No search fee. Required to search: name, years to search. Civil cases indexed by defendant, plaintiff. Civil records on computer from 1995, microfilm from 1984, prior on index books by docket number. Participates in the court records statewide Electronic Access Program; for signup, information and booklet call 609-292-4987.

General Information: Public Access terminal is available. This court does not handle criminal matters in the Special Civil Part. No fee to fax results. Copy fee: $.75 per page. Fee is for first 10 pages; $.50 per page next 10; each add'l $.25. Certification fee: $10.00. Payee: State of New Jersey. Personal checks accepted. Prepayment required. Mail turnaround time 1-2 weeks.

Camden County

Superior Court - Criminal Division Hall of Justice, 101 S 5th St, Camden, NJ 08103; 856-379-2200; Criminal phone: x3343; Fax: 856-379-2255. Hours: 8AM-4PM (EST). *Felony.*
www.judiciary.state.nj.us/camden/index.htm
Criminal Records: Access: Mail, fax, in person. Both court and visitors may perform in person searches. Search fee: None, but a fee is to be implemented. Required to search: name, years to search, DOB, SSN. Criminal records on computer from 1986, on docket books from 1970.
General Information: Public Access terminal is available. No sealed, expunged, dismissed, judges notes, PSI's or discovery packets records released. No copy fee. No certification fee. Prepayment required. Mail requests: SASE required. Mail turnaround time 3 days.

Superior Court - Civil Division Hall of Justice, 101 S 5th St, Camden, NJ 08103; 856-379-2200; Criminal phone: x3343; Fax: 856-379-2255. Hours: 8:30AM-4;30PM (EST). *Civil Actions Over $15,000, Probate.*
www.judiciary.state.nj.us/camden/index.htm
Civil Records: Access: Mail, online, in person. Both court and visitors may perform in person searches. No search fee. Required to search: name, years to search. Civil cases indexed by defendant, plaintiff. Civil records on computer from 1987. Participates in the court records statewide Electronic Access Program; for signup, information or booklet call 609-292-4987. Also, mail or in person judgment searches are directed to Trenton.
General Information: Public Access terminal is available. No sealed, dismissed, judges notes, or discovery packets records released. No copy fee. Payee: Clerk of Superior Court. Personal checks accepted. Prepayment required. Mail requests: SASE required. Mail turnaround time 5 days.

Superior Court Special Civil Part Hall of Justice Complex, 101 S. 5th St., Camden, NJ 08103; 856-379-2202. Hours: 8:30AM-4:30PM (EST). *Civil Actions Under $15,000, Eviction, Small Claims.*
www.judiciary.state.nj.us/camden/index.htm
Civil Records: Access: Mail, online, in person. Both court and visitors may perform in person searches. No search fee. Required to search: name, years to search. Civil cases indexed by defendant, plaintiff. Civil records on computer from 1988. Prior records on docket books. Participates in the court records statewide Electronic Access Program; for signup, information and booklet call 609-292-4987, or contact Admin Office of Court, Hughes Justice Complex, PO Box 981, Trenton, NJ 08625. In person access is limited to one name.
General Information: Public Access terminal is available. No adoption, sealed, juvenile, expunged,

restricted, or mental health records released. Copy fee: $.75 per page for the first ten, $.50 per page for the next ten, and $.25 per page thereafter. Certification fee: $5.00. Payee: Clerk Special Civil Part. Personal checks accepted. Prepayment required. Mail turnaround time varies.

Cape May County

Superior Court - Criminal Division 9 N Main St, Superior Court, Cape May Court House, NJ 08210; 609-463-6550; Fax: 609-463-6458. Hours: 8:30AM-4:30PM (EST). *Felony.*
www.judiciary.state.nj.us/atlantic/index.htm
Criminal Records: Access: In person only. Visitors must perform in person searches for themselves. No search fee. Required to search: name, years to search, DOB; also helpful: SSN. Criminal records on computer from 1985; on index books back to 1950.
General Information: Public Access terminal is available. No sealed, expunged, dismissed, judges notes, PSI's, or discovery packets records released. Copy fee: $.75 per page. Certification fee: $5.00. Payee: State of New Jersey. Personal checks accepted. Prepayment required.

Superior Court - Civil Division Civil/Equity Division-Law, DN-203, 9 N Main St, Cape May Court House, NJ 08210; 609-463-6506; Fax: 609-463-6465. Hours: 8:30AM-4:30PM (EST). *Civil Actions Over $15,000, Probate.*
www.judiciary.state.nj.us/atlantic/index.htm
Civil Records: Access: Online, in person. Visitors must perform in person searches for themselves. Search fee: none. Required to search: name, years to search. Civil cases indexed by defendant, plaintiff. Civil records on computer from 04/91, on index books and archived from 1900s. Participates in the court records statewide Electronic Access Program; for signup, information and booklet call 609-292-4987. A fee is charged for online access.
General Information: Public Access terminal is available. No sealed records released. Copy fee: pages 1-10, $.75 per pg; pgs 11-20, $.50 per pg; over 20 pgs $.25 per pg. Certification fee: First copy free; $5.00 1st 5 pgs; $.75 per pg each add'l pg. $5.00 minimum charge. Payee: Clerk of Superior Court. Personal checks accepted. Prepayment required.

Superior Court Special Civil Part DN-203, 9 N. Main St, Cape May Court House, NJ 08210; 609-463-6502; Fax: 609-463-6465. Hours: 8:30AM-4:30PM (EST). *Civil Actions Under $15,000, Eviction, Small Claims.*
www.judiciary.state.nj.us/atlantic/index.htm
Civil Records: Access: Online, in person. Visitors must perform in person searches for themselves. No search fee. Required to search: name, years to search; also helpful: address. Civil cases indexed by defendant, plaintiff. Civil records on computer from 4/1991, on index from 1973. Participates in the court records statewide Electronic Access Program; for signup, information and booklet call 609-292-4987. A fee is charged for remote online access.
General Information: Public Access terminal is available. No sealed records released. Copy fee: $.75 per page for the first ten pages, $.50 per page for the next ten, and $.25 per page thereafter. Certification fee: None if a party to the action; $5.00 if not. Payee: Clerk of the Special Civil Part. Personal checks accepted. Prepayment required.

Cumberland County

Superior Court - Criminal Division PO Box 757, Courthouse, Broad/Fayette Streets, Bridgeton, NJ 08302; 856-453-4300; Fax: 856-451-7152. Hours: 8:30AM-4:30PM (EST). *Felony.*
www.judiciary.state.nj.us/gloucester/cum/index.htm
Criminal Records: Access: Mail, in person. Both the court and visitors may perform in person searches. Search fee: $4.00 per name. Required to search: name, years to search, DOB, SSN, signed release; also helpful: address. Criminal records on computer from 1986, on index from 1900.
General Information: Public Access terminal is available. (Terminal in Law Library.) No sealed, expunged, dismissed, judges notes, PSI's, or discovery packets records released. Copy fee: $.25 per page. Certification fee: $5.00. Payee: State of New Jersey, Misc Fund. Personal checks accepted. Prepayment required. Mail requests: SASE Required. Mail turnaround time 1 week.

Superior Court - Civil Division PO Box 757, Bridgeton, NJ 08302; 856-453-4330; Criminal phone: 856-453-4300; Fax: 856-451-7152. Hours: 8:30AM-4:30PM (EST). *Civil Actions Over $15,000, Probate.*
www.judiciary.state.nj.us/gloucester/cum/index.htm
Civil Records: Access: Mail, online, in person. Search fee: $4.00 per name. Required to search: name, years to search. Civil records on computer from 1986, on index from 1900. Participates in the court records statewide Electronic Access Program; for signup, information and booklet call 609-292-4987.
General Information: Public Access terminal is available. No sealed, expunged, dismissed, judges notes, PSI's, or discovery packets records released. Copy fee: $.25 per page. Certification fee: $5.00. Payee: State of New Jersey, Misc Fund. Personal checks accepted. Prepayment required. Mail requests: SASE required. Mail turnaround time 1 week.

Superior Court Special Civil Part PO Box 10, Bridgeton, NJ 08302; 856-453-4350; Criminal phone: 856-453-4300. Hours: 8:30AM-4:30PM (EST). *Civil Actions Under $15,000, Eviction, Small Claims.*
www.judiciary.state.nj.us/gloucester/cum/index.htm
Civil Records: Access: Phone, mail, online, in person. Only the court performs in person searches; visitors may not. No search fee. Required to search: name, years to search. Civil cases indexed by defendant, plaintiff. Civil records on computer from 12/89, on docket books from 1949 to 11/89. Participates in the court records statewide Electronic Access Program; for signup, information and booklet call 609-292-4987. Phone access is limited to 1 or 2 searches.
General Information: No adoption, sealed, juvenile, expunged, dismissed, or mental illness records released. Copy fee: $.75 per page for the first ten, $.50 per page for the next ten, and $.25 per page thereafter. Certification fee: $5.00. Payee: Clerk, Special Civil Part. Personal checks accepted. Prepayment required. Mail requests: SASE requested. Mail turnaround time 1 week.

Essex County

Superior Court - Criminal Division 50 W Market St, Rm 100s, Essex County Court Bldg, Newark, NJ 07102-1681; 973-693-5965, 973-693-5700 (switchboard). Hours: 8:30AM-4:30PM (EST). *Felony.*
www.judiciary.state.nj.us/essex/index.htm
Criminal Records: Access: Mail, in person. Mail, in person. Both court and visitors may perform in person searches. Search fee: $3.00 per name.

Required to search: name, years to search, DOB, SSN. Criminal records on computer from 1985.

General Information: Public Access terminal is available. No sealed, expunged, dismissed, judges notes, PSI's, or discovery packets records released. Will fax results to local or toll free line. Copy fee: $.75 per page. Certification fee: $5.00. Payee: State of New Jersey Judiciary. Only cashiers checks and money orders accepted. Prepayment required. Mail requests: SASE required. Mail turnaround time 1 week.

Superior Court - Civil Division 465 Dr. Martin Luther King Blvd, Newark, NJ 07102-1681; 973-693-6460. Hours: 8:30AM-4:30PM (EST). *Civil Actions Over $15,000, Probate.*

www.judiciary.state.nj.us/essex/index.htm

Civil Records: Access: Online, in person. Only the court performs in person searches; visitors may not. No search fee. Required to search: name, years to search. Civil cases indexed by defendant, plaintiff. Civil records on computer from 1984, on index from 1930. Participates in the court records statewide Electronic Access Program; for signup, information and booklet call 609-292-4987.

General Information: No sealed, expunged, dismissed, judges notes, PSI's, or discovery packets records released. Will fax results $3.00 per page. Copy fee: $.75 per page. Certification fee: $5.00. Payee: State of New Jersey Judiciary. Business checks accepted. Prepayment required. Mail requests: SASE required. Mail turnaround time 1 week.

Superior Court Special Civil Part 465 Martin Luther King Blvd, Newark, NJ 07102; 973-693-6494; 693-6460; Fax: 973-621-5914. Hours: 8:30AM-4:30PM (EST). *Civil Actions Under $15,000, Eviction, Small Claims.*

www.judiciary.state.nj.us/essex/index.htm

Civil Records: Access: Mail, online, in person. Both court and visitors may perform in person searches. No search fee. Required to search: name, years to search. Civil cases indexed by defendant, plaintiff. Civil records on computer from 1986 and archived back to 1982. Participates in the court records statewide Electronic Access Program; for signup, information and booklet call 609-292-4987.

General Information: No adoption, sealed, juvenile, expunged, dismissed, or mental illness records released. Fee to fax results is $.75 per page. No certification fee. Payee: Essex County Special Civil Part. Personal checks accepted. Prepayment required. Mail requests: SASE required. Mail turnaround time 7-10 days.

Gloucester County

Superior Court - Criminal Division PO Box 187 (1 N Broad St), Woodbury, NJ 08096; 856-853-3531. Hours: 8:30AM-4:30 PM (EST). *Felony.*

www.judiciary.state.nj.us/gloucester/glo/index.htm

Criminal Records: Access: Mail, in person. Visitors must perform in person searches for themselves. Search fee: $4.00 per name. Required to search: name, years to search, DOB, SSN, signed release. Criminal records on computer from 1982, on index from 1955.

General Information: No sealed, expunged, dismissed, judges notes, PSI's, or discovery packets records released. Copy fee: $1.00 per page. Certification fee: $1.50. Payee: State of New Jersey, Miscellaneous. Personal checks accepted. Prepayment required. Mail requests: SASE required. Mail turnaround time 1-3 days.

Superior Court - Civil Division 1 North Broad St, Woodbury, NJ 08096; 856-853-3250. Hours: 8:30AM-4:30 PM (EST). *Civil Actions Over $15,000, Probate.*

www.judiciary.state.nj.us/gloucester/glo/index.htm

Civil Records: Access: Mail, online, in person. Only the court performs in person searches; visitors may not. No search fee. Required to search: name, years to search. Civil cases indexed by defendant, plaintiff. Civil records on computer from 1988, prior records on county books. Participates in the court records statewide Electronic Access Program; for signup, information and booklet call 609-292-4987.

General Information: No sealed, expunged, dismissed, judges notes, PSI's, or discovery packets records released. Copy fee: $.75 first 10; $.50 next 10; $.25 each add'l page. Certification fee: $1.50. Payee: State of New Jersey. Personal checks accepted. Prepayment required. Mail requests: SASE required. Mail turnaround time ASAP.

Superior Court Special Civil Part Old Courthouse, 1 N Broad St., Woodbury, NJ 08096; 856-853-3392; Fax: 856-853-3416. Hours: 8:30AM-4:30PM (EST). *Civil Actions Under $15,000, Eviction, Small Claims.*

www.judiciary.state.nj.us/gloucester/glo/index.htm

Civil Records: Access: Mail, online, in person. No search fee. Required to search: name, years to search. Civil cases indexed by defendant, plaintiff. Civil records on computer from 08/89, on index books from 1900. Participates in the court records statewide Electronic Access Program; for signup, information and booklet call 609-292-4987.

General Information: Copy fee: $.75 per page. Fee is for less after 10 pages. No certification fee. Payee: Clerk, Superior Court of NJ. Personal checks accepted. Prepayment required. Mail requests: SASE required.

Hudson County

Superior Court - Criminal Division 595 Newark Ave, Jersey City, NJ 07306; 201-795-6704; Fax: 201-217-5210. Hours: 8:30AM-4:30PM (EST). *Felony.*

www.judiciary.state.nj.us/hudson/index.htm

Criminal Records: Access: Mail, in person. Both court and visitors may perform in person searches. No search fee. Required to search: name, years to search, DOB, SSN. Criminal records on computer from 1985, on index books from 1900.

General Information: Public Access terminal is available. No sealed, expunged, dismissed, judges notes, PSI's, or discovery packets records released. Copy fee: $.75 per page for the first ten pages, $.50 per page for the next ten pages, and $.25 per page thereafter. Certification fee: $5.00. An uncertified copy of a judgment of conviction is $1.50. Payee: Treasurer, State of New Jersey. Personal checks accepted. Prepayment required. Mail turnaround time 1 week.

Superior Court - Civil Division 583 Newark Ave, Jersey City, NJ 07306; 201-271-5162; 201-217-5163 (Records Rm). Hours: 8:30AM-4:30PM (EST). *Civil Actions Over $15,000, Probate.*

www.judiciary.state.nj.us/hudson/index.htm

Civil Records: Access: Mail, in person. Both court and visitors may perform in person searches. No search fee. Required to search: name, years to search. Civil cases indexed by defendant, plaintiff. Civil records on computer for 18 months after disposition. Mail access is limited to one name. Participates in the court records statewide Electronic Access Program; for signup, info and booklet call 609-292-4987.

General Information: Public Access terminal is available. No sealed, expunged, dismissed, judges

notes, PSI's, or discovery packets records released. Copy fee: $.75 for 1-10pages; $.50 pages 11-20; $2.5 per page over 20. Certification fee: $5.00. Payee: Clerk of Superior Court. Personal checks accepted. Prepayment required. Mail turnaround time 1 week.

Superior Court Special Civil Part 595 Newark Ave, Jersey City, NJ 07306; 201-795-6680. Hours: 8:30AM-4:30PM (EST). *Civil Actions Under $15,000, Eviction, Small Claims.*

www.judiciary.state.nj.us/hudson/index.htm

Civil Records: Access: Online, in person. Visitors must perform in person searches for themselves. No search fee. Required to search: name, years to search, address. Civil cases indexed by defendant, plaintiff. Civil records on index cards from 1993, prior on docket books. Participates in the court records statewide Electronic Access Program; for signup, information and booklet call 609-292-4987.

General Information: Public Access terminal is available. No adoptions, sealed, juvenile, expunged, dismissed, or mental illness released. Copy fee: $.75 1-10 pages, $.50 11-20 pages; $.25 20 plus pages. Certification fee: $5.00. Payee: Clerk, Special Civil Part. Personal checks accepted. Prepayment required.

Hunterdon County

Superior Court - Criminal Division 65 Park Ave, Flemington, NJ 08822; 908-237-5840; Fax: 908-237-5841. Hours: 8:30AM-4:30PM (EST). *Felony.*

www.judiciary.state.nj.us/somerset/index.htm

Criminal Records: Access: Fax, mail, in person. Visitors must perform in person searches for themselves. Search fee: $6.00 per name. Required to search: name, years to search, DOB; also helpful: SSN. Criminal records on computer from 1987, prior on index books.

General Information: Public Access terminal is available. No sealed, expunged, dismissed, judges notes, PSI's, or discovery packets records released. Will fax results, no charge. Copy fee: $1.50 per page. Certification fee: $3.00. Payee: State of New Jersey. Personal checks accepted. Prepayment required. Mail requests: SASE required. Mail turnaround time 1-3 weeks.

Superior Court - Civil Division Hunterdon County Justice Center, 65 Park Ave, Flemington, NJ 08822; 908-237-5820; Probate phone: 908-788-1156. Hours: 8:30AM-4:30PM (EST). *Civil Actions Over $15,000, Probate.*

www.judiciary.state.nj.us/somerset/index.htm

Note: Probate records are indexed separately and are located on the 2nd Fl Surrogate/Probate office.

Civil Records: Access: Mail, online, in person, phone. Both court and visitors may perform in person searches. No search fee. Required to search: name, years to search. Civil cases indexed by defendant, plaintiff. Civil records on computer since 1990, on index from 1950. Participates in the court records statewide Electronic Access Program; for signup, information and booklet call 609-292-4987.

General Information: Public Access terminal is available. (Public terminal for civil only.) No sealed, expunged, dismissed, judges notes, PSI's, or discovery packets records released. Copy fee: $.75 per page 1st 10; $.50 for 2nd 10; $.25 each add'l. Certification fee: $5.00. Payee: State of New Jersey Judiciary. Personal checks accepted. Prepayment required. Mail requests: SASE required. Mail turnaround time 1-2 weeks.

Superior Court Special Civil Part Hunterdon County Justice Center, 65 Park Ave, 2nd Floor, Flemington, NJ 08822; 908-237-5820. Hours: 8:30AM-4:30PM (EST). *Civil Actions Under $15,000, Eviction, Small Claims.*

www.judiciary.state.nj.us/somerset/index.htm
Civil Records: Access: Phone, mail, online, in person. Both the court and visitors may perform in person searches. No search fee. Court will do one free search. Required to search: name, years to search. Civil cases indexed by defendant, plaintiff. Civil records on computer from 1991, on index books from 1900. Participates in the court records statewide Electronic Access Program; for signup, information and booklet call 609-292-4987.
General Information: Public Access terminal is available. (Public terminal for civil only.) No protective order files records released. Copy fee: $.75 per page for the first ten, $.50 per page for the next ten, and $.25 per page thereafter. Certification fee: $5.00. Payee: Superior Court of New Jersey. Personal checks accepted. Prepayment required. Mail requests: SASE required. Mail turnaround time 1-2 weeks.

Mercer County

Superior Court - Criminal Division 209 S. Broad, PO Box 8068, Trenton, NJ 08650-0068; 609-571-4000 ext 4. Hours: 8:30AM-4:30PM; Search Hours: 9AM-3:30PM (EST). *Felony.*
www.judiciary.state.nj.us/mercer/index.htm
Criminal Records: Access: In person only. Visitors must perform in person searches for themselves. No search fee. Required to search: name, years to search, DOB, SSN. Criminal records on computer from 1985, on docket books from 1900s.
General Information: No sealed, expunged, judges notes, PSI's, or discovery packets records released. Copy fee: $.75 per page. $5.00 minimum. Fee less after 10 pages. Certification fee: $5.00. Payee: Clerk of Superior Court. Personal checks accepted. Prepayment required. Mail requests: SASE required for Civil.

Superior Court - Civil Division 175 S Broad, PO Box 8068, Trenton, NJ 08650-0068; 609-571-4490; Fax: 609-571-4473. Hours: 8:30AM-4:30PM (EST). *Civil Actions Over $15,000, Probate.*
www.judiciary.state.nj.us/mercer/index.htm
Civil Records: Access: Fax, mail, online, in person. Only the court performs in person searches; visitors may not. No search fee. Required to search: name, years to search. Civil cases indexed by defendant, plaintiff. Civil records on computer since 1995, archived from 1972, on microfiche from 1965, prior indexed from 1894. Participates in the court records statewide Electronic Access Program; for signup, information and booklet call 609-292-4987.
General Information: No sealed, expunged, dismissed, judges notes, PSI's, or discovery packets records released. Copy fee: $.75 1-10 pages; $.50 11-20 pages; $.25 20 plus pages. Certification fee: $5.00. Payee: Clerk of Superior Court. Personal checks accepted. Prepayment required. Mail requests: SASE required for Civil. Turnaround time up to 2 weeks.

Superior Court Special Civil Part Box 8068, Trenton, NJ 08650; 609-571-4490 ext 1; Fax: 609-571-4489. Hours: 8:30AM-4:30PM (EST). *Civil Actions Under $15,000, Eviction, Small Claims.*
www.judiciary.state.nj.us/mercer/index.htm
Civil Records: Access: Mail, online, in person. Visitors must perform in person searches for themselves. No search fee. Required to search: name, years to search. Civil cases indexed by defendant, plaintiff. Civil records on computer from 1989, on index from 1984. Participates in the court records statewide Electronic Access Program; for signup, information and booklet call 609-292-4987.
General Information: Public Access terminal is available. No adoptions, sealed, juvenile, expunged, dismissed, or mental illness records released. Copy fee: $.75 per page for the first ten pages, $.50 per page

for the next ten, and $.25 per page thereafter. No certification fee. Payee: State of New Jersey. Only cashiers checks and money orders accepted. Prepayment required. Mail turnaround time 1 week.

Middlesex County

Superior Court - Criminal Division PO Box 964 (1 JFK Sq), New Brunswick, NJ 08903; 732-981-3128. 8:30AM-4:30PM (EST). *Felony.*
www.judiciary.state.nj.us/middlesex/index.htm
Criminal Records: Access: Mail, in person. Both court and visitors may perform in person searches; however, court will only search if provided with arrest date, summons, complaint or indictment number. No search fee. Required to search: name, years to search, DOB; also helpful: SSN, singed release. Criminal records on computer from 1981, prior on index books back to 1956.
General Information: Public Access terminal is available. No sealed, expunged, dismissed, judges notes, PSI's, on discovery packets records released. Copy fee: $.75 per page first 10, $.50 each next 10, then $.25 per page ofor all pages over 20. Certification fee: $5.00 per page of any document. Payee: State of New Jersey Judiciary. Cash, personal checks, or money orders accepted. Prepayment required. Mail requests: SASE required. Mail turnaround time up to 2 weeks.

Superior Court - Civil Division PO Box 2633 (1 JFK Sq, 2nd Floor Tower), New Brunswick, NJ 08903; 732-981-2464; Probate phone: 732-745-3055. Hours: 8:30AM-4:30PM (EST). *Civil Actions Over $15,000, Probate.*
www.judiciary.state.nj.us/middlesex/index.htm
Civil Records: Access: Mail, online, in person. Search fee: none. Required to search: name, years to search, if copies needed place request in writing. Civil cases indexed by defendant, plaintiff. Civil records on computer from 1992, on docket books from 1940. Participates in the court records statewide Electronic Access Program; for signup, information and booklet call 609-292-4987.
General Information: Public Access terminal is available. No sealed, expunged, dismissed, judges notes, PSI's, on discovery packets records released. Certification fee: $5.00. Payee: State of New Jersey, Clerk of Superior Court. Personal checks accepted. Prepayment required. Mail requests: SASE required. Mail turnaround time up to 3 weeks.

Superior Court Special Civil Part PO Box 1146 (1 JKF Sq, 3rd Fl Tower), New Brunswick, NJ 08903; 732-981-2044. 8:30AM-4:30PM (EST). *Civil Actions Under $15,000, Eviction, Small Claims.*
www.judiciary.state.nj.us/middlesex/index.htm
Civil Records: Access: Mail, online, in person. Both court and visitors may perform in person searches. No search fee. Required to search: name, years to search. Civil cases indexed by defendant, plaintiff. Civil records on computer from 1985, on docket books from 1960. Participates in the court records statewide Electronic Access Program; for signup, information and booklet call 609-292-4987.
General Information: Public Access terminal is available. No adoption, sealed, juvenile, expunged, dismissed, or mental health records released. Will not fax results. Copy fee: 1st page $1.00; 2-10 pages $.75; 11-20 pages $.50; 20 plus $.25. Certification fee: $5.00. Payee: Middlesex Special Civil Part. Personal checks accepted. Prepayment required. Mail turnaround time 30 days.

Monmouth County

Superior Court - Criminal Division 71 Monument Park, Rm 149, 1st Flr, E Wing, PO Box 1271, Freehold, NJ 07728-1271; 732-677-4300. Hours: 8:30AM-4:30PM (EST). *Felony.*
www.judiciary.state.nj.us/monmouth/index.htm
Criminal Records: Access: In person only. Visitors must perform in person searches for themselves. No search fee. Required to search: name, years to search. Criminal records on computer back to 1990, on index books from 1956.
General Information: Public Access terminal is available. (Criminal cases only.) No sealed, expunged, dismissed, judges notes, PSI's, or discovery packets records released. Copy fee: $.75 per page. Fee is for first 10 pages; $.50 per page next 10; each add'l $.25. Certification fee: $5.00. Payee: State of New Jersey. Personal checks accepted; ID required. Prepayment required.

Superior Court - Civil Division PO Box 1255, 71 Monument Pk, Freehold, NJ 07728-1255; 732-677-4268. Hours: 8:30AM-4:30PM (EST). *Civil Actions Over $15,000.*
www.judiciary.state.nj.us/monmouth/index.htm
Civil Records: Access: Mail, online, in person. Visitors must perform in person searches for themselves. No search fee. Required to search: name, years to search. Civil cases indexed by defendant, plaintiff. Civil records on computer from 1990, on index books from 1956. Participates in the court records statewide Electronic Access Program; for signup, information and booklet call 609-292-4987.
General Information: Public Access terminal is available. (Civil cases only.) No sealed, expunged, dismissed, judges notes, PSI's, or discovery packets records released. Copy fee: $.25. Certification fee: $5.00. Payee: Clerk of Superior Court. Personal checks accepted. Prepayment required.

Superior Court Special Civil Part Courthouse, 71 Monument Pk., PO Box 1270, Freehold, NJ 07728; 732-677-4223. Hours: 8:30AM-4:30PM (EST). *Civil Actions Under $15,000, Eviction, Small Claims.*
www.judiciary.state.nj.us/monmouth/index.htm
Civil Records: Access: Mail, online, in person. Both court and visitors may perform in person searches. No search fee. Required to search: name, years to search. Civil cases indexed by defendant, plaintiff. Civil records on computer from 1996, on index books from 1985, prior in archives. Participates in the court records statewide Electronic Access Program; for signup, information and booklet call 609-292-4987.
General Information: Public Access terminal is available. Copy fee: $.75 per page. Fee is for first 10 pages; $.50 per page next 10; each add'l $.25. Certification fee: $5.00. Payee: Monmouth Special Civil Part. Personal checks accepted. Prepayment required. Mail requests: SASE required. Mail turnaround time 1 day to weeks; longer if archived.

Morris County

Superior Court - Criminal Division PO Box 910 (Washington St), Morristown, NJ 07960-0910; 973-656-4115; Criminal phone: 973-656-4169; Fax: 973-656-4123. Hours: 8:30AM-4:30PM (EST). *Felony.*
www.judiciary.state.nj.us/morris/index.htm
Criminal Records: Access: Fax, mail, in person. Both court and visitors may perform in person searches. No search fee. Required to search: name, years to search, DOB, SSN, signed release. Criminal records on computer from 1984, on index books from 1966.

General Information: No sealed, expunged, dismissed, judges notes, PSI's, or discovery packets records released. Copy fee: $.75 per page. Fee is for first 10 pages; $.50 per page next 10; each add'l $.25. Certification fee: $5.00. Payee: State of New Jersey. Personal checks accepted. Prepayment required. Mail requests: SASE required. Mail turnaround: 1 week.

Superior Court - Civil Division PO Box 910 (Washington St), Morristown, NJ 07963-0910; 973-656-4115; Fax: 973-656-4123. Hours: 8:30AM-4:30PM (EST). *Civil Actions Over $15,000, Probate.* www.judiciary.state.nj.us/morris/index.htm

Civil Records: Access: Online, in person. Visitors must perform in person searches for themselves. No search fee. Required to search: name, years to search; also helpful: address. Civil cases indexed by defendant, plaintiff. Civil records on computer from 1984, on index books from 1966. Participates in the court records statewide Electronic Access Program; for signup, info and booklet call 609-292-4987.

General Information: Public Access terminal is available. No sealed, expunged, dismissed, judges notes, PSI's, or discovery packets records released. Copy fee: $.25 per page. Certification fee: $5.00. Payee: State of New Jersey. Personal checks accepted. Prepayment required.

Superior Court Special Civil Part PO Box 910 (Court St), Morristown, NJ 07963-0910; 973-656-4125. Hours: 8:30AM-4:30PM (EST). *Civil Actions Under $15,000, Eviction, Small Claims.* www.judiciary.state.nj.us/morris/index.htm

Civil Records: Access: Mail, online, in person. Visitors must perform in person searches for themselves. No search fee. Required to search: name, years to search. Civil cases indexed by defendant, plaintiff. Civil records on computer from 8/1988, on index books from 1979. Participates in the court records statewide Electronic Access Program; for signup, information and booklet call 609-292-4987.

General Information: Public Access terminal is available. No adoptions, sealed, juvenile, expunged, dismissed, or mental illness records released. Copy fee: $.75 per page for first 10, $.50 per page for next 10, and $.25 per page thereafter. Public copier is $.25 per copy. Certification fee: $5.00. Payee: State of New Jersey. Personal checks accepted. Prepayment required. Mail turnaround time 1 week.

Ocean County

Superior Court - Criminal Division PO Box 2191 (120 Hooper Ave), Justice Complex, Rm 220, Toms River, NJ 08754-2191; 732-929-2009. Hours: 8:30AM-4:30PM (EST). *Felony.* www.judiciary.state.nj.us/ocean/index.htm

Criminal Records: Access: Mail, in person. Both court and visitors may perform in person searches. Search fee: $3.00 per name if court performs search. Required to search: name, years to search; also helpful: address, DOB, SSN. Criminal records on computer from 1990, on index books from 1920.

General Information: Public Access terminal is available. (Terminal allows you to search statewide.) No sealed, expunged, judges notes, PSI's, or discovery packets records released. Will not fax results. Copy fee: $.75 per page, 11-20 pages $.50 per page, over 20 pages $.25 per page. Certification fee: $5.00. Payee: NJ State Treasurer. Personal checks accepted. Prepayment required. Mail turnaround time 1 week.

Superior Court - Civil Division 118 Washington #121, Toms River, NJ 08754; 732-929-2035. Hours: 8:30AM-4:30PM (EST). *Civil Actions Over $15,000, Probate.* www.judiciary.state.nj.us/ocean/index.htm

Civil Records: Access: Online, in person. Visitors must perform in person searches for themselves. No search fee. Required to search: name, years to search. Civil cases indexed by defendant, plaintiff. Civil records on computer from 1989, on index books from 1920. Participates in the court records statewide Electronic Access Program; for signup, information and booklet call 609-292-4987.

General Information: Public Access terminal is available. (Public terminal is located at 201 Courthouse Lane.) Copy fee: $.25. No certification fee. Payee: Superior Court Clerk. Personal checks accepted. Prepayment required. Mail turnaround time 1 week.

Superior Court Special Civil Part 118 Washington St, Toms River, NJ 08754; 732-929-2016; Fax: 732-506-5398. Hours: 8:30AM-4:30PM (EST). *Civil Actions Under $15,000, Eviction, Small Claims.* www.judiciary.state.nj.us/ocean/index.htm

Civil Records: Access: Online, in person. Both court and visitors may perform in person searches. No search fee. Required to search: name, years to search. Civil cases indexed by defendant, plaintiff. Civil records on computer from 1985, on index books from 1972, on microfilm prior. Participates in the court records statewide Electronic Access Program; for signup, information and booklet call 609-292-4987.

General Information: Public access terminal is located at 201 Courthouse Ln. No adoptions, sealed, juvenile, expunged, dismissed, or mental illness records released. Copy fee: $.25. Certification fee: $5.00. Payee: Ocean County Special Civil Part. Personal checks accepted. Prepayment required. Mail turnaround time 1-2 days.

Passaic County

Superior Court - Criminal Division 77 Hamilton St. 2nd Fl, Paterson, NJ 07505-2108; 973-247-8403; Fax: 973-247-8401. Hours: 8:30AM-4:30PM (EST). *Felony.* www.judiciary.state.nj.us/passaic/index.htm

Criminal Records: Access: Mail, in person. Both court and visitors may perform in person searches. Search fee: $5.00 per name. Required to search: name, years to search, DOB, SSN; also helpful: address. Criminal records on computer from 1986, on microfiche prior.

General Information: Public Access terminal is available. No sealed, expunged, dismissed, judges notes, PSI's, or discovery packets records released. Will fax results. Copy fee: $.75 per page for the first 10 pages, $.50 per page for the second set of 10 pages, and $.25 per page thereafter. Certification fee: $5.00. Payee: Superior Court of New Jersey. Personal checks accepted. Prepayment required. Mail turnaround time 3-4 days.

Superior Court - Civil Division 77 Hamilton St, Ist Fl, Paterson, NJ 07505-2108; 973-247-8215; Probate phone: 973-881-4760. Hours: 8:30AM-4:30PM (EST). *Civil Actions Over $15,000, Probate.* www.judiciary.state.nj.us/passaic/index.htm

Note: Probate is located on the 2nd Fl with the General Equity Division.

Civil Records: Access: Phone, mail, online, in person. Both court and visitors may perform in person searches. No search fee. Required to search: name, years to search. Civil cases indexed by defendant, plaintiff. Civil records on computer from 1986, on index books from 1979. Participates in the court records statewide Electronic Access Program; for signup, information and booklet call 609-292-4987. Phone access limited to short searches.

General Information: No sealed, expunged, dismissed, judges notes, PSI's, or discovery packets records released. Copy fee: $.25 per page. Certification fee: $5.00. Payee: State of New Jersey or Clerk of Superior Court. Personal checks accepted. Prepayment required. Mail turnaround time up to 1 week.

Superior Court Special Civil Part 71 Hamilton St., Old Courthouse, 2nd Fl, Paterson, NJ 07505; 973-247-8238. Hours: 8:30AM-4:30PM (EST). *Civil Actions Under $15,000, Eviction, Small Claims.* www.judiciary.state.nj.us/passaic/index.htm

Civil Records: Access: Mail, online, in person. Both court and visitors may perform in person searches. No search fee. Required to search: name, years to search. Civil cases indexed by defendant, plaintiff. Civil records on computer from 1993, on index from 1980, prior archived. Participates in the court records statewide Electronic Access Program; for signup, information and booklet call 609-292-4987. Include your phone number with written requests. It may take up to 2 days for court to retrieve case files.

General Information: Public Access terminal is available. No adoptions, sealed, juvenile, expunged, dismissed, or mental illness records released. Copy fee: $.75 per page. Fee is for first 10 pages; $.50 per page next 10; each add'l $.25. Certification fee: $5.00. Payee: Passaic County Special Civil Part. Personal checks accepted. Prepayment required. Mail turnaround time 2-3 days.

Salem County

Superior Court - Criminal Division PO Box 78 (92 Market St), Salem, NJ 08079-1913; 856-935-7510. Hours: 8:30AM-4:30PM (EST). *Felony.* www.judiciary.state.nj.us/gloucester/sal/index.htm

Criminal Records: Access: in person only. Visitors must perform in person criminal searches for themselves. No search fee. Required to search: name, years to search, DOB, SSN; also helpful-indictment number. Criminal records on computer back to 1989; indexed from 1957.

General Information: Public Access terminal is available. No sealed, expunged, dismissed, judges notes, PSI's, or discovery packets records released. Will not fax results. Copy fee: $.25 per page. Certification fee: $5.00. Payee: State of New Jersey. Personal checks accepted. Prepayment required. Mail requests: SASE required. Mail turnaround time 3-4 days.

Superior Court - Civil Division PO Box 29 (92 Market St), Salem, NJ 08079-1913; 856-935-7510 X8214; Probate phone: 856-935-7510 X8322; Fax: 856-935-6551. Hours: 8:30AM-4:30PM (EST). *Civil Actions Over $15,000, Probate.* www.judiciary.state.nj.us/gloucester/sal/index.htm

Note: Probate located at the County Surrogate's office at this 92 Market St. address in Salem.

Civil Records: Access: In person, online. Both the court and visitors perform in person searches. No search fee. Required to search: name, years to search. Civil cases indexed by defendant, plaintiff. Civil records on computer from 1987, indexed from 1953. Participates in the court records statewide Electronic Access Program; for signup, information and booklet call 609-292-4987. Searches for judgments are directed to the statewide system in Trenton.

General Information: Public Access terminal is available. No sealed, expunged, dismissed, judges notes, PSI's, or discovery packets records released. Copy fee: $.25 per page. Certification fee: $5.00. Payee: Superior Court of NJ. Personal checks accepted. Prepayment required.

Superior Court Special Civil Part PO Box 29 (92 Market St), Salem, NJ 08079; 856-935-7510 x8214; Fax: 856-935-6551. Hours: 8:30AM-4:30PM (EST). *Civil Actions Under $15,000, Eviction, Small Claims.*

www.judiciary.state.nj.us/gloucester/sal/index.htm

Civil Records: Access: Phone, fax, mail, online, in person. Both the court and visitors perform in person searches. No search fee. Required to search: name, years to search. Civil cases indexed by defendant, plaintiff. Civil records on computer from 1990, on index from 1953. Participates in the court records statewide Electronic Access Program; for signup, information and booklet call 609-292-4987.

General Information: Public Access terminal is available. No adoptions, sealed, juvenile, expunged, dismissed, or mental illness records released. Copy fee: $25 per page. Certification fee: $5.00. Payee: Special Civil Part. Personal checks accepted. Prepayment required. Mail turnaround time 1-2 days.

Somerset County

Superior Court - Criminal Division PO Box 3000 (20 N Bridge St, 2nd Fl), Somerville, NJ 08876-1262; 908-231-7600. Hours: 8:30AM-4:30PM (EST). *Felony.*

www.judiciary.state.nj.us/somerset/index.htm

Criminal Records: Access: Phone, fax, mail, in person. Both court and visitors may perform in person searches. Search fee: $6.00 per name. Required to search: name, years to search, DOB; also helpful: SSN. Criminal records on computer back to 1981, prior on index books. Public access terminal does not include criminal records.

General Information: Public Access terminal is available. (Only criminal available.) No sealed, expunged, judges notes, PSI's, or discovery packets records released. Copy fee: $.75 per page 1st 10 pages; $.50 pgs 11-20; $.25 per pg over 20. Certification fee: $3.00 plus $1.50 per page. Payee: State of New Jersey. Personal checks accepted. Prepayment required. Mail requests: SASE required. Mail turnaround time 2-3 days.

Superior Court - Civil Division Somerset Cty Courthouse, Civil Division, PO Box 3000 (Bridge & Main St), Somerville, NJ 08876-1262; 908-231-7054. Hours: 8:30AM-4:30PM (EST). *Civil Actions, Probate.*

www.judiciary.state.nj.us/somerset/index.htm

Civil Records: Access: Phone, mail, online, in person. Both court and visitors may perform in person searches. No search fee. Required to search: name; also helpful: years to search. Civil cases indexed by defendant, plaintiff. Civil records on computer from 1990. Participates in the court records statewide Electronic Access Program; for signup, information and booklet call 609-292-4987. Civil cases are archived 18 months after their last activity.

General Information: Public Access terminal is available. No sealed, expunged, dismissed, judges notes, PSI's, or discovery packets records released. Copy fee: $.75 per page. Fee after 1st 10 pages $.50 per pg up to 20 pgs, then $.25 per pg. Certification fee: $5.00 per page. Payee: Superior Court of NJ. Personal checks accepted. Prepayment required. Mail requests: SASE required. Mail turnaround time 1-2 days.

Superior Court Special Civil Part Somerset County Courthouse, Bridge and Main St, PO Box 3000, Somerville, NJ 08876-1262; 908-231-7014/7015. Hours: 8:30AM-4:30PM (EST). *Civil Actions Under $15,000, Eviction, Small Claims.*

www.judiciary.state.nj.us/somerset/index.htm

Civil Records: Access: Mail, online, in person. Visitors must perform in person searches for

themselves. No search fee. Required to search: name, years to search. Civil cases indexed by defendant, plaintiff. Civil records on computer from 1990, prior on index books. In person access requires an appointment. Participates in the court records statewide Electronic Access Program; for signup, information and booklet call 609-292-4987.

General Information: Public Access terminal is available. (Terminal at counter provides visitor with book lookup help only.) No adoptions, sealed, juvenile, expunged, dismissed, or mental illness records released. Will not fax results. Copy fee: $.75 per page for the first ten, $.50 per page for the next ten, and $.25 per page thereafter. No certification fee. Payee: Superior Court of New Jersey. Personal checks accepted. Prepayment required. Mail requests: SASE required. Mail turnaround time varies; may be lengthy.

Sussex County

Superior Court - Criminal Division 43-47 High St, Sussex Judicial Center, Newton, NJ 07860; 973-579-0696. 8:30AM-4:30PM (EST). *Felony.*

www.judiciary.state.nj.us/morris/index.htm

Criminal Records: Access: In person only. Visitors must perform in person searches for themselves. No search fee. Required to search: name, years to search, DOB, signed release; also helpful: SSN. Criminal records on computer from 1986, on docket books to 1950s.

General Information: Public Access terminal is available. No sealed, expunged, dismissed, judges notes, PSI's, or discovery packets records released. Copy fee: $.75 per page. Fee is for first 10 pages; $.50 per page next 10; each add'l $.25. Certification fee: $5.00. Payee: State of New Jersey Judiciary. Only cashiers checks and money orders accepted. Prepayment required. Mail turnaround time up to 1 week.

Superior Court - Civil Division 43-47 High St, Sussex Judicial Center, Newton, NJ 07860; 973-579-0914/0915. Hours: 8:30AM-4:30PM (EST). *Civil Actions Over $15,000, Probate.*

www.judiciary.state.nj.us/morris/index.htm

Civil Records: Access: Phone, mail, online, in person. Only the court performs in person searches; visitors may not. No search fee. Required to search: name, years to search. Civil cases indexed by defendant, plaintiff. Civil records on computer from 1989, on microfiche by plaintiff prior to 1989, closed cases archived yearly and sent to Trenton. Participates in the court records statewide Electronic Access Program; for signup, information and booklet call 609-292-4987.

General Information: No sealed, expunged, dismissed, judges notes, PSI's, or discovery packets records released. Will not fax results unless prepaid. Copy fee: $.75 per page for the first ten pages, $.50 per page for the next ten, and $.25 per page thereafter. Certification fee: $5.00. Payee: Clerk of Superior Court. Personal checks accepted. Prepayment required. Mail turnaround time up to 1 week.

Superior Court Special Civil Part 43-47 High St., Newton, NJ 07860; 973-579-0918; Fax: 973-579-0736. Hours: 8:30AM-4:30PM (EST). *Civil Actions Under $15,000, Eviction, Small Claims.*

www.judiciary.state.nj.us/morris/index.htm

Civil Records: Access: Phone, fax, mail, online, in person. Both court and visitors may perform in person searches. No search fee. Required to search: name, years to search. Civil cases indexed by defendant, plaintiff. Civil records on computer from mid 1989, on index books from 1940. Participates in the court records statewide Electronic Access Program; for signup, information and booklet call 609-292-4987.

Court will accept name phone and fax search requests for up to 3 names.

General Information: No adoptions, sealed, juvenile, expunged, dismissed, or mental illness records released. Copy fee: $.75 per page for first 10 pages; $.50 per page next 10; each add'l $.25. Certification fee: $5.00. Payee: State of New Jersey Judiciary. Personal checks accepted. Prepayment required. Mail turnaround time up to 2 weeks.

Union County

Superior Court - Criminal Division County Courthouse - Tower Building 5th Fl, Elizabeth, NJ 07207; Civil phone: 908-659-3844; Criminal phone: 908-659-3376; Probate phone: 908-527-4280; Fax: 908-659-3391 Crim. Hours: 8:30AM-4:30PM (EST). *Felony.*

www.judiciary.state.nj.us/union/index.htm

Criminal Records: Access: In person only. Visitors must perform in person searches for themselves. No search fee. Required to search: name, years to search; also helpful: DOB, SSN. Criminal records on computer from 1985 updated monthly, prior on index books from 1960. In person access 9AM-3:30PM. For requests regarding records prior to 1985, they recommend you contact the NJ State Police for a criminal history sheet, and from the IND/ACC# this court can quickly find the reference in their records.

General Information: Public Access terminal is available. No sealed, expunged, dismissed, judges notes, PSI's, or discovery packets records released. Will fax results for you. Copy fee: $.75 per page. Fee is for first 10 pages; $.50 per page next 10; each add'l $.25. Certification fee: $5.00. Payee: State of New Jersey Judiciary. Business checks and moaney orders accepted. Prepayment required. Mail turnaround time is a minimum of 5 business days.

Superior Court - Civil Division 2 Broad St, Elizabeth, NJ 07207; 908-659-4176; Fax: 908-659-4185. Hours: 8:30AM-4:30PM (EST). *Civil Actions Over $15,000.*

www.judiciary.state.nj.us/union/index.htm

Civil Records: Access: Phone, mail, online, in person. Visitors must perform in person searches for themselves. No search fee. Required to search: name, years to search. Civil cases indexed by defendant, plaintiff. Civil records on computer from 1988, prior records archived in Trenton NJ. Participates in the court records statewide Electronic Access Program; for signup, info and booklet call 609-292-4987.

General Information: Public Access terminal is available. No sealed, expunged, dismissed, judges notes, PSI's, or discovery packets records released. Copy fee: $.75 per page for the first ten pages, $.50 per page for the next ten, and $.25 per page thereafter. Certification fee: $5.00. Payee: Clerk of Superior Court. Personal checks accepted. Prepayment required. Mail turnaround time varies.

Superior Court Special Civil Part 2 Broad St, Elizabeth, NJ 07207; 908-659-3637/8. Hours: 8:30AM-4:30PM (EST). *Civil Actions Under $15,000, Eviction, Small Claims.*

www.judiciary.state.nj.us/union/index.htm

Civil Records: Access: Phone, mail, online, in person. Both court and visitors may perform in person searches. No search fee. Required to search: name, years to search. Civil cases indexed by defendant, plaintiff. Civil records on computer from 1993, on index books 1965, prior archived. Phone access limited to info after 11/93. Participates in the court records statewide Electronic Access Program; for signup, information and booklet call 609-292-4987.

General Information: No adoptions, sealed, juvenile, expunged, dismissed, or mental illness records released. Copy fee: $.75 per page. Fee is for first 10 pages; $.50 per page next 10; each add'l $.25. No certification fee. Payee: Special Civil Part. Personal checks accepted. Prepayment required. Mail turnaround time varies.

Warren County

Warren County Superior Court Criminal Case Management Division, PO Box 900, Belvidere, NJ 07823; 908-475-6990; Civil phone: 908-475-6140; Criminal phone: 908-475-6990; Probate phone: 908-475-6223; Fax: 908-475-6982. Hours: 8:30AM-4:30PM (EST). *Felony.*

www.judiciary.state.nj.us/somerset/index.htm

Criminal Records: Access: Phone, mail, fax, in person. Both court and visitors may perform in person searches. Search fee: $6.00 per name. Required to search: name, years to search, DOB; also helpful: SSN, signed release. Criminal records on computer back 10 years; prior on index cards to 1927.

General Information: Public Access terminal is available. No sealed, expunged, dismissed, judges notes, PSI's, or discovery packets records released. Will fax results to local or toll free line. Copy fee: $.75 up to 10 pages; $.50 11th-20th page; $.25 each

add'l page. Certification fee: $5.00. Payee: State of New Jersey Judiciary. Personal checks accepted. Prepayment required. Mail turnaround time 2 days.

Superior Court - Civil Division PO Box 900 (314 2nd St), Belvidere, NJ 07823; 908-475-6140. Hours: 8:30AM-4:30PM (EST). *Civil Actions Over $15,000, Probate.*

www.judiciary.state.nj.us/somerset/index.htm

Civil Records: Access: Mail, online, in person. Only the court performs in person searches; visitors may not. Search fee: None. Court will perfrom one search no fee. Required to search: name, years to search. Civil cases indexed by defendant, plaintiff. Civil records on computer from 1990, prior on index cards. Participates in the court records statewide Electronic Access Program; for signup, information and booklet call 609-292-4987.

General Information: No sealed, expunged, dismissed, judges notes, PSI's, or discovery packets records released. Copy fee: $.75 fee per page for first 10 pages; $.50 per page next 10; each add'l $.10. Certification fee: free for 1st page, next 5 pgs $5.00; each add'l pg $.75. Payee: Superior Court of New Jersey. Personal checks accepted. Prepayment required. Mail turnaround time 2 days.

Superior Court Special Civil Part PO Box 900 (314 2nd St), Belvidere, NJ 07823; 908-475-6140. Hours: 8:30AM-4:30PM (EST). *Civil Actions Under $15,000, Eviction, Small Claims.*

www.judiciary.state.nj.us/somerset/index.htm

Civil Records: Access: Mail, online, in person. Only the court performs in person searches; visitors may not. Search fee: None. Court will do one search no fee. Required to search: name, years to search. Civil cases indexed by defendant, plaintiff. Civil records on computer from 10/91, prior on index books from 1951. In person access requires an appointment. Participates in the court records statewide Electronic Access Program; for signup, information and booklet call 609-292-4987.

General Information: No adoptions, sealed, juvenile, expunged, dismissed, or mental illness records released. Copy fee: $.75 per page for the first ten pages, $.50 per page for the second ten pages, and $.25 per page thereafter. No certification fee. Payee: Superior Court of New Jersey. Personal checks accepted. Prepayment required. Mail requests: SASE required. Mail turnaround time 2-3 days.

New Jersey Recording Offices

ORGANIZATION: 21 counties, 21 recording offices. The recording officer title varies depending upon the county. It is either Register of Deeds or County Clerk. The Clerk of Circuit Court records the equivalent of some state's tax liens. The entire state is in the Eastern Time Zone (EST).

REAL ESTATE RECORDS: No counties will provide real estate searches. Copy and certification fees vary. Assessment and tax offices are at the municipal level.

UCC RECORDS: Financing statements are filed at the state level, except for real estate related collateral, which are filed with the County Clerk. However, prior to 07/2001, consumer goods and farm collateral were also filed at the County Clerk and these older records can be searched there. About half of the recording offices will perform UCC searches. Use search request form UCC-11. Search fees are usually $25.00 per debtor name and copy fees vary.

TAX LIEN RECORDS: All federal tax liens are filed with the County Clerk/Register of Deeds and are indexed separately from all other liens. State tax liens comprise two categories - certificates of debt are filed with the Clerk of Superior Court (some, called docketed judgments are filed specifically with the Trenton court), and warrants of execution are filed with the County Clerk/Register of Deeds. Few counties will provide tax lien searches. Refer to the County Court section for information about New Jersey Superior Courts.

OTHER LIENS: Judgment, mechanics, bail bond.

ONLINE ACCESS: A statewide database of property tax records can be accessed at http://taxrecords.com. Also, several county's property assessor and other info is available through a private company; for information, call Infocon at 814-472-6066 or www.ic-access.com.

Atlantic County

County Clerk, 5901 Main St, Courthouse, CN 2005, Mays Landing, NJ 08330-1797. **Phone**-609-625-4011; fax-609-625-4738; hours 8:30 AM-6:30 PM M W; 8:30AM-4:30PM T TH F
www.atlanticcountyclerk.org
Will search UCC records. Search per debtor- $25.00. Will not search real estate or tax lien records. Copy fee- $2.00 per page. Cert fee: $5.00 per cert. **Online Access to Property, Assessor, Inmate records:** Access to property data is free at http://tax1.co.monmouth.nj.us/cgi-bin/prc6.cgi. Use username "monm" and password "data" then select county. Also, see online notes in state summary at beginning of section. Also, search inmate info on private company website at www.vinelink.com/index.jsp.

Bergen County

County Clerk, One Bergen County Plaza, Hackensack, NJ 07601. **Phone**-201-336-7007; hours 9AM-4PM
Will not search UCC or real estate records. UCC copy- $1.00 per page. Cert fee: $1.00 per page. Payee: Bergen County Clerk. **Online Access to Property, Assessor records:** Access to property data is free at http://tax1.co.monmouth.nj.us/cgi-bin/prc6.cgi. Use username "monm" and password "data" then select county. Also, see online notes in state summary at beginning of section. **Other phones:** Assessor-201-336-6000; Treasurer-201-336-6000.

Burlington County

County Clerk, PO Box 6000, Mount Holly, NJ 08060. **Phone**-609-265-5122; fax-609-265-0696.
Will not search records. UCC copy- $.50 per page. **Online Access to Property, Assessor records:** Access to property data is free at http://tax1.co.monmouth.nj.us/cgi-bin/prc6.cgi. Use username "monm" and password "data" then select

county. Also, see online notes in state summary at beginning of section. **Other phones:** Assessor-609-265-5056.

Camden County

County Clerk, 520 Market St, Courthouse Rm 102, Camden, NJ 08102-1375. **Phone**-County Clerk, R/E & UCC Recording- 856-225-5300; fax-856-225-7100; hours 8AM-4PM
Will not search UCC or tax liens records. Computer index available for all real estate transactions after August, 1988 UCC copy- $1.00 per page. Cert fee: $2.00 per cert. Payee: Camden County Clerk. **Online Access to Property, Assessor records:** Access to property data is free at http://tax1.co.monmouth.nj.us/cgi-bin/prc6.cgi. Use username "monm" and password "data" then select county. Also, see online notes in state summary at beginning of section.

Cape May County

County Clerk, PO Box 5000, Cape May Court House, NJ 08210-5000. **Phone**-County Clerk, R/E & UCC Recording- 609-465-1010; fax-609-465-8625; hours 8:30AM-4:30PM www.capemaycountygov.net
Will not search UCC records or tax liens. Will not search real estate records. Copy fee- $2.00 per page. Cert fee: $10.00 per cert + $1.00 per page. Payee: Cape May County Clerk. **Online Access to Real Estate, Recording, Property records:** Property records for Cape May county are free to view online at http://209.204.84.120/ALIS/WW400R.PGM. To print and have full access to docs, registration and login is required. $1.00 per page copy and/or $10.00 certification fees apply to docs. Online docs go back to 1996, images to 2000. For assistance, telephone 609-465-1010. Land Records found at www.capemaycountygov.net. Also, see online notes in state summary at beginning of section. **Other phones:**

Assessor-609-465-1030; Treasurer-609-465-1170; Elections-609-465-1013; Vital Records-609-465-1023.

Cumberland County

County Clerk, PO Box 716, Bridgeton, NJ 08302. **Phone**-856-453-4864, R/E Recording-856-453-4860, UCC Recording-856-453-4860; fax-856-455-1410; hours 8:30AM-4PM
Will not search records. Copy fee- $2.00 per page. Cert fee: $10.00 per doc + $2.00 page fee. Payee: Cumberland County Clerk. **Online Access to Property, Assessor records:** Access to property data is free at http://tax1.co.monmouth.nj.us/cgi-bin/prc6.cgi. Use username "monm" and password "data" then select county. Also, see online notes in state summary at beginning of section. **Other phones:** Assessor-856-451-6699; Elections-856-453-4850.

Essex County

County Register of Deeds, 465 Martin Luther King Blvd, Hall of Records, Rm 130, Newark, NJ 07102. **Phone**-973-621-4960, R/E Recording-973-621-4960 x228, UCC Recording-973-621-4960 x225; fax-973-621-6114; hours 9AM-4PM www.essexregister.com
Will not search records. UCC copy- $3.00 per page. Cert fee: $4.00 1st page, $2.00 each add'l. Payee: Essex County Register of Deeds. **Online Access to Property, Assessor records:** Access to property data is free at http://tax1.co.monmouth.nj.us/cgi-bin/prc6.cgi. Use username "monm" and password "data" then select county. Also, see online notes in state summary at beginning of section. **Other phones:** Assessor-973-673-2344; Treasurer-973-621-4997.

Gloucester County

County Clerk, PO Box 129, Woodbury, NJ 08096-0129. **Phone-**County Clerk, R/E & UCC Recording-856-853-3230; fax-856-853-3327; hours 8:30AM-4PM www.co.gloucester.nj.us
Will search UCC records. Search per debtor- $25.00. Will not search real estate or tax lien records. RE record copy- $.50 Page. UCC copy- $.50 per page. Cert fee: $2.00 per cert. Payee: Gloucester County Clerk. **Online Access to Recording, Real Estate, Deed, Lien, UCC, Mortgage, Assessor, Property Tax records:** Access to property data is free at http://tax1.co.monmouth.nj.us/cgi-bin/prc6.cgi. Use username "monm" and password "data" then select county. Also, see online notes in state summary at beginning of section. **Other phones:** Assessor-856-384-6945; Treasurer-856-853-3353; Elections-856-384-4501; Tax Collector-856-853-6945.

Hudson County

County Clerk, 595 Newark Ave, Rm 105, Jersey City, NJ 07306. **Phone-**201-795-6571; fax-201-795-5177; hours 9AM-5PM. Will search UCC records. Search per debtor- $25.00. Will not search real estate records. UCC copy- $.25 per page. Cert fee: $10.50 per page $1.50 add'l. Payee: Hudson County Clerk. **Online Access to Property, Assessor records:** Access to property data is free at http://tax1.co.monmouth.nj.us/cgi-bin/prc6.cgi. Use username "monm" and password "data" then select county. Also, see online notes in state summary at beginning of section.

Hunterdon County

County Clerk, 71 Main St, Hall of Records, Flemington, NJ 08822. **Phone-**908-788-1221; fax-908-782-4068; hours 8:30AM-4PM. Will search UCC records. Search per debtor- $25.00. Will not search real estate or tax lien records. UCC copy- $.25 per page. Cert fee: $5.00. Payee: Hunterdon County Clerk. **Online Access to Property records:** See online notes in state summary at beginning of section. **Other phones:** Assessor-908-788-1173.

Mercer County

County Clerk, 209 S. Broad St, Courthouse, Rm 100, Trenton, NJ 08650. **Phone-**609-989-6466, R/E Recording-609-989-6487, UCC Recording-609-989-6487; fax-609-989-1111; hours 8:30AM-4:30PM www.mercercounty.org
Will not search records. Copy fee-$2.00 per page. Cert fee: $10.00 1st page; $1.50 each add'l. Payee: Mercer County Clerk. **Online Access to Property records:** See online notes in state summary at beginning of section. **Other phones:** Assessor-609-989-6704; Treasurer-609-989-6694; Elections-609-989-6495; Vital Records-609-292-4087.

Middlesex County

County Clerk, PO Box 1110, New Brunswick, NJ 08903. **Phone-**732-745-3204; hours 8:30AM-4PM
Will not search records. UCC copy- $2.00 per page. Cert fee: $10.00 per cert. Payee: Middlesex County Clerk. **Online Access to Recording, Deed, Lien, Judgment, Mortgage, Property records:** Access to the county public access system requires registration and password at http://mcrecords.co.middlesex.nj.us/. There is a sign up fee + $.25 per page, call clerk for more details. Also, see online notes in state summary at beginning of section. **Other phones:** Assessor-732-745-3000; Treasurer-732-754-3482.

Monmouth County

County Clerk, PO Box 1251, Freehold, NJ 07728. **Phone-**732-431-7324, R/E Recording-832-431-7321, UCC Recording-832-431-7321; hours 8:30AM-4:30PM www.co.monmouth.nj.us
Will search UCC records. Search per debtor- $25.00. Will not search real estate or tax lien records. RE record copy- $2.00 per page if not certified, $1.50 per page if certified. UCC copy- $2.00 per page. Cert fee: $10.00 per cert + $2.00 per page. Payee: Monmouth County Clerk. **Online Access to Real Estate, Deed, Mortgage, Grantor/Grantee, Property Tax, Assessor records:** Access to the county Online Public-Record Search System database is free at http://oprs.co.monmouth.nj.us/oprs/index.aspx. Records from 10/1/96 to present. Also, access to property data is free at http://tax1.co.monmouth.nj.us/cgi-bin/prc6.cgi. Use username "monm" and password "data" then select county. Also, see online notes in state summary at beginning of section. **Other phones:** Assessor-732-431-7404; Treasurer-732-431-7391; Appraiser/Auditor-732-431-7404; Elections-732-431-7780.

Morris County

County Clerk, PO Box 315, Morristown, NJ 07963-0315. **Phone-**973-285-6135; fax-973-285-5231; hours 8AM-4M M-F; 8AM-8PM W
Will not search records. UCC copy- $.25. Cert fee: $12.00. Payee: Morris County Clerk. **Online Access to Property, Assessor records:** Access to property data is free at http://tax1.co.monmouth.nj.us/cgi-bin/prc6.cgi. Use username "monm" and password "data" then select county. Also, see online notes in state summary at beginning of section.

Ocean County

County Clerk, PO Box 2191, Toms River, NJ 08754. **Phone-**732-929-2018; fax-732-349-4336; hours 8:30AM-4PM www.oceancountyclerk.com
Will search UCC records. Search per debtor- $25.00. Will not search real estate or tax lien records. UCC copy- $1.00 per page. Payee: Ocean County Clerk. **Online Access to Property Tax, Real Estate, Deed records:** Land records on the County Clerk database are free at www.oceancountyclerk.com/search.htm. Search by parties, doc or instrument type, or township. Tax records for Ocean county are also at http://oc.taxrecords.com. Search by name, address or property description. Also, see online notes at beginning of section.

Passaic County

County Clerk.Registry Division, 77 Hamilton St, Courthouse, Paterson, NJ 07505. **Phone-**973-881-4777; hours 8:30AM-4:30PM; Vault hours: 7:45AM-5:45PM. Will not search records. Copy fee- $2.00 per page. Cert fee: $10.00 1st page, $2.00 each add'l. Payee: Passaic County Clerk.

Salem County

County Clerk, 92 Market St, Salem, NJ 08079-1911. **Phone-**856-935-7510 x8218, R/E Recording-856-935-7510 x8206; fax-856-935-8882.
Will search UCC records. Search per debtor- $25.00. Will not search real estate or tax lien records. Copy fee- $2.00 per page. Cert fee: $5.00 per cert. Payee: Salem County Clerk. **Online Access to Property, Assessor records:** Access to property data is free at http://tax1.co.monmouth.nj.us/cgi-bin/prc6.cgi. Use username "monm" and password "data" then select county. Also, see online notes in state summary at beginning of section. **Other phones:** Assessor-856-935-9231; Treasurer-856-935--9036.

Somerset County

County Clerk, PO Box 3000, Somerville, NJ 08876. **Phone-**County Clerk, R/E & UCC Recording- 908-231-7006; fax-908-253-8853; hours 8:15AM-4PM www.co.somerset.nj.us
Will not search records. Copy fee- $2.00 per page. Cert fee: $2.00 per cert. Payee: Somerset County Clerk. **Online Access to Real Estate, Recording, Deed, Property Tax, Assessor records:** Access to the County Clerk's recordings database is free at http://209.92.88.21/. Registration required, or enter as "Guest." Index goes back to 1/93; images back to 6/11/01. Also, access to property data is free at http://tax1.co.monmouth.nj.us/cgi-bin/prc6.cgi. Use username "monm" and password "data" then select county. Also, see online notes in state summary at beginning of section. **Other phones:** Treasurer-908-231-7000 x7631; Elections-908-231-7084.

Sussex County

County Clerk, 4 Park Pl, Hall of Records, Newton, NJ 07860-1795. **Phone-**County Clerk, R/E & UCC Recording- 973-579-0900; fax-973-383-7493; hours 8:30AM-4:30PM www.sussexcountyclerk.com
Will search UCC records if debtors name, date, and docket number supplied. Will not search tax liens. Will search RE records only if book and page number, year and name are supplied. Record copy fee- $2.00 per page. Cert fee: $5.00. Payee: Sussex County Clerk. **Online Access to Property, Assessor, Real Estate, Recording, Deed records:** Access to property data is free at http://tax1.co.monmouth.nj.us/cgi-bin/prc6.cgi. Use username "monm" and password "data" then select county. Also, access to recorder records back to 1/1964 is at www.landaccess.com/proi/county.jsp?county=njsussex. They may begin charging a $250 sub fee. Also, see online notes in state summary at beginning of section. **Other phones:** Assessor-973-579-0970; Treasurer-973-579-0330; Elections-973-579-0950.

Union County

County Clerk, 2 Broad St, Courthouse, Rm 115, Elizabeth, NJ 07207. **Phone-**908-527-4794, R/E Recording-908-527-4787; fax-908-558-2589; hours 8:30AM-4:30PM www.unioncountynj.org/constit/clerk/record.html
Will not search records. Copy fee- $1.50 per page. Cert fee: $8.00 1st pg; $2.00 each add'l. Payee: Union County Clerk. **Online Access to Real Estate, Deed, Property Tax, Assessor records:** Search recorded real estate related docs at http://clerk.ucnj.org/UCPA/DocIndex. Access to property data is free at http://tax1.co.monmouth.nj.us/cgi-bin/prc6.cgi. Use username "monm" and password "data" then select county. **Other phones:** Elections-908-527-4996.

Warren County

County Clerk, 413 Second St, Courthouse, Belvidere, NJ 07823-1500. **Phone-**County Clerk, R/E & UCC Recording- 908-475-6211; hours 8:30AM-4PM
Will not search records. RE record copy- $2.00 per page, if reference is given. UCC copy- $2.00 per page. Cert fee: $5.00 per doc. Payee: Warren County Clerk. **Online Access to Property, Assessor records:** Access to property data is free at http://tax1.co.monmouth.nj.us/cgi-bin/prc6.cgi. Use username "monm" and password "data" then select county. Also, see online notes in state summary at beginning of section. **Other phones:** Assessor-908-475-6229; Treasurer-908-475-6542; Elections-908-475-6211.

New Jersey County Locator

You will usually be able to find the city name in the City/County Cross Reference below. In that case, it is a simple matter to determine the county from the cross reference. However, only the official US Postal Service city names are included in this index. We have also included a ZIP/City Cross Reference immediately following the City/County Cross Reference.

If you know the ZIP Code but the city name does not appear in the City/County Cross Reference index, look up the ZIP Code in the ZIP/City Cross Reference, find the city name, then look up the city name in the City/County Cross Reference.

New Jersey City/County Cross Reference

ABSECON Atlantic
ADELPHIA Monmouth
ALLAMUCHY Warren
ALLENDALE Bergen
ALLENHURST Monmouth
ALLENTOWN (08501) Monmouth(82),
    Burlington(10), Mercer(7)
ALLENWOOD Monmouth
ALLOWAY Salem
ALPINE Bergen
ANDOVER Sussex
ANNANDALE Hunterdon
ASBURY (08802) Hunterdon(67),
    Warren(32)
ASBURY PARK Monmouth
ATCO (08004) Camden(98), Burlington(1)
ATLANTIC CITY Atlantic
ATLANTIC HIGHLANDS Monmouth
AUDUBON Camden
AUGUSTA Sussex
AVALON Cape May
AVENEL Middlesex
AVON BY THE SEA Monmouth
BAPTISTOWN Hunterdon
BARNEGAT Ocean
BARNEGAT LIGHT Ocean
BARRINGTON Camden
BASKING RIDGE (07920) Somerset(98),
    Morris(1)
BAYONNE Hudson
BAYVILLE Ocean
BEACH HAVEN Ocean
BEACHWOOD Ocean
BEDMINSTER Somerset
BELFORD Monmouth
BELLE MEAD Somerset
BELLEVILLE Essex
BELLMAWR Camden
BELMAR Monmouth
BELVIDERE Warren
BERGENFIELD Bergen
BERKELEY HEIGHTS Union
BERLIN Camden
BERNARDSVILLE Somerset
BEVERLY Burlington
BIRMINGHAM Burlington
BLACKWOOD (08012) Camden(55),
    Gloucester(44)
BLAIRSTOWN Warren
BLAWENBURG Somerset
BLOOMFIELD Essex
BLOOMINGDALE Passaic
BLOOMSBURY (08804) Hunterdon(70),
    Warren(29)
BOGOTA Bergen
BOONTON Morris
BORDENTOWN Burlington
BOUND BROOK Somerset
BRADLEY BEACH Monmouth
BRANCHVILLE Sussex
BRICK Ocean
BRIDGEPORT Gloucester
BRIDGETON (08302) Cumberland(93),
    Salem(6)
BRIDGEWATER Somerset
BRIELLE Monmouth
BRIGANTINE Atlantic
BROADWAY Warren

BROOKSIDE Morris
BROWNS MILLS Burlington
BUDD LAKE Morris
BUENA Atlantic
BURLINGTON Burlington
BUTLER Morris
BUTTZVILLE Warren
CALDWELL Essex
CALIFON (07830) Hunterdon(88),
    Morris(11)
CAPE MAY Cape May
CAPE MAY COURT HOUSE Cape May
CAPE MAY POINT Cape May
CARLSTADT Bergen
CARTERET Middlesex
CEDAR BROOK Camden
CEDAR GROVE Essex
CEDAR KNOLLS Morris
CEDARVILLE Cumberland
CHANGEWATER Warren
CHATHAM Morris
CHATSWORTH Burlington
CHERRY HILL Camden
CHESTER Morris
CLARK Union
CLARKSBORO Gloucester
CLARKSBURG Monmouth
CLAYTON Gloucester
CLEMENTON Camden
CLIFFSIDE PARK Bergen
CLIFFWOOD Monmouth
CLIFTON Passaic
CLINTON Hunterdon
CLOSTER Bergen
COLLINGSWOOD Camden
COLOGNE Atlantic
COLONIA Middlesex
COLTS NECK Monmouth
COLUMBIA Warren
COLUMBUS Burlington
COOKSTOWN Burlington
CRANBURY (08512) Middlesex(68),
    Mercer(31)
CRANBURY Middlesex
CRANFORD Union
CREAM RIDGE (08514) Monmouth(70),
    Ocean(29)
CREAMRIDGE (08514) Monmouth(70),
    Ocean(29)
CRESSKILL Bergen
CROSSWICKS Burlington
DAYTON Middlesex
DEAL Monmouth
DEEPWATER Salem
DEERFIELD STREET Cumberland
DELAWARE Warren
DELMONT Cumberland
DEMAREST Bergen
DENNISVILLE Cape May
DENVILLE Morris
DIVIDING CREEK Cumberland
DORCHESTER Cumberland
DOROTHY Atlantic
DOVER Morris
DUMONT Bergen
DUNELLEN (08812) Somerset(51),
    Middlesex(48)
EAST BRUNSWICK Middlesex

EAST HANOVER Morris
EAST ORANGE Essex
EAST RUTHERFORD Bergen
EATONTOWN Monmouth
EDGEWATER Bergen
EDISON Middlesex
EGG HARBOR CITY (08215) Atlantic(94),
    Burlington(5)
EGG HARBOR TOWNSHIP Atlantic
ELIZABETH Union
ELMER Salem
ELMWOOD PARK Bergen
ELWOOD Atlantic
EMERSON Bergen
ENGLEWOOD Bergen
ENGLEWOOD CLIFFS Bergen
ENGLISHTOWN Monmouth
ESSEX FELLS Essex
ESTELL MANOR Atlantic
EWAN Gloucester
FAIR HAVEN Monmouth
FAIR LAWN Bergen
FAIRFIELD Essex
FAIRTON Cumberland
FAIRVIEW Bergen
FANWOOD Union
FAR HILLS Somerset
FARMINGDALE Monmouth
FLAGTOWN Somerset
FLANDERS Morris
FLEMINGTON Hunterdon
FLORENCE Burlington
FLORHAM PARK Morris
FORDS Middlesex
FORKED RIVER Ocean
FORT LEE Bergen
FORT MONMOUTH Monmouth
FORTESCUE Cumberland
FRANKLIN Sussex
FRANKLIN LAKES Bergen
FRANKLIN PARK Somerset
FRANKLINVILLE Gloucester
FREEHOLD Monmouth
FRENCHTOWN Hunterdon
GARFIELD Bergen
GARWOOD Union
GIBBSBORO Camden
GIBBSTOWN Gloucester
GILLETTE Morris
GLADSTONE Somerset
GLASSBORO Gloucester
GLASSER Sussex
GLEN GARDNER Hunterdon
GLEN RIDGE Essex
GLEN ROCK Bergen
GLENDORA Camden
GLENWOOD Sussex
GLOUCESTER CITY Camden
GOSHEN Cape May
GREAT MEADOWS Warren
GREEN CREEK Cape May
GREEN VILLAGE Morris
GREENDELL Sussex
GREENWICH Cumberland
GRENLOCH Gloucester
HACKENSACK Bergen
HACKETTSTOWN (07840) Warren(82),
    Morris(17)

HADDON HEIGHTS Camden
HADDONFIELD Camden
HAINESPORT Burlington
HALEDON Passaic
HAMBURG Sussex
HAMMONTON (08037) Atlantic(81),
    Camden(18)
HAMPTON (08827) Hunterdon(93),
    Warren(6)
HANCOCKS BRIDGE Salem
HARRINGTON PARK Bergen
HARRISON Hudson
HARRISONVILLE Gloucester
HASBROUCK HEIGHTS Bergen
HASKELL Passaic
HAWORTH Bergen
HAWTHORNE Passaic
HAZLET Monmouth
HEISLERVILLE Cumberland
HELMETTA Middlesex
HEWITT (07421) Passaic(98), Sussex(1)
HIBERNIA Morris
HIGH BRIDGE Hunterdon
HIGHLAND LAKES Sussex
HIGHLAND PARK Middlesex
HIGHLANDS Monmouth
HIGHTSTOWN Mercer
HILLSBOROUGH Somerset
HILLSDALE Bergen
HILLSIDE Union
HO HO KUS Bergen
HOBOKEN Hudson
HOLMDEL Monmouth
HOPATCONG Sussex
HOPE Warren
HOPEWELL (08525) Mercer(92),
    Hunterdon(6)
HOWELL Monmouth
IMLAYSTOWN Monmouth
IRONIA Morris
IRVINGTON Essex
ISELIN Middlesex
ISLAND HEIGHTS Ocean
JACKSON Ocean
JAMESBURG Middlesex
JERSEY CITY Hudson
JOBSTOWN Burlington
JOHNSONBURG Warren
JULIUSTOWN Burlington
KEANSBURG Monmouth
KEARNY Hudson
KEASBEY Middlesex
KENDALL PARK Middlesex
KENILWORTH Union
KENVIL Morris
KEYPORT (07735) Monmouth(92),
    Middlesex(7)
KINGSTON Somerset
KIRKWOOD VOORHEES Camden
LAFAYETTE Sussex
LAKE HIAWATHA Morris
LAKE HOPATCONG Morris
LAKEHURST Ocean
LAKEWOOD Ocean
LAMBERTVILLE (08530) Hunterdon(96),
    Mercer(3)
LANDING Morris
LANDISVILLE Atlantic

LANOKA HARBOR Ocean
LAVALLETTE Ocean
LAWNSIDE Camden
LAYTON Sussex
LEBANON Hunterdon
LEDGEWOOD Morris
LEEDS POINT Atlantic
LEESBURG Cumberland
LEONARDO Monmouth
LEONIA Bergen
LIBERTY CORNER Somerset
LINCOLN PARK Morris
LINCROFT Monmouth
LINDEN Union
LINWOOD Atlantic
LITTLE FALLS Passaic
LITTLE FERRY Bergen
LITTLE SILVER Monmouth
LITTLE YORK Hunterdon
LIVINGSTON Essex
LODI Bergen
LONG BRANCH Monmouth
LONG VALLEY Morris
LONGPORT Atlantic
LUMBERTON Burlington
LYNDHURST Bergen
LYONS Somerset
MADISON Morris
MAGNOLIA Camden
MAHWAH Bergen
MALAGA Gloucester
MANAHAWKIN Ocean
MANASQUAN Monmouth
MANTOLOKING Ocean
MANTUA Gloucester
MANVILLE Somerset
MAPLE SHADE Burlington
MAPLEWOOD Essex
MARGATE CITY Atlantic
MARLBORO Monmouth
MARLTON Burlington
MARMORA Cape May
MARTINSVILLE Somerset
MATAWAN (07747) Monmouth(65),
    Middlesex(34)
MAURICETOWN Cumberland
MAYS LANDING Atlantic
MAYWOOD Bergen
MC AFEE Sussex
MEDFORD Burlington
MENDHAM Morris
MERCHANTVILLE Camden
METUCHEN Middlesex
MICKLETON Gloucester
MIDDLESEX Middlesex
MIDDLETOWN Monmouth
MIDDLEVILLE Sussex
MIDLAND PARK Bergen
MILFORD Hunterdon
MILLBURN Essex
MILLINGTON Morris
MILLTOWN Middlesex
MILLVILLE Cumberland
MILMAY Atlantic
MINE HILL Morris
MINOTOLA Atlantic
MIZPAH Atlantic
MONMOUTH BEACH Monmouth
MONMOUTH JUNCTION Middlesex
MONROE TOWNSHIP Middlesex
MONROEVILLE (08343) Gloucester(58),
    Salem(41)
MONTAGUE Sussex
MONTCLAIR (07043) Essex(96),
    Passaic(3)
MONTCLAIR Essex
MONTVALE Bergen
MONTVILLE Morris
MOONACHIE Bergen
MOORESTOWN Burlington
MORGANVILLE Monmouth
MORRIS PLAINS Morris
MORRISTOWN Morris

MOUNT ARLINGTON Morris
MOUNT EPHRAIM Camden
MOUNT FREEDOM Morris
MOUNT HOLLY Burlington
MOUNT LAUREL Burlington
MOUNT ROYAL Gloucester
MOUNT TABOR Morris
MOUNTAIN LAKES Morris
MOUNTAINSIDE Union
MULLICA HILL Gloucester
MUSICAL HERITAGE Monmouth
NATIONAL PARK Gloucester
NAVESINK Monmouth
NEPTUNE Monmouth
NESHANIC STATION (08853)
    Somerset(86), Hunterdon(13)
NETCONG Morris
NEW BRUNSWICK Middlesex
NEW EGYPT (08533) Ocean(98),
    Burlington(1)
NEW GRETNA Burlington
NEW LISBON Burlington
NEW MILFORD Bergen
NEW PROVIDENCE Union
NEW VERNON Morris
NEWARK Essex
NEWFIELD (08344) Gloucester(65),
    Cumberland(24), Atlantic(6), Salem(3)
NEWFOUNDLAND Passaic
NEWPORT Cumberland
NEWTON Sussex
NEWTONVILLE Atlantic
NORMA Salem
NORMANDY BEACH Ocean
NORTH ARLINGTON Bergen
NORTH BERGEN Hudson
NORTH BRUNSWICK Middlesex
NORTHFIELD Atlantic
NORTHVALE Bergen
NORWOOD Bergen
NUTLEY Essex
OAK RIDGE (07438) Passaic(78),
    Morris(21)
OAKHURST Monmouth
OAKLAND Bergen
OAKLYN Camden
OCEAN CITY Cape May
OCEAN GATE Ocean
OCEAN GROVE Monmouth
OCEAN VIEW Cape May
OCEANPORT Monmouth
OCEANVILLE Atlantic
OGDENSBURG Sussex
OLD BRIDGE Middlesex
OLDWICK Hunterdon
ORADELL Bergen
ORANGE Essex
OSGLI Essex
OXFORD Warren
PALISADES PARK Bergen
PALMYRA Burlington
PARAMUS Bergen
PARK RIDGE Bergen
PARLIN Middlesex
PARSIPPANY Morris
PASSAIC Passaic
PATERSON Passaic
PAULSBORO Gloucester
PEAPACK Somerset
PEDRICKTOWN Salem
PEMBERTON Burlington
PENNINGTON Mercer
PENNS GROVE Salem
PENNSAUKEN Camden
PENNSVILLE Salem
PEQUANNOCK Morris
PERRINEVILLE Monmouth
PERTH AMBOY Middlesex
PHILLIPSBURG Warren
PICATINNY ARSENAL Morris
PINE BEACH Ocean
PINE BROOK Morris
PISCATAWAY Middlesex

PITMAN Gloucester
PITTSTOWN Hunterdon
PLAINFIELD (07063) Union(72),
    Somerset(27)
PLAINFIELD Union
PLAINSBORO Middlesex
PLEASANTVILLE Atlantic
PLUCKEMIN Somerset
POINT PLEASANT BEACH Ocean
POMONA Atlantic
POMPTON LAKES Passaic
POMPTON PLAINS Morris
PORT ELIZABETH Cumberland
PORT MONMOUTH Monmouth
PORT MURRAY Warren
PORT NORRIS Cumberland
PORT READING Middlesex
PORT REPUBLIC Atlantic
POTTERSVILLE Hunterdon
PRINCETON (08540) Mercer(72),
    Middlesex(15), Somerset(12)
PRINCETON JUNCTION Mercer
QUAKERTOWN Hunterdon
QUINTON Salem
RAHWAY Union
RAMSEY Bergen
RANCOCAS Burlington
RANDOLPH Morris
RARITAN Somerset
READINGTON Hunterdon
RED BANK Monmouth
RICHLAND Atlantic
RICHWOOD Gloucester
RIDGEFIELD Bergen
RIDGEFIELD PARK Bergen
RIDGEWOOD Bergen
RINGOES Hunterdon
RINGWOOD Passaic
RIO GRANDE Cape May
RIVER EDGE Bergen
RIVERDALE Morris
RIVERSIDE Burlington
RIVERTON Burlington
ROCHELLE PARK Bergen
ROCKAWAY Morris
ROCKY HILL Somerset
ROEBLING Burlington
ROOSEVELT Monmouth
ROSELAND Essex
ROSELLE Union
ROSELLE PARK Union
ROSEMONT Hunterdon
ROSENHAYN Cumberland
RUMSON Monmouth
RUNNEMEDE Camden
RUTHERFORD Bergen
SADDLE BROOK Bergen
SADDLE RIVER Bergen
SALEM Salem
SAYREVILLE Middlesex
SCHOOLEYS MOUNTAIN Morris
SCOTCH PLAINS Union
SEA GIRT Monmouth
SEA ISLE CITY Cape May
SEASIDE HEIGHTS Ocean
SEASIDE PARK Ocean
SECAUCUS Hudson
SERGEANTSVILLE Hunterdon
SEWAREN Middlesex
SEWELL Gloucester
SHILOH Cumberland
SHORT HILLS Essex
SHREWSBURY Monmouth
SICKLERVILLE (08081) Camden(96),
    Gloucester(3)
SKILLMAN (08558) Somerset(98),
    Mercer(1)
SOMERDALE Camden
SOMERS POINT Atlantic
SOMERSET Somerset
SOMERVILLE (08876) Somerset(98),
    Hunterdon(1)
SOUTH AMBOY Middlesex

SOUTH BOUND BROOK Somerset
SOUTH DENNIS Cape May
SOUTH HACKENSACK Bergen
SOUTH ORANGE Essex
SOUTH PLAINFIELD Middlesex
SOUTH RIVER Middlesex
SOUTH SEAVILLE Cape May
SPARTA Sussex
SPOTSWOOD Middlesex
SPRING LAKE Monmouth
SPRINGFIELD Union
STANHOPE Sussex
STANTON Hunterdon
STEWARTSVILLE Warren
STILLWATER Sussex
STIRLING Morris
STOCKHOLM (07460) Sussex(96),
    Morris(2)
STOCKTON Hunterdon
STONE HARBOR Cape May
STRATFORD Camden
STRATHMERE Cape May
SUCCASUNNA Morris
SUMMIT Union
SUSSEX Sussex
SWARTSWOOD Sussex
SWEDESBORO Gloucester
TEANECK Bergen
TENAFLY Bergen
TENNENT Monmouth
TETERBORO Bergen
THOROFARE Gloucester
THREE BRIDGES Hunterdon
TITUSVILLE Mercer
TOMS RIVER Ocean
TOTOWA Passaic
TOWACO Morris
TOWNSHIP OF WASHINGTON Bergen
TRANQUILITY Sussex
TRENTON (08620) Mercer(85),
    Burlington(14)
TRENTON (08691) Mercer(95),
    Monmouth(4)
TRENTON Burlington
TRENTON Mercer
TUCKAHOE Cape May
TUCKERTON (08087) Ocean(94),
    Burlington(5)
UNION Union
UNION CITY Hudson
VAUXHALL Union
VENTNOR CITY Atlantic
VERNON Sussex
VERONA Essex
VIENNA Warren
VILLAS Cape May
VINCENTOWN Burlington
VINELAND (08360) Cumberland(90),
    Atlantic(5), Gloucester(3)
VINELAND Cumberland
VOORHEES Camden
WALDWICK Bergen
WALLINGTON Bergen
WALLPACK CENTER Sussex
WANAQUE Passaic
WARETOWN Ocean
WARREN Somerset
WASHINGTON Warren
WATCHUNG Somerset
WATERFORD WORKS Camden
WAYNE Passaic
WEEHAWKEN Hudson
WENONAH Gloucester
WEST BERLIN Camden
WEST CREEK Ocean
WEST LONG BRANCH Monmouth
WEST MILFORD Passaic
WEST NEW YORK Hudson
WEST ORANGE Essex
WESTFIELD Union
WESTVILLE Gloucester
WESTWOOD Bergen
WHARTON Morris

WHIPPANY Morris
WHITEHOUSE Hunterdon
WHITEHOUSE STATION Hunterdon
WHITESBORO Cape May
WHITING Ocean
WICKATUNK Monmouth

WILDWOOD Cape May
WILLIAMSTOWN (08094) Gloucester(90), Atlantic(9)
WILLINGBORO Burlington
WINDSOR Mercer
WINSLOW Camden

WOOD RIDGE Bergen
WOODBINE (08270) Cape May(89), Atlantic(10)
WOODBRIDGE Middlesex
WOODBURY Gloucester
WOODBURY HEIGHTS Gloucester

WOODCLIFF LAKE Bergen
WOODSTOWN Salem
WRIGHTSTOWN Burlington
WYCKOFF Bergen
ZAREPHATH Somerset

New Jersey ZIP/City Cross Reference

07001-07001	AVENEL
07002-07002	BAYONNE
07003-07003	BLOOMFIELD
07004-07004	FAIRFIELD
07005-07005	BOONTON
07006-07007	CALDWELL
07008-07008	CARTERET
07009-07009	CEDAR GROVE
07010-07010	CLIFFSIDE PARK
07011-07015	CLIFTON
07016-07016	CRANFORD
07017-07019	EAST ORANGE
07020-07020	EDGEWATER
07021-07021	ESSEX FELLS
07022-07022	FAIRVIEW
07023-07023	FANWOOD
07024-07024	FORT LEE
07026-07026	GARFIELD
07027-07027	GARWOOD
07028-07028	GLEN RIDGE
07029-07029	HARRISON
07030-07030	HOBOKEN
07031-07031	NORTH ARLINGTON
07032-07032	KEARNY
07033-07033	KENILWORTH
07034-07034	LAKE HIAWATHA
07035-07035	LINCOLN PARK
07036-07036	LINDEN
07039-07039	LIVINGSTON
07040-07040	MAPLEWOOD
07041-07041	MILLBURN
07042-07043	MONTCLAIR
07044-07044	VERONA
07045-07045	MONTVILLE
07046-07046	MOUNTAIN LAKES
07047-07047	NORTH BERGEN
07050-07051	ORANGE
07052-07052	WEST ORANGE
07054-07054	PARSIPPANY
07055-07055	PASSAIC
07057-07057	WALLINGTON
07058-07058	PINE BROOK
07059-07059	WARREN
07060-07063	PLAINFIELD
07064-07064	PORT READING
07065-07065	RAHWAY
07066-07066	CLARK
07067-07067	COLONIA
07068-07068	ROSELAND
07069-07069	WATCHUNG
07070-07070	RUTHERFORD
07071-07071	LYNDHURST
07072-07072	CARLSTADT
07073-07073	EAST RUTHERFORD
07074-07074	MOONACHIE
07075-07075	WOOD RIDGE
07076-07076	SCOTCH PLAINS
07077-07077	SEWAREN
07078-07078	SHORT HILLS
07079-07079	SOUTH ORANGE
07080-07080	SOUTH PLAINFIELD
07081-07081	SPRINGFIELD
07082-07082	TOWACO
07083-07083	UNION
07086-07086	WEEHAWKEN
07087-07087	UNION CITY
07088-07088	VAUXHALL
07090-07091	WESTFIELD
07092-07092	MOUNTAINSIDE
07093-07093	WEST NEW YORK
07094-07094	SECAUCUS
07095-07095	WOODBRIDGE
07096-07096	SECAUCUS

07097-07097	JERSEY CITY
07098-07098	AVENEL
07099-07099	KEARNY
07100-07108	NEWARK
07109-07109	BELLEVILLE
07110-07110	NUTLEY
07111-07111	IRVINGTON
07112-07187	NEWARK
07187-07187	OSGLI
07188-07199	NEWARK
07200-07202	ELIZABETH
07203-07203	ROSELLE
07204-07204	ROSELLE PARK
07205-07205	HILLSIDE
07206-07216	ELIZABETH
07300-07399	JERSEY CITY
07401-07401	ALLENDALE
07403-07403	BLOOMINGDALE
07405-07405	BUTLER
07407-07407	ELMWOOD PARK
07410-07410	FAIR LAWN
07416-07416	FRANKLIN
07417-07417	FRANKLIN LAKES
07418-07418	GLENWOOD
07419-07419	HAMBURG
07420-07420	HASKELL
07421-07421	HEWITT
07422-07422	HIGHLAND LAKES
07423-07423	HO HO KUS
07424-07424	LITTLE FALLS
07428-07428	MC AFEE
07430-07430	MAHWAH
07432-07432	MIDLAND PARK
07435-07435	NEWFOUNDLAND
07436-07436	OAKLAND
07438-07438	OAK RIDGE
07439-07439	OGDENSBURG
07440-07440	PEQUANNOCK
07442-07442	POMPTON LAKES
07444-07444	POMPTON PLAINS
07446-07446	RAMSEY
07450-07451	RIDGEWOOD
07452-07452	GLEN ROCK
07456-07456	RINGWOOD
07457-07457	RIVERDALE
07458-07458	SADDLE RIVER
07460-07460	STOCKHOLM
07461-07461	SUSSEX
07462-07462	VERNON
07463-07463	WALDWICK
07465-07465	WANAQUE
07470-07477	WAYNE
07480-07480	WEST MILFORD
07481-07481	WYCKOFF
07495-07498	MAHWAH
07501-07505	PATERSON
07506-07507	HAWTHORNE
07508-07508	HALEDON
07509-07510	PATERSON
07511-07512	TOTOWA
07513-07533	PATERSON
07538-07538	HALEDON
07543-07544	PATERSON
07601-07602	HACKENSACK
07603-07603	BOGOTA
07604-07604	HASBROUCK HEIGHTS
07605-07605	LEONIA
07606-07606	SOUTH HACKENSACK
07607-07607	MAYWOOD
07608-07608	TETERBORO
07620-07620	ALPINE
07621-07621	BERGENFIELD
07624-07624	CLOSTER

07626-07626	CRESSKILL
07627-07627	DEMAREST
07628-07628	DUMONT
07630-07630	EMERSON
07631-07631	ENGLEWOOD
07632-07632	ENGLEWOOD CLIFFS
07640-07640	HARRINGTON PARK
07641-07641	HAWORTH
07642-07642	HILLSDALE
07643-07643	LITTLE FERRY
07644-07644	LODI
07645-07645	MONTVALE
07646-07646	NEW MILFORD
07647-07647	NORTHVALE
07648-07648	NORWOOD
07649-07649	ORADELL
07650-07650	PALISADES PARK
07652-07653	PARAMUS
07656-07656	PARK RIDGE
07657-07657	RIDGEFIELD
07660-07660	RIDGEFIELD PARK
07661-07661	RIVER EDGE
07662-07662	ROCHELLE PARK
07663-07663	SADDLE BROOK
07666-07666	TEANECK
07670-07670	TENAFLY
07675-07675	WESTWOOD
07676-07676	TOWNSHIP OF WASHINGTON
07677-07677	WOODCLIFF LAKE
07688-07688	TEANECK
07699-07699	TETERBORO
07701-07701	RED BANK
07702-07702	SHREWSBURY
07703-07703	FORT MONMOUTH
07704-07704	FAIR HAVEN
07709-07709	ALLENHURST
07710-07710	ADELPHIA
07711-07711	ALLENHURST
07712-07712	ASBURY PARK
07713-07713	MUSICAL HERITAGE
07715-07715	BELMAR
07716-07716	ATLANTIC HIGHLANDS
07717-07717	AVON BY THE SEA
07718-07718	BELFORD
07719-07719	BELMAR
07720-07720	BRADLEY BEACH
07721-07721	CLIFFWOOD
07722-07722	COLTS NECK
07723-07723	DEAL
07724-07724	EATONTOWN
07726-07726	ENGLISHTOWN
07727-07727	FARMINGDALE
07728-07728	FREEHOLD
07730-07730	HAZLET
07731-07731	HOWELL
07732-07732	HIGHLANDS
07733-07733	HOLMDEL
07734-07734	KEANSBURG
07735-07735	KEYPORT
07737-07737	LEONARDO
07738-07738	LINCROFT
07739-07739	LITTLE SILVER
07740-07740	LONG BRANCH
07746-07746	MARLBORO
07747-07747	MATAWAN
07748-07748	MIDDLETOWN
07750-07750	MONMOUTH BEACH
07751-07751	MORGANVILLE
07752-07752	NAVESINK
07753-07754	NEPTUNE
07755-07755	OAKHURST
07756-07756	OCEAN GROVE

07757-07757	OCEANPORT
07758-07758	PORT MONMOUTH
07760-07760	RUMSON
07762-07762	SPRING LAKE
07763-07763	TENNENT
07764-07764	WEST LONG BRANCH
07765-07765	WICKATUNK
07777-07777	HOLMDEL
07799-07799	EATONTOWN
07801-07802	DOVER
07803-07803	MINE HILL
07806-07806	PICATINNY ARSENAL
07820-07820	ALLAMUCHY
07821-07821	ANDOVER
07822-07822	AUGUSTA
07823-07823	BELVIDERE
07825-07825	BLAIRSTOWN
07826-07826	BRANCHVILLE
07827-07827	MONTAGUE
07828-07828	BUDD LAKE
07829-07829	BUTTZVILLE
07830-07830	CALIFON
07831-07831	CHANGEWATER
07832-07832	COLUMBIA
07833-07833	DELAWARE
07834-07834	DENVILLE
07836-07836	FLANDERS
07837-07837	GLASSER
07838-07838	GREAT MEADOWS
07839-07839	GREENDELL
07840-07840	HACKETTSTOWN
07842-07842	HIBERNIA
07843-07843	HOPATCONG
07844-07844	HOPE
07845-07845	IRONIA
07846-07846	JOHNSONBURG
07847-07847	KENVIL
07848-07848	LAFAYETTE
07849-07849	LAKE HOPATCONG
07850-07850	LANDING
07851-07851	LAYTON
07852-07852	LEDGEWOOD
07853-07853	LONG VALLEY
07855-07855	MIDDLEVILLE
07856-07856	MOUNT ARLINGTON
07857-07857	NETCONG
07860-07860	NEWTON
07863-07863	OXFORD
07865-07865	PORT MURRAY
07866-07866	ROCKAWAY
07869-07869	RANDOLPH
07870-07870	SCHOOLEYS MOUNTAIN
07871-07871	SPARTA
07874-07874	STANHOPE
07875-07875	STILLWATER
07876-07876	SUCCASUNNA
07877-07877	SWARTSWOOD
07878-07878	MOUNT TABOR
07879-07879	TRANQUILITY
07880-07880	VIENNA
07881-07881	WALLPACK CENTER
07882-07882	WASHINGTON
07885-07885	WHARTON
07890-07890	BRANCHVILLE
07901-07902	SUMMIT
07920-07920	BASKING RIDGE
07921-07921	BEDMINSTER
07922-07922	BERKELEY HEIGHTS
07924-07924	BERNARDSVILLE
07926-07926	BROOKSIDE
07927-07927	CEDAR KNOLLS
07928-07928	CHATHAM
07930-07930	CHESTER

Zip Range	City
07931-07931	FAR HILLS
07932-07932	FLORHAM PARK
07933-07933	GILLETTE
07934-07934	GLADSTONE
07935-07935	GREEN VILLAGE
07936-07936	EAST HANOVER
07938-07938	LIBERTY CORNER
07939-07939	LYONS
07940-07940	MADISON
07945-07945	MENDHAM
07946-07946	MILLINGTON
07950-07950	MORRIS PLAINS
07960-07963	MORRISTOWN
07970-07970	MOUNT FREEDOM
07974-07974	NEW PROVIDENCE
07976-07976	NEW VERNON
07977-07977	PEAPACK
07978-07978	PLUCKEMIN
07979-07979	POTTERSVILLE
07980-07980	STIRLING
07981-07999	WHIPPANY
08001-08001	ALLOWAY
08002-08003	CHERRY HILL
08004-08004	ATCO
08005-08005	BARNEGAT
08006-08006	BARNEGAT LIGHT
08007-08007	BARRINGTON
08008-08008	BEACH HAVEN
08009-08009	BERLIN
08010-08010	BEVERLY
08011-08011	BIRMINGHAM
08012-08012	BLACKWOOD
08014-08014	BRIDGEPORT
08015-08015	BROWNS MILLS
08016-08016	BURLINGTON
08018-08018	CEDAR BROOK
08019-08019	CHATSWORTH
08020-08020	CLARKSBORO
08021-08021	CLEMENTON
08022-08022	COLUMBUS
08023-08023	DEEPWATER
08025-08025	EWAN
08026-08026	GIBBSBORO
08027-08027	GIBBSTOWN
08028-08028	GLASSBORO
08029-08029	GLENDORA
08030-08030	GLOUCESTER CITY
08031-08031	BELLMAWR
08032-08032	GRENLOCH
08033-08033	HADDONFIELD
08034-08034	CHERRY HILL
08035-08035	HADDON HEIGHTS
08036-08036	HAINESPORT
08037-08037	HAMMONTON
08038-08038	HANCOCKS BRIDGE
08039-08039	HARRISONVILLE
08040-08040	KIRKWOOD VOORHEES
08041-08041	JOBSTOWN
08042-08042	JULIUSTOWN
08043-08043	VOORHEES
08045-08045	LAWNSIDE
08046-08046	WILLINGBORO
08048-08048	LUMBERTON
08049-08049	MAGNOLIA
08050-08050	MANAHAWKIN
08051-08051	MANTUA
08052-08052	MAPLE SHADE
08053-08053	MARLTON
08054-08054	MOUNT LAUREL
08055-08055	MEDFORD
08056-08056	MICKLETON
08057-08057	MOORESTOWN
08059-08059	MOUNT EPHRAIM
08060-08060	MOUNT HOLLY
08061-08061	MOUNT ROYAL
08062-08062	MULLICA HILL
08063-08063	NATIONAL PARK
08064-08064	NEW LISBON
08065-08065	PALMYRA
08066-08066	PAULSBORO
08067-08067	PEDRICKTOWN
08068-08068	PEMBERTON
08069-08069	PENNS GROVE
08070-08070	PENNSVILLE
08071-08071	PITMAN
08072-08072	QUINTON
08073-08073	RANCOCAS
08074-08074	RICHWOOD
08075-08075	RIVERSIDE
08076-08077	RIVERTON
08078-08078	RUNNEMEDE
08079-08079	SALEM
08080-08080	SEWELL
08081-08081	SICKLERVILLE
08083-08083	SOMERDALE
08084-08084	STRATFORD
08085-08085	SWEDESBORO
08086-08086	THOROFARE
08087-08087	TUCKERTON
08088-08088	VINCENTOWN
08089-08089	WATERFORD WORKS
08090-08090	WENONAH
08091-08091	WEST BERLIN
08092-08092	WEST CREEK
08093-08093	WESTVILLE
08094-08094	WILLIAMSTOWN
08095-08095	WINSLOW
08096-08096	WOODBURY
08097-08097	WOODBURY HEIGHTS
08098-08098	WOODSTOWN
08099-08099	BELLMAWR
08100-08105	CAMDEN
08106-08106	AUDUBON
08107-08107	OAKLYN
08108-08108	COLLINGSWOOD
08109-08109	MERCHANTVILLE
08110-08110	PENNSAUKEN
08201-08201	ABSECON
08202-08202	AVALON
08203-08203	BRIGANTINE
08204-08204	CAPE MAY
08205-08205	ABSECON
08210-08210	CAPE MAY COURT HOUSE
08212-08212	CAPE MAY POINT
08213-08213	COLOGNE
08214-08214	DENNISVILLE
08215-08215	EGG HARBOR CITY
08217-08217	ELWOOD
08218-08218	GOSHEN
08219-08219	GREEN CREEK
08220-08220	LEEDS POINT
08221-08222	LINWOOD
08223-08223	MARMORA
08224-08224	NEW GRETNA
08225-08225	NORTHFIELD
08226-08226	OCEAN CITY
08227-08227	LINWOOD
08230-08230	OCEAN VIEW
08231-08231	OCEANVILLE
08232-08233	PLEASANTVILLE
08234-08234	EGG HARBOR TOWNSHIP
08240-08240	POMONA
08241-08241	PORT REPUBLIC
08242-08242	RIO GRANDE
08243-08243	SEA ISLE CITY
08244-08244	SOMERS POINT
08245-08245	SOUTH DENNIS
08246-08246	SOUTH SEAVILLE
08247-08247	STONE HARBOR
08248-08248	STRATHMERE
08250-08250	TUCKAHOE
08251-08251	VILLAS
08252-08252	WHITESBORO
08260-08260	WILDWOOD
08270-08270	WOODBINE
08302-08302	BRIDGETON
08310-08310	BUENA
08311-08311	CEDARVILLE
08312-08312	CLAYTON
08313-08313	DEERFIELD STREET
08314-08314	DELMONT
08315-08315	DIVIDING CREEK
08316-08316	DORCHESTER
08317-08317	DOROTHY
08318-08318	ELMER
08319-08319	ESTELL MANOR
08320-08320	FAIRTON
08321-08321	FORTESCUE
08322-08322	FRANKLINVILLE
08323-08323	GREENWICH
08324-08324	HEISLERVILLE
08326-08326	LANDISVILLE
08327-08327	LEESBURG
08328-08328	MALAGA
08329-08329	MAURICETOWN
08330-08330	MAYS LANDING
08332-08332	MILLVILLE
08340-08340	MILMAY
08341-08341	MINOTOLA
08342-08342	MIZPAH
08343-08343	MONROEVILLE
08344-08344	NEWFIELD
08345-08345	NEWPORT
08346-08346	NEWTONVILLE
08347-08347	NORMA
08348-08348	PORT ELIZABETH
08349-08349	PORT NORRIS
08350-08350	RICHLAND
08352-08352	ROSENHAYN
08353-08353	SHILOH
08358-08358	CHERRY HILL
08360-08362	VINELAND
08370-08370	RIVERSIDE
08400-08401	ATLANTIC CITY
08402-08402	MARGATE CITY
08403-08403	LONGPORT
08404-08405	ATLANTIC CITY
08406-08406	VENTNOR CITY
08411-08411	ATLANTIC CITY
08501-08501	ALLENTOWN
08502-08502	BELLE MEAD
08504-08504	BLAWENBURG
08505-08505	BORDENTOWN
08510-08510	CLARKSBURG
08511-08511	COOKSTOWN
08512-08512	CRANBURY
08514-08514	CREAMRIDGE
08514-08514	CREAM RIDGE
08515-08515	CROSSWICKS
08518-08518	FLORENCE
08520-08520	HIGHTSTOWN
08525-08525	HOPEWELL
08526-08526	IMLAYSTOWN
08527-08527	JACKSON
08528-08528	KINGSTON
08530-08530	LAMBERTVILLE
08533-08533	NEW EGYPT
08534-08534	PENNINGTON
08535-08535	PERRINEVILLE
08536-08536	PLAINSBORO
08540-08544	PRINCETON
08550-08550	PRINCETON JUNCTION
08551-08551	RINGOES
08553-08553	ROCKY HILL
08554-08554	ROEBLING
08555-08555	ROOSEVELT
08556-08556	ROSEMONT
08557-08557	SERGEANTSVILLE
08558-08558	SKILLMAN
08559-08559	STOCKTON
08560-08560	TITUSVILLE
08561-08561	WINDSOR
08562-08562	WRIGHTSTOWN
08570-08570	CRANBURY
08600-08695	TRENTON
08701-08701	LAKEWOOD
08720-08720	ALLENWOOD
08721-08721	BAYVILLE
08722-08722	BEACHWOOD
08723-08724	BRICK
08730-08730	BRIELLE
08731-08731	FORKED RIVER
08732-08732	ISLAND HEIGHTS
08733-08733	LAKEHURST
08734-08734	LANOKA HARBOR
08735-08735	LAVALLETTE
08736-08736	MANASQUAN
08738-08738	MANTOLOKING
08739-08739	NORMANDY BEACH
08740-08740	OCEAN GATE
08741-08741	PINE BEACH
08742-08742	POINT PLEASANT BEACH
08750-08750	SEA GIRT
08751-08751	SEASIDE HEIGHTS
08752-08752	SEASIDE PARK
08753-08757	TOMS RIVER
08758-08758	WARETOWN
08759-08759	WHITING
08801-08801	ANNANDALE
08802-08802	ASBURY
08803-08803	BAPTISTOWN
08804-08804	BLOOMSBURY
08805-08805	BOUND BROOK
08807-08807	BRIDGEWATER
08808-08808	BROADWAY
08809-08809	CLINTON
08810-08810	DAYTON
08812-08812	DUNELLEN
08816-08816	EAST BRUNSWICK
08817-08820	EDISON
08821-08821	FLAGTOWN
08822-08822	FLEMINGTON
08823-08823	FRANKLIN PARK
08824-08824	KENDALL PARK
08825-08825	FRENCHTOWN
08826-08826	GLEN GARDNER
08827-08827	HAMPTON
08828-08828	HELMETTA
08829-08829	HIGH BRIDGE
08830-08830	ISELIN
08831-08831	JAMESBURG
08831-08831	MONROE TOWNSHIP
08832-08832	KEASBEY
08833-08833	LEBANON
08834-08834	LITTLE YORK
08835-08835	MANVILLE
08836-08836	MARTINSVILLE
08837-08837	EDISON
08840-08840	METUCHEN
08844-08844	HILLSBOROUGH
08846-08846	MIDDLESEX
08848-08848	MILFORD
08850-08850	MILLTOWN
08852-08852	MONMOUTH JUNCTION
08853-08853	NESHANIC STATION
08854-08854	PISCATAWAY
08857-08857	OLD BRIDGE
08858-08858	OLDWICK
08859-08859	PARLIN
08861-08862	PERTH AMBOY
08863-08863	FORDS
08865-08865	PHILLIPSBURG
08867-08867	PITTSTOWN
08868-08868	QUAKERTOWN
08869-08869	RARITAN
08870-08870	READINGTON
08871-08872	SAYREVILLE
08873-08875	SOMERSET
08876-08876	SOMERVILLE
08877-08877	SOUTH RIVER
08878-08879	SOUTH AMBOY
08880-08880	SOUTH BOUND BROOK
08882-08882	SOUTH RIVER
08884-08884	SPOTSWOOD
08885-08885	STANTON
08886-08886	STEWARTSVILLE
08887-08887	THREE BRIDGES
08888-08888	WHITEHOUSE
08889-08889	WHITEHOUSE STATION
08890-08890	ZAREPHATH
08896-08896	RARITAN
08899-08899	EDISON
08901-08901	NEW BRUNSWICK
08902-08902	NORTH BRUNSWICK
08903-08903	NEW BRUNSWICK
08904-08904	HIGHLAND PARK
08905-08989	NEW BRUNSWICK

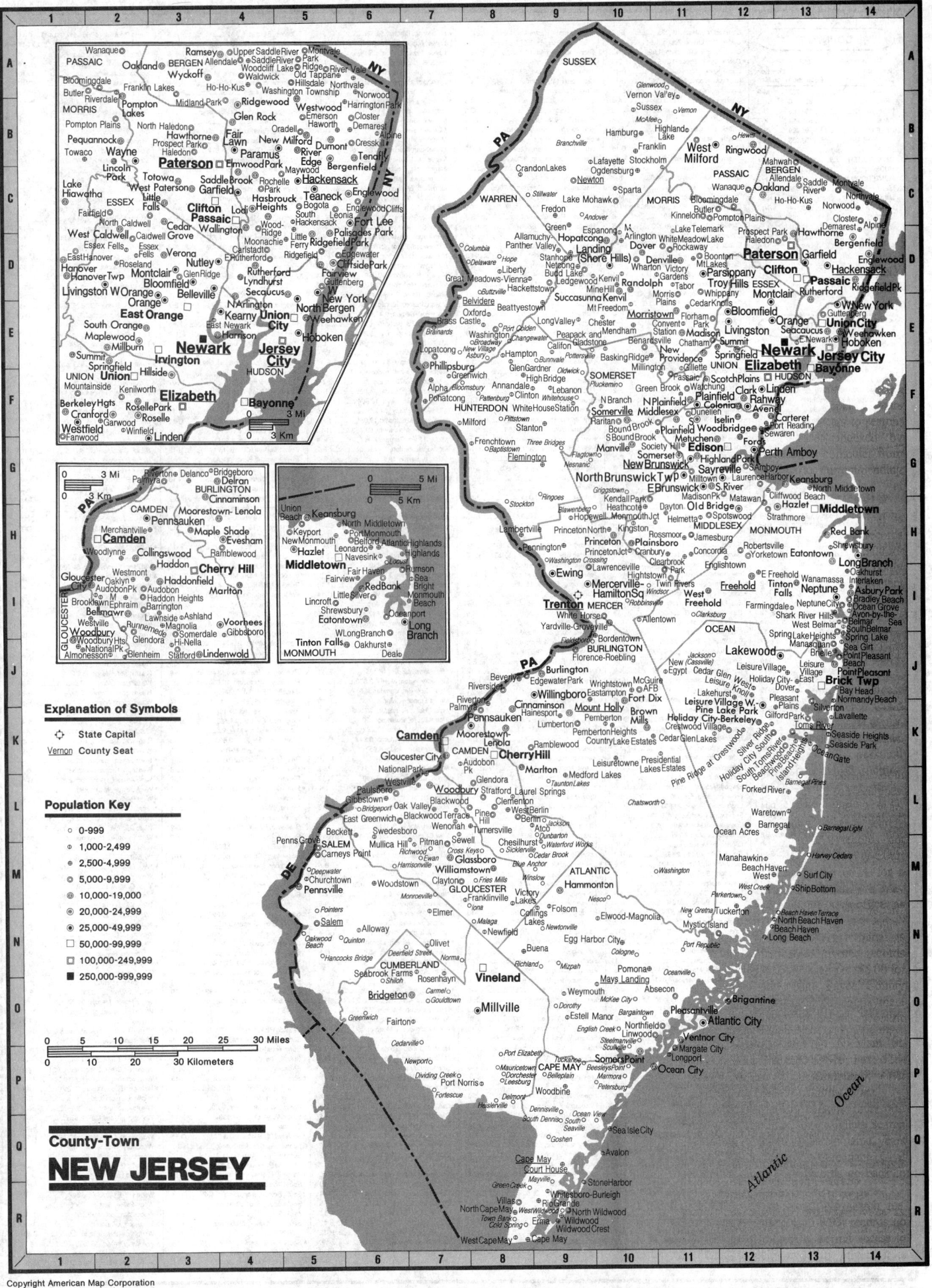

County-Town

NEW JERSEY

COUNTIES

(21 Counties)

Name of County	Population	Location on Map
ATLANTIC	224,327	M-9
BERGEN	825,380	C-12
BURLINGTON	395,066	J-9
CAMDEN	502,824	K-7
CAPE MAY	95,089	P-9
CUMBERLAND	138,053	N-6
ESSEX	778,206	D-12
GLOUCESTER	230,082	M-7
HUDSON	553,099	F-13
HUNTERDON	107,776	F-7
MERCER	325,824	H-9
MIDDLESEX	671,780	H-11
MONMOUTH	553,124	H-12
MORRIS	421,353	C-10
OCEAN	433,203	I-11
PASSAIC	453,060	B-11
SALEM	65,294	M-5
SOMERSET	240,279	F-10
SUSSEX	130,943	A-9
UNION	493,819	F-12
WARREN	91,607	C-8
TOTAL	7,730,188	

CITIES AND TOWNS

Note: The first name is that of the city or town, second, that of the county in which it is located, then the population and location on the map.

Aberdeen, Monmouth, 17,038 ... G-12
Absecon, Atlantic, 7,298 ... O-11
Alexandria, Hunterdon, 3,594 ... F-8
Allamuchy, Warren, 3,484 ... D-9
• Allamuchy-Panther Valley, Warren, 2,764 ... D-9
Allendale, Bergen, 5,900 ... C-13
Allentown, Monmouth, 1,828 ... I-10
• Alloway, Salem, 1,371 ... N-6
Alloway, Salem, 2,795 ... N-6
Almonesson, Gloucester ... J-2
Alpha, Warren, 2,530 ... F-7
Alpine, Bergen, 1,716 ... C-14
Andover, Sussex, 5,438 ... C-9
• Annandale, Hunterdon, 1,074 ... F-9
Asbury Park, Monmouth, 16,799 ... I-14
Ashland, Camden ... I-3
Atco, Camden ... L-9
Atlantic City, Atlantic, 37,986 ... O-11
Atlantic Highlands, Monmouth, 4,629 ... H-6
Audubon, Camden, 9,205 ... I-2
Audubon Park, Camden, 1,150 ... K-7
Avalon, Cape May, 1,809 ... Q-10
• Avenel, Middlesex, 15,504 ... F-12
Avon-by-the-Sea, Monmouth, 2,165 ... I-14
Barnegat, Ocean, 12,235 ... L-12
• Barnegat, Ocean, 1,160 ... L-12
Barrington, Camden, 6,774 ... I-2
Basking Ridge, Somerset ... E-10
Bass River, Burlington, 1,580 ... M-11
Bay Head, Ocean, 1,226 ... J-13
Bayonne, Hudson, 61,444 ... F-13
Beach Haven, Ocean, 1,475 ... N-12
• Beach Haven West, Ocean, 4,237 ... M-12
Beachwood, Ocean, 9,324 ... K-13
• Beattyestown, Warren, 3,966 ... E-9
• Beckett, Gloucester, 3,815 ... M-6
Bedminster, Somerset, 7,086 ... F-10
Belford, Monmouth ... H-6
• *Belleville, Essex, 34,213* ... D-3
Bellmawr, Camden, 12,603 ... I-2
Belmar, Monmouth, 5,877 ... I-14
▲ *Belvidere, Warren, 2,669* ... E-7
Bergenfield, Bergen, 24,458 ... D-14
Berkeley, Ocean, 37,319 ... K-13
• *Berkeley Heights, Union, 11,980* ... F-1
Berlin, Camden, 5,466 ... L-8
Berlin, Camden, 5,672 ... L-8
Bernards, Somerset, 17,199 ... F-10
Bernardsville, Somerset, 6,597 ... E-10
Bethlehem, Hunterdon, 3,104 ... F-8
Beverly, Burlington, 2,973 ... J-8
• Blackwood, Camden, 5,120 ... L-8
Blackwood Terrace, Gloucester ... L-7
Blairstown, Warren, 5,331 ... C-8
Blenheim, Camden ... J-2
• *Bloomfield, Essex, 45,061* ... E-12
Bloomingdale, Passaic, 7,530 ... C-12
Bogota, Bergen, 7,824 ... C-5
Boonton, Morris, 3,566 ... D-11
Boonton, Morris, 8,343 ... D-11
Bordentown, Burlington, 4,341 ... J-10
Bordentown, Burlington, 7,683 ... J-10
Bound Brook, Somerset, 9,487 ... F-11
Bradley Beach, Monmouth, 4,475 ... I-14
Branchburg, Somerset, 10,888 ... F-10
• Brass Castle, Warren, 1,419 ... E-8
• *Brick, Ocean, 66,473* ... J-13
Bridgeboro, Burlington ... G-3
Bridgeton, Cumberland, 18,942 ... O-7
Bridgewater, Somerset, 32,509 ... F-10
Brielle, Monmouth, 4,406 ... J-13
Brigantine, Atlantic, 11,354 ... O-12
Brooklawn, Camden, 1,805 ... I-2
• Brown Mills, Burlington, 11,429 ... K-10
• Budd Lake, Morris, 7,272 ... D-9
Buena, Atlantic, 4,441 ... N-8
Buena Vista, Atlantic, 7,655 ... N-9
Burlington, Burlington, 9,835 ... J-9
▲ *Burlington, Burlington, 12,454* ... J-9
Butler, Morris, 7,392 ... C-12
Byram, Sussex, 8,048 ... D-9
• *Caldwell, Essex, 7,549* ... D-2
Califon, Hunterdon, 1,073 ... E-9
Camden, Camden, 87,492 ... K-7
Cape May, Cape May, 4,668 ... R-8
• Cape May Court House, Cape May, 4,426 ... Q-9
Carlstadt, Bergen, 5,510 ... D-4
• Carneys Point, Salem, 7,686 ... M-5
Carneys Point, Salem, 8,443 ... M-5
Carteret, Middlesex, 19,025 ... F-12
• Cedar Glen Lakes, Ocean, 1,611 ... J-11
• Cedar Glen West, Ocean, 1,396 ... J-12
• *Cedar Grove, Essex, 12,053* ... C-3
Cedar Knolls, Morris ... E-11
Chatham, Morris, 8,007 ... E-11
Chatham, Morris, 9,361 ... E-11
• Cherry Hill, Camden, 69,319 ... K-8
Cherry Hill Township, Camden, 69,348 ... K-8
Chesilhurst, Camden, 1,526 ... M-9
Chester, Morris, 1,214 ... E-10
Chester, Morris, 5,958 ... E-10
Chesterfield, Burlington, 5,152 ... J-10
Churchtown, Salem ... M-5
• *Cinnaminson, Burlington, 14,583* ... K-8
• *Clark, Union, 14,629* ... F-12
Clayton, Gloucester, 6,155 ... M-7
• Clearbrook Park, Middlesex, 2,853 ... H-11
Clementon, Camden, 5,601 ... L-8
Cliffside Park, Bergen, 20,393 ... D-5
• Cliffwood Beach, Monmouth, 3,543 ... G-12
Clifton, Passaic, 71,742 ... D-13
Clinton, Hunterdon, 2,054 ... F-8
Clinton, Hunterdon, 10,816 ... E-9
Closter, Bergen, 8,094 ... C-14
• Collings Lakes, Atlantic, 2,046 ... N-9
Collingswood, Camden, 15,289 ... H-2
• Colonia, Middlesex, 18,238 ... F-12
Colts Neck, Monmouth, 8,559 ... I-13
Commercial, Cumberland, 5,026 ... P-8
• Concordia, Middlesex, 2,683 ... H-11
Convent Station, Morris ... E-11
• Country Lake Estates, Burlington, 4,492 ... K-10
▲ *Cranbury, Middlesex, 2,500* ... H-11
• Crandon Lakes, Sussex, 1,177 ... C-8
• Cranford, Union, 22,624 ... F-2
Cranford, Union, 22,633 ... F-2
Cresskill, Bergen, 7,558 ... B-6
• Crestwood Village, Ocean, 8,030 ... J-11
• Dayton, Middlesex, 4,321 ... H-11
Deal, Monmouth, 1,179 ... J-6
Deerfield, Cumberland, 2,933 ... O-7
• *Delanco, Burlington, 3,316* ... G-3
Delaware, Hunterdon, 4,512 ... G-8
▲ *Delran, Burlington, 13,178* ... G-4
Demarest, Bergen, 4,800 ... D-14
Dennis, Cape May, 5,574 ... P-9
▲ *Denville, Morris, 13,812* ... D-11
Deptford, Gloucester, 24,137 ... L-7
Dover, Morris, 15,115 ... D-10
Dover, Ocean, 76,371 ... K-12
Downe, Cumberland, 1,702 ... P-7
Dumont, Bergen, 17,187 ... B-5
Dunellen, Middlesex, 6,528 ... F-11
Eagleswood, Ocean, 1,476 ... M-12
East Amwell, Hunterdon, 4,332 ... G-9
• *East Brunswick, Middlesex, 43,548* ... G-11
• East Freehold, Monmouth, 3,842 ... I-12
▲ *East Greenwich, Gloucester, 5,258* ... L-7
• *East Hanover, Morris, 9,926* ... D-1
East Newark, Hudson, 2,157 ... E-13
East Orange, Essex, 73,552 ... E-3
East Rutherford, Bergen, 7,902 ... D-4
East Windsor, Mercer, 22,353 ... I-11
▲ *Eastampton, Burlington, 4,962* ... K-9
Eatontown, Monmouth, 13,800 ... H-13
Edgewater, Bergen, 5,001 ... D-5
• *Edgewater Park, Burlington, 8,388* ... J-8
• *Edison, Middlesex, 88,680* ... G-12
Egg Harbor, Atlantic, 24,544 ... O-10
Egg Harbor City, Atlantic, 4,583 ... N-10
Elizabeth, Union, 110,002 ... F-12
Elk, Gloucester, 3,806 ... M-7
Elmer, Salem, 1,571 ... N-7
Elmwood Park, Bergen, 17,623 ... C-4
Elsinboro, Salem, 1,170 ... N-5
• Elwood-Magnolia, Atlantic, 1,487 ... N-10
Emerson, Bergen, 6,930 ... B-5
Englewood, Bergen, 24,850 ... D-14
Englewood Cliffs, Bergen, 5,634 ... C-6
Englishtown, Monmouth, 1,268 ... H-12
• Erma, Cape May, 2,045 ... R-9
Espanong, Morris ... D-10
▲ *Essex Fells, Essex, 2,139* ... D-2
Estell Manor, Atlantic, 1,404 ... O-9
Evesham, Burlington, 35,309 ... L-9
• *Ewing, Mercer, 34,185* ... I-9
Fair Haven, Monmouth, 5,270 ... I-6
Fair Lawn, Bergen, 30,548 ... B-4
Fairfield, Cumberland, 5,699 ... O-6
• *Fairfield, Essex, 7,615* ... C-2
• Fairton, Cumberland, 1,359 ... O-7
Fairview, Bergen, 10,733 ... D-5
• Fairview, Monmouth, 3,853 ... I-6
Fanwood, Union, 7,115 ... G-1
Farmingdale, Monmouth, 1,462 ... I-13
Flemington, Hunterdon, 4,047 ... G-9
Florence, Burlington, 10,266 ... J-9
• Florence-Roebling, Burlington, 8,564 ... J-9
Florham Park, Morris, 8,521 ... E-11
Folsom, Atlantic, 2,181 ... N-9
• Fords, Middlesex, 14,392 ... G-12
• Forked River, Ocean, 4,243 ... L-13
• Fort Dix, Burlington, 10,205 ... J-10
Fort Lee, Bergen, 31,997 ... C-6
Frankford, Sussex, 5,114 ... B-10
Franklin, Gloucester, 14,482 ... N-8
Franklin, Hunterdon, 2,851 ... F-8
Franklin, Somerset, 42,780 ... G-10
Franklin, Sussex, 4,977 ... B-10
Franklin, Warren, 2,404 ... E-7
Franklin Lakes, Bergen, 9,873 ... A-3
Franklinville, Gloucester ... M-7
Fredon, Sussex, 2,763 ... C-9
Freehold, Monmouth, 10,742 ... I-12
Freehold, Monmouth, 24,710 ... I-12
Frelinghuysen, Warren, 1,779 ... D-9
Frenchtown, Hunterdon, 1,528 ... G-8
Galloway, Atlantic, 23,330 ... N-11
Garfield, Bergen, 26,727 ... D-13
Garwood, Union, 4,227 ... F-2
Gibbsboro, Camden, 2,383 ... I-4
• Gibbstown, Gloucester, 3,902 ... L-6
• Gilford Park, Ocean, 8,668 ... K-13
Gillette, Morris ... F-11
Glassboro, Gloucester, 15,614 ... M-7
Glen Gardner, Hunterdon, 1,665 ... E-8
• *Glen Ridge, Essex, 7,076* ... D-3
Glen Rock, Bergen, 10,883 ... B-4
• Glendora, Camden, 5,201 ... L-8
Gloucester, Camden, 53,797 ... L-8
Gloucester City, Camden, 12,649 ... K-7
• Great Meadows-Vienna, Warren, 1,108 ... D-8
Green, Sussex, 2,709 ... C-9
Green Brook, Somerset, 4,460 ... F-11
Greenwich, Gloucester, 5,102 ... L-6
▲ *Greenwich, Warren, 1,899* ... F-7
Guttenberg, Hudson, 8,268 ... E-13
Hackensack, Bergen, 37,049 ... C-5
Hackettstown, Warren, 8,120 ... D-9
▲ *Haddon, Camden, 14,837* ... I-2
Haddon Heights, Camden, 7,860 ... I-2
Haddonfield, Camden, 11,628 ... I-3
▲ *Hainesport, Burlington, 3,249* ... K-9
Haledon, Passaic, 6,951 ... B-3
Hamburg, Sussex, 2,566 ... B-10
Hamilton, Atlantic, 16,012 ... N-9
Hamilton, Mercer, 86,553 ... I-9
Hammonton, Atlantic, 12,208 ... M-9
Hampton, Hunterdon, 1,515 ... E-8
Hampton, Sussex, 4,438 ... C-9
• *Hanover, Morris, 11,538* ... D-1
Harding, Morris, 3,640 ... E-11
Hardwick, Warren, 1,235 ... C-8
Hardyston, Sussex, 5,275 ... B-10
Harmony, Warren, 2,653 ... E-7
Harrington Park, Bergen, 4,623 ... B-6
Harrison, Gloucester, 4,715 ... M-7
Harrison, Hudson, 13,425 ... E-4
Hasbrouck Heights, Bergen, 11,488 ... C-5
Haworth, Bergen, 3,384 ... B-5
Hawthorne, Passaic, 17,084 ... D-13
Hazlet, Monmouth, 21,976 ... H-13
• Heathcote, Middlesex, 3,112 ... H-10
Helmetta, Middlesex, 1,211 ... H-11
High Bridge, Hunterdon, 3,886 ... F-8
• Highland Lake, Sussex, 4,550 ... B-11
Highland Park, Middlesex, 13,279 ... G-11
Highlands, Monmouth, 4,849 ... H-6
Hightstown, Mercer, 5,126 ... I-11
Hillsborough, Somerset, 28,808 ... G-10
Hillsdale, Bergen, 9,750 ... A-5
• *Hillside, Union, 21,044* ... E-3
Hi-Nella, Camden, 1,045 ... J-3
Ho-Ho-Kus, Bergen, 3,935 ... C-13
Hoboken, Hudson, 33,397 ... E-13
• Holiday City-Berkeley, Ocean, 14,293 ... K-12
• Holiday City-Dover, Ocean, 2,391 ... J-13
• Holiday City South, Ocean, 5,452 ... K-12
Holland, Hunterdon, 4,892 ... F-7
Holmdel, Monmouth, 11,532 ... H-13
Hopatcong, Sussex, 15,586 ... D-10
Hope, Warren, 1,719 ... D-8
Hopewell, Cumberland, 4,215 ... O-7
Hopewell, Mercer, 1,968 ... H-9
Hopewell, Mercer, 11,590 ... H-9
Howell, Monmouth, 38,987 ... I-13
Independence, Warren, 3,940 ... E-8
• Irvington, Essex, 59,774 ... E-3
Irvington, Essex, 61,018 ... E-3
• Iselin, Middlesex, 16,141 ... F-12
Island Heights, Ocean, 1,470 ... K-13
Jackson, Ocean, 33,233 ... J-11
Jamesburg, Middlesex, 5,294 ... H-11
Jefferson, Morris, 17,825 ... C-10
Jersey City, Hudson, 228,537 ... E-13
Keansburg, Monmouth, 11,069 ... G-13
Kearny, Hudson, 34,874 ... E-4
• Kendall Park, Middlesex, 7,127 ... G-10
Kenilworth, Union, 7,574 ... F-2
Kenvil, Morris ... D-10
Keyport, Monmouth, 7,586 ... H-5
• Kingston, Middlesex, 1,047 ... H-10
Kingwood, Hunterdon, 3,325 ... G-8
Kinnelon, Morris, 8,470 ... C-11
Knowlton, Warren, 2,543 ... D-8
Lacey, Ocean, 22,141 ... L-12
Lafayette, Sussex, 1,902 ... C-10
Lake Hiawatha, Morris ... C-1
• Lake Mohawk, Sussex, 8,930 ... C-10
• Lake Telemark, Morris, 1,121 ... D-11
Lakehurst, Ocean, 3,078 ... J-12
• Lakewood, Ocean, 26,095 ... J-13
Lakewood, Ocean, 45,048 ... J-13
Lambertville, Hunterdon, 3,927 ... H-8
Landing (Shore Hills), Morris ... D-10
Laurel Springs, Camden, 2,341 ... L-8
• Laurence Harbor, Middlesex, 6,361 ... G-12
Lavallette, Ocean, 2,299 ... K-13
Lawnside, Camden, 2,841 ... I-3
Lawrence, Cumberland, 2,433 ... O-7
Lawrence, Mercer, 25,787 ... H-9
• Lawrenceville, Mercer, 6,446 ... H-9
Lebanon, Hunterdon, 1,036 ... F-9
Lebanon, Hunterdon, 5,679 ... E-8
Ledgewood, Morris ... D-10
• Leisure Knoll, Ocean, 2,707 ... J-12
• Leisure Village, Ocean, 4,295 ... J-13
• Leisure Village East, Ocean, 1,989 ... J-13
• Leisure Village West-Pine Lake Park, Ocean, 10,139 ... K-12
Leisuretowne, Burlington, 2,552 ... K-9
• Leonardo, Monmouth, 3,788 ... H-6
Leonia, Bergen, 8,365 ... C-5
▲ *Liberty, Warren, 2,493* ... D-8
Lincoln Park, Morris, 10,978 ... B-2
• Lincroft, Monmouth, 6,193 ... I-5
Linden, Union, 36,701 ... F-12
Lindenwold, Camden, 18,734 ... J-3
Linwood, Atlantic, 6,866 ... O-10
Little Egg Harbor, Ocean, 13,333 ... M-12
• *Little Falls, Passaic, 11,294* ... C-3
Little Ferry, Bergen, 9,989 ... D-5
Little Silver, Monmouth, 5,721 ... I-6
• *Livingston, Essex, 26,609* ... E-12
Lodi, Bergen, 22,355 ... C-4
Logan, Gloucester, 5,147 ... L-6
Long Beach, Ocean, 3,407 ... N-12
Long Branch, Monmouth, 28,658 ... H-14
▲ *Long Hill, Morris, 7,826* ... F-11
• Long Valley, Morris, 1,744 ... E-9
Longport, Atlantic, 1,224 ... P-11
▲ *Lopatcong, Warren, 5,052* ... F-7
Lower, Cape May, 20,820 ... R-9
Lower Alloways Creek, Salem, 1,858 ... N-5
▲ *Lumberton, Burlington, 6,705* ... K-9
• *Lyndhurst, Bergen, 18,262* ... D-4
Madison, Morris, 15,850 ... E-11
• Madison Park, Middlesex, 7,490 ... G-12
Magnolia, Camden, 4,861 ... I-3
Mahwah, Bergen ... C-13
Mahwah, Bergen, 17,905 ... C-13
• Manahawkin, Ocean, 1,594 ... M-12
Manalapan, Monmouth, 26,716 ... I-12
Manasquan, Monmouth, 5,369 ... J-13
Manchester, Ocean, 35,976 ... K-11
Mannington, Salem, 1,693 ... M-6
Mansfield, Burlington, 3,874 ... J-10
Mansfield, Warren, 7,154 ... E-8
Mantua, Gloucester, 10,074 ... M-7
Manville, Somerset, 10,567 ... G-10
• *Maple Shade, Burlington, 19,211* ... H-3
Maplewood, Essex, 21,652 ... E-2
• Maplewood, Essex, 21,756 ... E-2
Margate City, Atlantic, 8,431 ... P-11
Marlboro, Monmouth, 27,974 ... H-12
• Marlton, Burlington, 10,228 ... I-4
Matawan, Monmouth, 9,270 ... H-12
Maurice River, Cumberland, 6,648 ... O-8
• Mays Landing, Atlantic, 2,090 ... O-10
Maywood, Bergen, 9,473 ... C-5
• McGuire AFB, Burlington, 7,580 ... J-10
Medford, Burlington, 20,526 ... L-9
Medford Lakes, Burlington, 4,462 ... L-9
Mendham, Morris, 4,537 ... E-10
Mendham, Morris, 4,890 ... E-10
• Mercerville-Hamilton Square, Mercer, 26,873 ... I-9
Merchantville, Camden, 4,095 ... H-2
Metuchen, Middlesex, 12,804 ... G-12
Middle, Cape May, 14,771 ... Q-9
Middlesex, Middlesex, 13,055 ... F-11
Middletown, Monmouth, 68,183 ... H-13
Midland Park, Bergen, 7,047 ... B-4
Milford, Hunterdon, 1,273 ... F-7
• *Millburn, Essex, 18,630* ... E-2
Millington, Morris ... F-11
Millstone, Monmouth, 5,069 ... I-11
Milltown, Middlesex, 6,968 ... G-11
Millville, Cumberland, 25,992 ... O-8
▲ *Mine Hill, Morris, 3,333* ... D-10
Monmouth Beach, Monmouth, 3,303 ... I-7
• Monmouth Junction, Middlesex, 1,570 ... H-10
Monroe, Gloucester, 26,703 ... M-8
Monroe, Middlesex, 22,255 ... H-11
Montague, Sussex, 2,832 ... A-9
• *Montclair, Essex, 37,729* ... E-12
Montgomery, Somerset, 9,612 ... G-10
Montvale, Bergen, 6,946 ... C-14
Montville, Morris, 15,600 ... D-12
Moonachie, Bergen, 2,817 ... D-5
Moorestown, Burlington, 16,116 ... K-8
• Moorestown-Lenola, Burlington, 13,242 ... K-8
Morris, Morris, 19,952 ... E-11
Morris Plains, Morris, 5,219 ... E-11
▲ *Morristown, Morris, 16,189* ... E-11
Mount Arlington, Morris, 3,630 ... D-10
Mount Ephraim, Camden, 4,517 ... I-2
Mount Freedom, Morris ... E-10
• *Mount Holly, Burlington, 10,639* ... K-9
Mount Laurel, Burlington, 30,270 ... K-8
Mount Olive, Morris, 21,282 ... D-9
Mountain Lakes, Morris, 3,847 ... D-11
Mountainside, Union, 6,657 ... F-1
Mullica, Atlantic, 5,896 ... M-10
• Mullica Hill, Gloucester, 1,117 ... M-7
• Mystic Island, Ocean, 7,400 ... N-12
National Park, Gloucester, 3,413 ... L-7
Navesink, Monmouth ... H-6
Neptune, Monmouth, 28,148 ... I-13
Neptune City, Monmouth, 4,997 ... I-14
Netcong, Morris, 3,311 ... D-9
New Brunswick, Middlesex, 41,711 ... G-11
• New Egypt, Ocean, 2,327 ... J-11
New Hanover, Burlington, 9,546 ... J-10
New Milford, Bergen, 15,990 ... B-5
New Monmouth, Monmouth ... H-5
New Providence, Union, 11,439 ... E-11
Newark, Essex, 275,221 ... E-13
Newfield, Gloucester, 1,592 ... N-8
Newton, Sussex, 7,521 ... C-9
Normandy Beach, Ocean ... J-13
North Arlington, Bergen, 13,790 ... D-4
• North Beach Haven, Ocean, 2,413 ... N-12
• *North Bergen, Hudson, 48,414* ... D-5
North Branch, Somerset ... F-10
• *North Brunswick, Middlesex, 31,287* ... G-11
• *North Caldwell, Essex, 6,706* ... C-2
• North Cape May, Cape May, 3,574 ... R-8
North Haledon, Passaic, 7,987 ... B-3
North Hanover, Burlington, 9,994 ... J-10
• North Middletown, Monmouth, 3,160 ... G-13
North Plainfield, Somerset, 18,820 ... F-11
North Wildwood, Cape May, 5,017 ... R-9
Northfield, Atlantic, 7,305 ... O-11
Northvale, Bergen, 4,563 ... C-14
Norwood, Bergen, 4,858 ... C-14
• *Nutley, Essex, 27,099* ... D-4
• Oak Valley, Gloucester, 4,055 ... L-7
• Oakhurst, Monmouth, 4,130 ... J-6
Oakland, Bergen, 11,997 ... C-12
Oaklyn, Camden, 4,430 ... I-2
Ocean, Monmouth, 25,058 ... I-13
Ocean, Ocean, 5,416 ... L-12
• Ocean Acres, Ocean, 5,587 ... L-12
Ocean City, Cape May, 15,512 ... P-10
Ocean Gate, Ocean, 2,078 ... K-13
• Ocean Grove, Monmouth, 4,818 ... I-14
Oceanport, Monmouth, 6,146 ... I-6
Ogdensburg, Sussex, 2,722 ... C-10
• Old Bridge, Middlesex, 22,151 ... H-12
Old Bridge, Middlesex, 56,475 ... H-12
Old Tappan, Bergen, 4,254 ... A-5
Oldmans, Salem, 1,683 ... L-5
• Olivet, Salem, 1,315 ... N-7
Oradell, Bergen, 8,024 ... B-5
• *Orange, Essex, 29,925* ... E-12
• Oxford, Warren, 1,767 ... E-8
Oxford, Warren, 1,790 ... E-8
Palisades Park, Bergen, 14,536 ... D-5
Palmyra, Burlington, 7,056 ... K-8
Paramus, Bergen, 25,067 ... B-4
Park Ridge, Bergen, 8,102 ... A-5
• *Parsippany-Troy Hills Township, Morris, 48,478* ... D-11
Passaic, Passaic, 58,041 ... D-13
Paterson, Passaic, 140,891 ... D-13
Paulsboro, Gloucester, 6,577 ... L-6
Peapack and Gladstone, Somerset, 2,111 ... E-10
Pemberton, Burlington, 1,367 ... K-10
Pemberton, Burlington, 31,342 ... K-10
• Pemberton Heights, Burlington, 2,941 ... K-10
Pennington, Mercer, 2,537 ... H-9
Penns Grove, Salem, 5,228 ... M-5
• Pennsauken, Camden, 34,733 ... K-8
Pennsauken, Camden, 34,738 ... K-8
• Pennsville, Salem, 12,218 ... M-5
Pennsville, Salem, 13,794 ... M-5
• *Pequannock Township, Morris, 12,844* ... D-2
Perth Amboy, Middlesex, 41,967 ... G-12
Phillipsburg, Warren, 15,757 ... E-7
Pilesgrove, Salem, 3,250 ... M-6
Pine Beach, Ocean, 1,954 ... K-13
Pine Hill, Camden, 9,854 ... L-8
• Pine Ridge at Crestwood, Ocean, 2,372 ... K-12
Piscataway, Middlesex, 47,089 ... F-11
Pitman, Gloucester, 9,365 ... M-7
Pittsgrove, Salem, 8,121 ... N-7
Plainfield, Union, 46,567 ... F-11
▲ *Plainsboro, Middlesex, 14,213* ... H-10
• Pleasant Plains, Ocean, 2,577 ... K-12
Pleasantville, Atlantic, 16,027 ... O-11
Plumsted, Ocean, 6,005 ... J-11
▲ *Pohatcong, Warren, 3,591* ... F-7
Point Pleasant, Ocean, 18,177 ... J-13
Point Pleasant Beach, Ocean, 5,112 ... J-13
• Pomona, Atlantic, 2,624 ... N-10
Pompton Lakes, Passaic, 10,539 ... A-2
Pompton Plains, Morris ... B-2
• Port Monmouth, Monmouth, 3,558 ... H-6
• Port Norris, Cumberland, 1,701 ... P-8
• Port Reading, Middlesex, 3,977 ... F-12
• Presidential Lakes Estates, Burlington, 2,450 ... K-11
Princeton, Mercer, 12,016 ... H-10
Princeton, Mercer, 13,198 ... H-10
• Princeton Junction, Mercer, 2,362 ... H-10
• Princeton North, Mercer, 4,386 ... H-10
Prospect Park, Passaic, 5,053 ... D-13
Quinton, Salem, 2,511 ... N-6
Rahway, Union, 25,325 ... F-12
• Ramblewood, Burlington, 6,181 ... K-9
Ramsey, Bergen, 13,228 ... A-4
Randolph, Morris, 19,974 ... E-10
Raritan, Hunterdon, 15,616 ... G-9
Raritan, Somerset, 5,798 ... F-10
Readington, Hunterdon, 13,400 ... F-9
Red Bank, Monmouth, 10,636 ... H-13
Ridgefield, Bergen, 9,996 ... D-5
Ridgefield Park, Bergen, 12,454 ... D-14
Ridgewood, Bergen, 24,152 ... B-4
Ringwood, Passaic, 12,623 ... B-12
• Rio Grande, Cape May, 2,505 ... R-9
River Edge, Bergen, 10,603 ... B-5
• *River Vale, Bergen, 9,410* ... A-5
Riverdale, Morris, 2,370 ... A-2
• *Riverside, Burlington, 7,974* ... J-8
Riverton, Burlington, 2,775 ... K-8
• Robertsville, Monmouth, 9,841 ... H-12
• *Rochelle Park, Bergen, 5,587* ... C-4
Rockaway, Morris, 19,572 ... D-11
Rockaway, Morris, 6,243 ... D-11
Roseland, Essex, 4,847 ... D-2
Roselle, Union, 20,314 ... F-2
Roselle Park, Union, 12,805 ... F-2
• Rosenhayn, Cumberland, 1,053 ... N-7
• Rossmoor, Middlesex, 3,231 ... H-11
Roxbury, Morris, 20,429 ... D-10
Rumson, Monmouth, 6,701 ... I-6
Runnemede, Camden, 9,042 ... I-2
Rutherford, Bergen, 17,790 ... E-13
• *Saddle Brook, Bergen, 13,296* ... C-4
Saddle River, Bergen, 2,950 ... A-4
Salem, Salem, 6,883 ... N-5
Sandyston, Sussex, 1,732 ... A-9
Sayreville, Middlesex, 34,986 ... G-12
• *Scotch Plains, Union, 21,160* ... F-11
Sea Bright, Monmouth, 1,693 ... I-7
Sea Girt, Monmouth, 2,099 ... J-14
Sea Isle City, Cape May, 2,692 ... Q-10
• Seabrook Farms, Cumberland, 1,457 ... N-7
Seaside Heights, Ocean, 2,366 ... K-13
Seaside Park, Ocean, 1,871 ... K-13
Secaucus, Hudson, 14,061 ... D-5
• Sewaren, Middlesex, 2,569 ... F-12
Sewell, Gloucester ... L-7
Shamong, Burlington, 5,765 ... L-9
• Shark River Hills, Monmouth, 4,228 ... I-13
Ship Bottom, Ocean, 1,352 ... M-13
Shrewsbury, Monmouth, 1,098 ... I-6
Shrewsbury, Monmouth, 3,096 ... I-6
Silver Ridge, Ocean, 1,138 ... K-12
• Silverton, Ocean, 9,175 ... J-13
• Society Hill, Middlesex, 3,577 ... G-11
Somerdale, Camden, 5,440 ... J-3
Somers Point, Atlantic, 11,216 ... P-10
• Somerset, Somerset, 22,070 ... G-11
Somerville, Somerset, 11,632 ... F-10
South Amboy, Middlesex, 7,863 ... G-12
South Belmar, Monmouth, 1,482 ... I-14
South Bound Brook, Somerset, 4,185 ... G-11
South Brunswick, Middlesex, 25,792 ... H-11
▲ *South Hackensack, Bergen, 2,106* ... C-5
South Harrison, Gloucester, 1,919 ... M-6
• *South Orange, Essex, 16,390* ... E-2
South Plainfield, Middlesex, 20,489 ... F-11
South River, Middlesex, 13,692 ... G-11
South Toms River, Ocean, 3,869 ... K-13
Southampton, Burlington, 10,202 ... K-10
Sparta, Sussex ... C-10
Sparta, Sussex, 15,157 ... C-10
Spotswood, Middlesex, 7,983 ... H-11
Spring Lake, Monmouth, 3,499 ... I-14
Spring Lake Heights, Monmouth, 5,341 ... I-13
Springfield, Burlington, 3,028 ... J-10
• *Springfield, Union, 13,420* ... E-12
Stafford, Ocean, 13,325 ... M-12
Stanhope, Sussex, 3,393 ... D-9
Stanton, Hunterdon ... F-9
Stillwater, Sussex, 4,253 ... C-9
Stockholm, Sussex ... C-11
Stone Harbor, Cape May, 1,025 ... R-9
Stow Creek, Cumberland, 1,437 ... N-6
Stratford, Camden, 7,614 ... L-8
• Strathmore, Monmouth, 7,060 ... H-12
• Succasunna-Kenvil, Morris, 11,781 ... D-10
Summit, Union, 19,757 ... E-12
Surf City, Ocean, 1,375 ... M-13
Sussex, Sussex, 2,201 ... R-10
Swedesboro, Gloucester, 2,024 ... L-6
Tabernacle, Burlington, 7,360 ... L-10
Tabor (Mount Tabor), Morris ... D-11
• *Teaneck, Bergen, 37,825* ... C-5
Tenafly, Bergen, 13,326 ... B-6
Tewksbury, Hunterdon, 4,803 ... E-9
Tinton Falls, Monmouth, 12,361 ... I-13
• Toms River, Ocean, 7,524 ... K-13
Totowa, Passaic, 10,177 ... C-3
Towaco, Morris ... B-1
Trenton, Mercer, 88,675 ... I-9
Tuckerton, Ocean, 3,048 ... N-12
• Turnersville, Gloucester, 3,843 ... L-8
• Twin Rivers, Mercer, 7,715 ... I-11
Union, Hunterdon, 5,078 ... F-8
• *Union, Union, 50,024* ... F-2
Union Beach, Monmouth, 6,156 ... H-5
Union City, Hudson, 58,012 ... E-5
Upper, Cape May, 10,681 ... P-10
Upper Deerfield, Cumberland, 6,927 ... N-7
Upper Freehold, Monmouth, 3,277 ... I-11
Upper Pittsgrove, Salem, 3,140 ... M-7
Upper Saddle River, Bergen, 7,198 ... A-4
Ventnor City, Atlantic, 11,005 ... O-11
Vernon, Sussex, 21,211 ... B-11
• Vernon Valley, Sussex, 1,696 ... B-11
• *Verona, Essex, 13,597* ... D-3
Victory Gardens, Morris, 1,314 ... D-11
• Victory Lakes, Gloucester, 2,160 ... N-8
• Villas, Cape May, 8,136 ... R-8
Vineland, Cumberland, 54,780 ... N-8
▲ *Voorhees, Camden, 24,559* ... I-3
Waldwick, Bergen, 9,757 ... A-4
Wall, Monmouth, 20,244 ... I-13
Wallington, Bergen, 10,828 ... C-4
• Wanamassa, Monmouth, 4,530 ... I-14
Wanaque, Passaic, 9,711 ... C-12
Wantage, Sussex, 9,487 ... A-10
• Waretown, Ocean, 1,283 ... L-13
Warren, Somerset, 10,830 ... F-11
Washington, Gloucester, 41,960 ... L-7
Washington, Mercer, 5,815 ... I-10
Washington, Morris, 15,592 ... E-9
Washington, Warren, 5,367 ... E-8
Washington, Warren, 6,474 ... E-8
• *Washington Township, Bergen, 9,245* ... A-4
Watchung, Somerset, 5,110 ... F-11
Waterford, Camden, 10,940 ... M-9
• *Wayne, Passaic, 47,025* ... B-2
• *Weehawken, Hudson, 12,385* ... E-14
Wenonah, Gloucester, 2,331 ... L-7
West Amwell, Hunterdon, 2,251 ... H-8
• West Belmar, Monmouth, 2,498 ... I-13
West Berlin, Camden ... L-8
• *West Caldwell, Essex, 10,422* ... D-2
West Cape May, Cape May, 1,026 ... R-8
West Deptford, Gloucester, 19,380 ... L-7
• West Freehold, Monmouth, 11,166 ... I-11
West Long Branch, Monmouth, 7,690 ... I-6
• *West Milford, Passaic, 25,430* ... B-12
West New York, Hudson, 38,125 ... E-13
• *West Orange, Essex, 39,103* ... D-3
West Paterson, Passaic, 10,982 ... C-3
West Windsor, Mercer, 16,021 ... I-10
Westampton, Burlington, 6,004 ... J-9
Westfield, Union, 28,870 ... F-1
Westmont, Camden ... I-2
Westville, Gloucester, 4,573 ... L-7
Westwood, Bergen, 10,446 ... B-5
▲ *Weymouth, Atlantic, 1,957* ... O-9
Wharton, Morris, 5,405 ... D-10
Whippany, Morris ... D-11
White, Warren, 3,603 ... E-7
• White Horse, Mercer, 9,397 ... I-10
• White House Station, Hunterdon, 1,287 ... F-9
• White Meadow Lake, Morris, 8,002 ... D-11
• Whitesboro-Burleigh, Cape May, 2,080 ... R-9
Wildwood, Cape May, 4,484 ... R-9
Wildwood Crest, Cape May, 3,631 ... R-9
• Williamstown, Gloucester, 10,891 ... M-8
• *Willingboro, Burlington, 36,291* ... J-9
▲ *Winfield, Union, 1,576* ... F-2
Winslow, Camden, 30,087 ... M-9
Woodbine, Cape May, 2,678 ... P-9
• Woodbridge, Middlesex, 17,434 ... F-12
Woodbridge, Middlesex, 93,086 ... F-12
Woodbury, Gloucester, 10,904 ... L-7
Woodbury Heights, Gloucester, 3,392 ... J-1
Woodcliff Lake, Bergen, 5,303 ... A-5
Woodland, Burlington, 2,063 ... L-11
Woodlynne, Camden, 2,547 ... H-2
Wood-Ridge, Bergen, 7,506 ... C-4
Woolwich, Gloucester, 1,459 ... M-6
Wrightstown, Burlington, 3,843 ... J-10
• *Wyckoff, Bergen, 15,372* ... A-3
• Yardville-Groveville, Mercer, 9,248 ... I-10
• Yorktown, Monmouth, 6,313 ... M-12

Explanation of symbols: • – Census Designated Place (CDP) ▲ *italics* – Townships (shown on the map) • *italics* – Township shown which is also a CDP *italics* – Townships (not shown on the map)

New Mexico

General Help Numbers:

Governor's Office
State Capitol, Room 400　　　　505-476-2200
Santa Fe, NM 87503　　　　Fax 505-676-3026
www.governor.state.nm.us　　　　8AM-5PM

Attorney General's Office
PO Drawer 1508　　　　505-827-6000
Santa Fe, NM 87504-1508　　Fax 505-827-5826
www.ago.state.nm.us　　　　8AM-5PM

Legislative Records
Legislative Council Service
State Capitol Bldg, Room 411　　505-986-4600
Santa Fe, NM 87501　　　Fax 505-986-4610
http://legis.state.nm.us　　　　8AM-5PM

State Archives
1205 Camino Carlos Rey　　　505-476-7908
Santa Fe, NM 87505　　　Fax 505-476-7909
www.nmcpr.state.nm.us/　　　　8AM-5PM

State Specifics:

Capital:　　　　　　　　　　Santa Fe
　　　　　　　　　　　　Santa Fe County

Time Zone:　　　　　　　　　　MST

Number of Counties:　　　　　　　33

Population:　　　　　　　　1,874,614

Web Site:　　　　　　　　www.state.nm.us

State Agencies

Criminal Records

Department of Public Safety, Criminal Records Bureau, PO Box 1628, Santa Fe, NM 87504-1628 (Courier: 4491 Cerrillos Rd, Santa Fe, NM 87504); 505-827-9181, 505-827-3388 (Fax), 8AM-5PM.

www.dps.nm.org

Indexing & Storage: Records are available from 1935 on. It takes 2 to 4 weeks before new records are available for inquiry. Records are indexed on inhouse computer (93%); historical paper records are added to computer once requested. Records are normally destroyed after 99 years.

Searching: Fingerprint search requests are not available except for checks for childern or elderly-

related occupations mandated by state statute, and an FBI search can be done for those groups. The state's records are 100% fingerprint-supported. Include the following in your request-date of birth, Social Security Number, full name, signed release. The signed release from person of record authorizing the State of New Mexico to release records to specific requester must be notorized. A copy of the request form is found at www.dps.nm.org/faq/auth_release_info.pdf.

Access by: mail, in person, online.

Fee & Payment: The fee is $7.00 per individual. Fee payee: Department of Public Safety. Prepayment required. Must use cashiers check or money order. No credit cards accepted.

Mail search: Turnaround time: 1 to 2 weeks. Turnaround time is for "no record found." If records exist, turnaround time may be 3 to 4 weeks. A SASE is requested.

In person search: If records are found, they may be available in 5 to 7 working days.

Online search: Online access is available from www.osogrande.com/online-services.html. The fee is $10.00. You must set up an account to receive a password. When a record is found, a signed release from the subject must then be presented (faxed) to DPS in order to receive the detail page. For more information visit the website mentioned or call 505-345-6555.

Statewide Court Records

Administrative Office of the Courts, 237 Don Gaspar, Rm 25, Santa Fe, NM 87501; 505-827-4800, 505-827-4246 (Fax), 8AM-5PM.

www.nmcourts.com

Indexing & Storage: Records are available since 1997, in general. It takes 48 hours before new records are available for inquiry.

Access by: online. No searching by mail.

Online search: The www.nmcourts.com website offers free access to District and Magistrate Court case information, except Bernalillo Metro which has its own system. In general, records are available from June 1997 forward. Search by name or case #. The search is inclusive of all participating counties. The website also offers a DWI Offender History tool for researching an individual's DWI history. Search by name or SSN. Supreme Court opinions may be researched at www.supremecourt.nm.org/.

Sexual Offender Registry

Department of Public Safety, Records Bureau, PO Box 1628, Santa Fe, NM 87504-1628 (Courier: 4491 Cerrillos Rd, Santa Fe, NM 87504); 505-827-9297, 505-827-9193, 505-827-3388 (Fax), 8AM-5PM.

www.nmsexoffender.dps.state.nm.us/

Indexing & Storage: Records are available from 07/95. It takes 2 to 4 weeks before new records are available for inquiry. Records are normally destroyed after individual moves out of state.

Searching: The work address belonging to a sex offender is released if he/she will come into direct contact with children. The following data is not released: SSN

Access by: mail, phone, online.

Fee & Payment: There is no fee.

Mail search: Turnaround time: 1 to 2 weeks. A SASE is requested.

Phone search: Name searching available by phone.

Online search: The website offers a variety of search methods including by name, county, city, and ZIP Code. The site also offers a complete state list, also an absconder list.

Incarceration Records

New Mexico Corrections Department, Central Records Unit, PO Box 27116, Santa Fe, NM 87502; 505-827-8674, 505-827-8801 (Fax), 8AM-5PM.

http://corrections.state.nm.us/

Indexing & Storage: Records are available on current and former inmates. It takes 1-3 days before new records are available for inquiry. Records are normally destroyed after 50 years.

Searching: Include the following in your request-name; DOB and SSN are helpful. Location, conviction and sentencing information, behavior, release dates are provided.

Access by: mail, phone, online.

Fee & Payment: Fee is $.50 per copy. Fee payee: NM Department of Corrections

Mail search: Turnaround time: 7 to 10 days.

Phone search: Limited name searching available.

Online search: To search at the website, you must first click on Offender Information, then on Offender Search.

Corporation, Limited Liability Company Records

New Mexico Public Regulation Commission, Corporations Bureau, PO Box 1269, Santa Fe, NM 87504-1269 (Courier: 1120 Paseo de Peralta, Pera Bldg 4th Fl, Rm 413, Santa Fe, NM 87501); 505-827-4502 (Main Number), 800-947-4722 (In-state Only), 505-827-4510 (Good Standing), 505-827-4513 (Copy Request), 505-827-4387 (Fax), 8AM-12:00: 1PM-5PM.

www.nmprc.state.nm.us/corporations/corpshome.htm

Note: For Charter Requirement Information call 505-827-4511.

Indexing & Storage: Records are available for all entities. It takes 1-2 days before new records are available for inquiry. Records are indexed on microfilm. Records are normally destroyed after 5 years.

Searching: Include the following in your request-full name of business. In addition to the articles of incorporation, corporation records include the following information: Annual Reports, Officers, Directors, Prior (merged) names, Inactive, Registered and Reserved names. The following data is not released: financial information.

Access by: mail, phone, fax, in person, online.

Fee & Payment: There is no charge for a computer printout. Copies are $1.00 per page with minimum fee of $10.00 for for-profit companies or domestic LLCs and $5.00 for non-profit companies. Certification fee is $25.00, except for non-profits which is $10.00. Fee payee: Public Regulation Commission. Payment is due in 10 days. Personal checks accepted. No credit cards accepted.

Mail search: Turnaround time: 2 days. A SASE is requested.

Phone search: Limited information is given over the phone.

Fax search: Information can be requested by fax, but is returned by mail in 3-5 days.

In person search: Call is to schedule viewing time for microfilm.

Online search: There is no charge to view records at the Internet site, www.nmprc.state.nm.us/corporations/corpsinquiry.htm. Records can be searched by company name or by director name.

Other access: This agency makes the database available on electronic format using a 3480 tape cartridge. Fee is $3,600, monthly updates available for $600.

Trademarks/Servicemarks, Trade Names

Secretary of State, Trademarks Division, 325 Don Gaspar, #301, Santa Fe, NM 87503; 505-827-3609, 505-827-3611 (Fax), 8AM-5PM.

www.sos.state.nm.us/trade.htm

Note: Effective July 1, 1997, New Mexico no longer registers trade names. However, the agency will do searches for records on file.

Indexing & Storage: Records are available from 1980 to present. It takes 1 to 2 days before new records are available for inquiry. Records are indexed on inhouse computer.

Searching: Include the following in your request-trademark/servicemark name. Include your full name, address and telephone number.

Access by: mail, phone, fax, in person.

Fee & Payment: There is no search fee, copies are $.25 a page. Fee payee: Secretary of State. Personal checks accepted.

Mail search: Turnaround time: 2 to 3 days. No SASE is required. No fee for mail request.

Phone search: They will do a computer search and will give you the information over the phone for no fee.

Fax search: There is no fee. Turnaround time: 24 hours.

In person search: No fee for request. Turnaround time is usually immediate.

Uniform Commercial Code

UCC Division, Secretary of State, 325 Don GasparSt #300, Santa Fe, NM 87503; 505-827-3610, 505-827-3611 (Fax), 8AM-5PM.

www.sos.state.nm.us/ucc/ucchome.htm

Note: This agency will not conduct in-person searches. You must come in yourself, hire a local search company, or conduct your search at the agency website.

Indexing & Storage: Records are available from 1965. It takes 24 hours before new records are available for inquiry. Records are normally destroyed after six years.

Searching: Please note that all tax liens are filed at the county level. The system does not give information on collateral.

Access by: mail, in person, online.

Fee & Payment: Copies are $1.00 per page, plus $3.00 if certification requested. Fee payee: Secretary of State. Prepayment required. Personal checks accepted. No credit cards accepted.

Mail search: Turnaround time: 3 days. No name requests by mail, you must give specific document number.

In person search: You may use their in-house computer. For appointment only call 505-827-3614. You may view documents for free.

Online search: The website permits searching and provides a form to use to order copies of filings. You can also request records via email.

Other access: Microfilm and images (from 7/99) on disk may be purchased.

Federal Tax Liens, State Tax Liens

Records not maintained by a state level agency.

Note: Records are filed with the Clerk at the county level.

Sales Tax Registrations

Taxation & Revenue Department, Tax Administrative Services Division, PO Box 5374, Santa Fe, NM 87504 (Courier: Montoya Bldg,

1200 St Francis Drive, Santa Fe, NM 87501); 505-827-0700, 505-827-0614 (Fax), 8AM-5PM.

www.state.nm.us/tax

Note: New Mexico does not have a sales tax. It has a gross receipts tax instead.

Indexing & Storage: Records are available from 1988. It takes one week before new records are available for inquiry. Records are normally destroyed after 10 years.

Searching: This agency will only confirm that a business is registered and active. They will provide no other information. Include the following in your request-company name or ID#. The business name is required, the permit number and federal ID are optional.

Access by: mail, in person.

Fee & Payment: There is no search fee, copies are $.05 per page Prepayment is not required. Personal checks accepted. No credit cards accepted.

Mail search: Turnaround time: 6 to 12 weeks. A SASE is requested.

In person search: Simple requests processed immediately.

Expedited service: No expedited service available.

Birth Certificates

Department of Health, Bureau of Vital Records, PO Box 26110, Santa Fe, NM 87502 (Courier: 1105 South St Francis Dr, Santa Fe, NM 87502); 505-827-0121, 505-827-2338 (Information), 877-284-0963 (Order), 505-984-1048 (Fax), 8AM-5:00PM (Counter Service: 9AM-4PM).

www.health.state.nm.us

Note: All requesters must sign and date the request. It is a felony to obtain a record fraudulently.

Indexing & Storage: Records are available from 1920 on. New records are available for inquiry immediately. Records are indexed on microfiche, inhouse computer.

Searching: Records available only to immediate family members or those demonstrating legal tangible interest in the desired record. Sealed records (e.g. adoptions and paternity) are unavailable. Include the following in your request-full name, names of parents, mother's maiden name, date of birth, place of birth, relationship to person of record, reason for information request. Signature of requester and physical & mailing addresses are required.

Access by: mail, phone, fax, in person, online.

Fee & Payment: The search fee is $10.00 per record. There is an additional $15.00 fee if you order by phone or by fax for use of a credit card. Fee payee: NM Vital Records. Prepayment required. Personal checks accepted. Credit cards accepted: MasterCard, Visa, AmEx, Discover.

Mail search: Turnaround time: 3 weeks. No SASE is required.

Phone search: Records are available by phone.

Fax search: Same criteria as phone searches.

In person search: Turnaround time is usually less than 1/2 hour.

Online search: Records can be ordered at www.vitalchek.com, a state designated vendor.

Expedited service: Expedited service is available for online, phone and fax requests. Turnaround

time: 24 hours. Add use of credit card fee and add fee for delivery service. (Call for fees.)

Death Records

Department of Health, Bureau of Vital Records, PO Box 26110, Santa Fe, NM 87502 (Courier: 1105 South St Francis Dr, Santa Fe, NM 87502); 505-827-0121, 505827-2338 (Information), 877-284-0963 (Order), 505-984-1048 (Fax), 8AM-5PM (Counter Service: 9AM-4PM).

www.health.state.nm.us

Indexing & Storage: Records are available from 1920 to present. New records are available for inquiry immediately. Records are indexed on microfiche, inhouse computer.

Searching: Only immediate family member or a person with tangible interest can receive record. Include the following in your request-full name, date of death, place of death, Social Security Number, relationship to person of record, reason for information request. Age at death and name of mortuary must also be included for search.

Access by: mail, phone, fax, in person, online.

Fee & Payment: The fee is $5.00 per record. An additional fee may be charged if required information is not submitted. Use of credit card is an additional $15.00. Fee payee: NM Vital Records. Prepayment required. Credit cards are only used for phone and fax ordering. Personal checks accepted. Credit cards accepted: MasterCard, Visa, AmEx, Discover.

Mail search: Turnaround time: 3 to 4 weeks. No SASE is required.

Phone search: You must use a credit card.

Fax search: Same criteria as phone searches.

In person search: Turnaround time is usually 1 hour or less.

Online search: A free lookup is available at www.rootsweb.com/~usgenweb/nm/nmdi.htm. Records date from 1899 to 1940. Records can be ordered at www.vitalchek.com, a state designated vendor.

Expedited service: Expedited service is available for online, phone and fax requests. Turnaround time: 24 hours. Use of credit card required. Delivery fee is $13.25 minimum.

Marriage Certificates, Divorce Records

Records not maintained by a state level agency.

Note: Marriage and Divorce records are found at county of issue.

Workers' Compensation Records

Access to Records is Restricted

Workers Compensation Administration, PO Box 27198, Albuquerque, NM 87125-7198 (Courier: 2410 Centre Ave, SE, Albuquerque, NM 87106); 505-841-6000, 800-255-7965 (In-State Toll Free), 505-841-6060 (Fax), 8AM-5PM.

www.state.nm.us/wca/

Note: The subject must write the agency, provide proof of ID with a driver's license, and request the record, and pay a copy fee of $.25 per page. Most

records are confidential but access is permitted for all parties to a case and other cases involving the same worker. Only upon filing of rejection of a recommended resolution shall records be open to the public.

Driver Records

Motor Vehicle Division, Driver Services Bureau, PO Box 1028, Santa Fe, NM 87504-1028 (Courier: Joseph M. Montoya Bldg, 1100 S St. Francis Dr, 2nd Floor, Santa Fe, NM 87504); 505-827-2214, 505-827-2792 (Fax), 8AM-5PM.

www.state.nm.us/tax/mvd

Note: Copies of tickets may be obtained from the same address. There is no fee.

Indexing & Storage: Records are available for 3 years for moving violations; 25 years DWIs. Accidents are not reported on the record and neither are violations less than 10 mph over the limit in 55 or 65 zones. The driver's address is included on the record. It takes 30 to 40 days before new records are available for inquiry.

Searching: The law lists 9 permissible user groups and permits release of records with written consent. Purchasers may not use the information for direct mail solicitation or resell the reports after usage. The full name, DOB and either the license number or SSN is required when ordering. The following data is not released: Social Security Numbers, addresses or date of birth.

Access by: mail, in person, online.

Fee & Payment: There is no fee for mail or walk-in requests, as long as requester qualifies. Fee payee: Motor Vehicle Division. Prepayment required. Personal checks accepted. No credit cards accepted.

Mail search: Turnaround time: 3 to 5 days. No fee for manual search. A SASE is requested.

In person search: No fee for manual search. Up to 10 requests can be processed while you wait, the rest must be in writing and left overnight.

Online search: Records are available, for authorized users, from the state's designated vendors - Oso Grande (505-343-7639) and Samba (888-94-samba). Subscription fees are $2.50 per record for interactive, $1.50 per record for batch, plus a $.25 per minute network fee. The system is open 24 hours a day, batch requesters must wait 24 hours.

Vehicle and Vessel Ownership and Registration

Motor Vehicle Division, Vehicle Services Bureau, PO Box 1028, Santa Fe, NM 87504-1028 (Courier: Joseph M. Montoya Bldg, 1100 S St. Francis Dr, 2nd Floor, Santa Fe, NM 87504); 505-827-4636, 505-827-1004, 505-827-0395 (Fax), 8AM-5PM.

www.state.nm.us/tax/mvd

Indexing & Storage: Records are available for a minimum of 3 years on boats and 6 years on vehicles. All motorized boats, sailboats, and jet skis must be both titled and registered if over 10 ft, and only registered if 10 ft or less. It takes 30 days before new records are available for inquiry.

Searching: Authorized requesters are restricted to 9 user groups and must sign a contract that states purpose of request and subsequent use. Requesters may not use ownership and vehicle information to create a resalable database. UCCs on vehicles and vessels are located here. UCCs on jet skis are found at the Sec. of State's office. The following data is not released: addresses, Social Security Numbers or date of birth.

Access by: mail, in person, online.

Fee & Payment: There are no fees for mail or in person requests. A vehicle history search (microfilm) goes back 6 years. Fee payee: Department of Motor Vehicles. Prepayment required. Personal checks accepted. No credit cards accepted.

Mail search: Turnaround time: 3 to 4 weeks. A SASE is requested.

In person search: Up to ten requests will be processed while you wait.

Online search: Records are available, for authorized users, from the state's designated vendors - Oso Grande (505-343-7639) and Samba (888-94-samba). Go to www.osogrande.com or www.samba.biz.

Other access: Bulk requests for vehicle or ownership information must be approved by the Director's office. Once a sale is made, further resale is prohibited.

Accident Reports

Department of Public Safety, Attn: Records, PO Box 1628, Santa Fe, NM 87504-1628 (Courier: New Mexico State Police Complex, 4491 Cerrillos Rd, Santa Fe, NM 87504); 505-827-9181, 505-827-9189 (Fax), 8AM-5PM.

www.dps.nm.org

Indexing & Storage: Records are available up to 20 years to present in-house (on computer) and up to 25 years for fatalities. It takes up to 15 days before new records are available for inquiry.

Searching: Arrest information is not released. Include the following in your request-full name, date of accident, county, location of accident.

Access by: mail, phone, in person, online.

Fee & Payment: The fee is $1.00 per page plus $.25 each individual page. There is no fee for a no record found. There is no fee charged for persons directly involved in the accident. Fee payee: Department of Public Safety. Prepayment required. Personal checks accepted.

Mail search: Turnaround time: 2 weeks. A SASE is requested.

Phone search: No fee for telephone request.

In person search: Turnaround time is immediate if incident one year or less old.

Online search: Reports are at https://www.nmaccidentreports.com/index.jsp. The officer's diagram and narrative is included. There is a $1.00 fee. Credit cards are accepted.

Voter Registration
Access to Records is Limited

Secretary of State, Bureau of Elections, 325 Don Gaspar, #300, Santa Fe, NM 87503; 505-827-3620, 800-477-3632, 505-827-8403 (Fax), 8AM-5PM.

www.sos.state.nm.us/ELECTNET.HTM

Note: Individual look-ups must be done at the county clerk level. Addresses will be given. This agency maintains a limited database, not all counties upload information in a timely manner. The agency does sell statewide lists, such as they are, but only for restricted (political) purposes and not for commercial purposes.

GED Certificates

Department of Education, GED Testing Program, 300 Don Gaspar, Rm 122, Santa Fe, NM 87501-2786; 505-827-6702, 505-827-6616 (Fax), 8AM-5PM.

www.sde.state.nm.us/div/ais/assess/ged/

Note: Request forms may be downloaded from the website. Unless ordered by the subject, transcripts are mailed directly to institutions or employers only.

Indexing & Storage: Records are available from 1942 to present It takes 45 days before new records are available for inquiry.

Searching: Include the following in your request-name, DOB, SSN, and signed release (for either a verification or signed release).

Access by: mail, fax, in person.

Fee & Payment: There are no fees.

Mail search: Turnaround time: 2 weeks. No SASE is required.

Fax search: Same criteria as mail searching.

In person search: Simple requests may be processed while you wait.

Hunting and Fishing License Information

NM Dept of Game & Fish, PO Box 25112, Santa Fe, NM 87504 (Courier: #1 Wildlife Way, Santa Fe, NM 87507); 505-476-8000, 800-862-9310, 505-827-7915 (Fax), 8AM-12PM; 1PM-5PM.

www.wildlife.state.nm.us

Indexing & Storage: Records are available for last season only. Records are indexed on hard copy.

Searching: Include the following in your request-name.

Access by: mail, in person.

Fee & Payment: Fee is $60 per hour plus $.25 per copy. Fee payee: NM Dept of Fish & Game.

Mail search: Turnaround time: 1 to 2 weeks. Records are available by mail.

In person search: You may do the search yourself for no fee.

New Mexico State Licensing Agencies

Licenses Searchable Online

Acupuncturist #26..www.rld.state.nm.us/b&c/Acupuncture/Licensee%20Search/licensee_search.asp
Alcohol Server #14 ....www.rld.state.nm.us/AGD/Licensee%20Search/licensee_search_servers.asp
Announcer, Athletic Event (Ring) #39 ....www.rld.state.nm.us/b&c/Athletic%20Comm/Licensee%20Search/licensee_search.asp
Architect #17 ....www.nmbea.org/People/Aroster.htm
Art Therapist #57 ....www.rld.state.nm.us/b&c/counseling/Licensee%20Search/licensee_search.asp
Athletic Promoter/Matchmaker #39 ....www.rld.state.nm.us/b&c/Athletic%20Comm/Licensee%20Search/licensee_search.asp
Athletic Trainer #1 ....www.rld.state.nm.us/b&c/Athletic%20Trainers/Licensee%20Search/licensee_search.asp
Attorney #20 ....www.nmbar.org/template.cfm?section=attorney_firm_finder
Audiologist #11 ....www.rld.state.nm.us/b&c/speech/Licensee%20Search/licensee_search.asp
Bank #51 ....www.rld.state.nm.us/fid/Licensee%20Search/licensee_search_index.htm
Barber/Barber Shop/School #2 ....www.rld.state.nm.us/b&c/Barber%20&%20Cosmo/Licensee%20Search/licensee_search.asp
Boiler Operator Journeyman #33 ....www.contractorsnm.com/searchlic.html
Booking Agent #39 ....www.rld.state.nm.us/b&c/Athletic%20Comm/Licensee%20Search/licensee_search.asp
Boxing-related Occupation #39 ....www.rld.state.nm.us/b&c/Athletic%20Comm/Licensee%20Search/licensee_search.asp
Cemetery, Endowed/Perpetual Care #51..............www.rld.state.nm.us/fid/Licensee%20Search/licensee_search_index.htm
Chiropractor #3...www.rld.state.nm.us/b&c/Chiropractic/Licensee%20Search/licensee_search.asp
Clinical Nurse Specialist #19...............................www.state.nm.us/nursing/lookup.html
Collection Agency/Manager #51 ....www.rld.state.nm.us/fid/Licensee%20Search/licensee_search_index.htm
Consumer Credit Grantor/Loan Company #51........www.rld.state.nm.us/fid/Licensee%20Search/licensee_search_index.htm
Contractor #13..www.contractorsnm.com/searchlic.html
Cosmetologist / Cosmetology Shop/School #2 ......www.rld.state.nm.us/b&c/Barber%20&%20Cosmo/Licensee%20Search/licensee_search.asp
Counseling/Therapy Practice #57 ....www.rld.state.nm.us/b&c/counseling/Licensee%20Search/licensee_search.asp
Credit Union #51 ....www.rld.state.nm.us/fid/Licensee%20Search/licensee_search_index.htm
Crematory #12...www.rld.state.nm.us/b&c/thanato/Licensee%20Search/licensee_search_index.asp
Dentist / Dental Assistant / Dental Hygienist #4 ......www.rld.state.nm.us/b&c/dental/
Dietitian/Nutritionist #8 ....www.rld.state.nm.us
Direct Disposer (Funerary) #12............................www.rld.state.nm.us/b&c/thanato/Licensee%20Search/licensee_search_index.asp
Electrologist #2...www.rld.state.nm.us/b&c/Barber%20&%20Cosmo/Licensee%20Search/licensee_search.asp
Electrophysician #2...www.rld.state.nm.us/b&c/Barber%20&%20Cosmo/Licensee%20Search/licensee_search.asp
Engineer #44 ....www.state.nm.us/java-bin/peps/PEPSBoard/PEPSBoard.jsp
Escrow Company #51 ....www.rld.state.nm.us/fid/Licensee%20Search/licensee_search_index.htm
Esthetician #2...www.rld.state.nm.us/b&c/Barber%20&%20Cosmo/Licensee%20Search/licensee_search.asp
FSI (Funerary) #12 ....www.rld.state.nm.us/b&c/thanato/Licensee%20Search/licensee_search_index.asp
Funeral Director/Practitioner #12 ....www.rld.state.nm.us/b&c/thanato/Licensee%20Search/licensee_search_index.asp
Funeral Home #12...www.rld.state.nm.us/b&c/thanato/Licensee%20Search/licensee_search_index.asp
Funeral Service Intern #12 ....www.rld.state.nm.us/b&c/thanato/Licensee%20Search/licensee_search_index.asp
Hearing Aid Specialist #11 ....www.rld.state.nm.us/b&c/speech/Licensee%20Search/licensee_search.asp
Hemodialysis Technician #19................................www.state.nm.us/nursing/lookup.html
Insurance Agent #23 ....www.nmprc.state.nm.us/insurance/agents/agentshome.htm
Interior Designer #25...www.rld.state.nm.us/b&c/Interior/Licensee%20Search/licensee_search.asp
Journeyman Contractor #13.................................www.contractorsnm.com/searchlic.html
Landscape Architect #18......................................www.rld.state.nm.us/b&c/landscape/Licensee%20Search/licensee_search.asp
Loan Company, Small #51 ....www.rld.state.nm.us/fid/Licensee%20Search/licensee_search_index.htm
Lobbying Organization #32 ....http://web.state.nm.us/LOBBY/ORG.htm
Lobbyist #32 ....http://web.state.nm.us/LOBBY/LOB.htm
LPG Gas License #13 ....www.contractorsnm.com/searchlic.html
Manicurist #2...www.rld.state.nm.us/b&c/Barber%20&%20Cosmo/Licensee%20Search/licensee_search.asp
Marriage & Family Therapist #57 ....www.rld.state.nm.us/b&c/counseling/Licensee%20Search/licensee_search.asp
Martial Arts Contest #39......................................www.rld.state.nm.us/b&c/Athletic%20Comm/Licensee%20Search/licensee_search.asp
Massage Instructor/Practitioner/School #5............www.rld.state.nm.us/b&c/massage/Licnesee%20Search/licensee_search.asp
Massage Therapist #5..www.rld.state.nm.us/b&c/massage/Licnesee%20Search/licensee_search.asp
Medical Doctor #36 ....www.docboard.org/nm/
Medication Aide #19..www.state.nm.us/nursing/lookup.html
Mental Health Counselor #57...............................www.rld.state.nm.us/b&c/counseling/Licensee%20Search/licensee_search.asp
Money Order Agent/Company/ #51.......................www.rld.state.nm.us/fid/Licensee%20Search/licensee_search_index.htm
Mortgage Company/Loan Broker/Branch #51.........www.rld.state.nm.us/fid/Licensee%20Search/licensee_search_index.htm

Motor Vehicle Sales Finance Company #51	www.rld.state.nm.us/fid/Licensee%20Search/licensee_search_index.htm
Nurse Anesthetist #19	www.state.nm.us/nursing/lookup.html
Nurse-LPN / Nurse-RN / Nurse Practitioner #19	www.state.nm.us/nursing/lookup.html
Nursing Home Administrator #6	www.rld.state.nm.us/b&c/nhab/Licensee%20Search/licensee_search.asp
Occupational Therapist/Assistant #27	www.rld.state.nm.us/b&c/otb/Licensee%20Search/licensee_search.asp
Optometrist #40	www.rld.state.nm.us/b&c/optometry/Licensee%20Search/licensee_search.asp
Oriental Medicine Doctor #26	www.rld.state.nm.us/b&c/Acupuncture/Licensee%20Search/licensee_search.asp
Osteopathic Physician #7	www.rld.state.nm.us/b&c/osteo/Licensee%20Search/licensee_search.asp
Pharmacist #41	http://ec4.state.nm.us/pharmacy/
Pharmacy, Non-Residential #41	http://ec4.state.nm.us/pharmacy/
Physical Therapist/Assistant #28	www.rld.state.nm.us/b&c/ptb/Licensee%20Search/licensee_search.asp
Physician Assistant #36	www.docboard.org/nm/
Podiatrist #42	www.rld.state.nm.us/b&c/Podiatry/Licensee%20Search/licensee_search.asp
Psychologist #37	www.rld.state.nm.us/b&c/psychology/Licensee%20Search/licensee_search.asp
Psychologist Associate #37	www.rld.state.nm.us/b&c/psychology/Licensee%20Search/licensee_search.asp
Public Accountant-CPA #35	www.rld.state.nm.us/b&c/accountancy/Licensee%20Search/licensee_search.asp
Real Estate Agent/Broker/Salesperson #46	http://rld.state.nm.us/b&c/recom/Licensee%20Search/licensee_search.asp
Real Estate Appraiser #49	www.rld.state.nm.us/b&c/reappraisers/Licensee%20Search/licensee_search.asp
Referee #39	www.rld.state.nm.us/b&c/Athletic%20Comm/Licensee%20Search/licensee_search.asp
Respiratory Care Therapist #56	www.rld.state.nm.us/b&c/rcb/Licensee%20Search/licensee_search.asp
Savings & Loan #51	www.rld.state.nm.us/fid/Licensee%20Search/licensee_search_index.htm
School Administrator / School Counselor #24	www.ped.state.nm.us/
Social Worker (LBSW, LI, LM) #10	www.rld.state.nm.us/b&c/socialwk/index.htm
Social Worker, Provisional #10	www.rld.state.nm.us/b&c/socialwk/index.htm
Speech-Language Pathologist #11	www.rld.state.nm.us/b&c/speech/Licensee%20Search/licensee_search.asp
Substance Abuse Counselor/Intern #57	www.rld.state.nm.us/b&c/counseling/Licensee%20Search/licensee_search.asp
Surveyor, Land #44	www.state.nm.us/java-bin/peps/PEPSBoard/PEPSBoard.jsp
Teacher #24	www.ped.state.nm.us/
Trust Company #51	www.rld.state.nm.us/fid/Licensee%20Search/licensee_search_index.htm
Veterinarian/Veterinary Technician #55	www.state.nm.us/vetbd/
Veterinary Facility #55	www.state.nm.us/vetbd/
Wrestler #39	www.rld.state.nm.us/b&c/Athletic%20Comm/Licensee%20Search/licensee_search.asp

New Mexico Licensing Quick Finder

Acupuncturist #26	505-476-4630	
Alcohol Server #14	505-476-4875	
Animal Pregnancy Diagnosis #55	505-841-9112	
Announcer, Athletic Event (Ring) #39	505-827-7172	
Architect #17	505-827-6375	
Art Therapist #57	505-476-4610	
Artificial Inseminator #55	505-841-9112	
Athletic Promoter/Matchmaker #39	505-827-7172	
Athletic Trainer #1	505-476-7098	
Attorney #20	505-271-9706	
Audiologist #11	505-476-7098	
Bank #51	505-827-7100	
Barber #2	505-476-4690	
Barber Shop/School #2	505-476-4690	
Bingo/Raffles, Non-profit #14	505-476-4875	
Boiler Operator Journeyman #33	505-452-8311	
Booking Agent #39	505-827-7172	
Boxer #39	505-827-7172	
Boxer Manager #39	505-827-7172	
Boxing Judge/Timekeeper #39	505-827-7172	
Cemetery, Endowed/Perpetual Care #51		
	505-827-7100	
Chiropractor #3	505-476-7120	
Clinical Nurse Specialist #19	505-841-8340	
Collection Agency/Manager #51	505-827-7100	
Consumer Credit Grantor/Loan Company #51		
	505-827-7100	

Contractor #13	505-467-4700	
Cosmetologist #2	505-476-4690	
Cosmetology Shop/School #2	505-476-4690	
Counseling/Therapy Practice #57	505-476-4610	
Credit Union #51	505-827-7100	
Crematory #12	505-476-4870	
Dental Assistant #4	505-476-4680	
Dental Hygienist #4	505-476-4680	
Dentist #4	505-476-4680	
Dietitian/Nutritionist #8	505-476-7053	
Direct Disposer (Funerary) #12	505-476-4870	
Dispensing Physician #41	505-222-9130	
Electrologist #2	505-827-7550	
Electrophysician #2	505-476-4690	
Emergency Medical Technician #22	505-476-7701	
Engineer #44	505-827-7561	
Escrow Company #51	505-827-7100	
Esthetician #2	505-476-4690	
Fireworks Distributor Class C or B #54	505-827-3761	
Fireworks Manufacturer 1.4G #54	505-827-3761	
Fireworks Vendor #54	505-827-3761	
FSI (Funerary) #12	505-476-4870	
Funeral Director/Practitioner #12	505-476-4870	
Funeral Home #12	505-476-4870	
Funeral Service Intern #12	505-476-4870	
Gambling, Non-Profit #14	505-476-4875	
Hearing Aid Specialist #11	505-476-7098	

Hemodialysis Technician #19	505-841-8340	
Insurance Agent #23	505-827-4637	
Interior Designer #25	505-476-7078	
Investment Advisor/Rep. #32	505-476-4580	
Journeyman Contractor #13	505-467-4700	
Landscape Architect #18	505-476-4600	
Liquor Distributor #14	505-476-4875	
Loan Company, Small #51	505-827-7100	
Lobbying Organization #32	505-476-4580	
Lobbyist #32	505-476-4580	
LPG Gas License #13	505-467-4700	
Manicurist #2	505-476-4690	
Manufactured Housing Dealer/Broker #52		
	505-476-4770	
Mfg. Housing Installer/Repairman #52	505-476-4770	
Manufactured Housing Mfg./Seller #52	505-476-4770	
Marriage & Family Therapist #57	505-476-4610	
Martial Arts Contest #39	505-827-7172	
Massage Instr./Practitioner/School #5	505-476-7090	
Massage Therapist #5	505-476-7090	
Medical Doctor #36	505-827-6784	
Medical Researcher #41	505-222-9130	
Medical Wholesale Company #41	505-222-9130	
Medication Aide #19	505-841-8340	
Mental Health Counselor #57	505-476-4610	
Midwife #34	505-476-8908	
Midwife (CNM) #34	505-476-8908	

Money Order Agent/Company/Exempt Agent #51 505-827-7100

Mortgage Company/Loan Broker/Branch #51 505-827-7100

Motor Vehicle Sales Finance Company #51 505-827-7100

Notary Public #53 505-827-3605

Nuclear Medicine Technologist #38 505-476-3264

Nurse Anesthetist #19 505-841-8340

Nurse Practitioners #19 505-841-8340

Nurse-LPN #19 505-841-8340

Nurse-RN #19 505-841-8340

Nursing Home Administrator #6 505-476-4660

Occupational Therapist/Assistant #27 ..505-476-4880

Optometrist #40 505-476-4660

Oriental Medicine Doctor #26 505-476-4630

Osteopathic Physician #7 505-476-4695

Osteopathic Physician Assistant #7 505-476-4695

Patrol Operator, Private #9 505-476-4650

Pest Management Consultant #21 505-646-2133

Pesticide Applicator/Operator #21 505-646-2133

Pesticide Dealer #21 505-646-2133

Pharmacist #41 505-222-9130

Pharmacy, Non-Residential #41 505-222-9130

Physical Therapist/Assistant #28 505-476-4630

Physician Assistant #36 505-827-6784

Podiatrist #42 505-827-7120

Polygraph Examiner #9 505-476-4650

Private Investigator #9 505-476-4650

Psychologist #37 ....505-476-7078/ 7079

Psychologist Associate #37 ....505-476-7078/ 7079

Public Accountant-CPA #35 505-841-9108

Racing #45 505-841-6400

Radiation Therapy Technologist #38 ...505-476-3264

Radiologic Technologist #38 505-476-3264

Real Estate Agent/Salesperson #46 ...505-841-9120

Real Estate Appraiser #49 505-476-4611

Real Estate Broker #46 505-841-9120

Referee #39 505-827-7172

Respiratory Care Therapist #56 505-476-7121

Savings & Loan #51 505-827-7100

School Administrator #24 505-827-6587

School Counselor #24 505-827-6587

Securities Broker/Dealer #32 505-476-4580

Securities Division Agent #32 505-476-4580

Securities Sales Representative #32 ...505-476-4580

Security Guard #9 505-476-4650

Shorthand Reporter #16......................505-821-1440

Social Worker (LBSW, LI, LM) #10 505-476-4890

Social Worker, Provisional #10 505-476-4890

Speech-Language Pathologist #11 505-476-7098

Substance Abuse Counselor/Intern #57 505-476-4610

Surveyor, Land #44 505-827-7561

Teacher #24 505-827-6587

Trust Company #51............................505-827-7100

Veterinarian/Veterinary Tech. #55 505-841-9112

Veterinary Facility #55........................505-841-9112

Waste Water System Operator #38 505-476-3264

Wrestler #39 505-827-7172

New Mexico Licensing Agency Information

1 Regulation & Licensing Dept., Athletic Trainers Board, POB 2055 (2055 S Pacheco St #300), Santa Fe, NM 87505; 505-476-7098, Fax: 505-476-7094. www.rld.state.nm.us/b&c/Athletic%20Trainers/index.htm Email: AthleticTrainerBoard@state.nm.us Search Database at www.rld.state.nm.us/b&c/Athletic%20Trainers/Licensee%20Search/licensee_search.asp

2 Regulation & Licensing Dept., Board of Barbers & Cosmetologists, 2550 Cerrillos Rd, Santa Fe, NM 87505-3206; 505-476-4690, Fax: 505-476-4645. www.rld.state.nm.us/b&c/Barber%20&%20Cosmo/index.htm Search Database at www.rld.state.nm.us/b&c/Barber%20&%20Cosmo/Licensee%20Search/licensee_search.asp

3 Regulation & Licensing Dept., Board of Chiropractic Examiners, 2550 Cerrillos Rd 2nd Fl, Santa Fe, NM 87504; 505-476-4695, Fax: 505-476-4665. www.rld.state.nm.us/b&c/Chiropractic/index.htm Email: ChiroBoard@state.nm.us Search Database at www.rld.state.nm.us/b&c/Chiropractic/Licensee%20Search/licensee_search.asp Note: The lists provided online do not include sanctions.

4 Regulation & Licensing Dept., Board of Dental Health Care, PO Box 25101, Santa Fe, NM 87504-5101; 505-476-4680, Fax: 505-476-7095. www.rld.state.nm.us/b&c/dental/index.htm Email: Cynthia.Salazar@state.nm.us Search Database at www.rld.state.nm.us/b&c/dental/

5 Regulation & Licensing Dept., Massage Therapy Board, 2550 Cerrillos Road, Santa Fe, NM 87505; 505-476-7090, Fax: 505-476-7095. www.rld.state.nm.us/b&c/massage/index.htm Email: MassageBoard@state.nm.us Search Database at www.rld.state.nm.us/b&c/massage/Licensee%20Search/licensee_search.asp

6 Regulation & Licensing Dept., Nursing Home Administrators Board, 2550 Cerrillos Rd, Santa Fe, NM 87505-3260; 505-476-4660. www.rld.state.nm.us/b&c/nhab/index.htm Email: NursingHomeAdminBd@state.nm.us Search Database at www.rld.state.nm.us/b&c/nhab/Licensee%20Search/licensee_search.asp

7 Regulation & Licensing Dept., Board of Osteopathic Medical Examiners, 2550 Cerrillos Rd, Santa Fe, NM 87505-3260; 505-476-4695, Fax: 505-476-4665. www.rld.state.nm.us/b&c/osteo/index.htm Email: OsteoBoard@state.nm.us Search Database at www.rld.state.nm.us/b&c/osteo/Licensee%20Search/licensee_search.asp

8 Regulation & Licensing Dept., Nutrition & Dietetics Practice Board, 2550 Cerrillos Rd, Santa Fe, NM 87505-3206; 505-476-7053, Fax: 505-476-7094. www.rld.state.nm.us Email: NutritionDieteticsBd@state.nm.us

9 Regulation & Licensing Dept., Private Investigators & Polygraph Board, 2550 Cerrillos Rd, Santa Fe, NM 87505-3260; 505-476-4650, Fax: 505-476-4645. www.rld.state.nm.us/b&c/pipolygraph/index.htm Email: PIPolygraphBd@state.nm.us

10 Regulation & Licensing Dept., Social Work Examiners Board, 2550 Cerrillos Rd, Santa Fe, NM 87505-3206; 505-476-4890, Fax: 505-476-4620. www.rld.state.nm.us/b&c/socialwk/index.htm Email: SocialWorkBoard@state.nm.us Search Database at www.rld.state.nm.us/b&c/socialwk/index.htm Note: Verification $5.00 for first 5 names; $1.00 each addl. name. Lists, lables,or disc available.

11 Regulation & Licensing Dept., Speech, Language, Audiology, & Hearing Aid Board, 2550 Cerrillos Rd, Santa Fe, NM 87505-3260; 505-476-7098, Fax: 505-476-7094. www.rld.state.nm.us/b&c/speech/index.htm Email: Speech/Hearing@state.nm.us Search Database at www.rld.state.nm.us/b&c/speech/Licensee%20Search/licensee_search.asp

12 Regulation & Licensing Dept., Thanatopractice Board, 2550 Cerrillos Rd, Santa Fe, NM 87505-3260; 505-476-4870, Fax: 505-476-7069. www.rld.state.nm.us/b&c/thanato/ Email: FuneralBoard@state.nm.us Search Database at www.rld.state.nm.us/b&c/thanato/Licensee%20Search/licensee_search_index.asp

13 Regulation & Licensing Dept., Construction Industries Division, 2550 Cerrillos Rd, Sante Fe, NM 87505-3260; 505-467-4700, Fax: 505-765-5670. http://rld.state.nm.us/cid Email: rldcide@state.nm.us Search Database at www.contractorsnm.com/searchlic.html

14 Regulation & Licensing Dept., Alcohol & Gaming Division, 2550 Cerrillos Rd, Santa Fe, NM 87505-3260; 505-476-4875, Fax: 505-476-4595. Email: agd@state.nm.us www.rld.state.nm.us/agd/index.htm

16 Board Governing Recording of Judicial Proceedings, PO Box 92648, Albuquerque, NM 87125; 505-821-1440, Fax: 505-821-2940.

17 Board of Examiners for Architects, PO Box 509, Santa Fe, NM 87504; 505-827-6375, Fax: 505-827-6373. www.nmbea.org Search Database at www.nmbea.org/People/Aroster.htm

18 Board of Landscape Architects, 2550 Cerrillos Rd, Santa Fe, NM 87505-3260; 505-476-4600, Fax: 505-476-7087. www.rld.state.nm.us/b&c/landscape/index.htm Email: LandscapeArchitects@state.nm.us Search Database at www.rld.state.nm.us/b&c/landscape/Licensee%20Search/licensee_search.asp

19 Board of Nursing, 4206-A Lousiana NE Ste A, Albuquerque, NM 87109; 505-841-8340, Fax: 505-841-8347. www.state.nm.us/nursing Email: boardifnursing@state.nm.us Search at www.state.nm.us/nursing/lookup.html

20 Board of Bar Examiners, 9420 Indian School NE, Albuquerque, NM 87112; 505-271-9706, Fax: 505-271-9768. www.nmexam.org Email: info@nmexam.org Search Database at www.nmbar.org/template.cfm?section=attorney_firm_finder

21 Department of Agriculture, Pesticide Management Bureau, MSC 3AQ, PO Box 30005, Las Cruces, NM 88003-8005; 505-646-2133, Fax: 505-646-5977. http://nmdaweb.nmsu.edu/DIVISIONS/AES/pest.html Email: webmastr@nmsu.edu

22 Department of Health, Injury Prevention & EMS Bureau, 2500 Cerrillos Rd, Santa Fe, NM 87505; 505-476-7701, Fax: 505-476-7810.

23 Department of Insurance, Insurance Licensing Division, PO Box 1269, Santa Fe, NM 87504; 505-827-4637, Fax: 505-827-4551. www.nmprc.state.nm.us/insurance/agents/agentshome.htm

24 Education Department, Professional Licensure, 300 Don Gaspar, Education Bldg, Santa Fe, NM 87501-2786; 505-827-6587, Fax: 505-827-6696. www.sde.state.nm.us

25 Regulation & Licensing Dept., Board of Interior Design, 2550 Cerrillos Rd, Santa Fe, NM 87505-3260; 505-476-7078, Fax: 505-827-7087. www.rld.state.nm.us/b&c/Interior/index.htm Email: InteriorDesignBd@state.nm.us Search Database at www.rld.state.nm.us/b&c/Interior/Licensee%20Search/licensee_search.asp

26 Regulation & Licensing Dept., Acupuncture & Oriental Medicine Board, 2550 Cerrillos Rd, Santa Fe, NM 87505-3260; 505-476-4630, Fax: 505-476-4545. www.rld.state.nm.us/b&c/acupuncture/index.htm Email: AcuOrMedBoard@state.nm.us Search Database at www.rld.state.nm.us/b&c/Acupuncture/Licensee%20Search/licensee_search.asp

27 Regulation & Licensing Dept., Occupational Therapy Board, 2550 Cerrillos Rd, Santa Fe, NM 87505-3206; 505-476-4880, Fax: 505-476-7086. www.rld.state.nm.us/b&c/otb/index.htm Email: OccupationalTherapy@state.nm.us Search Database at www.rld.state.nm.us/b&c/otb/Licensee%20Search/licensee_search.asp

28 Regulation & Licensing Dept., Physical Therapy Board, P.O. Box 25101, Santa Fe, NM 87504-5101; 505-476-4630, Fax: 505-476-4545. www.rld.state.nm.us/b&c/ptb/index.htm Email: PhysicalThearpy@state.nm.us Search Database at www.rld.state.nm.us/b&c/ptb/Licensee%20Search/licensee_search.asp

32 Securities Division, Regulation and Licensing Dept., 2550 Cerrillos Rd, Santa Fe, NM 87505-3260; 505-476-4580, Fax: 505-984-0617. www.rld.state.nm.us/Securities/index.htm Email: rldsd@state.nm.us

33 Boiler Operator Journeyman Licensing Board, c/o Contractor Licensing Services, 3211 Coors Blvd SW #A3, Albuquerque, NM 87121; 505-452-8311, Fax: 505-452-8310. www.contractorsnm.com Search Database at www.contractorsnm.com/searchlic.html

34 Maternal Health Program, Family Health Bureau, PO Box 26110, Santa Fe, NM 87502; 505-476-8908, Fax: 505-476-8909. Email: rimav@doh.state.nm.us

35 Regulation & Licensing Dept., Accountancy Board, 1650 University Blvd. NE, #400A, Albuquerque, NM 87102; 505-841-9108, Fax: 505-841-9101. www.rld.state.nm.us/b&c/accountancy/ Email: publicaccountancyboard@state.nm.us Search Database at www.rld.state.nm.us/b&c/accountancy/Licensee%20Search/licensee_search.asp

36 Board of Medical Examiners, 491 Old Sante Fe Trail, Lamy Bldg, 2nd Fl, Santa Fe, NM 87501; 505-827-5022, Fax: 505-827-7377. www.state.nm.us/nmbme/ Search Database at www.docboard.org/nm/

37 Regulation & Licensing Dept., Board of Psychologist Examiners, 2550 Cerrillos Rd, Santa Fe, NM 87505; 505-476-7078/7079, Fax: 505-827-7017. www.rld.state.nm.us/b&c/psychology/index.htm Email: psychologistexaminers@state.nm.us Search Database at www.rld.state.nm.us/b&c/psychology/Licensee%20Search/licensee_search.asp

38 Environment Department, Radiation Protection Program, 1190 Saint Francis Dr, Santa Fe, NM 87502; 505-476-3264, Fax: 505-476-3015. www.nmenv.state.nm.us Email: stephen_sanchez@nmenv.state.nm.us

39 Regulation & Licensing Dept., Athletic Commission, 2550 Cerrillos Rd, Santa Fe, NM 87505-3260; 505-827-7124, Fax: 505-827-7095. www.rld.state.nm.us/b&c/Athletic%20Comm/ Email: henrietta.leos@state.nm.us Search Database at www.rld.state.nm.us/b&c/Athletic%20Comm/Licensee%20Search/licensee_search.asp

40 Regulation & Licensing Dept., Board of Examiners in Optometry, 2550 Cerrillos Road, Santa Fe, NM 87505-3260; 505-476-4660, Fax: 505-476-4620. www.rld.state.nm.us/b&c/optometry/index.htm Email: optometrybd@state.nm.us Search Database at www.rld.state.nm.us/b&c/optometry/Licensee%20Search/licensee_search.asp

41 Regulation & Licensing Dept., Pharmacy Board, 111 Loomis NW #412, Albuquerque, NM 87102; 505-222-9130, Fax: 505-222-9145. www.state.nm.us/pharmacy Email: NMBOP@nm-us.campuscwix.net Search Database at http://ec4.state.nm.us/pharmacy/

42 Regulation & Licensing Dept., Podiatry Board, 2550 Cerrillos Rd, Santa Fe, NM 87505-3260; 505-476-7120, Fax: 505-827-7094. www.rld.state.nm.us/b&c/Podiatry/index.htm Email: PodiatryBoard@state.nm.us Search Database at www.rld.state.nm.us/b&c/Podiatry/Licensee%20Search/licensee_search.asp

44 Professional Engineers & Surveyors Board, 1010 Marquez Pl, Santa Fe, NM 87501; 505-827-7561, Fax: 505-827-7566. www.state.nm.us/pepsboard Search Database at www.state.nm.us/java-bin/peps/PEPSBoard/PEPSBoard.jsp

45 Racing Commission, 300 San Mateo Blvd NE, #110, Albuquerque, NM 87108; 505-841-6400, Fax: 505-841-6413. www.nmprc.state.nm.us Email: nmrc@state.nm.us

46 Regulation & Licensing Dept., Real Estate Commission, 1650 University Blvd, #490, Albuquerque, NM 87102; 505-841-9120, 800-801-7505, Fax: 505-276-0725. www.state.nm.us/nmrec   Email: nmrec@state.nm.us Search Database at http://rld.state.nm.us/b&c/recom/Licensee%20Search/licensee_search.asp

49 Regulation & Licensing Dept., Real Estate Appraisers Board, 2550 Cerrillos Rd, Santa Fe, NM 87505-3260; 505-476-4611, Fax: 505-476-4645. www.rld.state.nm.us/b&c/reappraisers/index.htm Email: RobertaPerea@state.nm.us Search Database at www.rld.state.nm.us/b&c/reappraisers/Licensee%20Search/licensee_search.asp

51 Regulation & Licensing Dept., Financial Institutions Division, 2550 Cerrillos Rd 3rd Floor, Santa Fe, NM 87505-3260; 505-827-7100, Fax: 505-827-7107. www.rld.state.nm.us/fid/index.htm Email: rldfid@state.nm.us   Search Database at www.rld.state.nm.us/fid/Licensee%20Search/licensee_search_index.htm

52 Regulation & Licensing Dept., Manufactured Housing Division, 2550 Cerrillos Rd, Santa Fe, NM 87505-3260; 505-476-4770, Fax: 505-827-7074.   Email: MHD@state.nm.us www.rld.state.nm.us/mhd/index.htm

53 Secretary of State, Notary Public Section, State Capitol North Ste300, Santa Fe, NM 87503; 505-827-3600, Fax: 505-827-3611. www.sos.state.nm.us   Email: nm.notary@state.nm.us

54 State Fire Marshal, Public Regulation Commission, 142 West Palace Ave, P.O. Box 1269, Santa Fe, NM 87504; 505-827-3761, Fax: 505-827-3778.

55 Board of Veterinary Medicine, 7301 Jefferson St. NE Ste C, Albuquerque, NM 87109-4363; 505-841-9112, Fax: 505-841-9127. www.state.nm.us/vetbd   Search Database at www.state.nm.us/vetbd/ Note: To search, click on "license verification" at the website.

56 Regulation & Licensing Dept., Repiratory Care Advisory Board, 2550 Cerrillos Rd, Santa Fe, NM 87505; 505-476-4660, Fax: 505-476-7095. www.rld.state.nm.us/b&c/rcb/index.htm Email: respiratorycarebd@state.mt.us Search Database at www.rld.state.nm.us/b&c/rcb/Licensee%20Search/licensee_search.asp

57 Regulation & Licensing Dept., Counseling & Therapy Practice Board, 2550 Cerrillos Rd, Sante Fe, NM 87505-3260; 505-476-4610, Fax: 505-476-4633. www.rld.state.nm.us/b&c/counseling/index.htm Email: CounselingBoard@state.nm.us Search Database at www.rld.state.nm.us/b&c/counseling/Licensee%20Search/licensee_search.asp

New Mexico Federal Courts

The following list indicates the district and division name for each county in the state.

County/Court Cross Reference

Bernalillo	Albuquerque	McKinley	Albuquerque
Catron	Albuquerque	Mora	Albuquerque
Chaves	Albuquerque	Otero	Albuquerque
Cibola	Albuquerque	Quay	Albuquerque
Colfax	Albuquerque	Rio Arriba	Albuquerque
Curry	Albuquerque	Roosevelt	Albuquerque
De Baca	Albuquerque	San Juan	Albuquerque
Dona Ana	Albuquerque	San Miguel	Albuquerque
Eddy	Albuquerque	Sandoval	Albuquerque
Grant	Albuquerque	Santa Fe	Albuquerque
Guadalupe	Albuquerque	Sierra	Albuquerque
Harding	Albuquerque	Socorro	Albuquerque
Hidalgo	Albuquerque	Taos	Albuquerque
Lea	Albuquerque	Torrance	Albuquerque
Lincoln	Albuquerque	Union	Albuquerque
Los Alamos	Albuquerque	Valencia	Albuquerque
Luna	Albuquerque		

US District Court

Albuquerque Division 333 Lomas Blvd NW #270, Albuquerque, NM 87102-2274 (Use mail address for courier delivery) 505-348-2000, Fax: 505-348-2028. www.nmcourt.fed.us/dcdocs

Counties: All counties in New Mexico. Cases may be assigned to any of its three divisions - Santa Fe (505-988-6481), Las Cruces (505-528-1400), and Roswell (505-625-2388). Santa Fe and Las Cruces have searchable records; Roswell does not.

Indexing & Storage: New cases available in the index 2 days after filing date. Inquirer's phone number and the years to search are required to search for a record. Search records from 1990 to the present by plaintiff name. Prior records can be searched by defendant or case number.

Fee & Payment: Payment may be made by money order, cashier check, personal check. Copies are made through a copy service only. Payee: Clerk, U.S. District Court.

Phone Search: Only docket information available.

Mail Search: A SASE not required.

In Person Search: Fee charged if court conducts your in person search for you. Copying available from copy service.

PACER: There is no PACER access to this court.

Electronic Filing: This utilizes ACE (Advanced Court Engin.), and not the U.S. Courts standard CM/ECF system. Electronic filing information online at www.nmcourt.fed.us/dcdocs (Click on Electronic Filing)

Other Online Access: Submit a written request for an ACE (Advanced Court Engineering) user name and password in order to freely access court records, docket reports, and court opinions. See www.nmcourt.fed.us/web/DCDOCS/files/accountrequest.html.

U.S. Bankruptcy Court

District of New Mexico

Albuquerque Division PO Box 546, Albuquerque, NM 87103-0546 (courier address: 3rd Floor, Room 316, 421 Gold Ave SW, Albuquerque, NM 87102), 505-348-2500, Fax: 505-348-2473. www.nmcourt.fed.us/bkdocs

Counties: All counties in New Mexico. Judges do travel to Los Cruces and Roswell, however, bankruptcy records are not searchable at those courthouses.

Indexing & Storage: Cases indexed by debtor as well as by case number. New cases available in the index 24 hours after filing date. Card indexes are maintained on cases filed prior to May 26, 1987. Cases filed after that date are indexed in the computer.

Fee & Payment: Payment may be made by money order, cashier check, personal check, Visa or Mastercard. Debtor's checks are not accepted. Payee: Clerk, U.S. Bankruptcy Court.

Phone Search: Index, docket and claim information will be released over the phone. Automated voice case information service (VCIS) is available. VCIS 888-435-7822 or 505-248-6536.

Mail Search: Fee will be charged only when a case file search is required. Include SASE for return.

In Person Search: Fee charged if court conducts your in person search for you. There is a contract copy service, fax service and other related services located in the court. The copy service available by FAX. Call 505-842-9836 for info.

PACER: PACER is available online at http://pacer.nmb.uscourts.gov. New civil records are online after 1 day.

Electronic Filing: Currently in the process of implementing CM/ECF.

Other Online Access: Submit a written request for an ACE (Advanced Court Engineering) user name and password in order to freely access court records, docket reports, and court opinions. See www.nmcourt.fed.us/web/BCDOCS/bcindex.html.

Standards for Federal Courts: The search fee is $20.00 per item (one party name or case number). Certification fee is $7.00 per document. Copy fee is $.50 per page. All fees standard unless noted in profile. Mail Search: always enclose a stamped self addressed envelope unless otherwise noted. Most courts accept fax requests or will suggest a copying/search vendor. Before releasing records, all courts require prepayment unless noted in profile.

Open records are located at the court unless otherwise noted. District courts index by defendant and plaintiff as well as by case number. Bankruptcy courts usually index by debtor and case number. While most courts now have their indexes on computer, many still maintain index card files as well.

The universal PACER sign-up number is 800-676-6856. Find PACER and the Party/Case Index on the Web at http://pacer.psc.uscourts.gov. PACER dial-up access is $.60 per minute. Also, courts offering internet access via RACER, PACER, Web-PACER or the new CM-ECF charge $.07 per page fee unless noted as free.

New Mexico County Courts

Court	Jurisdiction	No. of Courts	How Organized
District Courts*	General	30	13 Districts
Magistrate Courts*	Limited	54	32 Magistrate Districts
Metropolitan Court of Bernalillo County*	Municipal	1	
Municipal Courts	Municipal	81	
Probate Courts	Probate	30	33 Counties

* Profiled in this Sourcebook.

Court	CIVIL								
	Tort	Contract	Real Estate	Min. Claim	Max. Claim	Small Claims	Estate	Eviction	Domestic Relations
District Courts*	X	X	X	$0	No Max	$10000	X		X
Magistrate Courts*	X	X	X	$0	$10000	$10000		X	
Metropolitan Court of Bernalillo County*	X	X	X	$0	$10000	$10000			
Municipal Courts									
Probate Courts*							X		

Court	CRIMINAL				
	Felony	Misdemeanor	DWI/DUI	Preliminary Hearing	Juvenile
District Courts*	X				X
Magistrate Courts*		X	X	X	
Metropolitan Court of Bernalillo County*		X	X	X	
Municipal Courts		Petty	X		
Probate Courts*					

ADMINISTRATION   Administrative Office of the Courts, 237 Don Gaspar, Rm 25, Santa Fe, NM, 87501; 505-827-4800, Fax: 505-827-7549. www.nmcourts.com/aoc.htm

COURT STRUCTURE   The 30 District Courts in 13 districts are the courts of general jurisdiction. The Magistrate Courts handle civil cases up to $10,000, and are refered to as Small Claims. Also, the Bernalillo Metropolitan Court has jurisdiction in cases up to $10,000. Municipal Courts handle petty misdemeanors, DWI/DUI, traffic violations and other municipal ordinance violations.

ONLINE ACCESS   The www.nmcourts.com web site offers free access to District and Magistrate Court case information, except Bernalillo Metro (see below). In general, records are available from June 1997 forward. The web site also offers a DWI Offender History tool for researching an individual's DWI history. Search by name or SSN. Supreme Court opinions may be researched at http://www.supremecourt.nm.org/.

A commercial online service is available for the Metropolitan Court of Bernalillo County. There is a $35.00 set up fee, a connect time fee based on usage. The system is available 24 hours a day. Call 505-345-6555 for more information.

ADDITIONAL INFORMATION   There are some "shared" courts in New Mexico, with one county handling cases arising in another. Records are held at the location(s) indicated in the text.

All magistrate courts and the Bernalillo Metropolitan Court have public access terminals to access civil records only.

PROBATE COURTS   County Clerks handle "informal" (uncontested) probate cases, and the District Courts handle "formal" (contested) probate cases.

Bernalillo County

2nd Judicial District Court PO Box 488, Albuquerque, NM 87103; 505-841-7425 (Administration); Civil phone: 505-841-7451; Criminal phone: 505-841-7542; Probate phone: 505-841-6787; Fax: 505-841-7446. Hours: 8AM-5PM (MST). *Felony, Civil.*
www.cabq.gov/cjnet/dst2alb
Civil Records: Access: Mail, online, in person. Both court and visitors may perform in person searches. Search fee: $1.50 per name. Required to search: name, years to search. Civil cases indexed by defendant, plaintiff. Civil records on computer from 1984, prior on docket books/microfiche. Online access is free at www.usnmcourts.com. Most data goes back to 6/1997.
Criminal Records: Access: Mail, online, in person. Both court and visitors may perform in person searches. Search fee: $1.50 per name. Required to search: name, years to search; also helpful: DOB, SSN. Criminal records on computer from 1979, prior on docket books/microfiche. Online access to criminal records is free at www.usnmcourts.com. Most data goes back to 6/1997.
General Information: Public Access terminal is available. No sequestered or juvenile records released. Copy fee: $.35 per page. Certification fee: $1.50. Payee: Clerk of the Court. Only cashiers checks and money orders accepted. Prepayment required. Mail requests: SASE required. Mail turnaround time up to 10 days.

Metropolitan Court 401 Lomas NW, Albuquerque, NM 87102; 505-841-8151/841-8160; Fax: 505-222-4800. Hours: 8AM-5PM (MST). *Misdemeanor, Civil Actions Under $10,000, Eviction, Small Claims.*
www.metrocourt.state.nm.us
Note: Records phone is 505-841-8240
Civil Records: Access: Phone, fax, mail, online, in person. Both court and visitors may perform in person searches. No search fee. Required to search: name, years to search. Civil cases indexed by defendant, plaintiff. Civil records on computer from 1987. Max. 5 years back except uncollected judgments which stay open 14 years from date of judgment. Access Metropolitan court civil records online at www.osogrande.com. There is set up fee plus a per minute charge based on usage. For information or to obtain an account call 505-345-6555. Also, search Metro Court civil cases for free at www.metrocourt.state.nm.us
Criminal Records: Access: Phone, fax, mail, online, in person. Both court and visitors may perform in person searches. No search fee. Required to search: name, SSN; also helpful: DOB. Criminal records on computer from 1983. Access to Metro Court criminal records is free at www.metrocourt.state.nm.us
General Information: Public Access terminal is available. (Only civil available.) No pre-sentence reports, psychological evaluations, confidential records released. Copy fee: $.50 per page. Computer printouts are $1.00 per page. Certification fee: $1.50. Payee: Metro Court. Personal checks accepted. Visa, MC accepted. Prepayment required. Mail requests: SASE required. Mail turnaround time 5-10 days.

County Clerk #1 Civic Plaza NW, 6th Fl, Albuquerque, NM 87102; 505-768-4247; Fax: 505-768-5180. Hours: 8AM-4:30PM (MST). *Probate.*

Catron County

7th Judicial District Court PO Drawer 1129, Socorro, NM 87801; 505-835-0050; Fax: 505-838-5217. Hours: 8AM-4PM (MST). *Felony, Civil.*
This court is also responsible for Socorro County.

Civil Records: Access: Phone, fax, mail, online, in person. Both court and visitors may perform in person searches. No search fee. Required to search: name, years to search. Civil cases indexed by defendant, plaintiff. Civil records on microfiche and hard copies from 1925; on computer back to 1997. Access to court records from 1997 forward is free at www.nmcourts.com.
Criminal Records: Access: Phone, fax, mail, online, in person. Both court and visitors may perform in person searches. No search fee. Required to search: name, years to search, DOB; also helpful-SSN, signed release. Criminal records on microfiche and hard copies from 1925; on computer back to 1997. Online access to criminal records is free at www.nmcourts.com.
General Information: Public Access terminal is available. No sequestered records released. Will fax results to local or toll free line. Copy fee: $.35 per page. Certification fee: $2.50. Payee: District Court Clerk. Business checks accepted. Prepayment required. Mail requests: SASE required. Mail turnaround time 1 day.

Quemado Magistrate Court PO Box 283, Quemado, NM 87829; 505-773-4604; Fax: 505-773-4688. Hours: 8AM-5PM (MST). *Misdemeanor, Civil Actions Under $10,000, Eviction, Small Claims.*
Civil Records: Access: Mail, fax, in online, person. Only the court performs in person searches; visitors may not. No search fee. Records computerized since 1997. Access to court records from 1997 forward is free at www.nmcourts.com.
Criminal Records: Access: Mail, fax, online, in person. Only the court performs in person searches; visitors may not. No search fee. Required to search: name, years to search, DOB; also helpful: SSN. Records computerized since 1997. Online access to criminal records is free at www.nmcourts.com.
General Information: Fee to fax results is $1.00 per page. Copy fee: $.10 per page. Certification fee: $.50. Payee: Magistrate Court. Prepayment required. Mail turnaround time 1-2 weeks.

Reserve Magistrate Court PO Box 447, Reserve, NM 87830; 505-533-6474; Fax: 505-533-6623. Hours: 8AM-5PM (MST). *Misdemeanor, Civil Actions Under $10,000, Eviction, Small Claims.*
Civil Records: Access: Mail, fax, in person, online. Both court and visitors may perform in person searches. No search fee. Records computerized since 1996. Access to court records from 1997 forward is free at www.nmcourts.com.
Criminal Records: Access: Mail, fax, in person, online. Both court and visitors may perform in person searches. No search fee. Required to search: name, years to search; also helpful: DOB, SSN. Records computerized since 1996. Online access to criminal records is free at www.nmcourts.com.
General Information: Public Access terminal is available. Will fax documents for $.50 per page. Copy fee: $.50 each. Certification fee: $1.00. Payee: Magistrate Court. Prepayment required. Mail turnaround time 1 week.

County Clerk PO Box I, Socorro, NM 87801; 505-835-0423; Fax: 505-835-1043. Hours: 8AM-5PM (MST). *Probate.*
Note: Local Probate Judge-505-533-6247, PO Box 663, Reserve NM 87830 by appointment.

Chaves County

5th Judicial District Court Box 1776, Roswell, NM 88202; 505-622-2212; Fax: 505-624-9510. 8AM-Noon,1-5PM (MST). *Felony, Civil.*
www.fifthdistrictcourt.com
Civil Records: Access: Online, in person. Visitors must perform in person searches for themselves. No

search fee. Required to search: name, years to search. Civil cases indexed by defendant, plaintiff. Civil records on computer from 1996, on microfiche and archived from 1891. Access to court records from 1997 forward is free at www.nmcourts.com.
Criminal Records: Access: Online, in person. Visitors must perform in person searches for themselves. No search fee. Required to search: name, years to search, DOB, aliases. Criminal records on computer from 1996, on microfiche and archived from 1891. Online access to criminal records is free at www.nmcourts.com.
General Information: Public Access terminal is available. No sequestered records released. Copy fee: $.35 per page. Certification fee: $1.50. Payee: District Court Clerk. Only cashiers checks and money orders accepted. Prepayment required.

Magistrate Court 200 E 4th St, Roswell, NM 88201; 505-624-6088; Fax: 505-624-6092. Hours: 8AM-4PM M, T, TH, F; 9AM-4PM W (MST). *Misdemeanor, Civil Actions Under $10,000, Eviction, Small Claims.*
www.nmcourts.com
Civil Records: Access: Online, in person. Both court and visitors may perform in person searches. No search fee. Access to court records from 1997 forward is free at www.nmcourts.com.
Criminal Records: Access: Online, in person. Both court and visitors may perform in person searches. No search fee. Required to search: name, years to search, DOB; also helpful: SSN. Online access to criminal records is free at www.nmcourts.com.
General Information: Public Access terminal is available. Copy fee: $.50 per page. Prepayment required.

County Clerk Box 580, Roswell, NM 88202; 505-624-6614; Fax: 505-624-6523. Hours: 7AM-5PM (MST). *Probate.*

Cibola County

13th Judicial District Court Box 758, Grants, NM 87020; 505-287-8831; Fax: 505-285-5755. Hours: 8AM-5PM (MST). *Felony, Civil, Probate.*
Civil Records: Access: Fax, mail, online, in person. Both court and visitors may perform in person searches. Search fee: $5.00 per name. Required to search: name, years to search. Civil cases indexed by defendant, plaintiff. Civil records on microfiche from 1981; prior to 1981 belong to Valencia County. Access to court records from 1997 forward is free at www.nmcourts.com.
Criminal Records: Access: Fax, mail, online, in person. Search fee: $5.00 per name. Required to search: name, years to search. Criminal records on microfiche from 1981; prior to 1981 belong to Valencia County. Online access to criminal records is free at www.nmcourts.com.
General Information: No sequestered records released. Will fax results: Unless a toll-free number provided, fee is $2.50 in-state; $5.00 out-of-state. Copy fee: $.35 per page. Certification fee: $1.50. Payee: District Court Clerk. Only cashier checks or money orders accepted. Prepayment required. Mail turnaround time 2-3 days.

Magistrate Court 515 W High, Grants, NM 87020; 505-285-4605. Hours: 8AM-4PM (MST). *Misdemeanor, Civil Actions Under $10,000, Eviction, Small Claims.*
Civil Records: Access: Fax, mail, in person, online. Both court and visitors may perform in person searches. No search fee. Access to court records from 1997 forward is free at www.nmcourts.com.
Criminal Records: Access: Fax, mail, in person, online. Court must perform searches. No search fee.

Required to search: name, years to search. Access to criminal records is free at www.nmcourts.com.

General Information: Copy fee: $.50. Mail requests: SASE required. Mail turnaround time up to 2 weeks.

County Clerk 515 W. High St, PO Box 190, Grants, NM 87020; 505-285-2535/285-2540; Fax: 505-285-2562. Hours: 8AM-5PM (MST). *Probate.*

Colfax County

8th Judicial District Court Box 160, Raton, NM 87740; 505-445-5585; Fax: 505-445-2626. Hours: 8AM-4PM (MST). *Felony, Civil.*

Civil Records: Access: Phone, mail, online, in person. Both court and visitors may perform in person searches. No search fee. Required to search: name, years to search. Civil cases indexed by defendant, plaintiff. Civil records archived from 1912. Access to court records from 1997 forward is free at www.nmcourts.com. Pleadings are unavailable.

Criminal Records: Access: Phone, mail, online, in person. Both court and visitors may perform in person searches. No search fee. Required to search: name, years to search; also helpful: DOB, SSN. Criminal records archived from 1912; computerized records go back to 1996/97. Access to criminal records is free at www.nmcourts.com. Pleadings are unavailable.

General Information: Public Access terminal is available. No adoption, mental, guardianship, children's cases (neglect & child in need of supervision) records released. Fee to fax results is $2.00 per page. Copy fee: $.35 per page. Certification fee: $1.50. Payee: District Court. Business checks accepted. Prepayment required. Mail requests: SASE required. Mail turnaround time 1 week.

Cimarron Magistrate Court PO Drawer 367, Highway 21, Cimarron, NM 87714; 505-376-2634; Fax: 505-376-9108. Hours: 8:30AM-3PM Weds only (MST). *Misdemeanor, Civil Actions Under $10,000, Eviction, Small Claims.*

On days when this court is not in session, you may call the Springer Magistrate Court at 505-483-2417

Civil Records: Access: In person, mail, online. Visitors must perform in person searches for themselves. No search fee. Required to search: Name, years to search; also helpful: DOB. Records searchable from 03/97 on computer. Access to court records 1997 forward is free at www.nmcourts.com.

Criminal Records: Access: In person, mail, online. Visitors must perform in person searches for themselves. Search fee: none. Required to search: name, years to search; also helpful: DOB. Records searchable from 03/97 on computer, except DUI. Online access to criminal records is free at www.nmcourts.com.

General Information: No copy fee. No certification fee. Mail requests: SASE not required. Mail turnaround time 10 days.

Raton Magistrate Court PO Box 68, Raton, NM 87740; 505-445-2220; Fax: 505-445-8966. Hours: 8AM-5PM (MST). *Misdemeanor, Civil Actions Under $10,000, Eviction, Small Claims.*

Civil Records: Access: Phone, mail, fax, in person, online. Only the court performs in person searches; visitors may not. No search fee. Required to search: name, years to search; also helpful: DOB, SSN. Records held for 14 years. Access to court records from 1997 forward is free at www.nmcourts.com.

Criminal Records: Access: Phone, mail, fax, in person, online. Only the court performs in person searches; visitors may not. No search fee. Required to search: name, years to search; also helpful: DOB, SSN. Online access to criminal records is free at www.nmcourts.com.

General Information: Copy fee: $.50. Prepayment required. Mail turnaround time within 1 week.

Springer Magistrate Court 300 Colbert Ave. PO Box 760, Springer, NM 87747; 505-483-2417; Fax: 505-483-0127. Hours: 8AM-4PM (MST). *Misdemeanor, Civil Actions Under $10,000, Eviction, Small Claims.*

Civil Records: Access: Online, in person. Both court and visitors may perform in person searches. Search fee: None. Required to search: name, years to search; also helpful: DOB. On computer back to 3/1997. Access to court records from 1997 forward is free at www.nmcourts.com.

Criminal Records: Access: Online, in person. Both court and visitors may perform in person searches. No search fee. Required to search: name, years to search; also helpful: DOB, SSN. On computer back to 3/1997, DUI kept longer. Online access to criminal records is free at www.nmcourts.com.

General Information: Public access terminal may be available. Copy fee: No charge. Certification fee: No charge. Mail requests: SASE not required. Mail turnaround time 3 days.

County Clerk PO Box 159, Raton, NM 87740; 505-445-5551; Fax: 505-445-4031. Hours: 8AM-5PM (MST). *Probate.*

Curry County

9th Judicial District Court Curry County Courthouse, 700 N Main, #11, Clovis, NM 88101; 505-762-9148; Fax: 505-763-5160. Hours: 8AM-4PM (MST). *Felony, Civil.*
www.nmcourts9thjdc.com

Civil Records: Access: Online, in person. Visitors must perform in person searches for themselves. No search fee. Required to search: name, years to search, address. Civil cases indexed by defendant, plaintiff. Civil records on computer from 1997, on microfiche and archived from 1910. Access to court records from 1997 forward is free at www.nmcourts.com.

Criminal Records: Access: Online, in person. Visitors must perform in person searches for themselves. No search fee. Required to search: name, years to search; also helpful: SSN. Criminal records on computer from 1997, on microfiche and archived from 1910. Online access to criminal records is free at www.nmcourts.com.

General Information: No adoptions, insanity, sequestered, neglect or abuse released. Copy fee: $.35 per page. Certification fee: $1.50. Payee: 9th Judicial District Court. Only cashiers checks and money orders accepted. Prepayment required.

Magistrate Court 221 Pile, Clovis, NM 88101; 505-762-3766; Fax: 505-769-1437. Hours: 8AM-4PM (MST). *Misdemeanor, Civil Actions Under $10,000, Eviction, Small Claims.*

Civil Records: Access: Phone, mail, fax, online, in person. Only the court performs in person searches; visitors may not. No search fee. Access to court records 1997 forward is free at www.nmcourts.com.

Criminal Records: Access: Phone, mail, fax, online, in person. Only the court performs in person searches; visitors may not. No search fee. Required to search: name, years to search; also helpful: DOB, SSN. Online access to criminal records is free at www.nmcourts.com.

General Information: Copy fee: $.50 per page. Certification fee: $.50 per page. Only cashiers checks and money orders accepted. Prepayment required. Mail turnaround time 1 week.

De Baca County

10th Judicial District Court Box 910, Ft. Sumner, NM 88119; 505-355-2896; Fax: 505-355-2899. Hours: 8AM-4:30PM (MST). *Felony, Civil.*

Civil Records: Access: Phone, mail, online, in person. Only the court performs in person searches;

visitors may not. No search fee. Required to search: name, years to search. Civil cases indexed by defendant, plaintiff. Civil records on index cards and docket books archived from 1917; on computer since 1997. Access to court records from 1997 forward is free at www.nmcourts.com.

Criminal Records: Access: Phone, mail, online, in person. Only the court performs in person searches; visitors may not. No search fee. Required to search: name, years to search. Criminal records on index cards and docket books archived from 1917; on computer since 1997. Online access to criminal records is free at www.nmcourts.com.

General Information: No mental, adoptions, or juvenile released. Fee to fax results is $1.00 per page. Copy fee: $.35 per page. Certification fee: $1.50. Payee: District Court. Only cashiers checks and money orders accepted. Prepayment required. Mail requests: SASE required. Mail turnaround: 2 days.

Magistrate Court Box 24, Ft Sumner, NM 88119; 505-355-7371; Fax: 505-355-7149. Hours: 8AM-5PM (MST). *Misdemeanor, Civil Actions Under $10,000, Eviction, Small Claims.*

Civil Records: Access: In person, mail, online. Both court and visitors may perform in person searches. No search fee. Required to search: name, COB; SSN is helpful. Online records go back to 1997. Access to court records from 1997 forward is free at www.nmcourts.com.

Criminal Records: Access: In person, mail, online. Both court and visitors may perform in person searches. No search fee. Required to search: name, years to search, DOB, SSN. Online records go back to 1997. Online access to criminal records is free at www.nmcourts.com.

General Information: Public Access terminal is available. Copy fee: $1.00. Prepayment required. Mail turnaround time is one week.

County Clerk 514 Ave C, PO Box 347, Ft. Sumner, NM 88119; 505-355-2601; Fax: 505-355-2441. Hours: 8AM-Noon, 1-4:30PM (MST). *Probate.*

Dona Ana County

3rd Judicial District Court 201 W Picacho, #A, Las Cruces, NM 88005; 505-523-8200; Fax: 505-523-8290. 8AM-Noon, 1-5PM (MST). *Felony, Civil.*
www.thirddistrictcourt.com/
Note: They also handle Domestic cases.

Civil Records: Access: Mail, online, in person. Both court and visitors may perform in person searches. Search fee: $1.50 per name. Required to search: name, years to search. Civil cases indexed by defendant, plaintiff. Civil records on computer from 1986, on microfiche and archived from 1912. Access to court records from 1997 forward is free at www.nmcourts.com.

Criminal Records: Access: Mail, online, in person. Both court and visitors may perform in person searches. Search fee: $1.50 per name. Required to search: name, years to search; also helpful: DOB, SSN. Criminal records on computer from 1986, on microfiche and archived from 1912. Online access to criminal records is free at www.nmcourts.com.

General Information: Public Access terminal is available. No adoption, mental health, or juvenile released. Copy fee: $.35 per page. Certification fee: $1.50. Payee: 3rd Judicial District. Only cashiers checks and money orders accepted. Prepayment required. Mail requests: SASE required. Mail turnaround time 2-3 days.

Anthony Magistrate Court PO Box 1259, Anthony, NM 88021; 505-233-3147. Hours: 8AM-Noon, 1-5PM (MST). *Misdemeanor, Civil Actions Under $10,000, Eviction, Small Claims.*

Civil Records: Access: Mail, in person, online. Only the court performs in person searches; visitors may not. No search fee. Access to court records from 1997 forward is free at www.nmcourts.com.

Criminal Records: Access: Mail, in person, online. Only the court performs in person searches; visitors may not. No search fee. Required to search: name, years to search, DOB, SSN. Online access to criminal records is free at www.nmcourts.com.

Hatch Magistrate Court PO Box 896, Hatch, NM 87937; 505-267-5202; Fax: 505-267-5088. 8:30AM-4PM Monday (MST). *Misdemeanor, Civil Actions Under $10,000, Eviction, Small Claims.*

Note: Note that this court is only open on Mondays.

Civil Records: Access: Mail, in person, online. Only the court performs in person searches; visitors may not. No search fee. Access to court records from 1997 forward is free at www.nmcourts.com.

Criminal Records: Access: Mail, in person, online. Only the court performs in person searches; visitors may not. No search fee. Required to search: name, years to search, DOB, SSN. Online access to criminal records is free at www.nmcourts.com.

General Information: Copy fee: $.50 per page. No certification fee. Payee: Magistrate Court. Only cashiers checks and money orders accepted. Mail requests: SASE required. Mail turnaround: 1 week.

Las Cruces Magistrate Court 151 N Church, Las Cruces, NM 88001; 505-524-2814; Fax: 505-525-2951. 8AM-4PM (MST). *Misdemeanor, Civil Actions Under $10,000, Eviction, Small Claims.*

Civil Records: Access: In person, mail, online. Both court and visitors may perform in person searches. No search fee. Access to court records from 1997 forward is free at www.nmcourts.com.

Criminal Records: Access: In person, mail, online. Both court and visitors may perform in person searches. No search fee. Required to search: name, years to search; also helpful: DOB, SSN. Access to criminal records is free at www.nmcourts.com.

General Information: Public Access terminal is available. Copy fee: $.50, if done by court $1.00. Payee: Magistrate Court. Turnaround time same day.

County Clerk c/o Third Judicial District, 201 W Picacho #A, Los Cruces, NM 88005; 505-523-8200; Fax: 505-523-8290. 8AM-5PM (MST). *Probate.*

Eddy County

5th Judicial District Court 102 N Canal St #240, Carlsbad, NM 88220; 505-885-4740; Fax: 505-887-7095. 8AM-Noon, 1-5PM (MST). *Felony, Civil.* www.fifthdistrictcourt.com

Civil Records: Access: In person, online. Visitors must perform in person searches for themselves. No search fee. Required to search: name, years to search. Civil cases indexed by defendant. Civil records on computer from 1986, microfiche from 1891. Access to court records from 1997 forward is free online at www.nmcourts.com/disclaim.html, or via the court website above.

Criminal Records: Access: In person, online. Visitors must perform in person searches for themselves. No search fee. Required to search: name, years to search, SSN or DOB. Criminal records on computer from 1986, microfiche from 1900s. Access to criminal records is free at www.nmcourts.com.

General Information: Public Access terminal is available. No adoption, SS case w/children, or guardianship released. Will fax results if urgent for $1.00 per page. Copy fee: $.35 per page. Certification

fee: $1.50. Payee: District Court Clerk. Only cashiers checks, money orders and law firm checks only. Prepayment required.

Artesia Magistrate Court 109 N 15th St, Artesia, NM 88210; 505-746-2481; Fax: 505-746-6763. Hours: 8AM-4PM (MST). *Misdemeanor, Civil Actions Under $10,000, Eviction, Small Claims.*

Note: This court also handles preliminary felonies, traffic, and DUI cases.

Civil Records: Access: Phone, mail, online. Only the court performs in person searches; visitors may not. No search fee. Records go back to 1992, computerized since 1996. Access to court records from 1997 forward is free at www.nmcourts.com.

Criminal Records: Access: Phone, mail, online. Only the court performs in person searches; visitors may not. No search fee. Required to search: name, years to search; also helpful: DOB, SSN. Records comupterized since 1996. Online access to criminal records is free at www.nmcourts.com.

General Information: Copy fee: $.50. Certification fee: $.50 per page. Prepayment required. Mail turnaround time 1-2 days.

Carlsbad Magistrate Court 1949 S Canal St, Carlsbad, NM 88220; 505-885-3218; Fax: 505-887-3460. Hours: 8AM-4PM (MST). *Misdemeanor, Civil Actions Under $10,000, Eviction, Small Claims.*

Civil Records: Access: Phone, mail, fax, in person, online. Only the court performs in person searches; visitors may not. No search fee. Records held 14 years, computerized since 1996. Access to court records 1997 forward is free at www.nmcourts.com.

Criminal Records: Visitors must perform in person searches for themselves. No search fee. Required to search: name, years to search, DOB, SSN. Records held 3 years, computerized since 1996. Online access to criminal records is free at www.nmcourts.com.

General Information: Copy fee: $.50. Turnaround time 1-5 days.

County Clerk Eddy County Probate Judge, 101 W. Green #312, Carlsbad, NM 88220; 505-885-3383; Fax: 505-234-1793. 8AM-5PM (MST). *Probate.*

Grant County

6th Judicial District Court Box 2339, Silver City, NM 88062; 505-538-3250; Fax: 505-388-5439. Hours: 8AM-5PM (MST). *Felony, Civil.*

Civil Records: Access: Fax, mail, online, in person. Both court and visitors may perform in person searches. No search fee. Required to search: name, years to search. Civil cases indexed by defendant, plaintiff. Civil records on microfiche from 1912-1977, on books from 1977; on computer back to 1996. Access to court records from 1997 forward is free at www.nmcourts.com.

Criminal Records: Access: Fax, mail, online, in person. Both court and visitors may perform in person searches. No search fee. Required to search: name, years to search. Criminal records on microfiche from 1912-1977, on books from 1977; on computer back to 1996. Online access to criminal records is free at www.nmcourts.com.

General Information: Public Access terminal is available. No adoptions or abuse records released. Fee to fax results is $2.50 per page. Copy fee: $.35 per page. Certification fee: $1.50. Payee: District Court Clerk. Only cashiers checks and money orders accepted. Prepayment required. Mail requests: SASE required. Mail turnaround time 1 day.

Bayard Magistrate Court PO Box 125, Bayard, NM 88023; 505-537-3042; Fax: 505-537-7365. Hours: 8AM-5PM (MST). *Misdemeanor, Civil Actions Under $10,000, Eviction, Small Claims.*

Civil Records: Access: Mail, fax, online, in person. Only the court performs in person searches; visitors may not. No search fee. Civil records go back to 1992. Access to court records from 1997 forward is free at www.nmcourts.com.

Criminal Records: Access: Mail, fax, in online, person. Only the court performs in person searches; visitors may not. No search fee. Required to search: name, years to search. Criminal records go back to 1999. Online access to criminal records is free at www.nmcourts.com.

General Information: Copy fee: $1.00. Certification fee: $1.00. Prepayment required. Mail turnaround time 10 days.

Silver City Magistrate Court 1620 E Pine St, Silver City, NM 88061; 505-538-3811; Fax: 505-538-8079. Hours: 8AM-5PM (MST). *Misdemeanor, Civil Actions Under $10,000, Eviction, Small Claims.*

Civil Records: Access: Mail, fax, in person, online. Only the court performs in person searches; visitors may not. No search fee. Required to search: years to search, DOB, SSN. Records computerized since 1995. Access to court records from 1997 forward is free at www.nmcourts.com.

Criminal Records: Access: Mail, fax, in person, online. Only the court performs in person searches; visitors may not. No search fee. Required to search: name, years to search, DOB; also helpful: SSN. Records held here from 1988, computerized since 6/16/95. Online access to criminal records is free at www.nmcourts.com.

General Information: Public Access terminal is available. Will fax back for $1.00 per page. Copy fee: $.50. Payee: Magistrate Court. Prepayment required. Mail turnaround time 2 days.

County Clerk Box 898, Silver City, NM 88061; 505-574-0042; Fax: 505-574-0076. Hours: 8AM-5PM (MST). *Probate.*

Note: Access to court records from 1997 forward are free online at www.nmcourts.com/disclaim.html.

Guadalupe County

4th Judicial District Court 420 Parker Ave #5, Guadalupe County Courthouse, Santa Rosa, NM 88435; 505-472-3888; Fax: 505-472-4451. Hours: 8AM-Noon; 1PM-5PM (MST). *Felony, Civil.*

Civil Records: Access: Online, in person. Visitors must perform in person searches for themselves. No search fee. Required to search: name, years to search. Civil cases indexed by defendant, plaintiff. Civil records on docket books from 1912. Access to court records 1997 forward is free at www.nmcourts.com.

Criminal Records: Access: Online, in person. Visitors must perform in person searches for themselves. No search fee. Required to search: name, years to search, DOB; also helpful: SSN. Criminal records on docket books from 1912. Online access to criminal records is free at www.nmcourts.com.

General Information: Public Access terminal is available. No adoption, insanity, juvenile, guardianship records released. Will not fax results. Copy fee: $.35 per page. Certification fee: $1.50. Payee: District Court Clerk Office. Only cashiers checks and money orders accepted. Prepayment required.

Santa Rosa Magistrate Court 603 Parker Ave, Santa Rosa, NM 88435; 505-472-3237. Hours: 8AM-4PM (MST). *Misdemeanor, Civil Actions Under $10,000, Eviction, Small Claims.*

Civil Records: Access: Mail, in person, online. Only the court performs in person searches; visitors may not. No search fee. Access to court records from 1997 forward is free at www.nmcourts.com.

Criminal Records: Access: Mail, in person, online. Only the court performs in person searches; visitors may not. No search fee. Required to search: name, years to search, DOB, offense, date of offense; also helpful: SSN. Online access to criminal records is free at www.nmcourts.com.

General Information: Copy fee: $.50 per copy. No certification fee. Prepayment required. Mail requests: SASE required. Mail turnaround time 7 days.

Vaughn Magistrate Court c/o Santa Rosa Justice Court, 603 Parker Av, Santa Rosa, NM 88435; 505-584-2345. Hours: 8AM-4PM (MST). *Misdemeanor, Civil Actions Under $10,000, Eviction, Small Claims.* Note: The Vaughn court is only open the 2nd Wednesday of the month. It is located at 8th & Calle De Carill, Vaughn, NM 88353. Most records are at Santa Rosa (phone # given here).

Civil Records: Access: Mail, in person, online. Both court and visitors may perform in person searches. No search fee. Access to court records from 1997 forward is free at www.nmcourts.com.

Criminal Records: Access: Mail, in person, online. Visitors must perform in person searches for themselves. No search fee. Required to search: name, years to search. Online access to criminal records is free at www.nmcourts.com.

General Information: Copy fee: $.50 per copy. No certification fee. Prepayment required. Mail requests: SASE required. Mail turnaround time is 7 days.

County Clerk 420 Parker Ave, Courthouse, Santa Rosa, NM 88435; 505-472-3791; Fax: 505-472-4791. Hours: 8AM-5PM (MST). *Probate.*

Harding County

10th Judicial District Court Box 1002, Mosquero, NM 87733; 505-673-2252; Fax: 505-673-2252. 9AM-3PM M-W,F (MST). *Felony, Civil.*

Civil Records: Access: Phone, fax, mail, online, in person. Only the court performs in person searches; visitors may not. No search fee. Required to search: name; also helpful: years to search. Civil cases indexed by defendant, plaintiff. Civil records on books from 1927. Computerized records go back to 1997. Access to court records from 1997 forward is free at www.nmcourts.com.

Criminal Records: Access: Phone, fax, mail, online, in person. Only the court performs in person searches; visitors may not. No search fee. Required to search: name, DOB, SSN; also helpful: years to search. Criminal records on books from 1927. Computerized records go back to 1992. Online access to criminal records is free at www.nmcourts.com.

General Information: No adoption records released. Will fax results for $1.00 per page. Copy fee: $.35 per page. Certification fee: $1.50. Payee: District Court Clerk. Business checks accepted from attorneys only. No personal checks. Prepayment required. Mail requests: SASE required. Mail turnaround time: 1 week.

Magistrate Court Box 9, Roy, NM 87743; 505-485-2549; Fax: 505-485-2407. Hours: 8AM-4PM (MST). *Misdemeanor, Civil Actions Under $10,000, Eviction, Small Claims.*

Civil Records: Access: Mail, phone, in person, online. Both court and visitors may perform in person searches. No search fee. Records computerized since 1996. Access to court records from 1997 forward is free at www.nmcourts.com.

Criminal Records: Access: Mail, phone, in person, online. Both court and visitors may perform in person searches. No search fee. Required to search: name, years to search, DOB; also helpful: address, SSN. Records computerized since 1996. Online access to criminal records is free at www.nmcourts.com.

General Information: Public Access terminal is available. Copy fee: $.50 per page. Payee: Magistrate Court. Prepayment required. Mail turnaround: 2 days.

County Clerk County Clerk, Box 1002, Mosquero, NM 87733; 505-673-2301; Fax: 505-673-2922. Hours: 8AM-4PM (MST). *Probate.*

Hidalgo County

6th Judicial District Court PO Box 608, Lordsburg, NM 88045; 505-542-3411; Fax: 505-542-3481. 8AM-Noon, 1-5PM (MST). *Felony, Civil.*

Civil Records: Access: Phone, fax, mail, online, in person. Only the court performs in person searches; visitors may not. No search fee. Required to search: name, years to search. Civil cases indexed by defendant, plaintiff. Civil records on microfiche and archived from 1920. Access to court records from 1997 forward is free at www.nmcourts.com.

Criminal Records: Access: Phone, fax, mail, online, in person. Only the court performs in person searches; visitors may not. No search fee. Required to search: name, years to search; also helpful: alias. Criminal records on microfiche and archived from 1920. Online access to criminal records is free at www.nmcourts.com.

General Information: No juvenile or adoption records released. Fee to fax results is $5.00 per document; will only fax results to toll-free numbers. Copy fee: $.35 per page. Certification fee: $1.50. Payee: District Court Clerk. Business checks accepted. No personal checks accepted. Prepayment required. Mail requests: SASE required. Mail turnaround time 3-5 days.

Magistrate Court 420 Wabash Ave, Lordsburg, NM 88045; 505-542-3582. Hours: 8AM-5PM (MST). *Misdemeanor, Civil Actions Under $10,000, Eviction, Small Claims.*

Civil Records: Access: Mail, in person, online. Only the court performs in person searches; visitors may not. No search fee. Access to court records from 1997 forward is free at www.nmcourts.com.

Criminal Records: Access: Mail, in person, fax, online. Only the court performs in person searches; visitors may not. No search fee. Required to search: name, years to search; also helpful: DOB, SSN. Online access to criminal records is free at www.nmcourts.com.

General Information: Copy fee: $.50. No certification fee. Payee: Magistrate Court. Only cashiers checks and money orders accepted. Prepayment required. Mail requests: SASE required. Mail turnaround time 1 week.

County Clerk 300 S Shakespeare, Lordsburg, NM 88045; 505-542-9213; Fax: 505-542-3193. Hours: 8AM-5PM (MST). *Probate.*

Lea County

5th Judicial District Court 100 N. Main, #6-C, Lovington, NM 88260; 505-396-8571; Fax: 505-396-2428. Hours: 8AM-5PM (MST). *Felony, Civil.* www.fifthdistrictcourt.com

Civil Records: Access: Fax, mail, online, in person. Both court and visitors may perform in person searches. No search fee. Required to search: name, years to search. Civil cases indexed by defendant, plaintiff. Civil records on computer from 1990, on microfiche from 1912. Access to court records from 1997 forward is free at www.nmcourts.com. Court refers search requests to a private researcher.

Criminal Records: Access: Fax, mail, online, in person. Both court and visitors may perform in person searches. No search fee. Required to search: name, years to search. Criminal records on computer from 1997, on microfiche from 1912. Online access to

criminal records is free at www.nmcourts.com. Court refers searches to a private researcher.

General Information: Public Access terminal is available. No adoptions, mental, abuse records released. Copy fee: $.35 per page. Certification fee: $1.50. Payee: District Court Clerk. Only cashiers checks and money orders accepted. Prepayment required. Mail requests: SASE required. Mail turnaround time 1-3 days.

Eunice Magistrate Court PO Box 240, Eunice, NM 88231; 505-394-3368; Fax: 505-394-3335. 8AM-4PM M,W,F (MST). *Misdemeanor, Civil Actions Under $10,000, Eviction, Small Claims.*

Civil Records: Access: Mail, in person, online. Only the court performs in person searches; visitors may not. No search fee. Access to court records from 1997 forward is free at www.nmcourts.com.

Criminal Records: Access: Mail, in person, online. Only the court performs in person searches; visitors may not. No search fee. Required to search: name, years to search, DOB; also helpful: SSN. Access to criminal records is free at www.nmcourts.com.

General Information: Copy fee: $1.00. Payee: Magistrate Court. Business checks accepted. Mail requests: SASE required. Mail turnaround: 3 days.

Hobbs Magistrate Court 2110 N Alto Dr, Hobbs, NM 88240-3455; 505-397-3621; Fax: 505-393-9121. 8AM-4PM (MST). *Misdemeanor, Civil Actions Under $10,000, Eviction, Small Claims.*

Civil Records: Access: Mail, online, in person. Only the court performs in person searches; visitors may not. No search fee. Civil records held 14 years, computerized since early 2002. Access to records from 1997 forward is free at www.nmcourts.com.

Criminal Records: Access: Mail, online, in person. Only the court performs in person searches; visitors may not. No search fee. Required to search: name, years to search, DOB; SSN and signed release helpful. Criminal records held 14 years, computerized since early 2002. Online access to criminal records is free at www.nmcourts.com.

General Information: Will fax results to local or toll free line. Certification fee: $.50 per page. Prepayment required. Mail turnaround time 3-5 days.

Jal Magistrate Court PO Box 507, Jal, NM 88252; 505-395-2740; Fax: 505-395-2595. Hours: 8-4pm T,Th (MST). *Misdemeanor, Civil Actions Under $10,000, Eviction, Small Claims.* Note: All record requests must be in writing.

Civil Records: Access: Mail, in person, online. Only the court performs in person searches; visitors may not. No search fee. Access to court records from 1997 forward is free at www.nmcourts.com.

Criminal Records: Access: Mail, in person, online. Only the court performs in person searches; visitors may not. No search fee. Required to search: name, years to search, DOB; also helpful: SSN. Access to criminal records is free at www.nmcourts.com.

General Information: Will fax results for $1.00 per page. Copy fee: $.50. Mail requests: SASE required. Mail turnaround time 3 days.

Lovington Magistrate Court 100 W Central, #D, Lovington, NM 88260; 505-396-6677; Fax: 505-396-6163. 8AM-4PM (MST). *Misdemeanor, Civil Actions Under $10,000, Eviction, Small Claims.* www.nmcourts.com

Civil Records: Access: Phone, fax, mail, in person, online. Both court and visitors may perform in person searches. No search fee. Required to search: name, years to search. Access to court records from 1997 forward is free at www.nmcourts.com.

Criminal Records: Access: Phone, fax, mail, in person, online. Both court and visitors may perform in person searches. No search fee. Required to search:

name, years to search, DOB. Online access to criminal records is free at www.nmcourts.com.

General Information: Public Access terminal is available. Will fax results per arrangement. Copy fee: $.50. Certification fee: $.50. Payee: Magistrate Court. Business checks accepted. Prepayment required. Mail requests: SASE required. Mail turnaround: 3 days.

Tatum Magistrate Court PO Box 918, Tatum, NM 88267; 505-398-5300; Fax: 505-398-5310. Hours: 8AM-4PM (MST). *Misdemeanor, Civil Actions Under $10,000, Eviction, Small Claims.*

Civil Records: Access: Phone, mail, fax, online, in person. Both court and visitors may perform in person searches. No search fee. Access to court records from 1997 forward is free at www.nmcourts.com.

Criminal Records: Access: Phone, mail, fax, online, in person. Both court and visitors may perform in person searches. No search fee. Required to search: name, years to search, DOB, SSN, signed release; also helpful: address. Criminal records go back to 1996. All DWI case are on file forever. Online access to criminal records is free at www.nmcourts.com. Phone access only on cases with final disposition.

General Information: Public Access terminal is available. Copy fee: $.50 per page. Certification fee: $2.50. Payee: Magistrate Court. Prepayment required. Mail requests: SASE required. Mail turnaround time 5 days.

County Clerk Box 1507, Lovington, NM 88260; 505-396-8619; Fax: 505-396-3293. Hours: 8AM-5PM (MST). *Probate.* www.leacounty-nm.org

Lincoln County

12th Judicial District Court Box 725, Carrizozo, NM 88301; 505-648-2432; Fax: 505-648-2581. Hours: 8AM-5PM (MST). *Felony, Civil.* www.12thdistrict.com

Civil Records: Access: Online, mail, in person. Both court and visitors may perform in person searches. No search fee. Required to search: name, years to search. Civil cases indexed by defendant, plaintiff. Civil records on computer from 1991, docket books from 1960, microfiche to 1960. Access to court records from 1997 forward is free at www.nmcourts.com.

Criminal Records: Access: Online, in person. Both court and visitors may perform in person searches. No search fee. Required to search: name, years to search. Criminal records on computer from 1991, docket books from 1960, microfiche to 1960. Online access to criminal records is free at www.nmcourts.com.

General Information: No juvenile, adoption, or mental records released. Will fax results to toll free number. Copy fee: $.35 per page. Certification fee: $1.50. Payee: District Court Clerk. Business checks accepted. Prepayment required. Mail turnaround time is 3 days.

Carrizozo Magistrate Court 310 11th St., Carrizozo, NM 88301; 505-648-2380; Civil phone: 505-378-7022. Hours: 8AM-12;00-1-4PM (MST). *Misdemeanor, Civil Actions Under $10,000, Eviction, Small Claims.*

Civil Records: Access: Mail, in person, online. Both court and visitors may perform in person searches. No search fee. Access to court records from 1997 forward is free at www.nmcourts.com.

Criminal Records: Access: Fax, in person, mail, online. Visitors must perform in person searches for themselves. Search fee: $7.00 per name, if more than 1 name. Required to search: name, years to search; also helpful: DOB, SSN. Access to criminal records for past 10 years is free at www.nmcourts.com.

General Information: Copy fee: $.50 per page. Payee: Magistrate Court. Mail requests: SASE required. Mail turnaround time 3 days.

Ruidoso Magistrate Court 301 W Highway 70 #2, Ruidoso, NM 88345; 505-378-7022; Fax: 505-378-8508. 8AM-4PM (MST). *Misdemeanor, Civil Actions Under $10,000, Eviction, Small Claims.*

Civil Records: Access: Mail, in person, online. Both court and visitors may perform in person searches. No search fee. Access to court records from 1997 forward is free at www.nmcourts.com.

Criminal Records: Access: Mail, in person, online. Visitors must perform in person searches for themselves. No search fee. Required to search: name, years to search; also helpful: DOB, SSN. Access to criminal records is free at www.nmcourts.com.

General Information: Copy fee: $.50 per page. Payee: Magistrate Court. Turnaround time 3 days.

County Clerk PO Box 338, Carrizozo, NM 88301; 505-648-2394; Fax: 505-648-2576. Hours: 8AM-5PM (MST). *Probate.* Note: This court will do searches

Los Alamos County

1st Judicial District Court c/o Santa Fe 1st District Court, PO Box 2268, Santa Fe, NM 87504. http://firstdistrictcourt.com Note: All civil and criminal cases handled by Santa Fe District Court.

Magistrate Court 1319 Trinity Dr, Los Alamos, NM 87544; 505-662-2727; Fax: 505-661-6258. Hours: 8AM-4PM (MST). *Misdemeanor, Civil Actions Under $10,000, Eviction, Small Claims.*

Civil Records: Access: Online, in person. Only the court performs in person searches; visitors may not. No search fee. Access to court records from 1997 forward is free at www.nmcourts.com.

Criminal Records: Access: Online, in person. Only the court performs in person searches; visitors may not. No search fee. Required to search: name, years to search, address, DOB, signed release; also helpful: SSN. Online access to criminal records is free at www.nmcourts.com.

County Clerk-Probate PO Box 30, Los Alamos, NM 87544; 505-662-8010; Fax: 505-662-8008. Hours: 7:30AM-5PM (MST). *Probate.*

Luna County

6th Judicial District Court Luna County Courthouse Rm 40, Deming, NM 88030; 505-546-9611; Fax: 505-546-0971. Hours: 8AM-4PM (MST). *Felony, Civil.*

Civil Records: Access: Mail, online, in person. Both court and visitors may perform in person searches. No search fee. Required to search: name, years to search. Civil cases indexed by defendant, plaintiff. Civil records on microfiche from 1911; on computer back to 1997. Access to court records from 1997 forward is free at www.nmcourts.com.

Criminal Records: Access: Mail, online, in person. Both court and visitors may perform in person searches. No search fee. Required to search: name, years to search. Criminal records on microfiche from 1911; on computer back to 1997. Online access to criminal records is free at www.nmcourts.com.

General Information: Public Access terminal is available. No adoptions, mental, sequestered or juvenile records released. Will fax results for $.35 per page. Copy fee: $.35 per page. Certification fee: $1.50. Payee: District Court Clerk. Only cashiers checks and money orders accepted. Prepayment required. Mail requests: SASE required. Mail turnaround time 5 days.

Magistrate Court 912 S Silver St, Deming, NM 88030; 505-546-9321; Fax: 505-546-4896. Hours: 8AM-Noon, 1-5PM (MST). *Misdemeanor, Civil Actions Under $10,000, Eviction, Small Claims.*

Civil Records: Access: Mail, in person, online. Only the court performs in person searches; visitors may not. No search fee. Access to court records from 1997 forward is free at www.nmcourts.com.

Criminal Records: Access: Mail, in person, online. Only the court performs in person searches; visitors may not. No search fee. Required to search: name, years to search. Online access to criminal records is free at www.nmcourts.com.

General Information: Will fax results for $1.00 per page. Copy fee: $.50 per page includes certification. Payee: Luna Magistrate Court. Prepayment required. Mail requests: SASE required. Mail turnaround time 2-3 days.

County Clerk PO Box 1838, Deming, NM 88031; 505-546-0491; Fax: 505-546-4708. Hours: 8AM-5PM (MST). *Probate.* Note: There can be some probate cases (those in dispute) at District Court level.

McKinley County

11th Judicial District Court 201 W. Hill, Rm 4, Gallup, NM 87301; 505-863-6816; Fax: 505-722-8401. 8AM-Noon, 1-5PM (MST). *Felony, Civil.*

Civil Records: Access: Phone, mail, online, in person. Both court and visitors may perform in person searches. No search fee. Required to search: name, years to search. Civil cases indexed by defendant, plaintiff. Civil records on computer from 1989, on microfiche from 1923. Access to court records from 1997 forward is free online at www.nmcourts.com. One name only by phone.

Criminal Records: Access: Phone, mail, online, in person. Both court and visitors may perform in person searches. No search fee. Required to search: name, years to search, DOB; also helpful: SSN. Criminal records on computer from 1989, on microfiche from 1923. Online access to criminal records is free at www.nmcourts.com. Will search one name only by phone.

General Information: Public Access terminal is available. No adoption or juvenile records released. Fee to fax results is $5.00 per call. Copy fee: $.35 per page. Certification fee: $1.50. Payee: McKinley County District Court. No personal checks accepted. Prepayment required. Mail requests: SASE required. Mail turnaround time 3-5 days.

Magistrate Court 285 Boardman Dr, Gallup, NM 87301; 505-722-6636; Fax: 505-863-3510. Hours: 8AM-4PM (MST). *Misdemeanor, Civil Actions Under $10,000, Eviction, Small Claims.* Note: Felony preliminary hearings held here.

Civil Records: Access: Online, in person. Only the court performs in person searches; visitors may not. No search fee. Access to court records from 1997 forward is free at www.nmcourts.com.

Criminal Records: Access: Online, in person. Only the court performs in person searches; visitors may not. No search fee. Required to search: name, years to search, DOB; also helpful: SSN. Online access to criminal records is free at www.nmcourts.com.

General Information: Prepayment required. Mail turnaround time 1-2 weeks.

County Clerk PO Box 1268, Gallup, NM 87305; 505-863-6866; Fax: 505-863-1419. Hours: 8AM-5PM (MST). *Probate.*

Thoreau Magistrate Court 39 First St., Thoreau, NM 87323; 505-862-7871; Fax: 505-862-8606. Hours: 8:30AM-4PM Every Other Friday (MST). *Misdemeanor, Civil Actions Under $10,000, Eviction, Small Claims.*

Note: Note this court is open only every other Friday.

Civil Records: Access: Mail, in person, online. Only the court performs in person searches; visitors may not. No search fee. Access to court records from 1997 forward is free at www.nmcourts.com.

Criminal Records: Access: Mail, in person, online. Only the court performs in person searches; visitors may not. No search fee. Required to search: name, years to search, DOB; also helpful: SSN. Access to criminal records is free at www.nmcourts.com.

General Information: Prepayment required. Mail turnaround time 1-2 weeks.

Mora County

4th Judicial District Court PO Box 1540, Las Vegas, NM 87701; 505-425-7281; Fax: 505-425-6307. 8AM-Noon, 1-4PM (MST). *Felony, Civil.*

Civil Records: Access: Online, in person. Both the court and visitors may perform in person searches. No search fee. Required to search: name, years to search. Civil cases indexed by defendant, plaintiff. Civil records on microfiche from 1912, archived before 1912. Access to court records from 1997 forward is free at www.nmcourts.com.

Criminal Records: Access: Online, in person, fax. Both the court and visitors may perform in person searches. No search fee. Required to search: name, years to search. Criminal records on microfiche from 1912, archived before 1912. Online access to criminal records is free at www.nmcourts.com.

General Information: Public Access terminal is available. No adoptions, insanity, or juvenile records released. Copy fee: $.35 per page. Certification fee: $1.50. Payee: 4th Judicial District Court. Only cashiers checks and money orders accepted. Prepayment required.

Magistrate Court 1927 7th St., Las Vegas, NM 87701-4957; 505-425-5204. Hours: 8AM-4PM (closed for lunch) (MST). *Misdemeanor, Civil Actions Under $10,000, Eviction, Small Claims.*

Civil Records: Access: Mail, in person, online. Both court and visitors may perform in person searches. No search fee. Access to court records from 1997 forward is free at www.nmcourts.com.

Criminal Records: Access: Mail, online, in person. Both court and visitors may perform in person searches. No search fee. Required to search: name, years to search. Online access to criminal records is free at www.nmcourts.com.

General Information: Copy fee: $.50 per page. No certification fee. Payee: Magistrate Court. Only cashiers checks and money orders accepted. Prepayment required. Mail requests: SASE required. Mail turnaround time 1-2 weeks.

Probate Court PO Box 360, Mora, NM 87732; 505-387-5014. Hours: 8AM-5PM (MST). *Probate.*

Otero County

12th Judicial District Court 1000 New York Ave, Rm 209, Alamogordo, NM 88310-6940; 505-437-7310; Fax: 505-434-8886. Hours: 8AM-5PM (MST). *Felony, Civil.* www.12thdistrict.net

Civil Records: Access: Online, in person. Visitors must perform in person searches for themselves. No search fee. Required to search: name, years to search. Civil cases indexed by defendant, plaintiff. Civil records on computer from 1991, on microfiche from 1926. Access to court records from 1997 forward is free at www.nmcourts.com. Also, current court dockets are at the court website. Phone & mail access limited to 5 names each.

Criminal Records: Access: Online, in person. Visitors must perform in person searches for themselves. No search fee. Required to search: name, years to search. Criminal records on computer from

1991, on microfiche from 1926. Online access to criminal records is free at www.nmcourts.com. Phone & mail access limited to 5 names each. Only court performs searches prior to March 1986.

General Information: Public Access terminal is available. No sealed, adoption records released. Copy fee: $.35 per page. Certification fee: $1.50. Payee: District Court. Only cashiers checks and money orders accepted. Prepayment required.

Magistrate Court 263 Robert H Bradley Dr, Alamogordo, NM 88310-8288; 505-437-9000 x256; Fax: 505-439-1365. Hours: 8AM-4PM (MST). *Misdemeanor, Civil Actions Under $10,000, Eviction, Small Claims.*

Civil Records: Access: Mail, in person, online. Only the court performs in person searches; visitors may not. No search fee. Records placed in storage after one year. Access to court records from 1997 forward is free at www.nmcourts.com.

Criminal Records: Access: Mail, in person, online. Only the court performs in person searches; visitors may not. No search fee. Required to search: name, years to search, DOB; also helpful: SSN. Records placed in storage after one year. Online access to criminal records is free at www.nmcourts.com.

General Information: Will fax results for $1.00 per page. Copy fee: $.50 per page. Certification fee: $1.00 per page. Payee: Magistrate Court. Prepayment required. Mail requests: SASE required. Mail turnaround time 1-2 weeks.

County Clerk 1000 New York Ave, Rm 108, Alamogordo, NM 88310-6932; 505-437-4942; Fax: 505-443-2922. 7:30AM-6PM (MST). *Probate.*

Quay County

10th Judicial District Court Box 1067, Tucumcari, NM 88401; 505-461-2764; Fax: 505-461-4498. Hours: 8AM-5PM (MST). *Felony, Civil.*

Civil Records: Access: Phone, fax, mail, online, in person. Both court and visitors may perform in person searches. No search fee. Required to search: name, years to search. Civil cases indexed by defendant, plaintiff. Civil records on hard copy file from 1995 to present, microfiche 1912 to 1994, archived from 1911, on computer back to 1997. Access to court records from 1997 forward is free at www.nmcourts.com.

Criminal Records: Access: Phone, fax, mail, online, in person. Both court and visitors may perform in person searches. No search fee. Required to search: name; also helpful: years to search, DOB, SSN. Criminal records on hard copy file from 1995 to present, microfiche 1912 to 1994, archived from 1911, on computer back to 1997. Online access to criminal records is free at www.nmcourts.com.

General Information: Public Access terminal is available. No adoptions, juvenile, insanity records released. Will fax results $2.00 1st page, $1.00 each add'l. Copy fee: $.35 per page. Certification fee: $1.50. Payee: District Court Clerk. Only cashiers checks and money orders accepted. Prepayment required. Mail requests: SASE required. Mail turnaround time same day.

Quay County

Tucumcari Magistrate Court PO Box 1301, Tucumcari, NM 88401; 505-461-1700; Fax: 505-461-4522. Hours: 8AM-4PM (MST). *Misdemeanor, Civil Actions Under $10,000, Eviction, Small Claims.*

Note: San Jon Magistrate Court (closed) records are found here.

Civil Records: Access: Online, in person. Only the court performs in person searches; visitors may not. No search fee. Access to court records from 1997 forward is free at www.nmcourts.com.

Criminal Records: Access: Online, in person. Only the court performs in person searches; visitors may not. No search fee. Required to search: name, years to search, DOB, SSN. Online access to criminal records is free at www.nmcourts.com.

General Information: Public Access terminal is available. (DWI Task Force only.). Will bill copy fees. Turnaround time same day.

County Clerk 300 S Third St, PO Box 1225, Tucumcari, NM 88401; 505-461-0510; Fax: 505-461-0513. Hours: 8AM-5PM (MST). *Probate.*

Rio Arriba County

1st Judicial District Court c/o Santa Fe 1st District Court, PO Box 2268, Santa Fe, NM 87504; 505-476-0189; Fax: 505-827-5055. *Felony, Misdemeanor, Probate.* http://firstdistrictcourt.com

Note: Most all major civil and criminal cases are handled by Santa Fe District Court.

Rio Arriba Magistrate Court - Division 1

PO Box 538 (1332 Hiway 17), Chama, NM 87520; 505-756-2278; Fax: 505-756-2477. Hours: 8AM-Noon, 1-5PM (MST). *Misdemeanor, Civil Actions Under $10,000, Eviction, Small Claims.*

Civil Records: Access: Mail, fax, in person, online. Both court and visitors may perform in person searches. No search fee. Required to search: name, years to search. On computer back to 1997. Access to court records from 1997 forward is free at www.nmcourts.com.

Criminal Records: Access: Mail, fax, in person, online. Only the court performs in person searches; visitors may not. No search fee. Required to search: name, years to search. On computer back to 1997. Online access to criminal records is free at www.nmcourts.com.

General Information: Copy fee: $.50 per page. Turnaround time 1 week.

Rio Arriba Magistrate Court - Division 2

410 Paseo de Onate, Espanola, NM 87532; 505-753-2532; Fax: 505-753-4802. Hours: 8AM-4PM (MST). *Misdemeanor, Civil Actions Under $10,000, Eviction, Small Claims.*

Civil Records: Access: Mail, in person, online. Only the court performs in person searches; visitors may not. No search fee. Access to court records from 1997 forward is free at www.nmcourts.com.

Criminal Records: Access: Mail, in person, online. Only the court performs in person searches; visitors may not. No search fee. Required to search: name, years to search. Online access to criminal records is free at www.nmcourts.com.

General information: Turnaround time within 1 week.

County Clerk PO Box 158, Tierra Amarilla, NM 87575; 505-588-7724; Fax: 505-588-7418. Hours: 8AM-5PM (MST). *Probate.*

Roosevelt County

9th Judicial District Court 109 West 1st St, #207, Portales, NM 88130; 505-356-4463; Fax: 505-359-2140. Hours: 8AM-4PM (MST). *Felony, Civil.*

Civil Records: Access: Online, in person. Visitors must perform in person searches for themselves. No search fee. Required to search: name, years to search. Civil cases indexed by defendant, plaintiff. Civil records on microfiche from 1912, archived before 1912. Access to court records from 1997 forward is free at www.nmcourts.com.

Criminal Records: Access: Online, in person. Visitors must perform in person searches for themselves. No search fee. Required to search: name, years to search. Criminal records on microfiche from

1912, archived before 1912. Online access to criminal records is free at www.nmcourts.com.

General Information: No adoption, guardianship, insanity records released. Copy fee: $.35 per page. Cert fee: $1.50. Payee: 9th Judicial District Court. Only cashiers checks and money orders accepted. Prepayment required.

Magistrate Court 42427 US Hwy 70, Portales, NM 88130; 505-356-8569; Fax: 505-359-6883. Hours: 8AM-4PM (MST). *Misdemeanor, Civil Actions Under $10,000, Eviction, Small Claims, Felonies.*

www.nmcourts.com

Civil Records: Access: Phone, mail, fax, in person, online. Only the court performs in person searches; visitors may not. No search fee. Records computerized since 1995. Access to court records from 1997 forward is free at www.nmcourts.com.

Criminal Records: Access: Phone, mail, fax, in person, online. Only the court performs in person searches; visitors may not. No search fee. Required to search: name, DOB; also helpful: SSN. Records computerized since 1995. Online access to criminal records is free at www.nmcourts.com.

General Information: Will fax results $1.00 per page. Copy fee: $1.00. Cert fee: $1.00. Prepayment required. Mail turnaround time 5 days.

County Clerk Roosevelt County Courthouse, 109 W First, Portales, NM 88130; 505-356-8562; Fax: 505-356-3560. Hours: 8AM-5PM (MST). *Probate.*

San Juan County

11th Judicial District Court 103 S. Oliver, Aztec, NM 87410; 505-334-6151; Fax: 505-334-1940. 8AM-Noon, 1-5PM (MST). *Felony, Civil.*

www.eleventhdistrictcourt.state.nm.us

Civil Records: Access: Online, in person. Visitors must perform in person searches for themselves. No search fee. Required to search: name, years to search; also helpful: address. Civil cases indexed by defendant, plaintiff. Civil records on computer from 1986, on microfiche from 1925, on cards from 1912. Access to court records from 1997 forward is free at www.nmcourts.com.

Criminal Records: Access: Online, in person, mail, fax. Both the court (if after 1986) and visitors may perform in person searches. No search fee. Required to search: name, years to search, DOB; also helpful: address, SSN. Criminal records on computer from 1986, on microfiche from 1925, on cards from 1912. Online access to criminal records is free at www.nmcourts.com.

General Information: Public Access terminal is available. No adoptions, insanity, sealed, expunged records released. Will fax results for $.35 per page. Copy fee: $.35 per page. Cert fee: $1.50 per page. Payee: Eleventh District Court. No personal or out-of-state checks accepted. Prepayment required. Mail requests: SASE required. Mail turnaround time is 3 days.

Aztec Magistrate Court 200 Gossett, Aztec, NM 87410; 505-334-9479; Fax: 505-334-2178. Hours: 8AM-4PM (MST). *Misdemeanor, Civil Actions Under $10,000, Eviction, Small Claims.*

Civil Records: Access: Online, in person. Both court and visitors may perform in person searches. No search fee. Access to court records from 1997 forward is free at www.nmcourts.com.

Criminal Records: Access: Online, in person. Both court and visitors may perform in person searches. No search fee. Required to search: name, years to search; also helpful: DOB, SSN. Online access to criminal records is free at www.nmcourts.com.

General Information: Public Access terminal is available.

Farmington Magistrate Court 950 W Apache St, Farmington, NM 87401; 505-326-4338; Fax: 505-325-2618. Hours: 8AM-4PM (MST). *Misdemeanor, Civil Actions Under $10,000, Eviction, Small Claims.*

www.nmcourts.com

Civil Records: Access: Online, in person. Both court and visitors may perform in person searches. No search fee. Civil records go back 12 years for open cases. Closed case records go back to 6-30-02. Access to court records from 1997 forward is free at www.nmcourts.com.

Criminal Records: Access: Online, in person. Both court and visitors may perform in person searches. No search fee. Required to search: name, years to search, DOB; also helpful: SSN. Criminal records go back to 6-30-02; DWI's 1986. Online access to criminal records is free at www.nmcourts.com.

General Information: Public Access terminal is available. Will fax results for $1.00 per page. Copy fee: $.50 per page. Prepayment required. Mail turnaround time same day.

County Clerk PO Box 550, Aztec, NM 87410; 505-334-9471; Fax: 505-334-3635. Hours: 7AM-5:30PM (MST). *Probate.*

San Miguel County

4th Judicial District Court PO Box 1540, Las Vegas, NM 87701; 505-425-7281; Fax: 505-454-8611. Hours: 8AM-Noon, 1-5PM (MST). *Felony, Civil, Probate.*

Note: Also handles cases for Mora County.

Civil Records: Access: Phone, mail, online, in person, fax. Visitors must perform in person searches for themselves. No search fee. Required to search: name, years to search. Civil cases indexed by defendant, plaintiff. Civil records on microfiche from 1912, archived before 1912. Access to court records from 1997 forward is free at www.nmcourts.com.

Criminal Records: Access: Online, in person. Visitors must perform in person searches for themselves. No search fee. Required to search: name, years to search. Criminal records on microfiche from 1912, archived before 1912. Online access to criminal records is free at www.nmcourts.com.

General Information: No adoptions, insanity, juvenile records released. Will fax results. Copy fee: $.35 per page. Cert fee: $1.50. Payee: 4th Judicial District Court Clerk. Only cashiers checks and money orders accepted. Prepayment required. Mail requests: SASE required.

Magistrate Court 1927 7th St, Las Vegas, NM 87701-4957; 505-425-5204; Fax: 505-425-0422. Hours: 8AM-4PM (MST). *Misdemeanor, Civil Actions Under $10,000, Eviction, Small Claims.*

Civil Records: Access: Online, in person. Only the court performs in person searches; visitors may not. No search fee. Access to court records from 1997 forward is free at www.nmcourts.com.

Criminal Records: Access: Online, in person. Only the court performs in person searches; visitors may not. No search fee. Required to search: name, years to search, DOB; also helpful: address, SSN. Online access to criminal records is free at www.nmcourts.com.

General information: Turnaround time 1-7 days.

County Clerk San Miguel County Clerk, 500 W. National Ave, #113, Las Vegas, NM 87701; 505-425-9331; Fax: 505-454-1799. Hours: 8AM-Noon, 1-5PM (MST). *Probate.*

Sandoval County

13th Judicial District Court 100 Avenida De Justicia, Bernalillo, NM 87004; 505-867-2376. Hours: 8AM-Noon, 1-5PM (MST). *Felony, Civil.*

Civil Records: Access: Fax, mail, online, in person. Both court and visitors may perform in person searches. Search fee: $5.00 search fee. Required to search: name, years to search. Civil cases indexed by defendant, plaintiff. Civil records indexed on computer back to 11/96; prior on microfiche. Access to court records from 1997 forward is free at www.nmcourts.com.

Criminal Records: Access: Fax, mail, online, in person. Both court and visitors may perform in person searches. Search fee: $5.00 per name. Required to search: name, years to search. Criminal records on computer back to 11/96. Online access to criminal records is free at www.nmcourts.com.

General Information: Public Access terminal is available. No adoption, neglect and abuse records released. Fee to fax results is $2.50 per page. Out of state $5.00 per page. Copy fee: $.35 per page. Microfilm copies $.50 per page (1991 and prior). Cert fee: $1.50. Payee: 13th Judicial District Court. Business checks accepted. Prepayment required. Mail turnaround time 2-3 days.

Bernalillo Magistrate Court PO Box 818, Bernalillo, NM 87004; 505-867-5202 X2-6; Fax: 505-867-0970. Hours: 8AM-4PM (MST). *Misdemeanor, Civil Actions Under $10,000, Eviction, Small Claims.*

Civil Records: Access: Mail, fax, in person, online. Both court and visitors may perform in person searches. No search fee. Civil records go back to 12/1996; prior destroyed. Access to court records from 1997 forward is free at www.nmcourts.com.

Criminal Records: Access: Mail, online, in person. Visitors must perform in person searches for themselves. No search fee. Required to search: name, years to search. Criminal records go back to 12/1996; prior destroyed. Online access to criminal records is free at www.nmcourts.com.

General Information: Public Access terminal is available. Copy fee: $.50 per page. Cert fee: $.50 per document. Payee: Magistrate Court. Turnaround time 1-2 weeks.

Cuba Magistrate Court PO Box 1497, Cuba, NM 87013; 505-289-3519; Fax: 505-289-3013. Hours: 8AM-Noon, 1-5PM (MST). *Misdemeanor, Civil Actions Under $10,000, Eviction, Small Claims.*

Civil Records: Access: Online, in person. Visitors must perform in person searches for themselves. No search fee. Access to court records from 1997 forward is free at www.nmcourts.com.

Criminal Records: Access: Online, in person. Visitors must perform in person searches for themselves. No search fee. Required to search: name, years to search. Online access to criminal records is free at www.nmcourts.com.

Probate Court PO Box 40, Bernalillo, NM 87004; 505-867-7572; Civil phone: 505-867-7645; Fax: 505-867-9365. Hours: 8AM-5PM (MST). *Probate.*

Santa Fe County

First Judicial District Court Box 2268, Santa Fe, NM 87504; 505-476-0189; Fax: 505-827-5055. Hours: 8AM-4PM (MST). *Felony, Civil.*

http://firstdistrictcourt.com

Note: Because this court also handles the counties of Los Alamos and Rio Arriba, you must indicate which county you are searching.

Civil Records: Access: Phone, mail, online, in person. Both court and visitors may perform in person searches. Search fee: none. Required to search: name, years to search. Civil cases indexed by defendant, plaintiff. Civil records on computer from 1984, older records on docket books. Request must be in writing. Access to index of court records from 1997 forward is free online at www.nmcourts.com.

Criminal Records: Access: Phone, mail, online, in person. Both court and visitors may perform in person searches. Search fee: none. Required to search: name, years to search; also helpful: DOB, SSN. Criminal records on computer from 1984, older records on docket books. Online access to index of criminal records is free at www.nmcourts.com.

General Information: Public Access terminal is available. No adoption, juvenile, mental or abuse records released. Copy fee: $.35 per page. Cert fee: $1.50 per seal. Payee: First Judicial District Court. Business checks accepted. Prepayment required. Mail requests: SASE required. Mail turnaround: 2 days.

Magistrate Court 2056 Galisteo St, Santa Fe, NM 87505; 505-984-9914; Fax: 505-986-5866. Hours: 8AM-4PM (MST). *Misdemeanor, Civil Actions Under $10,000, Eviction, Small Claims.*
Note: Also, the clerk for the Pojaoque Magistrate Court may be contacted here.

Civil Records: Access: Fax, mail, in person, online. Both court and visitors may perform in person searches. No search fee. Required to search: Name, years to search. Civil records on computer back to 1997. Access to court records from 1997 forward is free at www.nmcourts.com.

Criminal Records: Access: Fax, mail, in person, online. Both court and visitors may perform in person searches. No search fee. Required to search: name, years to search, DOB; also helpful: SSN. Criminal records on computer back to 1997. Online access to criminal records is free at www.nmcourts.com.

General Information: No cert fee. Mail turnaround time 1 week.

Pojoaque Magistrate Court 2052 Galisteo St, Santa Fe, NM 87505; 505-498-9914; Fax: 505-455-3053. Hours: 8AM-Noon,1-5PM (MST). *Misdemeanor, Civil Actions Under $10,000, Eviction, Small Claims.*
Note: The Court In Pojoaque is often closed; the clerk can be contacted at the Santa Fe Magistrate Court, 505-476-0189 (address above).

County Clerk Box 276, Santa Fe, NM 87504-0276; 505-986-6279; Fax: 505-986-6362. Hours: 8AM-5PM (MST). *Probate.*

Sierra County

7th Judicial District Court PO Box 3009, Truth or Consequences, NM 87901; 505-894-7167; Fax: 505-894-7168. Hours: 8AM-4PM (MST). *Felony, Civil.*
Civil Records: Access: Fax, mail, online, in person. Both the court and visitors may perform in person searches. No search fee. Required to search: name, years to search, address. Civil cases indexed by defendant, plaintiff. Civil records on microfiche from 1920, archived before 1920. Access to court records from 1997 forward is free at www.nmcourts.com.
Criminal Records: Access: Fax, mail, online, in person. Both the court and visitors may perform in person searches. No search fee. Required to search: name, years to search, address, SSN. Criminal records on microfiche from 1920, archived before 1920. Online access to criminal records is free at www.nmcourts.com.
General Information: Public Access terminal is available. No adoptions, insanity, juvenile, guardianship records released. Copy fee: $.35 per

page. Cert fee: $1.50. Payee: Sierra County District Court. Only cashiers checks and money orders accepted. Prepayment required. Mail requests: SASE required. Mail turnaround time 2 days.

Magistrate Court 155 W Barton, Truth or Consequences, NM 87901; 505-894-3051; Fax: 505-894-0476. Hours: 8AM-4PM (MST). *Misdemeanor, Civil Actions Under $10,000, Eviction, Small Claims.*
Civil Records: Access: Online, in person. Both court and visitors may perform in person searches. No search fee. Access to court records from 1997 forward is free at www.nmcourts.com.
Criminal Records: Access: Online, in person. Both court and visitors may perform in person searches. No search fee. Required to search: name, years to search, DOB, SSN. Online access to criminal records is free at www.nmcourts.com.
General information: Prepayment required. Mail turnaround time 3 weeks.

County Clerk 100 N Date St., (Probate Records), Truth or Consequences, NM 87901; 505-894-2840; Probate phone: 505-894-4416; Fax: 505-894-2516. Hours: 8AM-5PM (MST). *Probate.*

Socorro County

7th Judicial District Court District Court, PO Drawer 1129, Socorro, NM 87801; 505-835-0050 x10; Fax: 505-838-5217. *Felony, Civil Actions Over $7,500, Probate.*
Note: Although case hearings and trials are held here, all civil and criminal case files are housed at the Catron County District Court at the address above. The physical address for this court is 200 Church St, Socorro.

Magistrate Court 102 Winkler St, Socorro, NM 87801; 505-835-2500; Fax: 505-838-0428. Hours: 8AM-4PM (MST). *Misdemeanor, Civil Actions Under $10,000, Eviction, Small Claims.*
Civil Records: Access: Mail, in person, online. Only the court performs in person searches; visitors may not. No search fee. Access to court records from 1997 forward is free at www.nmcourts.com.
Criminal Records: Access: Mail, in person, online. Only the court performs in person searches; visitors may not. No search fee. Required to search: name, years to search; also helpful: DOB, SSN. Online access to criminal records is free at www.nmcourts.com.
General Information: Copy fee: $.50 per page. Cert fee: $1.00. Payee: Magistrate Court. Mail requests: SASE required. Mail turnaround time 1-5 days.

County Clerk 200 Church St, Socorro, NM 87801; 505-835-0423; Fax: 505-835-1043. Hours: 8AM-5PM (MST). *Probate.*

Taos County

8th Judicial District Court 105 Albright St #H, Taos, NM 87571; 505-758-3173; Fax: 505-751-1281. Hours: 8AM-4PM (MST). *Felony, Civil.*
Civil Records: Access: In person, online. Visitors must perform in person searches for themselves. No search fee. Required to search: name, years to search. Civil cases indexed by defendant, plaintiff. Civil records on computer since 1993, books since 1912, microfiche from 1912-1980. Access to court records from 1993 forward is free at www.nmcourts.com.
Criminal Records: Access: In person, online. Visitors must perform in person searches for themselves. No search fee. Required to search: name, years to search, DOB; also helpful: signed release, SSN. Criminal records on computer since 1993, books since 1912, microfiche from 1912-1950. Online

access to criminal records is free at www.nmcourts.com.
General Information: No adoption, juvenile, abuse or sequestered case records released. Copy fee: $.35 per page. Cert fee: $1.50. Payee: District Court. Only cashiers checks and money orders accepted. Prepayment required.

Questa Magistrate Court PO Box 586, Questa, NM 87556; 505-586-0761; Fax: 505-586-0428. Hours: 8AM-Noon,1-4PM (MST). *Misdemeanor, Civil Actions Under $10,000, Eviction, Small Claims.*
www.nmcourts.com
Civil Records: Access: Mail, in person, online. Both court and visitors may perform in person searches. No search fee. Civil records go back to 1984. Access to court records from 1997 forward is free at www.nmcourts.com.
Criminal Records: Access: Mail, in person, online. Both court and visitors may perform in person searches. No search fee. Required to search: name, years to search; also helpful: DOB, SSN. Criminal records go back to 1998. Online access to criminal records is free at www.nmcourts.com.
General Information: Public Access terminal is available. Fee to fax results is $1.00 per page. Copy fee: $.50 per page. No cert fee. Payee: Taos Circuit Court. Prepayment required. Mail turnaround 14 days.

Taos Magistrate Court 920 Salazar Rd #B, Taos, NM 87571; 505-758-4030; Fax: 505-751-0983. Hours: 8AM-4PM (MST). *Misdemeanor, Civil Actions Under $10,000, Eviction, Small Claims.*
Civil Records: Access: Online, in person. Both court and visitors may perform in person searches. No search fee. Civil records go back to 1997. Access to court records from 1997 forward is free at www.nmcourts.com.
Criminal Records: Access: Online, in person. Both court and visitors may perform in person searches. No search fee. Required to search: name, years to search, DOB; also helpful: SSN. Criminal records go back to 1997. Online access to criminal records is free at www.nmcourts.com.
General Information: Copy fee: $.50. Cert fee: $.50. Prepayment required. Mail turnaround time 3 days.

County Clerk 105 Albright, #E, Taos, NM 87551; 505-758-8266; Fax: 505-751-3391/737-6390. Hours: 8AM-Noon;1-5PM (MST). *Probate.*

Torrance County

7th Judicial District Court County Courthouse, PO Box 78, Estancia, NM 87016; 505-384-2974; Fax: 505-384-2229. Hours: 8AM-4PM (MST). *Felony, Civil.*
www.nmcourts.com
Civil Records: Access: Mail, online, in person. Both court and visitors may perform in person searches. No search fee. Required to search: name, years to search. Civil cases indexed by defendant, plaintiff. Civil records on hard copy until filmed, microfiche from 1912; on computer back to 1997. Access to court records from 1997 forward is free at www.nmcourts.com.
Criminal Records: Access: Mail, online, in person. Both court and visitors may perform in person searches. No search fee. Required to search: name, years to search; also helpful: SSN, DOB. Criminal records on hard copy until filmed, microfiche from 1912; on computer back to 1997. Online access to criminal records is free at www.nmcourts.com.
General Information: Public Access terminal is available. No juvenile, neglect, adoption, mental health records released. Will fax results to local or toll free line. Copy fee: $.35 per page. Cert fee: $1.50. Payee: Seventh Judicial District Court. Only cashiers

checks and money orders accepted. Prepayment required. Mail requests: SASE required. Mail turnaround time 1 day.

Estancia Magistrate Court
Neil Mertz Judicial Complex, PO Box 274, Estancia, NM 87016; 505-384-2926; Fax: 505-384-3157. Hours: 8AM-4PM (MST). *Misdemeanor, Civil Actions Under $10,000, Eviction, Small Claims.*
Note: All record requests must be in writing.

Civil Records: Access: Mail, fax, in person, online. Both court and visitors may perform in person searches. No search fee. Closed case files maintained 1 year then archived, record index on computer since 1997. Access to court records from 1997 forward is free at www.nmcourts.com.

Criminal Records: Access: Mail, fax, in person, online. Both court and visitors may perform in person searches. No search fee. Required to search: name, years to search; also helpful: DOB, SSN. Closed case files maintained 1 years then destroyed 1 year from date of closure, record index on computer since 1997. Online access to criminal records is free at www.nmcourts.com.

General Information: Public Access terminal is available. Will fax results for $1.00 per page. Cert fee: $.50. Payee: Magistrate court. Prepayment required. Mail turnaround time up to 3 days.

Moriarty Magistrate Court
PO Box 2027, Moriarty, NM 87035; 505-832-4476; Fax: 505-832-1563. Hours: 8AM-4PM (MST). *Misdemeanor, Civil Actions Under $10,000, Eviction, Small Claims.*

Civil Records: Access: Mail, fax, mail, in person, online. Both court and visitors may perform in person searches. No search fee. Closed case files maintained 1 year, record index on computer since 1997. Access to court records from 1997 forward is free at www.nmcourts.com.

Criminal Records: Access: In person, online. Both court and visitors may perform in person searches. No search fee. Required to search: name, years to search; also helpful: DOB, SSN. Closed case files maintained 1 year, record index on computer since 1997. Online access to criminal records is free at www.nmcourts.com.

General information: Prepayment required. Mail turnaround time up to 3 days.

County Clerk
PO Box 767, Estancia, NM 87016; 505-384-2221/1226; Fax: 505-384-4080. Hours: 8AM-5PM (MST). *Probate.*

Union County

8th Judicial District Court
Box 310, Clayton, NM 88415; 505-374-9577; Fax: 505-374-2089. Hours: 8AM-Noon, 1-5PM (MST). *Felony, Civil.*

Civil Records: Access: Mail, online, in person. Both court and visitors may perform in person searches. No search fee. Required to search: name, years to search. Civil cases indexed by defendant, plaintiff. Civil records on cards from 1981. Computerized records go to 1997. Access to court records from 1997 forward is free at www.nmcourts.com.

Criminal Records: Access: Mail, online, in person. Both court and visitors may perform in person searches. No search fee. Required to search: name, years to search. Criminal records on docket sheets from 1981. Computerized records go to 1997. Online access to criminal records is free at www.nmcourts.com.

General Information: Public Access terminal is available. No adoption, juvenile records released. Will fax results for $.35 per page. Copy fee: $.35 per page. Cert fee: $1.50. Payee: Clerk of District Court. Only cashiers checks and money orders accepted. Prepayment required. Mail requests: SASE required. Mail turnaround time 1-2 days.

Magistrate Court
836 Main St, Clayton, NM 88415; 505-374-9472; Fax: 505-374-9368. Hours: 8AM-Noon, 12:30-4:30PM (MST). *Misdemeanor, Civil Actions Under $10,000, Eviction, Small Claims.*
www.nmcourts.com/
Note: The court also handles preliminary felony hearings and felony probable cause.

Civil Records: Access: online, in person. Both court and visitors may perform in person searches. No search fee. Records available since 06/31/87, computerized since 03/13/97. Access to court records from 1997 forward is free at www.nmcourts.com.

Criminal Records: Access: online, in person. Both court and visitors may perform in person searches. No search fee. Required to search: name, years to search; also helpful: address, DOB, SSN. Records computerized since 03/13/97. Online access to criminal records is free at www.nmcourts.com.

General Information: Copy fee: $.50 per page. Prepayment required. Mail turnaround time 2 days.

County Clerk
PO Box 430, Clayton, NM 88415; 505-374-9491; Fax: 505-374-2763. Hours: 9AM-Noon, 1-5PM (MST). *Probate.*

Valencia County

13th Judicial District Court
Box 1089, Los Lunas, NM 87031; 505-865-4291; Fax: 505-865-8801. Hours: 8AM-5PM (MST). *Felony, Civil.*

Civil Records: Access: Fax, mail, online, in person. Both court and visitors may perform in person searches. Search fee: $5.00 for up to 2 names, $10.00 for 3-10 names. Required to search: name, years to search. Civil cases indexed by defendant, plaintiff. Civil records on microfiche from 1915. Access to court records from 1997 forward is free at www.nmcourts.com.

Criminal Records: Access: Mail, online, in person. Both court and visitors may perform in person searches. Search fee: $5.00 fee for 2 names, $10.00 for 3-10 names. Required to search: name, years to search. Criminal records on microfiche from 1915. Online access to criminal records is free at www.nmcourts.com.

General Information: Public Access terminal is available. No adoptions or juvenile records released. Will fax results for $2.50 in-state; $5.00 out-of-state. Copy fee: $.35 per page. Cert fee: $1.50. Payee: 13th Judicial District Court. Only cashiers checks and money orders accepted. Mail requests: SASE required. Mail turnaround time 2 days.

Belen Magistrate Court
901 W Castillo, Belen, NM 87002; 505-864-7509; Fax: 505-864-9532. Hours: 8AM-4PM (MST). *Misdemeanor, Civil Actions Under $10,000, Eviction, Small Claims.*

Civil Records: Access: online, in person. Only the court performs in person searches; visitors may not. No search fee. Access to court records from 1997 forward is free at www.nmcourts.com.

Criminal Records: Access: online, in person. Only the court performs in person searches; visitors may not. No search fee. Required to search: name, years to search, DOB, date of offense; also helpful: address, SSN. Online access to criminal records is free at www.nmcourts.com.

General Information: Copy fee: $.50. Prepayment required. Mail turnaround time 1 day.

Los Lunas Magistrate Court
1206 Main St, Los Lunas, NM 87031; 505-865-4637; Fax: 505-865-0639. Hours: 8AM-4PM (MST). *Misdemeanor, Civil Actions Under $10,000, Eviction, Small Claims.*

Civil Records: Access: online, in person. Only the court performs in person searches; visitors may not. No search fee. Access to court records from 1997 forward is free at www.nmcourts.com.

Criminal Records: Only the court performs in person searches; visitors may not. No search fee. Required to search: name, years to search, DOB; also helpful: SSN. Online access to criminal records is free at www.nmcourts.com.

General information: Prepayment required. Mail turnaround time 3-5 days.

County Clerk
PO Box 969, Los Lunas, NM 87031; 505-866-2073; Fax: 505-866-2023. Hours: 8AM-4:30PM (MST). *Probate.*
www.co.valencia.nm.us/Clerk.htm

New Mexico Recording Offices

ORGANIZATION: 33 counties, 33 recording offices. The recording officer is County Clerk. Most counties maintain a grantor/grantee index and a miscellaneous index. The entire state is in the Mountain Time Zone (MST).

REAL ESTATE RECORDS: Most counties will not perform real estate searches. Copy and certification fees vary.

UCC RECORDS: Financing statements are filed at the state level, except for real estate related collateral, which are filed with the County Clerk. However, prior to 07/2001, consumer goods and farm collateral were also filed at the County Clerk and these older records can be searched there. Only a few recording offices will perform UCC searches. Use search request form UCC-11. Search and copy fees vary widely.

TAX LIEN RECORDS: All federal and state tax liens are filed with the County Clerk. Most counties will not provide tax lien searches.

OTHER LIENS: Judgment, mechanics, lis pendens, contractors, hospital.

ONLINE ACCESS: Several counties offer online access, but there is no statewide system.

Bernalillo County

County Clerk, PO Box 542, Albuquerque, NM 87103-0542. **Phone-**505-768-4090, R/E Recording-505-768-4268, UCC Recording-505-768-4268; fax-505-768-4190; hours-8AM-5PM www.bernco.gov/live/depts_and_offices.asp
Will search UCC records. Tax liens not included in UCC search. Real estate record owner and mortgage searches available. RE record copy- $.50 per page. UCC copy- $1.00 per page. Cert fee: $.50 per doc. Payee: Bernalillo County. **Online Access to Real Estate, Property Assessor records:** Search assessor records at www.bernco.gov/property/default.asp?qpaction=search_form&type=situs. Also, the recorders data and Grantor/Grantee index is at http://cyclops.bernco.gov/splash.jsp. Free registration and password required. For more information call 505-768-4090. **Other phones:** Assessor-505-222-3700; Treasurer-505-768-4031.

Catron County

County Clerk, PO Box 197, Reserve, NM 87830-0197. **Phone-**County Clerk, R/E & UCC Recording- 505-533-6400; fax-505-533-6400; hours 8AM-4:30PM
May provide unofficial searches as a courtesy, and if mail and copy fees prepaid. Will not do official UCC records searches but may honor unofficial mail requests. Will not do an official tax lien search. May provide unofficial separate federal or state tax lien search. Will not perform official real estate record searches. RE record copy- $1.00 per page. UCC copy- $1.00 per page if mailed. Cert fee: $1.00 per doc. Payee: Catron County Clerk. **Other phones:** Assessor-505-533-6577; Treasurer-505-533-6384; Elections-505-533-6400.

Chaves County

County Clerk, Box 580, Roswell, NM 88202-0580. **Phone-**County Clerk, R/E & UCC Recording- 505-624-6614; fax-505-624-6523; hours 7AM-5PM
Will not search UCC or real estate records. Will search state/federal tax liens. RE record copy- $.25 per page. UCC copy- $1.00 per page. Cert fee: $1.00 per cert. Payee: Chaves County Clerk. **Other phones:** Assessor-505-624-6603; Treasurer-505-624-6618; Appraiser-505-624-6603; Elections-505-624-6614; Vital Records-505-827-0121.

Cibola County

County Clerk, PO Box 190, Grants, NM 87020. **Phone-**505-287-2539, R/E Recording-505-285-2539, UCC Recording-505-285-2539; fax-505-285-2562; hours 8AM-5PM

Will not search records. Copy fee- $1.00 per page. Cert fee: $2.00 per doc. Payee: Cibola County Clerk. **Other phones:** Assessor-505-285-2527; Treasurer-505-285-2520; Elections-505-285-2540.

Colfax County

County Clerk, PO Box 159, Raton, NM 87740-0159. **Phone-**County Clerk, R/E & UCC Recording- 505-445-5551; fax-505-445-4031; hours 8AM-5PM
Will not search records. RE record copy- $.35 per page. UCC copy- $1.00 per sheet. Cert fee: $1.00 per doc. Payee: County Clerk. **Other phones:** Assessor-505-445-2341; Treasurer-505-445-3171; Elections-505-445-5551; Vital Records-505-445-5551.

Curry County

County Clerk, PO Box 1168, Clovis, NM 88102-1168. **Phone-**County Clerk, R/E & UCC Recording- 505-763-5591; fax-505-763-4232; hours 8AM-5PM www.currycounty.org/clerk's.html
Will not search records. RE record copy- $.25 per page. UCC copy- $1.00 per page. Cert fee: $1.00 per doc + $.25 per page. Payee: Curry County Clerk. **Other phones:** Assessor-505-763-5731; Treasurer-505-763-3931; Appraiser-505-763-6581; Elections-505-763-5591; Vital Records-505-827-0121.

De Baca County

County Clerk, PO Box 347, Fort Sumner, NM 88119. **Phone-**County Clerk, R/E & UCC Recording- 505-355-2601; fax-505-355-2441; hours 8AM-N, 1-4:30PM. Will not search records. RE record copy- $.30 per page. UCC copy- $.30 per page. Cert fee: $1.50 per doc. Payee: De Baca County Clerk. **Other phones:** Assessor-505-355-7448; Treasurer-505-355-7395; Appraiser-505-355-7448; Elections-505-355-2601.

Dona Ana County

County Clerk, 251 W. Amador, Rm 103, Las Cruces, NM 88005-2893. **Phone-**505-647-7421, R/E Recording-505-647-7420; fax-505-647-7464; hours 8AM-5PM www.co.dona-ana.nm.us
Will not search records. RE record copy- $.25 per page. UCC copy- $1.00 per page. Cert fee: $1.50 per doc. Payee: Dona Ana County Clerk. **Online Access to Assessor, Real Estate, Personal Property, Voter Registration records:** Records on the Real Property database are free at www.co.dona-ana.nm.us/assr/search.html. Also, search the voter registration rolls for free at www.co.dona-ana.nm.us/boe/voter.html. **Other phones:** Assessor-505-647-7400; Treasurer-505-647-7433; Appraiser-505-647-7400; Elections-505-647-7466; Vital Records-505-827-0121.

Eddy County

County Clerk, 101 W. Greene St, Rm 312, Carlsbad, NM 88220. **Phone-**County Clerk, R/E & UCC Recording- 505-885-3383; fax-505-234-1793; hours 8AM-5PM. Will not search records. Copy fee- $.50 per page. Cert fee: $1.00 per doc. **Other phones:** Assessor-505-885-3813; Treasurer-505-885-3913; Appraiser-505-885-3813; Elections-505-885-3383; Vital Records-505-827-0121.

Grant County

County Clerk, PO Box 898, Silver City, NM 88062. **Phone-**County Clerk, R/E & UCC Recording- 505-574-0042; fax-505-574-0076; hours 8AM-5PM
Will not search records. RE record copy- $.25 per page. Cert fee: $1.00 per page. Payee: Grant County Clerk. **Other phones:** Assessor-505-574-0030; Treasurer-505-574-0055; Elections-505-574-0042; Vital Records-505-574-0042.

Guadalupe County

County Clerk, 420 Parker Ave, Courthouse, #1, Santa Rosa, NM 88435. **Phone-**County Clerk, R/E & UCC Recording- 505-472-3791; fax-505-472-3735; hours M-F 8AM-5PM
Will search UCC records. Search per debtor- $5.00. Will not search tax liens. Will search real estate records only 7 years back. Copy fee- $1.00 per page. Cert fee: $3.00 per doc. Payee: Guadalupe Co.Clerk. **Other phones:** Assessor-505-472-3738; Treasurer-505-472-3133; Elections-505-472-3741.

Harding County

County Clerk, PO Box 1002, Mosquero, NM 87733-1002. **Phone-**County Clerk, R/E & UCC Recording- 505-673-2301; fax-505-673-2922; hours 8AM-4PM
NM Vital Statistics, 1105 St Francis Dr PO Box 26110, Santa Fe, NM 87502. Will not search records. Record copy fees-$.25 if from book; $.50 if from microfiche or color copy. UCC copy- $1.00 per page. Cert fee: $1.00 per doc + $.25 or $.50 per page. Payee: Harding County Clerk. **Other phones:** Assessor-505-673-2926; Treasurer-505-673-2928; Appraiser-505-673-2926; Elections-505-673-2301; Vital Records-505-827-0121 (Info-505-827-2338).

Hidalgo County

County Clerk, 300 Shakespeare St, Lordsburg, NM 88045. **Phone-**505-542-9213; fax-505-542-3193; hours 8AM-5PM, Will not search records. Copy fee-$.25 per page. Cert fee: $1.25 per cert in person; $1.50 per page if mailed. Payee: Hidalgo County Clerk. **Other phones:** Assessor-505-542-3433; Treasurer-505-542-9313.

Lea County

County Clerk, PO Box 1507, Lovington, NM 88260. **Phone-**505-396-8614, R/E Recording-505-396-8531, UCC Recording-505-396-8531; fax-505-396-3293; hours 8AM-5PM www.leacounty-nm.org
Will search UCC records. UCC search per debtor- $20.00 per name. Will not search real estate records. UCC copy- None 1st 5 pages, over 5 pages $.50 per page. **Other phones:** Assessor-505-396-8527; Elections-505-396-8531.

Lincoln County

County Clerk, PO Box 338, Carrizozo, NM 88301. **Phone-**County Clerk, R/E & UCC Recording- 505-648-2394; fax-505-648-2576; hours 8AM-5PM
Will search UCC records. Will search tax liens. Will search for brief real estate records. Copy fee- $.25 per page. Cert fee: $1.50. Payee: Lincoln County Clerk. **Online Access to Assessor, Property records:** Access to the assessor property records is free at www.lincolncountynm.net/AssrOfficeFrPg.html; registration, software, username and password is required. Follow prompts at website. **Other phones:** Assessor-505-648-2306; Treasurer-505-648-2397; Appraiser-505-648-2306; Elections-505-648-2331; Vital Records-505-648-2394; Manager-505-648-2385.

Los Alamos County

County Clerk, PO Box 30, Los Alamos, NM 87544. **Phone-**County Clerk, R/E & UCC Recording- 505-662-8010; fax-505-662-8008; hours 7:30AM-5PM
Will not search records. RE record copy- $1.00 per page. UCC copy- $2.00 per page. Cert fee: $1.00 per cert. Payee: County Clerk. **Other phones:** Assessor-505-662-8030; Treasurer-505-662-8070; Elections-505-662-8011; Vital Records-505-827-2338.

Luna County

County Clerk, PO Box 1838, Deming, NM 88031-1838. **Phone-**County Clerk, R/E & UCC Recording-505-546-0491; fax-505-546-4708; hours 8AM-5PM
Will not search records. Copy fee- $.50 per page. Cert fee: $1.00 per doc. Payee: Luna County Clerk. **Other phones:** Assessor-505-546-0404; Treasurer-505-546-0401; Elections-505-546-0491; Vital Records-505-827-0121 (Santa Fe, NM).

McKinley County

County Clerk, PO Box 1268, Gallup, NM 87301. **Phone-**County Clerk, R/E & UCC Recording- 505-863-6866; fax-505-863-1419; hours 8AM-5PM
Will not search UCC or tax liens records. Real estate owner, mortgage, and property transfer searches available. RE record copy- $.35 per page. UCC copy- $1.00 per page. Cert fee: $2.00 per cert. Payee: McKinley County Clerk. **Other phones:** Assessor-505-863-3032; Treasurer-505-722-4459; Elections-505-722-4469; Vital Records-505-821-0121.

Mora County

County Clerk, PO Box 360, Mora, NM 87732-0360. **Phone-**County Clerk, R/E & UCC Recording- 505-387-2448; fax-505-387-9023; hours 8AM-N, 1-5PM
Will search UCC records. Search per debtor- $10.00 per 10 years. UCC search includes tax liens. Will search real estate records. Copy fee- $1.00 per page. **Other phones:** Assessor-505-387-5289; Treasurer-505-387-2756; Appraiser-505-387-5289; Elections-505-387-2448.

Otero County

County Clerk, 1000 New York Ave, Rm 108, Alamogordo, NM 88310-6932. **Phone-**County Clerk, R/E & UCC Recording- 505-437-4942; fax-505-443-2922; hours-7:30AM-6PM
www.oteroclerk@co.otero.nm.us

Will search UCC records, only one or two names. Will search tax liens. Only one or two names. Will search real estate records. Only one or two names. Copy fee- $.25 per page. Cert fee: $1.50 per certification. Payee: Otero County Clerk. **Other phones:** Assessor-505-437-5310; Treasurer-505-437-2030; Elections-505-437-4942.

Quay County

County Clerk, PO Box 1225, Tucumcari, NM 88401-1225. **Phone-**County Clerk, R/E & UCC Recording-505-461-0510; fax-505-461-0513; hours 8AM-5PM
Will search UCC records but will not certify. UCC search per debtor- no fee for uncertified search. Will not search real estate or tax lien records. Copy fee- $.50 per page. Cert fee: $1.50 per page. Payee: Quay County Clerk. **Other phones:** Assessor-505-461-1760; Treasurer-505-461-0470; Elections-505-461-0510; Vital Records-505-827-2338.

Rio Arriba County

County Clerk, PO Box 158, Tierra Amarilla, NM 87575. **Phone-**505-588-7724; fax-505-588-7418; hours 8AM-5PM. Will search UCC records. Search per debtor- $20.00. Will not search real estate or tax lien records. RE record copy- $1.00 per page. Copy fee-$1.00 per page. Cert fee: $.50 per cert. Payee: Rio Arriba County Clerk. **Other phones:** Assessor-505-588-7726; Treasurer-505-588-7727.

Roosevelt County

County Clerk, 101 W. 1st, Rm 106, Portales, NM 88130. **Phone-**505-356-8562; fax-505-356-3560; hours 8AM-5PM www.rooseveltcounty.com
Will not search records. RE record copy- $.50 per page. UCC copy- $1.00 per page. **Other phones:** Assessor-505-356-6971; Treasurer-505-356-4081.

San Juan County

County Clerk, PO Box 550, Aztec, NM 87410. **Phone-**County Clerk, R/E & UCC Recording- 505-334-9471; fax-505-334-3635; hours-7AM-5:30PM www.co.san-juan.nm.us
Will not search records. RE record copy- $.50 per page. UCC copy- $1.00 per page. Cert fee: $1.00 per cert. Payee: County Clerks Office. **Online Access to Real Estate, Assessor records:** Access to county real estate tax data is free at www.sjcounty.net/CountyTax/TaxHome.aspx. **Other phones:** Assessor-505-334-6157; Treasurer-505-334-9421; Elections-505-334-9471.

San Miguel County

County Clerk, Courthouse, Las Vegas, NM 87701. **Phone-**County Clerk, R/E & UCC Recording- 505-425-9331; fax-505-454-1799; hours 8AM-5PM
Will not search records. RE record copy- $.50 per copy. UCC copy- $.50 per copy. Cert fee: $2.00 per copy. Payee: San Miguel County. **Other phones:** Assessor-505-454-4980; Treasurer-505-425-9376; Elections-505-425-9331; Vital Records-505-425-9368.

Sandoval County

County Clerk, PO Box 40, Bernalillo, NM 87004. **Phone-**County Clerk, R/E & UCC Recording- 505-867-7572; fax-505-771-8610; hours 8AM-5PM
Will search UCC records. Search per debtor- $5.00. Will not search tax liens. Will search real estate records. RE record copy- $1.00 per page. UCC copy- $.25 per page. Cert fee: $.75 per doc. **Other phones:** Assessor-505-867-7562; Treasurer-505-867-7581; Appraiser-505-867-7503; Elections-505-867-7577; Vital Records-505-841-4185.

Santa Fe County

County Clerk, PO Box 1985, Santa Fe, NM 87504-1985. **Phone-**505-986-6280; fax-505-995-2767; hours

8AM-4PM. Will search UCC records from 1991 to present. Will search tax liens from 1991 to present. Federal/state combined tax lien search- $75 per copy. Will search real estate records 1991 to present. RE record copy- $.75 per copy, microfile xerox-$.50. UCC copy- $.50 per page; $.75 if from microfilm. Cert fee: $1.50 per doc + $.50 per page. Payee: Santa Fe County Clerk. **Online Access to Assessor, Property records:** Access to county property data at http://216.161.39.9/wick/Query1CompactHTMLInput.html requires Location ID or Tax Account ID that is found on a county tax bill. **Other phones:** Assessor-505-986-6308; Treasurer-505-986-6253; Appraiser-505-986-6300; Elections-505-986-6280; Vital Records-505-827-0121.

Sierra County

County Clerk, 100 Date St, Truth or Consequences, NM 87901. **Phone-**County Clerk, R/E & UCC Recording- 505-894-2840; fax-505-894-2516; 8AM-5PM. If asked, this agency will look in computer to see what is there for you, but they are not bonded to do searches. Will not search records. RE record copy-$.50 per copy. UCC copy- $.50 per copy. Cert fee: $1.00. Payee: Sierra County Clerk. **Other phones:** Assessor-505-894-2589; Treasurer-505-894-3524; Elections-505-894-2840; Vital Records-505-827-2338.

Socorro County

County Clerk, PO Box I, Socorro, NM 87801. **Phone-**505-835-3263, R/E Recording-505-835-0423, UCC Recording-505-835-0423; fax-505-835-1043; hours 8AM-5PM. Will not search records. **Other phones:** Assessor-505-835-0714; Treasurer-505-835-1701; Appraiser-505-835-0714; Elections-505-835-0423; Vital Records-505-835-0423.

Taos County

County Clerk, 105 Albright St, #D, Taos, NM 87571. **Phone-**505-737-6380, R/E Recording-505-751-8654, UCC Recording-505-751-8654; fax-505-737-6390; hours 8AM-5PM. Will not search records. UCC copy- $.25 per page. Cert fee: $1.50. Payee: Taos County Clerk. **Other phones:** Assessor-505-751-8651; Treasurer-505-751-8672; Appraiser-505-751-8554; Elections-505-751-8657.

Torrance County

County Clerk, PO Box 48, Estancia, NM 87016. **Phone-**505-384-2221; fax-505-384-4080; 8AM-5PM
Will not search records. RE record copy- $.50 per page. UCC copy- $1.00 per page. Cert fee: $1.00 per doc. Payee: County Clerk. **Other phones:** Assessor-505-384-2331; Treasurer-505-384-2241.

Union County

County Clerk, PO Box 430, Clayton, NM 88415. **Phone-**County Clerk, R/E & UCC Recording- 505-374-9491; fax-505-374-2763; hours 9AM-5PM
Will not search records. Copy fee- $1.00 per page. Cert fee: $1.00 per page. **Other phones:** Assessor-505-374-9441; Treasurer-505-374-2331; Appraiser-505-374-9441; Elections-505-374-9491.

Valencia County

County Clerk, PO Box 969, Los Lunas, NM 87031. **Phone-**County Clerk, R/E & UCC Recording- 505-866-2073; fax-505-866-2023; hours 8AM-4:30PM www.co.valencia.nm.us/CntyAgencies.htm
Will search UCC records. Will not search real estate or tax lien records. RE record copy- $2.50 per certified copy. Cert fee: $2.50. Payee: County Clerk. **Other phones:** Assessor-505-866-2065; Treasurer-505-866-2090; Elections-505-866-2080; Vital Records-505-841-4100.

New Mexico County Locator

You will usually be able to find the city name in the City/County Cross Reference below. In that case, it is a simple matter to determine the county from the cross reference. However, only the official US Postal Service city names are included in this index. There are an additional 40,000 place names that people use in their addresses. Therefore, we have also included a ZIP/City Cross Reference immediately following the City/County Cross Reference.

If you know the ZIP Code but the city name does not appear in the City/County Cross Reference index, look up the ZIP Code in the ZIP/City Cross Reference, find the city name, then look up the city name in the City/County Cross Reference. For example, you want to know the county for an address of Menands, NY 12204. There is no "Menands" in the City/County Cross Reference. The ZIP/City Cross Reference shows that ZIP Codes 12201-12288 are for the city of Albany. Looking back in the City/County Cross Reference, Albany is in Albany County.

New Mexico City/County Cross Reference

ABIQUIU Rio Arriba
ALAMOGORDO Otero
ALBUQUERQUE Bernalillo
ALBUQUERQUE Sierra
ALCALDE Rio Arriba
ALGODONES Sandoval
ALTO Lincoln
AMALIA Taos
AMISTAD Union
ANGEL FIRE Colfax
ANIMAS Hidalgo
ANTHONY (88021) Dona Ana(98), Otero(1)
ANTON CHICO Guadalupe
ARAGON Catron
ARENAS VALLEY Grant
ARREY Sierra
ARROYO HONDO Taos
ARROYO SECO Taos
ARTESIA Eddy
AZTEC San Juan
BARD Quay
BAYARD Grant
BELEN Valencia
BELL RANCH San Miguel
BELLVIEW Curry
BENT Otero
BERINO Dona Ana
BERNALILLO Sandoval
BINGHAM Socorro
BLANCO San Juan
BLOOMFIELD San Juan
BLUEWATER Cibola
BOSQUE (87006) Socorro(83), Valencia(16)
BOSQUE FARMS Valencia
BRIMHALL McKinley
BROADVIEW (88112) Quay(60), Curry(39)
BUCKHORN Grant
BUENA VISTA Mora
BUEYEROS Harding
CABALLO Sierra
CANJILON Rio Arriba
CANNON AFB Curry
CANONES Rio Arriba
CAPITAN Lincoln
CAPROCK Lea
CAPULIN Union
CARLSBAD Eddy
CARRIZOZO (88301) Lincoln(80), Torrance(20)
CARSON Taos
CASA BLANCA Cibola
CAUSEY Roosevelt
CEBOLLA Rio Arriba
CEDAR CREST Bernalillo
CEDARVALE Torrance
CERRILLOS Santa Fe
CERRO Taos
CHACON Mora
CHAMA Rio Arriba
CHAMBERINO Dona Ana
CHAMISAL Taos

CHAPARRAL (88081) Dona Ana(74), Otero(25)
CHIMAYO Rio Arriba
CHURCH ROCK McKinley
CIMARRON Colfax
CLAUNCH Socorro
CLAYTON Union
CLEVELAND Mora
CLIFF Grant
CLINES CORNERS Torrance
CLOUDCROFT Otero
CLOVIS Curry
COCHITI LAKE Sandoval
COCHITI PUEBLO Sandoval
COLUMBUS Luna
CONCHAS DAM San Miguel
CONTINENTAL DIVIDE McKinley
CORDOVA Rio Arriba
CORONA Lincoln
CORRALES (87048) Sandoval(85), Bernalillo(14)
COSTILLA Taos
COUNSELOR Sandoval
COYOTE Rio Arriba
CROSSROADS Lea
CROWNPOINT McKinley
CUBA Sandoval
CUBERO Cibola
CUCHILLO Sierra
CUERVO Guadalupe
DATIL Catron
DEMING Luna
DERRY Sierra
DES MOINES Union
DEXTER Chaves
DIXON Rio Arriba
DONA ANA Dona Ana
DORA Roosevelt
DULCE Rio Arriba
DURAN Torrance
EAGLE NEST Colfax
EDGEWOOD (87015) Santa Fe(69), Torrance(17), Bernalillo(12)
EL PRADO Taos
EL RITO Rio Arriba
ELEPHANT BUTTE Sierra
ELIDA (88116) Roosevelt(94), Chaves(5)
EMBUDO Rio Arriba
ENCINO (88321) Torrance(70), Guadalupe(29)
ESPANOLA Rio Arriba
ESTANCIA Torrance
EUNICE Lea
FAIRACRES Dona Ana
FARMINGTON San Juan
FAYWOOD Grant
FENCE LAKE Cibola
FLORA VISTA San Juan
FLOYD (88118) Roosevelt(94), Curry(5)
FLYING H Chaves
FOLSOM Union
FORT BAYARD Grant
FORT STANTON Lincoln

FORT SUMNER De Baca
FORT WINGATE McKinley
FRUITLAND San Juan
GALLINA Rio Arriba
GALLUP McKinley
GALLUP San Juan
GAMERCO McKinley
GARFIELD Dona Ana
GARITA San Miguel
GILA Grant
GLADSTONE Union
GLENCOE Lincoln
GLENRIO Quay
GLENWOOD Catron
GLORIETA Santa Fe
GONZALES RANCH San Miguel
GRADY (88120) Quay(57), Curry(42)
GRANTS Cibola
GRENVILLE Union
GUADALUPITA Mora
HACHITA Grant
HAGERMAN Chaves
HANOVER Grant
HATCH Dona Ana
HERNANDEZ Rio Arriba
HIGH ROLLS MOUNTAIN PARK Otero
HILLSBORO Sierra
HOBBS Lea
HOLLOMAN AIR FORCE BASE Otero
HOLMAN Mora
HONDO Lincoln
HOPE (88250) Chaves(62), Eddy(37)
HOUSE Quay
HURLEY Grant
ILFELD San Miguel
ISLETA Bernalillo
JAL Lea
JAMESTOWN McKinley
JARALES Valencia
JEMEZ PUEBLO Sandoval
JEMEZ SPRINGS Sandoval
KENNA Roosevelt
KIRTLAND San Juan
KIRTLAND AFB Bernalillo
LA JARA Sandoval
LA JOYA Socorro
LA LOMA Guadalupe
LA LUZ Otero
LA MADERA Rio Arriba
LA MESA Dona Ana
LA PLATA San Juan
LAGUNA Cibola
LAKE ARTHUR (88253) Chaves(96), Eddy(3)
LAKEWOOD Eddy
LAMY Santa Fe
LAS CRUCES Dona Ana
LAS TABLAS Rio Arriba
LAS VEGAS San Miguel
LEDOUX Mora
LEMITAR Socorro
LINDRITH Rio Arriba
LINGO Roosevelt

LLANO Taos
LOCO HILLS Eddy
LOGAN Quay
LORDSBURG Hidalgo
LOS ALAMOS Los Alamos
LOS LUNAS Valencia
LOS OJOS Rio Arriba
LOVING Eddy
LOVINGTON Lea
LUMBERTON Rio Arriba
LUNA Catron
MAGDALENA Socorro
MALAGA Eddy
MALJAMAR Lea
MAXWELL Colfax
MAYHILL (88339) Otero(77), Chaves(22)
MC ALISTER Quay
MC DONALD Lea
MC INTOSH Torrance
MEDANALES Rio Arriba
MELROSE (88124) Curry(83), Quay(11), Roosevelt(5)
MENTMORE McKinley
MESCALERO Otero
MESILLA Dona Ana
MESILLA PARK Dona Ana
MESQUITE Dona Ana
MEXICAN SPRINGS McKinley
MIAMI Colfax
MILAN Cibola
MILLS Harding
MILNESAND Roosevelt
MIMBRES Grant
MONTEZUMA San Miguel
MONTICELLO Sierra
MONUMENT Lea
MORA Mora
MORIARTY Torrance
MOSQUERO Harding
MOUNT DORA Union
MOUNTAINAIR Torrance
MULE CREEK Grant
NAGEEZI San Juan
NARA VISA Quay
NAVAJO (87328) McKinley(87), San Juan(12)
NAVAJO DAM San Juan
NEW LAGUNA Cibola
NEWCOMB San Juan
NEWKIRK Guadalupe
NOGAL Lincoln
OCATE Mora
OIL CENTER Lea
OJO CALIENTE Taos
OJO FELIZ Mora
OJO SARCO Rio Arriba
ORGAN Dona Ana
OROGRANDE Otero
PAGUATE Cibola
PECOS San Miguel
PENA BLANCA Sandoval
PENASCO Taos
PEP Roosevelt

PERALTA Valencia
PETACA Rio Arriba
PICACHO Lincoln
PIE TOWN Catron
PINEHILL Cibola
PINON (88344) Chaves(84), Otero(15)
PINOS ALTOS Grant
PLACITAS Sandoval
PLAYAS Hidalgo
POLVADERA Socorro
PONDEROSA Sandoval
PORTALES Roosevelt
PREWITT (87045) McKinley(78), Cibola(22)
PUEBLO OF ACOMA Valencia
QUAY Quay
QUEMADO Catron
QUESTA Taos
RADIUM SPRINGS Dona Ana
RAINSVILLE Mora
RAMAH (87321) Cibola(57), McKinley(42)
RANCHOS DE TAOS Taos
RATON Colfax
RED RIVER Taos
REDROCK Grant
REGINA Sandoval
REHOBOTH McKinley
RESERVE Catron
RIBERA San Miguel
RINCON Dona Ana
RIO RANCHO Sandoval
ROCIADA (87742) Mora(68), San Miguel(31)
RODARTE Taos

RODEO Hidalgo
ROGERS Roosevelt
ROSWELL Chaves
ROWE San Miguel
ROY Harding
RUIDOSO Lincoln
RUIDOSO DOWNS Lincoln
RUTHERON Rio Arriba
SACRAMENTO Otero
SAINT VRAIN Curry
SALEM Dona Ana
SAN ACACIA Socorro
SAN ANTONIO Socorro
SAN CRISTOBAL Taos
SAN FIDEL Cibola
SAN JON Quay
SAN JOSE San Miguel
SAN JUAN PUEBLO Rio Arriba
SAN MATEO Cibola
SAN MIGUEL Dona Ana
SAN PATRICIO Lincoln
SAN RAFAEL Cibola
SAN YSIDRO Sandoval
SANDIA PARK (87047) Bernalillo(70), Sandoval(18), Santa Fe(11)
SANOSTEE San Juan
SANTA CLARA Grant
SANTA CRUZ Santa Fe
SANTA FE Santa Fe
SANTA ROSA Guadalupe
SANTA TERESA Dona Ana
SANTO DOMINGO PUEBLO Sandoval
SAPELLO San Miguel
SEBOYETA Cibola

SEDAN Union
SENA San Miguel
SENECA Union
SERAFINA San Miguel
SHEEP SPRINGS San Juan
SHIPROCK San Juan
SILVER CITY Grant
SMITH LAKE McKinley
SOCORRO Socorro
SOLANO Harding
SPRINGER Colfax
STANLEY Santa Fe
STEAD Union
SUNLAND PARK Dona Ana
SUNSPOT Otero
TAIBAN (88134) De Baca(72), Roosevelt(20), Quay(8)
TAJIQUE Torrance
TAOS Taos
TAOS SKI VALLEY Taos
TATUM Lea
TERERRO San Miguel
TESUQUE Santa Fe
TEXICO Curry
THOREAU McKinley
TIERRA AMARILLA Rio Arriba
TIJERAS Bernalillo
TIMBERON Otero
TINNIE Lincoln
TOHATCHI McKinley
TOME Valencia
TORREON Torrance
TRAMPAS Taos
TREMENTINA San Miguel

TRES PIEDRAS Taos
TRUCHAS Rio Arriba
TRUTH OR CONSEQUENCES Sierra
TUCUMCARI Quay
TULAROSA Otero
TYRONE Grant
UTE PARK Colfax
VADITO Taos
VADO Dona Ana
VALDEZ Taos
VALLECITOS Rio Arriba
VALMORA Mora
VANADIUM Grant
VANDERWAGEN McKinley
VAUGHN Guadalupe
VEGUITA Socorro
VELARDE Rio Arriba
VILLANUEVA San Miguel
WAGON MOUND Mora
WATERFLOW San Juan
WATROUS Mora
WEED Otero
WHITE SANDS MISSILE RANGE Dona Ana
WHITES CITY Eddy
WILLARD Torrance
WILLIAMSBURG Sierra
WINSTON Sierra
YATAHEY McKinley
YESO De Baca
YOUNGSVILLE Rio Arriba
ZUNI McKinley

New Mexico ZIP/City Cross Reference

87001-87001	ALGODONES
87002-87002	BELEN
87004-87004	BERNALILLO
87005-87005	BLUEWATER
87006-87006	BOSQUE
87007-87007	CASA BLANCA
87008-87008	CEDAR CREST
87009-87009	CEDARVALE
87010-87010	CERRILLOS
87011-87011	CLAUNCH
87012-87012	COYOTE
87013-87013	CUBA
87014-87014	CUBERO
87015-87015	EDGEWOOD
87016-87016	ESTANCIA
87017-87017	GALLINA
87018-87018	COUNSELOR
87020-87020	GRANTS
87021-87021	MILAN
87022-87022	ISLETA
87023-87023	JARALES
87024-87024	JEMEZ PUEBLO
87025-87025	JEMEZ SPRINGS
87026-87026	LAGUNA
87027-87027	LA JARA
87028-87028	LA JOYA
87029-87029	LINDRITH
87031-87031	LOS LUNAS
87032-87032	MC INTOSH
87034-87034	PUEBLO OF ACOMA
87035-87035	MORIARTY
87036-87036	MOUNTAINAIR
87037-87037	NAGEEZI
87038-87038	NEW LAGUNA
87040-87040	PAGUATE
87041-87041	PENA BLANCA
87042-87042	PERALTA
87043-87043	PLACITAS
87044-87044	PONDEROSA
87045-87045	PREWITT
87046-87046	REGINA
87047-87047	SANDIA PARK
87048-87048	CORRALES

87049-87049	SAN FIDEL
87050-87050	SAN MATEO
87051-87051	SAN RAFAEL
87052-87052	SANTO DOMINGO PUEBLO
87053-87053	SAN YSIDRO
87055-87055	SEBOYETA
87056-87056	STANLEY
87057-87057	TAJIQUE
87059-87059	TIJERAS
87060-87060	TOME
87061-87061	TORREON
87062-87062	VEGUITA
87063-87063	WILLARD
87064-87064	YOUNGSVILLE
87068-87068	BOSQUE FARMS
87070-87070	CLINES CORNERS
87072-87072	COCHITI PUEBLO
87083-87083	COCHITI LAKE
87100-87116	ALBUQUERQUE
87117-87117	KIRTLAND AFB
87118-87123	ALBUQUERQUE
87124-87124	RIO RANCHO
87125-87140	ALBUQUERQUE
87144-87144	RIO RANCHO
87151-87158	ALBUQUERQUE
87174-87174	RIO RANCHO
87176-87201	ALBUQUERQUE
87300-87305	GALLUP
87310-87310	BRIMHALL
87311-87311	CHURCH ROCK
87312-87312	CONTINENTAL DIVIDE
87313-87313	CROWNPOINT
87315-87315	FENCE LAKE
87316-87316	FORT WINGATE
87317-87317	GAMERCO
87319-87319	MENTMORE
87320-87320	MEXICAN SPRINGS
87321-87321	RAMAH
87322-87322	REHOBOTH
87323-87323	THOREAU
87324-87324	GALLUP
87325-87325	TOHATCHI
87326-87326	VANDERWAGEN

87327-87327	ZUNI
87328-87328	NAVAJO
87347-87347	JAMESTOWN
87357-87357	PINEHILL
87364-87364	SHEEP SPRINGS
87365-87365	SMITH LAKE
87375-87375	YATAHEY
87401-87402	FARMINGTON
87410-87410	AZTEC
87412-87412	BLANCO
87413-87413	BLOOMFIELD
87415-87415	FLORA VISTA
87416-87416	FRUITLAND
87417-87417	KIRTLAND
87418-87418	LA PLATA
87419-87419	NAVAJO DAM
87420-87420	SHIPROCK
87421-87421	WATERFLOW
87455-87455	NEWCOMB
87461-87461	SANOSTEE
87499-87499	FARMINGTON
87500-87509	SANTA FE
87510-87510	ABIQUIU
87511-87511	ALCALDE
87512-87512	AMALIA
87513-87513	ARROYO HONDO
87514-87514	ARROYO SECO
87515-87515	CANJILON
87516-87516	CANONES
87517-87517	CARSON
87518-87518	CEBOLLA
87519-87519	CERRO
87520-87520	CHAMA
87521-87521	CHAMISAL
87522-87522	CHIMAYO
87523-87523	CORDOVA
87524-87524	COSTILLA
87525-87525	TAOS SKI VALLEY
87527-87527	DIXON
87528-87528	DULCE
87529-87529	EL PRADO
87530-87530	EL RITO
87531-87531	EMBUDO

87532-87533	ESPANOLA
87535-87535	GLORIETA
87536-87536	GONZALES RANCH
87537-87537	HERNANDEZ
87538-87538	ILFELD
87539-87539	LA MADERA
87540-87540	LAMY
87541-87541	LAS TABLAS
87543-87543	LLANO
87544-87545	LOS ALAMOS
87547-87547	LUMBERTON
87548-87548	MEDANALES
87549-87549	OJO CALIENTE
87550-87550	OJO SARCO
87551-87551	LOS OJOS
87552-87552	PECOS
87553-87553	PENASCO
87554-87554	PETACA
87556-87556	QUESTA
87557-87557	RANCHOS DE TAOS
87558-87558	RED RIVER
87560-87560	RIBERA
87561-87561	RODARTE
87562-87562	ROWE
87563-87563	RUTHERON
87564-87564	SAN CRISTOBAL
87565-87565	SAN JOSE
87566-87566	SAN JUAN PUEBLO
87567-87567	SANTA CRUZ
87568-87568	SENA
87569-87569	SERAFINA
87571-87571	TAOS
87573-87573	TERERRO
87574-87574	TESUQUE
87575-87575	TIERRA AMARILLA
87576-87576	TRAMPAS
87577-87577	TRES PIEDRAS
87578-87578	TRUCHAS
87579-87579	VADITO
87580-87580	VALDEZ
87581-87581	VALLECITOS
87582-87582	VELARDE
87583-87583	VILLANUEVA

87592-87594	SANTA FE
87701-87701	LAS VEGAS
87718-87718	EAGLE NEST
87722-87722	GUADALUPITA
87723-87723	HOLMAN
87724-87724	LA LOMA
87725-87725	LEDOUX
87728-87728	MAXWELL
87729-87729	MIAMI
87730-87730	MILLS
87731-87731	MONTEZUMA
87732-87732	MORA
87733-87733	MOSQUERO
87734-87734	OCATE
87735-87735	OJO FELIZ
87736-87736	RAINSVILLE
87740-87740	RATON
87742-87742	ROCIADA
87743-87743	ROY
87745-87745	SAPELLO
87746-87746	SOLANO
87747-87747	SPRINGER
87749-87749	UTE PARK
87750-87750	VALMORA
87752-87752	WAGON MOUND
87753-87753	WATROUS
87801-87801	SOCORRO
87815-87815	BINGHAM
87820-87820	ARAGON
87821-87821	DATIL
87823-87823	LEMITAR
87824-87824	LUNA
87825-87825	MAGDALENA
87827-87827	PIE TOWN
87828-87828	POLVADERA
87829-87829	QUEMADO
87830-87830	RESERVE
87831-87831	SAN ACACIA
87832-87832	SAN ANTONIO
87901-87901	TRUTH OR CONSEQUENCES
87910-87910	ALBUQUERQUE
87930-87930	ARREY
87931-87931	CABALLO
87932-87932	CUCHILLO
87933-87933	DERRY
87935-87935	ELEPHANT BUTTE
87936-87936	GARFIELD
87937-87937	HATCH
87939-87939	MONTICELLO
87940-87940	RINCON
87941-87941	SALEM
87942-87942	WILLIAMSBURG
87943-87943	WINSTON

87710-87710	ANGEL FIRE
87711-87711	ANTON CHICO
88000-88001	LAS CRUCES
88002-88002	WHITE SANDS MISSILE RANGE
88003-88007	LAS CRUCES
88008-88008	SANTA TERESA
88009-88009	PLAYAS
88011-88012	LAS CRUCES
88020-88020	ANIMAS
88021-88021	ANTHONY
88022-88022	ARENAS VALLEY
88023-88023	BAYARD
88024-88024	BERINO
88025-88025	BUCKHORN
88026-88026	SANTA CLARA
88027-88027	CHAMBERINO
88028-88028	CLIFF
88029-88029	COLUMBUS
88030-88031	DEMING
88032-88032	DONA ANA
88033-88033	FAIRACRES
88034-88034	FAYWOOD
88036-88036	FORT BAYARD
88038-88038	GILA
88039-88039	GLENWOOD
88040-88040	HACHITA
88041-88041	HANOVER
88042-88042	HILLSBORO
88043-88043	HURLEY
88044-88044	LA MESA
88045-88045	LORDSBURG
88046-88046	MESILLA
88047-88047	MESILLA PARK
88048-88048	MESQUITE
88049-88049	MIMBRES
88051-88051	MULE CREEK
88052-88052	ORGAN
88053-88053	PINOS ALTOS
88054-88054	RADIUM SPRINGS
88055-88055	REDROCK
88056-88056	RODEO
88058-88058	SAN MIGUEL
88061-88062	SILVER CITY
88063-88063	SUNLAND PARK
88065-88065	TYRONE
88072-88072	VADO
88073-88073	VANADIUM
88081-88081	CHAPARRAL
88101-88102	CLOVIS
88103-88103	CANNON AFB
88111-88111	BELLVIEW
88112-88112	BROADVIEW
88113-88113	CAUSEY

87712-87712	BUENA VISTA
87713-87713	CHACON
88114-88114	CROSSROADS
88115-88115	DORA
88116-88116	ELIDA
88118-88118	FLOYD
88119-88119	FORT SUMNER
88120-88120	GRADY
88121-88121	HOUSE
88122-88122	KENNA
88123-88123	LINGO
88124-88124	MELROSE
88125-88125	MILNESAND
88126-88126	PEP
88130-88130	PORTALES
88132-88132	ROGERS
88133-88133	SAINT VRAIN
88134-88134	TAIBAN
88135-88135	TEXICO
88136-88136	YESO
88201-88203	ROSWELL
88210-88211	ARTESIA
88213-88213	CAPROCK
88220-88221	CARLSBAD
88230-88230	DEXTER
88231-88231	EUNICE
88232-88232	HAGERMAN
88240-88244	HOBBS
88250-88250	HOPE
88252-88252	JAL
88253-88253	LAKE ARTHUR
88254-88254	LAKEWOOD
88255-88255	LOCO HILLS
88256-88256	LOVING
88260-88260	LOVINGTON
88262-88262	MC DONALD
88263-88263	MALAGA
88264-88264	MALJAMAR
88265-88265	MONUMENT
88266-88266	OIL CENTER
88267-88267	TATUM
88268-88268	WHITES CITY
88301-88301	CARRIZOZO
88310-88311	ALAMOGORDO
88312-88312	ALTO
88314-88314	BENT
88316-88316	CAPITAN
88317-88317	CLOUDCROFT
88318-88318	CORONA
88319-88319	DURAN
88321-88321	ENCINO
88322-88322	FLYING H
88323-88323	FORT STANTON
88324-88324	GLENCOE

87714-87714	CIMARRON
87715-87715	CLEVELAND
88325-88325	HIGH ROLLS MOUNTAIN PARK
88330-88330	HOLLOMAN AIR FORCE BASE
88336-88336	HONDO
88337-88337	LA LUZ
88338-88338	LINCOLN
88339-88339	MAYHILL
88340-88340	MESCALERO
88341-88341	NOGAL
88342-88342	OROGRANDE
88343-88343	PICACHO
88344-88344	PINON
88345-88345	RUIDOSO
88346-88346	RUIDOSO DOWNS
88347-88347	SACRAMENTO
88348-88348	SAN PATRICIO
88349-88349	SUNSPOT
88350-88350	TIMBERON
88351-88351	TINNIE
88352-88352	TULAROSA
88353-88353	VAUGHN
88354-88354	WEED
88355-88355	RUIDOSO
88401-88401	TUCUMCARI
88410-88410	AMISTAD
88411-88411	BARD
88412-88412	BUEYEROS
88414-88414	CAPULIN
88415-88415	CLAYTON
88416-88416	CONCHAS DAM
88417-88417	CUERVO
88418-88418	DES MOINES
88419-88419	FOLSOM
88421-88421	GARITA
88422-88422	GLADSTONE
88423-88423	GLENRIO
88424-88424	GRENVILLE
88426-88426	LOGAN
88427-88427	MC ALISTER
88429-88429	MOUNT DORA
88430-88430	NARA VISA
88431-88431	NEWKIRK
88432-88432	SANTA ROSA
88433-88433	QUAY
88434-88434	SAN JON
88435-88435	SANTA ROSA
88436-88436	SEDAN
88437-88437	SENECA
88438-88438	STEAD
88439-88439	TREMENTINA
88441-88441	BELL RANCH

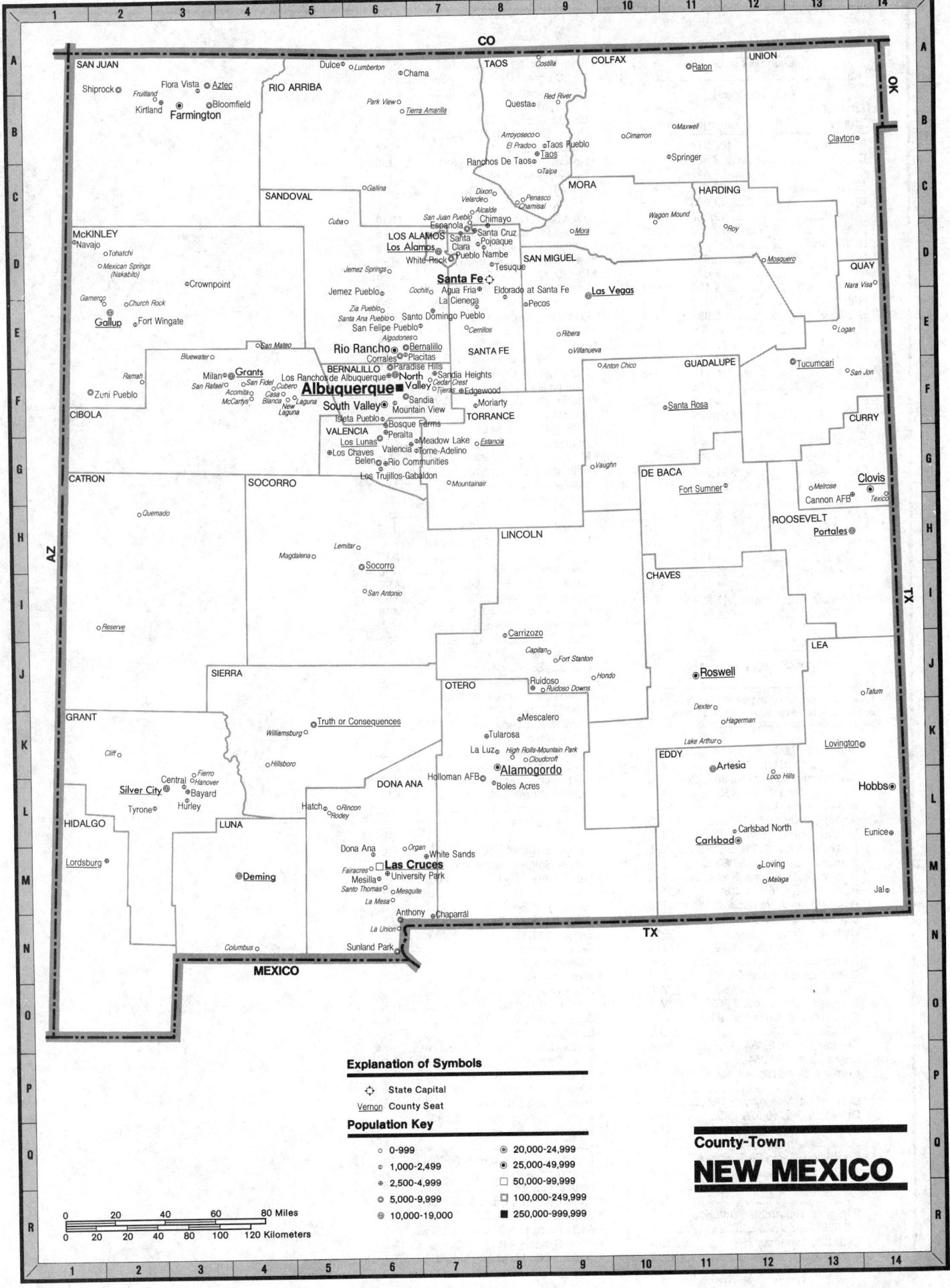

County-Town

NEW MEXICO

Explanation of Symbols

State Capital
Vernon   County Seat

Population Key

○ 0-999	⊕ 20,000-24,999
⊕ 1,000-2,499	◉ 25,000-49,999
⊕ 2,500-4,999	□ 50,000-99,999
◎ 5,000-9,999	▢ 100,000-249,999
◉ 10,000-19,000	■ 250,000-999,999

0   20   40   60   80 Miles
0   20   20   40   80   100   120 Kilometers

COUNTIES

(33 Counties)

Name of County	Population	Location on Map
BERNALILLO	480,577	F-5
CATRON	2,563	G-1
CHAVES	57,849	I-10
CIBOLA	23,794	F-1
COLFAX	12,925	A-9
CURRY	42,207	F-13
DEBACA	2,252	G-10
DONA ANA	135,510	L-6
EDDY	48,605	K-10
GRANT	27,676	K-1
GUADALUPE	4,156	F-11
HARDING	987	C-11
HIDALGO	5,958	L-1
LEA	55,765	J-13
LINCOLN	12,219	H-8
LOS ALAMOS	18,115	D-6
LUNA	18,110	L-3
MCKINLEY	60,686	D-1
MORA	4,264	C-3
OTERO	51,928	J-7
QUAY	10,823	D-14
RIO ARRIBA	34,365	A-4
ROOSEVELT	16,702	H-12
SAN JUAN	91,605	A-1
SAN MIGUEL	25,743	D-8
SANDOVAL	63,319	C-4
SANTA FE	98,928	D-7
SIERRA	9,912	J-3
SOCORRO	14,764	G-4
TAOS	23,118	A-8
TORRANCE	10,285	F-7
UNION	4,124	A-12
VALENCIA	45,235	F-5
TOTAL	**1,515,069**	

CITIES AND TOWNS

Note: The first name is that of the city or town, second, that of the county in which it is located, then the population and location on the map.

- Agua Fria, Santa Fe, 3,717 .... E-8
  Alamogordo, Otero, 27,596 .... K-8
  Albuquerque, Bernalillo, 384,736 .... F-6
- Anthony, Dona Ana, 5,160 .... N-6
  Artesia, Eddy, 10,610 .... K-11
  Aztec, San Juan, 5,479 .... A-3
  Bayard, Grant, 2,598 .... L-3
  Belen, Valencia, 6,547 .... G-6
  Bernalillo, Sandoval, 5,960 .... E-6
  Bloomfield, San Juan, 5,214 .... B-3
- Boles Acres, Otero, 1,409 .... L-8
  Bosque Farms, Valencia, 3,791 ...... F-6
- Cannon AFB, Curry, 3,312 .... H-13
  Carlsbad, Eddy, 24,952 .... M-12
- Carlsbad North, Eddy, 1,167 .... L-12
  Carrizozo, Lincoln, 1,075 .... J-8
  Central, Grant, 1,835 .... L-3
  Chama, Rio Arriba, 1,048 .... A-6
- Chaparral, Dona Ana, 2,962 .... M-7
- Chimayo, Rio Arriba/Santa Fe, 2,789 .... D-8
  Clayton, Union, 2,484 .... B-14
  Clovis, Curry, 30,954 .... G-14
  Corrales, Bernalillo/Sandoval, 5,453 .... E-6
- Crownpoint, McKinley, 2,108 .... D-3
  Deming, Luna, 10,970 .... M-4
- Dona Ana, Dona Ana, 1,202 .... M-6
- Dulce, Rio Arriba, 2,438 .... A-5
- Edgewood, Santa Fe/Torrance, 3,324 .... F-7
- Eldorado at Santa Fe, Santa Fe, 2,260 .... E-8
  Espanola, Rio Arriba/Santa Fe, 8,389 .... D-7
  Estancia, Torrance, 792 .... G-8
  Eunice, Lea, 2,676 .... L-14

  Farmington, San Juan, 33,997 .... B-3
- Flora Vista, San Juan, 1,021 .... A-3
  Fort Sumner, DeBaca, 1,269 .... G-11
  Fort Wingate, McKinley E-2
  Gallup, McKinley, 19,154 .... E-2
  Grants, Cibola, 8,626 .... F-4
  Hatch, Dona Ana, 1,136 .... L-5
  Hobbs, Lea, 29,115 .... L-14
- Holloman AFB, Otero, 5,891 .... L-8
  Hurley, Grant, 1,534 .... L-3
- Isleta Pueblo, Bernalillo/Valencia, 1,703 .... F-6
  Jal, Lea, 2,156 .... M-14
- Jemez Pueblo, Sandoval, 1,301 ..... D-6
- Kirtland, San Juan, 3,552 .... B-3
- La Cienega, Santa Fe, 1,066 .... E-8
- La Luz, Otero, 1,625 .... K-8
  Las Cruces, Dona Ana, 62,126 ..... M-6
  Las Vegas, San Miguel, 14,753 ..... E-9
  Lordsburg, Hidalgo, 2,951 .... M-2
- Los Alamos, Los Alamos, 11,455 ... D-7
- Los Chaves, Valencia, 3,872 .... G-5
  Los Lunas, Valencia, 6,013 .... G-6
  Los Ranchos de Albuquerque, Bernalillo, 3,955 .... F-6
- Los Trujillos-Gabaldon, Valencia, 1,841 .... G-6
  Loving, Eddy, 1,243 .... M-12
  Lovington, Lea, 9,322 .... K-14
- Meadow Lake, Valencia, 1,590 ...... G-6
- Mescalero, Otero, 1,159 .... K-8
  Mesilla, Dona Ana, 1,975 .... M-6
  Milan, Cibola, 1,911 .... F-4
  Mora, Mora, 1,911 .... D-9
  Moriarty, Torrance, 1,399 .... F-8
  Mosquero, Harding/San Miguel, 164 .... D-12
  Mountain View, Bernalillo F-6
- Nambe, Santa Fe, 1,246 .... D-8
- Navajo, McKinley, 1,985 .... D-1
- North Valley, Bernalillo, 12,507 ..... F-6
- Paradise Hills, Bernalillo, 5,513 ..... F-6
  Pecos, San Miguel, 1,012 .... E-8
- Peralta, Valencia, 3,182 .... F-6
- Placitas, Sandoval, 1,611 .... F-6
- Pojoaque, Santa Fe, 1,037 .... D-8
  Portales, Roosevelt, 10,690 .... H-13
  Questa, Taos, 1,707 .... B-8
- Ranchos De Taos, Taos, 1,779 ..... C-8
  Raton, Colfax, 7,372 .... A-11
  Reserve, Catron, 319 .... I-2
- Rio Communities, Valencia, 3,233 . G-6
  Rio Rancho, Sandoval, 32,505 ...... E-6
  Roswell, Chaves, 44,654 .... J-11
  Ruidoso, Lincoln, 4,600 .... J-8
- San Felipe Pueblo, Sandoval, 1,557 .... E-7
- Sandia, Bernalillo, 6,742 .... F-6
- Sandia Heights, Bernalillo, 3,519 .... F-7
- Santa Clara Pueblo, Rio Arriba, 1,156 .... C-7
- Santa Cruz, Santa Fe, 2,504 .... D-8
  Santa Fe, Santa Fe, 55,859 .... D-8
  Santa Rosa, Guadalupe, 2,263 ..... F-11
- Santo Domingo Pueblo, Sandoval, 2,866 .... E-7
- Shiprock, San Juan, 7,687 .... A-2
  Silver City, Grant, 10,683 .... L-3
  Socorro, Socorro, 8,159 .... H-6
- South Valley, Bernalillo, 35,701 ..... F-6
  Springer, Colfax, 1,262 .... C-11
  Sunland Park, Dona Ana, 8,179 ..... N-6
  Taos, Taos, 4,065 .... B-9
- Taos Pueblo, Taos, 1,187 .... B-9
- Tesuque, Santa Fe, 1,490 .... D-8
  Tierra Amarilla, Rio Arriba B-6
- Tome-Adelino, Valencia, 1,695 ...... G-7
  Truth or Consequences, Sierra, 6,221 .... K-5
  Tucumcari, Quay, 6,831 .... F-13
  Tularosa, Otero, 2,615 .... K-8
  Tyrone, Grant L-2
- University Park, Dona Ana, 4,520 .. M-6
- Valencia, Valencia, 3,917 .... G-7
- White Rock, Los Alamos, 6,192 ..... E-7
- White Sands, Dona Ana, 2,616 ...... M-7
- Zuni Pueblo, McKinley, 5,857 .... F-1

Explanation of symbols: ● – Census Designated Place (CDP)

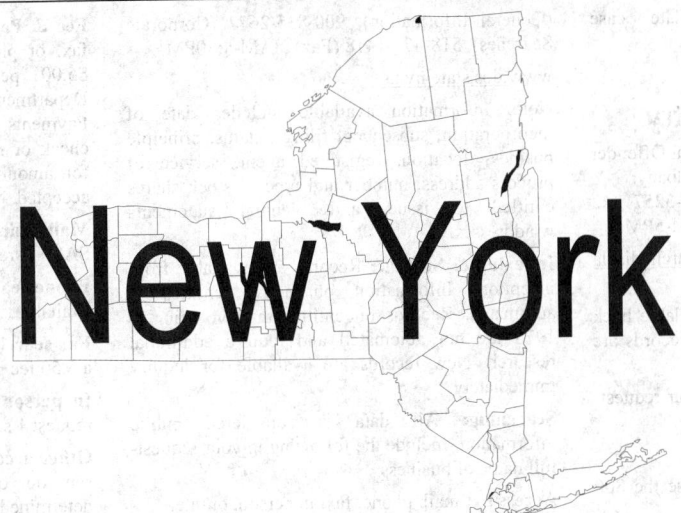

New York

General Help Numbers:

Governor's Office

Executive Chamber, State Capitol
Albany, NY 12224
www.state.ny.us/governor

518-474-8390
9AM-5PM

Attorney General's Office

State Capitol
Albany, NY 12224-0341
www.oag.state.ny.us

518-474-7330
Fax 518-473-9909
9AM-5:30PM

Legislative Records

State Capitol
State Street Rm 317
Albany, NY 12247
www.senate.state.ny.us

518-455-3216
Fax 518-426-6841
9AM-5PM

State Archives

Empire State Plaza
Cultural Education Center, 11D40
Albany, NY 12230
http://www.nysarchives.org/gindex.shtml

518-474-8955
Fax 518-473-9985
9AM-5PM

State Specifics:

Capital:	Albany
	Albany County
Time Zone:	EST
Number of Counties:	62
Population:	19,190,115
Web Site:	www.state.ny.us

State Agencies

Criminal Records

Access to Records is Restricted

Division of Criminal Justice Services, 4 Tower Place, Albany, NY 12203; 518-457-6043, 518-457-6550 (Fax), 8AM-5PM.

www.criminaljustice.state.ny.us

Note: Records are only released pursuant to court order, subpoena, to entities authorized by statute, or to person of record. 99% of records are fingerprint supported. The public must search at the county court level.

Statewide Court Records

NY State Office of Court Administration, New York City Office, 25 Beaver St, New York, NY 10004; 212-428-2100, 212-428-2990, 212-428-2190 (Fax), 9AM-5PM.

www.courts.state.ny.us

Searching: Include the following in your request- name, DOB, and SASE. OCA has mandated that all criminal record requests made to county Supreme Court Clerks and City Courts be forwarded to this office for processing.

Access by: mail, online.

Fee & Payment: The fee for a statewide search is $52.00.

Mail search: Turnaround time: 2 days or more. The search is a statewide search.

Online search: The OCA offers online access to approved requesters for criminal records. Requesters receive information back via email. Call the OCA for details on how to set up an account. The fee is $52.00 per record, the highest statewide record fee in the US. Civil Supreme Court case information for open cases is available for all 62 New York counties through the court system's website - http://e.courts.state.ny.us. Go to www.nycourts.gov/ctapps for appellate case summaries.

Sexual Offender Registry

Division of Criminal Justice Srvs, Sexual Offender Registry, 4 Tower Place, Rm 604, Albany, NY 12203; 518-457-6326 x1, 800-262-3257 x2 (Verification), 518-485-5805 (Fax), 8AM-5PM.

www.criminaljustice.state.ny.us/nsor/search_disclaimer.htm

Indexing & Storage: Records are available back to 01/22/96. It takes 1 day before new records are available for inquiry.

Searching: Include the following in your request- name, SSN, and DOB.

Access by: mail, phone, fax, online.

Fee & Payment: There is no fee to use the 800 telephone.

Mail search: Turnaround time: 1 week.

Phone search: Search requests can be done over the phone. Lengthy lists must be mailed.

Fax search: Will respond to a toll free or local fax line.

Online search: The sex offender registry Level 3 can be searched at the website. Requesters are required to register.

Incarceration Records

New York Department of Correctional Services, Building 2, 1220 Washington Ave, Albany, NY 12226-2050; 518-457-5000, 518-457-8126 (Contact phone), 518-485-9502 (Fax), 8AM-4PM.

www.docs.state.ny.us

Indexing & Storage: Records are available on current and former inmates. It takes 1 to 20 days before new records are available for inquiry.

Searching: Include the following in your request- full name; the DOB, SSN, and DIN (inmate number) are helpful. Location, DIN number, conviction and sentencing information, and release dates are provided.

Access by: mail, phone, fax, online.

Fee & Payment: There is no search fee. Copy fee is $.25 per page

Mail search: Turnaround time: 7 to 10 days. A SASE is requested.

Phone search: Limited name searching by phone is available from the agency. For information on the location of a NYS prison inmate, call 518-457-5000 during normal business hours.

Fax search: Requests accepted via fax.

Online search: Computerized inmate information is available from the Inmate Lookup at http://nysdocslookup.docs.state.ny.us/kinqw00 or follow "inmate lookup" link at main site. Records go back to early 1970s. To acquire inmate DIN number, you may call 518-457-5000.

Corporation, Limited Partnership, Limited Liability Company, Limited Liability Partnerships

Division of Corporations, Department of State, 41 State St, Albany, NY 12231; 518-473-2492

(General Information), 900-835-2677 (Corporate Searches), 518-474-1418 (Fax), 8AM-4:30PM.

www.dos.state.ny.us

Note: Information available includes date of incorporation, subsequent filings, status, principle business location, registered agent, service of process address, number and type of stock shares entitled to issue, and biennial statements w/addresses.

Indexing & Storage: Records are available from inception. Information on active entities is automated. Records on entities inactive prior to 1978 are not automated and require additional research. New records are available for inquiry immediately.

Searching: All data is considered public information. Include the following in your request- full name of business.

Access by: mail, phone, fax, in person, online.

Fee & Payment: There is no fee for basic information up to 5 names. Over 5 names, the fee is $5.00 per name. For documents, the certification fee is $10.00, $25.00 if SOS seal is required. The fee is $5.00 for every name availability checked. Fee payee: New York Department of State. Payments must be by check, money order, credit card or drawdown account. If amount is over $500, funds must be certified. Visa and MasterCard accepted.

Mail search: Turnaround time: 1 week. A SASE is requested.

Phone search: Call 1-900-TEL-CORP. You may search up to 5 names per call for a flat rate charge of $4.00 per call.

Fax search: Fax requests accepted.

In person search: The general public may obtain copies of documents and certificates under seal while they wait ONLY if expedited fees are paid.

Online search: A commercial account can be set up for direct access. Fee is $.75 per transaction through a drawdown account. There is an extensive amount of information available including historical information. Also, the Division's corporate and business entity database may be accessed via the Internet without charge at http://appsext4.dos.state.ny.us/corp_public/enter_search. The web has not-for-profit corporations, limited partnerships, limited liability companies and limited liability partnerships as well.

Other access: You may submit an email search request at corporations@dos.state.ny.us.

Expedited service: Expedited service is available for in person, mail and fax for searching and filing. Fees are $150 for 2-hour service; $75 for same day service and $25 for 24-hour service.

Trademarks/Servicemarks

Department of State, Miscellaneous Records Unit, 41 State St, Albany, NY 12231; 518-474-4770, 518-473-0730 (Fax), 8AM-4:30PM.

http://dos.state.ny.us

Indexing & Storage: Records are available for past 10 years. It takes 1 to 2 weeks before new records are available for inquiry. Records are normally destroyed after one year when expired.

Searching: Searches are only done on registered marks, not on pending marks. You need to provide written description of design or features of the mark.

Access by: mail, phone, fax, in person.

Fee & Payment: The first two requests by mail, fax, or phone are free. Additional requests cost $5.00 per search. Fee payee: New York Department of State. Prepayment required. Payments of more than $500.00 must be certified check or money order; personal checks accepted for amounts less than $500.00 Personal checks accepted. No credit cards accepted.

Mail search: Turnaround time: 2 to 3 days. A SASE is requested.

Phone search: Limited verification information is available.

Fax search: Turnaround time is 2-3 days. There is a $.50 fee per page to return results by fax.

In person search: No fee for request. You can request 1 search in person.

Other access: New marks can be photocopied and sent out on a regular monthly basis. Fees are determined by numbers of marks.

Uniform Commercial Code, Federal and State Tax Liens

Department of State, UCC Unit - Records, 41 State Street, Albany, NY 12231-0001; 518-474-4763, 518-474-5418, 518-474-4478 (Fax), 8AM-4:30PM.

www.dos.state.ny.us/corp/uccfaq.html

Indexing & Storage: Records are available from 1964. Records are computerized from 1/96. Records are indexed on computer, microfilm.

Searching: Use search request form UCC-11. Federal tax liens on businesses will be included. Lists of state tax liens (warrants) are available, but must be searched separately on premises. Federal tax liens on individuals are filed at the county level. Include the following in your request-debtor name. It is suggested for written requests that the form be 5" x 8" or use a UCC-11.

Access by: mail, in person, online.

Fee & Payment: UCC search is $25.00 per debtor name, one name per form. Individual debtor names should list addresses. The copy fee is $5.00 per file number, add $5.00 to certify. You can search state tax liens, in person, at no charge. Fee payee: Department of State. Prepayment required. All checks over $500.00 must be certified. The department will certify search listings for an additional $25.00. Credit cards (VISA & MC) are accepted.

Mail search: Turnaround time: 2 days. No SASE is required.

In person search: You may request information in person.

Online search: Free access at www.dos.state.ny.us/corp/corpwww.html. Seach financing statements and federal tax lien notices by by debtor name, or secured party name, or by filing number and date. Document images can be provided.

Other access: This agency offers its database for sale on microfilm.

Sales Tax Registrations

Sales Tax Registration Bureau, WA Harriman Campus, Building 8, Rm 957, Albany, NY 12227; 800-972-1233, 7AM-5PM.

www.nystax.gov/

Indexing & Storage: Records are available for current records only. Records are computerized since 1970.

Searching: This agency will confirm that a business is registered and release the legal name. Include the following in your request-business name. They will also search by tax permit number or federal tax number.

Access by: mail, phone, fax, in person.

Mail search: Turnaround time: 2 to 3 weeks. A SASE is requested. No fee for mail request.

Phone search: No fee for telephone request.

Fax search: Fax searching available.

In person search: No fee for request.

Birth Certificates

Vital Records Section, Certification Unit, 800 N Pearl St, Albany, NY 12204-1842; 518-474-3038, 518-474-3077, 877-854-4481 (Searching), 877-854-4607 (Fax), 8:30AM-4:30PM.

www.health.state.ny.us/nysdoh/consumer/vr.htm

Note: For records from New York City information, see that profile. Records may be ordered online from a vendor website www.vitalchek.com.

Indexing & Storage: Records are available from 1881 on. New records are available for inquiry immediately. Records are indexed on microfiche, inhouse computer.

Searching: May only obtain your own or a dependent child's records, without notarized release. They will not return records to a PO Box or an "in care of." Include the following in your request-full name, names of parents, mother's maiden name, date of birth, place of birth, relationship to person of record, reason for information request. Requester must show or include valid identification or 2 items showing proof of address (utility or telephone bill, etc.)

Access by: mail, phone, fax, in person.

Fee & Payment: The fee is $30.00 per name per record. Fee payee: New York State Department of Health. Prepayment required. Personal checks accepted. Credit cards accepted: MasterCard, Visa, AmEx, Discover.

Mail search: Turnaround time: 2 to 3 months. Turnaround time will be 2 weeks if you send your request by Express Mail, or if you pay an additional $15.00 for priority handling. A SASE is requested.

Phone search: See expedited service.

Fax search: See expedited service.

In person search: Results are still returned by mail.

Expedited service: Expedited service is available for phone and fax searches. Add $15.00 for prioity handling and $11.95 for use of credit card.

Death Records

Vital Records Section, Certification Unit, 800 N Pearl St, Albany, NY 12204-1842 (Courier: PO Box 2602, Albany, NY 12220-2602); 518-474-3038, 518-474-3077, 518-474-9168 (Fax), 8:30AM-4:30PM.

www.health.state.ny.us/nysdoh/consumer/vr.htm

Note: For New York City, see the separate entry. Records may be ordered online from website via Vitalchek.

Indexing & Storage: Records are available from 1880 on. New records are available for inquiry immediately. Records are indexed on microfiche, inhouse computer.

Searching: You must show cause why record is needed on letterhead, if not member of the immediate family. Include the following in your request-full name, date of death, place of death, relationship to person of record, reason for information request, and telephone number. Requester must show or include valid identification.

Access by: mail, phone, fax, in person.

Fee & Payment: The fee is $30.00 for searching and adidtional $15.00 if priority handling requested. Add $11.95 if credit card used. Fee payee: New York State Department of Health. Prepayment required. Personal checks accepted. Credit cards accepted: MasterCard, Visa, AmEx, Discover.

Mail search: Turnaround time: 2 to 3 months. Turnaround time will be 2 weeks if you send your request by Express Mail, or if you pay an additional $15.00 for priority handling. A SASE is requested.

Phone search: See expedited service.

Fax search: Same criteria as phone searches, use 518-432-6286.

In person search: Turnaround time shortened by mail time only.

Expedited service: Expedited service is available for mail, phone and fax searches. Turnaround time: 7 to 10 days. Add priority and credit card fees.

Marriage Certificates

Vital Records Section, Certification Unit, 800 N Pearl St, Albany, NY 12204-1842 (Courier: PO Box 2602, Albany, NY 12220-2602); 518-474-3038, 518-474-3077, 8:30AM-4:30PM.

www.health.state.ny.us/nysdoh/consumer/vr.htm

Note: For New York City information, see the separate entry. Records may be ordered online from website via Vitalchek.

Indexing & Storage: Records are available from 1881 on. New records are available for inquiry immediately. Records are indexed on microfiche, inhouse computer.

Searching: Must have a notarized release from persons of record or immediate family member for investigative purposes. Include the following in your request-names of husband and wife, date of marriage, place or county of marriage, relationship to person of record, reason for information request, wife's maiden name. Requester must show or include valid identification.

Access by: mail, phone, fax, in person.

Fee & Payment: The fee is $30.00 for searching and adidtional $15.00 if priority handling requested. Add $11.95 if credit card used. Fee payee: New York State Department of Health. Prepayment required. Personal checks accepted. Credit cards accepted: MasterCard, Visa, AmEx, Discover.

Mail search: Turnaround time: 2 to 3 months. Turnaround time will be 2 weeks if you send your request by Express Mail, or if you pay an additional $15.00 for priority handling. A SASE is requested.

Phone search: See expedited service.

Fax search: Same criteria as general searches, use 518-432-6286. Turnaround time is 1 week.

In person search: Turnaround time shortened by mail time only.

Expedited service: Expedited service is available for mail, phone and fax searches. Turnaround time: 7 to 10 days. Add priority and credit card fees.

Divorce Records

Vital Records Section, Certification Unit, 800 N Pearl St, Albany, NY 12204-1842 (Courier: PO Box 2602, Albany, NY 12220-2602); 518-474-3038, 518-474-3077, 8:30AM-4:30PM.

www.health.state.ny.us/nysdoh/consumer/vr.htm

Note: For New York City information, see the separate entry. To obtain a copy of a divorce decree, visit the county court where the document was filed.

Indexing & Storage: Records are available from 1963 on. New records are available for inquiry immediately. Records are indexed on microfiche, inhouse computer.

Searching: If you are not a party to the divorce you must have a court order to obtain records or show legal cause. Include the following in your request-names of husband and wife, date of divorce, place of divorce, relationship to person of record, reason for information request, and your telephone number.

Access by: mail, phone, fax, in person.

Fee & Payment: The fee is $30.00 for searching and adidtional $15.00 if priority handling requested. Add $11.95 if credit card used. Fee payee: New York State Department of Health. Prepayment required. Personal checks accepted. Credit cards accepted: MasterCard, Visa, AmEx, Discover.

Mail search: Turnaround time: 2 to 3 months. Turnaround time will be 2 weeks if you send your request by Express Mail, or if you pay an additional $15.00 for priority handling. A SASE is requested.

Phone search: See expedited service.

Fax search: Same criteria as phone searches, use 518-432-6286.

In person search: Turnaround time shortened by mail time only.

Expedited service: Expedited service is available for mail, phone and fax searches. Turnaround time: 7 to 10 days. Add priority and credit card fees.

Birth Certificate-New York City, Death Records-New York City

Department of Health, Bureau of Vital Records, 125 Worth St, Rm 133, New York, NY 10013; 212-788-4520, 212-442-1999, 212-962-6105 (Fax), 9AM-4PM.

www.nyc.gov/html/doh/

Note: Records may be ordered online from from an approved vendor at www.vitalchek.com. The fax number if calling outside NYC is 800-908-9146.

Indexing & Storage: Records are available from 1910 to present for birth and from 1949 forward for death. For prior records, call Municipal

Archives at 212-788-8580. It takes 2 months before new records are available for inquiry. Records are indexed on microfiche, inhouse computer.

Searching: Must have a notarized signed release from immediate family member. Include a copy of your photo ID. Include the following in your request-full name, date of birth, date of death, place of birth, place of death, reason for information request, name of the hospital. Parents' names are also required, mother's maiden name for birth.

Access by: mail, phone, fax, in person, online.

Fee & Payment: The fee is $15.00 per record plus $5.50 if using a credit card. Only those parties appearing on the birth record may order via a credit card. All other parties must order by mail or in-person and show cause or reason for the request. Fee payee: Department of Health. Prepayment required. Personal checks accepted. Credit cards accepted: MasterCard, Visa, AmEx, Discover.

Mail search: Allow 3-4 weeks for a birth record and 8-10 weeks for a death record. A SASE is requested.

Phone search: Birth only. Use of credit card is required. Turnaround time is 5-7 days.

Fax search: Same criteria as phone searching.

In person search: Turnaround time is usually while you wait.

Online search: Records may be requested via www.vitalchek.com. Use of credit card is required.

Expedited service: Expedited service is available for fax searches. Turnaround time: 1 to 2 days. Add $12.50 for overnight delivery service. The $15.00 search fee and $5.50 credit card fee must also be included.

Marriage Certificate-New York City

City Clerk's Office, Department of Records & Information Services, 1 Centre Street, Rm 252, New York, NY 10007; 212-669-8090, 8:30AM-3PM M-F.

Note: Records from 1866-1929 can be obtained from the Municipal Archives at 212-788-8580. Records from 1995 forward can be obtained from the City Clerk's Borough Office. Call this office for further information.

Indexing & Storage: Records are available from 1930 to present.

Searching: Current records (50 years or less) are not public information and are only available to the parties involved or their authorization or to legal representatives for litigation purposes. Otherwise, records are open. Include the following in your request-names and DOBs of parties, date of marriage, relationship of requester to involved parties, photo ID of requester.

Access by: mail, in person.

Fee & Payment: Search fee of $15.00 includes certification. Each additional year searched is add'l $1.00. Additional copies same search are $10.00 each. Fee payee: City Clerk. Prepayment required. No personal checks accepted, except attorneys.

Mail search: Turnaround time: 6-8 weeks.

In person search: Simple requests may be processed while you wait.

Divorce Records-New York City

New York County Clerk's Office, Divorce Records, 60 Centre Street, Rm 141B, New York City, NY 10007; 212-374-4376, 9AM-3PM, M-F.

Note: Records of divorces from 1981 to 1995 can be found at 31 Chambers St, Room 703. This is open Mon to Fri from 9-1 and 2-5. Call for specific details.

Indexing & Storage: Records are available from 1955 to 1970 on index cards, computerized since 1971. It takes 1 day before new records are available for inquiry.

Searching: Manhattan records are limited by statute to parties or attorneys of record or with notarized authorization from party involved.

Access by: mail, in person.

Fee & Payment: Fee is $8.00 for the search and a certified copy. Fee payee: New York County Clerk. Prepayment required. On site requests require cash; mail requests require postal money order or certified check. No credit cards accepted.

Mail search: Turnaround time: 6 weeks. SASE required.

In person search: You may make copies at $.25 per page. Credit cards accepted in person. Go to basement, either room 103 or room 141, or to 31 Chambers St #703. and bring identification

Workers' Compensation Records

NY Workers' Compensation Board, Office of General Counsel, 20 Park Street # 401, Albany, NY 12207; 518-474-6670, 9AM-5PM.

www.wcb.state.ny.us

Note: The Board maintains eleven district offices located in Albany, Binghamton, Brooklyn, Buffalo, Hauppague, Hempstead, Manhattan, Peekskill, Queens, Rochester and Syracuse.

Indexing & Storage: Records are available for up to 18 years after the case is closed. Older records are destroyed. New records are available for inquiry immediately. Records are indexed on inhouse computer.

Searching: Must have a notarized release from claimant naming requesting party and stating the purpose for which information is going to be used to access case files. Include the following in your request-claimant name, Social Security Number, claim number, date of accident. File copies of records are not released for employment purposes, even with a signed release.

Access by: mail, in person, online.

Fee & Payment: There is a $10.00 "mailing and handling fee" but no search fee. Copies are $.25 each. Fee payee: Workers' Compensation Board. Prepayment required. Personal checks accepted. No credit cards accepted.

Mail search: Turnaround time: 2 weeks. No SASE is required.

In person search: Turnaround time is while you wait.

Online search: Proof of coverage is available at www.wcb.state.ny.us/design/framework/ebiz.htm.

Driver Records

Department of Motor Vehicles, MV-15 Processing, 6 Empire State Plaza, Room 430, Albany, NY 12228; 518-473-5595, 800-225-5368 (In-state), 8AM-5PM.

www.nydmv.state.ny.us

Note: Copies of tickets may be purchased from the same address for a fee of $7.00 per ticket.

Indexing & Storage: Records are available for 3 years in addition to the current year for moving violations, 10 years for DWIs, and indefinitely for open (4 years for closed) suspensions. Most non-moving violations are not shown on record. It takes a few days after conviction before new records are available for inquiry. Records are normally destroyed after 5 years from expiration.

Searching: New York restricts the release of personal information on driving records to casual requesters. However, they will provide a "masked" abstract that contains no personal information. This record is only available from the DMV Albany Central Office. The driver's license number (ID#), name, and DOB are required when ordering a record. Use Form MV-15.

Access by: mail, phone, in person, online.

Fee & Payment: The fee is $6.00 per record, $5.00 if electronic. Form MV-15 lists all fees. Fee payee: Department of Motor Vehicles. Prepayment required. Escrow accounts can be set up for high volume users. Personal checks accepted. No credit cards accepted.

Mail search: Turnaround time: 4 to 6 weeks. Form MV-15 is required when ordering. A SASE is requested.

Phone search: Drivers wishing to obtain their own record or account holders may call. The DL# or name, DOB and sex are required when ordered. Payment by a credit card is required and an additional $5.00 is charged.

In person search: Records can be ordered from most any county-operated motor vehicle office and at the state offices in Albany. A photo ID of the requester and use of Form MV-15C is required.

Online search: NY has implemented a "Dial-In Inquiry" system which enables customers to obtain data online 24 hours a day. The DL# or name, DOB and sex are required to retrieve. If the DOB and sex are not entered, the system defaults to a limited group of 5 records. The fee is $5.00 per record. For more information, visit www.nysdmv.com/dialin.htm or call 518-474-4293. Note: You can use your Dial-in Search Account to request DMV records by mail.

Other access: This agency offers a program to employers whereby This agency will notify the employers when an event is posted to an employee's record. To find out about the "LENS" program, call 518-486-4480.

Vehicle and Vessel Ownership and Registration

Department of Motor Vehicles, Customer Service Center, 6 Empire State Plaza, Room 430, Albany, NY 12228; 518-474-0710, 518-474-8510, 8AM-5PM.

www.nydmv.state.ny.us

Indexing & Storage: Records are available for a minimum of 4 years on computer. All motorized vessels must be registered. Titles on boats are issued for model year 1987 and newer, if boat is at least 14 ft long. New records are available for inquiry immediately.

Searching: Generally, vehicle and ownership information is available. However, accessed is restricted in adherence to the Drivers' Privacy Protection Act and casual requesters cannot obtain records. Use of Form MV-15 required. The form is downloadable from the website.

Access by: mail, in person, online.

Fee & Payment: Mail requests are $6.00 per record, online inquiries are $5.00 per record. A copy of a registartion or title applicatrion is $7.00. A complete price list is on Form MV-15. Fee payee: Commissioner of Motor Vehicles. Prepayment required. For information regarding deposit accounts, call 518-474-4293. Personal checks accepted. No credit cards accepted.

Mail search: Turnaround time: 2 to 4 weeks. Include copy of requester's ID. Mail to MV-15 Form Processing for fastest turnaround time. A SASE is requested.

In person search: Results are returned by mail.

Online search: New York offers plate, VIN and ownership data through the same network discussed in the Driving Records Section. The system is interactive and open 24 hours a day. The fee is $5.00 per record. All accounts must be approved, requesters must follow DPPS guidelines. Call 518-474-4293 or visit www.nysdmv.com/dialin.htm for more information.

Accident Reports

DMV Certified Document Center, Accident Report Section, 6 Empire State Plaza, Swan St Bldg, Albany, NY 12228; 518-474-0710, 8AM-4:30PM.

www.nysdmv.com

Indexing & Storage: Records are available for 4 years to present. It takes 180 days after date of accident before new records are available for inquiry. Records are indexed on inhouse computer. Records are normally destroyed after 4 years.

Searching: Records are open to the public, but request must be in writing. Use of Form MV-198C is suggested. Release of records is restricted based on the Drivers' Privacy Protection Act. Include the following in your request-date of accident, location of accident, full name. Provide driver's address, if known.

Access by: mail, phone, fax.

Fee & Payment: The fees are $6.00 per search and $15.00 per accident report. Express mail is given priority. Fee payee: Commissioner of Motor Vehicle. Prepayment required. Personal checks accepted. No credit cards accepted.

Mail search: Turnaround time: 2 to 3 weeks. No SASE is required.

Phone search: There is an additional $5.00 fee if processed by phone.

Fax search: Fax requests accepted from ongoing accounts.

Voter Registration

Records not maintained by a state level agency.

Note: Records may only be viewed or purchased at the county level. Purchases are restricted for political purposes only.

GED Certificates

NY State Education Dept, GED Testing, PO Box 7348, Albany, NY 12224-0348; 518-474-5906, 518-474-3041 (Fax), 10AM-12PM, 1PM-3PM M-F.

www.emsc.nysed.gov/workforce/ged

Indexing & Storage: Records are available from 1985 to present. It takes 4 to 6 weeks, if paper before new records are available for inquiry.

Searching: To search, all of the following is required: full name when tested, data and location of test, SSN, and date of birth.

Access by: mail, phone.

Fee & Payment: There is no fee for verification. Copies of transcripts are $4.00 each. Copies of diplomas are $10.00 each. Fee payee: NY State Education Dept. Prepayment required. Money orders are accepted. No credit cards accepted.

Mail search: Turnaround time: 3 to 4 weeks. No SASE is required.

Phone search: Automated phone verifications can be accomplished for records that are from 1985 to 12/31/2001. A new system is being implemented to allow access to data from 2/2002 to present.

Expedited service: Will expedite if you provide a prepaid express envelope.

Hunting and Fishing License Information

Records not maintained by a state level agency.

New York State Licensing Agencies

Licenses Searchable Online

Accountant, CPA/Public #19 .... www.op.nysed.gov/opsearches.htm#nme
Acupuncturist/Acupuncturist Assistant #19 .... www.op.nysed.gov/opsearches.htm#nme
Addiction Treatment Center #31 .... www.oasas.state.ny.us/atc/atc.htm
Adult Care Med. Facility #38 .... www.health.state.ny.us/nysdoh/acf/map.htm
Adult Care Suspended List #38 .... www.health.state.ny.us/nysdoh/acf/memorandum.htm
Alarm Installer #10 .... http://appsext5.dos.state.ny.us/lcns_public/lcns_query.lic_name_search_frm
Alcohol Abuse Provider #31 .... http://aps.oasas.state.ny.us/providers/
Alcohol Beverage Bond Company #46 .... http://abc.state.ny.us/JSP/content/bonds.jsp
Alcohol Distiller/Whlser/Mfg #46 .... http://abc.state.ny.us/JSP/query/PublicQueryInstructPage.jsp
Alcohol Service Establishment #46 .... http://abc.state.ny.us/JSP/query/PublicQueryInstructPage.jsp
Apartment Manager/Vendor/Agent/Sharing Mgr. #10 .... http://appsext5.dos.state.ny.us/lcns_public/lcns_query.lic_name_search_frm
Appearance Enhancement Business/Professional #10 ..... http://appsext5.dos.state.ny.us/lcns_public/lcns_query.lic_name_search_frm
Architect #19 .... www.op.nysed.gov/opsearches.htm#nme
Armored Car/Car Carrier #10 .... http://appsext5.dos.state.ny.us/lcns_public/lcns_query.lic_name_search_frm
Athlete Agent #10 .... http://appsext5.dos.state.ny.us/lcns_public/lcns_query.lic_name_search_frm
Athletic Trainer #19 .... www.op.nysed.gov/opsearches.htm#nme
Attorney #18 .... www.nycourts.gov/attorneys/
Audiologist #19 .... www.op.nysed.gov/opsearches.htm#nme
Backflow Prevention Device Tester #13 .... www.health.state.ny.us
Bail Enforcement Agent #10 .... http://appsext5.dos.state.ny.us/lcns_public/lcns_query.lic_name_search_frm
Bank Branches, Foreign #23 .... www.banking.state.ny.us/sifbranc.htm
Bank Representative Office, Foreign #23 .... www.banking.state.ny.us/silicrepo.htm
Bank #23 .... www.banking.state.ny.us/sifagen.htm
Banker, Private #23 .... www.banking.state.ny.us/siprivat.htm
Banking Regulatory Action #23 .... www.banking.state.ny.us/ra.htm
Barber/Barber Shop/ Barber Apprentice #10 .... http://appsext5.dos.state.ny.us/lcns_public/lcns_query.lic_name_search_frm
Boat Launch Sites #50 .... www.nysparks.com/boats/mrv/reference.shtml#launchsites
Bottled Water Facility #13 .... www.health.state.ny.us
Budget Planner #23 .... www.banking.state.ny.us/sibudget.htm
Bulk Water Facility #13 .... www.health.state.ny.us
Check Casher #23 .... www.banking.state.ny.us/sicheckc.htm
Chiropractor #19 .... www.op.nysed.gov/opsearches.htm#nme
Cigarette/Tobacco Whlse/Retailer #52 .... http://www7.nystax.gov/CGTX/cgtxHome
Cigarette/Tobacco Tax Agent #52 .... http://www7.nystax.gov/CGTX/cgtxHome
Construction Plans Purchased #36 .... www.ogs.state.ny.us/dnc/EmpireStateBuilder/webplanspurchased.htm
Cosmetologist #10 .... http://appsext5.dos.state.ny.us/lcns_public/lcns_query.lic_name_search_frm
Court Reporter #19 .... www.op.nysed.gov/opsearches.htm#nme
Credit Union #23 .... www.banking.state.ny.us/sicredit.htm
Day Care, Farm Worker (ABCD) #29 .... www.agmkt.state.ny.us/programs/childdev.html
DEC Permit Application #11 .... www.dec.state.ny.us/apps/envapps/index.cfm?view=wizard
Dentist/Dental Assistant/ Dental Hygienist #19 .... www.op.nysed.gov/opsearches.htm#nme
Dietitian #19 .... www.op.nysed.gov/opsearches.htm#nme
Dispatch Facility (Alarm/Security/Fire) #10 .... http://appsext5.dos.state.ny.us/lcns_public/lcns_query.lic_name_search_frm
Dog License #27 .... www.agmkt.state.ny.us/AI/dog_pwd.htm
Domestic Out of State Bank Rep. Ofc. #23 .... www.banking.state.ny.us/sioosrep.htm
Engineer #19 .... www.op.nysed.gov/opsearches.htm#nme
Environmental Permit #11 .... www.dec.state.ny.us/apps/envapps/index.cfm?view=wizard
Esthetics Specialist #10 .... http://appsext5.dos.state.ny.us/lcns_public/lcns_query.lic_name_search_frm
Farm Products Dealer #26 .... www.agmkt.state.ny.us/AP/LicFarmProdDealersList.asp
Foreign Banking Agency #23 .... www.banking.state.ny.us/sifagen.htm
Greenhouse #26 .... www.agmkt.state.ny.us/nurseryDealers.html
Guard/Patrol Agency/Guard Dog #10 .... http://appsext5.dos.state.ny.us/lcns_public/lcns_query.lic_name_search_frm
Hair Styling, Natural #10 .... http://appsext5.dos.state.ny.us/lcns_public/lcns_query.lic_name_search_frm
Hearing Aid Dealer #10 .... http://appsext5.dos.state.ny.us/lcns_public/lcns_query.lic_name_search_frm
HMO (Insurance) #12 .... www.ins.state.ny.us/tocol4.htm
Holding Company #23 .... www.banking.state.ny.us/siholdmu.htm
Insurance Company #12 .... www.ins.state.ny.us/tocol4.htm
Interior Designer #19 .... www.op.nysed.gov/opsearches.htm#nme
Investment Company Article XII #23 .... www.banking.state.ny.us/siinvest.htm

Landscape Architect #19	www.op.nysed.gov/opsearches.htm#nme
Lender, Licensed #23	www.banking.state.ny.us/silicend.htm
Lobbyist #16	www.nylobby.state.ny.us/lobby_data.html
Lottery Claim Center #47	www.nylottery.org/ny/nyStore/cgi-bin/ProdSubEV_Cat_333605_NavRoot_306.htm#lcc
Massage Therapist #19	www.op.nysed.gov/opsearches.htm#nme
Medical Doctor #19	www.op.nysed.gov/opsearches.htm#nme
Medical Examiner, Independent #57	www.wcb.state.ny.us/content/main/hcpp/wc09000ime.htm
Medical Facility, Worker's Comp License #57	www.wcb.state.ny.us/content/main/hcpp/wc09000.htm
Mentally Retarded Health Facility/Service #49	www.omr.state.ny.us/ws/servlets/WsAdminServlet
Midwife #19	www.op.nysed.gov/opsearches.htm#nme
Minority/Woman-owned Business #35	http://205.232.252.35/
Money Transmitter #23	www.banking.state.ny.us/simoneyt.htm
Mortgage Banker/Broker #23	www.banking.state.ny.us/simbroke.htm
Nail Technologist #10	http://appsext5.dos.state.ny.us/lcns_public/lcns_query.lic_name_search_frm
Notary Public #10	http://appsext5.dos.state.ny.us/lcns_public/lcns_query.lic_name_search_frm
Nurse; Nurse-LPN, RPN #19	www.op.nysed.gov/opsearches.htm#nme
Nursery, Plant #26	www.agmkt.state.ny.us/nurseryDealers.html
Nutritionist #19	www.op.nysed.gov/opsearches.htm#nme
Occupational Therapist/Assistant #19	www.op.nysed.gov/opsearches.htm#nme
Off-Track Betting #15	http://licensing.racing.state.ny.us/license.cfm
Ophthalmic Dispenser #19	www.op.nysed.gov/opsearches.htm#nme
Optometrist #19	www.op.nysed.gov/opsearches.htm#nme
Pesticide-related Business #2	www.dec.state.ny.us/website/dshm/pesticid/appman.htm#top
Pharmacist #19	www.op.nysed.gov/opsearches.htm#nme
Physical Therapist/Assistant #19	www.op.nysed.gov/opsearches.htm#nme
Physician #19	www.op.nysed.gov/opsearches.htm#nme
Physician Assistant #19	www.op.nysed.gov/opsearches.htm#nme
Physicians Specialist Assistant #19	www.op.nysed.gov/opsearches.htm#nme
Plant Dealer #26	www.agmkt.state.ny.us/nurseryDealers.html
Podiatrist #19	www.op.nysed.gov/opsearches.htm#nme
Premium Finance Company #23	www.banking.state.ny.us/sipremfi.htm
Private Investigator #10	http://appsext5.dos.state.ny.us/lcns_public/lcns_query.lic_name_search_frm
Psychiatrist #19	www.nyspsych.org
Psychologist #19	www.op.nysed.gov/opsearches.htm#nme
Public Accountant-CPA #19	www.op.nysed.gov/opsearches.htm#nme
Racing Occupation #15	http://licensing.racing.state.ny.us/license.cfm
Radiologic Technology School #14	www.health.state.ny.us/nysdoh/radtech/schlist2.htm
Radon Testing Lab #14	www.wadsworth.org/labcert/elap/radon.html
Real Estate Agent/Broker/Office #10	http://appsext5.dos.state.ny.us/lcns_public/lcns_query.lic_name_search_frm
Real Estate Appraiser #10	http://appsext5.dos.state.ny.us/lcns_public/lcns_query.lic_name_search_frm
Respiratory Therapist/Therapy Technician #19	www.op.nysed.gov/opsearches.htm#nme
Safe Deposit Company #23	www.banking.state.ny.us/sisafede.htm
Sales Finance Company #23	www.banking.state.ny.us/sisalesf.htm
Savings & Loan #23	www.banking.state.ny.us/sisavloa.htm
Savings Bank #23	www.banking.state.ny.us/sisaving.htm
School, Non-Degree Granting/Proprietary #34	www.highered.nysed.gov/bpss/directory_main_page.htm
Security & Fire Alarm Installer #10	http://appsext5.dos.state.ny.us/lcns_public/lcns_query.lic_name_search_frm
Security Guard #10	http://appsext5.dos.state.ny.us/lcns_public/lcns_query.lic_name_search_frm
Social Worker #19	www.op.nysed.gov/opsearches.htm#nme
Speech Pathologist/Audiologist #19	www.op.nysed.gov/opsearches.htm#nme
State Bid Result #36	www.ogs.state.ny.us/dnc/EmpireStateBuilder/webbidresults.htm
State Telecommunication Contractor #37	www.ogs.state.ny.us/purchase/telecomContracts.asp
Substance Abuse Provider #31	http://aps.oasas.state.ny.us/providers/
Summer Camp for Mental Retarded #49	www.omr.state.ny.us/hp_camp_directory.jsp
Surveyor, Land #19	www.op.nysed.gov/opsearches.htm#nme
Teacher #17	www.highered.nysed.gov/tcert/respublic/ocvs.htm
Telemarketer Business #10	http://appsext5.dos.state.ny.us/lcns_public/lcns_query.lic_name_search_frm
Trust Company #23	www.banking.state.ny.us/sibank.htm
Uniform Procedures Act Permit #11	www.dec.state.ny.us/apps/envapps/index.cfm?view=wizard
Upholster & Bedding Industry #10	http://appsext5.dos.state.ny.us/lcns_public/lcns_query.lic_name_search_frm
Veterinarian/Veterinary Technician #19	www.op.nysed.gov/opsearches.htm#nme
Water Supply Permit #11	www.dec.state.ny.us/apps/envapps/index.cfm?view=wizard
Water Treatment Plant Operator #13	www.health.state.ny.us
Waxing License #10	http://appsext5.dos.state.ny.us/lcns_public/lcns_query.lic_name_search_frm
Weights/Measures Local Office #28	www.agmkt.state.ny.us/WM/wmdirlst.html

Woman-owned Business #35.............................. http://205.232.252.35/
Workers Comp 3rd Party Admin. #57 .... www.wcb.state.ny.us/content/main/SiLr/sec50_3bd.pdf
Workers Comp Claim Representative #57 .... www.wcb.state.ny.us/content/main/SiLr/sec24a.pdf
Workers Comp PPO Applicant #57 .... www.wcb.state.ny.us/content/main/ppopage/ppotrak1.pdf

New York Licensing Quick Finder

Accident/health Insurer #12 518-474-6623
Accountant, CPA/Public #19 518-474-3817
Acupuncturist/Acupuncturist Assist. #19 518-474-3817
Addiction Counselo #31 800-482-9564, 518-485-2057
Addiction Treatment Center #31 518-457-4384
Adoption Agency #24 800-345-5437
Adult Care Med. Facility #38 518-478-1101
Adult Care Suspended List #38............ 518-478-1101
Adult Family Home #24 518-474-7112
Alarm Installer #10 518-474-4429
Alcohol Abuse Provider #31 518-457-4384
Alcohol Beverage Bond Company #46 212-961-8385
Alcohol Distiller/Whlser/Mfg #46 212-961-8385
Alcohol Service Establishment #46 212-961-8385
Alcohol Service Permit #46 212-961-8385
Alcohol/Substance Abuse Counselor #31
.... 800-482-9564, 518-485-2057
Alcoholic Beverage Distributor #52 800-225-5829
Alternative-Fueling Site #37 518-862-1090
Ambulance Service #7 518-402-0996
Ambulatory Svc, Mentally Retarded #49 518-473-9689
Amusement Device #9 518-457-2735
Animal Disposal Plant #27 518-457-5459
Animal Transport Service #27 518-457-5459
Animals, Lab Permit #41 518-485-5378
Apartment Information Vendor #10 518-474-4429
Apartment Mgr./Vendor/Agent #10 518-474-4429
Apartment Sharing Manager #10 518-474-4429
Apiary #26 518-457-2087
Apparel Mfg Industry Certificate #9 518-457-1942
Appearance Enhancement Business /Profess'l #10
.... 518-474-4429
Aquaculture-related Permit #11 631-444-0483
Architect #19 518-474-3817
Armored Car/Car Carrier #10 518-474-4429
Asbestos Handler #9 518-457-2735
Asbestos Safety Training Certificate #39 518-402-7940
Athlete Agent #10 518-474-4429
Athletic Trainer #19 518-474-3817
ATM Machine #23 ..... 877-BANK-NYS, 212-709-1511
Attorney #18 212-428-2800
Audiologist #19 518-474-3817
Backflow Prevention Device Tester #13 518-402-7712
Bail Bond Agent #12 518-474-6630
Bail Enforcement Agent #10 518-474-4429
Bank, Domestic #23... 877-BANK-NYS, 212-709-1503
Bank, Foreign #23 .... 877-BANK-NYS, 212-709-1559
Banker, Private #23 877-BANK-NYS, 212-709-1503
Banking Regulatory Action #23 .... 877-BANK-NYS
Barber Apprentice #10 518-474-4429
Barber/Barber Shop #10 518-474-4429
Bathing Beach #40 518-402-7600
Bedding Manufacturing #10................ 518-474-4429
Beer/Malt Beverage Distributor #52 800-225-5829
Blaster #9 518-457-2735
Blood Alcohol Analysis Permit #41 518-474-0005
Blood Bank #41 518-485-5378
Boat Launch Sites #50 518-474-0445
Boating Permit (State Park) #50 518-474-0445
Boiler Inspector #8 518-457-2722
Bottled Water Facility #13 518-402-7712
Boxer #21 212-417-5700

Boxing/Wrestling-related Profess'l #21 212-417-5700
Breath Analysis Operator #41 518-474-2821
Brewer #46 212-961-8385
Budget Planner #23 .. 877-BANK-NYS, 212-709-5498
Building Permit #10 518-474-4429
Bulk Water Facility #13 518-402-7712
Business School Agent/Teacher #34 ... 518-474-3969
Canal Recreational Vessel Permit #32 . 518-436-2894
Care Facility (Family Board-sponsored) #25
.... 518-473-4630
Casino Employee #15 .... 518-453-8460 X2
Charitable Annuity #12 212-480-4778
Charitable Gaming #15 .... 518-453-8460 X2
Charity, Registered #44 212-416-8430
Check Casher #23 .... 877-BANK-NYS, 212-709-5494
Chemical Dependence Operating Certificate #31
.... 518-457-4384
Children's Overnight Camp #40 518-402-7600
Chiropractor #19 518-474-3817
Cigarette/Tobacco Whlse/Retailer #52 800-225-5829
Cigarette/Tobacco Tax Agent #52 800-225-5829
Clinical Lab Cirector/Assistant #41 518-485-5378
Clinical Lab/Blood Bank #41 518-485-5378
Coastal/Marine-related Permit #11 631-444-0470
Coin Processor #10 518-474-4429
Commercial Vessel (Canal) #32 518-471-5010
Commodity Investment Advisor #1 212-416-8222
Community Residence, Mental Health #48
.... 518-474-5570
Condominium #45 212-416-8122
Construction Permit #36.................... 518-474-1314
Construction Plans Purchased #36 518-474-1314
Controlled Substance Dispenser #42 ... 518-402-0707
Control'd Substance Lab/Importer #42 . 518-402-0707
Controlled Substance Mfg/Dist/Esporter #42
.... 518-402-0707
Controlled Substance Researcher #42 . 518-402-0707
Cooperative Insurance Company,
   Advance/Premium #12 212-480-5565
Cooperative, Housing #45 212-416-8122
Cosmetologist #10 518-474-4429
Court Reporter #19 518-474-3817
Crane Operator #9 518-457-2735
Credit Union #23 .... 877-BANK-NYS, 212-709-1511
Cytotechnologist #41 518-485-5378
Day Care Center #24 518-474-7112
Day Care, Farm Worker (ABCD) #29 ... 518-457-7076
Day Service Program #24 518-474-7112
DEC Permit Application #11................ 518-402-8985
Dental Hygienist #19 518-474-3817
Dentist/Dental Assistant #19 518-474-3817
Diagnostic/Treatment Ctr./Clinic #22 ... 518-402-0911
Dietitian #19 518-474-3817
Dispatch Facility (Alarm/Security/Fire) #10
.... 518-474-4429
Dog License #27 519-457-2728
Dog/Cat Breeder #27 518-457-2728
Domestic Out of State Bank Rep. Ofc. #23
.... 877-BANK-NYS
Domestic Violence Facility #24 518-474-7112
Drugs/Devices, Mfg/Whsle/Dist. #19 ... 518-474-3817
Electrician, Master #10 518-474-4429

Emergency Medical Technician #7 518-402-0996
Employment Agency/Manager #9........ 212-352-6079
Engineer #19 518-474-3817
Engineering Corportion #19 518-474-3817
English as a Second Language School #34
.... 518-474-3969
Environmental Permit #11 518-402-8985
Esthetics Specialist #10 518-474-4429
Euthanize Dogs/Cats #42 518-402-0707
Excavate/Remove/Dispose of Material #37
.... 518-474-2195
Excess Line Broker #12 518-474-6630
Explosive Registration/Handling #9 518-457-2735
Explosives Transport (Thruway) #55 ... 518-436-3079
Falconer #11 518-402-8843
Family Program, Interim #24 518-474-7112
Family/Group Day Care #24 518-474-7112
Farm Labor Camp/Store #9 518-457-4321
Farm Products Dealer #26 518-457-1954
Farmworker Specialty Certification #29 518-457-7076
Feed Facility #29 519-457-5457
Fertilizer Distributor #26 518-457-2087
Firearms Manufacturer #51................ 518-457-6721
First Responder #7 518-402-0996
Fish Processor #29 518-457-5459
Fishing Guide #3 518-402-8838
Food Inspector #29 518-457-5459
Food Processor #29 518-457-7139
Food Salvager #29 518-457-1215
Food Service Establishment #40 518-402-7630
Food Store, Retail #29 518-457-1215
Foreign Banking Agency #23
.... 877-bank-nys, 212-709-1559
Foster Care #24 518-474-7112
Franchise Sales #1......................... 212-416-8222
Franchise, Approved #1 212-416-8222
Fraternal Benefit Society #12 212-480-5027
Fund Raider, Professional #44 518-486-9797
Fund Raising Counsel #44 518-473-2374
Funeral Home/Director #6 518-402-0785
Game Bird Breeder #11 518-402-8985
Games of Chance Registration #10..... 518-474-4429
Greenhouse #26 518-457-2087
Guard Dog Agency #10..................... 518-474-4429
Guard/Patrol Agency #10 518-474-4429
Guide, Camping/Fishing/Hiking/Hunting #3
.... 518-402-8838
Guide. Rock/Ice Climbing #3 518-402-8838
Hair Styling, Natural #10 518-474-4429
Hauling Permit, Specialty Thruway #55 518-436-2793
Health Care Plan, Prepaid #43 518-473-4842
Health Club #10............................. 518-474-4429
Hearing Aid Dealer #10 518-474-4429
Heating Oil Seller #53 800-225-5829
Highway Use Tax Registration #53...... 800-748-3676
Hiking Guide #3 518-402-8838
HMO (Insurance) #12 518-474-6630
HMO (Medical Operation) #43 518-473-4842
Holding Company #23
.... 877-BANK-NYS, 212-709-1503
Home Care Service #38 518-478-1102
Home Health Agency #38 518-478-1102

Home Health Aide Training #38 ... 518-478-1060
Homeworker Industrial Distributor #9 ... 212-352-6032
Hospice #38 ... 518-478-1102
Hospital #38 ... 518-478-1102
Hotel.Motel Name Certificate #10 ... 518-474-4429
Hunting Guide #3 ... 518-402-8838
Insurance Adjuster #12 ... 518-474-6630
Insurance Agent/Consultant/Broker #12 518-474-6630
Insurance Appraiser #12 ... 518-474-6630
Insurance Company #12 ... 518-474-6630
Insurance Cont. Educ. Provider #12 ... 518-474-6630
Interior Designer #19 ... 518-474-3817
Investment Advisor #1 ... 212-416-8222
Investment Company Article XII #23 ... 877-BANK-NYS, 212-709-1503
Juvenile Detention Facility #25 ... 518-473-4630
Kosher Food #30 ... 718-722-2852
Landscape Architect #19 ... 518-474-3817
Laser Operator, Mobile #9 ... 518-457-2735
Lender, Licensed #23 877-BANK-NYS, 212-709-5496
Loan Broker #33 ... 518-473-7002
Lobbyist #16 ... 518-474-7126
Lottery Agent/Ticket Seller #47 ... 518-388-3300
Lottery Claim Center #47 ... 518-388-3300
LPG-related #53 ... 800-225-5829
Mass Gathering Permit #40 ... 518-402-7600
Massage Therapist #19 ... 518-474-3817
Medicaid Managed Care #43 ... 518-473-4842
Medical Certificate of Authoriz'n #57 ... 518-474-2036
Medical Delivery System #43 ... 518-473-4842
Medical Disciplinary Action #22 ... 800-663-6114
Medical Doctor #19 ... 518-474-3817
Medical Examiner, Independent #57 ... 518) 402-6190
Medical Facility, Worker's Comp License #5 7 ... 518-474-2036
Medical Personnel Profile #22 ... 888-338-6999
Mental Health Facility #48 ... 518-474-5570
Mentally Retarded Health Facility/Svc #49 ... 518-473-9689
Midwife #19 ... 518-474-3817
Migrant Farmworker Housing Facility #40 ... 518-402-7600
Milk Bacteriologist #27 ... 518-457-1772
Milk-related Dealer/Service #27 ... 518-457-5731
Mining/Exploration, State-owned Land #37 ... 518-473-1288
Minority/Woman-owned Business #35 . 518-292-5250
Mobile Home Park #40 ... 518-402-7600
Money Transmit'r #23 877-BANK-NYS, 212-709-5494
Mortgage Banker #23 877-BANK-NYS, 212-709-5574
Mortgage Broker #23 . 877-BANK-NYS, 212-709-5574
Mortgage Guaranty Insurance Agent #12 ... 518-474-6630
Mover #56 ... 518-457-6236
Municipal Health Benefit Plan #12 ... 212-480-5245
Nail Technologist #10 ... 518-474-4429
Notary Public #10 ... 518-474-4429
Nurse-LPN, RPN #19 ... 518-474-3817
Nursery, Plant #26 ... 518-457-2087
Nurses' Aide #5 ... 518-474-3817
Nursing Home #38 ... 518-478-1101
Nursing Home Administrator #5 ... 518-474-3817
Nutritionist #19 ... 518-474-3817
Occupational Therapist/Assistant #19 .. 518-474-3817
Off-Track Betting #15 ... 518-453-8460 X2
Ophthalmic Dispenser #19 ... 518-474-3817
Optometrist #19 ... 518-474-3817
Paramedic #7 ... 518-402-0996
Passenger Motor Carrier #56 ... 518-457-6503
Patient Service Center #41 ... 518-485-5378
Pesticide-related Business #2 ... 518-402-8748
Pet Cemetery/Crematory #10 ... 518-474-4429
Pet Dealer #27 ... 518-457-7749
Pet Food Producer #29 ... 519-457-5457
Petroleum/Fuel Product Dealer/Handler #53 ... 800-225-5829
Pharmacist / Pharmacy #19 ... 518-474-3817
Physical Therapist/Assistant #19 ... 518-474-3817
Physician #19 ... 518-474-3817
Physician Assistant #19 ... 518-474-3817
Physicians Specialist Assistant #19 ... 518-474-3817
Phytosanitary Certificate #26 ... 518-457-2087
Pistol Permit #51 ... 518-457-6721
Plant Dealer #26 ... 518-457-2087
Podiatrist #19 ... 518-474-3817
Premium Finance Company #23 ... 877-BANK-NYS, 212-709-5498
Private Investigator #10 ... 518-474-4429
Private School, Mentally Retarded #49 . 518-473-9689
Promoter, Entertainment #54 ... 800-225-5829
Psychiatrist #19 ... 518-474-3817
Psychologist #19 ... 518-474-3817
Public Accountant-CPA #19 ... 518-474-3817
Public Vessel (State Waters) #50 ... 518-474-0445
Racetrack #15 ... 518-453-8460 X2
Racing Occupation #15 ... 518-453-8460 X2
Radiation Device, General-use #9 ... 518-457-1202
Radiation Materials Permit #14 ... 518-402-7550
Radiation Safety Officer #14 ... 518-402-7580
Radiation Therapy Technologist #14 ... 518-402-7580
Radiologic Technologist #14 ... 518-402-7580
Radiologic Technology School #14 ... 518-402-7580
Radon Testing Lab #14 ... 518-402-7580
Rafting Guide, Whitewater #3 ... 518-402-8838
Railroad/Steamboat Policeman #10 ... 518-457-1932
Real Estate Agent/Broker/Office #10 ... 518-474-4429
Real Estate Appraiser #10 ... 518-474-4429
Real Estate Investment Trust #45 ... 212-416-8122
Real Estate Offering, Registered #45 .. 212-416-8122
Real Estate Syndication #45 ... 212-416-8122
Recreation Vehicle Permit #50 ... 518-474-0445
Regatta/Marina Permit #50 ... 518-474-0445
Reinsurance Intermediary #12 ... 518-474-6630
Reinsurer #12 ... 518-474-6623
Renderer #29 ... 518-457-1215
Rental Agency, Limited #12 ... 518-474-6630
Residential Facility #24 ... 518-474-7112
Respiratory Therapist/Therapy Technician #19 ... 518-474-3817
Restaurant Brewer #46 ... 212-961-8385
Rock and Ice Climbing Guide #3 ... 518-402-8838
Safe Deposit Co. #23 877-BANK-NYS, 212-709-1503
Sales Finance Company #23 ... 877-BANK-NYS, 212-709-5496
Sales Tax Permit #54 ... 800-225-5829
Savings & Loan #23 . 877-BANK-NYS, 212-709-1511
Savings Bank #23 ... 877-BANK-NYS, 212-709-1511
School Administrator/Supervisor #17 ... 518-474-3901
School Counselor #17 ... 518-474-3901
School Media Specialist #17 ... 518-474-3901
School, Non-Degree Granting/Proprietary #34 ... 518-474-3969
School, Private #34 ... 518-474-3969
School, Private, Director/Teacher #34 . 518-474-3969
Scientific Collection #11 ... 631-444-0483
Securities Broker/Dealer #1 ... 212-416-8222
Securities Salesperson #1 ... 212-416-8222
Security & Fire Alarm Installer #10 ... 518-474-4429
Security Guard #10 ... 518-474-4429
Self-Insured Carrier Rep. #57 ... 518-402-6190
Shellfish-related Permit #11 ... 631-444-0483
Short Hand Reporter #19 ... 518-474-3817
Show, Permit to Operate #54 ... 800-225-5829
Ski Tow #9 ... 518-457-2131
Slaughterhouse #27 ... 518-457-5459
Snowmobile Event #50 ... 518-474-0445
Snowmobile Instructor #50 ... 518-474-0445
Social Worker #19 ... 518-474-3817
Solicitor (Fund Raising) #44 ... 518-486-9797
Special Event, Serving Alcohol #46 ... 212-961-8385
Specialty Food Producer #29 ... 519-457-1215
Speech Pathologist/Audiologist #19 ... 518-474-3817
Sporting License #11 ... 518-402-8843
Sportsman License, Lifetime #11 ... 518-402-8843
State Bid Result #36 ... 518-474-1314
State Telecommunication Contr'r #37 .. 518-473-2658
Stevedore #20 ... 212-742-9280
Stock Life Insurer #12 ... 212-480-5038
Substance Abuse Provider #31 ... 518-457-4384
Summer Camp for Mental Retarded #49 ... 518-473-9689
Summer Day Camp #40 ... 518-402-7600
Surveyor, Land #19 ... 518-474-3817
Swimming Pool, Public/Group #40 ... 518-402-7600
Takeover Statement, Registration #1 .. 212-416-8222
Tandem Trailer Permit (Thruway) #55 . 518-436-3150
Teacher #17 ... 518-474-3901
Teacher, Proprietary School #34 ... 518-474-3969
Telemarketer Business #10 ... 518-474-4429
Terminal Operator #53 ... 800-225-5829
Theatrical Syndication #1 ... 212-416-8222
Ticket Distributor #1 ... 212-416-8222
Tour Vessel #32 ... 518-471-5010
Trading Stamp Registration #10 ... 518-474-4429
Tramway #9 ... 518-457-2131
Trapper #11 ... 518-402-8843
Traveling Summer Day Camp #40 ... 518-402-7600
Treatment Center/Clinic #22 ... 518-402-0911
Trust Company #23 ... 877-BANK-NYS, 212-709-1503
Underwater Land Lease #37 ... 518-474-2195
Uniform Procedures Act Permit #11 ... 518-402-8985
Upholster & Bedding Industry #10 ... 518-474-4429
Utilization Mgmt. Registration #43 ... 518-473-4842
Vessel Operator, Recreational/Touring #50 ... 518-474-0445
Veterinarian/Veterinary Tech. #19 ... 518-474-3817
Viatical Settlement Broker #12 ... 518-474-6630
Warehouse, Food #29 ... 518-457-1215
Warehouse, Refrigerated #29 ... 518-457-1215
Waste Water Treatment Plant Operator #4 ... 518-402-8177
Water Supply Permit #11 ... 518-402-8985
Water Treatment Plant Operator #13 ... 518-402-7712
Waxing License #10 ... 518-474-4429
Weighmaster #28 ... 518-457-3146
Weights/Measures Local Office #28 ... 518-457-3146
Wildlife Collector #11 ... 518-402-8985
Wildlife Rehabilitator #11 ... 518-402-8985
Window Cleaning Equipment #9 ... 518-457-1536
Woman-owned Business #35 ... 518-292-5250
Workers Comp 3rd Party Admin. #57 . 518) 402-6190
Workers Comp Claim Rep. #57 ... 518) 402-6190
Workers Comp PPO Applicant #57 ... 518-402-6190
Workers' Comp Preferred Provider #43 518-473-4842
Workplace Safety/Loss Prevention Consultant #9 ... 518-457-2735
Wrestler #21 ... 212-417-5700
Youth Shelter, Runaway/Homeless #24518-474-7112

New York Licensing Agency Information

1 Department of Law, Bureau of Investor Protection & Securities, 120 Broadway, 23rd Floor, New York, NY 10271; 212-416-8222, Fax: 212-416-8816. www.oag.state.ny.us

2 Department of Environmental Conservation, Bureau of Pesticide Management, 625 Broadway, Albany, NY 12233-7254; 518-402-8748, Fax: 518-402-9024. www.dec.state.ny.us Search Database at www.dec.state.ny.us/webs ite/dshm/pesticid/appman.htm#top Note: Permits are issued from various regional offices.

3 Department of Environmental Conservation, Division of Forest Protection & Fire Mgmt., 625 Broadway, 8th Fl, Albany, NY 12233-2560; 518-402-8838, Fax: 518-485-8458. www.dec.state.ny.us/website/protection/rangers/fr guid6.html   Email: dpaeweb@gw.dec.state.ny.us

4 Department of Environmental Conservation, Division of Water, Bureau of Watershed Compliance, 625 Broadway, Albany, NY 12233-3506; 518-402-8155, Fax: 518-402-8177. www.dec.state.ny.us Email: Webmaster@gw.dec.state.ny.us

5 Board of Examiners of Nursing Home Administrators, Bureau of Professional Credentialling, 161 Delaware Av, Delmar, NY 10254; 518-478-1060.

6 Department of Health, Bureau of Funeral Directing, 433 River St #303, Troy, NY 12180-2299; 518-402-0785, Fax: 518-402-0784.

7 Department of Health, Emergency Medical Services, 433 River St, #303, Troy, NY 12180; 518-402-0996, Fax: 518-402-0985. www.health.state.ny.us/nysdoh/ems/main.htm

8 Department of Labor, Boiler Safety Bureau, Bldg 12, Rm 165, Albany, NY 12240-0102; 518-457-2722, Fax: 518-485-9077.

9 Department of Labor, License & Certificate Unit, State Office Bldg Campus 12 Rm 166, Albany, NY 12240; 518-457-2735, Fax: 518-457-8452.   www.labor.state.ny.us

10 Department of State, Division of Licensing Services, 84 Holland Ave, Albany, NY 12208-3490; 518-474-4429, Fax: 518-473-6648. www.dos.state.ny.us/lcns/licensing.html Email: info@dos.state.ny.us Search Database at http://appsext5.dos.state.n y.us/lcns_public/lcns_query.lic_name_search_frm

11 Department of Environmental Conservation, Offices of Fish, Wildlife and Marine Resources, 625 Broadway, Albany, NY 12233-4750; 518-402-8985, Fax: 518-402-9027. www.dec.state.ny.us/website/dfwmr/index.html Email: fwinfo@gw.dec.state.ny.us <fwinfo@gw.dec.state.ny.us>

12 Insurance Department, Licensing Bureau Agency, Empire State Plaza, Bldg 1, Albany, NY 12257; 518-474-6630. www.ins.state.ny.us   Email: licensing@ins.state.ny.us

13 Department of Health, Bureau of Water Supply Protection, 547 River Street, Flanigan Square, Rm 400, Troy, NY 12180; 518-402-7712, Fax: 518-402-7599. www.health.state.ny.us/nysdoh/water/operate/oper ate.htm

14 Department of Health, Bureau of Environmental Radiation Protection, 547 River St, Flanigan Sq, Room 530, Troy, NY 12180-2216; 518-402-7580, Fax: 518-402-7575. www.health.state.ny.us/nysdoh/radtech/radtech.htm Email: berp@health.state.ny.us Search Database at www.health.state.ny.us/nysdoh/radtech/radtech.htm

15 Racing & Wagering Board, 1 Watervliet Av Extension #2, Albany, NY 12206; 518-453-8460 x2, Fax: 518-453-8492. www.racing.state.ny.us   Search Database at http://licensing.racing.state.ny.us/license.cfm

16 Temporary Commission on Lobbying, Agency Bldg #2, 17th Fl, Albany, NY 12223-1254; 518-474-7126, Fax: 518-473-6492. www.nylobby.state.ny.us Email: lobcom@emi.com   Search Database at www.nylobby.state.ny.us/lobby_data.html

17 State Education Department, Office of Teaching, 5N Education Bldg, Albany, NY 12234; 518-474-3901, Fax: 518-473-0271. www.highered.nysed.gov/tcert/ Search Database at www.highered.nysed.gov/tcert/respublic/ocvs.htm

18 Unified Court System, Attorney Registration Unit, PO Box 2806, Church Street Station, New York, NY 10008; 212-428-2800, Fax: 212-428-2804.   www.nycourts.gov Email: attyreg@courts.state.ny.us Search Database at www.nycourts.gov/attorneys/

19 Education Department, Office of the Professions, 89 Washington Ave, State Education Bldg, 2nd Fl, Albany, NY 12234; 518-474-3817, attendant available 9-11:45AM and 12:45-4:30PM ESTTDD 518-473-1426. www.op.nysed.gov Email: op4info@mail.nysed.gov Search Database at www.op.nysed.gov/opsearches.htm#nme

20 Division of Licenings & EIC, Waterfront Commission of New York Harbor, 39 Broadway, 4th Fl, New York, NY 10006; 212-742-9280, Fax: 212-905-9249. www.wcnynj.org

21 State Athletic Commission, Department of State, 123 Williams St, 20th Fl, New York, NY 10038; 212-417-5700, Fax: 212-417-4987. www.dos.state.ny.us/athletic/ Email: athletic@dos.state.ny.us

22 Department of Health, Office of Professional Medical Conduct, 433 River St. #303, Troy, NY 12180; 800-663-6114, 518-402-0836. www.health.state.ny.us/nysdoh/opmc/main.htm Email: opmc@health.state.ny.us Search Database at http://w3.health.state.ny.us/opmc/factions.nsf

23 State Banking Dept., Licensed Financial Svcs Division, One State St, 3rd Fl, New York, NY 10004-1417; 877-BANK-NYS, Fax: 212-709-3582.   www.banking.state.ny.us Search Database at www.banking.state.ny.us/supinst.htm

24 Office of Children and Family Services, Legal Division, 52 Washington St, Rensselaer, NY 12144; 518-474-7112. www.ocfs.state.ny.us

25 Office of Children and Family Services, Detention/Voluntary Agency Services Unit, 52 Washington St, Rensselaer, NY 12144; 518-473-4630. www.ocfs.state.ny.us

26 Department of Agriculture and Markets, Division of Plant Industry, 10B Airline Dr, Albany, NY 12235; 1-800-554-4501. www.agmkt.state.ny.us/ Note: User name and password required for dog license search.

27 Department of Agriculture and Markets, Division of Animal Industry, 10 B Airline Dr., Albany, NY 12235; 518-457-3502, Fax: 518-485-5816.   www.agmkt.state.ny.us/AI/AIHome.html

28 Department of Agriculture and Markets, Division of Weights and Measures, 1 Winners Circle, Albany, NY 12235-0001; 518-457-3146. www.agmkt.state.ny.us/WM/WMHome.html Email: agmweigh@agmkt.state.ny.us

29 Department of Agriculture and Markets, Division of Food Safety and Inspection, 1 Winners Circle, Albany, NY 12235; 518-457-1215, Fax: 518-457-8892. www.agmkt.state.ny.us/FS/FSHome.html

30 Department of Agriculture and Markets, Division of Kosher Law Enforcement, 55 Hanson Pl, Brooklyn, NY 11217; 718-722-2852. www.agmkt.state.ny.us/KO/KOHome.html

31 Office of Alcoholism and Substance Abuse Services, Bureau of Professional Development, 1450 Western Ave, Albany, NY 12203-3526; 518-473-3460. http://web2k.oasas.state.ny.us/oasas/home.cfm Email: Certification@oasas.state.ny.us

32 State Canal Corporation, Interchange 23, Rte 9W, Albany, NY 12201; 518-436-2700. www.canals.state.ny.us/

33 Office of the State Comptroller, Office of Unclaimed Funds, 110 State St, 8th Fl, Albany, NY 12236; 518-473-7002. www.osc.state.ny.us

34 State Education Department, Bureau of Proprietary School Supervision, Education Building Annex, Rm 974, Albany, NY 12234; 518-474-3969. www.highered.nysed.gov/bpss/ Email: bpss@mail.nysed.gov

35 Empire State Development, Division of Minority and Women's Business Development, 30 S Pearl St, Albany, NY 12245; 518-292-5250. www.nylovesbiz.com/Small_and_Growing_Busin esses/mwbe.asp Search Database at http://205.232.252.35/ Note: A second office is at 633 3rd Av, NY, NY 10017, phone 212-803-2414.

36 State Office of General Services, Design and Construction, 35th Floor Tower Bldg, Albany, NY 12242; 518-474-1314. www.ogs.state.ny.us/dnc/default.asp Email: design.construction@ogs.state.ny.us

37 State Office of General Services, Real Estate Development, 26th Fl Tower Bldg, Empire State Plaza, Albany, NY 12242; 518-474-2195. www.ogs.state.ny.us/building/flagpolicy/default.asp Email: real.property@ogs.state.ny.us

38 Department of Health, Office of Health Systems Management, 161 Delaware Ave, Delmar, NY 12054; 518-478-1101. Email: acfinfo@health.state.ny.us

39 State Department of Health, Bureau of Environmental Health, 547 River St, Rm 230, Flanagan Sq, Troy, NY 12180; 518-402-7940, Fax: 518-402-7949.

40 State Department of Health, Bureau of Community Sanitation and Food Protection, 547 River St. Flanagan Sq, Rm 515, Troy, NY 12180; 518-402-7600. www.health.state.ny.us

41 State Department of Health, Wadsworth Center, Empire State Plaza, Concourse Level, Rm. E324, Albany, NY 12201-0509; 518-474-0005. www.health.state.ny.us

42 Department of Health, Bureau of Controlled Substances, 433 River St, Troy, NY 12180; 518-402-0707, Fax: 518-402-0709. www.health.state.ny.us

43 State Department of Health, Bureau of Managed Care Certification & Surveillance, Corning Tower Bldg, Empire State Plaza, Rm 1911, Albany, NY 12237-0062; 518-473-4842. www.health.state.ny.us/nysdoh/mancare/mcmain.htm

44 Office of the Attorney General, Charities Bureau, 120 Broadway, 3rd Fl, New York, NY 10271; 212-416-8430. www.oag.state.ny.us/charities/charities.html Email: Charities.Bureau@oag.state.ny.us Note: There is a second office at the State Capitol in Albany, in telephone area code 518.

45 Office of the Attorney General, Bureau of Real Estate Finance, 120 Broadway, New York, NY 10271; 212-416-8122, Fax: 212-416-8179. www.oag.state.ny.us/realestate/realestate.html

46 State Liquor Authority, Divison of Alcoholic Beverage Control, 105 W 125th St. 4th Fl, New York, NY 10027; 212-961-8385, Fax: 212-961-8283. www.abc.state.ny.us Search Database at http://abc.state.ny.us/JSP/query/PublicQueryInstructPage.jsp Note: The Agency maintains three zone offices located in New York City, Albany (518-474-3114) and Buffalo (716-847-3035) and one satellite office in Syracuse (315-428-4198). Public Affairs office is 212-961-8300.

47 New York Lottery, 1 Broadway Center, Schenectady, NY 12301-7500; 518-388-3300, Fax: 518-388-3403. www.nylottery.org/index.php

48 State Office of Mental Health, Bureau of Inspection and Certification, 44 Holland Ave, Albany, NY 12229; 518-474-5570, Fax: 518-486-5587.

49 Office of Mental Retardation and Developmental Disabilities, Developmental Disabilities Service Office, 44 Holland Ave, Albany, NY 12229; 518-473-9689, Fax: 518-474-1335. www.omr.state.ny.us Note: There is also a New York City Office at 75 Morton St, 212-229-3231.

50 State Parks, Recreation and Historic Preservation, Bureau of Marine and Recreational Vehicles, Agency Building 1, 11th Fl, Empire State Plaza, Albany, NY 12238; 518-474-0445, Fax: 518-486-7378. www.nysparks.com/boats/mrv/ Note: Snowmobiles must be registered with state DMV.

51 State Police, BCI Section; Firearms Section, 1220 Washington Ave, Bldg 22, Albany, NY 12226; 518) 457-1932. www.troopers.state.ny.us Email: PIOOFFIC@troopers.state.ny.us

52 Department of Taxation and Finance, Registration and Bonding Tax Unit, Building 8, Rm 855, State Campus, Albany, NY 12227; 800-225-5829, Fax: 518-457-9807. www.tax.state.ny.us/sbc/

53 Department of Taxation & Finance, Registration & Data Services Bureau, Commodities Tax Unit, Building 8, Rm 400, State Campus, Albany, NY 12227; 800-225-5829. www.tax.state.ny.us

54 Department of Taxation & Finance, Sales Tax Registration Unit, Building 8, Rm 431, State Campus, Albany, NY; 800-225-5829. www.tax.state.ny.us

55 State Thruway Authority, Department Traffic Management, 200 Southern Blvd, Albany, NY 12201-0189; 518-436-3079. www.thruway.state.ny.us/commercial/index.html

56 State Department of Transportation, Passenger and Freight Safety Division, 50 Wolf Rd. Pod 53, Albany, NY 12232; 518-457-1016. www.dot.state.ny.us

57 State Workers' Compensation Board, Health Provider Administration, 20 Park St, Rm 211, Albany, NY 12207; 518-474-2036. www.wcb.state.ny.us

New York Federal Courts

The following list indicates the district and division name for each county in the state. If the bankruptcy court location is different from the district court, then the location of the bankruptcy court appears in parentheses.

County/Court Cross Reference

County	District	Location
Albany	Northern	Albany
Allegany	Western	Buffalo
Bronx	Southern	New York City
Broome	Northern	Binghamton (Utica)
Cattaraugus	Western	Buffalo
Cayuga	Northern	Syracuse (Utica)
Chautauqua	Western	Buffalo
Chemung	Western	Rochester
Chenango	Northern	Binghamton (Utica)
Clinton	Northern	Albany
Columbia	Northern (Southern)	Albany (Poughkeepsie)
Cortland	Northern	Syracuse (Utica)
Delaware	Northern	Binghamton (Utica)
Dutchess	Southern	White Plains (Poughkeepsie)
Erie	Western	Buffalo
Essex	Northern	Albany
Franklin	Northern	Binghamton (Albany)
Fulton	Northern	Syracuse (Albany)
Genesee	Western	Buffalo
Greene	Northern (Southern)	Albany (Poughkeepsie)
Hamilton	Northern	Syracuse (Utica)
Herkimer	Northern	Syracuse (Utica)
Jefferson	Northern	Binghamton (Albany)
Kings	Eastern	Brooklyn
Lewis	Northern	Binghamton (Utica)
Livingston	Western	Rochester
Madison	Northern	Syracuse (Utica)
Monroe	Western	Rochester
Montgomery	Northern	Syracuse (Albany)
Nassau	Eastern	Brooklyn (Westbury)
New York	Southern	New York City
Niagara	Western	Buffalo
Oneida	Northern	Utica
Onondaga	Northern	Syracuse (Utica)
Ontario	Western	Rochester
Orange	Southern	White Plains (Poughkeepsie)
Orleans	Western	Buffalo
Oswego	Northern	Syracuse (Utica)
Otsego	Northern	Binghamton (Utica)
Putnam	Southern	White Plains (Poughkeepsie)
Queens	Eastern	Brooklyn
Rensselaer	Northern	Albany
Richmond	Eastern	Brooklyn
Rockland	Southern	White Plains
Saratoga	Northern	Albany
Schenectady	Northern	Albany
Schoharie	Northern	Albany
Schuyler	Western	Rochester
Seneca	Western	Rochester
St. Lawrence	Northern	Binghamton (Albany)
Steuben	Western	Rochester
Suffolk	Eastern	Central Islip
Sullivan	Southern	White Plains (Poughkeepsie)
Tioga	Northern	Binghamton (Utica)
Tompkins	Northern	Syracuse (Utica)
Ulster	Northern (Southern)	Albany (Poughkeepsie)
Warren	Northern	Albany
Washington	Northern	Albany
Wayne	Western	Rochester
Westchester	Southern	White Plains
Wyoming	Western	Buffalo
Yates	Western	Rochester

Standards for Federal Courts: The search fee is $20.00 per item (one party name or case number). Certification fee is $7.00 per document. Copy fee is $.50 per page. All fees standard unless noted in profile. Mail Search: always enclose a stamped self addressed envelope unless otherwise noted. Most courts accept fax requests or will suggest a copying/search vendor. Before releasing records, all courts require prepayment unless noted in profile.

Notes: Open records are located at the court unless otherwise noted. District courts index by defendant and plaintiff as well as by case number. Bankruptcy courts usually index by debtor and case number. While most courts now have their indexes on computer, many still maintain index card files as well.

PACER: The universal PACER sign-up number is 800-676-6856. Find PACER and the Party/Case Index on the Web at http://pacer.psc.uscourts.gov. PACER dial-up access is $.60 per minute. Also, courts offering internet access via RACER, PACER, Web-PACER or the new CM-ECF charge $.07 per page fee unless noted as free.

US District Court

Eastern District of New York

Brooklyn Division Brooklyn Courthouse, 225 Cadman Plaza E, Room 130, Brooklyn, NY 11201 (courier address: Use mail address for courier delivery) 718-260-2600. www.nyed.uscourts.gov

Counties: Kings, Queens, Richmond. Cases from Nassau and Suffolk may also be filed here (but paper records and cases are heard in Central Islip Div.), but all records are available electronically trhough PACER from this Brooklyn Division.

Indexing & Storage: New cases available in the index 2 days after filing date.

Fee & Payment: Payment may be made by money order, cashier check, personal check. Payee: Clerk, U.S. District Court.

Phone Search: No searching by telephone.

Mail Search: Case records for Suffolk and Nassau counties are not physicly located here - see Central Islip Division. A SASE not required.

In Person Search: Fee charged if court conducts your in person search for you.

PACER: PACER is available online at http://pacer.nyed.uscourts.gov. This PACER system includes electronic records from Suffolk and Nassau Counties, Long Island. Case records go back to January 1, 1990. Records never purged. New records are online after 1 day.

Electronic Filing: Only law firms and practitioners may file cases electronically. Anyone can search online. Electronic filing information online at https://ecf.nyed.uscourts.gov

Central Islip Division 100 Federal Plaza, Central Islip, NY 17722-4438 (courier address: Use mail address for courier delivery) 613-712-6000. www.nyed.uscourts.gov

Counties: Nassau, Suffolk. Cases from these counties may be filed in Brooklyn Division, but heard in Central Islip. Central Islip cases can be found on Brooklyn's PACER system.

Indexing & Storage: New cases available in the index 2 days after filing date. Indexes and files are available here from 1987 on.

Fee & Payment: Payment may be made by money order, cashier check, personal check. Payee: Clerk, U.S. District Court.

Phone Search: Some limited docket information is available by phone.

In Person Search: Fee charged if court conducts your in person search for you.

PACER: PACER is available online at http://pacer.nyed.uscourts.gov. Case records go back to January 1, 1990. Records never purged. New records are online after 1 day.

Electronic Filing: Only law firms and practitioners may file cases electronically. Anyone can search online. Electronic filing information online at https://ecf.nyed.uscourts.gov

U.S. Bankruptcy Court

Eastern District of New York

Brooklyn Division 75 Clinton St, Brooklyn, NY 11201 (Use mail address for courier delivery) 718-330-2188. www.nyeb.uscourts.gov

Counties: Kings, Queens, Richmond. Kings and Queens County Chapter 11 cases may also be assigned to Westbury. Other Queens County cases may be assigned to Westbury Division. Nassau County Chapter 11 cases may be assigned here.

Indexing & Storage: Cases indexed by debtor as well as by case number. New cases available in the index 1 day after filing date. Older cases are indexed on microfiche.

Fee & Payment: Payment may be made by money order, cashier check, business check. Personal checks are not accepted. Payee: Clerk, U.S. Bankruptcy Court.

Phone Search: Only docket information available by phone. Automated voice case information service (VCIS) is available. Call VCIS at 800-252-2537 or 718-852-5726.

Mail Search: A SASE not required.

In Person Search: Fee charged if court conducts your in person search for you.

PACER: PACER is available online at http://pacer.nyeb.uscourts.gov. Records purged every year. New civil records are online after 3 days.

Electronic Filing: Electronic filing information online at https://ecf.nyeb.uscourts.gov

Central Islip Division Long Island Federal Courthouse, 290 Federal Plaza, 2nd Fl, Central Islip, NY 11722 (Use mail address for courier delivery) 631-712-6200. www.nyeb.uscourts.gov

Counties: Suffolk, Nassau.

Indexing & Storage: Cases indexed by debtor as well as by case number. New cases available in the index 1-2 days after filing date.

Fee & Payment: Payment may be made by money order, cashier check, personal check. Debtor's checks are not accepted. Enclose a FedEx package for expedited service. Payee: Clerk, U.S. Bankruptcy Court.

Phone Search: Basic docket information only available by phone. Automated voice case information service (VCIS) is available. Call VCIS at 800-252-2537 or 718-852-5726.

Mail Search: A SASE not required.

In Person Search: Fee charged if court conducts your in person search for you.

PACER: PACER is available online at http://pacer.nyeb.uscourts.gov. Records purged every year. New civil records are online after 3 days.

Electronic Filing: Electronic filing information online at https://ecf.nyeb.uscourts.gov

U.S. District Court

Northern District of New York

Albany Division 445 Broadway, Room 509, James T Foley Courthouse, Albany, NY 12207-2924 (Use mail address for courier delivery) 518-257-1800. www.nynd.uscourts.gov

Counties: Albany, Clinton, Columbia, Essex, Greene, Rensselaer, Saratoga, Schenectady, Schoharie, Ulster, Warren, Washington.

Indexing & Storage: New cases available in the index 1 day after filing date. Case indexes are available on computer terminal in any of the divisions in the Northern District.

Fee & Payment: Payment may be made by money order, cashier check, personal check. Payee: Clerk, U.S. District Court.

Phone Search: No searching by telephone.

Mail Search: A SASE not required.

In Person Search: Fee charged if court conducts your in person search for you.

PACER: PACER is available online at http://pacer.nynd.uscourts.gov. New records are online after 2 days.

Electronic Filing: Electronic filing information online at https://ecf.nynd.uscourts.gov

Binghamton Division 15 Henry St, Binghamton, NY 13902 (courier address: Use mail address for courier delivery) 607-773-2893. www.nynd.uscourts.gov

Counties: Broome, Chenango, Delaware, Franklin, Jefferson, Lewis, Otsego, St. Lawrence, TiogaThis court provides the judges for the Watertown Division.

Indexing & Storage: New cases available in the index 1 day after filing date.

Fee & Payment: Payment may be made by money order, cashier check, personal check. Payee: Clerk, U.S. District Court.

Phone Search: No searching by telephone. Only docket information available by phone.

In Person Search: Fee charged if court conducts your in person search for you.

PACER: PACER is available online at http://pacer.nynd.uscourts.gov. New records are online after 2 days.

Electronic Filing: Electronic filing information online at https://ecf.nynd.uscourts.gov

Syracuse Division PO Box 7367, Syracuse, NY 13261-7367 (courier address: 100 S Clinton St, Syracuse, NY 13261-7367), 315-234-8500. www.nynd.uscourts.gov

Counties: Cayuga, Cortland, Fulton, Hamilton, Herkimer, Madison, Montgomery, Onondaga, Oswego, Tompkins.

Indexing & Storage: New cases available in the index 1 day after filing date.

Fee & Payment: Payment may be made by money order, cashier check, personal check. Credit cards accepted in person only. Payee: Clerk, U.S. District Court.

Phone Search: No searching by telephone. Only docket information available by phone.

In Person Search: Fee charged if court conducts your in person search for you.

PACER: PACER is available online at http://pacer.nynd.uscourts.gov. New records are online after 2 days.

Electronic Filing: Electronic filing information online at https://ecf.nynd.uscourts.gov

Utica Division Alexander Pirnie Bldg, 10 Broad St, Utica, NY 13501 (courier address: Use mail address for courier delivery) 315-793-8151. www.nynd.uscourts.gov

Counties: Oneida.

Indexing & Storage: New cases available in the index 1 day after filing date. Indexes are on computer starting in 1991 and on cards prior to that. Closed case records from the other three Northern district courts were assembled here before going to the New York Federal Records Center. Starting in 1995, Albany and Binghamton and Syracuse are no longer sending their records to Utica.

Fee & Payment: Payment may be made by money order, cashier check, business check. Personal checks are not accepted. Payee: Clerk, U.S. District Court.

Phone Search: Information from the computer for 1991 forward is available by phone.

Mail Search: A SASE not required.

In Person Search: Fee charged if court conducts your in person search for you.

PACER: PACER is available online at http://pacer.nynd.uscourts.gov. New records are online after 2 days.

Electronic Filing: Electronic filing information online at https://ecf.nynd.uscourts.gov

U.S. Bankruptcy Court

Northern District of New York

Albany Division James T Foley Courthouse, 445 Broadway #330, Albany, NY 12207 (courier address: Use mail address for courier delivery) 518-257-1661. www.nynb.uscourts.gov

Counties: Albany, Clinton, Essex, Franklin, Fulton, Jefferson, Montgomery, Rensselaer, Saratoga, Schenectady, Schoharie, St. Lawrence, Warren, Washington.

Indexing & Storage: Cases indexed by debtor as well as by case number. New cases available in the index 48 hours after filing date. As of January 1, 1995, Jefferson and St. Lawrence Counties moved to Albany Division from Utica, while Broome, Chenango, Delaware, Otsego, Tioga and Tompkins Counties moved to Utica Division from Albany.

Fee & Payment: Payment may be made by money order, cashier check. Business checks are not accepted, Visa or Mastercard. Personal checks are not accepted. Credit cards are only accepted from in-person searchers. Payee: Clerk, U.S. Bankruptcy Court.

Phone Search: Only docket information available by phone. Automated voice case information service (VCIS) is available. Call VCIS at 800-206-1952.

Mail Search: If a case number is not known, the turnaround time may be as long as 5 days after the request is received. Include SASE for return.

In Person Search: Fee charged if court conducts your in person search for you.

PACER: PACER is available online at http://pacer.nynb.uscourts.gov. New civil records are online after 48 hours.

Electronic Filing: Electronic filing information online at https://ecf.nynb.uscourts.gov

Utica Division Room 230, 10 Broad St, Utica, NY 13501 (courier address: Use mail address for courier delivery) 315-793-8101, Fax: 315-793-8128. www.nynb.uscourts.gov

Counties: Broome, Cayuga, Chenango, Cortland, Delaware, Hamilton, Herkimer, Lewis, Madison, Oneida, Onondaga, Otsego, Oswego, Tioga, Tompkins.

Indexing & Storage: Cases indexed by debtor as well as by case number. New cases available in the index 24 hours after filing date. As of January 1, 1995, Jefferson and St. Lawrence Counties moved to Albany Division from Utica, while Broome, Chenango, Delaware, Otsego, Tioga and Tompkins Counties moved to Utica Division from Albany.

Fee & Payment: Payment may be made by money order, cashier check, personal check. Debtor's checks are not accepted. Payee: Clerk, U.S. Bankruptcy Court.

Phone Search: Only docket information available by phone. Automated voice case information service (VCIS) is available. Call VCIS at 800-206-1952.

Mail Search: A SASE not required.

In Person Search: Fee charged if court conducts your in person search for you. Visa/MC only accepted for in person searches.

PACER: PACER is available online at http://pacer.nynb.uscourts.gov. New civil records are online after 48 hours.

Electronic Filing: Electronic filing information online at https://ecf.nynb.uscourts.gov

U.S. District Court

Southern District of New York

New York City Division 500 Pearl St, New York, NY 10007 (courier address: Use mail address for courier delivery) 212-805-0136. www.nysd.uscourts.gov

Counties: Bronx, New York. A 2nd courthouse at 40 Centre St is an Appelate Division with some District Cases heard there; search both at Pearl St location. Some cases from the counties in the White Plains Division are also assigned to this New York Division.

Indexing & Storage: New cases available in the index 2 days after filing date.

Fee & Payment: Payment may be made by money order, cashier check. Business checks are not accepted. Personal checks are not accepted. Payee: Clerk of Court, S.D.N.Y.

Phone Search: No searching by telephone. Only docket information available by phone.

In Person Search: Fee charged if court conducts your in person search for you.

PACER: The old system replaced by new CM/ECF system. Records purged every six months. New records are online after 1 day.

Electronic Filing: Electronic filing information online at https://ecf.nysd.uscourts.gov

Opinions Online: Selected rulings are searchable online using CourtWeb. To download and view copies of rulings you must have Adobe Acrobat Reader. Court opinions are online at www.nysd.uscourts.gov/courtweb

White Plains Division U.S. Courthouse, 300 Quarropas St, White Plains, NY 10601 (courier address: Use mail address for courier delivery) 914-390-4100. www.nysd.uscourts.gov

Counties: Dutchess, Orange, Putnam, Rockland, Sullivan, Westchester. Some cases may be assigned to New York Division.

Indexing & Storage: New cases available in the index 2 days after filing date. Indexes have been automated since 1983.

Fee & Payment: Payment may be made by money order, cashier check. Business checks are not accepted. Personal checks are not accepted. Attorney checks are accepted. Payee: Clerk of Court, S.D.N.Y.

Phone Search: No searching by telephone.

In Person Search: Fee charged if court conducts your in person search for you.

PACER: The old system replaced by new CM/ECF system. Records purged every six months. New records are online after 1 day.

Electronic Filing: Electronic filing information online at https://ecf.nysd.uscourts.gov

Opinions Online: Selected rulings are searchable online using CourtWeb. To download and view copies of rulings you must have Adobe Acrobat Reader. Court opinions are online at www.nysd.uscourts.gov/courtweb

U.S. Bankruptcy Court

Southern District of New York

New York Division Room 534, 1 Bowling Green, New York, NY 10004-1408 (courier address: Use mail address for courier delivery) 212-668-2870. www.nysb.uscourts.gov

Counties: Bronx, New York.

Indexing & Storage: Cases indexed by debtor as well as by case number. New cases available in the index 1-3 days after filing date.

Fee & Payment: Payment may be made by money order, cashier check, business check. Personal checks are not accepted. Payee: Clerk, U.S. Bankruptcy Court.

Phone Search: Over the phone, this court will only provide whether a case is pending. A copy service is available at 212-480-0737 if you have the case number. Automated voice case information service (VCIS) is available. Call VCIS at 212-668-2772.

Mail Search: A SASE not required.

In Person Search: Permitted.

PACER: PACER is available online at https://ecf.nysb.uscourts.gov/cgi-bin/login.pl. Local access: 212-668-2896, 212-668-2897, 212-668-2898. Records purged every six months. New civil records are online after 2 days.

Electronic Filing: Electronic filing information online at http://ecf.nysb.uscourts.gov

Poughkeepsie Division 176 Church St, Poughkeepsie, NY 12601 (courier address: Use mail address for courier delivery) 845-452-4200, Fax: 845-452-8375. www.nysb.uscourts.gov

Counties: Columbia, Dutchess, Greene, Orange, Putnam, Sullivan, Ulster.

Indexing & Storage: Cases indexed by debtor as well as by case number. New cases available in the index 1-3 days after filing date.

Fee & Payment: Payment may be made by money order, cashier check, business check. Personal checks are not accepted. Payee: Clerk, U.S. Bankruptcy Court.

Phone Search: Over the phone, this court will only reveal whether the case is pending. Automated voice case information service (VCIS) is available. Call VCIS at 212-668-2772.

Mail Search: A SASE not required.

In Person Search: Fee charged if court conducts your in person search for you.

PACER: PACER is available online at https://ecf.nysb.uscourts.gov/cgi-bin/login.pl. Local access: 212-668-2896, 212-668-2897, 212-668-2898. Records purged every six months. New civil records are online after 2 days.

Electronic Filing: Electronic filing information online at http://ecf.nysb.uscourts.gov

White Plains Division 300 Quarropas St, White Plains, NY 10601 (courier address: Use mail address for courier delivery) 914-390-4060. www.nysb.uscourts.gov

Counties: Rockland, Westchester.

Indexing & Storage: Cases indexed by debtor as well as by case number. New cases available in the index 1-3 days after filing date. Records are also indexed on microfiche. District wide searches are available for cases from 1991 from this court.

Fee & Payment: Payment may be made by money order, business check. Personal checks are not accepted. Checks and credit cards are not accepted from debtors. Payee: Clerk, U.S. Bankruptcy Court.

Phone Search: Over the phone, this court will only reveal whether the case is pending. Automated voice case information service (VCIS) is available. Call VCIS at 212-668-2772.

In Person Search: Fee charged if court conducts your in person search for you. Visa/MC only accepted for in person searches.

PACER: PACER is available online at https://ecf.nysb.uscourts.gov/cgi-bin/login.pl. Local access: 212-668-2896, 212-668-2897, 212-668-2898. Records purged every six months. New civil records are online after 2 days.

Electronic Filing: Electronic filing information online at http://ecf.nysb.uscourts.gov

U.S. District Court
Western District of New York

Buffalo Division Room 304, 68 Court St, Buffalo, NY 14202 (courier address: Use mail address for courier delivery) 716-551-4211, Fax: 716-551-4850. www.nywd.uscourts.gov

Counties: Allegany, Cattaraugus, Chautauqua, Erie, Genesee, Niagara, Orleans, Wyoming. Prior to 1982, this division included what is now the Rochester Division.

Indexing & Storage: New cases available in the index 2 days after filing date.

Fee & Payment: Payment may be made by money order, cashier check, personal check. Payee: Clerk, U.S. District Court.

Phone Search: No searching by telephone.

Mail Search: A SASE not required.

In Person Search: Fee charged if court conducts your in person search for you.

PACER: PACER is available online at http://pacer.nywd.uscourts.gov. Case records go back to 1994. Records never purged. New civil records are online after 1 day. New criminal records online after 2 days.

Electronic Filing: Electronic filing information online at https://ecf.nywd.uscourts.gov

Rochester Division Room 2120, 100 State St, Rochester, NY 14614 (courier address: Use mail address for courier delivery) 585-263-6263, Fax: 585-263-3178. www.nywd.uscourts.gov

Counties: Chemung, Livingston, Monroe, Ontario, Schuyler, Seneca, Steuben, Wayne, Yates.

Indexing & Storage: New cases available in the index 1 day after filing date. This division was established in 1981. Cases closed from 1996 to present are also held here. Earlier case records and indexes are held in the Buffalo Division (Erie County).

Fee & Payment: Payment may be made by money order, cashier check, personal check. Payee: Clerk, U.S. District Court. Will fax results; call for instructions.

Phone Search: Simple docket information available by phone. Will fax results; call for instructions.

Mail Search: Mail searches including years prior to 1982 will be forwarded to the Buffalo Division. A SASE not required.

In Person Search: Fee charged if court conducts your in person search for you.

PACER: PACER is available online at http://pacer.nywd.uscourts.gov. Case records go back to 1994. Records never purged. New civil records are online after 1 day. New criminal records online after 2 days.

Electronic Filing: Electronic filing information online at https://ecf.nywd.uscourts.gov

U.S. Bankruptcy Court
Western District of New York

Buffalo Division Olympic Towers, 300 Pearl St #250, Buffalo, NY 14202-2501 (courier address: Use mail address for courier delivery) 716-551-4130. www.nywb.uscourts.gov

Counties: Allegany, Cattaraugus, Chautauqua, Erie, Genesee, Niagara, Orleans, Wyoming.

Indexing & Storage: Cases indexed by debtor as well as by case number. New cases available in the index 24 hours after filing date.

Fee & Payment: Payment may be made by money order, cashier check, business check. Personal checks are not accepted. Payee: Clerk, U.S. Bankruptcy Court.

Phone Search: Only docket information available by phone. Automated voice case information service (VCIS) is available. Call VCIS at 800-776-9578 or 716-551-5311.

In Person Search: Fee charged if court conducts your in person search for you.

PACER: PACER is available online at http://pacer.nywb.uscourts.gov. Case records go back to August 1987. Records never purged. New civil records are online after 1 day.

Electronic Filing: Electronic filing information online at https://ecf.nywb.uscourts.gov

Rochester Division Room 1220, 100 State St, Rochester, NY 14614 (courier address: Use mail address for courier delivery) 585-263-3148. www.nywb.uscourts.gov

Counties: Chemung, Livingston, Monroe, Ontario, Schuyler, Seneca, Steuben, Wayne, Yates.

Indexing & Storage: Cases indexed by debtor as well as by case number. New cases available in the index 24 hours after filing date. Records are also indexed on microfiche. District wide searches are available for information from August 1, 1987 from this division.

Fee & Payment: Payment may be made by money order, cashier check, business check. Personal checks are not accepted. The SASE should be large enough to hold all copies and have sufficient postage to send them. Payee: Clerk, U.S. Bankruptcy Court.

Phone Search: Only docket information available by phone. Automated voice case information service (VCIS) is available. Call VCIS at 800-776-9578 or 716-551-5311.

In Person Search: Fee charged if court conducts your in person search for you.

PACER: PACER is available online at http://pacer.nywb.uscourts.gov. Case records go back to August 1987. Records never purged. New civil records are online after 1 day

Electronic Filing: Electronic filing information online at https://ecf.nywb.uscourts.gov

New York County Courts

Court	Jurisdiction	No. of Courts	How Organized
Supreme Courts*	General	11	12 Districts
County Courts*	General	2	57 Counties
Combined Courts*	General	57	
City Courts*	Limited	61	61 Cities (outside of NYC)
District Courts*	Limited	10	Nassau, Suffolk Counties
Civil /Criminal Courts of the City of New York*	Municipal	6	Boroughs
Town and Village Justice Courts	Municipal	2173	
Surrogates' Courts*	Probate	62	62 Counties and Boroughs
Court of Claims	Limited	1	
Family Courts	Special	62	62 Counties and Boroughs

* Profiled in this Sourcebook.

Court	CIVIL								
	Tort	Contract	Real Estate	Min. Claim	Max. Claim	Small Claims	Estate	Eviction	Domestic Relations
Supreme Courts*	X	X	X	$25,000	No Max				X
County Courts*	X	X	X	$0	$25,000				
City Courts*	X	X	X	$0	$15,000	$3000		X	
District Courts*	X	X	X	$0	$15,000	$3000		X	
Civil /Criminal Courts of the City of New York*	X	X	X	$0	$25,000	$3000		X	
Town and Village Justice Courts	X	X	X	$0	$3000	$3000			
Surrogates' Courts*							X		X
Court of Claims	X	X	X	$0	No Max				
Family Courts									X

Court	CRIMINAL				
	Felony	Misdemeanor	DWI/DUI	Preliminary Hearing	Juvenile
Supreme Courts*	X				
County Courts*				X	
City Courts*	X	X	X	X	
District Courts*		X	X	X	
Civil /Criminal Courts of the City of New York*		X	X	X	
Town and Village Justice Courts		X	X	X	
Surrogates' Courts*					
Court of Claims					
Family Courts					X

ADMINISTRATION

Office of Court Administration, 25 Beaver St, New York, NY 10004, 212-428-2100. www.courts.state.ny.us

COURT STRUCTURE

"Supreme and County Courts" are the highest trial courts in the state, equivalent to Circuit or District Courts in other states. New York's Supreme and County Courts may be administered together or separately; when separate, there is a clerk for each. Supreme and/or County Courts are not appeals courts. Supreme Courts handle civil cases (usually civil cases over $25,000 but there are many exceptions). County Courts handle felony cases, and in many counties, these County Courts also handle misdemeanors.

City Courts handle misdemeanors and lower-value civil cases, small claims, and eviction cases. Not all counties have City Courts, thus cases there fall to the Supreme and County Courts respectively, or, in a many counties, to the small Town and Village Courts, which can number in the dozens within a county.

The staff at NY Superior, County, and City Courts are NY state employees. However, in some counties (usually smaller NY counties), the clerk for Supreme and County Courts may also be the "County Clerk" - these duo-role clerks are employed partly by the county, and partly by the state, which creates a question of whose "directives" and rules do they follow in regard to court record search procedures. More below.

Records for Supreme and County Courts are maintained by the County Clerks, who are county employees. There are exceptions. In New York City - with its five boroughs - the courts records are administered directly by the state OCA (Office of Court Administration). Also, there are a small number of upstate counties where the Supreme Court OR County Court records are maintained by their court clerk (state employee), and only an index list of cases and defendants is provided to the County Clerk (county employee).

You will find separate entries for "County Clerks" for most NY counties in this edition.. While the County Clerks are not courts, they do hold court records and the methods for searching at the County Clerk office are far different from searching at the Courts themselves. 1. In counties where the County Clerk and the Chief Court Clerk are one in the same, you will find only the standard Supreme & County Court listing. 2. In other counties - where the Supreme and County Courts direct all searches to the County Clerk - you will find the information for searching at the County Clerk office. 3. Because they are in different locations or maintain separate case indexes, the Supreme Court and the County Court may appear as separate entries in the profiles.

In some NY counties, the address for the County Clerk is the same as for the Supreme and County Courts. Exceptions are noted in the court profiles, and a separate profile is provided that lists the County Clerk and the "County" rules for a "countywide record search." Note also that, due to limitations in the receiving of records from the Chief Court Clerks, the County Clerk may only be able to do a civil record search, or, rarely, only a criminal record search. Each county is going to be different.

City Courts - While all City Courts are administered by state employees, there are a few City Courts that will do a city-only record check despite the edict to state employees that they must direct record searches to the OCA for the statewide record check. Records from City Courts do not go to the County Clerk. Records from City Courts go directly to the OCA.

In at least 20 New York Counties, misdemeanor records are only available at city, town, or village courts. This is also true of small claims and eviction records. Town and Village Courts are be listed at the end of each county section.

Now you have an overview of the confusing array of NY courts. You may have concluded that record searching would be a daunting task if you did not have the individual court profiles, updated progressively, provided here to aid you. You may also conclude that an accurate search for misdemeanor records is nearly impossible as there are over 1200 Town and Village Courts in NY which may or may not be accurately reporting their case records.

Understanding the court structure is important to record searchers, as explained below.

COURT RECORD SEARCHES: STATEWIDE VERSUS COUNTYWIDE

Effective July 14th, 2003, per Section 14 of Assembly Bill A02106, the NY Office of Court Administration (OCA) of the NY Unified Court System expanded its criminal record history search. What was formerly a single county search from one of thirteen counties in the New York City area suddenly became a statewide, all-counties inclusive search. The New York State Office of Court Administration-OCA (address below) has mandated that all criminal record requests made to the Supreme Court Clerk (or made to the County Court Clerk or City Court Clerk) be forwarded to the OCA office for processing. The OCA does not wish to have its clerks performing county only searches.

OCA will perform an electronic search for criminal history information from a database of criminal case records from all boroughs and all counties including Supreme Courts, County Courts, and City Courts. At press time, it is not clear that all City Courts submit all misdemeanors to this database. The search fee, payable by check, is $52.00 per name. The search is available by mail or in-person (6 to 24-hour turnaround time), or high volume requesters may order online with email return (same day if ordered by 2:30 pm).

Direct mail and in person requests to:

> Office of Court Administration (OCA)
> Criminal History Search
> 25 Beaver St, 8th Floor
> New York, NY 10004

However, Many Counties Still Offer a Countywide Criminal Record Search.

Each county has at least one Chief Court Clerk (sometimes called the Chief Clerk of the Court) who is an employee of the State Unified Court System. Remember, there are two courts - Supreme and County - so there may be a Chief Clerk at each, and each may act independently of the other. So, 1. Chief Court Clerk duties may coincide with the county Supreme Court, which is the general jurisdiction court, AND the County Court - OR 2. they may have separate Chief Clerks. Usually, it is smaller NY counties that combine the roles.

In counties outside of NYC, as cases are closed, the general rule is that the files are given to the County Clerk who is responsible for the public record. Each county has a County Clerk employed by the county (and in rare instances, the clerk may be both the state's Chief Court Clerk and the County's County Clerk). State edicts aside, the reality is that either type of clerk may "sell" county criminal and/or civil records. The County Clerk can because they are not state employees, and the Chief Court Clerk can - though they are told not to and seldom do - because it just makes life easier for everyone.

It is the Chief Court Clerks, who are state employees, who are "forbidden" by the state edict to sell their records even though those same records are shared and maintained by the County Clerk who, more often than not, does sell them for a handsome profit. Conversely, when the Chief Clerk follows the state's directive, the funds generated from the $52.00 statewide searches goes directly to the OCA.

Until the July 14th, 2003 OCA mandate, nearly all of the County Clerks permitted the public to perform their own searches of the criminal records, usually via an index found in books or public access terminal. Also, some County Clerks performed record searches for a fee. Prior to 07/14/03, a County Clerk's office either: 1) used the Chief Court Clerk's computer/ database to sell the record for the old $16.00 fee, and turned the money over to the Chief Court Clerk, or 2) performed the search using their own index and charged a fee of $5.00 per name for each 2 years searched, $16.00 for 7 years, or some other similar fee schedule.

Public Access Terminals- The County Clerks, since they already handle real estate, judgments, and lien records, can also provide access to these records AND the civil records (received from the Supreme Court Clerk) on their public access terminals. You will find, however, that there are far, far fewer County Clerks who offer access to criminal records on the county-owned public access terminals.

City Courts- The City Courts throughout the state do not provide public access terminals. However, plans are to add public access terminals at City Courts, but there is no promise on that nor is there a set timetable for plugging the public in.

Supreme Courts- Since most Supreme Court Clerks are well aware that their civil records are accessible on the County Clerk office (and in most cases on the County Clerk's public access terminals), the Supreme Court clerks do not provide public access terminals patched into their own Supreme Court computer systems.

County Courts- You will find that rarely does a County Court provide public access terminals where you can view their criminal records. It is also rare to find County Court criminal records on the County Clerk's public access terminal (How wise would it be to give that info away when you can charge at least $5.00 for it?). In some counties, the County Court provides the County Clerk with only a paper record of criminal indexes. (In the court profiles, you will find a public access terminal is indicated, but it may not indicate if or if not criminal records are available.)

OCA Unaware of County Clerk Search Procedures

What helped to contribute to the intrigue of "who gets the money for doing the search" is that the OCA administrators entrusted with instituting the policy changes (in July, 2003) literally had no idea about the County Clerks' searches. They did not realize that most County Clerks permit the public to search the county index and that a number of County Clerks perform record searching for a fee from a non-OCA database, i.e. the county clerk database.

The bottom line is that in many counties the OCA mandate will NOT affect what the County Clerks do regarding criminal or civil record searches. Although the OCA has asked the County Clerks to stop performing searches from their County Clerk indexes, OCA technically has no control over the County Clerks and their indices. Thus, many of the County Clerks who either permitted the public to do their own record searching or who performed the $5.00 (or higher) record search from their database will continue to do so. The July, 2003 OCA edict does not impede these services. This is a real benefit to the users of criminal records who wish to have only a county search, and also to the hands-on record retrievers who will be able to continue to perform in-person searches at the County Clerk offices outside of New York City. In fact, it has been found that more and more County Clerks are offering to perform countywide searches for you, and ignoring the profitless (for the clerk office) and costly (for the public) $52.00 OCA statewide record search.

Please note that nearly all the City Courts no longer do criminal record searchs and send misdemeanor record requesters to the OCA for the $52.00 statewide record search.

An Evolving Situation

We have indicated the counties where the County Clerks (and a limited number of Supreme and County Court Clerks) continue to provide countywide criminal record searches. We have also indicated when the County Clerk or Chief Clerk instructs criminal record searches to contact OCA. This information is subject to change, and does.

We urge those entities that use criminal records to utilize the services of professional researchers found in the *National Directory of Local Court and County Record Retrievers*.

ONLINE ACCESS

In addition to the $52.00 statewide record search that has been explained above, the OCA offers online access to "approved requesters" for criminal records. Requesters receive information back via email. Call the OCA for details on how to set up an account. The fee is the same $52.00 per record (the highest statewide record fee in the U.S.).

Civil Supreme Court case information is available for all 62 New York counties through the court system's website - http://e.courts.state.ny.us. Select decisions from New York Supreme Criminal Court and other criminal courts are also available. There is no charge for this information.

Also at http://e.courts.state.ny.us, you may search for future court dates for defendants in these 21 criminal courts: Bronx Criminal Court, Bronx Supreme Court, Dutchess County Court, Buffalo City Court, Erie County Court, Kings Criminal Court, Kings Supreme Court, Nassau County Court, Nassau District Court, New York Criminal Court, New York Supreme Court, Orange County Court, Putnam County, Queens Criminal Court, Queens Supreme Court, Richmond Criminal Court, Richmond Supreme Court, Rockland County Court, Suffolk County Court, Suffolk District Court, Westchester County Court.

ADDITIONAL INFORMATION

In all but a few NY counties, the Supreme and County Court records are maintained in some format in the County Clerk's office, which (with the exception of New York City and its boroughs) may index civil cases by defendant, whereas the courts themselves maintain only a plaintiff index. And, while most criminal courts in the state are indexed by defendant and plaintiff, many New York City courts are indexed by plaintiff only.

Almost all County Courts (felony records) will provide a Certificate of Disposition. This Certificate is a certified document from the court that indicates the disposition of a case. The fee for a Certificate of Disposition is either $5.00 or $6.00, depending upon the county. To obtain a Certificate of Disposition, you must prepay, you must include the name and an exact as possible date (either the disposition date or the arrest date - this requirement varies from county to county), or provide the case number. Some counties also ask for a signed release (this and other details will be noted in the individual court profiles.)

Probate is handled by Surrogate Courts. Surrogate Courts may also hear Domestic Relations cases in some counties.

Albany County

County Clerk Courthouse Rm 128, 16 Eagle St, Albany, NY 12207; 518-487-5118; Fax: 518-487-5099. Hours: 9AM-5PM (4:30 cut-off time) (EST). *Felony, Civil.*
www.albanycounty.com/clerk
Note: Countywide record search requests made to the County Clerk are processed in the manner described below.

Civil Records: Access: Mail, in person. Both court and visitors may perform in person searches. Search fee: $5.00 per name. Fee is for each two years requested. Required to search: name, years to search. Civil cases indexed by defendant, plaintiff. Civil records on computer from 1981, prior in books.
Criminal Records: Access: Mail, in person, online. Both court and visitors may perform in person searches. Search fee: $5.00 per name. Fee is per two years requested. Required to search: name, years to search, DOB. Criminal records on computer from 1981, prior in books. Search requests must be in writing. Access to current cases is at http://e.courts.state.ny.us/.
General Information: Public Access terminal is available. No sealed, expunged, adoption, sex offense, juvenile, mental health or divorce records released. Copy fee: $.65 per page. Cert fee: $5.00. Payee: County Clerk. Personal checks accepted. Prepayment required. Mail requests: SASE appreciated. Turnaround time 1-3 days.

Supreme & County Court Courthouse Rm 102, 16 Eagle St, Albany, NY 12207; 518-487-5010; Fax: 518-487-5020. Hours: 9AM-5PM (EST). *Felony, Civil.*
Note: Court-clerks direct record search requests to the OCA for a $52.00 statewide record check. For county only search requests, see the County Clerk in separate listing. Also, online access to current cases is available at http://e.courts.state.ny.us/.

Albany City Court - Civil Part City Hall Rm 209, Albany, NY 12207; 518-434-5115; Fax: 518-434-5034. Hours: 8:30AM-5PM (EST). *Civil Actions Under $15,000, Eviction, Small Claims.*
Civil Records: Access: Mail, in person. Only the court performs in person searches; visitors may not. No search fee. Required to search: name, years to search. Civil cases indexed by plaintiff. Civil records on computer from 1993, records go back 25 years.
General Information: No code enforcement records released. Will fax back results. Copy fee: $1.30 for first page, $.65 each add'l. Cert fee: $6.00. Payee: Albany City Court. Business checks accepted. Prepayment required. Mail requests: SASE required. Mail turnaround time varies.

Albany City Court - Misdemeanors Morton & Broad St, Albany, NY 12202; 518-462-6714; Fax: 518-447-8778. Hours: 8AM-4PM (EST). *Misdemeanor.*
Criminal Records: Access: Mail, in person. Only the court performs in person searches; visitors may not. Search fee: $5.00 per name per certificate. Required to search: name, years to search, DOB. Criminal records on computer since mid-'93, on index cards prior.
General Information: No sealed, expunged, adoption, sex offense, juvenile, or mental health records released without a signed release from the party. Copy fee: $.50 per page. Cert fee: $5.00. Payee: Albany City Court Criminal Part. Business checks accepted. Prepayment required. Mail requests: SASE required. Mail turnaround time 5 days.

Cohoes City Court PO Box 678, 97 Mohawk St, Cohoes, NY 12047-0678; 518-233-2133. Hours: 8AM-4PM (EST). *Misdemeanor, Civil Actions Under $15,000, Eviction, Small Claims.*
Civil Records: Access: In person only. Only the court performs in person searches; visitors may not. This court recommends searching for judgments through the County Clerk's office. No search fee. Required to search: name, years to search. Civil cases indexed by defendant, plaintiff. Civil records on computer from 1/95, prior in books, on cards.
Criminal Records: Access: None. No search fee. Will not permit access to records. All name searches forwarded to OCA for $52.00 statewide search unless specific docket number given.
General Information: No sealed or expunged records released. Copy fee: $.25 per page. Cert fee: $5.00. Payee: City Court. Only cashiers checks and money orders accepted. Prepayment required.

Watervliet City Court 2 Fifteenth St, Watervliet, NY 12189; 518-270-3803; Fax: 518-270-3812. Hours: 8AM-3PM (EST). *Misdemeanor, Civil Actions Under $15,000, Eviction, Small Claims.*
Civil Records: Access: Phone, fax, mail, in person. Only the court performs in person searches; visitors may not. Search fee: $5.00 per name per 2 year period. Required to search: name, years to search. Civil cases indexed by plaintiff. Civil records on computer from 1991, prior on index cards back to 1975.
Criminal Records: Access: Mail, in person. Only the court performs in person searches; visitors may not. No search fee. Required to search: name, years to search, DOB. Criminal records on computer from 1991, prior on index cards back to 1975. All name searches forwarded to OCA for $52.00 statewide search, unless specific docket number given.
General Information: Fee to fax results is $5.00 per document. Copy fee: $.65 per page. Cert fee: $6.00. Payee: City Court. Business checks accepted. Prepayment required. Mail requests: SASE required. Mail turnaround time 1-2 weeks.

Surrogate Court Courthouse, 16 Eagle St, Albany, NY 12207; 518-487-5393; Fax: 518-487-5087. Hours: 9AM-5PM (EST). *Probate.*
Note: Search fee is $25.00 for up to 25 year search; $70 if over.

Albany Town/Village Courts. *Misdemeanor- Civil Actions Under $3000- Small Claims.* Altamont Village Court- 518-861-8554, Berne Town Court- 518-872-1448, Bethlehem Town Court- 518-439-9717, Coeymans Town Court- 518-756-8480, Colonie Town Court- 518-783-2714, Green Island Town Court- 518-273-0661, Guilderland Town Court- 518-356-1980, Knox Town Court- 518-872-2551, Menands Village Court- 518-434-3992, New Scotland Town Court- 518-475-0493, Ravena Village Court- 518-756-2313, Rensselaerville Town Court- 518-239-4225, Voorheesville Village Court- 518-765-5524, Westerlo Town Court- 518-797-3239

Allegany County

County Clerk 7 Court St, Belmont, NY 14813; 585-268-9270; Fax: 585-269-9659. Hours: 9AM-5PM; 8:30AM-4PM Summer hours (EST). *Civil.*
Note: Felony records in Allegany County are managed by the County-Court Clerk who directs search requests to OCA for $52.00 statewide search.
Civil Records: Access: Phone, mail, in person, online. Both court and visitors may perform in person searches. Search fee: $5.00 for each 2-year period looked-up, if searched by staff. Required to search: name, years to search. Civil cases indexed by defendant. Civil records in books and computer. Access to current/pending Supreme Court civil cases is at http://e.courts.state.ny.us/.
General Information: No sealed records released. No fee to fax results. Will fax to toll free numbers only. Copy fee: $.65 per page; $1.30 minimum. Cert fee: $5.00 per doc; if doc over 5 pgs, add $1.25 each add'l page. Payee: County Clerk. Personal checks accepted. Prepayment required. Mail requests: SASE required. Mail turnaround time 7-10 days.

Supreme & County Court 7 Court St, Belmont, NY 14813; 585-268-5813; Fax: 585-268-7090. Hours: 9AM-5PM; 8:30AM-4PM Summer hours (EST). *Felony, Civil.*
Note: Direct civil record requests to County Clerk, see separate listing. The County-Court directs criminal search requests to the OCA for a $52.00 statewide record check. Access to current/pending civil cases is available at http://e.courts.state.ny.us/.

Surrogate Court Courthouse, 7 Court St, Belmont, NY 14813; 585-268-5815; Fax: 585-268-7090. Hours: 9AM-5PM Sept-May; 8:30AM-4PM June-Aug (EST). *Probate.*

Allegany Town/Village Courts. *Misdemeanor- Civil Actions Under $3000- Small Claims.* Alfred Town Court- 607-587-8524, Alfred Village Court- 607-587-9142, Allen Town Court- No Phone, Alma Town Court- 585-593-4021, Almond Town Court- 607-276-6665, Amity Town Court- 585-268-5305, Andover Town Court- 607-478-8446, Andover Village Court- 607-478-8455, Angelica Town Court- 585-466-7928, Angelica Village

Court- 585-966-7928, Belfast Town Court- 585-365-2623, Belmont Village Court- 716-268-5305, Birdsall Town Court- 607-545-6072, Bolivar Town Court- 585-928-1860, Bolivar Village Court- 585-928-2234, Burns Town Court- 607-545-8998, Caneadea Town Court- 585-365-8240, Centerville Town Court- 585-567-8425, Clarksville Town Court- 585-968-2031, Cuba Town Court- 585-968-1690, Friendship Town Court- 585-973-7566, Genesee Town Court- 716--928-1384, Granger Town Court- 716-567-4575, Grove Town Court- 607-545-8664, Hume Town Court- 585-567-2666, Independence Town Court- No Phone, New Hudson Town Court- 716-968-3288, Richburg Village Court- No Phone, Rushford Town Court- 585-437-2206, Scio Town Court- 585-593-5777, Ward Town Court- 585-593-7300, Wellsville Town Court- 716-593-1750, Wellsville Village Court- 585-593-5609, West Almond Town Court- 607-276-6680, Willing Town Court- No Phone, Wirt Town Court- 585-928-2130

Bronx Borough

Supreme Court - Civil Division 851 Grand Concourse, Mezzanine, Rm 118, Bronx, NY 10451; 718-590-3647 Clerk; Fax: 718-590-8122. Hours: 9AM-5PM (EST). *Civil Actions Over $25,000.* www.courts.state.ny.us/courts/12jd
Civil Records: Access: In person, online. Both court and visitors may perform in person searches. No search fee. Required to search: name, years to search. Civil cases indexed by defendant, plaintiff. Civil records on computer since 2001; prior records on archives. Archives are offsite. Access to current/pending civil cases and some closed cases is at http://e.courts.state.ny.us/.
General Information: Public Access terminal is available. (Terminal has records back to 2000-2001.) No marriage or divorce records released. Copy fee: $.75 per page; $.25 self serve. Cert fee: $6.00 per document. Payee: Bronx County Clerk. Only cashiers checks and money orders accepted. Prepayment required. Mail requests: SASE required. Mail turnaround time 7-10 days.

Supreme Court - Criminal Division 851 Grand Concourse, Rm 123, Bronx, NY 10451; 718-590-3803; Civil phone: 718-590-3722; Criminal phone: 718-590-2854; Probate phone: 718-590-4515; Fax: 718-590-3708. 9AM-5PM (EST). *Felony.* www.courts.state.ny.us/courts/12jd
Criminal Records: Access: Mail, in person. Only the court performs in person searches; visitors may not. No search fee. Required to search: name, years to search, DOB. Criminal records on computer back to 1977, prior on microfiche. Search online for future court appearances at http://e.courts.state.ny.us. Unless a specific docket number given, all criminal record name search requests are directed to the OCA for statewide record search, $52.00 search fee.
General Information: No sealed, expunged, juvenile or sex offense records released. Will not fax results. Copy fee: $.75 per page. Cert fee: $10.00. Payee: Bronx County Clerk. Only cashiers checks and money orders accepted. Prepayment required. Mail requests: SASE required.

Civil Court of the City of New York - Bronx Branch 851 Grand Concourse, Window 6, Basement, Bronx, NY 10451; 718-590-3601, 718-590-3597 records room. Hours: 9AM-5PM (EST). *Civil Actions Under $25,000, Eviction, Small Claims.* www.courts.state.ny.us/courts/12jd
Civil Records: Access: Phone, in person. Visitors must perform in person searches for themselves on public access terminal. No search fee. Required to search: name, years to search. Civil cases indexed by defendant, plaintiff. Small claims in docket books. Civil records in books, on file cards.records go back to the 1970s; computerized records since 1998. Records archived after five years, requiring 4-8 weeks (four to eight weeks) to requisition. To view files, call ahead

so that clerk can schedule a time and have files available. The advance time varies: the older the files searched, the longer the clerk's record retrieval time. Please use their form.
General Information: Public Access terminal is available. (Records on terminal go back to 1998.) Copy fee: $.25 per page self serve only. Cert fee: $6.00; See Window 8. Payee: Clerk of theCourt. Only money orders and cash accepted. Prepayment required.

Supreme Court - Criminal Div. - Misdemeanors Central Clerk's Office, 215 W 161st St, Bronx, NY 10451; 718-590-2853. Hours: 9AM-1PM, 2-5PM (EST). *Misdemeanor.* www.courts.state.ny.us/courts/12jd
Criminal Records: Access: Mail, in person. Only the court performs in person searches; visitors may not. No search fee. Required to search: name, years to search, DOB. Some criminal records on computer back to 1976, prior on microfiche. Search online for future court appearances at http://e.courts.state.ny.us. Unless a specific docket number given, all criminal record name search requests are directed to the OCA for statewide record search, $52.00 search fee.
General Information: No sealed, expunged, juvenile or sex offense records released. Cert fee: $5.00. Payee: Bronx Central Clerk's Office. Only cashiers checks and money orders accepted. Prepayment required. Mail requests: SASE required.

Surrogate Court 851 Grand Concourse, Bronx, NY 10451; 718-590-4515; Fax: 718-537-5158. Hours: 9AM-5PM (EST). *Probate.*

Broome County

County Clerk PO Box 2062, Broome County Clerk, County Office Bldg, Binghamton, NY 13902; 607-778-2255; Fax: 607-778-2243. 8AM-5PM; 7:30AM-4PM June-August (EST). *Felony, Civil.*
Note: Countywide record search requests made to the County Clerk are processed in the manner described below.
Civil Records: Access: Fax, mail, in person, online. Both court and visitors may perform in person searches. Search fee: $5.00 per name. Fee is per 2 years searched, 10 years maximum. Required to search: name, years to search. Civil cases indexed by defendant, plaintiff. Civil records on computer from 1985, prior in books. Access to current/pending civil cases and some closed cases is at http://e.courts.state.ny.us/. Also, access to civil (judgment) records are available; for registration information on the county clerk online system, call Mary at 607-778-2255.
Criminal Records: Access: Fax, mail, in person. Both court and visitors may perform in person searches. Search fee: $5.00 per name. Fee is per 2 years searched, 10 year maximum. Required to search: name, years to search, DOB. Criminal records on computer from 1985, prior in books. Access to criminal records may be available; for online date and registration information on the county clerk online system, call Mary at 607-778-2255.
General Information: Public Access terminal is available. No sealed or youthful offender records released. Will fax results for $1.00 per page. Copy fee: $.65 per page. $1.30 minimum. Cert fee: $5.20. Payee: Broome County Clerk. No personal checks over $1000.00. Prepayment required. Mail requests: SASE required. Mail turnaround time 3-5 days.

Supreme & County Court PO Box 1766, 92 Court St, Broome County Courthouse, Binghamton, NY 13902; 607-778-2448. Hours: 8AM-5PM; 7:30AM-4PM June-August (EST). *Felony, Civil.*
Note: The Supreme Court directs criminal record search requests to the OCA for processing.

Countywide search requests can be made to the County Clerk, see separate listing.

Binghamton City Court Governmental Plaza, Binghamton, NY 13901; 607-772-7006; Fax: 607-772-7041. Hours: 9AM-5PM (EST). *Misdemeanor, Civil Actions Under $15,000, Eviction, Small Claims.*
Civil Records: Access: Phone, mail, in person. Both court and visitors may perform in person searches. No search fee. Required to search: name, years to search. Civil cases indexed by defendant. Civil records on computer from 1990, prior in books, index cards. In person searching only for 04/21/99 forward.
Criminal Records: Access: Mail, in person. Only the court performs in person searches; visitors may not. No search fee. Required to search: notarized signature of requester (mail searches only), name, years to search, DOB. Criminal records on computer from 1990. Unless a specific docket number given, all criminal record name search requests are directed to the OCA for statewide record search, $52.00 fee.
General Information: Public Access terminal is available. (Only civil since 1996 available.) No sealed records released. Will not fax results. Copy fee: $.65 per page. $1.30 minimum. Cert fee: $5.00 per certificate. Payee: Binghamton City Court. Only cashiers checks and money orders accepted. Prepayment required. Mail requests: SASE required. Mail turnaround time 1-2 weeks.

Surrogate Court PO Box 1766, Binghamton, NY 13902; 607-778-2111; Fax: 607-778-2308. 9AM-5PM, Summer-8-4;July-Sept. (EST). *Probate.*
Note: $25 record search fee.

Broome Town/Village Courts. *Misdemeanor- Civil Actions Under $3000- Small Claims.* Barker Town Court-607-648-6961, Binghamton Town Court- 607-772-0357, Chenango Town Court- 607-722-4191, Colesville Town Court- 607-693-1172, Conklin Town Court- 607-775-5244, Deposit Village Court- 607-467-4240, Dickinson Town Court- 607-723-9403, Endicott Village Court- 607-757-2483, Fenton Town Court- 607-648-4801, Johnson City Village Court- 607-798-0002, Kirkwood Town Court- 607-775-2653, Lisle Town Court- 607-849-4685, Maine Town Court- 607-862-3427, Nanticoke Town Court- 607-692-4041, Sanford Town Court- 607-467-2516, Triangle Town Court- 607-692-4332, Union Town Court- 607-786-2965, Vestal Town Court- 607-748-1514, Windsor Town Court- 607-655-1973

Cattaraugus County

County Clerk 303 Court St, Little Valley, NY 14755; 716-938-9111 x2297; Probate phone: 716-938-2327; Fax: 716-938-2387. Hours: 9AM-5PM (EST). *Felony, Civil.*
Note: Countywide record search requests made to the County Clerk are processed in the manner described below.
Civil Records: Access: Mail, in person, online. Both court and visitors may perform in person searches. Search fee: $5.00 per name. Fee is per 2 years searched. Required to search: name, years to search. Civil cases indexed by defendant, plaintiff. Civil records on computer from 1989, prior in books, index cards from 1900. Access to current/pending Supreme Court civil cases is at http://e.courts.state.ny.us/.
Criminal Records: Access: Mail, in person. Both court and visitors may perform in person searches. Search fee: $5.00 per name. Fee is per 2 years searched. Required to search: name, years to search, DOB. Criminal records on computer from 1989, prior in books, index cards from 1900.
General Information: Public Access terminal is available. No sealed or youthful offender records released. Will fax results to local or toll free line for $3.00 (additional) per page. Copy fee: $1.00 per page. Cert fee: $5.00. Payee: County Clerk. Business checks

accepted. Prepayment required. Mail requests: SASE not required. Mail turnaround time 2-3 days.

Supreme & County Court 303 Court St, Little Valley, NY 14755; 716-938-9111 x2378; Fax: 716-938-6413. Hours: 9AM-5PM (EST). *Felony, Civil.*
Note: Court-clerks direct search requests to the OCA for a $52.00 statewide record check. For a countywide search, see the County Clerk in separate listing. Access to current/pending Supreme Court civil cases is available at http://e.courts.state.ny.us/.

Olean City Court PO Box 631, 101 E State St, Olean, NY 14760; 716-376-5620; Fax: 716-376-5623. Hours: 8:30AM-Noon, 1-5PM (EST). *Misdemeanor, Civil Actions Under $15,000, Eviction, Small Claims.*
Civil Records: Access: Mail, in person. Only the court performs in person searches; visitors may not. Search fee: $5.00 per name. Required to search: name, years to search, signed release; also helpful-case number. Civil cases indexed by defendant or docket number. Civil records on docket books.
Criminal Records: Access: None. Search fee: A Certificate of Disposition is $6.00. Criminal records on computer from 1990, prior in books. Unless a specific docket number given, all criminal record name search requests are directed to the OCA for statewide record search, $52.00 search fee.
General Information: No sealed or youthful offender records released. Will fax results to local or toll free line, if pre-paid. Copy fee: $1.00 per page. Cert fee: $6.00. Payee: Olean City Court. Business checks accepted. Prepayment required. Mail requests: SASE required. Mail turnaround time 4-5 days.

Salamanca City Court Municipal Center, 225 Wildwood Ave, Salamanca, NY 14779; 716-945-4153. Hours: 8AM-4PM (EST). *Misdemeanor, Civil Actions Under $15,000, Eviction, Small Claims.*
Civil Records: Access: Mail, in person. Only the court performs in person searches; visitors may not. No search fee. Required to search: name, years to search. Civil cases indexed by defendant. Civil records on dockets from 1930s; on computer back to 1995.
Criminal Records: Access: Mail, in person. Only the court performs in person searches; visitors may not. Search fee: A Certificate of Disposition is $6.00. Required to search: name, years to search, DOB, case number. Criminal records on dockets from 1930s; on computer back to 1995. Unless a specific docket number given, all criminal record name search requests are directed to the OCA for a $52.00 statewide record search.
General Information: No sealed records released. Will fax results. Copy fee: $.50 per page. Cert fee: $6.00. Payee: Salamanca City Court. No personal checks accepted. Prepayment required. Mail requests: SASE required. Mail turnaround time 1-2 weeks.

Surrogate Court 303 Court St, Little Valley, NY 14755; 716-938-9111; Fax: 716-938-6983. Hours: 9AM-5PM (EST). *Probate.*
Note: Public can search, but if court has to search there is a fee.

Cattaraugus Town/Village Courts. *Misdemeanor-Civil Actions Under $3000- Small Claims.* Allegany Town Court- 716-373-3670, Allegany Village Court- 716-373-1460, Ashford Town Court- No Phone, Carrollton Town Court- 716-925-8508, Coldspring Town Court- 716-354-5752, Conewango Town Court- 716-358-6386, Dayton Town Court- 716-532-3758, Delevan Village Court- , East Otto Town Court- No Phone, Ellicottville Town Court- 716-699-2240, Ellicottville Village Court- 716-699-4636, Farmersville Town Court- 716-676-3030, Franklinville Town Court- 716-676-3077, Freedom Town Court- 716-492-0961, Great Valley Town Court- 716-945-4200, Hinsdale Town Court- 716-557-2478, Humphrey Town Court- No Phone, Ischua Town Court- 716-557-2236, Leon Town Court- 716-296-8132,

Limestone Village Court- , Little Valley Town Court- 716-938-6882, Lyndon Town Court- 716-676-9928, Machias Town Court- 716-353-8207, Mansfield Town Court- No Phone, Napoli Town Court- 716-938-9418, New Albion Town Court- 716-257-3661, Olean Town Court- 716-373-0582, Otto Town Court- 716-257-3111, Perrysburg Town Court- 716-532-4090, Perrysburg Village Court- , Persia Town Court- 716-532-4042, Portville Town Court- 585-933-6658, Portville Village Court- 716-933-6288, Randolph Town Court- 716-358-4515, Red House Town Court- No Phone, Salamanca Town Court- No Phone, South Dayton Village Court- 716-988-3833, South Valley Town Court- 716-354-5854, Yorkshire Town Court- 716-492-1640

Cayuga County

County Clerk 160 Genesee St, Attn: County Clerk, Auburn, NY 13021; 315-253-1271; Fax: 315-253-1653. Hours: 9AM-5PM Sept-June; 8AM-4PM July-Aug (EST). *Felony, Misdemeanor, Civil.*
Note: If you have a specific case number, you can search countywide at the County Clerk office. The County Clerk will not do a criminal record name search.
Civil Records: Access: Mail, in person, online. Both court and visitors may perform in person searches. Search fee: $5.00 per name per 5 years searched. Required to search: name, years to search. Civil cases indexed by defendant, plaintiff. Civil records on computer from 1986, prior in books. Access to current/pending Supreme Court civil cases is at http://e.courts.state.ny.us/.
Criminal Records: Access: None. No search fee. Required to search: name, years to search, DOB. Criminal records names are computerized since 1930. Unless a specific case file number is given, access to records, including name searching, must be done at the OCA in New York City. The fees is $52.00 for a statewide search.
General Information: Public Access terminal is available. (The terminal is for civil records only.) No sealed records released. Copy fee: $.50 per page. Cert fee: $4.00 plus $.50 per page after first 8. Payee: County Clerk. Personal checks accepted. Prepayment required. Mail requests: SASE required. Mail turnaround time 1 day.

Supreme & County Court 154 Genesee St, Auburn, NY 13021-3424; 315-255-4320; Fax: 315-255-4322. Hours: 9AM-5PM Sept-June; 8AM-4PM July-Aug (EST). *Felony, Misdemeanor, Civil.*
Note: The County Clerk provides county only record searches, see separate entry. Also, access to current/pending Supreme Court civil cases is available at http://e.courts.state.ny.us/.

Auburn City Court 157 Genesee St, Auburn, NY 13021-3434; 315-253-1570; Fax: 315-253-1085. Hours: 8AM-4PM (EST). *Misdemeanor, Civil Actions Under $15,000, Eviction, Small Claims.*
Civil Records: Access: Mail, in person. Only the court performs in person searches; visitors may not. Search fee: None, but that is subject to change. Required to search: name, years to search. Civil cases indexed by defendant. Civil records on computer from 1986.
Criminal Records: Access: None. Search fee: A Certificate of Disposition is $5.00. The court refuses to permit access to records unless specific case file given. Searchers must use the OCA $52.00 statewide search.
General Information: No sealed, expunged, adoption, sex offense, juvenile or mental health records released. Copy fee: $1.30 1st page; $.65 each add'l page. Cert fee: $6.00. Payee: City Court Clerk. No personal checks. Prepayment required. Mail requests: SASE required. Mail turnaround 3 days.

Surrogate Court Courthouse, 152 Genesee St, Auburn, NY 13021-3471; 315-255-4316; Fax: 315-255-4322. Hours: 8:30AM-4:30PM; Summer hours 8AM-4:00PM (EST). *Probate.*
www.courts.state.ny.us/www/jd7/cayuga_surrogate.htm
Cayuga Town/Village Courts. *Misdemeanor- Civil Actions Under $3000- Small Claims.* Aurelius Town Court- 315-255-0065, Brutus Town Court- 315-834-6618, Cato Town Court- 315-626-6230, Cato Village Court- 315-626-2397, Conquest Town Court- 315-776-5288, Fleming Town Court- 315-252-8988, Genoa Town Court- 315-364-5516, Ira Town Court- 315-626-2154, Ledyard Town Court- 315-364-8169, Locke Town Court- 315-497-1932, Mentz Town Court- 315-776-8692, Meridian Village Court- 315-626-6230, Montezuma Town Court- 315-776-8822, Moravia Town Court- 315-497-0968, Moravia Village Court- 315-497-0968, Niles Town Court- 315-497-0066, Owasco Town Court- 315-255-0446, Port Byron Village Court- No Phone, Scipio Town Court- 315-364-5325, Semperonius Town Court- , Sennett Town Court- 315-253-7748, Springport Town Court- No Phone, Sterling Town Court- 315-865-5508, Summerhill Town Court- 315-497-3496, Throop Town Court- 315-252-7373, Venice Town Court- 315-364-6875, Victory Town Court- 315-626-6817, Weedsport Village Court- 315-834-8634

Chautauqua County

County Clerk Courthouse, PO Box 170, Mayville, NY 14757; 716-753-4331; Probate phone: 716-753-4339; Fax: 716-753-4293. Hours: 9AM-5PM/Summer 8:30AM-4:30PM (EST). *Felony, Civil.*
www.co.chautauqua.ny.us/clerk/clerkframe.htm
Note: Non in-person felony record requests are managed by the Supreme Court clerk who directs searches to OCA for $52.00 statewide search. Misdemeanor records are maintained by city, town and village courts.
Civil Records: Access: In person, online. Visitors must perform in person searches for themselves. No search fee. Required to search: name, years to search. Access to current/pending Supreme Court civil cases is at http://e.courts.state.ny.us/.
Criminal Records: Access: In person only. Visitors may perform in person searches for themselves. A Certificate of Conviction can be ordered for $5.00. Required to search: name, years to search, DOB. Criminal records on court's computer system from 1/1987. Court will not search felony records.
General Information: Public Access terminal is available. (Public terminal records go back to 1997.) No sealed records released. Copy fee: $4.00. Add $1.00 per page after first 4. No cert fee. Payee: County Clerk. Prepayment required.

Supreme & County Court - Criminal Courthouse, PO Box 292, Mayville, NY 14757; 716-753-4266; Probate phone: 716-753-4339; Fax: 716-753-4993. Hours: 9AM-5PM/Summer 8:30AM-4:30PM (EST). *Felony.*
Note: Misdemeanor records are maintained by city, town and village courts. The County-court directs search requests to the OCA for a $52.00 statewide record check.

Supreme & County Court - Civil PO Box 170, 1 N. Erie St, Mayville, NY 14757; 716-753-4331; Probate phone: 716-753-4339; Fax: 716-753-4293. Hours: 9AM-5PM/Summer 8:30AM-4:30PM (EST). *Civil.*
www.co.chautauqua.ny.us/clerk/clerkframe.htm
Civil Records: Access: Mail, in person. Visitors must perform in person searches for themselves. No search fee. Required to search: name, years to search. Civil cases indexed by plaintiff. Civil records in docket books or cards; on computer back to 8/1/1997. Access to current/pending Supreme Court civil cases is at http://e.courts.state.ny.us/.
General Information: Public Access terminal is available. (Terminal located in the county clerk office.) No sealed records released. Will not fax

results. Copy fee: $4.00. Add $1.00 per page after first 4. No cert fee. Payee: Chautauqua County Clerk. Personal checks accepted. Prepayment required. Mail requests: SASE required. Mail turnaround 1-2 days.

Dunkirk City Court City Hall, 342 Central Ave, Dunkirk, NY 14048; 716-366-2055; Fax: 716-366-3622. Hours: 9AM-5PM (EST). *Misdemeanor, Civil Actions Under $15,000, Eviction, Small Claims.*
Civil Records: Access: Mail, in person. Only the court performs in person searches; visitors may not. No search fee. Required to search: name, years to search. Civil cases indexed by defendant. Civil records on computer back to 1990, prior in books.
Criminal Records: Access: None. Search fee: A Certificate of Disposition is $6.00. Required to search: name, DOB, arrest date (for Cert of Disposition). The court refuses to permit access to records unless specific case file given. It is suggested to send requests to OCA for $52.00 statewide search.
General Information: No sealed, expunged, adoption, sex offense, juvenile or mental health records released. Copy fee: $.50 per page. Cert fee: $5.00. Payee: Dunkirk City Court. Only cashiers checks and money orders accepted. Prepayment required. Mail requests: SASE required. Mail turnaround time 1 week.

Jamestown City Court City Hall, Jamestown, NY 14701; 716-483-7561/7562; Fax: 716-483-7519. Hours: 8:30AM-5PM (EST). *Misdemeanor, Civil Actions Under $15,000, Eviction, Small Claims.*
Civil Records: Access: Fax, mail, in person. Both court and visitors may perform in person searches. Search fee: $5.00 per name per 2 years searched. Required to search: name, years to search. Civil cases indexed by defendant. Civil records on computer back to 1989, prior in books.
Criminal Records: Access: None. No search fee. Required to search: Name, DOB. Criminal records on computer back to 1989, prior in books to 1965. The court refuses to permit access to records unless specific case file given. It is suggested to send requests to OCA for $52.00 statewide search.
General Information: No sealed records released. Will fax results to local or toll free line. Copy fee: $.65 per page. Cert fee: $6.00. Payee: City Court. Business checks accepted. Prepayment required. Mail requests: SASE required. Mail turnaround 1 week.

Surrogate Court Gerace Office Bldg (3 N. Erie St), PO Box C, Mayville, NY 14757; 716-753-4339; Fax: 716-753-4600. Hours: 9AM-5PM Summer-8:30-4:30,July-Sept3 (EST). *Probate.*

Chautauqua Town/Village Courts. *Misdemeanor-Civil Actions Under $3000- Small Claims.* Arkwright Town Court- 716-679-4445, Brocton Village Court- 716-792-4189, Busti Town Court- 716-763-4695, Carroll Town Court- 716-569-5365, Charlotte Town Court- No Phone, Chautauqua Town Court- 716-753-5245, Cherry Creek Town Court- 716-296-5721, Clymer Town Court- 716-355-6331, Dunkirk Town Court- 716-366-3945, Ellery Town Court- 716-386-2521, Ellicott Town Court- 716-665-5319, Ellington Town Court- 716-287-2026, Fredonia Village Court- 716-679-2312, French Creek Town Court- 716-355-8801, Gerry Town Court- 716-985-5323, Hanover Town Court- 716-934-4770, Harmony Town Court- 716-488-1178, Kiantone Town Court- 716-488-0383, Mina Town Court- 716-769-7555, North Harmony Town Court- 716-789-3445, Poland Town Court- 716-267-2912, Pomfret Town Court- 716-672-6867, Portland Town Court- 716-792-4111, Ripley Town Court- 716-736-7575, Sheridan Town Court- 716-672-2600, Sherman Town Court- 716-761-6770, Silver Creek Village Court- 716-934-3558, Stockton Town Court- 716-595-2259, Villenova Town Court- 716-988-3678, Westfield Town Court- 716-326-6255, Westfield Village Court- 716-326-6135

Chemung County

Supreme & County Court - Criminal PO Box 588, Hazlett Bldg, 6th Fl, Elmira, NY 14902-0588; 607-737-2084; Probate phone: 607-737-2873. Hours: 9AM-5PM (EST). *Felony.*
Note: See County Clerk for Supreme court civil case records.
Criminal Records: Access: Mail, in person. Only the court performs in person searches; visitors may not. Search fee: $5.00 for every 2 years searched or $20.00 for a seven year search. Searches with both maiden and married names are considered two searches. Required to search: name, years to search, DOB, SSN. Criminal records in docket books back to 1979.
General Information: No sealed, divorce or adoption records released. Will fax results to local or toll free line. Copy fee: $.65 per page. Cert fee: $5.00. Payee: County Clerk. Personal checks accepted. Prepayment required. Mail requests: SASE required. Mail turnaround time 4-6 weeks.

County Clerk - Civil PO Box 588, 210 Lake St, Elmira, NY 14901; 607-737-2920; Fax: 607-737-2897. Hours: 8:30AM-4:30PM (EST). *Civil.*
www.chemungcounty.com
Civil Records: Access: Mail, fax, in person, online. Both court and visitors may perform in person searches. Search fee: $5.00 per name. Fee is per 2 years searched. Required to search: name, years to search. Civil cases indexed by defendant, plaintiff. Civil records on computer from 1994, prior in books to 1800s. Access to current/pending Supreme Court civil cases is at http://e.courts.state.ny.us/.
General Information: Public Access terminal is available. (Land records only from 1991 forward.) No sealed, divorce or adoption records released. Will fax results for $1.00 per page. Copy fee: $.65 per page. $1.30 minimum. Cert fee: $5.00 plus $1.25 per page after first 4. Payee: County Clerk. Personal checks accepted. Prepayment required. Mail requests: SASE required. Mail turnaround time 4-6 weeks.

Elmira City Court 317 E Church St, Elmira, NY 14901; 607-737-5681; Fax: 607-737-5820. Hours: 8AM-4PM (EST). *Misdemeanor, Civil Actions Under $15,000, Eviction, Small Claims.*
Civil Records: Access: In person. Visitors must perform in person searches for themselves. No search fee. Required to search: name, years to search. Civil cases indexed by defendant. Civil records on computer back to 1997; prior records on index cards.
Criminal Records: Access: None. Search fee: A Certificate of Disposition is $5.00. Required to search: name, years to search, date of arrest (for cert of disposition). Criminal records on computer back to 1987; prior on books. The court does not permit access to records unless specific case file given. It is suggested to send requests to OCA for $52.00 statewide search.
General Information: Public Access terminal is available. (Only civil available at terminal.) No sealed records released. Will fax results to lcoal or toll free line. Copy fee: $.65 per page; $1.30 minimum. Cert fee: $5.00. Payee: Elmira City Court. Personal checks accepted. Prepayment required.

Surrogate Court 224 Lake St, Elmira, NY 14902; 607-737-2946/2819; Fax: 607-737-2874. Hours: 9AM-5PM Summer-8:30-4:30 July-Sept 3 (EST). *Probate.*

Chemung Town/Village Courts. *Misdemeanor- Civil Actions Under $3000- Small Claims.* Ashland Town Court- 607-732-0723, Baldwin Town Court- No Phone, Big Flats Town Court- 607-562-8443 X223, Catlin Town Court- 607-739-5598, Chemung Town Court- 607-529-3322, Elmira Heights Village Court- 607-737-6750, Elmira Town Court- 607-734-5971, Erin Town Court- 607-739-8681, Horseheads Town Court- 607-739-2113, Horseheads Village Court- 607-739-0158, Millport

Village Court- No Phone, Southport Town Court- 607-734-4446, Van Etten Town Court- 607-589-4435, Veteran Town Court- 607-739-1476, Wellsburg Village Court- 607-733-8211

Chenango County

County Clerk County Office Bldg, 1st Fl, 5 Court St, Norwich, NY 13815-1676; 607-337-1450. Hours: 8:30AM-5PM (EST). *Felony, Civil.*
Note: Countywide record search requests made to the County Clerk are processed in the manner described below.
Civil Records: Access: Mail, in person, online. Both court and visitors may perform in person searches. Search fee: $5.00 per name. Fee is per 2 years searched. Required to search: name, years to search. Civil cases indexed by defendant, plaintiff. Civil records on computer from 1994, prior in books since 1880. Access to current/pending Supreme Court civil cases is at http://e.courts.state.ny.us/.
Criminal Records: Access: Mail, in person. Both court and visitors may perform in person searches. Search fee: $5.00 per name. Fee is per 2 years searched. Required to search: name, years to search, DOB. Criminal records in docket books.
General Information: Public Access terminal is available. No sealed, expunged, adoption, sex offense, juvenile or mental health records released. Copy fee: $.65 per page. $1.30 minimum. Cert fee: $1.25 per pg, $5.00 minimum. Payee: County Clerk. Personal checks accepted. Prepayment required. Mail requests: SASE required. Mail turnaround time 1 week.

Supreme & County Court County Office Bldg, 5 Court St, Norwich, NY 13815-1676; 607-337-1457. Hours: 9AM-5PM; 8:30AM-4:30PM Summer hours (EST). *Felony, Civil.*
Note: Direct all search requests to the County Clerk office, see separate listing. Online access to current/pending Supreme Court civil cases is available at http://e.courts.state.ny.us/.

Norwich City Court 1 Court Plaza, Norwich, NY 13815; 607-334-1224; Fax: 607-334-8494. Hours: 8:30AM-4:30PM (EST). *Misdemeanor, Civil Actions Under $15,000, Eviction, Small Claims.*
Civil Records: Access: Fax, mail, in person. Only the court performs in person searches; visitors may not. No search fee. Required to search: name, years to search. Civil cases indexed by defendant. Civil records on computer from 1990, prior in books.
Criminal Records: Access: In person only. Only the court performs in person searches; visitors may not. Search fee: $16.00 if computer generated.
General Information: No sealed, expunged, adoption, sex offense, juvenile or mental health records released. Will fax results to local or toll free line. Copy fee: $.65/page minimum $1.30. Cert fee: $5.00/2yr manual. Payee: City Court. Business checks accepted. Prepayment required. Mail requests: SASE required. Mail turnaround time 1 week.

Surrogate Court County Office Bldg, 5 Court St, Norwich, NY 13815; 607-337-1822/1827; Fax: 607-337-1834. Hours: 9AM-5PM Summer-8:30-4:30 July-Sept7TH (EST). *Probate.*

Chenango Town/Village Courts. *Misdemeanor- Civil Actions Under $3000- Small Claims.* Afton Town Court- No Phone, Afton Village Court- No Phone, Bainbridge Town Court- 607-967-7465, Bainbridge Village Court- 607-967-7465, Columbus Town Court- No Phone, Coventry Town Court- 607-656-8602, Earlville Village Court- 315-691-6020, German Town Court- No Phone, Greene Town Court- 607-656-4333, Greene Village Court- , Guilford Town Court- 607-895-6818, Lincklaen Town Court- 315-852-6128, Mcdonough Town Court- , New Berlin Town Court- 607-847-8962, New Berlin Village Court- 607-847-6249, North Norwich Town Court- 607-334-9224, Norwich Town Court- 607-337-2301, Otselic Town Court- 315-653-7201, Oxford Town Court- 607-843-9772, Oxford Village Court- 607-843-

9772, Pharsalia Town Court- 607-647-5203, Pitcher Town Court- 607-863-4929, Plymouth Town Court- No Phone, Preston Town Court- 607-336-1013, Sherburne Town Court- 607-674-4827, Sherburne Village Court- 607-674-4827, Smithville Town Court- 607-656-7969, Smyrna Town Court- No Phone

Clinton County

County Clerk County Government Center, 137 Margaret St, 1st Fl, Plattsburgh, NY 12901; 518-565-4701. Hours: 8AM-5PM (EST). *Civil.*

Note: The County Clerk does not have a seperate index of criminal records; see the Supreme and County Court.

Civil Records: Access: In person, online. Visitors must perform in person searches for themselves. No search fee. Required to search: name, years to search. Civil cases indexed by defendant. Civil records in docket books. Online access to current/pending civil cases is free at http://e.courts.state.ny.us/descCaseSearch.html.

General Information: No sealed or sex case records released. Will fax results to local or toll free line. Copy fee: $.50 per page. Cert fee: $5.00 up to 4 pages, then $1.25 per additional page. Payee: County Clerk. Personal checks accepted. Prepayment required.

Supreme & County Court County Government Center, 137 Margaret St, Plattsburgh, NY 12901; 518-565-4715; Fax: 518-565-4708. Hours: 9AM-noon, 1-5PM (EST). *Felony, Civil.*

Note: The County-court directs criminal search requestrs to the OCA for a $52.00 statewide record check. Civil records are with the County Clerk, see separate listing. Online access to current/pending civil cases is available at http://e.courts.state.ny.us.

Plattsburg City Court 24 US Oval, Plattsburgh, NY 12903; 518-563-7870; Fax: 518-563-3124. Hours: 8AM-4PM (EST). *Misdemeanor, Civil Actions Under $15,000, Eviction, Small Claims.*

Civil Records: Access: Mail, in person. Only the court performs in person searches; visitors may not. Search fee: $16.00 for computerized search. Required to search: name, years to search. Civil cases indexed by defendant. Civil records on computer back to 1986, prior in books.

Criminal Records: Access: None. No search fee. Records available here since 1986. The court will not support name searches unless specific case file given. Searchers must use the statewide search.

General Information: No sealed records released. Copy fee: $1.00 per page. Cert fee: $5.00. Payee: City Court. Only cashiers checks and money orders accepted. Prepayment required. Mail requests: SASE required. Mail turnaround time same day.

Surrogate Court 137 Margaret St, #315, Plattsburgh, NY 12901-2933; 518-565-4630; Fax: 518-565-4769. Hours: 8AM-5PM (EST). *Probate.*

Clinton Town/Village Courts. *Misdemeanor- Civil Actions Under $3000- Small Claims.* Altona Town Court- 518-236-7035, Au Sable Town Court- 518-834-9052, Beekmantown Town Court- 518-563-9930, Black Brook Town Court- 518-647-5412, Champlain Town Court- 518-298-2043, Champlain Village Court- 518-298-4088, Chazy Town Court- 518-846-8600, Clinton Town Court- 518-497-6133, Dannemora Town Court- 518-492-9751, Dannemora Village Court- 518-492-7000, Ellenburg Town Court- 518-594-7177, Keeseville Village Court- 518-834-9590, Mooers Town Court- 518-236-7927, Peru Town Court- 518-643-2745, Plattsburgh Town Court- 518-562-6870, Rouses Point Village Court- 518-297-6648, Saranac Town Court- 518-293-6666, Schuyler Falls Town Court- 518-563-1129

Columbia County

County Clerk 560 Warren St, Hudson, NY 12534; 518-828-3339; Fax: 518-828-5299. Hours: 9AM-5PM (EST). *Felony, Civil.*

Note: Countywide record search requests made to the County Clerk are processed in the manner described below.

Civil Records: Access: Mail, in person, online. Both court and visitors may perform in person searches. Search fee: $5.00 per name. Fee is per 2 years searched. Required to search: name, years to search. Civil cases indexed by defendant. Civil records on computer from 1993, prior on cards to 1985. Access to current/pending Supreme Court civil cases is at http://e.courts.state.ny.us/. Supreme and County courts are actually located at 401 Union in Hudson, but records for both courts are located at the County Clerk's Office as listed above.

Criminal Records: Access: Mail, in person. Both court and visitors may perform in person searches. Search fee: $5.00 per name. Fee is for 10 years searched. Required to search: name, years to search. Criminal records on computer from 1993, prior on cards to 1985. Supreme and County courts are actually located at 401 Union in Hudson, but records for both courts are located at the County Clerk's Office as listed above.

General Information: Public Access terminal is available. No sealed records released. Copy fee: $.25 per page. Cert fee: $4.00. Payee: County Clerk. Personal checks accepted. Prepayment required. Mail requests: SASE required. Mail turnaround 1 week.

Supreme & County Court 401 Union St, Hudson, NY 12534; 518-828-7858. Hours: 9AM-5PM (EST). *Felony, Civil.*

Note: Direct countywide search requests to the County Clerk, see separate listing. Also, access to current/pending Supreme Court civil cases is available at http://e.courts.state.ny.us/.

Hudson City Court 429 Warren St, Hudson, NY 12534; 518-828-3100; Fax: 518-828-3628. Hours: 8AM-3:45PM (EST). *Misdemeanor, Civil Actions Under $15,000, Eviction, Small Claims.* www.nycourts.gov/courts/3jd

Civil Records: Access: Fax, mail, in person. Only the court performs in person searches; visitors may not. Search fee: $16.00 per name. Required to search: name, years to search; also helpful: address. Civil cases indexed by defendant, plaintiff. Civil records on computer from 1991, prior in books.

Criminal Records: Access: None. No search fee. Criminal records on computer from 1991, prior in books. This court directs criminal records search requests to the OCA for a $52.00 statewide record check.

General Information: No sealed, expunged, adoption, sex offense, juvenile or mental health records released. Will fax results to local or toll free line. Copy fee: $.50 per page. Cert fee: $5.00. Payee: Hudson City Court. Business checks accepted. Prepayment required. Mail requests: SASE required. Mail turnaround time 1 week.

Surrogate Court Courthouse, 401 Union St, Hudson, NY 12534; 518-828-0414; Fax: 518-828-1603. Hours: 9AM-5PM (EST). *Probate.*

Columbia Town/Village Courts. *Misdemeanor- Civil Actions Under $3000- Small Claims.* Ancram Town Court- 518-329-6512, Austerlitz Town Court- 518-392-3260, Canaan Town Court- 518-781-4455, Chatham Town Court- 518-392-5440, Chatham Village Court- 518-392-9476, Claverack Town Court- 518-672-4468, Clermont Town Court- 518-537-6868, Copake Town Court- 518-329-1234, Gallatin Town Court- 518-398-7690, Germantown Town Court- 518-537-6687, Ghent Town Court- 518-392-4644, Greenport Town Court- 518-828-4656, Hillsdale Town Court- 518-325-5073,

Kinderhook Town Court- 518-784-2506, Kinderhook Village Court- No Phone, Livingston Town Court- 518-851-7210, New Lebanon Town Court- 518-794-9456, Philmont Village Court- 518-672-4886, Stockport Town Court- 518-828-9389, Stuyvesant Town Court- Taghkanic Town Court- 518-329-3030, Valatie Village Court- 518-758-9838

Cortland County

County Clerk 46 Greenbush St, #101, Cortland, NY 13045; 607-753-5021. Hours: 8:30PM-4:30PM (EST). *Felony, Civil.*

Note: Countywide record search requests made to the County Clerk are processed in the manner described below.

Civil Records: Access: Mail, in person. Both court and visitors may perform in person searches. Search fee: $5.00 per name per 2 year search. Required to search: name, years to search. Civil cases indexed by defendant, plaintiff. Civil records on computer from 5/94, prior in books. Access to current/pending Supreme Court civil cases and some closed cases is at http://e.courts.state.ny.us/.

Criminal Records: Access: Mail, in person. Only the court performs in person searches; visitors may not. Search fee: $5.00 per name per 2 years. Required to search: name, years to search, DOB. Criminal records in books.

General Information: No sealed or youthful offender records released. Will not fax results. Copy fee: $.65 per page, minimum $1.30. Cert fee: $5.00 per doc. Payee: County Clerk. Personal checks accepted. Prepayment required. Mail requests: SASE required. Mail turnaround time 2 days.

Supreme & County Court 46 Greenbush St, #301, Cortland, NY 13045; 607-753-5013, 753-5500. Hours: 8:30AM-4:30PM (EST). *Felony, Civil.*

Note: Direct record search requests to the County Clerk, see separate listing. Also, access to current/pending Supreme Court civil cases and some closed cases is at http://e.courts.state.ny.us/.

Cortland City Court 25 Court St, Cortland, NY 13045; 607-753-1811; Fax: 607-753-9932. Hours: 8:30AM-4:30PM (EST). *Misdemeanor, Civil Actions Under $15,000, Eviction, Small Claims.*

Civil Records: Access: Mail, in person. Only the court performs in person searches; visitors may not. Search fee: $5.00 per name per 2 years prior to 1991, $16 computer serach 1992 to present. Required to search: name, years to search. Civil cases indexed by defendant. Civil records on computer from 1991, prior in books.

Criminal Records: Access: Mail, in person. Only the court performs in person searches; visitors may not. Search fee: For low level misdemeanors only is $5.00 per name per 2 years. Required to search: name, years to search, DOB. Criminal records on computer from 1991, prior in books. The court does not permit access to "fingerprintable records" unless specific case file given. You must send requests to OCA for $52.00 statewide search.

General Information: No sealed records released. Will fax results to local or toll free line. Copy fee: $.65 per page. Cert fee: $5.00. Payee: Cortland City Court. Only cashiers checks and money orders accepted. Prepayment required. Mail requests: SASE required. Mail turnaround time 10 days.

Surrogate Court 46 Greenbush St, #301, Cortland, NY 13045; 607-753-5355; Fax: 607-756-3409. Hours: 9AM-5PM Summer-July-Sept 3-8:30-4:30 (EST). *Probate.* www.courts.state.ny.us/6jd

Cortland Town/Village Courts. *Misdemeanor- Civil Actions Under $3000- Small Claims.* Cincinnatus Town Court- 607-863-4220, Cortlandville Town Court- 607-756-2352, Cuyler Town Court- , Freetown Town Court- 607-849-3306, Harford Town Court- No Phone, Homer Town Court- 607-749-2326, Homer Village Court- 607-

749-2326, Lapeer Town Court- 607-849-3808, Marathon Town Court- 607-849-6966, Mcgraw Village Court- , Preble Town Court- 607-749-2377, Scott Town Court-607-749-2902, Solon Town Court- No Phone, Taylor Town Court- 607-863-3716, Truxton Town Court- 607-842-6291, Virgil Town Court- 607-835-6587, Willet Town Court- 607-863-3261

Delaware County

County Clerk 3 Court St, Delhi, NY 13753; 607-746-2123; Fax: 607-746-6924. Hours: 8:30AM-5PM (EST). *Felony, Civil.* Note: Countywide record search requests made to the County Clerk are processed in the manner described below.

Civil Records: Access: Mail, in person, online. Both court and visitors may perform in person searches. Search fee: $5.00 per name. Required to search: name, years to search. Civil cases indexed by defendant, plaintiff. Civil records in books. Access to current/pending Supreme Court civil cases and some closed cases is at http://e.courts.state.ny.us/.

Criminal Records: Access: Mail, in person. Both court and visitors may perform in person searches. Search fee: $10.00 per name. Required to search: name, years to search, DOB. Criminal records in books. Misdemeanor records are maintained by city, town and village courts.

General Information: No sealed records released. Copy fee: $.50 per page. Cert fee: $4.00 for up to 4 pages, then $1.00 per page. Payee: County Clerk. Personal checks accepted. Prepayment required. Mail requests: SASE required. Mail turnaround 2 days.

Supreme & County Court 3 Court St, Delhi, NY 13753; 607-746-2131. Hours: 9AM-5PM (EST). *Felony, Civil.*
Note: Direct record search requests to the County Clerk, see separate listing. Access to current/pending Supreme Court civil cases and some closed cases is available at http://e.courts.state.ny.us/.

Surrogate Court 3 Court St, Delhi, NY 13753; 607-746-2126; Fax: 607-746-3253. 9-5PM, Summer-July1-Sept 3; 9AM-4:30PM (EST). *Probate.*

Delaware Town/Village Courts. *Misdemeanor- Civil Actions Under $3000- Small Claims.* Andes Town Court-845-676-3550, Bovina Town Court- , Colchester Town Court- 845-498-5775, Davenport Town Court- None, Delhi Town & Village Court- 607-746-7161, Deposit Town Court- 607-467-3233, Franklin Town Court- 607-829-2211, Hamden Town Court- 607-746-6660, Hancock Town Court- 607-637-3651, Hancock Village Court- 607-637-5789, Harpersfield Town Court- 607-652-5060, Kortright Town Court- No Phone, Masonville Town Court- No Phone, Meredith Town Court- No Phone, Middletown Town Court- 845-586-2575, Roxbury Town Court- 607-588-7507, Sidney Town Court- 607-561-2309, Sidney Village Court- 607-561-2307, Stamford Town Court- 607-538-1825, Stamford Village Court- 607-652-6671, Tompkins Town Court- 607-865-4979, Walton Town Court- 607-865-5182, Walton Village Court- 607-865-6150

Dutchess County

County Clerk 22 Market St, Poughkeepsie, NY 12601-3203; 845-486-2139 (records); 486-2120 (main). Hours: 9AM-5PM (EST). *Felony, Civil.*
www.dutchessny.gov/dcclerk.htm
Note: Countywide record search requests made to the County Clerk are processed in the manner described below.

Civil Records: Access: In person, online. Visitors must perform in person searches for themselves. No search fee. Required to search: name, years to search. Civil cases indexed by defendant, plaintiff. Civil records in books back to 1847; on computer back to 1986. Access to current/pending Supreme Court civil cases is at http://e.courts.state.ny.us/.

Criminal Records: Access: Mail, in person. Both court and visitors may perform in person searches. Search fee: $5.00 per name per 2 years searched.

Required to search: name, years to search, aliases. Criminal records go back to 1847; on computer back to 1987. They will only create a certificate if their staff performs the search.

General Information: Public Access terminal is available. No sealed or youthful offender records released. Will not fax results. Copy fee: $.65 per copy. Cert fee: $5.00 per doc. Payee: Dutchess County Clerk. Personal checks accepted. Prepayment required. Mail requests: SASE required. Mail turnaround time 2 weeks.

Supreme & County Court 10 Market St, Poughkeepsie, NY 12601-3203; 845-486-2260. Hours: 9AM-5PM (EST). *Felony, Civil.*
Note: For countywide record search, see the County Clerk, otherwise this court recommends the $52.00 statewide search via the OCA. Also, access to current/pending civil cases is available at http://e.courts.state.ny.us/. Pending criminal cases also available.

Beacon City Court One Municipal Plaza, #2, Beacon, NY 12508; 845-838-5030; Fax: 845-838-5041. Hours: 8AM-4PM (EST). *Misdemeanor, Civil Actions Under $15,000, Eviction, Small Claims.*

Civil Records: Access: In person. Only the Court may perform searches. No search fee. Required to search: name, DOB, years to search; also helpful-address. Civil cases indexed by defendant, plaintiff. Civil records on computer from 1996, prior in books and cards.

Criminal Records: Access: None. Search fee: A Certificate of Disposition is $5.00. The court refuses to permit access to records unless specific case file given. Searchers must use the $52.00 statewide OCA search.

General Information: No sealed or youthful offender records released. Copy fee: $1.00 first page, $.50 every page thereafter. Cert fee: $5.00 for criminal; $6.00 if civil. Payee: City Court of Beacon. Only cashiers checks and money orders accepted. Prepayment required.

Poughkeepsie City Court Civic Center Plaza, PO Box 300, Poughkeepsie, NY 12602; 845-451-4091; Fax: 845-485-6795. Hours: 8AM-4PM (EST). *Misdemeanor, Civil Actions Under $15,000, Eviction, Small Claims.*

Civil Records: Access: Mail, in person. Both court and visitors may perform in person searches. Search fee: $5.00 per name per 2 years searched. $5.00 for certificate of disposition. Required to search: name, years to search. Civil cases indexed by defendant. Civil records on computer from 1993.

Criminal Records: Access: In person only. No search fee. Criminal records on computer from 1990. Direct criminal records search requests to OCA for $52.00 statewide search. Must go through state in order to get a certified disposition.

General Information: No sealed, expunged, adoption, sex offense, juvenile or mental health records released. Will not fax results. Copy fee: $.65 per page. Cert fee: $5.00. Payee: Poughkeepsie City Court. Only cashiers checks and money orders accepted. Prepayment required. Mail requests: SASE required. Mail turnaround time 1 week.

Surrogate Court 10 Market St, Poughkeepsie, NY 12601; 845-486-2235; Fax: 845-486-2234. Hours: 9AM-5PM (EST). *Probate.*

Dutchess Town/Village Courts. *Misdemeanor- Civil Actions Under $3000- Small Claims.* Beekman Town Court- 845-724-5581, Clinton Town Court- 845-266-5988, Dover Town Court- 845-832-3461, East Fishkill Town Court- 845-226-4229, Fishkill Town Court- 845-831-7860, Fishkill Village Court- 845-879-2103, Hyde Park Town Court- 845-229-2606/229-5210, La Grange Town Court- 845-452-1837, Milan Town Court- 845-758-

6960, Millbrook Village Court- 845-677-8277, Millerton Village Court, North East Town Court- 518-789-3080/584-3555, Pawling Town Court- 845-855-3516, Pawling Village Court- 845-855-5602, Pine Plains Town Court- 518-398-7194, Pleasant Valley Town Court- 845-635-2856, Poughkeepsie Town Court- 845-485-3690/3696, Red Hook Town Court- 845-758-4611/758-4609, Red Hook Village Court- 845-758-1081, Rhinebeck Town Court- 845-876-3858, Rhinebeck Village Court-845-876-4119, Stanford Town Court- 845-868-2269/2258, Tivoli Village Court- 845-757-3219, Union Vale Town Court- 845-724-3288/724-5600, Wappinger Town Court- 845-297-6070, Wappingers Falls Village Court- 845-297-6777, Washington Town Court- 845-677-6366

Erie County

County Clerk 25 Delaware Ave, 1st Fl, Buffalo, NY 14202; Civil phone: 716-858-7766; Criminal phone: 716-858-7877; Fax: 716-858-6550. Hours: 9AM-5PM; usually closed 1 hour for lunch but time varies. (EST). *Felony, Civil.*
www.erie.gov/depts/government/clerk/civil_criminal.phtml
Note: Countywide record search requests made to the County Clerk are processed in the manner described below.

Civil Records: Access: Mail, in person, online. Both court and visitors may perform in person searches. Search fee: $5.00 per name. Fee is per 2 years searched. Required to search: name, years to search. Civil cases indexed by defendant. Civil records on computer from 1994, prior in books back to 1900s. Online access to the county clerk's database of civil matters is free at http://ecclerk.erie.gov. Records go back to 2/1994. Also, access to current/pending Supreme Court civil cases is at http://e.courts.state.ny.us/.

Criminal Records: Access: In person only. No search fee. Required to search: name, years to search, DOB. Criminal records in books back to 1900s.

General Information: Public Access terminal is available. (Public terminal for civil in person searches.) No sealed records released. Will not fax results. Copy fee: $1.00 per page. Cert fee: $5.00. Payee: County Clerk. Personal checks accepted. Prepayment required. Mail requests: SASE required. Mail turnaround time 3-4 days.

Supreme & County Court 25 Delaware Ave, Ground Fl, Buffalo, NY 14202; 716-845-9301. Hours: 9AM-5PM; usually closed for lunch hour. (EST). *Felony, Civil.* www.erie.gov
Note: Court directs felony search requests to the OCA for a $52.00 statewide record check. See also County Clerk for access. Access to current/pending Supreme Court civil cases available at http://e.courts.state.ny.us/, also search pending criminal appearances.

Buffalo City Court 50 Delaware Ave, Buffalo, NY 14202; 716-845-2689; Civil phone: 716-845-2662; Criminal phone: 716-845-2661; Fax: 716-847-8257. Hours: 9AM-5PM (EST). *Misdemeanor, Civil Actions Under $15,000, Eviction, Small Claims.*

Civil Records: Access: Mail, fax, in person. Both court and visitors may perform in person searches. Search fee: $5.00 per name. Required to search: name, years to search. Civil cases indexed by defendant, plaintiff. Criminal records on computer back to 1983, prior in books back to 1974.

Criminal Records: Access: In person only. Only the court performs in person searches; visitors may not. Search fee: $5.00 per disposition. Required to search: name, DOB, date of offense. Criminal records on computer back to 1983, prior in books back to 1974. Search online for future court appearances at http://e.courts.state.ny.us. This court will perform a disposition search. No general searches are done; searches are directed to OCA in NYC.

General Information: No sealed or youthful offender records released. Copy fee: $1.00 per page. Cert fee: $5.00. Payee: City Court. Business checks accepted. Mail requests: SASE required. Mail turnaround time 7 days.

Lackawanna City Court 714 Ridge Rd, Rm 225, Lackawanna, NY 14218; 716-827-6486; Civil phone: 716-827-6661; Criminal phone: 716-827-6487; Fax: 716-825-1874. Hours: 8:30AM-4:30PM (EST). *Misdemeanor, Civil Actions Under $15,000, Eviction, Small Claims.*

Civil Records: Access: Mail, in person. Only the court may perform in person searches. Search fee: $16.00 per name. Required to search: name; also helpful: years to search. Civil cases indexed by defendant. Civil records on computer from 1994, prior on docket books. Mail access available to government agencies only.

Criminal Records: Access: None. No search fee. Criminal records on computer from 1994, prior on docket books. The court refuses to permit access to court records unless specific case file given. It is suggested to send requests to OCA for $52.00 statewide search.

General Information: No sealed or youthful offender records released. Will not fax results. Copy fee: $1.00 per page. Cert fee: $5.00. Payee: City Court. Only cashiers checks and money orders accepted. Prepayment required. Mail requests: SASE required. Mail turnaround time 2-3 days.

Tonawanda City Court 200 Niagara St, Tonawanda, NY 14150; 716-693-3484; Fax: 716-693-1612. Hours: 9AM-4PM (EST). *Misdemeanor, Civil Actions Under $15,000, Eviction, Small Claims, Criminal.*

Civil Records: Access: Mail, in person. Only the court performs in person searches; visitors may not. No search fee. Required to search: name, years to search. Civil cases indexed by defendant, plaintiff. Civil records on computer since 1997, prior on index cards, in books.

Criminal Records: Access: Mail, in person. Only the court performs in person searches; visitors may not. Search fee: $5.00 per name. A Certificate of Disposition is $5.00/$6.00. Required to search: name, years to search (case number, arrest date if Cert of Disposition). Criminal records on computer since 19867, prior on index cards, in books. As a rule, the court will not permit access to its records unless specific case file given. It is suggested to send requests to OCA for $52.00 statewide search. However, court will search older records for the fee listed below.

General Information: No sealed records released. Copy fee: $1.00 per page. Cert fee: $5.00. Payee: City Court of Tonawanda. Business checks accepted. Prepayment required. Mail requests: SASE not required. Mail turnaround time 3-5 days.

Surrogate Court 92 Franklin St, Buffalo, NY 14202; 716-854-2560; Fax: 716-853-3741. Hours: 9AM-5PM (EST). *Probate.*

Erie Town/Village Courts. *Misdemeanor- Civil Actions Under $3000- Small Claims.* Akron Village Court- 716-542 9636, Alden Town Court- 716-937-3411, Alden Village Court- 716-937-9216, Amherst Town Court- 716-689-4200, Angola Village Court- No Phone, Aurora Town Court- 716-457-3022, Blasdell Village Court- No Phone, Boston Town Court- 716-941-6115, Brant Town Court- 716-549-0300, Cheektowaga Town Court- 716-686-3437, Clarence Town Court- No Phone, Colden Town Court- 716-941-5012, Collins Town Court- 716-532-4887, Concord Town Court- 716-592-9898, Depew Village Court- 716-683-0978, Eden Town Court- 716-992-3559, Elma Town Court- 716-652-1855, Evans Town Court- 716-549-3707, Farnham Village Court- No Phone, Grand Island Town Court- 716-773-9650, Hamburg Town Court- 716-649-6111, Hamburg Village Court- 716-649-7204, Holland Town Court- No Phone,

Kenmore Village Court- No Phone, Lancaster Town Court- 716-683-1814, Lancaster Village Court- 716-683-6780, Marilla Town Court- 716-652-1213, Newstead Town Court- 716-542-4575, North Collins Town Court- 716-337-3712, Orchard Park Town Court- 716-662-6415, Orchard Park Village Court- 716-662-6415, Sardinia Town Court- 716-496-8900, Springville Village Court- , Tonawanda Town Court- 716-876-5536, Wales Town Court- 716-652-3320, West Seneca Town Court- 716-674-5600 Ext.246, Williamsville Village Court- 716-632-0450

Essex County

County Clerk PO Box 247, 7559 Court St, Essex County Government Ctr, Elizabethtown, NY 12932; Civil phone: 518-873-3600, 518-873-3601; Fax: 518-873-3548. Hours: 8AM-5PM (EST). *Civil, Felony.*

Note: County Clerk will not do criminal record searches for County-Court criminal records; clerk will only do civil record searches. You may search criminal books in person.

Civil Records: Access: Mail, in person, online. Both court and visitors may perform in person searches. No search fee. Required to search: name, years to search. Civil cases indexed by defendant, plaintiff. Civil records on computer from 11/93, prior in books. Access to current/pending Supreme Court civil cases is at http://e.courts.state.ny.us/.

Criminal Records: Access: In person only. Visitors must perform in person searches for themselves. No search fee. Required to search: name, years to search, DOB. Criminal records on computer from 1950s, prior in books; you may search the books.

General Information: Public Access terminal is available. No sealed or youthful offender records released. Will not fax results. Copy fee: $.65 per page; $1.30 minimum. Cert fee: $1.00 per page; minimum $5.00. Payee: Essex County Clerk. Personal checks accepted. Prepayment required. Mail requests: SASE required. Mail turnaround time same day.

Supreme & County Court PO Box 217, 7559 Court St, Essex County Government Ctr, Elizabethtown, NY 12932; Civil phone: 518-873-3612; Criminal phone: 518-873-3371, 518-873-3612. Hours: 8AM-5PM (EST). *Felony, Civil.*

Note: County-court directs criminal searches to the OCA for $52.00 statewide record check. Countywide record checks can be made at County Clerk, see separate listing. Access to current/pending Supreme Court civil cases available at http://e.courts.state.ny.us/.

Surrogate Court 7559 Court St, PO Box 505, Elizabethtown, NY 12932; 518-873-3384; Fax: 518-873-3731. Hours: 9AM-5PM (EST). *Probate.*

Essex Town/Village Courts. *Misdemeanor- Civil Actions Under $3000- Small Claims.* Chesterfield Town Court- 518-834-9211, Crown Point Town Court- 518-597-4144, Elizabethtown Town Court- 518-873-6555, Essex Town Court- 518-963-8016, Jay Town Court- 518 647 2204, Keene Town Court- 518-576-4444, Lake Placid Village Court- 518-523-2004; 2141, Lewis Town Court- 518-873-3204, Minerva Town Court- 518-251-2869, Moriah Town Court- No Phone, Newcomb Town Court- 518-582-2010, North Elba Town Court- 518-523-9516, North Hudson Town Court- 518-532-0587, Port Henry Village Court- , Schroon Town Court- 518-532-0569, St Armand Town Court- 518-891-3189, Ticonderoga Town Court- 518-585-7141, Westport Town Court- 518-962-4882, Willsboro Town Court- 518-963-8933, Wilmington Town Court- 518-946-2105

Franklin County

County Clerk 355 W Main St, Attn: County Clerk, Malone, NY 12953-1817; 518-481-1681. Hours: 9AM-5PM; 8AM-4PM Summer hours (EST). *Felony, Civil.*

Note: Felony records are managed by the Supreme Court clerk who directs search requests to OCA for a $52.00 statewide search. However, criminal records

are accessible in person here on the public access terminal.

Civil Records: Access: Mail, In person, online. Visitors must perform in person searches for themselves. Search fee: $5.00 per name per 2 years. Required to search: name, years to search. Civil cases indexed by defendant. Civil index of dockets on computer from 1996, prior in file folders in Clerk's office. Access to current/pending Supreme Court civil cases is at http://e.courts.state.ny.us/.

Criminal Records: Access: In person only. Visitors must perform in person searches for themselves. No search fee. Required to search: name, years to search, DOB. Criminal records on computer from 1962.

General Information: Public Access terminal is available. (There are separate terminals for criminal records and civil records.) No sealed or youthful offender records released. Copy fee: $.65 per page. Cert fee: $1.00 per page, 5 page minimum. Payee: County Clerk. Personal checks accepted. Prepayment required. Mail requests: SASE required. Mail turnaround time 1 week.

Supreme & County Court 355 W Main St, Court Clerk, Malone, NY 12953-1817; 518-481-1748; Criminal phone: 518-481-1749. Hours: 9AM-5PM; 8AM-4PM Summer hours (EST). *Felony, Civil.*

Note: Supreme Court directs criminal search requests to the OCA for a $52.00 statewide record check. Search civil records at County Clerk, see separate listing. Access to current/pending Supreme Court civil cases is available at http://e.courts.state.ny.us/.

Criminal Records: Access: Mail, in person. Visitors must perform in person searches for themselves. No search fee. Required to search: name, years to search, DOB. Criminal records on computer from 1962. Unless you search here in person, all criminal record name search requests are directed to the OCA for statewide record search, $52.00 search fee.

General Information: Public Access terminal is available. (Terminal is for criminal records only.) No sealed or youthful offender records released. Copy fee: $.65 per page. Cert fee: $1.00 per page, 5 page minimum. Payee: County Clerk. Personal checks accepted. Prepayment required. Mail requests: SASE required. Mail turnaround time 1 week.

Surrogate Court 355 W Main St, Malone, NY 12953-1817; 518-481-1736 & 1737; Fax: 518-483-7583. Hours: 8AM-5PM Summer,8:00-4PM JUN-AUG (EST). *Probate.*

Franklin Town/Village Courts. *Misdemeanor- Civil Actions Under $3000- Small Claims.* Altamont Town Court- 518-359-9278, Bangor Town Court- 518-481-6570, Bellmont Town Court- 518-425-3349, Bombay Town Court- 518-358-9939, Brandon Town Court- 518-327-3202, Brighton Town Court- 518-327-3202, Burke Town Court- 518-483-5497, Chateaugay Town Court- 518-497-6931, Constable Town Court- 518-481-6113, Dickinson Town Court- 518-856-9339, Duane Town Court- 518-483-0386, Fort Covington Town Court- 518-358-2047, Franklin Town Court- 518-841-3989, Harrietstown Town Court- 518-891-4500, Malone Town Court- 518-481-6634, Malone Village Court- 518-483-5210, Moira Town Court- 518-529-6080, Santa Clara Town Court- 518-891-1919, Saranac Lake Village Court- 518-891-4423, Tupper Lake Village Court- 518-359-9161, Waverly Town Court- 518-856-9482, Westville Town Court- 518-358-4180

Fulton County

Supreme & County Court 223 W Main St, County Bldg, Johnstown, NY 12095; 518-736-5539 (court) 518-736-5555 (county clerk). Hours: 9AM-5PM (EST). *Felony, Civil.*

Note: Hamilton County Supreme Court cases are heard here. Supreme court clerk directs criminal search requests to the OCA for a $52.00 statewide record check, however the County Clerk office (same location) may permit in person criminal record search requests.

Civil Records: Access: Phone, mail, fax, in person, online. Both court and visitors may perform in person searches. Search fee: $16.00 per name. Fee is $5.00 for in person searching, if record found. Required to search: name, years to search. Civil cases indexed by defendant, plaintiff. Civil records computerized since 1994. Access to current/pending Supreme Court civil cases is at http://e.courts.state.ny.us/.

Criminal Records: Access: In person only. Only the court may perform in person searches, visitors may not. Search fee: $5.00 if county clerk does in person search. Required to search: name, years to search, DOB. Criminal records in file folders since 1915, computerized since 1977.

General Information: No sealed, expunged, adoption, sex offense, juvenile or mental health records released. Copy fee: $1.00 per page. $.50 per page self service. Cert fee: $4.00. Payee: County Clerk. Business checks accepted. Prepayment required. Mail requests: SASE required. Mail turnaround time 1 week.

Gloversville City Court City Hall, Frontage Rd, Gloversville, NY 12078; 518-773-4527; Fax: 518-773-4599. Hours: 8AM-4PM (EST). *Misdemeanor, Civil Actions Under $15,000, Eviction, Small Claims.*

Civil Records: Access: Mail, in person. Only the court performs in person searches; visitors may not. No search fee. Required to search: name, years to search. Civil cases indexed by plaintiff. Civil records in books; on computer since.

Criminal Records: Access: None. Search fee: A Certificate of Disposition is $5.00. The court refuses to permit access to records unless specific case file given. Searchers must use the OCA $52.00 statewide search.

General Information: No sealed, youthful offender records released. Copy fee: $.65 per page. There is a $1.30 minimum. Cert fee: $5.00. Payee: Gloversville City Court. Only cashiers checks and money orders accepted. Prepayment required. Mail requests: SASE required. Mail turnaround time 2 weeks.

Surrogate Court 223 West Main St, Johnstown, NY 12095; 518-736-5685; Fax: 518-762-6372. Hours: 9AM-5PM (8AM-4PM July-August) (EST). *Probate.*

Fulton Town/Village Courts. *Misdemeanor- Civil Actions Under $3000- Small Claims.* Bleeker Town Court- 518-725-0859, Broadalbin Town Court- 518-883-5131, Broadalbin Village Court- 518-883-3353, Ephratah Town Court- 518-568-7560, Johnstown City Court- 518-762-0007, Johnstown Town Court- 518-762-7070, Mayfield Town Court- 518-661-5225, Oppenheim Town Court- 518-568-7503, Perth Town Court- 518-843-6977, Stratford Town Court- 315-429-8341

Genesee County

County Clerk PO Box 379 (15 Main St), Attn: County Clerk, Batavia, NY 14021-0379; 585-344-2550 x2243; Fax: 585-344-8551. Hours: 8:30AM-5PM (EST). *Felony, Civil.*

Note: Countywide criminal search requests made to the County Clerk are processed in the manner described below.

Civil Records: Access: Mail, in person, online. Both court and visitors may perform in person searches. Search fee: $10.00 per name per 5 year period. Required to search: name, years to search; also helpful: address. Civil cases indexed by defendant, plaintiff; indexed by defendant only prior to 1995. Civil records in books from 1802; on computer back to 1995. Access to current/pending Supreme Court civil cases is at http://e.courts.state.ny.us/.

Criminal Records: Access: Fax, mail, in person. Both court and visitors may perform in person searches. Search fee: $10.00 per name per 5 year period, $15.00 for 7 years, $20.00 for more. Required to search: name, years to search, DOB; also helpful: SSN. Criminal records in books from 1802; on computer back to 1995.

General Information: Public Access terminal is available. No sealed, expunged, adoption, sex offense, juvenile or mental health records released. Fee to fax results is $5.00 per document; no charge if to a toll free number. Copy fee: $1.30 for first page, $.65 each add'l. Cert fee: $4.00 plus $.50 per page in excess of 8 pages. Payee: County Clerk. Personal checks accepted. Prepayment required. Mail requests: SASE required. Mail turnaround time 1-3 days.

Supreme & County Court PO Box 379 (15 Main St), Attn: Court Clerk, Batavia, NY 14021-0379; 585-344-2550 x2239; Civil phone: x2243 for records info. Hours: 8:30AM-5PM (EST). *Felony, Civil.*

Note: The County-Court directs criminal search requests to the OCA for a $52.00 statewide record check. See also County Clerk, see separate listing. Access to current/pending Supreme Court civil cases is available at http://e.courts.state.ny.us/.

Batavia City Court Genesee County Courts Facility, 1 W Main St, Batavia, NY 14020; 585-344-2550 X2416, 2417, 2418; Fax: 585-344-8556. Hours: 9AM-5PM (EST). *Misdemeanor, Civil Actions Under $15,000, Eviction, Small Claims.*

Civil Records: Access: Fax, mail, in person. Both court and visitors may perform in person searches. Search fee: $6.00 per name. Required to search: name, years to search. Civil cases indexed by plaintiff. Civil records on computer from 1990, in books from 1957.

Criminal Records: Access: Mail, in person. Search fee: A Certificate of Disposition is available for $6.00. Required to search: name, years to search, DOB. Criminal records on computer from 1993, in books from 1947. All criminal record name search requests are directed to the OCA for statewide record search, $52.00 search fee.

General Information: No sealed, expunged, sex offense or mental health records released. Will fax results to local or toll free line only. Copy fee: $.50 per page. Cert fee: $6.00. Payee: City Court. Only cashiers checks and money orders accepted. Prepayment required. Mail requests: SASE required. Mail turnaround time 1-3 days.

Surrogate Court 1 West Main St, Batavia, NY 14020; 585-344-2550 ext 2237; Fax: 585-344-8517. Hours: 9AM-5PM Summer-8:30-4:30,JUN-Sept3 (EST). *Probate.* Note: $25.00 search fee.

Genesee Town/Village Courts. *Misdemeanor- Civil Actions Under $3000- Small Claims.* Alabama Town Court- No Phone, Alexander Town Court- 585-591-0908, Batavia Town Court- 585-343-1729, Bergen Town Court- 585-494-1121, Bethany Town Court- 585-343-3325, Byron Town Court- 585-548-7123, Corfu Village Court- 585-599-3327, Darien Town Court- 585-547-2274, Elba Town Court- 585-757-9200, Le Roy Town & Village Court- 585-768-6910/2527, Oakfield Town Court- 585-948-5835, Oakfield Village Court- 585-948-9588, Pavilion Town Court- 585-584-3850, Pembroke Town Court- 585-591-4892, Stafford Town Court- 585-344-4020

Greene County

Supreme & County Court Courthouse, County Clerk, 320 Main St, Catskill, NY 12414; 518-943-2050 x71 (county clerk) 518-943-2230 (court clerk); Fax: 518-943-2146. Hours: 9AM-5PM; 8:30AM-4:30PM Summer hours (EST). *Felony, Civil.*

Note: Search requests are processed by the County Clerk office in the manner described below.

Civil Records: Access: Phone, fax, mail, in person, online. Both court and visitors may perform in person searches. No search fee. Required to search: name, years to search. Civil cases indexed by defendant, plaintiff. Civil records in file folder, computerized since 06/13/97. Access to current/pending Supreme Court civil cases is at http://e.courts.state.ny.us/.

Criminal Records: Access: Fax, mail, in person. Only the court performs in person searches; visitors may not. Search fee: $5.00 per name for 2 years; $17.50 per name for 20 years. Required to search: name, years to search, DOB. Criminal records on index cards. Direct requests to the County Clerk's office 518-943-2050.

General Information: Public Access terminal is available. No sealed or youthful offender records released. Will fax results $1.00 per doc. Copy fee: $1.00 per page. Cert fee: $5.00. Payee: County Clerk. Personal checks accepted. Prepayment required. Mail requests: SASE required. Mail turnaround 1 week.

Surrogate Court Courthouse, 320 Main St, Catskill, NY 12414; 518-943-2484; Fax: 518-943-1864. Hours: 9AM-5PM (EST). *Probate.*

Greene Town/Village Courts. *Misdemeanor- Civil Actions Under $3000- Small Claims.* Ashland Town Court- 518-734-3636, Athens Town Court- 518-945-3360, Athens Village Court- No Phone, Cairo Town Court- 518-622-3388, Catskill Town Court- 518-943-2142, Catskill Village Court- 518-943-9544, Coxsackie Town Court- 518-731-6934, Coxsackie Village Court- 518-731-2225, Durham Town Court- 518-239-8260, Greenville Town Court- 518-966-4873, Halcott Town Court- No Phone, Hunter Town Court- 518-589-6150, Hunter Village Court- 518-263-4288, Jewett Town Court- 518-263-4626, Lexington Town Court- 518-989-6303, New Baltimore Town Court- 518-756-2079, Prattsville Town Court- 518-299-3125, Tannersville Village Court- 518-589-5858, Windham Town Court- 518-734-3431

Hamilton County

County Clerk & County Court Hamilton County Clerk, PO Box 204, Route 8, Lake Pleasant, NY 12108; 518-548-7111. Hours: 8:30AM-4:30PM (EST). *Felony, Civil.*

Note: Countywide record search requests are processed in the manner decribed below. Civil cases are heard in Fulton County (518-736-5539, Patricia, for info). Once closed, civil case records are returned to Hamilton County clerk.

Civil Records: Access: Mail, phone, in person, online. Both court and visitors may perform in person searches. No search fee. Required to search: name, years to search. Civil cases indexed by defendant. Civil records in books, records go back to 1850s. Access to current/pending Supreme Court civil cases is at http://e.courts.state.ny.us/.

Criminal Records: Access: Mail, in person. Only the court performs in person searches; visitors may not. Search fee: $5.00 per name. Fee is per two years searched. Required to search: name, years to search, DOB. Criminal records go back to 1878; no computerized records. Record search request must be in writing.

General Information: No sealed or youthful offender records released. Fee to fax results is $1.00 per document. Copy fee: $.65 per page. $1.30 minimum. Cert fee: $1.25 per page; $5.00 minimum. Payee: Hamilton County Clerk. Personal checks accepted. Prepayment required. Mail requests: SASE not required. Mail turnaround time 2-3 days.

Supreme Court Hamilton County Clerk, PO Box 204, Route 8, Lake Pleasant, NY 12108; 518-548-7111 (Hamilton county clerk) 518-736-5539 (Fulton court clerk). Hours: 8:30AM-4:30PM (EST). *Civil.*
Note: Supreme court (civil cases) in Hamilton County are heard in Fulton County. Civil records eventually returned to Hamilton County Clerk once the case is completed in Fulton. Original filings made in Hamilton, but subsequent filings usually made at Fulton.
Civil Records: Access: Mail, fax, phone, in person, online. Both court and visitors may perform in person searches. No search fee. Required to search: name, years to search. Civil cases indexed by defendant. Civil records in books, records go back to 1850s. Access to current/pending Supreme Court civil cases is at http://e.courts.state.ny.us/.
General Information: No sealed or youthful offender records released. Fee to fax results is $1.00 per document. Copy fee: $.65 per page. $1.30 minimum. Cert fee: $1.25 per page; $5.00 minimum. Payee: Hamilton County Clerk. Personal checks accepted. Prepayment required. Mail requests: SASE not required. Mail turnaround time 2-3 days. Public access terminal note- Hamilton county civil cases heard in Fulton county may be available on the Fulton county civil computer.

Surrogate Court PO Box 780, White Birch Lane, Indian Lake, NY 12842; 518-648-5411; Fax: 518-648-6286. 8:30AM-4:30PM (EST). *Probate.*
Note: Court is located in Hamilton County Ofc. Bldg.

Hamilton Town/Village Courts. *Misdemeanor- Civil Actions Under $3000- Small Claims.* Arietta Town Court- 518-548-6203, Benson Town Court- 518-863-8510, Hope Town Court- 518-924-2663, Indian Lake Town Court- 518-648-6226, Inlet Town Court- 315-357-6121, Lake Pleasant Town Court- 518-548-3625, Long Lake Town Court- No Phone, Morehouse Town Court- No Phone, Wells Town Court- 518-924-9285

Herkimer County

County Clerk 109 Mary St, Herkimer County Office Bldg, Herkimer, NY 13350-1993; 315-867-1133; Fax: 315-867-1349. Hours: 9AM-5PM Sept-May; 8:30AM-4PM June-Aug (EST). *Felony, Civil.*
Note: Countywide record search requests made to the County Clerk are processed in the manner described below. Misdemeanor records are maintained by city, town and village courts.
Civil Records: Access: Phone, mail, in person, online. Only the court performs in person searches; visitors may not. Search fee: $5.00 per name per 2 year period. Required to search: name, years to search. Civil cases indexed by defendant, plaintiff. Civil records on index books since 1800s. Access to current/pending Supreme Court civil cases is at http://e.courts.state.ny.us/.
Criminal Records: Access: mail, in person. Visitors may perform in person searches for themselves. Search fee: $5.00 per name per 2 year period. Required to search: name, years to search, DOB. Criminal records on index books since 1800s.
General Information: Public Access terminal is available. No sealed, expunged, adoption, sex offense, juvenile or mental health records released. Copy fee: $.65 per page, $1.30 minimum. Cert fee: $1.25 per page, $5.00 minimum. Payee: County Clerk. Personal checks accepted. Prepayment required. Mail requests: SASE required. Mail turnaround time varies.

Supreme & County Court 310 N Washington St, Herkimer, NY 13350-1993; 315-867-1282. Hours: 9AM-5PM; 8:30AM-4PM Summer hours (EST). *Felony, Civil.*
Note: The County-Court clerk directs felony requests to the OCA for a $52.00 statewide record check. See also separate listing for County Clerk. Access to current/pending Supreme Court civil cases is available at http://e.courts.state.ny.us/.

Little Falls City Court 659 E Main St, Little Falls, NY 13365; 315-823-1690; Fax: 315-823-1623. Hours: 8:30AM-4:30PM (EST). *Misdemeanor, Civil Actions Under $15,000, Eviction, Small Claims.*
Civil Records: Access: Mail, fax, in person. Only the court performs in person searches; visitors may not. Search fee: $5.00 per name. Required to search: name, years to search. Civil cases indexed by defendant. Civil records go back to 1973; on computer back to 4/02.
Criminal Records: Access: Mail, in person. Only the court performs in person searches; visitors may not. Search fee: $5.00 per name. Required to search: name, years to search, DOB, signed release. Criminal records go back to 1948; on computer back to 4/02.
General Information: No sealed, expunged, adoption, sex offense, juvenile or mental health records released. Will fax results to local or toll free line. Copy fee: $.50 per page; minimum $1.00. Cert fee: $5.00. Payee: City Court. Only cashiers checks and money orders accepted. Prepayment required. Mail requests: SASE required. Mail turnaround 1 wk.

Surrogate Court 301 N Washington St #5550, Herkimer, NY 13350; 315-867-1170. Hours: 9AM-5PM Sept-May; 8:30AM-4PM June-Aug (EST). *Probate.*

Herkimer Town/Village Courts. *Misdemeanor- Civil Actions Under $3000- Small Claims.* Cold Brook Village Court- 315-826-3432, Columbia Town Court- 315-866-1309, Danube Town Court- No Phone, Fairfield Town Court- 315-823-2747, Frankfort Town Court- 315-895-7267, Frankfort Village Court- 315-894-8513, German Flatts Town Court- 315-866-3571, Herkimer Town Court- 315-866-1280, Herkimer Village Court- 315-866-0604, Ilion Village Court- 315-894-4175, Litchfield Town Court- No Phone, Little Falls Town Court- 315-823-3390, Manheim Town Court- 315-429-9631, Middleville Village Court- No Phone, Mohawk Village Court- 315-866-4312, Newport Town Court- No Phone, Newport Village Court- 315-845-8938, Norway Town Court- 315-845-8272, Ohio Town Court- 315-826-7912, Poland Village Court- 315-826-3422, Russia Town Court- 315-826-3432, Salisbury Town Court- 315-429-8581, Schuyler Town Court- 315-733-1093, Stark Town Court- 315-858-2091, Warren Town Court- No Phone, Webb Town Court- 315-369-3321, Winfield Town Court- 315-822-4555

Jefferson County

Supreme & County Court Jefferson County Clerk's Office-Court Records, 175 Arsenal St, County Bldg, Watertown, NY 13601-3783; 315-785-3200 County Clerk; Probate phone: 315-785-3019; Fax: 315-785-5145. Hours: 9AM-5PM; 8:30AM-4PM July-Aug Summer hours (EST). *Felony, Civil.*
www.co.jefferson.ny.us/Jefflive.nsf/cclerk
Note: Countywide record search requests are processed in the manner described below by the County Clerk.
Civil Records: Access: In person, online. Visitors must perform in person searches for themselves. No search fee. Required to search: name, years to search. Civil cases indexed by defendant, plaintiff. Civil records on computer back to 1/1992; prior in books from 1805 by first defendant name only. Access to current/pending Supreme Court civil cases is at http://e.courts.state.ny.us/. Civil phone for the Supreme Court clerk 315-785-7912.
Criminal Records: Access: Mail, in person. Both court and visitors may perform in person searches.

Search fee: $5.00 per name. Fee is per 2 years searched. Required to search: name, years to search; also helpful: DOB, signed release. Criminal records on computer back to 1/1992; prior in books from 1805 by first defendant name only. Phone for the county court clerk is 315-785-3044.
General Information: Public Access terminal is available. No sealed, expunged, adoption, sex offense, juvenile or mental health records released. Will fax results. Copy fee: $.65 per page. The minimum copy fee is $1.30. Cert fee: w/o copy is $1.25 per page - $5.00 minimum; with copy, fee of $.65 per page, $5.20 minimum. Payee: County Clerk of Jefferson County. Personal checks accepted. Prepayment required. Mail requests: SASE required. Mail turnaround time 1 week.

Watertown City Court 245 Washington St, Municipal Bldg, Watertown, NY 13601; 315-785-7785; Fax: 315-785-7818. Hours: 8:30AM-4:30PM (EST). *Misdemeanor, Civil Actions Under $15,000, Eviction, Small Claims.*
Civil Records: Access: Mail, in person. Only the court performs in person searches; visitors may not. Search fee: $6.00 per name. Fee is per name & docket. Required to search: name, years to search. Civil cases indexed by defendant. Civil records in docket books.
Criminal Records: Access: None. No search fee. Criminal records in docket books. The court refuses to permit access to court records unless specific case file given. It is mandatory to send requests to OCA for $52.00 statewide search.
General Information: No sealed records released. Will fax results to local or toll free line. Copy fee: $.50 per page. Cert fee: $6.00. Payee: City Court. Only cashiers checks and money orders accepted. Prepayment required. Mail requests: SASE required. Mail turnaround time same day.

Surrogate Court County Court Complex, 163 Arsenal St, 3rd Fl, Watertown, NY 13601-2562; 315-785-3019; Fax: 315-785-5194. Hours: 9AM-4:30PM Sept-May; 8:30AM-4PM June-Aug (EST). *Probate.*

Jefferson Town/Village Courts. *Misdemeanor- Civil Actions Under $3000- Small Claims.* Adams Justice Court- 315-583-5085, Adams Village Court- 315-232-2632, Alexandria Bay Village Court- 315-482-4786, Alexandria Town Court- 315-482-9637, Antwerp Town Court- 315-659-2432, Brownville Fustice Court- 315-639-6266, Brownville Village Court- 315-782-7650, Cape Vincent Town Court- 315-654-2471, Carthage Village Court- 315-493-2890, Champion Town Court- 315-493-2687, Clayton Town Court- No Phone, Clayton Village Court- 315-686-2427, Dexter Village Court- No Phone, Ellisburg Town Court- 315-846-5116, Glen Park Village Court- 315-788-7889, Henderson Town Court- 315-938-5614, Hounsfield Town Court- 315-646-2030, Leray Town Court- 315-629-0228, Lorraine Town Court- 315-232-2548, Lyme Town Court- 315-893-7544, Orleans Town Court- 315-482-9210, Pamelia Town Court- 315-785-9794, Philadelphia Town Court- 315-642-3421, Philadelphia Village Court- 315-642-3452, Rodman Town Court- 315-232-4029, Rutland Town Court- 315-688-4248, Sackets Harbor Village Court- 315-646-3548, Theresa Town Court- No Phone, Watertown Town Court- No Phone, West Carthage Village Court- 315-493-6345, Wilna Town Court- 315-493-2771, Worth Town Court- No Phone

Kings Borough

Supreme Court - Civil Division 360 Adams St, Brooklyn, NY 11201; 718-643-5894; Fax: 718-643-8187. Hours: 9AM-3PM (EST). *Civil Actions Over $25,000.*
www.courts.state.ny.us/courts/2jd/kings.shtml#sup
Civil Records: Access: In person, online. Visitors must perform in person searches for themselves. Search fee: Free. Required to search: name, years to search; also helpful-index number. Civil cases indexed by defendant. Civil records on computer back to 1993; in books, on microfiche back to 1900s.

Access to current/pending Supreme Court civil cases is at http://e.courts.state.ny.us/. Picture ID required for in person searchers for matrimonial cases.

General Information: Public Access terminal is available. No sealed, expunged, adoption, sex offense, juvenile or mental health records released. Copy fee: $.65 per page. Cert fee: $8.00. Payee: County Clerk. Only cashiers checks and money orders accepted. Prepayment required.

Supreme Court - Criminal 120 Schermerhorn St, Brooklyn, NY 11210; 718-643-4044. Hours: 9:30AM-4:30PM (EST). *Felony, Misdemeanor.* www.courts.state.ny.us/courts/2jd/kings.shtml#sup Note: This court does not perform criminal searches; In person searches can be performed at OCA, 25 Beaver St, NYC, 212-428-2810. Also, search online for future court appearances at http://e.courts.state.ny.us.

Civil Court of the City of New York - Kings Branch 141 Livingston St, Brooklyn, NY 11201; 718-643-5069/643-8133 Clerk. Hours: 9AM-5PM (EST). *Civil Actions Under $25,000, Eviction, Small Claims.*

www.courts.state.ny.us/courts/2jd/kings.shtml#sup
Civil Records: Access: In person only. Visitors must perform in person searches for themselves. No search fee. Required to search: name, years to search. Civil cases indexed by plaintiff. Civil records on computer from 1987 for small claims, 1990 for tenant/landlord, and from January 1998 for civil.

General Information: Public Access terminal is available. (Landlord/tenant, civil, and small claims since 1998.) All records public. Copy fee: $.15 public copying machine fee. Cert fee: $6.00. Payee: NYC Civil Court. Only cashiers checks and money orders accepted. Prepayment required.

Surrogate Court 2 Johnson St, Brooklyn, NY 11201; 718-643-5262; Fax: 718-643-6237. Hours: 9AM-5PM (EST). *Probate.*
www.courts.state.ny.us/courtguides/Guide_24.pdf

Lewis County

Supreme & County Court Courthouse, County Clerk, PO Box 232, Lowville, NY 13367; 315-376-5333 (County); 315-376-5380 (Supreme); Probate phone: 315-376-5368; Fax: 315-376-3768. Hours: 8:30AM-4:30PM (EST). *Felony, Civil.*
Note: Countywide search requests are processed in the manner described below. Misdemeanor records are maintained by city, town and village courts.

Civil Records: Access: Mail, in person, online. Both court and visitors may perform in person searches. Search fee: $10.00 per name. Required to search: name, years to search. Civil cases indexed by defendant only. Civil records on index cards from 1935. Access to current/pending Supreme Court civil cases is at http://e.courts.state.ny.us/.
Criminal Records: Access: Mail, in person. Both court and visitors may perform in person searches. Search fee: $10.00 per name. Required to search: name, years to search. Criminal records on index cards from 1935.
General Information: Public Access terminal is available. No sealed, youthful offender or sex abuse case records released. Will fax results for $1.00 per page. Copy fee: $.65 per page. Cert fee: $5.00. Payee: County Clerk. Personal checks accepted. Prepayment required. Mail requests: SASE required. Mail turnaround time 2 days.

Surrogate Court Courthouse, 7660 State St, Lowville, NY 13367; 315-376-5344; Fax: 315-376-4145. Hours: 8:30AM-4:30PM, Summer-June,July,-Aug-8:30-4PM (EST). *Probate.* Note: Fee is $25 for under 25 years to $70 for over 70 years

Lewis Town/Village Courts. *Misdemeanor- Civil Actions Under $3000- Small Claims.* Croghan Town Court- 315-346-1212, Denmark Town Court- No Phone, Diana Town Court- 315-543-2628, Greig Town Court- No Phone, Lewis Town Court- No Phone, Leyden Town Court- 315-348-6215, Lowville Town Court- 315-376-8070, Lowville Village Court- 315-376-2834, Lyons Falls Village Court- 315-348-8971, Lyonsdale Town Court- No Phone, Martinsburg Town Court- 315-376-2458, New Bremen Town Court- 315-376-3752, Osceola Town Court- 315-599-8869, Pinckney Town Court- No Phone, Port Leyden Village Court- 315-348-6215, Turin Town Court- 315-348-6313, Watson Town Court- 315-376-3866, West Turin Town Court- 315-397-2786

Livingston County

County Clerk 6 Court St, Rm 201, Geneseo, NY 14454; 585-243-7010; Fax: 585-243-7928. Hours: 8:30AM-4:30PM Oct-May; 8AM-4PM June-Sept (EST). *Felony, Civil.*
Note: Countywide search requests made to the County Court Clerk are processed in the manner described below.

Civil Records: Access: Phone, mail, fax, in person, online. Both court and visitors may perform in person searches. Search fee: $2.50 per name per year if a written request. Required to search: name, years to search. Civil cases indexed by defendant only. Civil records on computer since 1996. Plaintiff index available only on computer searches. Access to current/pending Supreme Court civil cases is at http://e.courts.state.ny.us/.
Criminal Records: Access: Phone, mail, fax, in person. Both court and visitors may perform in person searches. Search fee: $2.50 per name per year if a written request. Phone requests: will search computer records back to 1996 only for no fee, but only a few requests. Required to search: name, years to search. Criminal records on computer since 1996. Plaintiff index available only on computer searches. Misdemeanor records are maintained by city, town and village courts. Fax requests accepted with payment.
General Information: Public Access terminal is available. No sealed or youthful offender records released. Will not fax results unless prepaid or to a toll-free number. Copy fee: $.65 per page. Cert fee: $5.00 plus $1.25 per page after first 4. Payee: County Clerk. Personal checks and money roders accepted. Prepayment required. Mail requests: SASE required. Mail turnaround time same day.

Supreme & County Court 2 Court St, Geneseo, NY 14454; 585-243-7060. Hours: 8:30AM-4:30PM; 8AM-4PM Summer (EST). *Felony, Civil.*
Note: County-Court directs felony search requests to the OCA for a $52.00 statewide search fee. See also County Clerk in separate listing. Access to current/pending Supreme Court civil cases is available at http://e.courts.state.ny.us/.

Surrogate Court 2 Court St, Geneseo, NY 14454; 585-243-7095; Fax: 585-243-7583. Hours: 9AM-5PM (EST). *Probate.*
Note: Search records over 25 years old is $70.00 search fee; if under 25 years old then $25.00 fee.

Livingston Town/Village Courts. *Misdemeanor- Civil Actions Under $3000- Small Claims.* Avon Town Court- 585-226-2130, Avon Village Court- 585-226-3660, Caledonia Town Court- 585-538-4927, Caledonia Village Court- 585-538-9810, Conesus Town Court- 585-346-3130, Dansville Village Court- 716-335-2460, Geneseo Town Court- 585-243-4530, Geneseo Village Court- 585-243-4350, Groveland Town Court- 585-243-3782, Leicester Town Court- 585-382-9419, Lima Town Court- 585-582-1011, Livonia Town Court- 585-346-

3710, Mount Morris Town Court- 585-658-2333, Mount Morris Village Court- 585-658-3249, North Dansville Town Court- 585-335-2460, Nunda Town Court- 585-468-2215, Ossian Town Court- No Phone, Portage Town Court- No Phone, Sparta Town Court- No Phone, Springwater Town Court- 585-669-2635, West Sparta Town Court- 585-335-2443, York Town Court- 585-243-0666

Madison County

County Clerk County Office Bldg, PO Box 668, Wampsville, NY 13163; 315-366-2261; Probate phone: 315-366-2392; Fax: 315-366-2615. Hours: 9AM-5PM (EST). *Felony, Civil.*
Note: Countywide search requests made to the County Clerk are processed in the manner described below. Misdemeanor records are maintained by city, town and village courts.

Civil Records: Access: Mail, in person, online. Both court and visitors may perform in person searches. Search fee: $5.00 per name. Fee is per 5 years searched. Required to search: name, years to search. Civil cases indexed by defendant. Judgment records on computer from 1992, prior in books. Access to current/pending Supreme Court civil cases and some closed cases is at http://e.courts.state.ny.us/.
Criminal Records: Access: Mail, in person. Only the court performs in person searches; visitors may not. Search fee: $5.00 per name per 5 years. Required to search: name, years to search, DOB. Criminal records on computer to 1989, previous years in books.
General Information: Public Access terminal is available. (Terminal has civil only, no criminal.) No sealed, expunged, adoption, sex offense, juvenile or mental health records released. Copy fee: $1.00 per page. Cert fee: Minimum $5.00; $1.00 per page if over 4 pages. Payee: County Clerk. Personal checks accepted. Prepayment required. Mail requests: SASE required. Mail turnaround time 2 days.

Supreme & County Court PO Box 545, Wampsville, NY 13163; 315-366-2267. Hours: 9AM-5PM (EST). *Felony, Civil.*
Note: Direct countywide search requests to County Clerk, see separate listing. Access to current/pending Supreme Court civil cases and some closed cases is available at http://e.courts.state.ny.us/. Misdemeanor records maintained by city, town, village courts.

Oneida City Court 109 N Main St, Oneida, NY 13421; 315-363-1310; Fax: 315-363-3230. Hours: 8:30AM-4:30PM (EST). *Misdemeanor, Civil Actions Under $15,000, Eviction, Small Claims.*
Civil Records: Access: Mail, in person. Only the court performs in person searches; visitors may not. Search fee: $5.00 per name per 2 years searched for records prior to 1990, other years are $16.00 per name. Required to search: name, years to search. Civil cases indexed by plaintiff. Civil records on computer from 1990, prior in books back to 1950s.
Criminal Records: Access: None. No search fee. Criminal records on computer back to 1989; prior in books back to 1950s. All criminal record search requests made to the Court Clerk are forwarded to the OCA for processing (see Introduction).
General Information: No sealed, expunged, sex offense, mental health or youthful offender records released. Will fax results to local or toll free line. Copy fee: $.65 per page. Cert fee: $6.00. Payee: City Court. Personal checks accepted. Prepayment required. Mail requests: SASE required. Mail turnaround time 1-2 days.

Surrogate Court PO Box 607, Wampsville, NY 13163; 315-366-2392; Fax: 315-366-2539. Hours: 9AM-5PM (EST). *Probate.*

Madison Town/Village Courts. *Misdemeanor- Civil Actions Under $3000- Small Claims.* Brookfield Town Court- No Phone, Canastota Village Court- 315-697-

9410, Cazenovia Town Court- 315-655-4011, Cazenovia Village Court- 315-655-4011, Chittenango Village Court- No Phone, De Ruyter Town Court- 315-852-9650, Eaton Town Court- 315-684-9111, Fenner Town Court- 315-655-2705, Georgetown Town Court- 315-837-4795, Hamilton Town Court- 315-824-3508, Hamilton Village Court- 315-824-3508, Lebanon Town Court- 315-837-4835, Lenox Town Court- No Phone, Lincoln Town Court- 315-697-7018, Madison Town Court- 315-893-7544, Madison Village Court- , Morrisville Village Court- 315-684-3154, Nelson Town Court- 315-655-8582, Smithfield Town Court- No Phone, Stockbridge Town Court- 315-495-3333, Sullivan Town Court- 315-687-3347, Wampsville Village Court- 315-363-5810

Monroe County

County Clerk County Office Bldg, County Clerk Office, 39 Main St West, Rochester, NY 14614; 585-428-5151; Fax: 716-428-4698. Hours: 9AM-5PM (EST). *Felony, Civil.* www.clerk.co.monroe.ny.us
Note: Countywide search requests made to the County Clerk are processed in the manner described below.

Civil Records: Access: Fax, mail, online, in person. Both court and visitors may perform in person searches. Search fee: $5.00 per name. Fee is per 2 years searched. Required to search: name, years to search. Civil cases indexed by defendant. Civil records on computer since 6/93, prior in books. Online access to felony, civil, and divorce records free online at www.clerk.co.monroe.ny.us. Records go back to 6/1993, and earlier film images are being added. Call 585-428-5151 for username, password, or more information. Also, access to current Supreme court cases and some closed cases is at http://e.courts.state.ny.us/.

Criminal Records: Access: Fax, mail, online, in person. Both court and visitors may perform in person searches. Search fee: $5.00 per name; fee is per 2 years searched. A $5.00 blanket index search is also available. Required to search: name, years to search, DOB. Criminal records on computer since 6/93, prior in books. Online access to criminal records is the same as civil.

General Information: Public Access terminal is available. No sealed, divorce records, confidential files released. Copy fee: $.65 per page. $1.30 minimum. Call Tom Fiorilli for more information. Cert fee: $5.00 plus $1.25 per page after first 4. Payee: County Clerk. Personal checks accepted. Prepayment required. Mail requests: SASE required. Mail turnaround time 2 weeks.

Supreme & County Court 545 Hall of Justice, 99 Exchange Blvd, Rochester, NY 14614; 585-428-5001. Hours: 9AM-5PM (EST). *Felony, Civil.* www.clerk.co.monroe.ny.us
Note: Direct countywide search requests to the County Clerk, see separate listing. Online access to courts records free online at www.clerk.co.monroe.ny.us. Current Supreme court cases and some closed cases is available at http://e.courts.state.ny.us/.

Rochester City Court - Civil 99 Exchange Blvd, Hall of Justice, Rm 6, Rochester, NY 14614; 585-428-2444; Fax: 585-428-2588. Hours: 9AM-5PM (EST). *Civil Actions Under $15,000, Eviction, Small Claims.*
Civil Records: Access: In person. Both court and visitors may perform in person searches. No search fee. Required to search: name, years to search. Civil cases indexed by defendant, plaintiff. Civil records on computer from 1983, prior in books from 1973.
General Information: Public Access terminal is available. No sealed, expunged, probation reports, adoption, sex offense, juvenile or mental health records released. Copy fee: $1.00 per page; add $2.00 if older records are located offsite. Cert fee: $6.00.

Only cashiers checks and money orders accepted. Prepayment required.

Rochester City Court - Criminal 150 S Plymouth, Rm 123, Public Safety Bldg, Rochester, NY 14614; 585-428-2447; Fax: 585-428-2732. Hours: 9AM-5PM (EST). *Misdemeanor.*
Criminal Records: Access: In person. Search fee: Certificate of disposition is $5.00. Required to search: Name, years to search, date (for Certificate of Disposition). Criminal records on computer since 1986, prior on books from 1973. The court directs name searches to the OCA for $52.00 statewide search, unless specific docket number given. In person searches limited to pending and current cases on the public access terminal.
General Information: Public Access terminal is available. (Terminal has pending cases only.) No sealed, expunged, probation reports, adoption, sex offense, juvenile or mental health records released. Copy fee: $1.00 per page (none of Certificate of Disposition). Cert fee: No charge. Payee: City Court. Only cashiers checks and money orders accepted. Prepayment required. Mail requests: SASE required. Mail turnaround time 1 week.

Surrogate Court Hall of Justice, Rm 541, 99 Exchange Blvd, Rochester, NY 14614; 585-428-5200; Fax: 585-428-2650. Hours: 9AM-5PM (EST). *Probate.*

Monroe Town/Village Courts. *Misdemeanor- Civil Actions Under $3000- Small Claims.* Brighton Town Court- 585-473-8849, Chili Town Court- 585-889-1999, Clarkson Town Court- 585-637-1134, East Rochester Town Court- 585-385-2576, Fairport Village Court- 585-223-0316, Gates Town Court- 585-247-6106, Greece Town Court- 585-227-3155, Hamlin Town Court- 585-964-8641, Henrietta Town Court- 585-359-2640, Honeoye Falls Village Court- 585-624-1711, Irondequoit Town Court- 585-336-6040, Mendon Town Court- 585-624-6064, Ogden Town Court- 716-352-3498, Parma Town Court- 585-392-9470, Penfield Town Court- 585-377-8623, Perinton Town Court- 585-223-0770, Pittsford Town Court- 585-248-6238, Riga Town Court- 716-193-3884, Rush Town Court- 716-533-1130, Sweden Town Court- 716-637-9157, Webster Town Court- 585-872-1000, Wheatland Town Court- 585-889-3074

Montgomery County

County Clerk PO Box 1500, 64 E Broadway, County Office Bldg, Fonda, NY 12068; 518-853-8113. Hours: 9AM-5PM; 8:30AM-4PM (civil) (EST). *Felony, Misdemeanor, Civil.* Note: Countywide record search requests made to the County Clerk are processed in the manner described below.
Civil Records: Access: Mail, in person, online. Both court and visitors may perform in person searches. Search fee: $5.00 per name. Fee is per 2 years searched. Required to search: name, years to search, address. Civil cases indexed by defendant, plaintiff. Civil records in books and on index cards back to 1965; on computer back to 1992. Access to current/pending Supreme Court civil cases is at http://e.courts.state.ny.us/.
Criminal Records: Access: In person only. Visitors must perform in person searches for themselves. No search fee. Required to search: name, years to search, DOB. Criminal records on computer back to 1992; file index back to 1965.
General Information: Public Access terminal is available. (Terminal is for civil cases only.) No sealed or youthful offender records released. Copy fee: $1.00 per page. Cert fee: $4.00 plus $1.00 per page after first. Payee: County Clerk. Personal checks accepted. Prepayment required. Mail requests: SASE required. Mail turnaround time 1 week.

Supreme & County Court PO Box 1500, Montgomery County Courthouse, Fonda, NY 12068; Civil phone: 518-853-4516; Fax: 518-853-3596. Hours: 9AM-5PM (EST). *Felony, Misdemeanor, Civil.*
Note: See County Clerk for civil search. See state OCA for $52.00 felony search. Court keeps its own Misdemeanor cases only; also search city, town, village courts. Access to current/pending Supreme Ct. civil cases is available at http://e.courts.state.ny.us/.

Amsterdam City Court Public Safety Bldg, Rm 208, One Guy Park Ave Ext, Amsterdam, NY 12010; 518-842-9510; Fax: 518-843-8474. Hours: 8AM-4PM (EST). *Misdemeanor, Civil Actions Under $15,000, Eviction, Small Claims.*
Civil Records: Access: Mail, in person. Only the court performs in person searches; visitors may not. Search fee: $16.00 per name. Required to search: name, years to search. Civil cases indexed by defendant. Civil records on computer since 1995, prior on index cards.
Criminal Records: Access: Mail, in person. Search fee: A Certificate of Disposition from this court is $6.00. Required to search: DOB and years to search. Criminal records on computer from 11/93, prior on index cards. All criminal record name search requests are directed to the OCA for statewide record search, $52.00 search fee. This court does not have acces to county records.
General Information: No sealed, expunged, adoption, sex offense, juvenile or mental health records released. Will fax results to local or toll free line. Copy fee: $.65 per page. Cert fee: $10.00. Payee: City Court. Only cashiers checks and money orders accepted. Prepayment required. Mail requests: SASE required. Mail turnaround time 1 week.

Surrogate Court 58 Broadway, PO Box 1500, Fonda, NY 12068; 518-853-8108; Fax: 518-853-8230. Hours: 9AM-5PM (EST). *Probate.*

Montgomery Town/Village Courts. *Misdemeanor- Civil Actions Under $3000- Small Claims.* Amsterdam Town Court- 518-842-7961, Canajoharie Town Court- 518-673-3013, Canajoharie Village Court- 518-673-5116, Charleston Town Court- 518-922-6771, Florida Town Court- 518-843-6468, Fultonville Village Court- 518-853-3166, Glen Town Court- 518-853-4825, Minden Town Court- 518-568-2728 Or 518-993-5180, Mohawk Town Court- 518-853-3031, Palatine Town Court- No Phone, Root Town Court- 518-673-3422, St Johnsville Justice Court- 518-568-2662, St Johnsville Village Court- 518-568-5298

Nassau County

County Clerk 240 Old Country Rd, Mineola, NY 11501; 516-571-2272. Hours: 9AM-5PM (EST). *Felony, Civil Actions Over $15,000.* www.co.nassau.ny.us/clerk/
Note: Holds records for the Supreme Court and for the County Court. As a rule, this office directs search requests to the OCA for the $52.00 statewide search, however, the records department can perform in person searches as described below.

Civil Records: Access: Mail, in person, online. Both court and visitors may perform in person searches. Search fee: $5.00 per name per 2 years. Required to search: name, years to search. Civil cases indexed by defendant, plaintiff. Civil records on computer from 1992, prior in books. Search supreme court decisions for free at http://www3.courts.state.ny.us/10jd/nassau/decisions/search/. Answers to record search questions-Bob at County Clerk office 516-571-1448.
Criminal Records: Access: None. The county clerk has felony case "minutes" from the County Court, but "minutes" data is only accessible by attorney's with a written letter of request. For full records, contact the County Court.

General Information: Public Access terminal is available. No sealed, expunged, adoption, sex offense, juvenile or mental health records released. Copy fee: $.65 per page; $1.30 minimum. Cert fee: $5.00. Includes up to 4 pages, then $1.25 per page additional. Includes copy fees. Payee: Nassau County Clerk's Office. Personal checks accepted. Prepayment required. Mail requests: SASE required. Mail turnaround time 3 weeks for cases prior to 1996.

Supreme Court Supreme Court Bldg, 100 Supreme Court Dr, Mineola, NY 11501; Civil phone: 516-571-2906. Hours: 9AM-5PM (EST). *Civil Actions Over $15,000.*
www.co.nassau.ny.us/clerk/
Note: All physical records are maintained at the County Clerk's Office (see entry for County Clerk) 240 Old Country Rd, Mineola, 516-571-2272. Also, search supreme court decisions for free at http://www3.courts.state.ny.us/10jd/nassau/decisions/search/.

County Court 262 Old Country Rd, Mineola, NY 11501; 516-571-2800; Fax: 516-571-2160. Hours: 9AM-5PM (EST). *Felony.*
www.co.nassau.ny.us/clerk
Criminal Records: Access: In person only. Only the court performs in person searches; visitors may not. Search fee: $2.00 here (search for older records) but is $52.00 statewide search if done by OCA. Required to search: name, years to search, DOB. Criminal records on computer from 1982, prior in archives or on microfilm. Search online for future court appearances at http://e.courts.state.ny.us. The County Court clerk directs felony search requests to the OCA for a statewide record search. However, the court will search pre-1982 records, which are on books only. Also, for "minutes," you may contact records section of the County Clerk office at 240 Old Country Rd, Mineola, NY, 11501, 516-571-2272. Minutes records are restricted to attorneys only.
General Information: No sealed, expunged, sex offense, juvenile, or mental health records released. Copy fee: $.65 per page. $1.30 minimum. Cert fee: $5.20. Payee: Clerk of Court. Only cashiers checks and money orders accepted. Prepayment required. Mail turnaround time up to 3 weeks for pre-1982 records only.

District Court - 1st & 2nd Districts 99 Main St, Hempstead, NY 11550; 516-572-2355; Civil phone: 516-572-2266. Hours: 9AM-5PM (EST). *Misdemeanor, Civil Actions Under $15,000, Eviction, Small Claims.*
Note: Records for 2nd District are separate prior to 1980. 1st District handles Misdemeanor case records.
Civil Records: Access: In person only. Only the court performs in person searches; visitors may not. Search fee: fee varies, but no guarantee when search will get done. Required to search: name, years to search. Civil cases indexed by defendant, plaintiff. Civil records on computer back to 1980, prior in books back to 1960.
Criminal Records: Access: None. No search fee. Criminal records on computer back to 1980, prior in books back to 1960. The court refuses to permit access to court records unless specific case file given. It is suggested to send requests to OCA for $52.00 statewide search. Search online for future court appearances at http://e.courts.state.ny.us.
General Information: No sealed records released. Copy fee: $1.30. Add $.65 per page after 2. Cert fee: $5.00. Payee: Clerk of Court. Only cashiers checks and money orders accepted. Prepayment required.

District Court - 3rd District 435 Middle Neck Rd, Great Neck, NY 11023; 516-571-8400/8401; Fax: 516-571-8403. Hours: 9AM-5PM (EST). *Misdemeanor, Civil Actions Under $15,000, Eviction, Small Claims.*
Note: Court has records only for its district. Records include Town of North Hempstead ordinance violations.
Civil Records: Access: In person only. Only the court performs in person searches; visitors may not. No search fee. Required to search: name, years to search. Civil cases indexed by defendant, plaintiff. Civil records on computer from 1989, prior in books. The court directs requests to OCA for $52.00 statewide search.
General Information: No sealed, expunged, adoption, sex offense, juvenile or mental health records released. Will not fax results. Copy fee: $.65 per page, $1.30 minimum. Cert fee: $6.00. Payee: Clerk of Court. Only cashiers checks and money orders accepted. Prepayment required.

District Court - 4th District PO Box 910, Hicksville, NY 11802-0910; 516-572-2355. Hours: 9AM-5PM (EST). *Civil Actions Under $15,000, Eviction, Small Claims.* Note: Court temporarily closed. Records at District Court 1st & 2nd District in Hempstead, 516-572-2355.

Glen Cove City Court 13 Glen St, Glen Cove, NY 11542-2704; 516-676-0109; Fax: 516-676-1570. Hours: 9AM-5PM (EST). *Misdemeanor, Civil Actions Under $15,000, Eviction, Small Claims.*
Civil Records: Access: Mail, fax, in person. Only the court performs in person searches; visitors may not. Search fee: $16.00 per name. Required to search: name, years to search. Civil records go back to 1970; on computer back to 1996.
Criminal Records: Access: None. No search fee. Criminal records go back to 1966; on computer back to 1996. The court refuses to permit access to court records unless specific case file given. It is suggested to send requests to OCA for $52.00 statewide search.
General Information: No sealed, expunged, adoption, sex offense, juvenile or mental health records released. Copy fee: $.65 per page; minimum $1.30. Cert fee: $5.00. Payee: Glen Cove City Court. Only cashiers checks and money orders accepted. Prepayment required. Mail requests: SASE required. Mail turnaround time 3-5 days.

Long Beach City Court 1 W Chester St, Long Beach, NY 11561; 516-431-1000; Fax: 516-889-3511. Hours: 9AM-5PM (EST). *Misdemeanor, Civil Actions Under $15,000, Eviction, Small Claims.*
Civil Records: Access: Mail, in person. Only the court performs in person searches; visitors may not. Search fee: $16.00 if case number not known. Required to search: name, years to search.
Criminal Records: Access: None. No search fee. Criminal records on computer from 1997. The court refuses to permit access to court records unless specific case file given. It is suggested to send requests to OCA for $52.00 statewide search.
General Information: No sealed, expunged, adoption, sex offense, juvenile or mental health records released. Copy fee: $.65 per copy, $1.30 minimum. Cert fee: $6.00. Payee: City Court of Long Beach. Only cashiers checks and money orders accepted. Prepayment required. Mail turnaround time 2 days.

Surrogate Court 262 Old Country Rd, Mineola, NY 11501; 516-571-2082; Fax: 516-571-3864. Hours: 9AM-5PM (EST). *Probate.*

Nassau Town/Village Courts. *Misdemeanor- Civil Actions Under $3000- Small Claims.* Atlantic Beach Village Court- 516-371-4552, Bayville Village Court- 516-628-1410, Bellerose Village Court- 516-358-2962,

Brookville Village Court- 516-922-8191, Cedarhurst Village Court- 516-295-5522, Centre Island Village Court- 516-922-0606, Cove Neck Village Court- 516-624-9600, East Hills Village Court- 516-621-4251, East Rockaway Village Court- No Phone, Farmingdale Village Court- 516-293-2292, Floral Park Village Court- 516-326-6325, Flower Hill Village Court- 516-627-8877, Freeport Village Court- 516-377-2329, Garden City Justice Court- 516-742-9886, Great Neck Estates Village Court- 516-482-6430, Great Neck Plaza Village Court- 516-482-4500, Great Neck Village Court- 516-487-0775, Hempstead Village Court- 516-489-3400, Hewlett Bay Park Village Court- 516-295-1400, Island Park Village Court- 516-431-0600, Kensington Village Court- 516-482-4409, Kings Point Village Court- 516-482-7872, Lake Success Village Court- 516-482-7430, Lattington Village Court- 516-681-9271, Laurel Hollow Village Court- 516-692-8826, Lawrence Village Court- 516-239-9166, Lynbrook Village Court- 516-599-0416, Malverne Village Court- 516-599-1200, Manorhaven Village Court- 516- 883-7000, Massapequa Park Village Court- 516-798-0244, Matinecock Village Court- 516-922-8198, Mill Neck Village Court- 516-922-6722, Mineola Village Court- 516-746-0754, Munsey Park Village Court- 516-365-7790, Muttontown Village Court- 516-364-2240, New Hyde Park Village Court- 516-354-6330, North Hills Village Court- 516- 627-3451, Old Brookville Village Court- (516) 624-6332, Old Westbury Village Court- 516-626-0809, Oyster Bay Cove Village Court- 516-681-9271, Plandome Heights Village Court- 516-627-1136, Plandome Manor Village Court- 516-627-3701, Plandome Village Court- 516-627-1748, Rockville Centre Village Court- 516-678-9233, Roslyn Estates Village Court- 516-621-3541, Roslyn Harbor Village Court- 516-621-7261, Roslyn Village Court- 516-621-1961, Russell Gardens Village Court- 516-482-8246, Saddle Rock Village Court- (516) 482-9400, Sands Point Village Court- 516-627-1748, Sea Cliff Village Court- 516-671-0328, South Floral Park Village Court- 516-353-8047, Stewart Manor Village Court- 516-354-1800, Thomaston Village Court- 516-482-3110, Upper Brookville Village Court- 516-676-5619, Valley Stream Village Court- 516- 825-4200, Westbury Village Court- 516-334-1700, Williston Park Village Court- 516-248-5150, Woodsburgh Village Court.

New York City

Supreme Court - Civil Division County Clerk, 60 Centre St, Rm 103, New York City, NY 10007; 212-374-4704/374-8339. Hours: 9AM-3PM (EST). *Civil Actions.*
www.nycourts.gov/supctmanh/
Note: Record search requests are managed by the County Clerk office; information here is for that County Clerk office.

Civil Records: Access: Mail, in person, online. Both court and visitors may perform in person searches. Search fee: $5.00 per name. Fee is per 2 years searched. Required to search: name, years to search. Civil cases indexed by defendant, plaintiff. Civil records on computer from 1993, prior in books; records go back to 1971. Access to current/pending Supreme Court civil cases is at http://e.courts.state.ny.us/. Statewide Commercial Division civil decisions may be searched online at http://decisions.courts.state.ny.us/nyscomdiv/search/comdivintro.htm. Case number or defendant/plaintiff name or judge. Also, search decisions at http://portal.courts.state.ny.us/pls/portal30/CMS_DEV.DECISIONS_NDAWCASE.show_parms.
General Information: Public Access terminal is available. (Terminal located in Rm 103B.) Copy fee: $.25 per page. Cert fee: $8.00 per document. Payee: County Clerk. Only cashiers checks and money orders accepted. Prepayment required. Mail requests: SASE required. Mail turnaround time 1 month.

Supreme Court - Criminal Division 100 Centre St, Rm 1000, New York, NY 10013; 212-374-4985; Criminal phone: 212-374-4190. Hours: 9AM-5PM (EST). *Felony, Misdemeanor.* Note: The Court will only process mail or in person requests for specific documents or papers related to felony cases.
Criminal Records: Access: Mail, in person. Visitors must perform in person searches themselves. No search fee if in person. A Certificate of Disposition is

$10.00. Required to search: name, years to search, DOB (case number or other date identifier is required for a Certificate of Disposition). Criminal records on computer from 1977, prior records archived. Search online for future court appearances at http://e.courts.state.ny.us. Written requests for name searches must be directed to OCA for $52.00 statewide record search. Will accept requests for specific documents via fax (must call first; they will not release fax number) or via email at asknyscr@courts.state.ny.us.

General Information: Public Access terminal is available. (A public terminal is planned and MAY be operational.) No sealed, expunged, adoption, sex offense, juvenile or mental health records released. Copy fee: $.15 per page self-serve. Cert fee: $8.00 per document; $10.00 for certificate of disposition. Payee: Office of Court Administration. No personal checks accepted. Prepayment required.

Civil Court of the City of New York 111

Centre St, New York, NY 10013; 212-374-4646; Fax: 212-374-5709. Hours: 9AM-5PM (EST). *Civil Actions Under $25,000, Eviction, Small Claims.*

Civil Records: Access: Mail, in person, phone. Visitors must perform in person searches for themselves. No search fee. Required to search: name, years to search; also helpful: address. Civil cases indexed by plaintiff; computerized records since 1994. Landlord/Tenant records on computer from 1984, civil from 1994, prior in books. Records are archived after 3 years; search by defendant available only from 6/94 on.

General Information: Public Access terminal is available. (Records go back to 1994.) no sealed records released. No copy fee. Cert fee: $6.00. Payee: Clerk of Civil Court. Only cashiers checks and money orders accepted. Attorney's and certified checks accepted. Prepayment required. Mail requests: SASE required.

Surrogate Court 31 Chambers St, New York

City, NY 10007; 212-374-8233, 374-8232. Hours: 9AM-5PM (EST). *Probate.*
www.courts.state.ny.us/courts/nyc/surrogates/index.shtml

Niagara County

County Clerk 175 Hawley St, Lockport, NY 14094; 716-439-7030; Probate phone: 716-439-7135; Fax: 716-439-7066. Hours: 9AM-5PM; 8:30AM-4:30PM Summer Hours (EST). *Felony, Civil Actions Over $25,000.*

Note: County Clerk maintains records for the Supreme Court (Civil) and the County Court (criminal).

Civil Records: Access: Mail, fax, in person, online. Both court and visitors may perform in person searches. Search fee: $5.00 per name per 2 years. Required to search: name, years to search. Civil cases indexed by defendant. Civil records in index books back to 1950, computerized since 1997. Access to current/pending Supreme Court civil cases is at http://e.courts.state.ny.us/. Will accept fax requests if payment arrangement is made in advance.

Criminal Records: Access: Mail, fax, in person. Both court and visitors may perform in person searches. Search fee: $5.00 per name per 2 years. Required to search: Name, years to search, DOB. Criminal records on computer since 1/96; prior records in books. Will accept fax requests if payment arrangement is made in advance.

General Information: Public Access terminal is available. No sealed or youthful offender records released. Will fax results for add'l $3.00 per name. Copy fee: $1.00 per page. Cert fee: $5.00. Payee: County Clerk. Personal checks and money orders accepted. Prepayment required. Mail requests: SASE not required. Mail turnaround time 3-5 days.

Supreme Court 775 3rd St, Niagara Falls, NY 14302; 716-278-1800; Probate phone: 716-439-7135; Fax: 716-278-1809. Hours: 9AM-5PM (EST). *Civil Actions Over $25,000.*

Note: All records are maintained at County Clerk office, 175 Hawley St, Lockport, NY 14094, 716-439-7030. Also, access to current/pending Supreme Court civil cases is available at http://e.courts.state.ny.us/.

County Court Courthouse, 175 Hawley St, Lockport, NY 14094; 716-439-7022; Probate phone: 716-439-7035; Fax: 716-439-7066. Hours: 9AM-5PM (EST). *Felony, Civil Actions Under $25,000.*

Note: All records are maintained at County Clerk office, 175 Hawley St, Lockport, NY 14094, 716-439-7030.

Lockport City Court Municipal Bldg, One Locks Plaza, Lockport, NY 14094; Civil phone: 716-439-6660; Criminal phone: 716-439-6671; Fax: 716-439-6684. Hours: 8AM-4:30PM (EST). *Misdemeanor, Civil Actions Under $15,000, Eviction, Small Claims.*

Civil Records: Access: Phone, fax, mail, in person. Both court and visitors may perform in person searches. Search fee: $16.00 per name. Required to search: name, years to search. Civil cases indexed by defendant. Civil records on computer from 1988, prior in books from 1900s.

Criminal Records: Access: None. No search fee. Criminal records in books from 1977 forward; computerized since 1988. The court refuses to permit access to criminal records unless specific case file given. It is suggested to send requests to OCA for $52.00 statewide search.

General Information: No sealed, expunged, adoption, sex offense, juvenile or mental health records released. Will fax results to local or toll free line. Copy fee: $1.00 per page. Cert fee: $5.00. Payee: City Court of Lockport. Only cashiers checks and money orders accepted. Prepayment required. Mail requests: SASE required. Mail turnaround 1 week.

Niagara Falls City Court PO Box 1586, Niagara Falls, NY 14302-2725; 716-278-9800; Civil phone: 716-278-9860; Criminal phone: 716-278-9800; Fax: 716-278-9809. Hours: 8:30AM-4:30PM (EST). *Misdemeanor, Civil Actions Under $15,000, Eviction, Small Claims.*

Civil Records: Access: Mail, in person. Both court and visitors may perform in person searches. Search fee: $5.00 per name for 2 years; computer search is $16.00. Required to search: name, years to search. Civil cases indexed by defendant. Civil records on microfilm from 1985, in books since 1970.

Criminal Records: Access: Mail, in person. Only the court performs in person searches; visitors may not. Search fee: A certificate of Disposition is $5.00. Criminal records in books from 1970. The court refuses to permit access to criminal court records unless specific case file given. All criminal record name search requests are directed to the OCA for statewide record search, $52.00 search fee.

General Information: No sealed, expunged, adoption, sex offense, juvenile or mental health records released. Copy fee: $1.00 per page. Payee: City Court of Niagara Falls. No checks accepted. Prepayment required. Mail requests: SASE required. Mail turnaround time 7-10 working days.

North Tonawanda City Court City Hall, North Tonawanda, NY 14120-5446; 716-693-1010; Fax: 716-743-1754. Hours: 8AM-5PM (EST). *Misdemeanor, Civil Actions Under $15,000, Eviction, Small Claims.*

Civil Records: Access: Mail, in person. Only the court performs in person searches; visitors may not.

Search fee: $5.00 for transcript. Required to search: name, years to search. Civil cases indexed by defendant. Civil records on computer from 1993, prior in books.

Criminal Records: Access: Mail, in person. Only the court performs in person searches; visitors may not. Search fee: $5.00 per name. Required to search: Name, exact date of arrest, DOB. Criminal records on computer from 1986, prior in books. This court will do a criminal search but they warn that the date of arrest must be included. The court suggests to send requests to OCA for $52.00 statewide search.

General Information: No sealed, expunged, adoption, sex offense, juvenile or mental health records released. Will fax results for $5.00 fee. Copy fee: $1.00 per page. Cert fee: $5.00. Payee: City Court. Only cashiers checks and money orders accepted. Prepayment required. Mail requests: SASE requested. Turnaround time 2-5 days.

Surrogate Court Niagara's County Courthouse, 175 Hawley St, Lockport, NY 14094; 716-439-7130/7131; Fax: 716-439-7319. Hours: 9AM-5PM (EST). *Probate.*

Niagara Town/Village Courts. *Misdemeanor- Civil Actions Under $3000- Small Claims.* Barker Village Court- 716-795-9193, Cambria Town Court- 716-433-7664, Hartland Town Court- 716-735-7239, Lewiston Town Court- 716-754-8213, Lockport Town Court- 716-439-9528, Newfane Town Court- 716-778-9292, Niagara Town Court- 716-215-1480, Pendleton Town Court- 716-625-8833, Porter Town Court- 716-745-7036 Ext 6, Royalton Town Court- 716-772-2588, Somerset Town Court- 716-795-9193, Wheatfield Town Court- 716-694-6793, Wilson Town Court- 716-751-0549, Wilson Village Court- 716-751-0549

Oneida County

County Clerk 800 Park Ave, Utica, NY 13501; Civil phone: 315-798-5776; Criminal phone: 315-798-5797; Fax: 315-798-6440. Hours: 8:30AM-5PM, 8:30AM-4:30PM Summer hours (EST). *Felony, Civil.*

Note: Search requests made to the County Clerk are processed in the manner described below.

Civil Records: Access: Mail, fax, in person, online. Both court and visitors may perform in person searches. Search fee: $5.00 per name. Fee is for 2 year search. Required to search: name, years to search. Civil cases indexed by defendant, plaintiff. Civil records on computer from 1992, prior in books by plaintiff only. Access to current/pending Supreme Court civil cases is at http://e.courts.state.ny.us/.

Criminal Records: Access: Mail, fax, in person. Both court and visitors may perform in person searches. Search fee: $5.00 per name. Fee is for 2 years searched. Required to search: name, years to search, DOB, signed release. Criminal records on computer from 1992, prior in books by defendant only.

General Information: Public Access terminal is available. No sealed, expunged, adoption, sex offense, juvenile or mental health records released. Will fax results for $1.00 per page plus copy fee. Copy fee: $.65 per page, $1.30 minimum. Cert fee: $5.00. Payee: County Clerk. Personal checks accepted. Prepayment required. Mail requests: SASE required. Mail turnaround time 1 week.

Supreme & County Court 200 Elizabeth St, Utica, NY 13501; 315-798-5889. Hours: 9AM-5PM; 8:30AM-4:30PM Summer hours (EST). *Felony, Civil.* Note: Direct record search requests to the County Clerk, see separate listing. Also, access to current/pending Supreme Court civil cases is available at http://e.courts.state.ny.us/.

Rome City Court 100 W Court St, Rome, NY 13440; 315-337-6440; Fax: 315-338-0343. Hours: 8:30AM-4:30PM; 8:30AM-4PM Summer Hours (EST). *Misdemeanor, Civil Actions Under $15,000, Eviction, Small Claims.*
Civil Records: Access: Mail, in person. Only the court performs in person searches; visitors may not. Search fee: $5.00 per name per 2 years. Required to search: name, years to search. Civil cases indexed by defendant, plaintiff. Civil records in books and some on computer.
Criminal Records: Access: In person. Only the court performs in person searches; visitors may not. Search fee: $5.00 per name per 2 years. Also, a Certificate of Disposition is $6.00. Required to search: name, years to search, (case number, arrest date for Cert. of Disposition). As a rule, this court does not permit access to court records unless specific case file given. It is suggested to send requests to OCA for $52.00 statewide search. However, aware that the state system does not include certain "violation" records, this court does allow an in person hand search.
General Information: No sealed or youthful offender records released. Will fax results to local or toll free line. Copy fee: $.50 per page. $1.00 minimum. Cert fee: $5.00. Payee: Rome City Court. Only cashiers checks and money orders accepted. Prepayment required. Mail requests: SASE required. Mail turnaround time 5-7 days.

Sherrill City Court 373 Sherrill Rd, Sherrill, NY 13461; 315-363-0996; Fax: 315-363-1176. Hours: 8AM-4PM (EST). *Misdemeanor, Civil Actions Under $15,000, Eviction, Small Claims.*
Civil Records: Access: Mail, in person. Only the court performs in person searches; visitors may not. Search fee: $5.00 per name per 2 year period. Required to search: name, years to search. Civil cases indexed by defendant only. Civil records in books since 1988, rest archived.
Criminal Records: Access: Mail, in person. Only the court performs in person searches; visitors may not. Search fee: $5.00 per name per 2 year period. Also, a Certificate of Disposition is $6.00. Required to search: name, DOB, years to search. Criminal records in books since 1800s. Though the court will do a name search of their records, they suggest to send requests to OCA for $52.00 statewide search.
General Information: No sealed, expunged, adoption, sex offense, juvenile or mental health records released. Copy fee: $.65 per page. Cert fee: $6.00. Payee: Sherrill City Court. Personal checks accepted. Prepayment required. Mail requests: SASE requested. Turnaround time 1-2 days.

Utica City Court 411 Oriskany St West, Utica, NY 13502; Civil phone: 315-724-8157; Criminal phone: 315-724-8227; Fax: 315-724-0762 (criminal)/792-8038 (civil). Hours: 8:30AM-4:30PM (EST). *Misdemeanor, Civil Actions Under $15,000, Eviction, Small Claims.*
Civil Records: Access: Mail, in person. Both court and visitors may perform in person searches. No search fee. Required to search: name, years to search, address. Civil cases indexed by defendant. Civil records in books from 1900s, computerized records back to 1980s.
Criminal Records: Access: None. Criminal records in books from 1900s, computerized records back to 1980s. The court refuses to permit access to court

records unless specific case file given. It is suggested to send requests to OCA for $52.00 statewide search.
General Information: No sealed, expunged, adoption, sex offense, juvenile or mental health records released. Copy fee: $.50 per page. $1.00 minimum. Cert fee: $5.00. Payee: City Court of Utica. Only cashiers checks and money orders accepted. Prepayment required. Mail requests: SASE required. Mail turnaround time 1-2 days.

Surrogate Court Oneida County Office Bldg - 8th Fl, 800 Park Ave, Utica, NY 13501; 315-797-923; Fax: 315-797-9237. Hours: 8:30AM-4:30PM Sept-May; 8:30AM-4PM June-Aug (EST). *Probate.*
Oneida Town/Village Courts. *Misdemeanor- Civil Actions Under $3000- Small Claims.* Annsville Town Court- 315-336-1295, Augusta Town Court- 315-843-4811, Ava Town Court- 315-942-6542, Boonville Town Court- 315-943-2071, Boonville Village Court- 315-943-2070, Bridgewater Town Court- 315-822-5909, Camden Town Court- 315-245-0817, Deerfield Town Court- 315-724-0605, Florence Town Court- No Phone, Floyd Town Court- 315-865-4256, Forestport Town Court- 315-392-2801, Kirkland Town Court- 315-853-4538, Lee Town Court- 315-336-1585, Marcy Town Court- , Marshall Town Court- 315-841-8515, New Hartford Town Court- 315-732-5924, New Hartford Village Court- 315-732-5924, New York Mills Village Court- 315-736-7811, Oriskany Village Court- 315-736-6349, Paris Town Court- 315-839-6208, Remsen Town Court- 315-831-5330, Sangerfield Town Court- 315-841-4108, Steuben Town Court- , Sylvan Beach Village Court- 315-762-4246, Trenton Town Court- 315-896-4510, Vernon Town & Village Court- 315-829-4481, Verona Town Court- 315-363-4394, Vienna Town Court- 315-245-2191, Waterville Village Court- 315-841-8007, Western Town Court- 315-827-4928, Westmoreland Town Court- 315-853-4333, Whitesboro Village Court- 315-736-4353, Whitestown Town Court- 315-736-1251

Onondaga County

County Clerk 401 Montgomery St, Rm 200, Syracuse, NY 13202; 315-435-8200; Civil phone: 315-435-2234; Criminal phone: 315-435-2236. Hours: 8AM-5PM (EST). *Felony, Civil.*
Note: Countywide record search requests made to the County Clerk are processed in the manner described below. All requests must be in writing.
Civil Records: Access: Mail, in person, online. Both court and visitors may perform in person searches. Search fee: $2.50 per name per year. Required to search: name, years to search. Civil cases indexed by defendant, plaintiff. Civil records on computer from 1989, prior in books but can only search by plaintiff name. Access to current/pending Supreme Court civil cases is at http://e.courts.state.ny.us/.
Criminal Records: Access: Mail, in person. Both court and visitors may perform in person searches. Search fee: $2.50 per name per year. Required to search: name, years to search; also helpful: DOB. Criminal records computerized from 1990, prior in books.
General Information: Public Access terminal is available. No sealed, divorce, judgment or sexual abuse records released. Will not fax results. Copy fee: $.65 per page. $1.30 minimum. Cert fee: $5.00 minimum; $1.25 add'l after 4 pages. Payee: County Clerk. Personal checks accepted; $60.00 limit. Prepayment required. Mail requests: SASE required. Mail turnaround time 2-3 days.

Supreme Court 401 Montgomery St, 3rd Fl, Syracuse, NY 13202; 315-671-1030. Hours: 8AM-5PM (EST). *Civil.*
Note: Search requests to Supreme Court forwarded to the OCA for processing. Countywide only searches can be performed at the County Clerk, see separate listing. Access to current/pending Supreme Court civil cases is available at http://e.courts.state.ny.us/.

County Court 505 S State St, Syracuse, NY 13202; 315-671-1020. 8AM-5PM (EST). *Felony.*
Note: Search requests made to County-Court are forwarded to the OCA for processing of $52.00 statewide record search. Countywide only searches can be performed at the County Clerk office, see separate listing.

Syracuse City Court 505 State St, Rm 130, Syracuse, NY 13202-2179; 315-671-2773; Civil phone: 315-671-2782; Criminal phone: 315-671-2760; Fax: 315-671-2742 Civil; 671-2744 criminal. Hours: 9AM-4PM (EST). *Misdemeanor, Civil Actions Under $15,000, Eviction, Small Claims.*
Note: Small claims phone is 315-671-2784; their fax is 315-671-2741
Civil Records: Access: Phone, fax, mail, in person. Only the court performs in person searches; visitors may not. Search fee: $5.00 per 2 years searched. Required to search: name, years to search; also helpful: address. Civil cases indexed by defendant, plaintiff or index #. Civil records on computer from 1993, from 1980-98 on fiche or microfilm.
Criminal Records: Access: Phone, fax, mail, in person. Only the court performs in person searches; visitors may not. No search fee. Required to search: name, years to search, DOB; also helpful: offense. Criminal records from 1960 to present are on either computer, dockets or manual books. If the case file is in electronic format, the court will direct searchers to the OCA staewide record search. Otherwise, search fee is $5.00 for each 2 years searched.
General Information: No sealed, expunged, adoption, sex offense, juvenile or mental health records released. Copy fee: $.50 per page. $1.00 minimum. Cert fee: $6.00 cert fee is for civil only; criminal records searched manully are certified as part of search fee. Payee: Syracuse City Court. Only cashiers checks, money orders and attorney checks accepted. Prepayment required. Mail requests: SASE required. Mail turnaround time 1-2 weeks.

Surrogate Court Onondaga Courthouse, Rm 209, 401 Montgomery St, Syracuse, NY 13202; 315-671-2100; Fax: 315-671-1162. Hours: 9AM-5PM (EST). *Probate.*
http://surrogate5th.courts.state.ny.us/public
Onadaga Town/Village Courts. *Misdemeanor- Civil Actions Under $3000- Small Claims.* Baldwinsville Village Court- 315-635-6355, Camillus Town Court- 315-487-7066, Cicero Town Court- 315-699-8478, Clay Town Court- 315-652-3800, De Witt Town Court- 315-446-9180, East Syracuse Village Court- 315-437-6456, Elbridge Town Court- 315-689-7380, Fabius Town Court- 315-696-8725, Fayetteville Village Court- 315-637-8070, Geddes Town Court- 315-468-3613, Jordan Village Court- 315-689-7350, La Fayette Town Court- 315-637-8070, Liverpool Village Court- 315-457-5379, Lysander Town Court- 315-638-1308, Manlius Town Court- 315-637-3251, Manlius Village Court- 315-682-7245, Marcellus Town Court- 315-673-1773, Minoa Village Court- 315-656-2203, North Syracuse Justice Court- 315-458-4695, Onondaga Town Court- 315-469-1674, Otisco Town Court- 315-696-6771, Pompey Town Court- 315-682-9877, Salina Town Court- 315-457 4252, Skaneateles Town Court- 315-685-5880, Solvay Village Court- 315-468-1608, Spafford Town Court- No Phone, Tully Town Court- 315-696-5884, Van Buren Town Court- 315-635-3523

Ontario County

County Clerk 20 Ontario St, Municipal Bldg, Canandaigua, NY 14424; Civil phone: 585-396-4205; Criminal phone: 585-393-2953; Fax: 585-393-2951. Hours: 8:30AM-5PM (EST). *Felony, Civil.*
Note: All criminal record search requests made to the Supreme Court Clerk are forwarded to the OCA for processing (see Introduction). Criminal search requests made to the County Court Clerk are processed in the manner described below.

Civil Records: Access: Fax, mail, in person, online. Both court and visitors may perform in person searches. No search fee. Required to search: name, years to search. Civil cases indexed by defendant, plaintiff. Civil records on computer from 1992, records go back to 1887. Access to current/pending Supreme Court civil cases is at http://e.courts.state.ny.us.

Criminal Records: Access: Fax, mail, in person. Both court and visitors may perform in person searches. Search fee: $5.00 per name. Required to search: name, years to search; also helpful-DOB. Criminal records on computer from 1990, records go back to 1919.

General Information: Public Access terminal is available. No sealed, youthful offender, sex abuse, sex crime, divorce or sealed records released. Will fax civil search results for fee of $1.50 1st page; $1.00 per pager thereafter. There is no fax fee to fax back criminal search results. Copy fee: $.65 per page, minimum $1.30. Cert fee: minimum $5.20 if you prepare ($.65 each copy); $5.00 minimum if they prepare ($1.25 each copy). Payee: County Clerk. Personal checks accepted. Prepayment required. Mail requests: SASE required. Mail turnaround 1 week.

Supreme & County Court 27 N Main St, Rm 130, Canandaigua, NY 14424-1447; 585-396-4239; Criminal phone: 585-396-4025; Fax: 585-396-4576. Hours: 8:30AM-5PM (EST). *Felony, Civil.*

Note: Direct search requests to the County Clerk, see separate listing. Also, access to current/pending Supreme Court civil cases is available at http://e.courts.state.ny.us.

Canandaigua City Court 2 N Main St, Canandaigua, NY 14424-1448; 585-396-5011; Fax: 585-396-5012. Hours: 8AM-4PM (EST). *Misdemeanor, Civil Actions Under $15,000, Eviction, Small Claims.*

Note: Court web site should be available in late 2004.

Civil Records: Access: Mail, in person. Only the court performs in person searches; visitors may not. Search fee: $5.00 per two years searched. Required to search: name, years to search. Civil cases indexed by defendant, plaintiff. Civil records on computer from 1986, prior in books from 1960.

Criminal Records: Access: None. No search fee. Criminal records on computer from 1986, prior in books from 1960. The court refuses to permit access to court records unless specific case file given. It is suggested to send requests to OCA for $52.00 statewide search.

General Information: No sealed, expunged, adoption, sex offense, juvenile or mental health records released. Copy fee: $.50 per page. Cert fee: $5.00. Payee: Canandaigua City Court. Only cashiers checks and money orders accepted. Prepayment required. Mail requests: SASE required. Mail turnaround time 1 week.

Geneva City Court 255 Exchange St, Geneva, NY 14456; 315-789-6560; Fax: 315-781-2802. Hours: 8AM-4PM (EST). *Misdemeanor, Civil Actions Under $15,000, Eviction, Small Claims.*

Civil Records: Access: Phone, mail, in person. Only the court performs in person searches; visitors may not. No search fee. Required to search: name, years to search. Civil cases indexed by plaintiff. Civil records on computer from 1992, prior in books.

Criminal Records: Access: None. No search fee. Criminal records on computer from 1992, prior in books. The court refuses to permit access to court records unless specific case file given. It is suggested to send requests to OCA for $52.00 statewide search. We do not do criminal record search. A statewide search procedure is now in efect (212) 428-2943.

General Information: No youthful offender records released. Will fax results to local or toll free line. Copy fee: $1.00 per page. Cert fee: $6.00. Payee: City Court. Only cashiers checks and money orders accepted. Prepayment required. Mail requests: SASE required. Mail turnaround time 1 month.

Surrogate Court 27 N Main St, Canandaigua, NY 14424-1447; 585-396-4055; Fax: 585-396-4576. Hours: 9AM-5PM (EST). *Probate.*

Ontario Town/Village Courts. *Misdemeanor- Civil Actions Under $3000- Small Claims.* Bristol Town Court- 585-229-4523, Canadice Town Court- 585-367-3590, Canandaigua Town Court- 585-394-9040, Clifton Springs Village Court- 315-462-3048, East Bloomfield Town Court- 585-657-7248, Farmington Town Court- 315-986-3113 Or 8195, Geneva Town Court- 315-789-1100, Gorham Town Court- 585-526-6298, Hopewell Town Court- 585-394-0036, Manchester Town Court- 585-289-6846, Naples Town Court- 585-374-2111, Phelps Town Court- 315-548-2090, Richmond Town Court- No Phone, Seneca Town Court- 585-526-4780, Shortsville Village Court- 585-289-3010, South Bristol Town Court- 585-374-6355, Victor Town Court- 585-924-5775, W Bloomfield Town Court- 716-624-7631

Orange County

County Clerk 255 Main St, Goshen, NY 10924; 845-291-3080; Fax: 845-291-2691. Hours: 9AM-5PM (EST). *Felony, Civil.*

Note: Search requests made to the County Clerk are processed in the manner described below. Misdemeanor records are maintained by city, town, and village courts.

Civil Records: Access: Fax, mail, in person. Both court and visitors may perform in person searches. Search fee: $2.50 per name; $5.00 per 2 years. Required to search: name, years to search. Civil cases indexed by defendant, plaintiff. Civil records on computer from 1993; prior indexed only by plaintiff.

Criminal Records: Access: Fax, mail, in person. Both court and visitors may perform in person searches. Search fee: $2.50 per name per year. Required to search: name, years to search, DOB. Criminal records on computer since 1993; prior on index Rolodex cards.

General Information: Public Access terminal is available. No sealed records released. Will not fax results. Copy fee: $.65 per page. $.25 for self serve. Cert fee: $5.00; $1.25 per page after first 4. Payee: County Clerk. Business checks accepted. Prepayment required. Mail requests: SASE required. Mail turnaround time 2 weeks.

Supreme & County Court 255 Main St, Goshen, NY 10924; Civil phone: 845-291-3111; Criminal phone: 845-291-3100. Hours: 9AM-5PM (EST). *Felony, Civil.*

Note: Direct search requests to County Clerk; see separate listing. The County-Court (criminal court) is at 285 Main St., but records at County Clerk office. Search future criminal court appearances and civil cases online at http://e.courts.state.ny.us.

Middletown City Court 2 James St, Middletown, NY 10940; 845-346-4050; Fax: 845-343-5737. Hours: 8:30AM-4PM (EST). *Misdemeanor, Civil Actions Under $15,000, Eviction, Small Claims.*

Civil Records: Access: Mail, in person. Both court and visitors may perform in person searches. Search fee: No fee unless extensive lists presented, then $16.00 per name. Prior to 1994 is $5.00 per name per 2 year search. Required to search: name, years to search. Civil cases indexed by defendant, plaintiff. Civil records on computer from 1994, prior on cards.

Criminal Records: Access: None. No search fee. Criminal records on computer from 1986, prior on cards. The court refuses to permit access to court

records unless specific case file given. It is suggested to send requests to OCA for $52.00 statewide search.

General Information: No sealed or youthful offender records released. Copy fee: $.65 per page. $1.30 minimum. Cert fee: $5.00. Payee: City Court of Middletown. Only cashiers checks and money orders accepted. Prepayment required. Mail requests: SASE required. Mail turnaround time 2-3 weeks.

Newburgh City Court 57 Broadway, Newburgh, NY 12550; 845-565-3208; Civil phone: 845-565-3074; Criminal phone: 845-565-3208. Hours: 8AM-4PM (EST). *Misdemeanor, Civil Actions Up to $15,000, Eviction, Small Claims.*

Civil Records: Access: Mail, in person. Only the court performs in person searches; visitors may not. Search fee: $5.00 per name per 2 years. Required to search: name, years to search; also helpful- case caption. Civil cases indexed by defendant. Civil records on computer from 1997, prior in docket books or on index cards.

Criminal Records: Access: None. No search fee. Criminal records on computer from 1986. The court refuses to permit access to court records unless specific case file given. It is suggested to send requests to OCA for $52.00 statewide search.

General Information: No sealed, youthful offender or sex abuse victim records released. Will fax results to local or toll free line. Copy fee: $.65 per page. Cert fee: $6.00. Payee: Newburgh City Court. Only cashiers checks and money orders accepted. Prepayment required. Mail requests: SASE required. Mail turnaround time 3-5 days.

Port Jervis City Court 14-18 Hammond St, Port Jervis, NY 12771-2495; 845-858-4034; Fax: 845-858-9883. Hours: 9AM-5PM (EST). *Misdemeanor, Civil Actions Under $15,000, Eviction, Small Claims.*

Civil Records: Access: Mail, in person. Both court and visitors may perform in person searches. No search fee. Required to search: name, years to search. Civil cases indexed by defendant. Civil records on dockets from 1978, computerized since 1996.

Criminal Records: Access: Mail, in person. Search fee: $5.00 per name per 2 years for "violations" only, no misdemeanors. Required to search: Name, years to search. Criminal records on dockets from 1978, computerized since 1996. The court refuses to permit access to misdemeanor records unless specific case file given. It is suggested to send requests to OCA for $52.00 statewide search.

General Information: No sealed, expunged, adoption, sex offense, juvenile or mental health records released. Will not fax results. Copy fee: $.65 per page, $1.30 minimum. Cert fee: $6.00. Payee: City Court of Port jervis. Only cashiers checks and money orders accepted. Prepayment required. Mail requests: SASE required. Mail turnaround 3 weeks.

Surrogate Court 30 Park Place, Surrogate's Courthouse, Goshen, NY 10924; 845-291-2193; Fax: 845-291-2196. Hours: 9AM-5PM; Vault closes at 4PM (EST). *Probate.*

Orange Town/Village Courts. *Misdemeanor- Civil Actions Under $3000- Small Claims.* Blooming Grove Town Court- 845-496-7631, Chester Town Court- 845-469-9541, Chester Village Court- 845-469-8584, Cornwall Town Court- 845-534-8717, Crawford Town Court- 845-744-1435, Deerpark Town Court- 845-856-2928, Florida Village Court- 845-651-4940, Goshen Town Court- 845-294-6477, Goshen Village Court- 845-294-5826, Greenville Town Court- 845-856-5588, Greenwood Lake Village Court- 845-477-9218, Hamptonburgh Town Court- 845-427-5432, Harriman Village Court- 845-782-6143, Highlands Town Court- 845-446-8666, Maybrook Village Court- 845-427-2224, Minisink Town Court- 845-726-3700, Monroe Town Court- 845-783-9733, Montgomery Town Court- 845-457-2620, Montgomery Village Court- 845-457-9037, Mount Hope Town Court- 845-386-5303, New Windsor

Town Court- 845-563-4682, Newburgh Town Court- 845-564-0960, Otisville Village Court- 845-386-1004, Tuxedo Park Village Court- 845-928-2311, Tuxedo Town Court- 845-351-5655, Unionville Village Court- No Phone, Walden Village Court- 845-778-1632, Wallkill Town Court- 845-692-5811, Warwick Town Court- 845-986-1128, Warwick Village Court- 845-986-7044, Washingtonville Village Court- 845-419-9797, Wawayanda Town Court- 845-355-1313, Woodbury Justice Court- 845-928-2311

Orleans County

County Clerk Courthouse, Attn: County Clerk, 3 S. Main, Albion, NY 14411-9998; 585-589-5334; Fax: 585-589-0181. Hours: 9AM-5PM; 8:30AM-4PM Summer hours (EST). *Civil.*
Note: Access civil records through the County Clerk's Office, 585-589-5334. Misdemeaner, Evictions and Small Claims are at Town and Village courts.

Civil Records: Access: Mail, in person, online. Both court and visitors may perform in person searches. Search fee: $5.00 per name. Fee is for 2 year search. Required to search: name, years to search. Civil cases indexed by defendant. Civil records in books to 1940s; on computer back to 1993. Access to current/pending Supreme Court civil cases is at http://e.courts.state.ny.us/.
Criminal Records: Access: In person, mail. Search fee: $52.00 OCA statewide search. Required to search: name, years to search, DOB. Criminal records in books to 1940s; on computer back to 1993. The clerk will only pull specific case files. All criminal record name search requests are directed to the OCA for statewide record search, $52.00 search fee.
General Information: No sealed or divorce records released. Will fax back results. Copy fee: $1.00 per page. Cert fee: $4.00 plus $1.00 per page after first 4. Payee: County Clerk. Personal checks accepted. Prepayment required. Mail requests: SASE required. Mail turnaround time 1 week.

Supreme & County Court Courthouse, 3 S. Main, Albion, NY 14411-9998; 585-589-54457; Fax: 585-589-0632. Hours: 9AM-5PM (EST). *Felony, Civil.*
Note: The court directs felony search requests to the OCA for a $52.00 statewide record search. Access civil records through the County Clerk, see separate entry. Access to current/pending Supreme Court civil cases is available at http://e.courts.state.ny.us/.

Surrogate Court 3 S Main St, Albion, NY 14411; 585-589-4457; Fax: 585-589-0632. Hours: 9AM-5PM (EST). *Probate.*

Orleans Town/Village Courts. *Misdemeanor- Civil Actions Under $3000- Small Claims.* Albion Town Court- 585-589-7048 Ext 18, Albion Village Court- 585-589-2335, Barre Town Court- 585-589-5100, Carlton Town Court- 585-682-3356, Clarendon Justice Court- 585-638-6371 Ext 5, Gaines Town Court- 716-589-4525, Kendall Town Court- 716-659-8540, Medina Village Court- 716-798-4875, Murray Town Court- 716-638-6727, Ridgeway Town Court- 585-798-3282, Shelby Town Court- 585-798-3120, Yates Town Court- 585-765-9603

Oswego County

County Clerk 46 E Bridge St, Oswego, NY 13126; 315-349-8616; Fax: 315-349-8692. Hours: 9AM-5PM (EST). *Felony, Civil.*
Note: Countywide search requests made to the County Court Clerk are processed in the manner described below.

Civil Records: Access: In person, online. Visitors must perform in person searches for themselves. No search fee. Required to search: name, years to search. Civil cases indexed by defendant and plaintiff. Civil records on computer from 1/90, prior in books from 1896. Access to current/pending Supreme Court civil cases is at http://e.courts.state.ny.us/.

Criminal Records: Access: Mail, in person. Only the court performs in person searches; visitors may not. Search fee: $5.00 per name for every 2 years searched. Required to search: name, years to search, DOB, signed release. Criminal records on computer from 1973; prior in docket books from 1939.
General Information: Public Access terminal is available. (The public access terminal is only for civil court records.) No sealed, youthful offender or divorce records released. Will not fax results. Copy fee: $.65 per page with a $1.30 minimum. Cert fee: $5.20 minimum; $1.30 per page after 4 pages. Payee: County Clerk. Personal checks accepted up to $200.00. Prepayment required. Mail requests: SASE required. Mail turnaround time 2-3 days.

Supreme & County Court 46 E Bridge St, Oswego, NY 13126; 315-349-3280. Hours: 9AM-4PM (EST). *Felony, Civil.*
Note: Direct search requests to the County Clerk, see separate listing. Also, access to current/pending Supreme Court civil cases is available at http://e.courts.state.ny.us/.

Fulton City Court 141 S 1st St, Fulton, NY 13069; 315-593-8400; Fax: 315-592-3415. Hours: 8:30AM-4:30PMSummer 8:30AM-4PM (EST). *Misdemeanor, Civil Actions Under $15,000, Eviction, Small Claims.*
Civil Records: Access: Mail, in person. Only the court performs in person searches; visitors may not. No search fee. Required to search: name, years to search. Civil cases indexed by defendant. Civil records on dockets from 1991; computerized records since 1998.
Criminal Records: Access: None. No search fee. Criminal records go back to 1918, computerized records since 1997, criminal records on dockets from 1987. The court refuses to permit access to court records unless specific case file given. It is suggested to send requests to OCA for $52.00 statewide search.
General Information: No sealed, expunged, adoption, sex offense, juvenile or mental health records released. Will fax results to a local or toll free line. Copy fee: $.65 per page. Cert fee: $6.00. Payee: Fulton City Court. Only cashiers checks and money orders accepted. Prepayment required. Mail requests: SASE not required. Mail turnaround time 1 week.

Oswego City Court Conway Muni. Bldg, 20 West Oneida St, Oswego, NY 13126; 315-343-0415; Fax: 315-343-0531. Hours: 8:30AM-5PM (EST). *Misdemeanor, Civil Actions Under $15,000, Eviction, Small Claims.*
Civil Records: Access: Mail, in person. Only the court performs in person searches; visitors may not. No search fee. Required to search: name, years to search. Civil cases indexed by defendant. Civil records on computer from 1987, prior in books.
Criminal Records: Access: None. No search fee. Criminal records on computer from 1987, prior in books. The court refuses to permit access to court records unless specific case file given. It is suggested to send requests to OCA for $52.00 statewide search.
General Information: No sealed or youthful offender records released. Copy fee: $.50 per page. Cert fee: $5.00 plus $.50 per page after first. Payee: Oswego City Court. Only cashiers checks and money orders accepted. Prepayment required. Mail requests: SASE required. Mail turnaround time 3-4 days.

Surrogate Court Courthouse, 25 E Oneida St, Oswego, NY 13126; 315-349-3295. Hours: 9AM-5PM Sept-May; 8:30AM-3:30 PM June-Aug (EST). *Probate.*
Oswego Town/Village Courts. *Misdemeanor- Civil Actions Under $3000- Small Claims.* Albion Town Court- 315-298-6325, Amboy Town Court- 315-964-1165, Boylston Town Court- No Phone, Central Square Village

Court- No Phone, Cleveland Village Court- 315-675-3556, Constantia Town Court- 315-623-7713, Granby Town Court- 315-598-2958, Hannibal Town Court- 315-564-6037, Hastings Town Court- 315-676-4317, Mexico Town Court- 315-963-3785, Minetto Town Court- 315-343-2393, New Haven Town Court- 315-298-5563, Orwell Town Court- 315-298-5563, Oswego Town Court- 315-343-7249, Palermo Town Court- 315-593-2333, Parish Town Court- 315-625-4592, Pulaski Village Court- 315-298-2526, Redfield Town Court- 315-599-7786, Richland Town Court- 315-298-5174, Sandy Creek Town Court- 315-387-5456, Schroeppel Town Court- 315-695-6177, Scriba Town Court- 315-343-3250, Volney Town Court- 315-593-8288, West Monroe Town Court- 315-676-3522, Williamstown Town Court- No Phone

Otsego County

County Clerk 197 Main St, Public Office Bldg, Cooperstown, NY 13326; 607-547-4276. Hours: 9AM-5PM; 8AM-5PM Summer hours. (EST). *Felony, Civil.* Note: Countywide record search requests made to the county clerk are processed in the manner described below.

Civil Records: Access: Mail, in person, online. Both court and visitors may perform in person searches. Search fee: $5.00 per name. Fee is for 2 years. Required to search: name, years to search. Civil cases indexed by defendant. Civil records on computer back to 1997; prior in books. Access to current/pending Supreme Court civil cases is at http://e.courts.state.ny.us/.
Criminal Records: Access: Mail, in person. Both court and visitors may perform in person searches. Search fee: $5.00 per name per 2 years. Required to search: name, years to search, address, DOB. Criminal records on computer back to 1997; prior in books. Misdemeanor records are maintained by city, town and village courts. In person criminal record searches should be performed at the Supreme and County Court office at the courthouse.
General Information: Public Access terminal is available. (County Clerk access terminal has civil cases only; search the criminal index at the Supreme and County Court only.) No sealed, expunged, adoption, sex offense, juvenile or mental health records released. Will fax results on criminal cases. Copy fee: $1.00 per page. Cert fee: $4.00. Payee: County Clerk. Business checks accepted. Prepayment required. Mail requests: SASE required. Mail turnaround time 1-2 days.

Supreme & County Court 193 Main St, Courthouse, Cooperstown, NY 13326; 607-547-4364; Probate phone: 607-547-4213; Fax: 607-547-7567. Hours: 9AM-5PM; 8AM-4PM Summer hours (EST). *Felony, Civil.*
www.nycourts.gov/6jd/CountyMaps/default.html
Note: In person criminal index searches can be made at this address. Direct all other types of search requests to the County Clerk office, see separate listing. Access to current/pending Supreme Court civil cases is available at http://e.courts.state.ny.us/.

Oneonta City Court 81 Main St, Oneonta, NY 13820; 607-432-4480; Fax: 607-432-2328. Hours: 8AM-4PM (EST). *Misdemeanor, Civil Actions Under $15,000, Eviction, Small Claims.*
Civil Records: Access: Mail, in person. Only the court performs in person searches; visitors may not. No search fee. Required to search: name, years to search. Civil cases indexed by defendant. Civil records on computer from 1987, prior in books.
Criminal Records: Access: None. Only the court performs Certicate of Disposition searches only. Search fee: A Certificate of Disposition is available for $5.00. Required to search: Name, case number, signed release. A release form is available from the clerk. Most records go back 6 years; DWAI 10 years. The court does not permit access to county records

unless a specific case file number given. To name search, requesters must use the OCA statewide search.

General Information: No sealed or youthful offender records released. Copy fee: $.65 per page. $1.30 minimum. Cert fee: $5.00. Payee: Oneonta City Court. Prefers certified funds only. Prepayment required. Mail requests: SASE required. Mail turnaround time 1 day.

Surrogate Court Surrogate's Office, 197 Main St, Cooperstown, NY 13326; 607-547-4338; Fax: 607-547-7566. Hours: 9AM-5PM (EST). *Probate.*

Otsego Town/Village Courts. *Misdemeanor- Civil Actions Under $3000- Small Claims.* Burlington Town Court- No Phone, Butternuts Town Court- 607-783-2758, Cherry Valley Town Court- 607-264-8324, Cherry Valley Village Court- 607-264-3791, Cooperstown Village Court- 607-547-9597, Decatur Town Court- 607-397-9116, Edmeston Town Court- 607-965-9823, Exeter Town Court- 315-858-3905, Hartwick Town Court- 607-293-8133, Laurens Town Court & Village Court- 607-433-1053, Maryland Town Court- 607-738-9495, Middlefield Town Court- 607-547-8800, Milford Town Court- 607-286-7773, Morris Town Court & Village Court- 607-263-2224, New Lisbon Town Court- 607-965-8627, Oneonta Town Court- 607-432-0124, Otego Town Court- 607-988-2698, Otsego Town Court- 607-547-5689, Pittsfield Town Court- 607-847-6524, Plainfield Town Court- No Phone, Richfield Springs Village Court- No Phone, Richfield Town Court- 315-858-2830, Roseboom Town Court- 607-264-3293, Springfield Town Court- 315-858-1508, Unadilla Town Court- 607-369-7458, Westford Town Court- 607-397-9210, Worcester Town Court- 607-397-8476

Putnam County

County Clerk 40 Gleneida Ave, County Clerk Office, Carmel, NY 10512; 845-225-3641 X307; Fax: 845-228-0231. Hours: 9AM-5PM; 8AM-4PM Summer hours (EST). *Felony, Civil.*

Note: Search online for future court appearances at http://e.courts.state.ny.us. Criminal search requests made to the County Court Clerk are processed in the manner described below.

Civil Records: Access: Mail, in person, online. Both court and visitors may perform in person searches. Search fee: $5.00 per name. Fee is per 2 years searched. Required to search: name, years to search. Civil cases indexed by defendant, plaintiff. Civil records on computer from 4/93, prior in books. Access to current/pending Supreme Court civil cases is at http://e.courts.state.ny.us/.

Criminal Records: Access: Mail, in person. Both court and visitors may perform in person searches. Search fee: $5.00 per name per certificate of disposition. Required to search: name, years to search, DOB. Criminal records computerized since 1983.

General Information: Public Access terminal is available. No sealed or youthful offender records released. Copy fee: $1.00 per page. Cert fee: $4.00. Payee: County Clerk. Personal checks accepted. Prepayment required. Mail requests: SASE required. Mail turnaround time 2 days.

Supreme & County Court 40 Gleneida Ave, Supreme and County Court, Carmel, NY 10512; 845-225-3641 X1008. Hours: 9AM-5PM (EST). *Felony, Civil.*

Note: For a county only record search, see the county clerk, see separate listing. Search online for future court appearances and for current/pending Supreme Court civil cases at http://e.courts.state.ny.us.

Surrogate's Court Historic Courthouse, 44 Gleneida Ave, Carmel, NY 10512; 845-225-3641 X295; Fax: 845-228-5761. Hours: 9AM-5PM (EST). *Probate.*

Putnam Town/Village Courts. *Misdemeanor- Civil Actions Under $3000- Small Claims.* Brewster Village Court- 845-279-4020, Carmel Town Court- 845-628-1500, Cold Spring Village Court- 845-265-9070, Kent Town Court- 845-225-1606, Nelsonville Village Court-

No Phone, Patterson Town Court- 845-878-1080, Philipstown Town Court- 845-265-2951, Putnam Valley Town Court- 845-526-3050, Southeast Town Court- 845-279-8939

Queens Borough

Supreme Court - Civil Division 88-11 Sutphin Blvd #106, Jamaica, NY 11435; 718-298-1000; Fax: 718-520-2204. Hours: 9AM-5PM, no cashier transactions after 4:45PM (EST). *Civil Actions Over $25,000.*

www.courts.state.ny.us/courts/11jd/index.shtml

Civil Records: Access: Mail, in person, online. Both court and visitors may perform in person searches. Search fee: $10.00 per name. Fee is for first two years. Add $5.00 per additional 2 years. Required to search: name, years to search, address. Civil cases indexed by plaintiff. Civil records on computer from 1992, prior in books. Access to current/pending Supreme Court civil cases is at http://e.courts.state.ny.us/.

General Information: Public Access terminal is available. No marriage or incompetence records released. Identification required to review confidential matrimonial case records. Copy fee: $4.00 per document. Cert fee: $8.00. Payee: County Clerk. Only cashiers checks and money orders accepted. Prepayment required. Mail requests: SASE required. Mail turnaround time 1 week.

Supreme Court - Criminal Division 125-01 Queens Blvd, Kew Gardens, NY 11415; 718-520-3542. Hours: 9:30AM-4:30PM (EST). *Felony, Misdemeanor.*

www.courts.state.ny.us/11jd/queens

Criminal Records: Access: None. No search fee. Search online for future court appearances at http://e.courts.state.ny.us. All criminal record search requests made to the Supreme Court Clerk are forwarded to the OCA for processing (see Introduction).

General Information: Public Access terminal is available. Copy fee: $.15 per page. Cert fee: $8.00 1st page, $1.00 each add'l. Payee: County Clerk. Personal checks accepted. Prepayment required. Mail requests: SASE required.

Supreme Court - Long Is. City 25-10 Court Sq, Long Island City, NY 11101; 718-520-3934; Fax: 718-520-2539. Hours: 9AM-5PM (EST). *Felony, Civil Actions over $25,000.*

www.courts.state.ny.us/11jd/queens/

Note: Trials only here; Criminal records available at Kew Gardens Criminal Court only; Court recommends the OCA $52.00 statewide criminal search. Civil records available only at Jamaica Civil Court only.

Civil Court of the City of New York - Queens Branch 89-17 Sutphin Blvd, Jamaica, NY 11435; 718-262-7100; Civil phone: 212-791-6000. Hours: 9AM-5PM (EST). *Civil Actions Under $25,000, Eviction, Small Claims.* Note: Housing court information telephone number is 212-791-6070.

Civil Records: Access: In person only. Visitors must perform in person searches for themselves. No search fee. Required to search: name, years to search. Civil cases indexed by plaintiff. Civil records on computer from 1997, prior in books.

General Information: Public Access terminal is available. (Housing and civil.) No sealed, youthful offender or sex victim records released. Will not fax results. Copy fee: $.25 per page. Cert fee: $6.00. Payee: Clerk of Civil Court. Only cashiers checks and money orders accepted. Prepayment required. Mail requests: SASE required. Mail turnaround time 3-5 days; 7-10 for older records.

Surrogate Court 88-11 Sutphin Blvd, Jamaica, NY 11435; 718-298-0500. Hours: 9AM-5PM (EST). *Probate.*

www.courts.state.ny.us/11jd/queens/contact_us.htm

Rensselaer County

County Clerk 105 3rd St, Troy, NY 12180; 518-270-4080; Fax: 518-271-7998. Hours: 8:30AM-5PM (EST). *Felony, Civil.*

www.rensco.com Note: Countywide record search requests made to the county clerk are processed in the manner described below.

Civil Records: Access: Mail, in person, online. Visitors must perform in person searches for themselves. Search fee: $10.00 per name. Required to search: name, years to search. Civil cases indexed by plaintiff pre-1996; by defendant & plaintiff after 1996. Civil records on computer back to 1997; prior in books to 1930s. Access to current/pending Supreme Court civil cases is at http://e.courts.state.ny.us/.

Criminal Records: Access: Mail, in person. Only the court performs in person searches; visitors may not. Search fee: $5.00 per name per 2 years. Required to search: name, years to search; also helpful- DOB. Criminal records on computer back to 1986; prior in books to 1976.

General Information: Public Access terminal is available. (Public terminal for civil in person searches only.) No sealed, open/pending cases, youthful offender records released. Copy fee: $1.00 per page. Cert fee: $4.00 plus $.50 per page after first 8. Payee: County Clerk. Personal checks accepted. Prepayment required. Mail requests: SASE required. Mail turnaround time 1 week.

Supreme & County Court 80 2nd St, Troy, NY 12180; 518-270-3711. Hours: 9AM-5PM (EST). *Felony, Civil.*

Note: Direct all search requests to the County Clerk office, see separate listing. Online access to current/pending Supreme Court civil cases is available at http://e.courts.state.ny.us/.

Rensselaer City Court City Hall, Rensselaer, NY 12144; 518-462-6751; Fax: 518-462-3307. Hours: 8AM-3:30PM (EST). *Misdemeanor, Civil Actions Under $15,000, Eviction, Small Claims.*

Civil Records: Access: Mail, in person. Only the court performs in person searches; visitors may not. No search fee. Required to search: name, years to search. Civil cases indexed by defendant. Civil records in books back 10 years; on computer back 2 years. All record name search requests are directed to the OCA for statewide record search, $52.00 search fee.

Criminal Records: Access: Mail, in person. Only the court performs in person searches; visitors may not. Search fee: $6.00 for a Certificate of Disposition only. Required to search: name, years to search, DOB, signed release. Criminal records in books go back 10 years; on computer back 7 years. Court will only confirm convictions with Certicate of Disposition. All criminal record name search requests are directed to the OCA for statewide record search, $52.00 search fee.

General Information: No sealed, expunged, adoption, sex offense, juvenile or mental health records released. Will not fax results. Copy fee: $.50 per page. Cert fee: $6.00. Payee: Rensselaer City Court. Only cashiers checks and money orders accepted. Prepayment required. Mail turnaround time 72 hours.

Troy City Court 51 State St, 2nd Fl, Troy, NY 12180; 518-271-1602; Fax: 518-274-2816. Hours: 9AM-3:30PM (EST). *Misdemeanor.*

Criminal Records: Access: Mail, in person. Only the court performs in person searches; visitors may not.

Search fee: $16.00 per name for certificate of disposition. Required to search: name, years to search, DOB, aliases, offense. Criminal records on computer from 1989, prior in books. Court will only confirm convictions. Name search requests are directed to the state OCA for a $52.00 statewide record check.
General Information: No sealed records released. Copy fee: Copies not made in court's office. Cert fee: $5.00. Payee: City Court. Personal checks accepted. Prepayment required. Mail requests: SASE required. Mail turnaround time 1 week.

Surrogate Court County Courthouse, 80 Second St, Troy, NY 12180; 518-270-3724; Fax: 518-272-5452. Hours: 9AM-5PM (EST). *Probate.*

Rensselaer Town/Village Courts. *Misdemeanor-Civil Actions Under $3000- Small Claims.* Berlin Town Court- 518-650-2020, Brunswick Town Court- 518-279-3461, Castleton-On-Hudson Village Court- 518-732-2211, East Greenbush Town Court- 518-477-5412, Grafton Town Court- 518-279-3565, Hoosick Falls Village Court- 518-686-4399, Hoosick Town Court- 518-686-3335, Nassau Town Court- 518-766-2813, Nassau Village Court- 518-766-3044, North Greenbush Town Court- No Phone, Petersburgh Town Court- 518-658-3777, Pittstown Town Court- No Phone, Poestenkill Town Court- 518-283-5100, Sand Lake Town Court- 518-674-3033, Schaghticoke Town Court- 518-753-6915, Schodack Town Court- 518-477-9390, Stephentown Town Court- 518-733-5636

Richmond County

Supreme Court - Civil Division 130 Stuyvesant Pl, c/o Richmond County Clerk, Staten Island, NY 10301; 718-390-5389 Court Desk; Civil phone: 718-390-5352. Hours: 9AM-5PM (EST). *Civil Actions Over $25,000.*
Civil Records: Access: In person only. Both court and visitors may perform in person searches. Search fee: $5.00 per name per two years. Required to search: name, years to search. Civil cases indexed by plaintiff. Civil records go back to 1990; on computer back to 1993. Access to current/pending Supreme Court civil cases is at http://e.courts.state.ny.us/.
General Information: Public Access terminal is available. No matrimonial records released. Will not fax results. Copy fee: $.25. Cert fee: $8.00. Payee: Richmond County Clerk. Only attorney's checks and money orders accepted. Prepayment required.

Supreme Court - Criminal Division 18 Richmond Terrace, Rm 110, Staten Island, NY 10301; 718-390-2739. Hours: 9AM-5PM, Closed 1-2PM (EST). *Felony, Misdemeanor.*
Criminal Records: Access: Mail, in person. Visitors must perform in person searches for themselves. Search fee: None, but court does not perform name only searches. Court will search for verified (known) cases only and will certify dispositions. Required to search: name, years to search, DOB. A notarized signed release is required for access to sealed records. Criminal records on computer back to 1975, prior archived bacl tp 1960. Search online for future court appearances at http://e.courts.state.ny.us. All criminal record name search requests are directed to the OCA for statewide record search, $52.00 search fee.
General Information: No sealed or youthful offender records released unless to subject. Will not fax results. Copy fee: $.50 per page. Cert fee: $10.00. Payee: County Clerk, Richmond County. Only cashiers checks and money orders accepted. Prepayment required. Mail requests: SASE required. Mail turnaround time 1-2 days.

Civil Court of the City of New York - Richmond Branch 927 Castleton Ave, Staten Island, NY 10310; 718-390-5417/5419. Hours: 9AM-4:30PM (EST). *Civil Actions Under $25,000, Eviction, Small Claims.*
Civil Records: Access: Mail, in person. Both court and visitors may perform in person searches. No search fee. Required to search: name. Civil cases indexed by plaintiff. Civil records on computer since 1999; prior on books.
General Information: Public Access terminal is available. No sealed records released. No copy fee. Cert fee: $6.00. Payee: Clerk Civil Court. Only cashiers checks and money orders accepted. Prepayment required. Mail requests: SASE required. Mail turnaround time 3-5 days.

Surrogate Court 18 Richmond Terrace, Rm 201, Staten Island, NY 10301; 718-390-5400; Fax: 718-390-8741. Hours: 9AM-5PM (EST). *Probate.*

Rockland County

County Clerk 1 S Main St #100, New City, NY 10956; 845-638-5070; Civil phone: x4; Criminal phone: x3. Hours: 7AM-6:30PM M-Th, 7AM-5:30PM F (EST). *Felony, Civil.*
www.rocklandcountyclerk.com
Note: Countywide record search requests made to the county clerk are processed here. Misdemeanor records maintained by city, town, village courts, but this clerk may have a misdemeanor record if you provide the index number.
Civil Records: Access: Mail, online, in person. Both court and visitors may perform in person searches. Search fee: $5.00 per each 2 years searched. Required to search: name, years to search. Civil cases indexed by defendant, plaintiff. Civil records on computer from 1982. Online access to county clerk's index is free at www.rocklandcountyclerk.com/court_records.html. Includes civil judgments, real estate records, tax warrants. Free registration required. Call 845-638-5221 for info. Also, access to current Supreme court cases is at http://e.courts.state.ny.us/.
Criminal Records: Access: Mail, online, in person. Both court and visitors may perform in person searches. Search fee: $5.00 per each 2 years searched. Required to search: name, years to search. Criminal records on computer from 1982. Access to county clerk index is free at www.rocklandcountyclerk.com/court_records.html. Includes criminal index back to 1982. Also, search for future court appearances at http://e.courts.state.ny.us.
General Information: Public Access terminal is available. No retention records released. Will not fax results. Copy fee: $1.25 per page; $5.00 minimum. Cert fee: $1.25 per page; $5.00 minimum. Payee: County Clerk. Personal checks accepted. Prepayment required. Mail requests: SASE required. Mail turnaround time 10 days.

Supreme & County Court 1 S Main St #200, New City, NY 10956; Civil phone: 845-638-5393; Criminal phone: 845-638-5363. Hours: 9AM-5PM (EST). *Felony, Civil.*
Note: Direct all search requests to the County Clerk office, see separate listing. Online access to current/pending Supreme Court civil cases is available at http://e.courts.state.ny.us/. See also county clerk for online access. County-Court is located in #400.

Surrogate Court 15 Main St, #270, New City, NY 10956; 845-638-5330; Fax: 845-638-5632. Hours: 9AM-5PM (EST). *Probate.*

Rockland Town/Village Courts. *Misdemeanor- Civil Actions Under $3000- Small Claims.* Chestnut Ridge Village Court- 845-425-3108, Clarkstown Town Court- 845-639-5960, Grand View-On-Hudson Village Court-

845-358-5078, Haverstraw Town Court- 845-354-7800, Haverstraw Village Court- 914-490-0303, Hillburn Village Court- 845-357-2036, New Hempstead Village Court- 845-354-8101, New Square Village Court- No Phone, Nyack Village Court- 845-358-4464, Orangetown Town Court- 845-359-5100, Piermont Village Court- 845-359-0345, Ramapo Town Court- 845-357-5100, Sloatsburg Village Court- 845-753-2727, South Nyack Village Court- 845-358-5078, Spring Valley Village Court- 845-352-1100, Stony Point Town Court- 845-786-2506, Suffern Village Court- 845-357-6424, Upper Nyack Village Court- 845-358-0084, Wesley Hills Village Court- 845-354-0404, West Haverstraw Village Court- 845-947-1013

Saratoga County

County Clerk 40 McMaster St, Ballston Spa, NY 12020; 518-885-2213 X4410; Fax: 518-884-4726. Hours: 9AM-5PM (EST). *Civil.*
Note: The county clerk does not have a seperate index of criminal records; see the Supreme and County Court.
Civil Records: Access: Mail, in person, online. Both court and visitors may perform in person searches. Search fee: $5.00 per name. Fee is per 2 years searched. Required to search: name, years to search; also helpful: address. Civil cases indexed by defendant, plaintiff. Civil records on computer from 03/88, prior in books. Access to current/pending Supreme Court civil cases is at http://e.courts.state.ny.us/.
General Information: Public Access terminal is available. No youthful offender or divorce records released. Copy fee: $1.25 per page. Cert fee: $5.00 for 1st 4 pages, $1.25 each add'l page. Payee: County Clerk. Personal checks accepted. Prepayment required. Mail requests: SASE required. Mail turnaround time 3-4 days.

Supreme & County Court 30 McMaster St, Ballston Spa, NY 12020; 518-885-2213 X2224. Hours: 9AM-5PM (EST). *Felony, Civil.*
Note: See County Clerk for Supreme court civil case records. Access to current/pending Supreme Court civil cases is available at http://e.courts.state.ny.us/. Misdemeanor records are maintained by city, town and village courts.
Criminal Records: Access: Mail, in person. Both court and visitors may perform in person searches. Search fee: $5.00 per name. Fee is per 2 years searched. Required to search: name, years to search, DOB; also helpful: address. Criminal records not computerized here, on books only. The County-Court directs criminal search requests to the OCA for a $52.00 statewide record check, however, you may search in person at the County-Court clerk office, as described below.
General Information: Public Access terminal is available. No youthful offender or divorce records released. Copy fee: $1.00 per page. Cert fee: $5.00 for 1st 4 pages, $1.25 each add'l page. Payee: County Court Clerk. Personal checks accepted. Prepayment required.

Mechanicville City Court 36 N Main St, Mechanicville, NY 12118; 518-664-9876; Fax: 518-664-8606. 8AM-4PM (EST). *Misdemeanor, Civil Actions Under $15,000, Eviction, Small Claims.*
Civil Records: Access: Mail, in person. Both court and visitors may perform in person searches. Search fee: $16.00 per name. Required to search: name, years to search. Civil cases indexed by defendant. Civil records on computer since 1/94; records go back to 1900.
Criminal Records: Access: None. No search fee. Criminal records on computer from 9/93; records go back to 1900. The court refuses to permit access to court records unless specific case file given. It is suggested to send requests to OCA for $52.00 statewide search.

General Information: No sealed, expunged, adoption, sex offense, juvenile or mental health records released. Will fax results to local or toll free line. Copy fee: $.65 per page; $1.30 minimum. Cert fee: $5.00. Payee: City Court. Personal checks accepted. Prepayment required. Mail requests: SASE required. Mail turnaround time 1 day.

Saratoga Springs City Court City Hall, 474 Broadway, Saratoga Springs, NY 12866; 518-581-1797. Hours: 8AM-4PM (EST). *Misdemeanor, Civil Actions Under $15,000, Eviction, Small Claims.*

Civil Records: Access: Mail, in person. Only the court performs in person searches; visitors may not. Search fee: $5.00 per name per 2 years or $16.00 computer search back to 10/94. Required to search: name, years to search. Civil cases indexed by defendant. Civil records on computer back to 10/94; prior records on index cards.

Criminal Records: Access: None. No search fee. Criminal records on computer back to 08/93. The court refuses to permit access to its records. It says it is required to direct requests to OCA for the $52.00 statewide search.

General Information: Sealed files not released. Will not fax results. Copy fee: $1.00 1st page; $.50 each add'l page. Cert fee: $5.00. Payee: City Court. Only cashiers checks and money orders accepted. Prepayment required. Mail requests: SASE required.

Surrogate Court 30 McMaster St, Bldg 3, Ballston Spa, NY 12020; 518-884-4722; Fax: 518-884-4774. Hours: 9AM-5PM (EST). *Probate.*

Saratoga Town/Village Courts. *Misdemeanor- Civil Actions Under $3000- Small Claims.* Ballston Spa Village Court- 518-885-8559, Ballston Town Court- 518-885-8559, Charlton Town Court- 518-882-1643, Clifton Park Town Court- 518-371-6668, Corinth Town Court- 518-654-6991, Day Town Court- 518-696-3789, Edinburg Town Court- 518-863-3154 Ext 15, Galway Town Court- 518-882-6070, Galway Village Court- 518-882-6070, Greenfield Town Court- 518-893-7432 Ext 310, Hadley Town Court- 518-696-4379, Halfmoon Town Court- 518-371-1592, Malta Town Court- 518-899-2687, Milton Town Court- 518-885-9267, Moreau Town Court- 518-745-0178, Northumberland Town Court- 518-745-0178, Providence Town Court- 518-828-4700, Saratoga Town Court- 518-695-3644, Stillwater Town Court- 518-664-6946, Stillwater Village Court- 518-664-5392, Waterford Town Court- 518-237-6788, Wilton Town Court- 518-587-1980

Schenectady County

County Clerk 620 State St, Attn: County Clerk, Schenectady, NY 12305; 518-388-4222; Fax: 518-388-4224. Hours: 9AM-5PM (EST). *Civil.*

Note: For felony records see the County-Court clerk at the Supreme and County Court in separate listing.

Civil Records: Access: Mail, in person, online. Both court and visitors may perform in person searches. Search fee: $5.00 per name. Fee is per 2 years searched. Required to search: name, years to search. Civil cases indexed by plaintiff. Civil records on computer from 1989, prior on index cards. In person access is only herea at the County Clerk, not the Supreme Court Clerk. Access to current/pending Supreme Court civil cases is at http://e.courts.state.ny.us/.

General Information: Public Access terminal is available. (Civil records only back to 1990.) No sealed, youthful offenders, infant compromise or divorce records released. Will fax results if all fees are paid, or to a toll-free number. Copy fee: $1.00 per page. Cert fee: $4.00; $1.00 each after 4th page. Payee: County Clerk. Personal checks accepted. Prepayment required. Mail requests: SASE required. Mail turnaround time 4 days. Will expedite requests if requested.

Supreme & County Court 612 State St, Schenectady, NY 12305; 518-388-4322; Fax: 518-388-4520. Hours: 9AM-5PM (EST). *Felony, Civil.*

Note: Direct civil record requests to County Clerk, see separate listing. Access to current/pending civil cases is available at http://e.courts.state.ny.us/.

Criminal Records: Access: Mail, in person. Both court and visitors may perform in person searches. Search fee: $5.00 per name per 2 years if done by County Clerk. Required to search: name, years to search, DOB. Criminal records on computer from 1989, prior in index books. The County-Court Clerk gives itself the option of referring criminal record search requests to the OCA for processing for $52.00 fee, or the County-Court may perform the search themselves as shown below.

General Information: No sealed, youthful offenders, infant compromise or divorce records released. Notarized, signed release required to access sealed records. Copy fee: $.50 per page. Cert fee: $5.00. Payee: County Clerk. Personal checks accepted. Prepayment required. Mail requests: SASE required. Mail turnaround time 4 days.

Schenectady City Court - Civil Jay St, City Hall #215, Schenectady, NY 12305; 518-382-5077; Fax: 518-382-5080. Hours: 8AM-4PM (EST). *Civil Actions Under $15,000, Eviction, Small Claims.*

Civil Records: Access: Mail, in person. Only the court performs in person searches; visitors may not. Search fee: $16.00 per name. Required to search: name, years to search. Civil cases indexed by defendant. Civil records on computer from 1981, prior in books.

General Information: No sealed or youthful offender records released. Copy fee: $.50 per page. Cert fee: $6.00. Payee: City Court. Only cashiers checks and money orders accepted. Prepayment required. Mail requests: SASE required. Mail turnaround time 2 weeks.

Schenectady City Court - Criminal 531 Liberty St, Schenectady, NY 12305; 518-382-5239; Fax: 518-382-5241. Hours: 8AM-4PM (EST). *Misdemeanor.*

Criminal Records: Access: None. Search fee: A Certicate of Disposition is $6.00. Required to search: Name, DOB, case number. Criminal records on computer from 1981, prior in books. The court directs name searches to the OCA for $52.00 statewide search, unless specific docket number given.

General Information: No sealed or youthful offender records released. Copy fee: $.50 per page. Cert fee: $6.00. Payee: City Court. Only cashiers checks and money orders accepted. Prepayment required.

Surrogate Court 612 State St, Judicial Bldg, Schenectady, NY 12305; 518-388-4293; Fax: 518-377-6378. Hours: 9AM-5PM (EST). *Probate.*

Schenectady Town/Village Courts. *Misdemeanor- Civil Actions Under $3000- Small Claims.* Duanesburg Town Court- 518-895-8922, Glenville Town Court- 518-382-3851, Niskayuna Town Court- 518-386-4560, Princetown Town Court- 518-864-5256, Rotterdam Town Court- 518-355-7911, Scotia Village Court- 518-374-2099

Schoharie County

Supreme & County Court PO Box 549, 284 Main St, Attn: County Clerk, Schoharie, NY 12157; 518-295-8316 (County Clerk); 518-295-8342 (Supreme); Fax: 518-295-8338. Hours: 8:30AM-5PM (EST). *Felony, Civil, Misdemeanor, Eviction, Small Claims.*

Note: Direct search requests to the County Clerk who pocesses requests in the manner described below.

Civil Records: Access: Fax, mail, in person, online. Both court and visitors may perform in person searches. Search fee: $5.00 per name. Required to search: name, years to search. Civil cases indexed by defendant, plaintiff. Civil records on computer from 1994, prior in books. Access to current/pending court civil cases is at http://e.courts.state.ny.us/.

Criminal Records: Access: Fax, mail, in person. Both court and visitors may perform in person searches. Search fee: $5.00 per name. Required to search: name, years to search, DOB or SSN. Criminal records in books back to 1930; on computer back to 1994.

General Information: Public Access terminal is available. No sealed criminal or divorce records released. Fee to fax results is $1.00 per page unless provided toll-free number. Copy fee: $.50 per page. Cert fee: $4.00. Payee: County Clerk. Personal checks accepted. Prepayment required. Mail requests: SASE required. Mail turnaround time same day.

Surrogate Court Courthouse, 290 Main St, PO Box 669, Schoharie, NY 12157; 518-295-8387. Hours: 9AM-5PM (EST). *Probate.*

Schoharie Town/Village Courts. *Misdemeanor- Civil Actions Under $3000- Small Claims.* Blenheim Town Court- 518-827-6157, Broome Town Court- 518-827-5074, Carlisle Town Court- 518-234-3486, Cobleskill Town And Village Court- 518-234-7886, Conesville Town Court- 607-588-7211, Esperance Town Court- 518-875-6109, Fulton Town Court- 518-827-6300, Gilboa Town Court- 607-588-7526, Jefferson Town Court- 607-652-2109, Middleburgh Town Court- 518-827-5100, Middleburgh Village Court- 518-827-5143, Richmondville Town Court- No Phone, Schoharie Town Court And Village Court- 518-295-7879, Seward Town Court- No Phone, Sharon Town Court- 518-284-3419, Summit Town Court- No Phone, Wright Town Court- 518-872-9726

Schuyler County

County Clerk Courthouse, 105 Ninth St, Unit #8, Watkins Glen, NY 14891; 607-535-8133. Hours: 9AM-5PM (EST). *Felony, Civil.*

Note: Countywide record search requests made to the county clerk are processed in the manner described below.

Civil Records: Access: Phone, mail, in person, online. Both court and visitors may perform in person searches. Search fee: $5.00 per name; a single name search is performed for free via telephone. Required to search: name, years to search. Civil cases indexed by defendant. Civil records are indexed in books; on computer back to 1987. Access to current/pending Supreme Court civil cases and some closed cases is at http://e.courts.state.ny.us/.

Criminal Records: Access: Phone, mail, in person. Only the court performs in person searches; visitors may not. Search fee: $5.00 per name; a single name search is performed for free via telephone. Required to search: name, years to search, DOB. Criminal records are indexed in books; on computer back to 1987. Misdemeanors go back to 1971.

General Information: No sealed or youthful offender records released. No fax at this office. Copy fee: $.65 per page. Cert fee: $5.00; $1.00 per page after 1st 4 pages. Payee: County Clerk. Personal checks accepted. Prepayment required. Mail requests: SASE required. Mail turnaround time 2-3 days.

Supreme & County Court Courthouse, 105 Ninth St, Unit #38, Watkins Glen, NY 14891; Civil phone: 607-535-7760; Criminal phone: 607-535-7015. Hours: 9AM-5PM (EST). *Felony, Civil.*

Note: Court-clerks direct record search requests to the OCA for a $52.00 statewide record check. For county only search requests (including free), see the County Clerk in separate listing. Online access to current cases is at http://e.courts.state.ny.us/.

Surrogate's Court County Courthouse, 105 Ninth St, Watkins Glen, NY 14891; 607-535-7144; Fax: 607-535-4918. 9AM-5PM (EST). *Probate.*

Schuyler Town/Village Courts. *Misdemeanor-Civil Actions Under $3000- Small Claims.* Catharine Town Court- 607-594-2233, Cayuta Town Court- 607-594-2507, Dix Town Court- 607-535-7973, Hector Town Court- 607-546-5286, Montour Falls Village Court- 607-535-7362, Montour Town Court- 607-535-7362, Odessa Village Court- No Phone, Orange Town Court- No Phone, Reading Town Court- No Phone, Tyrone Town Court- No Phone, Watkins Glen Village Court- 607-535-9717

Seneca County

County Clerk 1 DiPronio Dr, County Office Bldg, Attn: Seneca County Clerk, Waterloo, NY 13165-1396; 315-539-1771; Fax: 315-539-3789. Hours: 8:30AM-5PM (EST). *Felony, Civil.*
Note: Countywide record search requests made to the county clerk are processed in the manner described below.

Civil Records: Access: Mail, in person, online. Both court and visitors may perform in person searches. Search fee: $10.00 per name. Required to search: name, years to search. Civil cases indexed by defendant. Civil records on computer since March 1, 1997; prior records in books. Access to current/pending Supreme court civil cases and some closed cases is at http://e.courts.state.ny.us.
Criminal Records: Access: Mail, in person. Both court and visitors may perform in person searches. Search fee: $10.00 per name. Required to search: name, years to search, signed release. Criminal records on computer since March 1, 1997; prior records in books.
General Information: Public Access terminal is available. No divorce records released. Will fax results to local or toll free line. Copy fee: $.65 per page; $.40 per page if self serve. Cert fee: $5.00. Payee: Seneca County Clerk. Personal checks accepted. Prepayment required. Mail requests: SASE required. Mail turnaround time 1 week.

Supreme & County Court 48 Williams St, Courthouse, Waterloo, NY 13165; 315-539-7021; Fax: 315-539-7929. Hours: 9AM-5PM (EST). *Felony, Civil.*
Note: Direct all search requests to the County Clerk office, see separate listing. Online access to current/pending Supreme Court civil cases is available at http://e.courts.state.ny.us/.

Surrogate Court 48 W Williams St, Waterloo, NY 13165; 315-539-7531; Fax: 315-539-3267. Hours: 9AM-5PM (EST). *Probate.*

Seneca Town/Village Courts. *Misdemeanor- Civil Actions Under $3000- Small Claims.* Covert Town Court- 607-387-6802, Fayette Town Court- No Phone, Junius Town Court- 315-539-8910, Lodi Town Court- 607-532-9558, Ovid Town Court- 607-869-9845, Romulus Town Court- 607-869-9650, Seneca Falls Town Court- No Phone, Seneca Falls Village Court- No Phone, Tyre Town Court- No Phone, Varick Town Court- No Phone, Waterloo Town Court- 315-539-3213, Waterloo Village Court- 315-539-2512

St. Lawrence County

Supreme & County Court 48 Court St, Canton, NY 13617-1169; 315-379-2237 (couty clerk); 315-379-2219 (Court Clerk); Probate phone: 315-379-2217; Fax: 315-379-2302. Hours: 8:30AM-4:30PM (Thurs. til 7PM) (EST). *Felony, Civil.*
Note: Direct all search requests to the County Clerk office; information given here is for that County Clerk office.

Civil Records: Access: Fax, mail, in person, online. Both court and visitors may perform in person searches. Search fee: $5.00 per name. Required to search: name, years to search. Civil cases indexed by

defendant, plaintiff. Civil records go back to 1986; on computer since 1990, prior in books. Access to current/pending Supreme Court civil cases is at http://e.courts.state.ny.us/.
Criminal Records: Access: Fax, mail, in person. Both court and visitors may perform in person searches. Search fee: $5.00 per name. Required to search: name, years to search, DOB. Criminal records on computer since 1985, prior in books. Misdemeanor records are maintained by city, town and village courts.
General Information: Public Access terminal is available. (Civil records only on public access terminal.) No sealed or divorce records released. Will fax results $4.00 per document; no fee to toll-free numbers. Copy fee: $.65 per page. Cert fee: $5.00. Payee: County Clerk. Personal checks accepted. Prepayment required. Mail requests: SASE required. Mail turnaround time 2-3 days.

Ogdensburg City Court 330 Ford St, Ogdensburg, NY 13669; 315-393-3941; Fax: 315-393-6839. Hours: 8AM-4PM (EST). *Misdemeanor, Civil Actions Under $15,000, Eviction, Small Claims.*
Civil Records: Access: Mail, in person. Only the court performs in person searches; visitors may not. No search fee. Required to search: name, years to search. Civil cases indexed by defendant. Civil records on computer since 1995; prior records in books.
Criminal Records: Access: None. Search fee: A Certificate of Disposition is $6.00. Computerized records go back to 1992; archives back to 19th Century. The court does not permit access to county records unless a specific case file number given. Requesters must use the $52.00 OCA statewide search.
General Information: No youthful offender records released. Copy fee: $.50 per page. Cert fee: $5.00. Payee: City Court. Business checks accepted. Prepayment required. Mail requests: SASE required. Mail turnaround time 1 week.

Surrogate Court 48 Court St, Surrogate Bldg, Canton, NY 13617; 315-379-2217/9427. Hours: 9AM-5PM Sept-June; 8AM-4PM July-Aug (EST). *Probate.*

St Lawrence Town/Village Courts. *Misdemeanor-Civil Actions Under $3000- Small Claims.* Brasher Town Court- 315-769-5374, Canton Town Court- 315-379-9844, Canton Village Court- 315-379-9844, Clare Town Court- No Phone, Clifton Town Court- 315-848-5522, Colton Town Court- 315-262-2380, De Peyster Town Court- 315-344-7259, Dekalb Town Court- 315-347-2119, Edwards Town Court- 315-562-8113, Fine Town Court- 315-344-7284, Fowler Town Court- 315-287-0045, Gouverneur Town Court- 315-287-4623, Gouverneur Village Court- 315-287-0850, Hammond Town Court- 315-324-5321, Hermon Town Court- No Phone, Hopkinton Town Court- 315-328-4187, Lawrence Town Court- 315-389-4487, Lisbon Town Court- 315-393-0489, Louisville Town Court- 315-764-1424, Macomb Town Court- 315-344-7284, Madrid Town Court- 315-322-5760, Massena Town Court And Village Court- 315-769-5431, Morristown Town Court- 315-375-6510, Norfolk Town Court- 315-268-1722, Oswegatchie Town Court- 315-344-2400, Parishville Town Court- 315-268-1722, Piercefield Town Court- 518-359-7544, Pierrepont Town Court- 315-379-0415, Pitcairn Town Court- 315-543-2111, Potsdam Town Court- 315-265-4318, Potsdam Village Court- 315-265-5890, Rossie Town Court- 315-324-5166, Russell Town Court- 315-347-4825, Stockholm Justice Court- 315-389-5171, Waddington Town Court- 315-388-5629

Steuben County

Supreme & County Court 3 E Pulteney Sq - County Clerk, Bath, NY 14810; 607-776-9631 x3210 (County clerk); x3200 (Court Clerks); Fax: 607-776-2812. Hours: 8:30AM-5PM (EST). *Felony, Civil.*
Note: Direct all search requests to the County Clerk office; information given here is for that County Clerk office.

Civil Records: Access: Fax, mail, in person, online. Both court and visitors may perform in person searches. Search fee: $10.00 per name. Required to search: name, years to search. Civil cases indexed by defendant. Civil records on computer from 1960, in book from 1931, prior archived. Access to current/pending Supreme Court civil cases is at http://e.courts.state.ny.us/.
Criminal Records: Access: Fax, mail, in person. Both court and visitors may perform in person searches. Search fee: $10.00 per name. Required to search: name, years to search, DOB, SSN. Criminal records on computer from 1984, in book from 1931, prior archived.
General Information: Public Access terminal is available. (Terminal provides civil index data only.) No sealed, expunged, adoption, sex offense, juvenile or mental health records released. Will fax results for $3.00 per doc plus $1.00 per page. Copy fee: $.65 per page. Cert fee: $5.00. Payee: County Clerk. Personal checks accepted. Prepayment required. Mail requests: SASE required. Mail turnaround time 1 day.

Corning City Court 12 Civic Center Plaza, Corning, NY 14830-2884; 607-936-4111; Fax: 607-936-0519. Hours: 8AM-4PM (EST). *Misdemeanor, Civil Actions Under $15,000, Eviction, Small Claims.*
Civil Records: Access: Mail, in person. Only the court performs in person searches; visitors may not. Search fee: Fees subject to change; call for details. Required to search: name, years to search. Civil cases indexed by defendant. Civil records on computer from 1986, prior in books. Request must be in writing.
Criminal Records: Access: none. No search fee. Criminal records on computer from 1986, prior in books. The court refuses to permit access to court records unless specific case file given. Requesters are directed to OCA for $52.00 statewide search.
General Information: No sealed or youthful offender records released. Will fax results to local or toll free line. Copy fee: $5.00 per document. Cert fee: $5.00. Payee: Corning City Court. Prepayment required. Mail requests: SASE required. Mail turnaround time 1 week.

Hornell City Court PO Box 627 (82 Main St.), Hornell, NY 14843-0627; 607-324-7531; Fax: 607-324-6325. Hours: 8AM-3:30PM (EST). *Misdemeanor, Civil Actions Under $15,000, Eviction, Small Claims.*
www.nycourts.gov/courts/7jd/hornell/index.shtml
Civil Records: Access: In person. Only the court performs in person searches; visitors may not. No search fee. Required to search: name, years to search, DOB. Civil cases indexed by defendant, plaintiff. Civil records on computer from 1985, prior in books, folders and index cards go back 25 years. The court directs requesters to OCA for $52.00 statewide search.
Criminal Records: Access: None. No search fee. Criminal records on computer from 1985, records go back 25 years. The court will not permit access to court records. The court directs requesters to OCA for $52.00 statewide search.
General Information: No sealed or sexual offense records released. Will fax results to a local or toll free line. Copy fee: $.50 per page. Cert fee: $5.00. Payee: Hornell City Court. Only cashiers checks and money orders accepted. Prepayment required.

Surrogate Court 3 E Pulteney Sq, Bath, NY 14810-1598; 607-776-7126; Fax: 607-776-4987. Hours: 9AM-5PM (EST). *Probate.*

Steuben Town/Village Courts. *Misdemeanor- Civil Actions Under $3000- Small Claims.* Addison Town Court- 607-359-3615, Avoca Town Court And Village Court- 607-566-2093, Bath Town Court And Village Court- 607-776-3192, Bradford Town Court- 607-583-4270, Cameron Town Court- No Phone, Campbell Town Court- 607-527-8244, Canisteo Town Court- No Phone, Canisteo Village Court- 607-698-4378, Caton Town Court- 607-524-6772, Cohocton Town Court- 716-384-5252, Cohocton Village Court- No Phone, Corning Town Court- 607-936-9062, Dansville Town Court- 607-295-9917, Erwin Justice Court- 607-936-3122, Fremont Town Court- 607-324-0789, Greenwood Town Court- 607-225-4558, Hammondsport Village Court- No Phone, Hartsville Town Court- 607-698-2672, Hornby Town Court- 607-962-0683, Hornellsville Town Court- 607-295-7768, Howard Town Court- 607-566-8335, Jasper Town Court- 607-792-3338, Lindley Town Court- 607-523-8816, Prattsburgh Town Court- 607-522-3761, Pulteney Town Court- No Phone, Rathbone Town Court- No Phone, Savona Village Court- , Thurston Town Court- 607-776-9448, Troupsburg Town Court- 607-525-6403, Tuscarora Town Court- 607-359-2360, Urbana Town Court- 607-569-3738, Wayland Town Court And Village Court- 585-728-3504, Wayne Town Court- 607-292-3450, West Union Town Court- No Phone, Wheeler Town Court- No Phone, Woodhull Town Court- 607-458-5178

Suffolk County

Supreme & County Court - Main 310 Centre Dr, Attn: Court Actions, Riverhead, NY 11901; 631-852-3793, 631-852-1462 county; Civil phone: 631-852-3793; Criminal phone: 631-852-2016. Hours: 9AM-5PM (EST). *Felony, Civil.*
www.courts.state.ny.us/courts/10jd/suffolk/supreme.shtml
Civil Records: Access: Mail, in person, online. Both court and visitors may perform in person searches. Search fee: $5.00 per name. Fee is per 2 years searched. Required to search: name, years to search. Civil cases indexed by defendant, plaintiff. Civil records on computer back to 04/84; prior in books. Access to civil actions is free at www.co.suffolk.ny.us/clerk/clerkapp/index.htm.
Access to current/pending Supreme court civil cases and some closed cases is at http://e.courts.state.ny.us/.
Criminal Records: Access: Mail, in person. Both court and visitors may perform in person searches. Search fee: $52.00 statewide record search through OCA for 1985 to present; $5.00 per name per 2 years searched if prior to 1985. Required to search: name, years to search, DOB. Criminal records on computer back to 1984.
General Information: Public Access terminal is available. No sealed or divorce records released. Copy fee: $1.25 per page. Cert fee: $.50 per page, $5.00 minimum. Payee: County Clerk. Personal checks accepted. Prepayment required. Mail requests: SASE required. Mail turnaround time 7-10 days.

Supreme & County Court - Central Islip 400 Carleton Ave, Central Islip, NY 11722; 631-853-5423; Fax: 631-853-5462. Hours: 9AM-5PM (EST). *Felony, Civil.*
www.courts.state.ny.us/courts/10jd/suffolk/index.shtml
Note: Records are only at the Supreme Court in Riverhead.

1st District Court - Criminal 400 Carleton Ave, Central Islip, NY 11722; 631-853-7500 (all county District Courts). Hours: 9AM-5PM (EST). *Misdemeanor.*
http://courts.state.ny.us/courts/10jd/suffolk/dist
Criminal Records: Access: In person only. Court will pull record if docket number and proper identifiers are provided. No search fee. Required to search: Name, DOB. Criminal records go back to 1961; on computer back to 3/2000. Online access to criminal court dates only listed by defendant are free at http://e.courts.state.ny.us/crims. The court does not

permit access to court records unless specific case file is given. Requesters are directed to send requests to OCA for $52.00 statewide search. Also, a Suffolk County only search is through the local Police Department, 631-852-6015.
General Information: No sealed or youthful offender records released. Information for this court only is 631-853-3280. Copy fee: $.65 per page. Cert fee: $6.00. Payee: District Court Clerk. Personal checks accepted with proper ID. Prepayment required.

2nd District Court 375 Cormac Rd, Deer Park, NY 11702; 631-854-1950. Hours: 9AM-1PM, 2-5PM (EST). *Misdemeanor, Civil Actions Under $15,000, Eviction, Small Claims.*
http://courts.state.ny.us/courts/10jd/suffolk
Civil Records: Access: Mail, in person. Only the court performs in person searches; visitors may not. Search fee: $16.00 per name. Required to search: name, years to search. Civil cases indexed by plaintiff. Civil records on computer from 1989, prior in books, on cards.
Criminal Records: Access: None. Only the court performs Certicate of Disposition searches only. Search fee: A Certificate of Disposition is $6.00. Required to search: name, years to search; also helpful-case number. Criminal records on computer from 1989, prior in books, on cards. Online access to criminal court dates only listed by defendant are free at http://e.courts.state.ny.us/crims. The court does not permit access to court records unless specific case file given. Requesters are directed to send name search requests to OCA for $52.00 statewide search.
General Information: No sealed or youthful offender records released. Copy fee: $.65 per page. Cert fee: $6.00 per document. Payee: Clerk of Court. Only cashiers checks and money orders accepted. Prepayment required. Mail requests: SASE required. Mail turnaround time 1 week.

3rd District Court 1850 New York Ave, Huntington Station, NY 11746; 631-854-4545. Hours: 9AM-1PM, 2-4:30PM (EST). *Misdemeanor, Civil Actions Under $15,000, Eviction, Small Claims.*
http://courts.state.ny.us/courts/10jd/suffolk
Civil Records: Access: None. No search fee. Required to search: name, years to search. Civil cases indexed by defendant. Civil records on computer from 1988, prior in books, on microfilm. This court suggests a civil record search be performed at the County Clerk office. This court's civil records are indexed by key letters "HU".
Criminal Records: Access: In person. Only the court performs in person searches; visitors may not. No search fee. Required to search: name, years to search, DOB, SSN, signed release. Criminal records on computer from 1988, prior in books, on microfilm. Only misdemeanor records located here. Direct search requests to OCA for the $52.00 statewide record search for 1985 to present. For older records, you may search here in person; fees dependent on scope of search.
General Information: No sealed records released. Copy fee: $.65 per page. Cert fee: $6.00 per cert. Payee: Clerk of the Court. Business checks accepted. Attorney checks accepted. Prepayment required.

4th District Court North County Complex Bldg C158, Hauppauge, NY 11787; Civil phone: 631-853-5400; Criminal phone: 631-853-5357. Hours: 9AM-5PM (EST). *Misdemeanor, Civil Actions Under $15,000, Eviction, Small Claims.*
http://courts.state.ny.us/courts/10jd/suffolk
Civil Records: Access: Mail, in person. Only the court performs in person searches; visitors may not. Search fee: $16.00 per name. Required to search: name, years to search. Civil cases indexed by

defendant, plaintiff. Civil records on computer from 1987, prior in books.
Criminal Records: Access: None. Only the court performs in person searches; visitors may not. No search fee. Required to search: name, years to search, DOB. Criminal records on computer from 1987, prior in books. Online access to criminal court dates only listed by defendant are free at http://e.courts.state.ny.us/crims. All name searches forwarded to OCA for $52.00 statewide search unless specific docket number given.
General Information: No sealed records released. Will not fax results. Copy fee: $.65 per page. Cert fee: $6.00. Payee: Clerk of Court. Personal checks accepted. Prepayment required. Mail requests: SASE required. Mail turnaround time 1-2 weeks.

6th District Court 150 W Main St, Patchogue, NY 11772; 631-854-1440. Hours: 9AM-5PM (EST). *Misdemeanor, Civil Actions Under $15,000, Eviction, Small Claims.*
http://courts.state.ny.us/courts/10jd/suffolk/
Note: Criminal searches must be done at the OCA. The misdemeanor records here cover only Brookhaven Town Ordinance violations.

Civil Records: Access: Mail, in person. Only the court performs in person searches; visitors may not. Search fee: $16.00 per name. Required to search: name, years to search. Civil records on computer from 1989, prior on microfilm.
Criminal Records: Access: None. No search fee. Criminal records on computer from 1992, prior on microfilm. Online access to criminal court dates only listed by defendant are free at http://e.courts.state.ny.us/crims. The court does not permit access to court records unless specific case file given. It is suggested to send requests to OCA for $52.00 statewide search.
General Information: No sealed or youthful offender records released. Will not fax results. Copy fee: $.65 per page; $1.30 minimum. Cert fee: $6.00. Payee: Clerk of Court. Prepayment required. Mail requests: SASE required. Mail turnaround 3 days.

Suffolk District Courts 1 & 5 - Civil 3105-1 Veterans Memorial Hwy, Ronkonkoma, NY 11779-7614; 631-854-9676 (1st); 9673 (5th). Hours: 9AM-5PM (EST). *Civil Actions Under $15,000, Eviction, Small Claims.*
http://courts.state.ny.us/courts/10jd/suffolk
Civil Records: Access: Mail, in person. Only the court performs in person searches; visitors may not. Search fee: $16.00 per name. Required to search: name, years to search. Civil cases indexed by defendant. Civil records on computer back to 1989, prior in books back to 1969.
General Information: No sealed or youthful offender records released. Will fax results for no fee. Copy fee: $1.30 for one page, $.65 each for 2 or more pages. Cert fee: $6.00. Payee: Clerk of the Court. Cash, checks and money orders accepted. Prepayment required. Mail requests: SASE required. Mail turnaround time 2 weeks.

Surrogate Court 320 Centre Dr, Riverhead, NY 11901; 631-852-1745; Fax: 631-852-1777. Hours: 9AM-5PM (EST). *Probate.*

Suffolk Town/Village Courts. *Misdemeanor- Civil Actions Under $3000- Small Claims.* Amityville Village Court- 631-691-3303, Asharoken Village Court- 631-261-8677, Babylon Village Court- 631-669-1500, Belle Terre Village Court- 631-928-5105, Bellport Village Court- 631-286-0327, Brightwaters Village Court- 631-665-1281/1280, East Hampton Town Court- 631-324-4134, Greenport Village Court- 631-477-0248, Head of the Harbor Village Court- 631-584-5550, Huntington Bay Village Court- 631-427-2843, Islandia Village Court- 631-348-0470, Lake Grove Justice Court- 631-585-2008/2000, Lindenhurst Village Court- 631-957-7509,

Lloyd Harbor Village Court- no phone, Nissequogue Village Court- 631-862-8576, Northport Village Court- 631-757-0935, Ocean Beach Village Court- 631-583-0104, Old Field Village Court- 631-941-9416, Patchogue Village Court- 631-475-2753, Poquott Village Court- 631-331-0402, Port Jefferson Village Court- 631-473-8287, Quogue Village Court- 631-653-9400, Riverhead Justice Court- 631-727-3200, Saltaire Village Court- 631-583-8743, Shelter Island Town Court- 631-749-8989, Shoreham Village Court- 631-821-0680, Southampton Town Court- 631-283-6017, Southampton Village Court- 631-204-2140, Southold Town Court- 631-765-1852, The Branch Village Court- 631-265-3315

Sullivan County

County Clerk 100 North St, Sullivan Gov't Ctr, Monticello, NY 12701; 845-794-3000 x5012; Probate phone: 845-794-3000 x3450. Hours: 9AM-5PM (EST). *Felony, Civil.* Note: Countywide record search requests made to the county clerk are processed in the manner described below.

Civil Records: Access: Phone, mail, in person, online. Both court and visitors may perform in person searches. Search fee: $16.00 per name for 10 years with additional $5.00 for every 2 years prior. These fees ssubject to change. Required to search: name, years to search. Civil cases indexed by plaintiff. Civil records on computer from 1990, prior in books from 1800s. Access to current/pending Supreme Court civil cases is at http://e.courts.state.ny.us/.

Criminal Records: Access: In person only. Only the court performs in person searches; visitors may not. Search fee: None. A Certificate of Disposition is $6.00. Required to search: name, years to search, DOB. Criminal records go back to 1967; on computer back to 4/1990. For mail requests, the County-Court directs criminal search requests to the OCA for a $52.00 statewide record check. For in person requests, first name search the County Clerk index for case numbers. To retrieve case records, take case numbers to the Supreme & County Court (see separate listing) County-Court clerk who will pull cases records for you.

General Information: Public Access terminal is available. (Terminal has civil records only.) No sealed, expunged, adoption, sex offense, juvenile or mental health records released. Copy fee: $.50 per page; $.25 if self serve. Cert fee: $5.00; $5.20 if certification of prepared copy. Payee: County Clerk for civil; to Court Clerk for criminal. Personal checks accepted. Prepayment required. Mail requests: SASE not required. Mail turnaround time 1-2 weeks.

Supreme & County Court County Courthouse, 414 Broadway, Monticello, NY 12701; 845-794-4066; Probate phone: 845-794-3000 x3450. Hours: 9AM-5PM (EST). *Felony, Civil, Misdemeanor.*

Note: Civil records and criminal record index are maintained at County Clerk's office, see separate listing. However, actual felony records are located here at County-Court Clerk office.

Civil Records: Access: Mail, in person, online. Both court and visitors may perform in person searches. No search fee. Required to search: name, years to search. Civil cases indexed by plaintiff. Civil records on computer from 1990, prior in books from 1800s. Access to current/pending Supreme Court civil cases is at http://e.courts.state.ny.us/. Perform civil searches at the Court Clerk office.

Criminal Records: Access: Mail, in person. Only the court performs in person searches; visitors may not. No search fee for in person searches. Required to search: name, years to search, DOB. Criminal records go back to 1967; on computer back to 4/1990. For mail requests, the County-Court directs criminal search requests to the OCA for a $52.00 statewide record check. For in person searches, first find the case index number by performing a search at the

County Clerk office (see separate entry), then ask the county-court clerk office (address above) for case file. **General Information:** Public Access terminal is available. (Terminal has civil records only in County Clerk office.) No sealed, expunged, adoption, sex offense, juvenile or mental health records released. Copy fee: $.50 per page. Cert fee: $4.00. Payee: County Clerk for civil; to Court Clerk for criminal. Personal checks accepted. Prepayment required.

Surrogate Court County Government Center, 100 North St, Monticello, NY 12701; 845-794-3000 X3450/3451; Fax: 845-794-0310. Hours: 9AM-5PM (EST). *Probate.*

Sullivan Town/Village Courts. *Misdemeanor- Civil Actions Under $3000- Small Claims.* Bethel Town Court- 845-583-7420, Bloomingburg Justice Court- 845-733-1400, Callicoon Town Court- 845-482-5390 Ext 301, Cochecton Town Court- No Phone, Delaware Justice Court- 845-887-5250 Ext 8, Fallsburg Town Court- 845-434-4574, Forestburgh Town Court- 845-794-0679, Fremont Town Court- 845-687-4883, Highland Town Court- 845-557-8132, Liberty Justice Court- 845-292-0290, Liberty Town Court- 845-292-6980, Lumberland Town Court- 845-858-8548, Mamakating Town Court- No Phone, Monticello Village Court- , Neversink Town Court- 845-985-7685 Ext 311, Rockland Town Court- 607-498-4320, Thompson Town Court- 845-794-7130, Tusten Town Court- 845-252-3310 Ext 13, Woodridge Village Court- No Phone, Wurtsboro Village Court- No Phone

Tioga County

Court Clerk PO Box 307, 16 Court St, Owego, NY 13827; 607-687-8660; Fax: 607-687-8686. Hours: 9AM-5PM (EST). *Civil, Felony.*

Note: Countywide civil record search requests made to the county clerk are processed in the manner described below. County clerk has only a paper index list of felony proceedings. Felony records are managed by the County-Court Clerk, see separate listing.

Civil Records: Access: In person, online. Visitors must perform in person searches for themselves. No search fee. Required to search: name, years to search. Civil cases indexed by defendant. Civil records in books. Visitor can search in County Clerk's Office. Access to current/pending Supreme Court civil cases is at http://e.courts.state.ny.us/.

General Information: Public Access terminal is available. (Public terminal is newly installed; does not include criminal records.) No sealed, expunged, adoption, sex offense, juvenile or mental health records released. Will not fax results. Copy fee: $.50 per page. Cert fee: $5.00. Payee: County Clerk. Personal checks accepted. Prepayment required. Mail requests: SASE required. Mail turnaround time varies.

Supreme & County Court PO Box 307, 16 Court St, Owego, NY 13827; 607-687-0544; Fax: 607-687-3240. Hours: 8:30AM-4:30PM (EST). *Felony.*

Note: For civil records, see County Clerk. Also, access to current/pending Supreme Court civil cases is available at http://e.courts.state.ny.us/.

Criminal Records: Access: In person only. Both court and visitors may perform in person searches. Search fee: None if in person search. Required to search: name, years to search, DOB. Criminal records in books since 1984. Felony records are managed by the County-Court Clerk who directs search requests to OCA for $52.00 statewide search. You may also search County-court clerk felony files in person; details below.

General Information: No sealed, expunged, sex offense, or juvenile records released. Copy fee: $.50 per page. Cert fee: $5.00. Payee: County Clerk. Personal checks accepted. Prepayment required.

Surrogate Court PO Box 10; 20 Court St, Owego, NY 13827; 607-687-1303; Fax: 607-687-3240. Hours: 9AM-5PM (EST). *Probate.* Note: Court is located in the County Court Annex Bldg.

Tioga Town/Village Courts. *Misdemeanor- Civil Actions Under $3000- Small Claims.* Barton Town Court- 607-565-8609, Berkshire Town Court- 607-657-2705, Candor Town Court And Village Court- 607-659-3175, Newark Valley Town Court- 607-642-8746, Nichols Town Court- 607-642-5278, Owego Town Court- 607-687-2822, Owego Village Court- 607-687-2236, Richford Town Court- No Phone, Spencer Town Court- No Phone, Spencer Village Court- 607-589-4310, Tioga Town Court- 607-687-9577, Waverly Village Court- 607-565-4771

Tompkins County

Supreme & County Court Tomkins County Clerk, 320 N Tioga St, Ithaca, NY 14850; 607-274-5431 (County Clerk); 607-272-0466 (Count Clerks); Fax: 607-274-5445. Hours: 9AM-5PM (Court Clerks have Summer hours-8:30AM-4:30PM) (EST). *Felony, Civil.*

Note: Direct all search requests to the County Clerk office; information given here is for that County Clerk office.

Civil Records: Access: Fax, mail, in person, online. Both court and visitors may perform in person searches. Search fee: $5.00 per name if court does search. Fee is per 2 years searched. Required to search: name, years to search. Civil cases indexed by defendant, plaintiff. Civil records in books. Access to current/pending Supreme Court civil cases is at http://e.courts.state.ny.us/. Before faxing, you must first be approved with a credit account.

Criminal Records: Access: Fax, mail, in person. Only the court performs in person searches; visitors may not. Search fee: $5.00 per name if court does search. Fee is per 2 years searched. Required to search: name, years to search, signed release; also helpful: DOB, SSN. Felony records in books. Before faxing, you must first be approved with a credit account.

General Information: Public Access terminal is available. No sealed, expunged, adoption, sex offense, juvenile or mental health records released. Will fax results to local or toll free line. Copy fee: $.65 per page, $1.30 minimum. Cert fee: $5.00. Payee: County Clerk. Personal checks accepted. Prepayment required. Mail requests: SASE required. Mail turnaround time 1-2 days.

Ithaca City Court 118 E Clinton St, Ithaca, NY 14850; 607-273-2263. Hours: 8AM-4PM (EST). *Misdemeanor, Civil Actions Under $15,000, Eviction, Small Claims.* www.nycourts.gov/ithaca/city

Civil Records: Access: Mail, in person. Only the court performs in person searches; visitors may not. Search fee: $16.00 per name. For records prior to 1996, fee is $5.00 per each 2 year period searched. Required to search: name, years to search. Civil cases indexed by defendant. Civil records on computer since 1996; prior records in books.

Criminal Records: Access: None. No search fee. Criminal records on computer from 1990, prior in books. The court refuses to permit access to court records unless specific case file given. State policy requires requests be send to OCA for $52.00 statewide search.

General Information: No sealed, youthful offender records released. Will fax results to local or toll free line. Copy fee: $.65 per page. $1.30 minimum. Cert fee: $5.00. Payee: City Court. Only cashiers checks and money orders accepted. Prepayment required. Mail requests: SASE required. Mail turnaround time 1 week.

Surrogate Court 320 N Tioga St, Ithaca, NY 14850; 607-277-0622; Fax: 607-256-2572. Hours: 9AM-5PM (EST). *Probate.*

Tompkins Town/Village Courts. *Misdemeanor- Civil Actions Under $3000- Small Claims.* Caroline Town Court- 607-539-7796, Cayuga Heights Village Court- 607-257-3944, Danby Town Court- 607-277-4788, Dryden Town Court- 607-844-8621, Enfield Town Court- 607-272-6490, Groton Town Court- 607-898-5273, Ithaca Town Court- 607-273-1721, Lansing Town Court- 607-533-4776, Newfield Town Court- 607-564-9571, Ulysses Town Court- 607-387-5411

Ulster County

County Clerk PO Box 1800, 244 Fair St, Kingston, NY 12401; 845-340-3288 (Clerk); 845-340-3770 (Switchboard); Fax: 845-340-3299. Hours: 9AM-4:45PM (EST). *Felony, Civil.*
www.co.ulster.ny.us
Note: Countywide record search requests made to the County Clerk are processed in the manner described below.

Civil Records: Access: Phone, mail, in person. Both court and visitors may perform in person searches. Search fee: $5.00 per name per 2 years searched; county clerk may perform 1 search from 1987 forward for free over phone. Required to search: name, years to search. Civil cases indexed by defendant, plaintiff. Civil records on computer from 1987, in books from 1920s, prior archived. Access to current Supreme court cases is at http://e.courts.state.ny.us/.
Criminal Records: Access: Phone, mail, in person. Both court and visitors may perform in person searches. Search fee: $5.00 per name. Fee is per 2 years searched. Required to search: name, years to search. Criminal records on computer from 1987, in books from 1920s, prior archived.
General Information: Public Access terminal is available. No sealed, expunged, adoption, sex offense, juvenile or mental health records released. Copy fee: $.65 per page. Cert fee: $5.00. Payee: County Clerk. Personal checks accepted. Prepayment required. Mail requests: SASE not required. Mail turnaround 5 days.

Supreme & County Court 285 Wall St, Kingston, NY 12401; 845-340-3377. Hours: 9AM-5PM (EST). *Felony, Civil.*
Note: The Court Clerk directs record search requests to the County Clerk, see separate listing. Online access to current Supreme court cases is available at http://e.courts.state.ny.us/.

Kingston City Court One Garraghan Dr, Kingston, NY 12401; 845-338-2974. Hours: 8:30AM-4PM (EST). *Misdemeanor, Civil Actions Under $15,000, Eviction, Small Claims.*
Civil Records: Access: Mail, in person. Only the court performs in person searches; visitors may not. Search fee: $5.00 per name per 2 years. If pre-1995, fee is $16.00. Required to search: name, years to search. Civil cases indexed by plaintiff. Civil records on computer from 1995. Overall records go back to 1983. Request must be in writing.
Criminal Records: Access: None. No search fee. Criminal records on computer from 1995. Overall records go back to 1983. The court does not permit access to court records unless specific case file given. Requesters are directed to send requests to OCA for $52.00 statewide search.
General Information: No sealed or youthful offender records released. Copy fee: $1.00 per page. Cert fee: $5.00. Payee: City Court. Personal checks accepted. Prepayment required. Mail requests: SASE required. Mail turnaround time 2 weeks.

Surrogate Court PO Box 1800, 240 Fair St, Kingston, NY 12402; 845-340-3348; Fax: 845-340-3352. Hours: 9AM-5PM (EST). *Probate.*

Ulster Town/Village Courts. *Misdemeanor- Civil Actions Under $3000- Small Claims.* Crawford Town Court, Denning Town Court- 845-985-2411, Ellenville Village Court- 845-647-7080, Esopus Town Court- 845-331-3709, Gardiner Town Court- 845-255-9675, Hardenburgh Town Court- 845-586-3135, Hurley Town Court- 845-331-7474, Kingston Town Court- 845-336-8853, Lloyd Town Court- 845-691-8011, Marbletown Town Court- 845-687-7601, Marlborough Town Court- 845-795-5100, New Paltz Town Court- 845-255-0100, Olive Town Court- 845-657-2320, Plattekill Town Court- 845-883-7331, Rochester Town Court- 845-626-7384, Rosendale Town Court- 845-658-3159, Saugerties Town Court- 845-246-9989- 246-2800, Saugerties Village Court- 845-246-3958- 246-2321, Shandaken Town Court- 845-688-5004, Shawangunk Town Court- 845-895-2611, Ulster Town Court- 845-382-2455, Wawarsing Town Court- 845-647-6560

Warren County

County Clerk 1340 State Route 9, Attn: County Clerk, Lake George, NY 12845; 518-761-6420/6426. Hours: 9AM-5PM (EST). *Civil, Felony.*
Note: Countywide civil record search requests made to the county clerk are processed in the manner described below.

Civil Records: Access: Phone, mail, in person, online. Both court and visitors may perform in person searches. Search fee: $5.00 per name for each 2 years. Required to search: name, years to search. Civil cases indexed by plaintiff. Civil records index on computer from 1917 to present. Access to current/pending Supreme Court civil cases is at http://e.courts.state.ny.us.
Criminal Records: Access: In person only. Both court and visitors may perform in person searches. No search fee. Required to search: name, years to search, DOB. Criminal records not on computer, on index from 1929. First, name search the County Clerk index of dispositions for case numbers. To retrieve case records, take case numbers to the Supreme & County Court (see separate listing) County-Court clerk who will pull cases records for you.
General Information: Public Access terminal is available. No adoption, juvenile or mental health records released. Will not fax results. Copy fee: $.65 per page. Cert fee: $5.00 minimum. Payee: Warren County Clerk. Personal checks accepted. Prepayment required. Mail requests: SASE required. Mail turnaround time is 2-5 days.

Supreme & County Court 1340 State Route 9, Lake George, NY 12845; 518-761-6430/6431. Hours: 9AM-4:30 (EST). *Felony.*
Note: Direct civil searches to County Clerk only, see separate entry. Also, a criminal record disposition index is maintained at County Clerk's office. However, actual felony records are located here at Supreme & County Court County-Court Clerk office.
Criminal Records: Access: Mail, in person. Both court and visitors may perform in person searches. No search fee. Required to search: name, years to search, DOB, SSN, signed release. Criminal records on computer from 1986, prior on index from 1929. For mail requests, the County-Court directs criminal search requests to the OCA for a $52.00 statewide record check. For in person requests, first name search the County Clerk index for case numbers. To retrieve case records, take case numbers to the Supreme & County Court (see separate listing) County-Court clerk who will pull cases records for you.
General Information: No adoption, juvenile or mental health records released. Copy fee: $.50 per page. Cert fee: $4.00. Payee: Warren County Clerk. Personal checks accepted. Prepayment required. Mail

requests: SASE required. Mail turnaround time same day.

Glens Falls City Court 42 Ridge St, Glens Falls, NY 12801; 518-798-4714; Fax: 518-798-0137. Hours: 8:30AM-4:30PM (EST). *Misdemeanor, Civil Actions Under $15,000, Eviction, Small Claims.*
Civil Records: Access: Mail, in person. Only the court performs in person searches; visitors may not. Search fee: $16.00 per name. Fee is for computer search. No fee for manual search. Required to search: name, years to search. Civil cases indexed by defendant, plaintiff. Civil records go back to 1975; on computer from 1987, prior on microfilm.
Criminal Records: Access: None. No search fee. Criminal records go back to the late 1960s; on computer from 1990, prior on microfilm. The court does not permit access to court records unless specific case file given. Requesters are directed to OCA for $52.00 statewide search.
General Information: No sealed records released. Will fax results to local or toll free line. Copy fee: $.65 per page. There is a $1.30 minimum. Cert fee: $5.00. Payee: City Court. Only cashiers checks and money orders accepted. Prepayment required. Mail requests: SASE required. Mail turnaround time 1 week.

Surrogate Court 1340 State Route 9, County Muni. Ctr, Lake George, NY 12845; 518-761-6514/6515/6512; Fax: 518-761-6465 x6511. Hours: 9AM-5PM (EST). *Probate.*

Warren Town/Village Courts. *Misdemeanor- Civil Actions Under $3000- Small Claims.* Bolton Town Court- 518-644-2202, Chester Justice Ciurt, 518-494-3133, Hague Town Court- 518-543-6161, Horicon Town Court- 518-494-7958, Johnsburg Town Court- 518-251-3011, Lake George Town Court- 518-668-5420, Lake Luzerne Town Court- 518-696-4294, Queensbury Town Court- 518-745-5571, Stony Creek Town Court- 518-696-2508, Thurman Town Court- 518-623-9660, Warrensburg Town Court- 518-623-9776

Washington County

County Clerk 383 Broadway, Bldg A, Fort Edward, NY 12828; 518-746-2170; Fax: 518-746-2166. Hours: 8:30AM-4:30PM (EST). *Civil.*
Civil Records: Access: Mail, in person, online. Visitors must perform in person searches for themselves. Search fee: None. Generally, court will answer mailed civil records requests but you must at least provide year to search. Required to search: name, years to search. Civil cases indexed by defendant. Civil records on books from 1800s. Access to current/pending Supreme Court civil cases and some closed cases is at http://e.courts.state.ny.us/.
General Information: Public Access terminal is available. No sealed or youthful offender records released. Will not fax results. Copy fee: $1.00 per page. Cert fee: $5.00. Payee: County Clerk. Business checks accepted. Prepayment required. Mail requests: SASE required. Mail turnaround time 1-2 days.

Supreme & County Court 383 Broadway, Fort Edward, NY 12828; Civil phone: 518-746-2520; Criminal phone: 518-746-2521. Hours: 8:30AM-4:30PM (EST). *Felony, Civil.*
Note: Misdemeanor records maintained by city, town, village courts.

Civil Records: Access: In person only. No search fee. Required to search: name, years to search. Direct civil record search requests to the County Clerk, see separate listing. Access to current/pending Supreme Court civil cases and some closed cases is at http://e.courts.state.ny.us/.
Criminal Records: Access: In person only. Visitors may perform in person searches for themselves. Search fee: None to view indexes in person. Required to search: name, years to search. Criminal records on

books from 1800s. All criminal record name search requests are directed to the OCA for the $52.00 statewide record search.

General Information: No sealed or youthful offender records released. Copy fee: $1.00 per page. Cert fee: $4.00. Payee: County Clerk. Business checks accepted. Prepayment required.

Surrogate Court 383 Broadway, Fort Edward, NY 12828; 518-746-2546; Fax: 518-746-2547. Hours: 8:30AM-4:30PM (EST). *Probate.*

Washington Town/Village Courts. *Misdemeanor-Civil Actions Under $3000- Small Claims.* Argyle Town Court- 518-638-8681, Cambridge Town Court- 518-677-2444, Cambridge Village Court- 518-677-2414, Dresden Town Court- 518-499-2040, Easton Town Court- 518-692-0027, Fort Ann Town Court- 518-639-8929, Fort Edward Town And Village Court- 518-747-2252, Granville Town Court- 518-642-9243, Granville Village Court- 518-642-9386, Greenwich Town Court And Village Court- 518-692-7611, Hampton Town Court- 518-282-9830, Hartford Town Court- 518-632-5255, Hebron Town Court- 518-854-9300, Hudson Falls Village Court- 518-747-3292, Jackson Town Court- No Phone, Kingsbury Town Court- No Phone, Putnam Town Court- 518-547-8317, Salem Town Court- 518-854-9215, Salem Village Court- 518-854-9215, White Creek Town Court- 518-677-8545, Whitehall Town Court- 518-499-0772, Whitehall Village Court- 518-499-0772

Wayne County

Supreme & County Court 9 Pearl St, PO Box 608, Lyons, NY 14489-0608; 315-946-7470; Probate phone: 315-946-5430; Fax: 315-946-5978. 9AM-5PM (EST). *Felony, Civil, Eviction, Small Claims.*
Note: Direct all search requests to the County Clerk office; information given here is for that County Clerk office.

Civil Records: Access: Phone, fax, mail, in person, email, online. Both court and visitors may perform in person searches. Search fee: $5.00 per name per every 2 years. Required to search: name, years to search. Civil cases indexed by defendant, plaintiff. Civil records on computer back to 1985, prior in books. Access to current/pending Supreme Court civil cases is at http://e.courts.state.ny.us/.
Criminal Records: Access: Fax, mail, in person. Both court and visitors may perform in person searches. Search fee: $5.00 per name uncertified back to 1979. $5.00 per name for every 2 years certified search. Required to search: name, years to search, DOB; also helpful: gender. Criminal records on computer back to 1979.
General Information: Public Access terminal is available. No matrimonial records released. Fees to fax results: long distance within Wayne County $2.00 1st page, $1.00 each add'l page; long distance outside Wayne County $3.00 1st page, $1.00 each add'l page; no fax charge for 800 number. Copy fee: $.65 per page. $1.30 minimum. Cert fee: $5.00 plus $1.25 per page after first 4. Payee: County Clerk. Personal checks accepted. Prepayment required. Mail requests: SASE requested. Turnaround time 5-7 days.

Surrogate Court 54 Broad St #106, Hall of Justice, Lyons, NY 14489; 315-946-5430; Fax: 315-946-5433. Hours: 9AM-4PM (EST). *Probate.*

Wayne Town/Village Courts. *Misdemeanor- Civil Actions Under $3000- Small Claims.* Arcadia Town Court- 315-331-2744, Butler Town Court- 315-594-2719, Galen Town Court- 315-923-9375, Huron Town Court- 315-594-6511, Lyons Town Court- 315-946-4565, Lyons Village Court- 315-946-4565, Macedon Town Court- 315-986-9108 Ext 2, Macedon Village Court- 315-986-1597, Marion Town-No Phone, Newark Village Court- 315-331-5139, Ontario Justice Court- 315-524-6511 Ext 7, Palmyra Town Court- 315-597-5431, Rose Town Court- 315-587-4418, Savannah Town Court- 315-365-2811, Sodus Point Village Court- 315-483-6217, Sodus Town Court- 315-483-6807, Walworth Town Court- No Phone, Williamson Town Court- 315-589-8250, Wolcott Town Court- 315-594-8257, Wolcott Village Court- 315-594-6437

Westchester County

County Clerk 110 Dr Martin L King Blvd, Rm 330, White Plains, NY 10601; 914-995-3070; Fax: 914-995-3172. 8AM-4:45PM (EST). *Felony, Civil.*
www.westchester.com and www.courts.state.ny.us/courts/9jd/Westchester/supremecounty.shtml
Note: Record earch requests made to the County Clerk are processed in the manner described below.

Civil Records: Access: Mail, in person, online. Both court and visitors may perform in person searches. Search fee: $5.00 per name. Fee is per 2 years searched. Required to search: name, years to search. Civil cases indexed by defendant, plaintiff. Civil records on computer from 1986, prior in books from 1847. Access to current/pending Supreme court civil cases and some closed cases is at http://e.courts.state.ny.us/. Also, access judgments on the county clerk database search site at http://ccpv.westchesterclerk.com/StartMain.asp. Also, earch for future court appearances at http://e.courts.state.ny.us.
Criminal Records: Access: Mail, in person. Both court and visitors may perform in person searches. Search fee: $5.00 per name. Fee is per 2 years searched. Required to search: name, years to search. Criminal records on computer from 1986, prior in books from 1847.
General Information: Public Access terminal is available. No sealed, expunged, adoption, sex offense, juvenile or mental health records released. Will not fax results. Included in search fee Cert fee: $5.00. The fee covers up to 8 pages, each add'l page is $.50. Payee: County Clerk. Personal checks accepted. Prepayment required. Mail requests: SASE required. Mail turnaround time 1 week.

Supreme & County Court 111 Dr Martin L King Blvd, Rm 803, White Plains, NY 10601; Civil phone: 914-995-3800; Criminal phone: 914-995-3810. Hours: 9AM-5PM (EST). *Felony, Civil.*
www.westchesterclerk.com and www.courts.state.ny.us/courts/9jd/Westchester/supremecounty.shtml
Note: Direct search requests to the County Clerk, see separate listing, otherwise requests are directed to the OCA for the $52.00 statewide record search.

Mt Vernon City Court Municipal Bldg, Roosevelt Sq, Mt Vernon, NY 10550-2019; 914-665-2400; Criminal phone: 914-665-2409; Fax: 914-699-1230. Hours: 8:30AM-4:30PM (payments to 3:30PM only) (EST). *Misdemeanor, Civil Actions Under $15,000, Eviction, Small Claims.*
Note: Small claims phone is 665-2404; Landlord/Tenant is 665-2402; Traffic is 665-2405.

Civil Records: Access: Mail, in person. Only the court performs in person searches; visitors may not. No search fee. Required to search: name, years to search; also helpful: address. Civil cases indexed by defendant, plaintiff. Civil records on computer since 1986, prior in books.
Criminal Records: Access: In person only. Only the court performs in person searches; visitors may not. No search fee. Criminal records on computer since 1986, prior in books.
General Information: No sealed records released. Will not fax results. Copy fee: $1.30 1st page, $.65 each add'l page. Cert fee: $6.00. Payee: City Court. Only cashiers checks and money orders accepted. Prepayment required. Mail requests: SASE required. Mail turnaround time minimum 2 weeks.

New Rochelle City Court 475 North Ave, New Rochelle, NY 10801; Civil phone: 914-654-2299; Criminal phone: 914-654-2311; Fax: 914-654-0344. Hours: 9AM-5PM (EST). *Misdemeanor, Civil Actions Under $15,000, Small Claims.*
www.courts.state.ny.us/courts/9jd/Westchester/NewRochelle.shtml
Civil Records: Access: Mail, in person. Only the court performs in person searches; visitors may not. Search fee: $16.00 per name. Required to search: name, years to search. Civil records go back 20 years.
Criminal Records: Access: None. No search fee. The court does not permit access to court records unless specific case file given. Requesters are directed to OCA for $52.00 statewide search.
General Information: No sealed records released. Copy fee: $1.00 per page. Cert fee: $6.00 per doc. Payee: City Court of New Rochelle. Prepayment required.

Peekskill City Court 2 Nelson Ave, Peekskill, NY 10566; 914-737-3405. Hours: 9AM-5PM (EST). *Misdemeanor, Civil Actions Under $15,000, Eviction, Small Claims.*
Civil Records: Access: Mail, in person. Only the court performs in person searches; visitors may not. No search fee. Required to search: name, years to search. Civil cases indexed by plaintiff. Civil records on computer back to 1994, prior in books. Request must be in writing.
Criminal Records: Access: None. No search fee. The court does not permit access to court records unless specific case file given. Requesters are directed to OCA for $52.00 statewide search.
General Information: No sealed records released. Will not fax results. Copy fee: $.65 per page, $1.30 minimum. Cert fee: $6.00. Payee: Peekskill City Court. Only cash, cashiers checks or money orders accepted. Prepayment required. Mail requests: SASE required. Mail turnaround time 0-5 days.

Rye City Court 21 McCullough Place, Rye, NY 10580; 914-967-1599; Fax: 914-967-3308. Hours: 8:30AM-4:30PM (EST). *Misdemeanor, Civil Actions Under $15,000, Eviction, Small Claims.*
Civil Records: Access: Mail, in person. Only the court performs in person searches; visitors may not. Search fee: $5.00 per name. Required to search: name, years to search. Civil cases indexed by plaintiff. Civil records on computer from 1994, prior on index cards.
Criminal Records: Access: Mail, In person. Only the court performs in person searches; visitors may not. No search fee. Required to search: DOB, years to search. Criminal records on computer from 1986. The court will perform limited name searches. It is suggested to send requests to OCA for $52.00 statewide search.
General Information: No sealed records released. Copy fee: $.50 per page. Cert fee: $5.00. Payee: City Court. Only cashiers checks and money orders accepted. Prepayment required. Mail requests: SASE required. Mail turnaround time 1 month.

White Plains City Court 77 S Lexington Ave, White Plains, NY 10601; Civil phone: 914-422-6050; Criminal phone: 914-422-6075; Fax: 914-422-6058. Hours: 8:30AM-4:30PM (EST). *Misdemeanor, Civil Actions Under $15,000, Eviction, Small Claims.*
Civil Records: Access: Mail, fax, in person. Only the court performs in person searches; visitors may not. Search fee: $16.00 per name. Required to search: name, years to search. Civil cases indexed by defendant. Civil records on docket cards and computer.
Criminal Records: . The court does not permit access to court records unless specific case file given. Requesters are directed to OCA for $52.00 statewide

search. Criminal records on computer from 1988, prior on cards

General Information: No sealed, youthful offender or sex case records released. Will fax results no fee, if prepaid. Copy fee: $.25 per page. Cert fee: $5.00. Payee: City Court. Only cashiers checks and money orders accepted. Prepayment required. Mail requests: SASE required. Mail turnaround time 1-2 days.

Yonkers City Court 100 S Broadway, Yonkers, NY 10701; Civil phone: 914-377-6376; Criminal phone: 914-377-6352; Fax: 914-377-7966. Hours: 9AM-3:30PM (EST). *Misdemeanor, Civil Actions Under $15,000, Eviction, Small Claims.*

Civil Records: Access: Mail, in person. Only the court performs in person searches; visitors may not. Search fee: $16.00 per name. Required to search: name, years to search. Civil cases indexed by plaintiff. Civil records on computer since 01/95.

Criminal Records: Access: Mail, in person. No search fee. Criminal records on computer since 1993. The court does not permit access to court records unless specific case file given. Requesters are directed to the OCA for $52.00 statewide search.

General Information: No sealed records released. No copy fee. Cert fee: $5.00 per document. Payee: City Court. Only cashiers checks and money orders accepted. Prepayment required. Mail requests: SASE not required. Mail turnaround time 2-3 weeks.

Surrogate Court 140 Grand St, 8th Fl, White Plains, NY 10601; 914-995-3712; Fax: 914-995-3728. Hours: 9AM-5PM (EST). *Probate.*

Westchester Town/Village Courts. *Misdemeanor-Civil Actions Under $3000- Small Claims.* Ardsley Village Court- 914-693-1703, Bedford Town Court- 914-666-6965, Briarcliff Manor Village Court- 914-941-4800 Ext 4, Bronxville Village Court- 914-337-2454, Buchanan Village Court- 914-737-1033, Cortlandt Town Court- 914-734-1090, Croton-On-Hudson Village Court- 914-271-6266, Dobbs Ferry Village Court- 914-693-6161, Eastchester Town Court- 914-771-3354, Elmsford Village Court- 914-592-8949, Greenburgh Town Court- 914-682-5365, Harrison Town Court- 914-835-2000 Ext 3, Hastings-On-Hudson Village Court- 914-478-3403, Irvington Village Court- No Phone, Larchmont Village Court- 914-834-1826, Lewisboro Justice Court- 914-763-5417, Mamaroneck Town Court- 914-381-7875, Mamaroneck Village Court- 914-777-7710, Mount Kisco Town Court- 914-241-7033, Mount Pleasant Town Court- 914-742-2354, New Castle Justice Court- 914-238-4726, North Castle Justice Court- 914-273-8627, North Salem Town Court- 914-669-9691, North Tarrytown Village Court- 914-631-2783, Ossining Town Court- 914-762-8562, Ossining Village Court- 914-941-3067, Pelham Town Court- 914-738-7030, Pleasantville Village Court- 914-769-2027, Port Chester Justice Court- 914-939-8220, Pound Ridge Justice Court- 914-764-5511, Rye Town Court- 914-939-3305, Scarsdale Village Court- 914-723-5734, Somers Town Court- 914-277-8225, Tarrytown Village Court- 914-631-5215, Tuckahoe Village Court- 914-961-4787, Yorktown Town Court- 914-962-6216

Wyoming County

Supreme & County Court 143 N Main St, #104, Warsaw, NY 14569; 585-786-8810 county clerk, 585-786-2253 (court clerks); Fax: 585-786-3703 (county clerk), 585-786-2818. Hours: 9AM-5PM (EST). *Felony, Civil.*

Note: Direct all search requests to the County Clerk office; information given here is for that County Clerk office. Supreme and County Court office is at 147 Main St.

Civil Records: Access: Phone, fax, mail, in person, online. Both court and visitors may perform in person searches. Search fee: $5.00 per name. Required to search: name, years to search. Civil cases indexed by defendant. Civil records on computer back to 2/14/2001; prior on books. Access to current/pending Supreme court civil cases and some closed cases is at http://e.courts.state.ny.us/.

Criminal Records: Access: Phone, fax, mail, in person. Only the court may perform in person searches, visitors may not. Search fee: $10.00 for 1-5 years searched per name; 6-10 years is $15.00; 11-20 years is $20.00. Required to search: name, years to search, DOB. Criminal records in books. Address requests to County Clerk.

General Information: Public Access terminal is available. (Civil records only on terminal.) No sealed, divorce or sexual abuse records released. Fee to fax results is $1.00 per page. Copy fee: $.50 per page. Cert fee: $5.00. Payee: County Clerk. Personal checks accepted. Prepayment required. Mail requests: SASE required. Mail turnaround time 2-3 days.

Surrogate Court 147 N Main St, Warsaw, NY 14569; 585-786-3148; Fax: 585-786-3800. Hours: 9AM-5PM (EST). *Probate.*

Wyoming Town/Village Courts. *Misdemeanor- Civil Actions Under $3000- Small Claims.* Arcade Justice Court- 585-492-4479, Arcade Town Court- No Phone, Attica Town Court- No Phone, Attica Village Court- 585-591-2957, Bennington Town Court- 716-652-5585, Castile Town Court- 585-493-5875, Covington Town Court- 585-584-3565, Eagle Town Court- 585-322-7667, Gainesville Town Court- No Phone, Genesee Falls Town Court- No Phone, Java Town Court- 585-457-3233, Middlebury Town Court- 585-495-6300, Orangeville Town Court- 585-786-2883, Perry Town Court And Village Court- 585-237-2149, Pike Town Court- 585-493-5140, Sheldon Town Court- 585-535-7644, Silver Springs Village Court- 585-493-3395, Warsaw Town Court And Village Court- 585-786-3361, Wethersfield Town Court- No Phone

Yates County

County Clerk 417 Liberty St #1107, Penn Yan, NY 14527; 315-536-5120; Fax: 315-536-5545. Hours: 9AM-5PM; 8:30AM-4:30PM (EST). *Felony, Civil.*

Note: Countywide record search requests made to the County Clerk are processed in the manner described here, also see Supreme & County Court. Misdemeanor, Eviction, and Small Claims records are found at local Justice courts.

Civil Records: Access: In person, online. Both court and visitors may perform in person searches. No search fee. Required to search: name, years to search. Civil cases indexed by defendant, plaintiff. Civil record indices on computer back to 9/1987, prior in books. Access to current/pending Supreme Court civil cases is at http://e.courts.state.ny.us/.

Criminal Records: Access: Mail, fax, in person. Both court and visitors may perform in person searches. Search fee: $10.00 per name. Required to search: name, years to search. Criminal records on book index; not computerized.

General Information: Public Access terminal is available. (Terminal is for civil only.) No divorce records outside parties involved, sealed records released. Will fax results for $2.00 a page to non-toll-free number. Copy fee: $.65 per page, $1.30 minimum. Cert fee: $1.25 per page, $5.00 minimum. Payee: Yates County Clerk. Personal checks accepted. Prepayment required. Mail requests: SASE required. Mail turnaround time 2-3 days.

Supreme & County Court 415 Liberty St, Penn Yan, NY 14527; 315-536-5126/5129. Hours: 9AM-5PM; 8:30AM-4:30PM Summer Hours (EST). *Felony, Civil.*

Note: Direct civil search requests to the County Clerk office or http://e.courts.state.ny.us. This court directs felony searches to OCA for a $52.00 statewide search, however, a countywide search can be made at the County Clerk office, see separate listing.

Surrogate Court 415 Liberty St, Penn Yan, NY 14527; 315-536-5130; Fax: 315-536-5190. Hours: 9AM-5PM (EST). Probate

Yates Town/Village Courts. *Misdemeanor- Civil Actions Under $3000- Small Claims.* Barrington Town Court- 607-243-8958, Benton Town Court- 315-536-2320, Dundee Village Court- 607-243-5551, Italy Town Court- No Phone, Jerusalem Town Court- No Phone, Middlesex Town Court- 585-554-3607, Milo Town Court- 315-531-8816, Penn Yan Village Court- 315-536-7243, Potter Town Court- 585-554-6758, Starkey Town Court- No Phone, Torrey Town Court.

New York Recording Offices

ORGANIZATION: 62 counties, 62 recording offices. Recording officers are County Clerk (New York City Register in the counties of Bronx, Kings, New York, and Queens). Entire state is in the Eastern Time Zone (EST).

REAL ESTATE RECORDS: Some counties will perform real estate searches. Certified copy fees are usually $1.00 per page with a $4.00 minimum. Tax records are located at the Treasurer's Office.

UCC RECORDS: This was a dual filing state. Financing statements werefiled both at the state level and with the County Clerk, except for consumer goods, cooperatives (as in cooperative apartments), farm related and real estate related collateral, which were filed only with the County Clerk. Effective 07/2001, only real estate related collateral is filed at the county, but searches may still be done on all the records prior to 07/2001. All counties will perform UCC searches. Use search request form UCC-11. Search fees are $25.00 per debtor name. Copies usually cost $5.00 per document.

TAX LIEN RECORDS: Federal tax liens on personal property of businesses are filed with the Secretary of State. Other federal tax liens are filed with the County Clerk. State tax liens are filed with the County Clerk, with a master list - called state tax warrants - available at the Secretary of State's office. Federal tax liens are usually indexed with UCC Records. State tax liens are usually indexed with other miscellaneous liens and judgments. Some counties include federal tax liens as part of a UCC search, and others will search tax liens for a separate fee, or not search at all. Search fees and copy fees vary.

OTHER LIENS: Judgment, mechanics, welfare, hospital, matrimonial, wage assignment, lis pendens.

ONLINE ACCESS: A handful of counties and towns offering free Internet access to assessor records, and the number is growing. The NYC Register now offers free access to borough real estate records.

Albany County

County Clerk, County Courthouse, Rm 128, Albany, NY 12207. **Phone**-County Clerk, R/E & UCC Recording- 518-487-5120; fax-518-487-5099; hours 9AM-4:45PM www.albanycounty.com/departments UCC records search per debtor- $25.00. Will search real estate records. RE record copy- $.65 per page; $1.25 min. UCC copy- $5.00 per doc. Cert fee: $5.00 per doc. Payee: Albany County Clerk, 16 Eagle St. **Online Access to Naturalization, Property, Deed, Morgages, Recording, Assessor records:** Access to clerk's naturalization records from 1821-1991 are free at www.albanycounty.com/online/online.asp. Records are being added by volunteers. Also, access to deeds and mortgages access at https://access.albanycounty.com/clerk/deedsandmortgages/. Also, a private company offers property assessment data at www.uspdr.com/consumer/ownersearch.asp. **Other phones:** Assessor-518-487-5350; Treasurer-518-447-7070; Elections-518-487-5060; Vital Records-518-434-5045.

Allegany County

County Clerk, 7 Court St, Courthouse, Belmont, NY 14813-0087. **Phone**-County Clerk, R/E & UCC Recording- 585-268-9270; fax-585-268-9659; hours 9AM-5PM (June-August 8:30AM-4PM) www.alleganyco.com UCC records search per debtor- $25.00. UCC-11 search includes federal tax liens if requested. Will not search real estate records. UCC copy- $5.00 per doc. Cert fee: $5.00 per doc. Payee: Allegany County Clerk. **Online Access to Property records:** A private company offers property assessment data online at www.uspdr.com/consumer/ownersearch.asp. **Other phones:** Assessor-585-268-9381; Treasurer-585-268-9282; Elections-585-268-9294; Vital Records-each town/village have their own vital records.

Bronx County

City Register, 1932 Arthur Ave, Bronx, NY 10457. **Phone**-718-579-6827; hours 9AM-4PM UCC records search per debtor- $25.00. Will not search real estate or tax lien records. UCC copy- $5.00 per doc. Cert fee: $5.00 per doc. Payee:

NYC Dept. of Finance. **Online Access to Real Estate, Lien, Deed, Judgment, UCC, Deed, Mortgage, Tax Assessor, Property records:** Recording data from the City Register are free at http://a836-acris.nyc.gov/scripts/docsearch.dll/index. Also, for deeper financial data back 10 years, subscribe to the NYC Dept of Finance dial-up system; fee-$250 monthly and $5.00 per item. For info/signup, call Richard Reskin 718-935-6523. Also, property assessment rolls from NYC's Dept. of Finance are free http://nycserv.nyc.gov/nycproperty/nynav/jsp/selectbbl.jsp. No name searching. Also, they offer daily downloads for borough-wide transactions of UCCs, Fed Liens, deeds, real estate. Also, a private company offers property assessment data online at www.uspdr.com/consumer/ownersearch.asp. **Other phones:** Assessor-718-579-6879.

Broome County

County Clerk, PO Box 2062, Binghamton, NY 13902-2062. **Phone**-607-778-2451, R/E Recording-607-778-2255, UCC Recording-607-778-2255; fax-607-778-2243; hours 8AM-5PM (Memorial Day to Labor Day-7:30AM-4PM) www.gobroomecounty.com/clerk/index.php UCC records search per debtor- $25.00. Will search real estate records. RE record copy- $.65 per page. UCC copy- $5.00 per doc. Cert fee: $5.20 per doc. Payee: Broome County Clerk. **Online Access to Property, Deed, Mortgage records:** A private company offers property assessment data at www.uspdr.com/consumer/ownersearch.asp. **Other phones:** Assessor-607-778-2169; Treasurer-607-778-2161; Elections-607-778-2172; Secretary-607-778-2377.

Cattaraugus County

County Clerk, 303 Court St, Little Valley, NY 14755. **Phone**-County Clerk, R/E & UCC Recording- 716-938-9111; fax-716-938-6009; hours 9AM-5PM, M-F www.cattco.org Will search UCC records. Will not give results over phone. Search per debtor- $25.00 if you need answer in writing, if not, no fee. Federal/state combined tax lien search- $40.00 per debtor. Will not search real estate records. RE record copy- $1.00 per page. UCC copy- $5.00 per doc. Cert fee:

$5.00 per doc. Payee: County Clerk. **Online Access to Real Estate, Tax Assessor, Most Wanted, Warrant, Land records:** Records on the City of Olean assessor database are free at www.cityofolean.com/Assessor/main.htm. Also, you may search for property info on the interactive map at www.cattco.org/real-property/maphelp.htm. Make parcels visible at right. To name search, then click on Query button on lefthand toolbar. Also, the sheriff's most wanted and warrant list is at www.sheriff.cattco.org. Also, a private company offers property assessment data online at www.uspdr.com/consumer/ownersearch.asp. **Other phones:** Assessor-716-938-9111; Treasurer-716-938-9111.

Cayuga County

County Clerk, 160 Genesee St, Auburn, NY 13021. **Phone**-County Clerk, R/E & UCC Recording-315-253-1271; fax-315-253-1653. www.co.cayuga.ny.us/clerk UCC records search per debtor- $5.00. UCC search includes federal tax liens. Will not search real estate records. RE record copy- $.65 per page, $1.30 min. UCC copy- $1.00 per page. Cert fee: $5.00 per doc. Payee: Cayuga County Clerk. **Online Access to Property, Assessor, Real Estate, Deed, Lien records:** A private company offers property assessment data at www.uspdr.com/consumer/ownersearch.asp. Also, search real estate, deeds and liens at www.landaccess.com/proi/county.jsp?county=nycayuga. Free searching only until 10/1/2004. **Other phones:** Assessor-315-253-1270; Treasurer-315-253-1211; Elections-315-253-1285; Vital Records-315-255-4100.

Chautauqua County

County Clerk, PO Box 170, Mayville, NY 14757-0170. **Phone**-716-753-4980; fax-716-753-4310; hours 8:30AM-4:30PM www.co.chautauqua.ny.us UCC records search per debtor- $25.00. Will not search real estate or tax lien records. UCC copy- $5.00 per doc. Cert fee: $5.00 per doc. Payee: Chautauqua County Clerk. **Online Access to Property records:** A private company offers property assessment data at www.uspdr.com/consumer/ownersearch.asp. **Other phones:** Assessor-716-661-7223.

Chemung County

County Clerk, PO Box 588, Elmira, NY 14902-0588. **Phone**-607-737-2920; fax-607-737-2897; hours 8:30Am-4:30PM www.chemungcounty.com
UCC records search per debtor- $25.00. Tax lien search- $25.00 per debtor. Will not search real estate records. RE record copy- $.65 per page. UCC copy- $5.00 per doc. Cert fee: $5.00 per doc. Payee: Chemung Co. Clerk. **Online Access to Property records:** A private company offers property assessment data at www.uspdr.com/consumer/ownersearch.asp. **Other phones:** Assessor-607-737-2988; Treasurer-607-737-2927; Elections-607-737-5475; Vital Records-607-737-2018.

Chenango County

County Clerk, 5 Court St, Norwich, NY 13815. **Phone**-607-337-1452, R/E Recording-607-337-1450 UCC Recording-607-337-1450. hours 8:30AM-5PM www.co.chenango.ny.us
No phone searches accepted. UCC records search per debtor- $25.00. UCC search includes Federal (only) tax liens. Tax lien search- $25.00 per debtor. Will search real estate records. RE record copy- $.65 per page. UCC copy- $5.00 per doc. Cert fee: $5.00 per doc. Payee: Chenango County Clerk. **Online Access to Property records:** A private company offers property assessment data at www.uspdr.com/consumer/ownersearch.asp. **Other phones:** Assessor-607-337-1490; Treasurer-607-337-1414.

Clinton County

County Clerk, 137 Margaret St, Government Ctr, Plattsburgh, NY 12901-2974. **Phone**-County Clerk, R/E & UCC Recording- 518-565-4700, UCC Recording-518-565-4846; fax-518-565-4718; hours 8AM-5PM
www.co.clinton.ny.us/Departments/CC/CCHome.htm
UCC records search per debtor- $25.00. Will not search real estate or tax lien records. RE record copy- $1.00 per page, $4.00 min. UCC copy- $5.00 per doc. Cert fee: $5.00 per doc. Payee: Clinton County Clerk. **Online Access to Property records:** A private company offers property assessment data at www.uspdr.com/consumer/ownersearch.asp. **Other phones:** Assessor-518-565-4760; Treasurer-518-565-4730.

Columbia County

County Clerk, 560 Warren St., Hudson, NY 12534. **Phone**-County Clerk, R/E & UCC Recording- 518-828-3339; fax-518-828-5299; hours 9AM-5PM
UCC records search per debtor- $25.00. Will not search real estate or tax lien records. RE record copy- $.25 per page. UCC copy- $5.00 per doc. Cert fee: $4.00 per doc. Payee: Columbia County Clerk. **Online Access to Property records:** A private company offers property assessment data online at www.uspdr.com/consumer/ownersearch.asp. **Other phones:** Assessor-518-828-7334; Treasurer-518-828-0513; Elections-518-828-3115.

Cortland County

County Clerk, 46 Greenbush St #101, Cortland, NY 13045-3702. **Phone**-607-753-5021, R/E Recording-607-758-5021, UCC Recording-607-758-5021; fax-607-758-5500; hours-9AM-5PM
http://www2.cortland-co.org
UCC records search per debtor- $25.00. Will search tax liens including federal tax liens. Will search real estate records. UCC copy- $10.00 per doc. Cert fee: $5.00 per doc. **Online Access to Property records:** A private company offers property assessment data online at www.uspdr.com/consumer/ownersearch.asp. **Other phones:** Assessor-607-753-5040 (Real Property); Treasurer-607-753-5070; Elections-607-753-5032; Vital Records-607-756-6521.

Delaware County

County Clerk, PO Box 426, Delhi, NY 13753. **Phone**-County Clerk, R/E & UCC Recording- 607-746-2123; fax-607-746-6924; hours 8:30AM-5PM
UCC records search per debtor- $25.00. Tax lien search- $25.00 per search/doc. Will not search real estate records. RE record copy- $.50 per page. UCC copy- $5.00 per doc. Cert fee: $5.00 per doc. Payee: Delaware County Clerk. **Online Access to Property records:** A private company offers property assessment data at www.uspdr.com/consumer/ownersearch.asp. **Other phones:** Assessor-607-746-3747; Treasurer-607-746-2121; Elections-607-746-2315.

Dutchess County

County Clerk, 22 Market St, Poughkeepsie, NY 12601. **Phone**-County Clerk, R/E & UCC Recording- 845-486-2120, UCC Recording-845-486-2125; fax-845-486-2138; hours 9AM-4:45PM www.dutchessny.gov
UCC records search per debtor- $2.00 per name per year. Will not search real estate or tax lien records. UCC copy- $5.00 per doc. Cert fee: $5.00 per doc. Payee: Dutchess County Clerk. **Online Access to Property records:** A private company offers property assessment data at www.uspdr.com/consumer/ownersearch.asp. **Other phones:** Assessor-845-431-2140; Treasurer-845-431-2025; Elections-845-486-2480.

Erie County

County Clerk, 25 Delaware Ave, County Hall, Buffalo, NY 14202. **Phone**-County Clerk, R/E & UCC Recording- 716-858-6724, UCC Recording-716-858-6425; fax-716-858-6550. http://ecclerk.erie.gov
For information about searches, call 716-858-8785. UCC records search per debtor- $25.00. Will search state tax liens. Search per debtor-$5.00 per 2 years. Will search real estate records. Real estate copy fee-$1 per page. UCC copy- $5.00 per doc. Cert fee: $4.00 per doc. Payee: Erie County Clerk. **Online Access to Recording, Deed, Mortgage, Judgment, Property records:** Access to the county clerk's database is at http://ecclerk.erie.gov/CGI-BIN/DB2WWW/RECORDS.mbr/RECORDS. A private company offers property assessments at www.uspdr.com/consumer/ownersearch.asp. Also, find property data on the mapping site at http://erie-gis.co.erie.ny.us/website/erie_help/help.htm. Click on Internet Mapping System then "Locate Property.". **Other phones:** Assessor-716-858-8322; Treasurer-716-858-3236.

Essex County

County Clerk, PO Box 247, Elizabethtown, NY 12932. **Phone**-County Clerk, R/E & UCC Recording- 518-873-3601; fax-518-873-3548; hours 8AM-5PM www.co.essex.ny.us
UCC records search per debtor- $25.00. UCC search includes tax liens if requested. Separate federal/state combined tax lien search- $5.00 per debtor. Will not search real estate records. RE record copy- $1.25 per page after 4 if certified. UCC copy- $5.00 per doc or name. Cert fee: $1.25 per page if over 4 pages, flat fee of $5.00 if under 4 pages. Payee: Essex County Clerk. **Online Access to Property records:** A private company offers property assessment data online at www.uspdr.com/consumer/ownersearch.asp. **Other phones:** Assessor-518-873-3390; Treasurer-518-873-3310; Elections-518-873-3474.

Franklin County

County Clerk, PO Box 70, Malone, NY 12953. **Phone**-County Clerk, R/E & UCC Recording- 518-481-1681; fax-518-483-9143; hours 8AM-PM June-Aug; 9AM-5PM Sept-May. UCC records search per debtor-$25.00. UCC search includes tax liens. Will not search real estate records. UCC copy- $5.00 per doc uncertified, $10.00 for certified. Cert fee: $5.00 per doc. Payee: Franklin County Clerk. **Online Access to Property records:** A private company offers property assessment data at www.uspdr.com/consumer/ownersearch.asp. **Other phones:** Assessor-518-481-1502; Treasurer-518-481-1516; Elections-518-481-1662; Vital Records-518-481-1671.

Fulton County

County Clerk, PO Box 485, Johnstown, NY 12095. **Phone**-County Clerk, R/E & UCC Recording- 518-736-5555; fax-518-762-3839; hours 9AM-5PM
UCC records search per debtor- $25.00. Will not search real estate records. UCC copy- $5.00 per doc. Cert fee: $5.00 per doc. **Online Access to Auditor, Real Estate, Deed, UCC records:** Seatch county auditor information at http://66.194.132.76/. Search recorder docs at www.landaccess.com/sites/oh/disclaimer.php?county=ohfulton. **Other phones:** Assessor-518-736-5510; Treasurer-518-736-5580; Elections-518-736-5526; Vital Records-518-736-5555.

Genesee County

County Clerk, PO Box 379, Batavia, NY 14021-0379. **Phone**-585-344-2550 x2443, R/E Recording-585-344-2550 x2242, UCC Recording-585-344-2550 x2243; fax-585-344-8551; hours 8:30AM-5PM
UCC records search per debtor- $25.00. UCC search includes federal tax liens. Separate judgment search/state tax lien search-$5.00 per debtor per 5 years. Will not search real estate records. RE record copy- $.65 per page, $1.30 min. UCC copy- $5.00 per doc. Cert fee: $5.00 per doc. Payee: Genesee County Clerk. **Online Access to Property records:** A private company offers property assessment data online at www.uspdr.com/consumer/ownersearch.asp. **Other phones:** Assessor-585-344-2550 x2219; Treasurer- x2210; Elections- x2206.

Greene County

County Clerk, PO Box 446, Catskill, NY 12414. **Phone**-County Clerk, R/E & UCC Recording- 518-943-2050; fax-518-943-2146; hours 9AM-5PM (June-August 8:30AM-4:30PM)
UCC records search per debtor- $25.00. Will not search real estate or tax lien records. UCC copy- $5.00 per doc. Cert fee: $5.00 per doc. Payee: Greene County Clerk. **Online Access to Property records:** A private company offers property assessment data at www.uspdr.com/consumer/ownersearch.asp. **Other phones:** Assessor-518-943-6977; Treasurer-518-943-4152; Elections-518-943-4191.

Hamilton County

County Clerk, PO Box 204, Lake Pleasant, NY 12108. **Phone**-County Clerk, R/E & UCC Recording- 518-548-7111; fax-518-548-9740; hours 8:30AM-4:30PM
UCC records search per debtor- $25.00. Will not search real estate or tax lien records. RE record copy- $.50 per page, min. $1.00. UCC copy- $5.00 per doc. Cert fee: $5.00 per doc. Payee: Hamilton County Clerk. **Online Access to Property records:** A private company offers property assessment data online at www.uspdr.com/consumer/ownersearch.asp. **Other phones:** Assessor-518-548-5531; Treasurer-518-548-7911.

Herkimer County

County Clerk, 109 Mary St, #1111, Herkimer, NY 13350. **Phone**-315-867-1137; fax-315-867-1349; hours 9AM-5PM. UCC records search per debtor- $25.00. Will not search real estate records. UCC copy- $5.00 per doc. Cert fee: $10.00 per doc. Payee: Herkimer County Clerk. **Online Access to Property records:** A private company offers property assessment data at www.uspdr.com/consumer/ownersearch.asp. **Other phones:** Treasurer-315-867-1153; Elections-315-867-1102.

Jefferson County

County Clerk, 175 Arsenal St, Watertown, NY 13601-2555. **Phone**-County Clerk, R/E & UCC Recording-315-785-3081; fax-315-785-5145; hours 9AM-5PM; 8:30AM-4PM July & August
UCC records search per debtor- $25.00. Will not search real estate or tax lien records. RE record copy- $1.00 per page. UCC copy- $5.00 per doc. Cert fee: $5.00 per doc. Payee: Jefferson County Clerk. **Online Access to Property records:** A private company offers property assessment data online at www.uspdr.com/consumer/ownersearch.asp. **Other phones:** Assessor-315-785-3074; Treasurer-315-785-3055; Elections-315-785-5119.

Kings County

County Clerk, 210 Joralemon St, Municipal Bldg, 1st Fl, Rm 2, Brooklyn, NY 11201. **Phone**-718-802-3589; fax-718-802-3745; hours 9AM-4PM
UCC records search per debtor- $25.00. UCC search includes tax liens. Separate federal & state combined tax lien search- $25.00 per debtor Will not search real estate records. UCC copy- $5.00 per doc. Cert fee: $5.00 per doc. Payee: NYC Dept. of Finance. **Online Access to Real Estate, Lien, Deed, Judgment, UCC, Deed, Mortgage, Tax Assessor, Property records:** Recording data from the City Register are free at http://a836-acris.nyc.gov/scripts/docsearch.dll/index. Also, for deeper financial data back 10 years, subscribe to the NYC Dept of Finance dial-up system; fee-$250 monthly and $5.00 per item. For info/signup, call Richard Reskin 718-935-6523. Also, Dept. of Finance property assessment rolls are at http://nycserv.nyc.gov/nycproperty/nynav/jsp/selectbbl.jsp. No name searching. Also, a private company offers property assessment data at www.uspdr.com/consumer/ownersearch.asp. **Other phones:** Assessor-718-802-3560; Treasurer-718-669-2746.

Lewis County

County Clerk, PO Box 232, Lowville, NY 13367-0232. **Phone**-County Clerk, R/E & UCC Recording- 315-376-5333; fax-315-376-3768; hours 8:30AM-4:30PM
UCC records search per debtor- $25.00. UCC search includes federal tax liens. Will not search real estate records. RE record copy- $3.00 per page. UCC copy- $5.00 per doc. Cert fee: $5.00 per doc. Payee: Lewis County Clerk. **Online Access to Property records:** A private company offers property assessment data at www.uspdr.com/consumer/ownersearch.asp. **Other phones:** Assessor-315-376-5356; Treasurer-315-376-5326; Elections-315-376-5329.

Livingston County

County Clerk, 6 Court St, Rm 201, Government Ctr, Geneseo, NY 14454-1043. **Phone**-585-243-7010; fax-585-243-7928; hours 8:30AM-4:30PM Oct 1-May 30; 8AM-4PM June 1-Sept 30
UCC records search per debtor- $25.00. Will not search real estate or tax lien records. UCC copy- $5.00 per doc. Cert fee: $5.00 per doc. Payee: Livingston County Clerk. **Online Access to Property records:** A private company offers property assessment data at www.uspdr.com/consumer/ownersearch.asp. **Other phones:** Assessor-585-243-7192; Treasurer-585-243-7050.

Madison County

County Clerk, PO Box 668, Wampsville, NY 13163. **Phone**-County Clerk, R/E & UCC Recording- 315-366-2261, UCC Recording-315-366-2262; fax-315-366-2615; hours 9AM-4:45PM
UCC records search per debtor- $25.00. Tax liens not included in UCC search. Federal/state combined tax lien search- $10.00 per 5 years. Will search real estate records. RE record copy- $5.00 per 5 years. UCC copy- $5.00 per doc. Cert fee: $5.00 per doc.

Online Access to Property records: A private company offers property assessment data online at www.uspdr.com/consumer/ownersearch.asp. **Other phones:** Assessor-315-366-2346; Treasurer-315-366-2371; Elections-315-366-2231.

Monroe County

County Clerk, 39 W. Main St, Rochester, NY 14614. **Phone**-County Clerk, R/E & UCC Recording- 585-428-5151; fax-585-428-5447; hours 9AM-5PM www.co.monroe.ny.us
UCC records search per debtor- $25.00. Tax lien search- $5.00 for two years. Will not search real estate records. RE record copy- $.65 per page. UCC copy- $5.00 per doc. Cert fee: $5.00 per doc. **Online Access to Land, Judgment, UCC, Lien, Court, Property records:** Access the county clerk database online at www.clerk.co.monroe.ny.us. Includes mortgages, deeds, court records; free registration. Land records back to 1984. Liens, judgments, UCCS back to 5/1989. Court records - civil, felony, divorce - go back to June, 1993. Earlier microfilm images are being added as time permits. Also, a private company offers property assessment data at www.uspdr.com/consumer/ownersearch.asp. **Other phones:** Assessor-585-428-5290; Treasurer-585-428-5290; Elections-585-428-4550; Vital Records-585-274-6141.

Montgomery County

County Clerk, PO Box 1500, Fonda, NY 12068-1500. **Phone**-518-853-8115, R/E Recording-518-853-8111; hours 8:30AM-4PM
UCC records search per debtor- $40.00. UCC search includes only federal tax liens if requested. Separate federal/state combined tax lien search- $5.00 per 2 years. Will search real estate records if in writing. Copy fee-$1.00 per page. UCC copy- $5.00 per doc. Cert fee: $5.00 per doc. Payee: Montgomery County Clerk. **Online Access to Property records:** A private company offers property assessment data online at www.uspdr.com/consumer/ownersearch.asp. **Other phones:** Assessor-518-853-3996; Treasurer-518-853-8175.

Nassau County

County Clerk, 240 Old Country Rd, Mineola, NY 11501. **Phone**-516-571-2272; fax-516-742-4099; hours 9AM-4;45PM www.co.nassau.ny.us/clerk/index.html
UCC records search per debtor- $25.00. UCC copy-$5.00 per doc. Cert fee: $10.00 per doc. Payee: Nassau County Clerk. **Online Access to Real Estate, Assessor, Recording, Property records:** Access to the county assessor tax data for free at www.mynassauproperty.com. No name searching. Also, access to recorder images is through a private company at www.courthousedirect.com/pac-info/. Fee for data. Also, a private company offers property assessment data at www.uspdr.com/consumer/ownersearch.asp. **Other phones:** Assessor-516-571-2490; Treasurer-516-571-5021.

New York County

City Register, 66 John St, Rm 202, New York, NY 10007. **Phone**-212-361-7550; hours 9AM-4PM
UCC records search per debtor- $25.00. Will not search real estate or tax lien records. UCC copy-$5.00 per doc. Cert fee: $5.00 per doc. Payee: NYC Dept of Finance. **Online Access to Real Estate, Lien, Judgment, UCC, Deed, Mortgage, Tax Assessor, Most Wanted, Missing Person, Restaurant Insp. records:** Recording data from the City Register are free at http://a836-acris.nyc.gov/scripts/docsearch.dll/index. Also, for deeper financial data back 10 years, subscribe to the NYC Dept of Finance dial-up system; fee-$250 monthly and $5.00 per item. For info/signup, call Rich Reskin 718-935-6523. Also, assessment roll searches are free at

http://nycserv.nyc.gov/nycproperty/nynav/jsp/selectbbl.jsp; no name searching. Also, search assessments free at www.uspdr.com/consumer/ownersearch.asp. Search most wanted list at www.ci.nyc.ny.us/html/nypd/html/wanted/mwant.html; restaurant insp.-http://ibihost1.com/nycdoh/web/html/rii.pl. **Other phones:** Assessor-212-669-2387; Treasurer-212-669-3913.

Niagara County

County Clerk, PO Box 461, Lockport, NY 14095. **Phone**-716-439-7022, R/E Recording-716-439-7031, UCC Recording-716-439-7307; fax-716-439-7066; hours 9AM-5PM (Summer 8:30AM-4:30PM)
UCC records search per debtor- $25.00. Search request if there is real estate as collateral $40.00. UCC search includes tax liens if requested. Real estate record owner and mortgage searches available. RE record copy- $1.30 per page. UCC copy- $5.00 per doc. Cert fee: $5.00 per doc (5 pgs). Payee: Niagara County Clerk. **Online Access to Real Estate, Recording, Deed, Mortgage, Lien, Judgment records:** A private company offers access to county recorder docs at www2.landaccess.com:8003/. Username and password required; register online. Also, a private company offers property assessment data online at www.uspdr.com/consumer/ownersearch.asp. **Other phones:** Assessor-716-439-7077; Treasurer-716-439-7007; Elections-716-438-4040; Vital Records-716-439-6676.

Oneida County

County Clerk, 800 Park Ave, Utica, NY 13501. **Phone**-315-798-5792; fax-315-798-6440; hours 8:30AM-5PM www.oneidacounty.org/index1.htm
UCC records search per debtor- $25.00. UCC search includes only federal tax liens if requested. Separate federal/state combined tax lien search-$25.00 per debtor Real estate record owner and mortgage searches available. RE record copy- $1.30 per page. UCC copy- $5.00 per doc. Cert fee: $5.00 per doc. Payee: Oneida County Clerk. **Online Access to Property records:** A private company offers property assessment data at www.uspdr.com/consumer/ownersearch.asp. **Other phones:** Assessor-315-798-5750; Treasurer-315-798-5750; Elections-315-798-5763; Vital Records-315-798-5833.

Onondaga County

County Clerk, 401 Montgomery St, Rm 200, Syracuse, NY 13202. **Phone**-315-435-8200, R/E Recording-315-435-8250; fax-315-435-3455; hours 8AM-5PM
UCC records search per debtor- $25.00. UCC search includes Federal tax liens. Tax lien search- $25.00 per debtor. UCC copy- $5.00 per doc. Cert fee: $5.00 per doc. **Online Access to Property records:** A private company offers property assessment data online at www.uspdr.com/consumer/ownersearch.asp. **Other phones:** Assessor-315-448-8280 (City Syr), 315-435-2426 (outside city).

Ontario County

County Clerk, 20 Ontario St., Ontario County Muni. Bldg., Canandaigua, NY 14424. **Phone**-County Clerk, R/E & UCC Recording- 585-396-4200, UCC Recording-585-393-2952; fax-585-393-2951; hours 8:30AM-5PM www.co.ontario.ny.us
UCC records search per debtor- $25.00. Federal and UCC combined tax lien search- $25.00 per debtor. Will not search real estate records. RE record copy-$.65 per page. UCC copy- $5.00 per doc. Cert fee: $5.00 per doc up to 4 pages, $1.25 each add'l. Payee: Ontario County Clerk. **Online Access to Property records:** A private company offers property assessment data at www.uspdr.com/consumer/ownersearch.asp. **Other phones:** Assessor-585-396-4382; Treasurer-585-396-4432; Elections-585-396-4005.

Orange County

County Clerk, 255 Main St, Goshen, NY 10924. **Phone**-845-291-2690, R/E Recording-845-291-3062, UCC Recording-845-291-3062; fax-845-291-2691; hours 9AM-5PM www.co.orange.ny.us

UCC records search per debtor- $25.00. UCC search includes tax liens if requested. Real estate owner, mortgage, and property transfer searches available. RE record copy- $1.00 per page 1st 4 pages, $.50 each add'l. UCC copy- $5.00 per doc. Cert fee: $5.00 per doc. Payee: Orange County Clerk. **Online Access to Property records:** A private company offers property assessment data online at www.uspdr.com/consumer/ownersearch.asp. **Other phones:** Assessor-845-291-2480; Treasurer-845-291-2485; Elections-845-291-2444.

Orleans County

County Clerk, 3 S. Main St, Courthouse Sq, Albion, NY 14411-1498. **Phone**-County Clerk, R/E & UCC Recording- 585-589-5334; fax-585-589-0181; hours 8:30AM-4PM July-Aug; 9AM-5PM Sept-June

UCC records search per debtor- $7.00. Will not search real estate or tax lien records. RE record copy- $1.00 per page. UCC copy- $1.50 per doc. Cert fee: $5.00 per doc. **Online Access to Property records:** A private company offers property assessment data at www.uspdr.com/consumer/ownersearch.asp. **Other phones:** Assessor-585-589-5400; Treasurer-585-589-5353; Elections-585-589-7004; Vital Records-In each township in the county.

Oswego County

County Clerk, 46 E. Bridge St, Oswego, NY 13126. **Phone**-315-349-8385; fax-315-343-8383; 9AM-5PM

UCC records search per debtor- $25.00. UCC search includes tax liens if requested. UCC copy- $5.00 per doc. Cert fee: $5.00 per doc. Payee: Oswego County Clerk. **Online Access to Property records:** A private company offers property assessment data online at www.uspdr.com/consumer/ownersearch.asp. **Other phones:** Assessor-315-349-8315; Treasurer-315-349-8393.

Otsego County

County Clerk, PO Box 710, Cooperstown, NY 13326-0710. **Phone**-607-547-4278, R/E Recording-607-547-4277; fax-607-547-7544; hours 9AM-5PM Sept-June; 9AM-4PM July-Aug.

UCC records search per debtor- $25.00. Will not search real estate records. RE record copy- $1.00 per page. UCC copy- $5.00 per doc. Cert fee: $5.00 per doc. Payee: County Clerk. **Online Access to Property records:** A private company offers property assessment data at www.uspdr.com/consumer/ownersearch.asp. **Other phones:** Assessor-607-547-4222; Treasurer-607-547-4235; Appraiser-each town has own; Elections-607-547-4247.

Putnam County

County Clerk, 40 Gleneida Ave., Carmel, NY 10512. **Phone**-845-225-3641, R/E Recording-845-225-3641 x304, x305, UCC Recording-845-225-3641 x300; fax-845-228-0231; 9AM-5PM (Summer 8AM-4PM)

UCC records search per debtor- $25.00. UCC search includes tax liens if requested. Real estate record owner and mortgage searches available. RE record copy- $1.00. UCC copy- $5.00 per doc. Cert fee: $5.00 per doc. Payee: Putnam County Clerk. **Online Access to Real Estate, UCC, Lien, Property records:** County Recorder records are accessible through a private online service at www.landaccess.com; Registration is required. Also, a private company offers property assessment data online at www.uspdr.com/consumer/ownersearch.asp. **Other phones:** Assessor-845-225-3641 x310; Treasurer-845-225-3641 x321; Elections-845-278-6970.

Queens County

City Register, 144-06 94th Ave., Jamaica, NY 11435. **Phone**-718-298-7000; hours 9AM-4PM

UCC records search per debtor- $25.00. Will not search real estate or tax lien records. UCC copy- $5.00 per doc. Cert fee: $5.00 per doc. Payee: New York City Department of Finance. **Online Access to Real Estate, Lien, Deed, Judgment, UCC, Deed, Mortgage, Tax Assessor records:** Recording data from the City Register are free at http://a836-acris.nyc.gov/scripts/docsearch.dll/index. Also, for deeper financial data back 10 years, subscribe to the NYC Dept of Finance dial-up system; fee-$250 monthly and $5.00 per item. For info/signup, call Richard Reskin 718-935-6523. Also, property assessment rolls from NYC's Dept. of Finance are free http://nycserv.nyc.gov/nycproperty/nynav/jsp/selectbbl.jsp. No name searching. Also, a private company offers property assessment data online at www.uspdr.com/consumer/ownersearch.asp. **Other phones:** Assessor-718-658-4626.

Rensselaer County

County Clerk, Courthouse, Congress & 2nd St, Troy, NY 12180. **Phone**-518-270-4080; fax-518-271-7998; hours 8:30AM-5PM

UCC records search per debtor- $25.00. Will not search tax liens. Will search deeds and mortgages with name and year. RE record copy- $1.00 per page. UCC copy- $5.00 per doc. Cert fee: $5.00 per doc. Payee: Rensselaer County Clerk. **Online Access to Property, Assessor, Deed, Lien, Real Estate records:** A private company offers property assessment data online at www.uspdr.com/consumer/ownersearch.asp. Also, search real estate deeds and liens at www.nylandrecords.com. Registration is now required. Commercial users can subscribe for $25.00 per month and $.25 per search; Personal users can purchase docs for $5.00 each, no monthly fee. **Other phones:** Assessor-518-270-2751; Treasurer-518-270-2751.

Richmond County

County Clerk, 130 Stuyvesant Pl, Staten Island, NY 10301. **Phone**-718-390-5386, R/E Recording-718-390-5387; hours 9AM-5PM

UCC records search per debtor- $25.00. Will not search real estate or tax lien records. UCC copy- $5.00 per doc. Cert fee: $5.00 per doc. Payee: Richmond County Clerk. **Online Access to Real Estate, Lien, Deed, Judgment, UCC, Deed, Mortgage, Tax Assessor records:** Recording data from the City Register are free at http://a836-acris.nyc.gov/scripts/docsearch.dll/index. Also, for deeper financial data back 10 years, subscribe to the NYC Dept of Finance dial-up system; fee-$250 monthly and $5.00 per item. For info/signup, call Richard Reskin 718-935-6523. Also, property assessment rolls from NYC's Dept. of Finance are free http://nycserv.nyc.gov/nycproperty/nynav/jsp/selectbbl.jsp. No name searching. Also, a private company offers property assessment data online at www.uspdr.com/consumer/ownersearch.asp. **Other phones:** Assessor-718-815-8511.

Rockland County

County Clerk, 1 S. Main St #100, New City, NY 10956. **Phone**-845-638-5070, R/E Recording-845-638-5069, UCC Recording-845-708-7180; fax-845-638-5647; hours 7AM-7PM M-Th; 7AM-6PM F www.rocklandcountyclerk.com

UCC records search per debtor- $25.00. Tax liens not included in UCC search. Separate federal/state combined tax lien search- $25.00 per debtor. Real estate owner, mortgage, and property transfer searches available. RE record copy- $1.00 per page. UCC copy- $5.00 per doc. Cert fee: $5.00 per doc.

Payee: Rockland County Clerk. **Online Access to Real Estate, Lien, Deed, Court, Recording records:** Access is the county clerk's records index is free at www.rocklandcountyclerk.com/court_records.html. Includes criminal records back to 1982, civil judgments, real estate records, tax warrants. View images back to 6/96, and more are being added. Call Paul Pipearto at 845-638-5221 for more information. You can also search indices at http://204.253.88.241/Idxweb/Login.asp. Also, search for parcel info on the GIS site at http://idsigis.com/rockland/start.asp?tfw=400. Click on Start Search and "Search by Owner." Also, a private company offers property assessment data at www.uspdr.com/consumer/ownersearch.asp. **Other phones:** Assessor-845-638-5131; Elections-845-638-5712.

Saratoga County

County Clerk, 40 McMaster St, Ballston Spa, NY 12020. **Phone**-518-885-2213 ext 4411; fax-518-884-4726; hours Search hours: 8AM-5PM; UCC records search per debtor- $25.00. UCC search includes tax liens if requested. Real estate record owner and mortgage searches available. RE record copy- $1.00 per page. UCC copy- $5.00 per doc. Cert fee: $5.00 per doc. Payee: Saratoga County Clerk. **Online Access to Property records:** A private company offers property assessment data at www.uspdr.com/consumer/ownersearch.asp. **Other phones:** Assessor-518-885-5381 x455; Treasurer- x281.

Schenectady County

County Clerk, 620 State St, Schenectady, NY 12305-2114. **Phone**-518-388-4220; fax-518-388-4224; hours 9AM-5PM www.scpl.org

UCC records search per debtor- $25.00 + $5.00 per doc. Tax liens not included in UCC search. Separate federal tax lien search- $5.00 per 2 years. RE record copy- $1.00 per page. UCC copy- $1.50 per page. Cert fee: $5.00 per doc. **Online Access to Real Estate, Tax Assessor, Property records:** Records for approximately 2/5 of the county property assessments are free online on the library database at www.scpl.org/assessments. Includes Glenville and Niskayuna street name searching. Also, a private company offers property assessment data at www.uspdr.com/consumer/ownersearch.asp. **Other phones:** Assessor-518-388-4247; Treasurer-518-388-4262.

Schoharie County

County Clerk, PO Box 549, Schoharie, NY 12157. **Phone**-County Clerk, R/E & UCC Recording- 518-295-8316; fax-518-295-8338; hours 8:30AM-5PM

UCC records search per debtor- $7.00. Will search real estate records. Written requests only. RE record copy- $.50 per page. UCC copy- $1.50 per page. Cert fee: $4.00 per doc. **Online Access to Property records:** A private company offers property assessment data at www.uspdr.com/consumer/ownersearch.asp. **Other phones:** Assessor-518-295-7141; Treasurer-518-295-8386.

Schuyler County

County Clerk, 105 Ninth St Unit 8, County Office Bldg., Watkins Glen, NY 14891. **Phone**-County Clerk, R/E & UCC Recording- 607-535-8133; 9AM-5PM

UCC records search per debtor- $25.00. Will not search real estate or tax lien records. RE record copy- $.65 per page. UCC copy- $5.00 per doc. Cert fee: $5.00 per doc. Payee: Schuyler County Clerk. **Online Access to Property records:** A private company offers property assessment data at www.uspdr.com/consumer/ownersearch.asp. **Other phones:** Assessor-607-535-8118; Treasurer-607-535-8181.

Seneca County

County Clerk, 1 DiPronio Drive, Waterloo, NY 13165. **Phone**-315-539-1771, R/E Recording-315-539-1770,

UCC Recording-315-539-1772; fax-315-539-3789; hours 8:45AM-4:45PM
UCC records search per debtor- $25.00. Tax liens not included in UCC search. Tax lien search- $25.00. Will not search real estate records. UCC copy- $5.00 per doc. Cert fee: $5.00 per doc. **Online Access to Property records:** A private company offers property assessment data at www.uspdr.com/consumer/ownersearch.asp. **Other phones:** Assessor-315-539-1720; Treasurer-315-539-1738; Appraiser-315-539-1718; Elections-315-539-1762.

St. Lawrence County

County Clerk, 48 Court St, Canton, NY 13617-1198. **Phone-**County Clerk, R/E & UCC Recording- 315-379-2237; fax-315-379-2302; hours 8:30AM-4:30PM www.co.st-lawrence.ny.us/CoTOC2.htm
UCC records search per debtor- $25.00. Will not search real estate or tax lien records. RE record copy- $.65 per page. UCC copy- $5.00 per doc. Cert fee: $5.00 per doc. Payee: St. Lawrence County Clerk. **Online Access to Property records:** A private company offers property assessment data online at www.uspdr.com/consumer/ownersearch.asp. **Other phones:** Assessor-315-379-2272; Treasurer-315-379-2234; Elections-315-379-2202.

Steuben County

County Clerk, 3 E. Pulteney Sq, County Office Bldg., Bath, NY 14810. **Phone-**607-776-9631 x3210, R/E Recording-607-776-9631 x3203, UCC Recording-607-776-9631 x3203; fax-607-776-7158; hours 8:30AM-5PM www.steubencony.org
UCC records search per debtor- $25.00. Federal/state combined tax lien search- $20.00 per debtor Will search real estate records. RE record copy- $.65 per page. UCC copy- $5.00 per doc. Cert fee: $5.00 per doc. Payee: Steuben County Clerk. **Online Access to Tax Assessor, Property records:** A private company offers county property assessment data online at www.uspdr.com/consumer/ownersearch.asp. Also, Search Town of Erwin Real Property Assessment Roll free online at www.erwinny.org/ertxsrch.htm. **Other phones:** Assessor-607-324-3074; Treasurer-607-776-9631 x2488.

Suffolk County

Clerk's Office, 310 Center Drive, Riverhead, NY 11901-3392. **Phone-**631-852-2038, R/E Recording-631-852-2043; fax-631-852-2004; hours 8AM-5PM
UCC records search per debtor- $25.00. Will not search real estate or tax lien records. UCC copy- $5.00 per doc. Cert fee: $10.00 per doc. Payee: Suffolk County Clerk. **Online Access to Property, Most Wanted records:** Access the county most wanted list at www.co.suffolk.ny.us/police/cs/mwindex.asp. Also, a private company offers property assessment data at www.uspdr.com/consumer/ownersearch.asp. **Other phones:** Assessor-631-852-1551; Treasurer-631-852-1500.

Sullivan County

County Clerk, PO Box 5012, Monticello, NY 12701. **Phone-**845-794-3000 x3152; hours 9AM-5PM
UCC records search per debtor- $25.00. Will not search real estate or tax lien records. RE record copy- $1.00 per page. UCC copy- $5.00 per doc. Cert fee: $5.20 per doc. Payee: Sullivan County Clerk. **Online Access to Property records:** A private company offers property assessment data at www.uspdr.com/consumer/ownersearch.asp. **Other phones:** Assessor-845-794-3000 x5014; Treas.-845-794-3000.

Tioga County

County Clerk, PO Box 307, Owego, NY 13827. **Phone-**County Clerk, R/E & UCC Recording- 607-687-8660; fax-607-687-8686; hours 9AM-5PM

Will search UCC records. UCC search per debtor- $25.00 per name. Will not search real estate or tax lien records. UCC copy- $5.00 per doc. Cert fee: $5.00 per doc. Payee: Tioga County Clerk. **Online Access to Property records:** A private company offers property assessment data online at www.uspdr.com/consumer/ownersearch.asp. **Other phones:** Treasurer-607-687-8670; Elections-607-687-8261; Real Property Tax-607-687-8661.

Tompkins County

County Clerk, 320 N. Tioga St, Main Courthouse, Ithaca, NY 14850-4284. **Phone-**County Clerk, R/E & UCC Recording- 607-274-5431; fax-607-274-5445; hours 8:30AM-5PM www.tompkins-co.org
UCC records search per debtor- $25.00. UCC search includes federal tax liens. Real estate owner, mortgage, and property transfer searches available. RE record copy- $.50 per page, $1.00 min. UCC copy- $5.00 per doc. Cert fee: $5.00 per doc. Payee: Tompkins County Clerk. **Online Access to Real Estate, Assessor, Tentative Assessment records:** Access to property records on the ImageMate system at www.tompkins-co.org/assessment/online.html has two levels: basic free and a registration/password fee-based full system. There is no name searching on the free version. The fee service is $20 monthly or $200 per year. For information and registration for the latter, email assessment@tompkins-co.org. Also, a private company offers property assessment data at www.uspdr.com/consumer/ownersearch.asp. **Other phones:** Assessor-607-274-5517; Treasurer-607-274-5545; Elections-607-274-5522; Vital Records-607-274-642.

Ulster County

County Clerk, PO Box 1800, Kingston, NY 12402-0800. **Phone-**County Clerk, R/E & UCC Recording-845-340-3288; fax-845-340-3299; hours 9AM-4:45PM www.co.ulster.ny.us
UCC records search per debtor- $25.00. Tax liens not included in UCC search. Tax lien search- $5.00 per debtor. Real estate owner, mortgage, and property transfer searches available. RE record copy- $.65 per page. UCC copy- $5.00 per doc. Cert fee: $5.00 per doc. Payee: Ulster County Clerk. **Online Access to Real Estate, Lien, Property Tax, Voter Registration, Court records:** Two sources exist. Access to county online records requires a $33.33 (under 25 transactions) or $44.55 monthly fee; 12 month agreement required. Land Records date back to 1984. Includes county court records back to 7/1987. Lending agency information is available. For info, contact Valerie Harris at 845-334-5367. Also, a private company offers property assessment data at www.uspdr.com/consumer/ownersearch.asp. Also, the County Parcel Viewer at www.maphost.com/ulster provides free access to tax parcel information. Search by GIS map, parcel ID number, street name, or other criteria. **Other phones:** Assessor-845-340-3431; Treasurer-845-340-3431; Elections-845-340-5470.

Warren County

County Clerk, 1340 State Route 9, Municipal Ctr, Lake George, NY 12845. **Phone-**518-761-6426; fax-518-761-6551; hours 9-5PM
UCC records search per debtor- $25.00. Will not search real estate records. UCC copy- $5.00 per doc. Cert fee: $5.00 per doc. Payee: Warren County Clerk. **Online Access to Property records:** A private company offers property assessment data online at www.uspdr.com/consumer/ownersearch.asp. **Other phones:** Assessor-518-761-6465.

Washington County

County Clerk, 383 Broadway, Bldg A, Fort Edward, NY 12828. **Phone-**County Clerk, R/E & UCC Recording- 518-746-2170; fax-518-746-2166; hours

8:30AM-4:30PM. Will search UCC records affixed to real estate. Search per debtor- $25.00. Will do a federal tax lien search. Tax lien search- $25.00. UCC copy- $5.00 per doc. Payee: Washington County Clerk. **Online Access to Property records:** A private company offers property assessment data online at www.uspdr.com/consumer/ownersearch.asp. **Other phones:** Assessor-518-746-2130. Treasurer-518-746-2220; Elections-518-746-2180.

Wayne County

County Clerk, PO Box 608, Lyons, NY 14489-0608. **Phone-**County Clerk, R/E & UCC Recording- 315-946-7470; fax-315-946-5978; hours 9AM-5PM www.co.wayne.ny.us
UCC records search per debtor- $25.00. Separate federal tax lien search- $25.00 per debtor; state lien- $5.00 per debtor. UCC copy- $5.00 per doc. Cert fee: $5.00 per doc. Payee: Wayne County Clerk. **Online Access to Property records:** A private company offers property assessment data online at www.uspdr.com/consumer/ownersearch.asp. **Other phones:** Assessor-315-946-5916; Treasurer-315-946-7443; Elections-315-946-7400.

Westchester County

County Clerk, 110 Dr. Martin Luther King Jr. Blvd., White Plains, NY 10601. **Phone-**914-995-3098; fax-914-995-3172; hours 8AM-4:30PM
UCC records search per debtor- $25.00. Will not search real estate records. UCC copy- $5.00 per doc. Cert fee: $10.00 per doc. Payee: Westchester County Clerk. **Online Access to Property, Recordings, Deed, Land, Fictitious Names, Judgment, Lien, UCC records:** Access to the clerk's land record database is free at http://ccpv.westchesterclerk.com/StartMain.asp. There is also an advanced search that features images; registration is reuqired. Also, a private company offers property assessment data online at www.uspdr.com/consumer/ownersearch.asp. **Other phones:** Assessor-914-422-1223.

Wyoming County

County Clerk, 143 N Main St, #104, Warsaw, NY 14569. **Phone-**County Clerk, R/E & UCC Recording-585-786-8810; fax-585-786-3703; hours 9AM-5PM
UCC records search per debtor- $25.00. Tax liens not included in UCC search. Real estate owner, mortgage, and property transfer searches available. RE record copy- $.50 per page. UCC copy- $5.00 per doc. Cert fee: $5.00 per doc. Payee: Wyoming County Clerk. **Online Access to Real Estate, Recording, Property records:** County Recorder records are accessible through a private online service at www.landaccess.com; Fees and registration are required. Also, a private company offers property assessment data at www.uspdr.com/consumer/ownersearch.asp. **Other phones:** Assessor-585-786-8828; Treasurer-585-786-8812; Elections-585-786-8931.

Yates County

County Clerk, 417 Liberty St, Penn Yan, NY 14527. **Phone-**County Clerk, R/E & UCC Recording- 315-536-5120; fax-315-536-5545; hours 9AM-5PM www.yatescounty.org
UCC records search per debtor- $25.00. Will not search real estate or tax lien records. RE record copy- $.65 per page, min. $1.30. UCC copy- $5.00 per doc. Payee: Yates County Clerk. **Online Access to Property records:** A private company offers property assessment data at www.uspdr.com/consumer/ownersearch.asp. **Other phones:** Assessor-315-536-5165; Treasurer-315-536-5192; Elections-315-536-5135.

New York County Locator

You will usually be able to find the city name in the City/County Cross Reference below. In that case, it is a simple matter to determine the county from the cross reference. However, only the official US Postal Service city names are included in this index. There are an additional 40,000 place names that people use in their addresses. Therefore, we have also included a ZIP/City Cross Reference immediately following the City/County Cross Reference.

If you know the ZIP Code but the city name does not appear in the City/County Cross Reference index, look up the ZIP Code in the ZIP/City Cross Reference, find the city name, then look up the city name in the City/County Cross Reference. For example, you want to know the county for an address of Menands, NY 12204. There is no "Menands" in the City/County Cross Reference. The ZIP/City Cross Reference shows that ZIP Codes 12201-12288 are for the city of Albany. Looking back in the City/County Cross Reference, Albany is in Albany County.

New York City/County Cross Reference

ACCORD Ulster
ACRA Greene
ADAMS Jefferson
ADAMS BASIN Monroe
ADAMS CENTER Jefferson
ADDISON Steuben
ADIRONDACK Warren
AFTON (13730) Chenango(93), Broome(6)
AKRON (14001) Erie(92), Niagara(3), Genesee(3)
ALABAMA Genesee
ALBANY Albany
ALBERTSON Nassau
ALBION Orleans
ALCOVE Albany
ALDEN (14004) Erie(92), Wyoming(5), Genesee(2)
ALDER CREEK Oneida
ALEXANDER Genesee
ALEXANDRIA BAY Jefferson
ALFRED Allegany
ALFRED STATION (14803) Allegany(89), Steuben(10)
ALLEGANY Cattaraugus
ALLENTOWN Allegany
ALMA Allegany
ALMOND Allegany
ALPINE Schuyler
ALPLAUS Schenectady
ALTAMONT Albany
ALTMAR Oswego
ALTON Wayne
ALTONA Clinton
AMAGANSETT Suffolk
AMAWALK Westchester
AMENIA Dutchess
AMITYVILLE Suffolk
AMSTERDAM (12010) Montgomery(95), Schenectady(3), Fulton(1)
ANCRAM Columbia
ANCRAMDALE Columbia
ANDES Delaware
ANDOVER (14806) Allegany(83), Steuben(16)
ANGELICA Allegany
ANGOLA Erie
ANNANDALE ON HUDSON Dutchess
ANTWERP Jefferson
APALACHIN Tioga
APPLETON Niagara
APULIA STATION Onondaga
AQUEBOGUE Suffolk
ARCADE (14009) Wyoming(91), Cattaraugus(8)
ARDEN Orange
ARDSLEY Westchester
ARDSLEY ON HUDSON Westchester
ARGYLE Washington
ARKPORT (14807) Steuben(79), Allegany(20)
ARKVILLE (12406) Delaware(93), Ulster(6)
ARMONK Westchester
ASHLAND Greene
ASHVILLE Chautauqua

ATHENS Greene
ATHOL Warren
ATHOL SPRINGS Erie
ATLANTA Steuben
ATLANTIC BEACH Nassau
ATTICA (14011) Wyoming(91), Genesee(8)
AU SABLE FORKS (12912) Clinton(98), Essex(1)
AUBURN Cayuga
AURIESVILLE Montgomery
AURORA Cayuga
AUSTERLITZ Columbia
AVA Oneida
AVERILL PARK Rensselaer
AVOCA Steuben
AVON Livingston
BABYLON Suffolk
BAINBRIDGE (13733) Chenango(98), Delaware(1)
BAKERS MILLS Warren
BALDWIN Nassau
BALDWIN PLACE (10505) Westchester(83), Putnam(16)
BALDWINSVILLE Onondaga
BALLSTON LAKE Saratoga
BALLSTON SPA Saratoga
BALMAT St. Lawrence
BANGALL Dutchess
BANGOR Franklin
BARKER (14012) Niagara(95), Orleans(4)
BARNEVELD Oneida
BARRYTOWN Dutchess
BARRYVILLE Sullivan
BARTON Tioga
BASOM (14013) Genesee(98), Erie(1)
BATAVIA Genesee
BATH Steuben
BAY SHORE Suffolk
BAYPORT Suffolk
BAYSIDE Queens
BAYVILLE Nassau
BEACON Dutchess
BEAR MOUNTAIN Rockland
BEARSVILLE Ulster
BEAVER DAMS (14812) Schuyler(46), Chemung(30), Steuben(22)
BEAVER FALLS Lewis
BEDFORD Westchester
BEDFORD HILLS Westchester
BELFAST Allegany
BELLEVILLE Jefferson
BELLMORE Nassau
BELLONA Yates
BELLPORT Suffolk
BELLVALE Orange
BELMONT Allegany
BEMUS POINT Chautauqua
BERGEN (14416) Genesee(89), Monroe(9)
BERKSHIRE (13736) Tioga(94), Broome(4)
BERLIN Rensselaer
BERNE Albany
BERNHARDS BAY Oswego
BETHEL Sullivan
BETHPAGE Nassau

BIBLE SCHOOL PARK Broome
BIG FLATS (14814) Chemung(85), Steuben(14)
BIG INDIAN Ulster
BILLINGS Dutchess
BINGHAMTON Broome
BLACK CREEK Allegany
BLACK RIVER Jefferson
BLAUVELT Rockland
BLISS (14024) Wyoming(92), Allegany(7)
BLODGETT MILLS Cortland
BLOOMFIELD Ontario
BLOOMING GROVE Orange
BLOOMINGBURG (12721) Sullivan(93), Orange(6)
BLOOMINGDALE Essex
BLOOMINGTON Ulster
BLOOMVILLE Delaware
BLOSSVALE Oneida
BLUE MOUNTAIN LAKE Hamilton
BLUE POINT Suffolk
BOHEMIA Suffolk
BOICEVILLE Ulster
BOLIVAR Allegany
BOLTON LANDING Warren
BOMBAY Franklin
BOONVILLE Oneida
BOSTON Erie
BOUCKVILLE Madison
BOUQUET Essex
BOVINA CENTER Delaware
BOWMANSVILLE Erie
BRADFORD (14815) Schuyler(65), Steuben(34)
BRAINARD Rensselaer
BRAINARDSVILLE Franklin
BRANCHPORT (14418) Yates(90), Steuben(9)
BRANT Erie
BRANT LAKE Warren
BRANTINGHAM Lewis
BRASHER FALLS St. Lawrence
BREESPORT Chemung
BRENTWOOD Suffolk
BREWERTON Onondaga
BREWSTER Putnam
BRIARCLIFF MANOR Westchester
BRIDGEHAMPTON Suffolk
BRIDGEPORT (13030) Madison(56), Onondaga(43)
BRIDGEWATER Oneida
BRIER HILL St. Lawrence
BRIGHTWATERS Suffolk
BROADALBIN (12025) Fulton(84), Saratoga(15)
BROCKPORT Monroe
BROCTON Chautauqua
BRONX Bronx
BRONX New York
BRONXVILLE Westchester
BROOKFIELD Madison
BROOKHAVEN Suffolk
BROOKLYN Kings

BROOKTONDALE (14817) Tompkins(94), Tioga(5)
BROOKVIEW Rensselaer
BROWNVILLE Jefferson
BRUSHTON Franklin
BUCHANAN Westchester
BUFFALO Erie
BULLVILLE Orange
BURDETT Schuyler
BURKE Franklin
BURLINGHAM Sullivan
BURLINGTON FLATS Otsego
BURNT HILLS (12027) Saratoga(83), Schenectady(16)
BURT Niagara
BUSKIRK Rensselaer
BYRON (14422) Genesee(97), Orleans(2)
CADYVILLE Clinton
CAIRO Greene
CALCIUM Jefferson
CALEDONIA (14423) Livingston(98), Monroe(1)
CALLICOON Sullivan
CALLICOON CENTER Sullivan
CALVERTON Suffolk
CAMBRIA HEIGHTS Queens
CAMDEN Oneida
CAMERON Steuben
CAMERON MILLS Steuben
CAMILLUS Onondaga
CAMPBELL Steuben
CAMPBELL HALL Orange
CANAAN Columbia
CANAJOHARIE Montgomery
CANANDAIGUA Ontario
CANASERAGA (14822) Allegany(88), Livingston(11)
CANASTOTA Madison
CANDOR Tioga
CANEADEA Allegany
CANISTEO Steuben
CANTON St. Lawrence
CAPE VINCENT Jefferson
CARLE PLACE Nassau
CARLISLE Schoharie
CARMEL Putnam
CAROGA LAKE Fulton
CARTHAGE (13619) Lewis(97), St. Lawrence(2)
CASSADAGA Chautauqua
CASSVILLE Oneida
CASTILE Wyoming
CASTLE CREEK Broome
CASTLE POINT Dutchess
CASTLETON ON HUDSON Rensselaer
CASTORLAND Lewis
CATO (13033) Cayuga(96), Onondaga(2)
CATSKILL Greene
CATTARAUGUS Cattaraugus
CAYUGA Cayuga
CAYUTA (14824) Schuyler(72), Chemung(27)
CAZENOVIA (13035) Madison(96), Onondaga(3)

CEDARHURST Nassau
CELORON Chautauqua
CEMENTON Greene
CENTER MORICHES Suffolk
CENTEREACH Suffolk
CENTERPORT Suffolk
CENTERVILLE Allegany
CENTRAL BRIDGE Schoharie
CENTRAL ISLIP Suffolk
CENTRAL SQUARE Oswego
CENTRAL VALLEY Orange
CERES Allegany
CHADWICKS Oneida
CHAFFEE (14030) Erie(76),
   Cattaraugus(17), Wyoming(6)
CHAMPLAIN Clinton
CHAPPAQUA Westchester
CHARLOTTEVILLE Schoharie
CHASE MILLS St. Lawrence
CHATEAUGAY Franklin
CHATHAM Columbia
CHAUMONT Jefferson
CHAZY Clinton
CHELSEA Dutchess
CHEMUNG Chemung
CHENANGO BRIDGE Broome
CHENANGO FORKS Broome
CHERRY CREEK Chautauqua
CHERRY PLAIN Rensselaer
CHERRY VALLEY Otsego
CHESTER Orange
CHESTERTOWN Warren
CHICHESTER Ulster
CHILDWOLD St. Lawrence
CHIPPEWA BAY St. Lawrence
CHITTENANGO (13037) Madison(98),
   Onondaga(1)
CHURCHVILLE Monroe
CHURUBUSCO Clinton
CICERO Onondaga
CINCINNATUS Cortland
CIRCLEVILLE Orange
CLARENCE Erie
CLARENCE CENTER (14032) Erie(98),
   Niagara(1)
CLARENDON Orleans
CLARK MILLS Oneida
CLARKSON Monroe
CLARKSVILLE Albany
CLARYVILLE (12725) Sullivan(57),
   Ulster(42)
CLAVERACK Columbia
CLAY Onondaga
CLAYTON Jefferson
CLAYVILLE (13322) Herkimer(91),
   Oneida(8)
CLEMONS Washington
CLEVELAND (13042) Oswego(53),
   Oneida(46)
CLEVERDALE Warren
CLIFTON PARK Saratoga
CLIFTON SPRINGS Ontario
CLIMAX Greene
CLINTON Oneida
CLINTON CORNERS Dutchess
CLINTONDALE Ulster
CLOCKVILLE Madison
CLYDE (14433) Wayne(94), Seneca(5)
CLYMER Chautauqua
COBLESKILL Schoharie
COCHECTON Sullivan
COCHECTON CENTER Sullivan
COEYMANS Albany
COEYMANS HOLLOW (12046)
   Albany(90), Greene(9)
COHOCTON Steuben
COHOES Albany
COLD BROOK (13324) Herkimer(98),
   Hamilton(1)
COLD SPRING Putnam
COLD SPRING HARBOR Suffolk
COLDEN Erie
COLLIERSVILLE Otsego

COLLINS Erie
COLLINS CENTER Erie
COLTON St. Lawrence
COLUMBIAVILLE Columbia
COMMACK Suffolk
COMSTOCK Washington
CONESUS Livingston
CONEWANGO VALLEY (14726)
   Cattaraugus(90), Chautauqua(10)
CONGERS Rockland
CONKLIN Broome
CONNELLY Ulster
CONSTABLE Franklin
CONSTABLEVILLE Lewis
CONSTANTIA Oswego
COOPERS PLAINS Steuben
COOPERSTOWN Otsego
COPAKE Columbia
COPAKE FALLS Columbia
COPENHAGEN Lewis
COPIAGUE Suffolk
CORAM Suffolk
CORBETTSVILLE Broome
CORFU (14036) Genesee(97), Erie(2)
CORINTH Saratoga
CORNING (14830) Steuben(98),
   Chemung(1)
CORNING Steuben
CORNWALL Orange
CORNWALL ON HUDSON Orange
CORNWALLVILLE Greene
CORTLAND (13045) Cortland(91),
   Cayuga(6), Tompkins(1)
CORTLANDT MANOR Westchester
COSSAYUNA Washington
COTTEKILL Ulster
COWLESVILLE (14037) Wyoming(75),
   Erie(24)
COXSACKIE Greene
CRAGSMOOR Ulster
CRANBERRY LAKE St. Lawrence
CRARYVILLE Columbia
CRITTENDEN Erie
CROGHAN Lewis
CROMPOND Westchester
CROPSEYVILLE Rensselaer
CROSS RIVER Westchester
CROTON FALLS Westchester
CROTON ON HUDSON Westchester
CROWN POINT Essex
CUBA (14727) Allegany(79),
   Cattaraugus(20)
CUDDEBACKVILLE (12729) Orange(88),
   Sullivan(11)
CUTCHOGUE Suffolk
CUYLER (13050) Cortland(95),
   Onondaga(4)
DALE Wyoming
DALTON (14836) Livingston(57),
   Allegany(42)
DANNEMORA Clinton
DANSVILLE (14437) Livingston(90),
   Steuben(8)
DARIEN CENTER (14040) Genesee(87),
   Wyoming(12)
DAVENPORT (13750) Delaware(98),
   Otsego(1)
DAVENPORT CENTER Delaware
DAYTON Cattaraugus
DE KALB JUNCTION St. Lawrence
DE LANCEY Delaware
DE PEYSTER St. Lawrence
DE RUYTER (13052) Madison(52),
   Chenango(27), Cortland(18),
   Onondaga(1)
DEANSBORO Oneida
DEER PARK Suffolk
DEER RIVER Lewis
DEFERIET Jefferson
DELANSON (12053) Schenectady(86),
   Albany(13)
DELEVAN Cattaraugus
DELMAR Albany

DELPHI FALLS Onondaga
DENMARK Lewis
DENVER Delaware
DEPAUVILLE Jefferson
DEPEW Erie
DEPOSIT (13754) Broome(70),
   Delaware(29)
DERBY Erie
DEWITTVILLE Chautauqua
DEXTER Jefferson
DIAMOND POINT Warren
DICKINSON CENTER Franklin
DOBBS FERRY Westchester
DOLGEVILLE (13329) Herkimer(95),
   Fulton(4)
DORMANSVILLE Albany
DOVER PLAINS Dutchess
DOWNSVILLE Delaware
DRESDEN Yates
DRYDEN (13053) Tompkins(83),
   Cortland(16)
DUANESBURG Schenectady
DUNDEE (14837) Yates(74), Schuyler(20),
   Steuben(4)
DUNKIRK Chautauqua
DURHAM Greene
DURHAMVILLE Oneida
EAGLE BAY Herkimer
EAGLE BRIDGE Rensselaer
EAGLE HARBOR Orleans
EARLTON Greene
EARLVILLE (13332) Chenango(97),
   Madison(2)
EAST AMHERST Erie
EAST AURORA Erie
EAST BERNE Albany
EAST BETHANY (14054) Genesee(91),
   Wyoming(8)
EAST BLOOMFIELD Ontario
EAST BRANCH Delaware
EAST CHATHAM Columbia
EAST CONCORD Erie
EAST DURHAM Greene
EAST FREETOWN Cortland
EAST GREENBUSH Rensselaer
EAST GREENWICH Washington
EAST HAMPTON Suffolk
EAST HOMER Cortland
EAST ISLIP Suffolk
EAST JEWETT Greene
EAST MARION Suffolk
EAST MEADOW Nassau
EAST MEREDITH Delaware
EAST MORICHES Suffolk
EAST NASSAU (12062) Columbia(98),
   Rensselaer(1)
EAST NORTHPORT Suffolk
EAST NORWICH Nassau
EAST OTTO Cattaraugus
EAST PALMYRA Wayne
EAST PEMBROKE Genesee
EAST PHARSALIA Chenango
EAST QUOGUE Suffolk
EAST RANDOLPH Cattaraugus
EAST ROCHESTER Monroe
EAST ROCKAWAY Nassau
EAST SCHODACK Rensselaer
EAST SETAUKET Suffolk
EAST SPRINGFIELD Otsego
EAST SYRACUSE Onondaga
EAST WILLIAMSON Wayne
EAST WORCESTER Otsego
EASTCHESTER Westchester
EASTPORT Suffolk
EATON Madison
EDEN Erie
EDMESTON Otsego
EDWARDS St. Lawrence
ELBA (14058) Genesee(95), Orleans(4)
ELBRIDGE Onondaga
ELDRED Sullivan
ELIZABETHTOWN Essex
ELIZAVILLE Columbia

ELKA PARK Greene
ELLENBURG Clinton
ELLENBURG CENTER Clinton
ELLENBURG DEPOT Clinton
ELLENVILLE Ulster
ELLICOTTVILLE Cattaraugus
ELLINGTON Chautauqua
ELLISBURG Jefferson
ELMA Erie
ELMHURST Queens
ELMIRA Chemung
ELMONT Nassau
ELMSFORD Westchester
ENDICOTT (13760) Broome(90), Tioga(9)
ENDICOTT Broome
ENDWELL Broome
ERIEVILLE Madison
ERIN Chemung
ESOPUS Ulster
ESPERANCE Montgomery
ETNA Tompkins
EVANS MILLS Jefferson
FABIUS Onondaga
FAIR HAVEN (13064) Oswego(94),
   Onondaga(5)
FAIRFIELD Herkimer
FAIRPORT Monroe
FALCONER Chautauqua
FALLSBURG Sullivan
FANCHER Orleans
FAR ROCKAWAY Queens
FARMERSVILLE STATION (14060)
   Allegany(53), Cattaraugus(46)
FARMINGDALE (11735) Nassau(71),
   Suffolk(28)
FARMINGDALE Nassau
FARMINGTON Ontario
FARMINGVILLE Suffolk
FARNHAM Erie
FAYETTE Seneca
FAYETTEVILLE Onondaga
FELTS MILLS Jefferson
FERNDALE Sullivan
FEURA BUSH Albany
FILLMORE Allegany
FINDLEY LAKE Chautauqua
FINE St. Lawrence
FISHERS Ontario
FISHERS ISLAND Suffolk
FISHERS LANDING Jefferson
FISHKILL Dutchess
FISHS EDDY Delaware
FLEISCHMANNS (12430) Greene(59),
   Delaware(40)
FLORAL PARK (11001) Nassau(90),
   Queens(9)
FLORAL PARK Nassau
FLORAL PARK Queens
FLORIDA Orange
FLUSHING Queens
FLY CREEK Otsego
FONDA (12068) Montgomery(98), Fulton(1)
FORESTBURGH Sullivan
FORESTPORT Oneida
FORESTVILLE Chautauqua
FORT ANN Washington
FORT COVINGTON Franklin
FORT DRUM Jefferson
FORT EDWARD (12828) Washington(53),
   Saratoga(46)
FORT HUNTER Montgomery
FORT JACKSON St. Lawrence
FORT JOHNSON Montgomery
FORT MONTGOMERY Orange
FORT PLAIN (13339) Montgomery(73),
   Herkimer(15), Fulton(11)
FRANKFORT Herkimer
FRANKLIN Delaware
FRANKLIN SPRINGS Oneida
FRANKLIN SQUARE Nassau
FRANKLINVILLE (14737) Cattaraugus(98),
   Allegany(1)
FREDONIA Chautauqua

FREEDOM (14065) Cattaraugus(54), Allegany(45)
FREEHOLD Greene
FREEPORT Nassau
FREEVILLE Tompkins
FREMONT CENTER Sullivan
FREWSBURG (14738) Chautauqua(88), Cattaraugus(11)
FRIENDSHIP Allegany
FULTON Oswego
FULTONHAM Schoharie
FULTONVILLE Montgomery
GABRIELS Franklin
GAINESVILLE Wyoming
GALLUPVILLE Schoharie
GALWAY Saratoga
GANSEVOORT Saratoga
GARDEN CITY Nassau
GARDINER Ulster
GARNERVILLE Rockland
GARRATTSVILLE Otsego
GARRISON Putnam
GASPORT Niagara
GENESEO Livingston
GENEVA (14456) Ontario(92), Seneca(6)
GENOA Cayuga
GEORGETOWN (13072) Madison(96), Chenango(3)
GEORGETOWN Chenango
GERMANTOWN Columbia
GERRY Chautauqua
GETZVILLE Erie
GHENT Columbia
GILBERTSVILLE Otsego
GILBOA Schoharie
GLASCO Ulster
GLEN AUBREY Broome
GLEN COVE Nassau
GLEN HEAD Nassau
GLEN OAKS Queens
GLEN SPEY Sullivan
GLEN WILD Sullivan
GLENFIELD Lewis
GLENFORD Ulster
GLENHAM Dutchess
GLENMONT Albany
GLENS FALLS Warren
GLENWOOD Erie
GLENWOOD LANDING Nassau
GLOVERSVILLE Fulton
GODEFFROY Orange
GOLDENS BRIDGE Westchester
GORHAM Ontario
GOSHEN Orange
GOUVERNEUR St. Lawrence
GOWANDA (14070) Cattaraugus(57), Erie(42)
GRAFTON Rensselaer
GRAHAMSVILLE (12740) Sullivan(86), Ulster(13)
GRAND GORGE (12434) Delaware(92), Schoharie(7)
GRAND ISLAND Erie
GRANITE SPRINGS Westchester
GRANVILLE Washington
GREAT BEND Jefferson
GREAT NECK Nassau
GREAT RIVER Suffolk
GREAT VALLEY Cattaraugus
GREENE (13778) Chenango(66), Broome(33)
GREENFIELD CENTER Saratoga
GREENFIELD PARK Ulster
GREENHURST Chautauqua
GREENLAWN Suffolk
GREENPORT Suffolk
GREENVALE Nassau
GREENVILLE Greene
GREENWICH Washington
GREENWOOD Steuben
GREENWOOD LAKE Orange
GREIG Lewis

GROTON (13073) Tompkins(98), Cayuga(1)
GROVELAND Livingston
GUILDERLAND Albany
GUILDERLAND CENTER Albany
GUILFORD Chenango
HADLEY Saratoga
HAGAMAN Montgomery
HAGUE Warren
HAILESBORO St. Lawrence
HAINES FALLS Greene
HALCOTTSVILLE Delaware
HALL Ontario
HAMBURG Erie
HAMDEN Delaware
HAMILTON Madison
HAMLIN (14464) Monroe(97), Orleans(2)
HAMMOND St. Lawrence
HAMMONDSPORT (14840) Steuben(97), Schuyler(2)
HAMPTON Washington
HAMPTON BAYS Suffolk
HANCOCK Delaware
HANKINS Sullivan
HANNACROIX Greene
HANNAWA FALLS St. Lawrence
HANNIBAL Oswego
HARFORD Cortland
HARPERSFIELD Delaware
HARPURSVILLE Broome
HARRIMAN Orange
HARRIS Sullivan
HARRISON Westchester
HARRISVILLE (13648) St. Lawrence(84), Lewis(15)
HARTFORD Washington
HARTSDALE Westchester
HARTWICK Otsego
HARTWICK SEMINARY Otsego
HASTINGS Oswego
HASTINGS ON HUDSON Westchester
HAUPPAUGE Suffolk
HAVERSTRAW Rockland
HAWTHORNE Westchester
HECTOR Schuyler
HELENA St. Lawrence
HELMUTH Erie
HEMLOCK (14466) Ontario(58), Livingston(41)
HEMPSTEAD Nassau
HENDERSON Jefferson
HENDERSON HARBOR Jefferson
HENRIETTA Monroe
HENSONVILLE Greene
HERKIMER Herkimer
HERMON St. Lawrence
HEUVELTON St. Lawrence
HEWLETT Nassau
HICKSVILLE Nassau
HIGH FALLS Ulster
HIGHLAND Ulster
HIGHLAND FALLS Orange
HIGHLAND LAKE Sullivan
HIGHLAND MILLS Orange
HIGHMOUNT Ulster
HILLBURN Rockland
HILLSDALE Columbia
HILTON Monroe
HIMROD Yates
HINCKLEY Oneida
HINSDALE Cattaraugus
HOBART Delaware
HOFFMEISTER Hamilton
HOGANSBURG Franklin
HOLBROOK Suffolk
HOLLAND Erie
HOLLAND PATENT Oneida
HOLLEY (14470) Orleans(97), Monroe(2)
HOLLOWVILLE Columbia
HOLMES (12531) Dutchess(82), Putnam(17)
HOLTSVILLE Suffolk

HOMER (13077) Cortland(92), Onondaga(4), Cayuga(2)
HONEOYE Ontario
HONEOYE FALLS (14472) Monroe(90), Livingston(6), Ontario(2)
HOOSICK Rensselaer
HOOSICK FALLS Rensselaer
HOPEWELL JUNCTION (12533) Dutchess(98), Putnam(1)
HOPKINTON St. Lawrence
HORNELL Steuben
HORSEHEADS Chemung
HORTONVILLE Sullivan
HOUGHTON Allegany
HOWELLS Orange
HOWES CAVE Schoharie
HUBBARDSVILLE Madison
HUDSON Columbia
HUDSON FALLS Washington
HUGHSONVILLE Dutchess
HUGUENOT Orange
HULETTS LANDING Washington
HUME Allegany
HUNT (14846) Livingston(75), Allegany(24)
HUNTER Greene
HUNTINGTON Suffolk
HUNTINGTON STATION Suffolk
HURLEY Ulster
HURLEYVILLE Sullivan
HYDE PARK Dutchess
ILION Herkimer
INDIAN LAKE Hamilton
INDUSTRY Monroe
INLET Hamilton
INTERLAKEN Seneca
INWOOD Nassau
INWOOD Queens
IONIA (14475) Ontario(93), Monroe(6)
IRVING (14081) Chautauqua(50), Erie(47), Cattaraugus(2)
IRVINGTON Westchester
ISLAND PARK Nassau
ISLANDIA Suffolk
ISLIP Suffolk
ISLIP TERRACE Suffolk
ITHACA Tompkins
JACKSONVILLE Tompkins
JAMAICA Queens
JAMESPORT Suffolk
JAMESTOWN Chautauqua
JAMESVILLE Onondaga
JASPER Steuben
JAVA CENTER Wyoming
JAVA VILLAGE Wyoming
JAY Essex
JEFFERSON (12093) Schoharie(73), Delaware(26)
JEFFERSON VALLEY Westchester
JEFFERSONVILLE Sullivan
JERICHO Nassau
JEWETT Greene
JOHNSBURG Warren
JOHNSON Orange
JOHNSON CITY Broome
JOHNSONVILLE Rensselaer
JOHNSTOWN Fulton
JORDAN (13080) Onondaga(87), Cayuga(12)
JORDANVILLE Herkimer
KANONA Steuben
KATONAH Westchester
KATTSKILL BAY Warren
KAUNEONGA LAKE Sullivan
KEENE Essex
KEENE VALLEY Essex
KEESEVILLE (12944) Clinton(92), Essex(7)
KEESEVILLE Clinton
KENDALL (14476) Orleans(95), Monroe(4)
KENNEDY (14747) Chautauqua(90), Cattaraugus(9)
KENOZA LAKE Sullivan
KENT Orleans

KERHONKSON Ulster
KEUKA PARK Yates
KIAMESHA LAKE Sullivan
KILL BUCK Cattaraugus
KILLAWOG Broome
KINDERHOOK Columbia
KING FERRY Cayuga
KINGS PARK Suffolk
KINGSTON Ulster
KIRKVILLE (13082) Madison(57), Onondaga(42)
KIRKWOOD Broome
KNAPP CREEK Cattaraugus
KNOWLESVILLE Orleans
KNOX Albany
KNOXBORO Oneida
LA FARGEVILLE Jefferson
LA FAYETTE Onondaga
LACONA Oswego
LAGRANGEVILLE Dutchess
LAKE CLEAR Franklin
LAKE GEORGE Warren
LAKE GROVE Suffolk
LAKE HILL Ulster
LAKE HUNTINGTON Sullivan
LAKE KATRINE Ulster
LAKE LUZERNE Warren
LAKE PEEKSKILL Putnam
LAKE PLACID Essex
LAKE PLEASANT Hamilton
LAKE VIEW Erie
LAKEMONT Yates
LAKEVILLE Livingston
LAKEWOOD Chautauqua
LANCASTER Erie
LANESVILLE Greene
LANSING (14882) Tompkins(98), Cayuga(1)
LARCHMONT Westchester
LATHAM Albany
LAUREL Suffolk
LAURENS Otsego
LAWRENCE Nassau
LAWRENCEVILLE St. Lawrence
LAWTONS Erie
LAWYERSVILLE Schoharie
LE ROY (14482) Genesee(95), Livingston(3)
LEBANON Madison
LEBANON SPRINGS Columbia
LEE CENTER Oneida
LEEDS Greene
LEICESTER (14481) Livingston(98), Wyoming(1)
LEON Cattaraugus
LEONARDSVILLE Madison
LEVITTOWN Nassau
LEW BEACH (12753) Ulster(58), Sullivan(38), Delaware(4)
LEWIS Essex
LEWISTON Niagara
LEXINGTON Greene
LIBERTY Sullivan
LILY DALE Chautauqua
LIMA (14485) Livingston(93), Ontario(6)
LIMERICK Jefferson
LIMESTONE Cattaraugus
LINCOLNDALE Westchester
LINDENHURST Suffolk
LINDLEY Steuben
LINWOOD Genesee
LISBON St. Lawrence
LISLE Broome
LITTLE FALLS Herkimer
LITTLE GENESEE Allegany
LITTLE VALLEY Cattaraugus
LITTLE YORK Cortland
LIVERPOOL Onondaga
LIVINGSTON Columbia
LIVINGSTON MANOR (12758) Sullivan(91), Ulster(7)
LIVONIA (14487) Livingston(93), Ontario(6)
LIVONIA CENTER Livingston

LOCH SHELDRAKE Sullivan
LOCKE (13092) Tompkins(97), Cayuga(2)
LOCKPORT Niagara
LOCKWOOD (14859) Tioga(59), Chemung(40)
LOCUST VALLEY Nassau
LODI Seneca
LONG BEACH Nassau
LONG EDDY (12760) Delaware(67), Sullivan(32)
LONG ISLAND CITY Queens
LONG LAKE Hamilton
LORRAINE Jefferson
LOWMAN Chemung
LOWVILLE (13367) Lewis(94), Herkimer(5)
LYCOMING Oswego
LYNBROOK Nassau
LYNDONVILLE (14098) Orleans(98), Niagara(1)
LYON MOUNTAIN Clinton
LYONS (14489) Wayne(95), Ontario(2), Seneca(2)
LYONS FALLS Lewis
LYSANDER Onondaga
MACEDON (14502) Wayne(97), Monroe(2)
MACHIAS Cattaraugus
MADISON (13402) Madison(98), Oneida(1)
MADRID St. Lawrence
MAHOPAC (10541) Putnam(93), Westchester(6)
MAHOPAC FALLS Putnam
MAINE Broome
MALDEN BRIDGE Columbia
MALDEN ON HUDSON Ulster
MALLORY Oswego
MALONE Franklin
MALVERNE Nassau
MAMARONECK Westchester
MANCHESTER Ontario
MANHASSET Nassau
MANLIUS (13104) Onondaga(98), Madison(1)
MANNSVILLE Jefferson
MANORVILLE Suffolk
MAPLE SPRINGS Chautauqua
MAPLE VIEW Oswego
MAPLECREST Greene
MARATHON (13803) Cortland(94), Broome(5)
MARCELLUS Onondaga
MARCY Oneida
MARGARETVILLE (12455) Delaware(96), Ulster(3)
MARIETTA Onondaga
MARILLA Erie
MARION Wayne
MARLBORO (12542) Ulster(93), Orange(6)
MARTINSBURG Lewis
MARTVILLE (13111) Cayuga(87), Oswego(12)
MARYKNOLL Westchester
MARYLAND Otsego
MASONVILLE Delaware
MASSAPEQUA Nassau
MASSAPEQUA PARK Nassau
MASSENA St. Lawrence
MASTIC Suffolk
MASTIC BEACH Suffolk
MATTITUCK Suffolk
MATTYDALE Onondaga
MAYBROOK (12543) Orange(98), Dutchess(1)
MAYFIELD Fulton
MAYVILLE Chautauqua
MC CONNELLSVILLE Oneida
MC DONOUGH Chenango
MC GRAW Cortland
MC LEAN Tompkins
MECHANICVILLE (12118) Saratoga(98), Rensselaer(1)
MECKLENBURG Schuyler
MEDFORD Suffolk
MEDINA Orleans

MEDUSA Albany
MELLENVILLE Columbia
MELROSE Rensselaer
MELVILLE Suffolk
MEMPHIS Onondaga
MENDON Monroe
MERIDALE Delaware
MERIDIAN Cayuga
MERRICK Nassau
MEXICO Oswego
MID HUDSON Orange
MID ISLAND Suffolk
MIDDLE FALLS Washington
MIDDLE GRANVILLE Washington
MIDDLE GROVE Saratoga
MIDDLE ISLAND Suffolk
MIDDLE VILLAGE Queens
MIDDLEBURGH (12122) Albany(57), Schoharie(42)
MIDDLEPORT (14105) Niagara(94), Orleans(3), Genesee(1)
MIDDLESEX Yates
MIDDLETOWN (10940) Orange(98), Sullivan(1)
MIDDLETOWN Orange
MIDDLEVILLE Herkimer
MILFORD Otsego
MILL NECK Nassau
MILLBROOK Dutchess
MILLER PLACE Suffolk
MILLERTON (12546) Dutchess(96), Columbia(3)
MILLPORT (14864) Chemung(85), Schuyler(14)
MILLWOOD Westchester
MILTON Ulster
MINEOLA Nassau
MINERVA Essex
MINETTO Oswego
MINEVILLE Essex
MINOA Onondaga
MODEL CITY Niagara
MODENA Ulster
MOHAWK Herkimer
MOHEGAN LAKE Westchester
MOIRA Franklin
MONGAUP VALLEY Sullivan
MONROE Orange
MONSEY Rockland
MONTAUK Suffolk
MONTEZUMA Cayuga
MONTGOMERY Orange
MONTICELLO Sullivan
MONTOUR FALLS Schuyler
MONTROSE Westchester
MOOERS Clinton
MOOERS FORKS Clinton
MORAVIA Cayuga
MORIAH Essex
MORIAH CENTER Essex
MORICHES Suffolk
MORRIS Otsego
MORRISONVILLE Clinton
MORRISTOWN St. Lawrence
MORRISVILLE Madison
MORTON Orleans
MOTTVILLE Onondaga
MOUNT KISCO Westchester
MOUNT MARION Ulster
MOUNT MORRIS Livingston
MOUNT SINAI Suffolk
MOUNT TREMPER Ulster
MOUNT UPTON (13809) Chenango(66), Otsego(33)
MOUNT VERNON Westchester
MOUNT VISION Otsego
MOUNTAIN DALE Sullivan
MOUNTAINVILLE Orange
MUMFORD Monroe
MUNNSVILLE (13409) Madison(92), Oneida(7)
NANUET Rockland
NAPANOCH Ulster

NAPLES (14512) Ontario(75), Yates(19), Steuben(3)
NARROWSBURG Sullivan
NASSAU Rensselaer
NATURAL BRIDGE (13665) Jefferson(96), Lewis(3)
NEDROW Onondaga
NELLISTON Montgomery
NESCONSET Suffolk
NEVERSINK Sullivan
NEW BALTIMORE Greene
NEW BERLIN Chenango
NEW CITY Rockland
NEW HAMPTON Orange
NEW HARTFORD Oneida
NEW HAVEN Oswego
NEW HYDE PARK (11040) Nassau(96), Queens(3)
NEW HYDE PARK Nassau
NEW KINGSTON Delaware
NEW LEBANON Columbia
NEW LISBON Otsego
NEW MILFORD Orange
NEW PALTZ Ulster
NEW ROCHELLE Westchester
NEW RUSSIA Essex
NEW SUFFOLK Suffolk
NEW WINDSOR Orange
NEW WOODSTOCK (13122) Onondaga(65), Madison(34)
NEW YORK New York
NEW YORK MILLS Oneida
NEWARK (14513) Wayne(98), Ontario(1)
NEWARK VALLEY (13811) Tioga(93), Broome(6)
NEWBURGH Orange
NEWCOMB Essex
NEWFANE Niagara
NEWFIELD Tompkins
NEWPORT Herkimer
NEWTON FALLS St. Lawrence
NEWTONVILLE Albany
NIAGARA FALLS Niagara
NIAGARA UNIVERSITY Niagara
NICHOLS Tioga
NICHOLVILLE St. Lawrence
NINEVEH Broome
NIOBE Chautauqua
NIVERVILLE Columbia
NORFOLK St. Lawrence
NORTH BABYLON Suffolk
NORTH BANGOR Franklin
NORTH BAY Oneida
NORTH BLENHEIM Schoharie
NORTH BOSTON Erie
NORTH BRANCH Sullivan
NORTH BROOKFIELD Madison
NORTH CHATHAM Columbia
NORTH CHILI Monroe
NORTH CLYMER Chautauqua
NORTH COHOCTON Steuben
NORTH COLLINS Erie
NORTH CREEK Warren
NORTH EVANS Erie
NORTH GRANVILLE Washington
NORTH GREECE Monroe
NORTH HOOSICK Rensselaer
NORTH HUDSON Essex
NORTH JAVA Wyoming
NORTH LAWRENCE St. Lawrence
NORTH NORWICH Chenango
NORTH PITCHER Chenango
NORTH RIVER Warren
NORTH ROSE Wayne
NORTH SALEM Westchester
NORTH TONAWANDA Niagara
NORTHPORT Suffolk
NORTHVILLE Fulton
NORTON HILL Greene
NORWICH Chenango
NORWOOD St. Lawrence
NUNDA Livingston
NYACK Rockland

OAK HILL Greene
OAKDALE Suffolk
OAKFIELD Genesee
OAKS CORNERS Ontario
OBERNBURG Sullivan
OCEAN BEACH Suffolk
OCEANSIDE Nassau
ODESSA Schuyler
OGDENSBURG St. Lawrence
OLCOTT Niagara
OLD BETHPAGE Nassau
OLD CHATHAM Columbia
OLD FORGE Herkimer
OLD WESTBURY Nassau
OLEAN Cattaraugus
OLIVEBRIDGE Ulster
OLIVEREA Ulster
OLMSTEDVILLE Essex
ONCHIOTA Franklin
ONEIDA (13421) Madison(84), Oneida(15)
ONEONTA Otsego
ONTARIO (14519) Wayne(96), Monroe(3)
ONTARIO CENTER Wayne
ORAN Onondaga
ORANGEBURG Rockland
ORCHARD PARK Erie
ORIENT Suffolk
ORISKANY Oneida
ORISKANY FALLS (13425) Oneida(97), Madison(2)
ORWELL Oswego
OSSINING Westchester
OSWEGATCHIE St. Lawrence
OSWEGO Oswego
OTEGO (13825) Otsego(93), Delaware(6)
OTISVILLE (10963) Orange(97), Sullivan(2)
OTTO Cattaraugus
OUAQUAGA Broome
OVID Seneca
OWASCO Cayuga
OWEGO Tioga
OWLS HEAD Franklin
OXBOW Jefferson
OXFORD Chenango
OYSTER BAY Nassau
PAINTED POST (14870) Steuben(97), Schuyler(2)
PALATINE BRIDGE Montgomery
PALENVILLE Greene
PALISADES Rockland
PALMYRA (14522) Wayne(89), Ontario(10)
PANAMA Chautauqua
PARADOX Essex
PARIS Oneida
PARISH Oswego
PARISHVILLE St. Lawrence
PARKSVILLE Sullivan
PATCHOGUE Suffolk
PATTERSON Putnam
PATTERSONVILLE Schenectady
PAUL SMITHS Franklin
PAVILION (14525) Genesee(61), Wyoming(33), Livingston(5)
PAWLING Dutchess
PEARL RIVER Rockland
PECONIC Suffolk
PEEKSKILL Westchester
PELHAM Westchester
PENFIELD Monroe
PENN YAN Yates
PENNELLVILLE Oswego
PERKINSVILLE Steuben
PERRY Wyoming
PERRYSBURG Cattaraugus
PERRYVILLE Madison
PERU Clinton
PETERBORO Madison
PETERSBURG Rensselaer
PHELPS (14532) Ontario(94), Seneca(5)
PHILADELPHIA Jefferson
PHILLIPSPORT Sullivan
PHILMONT Columbia

PHOENICIA Ulster
PHOENIX (13135) Oswego(87),
   Onondaga(12)
PIERCEFIELD St. Lawrence
PIERMONT Rockland
PIERREPONT MANOR Jefferson
PIFFARD Livingston
PIKE Wyoming
PINE BUSH (12566) Ulster(58),
   Orange(37), Sullivan(3)
PINE CITY (14871) Chemung(83),
   Steuben(16)
PINE HILL Ulster
PINE ISLAND Orange
PINE PLAINS (12567) Dutchess(92),
   Columbia(7)
PINE VALLEY Chemung
PISECO Hamilton
PITCHER (13136) Chenango(96),
   Cortland(3)
PITTSFORD Monroe
PLAINVIEW Nassau
PLAINVILLE Onondaga
PLATTEKILL Ulster
PLATTSBURGH Clinton
PLEASANT VALLEY Dutchess
PLEASANTVILLE Westchester
PLESSIS Jefferson
PLYMOUTH Chenango
POESTENKILL Rensselaer
POINT LOOKOUT Nassau
POLAND (13431) Oneida(90), Herkimer(9)
POMONA Rockland
POMPEY Onondaga
POND EDDY Sullivan
POOLVILLE Madison
POPLAR RIDGE Cayuga
PORT BYRON Cayuga
PORT CHESTER Westchester
PORT CRANE Broome
PORT EWEN Ulster
PORT GIBSON Ontario
PORT HENRY Essex
PORT JEFFERSON Suffolk
PORT JEFFERSON STATION Suffolk
PORT JERVIS Orange
PORT KENT Essex
PORT LEYDEN Lewis
PORT WASHINGTON Nassau
PORTAGEVILLE (14536) Wyoming(74),
   Allegany(25)
PORTER CORNERS Saratoga
PORTLAND Chautauqua
PORTLANDVILLE Otsego
PORTVILLE (14770) Cattaraugus(75),
   Allegany(24)
POTSDAM St. Lawrence
POTTERSVILLE Warren
POUGHKEEPSIE Dutchess
POUGHQUAG Dutchess
POUND RIDGE Westchester
PRATTS HOLLOW Madison
PRATTSBURGH (14873) Steuben(98),
   Yates(1)
PRATTSVILLE (12468) Greene(95),
   Delaware(4)
PREBLE (13141) Cortland(63),
   Onondaga(36)
PRESTON HOLLOW (12469) Greene(95),
   Albany(4)
PROSPECT Oneida
PULASKI Oswego
PULTENEY Steuben
PULTNEYVILLE Wayne
PURCHASE Westchester
PURDYS Westchester
PURLING Greene
PUTNAM STATION Washington
PUTNAM VALLEY Putnam
PYRITES St. Lawrence
QUAKER STREET Schenectady
QUEENS VILLAGE Queens
QUEENSBURY Warren

QUOGUE Suffolk
RAINBOW LAKE Franklin
RANDOLPH Cattaraugus
RANSOMVILLE Niagara
RAQUETTE LAKE Hamilton
RAVENA Albany
RAY BROOK Essex
RAYMONDVILLE St. Lawrence
READING CENTER Schuyler
RED CREEK (13143) Wayne(98),
   Cayuga(1)
RED HOOK Dutchess
REDFIELD Oswego
REDFORD Clinton
REDWOOD Jefferson
REMSEN Oneida
REMSENBURG Suffolk
RENSSELAER Rensselaer
RENSSELAER FALLS St. Lawrence
RENSSELAERVILLE Albany
RETSOF Livingston
REXFORD (12148) Saratoga(96),
   Schenectady(3)
REXVILLE (14877) Steuben(98),
   Allegany(1)
RHINEBECK Dutchess
RHINECLIFF Dutchess
RICHBURG Allegany
RICHFIELD SPRINGS Otsego
RICHFORD (13835) Tioga(57),
   Broome(29), Cortland(12)
RICHLAND Oswego
RICHMOND HILL Queens
RICHMONDVILLE (12149) Schoharie(97),
   Otsego(2)
RICHVILLE St. Lawrence
RIDGE Suffolk
RIFTON Ulster
RIPARIUS Warren
RIPLEY Chautauqua
RIVERHEAD Suffolk
ROCHESTER Monroe
ROCK CITY FALLS Saratoga
ROCK HILL Sullivan
ROCK STREAM (14878) Schuyler(71),
   Yates(28)
ROCK TAVERN Orange
ROCKAWAY PARK Queens
ROCKLAND M P C Rockland
ROCKVILLE CENTRE Nassau
ROCKY POINT Suffolk
RODMAN Jefferson
RODMAN Lewis
ROME Oneida
ROMULUS Seneca
RONKONKOMA Suffolk
ROOSEVELT Nassau
ROOSEVELTOWN St. Lawrence
ROSCOE (12776) Sullivan(74),
   Delaware(25)
ROSE Wayne
ROSEBOOM Otsego
ROSENDALE Ulster
ROSLYN Nassau
ROSLYN HEIGHTS Nassau
ROSSBURG Allegany
ROTTERDAM JUNCTION Schenectady
ROUND LAKE Saratoga
ROUND TOP Greene
ROUSES POINT Clinton
ROXBURY Delaware
RUBY Ulster
RUSH Monroe
RUSHFORD Allegany
RUSHVILLE (14544) Yates(54),
   Ontario(45)
RUSSELL St. Lawrence
RYE Westchester
SABAEL Hamilton
SACKETS HARBOR Jefferson
SAG HARBOR Suffolk
SAGAPONACK Suffolk
SAINT BONAVENTURE Cattaraugus

SAINT JAMES Suffolk
SAINT JOHNSVILLE (13452)
   Montgomery(59), Fulton(40)
SAINT REGIS FALLS Franklin
SALAMANCA Cattaraugus
SALISBURY CENTER Herkimer
SALISBURY MILLS Orange
SALT POINT Dutchess
SANBORN Niagara
SAND LAKE Rensselaer
SANDUSKY Cattaraugus
SANDY CREEK Oswego
SANGERFIELD Oneida
SARANAC Clinton
SARANAC LAKE (12983) Franklin(82),
   Essex(17)
SARANAC LAKE Franklin
SARATOGA SPRINGS Saratoga
SARDINIA Erie
SAUGERTIES Ulster
SAUQUOIT (13456) Oneida(93),
   Herkimer(6)
SAVANNAH Wayne
SAVONA Steuben
SAYVILLE Suffolk
SCARSDALE Westchester
SCHAGHTICOKE Rensselaer
SCHENECTADY (12309) Schenectady(92),
   Albany(6)
SCHENECTADY Schenectady
SCHENEVUS Otsego
SCHODACK LANDING (12156)
   Rensselaer(91), Columbia(8)
SCHOHARIE Schoharie
SCHROON LAKE Essex
SCHUYLER FALLS Clinton
SCHUYLER LAKE Otsego
SCHUYLERVILLE Saratoga
SCIO Allegany
SCIPIO CENTER Cayuga
SCOTTSBURG Livingston
SCOTTSVILLE Monroe
SEA CLIFF Nassau
SEAFORD Nassau
SELDEN Suffolk
SELKIRK Albany
SENECA CASTLE Ontario
SENECA FALLS Seneca
SENNETT Cayuga
SEVERANCE Essex
SHANDAKEN (12480) Ulster(71),
   Greene(28)
SHARON SPRINGS (13459)
   Schoharie(94), Montgomery(5)
SHEDS Madison
SHELTER ISLAND Suffolk
SHELTER ISLAND HEIGHTS Suffolk
SHENOROCK Westchester
SHERBURNE (13460) Chenango(98),
   Madison(1)
SHERIDAN Chautauqua
SHERMAN Chautauqua
SHERRILL Oneida
SHINHOPPLE Delaware
SHIRLEY Suffolk
SHOKAN Ulster
SHOREHAM Suffolk
SHORTSVILLE Ontario
SHRUB OAK Westchester
SHUSHAN Washington
SIDNEY (13838) Delaware(94), Otsego(5)
SIDNEY CENTER Delaware
SILVER BAY Warren
SILVER CREEK Chautauqua
SILVER LAKE Wyoming
SILVER SPRINGS Wyoming
SINCLAIRVILLE Chautauqua
SKANEATELES (13152) Onondaga(92),
   Cayuga(7)
SKANEATELES FALLS Onondaga
SLATE HILL Orange
SLATERVILLE SPRINGS Tompkins
SLINGERLANDS Albany

SLOANSVILLE Schoharie
SLOATSBURG Rockland
SMALLWOOD Sullivan
SMITHBORO Tioga
SMITHS LANDING Greene
SMITHTOWN Suffolk
SMITHVILLE FLATS (13841) Cortland(80),
   Chenango(14), Broome(4)
SMYRNA Chenango
SODUS Wayne
SODUS CENTER Wayne
SODUS POINT Wayne
SOLSVILLE Madison
SOMERS Westchester
SONYEA Livingston
SOUND BEACH Suffolk
SOUTH BETHLEHEM Albany
SOUTH BUTLER Wayne
SOUTH BYRON Genesee
SOUTH CAIRO Greene
SOUTH COLTON St. Lawrence
SOUTH DAYTON (14138)
   Cattaraugus(65), Chautauqua(34)
SOUTH EDMESTON Otsego
SOUTH FALLSBURG Sullivan
SOUTH GLENS FALLS Saratoga
SOUTH JAMESPORT Suffolk
SOUTH KORTRIGHT Delaware
SOUTH LIMA Livingston
SOUTH NEW BERLIN Chenango
SOUTH OTSELIC Chenango
SOUTH PLYMOUTH Chenango
SOUTH RUTLAND Jefferson
SOUTH SALEM Westchester
SOUTH SCHODACK Rensselaer
SOUTH WALES Erie
SOUTH WESTERLO Albany
SOUTHAMPTON Suffolk
SOUTHFIELD Orange
SOUTHOLD Suffolk
SPARKILL Rockland
SPARROW BUSH (12780) Orange(82),
   Sullivan(17)
SPECULATOR Hamilton
SPENCER (14883) Tioga(79),
   Tompkins(20)
SPENCERPORT Monroe
SPENCERTOWN Columbia
SPEONK Suffolk
SPRAKERS Montgomery
SPRING BROOK Erie
SPRING GLEN Ulster
SPRING VALLEY Rockland
SPRINGFIELD CENTER Otsego
SPRINGVILLE (14141) Erie(94),
   Cattaraugus(5)
SPRINGWATER (14560) Ontario(51),
   Livingston(49)
STAATSBURG Dutchess
STAFFORD Genesee
STAMFORD (12167) Delaware(76),
   Schoharie(23)
STANFORDVILLE Dutchess
STANLEY (14561) Ontario(94), Yates(5)
STAR LAKE St. Lawrence
STATEN ISLAND Richmond
STEAMBURG Cattaraugus
STELLA NIAGARA Niagara
STEPHENTOWN Rensselaer
STERLING Cayuga
STERLING FOREST Orange
STILLWATER Saratoga
STITTVILLE Oneida
STOCKTON Chautauqua
STONE RIDGE Ulster
STONY BROOK Suffolk
STONY CREEK Warren
STONY POINT Rockland
STORMVILLE Dutchess
STOTTVILLE Columbia
STOW Chautauqua
STRATFORD (13470) Fulton(77),
   Herkimer(22)

STRYKERSVILLE (14145) Wyoming(92), Erie(7)
STUYVESANT Columbia
STUYVESANT FALLS Columbia
SUFFERN Rockland
SUGAR LOAF Orange
SUGARBUSH Franklin
SUMMIT Schoharie
SUMMITVILLE Sullivan
SUNDOWN Ulster
SURPRISE Greene
SWAIN Allegany
SWAN LAKE Sullivan
SYLVAN BEACH Oneida
SYOSSET Nassau
SYRACUSE Onondaga
TABERG Oneida
TALLMAN Rockland
TANNERSVILLE Greene
TAPPAN Rockland
TARRYTOWN Westchester
THENDARA Herkimer
THERESA Jefferson
THIELLS Rockland
THOMPSON RIDGE Orange
THOMPSONVILLE Sullivan
THORNWOOD Westchester
THOUSAND ISLAND PARK Jefferson
THREE MILE BAY Jefferson
TICONDEROGA Essex
TILLSON Ulster
TIOGA CENTER Tioga
TIVOLI (12583) Dutchess(62), Columbia(37)
TOMKINS COVE Rockland
TONAWANDA Erie
TREADWELL Delaware
TRIBES HILL Montgomery
TROUPSBURG Steuben
TROUT CREEK Delaware
TROY Albany
TROY Rensselaer
TRUMANSBURG (14886) Tompkins(61), Schuyler(26), Seneca(12)
TRUXTON (13158) Cortland(97), Madison(2)
TUCKAHOE Westchester
TULLY (13159) Onondaga(82), Cortland(17)
TUNNEL Broome
TUPPER LAKE (12986) Franklin(94), St. Lawrence(5)
TURIN Lewis
TUXEDO PARK Orange
TYRONE Schuyler
ULSTER PARK Ulster
UNADILLA Otsego
UNION HILL Wayne
UNION SPRINGS Cayuga
UNIONDALE Nassau
UNIONVILLE Orange

UPPER JAY Essex
UPTON Suffolk
UTICA (13501) Oneida(97), Herkimer(2)
UTICA Oneida
VAILS GATE Orange
VALATIE Columbia
VALHALLA Westchester
VALLEY COTTAGE Rockland
VALLEY FALLS Rensselaer
VALLEY STREAM Nassau
VALOIS (14888) Schuyler(82), Seneca(17)
VAN BUREN POINT Chautauqua
VAN ETTEN (14889) Chemung(87), Schuyler(6), Tioga(5)
VAN HORNESVILLE (13475) Herkimer(82), Otsego(17)
VARYSBURG Wyoming
VERBANK Dutchess
VERMONTVILLE Franklin
VERNON Oneida
VERNON CENTER Oneida
VERONA Oneida
VERONA BEACH Oneida
VERPLANCK Westchester
VERSAILLES Cattaraugus
VESTAL Broome
VICTOR (14564) Ontario(97), Monroe(2)
VICTORY MILLS Saratoga
VOORHEESVILLE Albany
WACCABUC Westchester
WADDINGTON St. Lawrence
WADHAMS Essex
WADING RIVER Suffolk
WAINSCOTT Suffolk
WALDEN Orange
WALES CENTER Erie
WALKER VALLEY Ulster
WALLKILL (12589) Ulster(78), Orange(21)
WALTON Delaware
WALWORTH Wayne
WAMPSVILLE Madison
WANAKENA St. Lawrence
WANTAGH Nassau
WAPPINGERS FALLS Dutchess
WARNERS Onondaga
WARNERVILLE Schoharie
WARRENSBURG Warren
WARSAW Wyoming
WARWICK Orange
WASHINGTON MILLS Oneida
WASHINGTONVILLE Orange
WASSAIC Dutchess
WATER MILL Suffolk
WATERFORD Saratoga
WATERLOO Seneca
WATERPORT Orleans
WATERTOWN Jefferson
WATERVILLE (13480) Oneida(95), Madison(4)
WATERVLIET Albany
WATKINS GLEN Schuyler

WAVERLY (14892) Tioga(91), Chemung(8)
WAWARSING Ulster
WAYLAND (14572) Steuben(79), Livingston(20)
WAYNE Schuyler
WEBSTER Monroe
WEBSTER CROSSING Livingston
WEEDSPORT (13166) Cayuga(97), Onondaga(2)
WELLESLEY ISLAND Jefferson
WELLS Hamilton
WELLS BRIDGE Otsego
WELLSBURG Chemung
WELLSVILLE Allegany
WEST BABYLON Suffolk
WEST BLOOMFIELD Ontario
WEST BURLINGTON Otsego
WEST CAMP Ulster
WEST CHAZY Clinton
WEST CLARKSVILLE Allegany
WEST COPAKE Columbia
WEST COXSACKIE Greene
WEST DANBY Tompkins
WEST DAVENPORT Delaware
WEST EATON Madison
WEST EDMESTON (13485) Madison(74), Otsego(24)
WEST EXETER Otsego
WEST FALLS Erie
WEST FULTON Schoharie
WEST HARRISON Westchester
WEST HAVERSTRAW Rockland
WEST HEMPSTEAD Nassau
WEST HENRIETTA Monroe
WEST HURLEY Ulster
WEST ISLIP Suffolk
WEST KILL Greene
WEST LEBANON Columbia
WEST LEYDEN (13489) Lewis(98), Oneida(1)
WEST MONROE Oswego
WEST NYACK Rockland
WEST ONEONTA Otsego
WEST PARK Ulster
WEST POINT Orange
WEST SAND LAKE Rensselaer
WEST SAYVILLE Suffolk
WEST SHOKAN Ulster
WEST STOCKHOLM St. Lawrence
WEST VALLEY Cattaraugus
WEST WINFIELD (13491) Herkimer(90), Otsego(6), Oneida(2)
WESTBROOKVILLE Sullivan
WESTBURY Nassau
WESTDALE (13483) Oneida(97), Oswego(2)
WESTERLO Albany
WESTERN Oneida
WESTERNVILLE Oneida
WESTFIELD Chautauqua
WESTFORD Otsego

WESTHAMPTON Suffolk
WESTHAMPTON BEACH Suffolk
WESTMORELAND Oneida
WESTONS MILLS Cattaraugus
WESTPORT Essex
WESTTOWN Orange
WEVERTOWN Warren
WHALLONSBURG Essex
WHIPPLEVILLE Franklin
WHITE LAKE Sullivan
WHITE PLAINS Westchester
WHITE SULPHUR SPRINGS Sullivan
WHITEHALL Washington
WHITESBORO Oneida
WHITESVILLE (14897) Allegany(93), Steuben(6)
WHITNEY POINT Broome
WILLARD Seneca
WILLET (13863) Cortland(98), Broome(1)
WILLIAMSON Wayne
WILLIAMSTOWN Oswego
WILLISTON PARK Nassau
WILLOW Ulster
WILLSBORO Essex
WILLSEYVILLE (13864) Tioga(67), Tompkins(32)
WILMINGTON (12997) Saratoga(84), Essex(15)
WILSON Niagara
WINDHAM Greene
WINDSOR Broome
WINGDALE Dutchess
WINTHROP St. Lawrence
WITHERBEE Essex
WOLCOTT Wayne
WOODBOURNE (12788) Sullivan(97), Ulster(2)
WOODBURY Nassau
WOODGATE Oneida
WOODHULL Steuben
WOODMERE Nassau
WOODRIDGE Sullivan
WOODSTOCK Ulster
WOODVILLE Jefferson
WORCESTER Otsego
WURTSBORO Sullivan
WYANDANCH Suffolk
WYNANTSKILL Rensselaer
WYOMING (14591) Wyoming(87), Genesee(12)
YAPHANK Suffolk
YONKERS Westchester
YORK Livingston
YORKSHIRE Cattaraugus
YORKTOWN HEIGHTS Westchester
YORKVILLE Oneida
YOUNGSTOWN Niagara
YOUNGSVILLE Sullivan
YULAN Sullivan

New York ZIP/City Cross Reference

00401-00401	PLEASANTVILLE
00501-00544	HOLTSVILLE
06390-06390	FISHERS ISLAND
09002-09894	APO or FPO
10000-10292	NEW YORK
10300-10314	STATEN ISLAND
10400-10499	BRONX
10501-10501	AMAWALK
10502-10502	ARDSLEY
10503-10503	ARDSLEY ON HUDSON
10504-10504	ARMONK
10505-10505	BALDWIN PLACE
10506-10506	BEDFORD
10507-10507	BEDFORD HILLS
10509-10509	BREWSTER
10510-10510	BRIARCLIFF MANOR
10511-10511	BUCHANAN
10512-10512	CARMEL

10514-10514	CHAPPAQUA
10516-10516	COLD SPRING
10517-10517	CROMPOND
10518-10518	CROSS RIVER
10519-10519	CROTON FALLS
10520-10521	CROTON ON HUDSON
10522-10522	DOBBS FERRY
10523-10523	ELMSFORD
10524-10524	GARRISON
10526-10526	GOLDENS BRIDGE
10527-10527	GRANITE SPRINGS
10528-10528	HARRISON
10530-10530	HARTSDALE
10532-10532	HAWTHORNE
10533-10533	IRVINGTON
10535-10535	JEFFERSON VALLEY
10536-10536	KATONAH
10537-10537	LAKE PEEKSKILL

10538-10538	LARCHMONT
10540-10540	LINCOLNDALE
10541-10541	MAHOPAC
10542-10542	MAHOPAC FALLS
10543-10543	MAMARONECK
10545-10545	MARYKNOLL
10546-10546	MILLWOOD
10547-10547	MOHEGAN LAKE
10548-10548	MONTROSE
10549-10549	MOUNT KISCO
10550-10559	MOUNT VERNON
10560-10560	NORTH SALEM
10562-10562	OSSINING
10566-10566	PEEKSKILL
10567-10567	CORTLANDT MANOR
10570-10572	PLEASANTVILLE
10573-10573	PORT CHESTER
10576-10576	POUND RIDGE

10577-10577	PURCHASE
10578-10578	PURDYS
10579-10579	PUTNAM VALLEY
10580-10581	RYE
10583-10583	SCARSDALE
10587-10587	SHENOROCK
10588-10588	SHRUB OAK
10589-10589	SOMERS
10590-10590	SOUTH SALEM
10591-10592	TARRYTOWN
10594-10594	THORNWOOD
10595-10595	VALHALLA
10596-10596	VERPLANCK
10597-10597	WACCABUC
10598-10598	YORKTOWN HEIGHTS
10600-10603	WHITE PLAINS
10604-10604	WEST HARRISON
10605-10650	WHITE PLAINS

10700-10705	YONKERS
10706-10706	HASTINGS ON HUDSON
10707-10707	TUCKAHOE
10708-10708	BRONXVILLE
10709-10709	EASTCHESTER
10710-10710	YONKERS
10800-10802	NEW ROCHELLE
10803-10803	PELHAM
10804-10805	NEW ROCHELLE
10901-10901	SUFFERN
10910-10910	ARDEN
10911-10911	BEAR MOUNTAIN
10912-10912	BELLVALE
10913-10913	BLAUVELT
10914-10914	BLOOMING GROVE
10915-10915	BULLVILLE
10916-10916	CAMPBELL HALL
10917-10917	CENTRAL VALLEY
10918-10918	CHESTER
10919-10919	CIRCLEVILLE
10920-10920	CONGERS
10921-10921	FLORIDA
10922-10922	FORT MONTGOMERY
10923-10923	GARNERVILLE
10924-10924	GOSHEN
10925-10925	GREENWOOD LAKE
10926-10926	HARRIMAN
10927-10927	HAVERSTRAW
10928-10928	HIGHLAND FALLS
10930-10930	HIGHLAND MILLS
10931-10931	HILLBURN
10932-10932	HOWELLS
10933-10933	JOHNSON
10940-10943	MIDDLETOWN
10950-10950	MONROE
10951-10951	ROCKLAND M P C
10952-10952	MONSEY
10953-10953	MOUNTAINVILLE
10954-10954	NANUET
10956-10956	NEW CITY
10958-10958	NEW HAMPTON
10959-10959	NEW MILFORD
10960-10960	NYACK
10962-10962	ORANGEBURG
10963-10963	OTISVILLE
10964-10964	PALISADES
10965-10965	PEARL RIVER
10968-10968	PIERMONT
10969-10969	PINE ISLAND
10970-10970	POMONA
10973-10973	SLATE HILL
10974-10974	SLOATSBURG
10975-10975	SOUTHFIELDS
10976-10976	SPARKILL
10977-10977	SPRING VALLEY
10979-10979	STERLING FOREST
10980-10980	STONY POINT
10981-10981	SUGAR LOAF
10982-10982	TALLMAN
10983-10983	TAPPAN
10984-10984	THIELLS
10985-10985	THOMPSON RIDGE
10986-10986	TOMKINS COVE
10987-10987	TUXEDO PARK
10988-10988	UNIONVILLE
10989-10989	VALLEY COTTAGE
10990-10990	WARWICK
10992-10992	WASHINGTONVILLE
10993-10993	WEST HAVERSTRAW
10994-10995	WEST NYACK
10996-10997	WEST POINT
10998-10998	WESTTOWN
11001-11002	FLORAL PARK
11003-11003	ELMONT
11004-11004	GLEN OAKS
11005-11005	FLORAL PARK
11010-11010	FRANKLIN SQUARE
11020-11027	GREAT NECK
11030-11030	MANHASSET
11040-11044	NEW HYDE PARK
11050-11055	PORT WASHINGTON
11096-11096	INWOOD
11099-11099	NEW HYDE PARK
11100-11120	LONG ISLAND CITY
11200-11256	BROOKLYN
11300-11359	BAYSIDE
11359-11359	BAYSIDE
11360-11379	FLUSHING
11379-11379	MIDDLE VILLAGE
11380-11380	FLUSHING
11380-11380	ELMHURST
11381-11390	FLUSHING
11400-11411	JAMAICA
11411-11411	CAMBRIA HEIGHTS
11412-11418	JAMAICA
11418-11418	RICHMOND HILL
11419-11427	JAMAICA
11427-11427	QUEENS VILLAGE
11428-11428	JAMAICA
11428-11428	QUEENS VILLAGE
11429-11499	JAMAICA
11501-11501	MINEOLA
11507-11507	ALBERTSON
11509-11509	ATLANTIC BEACH
11510-11510	BALDWIN
11514-11514	CARLE PLACE
11516-11516	CEDARHURST
11518-11518	EAST ROCKAWAY
11520-11520	FREEPORT
11530-11536	GARDEN CITY
11542-11542	GLEN COVE
11545-11545	GLEN HEAD
11547-11547	GLENWOOD LANDING
11548-11548	GREENVALE
11549-11551	HEMPSTEAD
11552-11552	WEST HEMPSTEAD
11553-11553	UNIONDALE
11554-11554	EAST MEADOW
11555-11556	UNIONDALE
11557-11557	HEWLETT
11558-11558	ISLAND PARK
11559-11559	LAWRENCE
11560-11560	LOCUST VALLEY
11561-11561	LONG BEACH
11563-11564	LYNBROOK
11565-11565	MALVERNE
11566-11566	MERRICK
11568-11568	OLD WESTBURY
11569-11569	POINT LOOKOUT
11570-11571	ROCKVILLE CENTRE
11572-11572	OCEANSIDE
11575-11575	ROOSEVELT
11576-11576	ROSLYN
11577-11577	ROSLYN HEIGHTS
11579-11579	SEA CLIFF
11580-11583	VALLEY STREAM
11588-11588	UNIONDALE
11590-11590	WESTBURY
11592-11592	ROCKVILLE CENTRE
11593-11595	WESTBURY
11596-11596	WILLISTON PARK
11597-11597	WESTBURY
11598-11598	WOODMERE
11599-11599	GARDEN CITY
11600-11694	FAR ROCKAWAY
11694-11694	ROCKAWAY PARK
11695-11695	FAR ROCKAWAY
11696-11696	INWOOD
11697-11697	FAR ROCKAWAY
11701-11701	AMITYVILLE
11702-11702	BABYLON
11703-11703	NORTH BABYLON
11704-11704	WEST BABYLON
11705-11705	BAYPORT
11706-11706	BAY SHORE
11707-11707	WEST BABYLON
11708-11708	AMITYVILLE
11709-11709	BAYVILLE
11710-11710	BELLMORE
11713-11713	BELLPORT
11714-11714	BETHPAGE
11715-11715	BLUE POINT
11716-11716	BOHEMIA
11717-11717	BRENTWOOD
11718-11718	BRIGHTWATERS
11719-11719	BROOKHAVEN
11720-11720	CENTEREACH
11721-11721	CENTERPORT
11722-11722	CENTRAL ISLIP
11724-11724	COLD SPRING HARBOR
11725-11725	COMMACK
11726-11726	COPIAGUE
11727-11727	CORAM
11729-11729	DEER PARK
11730-11730	EAST ISLIP
11731-11731	EAST NORTHPORT
11732-11732	EAST NORWICH
11733-11733	EAST SETAUKET
11735-11737	FARMINGDALE
11738-11738	FARMINGVILLE
11739-11739	GREAT RIVER
11740-11740	GREENLAWN
11741-11741	HOLBROOK
11742-11742	HOLTSVILLE
11743-11743	HUNTINGTON
11745-11745	SMITHTOWN
11746-11746	HUNTINGTON STATION
11747-11747	MELVILLE
11749-11749	FARMINGVILLE
11749-11749	ISLANDIA
11750-11750	HUNTINGTON STATION
11751-11751	ISLIP
11752-11752	ISLIP TERRACE
11753-11753	JERICHO
11754-11754	KINGS PARK
11755-11755	LAKE GROVE
11756-11756	LEVITTOWN
11757-11757	LINDENHURST
11758-11758	MASSAPEQUA
11760-11760	HAUPPAUGE
11760-11760	ISLANDIA
11762-11762	MASSAPEQUA PARK
11763-11763	MEDFORD
11764-11764	MILLER PLACE
11765-11765	MILL NECK
11766-11766	MOUNT SINAI
11767-11767	NESCONSET
11768-11768	NORTHPORT
11769-11769	OAKDALE
11770-11770	OCEAN BEACH
11771-11771	OYSTER BAY
11772-11772	PATCHOGUE
11773-11773	SYOSSET
11774-11774	FARMINGDALE
11775-11775	MELVILLE
11776-11776	PORT JEFFERSON STATION
11777-11777	PORT JEFFERSON
11778-11778	ROCKY POINT
11779-11779	RONKONKOMA
11780-11780	SAINT JAMES
11782-11782	SAYVILLE
11783-11783	SEAFORD
11784-11784	SELDEN
11786-11786	SHOREHAM
11787-11787	SMITHTOWN
11788-11788	HAUPPAUGE
11789-11789	SOUND BEACH
11790-11790	STONY BROOK
11791-11791	SYOSSET
11792-11792	WADING RIVER
11793-11793	WANTAGH
11794-11794	STONY BROOK
11795-11795	WEST ISLIP
11796-11796	WEST SAYVILLE
11797-11797	WOODBURY
11798-11798	WYANDANCH
11801-11802	HICKSVILLE
11803-11803	PLAINVIEW
11804-11804	OLD BETHPAGE
11805-11805	MID ISLAND
11815-11819	HICKSVILLE
11853-11853	JERICHO
11854-11855	HICKSVILLE
11901-11901	RIVERHEAD
11930-11930	AMAGANSETT
11931-11931	AQUEBOGUE
11932-11932	BRIDGEHAMPTON
11933-11933	CALVERTON
11934-11934	CENTER MORICHES
11935-11935	CUTCHOGUE
11937-11937	EAST HAMPTON
11939-11939	EAST MARION
11940-11940	EAST MORICHES
11941-11941	EASTPORT
11942-11942	EAST QUOGUE
11944-11944	GREENPORT
11946-11946	HAMPTON BAYS
11947-11947	JAMESPORT
11948-11948	LAUREL
11949-11949	MANORVILLE
11950-11950	MASTIC
11951-11951	MASTIC BEACH
11952-11952	MATTITUCK
11953-11953	MIDDLE ISLAND
11954-11954	MONTAUK
11955-11955	MORICHES
11956-11956	NEW SUFFOLK
11957-11957	ORIENT
11958-11958	PECONIC
11959-11959	QUOGUE
11960-11960	REMSENBURG
11961-11961	RIDGE
11962-11962	SAGAPONACK
11963-11963	SAG HARBOR
11964-11964	SHELTER ISLAND
11965-11965	SHELTER ISLAND HEIGHTS
11967-11967	SHIRLEY
11968-11969	SOUTHAMPTON
11970-11970	SOUTH JAMESPORT
11971-11971	SOUTHOLD
11972-11972	SPEONK
11973-11973	UPTON
11975-11975	WAINSCOTT
11976-11976	WATER MILL
11977-11977	WESTHAMPTON
11978-11978	WESTHAMPTON BEACH
11980-11980	YAPHANK
12007-12007	ALCOVE
12008-12008	ALPLAUS
12009-12009	ALTAMONT
12010-12010	AMSTERDAM
12015-12015	ATHENS
12016-12016	AURIESVILLE
12017-12017	AUSTERLITZ
12018-12018	AVERILL PARK
12019-12019	BALLSTON LAKE
12020-12020	BALLSTON SPA
12022-12022	BERLIN
12023-12023	BERNE
12024-12024	BRAINARD
12025-12025	BROADALBIN
12026-12026	BROOKVIEW
12027-12027	BURNT HILLS
12028-12028	BUSKIRK
12029-12029	CANAAN
12031-12031	CARLISLE
12032-12032	CAROGA LAKE
12033-12033	CASTLETON ON HUDSON
12035-12035	CENTRAL BRIDGE
12036-12036	CHARLOTTEVILLE
12037-12037	CHATHAM
12040-12040	CHERRY PLAIN
12041-12041	CLARKSVILLE
12042-12042	CLIMAX
12043-12043	COBLESKILL
12045-12045	COEYMANS
12046-12046	COEYMANS HOLLOW
12047-12047	COHOES
12050-12050	COLUMBIAVILLE
12051-12051	COXSACKIE
12052-12052	CROPSEYVILLE
12053-12053	DELANSON
12054-12054	DELMAR
12055-12055	DORMANSVILLE
12056-12056	DUANESBURG
12057-12057	EAGLE BRIDGE
12058-12058	EARLTON
12059-12059	EAST BERNE
12060-12060	EAST CHATHAM
12061-12061	EAST GREENBUSH
12062-12062	EAST NASSAU

12063-12063 EAST SCHODACK	12174-12174 STUYVESANT FALLS	12471-12471 RIFTON	12580-12580 STAATSBURG
12064-12064 EAST WORCESTER	12175-12175 SUMMIT	12472-12472 ROSENDALE	12581-12581 STANFORDVILLE
12065-12065 CLIFTON PARK	12176-12176 SURPRISE	12473-12473 ROUND TOP	12582-12582 STORMVILLE
12066-12066 ESPERANCE	12177-12177 TRIBES HILL	12474-12474 ROXBURY	12583-12583 TIVOLI
12067-12067 FEURA BUSH	12179-12183 TROY	12475-12475 RUBY	12584-12584 VAILS GATE
12068-12068 FONDA	12184-12184 VALATIE	12477-12477 SAUGERTIES	12585-12585 VERBANK
12069-12069 FORT HUNTER	12185-12185 VALLEY FALLS	12480-12480 SHANDAKEN	12586-12586 WALDEN
12070-12070 FORT JOHNSON	12186-12186 VOORHEESVILLE	12481-12481 SHOKAN	12588-12588 WALKER VALLEY
12071-12071 FULTONHAM	12187-12187 WARNERVILLE	12482-12482 SOUTH CAIRO	12589-12589 WALLKILL
12072-12072 FULTONVILLE	12188-12188 WATERFORD	12483-12483 SPRING GLEN	12590-12590 WAPPINGERS FALLS
12073-12073 GALLUPVILLE	12189-12189 WATERVLIET	12484-12484 STONE RIDGE	12592-12592 WASSAIC
12074-12074 GALWAY	12190-12190 WELLS	12485-12485 TANNERSVILLE	12593-12593 WEST COPAKE
12075-12075 GHENT	12192-12192 WEST COXSACKIE	12486-12486 TILLSON	12594-12594 WINGDALE
12076-12076 GILBOA	12193-12193 WESTERLO	12487-12487 ULSTER PARK	12600-12604 POUGHKEEPSIE
12077-12077 GLENMONT	12194-12194 WEST FULTON	12489-12489 WAWARSING	12701-12701 MONTICELLO
12078-12078 GLOVERSVILLE	12195-12195 WEST LEBANON	12490-12490 WEST CAMP	12719-12719 BARRYVILLE
12082-12082 GRAFTON	12196-12196 WEST SAND LAKE	12491-12491 WEST HURLEY	12720-12720 BETHEL
12083-12083 GREENVILLE	12197-12197 WORCESTER	12492-12492 WEST KILL	12721-12721 BLOOMINGBURG
12084-12084 GUILDERLAND	12198-12198 WYNANTSKILL	12493-12493 WEST PARK	12722-12722 BURLINGHAM
12085-12085 GUILDERLAND CENTER	12200-12288 ALBANY	12494-12494 WEST SHOKAN	12723-12723 CALLICOON
12086-12086 HAGAMAN	12300-12345 SCHENECTADY	12495-12495 WILLOW	12724-12724 CALLICOON CENTER
12087-12087 HANNACROIX	12401-12402 KINGSTON	12496-12496 WINDHAM	12725-12725 CLARYVILLE
12089-12089 HOOSICK	12404-12404 ACCORD	12498-12498 WOODSTOCK	12726-12726 COCHECTON
12090-12090 HOOSICK FALLS	12405-12405 ACRA	12501-12501 AMENIA	12727-12727 COCHECTON CENTER
12092-12092 HOWES CAVE	12406-12406 ARKVILLE	12502-12502 ANCRAM	12729-12729 CUDDEBACKVILLE
12093-12093 JEFFERSON	12407-12407 ASHLAND	12503-12503 ANCRAMDALE	12732-12732 ELDRED
12094-12094 JOHNSONVILLE	12409-12409 BEARSVILLE	12504-12504 ANNANDALE ON HUDSON	12733-12733 FALLSBURG
12095-12095 JOHNSTOWN	12410-12410 BIG INDIAN	12506-12506 BANGALL	12734-12734 FERNDALE
12106-12106 KINDERHOOK	12411-12411 BLOOMINGTON	12507-12507 BARRYTOWN	12736-12736 FREMONT CENTER
12107-12107 KNOX	12412-12412 BOICEVILLE	12508-12508 BEACON	12737-12737 GLEN SPEY
12108-12108 LAKE PLEASANT	12413-12413 CAIRO	12510-12510 BILLINGS	12738-12738 GLEN WILD
12110-12111 LATHAM	12414-12414 CATSKILL	12511-12511 CASTLE POINT	12739-12739 GODEFFROY
12113-12113 LAWYERSVILLE	12415-12415 CEMENTON	12512-12512 CHELSEA	12740-12740 GRAHAMSVILLE
12114-12114 LEBANON SPRINGS	12415-12415 SMITHS LANDING	12513-12513 CLAVERACK	12741-12741 HANKINS
12115-12115 MALDEN BRIDGE	12416-12416 CHICHESTER	12514-12514 CLINTON CORNERS	12742-12742 HARRIS
12116-12116 MARYLAND	12417-12417 CONNELLY	12515-12515 CLINTONDALE	12743-12743 HIGHLAND LAKE
12117-12117 MAYFIELD	12418-12418 CORNWALLVILLE	12516-12516 COPAKE	12745-12745 HORTONVILLE
12118-12118 MECHANICVILLE	12419-12419 COTTEKILL	12517-12517 COPAKE FALLS	12746-12746 HUGUENOT
12120-12120 MEDUSA	12420-12420 CRAGSMOOR	12518-12518 CORNWALL	12747-12747 HURLEYVILLE
12121-12121 MELROSE	12421-12421 DENVER	12520-12520 CORNWALL ON HUDSON	12748-12748 JEFFERSONVILLE
12122-12122 MIDDLEBURGH	12422-12422 DURHAM	12521-12521 CRARYVILLE	12749-12749 KAUNEONGA LAKE
12123-12123 NASSAU	12423-12423 EAST DURHAM	12522-12522 DOVER PLAINS	12750-12750 KENOZA LAKE
12124-12124 NEW BALTIMORE	12424-12424 EAST JEWETT	12523-12523 ELIZAVILLE	12751-12751 KIAMESHA LAKE
12125-12125 NEW LEBANON	12427-12427 ELKA PARK	12524-12524 FISHKILL	12752-12752 LAKE HUNTINGTON
12128-12128 NEWTONVILLE	12428-12428 ELLENVILLE	12525-12525 GARDINER	12753-12753 LEW BEACH
12130-12130 NIVERVILLE	12429-12429 ESOPUS	12526-12526 GERMANTOWN	12754-12754 LIBERTY
12131-12131 NORTH BLENHEIM	12430-12430 FLEISCHMANNS	12527-12527 GLENHAM	12758-12758 LIVINGSTON MANOR
12132-12132 NORTH CHATHAM	12431-12431 FREEHOLD	12528-12528 HIGHLAND	12759-12759 LOCH SHELDRAKE
12133-12133 NORTH HOOSICK	12432-12432 GLASCO	12529-12529 HILLSDALE	12760-12760 LONG EDDY
12134-12134 NORTHVILLE	12433-12433 GLENFORD	12530-12530 HOLLOWVILLE	12762-12762 MONGAUP VALLEY
12135-12135 NORTON HILL	12434-12434 GRAND GORGE	12531-12531 HOLMES	12763-12763 MOUNTAIN DALE
12136-12136 OLD CHATHAM	12435-12435 GREENFIELD PARK	12533-12533 HOPEWELL JUNCTION	12764-12764 NARROWSBURG
12137-12137 PATTERSONVILLE	12436-12436 HAINES FALLS	12534-12534 HUDSON	12765-12765 NEVERSINK
12138-12138 PETERSBURG	12438-12438 HALCOTTSVILLE	12537-12537 HUGHSONVILLE	12766-12766 NORTH BRANCH
12139-12139 PISECO	12439-12439 HENSONVILLE	12538-12538 HYDE PARK	12767-12767 OBERNBURG
12140-12140 POESTENKILL	12440-12440 HIGH FALLS	12540-12540 LAGRANGEVILLE	12768-12768 PARKSVILLE
12141-12141 QUAKER STREET	12441-12441 HIGHMOUNT	12541-12541 LIVINGSTON	12769-12769 PHILLIPSPORT
12143-12143 RAVENA	12442-12442 HUNTER	12542-12542 MARLBORO	12770-12770 POND EDDY
12144-12144 RENSSELAER	12443-12443 HURLEY	12543-12543 MAYBROOK	12771-12771 PORT JERVIS
12147-12147 RENSSELAERVILLE	12444-12444 JEWETT	12544-12544 MELLENVILLE	12775-12775 ROCK HILL
12148-12148 REXFORD	12446-12446 KERHONKSON	12545-12545 MILLBROOK	12776-12776 ROSCOE
12149-12149 RICHMONDVILLE	12448-12448 LAKE HILL	12546-12546 MILLERTON	12777-12777 FORESTBURGH
12150-12150 ROTTERDAM JUNCTION	12449-12449 LAKE KATRINE	12547-12547 MILTON	12778-12778 SMALLWOOD
12151-12151 ROUND LAKE	12450-12450 LANESVILLE	12548-12548 MODENA	12779-12779 SOUTH FALLSBURG
12153-12153 SAND LAKE	12451-12451 LEEDS	12549-12549 MONTGOMERY	12780-12780 SPARROW BUSH
12154-12154 SCHAGHTICOKE	12452-12452 LEXINGTON	12550-12552 NEWBURGH	12781-12781 SUMMITVILLE
12155-12155 SCHENEVUS	12453-12453 MALDEN ON HUDSON	12553-12553 NEW WINDSOR	12782-12782 SUNDOWN
12156-12156 SCHODACK LANDING	12454-12454 MAPLECREST	12555-12555 MID HUDSON	12783-12783 SWAN LAKE
12157-12157 SCHOHARIE	12455-12455 MARGARETVILLE	12561-12561 NEW PALTZ	12784-12784 THOMPSONVILLE
12158-12158 SELKIRK	12456-12456 MOUNT MARION	12563-12563 PATTERSON	12785-12785 WESTBROOKVILLE
12159-12159 SLINGERLANDS	12457-12457 MOUNT TREMPER	12564-12564 PAWLING	12786-12786 WHITE LAKE
12160-12160 SLOANSVILLE	12458-12458 NAPANOCH	12565-12565 PHILMONT	12787-12787 WHITE SULPHUR SPRINGS
12161-12161 SOUTH BETHLEHEM	12459-12459 NEW KINGSTON	12566-12566 PINE BUSH	12788-12788 WOODBOURNE
12162-12162 SOUTH SCHODACK	12460-12460 OAK HILL	12567-12567 PINE PLAINS	12789-12789 WOODRIDGE
12163-12163 SOUTH WESTERLO	12461-12461 OLIVEBRIDGE	12568-12568 PLATTEKILL	12790-12790 WURTSBORO
12164-12164 SPECULATOR	12462-12462 OLIVEREA	12569-12569 PLEASANT VALLEY	12791-12791 YOUNGSVILLE
12165-12165 SPENCERTOWN	12463-12463 PALENVILLE	12570-12570 POUGHQUAG	12792-12792 YULAN
12166-12166 SPRAKERS	12464-12464 PHOENICIA	12571-12571 RED HOOK	12801-12801 GLENS FALLS
12167-12167 STAMFORD	12465-12465 PINE HILL	12572-12572 RHINEBECK	12803-12803 SOUTH GLENS FALLS
12168-12169 STEPHENTOWN	12466-12466 PORT EWEN	12574-12574 RHINECLIFF	12804-12804 QUEENSBURY
12170-12170 STILLWATER	12468-12468 PRATTSVILLE	12575-12575 ROCK TAVERN	12808-12808 ADIRONDACK
12172-12172 STOTTVILLE	12469-12469 PRESTON HOLLOW	12577-12577 SALISBURY MILLS	12809-12809 ARGYLE
12173-12173 STUYVESANT	12470-12470 PURLING	12578-12578 SALT POINT	12810-12810 ATHOL

12811-12811	BAKERS MILLS
12812-12812	BLUE MOUNTAIN LAKE
12814-12814	BOLTON LANDING
12815-12815	BRANT LAKE
12816-12816	CAMBRIDGE
12817-12817	CHESTERTOWN
12819-12819	CLEMONS
12820-12820	CLEVERDALE
12821-12821	COMSTOCK
12822-12822	CORINTH
12823-12823	COSSAYUNA
12824-12824	DIAMOND POINT
12826-12826	EAST GREENWICH
12827-12827	FORT ANN
12828-12828	FORT EDWARD
12831-12831	GANSEVOORT
12832-12832	GRANVILLE
12833-12833	GREENFIELD CENTER
12834-12834	GREENWICH
12835-12835	HADLEY
12836-12836	HAGUE
12837-12837	HAMPTON
12838-12838	HARTFORD
12839-12839	HUDSON FALLS
12841-12841	HULETTS LANDING
12842-12842	INDIAN LAKE
12843-12843	JOHNSBURG
12844-12844	KATTSKILL BAY
12845-12845	LAKE GEORGE
12846-12846	LAKE LUZERNE
12847-12847	LONG LAKE
12848-12848	MIDDLE FALLS
12849-12849	MIDDLE GRANVILLE
12850-12850	MIDDLE GROVE
12851-12851	MINERVA
12852-12852	NEWCOMB
12853-12853	NORTH CREEK
12854-12854	NORTH GRANVILLE
12855-12855	NORTH HUDSON
12856-12856	NORTH RIVER
12857-12857	OLMSTEDVILLE
12858-12858	PARADOX
12859-12859	PORTER CORNERS
12860-12860	POTTERSVILLE
12861-12861	PUTNAM STATION
12862-12862	RIPARIUS
12863-12863	ROCK CITY FALLS
12864-12864	SABAEL
12865-12865	SALEM
12866-12866	SARATOGA SPRINGS
12870-12870	SCHROON LAKE
12871-12871	SCHUYLERVILLE
12872-12872	SEVERANCE
12873-12873	SHUSHAN
12874-12874	SILVER BAY
12878-12878	STONY CREEK
12879-12879	NEWCOMB
12883-12883	TICONDEROGA
12884-12884	VICTORY MILLS
12885-12885	WARRENSBURG
12886-12886	WEVERTOWN
12887-12887	WHITEHALL
12901-12903	PLATTSBURGH
12910-12910	ALTONA
12911-12911	KEESEVILLE
12912-12912	AU SABLE FORKS
12913-12913	BLOOMINGDALE
12914-12914	BOMBAY
12915-12915	BRAINARDSVILLE
12916-12916	BRUSHTON
12917-12917	BURKE
12918-12918	CADYVILLE
12919-12919	CHAMPLAIN
12920-12920	CHATEAUGAY
12921-12921	CHAZY
12922-12922	CHILDWOLD
12923-12923	CHURUBUSCO
12924-12924	KEESEVILLE
12926-12926	CONSTABLE
12927-12927	CRANBERRY LAKE
12928-12928	CROWN POINT
12929-12929	DANNEMORA
12930-12930	DICKINSON CENTER
12932-12932	ELIZABETHTOWN
12933-12933	ELLENBURG
12934-12934	ELLENBURG CENTER
12935-12935	ELLENBURG DEPOT
12936-12936	ESSEX
12937-12937	FORT COVINGTON
12938-12938	FORT JACKSON
12938-12938	NORTH LAWRENCE
12939-12939	GABRIELS
12940-12940	HOPKINTON
12941-12941	JAY
12942-12942	KEENE
12943-12943	KEENE VALLEY
12944-12944	KEESEVILLE
12945-12945	LAKE CLEAR
12946-12946	LAKE PLACID
12949-12949	LAWRENCEVILLE
12950-12950	LEWIS
12952-12952	LYON MOUNTAIN
12953-12953	MALONE
12955-12955	LYON MOUNTAIN
12956-12956	MINEVILLE
12957-12957	MOIRA
12958-12958	MOOERS
12959-12959	MOOERS FORKS
12960-12960	MORIAH
12961-12961	MORIAH CENTER
12962-12962	MORRISONVILLE
12964-12964	NEW RUSSIA
12965-12965	NICHOLVILLE
12966-12966	NORTH BANGOR
12967-12967	NORTH LAWRENCE
12968-12968	ONCHIOTA
12968-12968	SUGARBUSH
12968-12968	ONCHIOTA
12969-12969	OWLS HEAD
12970-12970	PAUL SMITHS
12972-12972	PERU
12973-12973	PIERCEFIELD
12974-12974	PORT HENRY
12975-12975	PORT KENT
12976-12976	RAINBOW LAKE
12977-12977	RAY BROOK
12978-12978	REDFORD
12979-12979	ROUSES POINT
12980-12980	SAINT REGIS FALLS
12981-12981	SARANAC
12982-12983	SARANAC LAKE
12985-12985	SCHUYLER FALLS
12986-12986	TUPPER LAKE
12987-12987	UPPER JAY
12989-12989	VERMONTVILLE
12990-12990	WADHAMS
12991-12991	BANGOR
12992-12992	WEST CHAZY
12993-12993	WESTPORT
12994-12994	BOUQUET
12994-12994	WHALLONSBURG
12995-12995	WHIPPLEVILLE
12996-12996	WILLSBORO
12997-12997	WILMINGTON
12998-12998	WITHERBEE
13020-13020	APULIA STATION
13021-13024	AUBURN
13026-13026	AURORA
13027-13027	BALDWINSVILLE
13028-13028	BERNHARDS BAY
13029-13029	BREWERTON
13030-13030	BRIDGEPORT
13031-13031	CAMILLUS
13032-13032	CANASTOTA
13033-13033	CATO
13034-13034	CAYUGA
13035-13035	CAZENOVIA
13036-13036	CENTRAL SQUARE
13037-13037	CHITTENANGO
13039-13039	CICERO
13040-13040	CINCINNATUS
13041-13041	CLAY
13042-13042	CLEVELAND
13043-13043	CLOCKVILLE
13044-13044	CONSTANTIA
13045-13045	CORTLAND
13050-13050	CUYLER
13051-13051	DELPHI FALLS
13052-13052	DE RUYTER
13053-13053	DRYDEN
13054-13054	DURHAMVILLE
13055-13055	EAST FREETOWN
13056-13056	EAST HOMER
13057-13057	EAST SYRACUSE
13060-13060	ELBRIDGE
13061-13061	ERIEVILLE
13062-13062	ETNA
13063-13063	FABIUS
13064-13064	FAIR HAVEN
13065-13065	FAYETTE
13066-13066	FAYETTEVILLE
13068-13068	FREEVILLE
13069-13069	FULTON
13071-13071	GENOA
13072-13072	GEORGETOWN
13073-13073	GROTON
13074-13074	HANNIBAL
13076-13076	HASTINGS
13077-13077	HOMER
13078-13078	JAMESVILLE
13080-13080	JORDAN
13081-13081	KING FERRY
13082-13082	KIRKVILLE
13083-13083	LACONA
13084-13084	LA FAYETTE
13085-13085	LEBANON
13087-13087	LITTLE YORK
13088-13090	LIVERPOOL
13092-13092	LOCKE
13093-13093	LYCOMING
13094-13094	LYSANDER
13101-13101	MC GRAW
13102-13102	MC LEAN
13103-13103	MALLORY
13104-13104	MANLIUS
13107-13107	MAPLE VIEW
13108-13108	MARCELLUS
13110-13110	MARIETTA
13111-13111	MARTVILLE
13112-13112	MEMPHIS
13113-13113	MERIDIAN
13114-13114	MEXICO
13115-13115	MINETTO
13116-13116	MINOA
13117-13117	MONTEZUMA
13118-13118	MORAVIA
13119-13119	MOTTVILLE
13120-13120	NEDROW
13121-13121	NEW HAVEN
13122-13122	NEW WOODSTOCK
13123-13123	NORTH BAY
13124-13124	NORTH PITCHER
13125-13125	ORAN
13126-13126	OSWEGO
13129-13129	GEORGETOWN
13130-13130	OWASCO
13131-13131	PARISH
13132-13132	PENNELLVILLE
13133-13133	PERRYVILLE
13134-13134	PETERBORO
13135-13135	PHOENIX
13136-13136	PITCHER
13137-13137	PLAINVILLE
13138-13138	POMPEY
13139-13139	POPLAR RIDGE
13140-13140	PORT BYRON
13141-13141	PREBLE
13142-13142	PULASKI
13143-13143	RED CREEK
13144-13144	RICHLAND
13145-13145	SANDY CREEK
13146-13146	SAVANNAH
13147-13147	SCIPIO CENTER
13148-13148	SENECA FALLS
13150-13150	SENNETT
13151-13151	SHEDS
13152-13152	SKANEATELES
13153-13153	SKANEATELES FALLS
13154-13154	SOUTH BUTLER
13155-13155	SOUTH OTSELIC
13156-13156	STERLING
13157-13157	SYLVAN BEACH
13158-13158	TRUXTON
13159-13159	TULLY
13160-13160	UNION SPRINGS
13162-13162	VERONA BEACH
13163-13163	WAMPSVILLE
13164-13164	WARNERS
13165-13165	WATERLOO
13166-13166	WEEDSPORT
13167-13167	WEST MONROE
13200-13210	SYRACUSE
13211-13211	MATTYDALE
13212-13290	SYRACUSE
13301-13301	ALDER CREEK
13302-13302	ALTMAR
13303-13303	AVA
13304-13304	BARNEVELD
13305-13305	BEAVER FALLS
13308-13308	BLOSSVALE
13309-13309	BOONVILLE
13310-13310	BOUCKVILLE
13312-13312	BRANTINGHAM
13313-13313	BRIDGEWATER
13314-13314	BROOKFIELD
13315-13315	BURLINGTON FLATS
13316-13316	CAMDEN
13317-13317	CANAJOHARIE
13318-13318	CASSVILLE
13319-13319	CHADWICKS
13320-13320	CHERRY VALLEY
13321-13321	CLARK MILLS
13322-13322	CLAYVILLE
13323-13323	CLINTON
13324-13324	COLD BROOK
13325-13325	CONSTABLEVILLE
13326-13326	COOPERSTOWN
13327-13327	CROGHAN
13328-13328	DEANSBORO
13329-13329	DOLGEVILLE
13331-13331	EAGLE BAY
13332-13332	EARLVILLE
13333-13333	EAST SPRINGFIELD
13334-13334	EATON
13335-13335	EDMESTON
13336-13336	FAIRFIELD
13337-13337	FLY CREEK
13338-13338	FORESTPORT
13339-13339	FORT PLAIN
13340-13340	FRANKFORT
13341-13341	FRANKLIN SPRINGS
13342-13342	GARRATTSVILLE
13343-13343	GLENFIELD
13345-13345	GREIG
13346-13346	HAMILTON
13348-13348	HARTWICK
13349-13349	HARTWICK SEMINARY
13350-13350	HERKIMER
13352-13352	HINCKLEY
13353-13353	HOFFMEISTER
13354-13354	HOLLAND PATENT
13355-13355	HUBBARDSVILLE
13357-13357	ILION
13360-13360	INLET
13361-13361	JORDANVILLE
13362-13362	KNOXBORO
13363-13363	LEE CENTER
13364-13364	LEONARDSVILLE
13365-13365	LITTLE FALLS
13367-13367	LOWVILLE
13368-13368	LYONS FALLS
13401-13401	MC CONNELLSVILLE
13402-13402	MADISON
13403-13403	MARCY
13404-13404	MARTINSBURG
13406-13406	MIDDLEVILLE
13407-13407	MOHAWK
13408-13408	MORRISVILLE
13409-13409	MUNNSVILLE
13410-13410	NELLISTON
13411-13411	NEW BERLIN
13413-13413	NEW HARTFORD

13415-13415 NEW LISBON	13624-13624 CLAYTON	13746-13746 CHENANGO FORKS	14006-14006 ANGOLA
13416-13416 NEWPORT	13625-13625 COLTON	13747-13747 COLLIERSVILLE	14008-14008 APPLETON
13417-13417 NEW YORK MILLS	13626-13626 COPENHAGEN	13748-13748 CONKLIN	14009-14009 ARCADE
13418-13418 NORTH BROOKFIELD	13627-13627 DEER RIVER	13749-13749 CORBETTSVILLE	14010-14010 ATHOL SPRINGS
13419-13419 WESTERN	13628-13628 DEFERIET	13750-13750 DAVENPORT	14011-14011 ATTICA
13420-13420 OLD FORGE	13630-13630 DE KALB JUNCTION	13751-13751 DAVENPORT CENTER	14012-14012 BARKER
13421-13421 ONEIDA	13631-13631 DENMARK	13752-13752 DE LANCEY	14013-14013 BASOM
13424-13424 ORISKANY	13632-13632 DEPAUVILLE	13753-13753 DELHI	14020-14021 BATAVIA
13425-13425 ORISKANY FALLS	13633-13633 DE PEYSTER	13754-13754 DEPOSIT	14024-14024 BLISS
13426-13426 ORWELL	13634-13634 DEXTER	13755-13755 DOWNSVILLE	14025-14025 BOSTON
13428-13428 PALATINE BRIDGE	13635-13635 EDWARDS	13756-13756 EAST BRANCH	14026-14026 BOWMANSVILLE
13429-13429 PARIS	13636-13636 ELLISBURG	13757-13757 EAST MEREDITH	14027-14027 BRANT
13431-13431 POLAND	13637-13637 EVANS MILLS	13758-13758 EAST PHARSALIA	14028-14028 BURT
13432-13432 POOLVILLE	13638-13638 FELTS MILLS	13760-13761 ENDICOTT	14029-14029 CENTERVILLE
13433-13433 PORT LEYDEN	13639-13639 FINE	13762-13762 ENDWELL	14030-14030 CHAFFEE
13434-13434 PRATTS HOLLOW	13640-13640 WELLESLEY ISLAND	13763-13763 ENDICOTT	14031-14031 CLARENCE
13435-13435 PROSPECT	13641-13641 FISHERS LANDING	13774-13774 FISHS EDDY	14032-14032 CLARENCE CENTER
13436-13436 RAQUETTE LAKE	13642-13642 GOUVERNEUR	13775-13775 FRANKLIN	14033-14033 COLDEN
13437-13437 REDFIELD	13643-13643 GREAT BEND	13776-13776 GILBERTSVILLE	14034-14034 COLLINS
13438-13438 REMSEN	13645-13645 HAILESBORO	13777-13777 GLEN AUBREY	14035-14035 COLLINS CENTER
13439-13439 RICHFIELD SPRINGS	13646-13646 HAMMOND	13778-13778 GREENE	14036-14036 CORFU
13440-13449 ROME	13647-13647 HANNAWA FALLS	13780-13780 GUILFORD	14037-14037 COWLESVILLE
13450-13450 ROSEBOOM	13648-13648 HARRISVILLE	13782-13782 HAMDEN	14038-14038 CRITTENDEN
13452-13452 SAINT JOHNSVILLE	13649-13649 HELENA	13783-13783 HANCOCK	14039-14039 DALE
13454-13454 SALISBURY CENTER	13650-13650 HENDERSON	13784-13784 HARFORD	14040-14040 DARIEN CENTER
13455-13455 SANGERFIELD	13651-13651 HENDERSON HARBOR	13786-13786 HARPERSFIELD	14041-14041 DAYTON
13456-13456 SAUQUOIT	13652-13652 HERMON	13787-13787 HARPURSVILLE	14042-14042 DELEVAN
13457-13457 SCHUYLER LAKE	13654-13654 HEUVELTON	13788-13788 HOBART	14043-14043 DEPEW
13459-13459 SHARON SPRINGS	13655-13655 HOGANSBURG	13790-13790 JOHNSON CITY	14047-14047 DERBY
13460-13460 SHERBURNE	13656-13656 LA FARGEVILLE	13794-13794 KILLAWOG	14048-14048 DUNKIRK
13461-13461 SHERRILL	13657-13657 LIMERICK	13795-13795 KIRKWOOD	14051-14051 EAST AMHERST
13464-13464 SMYRNA	13658-13658 LISBON	13796-13796 LAURENS	14052-14052 EAST AURORA
13465-13465 SOLSVILLE	13659-13659 LORRAINE	13797-13797 LISLE	14054-14054 EAST BETHANY
13466-13466 SOUTH EDMESTON	13660-13660 MADRID	13801-13801 MC DONOUGH	14055-14055 EAST CONCORD
13468-13468 SPRINGFIELD CENTER	13661-13661 MANNSVILLE	13802-13802 MAINE	14056-14056 EAST PEMBROKE
13469-13469 STITTVILLE	13662-13662 MASSENA	13803-13803 MARATHON	14057-14057 EDEN
13470-13470 STRATFORD	13664-13664 MORRISTOWN	13804-13804 MASONVILLE	14058-14058 ELBA
13471-13471 TABERG	13665-13665 NATURAL BRIDGE	13806-13806 MERIDALE	14059-14059 ELMA
13472-13472 THENDARA	13666-13666 NEWTON FALLS	13807-13807 MILFORD	14060-14060 FARMERSVILLE STATION
13473-13473 TURIN	13667-13667 NORFOLK	13808-13808 MORRIS	14061-14061 FARNHAM
13475-13475 VAN HORNESVILLE	13668-13668 NORWOOD	13809-13809 MOUNT UPTON	14062-14062 FORESTVILLE
13476-13476 VERNON	13669-13669 OGDENSBURG	13810-13810 MOUNT VISION	14063-14063 FREDONIA
13477-13477 VERNON CENTER	13670-13670 OSWEGATCHIE	13811-13811 NEWARK VALLEY	14065-14065 FREEDOM
13478-13478 VERONA	13671-13671 OXBOW	13812-13812 NICHOLS	14066-14066 GAINESVILLE
13479-13479 WASHINGTON MILLS	13672-13672 PARISHVILLE	13813-13813 NINEVEH	14067-14067 GASPORT
13480-13480 WATERVILLE	13673-13673 PHILADELPHIA	13814-13814 NORTH NORWICH	14068-14068 GETZVILLE
13482-13482 WEST BURLINGTON	13674-13674 PIERREPONT MANOR	13815-13815 NORWICH	14069-14069 GLENWOOD
13483-13483 WESTDALE	13675-13675 PLESSIS	13820-13820 ONEONTA	14070-14070 GOWANDA
13484-13484 WEST EATON	13676-13676 POTSDAM	13825-13825 OTEGO	14072-14072 GRAND ISLAND
13485-13485 WEST EDMESTON	13677-13677 PYRITES	13826-13826 OUAQUAGA	14075-14075 HAMBURG
13486-13486 WESTERNVILLE	13678-13678 RAYMONDVILLE	13827-13827 OWEGO	14079-14079 HELMUTH
13487-13487 WEST EXETER	13679-13679 REDWOOD	13830-13830 OXFORD	14080-14080 HOLLAND
13488-13488 WESTFORD	13680-13680 RENSSELAER FALLS	13832-13832 PLYMOUTH	14081-14081 IRVING
13489-13489 WEST LEYDEN	13681-13681 RICHVILLE	13833-13833 PORT CRANE	14082-14082 JAVA CENTER
13490-13490 WESTMORELAND	13682-13682 RODMAN	13834-13834 PORTLANDVILLE	14083-14083 JAVA VILLAGE
13491-13491 WEST WINFIELD	13683-13683 ROOSEVELTOWN	13835-13835 RICHFORD	14085-14085 LAKE VIEW
13492-13492 WHITESBORO	13684-13684 RUSSELL	13837-13837 SHINHOPPLE	14086-14086 LANCASTER
13493-13493 WILLIAMSTOWN	13685-13685 SACKETS HARBOR	13838-13838 SIDNEY	14091-14091 LAWTONS
13494-13494 WOODGATE	13687-13687 SOUTH COLTON	13839-13839 SIDNEY CENTER	14092-14092 LEWISTON
13495-13495 YORKVILLE	13688-13688 SOUTH RUTLAND	13840-13840 SMITHBORO	14094-14095 LOCKPORT
13500-13599 UTICA	13690-13690 STAR LAKE	13841-13841 SMITHVILLE FLATS	14098-14098 LYNDONVILLE
13601-13601 WATERTOWN	13691-13691 THERESA	13842-13842 SOUTH KORTRIGHT	14101-14101 MACHIAS
13602-13602 FORT DRUM	13692-13692 THOUSAND ISLAND PARK	13843-13843 SOUTH NEW BERLIN	14102-14102 MARILLA
13603-13603 WATERTOWN	13693-13693 THREE MILE BAY	13844-13844 SOUTH PLYMOUTH	14103-14103 MEDINA
13605-13605 ADAMS	13694-13694 WADDINGTON	13845-13845 TIOGA CENTER	14105-14105 MIDDLEPORT
13606-13606 ADAMS CENTER	13695-13695 WANAKENA	13846-13846 TREADWELL	14107-14107 MODEL CITY
13607-13607 ALEXANDRIA BAY	13696-13696 WEST STOCKHOLM	13847-13847 TROUT CREEK	14108-14108 NEWFANE
13608-13608 ANTWERP	13697-13697 WINTHROP	13848-13848 TUNNEL	14109-14109 NIAGARA UNIVERSITY
13609-13609 BALMAT	13698-13698 WOODVILLE	13849-13849 UNADILLA	14110-14110 NORTH BOSTON
13610-13610 RODMAN	13699-13699 POTSDAM	13850-13851 VESTAL	14111-14111 NORTH COLLINS
13611-13611 BELLEVILLE	13730-13730 AFTON	13856-13856 WALTON	14112-14112 NORTH EVANS
13612-13612 BLACK RIVER	13731-13731 ANDES	13859-13859 WELLS BRIDGE	14113-14113 NORTH JAVA
13613-13613 BRASHER FALLS	13732-13732 APALACHIN	13860-13860 WEST DAVENPORT	14120-14120 NORTH TONAWANDA
13614-13614 BRIER HILL	13733-13733 BAINBRIDGE	13861-13861 WEST ONEONTA	14125-14125 OAKFIELD
13615-13615 BROWNVILLE	13734-13734 BARTON	13862-13862 WHITNEY POINT	14126-14126 OLCOTT
13616-13616 CALCIUM	13736-13736 BERKSHIRE	13863-13863 WILLET	14127-14127 ORCHARD PARK
13617-13617 CANTON	13737-13737 BIBLE SCHOOL PARK	13864-13864 WILLSEYVILLE	14129-14129 PERRYSBURG
13618-13618 CAPE VINCENT	13738-13738 BLODGETT MILLS	13865-13865 WINDSOR	14130-14130 PIKE
13619-13619 CARTHAGE	13739-13739 BLOOMVILLE	13900-13905 BINGHAMTON	14131-14131 RANSOMVILLE
13620-13620 CASTORLAND	13740-13740 BOVINA CENTER	14001-14001 AKRON	14132-14132 SANBORN
13621-13621 CHASE MILLS	13743-13743 CANDOR	14003-14003 ALABAMA	14133-14133 SANDUSKY
13622-13622 CHAUMONT	13744-13744 CASTLE CREEK	14004-14004 ALDEN	14134-14134 SARDINIA
13623-13623 CHIPPEWA BAY	13745-13745 CHENANGO BRIDGE	14005-14005 ALEXANDER	14135-14135 SHERIDAN

14136-14136 SILVER CREEK	14139-14139 SOUTH WALES	14141-14141 SPRINGVILLE	14144-14144 STELLA NIAGARA
14138-14138 SOUTH DAYTON	14140-14140 SPRING BROOK	14143-14143 STAFFORD	14145-14145 STRYKERSVILLE
14150-14151 TONAWANDA	14507-14507 MIDDLESEX	14716-14716 BROCTON	14813-14813 BELMONT
14166-14166 VAN BUREN POINT	14508-14508 MORTON	14717-14717 CANEADEA	14814-14814 BIG FLATS
14167-14167 VARYSBURG	14510-14510 MOUNT MORRIS	14718-14718 CASSADAGA	14815-14815 BRADFORD
14168-14168 VERSAILLES	14511-14511 MUMFORD	14719-14719 CATTARAUGUS	14816-14816 BREESPORT
14169-14169 WALES CENTER	14512-14512 NAPLES	14720-14720 CELORON	14817-14817 BROOKTONDALE
14170-14170 WEST FALLS	14513-14513 NEWARK	14721-14721 CERES	14818-14818 BURDETT
14171-14171 WEST VALLEY	14514-14514 NORTH CHILI	14722-14722 CHAUTAUQUA	14819-14819 CAMERON
14172-14172 WILSON	14515-14515 NORTH GREECE	14723-14723 CHERRY CREEK	14820-14820 CAMERON MILLS
14173-14173 YORKSHIRE	14516-14516 NORTH ROSE	14724-14724 CLYMER	14821-14821 CAMPBELL
14174-14174 YOUNGSTOWN	14517-14517 NUNDA	14726-14726 CONEWANGO VALLEY	14822-14822 CANASERAGA
14200-14280 BUFFALO	14518-14518 OAKS CORNERS	14727-14727 CUBA	14823-14823 CANISTEO
14300-14305 NIAGARA FALLS	14519-14519 ONTARIO	14728-14728 DEWITTVILLE	14824-14824 CAYUTA
14410-14410 ADAMS BASIN	14520-14520 ONTARIO CENTER	14729-14729 EAST OTTO	14825-14825 CHEMUNG
14411-14411 ALBION	14521-14521 OVID	14730-14730 EAST RANDOLPH	14826-14826 COHOCTON
14413-14413 ALTON	14522-14522 PALMYRA	14731-14731 ELLICOTTVILLE	14827-14827 COOPERS PLAINS
14414-14414 AVON	14525-14525 PAVILION	14732-14732 ELLINGTON	14830-14831 CORNING
14415-14415 BELLONA	14526-14526 PENFIELD	14733-14733 FALCONER	14836-14836 DALTON
14416-14416 BERGEN	14527-14527 PENN YAN	14735-14735 FILLMORE	14837-14837 DUNDEE
14418-14418 BRANCHPORT	14529-14529 PERKINSVILLE	14736-14736 FINDLEY LAKE	14838-14838 ERIN
14420-14420 BROCKPORT	14530-14530 PERRY	14737-14737 FRANKLINVILLE	14839-14839 GREENWOOD
14422-14422 BYRON	14532-14532 PHELPS	14738-14738 FREWSBURG	14840-14840 HAMMONDSPORT
14423-14423 CALEDONIA	14533-14533 PIFFARD	14739-14739 FRIENDSHIP	14841-14841 HECTOR
14424-14424 CANANDAIGUA	14534-14534 PITTSFORD	14740-14740 GERRY	14842-14842 HIMROD
14425-14425 FARMINGTON	14536-14536 PORTAGEVILLE	14741-14741 GREAT VALLEY	14843-14843 HORNELL
14427-14427 CASTILE	14537-14537 PORT GIBSON	14742-14742 GREENHURST	14844-14845 HORSEHEADS
14428-14428 CHURCHVILLE	14538-14538 PULTNEYVILLE	14743-14743 HINSDALE	14846-14846 HUNT
14429-14429 CLARENDON	14539-14539 RETSOF	14744-14744 HOUGHTON	14847-14847 INTERLAKEN
14430-14430 CLARKSON	14541-14541 ROMULUS	14745-14745 HUME	14850-14853 ITHACA
14432-14432 CLIFTON SPRINGS	14542-14542 ROSE	14747-14747 KENNEDY	14854-14854 JACKSONVILLE
14433-14433 CLYDE	14543-14543 RUSH	14748-14748 KILL BUCK	14855-14855 JASPER
14435-14435 CONESUS	14544-14544 RUSHVILLE	14749-14749 KNAPP CREEK	14856-14856 KANONA
14437-14437 DANSVILLE	14545-14545 SCOTTSBURG	14750-14750 LAKEWOOD	14857-14857 LAKEMONT
14441-14441 DRESDEN	14546-14546 SCOTTSVILLE	14751-14751 LEON	14858-14858 LINDLEY
14442-14442 EAGLE HARBOR	14547-14547 SENECA CASTLE	14752-14752 LILY DALE	14859-14859 LOCKWOOD
14443-14443 EAST BLOOMFIELD	14548-14548 SHORTSVILLE	14753-14753 LIMESTONE	14860-14860 LODI
14444-14444 EAST PALMYRA	14549-14549 SILVER LAKE	14754-14754 LITTLE GENESEE	14861-14861 LOWMAN
14445-14445 EAST ROCHESTER	14550-14550 SILVER SPRINGS	14755-14755 LITTLE VALLEY	14863-14863 MECKLENBURG
14449-14449 EAST WILLIAMSON	14551-14551 SODUS	14756-14756 MAPLE SPRINGS	14864-14864 MILLPORT
14450-14450 FAIRPORT	14554-14554 SODUS CENTER	14757-14757 MAYVILLE	14865-14865 MONTOUR FALLS
14452-14452 FANCHER	14555-14555 SODUS POINT	14758-14758 NIOBE	14867-14867 NEWFIELD
14453-14453 FISHERS	14556-14556 SONYEA	14759-14759 NORTH CLYMER	14868-14868 NORTH COHOCTON
14454-14454 GENESEO	14557-14557 SOUTH BYRON	14760-14760 OLEAN	14869-14869 ODESSA
14456-14456 GENEVA	14558-14558 SOUTH LIMA	14766-14766 OTTO	14870-14870 PAINTED POST
14461-14461 GORHAM	14559-14559 SPENCERPORT	14767-14767 PANAMA	14871-14871 PINE CITY
14462-14462 GROVELAND	14560-14560 SPRINGWATER	14769-14769 PORTLAND	14872-14872 PINE VALLEY
14463-14463 HALL	14561-14561 STANLEY	14770-14770 PORTVILLE	14873-14873 PRATTSBURGH
14464-14464 HAMLIN	14563-14563 UNION HILL	14772-14772 RANDOLPH	14874-14874 PULTENEY
14466-14466 HEMLOCK	14564-14564 VICTOR	14774-14774 RICHBURG	14876-14876 READING CENTER
14467-14467 HENRIETTA	14568-14568 WALWORTH	14775-14775 RIPLEY	14877-14877 REXVILLE
14468-14468 HILTON	14569-14569 WARSAW	14776-14776 ROSSBURG	14878-14878 ROCK STREAM
14469-14469 BLOOMFIELD	14571-14571 WATERPORT	14777-14777 RUSHFORD	14879-14879 SAVONA
14470-14470 HOLLEY	14572-14572 WAYLAND	14778-14778 SAINT BONAVENTURE	14880-14880 SCIO
14471-14471 HONEOYE	14580-14580 WEBSTER	14779-14779 SALAMANCA	14881-14881 SLATERVILLE SPRINGS
14472-14472 HONEOYE FALLS	14584-14584 WEBSTER CROSSING	14781-14781 SHERMAN	14882-14882 LANSING
14474-14474 INDUSTRY	14585-14585 WEST BLOOMFIELD	14782-14782 SINCLAIRVILLE	14883-14883 SPENCER
14475-14475 IONIA	14586-14586 WEST HENRIETTA	14783-14783 STEAMBURG	14884-14884 SWAIN
14476-14476 KENDALL	14588-14588 WILLARD	14784-14784 STOCKTON	14885-14885 TROUPSBURG
14477-14477 KENT	14589-14589 WILLIAMSON	14785-14785 STOW	14886-14886 TRUMANSBURG
14478-14478 KEUKA PARK	14590-14590 WOLCOTT	14786-14786 WEST CLARKSVILLE	14887-14887 TYRONE
14479-14479 KNOWLESVILLE	14591-14591 WYOMING	14787-14787 WESTFIELD	14888-14888 VALOIS
14480-14480 LAKEVILLE	14592-14592 YORK	14788-14788 WESTONS MILLS	14889-14889 VAN ETTEN
14481-14481 LEICESTER	14600-14694 ROCHESTER	14801-14801 ADDISON	14891-14891 WATKINS GLEN
14482-14482 LE ROY	14701-14704 JAMESTOWN	14802-14802 ALFRED	14892-14892 WAVERLY
14485-14485 LIMA	14706-14706 ALLEGANY	14803-14803 ALFRED STATION	14893-14893 WAYNE
14486-14486 LINWOOD	14707-14707 ALLENTOWN	14804-14804 ALMOND	14894-14894 WELLSBURG
14487-14487 LIVONIA	14708-14708 ALMA	14805-14805 ALPINE	14895-14895 WELLSVILLE
14488-14488 LIVONIA CENTER	14709-14709 ANGELICA	14806-14806 ANDOVER	14896-14896 WEST DANBY
14489-14489 LYONS	14710-14710 ASHVILLE	14807-14807 ARKPORT	14897-14897 WHITESVILLE
14502-14502 MACEDON	14711-14711 BELFAST	14808-14808 ATLANTA	14898-14898 WOODHULL
14504-14504 MANCHESTER	14712-14712 BEMUS POINT	14809-14809 AVOCA	14900-14975 ELMIRA
14505-14505 MARION	14714-14714 BLACK CREEK	14810-14810 BATH	
14506-14506 MENDON	14715-14715 BOLIVAR	14812-14812 BEAVER DAMS	

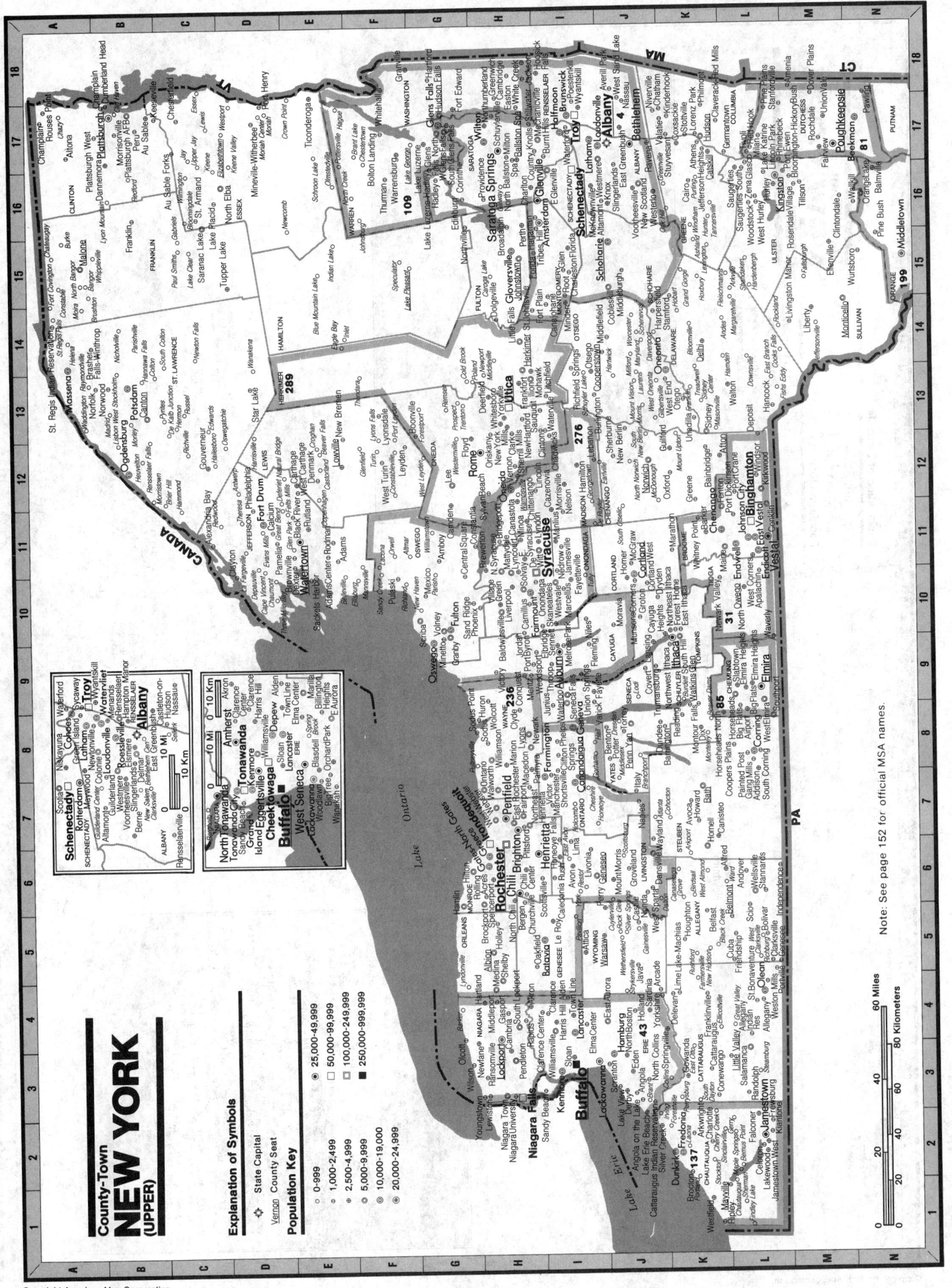

County-Town
NEW YORK
(UPPER)

Explanation of Symbols

✦ State Capital

Vernon ⊙ County Seat

Population Key

⊙ 0-999
● 1,000-2,499
● 2,500-4,999
● 5,000-9,999
● 10,000-19,000
⊙ 20,000-24,999

□ 25,000-49,999
□ 50,000-99,999
☐ 100,000-249,999
■ 250,000-999,999

Note: See page 152 for official MSA names.

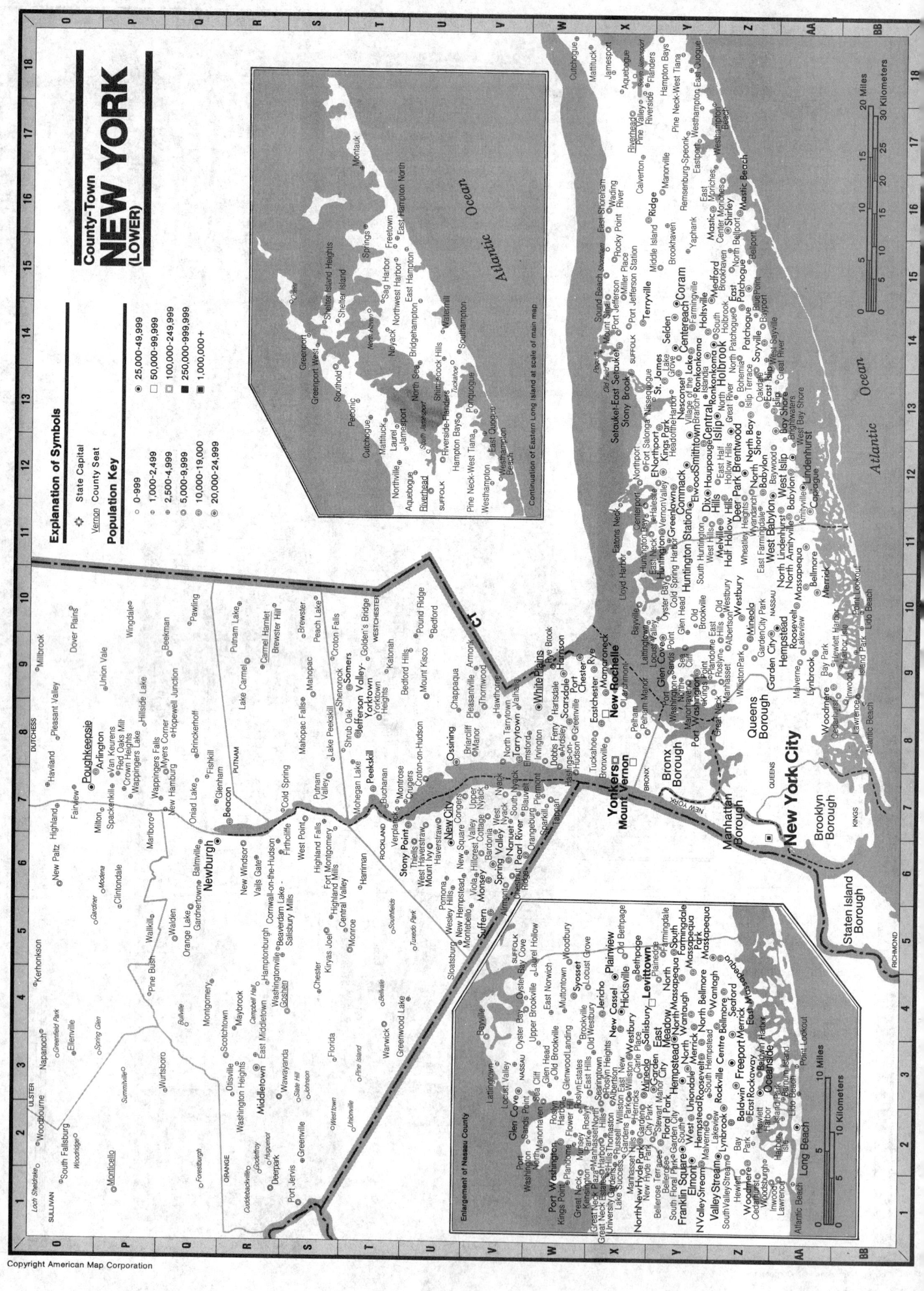

Explanation of symbols:

● — Census Designated Place (CDP)

▲ *italics* – Township (shown on the map)

● *italics* – Township shown which is also a CDP

italics – Township (not shown on the map)

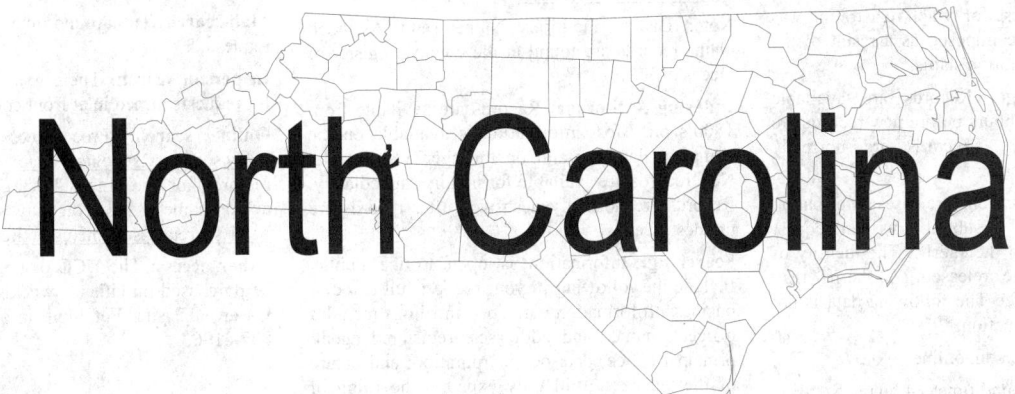

General Help Numbers:

Governor's Office

20301 Mail Service Center
Raleigh, NC 27699-0301
www.governor.state.nc.us

919-733-4240
Fax 919-715-3175
8AM-6PM

Attorney General's Office

Justice Department
PO Box 629
Raleigh, NC 27602-0629
www.jus.state.nc.us

919-716-6400
Fax 919-716-6750
8AM-5PM

Legislative Records

North Carolina General Assembly
16 W. Jones Street, Rm 2226
Raleigh, NC 27603
www.ncleg.net

919-733-7779
919-733-7778
8:30AM-5:30PM

State Archives

Archives & History Division
109 E Jones St
Raleigh, NC 27601-2807
www.ah.dcr.state.nc.us

919-733-7305
Fax 919-733-8807
8AM-5:30PM TU-F, 9-5 SA

State Specifics:

Capital:	Raleigh Wake County
Time Zone:	EST
Number of Counties:	100
Population:	8,407,248
Web Site:	www.ncgov.com

State Agencies

Criminal Records

Access to Records is Restricted

State Bureau of Investigation, Identification Section, PO Box 29500, Raleigh, NC 27626 (Courier: 3320 Garner Rd, Raleigh, NC 27626-0500); 919-662-4500 x6302, 919-662-4380 (Fax), 8AM-5PM.

http://sbi.jus.state.nc.us

Note: This agency and the Administrative Office of the Courts (AOC) have implemented a computer-to-computer interface, which provides all users with the capability to access statewide Clerk of Court criminal records. Record access is limited to criminal justice and other government agencies authorized by law. Employers are denied access unless subject is in a business desginated to receive records (i.e. health or child care). Contact agency for proper paperwork.

Statewide Court Records

Administrative Office of Courts, PO Box 2448, Raleigh, NC 27602-2448 (Courier: 2 E Morgan St, Raleigh, NC 27602-2448); 919-733-7107, 919-715-5779 (Fax), 8AM-5PM.

www.nccourts.org/Courts/

Access by: online. No searching by mail.

Online search: Search active District/Superior Court criminal calendars on a county or statewide basis at www1.aoc.state.nc.us/www/calendars/Civil.html. Also, appellate and supreme court opinions are available www.aoc.state.nc.us/www/public/html/opinions.htm.

Sexual Offender Registry

State Bureau of Investigation, Division of Criminal Information-SOR Unit, PO Box 29500, Raleigh, NC 27626 (Courier: 3320 Garner Rd, Raleigh, NC 27626-0500); 919-662-4500 x6257, 919-662-4619 (Fax), 8AM-5PM.

http://sbi.jus.state.nc.us

Note: Records are available for public inspection; name, sex, address, physical description, picture, conviction date, offense for which registration was required, the sentence imposed as a result of the conviction, and registration status.

Indexing & Storage: Records are available 01/01/96. It takes 24 hours before new records are available for inquiry. Records are normally destroyed after 105 years.

Searching: This office only releases information online. They suggest to submit a written request for the information to the sheriff. The identity of the victim cannot be released. A sheriff may charge a reasonable fee The following data is not released: victim information.

Access by: mail, in person, online.

Mail search: Turnaround time: 24 hours. SASE is required. Records are available by mail.

In person search: Records may be viewed in person at this office or at local law enforcement offices. There is a public access terminal.

Online search: Search Level 3 records at the website. Search by name or geographic region.

Other access: Agency can provide data on CD-Rom.

Incarceration Records

North Carolina Department of Corrections, Combined Records, 2020 Yonkers Road, 4226 MSC, Raleigh, NC 27699-4226; 919-716-3200, 919-716-3986 (Fax), 8AM-4:30PM.

www.doc.state.nc.us/

Indexing & Storage: Records are available on current and former inmates. It takes up to 10 days before new records are available for inquiry. Records are normally destroyed after 10 years (paper copies).

Searching: Computer records go back to 1973. Include the following in your request-full name. the DOB, SSN and DOC number are helpful. Location, physical identifiers, conviction and sentencing information, and release dates are provided.

Access by: mail, phone, fax, online.

Fee & Payment: The fee for copies is $1.00 for first page and $.25 each add'l. Fee payee: NC Dept of Corrections

Mail search: Turnaround time: 1 to 2 days. No SASE is required.

Phone search: Name searching available by phone.

Fax search: Search requests accepted by fax.

Online search: The web access allows searching by name or ID number for public information on inmates, probationers, or parolees since 1973. Also, a private company offers free web access to inmates at www.vinelink.com/index.jsp including state, DOC, and county jail systems.

Corporation, Limited Partnerships, Limited Liability Company Records, Trademarks/Servicemarks

Secretary of State, Corporations Division, PO Box 29622, Raleigh, NC 27626-0622 (Courier: 2 S Salisbury, Raleigh, NC 27601); 919-807-2225

(Corporations), 919-807-2162 (Trademarks), 888-246-7636, 919-807-2039 (Fax), 8AM-5PM.

www.secstate.state.nc.us/

Note: DBAs, Fictitious Names and Assumed Name records are found at the county Register of Deeds offices.

Indexing & Storage: Records are available from 1800's on. Most information is available on the computer database and on the agency's website. New records are available for inquiry immediately. Records are normally destroyed after records are not destroyed.

Searching: Information is open to the public. Include the following in your request-full name of business. Information contained in filings includes officers' names and addresses; registered agent; principal office; date of incorporation; and nature of the business. Will only expedite the filing of documents, not for searches.

Access by: mail, phone, fax, in person, online.

Fee & Payment: There is no search fee. Copies are $1.00 per page. Document certification is $15.00. Electronic certification is $10.00. Fee payee: Secretary of State. Prepayment required. Personal checks accepted. Credit cards accepted.

Mail search: Turnaround time: 2-3 days. Expect 6-10 day turnaround time for corporation documents, 2-3 day turnaround time for trademark documents. SASE not required.

Phone search: Copies may be ordered over the telephone.

Fax search: They will invoice.

In person search: Turnaround time is immediate. There is a public access terminal to view records.

Online search: The website at www.secretary.state.nc.us/corporations/ offers a free search of status, corporate documents, and registered agent by corporation name. The trademark database is not available online.

Other access: This agency makes database information available for purchase via an FTP site. Contact Bonnie Elek at 919-807-2196 for details.

Uniform Commercial Code, Federal Tax Liens

UCC Division, Secretary of State, PO Box 29626, Raleigh, NC 27626-0626 (Courier: 2 South Salisbury St, Raleigh, NC 27602); 919-807-2111, 919-807-2120 (Fax), 8AM-5PM.

www.secretary.state.nc.us/UCC

Indexing & Storage: Records are available from 1967. Records are computerized since 1985. It takes 72 hours before new records are available for inquiry. Records are normally destroyed after six years form lapse date.

Searching: Use search request form UCC-11. The search includes federal tax liens on businesses since 1985 if you request (add $5.00). You may search federal tax liens separately. Federal tax liens on individuals and all state tax liens are filed at Superior Courts. Include the following in your request-debtor name. Name will be searched as submitted; name variation printouts will be given.

Access by: mail, in person, online.

Fee & Payment: The search fee is $38.00 per debtor name plus $2.00 per page for copies or $2.00 per specific page request. $6.25 for certification plus $2.00 each additional page. $.50 per reader printer copy, from customer reader printers. Fee payee: Secretary of State. Prepayment

required. Prepayment is required. Underpayment requests will be rejected. Personal checks accepted. No credit cards accepted.

Mail search: Turnaround time: 3 days. A SASE is requested.

In person search: There is a $2.00 fee per page for requests turned in at front counter.

Online search: Free access is available at www.secretary.state.nc.us/ucc/. Click on "UCC research" or "Tax Liens." Search by ID number or debtor name. Also, you may search tax liens at www.secretary.state.nc.us/taxliens.

Other access: The UCC or tax lien database can be purchased on either a weekly or monthly basis via an FTP site. For more information, call 919-807-2196.

State Tax Liens

Records not maintained by a state level agency.

Note: Tax lien data is found at the county level.

Sales Tax Registrations

Access to Records is Restricted

Revenue Department, Sales & Use Tax Division, PO Box 25000, Raleigh, NC 27640 (Courier: 501 N Wilmington Street, Raleigh, NC 27604); 919-733-3661, 919-715-6086 (Fax), 8AM-5PM.

www.dor.state.nc.us

Birth Certificates

Center for health Statistics, Vital Records Branch, 1903 Mail Service Center, Raleigh, NC 27699-1903 (Courier: 225 N McDowell St, Raleigh, NC 27603); 919-733-3526, 800-669-8310 (Credit Card Orders), 919-829-1359 (Fax), 8AM-4PM.

http://vitalrecords.dhhs.state.nc.us/

Note: Anyone can order an non-certified copy of a record. Only family members can order a certified copy. The fee is the same.

Indexing & Storage: Records are available from 1913 to present. Prior to 1913, the state did not keep records of births. Recent records must be obtained at the county level. It takes 180 days after birth before new records are available for inquiry. Records are indexed on microfiche, inhouse computer.

Searching: Investigative searches are permitted, but only non-certified copies are provided. Otherwise, requester must state relationship to subject and why record is needed. Include the following in your request-full name, names of parents, mother's maiden name, date of birth, place of birth. The following data is not released: adoption records or medical records.

Access by: mail, phone, in person.

Fee & Payment: Search fee is $10.00 per 5 years searched. Add $9.95 for using a credit card. Add $5.00 per copy for additional copies. Add $15.00 for in person requests. Fee payee: North Carolina Vital Records. Prepayment required. Credit cards accepted for expedited service only. Personal checks accepted. Credit cards accepted: MasterCard, Visa.

Mail search: Turnaround time: 2 weeks. No SASE is required.

Phone search: See expedited service.

In person search: Walk-in services in the lobby is only for simple certificate requests. All other services (such as amending a certificate) will be conducted by appointment only. The walk-in service entails an additional $15.00 fee.

Expedited service: Expedited service is available requests using a credit card. Turnaround time: overnight delivery. Total fee is $55.45 and includes overnight delivery and credit card fee. Call 800-669-8310.

Death Records

Dept of Environment, Health & Natural Resources, Vital Records Section, 1903 Mail Service Center, Raleigh, NC 27699-1903 (Courier: 225 N McDowell St, Raleigh, NC 27603); 919-733-3526, 919-829-1359 (Fax), 8AM-4PM.

http://vitalrecords.dhhs.state.nc.us/

Note: Non-certified records may be obtained by the public; certified copies can only be purchased by family members. The fee is the same for either record.

Indexing & Storage: Records are available from 1930 to present. Recent records must be obtained at the county level. It takes 180 days after death before new records are available for inquiry. Records are indexed on microfiche, inhouse computer.

Searching: Investigative searches are permitted, but only non-certified copies are provided. Include the following in your request-full name, date of death, place of death. SSN is helpful.

Access by: mail, phone, in person.

Fee & Payment: The search fee is $15.00 for each 5 years searched. Add $9.95 for using a credit card. Add $5.00 per copy for additional copies. Add $15.00 for in person requests. Fee payee: North Carolina Vital Records. Prepayment required. Credit cards accepted for phone service only. Personal checks accepted. Credit cards accepted: MasterCard, Visa, AmEx, Discover.

Mail search: Turnaround time: 2 weeks. No SASE is required.

Phone search: See expedited service.

In person search: Walk-in services in the lobby is only for simple certificate requests. All other services (such as amending a certificate) will be conducted by appointment only. The walk-in service entails an additional $15.00 fee.

Expedited service: Expedited service is available requests using a credit card. Total fee is $55.45 and includes overnight delivery and fee for use of credit card. Call 800-669-8310.

Marriage Certificates

Dept of Environment, Health & Natural Resources, Vital Records Section, 1903 Mail Service Center, Raleigh, NC 27699-1903 (Courier: 225 N McDowell St, Raleigh, NC 27603); 919-733-3526, 919-829-1359 (Fax), 8AM-4PM.

http://vitalrecords.dhhs.state.nc.us/

Note: Non-certified copies may be purchased by the public. Certified copies can be obtained by family members. The fee is the same for either report.

Indexing & Storage: Records are available from 1962 to present. Recent records must be obtained at the county level. It takes 8 months before new records are available for inquiry. Records are indexed on microfiche, inhouse computer.

Searching: Investigative searches are permitted, but only non-certified copies are provided. Include the following in your request-names of husband and wife, date of marriage, place or county of marriage.

Access by: mail, phone, in person.

Fee & Payment: The search fee is $15.00 for each 5 years searched. Add $9.95 for using a credit card (expedited service only). Add $5.00 per copy for additional copies. Add $15.00 for in person requests. Fee payee: North Carolina Vital Records. Prepayment required. Personal checks accepted. Credit cards accepted: MasterCard, Visa, AmEx, Discover.

Mail search: Turnaround time: 2 weeks. No SASE is required.

Phone search: See expedited service.

In person search: Walk-in services in the lobby is only for simple certificate requests. All other services (such as amending a certificate) will be conducted by appointment only. The walk-in service entails an additional $15.00 fee.

Expedited service: Expedited service is available requests using a credit card. Total fee is $55.45 and includes overnight delivery and fee for use of credit card. Call 800-669-8310.

Divorce Records

Dept of Environment, Health & Natural Resources, Vital Records Section, 1903 Mail Service Center, Raleigh, NC 27699-1903 (Courier: 225 N McDowell St, Raleigh, NC 27603); 919-733-3526, 919-829-1359 (Fax), 8AM-4PM.

http://vitalrecords.dhhs.state.nc.us/

Note: Non-certified copies are available to the public, certified copies to family members. The fee is the same for either report.

Indexing & Storage: Records are available from 1958 to present. Recent records must be obtained at the county level. It takes up to 1 year before new records are available for inquiry. Records are indexed on microfiche, inhouse computer.

Searching: Investigative searches are permitted, but only non-certified copies are provided. Include the following in your request-names of husband and wife, date of divorce, place of divorce, case number (if known).

Access by: mail, phone, in person.

Fee & Payment: The search fee is $15.00 for each 5 years searched. Add $9.95 for using a credit card (expedited only). Add $5.00 per copy for additional copies. Add $15.00 for in person requests. Fee payee: North Carolina Vital Records. Prepayment required. Personal checks accepted. Credit cards accepted: MasterCard, Visa, AmEx, Discover.

Mail search: Turnaround time: 2 weeks. No SASE is required.

Phone search: See expedited service.

In person search: Walk-in services in the lobby is only for simple certificate requests. All other services (such as amending a certificate) will be conducted by appointment only. The walk-in service entails an additional $15.00 fee.

Expedited service: Expedited service is available requests using a credit card. Total fee is $55.45 and includes use of credit card and overnight delivery. Call 800-669-8310.

Workers' Compensation Records

NC Industrial Commission, Worker's Comp Records, 4340 Mail Service Center, Raleigh, NC 27699-4340; 919-807-2500, 800-688-8349 (Claims Questions), 919-715-0282 (Fax), 8AM-5PM.

www.comp.state.nc.us

Note: One may search the Workers' Compensation Name Search System at the web to find the addresses of employers, insurance companies, third party administrators, and the parties responsible for workers' compensation coverage at the time of an accident.

Indexing & Storage: Records are available from 1980.

Searching: Searches require a signed release or statement of purpose of request on letterhead. Only parties to claim will be allowed access. Per federal law, records may not be used for pre-employment screening.

Access by: mail, in person, online.

Fee & Payment: There is no search fee. There is no copy fee unless the file is over 20 pages, then the fee is $1.00 per page (over 20). Fee payee: NC Industrial Commission. Personal checks accepted. No credit cards accepted.

Mail search: Turnaround time: 2 to 3 days.

In person search: Generally turnaround time is immediate, unless the case is closed and records must be researched.

Online search: Extensive information about employers and insurerss may be searched online at www.comp.state.nc.us/iwcnss/. This site also gives access to court decisions involving worker's comp.

Driver Records

Division of Motor Vehicles, Driver's License Section, 3113 MSC, Raleigh, NC 27699 (Courier: 1100 New Bern Ave, Raleigh, NC 27697); 919-715-7000, 8AM-5PM.

www.ncdot.org/dmv/driver_services/

Note: Records available include a limited three year (insurance purposes) and a complete seven year (employment purposes) record.

Indexing & Storage: Records are available for 5 yrs or more for moving violations, 10 yrs or more for DWIs and suspensions. Surrendered license records are kept for 1 yr after the expiration date. This state utilizes two point systems-one for the DMV, one for insurance purposes. It takes minutes before new records are available for inquiry. Records are normally destroyed after 10 years, if not renewed.

Searching: Form DL-DPPA-1 is required. Casual requesters can obtain records, but no personal information is released. Include the following in your request-driver's license number, full name, date of birth. Some search modes will look at the driver's license number first, then the name and DOB as a secondary search. The following data is not released: medical information.

Access by: mail, in person, online.

Fee & Payment: The current fee is $5.00 per record. Certified records are an additional $2.00. Fee payee: Division of Motor Vehicles. Prepayment required. Personal checks accepted. No credit cards accepted.

Mail search: Turnaround time: 7 business days. No SASE is required.

In person search: Up to 2 requests will be processed across the counter; the rest are available the next day.

Online search: To qualify for online availability, a client must be an insurance agent or insurance company support organization. The mode is interactive and is open from 7 AM to 10 PM. The DL# and name are needed when ordering. Records are $5.00 each. A minimum $500 security deposit is required. Call 919-861-3062 for details.

Other access: Magnetic tape for high volume batch users is available. Requests must be pre-paid.

Vehicle Ownership, Vehicle Identification

Division of Motor Vehicles, Registration/Correspondence Unit, 1100 New Bern Ave, Rm 100, Raleigh, NC 27697-0001; 919-715-7000, 8AM-5PM.

www.dmv.dot.state.nc.us

Indexing & Storage: Records are available from their first records for title records (on microfilm). Computer records are purged periodically according to plate activity. Records are maintained for mobile homes and boat trailers, also.

Searching: The agency is in compliance with DPPA. Casual requesters receive records without personal information. Effective 01/01/00, only vehicle owners who have opted in are placed on marketing list requests. Include the following in your request-vehicle description, name, and signed release of subject on Form MVR-605A if not an ongoing requester.

Access by: mail, in person.

Fee & Payment: The fee is $1.00 per record (includes lien data) or $5.00 for a certified record. Fee payee: Department of Motor Vehicles. Prepayment required. Personal checks accepted. No credit cards accepted.

Mail search: Turnaround time: 3 days. The use of Form MVR-605A is helpful. The request requires the requester's signature. A SASE is requested.

In person search: Turnaround time is while you wait if you have the correct authorization.

Other access: North Carolina offers a bulk retrieval of ownership and registration information on magnetic tape. A written request specifying the purpose and details of the request is required. Request must comply with DPPA. For more information, call 919-861-3062.

Accident Reports

Division of Motor Vehicles, Traffic Records Section, 3105 Mail Service Center, Raleigh, NC 27699-3105; 919-861-3098, 919-733-9605 (Fax), 8AM-5PM.

www.ncdot.org/dmv/other_services/recordsstatistics/copyCrashReport.html

Indexing & Storage: Records are available from 1986 to present on computer, from 1990 to present on microfiche. Hard copies are available from 1995.

Searching: Records are not released on minor drivers. Using Form TR-67A, the requester should submit at least one of the names of the participants, the county of occurrence, date of occurrence, and the exception under which he/she qualifies to receive personal information in accordance with DPPA.

Access by: mail, in person.

Fee & Payment: The fee is $4.00 for a certified copy or no cost for a non-certified copy. Fee payee: Division of Motor Vehicles. Prepayment required. Personal checks accepted. No credit cards accepted.

Mail search: Turnaround time: 5 days.

In person search: Turnaround time is immediate if the record is available.

Other access: Bulk file purchase is available.

Vessel Ownership, Vessel Registration

North Carolina Wildlife Resources Commission, Transaction Management, 1709 Mail Service Center, Raleigh, NC 27699-1709 (Courier: 322 Chapanoke Road, Raleigh, NC 27603); 800-628-3773, 919-662-4379 (Fax), 8AM-5PM.

http://216.27.49.98/

Indexing & Storage: Records are available from 1970 and are computerized. This is an optional title state. Lien information will show if the vessel is titled. All motorized boats, including jet skis, and sailboats over 14 ft must be registered. New records are available for inquiry immediately.

Searching: Include the following in your request-Name, signed release. Submit the name or registration number or hull number.

Access by: mail, fax.

Fee & Payment: There is no search fee.

Mail search: Turnaround time: 1 to 2 weeks. No SASE is required.

Fax search: Turnaround time is several days.

Other access: The agency sells a CD-ROM disk with registration information for $20.00 per disk.

Other access: This agency will mail lists of bills on computer printouts.

Voter Registration

State Board of Elections, PO Box 27255, Raleigh, NC 27611-7255; 919-733-7173, 919-715-0135 (Fax), 8AM-5PM.

www.sboe.state.nc.us

Note: There is a statewide online system for record access. Records are open to the public.

Indexing & Storage: New records are available for inquiry immediately.

Access by: mail, phone, fax, in person, online.

Fee & Payment: The only fees are for either specialized reports or for actual costs to reproduces the records in the desired format.

Mail search: Turnaround time is variable, depending on workload.

Phone search: Records are available by phone.

Fax search: Records are available by fax.

In person search: Simple requests may be processed while you wait.

Online search: Online access to voter registration records is available free at www.app.sboe.state.nc.us/votersearch/seimsvot.htm. A DOB is needed.

Other access: The records are sold in CD format or sent via email. The maximum fee is $25.00. Request forms are available at the webpage.

GED Certificates

Department of Community Colleges, GED Office, 50164 Mail Service Center, Raleigh, NC 27699-5016; 919-733-7051 x744, 919-715-5351 (Fax), 8AM-5PM.

www.ncccs.cc.nc.us

Indexing & Storage: Records are available from the 1940s, from 09/77 on microfilm. It takes less than 1 day before new records are available for inquiry.

Searching: There are no fees for verification or copies of transcripts. Include the following in your request-signed release, Social Security Number, date of birth. The year of the test is helpful.

Access by: mail, fax, in person.

Mail search: Turnaround time: 1 week.

Fax search: available.

In person search: No fee for request.

Hunting and Fishing License Information

Wildlife Resource Commission, Archdale Bldg, 512 N Salisbury Street, Raleigh, NC 27604-0118; 919-662-4370, 919-661-4878 (Fax), 8AM-5PM.

http://216.27.49.98

Indexing & Storage: Records are available for the past four years. It takes 1 day before new records are available for inquiry.

Searching: Requests must be in writing.

Access by: mail, fax.

Fee & Payment: The fee is $20.00 per list. Fee payee: NC Wildlife Resources Commission

Mail search: Turnaround time: 3 days or less. You may call them after mailing your request.

Fax search: You may have to call back for results, once you have faxed the request.

Other access: A master CD list is available for $20.00.

North Carolina State Licensing Agencies

Licenses Searchable Online

Acupuncturist #40	http://ncaaom.org/directory.php
Amusement Device #24	www.nclabor.com/elevator/elevator.htm
Architect #3	www.member-base.com/ncbarch/public/lic/searchdb.asp
Architectural Firm #3	www.member-base.com/ncbarch/public/firms/searchdb.asp
Athletic Trainer #38	www.ncbate.org/trainers.html
Auction Company/Auctioneer/Apprentice #2	www.ncalb.org/scripts/members.asp
Auctioneer Disciplinary Action #2	www.ncalb.org/scripts/disciplinaryaction.asp
Bank #17	www.nccob.org/banks.htm
Boiler/Pressure Vessel Inspector #24	www.nclabor.com/boiler/boiler.htm
Building Inspector #23	www.ncdoi.com/OSFM/Documents/Engineering/InspectionDirectories/InspectorsByJurisdiction.pdf
Charitable/Sponsor Organization #52	www.secretary.state.nc.us/csl/search.asp
Check Casher #17	www.nccob.org/checkcas.htm
Consumer Financer #17	www.nccob.org/cf.htm
Contractor, General #32	www.nclbgc.org/lic_fr.html
Cosmetology Disciplinary Action #55	www.cosmetology.state.nc.us/newsletter/Disciplinary.pdf
Counselor, Professional #13	www.ncblpc.org/search.php
Crematory #7	www.ncbfs.org/dir_crematoriesdb.htm
Dental Hygienist #42	www.ncdentalboard.org/ncdbe_search.asp
Dentist #42	www.ncdentalboard.org/ncdbe_search.asp
DME (Rx Device) #11	www.ncbop.org/dme/
Electrical Contractor/Inspector #6	www.ncbeec.org/LicSearch.asp
Elevator Inspector #24	www.nclabor.com/elevator/elevator.htm
Embalmer #7	www.ncbfs.org/dir_licenseedb.htm
Engineer #48	www.member-base.com/ncbels-vs/public/searchdb.asp
Engineering/Surveying Firm #48	www.member-base.com/ncbels-vs/public/searchdb.asp
Fire Marshall #23	www.ncdoi.com/OSFM/Documents/FireRescueCommission/NCCFMAList.pdf
Fire Sprinkler Contractor/Technician #31	www.nclicensing.org/OnlineReg.htm
Fire Sprinkler Maintenance Technician #31	www.nclicensing.org/OnlineReg.htm
Forester #54	http://members.aol.com/ncbrf/roster_index.htm
Fund Raiser Consultant/Solicitor #52	www.secretary.state.nc.us/csl/search.asp
Funeral Chapel #7	www.ncbfs.org/dir_chapeldb.htm
Funeral Director/Service #7	www.ncbfs.org/dir_licenseedb.htm
Funeral Home #7	www.ncbfs.org/dir_funeralhomedb.htm
Funeral Trainee #7	www.ncbfs.org/dir_traineesdb.htm
Funeral Transport/Removal Svc #7	www.ncbfs.org/TransportServices.doc
Geologist #46	www.ncblg.org/licensees.html
Hearing Aid Dispenser/Fitter #43	www.nchalb.org/cgi-bin/sho_memb.pl
Heating Contractor #31	www.nclicensing.org/OnlineReg.htm
HMO #23	http://infoportal.ncdoi.net/cmp_lookup.jsp
Home Inspector #23	www.ncdoi.com/OSFM/Documents/Engineering/HILB/DirectoryAlpha.pdf
Insurance Company #23	http://infoportal.ncdoi.net/cmp_lookup.jsp
Insurer, Life/Health #23	http://infoportal.ncdoi.net/filelookup.jsp?divtype=3
Insurer, Property/Casualty #23	http://infoportal.ncdoi.net/filelookup.jsp?divtype=2
Investment Representative/Advisor #26	www.sosnc.com/
Landscape Architect #46	www.ncbola.org/rosternew.html
Loan Officer #17	https://www.nccob.com/online/LicenseSearch.aspx
Lobbyist #51	www.secretary.state.nc.us/lobbyists/Lsearch.asp
Manufactured Housing Retailer/Mfg/Contr. #23	www.ncdoi.com/OSFM/Home/Marshal.asp?PARAMSection=sidManufacturedBuilding&PARAMCategory=cidMBManufacturedHousing&PARAMSubCategory=scidHousingDirectory
Medical Doctor/Physician #47	www.ncmedboard.org/find.htm
Money Transmitter #17	www.nccob.org/mtlist.htm
Mortgage Lender/Broker #17	https://www.nccob.com/online/licensesearch.aspx
Nurse Practitioner #47	www.ncmedboard.org/find.htm
Nurse-LPN #8	https://www.ncbon.com/Lic-verif.asp
Nursing Home Administrator #5	www.ncbenha.org/searchdb.asp
Occupational Therapist/Therapist Assistant #9	www.ncbot.org/fpdb/otimport.html
Optometrist #18	www.ncoptometry.org/verify/index.asp
Osteopathic Physician #47	www.ncmedboard.org/find.htm
Pesticide Applicator #16	www.ncagr.com/aspzine/Fooddrug/data/advsearch.asp
Pesticide Dealer/Consultant #16	www.ncagr.com/aspzine/Fooddrug/data/advsearch.asp

Pharmacist #11 .... www.ncbop.org/names1.asp
Physical Therapist/Physical Therapist Assistant #49 ...... www.ncptboard.org/search.asp
Physician Assistant #47 .... www.ncmedboard.org/find.htm
Plumber #31 .... www.nclicensing.org/OnlineReg.htm
Podiatrist #12 .... www.ncbpe.org/search.php
Psychological Associate #36 .... www.ncpsychologyboard.org/search.htm
Psychologist #36 .... www.ncpsychologyboard.org/search.htm
Public Accountant-CPA #37 .... www.cpaboard.state.nc.us
RAL #17 .... www.nccob.org/rallist.htm
Real Estate Agent/Broker/Dealer #39 .... www.memberbase.com/ncrec-new/licdb/indv/searchdb.asp
Real Estate Firm #39 .... www.memberbase.com/ncrec-new/licdb/firms/searchdb.asp
Sanitarian #14 .... www.rsboard.com/rsweb/directory/directory.htm
Securities Agent/Broker #26 .... www.sosnc.com/
Soil Scientist #22 .... www.ncblss.org/director.html
Speech Pathologist/Audiologist #30 .... www.ncboeslpa.org
Surveyor, Land #48 .... www.member-base.com/ncbels-vs/public/searchdb.asp

North Carolina Licensing Quick Finder

Acupuncturist #40 919-773-0530
Alarm Installer #1 919-875-3611
Alarm System Business #1 919-875-3611
Alcoholic Beverage Control #20 919-779-0700
Ambulance Attendant #21 919-855-3750
Amusement Device #24 919-807-2770
Anesthetist Nurse #8 .... 919-782-3211x252
Architect #3 919-733-9544
Architectural Firm #3 919-733-9544
Armed Security Guard #53 919-875-3611
Armored Car #53 919-875-3611
Athletic Agent #51 919-807-2156
Athletic Trainer #38 919-821-4980
Attorney #45 919-828-4886
Auction Company #2 919-567-2844
Auctioneer Disciplinary Action #2 919-567-2844
Auctioneer/Auctioneer Apprentice #2 ... 919-567-2844
Bail Bond Runner #23 919-733-2200
Bank #27 919-508-5973
Bank #17 919-733-3016
Barber Inspector/Instructor #4 919-715-1159
Barber/Barber Apprentice #4 919-715-1159
Beauty Shop/Salon #55 919-733-4117
Boiler/Pressure Vessel Inspector #24 . 919-807-2760
Bondsman, Professional/Surety #23 919-733-2200
Building Inspector #23 919-733-3901
Cemetery #19 919-981-2536
Cemetery Salesperson #19 919-981-2536
Charitable/Sponsor Organization #52 .. 919-807-2214
Check Casher #17 919-733-3016
Chiropractor #41 704-793-1342
Clinical Nurse Specialist #8 .... 919-782-3211x252
Consumer Financer #17 919-733-3016
Contractor, General #32 919-571-4183
Cosmetologist Instructor/Apprentice/Practitioner #55
.... 919-733-4117
Cosmetology Disciplinary Action #55 ... 919-733-4117
Counselor, Professional #13 919-661-0820
Counter Intelligence Service #53 919-875-3611
Courier Service #53 919-875-3611
Crematory #7 919-733-9380
Dental Hygienist #42 919-678-8223
Dentist #42 919-678-8223
DME (Rx Device) #11 919-942-4454
EDM #21 919-855-3750
Electrical Contractor/Inspector #6 919-733-9042
Electrologist #35 336-574-1414
Electrology Instructor #35 336-574-1414
Elevator Inspector #24 919-807-2770
Embalmer #7 919-733-9380

Emergency Medical Service #21 919-855-3750
Emergency Medical Technician #21 919-855-3750
Engineer #48 919-781-9499
Engineering/Surveying Firm #48 919-781-9499
Esthetician Instructor/Apprentice/Practitioner #55
.... 919-733-4117
Family Therapist #33 336-794-3891
Fire Marshall #23 919-661-5880
Fire Sprinkler Contractor #31 919-875-3612
Fire Sprinkler Inspctr./ Contr. #31 . 919-875-3612
Fire Sprinkler Maintenance Tech. #31 . 919-875-3612
Fire/Rescue Instructor #23 919-661-5880
Firearms Trainer #53 919-875-3611
Forester #54 919-772-5883
Fund Raiser Consultant/Solicitor #52 ... 919-807-2214
Funeral Chapel #7 919-733-9380
Funeral Director/Service #7 919-733-9380
Funeral Home #7 919-733-9380
Funeral Preneed Seller #7 919-733-9380
Funeral Trainee #7 919-733-9380
Funeral Transport/Removal Svc #7 919-733-9380
Fur Dealer #25 919-661-4872
Game Bird Propagator #25 919-661-4872
Geologist #46 919-850-9669
Guard Dog Service #53 919-875-3611
Hearing Aid Dispenser/Fitter #43 252-752-6382
Heating Contractor #31 919-875-3612
HMO #23 919-733-7487
Home Inspector #23 919-733-3901
Hospital #21 919-855-3750
Hunting Preserve Operator #25 919-661-4872
Insurance Agent #23 .... 919-981-5244 option 1
Insurance Company #23 .... 919-981-5244 option 1
Insurer, Life/Health #23 919-733-7487
Insurer, Property/Casualty #23 919-733-7487
Investment Rep./Advisor #26 919-733-3924
Jailer #56 919-716-6460
Landscape Architect #46 919-850-9088
Librarian, Public #28 919-733-2570
Loan Officer #17 919-733-3016
Lobbyist #51 919-807-2156
Manicurist Instructor/Apprentice/Practitioner #55
.... 919-733-4117
Manufactured Housing Retailer/Mfg/Contractor #23
.... 919-733-7487
Marriage & Family Therapist #33 336-794-3891
Medical Doctor/Physician #47 919-326-1100
Medical Program Director #21 919-855-3750
Medical Responder #21 919-855-3750
Midwife Nurse #8 .... 919-782-3211x244

Money Transmitter #17 919-733-3016
Mortgage Lender/Broker #17 919-733-3016
Notary Public #58 919-733-3406
Nurse Practitioner #8 .... 919-782-3211x244
Nurse Practitioner #47 919-326-1100
Nurse-LPN #8 919-782-3211
Nursing Home #21 919-855-3750
Nursing Home Administrator #5 919-571-4164
Occupational Therapist/Therapist Assistant #9
.... 919-832-1380
Optician #10 919-733-9321
Optometrist #18 910-285-3160
Osteopathic Physician #47 919-326-1100
Paramedic #21 919-855-3750
Pesticide Applicator #16 919-733-3556
Pesticide Dealer/Consultant #16 919-733-3556
Pharmacist #11 919-942-4454
Pharmacy/Physician Pharmacy #11 919-942-4454
Physical Therapist #49 919-490-6393
Physical Therapist Assisant #49 919-490-6393
Physician Assistant #47 919-326-1100
Plumber #31 919-875-3612
Podiatrist #12 919-861-5583
Polygraph Examiner #53 919-875-3611
Private Investigator #53 919-875-3611
Psychological Associate #36 828-262-2258
Psychologist #36 828-262-2258
Public Accountant-CPA #37 919-733-4222
RAL #17 919-733-3016
Real Estate Agent/Broker/Dealer #39
.... 919-875-3700 x772
Real Estate Firm #39 .... 919-875-3700 x772
Sanitarian #14 336-656-0036
Securities Agent/Broker #26 919-733-3924
Security Guard & Patrol #53 919-875-3611
Shorthand Reporter #29 919-733-2927
Social Worker #15 336-625-1679
Soil Scientist #22 919-851-8963
Solid Waste Facility Operator #34 919-733-0379
Speech Pathologist/Audiologist #30 336-272-1828
Surveyor, Land #48 919-781-9499
Taxidermist #25 919-661-4872
Unarmed Security Guard #53 919-875-3611
Veterinarian #50 919-733-7689
Veterinary Technician #50 919-733-7689
Waste Water Treatment Plant Operator #34
.... 919-733-0379
Wildlife Collector #25 919-661-4872

North Carolina Licensing Agency Information

1 Alarm Systems Licensing Board, 1631 Midtown Pl #104, Raleigh, NC 27609; 919-875-3611, Fax: 919-875-3609.
Email: PPSASL@ncdoj.com

2 Auctioneer Licensing Board, 602 Stellata Drive, Fuquay-Varina, NC 27526;
919-567-2844, Fax: 919-567-2865.
www.ncalb.org   Email: info@ncalb.org
Search Database at
www.ncalb.org/scripts/members.asp

3 Board of Architecture, 127 Hargett St #304, Raleigh, NC 27601;
919-733-9544, Fax: 919-733-1272.
www.ncbarch.org   Email: ncba@earthlink.net
Search Database at www.ncbarch.org/dbase.asp
Note: Mailing lists are also available, see
"Directory" section at main website.

4 Board of Barber Examiners, 2321 Crabtree Blvd #110, Raleigh, NC 27604-2260;
919-715-1159, Fax: 919-715-4669.

5 Board of Examiners for Nursing Home Administrators, 3733 National Drive #228, Raleigh, NC 27612;
919-571-4164, Fax: 919-571-4166.
www.ncbenha.org   Search Database at
www.ncbenha.org/searchdb.asp

6 Public Board of Examiners of Electrical Contractors, PO Box 18727 (1299 Front St.), Raleigh, NC 27619;
919-733-9042, Fax: 919-733-6105.
www.ncbeec.org   Email: info@ncbeec.org
Search Database at
www.ncbeec.org/LicSearch.asp

7 Board of Funeral Service, 1033 Wade Avenue #108, Raleigh, NC 27605-1158; 919-733-9380, Fax: 919-733-8271.
http://ncbfs.org   Email: wpharris@ncbfs.org
Search Database at www.ncbfs.org/directory.htm

8 Board of Nursing, PO Box 2129 (3724 National Dr.), Raleigh, NC 27602;
919-782-3211, Fax: 919-781-9461.
www.ncbon.com   Search Database at
https://www.ncbon.com/Lic-verif.asp

9 Board of Occupational Therapy, PO Box 2280, Raleigh, NC 27602; 919-832-1380,
Fax: 919-833-1059.   www.ncbot.org
Email: administrator@ncbot.org   Search Database at
www.ncbot.org/fpdb/otimport.html

10 Board of Opticians, PO Box 25336, Raleigh, NC 27611-5336;
919-733-9321, Fax: 919-733-0040.

11 Board of Pharmacy, PO Box 4560, Chapel Hill, NC 27515-4560;
919-942-4454, Fax: 919-967-5757.
www.ncbop.org   Email: csmith@ncbog.org
Search Database at www.ncbop.org/names1.asp

12 Board of Podiatry Examiners, 1500 Sunday Dr #102, Raleigh, NC 27607-5151;
919-861-5583, Fax: 919-787-4916.
www.ncbpe.org   Email: info@ncbpe.org
Search Database at www.ncbpe.org/search.php

13 Board of Licensed Professional Counselors, PO Box 1369, Garner, NC 27529; 919-661-0820, Fax: 919-779-5642.   www.ncblpc.org
Search Database at www.ncblpc.org/search.php
Note: There is a $4.00 per name fee for verification request. Verifications are not given via phone.

14 Board of Sanitarian Examiners, 7171 Brown Summit Rd, Browns Summit, NC 27214; 336-656-0036, Fax: 336-656-0036.
www.rsboard.com   Email: rsboardcb@earthlink.net
Search Database at
www.rsboard.com/rsweb/directory/directory.htm

15 NC Social Work Certification & Licensure Board, PO Box 1043, Asheboro, NC 27204; 336-625-1679, Fax: 336-625-1680.
www.ncswboard.org   Email: swboard@asheboro.com

16 Department of Agriculture, Pesticide Section, 1090 Mail Service Ctr. (2109 Blue Ridge Rd), Raleigh, NC 27699-1090; 919-733-3556, Fax: 919-733-9796.   www.ncagr.com/pesticide
Search Database at www.ncagr.com/aspzine/Fooddrug/data/advsearch.asp

17 Department of Commerce, Commission of Banks, 4309 Mail Service Center (316 W. Edenton St), Raleigh, NC 27699; 919-733-3016, Fax: 919-733-6918.   www.nccob.org
Search Database at www.nccob.org

18 Board of Examiners in Optometry, 109 N. Graham Street, Wallace, NC 28466;
910-285-3160, Fax: 910-285-4546.
www.ncoptometry.org   Email: info@ncoptometry.org
Search Database at
www.ncoptometry.org/verify/index.asp

19 Department of Commerce, Cemetery Commission, 1000 Navaho Dr GL-2, Raleigh, NC 27609; 919-981-2536, Fax: 919-981-2538.

20 Alcoholic Beverage Control Commission, 4307 Mail Service Center, Raleigh, NC 27699-4307; 919-779-0700, Fax: 919-662-3583.
www.ncabc.com

21 Department of Health & Human Services, Division of Family Services, 2701 Mail Service Center (701 Barbour Drive), Raleigh, NC 27699-2701; 919-855-3750, Fax: 919-733-2757.
www.dhhs.state.nc.us/
Email: ed.browning@ncmail.net

22 Board For Licensing of Soil Scientists, 659 Cary Towne Blvd, PMB 281, Cary, NC 27511; 919-851-8963.   www.ncblss.org
Email: ncblss@earthlink.net
Search Database at www.ncblss.org

23 Department of Insurance, PO Box 26387, 430 N Salisbury St, Raleigh, NC 27611; 919-733-7487, 981-5244 Auto Verify number.
www.ncdoi.com

24 Department of Labor, 4 W Edenton St, Labor Bldg, Raleigh, NC 27601-1092; 919-807-2796, Fax: 919-733-6197.   www.dol.state.nc.us

25 Department of Natural Resources & Environment, Wildlife Resources Commission, 512 N Salisbury St, Raleigh, NC 27604-1188; 919-661-4872, Fax: 919-773-2955.
www.ncwildlife.org/fs_index_01_license.htm

26 Department of State, NC Secretary of State, P O Box 29622, Raleigh, NC 27626; 919-733-3924, Fax: 919-821-0818.
www.sosnc.com   Email: secdiv@sosnc.com
Search Database at www.sosnc.com/

27 Department of State Treasurer, Investment & Banking Division, 3250 N Salisbury St, Raleigh, NC 27603; 919-508-5176, Fax: 919-508-5167.
www.treasurer.state.nc.us

28 Division of State Library, Department of Cultural Resources, 109 E Jones St, Raleigh, NC 27601-2807; 919-733-2570, Fax: 919-733-8714.
http://statelibrary.dcr.state.nc.us

29 Examiners for Court Reporting Standards & Testing, PO Box 2448 (2 E Morgan St), Raleigh, NC 27602; 919-733-7107, Fax: 919-715-5779.

30 Examiners for Speech Pathologists & Audiologists, PO Box 16885, Greensboro, NC 27416-0885; 336-272-1828, Fax: 336-272-4353.
www.ncboeslpa.org
Email: ncboe@bellsouth.net
Search Database at www.ncboeslpa.org

31 Board of Examiners of Plumbing, Heating & Fire Sprinkler Contractors, 1109 Dresser Court, Raleigh, NC 27609;
919-875-3612, Fax: 919-875-3616.
www.nclicensing.org   Email: info@nclicensing.org
Search Database at
www.nclicensing.org/OnlineReg.htm

32 Licensing Board for General Contractors, PO Box 17187 (3739 National Dr #225), Raleigh, NC 27619; 919-571-4183, Fax: 919-571-4703.
www.nclbgc.net
Search Database at www.nclbgc.org/lic_fr.html

33 Marital & Family Therapy Certification Board, 3000 Bethesda Pl #503, Winston-Salem, NC 27103-3327; 336-794-3891.
http://jobs.esc.state.nc.us/lmi/ar/occuplic/MarFamTher.htm   Email: mftlb@bellsouth.net

34 Water Treatment Facility Operators, Certification Board, 1635 Mail Service Center, Raleigh, NC 27699-1635;
919-733-0379, Fax: 919-715-2726.

35 Board of Electrolysis Examiners, 2 Centerview Dr #34, Greensboro, NC 27407-3708;
336-574-1414, Fax: 336-574-1414.
Email: ncbeexam@yahoo.com

36 Psychology Board, 895 State Farm Road #101, Boone, NC 28607; 828-262-2258,
Fax: 828-265-8611.
www.ncpsychologyboard.org
Email: ncpsybd@charter.net   Search Database at
www.ncpsychologyboard.org/search.htm

37 Board of CPA Examiners, PO Box 12827 (1101 Oberlin Rd, #104), Raleigh, NC 27605-2827; 919-733-4222.
www.cpaboard.state.nc.us
Search Database at www.cpaboard.state.nc.us

38 Board of Athletic Trainer Examiners, PO Box 10769, Raleigh, NC 27605; 919-821-4980, Fax: 919-833-5743.   www.ncbate.org
Search Database at www.ncbate.org/trainers.html

39 Real Estate Commission, P.O. Box 17100 (1313 Navaho Dr), Raleigh, NC 27619-7100; 919-875-3700.
www.ncrec.state.nc.us
Email: records@ncrec.state.nc.us   Search Database at www.ncrec.state.nc.us/licensees/licensees.asp
Note: Online database contains only active licensees.

40 Acupuncture Licensing Board, 893 US Highway 70 West, Garner, NC 27529; 919-773-0530, Fax: 919-779-5642.
http://ncaaom.org
Search Database at
http://ncaaom.org/directory.php

41 Board of Chiropractic Examiners, 174 Church St N, Concord, NC 28025; 704-793-1342. http://ncchiroboard.com/ Email: ncchirobrd@juno.com

42 Board of Dental Examiners, 15100 Weston Parkway, Suite 101, Cary, NC 27513; 919-678-8223, Fax: 919-678-8472. www.ncdentalboard.org Email: info@ncdentalboard.org Search Database at www.ncdentalboard.org/ncdbe_search.asp

43 Board of Hearing Aid Dealers & Fitters, 2462 Stantonsburg Rd #214, Greenville, NC 27834; 252-752-6382, Fax: 252-752-6305. www.nchalb.org Email: info@nchalb.org Search Database at www.nchalb.org/cgi-bin/sho_memb.pl

45 Board of Law Examiners, PO Box 2946 (208 Fayetteville St Mall), Raleigh, NC 27602; 919-828-4886, Fax: 919-828-2251. www.ncble.org

46 Landscape Architecture & Geologists Board, PO Box 41225 (3733 Benson Dr), Raleigh, NC 27629; 919-850-9669, Fax: 919-872-1598. www.ncbola.org   Email: ncbla@bellsouth.net Search Database at www.ncbola.org/rosternew.html

47 Board of Medical Examiners, PO Box 20007 (1201 Front St, 27609), Raleigh, NC 27619; 919-326-1100, Fax: 919-326-1131. www.ncmedboard.org Email: info@ncmedboard.org

Search Database at www.ncmedboard.org/find.htm

48 Board of Examiners for Prof Engineers & Land Surveyors, 310 W Millbrook Rd, Raleigh, NC 27609; 919-841-4000, Fax: 919-841-4012. www.ncbels.org Email: lbpeace@ncbels.org Search Database at www.member-base.com/ncbels-vs/public/searchdb.asp

49 Examining Board of Physical Therapy, 18 W Colony Pl #140, Durham, NC 27705; 919-490-6393, Fax: 919-490-5106. www.ncptboard.org Email: NCPTBoard@mindspring.com Search Database at www.ncptboard.org/search.asp Note: Licensure lists for PT & PTA may be obtained for $60.00 each (disk or labels).

50 Veterinary Medical Board, PO Box 37549, Raleigh, NC 27627-7549; 919-733-7689. http://jobs.esc.state.nc.us/lmi/ar/occuplic/Veterinari.htm

51 Secretary of State, Lobbyist Registration, 2 N Salisbury St (PO Box 29622), Raleigh, NC 27626-0622; 919-807-2156, Fax: 919-807-2160. www.secstate.state.nc.us Email: mkelly@mail.secstate.state.nc.us Search Database at www.secretary.state.nc.us/lobbyists/Lsearch.asp

52 Secretary of State, Charitable Solicitation Licensing Section, PO Box 29622, Raleigh, NC 27626-0525; 919-807-2214, Fax: 919-807-2220. www.sosnc.com Email: csl@sosnc.com Search Database at www.secretary.state.nc.us/csl/search.asp

53 Private Protective Svcs Board, 1631 Midtown Pl #104, Raleigh, NC 27609; 919-875-3611, Fax: 919-875-3609. www.jus.state.nc.us/pps/ Email: PPSASL@ncdoj.com

54 Board of Registration of Forresters, PO Box 27393, Raleigh, NC 27611; 919-772-5883, Fax: 919-772-5883. http://members.aol.com/ncbrf/index.htm Email: ncbrf@aol.com Search Database at http://members.aol.com/ncbrf/roster_index.htm

55 Board of Cosmetic Arts Examiners, 1201 Front St., #110, Raleigh, NC 27609; 919-733-4117, Fax: 919-733-4127. www.cosmetology.state.nc.us

56 Department of Justice, Attorney General's Office, Sheriff's Standard Division, PO Drawer 629, Raleigh, NC 27602; 919-716-6460.

58 Secretary of State, Notary Public Section, PO Box 29622, Raleigh, NC 27626-0622; 919-807-2131. www.sosnc.com Email: noarty@sosnc.com

North Carolina Federal Courts

The following list indicates the district and division name for each county in the state. If the bankruptcy court location is different from the district court, then the location of the bankruptcy court appears in parentheses.

County/Court Cross Reference

County	District	Division
Alamance	Middle	Greensboro
Alexander	Western	Statesville (Charlotte)
Alleghany	Western	Statesville (Charlotte)
Anson	Western	Charlotte
Ashe	Western	Statesville (Charlotte)
Avery	Western	Asheville (Charlotte)
Beaufort	Eastern	Greenville-Eastern (Wilson)
Bertie	Eastern	Elizabeth City (Wilson)
Bladen	Eastern	Wilmington (Wilson)
Brunswick	Eastern	Wilmington (Wilson)
Buncombe	Western	Asheville (Charlotte)
Burke	Western	Shelby (Charlotte)
Cabarrus	Middle	Greensboro
Caldwell	Western	Statesville (Charlotte)
Camden	Eastern	Elizabeth City (Wilson)
Carteret	Eastern	Greenville-Eastern (Wilson)
Caswell	Middle	Greensboro
Catawba	Western	Statesville (Charlotte)
Chatham	Middle	Greensboro
Cherokee	Western	Bryson City (Charlotte)
Chowan	Eastern	Elizabeth City (Wilson)
Clay	Western	Bryson City (Charlotte)
Cleveland	Western	Shelby (Charlotte)
Columbus	Eastern	Wilmington (Wilson)
Craven	Eastern	Greenville-Eastern (Wilson)
Cumberland	Eastern	Greenville-Eastern (Wilson)
Currituck	Eastern	Elizabeth City (Wilson)
Dare	Eastern	Elizabeth City (Wilson)
Davidson	Middle	Greensboro (Winston-Salem)
Davie	Middle	Greensboro
Duplin	Eastern	Wilmington (Wilson)
Durham	Middle	Greensboro
Edgecombe	Eastern	Raleigh (Wilson)
Forsyth	Middle	Greensboro (Winston-Salem)
Franklin	Eastern	Raleigh
Gaston	Western	Charlotte
Gates	Eastern	Elizabeth City (Wilson)
Graham	Western	Bryson City (Charlotte)
Granville	Eastern	Raleigh
Greene	Eastern	Greenville-Eastern (Wilson)
Guilford	Middle	Greensboro
Halifax	Eastern	Greenville-Eastern (Wilson)
Harnett	Eastern	Raleigh
Haywood	Western	Asheville (Charlotte)
Henderson	Western	Asheville (Charlotte)
Hertford	Eastern	Elizabeth City (Wilson)
Hoke	Middle	Greensboro
Hyde	Eastern	Greenville-Eastern (Wilson)
Iredell	Western	Statesville (Charlotte)
Jackson	Western	Bryson City (Charlotte)
Johnston	Eastern	Raleigh
Jones	Eastern	Greenville-Eastern (Wilson)
Lee	Middle	Greensboro
Lenoir	Eastern	Greenville-Eastern (Wilson)
Lincoln	Western	Statesville (Charlotte)
Macon	Western	Bryson City (Charlotte)
Madison	Western	Asheville (Charlotte)
Martin	Eastern	Greenville-Eastern (Wilson)
McDowell	Western	Shelby (Charlotte)
Mecklenburg	Western	Charlotte
Mitchell	Western	Asheville (Charlotte)
Montgomery	Middle	Greensboro
Moore	Middle	Greensboro
Nash	Eastern	Raleigh (Wilson)
New Hanover	Eastern	Wilmington (Wilson)
Northampton	Eastern	Elizabeth City (Wilson)
Onslow	Eastern	Wilmington (Wilson)
Orange	Middle	Greensboro
Pamlico	Eastern	Greenville-Eastern (Wilson)
Pasquotank	Eastern	Elizabeth City (Wilson)
Pender	Eastern	Wilmington (Wilson)
Perquimans	Eastern	Elizabeth City (Wilson)
Person	Middle	Greensboro
Pitt	Eastern	Greenville-Eastern (Wilson)
Polk	Western	Shelby (Charlotte)
Randolph	Middle	Greensboro
Richmond	Middle	Greensboro
Robeson	Eastern	Wilmington (Wilson)
Rockingham	Middle	Greensboro
Rowan	Middle	Greensboro
Rutherford	Western	Shelby (Charlotte)
Sampson	Eastern	Wilmington (Wilson)
Scotland	Middle	Greensboro
Stanly	Middle	Greensboro
Stokes	Middle	Greensboro (Winston-Salem)
Surry	Middle	Greensboro (Winston-Salem)
Swain	Western	Bryson City (Charlotte)
Transylvania	Western	Asheville (Charlotte)
Tyrrell	Eastern	Elizabeth City (Wilson)
Union	Western	Charlotte
Vance	Eastern	Raleigh
Wake	Eastern	Raleigh
Warren	Eastern	Raleigh
Washington	Eastern	Elizabeth City (Wilson)
Watauga	Western	Statesville (Charlotte)
Wayne	Eastern	Raleigh (Wilson)
Wilkes	Western	Statesville (Charlotte)
Wilson	Eastern	Raleigh (Wilson)
Yadkin	Middle	Greensboro (Winston-Salem)
Yancey	Western	Asheville (Charlotte)

Standards for Federal Courts: See New York or North Dakota Federal Courts section for information on Federal Courts standards and fees.

US District Court

Eastern District of North Carolina

Eastern Division Room 209, 201 S Evans St, Greenville, NC 27858-1137 (courier address: Use mail address for courier delivery) 252-830-6009, Fax: 252-830-2793. www.nced.uscourts.gov

Counties: Beaufort, Carteret, Craven, Edgecombe, Greene, Halifax, Hyde, Jones, Lenoir, Martin, Pamlico, Pitt.

Indexing & Storage: New cases available in the index same day if possible after filing date. Civil records are retained for 2 years. All criminal records after 1979 are forwarded to Raleigh.

Fee & Payment: Payment may be made by money order, cashier check, business check. In state personal checks are also accepted. Payee: Clerk, U.S. District Court.

Phone Search: Only limited docket information is available by phone.

In Person Search: Fee charged if court conducts your in person search for you.

PACER: The RACER system is now administered by PACER, www.nced.uscourts.gov/Racer.htm for record access. Toll-free access: 800-995-0313. Local access: 919-856-4768. Records purged when necessary. New records are online after 3 days.

Northern Division c/o Raleigh Division, PO Box 25670, Raleigh, NC 27611 (courier address: Room 574, 310 New Bern Ave, Raleigh, NC 27601), 919-856-4370. www.nced.uscourts.gov

Counties: Bertie, Camden, Chowan, Currituck, Dare, Gates, Hertford, Northampton, Pasquotank, Perquimans, Tyrrell, Washington.

Indexing & Storage: Cases indexed by as well as by case number. New cases available in the index after filing date. Open records are located at the Raliegh Division.

Fee & Payment: Payment may be made by money order, cashier check, personal check.

Phone Search: No searching by telephone.

Mail Search: A SASE not required.

In Person Search: Permitted.

PACER: The RACER system is now administered by PACER, www.nced.uscourts.gov/Racer.htm for record access. Toll-free access: 800-995-0313. Local access: 919-856-4768. Records purged when necessary. New records are online after 3 days.

Southern Division Alton Lennon Fed. Bldg., '2 Princess Street, Wilmington, NC 28401 (courier address: Room 239, 2 Princess St, Wilmington, NC 28401), 910-815-4663, Fax: 910-815-4518. www.nced.uscourts.gov

Bladen, Brunswick, Columbus, Duplin, New Hanover, Onslow, Pender, Robeson, Sampson.

Indexing & Storage: New cases available in the index 1 day after filing date. Closed civil records are retained for 2 years. All criminal records after 1979 are located in Raleigh.

Fee & Payment: Payment may be made by money order, cashier check, personal check. Payee: Clerk, U.S. District Court.

Phone Search: Phone searches are only available for information from 1994 to the present.

Mail Search: A SASE not required.

In Person Search: Fee charged if court conducts your in person search for you.

PACER: The RACER system is now administered by PACER, www.nced.uscourts.gov/Racer.htm for record access. Toll-free access: 800-995-0313. Local access: 919-856-4768. Records purged when necessary. New records are online after 3 days.

Western Division Clerk's Office, PO Box 25670, Raleigh, NC 27611 (courier address: Room 574, 310 New Bern Ave, Raleigh, NC 27601), 919-645-1700, Fax: 919-645-1750. www.nced.uscourts.gov

Counties: Cumberland, Franklin, Granville, Harnett, Johnston, Nash, Vance, Wake, Warren, Wayne, Wilson.

Indexing & Storage: New cases available in the index 1 day after filing date. Records from a former office in Fayetteville that handled Cumberland and Harnett counties are maintained here. District wide searches are available after 1979 for criminal records through this court.

Fee & Payment: Payment may be made by money order, cashier check, business check. In state personal checks are also accepted. Payee: Clerk, U.S. District Court.

Phone Search: Only docket information available.

Mail Search: A SASE not required.

In Person Search: Fee charged if court conducts your in person search for you.

PACER: The RACER system is now administered by PACER, www.nced.uscourts.gov/Racer.htm for record access. Toll-free access: 800-995-0313. Local access: 919-856-4768. Records purged when necessary. New records are online after 3 days.

Greensboro Division Clerk's Office, PO Box 2708, Greensboro, NC 27402 (courier address: Room 401, 324 W Market St, Greensboro, NC 27401), 336-332-6000. www.ncmd.uscourts.gov

Alamance, Cabarrus, Caswell, Chatham, Davidson, Davie, Durham, Forsyth, Guilford, Hoke, Lee, Montgomery, Moore, Orange, Person, Randolph, Richmond, Rockingham, Rowan, Scotland, Stanly, Stokes, Surry, Yadkin.

Indexing & Storage: New cases available in the index 1 day after filing date. All other divisions in this district have been abolished as of July 1997.

Fee & Payment: Payment may be made by money order, cashier check, business check. In state personal checks are also accepted. Payee: Clerk, U.S. District Court.

Phone Search: No searching by telephone. Only docket information is available by case number over the phone.

Mail Search: A SASE not required.

In Person Search: Fee charged if court conducts your in person search for you.

PACER: PACER is available online at http://pacer.ncmd.uscourts.gov. Document images available. Case records go back to September 1991. Records never purged. New records are online after 2 days.

U.S. Bankruptcy Court

Eastern District of North Carolina

Raleigh Division PO Box 1441, Raleigh, NC 27602 (courier: Room 209, Century Station Bldg, 300 Fayetteville St Mall, Raleigh, NC 27602), 919-856-4752. www.nceb.uscourts.gov

Counties: Franklin, Granville, Harnett, Johnston, Vance, Wake, Warren.

Indexing & Storage: Cases indexed by debtor as well as by case number. New cases available in the index 1 day after filing date.

Fee & Payment: Payment may be made by money order, cashier check, business check, Visa or Mastercard. Personal checks are not accepted. Credit cards are accepted from companies only. Payee: Clerk, U.S. Bankruptcy Court.

Phone Search: Automated voice case information service (VCIS) is available. Call VCIS at 888-847-9138 or 252-234-7655.

In Person Search: Fee charged if court conducts your in person search for you.

PACER: Court uses new CM/ECF system..

Electronic Filing: For information on their electronic noticing and filing system using courtwatch.com, visit www.nceb.uscourts.gov/efiling.htm. Electronic filing information online at https://ecf.nceb.uscourts.gov

Other Online Access: Search records online using RACER at http://pacer.nceb.uscourts.gov. There is no fee. Document images available.

Wilson Division PO Drawer 2807, Wilson, NC 27894-2807 (courier: The Thomas Milton Moore Bldg, 1760 Parkwood Blvd, Wilson, NC 27894), 252-237-0248. www.nceb.uscourts.gov

Counties: Beaufort, Bertie, Bladen, Brunswick, Camden, Carteret, Chowan, Columbus, Craven, Cumberland, Currituck, Dare, Duplin, Edgecombe, Gates, Greene, Halifax, Hertford, Hyde, Jones, Lenoir, Martin, Nash, New Hanover, Northampton, Onslow, Pamlico, Pasquotank, Pender, Perquimans, Pitt, Robeson, Sampson, Tyrrell, Washington, Wayne, Wilson.

Indexing & Storage: Cases indexed by debtor as well as by case number. New cases available in the index 1 day after filing date.

Fee & Payment: Payment may be made by money order, cashier check, business check, Visa or Mastercard. Personal checks are not accepted. Payee: Clerk, U.S. Bankruptcy Court.

Phone Search: Only major dates such as the 341 date, discharge date and entry date will be released. Automated voice case information service (VCIS) is available. Call VCIS at 888-513-9765 or 252-234-7655.

In Person Search: Fee charged if court conducts your in person search for you.

PACER: Court uses new CM/ECF system..

Electronic Filing: For information on their electronic noticing and filing system using courtwatch.com, visit www.nceb.uscourts.gov/efiling.htm. Electronic filing information online at https://ecf.nceb.uscourts.gov

Other Online Access: Search records online using RACER at http://pacer.nceb.uscourts.gov. There is no fee. Document images available.

U.S. Bankruptcy Court

Middle District of North Carolina

Greensboro Division PO Box 26100, Greensboro, NC 27420-6100 (courier address: 101 S Edgeworth St, Greensboro, NC 27401), 336-333-5647. www.ncmb.uscourts.gov

Alamance, Cabarrus, Caswell, Chatham, Davidson, Davie, Durham, Guilford, Hoke, Lee, Montgomery, Moore, Orange, Person, Randolph, Richmond, Rockingham, Rowan, Scotland, Stanly.

Indexing & Storage: Cases indexed by debtor as well as by case number. New cases available in the index 1-2 days after filing date. Only pre-BANCAP cases (cases filed prior to 7/17/89) are indexed on a separate computer program. District wide searches are available for information on cases filed after July 17, 1989 from this division on their VCIS system.

Fee & Payment: Payment may be made by money order, cashier check, personal check. Debtor's checks are not accepted. Payee: Clerk, U.S. Bankruptcy Court.

Phone Search: Only the name of the debtor, case number, date filed, trustee and attorney for the debtor will be released over the phone. Automated voice case information service (VCIS) is available. Call VCIS at 888-319-0455 or 336-333-5532.

In Person Search: Fee charged if court conducts your in person search for you.

PACER: PACER is available online at http://pacer.ncmb.uscourts.gov. Document images available. Records purged every two years. New civil records are online after 1 day.

Electronic Filing: ECF images go back to 1999. Electronic filing information online at https://ecf.ncmb.uscourts.gov

Winston-Salem Division 226 S Liberty St, Winston-Salem, NC 27101 (courier address: Use mail address for courier delivery) 336-631-5340. www.ncmb.uscourts.gov

Counties: Forsyth, Stokes, Surry, Yadkin.

Indexing & Storage: Cases indexed by debtor as well as by case number. New cases available in the index 2 days after filing date.

Fee & Payment: Payment may be made by money order, cashier check, personal check. Debtor's checks are not accepted. Payee: Clerk, U.S. Bankruptcy Court.

Phone Search: Basic docket information only is available by phone. Automated voice case information service (VCIS) is available. Call VCIS at 888-319-0455 or 336-333-5532.

In Person Search: Fee charged if court conducts your in person search for you.

PACER: PACER is available online at http://pacer.ncmb.uscourts.gov. Document images available. Records purged every two years. New civil records are online after 1 day.

Electronic Filing: ECF images go back to 1999. Electronic filing information online at https://ecf.ncmb.uscourts.gov

U.S. District Court

Western District of North Carolina

Asheville Division Clerk of the Court, Room 309, U.S. Courthouse Bldg, 100 Otis St, Asheville, NC 28801-2611 (courier address: Use mail address for courier delivery) 828-771-7200, Fax: 828-271-4343. www.ncwd.uscourts.gov

Avery, Buncombe, Haywood, Henderson, Madison, Mitchell, Transylvania, Yancey.

Indexing & Storage: New cases available in the index 1 day after filing date. Not all records are entered on the in house automated system. This office also handles records for the Bryson City and Shelby Divisions.

Fee & Payment: Payment may be made by money order, cashier check, personal check. Payee: Clerk, U.S. District Court.

Phone Search: Only docket information available.

In Person Search: Fee charged if court conducts your in person search for you.

PACER: WebPACER is at www.ncwd.uscourts.gov/index.html. Document images available. New records are online after 2 days.

Bryson City Division c/o Asheville Division, Clerk of the Court, Room 309, U.S. Courthouse, 100 Otis St, Asheville, NC 28801-2611 (courier address: Use mail address for courier delivery) 828-771-7200. www.ncwd.uscourts.gov **Counties:** Cherokee, Clay, Graham, Jackson, Macon, Swain.

Indexing & Storage: New cases available in the index after filing date. Open records are located at the Asheville Division.

Fee & Payment: Payment may be made by money order, cashier check. Business checks are not accepted. Personal checks are not accepted.

Phone Search: No searching by telephone.

In Person Search: Permitted.

PACER: WebPACER is at www.ncwd.uscourts.gov/index.html. Document images available. New records are online after 2 days.

Charlotte Division Clerk, Room 210, 401 W Trade St, Charlotte, NC 28202 (courier address: Use mail address for courier delivery) 704-350-7400. www.ncwd.uscourts.gov

Counties: Anson, Gaston, Mecklenburg, Union.

Indexing & Storage: New cases available in the index 1-2 days after filing date. District wide searches are available for records from 1950 forward from this court. **Fee & Payment:** Payment by money order, cashier check, personal check. Payee: Clerk, U.S. District Court.

Phone Search: No searching by telephone. Only docket information available by phone. **Mail Search:** A SASE not required.

In Person Search: Fee charged if court conducts your in person search for you.

PACER: WebPACER is at www.ncwd.uscourts.gov/index.html. Document images available. New records are online after 2 days.

Shelby Division c/o Asheville Division, Clerk of the Court, Room 309, U.S. Courthouse, 100 Otis St, Asheville, NC 28801-2611 (courier address: Use mail address for courier delivery) 828-771-7200. www.ncwd.uscourts.gov

Burke, Cleveland, McDowell, Polk, Rutherford.

Indexing & Storage: Cases indexed by as well as by case number. New cases available in the index after filing date. Open records are located at the Asheville Division.

Fee & Payment: Payment may be made by money order, cashier check. Business checks are not accepted. Personal checks are not accepted.

Phone Search: No searching by telephone.

In Person Search: Permitted.

PACER: WebPACER is at www.ncwd.uscourts.gov/index.html. Document images available. New records are online after 2 days.

Statesville Division PO Box 466, Statesville, NC 28687 (courier address: Room 205, 200 W Broad St, Statesville, NC 28687), 704-883-1000. www.ncwd.uscourts.gov

Counties: Alexander, Alleghany, Ashe, Caldwell, Catawba, Iredell, Lincoln, Watauga, Wilkes.

Indexing & Storage: New cases available in the index 2 days after filing date.

Fee & Payment: Payment may be made by money order, cashier check, personal check. Payee: Clerk, U.S. District Court.

Phone Search: Only docket information available.

Mail Search: A SASE not required.

In Person Search: Fee charged if court conducts your in person search for you.

PACER: WebPACER is at www.ncwd.uscourts.gov/index.html. Document images available. New records are online after 2 days.

U.S. Bankruptcy Court

Western District of North Carolina

Charlotte Division P.O. Box 34189, Charlotte, NC 28234-4189 (courier address: 401 W Trade St, Charlotte, NC 28202), 704-350-7500. www.ncwb.uscourts.gov

Counties: Alexander, Alleghany, Anson, Ashe, Avery, Buncombe, Burke, Caldwell, Catawba, Cherokee, Clay, Cleveland, Gaston, Graham, Haywood, Henderson, Iredell, Jackson, Lincoln, Macon, Madison, McDowell, Mecklenburg, Mitchell, Polk, Rutherford, Swain, Transylvania, Union, Watauga, Wilkes, Yancey. There are five offices within this division; records for all may be searched here or at Asheville: 100 Otis St #112, Asheville, NC 28801, 828-771-7300.

Indexing & Storage: Cases indexed by debtor as well as by case number. New cases available in the index 1-2 days after filing date.

Fee & Payment: Payment may be made by money order, cashier check, business check. Personal checks are not accepted. Debtor's checks are not accepted. Payee: Clerk, U.S. Bankruptcy Court.

Phone Search: Only docket information available by telephone. Automated voice case information service (VCIS) is available. Call VCIS at 800-884-9868 or 704-350-7505.

In Person Search: Fee charged if court conducts your in person search for you.

PACER: Court uses new CM/ECF system.. Records purged every 2 years. New civil records are online after 1 day.

Electronic Filing: Electronic filing information online at https://ecf.ncwb.uscourts.gov

North Carolina County Courts

Court	Jurisdiction	No. of Courts	How Organized
Superior Courts*	General	0	46 Districts
District Courts*	Limited	0	39 Districts
Combined Courts*		100	

* Profiled in this Sourcebook.

Court	CIVIL								
	Tort	Contract	Real Estate	Min. Claim	Max. Claim	Small Claims	Estate	Eviction	Domestic Relations
Superior Courts*	X	X	X	$10,000	No Max		X		
District Courts*	X	X	X	$0	$10,000	4100		X	X

Court	CRIMINAL				
	Felony	Misdemeanor	DWI/DUI	Preliminary Hearing	Juvenile
Superior Courts*	X				
District Courts*		X	X	X	X

ADMINISTRATION Administrative Office of the Courts, Justice Bldg, 2 E Morgan St, Raleigh, NC, 27602; 919-733-7107, Fax: 919-715-5779. www.nccourts.org

COURT STRUCTURE The Superior Court is the court of general jurisdiction, the District Court is limited. The counties combine the courts, thus searching is done through one court, not two, within the county. Small claims court is part of the District Court Division. It handles civil cases where a plaintiff requests assignment to a magistrate and the amount in controversy is $4,000 or less. The principal relief sought in small claims court is money, the recovery of specific personal property, or summary ejectment (eviction).

ONLINE ACCESS While there is no statewide online access, web access to civil and criminal dockets are available at some individual courts.

Access active District/Superior Court criminal calendars on a county or statewide basis at www1.aoc.state.nc.us/www/calendars.html. Historical information is not available.

Go to www1.aoc.state.nc.us/www/calendars/Civil.html for Civil court calendars for 43 counties. Also, appellate and supreme court opinions are available on the Internet at www.aoc.state.nc.us/www/public/html/opinions.htm.

ADDITIONAL INFORMATION Many courts recommend that civil searches be done in person or by a retriever and that only criminal searches be requested in writing (for a $10.00 search fee, which is certified in most jurisdictions). Many courts have archived their records prior to 1968 in the Raleigh State Archives, 919-733-5722. A list of companies offering North Carolina criminal records online can be accessed at www.nccourts.org/Citizens/GoToCourt/ Default.asp?topic=1

PROBATE COURTS Probate is handled by County Clerks.

📖 📖 📖 📖 📖 📖

Alamance County

Superior-District Court - Criminal 212 West Elm St, #105, Graham, NC 27253; 336-438-1001. 8AM-5PM (EST). *Felony, Misdemeanor.* www.aoc.state.nc.us/www/public/courts/alamance.html
Note: Search civil and criminal court calendars at www1.aoc.state.nc.us/www/calendars.html.
Criminal Records: Access: Mail, in person. Both court and visitors may perform in person searches. Search fee: $10.00 per name. Required to search: name, years to search, DOB; also helpful: address, SSN. Criminal records on computer since 1985, on index cards back to 1975.

General Information: Public Access terminal is available. No sealed case records released. Copy fee: $1.50 for first page, $.25 each add'l. Certification fee: $3.00. Payee: Clerk of Superior Court. Only cashiers checks and money orders accepted. Prepayment required. Mail turnaround time 1 week.

Superior-District Court - Civil 1 Court Square, Graham, NC 27253; 336-438-1002; Civil phone: 336-438-1013; Criminal phone: 336-438-1001; Probate phone: 336-438-1008. Hours: 8AM-5PM (EST). *Civil, Eviction, Small Claims, Probate.*
Civil Records: Access: In person only. Visitors must perform in person searches for themselves. No search fee. Required to search: name, years to search. Civil

cases indexed by defendant, plaintiff. Civil records computerized since 1985, prior indexed on books.
General Information: Public Access terminal is available. No adoptions, sealed cases, juvenile, or mental records released. Copy fee: $2.00 for first page, $.25 each add'l. Certification fee: $3.00. Prepayment required.

Alexander County

Superior-District Court PO Box 100, Taylorsville, NC 28681; 828-632-2215; Fax: 828-632-3550. 8AM-5PM (EST). *Felony, Misdemeanor, Civil, Eviction, Small Claims, Probate.*
www.aoc.state.nc.us/www/public/courts/alexander.htm

Note: Search civil and criminal court calendars at www1.aoc.state.nc.us/www/calendars.html.

Civil Records: Access: Mail, in person. Both court and visitors may perform in person searches. Search fee: $5.00 per name. Required to search: name, years to search, address. Civil cases indexed by defendant, plaintiff. Civil records on computer since 10/1989, prior on books to 1865.

Criminal Records: Access: Mail, in person. Both court and visitors may perform in person searches. Search fee: $10.00 per name. Required to search: name, years to search, address, DOB, SSN. Criminal records on computer since 10/1989, prior on books to 1865

General Information: Public Access terminal is available. No adoptions, sealed cases, juvenile, sex offenders, mental, expunged records released. Copy fee: $.25 per page. Certification fee: $3.00. Payee: Clerk of Superior Court. Business checks accepted. Prepayment required. Mail requests: SASE required. Mail turnaround time 1-3 days.

Alleghany County

Superior-District Court PO Box 61, Sparta, NC 28675; 336-372-8949; Fax: 336-372-4899. Hours: 8AM-5PM (EST). *Felony, Misdemeanor, Civil, Eviction, Small Claims, Probate.*

www.aoc.state.nc.us/www/public/courts/alleghany.html
Note: Search the active Criminal Calendar at www1.aoc.state.nc.us/www/calendars/Criminal.html.

Civil Records: Access: In person only. Visitors must perform in person searches for themselves. Search fee: none. Required to search: name, years to search; also helpful: address. Civil cases indexed by defendant, plaintiff. Civil records on computer from 11/1988, index books prior.

Criminal Records: Access: Fax, mail, in person. Only the court performs in person searches; visitors may not. Search fee: $10.00 per name. Required to search: name, years to search, DOB; also helpful: address, SSN. Criminal records on computer from 11/1988, index books prior. **General Information:** Public Access terminal is available. No adoptions, sealed cases, juvenile, mental or expunged records released. Copy fee: $2.00 for first page, $.25 each add'l. Certification fee: $3.00. Payee: Clerk of Superior Court. Business checks accepted. Prepayment required. Mail requests: SASE required. Mail turnaround time 2 days.

Anson County

Superior-District Court PO Box 1064 (114 N Greene St), Wadesboro, NC 28170; 704-694-2314; Fax: 704-695-1161. Hours: 8AM-5PM (EST). *Felony, Misdemeanor, Civil, Eviction, Small Claims, Probate.*

www.aoc.state.nc.us/www/public/courts/anson.htm
Note: Search civil and criminal court calendars at www1.aoc.state.nc.us/www/calendars.html.

Civil Records: Access: Mail, in person. Visitors must perform in person searches for themselves. Search fee: $10.00 per name. Required to search: name, years to search. Civil cases indexed by defendant, plaintiff. Civil records on computer since Oct. 1989, in books prior.

Criminal Records: Access: Mail, in person. Only the court performs in person searches; visitors may not. Search fee: $10.00 per name. Required to search: name, years to search, DOB; also helpful: SSN. Criminal records on computer since 10/89, on microfilm 1982-89, in books prior.

General Information: Public Access terminal is available. (Estates/Special Proceedings only.) No adoptions, sealed cases, juvenile, mental, or expunged records released. Copy fee: $2.00 for first page, $.25 each add'l. Certification fee: $3.00. Payee: Clerk of

Superior Court. Business checks accepted. Prepayment required. Mail requests: SASE required. Mail turnaround time 2-5 days.

Ashe County

Superior-District Court 150 Government Circle #3100, Jefferson, NC 28640-9378; 336-246-5641; Fax: 336-246-4276. Hours: 8AM-5PM (EST). *Felony, Misdemeanor, Civil, Eviction, Small Claims, Probate.*

www.aoc.state.nc.us/www/public/courts/ashe.html
Note: Search civil and criminal court calendars at www1.aoc.state.nc.us/www/calendars.html.

Civil Records: Access: Mail, in person. Both court and visitors may perform in person searches. Search fee: $5.00 per name. Required to search: name, years to search. Civil cases indexed by defendant, plaintiff. Civil records on computer from 12/89, on index books back to 1900s.

Criminal Records: Access: Mail, in person. Both court and visitors may perform in person searches. Search fee: $10.00 per name. Required to search: name, years to search. Criminal records on computer from 12/89, on index books back to 1900s. Court will search records after 1988; visitors or researchers must search themselves for records prior to 1988.

General Information: Public Access terminal is available. No adoptions, sealed cases, juvenile, sex offenders, mental or expunged records released. Copy fee: $2.00 for first page, $.25 each add'l. Certification fee: $3.00. Payee: Clerk of Superior Court. Only cashiers checks and money orders accepted. Prepayment required. Mail turnaround time 1-3 days.

Avery County

Superior-District Court PO Box 115, Newland, NC 28657; 828-733-2900; Fax: 828-733-8410. 8AM-4:30PM (EST). *Felony, Misdemeanor, Civil, Eviction, Small Claims, Probate.*

www.aoc.state.nc.us/www/public/courts/avery.htm
Note: Search civil and criminal court calendars at www1.aoc.state.nc.us/www/calendars.html.

Civil Records: Access: In person only. Visitors must perform in person searches for themselves. Search fee: none. Required to search: name, years to search; also helpful: address. Civil cases indexed by defendant, plaintiff. Civil records on computer since 1988, on index books to 1968.

Criminal Records: Access: Mail, in person. Both court and visitors may perform in person searches. Search fee: $10.00 per name. Required to search: name, years to search; also helpful: address. Criminal records on computer from 11/88; on cards and books back to 1968.

General Information: Public Access terminal is available. No adoptions, sealed cases, juvenile, sex offenders, mental or expunged records released. Copy fee: $.25 per page. Certification fee: $3.00. Payee: Clerk of Superior Court. Only cashiers checks and money orders accepted. Prepayment required. Will bill copy fees. Turnaround time 2-3 days.

Beaufort County

Superior-District Court PO Box 1403, Washington, NC 27889; 252-946-5184; Civil phone: 252-974-7817. Hours: 8:30AM-5:30PM (EST). *Felony, Misdemeanor, Civil, Eviction, Small Claims, Probate.*

www.aoc.state.nc.us/www/public/courts/beaufort.html
Note: Search civil and criminal court calendars at www1.aoc.state.nc.us/www/calendars.html.

Civil Records: Access: In person only. Visitors must perform in person searches for themselves. No search fee. Required to search: name, years to search, address. Civil cases indexed by defendant, plaintiff.

Civil records on computer since 6/87, docket books to 1800s.

Criminal Records: Access: Mail, in person. Both court and visitors may perform in person searches. Search fee: $10.00 per name. Required to search: name, years to search, address, DOB, SSN. Criminal records on computer since 6/87, docket books to 1800s.

General Information: Public Access terminal is available. No adoptions, sealed cases, juvenile, sex offenders, mental or expunged records released. Copy fee: $2.00for first page, $.25 each add'l. Certification fee: $3.00. Payee: Clerk of Superior Court. Business checks accepted, personal checks are not. Prepayment required. Mail turnaround time 5 days.

Bertie County

Superior-District Court PO Box 370, Windsor, NC 27983; 252-794-3039; Fax: 252-794-2482. Hours: 8AM-5PM (EST). *Felony, Misdemeanor, Civil, Eviction, Small Claims, Probate.*

www.aoc.state.nc.us/www/public/courts/bertie.html
Note: Search civil and criminal court calendars at www1.aoc.state.nc.us/www/calendars.html.

Civil Records: Access: In person only. Visitors must perform in person searches for themselves. This court will do a civil search if it is conjuction with a criminal search. No search fee. Required to search: name, years to search. Civil cases indexed by defendant, plaintiff. Civil records on computer from 11/96, prior on books to 1968.

Criminal Records: Access: Mail, in person. Both court and visitors may perform in person searches. Search fee: $10.00 per name. Required to search: name, years to search, DOB; also helpful: address, SSN. Criminal records on computer from 3/89, prior on books to 1968.

General Information: Public Access terminal is available. No adoptions, sealed cases, juvenile, mental, expunged records released. Fee to fax results is $1.00 1st page; $.25 each add'l. Copy fee: $2.00 for first page of each document, $.25 each add'l. Certification fee: Court will not certify any in person searches, otherwise $3.00. Payee: Clerk of Superior Court. Only cashiers checks and money orders accepted. Prepayment required. Mail requests: SASE requested. Turnaround time 1-2 days.

Bladen County

Superior-District Court PO Box 2619, Elizabethtown, NC 28337; Civil phone: 910-862-2143; Criminal phone: 910-862-2818; Probate phone: 910-862-4911. Hours: 8:30AM-5PM (EST). *Felony, Misdemeanor, Civil, Eviction, Small Claims, Probate.*

www.aoc.state.nc.us/www/public/courts/bladen.html
Note: Search civil and criminal court calendars at www1.aoc.state.nc.us/www/calendars.html.

Civil Records: Access: In person only. Visitors must perform in person searches for themselves. No search fee. Required to search: name, years to search. Civil cases indexed by defendant, plaintiff. Civil records on computer since 1989, prior on judgment books back to 1896 (fire).

Criminal Records: Access: Mail, in person. Both court and visitors may perform in person searches. Search fee: $10.00 per name. Required to search: name, years to search, DOB. Criminal records on computer from 5/89, on books to 1968.

General Information: Public Access terminal is available. No adoptions, sealed cases, juvenile, sex offenders, mental or expunged records released. Copy fee: $1.50 for first page, $.25 each add'l. Certification fee: $3.00. Payee: Clerk of Superior Court. Only cashiers checks and money orders accepted. Prepayment required. Mail turnaround time 5 days.

Brunswick County

Superior-District Court 310 Goverment Center Dr.,unit 1, Bolivia, NC 28422; 910-253-8502; Fax: 910-253-7652. Hours: 8:30AM-5:00PM (EST). *Felony, Misdemeanor, Civil, Eviction, Small Claims, Probate.*
www.aoc.state.nc.us/www/public/courts/brunswick.html
Note: Search civil and criminal court calendars at www1.aoc.state.nc.us/www/calendars.html.
Civil Records: Access: In person only. Visitors must perform in person searches for themselves. No search fee. Required to search: name, years to search. Civil cases indexed by defendant, plaintiff. Civil records on computer since 1989, prior on books to 1968.
Criminal Records: Access: Mail, in person. Both court and visitors may perform in person searches. Search fee: $10.00 per name. Required to search: name, years to search. Criminal records on computer since 1989, prior on books to 1968.
General Information: Public Access terminal is available. No adoptions, sealed cases, juvenile, mental or expunged records. Copy fee: $2.00 for first page, $.25 each add'l. Certification fee: $3.00. Payee: Clerk of Court. Business checks accepted. Prepayment required. Mail turnaround time 1-2 days.

Buncombe County

Superior-District Court 60 Court Plaza, Asheville, NC 28801-3519; 828-232-2605; Civil phone: 828-232-2636; Criminal phone: 828-232-2652; Probate phone: 828-232-2694; Fax: 828-251-6257. 8:30AM-5PM (EST). *Felony, Misdemeanor, Civil, Eviction, Small Claims, Probate.*
www.nccourts.org/County/Buncombe/Default.asp
Note: Search civil and criminal court calendars at www1.aoc.state.nc.us/www/calendars.html.
Civil Records: Access: Mail, fax, in person. Both court and visitors may perform in person searches. Search fee: $5.00 per name. Required to search: name, years to search. Civil cases indexed by defendant, plaintiff. Civil records on computer since 1/88; on books or dockets to 1915; judgment books in archives.
Criminal Records: Access: Mail, fax, in person. Both court and visitors may perform in person searches. Search fee: $10.00 per name. Required to search: name, years to search, DOB. Criminal records on computer since 1/82; on books or dockets to 1970.
General Information: Public Access terminal is available. No adoptions, sealed cases, juvenile, sex offenders, mental or expunged records required. Fee to fax results is $1.00 1st page; $.25 each add'l. Copy fee: $2.00 for first page, $.25 each add'l. Certification fee: $3.00. Payee: Clerk of Court. Only cashiers checks and money orders accepted. Prepayment required. Mail requests: SASE required. Mail turnaround time 1 week.

Burke County

Superior-District Court PO Box 796, Morganton, NC 28680; 828-432-2800; Civil phone: 828-432-2805; Fax: 828-438-5460. Hours: 8AM-5PM (EST). *Felony, Misdemeanor, Civil, Eviction, Small Claims, Probate.*
www.aoc.state.nc.us/www/public/courts/burke.html
Note: Search civil and criminal court calendars at www1.aoc.state.nc.us/www/calendars.html.
Civil Records: Access: In person only. Visitors must perform in person searches for themselves. No search fee. Required to search: name, years to search; also helpful: address. Civil cases indexed by defendant, plaintiff. Civil records on computer since 10/88, on index books to 1890s.
Criminal Records: Access: Mail, in person. Both court and visitors may perform in person searches.

Search fee: $10.00 per name. Required to search: name, years to search, DOB; also helpful: address, SSN. Criminal records on computer since 6/86, on cards or books back to 1900s.
General Information: Public Access terminal is available. No adoptions, sealed cases, juvenile, sex offenders, mental or expunged records released. Fee to fax results is $3.00 per document. Copy fee: $1.50 for first page, $.25 each add'l. Certification fee: $5.00. Payee: Clerk of Court. Business checks accepted. Prepayment required. Mail requests: SASE required. Mail turnaround time 1-2 days.

Cabarrus County

Superior-District Court PO Box 70, Concord, NC 28026-0070; 704-786-4137 (Estates & Special Proceed); Civil phone: 704-786-4201; Criminal phone: 704-786-4138 (Superior); 786-4211 (Dist.). Hours: 8:30AM-5PM (EST). *Felony, Misdemeanor, Civil, Eviction, Small Claims, Probate.*
www.aoc.state.nc.us/www/public/courts/cabarrus.htm
Note: Search civil and criminal court calendars at www1.aoc.state.nc.us/www/calendars.html.
Civil Records: Access: In person only. Visitors must perform in person searches for themselves. No search fee. Required to search: name, years to search; also helpful: address. Civil cases indexed by defendant, plaintiff. Civil records go back to 1900s'; on computer since 2/13/89.
Criminal Records: Access: Mail, in person. Both court and visitors may perform in person searches. Search fee: $10.00 per name. Required to search: name, DOB; also helpful: address, SSN, maiden name. Criminal records go back to 12/70; on computer back to 01/1/85.
General Information: Public Access terminal is available. No adoptions, sealed cases, juvenile, sex offenders, mental or expunged records released. Copy fee: $2.00 for first page, $.25 each add'l. Certification fee: $3.00. Payee: Clerk of Superior Court. Only cashiers checks and money orders accepted. Prepayment required. Mail turnaround time 2-3 days.

Caldwell County

Superior-District Court PO Box 1376, Lenoir, NC 28645; 828-757-1373; Fax: 828-757-1479. Hours: 8AM-5PM (EST). *Felony, Misdemeanor, Civil, Eviction, Small Claims, Probate.*
www.aoc.state.nc.us/www/public/courts/caldwell.html
Note: Search civil and criminal court calendars at www1.aoc.state.nc.us/www/calendars.html.
Civil Records: Access: Mail, in person. Both court and visitors may perform in person searches. Search fee: $7.50 per name. Required to search: name, years to search. Civil cases indexed by defendant, plaintiff. Civil records on computer since Nov. 1988, prior on books to 1849.
Criminal Records: Access: Mail, in person. Both court and visitors may perform in person searches. Search fee: $10.00 per name. Required to search: name. Criminal records on computer from 8/86, prior in books to 1966.
General Information: Public Access terminal is available. No adoptions, sealed cases, juvenile, sex offenders, mental or expunged records released. Fee to fax results is $2.00 1st page; $.25 each add'l. Copy fee: $2.00 for first page, $.25 each add'l. Certification fee: $3.00. Payee: Clerk of Superior Court. Only cashiers checks and money orders accepted. Prepayment required. Mail turnaround time 1-2 days.

Camden County

Superior-District Court PO Box 219, Camden, NC 27921; 252-331-4871; Civil phone: 252-331-4871 ext 272 (District & Superior); Criminal phone: 252-331-4871 ext 270 (Superior) ext 269 (District); Probate phone: 252-331-4871 ext 273; Fax: 252-331-4827. 8AM-5PM (EST). *Felony, Misdemeanor, Civil, Eviction, Small Claims, Probate.*
www.aoc.state.nc.us/www/public/courts/camden.html
Note: Small Claims is ext 268
Search civil and criminal court calendars at www1.aoc.state.nc.us/www/calendars.html.
Civil Records: Access: In person only. Visitors must perform in person searches for themselves. No search fee. Required to search: name, years to search. Civil cases indexed by defendant, plaintiff. Civil records on computer since Nov. 27 1989, prior on index books to 1966.
Criminal Records: Access: Mail, fax, in person. Both court and visitors may perform in person searches. Search fee: $10.00 per name. Required to search: name, years to search, DOB. Criminal records on computer since Nov. 27 1989, prior on index books to 1966. Fax search requests must be prepaid.
General Information: Public Access terminal is available. No adoptions, sealed cases, juvenile, sex offenders, mental or expunged records released. Will fax results for no fee. Copy fee: $2.00 for first page, $.25 each add'l. Certification fee: $3.00 if you do search, otherwise cert fee is included in search fee. Payee: Clerk of Superior Court. Business checks accepted. Prepayment required. Mail turnaround time 1-2 days.

Carteret County

Superior-District Court Courthouse Square, Beaufort, NC 28516; 252-728-8500; Fax: 252-728-6502. 8AM-5PM (EST). *Felony, Misdemeanor, Civil, Eviction, Small Claims, Probate.*
www.aoc.state.nc.us/www/public/courts/carteret.html
Note: Search civil and criminal court calendars at www1.aoc.state.nc.us/www/calendars.html.
Civil Records: Access: In person only. Visitors must perform in person searches for themselves. No search fee. Required to search: name, years to search. Civil cases indexed by defendant, plaintiff. Civil records on computer back to 1988, prior on books to 1800s.
Criminal Records: Access: Mail, fax, in person. Both court and visitors may perform in person searches. Search fee: $10.00 per name. Required to search: name, years to search; also helpful: address, DOB, SSN. Criminal records on computer back to 1/87, prior on cards and books to 1800s.
General Information: Public Access terminal is available. No adoptions, sealed cases, juvenile, sex offenders, mental or expunged records released. Copy fee: $2.00 for first page, $1.00 each add'l. Certification fee: $3.00. Payee: Clerk of Superior Court. Business checks accepted. Prepayment required. Mail turnaround time 1-2 days.

Caswell County

Superior-District Court PO Drawer 790, Yanceyville, NC 27379; 336-694-4171; Fax: 336-694-7338. Hours: 8:30AM-5PM (EST). *Felony, Misdemeanor, Civil, Eviction, Small Claims, Probate.*
www.aoc.state.nc.us/www/public/courts/caswell.html
Note: Search civil and criminal court calendars at www1.aoc.state.nc.us/www/calendars.html.
Civil Records: Access: In person only. Visitors must perform in person searches for themselves. No search fee. Required to search: name, years to search. Civil cases indexed by defendant, plaintiff. Civil records on

computer from 3/89 to present, on index books back to 1970, prior records in civil summons book.

Criminal Records: Access: Mail, in person. Both court and visitors may perform in person searches. Search fee: $10.00 per name. Required to search: name, years to search, DOB; also helpful: address. Criminal records on computer since 5/88, prior on books and cards.

General Information: Public Access terminal is available. No adoptions, sealed cases, juvenile, mental or expunged records released. Copy fee: $2.00 for first page, $.25 each add'l. Certification fee: $3.00. Payee: Clerk of Superior Court. Business checks accepted. Prepayment required. Mail requests: SASE required; Mail only with stamped, self-addressed envelope. Turnaround time 1-2 days.

Catawba County

Superior-District Court PO Box 790, Newton, NC 28658; 828-466-6100; Civil phone: 828-466-6104; Criminal phone: 828-466-6106; Probate phone: 828-466-6103. Hours: 8AM-5PM (EST). *Felony, Misdemeanor, Civil, Eviction, Small Claims, Probate.*
www.co.catawba.nc.us/state/clerk/clerklst.htm
Note: Search civil and criminal court calendars at www1.aoc.state.nc.us/www/calendars.html.
Civil Records: Access: In person only. Visitors must perform in person searches for themselves. No search fee. Required to search: name, years to search. Civil cases indexed by defendant, plaintiff. Civil records on computer since 3/1988, prior on books.
Criminal Records: Access: Mail, in person. Both court and visitors may perform in person searches. Search fee: $10.00 per name. Required to search: name, years to search, DOB. Criminal records on computer since 4/85, on books to 1966, archived prior.
General Information: Public Access terminal is available. No adoptions, sealed cases, juvenile, sex offenders, mental or expunged records released. Copy fee: $2.00 for first page, $.25 each add'l. Certification fee: $3.00. Payee: Clerk of Court. Only cashiers checks and money orders accepted. Prepayment required. Mail requests: SASE required. Mail turnaround time 5 days.

Chatham County

Superior-District Court PO Box 369, Pittsboro, NC 27312; 919-542-3240; Fax: 919-542-1402. 8AM-5PM (EST). *Felony, Misdemeanor, Civil, Eviction, Small Claims, Probate.*
www.nccourts.org/County/Chatham/Default.asp
Note: Search civil and criminal court calendars at www1.aoc.state.nc.us/www/calendars.html.
Civil Records: Access: In person only. Both court and visitors may perform in person searches. Search fee: none. Required to search: name, years to search. Civil cases indexed by defendant, plaintiff. Civil records on computer since 4/89, prior on books, archived 1968 back in Raleigh.
Criminal Records: Access: Mail, in person. Both court and visitors may perform in person searches. Search fee: $10.00 per name. Required to search: name, years to search; also helpful: address, DOB, SSN. Criminal records on computer since 7/87, prior on books or cards to 1968.
General Information: Public Access terminal is available. No adoptions, sealed cases, juvenile, sex offenders, mental or expunged records released. Copy fee: Included in criminal search fee. Certification fee: $3.00 plus $.25 a page for criminal records. Will not certify civil. Payee: Clerk of Superior Court. Personal checks accepted. Prepayment required. Mail turnaround time 1 day.

Cherokee County

Superior-District Court 75 Peachtree St, Rm 201, Murphy, NC 28906; 828-837-2522; Fax: 828-837-8178. 8AM-5PM (EST). *Felony, Misdemeanor, Civil, Eviction, Small Claims, Probate.*
www.aoc.state.nc.us/www/public/courts/cherokee.html
Note: Search civil and criminal court calendars at www1.aoc.state.nc.us/www/calendars.html.
Civil Records: Access: Phone, fax, mail, in person. Both court and visitors may perform in person searches. Search fee: none. Required to search: name, years to search, address. Civil cases indexed by defendant, plaintiff. Civil records on computer since 5/89, on index books to 1867.
Criminal Records: Access: Mail, in person. Only the court performs in person searches; visitors may not. Search fee: $10.00 per name. Required to search: name, years to search, DOB. Criminal records on computer since 5/89, index cards to 1985, index books to 1966.
General Information: Public Access terminal is available. (Public access has civil records only, no criminal.) No adoptions, sealed cases, juvenile or mental records released. Fee to fax results is $2.00 1st page, $.25 each add'l. Will fax to toll-free number for no charge. Copy fee: $2.00 for first page, $.25 each add'l. Certification fee: $3.00. Payee: Clerk of Superior Court. No personal checks accepted. Prepayment required. Mail requests: SASE required. Mail turnaround time 1-2 days.

Chowan County

Superior-District Court N.C. Courier Box 106319, PO Box 588, Edenton, NC 27932; 252-482-2323; Fax: 252-482-2190. Hours: 9AM-5PM (EST). *Felony, Misdemeanor, Civil, Eviction, Small Claims, Probate.*
www.nccourts.org/County/Chowan/Default.asp
Note: Search civil and criminal court calendars at www1.aoc.state.nc.us/www/calendars.html.
Civil Records: Access: In person only. Visitors must perform in person searches for themselves. No search fee. Required to search: name, years to search; also helpful: address. Civil cases indexed by defendant, plaintiff. Civil records on computer since 1990, prior on books to 1800s.
Criminal Records: Access: Mail, in person. Both court and visitors may perform in person searches. Search fee: $10.00 per name. Required to search: name, years to search, DOB; also helpful: address, SSN. Criminal records on computer from 1/90, prior as civil.
General Information: Public Access terminal is available. No adoptions, sealed cases, juvenile, sex offenders, mental or expunged records released. Copy fee: $1.50 for first page, $.25 each add'l. Certification fee: $3.00. Payee: Clerk of Superior Court. Only cashiers checks and money orders accepted. Prepayment required. Mail requests: SASE required. Mail turnaround time 3-5 days.

Clay County

Superior-District Court PO Box 506, Hayesville, NC 28904; 828-389-8334; Fax: 828-389-3329. 8AM-5PM (EST). *Felony, Misdemeanor, Civil, Eviction, Small Claims, Probate.*
www.aoc.state.nc.us/www/public/courts/clay.html
Note: Search civil and criminal court calendars at www1.aoc.state.nc.us/www/calendars.html.
Civil Records: Access: Fax, mail, in person. Visitors must perform in person searches for themselves. Search fee: $5.00 per name. Required to search: name, years to search; also helpful: address. Civil cases indexed by defendant, plaintiff. Civil records on computer since 1989, on books since 1888.

Cleveland County

Superior-District Court 100 Justice Pl, Shelby, NC 28150; 704-484-4862; Fax: 704-480-5487. Hours: 8AM-5PM (EST). *Felony, Misdemeanor, Civil, Eviction, Small Claims, Probate.*
Note: Search civil and criminal court calendars at www1.aoc.state.nc.us/www/calendars.html.
Civil Records: Access: Mail, in person. Visitors must perform in person searches for themselves. No search fee. Required to search: name, years to search; also helpful: address. Civil cases indexed by defendant, plaintiff. Civil records on computer since 1988, books to 1968, archived prior.
Criminal Records: Access: Fax, mail, in person. Both court and visitors may perform in person searches. Search fee: $10.00 per name. Required to search: name, years to search, DOB; also helpful: address, SSN. Criminal records on computer since 6/86, on books to 1972, archived prior.
General Information: Public Access terminal is available. No adoptions, sealed cases, juvenile, sex offenders, mental or expunged records released. Will fax results $1.00 1st page, $.25 each add'l. Copy fee: $1.50 for first page, $.25 each add'l. Certification fee: $3.00. Payee: Clerk of Superior Court. No out-of-state checks accepted. Prepayment required. Mail requests: SASE requested. Turnaround time 1-2 days.

Columbus County

Superior-District Court PO Box 1587, Whiteville, NC 28472; Civil phone: 910-641-3000; Criminal phone: 910-641-3020; Probate phone: 910-641-3010; Fax: 910-641-3027. Hours: 8AM-5PM (EST). *Felony, Misdemeanor, Civil, Eviction, Small Claims, Probate.*
www.aoc.state.nc.us/www/public/courts/columbus.html
Note: Search civil and criminal court calendars at www1.aoc.state.nc.us/www/calendars.html.
Civil Records: Access: Mail, fax, in person. Visitors must perform in person searches for themselves. No search fee. Required to search: name, years to search; also helpful: address. Civil cases indexed by defendant, plaintiff. Civil records on computer from 1989, prior on books to 1968.
Criminal Records: Access: Mail, fax, in person. Both court and visitors may perform in person searches. Search fee: $10.00 per name. Required to search: name, years to search, DOB; also helpful: address, SSN. Criminal records on computer from 1987, prior on books or cards to 1968.
General Information: Public Access terminal is available. No adoptions, sealed, juvenile, sex offender, mental, expunged or dismissed. Will not fax results. Copy fee: $2.00 1st page, $.25 each add'l. Certification fee: $3.00 per copy. Payee: Clerk of Superior Court. Only cashiers checks and money orders accepted. Prepayment required. Mail requests: SASE required. Mail turnaround time 2-5 days.

Craven County

Superior-District Court PO Box 1187, New Bern, NC 28563; 252-514-4774; Civil phone: 252-514-4860; Criminal phone: 352-514-4777; Fax: 252-514-4891. Hours: 8AM-5PM (EST). *Felony, Misdemeanor, Civil, Eviction, Small Claims, Probate.*

www.aoc.state.nc.us/www/public/courts/craven.htm
Note: Search civil and criminal court calendars at www1.aoc.state.nc.us/www/calendars.html.
Civil Records: Access: Mail, in person. Both court and visitors may perform in person searches. Search fee: $7.50 per name. Required to search: name, years to search; also helpful: address. Civil cases indexed by defendant, plaintiff. Civil records on computer from 10/88, prior to 1968 are archived.
Criminal Records: Access: Mail, in person. Both court and visitors may perform in person searches. Search fee: $10.00 per name. Required to search: name, years to search, DOB; also helpful: address, SSN. Criminal records on computer since 1/87, prior on books and cards to 1968.
General Information: Public Access terminal is available. No adoptions, sealed cases, juvenile, sex, offenders, mental, expunged, or dismissed. Copy fee: $2.00 for first page, $.25 each add'l. Certification fee: $3.00. Payee: Clerk of Superior Court. Only cashiers checks and money orders accepted. Prepayment required. Mail requests: SASE required. Mail turnaround time 1-2 days.

Cumberland County

Superior-District Court PO Box 363, Fayetteville, NC 28302; 910-678-2902; Civil phone: 910-678-2909; Criminal phone: 910-678-2906. Hours: 8:30AM-5PM (EST). *Felony, Misdemeanor, Civil, Eviction, Small Claims, Probate.*

www.aoc.state.nc.us/district12
Note: Search civil and criminal court calendars at www1.aoc.state.nc.us/www/calendars.html.
Civil Records: Access: Mail, in person, online. Both court and visitors may perform in person searches. Search fee: $10.50 per name. Required to search: name, years to search; also helpful: address. Civil cases indexed by defendant, plaintiff. Civil records on computer since 1988, books back to 1956. The website presents a list of online vendors to instant record access.
Criminal Records: Access: Mail, in person. Both court and visitors may perform in person searches. Search fee: $10.00 per name. Required to search: name, years to search; also helpful: address, DOB, SSN. Criminal records on computer since 5/82, books and cards to 1920s.
General Information: Public Access terminal is available. No adoptions, sealed cases, juvenile, sex offenders, mental or expunged records released. Copy fee: $3.00 per page. Certification fee: Included in search fee. Payee: Clerk of Superior Court. Business checks accepted. Prepayment required. Mail turnaround time 2 weeks.

Currituck County

Superior-District Court PO Box 175, Currituck, NC 27929; 252-232-2010; Fax: 252-232-3722. 8AM-5PM (EST). *Felony, Misdemeanor, Civil, Eviction, Small Claims, Probate.*

www.aoc.state.nc.us/www/public/courts/currituck.html
Note: Search civil and criminal court calendars at www1.aoc.state.nc.us/www/calendars.html.
Civil Records: Access: Fax, mail, in person. Both court and visitors may perform in person searches. No search fee. Required to search: name, years to search. Civil cases indexed by defendant, plaintiff. Civil

records on computer back to 11/27/89, books to 1968, prior archived.
Criminal Records: Access: In person only. Both court and visitors may perform in person searches. Search fee: $10.00 per name. Required to search: name, years to search, DOB; also helpful-SSN, signed release. Criminal records on computer back to 11/27/89, books to 1968, prior archived
General Information: Public Access terminal is available. No adoptions, sealed cases, juvenile, sex offenders, mental or expunged records released. Copy fee: $2.50 for first page, $.25 each add'l. Certification fee: $4.00. Payee: Clerk of Superior Court. Only cashiers checks and money orders accepted. Prepayment required.

Dare County

Superior-District Court PO Box 1849, Manteo, NC 27954; 252-475-9100; Fax: 252-473-1620. 8:30AM-5PM (EST). *Felony, Misdemeanor, Civil, Eviction, Small Claims, Probate.*

www.aoc.state.nc.us/www/public/courts/dare.htm
Note: Search civil and criminal court calendars at www1.aoc.state.nc.us/www/calendars.html.
Civil Records: Access: Phone, mail, in person. Both court and visitors may perform in person searches. Search fee: $10.00 per name. Required to search: name, years to search; also helpful: address. Civil cases indexed by defendant, plaintiff. Civil records on computer since 1985, on books to 1966.
Criminal Records: Access: Mail, in person. Both court and visitors may perform in person searches. Search fee: $10.00 per name. Required to search: name, years to search, DOB. Criminal records on computer since 1987, on books and cards to 1966.
General Information: Public Access terminal is available. No adoptions, sealed cases, juvenile, sex offenders, mental or expunged records released. Fee to fax results is $.25 per page. Copy fee: $2.00 for first page, $.25 each add'l. Certification fee: $3.00. Payee: Superior District Court. Business checks accepted. No personal checks accepted. Prepayment required. Mail turnaround time 2 days.

Davidson County

Superior-District Court PO Box 1064, Lexington, NC 27293-1064; 336-249-0351; Fax: 336-249-6951. 8AM-5PM (EST). *Felony, Misdemeanor, Civil, Eviction, Small Claims, Probate.*

www.aoc.state.nc.us/www/public/courts/davidson.html
Note: Search civil and criminal court calendars at www1.aoc.state.nc.us/www/calendars.html.
Civil Records: Access: In person only. Visitors must perform in person searches for themselves. No search fee. Required to search: name, years to search; also helpful: address. Civil cases indexed by defendant, plaintiff. Civil records on computer since 5/16/88, prior on books.
Criminal Records: Access: Mail, in person. Both court and visitors may perform in person searches. Search fee: $10.00 per name. Required to search: name, years to search; also helpful: address, DOB, SSN. Criminal records on computer since 10/85, on books and cards to 1952.
General Information: Public Access terminal is available. No adoptions, sealed cases, juvenile, sex offenders, mental or expunged records released. Copy fee: $2.00 for first page, $.25 each add'l. Certification fee: $10.00. Payee: Clerk of Superior Court. Business checks accepted. Prepayment required. Mail requests: SASE requested. Turnaround time 2-3 days.

Davie County

Superior-District Court 140 S Main St, Mocksville, NC 27028; Civil phone: 336-751-3507; Criminal phone: 336-751-3508; Fax: 336-751-4720. Hours: 8:30AM-5PM (EST). *Felony, Misdemeanor, Civil, Eviction, Small Claims, Probate.*

www.aoc.state.nc.us/www/public/courts/davie.html
Note: Search civil and criminal court calendars at www1.aoc.state.nc.us/www/calendars.html.
Civil Records: Access: Mail, in person. Both court and visitors may perform in person searches. Search fee: $10.00 per name. Required to search: name, years to search. Civil cases indexed by defendant, plaintiff. Civil records on computer back to 10/89; on books to 1970.
Criminal Records: Access: Mail, in person. Both court and visitors may perform in person searches. Search fee: $10.00 per name. Required to search: name, years to search, DOB, signed release. Criminal records on computer back to 10/89; on books to 1970.
General Information: Public Access terminal is available. No adoptions, sealed cases, juvenile, sex offenders, mental or expunged records released. Copy fee: $2.00 for first page, $.25 each add'l. Certification fee: $3.00. Payee: Clerk of Superior Court. Personal checks accepted. Prepayment required. Mail requests: SASE required. Mail turnaround time 5 days.

Duplin County

Superior-District Court PO Box 189, Kenansville, NC 28349; Civil phone: 910-296-1686; Criminal phone: 910-296-2306; Fax: 910-296-2310. Hours: 8AM-5PM (EST). *Felony, Misdemeanor, Civil, Eviction, Small Claims, Probate.*

www.aoc.state.nc.us/www/public/courts/duplin.htm
Note: Search civil and criminal court calendars at www1.aoc.state.nc.us/www/calendars.html.
Civil Records: Access: Phone, fax, mail, in person. Both court and visitors may perform in person searches. Search fee: $5.00 per name. Required to search: name, years to search. Civil cases indexed by defendant, plaintiff. Civil records on computer since 1989, prior on books to early 1900s.
Criminal Records: Access: Mail, online, in person. Both court and visitors may perform in person searches. Search fee: $10.00 per name. Required to search: name, years to search, DOB. Criminal records on computer since 5/88, on cards and books to 1927.
General Information: Public Access terminal is available. No adoptions, sealed cases, juvenile, sex offenders, mental or expunged records released. Will fax results to local or toll free line. Copy fee: $1.50 for first page, $.25 each add'l. Certification fee: $3.00. Payee: Clerk of Superior Court. Personal checks not accepted. Prepayment required. Mail requests: SASE required. Mail turnaround time 1-2 days.

Durham County

Superior-District Court 201 E Main St, Durham, NC 27702; Civil phone: 919-564-7050; Criminal phone: 919-564-7270. Hours: 8:30AM-5PM (EST). *Felony, Misdemeanor, Civil, Eviction, Small Claims, Probate.*

www.nccourts.org/County/Durham/Default.asp
Note: Search civil and criminal court calendars at www1.aoc.state.nc.us/www/calendars.html.
Civil Records: Access: In person. Visitors must perform in person searches for themselves. No search fee. Required to search: name, years to search; also helpful: address. Civil cases indexed by defendant, plaintiff. Civil records on computer since 1/88, on books to late 1800s.
Criminal Records: Access: Mail, in person. Both court and visitors may perform in person searches. Search fee: $10.00 per name. Required to search:

name, years to search, DOB; also helpful: address. Criminal records on microfiche since 1982, prior on books to 1979.

General Information: Public Access terminal is available. No adoptions, sealed cases, juvenile, sex offenders, mental or expunged records released. Will not fax results. Copy fee: $2.00 for first page, $.25 each add'l. Certification fee: $3.00 for civil, but is included in search fee for criminal. Payee: Clerk of Superior Court. Only cashiers checks and money orders accepted. Prepayment required. Mail requests: SASE required. Mail turnaround time 3-4 days.

Edgecombe County

Superior-District Court PO Drawer 9, Tarboro, NC 27886; Civil phone: 252-823-6161; Criminal phone: 252-823-2056; Fax: 252-823-1278. Hours: 8AM-5PM (EST). *Felony, Misdemeanor, Civil, Eviction, Small Claims, Probate.*

www.aoc.state.nc.us/www/public/courts/edgecombe.htm
Note: Search civil and criminal court calendars at www1.aoc.state.nc.us/www/calendars.html.

Civil Records: Access: In person only. Visitors must perform in person searches for themselves. No search fee. Required to search: name, years to search, address. Civil cases indexed by defendant, plaintiff. Civil records on computer since 1988.

Criminal Records: Access: Mail, in person. Both court and visitors may perform in person searches. Search fee: $10.00 per name. Required to search: name, years to search, DOB, SSN; also helpful: address. Criminal records on computer since 4/87, on books and cards to 1900s.

General Information: Public Access terminal is available. No adoptions, sealed cases, juvenile, sex offenders, mental or expunged records required. Copy fee: $2.00 for first page, $.25 each add'l. Certification fee: $3.00. Payee: Clerk of Superior Court. Business checks accepted. Prepayment required. Mail turnaround time 1-2 days.

Forsyth County

Superior-District Court PO Box 20099, Winston Salem, NC 27120-0099; 336-761-2250; Civil phone: 336-761-2340; Criminal phone: 336-761-2366; Fax: 336-761-2018. Hours: 8AM-5PM (EST). *Felony, Misdemeanor, Civil, Eviction, Small Claims, Probate.*

www.aoc.state.nc.us/www/public/courts/forsyth.html
Note: Search civil and criminal court calendars at www1.aoc.state.nc.us/www/calendars.html.

Civil Records: Access: Mail, in person. Both court and visitors may perform in person searches. Search fee: $5.00 per name. Required to search: name, years to search. Civil cases indexed by defendant, plaintiff. Civil records on computer since 4/1988, prior on books to 1968, on microfiche prior.

Criminal Records: Access: Mail, in person. Both court and visitors may perform in person searches. Search fee: $10.00 per name. Required to search: name, years to search, DOB. Criminal records on computer since 10/1983, prior on books to 1968, on microfiche prior.

General Information: Public Access terminal is available. No adoptions, sealed cases, juvenile, sex offenders, mental or expunged records released. Copy fee: $1.50 for first page, $.25 each add'l. Certification fee: $3.00. Payee: Clerk of Superior Court. Business checks accepted. Prepayment required. Mail requests: SASE required. Mail turnaround time 1-2 days.

Franklin County

Superior-District Court 102 S Main St, Louisburg, NC 27549; 919-496-5104; Fax: 919-496-0407. 8:30AM-5PM (EST). *Felony, Misdemeanor, Civil, Eviction, Small Claims, Probate.*

www.aoc.state.nc.us/www/public/courts/franklin.html
Note: Search civil and criminal court calendars at www1.aoc.state.nc.us/www/calendars.html.

Civil Records: Access: Mail, in person. Visitors must perform in person searches for themselves. No search fee. Required to search: name, years to search; also helpful: address. Civil cases indexed by defendant, plaintiff. Civil records on computer since June 1989, prior on books.

Criminal Records: Access: Mail, in person. Both court and visitors may perform in person searches. Search fee: $10.00 per name. Required to search: name, years to search, DOB; also helpful: address. Criminal records on computer since 1980, on index books back to 1968.

General Information: Public Access terminal is available. No adoptions, sealed cases, juvenile, mental or expunged records released. Copy fee: $2.00 for first page, $.25 each add'l. Certification fee: $3.00. Payee: Clerk of Superior Court. Personal checks accepted. Prepayment required. Mail requests: SASE requested. Turnaround time 1-2 days.

Gaston County

Superior-District Court Gaston County Court House, 325 North Marietta St., Suit 1004, Gastonia, NC 28052-2331; 704-852-3100. Hours: 8:30AM-5PM (EST). *Felony, Misdemeanor, Civil, Eviction, Small Claims, Probate.*

www.aoc.state.nc.us/data/gaston/index.htm
Note: Search civil and criminal court calendars at www1.aoc.state.nc.us/www/calendars.html.

Civil Records: Access: In person only. Visitors must perform in person searches for themselves. No search fee. Required to search: name, years to search; also helpful: address. Civil cases indexed by defendant, plaintiff. Civil records on computer since 1988, prior on books to 1891.

Criminal Records: Access: Mail, in person. Both court and visitors may perform in person searches. Search fee: $10.00 per name. Required to search: name, address, DOB; also helpful: years to search, SSN. Criminal records on criminal terminal from 1/83, on books and microfilm to 1973.

General Information: Public Access terminal is available. No adoptions, sealed cases, juvenile, mental or expunged records released. Copy fee: $2.00 first page; $.25 addtl page. Certification fee: $3.00. Payee: Clerk of Superior Court. No out of state checks. Prepayment required. Mail turnaround time 1-2 days.

Gates County

Superior-District Court PO Box 31, Gatesville, NC 27938; 252-357-1365; Fax: 252-357-1047. 8AM-5PM (EST). *Felony, Misdemeanor, Civil, Eviction, Small Claims, Probate.*

www.aoc.state.nc.us/www/public/courts/gates.html
Note: Search civil and criminal court calendars at www1.aoc.state.nc.us/www/calendars.html.

Civil Records: Access: In person only. Visitors must perform in person searches for themselves. No search fee. Required to search: name, years to search; also helpful: address. Civil cases indexed by defendant, plaintiff. Civil records on computer since 1990, prior on books to 1966.

Criminal Records: Access: Mail, in person. Only the court performs in person searches; visitors may not. Search fee: $10.00 per name. Required to search: name, years to search, DOB; also helpful: address,

SSN. Criminal records on computer since 1990, prior on books to 1966.

General Information: Public Access terminal is available. (Civil only.) No adoptions, sealed cases, juvenile, sex offenders, mental or expunged records released. Copy fee: $2.00 for first page, $.25 each add'l. Certification fee: $3.00. Payee: Clerk of Superior Court. Business checks accepted. Prepayment required. Mail turnaround time 1-2 days.

Graham County

Superior-District Court PO Box 1179, Robbinsville, NC 28771; 828-479-7986; Civil phone: X7974; Criminal phone: X7975; Fax: 828-479-6417. Hours: 8AM-5PM (EST). *Felony, Misdemeanor, Civil, Eviction, Small Claims, Probate.*

www.aoc.state.nc.us/www/public/courts/graham.html
Note: Search civil and criminal court calendars at www1.aoc.state.nc.us/www/calendars.html.

Civil Records: Access: In person only. Visitors must perform in person searches for themselves. No search fee. Required to search: name, years to search. Civil cases indexed by defendant, plaintiff. Civil records on computer since 1989, on books since 1920s.

Criminal Records: Access: Mail, in person. Both court and visitors may perform in person searches. Search fee: $10.00 per name. Required to search: name, years to search; also helpful: address, DOB, SSN. Criminal records on computer since 1984, on books to 1920s.

General Information: Public Access terminal is available. No adoptions, sealed cases, juvenile, sex offenders, mental or expunged records released. Copy fee: $1.50 for first page, $.25 each add'l. Certification fee: $3.00. Payee: Clerk of Superior Court. Only cashiers checks and money orders accepted. Prepayment required. Mail requests: SASE required. Mail turnaround time 3-5 days.

Granville County

Superior-District Court Courthouse, 101 Main St., Oxford, NC 27565; 919-693-2649; Civil phone: Ext 1; Criminal phone: Ext 2; Fax: 919-693-8944. *Felony, Misdemeanor, Civil, Eviction, Small Claims, Probate.*

www.aoc.state.nc.us/www/public/courts/granville.html
Note: Search civil and criminal court calendars at www1.aoc.state.nc.us/www/calendars.html.

Civil Records: Access: Phone, mail, in person. No search fee. Required to search: name, years to search; also helpful: address. Civil cases indexed by defendant, plaintiff. Civil records on computer since June 12, 1989, on books to 1968, prior files destroyed.

Criminal Records: Access: Mail, in person. Both court and visitors may perform in person searches. Search fee: $10.00 per name. Required to search: name, years to search, DOB; also helpful: address. Criminal records on computer since Feb. 29, 1988, prior on books on cards to 1968.

General Information: Public Access terminal is available. No adoptions, sealed cases, juvenile, mental or expunged records released. Will not fax results. Copy fee: $2.00 for first page, $.25 each add'l. Certification fee: $3.00. Payee: Clerk of Superior Court. No personal checks accepted. Prepayment required. Mail requests: SASE helpful. Turnaround time 1 day.

Greene County

Superior-District Court PO Box 675, Snow Hill, NC 28580; 252-747-3505. Hours: 8AM-5PM (EST). *Felony, Misdemeanor, Civil, Eviction, Small Claims, Probate.*

www.nccourts.org/County/Greene/Default.asp
Note: Search civil and criminal court calendars at www1.aoc.state.nc.us/www/calendars.html.

Civil Records: Access: In person only. Visitors must perform in person searches for themselves. No search fee. Required to search: name, years to search; also helpful: address. Civil cases indexed by defendant, plaintiff. Civil records on computer since Oct. 1989, prior on books to 1865.

Criminal Records: Access: Mail, online, in person. Both court and visitors may perform in person searches. Search fee: $10.00 per name. Required to search: name, years to search; also helpful: address, DOB, SSN. Criminal records on computer since Oct. 1989, prior on books to 1865.

General Information: Public Access terminal is available. No adoptions, sealed cases, juvenile, sex offenders, mental or expunged records released. Will fax results for $2.00 1st page; $.25 each add'l. Copy fee: $2.00 for first page, $.25 each add'l. Certification fee: Included in search fee, unless in person then $3.00. Payee: Clerk of Superior Court. Business checks accepted. Prepayment required. Mail turnaround time 1-2 days.

Guilford County

Superior-District Court 201 S Eugene, PO Box 3008, Greensboro, NC 27402; Civil phone: 336-574-4305; Criminal phone: 336-574-4307. Hours: 8AM-5PM (EST). *Felony, Misdemeanor, Civil, Eviction, Small Claims, Probate.*
www.aoc.state.nc.us/www/public/courts/guilford.html
Note: Search civil and criminal court calendars at www1.aoc.state.nc.us/www/calendars.html.
Civil Records: Access: In person only. Visitors must perform in person searches for themselves. No search fee. Required to search: name, years to search; also helpful: address. Civil cases indexed by defendant, plaintiff. Civil records on computer since 9/88, on books to late 1800s.
Criminal Records: Access: Mail, in person. Both court and visitors may perform in person searches. Search fee: $10.00 per name. Required to search: name, years to search, DOB; also helpful: address, full name. Criminal records on computer since 5/83, on cards and books to late 1800s.
General Information: Public Access terminal is available. No adoptions, sealed cases, juvenile, sex offenders, mental or expunged records released. Copy fee: $2.00 for 1st, $.25 each add'l. Certification fee: $3.00. Payee: Clerk of Superior Court. Business checks accepted. Prepayment required. Mail requests: SASE required. Mail turnaround time 1 week.

Halifax County

Superior-District Court PO Box 66, Halifax, NC 27839; 252-583-5061; Fax: 252-583-1005. Hours: 8:30AM-5PM (EST). *Felony, Misdemeanor, Civil, Eviction, Small Claims, Probate.*
www.aoc.state.nc.us/data/HALIFAX/index.html
Note: Search civil and criminal court calendars at www1.aoc.state.nc.us/www/calendars.html.
Civil Records: Access: In person only. Visitors must perform in person searches for themselves. No search fee. Required to search: name, years to search; also helpful: address. Civil cases indexed by defendant, plaintiff. Civil records on computer since 1988, on books to 1968, prior archived.
Criminal Records: Access: Mail, in person. Both court and visitors may perform in person searches. Search fee: $10.00 per name. Required to search: name, years to search; also helpful: address, DOB, SSN. Criminal records on computer since 1988, on books to 1968, prior archived.
General Information: Public Access terminal is available. (Civil & Criminal only.) No adoptions, sealed cases, juvenile, sex offenders, mental or expunged records released. Copy fee: $1.50 for first page, $.25 each add'l. Certification fee: $3.00. Payee:

Clerk of Superior Court. Business checks accepted. Prepayment required. Mail turnaround time 1-2 days.

Harnett County

Superior-District Court 301 W Cornelius Blvd, Lillington, NC 27546; 910-814-4600; Civil phone: 910-814-4602; Criminal phone: 910-814-4601; Probate phone: 910-814-4603; Fax: 910-893-3683. 8:30AM-5PM (EST). *Felony, Misdemeanor, Civil, Eviction, Small Claims, Probate.*
www.aoc.state.nc.us/www/public/courts/harnett.html
Note: Search civil and criminal court calendars at www1.aoc.state.nc.us/www/calendars.html.
Civil Records: Access: In person only. Visitors must perform in person searches for themselves. No search fee. Required to search: name, years to search; also helpful: address. Civil cases indexed by defendant, plaintiff. Civil records on computer since April 17, 1989, prior on books from 1938.
Criminal Records: Access: Mail, in person. Both court and visitors may perform in person searches. Search fee: $10.00 per name. Required to search: name, years to search; also helpful: address, DOB, SSN. Criminal records on computer since 5/87, on books from 1968.
General Information: Public Access terminal is available. No adoptions, sealed cases, juvenile, mental or expunged records released. Will fax results for $2.00 1st page and $.25 each addtl page. Copy fee: $2.00 for first page, $.25 each add'l. Certification fee: $3.00. Payee: Clerk of Superior Court. Only cashiers checks and money orders accepted. Prepayment required. Mail requests: SASE required. Mail turnaround time 1 week-10 days.

Haywood County

Superior-District Court 215 N. Main, Waynesville, NC 28786; 828-456-3540; Criminal phone: 828-452-2578; Fax: 828-456-4937. Hours: 8AM-5PM (EST). *Felony, Misdemeanor, Civil, Eviction, Small Claims, Probate.*
www.aoc.state.nc.us/www/public/courts/haywood.html
Note: Search civil and criminal court calendars at www1.aoc.state.nc.us/www/calendars.html.
Civil Records: Access: In person only. Visitors must perform in person searches for themselves. No search fee. Required to search: name, years to search; also helpful: address. Civil cases indexed by defendant, plaintiff. Civil records on computer since Oct. 13, 1988, prior on books to 1955.
Criminal Records: Access: Mail, in person. Both court and visitors may perform in person searches. Search fee: $10.00 per name. Required to search: name, years to search, DOB; also helpful: address, SSN. Criminal records on computer from 5/87, on books or cards from 1800s.
General Information: Public Access terminal is available. No adoptions, sealed cases, juvenile, sex offenders, mental or expunged records released. Copy fee: $1.50 for first page, $.25 each add'l. Certification fee: $3.00. Payee: Clerk of Superior Court. Only cashiers checks and money orders accepted. Prepayment required. Mail requests: SASE required. Mail turnaround time 1-2 days.

Henderson County

Superior-District Court PO Box 965, Hendersonville, NC 28793; Civil phone: 828-697-4851; Criminal phone: 828-697-4859. Hours: 8:30AM-5PM (EST). *Felony, Misdemeanor, Civil, Eviction, Small Claims, Probate.*
www.aoc.state.nc.us/www/public/courts/henderson.html
Note: Search civil and criminal court calendars at www1.aoc.state.nc.us/www/calendars.html.
Civil Records: Access: Mail, in person. Both court and visitors may perform in person searches. No

search fee. Required to search: name, years to search; also helpful: address. Civil cases indexed by defendant, plaintiff. Civil records on computer back to 1988, prior on books to 1968.
Criminal Records: Access: Mail, in person. Both court and visitors may perform in person searches. Search fee: $10.00 per name. Required to search: name, years to search, DOB; also helpful: address, SSN. Criminal records on computer back to 09/89, prior on books to 1968.
General Information: Public Access terminal is available. No adoptions, sealed cases, juvenile, sex offenders, mental or expunged records released. Copy fee: $2.00 1st page; $.25 per add'l page. Certification fee: $3.00. Payee: Clerk of Superior Court. Personal checks accepted. Prepayment required. Mail requests: SASE required. Mail turnaround time 1 week.

Hertford County

Superior-District Court PO Box 86, Winton, NC 27986; 252-358-7845; Fax: 252-358-0793. Hours: 8AM-5PM (EST). *Felony, Misdemeanor, Civil, Eviction, Small Claims, Probate.*
www.aoc.state.nc.us/www/public/courts/hertford.html
Note: Search civil and criminal court calendars at www1.aoc.state.nc.us/www/calendars.html.
Civil Records: Access: In person only. Visitors must perform in person searches for themselves. No search fee. Required to search: name, years to search; also helpful: address. Civil cases indexed by defendant, plaintiff. Civil records on computer back to 4/1989, prior on index cards and judgment books to 1968.
Criminal Records: Access: Mail, in person. Both court and visitors may perform in person searches. Search fee: $10.00 per name. Required to search: name, years to search, DOB; also helpful: address, SSN. Criminal records on computer back to 4/1989, prior on index cards or judgment books to 1968.
General Information: Public Access terminal is available. No adoptions, sealed cases, juvenile, sex offenders, mental or expunged records released. Copy fee: $2.00 for first page, $.25 each add'l. Certification fee: Included in search fee, unless do it yourself then $3.00. Payee: Clerk of Superior Court. Only cashiers checks and money orders accepted. Prepayment required. Mail requests: SASE helpful. Turnaround time 1-2 days.

Hoke County

Superior-District Court PO Drawer 1569, Raeford, NC 28376; 910-875-3728; Fax: 910-904-1708. 8:30AM-5PM (EST). *Felony, Misdemeanor, Civil, Eviction, Small Claims, Probate.*
www.aoc.state.nc.us/www/public/courts/hoke.html
Note: Search civil and criminal court calendars at www1.aoc.state.nc.us/www/calendars.html.
Civil Records: Access: In person only. Visitors must perform in person searches for themselves. No search fee. Required to search: name, years to search; also helpful: address. Civil cases indexed by defendant, plaintiff. Civil records on computer since 10/89, on books to 1967.
Criminal Records: Access: Mail, in person. Both court and visitors may perform in person searches. Search fee: $10.00 per name. Required to search: name, years to search, DOB; also helpful: address, SSN. Criminal records on computer since 10/89, on books to 1967.
General Information: Public Access terminal is available. No adoptions, sealed cases, juvenile, mental or expunged records released. Will not fax results. Copy fee: $2.00 for first page, $.25 each add'l. Certification fee: $3.00. Payee: Clerk of Superior Court. Business checks accepted. Prepayment required. Mail requests: SASE required. Mail turnaround time 1-2 days.

Hyde County

Superior-District Court PO Box 337, Swanquarter, NC 27885; 252-926-4101; Fax: 252-926-1002. Hours: 8:00AM-5:00PM (EST). *Felony, Misdemeanor, Civil, Eviction, Small Claims, Probate.*

www.aoc.state.nc.us/www/public/courts/hyde.html

Note: Search civil and criminal court calendars at www1.aoc.state.nc.us/www/calendars.html.

Civil Records: Access: Mail, in person. Both court and visitors may perform in person searches. Search fee: $5.00 per name. Required to search: name, years to search. Civil cases indexed by defendant, plaintiff. Civil records on computer since 7/89, on books to 1968; estate and special proceedings back to 1996.

Criminal Records: Access: Phone, mail, in person. Both court and visitors may perform in person searches. Search fee: $10.00 per name. Required to search: name, years to search, DOB; also helpful-signed release. Criminal records on computer since 7/89, on books to 1968.

General Information: Public Access terminal is available. No adoptions, sealed cases, juvenile, sex offenders, mental or expunged records released. Fee to fax results is $1.50 1st page, $.25 each add'l. Copy fee: $1.50 for first page, $.25 each add'l. Certification fee: $3.00. Payee: Clerk of Superior Court. Only cashiers checks and money orders accepted. Prepayment required. Mail requests: SASE required. Mail turnaround time 2 days; phone results 15 minutes.

Iredell County

Superior-District Court PO Box 186, Statesville, NC 28687; Civil phone: 704-878-4306; Criminal phone: 704-878-4204; Probate phone: 704-878-4311; Fax: 704-878-3261. Hours: 8:30AM-5PM (EST). *Felony, Misdemeanor, Civil, Eviction, Small Claims, Probate.*

www.aoc.state.nc.us/www/public/courts/iredell.htm

Note: Search civil and criminal court calendars at www1.aoc.state.nc.us/www/calendars.html.

Civil Records: Access: Mail, in person. Both court and visitors may perform in person searches. Search fee: $10.00 per name. Required to search: name, years to search. Civil cases indexed by defendant, plaintiff. Civil records on computer since 1985, in books since, 1786, on microfiche since 1939.

Criminal Records: Access: Mail, in person. Both court and visitors may perform in person searches. Search fee: $10.00 per name. Required to search: name, years to search, DOB. Criminal records on computer since 1985, prior on books and cards to 1970.

General Information: Public Access terminal is available. No adoptions, sealed cases, juvenile, sex offenders, mental or expunged records released. Will fax results to local or toll free line, will not fax certified documents. Copy fee: $2.00 for first page, $.25 each add'l. Certification fee: $3.00. Payee: Clerk of Superior Court. Only cashiers checks and money orders accepted. Prepayment required. Mail requests: SASE required. Mail turnaround time 2 days.

Jackson County

Superior-District Court 401 Grindstaff Cove Rd, Sylva, NC 28779; 828-586-7512; Fax: 828-586-9009. 8:30AM-5PM (EST). *Felony, Misdemeanor, Civil, Eviction, Small Claims, Probate.*

www.aoc.state.nc.us/www/public/courts/jackson.html

Note: Search civil and criminal court calendars at www1.aoc.state.nc.us/www/calendars.html.

Civil Records: Access: In person only. Visitors must perform in person searches for themselves. No search fee. Required to search: name, years to search; also

helpful: address. Civil cases indexed by defendant, plaintiff. Civil records on computer since May 29, 1989, prior on books from 1966.

Criminal Records: Access: Mail, in person. Both court and visitors may perform in person searches. Search fee: $10.00 per name. Required to search: name, years to search, DOB; also helpful: address, SSN. Criminal records on computer since May 29, 1989, prior on books from 1966.

General Information: Public Access terminal is available. No adoptions, sealed cases, juvenile, mental or expunged records released. Copy fee: $1.50 for first page, $.25 each add'l. Certification fee: $3.00. Payee: Clerk of Superior Court. Only cashiers checks and money orders accepted. Prepayment required. Mail requests: SASE required. Mail turnaround time 1-2 days.

Johnston County

Superior-District Court PO Box 297, Smithfield, NC 27577; 919-934-3192; Fax: 919-934-5857. 8AM-5PM (EST). *Felony, Misdemeanor, Civil, Eviction, Small Claims, Probate.*

www.nccourts.org/County/Johnston/Default.asp

Note: The website shows current calendars.

Civil Records: Access: In person only. Visitors must perform in person searches for themselves. No search fee. Required to search: name, years to search; also helpful: address. Civil cases indexed by defendant, plaintiff. Civil records on computer since 1989, prior on books to 1930s.

Criminal Records: Access: Mail, in person. Both court and visitors may perform in person searches. Search fee: $10.00 per name. Required to search: name, DOB; also helpful: years to search, address, SSN. Criminal records on computer from 5/86, prior on books and cards to 1968.

General Information: Public Access terminal is available. No adoptions, sealed cases, juvenile, sex offenders, mental or expunged records released. Copy fee: $2.00 for first page, $.25 each add'l. Certification fee: $3.00. Payee: Clerk of Superior Court. Business checks accepted. Prepayment required. Mail requests: SASE requested. Turnaround time 1-2 days.

Jones County

Superior-District Court PO Box 280, Trenton, NC 28585; 252-448-7351; Fax: 252-448-1607. Hours: 8AM-5PM (EST). *Felony, Misdemeanor, Civil, Eviction, Small Claims, Probate.*

www.aoc.state.nc.us/www/public/courts/jones.html

Note: Search civil and criminal court calendars at www1.aoc.state.nc.us/www/calendars.html.

Civil Records: Access: In person. Visitors must perform in person searches for themselves. No search fee. Required to search: name, years to search. Civil cases indexed by defendant, plaintiff. Civil records on computer since 1989, prior on microfilm.

Criminal Records: Access: Mail, online, in person. Both court and visitors may perform in person searches. Search fee: $10.00 per name. Required to search: name, years to search, DOB. Criminal records on computer since 1989, prior on microfilm.

General Information: Public Access terminal is available. No adoptions, sealed cases, juvenile, sex offenders, mental or expunged records released. Will not fax results. Copy fee: $2.00 for first page, $.25 each add'l. Certification fee: $3.00. Payee: Clerk of Court. Only cashiers checks and money orders accepted. Prepayment required. Mail requests: SASE required. Mail turnaround time 5 days.

Lee County

Superior-District Court PO Box 4209, Sanford, NC 27331; 919-708-4400; Civil phone: 919-708-4402; Criminal phone: 919-708-4407; Probate phone: 919-708-4417; Fax: 919-775-3483. Hours: 8AM-5PM (EST). *Felony, Misdemeanor, Civil, Eviction, Small Claims, Probate.*

www.aoc.state.nc.us/www/public/courts/lee.html

Note: Search civil and criminal court calendars at www1.aoc.state.nc.us/www/calendars.html.

Civil Records: Access: In person only. Visitors must perform in person searches for themselves. No search fee. Required to search: name, years to search. Civil cases indexed by defendant, plaintiff. Civil records on computer since 1989, prior on books to 1967, index to 1907.

Criminal Records: Access: Mail, in person. Both court and visitors may perform in person searches. Search fee: $10.00 per name. Required to search: name, years to search, DOB. Criminal records on computer since 6/87, prior on books to 12/68, index to criminal actions books from 8/84 to 6/87.

General Information: Public Access terminal is available. No adoptions, sealed cases, juvenile, sex offenders, mental or expunged records released. Copy fee: $1.50 for first page, $.25 each add'l. Certification fee: $3.00. Payee: Clerk of Superior Court. Only cashiers checks and money orders accepted. Prepayment required. Mail turnaround time 1-3 days.

Lenoir County

Superior-District Court PO Box 68, Kinston, NC 28502-0068; 252-527-6231; Fax: 252-527-9154. Hours: 8AM-5PM (EST). *Felony, Misdemeanor, Civil, Eviction, Small Claims, Probate.*

www.nccourts.org/County/Lenoir/Default.asp

Note: Search civil and criminal court calendars at www1.aoc.state.nc.us/www/calendars.html.

Civil Records: Access: In person only. Both court and visitors may perform in person searches. No search fee. Required to search: name, years to search; also helpful: address. Civil cases indexed by defendant, plaintiff. Civil records on computer since Oct. 24, 1988, prior on books to 1900s, prior destroyed due to fire.

Criminal Records: Access: Mail, online, in person. Both court and visitors may perform in person searches. Search fee: $10.00 per name. Required to search: name, years to search, DOB; also helpful: address. Criminal records on computer since 8/86, prior records on books and cards to 1925.

General Information: Public Access terminal is available. No adoptions, sealed cases, juvenile, sex offenders, mental or expunged records released. Will fax results to local or toll free line. Copy fee: $2.00 for first page, $.25 each add'l. Certification fee: Included in search fee, unless do it yourself then $3.00. Payee: Clerk of Superior Court. Only cashiers checks and money orders accepted. Prepayment required. Mail requests: SASE required. Mail turnaround time 1-2 days.

Lincoln County

Superior-District Court PO Box 8, Lincolnton, NC 28093; Civil phone: 704-736-8563; Criminal phone: 704-736-8561; Probate phone: 704-736-8565; Fax: 704-736-8718. Hours: 8:30AM-5PM (EST). *Felony, Misdemeanor, Civil, Eviction, Small Claims, Probate.*

www.aoc.state.nc.us/www/public/courts/lincoln.htm

Note: Search civil and criminal court calendars at www1.aoc.state.nc.us/www/calendars.html.

Civil Records: Access: In person only. Visitors must perform in person searches for themselves. No search fee. Required to search: name, years to search. Civil

cases indexed by defendant, plaintiff. Civil records on computer since 11-1-87, in books since mid-1800s, on microfiche from 1-1-68 to present.

Criminal Records: Access: Mail, in person. Both court and visitors may perform in person searches. Search fee: $10.00 per name. Required to search: name, years to search, DOB. Criminal records on computer since 1987, prior on books and cards to 1968.

General Information: Public Access terminal is available. No adoptions, sealed cases, juvenile, sex offenders, mental or expunged records released. Copy fee: $2.00 for first page, $.25 each add'l. Certification fee: $3.00. Payee: Clerk of Court. Business checks accepted. No personal checks accepted. Prepayment required. Mail requests: SASE required. Mail turnaround time 2 days to 1 week.

Macon County

Superior-District Court PO Box 288, Franklin, NC 28744; 828-349-2000; Fax: 828-369-2515. Hours: 8:30AM-5PM (EST). *Felony, Misdemeanor, Civil, Eviction, Small Claims, Probate.*
www.aoc.state.nc.us/www/public/courts/macon.html
Note: Search civil and criminal court calendars at www1.aoc.state.nc.us/www/calendars.html.
Civil Records: Access: In person only. Visitors must perform in person searches for themselves. No search fee. Required to search: name, years to search; also helpful: address. Civil cases indexed by defendant, plaintiff. Civil records on computer since May 1989, prior on books to 1968.
Criminal Records: Access: Mail, in person. Only the court performs in person searches; visitors may not. Search fee: $10.00 per name. Required to search: name, DOB; also helpful: years to search, address. Criminal records on computer since May 1989, prior on books to 1968.
General Information: Public Access terminal is available. (Civil only.) No adoptions, sealed cases, juvenile, sex offenders, mental or expunged records released. Copy fee: $.25 per page. Certification fee: $3.00. Payee: Clerk of Superior Court. Local personal checks accepted. Prepayment required. Mail turnaround time 1-2 days.

Madison County

Superior-District Court PO Box 217, Marshall, NC 28753; 828-649-2531; Fax: 828-649-2829. 8AM-5PM (EST). *Felony, Misdemeanor, Civil, Eviction, Small Claims, Probate.*
www.aoc.state.nc.us/www/public/courts/madison.htm
Note: Search civil and criminal court calendars at www1.aoc.state.nc.us/www/calendars.html.
Civil Records: Access: In person only. Visitors must perform in person searches for themselves. No search fee. Required to search: name, years to search; also helpful: address. Civil cases indexed by defendant, plaintiff. Civil records on computer back to 10/88, prior on books to 1968.
Criminal Records: Access: Mail, in person. Only the court performs in person searches; visitors may not. Search fee: $10.00 per name. Required to search: name, DOB; also helpful: years to search. Criminal records on computer since 10/88, prior on books to 1968.
General Information: Public Access terminal is available. No adoptions, sealed cases, juvenile, sex offenders, mental, expunged, or dismissed records released. Copy fee: $2.00 for first page, $.25 each add'l. Certification fee: $3.00. Payee: Clerk of Superior Court. Only cashiers checks and money orders accepted. Prepayment required. Mail turnaround time 1-2 days.

Martin County

Superior-District Court PO Box 807, Williamston, NC 27892; 252-792-2515; Fax: 252-792-6668. 8AM-5PM (EST). *Felony, Misdemeanor, Civil, Eviction, Small Claims, Probate.*
www.aoc.state.nc.us/www/public/courts/martin.html
Note: Search civil and criminal court calendars at www1.aoc.state.nc.us/www/calendars.html.
Civil Records: Access: Mail, in person. Both court and visitors may perform in person searches. Search fee: $10.00 per name. Required to search: name, years to search, address. Civil cases indexed by defendant, plaintiff. Civil records go back to 1800s, civil records on computer since 1989, in books since 1968.
Criminal Records: Access: Mail, in person. Both court and visitors may perform in person searches. Search fee: $10.00 per name. Required to search: name, years to search, address, DOB; also helpful: SSN. Criminal records go back to 1800s criminal records on computer since 1996 in books since 1968.
General Information: Public Access terminal is available. No adoptions, sealed cases, juvenile, mental or expunged records released. Copy fee: $2.00 for first page, $.25 each add'l. Certification fee: $3.00. Payee: Clerk of Court. Only cashiers checks and money orders accepted. Prepayment required. Mail requests: SASE required. Mail turnaround time 1 week.

McDowell County

Superior-District Court 21 S Main St, Marion, NC 28752; 828-652-7717 x201; Civil phone: 828-652-7717 x208; Criminal phone: 828-652-7717 x228; Fax: 828-659-2641. Hours: 8:30AM-5PM (EST). *Felony, Misdemeanor, Civil, Eviction, Small Claims, Probate.*
www.aoc.state.nc.us/www/public/courts/mcdowell.html
Note: Search civil and criminal court calendars at www1.aoc.state.nc.us/www/calendars.html.
Civil Records: Access: Mail, in person. Both court and visitors may perform in person searches. No search fee. Required to search: name, years to search; also helpful: address. Civil cases indexed by defendant, plaintiff. Civil records on computer since 11/88, prior on books to 1930.
Criminal Records: Access: Mail, in person. Both court and visitors may perform in person searches. Search fee: $10.00 per name. Required to search: name, DOB; also helpful: years to search, address, SSN. Criminal records on computer since Oct. 1987, prior on books to 1968.
General Information: Public Access terminal is available. No adoptions, sealed cases, juvenile, sex offenders, mental or expunged records released. Copy fee: $1.50 for first page, $.25 each add'l. Certification fee: $3.00. Payee: Clerk of Superior Court. Business checks accepted. Prepayment required. Mail requests: SASE required. Mail turnaround time 1-2 days.

Mecklenburg County

Superior-District Court 800 E 4th St, PO Box 37971, Charlotte, NC 28237; Civil phone: 704-347-7814; Criminal phone: 704-347-7809. Hours: 8AM-5PM (EST). *Felony, Misdemeanor, Civil, Eviction, Small Claims, Probate.*
www.nccourts.org/County/Mecklenburg/Default.asp
Note: Search civil and criminal court calendars at www1.aoc.state.nc.us/www/calendars.html.
Civil Records: Access: In person only. Visitors must perform in person searches for themselves. No search fee. Required to search: name. Civil cases indexed by defendant, plaintiff. Civil records on computer since April 1988, prior on books to 1940s.
Criminal Records: Access: Mail, in person. Both court and visitors may perform in person searches. Search fee: $10.00 per name. Required to search:

name, years to search, address, DOB; also helpful: SSN. Criminal records on computer from 1/83, prior on cards and books to 1930s.
General Information: Public Access terminal is available. No adoptions, sealed cases, juvenile, sex offenders, mental or expunged records released. Copy fee: $1.50 for first page, $.25 each add'l. Certification fee: $3.00. Payee: Clerk of Superior Court. Only cashiers checks and money orders accepted. Prepayment required. Mail requests: SASE requested. Turnaround time 1-2 days.

Mitchell County

Superior-District Court PO Box 402, Bakersville, NC 28705; 828-688-2161; Fax: 828-688-2168. 8:30AM-5PM (EST). *Felony, Misdemeanor, Civil, Eviction, Small Claims, Probate.*
www.clerkofcourt.org
Note: Search civil and criminal court calendars at www1.aoc.state.nc.us/www/calendars.html.
Civil Records: Access: Mail, in person. Both court and visitors may perform in person searches. Search fee: $5.00 per name. Required to search: name, years to search; also helpful: address. Civil cases indexed by defendant, plaintiff. Civil records on computer since 1988, prior on books since 1968.
Criminal Records: Access: Mail, in person. Only the court performs in person searches; visitors may not. Search fee: $10.00 per name. Required to search: name, years to search, DOB, SSN; also helpful: address. Criminal records on computer since 1988, prior on books since 1968.
General Information: Public Access terminal is available. No adoptions, sealed cases, juvenile, sex offenders, mental or expunged records released. Copy fee: $2.00 for first page, $.25 each add'l. Certification fee: $3.00. Payee: Superior-District Court. Business checks accepted. Prepayment required. Mail requests: SASE required. Mail turnaround time 1-2 days.

Montgomery County

Superior-District Court PO Box 527, Troy, NC 27371; 910-576-4211; Fax: 910-576-5020. Hours: 8:30AM-5PM (EST). *Felony, Misdemeanor, Civil, Eviction, Small Claims, Probate.*
www.aoc.state.nc.us/www/public/courts/montgomery.html
Note: Search civil and criminal court calendars at www1.aoc.state.nc.us/www/calendars.html.
Civil Records: Access: In person only. Visitors must perform in person searches for themselves. No search fee. Required to search: name, years to search. Civil cases indexed by defendant, plaintiff. Civil records on computer since April 1989, on books to 170, archived in Raleigh to 1843, prior records destroyed in fire.
Criminal Records: Access: Phone, fax, mail, in person. Both court and visitors may perform in person searches. Search fee: $10.00 per name. Required to search: name, years to search, address, DOB, signed release. Criminal records on computer since April 1989, on books to 170, archived in Raleigh to 1843, prior records destroyed in fire.
General Information: Public Access terminal is available. No adoptions, sealed cases, juvenile, sex offenders, mental or expunged records released. Copy fee: $2.00 for 1st page, $.25 per page thereafter. Certification fee: $3.00. Payee: Clerk of Superior Court. Only cashiers checks and money orders accepted. Prepayment required. Mail turnaround time 1-2 days.

Moore County

Superior-District Court PO Box 936, Carthage, NC 28327; 910-947-2396; Fax: 910-947-1444. 8AM-5PM (EST). *Felony, Misdemeanor, Civil, Eviction, Small Claims, Probate.*
www.nccourts.org/County/Moore/Default.asp

Note: Search civil and criminal court calendars at www1.aoc.state.nc.us/www/calendars.html.

Civil Records: Access: Mail, in person. Both court and visitors may perform in person searches. No search fee. Civil cases indexed by defendant, plaintiff. Civil records on computer since March 1989, prior on books, older records in basement.

Criminal Records: Access: Mail, in person. Both court and visitors may perform in person searches. Search fee: $10.00 per name. Required to search: name, years to search, DOB, signed release; also helpful: address, SSN. Criminal records on computer since March 1989, prior on books to 1968, older records in basement.

General Information: Public Access terminal is available. No adoptions, sealed cases, juvenile, mental or expunged records released. Copy fee: $2.00 for first page, $.25 each add'l. Certification fee: $3.00. Payee: Clerk of Superior Court. Only cashiers checks and money orders accepted. Prepayment required. Mail turnaround time 2-4 days.

Nash County

Superior-District Court PO Box 759, Nashville, NC 27856; Civil phone: 252-459-4081; Criminal phone: 252-459-4085; Fax: 252-459-6050. Hours: 8AM-5PM (EST). *Felony, Misdemeanor, Civil, Eviction, Small Claims, Probate.*
www.aoc.state.nc.us/www/public/courts/nash.html
Note: Search civil and criminal court calendars at www1.aoc.state.nc.us/www/calendars.html.

Civil Records: Access: Mail, in person. Both court and visitors may perform in person searches. No search fee. Required to search: name, years to search; also helpful: address. Civil cases indexed by defendant, plaintiff. Civil records on computer since 6/88, prior in books to 1988.

Criminal Records: Access: Mail, in person. Both court and visitors may perform in person searches. Search fee: $10.00 per name. Required to search: name, years to search, DOB; also helpful: address. Criminal records on computer since 5/80, prior on books and cards dating back to late 1800s.

General Information: Public Access terminal is available. No adoptions, sealed cases, juvenile, mental or expunged records released. Copy fee: $2.00 for first page, $.25 each add'l. Certification fee: $3.00. Payee: Rachel M Joyner, CSC. Only cashiers checks and money orders accepted. Prepayment required. Mail requests: SASE required. Mail turnaround time 1 week.

New Hanover County

Superior-District Court PO Box 2023, Wilmington, NC 28402; 910-341-1111; Criminal phone: 910-341-1302; Fax: 910-251-2676. Hours: 8AM-5PM (EST). *Felony, Misdemeanor, Civil, Eviction, Small Claims, Probate.*
www.aoc.state.nc.us/www/public/courts/new_hanover.html
Note: Search civil and criminal court calendars at www1.aoc.state.nc.us/www/calendars.html.

Civil Records: Access: In person only. Visitors must perform in person searches for themselves. No search fee. Required to search: name, years to search; also helpful: address. Civil cases indexed by defendant, plaintiff. Civil records on computer since 1988, on books to late 1800s.

Criminal Records: Access: Mail, in person. Both court and visitors may perform in person searches. Search fee: $10.00 per name. Required to search: name, years to search, DOB; also helpful: address, SSN. Criminal records on computer since 11/83, prior on books and files to late 1800s.

General Information: Public Access terminal is available. No adoptions, sealed cases, juvenile, sex offenders, mental or expunged records released. Copy

---

fee: $1.50 for first page, $.25 each add'l. Certification fee: $3.00. Payee: Clerk of Superior Court. Only cashiers checks and money orders accepted. Prepayment required. Mail requests: SASE required. Mail turnaround time 1-2 days.

Northampton County

Superior-District Court PO Box 217, Jackson, NC 27845; 252-534-1631; Fax: 252-534-1308. Hours: 8:30AM-5PM (EST). *Felony, Misdemeanor, Civil, Eviction, Small Claims, Probate.*
www.aoc.state.nc.us/www/public/courts/northampton.html
Note: Search civil and criminal court calendars at www1.aoc.state.nc.us/www/calendars.html.

Civil Records: Access: Mail, in person. Both court and visitors may perform in person searches. No search fee. Required to search: name, years to search; also helpful: address. Civil cases indexed by defendant, plaintiff. Civil records on computer back to 1993, prior on books to 1968.

Criminal Records: Access: Mail, in person. Search fee: $10.00 per name. Required to search: name, years to search, DOB; also helpful: address, SSN. Criminal records on computer back to 1989, prior on books to 1968.

General Information: Public Access terminal is available. No adoptions, sealed cases, juvenile, sex offenders, mental or expunged records released. Copy fee: $1.50 for first page, $.25 each add'l. Certification fee: $3.00. Payee: Clerk of Superior Court. Business checks accepted. Prepayment required. Mail turnaround time is 3-10 days.

Onslow County

Superior-District Court 625 Court St, Jacksonville, NC 28540; 910-455-4458. Hours: 8AM-5PM (EST). *Felony, Misdemeanor, Civil, Eviction, Small Claims, Probate.*
www.aoc.state.nc.us/www/public/courts/onslow.htm
Note: Search civil and criminal court calendars at www1.aoc.state.nc.us/www/calendars.html.

Civil Records: Access: In person only. Visitors must perform in person searches for themselves. No search fee. Required to search: name, years to search; also helpful: address. Civil cases indexed by defendant, plaintiff. Civil records on computer since 1988, prior on books to 1920s.

Criminal Records: Access: Mail, in person. Both court and visitors may perform in person searches. Search fee: $10.00 per name. Required to search: name, years to search, DOB; also helpful: address, SSN. Criminal records on computer since 2/83, prior on books to 1920s.

General Information: Public Access terminal is available. No adoptions, sealed cases, juvenile, sex offenders, mental or expunged records released. Copy fee: $1.50 for first page, $.25 each add'l. Certification fee: $3.00. Payee: Clerk of Superior Court. Business checks accepted. Prepayment required. Mail turnaround time 1-2 days.

Orange County

Superior-District Court 106 E Margaret Lane, Hillsborough, NC 27278; Civil phone: 919-245-2210; Criminal phone: 919-245-2200; Probate phone: 919-245-2214; Fax: 919-644-3043. Hours: 8AM-5PM (EST). *Felony, Misdemeanor, Civil, Eviction, Small Claims, Probate.* www.nccourts.org
Note: Search civil and criminal court calendars at www1.aoc.state.nc.us/www/calendars.html.

Civil Records: Access: In person only. Both court and visitors may perform in person searches. No search fee. Required to search: name, years to search; also helpful: address. Civil cases indexed by defendant, plaintiff. Civil records on computer since May 1989, prior on books to early 1800s.

Criminal Records: Access: Mail, in person. Both court and visitors may perform in person searches. Search fee: $10.00 per name. Required to search: name, years to search, DOB; also helpful: address, SSN, race, sex. computer records go to 3/8.

General Information: Public Access terminal is available. No adoptions, sealed cases, juvenile, sex offenders, mental or expunged records released. Copy fee: $1.50 for first page, $.25 each add'l. Certification fee: $3.00. Payee: Clerk of Superior Court. Business checks accepted. Prepayment required. Mail requests: SASE required. Mail turnaround time 1-3 days.

Pamlico County

Superior-District Court PO Box 38, Bayboro, NC 28515; Civil phone: 252-745-6000; Criminal phone: 252-745-6001; Probate phone: 252-745-6002; Fax: 252-745-6018. Hours: 8AM-5PM (EST). *Felony, Misdemeanor, Civil, Eviction, Small Claims, Probate.*
www.aoc.state.nc.us/www/public/courts/pamlico.html
Note: Search civil and criminal court calendars at www1.aoc.state.nc.us/www/calendars.html.

Civil Records: Access: Mail, in person. Both court and visitors may perform in person searches. No search fee. Required to search: name, years to search, address. Civil cases indexed by defendant, plaintiff. Civil records go back to 1988; criminal records on computer since 9/89, prior on books to 1968.

Criminal Records: Access: Mail, in person. Both court and visitors may perform in person searches. Search fee: $10.00 per name. Required to search: name, years to search, DOB. Criminal records on computer since 9/84, prior on books to 1968.

General Information: Public Access terminal is available. No adoptions, sealed cases, juvenile, sex offenders, mental or expunged records released. Will fax results to local or toll free line. Copy fee: $1.50 for first page, $.25 each add'l. Certification fee: $3.00. Payee: Clerk of Court. Only cashiers checks and money orders accepted. Prepayment required. Mail requests: SASE required. Mail turnaround time 1-2 days.

Pasquotank County

Superior-District Court PO Box 449, Elizabeth City, NC 27907-0449; 252-331-4751. Hours: 8AM-5PM (EST). *Felony, Misdemeanor, Civil, Eviction, Small Claims, Probate.*
www.nccourts.org
Note: Search civil and criminal court calendars at www1.aoc.state.nc.us/www/calendars.html.

Civil Records: Access: In person only. Visitors must perform in person searches for themselves. No search fee. Required to search: name, years to search; also helpful: address. Civil cases indexed by defendant, plaintiff. Civil records on computer since March 6, 1989, books prior to 1800s (some in Raleigh).

Criminal Records: Access: Mail, in person. Both court and visitors may perform in person searches. Search fee: $10.00 per name. Required to search: name, years to search, DOB; also helpful: address, SSN, race, sex. Criminal records on computer since 4/88, prior on books and microfiche.

General Information: Public Access terminal is available. No adoptions, sealed cases, juvenile, sex offenders, mental or expunged records released. Copy fee: $1.50 for first page, $.25 each add'l. Certification fee: Included in search fee, court must do search. Payee: Clerk of Superior Court. Business checks accepted. Prepayment required. Mail turnaround time 2 days.

Pender County

Superior-District Court PO Box 310, Burgaw, NC 28425; 910-259-1229; Fax: 910-259-1292. Hours: 8:30AM-5PM (EST). *Felony, Misdemeanor, Civil, Eviction, Small Claims, Probate.*

www.aoc.state.nc.us/www/public/courts/pender.html
Note: Search civil and criminal court calendars at www1.aoc.state.nc.us/www/calendars.html.
Civil Records: Access: In person only. Visitors must perform in person searches for themselves. No search fee. Required to search: name, years to search; also helpful: address. Civil cases indexed by defendant, plaintiff. Civil records on computer since 9/89, prior in books from 1875.
Criminal Records: Access: Fax, mail, in person. Both court and visitors may perform in person searches. Search fee: $10.00 per name. Required to search: name, years to search, DOB; also helpful: address, SSN. Criminal records on computer since 9/89, prior in books from 1968.
General Information: Public Access terminal is available. No adoptions, sealed cases, juvenile, sex offenders, mental or expunged records released. Will fax results $1.00 1st page, $.25 each add'l. Copy fee: $2.00 for first page, $.25 each add'l. Certification fee: $3.00. Payee: Clerk of Superior Court. Business checks accepted. Prepayment required. Mail turnaround time 1 week.

Perquimans County

Superior-District Court PO Box 33, Hertford, NC 27944; 252-426-1505; Fax: 252-426-1901. Hours: 8AM-5PM (EST). *Felony, Misdemeanor, Civil, Eviction, Small Claims, Probate.*

www.aoc.state.nc.us/www/public/courts/perquimans.html
Note: Search civil and criminal court calendars at www1.aoc.state.nc.us/www/calendars.html.
Civil Records: Access: In person only. Visitors must perform in person searches for themselves. No search fee. Required to search: name, years to search. Civil cases indexed by defendant, plaintiff. Civil records on computer since 1989, prior in books to 1966, rest archived and must be searched in person only.
Criminal Records: Access: Mail, in person. Both court and visitors may perform in person searches. Search fee: $10.00 per name. Required to search: name, years to search, DOB. Criminal records on computer since 1989, prior in books to 1966, rest archived and must be searched in person only.
General Information: Public Access terminal is available. No adoptions, sealed cases, juvenile, sex offenders, mental or expunged records released. Copy fee: $1.50 for first page, $.25 each add'l. Certification fee: $3.00. Payee: Clerk of Superior Court. Only cashiers checks and money orders accepted. Prepayment required. Mail turnaround time 1-2 days.

Person County

Superior-District Court 105 S Main St, Roxboro, NC 27573; Civil phone: 336-597-0554; Criminal phone: 336-597-0556; Fax: 336-597-0568. Hours: 8:30AM-5PM (EST). *Felony, Misdemeanor, Civil, Eviction, Small Claims, Probate.*

www.aoc.state.nc.us/www/public/courts/person.html
Note: Search civil and criminal court calendars at www1.aoc.state.nc.us/www/calendars.html.
Civil Records: Access: In person only. Both court and visitors may perform in person searches. No search fee. Required to search: name, years to search. Civil cases indexed by defendant, plaintiff. Civil records on microfiche since 4/89, prior in index books to 1968.
Criminal Records: Access: Mail, in person. Both court and visitors may perform in person searches. Search fee: $10.00 per name. Required to search:

name, years to search, DOB. Criminal records on computer since 3/88, index cards and books prior to 1968.
General Information: Public Access terminal is available. No adoptions, sealed cases, juvenile, sex offenders, mental or expunged records released. Copy fee: $1.50 for first page, $.25 each add'l. Certification fee: Included in search fee, unless do it yourself then $2.00. Payee: Clerk of Superior Court. Business checks accepted. Prepayment required. Mail requests: SASE required. Mail turnaround time 1-2 days.

Pitt County

Superior - District Court PO Box 6067, Greenville, NC 27835; 252-695-7100; Civil phone: 252-695-7150; Criminal phone: 252-695-7117; Fax: 252-695-7376. Hours: 8AM-5PM (EST). *Felony, Misdemeanor, Civil, Eviction, Small Claims, Probate.*

www.aoc.state.nc.us/www/public/courts/pitt.htm
Note: Search civil and criminal court calendars at www1.aoc.state.nc.us/www/calendars.html.
Civil Records: Access: In person only. Visitors must perform in person searches for themselves. No search fee. Required to search: name, years to search; also helpful: address. Civil cases indexed by defendant, plaintiff. Civil records on computer back to 1988, on books to 1968.
Criminal Records: Access: Mail, in person. Both court and visitors may perform in person searches. Search fee: $10.00 per name. Required to search: name, years to search, DOB; also helpful: address, SSN. Criminal records on computer back to 2/85, on books and cards to early 1900s.
General Information: Public Access terminal is available. No adoptions, sealed cases, juvenile, sex offenders, mental or expunged records released. Copy fee: $1.50 for first page, $.25 each add'l. Certification fee: $5.00. Payee: Clerk of Court. Business checks accepted. Prepayment required. Mail turnaround time 1-2 days.

Polk County

Superior-District Court PO Box 38, Columbus, NC 28722; 828-894-8231; Fax: 828-894-5752. 8AM-5PM (EST). *Felony, Misdemeanor, Civil, Eviction, Small Claims, Probate.*

www.aoc.state.nc.us/www/public/courts/polk.html
Note: Search civil and criminal court calendars at www1.aoc.state.nc.us/www/calendars.html.
Civil Records: Access: Mail, in person. Both court and visitors may perform in person searches. Search fee: $5.00 per name. Required to search: name, years to search. Civil cases indexed by defendant, plaintiff. Civil records on computer since 5/89, prior on books to 1968.
Criminal Records: Access: Mail, in person. Only the court performs in person searches; visitors may not. Search fee: $10.00 per name. Required to search: name, years to search, DOB. Criminal records on computer since 5/89, prior on books to 1968.
General Information: Public Access terminal is available. No adoptions, sealed cases, juvenile, sex offenders, mental, expunged or dismissed records released. Copy fee: $1.50 for first page, $.25 each add'l. Certification fee: $3.00. Payee: Clerk of Superior Court. Business checks accepted. Prepayment required. Mail requests: SASE required. Mail turnaround time 1-2 days.

Randolph County

Superior-District Court 176 E Salisbury St #201, Asheboro, NC 27203; 336-328-3000; Civil phone: 336-328-3004; Criminal phone: 336-328-3005; Fax: 336-328-3131. Hours: 8AM-5PM (EST). *Felony, Misdemeanor, Civil, Eviction, Small Claims, Probate.*

www.aoc.state.nc.us/www/public/courts/randolph.htm
Note: Search civil and criminal court calendars at www1.aoc.state.nc.us/www/calendars.html.
Civil Records: Access: In person only. Visitors must perform in person searches for themselves. No search fee. Required to search: name, years to search. Civil cases indexed by defendant, plaintiff. Civil records on computer since 02/89, prior on books to 1800s.
Criminal Records: Access: Mail, in person. Only the court performs in person searches; visitors may not. Search fee: $10.00 per name. Required to search: name, years to search, address, DOB. Criminal records on computer since 06/85, prior on books and cards from 1970 to 1981. Microfilm from 1981 to 06/85.
General Information: Public Access terminal is available. (Civil only.) No adoptions, sealed cases, juvenile, sex offenders, mental or expunged records released. Will not fax results. Copy fee: $1.50 for first page, $.25 each add'l. Certification fee: $3.00. Payee: Clerk of Superior Court. Only cashiers checks and money orders accepted. Prepayment required. Mail requests: SASE required. Mail turnaround time 1-2 days.

Richmond County

Superior-District Court 114 E Franklin St #103, Rockingham, NC 28379; Civil phone: 910-997-9102; Criminal phone: 910-997-9101; Fax: 910-997-9126. 8AM-5PM (EST). *Felony, Misdemeanor, Civil, Eviction, Small Claims, Probate.*

www.aoc.state.nc.us/www/public/courts/richmond.htm
Note: Search civil and criminal court calendars at www1.aoc.state.nc.us/www/calendars.html.
Civil Records: Access: In person only. Visitors must perform in person searches for themselves. No search fee. Required to search: name, years to search; also helpful: address. Civil cases indexed by defendant, plaintiff. Civil records on computer since 4/89, prior on books since 1968.
Criminal Records: Access: Mail, in person. Both court and visitors may perform in person searches. Search fee: $10.00 per name. Required to search: name, years to search, DOB; also helpful: address, SSN. Criminal records on computer since 1977, cards to 1977, books to 1940, prior archived.
General Information: Public Access terminal is available. No adoptions, sealed cases, juvenile, sex offenders, mental or expunged records released. Copy fee: $1.50 for first page, $.25 each add'l. Certification fee: $3.00. Payee: Clerk of Superior Court. Business checks accepted. Prepayment required. Mail requests: SASE required. Mail turnaround time 1-2 days.

Robeson County

Superior-District Court PO Box 1084, Lumberton, NC 28359; 910-737-5035; Civil phone: 910-671-3372; Criminal phone: 910-671-3395; Fax: 910-618-5598. Hours: 8:15AM-5:15PM (EST). *Felony, Misdemeanor, Civil, Eviction, Small Claims, Probate.*

www.aoc.state.nc.us/www/public/courts/robeson.html
Note: Search civil and criminal court calendars at www1.aoc.state.nc.us/www/calendars.html.
Civil Records: Access: In person only. Visitors must perform in person searches for themselves. No search fee. Required to search: name, years to search; also helpful: address. Civil cases indexed by defendant,

plaintiff. Civil records on computer since 1988, prior on books since 1966. Court calanders may be viewed at the state court administration site.

Criminal Records: Access: Mail, in person. Both court and visitors may perform in person searches. Search fee: $10.00 per name. Required to search: name, years to search; also helpful: address, DOB. Criminal records on computer since 1983, index books prior

General Information: Public Access terminal is available. No sealed cases, juvenile, sex offenders, mental or expunged records released. Will not fax results. Copy fee: $2.00 for first page, $.25 each add'l. Certification fee: $3.00; Exemplification is $10.00. Payee: Clerk of Superior Court. Business checks accepted. Prepayment required. Mail requests: SASE required. Mail turnaround time 1-2 days.

Rockingham County

Superior-District Court PO Box 127, Wentworth, NC 27375; 336-342-8700; Civil phone: 336-342-8722; Criminal phone: 336-342-8706; Probate phone: 336-342-8703. Hours: 8AM-5PM (EST). *Felony, Misdemeanor, Civil, Eviction, Small Claims, Probate.* www.aoc.state.nc.us/www/public/courts/rockingham.html
Note: Search civil and criminal court calendars at www1.aoc.state.nc.us/www/calendars.html.
Civil Records: Access: In person only. Both court and visitors may perform in person searches. No search fee. Required to search: name, years to search. Civil cases indexed by defendant, plaintiff. Civil records on computer since 2/89, prior on books.
Criminal Records: Access: Mail, in person. Both court and visitors may perform in person searches. Search fee: $10.00 per name. Required to search: name, years to search, DOB. Criminal records on computer since 5/85, prior on cards and books.
General Information: Public Access terminal is available. No adoptions, sealed cases, juvenile, sex offenders, mental or expunged records released. Copy fee: $2.00 for first page, $.25 each add'l. Certification fee: $3.00. Payee: Clerk of Superior Court. Only cashiers checks and money orders accepted. Prepayment required. Mail turnaround time 1-2 days.

Rowan County

Superior-District Court PO Box 4599, 210 N Main St, Salisbury, NC 28144; 704-639-7505; Probate phone: 704-639-7680. Hours: 8AM-5PM (EST). *Felony, Misdemeanor, Civil, Eviction, Small Claims, Probate.*
www.aoc.state.nc.us/www/public/courts/rowan.html
Note: Crim District phone is 704-639-6766; for Superior is 704-639-7676.
Note: Search civil and criminal court calendars at www1.aoc.state.nc.us/www/calendars.html.
Civil Records: Access: In person only. Both court and visitors may perform in person searches. No search fee. Required to search: name, years to search; also helpful: address. Civil cases indexed by defendant, plaintiff. Civil records on computer since 1989, prior on books to 1800s.
Criminal Records: Access: Mail, in person. Both court and visitors may perform in person searches. Search fee: $10.00 per name. Required to search: name, DOB; also helpful: years to search, address, SSN. Criminal records on computer from 5/85, prior on books and cards to 1970.
General Information: No adoptions, sealed cases, juvenile, sex offenders, mental or expunged records released. Copy fee: $1.50 for first page, $.25 each add'l. Certification fee: Included in search fee, unless do it yourself then $2.00. Payee: Clerk of Superior Court. Business checks accepted. Prepayment required. Mail turnaround time 1-3 days.

Rutherford County

Superior-District Court PO Box 630, Rutherfordton, NC 28139; Civil phone: 828-286-9136; Criminal phone: 828-286-3243; Fax: 828-286-4322. 8:30AM-5PM (EST). *Felony, Misdemeanor, Civil, Eviction, Small Claims, Probate.*
www.aoc.state.nc.us/www/public/courts/rutherford.htm
Note: Search civil and criminal court calendars at www1.aoc.state.nc.us/www/calendars.html.
Civil Records: Access: In person only. Visitors must perform in person searches for themselves. No search fee. Required to search: name, years to search; also helpful: address. Civil cases indexed by defendant, plaintiff. Civil records on computer Oct. 1988, prior on books, some records to 1700s.
Criminal Records: Access: Mail, in person. Both court and visitors may perform in person searches. Search fee: $10.00 per name. Required to search: name, years to search, DOB; also helpful: address, SSN. Criminal records on computer since 6/87, prior on microfiche and books dating to 1800s.
General Information: Public Access terminal is available. No adoptions, sealed cases, juvenile, sex offenders, mental or expunged records released. Copy fee: $1.50 for first page, $.25 each add'l. Certification fee: $3.00. Payee: Clerk of Superior Court. Business checks accepted. Prepayment required. Mail turnaround time 1-2 days.

Sampson County

Superior-District Court Courthouse, Clinton, NC 28328; 910-592-5191; Civil phone: 910-592-5192; Criminal phone: 910-592-6981; Fax: 910-592-5502. 8AM-5PM (EST). *Felony, Misdemeanor, Civil, Eviction, Small Claims, Probate.*
www.sampsoncountyclerkofcourt.org
Note: Search civil and criminal court calendars at www1.aoc.state.nc.us/www/calendars.html.
Civil Records: Access: In person only. Visitors must perform in person searches for themselves. No search fee. Required to search: name, years to search; also helpful: address. Civil cases indexed by defendant, plaintiff. Civil records on computer since 1989, prior on books.
Criminal Records: Access: Phone, mail, in person. Both court and visitors may perform in person searches. Search fee: $10.00 per name. Required to search: name, years to search, DOB; also helpful: address, SSN. Criminal records on computer since 7/87, prior on books.
General Information: Public Access terminal is available. No adoptions, sealed cases, juvenile, sex offenders, mental or expunged records released. Will fax results. Copy fee: $2.00 for first page, $.25 each add'l. Certification fee: $3.00. Payee: Clerk of Superior Court. No personal checks accepted. Prepayment required. Mail requests: SASE requested. Turnaround time 1-2 days.

Scotland County

Superior-District Court PO Box 769, Laurinburg, NC 28353; 910-277-3240; Civil phone: 910-277-3265; Criminal phone: 910-277-3250; Probate phone: 910-277-3260. Hours: 8:30AM-5PM (EST). *Felony, Misdemeanor, Civil, Eviction, Small Claims, Probate.*
www.aoc.state.nc.us/www/public/courts/scotland.html
Note: Small claims phone is 910-277-3244.
Note: Search civil and criminal court calendars at www1.aoc.state.nc.us/www/calendars.html.
Civil Records: Access: Mail, in person. Both court and visitors may perform in person searches. Search fee: $5.00 per name. Required to search: name, years to search. Civil cases indexed by defendant, plaintiff.

Civil records on computer since 1988, in books since 1966, on microfiche since 1984.
Criminal Records: Access: Mail, in person. Both court and visitors may perform in person searches. Search fee: $10.00 per name. Required to search: name, years to search, DOB; SSN helpful. Criminal records on computer since 1988, in books 1966-1988, on microfiche 1984-1988.
General Information: Public Access terminal is available. No adoptions, sealed cases, juvenile, sex offenders, mental or expunged records released. Will not fax results. Copy fee: $1.50 for first page, $.25 each add'l. Certification fee: $3.00. Payee: Clerk of Court. Only cashiers checks and money orders accepted. Prepayment required. Mail requests: SASE required. Mail turnaround time 1-2 days.

Stanly County

Superior-District Court PO Box 668, Albemarle, NC 28002-0668; 704-982-2161; Fax: 704-982-8107. Hours: 8:30AM-5PM (EST). *Felony, Misdemeanor, Civil, Eviction, Small Claims, Probate.*
www.aoc.state.nc.us/www/public/courts/stanly.htm
Note: Search civil and criminal court calendars at www1.aoc.state.nc.us/www/calendars.html.
Civil Records: Access: In person only. Visitors must perform in person searches for themselves. No search fee. Required to search: name, years to search; also helpful: address. Civil cases indexed by defendant, plaintiff. Civil records on computer since 1989, books to 1968.
Criminal Records: Access: Mail, in person. Both court and visitors may perform in person searches. Search fee: $10.00 per name. Required to search: name, years to search, DOB; also helpful: address, SSN. Criminal records on computer since 1989, books to 1968.
General Information: Public Access terminal is available. No adoptions, sealed cases, juvenile, sex offenders, mental or expunged records released. Copy fee: $2.00 for first page, $.25 each add'l. Certification fee: $3.00. Payee: Clerk of Superior Court. Only cashiers checks and money orders accepted. Prepayment required. Mail requests: SASE required. Mail turnaround time 1-2 days.

Stokes County

Superior-District Court PO Box 250, Danbury, NC 27016; 336-593-9173; Fax: 336-593-5459. 8AM-5PM (EST). *Felony, Misdemeanor, Civil, Eviction, Small Claims, Probate.*
www.aoc.state.nc.us/www/public/courts/stokes.html
Note: Search civil and criminal court calendars at www1.aoc.state.nc.us/www/calendars.html.
Civil Records: Access: In person only. Visitors must perform in person searches for themselves. No search fee. Required to search: name, years to search; also helpful: address. Civil cases indexed by defendant, plaintiff. Civil records on computer since 9/1988, prior on books to early 1900s. Civil background checks not performed.
Criminal Records: Access: Mail, in person. Both court and visitors may perform in person searches. Search fee: $10.00 per name. Required to search: name, years to search; also helpful: address, DOB. Criminal records on computer since 9/1988, prior on books to early 1900s.
General Information: Public Access terminal is available. No adoptions, sealed cases, juvenile, sex offenders, mental or expunged records released. Copy fee: $1.50 for first page, $.25 each add'l. Certification fee: Included in search fee, unless do it yourself then $2.00. Payee: Clerk of Superior Court. Only cashiers checks and money orders accepted. Prepayment

required. Mail requests: SASE required. Mail turnaround time 1 week.

Surry County

Superior-District Court PO Box 345, Dobson, NC 27017; 336-386-3700; Fax: 336-386-9879. Hours: 8AM-5PM (EST). *Felony, Misdemeanor, Civil, Eviction, Small Claims, Probate.*
www.aoc.state.nc.us/www/public/courts/surry.html
Note: Search civil and criminal court calendars at www1.aoc.state.nc.us/www/calendars.html.
Civil Records: Access: In person, mail. Visitors must perform in person searches for themselves. No search fee. Required to search: name, years to search, DOB; also helpful: address. Civil cases indexed by defendant, plaintiff. Civil records on computer since 10/88, on books to 1970, must know township for earlier records.
Criminal Records: Access: Mail, in person. Both court and visitors may perform in person searches. Search fee: $10.00 per name. Required to search: name, years to search, DOB. Criminal records on computer since 10/88, on books to 1970, must know township for earlier records.
General Information: Public Access terminal is available. No adoptions, sealed cases, juvenile, sex offenders, mental or expunged records released. Copy fee: $1.50 for first page, $.25 each add'l. Certification fee: $3.00. Payee: Clerk of Superior Court. Business checks accepted. Prepayment required. Mail requests: SASE required. Mail turnaround time 1-2 days.

Swain County

Superior-District Court Clerk of Superior Court, PO Box 1397, Bryson City, NC 28713; 828-488-2288; Fax: 828-488-9360. Hours: 8:30AM-5PM (EST). *Felony, Misdemeanor, Civil, Eviction, Small Claims, Probate.*
www.aoc.state.nc.us/www/public/courts/swain.html
Note: Search civil and criminal court calendars at www1.aoc.state.nc.us/www/calendars.html.
Civil Records: Access: In person only. Both court and visitors may perform in person searches. Search fee: none. Required to search: name, years to search. Civil cases indexed by defendant, plaintiff. Civil records on computer since 5/1989, prior on books to 1920.
Criminal Records: Access: In person only. Only the court performs in person searches; visitors may not. Search fee: $10.00 per name. Required to search: name, years to search, DOB; also helpful-SSN, signed release. Criminal records on computer back to 1989, prior on books to 1969.
General Information: Public Access terminal is available. (Civil only.) No adoptions, sealed cases, juvenile, mental or expunged records released. Will fax results for $10.00 per page. Fee must be paid in advance. Copy fee: $.25. Certification fee: $1.00 first page, $.25 each add'l. Payee: Clerk of Superior Court. Only cashiers checks and money orders accepted. Prepayment required.

Transylvania County

Superior-District Court 12 E Main St, Brevard, NC 28712; 828-884-3120; Fax: 828-883-2161. 8AM-5PM (EST). *Felony, Misdemeanor, Civil, Eviction, Small Claims, Probate.* www.aoc.stat e.nc.us/www/public/courts/transylvania.html
Note: Search civil and criminal court calendars at www1.aoc.state.nc.us/www/calendars.html.
Civil Records: Access: In person only. Visitors must perform in person searches for themselves. No search fee. Required to search: name, years to search; also helpful: address. Civil cases indexed by defendant, plaintiff. Civil records on computer from 11/99, on books from 1968.

Criminal Records: Access: Mail, in person. Visitors must perform in person searches themselves. Search fee: $10.00 per name. Fee is for certified record check. Required to search: name, years to search, DOB; also helpful: address, SSN. Criminal records on computer from 6/89, on books 1968-1989.
General Information: Public Access terminal is available. No adoptions, sealed cases, juvenile, mental or expunged records released. Copy fee: $1.50 for first page, $.25 each add'l. Certification fee: $3.00. Payee: Clerk of Superior Court. Personal checks accepted. Prepayment required. Mail requests: SASE required. Mail turnaround time 1-3 days.

Tyrrell County

Superior-District Court PO Box 406, Columbia, NC 27925; 252-796-6281; Fax: 252-796-0008. 8:30AM-5PM (EST). *Felony, Misdemeanor, Civil, Eviction, Small Claims, Probate.*
www.aoc.state.nc.us/www/public/courts/tyrrell.html
Note: Search civil and criminal court calendars at www1.aoc.state.nc.us/www/calendars.html.
Civil Records: Access: In person only. Visitors must perform in person searches for themselves. No search fee. Required to search: name, years to search; also helpful: address. Civil cases indexed by defendant, plaintiff. Civil records on computer since 10/89, prior on microfilm to 1968.
Criminal Records: Access: Mail, in person. Both court and visitors may perform in person searches. Search fee: $10.00 per name. Required to search: name, years to search, DOB; also helpful: address, SSN. Criminal records on computer since 10/89, prior on books to 1968.
General Information: Public Access terminal is available. No adoptions, sealed cases, juvenile, sex offenders, mental records expunged. Copy fee: $1.50 for first page, $.25 each add'l. Certification fee: $3.00. Payee: Clerk of Superior Court. Business checks accepted. Prepayment required. Mail turnaround time 1-2 days.

Union County

Superior-District Court PO Box 5038, Monroe, NC 28111; 704-283-4313; Fax: 704-289-2444. 8AM-5PM (EST). *Felony, Misdemeanor, Civil, Eviction, Small Claims, Probate.*
www.aoc.state.nc.us/www/public/courts/union.htm
Note: Search civil and criminal court calendars at www1.aoc.state.nc.us/www/calendars.html.
Civil Records: Access: In person only. Visitors must perform in person searches for themselves. No search fee. Required to search: name, years to search; also helpful: address. Civil cases indexed by defendant, plaintiff. Civil records on computer since 1987, prior on books to 1968.
Criminal Records: Access: Mail, in person. Both court and visitors may perform in person searches. Search fee: $10.00 per name. Required to search: name, years to search; also helpful: address, DOB, SSN. Criminal record on computer since 1987; prior on books to 1968.
General Information: Public Access terminal is available. No adoptions, sealed cases, juvenile, sex offenders, mental or expunged records released. Copy fee: $1.50 for first page, $.25 each add'l. Certification fee: Included in copy fee or search fee. Payee: Clerk of Superior Court. Will accept local business checks. Prepayment required. Mail turnaround time 1-2 days.

Vance County

Superior-District Court 156 Church St. #101, Henderson, NC 27536; 252-738-9000. Hours: 8AM-5PM (EST). *Felony, Misdemeanor, Civil, Eviction, Small Claims, Probate.*
www.aoc.state.nc.us/www/public/courts/vance.html

Note: Search civil and criminal court calendars at www1.aoc.state.nc.us/www/calendars.html.
Civil Records: Access: In person only. Visitors must perform in person searches for themselves. No search fee. Required to search: name, years to search; also helpful: address. Civil cases indexed by defendant, plaintiff. Civil records on computer since 1989, prior on books to 1881.
Criminal Records: Access: Mail, in person. Both court and visitors may perform in person searches. Search fee: $10.00 per name. Required to search: name, years to search, address, DOB; also helpful: SSN. Criminal records on computer to 12/80, prior on books and cards to 1881.
General Information: Public Access terminal is available. No adoptions, sealed cases, juvenile, sex offenders, mental or expunged records released. Copy fee: $1.50 for first page, $.25 each add'l. Certification fee: Included in search fee, unless do it yourself then $2.00. Payee: Clerk of Superior Court. Business checks accepted. Prepayment required. Mail turnaround time 1-2 days.

Wake County

Superior-District Court PO Box 351, Raleigh, NC 27602; 919-755-4105; Civil phone: 919-755-4108; Criminal phone: 919-755-4112. Hours: 8:30AM-5:00PM (EST). *Felony, Misdemeanor, Civil, Eviction, Small Claims, Probate.*
http://web.co.wake.nc.us/courts
Note: Search civil and criminal court calendars at www1.aoc.state.nc.us/www/calendars.html.
Civil Records: Access: In person only. Visitors must perform in person searches for themselves. No search fee. Required to search: name, years to search. Civil cases indexed by defendant, plaintiff. Civil records on computer since 1988, prior on books to 1920s.
Criminal Records: Access: Mail, in person. Both court and visitors may perform in person searches. Search fee: $10.00 per name. Required to search: name, years to search. Criminal records on computer from 5/82, prior on books and cards from 1968.
General Information: Public Access terminal is available. Juvenile, judicial waivers, involuntary commitments are confidential. No sealed cases, juvenile, mental or expunged records released. Copy fee: $2.00 for first page, $.25 each add'l. Certification fee: $3.00. Payee: Clerk of Superior Court. Business checks accepted with prior registration. No personal checks accepted. Prepayment required. Mail turnaround time 1-2 days.

Warren County

Superior-District Court PO Box 709, Warrenton, NC 27589; 252-257-3261; Fax: 252-257-5529. 8:30AM-5PM (EST). *Felony, Misdemeanor, Civil, Eviction, Small Claims, Probate.*
www.aoc.state.nc.us/www/public/courts/warren.htm
Note: Search civil and criminal court calendars at www1.aoc.state.nc.us/www/calendars.html.
Civil Records: Access: In person only. Visitors must perform in person searches for themselves. No search fee. Required to search: name, years to search. Civil cases indexed by defendant, plaintiff. Civil records on computer since 1989, prior on books to 1968.
Criminal Records: Access: Mail, in person. Both court and visitors may perform in person searches. Search fee: $10.00 per name. Required to search: name, years to search, DOB. Criminal records on computer from 5/81, prior on books to 1968.
General Information: Public Access terminal is available. No adoptions, sealed cases, juvenile, sex offenders, mental or expunged records released. Copy fee: $1.50 for first page, $.25 each add'l. Certification fee: $3.00. Payee: Clerk of Superior Court. Business

checks accepted. Prepayment required. Mail turnaround time 1-2 days.

Washington County

Superior-District Court PO Box 901, Plymouth, NC 27962; 252-793-3013; Fax: 252-793-1081. 8AM-5PM (EST). *Felony, Misdemeanor, Civil, Eviction, Small Claims, Probate.* www.aoc.state.nc.us/www/public/courts/washington.html
Note: Search civil and criminal court calendars at www1.aoc.state.nc.us/www/calendars.html.
Civil Records: Access: In person only. Visitors must perform in person searches for themselves. No search fee. Required to search: name, years to search. Civil cases indexed by defendant, plaintiff. Civil records on computer back to 12/89, prior on books.
Criminal Records: Access: Mail, in person. Both court and visitors may perform in person searches. Search fee: $10.00 per name. Required to search: name, years to search; also helpful: address, DOB, SSN. Criminal records on computer back to 12/89, prior on books.
General Information: Public Access terminal is available. No adoptions, sealed, juvenile, mental health, expunged or dismissed records released. Copy fee: $1.50 for first page, $.25 each add'l. Certification fee: $3.00. Payee: Clerk of Court. Business checks accepted. Prepayment required. Mail requests: SASE required. Mail turnaround time 2-3 days.

Watauga County

Superior-District Court Courthouse #13, 842 West King St, Boone, NC 28607-3525; 828-265-5364; Civil phone: 828-265-5432; Criminal phone: 828-265-5430; Probate phone: 828-265-5443; Fax: 828-262-5753. 8AM-5PM *Felony, Misdemeanor, Civil, Eviction, Small Claims, Probate.* www.aoc.state.nc.us/www/public/courts/watauga.htm
Note: Search civil and criminal court calendars at www1.aoc.state.nc.us/www/calendars.html.
Civil Records: Access: Mail, in person. Both court and visitors may perform in person searches. Search fee: $5.00 per name. Required to search: name, years to search. Civil cases indexed by defendant, plaintiff. Civil records on computer since 12/5/88, on books to 1872, prior destroyed by fire.
Criminal Records: Access: Mail, in person. Both court and visitors may perform in person searches. Search fee: $10.00 per name. Required to search: name, years to search, DOB, SSN. Criminal records on computer from 11/88, prior on cards and books to 1968.
General Information: Public Access terminal is available. No adoptions, sealed, juvenile, sex offenders, mental, expunged or dismissed records released. Copy fee: $1.50 for first page, $.25 each add'l. Certification fee: $3.00. Payee: Clerk of Court. Only cashiers checks and money orders accepted. Prepayment required. Mail requests: SASE requested. Turnaround time 1-2 days.

Wayne County

Superior-District Court PO Box 267, Goldsboro, NC 27530; 919-731-7921; Civil phone: 919-731-7919; Criminal phone: 919-731-7910; Fax: 919-731-2037. 8AM-5PM *Felony, Misdemeanor, Civil, Eviction, Small Claims, Probate.* www.nccourts.org/County/Wayne/Default.asp
Note: Court calendar appears on the Internet.

Civil Records: Access: In person only. Visitors must perform in person searches for themselves. No search fee. Required to search: name, years to search; also helpful: address. Civil cases indexed by defendant, plaintiff. Civil records on computer since 7-18-88, on books since 1968, open to public prior. The court will not do a search unless book and page number or a year of judgment given.
Criminal Records: Access: Mail, in person. Both court and visitors may perform in person searches. Search fee: $10.00 per name. Required to search: name, years to search, DOB; also helpful: address, SSN, aliases. Criminal records on computer since 7-18-88, on books since 1985, open to public prior.
General Information: Public Access terminal is available. No adoptions, sealed, juvenile, sex offenders, mental, expunged or dismissed. Copy fee: $2.00 for first page, $.25 each add'l. Certification fee: $3.00. Payee: Clerk of Superior Court. Business checks accepted. Prepayment required. Mail requests: SASE requested. Turnaround time 1-2 days.

Wilkes County

Superior-District Court 500 Courthouse Drive, #1115, Wilkesboro, NC 28697; Civil phone: 336-667-1201; Criminal phone: 336-667-5266; Fax: 336-667-1985. 8AM-5PM (EST). *Felony, Misdemeanor, Civil, Eviction, Small Claims, Probate.* www.nccourts.org/County/Wilkes/Default.asp
Note: Search civil and criminal court calendars at www1.aoc.state.nc.us/www/calendars.html.
Civil Records: Access: In person only. Visitors must perform in person searches for themselves. No search fee. Required to search: name, years to search. Civil cases indexed by defendant, plaintiff. Civil records on computer since 12/88, prior on books to early 1900s.
Criminal Records: Access: Mail, online, in person. Both court and visitors may perform in person searches. Search fee: $10.00 per name. Required to search: name, years to search, DOB; also helpful: address. Criminal records on computer since 12/88, prior on books to early 1900s.
General Information: Public Access terminal is available. No adoptions, sealed cases, juvenile, sex offenders, mental or expunged records released. Copy fee: $2.00 for first page, $.25 each add'l. Certification fee: $3.00. Payee: Clerk of Superior Court. Only cashiers checks and money orders accepted. Prepayment required. Mail requests: SASE requested. Turnaround time 1-2 days.

Wilson County

Superior-District Court PO Box 1608, Wilson, NC 27894; 252-291-7500; Civil phone: 252-291-7502; Probate phone: 252-291-7502; Fax: 252-291-8049 (Criminal) 291-8635 (Civil). Hours: 9AM-5PM (EST). *Felony, Misdemeanor, Civil, Eviction, Small Claims, Probate.* www.aoc.state.nc.us/www/public/courts/wilson.html
Note: Search civil and criminal court calendars at www1.aoc.state.nc.us/www/calendars.html.
Civil Records: Access: In person only. Visitors must perform in person searches for themselves. No search fee. Required to search: name, years to search; also helpful: address. Civil cases indexed by defendant, plaintiff. Civil records on computer since 8/88, prior on books to 1968, public viewing from 1915 to 1968.
Criminal Records: Access: Mail, fax, in person. Both court and visitors may perform in person searches. Search fee: $10.00 per name. Required to search: name, years to search, DOB; also helpful:

address, SSN. Criminal records on computer since 5/86, Index cards to 9/76, books to 1918.
General Information: Public Access terminal is available. No adoptions, sealed cases, juvenile, sex offenders, mental, or expunged records released. Will not fax results. Copy fee: $2.00 for first page, $.25 each add'l. Certification fee: $3.00. Payee: Clerk of Court. Only cashiers checks and money orders accepted. Prepayment required. Mail requests: SASE requested. Turnaround time 2-4 days.

Yadkin County

Superior-District Court PO Box 95, Yadkinville, NC 27055; 336-679-8838; Fax: 336-679-4378. 8AM-5PM (EST). *Felony, Misdemeanor, Civil, Eviction, Small Claims, Probate.* www.aoc.state.nc.us/www/public/courts/yadkin.htm
Note: Search civil and criminal court calendars at www1.aoc.state.nc.us/www/calendars.html.
Civil Records: Access: In person only. Visitors must perform in person searches for themselves. No search fee. Required to search: name, years to search; also helpful: address. Civil cases indexed by defendant, plaintiff. Civil records on computer since 8/89, prior on books to 1970.
Criminal Records: Access: Mail, in person. Both court and visitors may perform in person searches. Search fee: $10.00 per name. Required to search: name, years to search, DOB; also helpful: address. Criminal records on computer since 8/89, prior on books to 1970.
General Information: Public Access terminal is available. No adoptions, sealed cases, juvenile, sex offenders, mental or expunged records released. Copy fee: $2.00 for first page, $.25 each add'l. Certification fee: $3.00. Payee: Clerk of Superior Court. Business checks accepted. Prepayment required. Mail requests: SASE required. Mail turnaround time 1-2 days.

Yancey County

Superior-District Court 110 Town Square, Burnsville, NC 28714; 828-682-2122; Fax: 828-682-6296. 8:30AM-5PM (EST). *Felony, Misdemeanor, Civil, Eviction, Small Claims, Probate.* www.aoc.state.nc.us/www/public/courts/yancey.htm
Note: Search civil and criminal court calendars at www1.aoc.state.nc.us/www/calendars.html.
Civil Records: Access: In person only. Visitors must perform in person searches for themselves. No search fee. Required to search: name, years to search; also helpful: address. Civil cases indexed by defendant, plaintiff. Civil records on computer since 1988, prior on books.
Criminal Records: Access: Mail, in person. Only the court performs in person searches; visitors may not. Search fee: $10.00 per name. Required to search: name, years to search, DOB; also helpful: address, SSN. Criminal records on computer since 1988, prior on books.
General Information: Public Access terminal is available. (Civil only.) No adoptions, sealed cases, juvenile, sex offenders, mental, expunged or dismissed records released. Copy fee: $1.50 for first page, $.25 each add'l. Certification fee: $3.00. Payee: Clerk of Superior Court. Business checks accepted. Prepayment required. Mail turnaround time depends on ease of access, can take up to 2 weeks.

North Carolina Recording Offices

ORGANIZATION: 100 counties, 100 recording offices. The recording officers are Register of Deeds and Clerk of Superior Court (tax liens). The entire state is in the Eastern Time Zone (EST).

REAL ESTATE RECORDS: Counties will not perform real estate searches. Copy fees are usually $1.00 per page. Certification usually costs $5.00 for the first page and $2.00 for each additional page of a document.

UCC RECORDS: This was a dual filing state. Financing statements are were both at the state level and with the Register of Deeds, except for consumer goods, farm related and real estate related collateral. As of 7/1/2001, only real estate related collateral is filed at the county level. All counties will perform UCC searches on the records recorded prior to 7/1/2001. Use search request form UCC-11. Search fees were raised in 2001 to $30.00 per debtor name. Copies usually cost $1.00 per page.

TAX LIEN RECORDS: Federal tax liens on personal property of businesses are filed with the Secretary of State. Other federal and all state tax liens are filed with the county Clerk of Superior Court, not with the Register of Deeds. (Oddly, even tax liens on real property are also filed with the Clerk of Superior Court, not with the Register of Deeds.)

OTHER LIENS: Judgment, mechanics (all at Clerk of Superior Court).

ONLINE ACCESS: A growing number of counties offer free access to assessor and real estate records via the web.

Alamance County

Register of Deeds, PO Box 837, Graham, NC 27253. **Phone**-336-570-6565, R/E Recording-336-228-1312; hours 8AM-5PM. Will search UCC records prior to 7/2001 and current fixture (land) files. Search per debtor- $30.00. Will not search real estate records. UCC copy- $1.00 per page. Cert fee: $5.00 per cert. Payee: Alamance County Register of Deeds. **Other phones:** Assessor-336-228-1318; Treasurer-336-570-1318.

Alexander County

Register of Deeds, 75 1st St SW, #1, Taylorsville, NC 28681-2504. **Phone**-828-632-3152, R/E Recording-704-632-3152; fax-828-632-1119; hours 8AM-5PM Will search UCC records prior to 7/2001 and current fixture (land) files. Will not search real estate records. UCC copy- $1.00 per page. Cert fee: $5.00 1st pg, $1.00 each add'l. Payee: Alexander County Register of Deeds.

Alleghany County

Register of Deeds, PO Box 186, Sparta, NC 28675. **Phone**-Register of Deeds, R/E & UCC Recording- 336-372-4342; fax-336-372-2061; hours 8AM-5PM www.allcorod.com Will search UCC records prior to 7/2001 and current fixture (land) files. Search per debtor- $30.00. Will not search real estate records. RE record copy- $.25 per copy. UCC copy- $1.00 per page. Cert fee: $3.00 1st pg, $2.00 each add'l. Payee: County Register of Deeds. **Online Access to Real Estate, Grantor/Grantee, Property, GIS records:** Access to the Register of Deeds database is free at www.allcorod.com. Click on "View & Search records online." Records go back to 1/1/1993. Also, search for property data on a GIS site at http://arcims.webgis.net/nc/Alleghany/default.asp. Name search- click on magnifying glass with ? in it. **Other phones:** Assessor-336-372-8291; Treasurer-336-372-4179; Appraiser-336-372-8291; Elections-336-372-4557; Vital Records-336-372-4342.

Anson County

Register of Deeds, PO Box 352, Wadesboro, NC 28170-0352. **Phone**-Register of Deeds, R/E & UCC Recording- 704-694-3212, UCC Recording-704-694-7594; fax-704-694-6135; hours 8:30AM-5PM www.co.anson.nc.us/services.php Will search UCC records prior to 7/2001 and current fixture (land) files. Search per debtor- $30.00. Will not search real estate records. RE record copy- $.50 per page. UCC copy- $1.00 per page. Cert fee: $5.00 per cert for 1st 10 pages, $2.00 each add'ls. Payee: Anson County Register of Deeds. **Online Access to Assessor, Real Estate, 911 Address Converter, Tax Collection records:** Records on the county Online Tax Inquiry System are free at www.co.anson.nc.us/pubcgi/taxinq. There is a tax collections search at www.co.anson.nc.us/pubcg i/colinq/. Also, there is an 911 address converter at www.co.anson.nc.us/pubcgi/911addresslookup/. **Other phones:** Assessor-704-694-2918; Treasurer-704-694-6219; Appraiser-704-694-3072; Elections-704-694-7593; Vital Records-704-694-7593.

Ashe County

Register of Deeds, 150 Government Circle, #2300, Jefferson, NC 28640. **Phone**-Register of Deeds, R/E & UCC Recording- 336-219-2540; fax-336-219-2564; hours 8AM-4:30PM. ll search UCC records prior to 7/2001 and current fixture (land) files. Search per debtor- $30.00. Will not search real estate records. RE record copy- $.25 per page. UCC copy- $1.00 per page. Cert fee: $5.00 1st page, $2.00 each add'l. Payee: Ashe County Register of Deeds. **Online Access to Assessor, Real Estate, Grantor/Grantee, Property records:** Access to the register of deeds real estate data is free at www.ashencrod.org/Opening.asp. Full index goes back to 1/1995; images to 3/1979. Also, access to records on the county Tax Parcel Information System is free at http://arcims2.webgis.net/ashe/default.asp. Click on the "Search" button. **Other phones:** Assessor-336-219-2554; Treasurer-336-219-2560; Elections-336-219-2570; Vital Records-336-219-2540.

Avery County

Register of Deeds, PO Box 87, Newland, NC 28657. **Phone**-828-733-8260; fax-828-733-8261; hours 8AM-4:30PM www.averyrod.com Will search UCC records prior to 7/2001 and current fixture (land) files. Search per debtor- $38.00. Will not search real estate records. RE record copy- $.25 per page. UCC copy- $1.00 per page. Cert fee: $3.00 per cert. Payee: Avery County Register of Deeds. **Online Access to Recording, Grantor/Grantee, Property records:** Search the recorders database free at www.averyrod.com/view/disclaimer.html. Also, search for property info on the GIS site free at http://arcims2.webgis.net/avery/default.asp. To name search- click on magnifying glass with ? in it. **Other phones:** Assessor-828-733-8216; Treasurer-828-732-8200.

Beaufort County

Register of Deeds, PO Box 514, Washington, NC 27889. **Phone**-Register of Deeds, R/E & UCC Recording- 252-946-2323; hours 8:30AM-5PM Will search UCC records prior to 7/2001. Search per debtor- $30.00. Will not search real estate records. RE record copy- $.25 per page. UCC copy- $1.00 per page. Cert fee: $5.00 1st page; $2.00 each add'l. Payee: County Register of Deeds. Other phones: Vital Records-252-946-2323.

Bertie County

Register of Deeds, PO Box 340, Windsor, NC 27983. **Phone**-252-794-5309; fax-252-794-5374; hours 8:30AM-5PM. Will search UCC records prior to 7/2001 and current fixture (land) files. Search per debtor- $30.00. Will not search real estate records. UCC copy- $1.00 per copy. **Other phones:** Assessor-252-794-5310; Elections-252-794-5306; Vital Records-252-794-5309.

Bladen County

Register of Deeds, PO Box 247, Elizabethtown, NC 28337. **Phone**-Register of Deeds, R/E & UCC Recording- 910-862-6710; fax-910-862-6714. Will search UCC records prior to 7/2001 and current fixture (land) files. Search per debtor- $30.00. Will not search real estate records. RE record copy- $.25 per page. UCC copy- $1.00 per page. Cert fee: $5.00 1st page; $2.00 each add'l. Payee: Register of Deeds. **Other phones:** Assessor-910-862-6748.

Brunswick County

Register of Deeds, PO Box 87, Bolivia, NC 28422-0087. **Phone**-877-625-9310, 910-253-2690, fax-910-253-2703. http://rod.brunsco.net Will search UCC records prior to 7/2001 and current fixture (land) files. Search per debtor- $30.00. Will not search real estate records. **Online Access to Recording, Deed, Lien, Property Tax records:** Access to the recorder database is free at http://rod.brunsco.net. Free registration, logon and password are required. Records updated 3 times a month. Also, search the tax administration data for free at www.brunsconctax.org/. **Other phones:** Assessor-910-253-4351; Treasurer-910-253-4331.

Buncombe County

Register of Deeds, 60 Court Plaza, Rm 110, Asheville, NC 28801-3563. **Phone**-828-250-4300, R/E Recording-828-250-4305, UCC Recording-828-250-

4302; fax-828-255-5829; hours 8:30AM-5PM www.buncombecounty.org

Will search UCC records prior to 7/2001 and current fixture (land) files. Search per debtor- $30.00. Will not search real estate records. UCC copy- $1.00 per page. **Online Access to Assessor, Property Tax, Real Estate, Recording, Marriage, Death, Corporation, Fictitious Name, Deed records:** Access to county Register of Deeds records is free at http://registerofdeeds.buncombe county.org/resolution/login.asp. Free registration is required; includes marriages, deaths, fictitious names, deeds. Access to county property information is free at www.buncombegis.org/owner.htm. This is an owner search on the gis-mapping system. Also, county assessor tax records are free at www.buncombetax.org. http://registerofdeeds.buncombecounty.org/resolution/login.asp. **Other phones:** Assessor-828-250-4940; Appraiser-828-250-4900; Elections-828-250-4200; Vital Records-828-250-4301.

Burke County

Register of Deeds, PO Box 936, Morganton, NC 28680. **Phone-**Register of Deeds, R/E- 828-438-5450, UCC Recording-828-438-5456; fax-828-438-5463; hours 8AM-5PM www.co.burke.nc.us

Will search UCC records prior to 7/2001 and current fixture (land) files. Search per debtor- $30.00. Will not search real estate records. UCC copy- $1.00 per page. Payee: Burke County Register of Deeds. **Online Access to Property, Assessor records:** Access to the property information is free on the GIS mapping site at http://arcims.webg is.net/nc/Burke/default.asp. Name search- click on magnifying glass with ? in it. **Other phones:** Assessor-828-438-5444; Treasurer-828-438-5446; Appraiser-828-438-5403; Elections-828-433-1703; Vital Records-828-438-5453; Liens/Judgments-828-432-2804.

Cabarrus County

Register of Deeds, PO Box 707, Concord, NC 28026. **Phone-**704-920-2112; fax-704-920-2898; hours 8AM-5PM www.co.cabarrus.nc.us

Will search UCC records prior to 7/2001. Search per debtor- $30.00. Will not search real estate records. Cert fee: $5.00 1st page, $2.00 each add'l. **Online Access to Assessor, Real Estate, Recorder, Deed, Lien, Grantor/Grantee, UCC, Tax Roll records:** Access to the recorder records is free at www.cabarrusncrod.org by two methods: full system or image-only system. You can name search the former; book & page number required for the latter. Land records go back to 1983; images to 2001. Also, search the tax assessor database for free online at http://166.82.128.222/ParcelInfo.html. Also, search the tax bill scroll for free at http://co.cabarrus.nc.us/TaxScroll/index.html. **Other phones:** Assessor-704-920-2166.

Caldwell County

Register of Deeds, 905 West Ave N.W., County Office Bldg., Lenoir, NC 28645. **Phone-**828-757-1399, R/E Recording-828-757-1311, UCC Recording-828-757-1311; fax-828-757-1294; hours 8:00AM-5:00PM www.co.caldwell.nc.us

Will search UCC records prior to 7/2001 and current fixture (land) files. Search per debtor- $30.00. Will not search real estate records. UCC copy- $1.00 per page. Cert fee: $5.00 1st page, $2.00 each add'l. Payee: Register of Deeds. **Online Access to Property, Assessor, Real Estate, Birth, Death, Marriage, Notary, Business Name records:** Records on the county GIS map server site are free at http://maps.co.caldwell.nc.us. Click on "Start Spatial-data Explorer" then find query field at bottom of next page. Also, access to register of deeds recording data is for free at http://rod.co.caldwell.nc.us/resolution/.

Choose advanced or simple search; online registration is required. **Other phones:** Vital Records-828-757-1310.

Camden County

Register of Deeds, PO Box 190, Camden, NC 27921. **Phone-**252-338-1919; hours 8AM-5PM

Will search UCC records prior to 7/2001 and current fixture (land) files. Search per debtor- $38.00. Real estate record owner searches available. UCC copy- $1.00 per page. Cert fee: $5.00. Payee: Camden County Register of Deeds. **Other phones:** Assessor-252-338-0066.

Carteret County

Register of Deeds, Courthouse Sq, Beaufort, NC 28516-1898. **Phone-**Register of Deeds, R/E & UCC Recording- 252-728-8474; fax-252-728-7693; hours 8AM-5PM. Will search UCC records prior to 7/2001 and current fixture (land) files. Search per debtor- $38.00. Will not search real estate records. UCC copy- $1.00 per page. Cert fee: $5.00 add'l $2.00 per page. Payee: Carteret County Register of Deeds. **Other phones:** Vital Records-252-728-8474.

Caswell County

Register of Deeds, PO Box 98, Yanceyville, NC 27379. **Phone-**336-694-4197; fax-336-694-1405; 8AM-5PM Will search UCC records prior to 7/2001 and current fixture (land) files. Search per debtor- $30.00. Will not search real estate or tax lien records. RE record copy- $.50 per page. UCC copy- $1.00 per page. Cert fee: $5.00 1st pg, $2.00 each add'l. Payee: Caswell County Register of Deeds.

Catawba County

Register of Deeds, PO Box 65, Newton, NC 28658-0065. **Phone-**828-465-1573; hours 8AM-5PM www.co.catawba.nc.us

Will search UCC records prior to 7/2001 and current fixture (land) files. Search per debtor- $38.00. Will not search real estate records. UCC copy- $2.00 per page. Cert fee: $5.00 1st page, $2.00 each add'l. Payee: Catawba County Register of Deeds. **Online Access to Assessor, Property, Grantor/Grantee, Real Estate, Deed records:** Records on the County Geographic Info System database are free at www.gis.catawba.nc.us/. Click on "Online Mapping" then choose "Real Estate" then search using query fields. Also, access to the register of deeds online deed information is at http://204.211.226.33/rod/index.html. **Other phones:** Assessor-828-465-8421; Elections-828-464-2424.

Chatham County

Register of Deeds, PO Box 756, Pittsboro, NC 27312. **Phone-**Register of Deeds, R/E & UCC Recording- 919-542-8235; hours 8AM-4:30PM

Will search UCC records prior to 7/2001 and current fixture (land) files. Search per debtor- $30.00. Will not search real estate records. RE record copy- $.25 per page. UCC copy- $1.00 per page. Cert fee: $5.00 1st pg, $2.00 each add'l. Payee: Chatham County Register of Deeds. **Other phones:** Assessor-919-542-8250; Treasurer-919-542-8210; Appraiser-919-542-8287; Elections-919-542-8206; Vital Records-919-542-8235; County Manager-919-542-8200.

Cherokee County

Register of Deeds, 53 Peachtree St, Murphy, NC 28906. **Phone-**Register of Deeds 828-837-2613; fax-828-837-8414. www.cherokeecounty-nc.org

Will search UCC records prior to 7/2001 and current fixture (land) files. Search per debtor- $30.00. Will not search real estate records. RE record copy- $.25 per page. Cert fee: $5.00 per doc. **Online Access to Real Estate records:** At present, the county offers only a GIS mapping site for searching for parcel and property information at

http://204.211.88.251/index.htm. There is no name searching and search tools are limited. **Other phones:** Assessor-828-837-6626; Elections-828-837-6670.

Chowan County

Register of Deeds, PO Box 487, Edenton, NC 27932-0487. **Phone-**252-482-2619; hours 8AM-5PM Will search UCC records prior to 7/2001 and current fixture (land) files. Search per debtor- $38.00. Will not search real estate records. RE record copy- $.50 per page. UCC copy- $2.00 per page. Cert fee: $5.00 1st pg, $2.00 each add'l. Payee: Chowan County Register of Deeds.

Clay County

Register of Deeds, PO Box 118, Hayesville, NC 28904. **Phone-**828-389-0087; fax-828-389-9749; 8AM-5PM Will search UCC records prior to 7/2001 and current fixture (land) files. Search per debtor- $30.00. Will not search real estate records. RE record copy- $.25 per page. UCC copy- $1.00 per page. Cert fee: $5.00 1st pg, $2.00 each add'l. Payee: Clay County Register of Deeds. **Other phones:** Assessor-828-389-1266.

Cleveland County

Register of Deeds, PO Box 1210, Shelby, NC 28151-1210. **Phone-**Register of Deeds, R/E & UCC Recording- 704-484-4834; fax-704-484-4909; hours 8AM-5PM www.clevelandcounty.com

Will search UCC records prior to 7/2001 and current fixture (land) files. Search per debtor- $30.00. Will not search real estate records. Copy fee is $1.00 per page. **Online Access to Real Estate, Assessor, Real Estate, Grantor/Grantee records:** Access to property information on a gis mapping site is free at http://arcims2.webgis.net/nc/Cleveland/default.asp. Also, access to register of deeds grantor/grantee index is free at http://cleveland.parker-lowe.net/view/softlic.html. **Other phones:** Assessor-704-484-4847; Treasurer-704-484-4807; Vital Records-704-484-4834.

Columbus County

Register of Deeds, PO Box 1086, Whiteville, NC 28472-1086. **Phone-**910-640-6625; fax-910-640-2547; hours 8:30AM-5PM. Will not search UCC or real estate records. UCC copy- $1.00 per page. Cert fee: $5.00. Payee: Columbus County Register of Deeds. **Online Access to Recording, Deed, Lien, Real Estate, Assumed Name, Corporation, UCC records:** Access to the Recorder's database is free at http://198.143.202.5/. User-ID is "public" and you should be able to logon for free. **Other phones:** Assessor-910-640-6635.

Craven County

Register of Deeds, 226 Pollock St, New Bern, NC 28560. **Phone-**Register of Deeds, R/E & UCC Recording- 252-636-6617; fax-252-636-1937; hours 8AM-5PM www.co.craven.nc.us

Will search UCC records prior to 7/2001 and current fixture (land) files. Search per debtor- $30.00. Will not search real estate records. RE record copy- $.25 per page. UCC copy- $1.00 per page. Cert fee: $5.00 per doc. Payee: Register of Deeds. **Online Access to Real Estate, Recording, Deed, Tax Assessor, Boat, Mobile Home, Foreclosure, GIS records:** Access to the county Public Inquiry System is free at www.co.craven.nc.us/depts/reg/regwwwdis claimer.htm. Also, access to assessor and property data is at http://gismaps2.cravencounty.com/maps/map.asp. **Other phones:** Assessor-252-636-6605; Treasurer-252-636-6603; Appraiser-252-636-6640; Elections-252-636-6610; Vital Records-252-636-6617.

Cumberland County

Register of Deeds, PO 2039, Fayetteville, NC 28302-2039. **Phone-**910-678-7775, R/E Recording-910-678-

7783, UCC Recording-910-678-7718; fax-910-323-1456; hours 8AM-5PM www.ccrod.org

Will search UCC records prior to 7/2001 and current fixture (land) files. Search per debtor- $30.00. Will not search real estate records. UCC copy- $1.00 per page. Cert fee: $5.00 1st pg, $2.00 each add'l. Payee: Cumberland County Register of Deeds. **Online Access to Land, Deed, Recording, UCC, Property Tax, Assessor records:** Search two systems free at www.ccrodinternet.org. The land records index and images go back to 1978; images go back to 1/21/1972; UCCs are from 1995 to June 29, 2001. Also, the county tax assessor real estate search is free at http://mainfr.co.cumberland.nc.us/oasearch.htm. **Other phones:** Assessor-910-678-7507; Elections-910-678-7733; Vital Records-910-678-7767.

Currituck County

Register of Deeds, PO Box 71, Currituck, NC 27929. **Phone-**252-232-3297; fax-252-232-3906; 8AM-5PM Will search UCC records prior to 7/2001. Search per debtor- $30.00. Will not search real estate records. RE record copy- $.25 per page. $1.00 per page to mail. UCC copy- $1.00 per page. Cert fee: $5.00 per cert, $2.00 per page. Payee: Currituck County Register of Deeds. **Other phones:** Assessor-252-232-3005.

Dare County

Register of Deeds, PO Box 70, Manteo, NC 27954. **Phone-**252-473-3438, R/E Recording-252-475-5970, UCC Recording-252-475-5970; hours 8:30AM-5PM www.co.dare.nc.us

Will search UCC records prior to 7/2001 and current fixture (land) files. Search per debtor- $38.00. Will not search real estate records. RE record copy- $.25 per page. UCC copy- $1.00 per page. Cert fee: $5.00 per cert. Payee: County Register of Deeds. **Online Access to Assessor, Real Estate, Marriage, UCC records:** Assessor records are at www.co.dare.nc.us/public/TaxInquiry.htm. Other records are free at www.co.dare.nc.us/public/index.htm. Real estate from 1976 forward, UCC from 1989 forward, and marriage 1990 forward. Tax files can be downloaded. **Other phones:** Assessor-252-475-5952; Treasurer-252-475-5930; Appraiser-252-475-5940; Elections-252-475-5630; Vital Records-252-475-5970.

Davidson County

Register of Deeds, PO Box 464, Lexington, NC 27293-0464. **Phone-**Register of Deeds, R/E & UCC Recording- 336-242-2150; fax-336-238-2318; hours 8AM-5PM www.co.davidson.nc.us

Will search UCC records prior to 7/2001 and current fixture (land) files. Search per debtor- $30.00. Will not search real estate records. RE record copy- $1.00 1st page, $.25 each add'l. Copy fee is $1.00 per page. Cert fee: $5.00 per doc. Payee: Register of deeds. **Online Access to Property, Assessor, Real Estate records:** Records on the county Tax Department database are free at www.co.davidson.nc.us/dc/. Click on County Tax Records. Also, search for property info on the GIS site for free at http://arcims2.webgis.net/davidson/default.asp. Name search- click on magnifying glass with ? in it. **Other phones:** Vital Records-336-242-2150.

Davie County

Register of Deeds, 123 S. Main St, Mocksville, NC 27028. **Phone-**336-634-2513; hours 8:30AM-5PM www.co.davie.nc.us

Will search UCC records prior to 7/2001. Search per debtor- $30.00. Will not search real estate records. RE record copy- $.25 per page. UCC copy- $.25 per page. Cert fee: $5.00 1st pg, $2.00 each add'l. Payee: Davie County Register of Deeds. **Online Access to Real Estate, GIS-mapping records:** Access to county property data on the GIS-mapping site

is free at www.roktech.net/DavieNC/. Click on "Start Spatial Data Explorer" then search at bottom of page. **Other phones:** Assessor-336-634-3416.

Duplin County

Register of Deeds, PO Box 970, Kenansville, NC 28349. **Phone-**Register of Deeds, R/E & UCC Recording- 910-296-2108; fax-910-296-2344; hours 8AM-5PM http://rod.duplincounty.org

Will search UCC records prior to 7/2001 and current fixture (land) files. Search per debtor- $30.00. Will not search real estate records. UCC copy- $1.00 per page. Cert fee: $5.00 1st page; $2.00 each add'l. Payee: Register of Deeds. **Online Access to Real Property, Deed, Lien, Judgment, Mortgage, Marriage, Death, Notary, Military Discharge records:** Access to the Register's multiple databases is free at http://rod.duplincounty.org. **Other phones:** Assessor-910-296-2110; Appraiser-910-296-2110; Elections-910-296-2170; Vital Records-910-296-2108.

Durham County

Register of Deeds, PO Box 1107, Durham, NC 27702. **Phone-**919-560-0494, R/E Recording-919-560-0480, UCC Recording-919-560-0480; fax-919-560-0497; hours 8:30AM-5PM www.co.durham.nc.us/rgds

Will search UCC records prior to 7/2001. Search per debtor- $30.00. Will not search real estate records. RE record copy- $1.00 per page. Copy fee is $1.00 per page. Cert fee: $5.00 1st page, $2.00 per add'l. Payee: Register of Deeds. **Online Access to Real Estate, Deed, Judgment, Recording, Voter Registration records:** Access to the Register of Deeds database is free at http://207.4.222.118. Access to tax assessor data is free at www.co.durham.nc.us/departments/txad/TaxDB/. Also, search property records from the GIS mapping site free at http://gisweb2.ci.durham.nc.us/sdx/. After the disclaimer, click on "Spatial Data Explorer" to search. Also, search voter registration free at www.co.durham.nc.us/departments/elec/votersearch/VoterRecSearch.cfm. **Other phones:** Assessor-919-560-0300; Vital Records-919-560-7670 (births/deaths); Vital Records (Marriages)-919-560-0480.

Edgecombe County

Register of Deeds, PO Box 386, Tarboro, NC 27886. **Phone-**Register of Deeds, R/E & UCC Recording- 252-641-7924; fax-252-641-1771; hours 7:30AM-5:00PM Will search UCC records file fixture only - search not available after 7/2001. Search per debtor- $38.00 1-2 pcs, 3-10 $45.00, Will not search real estate records. RE record copy- $1.00 2st page; $.05 each add'l if SASE provided. UCC copy- $1.00 per page. Cert fee: $5.00 1st page; $2.00 each add'l. Payee: Register of Deeds. **Other phones:** Assessor-252-641-7855; Treasurer-252-641-7834; Appraiser-252-641-7858; Elections-252-641-7854; Vital Records-252-641-7924.

Forsyth County

Register of Deeds, PO Box 20639, Winston-Salem, NC 27120-0639. **Phone-**336-727-2903; fax-336-727-2341; hours 8AM-5PM. Will search UCC records prior to 7/2001 and current fixture (land) files. Search per debtor- $30.00. Will not search real estate records. UCC copy- $1.00 per page. Cert fee: $5.00. Payee: County Register of Deeds. **Online Access to Real Estate, Land, Lien records:** Access to the county Geo-Data Explorer database is free online at http://maps.co.forsyth.nc.us. Address and Parcel ID searching only. Includes Board of Adjustment and building permit records. Also, Register of Deed records are on CD-ROM. Also, search tax liens by name lists free at www.co.forsyth.nc.u s/tax/header.htm. Also, access to property and deeds indexes and images is via a private company at www.titlesearcher.com or support@TitleSearcher.com. Fee/registration required;

monthly and per day access available. **Other phones:** Assessor-336-727-2513; Treasurer-336-727-2655.

Franklin County

Register of Deeds, PO Box 545, Louisburg, NC 27549-0545. **Phone-**Register of Deeds, R/E & UCC Recording- 919-496-3500; fax-919-496-1457; hours 8AM-5PM www.co.franklin.nc.us

Will search UCC records prior to 7/2001 and current fixture (land) files. Search per debtor- $30.00. Will not search real estate records. RE record copy- $.25 per page. UCC copy- $1.00 per page. **Online Access to Real Property records:** Access to the county spatial data explorer database is free at www.co.franklin.nc.us/docs/frame_tax.htm. Search the gis map or click on "text search" for name searching. **Other phones:** Assessor-919-496-1497; Elections-919-496-3710.

Gaston County

Register of Deeds, PO Box 1578, Gastonia, NC 28053. **Phone-**R/E Recording-704-866-3181, UCC Recording-704-862-7583; fax-704-862-7519; 8:30AM-5PM

Will search UCC records prior to 7/2001 and current fixture (land) files. Search per debtor- $30.00. Will not search real estate records. Copy fee is $1.00 per page. Cert fee: $5.00 for 1st pg., $2.00 each add'l pg. Payee: Gaston County Register of Deeds. **Other phones:** Assessor-704-810-5838; Treasurer-704-866-3034; Appraiser-704-810-5809; Elections-704-864-5858; Vital Records-704-862-7687; Deed Room-704-862-7683.

Gates County

Register of Deeds, PO Box 471, Gatesville, NC 27938-0471. **Phone-**Register of Deeds, R/E & UCC Recording- 252-357-0850; fax-252-357-0850; hours 9AM-5PM. Will search UCC records prior to 7/2001 and current fixture (land) files. Search per debtor- $30.00. Will not search real estate records. **Other phones:** Assessor-252-357-1360; Treasurer-252-357-1240; Appraiser-252-357-1360; Elections-252-357-1780; Vital Records-252-357-0850.

Graham County

Register of Deeds, PO Box 406, Robbinsville, NC 28771-0406. **Phone-**Register of Deeds, R/E & UCC Recording- 828-479-7971; fax-828-479-7988. Will not search records. UCC copy- $1.00 per page. **Other phones:** Assessor-828-479-7965; Treasurer-828-479-7962; Appraiser-828-479-7963; Elections-828-479-7969; Vital Records-828-479-7971.

Granville County

Register of Deeds, PO Box 427, Oxford, NC 27565. **Phone-**Register of Deeds, R/E & UCC Recording- 919-693-6314; hours 8:30am-5PM

Will search UCC records prior to 7/2001. Search per debtor- $30.00. Will not search real estate records. RE record copy- $1.00 1st page, $.25 each add'l. UCC copy- $1.00 per page. Cert fee: $5.00 1st page, $2.00 each add'l. Payee: Register of Deeds. **Other phones:** Assessor-919-693-4181; Treasurer-919-603-1301 (Finance); Elections-919-693-2515; Vital Records-919-693-6314.

Greene County

Register of Deeds, PO Box 86, Snow Hill, NC 28580. **Phone-**252-747-3620, R/E Recording-919-747-3620; hours 8AM-5PM. Will search UCC records prior to 7/2001 and current fixture (land) files. Search per debtor- $30.00. Will not search real estate records. UCC copy- $1.00 per page. Cert fee: $5.00 1st pg, $2.00 each add'l. Payee: Greene County Register of Deeds.

Guilford County

Register of Deeds, PO Box 1467, High Point, NC 27261-1467. **Phone**-Register of Deeds 336-845-7931; 8AM-5PM www.co.guilford.nc.us
Will search UCC records prior to 7/2001 and current fixture (land) files. Search per debtor- $30.00. Will not search real estate records. RE record copy- $1.00 per page (mail request). UCC copy- $1.00 per page. Cert fee: $5.00 1st page, $2.00 each add'l. Payee: Guilford County Register of Deeds. **Online Access to Recorder, Assessor, Property, UCC, Vital Statistic, Military Discharge records:** Access to the county e-gov databases is free at www.co.guilford.nc.us/ego v/index.html. Also, you may search Birth, Death, Marriage, and military records directly at www.co.guilford.nc.us/novation/rodvrpub.html. Search page found at www.co.guilford.nc.us/governme nt/deeds/. **Other phones:** Assessor-336-845-7911; Treasurer-336-845-7911; Appraiser-336-845-3330; Elections-336-845-3836; Vital Records-336-845-7931.

Halifax County

Register of Deeds, PO Box 67, Halifax, NC 27839-0067. **Phone**-Register of Deeds, R/E & UCC Recording- 252-583-2101; fax-252-583-1273; hours 8:30AM-5PM www.halifaxnc.com/halinav.html
Will search UCC records prior to 7/2001 and current fixture (land) files. Search per debtor- $30.00. Will not search real estate records. RE record copy- $.25 per page. Cert fee: $5.00 1st page, $2.00 each add'l. Payee: Register of Deeds. **Other phones:** Assessor-252-583-2121; Treasurer-252-583-3771; Elections-252-583-4391; Vital Records-252-583-2101.

Harnett County

Register of Deeds, PO Box 279, Lillington, NC 27546. **Phone**-Register of Deeds, R/E & UCC Recording- 910-893-7540; fax-910-814-3841; hours 8AM-5PM www.harnett.org/harnett/departments/rod.html
Will search UCC records prior to 7/2001 and current fixture (land) files. Search per debtor- $30.00. Will not search real estate records. RE record copy- $.10 per page. UCC copy- $1.00 per page. Cert fee: $5.00 1st pg, $2.00 each add'l. Payee: Harnett County Register of Deeds. **Online Access to Real Estate, Grantor/Grantee, Vital Statistic, Military Discharge, UCC records:** County real estate and property tax information is free online at http://rod.harnett.org. Search Births, Deaths, Marriages, military discharges, UCCs and official public records Also, search the GIS/Rel Property database for free at www.harnett.org/sdx/index.html. **Other phones:** Vital Records-910-893-7542.

Haywood County

Register of Deeds, 215 N Main St, Courthouse, Waynesville, NC 28786. **Phone**-Register of Deeds 828-452-6635; fax-828-452-6762; hours 8AM-5PM
Will search UCC records prior to 7/2001 and current fixture (land) files. Search per debtor- $38.00. Will not search real estate records. UCC copy- $1.00 per page. Cert fee: no fee. Payee: Haywood County Register of Deeds. **Online Access to Real Estate, Deed, Property, GIS-mapping records:** Records on the Register of Deeds database are at http://rodweb.gov.co.haywood.nc.us. Real estate records go back to 1986. Also, search for property data on the GIS-mapping site for free at http://lrgis.gov.co.haywood.nc.us/hayweb/haywood.ht ml. **Other phones:** Assessor-828-452-6641; Treasurer-828-452-6643.

Henderson County

Register of Deeds, 200 N. Grove St, #129, Hendersonville, NC 28792. **Phone**-828-697-4901; hours 9AM-5PM

Will search UCC records prior to 7/2001 and current fixture (land) files. Search per debtor- $38.00. Will not search real estate records. UCC copy- $2.00 per page. Cert fee: $5.00. Payee: Henderson County Register of Deeds. **Online Access to Real Estate, GIS-mapping records:** Search property records at the GIS site free at http://gis.hendersoncountync.org/prc/. **Other phones:** Assessor-828-697-4870.

Hertford County

Register of Deeds, PO Box 36, Winton, NC 27986. **Phone**-Register of Deeds, R/E & UCC Recording- 252-358-7850; fax-252-358-7806; hours 8:30AM-5PM
Will search UCC records prior to 7/2001 and current fixture (land) files. Search per debtor- $30.00. Will not search real estate records. **Other phones:** Assessor-252-358-7810; Treasurer-252-358-7815; Elections-252-358-7812; Vital Records-252-358-7850.

Hoke County

Register of Deeds, 113 Campus Ave, Raeford, NC 28376. **Phone**-Register of Deeds, R/E & UCC Recording- 910-875-2035, UCC Recording-910-875-0235; fax-910-875-9554; hours 8AM-5PM
May or may not search UCC records. Search per debtor- $30.00. Will not search real estate records. UCC copy- $1.00 per page. Cert fee: $3.00. Payee: Hoke County Register of Deeds. **Other phones:** Assessor-910-875-8751; Appraiser-910-875-8751; Elections-910-875-8751; Vital Records-910-875-2035.

Hyde County

Register of Deeds, PO Box 294, Swanquarter, NC 27885. **Phone**-252-926-4181, R/E Recording-252-926-3011; fax-252-926-3082.
UCC records search per debtor- $30.00. Will not search real estate records. Payee: Hyde County Register of Deeds. **Online Access to Real Property, Grantor/Grantee records:** Access Register of Deeds real property records free at www.h yderod.com/view/disclaimer.html. **Other phones:** Assessor-252-926-5151; Treasurer-252-926-4101.

Iredell County

Register of Deeds, PO Box 904, Statesville, NC 28687. **Phone**-704-872-7468; fax-704-878-3055; hours 8AM-5PM www.co.iredell.nc.us
Will search UCC records prior to 7/2001 and current fixture (land) files. Search per debtor- $38.00. Will not search real estate records. Copy fee- $1.00 per page. Cert fee: $5.00 1st page, $2.00 each add'l. Payee: Iredell County Register of Deeds. **Other phones:** Assessor-704-872-3021.

Jackson County

Register of Deeds, 401 Grindstaff Cove Rd. #103, Sylva, NC 28779. **Phone**-Register of Deeds, R/E & UCC Recording- 828-586-7530; fax-828-586-6879; hours 8:30AM-5PM www.jacksonnc.org
Will search UCC records prior to 7/2001 and current fixture (land) files. Search per debtor- $30.00. Will not search real estate records. RE record copy- $3.00 per doc; $.30 self-serve. UCC copy- $1.00 per page if mailed; $.30 self-serve. Cert fee: $5.00 1st page; $2.00 each add'l. Payee: Register of Deeds. **Other phones:** Assessor-828-586-4055; Treasurer-828-586-7501; Appraiser-828-586-7542; Vital Records-828-568-7530.

Johnston County

Register of Deeds, Box 118, Smithfield, NC 27577. **Phone**-Register of Deeds, R/E & UCC Recording- 919-989-5160, UCC Recording-919-989-5167; fax-919-989-5728; hours 8AM-5PM www.johnstonnc.com
Will search UCC records prior to 7/2001 and current fixture (land) files. Search per debtor- $30.00. Will not search real estate records. RE record copy- $.10 per page. UCC copy- $1.00 for searches, $.10 per

copy. Cert fee: $5.00 1st pg, $2.00 each add'l. Payee: Johnston County Register of Deeds. **Online Access to Real Estate, UCC, Deed records:** Access to Register's indexes is free at http://johnstonnc.com/deedsearch. Land records go back to 1972; UCCs back to 7/1997. **Other phones:** Elections-919-989-5095; Vital Records-919-989-5160; Deed Vault-919-989-5165.

Jones County

Register of Deeds, PO Box 189, Trenton, NC 28585-0189. **Phone**-252-448-2551; fax-252-448-1357; hours 8AM-5PM www.jonesrod.com
Will search UCC records prior to 7/2001 and current fixture (land) files. Search per debtor- $30.00. Will not search real estate records. RE record copy- $.25 per page. UCC copy- $1.00 per page. Cert fee: $3.00 1st pg, $1.00 each add'l. Payee: County Register of Deeds. **Other phones:** Assessor-252-448-2546; Vital Records-252-448-2551.

Lee County

Register of Deeds, PO Box 2040, Sanford, NC 27331-2040. **Phone**-Register of Deeds, R/E & UCC Recording- 919-774-4821; fax-919-774-5063; hours 8AM-5PM www.leencrod.org
Will not search UCC or real estate records. RE record copy- $.25 per copy. UCC copy- $1.00 per page. Cert fee: $5.00 for 1st pg., $2.00 each add'l pg. Payee: Register of Deeds. **Online Access to Real Estate, Grantor/Grantee, Deed, Lien records:** Access to the Register of Deeds index and images are free at www.leencrod.org/welcome.asp. Land record index goes back to 1985; images to 1971. Plat images goe back to 1975. **Other phones:** Assessor-919-718-4600; Appraiser-919-718-4661; Elections-919-776-0515; Vital Records-919-774-4821.

Lenoir County

Register of Deeds, PO Box 3289, Kinston, NC 28502. **Phone**-Register of Deeds, R/E & UCC Recording- 252-559-6420; fax-252-523-6139; hours 8:30AM-5PM
Will search UCC records prior to 7/2001 and current fixture (land) files. Search per debtor- $30.00. Will not search real estate records. UCC copy- $1.00 per page. **Other phones:** Assessor-252-527-7174; Treasurer-252-527-7174; Vital Records-252-559-6420.

Lincoln County

Register of Deeds, PO Box 218, Lincolnton, NC 28093-0218. **Phone**-704-736-8530, R/E Recording-704-736-8535, UCC Recording-704-736-8533; fax-704-732-9049; 8AM-5PM www.co.lincoln.nc.us/
Will search UCC records prior to 7/2001 and current fixture (land) files. Search per debtor- $30.00. Will not search real estate records. Copy fee- $1.00 per page. Cert fee: $5.00 per doc + $2.00 per page. Payee: Register of Deeds. **Online Access to Real Estate, Deed, Lien, Mapping, UCC, Property Tax records:** Tax and property data is free at http://207.4.172.205/Lincoln_TaxCached.html. Enable browser for Java. Grantor/Grantee indices go back to 1993. Images go back to Book 186. Search either of the 2 databases. Also, access county GIS Land System free at www.co.lincoln.nc.us/County/gisd.htm. At the website, under Data Tools, click on Search. **Other phones:** Assessor-704-736-8540; Elections-704-736-8480; Vital Records-704-736-8530.

Macon County

Register of Deeds, 5 W. Main St, Franklin, NC 28734. **Phone**-828-349-2095, R/E Recording-828-524-6421; fax-828-349-6382.
Will search UCC records prior to 7/2001 and current fixture (land) files. Search per debtor- $30.00. Will not search real estate records. **Online Access to Property, Deed Image records:** Access to county property data is free at

http://63.167.19.252/dbp/deed.asp. **Other phones:** Assessor-828-524-6421; Elections-828-349-2034.

Madison County

Register of Deeds, PO Box 66, Marshall, NC 28753. **Phone**-Register of Deeds, R/E & UCC Recording- 828-649-3131; hours 8:30AM-5PM

UCC records search per debtor- $30.00. Will not search real estate records. RE record copy- $.25 per page. UCC copy- $3.00 1st page, $1.00 each add'l. Cert fee: $5.00 1st pg, $2.00 each add'l. Payee: Madison County Register of Deeds. **Other phones:** Assessor-828-649-3014; Treasurer-828-649-2521; Appraiser-828-649-3014; Elections-828-649-3731; Vital Records-828-649-3131.

Martin County

Register of Deeds, PO Box 348, Williamston, NC 27892. **Phone**-Register of Deeds, R/E & UCC Recording- 252-792-1683; fax-252-792-1684; hours 8AM-5PM

Will search UCC records prior to 7/2001 only. Search per debtor- $30.00. Will not search real estate records. RE record copy- $.25 per sheet. UCC copy- $1.00 per sheet. Cert fee: $5.00 1st page, $2.00 each add'l. Payee: Martin County Register of Deeds. **Other phones:** Assessor-252-792-1031; Elections-252-792-5845; Vital Records-252-792-1683; Collector-252-792-2167.

McDowell County

Register of Deeds, 21 S. Main St, Courthouse, Marion, NC 28752-3992. **Phone**-828-652-4727; fax-828-652-1537; hours 8:30AM-5PM

Will not search UCC or real estate records. UCC copy- $.35 per page. Cert fee: $14.00 add'l $3.00. Payee: McDowell County Clerk. **Online Access to Land, Deed records:** Access to property and deeds indexes and images is via a private company at www.titlesearcher.com. Fee/registration required; see state introduction. Images go back to 1/1971. **Other phones:** Assessor-828-652-7121; Treasurer-828-652-7121; Elections-828-652-7121; Vital Records-828-652-4727.

Mecklenburg County

Register of Deeds, 720 E. 4th St, #103, Charlotte, NC 28202. **Phone**-704-336-2443; fax-704-336-7699; hours 8:30AM-4:30PM http://meckrod.hartic.com

Will search UCC records prior to 7/2001 and current fixture (land) files. Search per debtor- $30.00. Tax liens with Clerk of Superior Court and County Tax Dept. Will not search real estate records. UCC copy- $1.00 per page. Cert fee: $4.00 1st pg, $2.00 each add'l. Payee: Mecklenburg County Register of Deeds, **Online Access to Assessor, Real Estate, Grantor/Grantee, Judgment, Lien, Vital Statistic, Personal Property, Accident Report records:** Access to birth, death, marriage, recordings, judgments, liens, and grantor/grantee indices are free at http://meckrod.hartic.com/default.asp. There is also a real estate lookup at http://meckcama.co.meckl enburg.nc.us/relookup/. Also, online access to the assessors records for real estate, personal property, and tax bills are free at http://mcmf.co.mecklenb urg.nc.us:3007/cics/txar/txar00i/. The sheriff's inmate lookup is at http://mcmf.co.mecklenburg.nc.us:3007/ cjjl01w/cjjl/webnull. Search warrants at http://mcmf.co.mecklenburg.nc.us:3007/cjcr01w/cjjl/we bnull. Accident reports are at http://accident.ci.charlotte.nc.us/index.htm.

Mitchell County

Register of Deeds, 26 Crimson Laurel Cir. #4, Bakersville, NC 28705-9510. **Phone**-828-688-2139, R/E Recording-828-688-2139 x118, UCC Recording-828-688-2139 x118; fax-828-688-3666; 8AM-5PM

Will search UCC records prior to 7/2001 and current fixture (land) files. Search per debtor- $30.00. Will not search real estate records. Record copy- $1.00 per page. Cert fee: $5.00 for 1st page, $2 each add'l. Payee: Mitchell County Register of Deeds. **Other phones:** Assessor-828-688-2139 x115; Treasurer-828-688-2139 x125; Appraiser-828-688-2139 x115; Elections-828-688-3101; Vital Records-828-688-2139 x118.

Montgomery County

Register of Deeds, PO Box 695, Troy, NC 27371-0695. **Phone**-Register of Deeds, R/E & UCC Recording- 910-576-4271; fax-910-576-2209; hours 8AM-5PM

Will search UCC records prior to 7/2001 and current fixture (land) files. Search per debtor- $30.00. Will not search real estate records. RE record copy- $.25 per page. UCC copy- $1.00 per page. Cert fee: $5.00 1st pg, $3.00 each add'l. Payee: Montgomery County Register of Deeds. **Other phones:** Assessor-910-576-4311; Treasurer-910-572-4221; Appraiser-910-576-4311; Elections-910-572-2024; Vital Records-910-576-4271.

Moore County

Register of Deeds, PO Box 1210, Carthage, NC 28327. **Phone**-910-947-6370, R/E Recording-910-947-6372, UCC Recording-910-947-6372; fax-910-947-6396; hours 8AM-5PM www.co.moore.nc.us

Will search UCC records prior to 7/2001 and current fixture (land) files through 6/30/01. Search per debtor- $30.00. Will not search real estate records. UCC copy- $1.00 per copy. **Online Access to Real Estate, Lien, Grantor/Grantee, Vital Statistic, DD214, Property Tax, Land Record, Restaurant Grade records:** Access to the recorder's Online Public Records (OPR) database is free at http://rod.co.moore.nc.us/nc32. Also, access to county deed, property and tax data is free online at www.co.moore.nc.us/main/page.asp?rec=/pages/proper tyinfo/propertyinfo.asp. Also, check county restaurant grades at www.co.moore.nc.us/main/page.asp?re c=/pages/rgrades/restrt.asp. **Other phones:** Treasurer-910-947-6310; Appraiser-910-947-6412; Elections-910-947-3868; Vital Records-910-947-6370.

Nash County

Register of Deeds, PO Box 974, Nashville, NC 27856. **Phone**-Register of Deeds, R/E & UCC Recording- 252-459-9836, UCC Recording-252-459-9825; fax-252-459-9889; hours-8AM-4:30PM www.deeds.co.nash.nc.us/resolution

Will search UCC records prior to 7/2001 and current fixture (land) files. Search per debtor- $38.00. Will not search real estate records. Copy fee- $1.00 per page. Cert fee: $5.00 1st page, $2.00 each add'l. **Other phones:** Assessor-252-459-9824; Vital Records-252-459-9839.

New Hanover County

Register of Deeds, 216 N. 2nd St., Wilmington, NC 28401. **Phone**-Register of Deeds, R/E & UCC Recording- 910-798-4530; fax-910-798-4586; hours 8AM-5PM www.nhcgov.com

Until further notice, real estate records are located at 216 N 2nd St. Will search UCC records prior to 7/2001 and current fixture (land) files. Search per debtor- $30.00. No tax liens filed here; contact Clerk of Superior Court. Will not search real estate records. Record copy fee- $1.00 per page. Cert fee: $5.00 1st page; $2.00 each add'l. **Online Access to Real Estate, Assessor, Grantor/Grantee, Lien, UCC, Judgment, Marriage, Military Discharge records:** Access to the Register of Deeds database is free at http://srvrodweb.nhcgov.com. Also, online access to the real estate tax database is free at www.nhcgov.com/Oasinq/Oasinput.jsp. Also, you may search for property information on the GIS-mappings

site at www.nhcgov.com/GIS/GISservices.asp. **Other phones:** Elections-910-798-4060; Vital Records-910-798-4547.

Northampton County

Register of Deeds, PO Box 128, Jackson, NC 27845. **Phone**-252-534-2511; fax-252-534-1580; 8AM-5PM

Will search UCC records prior to 7/2001 and current fixture (land) files. Search per debtor- $30.00. Will not search real estate records. RE record copy- $.25 per page. UCC copy- $1.00 per page. Cert fee: $5.00 1st pg, $2.00 each add'l. Payee: Northampton County Register of Deeds. **Other phones:** Assessor-252-534-2511.

Onslow County

Register of Deeds, 109 Old Bridge St, Jacksonville, NC 28540. **Phone**-910-347-3451; fax-910-347-3340; hours 8AM-5PM http://co.onslow.nc.us/register_of_deeds

Will search UCC records prior to 7/2001 and current fixture (land) files. Search per debtor- $30.00. Will not search real estate records. UCC copy- $1.00 per page. Cert fee: $5.00 1st page, $2 each add'l. Payee: Onslow County Register of Deeds. **Online Access to Real Estate records:** Access is to property information is free at www.roktech.net/onslow/. Enter the site and name search using the advanced search in the Parcel Query box.

Orange County

Register of Deeds, PO Box 8181, Hillsborough, NC 27278-8181. **Phone**-919-732-8181, R/E Recording-919-245-2675; fax-919-644-3018; hours 8AM-5PM www.co.orange.nc.us/deeds/

Will search UCC records prior to 7/2001 and current fixture (land) files. Search per debtor- $38.00 3 pgs, $45.00 3-10 pgs, $2.00 each add'l pg. Will not search real estate records. UCC copy- $1.00 per page. Cert fee: $5.00 1st 5 pages, $.50 each add'l. **Online Access to Property records:** Access to property records on the GIS mapping site is free at http://gis.co.orange.n c.us/gisdisclaimer.htm. **Other phones:** Assessor-919-245-2101; Elections-919-245-2350.

Pamlico County

Register of Deeds, PO Box 433, Bayboro, NC 28515. **Phone**-252-745-4421; hours 8AM-5PM

Will search UCC records prior to 7/2001 and current fixture (land) files. Search per debtor- $30.00. Will not search real estate records. RE record copy- $.25 per page. UCC copy- $1.00 per page. Cert fee: $5.00 1st pg, $2.00 each add'l. Payee: Pamlico County Register of Deeds. **Other phones:** Assessor-252-745-4125 x33.

Pasquotank County

Register of Deeds, PO Box 154, Elizabeth City, NC 27907-0154. **Phone**-Register of Deeds, R/E & UCC Recording- 252-335-4367; fax-252-335-5106; hours summerourd@co.pasquotank.nc.us

UCC records search per debtor- $30.00. Will not search real estate records. **Online Access to Property, Assessor records:** Access to the county tax parcel database is at www.co.pasquotank.n c.us/departments/GIS/taxquery.cfm. **Other phones:** Assessor-252-338-5169; Treasurer-252-335-4580; Elections-252-335-1739; Vital Records-252-335-4367.

Pender County

Register of Deeds, PO Box 43, Burgaw, NC 28425. **Phone**-910-259-1225; fax-910-259-1299; 8AM-5PM

Will not search UCC or real estate records. UCC copy- $1.00 per page. Cert fee: $2.00. Payee: Pender County Clerk. **Online Access to Property records:** Access to property data on the Oasis.Webview system is free at www.undersys.com/penderweb/pender.html.

Other phones: Assessor-910-259-1225; Elections-910-259-1225; Vital Records-910-259-1458.

Perquimans County

Register of Deeds, PO Box 74, Hertford, NC 27944. **Phone-**Register of Deeds, R/E & UCC Recording- 252-426-5660; fax-252-426-7443; hours 8AM-5PM
Will search UCC records prior to 7/2001 and current fixture (land) files. Search per debtor- $30.00. Will not search real estate records. Record copy- $1.00 per page. Cert fee: $3.00 1st pg, $1.00 each add'l. Payee: County Register of Deeds. **Other phones:** Assessor-252-426-5564.

Person County

Register of Deeds, Courthouse Sq, Roxboro, NC 27573. **Phone-**Register of Deeds, R/E & UCC Recording- 336-597-1733; hours 8:30AM-5PM www.personcounty.net
Will search UCC records prior to 7/2001. Search per debtor- $30.00. Will not search real estate records. Record copy- $1.00 per page. Cert fee: $5.00 for 1st page; $2.00 each add'l. Payee: Person County Register of Deeds. **Online Access to Real Estate, Recording, Grantor/Grantee records:** Access to county real estate records is free at www.personrod.com/v iew/disclaimer.html. Index goes back to 1/1/1995. **Other phones:** Assessor-336-597-1712; Elections-336-597-1727; Vital Records-336-597-1733; Deed Vault-336-597-1729.

Pitt County

Register of Deeds, PO Box 35, Greenville, NC 27835-0035. **Phone-**252-830-4128, R/E Recording-252-830-4138, UCC Recording-252-830-4138; hours 8AM-5PM www.co.pitt.nc.us/depts/
UCC records search per debtor- $30.00. Will not search real estate records. Record copy- $1.00 per page. Cert fee: $5.00 1st pg, $2.00 each add'l. Payee: Pitt County Register of Deeds. **Online Access to Property, Tax Sale records:** Access to property information on the GIS-mapping site is free at http://opis.co.pitt.nc.us/opis/. Also, online access to the county tax sales list is free at www.co.pitt.nc.us/foreclosure/. **Other phones:** Assessor-252-830-4138.

Polk County

Register of Deeds, PO Box 308, Columbus, NC 28722. **Phone-**828-894-8450; fax-828-894-5781; hours 8:30-5PM www.polkrod.com
Will search UCC records prior to 7/2001 and current fixture (land) files. Search per debtor- $30.00. Will not search real estate records. UCC copy- $.25 per page. Cert fee: $5.00. **Other phones:** Assessor-828-894-8500; Treasurer-828-894-8500.

Randolph County

Register of Deeds, PO Box 4066, Asheboro, NC 27204. **Phone-**Register of Deeds, R/E & UCC Recording- 336-318-6960; hours 8AM-5PM www.co.randolph.nc.us
Will search UCC records prior to 7/2001 and current fixture (land) files. Search per debtor- $30.00. Will not search real estate records. RE record copy- $.50 per page. UCC copy- $1.00 per page. Cert fee: $5.00 1st page, $2.00 each add'l. Payee: Randolph County Register of Deeds. **Online Access to Real Property records:** Access to the county GIS database is free at www.co.randolph.nc.us/gis.htm. In the "Search functions" on the map page, click on "parcel owner." Real Estate records access at www.randrod.com. **Other phones:** Vital Records-336-318-6960.

Richmond County

Register of Deeds, 114 E Franklin St, #101, Rockingham, NC 28379-3601. **Phone-**910-997-8250; fax-910-997-8499; hours 8AM-5PM

Will search UCC records prior to 7/2001. Search per debtor- $30.00. Will not search real estate records. Copy fee is $1.00 per page. Cert fee: $5.00 1st page; $2.00 each add'l. Payee: Register of Deeds. **Online Access to Property records:** Access to County property records is via a subscription service; registration and fees are required. For information, call 334-344-3333. **Other phones:** Assessor-910-997-8274; Vital Records-910 997-8251.

Robeson County

Register of Deeds, Box 22 Courthouse-Rm102, Lumberton, NC 28358. **Phone-**910-671-3046, R/E Recording-910-671-3043; fax-910-671-3041; hours 8:15AM-5:15PM
Will search UCC records prior to 7/2001 and current fixture (land) files. Search per debtor- $38.00 per request. Price vary by the amount of requests. Will not search real estate records. UCC copy- $1.00 per page. **Other phones:** Assessor-910-671-3060; Elections-910-671-3080; Vital Records-910-671-4045; Deed Vault-910-671-3049.

Rockingham County

Register of Deeds, PO Box 56, Wentworth, NC 27375-0056. **Phone-**Register of Deeds, R/E & UCC Recording- 336-342-8820; fax-336-342-6209; hours 8AM-5PM www.rockinghamcorod.org
Will search UCC records prior to 7/2001 and current fixture (land) files. Search per debtor- $30.00. Will not search real estate records. RE record copy- $.25 per sheet. UCC copy- $1.00 per page. Cert fee: $5.00 1st pg, $2.00 each add'l. Payee: Rockingham County Register of Deeds. **Online Access to Land, Grantor/Grantee, Judgment, Tax Sale, Property, GIS records:** Access to Register of Deeds database is free at www.rockinghamcorod.org. Land indexes 1996 to present; and record images 1984 to present; plats 1907 to present. Also, online access to real estate (1996 forward) and tax appraiser data is free at www.co.rockingham.nc.us/taxinfo2.html. Also, search property data free at the GIS site at http://arcims.webgis.net/nc/rockingham/default.asp. Name search- click on magnifying glass with ? in it. Also, online access to the tax sales property is at www.co.rockingham.nc.us/forecl.htm. **Other phones:** Assessor-336-342-8280; Treasurer-336-342-8120; Appraiser-336-342-8280; Elections-336-342-8107; Vital Records-336-342-8820.

Rowan County

Register of Deeds, PO Box 2568, Salisbury, NC 28145. **Phone-**704-638-3102; hours-8AM-5PM www.co.rowan.nc.us/rod
Will search UCC records prior to 7/2001 and current fixture (land) files. Search per debtor- $30.00. Will not search real estate records. RE record copy- $.50 per page. UCC copy- $1.00 per page. Cert fee: $3.00 1st pg, $1.00 each add'l. Payee: Rowan County Register of Deeds. **Online Access to Real Estate, Recording, Property records:** Access to the Register of Dees land records database is free at http://rod.co.rowan.nc.us. Records go back to 1975; financing statements back to 1993; images back to 2000 (eventually to 1990). Also, access to the county GIS mapping site is free at http://arcims2.webgis.net/nc/Rowan/default.asp. Name search- click on magnifying glass with ? in it. **Other phones:** Assessor-704-633-4601; Treasurer-704-633-3871; Elections-704-633-6231.

Rutherford County

Register of Deeds, PO Box 551, Rutherfordton, NC 28139. **Phone-**Register of Deeds, R/E & UCC Recording- 828-287-6155; fax-828-287-1229; hours 8:30AM-5PM
Will search UCC records prior to 7/2001 and current fixture (land) files. Search per debtor- $38.00. Will

not search real estate records. UCC copy- $1.00 per page. Cert fee: $5.00 per cert. Payee: Rutherford County Register of Deeds. **Other phones:** Assessor-828-287-6215.

Sampson County

Register of Deeds, PO Box 256, Clinton, NC 28329. **Phone-**Register of Deeds, R/E & UCC Recording- 910-592-8026; fax-910-592-1803; hours 8AM-5:15PM www.sampsonrod.org
Will search UCC records prior to 7/2001 and current fixture (land) files. Search per debtor- $30.00. Will not search real estate records. RE record copy- $.50 per page. UCC copy- $1.00 per page. Cert fee: $5.00 1st page; $2.00 each add'l. Payee: Sampson County Register of Deeds. **Online Access to Real Estate, Recorder, Deed, Grantor/Grantee records:** Access to county Register of Deeds land data is free at www.sampsonrod.org/welcome.asp. Index goes back to 1/1/1998; images to 1/22/1998. **Other phones:** Vital Records-910-592-8026.

Scotland County

Register of Deeds, PO Box 769, Laurinburg, NC 28353. **Phone-**Register of Deeds, R/E & UCC Recording- 910-277-2575, UCC Recording-910 277-2575; fax-910-277-3133; hours 8AM-5PM
Will search UCC records prior to 7/2001 and current fixture (land) files. Search per debtor- $30.00. Will not search real estate records. RE record copy- $.25 per page. UCC copy- $1.00 per copy. Cert fee: $5.00 1st page; $2.00 each add'l. Payee: Scotland County Register of Deeds. **Other phones:** Assessor-910-277-3270; Treasurer-910-277-2410; Appraiser-910-277-2566; Elections-910-277-2595; Vital Records-910-277-2575.

Stanly County

Register of Deeds, PO Box 97, Albemarle, NC 28002-0097. **Phone-**Register of Deeds, R/E & UCC Recording- 704-986-3640; hours 8:30AM-5PM www.co.stanly.nc.us
Will search UCC records prior to 7/2001. Search per debtor- $30.00. Will not search real estate records. UCC copy- $1.00 per page. Cert fee: $5.00 1st pg, $2.00 each add'l. Payee: Stanly County Register of Deeds. **Online Access to Real Estate, Assessor records:** Access the county Property database free on the gis mapping site at www.webgis.net/stanly. Click on "Continue to the GIS". Provides parcel ID and tax numbers, owner, address, year, land and building values. Also go to http://205.244.106.228/login.asp?password=stqn342&accountid=stanlyhome for an index search. **Other phones:** Assessor-704-586-3626; Treasurer-704-986-3618; Appraiser-704-986-3629; Elections-704-986-3647; Vital Records-704-986-3640.

Stokes County

Register of Deeds, PO Box 67, Danbury, NC 27016. **Phone-**Register of Deeds, R/E & UCC Recording- 336-593-2811; fax-336-593-9360; hours 8:30AM-5PM www.stokescorod.org
Will search UCC records prior to 7/2001 and current fixture (land) files only. Search per debtor- $30.00. Will not search real estate records. RE record copy- $.50 per page by mail, $.25 per page if you go in-person. UCC copy- $1.00 per page. Cert fee: $5.00 1st page; $2.00 each add'l. Payee: Register of Deeds. **Online Access to Grantor/Grantee, Deed, UCC, Property records:** Access to the Register of Deeds Remote Access site is free at www.stokescorod.org/welc ome.asp. Land records go back to 1993, images to mid-1985; UCCs back to 1994. Also, access property info on the GIS mapping site free at http://arcims2.we gis.net/stokes/default.asp. Name search- click on magnifying glass with ? in it. **Other phones:** Assessor-336-593-2811; Elections-336-593-2811; Vital Records-336-593-2811.

Surry County

Register of Deeds, PO Box 303, Dobson, NC 27017-0303. **Phone-**336-401-8150, R/E Recording-336-386-9201; fax-336-401-8151; hours 8:15AM-5PM www.co.surry.nc.us
Will search UCC records prior to 7/2001. Search per debtor- $30.00. Will not search real estate records. Copy fee is $1.00 per page. **Online Access to Tax Map records:** Tax maps located at http://arcims.webgis.net/nc/surry/. **Other phones:** Assessor-336-401-8100; Treasurer-336-386-9230; Elections-336-401-8225.

Swain County

Register of Deeds, PO Box 1183, Bryson City, NC 28713. **Phone-**828-488-9273 x207, R/E Recording-828-488-9273 x205; fax-828-488-6947; hours 8AM-5PM www.swaincounty.org/page5.html
Will search UCC records prior to 7/2001 and current fixture (land) files. Search per debtor- $30.00. Will not search real estate or tax lien records. UCC copy- $1.00 per page. **Other phones:** Assessor-828-488-9273 x223; Elections-828-488-6177; Vital Records-828-488-9273 x205.

Transylvania County

Register of Deeds, 12 E Main St, Courthouse, Brevard, NC 28712. **Phone-**Register of Deeds, R/E & UCC Recording- 828-884-3162; hours 8:30AM-5PM www.landofsky.org
Will search UCC records prior to July 1, 2001. Search per debtor- $30.00. Will not search real estate records. UCC copy- $1.00 per page. Cert fee: $5.00 1st page, $2.00 each add'l. Payee: Transylvania County Register of Deeds. **Other phones:** Assessor-828-884-3200; Treasurer-828-884-3104; Elections-828-884-3114; Vital Records-828-884-3162.

Tyrrell County

Register of Deeds, PO Box 449, Columbia, NC 27925. **Phone-**252-796-2901; fax-252-796-0148; hours 9AM-5PM www.tyrrellrod.com
Will search UCC records prior to 7/2001 and current fixture (land) files. Search per debtor- $30.00. Will not search real estate records. RE record copy- $.25 per page. UCC copy- $1.00 per page. Cert fee: $5.00 for 1st pg, $2.00 each add'l pg. Payee: Register of Deeds. **Online Access to Real Estate, Grantor/Grantee, Deed records:** Access to Register of Deeds real estate records is free at www.tyrrellrod.com/view/disclaimer.html. Records go back to 1997; images are from Book 160 forward. **Other phones:** Assessor-252-796-1371; Elections-252-796-0775.

Union County

Register of Deeds, PO Box 248, Monroe, NC 28111-0248. **Phone-**Register of Deeds, R/E & UCC Recording- 704-283-3727, UCC Recording-704-283-3610; hours 8AM-5PM
Will search UCC records prior to 7/2001 and current fixture (land) files. Search per debtor- $30.00. Will not search real estate records. UCC copy- $1.00 per page. Cert fee: $3.00 1st pg, $1.00 each add'l. Payee: Union County Register of Deeds. **Other phones:** Vital Records-704-283-3610; Land Records-704-283-3728.

Vance County

Register of Deeds, 122 Young St, Courthouse, #F, Henderson, NC 27536. **Phone-**252-738-2110; hours 8:30AM-5PM
Will search UCC records prior to 7/2001. Search per debtor- $30.00. Will not search real estate records. UCC copy- $1.00 per page. Cert fee: $5.00 per cert

for 1st page, $2.00 each add'l. Payee: Vance County Register of Deeds.

Wake County

Register of Deeds, PO Box 1897, Raleigh, NC 27602. **Phone-**Register of Deeds, R/E & UCC Recording-919-856-5460, UCC Recording-919-856-5464; fax-919-856-5467; hours-8:30AM-5:15PM http://web.co.wake.nc.us/rdeeds/
Will search UCC records prior to 7/2001 and current fixture (land) files. Search per debtor- $30.00. Will not search real estate records. UCC copy- $1.00 per page. Cert fee: $5.00 1st page, $2.00 each add'l. Payee: Wake County Register of Deeds. **Online Access to Real Estate, Assessor, Deed, Judgment, Lien, Voter Registration records:** Records from the County Department of Revenue are downloadable by township for free at http://web.co.wake.nc.us/revenue/wcmap.html. Also, a free real estate property search is at http://aws1.co.wake.nc.us/realestate/search.asp. Also, online access to the Register of Deeds database is free at http://rodweb01.co.wake.nc.us/books/genext/genextsearch.asp. Records go back to 10/1991. Registered voters can be found at http://msweb03.co.wake.nc.us/bordelec/Waves/WavesOptions.asp. Also, access to Town of Cary property info is free http://arcims2.webgis.net/nc/cary/default.asp. **Other phones:** Assessor-919-856-6600; Treasurer-919-856-6600; Vital Records-919-733-3526.

Warren County

Register of Deeds, PO Box 506, Warrenton, NC 27589. **Phone-**Register of Deeds, R/E & UCC Recording- 252-257-3265; fax-252-257-7011; hours 8:30AM-5PM
Will not search UCC or real estate records. UCC copy- $.25 per page. Cert fee: $5.00. Payee: Warren County Register of Deeds. **Other phones:** Assessor-252-257-4158; Treasurer-252-257-3337; 2nd fax-252-257-7011.

Washington County

Register of Deeds, PO Box 1007, Plymouth, NC 27962. **Phone-**252-793-2325; fax-252-793-6982; hours 8:30AM-5PM www.washingtoncountygov.com
Will search UCC records prior to 7/2001. Search per debtor- $30.00. Will not search real estate records. RE record copy- $.25 per page. UCC copy- $1.00 per page. Cert fee: $5.00 1st pg, $2.00 each add'l. Payee: Washington County Register of Deeds. **Other phones:** Assessor-252-793-1176.

Watauga County

Register of Deeds, 842 W. King St, #9, Boone, NC 28607-3585. **Phone-**Register of Deeds, R/E & UCC Recording- 828-265-8052, UCC Recording-828-265-8056; fax-828-265-7632; hours 8AM-5PM www.wataugacounty.org/deeds/index.html
Will search UCC records prior to 7/2001 and current fixture (land) files. Search per debtor- $30.00. Will not search real estate records. UCC copy- $1.00 per page. **Online Access to Grantor/Grantee, Deed, UCC, Assessor, Property records:** Access to register of deeds database is free at www.wataugacounty.org/deeds/disclaimer.shtml. Also, online access to county tax search data is free at www.wataugacounty.org/tax/search_tax.shtml. Also, search Town of Blowing Rock property info at http://arcims2.webgis.net/blowingrock/default.asp. Name search- click on magnifying glass with ? in it. **Other phones:** Assessor-828-265-8036; Appraiser-828-265-8141; Elections-828-265-8061; Vital Records-828-265-8052.

Wayne County

Register of Deeds, PO Box 267, Goldsboro, NC 27533-0267. **Phone-**919-731-1449; fax-919-731-1441; hours 8AM-5PM www.waynegov.com
Will search UCC records prior to 7/2001 and current fixture (land) files. Search per debtor- $30.00. Will not search real estate records. UCC copy- $1.00 per page. Cert fee: $3.00 per cert. Payee: Wayne County Register of Deeds. **Online Access to Real Estate, Deed, Grantor/Grantee records:** Access to the registers CRP, financing statement, and real estate (back to 1969) databases are free at http://152.34.232.92/resolution/. **Other phones:** Assessor-919-731-1461.

Wilkes County

Register of Deeds, 500 Courthouse Dr, #1000, Wilkesboro, NC 28697. **Phone-**Register of Deeds, R/E & UCC Recording- 336-651-7351; 8:30AM-5PM
Will search UCC records prior to 7/2001 and current fixture (land) files. Search per debtor- $30.00. Will not search real estate records. RE record copy- $1.00 per page if mailed; $.25 per page otherwise. UCC copy- $1.00 per page. Cert fee: $5.00 1st pg, $2.00 each add'l. Payee: Wilkes County Register of Deeds. **Online Access to Property, GIS-mapping records:** Access to porperty data is free on the GIS-site at www.undersys.com/wilkesweb/wilkes.html. **Other phones:** Vital Records-336-651-7351.

Wilson County

Register of Deeds, PO Box 1728, Wilson, NC 27893. **Phone-**Register of Deeds, R/E & UCC Recording- 252-399-2935; fax-252-399-2942; hours 8AM-5PM www.wilson-co.com/rod.html
Will search UCC records prior to 7/2001 and current fixture (land) files. Search per debtor- $30.00. Will not search real estate records. RE record copy- $.50 per copy. UCC copy- $1.00 per page. $.50 each reader printer copy from customer. **Online Access to Assessor, Real Estate, Voter Registration, Property, Deed records:** Records on the county Geolink property tax database are free at www.wilson-co.com/intro.html. Records on the county registered voter database are at www.wilson-co.com/wcbe_search.cfm. Also, search the Register of Deeds search site at www.wilson-co.com/wcjav_begin.html. If using property search function, username or password required; deeds section does not. Search voter registration records at www.wilson-co.com/wcbe_search.cfm. **Other phones:** Assessor-252-399-2901; Treasurer-252-399-2902; Elections-252-399-2836; Vital Records-252-399-2935.

Yadkin County

Register of Deeds, PO Box 211, Yadkinville, NC 27055. **Phone-**Register of Deeds, R/E & UCC Recording- 336-679-4225; fax-336-679-3239; hours 8AM-5PM www.yadkincounty.gov/RegDeed.htm
Will search UCC records prior to 7/2001. Search per debtor- $30.00. Will not search real estate records. RE record copy- $.25 per page. UCC copy- $1.00 per page. Cert fee: $10.00 per cert. Payee: Yadkin County Register of Deeds. **Other phones:** Assessor-336-679-4221; Treasurer-336-679-4223; Appraiser-336-679-2308; Elections-336-679-4227; Vital Records-336-679-4225.

Yancey County

Register of Deeds, Courthouse, Rm #4, 110 Town Sq, Burnsville, NC 28714. **Phone-**828-682-2174, R/E Recording-704-682-2174; fax-828-682-4520; hours 8:30AM-5PM
Will not search UCC or real estate records. UCC copy- $1.00 per page. Cert fee: $5.00 1st pg, $2.00 each add'l. Payee: Yancey County Register of Deeds.

North Carolina County Locator

You will usually be able to find the city name in the City/County Cross Reference below. In that case, it is a simple matter to determine the county from the cross reference. However, only the official US Postal Service city names are included in this index. There are an additional 40,000 place names that people use in their addresses. Therefore, we have also included a ZIP/City Cross Reference immediately following the City/County Cross Reference.

If you know the ZIP Code but the city name does not appear in the City/County Cross Reference index, look up the ZIP Code in the ZIP/City Cross Reference, find the city name, then look up the city name in the City/County Cross Reference. For example, you want to know the county for an address of Menands, NY 12204. There is no "Menands" in the City/County Cross Reference. The ZIP/City Cross Reference shows that ZIP Codes 12201-12288 are for the city of Albany. Looking back in the City/County Cross Reference, Albany is in Albany County.

North Carolina City/County Cross Reference

ABERDEEN (28315) Moore(76), Hoke(23)
ADVANCE Davie
AHOSKIE Hertford
ALAMANCE Alamance
ALBEMARLE Stanly
ALBERTSON Duplin
ALEXANDER Buncombe
ALEXIS Gaston
ALLIANCE Pamlico
ALMOND Swain
ALTAMAHAW Alamance
ANDREWS Cherokee
ANGIER (27501) Harnett(73), Johnston(25), Wake(1)
ANSONVILLE Anson
APEX (27523) Wake(66), Chatham(33)
APEX Wake
AQUONE Macon
ARAPAHOE Pamlico
ARARAT Surry
ARDEN (28704) Buncombe(91), Henderson(8)
ASH Brunswick
ASHEBORO Randolph
ASHEVILLE Buncombe
ATKINSON Pender
ATLANTIC Carteret
ATLANTIC BEACH Carteret
AULANDER (27805) Bertie(68), Hertford(31)
AURORA Beaufort
AUTRYVILLE (28318) Sampson(87), Cumberland(12)
AVON Dare
AYDEN (28513) Pitt(94), Greene(5)
AYDLETT Currituck
BADIN Stanly
BAHAMA Durham
BAILEY (27807) Nash(64), Wilson(35)
BAKERSVILLE Mitchell
BALSAM Jackson
BALSAM GROVE Transylvania
BANNER ELK (28604) Watauga(61), Avery(38)
BARBER Rowan
BARCO Currituck
BARIUM SPRINGS Iredell
BARNARDSVILLE Buncombe
BARNESVILLE Robeson
BAT CAVE Henderson
BATH Beaufort
BATTLEBORO (27809) Nash(53), Edgecombe(46)
BAYBORO Pamlico
BEAR CREEK Chatham
BEAUFORT Carteret
BELEWS CREEK Forsyth
BELHAVEN Beaufort
BELLARTHUR Pitt
BELMONT Gaston
BELVIDERE (27919) Perquimans(89), Chowan(6), Gates(3)

BENNETT (27208) Chatham(95), Moore(2), Randolph(1)
BENSON (27504) Johnston(97), Harnett(2)
BESSEMER CITY Gaston
BETHANIA Forsyth
BETHEL (27812) Pitt(95), Edgecombe(4)
BEULAVILLE (28518) Duplin(90), Onslow(9)
BISCOE (27209) Montgomery(81), Moore(18)
BLACK CREEK Wilson
BLACK MOUNTAIN Buncombe
BLADENBORO (28320) Bladen(91), Columbus(8)
BLANCH Caswell
BLOUNTS CREEK Beaufort
BLOWING ROCK Watauga
BOILING SPRINGS Cleveland
BOLIVIA Brunswick
BOLTON (28423) Columbus(95), Bladen(4)
BONLEE Chatham
BOOMER Wilkes
BOONE Watauga
BOONVILLE Yadkin
BOSTIC Rutherford
BRASSTOWN (28902) Clay(94), Cherokee(5)
BREVARD Transylvania
BRIDGETON Craven
BROADWAY (27505) Harnett(80), Lee(19)
BROWNS SUMMIT Guilford
BRUNSWICK Columbus
BRYSON CITY Swain
BUIES CREEK Harnett
BULLOCK (27507) Granville(93), Vance(6)
BUNN Franklin
BUNNLEVEL Harnett
BURGAW Pender
BURLINGTON (27217) Alamance(92), Caswell(7)
BURLINGTON Alamance
BURNSVILLE Yancey
BUTNER Granville
BUTTERS Bladen
BUXTON Dare
BYNUM Chatham
CALABASH Brunswick
CALYPSO Duplin
CAMDEN Camden
CAMERON (28326) Harnett(45), Moore(34), Lee(20)
CAMP LEJEUNE Onslow
CANDLER Buncombe
CANDOR Montgomery
CANTON Haywood
CAROLEEN Rutherford
CAROLINA BEACH New Hanover
CARRBORO Orange
CARTHAGE Moore
CARY (27519) Wake(97), Durham(1)
CARY Wake
CASAR (28020) Cleveland(85), Rutherford(14)

CASHIERS Jackson
CASTALIA (27816) Nash(76), Franklin(23)
CASTLE HAYNE New Hanover
CATAWBA Catawba
CEDAR FALLS Randolph
CEDAR GROVE Orange
CEDAR ISLAND Carteret
CEDAR MOUNTAIN Transylvania
CERRO GORDO Columbus
CHADBOURN Columbus
CHAPEL HILL (27517) Chatham(40), Orange(39), Durham(20)
CHAPEL HILL (27516) Orange(87), Chatham(12)
CHAPEL HILL Orange
CHARLOTTE (28215) Mecklenburg(94), Cabarrus(5)
CHARLOTTE Mecklenburg
CHEROKEE Swain
CHERRY POINT Craven
CHERRYVILLE (28021) Gaston(85), Lincoln(11), Cleveland(3)
CHIMNEY ROCK Rutherford
CHINA GROVE Rowan
CHINQUAPIN (28521) Duplin(95), Onslow(4)
CHOCOWINITY Beaufort
CLAREMONT Catawba
CLARENDON Columbus
CLARKTON (28433) Bladen(67), Columbus(32)
CLAYTON Johnston
CLEMMONS (27012) Forsyth(75), Davidson(24)
CLEVELAND (27013) Rowan(90), Iredell(9)
CLIFFSIDE Rutherford
CLIMAX (27233) Randolph(66), Guilford(33)
CLINTON Sampson
CLYDE Haywood
COATS Harnett
COFIELD Hertford
COINJOCK Currituck
COLERAIN Bertie
COLFAX Guilford
COLLETTSVILLE (28611) Caldwell(94), Avery(6)
COLUMBIA Tyrrell
COLUMBUS Polk
COMFORT Jones
COMO Hertford
CONCORD Cabarrus
CONETOE Edgecombe
CONNELLYS SPRINGS (28612) Burke(98), Catawba(1)
CONOVER Catawba
CONWAY Northampton
COOLEEMEE Davie
CORAPEAKE Gates
CORDOVA Richmond
CORNELIUS Mecklenburg
COROLLA Currituck
COUNCIL Bladen

COVE CITY Craven
CRAMERTON Gaston
CRANBERRY Avery
CREEDMOOR (27522) Granville(89), Wake(10)
CRESTON Ashe
CRESWELL (27928) Washington(96), Tyrrell(3)
CROSSNORE Avery
CROUSE (28033) Lincoln(90), Gaston(9)
CRUMPLER Ashe
CULBERSON Cherokee
CULLOWHEE Jackson
CUMBERLAND Cumberland
CUMNOCK Lee
CURRIE Pender
CURRITUCK Currituck
DALLAS Gaston
DANA Henderson
DANBURY Stokes
DAVIDSON (28036) Mecklenburg(73), Cabarrus(25), Iredell(1)
DAVIDSON Mecklenburg
DAVIS Carteret
DEEP GAP Watauga
DEEP RUN (28525) Lenoir(89), Duplin(10)
DELCO Columbus
DENTON (27239) Davidson(77), Randolph(22)
DENVER (28037) Lincoln(83), Catawba(16)
DILLSBORO Jackson
DOBSON Surry
DOVER (28526) Craven(83), Jones(13), Lenoir(2)
DREXEL Burke
DUBLIN Bladen
DUDLEY Wayne
DUNN (28334) Harnett(63), Sampson(28), Johnston(6), Cumberland(1)
DUNN Harnett
DURANTS NECK Perquimans
DURHAM (27707) Durham(98), Orange(1)
DURHAM (27713) Durham(98), Chatham(1)
DURHAM Durham
EAGLE ROCK (27523) Wake(66), Chatham(33)
EAGLE SPRINGS Moore
EARL Cleveland
EAST BEND Yadkin
EAST FLAT ROCK Henderson
EAST SPENCER Rowan
EDEN Rockingham
EDENTON Chowan
EDNEYVILLE Henderson
EDWARD Beaufort
EFLAND Orange
ELIZABETH CITY Pasquotank
ELIZABETHTOWN Bladen
ELK PARK Avery
ELKIN (28621) Surry(64), Wilkes(35)
ELLENBORO Rutherford
ELLERBE Richmond

ELM CITY (27822) Wilson(89), Nash(6), Edgecombe(3)
ELON COLLEGE (27244) Alamance(95), Guilford(4)
EMERALD ISLE Carteret
ENFIELD Halifax
ENGELHARD Hyde
ENKA Buncombe
ENNICE Alleghany
ERNUL Craven
ERWIN Harnett
ETHER Montgomery
ETOWAH Henderson
EURE Gates
EVERETTS Martin
EVERGREEN Columbus
FAIR BLUFF Columbus
FAIRFIELD (27826) Hyde(87), Tyrrell(12)
FAIRMONT Robeson
FAIRVIEW Buncombe
FAISON (28341) Sampson(77), Duplin(22)
FAITH Rowan
FALCON Cumberland
FALKLAND Pitt
FALLSTON Cleveland
FARMVILLE Pitt
FAYETTEVILLE (28304) Cumberland(98), Hoke(1)
FAYETTEVILLE (28312) Cumberland(91), Bladen(8)
FAYETTEVILLE Cumberland
FERGUSON Wilkes
FLAT ROCK Henderson
FLEETWOOD Ashe
FLETCHER (28732) Henderson(76), Buncombe(22)
FONTANA DAM Graham
FOREST CITY Rutherford
FORT BRAGG Cumberland
FOUNTAIN (27829) Wilson(72), Pitt(22), Edgecombe(5)
FOUR OAKS (27524) Johnston(97), Wayne(2)
FRANKLIN Macon
FRANKLINTON (27525) Franklin(74), Granville(25)
FRANKLINVILLE Randolph
FREMONT (27830) Wayne(95), Wilson(4)
FRISCO Dare
FUQUAY VARINA (27526) Wake(71), Harnett(28)
GARLAND (28441) Sampson(59), Bladen(39)
GARNER (27529) Wake(77), Johnston(22)
GARYSBURG Northampton
GASTON Northampton
GASTONIA Gaston
GATES Gates
GATESVILLE Gates
GERMANTON (27019) Stokes(74), Forsyth(25)
GERTON Henderson
GIBSON Scotland
GIBSONVILLE (27249) Guilford(63), Alamance(28), Caswell(5), Rockingham(2)
GLADE VALLEY Alleghany
GLEN ALPINE Burke
GLENDALE SPRINGS Ashe
GLENDON Moore
GLENVILLE Jackson
GLENWOOD McDowell
GLOUCESTER Carteret
GODWIN (28344) Sampson(80), Cumberland(19)
GOLD HILL (28071) Rowan(49), Cabarrus(29), Stanly(21)
GOLDSBORO Wayne
GOLDSTON Chatham
GRAHAM Alamance
GRANDY Currituck
GRANITE FALLS Caldwell
GRANITE QUARRY Rowan

GRANTSBORO Pamlico
GRASSY CREEK (28631) Ashe(98), Alleghany(1)
GRAYSON Ashe
GREEN MOUNTAIN Yancey
GREENMOUNTAIN Yancey
GREENSBORO Guilford
GREENVILLE Pitt
GRIFTON (28530) Pitt(46), Lenoir(26), Craven(23), Greene(3)
GRIMESLAND (27837) Pitt(94), Beaufort(5)
GROVER Cleveland
GULF Chatham
GUMBERRY Northampton
HALIFAX Halifax
HALLSBORO Columbus
HAMILTON Martin
HAMLET (28345) Richmond(98), Scotland(1)
HAMPSTEAD Pender
HAMPTONVILLE (27020) Yadkin(76), Wilkes(17), Iredell(6)
HARBINGER Currituck
HARKERS ISLAND Carteret
HARMONY (28634) Iredell(93), Davie(6)
HARRELLS (28444) Bladen(53), Sampson(44), Duplin(1)
HARRELLSVILLE Hertford
HARRIS Rutherford
HARRISBURG Cabarrus
HASSELL Martin
HATTERAS Dare
HAVELOCK Craven
HAW RIVER Alamance
HAYESVILLE Clay
HAYS Wilkes
HAZELWOOD Haywood
HENDERSON (27537) Vance(94), Franklin(3), Warren(1)
HENDERSON Vance
HENDERSONVILLE Henderson
HENRICO (27842) Northampton(97), Warren(2)
HENRIETTA Rutherford
HERTFORD Perquimans
HICKORY (28601) Catawba(96), Caldwell(2)
HICKORY (28602) Catawba(95), Burke(4)
HICKORY Catawba
HIDDENITE (28636) Alexander(96), Iredell(3)
HIGH POINT (27265) Guilford(76), Davidson(22), Forsyth(1)
HIGH POINT (27263) Randolph(59), Guilford(40)
HIGH POINT Guilford
HIGH SHOALS Gaston
HIGHFALLS Moore
HIGHLANDS Macon
HILDEBRAN (28637) Burke(98), Catawba(1)
HILLSBOROUGH (27278) Orange(96), Durham(3)
HOBBSVILLE (27946) Gates(97), Chowan(1)
HOBGOOD (27843) Halifax(90), Edgecombe(8)
HOBUCKEN Pamlico
HOFFMAN (28347) Richmond(92), Moore(7)
HOLLISTER Halifax
HOLLY RIDGE (28445) Onslow(57), Pender(42)
HOLLY SPRINGS (27540) Wake(89), Harnett(10)
HOOKERTON (28538) Greene(79), Lenoir(20)
HOPE MILLS Cumberland
HORSE SHOE Henderson
HOT SPRINGS Madison
HUBERT Onslow
HUDSON Caldwell
HUNTERSVILLE Mecklenburg

HURDLE MILLS (27541) Person(50), Orange(49)
HUSK Ashe
ICARD Burke
INDIAN TRAIL Union
INGOLD Sampson
IRON STATION (28080) Lincoln(98), Gaston(1)
IVANHOE (28447) Sampson(35), Pender(32), Bladen(31)
JACKSON Northampton
JACKSON SPRINGS (27281) Moore(58), Montgomery(35), Richmond(6)
JACKSONVILLE Onslow
JAMESTOWN Guilford
JAMESVILLE Martin
JARVISBURG Currituck
JEFFERSON (28640) Ashe(97), Wilkes(2)
JONAS RIDGE Burke
JONESVILLE (28642) Yadkin(93), Wilkes(6)
JULIAN (27283) Guilford(85), Randolph(14)
KANNAPOLIS (28083) Cabarrus(73), Rowan(26)
KANNAPOLIS Cabarrus
KELFORD Bertie
KELLY Bladen
KENANSVILLE Duplin
KENLY (27542) Wilson(50), Johnston(44), Wayne(5)
KERNERSVILLE (27284) Forsyth(93), Guilford(4), Davidson(2)
KERNERSVILLE Forsyth
KILL DEVIL HILLS Dare
KING (27021) Stokes(97), Forsyth(2)
KINGS MOUNTAIN Cleveland
KINSTON (28501) Lenoir(97), Jones(2)
KINSTON Lenoir
KIPLING Harnett
KITTRELL (27544) Vance(89), Granville(10)
KITTY HAWK Dare
KNIGHTDALE Wake
KNOTTS ISLAND Currituck
KURE BEACH New Hanover
LA GRANGE (28551) Lenoir(66), Wayne(26), Greene(6)
LAKE JUNALUSKA Haywood
LAKE LURE Rutherford
LAKE TOXAWAY Transylvania
LAKE WACCAMAW Columbus
LAKEVIEW Moore
LANDIS Rowan
LANSING Ashe
LASKER Northampton
LATTIMORE Cleveland
LAUREL HILL Scotland
LAUREL SPRINGS (28644) Alleghany(58), Ashe(38), Wilkes(2)
LAURINBURG Scotland
LAWNDALE (28090) Cleveland(90), Lincoln(8)
LAWSONVILLE Stokes
LEASBURG Caswell
LEICESTER Buncombe
LELAND Brunswick
LEMON SPRINGS Lee
LENOIR (28645) Caldwell(98), Wilkes(1)
LENOIR Caldwell
LEWISTON WOODVILLE Bertie
LEWISVILLE Forsyth
LEXINGTON Davidson
LIBERTY (27298) Randolph(59), Alamance(30), Guilford(8), Chatham(1)
LILESVILLE Anson
LILLINGTON Harnett
LINCOLNTON (28092) Lincoln(94), Gaston(4), Catawba(1)
LINCOLNTON Lincoln
LINDEN (28356) Cumberland(68), Harnett(31)
LINVILLE Avery
LINVILLE FALLS Burke

LINWOOD Davidson
LITTLE SWITZERLAND McDowell
LITTLETON (27850) Halifax(83), Warren(16)
LOCUST Stanly
LONGISLAND Catawba
LONGWOOD Brunswick
LOUISBURG Franklin
LOWELL Gaston
LOWGAP Surry
LOWLAND Pamlico
LUCAMA Wilson
LUMBER BRIDGE (28357) Robeson(54), Hoke(45)
LUMBERTON Robeson
LYNN Polk
MACCLESFIELD (27852) Wilson(81), Edgecombe(18)
MACON Warren
MADISON (27025) Rockingham(73), Stokes(26)
MAGGIE VALLEY Haywood
MAGNOLIA (28453) Duplin(73), Sampson(26)
MAIDEN Catawba
MAMERS Harnett
MANNS HARBOR Dare
MANSON (27553) Vance(65), Warren(34)
MANTEO Dare
MAPLE Currituck
MAPLE HILL (28454) Pender(77), Onslow(22)
MARBLE Cherokee
MARGARETTSVILLE Northampton
MARIETTA Robeson
MARION McDowell
MARS HILL (28754) Madison(88), Yancey(11)
MARSHALL Madison
MARSHALLBERG Carteret
MARSHVILLE (28103) Union(98), Anson(1)
MARSTON (28363) Scotland(57), Richmond(42)
MATTHEWS (28105) Mecklenburg(97), Union(2)
MATTHEWS (28104) Union(93), Mecklenburg(6)
MATTHEWS Mecklenburg
MAURY Greene
MAXTON (28364) Robeson(73), Scotland(26)
MAYODAN Rockingham
MAYSVILLE (28555) Onslow(75), Jones(24)
MC ADENVILLE Gaston
MC FARLAN Anson
MC GRADY Wilkes
MC LEANSVILLE Guilford
MCCAIN Hoke
MCCUTCHEON FIELD Onslow
MEBANE (27302) Alamance(60), Orange(26), Caswell(13)
MERRITT Pamlico
MERRY HILL Bertie
MICAVILLE Yancey
MICRO Johnston
MIDDLEBURG Vance
MIDDLESEX (27557) Johnston(51), Nash(46), Wilson(1)
MIDLAND (28107) Cabarrus(88), Mecklenburg(6), Stanly(3), Union(1)
MIDWAY PARK Onslow
MILL SPRING (28756) Polk(97), Rutherford(2)
MILLERS CREEK Wilkes
MILTON (27305) Caswell(98), Person(1)
MILWAUKEE Northampton
MINERAL SPRINGS Union
MINNEAPOLIS Avery
MISENHEIMER Stanly
MOCKSVILLE Davie
MONCURE Chatham
MONROE Union

MONTEZUMA Avery
MONTREAT Buncombe
MOORESBORO (28114) Rutherford(54),
    Cleveland(45)
MOORESVILLE (28115) Iredell(86),
    Rowan(13)
MOORESVILLE Iredell
MORAVIAN FALLS Wilkes
MOREHEAD CITY Carteret
MORGANTON Burke
MORRISVILLE (27560) Wake(94),
    Durham(5)
MORVEN Anson
MOUNT AIRY (27030) Surry(97), Stokes(2)
MOUNT GILEAD (27306) Richmond(59),
    Montgomery(40)
MOUNT HOLLY Gaston
MOUNT MOURNE Iredell
MOUNT OLIVE (28365) Wayne(65),
    Duplin(30), Sampson(4)
MOUNT PLEASANT Cabarrus
MOUNT ULLA (28125) Rowan(94),
    Iredell(5)
MOUNTAIN HOME Henderson
MOYOCK Currituck
MURFREESBORO (27855) Hertford(96),
    Northampton(3)
MURPHY Cherokee
NAGS HEAD Dare
NAKINA Columbus
NAPLES Henderson
NASHVILLE Nash
NEBO (28761) McDowell(83), Burke(16)
NEW BERN (28560) Craven(89),
    Pamlico(10)
NEW BERN (28562) Craven(96), Jones(3)
NEW BERN Craven
NEW HILL (27562) Wake(55),
    Chatham(43)
NEW LONDON (28127) Stanly(60),
    Montgomery(33), Davidson(5)
NEWELL Mecklenburg
NEWLAND (28657) Avery(88), Burke(11)
NEWPORT Carteret
NEWTON Catawba
NEWTON GROVE (28366) Sampson(81),
    Johnston(18)
NORLINA Warren
NORMAN Richmond
NORTH WILKESBORO Wilkes
NORTHSIDE Granville
NORWOOD Stanly
OAK CITY Martin
OAK ISLAND Brunswick
OAK RIDGE Guilford
OAKBORO Stanly
OCEAN ISLE BEACH Brunswick
OCRACOKE Hyde
OLD FORT McDowell
OLIN Iredell
OLIVIA Harnett
ORIENTAL Pamlico
ORRUM Robeson
OTTO Macon
OXFORD (27565) Granville(92), Vance(6),
    Person(1)
PALMYRA Halifax
PANTEGO Beaufort
PARKTON (28371) Robeson(83),
    Cumberland(16)
PARMELE Martin
PATTERSON Caldwell
PAW CREEK Mecklenburg
PEACHLAND (28133) Anson(90), Union(9)
PELHAM (27311) Caswell(93),
    Rockingham(6)
PEMBROKE Robeson
PENDLETON Northampton
PENLAND Mitchell
PENROSE (28766) Transylvania(78),
    Henderson(21)
PFAFFTOWN Forsyth

PIKEVILLE (27863) Wayne(70),
    Greene(29)
PILOT MOUNTAIN (27041) Surry(67),
    Stokes(32)
PINE HALL Stokes
PINE LEVEL Johnston
PINEBLUFF Moore
PINEHURST Moore
PINEOLA Avery
PINETOPS Edgecombe
PINETOWN Beaufort
PINEVILLE Mecklenburg
PINEY CREEK Alleghany
PINK HILL (28572) Duplin(55), Lenoir(36),
    Jones(7)
PINNACLE Stokes
PISGAH FOREST Transylvania
PITTSBORO Chatham
PLEASANT GARDEN (27313) Guilford(59),
    Randolph(40)
PLEASANT HILL Northampton
PLUMTREE Avery
PLYMOUTH Washington
POINT HARBOR Currituck
POLKTON Anson
POLKVILLE Cleveland
POLLOCKSVILLE (28573) Jones(98),
    Craven(1)
POPE A F B Cumberland
POPLAR BRANCH Currituck
POTECASI Northampton
POWELLS POINT Currituck
POWELLSVILLE Bertie
PRINCETON (27569) Johnston(88),
    Wayne(11)
PROCTORVILLE Robeson
PROSPECT HILL Caswell
PROVIDENCE Caswell
PURLEAR Wilkes
RAEFORD Hoke
RALEIGH (27603) Wake(98), Johnston(1)
RALEIGH (27613) Wake(97), Durham(2)
RALEIGH Wake
RAMSEUR Randolph
RANDLEMAN (27317) Randolph(98),
    Guilford(1)
RED OAK Nash
RED SPRINGS (28377) Robeson(62),
    Hoke(37)
REIDSVILLE (27320) Rockingham(90),
    Caswell(9)
REIDSVILLE Rockingham
REX Robeson
RHODHISS Caldwell
RICH SQUARE Northampton
RICHFIELD (28137) Rowan(50), Stanly(49)
RICHLANDS (28574) Onslow(94),
    Duplin(3), Jones(2)
RIDGECREST Buncombe
RIDGEWAY Warren
RIEGELWOOD (28456) Columbus(51),
    Bladen(42), Brunswick(6)
ROANOKE RAPIDS Halifax
ROARING GAP Alleghany
ROARING RIVER Wilkes
ROBBINS Moore
ROBBINSVILLE Graham
ROBERSONVILLE (27871) Pitt(83),
    Martin(16)
ROCKINGHAM Richmond
ROCKWELL (28138) Rowan(81),
    Cabarrus(18)
ROCKY MOUNT (27803) Nash(89),
    Wilson(10)
ROCKY MOUNT Edgecombe
ROCKY MOUNT Nash
ROCKY POINT Pender
RODANTHE Dare
RODUCO Gates
ROLESVILLE Wake
RONDA Wilkes
ROPER Washington

ROSE HILL (28458) Duplin(69),
    Sampson(30)
ROSEBORO (28382) Sampson(80),
    Cumberland(19)
ROSMAN Transylvania
ROUGEMONT (27572) Orange(40),
    Person(31), Durham(23), Granville(4)
ROWLAND Robeson
ROXBORO Person
ROXOBEL Bertie
RUFFIN (27326) Rockingham(60),
    Caswell(40)
RURAL HALL (27045) Forsyth(94),
    Stokes(5)
RURAL HALL Forsyth
RUTHERFORD COLLEGE Burke
RUTHERFORDTON Rutherford
SAINT PAULS (28384) Robeson(87),
    Bladen(11)
SALEMBURG Sampson
SALISBURY Rowan
SALTER PATH Carteret
SALUDA (28773) Polk(84), Henderson(15)
SALVO Dare
SANDY RIDGE Stokes
SANFORD (27330) Lee(91), Chatham(6)
SANFORD (27332) Lee(58), Harnett(41)
SANFORD Lee
SAPPHIRE (28774) Jackson(72),
    Transylvania(27)
SARATOGA Wilson
SAXAPAHAW Alamance
SCALY MOUNTAIN Macon
SCOTLAND NECK Halifax
SCOTTS Iredell
SCOTTVILLE Ashe
SCRANTON Hyde
SEABOARD (27876) Northampton(88),
    Pitt(11)
SEAGROVE (27341) Randolph(69),
    Moore(20), Montgomery(10)
SEALEVEL Carteret
SEDALIA Guilford
SELMA Johnston
SEMORA (27343) Person(67), Caswell(32)
SEVEN SPRINGS (28578) Wayne(69),
    Lenoir(17), Duplin(13)
SEVERN Northampton
SHALLOTTE Brunswick
SHANNON (28386) Robeson(61),
    Hoke(38)
SHARPSBURG Nash
SHAWBORO (27973) Camden(72),
    Currituck(27)
SHELBY Cleveland
SHERRILLS FORD (28673) Catawba(97),
    Lincoln(2)
SHILOH Camden
SILER CITY (27344) Chatham(98),
    Randolph(1)
SILOAM Surry
SIMPSON Pitt
SIMS (27880) Wilson(92), Nash(7)
SKYLAND Buncombe
SMITHFIELD Johnston
SMYRNA Carteret
SNEADS FERRY Onslow
SNOW CAMP (27349) Alamance(78),
    Chatham(21)
SNOW HILL Greene
SOPHIA Randolph
SOUTH BRUNSWICK Brunswick
SOUTH MILLS Camden
SOUTHERN PINES Moore
SOUTHMONT Davidson
SOUTHPORT Brunswick
SPARTA Alleghany
SPEED Edgecombe
SPENCER Rowan
SPINDALE Rutherford
SPRING HOPE Nash
SPRING LAKE (28390) Harnett(53),
    Cumberland(46)

SPRUCE PINE Mitchell
STACY Carteret
STALEY (27355) Randolph(71),
    Chatham(28)
STANFIELD Stanly
STANLEY (28164) Gaston(78), Lincoln(21)
STANTONSBURG (27883) Wilson(70),
    Wayne(18), Greene(11)
STAR (27356) Montgomery(85), Moore(14)
STATE ROAD (28676) Wilkes(95), Surry(4)
STATESVILLE Iredell
STEDMAN Cumberland
STELLA (28582) Onslow(63), Carteret(36)
STEM Granville
STOKES Pitt
STOKESDALE (27357) Rockingham(67),
    Guilford(32)
STONEVILLE Rockingham
STONEWALL Pamlico
STONY POINT Alexander
STOVALL Granville
STUMPY POINT Dare
SUGAR GROVE Watauga
SUMMERFIELD (27358) Guilford(67),
    Rockingham(32)
SUNBURY Gates
SUNSET BEACH Brunswick
SUPPLY Brunswick
SWANNANOA Buncombe
SWANQUARTER Hyde
SWANSBORO (28584) Carteret(60),
    Onslow(39)
SWEPSONVILLE Alamance
SYLVA Jackson
TABOR CITY Columbus
TAPOCO Graham
TAR HEEL Bladen
TARAWA TERRACE Onslow
TARBORO Edgecombe
TAYLORSVILLE Alexander
TEACHEY Duplin
TERRELL Catawba
THOMASVILLE (27360) Davidson(94),
    Randolph(5)
THOMASVILLE Davidson
THURMOND Wilkes
TILLERY Halifax
TIMBERLAKE (27583) Person(98),
    Orange(1)
TOAST Surry
TOBACCOVILLE (27050) Forsyth(85),
    Stokes(14)
TODD (28684) Ashe(53), Watauga(46)
TOPTON (28781) Macon(51),
    Cherokee(48)
TOWNSVILLE Vance
TRAPHILL Wilkes
TRENTON Jones
TRINITY Randolph
TRIPLETT Watauga
TROUTMAN Iredell
TROY (27371) Montgomery(86),
    Randolph(13)
TRYON Polk
TUCKASEGEE Jackson
TURKEY Sampson
TURNERSBURG Iredell
TUXEDO Henderson
TYNER Chowan
UNION GROVE Iredell
UNION MILLS Rutherford
VALDESE Burke
VALE (28168) Lincoln(55), Catawba(43)
VALLE CRUCIS Watauga
VANCEBORO (28586) Craven(87), Pitt(6),
    Beaufort(5)
VANDEMERE Pamlico
VASS Moore
VAUGHAN Warren
VILAS Watauga
WACO Cleveland
WADE Cumberland
WADESBORO Anson

WAGRAM Scotland
WAKE FOREST (27587) Wake(94),
   Granville(3), Franklin(2)
WAKE FOREST Wake
WAKULLA Robeson
WALKERTOWN Forsyth
WALLACE (28466) Duplin(78), Pender(20),
   Sampson(1)
WALLBURG Davidson
WALNUT COVE (27052) Stokes(89),
   Forsyth(10)
WALSTONBURG (27888) Wilson(51),
   Greene(45), Pitt(2)
WANCHESE Dare
WARNE Clay
WARRENSVILLE Ashe
WARRENTON (27589) Warren(97),
   Franklin(2)
WARSAW Duplin
WASHINGTON (27889) Beaufort(97),
   Pitt(2)

WATHA Pender
WAVES Dare
WAXHAW Union
WAYNESVILLE Haywood
WEAVERVILLE (28787) Buncombe(95),
   Madison(4)
WEBSTER Jackson
WELCOME Davidson
WELDON Halifax
WENDELL (27591) Wake(77),
   Johnston(22)
WENTWORTH Rockingham
WEST END Moore
WEST JEFFERSON Ashe
WESTFIELD Surry
WHITAKERS (27891) Nash(90),
   Edgecombe(8), Halifax(1)
WHITE OAK Bladen
WHITE PLAINS Surry
WHITEHEAD Alleghany
WHITEVILLE Columbus

WHITSETT Guilford
WHITTIER Jackson
WILBAR Wilkes
WILKESBORO Wilkes
WILLARD (28478) Pender(96),
   Sampson(3)
WILLIAMSTON Martin
WILLISTON Carteret
WILLOW SPRING (27592) Wake(52),
   Johnston(43), Harnett(3)
WILMINGTON (28411) New Hanover(88),
   Pender(11)
WILMINGTON Brunswick
WILMINGTON New Hanover
WILSON (27896) Wilson(84), Nash(15)
WILSON Wilson
WILSONS MILLS Johnston
WINDSOR Bertie
WINFALL Perquimans
WINGATE Union
WINNABOW Brunswick

WINSTON SALEM (27127) Forsyth(89),
   Davidson(10)
WINSTON SALEM Forsyth
WINSTON-SALEM Forsyth
WINTERVILLE Pitt
WINTON Hertford
WISE Warren
WOODLAND (27897) Northampton(92),
   Hertford(7)
WOODLEAF Rowan
WRIGHTSVILLE BEACH New Hanover
YADKINVILLE Yadkin
YANCEYVILLE Caswell
YOUNGSVILLE (27596) Franklin(87),
   Wake(8), Granville(3)
ZEBULON (27597) Wake(76), Franklin(14),
   Johnston(4), Nash(4)
ZIONVILLE (28698) Watauga(98), Ashe(1)
ZIRCONIA Henderson

North Carolina ZIP/City Cross Reference

ZIP	City
27006-27006	ADVANCE
27007-27007	ARARAT
27008-27008	BARBER
27009-27009	BELEWS CREEK
27010-27010	BETHANIA
27011-27011	BOONVILLE
27012-27012	CLEMMONS
27013-27013	CLEVELAND
27014-27014	COOLEEMEE
27016-27016	DANBURY
27017-27017	DOBSON
27018-27018	EAST BEND
27019-27019	GERMANTON
27020-27020	HAMPTONVILLE
27021-27021	KING
27022-27022	LAWSONVILLE
27023-27023	LEWISVILLE
27024-27024	LOWGAP
27025-27025	MADISON
27027-27027	MAYODAN
27028-27028	MOCKSVILLE
27030-27030	MOUNT AIRY
27031-27031	WHITE PLAINS
27040-27040	PFAFFTOWN
27041-27041	PILOT MOUNTAIN
27042-27042	PINE HALL
27043-27043	PINNACLE
27045-27045	RURAL HALL
27046-27046	SANDY RIDGE
27047-27047	SILOAM
27048-27048	STONEVILLE
27049-27049	TOAST
27050-27050	TOBACCOVILLE
27051-27051	WALKERTOWN
27052-27052	WALNUT COVE
27053-27053	WESTFIELD
27054-27054	WOODLEAF
27055-27055	YADKINVILLE
27094-27099	RURAL HALL
27100-27100	WINSTON-SALEM
27100-27100	WINSTON SALEM
27100-27100	WINSTON-SALEM
27101-27199	WINSTON SALEM
27201-27201	ALAMANCE
27202-27202	ALTAMAHAW
27203-27205	ASHEBORO
27207-27207	BEAR CREEK
27208-27208	BENNETT
27209-27209	BISCOE
27212-27212	BLANCH
27213-27213	BONLEE
27214-27214	BROWNS SUMMIT
27215-27220	BURLINGTON
27228-27228	BYNUM
27229-27229	CANDOR
27230-27230	CEDAR FALLS
27231-27231	CEDAR GROVE
27233-27233	CLIMAX
27235-27235	COLFAX
27237-27237	CUMNOCK
27239-27239	DENTON
27242-27242	EAGLE SPRINGS
27243-27243	EFLAND
27244-27244	ELON COLLEGE
27247-27247	ETHER
27248-27248	FRANKLINVILLE
27249-27249	GIBSONVILLE
27251-27251	GLENDON
27252-27252	GOLDSTON
27253-27253	GRAHAM
27256-27256	GULF
27258-27258	HAW RIVER
27259-27259	HIGHFALLS
27260-27265	HIGH POINT
27278-27278	HILLSBOROUGH
27281-27281	JACKSON SPRINGS
27282-27282	JAMESTOWN
27283-27283	JULIAN
27284-27285	KERNERSVILLE
27288-27289	EDEN
27291-27291	LEASBURG
27292-27295	LEXINGTON
27298-27298	LIBERTY
27299-27299	LINWOOD
27301-27301	MC LEANSVILLE
27302-27302	MEBANE
27305-27305	MILTON
27306-27306	MOUNT GILEAD
27310-27310	OAK RIDGE
27311-27311	PELHAM
27312-27312	PITTSBORO
27313-27313	PLEASANT GARDEN
27314-27314	PROSPECT HILL
27315-27315	PROVIDENCE
27316-27316	RAMSEUR
27317-27317	RANDLEMAN
27320-27323	REIDSVILLE
27325-27325	ROBBINS
27326-27326	RUFFIN
27330-27332	SANFORD
27340-27340	SAXAPAHAW
27341-27341	SEAGROVE
27342-27342	SEDALIA
27343-27343	SEMORA
27344-27344	SILER CITY
27349-27349	SNOW CAMP
27350-27350	SOPHIA
27351-27351	SOUTHMONT
27355-27355	STALEY
27356-27356	STAR
27357-27357	STOKESDALE
27358-27358	SUMMERFIELD
27359-27359	SWEPSONVILLE
27360-27361	THOMASVILLE
27370-27370	TRINITY
27371-27371	TROY
27373-27373	WALLBURG
27374-27374	WELCOME
27375-27375	WENTWORTH
27376-27376	WEST END
27377-27377	WHITSETT
27379-27379	YANCEYVILLE
27400-27499	GREENSBORO
27501-27501	ANGIER
27502-27502	APEX
27503-27503	BAHAMA
27504-27504	BENSON
27505-27505	BROADWAY
27506-27506	BUIES CREEK
27507-27507	BULLOCK
27508-27508	BUNN
27509-27509	BUTNER
27510-27510	CARRBORO
27511-27513	CARY
27514-27517	CHAPEL HILL
27518-27519	CARY
27520-27520	CLAYTON
27521-27521	COATS
27522-27522	CREEDMOOR
27523-27523	EAGLE ROCK
27523-27523	APEX
27524-27524	FOUR OAKS
27525-27525	FRANKLINTON
27526-27526	FUQUAY VARINA
27527-27528	CLAYTON
27529-27529	GARNER
27530-27534	GOLDSBORO
27536-27537	HENDERSON
27539-27539	APEX
27540-27540	HOLLY SPRINGS
27541-27541	HURDLE MILLS
27542-27542	KENLY
27543-27543	KIPLING
27544-27544	KITTRELL
27545-27545	KNIGHTDALE
27546-27546	LILLINGTON
27549-27549	LOUISBURG
27551-27551	MACON
27552-27552	MAMERS
27553-27553	MANSON
27555-27555	MICRO
27556-27556	MIDDLEBURG
27557-27557	MIDDLESEX
27559-27559	MONCURE
27560-27560	MORRISVILLE
27562-27562	NEW HILL
27563-27563	NORLINA
27564-27564	NORTHSIDE
27565-27565	OXFORD
27568-27568	PINE LEVEL
27569-27569	PRINCETON
27570-27570	RIDGEWAY
27571-27571	ROLESVILLE
27572-27572	ROUGEMONT
27573-27574	ROXBORO
27576-27576	SELMA
27577-27577	SMITHFIELD
27581-27581	STEM
27582-27582	STOVALL
27583-27583	TIMBERLAKE
27584-27584	TOWNSVILLE
27586-27586	VAUGHAN
27587-27588	WAKE FOREST
27589-27589	WARRENTON
27591-27591	WENDELL
27592-27592	WILLOW SPRING
27593-27593	WILSONS MILLS
27594-27594	WISE
27596-27596	YOUNGSVILLE
27597-27597	ZEBULON
27599-27599	CHAPEL HILL
27600-27699	RALEIGH
27700-27722	DURHAM
27801-27804	ROCKY MOUNT
27805-27805	AULANDER
27806-27806	AURORA
27807-27807	BAILEY
27808-27808	BATH
27809-27809	BATTLEBORO
27810-27810	BELHAVEN
27811-27811	BELLARTHUR
27812-27812	BETHEL
27813-27813	BLACK CREEK
27814-27814	BLOUNTS CREEK
27816-27816	CASTALIA
27817-27817	CHOCOWINITY
27818-27818	COMO
27819-27819	CONETOE
27820-27820	CONWAY
27821-27821	EDWARD
27822-27822	ELM CITY
27823-27823	ENFIELD
27824-27824	ENGELHARD
27825-27825	EVERETTS
27826-27826	FAIRFIELD
27827-27827	FALKLAND
27828-27828	FARMVILLE
27829-27829	FOUNTAIN
27830-27830	FREMONT
27831-27831	GARYSBURG
27832-27832	GASTON
27833-27836	GREENVILLE
27837-27837	GRIMESLAND
27838-27838	GUMBERRY

27839-27839	HALIFAX
27840-27840	HAMILTON
27841-27841	HASSELL
27842-27842	HENRICO
27843-27843	HOBGOOD
27844-27844	HOLLISTER
27845-27845	JACKSON
27846-27846	JAMESVILLE
27847-27847	KELFORD
27848-27848	LASKER
27849-27849	LEWISTON WOODVILLE
27850-27850	LITTLETON
27851-27851	LUCAMA
27852-27852	MACCLESFIELD
27853-27853	MARGARETTSVILLE
27854-27854	MILWAUKEE
27855-27855	MURFREESBORO
27856-27856	NASHVILLE
27857-27857	OAK CITY
27858-27858	GREENVILLE
27859-27859	PALMYRA
27860-27860	PANTEGO
27861-27861	PARMELE
27862-27862	PENDLETON
27863-27863	PIKEVILLE
27864-27864	PINETOPS
27865-27865	PINETOWN
27866-27866	PLEASANT HILL
27867-27867	POTECASI
27868-27868	RED OAK
27869-27869	RICH SQUARE
27870-27870	ROANOKE RAPIDS
27871-27871	ROBERSONVILLE
27872-27872	ROXOBEL
27873-27873	SARATOGA
27874-27874	SCOTLAND NECK
27875-27875	SCRANTON
27876-27876	SEABOARD
27877-27877	SEVERN
27878-27878	SHARPSBURG
27879-27879	SIMPSON
27880-27880	SIMS
27881-27881	SPEED
27882-27882	SPRING HOPE
27883-27883	STANTONSBURG
27884-27884	STOKES
27885-27885	SWANQUARTER
27886-27886	TARBORO
27887-27887	TILLERY
27888-27888	WALSTONBURG
27889-27889	WASHINGTON
27890-27890	WELDON
27891-27891	WHITAKERS
27892-27892	WILLIAMSTON
27893-27896	WILSON
27897-27897	WOODLAND
27906-27909	ELIZABETH CITY
27910-27910	AHOSKIE
27915-27915	AVON
27916-27916	AYDLETT
27917-27917	BARCO
27919-27919	BELVIDERE
27920-27920	BUXTON
27921-27921	CAMDEN
27922-27922	COFIELD
27923-27923	COINJOCK
27924-27924	COLERAIN
27925-27925	COLUMBIA
27926-27926	CORAPEAKE
27927-27927	COROLLA
27928-27928	CRESWELL
27929-27929	CURRITUCK
27930-27930	DURANTS NECK
27932-27932	EDENTON
27935-27935	EURE
27936-27936	FRISCO
27937-27937	GATES
27938-27938	GATESVILLE
27939-27939	GRANDY
27941-27941	HARBINGER
27942-27942	HARRELLSVILLE
27943-27943	HATTERAS
27944-27944	HERTFORD

27946-27946	HOBBSVILLE
27947-27947	JARVISBURG
27948-27948	KILL DEVIL HILLS
27949-27949	KITTY HAWK
27950-27950	KNOTTS ISLAND
27953-27953	MANNS HARBOR
27954-27954	MANTEO
27956-27956	MAPLE
27957-27957	MERRY HILL
27958-27958	MOYOCK
27959-27959	NAGS HEAD
27960-27960	OCRACOKE
27962-27962	PLYMOUTH
27964-27964	POINT HARBOR
27965-27965	POPLAR BRANCH
27966-27966	POWELLS POINT
27967-27967	POWELLSVILLE
27968-27968	RODANTHE
27969-27969	RODUCO
27970-27970	ROPER
27972-27972	SALVO
27973-27973	SHAWBORO
27974-27974	SHILOH
27976-27976	SOUTH MILLS
27978-27978	STUMPY POINT
27979-27979	SUNBURY
27980-27980	TYNER
27981-27981	WANCHESE
27982-27982	WAVES
27983-27983	WINDSOR
27985-27985	WINFALL
27986-27986	WINTON
28001-28002	ALBEMARLE
28006-28006	ALEXIS
28007-28007	ANSONVILLE
28009-28009	BADIN
28010-28010	BARIUM SPRINGS
28012-28012	BELMONT
28016-28016	BESSEMER CITY
28017-28017	BOILING SPRINGS
28018-28018	BOSTIC
28019-28019	CAROLEEN
28020-28020	CASAR
28021-28021	CHERRYVILLE
28023-28023	CHINA GROVE
28024-28024	CLIFFSIDE
28025-28027	CONCORD
28031-28031	CORNELIUS
28032-28032	CRAMERTON
28033-28033	CROUSE
28034-28034	DALLAS
28035-28036	DAVIDSON
28037-28037	DENVER
28038-28038	EARL
28039-28039	EAST SPENCER
28040-28040	ELLENBORO
28041-28041	FAITH
28042-28042	FALLSTON
28043-28043	FOREST CITY
28051-28056	GASTONIA
28070-28070	HUNTERSVILLE
28071-28071	GOLD HILL
28072-28072	GRANITE QUARRY
28073-28073	GROVER
28074-28074	HARRIS
28075-28075	HARRISBURG
28076-28076	HENRIETTA
28077-28077	HIGH SHOALS
28078-28078	HUNTERSVILLE
28079-28079	INDIAN TRAIL
28080-28080	IRON STATION
28081-28083	KANNAPOLIS
28086-28086	KINGS MOUNTAIN
28088-28088	LANDIS
28089-28089	LATTIMORE
28090-28090	LAWNDALE
28091-28091	LILESVILLE
28092-28093	LINCOLNTON
28097-28097	LOCUST
28098-28098	LOWELL
28101-28101	MC ADENVILLE
28102-28102	MC FARLAN
28103-28103	MARSHVILLE

28104-28106	MATTHEWS
28107-28107	MIDLAND
28108-28108	MINERAL SPRINGS
28109-28109	MISENHEIMER
28110-28112	MONROE
28114-28114	MOORESBORO
28115-28117	MOORESVILLE
28119-28119	MORVEN
28120-28120	MOUNT HOLLY
28123-28123	MOUNT MOURNE
28124-28124	MOUNT PLEASANT
28125-28125	MOUNT ULLA
28126-28126	NEWELL
28127-28127	NEW LONDON
28128-28128	NORWOOD
28129-28129	OAKBORO
28130-28130	PAW CREEK
28133-28133	PEACHLAND
28134-28134	PINEVILLE
28135-28135	POLKTON
28136-28136	POLKVILLE
28137-28137	RICHFIELD
28138-28138	ROCKWELL
28139-28139	RUTHERFORDTON
28144-28147	SALISBURY
28150-28152	SHELBY
28159-28159	SPENCER
28160-28160	SPINDALE
28163-28163	STANFIELD
28164-28164	STANLEY
28166-28166	TROUTMAN
28167-28167	UNION MILLS
28168-28168	VALE
28169-28169	WACO
28170-28170	WADESBORO
28173-28173	WAXHAW
28174-28174	WINGATE
28200-28299	CHARLOTTE
28301-28306	FAYETTEVILLE
28307-28307	FORT BRAGG
28308-28308	POPE A F B
28309-28309	FAYETTEVILLE
28310-28310	FORT BRAGG
28311-28314	FAYETTEVILLE
28315-28315	ABERDEEN
28318-28318	AUTRYVILLE
28319-28319	BARNESVILLE
28320-28320	BLADENBORO
28323-28323	BUNNLEVEL
28324-28324	BUTTERS
28325-28325	CALYPSO
28326-28326	CAMERON
28327-28327	CARTHAGE
28328-28329	CLINTON
28330-28330	CORDOVA
28331-28331	CUMBERLAND
28332-28332	DUBLIN
28333-28333	DUDLEY
28334-28335	DUNN
28337-28337	ELIZABETHTOWN
28338-28338	ELLERBE
28339-28339	ERWIN
28340-28340	FAIRMONT
28341-28341	FAISON
28342-28342	FALCON
28343-28343	GIBSON
28344-28344	GODWIN
28345-28345	HAMLET
28347-28347	HOFFMAN
28348-28348	HOPE MILLS
28349-28349	KENANSVILLE
28350-28350	LAKEVIEW
28351-28351	LAUREL HILL
28352-28353	LAURINBURG
28355-28355	LEMON SPRINGS
28356-28356	LINDEN
28357-28357	LUMBER BRIDGE
28358-28360	LUMBERTON
28361-28361	MCCAIN
28362-28362	MARIETTA
28363-28363	MARSTON
28364-28364	MAXTON
28365-28365	MOUNT OLIVE

28366-28366	NEWTON GROVE
28367-28367	NORMAN
28368-28368	OLIVIA
28369-28369	ORRUM
28370-28370	PINEHURST
28371-28371	PARKTON
28372-28372	PEMBROKE
28373-28373	PINEBLUFF
28374-28374	PINEHURST
28375-28375	PROCTORVILLE
28376-28376	RAEFORD
28377-28377	RED SPRINGS
28378-28378	REX
28379-28380	ROCKINGHAM
28382-28382	ROSEBORO
28383-28383	ROWLAND
28384-28384	SAINT PAULS
28385-28385	SALEMBURG
28386-28386	SHANNON
28387-28388	SOUTHERN PINES
28390-28390	SPRING LAKE
28391-28391	STEDMAN
28392-28392	TAR HEEL
28393-28393	TURKEY
28394-28394	VASS
28395-28395	WADE
28396-28396	WAGRAM
28397-28397	WAKULLA
28398-28398	WARSAW
28399-28399	WHITE OAK
28401-28412	WILMINGTON
28420-28420	ASH
28421-28421	ATKINSON
28422-28422	BOLIVIA
28423-28423	BOLTON
28424-28424	BRUNSWICK
28425-28425	BURGAW
28428-28428	CAROLINA BEACH
28429-28429	CASTLE HAYNE
28430-28430	CERRO GORDO
28431-28431	CHADBOURN
28432-28432	CLARENDON
28433-28433	CLARKTON
28434-28434	COUNCIL
28435-28435	CURRIE
28436-28436	DELCO
28438-28438	EVERGREEN
28439-28439	FAIR BLUFF
28441-28441	GARLAND
28442-28442	HALLSBORO
28443-28443	HAMPSTEAD
28444-28444	HARRELLS
28445-28445	HOLLY RIDGE
28446-28446	INGOLD
28447-28447	IVANHOE
28448-28448	KELLY
28449-28449	KURE BEACH
28450-28450	LAKE WACCAMAW
28451-28451	LELAND
28452-28452	LONGWOOD
28453-28453	MAGNOLIA
28454-28454	MAPLE HILL
28455-28455	NAKINA
28456-28456	RIEGELWOOD
28457-28457	ROCKY POINT
28458-28458	ROSE HILL
28459-28459	SHALLOTTE
28460-28460	SNEADS FERRY
28461-28461	SOUTHPORT
28462-28462	SUPPLY
28463-28463	TABOR CITY
28464-28464	TEACHEY
28465-28465	OAK ISLAND
28466-28466	WALLACE
28467-28467	CALABASH
28468-28468	SUNSET BEACH
28469-28469	OCEAN ISLE BEACH
28470-28470	SOUTH BRUNSWICK
28471-28471	WATHA
28472-28472	WHITEVILLE
28478-28478	WILLARD
28479-28479	WINNABOW
28480-28480	WRIGHTSVILLE BEACH

28501-28504	KINSTON
28508-28508	ALBERTSON
28509-28509	ALLIANCE
28510-28510	ARAPAHOE
28511-28511	ATLANTIC
28512-28512	ATLANTIC BEACH
28513-28513	AYDEN
28515-28515	BAYBORO
28516-28516	BEAUFORT
28518-28518	BEULAVILLE
28519-28519	BRIDGETON
28520-28520	CEDAR ISLAND
28521-28521	CHINQUAPIN
28522-28522	COMFORT
28523-28523	COVE CITY
28524-28524	DAVIS
28525-28525	DEEP RUN
28526-28526	DOVER
28527-28527	ERNUL
28528-28528	GLOUCESTER
28529-28529	GRANTSBORO
28530-28530	GRIFTON
28531-28531	HARKERS ISLAND
28532-28532	HAVELOCK
28533-28533	CHERRY POINT
28537-28537	HOBUCKEN
28538-28538	HOOKERTON
28539-28539	HUBERT
28540-28541	JACKSONVILLE
28542-28542	CAMP LEJEUNE
28543-28543	TARAWA TERRACE
28544-28544	MIDWAY PARK
28545-28545	MCCUTCHEON FIELD
28546-28546	JACKSONVILLE
28547-28547	CAMP LEJEUNE
28551-28551	LA GRANGE
28552-28552	LOWLAND
28553-28553	MARSHALLBERG
28554-28554	MAURY
28555-28555	MAYSVILLE
28556-28556	MERRITT
28557-28557	MOREHEAD CITY
28560-28564	NEW BERN
28570-28570	NEWPORT
28571-28571	ORIENTAL
28572-28572	PINK HILL
28573-28573	POLLOCKSVILLE
28574-28574	RICHLANDS
28575-28575	SALTER PATH
28577-28577	SEALEVEL
28578-28578	SEVEN SPRINGS
28579-28579	SMYRNA
28580-28580	SNOW HILL
28581-28581	STACY
28582-28582	STELLA
28583-28583	STONEWALL
28584-28584	SWANSBORO
28585-28585	TRENTON
28586-28586	VANCEBORO
28587-28587	VANDEMERE
28589-28589	WILLISTON
28590-28590	WINTERVILLE
28594-28594	EMERALD ISLE

28601-28603	HICKORY
28604-28604	BANNER ELK
28605-28605	BLOWING ROCK
28606-28606	BOOMER
28607-28608	BOONE
28609-28609	CATAWBA
28610-28610	CLAREMONT
28611-28611	COLLETTSVILLE
28612-28612	CONNELLYS SPRINGS
28613-28613	CONOVER
28614-28614	CRANBERRY
28615-28615	CRESTON
28616-28616	CROSSNORE
28617-28617	CRUMPLER
28618-28618	DEEP GAP
28619-28619	DREXEL
28621-28621	ELKIN
28622-28622	ELK PARK
28623-28623	ENNICE
28624-28624	FERGUSON
28625-28625	STATESVILLE
28626-28626	FLEETWOOD
28627-28627	GLADE VALLEY
28628-28628	GLEN ALPINE
28629-28629	GLENDALE SPRINGS
28630-28630	GRANITE FALLS
28631-28631	GRASSY CREEK
28632-28632	GRAYSON
28633-28633	LENOIR
28634-28634	HARMONY
28635-28635	HAYS
28636-28636	HIDDENITE
28637-28637	HILDEBRAN
28638-28638	HUDSON
28639-28639	HUSK
28640-28640	JEFFERSON
28641-28641	JONAS RIDGE
28642-28642	JONESVILLE
28643-28643	LANSING
28644-28644	LAUREL SPRINGS
28645-28645	LENOIR
28646-28646	LINVILLE
28647-28647	LINVILLE FALLS
28648-28648	LONGISLAND
28649-28649	MC GRADY
28650-28650	MAIDEN
28651-28651	MILLERS CREEK
28652-28652	MINNEAPOLIS
28653-28653	MONTEZUMA
28654-28654	MORAVIAN FALLS
28655-28655	MORGANTON
28656-28656	NORTH WILKESBORO
28657-28657	NEWLAND
28658-28658	NEWTON
28659-28659	NORTH WILKESBORO
28660-28660	OLIN
28661-28661	PATTERSON
28662-28662	PINEOLA
28663-28663	PINEY CREEK
28664-28664	PLUMTREE
28665-28665	PURLEAR
28666-28666	ICARD
28667-28667	RHODHISS

28668-28668	ROARING GAP
28669-28669	ROARING RIVER
28670-28670	RONDA
28671-28671	RUTHERFORD COLLEGE
28672-28672	SCOTTVILLE
28673-28673	SHERRILLS FORD
28674-28674	NORTH WILKESBORO
28675-28675	SPARTA
28676-28676	STATE ROAD
28677-28677	STATESVILLE
28678-28678	STONY POINT
28679-28679	SUGAR GROVE
28680-28680	MORGANTON
28681-28681	TAYLORSVILLE
28682-28682	TERRELL
28683-28683	THURMOND
28684-28684	TODD
28685-28685	TRAPHILL
28686-28686	TRIPLETT
28687-28687	STATESVILLE
28688-28688	TURNERSBURG
28689-28689	UNION GROVE
28690-28690	VALDESE
28691-28691	VALLE CRUCIS
28692-28692	VILAS
28693-28693	WARRENSVILLE
28694-28694	WEST JEFFERSON
28695-28695	WHITEHEAD
28696-28696	WILBAR
28697-28697	WILKESBORO
28698-28698	ZIONVILLE
28699-28699	SCOTTS
28701-28701	ALEXANDER
28702-28702	ALMOND
28703-28703	AQUONE
28704-28704	ARDEN
28705-28705	BAKERSVILLE
28707-28707	BALSAM
28708-28708	BALSAM GROVE
28709-28709	BARNARDSVILLE
28710-28710	BAT CAVE
28711-28711	BLACK MOUNTAIN
28712-28712	BREVARD
28713-28713	BRYSON CITY
28714-28714	BURNSVILLE
28715-28715	CANDLER
28716-28716	CANTON
28717-28717	CASHIERS
28718-28718	CEDAR MOUNTAIN
28719-28719	CHEROKEE
28720-28720	CHIMNEY ROCK
28721-28721	CLYDE
28722-28722	COLUMBUS
28723-28723	CULLOWHEE
28724-28724	DANA
28725-28725	DILLSBORO
28726-28726	EAST FLAT ROCK
28727-28727	EDNEYVILLE
28728-28728	ENKA
28729-28729	ETOWAH
28730-28730	FAIRVIEW
28731-28731	FLAT ROCK
28732-28732	FLETCHER

28733-28733	FONTANA DAM
28734-28734	FRANKLIN
28735-28735	GERTON
28736-28736	GLENVILLE
28737-28737	GLENWOOD
28738-28738	HAZELWOOD
28739-28739	HENDERSONVILLE
28740-28740	GREENMOUNTAIN
28740-28740	GREEN MOUNTAIN
28741-28741	HIGHLANDS
28742-28742	HORSE SHOE
28743-28743	HOT SPRINGS
28744-28744	FRANKLIN
28745-28745	LAKE JUNALUSKA
28746-28746	LAKE LURE
28747-28747	LAKE TOXAWAY
28748-28748	LEICESTER
28749-28749	LITTLE SWITZERLAND
28750-28750	LYNN
28751-28751	MAGGIE VALLEY
28752-28752	MARION
28753-28753	MARSHALL
28754-28754	MARS HILL
28755-28755	MICAVILLE
28756-28756	MILL SPRING
28757-28757	MONTREAT
28758-28758	MOUNTAIN HOME
28760-28760	NAPLES
28761-28761	NEBO
28762-28762	OLD FORT
28763-28763	OTTO
28765-28765	PENLAND
28766-28766	PENROSE
28768-28768	PISGAH FOREST
28770-28770	RIDGECREST
28771-28771	ROBBINSVILLE
28772-28772	ROSMAN
28773-28773	SALUDA
28774-28774	SAPPHIRE
28775-28775	SCALY MOUNTAIN
28776-28776	SKYLAND
28777-28777	SPRUCE PINE
28778-28778	SWANNANOA
28779-28779	SYLVA
28780-28780	TAPOCO
28781-28781	TOPTON
28782-28782	TRYON
28783-28783	TUCKASEGEE
28784-28784	TUXEDO
28785-28786	WAYNESVILLE
28787-28787	WEAVERVILLE
28788-28788	WEBSTER
28789-28789	WHITTIER
28790-28790	ZIRCONIA
28791-28793	HENDERSONVILLE
28800-28816	ASHEVILLE
28901-28901	ANDREWS
28902-28902	BRASSTOWN
28903-28903	CULBERSON
28904-28904	HAYESVILLE
28905-28905	MARBLE
28906-28906	MURPHY
28909-28909	WARNE

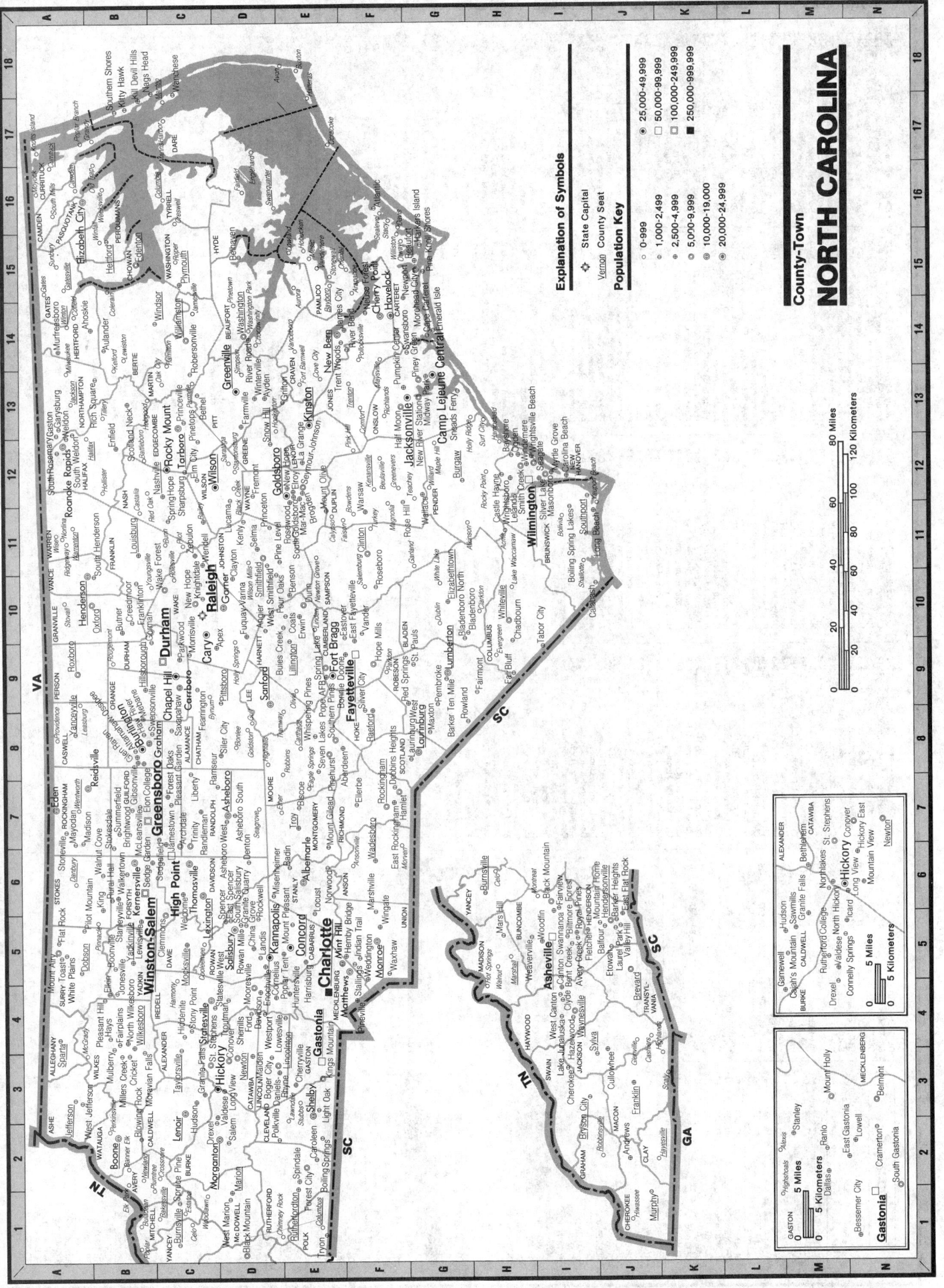

NORTH CAROLINA

County-Town

Explanation of Symbols

⊕ State Capital
Vernon   County Seat

Population Key

● 25,000-49,999		
□ 50,000-99,999		
▢ 100,000-249,999		
■ 250,000-999,999		

○ 0-999
⊙ 1,000-2,499
⊕ 2,500-4,999
⊙ 5,000-9,999
◉ 10,000-19,000
◉ 20,000-24,999

COUNTIES

(100 Counties)

Name of County	Population	Location on Map
ALAMANCE	108,213	C-8
ALEXANDER	27,544	C-3
ALLEGHANY	9,590	A-3
ANSON	23,474	F-6
ASHE	22,209	A-2
AVERY	14,867	B-2
BEAUFORT	42,283	D-14
BERTIE	20,388	B-13
BLADEN	28,663	F-9
BRUNSWICK	50,985	I-11
BUNCOMBE	174,821	H-5
BURKE	75,744	C-2
CABARRUS	98,935	E-5
CALDWELL	70,709	B-2
CAMDEN	5,904	A-15
CARTERET	52,556	F-14
CASWELL	20,693	A-8
CATAWBA	118,412	D-3
CHATHAM	38,759	C-8
CHEROKEE	20,170	J-1
CHOWAN	13,506	B-15
CLAY	7,155	J-2
CLEVELAND	84,714	D-2
COLUMBUS	49,587	H-9
CRAVEN	81,613	E-13
CUMBERLAND	274,566	E-9
CURRITUCK	13,736	A-16
DARE	22,746	C-17
DAVIDSON	126,677	C-6
DAVIE	27,859	C-5
DUPLIN	39,995	E-11
DURHAM	181,835	B-9
EDGECOMBE	56,558	C-12
FORSYTH	265,878	B-6
FRANKLIN	36,414	B-11
GASTON	175,093	E-3
GATES	9,305	A-14
GRAHAM	7,196	I-2
GRANVILLE	38,345	A-10
GREENE	15,384	D-12
GUILFORD	347,420	B-7
HALIFAX	55,516	A-12
HARNETT	67,822	D-9
HAYWOOD	46,942	H-4
HENDERSON	69,285	I-5
HERTFORD	22,523	A-14
HOKE	22,856	F-8
HYDE	5,411	D-15
IREDELL	92,931	C-4
JACKSON	26,846	I-3
JOHNSTON	81,306	D-11
JONES	9,414	E-13
LEE	41,374	D-9
LENOIR	57,274	E-12
LINCOLN	50,319	D-3
MACON	23,499	J-2
MADISON	16,953	H-5
MARTIN	25,078	C-13
MCDOWELL	35,681	D-1
MECKLENBURG	511,433	E-4
MITCHELL	14,433	B-1
MONTGOMERY	23,346	E-7
MOORE	59,013	D-7
NASH	76,677	B-12
NEW HANOVER	120,284	I-12
NORTHAMPTON	20,798	A-13
ONSLOW	149,838	F-13
ORANGE	93,851	B-9
PAMLICO	11,372	E-14
PASQUOTANK	31,298	A-15
PENDER	28,855	G-11
PERQUIMANS	10,447	B-15
PERSON	30,180	A-9
PITT	107,924	D-13
POLK	14,416	E-1
RANDOLPH	106,546	C-7
RICHMOND	44,518	E-7
ROBESON	105,179	F-9
ROCKINGHAM	86,064	A-7
ROWAN	110,605	C-5
RUTHERFORD	56,918	D-1
SAMPSON	47,297	E-10
SCOTLAND	33,754	F-8
STANLY	51,765	E-6
STOKES	37,223	A-6
SURRY	61,704	A-4
SWAIN	11,268	I-3
TRANSYLVANIA	25,520	J-4
TYRRELL	3,856	C-16
UNION	84,211	F-5
VANCE	38,892	A-10
WAKE	423,380	C-10
WARREN	17,265	A-11
WASHINGTON	13,997	C-15
WATAUGA	36,952	B-2
WAYNE	104,666	D-12
WILKES	59,393	B-3
WILSON	66,061	C-12
YADKIN	30,488	B-4
YANCEY	15,419	C-1
TOTAL	6,628,637	

CITIES AND TOWNS

Note: The first name is that of the city or town, second, that of the county in which it is located, then the population and location on the map.

City or Town, County, Population	Location on Map
Aberdeen, Moore, 2,700	E-8
Ahoskie, Hertford, 4,391	B-14
Albemarle, Stanly, 14,939	E-6
• Altamahaw-Ossipee, Alamance, 1,076	B-8
Andrews, Cherokee, 2,551	J-2
Angier, Harnett, 2,235	D-10
Apex, Wake, 4,968	D-9
Archdale, Guilford/Randolph, 6,913	C-7
Asheboro, Randolph, 16,362	D-7
Asheville, Buncombe, 61,607	I-5
Atlantic Beach, Carteret, 1,938	F-15
Aulander, Bertie, 1,209	B-14
• Avery Creek, Buncombe, 1,144	J-5
Ayden, Pitt, 4,740	D-13
• Badin, Stanly, 1,481	E-6
Bakersville, Mitchell, 332	C-1
• Balfour, Henderson, 1,118	J-5
• Barker Heights, Henderson, 1,137	J-5
• Barker Ten Mile, Robeson, 1,087	G-9
Bayboro, Pamlico, 733	E-15
• Bayshore, New Hanover, 1,661	H-12
Beaufort, Carteret, 3,808	G-15
Belhaven, Beaufort, 2,269	D-15
Belmont, Gaston, 8,434	N-3
Benson, Johnston, 2,810	E-10
• Bent Creek, Buncombe, 1,487	I-5
Bessemer City, Gaston, 4,698	N-1
Bethel, Pitt, 1,842	C-13
• Bethlehem, Alexander, 3,186	M-6
Biltmore Forest, Buncombe, 1,327	I-5
Biscoe, Montgomery, 1,484	E-7
Black Mountain, Buncombe, 5,418	I-6
Bladenboro, Bladen, 1,821	G-10
Bladenboro North, Bladen	G-10
Blowing Rock, Caldwell/Watauga, 1,257	B-2
• Boger City, Lincoln, 1,373	D-3
Boiling Spring Lakes, Brunswick, 1,650	I-12
Boiling Springs, Cleveland, 2,445	E-2
• Bonnie Doone, Cumberland, 3,893	F-9
Boone, Watauga, 12,915	B-2
Boonville, Yadkin, 1,009	B-5
Brevard, Transylvania, 5,388	J-5
Brightwood, Guilford	B-7
• Brogden, Wayne, 3,246	E-12
Bryson City, Swain, 1,145	I-3
• Buies Creek, Harnett, 2,085	E-10
Burgaw, Pender, 1,807	G-12
Burlington, Alamance, 39,498	B-8
Burnsville, Yancey, 1,482	C-1
• Butner, Granville, 4,679	B-10
Cajah's Mountain, Caldwell, 2,429	M-5
Calabash, Brunswick, 1,210	I-11
Camden, Camden	A-16
• Camp Lejeune Central, Onslow, 36,716	G-13
Canton, Haywood, 3,790	I-4
Cape Carteret, Carteret, 1,008	G-14
Caroleen, Rutherford	E-2
Carolina Beach, New Hanover, 3,630	I-12
Carrboro, Orange, 11,553	C-9
Carthage, Moore, 976	E-8
Cary, Wake, 43,858	C-10
• Castle Hayne, New Hanover, 1,182	H-12
Chadbourn, Columbus, 2,005	H-9
Chapel Hill, Durham/Orange, 38,719	C-9
Charlotte, Mecklenburg, 395,934	E-4
Cherokee, Swain	I-3
Cherry Point, Craven	F-14
Cherryville, Gaston, 4,756	E-3
China Grove, Rowan, 2,732	D-5
Clayton, Johnston, 4,756	D-10
Clemmons, Forsyth, 6,020	C-6
Clinton, Sampson, 8,204	F-11
Clyde, Haywood, 1,041	I-4
Coats, Harnett, 1,493	E-10
Columbia, Tyrrell, 836	C-16
Columbus, Polk, 812	E-1
Concord, Cabarrus, 27,347	E-5
Connelly Springs, Burke, 1,349	N-5
Conover, Catawba, 5,465	D-3
Cornelius, Mecklenburg, 2,581	D-4
Cramerton, Gaston, 2,371	N-2
Creedmoor, Granville, 1,504	B-10
• Cricket, Wilkes, 2,015	B-3
• Cullowhee, Jackson, 4,029	J-4
Currituck, Currituck	A-16
Dallas, Gaston, 3,012	M-2
Danbury, Stokes, 119	A-6
Daniels-Rhyne, Lincoln	D-3
Davidson, Iredell/Mecklenburg, 4,046	D-4
Denton, Davidson, 1,292	D-6
Dobbins Heights, Richmond, 1,144	F-7
Dobson, Surry, 1,195	A-5
Drexel, Burke, 1,746	C-2
Dunn, Harnett, 8,336	E-10
Durham, Durham/Orange, 136,611	C-9
East Fayetteville, Cumberland	F-10
• East Flat Rock, Henderson, 3,218	J-5
East Gastonia, Gaston	N-2
• East Rockingham, Richmond, 4,158	F-7
East Spencer, Rowan, 2,055	D-5
• Eastover, Cumberland, 1,243	F-10
Eden, Rockingham, 15,238	A-7
Edenton, Chowan, 5,268	B-15
Elizabeth City, Camden/Pasquotank, 14,292	A-16
Elizabethtown, Bladen, 3,704	G-10
Elkin, Surry/Wilkes, 3,790	B-4
Ellerbe, Richmond, 1,132	F-7
Elm City, Wilson, 1,624	C-12
Elon College, Alamance, 4,394	B-8
• Elroy, Wayne, 4,028	E-12
Emerald Isle, Carteret, 2,434	G-14
Enfield, Halifax, 3,082	B-12
• Enochville, Rowan, 2,901	D-5
Erwin, Harnett, 4,061	E-10
• Etowah, Henderson, 1,997	J-5
Fair Bluff, Columbus, 1,068	H-9
Fairmont, Robeson, 2,489	H-9
• Fairplains, Wilkes, 2,339	B-4
• Fairview, Buncombe, 1,830	I-6
Farmville, Pitt, 4,392	D-13
Fayetteville, Cumberland, 75,695	F-9
• Fearrington, Chatham, 1,101	C-8
• Flat Rock, Surry, 1,812	A-5
Fletcher, Henderson, 2,787	I-5
Forest City, Rutherford, 7,475	E-2
• Forest Oaks, Guilford, 3,054	C-7
• Fort Bragg, Cumberland, 34,744	E-9
Four Oaks, Johnston, 1,308	D-10
Franklin, Macon, 2,873	J-3
Franklinton, Franklin, 1,615	B-10
Fremont, Wayne, 1,710	D-12
Fuquay-Varina, Wake, 4,562	D-10
Gamewell, Caldwell, 3,357	M-5
Garner, Wake, 14,967	D-10
Garysburg, Northampton, 1,057	A-13
Gaston, Northampton, 1,003	A-13
Gastonia, Gaston, 54,732	E-3
Gatesville, Gates, 308	A-15
Gibsonville, Alamance/Guilford, 3,441	B-8
• Glen Raven, Alamance, 2,616	B-8
Goldsboro, Wayne, 40,709	E-12
• Gorman, Durham, 1,090	C-10
Graham, Alamance, 10,426	B-8
Granite Falls, Caldwell, 3,253	C-3
Granite Quarry, Rowan, 1,646	D-5
Greensboro, Guilford, 183,521	B-7
Greenville, Pitt, 44,972	D-13
Grifton, Lenoir/Pitt, 2,393	E-13
• Half Moon, Onslow, 6,306	F-13
Halifax, Halifax, 327	B-12
Hamlet, Richmond, 6,196	F-7
• Harkers Island, Carteret, 1,759	G-15
Harrisburg, Cabarrus, 1,625	E-5
Havelock, Craven, 20,268	F-14
Haw River, Alamance, 1,855	B-8
Hayesville, Clay, 279	J-2
• Hays, Wilkes, 1,522	B-4
Hazelwood, Haywood, 1,678	I-4
• Hemby Bridge, Union, 2,876	E-5
Henderson, Vance, 15,655	A-10
Hendersonville, Henderson, 7,284	J-5
Hertford, Perquimans, 2,105	B-15
Hickory, Burke/Catawba, 28,301	C-3
Hickory East, Catawba	N-6
Hiddenite, Alexander	C-4
High Point, Davidson/Forsyth/Guilford/Randolph, 69,496	C-6
Hillsborough, Orange, 4,263	B-9
Hope Mills, Cumberland, 8,184	F-9
Hudson, Caldwell, 2,819	C-3
Huntersville, Mecklenburg, 3,014	E-4
• Icard, Burke, 2,553	N-5
Indian Trail, Union, 1,942	F-5
Jackson, Northampton, 592	A-13
Jacksonville, Onslow, 30,013	G-13
• James City, Craven, 4,279	F-14
Jamestown, Guilford, 2,600	C-7
Jefferson, Ashe, 1,300	A-3
Jonesville, Yadkin, 1,549	B-4
Kannapolis, Cabarrus/Rowan, 29,696	D-5
Kenansville, Duplin, 856	F-12
Kenly, Johnston/Wilson, 1,549	D-11
Kernersville, Forsyth/Guilford, 10,836	B-6
Kill Devil Hills, Dare, 4,238	B-17
King, Forsyth/Stokes, 4,059	B-6
Kings Mountain, Cleveland/Gaston, 8,763	E-3
Kinston, Lenoir, 25,295	E-13
Kitty Hawk, Dare, 1,937	B-17
Knightdale, Wake, 1,884	C-10
La Grange, Lenoir, 2,805	E-12
• Lake Junaluska, Haywood, 2,482	I-4
Landis, Rowan, 2,333	D-5
Landis Northeast, Rowan	D-5
Laurel Park, Henderson, 1,322	J-5
Laurinburg, Scotland, 11,643	G-8
Laurinburg West, Scotland	G-8
Leland, Brunswick, 1,801	H-12
Lenoir, Caldwell, 14,192	C-3
• Lewisville, Forsyth, 3,206	B-5
Lexington, Davidson, 16,581	C-6
Liberty, Randolph, 2,047	C-8
• Light Oak, Cleveland, 1,339	E-3
Lillington, Harnett, 2,048	E-9
Lincolnton, Lincoln, 6,847	D-3
Locust, Stanly, 1,940	E-6
Long Beach, Brunswick, 3,816	I-11
Long View, Burke/Catawba, 3,229	D-3
Louisburg, Franklin, 3,037	B-11
Lowell, Gaston, 2,704	N-2
• Lowesville, Lincoln, 1,092	D-4
Lumberton, Robeson, 18,601	G-9
Madison, Rockingham, 2,371	A-7
Maiden, Catawba/Lincoln, 2,574	D-3
Manteo, Dare, 991	C-17
• Mar-Mac, Wayne, 3,282	E-12
Marion, McDowell, 4,765	D-1
Mars Hill, Madison, 1,611	H-5
Marshall, Madison, 809	H-5
Marshville, Union, 2,020	F-5
• Masonboro, New Hanover, 7,010	I-12
Matthews, Mecklenburg, 13,651	E-5
Maxton, Robeson/Scotland, 2,373	G-8
Mayodan, Rockingham, 2,471	A-7
• McLeansville, Guilford, 1,154	B-7
Mebane, Alamance/Orange, 4,754	B-8
Midway Park, Onslow	G-13
• Millers Creek, Wilkes, 1,787	B-3
Mint Hill, Mecklenburg, 11,567	E-5
Misenheimer, Stanly	D-6
Mocksville, Davie, 3,399	C-5
Monroe, Union, 16,127	F-5
Mooresville, Iredell, 9,317	D-4
• Moravian Falls, Wilkes, 1,736	B-3
Morehead City, Carteret, 6,046	G-15
Morganton, Burke, 15,085	C-2
Morrisville, Durham/Wake, 1,022	C-9
Mount Airy, Surry, 7,156	A-5
Mount Gilead, Montgomery, 1,336	E-7
Mount Holly, Gaston, 7,710	M-3
Mount Olive, Duplin/Wayne, 4,582	E-11
Mount Pleasant, Cabarrus, 1,027	E-5
• Mountain Home, Henderson, 1,898	J-5
• Mountain View, Catawba, 3,697	N-6
• Mulberry, Wilkes, 2,339	B-4
Murfreesboro, Hertford, 2,580	A-14
Murphy, Cherokee, 1,575	J-1
• Myrtle Grove, New Hanover, 4,275	I-12
Nags Head, Dare, 1,838	C-18
Nashville, Nash, 3,617	C-12
• Neuse Forest, Craven, 1,110	F-14
New Bern, Craven, 17,363	E-14
• New Hope, Wake, 5,694	C-10
• New Hope, Wayne, 4,491	E-12
• New River Station, Onslow, 9,732	G-13
Newland, Avery, 645	B-2
Newport, Carteret, 2,516	F-15
Newton, Catawba, 9,304	D-3
• North Hickory, Catawba, 4,299	M-6
North Wilkesboro, Wilkes, 3,384	B-4
• Northlakes, Caldwell, 1,219	M-6
Norwood, Stanly, 1,617	E-6
• Ogden, New Hanover, 3,228	H-12
Oxford, Granville, 7,913	B-10
• Parkwood, Durham, 4,123	C-9
Pembroke, Robeson, 2,241	G-9
Pilot Mountain, Surry, 1,181	A-5
Pine Knoll Shores, Carteret, 1,360	G-15
Pine Level, Johnston, 1,217	E-11
Pinehurst, Moore, 5,103	E-8
Pinetops, Edgecombe, 1,514	C-12
Pineville, Mecklenburg, 2,970	F-4
• Piney Green, Onslow, 8,999	G-13
Pittsboro, Chatham, 1,436	D-9
• Pleasant Garden, Guilford, 2,228	C-7
• Pleasant Hill, Wilkes, 1,114	B-4
Plymouth, Washington, 4,328	C-15
Polkville, Cleveland, 1,514	D-2
• Pope AFB, Cumberland, 2,857	E-9
• Poplar Tent, Cabarrus, 3,872	E-5
Princeton, Johnston, 1,181	D-11
Princeville, Edgecombe, 1,652	C-13
• Pumpkin Center, Onslow, 2,857	G-13
Raeford, Hoke, 3,469	F-8
Raleigh, Wake, 207,951	C-10
Ramseur, Randolph, 1,186	D-7
Randleman, Randolph, 2,612	C-7
Ranlo, Gaston, 1,650	M-2
Red Springs, Robeson, 3,799	G-9
Reidsville, Rockingham, 12,183	A-7
Rich Square, Northampton, 1,058	B-13
River Bend, Craven, 2,408	F-14
• River Road, Beaufort, 3,892	D-15
Roanoke Rapids, Halifax, 15,722	A-12
Robbinsville, Graham, 709	J-2
Robersonville, Martin, 1,940	C-13
Rockingham, Richmond, 9,399	F-7
Rockwell, Rowan, 1,598	D-5
Rocky Mount, Edgecombe/Nash, 48,997	C-12
Rose Hill, Duplin, 1,287	F-12
Roseboro, Sampson, 1,441	F-10
Rowan Mill, Rowan	D-5
Rowland, Robeson, 1,139	G-8
Roxboro, Person, 7,332	A-9
• Royal Pines, Buncombe, 4,418	I-5
Rural Hall, Forsyth, 1,652	B-6
Rutherford College, Burke, 1,126	M-5
Rutherfordton, Rutherford, 3,617	E-1
Saint Pauls, Robeson, 1,992	G-9
• Saint Stephens, Catawba, 8,734	M-7
• Salem, Burke, 2,271	D-2
Salisbury, Rowan, 23,087	D-5
Sanford, Lee, 14,475	D-9
Sawmills, Caldwell, 4,088	M-5
• Saxapahaw, Alamance, 1,178	C-8
Scotland Neck, Halifax, 2,575	B-13
• Seagate, New Hanover, 5,444	H-12
• Sedge Garden, Forsyth, 2,784	B-6
Sedgefield, Guilford	C-7
Selma, Johnston, 4,600	D-11
• Seven Lakes, Moore, 2,049	E-7
Seymour-Johnson, Wayne	E-12
Sharpsburg, Edgecombe/Nash/Wilson, 1,536	C-12
Shelby, Cleveland, 14,669	E-3
• Sherrills Ford, Catawba, 3,185	D-4
Siler City, Chatham, 4,808	D-8
• Silver City, Hoke, 1,343	F-8
• Silver Lake, New Hanover, 4,071	I-12
• Smith Creek, New Hanover, 7,461	H-12
Smithfield, Johnston, 7,540	D-11
• Sneads Ferry, Onslow, 2,031	G-13
Snow Hill, Greene, 1,378	D-12
• South Gastonia, Gaston, 5,487	N-2
South Goldsboro, Wayne	E-12
• South Henderson, Vance, 1,374	B-10
• South Rosemary, Halifax, 1,955	A-12
South Salisbury, Rowan	D-5
• South Weldon, Halifax, 1,640	A-13
Southern Pines, Moore, 9,129	E-8
Southern Shores, Dare, 1,447	B-17
Southport, Brunswick, 2,369	I-12
Sparta, Alleghany, 1,957	A-4
Spencer, Rowan, 3,219	D-5
Spindale, Rutherford, 4,040	E-2
Spring Hope, Nash, 1,221	C-11
Spring Lake, Cumberland, 7,524	E-9
Spruce Pine, Mitchell, 2,010	C-1
Stallings, Union, 2,132	F-5
Stanley, Gaston, 2,823	M-2
• Stanleyville, Forsyth, 4,779	B-6
Statesville, Iredell, 17,567	C-4
Stokesdale, Guilford, 2,134	B-7
Stoneville, Rockingham, 1,109	A-7
• Stony Point, Alexander/Iredell, 1,286	C-4
• Summerfield, Guilford, 2,051	B-7
• Swannanoa, Buncombe, 3,538	I-5
Swanquarter, Hyde	D-16
Swansboro, Onslow, 1,165	G-14
• Swepsonville, Alamance, 1,195	B-8
Sylva, Jackson, 1,809	I-3
Tabor City, Columbus, 2,330	I-9
Tarboro, Edgecombe, 11,037	C-13
Taylorsville, Alexander, 1,566	C-4
Thomasville, Davidson, 15,915	C-6
• Toast, Surry, 2,125	A-5
Trent Woods, Craven, 2,366	F-14
Trenton, Jones, 248	F-13
• Trinity, Randolph, 5,469	C-7
Troutman, Iredell, 1,493	D-4
Troy, Montgomery, 3,404	E-7
Tryon, Polk, 1,680	E-1
Valdese, Burke, 3,914	C-3
• Valley Hill, Henderson, 1,802	J-5
• Vander, Cumberland, 1,179	F-10
Wadesboro, Anson, 3,645	F-6
Wake Forest, Wake, 5,769	C-10
Walkertown, Forsyth, 1,200	B-6
Wallace, Duplin/Pender, 2,939	G-12
Walnut Cove, Stokes, 1,088	B-6
• Wanchese, Dare, 1,380	C-18
Warrenton, Warren, 949	A-11
Warsaw, Duplin, 2,859	F-11
Washington, Beaufort, 9,075	D-14
Waxhaw, Union, 1,294	F-5
Waynesville, Haywood, 6,758	I-4
Weaverville, Buncombe, 2,107	H-5
Weddington, Mecklenburg/Union, 3,803	F-5
• Welcome, Davidson, 3,377	C-6
Weldon, Halifax, 1,392	A-13
Wendell, Wake, 2,822	C-11
Wentworth, Rockingham	A-7
• West Canton, Haywood, 1,119	I-4
West Jefferson, Ashe, 1,002	A-3
• West Marion, McDowell, 1,291	D-1
• West Smithfield, Johnston, 2,411	E-11
• Westport, Lincoln, 1,280	D-4
Whispering Pines, Moore, 1,243	E-8
• White Plains, Surry, 1,027	A-5
Whiteville, Columbus, 5,078	H-10
Wilkesboro, Wilkes, 2,573	B-4
Williamston, Martin, 5,503	C-14
Wilmington, New Hanover, 55,530	H-12
Wilson, Wilson, 36,930	D-12
• Windemere, New Hanover, 4,604	H-12
Windsor, Bertie, 2,056	C-14
Wingate, Union, 2,821	F-5
Winston-Salem, Forsyth, 143,485	B-6
Winterville, Pitt, 2,816	D-13
Winton, Hertford, 796	A-14
Woodfin, Buncombe, 2,736	I-5
• Wrightsboro, New Hanover, 4,752	H-12
Wrightsville Beach, New Hanover, 2,937	H-12
Yadkinville, Yadkin, 2,525	B-5
Yanceyville, Caswell, 1,973	A-8
Zebulon, Wake, 3,173	C-11

Explanation of symbols: • – Census Designated Place (CDP)

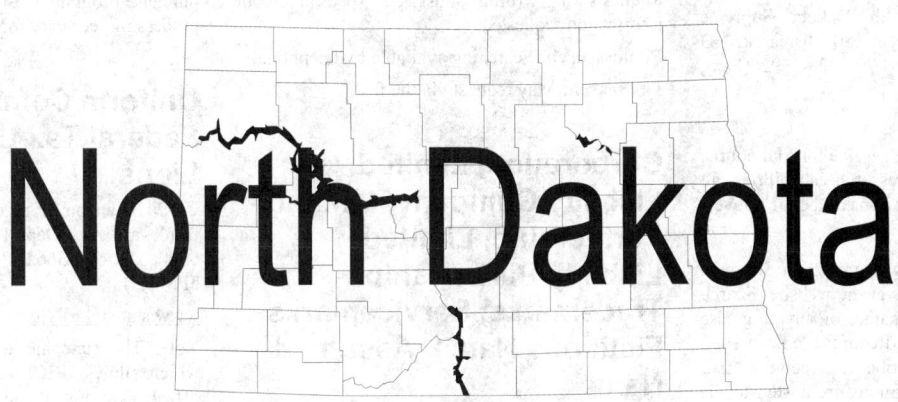

General Help Numbers:

Governor's Office
State Capitol   701-328-2200
600 E Boulevard Ave, 1st Floor   Fax 701-328-2205
Bismarck, ND 58505-0001   8AM-5PM
www.governor.state.nd.us

Attorney General's Office
State Capitol - Dept 125   701-328-2210
600 E Boulevard Ave   Fax 701-328-2226
Bismarck, ND 58505-0040   8AM-5PM
www.ag.state.nd.us

Legislative Records
North Dakota Legislative Council   701-328-2916
600 E Blvd Ave
Bismarck, ND 58505   8AM-5PM
www.state.nd.us/lr

State Archives
State Archives &   701-328-2666
Historical Research Library   Fax 701-328-3710
N Dakota Heritage Center, 612 E Blvd Ave   8AM-5PM
Bismarck, ND 58505-0830
www.state.nd.us/hist/sal.htm

State Specifics:

Capital: **Bismark**
Burleigh County

Time Zone: CST

Number of Counties: 53

Population: 633,837

Web Site: http://discovernd.com

State Agencies

Criminal Records

Bureau of Criminal Investigation, Criminal Records Section, PO Box 1054, Bismarck, ND 58502-1054 (Courier: 4205 N State St, Bismarck, ND 58501); 701-328-5500, 701-328-5510 (Fax), 8AM-5PM.

www.ag.state.nd.us

Indexing & Storage: Records are available from 1930 to present. It takes 6 to 10 days before new records are available for inquiry. Records are indexed on computer if DOB is 1940 to present;

prior in paper files. Records are normally destroyed after (records maintained indefinitely).

Searching: Subject will be notified of the request. Include the following in your request-signed release from subject, name, DOB, current address, Social Security Number. Fingerprints optional, for add'l fee to certain entities, but fingerprint searches are not available to public. 100% of the records are fingerprint-supported. The following data is not released: cases dismissed or scaled

Access by: mail, in person.

Fee & Payment: The search fee is $30.00 per name. Fee payee: ND Attorney General. Prepayment required. Personal checks accepted. No credit cards accepted.

Mail search: Turnaround time: 3 to 5 days. No SASE is required.

In person search: Turnaround time while you wait.

Statewide Court Records

Court Administrator, North Dakota Supreme Court, 600 E Blvd Ave, Dept 180, Bismarck, ND 58505-0530; 701-328-4216, 701-328-2092 (Fax), 8AM-5PM.

www.ndcourts.com/

Note: There is no statewide service for trial courts. Except for certain online research capabilities, all court record access must be done at the local level.

Access by: online.

Online search: You may search ND Supreme Court dockets and opinions at the website. Search by docket number, party name, or anything else that may appear in the text. Records are from 1982 forward. You may subscribe to receive e-mail notification when new Opinions are posted to the North Dakota Supreme Court website, and to be informed when Supreme Court Notices (of proposed or new rules, and the like) are posted.

Sexual Offender Registry

Bureau of Criminal Investigation, SOR Unit, PO Box 1054, Bismarck, ND 58502-1054 (Courier: 4205 N State St, Bismarck, ND 58501); 701-328-5500, 701-328-5510 (Fax), 8AM-5PM.

www.ndsexoffender.com/

Indexing & Storage: Records are available from 1991. It takes 6 to 10 days before new records are available for inquiry.

Searching: Offender information may be requested by city, county, or the entire state.

Access by: mail, phone, in person, online.

Fee & Payment: There is no fee.

Mail search: Turnaround time: 1 to 2 days. No SASE is required.

Phone search: Limited name searching available. Call for lists.

In person search: Turnaround time while you wait.

Online search: Access is available from the website. The online listings include offenders who are identified as lifetime registrants as defined by law, or have been designated as high-risk offenders by the Attorney General's Risk Level Committee.

Incarceration Records

Department of Corrections and Rehabilitation, Records Clerk, PO Box 5521, Bismarck, ND 58506 (Courier: 3100 E Railroad Ave, Bismarck, ND 58506); 701-328-6122, 701-328-6640 (Fax), 8AM-5PM.

www.state.nd.us/docr/

Note: Employees of the Prisons Division may not disclose inmate information except as granted in North Dakota Century Code 12-47-36.

Indexing & Storage: Records are available on current and former inmates. It takes about 3 days before new records are available for inquiry. Records are normally destroyed after 7 years after discharge.

Searching: Include the following in your request-first and last name. DOB is helpful. Location, conviction and sentencing information, and release dates are provided.

Access by: mail, phone, fax.

Fee & Payment: There is no fee.

Mail search: Turnaround time: 5 to 7 days. Requests in writing must be specific about information requested.

Phone search: Searching available by telephone.

Fax search: May request via the fax.

Corporation, Limited Liability Company, Limited Partnership, Limited Liability Partnership, Trademarks, Servicemarks, Fictitious Name, Assumed Name

Secretary of State, Business Information/Registration, 600 E Boulevard Ave, Dept 108, Bismarck, ND 58505-0500; 701-328-4284, 800-352-0867, 701-328-2992 (Fax), 8AM-5PM.

www.state.nd.us/sec

Indexing & Storage: Records are available from 1890's on. Records are computerized since 1989. Records inactive prior to 1989 are maintained by state archives, and may take as long as two weeks to search. New records are available for inquiry immediately. Records are indexed on index cards, inhouse computer.

Searching: Include the following in your request-full name of business. In addition to the articles of incorporation, corporation records include the following information: Annual Reports, Officers, Directors, DBAs, Prior (merged) names, Inactive names, and Reserved names. The following data is not released: financial information.

Access by: mail, phone, fax, in person, online.

Fee & Payment: There is a search fee of $5.00 if a written confirmation is required or if data must be retrieved from the archives. Copies cost $1.00 for each 4 pages or fraction thereof. Certification is an additional $15.00. Fee payee: Secretary of State. Prepayment required. Personal checks accepted. Credit cards accepted: MasterCard, Visa, Discover.

Mail search: Turnaround time: 3 to 5 days. No SASE is required.

Phone search: There is no fee for verbal confirmation on an active record, otherwise there is a $5.00 fee.

Fax search: Same fees as phone searching. Turnaround time is 1-3 days if written confirmation required. Add $1.00 per page for fax results.

In person search: No fee on active records, $5.00 fee on inactive records or if in archives. Turnaround time is usually while you wait.

Online search: The Secretary of State's registered business database may be viewed at the Internet for no charge. Records include corporations, limited liability companies, limited partnerships, limited liability partnerships, limited limited partnerships, partnership fictitious names, trade names, trademarks, and real estate investment trusts. The database includes all active records and records inactivated within past twelve months. Access by the first few words of a business name, a significant word in a business name, or by the record ID number assigned. If questions, email sosbir@state.nd.us.

Other access: This agency provides a database purchase program. Cost is $35.00 per database and processing fees vary for type of media.

Uniform Commercial Code, Federal Tax Liens, State Tax Liens

UCC Division, Secretary of State, 600 E Boulevard Ave Dept 108, Bismarck, ND 58505-0500; 701-328-3662, 701-328-4214 (Fax), 8AM-5PM.

www.state.nd.us/sec

Note: The state has a Central Indexing System which allows UCC and tax lien searches at this office or at any of the county Register of Deeds (53).

Indexing & Storage: Records are available from 1966. Records are computerized on index statewide since 1992. It takes less than 1 day before new records are available for inquiry. Records are indexed on inhouse computer. Records are normally destroyed after 1 year after expiration date.

Searching: Use search request form UCC-11. Include the following in your request-debtor name.

Access by: mail, phone, fax, in person, online.

Fee & Payment: The search fee is $7.00 for the first 5 entries and $2.00 for each additional 5 entries or fraction thereof. A copy request with certificate is $7.00 for first 3 copies and $2.00 for each additional. All tax liens will show on the record request. Fee payee: Secretary of State. Will invoice, if requested. Monthly billing is offered to ongoing requesters. Personal checks accepted. Credit cards accepted: MasterCard, Visa, Discover.

Mail search: Turnaround time: 1 day. A SASE is requested.

Phone search: General information is available without charge.

Fax search: There is an additional fee of $3.00 (maximum 20 pages). Please allow 20 minutes to 1 hour.

In person search: You may request information in person.

Online search: There is a limited free public search and a commercial system for professionals. Sign-up for access to the Central Indexing System includes an annual subscription $150 fee and a one-time $50.00 registration fee. The $7.00 fee applies, but documents will not be certified. Searches include UCC-11 information listing and farm product searches.

Sales Tax Registrations

Office of State Tax Commissioner, Sales & Special Taxes Division, State Capitol, 600 E Boulevard Ave, Bismarck, ND 58505-0599; 701-328-3470, 701-328-3700 (Fax), 8AM-5PM.

www.state.nd.us/taxdpt

Indexing & Storage: Records are available from 1998 to present, including inactive records. It takes hours before new records are available for inquiry. Records are indexed on computer. Records are normally destroyed after 6 years.

Searching: This agency will only confirm if a business is registered and active. They will provide no other information as it is confidential. Include the following in your request-business name. They will also search by tax permit number or owner name.

Access by: mail, phone, fax, online.

Mail search: Turnaround time: 7 to 10 days. A SASE is requested. No fee for mail request.

Phone search: No fee for telephone request.

Fax search: There is no fee.

Online search: A permit number may be verified online at website. System indicates valid permit registered to company name.

Birth Certificates

ND Department of Health, Vital Records, State Capitol, 600 E Blvd, Dept 301, Bismarck, ND 58505-0200; 701-328-2360, 701-328-1850 (Fax), 7:30AM-5PM.

www.vitalnd.com

Indexing & Storage: Records are available from 1870 on. New records are available for inquiry immediately. Records are indexed on inhouse computer.

Searching: Must have a signed release from person of record if it is an out-of-wedlock birth. If under 18, parent or legal guardian signature needed. Include the following in your request-full name, names of parents, mother's maiden name, date of birth, place of birth, relationship to person of record, reason for information request.

Access by: mail, fax, in person, online.

Fee & Payment: The fee is $7.00 per name. Add $4.00 per name for second copies. Fee payee: North Dakota Department of Health. Prepayment required. Personal checks accepted. Credit cards accepted: MasterCard, Visa, Discover.

Mail search: Turnaround time: 5 to 7 days. No SASE is required.

Fax search: Use of credit card required. Turnaround time is same day if received by 10AM and request is marked for FedEx or UPS.

In person search: Turnaround time is less than 15 minutes.

Online search: Records may be ordered online from the Internet site or from vitalchek.com. Records are not returned online.

Expedited service: Expedited service is available for fax or online searches. Turnaround time: overnight delivery. Expedited service options are available using a credit card and an additional $13.00 fee for shipping.

Death Records

ND Department of Health, Vital Records, State Capitol, 600 E Blvd, Dept 301, Bismarck, ND 58505-0200; 701-328-2360, 701-328-1850 (Fax), 7:30AM-5PM.

www.vitalnd.com

Indexing & Storage: Records are available from 1881 on. Early records are few. New records are available for inquiry immediately. Records are indexed on inhouse computer.

Searching: Cause of death not shown on copy of Death Certificate if not a family member. Include the following in your request-full name, date of death, place of death, relationship to person of record, reason for information request.

Access by: mail, fax, in person, online.

Fee & Payment: The fee is $5.00 per name. Add $2.00 per name for second copies. Fee payee:

North Dakota Department of Health. Prepayment required. Personal checks accepted. Credit cards accepted: MasterCard, Visa, Discover.

Mail search: Turnaround time: 5 to 7 days. A SASE is requested.

Fax search: This is considered expedited service. Turnaround time is same day if received by 10AM noon and request is marked for FedEx or UPS.

In person search: Turnaround time is 10 to 15 minutes.

Online search: Records may be ordered online from the Internet site.

Expedited service: Expedited service is available for fax searches. Turnaround time: overnight delivery. Expedited service options are available using a credit card and an additional $13.00 fee for shipping.

Marriage Certificates

ND Department of Health, Vital Records, State Capitol, 600 E Blvd, Dept 301, Bismarck, ND 58505-0200; 701-328-2360, 701-328-1850 (Fax), 7:30AM-5PM.

www.vitalnd.com

Indexing & Storage: Records are available from July 1, 1925 to present. New records are available for inquiry immediately. Records are indexed on inhouse computer.

Searching: Include the following in your request-names of husband and wife, date of marriage, place or county of marriage, relationship to person of record, reason for information request, wife's maiden name.

Access by: mail, fax, in person, online.

Fee & Payment: The fee is $5.00 per name. Add $2.00 per name for second copies. Fee payee: North Dakota Department of Health. Prepayment required. Personal checks accepted. Credit cards accepted: MasterCard, Visa, AmEx, Discover.

Mail search: Turnaround time: 5 to 7 days. No SASE is required.

Fax search: Turnaround time is same day if received by 10 AM and request is being returned by FedEx or UPS.

In person search: Turnaround time is 10 to 15 minutes.

Online search: Records may be ordered online from the Internet site.

Expedited service: Expedited service is available for fax or online searches. Turnaround time: overnight delivery. Expedited service options are available using a credit card and an additional $13.00 fee for shipping.

Divorce Records

Access to Records is Restricted

ND Department of Health, Vital Records, State Capitol, 600 E Blvd, Dept 301, Bismarck, ND 58505-0200; 701-328-2360, 701-328-1850 (Fax), 7:30AM-5PM.

www.vitalnd.com

Note: The state has an index to direct people to which county has the records. The index contains records from July 1, 1949 to present. Call or e-mail vitalrec@state.nd.us.

Workers' Compensation Records

Workforce Safety & Insurance, Workers' Compensation Records, PO Box 5585, Bismarck ND 58506-5585 (Courier: 1600 East Century Avenue, Suite 1, Bismarck, ND 58503-0644); 701-328-3800, 800-777-5033, 701-328-3750 (Fax), 7:30AM-5PM.

www.workforcesafety.com/

Indexing & Storage: Records are available from 1919 but more reliable information is from 1975 on. It takes 24 hours before new records are available for inquiry. Records are indexed on inhouse computer.

Searching: Must have a signed release from person of record stating exactly what information is requested. Include the following in your request-claimant name, Social Security Number, date of birth. Also, a signed release by the subject is required, unless the requester is involved within the case.

Access by: mail.

Fee & Payment: Copies are $.35 per page. There is no search fee, unless file needs to be retrieved from off-site, then $5.00 is charged. Fee payee: Worker's Compensation Bureau. Prepayment required. Personal checks accepted.

Mail search: Turnaround time: 5 days. A SASE is requested.

Driver Records

Department of Transportation, Driver License & Traffic Safety Division, 608 E Boulevard Ave, Bismarck, ND 58505-0700; 701-328-2603, 701-328-2435 (Fax), 8AM-5PM.

www.state.nd.us/dot

Note: Copies of tickets must be obtained from the local courts.

Indexing & Storage: Records are available for 3 yrs for moving violations, DWI and suspensions. Records available to the public show neither violations less than 2 points nor accidents. The record will not show driver's address to casual requesters without consent. It takes 1 day before new records are available for inquiry. Records are normally destroyed after three years.

Searching: The Division sends an additional copy of the abstract to the driver whose record was requested, accompanied by a statement identifying the requester. Include the following in your request-license number, name, and DOB are required when ordering, but "two out of three" may produce a "hit." Written requests must also include reason for request.

Access by: mail, in person, online.

Fee & Payment: The fee is $3.00 per record. Fee payee: Driver License & Traffic Safety. Prepayment required. Personal checks accepted. Credit cards accepted: MasterCard, Visa, Discover.

Mail search: Turnaround time: 3 days. A SASE is requested.

In person search: Up to eight requests will be processed while you wait.

Online search: The website offers record ordering at https://secure.apps.state.nd.us/dot/dlts/dlos/welcome.htm. Fee is $3.00 per record, record is returned by mail. If you are not ordering your own record, you must qualify per DPPA. Ongoing, approved commercial accounts may request records with personal information via a commercial system. There is a minimum of 100 requests per month. For more information, call 701-328-4790.

Other access: Magnetic tape ordering is available for high volume users.

Vehicle Ownership, Vehicle Identification

Department of Transportation, Records Section/Motor Vehicle Div., 608 E Boulevard Ave, Bismarck, ND 58505-0780; 701-328-2725, 701-328-1285 (TTY:), 701-328-1487 (Fax), 8AM-4:50PM.

www.state.nd.us/dot/

Note: Records on mobile homes are also maintained by this agency.

Indexing & Storage: Records are available from 1911 for license plate numbers. It takes 10 to 14 days before new records are available for inquiry. Records are normally destroyed after several years, but they are imaged first.

Searching: Records are available with the prior authorization. Personal information is not released to casual requesters without consent. A written request or use of Form SFN-51269A is required. Requester must initial one of 12 categories. The following data is not released: Social Security Numbers or medical records.

Access by: mail, fax, in person.

Fee & Payment: The fee is $3.00 per vehicle (includes lien data). There is a fee for a no record found. Fee payee: Motor Vehicle Division. Prepayment required. Personal checks accepted. Credit cards accepted: MasterCard, Visa.

Mail search: Turnaround time: same day. A SASE is helpful.

Fax search: fax requesting is available for pre-approved commercial accounts.

In person search: The state may limit the number of requests processed immediately, if busy.

Other access: North Dakota offers bulk or batch retrieval of VIN or ownership information of vehicles. The requester must explain purpose and intent; however, there are no restrictions placed upon requests of a legal nature. Customized or special runs are available.

Accident Reports

Driver License & Traffic Safety Division, Traffic Records Section, 608 E Boulevard Ave, Bismarck, ND 58505-0780; 701-328-4397, 701-328-2601, 701-328-2435 (Fax), 8AM-5PM.

www.state.nd.us/dot

Indexing & Storage: Records are available from 1996. Records are computer indexed since 1996. It takes 1-2 months before new records are available for inquiry. Records are normally destroyed after 5 years.

Searching: The front page which includes drivers, witnesses, and insurance information, can be ordered by anyone with a written request. The investigating officer's report is also only to parties involved or their legal representative or insurer.

Include the following in your request-date of accident, location of accident, full name of at least one driver, reason for information request.

Access by: mail, in person.

Fee & Payment: Fee is $3.00 for front page record (drivers, witnesses, etc.). Add $5.00 to receive the investigating officer's report. Fee payee: Driver License & Traffic Safety Division. Prepayment required. Personal checks accepted. Credit cards accepted: MasterCard, Visa.

Mail search: Turnaround time: 5 days. A SASE is requested.

In person search: Turnaround time while you wait.

Vessel Ownership, Vessel Registration

North Dakota Game & Fish Department, Boat Registrations, 100 N Bismarck Expressway, Bismarck, ND 58501; 701-328-6335, 701-328-6374 (Fax), 8AM-5PM.

www.state.nd.us/gnf

Note: Liens are filed at same locations as UCCs. Owners of any watercraft propelled by motors must register their vessels with the Game and Fish Department.

Indexing & Storage: Records are available from 1975 to present. Records are computer indexed for the last five years. No titles are issued. It takes 2 weeks before new records are available for inquiry. Records are normally destroyed after 10 years.

Searching: Include the following in your request-one of the following is required: hull ID #, registration #, decal #, or name. The agency does NOT follow DPPA. All records are open to the public.

Access by: mail, phone, fax, in person, online.

Fee & Payment: There is no fee for 1-2 names.

Mail search: Turnaround time: 1 day. No SASE is required.

Phone search: Records are available by phone.

Fax search: Results can be faxed, mailed, or phoned.

In person search: Turnaround time is usually immediate.

Online search: There is a free public inquiry system at https://secure.apps.state.nd.us/gnf/inquiry/pubsysinq-boat.htm (or access via the agency web page). One can also search lottery hunting permit applications and hunter safety listings.

Other access: A printed list is available of all registered vessels.

Voter Registration

Records not maintained by a state level agency.

Note: Records are maintained at the county level by the County Auditors in poll books. Records are open to the public.

GED Certificates

Department of Public Instruction, GED Testing, 600 E Blvd Ave, Bismarck, ND 58505-0440; 701-328-2393, 701-328-4770 (Fax), 8AM-4:30PM.

www.dpi.state.nd.us

Searching: A verification will only verify that a test was taken, but not if the subject passed the test. Include the following in your request-name, signed release, Social Security Number, date of birth.

Access by: mail, fax, in person, online.

Fee & Payment: There is no fee for a verification and a $2.00 fee for a copy of a transcript. Fee payee: Dept of Public Instruction. Prepayment required. Money orders and business checks accepted. No credit cards accepted.

Mail search: Turnaround time: 1 week. No SASE is required.

Fax search: Used only for verification.

In person search: Picture ID required.

Online search: One may request records via email at JMarcell@state.nd.us. There is no fee, unless a transcript is ordered.

Hunting and Fishing License Information

ND Game & Fish Department, 100 N Bismarck Expressway, Bismarck, ND 58501-5095; 701-328-6300, 701-328-6335 (Licensing), 701-328-6352 (Fax), 8AM-5PM.

www.state.nd.us/gnf

Indexing & Storage: Records are available from 1992 on computer. Big Game Lottery Permits are only available for the current season. Records are indexed on inhouse computer.

Searching: Include the following in your request-full name, date of birth, Social Security Number. This agency also registers boats.

Access by: mail, fax, in person, online.

Fee & Payment: There is no search fee.

Mail search: Turnaround time: 1 to 3 days. A SASE is requested.

Fax search: Same criteria as mail searches.

In person search: You can go in and access their records. They also make the boat registrations available.

Online search: From the web site, one can search to see if a person has been chosen (lottery) for a specific hunt or passed hunter safety. Go to Public Inquiry System.

Other access: They sell mailing lists. Call Paul Schadewald at 701-328-6328 for more information.

North Dakota State Licensing Agencies

Licenses Searchable Online

Alcoholic Beverage Control #3	www.ag.state.nd.us/Licensing/Beverage/Beverage.htm
Amusement Device, Coin-Operated #3	www.ag.state.nd.us/Licensing/Amusement/Amusement.htm
Asbestos-related Occupation #27	www.health.state.nd.us/ndhd/environ/ee/rad/asb/
Attorney #41	www.court.state.nd.us/court/lawyers/index/frameset.htm
Auction Clerk #34	www.psc.state.nd.us/psc/jurisdiction/auctioneers-entities.html
Auctioneer #34	www.psc.state.nd.us/psc/jurisdiction/auctioneers-entities.html
Bank, Commercial #20	www.state.nd.us/dfi/regulate/reg/regulated.asp
Charitable Solicitation #39	www.state.nd.us/sec/charitableorg/search.htm
Coal Mine, Surface #34	www.psc.state.nd.us/psc/jurisdiction/reclamation-list.html
Collection Agency #20	www.state.nd.us/dfi/regulate/reg/regulated.asp
Consumer Finance Company #20	www.state.nd.us/dfi/regulate/reg/regulated.asp
Contractor #27	www.health.state.nd.us/ndhd/environ/ee/rad/asb/
Contractor/General Contractor #39	www.state.nd.us/sec/licensing/search.html
Credit Union #20	www.state.nd.us/dfi/regulate/reg/regulated.asp
Debt Collector #20	www.state.nd.us/dfi/regulate/reg/regulated.asp
Deferred Presentment Provider #20	www.state.nd.us/dfi/regulate/reg/regulated.asp
Drug Manufacturer/Wholesaler #14	www.nodakpharmacy.com
Engineer #36	www.ndpelsboard.org
Fireworks, Wholesale #3	www.ag.state.nd.us/Licensing/Fireworks/Fireworks.htm
Gaming #3	www.ag.state.nd.us/Gaming/listorg.PDF
Gaming Distributor #3	www.ag.state.nd.us/Gaming/distlist.PDF
Gaming Manufacturer #3	www.ag.state.nd.us/Gaming/manlst.PDF
Grain Buyer #34	www.psc.state.nd.us/psc/jurisdiction/grain-entities.html
Grain Warehouse/Elevator #34	www.psc.state.nd.us/psc/jurisdiction/grain-entities.html
Investment Advisor #40	www.ndsecurities.com
Land Surveyor #36	www.ndpelsboard.org
Livestock Agent #19	www.agdepartment.com/Programs/Livestock/Agents.html
Livestock Auction Market #19	www.agdepartment.com/Programs/Livestock/markets.html
Livestock Dealer #19	www.agdepartment.com/Programs/Livestock/Dealers.html
Lobbyist #39	www.state.nd.us/sec/lobbylegislate/lobbying/reg-mnu.html
Medical Doctor #47	www.ndbomex.com
Money Broker Firm #20	www.state.nd.us/dfi/regulate/reg/regulated.asp
Nurse Assistant #31	www.ndbon.org
Nurse-Advanced Practice #31	www.ndbon.org
Nurse-LPN/Nurse-RN #31	www.ndbon.org
Optometrist #49	www.ndsbopt.org/directory.asp
Osteopathic Physician #47	www.ndbomex.com
Pharmacist #14	www.nodakpharmacy.com
Pharmacy #14	www.nodakpharmacy.com
Pharmacy Technician/Intern #14	www.nodakpharmacy.com
Physician Assistant #47	www.ndbomex.com
Polygraph Examiner #3	www.ag.state.nd.us/Licensing/Polygraph/Polygraph.htm
Private Investigation Agency #33	www.state.nd.us/pisb/holders.html
Private Investigator #33	www.state.nd.us/pisb/holders.html
Public Accountant-CPA/ Public Accounting Firm #42	www.state.nd.us/ndsba/database/sbasearch.asp
Racing #3	www.ndracingcommission.com/Forms.htm
Sale of Check #20	www.state.nd.us/dfi/regulate/reg/regulated.asp
Securities Agent/Dealer #40	www.ndsecurities.com
Security Provider/Company #33	www.state.nd.us/pisb/holders.html
Social Worker #18	www.ndbswe.com
Soil Classifier #17	www.soilsci.ndsu.nodak.edu/soilclassifiers/pscand.htm
Speech-Language Pathologist/Audiologist #12	http://governor.state.nd.us/boards/bcpublicsearch.asp?searchtype=member
Telecommunications Company #34	www.psc.state.nd.us/psc/jurisdiction/telecom-consinfo.html
Tobacco, Retail/Wholesale #3	www.ag.state.nd.us/Licensing/Tobacco/Tobacco.htm
Transient Merchant #3	www.ag.state.nd.us/Licensing/Transient/TransientMerchant.htm
Trust Company #20	www.state.nd.us/dfi/regulate/reg/regulated.asp
Water Well Driller/Pump & Pitless Unit #50	www.health.state.nd.us/wq/gw/wells.htm
Weighing Device Company #34	www.psc.state.nd.us/psc/jurisdiction/weights-list.html
Well Contractor, Monitoring #50	www.health.state.nd.us/wq/gw/wells.htm

North Dakota Licensing Quick Finder

Abstractor/Abstractor Company #1 701-947-2446
Adoption Service #22 701-328-4805
Aerial Applicator #30 701-328-9650
Aircraft Dealer #30 701-328-9650
Aircraft Registration #30 701-328-9650
Alcoholic Beverage Control #3 701-328-2329
Amusement Device, Coin-Operated #3 . 701-328-2329
Architect #43 701-223-3184
Asbestos-related Occupation #27 701-328-5188
Athletic Trainer #5 701-476-7335
Attorney #41 701-328-4201
Auction Clerk #34 701-328-4097
Auctioneer #34 701-328-4097
Bank, Commercial #20 701-328-9933
Barber #6 701-232-8394
Barber Shop #6 701-232-8394
Boxer/Boxing Professional #38 701-328-3665
Broker, Corporate #28 .... 701-328-3548 x2
Charitable Solicitation #39 701-328-3665
Chiropractor #7 701-352-1690
Coal Mine, Surface #34 701-328-4096
Collection Agency #20 701-328-9933
Consumer Finance Company #20 701-328-9933
Contractor #27 701-328-5188
Contractor/General Contractor #39 701-328-3665
Cosmetologist/Cosmetologist Instructor #8
 701-224-9800
Counselor, Addiction #4 701-255-1439
Counselor, Professional #9 701-667-5969
Credit Union #20 701-328-9933
Crematorium #44 701-873-7700
Day Care Service #22 701-328-4809
Debt Collector #20 701-328-9933
Deferred Presentment Provider #20 701-328-9933
Dental Assistant /Dental Hygienist #10 701-258-8600
Dentist #10 701-258-8600
Dietitian/Nutritionist #11 701-746-9171
Drug Mfg./Wholesaler #14 701-328-9535
Electrician #25 701-328-9522
Electrician Apprentice #25 701-328-9522
Embalmer #44 701-873-7700
Employment Agency #23 701-328-2660
Engineer #36 701-258-0786
Esthetician #8 701-224-9800

Fireworks, Wholesale #3 701-328-2329
Fishing Guide #26 701-328-6300
Foster Care Program #22 701-328-3587
Fund Raiser, Professional #39 701-328-3665
Funeral Director /Funeral Home #44 701-873-7700
Gaming #3 701-328-2329
Gaming Distributor /Manufacturer #3 ... 701-328-2329
Grain Buyer #34 701-328-4097
Grain Warehouse/Elevator #34 701-328-4097
Hearing Aid Dealer/Fitter #45 701-237-9977
Hunting Guide #26 701-328-6300
Hunting/Fishing Guide Combo #26 701-328-6300
Insurance Agency/Agent #28 .... 701-328-3548 x2
Insurance Broker #28 .... 701-328-3548 x2
Investment Advisor #40 701-328-4698
Kickboxer #38 701-328-3665
Laboratory Clinician #53 701-530-0199
Land Surveyor #36 701-258-0786
Livestock Agent #19 701-328-4761
Livestock Auction Market /Dealer #19 .. 701-328-4761
Lobbyist #39 701-328-3665
Manicurist #8 701-224-9800
Massage Therapist #46 701-872-4895
Medical Doctor #47 701-328-6500
Money Broker Firm #20 701-328-9933
Mortician #44 701-873-7700
Notary Public #39 701-328-2901
Nurse Assistant #31 701-328-9780
Nurse-Advanced Practice #31 701-328-9777
Nurse-LPN /Nurse-RN #31 701-328-9777
Nursing Home Administrator #13 701-222-4867
Nutritionist #11 701-746-9171
Occupational Therapist #48 701-250-0847
Occupational Therapy Assistant #48 ... 701-250-0847
Oil & Gas Broker #40 701-328-2910
Oil & Gas Wellhead Welder #40 701-328-2910
Optometrist #49 701-225-9333
Osteopathic Physician #47 701-328-6500
Pharmacist /Pharmacy #14 701-328-9535
Pharmacy Technician/Intern #14 701-328-9535
Physical Therapist/Assistant #51 701-352-0125
Physician Assistant #47 701-328-6500
Plumber Journeyman/Apprentice/Master #32
 701-328-9977

Podiatrist #15 701-483-6986
Polygraph Examiner #3 701-328-2329
Private Investigation Agency #33 701-222-3063
Private Investigator #33 701-222-3063
Psychologist #16 701-250-8691
Public Accountant-CPA #42 800-532-5904
Public Accounting Firm #42 800-532-5904
Racing #3 701-328-4633
Real Estate Agent/Broker License/Regulation #35
 701-328-9749
Respiratory Care Practitioner #37 701-222-1564
Sale of Check #20 701-328-9933
School Counselor/Designate #24 701-328-2260
School Media Specialist #24 701-328-2260
School Principal/Assistant #24 701-328-2260
School Superintendent/Assistant #24 .. 701-328-2260
Securities Agent/Dealer #40 701-328-4698
Security Employee #33 701-222-2063
Security Provider/Company #33 701-222-3063
Sewer & Water Contractor/Instal. #32 . 701-328-9977
Social Worker #18 701-222-0255
Soil Classifier #17 701-530-2020
Speech-Language Pathologist/Audiologist #12
 701-777-4421
Taxidermist #26 701-328-6300
Teacher #24 701-328-2260
Telecommunications Company #34 701-328-4076
Telecommunications Personnel #34 701-328-4076
Tobacco, Retail/Wholesale #3 701-328-2329
Transient Merchant #3 701-328-2329
Trust Company #20 701-328-9933
Veterinarian #29 701-328-9540
Veterinary Technician #29 701-328-9540
Waste Water System Operator #21 701-328-5211
Water Conditioning Contr./Instal. #32 .. 701-328-9977
Water Distri. System Operator #21 701-328-5211
Water Well Driller #50 701-328-2754
Water Well Pump & Pitless Unit #50 701-328-2754
Weather Modifier #2 701-328-2788
Weighing Device Company #34 701-328-2400
Weighing Device Tester #34 701-328-2400
Well Contractor, Monitoring #50 701-328-2754

North Dakota Licensing Agency Information

1 Abstractors Board of Examiners, PO Box 551, New Rockford, ND 58356; 701-947-2446, Fax: 701-947-2443. http://governor.state.nd.us/boards/boards-query.asp?Board_ID=1

2 Atmospheric Resource Board, Water Commission, 900 E Boulevard Ave, Bismarck, ND 58505; 701-328-4940, Fax: 701-328-4749. www.swc.state.nd.us/index.html

3 Attorney General's Office, Licensing Division, 600 E Boulevard Ave, Dept 125, Bismarck, ND 58505-0040; 701-328-4848, Fax: 701-328-3535. www.ag.state.nd.us

4 Board of Addiction Counseling Examiners, PO Box 975, Bismarck, ND 58502-0975; 701-255-1439, Fax: 701-224-9824. www.ndbace.org   Email: ndbace@aptnd.com Note: The Board can sell lists for $20.00. Can be sent by e-mail, labels or a list.

5 Board of Athletic Trainers, 336 4th Street NW, PO Box 5020, Valley City, ND 58702; 701-476-7335, Fax: 701-857-5694. http://governor.state.nd.us/boards/boards-query.asp?Board_ID=12

6 Board of Barber Examiners, 1146 3rd Street North, Fargo, ND 58102; 701-232-8394.

7 c/o Jerry Blanchard, Board of Chiropractic Examiners, PO Box 185, Grafton, ND 58237; 701-352-1690, Fax: 701-352-2258.

8 Board of Cosmetology, PO Box 2177 (1102 S Washington #200), Bismarck, ND 58502; 701-224-9800, Fax: 701-222-8756. Email: cosmo@qcentral.com

9 Board of Counselor Examiners, 2112 10th Av SE, Mandan, ND 58554-5066; 701-667-5969. www.sendit.nodak.edu/ndbce/ Email: ndbce@btigate.com

10 Board of Dental Examiners, PO Box 7246, Bismarck, ND 58507-7246; 701-258-8600, Fax: 701-224-9824.   www.nddentalboard.org Email: ndsbde@aptnd.com Note: Lists available on disk, labels, email, or printed.

11 Board of Dietetic Practice, PO Box 6142, Grand Forks, ND 58206-6142; 701-777-2539, Fax: 701-777-3268. http://governor.state.nd.us/boards/boards-query.asp?Board_ID=33

12 Board of Examiners in Audiology/Speech Pathology, 720 4th St N, Fargo, ND 58122; 701-777-4421, Fax: 701-777-4365. http://governor.state.nd.us/boards/boards-query.asp?Board_ID=14

13 Board of Examiners in Nursing Home Adminstrators, 1900 N 11th St, Bismarck, ND 58501-1914; 701-222-4867, Fax: 701-223-0977. www.ndboenha.org   Email: bev@ndltca.org

14 Board of Pharmacy, PO Box 1354, Bismarck, ND 58502-1354; 701-328-9535, Fax: 701-258-9312. www.nodakpharmacy.com Email: ndboph@btinet.net

15 Dr. Mathews, Board of Podiatric Medicine, 2400 32nd Ave S, Fargo, ND 58103; 701-234-8770.

16 Board of Psychologist Examiners, PO Box 7458, Bismarck, ND 58507-7458; 701-250-8691, Fax: 701-250-8611. www.governor.state.nd.us/boards/boards-query.asp?Board_ID=88

17 Board of Registry for Professional Soil Classifier, 202 E Divide Ave, Bismarck, ND 58501; 701-530-2020.
www.governor.state.nd.us/boards/
Email: mike.ulmer@nd.udsa.gov

18 Board of Social Worker Examiners, PO Box 914, Bismarck, ND 58502-0914; 701-222-0255, Fax: 701-224-9824.
www.ndbswe.com   Email: ndbswe@aptnd.com
Search Database at www.ndbswe.com Note: Also sell lists for $100.00 by email, disk list or labels - for continuing ed or research purposes only.

19 Department of Agriculture, Livestock & Pesticide Programs, 600 E Boulevard Ave,Dept 602, Bismarck, ND 58505-0020; 701-328-2231, Fax: 701-328-4567. www.agdepartment.com
Email: wcarlson@state.nd.us   Search Database at www.agdepartment.com/Programs/Livestock/Livestock.html

20 Department of Financial Institutions, 2000 Schafer St. #G, Bismarck, ND 58501-1204; 701-328-9933, Fax: 701-328-9955.
www.discovernd.com/dfi
Email: dfi@state.nd.us   Search Database at www.state.nd.us/dfi/regulate/reg/regulated.asp

21 Department of Health, Municipal Facilities, 1200 Missouri Av, Bismarck, ND 58506-5520; 701-328-5211, Fax: 701-328-5200. www.health.state.nd.us/ndhd/environ/mf/Index.htm

22 Department of Human Services, Children & Family Services, 600 E Boulevard Ave, Bismarck, ND 58505-0250; 701-328-2310, Fax: 701-328-2359.   www.state.nd.us/humanservices

23 Department of Labor, 600 E Blvd Ave, Dept 406, Bismarck, ND 58505-0340; 701-328-2660, Fax: 701-328-2031.
www.state.nd.us/labor/services/ea-licensing/
Email: labor@state.nd.us

24 Department of Public Instruction, 600 E Boulevard Ave, 1st Fl-Judicial Wing, Bismarck, ND 58505-0440; 701-328-2260, Fax: 701-328-2461. www.dpi.state.nd.us

25 Electrical Board, PO Box 857 (721 Memorial Highway), Bismarck, ND 58502; 701-328-9522, Fax: 701-328-9524. www.state.nd.us/electric
Email: electric@state.nd.us

26 Game & Fish Department, 100 N Bismarck Exprwy, Bismarck, ND 58501-5095; 701-328-6300, Fax: 701-328-6352.
www.state.nd.us/gnf/   Email: ndgf@state.nd.us

27 Department of Health, Asbestos Control Program, PO Box 5520 (1200 Missouri Ave), Bismarck, ND 58506-5520; 701-328-5188, Fax: 701-328-5200.
www.health.state.nd.us/ndhd/environ/ee/rad/asb/
Email: kwangler@state.nd.us   Search Database at www.health.state.nd.us/ndhd/environ/ee/rad/asb/

28 Insurance Department, Producer/Agent Information, 600 E Boulevard Ave, Capitol Bldg, 1st Fl, Bismarck, ND 58505-0320; 701-328-2440, Fax: 701-328-4880.
www.state.nd.us/ndins   Email: insuranc@state.nd.us

29 Board of Veterinarian ExaminERS, PO Box 5001, Bismarck, ND 58502-5001; 701-328-9540, Fax: 701-224-0435.   Email: ndbvme@state.nd.us

30 Aeronautics Commission, PO Box 5020, Bismarck, ND 58502-5020; 701-328-9650, Fax: 701-328-9656.
www.state.nd.us/ndaero/   Email: ndaero@state.nd.us

31 Board of Nursing, 919 S 7th St #504, Bismarck, ND 58504-5881; 701-328-9777, Fax: 701-328-9785.
www.ndbon.org

32 State Board of Plumbing, 204 W Thayer Av, Bismarck, ND 58501; 701-328-9977, Fax: 701-328-9979.
http://governor.state.nd.us/boards/boards-query.asp?Board_ID=83
Email: ndplumb@state.nd.us

33 Private Investigation & Security Board, Private Investigators Licensing, 513 E Bismarck Expy, #5, Bismarck, ND 58504-6577; 701-222-3063, Fax: 701-222-3063.
www.state.nd.us./pisb   Email: ndpisb@midco.net
Search Database at www.state.nd.us/pisb/holders.html

34 Public Service Commission, 600 E Boulevard Ave, Dept 408, Bismarck, ND 58505-0480; 701-328-4097, Fax: 701-328-2410.
www.psc.state.nd.us   Email: skr@psc.state.nd.us
Search at www.psc.state.nd.us/psc/jurisdiction/
Note: Lists are provided online.

35 Real Estate Commission, PO Box 727, Bismarck, ND 58502-0727; 701-328-9749, Fax: 701-328-9750.
Email: pjergenson@state.nd.us

36 Registration for Prof. Engineers & Land Surveyors, PO Box 1357, Bismarck, ND 58502-1357; 701-258-0786, Fax: 701-258-7471.
www.ndpelsboard.org
Email: brdofreg@bt.igate.net

37 Respiratory Care Examining Board, PO Box 2223, Bismarck, ND 58502; 701-222-1564, Fax: 701-255-9149.
www.governor.state.nd.us/boards/boards-query.asp?Board_ID=96
Email: ndsbrc@btigate.com

38 Secretary of State, Athletic Commissioner, Licensing Division, 600 East Blvd Ave, Dept 108, Bismarck, ND 58505-0040; 701-328-2900, Fax: 701-328-1690.
www.state.nd.us/sec/   Email: sosadlic@state.nd.us

39 Secretary of State, Licensing Division, 600 East Blvd Ave, Dept 108, Bismarck, ND 58505-0500; 701-328-3665, Fax: 701-328-1690.
www.state.nd.us/sec/
Email: sosadlic@state.nd.us

40 Securities Department, 600 E Blvd Ave, Dept 414, State Capitol, 5th Fl, Bismarck, ND 58505-0510; 701-328-2910, Fax: 701-328-2946.
www.ndsecurities.com
Email: ndsecurities@state.nd.us
Search Database at http://pdpi.nasdr.com/PDPI/

41 State Board of Law Examiners, 600 E Boulevard Ave, Dept. 180, Bismarck, ND 58505-0530; 701-328-4201, Fax: 701-328-4480.
www.ndcourts.com/lawyers/
Search Database at www.court.state.nd.us/court/lawyers/index/frameset.htm

42 Board of Accountancy, 2701 S Columbia Rd, Grand Forks, ND 58201-6029; 800-532-5904, Fax: 701-775-7430. www.state.nd.us/ndsba
Email: ndsba@state.nd.us   Search Database at www.state.nd.us/ndsba/database/sbasearch.asp

43 Board of Architects, PO Box 7370, Bismarck, ND 58507-7370; 701-223-3184, Fax: 701-223-8154.

44 Board of Funeral Service, PO Box 633, Devil's Lake, ND 58301; 701-662-2511, Fax: 701-662-2501.   Email: sfh@westriv.com

45 Board of Hearing Instrument Specialists, 825 25th St SW, Fargo, ND 58103; 701-237-9977.
http://governor.state.nd.us/boards/boards-query.asp?Board_ID=47

46 Board of Massage, PO Box0218, Beach, ND 58621; 701-872-4895, Fax: 701-872-4895.
www.ndboardofmassage.com
Email: k_wojahn@yahoo.com

47 Board of Medical Examiners, 418 E. Broadway #12, Bismarck, ND 58501; 701-328-6500, Fax: 701-328-6505.
www.ndbomex.com
Email: medbd@tic.bisman.com   Search Database at www.sdofnd.com/cart/ndbomex/Search%20Page.asp Note: Order form needed. For bulk users, a $15.00 setup fee plus $.05 per name billed after order is filled.

48 Board of Occupational Therapy Practice, PO Box 4005, Bismarck, ND 58502-4005; 701-250-0847, Fax: 701-224-9824.
www.ndotboard.com   Email: ndotboard@aptnd.com

49 Board of Optometry, 341 1st St E, Dickinson, ND 58601; 701-483-9141, Fax: 701-483-9501.
www.ndsbopt.org Email: ndsbopt@dickinson.ctctel.com
Search Database at www.ndsbopt.org/directory.asp

50 Board of Water Well Contractors, 900 E Boulevard Ave, Bismarck, ND 58505; 701-328-2754, Fax: 701-328-3696.
http://governor.state.nd.us/boards/boards-query.asp?Board_ID=111

51 Examining Committee of Physical Therapists, PO Box 69, Grafton, ND 58237; 701-352-0125, Fax: 701-352-3093.   Email: ndsecpt@gft.midco.net

53 Board of Clinical Laboratory Practice, PO Box 4103, Bismarck, ND 58502-4103; 701-530-0199, Fax: 701-224-9824.
www.ndclinlab.com   Email: ndbclp@aptnd.com

North Dakota Federal Courts

The following list indicates the district and division name for each county in the state. If the bankruptcy court location is different from the district court, then the location of the bankruptcy court appears in parentheses.

County/Court Cross Reference

County	Court	County	Court
Adams	Bismarck-Southwestern (Fargo)	McLean	Bismarck-Southwestern (Fargo)
Barnes	Fargo-Southeastern (Fargo)	Mercer	Bismarck-Southwestern (Fargo)
Benson	Grand Forks-Northeastern (Fargo)	Morton	Bismarck-Southwestern (Fargo)
Billings	Bismarck-Southwestern (Fargo)	Mountrail	Minot-Northwestern (Fargo)
Bottineau	Minot-Northwestern (Fargo)	Nelson	Grand Forks-Northeastern (Fargo)
Bowman	Bismarck-Southwestern (Fargo)	Oliver	Bismarck-Southwestern (Fargo)
Burke	Minot-Northwestern (Fargo)	Pembina	Grand Forks-Northeastern (Fargo)
Burleigh	Bismarck-Southwestern (Fargo)	Pierce	Minot-Northwestern (Fargo)
Cass	Fargo-Southeastern (Fargo)	Ramsey	Grand Forks-Northeastern (Fargo)
Cavalier	Grand Forks-Northeastern (Fargo)	Ransom	Fargo-Southeastern (Fargo)
Dickey	Fargo-Southeastern (Fargo)	Renville	Minot-Northwestern (Fargo)
Divide	Minot-Northwestern (Fargo)	Richland	Fargo-Southeastern (Fargo)
Dunn	Bismarck-Southwestern (Fargo)	Rolette	Minot-Northwestern (Fargo)
Eddy	Fargo-Southeastern (Fargo)	Sargent	Fargo-Southeastern (Fargo)
Emmons	Bismarck-Southwestern (Fargo)	Sheridan	Minot-Northwestern (Fargo)
Foster	Fargo-Southeastern (Fargo)	Sioux	Bismarck-Southwestern (Fargo)
Golden Valley	Bismarck-Southwestern (Fargo)	Slope	Bismarck-Southwestern (Fargo)
Grand Forks	Grand Forks-Northeastern (Fargo)	Stark	Bismarck-Southwestern (Fargo)
Grant	Bismarck-Southwestern (Fargo)	Steele	Fargo-Southeastern (Fargo)
Griggs	Fargo-Southeastern (Fargo)	Stutsman	Fargo-Southeastern (Fargo)
Hettinger	Bismarck-Southwestern (Fargo)	Towner	Grand Forks-Northeastern (Fargo)
Kidder	Bismarck-Southwestern (Fargo)	Traill	Grand Forks-Northeastern (Fargo)
La Moure	Fargo-Southeastern (Fargo)	Walsh	Grand Forks-Northeastern (Fargo)
Logan	Bismarck-Southwestern (Fargo)	Ward	Minot-Northwestern (Fargo)
McHenry	Minot-Northwestern (Fargo)	Wells	Minot-Northwestern (Fargo)
McIntosh	Bismarck-Southwestern (Fargo)	Williams	Minot-Northwestern (Fargo)
McKenzie	Minot-Northwestern (Fargo)		

Standards for Federal Courts: The search fee is $20.00 per item (one party name or case number). Certification fee is $7.00 per document. Copy fee is $.50 per page. All fees standard unless noted in profile. Mail Search: always enclose a stamped self addressed envelope unless otherwise noted. Most courts accept fax requests or will suggest a copying/search vendor. Before releasing records, all courts require prepayment unless noted in profile.

Open records are located at the court unless otherwise noted. District courts index by defendant and plaintiff as well as by case number. Bankruptcy courts usually index by debtor and case number. While most courts now have their indexes on computer, many still maintain index card files as well.

PACER: The universal PACER sign-up number is 800-676-6856. Find PACER and the Party/Case Index on the Web at http://pacer.psc.uscourts.gov. PACER dial-up access is $.60 per minute. Also, courts offering internet access via RACER, PACER, Web-PACER or the new CM-ECF charge $.07 per page fee unless noted as free.

US District Court

District of North Dakota

Bismarck-Southwestern Division PO Box 1193, Bismarck, ND 58502 (courier address: 220 E Rosser Ave, Room 476, Bismarck, ND 58501), 701-530-2300, Fax: 701-530-2312. www.ndd.uscourts.gov

Counties: Adams, Billings, Bowman, Burleigh, Dunn, Emmons, Golden Valley, Grant, Hettinger, Kidder, Logan, McIntosh, McLean, Mercer, Morton, Oliver, Sioux, Slope, Stark.

Indexing & Storage: New cases available in the index 24 hours after filing date. Records are on computer and stored as hard copy records.

Fee & Payment: Payment may be made by money order, cashier check, in-state business check. In state personal checks are also accepted. Court will bill for copies. Payee: Clerk, U.S. District Court. Will fax results $1.50 per page.

Phone Search: Only docket information available by phone. Will fax results $1.50 per page.

Mail Search: A SASE not required.

In Person Search: Fee charged if court conducts your in person search for you.

PACER: PACER is available online at http://pacer.ndd.uscourts.gov. Case records go back to October 1990. Records never purged. New records are online after 1 day.

Fargo-Southeastern Division PO Box 870, Fargo, ND 58107 (courier address: 655 1st Ave N, Fargo, ND 58102), 701-297-7000, Fax: 701-297-7005. www.ndd.uscourts.gov

Counties: Barnes, Cass, Dickey, Eddy, Foster, Griggs, La Moure, Ransom, Richland, Sargent, Steele, Stutsman. Rolette County cases prior to 1995 may be located here.

Indexing & Storage: New cases available in the index 1 day after filing date. Civil cases prior to 10/90 are on index cards as well as all criminal records. Current records are on computer and stored as hard copy records.

Fee & Payment: Payment may be made by money order, cashier check, in-state business check. In state personal checks are also accepted. Payee:

Clerk, U.S. District Court. Will fax results at $.50 per page, prepaid.

Phone Search: Only docket information available by phone. Will fax results at $.50 per page, prepaid.

Mail Search: A SASE not required.

In Person Search: Fee charged if court conducts your in person search for you.

PACER: PACER is available online at http://pacer.ndd.uscourts.gov. Case records go back to October 1990. Records never purged. New records are online after 1 day.

Grand Forks-Northeastern Division c/o Fargo-Southeastern Division, 102 N 4th St, Grand Forks, ND 58201 (courier address: 655 1st Ave N, Fargo, ND 58102), 701-772-0511, Fax: 701-746-7544. www.ndd.uscourts.gov

Counties: Benson, Cavalier, Grand Forks, Nelson, Pembina, Ramsey, Towner, Traill, Walsh.

Indexing & Storage: Cases indexed by as well as by case number. New cases available in the index after filing date. Open records are located at the Fargo-SE Division.

Fee & Payment: Payment may be made by money order, cashier check. Business checks are not accepted. Personal checks are not accepted.

Phone Search: No searching by telephone.

Mail Search: A SASE not required.

In Person Search: Permitted.

PACER: PACER is available online at http://pacer.ndd.uscourts.gov. Case records go back to October 1990. Records never purged. New records are online after 1 day.

Minot-Northwestern Division c/o Bismarck Division, PO Box 1193, Bismarck, ND 58502 (courier address: 100 1st St SW, Minot, ND 58701), 701-839-6251, Fax: 701-838-3276. www.ndd.uscourts.gov

Counties: Bottineau, Burke, Divide, McHenry, McKenzie, Mountrail, Pierce, Renville, Rolette, Sheridan, Ward, Wells, Williams. Case records from Rolette County prior to 1995 may be located in Fargo-Southeastern Division.

Indexing & Storage: Cases indexed by as well as by case number. New cases available in the index

after filing date. Open records are located at the Bismarck Division.

Fee & Payment: Payment may be made by money order, cashier check. Business checks are not accepted. Personal checks are not accepted.

Phone Search: No searching by telephone.

Mail Search: A SASE not required.

In Person Search: Permitted.

PACER: PACER is available online at http://pacer.ndd.uscourts.gov. Case records go back to October 1990. Records never purged. New records are online after 1 day.

U.S. Bankruptcy Court

District of North Dakota

Fargo Division 655 1st Ave N. #210, Fargo, ND 58102-4932 (courier address: Room 236, Federal Bldg & U.S. Courthouse, Fargo, ND 58102), 701-297-7100, Fax: 701-297-7104. www.ndb.uscourts.gov

Counties: All counties in North Dakota.

Indexing & Storage: Cases indexed by debtor as well as by case number. New cases available in the index 1 day after filing date.

Fee & Payment: Payment may be made by money order, cashier check, business check. Personal checks are not accepted. Exemplification costs $10.00 per document. Fax available in emergencies for $.50 per page sending or receiving. Payee: Clerk, U.S. Bankruptcy Court.

Phone Search: Only docket information available by telephone. Automated voice case information service (VCIS) is available. Call VCIS at 701-297-7166.

Mail Search: A SASE not required.

In Person Search: Fee charged if court conducts your in person search for you.

PACER: PACER is available online at http://pacer.okwd.uscourts.gov. New civil records are online after 1 day.

Electronic Filing: Electronic filing information online at https://ecf.ndb.uscourts.gov

Other Online Access: RACER is no longer available and has been replaced by a new PACER system.

North Dakota County Courts

Court	Jurisdiction	No. of Courts	How Organized
District Courts*	General	53	7 Judicial Districts
Municipal Courts	Municipal	76	76 Cities

* Profiled in this Sourcebook.

	CIVIL								
Court	Tort	Contract	Real Estate	Min. Claim	Max. Claim	Small Claims	Estate	Eviction	Domestic Relations
District Courts*	X	X	X	$0	No Max	$5000	X	X	X
Municipal Courts									

	CRIMINAL				
Court	Felony	Misdemeanor	DWI/DUI	Preliminary Hearing	Juvenile
District Courts*	X	X	X	X	X
Municipal Courts			X		

ADMINISTRATION   State Court Administrator, North Dakota Judiciary, 600 E Blvd, 1st Floor Judicial Wing, Dept. 180, Bismarck, ND, 58505-0530; 701-328-4216, Fax: 701-328-2092. www.ndcourts.com or www.court.state.nd.us

COURT STRUCTURE   In 1995, the County Courts merged with the District Courts statewide. County court records are maintained by the 53 District Court Clerks in the seven judicial districts. We recommend stating "include all County Court cases" in search requests. There are 76 Municipal Courts that handle traffic cases.

ONLINE ACCESS   A statewide computer system for internal purposes is in operation in most counties. You may now search North Dakota Supreme Court dockets and opinions at www.ndcourts.com. Search by docket number, party name, or anything else that may appear in the text. Records are from 1982 forward. Email notification of new opinions is also available.

ADDITIONAL INFORMATION   In the summer of 1997, the standard search fee in District Courts increased to $10.00 per name, and the certification fee increased to $10.00 per document. Copy fees remain at $.50 per page, but many courts charge only $.25.

📖 📖 📖 📖 📖 📖

Adams County

Southwest Judicial District Court 602 Adams Ave, PO Box 469, Hettinger, ND 58639; 701-567-2460; Fax: 701-567-2910. Hours: 8:30AM-5PM (MST). *Felony, Misdemeanor, Civil, Eviction, Small Claims, Probate.*

Note: Search requests must be in writing.

Civil Records: Access: Fax, mail, in person. Both court and visitors may perform in person searches. Search fee: $10.00 per name. Required to search: name, years to search; also helpful: address. Civil cases indexed by defendant, plaintiff. Civil records on index cards from 1990, on docket books in vault from 1900s.

Criminal Records: Access: Fax, mail, in person. Both court and visitors may perform in person searches. Search fee: $10.00 per name. Required to search: name, years to search, DOB; also helpful: address. Criminal records on index cards from 1990, on docket books in vault from 1900s.

General Information: No adoptions, sealed, juvenile, mental health, expunged, DV or dismissed records released. Fee to fax results is $3.00 1st 2

pages, $.50 each add'l. Copy fee: $.25 per page. Certification fee: $10.00. Payee: Clerk of District Court. Personal checks accepted. Prepayment required. Mail requests: SASE required. Mail turnaround time 1-2 days.

Barnes County

Southeast Judicial District Court PO Box 774, Valley City, ND 58072; 701-845-8512; Fax: 701-845-1341. Hours: 8AM-5PM (CST). *Felony, Misdemeanor, Civil, Eviction, Small Claims, Probate.*

Civil Records: Access: Fax, mail, in person. Only the court performs in person searches; visitors may not. Search fee: $10.00 per name. Required to search: name, years to search; also helpful: address. Civil cases indexed by defendant, plaintiff. Civil records on index books from early 1900s; on computer back to 1996.

Criminal Records: Access: Fax, mail, in person. Only the court performs in person searches; visitors may not. Search fee: $10.00 per name. Required to search: name, years to search; also helpful: address, DOB, SSN. Criminal records maintained here for 10

years, archived on index books from early 1900s; on computer back to 1996.

General Information: No adoptions, paternity, sealed, juvenile, mental health, expunged or dismissed records released. Will fax results $10.00 per doc. Copy fee: $.25 per page. Certification fee: $10.00. $5.00 for second copy. Payee: Clerk of District Court. Personal checks accepted. Prepayment required. Mail requests: SASE required. Mail turnaround: 1-2 days.

Benson County

Northeast Judicial District Court PO Box 213, Minnewaukan, ND 58351; 701-473-5345; Fax: 701-473-5571. Hours: 8:30AM-4:30PM (CST). *Felony, Misdemeanor, Civil, Eviction, Small Claims, Probate.*

Civil Records: Access: Fax, mail, in person. Only the court performs in person searches; visitors may not. Search fee: $10.00 per name. Required to search: name, years to search; also helpful: address. Civil cases indexed by defendant, plaintiff. Civil records on docket books and index books from early 1900s, on index cards from 6/10/91.

Criminal Records: Access: Fax, mail, in person. Only the court performs in person searches; visitors may not. Search fee: $10.00 per name. Required to search: name, years to search, DOB, signed release; also helpful: address. Criminal records on docket books and index books from early 1900s, on index cards from 6/10/91. Signed release required for juvenile cases.

General Information: No adoptions, sealed, juvenile, mental health, expunged or dismissed records released. Will fax results for $1.00 per page. Copy fee: $1.00 per page. Certification fee: $10.00. Payee: Benson County Court. Personal checks accepted. Prepayment required. Mail requests: SASE required. Mail turnaround time 5 days.

Billings County

Southwest Judicial District Court PO Box 138, Medora, ND 58645; 701-623-4492; Fax: 701-623-4896. Hours: 9AM-Noon, 1-5PM (MST). *Felony, Misdemeanor, Civil, Eviction, Small Claims, Probate.*

Civil Records: Access: Fax, mail, in person. Both court and visitors may perform in person searches. Search fee: $10.00 per name. Required to search: name, years to search; also helpful: address. Civil cases indexed by defendant, plaintiff. Civil records on index books from 1800s.

Criminal Records: Access: Fax, mail, in person. Both court and visitors may perform in person searches. Search fee: $10.00 per name. Required to search: name, years to search; also helpful: address, DOB, SSN. Criminal records in books.

General Information: No adoptions, sealed, juvenile, mental health, expunged or dismissed records released. Will fax results for $2.00 1st 4 pages, $.50 each add'l. Copy fee: $.25 per page. Certification fee: $10.00 plus $5.00 each add'l page. Payee: Clerk of District Court. No out-of-state checks accepted unles pre-approved. Prepayment required. Mail requests: SASE required. Mail turnaround time 2-3 days.

Bottineau County

Northeast Judicial District Court 314 W 5th St, Bottineau, ND 58318; 701-228-3983; Fax: 701-228-2336. Hours: 8:30AM-5PM (CST). *Felony, Misdemeanor, Civil, Eviction, Small Claims, Probate.*

Civil Records: Access: Fax, mail, in person. Only the court performs in person searches; visitors may not. Search fee: $10.00 per name. Required to search: name, years to search; also helpful: address. Civil cases indexed by defendant, plaintiff. Civil records on index cards from 1987, on docket books from 1972.

Criminal Records: Access: Fax, mail, in person. Only the court performs in person searches; visitors may not. Search fee: $10.00 per name. Required to search: name, years to search; also helpful: address, DOB, SSN. Criminal records on docket books from 1885.

General Information: No adoptions, paternity, sealed, juvenile, mental health, expunged or dismissed records released. Will fax results $4.00 for 1st page, $2.00 each add'l. Copy fee: $.25 per page. Certification fee: $10.00. Payee: Clerk of the Court. Personal checks accepted. Prepayment required. Mail requests: SASE required. Mail turnaround time 1 day.

Bowman County

Southwest Judicial District Court PO Box 379, Bowman, ND 58623; 701-523-3450; Fax: 701-523-5443. Hours: 8:00AM-Noon, 1-4:30PM (MST). *Felony, Misdemeanor, Civil, Eviction, Small Claims, Probate.*

Civil Records: Access: Mail, in person, phone, fax. Both court and visitors may perform in person searches. Search fee: $10.00 per name. Required to search: name, years to search; also helpful: address. Civil cases indexed by defendant, plaintiff. Civil records on dockets from 1907; computerized records back to 1995.

Criminal Records: Access: Mail, in person. Both court and visitors may perform in person searches. Search fee: $10.00 per name. Required to search: name, years to search, DOB; also helpful: address. Criminal records on microfiche from 1978, on dockets from 1907; computerized records back to 1995.

General Information: No adoptions, sealed, juvenile, mental health, expunged or dismissed records released. Will fax results to local or toll free line. Copy fee: $1.00 per page. Certification fee: $10.00. Payee: Clerk of Court. Personal checks accepted. Prepayment required. Mail requests: SASE required. Mail turnaround time 1-2 days.

Burke County

Northwest Judicial District Court PO Box 219, Bowbells, ND 58721; 701-377-2718; Fax: 701-377-2020. Hours: 8:30AM-Noon, 1-5 PM (CST). *Felony, Misdemeanor, Civil, Eviction, Small Claims, Probate.*

Civil Records: Access: Mail, in person. Both court and visitors may perform in person searches. Search fee: $10.00 if a written reply is required. Required to search: name, years to search; also helpful: address. Civil cases indexed by defendant, plaintiff. Civil records for county civil, probate, and district from 1910, county criminal and small claims from 1980.

Criminal Records: Access: Mail, in person. Both court and visitors may perform in person searches. Search fee: $10.00 if a written reply is required. Required to search: name, years to search; also helpful: address, DOB, SSN. Criminal records for county civil, probate, and district from 1910, county criminal and small claims from 1980.

General Information: No adoptions, sealed, juvenile, mental health, expunged or dismissed records released. Fee to fax results is $2.00 per page. Copy fee: $.50 per page. Certification fee: $10.00. Payee: Clerk of Court. Personal checks accepted. Prepayment required. Mail requests: SASE not required. Mail turnaround time 1-3 days.

Burleigh County

South Central Judicial District Court PO Box 1055, Bismarck, ND 58502; 701-222-6690; Criminal phone: Fax: 701-222-6758; Fax: 701-221-3756. 8AM-5PM (CST). *Felony, Misdemeanor, Civil, Eviction, Small Claims, Probate.*

Civil Records: Access: Mail, in person. Both court and visitors may perform in person searches. Search fee: $10.00 per name. Required to search: name; also helpful: years to search. Civil cases indexed by defendant, plaintiff. Civil records on computer back to 1/91; in books from 1800s.

Criminal Records: Access: Mail, in person. Both court and visitors may perform in person searches. Search fee: $10.00 per name. Required to search: name; also helpful: years to search, address, DOB, SSN. Criminal records on computer back to 1/91; in books from early 1900s.

General Information: Public Access terminal is available. No adoptions, sealed, juvenile, mental health, expunged or dismissed records released. Will fax results to local or toll free line. Copy fee: $.10 per page; $1 minimum. Certification fee: $10.00 plus $5.00 each add'l copy of same document, if needed. Payee: Clerk of Court. Personal checks accepted.

Prepayment required. Mail requests: SASE required. Mail turnaround time 1-2 days.

Cass County

East Central Judicial District Court PO Box 2806, Fargo, ND 58108; Civil phone: 701-241-5645; Criminal phone: 701-241-5660; Probate phone: 701-241-5655; Fax: 701-241-5636. Hours: 8AM-5PM (CST). *Felony, Misdemeanor, Civil, Eviction, Small Claims, Probate.*

Civil Records: Access: Mail, fax, in person, online. Both court and visitors may perform in person searches. Search fee: $10.00 per name. Required to search: name, years to search; also helpful: address. Civil cases indexed by defendant, plaintiff. Civil records on computer from 1988, on index books from late 1800s. Probate is online at www.lib.ndsu.no dak.edu/ndirs/databases/probate.php. There is no fee.

Criminal Records: Access: Mail, fax, in person. Both court and visitors may perform in person searches. Search fee: $10.00 per name. Required to search: name, years to search; also helpful: address, DOB, SSN. Criminal records on computer from 1988, on index cards from 1980.

General Information: Public Access terminal is available. No adoptions, sealed, juvenile, mental health, expunged or dismissed records released. Copy fee: $.10 per page. $1.00 minimum. Certification fee: $10.00. Payee: Clerk of District Court. Personal checks accepted. Prepayment required. Mail requests: SASE required. Mail turnaround time 3-5 days.

Cavalier County

Northeast Judicial District Court 901 Third St, Langdon, ND 58249; 701-256-2124; Fax: 701-256-2124. Hours: 8:30AM-4:30PM (CST). *Felony, Misdemeanor, Civil, Eviction, Small Claims, Probate.*

Civil Records: Access: Fax, mail, in person. Only the court performs in person searches; visitors may not. Search fee: $10.00 per name. Required to search: name, years to search; also helpful: address. Civil cases indexed by defendant, plaintiff. Civil records going on computer, prior stored.

Criminal Records: Access: Fax, mail, in person. Only the court performs in person searches; visitors may not. Search fee: $10.00 per name. Required to search: name, years to search; also helpful: address, DOB, SSN. Criminal records for District Court on index books from 1937, for County Court on index books from 1983, prior stored.

General Information: No adoptions, sealed, juvenile, mental health, expunged or dismissed records released. No fee to fax results. Copy fee: $.25 per page. Certification fee: $10.00. Payee: Clerk of Court. Personal checks accepted. Prepayment required. Mail requests: SASE required. Mail turnaround time 1 week.

Dickey County

Southeast Judicial District Court Clerk of Court, PO Box 336, Ellendale, ND 58436; 701-349-3249 X4; Fax: 701-349-3560. Hours: 9AM-Noon, 1-5PM (CST). *Felony, Misdemeanor, Civil, Eviction, Small Claims, Probate.*

Civil Records: Access: Mail, in person. Only the court performs in person searches; visitors may not. Search fee: $10.00 per name. Required to search: name, years to search; also helpful: address. Civil cases indexed by defendant, plaintiff. Civil records on index books to 1983; 1997-present. Probate from 1800s. Old district court records have no index and are very hard to search.

Criminal Records: Access: Mail, in person. Only the court performs in person searches; visitors may not. Search fee: $10.00 per name. Required to search:

name, years to search, DOB; also helpful: address, SSN. Criminal records on index books to 1983, 1997-present. Old district court records have no index and are very hard to search.

General Information: No adoptions, sealed, juvenile, mental health, expunged or dismissed records released. Will fax results to local or toll free line. Copy fee: $.25 per page. Certification fee: $10.00. Payee: Clerk of Court. Personal checks accepted. Prepayment required. Mail requests: SASE not required. Mail turnaround time 1-2 days.

Divide County

Northwest Judicial District Court PO Box 68, Crosby, ND 58730; 701-965-6831; Fax: 701-965-6943. Hours: 8:30AM-Noon, 1-5PM (CST). *Felony, Misdemeanor, Civil, Eviction, Small Claims, Probate.*

Civil Records: Access: Fax, mail, in person. Only the court performs in person searches; visitors may not. Search fee: $10.00 per name. Required to search: name, years to search; also helpful: address. Civil cases indexed by defendant, plaintiff. Civil records on index books from 1910. Visitor can check for judgments. Records for eviction, smalll claims and probate are an additonal $10.00 if full certification needed.

Criminal Records: Access: Fax, mail, in person. Only the court performs in person searches; visitors may not. Search fee: $10.00 per name. Required to search: name, years to search; also helpful: address, DOB, SSN. Criminal records on index books from 1910.

General Information: No adoptions, sealed, juvenile, mental health, expunged or dismissed records released. Will fax results $3.00 1st page, $1.00 each add'l. Also a charge of $1.00 per incoming fax page. Copy fee: $.25 per page. $1.00 minimum. Certification fee: Included in search fee. Payee: Clerk of District Court. Personal checks accepted. Prepayment required. Mail requests: SASE required. Mail turnaround time 1-2 days.

Dunn County

District Court PO Box 136, Manning, ND 58642-0136; 701-573-4447; Fax: 701-573-4444. Hours: 8AM-Noon,12:30-4:30PM (MST). *Felony, Misdemeanor, Civil, Small Claims, Probate.*

Civil Records: Access: Fax, mail, in person. Both court and visitors may perform in person searches. Search fee: $10.00 per name. Required to search: name, years to search; also helpful: address. Civil cases indexed by defendant, plaintiff. Civil records on plaintiff/defendant index cards from 1988, on docket books from 1900s, on computer since 01/97. Fax requests must fax copy of the check to be mailed.

Criminal Records: Access: Fax, mail, in person. Both court and visitors may perform in person searches. Search fee: $10.00 per name. Required to search: name, years to search, DOB; also helpful: address, SSN. Criminal records on plaintiff/defendant index cards from 1988, on docket books from 1900s, on computer since 01/97. Fax requesters must fax copy of the check, which can be mailed.

General Information: Public Access terminal is available. Adoptions, paternity, juvenile, mental health, deferred impositions, and termination of parental rights are restricted access files. Will fax results $2.00 plus $1.00 per page. Copy fee: $2.00 plus $.50 each page (mailed copies). Certification fee: $10.00. Payee: Dunn County Clerk of Court. In state personal checks accepted. Prepayment required. Mail requests: SASE not required. Mail turnaround time 2 days.

Eddy County

Southeast Judicial District Court 524 Central Ave, New Rockford, ND 58356; 701-947-2813 x2013; Fax: 701-947-2067. Hours: 8AM-4PM (CST). *Felony, Misdemeanor, Civil, Eviction, Small Claims, Probate.*

Civil Records: Access: Fax, mail, in person. Only the court performs in person searches; visitors may not. Search fee: $10.00 per name. Required to search: name, years to search; also helpful: address. Civil cases indexed by defendant, plaintiff. Civil records on index cards from 4/92, on index books from early 1900s. All requests must be in writing.

Criminal Records: Access: Fax, mail, in person. Only the court performs in person searches; visitors may not. Search fee: $10.00 per name. Required to search: name, years to search; also helpful: address, DOB, SSN. Criminal records on index cards from 4/92, on index books from early 1900s. All requests must be in writing.

General Information: No adoptions, sealed, juvenile, mental health, expunged or dismissed records released. Fee to fax results is $4.00 1st 3 pages, $1.00 each add'l page. Copy fee: $1.00 per document. Certification fee: $10.00. Payee: Eddy County District Court. Personal checks accepted. Prepayment required. Mail requests: SASE required. Mail turnaround time 1-2 days.

Emmons County

South Central Judicial District Court PO Box 905, Linton, ND 58552; 701-254-4812; Fax: 701-254-4012. Hours: 8:30AM-Noon, 1-5PM (CST). *Felony, Misdemeanor, Civil, Eviction, Small Claims, Probate.*

Civil Records: Access: Fax, mail, in person. Only the court performs in person searches; visitors may not. Search fee: $10.00 per name. Required to search: name, years to search; also helpful: address. Civil cases indexed by defendant, plaintiff. Civil records on index cards from 1988, on index books from 1914, on computer back to 1995.

Criminal Records: Access: Fax, mail, in person. Only the court performs in person searches; visitors may not. Search fee: $10.00 per name. Required to search: name, years to search, DOB; also helpful: address, SSN. Criminal records on index books back to 1983; on computer back to 1995.

General Information: No adoptions, sealed, juvenile, mental health, expunged or dismissed records released. Fee to fax results is $3.00 1st page, $1.00 each add'l. Copy fee: $.20 per page. Certification fee: $10.00. Payee: Clerk of Courts. Personal checks accepted. Prepayment required. Mail requests: SASE required. Mail turnaround time 1-2 days.

Foster County

Southeast Judicial District Court PO Box 257, Carrington, ND 58421; 701-652-1001; Fax: 701-652-2173. Hours: 8:30AM-4:30PM (CST). *Felony, Misdemeanor, Civil, Eviction, Small Claims, Probate.*

Civil Records: Access: Mail, in person. Both court and visitors may perform in person searches. Search fee: $10.00 per name if court performs search. Required to search: name, years to search; also helpful: address. Civil cases indexed by defendant, plaintiff. Civil records on index books from early 1900s.

Criminal Records: Access: Mail, in person. Both court and visitors may perform in person searches. Search fee: $10.00 per name if court performs search. Required to search: name, years to search, DOB; also

helpful: address. Criminal records on index books from early 1900s.

General Information: No adoptions, sealed, juvenile, mental health, expunged or dismissed records released. Will fax results $3.00 per doc. Copy fee: $1.00 per page. Certification fee: $10.00. Payee: Clerk of Courts. Personal checks accepted. Prepayment required. Mail requests: SASE required. Mail turnaround time 1-2 days.

Golden Valley County

Southwest Judicial District Court PO Box 9, Beach, ND 58621-0009; 701-872-3713; Fax: 701-872-4383. Hours: 8-Noon, 1-4PM (MST). *Felony, Misdemeanor, Civil, Eviction, Small Claims, Probate.*

Civil Records: Access: Fax, mail, in person. Only the court performs in person searches; visitors may not. Search fee: $10.00 per name. Required to search: name, years to search; also helpful: address. Civil cases indexed by defendant, plaintiff. Civil records on index cards from 1987, on index books from 1913 to 1960. From 1960 to 1987, records are hard to find; there is no indexing and files are filed by number. Fax request must include copy of check.

Criminal Records: Access: Fax, mail, in person. Only the court performs in person searches; visitors may not. Search fee: $10.00 per name. Required to search: name, years to search, DOB; also helpful: address, SSN. Criminal records on index cards from 1987, on index books from 1913 to 1960. From 1960 to 1987, records are hard to find; there is no indexing and files are filed by number. Fax request must include copy of check. Statewide records on comuputer since 04/04/03.

General Information: No adoptions, sealed, juvenile, mental health, expunged or dismissed records released. Will fax results $1.00 per page. Copy fee: $.50 per page. Certification fee: $10.00. Payee: Clerk of Court. Personal checks accepted. Prepayment required. Mail requests: SASE required. Mail turnaround time 3-4 days.

Grand Forks County

Northeast Central Judicial District Court PO Box 5939, Grand Forks, ND 58206-5939; 701-780-8214; Fax: 701-780-8217. Hours: 8AM-5PM (CST). *Felony, Misdemeanor, Civil, Eviction, Small Claims, Probate.*

Civil Records: Access: Mail, in person. Both the court and visitors may perform in person searches. Search fee: $10.00 per name. Required to search: name, years to search; also helpful: address. Civil cases indexed by defendant, plaintiff. Civil records on computer from 10/91, on index books from early 1900s.

Criminal Records: Access: Mail, in person. Both the court and visitors may perform in person searches. Search fee: $10.00 per name. Required to search: name, years to search, DOB, signed release; also helpful: address, SSN. Criminal records on computer from 10/91, on index books from early 1900s.

General Information: Public Access terminal is available. No adoptions, sealed, juvenile, mental health, expunged or dismissed records released. Will fax results for no charge. Copy fee: $.10 per page; $1.00 minimum. Certification fee: $10.00. Payee: Clerk of District Court. Personal checks accepted. Prepayment required. Mail requests: SASE required. Mail turnaround time 1-2 days.

Grant County

South Central Judicial District Court PO Box 258, Carson, ND 58529; 701-622-3615; Fax: 701-622-3717. Hours: 8AM-Noon, 12:30-4PM (MST). *Felony, Misdemeanor, Civil, Eviction, Small Claims, Probate.*

Civil Records: Access: Fax, mail, in person. Both court and visitors may perform in person searches. Search fee: $10.00 per name. Required to search: name, years to search; also helpful: address. Civil cases indexed by defendant, plaintiff. Civil records on index cards from 1990, on docket books in vault from 1900s.

Criminal Records: Access: Fax, mail, in person. Both court and visitors may perform in person searches. Search fee: $10.00 per name. Required to search: name, years to search; also helpful: address, DOB, SSN. Criminal records on index cards from 1990, on docket books in vault from 1900s.

General Information: No adoptions, sealed, juvenile, mental health, expunged or dismissed records released. Will fax results $3.00 per doc. Copy fee: $.25 per page. Certification fee: $10.00. Payee: Clerk of Grant County Court. Personal checks accepted. Prepayment required. Mail requests: SASE not required. Mail turnaround time 1 day.

Griggs County

Southeast Judicial District Court PO Box 326, Cooperstown, ND 58425; 701-797-2772; Fax: 701-797-3587. Hours: 8AM-Noon, 1-4:30PM (CST). *Felony, Misdemeanor, Civil, Eviction, Small Claims, Probate.*

Civil Records: Access: Fax, mail, in person. Both court and visitors may perform in person searches. Search fee: $10.00 per name. Required to search: name, years to search; also helpful: address. Civil cases indexed by defendant, plaintiff. Civil records in docket books from 1890 to 2001 and UCIS 2001 to present. Phone access discouraged.

Criminal Records: Access: Fax, mail, in person. Both court and visitors may perform in person searches. Search fee: $10.00 per name. Required to search: name, years to search; also helpful: address, DOB, SSN. Criminal records on docket books from 1890 to 2001 and UCIS 2001 to present. Phone access discouraged.

General Information: No adoptions, sealed, juvenile, mental health, expunged or dismissed records released. Will fax results $1.00 per page. Incoming fax- $1.00 per page; free for state attorneys. Copy fee: $.25 per page. Certification fee: $10.00. Payee: Clerk of Courts. Personal checks accepted. Prepayment required. Mail requests: SASE required. Mail turnaround time 1-2 days.

Hettinger County

Southwest Judicial District Court PO Box 668, Mott, ND 58646; 701-824-2645; Fax: 701-824-2717. Hours: 8AM-Noon, 1-4:30PM (MST). *Felony, Misdemeanor, Civil, Eviction, Small Claims, Probate.*

Civil Records: Access: Fax, mail, in person. Both court and visitors may perform in person searches. Search fee: $10.00 per name. Required to search: name, years to search; also helpful: address. Civil cases indexed by defendant, plaintiff. Civil records on index cards from 1987, on index books from 1908.

Criminal Records: Access: Fax, mail, in person. Both court and visitors may perform in person searches. Search fee: $10.00 per name. Required to search: name, years to search, DOB; also helpful: address. Criminal records on index cards from 1987, on index books from 1908.

General Information: No adoptions, sealed, juvenile, mental health, expunged or dismissed records released. Will fax results $3.00 per doc. Fee is for up to 20 pages. Copy fee: $.25 per page. Certification fee: $10.00. Payee: Hettinger Court Clerk. Personal checks accepted. Prepayment required. Mail requests: SASE required. Mail turnaround time 1 day.

Kidder County

District Court PO Box 66, Steele, ND 58482; 701-475-2632; Fax: 701-475-2202. Hours: 9AM-5PM (CST). *Felony, Misdemeanor, Civil, Eviction, Small Claims, Probate.*

Civil Records: Access: Fax, mail, in person. Both court and visitors may perform in person searches. Search fee: $10.00 per name. Required to search: name, years to search; also helpful: address. Civil cases indexed by defendant, plaintiff. Civil records on index book from 1800s, on computer since 1990.

Criminal Records: Access: Mail, in person. Both court and visitors may perform in person searches. Search fee: $10.00 per name. Required to search: name, years to search, DOB; also helpful: address. Records on index book from 1900s, on computer since 1990.

General Information: Public Access terminal is available. No adoptions, sealed, juvenile, mental health, expunged or dismissed records released. Will fax results for $3.00 per document. Copy fee: $1.00 per page. Certification fee: $10.00. Payee: Clerk of Court. Personal checks accepted. Prepayment required. Mail requests: SASE required. Mail turnaround time 1-2 days.

La Moure County

Southeast Judicial District Court PO Box 128, LaMoure, ND 58458; 701-883-5193; Fax: 701-883-4240. Hours: 9AM-Noon, 1-5PM (CST). *Felony, Misdemeanor, Civil, Eviction, Small Claims, Probate.*

Civil Records: Access: Fax, mail, in person. Both court and visitors may perform in person searches. Search fee: $10.00 per name. Required to search: name, years to search; also helpful: address. Civil cases indexed by defendant, plaintiff. Civil records on docket books from 1800s; on computer back to 2002.

Criminal Records: Access: Fax, mail, in person. Both court and visitors may perform in person searches. Search fee: $10.00 per name. Required to search: name, years to search; also helpful: address, DOB. Criminal records go back to 1987.

General Information: No adoptions, sealed, juvenile, mental health, expunged or dismissed records released. Will not fax results without prepayment or copy of payment check. Copy fee: $.25 for first page, $.10 each add'l. Certification fee: $10.00. Payee: Clerk of Court. Personal checks accepted. Prepayment required. Mail requests: SASE required. Mail turnaround time 1 day.

Logan County

South Central Judicial District Court PO Box 6, Napoleon, ND 58561; 701-754-2751; Fax: 701-754-2270. Hours: 8:30AM-4:30PM (CST). *Felony, Misdemeanor, Civil, Eviction, Small Claims, Probate.*

Civil Records: Access: Fax, mail, in person. Both court and visitors may perform in person searches. Search fee: $10.00 per name. Required to search: name, years to search; also helpful: address, signed release. Civil cases indexed by defendant, plaintiff. Civil records on index books from 1884.

Criminal Records: Access: Fax, mail, in person. Only the court performs in person searches; visitors may not. Search fee: $10.00 per name. Required to

search: name, years to search, DOB; also helpful: address, signed release. Criminal records on index books from 1890.

General Information: No adoptions, sealed, juvenile, mental health, expunged or dismissed records released. Fee to fax results is $3.00 1st page, $1.00 each add'l. Copy fee: $1.00 per page. Certification fee: $10.00. Payee: Clerk of Court. Business checks accepted. Prepayment required. Mail requests: SASE required. Mail turnaround time 1-2 days.

McHenry County

Northeast Judicial District Court PO Box 117, Towner, ND 58788; 701-537-5729; Fax: 701-537-5969. Hours: 8AM-4:30PM (CST). *Felony, Misdemeanor, Civil, Eviction, Small Claims, Probate.*

Civil Records: Access: Fax, mail, in person. Both court and visitors may perform in person searches. Search fee: $10.00 per name. Required to search: name, years to search; also helpful: address. Civil cases indexed by defendant, plaintiff. Civil records on index cards from 1991, on index books from 1905.

Criminal Records: Access: Fax, mail, in person. Both court and visitors may perform in person searches. Search fee: $10.00 per name. Required to search: name, years to search; also helpful: address, DOB, SSN. Criminal records on index cards from 1991, on index books from 1905.

General Information: No adoptions, sealed, juvenile, mental health, expunged or dismissed records released. Will fax results $1.00 1st page, $.25 each add'l. Copy fee: $.25 per page. Certification fee: $10.00. Payee: Clerk of Courts. Personal checks accepted. Prepayment required. Mail requests: SASE required. Mail turnaround time 1-2 days.

McIntosh County

South Central Judicial District Court PO Box 179, Ashley, ND 58413; 701-288-3450; Fax: 701-288-3671. Hours: 8AM-4:30PM (CST). *Felony, Misdemeanor, Civil, Eviction, Small Claims, Probate.*

Civil Records: Access: Phone, fax, mail, in person. Visitors must perform in person searches for themselves. Search fee: $10.00 per name. Required to search: name, years to search; also helpful: address. Civil cases indexed by defendant, plaintiff. Civil records on index cards from 1987, on index books from 1930s.

Criminal Records: Access: Fax, mail, in person. Both court and visitors may perform in person searches. Search fee: $10.00 per name. Required to search: name, years to search, DOB; also helpful: address. Criminal records on index cards from 1987, on index books from 1930s.

General Information: No adoptions, sealed, juvenile, mental health, expunged or dismissed records released. Will fax results to local or toll free line. Copy fee: $.25 per page. Certification fee: $10.00. Payee: Clerk of Court. Only cashiers checks and money orders accepted. Prepayment required. Mail requests: SASE not required. Mail turnaround time 1-2 days.

McKenzie County

Northwest Judicial District Court PO Box 524, Watford City, ND 58854; 701-444-3452; Fax: 701-444-3916. Hours: 8:30AM-Noon, 1-5PM (CST). *Felony, Misdemeanor, Civil, Eviction, Small Claims, Probate.*

Civil Records: Access: Mail, in person. Both court and visitors may perform in person searches. Search fee: $10.00 per name. Required to search: name, years to search; also helpful: address, SSN. Civil cases indexed by defendant, plaintiff. Civil records on computer back to 01/96.

Criminal Records: Access: Mail, in person. Only the court performs in person searches; visitors may not. Search fee: $10.00 per name. Required to search: name, years to search, DOB, SSN. Criminal records on computer back to 12/87; on books back to 1908.

General Information: No adoptions, juvenile, mental health, expunged or dismissed records released. Fee to fax results is $2.00 per page. Copy fee: $.25 per page. Certification fee: $10.00. Payee: Clerk of Court, McKenzie County. Personal checks accepted. Prepayment required. Mail requests: SASE required. Mail turnaround time 1-2 days.

McLean County

South Central Judicial District Court PO Box 1108, Washburn, ND 58577; 701-462-8541; Fax: 701-462-8212. Hours: 8AM-Noon, 12:30-4:30PM (CST). *Felony, Misdemeanor, Civil, Eviction, Small Claims, Probate.*

Civil Records: Access: Mail, in person. Both court and visitors may perform in person searches. Search fee: $10.00 per name. Required to search: name, years to search; also helpful: address. Civil cases indexed by defendant, plaintiff. Civil records on index books from early 1900s; on computer back to 1996.

Criminal Records: Access: Mail, in person. Both court and visitors may perform in person searches. Search fee: $10.00 per name. Required to search: name, years to search, DOB; also helpful: address, SSN. Criminal records on index cards from 1983, on index books from early 1900s; on computer back to 1996.

General Information: Public Access terminal is available. No adoptions, sealed, juvenile, mental health, expunged or deferred imposition dismissed records released. Will fax results to toll free line. Copy fee: $.25 per page. Certification fee: $10.00. Payee: Clerk of Courts. Personal checks accepted. Prepayment required. Mail requests: SASE required. Mail turnaround time 1-2 days.

Mercer County

District Court PO Box 39, Stanton, ND 58571; 701-745-3262; Fax: 701-745-3710. Hours: 8AM-4PM (MST). *Felony, Misdemeanor, Civil, Eviction, Small Claims, Probate.*

Civil Records: Access: Fax, mail, in person. Both court and visitors may perform in person searches. Search fee: $10.00 per name. Required to search: name, years to search; also helpful: address. Civil cases indexed by defendant, plaintiff. Civil records on index cards from 1979, on index books from 1889, computerized since 1990.

Criminal Records: Access: Fax, mail, in person. Both court and visitors may perform in person searches. Search fee: $10.00 per name. Required to search: name, years to search, signed release; also helpful: address, DOB, SSN. Criminal records on index cards from 1979, on index books from 1889, computerized since 1990.

General Information: Public Access terminal is available. No adoptions, sealed, juvenile, mental health, expunged or dismissed records released. Will fax results $5.00 per doc. Copy fee: $.25 per page. Certification fee: $10.00. Payee: Mercer County Clerk of Court. Personal checks accepted. Prepayment required. Mail requests: SASE required. Mail turnaround time 1-2 days.

Morton County

South Central Judicial District Court 210 2nd Ave NW, Mandan, ND 58554; 701-667-3358; Criminal phone: 701-667-3355. Hours: 8AM-5PM (MST). *Felony, Misdemeanor, Civil, Eviction, Small Claims, Probate.*

Civil Records: Access: Mail, in person. Both court and visitors may perform in person searches. Search fee: $10.00 per name. Fee is for written search request. Required to search: name, years to search; also helpful: address. Civil cases indexed by defendant, plaintiff. Civil records on computer from 1990; on index books from 1985.

Criminal Records: Access: Mail, in person. Both court and visitors may perform in person searches. Search fee: $10.00 per name. Fee is for written search request. Required to search: name, years to search, DOB; also helpful: address. Criminal records on computer from 1990, on index books from 1985.

General Information: Public Access terminal is available. No adoptions, sealed, juvenile, mental health, expunged or dismissed records released. Will fax case files to local or toll free number. Copy fee: $5.00 per document. Certification fee: $10.00. Payee: Clerk of District Court. Personal checks accepted. Prepayment required. Mail requests: SASE required. Mail turnaround time 1-2 days.

Mountrail County

Northwest Judicial District Court PO Box 69, Stanley, ND 58784; 701-628-2915; Fax: 701-628-2276. Hours: 8:30AM-4:30PM (CST). *Felony, Misdemeanor, Civil, Eviction, Small Claims, Probate.*

Civil Records: Access: Mail, in person, fax, phone. Both court and visitors may perform in person searches. Search fee: $10.00 per name. Fee is for written search. Required to search: name, years to search; also helpful: address. Civil cases indexed by defendant, plaintiff. Civil records on index books from 1909; on computer back to 1998.

Criminal Records: Access: Mail, in person. Both court and visitors may perform in person searches. Search fee: $10.00 per name. Fee is for written search. Required to search: name, years to search, DOB. Criminal records on index books from 1909; on computer back to 1998.

General Information: Public Access terminal is available. No adoptions, sealed, juvenile, mental health, expunged or dismissed records released. No fee to fax results. Copy fee: $.30 per page. Certification fee: $10.00. Payee: Clerk of District Court. Personal checks accepted. Prepayment required. Mail requests: SASE not required. Mail turnaround time 1-2 days.

Nelson County

Northeast Central Judicial District Court Nelson County Recorder-Clerk of Court, 210 B Ave W, #203, Lakota, ND 58344-7410; 701-247-2462; Fax: 701-247-2412. Hours: 8:30AM-Noon; 1PM-4:30PM (CST). *Felony, Misdemeanor, Civil, Eviction, Small Claims, Probate.*

Civil Records: Access: Fax, mail, in person, email. Both court and visitors may perform in person searches. Search fee: $10.00 per name. Required to search: name, years to search; also helpful: address. Civil cases indexed by defendant, plaintiff. Civil records on index books from 1883. Will accept email record requests at rstevens@pioneer.state.nd.us.

Criminal Records: Access: Fax, mail, in person, email. Only the court performs in person searches; visitors may not. Search fee: $10.00 per name. Required to search: name, years to search, DOB; also helpful: address, SSN. Criminal records on index

books from 1883. Will accept email record requests at rstevens@pioneer.state.nd.us.

General Information: Public Access terminal is available. (Civil records only.) No adoptions, sealed, juvenile, mental health, expunged or dismissed records released. Will fax results $3.00 per doc. Copy fee: $1.00 per page. Certification fee: $10.00. Payee: Clerk of Courts. Personal checks accepted. Prepayment required. Mail requests: SASE required. Mail turnaround time 1-2 days.

Oliver County

South Central Judicial District Court Box 125, Center, ND 58530; 701-794-8777; Fax: 701-794-3476. Hours: 8AM-4PM (CST). *Felony, Misdemeanor, Civil, Eviction, Small Claims, Probate.*

Civil Records: Access: Fax, mail, in person. Only the court performs in person searches; visitors may not. Search fee: $10.00 per name. Required to search: name, years to search; also helpful: address. Civil cases indexed by defendant. Civil records on docket books from 1920s.

Criminal Records: Access: Fax, mail, in person. Only the court performs in person searches; visitors may not. Search fee: $10.00 per name. Required to search: name, years to search, DOB; also helpful: address. Criminal records on docket books from 1920s.

General Information: No adoptions, sealed, juvenile, mental health, expunged or dismissed records released. Will fax results $1.00 1st page, $.50 each add'l. Copy fee: $.25 per page. Certification fee: $10.00. Payee: Clerk of Court. Personal checks accepted. Prepayment required. Mail requests: SASE required. Mail turnaround time 1-2 days.

Pembina County

Pembina County District Court 301 Dakota St West #6, Cavalier, ND 58220-4100; 701-265-4275; Fax: 701-265-4876. Hours: 8:30AM-5PM (CST). *Felony, Misdemeanor, Civil, Eviction, Small Claims, Probate.*

Civil Records: Access: Fax, mail, in person. Both court and visitors may perform in person searches. Search fee: $10.00 per name. Required to search: name, years to search; also helpful: address, DOB, SSN. Civil cases indexed by defendant, plaintiff. Civil records on index books from 1880s; computerized records go back to 1992.

Criminal Records: Access: Fax, mail, in person. Both the court and visitors may perform in person searches. Search fee: $10.00 per name. Required to search: name, years to search, DOB; also helpful: address, SSN. Felony records kept for 21 years, misdemeanor for 15 years; computerized records go back to 1997.

General Information: Public Access terminal is available. No adoptions, sealed, juvenile, mental health, expunged or dismissed records released. Will fax results to local or toll free line. Copy fee: $.25 per page. Certification fee: $10.00. Payee: Pembina County Clerk of Court. Personal checks accepted. Prepayment required. Mail requests: SASE requested. Turnaround time 1-2 days.

Pierce County

Northeast Judicial District Court 240 SE 2nd St, Rugby, ND 58368; 701-776-6161; Fax: 701-776-5707. Hours: 9AM-5PM (CST). *Felony, Misdemeanor, Civil, Eviction, Small Claims, Probate.*

Civil Records: Access: Fax, mail, in person. Only the court performs in person searches; visitors may not. Search fee: $10.00 per name. Required to search: name, years to search; also helpful: address. Civil cases indexed by defendant, plaintiff. Civil records on computer from 1986, on index books and docket books from early 1900s.

Criminal Records: Access: Fax, mail, in person. Only the court performs in person searches; visitors may not. Search fee: $10.00 per name. Required to search: name, years to search, DOB; also helpful: address, SSN. Criminal records on computer from 1986, on index books and docket books from early 1900s.

General Information: No adoptions, sealed, juvenile, mental health, expunged or dismissed records released. Will fax results $5.00 per doc. Copy fee: $.25 per page. Certification fee: $10.00. Payee: Clerk of Courts. Personal checks accepted. Prepayment required. Mail requests: SASE helpful. Turnaround time 1-2 days.

Ramsey County

District Court 524 4th Ave #4, Devils Lake, ND 58301; 701-662-1309; Fax: 701-662-1303. Hours: 8AM-Noon; 1:00PM-5:00PM (CST). *Felony, Misdemeanor, Civil, Eviction, Small Claims, Probate.*

Civil Records: Access: Fax, mail, in person. Only the court performs in person searches; visitors may not. Search fee: $10.00 per name. Required to search: name; also helpful: years to search. Civil cases indexed by defendant, plaintiff. Civil records on index cards from 1985, on index books from early 1900s.

Criminal Records: Access: Fax, mail, in person. Only the court performs in person searches; visitors may not. Search fee: $10.00 per name. Required to search: name; also helpful: years to search, address, DOB, SSN. Criminal records on index cards from 1985, on index books from early 1900s.

General Information: No adoptions, sealed, juvenile, mental health, expunged or dismissed records released. No fee to fax results. Fax only available to businesses. Copy fee: $.50 per page. Certification fee: $10.00. Payee: Clerk of Courts. Personal checks accepted. Prepayment required. Mail requests: SASE required. Mail turnaround time 1-2 days.

Ransom County

Southeast Judicial District Court PO Box 626, Lisbon, ND 58054; 701-683-5823 X120; Criminal phone: 701-683-5823 x142; Fax: 701-683-5826. Hours: 8:30AM-5PM (CST). *Felony, Misdemeanor, Civil, Eviction, Small Claims, Probate.*

Civil Records: Access: Fax, mail, in person. Both court and visitors may perform in person searches. Search fee: $10.00 per name. Required to search: name, years to search; also helpful: address. Civil cases indexed by defendant, plaintiff. Civil records computerized from 2000.

Criminal Records: Access: Fax, mail, in person. Both court and visitors may perform in person searches. Search fee: $10.00 per name. Required to search: name, years to search, DOB; also helpful: address. Criminal records computerized from 2000.

General Information: No adoptions, sealed, juvenile, mental health, expunged or dismissed records released. No fee to fax results. Copy fee: $.20 per page. Certification fee: $10.00. Payee: Clerk of Court. Personal checks accepted. Prepayment required. Mail requests: SASE required. Mail turnaround time 3-4 days.

Renville County

Northeast Judicial District Court PO Box 68, Mohall, ND 58761; 701-756-6398; Fax: 701-756-6398. Hours: 9AM-4:30PM (CST). *Felony, Misdemeanor, Civil, Eviction, Small Claims, Probate.*

Civil Records: Access: Fax, mail, in person. Both court and visitors may perform in person searches. Search fee: $10.00 per name. Required to search: name, years to search; also helpful: address. Civil cases indexed by defendant, plaintiff. Civil records on index books from 1910.

Criminal Records: Access: Fax, mail, in person. Both court and visitors may perform in person searches. Search fee: $10.00 per name. Required to search: name, years to search, DOB; also helpful: address. Criminal records on computer from 1/88, on index books from 1910 but not reliable before 1940.

General Information: No adoptions, sealed, juvenile, mental health, expunged or dismissed records released. Will fax results $3.00 1st page, $1.00 each add'l. Copy fee: $.25 per page. Certification fee: $10.00. Payee: Clerk of Courts. Personal checks accepted. Prepayment required. Mail requests: SASE required. Mail turnaround time 1-2 days.

Richland County

Southeast Judicial District Court 418 2nd Ave North, Wahpeton, ND 58074; 701-671-1524; Fax: 701-671-1512. Hours: 8AM-5PM (CST). *Felony, Misdemeanor, Civil, Eviction, Small Claims, Probate.*

Civil Records: Access: Mail, fax, in person. Both court and visitors may perform in person searches. Search fee: $10.00 per name. Required to search: name, years to search; also helpful: address. Plaintiff and defendant names required to search. Civil records on index cards and computer. Plaintiff and defendant names required to search.

Criminal Records: Access: Mail, fax, in person. Both court and visitors may perform in person searches. Search fee: $10.00 per name. Required to search: name, years to search, DOB, SSN; also helpful: address. Criminal records on docket books and computer.

General Information: Public Access terminal is available. (Public access includes 1998 to present.) No adoptions, sealed, juvenile, mental health, expunged or dismissed records released. Will fax results to toll-free number, otherwise fee is $.25 per page, $1.00 minimum. Copy fee: $.10 per page; $1.00 minimum. Certification fee: $10.00. Payee: Clerk of District Court. Personal checks accepted. Prepayment required. Mail requests: SASE required. Mail turnaround time 1-2 days.

Rolette County

Northeast Judicial District Court PO Box 460, Rolla, ND 58367; 701-477-3816; Fax: 701-477-5770. Hours: 8:30AM-4:30PM (CST). *Felony, Misdemeanor, Civil, Eviction, Small Claims, Probate.*

Civil Records: Access: Fax, mail, in person. Both court and visitors may perform in person searches. Search fee: $10.00 per name. Required to search: name, years to search; also helpful: address. Civil cases indexed by defendant, plaintiff, stored since 1889; computerized since 2000.

Criminal Records: Access: Fax, mail, in person. Both court and visitors may perform in person searches. Search fee: $10.00 per name. Required to search: name, years to search; also helpful: address, DOB, SSN. Criminal records on dockets from 1970,

computerized since 2000. Prior to 1970, records hard to find and not very accurate.

General Information: No adoptions, sealed, juvenile, mental health, expunged or dismissed records released. Will fax results $5.00 per doc. Copy fee: $.50 per page. Certification fee: $10.00. Payee: Clerk of Court. Business checks accepted. Prepayment required. Mail requests: SASE required. Mail turnaround time 1-2 days.

Sargent County

Southeast Judicial District Court PO Box 176 (355 Main St), Forman, ND 58032; 701-724-6241 X115; Fax: 701-724-6244. Hours: 9AM-Noon, 12:30-4:30PM (CST). *Felony, Misdemeanor, Civil, Eviction, Small Claims, Probate.*

Civil Records: Access: Fax, mail, in person. Both court and visitors may perform in person searches. Search fee: $10.00 per name. Required to search: name, years to search; also helpful: address. Civil cases indexed by defendant. Civil records on books from early 1800s.

Criminal Records: Access: Fax, mail, in person. Both court and visitors may perform in person searches. Search fee: $10.00 per name. Required to search: name, years to search; also helpful-DOB. Criminal records on books from early 1800s.

General Information: No adoptions, sealed, juvenile, mental health, expunged or dismissed records released. Will fax results $3.00 1st page, $1.00 each add'l. Copy fee: $.10 per page. Certification fee: $10.00. Payee: Clerk of Court. Personal checks accepted. Prepayment required. Mail requests: SASE not required. Mail turnaround time 1-2 days.

Sheridan County

South Central Judicial District Court PO Box 409, McClusky, ND 58463; 701-363-2207; Fax: 701-363-2953. Hours: 9AM-Noon, 1-5PM (CST). *Felony, Misdemeanor, Civil, Eviction, Small Claims, Probate.*

Civil Records: Access: Mail, in person. Both court and visitors may perform in person searches. Search fee: $10.00 per name. Required to search: name, years to search; also helpful: address. Civil cases indexed by defendant, plaintiff. Civil records on index books from 1909.

Criminal Records: Access: Mail, in person. Both court and visitors may perform in person searches. Search fee: $10.00 per name. Required to search: name, years to search, signed release; also helpful: address, DOB, SSN. Criminal records on index books from 1909.

General Information: No adoptions, sealed, juvenile, mental health, expunged or dismissed records released. Copy fee: $.25 per page. Certification fee: $10.00. Payee: Clerk of District Court. Business checks accepted. Prepayment required. Mail requests: SASE not required. Mail turnaround time 1-2 days.

Sioux County

South Central Judicial District Court Box L, Fort Yates, ND 58538; 701-854-3853; Fax: 701-854-3854. Hours: 9AM-4:30PM (CST). *Felony, Misdemeanor, Civil, Eviction, Small Claims, Probate.*

Civil Records: Access: Fax, mail, in person. Both court and visitors may perform in person searches. Search fee: $10.00 per name per year. Required to search: name, years to search; also helpful: address. Civil cases indexed by defendant, plaintiff. Civil records on index books from 1914.

Criminal Records: Access: Mail, in person. Both court and visitors may perform in person searches.

Search fee: $10.00 per name per year. Required to search: name, years to search; also helpful: address, DOB, SSN. Criminal records on index books from 1914.

General Information: No adoptions, sealed, juvenile, mental health, expunged or dismissed records released. Fee to fax results is $3.00 per document. Copy fee: $.50 per page. Certification fee: $10.00. Payee: Clerk of Court. Personal checks accepted. Prepayment required. Mail requests: SASE required. Mail turnaround time 1-2 days.

Slope County

Southwest Judicial District Court PO Box JJ, Amidon, ND 58620; 701-879-6275; Fax: 701-879-6278. Hours: 8:00AM-Noon; 1:00PM-5:00PM (MST). *Felony, Misdemeanor, Civil, Eviction, Small Claims, Probate.*

Civil Records: Access: Fax, mail, in person. Both court and visitors may perform in person searches. Search fee: $10.00 per name. Required to search: name, years to search; also helpful: address. Civil cases indexed by defendant, plaintiff. Civil records on index cards from 1989.

Criminal Records: Access: Fax, mail, in person. Both court and visitors may perform in person searches. Search fee: $10.00 per name. Required to search: name, years to search, DOB; also helpful: address. Criminal records on index books from 1915.

General Information: No adoptions, sealed, juvenile, mental health, expunged or dismissed records released. Will fax results $3.00 per doc. Copy fee: $.50 per page. Certification fee: $10.00. Payee: Clerk of Court. Personal checks accepted. Prepayment required. Mail requests: SASE required. Mail turnaround time 1-2 days.

Stark County

District Court 51 Third St #106, Dickinson, ND 58602; 701-227-3184; Civil phone: 701-227-3182; Criminal phone: 701-227-3180; Probate phone: 701-227-3181; Fax: 701-227-3185. Hours: 7AM-5PM (MST). *Felony, Misdemeanor, Civil, Eviction, Small Claims, Probate.*

Civil Records: Access: Mail, in person. Both court and visitors may perform in person searches. Search fee: $10.00 per name. Required to search: name, years to search. Civil cases indexed by defendant, plaintiff. Civil records on computer since 1/92, index cards since 1800s.

Criminal Records: Access: Mail, in person. Both court and visitors may perform in person searches. Search fee: $10.00 per name. Required to search: name, years to search, DOB; also helpful: SSN. Criminal records on computer since 1/92, index cards since 1800s.

General Information: Public Access terminal is available. No adoptions, sealed, juvenile, mental health, expunged or dismissed records. Will fax results for $.25 per page, $1.00 minimum. Copy fee: $.25 per page; $1.00 minimum. Certification fee: $10.00. Payee: Clerk of Court. Personal checks accepted. Prepayment required. Mail requests: SASE required. Mail turnaround time 1-2 days.

Steele County

East Central Judicial District Court PO Box 296, Finley, ND 58230; 701-524-2152; Fax: 701-524-1325. Hours: 8AM-Noon; 1-4:30PM (CST). *Felony, Misdemeanor, Civil, Eviction, Small Claims, Probate.*

Civil Records: Access: Mail, in person. Only the court performs in person searches; visitors may not. Search fee: $10.00 per name. Required to search: name, years to search; also helpful: address. Civil

cases indexed by defendant, plaintiff. Civil records on docket books from approx 1894.

Criminal Records: Access: Mail, in person. Only the court performs in person searches; visitors may not. Search fee: $10.00 per name. Required to search: name, years to search, DOB, signed release; also helpful: address. Criminal records on docket books from approx 1894.

General Information: Public Access terminal is available. No adoptions, sealed, juvenile, mental health, expunged or dismissed records released. Copy fee: $1.00 per page. Certification fee: $10.00. Payee: Clerk of Court. Business checks accepted. Prepayment required. Mail requests: SASE required. Mail turnaround time 1-2 days.

Stutsman County

Southeast Judicial District Court 511 2nd Ave SE, Jamestown, ND 58401; 701-252-9042; Fax: 701-251-1006. Hours: 8AM-5PM (CST). *Felony, Misdemeanor, Civil, Eviction, Small Claims, Probate.*

Civil Records: Access: Mail, fax, in person. Only the court performs in person searches; visitors may not. Search fee: $10.00 per name. Required to search: name, years to search; also helpful: address. Civil records on computer back to 1/87, on index books from 1800s.

Criminal Records: Access: Mail, fax, in person. Only the court performs in person searches; visitors may not. Search fee: $10.00 per name. Required to search: name, years to search, DOB; also helpful: address. Criminal records on computer back to 1/96, on index books from 1800s.

General Information: No adoptions, sealed, juvenile, mental health, expunged or dismissed records released. Will fax results to local or toll free line. Copy fee: $.10 per page, minimum charge is $1.00. Certification fee: $10.00. Payee: Clerk of Court. Personal checks accepted. Prepayment required. Mail requests: SASE required. Mail turnaround time 1-2 days.

Towner County

Northeast Judicial District Court Box 517, Cando, ND 58324; 701-968-4340 Ext 3; Fax: 701-968-4344. Hours: 8:30AM-Noon; 1:00PM-5:00PM (CST). *Felony, Misdemeanor, Civil, Eviction, Small Claims, Probate.*

Civil Records: Access: Fax, mail, in person. Only the court performs in person searches; visitors may not. Search fee: $10.00 per name. Required to search: name, years to search; also helpful: address. Civil cases indexed by defendant, plaintiff. Civil records on index books from 1800s.

Criminal Records: Access: Fax, mail, in person. Only the court performs in person searches; visitors may not. Search fee: $10.00 per name. Required to search: name, years to search; also helpful: address, DOB, SSN.

General Information: No adoptions, sealed, juvenile, mental health, expunged or dismissed records released. Will fax results $3.00 per doc. Copy fee: $1.00 per page. Certification fee: $10.00. Payee: Clerk of District Court. Personal checks accepted. Prepayment required. Mail requests: SASE required. Mail turnaround time 1-2 days.

Traill County

East Central Judicial District Court PO Box 805, Hillsboro, ND 58045; 701-636-4454; Fax: 701-636-5124. Hours: 8AM-4:30PM (CST). *Felony, Misdemeanor, Civil, Eviction, Small Claims, Probate.*

Civil Records: Access: Phone, fax, mail, in person. Only the court performs in person searches; visitors

may not. Search fee: $10.00 per name. Required to search: name, years to search; also helpful: address. Civil cases indexed by defendant, plaintiff. Civil records on index books from 1800s.

Criminal Records: Access: Phone, fax, mail, in person. Only the court performs in person searches; visitors may not. Search fee: $10.00 per name. Required to search: name, years to search; also helpful: address, DOB, SSN. Criminal records on index books from 1800s.

General Information: No adoptions, sealed, juvenile, mental health, expunged or dismissed records released. Will fax results $1.00 per page. Copy fee: $.25 per page. Certification fee: $10.00. Payee: Clerk of Court. Personal checks accepted. Prepayment required. Mail requests: SASE required. Mail turnaround time 1-2 days.

Walsh County

Northeast Judicial District Court 600 Cooper Ave, Grafton, ND 58237; 701-352-0350; Fax: 701-352-4466. Hours: 8:30AM-5PM (CST). *Felony, Misdemeanor, Civil, Eviction, Small Claims, Probate.*

Civil Records: Access: Mail, in person. Both court and visitors may perform in person searches. Search fee: $10.00 per name. Required to search: name, years to search; also helpful: address. Civil cases indexed by defendant, plaintiff. Civil records on index books from early 1900s; on computer from 11/97.

Criminal Records: Access: Mail, in person. Both court and visitors may perform in person searches. Search fee: $10.00 per name. Required to search: name, years to search, DOB; also helpful: address, SSN. Criminal records on index books from early 1900s; on computer from 11/97.

General Information: Public Access terminal is available. No adoptions, sealed, juvenile, mental health, expunged or dismissed records released. Fee to fax results is $5.00 per document. Copy fee: $.10 per page; $1.00 minimum. Certification fee: $10.00, then $5.00 each add'l page. Payee: Clerk of Court. Personal checks accepted. Prepayment required. Mail requests: SASE required. Mail turnaround time 2-3 days.

Ward County

Northwest Judicial District Court PO Box 5005, Minot, ND 58702-5005; 701-857-6460; Fax: 701-857-6468. Hours: 8AM-4:30PM (CST). *Felony, Misdemeanor, Civil, Eviction, Small Claims, Probate.*

Civil Records: Access: Mail, in person. Both court and visitors may perform in person searches. Search fee: $10.00 per name. Required to search: name, years to search; also helpful: address. Civil cases indexed by defendant, plaintiff. Civil records on index cards from 1990, on index books from 1800s; computerized records go back to 1994.

Criminal Records: Access: Mail, in person. Both court and visitors may perform in person searches. Search fee: $10.00 per name. Required to search: name, years to search; also helpful: address, DOB, SSN. Criminal records on index cards from 1990, on index books from 1800s; computerized records go back to 1994.

General Information: Public Access terminal is available. No adoptions, sealed, juvenile, mental health, expunged or dismissed records released. Copy fee: $.10 per page (minimum $1.00). Certification fee: $10.00. Payee: Clerk of District Court. Business checks accepted. Prepayment required. Mail requests: SASE required. Mail turnaround time 5 days.

Wells County

Southeast Judicial District Court PO Box 155, Fessenden, ND 58438; 701-547-3840; Fax: 701-547-3719. 8AM-4:30PM. *Felony, Misdemeanor, Civil, Eviction, Small Claims, Probate.*

Civil Records: Access: Mail, in person. Only the court performs in person searches; visitors may not. Search fee: $10.00 per name. Required to search: name, years to search; also helpful: address. Civil cases indexed by defendant, plaintiff. Civil records on index books.

Criminal Records: Access: Mail, in person. Only the court performs in person searches; visitors may not. Search fee: $10.00 per name. Required to search: name, years to search; also helpful: address, DOB, SSN. Criminal records on index books from 1980.

General Information: No adoptions, sealed, juvenile, mental health, expunged or dismissed records released. Will fax results to local or toll free line. Copy fee: $1.00 per document. Certification fee: $10.00. Payee: District Court. Personal checks accepted. Prepayment required. Mail requests: SASE required. Mail turnaround time 1-2 days.

Williams County

Northwest Judicial District Court PO Box 2047, Williston, ND 58802; 701-774-4374; Fax: 701-774-4379. 8AM-5PM (CST). *Felony, Misdemeanor, Civil, Eviction, Small Claims, Probate.*

Civil Records: Access: Mail, in person. Both court and visitors may perform in person searches. Search fee: $10.00 per name. Required to search: name, years to search; also helpful: address. Civil cases indexed by defendant, plaintiff. Civil records computerized since 1/98, on index cards from 1/92, on index books from 1899.

Criminal Records: Access: Mail, in person. Both court and visitors may perform in person searches. Search fee: $10.00 per name. Required to search: name, years to search; also helpful: address, DOB, SSN. Criminal records computerized since 1/98, on index cards from 1/92, on index books from 1899.

General Information: Public Access terminal is available. No adoptions, sealed, juvenile, mental health, expunged or dismissed records released. Will fax results. Copy fee: $.10 per page with $1 minimum. Certification fee: $10.00. Payee: Clerk of Court. Personal checks accepted. Prepayment required. Mail requests: SASE required. Mail turnaround time 1-2 days.

North Dakota Recording Offices

ORGANIZATION: 53 counties, 53 recording offices. The recording officer is the Register of Deeds. The entire state is in the Central Time Zone (CST).

REAL ESTATE RECORDS: Some counties will perform real estate searches by name or by legal description. Copy fees are usually $1.00 per page. Certified copies usually cost $5.00 for the first page and $2.00 for each additional page. Copies may be faxed.

UCC RECORDS: Since 07/1/2001, all financing statements must be filed at the state level, except for real estate related collateral, which are filed only with the Register of Deeds. Previously, the state was a dual filing state and reocrd could be filed at either place. The good news is that all counties access a statewide computer database of filings and will perform UCC searches. Use search request form UCC-11. Various search options are available, including by federal tax identification number or Social Security number The search with copies costs $7.00 per debtor name, including three pages of copies and $1.00 per additional page. Copies may be faxed for an additional fee of $3.00.

TAX LIEN RECORDS: Federal tax liens on personal property of businesses are filed with the Secretary of State. Other federal and all state tax liens are filed with the county Register of Deeds. All counties will perform tax lien searches. Some counties automatically include business federal tax liens as part of a UCC search because they appear on the statewide database. (Be careful - federal tax liens on individuals may only be in the county lien books, not on the statewide system.) Separate searches are usually available at $5.00-7.00 per name. Copy fees vary. Copies may be faxed.

OTHER LIENS: Mechanics, judgment, hospital, repair, egg cutter.

ONLINE ACCESS: The North Dakota Recorders Information Network (NDRIN) is a electronic central repository representing a number of ND counties participating in Internet access to to records. There is a $200 set-up fee and $50 monthly with $1.00 charge per image printed. Register or request information via the web site at www.ndrin.com

Adams County

County Recorder, PO Box 469, Hettinger, ND 58639-0469. **Phone-**701-567-2460; fax-701-567-2910; hours 8:30AM-Noon, 1-5PM
Will search UCC records. Copy request with certificate (per debtor)- $7.00. Fee depends on number of offerings. Tax lien search- $10.00 per debtor. Will search real estate records. RE record copy- $1.00 per doc. UCC copy- $1.00 per doc. Cert fee: $5.00 1st page; $2.00 each add'l. Payee: Adams County Recorder. **Other phones:** Assessor-701-567-2900; Treasurer-701-567-2537; Elections-701-567-4363.

Barnes County

Register of Deeds, 230 4th St NW, #201, Valley City, ND 58072. **Phone-**Register of Deeds, R/E & UCC Recording- 701-845-8506, UCC Recording-701-845-8507; fax-701-845-8538; hours 8AM-5PM
Participates in the ND Recorders Information Network, www.ndrin.com. Will search UCC records. Copy request with certificate (per debtor)- $7.00. Federal/state combined tax lien search- $7.00+. Will not search real estate records. Copy fee- $1.00 per page. Cert fee: $5.00 per page, $2.00 each add'l. Payee: Barnes County Recorders. **Other phones:** Assessor-701-845-8515; Treasurer-701-845-8505; Elections-701-845-8500; Vital Records-701-845-8512.

Benson County

County Recorder, PO Box 193, Minnewaukan, ND 58351. **Phone-**701-473-5332; fax-701-473-5571.
Will search UCC records. Copy request with certificate (per debtor)- $7.00. Will search real estate records. Copy fee-$2.00 per doc. Copy fee is $2.00 per copy. **Other phones:** Assessor-701-473-5524; Treasurer-701-473-5458; Elections-701-473-5340; Vital Records-701-473-5345.

Billings County

County Recorder, PO Box 138, Medora, ND 58645-0138. **Phone-**701-623-4491; fax-701-623-4896; hours 9AM-Noon; 1PM-5PM
Will search UCC records. Copy request with certificate (per debtor)- $7.00. Tax lien search- $7.00 per debtor. Will not search real estate records. Copy fee- $1.00 per page. Cert fee: $5.00 for 1st pg,$1.00 each add'l pg. Payee: Billings County. **Other phones:** Assessor-701-623-4810; Treasurer-701-623-4484; Elections-701-623-4377.

Bottineau County

County Recorder, 314 W. 5th St, Bottineau, ND 58318-1265. **Phone-**701-228-2786; fax-701-228-3658; hours 8:30AM-5PM
Will search UCC records. Copy request with certificate (per debtor)- $7.00. Tax lien search- $7.00 per debtor. Will not search real estate records except for last document of record. RE record copy- $1.00 per doc. UCC copy- $1.00 per page. Cert fee: $7.00 1st pg; $1.00 each add'l. **Other phones:** Treasurer-701-228-2035; Elections-701-228-2225.

Bowman County

County Recorder, PO Box 379, Bowman, ND 58623. **Phone-**County Recorder, R/E & UCC Recording- 701-523-3450; fax-701-523-5443; hours 8AM-4:30PM
Will search UCC records. Copy request with certificate (per debtor)- $7.00. UCC search includes tax liens. Will search real estate records. RE record copy- $1.00 per page. UCC copy- $2.00 per record. Cert fee: $5.00 1st page; $2.00 each add'l. Payee: County Recorder. **Other phones:** Assessor-701-523-3129; Treasurer-701-523-3665; Appraiser/Auditor-701-523-3129; Elections-701-523-3130; Vital Records-701-328-2360; Auditor-701-523-3130.

Burke County

Register of Deeds, PO Box 219, Bowbells, ND 58721-0219. **Phone-**Register of Deeds, R/E & UCC Recording- 701-377-2818; fax-701-377-2020; hours 8:30AM-5PM
Will search UCC records. Copy request with certificate (per debtor)- $7.00 1st 5 entries; $2.00 each add'l entry. Federal/state combined tax lien search- $7.00 per debtor Will search real estate records only on a very limited basis. RE record copy-$.50 per page. UCC copy- $1.00 per page. Cert fee: $5.00 for 1st page; $2.00 each add'l. Payee: County Recorder. **Other phones:** Assessor-701-377-2661; Treasurer-701-377-2917; Appraiser/ Auditor-701-377-2661; Elections-701-377-2861; Vital Records-701-377-2718.

Burleigh County

County Recorder, PO Box 5518, Bismarck, ND 58506-5518. **Phone-**County Recorder, R/E & UCC Recording- 701-222-6749; fax-701-222-6717; hours 8AM-5PM www.ndrin.com
Will search UCC records. Copy request with certificate (per debtor)- $7.00 min. Federal/state combined tax lien search- $7.00 per debtor. Will not search real estate records. UCC copy- $1.00 per page. **Online Access to Real Estate, Treasurer/Auditor, Property records:** Subscription access the recorder's land records is via NDRIN's central repository at www.ndrin.com. See section introduction. Also, access to treasurer and auditor property data is free at https://burleigh.nd.ezov.com/ezproperty/review_search.jsp. No name searching. **Other phones:** Assessor-701-222-6691; Treasurer-701-222-6696; Appraiser/ Auditor-701-222-6691; Elections-701-222-6718; Vital Records-701-222-2360.

Cass County

Register of Deeds, PO Box 2806, Fargo, ND 58108-2806. **Phone**-701-241-5620; fax-701-241-5621; hours 8AM-5PM

Will search UCC records. Copy request with certificate (per debtor)- $7.00. Separate federal & state combined tax lien search- $7.00 Will not search real estate records. UCC copy- $1.00 per page. Cert fee: $5.00. Payee: Cass County Register of Deeds. **Online Access to Real Estate records:** Subscription access the recorder's land records is via NDRIN's central repository at www.ndrin.com. See section introduction. **Other phones:** Assessor-701-241-5611; Treasurer-701-241-5611; Elections-701-241-5601.

Cavalier County

Register of Deeds, 901 3rd St #13, Langdon, ND 58249. **Phone**-Register of Deeds, R/E & UCC Recording- 701-256-2136; fax-701-256-2566; hours 8:30AM-4:30PM

Participates in the ND Recorders Information Network, www.ndrin.com. Will search UCC records. Copy request with certificate (per debtor)- $7.00. Will not search real estate records. RE record copy- $1.00 per page. UCC copy- $1.00 per UCC. **Other phones:** Assessor-701-256-3826; Treasurer-701-256-2549; Elections-701-256-2229; Vital Records-701-256-2124.

Dickey County

Register of Deeds, PO Box 148, Ellendale, ND 58436. **Phone**-Register of Deeds, R/E & UCC Recording- 701-349-3249; fax-701-349-4639; hours 8AM-4:30PM

Will search UCC records. Copy request with certificate (per debtor)- $7.00. UCC search includes tax liens if requested. Separate federal & state combined tax lien search- $7.00 Will search real estate records. UCC copy- $1.00 per page. Cert fee: $5.00. Payee: Dickey County. **Other phones:** Assessor-701-349-3218; Elections-701-349-3249.

Divide County

Register of Deeds, PO Box 68, Crosby, ND 58730. **Phone**-701-965-6661; fax-701-965-6943; hours 8:30-12;00-1-5PM

Will search UCC records. Copy request with certificate (per debtor)- $7.00 per entry. UCC search includes tax liens if requested. Will not search real estate records. UCC copy- $2.00 per page. Cert fee: $5.00. Payee: Webster County Recorder. **Other phones:** Assessor-701-965-6351; Treasurer-701-965-6312; Elections-701-965-6351.

Dunn County

Register of Deeds, PO Box 106, Manning, ND 58642-0106. **Phone**-Register of Deeds, R/E & UCC Recording- 701-573-4443; fax-701-573-4444; hours 8AM-Noon, 12:30 PM-4:30PM www.ndrin.com

Will search UCC records. Copy request with certificate (per debtor)-. Will not search real estate or tax lien records. RE record copy- $1.00 per copy. UCC copy- $1.00 per copy. Cert fee: $10.00 per cert. Payee: Dunn County Recorder. **Online Access to Real Estate, Mrotgage records:** Subscription access the recorder's land records is via NDRIN's central repository at www.ndrin.com. See section introduction. **Other phones:** Assessor-701-573-4445; Treasurer-701-573-4446; Elections-701-573-4448 (Auditor); Vital Records-701-328-2360.

Eddy County

Register of Deeds, 524 Central Ave, New Rockford, ND 58356-1698. **Phone**-701-947-2813; fax-701-947-2067; hours 8:00AM-Noon; 12:30PM-4:00PM

Will search UCC records. Copy request with certificate (per debtor)- $10.00. UCC search includes tax liens if requested. Separate federal & state combined tax lien search- $10.00 Will not search real estate records. UCC copy- $.25 per page. Cert fee: $10.00. Payee: Eddy County. **Other phones:** Assessor-701-947-5220; Treasurer-701-947-5315; Elections-701-947-2434.

Emmons County

County Recorder, PO Box 905, Linton, ND 58552. **Phone**-701-254-4812; fax-701-254-4012; hours 8:30AM-Noon, 1PM-5PM

Will search UCC records. Copy request with certificate (per debtor)- $7.00. Will not search real estate records. RE record copy- $1.00 per page. Cert fee: $10.00 per cert. Payee: Emmons County Recorder. **Other phones:** Assessor-701-254-4417; Treasurer-701-254-4802; Elections-701-254-4807.

Foster County

Recorder, PO Box 76, Carrington, ND 58421. **Phone**-701-652-2491; fax-701-652-2173; 8:30AM-4:30PM

Will search UCC records. Copy request with certificate (per debtor)- Amt varies depending on number of UCC's recorded. Will search tax liens. Tax lien search-varies. Will search real estate records. RE record copy- $1.00 per doc. Cert fee: $5.00 for 1st page/$2.00 per add'ls. Payee: Foster County Recorder. **Other phones:** Assessor-701-652-2441; Treasurer-701-652-2322; Elections-701-652-2441.

Golden Valley County

County Recorder, PO Box 130, Beach, ND 58621-0130. **Phone**-County Recorder, R/E & UCC Recording- 701-872-3713; fax-701-872-4383; hours 8AM-Noon, 1PM-4PM. Will search UCC records. Copy request with certificate (per debtor)- $7.00. If "all" is checked on request form, then tax liens will be searched. Will not search real estate records. RE record copy- $1.00 per page. Copy fee is $1.00 per page. Cert fee: $5.00 1st page, $2.00 each add'l. Payee: County Recorder. **Other phones:** Assessor-701-872-4673; Treasurer-701-872-4411; Elections-701-872-4331; Vital Records-701-328-2360; Auditor-701-872-4331.

Grand Forks County

Register of Deeds, PO Box 5066, Grand Forks, ND 58206. **Phone**-701-780-8259, R/E Recording-701-780-8200; fax-701-780-8212; hours 8AM-5PM www.co.grand-forks.nd.us/homepage.htm

Will search UCC records. Copy request with certificate (per debtor)- $7.00. Will not search real estate records. **Online Access to Real Estate, Recording, Deed, Death, Judgment, Lien records:** Access to county property information is free at www.co.grand-forks.nd.us/search.htm. Also, access to the recorder's database is free at www.co.grand-forks.nd.us/recorders%20search.htm. **Other phones:** Assessor-701-780-8261; Treasurer-701-780-8295; Elections-701-780-8200.

Grant County

Register of Deeds, PO Box 258, Carson, ND 58529. **Phone**-701-622-3544; fax-701-622-3717; 8AM-4PM
Will search UCC records. Copy request with certificate (per debtor)- $7.00. UCC search includes tax liens if requested. Separate federal/state combined tax lien search- $7.00 Will not search real estate records. UCC copy- $1.00 per page. Cert fee: $10.00. Payee: Grant County Register of Deeds. **Other phones:** Assessor-701-622-3275; Treasurer-701-622-3422; Elections-701-622-3275.

Griggs County

Register of Deeds, PO Box 237, Cooperstown, ND 58425. **Phone**-701-797-2771; fax-701-797-3587; hours 8AM-1200-1-4:30

Participates in the ND Recorders Information Network, www.ndrin.com. Will search UCC records. Copy request with certificate (per debtor)- $11.00. Federal/state combined tax lien search- $11.00 Will not search real estate records. UCC copy- $1.00 per page. Cert fee: $5.00. Payee: County Register of Deeds. **Other phones:** Assessor-701-797-3211; Treasurer-701-797-2411; Elections-701-797-3117.

Hettinger County

County Recorder, PO Box 668, Mott, ND 58646. **Phone**-701-824-2545/2645, R/E Recording-701-824-2545, UCC Recording-701-824-2545; fax-701-824-2717. Will search UCC records. Copy request with certificate (per debtor)- $7.00. Will do tax lien search. Will perform a separate federal & state combined tax lien search; fee varies. Will not search real estate records. RE record copy- $1.00 per copy. UCC copy- varies. Cert fee: $7.00 1st pg; $2.00 each add'l. **Other phones:** Assessor-701-824-2515; Treasurer-701-824-2655; Appraiser/ Auditor-701-824-2515; Elections-701-824-2515; Vital Records-701-824-2545.

Kidder County

County Recorder, PO Box 66, Steele, ND 58482. **Phone**-County Recorder, R/E & UCC Recording- 701-475-2632; fax-701-475-2202; 9AM-12PM; 1-5PM

Will search UCC records. Copy request with certificate (per debtor)- $7.00. UCC search includes tax liens. Separate federal/state combined tax lien search- $7.00 per search. Will not search real estate records. RE record copy- $1.00 per doc. Cert fee: $5.00 1st page; $2.00 each add'l. Payee: County Recorder. **Other phones:** Assessor-701-475-2632; Treasurer-701-475-2632; Elections-701-475-2632.

La Moure County

County Recorder, PO Box 128, La Moure, ND 58458-0128. **Phone**-County Recorder, R/E & UCC Recording- 701-883-5301 x6; fax-701-883-4220; hours 9AM-Noon, 1-5PM (Summer hours 8AM-Noon, 1PM-4PM) http://lamoco.drtel.net/countyrecorder.html

Will search UCC records. Copy request with certificate (per debtor)- $7.00 per 5 entities. Federal/state combined tax lien search- $7.00 per debtor Will search real estate records. Copy fee-$1.00 per doc. Copy fee is $1.00 per doc. Cert fee: $10.00 1st page, $3.00 each add'l. Payee: County Recorder. **Other phones:** Assessor-701-883-5301; Treasurer-701-883-5101; Elections-701-883-5301.

Logan County

Register of Deeds, PO Box 6, Napoleon, ND 58561-0006. **Phone**-Register of Deeds, R/E & UCC Recording- 701-754-2751; fax-701-754-2270; hours 8:30AM-Noon, 1-4:30PM

Will search UCC records. Copy request with certificate (per debtor)- $7.00. UCC search includes federal tax liens if requested. Separate federal/state combined tax lien search- $7.00 per search. Real estate record owner and mortgage searches available. RE record copy- $1.00 per doc. UCC copy- $1.00 with search (after three pages). Cert fee: $7.00 1st 3 pgs, $2.00 each add'l. Payee: Logan County Recorder. **Other phones:** Assessor-701-754-2239; Treasurer-701-754-2286; Elections-701-754-2425.

McHenry County

County Recorder, PO Box 149, Towner, ND 58788. **Phone**-County Recorder, R/E & UCC Recording- 701-537-5634; fax-701-537-5969; hours 8AM-N, 1-4:30PM www.state.nd.us

Will search UCC records. Copy request with certificate (per debtor)- $7.00 for 1st 3 pages, $2.00 each add'l. Tax lien search- $7.00 per debtor for 1st 3 pages; $2.00 each add'l. Will search real estate records. RE record copy- $1.00 per copy. UCC copy fee-. **Online Access to Deed, Mortgage records:** Subscription access the recorder's land records is via NDRIN's central repository at www.ndrin.com. See section introduction. **Other phones:** Assessor-701-537-5359; Treasurer-701-537-5731; Elections-701-537-5724; Vital Records-701-537-5729.

McIntosh County

County Recorder, PO Box 179, Ashley, ND 58413. **Phone-**701-288-3589/3450, R/E Recording-701-288-3589; fax-701-288-3671; hours 8AM-4:30PM Will search UCC records. Copy request with certificate (per debtor)- $7.00. Will not search tax liens. Will search real estate records. RE record copy- $1.00 per page. Cert fee: $5.00 + $2.00 each add'l. Payee: County Recorder. **Other phones:** Assessor-701-288-3347; Treasurer-701-288-3342; Elections-701-288-3347.

McKenzie County

County Recorder, PO Box 523, Watford City, ND 58854. **Phone-**County Recorder, R/E & UCC Recording- 701-444-3453; fax-701-844-3902; hours 8:30AM-5PM   www.4eyes.net/county.htm   and www.ndrin.com Will search UCC records. Copy request with certificate (per debtor)- $7.00. Will search tax liens including federal tax liens. Tax lien search- $7.00 per debtor. Will not do a real estate record name search; will only search for last deed of record. Copy fee- $1.00 per page. Cert fee: $5.00 1st page + $2.00 each add'l. Payee: County Recorder. **Online Access to Real Estate records:** Access the recorder's land records 5/1998 to present by subscription via NDRIN's central repository at www.ndrin.com. See section introduction. **Other phones:** Assessor-701-444-6852; Treasurer-701-444-3457; Appraiser/ Auditor-701-444-6852; Elections-701-444-3616; Vital Records-701-444-3452.

McLean County

County Recorder, PO Box 1108, Washburn, ND 58577-1108. **Phone-**701-462-8541 x226/5, R/E Recording-701-462-8541 X226, x225, UCC Recording-701-462-8541; fax-701-462-3633; 8AM-N, 12:30-4:30PM www.visitmcleancounty.com Will search UCC records. Copy request with certificate (per debtor)- $7.00 (includes 1st 3 pages). Will not search tax liens. Will search real estate records depending on nature of request. RE record copy- $.50 per page. UCC copy- $1.00 per page. Cert fee: $7.00 per doc. Payee: McLean County Recorder. **Online Access to Real Estate records:** Subscription access the recorder's land records is via NDRIN's central repository at www.ndrin.com. See section introduction. **Other phones:** Assessor-701-462-8541; Treasurer-701-462-8541 x223; Elections-701-462-8541 x216; Vital Records-701-462-8541 x228.

Mercer County

County Recorder, PO Box 39, Stanton, ND 58571. **Phone-**County Recorder, R/E & UCC Recording- 701-745-3272; fax-701-745-3364; hours 8AM-4PM Will search UCC records. Copy request with certificate (per debtor)- $7.00 per 2 records. Will search tax liens including federal tax liens. Will not search real estate records. **Other phones:** Assessor-701-745-3294; Treasurer-701-745-3323; Elections-701-745-3292.

Morton County

Register of Deeds, 210 2nd Ave, Mandan, ND 58554. **Phone-**701-667-3305; fax-701-667-3453; 8AM-5PM Participates in the ND Recorders Information Network, www.ndrin.com. Will search UCC records. Copy request with certificate (per debtor)- $7.00. UCC search includes tax liens if requested. Separate federal/state combined tax lien search- $7.00 Will not search real estate records. UCC copy- $2.00 per page. Cert fee: $5.00. Payee: Morton County Register of Deeds. **Other phones:** Assessor-701-667-3300; Treasurer-701-667-3310; Elections-701-667-3300; Auditor-701-667-3300.

Mountrail County

Register of Deeds, PO Box 69, Stanley, ND 58784. **Phone-**Register of Deeds, R/E & UCC Recording- 701-628-2945; fax-701-628-2276. Will search UCC records. Copy request with certificate (per debtor)- $7.00. Will not search real estate records. **Other phones:** Assessor-701-826-2425; Treasurer-701-628-2935; Elections-701-628-2145.

Nelson County

Coounty Recorder, 210 B Ave. West, #203, Lakota, ND 58344. **Phone-**Coounty Recorder, R/E & UCC Recording- 701-247-2433; fax-701-247-2412; hours 8AM-Noon, 1PM-4:30PM Participates in the ND Recorders Information Network, www.ndrin.com. Will search UCC records. Copy request with certificate (per debtor)- $7.00. Will search tax liens including federal tax liens. Tax lien search- $7.00 per debtor. Will not search real estate records. RE record copy- $1.00 per doc. UCC copy- $1.00 per page. Cert fee: UCC $7.00 per 5 entries. Payee: Nelson County Recorder. **Other phones:** Assessor-701-247-2840; Treasurer-701-247-2453; Elections-701-247-2463; Vital Records-701-247-2462.

Oliver County

Register of Deeds, PO Box 125, Center, ND 58530-0125. **Phone-**701-794-8777; fax-701-794-3476; hours 8AM-N, 1-4PM Will search UCC records. Copy request with certificate (per debtor)- $7.00. Will not search tax liens. Will search real estate records. RE record copy- $.25 per page. Copy fee is $1.00 per page. Cert fee: $5.00. Payee: County Recorder. **Other phones:** Assessor-701-794-8721; Treasurer-701-794-8737; Elections-701-794-8721.

Pembina County

Clerk/Recorder, 301 Dakota St W. #10, Cavalier, ND 58220. **Phone-**Clerk/Recorder, R/E & UCC Recording-701-265-4373; fax-701-265-4876; hours 8AM-5PM www.pembinacountynd.gov Will search UCC records. Copy request with certificate (per debtor)- $7.00 min. Will search tax liens including federal tax liens. Tax lien search- $7.00 per debtor (mimumin fee). Will not search real estate records. RE record copy- $1.00 per doc. UCC copy- $1.00 per page. Cert fee: $5.00 1st page, $2.00 each add'l. Payee: Pembina County. **Online Access to Real Estate records:** Subscription access the recorder's land records is via NDRIN's central repository at www.ndrin.com. See section introduction. **Other phones:** Assessor-701-265-4697; Treasurer-701-265-4465; Elections-701-265-4231.

Pierce County

Register of Deeds, 240 S.E. 2nd St, Rugby, ND 58368. **Phone-**701-776-5206; fax-701-776-5707; 9AM-5PM Will search UCC records. Copy request with certificate (per debtor)- $15.00. Federal/state combined tax lien search- $7.00 Will not search real estate records. UCC copy- $1.00 per page. Cert fee:

$7.00. Payee: Pierce County Register of Deeds. **Other phones:** Assessor-701-776-5225; Treasurer-701-776-6841; Elections-701-776-5225.

Ramsey County

Register of Deeds, 524 4th Ave #30, Devils Lake, ND 58301. **Phone-**Register of Deeds, R/E & UCC Recording- 701-662-7018; fax-701-662-7093; hours 8AM-5PM www.co.ramsey.nd.us Will search UCC records. Copy request with certificate (per debtor)- $7.00. Tax lien search- $7.00 per debtor. Will not search real estate records. RE record copy- $2.00 per doc. UCC copy- $1.00 per page. Cert fee: $7.00 per page. Payee: Ramsey County Recorder. **Other phones:** Assessor-701-662-7012; Treasurer-701-662-7021; Elections-701-662-7007; Vital Records-701-662-7018.

Ransom County

County Recorder, PO Box 666, Lisbon, ND 58054-0666. **Phone-**701-683-5823, R/E Recording-701-683-5823 x115, UCC Recording-701-683-5823 x115; fax-701-683-5827; hours 8:30AM-5PM Participates in the ND Recorders Information Network, www.ndrin.com. Will search UCC records. Copy request with certificate (per debtor)- $7.00 min. charge. Will search tax liens including federal tax liens. Federal/state combined tax lien search- $7.00 per debtor. Will search real estate records. RE record copy- $1.00 per doc per each 3 pages. UCC copy- $1.00 per filing. Cert fee: $5.00 1st page, #2.00 each add'l. Payee: Ransom County Recorder. **Online Access to Real Estate records:** Subscription access the recorder's land records is via NDRIN's central repository at www.ndrin.com. See section introduction. **Other phones:** Assessor-701-683-5823 x111; Treasurer- x118; Elections- x113; Vital Records- x120.

Renville County

Register of Deeds, PO Box 68, Mohall, ND 58761-0068. **Phone-**Register of Deeds, R/E & UCC Recording- 701-756-6398; fax-701-756-7158; hours 9AM-4:30PM www.renvillecounty.org Will search UCC records. Copy request with certificate (per debtor)- $7.00. UCC search includes federal tax liens. Will not search real estate records. RE record copy- $1.00 per page. UCC copy- $1.00 with search (after three pages). Cert fee: $7.00 1st pg, $3.00 each add'l. Payee: Renville County Register of Deeds. **Other phones:** Assessor-701-756-6368; Treasurer-701-756-6304; Appraiser/ Auditor-701-756-6368; Elections-701-756-6301; Vital Records-701-756-6398.

Richland County

County Recorder, 418 2nd Ave North, Courthouse, Wahpeton, ND 58075-4400. **Phone-**County Recorder, R/E & UCC Recording- 701-642-7800; fax-701-642-7820; hours 8:00AM-5:00PM Participates in the ND Recorders Information Network, www.ndrin.com. Will search UCC records. Copy request with certificate (per debtor)- $7.00. Will search tax liens. Will search real estate records. Real estate copy fee- $1.00 per page. UCC copy- $1.00 per doc. Cert fee: $7.00 1st page; $2.00 each add'l. **Other phones:** Assessor-701-642-7805; Treasurer-701-642-7705; Elections-701-642-7700; Vital Records-701-642-7800.

Rolette County

Recorder, PO Box 276, Rolla, ND 58367. **Phone-**Recorder, R/E & UCC Recording- 701-477-3166; fax-701-477-5770; hours 8:30AM-4:30PM Will search UCC records. Copy request with certificate (per debtor)- $7.00. Tax lien search- $7.00 per debtor. Will search real estate records. Copy fee-$1.00 per doc. Copy fee is $1.00 per page. Cert fee: $7.00 per 1st page; $2.00 each add'l. Payee: Recorder. **Other phones:** Assessor-701-477-5665; Treasurer-701-477-3207; Elections-701-477-5665; Vital Records-701-477-3816.

Sargent County

Register of Deeds, PO Box 176, Forman, ND 58032-0176. **Phone-**701-724-6241, R/E Recording-701-724-6241 x117; fax-701-724-6244.
Will search UCC records. Copy request with certificate (per debtor)- $7.00. Tax lien search- $7.00 per debtor. Will not search real estate records. UCC copy- $1.00 per copy. Cert fee: $5.00 per doc. Payee: County Recorder. **Other phones:** Assessor-701-724-6241 x15; Treasurer-701-724-6241 x13,14; Elections-701-724-6241.

Sheridan County

Register of Deeds, PO Box 668, McClusky, ND 58463-0668. **Phone-**Register of Deeds, R/E & UCC Recording- 701-363-2207; fax-701-363-2953; hours 9AM-N, 1-5PM
Will search UCC records. Copy request with certificate (per debtor)- $7.00. Request without certificate-1st 3 pages $2.00 each additional page. Will search tax liens including federal tax liens. Separate federal & state combined tax lien search- $7.00 per search. Will search real estate records. RE record copy- $1.00 per doc. UCC copy- $1.00 per page. Cert fee: $5.00 1st page, $2.00 each add'l. Payee: Sheridan County Recorder. **Other phones:** Assessor-701-363-2201; Treasurer-701-363-2206; Elections-701-363-2205; Vital Records-603-895-2207.

Sioux County

Register of Deeds, PO Box L, Fort Yates, ND 58538. **Phone-**701-854-3853; fax-701-854-3854; hours 8AM-4:30PM
Will search UCC records. Copy request with certificate (per debtor)- $7.00. Will not search real estate records. UCC copy- $2.00 per page. Cert fee: $5.00. Payee: Sioux County Register of Deeds. **Other phones:** Assessor-701-854-3424; Elections-701-854-3481.

Slope County

County Recorder, PO Box JJ, Amidon, ND 58620-0445. **Phone-**701-879-6275; fax-701-879-6278.
Will search UCC records. Copy request with certificate (per debtor)- $7.00. Will not search real estate or tax lien records. RE record copy- $.50 per page. Cert fee: $10.00. Payee: County Recorder. **Other phones:** Assessor-701-879-6370; Treasurer-701-879-6272; Elections-701-879-6276.

Stark County

County Recorder, PO Box 130, Dickinson, ND 58601. **Phone-**County Recorder, R/E & UCC Recording- 701-456-7645; fax-701-456-7628; hours 8AM-5PM
Will search UCC records. Copy request with certificate (per debtor)- $7.00 for 1st 5 entries; $2.00 for each add'l entry. UCC search includes tax liens. Separate federal/state combined tax lien search- $7.00 per debtor. Will not search real estate records. RE record copy- $.50 in office; $1.00 per copy if mailed or faxed; fee to fax results is $3.00 per doc. UCC copy- $1.00 per page. Payee: Stark County Recorder. **Online Access to Real Estate records:** Subscription access the recorder's land records is via NDRIN's central repository at

www.ndrin.com. See section introduction. **Other phones:** Assessor-701-456-7671; Elections-701-456-7630; Vital Records-701-456-7645.

Steele County

Register of Deeds, PO Box 296, Finley, ND 58230. **Phone-**701-524-2152, R/E Recording-701-524-2790; fax-701-524-1325; hours 8AM-12;00-1-4:30PM
Will search UCC records. Copy request with certificate (per debtor)- $7.00 MIN. Will not search real estate or tax lien records. UCC copy- $1.00 per page. Cert fee: $5.00. Payee: Steele County Register of Deeds. **Online Access to Real Estate records:** Subscription access the recorder's land records is via NDRIN's central repository at www.ndrin.com. See section introduction. **Other phones:** Assessor-701-524-2110; Treasurer-701-524-2890; Elections-701-524-2110.

Stutsman County

County Recorder, 511 2nd Ave S.E., Courthouse, Jamestown, ND 58401. **Phone-**County Recorder, R/E & UCC Recording-701-252-9034; fax-701-251-1603; hours 8AM-5PM
Participates in the ND Recorders Information Network, www.ndrin.com. Will search UCC records. Copy request with certificate (per debtor)- $7.00. Information request with certificate:$7.00 for 1st 5 entries; $2.00 for each add'l entry. UCC search includes tax liens. Will not search real estate records. RE record copy- 1.00 per four pages. UCC copy- $1.00 per page. Cert fee: $7.00 per cert + $1.00 per page afrter 1st. Payee: Stutsam County Recorder. **Other phones:** Assessor-701-252-9032; Treasurer-701-252-9036; Elections-701-252-9035; Vital Records-701-252-9034.

Towner County

Recorder, PO Box 517, Cando, ND 58324. **Phone-**Recorder, R/E & UCC Recording- 701-968-4340 x5; fax-701-968-4344.
Will search UCC records. Copy request with certificate (per debtor)- $7.00. Will do tax lien search. Federal/state combined tax lien search- $7.00 1st sentries. Will not search real estate records. Copy fee- $1.00 per page. Cert fee: $7.00 per doc; $1.00 each add'l. **Other phones:** Assessor-701-968-4352; Treasurer-701-968-4347; Elections-701-968-4340.

Traill County

County Recorder, PO Box 399, Hillsboro, ND 58045. **Phone-**701-636-4457, R/E Recording-701-436-4457, UCC Recording-701-436-4457; fax-701-636-4457; hours 8AM-Noon 12:30PM-4:30PM
Will search UCC records. Copy request with certificate (per debtor)- $7.00. **Other phones:** Assessor-701-436-5950; Treasurer-701-436-4459; Elections-701-436-4458; Vital Records-701-436-4454.

Walsh County

County Recorder, 600 Cooper Ave, Courthouse, Grafton, ND 58237. **Phone-**County Recorder, R/E & UCC Recording- 701-352-2380; fax-701-352-3340; hours 8AM-Noon, 12:30PM-4:30PM
Will search UCC records. Copy request with certificate- $7.00 for 1st 5, $2.00 each additional. Will search tax liens. Will not search real estate records. RE record copy- $1.00 per doc. UCC copy- $1.00 per page. Cert fee: $5.00 1st page, $2.00

each add'l. Payee: Walsh County Recorder. **Online Access to Real Estate records:** Access the recorder's land records are by subscription to NDRIN's central repository at www.ndrin.com. See section introduction. **Other phones:** Assessor-701-352-1077; Treasurer-701-352-2541; Elections-701-352-2851; Vital Records-701-352-2380.

Ward County

Register of Deeds, PO Box 5005, Minot, ND 58705-5005. **Phone-**701-857-6410, R/E Recording-701-857-6420; fax-701-857-6414; hours 8AM-4:30PM
Will search UCC records. Copy request with certificate (per debtor)- $7.00. UCC search includes tax liens if requested. Separate federal & state combined tax lien search- $7.00 Will not search real estate records. UCC copy- $1.00 per page. Cert fee: $7.00. Payee: Ward County Register of Deeds. **Online Access to Real Estate, Property Tax records:** Subscription access the recorder's land records is via NDRIN's central repository at www.ndrin.com. See section introduction. Also, access to property tax data is free at www.co.ward.nd.us/ext/PropertyTax.htm. **Other phones:** Assessor-701-857-6430; Elections-701-857-6420.

Wells County

County Recorder, PO Box 125, Fessenden, ND 58438-0125. **Phone-**County Recorder, R/E & UCC Recording- 701-547-3141; fax-701-547-3719; hours 8AM-N, 12:30-4PM
http://mylocalgov.com/wellscountynd
Will search UCC records. Copy request with certificate (per debtor)- $7.00 for certificate and 1st 3 pages. $2.00 per page thereafter. Must use a UCC-11 form. Tax lien search- $7.00 for 1st 5 entries; $2.00 each add'l entry. Will search real estate records. Copy fee- $1.00 per page. Cert fee: $7.00 for 1st page; $2.00 each add'l. Payee: Well County Recorder. **Online Access to Real Estate records:** Subscription access the recorder's land records is via NDRIN's central repository at www.ndrin.com. See section introduction. **Other phones:** Assessor-701-547-3220; Treasurer-701-547-3161; Elections-701-547-3521; Vital Records-701-547-3122; State Vital Records-701-328-2360.

Williams County

Recorder, PO Box 2047, Williston, ND 58802-2047. **Phone-**Recorder, R/E & UCC Recording- 701-577-4540; fax-701-577-4535; hours 8AM-5PM
www.williamsnd.com
Participates in the ND Recorders Information Network, www.ndrin.com. Will search UCC records. Copy request with certificate (per debtor)- $7.00. UCC search includes tax liens. Tax lien search-starts at $7.00 per debtor. Will not search real estate records. RE record copy- $.50 per page. UCC copy- $1.00 per page. Cert fee: $5.00 1st page; $2.00 each add'l. Payee: Williams County Recorder. **Online Access to Property Tax, Treasurer records:** Access to the county property tax data is free at www.williamsnd.com/taxes/search/default.asp. **Other phones:** Assessor-701-577-4555; Treasurer-701-577-4530; Elections-701-577-4500; Vital Records-701-577-4580.

North Dakota County Locator

You will usually be able to find the city name in the City/County Cross Reference below. In that case, it is a simple matter to determine the county from the cross reference. However, only the official US Postal Service city names are included in this index. There are an additional 40,000 place names that people use in their addresses. Therefore, we have also included a ZIP/City Cross Reference immediately following the City/County Cross Reference. If you know the ZIP Code but the city name does not appear in the City/County Cross Reference index, look up the ZIP Code in the ZIP/City Cross Reference, find the city name, then look up the city name in the City/County Cross Reference.

North Dakota City/County Cross Reference

ABERCROMBIE Richland
ABSARAKA Cass
ADAMS Walsh
AGATE Rolette
ALAMO (58830) Williams(60), Divide(39)
ALEXANDER McKenzie
ALFRED La Moure
ALICE Cass
ALMONT (58520) Morton(73), Grant(26)
ALSEN Cavalier
AMBROSE Divide
AMENIA Cass
AMIDON (58620) Slope(97), Billings(2)
ANAMOOSE (58710) McHenry(61), Sheridan(22), Pierce(16)
ANETA (58212) Nelson(63), Griggs(25), Grand Forks(9), Steele(1)
ANTLER Bottineau
ARDOCH Walsh
ARENA (58412) Burleigh(98), Kidder(1)
ARGUSVILLE Cass
ARNEGARD McKenzie
ARTHUR Cass
ARVILLA Grand Forks
ASHLEY (58413) McIntosh(93), Dickey(6)
AYR Cass
BALDWIN Burleigh
BALFOUR McHenry
BALTA Pierce
BANTRY McHenry
BARNEY Richland
BARTON Pierce
BATHGATE Pembina
BEACH (58621) Golden Valley(96), McKenzie(2)
BELCOURT Rolette
BELFIELD (58622) Stark(72), Billings(27)
BENEDICT (58716) McLean(81), Ward(18)
BERLIN (58415) La Moure(98), Dickey(1)
BERTHOLD (58718) Ward(73), Mountrail(23), Renville(2)
BEULAH (58523) Mercer(94), Oliver(5)
BINFORD (58416) Griggs(97), Nelson(2)
BISBEE (58317) Towner(95), Rolette(3)
BISMARCK Burleigh
BLAISDELL Mountrail
BLANCHARD Traill
BOTTINEAU Bottineau
BOWBELLS (58721) Burke(96), Ward(3)
BOWBELLS Burke
BOWDON (58418) Wells(92), Kidder(7)
BOWMAN (58623) Bowman(91), Slope(8)
BRADDOCK (58524) Emmons(67), Kidder(21), Burleigh(10)
BREMEN Wells
BRINSMADE Benson
BROCKET (58321) Ramsey(50), Nelson(27), Walsh(21)
BUCHANAN Stutsman
BUFFALO Cass
BURLINGTON Ward
BUTTE (58723) Sheridan(44), McLean(44), McHenry(11)
BUXTON Traill
CALEDONIA Traill
CALVIN (58323) Cavalier(71), Towner(28)
CANDO Towner
CANNON BALL Sioux
CARPIO (58725) Renville(53), Ward(46)

CARRINGTON (58421) Foster(95), Stutsman(2), Wells(1)
CARSON Grant
CARTWRIGHT McKenzie
CASSELTON Cass
CATHAY Wells
CAVALIER Pembina
CAYUGA Sargent
CENTER Oliver
CHAFFEE Cass
CHASELEY (58423) Wells(84), Kidder(15)
CHRISTINE (58015) Richland(97), Cass(2)
CHURCHS FERRY (58325) Ramsey(61), Benson(38)
CLEVELAND Stutsman
CLIFFORD (58016) Traill(66), Steele(33)
COGSWELL Sargent
COLEHARBOR McLean
COLFAX Richland
COLUMBUS Burke
COOPERSTOWN Griggs
COURTENAY (58426) Stutsman(98), Foster(1)
CRARY Ramsey
CROSBY Divide
CRYSTAL Pembina
CRYSTAL SPRINGS Kidder
CUMMINGS Traill
DAHLEN (58224) Nelson(95), Walsh(4)
DAVENPORT Cass
DAWSON Kidder
DAZEY (58429) Barnes(97), Griggs(2)
DEERING (58731) McHenry(95), Ward(4)
DENHOFF Sheridan
DES LACS Ward
DEVILS LAKE Ramsey
DICKEY La Moure
DICKINSON (58601) Stark(96), Dunn(3)
DICKINSON Stark
DODGE (58625) Dunn(70), Mercer(29)
DONNYBROOK (58734) Ward(42), Mountrail(38), Renville(19)
DOUGLAS (58735) Ward(58), McLean(41)
DOYON Ramsey
DRAKE (58736) McHenry(88), Sheridan(11)
DRAYTON (58225) Pembina(87), Walsh(12)
DRISCOLL (58532) Burleigh(75), Kidder(24)
DUNN CENTER Dunn
DUNSEITH (58329) Rolette(83), Bottineau(16)
ECKELSON Barnes
EDGELEY (58433) La Moure(89), Dickey(10)
EDINBURG (58227) Walsh(62), Pembina(32), Cavalier(5)
EDMORE (58330) Ramsey(93), Walsh(4), Cavalier(2)
EGELAND Towner
ELGIN Grant
ELLENDALE Dickey
EMERADO Grand Forks
ENDERLIN (58027) Ransom(74), Cass(19), Barnes(5)
EPPING Williams
ERIE Cass
ESMOND (58332) Benson(87), Pierce(12)

FAIRDALE (58229) Walsh(75), Cavalier(20), Ramsey(3)
FAIRFIELD Billings
FAIRMOUNT Richland
FARGO Cass
FESSENDEN Wells
FINGAL (58031) Barnes(60), Cass(39)
FINLEY Steele
FLASHER (58535) Morton(78), Grant(21)
FLAXTON Burke
FORBES Dickey
FORDVILLE (58231) Walsh(73), Grand Forks(26)
FOREST RIVER (58233) Walsh(90), Grand Forks(9)
FORMAN Sargent
FORT RANSOM (58033) Ransom(98), La Moure(1)
FORT RICE Morton
FORT TOTTEN Benson
FORT YATES Sioux
FORTUNA Divide
FOXHOLM Ward
FREDONIA (58440) Logan(70), McIntosh(29)
FULLERTON Dickey
GACKLE (58442) Logan(85), Stutsman(14)
GALESBURG (58035) Traill(60), Cass(25), Steele(14)
GARDENA Bottineau
GARDNER Cass
GARRISON McLean
GILBY Grand Forks
GLADSTONE (58630) Stark(75), Dunn(24)
GLASSTON Pembina
GLEN ULLIN (58631) Morton(80), Grant(11), Mercer(7), Oliver(1)
GLENBURN (58740) Renville(70), Ward(25), Bottineau(1), McHenry(1)
GLENFIELD (58443) Foster(98), Griggs(1)
GOLDEN VALLEY Mercer
GOLVA Golden Valley
GOODRICH (58444) Sheridan(94), Burleigh(5)
GRACE CITY (58445) Foster(87), Eddy(12)
GRAFTON Walsh
GRAND FORKS Grand Forks
GRAND FORKS AFB Grand Forks
GRANDIN (58038) Cass(75), Traill(25)
GRANVILLE McHenry
GRASSY BUTTE (58634) McKenzie(92), Billings(7)
GREAT BEND Richland
GRENORA (58845) Williams(57), Divide(42)
GUELPH Dickey
GWINNER Sargent
HAGUE Emmons
HALLIDAY (58636) Dunn(97), Mercer(2)
HAMBERG Wells
HAMILTON Pembina
HAMPDEN (58338) Ramsey(54), Cavalier(45)
HANKINSON Richland
HANNAFORD (58448) Griggs(98), Barnes(1)
HANNAH Cavalier
HANSBORO Towner

HARVEY (58341) Wells(88), Pierce(9), Benson(1)
HARWOOD Cass
HATTON (58240) Traill(73), Steele(16), Grand Forks(10)
HAVANA Sargent
HAZELTON Emmons
HAZEN (58545) Mercer(94), Oliver(5)
HEATON (58450) Wells(86), Kidder(13)
HEBRON (58638) Morton(77), Mercer(9), Stark(8), Dunn(3)
HEIMDAL Wells
HENSEL Pembina
HENSLER Oliver
HETTINGER Adams
HILLSBORO Traill
HOOPLE (58243) Walsh(88), Pembina(12)
HOPE (58046) Steele(73), Barnes(23), Cass(3)
HORACE Cass
HUNTER (58048) Cass(95), Traill(4)
HURDSFIELD (58451) Wells(97), Sheridan(2)
INKSTER (58244) Grand Forks(96), Walsh(3)
JAMESTOWN Stutsman
JESSIE Griggs
JOLIETTE Pembina
JUD (58454) La Moure(80), Stutsman(19)
KARLSRUHE McHenry
KATHRYN (58049) Barnes(77), Ransom(16), La Moure(5)
KEENE McKenzie
KENMARE (58746) Ward(76), Renville(12), Burke(10)
KENSAL (58455) Stutsman(81), Foster(18)
KIEF (58747) Sheridan(70), McHenry(29)
KILLDEER (58640) Dunn(97), McKenzie(1)
KINDRED (58051) Cass(79), Richland(20)
KINTYRE (58549) Emmons(58), Logan(37), Kidder(3)
KNOX Benson
KRAMER (58748) Bottineau(96), McHenry(3)
KULM (58456) La Moure(77), Dickey(16), McIntosh(6)
LAKOTA (58344) Nelson(96), Ramsey(3)
LAMOURE (58458) La Moure(98), Dickey(1)
LANGDON Cavalier
LANKIN Walsh
LANSFORD (58750) Bottineau(64), Renville(35)
LARIMORE Grand Forks
LAWTON (58345) Ramsey(61), Walsh(38)
LEEDS (58346) Benson(92), Towner(7)
LEFOR Stark
LEHR (58460) McIntosh(55), Logan(44)
LEITH Grant
LEONARD (58052) Cass(80), Richland(15), Ransom(3)
LIDGERWOOD (58053) Richland(84), Sargent(15)
LIGNITE Burke
LINTON Emmons
LISBON Ransom
LITCHVILLE (58461) Barnes(74), La Moure(25)

LUVERNE (58056) Barnes(56), Steele(30), Griggs(12)
MADDOCK (58348) Benson(92), Wells(7)
MAIDA Cavalier
MAKOTI (58756) Ward(78), Mountrail(15), McLean(5)
MANDAN Morton
MANDAREE (58757) McKenzie(52), Dunn(47)
MANFRED Wells
MANNING (58642) Dunn(93), Billings(6)
MANTADOR Richland
MANVEL Grand Forks
MAPLETON Cass
MARION (58466) La Moure(77), Barnes(20), Stutsman(1)
MARMARTH (58643) Bowman(67), Slope(32)
MARSHALL Dunn
MARTIN (58758) Sheridan(66), Pierce(17), Wells(15)
MAX (58759) Ward(56), McLean(43)
MAXBASS Bottineau
MAYVILLE Traill
MCCANNA Grand Forks
MCCLUSKY Sheridan
MCGREGOR (58755) Williams(65), Divide(26), Burke(8)
MCHENRY (58464) Foster(52), Eddy(40), Griggs(7)
MCKENZIE Burleigh
MCLEOD (58057) Richland(72), Ransom(28)
MCVILLE Nelson
MEDINA (58467) Stutsman(94), Kidder(5)
MEDORA (58645) Billings(93), Golden Valley(6)
MEKINOCK Grand Forks
MENOKEN Burleigh
MERCER (58559) McLean(88), Sheridan(11)
MERRICOURT Dickey
MICHIGAN Nelson
MILNOR (58060) Sargent(80), Ransom(18)
MILTON (58260) Cavalier(93), Walsh(6)
MINNEWAUKAN (58351) Benson(95), Ramsey(4)
MINOT Ward
MINOT AFB Ward
MINTO (58261) Walsh(87), Grand Forks(12)
MOFFIT (58560) Burleigh(82), Emmons(17)
MOHALL (58761) Renville(72), Bottineau(27)
MONANGO Dickey
MONTPELIER (58472) Stutsman(69), La Moure(30)
MOORETON Richland

MOTT (58646) Hettinger(97), Adams(2)
MOUNTAIN (58262) Pembina(95), Cavalier(4)
MUNICH (58352) Cavalier(93), Towner(6)
MYLO Rolette
NAPOLEON Logan
NECHE Pembina
NEKOMA Cavalier
NEW ENGLAND (58647) Hettinger(66), Slope(26), Stark(7)
NEW LEIPZIG (58562) Grant(88), Hettinger(7), Adams(3)
NEW ROCKFORD (58356) Eddy(94), Wells(3), Foster(1)
NEW SALEM (58563) Morton(81), Oliver(17)
NEW TOWN (58763) Mountrail(77), McKenzie(22)
NEWBURG (58762) Bottineau(85), McHenry(14)
NIAGARA (58266) Grand Forks(82), Nelson(17)
NOME (58062) Barnes(80), Ransom(19)
NOONAN Divide
NORTHWOOD (58267) Grand Forks(98), Steele(1)
NORWICH (58768) McHenry(54), Ward(45)
OAKES (58474) Dickey(96), Sargent(3)
OBERON Benson
ORISKA Barnes
ORRIN Pierce
OSNABROCK Cavalier
OVERLY Bottineau
PAGE (58064) Cass(89), Barnes(8), Steele(1)
PALERMO Mountrail
PARK RIVER Walsh
PARSHALL (58770) Mountrail(82), McLean(17)
PEKIN Nelson
PEMBINA Pembina
PENN Ramsey
PERTH (58363) Towner(85), Rolette(14)
PETERSBURG Nelson
PETTIBONE (58475) Kidder(94), Stutsman(5)
PILLSBURY Barnes
PINGREE Stutsman
PISEK Walsh
PLAZA (58771) Mountrail(78), Ward(18), McLean(2)
PORTAL Burke
PORTLAND (58274) Traill(85), Steele(14)
POWERS LAKE (58773) Burke(73), Mountrail(26)
RALEIGH Grant
RAY Williams
REEDER (58649) Adams(85), Hettinger(7), Bowman(6)

REGAN Burleigh
REGENT (58650) Hettinger(94), Adams(5)
REYNOLDS (58275) Grand Forks(57), Traill(42)
RHAME (58651) Bowman(69), Slope(30)
RICHARDTON (58652) Stark(89), Dunn(10)
RIVERDALE McLean
ROBINSON Kidder
ROCKLAKE Towner
ROGERS Barnes
ROLETTE (58366) Rolette(97), Pierce(2)
ROLLA (58367) Rolette(91), Towner(8)
ROSEGLEN McLean
ROSS Mountrail
RUGBY (58368) Pierce(95), McHenry(2), Benson(2)
RUSO (58778) McLean(95), McHenry(4)
RUTLAND Sargent
RYDER (58779) McLean(54), Ward(45)
SAINT ANTHONY Morton
SAINT JOHN Rolette
SAINT MICHAEL Benson
SAINT THOMAS Pembina
SANBORN Barnes
SARLES (58372) Towner(51), Cavalier(48)
SAWYER Ward
SCRANTON (58653) Bowman(90), Slope(9)
SELFRIDGE Sioux
SELZ Pierce
SENTINEL BUTTE Golden Valley
SHARON Steele
SHELDON (58068) Ransom(98), Cass(1)
SHERWOOD (58782) Renville(95), Bottineau(4)
SHEYENNE (58374) Eddy(59), Benson(31), Wells(8)
SHIELDS Grant
SOLEN (58570) Morton(58), Sioux(41)
SOURIS Bottineau
SOUTH HEART Stark
SPIRITWOOD (58481) Stutsman(51), Barnes(48)
STANLEY (58784) Mountrail(95), Burke(4)
STANTON (58571) Mercer(76), Oliver(23)
STARKWEATHER (58377) Ramsey(81), Towner(11), Cavalier(7)
STEELE Kidder
STERLING Burleigh
STIRUM (58069) Sargent(95), Ransom(4)
STRASBURG Emmons
STREETER (58483) Stutsman(66), Logan(21), Kidder(12)
SURREY Ward
SUTTON (58484) Griggs(81), Foster(18)
SYKESTON (58486) Wells(92), Stutsman(7)
TAPPEN Kidder

TAYLOR (58656) Stark(83), Dunn(16)
THOMPSON Grand Forks
TIOGA (58852) Williams(91), Mountrail(8)
TOKIO Benson
TOLLEY (58787) Renville(96), Ward(3)
TOLNA (58380) Nelson(47), Eddy(43), Benson(8)
TOWER CITY (58071) Cass(80), Barnes(19)
TOWNER (58788) McHenry(95), Pierce(4)
TRENTON Williams
TROTTERS Golden Valley
TURTLE LAKE McLean
TUTTLE Kidder
UNDERWOOD McLean
UNION Cavalier
UPHAM (58789) McHenry(90), Bottineau(9)
VALLEY CITY Barnes
VELVA (58790) McHenry(92), Ward(7)
VENTURIA McIntosh
VERONA (58490) La Moure(86), Ransom(13)
VOLTAIRE McHenry
WAHPETON Richland
WALCOTT Richland
WALES Cavalier
WALHALLA (58282) Pembina(86), Cavalier(13)
WARWICK (58381) Benson(53), Eddy(46)
WASHBURN McLean
WATFORD CITY McKenzie
WEBSTER Ramsey
WEST FARGO Cass
WESTHOPE Bottineau
WHEATLAND Cass
WHITE EARTH (58794) Mountrail(98), Williams(1)
WILDROSE (58795) Divide(52), Williams(47)
WILLISTON Williams
WILLOW CITY (58384) Bottineau(65), Pierce(17), McHenry(11), Rolette(5)
WILTON (58579) McLean(51), Burleigh(48)
WIMBLEDON (58492) Barnes(78), Stutsman(12), Griggs(8)
WING Burleigh
WISHEK (58495) McIntosh(84), Logan(15)
WOLFORD (58385) Pierce(91), Rolette(8)
WOODWORTH Stutsman
WYNDMERE Richland
YORK (58386) Benson(74), Pierce(25)
YPSILANTI (58497) Stutsman(93), Barnes(6)
ZAHL (58856) Williams(65), Divide(34)
ZAP Mercer
ZEELAND McIntosh

North Dakota ZIP/City Cross Reference

58001-58001	ABERCROMBIE	58030-58030	FAIRMOUNT	58054-58054	LISBON	58081-58081	WYNDMERE
58002-58002	ABSARAKA	58031-58031	FINGAL	58056-58056	LUVERNE	58102-58126	FARGO
58003-58003	ALICE	58032-58032	FORMAN	58057-58057	MCLEOD	58201-58203	GRAND FORKS
58004-58004	AMENIA	58033-58033	FORT RANSOM	58058-58058	MANTADOR	58204-58205	GRAND FORKS AFB
58005-58005	ARGUSVILLE	58035-58035	GALESBURG	58059-58059	MAPLETON	58206-58208	GRAND FORKS
58006-58006	ARTHUR	58036-58036	GARDNER	58060-58060	MILNOR	58210-58210	ADAMS
58007-58007	AYR	58038-58038	GRANDIN	58061-58061	MOORETON	58212-58212	ANETA
58008-58008	BARNEY	58039-58039	GREAT BEND	58062-58062	NOME	58213-58213	ARDOCH
58009-58009	BLANCHARD	58040-58040	GWINNER	58063-58063	ORISKA	58214-58214	ARVILLA
58011-58011	BUFFALO	58041-58041	HANKINSON	58064-58064	PAGE	58216-58216	BATHGATE
58012-58012	CASSELTON	58042-58042	HARWOOD	58065-58065	PILLSBURY	58218-58218	BUXTON
58013-58013	CAYUGA	58043-58043	HAVANA	58067-58067	RUTLAND	58219-58219	CALEDONIA
58014-58014	CHAFFEE	58045-58045	HILLSBORO	58068-58068	SHELDON	58220-58220	CAVALIER
58015-58015	CHRISTINE	58046-58046	HOPE	58069-58069	STIRUM	58222-58222	CRYSTAL
58016-58016	CLIFFORD	58047-58047	HORACE	58071-58071	TOWER CITY	58223-58223	CUMMINGS
58017-58017	COGSWELL	58048-58048	HUNTER	58072-58072	VALLEY CITY	58224-58224	DAHLEN
58018-58018	COLFAX	58049-58049	KATHRYN	58074-58076	WAHPETON	58225-58225	DRAYTON
58021-58021	DAVENPORT	58051-58051	KINDRED	58077-58077	WALCOTT	58227-58227	EDINBURG
58027-58027	ENDERLIN	58052-58052	LEONARD	58078-58078	WEST FARGO	58228-58228	EMERADO
58029-58029	ERIE	58053-58053	LIDGERWOOD	58079-58079	WHEATLAND	58229-58229	FAIRDALE

58230-58230 FINLEY	58363-58363 PERTH	58492-58492 WIMBLEDON	58701-58703 MINOT
58231-58231 FORDVILLE	58365-58365 ROCKLAKE	58494-58494 WING	58704-58705 MINOT AFB
58233-58233 FOREST RIVER	58366-58366 ROLETTE	58495-58495 WISHEK	58707-58707 MINOT
58235-58235 GILBY	58367-58367 ROLLA	58496-58496 WOODWORTH	58710-58710 ANAMOOSE
58236-58236 GLASSTON	58368-58368 RUGBY	58497-58497 YPSILANTI	58711-58711 ANTLER
58237-58237 GRAFTON	58369-58369 SAINT JOHN	58501-58507 BISMARCK	58712-58712 BALFOUR
58238-58238 HAMILTON	58370-58370 SAINT MICHAEL	58520-58520 ALMONT	58713-58713 BANTRY
58239-58239 HANNAH	58372-58372 SARLES	58521-58521 BALDWIN	58716-58716 BENEDICT
58240-58240 HATTON	58373-58373 SELZ	58523-58523 BEULAH	58718-58718 BERTHOLD
58241-58241 HENSEL	58374-58374 SHEYENNE	58524-58524 BRADDOCK	58720-58720 BLAISDELL
58243-58243 HOOPLE	58377-58377 STARKWEATHER	58528-58528 CANNON BALL	58721-58721 BOWBELLS
58244-58244 INKSTER	58379-58379 TOKIO	58529-58529 CARSON	58722-58722 BURLINGTON
58246-58246 JOLIETTE	58380-58380 TOLNA	58530-58530 CENTER	58723-58723 BUTTE
58249-58249 LANGDON	58381-58381 WARWICK	58531-58531 COLEHARBOR	58725-58725 CARPIO
58250-58250 LANKIN	58382-58382 WEBSTER	58532-58532 DRISCOLL	58727-58727 COLUMBUS
58251-58251 LARIMORE	58384-58384 WILLOW CITY	58533-58533 ELGIN	58728-58728 BOWBELLS
58253-58253 MCCANNA	58385-58385 WOLFORD	58535-58535 FLASHER	58730-58730 CROSBY
58254-58254 MCVILLE	58386-58386 YORK	58537-58537 FORT RICE	58731-58731 DEERING
58255-58255 MAIDA	58401-58405 JAMESTOWN	58538-58538 FORT YATES	58733-58733 DES LACS
58256-58256 MANVEL	58411-58411 ALFRED	58540-58540 GARRISON	58734-58734 DONNYBROOK
58257-58257 MAYVILLE	58412-58412 ARENA	58541-58541 GOLDEN VALLEY	58735-58735 DOUGLAS
58258-58258 MEKINOCK	58413-58413 ASHLEY	58542-58542 HAGUE	58736-58736 DRAKE
58259-58259 MICHIGAN	58415-58415 BERLIN	58544-58544 HAZELTON	58737-58737 FLAXTON
58260-58260 MILTON	58416-58416 BINFORD	58545-58545 HAZEN	58738-58738 FOXHOLM
58261-58261 MINTO	58418-58418 BOWDON	58547-58547 HENSLER	58739-58739 GARDENA
58262-58262 MOUNTAIN	58420-58420 BUCHANAN	58549-58549 KINTYRE	58740-58740 GLENBURN
58265-58265 NECHE	58421-58421 CARRINGTON	58551-58551 LEITH	58741-58741 GRANVILLE
58266-58266 NIAGARA	58422-58422 CATHAY	58552-58552 LINTON	58744-58744 KARLSRUHE
58267-58267 NORTHWOOD	58423-58423 CHASELEY	58553-58553 MCKENZIE	58746-58746 KENMARE
58269-58269 OSNABROCK	58424-58424 CLEVELAND	58554-58554 MANDAN	58747-58747 KIEF
58270-58270 PARK RIVER	58425-58425 COOPERSTOWN	58558-58558 MENOKEN	58748-58748 KRAMER
58271-58271 PEMBINA	58426-58426 COURTENAY	58559-58559 MERCER	58750-58750 LANSFORD
58272-58272 PETERSBURG	58427-58427 CRYSTAL SPRINGS	58560-58560 MOFFIT	58752-58752 LIGNITE
58273-58273 PISEK	58428-58428 DAWSON	58561-58561 NAPOLEON	58755-58755 MCGREGOR
58274-58274 PORTLAND	58429-58429 DAZEY	58562-58562 NEW LEIPZIG	58756-58756 MAKOTI
58275-58275 REYNOLDS	58430-58430 DENHOFF	58563-58563 NEW SALEM	58757-58757 MANDAREE
58276-58276 SAINT THOMAS	58431-58431 DICKEY	58564-58564 RALEIGH	58758-58758 MARTIN
58277-58277 SHARON	58432-58432 ECKELSON	58565-58565 RIVERDALE	58759-58759 MAX
58278-58278 THOMPSON	58433-58433 EDGELEY	58566-58566 SAINT ANTHONY	58760-58760 MAXBASS
58279-58279 UNION	58436-58436 ELLENDALE	58568-58568 SELFRIDGE	58761-58761 MOHALL
58281-58281 WALES	58438-58438 FESSENDEN	58569-58569 SHIELDS	58762-58762 NEWBURG
58282-58282 WALHALLA	58439-58439 FORBES	58570-58570 SOLEN	58763-58763 NEW TOWN
58301-58301 DEVILS LAKE	58440-58440 FREDONIA	58571-58571 STANTON	58765-58765 NOONAN
58310-58310 AGATE	58441-58441 FULLERTON	58572-58572 STERLING	58768-58768 NORWICH
58311-58311 ALSEN	58442-58442 GACKLE	58573-58573 STRASBURG	58769-58769 PALERMO
58313-58313 BALTA	58443-58443 GLENFIELD	58575-58575 TURTLE LAKE	58770-58770 PARSHALL
58315-58315 BARTON	58444-58444 GOODRICH	58576-58576 UNDERWOOD	58771-58771 PLAZA
58316-58316 BELCOURT	58445-58445 GRACE CITY	58577-58577 WASHBURN	58772-58772 PORTAL
58317-58317 BISBEE	58447-58447 GUELPH	58579-58579 WILTON	58773-58773 POWERS LAKE
58318-58318 BOTTINEAU	58448-58448 HANNAFORD	58580-58580 ZAP	58775-58775 ROSEGLEN
58319-58319 BREMEN	58450-58450 HEATON	58581-58581 ZEELAND	58776-58776 ROSS
58320-58320 BRINSMADE	58451-58451 HURDSFIELD	58601-58602 DICKINSON	58778-58778 RUSO
58321-58321 BROCKET	58452-58452 JESSIE	58620-58620 AMIDON	58779-58779 RYDER
58323-58323 CALVIN	58454-58454 JUD	58621-58621 BEACH	58781-58781 SAWYER
58324-58324 CANDO	58455-58455 KENSAL	58622-58622 BELFIELD	58782-58782 SHERWOOD
58325-58325 CHURCHS FERRY	58456-58456 KULM	58623-58623 BOWMAN	58783-58783 SOURIS
58327-58327 CRARY	58458-58458 LAMOURE	58625-58625 DODGE	58784-58784 STANLEY
58328-58328 DOYON	58460-58460 LEHR	58626-58626 DUNN CENTER	58785-58785 SURREY
58329-58329 DUNSEITH	58461-58461 LITCHVILLE	58627-58627 FAIRFIELD	58787-58787 TOLLEY
58330-58330 EDMORE	58463-58463 MCCLUSKY	58630-58630 GLADSTONE	58788-58788 TOWNER
58331-58331 EGELAND	58464-58464 MCHENRY	58631-58631 GLEN ULLIN	58789-58789 UPHAM
58332-58332 ESMOND	58465-58465 MANFRED	58632-58632 GOLVA	58790-58790 VELVA
58335-58335 FORT TOTTEN	58466-58466 MARION	58634-58634 GRASSY BUTTE	58792-58792 VOLTAIRE
58337-58337 HAMBERG	58467-58467 MEDINA	58636-58636 HALLIDAY	58793-58793 WESTHOPE
58338-58338 HAMPDEN	58469-58469 MERRICOURT	58638-58638 HEBRON	58794-58794 WHITE EARTH
58339-58339 HANSBORO	58471-58471 MONANGO	58639-58639 HETTINGER	58795-58795 WILDROSE
58341-58341 HARVEY	58472-58472 MONTPELIER	58640-58640 KILLDEER	58801-58802 WILLISTON
58342-58342 HEIMDAL	58474-58474 OAKES	58641-58641 LEFOR	58830-58830 ALAMO
58343-58343 KNOX	58475-58475 PETTIBONE	58642-58642 MANNING	58831-58831 ALEXANDER
58344-58344 LAKOTA	58476-58476 PINGREE	58643-58643 MARMARTH	58833-58833 AMBROSE
58345-58345 LAWTON	58477-58477 REGAN	58644-58644 MARSHALL	58835-58835 ARNEGARD
58346-58346 LEEDS	58478-58478 ROBINSON	58645-58645 MEDORA	58838-58838 CARTWRIGHT
58348-58348 MADDOCK	58479-58479 ROGERS	58646-58646 MOTT	58843-58843 EPPING
58351-58351 MINNEWAUKAN	58480-58480 SANBORN	58647-58647 NEW ENGLAND	58844-58844 FORTUNA
58352-58352 MUNICH	58481-58481 SPIRITWOOD	58649-58649 REEDER	58845-58845 GRENORA
58353-58353 MYLO	58482-58482 STEELE	58650-58650 REGENT	58847-58847 KEENE
58355-58355 NEKOMA	58483-58483 STREETER	58651-58651 RHAME	58849-58849 RAY
58356-58356 NEW ROCKFORD	58484-58484 SUTTON	58652-58652 RICHARDTON	58852-58852 TIOGA
58357-58357 OBERON	58486-58486 SYKESTON	58653-58653 SCRANTON	58853-58853 TRENTON
58359-58359 ORRIN	58487-58487 TAPPEN	58654-58654 SENTINEL BUTTE	58854-58854 WATFORD CITY
58360-58360 OVERLY	58488-58488 TUTTLE	58655-58655 SOUTH HEART	58856-58856 ZAHL
58361-58361 PEKIN	58489-58489 VENTURIA	58656-58656 TAYLOR	
58362-58362 PENN	58490-58490 VERONA	58657-58657 TROTTERS	

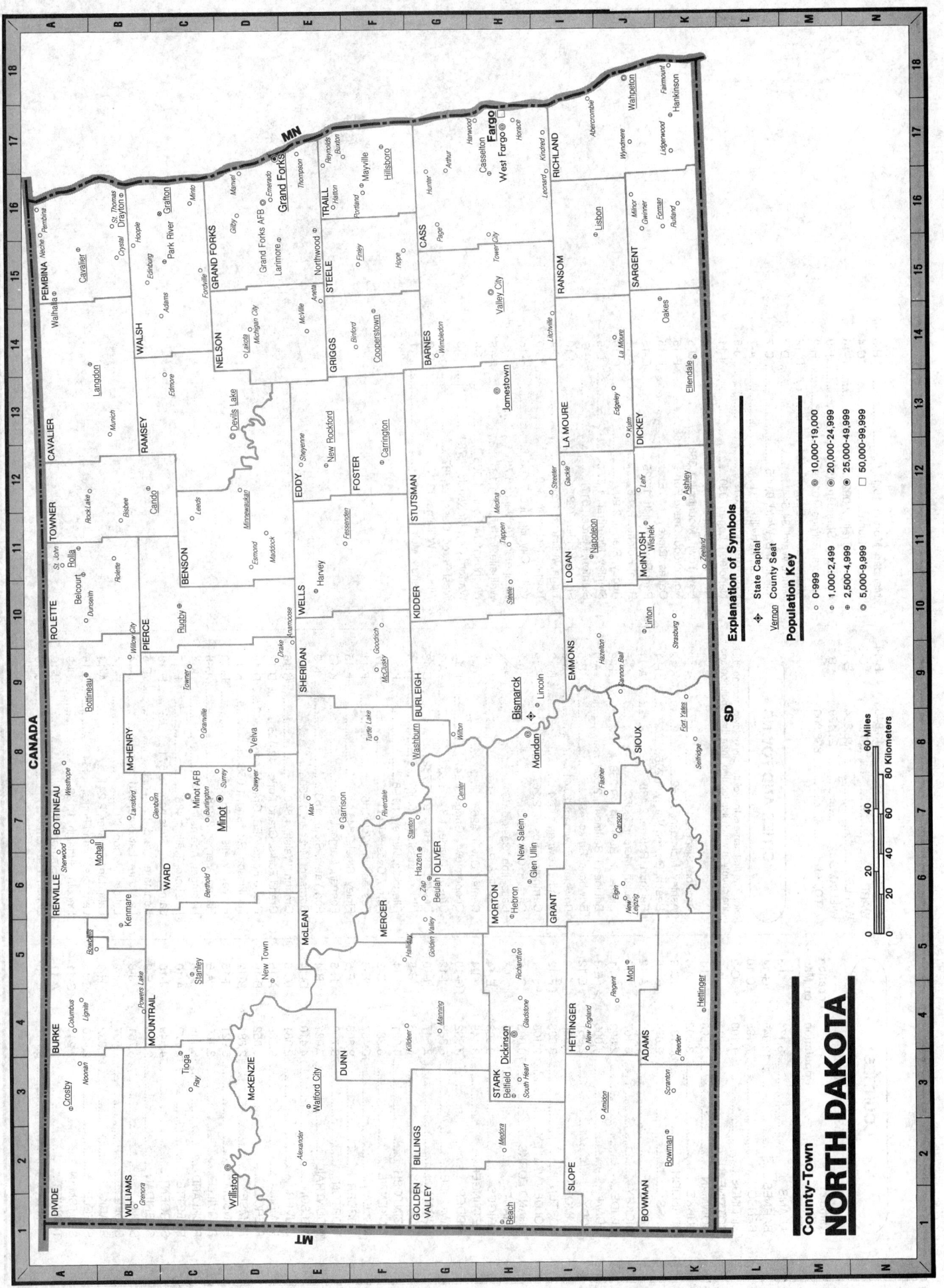

County-Town
NORTH DAKOTA

COUNTIES

(53 Counties)

Name of County	Population	Location on Map
ADAMS	3,174	J-3
BARNES	12,545	G-14
BENSON	7,198	C-10
BILLINGS	1,108	G-2
BOTTINEAU	8,011	A-7
BOWMAN	3,596	J-1
BURKE	3,002	A-4
BURLEIGH	60,131	G-9
CASS	102,874	G-15
CAVALIER	6,064	A-12
DICKEY	6,107	J-12
DIVIDE	2,899	A-1
DUNN	4,005	E-3
EDDY	2,951	E-12
EMMONS	4,830	I-9
FOSTER	3,983	F-12
GOLDEN VALLEY	2,108	G-1
GRAND FORKS	70,683	C-15
GRANT	3,549	I-5
GRIGGS	3,303	E-14
HETTINGER	3,445	I-4
KIDDER	3,332	G-10
LAMOURE	5,383	I-12
LOGAN	2,847	I-10
MCHENRY	6,528	B-8
MCINTOSH	4,021	J-11
MCKENZIE	6,383	D-3
MCLEAN	10,457	E-5
MERCER	9,808	F-5
MORTON	23,700	H-5
MOUNTRAIL	7,021	B-4
NELSON	4,410	D-14
OLIVER	2,381	G-6
PEMBINA	9,238	A-15
PIERCE	5,052	B-10
RAMSEY	12,681	B-12
RANSOM	5,921	I-15
RENVILLE	3,160	A-6
RICHLAND	18,148	I-16
ROLETTE	12,772	A-10
SARGENT	4,549	J-15
SHERIDAN	2,148	E-9
SIOUX	3,761	J-8
SLOPE	907	I-2
STARK	22,832	H-3
STEELE	2,420	E-15
STUTSMAN	22,241	G-11
TOWNER	3,627	A-11
TRAILL	8,752	E-16
WALSH	13,840	B-14
WARD	57,921	C-6
WELLS	5,864	E-10
WILLIAMS	21,129	B-1
TOTAL	**638,800**	

CITIES AND TOWNS

Note: The first name is that of the city or town, second, that of the county in which it is located, then the population and location on the map.

Amidon, Slope, 24	I-3
Ashley, McIntosh, 1,052	K-12
Beach, Golden Valley, 1,205	H-1
● Belcourt, Rolette, 2,458	A-11
Beulah, Mercer, 3,363	G-6
Bismarck, Burleigh, 49,256	H-8
Bottineau, Bottineau, 2,598	A-9
Bowbells, Burke, 498	B-5
Bowman, Bowman, 1,741	K-2
Cando, Towner, 1,564	B-12
Carrington, Foster, 2,267	F-12
Carson, Grant, 383	J-7
Casselton, Cass, 1,601	H-16
Cavalier, Pembina, 1,508	A-15
Center, Oliver, 826	G-7
Cooperstown, Griggs, 1,247	F-14
Crosby, Divide, 1,312	A-3
Devils Lake, Ramsey, 7,782	D-13
Dickinson, Stark, 16,097	H-4
Ellendale, Dickey, 1,798	K-14
Fargo, Cass, 74,111	H-17
Fessenden, Wells, 655	F-11
Finley, Steele, 543	F-15
Forman, Sargent, 586	K-16
Fort Yates, Sioux, 183	K-9
Garrison, McLean, 1,530	E-7
Grafton, Walsh, 4,840	C-16
Grand Forks, Grand Forks, 49,425	D-17
● Grand Forks AFB, Grand Forks, 9,343	D-16
Hankinson, Richland, 1,038	K-17
Harvey, Wells, 2,263	E-10
Hazen, Mercer, 2,818	G-6
Hettinger, Adams, 1,574	K-4
Hillsboro, Traill, 1,488	F-17
Jamestown, Stutsman, 15,571	H-13
Kenmare, Ward, 1,214	B-5
La Moure, LaMoure, 970	J-14
Lakota, Nelson, 898	D-14
Langdon, Cavalier, 2,241	A-14
Larimore, Grand Forks, 1,464	D-15
Lincoln, Burleigh, 1,132	I-9
Linton, Emmons, 1,410	J-10
Lisbon, Ransom, 2,177	J-16
Mandan, Morton, 15,177	H-8
Manning, Dunn	G-4
Mayville, Traill, 2,092	F-16
McClusky, Sheridan, 492	F-9
Medora, Billings, 101	H-2
Minnewaukan, Benson, 401	D-12
Minot, Ward, 34,544	D-7
● Minot AFB, Ward, 9,095	C-7
Mohall, Renville, 931	A-7
Mott, Hettinger, 1,019	J-5
Napoleon, Logan, 930	I-11
New Rockford, Eddy, 1,604	E-12
New Town, Mountrail, 1,388	D-5
Northwood, Grand Forks, 1,166	E-16
Oakes, Dickey, 1,775	K-15
Park River, Walsh, 1,725	C-15
Rolla, Rolette, 1,286	A-11
Rugby, Pierce, 2,909	C-10
Stanley, Mountrail, 1,371	C-5
Stanton, Mercer, 517	G-7
Steele, Kidder, 762	H-10
Tioga, Williams, 1,278	C-4
Towner, McHenry, 669	C-9
Valley City, Barnes, 7,163	H-15
Wahpeton, Richland, 8,751	J-18
Walhalla, Pembina, 1,131	A-15
Washburn, McLean, 1,506	G-8
Watford City, McKenzie, 1,784	E-3
West Fargo, Cass, 12,287	H-17
Williston, Williams, 13,131	D-2
Wishek, McIntosh, 1,171	J-11

General Help Numbers:

Governor's Office
77 S High St, 30th Floor
Columbus, OH 43215
http://governor.ohio.gov/

614-466-3555
Fax 614-466-9354
8AM-5PM

Attorney General's Office
State Office Tower
30 E Broad St, 17th Floor
Columbus, OH 43215-3428
www.ag.state.oh.us

614-466-4320
Fax 614-644-6135
8AM-5PM

Legislative Records
Ohio House of Representatives
77 S High Street
Columbus, OH 43266
www.legislature.state.oh.us

614-466-9745
Fax 614-644-8744
8:30AM-5PM

State Archives
Archives/Library
1982 Velma Ave
Columbus, OH 43211-2497   9AM-5PM TH-SA: 10-5 SU
www.ohiohistory.org/ar_tools.html

614-297-2300
Fax 614-297-2546

State Specifics:

Capital:	Columbus Franklin County
Time Zone:	EST
Number of Counties:	88
Population:	11,435,798
Web Site:	www.state.oh.us

State Agencies

Criminal Records

Ohio Bureau of Investigation, Civilian Background Section, PO Box 365, London, OH 43140 (Courier: 1560 State Rte 56, London, OH 43140); 740-845-2000 (General Info), 740-845-2375 (Civilian Background Cks), 740-845-2633 (Fax), 8AM-4:45PM.

www.webcheck.ag.state.oh.us

Note: The state has an innovative system over the web for electronic transfer of fingerprints. See Online Access below.

Indexing & Storage: Records are available from 1921 on. Records from 1972 on are computerized.

It takes 5 days, 15 with fingerprints before new records are available for inquiry. Records are indexed on inhouse computer. Records are normally destroyed after (records maintained indefinitely).

Searching: Include the following in your request-witnessed signed release from subject, fingerprints, name DOB, SSN. 100% of the records are fingerprint supported.

Access by: mail, online.

Fee & Payment: The search fee is $15.00 per record. Stautorily-required checks may include an FBI fingerprint check for an additional $24.00. Fee

payee: Treasurer - State of Ohio. Prepayment required. No credit cards accepted.

Mail search: Turnaround time: 30 days. No SASE is required.

Online search: WebCheck is an Internet-based request program for civilian background checks for school districts, education associations, children's hospitals, and public institutions. Results are NOT returned via the Internet. Agencies can send fingerprint images and other data via the Internet using a single digit fingerprint scanner and a driver's license magnetic strip reader. Within two business days, the school or daycare center will receive their results of their background check requests.

Statewide Court Records

Administrative Director, Supreme Court of Ohio, 65 S Front Street, Columbus, OH 43215-3431; 614-387-9000, 800-826-9010, 8AM-5PM.

www.sconet.state.oh.us

Note: This office does not provide access to county court records. Except for certain online research capabilities, all court record access must be done at the local level.

Access by: online.

Online search: Appellate and Supreme Court opinions may be researched from the website.

Sexual Offender Registry Access to Records is Restricted

Ohio Bureau of Investigation, Sexual Offender Registry, PO Box 365, London, OH 43140 (Courier: 1560 State Rte 56 SW, London, OH 43140); 740-845-2221, 740-845-2223, 740-845-2633 (Fax), 8AM-4:45PM.

www.esorn.ag.state.oh.us/Secured/p1.aspx

Note: O.R.C. 2950.13 requires that the public eSORN database contain information on every person convicted as an adult and registered in the state registry of sex offenders and child-victim offenders. The database that contains information regarding all registered sex offenders in the State of Ohio is known as eSORN.

Incarceration Records

Ohio Department of Rehabilitation and Correction, Bureau of Records Management, 1050 Freeway Drive, N., Columbus, OH 43229; 614-752-1076, 614-752-1086 (Fax), 8:30AM-5PM M-F.

www.drc.state.oh.us/

Indexing & Storage: Records are available on current and former inmates, except online is current only. It takes 1 to 5 days before new records are available for inquiry. Records are normally destroyed after 10 years.

Searching: Include the following in your request- first and last name or Offender Number. The DOB and SSN are helpful. Location, physical identifiers, conviction and sentencing information, and release dates are provided.

Access by: mail, phone, fax, online.

Mail search: Turnaround time: 1 to 2 weeks. No SASE is required.

Phone search: Record inquiry available by phone. To obtain information on offenders previously under the supervision of the Department, call 614-752-1159 and choose option 3.

Fax search: Fax requests are accepted.

Online search: From the website, in the Select a Destination box, select Offender Search. You can search by name or inmate number. The Offender Search includes all offenders currently incarcerated or under some type of Department supervision (parole, post-release control, or transitional control).

Corporation, Fictitious Name, Limited Partnership Records, Assumed Name, Trademarks, Servicemarks, Limited Liability Company

Secretary of State, Corporate Records Access, PO Box 130, Columbus, OH 43215 (Courier: 180 E Broad Street, 16th Fl, Columbus, OH 43215); 877-767-3453, 614-466-3910, 614-466-3899 (Fax), 8AM-5PM.

www.sos.state.oh.us/sos/

Note: Information regarding officers is available from the Department of Taxation at 614-438-5339. The Dept of Commerce offers a statewide search for unclaimed funds at www4.state.oh.us/com/unfd/qry1.asp.

Indexing & Storage: Records are available from the 1800's. New records are available for inquiry immediately. Records are indexed on microfilm, index cards, inhouse computer.

Searching: Include the following in your request- full name of business. Use the request form for certifed documents (available from web). In addition to the articles of incorporation, corporation records include the following information: Annual Reports, Prior (merged) names, Inactive and Reserved names.

Access by: mail, phone, fax, in person, online.

Fee & Payment: There is no search fee, The certification fee is $5.00, a Good Standing is also $5.00. Copy fees are no charge up to 34 pages, $1.05 for the 35th, and $.03 per copy thereafter. There is no fee for a corporate printout of limited information. Fee payee: Secretary of State. Prepayment required. Personal checks accepted. No credit cards accepted.

Mail search: Turnaround time: 2 days. No SASE is required.

Phone search: They will release limited information over the phone.

Fax search: No fee, turnaround time is 2 days. Do not fax for plain copy requests.

In person search: There is no fee to look at records.

Online search: The agency provides free Internet searching for business and corporation records at www.sos.state.oh.us/sos/busiserv/index.html. The site also includes UCC and campaign finance. Images are available, as well as Good Standings.

Other access: This agency makes the database available for purchase, call for details.

Uniform Commercial Code

UCC Records, Secretary of State, PO Box 2795, Columbus, OH 43216 (Courier: 180 E Broad Street, 16th Fl, Columbus, OH 43215); 877-767-3453, 614-466-3910, 614-466-2892 (Fax), 8AM-5PM.

www.sos.state.oh.us/sos/ucc/index.html

Indexing & Storage: Records are available for only current or active filings. Records are indexed on inhouse computer.

Searching: Use search form UCC-11. All tax liens are filed at the county level. Include the following in your request-debtor name. Be sure to include the words "any and all addresses" in your search request.

Access by: mail, phone, fax, in person, online.

Fee & Payment: The search fee is $20.00 per debtor name, copies included. Fee payee: Secretary of State. Prepayment required. Personal checks accepted. No credit cards accepted.

Mail search: Turnaround time: 2 days.

Phone search: Calls are limited to 10 filings, 3 debtor names per call. There is no charge for verbal information.

Fax search: Only available for prepaid accounts.

In person search: Simple requests may be processed while you wait.

Online search: The Internet site offers free online access to records. Search by debtor, secured party, or financing statement number.

Other access: The complete database is available on electronic media with weekly updates. Call for current pricing.

Federal Tax Liens, State Tax Liens

Records not maintained by a state level agency.

Note: Records are not housed by a state agency. You must secure from the local county recorder offices.

Sales Tax Registrations

Access to Records is Restricted

Taxation Department, Sale & Use Tax Division, 30 E Broad St, 20th Floor, Columbus, OH 43215; 614-466-7351, 888-405-4039, 614-466-4977 (Fax), 8AM-5PM M-F.

http://tax.ohio.gov

Note: This agency refuses to release any information about registrants.

Birth Certificates

Ohio Department of Health, Bureau of Vital Statistics, PO Box 15098, Columbus, OH 43215-0098 (Courier: 246 N High St, 1st Fl, Revenue Room, Columbus, OH 43215); 614-466-2531, 877-828-3101, 877-553-2439 (Fax), 7:45AM-4:30PM.

www.odh.state.oh.us/VitStats/birth1.htm

Indexing & Storage: Records are available from 01/45 1908 to present. Records from 12/20/08 to 12/44 are at the Ohio Historical Society at 614-297-2510. It takes 3 months before new records are available for inquiry.

Searching: Include the following in your request- full name, names of parents including mother's maiden name, date of birth, city and county of birth.

Access by: mail, fax, in person.

Fee & Payment: The fee is $15.00 for a certified copy, or $3.00 uncertified, for each 10 years searched. There is an additional $3.00 for each additional 10 years searched. Fee payee: Treasurer, State of Ohio Prepayment required. Credit card use only for expedited service. Personal checks accepted. Credit cards accepted: MasterCard, Visa, AmEx, Discover.

Mail search: Turnaround time: 4 to 6 weeks. No SASE is required.

Fax search: See expedited service below.

In person search: Turnaround time 7 to 10 days.

Expedited service: For fax and phone requests. Turnaround time: 2 to 3 days. This is available from VitalChek.com. There is an additional $9.95 fee to use a credit card, add overnight shiipping costs if desired. You can also order online.

Death Records

Ohio Department of Health, Bureau of Vital Statistics, PO Box 15098, Columbus, OH 43215-0098 (Courier: 246 N High Street, 1st Fl, Revenue Room, Columbus, OH 43215); 614-466-2531, 877-828-3101, 877-553-2439 (Fax), 7:45AM-4:30PM.

www.odh.state.oh.us/VitStats/death1.htm

Indexing & Storage: Records are available from 1953 to May 2003. Death records from 1908 to 1953 are found at Ohio Historical Society, 1982 Velma Ave, Columbus, OH 43211. Records prior to 1908 are located at the county level. It takes 3 months before new records are available for inquiry.

Searching: Requests must be in writing. Include the following in your request-full name, date of death, city and county of death.

Access by: mail, fax, in person, online.

Fee & Payment: The search fee is $3.00 for each 10 years searched, if year not known. Certification is $15.00. Fee payee: Treasurer, State of Ohio. Prepayment required. Credit cards only accepted for expedited service. Personal checks accepted. Credit cards accepted: MasterCard, Visa, AmEx, Discover.

Mail search: Turnaround time: 4 to 6 weeks. No SASE is required.

Fax search: See expedited service.

In person search: Turnaround time is 7 to 10 days.

Online search: The Ohio Historical Society Death Certificate Index Searchable Database at www.ohiohistory.org/dindex/search.cfm permits searching by name, county, index. Data is available from 1913 to 1937 only.

Expedited service: For fax and phone requests. Turnaround time: 2 to 3 days. This is available from VitalChek.com. There is an additional $9.95 fee to use a credit card, add overnight shiipping costs if desired. You can also order online.

Marriage Certificates, Divorce Records

Access to Records is at County

Ohio Department of Health, Bureau of Vital Statistics, PO Box 15098, Columbus, OH 43215-0098; 614-466-2531.

www.odh.state.oh.us/VitStats/searchpro.htm

Note: Marriage and Divorce records are found at county of issue. This agency will only do a search of the index from 1953 forward. To request a 10-year search, a $3 fee is assessed for every 10-year period searched.

Workers' Compensation Records

Bureau of Workers Compensation, Customer Contact Center, 30 W Spring St, Fl 10, Columbus, OH 43215-2241; 800-644-6292, 877-520-6446 (Fax), 7:30AM-5:30PM.

www.ohiobwc.com

Indexing & Storage: Records are available for the past 10 years. Records are indexed on inhouse computer. Records are normally destroyed after 10 years if records are inactive.

Searching: All information is public except injured worker medical report and information pertaining to the employer's financial condition. Include the following in your request-claimant name, Social Security Number. Claim number is helpful. All requests must be in writing.

Access by: mail, phone, fax, in person, online.

Fee & Payment: There is no search fee, copy fee is $.05 per page. Fee payee: Ohio Bureau of Workers Compensation. Prepayment required. Personal checks accepted. No credit cards accepted.

Mail search: Turnaround time: 1 week. A SASE is requested.

Phone search: They will provide the information immediately unless file is lengthy or excessive.

Fax search: Service is available with a 24 hour turnaround time.

In person search: Call for location of records before going in because there are 22 different office locations.

Online search: Injured workers, injured worker designees, representatives and managed care organizations (MCOs) can view a list of all claims associated with a given SSN, but are limited to viewing only the claims with which they are associated. Employers, their representatives or designees, and managed care organizations can view a list of all claims associated to their BWC policy number. Medical providers can view all claims associated with any given SSN. Access is through the website listed above.

Other access: Bulk data is released to approved accounts; however, the legal department must approve requesters. The agency has general information available on a website.

Driver Records

Department of Public Safety, Bureau of Motor Vehicles, 1970 W Broad St, Columbus, OH 43223-1102; 614-752-7600, 614-752-7987 (Fax), 8AM-5:30PM M-T-W; 8AM-4:30PM TH-F.

www.ohiobmv.com/

Note: Copies of tickets are available from the Bureau of Motor Vehicles, Transcript Records, PO Box 16520, Columbus 43266-0020. The fee is $1.00 per page.

Indexing & Storage: Records are available for 3 years for moving violations, DWI's and suspensions. Records are purged from public view after 3 years; insurance laws require 36 months of availability. It takes 2 to 5 weeks before new records are available for inquiry.

Searching: Use Record Request Form 1173 (downloadable from Internet). If requester does not have permissible use per DPPA, Form BMV 5008 is also required, which requires notarized consent of subject. Records w/o personal information are not released to the public. Include the following in your request-driver's license number, full name, date of birth, Social Security Number. Driver's address is included as part of the search report for permissible requesters, except for requests received from California. The following data is not released: mental health records, SSNs

unless provided by requester (except government agency requesters).

Access by: mail, phone, fax, in person, online.

Fee & Payment: The fee is $2.00 per record. A license status check is available for $2.00. Fee payee: Treasurer, State of Ohio. Prepayment required. Personal checks accepted. No credit cards accepted.

Mail search: Turnaround time: 1 to 3 days. A SASE is requested.

Phone search: Qualified, pre-approved accounts may order by phone. There is a $200.00 deposit.

Fax search: Same criteria as phone searches.

In person search: Up to eight records will be processed while you wait.

Online search: The Online Abstract System suggested for requesters who order 100 or more motor vehicle reports per day in batch mode. Turnaround is in 4-8 hours. The DL# or SSN and name are needed when ordering. Fee is $2.00 per record. For more information, call 614-752-2091.

Other access: Overnight CD service is available for larger accounts.

Vehicle Ownership, Vehicle Identification

Bureau of Motor Vehicles, Motor Vehicle Title Records, 1970 W Broad St, Columbus, OH 43223-1102; 614-752-7671, 614-752-8929 (Fax), 7:30AM-4:45PM.

www.ohiobmv.com

Indexing & Storage: Records are available for the current year plus six. It takes 1 to 2 days normally before new records are available for inquiry.

Searching: Use Record Request Form 1173 (downloadable from Internet). If requester does not have permissible use per DPPA, Form BMV 5008 is also required, which requires notarized consent of subject. Records w/o personal information are not released to the public. Include the following in your request-name, year, make VIN, license plate number if known. Lien information is not recorded on vehicle registration records in Ohio. The following data is not released: Social Security Numbers, unless included in request.

Access by: mail, phone, fax, in person, online.

Fee & Payment: The fee is $2.00 or each record searched. Fee payee: Treasurer, State of Ohio. Prepayment required. Personal checks accepted. No credit cards accepted.

Mail search: Turnaround time: 1 to 3 days. A SASE is requested.

Phone search: There is a pre-paid Search Account for addresses only. Call Fiscal Section at 614-752-2091 to establish an account.

Fax search: Records are available only for pre-approved accounts with funds on file.

In person search: There may be a limit on the number of requests processed immediately, most are not available until the next day.

Online search: Ohio offers online access through AAMVAnet. All requesters must comply with a contractual agreement prior to release of data, which complies with DPPA regulations. Fee is $2.00 per record. Call 614-752-7671 for more information. The website offers free access to title records for vehicles and watercraft. No personal informaion is release. Search by ttile number or

ID. Also search at https://www.dps.state.oh.us/atps/.

Other access: Bulk records are available for purchase, per DPPA guidelines.

Accident Reports

Department of Public Safety, OSHP Central Records, 1st Fl, PO Box 182074, Columbus, OH 43218-2074; 614-752-1583, 614-644-9749 (Fax), 8AM-4:45PM.

http://statepatrol.ohio.gov/crash.htm

Indexing & Storage: Records are available for 5 years to present. Records are indexed on computer. It takes 7 to 10 days before new records are available for inquiry. Records are normally destroyed after 5 years.

Searching: OSHP will assist to find correct report, but will not accept phone orders. Include the following in your request-full name, date of accident county of occurrence, or crash number if known. Submitting the driver's license number or SSN is very helpful for reports older than 2001. The following data is not released: Social Security Numbers.

Access by: mail, in person, online.

Fee & Payment: The fee is $4.00 per record. There is a charge for a no record found. Fee payee: Ohio State Highway Patrol Prepayment required. Personal checks accepted. No credit cards accepted.

Mail search: Turnaround time: 3-4 weeks.

In person search: Public access terminals are available in the lobby. Turnaround time is immediate if the record is on file. Assistance is available.

Online search: Crash reports purchased online will be sent to your e-mail account the same day. Crash photographs purchased online will be sent in the mail. Online crash reports are available for crashes that occurred on or after August 5, 2001. Crash reports prior to August 5, 2001 are available by mail-in request. Reports must be purchased using a credit card.

Vessel Ownership, Vessel Registration

NRD-Division of Watercraft, Titles and Registration, 4435 Fountain Square Dr Bldg A, Columbus, OH 43224-1362; 614-265-6480, 877-426-2837 (Titles), 614-267-8883 (Fax), 8AM-5PM.

www.dnr.state.oh.us/watercraft/

Note: Liens are included on title histories, but you must first request the lien history in writing.

Indexing & Storage: Records are available from 1960 to the present. Records are indexed on computer for the last 3 years. Any boat operated on public waters must be registered. All boats 14 ft or longer or having a 10+ hp motor must be titled.

Searching: To search, one of the following is required: name, hull ID #, registration #, or serial #. The following data is not released: Social Security Numbers.

Access by: mail, phone, fax, in person, online.

Fee & Payment: There is no search fee for registration records. There is a $2.00 fee for a title search. Fee payee: Division of Watercraft. Prepayment required. Personal checks accepted. No credit cards accepted.

Mail search: Turnaround time: 2 to 4 days. No SASE is required.

Phone search: There is a limit of five names per call for registration information.

Fax search: Same criteria as mail searching.

In person search: Simple requests may be processed while you wait.

Online search: No online access available.

Voter Registration

Secretary of State, Elections Division, 180 E Broad St, 15th Fl, Columbus, OH 43215; 614-466-2585, 614-752-4360 (Fax), 8AM-5PM.

www.state.oh.us/sos

Note: Records are open. This agency will sell the votor file to individuals and businesses. Single name search requests are better served at the local level.

Indexing & Storage: Records are available for 6 years. It takes 1 day before new records are available for inquiry.

Searching: The agency suggests that all individual requests be done at the county Board of Elections.

Access by: mail, in person.

Fee & Payment: There is no fee, unless lists or extensive research is involved. Fee payee: Secretary of State. Prepayment required. No credit cards accepted.

Mail search: Turnaround time: 1 week to 10 days. No SASE is required.

In person search: The state is not prepared to handle look-ups, but will assist as necessary.

Other access: Records may be purchased in a variety of formats. Lists are arranged in alpha order within precinct, unless otherwise indicated.

For further information, contact Audrey Hatchett at 614-466-8895.

GED Certificates

GED Transcript Office, 25 S Front St, 1st Fl, Columbus, OH 43215-4183; 614-466-1577, 614-752-9445 (Fax), 8AM-4:30PM.

www.ode.state.oh.us/curriculum-assessment/assessment/ged

Indexing & Storage: Records are available from 1984 to present. Prior records are on microfilm. It takes 3 to 4 weeks before new records are available for inquiry.

Searching: Include the following in your request-date of birth, Social Security Number, signed release, approx date of test. DOB, city of test, previous names are helpful.

Access by: mail, fax, in person.

Fee & Payment: There is no fee for a verification, a $5.00 fee is charged for a copy of a transcript. Fee payee: Oh Testing Services Prepayment required. Personal checks and credit cards not accepted.

Mail search: Turnaround time: 7 to 10 days. No SASE is required.

Fax search: Same criteria as mail searching.

In person search: Simple requests may be processed while you wait.

Hunting and Fishing License Information

Ohio Department of Natural Resources, Division of Wildlife, 1840 Belcher Drive, Columbus, OH 43224; 614-265-6300, 8AM-5PM.

www.dnr.state.oh.us/wildlife/default.htm

Indexing & Storage: Records are available from 1999 forward. It takes 2 days before new records are available for inquiry. Records are normally destroyed after 3 years.

Searching: Request must be in writing, suggest placing "Attn: Cheryl" on envelope. Include the following in your request-SSN, DOB. The agency will charge up to a fee for $50.00 for searching records.

Access by: mail.

Fee & Payment: There is no fee.

Mail search: Turnaround time: 1 to 3 days.

Ohio State Licensing Agencies

Licenses Searchable Online

Accounting Firm #1	http://acc.ohio.gov/lookup.html
Acupuncturist #28	http://license.ohio.gov/lookup/default.asp
Anesthesiologist Assistant #28	http://license.ohio.gov/lookup/default.asp
Architect #2	www.arc.ohio.gov//license/query.asp
Athletic Trainer #29	www.state.oh.us/scripts/pyt/query.asp
Attorney (Bar Assoc./by type) #13	www.ohiobar.org/memdir/
Audiologist/Audiologist Aide #8	http://license.ohio.gov/lookup/
Backflow Prevention Assembly Insp. #34	www.com.state.oh.us/odoc/dic/default.htm
Backflow Tester #14	www.com.state.oh.us/ODOC/dic/plans/scripts/bkfloqy.htm
Barber School #26	www.state.oh.us/brb/barbsch.htm
Boiler Contractor #14	www.com.state.oh.us/odoc/dic/scripts/boilerctrqy.htm
Boiler Contractor #3	www.com.state.oh.us/odoc/dic/scripts/boilerctrqy.htm
Cemetery #15	www.com.state.oh.us/odoc/real/scripts/searchcriteria.htm
Check Cashing Service #17	https://www.com.state.oh.us/dfi/scripts/cnfnqy.htm
Check Lending Service #17	https://www.com.state.oh.us/dfi/scripts/cnfnqy.htm
Child Care Type A or B House #19	www.odjfs.state.oh.us/cdc/query.asp
Child Day Care Facility #19	www.odjfs.state.oh.us/cdc/query.asp
Chiropractor #9	http://156.63.245.111/default.htm
Clinical Nurse Specialist #6	www.nursing.ohio.gov/verification.stm
Coil Cleaner (Liquor/Beverage) #27	www.state.oh.us/com/liquor/liquor13.htm
Consumer Finance Company #17	https://www.com.state.oh.us/dfi/scripts/cnfnqy.htm
Contractor #14	www.com.state.oh.us/odoc/dic/scripts/ociebqy.htm
Cosmetic Therapist #28	http://license.ohio.gov/lookup/default.asp
Cosmetologist/Managing Cosmetologist #4	http://license.ohio.gov
Cosmetology Instructor #4	http://license.ohio.gov
Counselor #11	http://cswmft.ohio.gov/query.asp
Day Camp, Childrens #19	www.odjfs.state.oh.us/cdc/query.asp
Dental Assistant Radiologist #33	www.state.oh.us/scripts/den/query.stm
Dentist / Dental Hygienist #33	www.state.oh.us/scripts/den/query.stm
Dialysis Technician #6	www.nursing.ohio.gov/verification.stm
Dietitian #31	www.dietetics.ohio.gov
Drug Wholesaler/Distributor #7	www.ohio.gov/pharmacy/license.htm
Electrical Safety Inspector #3	www.com.state.oh.us/odoc/dic/default.htm
Electrician #14	www.com.state.oh.us/odoc/dic/scripts/ociebqy.htm
Emergency Medical Technician / Instructor #22	https://www.dps.state.oh.us/ems/cert.asp
Engineer #23	www.ohiopeps.org/search.html
Engineering/Surveying Company #23	www.ohiopeps.org/search.html
Esthetician/Managing Esthetician #4	http://license.ohio.gov
Fire Protection System Designer #3	www.com.state.oh.us/odoc/dic/default.htm
Firefighter/Firefighter Instructor #22	https://www.dps.state.oh.us/ems/cert.asp
Foreign Real Estate Property #15	www.com.state.oh.us/odoc/real/scripts/searchcriteria.htm
Heating/Refrigeration (HVAC) #14	www.com.state.oh.us/odoc/dic/scripts/ociebqy.htm
Horse Racing Facility/Owner #41	www.state.oh.us/rac/license.stm
Hydronic-related Occupation #14	www.com.state.oh.us/odoc/dic/scripts/ociebqy.htm
Insurance Agent #20	www.ohioinsurance.gov/ConsumServ/ocs/agentloc.asp
Landscape Architect #2	www.arc.ohio.gov//license/query.asp
Legislative Agent/Agent Employer #30	www.jlec-olig.state.oh.us/agent_search_form.cfm
Liquor Distributor #27	www.state.oh.us/com/liquor/liquor15.htm
Liquor License #27	www.state.oh.us/com/liquor/phone.txt
Liquor License Cancellation #27	www.liquorcontrol.ohio.gov/canceled.txt
Liquor Permit #27	www.liquorcontrol.ohio.gov/liquor5a.html
Liquor Store #27	www.liquorcontrol.ohio.gov/phone.txt
Lobbyist/Lobbyist Employer #30	www.jlec-olig.state.oh.us/agent_search_form.cfm
Lottery Retailer #35	www.ohiolottery.com/frameset/games/retailer.html
Manicuring/Esthetician Instructor #4	http://license.ohio.gov
Manicurist/Managing Manicurist #4	http://license.ohio.gov
Marriage and Family Therapist #11	http://cswmft.ohio.gov/query.asp
Massage Therapist #28	http://license.ohio.gov/lookup/default.asp
Mechanotherapist #28	http://license.ohio.gov/lookup/default.asp
Medical Doctor #28	http://license.ohio.gov/lookup/default.asp

Midwife Nurse #6 .... www.nursing.ohio.gov/verification.stm
Mortgage Broker #17 .... https://www.com.state.oh.us/dfi/scripts/cnfnqy.htm
Naprapath #28 .... http://license.ohio.gov/lookup/default.asp
Nurse Anesthetist #6 .... www.nursing.ohio.gov/verification.stm
Nurse Practitioner #6 .... www.nursing.ohio.gov/verification.stm
Nurse-RN/LPN #6 .... www.nursing.ohio.gov/verification.stm
Occupational Therapist/Assistant #29 .... www.state.oh.us/scripts/pyt/query.asp
Ocularist/Ocularist Apprentice #39 .... www.license.ohio.gov/lookup/
Optical Dispenser #39 .... www.license.ohio.gov/lookup/
Optician/Optician Apprentice #39 .... www.license.ohio.gov/lookup/
Optometrist #37 .... www.optometry.ohio.gov/query.asp
Osteopathic Physician #28 .... http://license.ohio.gov/lookup/default.asp
Pawnbroker #17 .... https://www.com.state.oh.us/dfi/scripts/cnfnqy.htm
Pesticide Applicator Business #40 .... www.ohioagriculture.gov/pubs/divs/plnt/plnt-licensing.stm
Pesticide-related Occupation #40 .... www.ohioagriculture.gov/pubs/divs/plnt/plnt-licensing.stm
Pharmacist/Pharmacy/Pharmacy Dispensary #7 www.ohio.gov/pharmacy/license.htm
Physical Therapist/Assistant #29 .... www.state.oh.us/scripts/pyt/query.asp
Physician Assistant #28 .... http://license.ohio.gov/lookup/default.asp
Plumber #14 .... www.com.state.oh.us/odoc/dic/scripts/ociebqy.htm
Plumbing Inspector #3 .... www.com.state.oh.us/odoc/dic/default.htm
Podiatrist #28 .... http://license.ohio.gov/lookup/default.asp
Polygraph Examiner #46 .... http://polygraph.org/states/oape/directory.htm
Precious Metals Dealer #17 .... https://www.com.state.oh.us/dfi/scripts/cnfnqy.htm
Premium Finance Company #17 .... https://www.com.state.oh.us/dfi/scripts/cnfnqy.htm
Prescriptive Authority #6 .... www.nursing.ohio.gov/verification.stm
Private Investigator #15 .... www.com.state.oh.us/odoc/real/scripts/searchcriteria.htm
Psychologist #36 .... www.psychology.ohio.gov/LicenseLookup/query.asp
Public Accountant-CPA #1 .... http://acc.ohio.gov/lookup.html
Racetrack-related Occupation #41 .... www.state.oh.us/rac/license.stm
Racing Permit #41 .... www.state.oh.us/rac/license.stm
Real Estate Agent/Broker/Sales #15 .... www.com.state.oh.us/odoc/real/scripts/searchcriteria.htm
Real Estate Appraiser #15 .... www.com.state.oh.us/odoc/real/scripts/searchcriteria.htm
Respiratory Therapist/Student #42 .... www.state.oh.us/scripts/rsp/license/query.asp
Savings & Loan Association #17 .... https://www.com.state.oh.us/dfi/scripts/cnfnqy.htm
Savings Bank #17 .... https://www.com.state.oh.us/dfi/scripts/cnfnqy.htm
School Psychologist #36 .... www.psychology.ohio.gov/LicenseLookup/query.asp
Securities Filing #16 .... www.securities.state.oh.us/secu_apps/offering/disclaimer.aspx
Security Guard #15 .... www.com.state.oh.us/odoc/real/scripts/searchcriteria.htm
Social Worker #11 .... http://cswmft.ohio.gov/query.asp
Speech Pathologist/Audiologist #8 .... http://license.ohio.gov/lookup/
Storage Tank Corrective Action #34 .... https://www.com.state.oh.us/odoc/sfm/bustr/CorrectiveActions.htm
Surveyor, Land #23 .... www.ohiopeps.org/search.html
Teacher/Teacher's Aide #43 .... https://www.ode.state.oh.us/Teaching-Profession/Teacher/Certification_Licensure/certifact.asp
Underground Storage Tank #34 .... https://www.com.state.oh.us/odoc/sfm/bustr/PublicInquiry.htm
Underground Tank Inspector/Installer #34 .... https://www.com.state.oh.us/odoc/sfm/bustr/PDFs/Data/WEBInspectorList
Underground Tank Instructor #34 .... https://www.com.state.oh.us/odoc/sfm/bustr/PDFs/TrainerApprovedlist.xls
Veterinarian/Veterinary Technician #45 .... www.ovmlb.ohio.gov/

Ohio Licensing Quick Finder

Accounting Firm #1 614-466-4135
Acupuncturist #28 614-466-3934
Adoption Agency #19 614-466-9274
Adult Care Home #18 614-466-7713
Airline Liquor Permit #27 614-644-2360
Anesthesiologist Assistant #28 614-466-3934
Architect #2 614-466-2316
Athlete Agent #32 216-518-9497
Athletic Trainer #29 614-466-3774
Attorney (Bar Assoc./by type) #13 800-282-6556
Attorney (State) #44 614-461-1553
Audiologist/Audiologist Aide #8 614-466-3145
Backflow Prevention Inspector #34 614-644-2223
Backflow Tester #14 614-644-2223
Bank #17 614-728-8400
Barber #26 614-466-5003
Barber Instructor #26 614-466-5003

Barber School / Shop #26 614-466-5003
Bedding/Furniture Dealer/Dist. #38 614-644-2233
Bedding/Furniture Mfg/Renovator #38 . 614-644-2233
Boiler Contractor #14 614-644-3493
Boiler Contractor #3 614-644-2613
Boiler Inspector #34 614-644-2223
Boiler Operator #34 614-644-2223
Boxer/Boxing Professional #32 216-518-9497
Boxing Event #32 216-518-9497
Building Inspector #3 614-644-2613
Building Official #3 614-644-2613
Cemetery #15 216-787-3100
Check Cashing Service #17 614-728-8400
Check Lending Service #17 614-728-8400
Child Care Type A or B House #19 614-466-3822
Child Day Care Facility #19 614-466-3822
Children's Residential Center #19 614-466-5392

Children's Services Agency #19 614-466-5392
Chiropractor #9 614-644-7032
Clinical Nurse Specialist #6 614-466-3947
Coil Cleaner (Liquor/Beverage) #27 614-644-2360
Consumer Finance Company #17 614-728-8400
Contractor #14 614-644-3493
Cosmetic Therapist #28 614-466-3934
Cosmetologist/Mgr'g Cosmetologist #4 614-644-3834
Cosmetology Instructor #4 614-644-3834
Counselor #11 614-466-0912
Crematory #5 614-466-4252
Dairy Farm #12 614-466-5550
Day Camp, Childrens #19 614-466-3822
Dental Assistant Radiologist #33 614-466-2580
Dental Hygienist #33 614-466-2580
Dentist #33 614-466-2580
Dialysis Technician #6 614-466-3947

Dietitian #31	614-466-3291
Drug Wholesaler/Distributor #7	614-466-4143
Electrical Safety Inspector #3	614-644-2613
Electrical Safety Trainee #3	614-644-2613
Electrician #14	614-644-3493
Elevator Inspector #38	614-644-3524
Embalmer/Embalming Facility #5	614-466-4252
Emergency Medical Tech. Instr. #22	614-466-9447
Emergency Medical Technician #22	614-466-9447
Engineer #23	614-466-3650
Engineering/Surveying Company #23	614-466-3650
Esthetician/Managing Esthetician #4	614-644-3834
Explosives #34	614-752-7126
Family Foster Home #19	614-466-5392
Fire Alarm & Detection Inspector #34	614-644-7126
Fire Extinguisher Inspector #34	614-644-7126
Fire Extinguisher Equip. Inspector #34	614-644-7126
Fire Protection System Designer #3	614-644-2613
Firefighter/Firefighter Instructor #22	614-466-9447
Fireworks Exhibitor/Assistant #34	614-752-7126
Fishing Guide #21	419-625-8062
Foreign Real Estate Property #15	614-466-4100
Funeral Director/Funeral Home #5	614-466-4252
Group Home Operator #19	614-466-5392
Health Care Facility #18	614-466-7713
Hearing Aid Dealer/Fitter #25	614-466-5215
Heating/Refrigeration (HVAC) #14	614-644-3493
Horse Racing Facility/Owner #41	614-466-2757
Hotel/Motel #34	614-752-7126
Hydronic-related Occupation #14	614-644-3493
Independent Living Arranger #19	614-466-9274
Insurance Agent #20	614-644-2665
Insurance Broker, Non-Resident #20	614-644-2665
Insurance Solicitor #20	614-644-2665
Investment Advisor/Advisor Rep. #16	614-644-3466
Landscape Architect #2	614-466-2316
Legislative Agent/Agent Employer #30	614-728-5100
Liquor Distributor #27	614-644-2360
Liquor License #27	614-644-2360
Liquor License Cancellation #27	614-644-2360
Liquor Permit #27	614-644-2360
Liquor Store #27	614-644-2360
Lobbyist/Lobbyist Employer #30	614-728-5100
Lottery Retailer #35	216-787-3200
Manicuring/Esthetician Instructor #4	614-644-3834
Manicurist/Managing Manicurist #4	614-644-3834
Marriage and Family Therapist #11	614-466-0912
Massage Therapist #28	614-466-3934
Mechanical Inspector #3	614-644-2613
Mechanotherapist #28	614-466-3934
Medical Doctor #28	614-466-3934
Midwife Nurse #6	614-466-3947
Milk Hauler #12	614-466-5550
Milk Processor/Producer/Plant #12	614-466-5550
Milk Tester/Sampler #12	614-466-5550
Mortgage Broker #17	614-728-8400
Naprapath #28	614-466-3934
Notary Public #10	614-644-4559
Nurse Anesthetist #6	614-466-3947
Nurse Practitioner #6	614-466-3947
Nurse-RN/LPN #6	614-466-3947
Nursing Home #18	614-466-7713
Nursing Home Administrator #18	614-466-5114
Occupational Therapist/Assistant #29	614-466-3774
Ocularist/Ocularist Apprentice #39	614-466-9709
Optical Dispenser #39	614-466-9709
Optician/Optician Apprentice #39	614-466-9709
Optometrist #7	614-466-5115
Osteopathic Physician #28	614-466-3934
Pawnbroker #17	614-728-8400
Pesticide Applicator Business #40	614-728-6987
Pesticide-related Occupation #40	614-728-6987
Pharmacist #7	614-466-4143
Pharmacy/Pharmacy Dispensary #7	614-466-4143
Physical Therapist/Assistant #29	614-466-3774
Physician Assistant #28	614-466-3934
Plan Examiner #3	614-644-2613
Plumber #14	614-644-3493
Plumbing Inspector #3	614-644-2613
Podiatrist #28	614-466-3934
Polygraph Examiner #46	614-645-4174
Precious Metals Dealer #17	614-728-8400
Premium Finance Company #17	614-466-2221
Prescriptive Authority #6	614-466-3947
Pressure Piping Inspector #34	614-644-2223
Private Investigator #15	614-466-4130
Psychologist #36	614-466-8808
Public Accountant-CPA #1	614-466-4135
Public Adjuster #20	614-644-2665
Racetrack-related Occupation #41	614-466-2757
Racing Permit #41	614-466-2757
Real Estate Agent/Broker/Sales #15	614-466-4100
Real Estate Appraiser #15	216-787-3100
Residential Care Facility #18	614-466-7713
Residential Parenting Organization #19	614-466-9274
Respiratory Therapist/Student #42	614-752-9218
Savings & Loan Association #17	614-728-8400
Savings Bank #17	614-728-8400
School Counselor #43	614-466-3593
School Principal/Administrator #43	614-466-3593
School Psychologist #36	614-466-8808
School Treasurer/Business Mgr. #43	614-466-3593
Scientific Collection Permit #21	614-265-6320
Securities Filing #16	614-644-3466
Securities Salesperson/Dealer #16	614-644-3466
Security Guard #15	614-466-4130
Social Worker #11	614-466-0912
Solid Waste Facility Operator #24	614-644-2621
Speech Pathologist Aide #8	614-466-3145
Speech Pathologist/Audiologist #8	614-466-3145
Sprinkler Equipment Inspector #34	614-644-7126
Sprinkler Inspector #3	614-644-2613
Sprinkler, Fire Alarm, Hazardous Designer #3	614-644-2613
Steam Engineer #34	614-644-2223
Steam, Stationary #34	614-644-2223
Storage Tank Corrective Action #34	614-752-7921
Surveyor, Land #23	614-466-3650
Teacher/Teacher's Aide #43	614-466-3593
Tough-Person Promoter #32	216-518-9497
Tour Promoter #34	614-644-2223
Travel Agent #34	614-644-2223
Underground Tan-related Occupation #34	614-752-7921
Veterinarian/Veterinary Tech. #45	614-644-5281
Water Supply Equipment Inspct. #34	614-644-2223

Ohio Licensing Agency Information

1 Accountancy Board of Ohio, 77 S High St, 18th Fl, Columbus, OH 43215-6128; 614-466-4135, Fax: 614-466-2628.
www.state.oh.us/acc
Search Database at http://acc.ohio.gov/lookup.html

2 Architects Board of Ohio, 77 S High St, 16th Fl, Columbus, OH 43266-0303;
614-466-2316, Fax: 614-644-9048.
www.arc.ohio.gov Email: cmharch@aol.com
Search Database at
www.arc.ohio.gov//license/query.asp

3 Department of Commerce, Board of Building Standards, 6606 Tussing Rd (PO Box 4009), Reynoldsburg, OH 43068;
614-644-2613, Fax: 614-644-3147.
www.com.state.oh.us/odoc/dic/dicbbs.htm
Email: jwbrant@com.state.oh.us Search Database at
www.com.state.oh.us/odoc/dic/default.htm

4 Board of Cosmetology, Suite 101 Southland Mall, 3700 South High Street, Columbus, OH 43207-4041; 614-466-3834, Fax: 614-466-6880.
http://cos.ohio.gov email: ohiocosbd@cos.state.oh.us
Search Database at http://license.ohio.gov

5 Board of Embalmers & Funeral Directors of Ohio, 77 S High St, 16th Fl, Columbus, OH 43215-6108; 614-466-4252, Fax: 614-728-6825.
www.state.oh.us/fun
Email: oh.emb.bd@exchange.state.oh.us

6 Board of Nursing, 17 S High St #400, Columbus, OH 43215; 614-466-3947, Fax: 614-466-0388.
www.nursing.ohio.gov Search Database at www.nursing.ohio.gov/verification.stm
Note: Must search by license number or SSN. Prescriptive authority needs name or COA#.

7 Board of Pharmacy, 77 S High St, 17th Fl, Columbus, OH 43266-0320;
614-466-4143, Fax: 614-752-4836.
www.wvinsurance.gov
Email: agent.licensing@wvinsurance.gov
Search Database at
www.state.oh.us/pharmacy/license.htm

8 Board of Speech Pathology & Audiology, 77 S High St, 16th Fl, Columbus, OH 43215; 614-466-3145, Fax: 614-995-2286.
www.slpaud.ohio.gov
Email: michael.setty@splaud.state.oh.us
Search Database at
http://license.ohio.gov/lookup/default.asp

9 Chiropractic Board, 77 S High St, 16th Fl, Columbus, OH 43215-6108;
614-644-7032, Fax: 614-752-2539.
www.state.oh.us/chr/
Email: chirobd@mail.peps.state.oh.us
Search Database at
http://156.63.245.111/default.htm

10 Commission Clerk, PO Box 1658, Columbus, OH 43215; 614-644-4559, Fax: 614-644-8820.
www.sos.state.oh.us/sos/Notary_FAQ.htm

11 Counselor & Social Worker Board, 77 S High St, 16th Fl, Columbus, OH 43266-0340;
614-466-0912, Fax: 614-728-7790.
www.state.oh.us/csw Email: csw_hackett@ohio.gov
Search Database at
http://cswmft.ohio.gov/query.asp

12 Department of Agriculture, 8995 E Main St, Reynoldsburg, OH 43068-3399; 614-466-5550, Fax: 614-728-2652.
www.state.oh.us/agr/
Email: agri@odant.agri.state.oh.us

13 State Bar Association, 1700 Lake Shore Dr, Columbus, OH 43204; 800-282-6556, 614-487-2050, Fax: 614-487-1008.
www.ohiobar.org Email: osba@ohiobar.org
Search Database at www.ohiobar.org/memdir/

14 Ohio Department of Commerce, Construction Industry Examination Board, 6606 Tussing Rd, Reynoldsburg, OH 43068-9009;
614-644-3493, Fax: 614-728-1200.
www.com.state.oh.us/odoc/dic/default.htm
Search Database at
www.com.state.oh.us/odoc/dic/scripts/ociebqy.htm

15 Department of Commerce, Division of Real Estate & Professional Licensing, 77 S High St, 20th Fl, Columbus, OH 43215-6133; 614-466-4190, Fax: 614-644-0584. www.com.state.oh.us/real Email: repld@com.state.oh.us   Search Database at www.com.state.oh.us/odoc/real/scripts/searchcriteria.htm

16 Department of Commerce, Division of Securities, 77 S High St, 22nd Fl, Columbus, OH 43215-0548; 614-644-7381, Fax: 614-466-3316. www.securities.state.oh.us

17 Department of Commerce, Division of Financial Institutions, 77 S High St, 21st Fl, Columbus, OH 43266-0121; 614-728-8400, Fax: 614-466-1631. www.com.state.oh.us/dfi/default.htm Email: WebMaster@com.state.oh.us Search Database at https://www.com.state.oh.us/dfi/scripts/cnfnqy.htm

18 Department of Health, Health Care Facility Program, PO Box 118, Columbus, OH 43216-0118; 614-466-5114, Fax: 614-466-0271. www.ohiobenha.org/

19 Office For Children & Families, Bureau of Family Svcs, 255 E Main, 3rd Fl, Columbus, OH 43215; 614-466-9274, Fax: 614-728-6726. http://jfs.ohio.gov/ocf/

20 Department of Insurance, 2100 Stella Ct, Columbus, OH 43215-1067; 614-644-2665, Fax: 614-644-3475. www.ohioinsurance.gov Search Database at www.ohioinsurance.gov/ConsumServ/ocs/agentloc.asp

21 Department of Natural Resources, 1840 Belcher Dr, Columbus, OH 43224; 1-800-945-3543, Fax: 614-262-1143. www.dnr.state.oh.us/wildlife/default.htm

22 Department of Public Safety, Emergency Medical Services Division, PO Box 182073, Columbus, OH 43218-2073; 614-466-9447, Fax: 614-466-9461. http://ems.ohio.gov Email: rnrucker@dps.state.oh.us Search Database at https://www.dps.state.oh.us/ems/cert.asp

23 Engineers & Surveyors Board, 77 S High St, 16th Fl, Rm 1698, Columbus, OH 43266-0314; 614-466-3650, Fax: 614-728-3059. www.ohiopeps.org Email: board@mail.peps.state.oh.us Search Database at www.ohiopeps.org/search.html

24 Hazardous Waste Facility Board, 122 S Front St, Columbus, OH 43215; 614-644-2621, Fax: 614-728-5315. www.epa.state.oh.us/dsiwm

25 Hearing Aid Dealers & Fitters Board, 246 N High St (PO Box 118), Columbus, OH 43216-0118; 614-466-5215, Fax: 614-466-8692. www.odh.state.oh.us/index.asp Email: hearing@gw.odh.state.oh.us

26 Licensing Boards, Barber Board, 77 S High St, 16th Fl, Columbus, OH 43215; 614-466-5003, Fax: 614-387-1694. www.state.oh.us/brb

27 Division of Liquor Control, 6606 Tussing Rd, Reynoldsburg, OH 43068-9005; 614-644-2360, Fax: 614-644-2480. www.state.oh.us/com/liquor/liquororiginal.htm Email: agencyops@liquor.state.oh.us

28 Medical Board of Ohio, 77 S High St, 17th Fl, Columbus, OH 43266-0315; 614-466-3934, Fax: 614-728-5946. www.med.ohio.gov Email: kay.rieve@med.state.oh.us Search Database at http://license.ohio.gov/lookup/default.asp

29 OTPTAT - Occupational Therapy - Physical Therapy Board, 77 S High St, 16th Fl, Columbus, OH 43266-0317; 614-466-3774, Fax: 614-995-0816. www.state.oh.us/pyt Search Database at www.state.oh.us/scripts/pyt/query.asp

30 Office of Legislative Inspector General, 50 W Broad St, #1308, Columbus, OH 43215-3365; 614-728-5100, Fax: 614-728-5074. www.jlec-olig.state.oh.us Email: info@jlec-olig.state.oh.us Search Database at www.jlec-olig.state.oh.us/agent_search_form.cfm

31 Board of Dietetics, 77 S High St, 18th Fl, Columbus, OH 43266-0337; 614-466-3291, Fax: 614-728-0723. www.dietetics.ohio.gov Email: obd_mavko@ohio.gov

32 Boxing Commission, 2545 Belmont Ave, Union Square Plaza, Youngstown, OH 44505; 216-518-9479, Fax: 216-518-9619. Email: paul.amodio@exchange.state.oh.us

33 Dental Board, 77 S High St, 18th Fl, Columbus, OH 43215-6135; 614-466-2580, Fax: 614-752-8995. www.state.oh.us/den Search Database at www.state.oh.us/scripts/den/query.stm

34 Ohio Department of Commerce, Testing and Registration, PO Box 4009, (6606 Tussing Rd), Reynoldsburg, OH 43068-9009; 614-644-2223, Fax: 614-644-2428. www.com.state.oh.us/odoc/dic/default.htm Email: ic@com.state.oh.us Search Database at www.com.state.oh.us/odoc/dic/default.htm

35 Lottery Commission, 615 W Superior Ave, NW Frank J. Lausche Bldg, Cleveland, OH 44113; 216-787-3200, Fax: 216-787-3718. www.ohiolottery.com Email: olcwebmail@olc.state.oh.us Search Database at www.ohiolottery.com/frameset/games/retailer.html

36 State Board of Psychology, 77 S High St, Ste 1830, Columbus, OH 43215-6108; 614-466-8808, Fax: 614-728-7081. www.state.oh.us/psy Email: optometry.board@exchange.state.oh.us Search Database at www.psychology.ohio.gov/LicenseLookup/query.asp Note: If "SP" is part of a license number, that indicates a "school psychologist."

37 Board of Optometry, 77 S High St, 16th Fl, Columbus, OH 43215-6108; 614-466-5115, Fax: 614-644-3937. www.optometry.ohio.gov Email: optometry.board@exchange.state.oh.us Search Database at www.optometry.ohio.gov/query.asp Note: Will sell rosters and labels on disk.

38 Bedding, Stuffed Toys & Upholstered Furniture Div., Industrial Complaince Division; Operations & Maintenance, 6606 Tussing Rd (PO Box 4009), Reynoldsburg, OH 43068-9009; 614-644-3964, Fax: 614-644-8658. www.com.state.oh.us/odoc/dic/dicbedding.htm

39 Optical Dispensers Board, 77 S High St, 16th Fl, Columbus, OH 43215-6108; 614-466-9709, Fax: 614-995-5392. www.optical.ohio.gov Email: ohioopticalboard@hotmail.com Search Database at www.license.ohio.gov/lookup/

40 Pesticide Regulations, 8995 E Main St, Reynoldsburg, OH 43068-3399; 614-728-6200, Fax: 614-728-4235. www.ohioagriculture.gov Search Database at www.ohioagriculture.gov/pubs/divs/plnt/plnt-licensing.stm

41 Racing Commission, 77 S High St, 18th Fl, Columbus, OH 43215-6108; 614-466-2757, Fax: 614-466-1900. www.state.oh.us/rac/keypersonnel.stm Search Database at www.state.oh.us/rac/license.stm

42 Respiratory Care Board, 77 S High St, 16th Fl, Columbus, OH 43215-6108; 614-752-9218, Fax: 614-728-8691. www.state.oh.us/rsp/ Email: rcb.logsdon@rcb.state.oh.us Search Database at www.state.oh.us/scripts/rsp/license/query.asp

43 Department of Education, Office of Certification/Licensure, 25 S Front St, Columbus, OH 43215-4183; 614-466-3593, Fax: 614-466-1999. https://www.ode.state.oh.us Search Database at https://www.ode.state.oh.us/Teaching-Profession/Teacher/Certification_Licensure/certifact.asp

44 Supreme Court, 30 E Broad St, Columbus, OH 43266-0419; 614-466-1553, Fax: 614-728-0930.

45 Veterinary Medical Board, 77 S High St, 16th Fl, Columbus, OH 43266-0116; 614-644-5281, Fax: 614-644-9038. www.ovmlb.ohio.gov/ Email: info@ovmlb.state.oh.us Search Database at www.ovmlb.ohio.gov/ Note: Searching will be available at search site.

46 Association of Polygraph Examiners, c/o Phillip Osborne, Columbus PD, 120 Marconi Blvd. 7th Fl, Columbus, OH 43215; 614-645-4174, Fax: 614-781-0257. http://polygraph.org/states/oape/index.htm Email: posborne@insight.rr.com Search Database at http://polygraph.org/states/oape/directory.htm

Ohio Federal Courts

The following list indicates the district and division name for each county in the state. If the bankruptcy court location is different from the district court, then the location of the bankruptcy court appears in parentheses.

County/Court Cross Reference

County	District	Division
Adams	Southern	Cincinnati
Allen	Northern	Toledo
Ashland	Northern	Cleveland (Canton)
Ashtabula	Northern	Cleveland (Youngstown)
Athens	Southern	Columbus
Auglaize	Northern	Toledo
Belmont	Southern	Columbus
Brown	Southern	Cincinnati
Butler	Southern	Cincinnati (Dayton)
Carroll	Northern	Akron (Canton)
Champaign	Southern	Dayton
Clark	Southern	Dayton
Clermont	Southern	Cincinnati
Clinton	Southern	Cincinnati (Dayton)
Columbiana	Northern	Youngstown
Coshocton	Southern	Columbus
Crawford	Northern	Cleveland (Canton)
Cuyahoga	Northern	Cleveland
Darke	Southern	Dayton
Defiance	Northern	Toledo
Delaware	Southern	Columbus
Erie	Northern	Toledo
Fairfield	Southern	Columbus
Fayette	Southern	Columbus
Franklin	Southern	Columbus
Fulton	Northern	Toledo
Gallia	Southern	Columbus
Geauga	Northern	Cleveland
Greene	Southern	Dayton
Guernsey	Southern	Columbus
Hamilton	Southern	Cincinnati
Hancock	Northern	Toledo
Hardin	Northern	Toledo
Harrison	Southern	Columbus
Henry	Northern	Toledo
Highland	Southern	Cincinnati
Hocking	Southern	Columbus
Holmes	Northern	Akron (Canton)
Huron	Northern	Toledo
Jackson	Southern	Columbus
Jefferson	Southern	Columbus
Knox	Southern	Columbus
Lake	Northern	Cleveland
Lawrence	Southern	Cincinnati
Licking	Southern	Columbus
Logan	Southern	Columbus
Lorain	Northern	Cleveland
Lucas	Northern	Toledo
Madison	Southern	Columbus
Mahoning	Northern	Youngstown
Marion	Northern	Toledo
Medina	Northern	Cleveland (Akron)
Meigs	Southern	Columbus
Mercer	Northern	Toledo
Miami	Southern	Dayton
Monroe	Southern	Columbus
Montgomery	Southern	Dayton
Morgan	Southern	Columbus
Morrow	Southern	Columbus
Muskingum	Southern	Columbus
Noble	Southern	Columbus
Ottawa	Northern	Toledo
Paulding	Northern	Toledo
Perry	Southern	Columbus
Pickaway	Southern	Columbus
Pike	Southern	Columbus
Portage	Northern	Akron
Preble	Southern	Dayton
Putnam	Northern	Toledo
Richland	Northern	Cleveland (Canton)
Ross	Southern	Columbus
Sandusky	Northern	Toledo
Scioto	Southern	Cincinnati
Seneca	Northern	Toledo
Shelby	Southern	Dayton
Stark	Northern	Akron (Canton)
Summit	Northern	Akron
Trumbull	Northern	Youngstown
Tuscarawas	Northern	Akron (Canton)
Union	Southern	Columbus
Van Wert	Northern	Toledo
Vinton	Southern	Columbus
Warren	Southern	Cincinnati (Dayton)
Washington	Southern	Columbus
Wayne	Northern	Akron (Canton)
Williams	Northern	Toledo
Wood	Northern	Toledo
Wyandot	Northern	Toledo

Standards for Federal Courts: The search fee is $20.00 per item (one party name or case number). Certification fee is $7.00 per document. Copy fee is $.50 per page. All fees standard unless noted in profile. Mail Search: always enclose a stamped self addressed envelope unless otherwise noted. Most courts accept fax requests or will suggest a copying/search vendor. Before releasing records, all courts require prepayment unless noted in profile.

Open records are located at the court unless otherwise noted. District courts index by defendant and plaintiff as well as by case number. Bankruptcy courts usually index by debtor and case number. While most courts now have their indexes on computer, many still maintain index card files as well.

The universal PACER sign-up number is 800-676-6856. Find PACER and the Party/Case Index on the Web at http://pacer.psc.uscourts.gov. PACER dial-up access is $.60 per minute. Also, courts offering internet access via RACER, PACER, Web-PACER or the new CM-ECF charge $.07 per page fee unless noted as free.

US District Court

Eastern Division

Akron Division 568 U.S. Courthouse, 2 S Main St, Akron, OH 44308 (courier address: Use mail address for courier delivery) 330-375-5705. www.ohnd.uscourts.gov

Counties: Carroll, Holmes, Portage, Stark, Summit, Tuscarawas, Wayne. Cases filed prior to 1995 for counties in the Youngstown Division may be located here.

Indexing & Storage: New cases available in the index immediately after filing date. Open cases may be located in another division in this district, depending on the judge assigned.

Fee & Payment: Payment may be made by money order, cashier check, personal check. Payee: Clerk, U.S. District Court.

Phone Search: Only docket information available.

In Person Search: Fee charged if court conducts your in person search for you.

PACER: PACER is available online at http://pacer.ohnd.uscourts.gov. Use the CM/ECF system (below) when PACER is phased out. Many cases prior to the indicated dates are also online. Case records go back to January 1, 1990. Records never purged. New records are online after 1 day.

Electronic Filing: Electronic filing information online at http://ecf.ohnd.uscourts.gov

Cleveland Division 801 West Superior Ave, Cleveland, OH 44114-1830 (courier address: Use mail address for courier delivery) 216-357-7000. www.ohnd.uscourts.gov

Counties: Ashland, Ashtabula, Crawford, Cuyahoga, Geauga, Lake, Lorain, Medina, Richland. Cases prior to July 1995 for the counties

of Ashland, Crawford, Medina and Richland are located in the Akron Division. Cases filed prior to 1995 from the counties in the Youngstown Division may be located here.

Indexing & Storage: New cases available in the index immediately after filing date. Open cases may be located in other divisions in this district, depending on the judge assigned.

Fee & Payment: Payment may be made by money order, cashier check, personal check. Payee: Clerk, U.S. District Court.

Phone Search: Only docket information available by phone.

Mail Search: A SASE not required.

In Person Search: Fee charged if court conducts your in person search for you.

PACER: PACER is available online at http://pacer.ohnd.uscourts.gov. Use the CM/ECF system (below) when PACER is phased out. Many cases prior to the indicated dates are also online. Case records go back to January 1, 1990. Records never purged. New records are online after 1 day.

Electronic Filing: Electronic filing information online at http://ecf.ohnd.uscourts.gov

Toledo Division 114 U.S. Courthouse, 1716 Spielbusch, Toledo, OH 43624 (Use mail address for courier delivery); 419-259-6412. www.ohnd.uscourts.gov

Counties: Allen, Auglaize, Defiance, Erie, Fulton, Hancock, Hardin, Henry, Huron, Lucas, Marion, Mercer, Ottawa, Paulding, Putnam, Sandusky, Seneca, Van Wert, Williams, Wood, Wyandot.

Indexing & Storage: New cases available in the index 1 day after filing date.

Fee & Payment: Payment may be made by money order, cashier check, personal check. Payee: Clerk, U.S. District Court.

Phone Search: Only docket information available.

In Person Search: Fee charged if court conducts your in person search for you.

PACER: PACER is available online at http://pacer.ohnd.uscourts.gov. Use the CM/ECF system (below) when PACER is phased out. Many cases prior to the indicated dates are also online. Case records go back to January 1, 1990. Records never purged. New records are online after 1 day.

Electronic Filing: Electronic filing information online at http://ecf.ohnd.uscourts.gov

Youngstown Division 337 Federal Bldg, 125 Market St, Youngstown, OH 44503-1780 (courier address: Use mail address for courier delivery) 330-746-1906, Fax: 330-746-2027. www.ohnd.uscourts.gov

Counties: Columbiana, Mahoning, Trumbull. This division was re-activated in the middle of 1995. Older cases will be found in Akron or Cleveland.

Indexing & Storage: New cases available in the index immediately after filing date. Open cases may also be located in other divisions in this district, depending upon the judge assigned.

Fee & Payment: Payment may be made by money order, cashier check, personal check. Payee: Clerk, U.S. District Court.

Phone Search: Only docket information available.

In Person Search: Fee charged if court conducts your in person search for you.

PACER: PACER is available online at http://pacer.ohnd.uscourts.gov. Use the CM/ECF

system (below) when PACER is phased out. Many cases prior to the indicated dates are also online. Case records go back to January 1, 1990. Records never purged. New records are online after 1 day.

Electronic Filing: Electronic filing information online at http://ecf.ohnd.uscourts.gov

U.S. Bankruptcy Court

Northern District of Ohio

Akron Division 455 U.S. Courthouse, 2 S Main, Akron, OH 44308 (courier address: Use mail address for courier delivery) 330-375-5840. www.ohnb.uscourts.gov

Counties: Medina, Portage, Summit.

Indexing & Storage: Cases indexed by debtor as well as by case number. New cases available in the index 1-2 days after filing date. Case records closed before 1993 were sent to the Chicago Federal Records Center. In Spring 1995, the 1994 closed cases were sent to Dayton.

Fee & Payment: Payment may be made by money order, cashier check, personal check, Visa or Mastercard. Payee: Clerk, U.S. Bankruptcy Court.

Phone Search: Automated voice case information service (VCIS) is available. Call VCIS at 800-898-6899 or 330-489-4731.

In Person Search: Fee charged if court conducts your in person search for you.

PACER: PACER is available online at http://pacer.ohnb.uscourts.gov. Records purged only up to September 1990. New civil records are online after 2 days.

Electronic Filing: Electronic filing information online at https://ecf.ohnb.uscourts.gov

Canton Division Frank T Bow Federal Bldg, 201 Cleveland Ave SW, Canton, OH 44702 (courier address: Use mail address for courier delivery) 330-489-4426, Fax: 330-489-4434. www.ohnb.uscourts.gov

Counties: Ashland, Carroll, Crawford, Holmes, Richland, Stark, Tuscarawas, Wayne.

Indexing & Storage: Cases indexed by debtor as well as by case number. New cases available in the index 48 hours after filing date. Records are indexed on computer from 1985 to the present. Records are indexed on index cards from 1982 to 1984, and also journalized in books from 1984 to 1990. Prior to 1995, closed case records were sent to the Chicago Federal Records Center.

Fee & Payment: Payment may be made by money order, cashier check, personal check, Visa or Mastercard. Debtor's checks are not accepted. Payee: Clerk, U.S. Bankruptcy Court.

Phone Search: Automated voice case information service (VCIS) is available. Call VCIS at 800-898-6899 or 330-489-4731.

In Person Search: Fee charged if court conducts your in person search for you.

PACER: PACER is available online at http://pacer.ohnb.uscourts.gov. Records purged only up to September 1990. New civil records are online after 2 days.

Electronic Filing: Electronic filing information online at https://ecf.ohnb.uscourts.gov

Cleveland Division Key Tower, Room 3001, 127 Public Square, Cleveland, OH 44114 (courier address: Use mail address for courier delivery) 216-522-4373. www.ohnb.uscourts.gov

Counties: Cuyahoga, Geauga, Lake, Lorain.

Indexing & Storage: Cases indexed by debtor as well as by case number. New cases available in the index 2 days after filing date. Records are also indexed on microfiche. Prior to 1995, closed case records were sent to the Chicago Federal Records Center.

Fee & Payment: Payment may be made by money order, personal check. Debtor's checks are not accepted. Payee: Clerk, U.S. Bankruptcy Court.

Phone Search: Automated voice case information service (VCIS) is available. Call VCIS at 800-898-6899 or 330-489-4731.

In Person Search: Fee charged if court conducts your in person search for you. Outside copy service available.

PACER: PACER is available online at http://pacer.ohnb.uscourts.gov. Records purged only up to September 1990. New civil records are online after 2 days.

Electronic Filing: Electronic filing information online at https://ecf.ohnb.uscourts.gov

Toledo Division Room 411, 1716 Spielbusch Ave, Toledo, OH 43624 (courier address: Use mail address for courier delivery) 419-259-6440. www.ohnb.uscourts.gov

Counties: Allen, Auglaize, Defiance, Erie, Fulton, Hancock, Hardin, Henry, Huron, Lucas, Marion, Mercer, Ottawa, Paulding, Putnam, Sandusky, Seneca, Van Wert, Williams, Wood, Wyandot.

Indexing & Storage: Cases indexed by debtor as well as by case number. New cases available in the index 24 hours after filing date. Prior to 1995, closed case records were sent to the Chicago Federal Records Center.

Fee & Payment: Payment may be made by money order, cashier check, business check, Visa or Mastercard. Personal checks are not accepted. Payee: Clerk, U.S. Bankruptcy Court.

Phone Search: Automated voice case information service (VCIS) is available. Call VCIS at 800-898-6899 or 330-489-4731.

In Person Search: Fee charged if court conducts your in person search for you.

PACER: PACER is available online at http://pacer.ohnb.uscourts.gov. Records purged only up to September 1990. New civil records are online after 2 days.

Electronic Filing: Electronic filing information online at https://ecf.ohnb.uscourts.gov

Youngstown Division U.S. Courthouse, 10 East Commerce Street, Youngstown, OH 44501, 330-746-7027. www.ohnb.uscourts.gov

Counties: Ashtabula, Columbiana, Mahoning, Trumbull.

Indexing & Storage: Cases indexed by debtor and creditors as well as by case number. New cases available in the index 24 hours after filing date. Prior to 1995, closed cases were sent to the Chicago Federal Records Center. Now case records are sent to the Dayton Federal Records Center every few years.

Fee & Payment: Payment may be made by money order, cashier check, business check, Visa or

Mastercard. Personal checks are not accepted. Payee: Clerk, U.S. Bankruptcy Court.

Phone Search: Automated voice case information service (VCIS) is available. Call VCIS at 800-898-6899 or 330-489-4731.

Mail Search: A SASE not required.

In Person Search: Fee charged if court conducts your in person search for you.

PACER: PACER is available online at http://pacer.ohnb.uscourts.gov. Records purged only up to September 1990. New civil records are online after 2 days.

Electronic Filing: Electronic filing information online at https://ecf.ohnb.uscourts.gov

U.S. District Court

Southern District of Ohio

Cincinnati Division Clerk, U.S. District Court, Potter Stewart Courthouse Rm 324, 100 E 5th St, Cincinnati, OH 45202 (courier address: Use mail address for courier delivery) 513-564-7500, Fax: 513-564-7505. www.ohsd.uscourts.gov

Counties: Adams, Brown, Butler, Clermont, Clinton, Hamilton, Highland, Lawrence, Scioto, Warren.

Indexing & Storage: New cases available in the index immediately after filing date.

Fee & Payment: Payment may be made by money order, cashier check, personal check. Give FedEx account number for expedited copy delivery. Payee: Clerk, U.S. District Court.

Phone Search: Only docket information available by phone.

Mail Search: A SASE not required.

In Person Search: Fee charged if court conducts your in person search for you.

PACER: PACER is available online at http://pacer.ohsd.uscourts.gov. Case records go back to 1994. Records never purged. New records are online after 1 day.

Electronic Filing: Electronic filing information online at https://ecf.ohsd.uscourts.gov

Columbus Division Office of the clerk, Room 260, 85 Marconi Blvd, Columbus, OH 43215 (Use mail address for courier delivery) 614-719-3000, Fax: 614-469-5953. www.ohsd.uscourts.gov

Counties: Athens, Belmont, Coshocton, Delaware, Fairfield, Fayette, Franklin, Gallia, Guernsey, Harrison, Hocking, Jackson, Jefferson, Knox, Licking, Logan, Madison, Meigs, Monroe, Morgan, Morrow, Muskingum, Noble, Perry, Pickaway, Pike, Ross, Union, Vinton, Washington.

Indexing & Storage: New cases available in the index 1-2 days after filing date. Records are also indexed on microfiche back to 1982. District wide searches are available from this division.

Fee & Payment: Payment may be made by money order, cashier check, business check. Personal checks are not accepted. Payee: Clerk, U.S. District Court.

Phone Search: Only docket information available by phone.

In Person Search: Fee charged if court conducts your in person search for you.

PACER: PACER is available online at http://pacer.ohsd.uscourts.gov. Case records go back to 1994. Records never purged. New records are online after 1 day.

Electronic Filing: Electronic filing information online at https://ecf.ohsd.uscourts.gov

Dayton Division Federal Bldg, 200 W 2nd, Room 712, Dayton, OH 45402 (courier address: Use mail address for courier delivery) 937-512-1400. www.ohsd.uscourts.gov

Counties: Champaign, Clark, Darke, Greene, Miami, Montgomery, Preble, Shelby.

Indexing & Storage: New cases available in the index 1 day after filing date. Records are also indexed on microfiche. The computer is only valid for cases that were open and pending from 1/90 to present. A view box is available to the public for cases filed for the present day that have not been entered into the computer.

Fee & Payment: Payment may be made by money order, cashier check, business check. Personal checks are not accepted. The Clerk's office will not respond to telephone requests that involve copywork. The searcher must provide a wide envelope for return of documents or, if documents are bulky, the searcher must provide access for bulk mailing. Payee: Clerk, U.S. District Court.

Phone Search: Over the phone, this court will only reveal whether a case has been filed.

In Person Search: Fee charged if court conducts your in person search for you.

PACER: PACER is available online at http://pacer.ohsd.uscourts.gov. Case records go back to 1994. Records never purged. New records are online after 1 day.

Electronic Filing: Electronic filing information online at https://ecf.ohsd.uscourts.gov

U.S. Bankruptcy Court

Southern District of Ohio

Cincinnati Division Atrium Two, Suite 800, 221 E Fourth St, Cincinnati, OH 45202 (courier address: Use mail address for courier delivery) 513-684-2572. www.ohsb.uscourts.gov

Counties: Adams, Brown, Clermont, Hamilton, Highland, Lawrence, Scioto and a part of Butler.

Indexing & Storage: Cases indexed by debtor as well as by case number. New cases available in the index 2 days after filing date. Prior to 1993, closed case records were sent to the Chicago Federal Records Center.

Fee & Payment: Payment may be made by money order, cashier check. Business checks are not accepted, Visa, Mastercard. Personal checks are not accepted. Credit cards are accepted only from law firms. Debtor checks are not accepted. Payee: Clerk, U.S. Bankruptcy Court.

Phone Search: Only docket information available by phone. Automated voice case information service (VCIS) is available. Call VCIS at 800-726-1004 or 937-225-2544.

In Person Search: Fee charged if court conducts your in person search for you.

PACER: PACER is available online at http://pacer.ohsb.uscourts.gov. Records purged every six months. New civil records are online after 1 day.

Electronic Filing: Electronic filing information online at https://ecf.ohsb.uscourts.gov

Columbus Division
170 N High St, Columbus, OH 43215 (courier address: Use mail address for courier delivery) 614-469-6638. www.ohsb.uscourts.gov

Counties: Athens, Belmont, Coshocton, Delaware, Fairfield, Fayette, Franklin, Gallia, Guernsey, Harrison, Hocking, Jackson, Jefferson, Knox, Licking, Logan, Madison, Meigs, Monroe, Morgan, Morrow, Muskingum, Noble, Perry, Pickaway, Pike, Ross, Union, Vinton, Washington.

Indexing & Storage: Cases indexed by as well as by case number. New cases available in the index 1 day after filing date. Prior to 1993, closed cases were sent to the Chicago Federal Records Facility.

Fee & Payment: Payment may be made by money order, cashier check, business check. Personal checks are not accepted. Debtor's checks are not accepted. Payee: Clerk, U.S. Bankruptcy Court.

Phone Search: Automated voice case information service (VCIS) is available. Call VCIS at 800-726-1006 or 513-225-2562.

Mail Search: A SASE not required.

In Person Search: Permitted. Court also offers on-site copy service to provide copies from case records, fee not to exceed $.50 per page. Call West Coast Copy Svc., 614-228-8812.

PACER: PACER is available online at http://pacer.ohsb.uscourts.gov. Records purged every six months. New civil records are online after 1 day.

Electronic Filing: Electronic filing information online at https://ecf.ohsb.uscourts.gov

Dayton Division
120 W 3rd St, Dayton, OH 45402 (Use mail address for courier delivery) 937-225-2516. www.ohsb.uscourts.gov

Counties: Butler, Champaign, Clark, Clinton, Darke, Greene, Miami, Montgomery, Preble, Shelby, Warren; parts of Butler County are handled by Cincinnati Division.

Indexing & Storage: Cases indexed by debtor as well as by case number. New cases available in the index 1 day after filing date. Cases closed before June 1991 were sent to the Chicago Federal Records Facility.

Fee & Payment: Payment may be made by money order, cashier check, in-state business check. Personal checks are not accepted. Debtor's checks are not accepted. Payee: Clerk, U.S. Bankruptcy Court.

Phone Search: Only docket information available by phone. Automated voice case information service (VCIS) is available. Call VCIS at 800-726-1004 or 937-225-2544.

In Person Search: Fee charged if court conducts your in person search for you.

PACER: PACER is available online at http://pacer.ohsb.uscourts.gov. Records purged every six months. New civil records are online after 1 day.

Electronic Filing: Electronic filing information online at https://ecf.ohsb.uscourts.gov

Ohio County Courts

Court	Jurisdiction	No. of Courts	How Organized
Court of Common Pleas*	General	88	county
County Courts*	Limited	47	
Municipal Courts*	Municipal	118	
Mayors Courts	Municipal	400	
Court of Claims	Special	1	

* Profiled in this Sourcebook.

Court	CIVIL								
	Tort	Contract	Real Estate	Min. Claim	Max. Claim	Small Claims	Estate	Eviction	Domestic Relations
Court of Common Pleas*	X	X	X	$3000/ $10,000	No Max		X		X
County Courts*	X	X	X	$0	$15,000	$3000		X	
Municipal Courts*	X	X	X	$0	$15,000	$3000		X	
Mayors Courts									
Court of Claims					No Max				

Court	CRIMINAL				
	Felony	Misdemeanor	DWI/DUI	Preliminary Hearing	Juvenile
Court of Common Pleas*	X		Juvenile		X
County Courts*		X	X	X	
Municipal Courts*		X	X	X	
Mayors Courts		X	X		
Court of Claims					

ADMINISTRATION   Administrative Director, Supreme Court of Ohio, 30 E Broad St, 3rd Fl, Columbus, OH, 43266-0419; 614-466-2653, Fax: 614-752-8736. www.sconet.state.oh.us

COURT STRUCTURE   The Court of Common Pleas is the general jurisdiction court and County Courts have limited jurisdiction. Effective July 1, 1997, the dollar limits for civil cases in County and Municipal Courts were raised as follows: County Court - from $3,000 to $15,000; Municipal Court - from $10,000 to $15,000. In addition the small claims limit was raised from $2,000 to $3,000.

Effective in 2001, Ohio Common Pleas Courts may name their own civil action limits, though most of these courts have yet to make changes. In effect, these Common Pleas courts may take any civil cases. However, civil maximum limits for Ohio's County Courts and Municipal Courts remains the same: $15,000.

ONLINE ACCESS   There is no statewide computer system, but a number of counties offer online access. Appellate and Supreme Court opinions may be researched from the web site.

PROBATE COURTS   Probate courts are separate from the Court of Common Pleas, but Probate Court phone numbers are given with that court in each county.

Adams County

Common Pleas Court 110 W Main, Rm 207, West Union, OH 45693; 937-544-2344; Probate phone: 937-544-2368; Fax: 937-544-8271. Hours: 8:30AM-4PM (EST). *Felony, Civil Actions Over $3,000, Probate.*

Civil Records: Access: In person only. Visitors must perform in person searches for themselves. No search fee. Required to search: name, years to search. Civil cases indexed by defendant, plaintiff. Civil records on computer from April, 93, prior in books, archived from 1910.

Criminal Records: Access: Mail, in person. Visitors must perform in person searches for themselves. Search fee: $10.00. Required to search: name, years to search, signed release; also helpful: DOB, SSN. Criminal records on computer from April, 93, prior in books, archived from 1910.

General Information: Public Access terminal is available. Will fax results to local or toll free line. Copy fee: $.25 per page. Cert fee: $1.00. Payee: Clerk of Court. Personal checks accepted. Prepayment required.

County Court 110 W Main, Rm 25, West Union, OH 45693; 937-544-2011; Fax: 937-544-8911. Hours: 8AM-4PM (EST). *Misdemeanor, Civil Actions Under $15,000, Small Claims.*

Civil Records: Access: Mail, in person. Both court and visitors may perform in person searches. Search fee: $10.00 per name. Required to search: name, years to search. Civil cases indexed by defendant, plaintiff. Civil records on computer from March, 93, index from 1958, prior on dockets and microfilm.

Criminal Records: Access: Mail, in person. Both court and visitors may perform in person searches. Search fee: $10.00 per name. Required to search: name, years to search; also helpful: SSN. Criminal records on computer from March, 93, index from 1958, prior on dockets and microfilm.

General Information: Public Access terminal is available. Copy fee: $.50 per page. Cert fee: $1.00. Payee: Adams County Court. Business checks accepted. Prepayment required. Mail requests: SASE required. Mail turnaround time 1-2 days.

Allen County

Common Pleas Court PO Box 1243, 301 N. Main, Lima, OH 45802; 419-228-3700; Fax: 419-222-8427. Hours: 8AM-4:30PM (EST). *Felony, Civil Actions Over $15,000, Probate.*

Note: Probate is a separate court.

Civil Records: Access: In person. Visitors must perform in person searches for themselves. No search fee. Required to search: name; also helpful: years to search, address. Civil cases indexed by defendant, plaintiff. Civil records on computer back to 1986; in books and archived prior.

Criminal Records: Access: In person only. Visitors must perform in person searches themselves. No search fee. Required to search: name, years to search; also helpful: address, DOB, SSN. Criminal records on computer back to 1986; in books and archived prior.

General Information: Public Access terminal is available. No secret indictment records released. Copy fee: $1.00 for first page, $.25 each add'l. Cert fee: $3.00. Payee: Clerk of Court. Personal checks accepted. Prepayment required.

Lima Municipal Court 109 N Union St (PO Box 1529), Lima, OH 45802; 419-221-5275; Civil phone: 419-221-5250; Fax: 419-998-5526. Hours: 8AM-5PM (EST). *Misdemeanor, Civil Actions Under $15,000, Eviction, Small Claims.*

www.limamunicipalcourt.org

Civil Records: Access: Phone, fax, mail, in person, email, online. Both court and visitors may perform in person searches. No search fee. Required to search: name, years to search; also helpful: address. Civil cases indexed by defendant, plaintiff. Civil records on computer from April, 90, microfilm from 1975, books and archived prior. Search index information from the website, click on Case Inquiry.

Criminal Records: Access: Phone, fax, mail, in person, email, online. Both court and visitors may perform in person searches. No search fee. Required to search: name, years to search; also helpful: address, DOB, SSN. Criminal records on computer from April, 90, microfilm from 1975, books and archived prior. Search index information from the website, click on Case Inquiry.

General Information: Public Access terminal is available. Fee to fax results is $.25 per page. Copy fee: $.25 per page. Cert fee: $2.00. Payee: Clerk of Court. Business checks accepted. Visa, MC accepted. Prepayment required. Mail requests: SASE required. Mail turnaround time same day.

Ashland County

Common Pleas Court 142 W 2nd St, Ashland, OH 44805; 419-282-4242; Probate phone: 419-282-4284; Fax: 419-282-4240. Hours: 8AM-4PM (EST). *Felony, Civil Actions Over $10,000, Probate.*

www.ashlandcounty.org/clerkofcourts

Note: Probate court is a separate court at the same address.

Civil Records: Access: In person, online. Visitors must perform in person searches for themselves. Search fee: none. Required to search: name or case number. Civil cases indexed by defendant, plaintiff. Civil records on microfilm from 1800s. Access records at www.ashlandcountycpcourt.org. Computerized court records go back to June 7th, 1995.

Criminal Records: Access: In person, online. Visitors must perform in person searches for themselves. No search fee. Required to search: name or case number. Criminal records on microfilm from 1800s. Access records at www.ashlandcountycpcourt.org. Computerized court records go back to June 7th, 1995.

General Information: Public Access terminal is available. Copy fee: $.10 per page. Cert fee: $1.00. Payee: Clerk of Court. Personal checks accepted. Prepayment required.

Ashland Municipal Court 1209 E Main St, Ashland, OH 44805; 419-289-8137x; Fax: 419-289-8545. Hours: 8AM-5PM (EST). *Misdemeanor, Civil Actions Under $15,000, Eviction, Small Claims.*

www.ashland-ohio.com

Civil Records: Access: Phone, mail, fax, in person. Both court and visitors may perform in person searches. No search fee. Required to search: name, years to search. Civil cases indexed by defendant, plaintiff. Civil records on docket books from 1952, computerized since 1995.

Criminal Records: Access: Phone, mail, fax, in person. Both court and visitors may perform in person searches. No search fee. Required to search: name, years to search, SSN. Criminal records on docket books from 1952, computerized since 1995.

General Information: Public Access terminal is available. Fee to fax results is $1.00 per page. Copy fee: $.03 per page. Cert fee: $1.00. Payee: Municipal Court. Personal checks accepted. Prepayment required. Mail requests: SASE required. Mail turnaround time 1-3 days.

Ashtabula County

Common Pleas Court 25 W Jefferson St, Jefferson, OH 44047; 440-576-3637; Probate phone: 440-576-3451; Fax: 440-576-2819. Hours: 8AM-4:30PM (EST). *Felony, Civil Actions Over $10,000, Probate.*

Note: Probate is a separate office at the same location. Probate fax is 440-576-3633.

Civil Records: Access: In person, online. Visitors must perform in person searches for themselves. No search fee. Required to search: name, years to search; also helpful: address. Civil cases indexed by defendant, plaintiff. Civil records on computer back to 5/93, in books back to the 1800s. Access to records is free at http://courts.co.ashtabula.oh.us/pa.htm.

Criminal Records: Access: In person, online. Visitors must perform in person searches for themselves. No search fee. Required to search: name, years to search; also helpful: address, DOB, SSN. Criminal records on computer back to 5/93, in books back to the 1800s. Access to records is free at http://courts.co.ashtabula.oh.us/pa.htm.

General Information: Public Access terminal is available. No expungments released. Will not fax results. Copy fee: $.25 per page. Cert fee: $1.00. Payee: Clerk of Court. Personal checks accepted. Prepayment required.

County Court Eastern Division 25 W Jefferson St, Jefferson, OH 44047; 440-576-3617. Hours: 8AM-4:30PM (EST). *Misdemeanor, Civil Actions Under $15,000, Eviction, Small Claims.*

www.co.ashtabula.oh.us

Civil Records: Access: Mail, fax, in person, online. Both court and visitors may perform in person searches. No search fee. Required to search: name, years to search. Civil cases indexed by defendant, plaintiff. Civil records on computer since 01/09/95; in books back to 1960s. Access to records is free at http://courts.co.ashtabula.oh.us/pa.htm.

Criminal Records: Access: Mail, fax, in person, online. Both court and visitors may perform in person searches. No search fee. Required to search: name, years to search, DOB or SSN. Criminal records on computer since 01/09/95; in books back to 1960s. Access to records is free at http://courts.co.ashtabula.oh.us/pa.htm.

General Information: Public Access terminal is available. Fee to fax results is $.50 per page. Copy fee: $.50 per page. Cert fee: $1.50. Payee: Eastern County Court. Only cashiers checks and money orders accepted. Prepayment required. Mail requests: SASE required. Mail turnaround time 1-2 days.

County Court Western Division 117 W Main St, Geneva, OH 44041; 440-466-1184; Fax: 440-466-7171. Hours: 8AM-4:30PM (EST). *Misdemeanor, Civil Actions Under $15,000, Small Claims.*

Civil Records: Access: In person, mail, fax, online. Visitors must perform in person searches for themselves. No search fee. Required to search: name, years to search. Civil cases indexed by defendant, plaintiff. Civil records on computer back to 1995; prior records on docket books. Access to records is free at http://courts.co.ashtabula.oh.us/pa.htm.

Criminal Records: Access: In person, mail, fax, online. Visitors must perform in person searches for themselves. No search fee. Required to search: name, years to search, DOB, SSN, signed release. Criminal records on computer back to 1995; prior records on docket books. Access to records is free at http://courts.co.ashtabula.oh.us/pa.htm.

General Information: Public Access terminal is available. No confidential records released. Will not fax results. Copy fee: $.25 per page. Cert fee: $1.00 per page. Payee: Western County Court. Only cashiers checks and money orders accepted. Prepayment required. Mail requests: SASE required. Mail turnaround time is 72 hours.

Ashtabula Municipal Court
110 W 44th St, Ashtabula, OH 44004; 440-992-7110; Fax: 440-998-5786. Hours: 8AM-4:30PM (EST). *Misdemeanor, Civil Actions Under $15,000, Eviction, Small Claims.*
www.ashtabulamunicipalcourt.com
Note: 440-992-7109 gives a directory.

Civil Records: Access: In person, online. Visitors must perform in person searches for themselves. No search fee. Required to search: name, years to search. Civil cases indexed by defendant, plaintiff. Civil records on computer from 1992, books back to 1971. Online access to court cases is free at www.ashtabulamunicipalcourt.com.

Criminal Records: Access: In person, online. Visitors must perform in person searches for themselves. No search fee. Required to search: name, years to search, DOB, SSN, signed release. Criminal records on computer from 1992, books back to 1971. Online access to court cases, including traffic, is free at www.ashtabulamunicipalcourt.com.

General Information: Public Access terminal is available. No expunged records released. Will fax back results for $1.00 per document. Copy fee: $1.00 per page. Cert fee: $5.00. Payee: Municipal Court. Personal checks accepted. Prepayment required.

Athens County

Common Pleas Court
PO Box 290, Athens, OH 45701-0290; 740-592-3242; Probate phone: 740-592-3251. Hours: 8AM-4PM (EST). *Felony, Civil Actions Over $10,000, Probate.*
www.athenscountycpcourt.org

Civil Records: Access: In person, online. Visitors must perform in person searches for themselves. No search fee. Required to search: name, years to search; also helpful: address. Civil cases indexed by defendant, plaintiff. Civil records on computer back to 1/92; prior in books. Online access to the CP court records is free at www.athenscountycpcourt.org/genrlmnu.htm.

Criminal Records: Access: In person, online. Visitors must perform in person searches for themselves. No search fee. Required to search: name, years to search; also helpful: address, DOB, SSN. Criminal records on computer back to 1/92; prior in books. Online access to criminal records is the same as civil.

General Information: Public Access terminal is available. Copy fee: $.25 per page. Cert fee: $1.00. Payee: Clerk of Court. Business checks accepted. Prepayment required.

Athens Municipal Court
City Hall, 8 E Washington St, Athens, OH 45701; 740-592-3328; Fax: 740-592-3331. Hours: 8AM-4PM (EST). *Misdemeanor, Civil Actions Under $15,000, Eviction, Small Claims.*

Civil Records: Access: Mail, in person. Visitors must perform in person searches for themselves. No search fee. Required to search: name, years to search; also helpful: address. Civil cases indexed by defendant, plaintiff. Civil records on computer back to 1994, prior in books.

Criminal Records: Access: Mail, in person. Visitors must perform in person searches for themselves. No search fee. Required to search: name, years to search; also helpful: address, DOB, SSN. Criminal records on computer back to 7/1993, prior in books back to 1974.

General Information: Public Access terminal is available. No expunged or sealed records released. Copy fee: self serve copies: $.05. Cert fee: $1.00. Payee: ACMC. Personal checks accepted. Visa, MC

accepted. Prepayment required. Mail turnaround time is 10 days.

Auglaize County

Common Pleas Court
PO Box 409, Wapakoneta, OH 45895; 419-738-4219 or 419-738-4280; Probate phone: 419-738-7710; Fax: 419-738-7953. Hours: 8AM-4:30PM (EST). *Felony, Civil Actions Over $10,000, Probate.*

Civil Records: Access: Fax, in person. Visitors must perform in person searches for themselves. No search fee. Required to search: name, years to search; also helpful: address. Civil cases indexed by defendant, plaintiff. Civil records on dockets from 1850, computerized since 02/00. Fax requests must be on company letterhead.

Criminal Records: Access: Fax, in person. Visitors must perform in person searches for themselves. No search fee. Required to search: name, years to search; also helpful: address, DOB, SSN. Criminal records on dockets from 1850, computerized since 02/00. Fax requests must be on company letterhead.

General Information: Public Access terminal is available. Fee to fax results is $2.00 per page, plus $.25 each copy fee. Copy fee: $.25 per page. Cert fee: $1.00. Payee: Clerk of Court. Personal checks accepted. Prepayment required.

Auglaize County Municipal Court
PO Box 409, Wapakoneta, OH 45895; 419-738-2923; Civil phone: 419-738-2917. Hours: 8AM-4:30PM (EST). *Misdemeanor, Civil Actions Under $15,000, Eviction, Small Claims.*

Civil Records: Access: In person only. Visitors must perform in person searches for themselves. No search fee. Required to search: name, years to search; also helpful: address. Civil cases indexed by defendant, plaintiff. Civil records on computer from April, 1994, docket back to 1976.

Criminal Records: Access: In person only. Visitors must perform in person searches for themselves. No search fee. Required to search: name, years to search, signed release; also helpful: address, DOB, SSN. Criminal records on computer from October, 1993, docket back to 1976.

General Information: Public Access terminal is available. No records released. Copy fee: $.25 per page. Cert fee: $2.00. Payee: Clerk of Court. Personal checks accepted. Prepayment required.

Belmont County

Common Pleas Court
Belmont County Clerk of Courts, Main St, Courthouse, St Clairsville, OH 43950; 740-695-2121; Civil phone: 740-695-2169; Probate phone: 740-695-2121 X202. Hours: 8:30AM-4:30PM (EST). *Felony, Civil Actions Over $3,000, Probate.*

Civil Records: Access: Mail, in person. Both court and visitors may perform in person searches. Search fee: $3.00 per name. Required to search: name, years to search. Civil cases indexed by defendant, plaintiff. Civil records in books, archived from 1896; computerized from 1995.

Criminal Records: Access: Mail, in person. Both court and visitors may perform in person searches. Search fee: $3.00 per name. Required to search: name, years to search. Criminal records in books, archived from 1896; computerized from 1995.

General Information: Public Access terminal is available. No secret criminal records released. Will fax results to local or toll free line. Copy fee: $1.00 per page. Cert fee: $5.00. Payee: Clerk of Court. Personal checks accepted. Prepayment required. Mail requests: SASE required. Mail turnaround time 1 day.

County Court Eastern Division
400 W 26th St, Bellaire, OH 43906; 740-676-4490. Hours: 8AM-4PM (EST). *Misdemeanor, Civil Actions Under $15,000, Small Claims.*

Civil Records: Access: Mail, in person. Both court and visitors may perform in person searches. No search fee. Required to search: name, years to search. Civil cases indexed by defendant, plaintiff. Civil records on computer from September, 94, books back to 1950s. Mail access for attorneys only.

Criminal Records: Access: Mail, in person. Both court and visitors may perform in person searches. No search fee. Required to search: name, years to search; also helpful: DOB, SSN. Criminal records on computer from September, 94, books back to 1950s.

General Information: Public Access terminal is available. No sealed or confidential records released. No copy fee. Cert fee: $1.00 per page. Payee: Eastern Division. Only cashiers checks and money orders accepted. Prepayment required. Mail requests: SASE required.

County Court Northern Division
PO Box 40, Martins Ferry, OH 43935; 740-633-3147; Fax: 740-633-6631. Hours: 8AM-4PM (EST). *Misdemeanor, Civil Actions Under $15,000, Small Claims.*

Civil Records: Access: Mail, fax, in person. Both court and visitors may perform in person searches. No search fee. Required to search: name, years to search. Civil cases indexed by defendant, plaintiff. Civil records on computer from June, 1994, books back to 1950s.

Criminal Records: Access: Mail, fax, in person. Both court and visitors may perform in person searches. No search fee. Required to search: name, years to search, DOB; also helpful: SSN, sex, signed release. Criminal records on computer from June, 1994, books back to 1950s.

General Information: Public Access terminal is available. Will fax results for no fee. No copy fee. No cert fee. Mail requests: SASE not required. Mail turnaround time 5-7 days.

County Court Western Division
147 W Main St, St Clairsville, OH 43950; 740-695-2875; Fax: 740-695-7285. Hours: 8AM-4PM (EST). *Misdemeanor, Civil Actions Under $15,000, Small Claims.*

Civil Records: Access: Fax, mail, in person. Both court and visitors may perform in person searches. No search fee. Required to search: name, years to search, address. Civil cases indexed by defendant, plaintiff. Civil records on computer from 1994, books back to 1950s.

Criminal Records: Access: Fax, mail, in person. Both court and visitors may perform in person searches. No search fee. Required to search: name, years to search, address, DOB, SSN. Criminal records on computer from 1994, books back to 1950s.

General Information: Public Access terminal is available. Pending case information not released. No fee to fax results. Cert fee: $1.00. Payee: Western Division Court. Only cashiers checks and money orders accepted. Prepayment required. Mail requests: SASE required. Mail turnaround time 1 week.

Brown County

Common Pleas Court
101 S Main, Georgetown, OH 45121; 937-378-3100; Probate phone: 937-378-6549. Hours: 7:30AM-4:30PM (EST). *Felony, Civil Actions Over $3,000, Probate.*

Civil Records: Access: in person only. Visitors must perform in person searches for themselves. No search fee. Required to search: name, years to search; also helpful: address. Civil cases indexed by defendant, plaintiff. Civil records on computer since 1995, in books back to 1860s.

Criminal Records: Access: In person only. Visitors must perform in person searches for themselves. No search fee. Required to search: name, years to search; also helpful: address, DOB, SSN. Criminal records on computer since 1995, in books back to 1860s.

General Information: Public Access terminal is available. No criminal expungment records released. Copy fee: $.25 per page. Cert fee: $1.00. Payee: Clerk of Court. Personal checks accepted. Prepayment required.

County Municipal Court 770 Mount Orab Pike, Georgetown, OH 45121; 937-378-6358; Fax: 937-378-2462. Hours: 7:30AM-4:30PM M-F; 9AM-Noon S (EST). *Misdemeanor, Civil Actions Under $15,000, Eviction, Small Claims.*
www.browncountycourt.org
Civil Records: Access: Mail, in person, online. Both court and visitors may perform in person searches. No search fee. Required to search: name, years to search. Civil cases indexed by defendant, plaintiff. Civil records in books back to 1958, computerized since 1995. Access to records is free at www.browncountycourt.org/srchmain.html.
Criminal Records: Access: Mail, in person, online. Both court and visitors may perform in person searches. No search fee. Required to search: name, years to search, DOB; also helpful: SSN. Criminal records in books back to 1958, computerized since 1995. Access to records is free at www.browncountycourt.org/srchmain.html.
General Information: Public Access terminal is available. Will not fax results. Copy fee: $.10. No cert fee. Payee: Brown County Muni. Court. Only cashiers checks and money orders accepted. Prepayment required. Mail requests: SASE required.

Butler County

Common Pleas Court 315 High St, General Division, Government Services Ctr, 3rd Fl, Hamilton, OH 45011; 513-887-3287; Probate phone: 513-887-3294; Fax: 513-887-3089. Hours: 8:30AM-4:30PM (EST). *Felony, Civil Actions Over $3,000, Probate.*
www.butlercountyclerk.org/
Note: Government Service Center phone number is 513-887-3288.
Civil Records: Access: Online, in person. Visitors must perform in person searches for themselves. No search fee. Required to search: name, years to search. Civil cases indexed by defendant, plaintiff. Civil records on computer from 1988, records go back to 1987. Online access to County Clerk of Courts records is free at www.butlercountyclerk.org/pa/pa.urd/pamw6500-display. Search by name, dates, or case number and type. Online access to Probate Court records is free at www.butlercountyohio.org/probate/estate.cfm. Search the Estate or Guardianship databases.
Criminal Records: Access: Online, in person. Visitors must perform in person searches for themselves. No search fee. Required to search: name, years to search, DOB; also helpful: SSN. Criminal records on computer from 1988, prior in books. Online access to criminal records is the same as civil.
General Information: Public Access terminal is available. Copy fee: $.25 per page. Cert fee: $2.00. Payee: Butler County Clerk of Court. Personal checks accepted. Prepayment required.

County Court Area #1 118 West High, Oxford, OH 45056; 513-523-4748; Fax: 513-523-4737. Hours: 8:30AM-5PM (EST). *Misdemeanor, Civil Actions Under $15,000, Small Claims.*
Civil Records: Access: Phone, mail, in person. Both court and visitors may perform in person searches. No search fee. Required to search: name, years to search.

Civil cases indexed by defendant, plaintiff. Civil records on index back to 1983.
Criminal Records: Access: Mail, in person, phone. Both court and visitors may perform in person searches. No search fee. Required to search: name, years to search, DOB. Criminal records on index back to 1983.
General Information: No sealed records released. No copy fee. No cert fee. Mail requests: SASE required. Mail turnaround time 1-5 days.

County Court Area #2 Butler County Courthouse, 101 High St, 1st Fl, Hamilton, OH 45011; 513-887-3459. Hours: 8AM-5PM (EST). *Misdemeanor, Civil Actions Under $15,000, Small Claims.*
Civil Records: Access: Phone, in person. Visitors must perform in person searches for themselves. No search fee. Required to search: name, years to search. Civil cases indexed by defendant, plaintiff. Civil records on computer from 1993, books back to 1983.
Criminal Records: Access: Phone, in person, mail. Visitors must perform in person searches for themselves. No search fee. Required to search: name, years to search. Criminal records on computer from 1993, books back to 1983.
General Information: Public Access terminal is available. No sealed records released. No copy fee. No cert fee. Only cashiers checks and money orders accepted. Prepayment required. Mail requests: SASE required. Mail turnaround time is 2 days.

County Court Area #3 9113 Cincinnati, Dayton Rd, West Chester, OH 45069; 513-867-5070; Fax: 513-777-0558. Hours: 8:AM-5PM (EST). *Misdemeanor, Civil Actions Under $15,000, Small Claims.*
Civil Records: Access: Mail, in person. Both court and visitors may perform in person searches. No search fee. Required to search: name, years to search. Civil cases indexed by defendant, plaintiff. Civil records on computer from 1993, books back to 1983.
Criminal Records: Access: Mail, in person. Both court and visitors may perform in person searches. No search fee. Required to search: name, years to search. Criminal records on computer from 1993, books back to 1983.
General Information: Public Access terminal is available. No copy fee. Cert fee: $1.00. Payee: Area #3 Court. Personal checks accepted. Prepayment required. Mail requests: SASE required. Mail turnaround time 2-3 days.

Hamilton Municipal Court 345 High St, #2, Hamilton, OH 45011; 513-785-7300; Fax: 513-785-7315. Hours: 8AM-5PM (EST). *Misdemeanor, Civil Actions Under $15,000, Small Claims.*
www.hamiltonmunicipalcourt.org
Civil Records: Access: Phone, in person, online. Both court and visitors may perform in person searches. No search fee. Required to search: name, years to search. Civil cases indexed by defendant, plaintiff. Civil records on computer from 1993, books back to 1983. Record access at the website at no fee.
Criminal Records: Access: Phone, in person, online. Both court and visitors may perform in person searches. No search fee. Required to search: name, years to search. Criminal records on computer from 1993, books back to 1983. Misdemeanor and traffic record access at the website at no fee.
General Information: Public Access terminal is available. No sealed records released. Will fax results to local or toll free line. Copy fee: $.05 per page. No cert fee. Prepayment required.

Carroll County

Common Pleas Court PO Box 367, Carrollton, OH 44615; 330-627-4886; Probate phone: 330-627-2323; Fax: 330-627-6737. Hours: 8AM-4PM (EST). *Felony, Civil Actions Over $15,000, Probate.*
Note: Probate Court address is 119 Public Sq, Courthouse, Carrollton, OH.
Civil Records: Access: In person only. Visitors must perform in person searches for themselves. No search fee. Required to search: name, years to search. Civil cases indexed by defendant, plaintiff. Civil records in books back to 1900s.
Criminal Records: Access: In person only. Visitors must perform in person searches for themselves. No search fee. Required to search: name, years to search; also helpful: DOB, SSN. Criminal records in books back to 1900s.
General Information: Public Access terminal is available. Copy fee: $.05 per page. Cert fee: $1.00. Payee: Clerk of Court. Personal checks accepted. Prepayment required.

County Court 119 S Lisbon St #301, Carrollton, OH 44615; 330-627-5049; Fax: 330-627-3662. Hours: 8AM-4PM (EST). *Misdemeanor, Civil Actions Under $15,000, Small Claims, Evictions.*
Civil Records: Access: In person only. Visitors must perform in person searches for themselves. No search fee. Required to search: name, years to search. Civil cases indexed by defendant, plaintiff. Civil records in books from 1958; on computer since 11/95.
Criminal Records: Access: In person only. Visitors must perform in person searches for themselves. No search fee. Required to search: name, years to search, DOB. Criminal records in books from 1958; on computer since 11/95.
General Information: Public Access terminal is available. No confidential records released. Copy fee: $.25 per page. Cert fee: $2.00. Payee: Carroll County Court. Personal checks accepted. Prepayment required.

Champaign County

Common Pleas Court 200 N Main St, Urbana, OH 43078; 937-653-2746; Probate phone: 937-652-2108. Hours: 8AM-4PM (EST). *Felony, Civil Actions Over $10,000, Probate.*
Note: Probate is separate court at phone number given.
Civil Records: Access: Phone, mail, in person. Visitors must perform in person searches for themselves. No search fee. Required to search: name, years to search. Civil cases indexed by defendant, plaintiff. Civil records on computer from 06/92, books back to late 1800'. Will only do phone or mail searches with a case number. Even in this situation, requesters are limited to 10 files per month if acting as a retriever.
Criminal Records: Access: Phone, mail, in person. Visitors must perform in person searches for themselves. No search fee. Required to search: name, years to search, DOB, SSN, signed release. Criminal records on computer from 06/92, books back to late 1800s. Will only do mail or phone searches with a case number. Even in this situation, requesters are limited to 10 files per month if acting as a retriever.
General Information: Public Access terminal is available. All records are public. Copy fee: $.25 per page. Cert fee: $1.00. Payee: Clerk of Court. Personal checks over $10.00 not accepted. Prepayment required. Mail requests: SASE required.

Champaign County Municipal Court PO Box 85, Urbana, OH 43078; 937-653-7376. Hours: 8AM-4PM (EST). *Misdemeanor, Civil Actions Under $15,000, Eviction, Small Claims.*

Civil Records: Access: Mail, in person. Both court and visitors may perform in person searches. No search fee. Required to search: name, years to search. Civil cases indexed by defendant, plaintiff. Civil records on computer from June, 93, books back to late 1800s.

Criminal Records: Access: Mail, in person. Both court and visitors may perform in person searches. No search fee. Required to search: name, years to search; also helpful: DOB, SSN. Criminal records on computer from June, 93, books back to late 1800s.

General Information: No sealed records released. Copy fee: $.25 per page. Cert fee: $2.50. Payee: Municipal Court. Only cashiers checks and money orders accepted. Prepayment required. Mail requests: SASE required. Mail turnaround time 2-3 days.

Clark County

Common Pleas Court 101 N Limestone St, Springfield, OH 45502; 937-328-2458; 937-328-4648 (Domestic); Probate phone: 937-328-2434; Fax: 937-328-2436. Hours: 8AM-4:30PM (EST). *Felony, Civil Actions Over $10,000, Probate.*
www.co.clark.oh.us

Note: Probate Court and records are at the same address, separate office and phone.

Civil Records: Access: In person, online. Visitors must perform in person searches for themselves. No search fee. Required to search: name, years to search. Civil cases indexed by defendant. Civil records on computer back to 1990, prior in index books. Online access to clerk's records is free at http://64.56.97.140/.

Criminal Records: Access: In person, online. Visitors must perform in person searches for themselves. No search fee. Required to search: name, years to search. Criminal records on computer back to 1990, prior in index books. Online access to clerk's records are free at http://64.56.97.140/. The Sheriff's most wanted list is found at www.clarkcountysheriff.com.

General Information: Public Access terminal is available. Copy fee: $.25 per page. Cert fee: $1.00. Payee: Clerk of Court. Business checks accepted. Prepayment required.

Clark County Municipal Court 50 E Columbia St, Springfield, OH 45502; 937-328-3700; Civil phone: 937-328-3715; Criminal phone: 937-328-3726. Hours: 8AM-5PM (EST). *Misdemeanor, Civil Actions Under $15,000, Eviction, Small Claims.*
www.clerkofcourts.municipal.co.clark.oh.us

Civil Records: Access: Phone, mail, in person, online. Both court and visitors may perform in person searches. No search fee. Required to search: name, years to search. Civil cases indexed by defendant, plaintiff. Civil records on computer since 3/90; prior records go back to 6/87. Online access to case information is free at www.clerkofcourts.municipal.co.clark.oh.us/cases/courtcases.nsf. Name searching on "New Cases" other types require a case number.

Criminal Records: Access: Mail, in person, online. Both court and visitors may perform in person searches. No search fee. Required to search: name, years to search; also helpful: DOB, SSN. Criminal records on computer since 3/90; prior records go back to 6/87. Access to criminal records is the same as civil.

General Information: Public Access terminal is available. Copy fee: $.50 per page. Cert fee: $2.00. Payee: Clerk of Court. Personal checks not accepted.

Prepayment required. Mail requests: SASE required. Mail turnaround time 2-3 days.

Clermont County

Common Pleas Court 270 Main St, Batavia, OH 45103; 513-732-7130; Probate phone: 513-732-7243; Fax: 513-732-7050. Hours: 8:30AM-4:30PM (EST). *Felony, Civil Actions Over $10,000, Probate.*

Note: Probate court is located at 76 S Riverside Dr, Batavia 45103

Civil Records: Access: In person, online. Visitors must perform in person searches for themselves. No search fee. Required to search: name, years to search; also helpful: address. Civil cases indexed by defendant, plaintiff. Civil records on computer from 1987, some on microfiche from 1920s, index books from 1959. Online access to civil records is the same as criminal, see following.

Criminal Records: Access: In person, online. Visitors must perform in person searches for themselves. No search fee. Required to search: name, years to search, DOB; also helpful: address, SSN. Criminal records on computer from 1987, some on microfiche from 1920s, index books from 1959. Online access to court records is free at www.clermontclerk.org/Case_Access.htm. Online records go back to 1/1998. Includes later Municipal Court records. The clerk refers criminal record requests to the Sheriff (513-732-7500) who will do searches for $5.00 per name.

General Information: Public Access terminal is available. Copy fee: $.10 per page. Cert fee: $1.00 per page. Payee: Clerk of Court. Business checks accepted. Prepayment required.

Clermont County Municipal Court 289 Main St, Civil court: 66 S Riverside Rd, Batavia, OH 45103; Civil phone: 513-732-7292; Criminal phone: 513-732-7290. Hours: 8AM-5PM (EST). *Misdemeanor, Civil Actions Under $15,000, Eviction, Small Claims.*
www.clermontclerk.org

Civil Records: Access: Mail, in person, online. Visitors must perform in person searches for themselves. Search fee: none. Required to search: name, years to search. Civil cases indexed by defendant, plaintiff. Computerized records from 5/96, civil records in books and microfiche from 1959, docket books back to 1800s. Online access to court records is the same as criminal, see following.

Criminal Records: Access: Mail, in person, online. Visitors must perform in person searches for themselves. Search fee: none. Required to search: name, years to search, DOB; also helpful: SSN. Computerized records back to 5/96, criminal records in books and microfiche from 1957, docket books back to 1800s. Online access to court records is free at www.clermontclerk.org/Case_Access.htm. Online records go back to 5/1/1996. Includes Common Pleas court records.

General Information: Public Access terminal is available. Copy fee: $.25 per page. Cert fee: $4.00. Payee: Clerk of Court. Only cashiers checks and money orders accepted. Prepayment required. Mail requests: SASE required.

Clinton County

Common Pleas Court 46 S South St, Wilmington, OH 45177; 937-382-2316; Probate phone: 937-382-2280; Fax: 937-383-3455. Hours: 7:30AM-4:30PM (EST). *Felony, Civil Actions Over $15,000, Probate.*

Note: Probate fax is 937-383-1158; hours are 8AM-4:30PM.

Civil Records: Access: Fax, mail, in person. Both court and visitors may perform in person searches. No search fee. Required to search: name, years to search;

also helpful: address. Civil cases indexed by defendant, plaintiff. Civil records on computer since 1995; prior in books back to 1810.

Criminal Records: Access: Mail, in person. Both court and visitors may perform in person searches. Search fee: $5.00 per name. Required to search: name, years to search, DOD, SSN; also helpful: address. Criminal records on computer since 1995; prior in books back to 1810.

General Information: Public Access terminal is available. No confidential records released. Will fax results for $5.00 per name. Copy fee: $.25 per page. Cert fee: $1.00. Payee: Clerk of Court. Personal checks accepted. Prepayment required. Mail requests: SASE required. Mail turnaround time 1 week.

Clinton County Municipal Court 69 N South St, PO Box 71, Wilmington, OH 45177; 937-382-8985; Fax: 937-383-0130. Hours: 8AM-4PM (EST). *Misdemeanor, Civil Actions Under $15,000, Eviction, Small Claims.*

Civil Records: Access: Fax, mail, in person. Both court and visitors may perform in person searches. No search fee. Required to search: name, years to search. Civil cases indexed by defendant, plaintiff. Civil records in books from 1960; computerized records go back to 1995.

Criminal Records: Access: Fax, mail, in person. Both court and visitors may perform in person searches. No search fee. Required to search: name, years to search, DOB; also helpful: SSN. Criminal records in books from 1960; computerized records go back to 1995.

General Information: Public Access terminal is available. Will fax results to local or toll free line. Copy fee: $.25 per page after 10 pages. No cert fee. Payee: Clerk of Court. Only cashiers checks and money orders accepted. Prepayment required. Mail requests: SASE required. Mail turnaround time 1 day.

Columbiana County

Common Pleas Court 105 S Market St, Lisbon, OH 44432; 330-424-7777; Fax: 330-424-3960. Hours: 8AM-4PM (EST). *Felony, Civil Actions Over $15,000, Probate.*
www.ccclerk.org

Civil Records: Access: In person, online. Visitors must perform in person searches for themselves. No search fee. Required to search: name, years to search; also helpful: address. Civil cases indexed by defendant, plaintiff. Civil records on computer since 1993; prior in books from 1968, archived back to 1800s. Online access free to all county court index and docket records at www.ccclerk.org/case_access.htm. Includes probate.

Criminal Records: Access: In person, online. Visitors must perform in person searches for themselves. No search fee. Required to search: name, years to search, DOB; also helpful: address, SSN. Criminal records on computer since 1993; prior in books from 1968, archived back to 1800s. Free online access to all county court index and docket records is at www.ccclerk.org/case_access.htm.

General Information: Public Access terminal is available. No secret indictment records released. Copy fee: $.05 per page. Cert fee: $1.00 per page. Payee: Clerk of Court. Personal checks accepted. Prepayment required.

Municipal Court Eastern Area 31 N Market St, East Palestine, OH 44413; 330-426-3774; Fax: 330-426-6328. Hours: 8AM-4PM (EST). *Misdemeanor, Civil Actions Under $15,000, Small Claims.*
www.ccclerk.org/the_courts.htm

Civil Records: Access: In person, online. Visitors must perform in person searches for themselves. No search fee. Required to search: name, years to search.

Civil cases indexed by defendant, plaintiff. Civil records in books from 1950s, archived from 1800s, recent records computerized. Online access free to all county court index and docket records at www.ccclerk.org/the_courts.htm.

Criminal Records: Access: In person, online. Visitors must perform in person searches for themselves. No search fee. Required to search: name, years to search. Criminal records in books from 1950s, archived from 1800s, recent records computerized. Free online access to all county court index and docket records at www.ccclerk.org/the_courts.htm.

General Information: Public Access terminal is available. No fee to fax to a toll-free number. Copy fee: $.25 per page. Cert fee: $1.00. Payee: Clerk of Court. Only cashiers checks and money orders accepted. Prepayment required.

Municipal Court Northwest Area 130 Penn
Ave, Salem, OH 44460; 330-332-0297. Hours: 8AM-4PM (EST). *Misdemeanor, Civil Actions Under $15,000, Small Claims.*
www.ccclerk.org
Civil Records: Access: In person, online. Both court and visitors may perform in person searches. No search fee. Required to search: name, years to search. Civil cases indexed by defendant, plaintiff. Civil records in books from 1950s, archived from 1800s, computerized since 11/94. Online access free to all county court index and docket records at www.ccclerk.org/the_courts.htm.
Criminal Records: Access: Mail, in person, online. Both court and visitors may perform in person searches. No search fee. Required to search: name, years to search; also helpful: DOB. Criminal records in books from 1950s, archived from 1800s, computerized back to 11/94. Free online access to all county court index and docket records at www.ccclerk.org/the_courts.htm.
General Information: Public Access terminal is available. Will only fax to government agencies. Copy fee: $.25 per page. Cert fee: $1.00. Payee: Northwest Area Court. Only cashiers checks and money orders accepted. Prepayment required. Mail requests: SASE required. Mail turnaround time 2-3 days.

Municipal Court Southwest Area 41 N
Park Ave, Lisbon, OH 44432; 330-424-5326; Fax: 330-424-6658. Hours: 8AM-4PM (EST). *Misdemeanor, Civil Actions Under $15,000, Small Claims.*
www.ccclerk.org/the_courts.htm
Civil Records: Access: In person, online. Visitors must perform in person searches for themselves. No search fee. Required to search: name, years to search. Civil cases indexed by defendant, plaintiff. Civil records in books from 1950s, archived back to 1800s; on comptuer back to 1994. Online access free to all county court index and docket records at www.ccclerk.org/the_courts.htm.
Criminal Records: Access: In person, online. Visitors must perform in person searches for themselves. No search fee. Required to search: name, years to search; also helpful: DOB, SSN. Criminal records in books from 1950s, archived back to 1800s; on computer back to 1994. Free online access to all county court index and docket records at www.ccclerk.org/the_courts.htm.
General Information: Public Access terminal is available. No expungment records released. Copy fee: $.50 per page. Cert fee: $1.00. Payee: Southwest Court. Only cashiers checks and money orders accepted. Prepayment required.

East Liverpool Municipal Court 126 W 6th
St, East Liverpool, OH 43920; 330-385-5151; Fax: 330-385-1566. Hours: 8AM-4PM (EST). *Misdemeanor, Civil Actions Under $15,000, Eviction, Small Claims.*
www.eastliverpool.com/court.html
Civil Records: Access: Phone, fax, mail, in person, online. Both court and visitors may perform in person searches. No search fee. Required to search: name, years to search. Civil cases indexed by defendant, plaintiff. Civil records in books from 1968, archived back to 1800s, computerized since 11/92. Online access free to all county court index and docket records at www.ccclerk.org/the_courts.htm.
Criminal Records: Access: Phone, fax, mail, in person, online. Both court and visitors may perform in person searches. No search fee. Required to search: name, years to search, signed release; also helpful: DOB, SSN. Criminal records in books from 1968, archived back to 1800s, computerized since 11/92. Free online access to all county court index and docket records at www.ccclerk.org/the_courts.htm.
General Information: Public Access terminal is available. No expungement records released. No fee to fax results. Copy fee: $.25 per page. Cert fee: $3.00. Payee: East Liverpool Muni. Court. No business or personal checks accepted. Prepayment required. Mail requests: SASE required. Mail turnaround time 1-2 days.

Coshocton County

Common Pleas Court 318 Main St,
Coshocton, OH 43812; 740-622-1456; Probate phone: 740-622-1837. Hours: 8AM-4PM (EST). *Felony, Civil Actions Over $10,000, Probate.*
Civil Records: Access: Mail, in person. Both court and visitors may perform in person searches. No search fee. Required to search: name, years to search. Civil cases indexed by defendant, plaintiff. Civil records in books, microfilm back to 1985, archived back to 1800s; on computer back to 1998.
Criminal Records: Access: Mail, in person. Both court and visitors may perform in person searches. No search fee. Required to search: name, years to search, DOB; also helpful: SSN. Criminal records in books, microfilm back to 1985, archived back to 1800s; on computer back to 1998.
General Information: Public Access terminal is available. No expunged records released. Copy fee: $.25 per page. Cert fee: $1.00. Payee: Clerk of Court. Personal checks accepted. Prepayment required. Mail requests: SASE not required. Mail turnaround time 2 days.

Coshocton Municipal Court 760 Chesnut St,
Coshocton, OH 43812; 740-622-2871; Fax: 740-623-5928. Hours: 8AM-4:30PM M-W,F; 8AM-Noon Th (EST). *Misdemeanor, Civil Actions Under $15,000, Eviction, Small Claims.*
www.coshoctonmunicipalcourt.com
Civil Records: Access: Phone, fax, mail, in person, online. Both court and visitors may perform in person searches. No search fee. Required to search: name, years to search. Civil cases indexed by defendant, plaintiff. Civil records on computer from 1989, books back to 1952. Online access to civil records is at the website. Search by name, case number, attorney, date.
Criminal Records: Access: Phone, fax, mail, in person, online. Both court and visitors may perform in person searches. No search fee. Required to search: name, years to search; also helpful: DOB, SSN. Criminal records on computer from 1989, books back to 1952. Online access to criminal records is the same as civil. Search by name, attorney, citation or case number.
General Information: Public Access terminal is available. No expunged records released. No fee to

fax results. Copy fee: $.50 per page. Cert fee: $5.00. Payee: Clerk of Court. Personal checks accepted. Prepayment required. Mail requests: SASE required. Mail turnaround time same day.

Crawford County

Common Pleas Court 112 E Mansfield St
#204, Bucyrus, OH 44820; 419-562-2766; Probate phone: 419-562-8891; Fax: 419-562-8011. Hours: 8:30AM-4:30PM (EST). *Felony, Civil Actions Over $3,000, Probate.*
www.crawford-co.org/Clerk/default.html
Civil Records: Access: Phone, mail, in person, online. Both court and visitors may perform in person searches. Search fee: $5.00 per name. Required to search: name, years to search; also helpful: address. Civil cases indexed by defendant, plaintiff. Civil records on computer back to 1990, some on microfiche and index books from 1800s. Online access to Common Please court records is free at www.crawford-co.org/Clerk/default.html and click on "Internet Inquiry."
Criminal Records: Access: Mail, in person, online. Both court and visitors may perform in person searches. Search fee: $5.00 per name. Required to search: name, years to search; also helpful: address, DOB, SSN. Criminal records on computer back to 1990, some on microfiche and index books from 1800s. Online access to criminal cases is the same as civil.
General Information: Public Access terminal is available. No divorce investigations. Will fax results for no fee. No copy fee. Cert fee: $1.00. Payee: Clerk of Court. Personal checks accepted. Prepayment required. Mail requests: SASE required. Mail turnaround time 1-2 days.

Crawford County Municipal Court PO Box
550, Bucyrus, OH 44820; 419-562-2731; Fax: 419-562-7064. Hours: 8:30AM-4:30PM (EST). *Misdemeanor, Civil Actions Under $15,000, Eviction, Small Claims.*
Civil Records: Access: Phone, fax, mail, in person. Both court and visitors may perform in person searches. No search fee. Required to search: name, years to search. Civil cases indexed by defendant, plaintiff. Civil records in books back to 1978.
Criminal Records: Access: Mail, in person. Both court and visitors may perform in person searches. No search fee. Required to search: name, years to search, DOB. Criminal records in books back to 1978; on computer back to 1996.
General Information: Public Access terminal is available. No counseling report records released. Will fax results to toll free line. Copy fee: $.10 per page. Cert fee: $2.00. Business checks accepted. Crawford county business checks accepted. Prepayment required. Mail requests: SASE not required. Mail turnaround time within 1 week.

Crawford County Municipal Court
Eastern Division 301 Harding Way East, Galion, OH 44833; 419-468-6819; Fax: 419-468-6828. Hours: 8AM-5PM (EST). *Misdemeanor, Civil Actions Under $15,000, Eviction, Small Claims.*
Civil Records: Access: Mail, in person. Both court and visitors may perform in person searches. No search fee. Required to search: name, years to search. Civil cases indexed by defendant, plaintiff. Civil records in books back to 1800s.
Criminal Records: Access: Mail, in person. Both court and visitors may perform in person searches. No search fee. Required to search: name, years to search, DOB, SSN, signed release. Criminal records in books back to 1800s.
General Information: Public Access terminal is available. Copy fee: $.10 per page. Cert fee: $3.00. Payee: Municipal Court. Only cashiers checks and

money orders accepted. Prepayment required. Mail requests: SASE required. Mail turnaround time 2-3 days.

Cuyahoga County

Common Pleas Court - General Division

1200 Ontario St, Cleveland, OH 44113; 216-443-8560; Civil phone: 216-443-7966; Criminal phone: 216-443-7985; Probate phone: 216-443-8764; Fax: 216-443-5424. Hours: 8:30AM-4:30PM (EST). *Felony, Civil Actions Over $10,000, Probate.*
www.cuyahoga.oh.us/common/default.htm
Note: Probate is a separate division with separate records and personnel.

Civil Records: Access: Phone, mail, in person, online. Both court and visitors may perform in person searches. No search fee. Required to search: name, years to search; also helpful: address. Civil cases indexed by defendant, plaintiff. Civil records on index and dockets from 1968, archived from 1800s; computerized since 1975. Online access to Common Pleas civil courts; click on Civil Case Dockets at http://cpdocket.cuyahoga.oh.us/cjisjs/servlet/cjis.urd/run/cmsw101. Access or Probate is at http://probate.cuyahogacounty.us/pa/. Phone requests to 216-443-7966. Address mail requests to Gerald Fuerst, 1st Fl, Index Dept.

Criminal Records: Access: In person only. Visitors must perform in person searches for themselves. No search fee. Required to search: name, years to search; also helpful: address, DOB, SSN. Criminal records on index and dockets from 1968, archived from 1800s; computerized since 1975. Online access to criminal records dockets is free at http://cpdocket.cuyahoga.oh.us/cjisjs/servlet/cjis.urd/run/cmsw101. Address mail requests to Criminal Dept, 2nd Fl. Phone requests must have case number.

General Information: Public Access terminal is available. No expungments or sealed records released. Copy fee: $.25 per page. Cert fee: $1.00 per page. Payee: Clerk of Court. Business checks accepted. Prepayment required. Mail requests: SASE required.

Cleveland Municipal Court - Civil Division

1200 Ontario St, Cleveland, OH 44113; 216-664-4870; Fax: 216-664-4065. Hours: 8AM-3:50PM (EST). *Civil Actions Under $15,000, Eviction, Small Claims.*
http://clevelandmunicipalcourt.org/home.html
Note: The court plan to have online access to case information in the near future.

Civil Records: Access: Fax, mail, in person. Both court and visitors may perform in person searches. No search fee. Required to search: name, years to search; also helpful: address. Civil cases indexed by defendant, plaintiff. Civil records on computer from 1988, docket books and index from 1950s, prior archived.
General Information: Public Access terminal is available. Copy fee: $.25 per page. Cert fee: $1.00. Payee: Municipal Court. Personal checks accepted. Prepayment required. Mail requests: SASE required. Mail turnaround time 2 days.

Cleveland Municipal Court - Criminal Division

1200 Ontario St, Cleveland, OH 44113; 216-664-3268. Hours: 8AM-3:50PM (EST). *Misdemeanor.*
http://clevelandmunicipalcourt.org/home.html
Note: The court plan to have online access to case information in the near future.

Criminal Records: Access: In person. Both court and visitors may perform in person searches. No search fee. Required to search: name, years to search, DOB, SSN, signed release. Criminal records on computer since 1988, on books to 1950s, archived prior.

General Information: No adoption or juvenile records released. Copy fee: $.25 per page. Cert fee: $3.00. Payee: Municipal Court. Personal checks accepted. Prepayment required. Mail requests: SASE required. Mail turnaround time 3-4 days.

Bedford Municipal Court
165 Center Rd., Bedford, OH 44146; 440-232-3420; Fax: 440-232-2510. Hours: 8:30AM-4:30PM (EST). *Misdemeanor, Civil Actions Under $15,000, Eviction, Small Claims.*
www.bedfordmuni.org
Civil Records: Access: Fax, mail, in person, online. Both court and visitors may perform in person searches. No search fee. Required to search: name, years to search. Civil cases indexed by defendant, plaintiff. Civil records on computer from 1990 docket books and index from 1970s, prior archived. Access index to court records at the web page.
Criminal Records: Access: Fax, mail, in person, online. Both court and visitors may perform in person searches. No search fee. Required to search: name, years to search. Criminal records on computer from 2000, docket books and index from 1970s, prior archived. Access index to court records at the web page.
General Information: No fee to fax results. Copy fee: $.50 per page. Cert fee: $2.00. Payee: Municipal Court. Only cashiers checks and money orders accepted. Prepayment required. Mail requests: SASE required. Mail turnaround time 3 days.

Berea Municipal Court
11 Berea Commons, Berea, OH 44017; Civil phone: 440-826-5860; Criminal phone: 440-826-5862; Fax: 440-891-3387-civ; 440-234-2768-crim/traffic. Hours: 8AM-4:30PM (EST). *Misdemeanor, Civil Actions Under $15,000, Eviction, Small Claims.*
www.bereamunicourt.org
Civil Records: Access: Mail, fax, in person, online. Both court and visitors may perform in person searches. No search fee. Required to search: name, years to search. Civil cases indexed by defendant, plaintiff. Civil records on computer back to 1991, prior in books and archived. Search docket information at the website.
Criminal Records: Access: Fax, mail, in person, online. Both court and visitors may perform in person searches. Search fee: $5.00 per name. Required to search: name, years to search; also helpful: address, DOB, SSN. Criminal records on computer back to 1991, prior in books and archived. Search docket information at the website.
General Information: No probation records released. No fee to fax results. Copy fee: $1.00 per page. Cert fee: $5.00. Payee: Berea Municipal Court. Personal checks accepted. Visa, MC accepted. Prepayment required. Mail requests: SASE required. Mail turnaround time 1 week-10 days.

Cleveland Heights Municipal Court
40 Severance Circle, Cleveland Heights, OH 44118; 216-291-4901; Fax: 216-291-2459. Hours: 8AM-5PM (EST). *Misdemeanor, Civil Actions Under $15,000, Eviction, Small Claims.*
www.clevelandheightscourt.com
Civil Records: Access: Online, in person. Visitors must perform in person searches for themselves. No search fee. Required to search: name, years to search; also helpful: address. Civil cases indexed by defendant, plaintiff. Civil records on computer from 1990, prior in books to 1980. Civil (to $15,000) or misdemeanor docket records for Municipal Court are on the website. Search by name or case number.
Criminal Records: Access: Online, in person. Visitors must perform in person searches for themselves. No search fee. Required to search: name, years to search; also helpful: address, DOB, SSN.

Criminal records on computer from 1990, prior in books to 1980s. Online access to criminal records is the same as civil.
General Information: Public Access terminal is available. No expungments or search warrant records released. Copy fee: $.10 per page. Cert fee: $3.00. Payee: Municipal Court. Personal checks accepted. Visa, MC accepted. Visa, MC in person only. Prepayment required.

East Cleveland Municipal Court
14340 Euclid Ave, East Cleveland, OH 44112; 216-681-2021/2022. Hours: 8:30AM-4:30PM (EST). *Misdemeanor, Civil Actions Under $15,000, Eviction, Small Claims.*
Civil Records: Access: In person only. Visitors must perform in person searches for themselves. No search fee. Required to search: name, years to search. Civil cases indexed by defendant, plaintiff. Civil records go back to 1979; on computer from 1989, docket books and index from 1950s, prior archived.
Criminal Records: Access: Mail, in person. Visitors must perform in person searches for themselves. No search fee. Required to search: name, years to search, DOB, SSN, signed release; also helpful: address. Criminal records on computer from 1997, docket books and index from 1950s, prior archived. Address mail requests to Police Record Room.
General Information: Copy fee: $1.00 per page. Cert fee: $3.00. Payee: Municipal Court. Personal checks not accepted on criminal cases. Prepayment required. Mail requests: SASE required. Mail turnaround time 1-2 weeks.

Euclid Municipal Court
555 E 222 St, Euclid, OH 44123-2099; 216-289-2888; Fax: 216-289-8254. Hours: 8:30AM-4:30PM (EST). *Misdemeanor, Civil Actions Under $15,000, Eviction, Small Claims.*
Civil Records: Access: Mail, in person. Both court and visitors may perform in person searches. Search fee: $5.00 per name. Required to search: name, years to search. Civil cases indexed by defendant, plaintiff. Civil records on computer from 2004, docket books and index from 1950s, prior archived.
Criminal Records: Access: Mail, in person. Both court and visitors may perform in person searches. Search fee: $5.00 per name. Required to search: name, years to search, DOB; also helpful: address, SSN. Criminal records on computer from 1995, docket books and index from 1950s, prior archived.
General Information: Public Access terminal is available. No expunged records released. Copy fee: $1.00 per page. Cert fee: $5.00 (included in search fee). Payee: Municipal Court. Personal checks accepted. Prepayment required. Mail requests: SASE required. Mail turnaround time 1 week.

Garfield Heights Municipal Court
5555 Turney Rd, Garfield Heights, OH 44125; 216-475-1900. Hours: 8:30AM-4:30PM (EST). *Misdemeanor, Civil Actions Under $15,000, Eviction, Small Claims.*
www.ghmc.org
Civil Records: Access: Phone, mail, in person, online. Both court and visitors may perform in person searches. No search fee. Required to search: name, years to search; also helpful: address. Civil cases indexed by defendant, plaintiff. Civil records on computer from 11/91, docket books and index from 1996, prior archived. Online access is limited to current dockets; search by name, date or case number at www.ghmc.org/docket.html. Phone access depends on age of case.
Criminal Records: Access: Phone, mail, in person, online. Both court and visitors may perform in person searches. No search fee. Required to search: name, years to search, DOB; also helpful: address, SSN, signed release. Criminal records on computer from

1996, docket books and index from 1995, prior archived. Online access to criminal records is the same as civil.

General Information: Public Access terminal is available. No expunged records released. Copy fee: $.05 per page. Cert fee: $1.00. Payee: Municipal Court. Personal checks accepted. Prepayment required. Mail requests: SASE required. Mail turnaround time 2 weeks.

Lakewood Municipal Court 12650 Detroit Ave, Lakewood, OH 44107; 216-529-6700; Fax: 216-529-7687. Hours: 8AM-5PM (EST). *Misdemeanor, Civil Actions Under $15,000, Eviction, Small Claims.*

www.lakewoodcourtoh.com

Civil Records: Access: Phone, fax, mail, in person, online. Both court and visitors may perform in person searches. No search fee. Required to search: name, years to search; also helpful: address. Civil cases indexed by defendant, plaintiff. Civil records on computer from 1987, prior in books. Weekly dockets only are at www.lakewoodcourtoh.com/CourtDockets.htm.

Criminal Records: Access: Fax, mail, in person, online. Both court and visitors may perform in person searches. No search fee. Required to search: name, years to search, DOB; also helpful: address, SSN. Criminal records on computer since 1983, prior in books. Weekly dockets only are at www.lakewoodcourtoh.com/CourtDockets.htm.

General Information: No confidential records released. No fee to fax results. Local faxing only. Copy fee: $.25 per page. Cert fee: $3.00. Payee: Municipal Court. Personal checks accepted. Prepayment required. Mail requests: SASE required. Mail turnaround time 1 week.

Lyndhurst Municipal Court 5301 Mayfield Rd, Lyndhurst, OH 44124; 440-461-6500; Fax: 440-442-1910. Hours: 8:30AM-5PM M-TH; -4PM F (EST). *Misdemeanor, Civil Actions Under $15,000, Eviction, Small Claims.*

Civil Records: Access: Mail, in person. Both court and visitors may perform in person searches. No search fee. Required to search: name, years to search; also helpful: address. Civil cases indexed by defendant, plaintiff. Civil records on computer from 1991, prior in books.

Criminal Records: Access: Mail, in person. Both court and visitors may perform in person searches. No search fee. Required to search: name, years to search, signed release; also helpful: address, DOB, SSN, location. Criminal records on computer from 1991, prior in books.

General Information: Will fax results to local or toll free line. Copy fee: $1.00 per page. Cert fee: $5.00 per page. Payee: Municipal Court. Personal checks accepted. Prepayment required. Mail requests: SASE required. Mail turnaround time 1 week.

Parma Municipal Court 5555 Powers Blvd, Parma, OH 44125; 440-887-7400; Fax: 440-887-7485. Hours: 8:30AM-4:30PM (EST). *Misdemeanor, Civil Actions Under $15,000, Eviction, Small Claims.*

Note: The court is making changes to block the SSN from appearing on record requests.

Civil Records: Access: Phone, fax, mail, in person. Both court and visitors may perform in person searches. Search fee: $1.00 for copy. Required to search: name, years to search; also helpful: address. Civil cases indexed by defendant, plaintiff. Civil records on computer from 1993, prior in books to 1977.

Criminal Records: Access: Phone, fax, mail, in person. Both court and visitors may perform in person searches. Search fee: $1.00 for copy. Required to

search: name, years to search, DOB; also helpful: address, SSN. Criminal records on computer from 1993, prior in books to 1992.

General Information: Public Access terminal is available. (The terminal is only for civil records.) Copy fee: $.05 per page. Cert fee: $1.00. Payee: Municipal Court. Personal checks accepted. Prepayment required. Mail requests: SASE required. Mail turnaround time up to 1 week.

Rocky River Municipal Court 21012 Hilliard Blvd, Rocky River, OH 44116; 440-333-0066; Fax: 440-356-5613. Hours: 8:30AM-4:30PM (EST). *Misdemeanor, Civil Actions Under $15,000, Eviction, Small Claims.*

www.rrcourt.net

Civil Records: Access: Phone, fax, mail, in person, online. Visitors must perform in person searches for themselves. No search fee. Required to search: name, years to search. Civil cases indexed by defendant, plaintiff. Civil records on computer from 1987, prior in books to 1977. Public access to record index at the web page.

Criminal Records: Access: Phone, fax, mail, in person, online. Visitors must perform in person searches for themselves. No search fee. Required to search: name, years to search, DOB. Criminal records on computer back to 1987, prior in books to 1977. Public access to record index is at the web page.

General Information: Public Access terminal is available. Will fax results to toll free line. Copy fee: $.10 per page. Cert fee: $10.00. Payee: Municipal Court. Personal checks accepted. Prepayment required. Mail requests: SASE required. Mail turnaround time 2 days.

Shaker Heights Municipal Court 3355 Lee Rd, Shaker Heights, OH 44120; 216-491-1300; Fax: 216-491-1314. Hours: 8:30AM-4:30PM (EST). *Misdemeanor, Civil Actions Under $15,000, Eviction, Small Claims.*

www.shakerheightscourt.org

Note: Criminal Clerk open until 6:30PM on Mondays.

Civil Records: Access: Mail, fax, in person. Both court and visitors may perform in person searches. No search fee. Required to search: name, years to search; also helpful: address. Civil cases indexed by defendant, plaintiff. Civil records on computer from 06/86, prior in books for at least 25 years.

Criminal Records: Access: Phone, fax, mail, in person. Both court and visitors may perform in person searches. Search fee: None, however complete dockets are $10.00. Required to search: name, years to search, DOB or SSN. Criminal records on computer from 06/86, prior in books. For records prior to 1986 provide month & year to search. Phone access limited to gov't agencies.

General Information: No medical or LEADS print-out records released. Fee to fax results is $.50 per page. Copy fee: $.05 per page. Cert fee: $5.00. Payee: Shaker Heights Municipal Court. Personal checks accepted. Credit cards accepted: Visa, MC, AmEx. Visa, MC, Amex, accepted in person only. Prepayment required. Mail requests: SASE required. Mail turnaround time 2 days.

South Euclid Municipal Court 1349 S Green Rd, South Euclid, OH 44121; 216-381-2880; Fax: 216-381-1195. Hours: 8:30AM-5PM (EST). *Misdemeanor, Civil Actions Under $15,000, Eviction, Small Claims.*

Civil Records: Access: Phone, fax, mail, in person. Both court and visitors may perform in person searches. No search fee. Required to search: name, years to search; also helpful: address. Civil cases indexed by defendant, plaintiff. Civil records on computer back to 10/97; prior in docket books to 1960s.

Criminal Records: Access: Mail, in person. Both court and visitors may perform in person searches. No search fee. Required to search: name, years to search, DOB, SSN, signed release; also helpful: address. Criminal records on computer back to 10/97; prior in docket books to 1960s.

General Information: Public Access terminal is available. Will fax results to local or toll free line. Copy fee: No charge until at least 10 pages, then $.10 per copy. Cert fee: $1.00 per page. Payee: Clerk of Court, South Euclid Municipal Court. Personal checks accepted. Visa/MC accepted. Prepayment required. Mail requests: SASE required. Mail turnaround time 1 week.

Darke County

Common Pleas Court Courthouse, Greenville, OH 45331; 937-547-7335; Probate phone: 937-547-7345; Fax: 937-547-7305. Hours: 8:30AM-4:30PM (EST). *Felony, Civil Actions Over $15,000, Probate.*

Note: Probate is a separate court located at 300 Garst Ave at the number given.

Civil Records: Access: Mail, in person. Both court and visitors may perform in person searches. Search fee: $5.00 per name. Required to search: name, years to search. Civil cases indexed by defendant, plaintiff. Civil records in books to 1832, on microfiche from 1940s, computerized since 1993.

Criminal Records: Access: Mail, in person. Both court and visitors may perform in person searches. Search fee: $5.00 per name. Required to search: name, years to search. Criminal records in books to 1832, on microfiche from 1940s, computerized since 1987.

General Information: Public Access terminal is available. No secret indictment records released. Will fax results to local or toll free line. Copy fee: $.25 per page. Cert fee: $1.00. Payee: Clerk of Court. Business checks accepted. Prepayment required. Mail requests: SASE required. Mail turnaround time 1-2 days.

County Court Courthouse, Greenville, OH 45331-1990; 937-547-7340; Fax: 937-547-7378. Hours: 8:30AM-4:30PM (EST). *Misdemeanor, Civil Actions Under $15,000, Small Claims.*

Civil Records: Access: Mail, in person. Both court and visitors may perform in person searches. Search fee: $5.00 per name. Required to search: name, years to search. Civil cases indexed by defendant, plaintiff. Civil records in books since 1959, computerized since 1996.

Criminal Records: Access: Mail, in person. Both court and visitors may perform in person searches. Search fee: $5.00 per name. Required to search: name, years to search, DOB; also helpful: SSN. Criminal records in books since 1959.

General Information: Public Access terminal is available. No sealed or confidential records released. Will fax result for no fee. Copy fee: $.25 per page. Cert fee: $5.00. Payee: Clerk of Court, Darke County. Only cashiers checks and money orders accepted. Visa, MC accepted. Prepayment required. Mail requests: SASE required. Mail turnaround time 1 week.

Defiance County

Common Pleas Court PO Box 716, Defiance, OH 43512; 419-782-1936; Probate phone: 419-782-4181. Hours: 8:30AM-4:30PM (EST). *Felony, Civil Actions Over $10,000, Probate.*

Civil Records: Access: Phone, in person. Visitors must perform in person searches for themselves. No search fee. Required to search: name, years to search; also helpful: address. Civil cases indexed by defendant, plaintiff. Civil Records on computer since 1995. Most recent records are kept here.

Criminal Records: Access: Phone, in person. Visitors must perform in person searches for themselves. No search fee. Required to search: name, years to search; also helpful: address, DOB, SSN. Criminal records on computer since 1995; prior records on docket books.

General Information: Public Access terminal is available. Will fax results $3.00 1st page, $1.00 each add'l. Copy fee: $.25 per page. Cert fee: $1.00. Payee: Clerk of Court. Personal checks accepted. Prepayment required. Mail turnaround time 4-5 days.

Defiance Municipal Court 324 Perry St, Defiance, OH 43512; 419-782-5756; Civil phone: 419-782-4092; Fax: 419-782-2018. Hours: 8AM-5PM (EST). *Misdemeanor, Civil Actions Under $15,000, Eviction, Small Claims.*

Civil Records: Access: Mail, in person. Both court and visitors may perform in person searches. Search fee: $8.00 per name. Fee only for records prior to 1989. Required to search: name, years to search; also helpful: DOB, SSN, address. Civil cases indexed by defendant, plaintiff. Civil records on computer from 12/89, prior in books to 1958.

Criminal Records: Access: Mail, in person. Both court and visitors may perform in person searches. Search fee: $9.80 per name, but only for records prior to 1992. Required to search: name, years to search; also helpful: address, DOB, SSN. Criminal records on computer from 10/89, prior in books to 1958.

General Information: Public Access terminal is available. No confidential records released. Copy fee: $.50 per page. Cert fee: $1.00. Payee: Municipal Court. Personal checks accepted. Credit cards accepted. Prepayment required. Mail requests: SASE required. Mail turnaround time 14 days.

Delaware County

Common Pleas Court 91 N Sandusky, Delaware, OH 43015; 740-833-2500; Probate phone: 740-833-2680; Fax: 740-833-2499. Hours: 8:30AM-4:30PM (EST). *Felony, Civil Actions Over $15,000, Probate.*

www.delawarecountyclerk.org

Note: Probate Court is separate and located at 88 N Sandusky St; Probate hours are 8:30AM-4:30PM (Fax number for Probate is not available.)

Civil Records: Access: Mail, in person, online. Both court and visitors may perform in person searches. No search fee. Required to search: name, years to search; also helpful: address. Civil cases indexed by defendant, plaintiff. Civil records on computer from 1992, prior books go back to 1800s. Access to court records is free at www.delawarecountyclerk.org. Probate court index from 1852 to 1920 is free at www.midohio.net/dchsdcgs/probate.html.

Criminal Records: Access: Mail, in person. Both court and visitors may perform in person searches. No search fee. Required to search: name, years to search, DOB; also helpful: address, SSN. Criminal records on computer from 1992, prior books go back to 1800s. Access to court records is free at www.delawarecountyclerk.org. Search the sheriff's county database of sex offenders, deadbeat parents, and most wanted list for free at www.delawarecountysheriff.com.

General Information: Public Access terminal is available. No grand jury proceedings or expungment records released. Will not fax results. Copy fee: $.05 per page self-serve. Cert fee: $1.00. Payee: Clerk of Court. Personal checks accepted. Prepayment required. Mail requests: SASE required. Mail turnaround time 1-2 days.

Delaware Municipal Court 70 N Union St, Delaware, OH 43015; 740-548-6707; Civil phone: 740-368-1550; Criminal phone: 740-368-1555; Fax: 740-368-1583. Hours: 8AM-4:30PM (EST). *Misdemeanor, Civil Actions Under $15,000, Eviction, Small Claims.*

www.municipalcourt.org

Civil Records: Access: Phone, mail, in person, online. Both court and visitors may perform in person searches. No search fee. Required to search: name, years to search. Civil cases indexed by defendant, plaintiff. Civil records on computer from 1992, prior in books. Muncipal courts records are at www.municipalcourt.org:81/connection/court/.

Criminal Records: Access: Phone, mail, in person, online. Both court and visitors may perform in person searches. No search fee. Required to search: name, years to search, DOB; also helpful: SSN. Criminal records on computer from 1992, prior in books. Misdemeanor and traffic case records are free at www.municipalcourt.org:81/connection/court/lookup.xsp?in=ct. Also, search the court's DUI list at www.municipalcourt.org/main_dui.asp.

General Information: Public Access terminal is available. No assessment results or probation records released. Will not fax results. Copy fee: $.05 per page. Cert fee: $1.00. Payee: Delaware Municipal Court. Delaware County personal checks accepted. Prepayment required. Mail requests: SASE required. Mail turnaround time 1-2 weeks.

Erie County

Common Pleas Court 323 Columbus Ave, 1st Fl, Sandusky, OH 44870; 419-627-7705; Probate phone: 419-627-7759; Fax: 419-627-6873. Hours: 8AM-4PM M-Th/8AM-5PM F (EST). *Felony, Civil Actions Over $10,000, Probate.*

Civil Records: Access: In person only. Visitors must perform in person searches for themselves. No search fee. Required to search: name, years to search. Civil cases indexed by defendant, plaintiff. Civil records on books.

Criminal Records: Access: In person only. Visitors must perform in person searches for themselves. No search fee. Required to search: name, years to search, DOB, SSN, signed release. Criminal records on books; computerized records since 2001.

General Information: Public Access terminal is available. Passports and expungments not released. Copy fee: $.25 per page. Cert fee: $1.00 for 1st page, $.25 each add'l page. Payee: Clerk of Court. Personal checks accepted. Prepayment required.

Erie County Court 150 W Mason Rd, Milan, OH 44846; 419-499-4689; Fax: 419-499-3300. Hours: 8AM-4PM (EST). *Misdemeanor, Civil Actions Under $15,000, Small Claims.*

Civil Records: Access: Mail, in person. Both court and visitors may perform in person searches. No search fee. Required to search: name, years to search; also helpful: address. Civil cases indexed by defendant, plaintiff. Civil records on computer back to 1990, microfiche back to 1982.

Criminal Records: Access: Mail, in person. Both court and visitors may perform in person searches. No search fee. Required to search: name, years to search; also helpful: address, DOB. Criminal records on computer back to 1990, microfiche back to 1982.

General Information: Public Access terminal is available. No sealed records released. Copy fee: $.10 per page. No cert fee. Payee: County Court. Business checks accepted. Prepayment required. Mail requests: SASE required. Mail turnaround time 3-4 days.

Sandusky Municipal Court 222 Meigs St, Sandusky, OH 44870; 419-627-5926; Civil phone: 419-627-5914; Criminal phone: 419-627-5975; Fax: 419-627-5950. Hours: 7AM-4PM (EST). *Misdemeanor, Civil Actions Under $15,000, Eviction, Small Claims.*

Civil Records: Access: Phone, fax, mail, in person. Both court and visitors may perform in person searches. No search fee. Required to search: name, years to search; also helpful: case number. Civil cases indexed by defendant, plaintiff. Civil records on computer from 1987, prior in books.

Criminal Records: Access: Phone, fax, mail, in person. Both court and visitors may perform in person searches. No search fee. Required to search: name, years to search, DOB; also helpful: SSN, case number. Criminal records on computer from 1987, prior in books.

General Information: Public Access terminal is available. No pending, (some) crimes of violence records, or expunged records released. Will fax results for $0.10 per page. Copy fee: $.10 per page. Cert fee: $4.00. Payee: Sandusky Municipal Court. Prepayment required. Mail requests: SASE requested. Turnaround time 3-4 days.

Vermilion Municipal Court 687 Decatur St, Vermilion, OH 44089; 440-967-6543; Fax: 440-967-1467. Hours: 8AM-4PM (EST). *Misdemeanor, Civil Actions Under $15,000, Eviction, Small Claims.*

www.vermilionmunicipalcourt.org

Civil Records: Access: Fax, mail, in person, online. Both court and visitors may perform in person searches. No search fee. Required to search: name, years to search. Civil cases indexed by defendant, plaintiff. Civil records on computer from 1992, prior in books. Online access to municipal court records is at the website or directly at http://209.142.158.114/search.html.

Criminal Records: Access: Fax, mail, in person, online. Both court and visitors may perform in person searches. No search fee. Required to search: name, years to search, DOB; also helpful: SSN. Criminal records on computer from 1992, prior in books. Online access to criminal records is the same as civil.

General Information: Public Access terminal is available. Copy fee: $1.00 per page. The fee is for a computer printout. Cert fee: $2.00. Payee: Vermilion Municipal Court. Only cashiers checks and money orders accepted. Visa, MC accepted. Prepayment required. Mail requests: SASE required. Mail turnaround time 1-5 days.

Fairfield County

Common Pleas Court 224 E Main, Clerk's Office, Lancaster, OH 43130-0370; 740-687-7030; Probate phone: 740-687-7093. Hours: 8AM-4PM (EST). *Felony, Civil Actions Over $10,000, Probate.*

www.fairfieldcountyclerk.com/

Note: Probate Court is separate from this court, at the same address and at the Probate phone number above.

Civil Records: Access: fax, mail, in person, online. Visitors must perform in person searches for themselves. No search fee. Required to search: name, years to search; also helpful: address. Civil cases indexed by defendant, plaintiff. Civil records on computer from 10/93, in books to 1970, archived to 1800s. Online access to County Clerk's court records database is free at www.fairfieldcountyclerk.com/Search/.

Criminal Records: Access: In person, online. Visitors must perform in person searches for themselves. No search fee. Required to search: name, years to search; also helpful: address, DOB, SSN. Criminal records on computer from 10/93, in books to 1970, prior archived to 1800s. Online access to

County Clerk's court records database is free at www.fairfieldcountyclerk.com/Search/.

General Information: Public Access terminal is available. No adoption or juvenile records released. Copy fee: $.05 per page. Cert fee: $5.00. Payee: Clerk of Court. Personal checks accepted. Credit cards accepted: Visa. Credit cards not accepted over the phone. Prepayment required. Mail requests: SASE required. Mail turnaround time is 2-3 weeks.

Fairfield County Municipal Court PO Box 2390, Lancaster, OH 43130; 740-687-6621. Hours: 8AM-4PM (EST). *Misdemeanor, Civil Actions Under $15,000, Eviction, Small Claims.*
www.fairfieldcountymunicipalcourt.org

Civil Records: Access: Mail, in person, online. Both court and visitors may perform in person searches. No search fee. Required to search: name, years to search. Civil cases indexed by defendant, plaintiff. Civil records on computer from 1990, prior in books. Cases may be searched online from the website.

Criminal Records: Access: Mail, in person, online. Both court and visitors may perform in person searches. No search fee. Required to search: name, years to search. Criminal records on computer from 1989, prior in books. Cases may be searched online from the website.

General Information: Public Access terminal is available. Will fax results to local or toll free line. No copy fee. Cert fee: $1.00. Payee: Fairfiled County Court. Personal checks accepted. Prepayment required. Mail requests: SASE required. Mail turnaround time 2 days.

Fayette County

Common Pleas Court 110 E Court St, Washington Court House, OH 43160; 740-335-6371; Probate phone: 740-335-0640. Hours: 9AM-4PM (EST). *Felony, Civil Actions Over $10,000, Probate.*
Note: Probate is a separate court at number given.

Civil Records: Access: Mail, in person. Visitors must perform in person searches for themselves. No search fee. Required to search: name, years to search. Civil cases indexed by defendant, plaintiff. Civil records on computer from 1992, prior in books to 1800s.

Criminal Records: Access: Mail, in person. Visitors must perform in person searches for themselves. No search fee. Required to search: name, years to search, DOB, SSN. Criminal records on computer from 1992, prior in books to 1800s.

General Information: Public Access terminal is available. No records released. Fee to fax results is $1.00 per page, plus $2.00 for cover page. Copy fee: $1.00 per page. Cert fee: $1.00. Payee: Clerk of Court. Personal checks accepted. Prepayment required. Mail requests: SASE required. Mail turnaround time varies.

Municipal Court Washington Courthouse, 119 N Main St, Washington Court House, OH 43160; 740-636-2350; Fax: 740-636-2359. Hours: 8AM-4PM (EST). *Misdemeanor, Civil Actions Under $15,000, Eviction, Small Claims.*

Civil Records: Access: Mail, in person. Both court and visitors may perform in person searches. No search fee. Required to search: name, years to search. Civil cases indexed by defendant, plaintiff. Civil records on computer from 1990, prior in books to 1950s.

Criminal Records: Access: Mail, in person. Both court and visitors may perform in person searches. No search fee. Required to search: name, years to search, DOB; also helpful: SSN. Criminal records on computer from 1990, prior in books to 1950s.

General Information: Public Access terminal is available. No records protected by the privacy act released. No copy fee. Cert fee: $5.00. Payee: Clerk of Court. Only cashiers checks and money orders

accepted. Prepayment required. Mail requests: SASE required. Mail turnaround time 1 week.

Franklin County

Common Pleas Court 369 S High St, Columbus, OH 43215-6311; 614-462-3600; Civil phone: 614-462-3621; Criminal phone: 614-462-3650; Probate phone: 614-462-3894; Fax: 614-462-4325 Civil; 614-462-6661 Crim. Hours: 8AM-5PM (EST). *Felony, Civil Actions Over $15,000.*
www.franklincountyclerk.com

Civil Records: Access: Online, in person. Visitors must perform in person searches for themselves. No search fee. Required to search: name, years to search. Civil cases indexed by defendant, plaintiff. Civil records go back to 1820. Access records via the website. Java-enable web browser required.

Criminal Records: Access: Mail, in person. Both court and visitors may perform in person searches. No search fee. Required to search: name, years to search. Criminla records availablle since 1935.

General Information: Public Access terminal is available. No psych, adoption or estate tax records released. Copy fee: $.10 per page. Cert fee: $1.00 per entry. Payee: Franklin County Clerk of Courts. Only cashiers checks and money orders accepted. Prepayment required. Mail requests: SASE required. Mail turnaround time up to 7 days.

Franklin County Municipal Court - Civil Division 375 S High St, 3rd Flr, Columbus, OH 43215; 614-645-7220; Civil phone: 614-645-8161-file room; Fax: 614-645-6919 (for filings only). Hours: 8AM-5PM (EST). *Civil Actions Under $15,000, Eviction, Small Claims.*
www.fcmcclerk.com

Civil Records: Access: Phone, fax, mail, online, in person. Both court and visitors may perform in person searches. No search fee. Required to search: name, years to search. Civil cases indexed by defendant, plaintiff. Civil records on computer from 1992, prior in books to 1974. Records from the Clerk of Court Courtview database free online at www.fcmcclerk.com/pa/pa.htm. Search by name or case number.

General Information: Public Access terminal is available. No sealed or expunged records released. Will fax results for free. Copy fee: First 25 copies are free, then $.05 each. No cert fee. Payee: Franklin County Municipal Court. Personal checks accepted. Visa, MC, Discover accepted. Prepayment required. Mail requests: SASE required. Mail turnaround time 2-3 days.

Franklin County Municipal Court - Criminal Division 375 S High St, 2nd Fl, Columbus, OH 43215; 614-645-8186. Hours: Open 24 hours a day (EST). *Misdemeanor.*
www.fcmcclerk.com

Criminal Records: Access: Mail, online, in person. Both court and visitors may perform in person searches. No search fee. Required to search: name, years to search; also helpful: DOB, SSN. Criminal records go back to 1987; on computer back to 1992. Criminal and traffic records from the Clerk of Court Courtview database free online at www.fcmcclerk.com/pa/pa.htm. Search by name, SSN, dates, ticket, DL or case numbers.

General Information: Public Access terminal is available. No sealed or expunged records released. Copy fee: $.25 per page. Cert fee: $1.00. Payee: Franklin County Municipal Court. Personal checks accepted. Visa, MC accepted. Prepayment required. Mail requests: SASE required. Mail turnaround time 7 days.

Probate Court 373 S High St, 22nd Fl, Columbus, OH 43215-6311; 614-462-3894; Fax: 740-393-6832. Hours: 8AM-5PM (EST). *Probate.*
Note: Search online at www.co.franklin.oh.us/probate/ProbateSearch.html.

Fulton County

Common Pleas Court 210 S Fulton, Wauseon, OH 43567; 419-337-9230; Probate phone: 419-337-9242. Hours: 8:30AM-4:30PM (EST). *Felony, Civil Actions Over $3,000, Probate.*

Civil Records: Access: In person only. Visitors must perform in person searches for themselves. No search fee. Required to search: name, years to search. Civil cases indexed by defendant, plaintiff. Civil records on computer from 9/88, prior in books to 1968, archived to 1800s.

Criminal Records: Access: In person only. Visitors must perform in person searches for themselves. No search fee. Required to search: name, years to search, DOB; also helpful: SSN. Criminal records on computer from 9/88, prior in books to 1968, archived to 1800s.

General Information: Public Access terminal is available. Copy fee: $.25 per page. Cert fee: $1.00 per page. Payee: Mary Gype Clerk of Court. Personal checks accepted. Prepayment required.

County Court Eastern District 204 S Main St, Swanton, OH 43558; 419-826-5636; Fax: 419-825-3324. Hours: 8:30AM-4:30PM (EST). *Misdemeanor, Civil Actions Under $15,000, Small Claims.*
www.fultoncountyoh.com/courts.htm

Civil Records: Access: Mail, fax, in person. Both court and visitors may perform in person searches. No search fee. Required to search: name, years to search. Civil cases indexed by defendant, plaintiff. Civil records on computer from 1988, prior in books.

Criminal Records: Access: Mail, in person. Only the court performs in person searches; visitors may not. No search fee. Required to search: name, years to search, DOB; signed release requested. Criminal records on computer from 1988, prior in books.

General Information: No pending case records released. Copy fee: None, but must supply own paper for copies. No cert fee. Only cashiers checks and money orders accepted. Mail requests: SASE required. Mail turnaround time 2 weeks.

County Court Western District 224 S Fulton St, Wauseon, OH 43567; 419-337-9212; Fax: 419-337-9286. Hours: 8:30AM-4:30PM (EST). *Misdemeanor, Civil Actions Under $15,000, Small Claims.*

Civil Records: Access: Mail, in person. Both court and visitors may perform in person searches. No search fee. Required to search: name, years to search. Civil cases indexed by defendant, plaintiff. Civil records on computer from 1989, prior in books. In-person searchers should call first; Tuesdays are court day and computers in use.

Criminal Records: Access: Mail, in person. Both court and visitors may perform in person searches. No search fee. Required to search: name, years to search, DOB; also helpful: SSN. Criminal records on computer after 1988, indexed by name and DOB. In-person searchers should call first; be aware Tuesdays are busy and hard to get on computer to search.

General Information: Public Access terminal is available. No pending case records released. Copy fee: $.10 per page. Cert fee: $1.00. Payee: County Court Western District. No personal checks. Prepayment required. Mail requests: SASE required. Mail turnaround time 2-3 days.

Gallia County

Common Pleas Court - Gallia County Courthouse 18 Locust St, Rm 1290, Gallipolis, OH 45631-1290; 740-446-4612 x223; Probate phone: 740-446-4612 x240; Fax: 740-441-2094. Hours: 8AM-4PM (EST). *Felony, Civil Actions Over $10,000, Probate.*

Civil Records: Access: In person only. Visitors must perform in person searches for themselves. No search fee. Required to search: name, years to search. Civil cases indexed by defendant, plaintiff. Civil records on computer from 7/91, in books to 1968, archived to 1800s. Will fax copies for $1.00 per page if pre-paid.

Criminal Records: Access: In person only. Visitors must perform in person searches for themselves. No search fee. Required to search: name, years to search. Criminal records on computer from 7/91, in books to 1968, archived to 1800s. Will fax copies for $1.00 per page if pre-paid.

General Information: Public Access terminal is available. No records released. Copy fee: $.25 per page. Cert fee: $1.00. Payee: Clerk of Court. Personal checks accepted. Prepayment required.

Gallipolis Municipal Court 518 2nd Ave, Gallipolis, OH 45631; 740-446-9400; Fax: 740-441-2070. Hours: 7:30AM-5PM (EST). *Misdemeanor, Civil Actions Under $15,000, Eviction, Small Claims.*

Civil Records: Access: Phone, mail, in person. Both court and visitors may perform in person searches. No search fee. Required to search: name, years to search; also helpful: address. Civil cases indexed by defendant, plaintiff. Civil records on computer from 8/93, prior in books.

Criminal Records: Access: Phone, mail, in person. Both court and visitors may perform in person searches. No search fee. Required to search: name, years to search; also helpful: address, DOB, SSN. Criminal records on computer from 8/93, prior in books.

General Information: Public Access terminal is available. No expunged records released. Will not fax results. Copy fee: $.25 per page. Cert fee: $2.00. Payee: Municipal Court. Personal checks accepted. Prepayment required. Mail requests: SASE required. Mail turnaround time 1 week.

Geauga County

Common Pleas Court 100 Short Court, Chardon, OH 44024; 440-285-2222 X2380; Probate phone: 440-285-2222 X2000; Fax: 440-286-2127. Hours: 8AM-4:30PM (EST). *Felony, Civil Actions Over $10,000, Probate.*
www.co.geauga.oh.us

Civil Records: Access: In person, online. Visitors must perform in person searches for themselves. No search fee. Required to search: name, years to search. Civil cases indexed by defendant, plaintiff. Civil records on computer from 1990, in books from 1968, prior archived. Online access is free from the Clerk of Courts at www.co.geauga.oh.us/departments/clerk_of_courts/docket/Courtintro.asp. Online records go back to 1990. Includes domestic cases.

Criminal Records: Access: In person, online. Visitors must perform in person searches for themselves. No search fee. Required to search: name, years to search. Criminal records on computer from 1990, in books from 1968, prior archived. Online access is free from the Clerk of Courts at www.co.geauga.oh.us/departments/clerk_of_courts/docket/Courtintro.asp. Online records go back to 1990.

General Information: Public Access terminal is available. no sealed records released. Will not fax results. Copy fee: $.25 per page. Cert fee: $1.00.

Payee: Clerk of Court. Personal checks accepted. Credit cards accepted. Prepayment required.

Chardon Municipal Court 111 Water St, Chardon, OH 44024; 440-286-2670/2684; Fax: 440-286-2679. Hours: 8AM-4:30PM (EST). *Misdemeanor, Civil Actions Under $15,000, Eviction, Small Claims.*
www.co.geauga.oh.us/departments/muni_court.htm

Civil Records: Access: Mail, in person. Both court and visitors may perform in person searches. No search fee. Required to search: name, years to search; also helpful: address. Civil cases indexed by defendant, plaintiff. Civil records on computer from 1990, prior in books.

Criminal Records: Access: Mail, in person. Both court and visitors may perform in person searches. No search fee. Required to search: name, years to search; also helpful: address, DOB, SSN. Criminal records on computer from 1988, prior in books to 1965.

General Information: Public Access terminal is available. (Available 8AM-4:30PM; 2 hour maximum.) No expunged records released. Will fax results to local or toll free line. Copy fee: $.25 per page. Cert fee: $1.50. Payee: Chardon Municipal Court. Personal checks accepted. Visa, MC accepted. Accepted for criminal only. Prepayment required. Mail requests: SASE required. Mail turnaround time 2-4 days.

Greene County

Common Pleas Court 45 N Detroit St (PO Box 156), Xenia, OH 45385; 937-562-5290; Probate phone: 937-376-5280; Fax: 937-562-5309. Hours: 8AM-4:30PM (EST). *Felony, Civil Actions Over $10,000, Probate.*
www.co.greene.oh.us/clerk.htm

Civil Records: Access: In person, online. Visitors must perform in person searches for themselves. No search fee. Required to search: name, years to search. Civil cases indexed by defendant, plaintiff. Civil records on computer from 1982, prior in books and on microfiche. Online access to clerk of court records is free at http://198.30.12.230/pa/pa.htm. Search by name or case number.

Criminal Records: Access: In person, online. Visitors must perform in person searches for themselves. No search fee. Required to search: name, years to search; also helpful: DOB, SSN, case number. Criminal records on computer from 1982, prior in books and on microfiche. Online access to clerk of court records is free at http://198.30.12.230/pa/pa.htm. Search by name or case number.

General Information: Public Access terminal is available. No sealed records released. Will fax specifc case file requests for $2.00 per page. Copy fee: $.25 per page. Cert fee: $1.00 per page. Payee: Clerk of Court. Personal checks accepted. Visa, MC accepted. Prepayment required.

Fairborn Municipal Court 44 W Hebble Ave, Fairborn, OH 45324; Civil phone: 937-754-3044; Criminal phone: 937-754-3040; Fax: 937-879-4422. Hours: 7:30AM-4:30PM (EST). *Misdemeanor, Civil Actions Under $20,000, Eviction, Small Claims.*
http://ci.fairborn.oh.us/Court/municipal_court.htm

Civil Records: Access: Mail, in person, online. Both court and visitors may perform in person searches. No search fee. Required to search: name, years to search; also helpful: address. Civil cases indexed by defendant, plaintiff. Civil records on computer from 1991, records go back to 1976. The web page offers free online access to civil, misdemeanor and traffic records.

Criminal Records: Access: Mail, in person, online. Both court and visitors may perform in person searches. No search fee. Required to search: name,

years to search, SSN; also helpful: address, DOB. Criminal records on computer from mid 1991, records go back to 1976. Online access same as civil.

General Information: Public Access terminal is available. Will not fax results. Copy fee: $.25 per page. Cert fee: $2.00. Payee: Municipal Court. Personal checks accepted. Prepayment required. Mail requests: SASE required. Mail turnaround time 1 week.

Xenia Municipal Court 101 N Detroit, Xenia, OH 45385; 937-376-7294; 376-7297 (Civil Clerk); Fax: 937-376-7288. Hours: 8AM-4:30PM (EST). *Misdemeanor, Civil Actions Under $15,000, Eviction, Small Claims.*
http://xmcwa.ci.xenia.oh.us

Civil Records: Access: Fax, mail, in person, online. Both court and visitors may perform in person searches. No search fee. Required to search: name, years to search; also helpful: address. Civil cases indexed by defendant, plaintiff. Civil records on computer from 1994, prior in books to 1966. Online access to Municipal Court records is free through CourtView at http://xmcwa.ci.xenia.oh.us.

Criminal Records: Access: Fax, mail, in person, online. Both court and visitors may perform in person searches. No search fee. Required to search: name, years to search; also helpful: address, DOB, SSN. Criminal records on computer from 1994, prior in books to 1966. Access to criminal records is the same as civil.

General Information: Public Access terminal is available. No search warrant records released. No fee to fax results. Copy fee: $.10 per page. Cert fee: $2.00. Payee: Municipal Court. Business checks accepted. Visa, MC accepted. Visa, MC. Prepayment required. Mail requests: SASE required.

Guernsey County

Common Pleas Court 801 E Wheeling Ave D-300, Cambridge, OH 43725; 740-432-9230; Probate phone: 740-432-9262; Fax: 740-432-7807. Hours: 8:30AM-4PM (EST). *Felony, Civil Actions Over $10,000, Probate.*
www.guernseycountycpcourt.org/

Note: Probate is a separate division with separate records and personnel.

Civil Records: Access: Online, in person. Visitors must perform in person searches for themselves. No search fee. Required to search: name, years to search. Civil cases indexed by defendant, plaintiff. Civil records on computer from 1990, prior in books, archived to 1800s. Access case index data online at the website.

Criminal Records: Access: Online, in person. Visitors must perform in person searches for themselves. No search fee. Required to search: name, years to search, DOB, SSN, signed release. Criminal records on computer from 1990, prior in books, archived to 1800s. Access case index data online at the website.

General Information: Public Access terminal is available. No expunged records released. Copy fee: $.25 per page. Cert fee: $2.00. Payee: Clerk of Court. Personal checks accepted. Prepayment required.

Cambridge Municipal Court 134 Southgate Parkway, Cambridge, OH 43725; 740-439-5585; Civil phone: x240; Criminal phone: x226; Fax: 740-439-5666. Hours: 8:30AM-4:30PM (EST). *Misdemeanor, Civil Actions Under $15,000, Eviction, Small Claims.*

Civil Records: Access: Mail, in person, fax. Both court and visitors may perform in person searches. Search fee: none. Required to search: name, years to search; also helpful: address. Civil cases indexed by defendant, plaintiff. Civil records on computer from

1988, prior in books. Fax civil court requests to 740-439-9405.

Criminal Records: Access: Mail, in person, fax. Visitors must perform in person searches for themselves. Search fee: none. Required to search: name, years to search, DOB, SSN; also helpful: address. Criminal records on computer from 1988, prior in books.

General Information: Public Access terminal is available. No confidential records released. Will fax results to toll-free number only. No copy fee. Cert fee: $2.00. Payee: Cambridge Municipal Court. Personal checks accepted. Visa, MC accepted. Prepayment required. Mail requests: SASE required. Mail turnaround time 3-5 days.

Hamilton County

Common Pleas Court 1000 Main St, Rm 315, Cincinnati, OH 45202; Civil phone: 513-946-5635; Criminal phone: 513-946-5671; Probate phone: 513-946-3580. Hours: 8AM-4PM (EST). *Felony, Civil Actions Over $10,000, Probate.*
www.courtclerk.org
Note: Probate is separate court at telephone number given.

Civil Records: Access: Mail, online, in person. Both court and visitors may perform in person searches. No search fee. Required to search: name, years to search. Civil cases indexed by defendant, plaintiff. Civil records indexed on computer since 1960s, prior in books and files. Records from the court clerk are free online at the website or www.courtclerk.org/queries.htm. Online civil index goes back to 1991. Also, search probate records free at www.probatect.org/case_search/casesearch.asp.

Criminal Records: Access: Mail, online, in person. Both court and visitors may perform in person searches. No search fee. Required to search: name, years to search, signed release; also helpful: DOB, SSN. Criminal records indexed on computer since 1960s, prior in books and files. Online access to criminal records is the same as civil. Online criminal index goes back to 1986.

General Information: Public Access terminal is available. Criminal histories not released. Copy fee: Fees vary by storage media of original. Cert fee: $1.00. Payee: Clerk of Court. Personal checks accepted. Credit cards accepted. Prepayment required. Mail requests: SASE required. Mail turnaround time 2-3 days.

Hamilton County Municipal Court - Civil 1000 Main St, Rm 115, Cincinnati, OH 45202; 513-946-5700; Criminal phone: 513-946-6029; Fax: 513-946-5710. Hours: 8AM-4PM (EST). *Civil Actions Under $15,000, Eviction, Small Claims.*
www.courtclerk.org
Civil Records: Access: Fax, mail, online, in person. Both court and visitors may perform in person searches. No search fee. Required to search: name; also helpful: years to search. Civil cases indexed by defendant, plaintiff. Civil records on computer from 1989, prior on microfilm. Records from the court clerk are free online at the website or www.courtclerk.org/queries.htm.
General Information: Public Access terminal is available. No expungement records released. No fee to fax results. Copy fee: $.25 per page. $4.00 for docket sheet (civil). Cert fee: $5.00. Payee: Clerk of Courts. Personal checks accepted. Visa, MC accepted. Prepayment required. Mail turnaround time 5 days.

Hamilton County Municipal Court - Criminal 1000 Sycamore St #111, Cincinnati, OH 45202; 513-946-6029/6040. Hours: 8AM-4PM (EST). *Misdemeanor.*
www.courtclerk.org

Criminal Records: Access: In person, online. Visitors must perform in person searches for themselves. No search fee. Required to search: name, years to search, DOB; also helpful: SSN. Criminal records on computer back to 2000, prior on microfiche back to 1973. Records from the court clerk are free online at www.courtclerk.org/queries.htm.
General Information: Public Access terminal is available. Copy fee: $.10 per page. No cert fee. Payee: Clerk of Courts. Personal checks accepted. Visa, MC accepted. Prepayment required.

Hancock County

Common Pleas Court 300 S Main St, Findlay, OH 45840; 419-424-7037/7008; Probate phone: 419-424-7079. Hours: 8:30AM-4:30PM (EST). *Felony, Civil Actions Over $10,000, Probate.*
www.co.hancock.oh.us/commonpleas
Civil Records: Access: Mail, in person, online. Both court and visitors may perform in person searches. Search fee: $10.00 per name. Required to search: name, years to search. Civil cases indexed by defendant, plaintiff. Civil records on computer from 1985, microfiche from 1974, dockets archived to 1800s. Search records online back to 1985 at web page.
Criminal Records: Access: Mail, in person, online. Both court and visitors may perform in person searches. Search fee: $10.00 per name. Required to search: name, years to search. Criminal records on computer from 1985, microfiche from 1974, dockets archived to 1800s. Search records online back to 1985 at web page.
General Information: Public Access terminal is available. No home investigations, medical records released. Cert fee: $1.00. Payee: Clerk of Court. Personal checks accepted. Prepayment required. Mail requests: SASE required. Mail turnaround time 1-2 days.

Findlay Municipal Court PO Box 826, Findlay, OH 45839; Civil phone: 419-424-7143; Criminal phone: 419-424-7141; Fax: 419-424-7803. Hours: 8AM-5PM; 8AM-7PM Tuesday only (EST). *Misdemeanor, Civil Actions Under $15,000, Eviction, Small Claims.*
Civil Records: Access: Mail, in person. Both court and visitors may perform in person searches. Search fee: $2.00 per name. Required to search: name, years to search. Civil cases indexed by defendant, plaintiff. Civil records on computer from 1984.
Criminal Records: Access: Mail, in person. Both court and visitors may perform in person searches. Search fee: $2.00 per name. Required to search: name, years to search, DOB, SSN. Criminal records on computer from 1984.
General Information: Public Access terminal is available. Will not fax results. Copy fee: $.25 per page. Cert fee: $1.00. Payee: Findlay Municipal Court. Local (Hancock County) personal checks accepted. Visa, Mc accepted. Prepayment required. Mail requests: SASE required.

Hardin County

Common Pleas Court Courthouse, #310, Kenton, OH 43326; 419-674-2278; Probate phone: 419-674-2230; Fax: 419-674-2273. Hours: 8:30AM-4PM (EST). *Felony, Civil Actions Over $10,000.*
Civil Records: Access: Mail, in person. Both court and visitors may perform in person searches. No search fee. Required to search: name, years to search. Civil cases indexed by defendant, plaintiff. Current records on computer as of 1/95. Overall records go back to 1885.
Criminal Records: Access: Mail, fax, in person. Both court and visitors may perform in person searches. No search fee. Required to search: name,

years to search, DOB, signed release; also helpful: SSN. Current records on computer as of 1/95. Overall records go back to 1885.
General Information: Public Access terminal is available. Will fax results $2.00 1st page, $1.00 each add'l. Copy fee: $.25 per page. Certified copies $1.00 per page. Cert fee: $1.00 per page. Payee: Clerk of Court. Business checks accepted. Prepayment required. Mail requests: SASE required. Mail turnaround time 2-4 days.

Hardin County Municipal Court PO Box 250, Kenton, OH 43326; 419-674-4362; Fax: 419-674-4096. Hours: 8:30AM-4PM (EST). *Misdemeanor, Civil Actions Under $15,000, Eviction, Small Claims.*
Civil Records: Access: Mail, in person. Both court and visitors may perform in person searches. Search fee: $5.00. Required to search: name, years to search. Civil cases indexed by defendant, plaintiff. Civil records on computer since 1989, prior on books.
Criminal Records: Access: Mail, in person. Both court and visitors may perform in person searches. Search fee: $5.00. Required to search: name, years to search; also helpful: SSN. Criminal records on computer since 1989, prior on books.
General Information: Public Access terminal is available. Copy fee: $.25 per page. Cert fee: $2.00. Payee: Hardin County Municipal Court. Business checks accepted. Prepayment required. Mail requests: SASE required. Mail turnaround time 1-2 days.

Harrison County

Common Pleas Court 100 W Market, Cadiz, OH 43907; 740-942-8500; Probate phone: 740-942-8868; Fax: 740-942-3006. Hours: 8:30AM-4:30PM (EST). *Felony, Civil Actions Over $3,000, Probate.*
Civil Records: Access: Phone, fax, mail, in person. Both court and visitors may perform in person searches. No search fee. Required to search: name, years to search; also helpful: address. Civil cases indexed by defendant, plaintiff. Civil records on computer since 1994, in books back to 1800s.
Criminal Records: Access: In person only. Visitors must perform in person searches for themselves. No search fee. Required to search: name, years to search; also helpful: address, DOB, SSN. Criminal records on computer since 1994, in books back to 1800s.
General Information: Public Access terminal is available. No secret records released. Will fax results $.25 per page. Copy fee: $.25 per page. Cert fee: $1.00. Payee: Clerk of Court. Personal checks accepted. Prepayment required. Mail requests: SASE required. Mail turnaround time 1-2 days.

Harrison County Court Courthouse, 100 W Market St, Cadiz, OH 43907; 740-942-8865; Fax: 740-942-3541. Hours: 8:00AM-4:30PM (EST). *Misdemeanor, Civil Actions Under $15,000, Small Claims.*
Civil Records: Access: In person only. Visitors must perform in person searches for themselves. No search fee. Required to search: name, years to search. Civil cases indexed by defendant, plaintiff. Civil records in books; on computer back to 1/2000 (older records being added).
Criminal Records: Access: In person only. Visitors must perform in person searches for themselves. No search fee. Required to search: name, years to search, DOB; also helpful: SSN. Criminal records in books; on computer back to 1/2000 (older records being added).
General Information: Public Access terminal is available. Copy fee: $.25 per page. Cert fee: $1.00. Payee: Harrison County Court. Only cashiers checks and money orders accepted. Prepayment required.

Henry County

Common Pleas Court PO Box 70, Napoleon, OH 43545; 419-592-5926; Probate phone: 419-592-7771; Fax: 419-592-0803. Hours: 8:30AM-4:30PM (EST). *Felony, Civil Actions Over $10,000, Probate.* Note: Probate Court's address is PO Box 70, fax is 419-592-7000.

Civil Records: Access: Fax, mail, in person. Visitors must perform in person searches for themselves. No search fee. Required to search: name, years to search. Civil cases indexed by defendant, plaintiff. Civil records on computer from 10/94, prior in books.

Criminal Records: Access: Fax, mail, in person. Visitors must perform in person searches for themselves. No search fee. Required to search: name, years to search. Criminal records on computer from 10/94, prior in books.

General Information: Public Access terminal is available. No adoption or mental records released. Will fax results $3.00 1st page, $1.00 each add'l. Copy fee: $1.00 per page. Cert fee: $1.00. Payee: Clerk of Court. Personal checks accepted. Prepayment required. Mail requests: SASE required.

Napoleon Municipal Court PO Box 502, Napoleon, OH 43545; 419-592-2851; Fax: 419-592-1805. Hours: 8AM-5PM (EST). *Misdemeanor, Civil Actions Under $15,000, Eviction, Small Claims.*

Civil Records: Access: Phone, fax, mail, in person. Both court and visitors may perform in person searches. No search fee. Required to search: name, years to search. Civil cases indexed by defendant, plaintiff. Civil records on computer from 1990, prior in books.

Criminal Records: Access: Phone, fax, mail, in person. Both court and visitors may perform in person searches. No search fee. Required to search: name, years to search, DOB; also helpful: SSN. Criminal records on computer from 1990, prior in books.

General Information: No alcohol treatment records released. Copy fee: $.05 per page. Cert fee: $1.00. Payee: Clerk of Court. Personal checks accepted. Visa, MC accepted. Prepayment required. Mail requests: SASE required. Mail turnaround time 1-2 days.

Highland County

Common Pleas Court PO Box 821, Hillsboro, OH 45133; 937-393-9957; Probate phone: 937-393-9981; Fax: 937-393-9878. Hours: 8AM-4:30PM (EST). *Felony, Civil Actions Over $10,000, Probate.* Note: Probate is a separate court.

Civil Records: Access: Mail, fax, in person. Both court and visitors may perform in person searches. No search fee. Required to search: name, years to search; also helpful: address. Civil cases indexed by defendant, plaintiff. Civil records in books since 1800s; on computer since 1995.

Criminal Records: Access: Mail, fax, in person. Both court and visitors may perform in person searches. No search fee. Required to search: name, years to search, DOB, signed release; also helpful: SSN. Criminal records in books since 1800s; on computer since 1990.

General Information: Public Access terminal is available. no sealed records released. Will fax results to local or toll free line. Copy fee: $.10 per page. Cert fee: $1.00 per page. Payee: Clerk of Court. Personal checks accepted. Mail requests: SASE required. Mail turnaround time same day.

Hillsboro County Municipal Court 130 Homestead Ave, Hillsboro, OH 45133; 937-393-3022; Fax: 937-393-0517. Hours: 7AM-3:30PM M,T,Th,F; 7AM-Noon W (EST). *Misdemeanor, Civil Actions Under $15,000, Eviction, Small Claims.*

Civil Records: Access: Phone, fax, mail, in person. Only the court performs in person searches; visitors may not. No search fee. Required to search: name, years to search. Civil cases indexed by defendant, plaintiff. Civil records on computer from 1991, prior in books.

Criminal Records: Access: Phone, fax, mail, in person. Only the court performs in person searches; visitors may not. No search fee. Required to search: name, years to search, DOB, SSN. Criminal records on computer from 1991, prior in books.

General Information: No expunged records released. No fee to fax results. Local or toll free calls only. Copy fee: $.15 per page. No cert fee. Payee: Hillsboro Municipal Court. Personal checks accepted. Prepayment required. Mail turnaround time 1-2 days.

Hocking County

Common Pleas Court PO Box 108, Logan, OH 43138; 740-385-2616; Probate phone: 740-385-3022; Fax: 740-385-1822. Hours: 8:30AM-4PM (EST). *Felony, Civil Actions Over $10,000.* Note: Probate is a separate court at the number given.

Civil Records: Access: Phone, fax, mail, in person. Both court and visitors may perform in person searches. No search fee. Required to search: name, years to search; also helpful: address. Civil cases indexed by defendant, plaintiff. Civil records on computer since 1996, in books to late 1800s.

Criminal Records: Access: Phone, fax, mail, in person. Both court and visitors may perform in person searches. No search fee. Required to search: name, years to search; also helpful: address, DOB, SSN. Criminal records date back to 1980 on docket books.

General Information: Public Access terminal is available. No secret records released. Will fax results $1.00 per page. Copy fee: $1.00 per page. Cert fee: $1.00. Payee: Clerk of Court. Business checks accepted. Prepayment required. Mail requests: SASE required. Mail turnaround time 1-2 days.

Hocking County Municipal Court PO Box 950, Logan, OH 43138-1278; 740-385-2250; Fax: 740-385-3826. Hours: 8:30AM-4PM (EST). *Misdemeanor, Civil Actions Under $15,000, Eviction, Small Claims.*
www.Hocking County Municipal Court

Civil Records: Access: Mail, in person, fax. Only the court performs in person searches; visitors may not. No search fee. Required to search: name, years to search. Civil cases indexed by defendant, plaintiff. Civil records on computer from 1991, prior in books.

Criminal Records: Access: Mail, in person, fax. Only the court performs in person searches; visitors may not. No search fee. Required to search: name, years to search, DOB, SSN, signed release. Criminal records on computer from 1991 prior in books.

General Information: Copy fee: $.10 per page. Cert fee: $1.00 per page. Payee: Municipal Court. Personal checks accepted. Prepayment required. Mail requests: SASE required. Mail turnaround time 1-2 days.

Holmes County

Common Pleas Court 1 E Jackson St #306, Millersburg, OH 44654; 330-674-1876; Probate phone: 330-674-5881; Fax: 330-674-0289. Hours: 8:30AM-4:30PM (EST). *Felony, Civil Actions Over $10,000, Probate.* Note: Juvenile and probate court at #201.

Civil Records: Access: Fax, mail, in person. Both court and visitors may perform in person searches. Search fee: $5.00 per name. Required to search: name, years to search; also helpful: address. Civil cases indexed by defendant, plaintiff. Civil records on computer from 6/30/94, prior in books to 1850.

Criminal Records: Access: Fax, mail, in person. Both court and visitors may perform in person

searches. Search fee: $5.00 per name. Required to search: name, years to search; also helpful: address, DOB, SSN. Criminal records on computer from 6/30/94, prior in books to 1850.

General Information: Public Access terminal is available. No court order, expunged records released. Fee to fax results is $1.00 per page. Copy fee: $.25 per page. Cert fee: $1.00. Payee: Clerk of Court. Personal checks accepted. Prepayment required. Mail requests: SASE required. Mail turnaround time 1-2 days.

County Court 1 E Jackson St, #101, Millersburg, OH 44654; 330-674-4901; Fax: 330-674-5514. Hours: 8:30AM-4:30PM (EST). *Misdemeanor, Civil Actions Under $15,000, Small Claims.*

Civil Records: Access: Phone, fax, mail, in person. Both court and visitors may perform in person searches. Search fee: $1.00 per name. Required to search: name, years to search. Civil cases indexed by defendant, plaintiff. Civil records in books going back to 1813; computerized records since 1994. Phone & fax access limited to 1 name.

Criminal Records: Access: Phone, fax, mail, in person. Both court and visitors may perform in person searches. Search fee: $1.00 per name. Required to search: name, years to search. Criminal records in books going back to 1813; computerized records since 1994. Same as civil.

General Information: Public Access terminal is available. No search warrant records released. Copy fee: $.15 1-10 pages; $.10 10 plus pages. Cert fee: $1.00 per page. Payee: Holmes County Court. Personal checks accepted. Prepayment required. Mail requests: SASE required. Mail turnaround time 2-5 days.

Huron County

Common Pleas Court 2 E Main St, Norwalk, OH 44857; 419-668-5113; Probate phone: 419-668-4383. Hours: 8AM-4:30PM (EST). *Felony, Civil Actions Over $10,000, Probate.*
www.huroncountyclerk.com
Note: Probate is separate court at phone number given.

Civil Records: Access: In person, online. Both court and visitors may perform in person searches. Search fee: $1.00 per name. Required to search: name, years to search; also helpful: address. Civil cases indexed by defendant, plaintiff. Civil records on computer from 1989, prior in books and on microfiche. Search court dockets and public records free at the website or http://64.186.204.42/search.shtml.

Criminal Records: Access: In person, online. Both court and visitors may perform in person searches. Search fee: $1.00 per name. Required to search: name, years to search, offense, date of offense; also helpful: address, DOB, SSN. Criminal records on computer since 1989, records from 1985 to present in actual files, 1930 to 1985 on microfiche. Search court dockets and public records free at the website or http://64.186.204.42/search.shtml.

General Information: Public Access terminal is available. No secret records released. Copy fee: $.25 per page. Cert fee: $1.00. Payee: Clerk of Court. Personal checks accepted. Prepayment required.

Bellevue Municipal Court 3000 Seneca Industrial Pky, Bellevue, OH 44811; 419-483-5880; Fax: 419-484-8060. Hours: 8:30AM-4:30PM (EST). *Misdemeanor, Civil Actions Under $15,000, Eviction, Small Claims.*

Civil Records: Access: Phone, mail, in person. Both court and visitors may perform in person searches. No search fee. Required to search: name, years to search. Civil cases indexed by defendant, plaintiff. Civil records on index from 1988, prior in books. Will only do phone searching if not busy.

Criminal Records: Access: Phone, mail, in person. Both court and visitors may perform in person searches. No search fee. Required to search: name, years to search, DOB; also helpful: SSN. Criminal records on computer from 8/93. Court searches back to 8/93 only. Use an abstractor to go back further.

General Information: Will fax results to local or toll free line. Copy fee: depends on copies, no fee if less than 5 copies. Cert fee: $1.00. Payee: Bellevue Municipal Court. Only cashiers checks and money orders accepted. Prepayment required. Mail requests: SASE required. Mail turnaround time 3-7 days.

Norwalk Municipal Court 45 N Linwood, Norwalk, OH 44857; 419-663-6750; Fax: 419-663-6749. Hours: 8:30AM-4:30PM (EST). *Misdemeanor, Civil Actions Under $15,000, Eviction, Small Claims.*
www.norwalkmunicourt.com
Civil Records: Access: Fax, mail, in person. Both court and visitors may perform in person searches. Search fee: $1.00 per name. Required to search: name, years to search; also helpful: address. Civil cases indexed by defendant, plaintiff. Civil records on computer from 7/88; prior on docket book to 1976.
Criminal Records: Access: Fax, mail, in person. Both court and visitors may perform in person searches. Search fee: $1.00 per name. Required to search: name, years to search, DOB, SSN; also helpful: address. Criminal records on computer from 7/88, prior on docket books to 1976.
General Information: Public Access terminal is available. Fee to fax results is $1.00 per page. Copy fee: $.05 per page. Cert fee: $1.00 per page. Payee: Municipal Court. Personal checks accepted. Prepayment required. Mail requests: SASE required. Mail turnaround time 2-7 days.

Jackson County

Common Pleas Court 226 Main St, Jackson, OH 45640; 740-286-2006; Probate phone: 740-286-1401; Fax: 740-286-4061. Hours: 8AM-4PM (EST). *Felony, Civil Actions Over $10,000, Probate.*
Civil Records: Access: Mail, fax, in person. Both court and visitors may perform in person searches. No search fee. Required to search: name, years to search; also helpful: address. Civil cases indexed by defendant, plaintiff. Civil records go back to 1800s, computerized since 06/20/97.
Criminal Records: Access: Mail, fax, in person. Both court and visitors may perform in person searches. Search fee: Searches only performed in emergency situations. Required to search: name, years to search; also helpful: address, DOB, SSN. Criminal records go back to 1/83; computerized since 06/20/97.
General Information: Public Access terminal is available. No juvenile or search warrant record released. Will fax results for $3.00 fee. Copy fee: $.50 per page. Cert fee: $1.00. Payee: Clerk of Court. Personal checks accepted. Prepayment required. Mail requests: SASE required. Mail turnaround time varies.

Jackson County Municipal Court 350 Portsmouth St #101, Jackson, OH 45640-1764; 740-286-2718; Fax: 740-286-0679. Hours: 8AM-4PM (EST). *Misdemeanor, Civil Actions Under $15,000, Eviction, Small Claims.*
Civil Records: Access: In person only. Visitors must perform in person searches for themselves. No search fee. Required to search: name, years to search. Civil cases indexed by defendant, plaintiff. Civil records in books readily available for 8-10 years, prior archived.
Criminal Records: Access: In person only. Visitors must perform in person searches for themselves. No search fee. Required to search: name, years to search, DOB, SSN. Criminal records in books readily available for 8-10 years, prior archived.

General Information: Public Access terminal is available. No victim records released. Copy fee: $.10 per page. No cert fee. Payee: Clerk of Municipal Court. Only cashiers checks and money orders accepted. Prepayment required.

Jefferson County

Common Pleas Court 301 Market St (PO Box 1326), Steubenville, OH 43952; 740-283-8583. Hours: 8:30AM-4:30PM (EST). *Felony, Civil Actions Over $500, Probate.*
Note: Probate is at PO Box 649 and can be reached at 740-283-8653.
Civil Records: Access: Mail, in person. Both court and visitors may perform in person searches. Search fee: $5.00 per name. Required to search: name, years to search. Civil cases indexed by defendant, plaintiff. Civil records on computer back 10 years or so, prior archived. Computerized domestic records go back to 1972.
Criminal Records: Access: Mail, in person. Both court and visitors may perform in person searches. Search fee: $5.00 per name. Required to search: name, years to search, DOB, offense, date of offense; also helpful-SSN. Criminal records on books for 10 years or so, prior archived.
General Information: Public Access terminal is available. No sealed records released. Will not fax results. Copy fee: $.25 per page. Cert fee: $1.00 per page. Payee: Jefferson County Clerk of Courts. Business checks accepted. Prepayment required. Mail requests: SASE required. Mail turnaround time 1-2 days.

County Court #1 1007 Franklin Ave, Toronto, OH 43964; 740-537-2020. Hours: 8AM-4PM (EST). *Misdemeanor, Civil Actions Under $15,000, Small Claims.*
www.uov.net/jeffcodp/court1.htm
Civil Records: Access: Mail, in person. Both court and visitors may perform in person searches. Search fee: $5.00 per name. Required to search: name, years to search. Civil cases indexed by defendant, plaintiff. Civil records in books, dating from 1813, computerized records from 6/98.
Criminal Records: Access: Mail, in person. Both court and visitors may perform in person searches. Search fee: $5.00 per name. Required to search: name, years to search, DOB, also helpful: SSN, sex, signed release. Criminal records in books, dating from 1813, computerized records from 6/98.
General Information: Public Access terminal is available. All records are public. Will fax results to local or toll free line. No copy fee. No cert fee. Payee: Jefferson County Court #1. Only cashiers checks and money orders accepted. Mail requests: SASE required. Mail turnaround time 1-2 days.

County Court #2 PO Box 2207, Wintersville, OH 43953; 740-264-7644. Hours: 8AM-4PM (EST). *Misdemeanor, Civil Actions Under $15,000, Small Claims.*
www.uov.net/jeffcodp/court1.htm
Civil Records: Access: Mail, in person. Both court and visitors may perform in person searches. Search fee: $5.00 per name. Required to search: name, years to search. Civil cases indexed by defendant, plaintiff. Civil records on computer back to 1998; in books from 1950s, prior archived.
Criminal Records: Access: Mail, in person. Both court and visitors may perform in person searches. Search fee: $5.00 per name. Required to search: name, years to search, DOB or SSN. Criminal records on computer back to 1998; in books from 1950s, prior archived.
General Information: Public Access terminal is available. Will fax results to local or toll free line.

Copy fee: $.25 per page. Cert fee: $1.00 per page. Payee: County Court #2. Only cashiers checks and money orders accepted. Prepayment required. Mail requests: SASE required. Mail turnaround time 1-2 days.

County Court #3 PO Box 495, Dillonvale, OH 43917; 740-769-2903. Hours: 8AM-4PM (EST). *Misdemeanor, Civil Actions Under $15,000, Small Claims.*
www.uov.net/jeffcodp/court1.htm
Civil Records: Access: Mail, fax, in person. Both court and visitors may perform in person searches. Search fee: $5.00. Required to search: name, years to search. Civil cases indexed by defendant, plaintiff. Civil records on computer from 1998, prior manual dockets.
Criminal Records: Access: Mail, in person. Both court and visitors may perform in person searches. Search fee: $5.00. Required to search: name, years to search, DOB; also helpful: SSN. Criminal records on computer from 1998, prior manual dockets.
General Information: Public Access terminal is available. Will fax results for $1.00 per page. Copy fee: $1.00 per page. Cert fee: $1.00 per page. Payee: County Court #3. Only cashiers checks and money orders accepted. Prepayment required. Mail requests: SASE required. Mail turnaround time 1-2 days.

Steubenville Municipal Court 123 S 3rd St, Steubenville, OH 43952; 740-283-6020; Fax: 740-283-6167. Hours: 8:30AM-4PM (EST). *Misdemeanor, Civil Actions Under $15,000, Eviction, Small Claims.*
www.uov.net/jeffcodp/court1.htm
Civil Records: Access: Mail, in person. Both court and visitors may perform in person searches. No search fee. Required to search: name, years to search; also helpful: address. Civil cases indexed by defendant, plaintiff. Civil records on computer from 1991, prior in books.
Criminal Records: Access: Mail, in person. Both court and visitors may perform in person searches. No search fee. Required to search: name, years to search; also helpful: address, DOB, SSN. Criminal records on computer from 1991, prior in books.
General Information: No expunged records released. Will fax results to local or toll free line. Copy fee: $1.00 per page. Cert fee: $2.00. Payee: Steubenville Municipal Court. Only cashiers checks and money orders accepted. Prepayment required. Mail requests: SASE required. Mail turnaround time 1-5 days.

Knox County

Common Pleas Court Knox County Clerk of Courts, 117 E High St #201, Mt Vernon, OH 43050; 740-393-6788; Probate phone: 740-393-6798. Hours: 8AM-4PM (EST). *Felony, Civil Actions Over $10,000.*
www.knoxcountyclerk.org
Note: Probate is separate farm this office, and is located at 111 E High St.
Civil Records: Access: Online, in person. Visitors must perform in person searches for themselves. No search fee. Required to search: name, years to search. Civil cases indexed by defendant, plaintiff. Civil records on computer since 9/86, on microfilm from 1960, prior archived. Search court index, dockets, calendars free online at www.knoxcountycpcourt.org. Search by name or case number.
Criminal Records: Access: Online, in person. Visitors must perform in person searches for themselves. No search fee. Required to search: name, years to search. Criminal records on computer since 9/86, on microfilm from 1960, prior archived. Online access to criminal records is the same as civil.

General Information: Public Access terminal is available. If exact case number given, clerk will return pages by fax for $3.00 1st page and $1.00 each additional. Copy fee: $.25 per page. Cert fee: $1.00. Payee: Common Pleas Court. Personal checks accepted.

Mount Vernon Municipal Court 5 N Gay St, Mount Vernon, OH 43050; 740-393-9510; Fax: 740-393-5349. Hours: 8AM-4PM (EST). *Misdemeanor, Civil Actions Under $15,000, Eviction, Small Claims.*
www.mountvernonmunicipalcourt.org
Civil Records: Access: Phone, fax, mail, in person, online. Both court and visitors may perform in person searches. No search fee. Required to search: name, years to search. Civil cases indexed by defendant, plaintiff. Civil records on computer from 06/89, prior in books. Access to the clerk's civil records are free at www.mountvernonmunicipalcourt.org/cmiflash/court/home.html.
Criminal Records: Access: Phone, fax, mail, in person, online. Both court and visitors may perform in person searches. No search fee. Required to search: name, years to search. Criminal records on computer from 06/89, prior in books. Access to the clerk's criminal and traffic records are free at www.mountvernonmunicipalcourt.org/cmiflash/court/home.html.
General Information: Will fax results. No copy fee. No cert fee. Payee: Mt Vernon Municipal Ct. Personal checks accepted. Credit cards accepted in some cases. Mail requests: SASE required. Mail turnaround time 1 week.

Probate Court 111 E High St, Mt Vernon, OH 43050; 740-393-6796; Fax: 740-393-6832. Hours: 8AM-4PM, 8AM-6PM Tues. (EST). *Probate.*

Lake County

Common Pleas Court PO Box 490, Painesville, OH 44077; 440-350-2626; Probate phone: 440-350-2624. Hours: 8AM-4:30PM (EST). *Felony, Civil Actions Over $10,000, Probate.*
www.lakecountyohio.org
Civil Records: Access: In person, online. Visitors must perform in person searches for themselves. No search fee. Required to search: name, years to search; also helpful: address. Civil cases indexed by defendant, plaintiff. Civil records on computer from 1990, microfilm from 1960, prior archived. Online access to court records, dockets, and quick index are free at http://clerk.lakecountyohio.org/clerk/. Includes domestic and appeals cases. Access probate online at http://probate.lakecountyohio.org/probate/.
Criminal Records: Access: In person, online. Visitors must perform in person searches for themselves. No search fee. Required to search: name, years to search; also helpful: address, DOB, SSN. Criminal records on computer from 1990, microfilm from 1960, prior archived. Online access to criminal records is the same as civil.
General Information: Public Access terminal is available. No adoption or juvenile records released. Will not fax results. Copy fee: $.25 per page. Cert fee: $1.00. Payee: Clerk of Court. Business checks accepted. Prepayment required.

Mentor Municipal Court 8500 Civic Center Blvd, Mentor, OH 44060-2418; Civil phone: 440-974-5744; Criminal phone: 440-974-5745; Fax: 440-974-5742. Hours: 8AM-4PM daily except Wed 8AM-6PM (EST). *Misdemeanor, Civil Actions Under $15,000, Eviction, Small Claims.*
Civil Records: Access: In person only. Visitors must perform in person searches for themselves. No search fee. Required to search: name. Civil cases indexed by

defendant, plaintiff. Civil records go back to 1972; on computer back to 11/1995.
Criminal Records: Access: In person only. Visitors must perform in person searches for themselves. No search fee. Required to search: name, years to search; also helpful: DOB. Criminal records go back to 1972; on computer back to 11/1995.
General Information: Public Access terminal is available. Copy fee: $1.00 per page. Cert fee: $1.00. Payee: Mentor Municipal Court. Only cashiers checks and money orders accepted. Prepayment required.

Painesville Municipal Court 7 Richmond St (PO Box 601), Painesville, OH 44077; 440-392-5900; Fax: 440-352-0028. Hours: 8AM-4:30PM (EST). *Misdemeanor, Civil Actions Under $15,000, Eviction, Small Claims.*
www.painesvillemunicipalcourt.org/
Note: Probation fax is 440-639-4932.
Civil Records: Access: Fax, mail, in person, online. Visitors must perform in person searches for themselves. No search fee. Required to search: name, years to search; also helpful: address. Civil cases indexed by defendant, plaintiff. Civil records on computer from 7/90 (all divisions), prior on books or archived. Free online access to records at www.pmcourt.com/search.html.
Criminal Records: Access: Fax, mail, in person, online. Visitors must perform in person searches for themselves. No search fee. Required to search: name, years to search, address; also helpful: DOB, SSN. Criminal records on computer from 7/90 (all divisions), prior on books or archived. Free online access to records at www.pmcourt.com/search.html.
General Information: Public Access terminal is available. Will fax results: local $1.00 per pg; long distance $3.00 per pg. Copy fee: $1.00 first page. $.20 each addl. Cert fee: $2.00 plus $1.00 per page after first. Payee: Municipal Court. Personal checks accepted. Visa, MC accepted. Prepayment required. Mail requests: SASE required. Mail turnaround time 1 week.

Willoughby Municipal Court One Public Sq, Willoughby, OH 44094-7888; 440-953-4150; Civil phone: 440-953-4170; Fax: 440-953-4149. Hours: 7:30AM-4:30 PM (till 7:30 on Mon) (EST). *Misdemeanor, Civil Actions Under $15,000, Eviction, Small Claims.*
www.willoughbycourt.com
Note: This court serves these communites: Eastlake, Kirtland, Kirtland Hills, Lakeland Community College, Lakeline, Timberlake, Waite Hill, Wickliffe, Willoughby, Willoughby Hills, and Willowick.
Civil Records: Access: Mail, in person. Both court and visitors may perform in person searches. No search fee. Required to search: name, years to search. Civil cases indexed by defendant. Civil records on docket books since 1960, computerized back to 1986.
Criminal Records: Access: Mail, in person. Both court and visitors may perform in person searches. No search fee. Required to search: name; also helpful: DOB, SSN. Criminal records in docket books since 1960, computerized bacl to 1988.
General Information: Public Access terminal is available. Copy fee: $.25. Cert fee: $1.00 per page. Payee: Willoughby Municipal Court. Personal checks accepted. Prepayment required. Mail turnaround time 2-3 days.

Lawrence County

Common Pleas Court Clerk of the Courts, PO Box 208, Ironton, OH 45638; 740-533-4355/4329; Probate phone: 740-533-4340; Fax: 740-533-4383. Hours: 8:30AM-4PM (EST). *Felony, Civil Actions.*
www.lawrencecountyclkofcrt.org

Note: Probate is a separate court at Veterans Sq in Ironton.
Civil Records: Access: In person, online. Visitors must perform in person searches for themselves. Search fee: none. Required to search: name, years to search; also helpful: address. Civil cases indexed by defendant, plaintiff. Civil records on computer back to 6/88, prior in books going back to 1800s. Online access to civil records is free at the website.
Criminal Records: Access: In person, online. Visitors must perform in person searches for themselves. No search fee. Required to search: name, years to search; also helpful: address, DOB, SSN. Criminal records on computer back to 1/88, prior in books going back to 1800s. Online access to criminal records is free at www.lawrencecountyclkofcrt.org.
General Information: Public Access terminal is available. Copy fee: $.25 per page. Cert fee: $1.00. Payee: Clerk of Court. Personal checks accepted. Prepayment required.

Lawrence County Municipal Court PO Box 126, Chesapeake, OH 45619; 740-867-3128/3127; Fax: 740-867-3547. Hours: 8:30AM-4PM (EST). *Misdemeanor, Civil Actions Under $15,000, Eviction, Small Claims.*
Civil Records: Access: Phone, fax, mail, in person. Both court and visitors may perform in person searches. Search fee: $5.00 per name. Required to search: name, years to search. Civil cases indexed by defendant, plaintiff. Civil records on computer from 1991.
Criminal Records: Access: Phone, fax, mail, in person. Both court and visitors may perform in person searches. Search fee: $5.00 per name. Required to search: name, years to search, DOB; also helpful: SSN. Criminal records on computer from 1991.
General Information: All records public. Copy fee: $.10 per page. Cert fee: $2.00. Payee: Lawrence County Municipal Court. Personal checks accepted. Prepayment required. Mail requests: SASE required. Mail turnaround time 7-10 days.

Ironton Municipal Court PO Box 237, Ironton, OH 45638; 740-532-3062; Fax: 740-533-6088. Hours: 8:30AM-4PM (EST). *Misdemeanor, Civil Actions Under $15,000, Eviction, Small Claims.*
Civil Records: Access: Mail, in person. Both court and visitors may perform in person searches. No search fee. Required to search: name, years to search; also helpful: address. Civil cases indexed by defendant, plaintiff. Civil records on computer from 7/89, prior in books.
Criminal Records: Access: Mail, in person. Both court and visitors may perform in person searches. No search fee. Required to search: name, years to search; also helpful: address, DOB, SSN, singed release. Criminal records on computer from 7/89, prior in books.
General Information: Public Access terminal is available. Copy fee: Varies. Cert fee: $1.00 per page. Payee: Municipal Court. Prepayment required. Mail requests: SASE required. Mail turnaround time 1-2 weeks.

Licking County

Common Pleas Court PO Box 4370, Newark, OH 43058-4370; 740-349-6171; Probate phone: 740-349-6141; Fax: 740-349-6945. Hours: 8AM-4:30PM (EST). *Felony, Civil Actions Over $15,000, Probate.*
www.lcounty.com/clerkofcourts/
Note: Probate court has a separate clerk at the same address.

Civil Records: Access: In person, online. Visitors must perform in person searches for themselves. No search fee. Required to search: name, years to search; also helpful: address. Civil cases indexed by defendant, plaintiff. Civil records on computer from 1992, prior in books. The county clerk's office offers free Internet access to current records at the website. Click on "Courtview 2000".

Criminal Records: Access: In person, online. Visitors must perform in person searches for themselves. No search fee. Required to search: name, years to search, DOB; also helpful: address, SSN. Criminal records on computer from 1992, prior in books. The county clerk's office offers free Internet access to current records at the website. Click on "Courtview 2000".

General Information: Public Access terminal is available. No sealed records released. Copy fee: $.05 per page. Cert fee: $1.00. Payee: Clerk of Court. Business checks accepted. Prepayment required.

Licking County Municipal Court 40 W Main St, Newark, OH 43055; Civil phone: 740-349-6631; Criminal phone: 740-349-6627. Hours: 8AM-4:30PM (EST). *Misdemeanor, Civil Actions Under $15,000, Eviction, Small Claims.*
www.newarkohio.net/municipal/index.html
Civil Records: Access: Phone, fax, mail, in person, online. Both court and visitors may perform in person searches. No search fee. Required to search: name, years to search. Civil cases indexed by defendant, plaintiff. Civil records on computer from 1990, prior in books. Online access to Municipal Court records is free at http://209.239.139.169/connection/court/.
Criminal Records: Access: Phone, fax, mail, in person, online. Both court and visitors may perform in person searches. No search fee. Required to search: name, years to search. Criminal records on computer from 1990, prior in books. Online access to criminal records is the same as civil.
General Information: Public Access terminal is available. No sealed records released. Will not fax results. Copy fee: $.05 per page. Cert fee: $2.00. Payee: Licking County Municipal Court. Personal checks accepted. Prepayment required. Mail requests: SASE required. Mail turnaround time 2-3 days.

Logan County

Common Pleas Court 101 S Main St Rm 18, Bellefontaine, OH 43311-2097; 937-599-7260. Hours: 8:30AM-4:30PM (EST). *Felony, Civil Actions Over $10,000.*
www.co.logan.oh.us/clerkofcourts
Civil Records: Access: In person only. Visitors must perform in person searches for themselves. Search fee: none. Required to search: name, years to search; also helpful: address. Civil cases indexed by defendant, plaintiff. Civil records on computer from 6/88, prior in books to 1943.
Criminal Records: Access: In person only. Visitors must perform in person searches for themselves. Search fee: none. Required to search: name, years to search, DOB; also helpful: address, SSN. Criminal records on computer from 6/88, prior in books to 1943.
General Information: Public Access terminal is available. All records public. Copy fee: $.25 per page after first 25 pages. Cert fee: $1.00 per page. Payee: Clerk of Court. Only cashiers checks and money orders accepted. Prepayment required.

Bellefontaine Municipal Court 226 W Columbus Ave, Bellefontaine, OH 43311; 937-599-6127. Hours: 8AM-4:30PM (EST). *Misdemeanor, Civil Actions Under $15,000, Eviction, Small Claims.*
Civil Records: Access: In person, fax, mail. Visitors must perform in person searches for themselves. No search fee. Required to search: name, years to search. Civil cases indexed by defendant, plaintiff. Civil records on computer from 1986, prior in books.

Criminal Records: Access: In person, fax, mail. Visitors must perform in person searches for themselves. No search fee. Required to search: name, years to search, DOB, SSN, signed release; also helpful: address. Criminal records on computer from 1986, prior in books.
General Information: Public Access terminal is available. All records are public. Copy fee: $.05 per page. Cert fee: $1.00. Payee: Bellefontaine Municipal Court. Local checks accepted. Visa, MC accepted. Accepted for traffic & criminal only. Prepayment required. Mail requests: SASE required. Mail turnaround time is 1-2 days.

Lorain County

Common Pleas Court 225 Court St., Elyria, OH 44035; 440-329-5536; Probate phone: 440-329-5175; Fax: 440-329-5404. Hours: 8AM-4:30PM (EST). *Felony, Civil Actions Over $10,000, Probate.*
www.loraincounty.com/clerk
Civil Records: Access: Online, in person. Both court and visitors may perform in person searches. No search fee. Required to search: name, years to search. Civil cases indexed by defendant, plaintiff. Civil records on computer from 1988, prior in books archived to 1800s. Some records on microfiche to 1960. The website offers free access to indices and dockets for civil and domestic relationship cases. Access probate records at www.loraincounty.com/probate/search.shtml. Court will not do index searching, but they will pull specified records.
Criminal Records: Access: Online, in person. Both court and visitors may perform in person searches. No search fee. Required to search: name, years to search. Criminal records on computer from 1988, prior in books archived to 1800s. Some records on microfiche to 1960. Online access to criminal records is the same as civil. Court will not do index searching, but they will pull specified records.
General Information: Public Access terminal is available. No juvenile records released. Copy fee: $.10 per page. Cert fee: $1.00. Payee: Clerk of Court. Personal checks accepted. Prepayment required.

Avon Lake Municipal Court 32855 Walker Rd, Avon Lake, OH 44012; 440-930-4103. Hours: 8:30AM-4:30PM (EST). *Misdemeanor, Civil Actions Under $15,000, Eviction, Small Claims.*
Civil Records: Access: Phone, mail, in person. Both court and visitors may perform in person searches. No search fee. Required to search: name, years to search. Civil cases indexed by defendant, plaintiff. Civil records on computer from 5/92, records go back to 1976.
Criminal Records: Access: Phone, mail, in person. Both court and visitors may perform in person searches. No search fee. Required to search: name, years to search, DOB; also helpful: SSN. Criminal records on computer from 7/92, records go back to 1976.
General Information: Public Access terminal is available. No non-public records released. Fee to fax results is $3.00 per document. Copy fee: $.25 per page. Cert fee: $1.00. Payee: Avon Lake Municipal Court. Personal checks accepted. Prepayment required. Mail requests: SASE required. Mail turnaround time 1-2 days.

Elyria Municipal Court 328 Broad St (PO Box 1498), Elyria, OH 44036; 440-323-5743; Criminal phone: 440-323-1328; Fax: 440-323-0785-Civil, 440-323-8095-Criminal. Hours: 8AM-4:30PM (EST). *Misdemeanor, Civil Actions Under $15,000, Eviction, Small Claims.*
www.elyriamunicourt.org
Civil Records: Access: Fax, mail, online, in person. Both court and visitors may perform in person

searches. No search fee. Required to search: name, years to search; also helpful: address. Civil cases indexed by defendant, plaintiff. Civil records in books to 1956, computer from 1996. Search at the Internet site, also you can reqeust information by email to civil@elyriamunicourt.org.
Criminal Records: Access: Fax, mail, in person. Both court and visitors may perform in person searches. No search fee. Required to search: name, years to search; also helpful: address, DOB, SSN. Criminal records in books to 1956, computer from 1996. Search misdemeanor and traffic records at the website, also send email requests to crtr@elyriamunicourt.org.
General Information: Public Access terminal is available. All records are public. No copy fee. Cert fee: $2.00. Personal checks accepted. Mail requests: SASE required. Mail turnaround time 5 days.

Lorain Municipal Court 200 W Erie Ave, Lorain, OH 44052; 440-204-2140; Fax: 440-204-2146. Hours: 8:30AM-4:30PM (EST). *Misdemeanor, Civil Actions Under $15,000, Eviction, Small Claims.*
www.lorainmunicourt.org
Civil Records: Access: Online, in person. Visitors must perform in person searches for themselves. No search fee. Required to search: name, years to search; also helpful: address. Civil cases indexed by defendant, plaintiff. Civil records in books. Online access to municipal court records free at www.lorainmunicourt.org/search.shtml. Search by name, date, case number, driver license number or attorney.
Criminal Records: Access: Online, in person. Visitors must perform in person searches for themselves. No search fee. Required to search: name, years to search; also helpful: address, DOB, SSN. Criminal records in books. Online access to criminal records is the same as civil.
General Information: Public Access terminal is available. Copy fee: $1.00 per page. Cert fee: $2.00. Payee: Municipal Court. Prepayment required.

Oberlin Municipal Court 85 S Main St, Oberlin, OH 44074; 440-775-1751; Fax: 440-775-0619. Hours: 8AM-4PM (EST). *Misdemeanor, Civil Actions Under $15,000, Eviction, Small Claims.*
Civil Records: Access: In person only. Visitors must perform in person searches for themselves. No search fee. Required to search: name, years to search; also helpful: address. Civil cases indexed by defendant, plaintiff. Civil records on computer from 1991, prior in books.
Criminal Records: Access: In person only. Visitors must perform in person searches for themselves. No search fee. Required to search: name, years to search; also helpful: address, DOB, SSN. Criminal records on computer from 1991, prior in books.
General Information: Public Access terminal is available. Copy fee: $.10 per page. Cert fee: $1.00. Payee: Oberlin Municipal Court. Business checks accepted. Visa, MC accepted. Prepayment required.

Vermilion Municipal Court 687 Decatour St, Vermilion, OH 44089-1152; 440-967-6543; Fax: 440-967-1467. Hours: 8AM-4PM (EST). *Misdemeanor, Civil Actions Under $15,000, Eviction, Small Claims.*
www.vermilionmunicipalcourt.org
Civil Records: Access: Fax, mail, in person, online. Both court and visitors may perform in person searches. No search fee. Required to search: name, years to search; also helpful: address. Civil cases indexed by defendant, plaintiff. Civil records on computer since late 1991, indexed in books since 1966. Online access to municipal court records is at

the website or directly at http://209.142.158.114/search.html.
Criminal Records: Access: Fax, mail, in person, online. Both court and visitors may perform in person searches. No search fee. Required to search: name, years to search; also helpful: SSN. Criminal records on computer since late 1991, indexed in books since 1966. Online access to criminal records is the same as civil.
General Information: Public Access terminal is available. no addresses, victim info or confidential report records released. No fee to fax results. Copy fee: $.10 per page. Cert fee: $2.00. Payee: Municipal Court. Personal checks accepted. Visa, MC accepted. Prepayment required.

Lucas County

Common Pleas Court 700 Adams, Courthouse, Toledo, OH 43624; 419-213-4483 & 4484; Probate phone: 419-213-4775; Fax: 419-213-4487. Hours: 8AM-4:45PM (EST). *Felony, Civil Actions Over $10,000, Probate.*
www.co.lucas.oh.us/clerk
Note: Probate records must be searched separately; probate hours are 8:30-4:30 at the courthouse.
Civil Records: Access: Fax, mail, in person, online. Both court and visitors may perform in person searches. Search fee: $2.00 per name. Required to search: name, years to search. Civil cases indexed by defendant, plaintiff. Civil records computer from 1987, records go back to 1948, prior in books and on film. Online access to clerk of courts dockets is free at www.co.lucas.oh.us/Clerk/dockets.asp. Online records go back to 9/1997. Search probate records at www.lucas-co-probate-ct.org/.
Criminal Records: Access: Fax, mail, in person, online. Both court and visitors may perform in person searches. Search fee: $5.00 per name. Required to search: name, years to search, DOB, SSN; also helpful: sex, signed release. Criminal records computer from 1987, records go back to 1948, prior in books and on film. Online access to clerk of courts dockets is free at www.co.lucas.oh.us/Clerk/dockets.asp. Online record go back to 9/1997. Search sex offenders at www.lucascountysheriff.org/sheriff/disclaimer.asp.
General Information: Public Access terminal is available. No expunged records released. Will fax results $1.00 per page plus $3.00 transmittal fee. Copy fee: $.25 per page. Cert fee: $3.00. Payee: Clerk of Court. Only cashiers checks and money orders accepted. Prepayment required. Mail requests: SASE not required. Mail turnaround time 3 days.

Maumee Municipal Court 400 Conant St, Maumee, OH 43537-3397; Civil phone: 419-897-7145; Criminal phone: 419-897-7136; Fax: 419-897-7129. Hours: 8AM-4:30PM (EST). *Misdemeanor, Civil Actions Under $15,000, Eviction, Small Claims.*
www.maumee.org/city/municipalclerk.htm
Civil Records: Access: Phone, fax, mail, in person, online. Both court and visitors may perform in person searches. No search fee. Required to search: name; also helpful: years to search. Civil cases indexed by defendant, plaintiff. Civil records in docket books since 1964, on computer since 1989. Online access to the interactive web court system database is free at www.maumee.org/municipal/caseinfo.htm.
Criminal Records: Access: Phone, fax, mail, in person, online. Both court and visitors may perform in person searches. No search fee. Required to search: name, years to search, DOB; also helpful: SSN. Criminal records in docket books since 1964, on computer since 1987. Online access to criminal records is the same as civil.

General Information: Public Access terminal is available. Will fax results $3.00 plus toll call charge. Copy fee: $.25 per page. Cert fee: $1.50. Payee: Maumee Municipal Court. Personal checks accepted. Visa, MC accepted. Credit cards not accepted for phone orders. Prepayment required. Mail turnaround time 1 week.

Oregon Municipal Court 5330 Seaman Rd, Oregon, OH 43616; Civil phone: 419-698-7008; Criminal phone: 419-698-7173; Fax: 419-698-7013. Hours: 8:30AM-4:30PM (EST). *Misdemeanor, Civil Actions Under $15,000, Eviction, Small Claims, Traffic.*
www.ci.oregon.oh.us/ctydpt/court/court.htm
Civil Records: Access: Phone, fax, mail, in person, email. Both court and visitors may perform in person searches. No search fee. Required to search: name, years to search. Civil cases indexed by defendant, plaintiff. Civil records on books since 1960, computerized since 1989.
Criminal Records: Access: Phone, fax, mail, in person. Both court and visitors may perform in person searches. No search fee. Required to search: name, years to search; also helpful: DOB, SSN. Criminal records on books since 1960, computerized since 1989.
General Information: No fee to fax results. Must be local call. Copy fee: $.50 for first page, $.10 each add'l. Cert fee: $2.50 for first page, $.10 each add'l. Payee: Oregon Municipal Court. Personal checks accepted. Visa, MC cards accepted for criminal records only. For in person searching only. Prepayment required. Mail requests: SASE required. Mail turnaround time 1-2 days.

Sylvania Municipal Court 6700 Monroe St, Sylvania, OH 43560-1995; 419-885-8975; Civil phone: 419-885-8985; Criminal phone: 419-885-8975; Fax: 419-885-8987. Hours: 7:30AM-4PM (EST). *Misdemeanor, Civil Actions Under $15,000, Eviction, Small Claims.*
www.sylvaniacourt.com
Civil Records: Access: Fax, mail, in person, online. Visitors must perform in person searches for themselves. No search fee. Required to search: name, years to search. Civil cases indexed by defendant, plaintiff. Civil records on books since 1964, computerized since 1987. Search records from the web page.
Criminal Records: Access: Fax, mail, in person, online. Visitors must perform in person searches for themselves. No search fee. Required to search: name, years to search, DOB, SSN. Criminal records on books since 1964, computerized since 1987. Search records from the web page.
General Information: Public Access terminal is available. Will fax results to local or toll free line. Copy fee: $.10 per page. Cert fee: $2.00 per page. Payee: Clerk of Court. Business checks accepted. Prepayment required. Mail turnaround time 1 week.

Toledo Municipal Court 555 N Erie St, Toledo, OH 43624-1391; 419-245-1926 (Small Claims); Civil phone: 419-245-1927; Criminal phone: 419-936-3650; Fax: 419-245-1801. Hours: 8AM-4:30PM civil; 6AM-6PM M-F, 6-11:30AM Sat crim & traffic (EST). *Misdemeanor, Civil Actions Under $15,000, Eviction, Small Claims.*
www.tmc-clerk.com
Note: A second web site is at www.toledomunicipalcourt.org.
Civil Records: Access: Mail, fax, in person, email. Both court and visitors may perform in person searches. No search fee. Required to search: name, years to search. Civil cases indexed by defendant. Civil records on computer back to 1986, prior in books since 1960s. The daily docket is online at the

website. Direct email requests to clerk@tmc-clerk.com.
Criminal Records: Access: Mail, fax, in person, email, online. Both court and visitors may perform in person searches. No search fee. Required to search: name, years to search, DOB, SSN; also helpful: address. Criminal records on computer back to 1985, prior in books since 1960s. The daily docket is online at the website. Direct email requests to clerk@tmc-clerk.com. Have either date of birth or SSN to request a search.
General Information: Public Access terminal is available. (Civil only available.) No expunged records released. Copy fee: $.25 per page. Cert fee: $6.00. Payee: Toledo Municipal Court. Personal checks accepted. Credit cards accepted for criminal only. Prepayment required. Mail requests: SASE required. Mail turnaround time 3 to 5 days.

Madison County

Common Pleas Court PO Box 557, London, OH 43140; 740-852-9776; Probate phone: 740-852-0756; Fax: 740-845-1778. Hours: 8AM-4PM (EST). *Felony, Civil Actions Over $10,000, Probate.*
Civil Records: Access: In person only. Visitors must perform in person searches for themselves. No search fee. Required to search: name, years to search. Civil cases indexed by defendant, plaintiff. Civil records in books since 1981. Search probate records (not civil records) at www.madisonprobate.org/Search/.
Criminal Records: Access: In person only. Visitors must perform in person searches for themselves. No search fee. Required to search: name, years to search; also helpful: address, DOB, SSN. Criminal records in books since 1981.
General Information: Public Access terminal is available. No secret indictment records released. Copy fee: $.25 per page. No cert fee. Payee: Clerk of Court. Personal checks accepted. Prepayment required.

Madison County Municipal Court Main & High St, PO Box 646, London, OH 43140; 740-852-1669; Fax: 740-852-0812. Hours: 8AM-4PM (EST). *Misdemeanor, Civil Actions Under $15,000, Eviction, Small Claims.*
Civil Records: Access: Phone, fax, mail, in person. Both court and visitors may perform in person searches. No search fee. Required to search: name, years to search. Civil cases indexed by defendant, plaintiff. Civil records on computer from 1989, prior in books indexed from 1958.
Criminal Records: Access: Phone, fax, mail, in person. Both court and visitors may perform in person searches. No search fee. Required to search: name, years to search, DOB; also helpful: SSN. Criminal records on computer from 1989, prior in books indexed from 1958.
General Information: Public Access terminal is available. No probation records released. No fee to fax results. Copy fee: $.25 per page. Cert fee: $1.00. Payee: Madison County Municipal Court. Only cashiers checks and money orders accepted. Prepayment required. Mail requests: SASE required. Mail turnaround time up to 1 week.

Mahoning County

Common Pleas Court 120 Market St, Youngstown, OH 44503; 330-740-2103; Probate phone: 330-740-2312; Fax: 330-740-2105. Hours: 8AM-4PM (EST). *Felony, Civil Actions Over $15,000, Probate.*
Civil Records: Access: In person only. Visitors must perform in person searches for themselves. No search fee. Required to search: name, years to search; also helpful: address. Civil cases indexed by defendant, plaintiff. Civil records on computer from 1989, prior in books indexed from 1946.

Criminal Records: Access: Phone, fax, mail, in person. Both court and visitors may perform in person searches. No search fee. Required to search: name, years to search; also helpful: address, DOB, SSN. Criminal records on computer from 1989, prior in books indexed from 1946.

General Information: Public Access terminal is available. No secret indictment records released. Will fax results $2.00 1st page, $1.00 each add'l. Copy fee: $.10 per page. Cert fee: $1.00. Payee: Clerk of Court. Personal checks accepted. Prepayment required. Mail requests: SASE required. Mail turnaround time 1 week.

County Court #2 127 Boardman Canfield Rd, Boardman, OH 44512; 330-726-5546; Fax: 330-740-2035. Hours: 8:30AM-4PM (EST). *Misdemeanor, Civil Actions Under $15,000, Small Claims.*
Civil Records: Access: Mail, fax, in person. Both court and visitors may perform in person searches. No search fee. Required to search: name, years to search. Civil cases indexed by defendant, plaintiff. Civil records in books and dockets from 1960; on computer back to 1995.
Criminal Records: Access: Mail, fax, in person. Both court and visitors may perform in person searches. No search fee. Required to search: name, years to search, DOB, SSN, signed release. Criminal records in books and dockets from 1960; on computer back to 1995. Court will not perform party names searches for in-person requesters.
General Information: Public Access terminal is available. Expunged records are not released. Copy fee: $.25 per page. Cert fee: $1.00. Payee: County Court #2. Personal checks accepted. Prepayment required. Mail requests: SASE required. Mail turnaround time 5-10 days.

County Court #3 605 E Ohio Ave, Sebring, OH 44672; 330-938-9873; Fax: 330-938-6518. Hours: 8:30AM-4PM (EST). *Misdemeanor, Civil Actions Under $15,000, Small Claims.*
Civil Records: Access: Mail, in person. Both court and visitors may perform in person searches. No search fee. Required to search: name, years to search. Civil cases indexed by defendant, plaintiff. Civil records in books from 1958; on computer back to 8/95.
Criminal Records: Access: Mail, in person. Both court and visitors may perform in person searches. No search fee. Required to search: name, years to search, DOB; also helpful: SSN. Criminal records in books from 1989; on computer back to 8/95.
General Information: Public Access terminal is available. No expunged records released. Copy fee: $.10 per page. Cert fee: $1.00 per page. Payee: Mahoning County Court #3. Personal checks accepted. Prepayment required. Mail requests: SASE required. Mail turnaround time 1 week.

County Court #4 6000 Mahoning Ave, Youngstown, OH 44515-2288; 330-740-2001; Fax: 330-740-2036. Hours: 8:30AM-4PM (EST). *Misdemeanor, Civil Actions Under $15,000, Small Claims.*
Civil Records: Access: Fax, mail, in person. Both court and visitors may perform in person searches. No search fee. Required to search: name, years to search. Civil cases indexed by defendant, plaintiff. Civil records in books from the 1940s, on microfiche recent; computerized records since 1996. Phone, fax and mail access limited to out of town requests.
Criminal Records: Access: Fax, mail, in person. Both court and visitors may perform in person searches. No search fee. Required to search: name, years to search, DOB, SSN, signed release. Criminal records in books from the 1940s, on microfiche rec; computerized records since 1996.

General Information: Public Access terminal is available. No expunged records released. Will fax results $2.00 1st page, $.50 each add'l. Copy fee: $.10 per page. Cert fee: $1.00. Payee: County Court #4. Personal checks accepted. Prepayment required. Mail requests: SASE required. Mail turnaround time same day.

County Court #5 72 N Broad St, Canfield, OH 44406; 330-533-3643; Fax: 330-740-2034. Hours: 8:30AM-4PM (EST). *Misdemeanor, Civil Actions Under $15,000, Small Claims.*
Civil Records: Access: Fax, mail, in person. Visitors must perform in person searches for themselves. No search fee. Required to search: name, years to search; also helpful: address. Civil cases indexed by defendant, plaintiff. Civil records on computer since 1995; overall records go back to 1991.
Criminal Records: Access: Fax, mail, in person. Both court and visitors may perform in person searches. Search fee: $5.00 per name. Fee includes certification. Required to search: name, years to search; also helpful: DOB, SSN. Criminal records on computer since 1995; overall records go back to 1991.
General Information: Public Access terminal is available. No LEADS printout records released. Will fax results $2.00 1st page, $1.00 each add'l. Copy fee: $.10 per page. Cert fee: $1.00. Payee: County Court #5. Only cashiers checks and money orders accepted. Prepayment required. Mail requests: SASE required. Mail turnaround time 1-2 days.

Campbell Municipal Court 351 Tenney Ave, Campbell, OH 44405; 330-755-2165; Fax: 330-750-3058. Hours: 8AM-4PM (EST). *Misdemeanor, Civil Actions Under $15,000, Eviction, Small Claims.*
Civil Records: Access: Fax, mail, in person. Only the court performs in person searches; visitors may not. No search fee. Required to search: name, years to search. Civil cases indexed by defendant, plaintiff. Civil records in books from 1950s; on computer back to 1999. Mail and fax access limited to short searches.
Criminal Records: Access: Fax, mail, in person. Only the court performs in person searches; visitors may not. No search fee. Required to search: name, years to search; also helpful: DOB, SSN, signed release. Criminal records in books from 1950s; on computer back to 7/1999.
General Information: No sealed records released. Will fax results to police agencies only. Copy fee: $.50 per page. Cert fee: $20.00. Payee: Campbell Municipal Court. Only cashiers checks and money orders accepted. Prepayment required. Mail requests: SASE required. Mail turnaround time depends on workload.

Struthers Municipal Court 6 Elm St, Struthers, OH 44471; 330-755-1800; Fax: 330-755-2790. Hours: 8AM-4PM; Public access only on Tuesday and Thursday (EST). *Misdemeanor, Civil Actions Under $15,000, Eviction, Small Claims.*
Civil Records: Access: Mail, in person. Both court and visitors may perform in person searches. No search fee. Required to search: name, years to search. Civil cases indexed by defendant, plaintiff. Civil records in books since 1965; on computer since 1996.
Criminal Records: Access: Mail, in person. Both court and visitors may perform in person searches. No search fee. Required to search: name, years to search; also helpful: SSN, DOB, signed release. Criminal records in books since 1965; on computer since 1996.
General Information: Public Access terminal is available. (Terminal up on Tuesdays and Thursdays.) No pending case records released. No copy fee. Cert fee: $10.00. Payee: Municipal Court. Only cashiers checks and money orders accepted. Prepayment required. Mail requests: SASE required. Mail turnaround time 2-3 days.

Youngstown Municipal Court - Civil Records PO Box 6047, Youngstown, OH 44501-6047; 330-742-8863; Fax: 330-742-8786. Hours: 8AM-4PM (EST). *Civil Actions Under $15,000, Eviction, Small Claims.*
Civil Records: Access: Phone, fax, mail, in person. Both court and visitors may perform in person searches. No search fee. Required to search: name, years to search; also helpful: address. Civil cases indexed by defendant, plaintiff. Civil records in books since 1970; on computer since 1998.
General Information: Public Access terminal is available. All records are public. Copy fee: $.10 per page. Cert fee: $1.00. Payee: Municipal Court. Personal checks accepted. Prepayment required. Mail requests: SASE required. Mail turnaround time 1-2 days.

Youngstown Municipal Court - Criminal Records 26 S Phelps St, Youngstown, OH 44503; 330-742-8860; Fax: 330-742-8786. Hours: 8AM-4PM (EST). *Misdemeanor.*
Criminal Records: Access: Fax, mail, in person. Both court and visitors may perform in person searches. No search fee. Required to search: name, years to search, DOB; also helpful: SSN. Criminal records go back to 1966; kept available since 1981 on docket books, microfiche; also on computer since 1998.
General Information: Public Access terminal is available. No records released. Will fax results to local or toll free line. Copy fee: $.10 per page. Cert fee: $1.00. Payee: Municipal Court. Only cashiers checks and money orders accepted. Prepayment required. Mail requests: SASE required. Mail turnaround time 1 day.

Marion County

Common Pleas Court 100 N Main St, Marion, OH 43301-1823; 740-223-4270; Probate phone: 740-232-4260; Fax: 740-223-4279. Hours: 8:30AM-4:30PM (EST). *Felony, Civil Actions Over $10,000.*
Civil Records: Access: Mail, in person. Visitors must perform in person searches for themselves. No search fee. Required to search: name, years to search. Civil cases indexed by defendant, plaintiff. Civil records on computer from 1991, prior in books since 1886. Mail is only used if you have the case number and request a specific document.
Criminal Records: Access: Mail, in person. Visitors must perform in person searches for themselves. No search fee. Required to search: name, years to search; also helpful: DOB, SSN. Criminal records on computer from 1991, prior in books since 1886. Mail is only used if you have the case number and request a specific document.
General Information: Public Access terminal is available. No sealed, expunged records released. Fee to fax results is $2.00 per transmission and $1.00 per page. Copy fee: $.10 per page. Cert fee: $1.00. Payee: Marion County Clerk of Courts. Personal checks accepted. Prepayment required. Mail requests: SASE required. Mail turnaround time 1-3 days.

Marion Municipal Court 233 W Center St, Marion, OH 43302-0326; 740-387-0439; Civil phone: 740-383-5515; Criminal phone: 740-382-4031; Fax: 740-382-5274. Hours: 8:30AM-4:30PM (EST). *Misdemeanor, Civil Actions Under $15,000, Eviction, Small Claims.*
Civil Records: Access: In person only. Visitors must perform in person searches for themselves. No search fee. Required to search: name, years to search. Civil cases indexed by defendant, plaintiff. Civil records on computer since 1995.
Criminal Records: Access: Mail, in person. Both court and visitors may perform in person searches. No

search fee. Required to search: name, years to search; also helpful: DOB, SSN. Criminal records on computer from 1986, prior in books.

General Information: Copy fee: $.25 per page. Cert fee: $5.00. Payee: Municipal Court. Only cashiers checks and money orders accepted. Prepayment required. Mail requests: SASE required. Mail turnaround time 7 days.

Medina County

Common Pleas Court 93 Public Sq, Medina, OH 44256; 330-725-9720; Probate phone: 330-725-9703; Fax: 330-764-8454. Hours: 8AM-4:30PM (EST). *Felony, Civil Actions Over $10,000, Probate.* www.medinacommonpleas.com

Civil Records: Access: Mail, in person, online. No search fee. Required to search: name, years to search. Civil cases indexed by defendant, plaintiff. Civil records on computer from 10/92, in books to early 1960s, prior archived. Search court documents, motion dockets and court notices at the web page.

Criminal Records: Access: Mail, in person, online. Both court and visitors may perform in person searches. No search fee. Required to search: name, years to search. Criminal records on computer from 10/92, in books to early 1960s, prior archived. Online access same as civil.

General Information: Public Access terminal is available. Copy fee: $.25 per page. Cert fee: $1.00. Payee: Clerk of Court. Personal checks accepted. Prepayment required. Mail requests: SASE required. Mail turnaround time 1-2 days.

Medina Municipal Court 135 N Elmwood, Medina, OH 44256; 330-723-3287; Fax: 330-225-1108. Hours: 8AM-4:30PM (EST). *Misdemeanor, Civil Actions Under $15,000, Eviction, Small Claims.* www.medinamunicipalcourt.org

Civil Records: Access: Mail, online, in person. Both court and visitors may perform in person searches. No search fee. Required to search: name, years to search. Civil cases indexed by defendant, plaintiff. Civil records on computer from 1986, prior in books. There are two systems, one is via the website, and the other is dial-up system. Both contain records from 1986 to present. Access to the dial-up system requires Procomm Plus. There are no fees. Search by name or case number. The computer access number is 330-723-4337. For more information, call Rich Armstrong at 330-723-3287, ext. 230.

Criminal Records: Access: Mail, online, in person. Visitors must perform in person searches for themselves. No search fee. Required to search: name, years to search; also helpful: address, DOB, SSN. Criminal records on computer from 1986, prior in books. Online access to traffic records is the same as civil.

General Information: Public Access terminal is available. No expunged records released. Copy fee: $.25 per page. Cert fee: $1.50. Payee: Municipal Court. Personal checks accepted. Visa, MC accepted for criminal and traffic records only. Prepayment required. Mail requests: SASE required. Mail turnaround time is 7-14 days.

Wadsworth Municipal Court 120 Maple St, Wadsworth, OH 44281-1825; 330-335-1596; Fax: 330-335-2723. Hours: 8AM-4PM (EST). *Misdemeanor, Civil Actions Under $15,000, Eviction, Small Claims.* www.wadsworthmunicipalcourt.com/main.htm

Note: Covers Villages of Gloria Glens, Lodi, Seville, Westfield Center; Townships of: Guilford, Harrisville, Homer, Sharon, Wadsworth, and Westfield.

Civil Records: Access: Fax, mail, in person. Both court and visitors may perform in person searches. No

search fee. Required to search: name, years to search. Civil cases indexed by defendant, plaintiff. Civil records on computer from 3/90, prior in books.

Criminal Records: Access: Fax, mail, in person. Both court and visitors may perform in person searches. No search fee. Required to search: name, years to search; also helpful: address, DOB, SSN. Criminal records on computer from 3/90, prior in books.

General Information: Public Access terminal is available. No search warrant records released. No fee to fax results. Local faxing only. Copy fee: $.25 per page. Cert fee: $1.00. Payee: Wadsworth Muni. Court. Personal checks accepted. Prepayment required. Mail requests: SASE required. Mail turnaround time up to 1 week.

Meigs County

Common Pleas Court PO Box 151, Pomeroy, OH 45769; 740-992-5290; Probate phone: 740-992-3096; Fax: 740-992-4429. Hours: 8:30AM-4:30PM (EST). *Felony, Civil Actions Over $3,000, Probate.* Note: Probate fax is 740-992-6727.

Civil Records: Access: In person only. Visitors must perform in person searches for themselves. No search fee. Required to search: name, years to search; also helpful: address. Civil cases indexed by defendant, plaintiff. Civil records on computer since 1996, in books to 1800s.

Criminal Records: Access: In person only. Visitors must perform in person searches for themselves. No search fee. Required to search: name, years to search, DOB; also helpful: address, SSN. Criminal records on computer since 1996, in books to 1800s.

General Information: Public Access terminal is available. No secret records released. Will fax specific document to local or toll-free number. Copy fee: $.25 per page. Cert fee: $1.00. Payee: Clerk of Court. Personal checks accepted. Prepayment required.

Meigs County Court 2nd St Courthouse, Pomeroy, OH 45769; 740-992-2279; Fax: 740-992-4570. Hours: 8:30AM-4:30PM (EST). *Misdemeanor, Civil Actions Under $15,000, Small Claims.*

Civil Records: Access: In person only. Visitors must perform in person searches for themselves. No search fee. Required to search: name, years to search. Civil cases indexed by defendant, plaintiff. Civil records on computer from 8/90, prior in docket books. Phone access limited to records from 1990 to present.

Criminal Records: Access: In person only. Visitors must perform in person searches for themselves. No search fee. Required to search: name, years to search, DOB, SSN, signed release. Criminal records on computer from 8/90, prior in docket books. Phone access limited to records from 1990 to present.

General Information: No sealed records released. Copy fee: $.10 per page. Cert fee: $2.00. Payee: Meigs County Court. Personal checks accepted. Out of state checks not accepted. Prepayment required.

Mercer County

Common Pleas Court 101 N Main St, Rm 205, PO Box 28, Celina, OH 45822; 419-586-6461; Probate phone: 419-586-2418; Fax: 419-586-5826. Hours: 8:30AM-4PM (EST). *Felony, Civil Actions Over $10,000, Probate.*

Civil Records: Access: In person only. Visitors must perform in person searches for themselves. No search fee. Required to search: name, years to search; also helpful: address. Civil cases indexed by defendant, plaintiff. Civil records on computer back to 1997, microfiche up to and including 1985, prior in books.

Criminal Records: Access: In person only. Visitors must perform in person searches for themselves. No search fee. Required to search: name, years to search; also helpful: address, DOB, SSN. Criminal records on

computer back to 1997, microfiche up to and including 1985, prior in books.

General Information: Public Access terminal is available. No juvenile or sealed records released. Will fax specific document for $3.00 for 1st page; $1.00 for each add'l page. Copy fee: $.25 per page. Cert fee: $1.00. Payee: Clerk of Court. Personal checks accepted. Prepayment required.

Celina Municipal Court PO Box 362, Celina, OH 45822; 419-586-6491; Fax: 419-586-4735. Hours: 8AM-5PM (EST). *Misdemeanor, Civil Actions Under $15,000, Small Claims.*

Civil Records: Access: Fax, mail, in person. Both court and visitors may perform in person searches. No search fee. Required to search: name, years to search; also helpful: address. Civil cases indexed by defendant, plaintiff. Civil records on computer from 1990, prior in books.

Criminal Records: Access: Fax, mail, in person. Both court and visitors may perform in person searches. No search fee. Required to search: name, years to search; also helpful: address, DOB, SSN. Criminal records are on computer since 1989, prior found in books and files.

General Information: Public Access terminal is available. No confidential information released. Will fax results to local or toll free line. Copy fee: $.05 per page. Cert fee: $1.00. Payee: Municipal Court. Personal checks accepted. Prepayment required. Mail requests: SASE required. Mail turnaround time 2-3 days.

Miami County

Common Pleas Court & Court of Appeals Safety Bldg, 201 W Main St, 3rd Flr, Troy, OH 45373; 937-440-6010; Probate phone: 937-440-6050; Fax: 937-440-6011. Hours: 8AM-4PM (EST). *Felony, Civil Actions Over $10,000, Probate.* www.onthesquare.com/muni/index.htm

Note: Probate is a separate division on the second floor at the address above. Phone number given above.

Civil Records: Access: Fax, mail, in person. Both court and visitors may perform in person searches. Search fee: $5.00 per name. Required to search: name, years to search; also helpful: address. Civil cases indexed by defendant, plaintiff. Civil records in books for past 30 years, prior are archived; on computer since 1984.

Criminal Records: Access: Fax, mail, in person. Both court and visitors may perform in person searches. Search fee: $5.00 per name. Required to search: name, years to search, DOB, SSN; also helpful: address. Criminal records in books for past 30 years, prior are archived; on computer since 1984.

General Information: Public Access terminal is available. No expunged or sealed records released. Will fax results $1.00 per doc. Copy fee: $.25 per page. Cert fee: $1.00. Payee: Miami County Clerk of Courts. Personal checks accepted. Prepayment required. Mail turnaround time 1-2 days.

Miami County Municipal Court 201 W Main St, Troy, OH 45373; 937-440-3910; Civil phone: 937-440-3918; Criminal phone: 937-440-3910; Fax: 937-440-3911. Hours: 8AM-4PM (EST). *Misdemeanor, Civil Actions Under $15,000, Eviction, Small Claims.* www.co.miami.oh.us/muni/index.htm

Note: If the SSN is not provided by the party doing the search, the court personnel will mask the SSN before providing copies.

Civil Records: Access: Mail, in person, online. Both court and visitors may perform in person searches. Search fee: $5.00 per name. Required to search: name, years to search. Civil cases indexed by defendant, plaintiff. Civil records in books go back 25 years; on computer back to 11/89. Online access to records is free at www.co.miami.oh.us/pa/index.htm.

Criminal Records: Access: Mail, in person, online. Both court and visitors may perform in person searches. Search fee: $5.00 per name. Required to search: name, years to search, SSN. Criminal records on computer back to 1985, prior in books. Online access to records is free at www.co.miami.oh.us/pa/index.htm.

General Information: Public Access terminal is available. No search warrant records released. Copy fee: $.25 per page. Cert fee: $2.00. Payee: Municipal Court. Visa, MC accepted. Prepayment required. Mail requests: SASE required. Mail turnaround time 2-3 days.

Monroe County

Common Pleas Court 101 N Main St Rm 26, Woodsfield, OH 43793; 740-472-0761; Probate phone: 740-472-1654; Fax: 740-472-2549. Hours: 8:30AM-4:30PM (EST). *Felony, Civil Actions Over $3,000, Probate.*

Civil Records: Access: In person only. Visitors must perform in person searches for themselves. No search fee. Required to search: name, years to search; also helpful: address. Civil cases indexed by defendant, plaintiff. Civil records in books since 1800; computerized records from 11/18/02 to present.

Criminal Records: Access: Mail, fax, in person. Both court and visitors may perform in person searches. Search fee: $2.00 per name. Clerk of Courts will search more than one name but we do charge $2.00 per name!!!. Required to search: name, years to search; also helpful: address, DOB, SSN. Criminal records in books since 1800; computerized records from 11/18/02 to present. The court will not do party names searches for in-person requesters.

General Information: Public Access terminal is available. No secret indictment records released. Fee to fax results is $2.00 per page. Copy fee: $.25 per page. Cert fee: $1.00. Payee: Clerk of Court. Personal checks accepted. Prepayment required. Mail requests: SASE required. Mail turnaround time 3 days.

County Court 101 N Main St, Rm 35, Woodsfield, OH 43793; 740-472-5181. Hours: 9AM-4:30PM (EST). *Misdemeanor, Civil Actions Under $15,000, Small Claims.*

Civil Records: Access: Phone, mail, in person. Both court and visitors may perform in person searches. No search fee. Required to search: name, years to search. Civil cases indexed by defendant, plaintiff. Civil records in books, indexed back to 1950; on computer back to 8/1999.

Criminal Records: Access: Phone, mail, in person. Both court and visitors may perform in person searches. No search fee. Required to search: name, years to search. Criminal records in books, indexed back to 1979; on computer back to 1999.

General Information: Public Access terminal is available. No copy fee. No cert fee. Mail requests: SASE required. Mail turnaround time 1-2 days.

Montgomery County

Common Pleas Court 41 N Perry St, Dayton, OH 45422; 937-225-4512; Criminal phone: 937-225-4536; Probate phone: 937-225-4640; Fax: 937-496-7389/7220. Hours: 8:30AM-4:30PM (EST). *Felony, Civil Actions Over $10,000, Probate.*
www.clerk.co.montgomery.oh.us

Civil Records: Access: Fax, mail, in person, online. Both court and visitors may perform in person searches. No search fee. Required to search: name, years to search; also helpful: address. Civil cases indexed by defendant, plaintiff. Civil records on computer from 1970s, prior in books. Online access to

the Courts county-wide PRO system is free at www.clerk.co.montgomery.oh.us/pro/index.cfm. Address mail requests to Montgomery County Clerk of Court "Civil Records."

Criminal Records: Access: In person, online. Visitors must perform in person searches for themselves. No search fee. Required to search: name, years to search; also helpful: address, DOB, SSN. Criminal records on computer from 1970s, prior in books. Online access to criminal and traffic records is the same as civil.

General Information: Public Access terminal is available. No sealed records released. Copy fee: $.10 per page. Cert fee: $1.00 per page. Payee: Clerk of Court. Personal checks accepted. Prepayment required.

County Court - Area 1 195 S Clayton Rd, New Lebanon, OH 45345-9601; 937-687-9099; Fax: 937-687-7119. Hours: 8AM-4PM; (12PM-7PM, M); (9-4PM, F) (EST). *Misdemeanor, Civil Actions Under $15,000, Small Claims.*
www.clerk.co.montgomery.oh.us

Civil Records: Access: Mail, in person, online. Both court and visitors may perform in person searches. No search fee. Required to search: name, years to search. Civil cases indexed by defendant, plaintiff. Civil records on computer from 2/92, prior in books, Archives 937-225-6366. Search county-wide records online at www.clerk.co.montgomery.oh.us/areacourt/pro/.

Criminal Records: Access: Mail, in person, online. Both court and visitors may perform in person searches. No search fee. Required to search: name, years to search; also helpful: SSN. Criminal records on computer from 2/92, prior in books, Archives 937-225-6366. Online access to criminal records is the same as civil.

General Information: Public Access terminal is available. No medical, PSI report or LEADS print-out records released. Copy fee: $.75 per page. Cert fee: $1.00. Payee: Montgomery County Court Area One. Only cashiers checks and money orders accepted. Prepayment required. Mail requests: SASE required. Mail turnaround time 2-3 days.

County Court - Area 2 6111 Taylorsville Rd, Huber Heights, OH 45424; 937-496-7231; Fax: 937-496-7236. Hours: 9AM-4PM (EST). *Misdemeanor, Civil Actions Under $15,000, Small Claims under $3,000.*
http://countycourt.dynip.com

Civil Records: Access: Phone, fax, mail, in person, online, email. Both court and visitors may perform in person searches. No search fee. Required to search: name, years to search; also helpful: address. Civil cases indexed by defendant, plaintiff. Civil records on computer from 1992, prior in books back to 1974. Search county-wide records online at www.clerk.co.montgomery.oh.us/areacourt/pro/.

Criminal Records: Access: Phone, fax, mail, in person, online, email. Both court and visitors may perform in person searches. No search fee. Required to search: name, years to search; also helpful: address, DOB, SSN. Criminal records on computer from 1992, prior in books back to 1974. Online access to criminal records is the same as civil.

General Information: Public Access terminal is available. No confidential, forensic evaluation or medical records released. No fee to fax results. Copy fee: $.25 per page. Cert fee: $1.00. Fee is for civil only. $1.00 fee for criminal/traffic. Payee: County Court Area Two. Business checks accepted. Prepayment required. Mail requests: SASE required. Mail turnaround time 2-7 days.

Dayton Municipal Court - Civil Division 301 W 3rd St, PO Box 968, Dayton, OH 45402-0968; 937-333-4471; Fax: 937-333-4468. Hours: 8AM-4:30PM (EST). *Civil Actions Under $15,000, Eviction, Small Claims.*
www.daytonmunicipalcourt.org

Civil Records: Access: Phone, mail, in person, online. Both court and visitors may perform in person searches. No search fee. Required to search: name, years to search; also helpful: address. Civil cases indexed by defendant, plaintiff. Civil records on computer back to 1998, prior in books to 1977. Online access to municipal court records is free at www.daytonmunicipalcourt.org/scripts/rgw.dll/Docket; includes traffic and criminal.

General Information: Public Access terminal is available. No expunged case records released. Copy fee: $.25 per page. No cert fee. Payee: Clerk of Court. Personal checks accepted. Prepayment required. Mail requests: SASE required. Mail turnaround time 2-3 days.

Dayton Municipal Court - Criminal Division 301 W 3rd St, Rm 331, Dayton, OH 45402; 937-333-4315; Fax: 937-333-4490. Hours: 8AM-4:30PM (EST). *Misdemeanor.*
www.daytonmunicipalcourt.org

Criminal Records: Access: In person, online. Visitors must perform in person searches for themselves. No search fee. Required to search: name, years to search, DOB; also helpful: address, SSN, signed release. Criminal records on computer back to 1992, prior in books. Online access to municipal court records is free at www.daytonmunicipalcourt.org/scripts/rgw.dll/Docket; includes traffic and civil. Phone access is limited.

General Information: Public Access terminal is available. All records are public. Copy fee: $.25 per page. No cert fee. Payee: Dayton Municipal Court. Personal checks accepted. Visa, MC accepted. Prepayment required. Mail requests: SASE required.

Dayton Municipal Court - Traffic Division 301 W 3rd St (PO Box 10700), Dayton, OH 45402; 937-333-4313; Fax: 937-333-7558. Hours: 8AM-4:30PM (EST). *Misdemeanor.*
www.daytonmunicipalcourt.org

Note: It is difficult for the court to provide case information prior to 1995.

Kettering Municipal Court 3600 Shroyer Rd, Kettering, OH 45429; 937-296-2461; Fax: 937-534-7017. Hours: 8:30AM-4:30PM (EST). *Misdemeanor, Civil Actions Under $15,000, Eviction, Small Claims.*
www.ketteringcourt.org

Civil Records: Access: Phone, mail, fax, in person. Both court and visitors may perform in person searches. No search fee. Required to search: name, years to search. Civil cases indexed by defendant, plaintiff. Civil records on computer from 1989, prior in books.

Criminal Records: Access: Phone, mail, in person. Both court and visitors may perform in person searches. No search fee. Required to search: name, years to search, DOB; also helpful: SSN. Criminal records on computer from 1988.

General Information: No expungment records released. Will fax results to local or toll free line. Copy fee: $.05 per page. Cert fee: $2.50 per page. Payee: Kettering Municipal Court. Business checks accepted. Attorney checks accepted. Visa, MC accepted. Mail requests: SASE required. Mail turnaround time 1-5 days.

Miamisburg Municipal Court 10 N First St, Miamisburg, OH 45342; 937-866-2203; Fax: 937-866-0135. Hours: 8AM-4PM (EST). *Misdemeanor, Civil Actions Under $15,000, Eviction, Small Claims.*

Civil Records: Access: Mail, in person. Both court and visitors may perform in person searches. No search fee. Required to search: name, years to search; also helpful: address. Civil cases indexed by defendant, plaintiff. Civil records on computer from 1988, prior in books. Call in advance to schedule in person searching. Mail request requires SASE.

Criminal Records: Access: Mail, in person. Only the court may perform in person searches. No search fee. Required to search: name, years to search; also helpful: address, DOB, SSN. Criminal records on computer from 1988, prior in books. Call in advance to schedule in person searching. Mail request requires SASE.

General Information: No police reports, search warrants with no returns records released. Will fax results to local or toll free line. Copy fee: $.25 per page. No cert fee. Payee: Clerk of Court. Personal checks accepted. Prepayment required. Mail requests: SASE required. Mail turnaround time 1-2 weeks.

Oakwood Municipal Court 30 Park Ave, Dayton, OH 45419; 937-293-3058; Fax: 937-297-2939. Hours: 8:30AM-4PM (EST). *Misdemeanor, Civil Actions Under $15,000, Eviction, Small Claims.*

Civil Records: Access: Mail, in person. Only the court performs in person searches; visitors may not. No search fee. Required to search: name, years to search; also helpful: address. Civil cases indexed by defendant, plaintiff. Civil records in books since 1976.

Criminal Records: Access: In person, mail. Only the court performs in person searches; visitors may not. No search fee. Required to search: name, years to search; also helpful: address, DOB, SSN. Criminal records in books since 1976. Address mail search requests to the Police Records Section.

General Information: No sealed, expunged or confidential records released. Will fax results to local or toll free line. No copy fee. No cert fee. Local checks accepted. Mail requests: SASE required. Mail turnaround time 1-2 weeks.

Vandalia Municipal Court PO Box 429, Justice Center, 2nd Fl, Vandalia, OH 45377; 937-898-3996; Fax: 937-898-6648. Hours: 8AM-4PM (EST). *Misdemeanor, Civil Actions Under $15,000, Eviction, Small Claims.* www.vandaliacourt.com

Civil Records: Access: Phone, fax, mail, in person, online. Both court and visitors may perform in person searches. Search fee: $1.00 per page for complete print out. Required to search: name, years to search. Civil cases indexed by defendant, plaintiff. Civil records on computer from 1986, prior in books. Search records, including traffic, at http://64.108.110.4/cmiflash/court/.

Criminal Records: Access: Fax, mail, in person, online. Both court and visitors may perform in person searches. No search fee. Required to search: name, years to search, DOB, SSN. Criminal records on computer from 1986, prior in books. Search records, including traffic, at http://64.108.110.4/cmiflash/court/.

General Information: Public Access terminal is available. No medical, psychological reports or domestic violence report records released. Copy fee: $1.00 per page. No cert fee. Payee: Clerk of Court. Business checks accepted. Credit cards accepted. Prepayment required. Mail requests: SASE required. Mail turnaround time is 7 days.

Morgan County

Common Pleas Court 19 E Main St, McConnelsville, OH 43756; 740-962-4752; Probate phone: 740-962-2861; Fax: 740-962-4589. Hours: 8AM-4PM M-Th; 8AM-5PM F (EST). *Felony, Civil Actions Over $3,000, Probate.*

Note: Above number is for Clerk. The Common Pleas Court can be reached at 740-962-3371.

Civil Records: Access: Mail, in person. Visitors must perform in person searches for themselves. Search fee: $2.00 per name. Required to search: name, years to search; also helpful: address. Civil cases indexed by defendant, plaintiff. Civil records in books, some back to 1850.

Criminal Records: Access: Mail, in person. Both court and visitors may perform in person searches. Search fee: $2.00 per name. Required to search: name, years to search; also helpful: address, DOB, SSN. Criminal records in books, some back to 1850.

General Information: Public Access terminal is available. No secret indictment records released. No copy fee. Cert fee: $1.00 per page. Payee: Clerk of Court. Personal checks accepted. Prepayment required. Mail requests: SASE required. Mail turnaround time 1-3 days.

Morgan County Court 37 E Main St, McConnelsville, OH 43756; 740-962-4031; Fax: 740-962-2895. Hours: 8AM-4PM (EST). *Misdemeanor, Civil Actions Under $15,000, Small Claims.*

Civil Records: Access: Fax, mail, in person. Both court and visitors may perform in person searches. No search fee. Required to search: name, years to search. Civil cases indexed by defendant, plaintiff. Civil records in books from 1950, computerized since 12/02.

Criminal Records: Access: Fax, mail, in person. Both court and visitors may perform in person searches. No search fee. Required to search: name, years to search, DOB; also helpful: SSN. Criminal records in books from 1950, computerized since 12/02.

General Information: Public Access terminal is available. No fee to fax results. Copy fee: $.10 per page. Cert fee: $1.00. Payee: Morgan County Court. Personal checks accepted. Prepayment required. Mail requests: SASE required. Mail turnaround time 1-2 days.

Morrow County

Common Pleas Court 48 E High St, Mount Gilead, OH 43338; 419-947-2085; Probate phone: 419-947-5575; Fax: 419-947-5421. Hours: 8AM-4:30PM (EST). *Felony, Civil Actions Over $3,000, Probate.*

Civil Records: Access: Phone, fax, mail, in person. Both court and visitors may perform in person searches. No search fee. Required to search: name, years to search; also helpful: address. Civil cases indexed by defendant, plaintiff. Civil records in books from 1960, computerized since 01/02.

Criminal Records: Access: Phone, fax, mail, in person. Both court and visitors may perform in person searches. No search fee. Required to search: name, years to search; also helpful: address, DOB, SSN. Criminal records in books from 1960, computerized since 01/02.

General Information: Public Access terminal is available. Copy fee: $1.00 per page. Cert fee: $1.00. Payee: Clerk of Court. Personal checks accepted. Prepayment required. Mail requests: SASE required. Mail turnaround time 1 day.

Municiapl Court 48 E High St, Mount Gilead, OH 43338; 419-947-5045; Fax: 419-947-9161. Hours: 7:30AM-5PM (EST). *Misdemeanor, Civil Actions Under $15,000, Small Claims.*

Civil Records: Access: Mail, in person. Both court and visitors may perform in person searches. No search fee. Required to search: name, years to search; also helpful-DOB or SSN. Civil cases indexed by defendant, plaintiff. Civil records on computer back to 1997, indexed on books from 1970s, archived from 1800s.

Criminal Records: Access: Mail, in person. Both court and visitors may perform in person searches. No search fee. Required to search: name, years to search, DOB, SSN. Criminal records on computer since 1990, indexed on books from 1970s, archived from 1800s.

General Information: No confidential records released. Copy fee: $1.00 per page. Cert fee: $2.00. Turnaround time 1-2 days.

Muskingum County

Common Pleas Court 401 Main St, Zanesville, OH 43701; 740-455-7104; Probate phone: 740-455-7113. Hours: 8:30AM-4:30PM (EST). *Felony, Civil Actions, Probate.*

Note: As of 1/1/2001, there is no dollar limit on civil actions; prior, the civil action minimum was $15,000.

Civil Records: Access: Mail, in person. Both court and visitors may perform in person searches. No search fee. Required to search: name, years to search; also helpful: address. Civil cases indexed by defendant, plaintiff. Civil records in original files back to 1800s.

Criminal Records: Access: Mail, in person. Both court and visitors may perform in person searches. No search fee. Required to search: name, years to search, DOB; also helpful: address, SSN. Criminal records on docket books to 1960, original files back to 1800s.

General Information: Public Access terminal is available. No grand jury records released. Will not fax results. Copy fee: $.25 per page. Cert fee: $1.00 per page. Payee: Clerk of Court. Personal checks accepted. Visa/MC accepted. Prepayment required. Mail requests: SASE required. Mail turnaround time 2 weeks.

County Court 27 N 5th St, Zanesville, OH 43701; 740-455-7138; Fax: 740-455-7157. Hours: 8AM-4PM (EST). *Misdemeanor, Civil Actions Under $15,000, Small Claims.* www.muskingumcountycourt.org

Civil Records: Access: Fax, mail, in person, online. Both court and visitors may perform in person searches. No search fee. Required to search: name, years to search; also helpful: address. Civil cases indexed by defendant, plaintiff. Civil records in books from 1958; on computer back to 1995. Access to county court records is free at www.muskingumcountycourt.org/sear.html.

Criminal Records: Access: Fax, mail, in person, online. Both court and visitors may perform in person searches. No search fee. Required to search: name, years to search, DOB; also helpful: address, SSN. Criminal records in books from 1958; on computer back to 1995. Access to county court records is free at www.muskingumcountycourt.org/sear.html.

General Information: Public Access terminal is available. No expunged records released. No fee to fax results. Fax available in emergency only. Copy fee: There is a $1.00 fee for certified copies, but no fee for uncertified. Cert fee: $1.00. Payee: Muskingum County Clerk. Personal checks accepted. Prepayment required. Mail requests: SASE required. Mail turnaround time up to 1 week.

Zanesville Municipal Court PO Box 566, Zanesville, OH 43702; 740-454-3269; Fax: 740-455-0739. Hours: 9AM-4:30PM (EST). *Misdemeanor, Civil Actions Under $15,000, Eviction, Small Claims.*

Civil Records: Access: Mail, in person. Both court and visitors may perform in person searches. No search fee. Required to search: name, years to search; also helpful: address. Civil cases indexed by defendant, plaintiff. Civil records on computer since 1987.

Criminal Records: Access: Mail, in person, fax. Both court and visitors may perform in person searches. No search fee. Required to search: name, years to search; also helpful: address, DOB, SSN. Criminal records on computer since 1993.

General Information: Public Access terminal is available. No copy fee. Cert fee: $1.00. Payee: Municipal Court. Personal checks accepted. Prepayment required. Mail requests: SASE required. Mail turnaround time 1 week.

Noble County

Common Pleas Court 350 Courthouse, Caldwell, OH 43724; 740-732-4408; Probate phone: 740-732-5047; Fax: 740-732-0100. Hours: 8-11:30AM,12:30-4PM M-W; 8-Noon Th; 8-11:30AM, 12:30-6PM F (EST). *Felony, Civil Actions Over $3,000.*

Note: Probate office is separate from this court at noble County Probate Court, 270 Courthouse, Caldwell, OH 43724.

Civil Records: Access: Phone, fax, mail, in person. Both court and visitors may perform in person searches. No search fee. Required to search: name, years to search; also helpful: address. Civil cases indexed by defendant, plaintiff. Civil records in books, archived back to mid-1800s. Recent civil records are computerized.

Criminal Records: Access: Phone, fax, mail, in person. Both court and visitors may perform in person searches. No search fee. Required to search: name, years to search; also helpful: address, DOB, SSN. Criminal records in books, archived back to 1800s. Recent civil records are computerized.

General Information: Public Access terminal is available. No sealed records released. No fee to fax results. Copy fee: $.50 per page. Payee: Clerk of Court. Personal checks accepted. Will bill all court rule copies. Mail requests: SASE required. Mail turnaround time 1-2 days.

Noble County Court 100 Courthouse, Caldwell, OH 43724; 740-732-5795; Fax: 740-732-1435. Hours: 8:30AM-4PM M-W,F; 8:30-N Th (EST). *Misdemeanor, Civil Actions Under $15,000, Small Claims.*

Civil Records: Access: Phone, fax, mail, in person. Both court and visitors may perform in person searches. No search fee. Required to search: name, years to search. Civil cases indexed by defendant, plaintiff. Civil records in books since 1960, on computer back to 2002.

Criminal Records: Access: Fax, mail, in person. Both court and visitors may perform in person searches. No search fee. Required to search: name, years to search, DOB; also helpful- SSN, signed release. Criminal records in books since 1960; on computer back to 2002.

General Information: Will fax results to local or toll free line. Copy fee: $.50 per page. Cert fee: $5.00. Payee: County Court. Only cashiers checks and money orders accepted. Prepayment required. Mail requests: SASE required. Mail turnaround time up to 1 week.

Ottawa County

Common Pleas Court 315 Madison St, 3rd Fl, Port Clinton, OH 43452; 419-734-6755 (General Division); Probate phone: 419-734-6830. Hours: 8:30AM-4:30PM (EST). *Felony, Civil Actions Over $10,000, Probate.*

www.ottawacocpcourt.com

Note: Probate is a separate court at 315 Madison St., Rm 306.

Civil Records: Access: In person only. Visitors must perform in person searches for themselves. No search fee. Required to search: name, years to search; also helpful: address. Civil cases indexed by defendant, plaintiff. Civil records on computer from 8/89, prior in books to 1842.

Criminal Records: Access: In person only. Visitors must perform in person searches for themselves. No search fee. Required to search: name, years to search; also helpful: address, DOB, SSN. Criminal records on computer from 8/89, prior in books to 1842.

General Information: Public Access terminal is available. No sealed records released. Will fax specific case documents for $3.00. Copy fee: $1.00 per page. Cert fee: $1.00. Payee: Clerk of Courts. Personal checks accepted. Prepayment required.

Ottawa County Municipal Court 1860 E Perry St, Port Clinton, OH 43452; 419-734-4143; Fax: 419-732-2862. Hours: 8:30AM-4:30PM (EST). *Misdemeanor, Civil Actions Under $15,000, Eviction, Small Claims.*

www.ottawacountymunicipalcourt.com

Civil Records: Access: In person, online. Visitors must perform in person searches for themselves. No search fee. Required to search: name, years to search; also helpful: address. Civil cases indexed by defendant, plaintiff. Civil records on computer from 1989, prior in books. Record index is at www.ottawacountymunicipalcourt.com/search.html.

Criminal Records: Access: In person, online. Visitors must perform in person searches for themselves. No search fee. Required to search: name, years to search, DOB; also helpful: address, SSN. Criminal records on computer from 1989, prior in books. Record index is at www.ottawacountymunicipalcourt.com/search.html.

General Information: Public Access terminal is available. No sealed records released. Copy fee: $.25 per page. Cert fee: $3.00. Payee: Municipal Court. Only cashiers checks and money orders accepted. Prepayment required.

Paulding County

Common Pleas Court 115 N Williams St Rm 104, Paulding, OH 45879; 419-399-8210; Probate phone: 419-339-8256; Fax: 419-399-8248. Hours: 8AM-4PM (EST). *Felony, Civil Actions Over $3,000, Probate.*

Civil Records: Access: Fax, mail, in person. Both court and visitors may perform in person searches. Search fee: $5.00 per name. Required to search: name, years to search. Civil cases indexed by defendant, plaintiff. Civil records in books, archived from 1800s.

Criminal Records: Access: Fax, mail, in person. Both court and visitors may perform in person searches. Search fee: $5.00 per name. Required to search: name, years to search; also helpful: address, DOB, SSN. Criminal records in books, archived from 1800s.

General Information: Public Access terminal is available. No mental, adoption records released. No fee to fax results. Copy fee: $.25 per page. Cert fee: $1.00. Payee: Clerk of Court. Personal checks accepted. Prepayment required. Mail requests: SASE required. Mail turnaround time same day.

County Court 201 E Carolina St, #2, Paulding, OH 45879; 419-399-2792; Fax: 419-399-3421. Hours: 8AM-4PM (EST). *Misdemeanor, Civil Actions Under $15,000, Small Claims.*

www.pauldingcountycourt.com

Civil Records: Access: Fax, mail, in person. Both court and visitors may perform in person searches. Search fee: $5.00 per name. Required to search: name, years to search; also helpful: address. Civil cases indexed by defendant, plaintiff. Civil records in books since 1985; computerized records since 1997. Access to civil records is at www.pauldingcountycourt.com/.

Criminal Records: Access: Fax, mail, in person. Both court and visitors may perform in person searches. Search fee: $5.00 per name. Required to search: name, years to search; also helpful: address, DOB, SSN. Criminal records in books since 1985; computerized records since 1997. Access to criminal records is at www.pauldingcountycourt.com/.

General Information: Public Access terminal is available. No fee to fax results. Copy fee: $.50 per page. Cert fee: $2.00. Payee: County Court. Personal checks accepted. Prepayment required. Mail requests: SASE required. Mail turnaround time 2-4 days.

Perry County

Common Pleas Court PO Box 67, New Lexington, OH 43764; 740-342-1022; Probate phone: 740-342-1493; Fax: 740-342-5527. Hours: 8AM-4PM (EST). *Felony, Civil Actions Over $3,000, Probate.*

www.lawrencecountyclkofcrt.org

Civil Records: Access: In person only. Visitors must perform in person searches for themselves. No search fee. Required to search: name, years to search; also helpful: address. Civil cases indexed by defendant, plaintiff. Civil records on computer since 3/96, in case files prior, indexed from 1940.

Criminal Records: Access: In person only. Visitors must perform in person searches for themselves. Search fee: n/z. Required to search: name, years to search; also helpful: address, DOB, SSN. Criminal records on computer since 3/96, in case files prior, indexed from 1940.

General Information: Public Access terminal is available. Copy fee: $.05 per page. Cert fee: $1.00 per certification. Payee: Clerk of Court. Personal checks accepted. Prepayment required.

Perry County Court PO Box 207, New Lexington, OH 43764-0207; 740-342-3156; Fax: 740-342-2188. Hours: 8:30AM-4:30PM M,W,F (EST). *Misdemeanor, Civil Actions Under $15,000, Small Claims.*

Civil Records: Access: In person only. Visitors must perform in person searches for themselves. No search fee. Required to search: name, years to search. Civil cases indexed by defendant, plaintiff. Civil records in books 10 to 12 years, computerized since 04/97.

Criminal Records: Access: In person only. Visitors must perform in person searches for themselves. No search fee. Required to search: name, years to search, DOB, SSN, signed release. Criminal records in books 10 to 12 years, computerized since 04/97.

General Information: Public Access terminal is available. All records are public. Copy fee: $1.00 per page. Cert fee: $1.00. Payee: Perry County Court. Personal checks accepted. Prepayment required.

Pickaway County

Common Pleas Court County Courthouse, 207 Court St PO Box 270, Circleville, OH 43113; 740-474-5231; Probate phone: 740-474-3950. Hours: 8AM-4PM (EST). *Felony, Civil Actions Over $10,000, Probate.*

www.pickawaycountycpcourt.org

Civil Records: Access: Mail, in person, online. Both court and visitors may perform in person searches. No search fee. Required to search: name, years to search; also helpful: address. Civil cases indexed by defendant. Civil records on computer back to 1988, indexed to 1940s, archived from 1800s. Search docket information at the website.

Criminal Records: Access: Mail, in person, online. Both court and visitors may perform in person searches. No search fee. Required to search: name, years to search; also helpful: address, DOB, SSN. Criminal records on computer back to 1988, indexed to 1940s, archived from 1800s. Search docket information at the website.

General Information: Public Access terminal is available. Copy fee: $.25 per page. Cert fee: $1.00 per page. Payee: Clerk of Court. Prepayment required. Mail requests: SASE required. Mail turnaround time 2-3 days.

Circleville Municipal Court PO Box 128, Circleville, OH 43113; 740-474-3171; Fax: 740-477-8291. Hours: 8AM-4PM (EST). *Misdemeanor, Civil Actions Under $15,000, Eviction, Small Claims.*

www.circlevillecourt.com

Civil Records: Access: Phone, fax, mail, in person, online. Both court and visitors may perform in person searches. No search fee. Required to search: name, years to search. Civil cases indexed by defendant, plaintiff. Civil records on computer from 1989, prior in books. Search online at www.circlevillecourt.com/AccessCourtRecords.asp.

Criminal Records: Access: Phone, fax, mail, in person, online. Both court and visitors may perform in person searches. No search fee. Required to search: name, years to search; also helpful: SSN. Criminal records on computer from 1987, prior in books back to 1983. Search online at www.circlevillecourt.com/AccessCourtRecords.asp.

General Information: Public Access terminal is available. No warrant records released. Copy fee: $.50 per page. No cert fee. Payee: Circleville Municipal Court. Personal checks accepted. Visa, MC accepted. Prepayment required. Mail requests: SASE required. Mail turnaround time 1-2 days.

Pike County

Common Pleas Court 100 E 2nd St, 2nd Fl, Waverly, OH 45690; 740-947-2715; Probate phone: 740-947-2560; Fax: 740-947-1729. Hours: 8:30AM-4PM (EST). *Felony, Civil Actions Over $15,000, Probate.*

Note: Probate is a separate court at 230 Waverly Plaza, #600.

Civil Records: Access: In person only. Visitors must perform in person searches for themselves. No search fee. Required to search: name, years to search; also helpful: address. Civil cases indexed by defendant, plaintiff. Civil records in books back to 1815; on comptuer back to 1999.

Criminal Records: Access: In person only. Visitors must perform in person searches for themselves. No search fee. Required to search: name, years to search; also helpful: address, DOB, SSN. Criminal records in books back to 1815; on computer back to 1999.

General Information: Public Access terminal is available. No grand jury secret indictment records released. Copy fee: $.25 per page. Cert fee: $1.00. Payee: Clerk of Court. Personal checks accepted. Prepayment required.

Pike County Court 230 Waverly Plaza, #900, Waverly, OH 45690; Criminal phone: 740-947-4003. Hours: 8:30AM-4PM (EST). *Misdemeanor, Civil Actions Under $15,000, Small Claims.*

Civil Records: Access: Phone, fax, mail, in person. Both court and visitors may perform in person

searches. No search fee. Required to search: name, years to search. Civil cases indexed by defendant, plaintiff. Civil records in books indexed to 1958, computerized since 1996.

Criminal Records: Access: Phone, fax, mail, in person. Both court and visitors may perform in person searches. No search fee. Required to search: name, years to search. Criminal records in books indexed to 1958, computerized since 1996.

General Information: Public Access terminal is available. No sealed or expunged records released. Will fax results to local or toll free line. Copy fee: $1.00 per page. No cert fee. Payee: Pike County Court. Personal checks accepted. Prepayment required. Mail requests: SASE required. Mail turnaround time 1 week.

Portage County

Common Pleas Court PO Box 1035, Ravenna, OH 44266; 330-297-3644; Civil phone: 330-297-3644; Criminal phone: 330-297-3640; Probate phone: 330-297-3870; Fax: 330-297-4554. Hours: 8AM-4PM (EST). *Felony, Civil Actions Over $10,000, Probate.*

Note: Probate Court address is 203 W Main, Ravenna, OH 44266-0936.

Civil Records: Access: In person, online. Visitors must perform in person searches for themselves. No search fee. Required to search: name, years to search; also helpful: address. Civil cases indexed by defendant, plaintiff. Civil records on computer back to 11/1991, prior in books back to 1977; Judgments back to 1/1982. For records from 1992 forward, go to http://67.39.103.41/pa/pa.htm.

Criminal Records: Access: In person, online. Visitors must perform in person searches for themselves. No search fee. Required to search: name, years to search; also helpful: address, DOB. Criminal records on computer back to 1977, prior in books. For records from 1992 forward, go to http://67.39.103.41/pa/pa.htm. (Direct questions about online access to Pam Christy at 330-297-3646.).

General Information: Public Access terminal is available. Copy fee: $.10 per page. Cert fee: $1.00 per page. Payee: Clerk of Court. Personal checks accepted. Prepayment required. Monthly accounts available.

Portage County Municipal Court PO Box 958, Ravenna, OH 44266; Civil phone: 330-297-3635; Criminal phone: 330-297-3639; Fax: 330-297-3526 (civ); 297-5867 (crim). Hours: 8AM-4PM (EST). *Misdemeanor, Civil Actions Under $15,000, Eviction, Small Claims.*

www.co.portage.oh.us

Civil Records: Access: Mail, in person, online. Visitors must perform in person searches for themselves. Search fee: $5.00. Required to search: name, years to search; also helpful: address. Civil cases indexed by defendant, plaintiff. Civil records on computer from 1992. For records from 1992 forward, go to http://67.39.103.41/pa/pa.htm.

Criminal Records: Access: Mail, in person, online. Visitors must perform in person searches for themselves. Search fee: $5.00. Required to search: name, years to search; also helpful: address, DOB, SSN. Criminal records on computer from 1992. For records from 1992 forward, go to http://67.39.103.41/pa/pa.htm. (Direct questions about online access to Pam Christy at 330-297-3646.).

General Information: Public Access terminal is available. No records released. Copy fee: $.10 per page. Cert fee: $1.00. Payee: Municipal Court. Personal checks accepted. Prepayment required. Mail turnaround time is 2 days.

Portage Municipal Court - Kent Branch 214 S Water, Kent, OH 44240; 330-678-9170; Civil phone: 330-678-9170; Criminal phone: 330-678-9100; Fax: 330-677-9944. Hours: 8AM-4PM (EST). *Misdemeanor, Civil Actions Under $15,000, Eviction, Small Claims.*

www.co.portage.oh.us

Civil Records: Access: In person, online. Search fee: $5.00 per name. Required to search: name, years to search; also helpful: address. Civil cases indexed by defendant, plaintiff. Civil records on computer from 1992, prior in books. For records from 1992 forward, go to http://67.39.103.41/pa/pa.htm.

Criminal Records: Access: In person, online. Both court and visitors may perform in person searches. Search fee: $5.00 per name. Required to search: name, years to search; also helpful: address, DOB, SSN. Criminal records on computer from 1992, prior in books. For records from 1992 forward, go to http://67.39.103.41/pa/pa.htm. (Direct questions about online access to Pam Christy at 330-297-3646.).

General Information: Public Access terminal is available. No expunged records released. Will fax case file documents for $1.00 per page. Copy fee: $.10 per page. Cert fee: $1.00. Payee: Portage County Municipal Court. Personal checks accepted. Visa/MC cards accepted (plus 4% fee). Accepted for criminal only, and only if "in person". Prepayment required.

Preble County

Common Pleas Court 101 E Main, 3rd Fl, Eaton, OH 45320; 937-456-8160; 456-8165 (common pleas); Probate phone: 937-456-8138; Fax: 937-456-9548. Hours: 8AM-4:30PM (EST). *Felony, Civil, Probate.*

Note: Probate office is separate from this court.

Civil Records: Access: In person only. Visitors must perform in person searches for themselves. No search fee. Required to search: name, years to search; also helpful: address. Civil cases indexed by defendant, plaintiff. Civil records on computer from 11/89, prior in books indexed to 1940s.

Criminal Records: Access: Mail, in person. Both court and visitors may perform in person searches. Search fee: $3.00 per name. Required to search: name, years to search; also helpful: address, DOB, SSN. Criminal records on computer from 11/89, prior in books indexed to 1940s.

General Information: Public Access terminal is available. No secret records released. Copy fee: $.50 per page. Cert fee: $1.00. Payee: Clerk of Court. Personal checks accepted. Prepayment required. Mail requests: SASE required. Mail turnaround time 1 day.

Eaton Municipal Court PO Box 65 (101 E Main St), Eaton, OH 45320; 937-456-4941/6204; Fax: 937-456-4685. Hours: 8AM-Noon, 1-4:30PM (EST). *Misdemeanor, Civil Actions Under $15,000, Eviction, Small Claims.*

www.eatonmunicipalcourt.com

Civil Records: Access: Mail, in person, online. Both court and visitors may perform in person searches. No search fee. Required to search: name, years to search. Civil cases indexed by defendant, plaintiff. Civil records on computer from 1989, prior in books indexed to 1959. Search by name or case number at the website. Records back to 1992.

Criminal Records: Access: Mail, in person, online. Both court and visitors may perform in person searches. No search fee. Required to search: name, years to search; also helpful: SSN. Criminal records on computer from 1989, prior in books indexed to 1959. Search by name or case number at the website. Computerized records begin in 1992 for civil, criminal and traffic cases.

General Information: Public Access terminal is available. (Criminal records only.) No driving records released. Copy fee: $1.00 per page. Cert fee: $1.00. Payee: Eaton Municipal Court. Personal checks accepted. Visa, MC accepted. Prepayment required. Mail requests: SASE required. Mail turnaround time 1 week.

Putnam County

Common Pleas Court 245 E Main, Rm 301, Ottawa, OH 45875; 419-523-3110; Probate phone: 419-523-3012; Fax: 419-523-5284. Hours: 8:30AM-4:30PM (EST). *Felony, Civil Actions Over $10,000, Probate.*

Note: Probate is a separate court at number given.

Civil Records: Access: Fax, mail, in person. Both court and visitors may perform in person searches. Search fee: $10.00 per name. Required to search: name, years to search. Civil cases indexed by defendant, plaintiff. Civil records on computer from 1992 indexed on docket books back to 1800s.

Criminal Records: Access: Fax, mail, in person. Both court and visitors may perform in person searches. Search fee: $10.00 per name. Required to search: name, years to search; also helpful: address, DOB, SSN. Criminal records on computer from 1992 indexed on docket books back to 1800s.

General Information: Public Access terminal is available. No sealed records released. Will fax results for $3.00 per transmission plus $1.00 per page. Copy fee: $.25 per page. Cert fee: $1.00. Payee: Clerk of Court. Putnam County personal checks accepted. Prepayment required. Mail requests: SASE required. Mail turnaround time 1-4 days.

Putnam County Court 245 E Main, Rm 303, Ottawa, OH 45875; 419-523-3110; Fax: 419-523-5284. Hours: 8:30AM-4:30PM (EST). *Misdemeanor, Civil Actions Under $10,000, Small Claims.*

Civil Records: Access: Mail, in person, fax. Both court and visitors may perform in person searches. Search fee: $10.00 per name. Required to search: name, years to search. Civil cases indexed by defendant, plaintiff. Civil records go back to 1800s; computerized records go back to 1992.

Criminal Records: Access: Mail, in person. Both court and visitors may perform in person searches. Search fee: $10.00 per name. Required to search: name, years to search. Criminal records go back to 1826; computerized records go back to 1992.

General Information: Public Access terminal is available. Will fax results for $3.00 per fax plus $1.00 per page. Copy fee: $.25 per page. Cert fee: $1.00. Payee: Clerk of Court. Only cashiers checks and money orders accepted. Prepayment required. Mail requests: SASE required. Mail turnaround time up to 4 days.

Richland County

Common Pleas Court 50 Park Ave E, 2nd Fl, PO Box 127, Mansfield, OH 44901; 419-774-5549; Probate phone: 419-755-5583. Hours: 8AM-4PM (EST). *Felony, Civil Actions Over $10,000, Probate.* www.richlandcountyoh.us/coc.htm

Civil Records: Access: In person, mail, fax, online. Both court and visitors may perform in person searches. No search fee. Required to search: name, years to search; also helpful: address. Civil cases indexed by defendant, plaintiff. Civil records on computer from 1989, prior in books and on microfiche to 1960. Access to civil records is at www.richlandcountyoh.us/courtv.htm.

Criminal Records: Access: In person, mail. Both court and visitors may perform in person searches. No search fee. Required to search: name, years to search, DOB, SSN, signed release; also helpful: address. Criminal records on computer from 1991, prior in books and on microfiche to 1960. Access to criminal records at www.richlandcountyoh.us.

General Information: Public Access terminal is available. No sealed records released. Copy fee: $.25 per page. Cert fee: $5.00. Payee: Clerk of Court. Personal checks accepted. Prepayment required.

Mansfield Municipal Court PO Box 1228, Mansfield, OH 44901; 419-755-9617; Fax: 419-755-9647. Hours: 8AM-4PM (EST). *Misdemeanor, Civil Actions Under $15,000, Eviction, Small Claims.*

Civil Records: Access: Phone, fax, mail, in person, online. Both court and visitors may perform in person searches. No search fee. Required to search: name, years to search; also helpful: address. Civil cases indexed by defendant, plaintiff. Criminal records on computer from 1989. Overall records go back to 1940. Phone & fax access limited to short searches. Online access at www6.mapstrategies.com/mansfield/index.html for records from 1992 forward.

Criminal Records: Access: Phone, fax, mail, in person, online. Both court and visitors may perform in person searches. No search fee. Required to search: name, years to search; also helpful: address, DOB, SSN. Criminal records on computer from 1989. Overall records go back to 1940. Online access at www6.mapstrategies.com/mansfield/index.html for records from 1992 forward.

General Information: Public Access terminal is available. No lead print out records released. No fee to fax results. Copy fee: $.25 per page. Cert fee: $1.00. Payee: Clerk of Court or Mansfield Municipal Court. Personal checks accepted. Prepayment required. Mail requests: SASE required. Mail turnaround time 2-3 days.

Ross County

Common Pleas Court County Courthouse, 2 N Paint St, #A, Chillicothe, OH 45601; 740-702-3010; Probate phone: 740-774-1179; Fax: 740-702-3018. Hours: 8AM-4PM (EST). *Felony, Civil Actions Over $10,000, Probate.* www.co.ross.oh.us

Civil Records: Access: In person only, online. Both court and visitors may perform in person searches. No search fee. Required to search: name, years to search; also helpful: address. Civil cases indexed by defendant, plaintiff. Civil records on computer from 1989, prior in books to 1800s. Search records back to 11/89 at the website.

Criminal Records: Access: In person, online. Both court and visitors may perform in person searches. No search fee. Required to search: name, years to search; also helpful: address, DOB, SSN. Criminal records on computer from 1989, prior in books to 1800s. Search records back to 11/89 at the website.

General Information: Public Access terminal is available. No secret indictment records released. Will fax results to local or toll free line. Copy fee: $.05 per page. Cert fee: $1.00. Payee: Clerk of Court. Personal checks accepted. Prepayment required.

Chillicothe Municipal Court 26 S Paint St, Chillicothe, OH 45601; 740-773-3515; Fax: 740-774-1101. Hours: 7:30AM-4:30PM (EST). *Misdemeanor, Civil Actions Under $15,000, Eviction, Small Claims.* www.chillicothemunicipalcourt.org

Civil Records: Access: Mail, in person, online. Both court and visitors may perform in person searches. No search fee. Required to search: name, years to search; also helpful: address. Civil cases indexed by defendant, plaintiff. Civil records on computer from 6/93, prior in books. Search docket information from http://216.201.21.130/Search/.

Criminal Records: Access: Mail, in person, online. Both court and visitors may perform in person searches. No search fee. Required to search: name, years to search, DOB, SSN; also helpful: address.

Criminal records on computer from 6/93, prior in books. Search docket information from http://216.201.21.130/Search/.

General Information: Public Access terminal is available. No confidential records released. Will not fax results. Copy fee: $.05 per page. Cert fee: $1.00 per page (includes the $.05 copy fee). Payee: Municipal Court. Business checks accepted. Prepayment required. Mail requests: SASE required. Mail turnaround time 10 days.

Sandusky County

Common Pleas Court 100 N Park Ave, #320, Fremont, OH 43420; 419-334-6161/6163; Probate phone: 419-334-6217; Fax: 419-334-6164. Hours: 8AM-4:30PM (EST). *Felony, Civil Actions Over $3,000, Probate.*

Civil Records: Access: In person only. Visitors must perform in person searches for themselves. No search fee. Required to search: name, years to search; also helpful: address. Civil cases indexed by defendant, plaintiff. Civil records on computer from 1988, prior in books to 1800s.

Criminal Records: Access: In person only. Visitors must perform in person searches for themselves. No search fee. Required to search: name, years to search; also helpful: address, DOB, SSN. Criminal records on computer from 1988, prior in books to 1800s.

General Information: Public Access terminal is available. No search warrant records released. Copy fee: $.10 per page. Cert fee: $1.00. Payee: Clerk of Court. Personal checks accepted. Prepayment required.

County Court #1 847 E McPherson Hwy (PO Box 267), Clyde, OH 43410; 419-547-0915; Fax: 419-547-9198. Hours: 8AM-4:30PM (EST). *Misdemeanor, Civil Actions Under $15,000, Small Claims.* www.co.sandusky.oh.us

Civil Records: Access: Phone, fax, mail, in person. Both court and visitors may perform in person searches. No search fee. Required to search: name, years to search; also helpful: address. Civil cases indexed by defendant, plaintiff. Civil records on computer from 1998, prior in books for 25 years.

Criminal Records: Access: Phone, fax, mail, in person. Both court and visitors may perform in person searches. No search fee. Required to search: name, years to search, DOB, SSN; also helpful: address. Criminal records on computer from 1998, prior in books for 25 years.

General Information: No fee to fax results to toll-free number. Copy fee: $.10 per page. Cert fee: $1.00. Payee: County Court. Personal checks accepted. Visa, MC accepted. Prepayment required. Mail requests: SASE required. Mail turnaround time 2-3 days.

County Court #2 215 W Main St, Woodville, OH 43469; 419-849-3961; Fax: 419-849-3932. Hours: 8AM-4:30PM (EST). *Misdemeanor, Civil Actions Under $15,000, Small Claims.* www.sandusky-county.org

Civil Records: Access: Phone, fax, mail, in person. Both court and visitors may perform in person searches. No search fee. Required to search: name, years to search; also helpful: address. Civil cases indexed by defendant, plaintiff. Civil records go back to 1983; on computer back to 1998.

Criminal Records: Access: Phone, fax, mail, in person. Only the court performs in person searches. No search fee. Required to search: name, years to search, DOB, SSN. Criminal records go back to 1995; on computer back to 1998.

General Information: No confidential records released. Will fax results $5.00 per doc. Copy fee: $.10 per page. Cert fee: $1.00. Payee: County Court. Personal checks accepted. Visa, MC accepted.

Prepayment required. Mail requests: SASE required. Mail turnaround time 10 days; by phone 3 hours.

Fremont Municipal Court
PO Box 886, Fremont, OH 43420-0071; 419-332-1579; Fax: 419-332-1570. Hours: 8AM-4:30PM (EST). *Misdemeanor, Civil Actions Under $15,000, Eviction, Small Claims.*
Civil Records: Access: Fax, mail, in person. Both court and visitors may perform in person searches. No search fee. Required to search: name, years to search. Civil cases indexed by defendant, plaintiff. Civil records in books from 1960, computerized since 1992.
Criminal Records: Access: Fax, mail, in person. Both court and visitors may perform in person searches. No search fee. Required to search: name, years to search; also helpful: DOB, SSN. Criminal records in books from 1960, computerized since 1992.
General Information: Public Access terminal is available. No fee to fax results. Local faxing only. Copy fee: $.25 per page. No cert fee. Payee: Fremont Municipal Court. Only cashiers checks and money orders accepted. Prepayment required. Mail turnaround time 2 days.

Scioto County

Common Pleas Court
602 7th St, Rm 205, Portsmouth, OH 45662; 740-355-8226; Probate phone: 740-355-8243; Fax: 740-354-2057. Hours: 8AM-4:30PM (EST). *Felony, Civil Actions Over $15,000, Probate.*
www.sciotocountycpcourt.org
Note: Probate is a separate office at the same address in Rm 201.
Civil Records: Access: In person, online. Both court and visitors may perform in person searches. No search fee. Required to search: name, years to search; also helpful: address. Civil cases indexed by defendant, plaintiff. Civil records on computer from 1986, dockets to 1800s. Online access to civil records is free at www.sciotocountycpcourt.org/search.htm. Search by court calendar, quick index, general index or docket sheet.
Criminal Records: Access: In person, online. Both court and visitors may perform in person searches. No search fee. Required to search: name, years to search; also helpful: address, DOB. Criminal records on computer from 1986, dockets to 1800s. Online access to criminal records is the same as civil.
General Information: Public Access terminal is available. No sealed or secret records released. Will fax specifc case file requests for $1.00 per page. Copy fee: $1.00 per page. Cert fee: $1.00 per page. Payee: Clerk of Court. Personal checks accepted. Prepayment required.

Portsmouth Municipal Court
728 2nd St, Portsmouth, OH 45662; 740-354-3283; Fax: 740-353-6645. Hours: 8AM-4PM (EST). *Misdemeanor, Civil Actions Under $15,000, Eviction, Small Claims.*
www.portsmouth-municipal-court.com
Civil Records: Access: Mail, in person, online. Both court and visitors may perform in person searches. Search fee: No fee for computer records search 1989 forward. Required to search: name, years to search. Civil cases indexed by defendant, plaintiff. Criminal records go back to 1985; on computer back to 1995. Online access is free at www.portsmouth-municipal-court.com/disc.html.
Criminal Records: Access: Mail, in person, online. Both court and visitors may perform in person searches. Search fee: $20.00 per name if search includes years prior to 1989. No fee for computer records search 1989 forward. Required to search: name, years to search, SSN. Criminal records go back to 1985; on computer back to 1995. Online access to

criminal records is free at www.portsmouth-municipal-court.com/disc.html.
General Information: Public Access terminal is available. No competency hearing, protection order records released. No fee to fax results. No copy fee. Cert fee: $1.00 per page. Payee: Portsmouth Municipal Court. Prepayment required. Mail requests: SASE required. Mail turnaround time 2-3 days; older records up to 2 weeks.

Seneca County

Common Pleas Court
117 E. Market, Tiffin, OH 44883; 419-447-0671; Probate phone: 419-447-3121; Fax: 419-443-7919. Hours: 8:30AM-4:30PM (EST). *Felony, Civil Actions Over $10,000, Probate.*
Civil Records: Access: Phone, fax, mail, in person. Both court and visitors may perform in person searches. No search fee. Required to search: name, years to search; also helpful: address. Civil cases indexed by defendant, plaintiff. Civil records on computer from 1/93, prior in books to 1900s, archived to 1800s.
Criminal Records: Access: Phone, fax, mail, in person. Both court and visitors may perform in person searches. No search fee. Required to search: name, years to search, SSN, date of offense. Criminal records on computer from 1/93, prior in books to 1900s, archived to 1800s.
General Information: Public Access terminal is available. (Terminal is located in the Recorder's Office; docket sheets can be printed out for $.25 per page in clerk's office.) No sealed records released. Fee to fax results is $2.00 per transmission. Copy fee: $.25 per page. Cert fee: $1.00. Payee: Clerk of Court. Personal checks accepted. Prepayment required. Mail requests: SASE required. Mail turnaround time 1 week.

Fostoria Municipal Court
PO Box 985, Fostoria, OH 44830; 419-435-8139; Fax: 419-435-1150. Hours: 8:30AM-5PM, Wed. 8:30AM-Noon (EST). *Misdemeanor, Civil Actions Under $15,000, Eviction, Small Claims.*
Civil Records: Access: Phone, fax, mail, in person. Both court and visitors may perform in person searches. No search fee. Required to search: name, years to search. Civil cases indexed by defendant, plaintiff. Civil records computerized since 1987.
Criminal Records: Access: Phone, fax, mail, in person. Both court and visitors may perform in person searches. No search fee. Required to search: name, years to search; also helpful: SSN. Criminal records computerized since 1987.
General Information: Public Access terminal is available. No fee if faxed to local or toll free number. Copy fee: $.10 per page. Cert fee: $1.00 per page. Payee: Fostoria Municipal Court. Personal checks accepted. Prepayment required. Mail turnaround time 1-2 days.

Tiffin Municipal Court
PO Box 694, Tiffin, OH 44883; 419-448-5412; Civil phone: 419-448-5418; Criminal phone: 419-448-5411; Fax: 419-448-5419. Hours: 8:30AM-4:30PM (EST). *Misdemeanor, Civil Actions Under $15,000, Eviction, Small Claims.*
Civil Records: Access: Fax, mail, in person. Both court and visitors may perform in person searches. No search fee. Required to search: name, years to search; also helpful: address. Civil cases indexed by defendant, plaintiff. Civil records on computer from 8/90, prior in books.
Criminal Records: Access: Fax, mail, in person. Both court and visitors may perform in person searches. No search fee. Required to search: name, years to search, DOB, SSN, signed release; also helpful: address. Criminal records on computer from 8/90, prior in books.

General Information: Public Access terminal is available. No expunged records released. Fee to fax back results is $.25 per page. Copy fee: $.05 per page. Cert fee: $1.00. Payee: Municipal Court. Personal checks accepted. Prepayment required. Mail requests: SASE required. Mail turnaround time 3 days.

Shelby County

Common Pleas Court
PO Box 809, Sidney, OH 45365; 937-498-7221; Fax: 937-498-4840. Hours: 8AM-4PM (EST). *Felony, Civil Actions Over $10,000, Probate.*
http://co.shelby.oh.us/commonpleas
Civil Records: Access: Fax, mail, in person. Both court and visitors may perform in person searches. Search fee: $1.00 per name. Required to search: name, years to search; also helpful: address. Civil cases indexed by defendant, plaintiff. Civil records on computer from 1987, on indexes from 1819.
Criminal Records: Access: Mail, in person. Visitors must perform in person searches for themselves. Search fee: $1.00 per name. Required to search: name, years to search DOB, SSN; also helpful: address. Criminal records on computer from 1987, on indexes from 1819.
General Information: Public Access terminal is available. No grand jury tapes released. Fee to fax results is $3.00 per page. Copy fee: $.25 per page. Cert fee: $4.00. Payee: Shelby County Clerk of Courts. Personal checks accepted. Prepayment required. Mail requests: SASE required. Mail turnaround time 5 days.

Sidney Municipal Court
201 W Poplar, Sidney, OH 45365; 937-498-0011; Fax: 937-498-8179. Hours: 8AM-4:30PM (EST). *Misdemeanor, Civil Actions Under $15,000, Eviction, Small Claims.*
www.sidneyoh.com
Note: Send mail requests to the address above; phone and in person searches are made at the court at 110 W Court St.
Civil Records: Access: Phone, fax, mail, in person. Both court and visitors may perform in person searches. No search fee. Required to search: name, years to search. Civil cases indexed by defendant, plaintiff. Civil records on computer from 1988; prior on books to 1958.
Criminal Records: Access: Phone, fax, mail, in person. Both court and visitors may perform in person searches. No search fee. Required to search: name, years to search; also helpful: address, DOB, SSN. Criminal records on computer from 1988; prior on books to 1958.
General Information: Public Access terminal is available. Confidential and probation records are not released. Copy fee: $.10 per page. Cert fee: $1.00 per page. Payee: Municipal Court. Personal checks accepted. Prepayment required. Mail requests: SASE not required. Mail turnaround time 2 days.

Stark County

Alliance Municipal Court
470 E Market St, Rm 16, Alliance, OH 44601; 330-823-6600; Fax: 330-829-2231. Hours: 8:30AM-4:30PM (EST). *Misdemeanor, Civil Actions Under $15,000, Eviction, Small Claims.*
www.starkcountycjis.org/alliance/
Note: Jurisdiction Includes Alliance, Lexington, Marlboro, Washignton, Paris, Uniontown, Minerva, Limaville, and Robertsville.
Civil Records: Access: Fax, mail, in person, online. Both court and visitors may perform in person searches. No search fee. Required to search: name. Civil cases indexed by defendant, plaintiff. Civil records go back to 1993. Search the Online Case Docket of the Alliance Court at

www.starkcountycjis.org/alliance/docket/search_large_frame.html.

Criminal Records: Access: Fax, mail, in person, online. Both court and visitors may perform in person searches. No search fee. Required to search: name, years to search; also helpful: DOB, SSN. computerized since 1991. Search the Online Case Docket of the Massillon Court at www.starkcountycjis.org/alliance/docket/search_large_frame.html, includes traffic and misdemeanor records.

General Information: Public Access terminal is available. No fee to fax results. Copy fee: $.25 per page. Cert fee: $3.00 per page. Payee: Alliance Municipal Court. Personal checks accepted. Prepayment required. Mail turnaround time 1 day.

Common Pleas Court - Civil Division PO Box 21160, Canton, OH 44701; 330-451-7795; Fax: 330-451-7853. Hours: 8:30AM-4:30PM (EST). *Civil Actions Over $15,000.*
www.starkclerk.org

Civil Records: Access: Phone, fax, mail, in person, online. Both court and visitors may perform in person searches. No search fee. Required to search: name, years to search. Civil cases indexed by defendant, plaintiff. Civil records on computer from 1985, prior in books form 1940s. Online access to the county online case docket database is free at www.starkcourt.org/docket/index.html. Search by name or case number.

General Information: Public Access terminal is available. No sealed records released. Fee to fax results is $2.00 for 1st page, $1.00 each add'l. Copy fee: $.10 per page. Cert fee: $1.00. Payee: Clerk of Court. Personal checks accepted. Prepayment required. Mail requests: SASE required. Mail turnaround time up to 1 week.

Common Pleas Court - Criminal Division PO Box 21160, Canton, OH 44701-1160; 330-451-7929; Fax: 330-451-7853. Hours: 8:30AM-4:30PM (EST). *Felony.*
www.starkclerk.org

Criminal Records: Access: Mail, in person, online. Both court and visitors may perform in person searches. No search fee. Required to search: name, years to search, DOB, SSN. Criminal records on computer back to 1985, prior in books to 1940s. Online access to the county online case docket database is free at www.starkcourt.org/docket/index.html. Search by name, case number or SSN.

General Information: Public Access terminal is available. No secret indictments, expungment records released. Will fax results. Copy fee: $.10 per page. Cert fee: $1.00. Payee: Clerk of Courts. Personal checks accepted. Prepayment required. Mail requests: SASE required. Mail turnaround time up to 2 weeks.

Canton Municipal Court 218 Cleveland Ave SW, PO Box 24218, Canton, OH 44702-4218; 330-489-3203; Fax: 330-489-3075 (civil) 489-3372 (criminal). Hours: 8AM-4:30PM (EST). *Misdemeanor, Civil Actions Under $15,000, Eviction, Small Claims.*
www.cantoncourt.org
Note: Jurisdiction includes Canton, North Canton, Louisville, Lake, Plain, Nimishillen, Osnaburg, Pike, Sandy, Hartville, E Canton, Myers Lake, E Sparta, Waynesburg, and Magnolia.

Civil Records: Access: Phone, fax, mail, in person, online. Both court and visitors may perform in person searches. No search fee. Required to search: name, years to search. Civil cases indexed by defendant, plaintiff. Civil records on computer from 1991, prior in books to 1928. Search docket information at www.cantoncourt.org/docket.html.

Criminal Records: Access: Phone, fax, mail, in person, online. Both court and visitors may perform in person searches. No search fee. Required to search: name, years to search; also helpful: DOB, SSN. Criminal records on computer from 1986, books to 1928. Search docket information at www.cantoncourt.org/docket.html. Includes traffic.

General Information: Public Access terminal is available. No sealed records released. No fee to fax results. Copy fee: $.25 per page. Cert fee: $1.00. Payee: Municipal Court. Personal checks accepted. Prepayment required. Mail requests: SASE required. Mail turnaround time 1-2 days.

Massillon Municipal Court Two James Duncan Plaza, Massillon, OH 44646-6690; 330-830-2591; Civil phone: 330-830-1731; Criminal phone: 330-830-1732; Fax: 330-830-3648. Hours: 8:30AM-4:30PM (EST). *Misdemeanor, Civil Actions Under $15,000, Eviction, Small Claims.*
www.massilloncourt.org/
Note: Jurisdiction includes Massillon, Canal Fulton, Bethlehem, Jackson, Lawrence, Perry, Sugarcreek, Tuscarawas, Beach City, Brewster, Hills and Dales, Navarre, and Wilmot.

Civil Records: Access: Fax, mail, in person, online. Both court and visitors may perform in person searches. No search fee. Required to search: name. Civil cases indexed by defendant, plaintiff. Civil records on docket books from 1986, computerized since 1991. Search the Online Case Docket of the Massillon Court at www.massilloncourt.org.

Criminal Records: Access: Fax, mail, in person, online. Both court and visitors may perform in person searches. No search fee. Required to search: name, years to search; also helpful: DOB, SSN. computerized since 1991. Search the Online Case Docket of the Massillon Court at the website, includes traffic and misdemeanor records.

General Information: Public Access terminal is available. No fee to fax results. Copy fee: $.05 per page. Cert fee: $2.00 per page. Payee: Massillon Municipal Court. Personal checks accepted. Prepayment required. Mail turnaround time 1 week.

Summit County

Common Pleas Court 209 S High St, Akron, OH 44308; 330-643-2201 (Divorce); Civil phone: 330-643-2217; Criminal phone: 330-643-2282; Probate phone: 330-643-2350; Fax: 330-643-7772. Hours: 9:30AM-4:15PM (EST). *Felony, Civil Actions Over $10,000, Probate.*
www.cpclerk.co.summit.oh.us
Note: Mail requests to Clerk at 53 Univeristy Ave, Akron 44308 for fatser mail service. Probate is a separate court at the phone number above.

Civil Records: Access: Mail, in person, online. Both court and visitors may perform in person searches. No search fee. Required to search: name, years to search. Civil cases indexed by defendant, plaintiff. Civil records on computer from 1982, prior in books, some microfiche. Access to county clerk of courts records is free at www.cpclerk.co.summit.oh.us. Click on "Case Search." Access to probate records at http://probatecourt.summitoh.net/CaseAccess.htm.

Criminal Records: Access: Mail, in person, online. Both court and visitors may perform in person searches. Search fee: $2.00 per name. Required to search: name, years to search, DOB; also helpful: SSN. Criminal records on computer from 1982, prior in books, some microfiche. Access to county clerk of courts records is free at www.cpclerk.co.summit.oh.us. Click on "Case Search."

General Information: Public Access terminal is available. No secret indictment records released. Copy fee: $.05 per page. Cert fee: $1.00 per page. Payee:

Clerk of Court. Only cashiers checks and money orders accepted. Prepayment required. Mail requests: SASE required. Mail turnaround time 1 week.

Akron Municipal Court 217 S High St, Rm 837, Akron, OH 44308; Civil phone: 330-375-2920; Criminal phone: 330-375-2263; Fax: 330-375-2427. Hours: 8AM-4:30PM (EST). *Misdemeanor, Civil Actions Under $15,000, Eviction, Small Claims.*
http://courts.ci.akron.oh.us

Civil Records: Access: Mail, in person, online. Both court and visitors may perform in person searches. No search fee. Required to search: name, years to search. Civil cases indexed by defendant, plaintiff. Civil records on computer from 1988, prior in books to 1975. Online access to court records is free at http://courts.ci.akron.oh.us/disclaimer.htm.

Criminal Records: Access: Mail, in person, online. Both court and visitors may perform in person searches. No search fee. Required to search: name, years to search, DOB, SSN. Criminal records on computer from 1988, prior in books to 1960. Online access to court records is free at http://courts.ci.akron.oh.us/disclaimer.htm.

General Information: Public Access terminal is available. No sealed records released. Will not fax results. Copy fee: $.25 per page. Cert fee: $1.00. Payee: Municipal Court. Personal checks accepted. Prepayment required. Mail requests: SASE required. Mail turnaround time up to 1 week.

Barberton Municipal Court Municipal Bldg, 576 W Park Ave, Barberton, OH 44203-2584; 330-753-2261; Fax: 330-848-6779. Hours: 8AM-5PM (civ); Crim/traffic to 8PM (EST). *Misdemeanor, Civil Actions Under $15,000, Eviction, Small Claims.*
www.cityofbarberton.com/clerkofcourts

Civil Records: Access: Phone, fax, mail, in person, online. Both court and visitors may perform in person searches. No search fee. Required to search: name, years to search. Civil cases indexed by defendant, plaintiff. Civil records computerized since 1994. Online records for Barberton, Green, Norton, Franklin, Clinton, Copley and Coventry are free at http://24.93.200.18/.

Criminal Records: Access: Phone, fax, mail, in person, online. Both court and visitors may perform in person searches. No search fee. Required to search: name, years to search; also helpful: DOB, SSN. Criminal records computerized since 1994. Online records for Barberton, Green, Norton, Franklin, Clinton, Copley and Coventry are free at http://24.93.200.18/.

General Information: Public Access terminal is available. No fee to fax results. Copy fee: $.10 per page. Cert fee: $1.00 per page. Payee: Barberton Municipal Court. Personal checks accepted. Prepayment required. Mail turnaround time 1 week.

Cuyahoga Falls Municipal Court 2310 Second St, Cuyahoga Falls, OH 44221; 330-971-8110; Civil phone: 330-971-8108; Criminal phone: 330-971-8109; Fax: 330-971-8114. Hours: 8AM-8PM (Criminal), 8AM-4:30PM (Civil) (EST). *Misdemeanor, Civil Actions Under $15,000, Eviction, Small Claims.*
www.cfmunicourt.com

Civil Records: Access: Phone, mail, in person, online. Both court and visitors may perform in person searches. No search fee. Required to search: name, years to search. Civil cases indexed by defendant, plaintiff, or case number. Civil records indexed back to 1954. Court docket information is free at the website.

Criminal Records: Access: Phone, mail, in person, online. Both court and visitors may perform in person searches. No search fee. Required to search: name or case number. Criminal records indexed back to 1954. Court docket information is free at the website.

General Information: Public Access terminal is available. Copy fee: $.05 per page. Cert fee: $1.00 per page. Payee: Cuyahoga Falls Municipal Court. Business checks accepted. Prepayment required. Mail turnaround time 1 week.

Trumbull County

Common Pleas Court 161 High St, Warren, OH 44481; 330-675-2557; Probate phone: 330-675-2521. Hours: 8:30AM-4:30PM (EST). *Felony, Civil Actions Over $10,000, Probate.*
www.clerk.co.trumbull.oh.us
Civil Records: Access: Phone, mail, in person, online. Both court and visitors may perform in person searches. Search fee: $5.00 per name. Required to search: name, years to search. Civil cases indexed by defendant, plaintiff. Civil records indexed in books from 1977, archived from 1800s; on computer back to 5/96. Online access to court records is free at www.clerk.co.trumbull.oh.us/search/search.htm. Records go back to May, 1996. Online access access to probate court records is free at www.trumbullprobate.org/paccessfront.htm.
Criminal Records: Access: Mail, in person, online. Both court and visitors may perform in person searches. Search fee: $5.00 per name. Required to search: name, years to search, DOB, SSN, signed release. Criminal records indexed in books from 1977, archived from 1800s; on computer back to 5/96. Online access to criminal records is the same as civil.
General Information: Public Access terminal is available. No secret or sealed records released. Copy fee: $.10 per page. Cert fee: $1.00 per page. Payee: Clerk of Court. Business checks accepted. Prepayment required. Mail requests: SASE required. Mail turnaround time 1 week.

Trumbull County Court Central 180 N Mecca St, Cortland, OH 44410; 330-637-5023; Fax: 330-637-5021. Hours: 8AM-4PM (EST). *Misdemeanor, Civil Actions Under $15,000, Eviction, Small Claims.*
Civil Records: Access: Phone, fax, mail, in person. Both court and visitors may perform in person searches. No search fee. Required to search: name, years to search. Records available since 1983.
Criminal Records: Access: Phone, fax, mail, in person. Both court and visitors may perform in person searches. No search fee. Required to search: name, years to search; also helpful: DOB, SSN. Same record keeping as civil.
General Information: Public Access terminal is available. No fee to fax results. Local faxing only. Copy fee: $.25 per page. Cert fee: $2.00 per page. Payee: Trumbull County Court Central. Personal checks accepted. Visa, MC accepted. In person only. Prepayment required. Mail turnaround time is 1-2 days.

Trumbull County Court East 7130 Brookwood Dr, Brookfield, OH 44403; 330-448-1726; Fax: 330-448-6310. Hours: 8:30AM-4:30PM (EST). *Misdemeanor, Civil Under $15,000, Eviction, Small Claims.*
Civil Records: Access: Phone, fax, mail, in person. Both court and visitors may perform in person searches. No search fee. Required to search: name, years to search. Civil records go back to 1994.
Criminal Records: Access: Phone, fax, mail, in person. Both court and visitors may perform in person searches. No search fee. Required to search: name, years to search; also helpful: DOB, SSN. Criminal Records in docket books since 1990, computerized since 1994.
General Information: Public Access terminal is available. No fee to fax results. Local faxing only.

Copy fee: $.25 per page. No cert fee. Payee: Trumbull County Court East. Personal checks accepted. Visa, MC accepted. Prepayment required. Mail turnaround time 1-2 days.

Girard Municipal Court City Hall, 100 N Market St, #A, Girard, OH 44420-2559; Civil phone: 330-545-3177; Criminal phone: 330-545-0069; Fax: 330-545-7045. Hours: 8AM-4PM (EST). *Misdemeanor, Civil Actions Under $15,000, Eviction, Small Claims.*
Note: Traffic Records phone is 330-545-3049.
Civil Records: Access: Fax, mail, in person. Both court and visitors may perform in person searches. No search fee. Required to search: name, years to search. Civil cases indexed by defendant, plaintiff. Civil records on books since 1964, computerized since 09/96.
Criminal Records: Access: Fax, mail, in person. Both court and visitors may perform in person searches. No search fee. Required to search: name, years to search; also helpful: DOB, SSN. Criminal records on books since 1964, computerized since 09/96.
General Information: Public Access terminal is available. No fee to fax results. Copy fee: 1st 10 free; $.10 per page each add'l. Cert fee: $10.00 per page. Payee: Girard Municipal Court. Business checks accepted. Prepayment required. Mail turnaround time 1 week.

Newton Falls Municipal Court 19 N Canal St, Newton Falls, OH 44444-1302; 330-872-0302; Fax: 330-872-3899. Hours: 7:30AM-4:00PM (EST). *Misdemeanor, Civil Actions Under $15,000, Eviction, Small Claims.*
Civil Records: Access: Fax, mail, in person. Only the court performs in person searches; visitors may not. No search fee. Required to search: name, years to search. Civil cases indexed by defendant, plaintiff. Civil records in books since 1970, computerized since 1992.
Criminal Records: Access: Fax, mail, in person. Only the court performs in person searches; visitors may not. No search fee. Required to search: name, years to search; also helpful: DOB, SSN. Criminal records in books since 1970, computerized since 1992.
General Information: No fee to fax results. Local faxing only. Copy fee: $.10 per page. Cert fee: $1.00. Payee: Newton Falls Municipal Court. Only cashiers checks and money orders accepted. Prepayment required. Mail turnaround time varies, but usually 1 week or less.

Niles Municipal Court 15 E State St, Niles, OH 44446-5051; 330-652-5863; Fax: 330-544-9025. Hours: 8AM-4PM (EST). *Misdemeanor, Civil Actions Under $15,000, Eviction, Small Claims.*
www.nilesmunicourt.org
Civil Records: Access: Fax, mail, in person. Both court and visitors may perform in person searches. No search fee. Required to search: name, years to search. Civil cases indexed by defendant, plaintiff. Civil records on computer since 10/96, in books since 1990, in storage from 1930.
Criminal Records: Access: Fax, mail, in person. Both court and visitors may perform in person searches. No search fee. Required to search: name, years to search; also helpful: DOB, SSN. Criminal records on computer since 10/96, in books since 1990, in storage from 1930.
General Information: Public Access terminal is available. No fee to fax results. Local faxing only. Copy fee: $.25 per page. No cert fee. Payee: Niles Municipal Court. Only cashiers checks and money orders accepted. Prepayment required. Mail turnaround times will vary.

Warren Municipal Court 141 South St SE (PO Box 1550), Warren, OH 44482; 330-841-2525; Civil phone: 330-841-2525 x112-115; Criminal phone: 330-841-2525 x105-110; Fax: 330-841-2760. Hours: 8AM-4:30PM (EST). *Misdemeanor, Civil Actions Under $15,000, Eviction, Small Claims.*
Civil Records: Access: Fax, mail, in person. Both court and visitors may perform in person searches. No search fee. Required to search: name, years to search; also helpful: address. Civil cases indexed by defendant, plaintiff. Civil records on computer since 1995; prior in books to 1978.
Criminal Records: Access: Fax, mail, in person. Both court and visitors may perform in person searches. No search fee. Required to search: name, years to search, DOB, SSN, signed release; also helpful: address. Criminal records on computer since 1995; prior in books to 1978.
General Information: Public Access terminal is available. No open case records released. No fee to fax results. Copy fee: $.05 per page. Cert fee: $1.00 per document. Payee: Warren Municipal Court. Personal checks accepted. Visa, MC accepted. Prepayment required. Mail requests: SASE required. Mail turnaround time 1-5 days.

Tuscarawas County

Common Pleas Court 125 E High (PO Box 628), New Philadelphia, OH 44663; 330-365-3243; Probate phone: 330-365-3266; Fax: 330-343-4682. Hours: 8AM-4:30PM (EST). *Felony, Civil Actions Over $15,000, Probate.*
www.co.tuscarawas.oh.us
Note: Probate is a separate court at 101 E High Ave.
Civil Records: Access: In person, online. Visitors must perform in person searches for themselves. No search fee. Required to search: name, years to search; also helpful: address. Civil cases indexed by defendant, plaintiff. Civil records on computer from 1987, prior in books to 1808, archived prior. Search dockets online at www.co.tuscarawas.oh.us/ClerkofCourts/DocketSearch.htm.
Criminal Records: Access: In person, online. Visitors must perform in person searches for themselves. No search fee. Required to search: name, years to search; also helpful: address, DOB, SSN. Criminal recods go back to 1868, criminal records on computer from 1987, prior in books to 1808, archived prior. Search dockets online at www.co.tuscarawas.oh.us/ClerkofCourts/DocketSearch.htm.
General Information: Public Access terminal is available. Will fax results for $2.00 transmission fee plus $1.00 per page. Copy fee: $.10 per page. Cert fee: $1.00 per page. Payee: Clerk of Court. Personal checks accepted. Visa, MC accepted. Visa, MC. Prepayment required.

County Court 220 E 3rd, Uhrichsville, OH 44683; 740-922-4795; Fax: 740-922-7020. Hours: 8AM-4:30PM (EST). *Misdemeanor, Civil Actions Under $15,000, Small Claims.*
Note: Probation Office phone: 740-922-3653 & 922-4360. Probation Office hours: 8AM-4:30PM.
Civil Records: Access: Fax, mail, in person, fax. Both court and visitors may perform in person searches. No search fee. Required to search: name, years to search. Civil cases indexed by defendant, plaintiff. Civil records go back toi 19700s, civil records on computer from 2/94, prior in books. Search dockets online at www.co.tuscarawas.oh.us/Clerk%20of%20Courts/Docket%20Search.htm.
Criminal Records: Access: Fax, mail, in person. Both court and visitors may perform in person searches. No search fee. Required to search: name,

years to search, DOB; also helpful: SSN. Criminal records on computer from 2/94, prior in books. Search dockets online at www.co.tuscarawas.oh.us/Clerk%20of%20Courts/Docket%20Search.htm.

General Information: Public Access terminal is available. No fee to fax results. Local faxing only. Copy fee: $1.00 per page. No cert fee. Payee: Tuscarawas County Court. Only Tuscarawas County personal checks accepted. Prepayment required. Mail requests: SASE required. Mail turnaround time 1-2 days.

New Philadelphia Municipal Court 166 E High Ave, New Philadelphia, OH 44663; 330-343-6797; Civil phone: 330-231-6797; Criminal phone: 330-234-6797; Fax: 330-364-6885. Hours: 8AM-4:30PM (EST). *Misdemeanor, Civil Actions Under $15,000, Eviction, Small Claims.*
www.npmunicipalcourt.org/
Note: The New Philadelphia Municipal Court has territorial jurisdiction within the municipal corporations of New Philadelphia and Dover, and the villages of Baltic, Bolivar, Midvale, Mineral City, Roswell, Stonecreek, Strasburg, Sugarcreek, and Zoar.

Civil Records: Access: Mail, in person. Visitors must perform in person searches for themselves. No search fee. Required to search: name, years to search. Civil cases indexed by defendant, plaintiff. Civil records on computer back to 4/91, prior in books to 1976.

Criminal Records: Access: In person only. Visitors must perform in person searches for themselves. No search fee. Required to search: name, years to search, SSN. Criminal records on computer back to 4/91, prior in books to 1976.

General Information: Public Access terminal is available. Copy fee: $.25 per page after first 10 free. Cert fee: $1.00 per page. Payee: Municipal Court. Personal checks accepted. Credit cards accepted in person: Visa, MC. Prepayment required. Mail requests: SASE required. Mail turnaround time 5-7 days.

Union County

Common Pleas Court County Courthouse, Clerk of Courts, 215 W 5th 2nd Fl, Marysville, OH 43040; 937-645-3006; Civil phone: 937-645-3145; Criminal phone: 937-645-3140; Probate phone: 937-645-3029; Fax: 937-645-3162. Hours: 8:30AM-4PM (EST). *Felony, Civil Actions Over $10,000, Probate.*
www.co.union.oh.us/Clerk_of_Courts/clerk_of_courts.html
Note: Forms are available at the website. Probate is located at the same address, separate office. Probate fax is 937-645-3160.

Civil Records: Access: In person, online. Visitors must perform in person searches for themselves. No search fee. Required to search: name, years to search; also helpful: address. Civil cases indexed by defendant, plaintiff. Civil records on computer from 1990, records go back to 1850. Online access to the court clerk's public record and index is free at http://www2.co.union.oh.us/clerkofcourts/SelectSearch.htm. Records go back to 1/1990, older records added as accessed. Images go back to 1/2002.

Criminal Records: Access: In person, online. Visitors must perform in person searches for themselves. Search fee: $5.00 per name. Required to search: name, years to search, DOB, SSN; also helpful: address. Criminal records on computer from 1990, records go back to 1850. Online access to the court clerk's public record and index is free at http://www2.co.union.oh.us/clerkofcourts/SelectSearch.htm. Records go back to 1/1990, older records added as accessed. Images go back to 1/2002.

General Information: Public Access terminal is available. Fee to fax results is $2.00 per page. Copy fee: $.50 per page. Cert fee: $1.00. Payee: Clerk of Court. Only cashiers checks and money orders accepted. Prepayment required.

Marysville Municipal Court City Hall Bldg, 125 E 6th St, Marysville, OH 43040; 937-644-9102; Fax: 937-644-1228. Hours: 8AM-4PM (EST). *Misdemeanor, Civil Actions Under $15,000, Eviction, Small Claims.*

Civil Records: Access: Phone, fax, mail, in person. Both court and visitors may perform in person searches. No search fee. Required to search: name, years to search. Civil cases indexed by defendant, plaintiff. Civil records on computer from 1989, prior on microfilm.

Criminal Records: Access: Phone, fax, mail, in person. Both court and visitors may perform in person searches. No search fee. Required to search: name, years to search; also helpful: SSN. Criminal records on computer from 1989, prior on microfilm.

General Information: Public Access terminal is available. No probation records released. No fee to fax results. No copy fee. No cert fee. Mail requests: SASE required. Mail turnaround time 1-2 days.

Van Wert County

Common Pleas Court 305 Courthouse, 121 E Main St, Van Wert, OH 45891; 419-238-6935; Probate phone: 419-238-0027; Fax: 419-238-2874; Clerk- 238-4760. Hours: 8AM-4PM (EST). *Felony, Civil Actions, Probate.*
www.vwcommonpleas.org
Note: Probate records are at the same address; call 419-238-0027. Address; 108 Main St.,Van Wert,Oh.45891

Civil Records: Access: In person only. Visitors must perform in person searches for themselves. No search fee. Required to search: name, years to search. Civil cases indexed by defendant, plaintiff. Some early records on microfiche, have docket books and files, indexed on computer since 05/98. Court calendars available online.

Criminal Records: Access: In person only. Visitors must perform in person searches for themselves. No search fee. Required to search: name, years to search; also helpful: address, DOB, SSN. Some early years on microfiche, have docket books and files, indexed on computer since 05/98. Court calendar available online.

General Information: Public Access terminal is available. (Records go back to 05/98.) All records public. Copy fee: $.25 per page. Cert fee: $1.00. Payee: Clerk of Court. Personal checks accepted. Prepayment required.

Van Wert Municipal Court 124 S Market, Van Wert, OH 45891; 419-238-5767. Hours: 8AM-4PM (EST). *Misdemeanor, Civil Actions Under $15,000, Eviction, Small Claims.*
http://vanwert.org/gov/court/index.htm

Civil Records: Access: Mail, in person. Both court and visitors may perform in person searches. No search fee. Required to search: name, years to search. Civil cases indexed by defendant, plaintiff. Civil records on computer from 1989.

Criminal Records: Access: Mail, in person. Both court and visitors may perform in person searches. No search fee. Required to search: name, years to search; also helpful: SSN. Criminal records on computer from 1989.

General Information: Public Access terminal is available. Fee to fax results is $1.00 per page. Copy fee: $1.00 per page. Cert fee: $1.00. Payee: Municipal Court. Personal checks accepted. Prepayment

Vinton County

Common Pleas Court County Courthouse, 100 E Main St, McArthur, OH 45651; 740-596-3001; Probate phone: 740-596-3438; Fax: 740-596-9611. Hours: 8:30AM-4PM M-F (EST). *Felony, Civil Actions Over $3,000, Probate.*

Civil Records: Access: In person only. Both court and visitors may perform in person searches. No search fee. Required to search: name, years to search. Civil cases indexed by defendant, plaintiff. Civil records in books since 1850.

Criminal Records: Access: In person only. Both court and visitors may perform in person searches. No search fee. Required to search: name, years to search; also helpful: DOB, SSN. Criminal records in books since 1850.

General Information: Public Access terminal is available. No sealed records released. Copy fee: $.25 per page. Cert fee: $2.00. Payee: Clerk of Court. Personal checks accepted. Prepayment required.

Vinton County Court County Courthouse, McArthur, OH 45651; 740-596-5000; Fax: 740-596-9721. Hours: 8:30AM-4PM (EST). *Misdemeanor, Civil Actions Under $15,000, Small Claims$3,000.*

Civil Records: Access: Phone, mail, in person. Both court and visitors may perform in person searches. No search fee. Required to search: name, years to search. Civil cases indexed by defendant, plaintiff. Civil records in books from 1980s, archived from 1800s.

Criminal Records: Access: Phone, mail, in person. Both court and visitors may perform in person searches. No search fee. Required to search: name, years to search, DOB; also helpful: SSN. Criminal records in books from 1980s, archived from 1800s.

General Information: No copy fee. No cert fee. Mail requests: SASE required. Mail turnaround time 1-2 days.

Warren County

Common Pleas Court PO Box 238, Lebanon, OH 45036; 513-695-1120; Probate phone: 513-695-1180; Fax: 513-695-2965. Hours: 8:30AM-4:30PM (EST). *Felony, Civil Actions Over $3,000, Probate.*
www.co.warren.oh.us/clerkofcourt

Civil Records: Access: Phone, mail, in person, online. Both court and visitors may perform in person searches. Search fee: $4.00 per name. Required to search: name, years to search. Civil cases indexed by defendant, plaintiff. Civil records on computer from 1974, archived from 1850. Access to court records is free at www.co.warren.oh.us/clerkofcourt/Courts/CtDispat.EXE. Index goes back to 1980.

Criminal Records: Access: Mail, in person, online. Both court and visitors may perform in person searches. Search fee: $4.00 per name. Required to search: name, years to search, DOB, signed release; also helpful: SSN. Criminal records on computer from 1974, archived from 1850. Access to court records is free at www.co.warren.oh.us/clerkofcourt/Courts/CtDispat.EXE. Index goes back to 1980.

General Information: Public Access terminal is available. Will fax results for $2.00 per fax plus $1.00 per page. Copy fee: $.20 per page. Cert fee: $1.00. Payee: Clerk of Court. Personal checks accepted. Prepayment required. Mail requests: SASE required. Mail turnaround time 1-4 days.

County Court 550 Justice Dr, Lebanon, OH 45036; 513-695-1370. Hours: 8AM-4:30PM (EST). *Misdemeanor, Civil Actions Under $15,000, Small Claims under $3000.*
www.co.warren.oh.us/countycourt

Civil Records: Access: Phone, mail, in person. Both court and visitors may perform in person searches. No search fee. Required to search: name, years to search; also helpful: address. Civil cases indexed by defendant, plaintiff. Civil records on computer from 1990, prior in books. No in person searches on Tuesdays or Thursdays.

Criminal Records: Access: Phone, mail, in person. Both court and visitors may perform in person searches. No search fee. Required to search: name, years to search, DOB; also helpful: SSN, address. Criminal records on computer from 1990, prior in books. No in person searches on Tuesdays or Thursdays.

General Information: Public Access terminal is available. Will not fax results. Copy fee: $.05 per page. No cert fee. Warren County checks accepted. Visa/MC accepted. Prepayment required. Mail requests: SASE required. Mail turnaround time 1-2 weeks.

Franklin Municipal Court
1 Benjamin Franklin Way, Franklin, OH 45005; 937-746-2858; Fax: 937-743-7751. Hours: 8:30AM-5PM (EST). *Misdemeanor, Civil Actions Under $15,000, Eviction, Small Claims.*

Civil Records: Access: Phone, mail, in person. Both court and visitors may perform in person searches. No search fee. Required to search: name, years to search. Civil cases indexed by defendant, plaintiff. Civil records on computer back to 1990.

Criminal Records: Access: Phone, mail, in person. Both court and visitors may perform in person searches. No search fee. Required to search: name, years to search, signed release; also helpful: DOB, SSN. Criminal records on computer back to 1990.

General Information: Will fax back results. Copy fee: $.50 per page. Cert fee: $5.00. Payee: Franklin Municipal Court. Personal checks accepted. In person only. Prepayment required. Mail turnaround time 1-2 days.

Lebanon Muncipal Court
City Bldg, 50 S Broadway, Lebanon, OH 45036-1777; 513-932-3060; Fax: 513-933-7212. Hours: 8AM-4PM (EST). *Misdemeanor, Civil Actions, Eviction, Small Claims.*
www.ci.lebanon.oh.us/departments/courts/courts.htm

Civil Records: Access: Fax, mail, in person. Both court and visitors may perform in person searches. No search fee. Required to search: name, years to search. Civil cases indexed by defendant, plaintiff. Civil records on books since 1956, computerized since 1990.

Criminal Records: Access: Fax, mail, in person. Both court and visitors may perform in person searches. No search fee. Required to search: name, years to search; also helpful: DOB, SSN. Criminal records on books since 1956, computerized since 1990.

General Information: Public Access terminal is available. No fee to fax results. Local faxing only. No cert fee. Only for criminal record searching, not civil. Turnaround time 2 days.

Mason Municipal Court
5950 S Mason Montgomery Rd, Mason, OH 45040-3712; 513-398-7901; Fax: 513-459-8085. Hours: 7:30AM-4PM (EST). *Misdemeanor, Civil Actions Under $15,000, Eviction, Small Claims.*
www.masonmunicipalcourt.org

Civil Records: Access: Phone, fax, mail, in person, online. Both court and visitors may perform in person searches. Search fee: none. Required to search: name, years to search. Civil cases indexed by defendant, plaintiff. Civil records in docket books since 1985, computerized since 1988. Online access to court records is free at

http://courtconnect.masonmunicipalcourt.org/connection/court/.

Criminal Records: Access: Phone, fax, mail, in person, online. Both court and visitors may perform in person searches. Search fee: none. Required to search: name, years to search; also helpful: SSN. Criminal records in docket books since 1985, computerized since 1988. Online access to court records is free at http://courtconnect.masonmunicipalcourt.org/connection/court/.

General Information: No fee to fax results. Local faxing only. Cert fee: $3.00 per page. Payee: Mason Municipal Court. Only cashiers checks and money orders accepted. Visa, MC accepted. In person criminal searching only. Prepayment required. Mail turnaround time 1-2 weeks.

Washington County

Common Pleas Court
205 Putnam St, Marietta, OH 45750; 740-373-6623; Probate phone: 740-373-6623. Hours: 8AM-4:15PM (EST). *Felony, Civil Actions Over $10,000, Probate.*
www.washingtongov.org

Civil Records: Access: In person only. Visitors must perform in person searches for themselves. No search fee. Required to search: name, years to search. Civil cases indexed by defendant, plaintiff. Civil records on computer since 1985, microfilm to 1977, index in books prior to 1795.

Criminal Records: Access: In person only. Visitors must perform in person searches for themselves. No search fee. Required to search: name, years to search. Criminal records on computer since 1985, microfilm to 1977, index in books prior to 1795.

General Information: Public Access terminal is available. No sealed, expunged records released. Copy fee: $.10 per page if 10 pages or over. Cert fee: $1.00. Payee: Clerk of Court. Personal checks and credit cards accepted. Prepayment required.

Marietta Municipal Court
301 Putnam (PO Box 615), Marietta, OH 45750; 740-373-4474; Fax: 740-373-2547. Hours: 8AM-5PM (EST). *Misdemeanor, Civil Actions Under $15,000, Eviction, Small Claims.*
www.mariettacourt.com

Civil Records: Access: Mail, in person, online. Both court and visitors may perform in person searches. No search fee. Required to search: name, years to search. Civil cases indexed by defendant, plaintiff. Civil records on computer from 11/91, prior in books. Online access to from 1992 of court dockets is free at www.mariettacourt.com.

Criminal Records: Access: Mail, in person, online. Both court and visitors may perform in person searches. No search fee. Required to search: name, years to search. Criminal records on computer from 11/91, prior in books back to 1975. Online access to criminal records is the same as civil.

General Information: Public Access terminal is available. Copy fee: $.05 per page. Cert fee: $1.50. Payee: Municipal Court. Personal checks accepted. Prepayment required. Mail requests: SASE required. Mail turnaround time 1 week.

Wayne County

Common Pleas Court
PO Box 507, Wooster, OH 44691; 330-287-5590; Probate phone: 330-287-5575; Fax: 330-287-5416. Hours: 8AM-4:30PM (EST). *Felony, Civil Actions Over $15,000, Probate.*
http://waynecountyclerkofcourts.org
Note: Probate is a separate court at number given.

Civil Records: Access: Mail, in person. Visitors must perform in person searches for themselves. No search fee. Required to search: name, years to search. Civil cases indexed by defendant, plaintiff. Civil records on

computer since 1995, in books to 1800s. No name searches are performed by mail.

Criminal Records: Access: Mail, in person. Visitors must perform in person searches for themselves. No search fee. Required to search: name, years to search. Criminal records on computer since 1995, in books to 1800s.

General Information: Public Access terminal is available. No grand jury indictment records released. Will not fax results. Copy fee: $.05 per page. Cert fee: $2.00. Payee: Clerk of Court. Personal checks accepted. Prepayment required. Mail turnaround time 1 week.

Wayne County Municipal Court Clerk
215 N Grant St, Wooster, OH 44691-4817; 330-287-5650; Fax: 330-263-4043. Hours: 8AM-4:30PM (EST). *Misdemeanor, Civil Actions Under $15,000, Eviction, Small Claims.*

Civil Records: Access: In person only. Visitors must perform in person searches for themselves. Search fee: none. Required to search: name, years to search. Civil cases indexed by defendant, plaintiff. Civil records on computer back to 9/94; in books from 1975.

Criminal Records: Access: In person only. Visitors must perform in person searches for themselves. No search fee. Required to search: name, years to search, offense, date of offense. Criminal records on computer back to 9/94; in books from 1975.

General Information: Public Access terminal is available. Copy fee: $.10 per page. Cert fee: $1.00. Payee: Wayne County Municipal Court. In state personal checks accepted. Prepayment required.

Williams County

Common Pleas Court
1 Courthouse Sq, Clerk of Court of Common Pleas, Bryan, OH 43506; 419-636-1551; Probate phone: 419-636-1548; Fax: 419-636-7877. Hours: 8:30AM-4:30PM (EST). *Felony, Civil Actions Over $10,000, Probate.*
Note: Probate Court is at the same address, different phone number.

Civil Records: Access: Phone, fax, mail, in person. Both court and visitors may perform in person searches. No search fee. Required to search: name, years to search. Civil cases indexed by defendant, plaintiff. Civil records on computer from 1988, records go back to 1840.

Criminal Records: Access: Mail, in person. Both court and visitors may perform in person searches. No search fee. Required to search: name, years to search. Criminal records on computer from 1988, records go back to 1840.

General Information: Public Access terminal is available. No expunged records released. Will fax results. Copy fee: $.25 per page. Cert fee: $1.00 per page. Payee: Clerk of Court. Personal checks accepted. Prepayment required. Mail requests: SASE required. Mail turnaround time 1-2 days.

Bryan Municipal Court
1399 E High, PO Box 546, Bryan, OH 43506; 419-636-6939; Fax: 419-636-3417. Hours: 8:30AM-4:30PM (EST). *Misdemeanor, Civil Actions Under $15,000, Eviction, Small Claims.*

Civil Records: Access: Fax, mail, in person. Both court and visitors may perform in person searches. Search fee: None. Required to search: name, years to search. Civil cases indexed by defendant, plaintiff. Civil records on computer from 1988, prior in books to 1966, indexed prior.

Criminal Records: Access: Fax, mail, in person. Both court and visitors may perform in person searches. Search fee: None. Required to search: name, years to search, DOB; also helpful: SSN. Criminal records on computer from 1988, prior in books to 1966, indexed prior.

General Information: Public Access terminal is available. Will fax results $2.00. Payee: Municipal Court. Personal checks accepted. Visa, MC accepted. Prepayment required. Mail requests: SASE required. Mail turnaround time 5 days.

Wood County

Common Pleas Court Courthouse Sq, Bowling Green, OH 43402; 419-354-9280; Probate phone: 419-354-9230; Fax: 419-354-9241. Hours: 8:30AM-4:30PM (EST). *Felony, Civil Actions Over $10,000, Probate.*

Note: Probate record searching and copy fees are different than those listed for civil and criminal records.

Civil Records: Access: Phone, fax, mail, in person, online. Both court and visitors may perform in person searches. Search fee: $3.00 per name. Required to search: name, years to search. Civil cases indexed by defendant, plaintiff. Civil records on computer from 7/90, in books and on microfilm from 1800s, docket books, journals and microfilm back to 1800s. Search probate records online at www.probate-court.co.wood.oh.us.

Criminal Records: Access: Fax, mail, in person. Both court and visitors may perform in person searches. Search fee: $3.00 per name. Required to search: name, years to search; also helpful: SSN. Criminal records on computer from 7/90, in books and on microfilm from 1980, docket books, journals and microfilm back to 1800s.

General Information: Public Access terminal is available. No adoption commitment, parental rights, juvenile, mental illness records released. No fee to fax results. Copy fee: $.25 per page first 25 pages, $.10 thereafter. Cert fee: $1.00. Payee: Common Pleas Court. Business checks accepted. Prepayment required. Mail requests: SASE required. Mail turnaround time same day.

Bowling Green Municipal Court PO Box 326, Bowling Green, OH 43402; 419-352-5263; Fax: 419-352-9407. Hours: 8:30AM-4:30PM (EST). *Misdemeanor, Civil Actions Under $15,000, Eviction, Small Claims.*
www.bgcourt.org

Civil Records: Access: Phone, fax, mail, in person, online. Both court and visitors may perform in person searches. No search fee. Required to search: name,

years to search. Civil cases indexed by defendant, plaintiff. Civil records on computer from 1988. Access is free to civil records at http://157.134.164.156/cmiflash/court/.

Criminal Records: Access: Phone, fax, mail, in person, online. Both court and visitors may perform in person searches. No search fee. Required to search: name, years to search, DOB; also helpful: SSN. Criminal records on computer from 1988. Free access to criminal and traffic records from http://157.134.164.156/cmiflash/court/.

General Information: Public Access terminal is available. No fee to fax results. Local faxing only. Copy fee: $.05 per page. No cert fee. Payee: Municipal Court. Personal checks accepted. Visa, MC accepted. Mail requests: SASE required. Mail turnaround time 3 days.

Perrysburg Municipal Court 300 Walnut St, Perrysburg, OH 43551; 419-872-7900; Fax: 419-872-7905. Hours: 8AM-4:30PM (8AM-7PM Tues.) (EST). *Misdemeanor, Civil Actions Under $15,000, Eviction, Small Claims.*
www.perrysburgcourt.com

Civil Records: Access: Phone, fax, mail, online, in person. Both court and visitors may perform in person searches. Search fee: $3.00 per name. Fee is $15.00 to look in closed, stored files. Required to search: name, years to search; also helpful: address. Civil cases indexed by defendant, plaintiff. Civil records on computer from 1989, prior in books to 1982, archived from 1972. Online access to court records is free at www.perrysburgcourt.com/disc.html.

Criminal Records: Access: Phone, fax, mail, online, in person. Both court and visitors may perform in person searches. Search fee: $3.00 per name. Fee is $15.00 to look in closed, stored files. Required to search: name, years to search; also helpful: DOB, SSN. Criminal records on computer from 1989, prior in books to 1982, archived from 1972. Online access to court records is free at www.perrysburgcourt.com/disc.html.

General Information: No expunged records released. Fee to fax results is $5.00 per document. Copy fee: $.10 per page. Cert fee: $3.00. Payee: Municipal Court. Personal checks accepted. Visa, MC accepted. Not accepted over the phone. Prepayment required. Mail requests: SASE required. Mail turnaround time 2 days.

Wyandot County

Common Pleas Court 109 S Sandusky Ave, Rm 31, Upper Sandusky, OH 43351; 419-294-1432; Probate phone: 419-294-2302; Fax: 419-294-6414. Hours: 8:30AM-4:30PM (EST). *Felony, Civil Actions Over $10,000, Probate.*
www.co.wyandot.oh.us/clerk/index.html

Civil Records: Access: In person. Visitors must perform in person searches for themselves. No search fee. Required to search: name, years to search. Civil cases indexed by defendant, plaintiff. Civil records on computer from 1990, prior in books from late 1800s.

Criminal Records: Access: Fax, mail, in perso, phone. Both court and visitors may perform in person searches. No search fee. Required to search: name, years to search; also helpful: SSN. Criminal records on computer from 1990, prior in books from late 1800s.

General Information: Public Access terminal is available. No fee to fax results. Copy fee: $.25 per page. Cert fee: $1.00 per page. Payee: Clerk of Court. Personal checks accepted. Prepayment required. Mail requests: SASE required. Mail turnaround time 1-2 days.

Upper Sandusky Municipal Court 119 N 7th St, Upper Sandusky, OH 43351; 419-294-3809; Fax: 419-09-0474. Hours: 8AM-4:30PM (EST). *Misdemeanor, Civil Actions Under $15,000, Eviction, Small Claims.*

Civil Records: Access: Mail, in person. Both court and visitors may perform in person searches. Search fee: $10.00 per name. Required to search: name, years to search. Civil cases indexed by defendant, plaintiff. Civil records on computer from 5/90, prior in books.

Criminal Records: Access: Mail, in person. Both court and visitors may perform in person searches. Search fee: $10.00 per name. Required to search: name, years to search; also helpful: SSN. Criminal records on computer from 5/90, prior in books.

General Information: Public Access terminal is available. No sealed records released. Will fax results for $10.00 per name. Copy fee: $.50 per page. Cert fee: $1.00. Payee: Upper Sandusky. Personal checks accepted. Visa, MC accepted. Not accepted over the phone. Prepayment required. Mail requests: SASE required. Mail turnaround time 1-2 days.

Ohio Recording Offices

ORGANIZATION: 88 counties, 88 recording offices. The recording officer is County Recorder and Clerk of Common Pleas Court (state tax liens). The entire state is in the Eastern Time Zone (EST).

REAL ESTATE RECORDS: Counties will not perform real estate searches. Copy fees are usually $2.00 per page. Certification usually costs $1.00 per document. Tax records are located at the Auditor's Office.

UCC RECORDS: This was a dual filing state. Financing statements were filed both at the state level and with the County Recorder, except for consumer goods, farm related and real estate related collateral, which were filed only with the County Recorder. As of 7/1/2001, only real estate related collateral is filed at the county level. All counties will perform UCC searches. Use search request form UCC-11. Search fees are usually $20.00 per debtor name. Copies usually cost $2.00 per page.

TAX LIEN RECORDS: All federal tax liens are filed with the County Recorder. All state tax liens are filed with the Clerk of Common Pleas Court. Refer to County Court section for information about Ohio courts. Federal tax liens are filed in the "Official Records" of each county. Most counties will not perform a federal tax lien search.

OTHER LIENS: Mechanics, workers compensation, judgment.

ONLINE ACCESS: A growing number of Ohio counties offer online access via the Internet to assessor/real estate data.

Adams County

County Recorder, 110 W. Main, Courthouse, West Union, OH 45693. **Phone**-937-544-2513, R/E and UCC Recording-937-258-3315; fax-937-544-4616; hours 8AM-4PM
Will search UCC records. Search per debtor- $20.00. Will search tax liens; provide date and name. Will not search real estate records. Copy fee- $2.00 per page. Cert fee: $1.00 per cert. Payee: Adams County Recorder. **Online Access to Property Tax, Sex Offender records:** Access to the treasurer and auditor property tax data is free at http://adamspropertymax.governmaxa.com/propertymax/rover30.asp. **Other phones:** Assessor-937-544-2364; Treasurer-937-544-2317; Auditor-937-544-2364; Elections-937-544-2633; Vital Records-937-544-5547.

Allen County

County Recorder, PO Box 1243, Lima, OH 45802. **Phone**-419-223-8517; fax-419-222-8427; hours 8:30AM-4:30PM www.co.allen.oh.us/rec.php
Will search UCC records. Search per debtor- $20.00. Will not do federal tax lien search. Will not search real estate records. UCC copy- $2.00 per page. Cert fee: $1.00 per cert. Payee: Allen County Recorder. **Online Access to Property, Auditor, Property Sale, Cemetery, War Casualty, Death records:** Access to the auditor property data is free at www.allencountyauditorohio.com/Allen208/LandRover.asp Also, search cemetery, war, and death records free at www.delphos-ohio.com/history/cemeteri.htm. **Other phones:** Treasurer-419-223-8515.

Ashland County

County Recorder, 142 W. 2nd St., Courthouse, Ashland, OH 44805-2193. **Phone**-County Recorder, R/E & UCC Recording- 419-282-4238; fax-419-281-5715; hours-8AM-4PM www.ashlandcounty.org/recorder/index.htm
Will search UCC records. Search per debtor- $20.00. Will not search real estate or tax liens records. Copy fee- $2.00 per page. Cert fee: $1.00 per cert. Payee: Ashland County Recorder. **Online Access to Real Estate, Auditor, Property Sale, Sex Offender records:** Property records on the county Auditor's database are free at www.ashlandcoauditor.org/ashland208/landrover.asp. Search the county sex offender list for free at www.ashlandcounty.org/sheriff/offenders.cfm. **Other phones:** Assessor-419-282-4330; Treasurer-419-282-4229; Auditor-419-282-4330; Elections-419-282-4224; Vital Records-419-282-4226.

Ashtabula County

County Recorder, 25 W. Jefferson St, Jefferson, OH 44047. **Phone**-County Recorder, R/E & UCC Recording- 440-576-3762; fax-440-576-3231; hours 8AM-4:30PM www.co.ashtabula.oh.us
Will search UCC records. Search per debtor- $20.00. Will not search tax liens. Can give specific real estate information - filed date, deed volume/page, etc.- over phone. Copy fee- $2.00 per page. Cert fee: $1.00 per cert. **Online Access to Real Estate, Auditor, Property Sale records:** Property records on the county Auditor's database are free at http://216.28.192.48/ashtabula208/LandRover.asp. Sheriff's poperty sale list is at www.ashtabulacountyauditor.org/property.pdf. **Other phones:** Assessor-440-576-3789; Treasurer-440-576-3727; Auditor-440-576-3789; Elections-440-576-6915; Vital Records-440-576-3627; Auditor-440-576-3783.

Athens County

County Recorder, 15 S Court St, Rm 236, Athens, OH 45701. **Phone**-County Recorder, R/E & UCC Recording- 740-592-3228; fax-740-592-3229; hours 8AM-4PM www.athenscountygovernment.com
Will search UCC records. Search per debtor- $20.00. Will not search real estate or tax liens records. UCC copy- $2.00 per page. Cert fee: $1.00 per cert. **Online Access to Property, Deed, UCC, Inmate, Mapping records:** Access to county land and UCC records is free at www.landaccess.com. Records go back to 1/1981. Also, search the GIS site by name at http://132.235.241.200/website/athens_v1/viewer.htm. Also, search the inmate list for free at http://xw.textdata.com:81/cgi/progcgi.exe?program=search. **Other phones:** Assessor-740-592-3223; Treasurer-740-592-3231; Auditor-740-592-3223; Elections-740-592-3201; Vital Records-740-592-3251; Auditor-740-592-3223; Microfilm Dept-740-592-3271.

Auglaize County

County Recorder, 209 S Blackhoof St, Rm 103, Wapakoneta, OH 45895-1972. **Phone**-419-739-6735; fax-419-739-6736. Will search UCC records. Search per debtor- $20.00. Will not search real estate or tax liens records. Copy fee- $2.00 per page. Cert fee: $1.00 per cert. **Online Access to Property, Sex Offender records:** Access county property data for free at http://auglaizeauditor.ddti.net/. Search the sex offender list for free at www.bright.net/~sheriff6/sexpred.htm. **Other phones:** Treasurer-419-739-6745; Elections-419-739-6720; Auditor-419-739-6705.

Belmont County

County Recorder, 101 Main St, Courthouse, Rm 105, St. Clairsville, OH 43950. **Phone**-740-699-2121, UCC Recording-740-699-2140; fax-740-699-2140 x198; hours-8:30AM-4:30PM
www.belmontcountyohio.org/recorder/index.html
Will search UCC records. Search per debtor- $20.00. Will not search tax liens. Mortgage searches available. UCC copy- $2.00 per page. Cert fee: $1.00 per cert. Payee: Belmont County Recorder. **Online Access to Deed, Property records:** Access to recorder deed information is free at http://landmarc.landaccess.com/sites/oh/disclaimer.php?county=ohbelmont. Also, search auditor records at www.belmontcountyohio.org/auditor.htm. **Other phones:** Assessor-740-699-2130; Treasurer-740-695-2120 x211; Auditor-740-695-2120 x257.

Brown County

County Recorder, PO Box 149, Georgetown, OH 45121. **Phone**-937-378-6478, UCC Recording-937-378-6478; fax-937-378-2848; hours 8AM-4PM
Will search UCC records. Search per debtor- $20.00. Will not search real estate or tax liens records. Copy fee- $2.00 per page. Cert fee: $1.00 per cert. Payee: Brown County Recorder. **Online Access to Property, Deed, UCC records:** Access to recordings is free at www.landaccess.com/sites/oh/disclaimer.php?county=ohbrown. **Other phones:** Treasurer-937-378-6705; Auditor-937-378-6398.

Butler County

County Recorder, 130 High St, Hamilton, OH 45011. **Phone**-513-887-3192; fax-513-887-3198; hours 8AM-4:30PM www.butlercountyohio.org/recorder
Will search UCC records. Search per debtor- $20.00. Will not do federal tax lien search. Will not search real estate records. UCC copy- $2.00 per page. Cert fee: $1.00 per cert. Payee: Butler County Recorder. **Online Access to Property, Deed, UCC, Probate, Voter Registration, Tax Sale, Sex Offender records:** County voter records are at www.butlercountyohio.org/elections/search/search.asp. County probate records are at www.butlercountyohio.org/probate/estate.cfm. Search auditor records at http://propertysearch.butlercountyohio.org/butler/. Also, access to county land and UCC records is free at www.landaccess.com. Records go back to 1/1987. Also, search county available property at www.butlercountyohio.org/edabc/availand_index.html.

The sheriff's tax sale and sex offender lists are at www.butlersheriff.org. Search vendors at www.butlercountyohio.org/auditor/vl_search.cfm. **Other phones:** Treasurer-513-887-3181; Auditor-513-887-3147; Elections-513-887-3700; Vital Records-513-863-1770; Auditor-513-887-3295.

Carroll County

County Recorder, PO Box 550, Carrollton, OH 44615-0550. **Phone-**330-627-4545; fax-330-627-4295; hours 8AM-4PM www.ohiorecorders.com
Will search UCC records. Search per debtor- $20.00. Will not search real estate or tax lien records. Copy fee- $2.00 per page. Cert fee: $1.00 per cert. Payee: Carroll County Recorder. **Online Access to Auditor, Property records:** Access to the Auditor's property data is free at http://carrollpropertymax.governmaxa.com/propertymax/rover30.asp.
Other phones: Assessor-330-327-2250; Treasurer-330-627-4221; Auditor-330-627-2250; Elections-330-627-2610.

Champaign County

County Recorder, 512 S US Hwy 68 #B200, Urbana, OH 43078. **Phone-**937-652-2263; fax-937-652-1515. www.co.champaign.oh.us/auditor/
Will search UCC records. Search per debtor- $20.00. UCC copy- $2.00 per page. Cert fee: $1.00 per cert. **Online Access to Real Estate records:** Auditor real estate data is free at http://champaignoh.ddti.net/. **Other phones:** Treasurer-937-484-1640; Auditor-937-652-2264.

Clark County

County Recorder, PO Box 1406, Springfield, OH 45501. **Phone-**County Recorder, R/E & UCC Recording- 937-328-2445; fax-937-328-4620; hours 8AM-4:30PM www.co.clark.oh.us/
Will not search records. Copy fee- $2.00 per page. Cert fee: $1.00 per cert. Payee: Clark County Recorder. **Online Access to Property, Deed, UCC, Sheriff Real Estate Sale, Tax Sale, Sex Offender records:** Access to county land and UCC records is free at www.landaccess.com. Records go back to 1/1988. Also, the sheriff's real estate sale, tax sale, sex offender and most wanted lists are at www.clarkcountysheriff.com. Also, search cemeteries for free at www.geocities.com/Heartland/Garden/3458/Cemeteries.htm. Search obituaries at http://guardian.ccpl.lib.oh.us/obits/. **Other phones:** Treasurer-937-328-2432; Auditor-937-328-2423.

Clermont County

County Recorder, 101 E. Main St, Batavia, OH 45103-2958. **Phone-**County Recorder, R/E & UCC Recording- 513-732-7236; fax-513-732-7891; hours 8AM-4:30PM http://recorder.co.clermont.oh.us/
Will search UCC records. Search per debtor- $20.00. Will not do a state tax lien search. Will not search real estate records. Copy fee- $2.00 per page. Cert fee: $1.00 per doc. Payee: Clermont County Treasurer. **Online Access to Property, Deed, UCC, Property Tax, Auditor, Sex Offender, Child Support records:** Records from the auditor's county property database are free at www.clermontauditorrealestate.org. Also, free access to the recorder's property, deed, and UCC records is at www.landaccess.com. Dog licenses and public officials directory is also online at www.co.clermont.oh.us. Also, search county sex offenders database free at www.clermontsheriff.org/registered_sex_offenders.htm. Search child support wants at www.clermontsupportskids.org. **Other phones:** Assessor-513-732-7150; Treasurer-513-732-7254; Elections-513-732-7275; Auditor-513-732-7150; Commissioners-513-732-7300.

Clinton County

County Recorder, 46 S. South St, Courthouse, Wilmington, OH 45177. **Phone-**937-382-2067; fax-937-382-8097; hours-8AM-4PM www.co.clinton.oh.us/default.htm
Will search UCC records. Search per debtor- $20.00. Will not do federal tax lien search. Will not search real estate records. Copy fee- $2.00 per page. Cert fee: $1.00 per page. Payee: Clinton County Recorder. **Online Access to Auditor, Property records:** Access the Auditor's property database for free at www.co.clinton.oh.us/auditor/iView/iView.asp. **Other phones:** Treasurer-937-382-2224; Elections-937-382-3537; Vital Records-937-382-3829; Auditor-937-382-2250.

Columbiana County

County Recorder, 105 S. Market St., County Courthouse, Rm 104, Lisbon, OH 44432. **Phone-**330-424-9517 x641; fax-330-424-5067; hours 8am-4pm M-F
Will search UCC records. Search per debtor- $20.00 (index printout only). Will not search real estate or tax lien records. RE record copy- $2.00 per page. Copy fee-$2.00 per page. Cert fee: $1.00 per cert. Payee: Columbiana County Recorder. **Online Access to Real Estate, Auditor, Forfeited Land Sale records:** Property records on the county Auditor's database are available free at www.columbianacntyauditor.org/columbv208/LandRover.asp. Both the Auditor and Sheriff's sales can be accessed here.

Coshocton County

County Recorder, PO Box 817, Coshocton, OH 43812. **Phone-**County Recorder, R/E & UCC Recording- 740-622-2817; fax-740-295-7352; hours 8AM-4PM www.co.coshocton.oh.us/
Will search UCC records. Search per debtor- $20.00. Will not search real estate or tax lien records. Copy fee- $2.00 per page. Cert fee: $1.00 per cert. Payee: County Recorder. **Online Access to Property, Deed, UCC, Auditor, Property Tax, Sex Offender records:** Access to county land and UCC records is free at www.landaccess.com. Records go back to 1/1980. Also, search property tax records for free at www.coshcoauditor.org; click on "Property Search." The sex offender list can be searched at www.coshoctonsheriff.com/sexualpred.cfm. **Other phones:** Treasurer-740-622-2713; Elections-740-622-1117; Auditor-740-622-1243.

Crawford County

County Recorder, PO Box 788, Bucyrus, OH 44820-0788. **Phone-**County Recorder, R/E & UCC Recording- 419-562-6961; fax-419-562-6061; hours 8:30-4:30PM
Will search UCC records. Search per debtor- $20.00. Will not search real estate or tax lien records. Copy fee- $2.00 per page. Cert fee: $1.00 per cert. Payee: Crawford County Recorder. **Online Access to Auditor, Real Estate, Dog Tag records:** Access to the auditor database is free at www.crawford-co.org/auditor/default.html. **Other phones:** Treasurer-419-562-7861; Auditor-419-562-7941; Elections-419-562-8721.

Cuyahoga County

County Recorder, 1219 Ontario St, Rm 220, Cleveland, OH 44113. **Phone-**216-443-7316, R/E Recording-216-443-7300, 216-443-8194, UCC Recording-216-443-7300; fax-216-443-8193; hours 8:30AM-4:30PM www.recorder.cuyahogacounty.com
Will search UCC records. Search per debtor- $20.00. Will not do federal tax lien search. Will search real estate records. Copy fee-$2.00 per page. UCC copy-$2.00 per page. Cert fee: #1.00 per cert. Payee:

Cuyahoga County Recorder. **Online Access to Auditor, Probate, Marriage, Real Estate, Tax Lien, Recording, Cemetery, Most Wanted, Sexual Predator records:** Access the Recorders database is free at http://recorder.cuyahoga.oh.us/general.cfm. The Recorder's data includes land docs from 1925-2003. Search the auditor property tax database free at http://auditor.cuyahoga.oh.us/auditor/repi/default.asp. Also, search 22 categories of Probate records including marriages free online at http://probate.cuyahogacounty.us/pa/. Obits and death notices are at www.cleveland.com/obits/archives/. Also, sexual predator/most wanted lists at www.cuyahoga.oh.us/sheriff/sou/default.asp. Foreclosure sales: www.cuyahoga.oh.us/sheriff/foreclosures/sales.htm. Cemetery: www.geocities.com/micheledanielle/cemetery.html.
Other phones: Auditor-216-443-7092; Vital Records-216-664-2317.

Darke County

County Recorder, 504 S Broadway, Courthouse, Greenville, OH 45331. **Phone-**County Recorder, R/E & UCC Recording- 937-547-7390; hours 8:30AM-4:30PM www.co.darke.oh.us/links.htm
Will search UCC records. Search per debtor- $12.00. Will not do federal tax lien search. Will not search real estate records. UCC copy- $2.00 per copy. Cert fee: $1.00 per doc. Payee: Darke County Recorder. **Online Access to Real Estate, Deed, UCC, Property Tax records:** Property and property tax records on the Darke County database are free at http://darkepropertymax.governmax.com/propertymax/rover30.asp?. Also, online access to the recorder's county land and UCC records is free at www.landaccess.com. Records go back to 1/1996. **Other phones:** Treasurer-937-547-7365; Auditor-937-547-7310.

Defiance County

County Recorder, 221 Clinton St, Courthouse, Defiance, OH 43512. **Phone-**County Recorder, R/E & UCC Recording- 419-782-4741; fax-419-782-3421; hours 8:30AM-4:30PM www.defiance-county.com/recorder.html
Will search UCC records. Search per debtor- $20.00. Will not do federal tax lien search. Will not search real estate records. Copy fee- $2.00 per page. Cert fee: $1.00 per cert. Payee: Defiance County Recorder. **Online Access to Auditor, Real Estate records:** Assess to the auditor real estate data is at www.defiance-county.com/realestatesearch.html. Call 800-875-3953 or 419-784-3111 for necessary password. **Other phones:** Assessor-419-784-3111; Treasurer-419-782-8741; Auditor-419-784-3111.

Delaware County

County Recorder, 91 N. Sandusky St, Courthouse, Delaware, OH 43015. **Phone-**740-833-2460; fax-740-833-2459; 8:30AM-4:30PM www.co.delaware.oh.us
Will search UCC records. Search per debtor- $20.00. Will not do federal tax lien search. Tax lien search- $2.00 per page. Will not search real estate records. UCC copy- $2.00 per page. Cert fee: $1.00 per cert. Payee: Delaware County Recorder. **Online Access to Real Estate, Deed, UCC Auditor, Property Sale, Sheriff Sale, Most Wanted, Sex Offender, DUI records:** Access to the Recorder's data plus UCCs is free at www.landaccess.com. Also, access to auditor's property and sales information is free at www.delawarecountyauditor.org/propertymax/rover30.asp?. Also, Sheriff sales, Most Wanted, Sex Offender information is free at www.delawarecountysheriff.com. Also, search the municipal court DUI list at www.municipalcourt.org/main_dui.asp. Also, search cemeteries at http://delcohist.tripod.com/burials.htm.
Other phones: Treasurer-740-833-2460; Auditor-740-833-2460.

Erie County

County Recorder, 247 Columbus Ave., Erie County Office Bldg, Rm 225, Sandusky, OH 44870-2635. **Phone**-419-627-7686; fax-419-627-6639; hours 8AM-4PM www.erie-county-ohio.net/officials.htm
Will search UCC records. Search per debtor- $20.00. UCC search does not include federal tax liens. Will not search real estate records. UCC copy- $2.00 per page. Cert fee: $1.00 per doc. Payee: Erie County Recorder. **Online Access to Auditor, Property, Deed, Recorder records:** Access the auditor property database for free at www.erie.iviewtaxmaps.com/iView/iView.asp. Access recorded documents at www.co-erie-oh-us-recorder.com. **Other phones:** Treasurer-419-627-7201; Auditor-419-627-7746; Auditor-419-627-7741.

Fairfield County

County Recorder, PO Box 2420, Lancaster, OH 43130-5420. **Phone**-740-687-7100; fax-740-687-7104; hours 8AM-4PM www.co.fairfield.oh.us
Will search UCC records. Search per debtor- $20.00. Will not do federal tax lien search. Will not search real estate records. UCC copy- $2.00 per page. Cert fee: $1.00 per cert. Payee: Fairfield County Recorder. **Online Access to Property, Deed, UCC, Auditor, Property Sale, Inmate, Sex Offender records:** Access to county land and UCC records is free at www.landaccess.com. Records go back to 8/1996. Also, online access to the Auditor's property and sales database is free at http://realestate.co.fairfield.oh.us/. Also, access to the sheriff's real estate sale list and sex offenders list is free at www.sheriff.fairfield.oh.us/. Search inmates list at http://xw.textdata.com:81/cgi/progcgi.exe?program=search3. Search sheriff's sex offender list at. **Other phones:** Treasurer-740-687-7094; Auditor-740-687-7090.

Fayette County

County Recorder, 133 S Main St, Courthouse Bldg., Washington Court House, OH 43160-1393. **Phone**-County Recorder, R/E & UCC Recording- 740-335-1770; fax-740-333-3521; hours 9AM-4PM www.fayette-co-oh.com/
Will search UCC records. Search per debtor- $20.00. Will not search real estate or tax lien records. RE record copy- $2.00 per page. Copy fee is $2.00 per page. Cert fee: $1.00 per cert. Payee: Recorder. **Online Access to Recorder, Deed, Lien, Judgment, Birth, Auditor, Property, Sale, Sex Offender, Sheriff Sale records:** Search the auditor's database for property information at http://fayettepropertymax.governmax.com/propertymax/rover30.asp. Also, access to recorders index database is through a private company for free at www.landaccess.com. Images go back to 5/20/02. Also, search the sheriff's lists for free at www.faycoso.com. **Other phones:** Assessor-740-335-6461; Treasurer-740-335-4961; Elections-740-335-1190; Vital Records-740-335-5910.

Franklin County

County Recorder, 373 S. High St, 18th Fl, Columbus, OH 43215-6307. **Phone**-614-462-3930, 614-462-3378, R/E Recording-614-462-3930, UCC Recording-614-462-3937; fax-614-462-4312, 614-462-4299; hours 8:AM-5PM www.co.franklin.oh.us/recorder/
Will search UCC records. Search per debtor- $20.00. Will not search real estate or tax lien records. UCC copy- $2.00 per page. Cert fee: $1.00 per cert. **Online Access to Recorder, Property, Auditor, Unclaimed Funds, Marriage, Treasurer Refund, Most Wanted, Sheriif Sale, Sex Offender records:** Access to the recorders data is free at www.co.franklin.oh.us/recorder/documents.html. Free registration required. Search veterans graves at www.co.franklin.oh.us/main/vetsTransPage.htm.

Search marriage licenses back to 1995 at www.co.franklin.oh.us/probate/PBMLSearch.html. Search unclaimed funds at www.franklincountyohio.gov/clerk/UnclaimedFunds.htm. Most wanted, sex offenders, sheriff sales at www.faycoso.com Also, auditor's property data is at http://franklin.governmaxa.com/propertymax/rover30.asp. Other county/municipal databases are free at www.co.franklin.oh.us. Real estate refund search www.co.franklin.oh.us/treasurer/refunds/search.asp. **Other phones:** ; Auditor-614-462-3894.

Fulton County

County Recorder, 152 S Fulton St #175, Wauseon, OH 43567. **Phone**-County Recorder, R/E & UCC Recording- 419-337-9232; fax-419-337-9282; hours 8:30AM-4:30PM www.fultoncountyoh.com
Will search UCC records. Search per debtor- $20.00. Will not search real estate or tax lien records. Copy fee- $2.00 per page. Cert fee: $1.00 per cert. Payee: Fulton County Recorder. **Online Access to Property, Deed, Recorder, UCC, Auditor, Real Estate records:** Access to property, deed, and UCC records is to be free at www.landaccess.com/sites/oh/disclaimer.php?county=ohfulton. Also, search the auditor property data for free at http://fultonpropertymax.governmax.com/propertymax/rover30.asp. **Other phones:** Treasurer-419-337-9252; Elections-419-335-6841; Auditor-419-337-9200.

Gallia County

County Recorder, 18 Locust St, Rm 1265, Gallipolis, OH 45631-1265. **Phone**-740-446-4612 x248, R/E Recording-740-446-4612 x246, UCC Recording-740-446-4612; fax-740-446-4804; hours 8AM-4PM www.galliacounty.org/government/government.html
Will search UCC records. Search per debtor- $20.00. Will not search real estate or tax lien records. Copy fee- $2.00 per page. Cert fee: $1.00 per cert. Payee: Gallia County Recorder. **Online Access to Property, Real Estate, Most Wanted, Sex Offender, Inmate records:** Property records on the county auditor real estate database are free at http://galliaauditor.ddti.net. Click on "attributes" for property information; click on "sales" to search by real estate attributes. Also, search the sheriff's database for inmates, sex offenders, ner'do'wells, etc at www.galliasheriff.org. **Other phones:** Assessor-740-446-4612 x218; Treasurer-740-446-6004; Auditor-740-446-4612 x218.

Geauga County

County Recorder, 231 Main St, #1C, Courthouse Annex, Chardon, OH 44024-1235. **Phone**-County Recorder, R/E & UCC Recording- 440-285-2222 x3680; hours 8AM-4:30PM www.co.geauga.oh.us
Will search UCC records. Search per debtor- $20.00. Will search federal tax liens. Will not search real estate records. Copy fee- $2.00 per page. Cert fee: $1.00 per cert. Payee: Geauga County Recorder. **Online Access to Delinquent Property Tax, Tax Sale, Auditor, Property, Most Wanted, Sex Offender records:** Search Auditor's property database at www.co.geauga.oh.us/departments/auditor/ag/. No name searching. Also, search the auditor's records at www.auditor.co.geauga.oh.us/ag/. Also, search the sheriff's tax sale, most wanted and sex offender lists for free at www.sheriff.geauga.oh.us. Also, the treasurer's delinquent tax list is in pdf format at www.co.geauga.oh.us/departments/treasurer/delinquent.htm. **Other phones:** Assessor-440-285-2222 x3450; Treasurer-440-285-2222 x3850; Auditor-440-285-2222 x4490; Elections-440-285-2222 x4020; Vital Records-440-285-2222 x6407.

Greene County

County Recorder, PO Box 100, Xenia, OH 45385-0100. **Phone**-937-376-5270, R/E Recording-937-562-

5270, UCC Recording-937-562-5275; fax-937-376-5386; hours-8AM-4:30PM
www.co.greene.oh.us/recorder.htm
Will search UCC records. Search per debtor- $20.00. Will not do federal tax lien search. Will not search real estate records. Copy fee- $2.00 per page. Cert fee: $1.00 per cert. Payee: Greene County Recorder. **Online Access to Real Estate, Auditor, Recording, Deed, Mortgage, Grantor/Grantee, Sheriff Sale, Sex Offender records:** Access to the recorders data is free at www.co.greene.oh.us/recorder/documentSearch.asp. Also, records on the county Internet Map Server are free at www.co.greene.oh.us/gismapserver.htm. Click on "Click here to enter. Server Site #1". Data includes owner, address, valuation, taxes, sales data, and parcel ID number. Also, search the sheriff's sales and sex offender list at www.co.greene.oh.us/sheriff/. **Other phones:** Assessor-937-562-5017; Treasurer-937-562-5017; Auditor-937-562-5278; Elections-937-562-5261; Vital Records-937-562-5686; Auditor-937-562-5065.

Guernsey County

County Recorder, 801 Wheeling Ave, Courthouse D-202, Cambridge, OH 43725. **Phone**-County Recorder, R/E & UCC Recording- 740-432-9275; fax-740-439-6258; hours 8AM-4PM
Will search UCC records. Search per debtor- $20.00. Will not search real estate or tax lien records. RE record copy- #2.00 per page. UCC copy- $2.00 per page. Cert fee: $1.00 per cert. Payee: Guernsey County Recorder. **Online Access to Sex Offender records:** Search for sex offendors at www.guernseysheriff.com/sexoffenders.htm. **Other phones:** Assessor-740-432-9243; Treasurer-740-432-9278; Auditor-740-432-9243; Elections-740-432-2680; Vital Records-740-432-3577.

Hamilton County

County Recorder, 138 E Court St, Rm 101-A, Cincinnati, OH 45202. **Phone**-513-946-4570; fax-513-946-4577; hours-8AM-4PM
www.recordersoffice.hamilton-co.org
Will search UCC records. Search per debtor- $20.00. UCC search does not include federal tax liens. Will not search real estate records. Copy fee- $2.00 per page. Cert fee: $1.00 per page. Payee: Hamilton County Recorder. **Online Access to Real Estate, Lien, Recording, Lien, Deed, Mortgage, UCC, Auditor, Sex Offender, Most Wanted, Missing, Sheriff Sale. Marriage records:** Access to county recorder records is free at www.recordersoffice.hamilton-co.org. Search the marriage license database at www.probatect.org/case_search/cs-scripts/ml_Input.asp. Also, online access to the auditor's tax records database is free at www.hamiltoncountyauditor.org./realestate/. Also, search probate records back to 1/2000 at www.probatect.org/case_search/cs-scripts/pimain.html. Also, search lists for most wanted, sex offender, deadbeat parents, missing persons, and sheriff's sale on the sheriff's site under "Public Services" at www.hcso.org. **Other phones:** Treasurer-513-946-4800; Auditor-513-946-4000.

Hancock County

County Recorder, 300 S. Main St, Courthouse, Findlay, OH 45840. **Phone**-County Recorder, R/E & UCC Recording- 419-424-7091; fax-419-423-3017; hours 8:30AM-4:30PM
http://co.hancock.oh.us/recorder/recorder.htm
Will search UCC records. Search per debtor- $20.00. Must be on UCC-11 form. Will not search real estate or tax lien records. Copy fee- $2.00 per page. Cert fee: $1.00 per cert. Payee: Hancock County Recorder. **Online Access to Property, Auditor, Sex Offender, Real estate, Recorder, Deed,**

UCC records: Search the auditor's property database free at http://hancock.iviewauditor.com. No name searching. Also, access to recorder records is free at www.landaccess.com. Index goes back to 1986; images to 5/2001. Also, search the sheriff's sex offender list at www.hancocksheriff.org/info/sexoffenders.htm. **Other phones:** Treasurer-419-424-7213; Auditor-419-424-7015; Elections-419-422-3245; Vital Records-419-424-7869; Auditor-419-424-7083.

Hardin County

County Recorder, One Courthouse Sq, #220, Kenton, OH 43326. **Phone-**County Recorder, R/E & UCC Recording- 419-674-2250; fax-419-675-2802; hours 8:30AM-4PM; 8:30AM-5PM Friday www.co.hardin.oh.us

Will search UCC records. Search per debtor- $20.00. Will not do federal tax lien search. Will not search real estate records. Copy fee- $2.00 per page. Cert fee: $1.00 per cert. Payee: Hardin County Recorder. **Online Access to Auditor, Property, Sex Offender records:** Property records from the county database are at www.co.hardin.oh.us. Click on "Real Estate Internet Inquiry." Also, check a dog tag number for its owner's name here. Also, find property data for free at http://198.30.105.171/. No name search. Also, search the sheriff's county sex offender list at www.hardinsheriff.com/offenders/default_soc.htm. **Other phones:** Treasurer-419-674-2246; Auditor-419-674-2239.

Harrison County

County Recorder, 100 W. Market St, Courthouse, Cadiz, OH 43907. **Phone-**County Recorder, R/E & UCC Recording- 740-942-8869; fax-740-942-4693; hours 8:30AM-4:30PM www.harrisoncountyohio.org/ Will search UCC records. Search per debtor- $20.00. Will not do federal tax lien search. Will search real estate records. Copy fee- $2.00 per page. Cert fee: $1.00 per cert. Payee: Harrison County Recorder. **Other phones:** Treasurer-740-942-8864; Elections-740-942-8866; Vital Records-740-942-8868; Auditor-740-942-8861; Engineer-740-942-8867.

Henry County

County Recorder, 660 N. Perry St., Courthouse, Rm 202, Napoleon, OH 43545-1747. **Phone-**County Recorder, R/E & UCC Recording- 419-592-1766; fax-419-592-1652; hours-8:30AM-4:30PM www.ohiorecorders.com

Will search UCC records. Search per debtor- $20.00. Will not do federal tax lien search. Will not search real estate records. Copy fee- $2.00 per page. Cert fee: $1.00 per cert. Payee: Henry County Recorder. **Online Access to Sheriff Sale, Sex Offender records:** Search the county sex offender and sheriff sales lists for free at www.henrycountysheriff.com. **Other phones:** Assessor-419-492-1956; Treasurer-419-592-1851; Elections-419-592-7956; Vital Records-419-599-5545.

Highland County

County Recorder, PO Box 804, Hillsboro, OH 45133. **Phone-**County Recorder, R/E & UCC Recording- 937-393-9954; fax-937-393-5855; hours 8:30AM-4PM www.ohiorecorders.com

Will search UCC records. Search per debtor- $20.00. Will search federal tax liens. Will not search real estate records. RE record copy- $2.00 per page. UCC copy- $2.00 per item/page. Cert fee: $1.00 per cert. Payee: Highland County Recorder. **Online Access to Property, Deed, UCC, Auditor, Property Sale, Sex Offender, Sheriff Sale records:** Access to recorders database is free at www.landaccess.com/sites/oh/highland/index.php.

Also, search the auditor's data for free at http://highlandpropertymax.governmaxa.com/property max/rover30.asp. The sheriff's sex offender and sales lists are free at www.highlandcoso.com/rso.htm. **Other phones:** Assessor-937-393-1915; Treasurer-937-393-9951; Auditor-937-393-1915; Elections-937-393-9961; Vital Records-937-393-1941.

Hocking County

County Recorder, PO Box 949, Logan, OH 43138-0949. **Phone-**County Recorder, R/E & UCC Recording- 740-385-2031; fax-740-385-0377; hours 8:30AM - 4PM www.co.hocking.oh.us/

Will search UCC records. Search per debtor- $20.00. Will not search real estate or tax lien records. Copy fee- $2.00 per page. Cert fee: $1.00 per cert. Payee: Recorder. **Online Access to Property, Auditor, Sexual Offender, Inmate records:** Accesss to the auditor's real estate data (and dog tag ownership) is free at www.realestate.co.hocking.oh.us. Also, search the sheriff list of sexual offenders at www.hockingsheriff.org. Search county inmates at http://xw.textdata.com:81/cgi/progcgi.exe?program=search3. **Other phones:** Assessor-740-385-2127; Treasurer-740-385-3517; Auditor-740-385-2127; Elections-740-380-8683; Vital Records-740-385-3030; Clerk of Coruts-740-385-2616.

Holmes County

County Recorder, PO Box 213, Millersburg, OH 44654. **Phone-**330-674-5916; 8AM-4:30PM Will search UCC records. Search per debtor- $20.00. Will not do federal tax lien search. Will not search real estate records. UCC copy- $2.00 per page. Cert fee: $1.00 per cert. Payee: Holmes County Recorder. **Online Access to Property, Auditor, Sale records:** Access to the auditor's property data is free at www.holmescountyauditor.org. **Other phones:** Treasurer-330-674-1896; Auditor-330-674-1896.

Huron County

County Recorder, PO Box 354, Norwalk, OH 44857. **Phone-**County Recorder, R/E & UCC Recording- 419-668-1916; fax-419-663-4052; hours 8AM-4:30PM Will search UCC records. Search per debtor- $20.00. Will not search real estate or tax lien records. UCC copy- $2.00 per page. Cert fee: $1.00 per cert. **Online Access to Property, Auditor, Sale records:** Access to the auditor data is free at www.huroncountyauditor.org. **Other phones:** Assessor-419-668-4304; Treasurer-419-668-2090; Elections-419-668-8238; Vital Records-419-668-1652; Auditor-419-668-4304.

Jackson County

County Recorder, 226 E. Main St., Courthouse, #1, Jackson, OH 45640. **Phone-**County Recorder, R/E & UCC Recording- 740-286-1919; hours 8AM-4PM Will search UCC records. Search per debtor- $20.00. Will not do federal tax lien search. Will not search real estate records. Copy fee- $2.00 per page. Cert fee: $1.00 per cert. Payee: Jackson County Recorder. **Online Access to Inmates, Sex Offender records:** Access to the county inmate search is free at http://xw.textdata.com:81/cgi/progcgi.exe?program=search3. **Other phones:** Treasurer-740-286-2402; Elections-740-286-2905; Auditor-740-286-4231.

Jefferson County

County Recorder, Jefferson County Recorder 301 Market St., Steubenville, OH 43952. **Phone-**740-283-8566; fax-none; hours 8:30AM-4:30PM Will search UCC records. Search per debtor- $20.00. Will not search real estate or tax lien records. UCC copy- $2.00 per page. Cert fee: $2.00 per cert. Payee: Jefferson County Recorder. **Online Access to Property, Auditor records:** Access to the county auditor property data is free at http://public.jeffersoncountyoh.com/tax/. **Other phones:** Assessor-614-283-8518; Treasurer-614-283-8511; Auditor-614-283-8511.

Knox County

County Recorder, 117 E. High St, Mount Vernon, OH 43050. **Phone-**County Recorder, R/E & UCC Recording- 740-393-6755; hours 8AM-4PM www.knoxcountyohio.org/CountyOffices.htm

Will search UCC records. Search per debtor- $20.00. Will not search real estate or tax lien records. Copy fee- $2.00 per page. Cert fee: $1.00 per cert. Payee: Knox County Recorder. **Online Access to Property, records:** Records on the auditor database are free at http://knoxpropertymax.governmax.com/propertymax/rover30.asp. Also, Civil, Criminal, Domestic Relations & Court of Appeals Cases found free at www.knoxcountycpcourt.org. **Other phones:** Assessor-740-397-6291; Treasurer-740-393-6735; Auditor-740-393-6750; Elections-740-393-6716; Vital Records-740-393-2200; Records Center 740-393-6781-

Lake County

County Recorder, PO Box 490, Painesville, OH 44077-0490. **Phone-**County Recorder, R/E & UCC Recording- 440-350-2510, UCC Recording-440-350-2511; fax-440-350-5940; hours 8AM-4PM www.lakecountyrecorder.org

Will search UCC records. Search per debtor- $20.00. Will not search real estate or tax lien records. Copy fee- $2.00 per page. Cert fee: $1.00 per doc. Payee: Lake County Recorder. **Online Access to Recording, Lien, Deed, UCC, Land Bank Sale records:** Access to the Recorder's Document Index database is free at www.lakecountyrecorder.org. Records go back to 1986. UCCs are index only. Also, access to the treasurer and auditor's real estate databases is free at www.lake.iviewauditor.com. Also, online access to Land Bank sales is at www.lakecountyohio.org/auditor/index.htm and click on "Land Bank Sales". **Other phones:** Treasurer-440-350-2517; Elections-440-350-2700; Vital Records-440-350-2549; Auditor-440-350-2528.

Lawrence County

County Recorder, PO Box 77, Ironton, OH 45638. **Phone-**County Recorder, R/E & UCC Recording- 740-533-4314; fax-740-533-4411; hours 8AM-4PM http://63.239.104.62 Will search UCC records. Search per debtor- $20.00. UCC search includes tax liens if requested. Will not search real estate records. UCC copy- $2.00 per page. Cert fee: $1.00 per cert. **Online Access to Auditor, Property, Real Estate, Deed, Lien, Recording records:** Access to the recorders database is free at http://63.239.104.62/record_search.htm. Deeds go back to 1984; mortgages to 1988; liens to 1981. Also, the auditor's data is free at www.lawrencecountyauditor.org.

Licking County

County Recorder, PO Box 520, Newark, OH 43058. **Phone-**740-349-6060, R/E Recording-740-349-6061, UCC Recording-740-349-6061; fax-740-349-1415; hours 8:30AM-4:30PM www.lcounty.com/rec/

Will search UCC records. Search per debtor- $20.00. Will not do federal tax lien search. Will not search real estate records. UCC copy- $2.00 per page. Cert fee: $2.00 per cert. Payee: Licking County Recorder. **Online Access to Real Estate, Tax Lien, Recording, Property Tax, Cemetery, Genealogy, Sex Offender records:** Access to the county recorders database is free at www.lcounty.com/recordings/. Records with images go back to 1997. Also, online access to the Auditor's county property database is free at www.lcounty.com/licking208/. Search the sheriff's sex offender lists for free at www.lcounty.com/sheriff/sex_offenders/. Also, search cemetery names free on private company site at www.rootsweb.com/~cemetery/ohio/licking.htm. Search the genealogy site for the county at www.rootsweb.com/~ohlickin/#data. **Other phones:** Assessor-740-349-6026; Treasurer-740-349-6046; Auditor-740-349-6026; Elections-740-349-8683.

Logan County

County Recorder, 100 S Madriver, #A, Bellefontaine, OH 43311-2075. **Phone**-937-599-7201; fax-937-599-7287; hours-8:30AM-4:30PM www.co.logan.oh.us/Recorder/index.html Will search UCC records. Search per debtor- $20.00. Will not search real estate or tax lien records. Copy fee- $2.00 per page. Cert fee: $1.00 per cert. Payee: Logan County Recorder. **Online Access to Real Estate, Auditor, Recording, Deed, Lien, Jail Inmate, Sex Offender records:** Records on the County Auditor's database are free at www2.co.logan.oh.us/logan208/LandRover.asp. Also, online access to the recorders database is free at www3.co.logan.oh.us/record30.asp. Click on "Document Search." Also, search the sheriff's inmate and sex offender lists at www.co.logan.oh.us/sheriff/. **Other phones:** Treasurer-937-599-7223; Elections-937-599-7255; Auditor-937-599-7213.

Lorain County

County Recorder, 226 Middle Ave, Elyria, OH 44035. **Phone**-County Recorder, R/E & UCC Recording- 440-329-5148, UCC Recording-440-329-514; fax-440-329-5477; hours-8AM-4:30PM Will search UCC records. Search per debtor- $20.00. Will not search real estate or tax lien records. Copy fee- $2.00 per page. Cert fee: $1.00 per cert. **Online Access to Real Estate, Lien, Auditor, Property Sale, Unclaimed Funds, Sheriff Sale, Sex Offender records:** Access to the assessor database is free at www.loraincounty.com/recorder/register. Free registration is required. Also, access records on the County Auditor's database for a fee at www.loraincountyauditor.org/lorain208/LandRover.asp. Search the unclaimed funds list at www.loraincounty.com/clerk/unclaimedfunds.html. Search the sex offender and sheriff sales lists for free at www.loraincountysheriff.com. **Other phones:** Auditor-440-329-5207.

Lucas County

County Recorder, 1 Government Ctr #700, Jackson St, Toledo, OH 43604. **Phone**-419-213-4400; fax-419-213-4284; hours 8AM-5PM www.co.lucas.oh.us/ Will search UCC records. Search per debtor- $20.00. Will not search real estate records. Copy fee- $2.00 per page. Cert fee: $2.00 per cert. Payee: Lucas County Recorder. **Online Access to Real Estate, Auditor, Unclaimed Funds, Sheriff Sale, Sex Offender records:** Property records on the County Auditor's Real Estate info System (AREIS) database are free at www.co.lucas.oh.us/Areis/areismain.asp. This replaces the old system. Also, access to recorder real estate records is free with registration at www.co.lucas.oh.us/recordings/logon.asp. Also, online access to the treasurer's unclaimed funds and sheriff sale lists are free at www.raytkest.com. Search the sheriff's sex offender list at www.lucascountysheriff.org/sheriff/disclaimer.asp. **Other phones:** Treasurer-419-213-4303; Vital Records-419-213-4100; Auditor-419-213-4420.

Madison County

County Recorder, 1 N Main St, Rm 40, Courthouse, London, OH 43140. **Phone**-County Recorder, R/E & UCC Recording- 740-852-1854; fax-740-845-1776; hours 8AM-4PM www.co.madison.oh.us Will search UCC records. Search per debtor- $20.00. Will not search real estate or tax lien records. Copy fee- $2.00 per page. Cert fee: $1.00 per cert. Payee: Madison County Recorder. **Online Access to Real Estate, Auditor, Deed, UCC, Recording, Sex Offender, Sheriff Sale records:** Records on the

County Auditor's database are free at www.co.madison.oh.us/auditor/iView/iView.asp. Also, online access to county land and UCC records is free at www.landaccess.com/sites/oh/madison/index.php. Records go back to 5/1994. Also, access to the sheriff's sale and sex offender lists are at www.madisonsheriff.org. **Other phones:** Treasurer-740-852-1936; Auditor-740-852-9717.

Mahoning County

County Recorder, PO Box 928, Youngstown, OH 44501. **Phone**-County Recorder, R/E & UCC Recording- 330-740-2345; fax-330-740-2006. www.mahoningcountyauditor.org Will search UCC records. Search per debtor- $20.00. Will not do a state tax lien search. UCC copy- $2.00 per page. Cert fee: $1.00 per cert. **Online Access to Real Estate, Auditor, Property Sale, Deed, UCC, Lien, Judgment, Recording records:** Access to recorder's property, deed, and UCC records is to be at www.landaccess.com/sites/oh/mahoning/index.php. Records go back to 1985. Also, property tax records on the County Auditor's database are free at www.mahoningcountyauditor.org. **Other phones:** Assessor-330-740-2010; Treasurer-330-740-2460; Auditor-330-740-2010; Elections-330-783-2474; Vital Records-330-743-3333 x231; Auditor-330-740-2010.

Marion County

County Recorder, 222 W Center St, Marion, OH 43302-3646. **Phone**-County Recorder, R/E & UCC Recording- 740-223-4100; hours 8:30AM-4:30PM www.co.marion.oh.us Will search UCC records. Search per debtor- $20.00. Will not search real estate or tax lien records. Copy fee- $2.00 per page. Cert fee: $1.00 per cert. Payee: Marion County Recorder. **Online Access to Real Estate, Auditor records:** Access to the county auditor real estate database is free at www.co.marion.oh.us. Click on "Real Estate Inquiry.". **Other phones:** Assessor-740-223-4020; Treasurer-740-223-4030; Auditor-740-223-4020; Elections-740-223-4090; Auditor-740-223-4020.

Medina County

County Recorder, 144 N. Broadway, County Admin. Bldg, Medina, OH 44256-2295. **Phone**-County Recorder, R/E & UCC Recording- 330-725-9782, UCC Recording-330-725-9783; hours 8AM-4:30PM www.recorder.co.medina.oh.us Will search UCC records. Search per debtor- $20.00. Will not do federal tax lien search. Will not search real estate records. Copy fee- $2.00 per page. Cert fee: $1.00 per cert. Payee: Medina County Recorder. **Online Access to Real Estate, Auditor, Property Transfer, Sex Offender, records:** Access to indexes 1983 to present on the Recorder database is free at www.recorder.co.medina.oh.us/fcquery.htm. Also, online access to property records on the Medina County Auditor database are free at www.medinacountyauditor.org/pptylook.htm. Also, search property transfers at www.medinacountyauditor.org/trbytd2.htm. Also, find a lost dog's owner at www.medinacountyauditor.org/finddog.htm. The sheriff's sex offender list is via www.medinasheriff.com; the county tax sale list is at www.medinacountyauditor.org/sheriff.htm#delinq. **Other phones:** Assessor-330-725-9754.

Meigs County

County Recorder, 100 E. Second St, Courthouse, Pomeroy, OH 45769. **Phone**-740-992-3806; fax-740-992-2867; hours 8:30AM-4:30PM Will search UCC records. Search per debtor- $20.00. Will not do federal tax lien search. Will not search real estate records. RE record copy- $2.00 per side. UCC copy- $2.00 per page. Cert fee: $1.00 per

cert. Payee: Meigs County Recorder. **Other phones:** Treasurer-740-992-2004; Auditor-740-992-2004; Auditor-740-992-5290.

Mercer County

County Recorder, 101 N. Main St, Courthouse Sq, Rm 203, Celina, OH 45822. **Phone**-County Recorder, R/E & UCC Recording- 419-586-4232; fax-419-586-3541; hours 8:30AM-5PM M; 8:30AM-4PM T-F Will search UCC records. Search per debtor- $20.00. Will not search tax liens. Will search real estate records. RE record copy- $2.00 per page only if you have volume and page #. UCC copy- $2.00 per page. Cert fee: $1.00 per cert. Payee: Mercer County Recorder. **Online Access to Real Estate, Auditor, Property Sale, Sex Offender records:** Property records on the County Auditor Real Estate Department database are free at www.mercercountyohio.org/auditor/ParcelSearch/. Also, search the county sheriff sex offender list at www.mercercountyohio.org/sheriff/SEX_OFF_HOME .htm. **Other phones:** Treasurer-419-586-2259; Auditor-419-586-6402; Elections-419-586-2215; Auditor-419-586-2259.

Miami County

County Recorder, PO Box 653, Troy, OH 45373. **Phone**-937-332-6893, R/E Recording-937-440-6040, UCC Recording-937-440-6040; fax-937-332-6806; hours 7:30AM-4:30PM Will search UCC records. Search per debtor- $20.00. Will not do federal tax lien search. Will not search real estate records. UCC copy- $2.00 per page. Cert fee: $1.00 per cert. Payee: Miami County Recorder. **Other phones:** Assessor-937-440-5925; Treasurer-937-440-6045; Auditor-937-440-5925; Elections-937-440-3900; Auditor-937-440-5925.

Monroe County

County Recorder, PO Box 152, Woodsfield, OH 43793-0152. **Phone**-740-472-5264; fax-740-472-2523; hours 8AM-4PM Will search UCC records. Search per debtor- $24.00. Will not do federal tax lien search. Will not search real estate records. UCC copy- $2.00 per page. Cert fee: $1.00 per cert. Payee: Monroe County Recorder. **Online Access to Property, Auditor records:** Access to the auditor's property data is free at http://monroecountyauditor.org. Use Quick Search or Attribute Search. **Other phones:** Assessor-740-472-0763; Treasurer-740-472-1521; Auditor-740-472-0873.

Montgomery County

County Recorder, PO Box 972, Dayton, OH 45422. **Phone**-937-225-4275; fax-937-225-5980; hours 8AM-4:30PM www.mcohio.org/departments.html Will search UCC records. Search per debtor- $20.00. Will not search real estate or tax lien records. UCC copy- $2.00 per page. Cert fee: $1.00 per cert. **Online Access to Property, Real Estate, Lien, Recording, Auditor records:** Access recorders data free at www.mcrecorder.org/search_selection.cfm. Also, search the auditor's property records for free at www.mcauditor.org/realestate/. Also, property tax records on the county treasurer real estate tax information database are free at www.mctreas.org. also, search the sheriff's site for missing persons, property sales, sex offenders at www.co.montgomery.oh.us/Sheriff/. **Other phones:** Auditor-937-225-4002.

Morgan County

County Recorder, 155 E Main St, RM 160, McConnelsville, OH 43756. **Phone**-County Recorder, R/E & UCC Recording- 740-962-4051; fax-740-962-3364; hours 8AM-4PM Will search UCC records. Search per debtor- $20.00. Will not search real estate or tax lien records. Copy fee- $2.00 per page. Cert fee: $1.00 per cert.

Payee: Morgan County Recorder. **Online Access to Property, Auditor, Inmate records:** Access to the auditor property data is free at http://morgancountyauditor.org. Use Quick search or Attribute Search. Also, search the county past inmate list at http://xw.textdata.com:81/cgi/progcgi.exe?program=search3. Engineer-www.morgancoengineer.com. **Other phones:** Treasurer-740-962-3561; Elections-740-962-3116; Vital Records-740-962-4572; Auditor-740-962-4475; Engineer-740-962-3171.

Morrow County

County Recorder, 48 E. High St, Mount Gilead, OH 43338. **Phone-**County Recorder, R/E & UCC Recording-419-947-3060; fax-419-947-3709; hours 8:00AM-4:00PM
www.morrowcounty.info/morrowoff.htm
Will search UCC records. Search per debtor- $20.00. Will not search real estate or tax lien records. Copy fee- $2.00 per page. Cert fee: $1.00 per cert. Payee: Morrow County Recorder. **Online Access to Real Estate, Appraisal, Property Sale records:** Access to the county auditor database is free at http://auditor.co.morrow.oh.us/iView/. Includes land sales data. **Other phones:** Treasurer-419-947-6070; Auditor-419-947-4060.

Muskingum County

County Recorder, PO Box 2333, Zanesville, OH 43702-2333. **Phone-**County Recorder, R/E & UCC Recording- 740-455-7107; fax-740-455-7943; hours 8:30AM-4:30PM
Will search UCC records. Search per debtor- $20.00. Will not search real estate or tax lien records. RE record copy- $2.00 per page. Copy fee is $2.00 per page. Cert fee: $1.00 per cert. Payee: Muskingum County Recorder. **Online Access to Real Estate, Assessor, Sheriff Sale, Sex Offender records:** Records on the county auditor database are free at www.muskingumcountyauditor.org/iView/iView.asp. Also, the sheriff's site provides sale lists and sex offender info at www.ohiomuskingumsheriff.org. **Other phones:** Assessor-740-455-7109; Treasurer-740-455-7118; Auditor-740-455-7109; Elections-740-455-7120; Auditor-740-455-7109.

Noble County

County Recorder, 260 Courthouse, Rm 2E, Caldwell, OH 43724. **Phone-**County Recorder, R/E & UCC Recording- 740-732-4319; hours 8AM-4PM M-W; 8-12:00AM Th; 8AM-6PM
Will search UCC records. No certification of UCC searches by county recorders. Search per debtor- $20.00. Will not search real estate or tax lien records. Copy fee- $2.00 per page. Payee: Noble County Recorder. **Other phones:** Treasurer-740-732-2457; Elections-740-732-2057; Vital Records-740-732-5047.

Ottawa County

County Recorder, 315 Madison St, Rm 204, Port Clinton, OH 43452. **Phone-**419-734-6730, R/E Recording-419-734-6735, UCC Recording-419-734-6735; fax-419-734-6919; hours 8:30AM-4:30PM
Will search UCC records. Search per debtor- $20.00. Will not search real estate or tax lien records. UCC copy- $2.00 per page. Cert fee: $1.00 per cert. Payee: Ottawa County Recorder. **Online Access to Property, Auditor, Cemetery, Sex Offender records:** Access to the auditor's property database is free at www.ottawacountyauditor.org. Also, search cemetary registrations for free on private company website at www.rootsweb.com/~cemetery/ohio/ottawa.htm. Search the sheriff's sex offender list for free at www.ottawacountysheriff.org/sorn.html. **Other phones:** Treasurer-419-734-6750; Auditor-419-734-6740; Vital Records-419-734-6800.

Paulding County

County Recorder, 115 N Williams St, Paulding, OH 45879. **Phone-**County Recorder, R/E & UCC Recording- 419-399-8275; fax-419-399-2862; hours 8AM-4PM. Will search UCC records. Search per debtor- $20.00. Will not search real estate or tax lien records. Copy fee- $2.00 per page. Cert fee: $1.00 per cert. Payee: County Recorder. **Other phones:** Assessor-419-399-8205; Treasurer-419-399-8280; Auditor-419-399-8205; Elections-419-399-8230; Vital Records-419-399-3921.

Perry County

County Recorder, PO Box 147, New Lexington, OH 43764. **Phone-**740-342-2494, R/E Recording-740-342-2444; fax-740-342-5539; hours 8:30AM-4:30PM
Will search UCC records. Search per debtor- $20.00. Will not do federal tax lien search. Will not search real estate records. Copy fee- $2.00 per page. Cert fee: $1.00 per cert. Payee: Perry County Recorder. **Online Access to Inmate records:** Access to the county inmates search is free at http://xw.textdata.com:81/cgi/progcgi.exe?program=search3. **Other phones:** Treasurer-740-342-2074; Auditor-740-342-2074.

Pickaway County

County Recorder, 207 S. Court St, Circleville, OH 43113. **Phone-**740-474-5826; fax-740-477-6361; hours 8AM-4PM
Will search UCC records. Search per debtor- $20.00. Will not search real estate or tax lien records. Copy fee- $2.00 per page. Cert fee: $1.00 per doc. Payee: Pickaway County Recorder. **Online Access to Property, Auditor, Real Estate, Recorder, Deed, UCC records:** Access to the county auditor property data is free at http://pickaway.iviewauditor.com/iView/. Also, search the recorder database free at www.landaccess.com/sites/oh/pickaway/index.php. **Other phones:** Assessor-740-474-4765; Treasurer-740-474-2370; Elections-740-474-1100; Auditor-740-474-4765.

Pike County

County Recorder, 230 Waverly Plaza #500, Courthouse, Waverly, OH 45690. **Phone-**740-947-2622; fax-740-947-7997; hours 8:30AM-4PM
Will search UCC records. Search per debtor- $20.00. Will not search real estate or tax lien records. UCC copy- $2.00 per copy. Cert fee: $1.00 per cert. Payee: Pike County Recorder. **Online Access to Recorder, Deed, Lien, UCC, Real Estate, Auditor, Inmate records:** Access to the recorder's database is free at www.landaccess.com/sites/oh/pike/index.php. Also, access to the county auditor property tax data is free at http://207.90.76.229/pikeweb/browser/. Also, search the inmate list for free at http://xw.textdata.com:81/cgi/progcgi.exe?program=search3. **Other phones:** Assessor-740-947-4125; Treasurer-740-947-2713; Auditor-614-947-2713.

Portage County

County Recorder, 449 S. Meridian St, Ravenna, OH 44266. **Phone-**330-297-3554, R/E Recording-330-297-3553; fax-330-297-7349; hours 8AM-4:30PM
www.co.portage.oh.us
Will search UCC records. Search per debtor- $20.00. Will not search real estate or tax lien records. Copy fee- $2.00 per page. Cert fee: $1.00 per cert. Payee: Portage County Recorder. **Online Access to Property, Auditor, Property Sale, Sheriff Sale, Sex Offender records:** Access to the auditor's property records is free at http://portagepropertymax.govemmaxa.com/propertymax/rover30.asp. Also, access to the sheriff's property sales and sex offender lists is free at www.co.portage.oh.us. **Other phones:** Treasurer-330-297-3586; Auditor-330-297-3569.

Preble County

County Recorder, PO Box 371, Eaton, OH 45320-0371. **Phone-**937-456-8173; hours 8AM-4:30PM
www.ohiorecorders.com
Will search UCC records. Search per debtor- $20.00. Will not search real estate or tax lien records. Copy fee- $2.00 per page. Cert fee: $1.00 per cert. Payee: Preble County Recorder. **Online Access to Real Estate, Auditor, Obituary records:** Property records on the County Auditor's database are free at www.preblecountyauditor.org/preble208/LandRover.asp. Also, search the 1980-1995 obituary list compiled by the Preble County Room for free at www.pcdl.lib.oh.us/getobit.htm. **Other phones:** Assessor-937-456-8148.

Putnam County

County Recorder, 245 E. Main St, Courthouse - #202, Ottawa, OH 45875-1959. **Phone-**419-523-6490; fax-419-523-4403; hours 8:30AM-4:30PM
Will search UCC records. Search per debtor- $20.00. Will not search tax liens or real estate records. UCC copy- $2.00 per copy. Cert fee: $1.00 per cert. Payee: Putnam County Recorder. **Online Access to Property, Auditor, Property Sale records:** Access to the county auditor property data is free at www.putnam.iviewauditor.com/iView.asp. **Other phones:** Auditor-419-523-6686; Elections-419-523-3343.

Richland County

County Recorder, 50 Park Ave East, Mansfield, OH 44902. **Phone-**419-774-5602/5600, R/E Recording-419-774-5599, UCC Recording-419-774-5601; fax-419-774-5603; hours-8AM-4PM
www.richlandcountyauditor.org
Will search UCC records. Search per debtor- $20.00. Will not search real estate or tax lien records. Copy fee- $2.00 per page. Cert fee: $1.00 per cert. Payee: Richland County Recorder. **Online Access to Real Estate, Auditor, Deed, UCC, Property Sale, Sheriff Sale, Sex Offender records:** Property records from the County Auditor database are free at www.richlandcountyauditor.org. Also, online access to county land and UCC records is free at www.landaccess.com. Records go back to 4/1989. Also, search the sheriff sales and sex offender lists for free at www.sheriffrichlandcounty.com. **Other phones:** Assessor-419-774-5502; Treasurer-419-774-5622; Auditor-419-774-5503; Elections-419-774-5530; Vital Records-419-774-4500.

Ross County

County Recorder, PO Box 6162, Chillicothe, OH 45601. **Phone-**740-702-3000; fax-740-702-3006; hours 8:30AM-4:30PM www.co.ross.oh.us/
Will search UCC records. Search per debtor- $20.00. Will not do federal tax lien search. Will not search real estate records. Copy fee- $2.00 per page. Cert fee: $2.00 per cert. Payee: Ross County Recorder. **Online Access to Property, Deed, UCC, Auditor, Recorder records:** Access to county land, recording and UCC records is free at www.landaccess.com. Records go back to 1/1974. Also, access to the auditor's property and sales data is free at www.co.ross.oh.us/auditor/iView/iView.asp. **Other phones:** Assessor-740-702-3080; Treasurer-740-702-3080; Auditor-740-702-3080.

Sandusky County

County Recorder, 100 N. Park Ave., Courthouse, Fremont, OH 43420-2477. **Phone-**419-334-6226; hours 8AM-4:30PM www.sandusky-county.org/County_Recorder.asp
Will search UCC records. Search per debtor- $20.00. Will not do federal tax lien search. Will not search real estate records. Copy fee- $2.00 per page. Cert

fee: $1.00 per cert + $2.00 per page copy. Payee: Sandusky County Recorder. **Online Access to Property, Auditor, Treasurer records:** Access to county auditor and treasurer property data is free at http://ohsanduskypropertymax.governmaxa.com/propertymax/rover30.asp. Click on "Property Search" and shoose to search by name. **Other phones:** Treasurer-419-334-6233; Auditor-419-334-6123.

Scioto County

County Recorder, 602 7th St, Rm 110, Rm 110, Portsmouth, OH 45662-3950. **Phone-**County Recorder, R/E & UCC Recording- 740-355-8304; fax-740-353-7358;   hours-8AM-4:30PM www.sciotocountyohio.com/
Will search UCC records. Search per debtor- $20.00. Will not search real estate or tax lien records. Copy fee- $2.00 per page. Cert fee: $1.00 per cert. Payee: Recorder. **Online Access to Property, Auditor records:** Access to the auditor's property data is free at www.sciotocountyauditor.org/scioto208/LandRover.asp. **Other phones:** Assessor-740-355-8264; Treasurer-740-355-8296; Auditor-740-355-8264; Elections-740-355-8217; City Birth or Death-740-353-5153; County Birth or Death-740-354-3241.

Seneca County

County Recorder, 109 S. Washington St #2104, Tiffin, OH 44883. **Phone-**419-447-4434; hours 8:30AM-4:30PM
Will search UCC records. Search per debtor- $20.00. Will not do federal tax lien search. Will not search real estate records. Copy fee- $2.00 per page. Cert fee: $1.00 per cert. Payee: Seneca County Recorder. **Online Access to Property, Most Wanted, Missing Person records:** Access the sheriff's missing person and most wanted lists is free at www.bright.net/~senecaso/. Also, property data may be accessible via www.landaccess.com. **Other phones:** Assessor-419-447-1584;   Treasurer-419-447-1584; Auditor-419-447-0692; Vital Records-419-447-3691.

Shelby County

County Recorder, 129 E. Court St, Shelby County Annex, Sidney, OH 45365. **Phone-**County Recorder, R/E & UCC Recording- 937-498-7270; fax-937-498-7272;   hours-7:30AM-4:30PM www.co.shelby.oh.us/Recorder.asp
Will search UCC records. Search per debtor- $20.00 to start search. Will not search real estate or tax lien records. Copy fee- $2.00 per page. Cert fee: $1.00 per doc. Payee: Shelby County Recorder. **Online Access to Sheriff Sale, Sex Offender records:** Access to the sheriff's sales and sex offender lists is free at http://shelbycountysheriff.com/index2.htm. **Other phones:** Treasurer-937-498-7281; Auditor-937-498-7202; Elections-937-498-7208 or 7209; Vital Records-937-498-7249 (Birth & Death Certificates); Probate (Wills)-937-498-7263; Clerk of Courts-Divorce & judgments-937-498-7221.

Stark County

County Recorder, 110 Central Plaza South, #170, Canton, OH 44702-1409. **Phone-**330-451-7443, R/E Recording-330-451-7443 x4464, UCC Recording-330-451-7443 x7933; fax-330-451-7394; hours 8:30AM-4:30PM (Recording: til 4PM) www.co.stark.oh.us
Will search UCC records. Search per debtor- $20.00. Will not do federal tax lien search. Will not search real estate records. UCC copy- $2.00 per page. Cert fee: $1.00 per cert. Payee: Stark County Recorder. **Online Access to Real Estate, Deed, Recording, Auditor, Property, Sheriff Sale, Delinquent Taxpayer, Sex Offender, Unclaimed Funds records:** Access to the recorder's database is free at www.recorder.co.stark.oh.us/DTS/. Chose from simple, advanced or instrument search. Also, search the auditor's property data for free at

www.auditor.co.stark.oh.us/AUDsearch.asp. Also, elected officials list is at www.stark.lib.oh.us/officials.html. A weekly delinquent taxpayers list is at www.starktaxes.com/list.cgi. Access sheriff sales lists at www.sheriff.co.stark.oh.us/RealEstate.htm. Sex offenders list is at www.sheriff.co.stark.oh.us/OffenderLinks.htm. Unclaimed funds at www.starkcourt.org/perl/starkcrt/pdfarchive/uf/uf_pdflist.cgi. City of Louisville library obituary list can be searched at www.louisville.lib.oh.us/genealogy/. **Other phones:** Treasurer-330-451-7814; Auditor-330-451-7814.

Summit County

Fiscal Officer, Recording Department, 175 S Main St, Akron, OH 44308-1355. **Phone-**Fiscal Officer, Recording Department, R/E & UCC Recording- 330-643-2720, UCC Recording-330-643-2717; hours 7:30AM-4PM www.co.summit.oh.us/fiscaloffice
Will search UCC records. Search per debtor- $20.00. Will not do federal tax lien search. Will not search real estate records. Copy fee- $2.00 per page. Cert fee: $1.00 per page. Payee: Summit County Fiscal Officer. **Online Access to Real Estate, Auditor, Property Tax, Recording, Deed, Sex Offender, Most Wanted, Sheriff Sale records:** Tax map information from the county fiscal officer is free online at www.co.summit.oh.us/fiscalofficer (choose: Public Access Web Services), also property appraisal, images and tax information are at above site. Access to the full images requires registration, password. Call Summit County Data Ctr Help Desk at 330-643-2013 for info and sign-up. Also search property tax records at http://megatron.summitoh.net/summit/html/webintg.html. Recorder images are at www.co.summit.oh.us/fiscalofficer. Password required; obtain password from Fiscal Officer. No name searching. Also search sex offenders, most wanted, and sheriff tax sale lists for free at www.co.summit.oh.us/sheriff. **Other phones:** Treasurer-330-643-2587; Auditor-330-643-2638; Fiscal Officer-330-643-2630.

Trumbull County

County Recorder, 160 High St NW, Warren, OH 44481. **Phone-**330-675-2401, 330-393-2707, R/E Recording-330-675-2401, UCC Recording-330-675-2798; fax-330-675-2404; hours 8:30AM-4:30PM www.tcrecorder.co.trumbull.oh.us
Will search UCC records. Search per debtor- $20.00. Will not do federal tax lien search. Will not search real estate records. Copy fee- $2.00 per page. Cert fee: $1.00 per seal. Payee: Trumbull County Recorder. **Online Access to Auditor, Property Tax, Recording, Deed, Mortgage, Lien, Unclaimed Fund, Warrant records:** Access to the recorder's database requires free registration and password at http://tcrecorder.co.trumbull.oh.us/index.cfm. Dog tags at www.dogtagsplus.com/Start.asp?CountyID=2. Also, real estate records from the County Auditor are free at www.co.auditor.trumbull.oh.us/iView/. Also, unclaimed funds list from probate court is at www.trumbullprobate.org/UnclaimedFunds.htm. The Sheriff's warrants list is at www.sheriff.co.trumbull.oh.us/warrants.htm. **Other phones:** Treasurer-330-675-2736; Auditor-330-675-2420; Elections-330-675-4050; Auditor-330-675-2420.

Tuscarawas County

County Recorder, 125 E. High Ave, New Philadelphia, OH 44663. **Phone-**330-365-3284; hours 8AM-4:30PM www.co.tuscarawas.oh.us
Will search UCC records. Search per debtor- $20.00. Will not do federal tax lien search. Will not search real estate records. Copy fee- $2.00 per page. Cert fee: $1.00 per cert. Payee: Tuscarawas County Recorder. **Online Access to Real Estate, Unclaimed

Funds, records: County real estate records are free at www.co.tuscarawas.oh.us/tusca208/LandRover.asp. The auditor's delinquent tax list is updated in September. Also, the clerk of court's page (see county main website) can be searched free for unclaimed funds and outstanding checks. **Other phones:** Treasurer-330-365-3254; Auditor-330-365-3220; Auditor-330-364-8811 x220.

Union County

County Recorder, 233 W. Sixth St., Marysville, OH 43040. **Phone-**County Recorder, R/E & UCC Recording- 937-645-3032; fax-937-642-3397; hours 8:30AM-4PM www.co.union.oh.us/Recorder/recorder.html
Will search UCC records. Search per debtor- $20.00. Will not do federal tax lien search. Will not search real estate records. UCC copy- $2.00 per page. Cert fee: $1.00 per cert. Payee: Union County Recorder. **Online Access to Auditor, Property Tax, Real Estate, Recording, Delinquent Taxpayer records:** Access to the Auditors tax assessment/property records database and the appraiser property information database is free at www2.co.union.oh.us/PropInfoGuide.htm. You may also search for property information via the online GIS map. Search recorded documents at www.co.union.oh.us/Recorder/disclaimer.htm. Search the treasurers' list of delinquent taxpayers at www.co.union.oh.us/Treasurer/List_of_Delinquent_Taxpayers/list_of_delinquent_taxpayers.html. **Other phones:** Treasurer-937-645-3029; Auditor-937-645-3003.

Van Wert County

County Recorder, 121 E Main St, Courthouse - Rm 206, Van Wert, OH 45891-1729. **Phone-**County Recorder, R/E & UCC Recording- 419-238-2558; fax-419-238-5410; hours 8:30AM-5PM M; 8:30AM-4PM T-F www.ohiorecorders.com
Will search UCC records. Search per debtor- $20.00. Will not do federal tax lien search. Will not search real estate records. RE record copy- $2.00 per copy. UCC copy- $2.00 per page. Cert fee: $1.00 per cert. Payee: Van Wert County Recorder. **Online Access to Property, Deed, UCC, Recording, Auditor records:** Access to county land and UCC records is free at www.landaccess.com. Records go back to 1/1994. Also, access to the auditor's property records is free at http://realestate.co.vanwert.oh.us. **Other phones:** Assessor-419-238-0843;   Treasurer-419-238-5177; Auditor-419-238-0843; Elections-419-238-4192; Vital Records-419-238-0808; Auditor-419-238-0843.

Vinton County

County Recorder, 100 E Main St, McArthur, OH 45651. **Phone-**County Recorder, R/E & UCC Recording- 740-596-4314; fax-740-596-2265; hours 8:30AM-4PM
Will search UCC records. Search per debtor- $20.00. Will not search real estate or tax lien records. UCC copy- $2.00 per page. Cert fee: $1.00 per page. Payee: Vinton County Recorder. **Online Access to Inmate records:** Access to the county past inmate list is free at http://xw.textdata.com:81/cgi/progcgi.exe?program=search3. **Other phones:** Assessor-740-596-5445; Treasurer-740-596-5690; Auditor-740-596-5445; Elections-740-596-5855; Vital Records-740-596-5480; Auditor-740-596-5445.

Warren County

County Recorder, 406 Justice Dr., Lebanon, OH 45036. **Phone-**County Recorder, R/E & UCC Recording- 513-695-1382, UCC Recording-513-695-2638; fax-513-695-2949; hours 8AM-4:30PM www.co.warren.oh.us
Will search UCC records. Search per debtor- $20.00. Will not search real estate or tax lien records. Copy fee- $2.00 per page. Cert fee: $1.00 per page (must

copy entire doc). Payee: Recorder. **Online Access to Property, Auditor, Mapping, Sex Offender records:** Access to the county auditor database is at http://gisweb.woolpert.com/warrencounty/html/locator.asp. Also, search the sheriff's sex offender list at www.wcsooh.org/sheriff/sex_offenders_disclaimer.htm. Recorders Records access since 1979 found at www.co.warren.oh.us/recorder. **Other phones:** Assessor-513-695-1235;   Treasurer-513-695-1300; Auditor-513-695-1218;   Elections-513-695-1358; Auditor-513-695-1235.

Washington County

County Recorder, 205 Putnam St, Courthouse, Marietta, OH 45750. **Phone-**740-373-6623 x235 or 236, R/E Recording-740-373-6623 x235; fax-740-373-9643; hours 8AM-5PM www.ohiorecorders.com
Will search UCC records. Search per debtor- $20.00. Will not search real estate or tax lien records. UCC copy- $2.00 per page. Cert fee: $2.00 per page. **Online Access to Property, Auditor, Deed, UCC, Recorder, Real Estate records:** Access to the county auditor's Property search database is free at www.washingtoncountyauditor.org/washington208/LandRover.asp. Also, access to property, deed, and UCC records is free at www.landaccess.com/sites/oh/washington/index.php. **Other phones:** Treasurer-740-373-6623 x256; Auditor-740-373-6623 x263.

Wayne County

County Recorder, 428 W Liberty St, Wooster, OH 44691-5097. **Phone-**County Recorder, R/E & UCC Recording- 330-287-5460; fax-330-287-5685; hours 8AM-4:30PM www.co.wayne.oh.us
Will search UCC records. Search per debtor- $20.00. Will not search real estate or tax lien records. Copy fee- $2.00 per page. Cert fee: $1.00 per cert. Payee: Wayne County Recorder. **Online Access to Property, Auditor, Sex Offender, Late Taxpayer records:** Access to the auditor's property data should be free at www.waynecountyauditor.org. The late taxpayer list should soon be appear at the treasurer's website, www.co.wayne.oh.us. Also, search the sheriff's sex offender list for free at www.waynecountysheriff.com/sexoffenders.htm.
Other phones: Treasurer-330-287-5450; Elections-330-287-5480; Auditor-330-287-5430.

Williams County

County Recorder, 1 Courthouse Sq, Bryan, OH 43506. **Phone-**419-636-3259; hours 8:30AM-4:30PM
Will search UCC records. Search per debtor- $20.00. Will not do federal tax lien search. Will not search real estate records. Copy fee- $2.00 per page. Cert fee: $1.00 per cert. Payee: Williams County Recorder. **Online Access to Property, Auditor, Property Sale records:** Access to the auditor's property data is free at www.co.williams.oh.us/realestate/LandRover.asp.
Other phones: ; Auditor-419-636-5639.

Wood County

County Recorder, 1 Courthouse Sq, Bowling Green, OH 43402-2427. **Phone-**County Recorder, R/E & UCC Recording- 419-354-9140; hours 8:30AM-4:30PM www.co.wood.oh.us/recorder
Will search UCC records. Search per debtor- $20.00. Will not search real estate or tax lien records. Copy fee- $2.00 per page. Cert fee: $1.00 per cert. Payee: Wood County Recorder. **Online Access to Property, Auditor, Obituary, Treasurer Tax records:** Access to the auditor's property data is free at http://auditor.co.wood.oh.us/. No name searching. Also, search the treasurer's tax data for free at http://woodtaxcollector.governmax.com/collectmax/collect30.asp? Also, search the library's obituaries from 1848 to present for free at http://wcdpl.lib.oh.us/databases/obitsearch.asp. **Other phones:** Assessor-419-354-9150; Treasurer-419-354-9130; Auditor-419-354-9150; Elections-419-354-9120; Vital Records-419-354-9130.

Wyandot County

County Recorder, 109 S. Sandusky Ave., Courthouse, Upper Sandusky, OH 43351. **Phone-**County Recorder, R/E & UCC Recording- 419-294-1442; fax-419-294-6405; hours 8:30AM-4:30PM
Will search UCC records. Search per debtor- $20.00. Will not search real estate or tax lien records. Copy fee- $2.00 per page. Cert fee: $1.00 per cert. Payee: Wyandot County. **Online Access to Property, Auditor records:** Access to the Auditor's real estate database is free at www.co.wyandot.oh.us/auditor/default.html. Click on "Real Estate Internet Inquiry.". **Other phones:** Assessor-419-294-1531;   Treasurer-419-294-2131; Elections-419-294-1226; Vital Records-419-294-2302.

Ohio County Locator

You will usually be able to find the city name in the City/County Cross Reference below. In that case, it is a simple matter to determine the county from the cross reference. However, only the official US Postal Service city names are included in this index. There are an additional 40,000 place names that people use in their addresses. Therefore, we have also included a ZIP/City Cross Reference immediately following the City/County Cross Reference.

If you know the ZIP Code but the city name does not appear in the City/County Cross Reference index, look up the ZIP Code in the ZIP/City Cross Reference, find the city name, then look up the city name in the City/County Cross Reference. For example, you want to know the county for an address of Menands, NY 12204. There is no "Menands" in the City/County Cross Reference. The ZIP/City Cross Reference shows that ZIP Codes 12201-12288 are for the city of Albany. Looking back in the City/County Cross Reference, Albany is in Albany County.

Ohio City/County Cross Reference

ABERDEEN (45101) Brown(97), Adams(2)
ADA (45810) Hardin(94), Hancock(2), Allen(2)
ADAMSVILLE Muskingum
ADDYSTON Hamilton
ADELPHI Ross
ADENA (43901) Jefferson(77), Harrison(12), Belmont(10)
ADRIAN Seneca
AKRON Summit
ALBANY (45710) Athens(59), Meigs(23), Vinton(16)
ALEXANDRIA Licking
ALGER (45812) Hardin(93), Allen(6)
ALLEDONIA Belmont
ALLIANCE (44601) Stark(90), Mahoning(6), Columbiana(2)
ALPHA Greene
ALVADA (44802) Seneca(61), Hancock(38)
ALVORDTON Williams
AMANDA (43102) Fairfield(90), Hocking(7), Pickaway(1)
AMELIA Clermont
AMESVILLE (45711) Athens(91), Washington(6), Morgan(2)
AMHERST Lorain
AMLIN Franklin
AMSDEN Seneca
AMSTERDAM (43903) Carroll(54), Jefferson(45)
ANDOVER Ashtabula
ANNA Shelby
ANSONIA Darke
ANTWERP (45813) Paulding(98), Defiance(1)
APPLE CREEK Wayne
ARCADIA Hancock
ARCANUM (45304) Darke(98), Preble(1)
ARCHBOLD (43502) Fulton(89), Henry(9)
ARLINGTON Hancock
ASHLAND (44805) Ashland(98), Richland(1)
ASHLEY (43003) Delaware(73), Morrow(26)
ASHTABULA Ashtabula
ASHVILLE Pickaway
ATHENS Athens
ATTICA (44807) Seneca(86), Huron(13)
ATWATER (44201) Portage(96), Stark(3)
AUGUSTA Carroll
AURORA (44202) Portage(89), Summit(8), Geauga(2)
AUSTINBURG Ashtabula
AVA Noble
AVON Lorain
AVON LAKE Lorain
B F GOODRICH CO Summit
BAINBRIDGE (45612) Ross(69), Pike(20), Highland(9)
BAKERSVILLE Coshocton
BALTIC (43804) Holmes(52), Tuscarawas(25), Coshocton(21)
BALTIMORE Fairfield
BANNOCK Belmont
BARBERTON Summit

BARLOW Washington
BARNESVILLE Belmont
BARTLETT Washington
BARTON Belmont
BASCOM Seneca
BATAVIA Clermont
BATH Summit
BAY VILLAGE Cuyahoga
BEACH CITY (44608) Stark(75), Tuscarawas(24)
BEACHWOOD Cuyahoga
BEALLSVILLE (43716) Monroe(73), Belmont(26)
BEAVER (45613) Pike(82), Jackson(17)
BEAVERDAM Allen
BEDFORD Cuyahoga
BELLAIRE Belmont
BELLBROOK Greene
BELLE CENTER (43310) Logan(75), Hardin(24)
BELLE VALLEY Noble
BELLEFONTAINE Logan
BELLEVUE (44811) Huron(41), Sandusky(41), Seneca(11), Erie(6)
BELLVILLE (44813) Richland(85), Knox(7), Morrow(6)
BELMONT Belmont
BELMORE Putnam
BELOIT (44609) Mahoning(60), Columbiana(39)
BELPRE Washington
BENTON RIDGE Hancock
BENTONVILLE Adams
BEREA Cuyahoga
BERGHOLZ (43908) Jefferson(95), Carroll(4)
BERKEY (43504) Lucas(95), Fulton(4)
BERLIN Holmes
BERLIN CENTER Mahoning
BERLIN HEIGHTS Erie
BETHEL (45106) Clermont(86), Brown(13)
BETHESDA Belmont
BETTSVILLE Seneca
BEVERLY (45715) Washington(97), Morgan(2)
BIDWELL Gallia
BIG PRAIRIE (44611) Holmes(94), Wayne(5)
BIRMINGHAM Erie
BLACKLICK Franklin
BLADENSBURG Knox
BLAINE Belmont
BLAKESLEE Williams
BLANCHESTER (45107) Clinton(83), Warren(8), Clermont(4), Brown(3)
BLISSFIELD Coshocton
BLOOMDALE (44817) Wood(91), Hancock(8)
BLOOMINGBURG Fayette
BLOOMINGDALE (43910) Jefferson(96), Harrison(3)
BLOOMVILLE (44818) Seneca(62), Crawford(37)
BLUE CREEK (45616) Adams(82), Scioto(17)

BLUE ROCK (43720) Muskingum(91), Morgan(8)
BLUFFTON (45817) Allen(82), Hancock(15), Putnam(1)
BOLIVAR (44612) Tuscarawas(95), Stark(4)
BOTKINS (45306) Shelby(95), Auglaize(4)
BOURNEVILLE Ross
BOWERSTON (44695) Harrison(56), Carroll(43)
BOWERSVILLE Greene
BOWLING GREEN Wood
BRADFORD (45308) Darke(54), Miami(45)
BRADNER (43406) Wood(92), Sandusky(7)
BRADY LAKE Portage
BRECKSVILLE (44141) Cuyahoga(93), Summit(6)
BREMEN (43107) Fairfield(92), Hocking(5), Perry(2)
BREWSTER Stark
BRICE Franklin
BRIDGEPORT Belmont
BRILLIANT Jefferson
BRINKHAVEN (43006) Coshocton(40), Holmes(40), Knox(19)
BRISTOLVILLE Trumbull
BROADVIEW HEIGHTS Cuyahoga
BROADWAY Union
BROOKFIELD Trumbull
BROOKPARK Cuyahoga
BROOKVILLE Montgomery
BROWNSVILLE Licking
BRUNSWICK Medina
BRYAN (43506) Williams(93), Defiance(6)
BUCHTEL Athens
BUCKEYE LAKE Licking
BUCKLAND Auglaize
BUCYRUS Crawford
BUFFALO Guernsey
BUFORD Highland
BURBANK (44214) Wayne(72), Medina(27)
BURGHILL Trumbull
BURGOON (43407) Sandusky(97), Seneca(2)
BURKETTSVILLE Mercer
BURTON Geauga
BUTLER (44822) Richland(60), Knox(38)
BYESVILLE Guernsey
CABLE Champaign
CADIZ (43907) Harrison(98), Jefferson(1)
CAIRO Allen
CALDWELL (43724) Noble(97), Morgan(1)
CALEDONIA (43314) Marion(87), Morrow(6), Crawford(5)
CAMBRIDGE Guernsey
CAMDEN Preble
CAMERON Monroe
CAMP DENNISON Hamilton
CAMPBELL Mahoning
CANAL FULTON (44614) Stark(97), Summit(1), Wayne(1)
CANAL WINCHESTER (43110) Franklin(73), Fairfield(26)
CANFIELD Mahoning

CANTON (44720) Stark(92), Summit(7)
CANTON (44730) Stark(98), Carroll(1)
CANTON Stark
CARBON HILL Hocking
CARBONDALE Athens
CARDINGTON (43315) Morrow(93), Marion(6)
CAREY (43316) Wyandot(84), Seneca(13), Hancock(1)
CARROLL Fairfield
CASSTOWN (45312) Miami(98), Champaign(1)
CASTALIA (44824) Erie(96), Sandusky(3)
CATAWBA Clark
CECIL (45821) Paulding(89), Defiance(10)
CEDARVILLE (45314) Greene(98), Clark(1)
CELINA Mercer
CENTERBURG (43011) Knox(69), Morrow(11), Delaware(10), Licking(7)
CHAGRIN FALLS (44022) Cuyahoga(77), Geauga(22)
CHAGRIN FALLS Geauga
CHANDLERSVILLE Muskingum
CHARDON (44024) Geauga(97), Lake(2)
CHARM Holmes
CHATFIELD Crawford
CHAUNCEY Athens
CHERRY FORK Adams
CHESAPEAKE Lawrence
CHESHIRE (45620) Gallia(96), Meigs(3)
CHESTER Meigs
CHESTERHILL (43728) Morgan(96), Athens(3)
CHESTERLAND Geauga
CHESTERVILLE Morrow
CHICKASAW Mercer
CHILLICOTHE Ross
CHILO Clermont
CHIPPEWA LAKE Medina
CHRISTIANSBURG Champaign
CINCINNATI (45241) Hamilton(72), Butler(26), Warren(1)
CINCINNATI (45244) Hamilton(57), Clermont(42)
CINCINNATI (45246) Hamilton(92), Butler(7)
CINCINNATI (45249) Hamilton(96), Warren(3)
CINCINNATI (45255) Hamilton(64), Clermont(35)
CINCINNATI Clermont
CINCINNATI Hamilton
CIRCLEVILLE Pickaway
CLARINGTON Monroe
CLARKSBURG (43115) Ross(77), Pickaway(22)
CLARKSVILLE (45113) Clinton(62), Warren(37)
CLAY CENTER Ottawa
CLAYTON Montgomery
CLEVELAND Cuyahoga
CLEVES Hamilton
CLIFTON Greene
CLINTON (44216) Summit(89), Stark(9)

CLOVERDALE (45827) Putnam(84), Paulding(15)
CLYDE (43410) Sandusky(96), Seneca(3)
COAL RUN Washington
COALTON Jackson
COLDWATER Mercer
COLERAIN Belmont
COLLEGE CORNER Butler
COLLINS (44826) Huron(84), Erie(15)
COLLINSVILLE Butler
COLTON Henry
COLUMBIA STATION Lorain
COLUMBIANA (44408) Columbiana(85), Mahoning(14)
COLUMBUS Delaware
COLUMBUS Franklin
COLUMBUS GROVE (45830) Putnam(79), Allen(20)
COMMERCIAL POINT Pickaway
CONESVILLE (43811) Coshocton(98), Muskingum(1)
CONNEAUT Ashtabula
CONOVER (45317) Champaign(47), Miami(40), Shelby(11)
CONTINENTAL (45831) Putnam(96), Defiance(2), Paulding(1)
CONVOY (45832) Van Wert(98), Paulding(1)
COOLVILLE (45723) Athens(87), Meigs(10), Washington(1)
CORNING (43730) Perry(97), Morgan(2)
CORTLAND Trumbull
COSHOCTON Coshocton
COVINGTON Miami
CREOLA (45622) Vinton(97), Hocking(2)
CRESTLINE (44827) Crawford(90), Richland(9)
CRESTON (44217) Wayne(89), Medina(10)
CROOKSVILLE (43731) Perry(85), Morgan(14)
CROTON (43013) Licking(98), Delaware(1)
CROWN CITY (45623) Gallia(83), Lawrence(16)
CUBA Clinton
CUMBERLAND (43732) Guernsey(74), Noble(16), Muskingum(6), Morgan(1)
CURTICE (43412) Lucas(56), Ottawa(43)
CUSTAR (43511) Wood(72), Henry(27)
CUTLER (45724) Washington(98), Athens(1)
CUYAHOGA FALLS Summit
CYGNET Wood
CYNTHIANA Pike
DALTON (44618) Wayne(92), Stark(7)
DAMASCUS Mahoning
DANVILLE Knox
DAYTON (45434) Greene(98), Montgomery(1)
DAYTON (45440) Montgomery(62), Greene(37)
DAYTON (45458) Montgomery(92), Warren(5), Greene(1)
DAYTON (45459) Montgomery(98), Greene(1)
DAYTON Greene
DAYTON Montgomery
DE GRAFF (43318) Logan(79), Champaign(20)
DECATUR Brown
DEERFIELD Portage
DEERSVILLE Harrison
DEFIANCE (43512) Defiance(95), Paulding(3)
DELLROY Carroll
DELPHOS (45833) Allen(56), Van Wert(40), Putnam(3)
DELTA Fulton
DENNISON (44621) Tuscarawas(90), Harrison(8), Carroll(1)
DERBY Pickaway
DERWENT Guernsey
DESHLER (43516) Henry(81), Wood(12), Putnam(4), Hancock(1)

DEXTER CITY Noble
DIAMOND (44412) Portage(80), Mahoning(19)
DILLONVALE (43917) Jefferson(68), Belmont(31)
DOLA Hardin
DONNELSVILLE Clark
DORSET Ashtabula
DOVER Tuscarawas
DOYLESTOWN (44230) Wayne(97), Medina(2)
DRESDEN (43821) Muskingum(86), Coshocton(13)
DUBLIN (43017) Franklin(87), Delaware(11)
DUNBRIDGE Wood
DUNCAN FALLS Muskingum
DUNDEE (44624) Tuscarawas(60), Holmes(27), Wayne(11)
DUNKIRK Hardin
DUPONT Putnam
EAST CLARIDON Geauga
EAST FULTONHAM Muskingum
EAST LIBERTY (43319) Logan(96), Union(3)
EAST LIVERPOOL Columbiana
EAST PALESTINE Columbiana
EAST ROCHESTER (44625) Columbiana(81), Carroll(18)
EAST SPARTA (44626) Stark(94), Tuscarawas(5)
EAST SPRINGFIELD Jefferson
EASTLAKE Lake
EATON Preble
EDGERTON (43517) Williams(78), Defiance(21)
EDISON Morrow
EDON Williams
ELDORADO Preble
ELGIN Van Wert
ELKTON Columbiana
ELLSWORTH Mahoning
ELMORE (43416) Ottawa(93), Sandusky(6)
ELYRIA Lorain
EMPIRE Jefferson
ENGLEWOOD (45322) Montgomery(97), Miami(2)
ENON Clark
ETNA Licking
EUCLID Cuyahoga
EVANSPORT Defiance
FAIRBORN (45324) Greene(96), Clark(3)
FAIRFIELD Butler
FAIRLAWN Summit
FAIRPOINT Belmont
FAIRVIEW Guernsey
FARMDALE Trumbull
FARMER Defiance
FARMERSVILLE (45325) Montgomery(96), Preble(3)
FAYETTE (43521) Fulton(97), Williams(2)
FAYETTEVILLE (45118) Brown(94), Highland(2), Clermont(2)
FEESBURG Brown
FELICITY (45120) Clermont(73), Brown(26)
FINDLAY Hancock
FLAT ROCK Seneca
FLEMING Washington
FLETCHER Miami
FLUSHING (43977) Belmont(80), Harrison(19)
FOREST (45843) Hardin(61), Wyandot(19), Hancock(18)
FORT JENNINGS (45844) Putnam(90), Allen(4), Van Wert(4)
FORT LORAMIE (45845) Shelby(95), Auglaize(3)
FORT RECOVERY (45846) Mercer(84), Darke(15)
FORT SENECA Seneca
FOSTORIA (44830) Seneca(65), Hancock(17), Wood(16)
FOWLER Trumbull

FRANKFORT Ross
FRANKLIN Warren
FRANKLIN FURNACE (45629) Scioto(93), Lawrence(6)
FRAZEYSBURG (43822) Muskingum(61), Licking(19), Coshocton(12), Knox(6)
FREDERICKSBURG (44627) Wayne(68), Holmes(31)
FREDERICKTOWN (43019) Knox(84), Morrow(14)
FREEPORT (43973) Guernsey(52), Harrison(46)
FREMONT Sandusky
FRESNO (43824) Coshocton(91), Tuscarawas(8)
FRIENDSHIP Scioto
FULTON Morrow
FULTONHAM Muskingum
GALENA Delaware
GALION (44833) Crawford(85), Morrow(9), Richland(3), Marion(1)
GALLIPOLIS Gallia
GALLOWAY (43119) Franklin(95), Madison(4)
GAMBIER Knox
GARRETTSVILLE (44231) Portage(88), Geauga(10)
GATES MILLS (44040) Cuyahoga(98), Geauga(1)
GENEVA (44041) Ashtabula(98), Lake(1)
GENOA (43430) Ottawa(94), Wood(3), Sandusky(1)
GEORGETOWN (45121) Brown(98), Clermont(1)
GERMANTOWN (45327) Montgomery(97), Preble(1)
GETTYSBURG Darke
GIBSONBURG (43431) Sandusky(98), Wood(1)
GIRARD Trumbull
GLANDORF Putnam
GLENCOE Belmont
GLENFORD (43739) Perry(64), Licking(35)
GLENMONT (44628) Holmes(61), Knox(38)
GLOUSTER (45732) Athens(92), Perry(5), Hocking(2)
GNADENHUTTEN Tuscarawas
GOMER Allen
GORDON Darke
GOSHEN (45122) Clermont(91), Warren(8)
GRAFTON Lorain
GRAND RAPIDS (43522) Wood(48), Lucas(45), Henry(6)
GRAND RIVER Lake
GRANVILLE Licking
GRATIOT Licking
GRATIS Preble
GRAYSVILLE (45734) Monroe(78), Washington(21)
GRAYTOWN Ottawa
GREEN Summit
GREEN CAMP Marion
GREEN SPRINGS (44836) Seneca(65), Sandusky(34)
GREENFIELD (45123) Highland(55), Ross(25), Fayette(18)
GREENFIELD Highland
GREENFORD Mahoning
GREENTOWN Stark
GREENVILLE Darke
GREENWICH (44837) Huron(75), Richland(12), Ashland(12)
GRELTON Henry
GROVE CITY Franklin
GROVEPORT (43125) Franklin(98), Pickaway(1)
GROVEPORT Franklin
GROVER HILL (45849) Paulding(63), Van Wert(34), Putnam(1)
GUYSVILLE (45735) Athens(94), Meigs(5)
GYPSUM Ottawa
HALLSVILLE Ross

HAMDEN Vinton
HAMERSVILLE (45130) Brown(89), Clermont(10)
HAMILTON Butler
HAMLER Henry
HAMMONDSVILLE (43930) Jefferson(83), Columbiana(16)
HANNIBAL Monroe
HANOVERTON Columbiana
HARBOR VIEW Lucas
HARLEM SPRINGS Carroll
HARPSTER (43323) Wyandot(93), Marion(6)
HARRISBURG Franklin
HARRISON Hamilton
HARRISVILLE Harrison
HARROD (45850) Allen(81), Hardin(12), Auglaize(6)
HARTFORD Trumbull
HARTVILLE (44632) Stark(95), Portage(4)
HARVEYSBURG Warren
HASKINS Wood
HAVERHILL Scioto
HAVILAND Paulding
HAYDENVILLE Hocking
HAYESVILLE Ashland
HEBRON Licking
HELENA Sandusky
HICKSVILLE (43526) Defiance(96), Paulding(3)
HIGGINSPORT Brown
HIGHLAND Highland
HILLIARD Franklin
HILLSBORO (45133) Highland(97), Pike(2)
HINCKLEY Medina
HIRAM (44234) Portage(55), Geauga(44)
HOCKINGPORT Athens
HOLGATE (43527) Henry(89), Defiance(10)
HOLLAND Lucas
HOLLANSBURG Darke
HOLLOWAY Belmont
HOLMESVILLE Holmes
HOMER Licking
HOMERVILLE Medina
HOMEWORTH (44634) Columbiana(80), Stark(19)
HOOVEN Hamilton
HOPEDALE (43976) Harrison(98), Jefferson(1)
HOPEWELL (43746) Muskingum(90), Licking(10)
HOUSTON Shelby
HOWARD Knox
HOYTVILLE Wood
HUBBARD Trumbull
HUDSON (44236) Summit(98), Portage(1)
HUDSON Summit
HUNTSBURG (44046) Geauga(98), Ashtabula(1)
HUNTSVILLE Logan
HURON Erie
IBERIA Morrow
INDEPENDENCE Cuyahoga
IRONDALE (43932) Jefferson(92), Columbiana(7)
IRONTON (45638) Lawrence(94), Scioto(5)
IRWIN (43029) Union(75), Madison(24)
ISLE SAINT GEORGE Ottawa
JACKSON Monroe
JACKSON CENTER (45334) Shelby(88), Auglaize(7), Logan(3)
JACKSONTOWN Licking
JACKSONVILLE Athens
JACOBSBURG Belmont
JAMESTOWN (45335) Greene(95), Clinton(2), Fayette(1)
JASPER Pike
JEFFERSON Ashtabula
JEFFERSONVILLE Fayette
JENERA (45841) Hancock(94), Hardin(5)
JEROMESVILLE (44840) Ashland(98), Wayne(1)

JERRY CITY Wood
JERUSALEM (43747) Monroe(64), Belmont(35)
JEWELL Defiance
JEWETT (43986) Harrison(91), Carroll(8)
JOHNSTOWN (43031) Licking(97), Delaware(2)
JUNCTION CITY Perry
KALIDA Putnam
KANSAS (44841) Seneca(69), Sandusky(30)
KEENE Coshocton
KELLEYS ISLAND Erie
KENSINGTON (44427) Columbiana(57), Carroll(42)
KENT (44240) Portage(98), Summit(1)
KENT Portage
KENTON Hardin
KERR Gallia
KETTLERSVILLE Shelby
KIDRON Wayne
KILBOURNE Delaware
KILLBUCK (44637) Holmes(83), Coshocton(16)
KIMBOLTON (43749) Guernsey(92), Coshocton(4), Tuscarawas(2)
KINGS MILLS Warren
KINGSTON (45644) Ross(64), Pickaway(35)
KINGSVILLE Ashtabula
KINSMAN (44428) Trumbull(96), Ashtabula(3)
KIPLING Guernsey
KIPTON Lorain
KIRBY Wyandot
KIRKERSVILLE Licking
KITTS HILL Lawrence
KUNKLE Williams
LA RUE (43332) Marion(90), Hardin(7), Wyandot(1)
LACARNE Ottawa
LAFAYETTE Allen
LAFFERTY Belmont
LAGRANGE Lorain
LAINGS Monroe
LAKE MILTON (44429) Mahoning(98), Portage(1)
LAKEMORE Summit
LAKESIDE MARBLEHEAD Ottawa
LAKEVIEW (43331) Logan(94), Auglaize(4), Hardin(1)
LAKEVILLE (44638) Holmes(79), Ashland(14), Wayne(7)
LAKEWOOD Cuyahoga
LANCASTER Fairfield
LANGSVILLE Meigs
LANSING Belmont
LATHAM Pike
LATTY Paulding
LAURA (45337) Miami(86), Darke(13)
LAURELVILLE (43135) Hocking(75), Ross(12), Pickaway(11)
LEAVITTSBURG Trumbull
LEBANON Warren
LEES CREEK Clinton
LEESBURG (45135) Highland(77), Fayette(15), Clinton(6)
LEESVILLE Carroll
LEETONIA Columbiana
LEIPSIC (45856) Putnam(97), Henry(2)
LEMOYNE Wood
LEWIS CENTER Delaware
LEWISBURG Preble
LEWISTOWN Logan
LEWISVILLE Monroe
LIBERTY CENTER (43532) Henry(89), Fulton(7), Lucas(3)
LIMA (45806) Allen(94), Auglaize(5)
LIMA Allen
LIMAVILLE Stark
LINDSEY (43442) Sandusky(96), Ottawa(3)
LISBON Columbiana

LITCHFIELD (44253) Medina(82), Lorain(17)
LITHOPOLIS Fairfield
LITTLE HOCKING (45742) Washington(91), Athens(8)
LOCKBOURNE (43137) Franklin(51), Pickaway(48)
LODI Medina
LOGAN (43138) Hocking(98), Perry(1)
LONDON Madison
LONDONDERRY Ross
LONG BOTTOM Meigs
LORAIN Lorain
LORE CITY Guernsey
LOUDONVILLE (44842) Ashland(89), Holmes(9)
LOUISVILLE Stark
LOVELAND (45140) Clermont(40), Hamilton(30), Warren(29)
LOWELL (45744) Morgan(54), Washington(40), Noble(5)
LOWELLVILLE Mahoning
LOWER SALEM (45745) Noble(73), Monroe(14), Washington(12)
LUCAS (44843) Richland(97), Ashland(2)
LUCASVILLE (45648) Scioto(70), Pike(29)
LUCASVILLE Scioto
LUCKEY (43443) Wood(98), Sandusky(1)
LUDLOW FALLS Miami
LYNCHBURG (45142) Highland(90), Clinton(9)
LYNX Adams
LYONS Fulton
MACEDONIA Summit
MACKSBURG (45746) Noble(80), Washington(19)
MADISON Lake
MAGNETIC SPRINGS Union
MAGNOLIA (44643) Stark(42), Tuscarawas(36), Carroll(20)
MAINEVILLE (45039) Warren(98), Hamilton(1)
MALAGA Monroe
MALINTA Henry
MALTA Morgan
MALVERN Carroll
MANCHESTER Adams
MANSFIELD (44904) Richland(89), Morrow(10)
MANSFIELD Richland
MANTUA (44255) Portage(86), Geauga(13)
MAPLE HEIGHTS Cuyahoga
MAPLEWOOD Shelby
MARATHON Clermont
MARENGO (43334) Morrow(94), Delaware(5)
MARIA STEIN (45860) Mercer(98), Darke(1)
MARIETTA Washington
MARK CENTER Defiance
MARSHALLVILLE (44645) Wayne(97), Stark(2)
MARTEL Marion
MARTIN (43445) Ottawa(69), Lucas(30)
MARTINS FERRY Belmont
MARTINSBURG Knox
MARTINSVILLE Clinton
MARYSVILLE Union
MASON Warren
MASSILLON Stark
MASURY Trumbull
MAXIMO Stark
MAYNARD Belmont
MC ARTHUR Vinton
MC CLURE (43534) Henry(97), Wood(2)
MC COMB (45858) Hancock(97), Putnam(2)
MC CONNELSVILLE Morgan
MC CUTCHENVILLE (44844) Wyandot(65), Seneca(34)
MC DERMOTT Scioto

MC DONALD (44437) Trumbull(97), Mahoning(2)
MC GUFFEY Hardin
MECHANICSBURG (43044) Champaign(81), Clark(12), Madison(5)
MECHANICSTOWN Carroll
MEDINA Medina
MEDWAY Clark
MELMORE Seneca
MELROSE Paulding
MENDON (45862) Mercer(92), Auglaize(7)
MENTOR Lake
MESOPOTAMIA Trumbull
METAMORA Fulton
MIAMISBURG Montgomery
MIAMITOWN Hamilton
MIAMIVILLE Clermont
MIDDLE BASS Ottawa
MIDDLE POINT Van Wert
MIDDLEBRANCH Stark
MIDDLEBURG Logan
MIDDLEFIELD (44062) Geauga(80), Trumbull(16), Ashtabula(2)
MIDDLEPORT Meigs
MIDDLETOWN Butler
MIDLAND (45148) Clinton(93), Brown(6)
MIDVALE Tuscarawas
MILAN (44846) Erie(92), Huron(7)
MILFORD Clermont
MILFORD CENTER (43045) Union(95), Champaign(4)
MILLBURY (43447) Wood(80), Ottawa(19)
MILLEDGEVILLE Fayette
MILLER CITY Putnam
MILLERSBURG (44654) Holmes(97), Coshocton(2)
MILLERSPORT (43046) Fairfield(91), Licking(8)
MILLFIELD Athens
MILTON CENTER Wood
MINERAL CITY (44656) Tuscarawas(96), Carroll(3)
MINERAL RIDGE (44440) Trumbull(83), Mahoning(16)
MINERVA (44657) Stark(50), Carroll(34), Columbiana(14)
MINFORD Scioto
MINGO Champaign
MINGO JUNCTION Jefferson
MINSTER (45865) Auglaize(78), Shelby(20)
MOGADORE (44260) Portage(70), Summit(24), Stark(5)
MONCLOVA Lucas
MONROE Butler
MONROEVILLE (44847) Huron(70), Erie(29)
MONTEZUMA Mercer
MONTPELIER Williams
MONTVILLE (44064) Geauga(97), Ashtabula(2)
MORRAL (43337) Marion(83), Wyandot(16)
MORRISTOWN Belmont
MORROW Warren
MOSCOW Clermont
MOUNT BLANCHARD (45867) Hancock(94), Wyandot(5)
MOUNT CORY (45868) Hancock(96), Putnam(3)
MOUNT EATON Wayne
MOUNT GILEAD Morrow
MOUNT HOPE Holmes
MOUNT LIBERTY Knox
MOUNT ORAB Brown
MOUNT PERRY (43760) Perry(66), Muskingum(29), Licking(3)
MOUNT PLEASANT Jefferson
MOUNT SAINT JOSEPH Hamilton
MOUNT STERLING (43143) Madison(75), Pickaway(16), Fayette(7)
MOUNT VERNON Knox
MOUNT VICTORY (43340) Hardin(89), Union(10)

MOWRYSTOWN Highland
MOXAHALA Perry
MUNROE FALLS Summit
MURRAY CITY Hocking
NANKIN Ashland
NAPOLEON (43545) Henry(98), Defiance(1)
NASHPORT (43830) Muskingum(88), Licking(11)
NASHVILLE Holmes
NAVARRE (44662) Stark(97), Wayne(2)
NEAPOLIS Lucas
NEFFS Belmont
NEGLEY Columbiana
NELSONVILLE (45764) Athens(88), Hocking(11)
NEVADA (44849) Wyandot(87), Crawford(12)
NEVILLE Clermont
NEW ALBANY Franklin
NEW ATHENS Harrison
NEW BAVARIA (43548) Henry(94), Defiance(2), Putnam(2)
NEW BLOOMINGTON Marion
NEW BREMEN (45869) Auglaize(91), Shelby(4), Mercer(4)
NEW CARLISLE (45344) Clark(82), Miami(14), Montgomery(2)
NEW CONCORD (43762) Muskingum(82), Guernsey(17)
NEW HAMPSHIRE Auglaize
NEW HAVEN Huron
NEW HOLLAND (43145) Pickaway(66), Fayette(33)
NEW KNOXVILLE (45871) Auglaize(77), Shelby(22)
NEW LEBANON Montgomery
NEW LEXINGTON Perry
NEW LONDON (44851) Huron(82), Lorain(12), Ashland(4)
NEW MADISON Darke
NEW MARSHFIELD (45766) Athens(89), Vinton(10)
NEW MATAMORAS (45767) Monroe(66), Washington(33)
NEW MIDDLETOWN Mahoning
NEW PARIS (45347) Preble(93), Darke(6)
NEW PHILADELPHIA Tuscarawas
NEW PLYMOUTH (45654) Vinton(72), Hocking(27)
NEW RICHMOND Clermont
NEW RIEGEL Seneca
NEW RUMLEY Harrison
NEW SPRINGFIELD (44443) Mahoning(95), Columbiana(4)
NEW STRAITSVILLE (43766) Perry(84), Hocking(15)
NEW VIENNA (45159) Clinton(95), Highland(4)
NEW WASHINGTON (44854) Crawford(95), Seneca(4)
NEW WATERFORD Columbiana
NEW WESTON (45348) Darke(98), Mercer(1)
NEWARK Licking
NEWBURY Geauga
NEWCOMERSTOWN (43832) Tuscarawas(84), Coshocton(13), Guernsey(2)
NEWTON FALLS (44444) Trumbull(94), Portage(4), Mahoning(1)
NEWTONSVILLE Clermont
NEY Defiance
NILES Trumbull
NORTH BALTIMORE (45872) Wood(98), Hancock(1)
NORTH BEND Hamilton
NORTH BENTON (44449) Portage(52), Mahoning(47)
NORTH BLOOMFIELD Trumbull
NORTH FAIRFIELD Huron
NORTH GEORGETOWN Columbiana
NORTH HAMPTON Clark

NORTH JACKSON Mahoning
NORTH KINGSVILLE Ashtabula
NORTH LAWRENCE (44666) Stark(80),
   Wayne(19)
NORTH LEWISBURG (43060) Union(51),
   Champaign(34), Logan(14)
NORTH LIMA Mahoning
NORTH OLMSTED Cuyahoga
NORTH RIDGEVILLE Lorain
NORTH ROBINSON Crawford
NORTH ROYALTON Cuyahoga
NORTH STAR Darke
NORTHFIELD Summit
NORTHWOOD Wood
NORWALK (44857) Huron(98), Erie(1)
NORWICH Muskingum
NOVA (44859) Ashland(92), Lorain(7)
NOVELTY Geauga
OAK HARBOR (43449) Ottawa(97),
   Sandusky(2)
OAK HILL (45656) Jackson(87), Gallia(7),
   Lawrence(4)
OAKWOOD Paulding
OBERLIN Lorain
OCEOLA Crawford
OHIO CITY Van Wert
OKEANA Butler
OKOLONA Henry
OLD FORT Seneca
OLD WASHINGTON Guernsey
OLMSTED FALLS Cuyahoga
ONTARIO Richland
ORANGEVILLE Trumbull
OREGON Lucas
OREGONIA Warren
ORIENT (43146) Pickaway(76),
   Franklin(21), Madison(1)
ORRVILLE Wayne
ORWELL (44076) Ashtabula(91),
   Trumbull(8)
OSGOOD Darke
OSTRANDER (43061) Delaware(82),
   Union(17)
OTTAWA Putnam
OTTOVILLE Putnam
OTWAY (45657) Scioto(80), Adams(17),
   Pike(2)
OVERPECK Butler
OWENSVILLE Clermont
OXFORD Butler
PAINESVILLE Lake
PALESTINE Darke
PANDORA (45877) Putnam(93), Allen(4),
   Hancock(1)
PARIS Stark
PARKMAN Geauga
PATASKALA Licking
PATRIOT Gallia
PAULDING Paulding
PAYNE Paulding
PEDRO Lawrence
PEEBLES (45660) Adams(87), Pike(10),
   Highland(2)
PEMBERTON Shelby
PEMBERVILLE Wood
PENINSULA Summit
PERRY Lake
PERRYSBURG Wood
PERRYSVILLE (44864) Ashland(61),
   Richland(38)
PETERSBURG (44454) Mahoning(84),
   Columbiana(15)
PETTISVILLE Fulton
PHILLIPSBURG Montgomery
PHILO Muskingum
PICKERINGTON Fairfield
PIEDMONT (43983) Belmont(57),
   Guernsey(29), Harrison(14)
PIERPONT Ashtabula
PIKETON Pike
PINEY FORK Jefferson
PIONEER Williams
PIQUA (45356) Miami(96), Shelby(3)

PITSBURG Darke
PLAIN CITY (43064) Madison(52),
   Union(45), Franklin(1)
PLAINFIELD Coshocton
PLEASANT CITY (43772) Guernsey(58),
   Noble(41)
PLEASANT HILL Miami
PLEASANT PLAIN (45162) Warren(97),
   Clermont(2)
PLEASANTVILLE (43148) Fairfield(90),
   Perry(9)
PLYMOUTH (44865) Richland(49),
   Huron(45), Crawford(4)
POLK Ashland
POMEROY Meigs
PORT CLINTON Ottawa
PORT JEFFERSON Shelby
PORT WASHINGTON (43837)
   Tuscarawas(96), Guernsey(3)
PORT WILLIAM Clinton
PORTAGE Wood
PORTLAND Meigs
PORTSMOUTH Scioto
POTSDAM Miami
POWELL (43065) Delaware(85),
   Franklin(14)
POWHATAN POINT (43942) Belmont(92),
   Monroe(7)
PROCTORVILLE Lawrence
PROSPECT (43342) Marion(91),
   Delaware(6), Union(2)
PUT IN BAY Ottawa
QUAKER CITY (43773) Guernsey(54),
   Noble(39), Belmont(2), Monroe(2)
QUINCY (43343) Logan(89),
   Champaign(6), Shelby(3)
RACINE Meigs
RADCLIFF Vinton
RADNOR Delaware
RANDOLPH Portage
RARDEN (45671) Scioto(66), Pike(20),
   Adams(8), Fairfield(4)
RAVENNA Portage
RAWSON Hancock
RAY (45672) Vinton(68), Jackson(26),
   Ross(4)
RAYLAND (43943) Jefferson(96),
   Belmont(3)
RAYMOND Union
REEDSVILLE Meigs
REESVILLE Clinton
RENO Washington
REPUBLIC Seneca
REYNOLDSBURG (43068) Franklin(74),
   Licking(18), Fairfield(7)
REYNOLDSBURG Franklin
RICHFIELD Summit
RICHMOND Jefferson
RICHMOND DALE Ross
RICHWOOD (43344) Union(96),
   Delaware(2)
RIDGEVILLE CORNERS Henry
RIDGEWAY (43345) Hardin(61), Logan(38)
RIO GRANDE Gallia
RIPLEY Brown
RISINGSUN (43457) Wood(69),
   Sandusky(26), Seneca(4)
RITTMAN (44270) Wayne(94), Medina(5)
ROBERTSVILLE Stark
ROCK CAMP Lawrence
ROCK CREEK Ashtabula
ROCKBRIDGE Hocking
ROCKFORD (45882) Mercer(94), Van
   Wert(5)
ROCKY RIDGE Ottawa
ROCKY RIVER Cuyahoga
ROGERS Columbiana
ROME Ashtabula
ROOTSTOWN Portage
ROSEVILLE (43777) Muskingum(55),
   Perry(44)
ROSEWOOD Champaign
ROSS Butler

ROSSBURG Darke
ROSSFORD Wood
ROUNDHEAD Hardin
RUDOLPH Wood
RUSHSYLVANIA (43347) Logan(89),
   Hardin(10)
RUSHVILLE (43150) Fairfield(67),
   Perry(32)
RUSSELLS POINT Logan
RUSSELLVILLE Brown
RUSSIA Shelby
RUTLAND Meigs
SABINA (45169) Clinton(98), Fayette(1)
SAINT CLAIRSVILLE Belmont
SAINT HENRY Mercer
SAINT JOHNS Auglaize
SAINT LOUISVILLE Licking
SAINT MARYS Auglaize
SAINT PARIS Champaign
SALEM (44460) Columbiana(88),
   Mahoning(11)
SALESVILLE (43778) Guernsey(97),
   Noble(2)
SALINEVILLE (43945) Columbiana(71),
   Carroll(19), Jefferson(9)
SANDUSKY Erie
SANDYVILLE Tuscarawas
SARAHSVILLE Noble
SARDINIA Brown
SARDIS Monroe
SAVANNAH Ashland
SCIO (43988) Harrison(71), Carroll(28)
SCIOTO FURNACE Scioto
SCOTT (45886) Van Wert(55),
   Paulding(45)
SCOTTOWN (45678) Lawrence(80),
   Gallia(19)
SEAMAN (45679) Adams(92), Highland(7)
SEBRING Mahoning
SEDALIA Madison
SENECAVILLE (43780) Guernsey(69),
   Noble(30)
SEVEN MILE Butler
SEVILLE Medina
SHADE (45776) Meigs(52), Athens(47)
SHADYSIDE Belmont
SHANDON Butler
SHARON CENTER Medina
SHARPSBURG Athens
SHAUCK Morrow
SHAWNEE Perry
SHEFFIELD LAKE Lorain
SHELBY (44875) Richland(97),
   Crawford(2)
SHERRODSVILLE (44675) Carroll(70),
   Tuscarawas(29)
SHERWOOD Defiance
SHILOH (44878) Richland(90), Huron(6),
   Ashland(3)
SHORT CREEK Harrison
SHREVE (44676) Wayne(82), Holmes(17)
SIDNEY Shelby
SINKING SPRING Highland
SMITHFIELD Jefferson
SMITHVILLE Wayne
SOLON Cuyahoga
SOMERDALE Tuscarawas
SOMERSET Perry
SOMERVILLE Butler
SOUTH BLOOMINGVILLE (43152)
   Hocking(81), Vinton(18)
SOUTH CHARLESTON (45368) Clark(97),
   Greene(2)
SOUTH LEBANON Warren
SOUTH POINT Lawrence
SOUTH SALEM Ross
SOUTH SOLON (43153) Madison(76),
   Fayette(10), Clark(7), Greene(4)
SOUTH VIENNA Clark
SOUTH WEBSTER (45682) Scioto(96),
   Jackson(2)
SOUTHINGTON (44470) Trumbull(98),
   Portage(1)

SPARTA Morrow
SPENCER (44275) Medina(93), Lorain(6)
SPENCERVILLE (45887) Allen(75),
   Auglaize(14), Van Wert(7), Mercer(2)
SPRING HILL NURSERIES Miami
SPRING VALLEY Greene
SPRINGBORO Warren
SPRINGFIELD (45502) Clark(97),
   Champaign(2)
SPRINGFIELD Clark
STAFFORD Monroe
STERLING Wayne
STEUBENVILLE Jefferson
STEWART Athens
STEWARTSVILLE Belmont
STILLWATER Tuscarawas
STOCKDALE Pike
STOCKPORT (43787) Morgan(92),
   Washington(7)
STOCKPORT Morgan
STONE CREEK (43840) Coshocton(70),
   Tuscarawas(29)
STONY RIDGE Wood
STOUT (45684) Scioto(67), Adams(32)
STOUTSVILLE (43154) Fairfield(78),
   Pickaway(21)
STOW Summit
STRASBURG Tuscarawas
STRATTON Jefferson
STREETSBORO Portage
STRONGSVILLE Cuyahoga
STRUTHERS Mahoning
STRYKER (43557) Williams(81),
   Henry(12), Fulton(5)
SUGAR GROVE (43155) Fairfield(74),
   Hocking(25)
SUGARCREEK (44681) Tuscarawas(77),
   Holmes(22)
SULLIVAN (44880) Ashland(81),
   Lorain(15), Medina(2)
SULPHUR SPRINGS Crawford
SUMMERFIELD (43788) Noble(76),
   Monroe(23)
SUMMIT STATION Licking
SUMMITVILLE Columbiana
SUNBURY (43074) Delaware(98),
   Licking(1)
SWANTON (43558) Fulton(57), Lucas(42)
SYCAMORE (44882) Wyandot(65),
   Crawford(29), Seneca(5)
SYCAMORE VALLEY Monroe
SYLVANIA Lucas
SYRACUSE Meigs
TALLMADGE (44278) Summit(97),
   Portage(2)
TARLTON Pickaway
TERRACE PARK Hamilton
THE PLAINS Athens
THOMPSON (44086) Geauga(79),
   Lake(15), Ashtabula(5)
THORNVILLE (43076) Perry(45),
   Licking(30), Fairfield(23)
THURMAN (45685) Gallia(72), Jackson(27)
THURSTON Fairfield
TIFFIN Seneca
TILTONSVILLE Jefferson
TIPP CITY (45371) Miami(98),
   Montgomery(1)
TIPPECANOE (44699) Harrison(72),
   Tuscarawas(24), Guernsey(2)
TIRO Crawford
TOLEDO (43605) Lucas(97), Wood(2)
TOLEDO Lucas
TOLEDO Wood
TONTOGANY Wood
TORCH Athens
TORONTO Jefferson
TREMONT CITY Clark
TRENTON Butler
TRIMBLE Athens
TRINWAY Muskingum
TROY Miami
TUPPERS PLAINS Meigs

TUSCARAWAS Tuscarawas
TWINSBURG Summit
UHRICHSVILLE (44683) Tuscarawas(91), Harrison(8)
UNION CITY Darke
UNION FURNACE Hocking
UNIONPORT Jefferson
UNIONTOWN (44685) Stark(51), Summit(48)
UNIONVILLE Ashtabula
UNIONVILLE CENTER Union
UNIOPOLIS Auglaize
UPPER SANDUSKY Wyandot
UTICA (43080) Licking(70), Knox(29)
VALLEY CITY (44280) Medina(95), Lorain(4)
VAN BUREN Hancock
VAN WERT Van Wert
VANDALIA Montgomery
VANLUE Hancock
VAUGHNSVILLE Putnam
VENEDOCIA (45894) Van Wert(96), Mercer(2)
VERMILION (44089) Erie(56), Lorain(43)
VERONA Preble
VERSAILLES Darke
VICKERY (43464) Sandusky(76), Erie(23)
VIENNA Trumbull
VINCENT Washington
VINTON Gallia
WADSWORTH Medina
WAKEFIELD Pike
WAKEMAN (44889) Huron(58), Erie(31), Lorain(10)
WALBRIDGE Wood
WALDO (43356) Marion(77), Delaware(14), Morrow(7)
WALHONDING (43843) Coshocton(65), Knox(34)

WALNUT CREEK Holmes
WAPAKONETA (45895) Auglaize(98), Logan(1)
WARNOCK Belmont
WARREN (44481) Trumbull(98), Mahoning(1)
WARREN Trumbull
WARSAW (43844) Coshocton(95), Knox(4)
WASHINGTON COURT HOUSE (43160) Fayette(98), Ross(1)
WASHINGTONVILLE Columbiana
WATERFORD (45786) Washington(93), Morgan(6)
WATERLOO (45688) Lawrence(93), Gallia(6)
WATERTOWN Washington
WATERVILLE Lucas
WAUSEON Fulton
WAVERLY (45690) Pike(92), Ross(7)
WAYLAND Portage
WAYNE Wood
WAYNESBURG (44688) Stark(88), Carroll(11)
WAYNESFIELD (45896) Auglaize(77), Hardin(11), Allen(10)
WAYNESVILLE Warren
WELLINGTON Lorain
WELLSTON Jackson
WELLSVILLE Columbiana
WEST ALEXANDRIA (45381) Preble(93), Montgomery(6)
WEST CHESTER Butler
WEST ELKTON Preble
WEST FARMINGTON (44491) Trumbull(82), Geauga(14), Portage(2)
WEST JEFFERSON Madison
WEST LAFAYETTE Coshocton
WEST LIBERTY (43357) Logan(75), Champaign(24)

WEST MANCHESTER (45382) Preble(77), Darke(22)
WEST MANSFIELD (43358) Logan(57), Union(42)
WEST MILLGROVE Wood
WEST MILTON Miami
WEST POINT Columbiana
WEST PORTSMOUTH Scioto
WEST RUSHVILLE Fairfield
WEST SALEM (44287) Wayne(63), Ashland(29), Medina(6)
WEST UNION Adams
WEST UNITY (43570) Williams(94), Fulton(5)
WESTERVILLE Delaware
WESTERVILLE Franklin
WESTFIELD CENTER Medina
WESTLAKE Cuyahoga
WESTON Wood
WESTVILLE Champaign
WHARTON Wyandot
WHEELERSBURG Scioto
WHIPPLE Washington
WHITE COTTAGE Muskingum
WHITEHOUSE Lucas
WICKLIFFE Lake
WILBERFORCE Greene
WILKESVILLE Vinton
WILLARD Huron
WILLIAMSBURG Clermont
WILLIAMSFIELD Ashtabula
WILLIAMSPORT (43164) Pickaway(95), Ross(4)
WILLIAMSTOWN Hancock
WILLISTON Ottawa
WILLOUGHBY Lake
WILLOW WOOD Lawrence
WILLSHIRE (45898) Van Wert(70), Mercer(29)

WILMINGTON Clinton
WILMOT (44689) Holmes(70), Stark(29)
WINCHESTER (45697) Adams(62), Brown(25), Highland(12)
WINDHAM (44288) Portage(98), Trumbull(1)
WINDSOR (44099) Ashtabula(87), Geauga(12)
WINESBURG Holmes
WINGETT RUN (45789) Washington(96), Monroe(3)
WINONA Columbiana
WINTERSVILLE Jefferson
WOLF RUN Jefferson
WOODSFIELD Monroe
WOODSTOCK (43084) Champaign(91), Union(8)
WOODVILLE (43469) Sandusky(93), Ottawa(5), Wood(1)
WOOSTER Wayne
WREN Van Wert
XENIA Greene
YELLOW SPRINGS (45387) Greene(92), Clark(7)
YORKSHIRE (45388) Darke(95), Mercer(2), Shelby(2)
YORKVILLE (43971) Jefferson(65), Belmont(34)
YOUNGSTOWN (44505) Mahoning(65), Trumbull(34)
YOUNGSTOWN Mahoning
ZALESKI Vinton
ZANESFIELD Logan
ZANESVILLE Muskingum
ZOAR Tuscarawas

Ohio ZIP/City Cross Reference

43001-43001	ALEXANDRIA
43002-43002	AMLIN
43003-43003	ASHLEY
43004-43004	BLACKLICK
43005-43005	BLADENSBURG
43006-43006	BRINKHAVEN
43007-43007	BROADWAY
43008-43008	BUCKEYE LAKE
43009-43009	CABLE
43010-43010	CATAWBA
43011-43011	CENTERBURG
43013-43013	CROTON
43014-43014	DANVILLE
43015-43015	DELAWARE
43016-43017	DUBLIN
43018-43018	ETNA
43019-43019	FREDERICKTOWN
43021-43021	GALENA
43022-43022	GAMBIER
43023-43023	GRANVILLE
43025-43025	HEBRON
43026-43026	HILLIARD
43027-43027	HOMER
43028-43028	HOWARD
43029-43029	IRWIN
43030-43030	JACKSONTOWN
43031-43031	JOHNSTOWN
43032-43032	KILBOURNE
43033-43033	KIRKERSVILLE
43035-43035	LEWIS CENTER
43036-43036	MAGNETIC SPRINGS
43037-43037	MARTINSBURG
43040-43041	MARYSVILLE
43044-43044	MECHANICSBURG
43045-43045	MILFORD CENTER
43046-43046	MILLERSPORT
43047-43047	MINGO
43048-43048	MOUNT LIBERTY
43050-43050	MOUNT VERNON
43054-43054	NEW ALBANY

ZIP Range	City
43055-43058	NEWARK
43060-43060	NORTH LEWISBURG
43061-43061	OSTRANDER
43062-43062	PATASKALA
43064-43064	PLAIN CITY
43065-43065	POWELL
43066-43066	RADNOR
43067-43067	RAYMOND
43068-43069	REYNOLDSBURG
43070-43070	ROSEWOOD
43071-43071	SAINT LOUISVILLE
43072-43072	SAINT PARIS
43073-43073	SUMMIT STATION
43074-43074	SUNBURY
43076-43076	THORNVILLE
43077-43077	UNIONVILLE CENTER
43078-43078	URBANA
43080-43080	UTICA
43081-43082	WESTERVILLE
43083-43083	WESTVILLE
43084-43084	WOODSTOCK
43085-43085	COLUMBUS
43086-43086	WESTERVILLE
43093-43093	NEWARK
43098-43098	HEBRON
43099-43099	BLACKLICK
43101-43101	ADELPHI
43102-43102	AMANDA
43103-43103	ASHVILLE
43105-43105	BALTIMORE
43106-43106	BLOOMINGBURG
43107-43107	BREMEN
43109-43109	BRICE
43110-43110	CANAL WINCHESTER
43111-43111	CARBON HILL
43112-43112	CARROLL
43113-43113	CIRCLEVILLE
43115-43115	CLARKSBURG
43116-43116	COMMERCIAL POINT
43117-43117	DERBY

ZIP Range	City
43119-43119	GALLOWAY
43123-43123	GROVE CITY
43125-43125	GROVEPORT
43126-43126	HARRISBURG
43127-43127	HAYDENVILLE
43128-43128	JEFFERSONVILLE
43130-43132	LANCASTER
43135-43135	LAURELVILLE
43136-43136	LITHOPOLIS
43137-43137	LOCKBOURNE
43138-43138	LOGAN
43140-43140	LONDON
43142-43142	MILLEDGEVILLE
43143-43143	MOUNT STERLING
43144-43144	MURRAY CITY
43145-43145	NEW HOLLAND
43146-43146	ORIENT
43147-43147	PICKERINGTON
43148-43148	PLEASANTVILLE
43149-43149	ROCKBRIDGE
43150-43150	RUSHVILLE
43151-43151	SEDALIA
43152-43152	SOUTH BLOOMINGVILLE
43153-43153	SOUTH SOLON
43154-43154	STOUTSVILLE
43155-43155	SUGAR GROVE
43156-43156	TARLTON
43157-43157	THURSTON
43158-43158	UNION FURNACE
43160-43160	WASHINGTON COURT HOUSE
43162-43162	WEST JEFFERSON
43163-43163	WEST RUSHVILLE
43164-43164	WILLIAMSPORT
43195-43199	GROVEPORT
43200-43299	COLUMBUS
43301-43307	MARION
43310-43310	BELLE CENTER
43311-43311	BELLEFONTAINE
43314-43314	CALEDONIA

ZIP Range	City
43315-43315	CARDINGTON
43316-43316	CAREY
43317-43317	CHESTERVILLE
43318-43318	DE GRAFF
43319-43319	EAST LIBERTY
43320-43320	EDISON
43321-43321	FULTON
43322-43322	GREEN CAMP
43323-43323	HARPSTER
43324-43324	HUNTSVILLE
43325-43325	IBERIA
43326-43326	KENTON
43330-43330	KIRBY
43331-43331	LAKEVIEW
43332-43332	LA RUE
43333-43333	LEWISTOWN
43334-43334	MARENGO
43335-43335	MARTEL
43336-43336	MIDDLEBURG
43337-43337	MORRAL
43338-43338	MOUNT GILEAD
43340-43340	MOUNT VICTORY
43341-43341	NEW BLOOMINGTON
43342-43342	PROSPECT
43343-43343	QUINCY
43344-43344	RICHWOOD
43345-43345	RIDGEWAY
43346-43346	ROUNDHEAD
43347-43347	RUSHSYLVANIA
43348-43348	RUSSELLS POINT
43349-43349	SHAUCK
43350-43350	SPARTA
43351-43351	UPPER SANDUSKY
43356-43356	WALDO
43357-43357	WEST LIBERTY
43358-43358	WEST MANSFIELD
43359-43359	WHARTON
43360-43360	ZANESFIELD
43402-43403	BOWLING GREEN
43406-43406	BRADNER

ZIP Range	City
43407-43407	BURGOON
43408-43408	CLAY CENTER
43410-43410	CLYDE
43412-43412	CURTICE
43413-43413	CYGNET
43414-43414	DUNBRIDGE
43416-43416	ELMORE
43420-43420	FREMONT
43430-43430	GENOA
43431-43431	GIBSONBURG
43432-43432	GRAYTOWN
43433-43433	GYPSUM
43434-43434	HARBOR VIEW
43435-43435	HELENA
43436-43436	ISLE SAINT GEORGE
43437-43437	JERRY CITY
43438-43438	KELLEYS ISLAND
43439-43439	LACARNE
43440-43440	LAKESIDE MARBLEHEAD
43441-43441	LEMOYNE
43442-43442	LINDSEY
43443-43443	LUCKEY
43445-43445	MARTIN
43446-43446	MIDDLE BASS
43447-43447	MILLBURY
43449-43449	OAK HARBOR
43450-43450	PEMBERVILLE
43451-43451	PORTAGE
43452-43452	PORT CLINTON
43456-43456	PUT IN BAY
43457-43457	RISINGSUN
43458-43458	ROCKY RIDGE
43460-43460	ROSSFORD
43462-43462	RUDOLPH
43463-43463	STONY RIDGE
43464-43464	VICKERY
43465-43465	WALBRIDGE
43466-43466	WAYNE
43467-43467	WEST MILLGROVE
43468-43468	WILLISTON
43469-43469	WOODVILLE
43501-43501	ALVORDTON
43502-43502	ARCHBOLD
43504-43504	BERKEY
43505-43505	BLAKESLEE
43506-43506	BRYAN
43510-43510	COLTON
43511-43511	CUSTAR
43512-43512	DEFIANCE
43515-43515	DELTA
43516-43516	DESHLER
43517-43517	EDGERTON
43518-43518	EDON
43519-43519	EVANSPORT
43520-43520	FARMER
43521-43521	FAYETTE
43522-43522	GRAND RAPIDS
43523-43523	GRELTON
43524-43524	HAMLER
43525-43525	HASKINS
43526-43526	HICKSVILLE
43527-43527	HOLGATE
43528-43528	HOLLAND
43529-43529	HOYTVILLE
43530-43530	JEWELL
43531-43531	KUNKLE
43532-43532	LIBERTY CENTER
43533-43533	LYONS
43534-43534	MC CLURE
43535-43535	MALINTA
43536-43536	MARK CENTER
43537-43537	MAUMEE
43540-43540	METAMORA
43541-43541	MILTON CENTER
43542-43542	MONCLOVA
43543-43543	MONTPELIER
43545-43545	NAPOLEON
43547-43547	NEAPOLIS
43548-43548	NEW BAVARIA
43549-43549	NEY
43550-43550	OKOLONA
43551-43552	PERRYSBURG
43553-43553	PETTISVILLE
43554-43554	PIONEER
43555-43555	RIDGEVILLE CORNERS
43556-43556	SHERWOOD
43557-43557	STRYKER
43558-43558	SWANTON
43560-43560	SYLVANIA
43565-43565	TONTOGANY
43566-43566	WATERVILLE
43567-43567	WAUSEON
43569-43569	WESTON
43570-43570	WEST UNITY
43571-43571	WHITEHOUSE
43600-43615	TOLEDO
43616-43616	OREGON
43617-43617	TOLEDO
43618-43618	OREGON
43619-43619	NORTHWOOD
43620-43699	TOLEDO
43701-43702	ZANESVILLE
43711-43711	AVA
43713-43713	BARNESVILLE
43716-43716	BEALLSVILLE
43717-43717	BELLE VALLEY
43718-43718	BELMONT
43719-43719	BETHESDA
43720-43720	BLUE ROCK
43721-43721	BROWNSVILLE
43722-43722	BUFFALO
43723-43723	BYESVILLE
43724-43724	CALDWELL
43725-43725	CAMBRIDGE
43727-43727	CHANDLERSVILLE
43728-43728	CHESTERHILL
43730-43730	CORNING
43731-43731	CROOKSVILLE
43732-43732	CUMBERLAND
43733-43733	DERWENT
43734-43734	DUNCAN FALLS
43735-43735	EAST FULTONHAM
43736-43736	FAIRVIEW
43738-43738	FULTONHAM
43739-43739	GLENFORD
43740-43740	GRATIOT
43746-43746	HOPEWELL
43747-43747	JERUSALEM
43748-43748	JUNCTION CITY
43749-43749	KIMBOLTON
43750-43750	KIPLING
43752-43752	LAINGS
43754-43754	LEWISVILLE
43755-43755	LORE CITY
43756-43756	MC CONNELSVILLE
43757-43757	MALAGA
43758-43758	MALTA
43759-43759	MORRISTOWN
43760-43760	MOUNT PERRY
43761-43761	MOXAHALA
43762-43762	NEW CONCORD
43764-43764	NEW LEXINGTON
43766-43766	NEW STRAITSVILLE
43767-43767	NORWICH
43768-43768	OLD WASHINGTON
43770-43770	STOCKPORT
43771-43771	PHILO
43772-43772	PLEASANT CITY
43773-43773	QUAKER CITY
43777-43777	ROSEVILLE
43778-43778	SALESVILLE
43779-43779	SARAHSVILLE
43780-43780	SENECAVILLE
43782-43782	SHAWNEE
43783-43783	SOMERSET
43786-43786	STAFFORD
43787-43787	STOCKPORT
43788-43788	SUMMERFIELD
43789-43789	SYCAMORE VALLEY
43791-43791	WHITE COTTAGE
43793-43793	WOODSFIELD
43802-43802	ADAMSVILLE
43803-43803	BAKERSVILLE
43804-43804	BALTIC
43805-43805	BLISSFIELD
43811-43811	CONESVILLE
43812-43812	COSHOCTON
43821-43821	DRESDEN
43822-43822	FRAZEYSBURG
43824-43824	FRESNO
43828-43828	KEENE
43830-43830	NASHPORT
43832-43832	NEWCOMERSTOWN
43836-43836	PLAINFIELD
43837-43837	PORT WASHINGTON
43840-43840	STONE CREEK
43842-43842	TRINWAY
43843-43843	WALHONDING
43844-43844	WARSAW
43845-43845	WEST LAFAYETTE
43901-43901	ADENA
43902-43902	ALLEDONIA
43903-43903	AMSTERDAM
43905-43905	BARTON
43906-43906	BELLAIRE
43907-43907	CADIZ
43908-43908	BERGHOLZ
43909-43909	BLAINE
43910-43910	BLOOMINGDALE
43912-43912	BRIDGEPORT
43913-43913	BRILLIANT
43914-43914	CAMERON
43915-43915	CLARINGTON
43916-43916	COLERAIN
43917-43917	DILLONVALE
43920-43920	EAST LIVERPOOL
43925-43925	EAST SPRINGFIELD
43926-43926	EMPIRE
43927-43927	FAIRPOINT
43928-43928	GLENCOE
43930-43930	HAMMONDSVILLE
43931-43931	HANNIBAL
43932-43932	IRONDALE
43933-43933	JACOBSBURG
43934-43934	LANSING
43935-43935	MARTINS FERRY
43937-43937	MAYNARD
43938-43938	MINGO JUNCTION
43939-43939	MOUNT PLEASANT
43940-43940	NEFFS
43941-43941	PINEY FORK
43942-43942	POWHATAN POINT
43943-43943	RAYLAND
43944-43944	RICHMOND
43945-43945	SALINEVILLE
43946-43946	SARDIS
43947-43947	SHADYSIDE
43948-43948	SMITHFIELD
43950-43950	SAINT CLAIRSVILLE
43951-43951	LAFFERTY
43952-43952	STEUBENVILLE
43953-43953	WINTERSVILLE
43960-43960	STEWARTSVILLE
43961-43961	STRATTON
43962-43962	SUMMITVILLE
43963-43963	TILTONSVILLE
43964-43964	TORONTO
43966-43966	UNIONPORT
43967-43967	WARNOCK
43968-43968	WELLSVILLE
43970-43970	WOLF RUN
43971-43971	YORKVILLE
43972-43972	BANNOCK
43973-43973	FREEPORT
43974-43974	HARRISVILLE
43976-43976	HOPEDALE
43977-43977	FLUSHING
43981-43981	NEW ATHENS
43983-43983	PIEDMONT
43984-43984	NEW RUMLEY
43985-43985	HOLLOWAY
43986-43986	JEWETT
43988-43988	SCIO
43989-43989	SHORT CREEK
44001-44001	AMHERST
44003-44003	ANDOVER
44004-44005	ASHTABULA
44010-44010	AUSTINBURG
44011-44011	AVON
44012-44012	AVON LAKE
44017-44017	BEREA
44021-44021	BURTON
44022-44023	CHAGRIN FALLS
44024-44024	CHARDON
44026-44026	CHESTERLAND
44028-44028	COLUMBIA STATION
44030-44030	CONNEAUT
44032-44032	DORSET
44033-44033	EAST CLARIDON
44035-44036	ELYRIA
44039-44039	NORTH RIDGEVILLE
44040-44040	GATES MILLS
44041-44041	GENEVA
44044-44044	GRAFTON
44045-44045	GRAND RIVER
44046-44046	HUNTSBURG
44047-44047	JEFFERSON
44048-44048	KINGSVILLE
44049-44049	KIPTON
44050-44050	LAGRANGE
44052-44053	LORAIN
44054-44054	SHEFFIELD LAKE
44055-44055	LORAIN
44056-44056	MACEDONIA
44057-44057	MADISON
44060-44061	MENTOR
44062-44062	MIDDLEFIELD
44064-44064	MONTVILLE
44065-44065	NEWBURY
44067-44067	NORTHFIELD
44068-44068	NORTH KINGSVILLE
44070-44070	NORTH OLMSTED
44072-44073	NOVELTY
44074-44074	OBERLIN
44076-44076	ORWELL
44077-44077	PAINESVILLE
44080-44080	PARKMAN
44081-44081	PERRY
44082-44082	PIERPONT
44084-44084	ROCK CREEK
44085-44085	ROME
44086-44086	THOMPSON
44087-44087	TWINSBURG
44088-44088	UNIONVILLE
44089-44089	VERMILION
44090-44090	WELLINGTON
44092-44092	WICKLIFFE
44093-44093	WILLIAMSFIELD
44094-44094	WILLOUGHBY
44095-44095	EASTLAKE
44096-44096	WILLOUGHBY
44097-44097	EASTLAKE
44099-44099	WINDSOR
44100-44106	CLEVELAND
44107-44107	LAKEWOOD
44108-44115	CLEVELAND
44116-44116	ROCKY RIVER
44117-44117	EUCLID
44118-44121	CLEVELAND
44122-44122	BEACHWOOD
44123-44123	EUCLID
44124-44130	CLEVELAND
44131-44131	INDEPENDENCE
44132-44132	EUCLID
44133-44133	NORTH ROYALTON
44134-44135	CLEVELAND
44136-44136	STRONGSVILLE
44137-44137	MAPLE HEIGHTS
44138-44138	OLMSTED FALLS
44139-44139	SOLON
44140-44140	BAY VILLAGE
44141-44141	BRECKSVILLE
44142-44142	BROOKPARK
44143-44144	CLEVELAND
44145-44145	WESTLAKE
44146-44146	BEDFORD
44147-44147	BROADVIEW HEIGHTS
44149-44149	STRONGSVILLE
44177-44199	CLEVELAND
44201-44201	ATWATER
44202-44202	AURORA
44203-44203	BARBERTON

44210-44210	BATH	44445-44445	NEW WATERFORD	44682-44682	TUSCARAWAS	45005-45005	FRANKLIN
44211-44211	BRADY LAKE	44446-44446	NILES	44683-44683	UHRICHSVILLE	45011-45013	HAMILTON
44212-44212	BRUNSWICK	44449-44449	NORTH BENTON	44685-44685	UNIONTOWN	45014-45014	FAIRFIELD
44214-44214	BURBANK	44450-44450	NORTH BLOOMFIELD	44687-44687	WALNUT CREEK	45015-45015	HAMILTON
44215-44215	CHIPPEWA LAKE	44451-44451	NORTH JACKSON	44688-44688	WAYNESBURG	45018-45018	FAIRFIELD
44216-44216	CLINTON	44452-44452	NORTH LIMA	44689-44689	WILMOT	45020-45026	HAMILTON
44217-44217	CRESTON	44453-44453	ORANGEVILLE	44690-44690	WINESBURG	45030-45030	HARRISON
44221-44223	CUYAHOGA FALLS	44454-44454	PETERSBURG	44691-44691	WOOSTER	45032-45032	HARVEYSBURG
44224-44224	STOW	44455-44455	ROGERS	44693-44693	DEERSVILLE	45033-45033	HOOVEN
44230-44230	DOYLESTOWN	44460-44460	SALEM	44695-44695	BOWERSTON	45034-45034	KINGS MILLS
44231-44231	GARRETTSVILLE	44470-44470	SOUTHINGTON	44697-44697	ZOAR	45036-45036	LEBANON
44232-44232	GREEN	44471-44471	STRUTHERS	44699-44699	TIPPECANOE	45039-45039	MAINEVILLE
44233-44233	HINCKLEY	44473-44473	VIENNA	44700-44799	CANTON	45040-45040	MASON
44234-44234	HIRAM	44481-44488	WARREN	44801-44801	ADRIAN	45041-45041	MIAMITOWN
44235-44235	HOMERVILLE	44490-44490	WASHINGTONVILLE	44802-44802	ALVADA	45042-45044	MIDDLETOWN
44236-44238	HUDSON	44491-44491	WEST FARMINGTON	44803-44803	AMSDEN	45050-45050	MONROE
44240-44240	KENT	44492-44492	WEST POINT	44804-44804	ARCADIA	45051-45051	MOUNT SAINT JOSEPH
44241-44241	STREETSBORO	44493-44493	WINONA	44805-44805	ASHLAND	45052-45052	NORTH BEND
44242-44243	KENT	44500-44599	YOUNGSTOWN	44807-44807	ATTICA	45053-45053	OKEANA
44250-44250	LAKEMORE	44601-44601	ALLIANCE	44809-44809	BASCOM	45054-45054	OREGONIA
44251-44251	WESTFIELD CENTER	44606-44606	APPLE CREEK	44811-44811	BELLEVUE	45055-45055	OVERPECK
44253-44253	LITCHFIELD	44607-44607	AUGUSTA	44813-44813	BELLVILLE	45056-45056	OXFORD
44254-44254	LODI	44608-44608	BEACH CITY	44814-44814	BERLIN HEIGHTS	45061-45061	ROSS
44255-44255	MANTUA	44609-44609	BELOIT	44815-44815	BETTSVILLE	45062-45062	SEVEN MILE
44256-44259	MEDINA	44610-44610	BERLIN	44816-44816	BIRMINGHAM	45063-45063	SHANDON
44260-44260	MOGADORE	44611-44611	BIG PRAIRIE	44817-44817	BLOOMDALE	45064-45064	SOMERVILLE
44262-44262	MUNROE FALLS	44612-44612	BOLIVAR	44818-44818	BLOOMVILLE	45065-45065	SOUTH LEBANON
44264-44264	PENINSULA	44613-44613	BREWSTER	44820-44820	BUCYRUS	45066-45066	SPRINGBORO
44265-44265	RANDOLPH	44614-44614	CANAL FULTON	44822-44822	BUTLER	45067-45067	TRENTON
44266-44266	RAVENNA	44615-44615	CARROLLTON	44824-44824	CASTALIA	45068-45068	WAYNESVILLE
44270-44270	RITTMAN	44617-44617	CHARM	44825-44825	CHATFIELD	45069-45069	WEST CHESTER
44272-44272	ROOTSTOWN	44618-44618	DALTON	44826-44826	COLLINS	45070-45070	WEST ELKTON
44273-44273	SEVILLE	44619-44619	DAMASCUS	44827-44827	CRESTLINE	45071-45071	WEST CHESTER
44274-44274	SHARON CENTER	44620-44620	DELLROY	44828-44828	FLAT ROCK	45073-45099	MONROE
44275-44275	SPENCER	44621-44621	DENNISON	44829-44829	FORT SENECA	45101-45101	ABERDEEN
44276-44276	STERLING	44622-44622	DOVER	44830-44830	FOSTORIA	45102-45102	AMELIA
44278-44278	TALLMADGE	44624-44624	DUNDEE	44833-44833	GALION	45103-45103	BATAVIA
44280-44280	VALLEY CITY	44625-44625	EAST ROCHESTER	44836-44836	GREEN SPRINGS	45105-45105	BENTONVILLE
44281-44282	WADSWORTH	44626-44626	EAST SPARTA	44837-44837	GREENWICH	45106-45106	BETHEL
44285-44285	WAYLAND	44627-44627	FREDERICKSBURG	44838-44838	HAYESVILLE	45107-45107	BLANCHESTER
44286-44286	RICHFIELD	44628-44628	GLENMONT	44839-44839	HURON	45110-45110	BUFORD
44287-44287	WEST SALEM	44629-44629	GNADENHUTTEN	44840-44840	JEROMESVILLE	45111-45111	CAMP DENNISON
44288-44288	WINDHAM	44630-44630	GREENTOWN	44841-44841	KANSAS	45112-45112	CHILO
44300-44317	AKRON	44631-44631	HARLEM SPRINGS	44842-44842	LOUDONVILLE	45113-45113	CLARKSVILLE
44318-44318	B F GOODRICH CO	44632-44632	HARTVILLE	44843-44843	LUCAS	45114-45114	CUBA
44319-44334	AKRON	44633-44633	HOLMESVILLE	44844-44844	MC CUTCHENVILLE	45115-45115	DECATUR
44334-44334	FAIRLAWN	44634-44634	HOMEWORTH	44845-44845	MELMORE	45118-45118	FAYETTEVILLE
44372-44399	AKRON	44636-44636	KIDRON	44846-44846	MILAN	45119-45119	FEESBURG
44401-44401	BERLIN CENTER	44637-44637	KILLBUCK	44847-44847	MONROEVILLE	45120-45120	FELICITY
44402-44402	BRISTOLVILLE	44638-44638	LAKEVILLE	44848-44848	NANKIN	45121-45121	GEORGETOWN
44403-44403	BROOKFIELD	44639-44639	LEESVILLE	44849-44849	NEVADA	45122-45122	GOSHEN
44404-44404	BURGHILL	44640-44640	LIMAVILLE	44850-44850	NEW HAVEN	45123-45123	GREENFIELD
44405-44405	CAMPBELL	44641-44641	LOUISVILLE	44851-44851	NEW LONDON	45130-45130	HAMERSVILLE
44406-44406	CANFIELD	44643-44643	MAGNOLIA	44853-44853	NEW RIEGEL	45131-45131	HIGGINSPORT
44408-44408	COLUMBIANA	44644-44644	MALVERN	44854-44854	NEW WASHINGTON	45132-45132	HIGHLAND
44410-44410	CORTLAND	44645-44645	MARSHALLVILLE	44855-44855	NORTH FAIRFIELD	45133-45133	HILLSBORO
44411-44411	DEERFIELD	44646-44648	MASSILLON	44856-44856	NORTH ROBINSON	45135-45135	LEESBURG
44412-44412	DIAMOND	44650-44650	MAXIMO	44857-44857	NORWALK	45138-45138	LEES CREEK
44413-44413	EAST PALESTINE	44651-44651	MECHANICSTOWN	44859-44859	NOVA	45140-45140	LOVELAND
44415-44415	ELKTON	44652-44652	MIDDLEBRANCH	44860-44860	OCEOLA	45142-45142	LYNCHBURG
44416-44416	ELLSWORTH	44653-44653	MIDVALE	44861-44861	OLD FORT	45144-45144	MANCHESTER
44417-44417	FARMDALE	44654-44654	MILLERSBURG	44862-44862	ONTARIO	45145-45145	MARATHON
44418-44418	FOWLER	44656-44656	MINERAL CITY	44864-44864	PERRYSVILLE	45146-45146	MARTINSVILLE
44420-44420	GIRARD	44657-44657	MINERVA	44865-44865	PLYMOUTH	45147-45147	MIAMIVILLE
44422-44422	GREENFORD	44659-44659	MOUNT EATON	44866-44866	POLK	45148-45148	MIDLAND
44423-44423	HANOVERTON	44660-44660	MOUNT HOPE	44867-44867	REPUBLIC	45150-45150	MILFORD
44424-44424	HARTFORD	44661-44661	NASHVILLE	44870-44871	SANDUSKY	45152-45152	MORROW
44425-44425	HUBBARD	44662-44662	NAVARRE	44874-44874	SAVANNAH	45153-45153	MOSCOW
44427-44427	KENSINGTON	44663-44663	NEW PHILADELPHIA	44875-44875	SHELBY	45154-45154	MOUNT ORAB
44428-44428	KINSMAN	44665-44665	NORTH GEORGETOWN	44878-44878	SHILOH	45155-45155	MOWRYSTOWN
44429-44429	LAKE MILTON	44666-44666	NORTH LAWRENCE	44880-44880	SULLIVAN	45156-45156	NEVILLE
44430-44430	LEAVITTSBURG	44667-44667	ORRVILLE	44881-44881	SULPHUR SPRINGS	45157-45157	NEW RICHMOND
44431-44431	LEETONIA	44669-44669	PARIS	44882-44882	SYCAMORE	45158-45158	NEWTONSVILLE
44432-44432	LISBON	44670-44670	ROBERTSVILLE	44883-44883	TIFFIN	45159-45159	NEW VIENNA
44436-44436	LOWELLVILLE	44671-44671	SANDYVILLE	44887-44887	TIRO	45160-45160	OWENSVILLE
44437-44437	MC DONALD	44672-44672	SEBRING	44888-44888	WILLARD	45162-45162	PLEASANT PLAIN
44438-44438	MASURY	44675-44675	SHERRODSVILLE	44889-44889	WAKEMAN	45164-45164	PORT WILLIAM
44439-44439	MESOPOTAMIA	44676-44676	SHREVE	44890-44890	WILLARD	45165-45165	GREENFIELD
44440-44440	MINERAL RIDGE	44677-44677	SMITHVILLE	44900-44999	MANSFIELD	45166-45166	REESVILLE
44441-44441	NEGLEY	44678-44678	SOMERDALE	45001-45001	ADDYSTON	45167-45167	RIPLEY
44442-44442	NEW MIDDLETOWN	44679-44679	STILLWATER	45002-45002	CLEVES	45168-45168	RUSSELLVILLE
44443-44443	NEW SPRINGFIELD	44680-44680	STRASBURG	45003-45003	COLLEGE CORNER	45169-45169	SABINA
44444-44444	NEWTON FALLS	44681-44681	SUGARCREEK	45004-45004	COLLINSVILLE	45171-45171	SARDINIA

45172-45172 SINKING SPRING	45389-45389 CHRISTIANSBURG	45719-45719 CHAUNCEY	45856-45856 LEIPSIC
45174-45174 TERRACE PARK	45390-45390 UNION CITY	45720-45720 CHESTER	45858-45858 MC COMB
45176-45176 WILLIAMSBURG	45401-45490 DAYTON	45721-45721 COAL RUN	45859-45859 MC GUFFEY
45177-45177 WILMINGTON	45500-45506 SPRINGFIELD	45723-45723 COOLVILLE	45860-45860 MARIA STEIN
45200-45299 CINCINNATI	45601-45601 CHILLICOTHE	45724-45724 CUTLER	45861-45861 MELROSE
45301-45301 ALPHA	45612-45612 BAINBRIDGE	45727-45727 DEXTER CITY	45862-45862 MENDON
45302-45302 ANNA	45613-45613 BEAVER	45729-45729 FLEMING	45863-45863 MIDDLE POINT
45303-45303 ANSONIA	45614-45614 BIDWELL	45730-45730 JACKSON	45864-45864 MILLER CITY
45304-45304 ARCANUM	45616-45616 BLUE CREEK	45732-45732 GLOUSTER	45865-45865 MINSTER
45305-45305 BELLBROOK	45617-45617 BOURNEVILLE	45734-45734 GRAYSVILLE	45866-45866 MONTEZUMA
45306-45306 BOTKINS	45618-45618 CHERRY FORK	45735-45735 GUYSVILLE	45867-45867 MOUNT BLANCHARD
45307-45307 BOWERSVILLE	45619-45619 CHESAPEAKE	45739-45739 HOCKINGPORT	45868-45868 MOUNT CORY
45308-45308 BRADFORD	45620-45620 CHESHIRE	45740-45740 JACKSONVILLE	45869-45869 NEW BREMEN
45309-45309 BROOKVILLE	45621-45621 COALTON	45741-45741 LANGSVILLE	45870-45870 NEW HAMPSHIRE
45310-45310 BURKETTSVILLE	45622-45622 CREOLA	45742-45742 LITTLE HOCKING	45871-45871 NEW KNOXVILLE
45311-45311 CAMDEN	45623-45623 CROWN CITY	45743-45743 LONG BOTTOM	45872-45872 NORTH BALTIMORE
45312-45312 CASSTOWN	45624-45624 CYNTHIANA	45744-45744 LOWELL	45873-45873 OAKWOOD
45314-45314 CEDARVILLE	45628-45628 FRANKFORT	45745-45745 LOWER SALEM	45874-45874 OHIO CITY
45315-45315 CLAYTON	45629-45629 FRANKLIN FURNACE	45746-45746 MACKSBURG	45875-45875 OTTAWA
45316-45316 CLIFTON	45630-45630 FRIENDSHIP	45750-45750 MARIETTA	45876-45876 OTTOVILLE
45317-45317 CONOVER	45631-45631 GALLIPOLIS	45760-45760 MIDDLEPORT	45877-45877 PANDORA
45318-45318 COVINGTON	45633-45633 HALLSVILLE	45761-45761 MILLFIELD	45879-45879 PAULDING
45319-45319 DONNELSVILLE	45634-45634 HAMDEN	45764-45764 NELSONVILLE	45880-45880 PAYNE
45320-45320 EATON	45636-45636 HAVERHILL	45766-45766 NEW MARSHFIELD	45881-45881 RAWSON
45321-45321 ELDORADO	45638-45638 IRONTON	45767-45767 NEW MATAMORAS	45882-45882 ROCKFORD
45322-45322 ENGLEWOOD	45640-45640 JACKSON	45768-45768 NEWPORT	45883-45883 SAINT HENRY
45323-45323 ENON	45642-45642 JASPER	45769-45769 POMEROY	45884-45884 SAINT JOHNS
45324-45324 FAIRBORN	45643-45643 KERR	45770-45770 PORTLAND	45885-45885 SAINT MARYS
45325-45325 FARMERSVILLE	45644-45644 KINGSTON	45771-45771 RACINE	45886-45886 SCOTT
45326-45326 FLETCHER	45645-45645 KITTS HILL	45772-45772 REEDSVILLE	45887-45887 SPENCERVILLE
45327-45327 GERMANTOWN	45646-45646 LATHAM	45773-45773 RENO	45888-45888 UNIOPOLIS
45328-45328 GETTYSBURG	45647-45647 LONDONDERRY	45775-45775 RUTLAND	45889-45889 VAN BUREN
45329-45329 GORDON	45648-45648 LUCASVILLE	45776-45776 SHADE	45890-45890 VANLUE
45330-45330 GRATIS	45650-45650 LYNX	45777-45777 SHARPSBURG	45891-45891 VAN WERT
45331-45331 GREENVILLE	45651-45651 MC ARTHUR	45778-45778 STEWART	45893-45893 VAUGHNSVILLE
45332-45332 HOLLANSBURG	45652-45652 MC DERMOTT	45779-45779 SYRACUSE	45894-45894 VENEDOCIA
45333-45333 HOUSTON	45653-45653 MINFORD	45780-45780 THE PLAINS	45895-45895 WAPAKONETA
45334-45334 JACKSON CENTER	45654-45654 NEW PLYMOUTH	45781-45781 TORCH	45896-45896 WAYNESFIELD
45335-45335 JAMESTOWN	45656-45656 OAK HILL	45782-45782 TRIMBLE	45897-45897 WILLIAMSTOWN
45336-45336 KETTLERSVILLE	45657-45657 OTWAY	45783-45783 TUPPERS PLAINS	45898-45898 WILLSHIRE
45337-45337 LAURA	45658-45658 PATRIOT	45784-45784 VINCENT	45899-45899 WREN
45338-45338 LEWISBURG	45659-45659 PEDRO	45786-45786 WATERFORD	45944-45999 CINCINNATI
45339-45339 LUDLOW FALLS	45660-45660 PEEBLES	45787-45787 WATERTOWN	
45340-45340 MAPLEWOOD	45661-45661 PIKETON	45788-45788 WHIPPLE	
45341-45341 MEDWAY	45662-45662 PORTSMOUTH	45789-45789 WINGETT RUN	
45342-45343 MIAMISBURG	45663-45663 WEST PORTSMOUTH	45801-45807 LIMA	
45344-45344 NEW CARLISLE	45669-45669 PROCTORVILLE	45808-45808 BEAVERDAM	
45345-45345 NEW LEBANON	45670-45670 RADCLIFF	45809-45809 GOMER	
45346-45346 NEW MADISON	45671-45671 RARDEN	45810-45810 ADA	
45347-45347 NEW PARIS	45672-45672 RAY	45812-45812 ALGER	
45348-45348 NEW WESTON	45673-45673 RICHMOND DALE	45813-45813 ANTWERP	
45349-45349 NORTH HAMPTON	45674-45674 RIO GRANDE	45814-45814 ARLINGTON	
45350-45350 NORTH STAR	45675-45675 ROCK CAMP	45815-45815 BELMORE	
45351-45351 OSGOOD	45677-45677 SCIOTO FURNACE	45816-45816 BENTON RIDGE	
45352-45352 PALESTINE	45678-45678 SCOTTOWN	45817-45817 BLUFFTON	
45353-45353 PEMBERTON	45679-45679 SEAMAN	45819-45819 BUCKLAND	
45354-45354 PHILLIPSBURG	45680-45680 SOUTH POINT	45820-45820 CAIRO	
45356-45356 PIQUA	45681-45681 SOUTH SALEM	45821-45821 CECIL	
45358-45358 PITSBURG	45682-45682 SOUTH WEBSTER	45822-45822 CELINA	
45359-45359 PLEASANT HILL	45683-45683 STOCKDALE	45826-45826 CHICKASAW	
45360-45360 PORT JEFFERSON	45684-45684 STOUT	45827-45827 CLOVERDALE	
45361-45361 POTSDAM	45685-45685 THURMAN	45828-45828 COLDWATER	
45362-45362 ROSSBURG	45686-45686 VINTON	45830-45830 COLUMBUS GROVE	
45363-45363 RUSSIA	45687-45687 WAKEFIELD	45831-45831 CONTINENTAL	
45365-45365 SIDNEY	45688-45688 WATERLOO	45832-45832 CONVOY	
45366-45366 SPRING HILL NURSERIES	45690-45690 WAVERLY	45833-45833 DELPHOS	
45367-45367 SIDNEY	45692-45692 WELLSTON	45835-45835 DOLA	
45368-45368 SOUTH CHARLESTON	45693-45693 WEST UNION	45836-45836 DUNKIRK	
45369-45369 SOUTH VIENNA	45694-45694 WHEELERSBURG	45837-45837 DUPONT	
45370-45370 SPRING VALLEY	45695-45695 WILKESVILLE	45838-45838 ELGIN	
45371-45371 TIPP CITY	45696-45696 WILLOW WOOD	45839-45840 FINDLAY	
45372-45372 TREMONT CITY	45697-45697 WINCHESTER	45841-45841 JENERA	
45373-45374 TROY	45698-45698 ZALESKI	45843-45843 FOREST	
45377-45377 VANDALIA	45699-45699 LUCASVILLE	45844-45844 FORT JENNINGS	
45378-45378 VERONA	45701-45701 ATHENS	45845-45845 FORT LORAMIE	
45380-45380 VERSAILLES	45710-45710 ALBANY	45846-45846 FORT RECOVERY	
45381-45381 WEST ALEXANDRIA	45711-45711 AMESVILLE	45848-45848 GLANDORF	
45382-45382 WEST MANCHESTER	45712-45712 BARLOW	45849-45849 GROVER HILL	
45383-45383 WEST MILTON	45713-45713 BARTLETT	45850-45850 HARROD	
45384-45384 WILBERFORCE	45714-45714 BELPRE	45851-45851 HAVILAND	
45385-45385 XENIA	45715-45715 BEVERLY	45853-45853 KALIDA	
45387-45387 YELLOW SPRINGS	45716-45716 BUCHTEL	45854-45854 LAFAYETTE	
45388-45388 YORKSHIRE	45717-45717 CARBONDALE	45855-45855 LATTY	

Explanation of Symbols

✦ State Capital

Vernon County Seat

Population Key

○ 0-999	◉ 20,000-24,999
◔ 1,000-2,499	◉ 25,000-49,999
◓ 2,500-4,999	☐ 50,000-99,999
◕ 5,000-9,999	◰ 100,000-249,999
◉ 10,000-19,000	■ 250,000-999,999

County-Town
OHIO

0	10	20	30	40	50 Mi

0	20	40	60 Kilometers

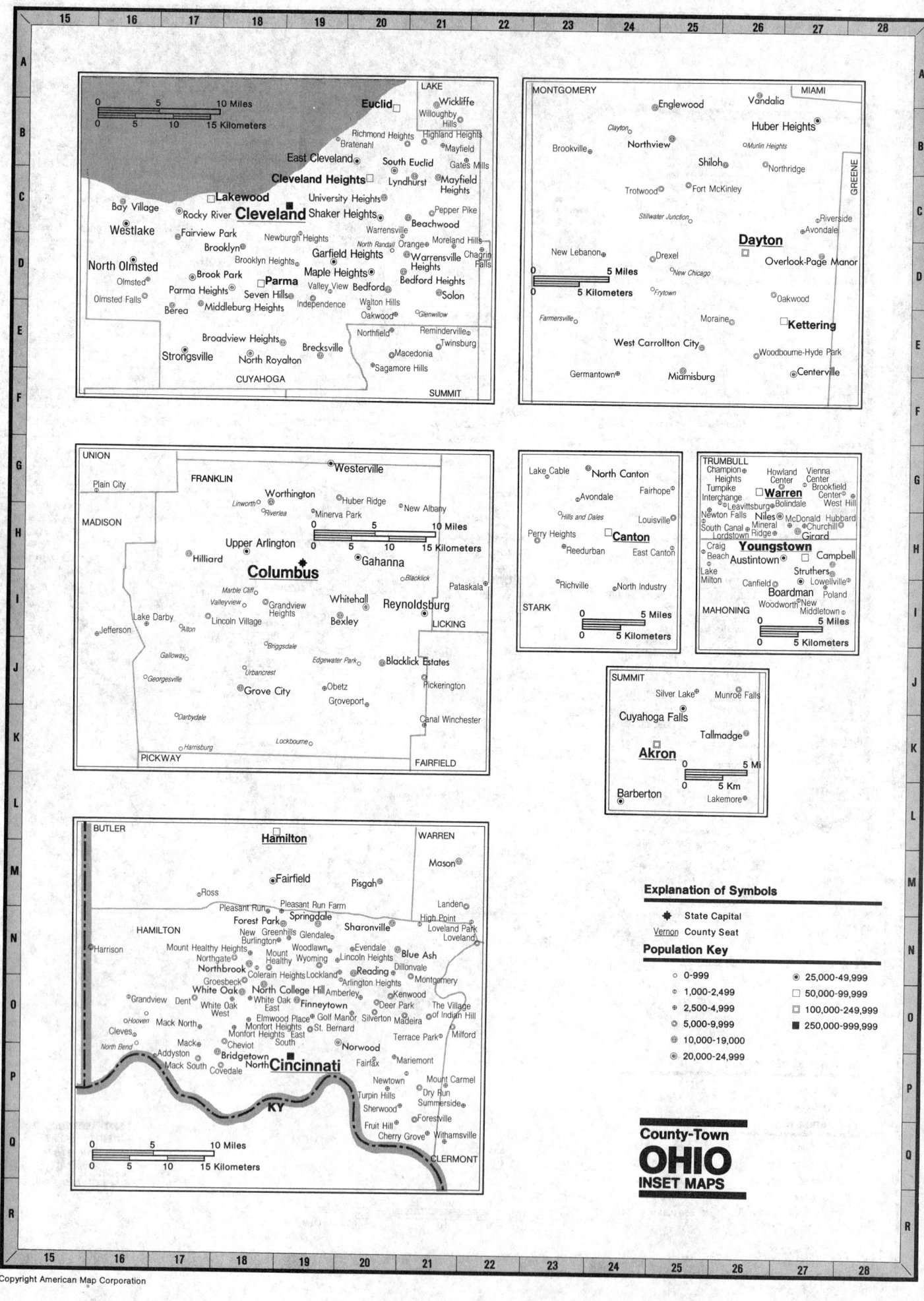

County-Town
OHIO
INSET MAPS

COUNTIES

(88 Counties)

Name of County	Population	Location on Map
ADAMS	25,371	M-4
ALLEN	109,755	E-3
ASHLAND	47,507	F-9
ASHTABULA	99,821	B-13
ATHENS	59,549	L-9
AUGLAIZE	44,585	F-2
BELMONT	71,074	I-12
BROWN	34,966	M-4
BUTLER	291,479	J-1
CARROLL	26,521	G-12
CHAMPAIGN	36,019	H-3
CLARK	147,548	I-4
CLERMONT	150,187	M-3
CLINTON	35,415	K-4
COLUMBIANA	108,276	E-13
COSHOCTON	35,427	G-9
CRAWFORD	47,870	E-7
CUYAHOGA	1,412,140	B-11
DARKE	53,619	G-1
DEFIANCE	39,350	C-1
DELAWARE	66,929	G-6
ERIE	76,779	C-7
FAIRFIELD	103,461	J-8
FAYETTE	27,466	J-5
FRANKLIN	961,437	I-7
FULTON	38,498	B-2
GALLIA	30,954	N-9
GEAUGA	81,129	C-12
GREENE	136,731	J-4
GUERNSEY	39,024	H-11
HAMILTON	866,228	K-1
HANCOCK	65,536	D-4
HARDIN	31,111	F-4
HARRISON	16,085	G-12
HENRY	29,108	D-3
HIGHLAND	35,728	L-5
HOCKING	25,533	K-7
HOLMES	32,849	G-9
HURON	56,240	D-7
JACKSON	30,230	L-7
JEFFERSON	80,298	F-13
KNOX	47,473	G-9
LAKE	215,499	B-12
LAWRENCE	61,834	N-8
LICKING	128,300	H-7
LOGAN	42,310	G-4
LORAIN	271,126	D-9
LUCAS	462,361	B-4
MADISON	37,068	H-5
MAHONING	264,806	D-13
MARION	64,274	F-5
MEDINA	122,354	D-10
MEIGS	22,987	L-9
MERCER	39,443	F-1
MIAMI	93,182	H-3
MONROE	15,497	J-12
MONTGOMERY	573,809	J-2
MORGAN	14,194	J-10
MORROW	27,749	F-7
MUSKINGUM	82,068	I-10
NOBLE	11,336	J-12
OTTAWA	40,029	B-6
PAULDING	20,488	D-1
PERRY	31,557	J-9
PICKAWAY	48,255	J-6
PIKE	24,249	L-5
PORTAGE	142,585	D-12
PREBLE	40,113	J-1
PUTNAM	33,819	D-2
RICHLAND	126,137	E-8
ROSS	69,330	K-6
SANDUSKY	61,963	C-6
SCIOTO	80,327	M-6
SENECA	59,733	D-7
SHELBY	44,915	H-3
STARK	367,585	F-11
SUMMIT	514,990	C-11
TRUMBULL	227,813	C-14
TUSCARAWAS	84,090	H-11
UNION	31,969	G-5
VAN WERT	30,464	E-1
VINTON	11,098	K-8
WARREN	113,909	K-3
WASHINGTON	62,254	K-10
WAYNE	101,461	F-10
WILLIAMS	36,956	B-1
WOOD	113,269	D-4
WYANDOT	22,254	F-5
TOTAL	10,847,115	

CITIES AND TOWNS

Note: The first name is that of the city or town, second, that of the county in which it is located, then the population and location on the map.

Aberdeen, Brown, 1,329 .... W-4
Ada, Hardin, 5,413 .... E-4
Addyston, Hamilton, 1,198 .... P-17
Akron, Summit, 223,019 .... D-11
Alliance, Mahoning/Stark, 23,376 .... E-12
Amberley, Hamilton, 3,108 .... O-20
Amelia, Clermont, 1,837 .... L-3
Amherst, Lorain, 10,332 .... C-9
Andover, Ashtabula, 1,216 .... B-14
Anna, Shelby, 1,164 .... G-3
Ansonia, Darke, 1,279 .... H-1
Antwerp, Paulding, 1,677 .... D-1
Arcanum, Darke, 1,953 .... I-2
Archbold, Fulton, 3,440 .... B-2
Arlington, Hancock, 1,267 .... E-4
Arlington Heights, Hamilton, 1,084 .. O-20
Ashland, Ashland, 20,079 .... E-9
Ashley, Delaware, 1,059 .... G-7
Ashtabula, Ashtabula, 21,633 .... A-13
Ashville, Pickaway, 2,254 .... J-7
Athens, Athens, 21,265 .... K-9
Aurora, Portage, 9,192 .... C-12
• Austintown, Mahoning, 32,371 .... G-25
Avon, Lorain, 7,337 .... C-9
Avon Lake, Lorain, 15,066 .... B-10
Avondale, Montgomery C-27
Avondale, Stark G-23
• Bainbridge, Geauga, 3,602 .... C-12
• Ballville, Sandusky, 3,083 .... C-6
Baltimore, Fairfield, 2,971 .... I-8
Barberton, Summit, 27,623 .... L-24
Barnesville, Belmont, 4,326 .... H-12
Batavia, Clermont, 1,700 .... L-3
Bay Village, Cuyahoga, 17,000 .... C-16
Beach City, Stark, 1,051 .... F-11
Beachwood, Cuyahoga, 10,677 ...... C-21
Beavercreek, Greene, 33,626 .... J-3
• Beckett Ridge, Butler, 4,505 .... K-2
Bedford, Cuyahoga, 14,822 .... E-20
Bedford Heights, Cuyahoga, 12,131 D-20
• Beechwood Trails, Licking, 1,875 .... I-8
Bellaire, Belmont, 6,028 .... H-14
Bellbrook, Greene, 6,511 .... J-3
Bellefontaine, Logan, 12,142 .... G-4
Bellevue, Huron/Sandusky, 8,146 ...... C-7
Bellville, Richland, 1,568 .... F-8
Beloit, Mahoning, 1,037 .... E-13
Belpre, Washington, 6,796 .... K-11
Berea, Cuyahoga, 19,051 .... E-17
Bethel, Clermont, 2,407 .... M-3
Bethesda, Belmont, 1,161 .... H-13
Beverly, Washington, 1,444 .... J-11
Bexley, Franklin, 13,088 .... I-19
• Blacklick Estates, Franklin, 10,080 ... J-20
Blanchester, Clinton/Warren, 4,206 ... K-3
Blue Ash, Hamilton, 11,860 .... N-21
Bluffton, Allen/Hancock, 3,367 .... E-4
• Boardman, Mahoning, 38,596 .... H-26
• Bolindale, Trumbull, 2,827 .... G-26
Botkins, Shelby, 1,340 .... G-3
Bowling Green, Wood, 28,176 .... C-4
Bradford, Darke/Miami, 2,005 .... H-2
Bradner, Wood, 1,093 .... C-5
Bratenahl, Cuyahoga, 1,356 .... B-19
Brecksville, Cuyahoga, 11,818 .... E-19
Bremen, Fairfield, 1,386 .... J-8
• Brentwood, Jefferson, 3,568 .... G-14
Brewster, Stark, 2,307 .... F-11
Bridgeport, Belmont, 2,318 .... H-14
• Bridgetown North, Hamilton, 11,748 P-17
Brilliant, Jefferson, 1,672 .... G-14
• Brimfield, Portage, 3,223 .... D-12
Broadview Heights, Cuyahoga, 12,219 .... C-11
Brook Park, Cuyahoga, 22,865 .... D-17
• Brookfield Center, Trumbull, 1,396 .. G-27
Brooklyn, Cuyahoga, 11,706 .... D-18
Brooklyn Heights, Cuyahoga, 1,450 D-19
Brookville, Montgomery, 4,621 .... I-2
Brunswick, Medina, 28,230 .... D-10
Bryan, Williams, 8,348 .... C-2
Buckeye Lake, Licking, 2,986 .... I-8
Bucyrus, Crawford, 13,496 .... E-7
• Burlington, Lawrence, 3,003 .... O-8
Burton, Geauga, 1,349 .... B-12
Byesville, Guernsey, 2,435 .... I-11
Cadiz, Harrison, 3,439 .... G-13
• Calcutta, Columbiana, 1,212 .... F-14
Caldwell, Noble, 1,786 .... I-11
Cambridge, Guernsey, 11,748 .... H-11
Camden, Preble, 2,210 .... J-1
Campbell, Mahoning, 10,038 .... H-27
Canal Fulton, Stark, 4,157 .... E-11
Canal Winchester, Fairfield/Franklin, 2,617 .... I-21
Canfield, Mahoning, 5,409 .... H-25
Canton, Stark, 84,161 .... E-12
Cardington, Morrow, 1,770 .... G-7
Carey, Wyandot, 3,684 .... E-5
Carlisle, Montgomery/Warren, 4,872 .. J-2
Carrollton, Carroll, 3,042 .... F-13
Cedarville, Greene, 3,210 .... J-4
Celina, Mercer, 9,650 .... F-1
Centerburg, Knox, 1,323 .... G-7
Centerville, Montgomery, 21,082 ..... E-27
Chagrin Falls, Cuyahoga, 4,146 .... D-22
• Champion Heights, Trumbull, 4,665 .... C-13
Chardon, Geauga, 4,446 .... B-12
• Cherry Grove, Hamilton, 4,972 .... Q-21
Chesapeake, Lawrence, 1,073 .... O-8
• Chesterland, Geauga, 2,078 .... B-12
Cheviot, Hamilton, 9,616 .... O-18
Chillicothe, Ross, 21,923 .... K-6
Chillicothe West, Ross K-6
• Chocktou Lake, Madison, 1,234 .... I-6
• Churchill, Trumbull, 2,691 .... D-14
Cincinnati, Hamilton, 364,040 .... L-2
Circleville, Pickaway, 11,666 .... J-7
Cleveland, Cuyahoga, 505,616 .... C-11
Cleveland Heights, Cuyahoga, 54,052 .... C-20
Cleves, Hamilton, 2,208 .... L-1
Clinton, Summit, 1,175 .... E-11
Clyde, Sandusky, 5,776 .... C-7
Coal Grove, Lawrence, 2,251 .... N-8
Coldwater, Mercer, 4,335 .... G-1
Colerain Heights, Hamilton N-18
Columbiana, Columbiana/Mahoning, 4,961 .... E-14
Columbus, Fairfield/Franklin, 632,910 .... H-7
Columbus Grove, Putnam, 2,231 .... E-3
Conneaut, Ashtabula, 13,241 .... A-14
Continental, Putnam, 1,214 .... D-3
Convoy, Van Wert, 1,200 .... E-1
Copley, Summit D-11
Cortland, Trumbull, 5,666 .... C-14
Coshocton, Coshocton, 12,193 .... G-10
• Covedale, Hamilton, 6,669 .... L-1
Covington, Miami, 2,603 .... H-2
Craig Beach, Mahoning, 1,402 .... D-13
Crestline, Crawford/Richland, 4,934 .. E-7
Creston, Wayne, 1,848 .... E-10
Cridersville, Auglaize, 1,885 .... F-3
Crooksville, Perry, 2,601 .... I-9
• Crystal Lakes, Clark, 1,613 .... I-3
Cuyahoga Falls, Summit, 48,950 ...... J-25
Dalton, Wayne, 1,377 .... E-11
Danville, Knox, 1,001 .... G-9
• Day Heights, Clermont, 2,812 .... L-2
Dayton, Montgomery, 182,044 .... J-3
De Graff, Logan, 1,331 .... G-4
Deer Park, Hamilton, 6,181 .... O-20
Defiance, Defiance, 16,768 .... C-2
Delaware, Delaware, 20,030 .... G-6
Delphos, Allen/Van Wert, 7,093 .... E-2
Delta, Fulton, 2,849 .... B-3
Dennison, Tuscarawas, 3,282 .... G-12
• Dent, Hamilton, 6,416 .... O-17
Deshler, Henry, 1,876 .... D-3
• Devola, Washington, 2,736 .... K-11
• Dillonvale, Hamilton, 4,209 .... N-20
Dover, Tuscarawas, 11,329 .... F-11
Doylestown, Wayne, 2,668 .... E-11
Dresden, Muskingum, 1,581 .... H-10
• Drexel, Montgomery, 5,143 .... D-24
• Dry Run, Hamilton, 5,389 .... P-21
Dublin, Delaware/Franklin/Union, 16,366 .... H-6
Duncan Falls, Muskingum I-10
East Canton, Stark, 1,742 .... H-25
East Cleveland, Cuyahoga, 33,096 . B-20
East Liverpool, Columbiana, 13,654 .... F-14
East Liverpool North, Columbiana ... F-14
East Palestine, Columbiana, 5,168 .. E-14
Eastlake, Lake, 21,161 .... B-11
Eaton, Preble, 7,396 .... J-1
• Eaton Estates, Lorain, 1,586 .... C-10
Edgerton, Williams, 1,896 .... C-1
• Edgewood, Ashtabula, 5,189 .... A-13
Elida, Allen, 1,486 .... E-3
Elmore, Ottawa, 1,334 .... C-6
Elmwood Place, Hamilton, 2,937 ..... O-19
Elyria, Lorain, 56,746 .... C-9
Englewood, Montgomery, 11,432 .... B-24
Enon, Clark, 2,605 .... I-4
Euclid, Cuyahoga, 54,875 .... B-11
Evendale, Hamilton, 3,175 .... N-20
Fairborn, Greene, 31,300 .... I-3
Fairfax, Hamilton, 2,029 .... P-20
Fairfield, Butler/Hamilton, 39,729 ...... K-2
• Fairfield Beach, Fairfield, 1,084 .... I-8
Fairhope, Stark G-25
Fairlawn, Summit, 5,779 .... D-11
Fairport Harbor, Lake, 2,978 .... A-12
• Fairview Lanes, Erie, 1,120 .... C-8
Fairview Park, Cuyahoga, 18,028 .... C-17
Fayette, Fulton, 1,248 .... B-2
Findlay, Hancock, 35,703 .... D-4
• Finneytown, Hamilton, 13,096 .... O-19
• Five Points, Warren, 1,554 .... J-2
Flushing, Belmont, 1,042 .... H-13
Forest, Hardin, 1,594 .... E-5
Forest Park, Hamilton, 18,609 .... N-19
• Forestville, Hamilton, 9,185 .... Q-21
Fort Loramie, Shelby, 1,042 .... G-2
• Fort McKinley, Montgomery, 9,740 .. C-25
Fort Recovery, Mercer, 1,313 .... G-1
Fort Shawnee, Allen, 4,128 .... F-3
Fostoria, Hancock/Seneca/Wood, 14,983 .... D-5
Frankfort, Ross, 1,065 .... K-6
Franklin, Warren, 11,026 .... J-2
• Franklin Furnace, Scioto, 1,212 .... N-7
Frazeysburg, Muskingum, 1,165 .... H-9
Fredericktown, Knox, 2,443 .... G-8
Fremont, Sandusky, 17,648 .... C-6
• Fruit Hill, Hamilton, 4,101 .... Q-20
Gahanna, Franklin, 27,791 .... H-20
Galion, Crawford, 11,859 .... F-7
Gallipolis, Gallia, 4,831 .... M-9
Gambier, Knox, 2,073 .... G-8
Garfield Heights, Cuyahoga, 31,739 .... D-19
Garrettsville, Portage, 2,014 .... C-13
Gates Mills, Cuyahoga, 2,508 .... B-21
Geneva, Ashtabula, 6,597 .... A-13
Geneva-on-the-Lake, Ashtabula, 1,626 .... A-13
Genoa, Ottawa, 2,262 .... B-5
Georgetown, Brown, 3,627 .... M-4
Germantown, Montgomery, 4,916 .... E-24
Gibsonburg, Sandusky, 2,579 .... C-6
Girard, Trumbull, 11,304 .... D-14
Glendale, Hamilton, 2,445 .... N-19
• Glenmoor, Columbiana, 2,307 .... F-14
Glouster, Athens, 2,001 .... J-9
Gnadenhutten, Tuscarawas, 1,226 .. G-12
Golf Manor, Hamilton, 4,154 .... O-20
Goshen, Clermont L-3
Grafton, Lorain, 3,344 .... C-9
• Grandview, Hamilton, 1,301 .... O-16
Grandview Heights, Franklin, 7,010 .. I-18
Granville, Licking, 4,353 .... H-8
• Granville South, Licking, 1,124 .... H-8
Green, Summit, 3,553 .... E-11
• Green Meadows, Clark, 2,526 .... I-4
Green Springs, Sandusky/Seneca, 1,446 .... D-6
Greenfield, Highland, 5,172 .... K-5
Greenhills, Hamilton, 4,393 .... N-19
• Greensburg, Summit, 3,306 .... E-11
• Greentown, Stark, 1,856 .... E-11
Greenville, Darke, 12,863 .... H-1
Greenwich, Huron, 1,442 .... D-8
• Groesbeck, Hamilton, 6,684 .... O-18
Grove City, Franklin, 19,661 .... I-6
Groveport, Franklin, 2,948 .... J-20
Hamilton, Butler, 61,368 .... K-2
• Harbor Hills, Licking, 1,372 .... I-8
Harrison, Hamilton, 7,518 .... K-1
Hartville, Stark, 2,031 .... E-12
Heath, Licking, 7,231 .... H-8
Hebron, Licking, 2,076 .... I-8
Hicksville, Defiance, 3,664 .... C-1
High Point, Hamilton N-21
Highland Heights, Cuyahoga, 6,249 B-21
Hilliard, Franklin, 11,796 .... H-17
Hillsboro, Highland, 6,235 .... L-5
Hiram, Portage, 1,330 .... C-12
Holgate, Henry, 1,290 .... D-3
• Holiday Valley, Clark, 1,243 .... I-2
Holland, Lucas, 1,210 .... B-4
• Howland Center, Trumbull, 6,732 ..... C-27
Howland Corners, Trumbull C-14
Hubbard, Trumbull, 8,248 .... D-14
Huber Heights, Miami/Montgomery, 38,696 .... B-27
• Huber Ridge, Franklin, 5,255 .... G-19
Hudson, Summit, 5,159 .... D-11
Huron, Erie, 7,030 .... C-8
Independence, Cuyahoga, 6,500 ..... D-19
Ironton, Lawrence, 12,751 .... N-8
Jackson, Jackson, 6,144 .... L-8
Jackson Center, Shelby, 1,398 .... G-3
Jamestown, Greene, 1,794 .... J-4
Jefferson, Ashtabula, 3,331 .... A-13
Jefferson, Madison, 4,505 .... I-6
Jeffersonville, Fayette, 1,281 .... J-5
Johnstown, Licking, 3,237 .... H-8
Kent, Portage, 28,835 .... D-12
Kenton, Hardin, 8,356 .... F-5
• Kenwood, Hamilton, 7,469 .... O-20
Kettering, Greene/Montgomery, 60,569 .... E-27
Kingston, Ross, 1,153 .... K-7
Kirtland, Lake, 5,881 .... B-12
Krumroy, Summit D-11
• La Croft, Columbiana, 1,427 .... F-14
Lagrange, Lorain, 1,199 .... D-9

Explanation of symbols: • – Census Designated Place (CDP)

Explanation of symbols: ● – Census Designated Place (CDP)

Oklahoma

General Help Numbers:

Governor's Office
State Capitol, Suite 212
Oklahoma City, OK 73105
http://www.governor.state.ok.us

405-521-2342
Fax 405-521-3353
8AM-5PM

Attorney General's Office
2300 N Lincoln, #112
Oklahoma City, OK 73105
www.oag.state.ok.us/
explorer.index.html

405-521-3921
Fax 405-521-6246
8:30AM-5PM

Legislative Records
Oklahoma Legislature, State Capitol,
Bill Status Info-Rm B-30, Copies-Rm 310
Oklahoma City, OK 73105
www.lsb.state.ok.us

405-521-5642
Fax 405-521-5507
8:30AM-4:30PM

State Archives
Archives & Records Mgt Divisions
200 NE 18th
Oklahoma City, OK 73105-3298
www.odl.state.ok.us

405-522-3577
Fax 405-525-7804
8AM-5PM

State Specifics:

Capital:	Oklahoma City
	Oklahoma County
Time Zone:	CST
Number of Counties:	77
Population:	3,511,532
Web Site:	www.state.ok.us

State Agencies

Criminal Records

OK State Bureau of Investigation, Criminal History Reporting, 6600 N Harvey, Oklahoma City, OK 73116; 405-848-6724, 405-879-2503 (Fax), 8AM-5PM.

www.osbi.state.ok.us

Note: A record request form is available at the website.

Indexing & Storage: Records are available from 1925 on. It takes 5 to 7 days before new records are available for inquiry. Records are maintained indefinitely.

Searching: Include the following in your request-DOB or approximate age. The SSN, sex or race are helpful and provide a better search, but not required. Fingerprints are optional. 100% of the records are fingerprint-supported. The following data is not released: juvenile records.

Access by: mail, fax, in person.

Fee & Payment: The fee for a computer name search is $15.00. The fee for the fingerprint search is $19.00. Fingerprint search does not include FBI fingerprint search; agency will not conduct an FBI search. Copies are $.25 per page. Fee payee: O.S.B.I. Prepayment required. Personal checks not

accepted. Credit cards accepted: MasterCard, Visa, Discover.

Mail search: Turnaround time: 2 weeks. A SASE is requested.

Fax search: Use of credit card and their "Credit Card Fax Form" is required. Call to have them fax you the form or download from web.

In person search: Name requests take 20 minutes, fingerprint searches take up to ten days to process.

Statewide Court Records

Administrative Director of Courts, 1915 N Stiles, #305, Oklahoma City, OK 73105; 405-521-2450, 405-521-6815 (Fax), 8AM-5PM.

www.oscn.net

Access by: online. No searching by mail.

Online search: Free Internet access is available for District Courts in 12 counties and all Appellate courts at www.oscn.net. Both civil and criminal docket information is available for the counties invoved. Also, the Oklahoma District Court Records free website at www.odcr.com offers searching from over 30 District Courts. More counties are being added as they are readied; they hope to eventually feature all OK District Courts. Please note many of the county records in this system do not go back 7 years.

Sexual Offender Registry

Oklahoma Department fo Corrections, Sex Offender Registry, PO Box 11400, Oklahoma City, OK 73136-0400; 405-962-6104, 8AM-5PM.

www.doc.state.ok.us/DOCS/offender_info.htm

Access by: mail, online.

Mail search: Turnaround time: 1-3 days. Names searches and geographic lists are available by mail.

Online search: Searching is available from the website. The Sex Offender Lookup only lists lifetime (habitual and aggravated) sex offenders, all others have not been put on the site yet. There are a number of search options.

Incarceration Records

Oklahoma Department of Corrections, Offender Records, PO Box 11400, Oklahoma City, OK 73136 (Courier: 3400 Martin Luther King Avenue, Oklahoma City, OK 73136); 405-425-2500, 405-425-2608 (Fax), 8AM-4:30PM.

www.doc.state.ok.us/

Indexing & Storage: Records are available on current and former inmates. It takes 10 days before new records are available for inquiry.

Searching: Records are maintained indefinitely. Include the following in your request-provide first and last name, but the DOB, SSN and DOC number helpful. You can search online by either the name or DOC number. Location, DOC number, physical identifiers, conviction and sentencing information, and release dates are provided. The following data is not released: SSN, offender home address.

Access by: mail, phone, fax, online.

Mail search: Turnaround time: 5 to 10 working days.

Phone search: Limited phone searching available.

Fax search: May request via the fax.

Online search: At the main website, click on Offender Information. The online system is shut down from 3AM until 3:30 AM.

Corporation, Limited Liability Company, Limited Partnerships, Trademarks, Servicemarks, Limited Liability Partnerships

Secretary of State, Business Records Department, 2300 N Lincoln Blvd, Rm 101, Oklahoma City, OK 73105-4897; 405-522-4582 (Records), 900-825-2424 (Records), 405-521-3771 (Fax), 8AM-5PM.

www.sos.state.ok.us/

Note: Officers are available from the Franchise Tax Dept. of the Oklahoma Tax Commission, 405-521-3161.

Indexing & Storage: Records are available from late 1800's on. Older records are kept at the State Archives. More recent records are maintained on a mainframe. New records are available for inquiry immediately.

Searching: The search includes correct name, status, date of registration, service agent and address, state of domicile, authorized shares and par value, amendments, name changes, mergers, and trade names. The records do not include owner. Include the following in your request-full name of business. Records include:corporations, limited partnerships, limited liability companies, limited liability partnerships, certificate of partnership fictitious name for general partnerships and trade names.

Access by: mail, phone, fax, in person, online.

Fee & Payment: The search fee is $5.00. Copies are provided by the Certification Dept at $1.00 per page. Fee payee: Secretary of State. Prepayment required. Personal checks accepted. The Discover Card is accepted.

Mail search: Turnaround time: 1 to 2 days. A SASE is requested.

Phone search: Dial 1-900-555-2424. The fee is $5.00 per call and you are allowed up to 3 record searches per call. Dial 405-522-4582 and purchase records using a credit card. $5.00 also applies, one fee per record.

Fax search: Turnaround time 1 to 2 days.

In person search: There is no fee to search records on a public access terminal.

Online search: Visit SOONERAccess at https://www.sooneraccess.state.ok.us/ for free lookups on names and entities, including registered agents and Trademarks. Customers may also order and receive status certificates as well as certified and plain copies from this system.

Other access: A copy of the corporation database is available on cartridges or on magnetic tape for $500.

Uniform Commercial Code

UCC Central Filing Office, Oklahoma County Clerk, 320 R.S. Kerr Ave, County Office Bldg, Rm 105, Oklahoma City, OK 73102; 405-713-1521, 405-713-1810 (Fax), 8AM-5PM.

www.oklahomacounty.org/countyclerk

Note: This county agency is the central filing agency for the state.

Indexing & Storage: Records are available for since 2/91 on UCC, 10 years on tax liens on computer. Records are on microfiche from 1977 to present. It takes 2 to 3 days before new records are available for inquiry. Records are normally destroyed after one year form lapse.

Searching: Use search request form UCC-11, national standard form. Include the following in your request-debtor name.

Access by: mail, in person, online.

Fee & Payment: The search fee is $10.00 per debtor name, the copy fee is $1.00 per page, to certify the document add $1.00. Fee payee: Oklahoma County Clerk. Prepayment required. Personal checks accepted. No credit cards accepted, but may start inlate 2004.

Mail search: Turnaround time: 2 days.

In person search: Turnaround time is while you wait.

Online search: Records of all UCC financing statements may be viewed free on the Internet at www.oklahomacounty.org/coclerk/default.htm. Neither certified searches nor record requests are accepted at the web. Search by debtor or secured party.

Other access: The entire database is available on microfilm or computer tapes, prices start at $500.

Federal Tax Liens, State Tax Liens

Records not maintained by a state level agency.

Note: All state tax liens and federal tax liens are filed at the local level. Federal tax liens on businesses are filed with the Clerk of Oklahoma County.

Sales Tax Registrations

Taxpayer Assistance, Sale Tax Registration Records, 2501 N Lincoln Blvd, Oklahoma City, OK 73194; 405-521-3160, 405-521-3200, 405-521-3826 (Fax), 7:30AM-4:30PM.

www.oktax.state.ok.us/salesuse.html

Indexing & Storage: Records are available for the most recent 10 years on computer, microfilmed back to the 1970's.

Searching: This agency will provide any information found on the face of the permit-business name, address, tax permit number, and SIC code. Payment history is not released. Include the following in your request-permit number or business name. They will also search by owner name, federal tax ID, or by tax permit number.

Access by: mail, phone, in person.

Fee & Payment: No search fees, but there is a copy fee of $.25 per page. Fee payee: Oklahoma Tax Commission. Prepayment required. If the card is used, there is an additional fee equal to 1.35% of the purchase. Personal checks accepted. No credit cards accepted.

Mail search: Turnaround time: within 2 weeks. A SASE is requested.

Phone search: Tax permit numbers can be verified by phone, via an automated system.

In person search: Copies cost $.25 per page.

Other access: Current sales tax permit holders are permitted to purchase the sales tax database on microfiche or on 3.5 inch floppies. The annual subscription is $150.00 and is updated monthly.

Birth Certificates

State Department of Health, Vital Records Service, PO Box 53551, Oklahoma City, OK 73152-3551 (Courier: 1000 NE 10th St, Oklahoma City, OK 73117); 405-271-4040, 405-271-1646 (Order Line), 405-232-3311 (Fax), 8:30AM-4PM.

www.health.state.ok.us/program/vital/brec.html

Indexing & Storage: Records are available from 1908 on. Records are computerized since 1930. New records are available for inquiry immediately. Records are indexed on inhouse computer.

Searching: Must have a signed release from person of record or immediate family member. Include the following in your request-full name, names of parents, mother's maiden name, date of birth, place of birth, reason for information request, and copy of ID of requester. Also, daytime phone number.

Access by: mail, phone, fax, in person.

Fee & Payment: Fee is $10.00. Fee payee: Oklahoma State Health Department. Prepayment required. Personal checks accepted. Credit cards accepted: MasterCard, Visa.

Mail search: Turnaround time: 1 to 2 weeks. A SASE is requested.

Phone search: See expedited service.

Fax search: See expedited service.

In person search: Turnaround time is while you wait.

Expedited service: Expedited service is available for fax and phone searches. Turnaround time: 1-2 days. Add $15.50 for express delivery. Use of credit card required, for an additional $10.95 fee.

Death Records

State Department of Health, Vital Records Service, PO Box 53551, Oklahoma City, OK 73152-3551 (Courier: 1000 NE 10th St, Oklahoma City, OK 73117); 405-271-4040, 405-271-1646 (Order Line), 405-232-3311 (Fax), 8:30AM-4PM.

www.health.state.ok.us/program/vital/brec.html

Indexing & Storage: Records are available from October 1908 on. Records are computerized since 1930. New records are available for inquiry immediately. Records are indexed on microfiche, inhouse computer.

Searching: Records are open to the public. Include the following in your request-full name, date of death, place of death, copy of ID of requester. Also, daytime phone number.

Access by: mail, phone, fax, in person.

Fee & Payment: Fee is $10.00 per record. Fee payee: Oklahoma State Health Department. Prepayment required. Personal checks accepted. No credit cards accepted.

Mail search: Turnaround time: 1 to 2 weeks. A SASE is requested.

Phone search: See expedited service.

Fax search: See expedited service.

In person search: Turnaround time is while you wait.

Expedited service: Expedited service is available for fax and phone searches. Turnaround time: 1-2 days. Add $15.50 for express delivery. Use of credit card required, for an additional $10.95 fee.

Marriage Certificates, Divorce Records

Records not maintained by a state level agency.

Note: Marriage and Divorce records are found at county level. The record should be requested from the county courthouse in the county where the marriage or divorce was filed or granted.

Workers' Compensation Records

Workers Compensation Court, Records, 1915 N Stiles Ave, Oklahoma City, OK 73105-4918; 405-522-8600, 405-522-8640 (Records Dept), 800-269-5353 (Enforcement), 405-552-8647 (Fax), 8AM-5PM.

www.owcc.state.ok.us

Indexing & Storage: Records are available since 1989 on computer. Index to case files are on print-outs and cards since the 1930's. It takes one day before new records are available for inquiry. Records are normally destroyed after ten years.

Searching: Claims information is considered public record. Anyone having a correct case number can access and review files. There are 2 searches involved-1st to get case number, then to do search. Any requests must be on their forms. Pending cases are available. Include the following in your request-claimant name, Social Security Number, claim number, date of birth, date of accident. To get the claim number, send a written request (Attn: Prior Claims) on their "Request for Information Form," and they will notify you of the case number. With a case number, you can request copies, but you must use their form.

Access by: mail, in person.

Fee & Payment: Using their "Request for Information Form" (index card), include a $1.00 search fee to get the case number, unless you are statutorily exempt. The copy fee is $1.00 for the first page and $.50 each add'l page if done by staff; $.25 if by searcher. Fee payee: Workers' Compensation Court. Prepayment required. In-state businesses can set up charge accounts for copies only; payment due within 30 days. Personal checks accepted. No credit cards accepted.

Mail search: Turnaround time: 5 days. Frequent requesters should set up an account. If payment not included, party will be billed and funds must be received before documents are mailed. A SASE is requested.

In person search: One may search on the in-house computer in the basement level and also request and review a file ($1.00 per file). Files are pulled for the public from 8:15AM to 4:45PM.

Other access: PDF versions of most forms are available at the website.

Driver Records

MVR Desk, Records Management Division, PO Box 11415, Oklahoma City, OK 73136-0415 (Courier: 3600 Martin Luther King Blvd, Rm 206, Oklahoma City, OK 73111); 405-425-2262, 8AM-4:45PM.

www.dps.state.ok.us/dls

Note: Copies of tickets may be obtained for $.25 per page from the address listed above. Most tickets are two pages. For certification of copies, add $3.00.

Indexing & Storage: Records are available for 3 years for moving violations, DWIs and suspensions. All violations, except speeding less than ten mph over the limit, appear on the driving record. Accidents are reported if there is a conviction of citation. It takes 10 days to 6 months before new records are available for inquiry.

Searching: Information is available for law enforcement purposes. Anyone else requesting an MVR for another person is required to submit a consent to release records form signed by both parties. Ask for a State of Oklahoma Records Request Form. Include the following in your request-full name and date of birth, or driver's license number. Requesters can also visit "local tag agencies" to obtain record information. The following data is not released: medical records, Social Security Numbers, addresses or personal information (height, weight, sex, eye color, etc.).

Access by: mail, in person, online.

Fee & Payment: The fee is $10.00 per driving record. There is a full fee for a no record found. Online access is slightly higher ($12.50). Fee payee: Department of Public Safety. Prepayment required. Personal checks accepted. No credit cards accepted.

Mail search: Turnaround time: 1 week to 10 days. This agency offers a monthly billing system for high volume requesters. A SASE is requested.

In person search: Records may be requested at any Oklahoma Tag Agency statewide. Up to ten requests may be processed in one day or less. Many MV offices across the state will sell records.

Online search: Online access is available for qualified, approved users through www.youroklahoma.com. This is a batch mode process with plans for interactive service in the future. The $12.50 fee includes a $2.50 service fee. For further information, call 800-955-3468.

Vehicle and Vessel Ownership and Registration

Oklahoma Tax Commission, Motor Vehicle Division, Attn: Research, 2501 N Lincoln Blvd, Oklahoma City, OK 73194; 405-521-3770, 7:30AM-4:30PM.

www.oktax.state.ok.us/mvhome.html

Indexing & Storage: Records are available for 3 years (registration records); the state keeps title records internally for 20 years. All watercraft must be titled and registered. All motors in excess of 10 HP must be titled. Lien information appears on title records. It takes 2 up to 5 weeks before new records are available for inquiry.

Searching: Records are not released to casual requesters. Approved requesters must use the Vehicle Information Request Form 769 completed front and back. Name searches are not performed. The title number, VIN or current plate number is needed for a search. Actual signature on each form required.

Access by: mail, in person.

Fee & Payment: Current ownerhip/lienholder data is $1.00. A computer generated title history is $5.00 (models 1992 & newer), a microfilm title history is $7.50, and a certified microfilm title history is $10.00. Fee payee: Oklahoma Tax Commission, MVD. Prepayment required.

Personal checks accepted. No credit cards accepted.

Mail search: Turnaround time: 7 to 10 days.

In person search: Turnaround time is while you wait, depending on the workload.

Other access: Oklahoma does not offer bulk delivery of vehicle and ownership information except for purposes such as vehicle recall.

Accident Reports

Department of Public Safety, Records Management Division, PO Box 11415, Oklahoma City, OK 73136 (Courier: 3600 Martin Luther King Blvd, Room 206, Oklahoma City, OK 73111); 405-425-2192, 405-425-2046 (Fax), 8AM-4:45PM.

www.dps.state.ok.us

Note: This agency refers to these reports as Collision Reports. Reports are held 60 days before release to the public.

Indexing & Storage: Records are available for 3 years to present. It takes 10 to 14 days before new records are available for inquiry. Records are indexed on inhouse computer.

Searching: Include the following in your request-date of accident, location of accident, full name, county. Qualified requesters include those uses listed under DPPA and members of the media.

Access by: mail, phone, in person.

Fee & Payment: The fee is $7.00 for an uncertified copy and $10.00 for a certified copy. There is no charge for a no record found. Fee payee: Department of Public Safety. Prepayment required. Personal checks accepted. No credit cards accepted.

Mail search: Turnaround time: 24 hours. A SASE is requested.

Phone search: No fee for telephone request. This agency will reveal whether there is an accident over the phone. No other information will be revealed over the phone.

In person search: Normal turnaround time is while you wait.

Voter Registration

State Election Board, PO Box 53156, Oklahoma City, OK 73152 (Courier: State Capitol-Rm B6, Oklahoma City, OK 73105); 405-521-2391, 405-521-6457 (Fax), 8AM-5PM.

www.elections.state.ok.us

Indexing & Storage: Records are available for 4 years. It takes 7 to 10 days before new records are available for inquiry.

Searching: Records are open to the public and can be accessed at both the state and county levels. Include the following in your request-subject name, address and DOB. The following data is not released: phone numbers.

Access by: mail, phone, fax, in person.

Fee & Payment: There is no fee for look-ups. Fee payee: OK State Election Board Certified funds or cashier's checks are preferred for database sales. A 2-week hold is placed on order paid for using personal check. No credit cards accepted.

Mail search: Turnaround time: 2 to 5 days. No SASE is required.

Phone search: Limited information is given, depending on staff availability.

Fax search: available.

In person search: Simple requests may be processed while you wait.

Other access: A statewide database can be purchased on CD for a fee of $150. Large counties are available on CD for $50-75, and smaller counties or precincts or district are available on disk for $10-35.

GED Certificates

State Dept of Education, Lifelong Learning, 2500 N Lincoln Blvd, Rm 115, Oklahoma City, OK 73105; 405-521-3321, 405-522-5394 (Fax).

http://sde.state.ok.us

Searching: To search, all of the following is required: name, approximate year of test, date of birth, and SSN.

Access by: mail, phone, fax, in person.

Fee & Payment: There is no fee for a verification. There is a $5.00 fee to obtain a transcript. If a duplicate certification is needed, that is $5.00 plus you must also purchase the transcript for $5.00. Fee payee: State Dept of Education. Prepayment required. Money orders and business checks are accepted. No credit cards accepted.

Mail search: Turnaround time: 1 to 2 days. No SASE is required.

Phone search: This is for verification only.

Fax search: The will accept requests for verifications only, not for transcripts.

In person search: Turnaround time is typically 30 minutes for verification.

Hunting and Fishing License Information

Access to Records is Restricted

Department of Wildlife Conservation, Fish & Game Records, PO Box 53465, Oklahoma City, OK 73152; 405-521-3852, 405-521-6535 (Fax), 8AM-4:30PM.

www.wildlifedepartment.com

Note: They have a central database, but do not release information to the public.

Oklahoma State Licensing Agencies

Licenses Searchable Online

Accounting Firm #15	www.youroklahoma.com/oab/search.php
Advanced Registered Nurse Practitioner #30	www.youroklahoma.com/nursing/verify/
Alarm Company #37	www.health.state.ok.us/program/ol/OklahomaLicensedAlarmCompanies.pdf
Alarm Company Employee #37	www.health.state.ok.us/program/ol/AlarmIndividualsByCompanys.pdf
Architect #23	www.youroklahoma.com/architects/index.php?s=license.html
Athletic Trainer/Apprentice #8	www.okmedicalboard.org/display.php?content=md_search_advanced:md_search_advanced
Attorney #28	www.oklahomafindalawyer.com/find
Audiologist #6	www.obespa.state.ok.us/License%20Data.htm
Bank #35	www.state.ok.us/~osbd/
Certified Nurse Midwife #30	www.youroklahoma.com/nursing/verify/
Certified Registered Nurse Anesthetist #30	www.youroklahoma.com/nursing/verify/
Clinical Nurse Specialist #30	www.youroklahoma.com/nursing/verify/
Consumer Finance Company #20	www.okdocc.state.ok.us/
Credit Services Organization #20	www.okdocc.state.ok.us/
Credit Union #35	www.state.ok.us/~osbd/
Dental Laboratory #29	www.dentist.state.ok.us/lists/index.htm
Dentist/Dental Assistant/Hygenist #29	www.dentist.state.ok.us/lists/index.htm
Dietitian/Provisional Licensed Dietitian #8	www.okmedicalboard.org/display.php?content=md_search_advanced:md_search_advanced
Electrologist #8	www.okmedicalboard.org/display.php?content=md_search_advanced:md_search_advanced
Engineer #13	www.pels.state.ok.us/roster/index.html
Funeral Home #5	www.okfuneral.com/funeralhomedirectory/index.htm
Health Spa #20	www.okdocc.state.ok.us/
Home Inspector #37	www.health.state.ok.us/program/ol/home-inspector-list.pdf
Investment Company #34	www.securities.state.ok.us/_private/DB_Query/Corp_Fin_Search.htm
Landscape Architect #23	www.youroklahoma.com/architects/index.php?s=license.html
Lobbyist #42	www.state.ok.us/~ethics/lobbyist.html
Medical Doctor #8	www.okmedicalboard.org/display.php?content=md_search_advanced:md_search_advanced
Money Order Agent #35	www.state.ok.us/~osbd/
Mortgage Broker #20	www.okdocc.state.ok.us/
Notary Public #26	https://www.sooneraccess.state.ok.us/notary/notary_search-menu.asp
Nurse-RN/LPN #30	www.youroklahoma.com/nursing/verify/
Occupational Therapist/Assistant #8	www.okmedicalboard.org/display.php?content=md_search_advanced:md_search_advanced
Optometrist #7	www.arbo.org/odfinder/LicSearch.asp
Orthotist/Prosthetist #8	www.okmedicalboard.org/display.php?content=md_search_advanced:md_search_advanced
Osteopathic Physician #10	www.docboard.org/ok/df/oksearch.htm
Pawnbroker #20	www.okdocc.state.ok.us/
Payday Lender #20	www.okdocc.state.ok.us/
Perdorthist #8	www.okmedicalboard.org/display.php?content=md_search_advanced:md_search_advanced
Perfusionist #8	www.okmedicalboard.org/display.php?content=md_search_advanced:md_search_advanced
Pesticide Applicator #27	http://kellysolutions.com/ok/
Pesticide Certification/Registration #27	http://kellysolutions.com/ok/
Pesticide Dealers #27	http://kellysolutions.com/ok/
Pharmacy Intern /Technician #11	http://lv.pharmacy.state.ok.us/osbpinquire/
Physical Therapist/Assistant #8	www.okmedicalboard.org/display.php?content=md_search_advanced:md_search_advanced
Physician Assistant #8	www.okmedicalboard.org/display.php?content=md_search_advanced:md_search_advanced
Podiatrist #12	www.okmedicalboard.org/display.php?content=md_search_advanced:md_search_advanced
Precious Metals & Gem Dealer #20	www.okdocc.state.ok.us/
Private Investigator Individual/Agency #19	www.opia.com/find_a_pi/default.asp
Prosthetist #8	www.okmedicalboard.org/display.php?content=md_search_advanced:md_search_advanced
Public Accountant-CPA #15	www.youroklahoma.com/oab/search.php
Real Estate Agent/Broker/Sales #38	www.orec.state.ok.us/agents2.html
Real Estate Appraiser #33	www.asc.gov/content/category1/appr_by_state.asp
Real Estate Corp./Partnership #38	www.orec.state.ok.us/agents2.html
Rent to Own Dealer #20	www.okdocc.state.ok.us/
Respiratory Care Practitioner #8	www.okmedicalboard.org/display.php?content=md_search_advanced:md_search_advanced
Savings & Loan Association #35	www.state.ok.us/~osbd/
Speech Pathologist #6	www.obespa.state.ok.us/License%20Data.htm
Surveyor, Land #13	www.pels.state.ok.us/roster/index.html
Trust Company #35	www.state.ok.us/~osbd/

Oklahoma Licensing Quick Finder

Accounting Firm #15 405-521-2397	Facial Operator/Esthetician #4 405-521-2441	Payday Lender #20 405-521-3653
Advanced Registered Nurse Practitioner #30 405-962-1800	Feed/Seed #27 405-522-5894	Perdorthist #8 .... 405-848-6841 x113
Alarm Company #37 405-271-5217	Fertilizer #27 405-522-5985	Perfusionist #8 .... 405-848-6841 x113
Alarm Company Employee #37 405-271-5217	Firearm Permit for Retired Police Officer #19 405-425-2484	Pesticide Applicator #27 405-522-5984
Alcohol & Drug Influence Tester #17 405-425-2460	Forester #16 405-522-6147	Pesticide Certification/Registration #27 405-522-5950
Animal Technician #18 405-524-9006	Funeral Director #5 405-522-1790	Pesticide Dealers #27 405-522-5984
Architect #23 405-949-2383	Funeral Home #5 405-522-1790	Pharmacist #11 405-521-3815
Asbestos Abatement Worker #44. 405-528-1500 x326	Ground Water & Observation Water Well Driller #39 405-530-8800	Pharmacy #11 405-521-3815
Athletic Trainer/Apprentice #8 .... 405-848-6841 x113	Groundwater Right Permitting #39 405-530-8800	Pharmacy Intern #11 405-521-3815
Attorney #28 405-416-7000	Hairbraider #4 405-521-2441	Pharmacy Technician #11 405-521-3815
Audiologist #6 405-840-2774	Health Spa #20 405-521-3653	Physical Therapist/Assistant #8 .. 405-848-6841 x113
Bail Bondsman #32 405-521-6610	Hearing Aid Dealer/Fitter #37 405-271-5217	Physician Assistant #8 .... 405-848-6841 x113
Bank #35 405-521-2783	Home Inspector #37 405-271-5217	Placement Agency #21 405-521-3561
Barber Instructor #37 405-271-5217	Horse Racing #31 405-943-6472	Plumbing Contractor/Inspector #36 405-271-5217
Barber Shop #37 405-271-5217	Horse Racing Professional #31 405-943-6472	Podiatrist #12 405-848-6841
Barber/Barber Apprentice #37 405-271-5217	Horse Trainer #31 405-943-6472	Police Officer #19 405-425-2755
Beauty School #4 405-521-2441	Insurance Adjuster #32 405-521-2828	Polygraph Examiner/Intern #40 405-425-2772
Beauty Shop/Salon #4 405-521-2441	Insurance Agent/Rep. #32 405-521-2828	Polygraph Operator #19 405-425-2778
Blacksmith #31 405-943-6472	Insurance Consultant #32 405-521-2828	Precious Metals & Gem Dealer #20.. 405-521-3653
Building Inspector #37 405-271-5217	Investment Adviser / Rep. #34 405-280-7700	Private Investigator/Agency #19 405-425-2775
Burglar Alarm Salesman #37 405-271-5217	Investment Company #34 405-280-7700	Prosthetist #8 .... 405-848-6841 x113
Burglar Alarm Service/Installer #37 405-271-5217	Issuer Agent #34 405-280-7700	Psychologist #14 405-524-9094
Cemetery #35 405-521-2783	Jockey #31 405-943-6472	Public Accountant-CPA #15.... 405-521-2397
Certified Nurse Midwife #30 405-962-1800	Jockey Agent #31 405-943-6472	Pump Installer #39 405-530-8800
Certified Registered Nurse Anesthetist #30 405-962-1800	Journeyman #36 405-271-5217	Real Estate Agent/Broker/Sales #38 ... 405-521-3387
	Land Sales Agent #34 405-280-7700	Real Estate Appraiser #33 405-521-6636
Children & Youth Agency, Private/Public #21 405-521-3561	Landscape Architect #23 405-949-2383	Real Estate Corp./Partnership #38 405-521-3387
Chiropractor #3 405-524-6223	Liquor Industry #1 405-521-3484	Rent to Own Dealer #20 405-521-3653
Clinical Nurse Specialist #30 405-962-1800	Lobbyist #42 405-521-3451	Residential Child Care Facility #21 405-521-3561
Consumer Finance Company #20 405-521-3653	LPG-Liquefied Petroleum Dealer/Mfg./Mgr #25 405-521-2458	Respiratory Care Practitioner #8.. 405-848-6841 x113
Cosmetician/Dry Hair Stylist #4 405-521-2441		Sanitarian/Environmental Spec'l #37 ... 405-271-5217
Cosmetology Instructor #4 405-521-2441	LPG-Liquef'd Petrol. System Instal. #25 405-521-2458	Savings & Loan Association #35 405-521-2783
Cosmetology Student/Apprentice #4 ... 405-521-2441	Manicurist #4 405-521-2441	School Accreditation #41 405-521-3301
Counselor LPC/LM&T #43 405-271-6030	Mechanical Contractor #36 405-271-5217	School Transportation #41 405-521-3301
Credit Services Organization #20 405-521-3653	Mechanical Inspector #36 405-271-5217	Securities Broker-Dealer #34 405-280-7700
Credit Union #35 405-521-2783	Medical Doctor #8 .... 405-848-6841 x113	Security Guard/Agency #19 405-425-2775
Dental Hygienist #29 .405-524-9037/ 1-866-534-9037	Mining Operation #22 405-521-3859	Self Defense Act Instructor #19 405-425-2760
Dental Lab #29 ...... 405-524-9037/ 1-866-534-9037	Money Order Agent #35 405-521-2783	Shorthand Reporter #9 405-521-2450
Dentist/Dental Assist.#29 405-524-9037/ 866-534-9037	Mortgage Broker #20 405-521-3653	Social Worker #24 405-946-7230
Dietitian/Prov'l Dietitian #8 .... 405-848-6841 x113	Notary Public #26 405-521-2516	Speech Pathologist #6 405-840-2774
Electrical Contractor #37 405-271-5217	Nurse-RN/LPN #30 405-962-1800	Surface Wat Right Permit #39 405-530-8800
Electrical Inspector #37 405-271-5217	Nursery, Plant #27 405-522-5953	Surveyor, Land #13 405-521-2874
Electrician, Journeyman #37 405-271-5217	Nursing Home Administrator #2 405-521-0991	Teacher #41 405-521-3301
Electrologist #8 .... 405-848-6841 x113	Occupational Therapist/Assist.#8. 405-848-6841 x113	Trust Company #35 405-521-2783
Embalmer #5 405-522-1790	Optometrist #7 405-733-7836	Veterinarian #18 405-524-9006
Emergency Medical Tech. #37 405-271-4240	Orthotist/Prosthetist #8 .... 405-848-6841 x113	Veterinary Technician #18 405-524-9006
Engineer #13 405-521-2874	Osteopathic Physician #10 405-528-8625	Waste Water Operator #45 405-702-1000
Facial Operator School/Instructor #4 405-521-2441	Pawnbroker #20 405-521-3653	Weights & Measures, Agricultural #27. 405-522-5870
		Well Driller/Monitor #39 405-530-8800

Oklahoma Licensing Agency Information

1 Alcoholic Beverage Laws Enforcement Commission, 4545 N Lincoln Blvd, #270, Oklahoma City, OK 73105; 405-521-3484, Fax: 405-521-6578. www.able.state.ok.us Email: ablecomm@mhs.oklaosf.state.ok.us

2 Board for Nursing Home Administrators, 3033 N Walnut, #100E, Oklahoma City, OK 73105; 405-521-0991, Fax: 405-528-3483. Email: jclark@oklaosf.state.ok.us

3 Board of Chiropractic Examiners, 201 N.E. 38th Terrace, Suite 3, Oklahoma City, OK 73105; 405-524-6223, Fax: 405-524-9542. www.state.ok.us/~chiro/obce.htm Email: bkelly@chiro.state.ok.us

4 Board of Cosmetology, 2401 NW 23rd St #84, Oklahoma City, OK 73107-2431; 405-521-2441, Fax: 405-521-2440. www.state.ok.us/~cosmo

5 Board of Embalmers & Funeral Directors, 4545 N Lincoln Blvd, #175, Oklahoma City, OK 73105; 405-522-1790, Fax: 405-522-1797. www.okfuneral.com Email: info@okfuneral.com

6 Board of Examiners for Speech Pathology/Audiology, 1140 NW 63rd, #305 (PO Box 53592), Oklahoma City, OK 73152-3592; 405-840-2774, Fax: 405-843-3489. www.obespa.state.ok.us Email: obespa@oklaosf.state.ok.us   Search Database at www.obespa.state.ok.us/License%20Data.htm

7 Board of Examiners in Optometry, 6912 E Reno Ave #302, Midwest City, OK 73110-2162; 405-733-7836, Fax: 405-741-3060. www.state.ok.us/~optometry Email: optboard@oklaosf.state.ok.us Search Database at www.arbo.org/odfinder/LicSearch.asp

8 Board of Medical Licensure & Supervision, 5104 N Francis, #C (POB 18256 OK, OK 73154), Oklahoma City, OK 73118-0256; 405-848-6841 x113, Fax: 405-848-8240. www.okmedicalboard.org/index.php Email: licensing@okmedicalboard.org Search Database at www.okmedicalboard.o rg/index.php ("Find a Doctor")

9 Board of Official Shorthand Reporters, 1915 N Stiles, Rm 305, Oklahoma City, OK 73105; 405-521-2450, Fax: 405-521-9688. www.oscn.net

10 Board of Osteopathic Examiners, 4848 N Lincoln, #100, Oklahoma City, OK 73105; 405-528-8625, Fax: 405-557-0653. www.docboard.org/ok/ok.htm Search Database at www.docboard.org/ok/df/oksearch.htm

11 Oklahoma Board of Pharmacy, 4545 N Lincoln Blvd #112, Oklahoma City, OK 73105-3488; 405-521-3815, Fax: 405-521-3758. www.pharmacy.state.ok.us/
Email: pharmacy@oklaosf.state.ok.us

12 Board of Podiatry, 5104 N Francis, #C, Oklahoma City, OK 73154-0256; 405-848-6841, Fax: 405-848-8240.
Email: executive@osbmis.state.ok.us
Search Database at www.okmedicalboard.org/display.php?content=md_search_advanced:md_search_advanced Note: May purchase information on discs or hardcopy.

13 Board of Professional Engineers & Land Surveyors, 201 NE 27th St, Oklahoma City, OK 73105; 405-521-2874, Fax: 405-523-2135. www.pels.state.ok.us
Email: okpels@pels.state.ok.us Search Database at www.pels.state.ok.us/roster/index.html

14 Board of Psychologists Examiners, 201 NE 38th Terr #3, Oklahoma City, OK 73105; 405.524.9094. www.youroklahoma.com/agencies/contact.php?page=135

15 Board of Public Accountancy, 4545 N Lincoln Blvd, #165, Oklahoma City, OK 73105; 405-521-2397, Fax: 405-521-3118.
www.youroklahoma.com/oab/
Email: okaccybd@oklaosf.state.ok.us
Search Database at www.youroklahoma.com/oab/search.php

16 Board of Registration for Foresters, 2800 N Lincoln Blvd, Agriculture Bldg, Oklahoma City, OK 73105-4298; 405-522-6147, Fax: 405-522-4583.
Email: kurt@oda.state.ok.us Note: Will provide list of registered foresters.

17 Board of Tests for Alcohol & Drug Influence, PO Box 11415, Oklahoma City, OK 73136-0415; 405-425-2460, Fax: 405-425-2490.
Email: msample@dos.state.ok.us

18 Board of Veterinary Medical Examiners, 201 NE 38th Terr. #1, Oklahoma City, OK 73105; 405-524-9006, Fax: 405-524-9012.
www.okvetboard.com
Email: information@okvetboard.com

19 Council on Law Enforcement Education & Training, 3530 N Martin Luther King Ave, Oklahoma City, OK 73136-0476; 405-425-2750, Fax: 405-425-2773.
www.cleet.state.ok.us
Email: nfloyd@cleet.state.ok.us

20 Department of Consumer Credit, 4545 N Lincoln Blvd, #104, Oklahoma City, OK 73105; 405-521-3653, Fax: 405-521-6740.
www.okdocc.state.ok.us/
Email: kbanks@okdocc.state.ok.us
Search Database at www.okdocc.state.ok.us/

21 Department of Human Services, PO Box 25352, Oklahoma City, OK 73125; 405-521-3561, Fax: 405-522-2564.
www.okdhs.org/childcare/

22 Department of Mines, Mining Commission, 4040 N Lincoln, #107, Oklahoma City, OK 73105; 405-521-3859, Fax: 405-427-9646.
www.odl.state.ok.us/sginfo/oksg/ok_mines.htm

23 Board of Governors/Licensed Architects & Landscape Architects, PO Box 53430 (3555 NW 58th St #640), Oklahoma City, OK 73152; 405-949-2383, Fax: 405-949-1690.
www.state.ok.us/~architects/
Search Database at www.state.ok.us/~architects/

24 Licensed Social Workers Registration Board, 5104 North Francis, Suite E, Oklahoma City, OK 73112; 405-946-7230, Fax: 405-942-1070.
www.state.ok.us/~osblsw/
Email: socialwork@oswb.state.ok.us

25 Liquefied Petroleum Gas Board, 2101 N Lincoln Blvd, Jim Thorpe Bldg, Rm B-45, Oklahoma City, OK 73105-4990; 405-521-2458, Fax: 405-521-6037.
Email: lpgasinfo@lpgas.state.ok.us

26 Office of Secretary of State, Notary Public Department, 2300 N. Lincoln Blvd., Suite 101, Oklahoma City, OK 73105; 405-521-2516, Fax: 405-522-3555.
www.sos.state.ok.us
Email: mary.a.watts@oklaosf.state.ok.us
Search Database at https://www.sooneraccess.state.ok.us/notary/notary_search-menu.asp

27 Department of Agriculture, Food & Forestry, Plant Industry & Comsumer Services Division, 2800 N Lincoln Blvd, Oklahoma City, OK 73105-4298; 405-521-3864, Fax: 405-922-0909.
www.oda.state.ok.us/pics-home.htm

28 Bar Association, Attorney Certification, 1901 Lincoln Blvd, Oklahoma City, OK 73105; 405-416-7080, Fax: 405-524-7001.
www.okbar.org
Email: jennyg@okbar.org
Search Database at www.oklahomafindalawyer.com/find Note: They sell labels @ $.15 per name.

29 Board of Dentistry, 201 N.E. 38th Terr, #2, Oklahoma City, OK 73105; 405-524-9037, Fax: 405-524-2223.
www.state.ok.us/~dentist/
Email: dentist@oklaosf.state.ok.us
Search Database at www.dentist.state.ok.us/lists/index.htm

30 Board of Nursing, 2915 N Classen Blvd, #524, Oklahoma City, OK 73106; 405-962-1800, Fax: 405-962-1821.
www.youroklahoma.com/nursing/
Email: oklahoma@ncsbn.org
Search Database at www.youroklahoma.com/nursing/verify/

31 Horse Racing Commission, Shepherd Mall 2401 NW 23rd St, # 78, Oklahoma City, OK 73107; 405-943-6472, Fax: 405-943-6474.
www.state.ok.us/~ohrc
Email: ohrc@socket.net

32 Insurance Department, PO Box 53408 (2401 N.W. 23 St #28), Oklahoma City, OK 73152-3408; 405-521-2828, Fax: 405-521-6652.
www.oid.state.ok.us Note: Tulsa office is 3105 E. Skelly Dr #305, Tulsa OK 74105, 918/747-7700.

33 Real Estate Appraiser Board, PO Box 53408, Oklahoma City, OK 73152-3408; 405-521-6636, Fax: 405-522-6909.
www.oid.state.ok.us/agentbrokers/index.html
Email: reab@insurance.state.ok.us

34 Securities Commission, Department of Securities, 120 N Robinson, 1st National Center #860, Oklahoma City, OK 73102; 405-280-7700, Fax: 405-280-7742.
www.securities.state.ok.us
Email: jku@securities.state.ok.us

35 Banking Department, 4545 N Lincoln Blvd, #164, Oklahoma City, OK 73105-3427; 405-521-2782, Fax: 405-522-2993.
www.state.ok.us/~osbd
Search Database at www.state.ok.us/~osbd

37 Department of Health, Occupational Licensing, 1000 NE 10th St, Oklahoma City, OK 73117-1299; 405-271-5600, Fax: 405-271-5254.
www.health.state.ok.us
Email: rockym@health.state.ok.us

38 Real Estate Commission, 2401 NW 23rd St #18, Oklahoma City, OK 73107; 405-521-3387, Fax: 405-521-2189. www.orec.state.ok.us
Email: orec.help@orec.state.ok.us
Search Database at www.orec.state.ok.us/agents2.html

39 Water Resources Board, 3800 N Classen Blvd, Oklahoma City, OK 73118; 405-530-8800, Fax: 405-530-8900. www.owrb.state.ok.us

40 Polygraph Examiners Board, PO Box 11476, Oklahoma City, OK 73136-0476; 405-425-2778, Fax: 405-425-7314.

41 Department of Education, 2500 N Lincoln Blvd, Oklahoma City, OK 73105-4599; 405-521-3301, Fax: 405-521-6205.
www.sde.state.ok.us/home/defaultie.html

42 Ethics Commission, Lobbyist Registration, Sec. of State, 2300 N Lincoln Blvd, RM B5, Oklahoma City, OK 73105-4812; 405-521-3451, Fax: 405-521-4905.
www.ethics.state.ok.us/home.html.
Search Database at www.state.ok.us/~ethics/lobbyist.html

43 Department of Health, Professional Counselor Licensing, 1000 NE 10th, Oklahoma City, OK 73117-1299; 405-271-6030, Fax: 405-271-1918.
www.health.state.ok.us

44 Department of Labor, Asbestos Division, 4001 N Lincoln Blvd, Oklahoma City, OK 73105-5212; 405-528-1500, Fax: 405-528-3412.

45 Department of Environmental Quality, 707 N Robinson, Oklahoma City, OK 73102; 405-702-1000.

Oklahoma Federal Courts

The following list indicates the district and division name for each county in the state. If the bankruptcy court location is different from the district court, then the location of the bankruptcy court appears in parentheses.

County/Court Cross Reference

County	District	Location
Adair	Eastern	Muskogee (Okmulgee)
Alfalfa	Western	Oklahoma City
Atoka	Eastern	Muskogee (Okmulgee)
Beaver	Western	Oklahoma City
Beckham	Western	Oklahoma City
Blaine	Western	Oklahoma City
Bryan	Eastern	Muskogee (Okmulgee)
Caddo	Western	Oklahoma City
Canadian	Western	Oklahoma City
Carter	Eastern	Muskogee (Okmulgee)
Cherokee	Eastern	Muskogee (Okmulgee)
Choctaw	Eastern	Muskogee (Okmulgee)
Cimarron	Western	Oklahoma City
Cleveland	Western	Oklahoma City
Coal	Eastern	Muskogee (Okmulgee)
Comanche	Western	Oklahoma City
Cotton	Western	Oklahoma City
Craig	Northern	Tulsa
Creek	Northern	Tulsa
Custer	Western	Oklahoma City
Delaware	Northern	Tulsa
Dewey	Western	Oklahoma City
Ellis	Western	Oklahoma City
Garfield	Western	Oklahoma City
Garvin	Western	Oklahoma City
Grady	Western	Oklahoma City
Grant	Western	Oklahoma City
Greer	Western	Oklahoma City
Harmon	Western	Oklahoma City
Harper	Western	Oklahoma City
Haskell	Eastern	Muskogee (Okmulgee)
Hughes	Eastern	Muskogee (Okmulgee)
Jackson	Western	Oklahoma City
Jefferson	Western	Oklahoma City
Johnston	Eastern	Muskogee (Okmulgee)
Kay	Western	Oklahoma City
Kingfisher	Western	Oklahoma City
Kiowa	Western	Oklahoma City
Latimer	Eastern	Muskogee (Okmulgee)
Le Flore	Eastern	Muskogee (Okmulgee)
Lincoln	Western	Oklahoma City
Logan	Western	Oklahoma City
Love	Eastern	Muskogee (Okmulgee)
Major	Western	Oklahoma City
Marshall	Eastern	Muskogee (Okmulgee)
Mayes	Northern	Tulsa
McClain	Western	Oklahoma City
McCurtain	Eastern	Muskogee (Okmulgee)
McIntosh	Eastern	Muskogee (Okmulgee)
Murray	Eastern	Muskogee (Okmulgee)
Muskogee	Eastern	Muskogee (Okmulgee)
Noble	Western	Oklahoma City
Nowata	Northern	Tulsa
Okfuskee	Eastern	Muskogee (Okmulgee)
Oklahoma	Western	Oklahoma City
Okmulgee	Northern (Eastern)	Tulsa (Okmulgee)
Osage	Northern	Tulsa
Ottawa	Northern	Tulsa
Pawnee	Northern	Tulsa
Payne	Western	Oklahoma City
Pittsburg	Eastern	Muskogee (Okmulgee)
Pontotoc	Eastern	Muskogee (Okmulgee)
Pottawatomie	Western	Oklahoma City
Pushmataha	Eastern	Muskogee (Okmulgee)
Roger Mills	Western	Oklahoma City
Rogers	Northern	Tulsa
Seminole	Eastern	Muskogee (Okmulgee)
Sequoyah	Eastern	Muskogee (Okmulgee)
Stephens	Western	Oklahoma City
Texas	Western	Oklahoma City
Tillman	Western	Oklahoma City
Tulsa	Northern	Tulsa
Wagoner	Eastern	Muskogee (Okmulgee)
Washington	Northern	Tulsa
Washita	Western	Oklahoma City
Woods	Western	Oklahoma City
Woodward	Western	Oklahoma City

Standards for Federal Courts: The search fee is $20.00 per item (one party name or case number). Certification fee is $7.00 per document. Copy fee is $.50 per page. All fees standard unless noted in profile. Mail Search: always enclose a stamped self addressed envelope unless otherwise noted. Most courts accept fax requests or will suggest a copying/search vendor. Before releasing records, all courts require prepayment unless noted in profile. Open records are located at the court unless otherwise noted. District courts index by defendant and plaintiff as well as by case number. Bankruptcy courts usually index by debtor and case number. While most courts now have their indexes on computer, many still maintain index card files as well.

The universal PACER sign-up number is 800-676-6856. Find PACER and the Party/Case Index on the Web at http://pacer.psc.uscourts.gov. PACER dial-up access is $.60 per minute. Also, courts offering internet access via RACER, PACER, Web-PACER or the new CM-ECF charge $.07 per page fee unless noted as free.

US District Court

Eastern District of Oklahoma

Muskogee Division Clerk, PO Box 607, Muskogee, OK 74401 (courier address: 101 N 5th, Muskogee, OK 74401), 918-684-7920, Fax: 918-684-7902. www.oked.uscourts.gov

Counties: Adair, Atoka, Bryan, Carter, Cherokee, Choctaw, Coal, Haskell, Hughes, Johnston, Latimer, Le Flore, Love, McCurtain, McIntosh, Marshall, Murray, Muskogee, Okfuskee, Pittsburg, Pontotoc, Pushmataha, Seminole, Sequoyah, Wagoner.

Indexing & Storage: New cases available in the index 1 day after filing date.

Fee & Payment: Payment may be made by money order, cashier check. Business checks are not accepted. Personal checks are not accepted. Will bill law firms. Payee: Clerk, U.S. District Court.

Phone Search: Only docket information available.

Mail Search: A SASE not required.

In Person Search: Fee charged if court conducts your in person search for you.

PACER: PACER is available online at http://pacer.oked.uscourts.gov. Toll-free access: 866-863-3767. Local access: 918-687-2166. Case records go back to 1996. Records never purged. New records are online after 1 day.

U.S. Bankruptcy Court

Eastern District of Oklahoma

Okmulgee Division PO Box 1347, Okmulgee, OK 74447 (courier address: PO & Federal Bldg, 111 W 4th St, Room 229, Okmulgee, OK 74447), 918-758-0126, Fax: 918-756-9248. www.okeb.uscourts.gov

Counties: Adair, Atoka, Bryan, Carter, Cherokee, Choctaw, Coal, Haskell, Hughes, Johnston, Latimer, Le Flore, Love, Marshall, McCurtain, McIntosh, Murray, Muskogee, Okfuskee, Okmulgee, Pittsburg, Pontotoc, Pushmataha, Seminole, Sequoyah, Wagoner.

Indexing & Storage: Cases indexed by debtor as well as by case number. New cases available in the index immediately after filing date.

Fee & Payment: Payment may be made by money order, cashier check, personal check. Debtor's checks are not accepted. Payee: Clerk, U.S. Bankruptcy Court. Will fax back $2.00 per page.

Phone Search: Only docket information available by phone. Automated voice case information service (VCIS) is available. Call VCIS at 877-377-1221 or 918-756-8617.

In Person Search: Fee charged if court conducts your in person search for you.

PACER: PACER is available online at http://pacer.okeb.uscourts.gov. Document images available. Records purged every six months. New civil records are online after 1 day.

Electronic Filing: Electronic filing information online at https://ecf.okeb.uscourts.gov

U.S. District Court

Northern District of Oklahoma

Tulsa Division 411 U.S. Courthouse, 333 W 4th St, Tulsa, OK 74103 (courier address: Use mail address for courier delivery) 918-699-4700, Fax: 918-699-4756. www.oknd.uscourts.gov

Counties: Craig, Creek, Delaware, Mayes, Nowata, Okmulgee, Osage, Ottawa, Pawnee, Rogers, Tulsa, Washington.

Indexing & Storage: New cases available in the index immediately after filing date.

Fee & Payment: Payment may be made by money order, cashier check, personal check, Visa, MC. Credit cards are only accepted from in-person searchers. Payee: Clerk, U.S. District Court.

Phone Search: Only docket information available.

In Person Search: Fee charged if court conducts your in person search for you.

PACER: PACER is available online at http://pacer.oknd.uscourts.gov. New records are online after 1 day.

Electronic Filing: Currently in the process of implementing CM/ECF.

Other Online Access: Search using RACER at www.oknd.uscourts.gov/perl/bkplog.html. Access fee is $.07 per page. Document images available.

U.S. Bankruptcy Court

Northern District of Oklahoma

Tulsa Division 224 S. Boulder Ave, Tulsa, OK 74103 (courier address: Use mail address for courier delivery) 918-699-4000, Fax: 918-699-4051. www.oknb.uscourts.gov

Counties: Craig, Creek, Delaware, Mayes, Nowata, Osage, Ottawa, Pawnee, Rogers, Tulsa, Washington.

Indexing & Storage: Cases indexed by debtor as well as by case number. New cases available in the index same day if possible after filing date. District wide searches are available from this court.

Fee & Payment: Payment may be made by money order, cashier check, personal check. Debtor's checks are not accepted. Payee: Clerk, U.S. Bankruptcy Court. No fee to fax results if copy fees prepaid.

Phone Search: Only docket information available by phone, and only if it takes a minimum amount of time. Automated voice case information service (VCIS) is available. Call VCIS at 888-501-6977 or 918-699-4001.

Mail Search: A SASE not required.

In Person Search: Fee charged if court conducts your in person search for you.

PACER: PACER is available online at https://pacer.login.uscourts.gov/cgi-bin/login.pl?court_id=OKNBK. Document images available. Case records go back to 1994. Records never purged. New civil records are online after 1 day.

Electronic Filing: Electronic filing information online at https://ecf.oknb.uscourts.gov

Other Online Access: The court suggests using WebPACER instead of RACER at www.oknb.uscourts.gov/perl/bkplog.html. RACER data has a 24-hour lag time. There is an email new case notification system available, see www.oknb.uscourts.gov/ebn%20intro.pdf.

U.S. District Court

Western District of Oklahoma

Oklahoma City Division Clerk, Room 1210, 200 NW 4th St, Oklahoma City, OK 73102 (courier address: Use mail address for courier delivery) 405-609-5000, Fax: 405-609-5099. www.okwd.uscourts.gov

Counties: Alfalfa, Beaver, Beckham, Blaine, Caddo, Canadian, Cimarron, Cleveland, Comanche, Cotton, Custer, Dewey, Ellis, Garfield, Garvin, Grady, Grant, Greer, Harmon, Harper, Jackson, Jefferson, Kay, Kingfisher, Kiowa, Lincoln, Logan, McClain, Major, Noble, Oklahoma, Payne, Pottawatomie, Roger Mills, Stephens, Texas, Tillman, Washita, Woods, Woodward.

Indexing & Storage: New cases available in the index immediately after filing date. Records are also indexed on microfiche. District wide searches

are available for records from 1907 from this court.

Fee & Payment: Payment may be made by money order, cashier check, personal check. Will bill in some circumstances. Payee: Clerk, U.S. District Court.

Phone Search: Information relating to docket entries will be given over the phone.

Mail Search: A SASE not required.

In Person Search: Fee charged if court conducts your in person search for you.

PACER: PACER is available online at http://pacer.okwd.uscourts.gov. Document images available on the RACER system. Case records go back to 1994. Records never purged. New records are online after 2 days.

Electronic Filing: Electronic filing information online at https://ecf.okwd.uscourts.gov

U.S. Bankruptcy Court

Western District of Oklahoma

Oklahoma City Division 1st Floor, Old Post Office Bldg, 215 Dean A McGee Ave, Oklahoma City, OK 73102 (courier address: Use mail address for courier delivery) 405-609-5700, Fax: 405-609-5752. www.okwb.uscourts.gov

Counties: Alfalfa, Beaver, Beckham, Blaine, Caddo, Canadian, Cimarron, Cleveland, Comanche, Cotton, Custer, Dewey, Ellis, Garfield, Garvin, Grady, Grant, Greer, Harmon, Harper, Jackson, Jefferson, Kay, Kingfisher, Kiowa, Lincoln, Logan, Major, McClain, Noble, Oklahoma, Payne, Pottawatomie, Roger Mills, Stephens, Texas, Tillman, Washita, Woods, Woodward.

Indexing & Storage: Cases indexed by debtor as well as by case number. New cases available in the index 24 hours after filing date. Cases are also indexed by social security number.

Fee & Payment: Payment may be made by money order, cashier check, personal check. Debtor's checks are not accepted. Payee: Clerk, U.S. Bankruptcy Court.

Phone Search: Docket information is available by phone. Automated voice case information service (VCIS) is available. Call VCIS at 800-872-1348 or 405-231-4768.

In Person Search: Fee charged if court conducts your in person search for you.

PACER: No PACER access for this court; free searching available. There is no PACER access to this court.

Other Online Access: Internet access to court records is free at www.okcbankr.com; registration and username required. For information, call 405-609-5700 or 405-609-5746.

Oklahoma County Courts

Court	Jurisdiction	No. of Courts	How Organized
District Courts*	General	82	26 Districts
Municipal Courts of Record	Municipal	2	
Municipal Courts Not of Record	Municipal	340	
Workers' Compensation Court	Special	1	

* Profiled in this Sourcebook.

Court	CIVIL								
	Tort	Contract	Real Estate	Min. Claim	Max. Claim	Small Claims	Estate	Eviction	Domestic Relations
District Courts*	X	X	X	$0	No Max	$4500	X	X	X
Municipal Courts of Record									
Municipal Courts Not of Record									
Workers' Compensation Court									

Court	CRIMINAL				
	Felony	Misdemeanor	DWI/DUI	Preliminary Hearing	Juvenile
District Courts*	X	X	X	X	X
Municipal Courts of Record			X		
Municipal Courts Not of Record			X		
Workers' Compensation Court					

ADMINISTRATION

Administrative Director of Courts, 1915 N Stiles #305, Oklahoma City, OK, 73105; 405-521-2450, Fax: 405-521-6815. www.oscn.net

COURT STRUCTURE

There are 82District Courts in 26 judicial districts. Cities with populations in excess of 200,000 (Oklahoma City and Tulsa) have municipal criminal courts of record. Cities with less than 200,000 do not have such courts.

The small claims limit was raised from $3000 to $4500 in 1998.

ONLINE ACCESS

Free Internet access is available for District Courts in 12 counties and all Appellate courts at www.oscn.net. Both civil and criminal docket information is available for the counties invoved. Also, one can search the Oklahoma Supreme Court Network by single cite or multiple cite (no name searches) from the www.oscn.net Internet site .

Case information is available in bulk form for downloading to computer. For information, call the Administrative Director of Courts, 405-521-2450.

Also, the Oklahoma District Court Records free website at www.odcr.com offers searching from over 30 District Courts. More counties are being added as they are readied; they hope to eventually feature all OK District Courts. Please note many of the county records in this system do not go back 7 years.

Adair County

15th Judicial District Court PO Box 426 (220 W Division), Stilwell, OK 74960; 918-696-7633. Hours: 8AM-4:30PM (CST). *Felony, Misdemeanor, Civil, Eviction, Small Claims, Probate.*

Civil Records: Access: Phone, fax, mail, in person. Both court and visitors may perform in person searches. Search fee: $5.00 per name. Fee is for 7 year search. Required to search: name, years to search. Civil cases indexed by defendant, plaintiff. Civil records archived since 1907.

Criminal Records: Access: Phone, fax, mail, in person. Both court and visitors may perform in person searches. Search fee: $5.00 per name. Fee is for 7 year search. Required to search: name, years to search, DOB; also helpful: SSN. Criminal records archived since 1907.

General Information: Public Access terminal is available. No juvenile, mental health or guardianship records released. Will fax results to local or toll free line. Copy fee: $1.00 for first page, $.50 each add'l. Cert fee: $.50 per page. Payee: Adair County Court Clerk. Personal checks accepted. Prepayment required. Mail requests: SASE required. Mail turnaround time 1 day.

Alfalfa County

4th Judicial District Court County Courthouse, 300 S Grand, Cherokee, OK 73728; 580-596-3523. Hours: 8:30AM-4:30PM (CST). *Felony, Misdemeanor, Civil, Eviction, Small Claims, Probate.*

Civil Records: Access: Mail, in person. Both court and visitors may perform in person searches. Search fee: $5.00 per name. Required to search: name, years to search. Civil cases indexed by defendant, plaintiff. Civil records archived to 1907; on computer back to 1998.

Criminal Records: Access: Mail, in person. Both court and visitors may perform in person searches. Search fee: $5.00 per name. Required to search: name, years to search. Criminal records archived to 1907; on computer back to 1998.

General Information: Public Access terminal is available. No confidential or guardianship records not released. Fee to fax results is $4.00 per page; $2.00 each add'l. Copy fee: $1.00 for first page, $.50 each add'l. Cert fee: $.50 per page. Payee: Court Clerk. Only cashiers checks and money orders accepted. Prepayment required. Mail requests: SASE required. Mail turnaround time 1 day.

Atoka County

25th Judicial District Court 200 E. Court St, Atoka, OK 74525; 580-889-3565. Hours: 8:30AM-4:30PM (CST). *Felony, Misdemeanor, Civil, Eviction, Small Claims, Probate.*

Civil Records: Access: Mail, in person. Both court and visitors may perform in person searches. Search fee: $5.00 per name. Required to search: name, years to search. Civil cases indexed by defendant, plaintiff. Civil records on computer back to 1998; prior on books.

Criminal Records: Access: Mail, in person. Both court and visitors may perform in person searches. Search fee: $5.00 per name. Required to search: name, years to search, DOB or SSN. Criminal records on books from 1920; on computer back to 1998.

General Information: Public Access terminal is available. No adoption, mental health or juvenile records released. Copy fee: $1.00 for first page, $.50 each add'l. Cert fee: $.50 per page. Payee: Court Clerk. Personal checks accepted. Prepayment required. Mail requests: SASE required. Mail turnaround time 1-2 days.

Beaver County

1st Judicial District Court PO Box 237 (111 W 2nd), Beaver, OK 73932; 580-625-3191. Hours: 9AM-Noon, 1-5PM (CST). *Felony, Misdemeanor, Civil, Eviction, Small Claims, Probate.*

Civil Records: Access: Phone, mail, in person. Both court and visitors may perform in person searches. Search fee: $5.00 per name. Required to search: name, years to search. Civil cases indexed by defendant, plaintiff. Civil records on microfilm and archives from late 1800s, computerized back to 1997.

Criminal Records: Access: Mail, in person. Both court and visitors may perform in person searches. Search fee: $5.00 per name. Required to search: name, years to search. Criminal records on microfilm and archives from late 1800s, computerized back to 1997.

General Information: Public Access terminal is available. No adoption, mental health or juvenile records released. Copy fee: $1.00 for first page, $.50 each add'l. Cert fee: $.50. Payee: Court Clerk. Personal checks accepted. Prepayment required. Mail requests: SASE required. Mail turnaround time 1-3 days.

Beckham County

2nd Judicial District Court PO Box 520 (302 E Main St), Sayre, OK 73662; 580-928-3330; Fax: 580-928-9278. Hours: 9AM-5PM (CST). *Felony, Misdemeanor, Civil, Eviction, Small Claims, Probate.*

Civil Records: Access: Fax, mail, in person, online. Both court and visitors may perform in person searches. Search fee: $5.00 per name. Required to search: name, years to search. Civil cases indexed by defendant, plaintiff. Civil records on microfiche back to 1907; on computer back to 1997. Search records from 01/01/00 forward at www.odcr.com. There is no fee.

Criminal Records: Access: Fax, mail, in person, online. Both court and visitors may perform in person searches. Search fee: $5.00 per name. Required to search: name, years to search. Criminal records on microfiche; on computer back to 1997. Search records from 01/01/00 forward at www.odcr.com. There is no fee.

General Information: Public Access terminal is available. No juvenile, adoption or expunged records released. Fee to fax results is $1.00 per page. Copy fee: $1.00 for first page, $.50 each add'l. Cert fee: $.50. Payee: Court clerk. Personal checks accepted. Prepayment required. Mail requests: SASE required. Mail turnaround time 2 weeks.

Blaine County

4th Judicial District Court 212 N. Weigle St, Watonga, OK 73772; 580-623-5970. Hours: 8AM-4PM (CST). *Felony, Misdemeanor, Civil, Eviction, Small Claims, Probate.*

Civil Records: Access: Mail, in person, online. Both court and visitors may perform in person searches. Search fee: $5.00 per name. Required to search: name, years to search. Civil cases indexed by defendant, plaintiff. Civil records archived from 1900; on computer back to 1998. Search records from 08/98 forward at www.odcr.com. There is no fee.

Criminal Records: Access: Mail, in person, online. Both court and visitors may perform in person searches. Search fee: $5.00 per name. Required to search: name, years to search. Criminal records archived from 1900; on computer back to 1998. Search records from 08/98 forward at www.odcr.com. There is no fee.

General Information: Public Access terminal is available. No juvenile or expunged records released. Copy fee: $1.00 for first page, $.50 each add'l. Cert

fee: $.50. Payee: Court Clerk. Personal checks accepted. Prepayment required. Mail requests: SASE required. Mail turnaround time 7-10 days.

Bryan County

19th Judicial District Court Courthouse 3rd Fl, 402 W Evergreen St, Durant, OK 74701; 580-924-1446. Hours: 8:00AM-12:00PM,1:00PM-5:00PM (CST). *Felony, Misdemeanor, Civil, Eviction, Small Claims, Probate.*

Civil Records: Access: Mail, in person, online. Both court and visitors may perform in person searches. Search fee: $5.00 per name. Required to search: name, years to search, DOB. Civil cases indexed by defendant, plaintiff. Civil records archived from 1907; on comptuer back to 1994. Search records from 07/94 forward at www.odcr.com. There is no fee.

Criminal Records: Access: Mail, in person, online. Both court and visitors may perform in person searches. Search fee: $5.00 per name. Required to search: name, DOB, SSN, signed release. Criminal records archived from 1907; on comptuer back to 1994. Search records from 07/94 forward at www.odcr.com. There is no fee.

General Information: Public Access terminal is available. No juvenile, mental health or adoption records released. Copy fee: $1.00 for first page, $.50 each add'l. Cert fee: $.50. Payee: Bryan County Court Clerk. Only cashiers checks and money orders accepted. Prepayment required. Mail requests: SASE required. Mail turnaround time 2 days.

Caddo County

6th Judicial District Court PO Box 10 (201 W Oklahoma Ave), Anadarko, OK 73005; 405-247-3393. Hours: 8:30AM-4:30PM (CST). *Felony, Misdemeanor, Civil, Eviction, Small Claims, Probate.*

Civil Records: Access: Mail, in person. Both court and visitors may perform in person searches. Search fee: $10.00 per hour. Required to search: name, years to search. Civil cases indexed by defendant, plaintiff. Civil records on computer since 1997; prior on docket books to 1901.

Criminal Records: Access: Mail, in person. Both court and visitors may perform in person searches. Search fee: $10.00 per hour. Required to search: name, years to search. Criminal records on computer since 1997, prior on docket books to 1901.

General Information: Public Access terminal is available. No adoption, mental health, juvenile, and some guardianship records released. Copy fee: $1.00 for first page, $.50 each add'l. Cert fee: $.50. Payee: Court Clerk. No foreign checks accepted. Prepayment required. Mail requests: SASE helpful. Turnaround time 1 week.

Canadian County

26th Judicial District Court PO Box 730 (301 N Choctaw St), El Reno, OK 73036; 405-262-1070. Hours: 8AM-4:30PM (CST). *Felony, Misdemeanor, Civil, Eviction, Small Claims, Probate.*

Note: Use ext 168 for civil; 165 for criminal; and 170 for probate.

Civil Records: Access: Mail, online, in person. Both court and visitors may perform in person searches. Search fee: $5.00 per name. Required to search: name, years to search. Civil cases indexed by defendant, plaintiff. Civil records on computer back to 1993, archived from 1907. Online access to court dockets is free at www.oscn.net/applications/oscn/casesearch.asp. Dockets go back to 3/1993.

Criminal Records: Access: Mail, online, in person. Both court and visitors may perform in person searches. Search fee: $5.00 per name. Required to search: name, years to search, DOB or SSN. Criminal records on computer back to 1993, archived from 1907. Online access to criminal dockets is same as civil.

General Information: Public Access terminal is available. No expunged criminal cases, juvenile, adoption, confidential portion of guardianship records released. Copy fee: $1.00 for first page, $.50 each add'l. Cert fee: $.50 per page. Payee: Court Clerk. Personal checks accepted. Prepayment required. Mail turnaround time is 2-3 days.

Carter County

20th Judicial District Court PO Box 37 (First & B Southwest), Court Clerk, Ardmore, OK 73402; 580-223-5253. Hours: 8AM-Noon, 1-5PM (CST). *Felony, Misdemeanor, Civil, Eviction, Small Claims, Probate.*

www.brightok.net/cartercounty/CarterCountyCourtClerk.html

Civil Records: Access: Mail, in person. Both court and visitors may perform in person searches. Search fee: $5.00 per name. Required to search: name, years to search. Civil cases indexed by defendant, plaintiff. Civil records archived from 1907; on computer back to 1997. Only current week dockets are online at clerk's website.

Criminal Records: Access: Mail, in person. Both court and visitors may perform in person searches. Search fee: $5.00 per name. Required to search: name, years to search. Criminal records archived from 1907; on computer back to 1997. Only current week dockets and bench warrants are online at clerk's website.

General Information: Public Access terminal is available. No juvenile, mental health, or adoption records released. The copy room is filled with Elvis memorabilia. Copy fee: $1.00 for first page, $.50 each add'l. Cert fee: $.50. Payee: Carter County Court Clerk. Personal checks accepted. Prepayment required. Mail requests: SASE required. Mail turnaround time 2 weeks.

Cherokee County

15th Judicial District Court 213 W. Delaware, Rm 302, Tahlequah, OK 74464; 918-456-0691; Fax: 918-458-6587. Hours: 8AM-4:30PM (CST). *Felony, Misdemeanor, Civil, Eviction, Small Claims, Probate.*

Civil Records: Access: Phone, mail, in person, online. Both court and visitors may perform in person searches. Search fee: $5.00 per name. Required to search: name, years to search. Civil cases indexed by defendant, plaintiff. Civil records on microfiche from 1907 (civil, probate, vital), computerized since 1997. Search records from 01/97 forward at www.odcr.com. There is no fee.

Criminal Records: Access: Phone, mail, in person, online. Both court and visitors may perform in person searches. Search fee: $5.00 per name. Required to search: name, years to search, DOB. Criminal records kept form 1907. Search records from 01/97 forward at www.odcr.com. There is no fee.

General Information: Public Access terminal is available. No juvenile, adoption or mental health released. Copy fee: $1.00 for first page, $.50 each add'l. Cert fee: $.50 per page. Payee: Court Clerk. Personal checks accepted. Prepayment required. Mail requests: SASE required. Mail turnaround time 1-2 days.

Choctaw County

17th Judicial District Court 300 E. Duke, Hugo, OK 74743; 580-326-7554 & 7555. Hours: 8AM-4PM (CST). *Felony, Misdemeanor, Civil, Eviction, Small Claims, Probate.*

Civil Records: Access: Phone, fax, mail, in person. Both court and visitors may perform in person searches. Search fee: $10.00 per name. Required to search: name, years to search. Civil cases indexed by defendant, plaintiff. Civil records archived from 1907.

Criminal Records: Access: Phone, fax, mail, in person. Both court and visitors may perform in person searches. Search fee: $10.00 per name. Required to search: name, years to search, DOB. Criminal records archived from 1907.

General Information: Public Access terminal is available. No juvenile, adoption, guardianship, wills or expunged records released. Will fax results $7.50 fee. Copy fee: $1.00 for first page, $.50 each add'l. Cert fee: $.50. Payee: Court Clerk. Personal checks accepted. Prepayment required. Mail requests: SASE required. Mail turnaround time 1 day.

Cimarron County

1st Judicial District Court PO Box 788, Boise City, OK 73933; 580-544-2221. Hours: 9AM-Noon,1-5PM (CST). *Felony, Misdemeanor, Civil, Eviction, Small Claims, Probate.*

Civil Records: Access: Phone, mail, in person. Only the court performs in person searches; visitors may not. Search fee: none. Required to search: name, years to search. Civil cases indexed by defendant, plaintiff. Civil records archived from 1907; on computer back to 8/2001.

Criminal Records: Access: Phone, mail, in person. Only the court performs in person searches; visitors may not. Search fee: none. Required to search: name, years to search. Criminal records archived from 1907.

General Information: No juvenile, adoption or mental health records released. Will fax results for $1.00 per page. Copy fee: $1.00 for first page, $.50 each add'l. Cert fee: $.50. Payee: Court Clerk. Personal checks accepted. Prepayment required. Mail requests: SASE requested. Turnaround time 1 day.

Cleveland County

21st Judicial District Court - Civil Branch 200 S. Peters, Norman, OK 73069; 405-321-6402. Hours: 8AM-5PM (CST). *Civil, Eviction, Small Claims, Probate.*

Civil Records: Access: Mail, online, in person. Both court and visitors may perform in person searches. No search fee. Required to search: name, years to search. Civil cases indexed by defendant, plaintiff. Civil records on computer from 1989, on microfiche from 1800s, archived since 1970. Online access to court dockets is free at www.oscn.net/applications/oscn/casesearch.asp. Dockets go back to 1/1989.

General Information: Public Access terminal is available. No expunged, sealed records released. Copy fee: $1.00 for first page, $.50 each add'l. Cert fee: $.50. Payee: Court Clerk. Personal checks accepted. Prepayment required. Mail requests: SASE required. Mail turnaround time 7-10 days.

21st Judicial District Court - Criminal 200 S. Peters, Norman, OK 73069; 405-321-6402. Hours: 8AM-5PM (CST). *Felony, Misdemeanor.*

Criminal Records: Access: Mail, online, in person. Both court and visitors may perform in person searches. No search fee. Required to search: name, years to search. Criminal records on computer from 1989, on microfiche from 1800s. Online access to court dockets is free at www.oscn.net/applications/oscn/casesearch.asp. Dockets go back to 1/1989.

General Information: Public Access terminal is available. No juvenile, adoption, or guardianship records released. Copy fee: $1.00 for first page, $.50 each add'l. Cert fee: $.50. Payee: Cleveland County Court Clerk. Local personal checks accepted.

Prepayment required. Mail turnaround time 7-10 days.

Coal County

25th Judicial District Court 4 N Main St, Coalgate, OK 74538; 580-927-2281. Hours: 8AM-4PM (CST). *Felony, Misdemeanor, Civil, Eviction, Small Claims, Probate.*

Civil Records: Access: In person, mail. Visitors must perform in person searches for themselves. No search fee. Required to search: name, years to search. Civil cases indexed by defendant, plaintiff. Civil records archived since 1907; computerized back to 1999.

Criminal Records: Access: In person, mail. Visitors must perform in person searches for themselves. No search fee. Required to search: name, years to search. Criminal records archived since 1907; computerized back to 1999.

General Information: Public Access terminal is available. No juvenile, adoption, mental health, guardianship, wills or expunged records released. Copy fee: $1.00 for first page, $.50 each add'l. Cert fee: $.50. Payee: Court Clerk. Only cashiers checks and money orders accepted. Prepayment required. Mail requests: SASE required. Mail turnaround time is 2-3 days.

Comanche County

5th Judicial District Court 315 SW 5th St, Rm 504, Lawton, OK 73501-4390; 580-355-4017. Hours: 8AM-5PM (CST). *Felony, Misdemeanor, Civil, Eviction, Small Claims, Probate.*

Note: Traffic and marriage licenses also handled here.

Civil Records: Access: Phone, mail, online, in person. Only the court performs in person searches; visitors may not. Search fee: $10.00 per name. Required to search: name, years to search. Civil cases indexed by defendant, plaintiff. Civil records on computer from 8/88, prior in books to 1901. Online access to court dockets is free at www.oscn.net/applications/oscn/casesearch.asp. Dockets go back to 8/1988.

Criminal Records: Access: Mail, online, in person. Only the court performs in person searches on computer; visitors may not. Search fee: $10.00 per name. Required to search: name, years to search; also helpful: DOB, SSN. Criminal records on computer from 8/88, prior in books to 1901. Online access to court dockets is free at www.oscn.net/applications/oscn/casesearch.asp. Dockets go back to 8/1988.

General Information: No juvenile, mental health, adoption or some probate records released. Copy fee: $1.00 for first page, $.50 each add'l. Cert fee: $.50 per page. Payee: District Court Clerk. Business checks accepted. Prepayment required. Mail requests: SASE required. Mail turnaround time 1 day.

Cotton County

5th Judicial District Court 301 N. Broadway, Walters, OK 73572; 580-875-3029. Hours: 8AM-4PM (CST). *Felony, Misdemeanor, Civil, Eviction, Small Claims, Probate.*

Civil Records: Access: Mail, in person, online. Both court and visitors may perform in person searches. Search fee: $5.00 per name. Required to search: name, years to search. Civil cases indexed by defendant, plaintiff. Civil records archived from 1912; computerized back to 1997. Search records from 01/97 forward at www.odcr.com. There is no fee.

Criminal Records: Access: Mail, in person, online. Both court and visitors may perform in person searches. Search fee: $5.00 per name. Required to search: name, years to search, DOB. Criminal records archived from 1912; computerized back to 1997.

Search records from 01/97 forward at www.odcr.com. There is no fee.

General Information: Public Access terminal is available. No adoption, juvenile, and some guardianship records released. Copy fee: $1.00 for first page, $.50 each add'l. Cert fee: $.50. Payee: Court Clerk. Personal checks accepted. Prepayment required. Mail requests: SASE not required. Mail turnaround time 2 days.

Craig County

12th Judicial District Court 301 W. Canadian, Vinita, OK 74301; 918-256-6451. Hours: 8:30AM-4:30PM (CST). *Felony, Misdemeanor, Civil, Eviction, Small Claims, Probate.*
Note: SSNs are released to the public on criminal case matters, but not for civil cases.

Civil Records: Access: Mail, in person, online. Both court and visitors may perform in person searches. Search fee: $5.00 per name. Required to search: name, years to search. Civil cases indexed by defendant, plaintiff. Civil records on microfilm from 1902; on computer since 4/97. Search records from 04/97 forward at www.odcr.com. There is no fee.

Criminal Records: Access: Mail, in person, online. Both court and visitors may perform in person searches. Search fee: $5.00 per name. Required to search: name, years to search; also helpful: SSN, DOB, sex. Criminal records on microfilm from 1902; on computer since 4/97. Search records from 04/97 forward at www.odcr.com. There is no fee.

General Information: Public Access terminal is available. No mental, guardianship, adoption, or juvenile records released. Copy fee: $1.00 for first page, $.50 each add'l. Cert fee: $.50. Payee: Court Clerk. Personal checks accepted. Prepayment required. Mail requests: SASE required. Mail turnaround time 1-3 days.

Creek County

24th Judicial District Court 222 E Dewey Ave, #201, Sapulpa, OK 74066; 918-227-2525; Fax: 918-227-5030. Hours: 8AM-5PM (CST). *Felony, Misdemeanor, Civil, Eviction, Small Claims, Probate.*
Note: All three courts in this county should be searched, there is not overall countywide database.

Civil Records: Access: In person, online. Visitors must perform in person searches for themselves. No search fee. Required to search: name, years to search; also helpful: address. Civil cases indexed by defendant, plaintiff. Computerized records back to 1998, civil records on docket books and files back to 1907. Search records from 03/98 forward at www.odcr.com. There is no fee.

Criminal Records: Access: In person, online. Visitors must perform in person searches for themselves. No search fee. Required to search: name, years to search; also helpful: address, DOB, SSN. Criminal records on docket books and files. They go back "many years, no exact date known". Search records from 03/98 forward at www.odcr.com. There is no fee.

General Information: Public Access terminal is available. No juvenile, mental health, or adoption records released. Copy fee: $1.00 for first page, $.50 each add'l. Cert fee: $.50. Payee: Creek County Court Clerk. Personal checks accepted. Prepayment required.

24th Judicial District Court PO Box 1055, Bristow, OK 74010; 918-367-5537; Fax: 918-367-5505. Hours: 8AM-5PM (CST). *Felony, Misdemeanor, Civil, Eviction, Small Claims, Probate.*
Note: All three courts in this county should be searched, there is not overall countywide database.

Civil Records: Access: In person, mail, online. Both court and visitors may perform in person searches. No search fee. Required to search: name, years to search; also helpful: address. Civil cases indexed by defendant, plaintiff. Computerized records back to Computerized records back to 1998, civil records on docket books and files back to 1907. Search records from 10/99 forward at www.odcr.com. There is no fee.

Criminal Records: Access: In person, mail, online. Both court and visitors may perform in person searches. No search fee. Required to search: name, years to search; also helpful: address, DOB, SSN. Criminal records on docket books and files. They go back "many years, no exact date known". Search records from 10/99 forward at www.odcr.com. There is no fee.

General Information: Public Access terminal is available. No juvenile, mental health, or adoption records released. Copy fee: $1.00 for first page, $.50 each add'l. Cert fee: $.50. Payee: Creek County Court Clerk. Personal checks accepted. Prepayment required.

24th Judicial District Court 222 E Dewey Ave, #201, Drumright, OK 74030; 918-352-2575. Hours: 8AM-5PM (CST). *Felony, Misdemeanor, Civil, Eviction, Small Claims, Probate.*
Note: All three courts in this county should be searched, there is not overall countywide database.

Civil Records: Access: In person only. Visitors must perform in person searches for themselves. No search fee. Required to search: name, years to search; also helpful: address. Civil cases indexed by defendant, plaintiff. Civil records on docket books and files back at least 20 years.

Criminal Records: Access: In person only. Visitors must perform in person searches for themselves. No search fee. Required to search: name, years to search; also helpful: address, DOB, SSN. Criminal records on docket books and files. They go back "many years, no exact date known".

General Information: No juvenile, mental health, or adoption records released. Copy fee: $1.00 for first page, $.50 each add'l. Cert fee: $.50. Payee: Creek County Court Clerk. Personal checks accepted. Prepayment required.

Custer County

2nd Judicial District Court PO Box D (3rd & B St), Arapaho, OK 73620; 580-323-3233; Fax: 580-331-1121. Hours: 8AM-4PM (CST). *Felony, Misdemeanor, Civil, Eviction, Small Claims, Probate.*
Civil Records: Access: In person, online. Visitors must perform in person searches for themselves. Search fee: Court will not perform civil searches, but may assist. Required to search: name, years to search; also helpful: address. Civil cases indexed by defendant, plaintiff. Civil records go back to 1900s; records on computer go back to 1/95. Search records from 08/01 forward at www.odcr.com. There is no fee.

Criminal Records: Access: Mail, in person, online. Both court and visitors may perform in person searches. Search fee: $5.00 per name. Required to search: name, years to search; also helpful: DOB, SSN. Criminal records go back to 1900s; records on computer go back to 1/95. Search records from 08/01 forward at www.odcr.com. There is no fee.

General Information: Public Access terminal is available. No adoptions, juvenile, or mental records released. Will fax results to local or toll free line. Copy fee: $1.00 for first page, $.50 each add'l. Cert fee: $.50. Payee: Court Clerk. Personal checks accepted. Prepayment required. Mail requests: SASE requested. Turnaround time 2-3 days.

Delaware County

13th Judicial District Court Box 407 (Whitehead & Krause St), Jay, OK 74346; 918-253-4420. Hours: 8AM-4:30PM (CST). *Felony, Misdemeanor, Civil, Eviction, Small Claims, Probate.*
Civil Records: Access: Mail, in person, online. Both court and visitors may perform in person searches. Search fee: $5.00 per name. Required to search: name, years to search. Civil cases indexed by defendant, plaintiff. Civil records on computer since 1996 and on microfilm from 1913. Search records from 06/91 forward at www.odcr.com. There is no fee.

Criminal Records: Access: Mail, in person, online. Both court and visitors may perform in person searches. Search fee: $5.00 per name. Required to search: name, years to search; also helpful: DOB, SSN. Criminal records on computer since 1991. Search records from 06/91 forward at www.odcr.com. There is no fee.

General Information: Public Access terminal is available. No juvenile, adoption, guardianship or search warrant records released. Will fax results. Copy fee: $1.00 for first page, $.50 each add'l. Cert fee: $.50. Payee: Delaware County Court Clerk. Business checks accepted. Prepayment required. Mail requests: SASE requested. Turnaround time 1-2 weeks.

Dewey County

4th Judicial District Court Box 278 (Broadway & Ruble), Taloga, OK 73667; 580-328-5521. Hours: 8AM-4PM (CST). *Felony, Misdemeanor, Civil, Small Claims, Probate.*
Civil Records: Access: Mail, in person. Both court and visitors may perform in person searches. No search fee. Required to search: name, years to search. Civil cases indexed by defendant, plaintiff. Civil records archived from late 1800s, computerized records go back to 1995. All requests must be in writing.

Criminal Records: Access: Mail, in person. Both court and visitors may perform in person searches. No search fee. Required to search: name, years to search; also helpful: SSN. Criminal records archived from late 1800s, computerized records go back to 1995. All requests must be in writing.

General Information: No expunged, adoption, mental, guardianship, juvenile records released. Copy fee: $1.00 for first page, $.50 each add'l. Cert fee: $.50. Payee: Dewey County Court Clerk. Personal checks accepted. Prepayment required. Mail requests: SASE requested. Turnaround time 2 days.

Ellis County

2nd Judicial District Court Box 217 ((100 S Washington St), Arnett, OK 73832; 580-885-7255. Hours: 8:30AM-4:30PM (CST). *Felony, Misdemeanor, Civil, Eviction, Small Claims, Probate.*
Civil Records: Access: Phone, mail, in person, online. Both court and visitors may perform in person searches. No search fee. Required to search: name, years to search. Civil cases indexed by defendant, plaintiff. Civil records on docket books from 1900. Online access to court dockets is free at www.oscn.net/applications/oscn/casesearch.asp.

Criminal Records: Access: Phone, mail, in person, online. Both court and visitors may perform in person searches. Search fee: $5.00 per name. Required to search: name, years to search; also helpful: SSN. Criminal records on docket books from 1900. Online access to court dockets is free at www.oscn.net/applications/oscn/casesearch.asp.

General Information: Public Access terminal is available. No expunged records released. Will fax results to local or toll free line. Copy fee: $1.00 for first page, $.50 each add'l. Cert fee: $.50. Payee: Ellis County Court Clerk. Personal checks accepted. Prepayment required. Mail requests: SASE required. Mail turnaround time 1 day.

Garfield County

4th Judicial District Court 114 W Broadway, Enid, OK 73701-4024; 580-237-0232. Hours: 8AM-4:30PM (CST). *Felony, Misdemeanor, Civil, Eviction, Small Claims, Probate.*

Civil Records: Access: Online, in person. Both court and visitors may perform in person searches. Search fee: $5.00. Required to search: name, years to search. Civil cases indexed by defendant, plaintiff. Civil records on computer from 3-89, on microfiche from 1893. Online access to court dockets is free at www.oscn.net/applications/oscn/casesearch.asp. Dockets go back to 3/1989.

Criminal Records: Access: Online, in person. Both court and visitors may perform in person searches. Search fee: $5.00. Required to search: name, years to search, SSN. Criminal records on computer from 1989, on microfiche from 1893. Online access to criminal dockets is same as civil.

General Information: Public Access terminal is available. No juvenile, mental health, or adoption records released. Copy fee: $1.00 for first page, $.50 each add'l. Cert fee: $.50. Payee: Court Clerk. Personal checks accepted. Prepayment required.

Garvin County

21st Judicial District Court PO Box 239 (201 W Grant), Pauls Valley, OK 73075; 405-238-5596. Hours: 8:30AM-4:30PM (CST). *Felony, Misdemeanor, Civil, Eviction, Small Claims, Probate.*

Civil Records: Access: Mail, in person, online. Both court and visitors may perform in person searches. Search fee: $10.00 per name. SASE enclosed. Required to search: name, years to search. Civil cases indexed by defendant, plaintiff. Civil records on computer since 1994, docket books from 1907. Online access to court dockets is free at www.oscn.net/applications/oscn/casesearch.asp. Also, search records from 01/95 forward at www.odcr.com/. There is no fee.

Criminal Records: Access: Mail, in person, online. Both court and visitors may perform in person searches. Search fee: $10.00 per name. SASE enclosed. Required to search: name, years to search; also helpful: SSN, DOB. Criminal records on computer since 1994, docket books from 1907. Online access to criminal dockets is same as civil.

General Information: Public Access terminal is available. No juvenile, adoption or guardianship released. Will fax results to local or toll free line. Copy fee: $1.00 for first page, $.50 each add'l. Cert fee: $.50 per page. Payee: Garvin County Court Clerk. Only cashiers checks and money orders accepted. Prepayment required. Mail requests: SASE required. Mail turnaround time 1 day.

Grady County

6th Judicial District Court PO Box 605 (4th & Choctaw Ave), Chickasha, OK 73023; 405-224-7446. Hours: 8AM-4:30PM (CST). *Felony, Misdemeanor, Civil, Eviction, Small Claims, Probate.*

Civil Records: Access: In person only. Visitors must perform in person searches for themselves. No search fee. Required to search: name, years to search. Civil cases indexed by defendant, plaintiff. Civil records on microfiche from 1982, archived from 1907.

Criminal Records: Access: In person only. Visitors must perform in person searches for themselves. No search fee. Required to search: name, years to search; also helpful: address, DOB, SSN. Criminal records on microfiche from 1982, archived from 1907.

General Information: Public Access terminal is available. No juvenile, adoption, guardianship or mental health records released. Copy fee: $1.00 for first page, $.50 each add'l. Cert fee: $.50 per document. Payee: Court Clerk. Personal checks accepted. Prepayment required.

Grant County

4th Judicial District Court 112 E Guthrie, Medford, OK 73759; 580-395-2828. Hours: 8AM-4:30PM (CST). *Felony, Misdemeanor, Civil, Eviction, Small Claims, Probate.*

Civil Records: Access: Mail, in person, online. Both court and visitors may perform in person searches. Search fee: $5.00 per name. Required to search: name, years to search. Civil cases indexed by defendant, plaintiff. Civil records archived from 1893, in books since 1898. Search records from 10/97 forward at www.odcr.com. There is no fee.

Criminal Records: Access: Mail, in person, online. Both court and visitors may perform in person searches. Search fee: $5.00 per name. Required to search: name, years to search; also helpful: SSN. Criminal records archived from 1893, in books since 1898. Search records from 10/97 forward at www.odcr.com. There is no fee.

General Information: Public Access terminal is available. No juvenile, adoption, mental health, some guardianship or wills released. Copy fee: $1.00 for first page, $.50 each add'l. Cert fee: $.50 per page. Payee: Court Clerk. No out of state personal checks accepted. Prepayment required. Mail requests: SASE helpful. Turnaround time 1-3 days.

Greer County

2nd Judicial District Court PO Box 216 (Courthouse Sq), Mangum, OK 73554; 580-782-3665. Hours: 9AM-5PM (CST). *Felony, Misdemeanor, Civil, Eviction, Small Claims, Probate.*

Civil Records: Access: Mail, in person. Both court and visitors may perform in person searches. Search fee: $5.00 per name. Required to search: name, years to search. Civil cases indexed by defendant, plaintiff. Civil records on docket books from 1901; on computer back to 1997.

Criminal Records: Access: Mail, in person. Both court and visitors may perform in person searches. Search fee: $5.00 per name. Required to search: name, years to search, DOB; also helpful: SSN. Criminal records on docket books from 1901; on computer back to 1997.

General Information: Public Access terminal is available. No juvenile, mental health, adoption or guardianship records released. Fee to fax results is $1.00 per document. Copy fee: $1.00 for first page, $.50 each add'l. Cert fee: $.50. Payee: Court Clerk. Only cash, cashiers checks or money orders accepted. Prepayment required. Mail requests: SASE required. Mail turnaround time 1-2 days.

Harmon County

3rd Judicial District Court 114 W. Hollis, Hollis, OK 73550; 580-688-3617; Fax: 580-688-2900. Hours: 8AM-5PM (CST). *Felony, Misdemeanor, Civil, Eviction, Small Claims, Probate.*

Civil Records: Access: Mail, fax, in person. Both court and visitors may perform in person searches. Search fee: $5.00 per name. Required to search: name, years to search. Civil cases indexed by

defendant, plaintiff. Civil records on docket books from 1909; on computer since 1996.

Criminal Records: Access: Mail, fax, in person. Both court and visitors may perform in person searches. Search fee: $5.00 per name. Required to search: name, years to search; also helpful: DOB, SSN, sex. Criminal records on docket books from 1909; on computer since 1996.

General Information: No juvenile, adoption, mental health, or guardianship records released. Will fax results if prepaid or you provide proof of payment, facsimile of check, etc. Copy fee: $1.00 for first page, $.50 each add'l. Cert fee: $.50 per page. Payee: Harmon County Court Clerk. Personal checks accepted. Prepayment required. Mail requests: SASE requested. Turnaround time 1-2 days.

Harper County

1st Judicial District Court Box 347 (311 Southeast 1st St), Buffalo, OK 73834; 580-735-2010. Hours: 8AM-4PM (CST). *Felony, Misdemeanor, Civil, Eviction, Small Claims, Probate.*

Civil Records: Access: Mail, in person. Both court and visitors may perform in person searches. Search fee: $5.00 per name. Required to search: name, years to search. Civil cases indexed by defendant, plaintiff. Civil records on docket books from 1907.

Criminal Records: Access: Mail, in person. Both court and visitors may perform in person searches. Search fee: $5.00 per name. Required to search: name, years to search. Criminal records on docket books from 1907.

General Information: No adoption, juvenile, conservatorship, mental health, guardianship, or expunged records released. Copy fee: $1.00 for first page, $.50 each add'l. Cert fee: $.50 per page. Payee: Harper County Court Clerk. Personal checks not accepted. Cashier's check or money order. Prepayment required. Mail requests: SASE requested. Turnaround time 3 or 4 days.

Haskell County

16th Judicial District Court 202 E. Main, Stigler, OK 74462; 918-967-3323; Fax: 918-967-2819. Hours: 8AM-4:30PM (CST). *Felony, Misdemeanor, Civil, Eviction, Small Claims, Probate.*

Civil Records: Access: Phone, fax, mail, in person, online. Both court and visitors may perform in person searches. Search fee: $5.00. Required to search: name, years to search. Civil cases indexed by defendant, plaintiff. Civil records archived from 1907, they are in the process of placing files on microfiche starting with 1994; computerized since 1997. Access to the OK Dist. Ct. Records site is free at www.odcr.com.

Criminal Records: Access: Phone, fax, mail, in person, online. Both court and visitors may perform in person searches. Search fee: $5.00. Required to search: name, years to search; also helpful: SSN. Criminal records archived from 1907, they are in the process of placing files on microfiche starting with 1994; computerized since 1997. Access to the OK Dist. Ct. Records site is free at www.odcr.com.

General Information: Public Access terminal is available. No juvenile, adoption or mental health records released. Copy fee: $1.00 for first page, $.50 each add'l. Cert fee: $2.00. Payee: Haskell County Court Clerk. Personal checks accepted. Mail requests: SASE required. Mail turnaround time 1 week.

Hughes County

22nd Judicial District Court 200 N Broadway, Box 32, Holdenville, OK 74848; 405-379-3384. Hours: 8AM-4:30PM (CST). *Felony, Misdemeanor, Civil, Eviction, Small Claims, Probate.*

Civil Records: Access: Mail, in person, online. Both court and visitors may perform in person searches. Search fee: $5.00 per name. Required to search: name, years to search. Civil cases indexed by defendant, plaintiff. Civil records archived from 1907, computerized records go back to 1998. Search records from 12/98 forward at www.odcr.com. There is no fee.

Criminal Records: Access: Mail, in person, online. Both court and visitors may perform in person searches. Search fee: $5.00 per name. Required to search: name, years to search; also helpful: SSN. Criminal records archived from 1907. Search records from 12/98 forward at www.odcr.com. There is no fee.

General Information: Public Access terminal is available. No juvenile or adoption records released. Copy fee: $1.00 for first page, $.50 each add'l. Cert fee: $.50. Payee: Hughes County Court Clerk. Personal checks accepted. Prepayment required. Mail requests: SASE required. Mail turnaround time 2 days.

Jackson County

3rd Judicial District Court PO Box 616 (101 N. Main, Rm. 303), Jackson County Courthouse, Altus, OK 73522; 580-482-0448. Hours: 8AM-4PM (CST). *Felony, Misdemeanor, Civil, Eviction, Small Claims, Probate.*

Civil Records: Access: Mail, in person. Both court and visitors may perform in person searches. Search fee: $5.00 per name. Required to search: name, years to search. Civil cases indexed by defendant, plaintiff. Civil records archived from early 1900; computerized records since 7/97.

Criminal Records: Access: Mail, in person. Both court and visitors may perform in person searches. Search fee: $5.00 per name. Required to search: name, years to search; also helpful: SSN. Criminal records archived from early 1900; computerized records since 7/97.

General Information: Public Access terminal is available. No adoption, juvenile, mental health, or guardianship records released. Copy fee: $1.00 for first page, $.50 each add'l. Cert fee: $.50. Payee: Jackson County Court Clerk. Business checks accepted. Prepayment required. Mail requests: SASE required. Mail turnaround time 3-4 days.

Jefferson County

5th Judicial District Court 220 N. Main, Rm 302, Waurika, OK 73573; 580-228-2961; Fax: 580-228-2185. Hours: 8AM-4PM (CST). *Felony, Misdemeanor, Civil, Eviction, Small Claims, Probate.*

Civil Records: Access: Mail, in person. Both court and visitors may perform in person searches. Search fee: $5.00 per name. Required to search: name, years to search, DOB or SSN. Civil cases indexed by defendant, plaintiff. Civil records on docket books from 1907; on computer since October, 1997.

Criminal Records: Access: Mail, in person. Both court and visitors may perform in person searches. Search fee: $5.00 per name. Required to search: name, years to search, DOB; also helpful: SSN. Criminal records on docket books from 1907; on computer since October, 1997.

General Information: Public Access terminal is available. No juvenile, adoption or guardianship records released. Copy fee: $1.00 for first page, $.50 each add'l. Cert fee: $.50. Payee: Court Clerk. Personal checks accepted. Prepayment required. Mail requests: SASE required. Mail turnaround time 1 week.

Johnston County

20th Judicial District Court 403 W Main, #201, Tishomingo, OK 73460; 580-371-3281. Hours: 8:30AM-4:30PM (CST). *Felony, Misdemeanor, Civil, Eviction, Small Claims, Probate.*

Civil Records: Access: Phone, mail, in person. Both court and visitors may perform in person searches. Search fee: $5.00 per name. Required to search: name, years to search. Civil cases indexed by defendant, plaintiff. Civil records on docket books from 1907; on computer back to 1997. All requests must be in writing.

Criminal Records: Access: Mail, in person. Both court and visitors may perform in person searches. Search fee: $5.00 per name. Required to search: name, years to search; also helpful: DOB, SSN. Criminal records on docket books from 1907; on computer back to 1997. All requests must be in writing.

General Information: Public Access terminal is available. No juvenile or mental health records released. Copy fee: $1.00 for first page, $.50 each add'l. Cert fee: $.50. Payee: Court. Personal checks accepted. Prepayment required. Mail requests: SASE required. Mail turnaround time 2 days.

Kay County

8th Judicial District Court Box 428, Newkirk, OK 74647; 580-362-3350. Hours: 8:00AM-4:30PM (CST). *Felony, Misdemeanor, Civil, Eviction, Small Claims, Probate.*
www.courthouse.kay.ok.us/home.html
Note: This courthouse holds the closed case files for the satelite courts in Ponca City (580-762-2148) and Blackwell (580-363-2080).

Civil Records: Access: Phone, mail, in person, online. Both court and visitors may perform in person searches. Search fee: $5.00 per name. Required to search: name, years to search. Civil cases indexed by defendant, plaintiff. Civil records on microfiche and original records; computerized records since 1995. Search records from 01/95 forward at www.odcr.com. There is no fee.

Criminal Records: Access: Phone, mail, in person, online. Both court and visitors may perform in person searches. Search fee: $5.00 per name. Required to search: name, years to search; also helpful: DOB, SSN. Criminal records on microfiche and original records; computerized records since 1995. Search records from 01/95 forward at www.odcr.com. There is no fee.

General Information: Public Access terminal is available. No juvenile, adoption, mental health, or sealed records released. Copy fee: $1.00 for first page, $.50 each add'l. Cert fee: $.50. Payee: Kay County Court Clerk. Personal checks accepted. Prepayment required. Mail turnaround time 1 day.

Kingfisher County

4th Judicial District Court Box 328 (101 S Main St), Kingfisher, OK 73750; 405-375-3813. Hours: 8:00AM-4:30PM (CST). *Felony, Misdemeanor, Civil, Eviction, Small Claims, Probate.*

Civil Records: Access: Phone, mail, in person, online. Both court and visitors may perform in person searches. Search fee: $5.00. Required to search: name, years to search. Civil cases indexed by defendant, plaintiff. Civil records archived from 1900, computerized since 1998. Search records from 10/97 forward at www.odcr.com. There is no fee.

Criminal Records: Access: Mail, in person, online. Both court and visitors may perform in person searches. Search fee: $5.00. Required to search: name, years to search; also helpful: SSN. Criminal records archived from 1900, comuterized since 1998. Search

records from 10/97 forward at www.odcr.com. There is no fee.

General Information: Public Access terminal is available. No juvenile, mental or guardianship records released. Copy fee: $1.00 for first page, $.50 each add'l. Cert fee: $.50. Payee: Court Clerk. Personal checks accepted. Prepayment required. Mail turnaround time 1-2 days.

Kiowa County

3rd Judicial District Court Box 854 (316 S Main St), Hobart, OK 73651; 580-726-5125. Hours: 9AM-5PM (CST). *Felony, Misdemeanor, Civil, Eviction, Small Claims, Probate.*

Civil Records: Access: Phone, mail, in person. Both court and visitors may perform in person searches. Search fee: $5.00 per name. Required to search: name, years to search. Civil cases indexed by defendant, plaintiff. Civil records archived from 1900, computerized reocrds from1996.

Criminal Records: Access: Phone, mail, in person. Both court and visitors may perform in person searches. Search fee: $5.00 per name. Required to search: name, years to search; also helpful: SSN. Criminal records archived from 1900, computerized records from 1996.

General Information: No juvenile or adoptions records released. Copy fee: $1.00 for first page, $.50 each add'l. Cert fee: $.50. Payee: Court Clerk. Only cashiers checks and money orders accepted. Prepayment required. Mail requests: SASE required. Mail turnaround time 1-2 days.

Latimer County

16th Judicial District Court 109 N. Central, Rm 200, Wilburton, OK 74578; 918-465-2011. Hours: 8AM-4:30PM (CST). *Felony, Misdemeanor, Civil, Eviction, Small Claims, Probate.*

Civil Records: Access: Phone, mail, in person. Both court and visitors may perform in person searches. Search fee: $5.00 per name. Required to search: name, years to search. Civil cases indexed by defendant, plaintiff. Civil records in original files from 1907, computerized from 1999.

Criminal Records: Access: Mail, in person. Both court and visitors may perform in person searches. Search fee: $5.00 per name. Required to search: name, years to search; also helpful: DOB, SSN. Criminal records in original files from 1907, computerized from 1999.

General Information: Public Access terminal is available. No guardianship or juvenile records released. Will not fax results. Copy fee: $1.00 for first page, $.50 each add'l. Cert fee: $.50. Payee: Latimer County Court Clerk. Personal checks accepted. Prepayment required. Will bill search fee to law firms. Mail requests: SASE not required. Mail turnaround time 2 days.

Le Flore County

16th Judicial District Court PO Box 688 (110 Front St), Poteau, OK 74953; 918-647-3181. Hours: 8AM-4:30PM (CST). *Felony, Misdemeanor, Civil, Eviction, Small Claims, Probate.*

Civil Records: Access: Mail, in person. Both court and visitors may perform in person searches. Search fee: $5.00 per name. Required to search: name, years to search. Civil cases indexed by defendant, plaintiff. Civil records on computer since July 1, 1997; prior records archived since 1904 in files and books.

Criminal Records: Access: Mail, in person. Both court and visitors may perform in person searches. Search fee: $5.00 per name. Required to search: name, years to search; also helpful: SSN. Criminal records on computer since July 1, 1997; prior records archived since 1904 in files and books.

General Information: Public Access terminal is available. No juvenile, adoptions, mental health or guardian records released. Copy fee: $1.00 for first page, $.50 each add'l. Cert fee: $.50. Payee: Court Clerk. Personal checks accepted. Prepayment required. Mail requests: SASE required. Mail turnaround time 1 week.

Lincoln County

23rd Judicial District Court PO Box 307 (811 Manvel Ave), Chandler, OK 74834; 405-258-1309. Hours: 8:30AM-4:30PM (CST). *Felony, Misdemeanor, Civil, Eviction, Small Claims, Probate.*

Civil Records: Access: Mail, in person, online. Both court and visitors may perform in person searches. Search fee: $5.00 per name. Required to search: name, years to search. Civil cases indexed by defendant, plaintiff. Civil records archived since 1891. Search records from 07/94 forward at www.odcr.com. There is no fee.

Criminal Records: Access: Mail, in person, online. Both court and visitors may perform in person searches. Search fee: $5.00 per name. Required to search: name, years to search, DOB, signed release; also helpful: SSN. Criminal records archived since 1891. Search records from 07/94 forward at www.odcr.com. There is no fee.

General Information: Public Access terminal is available. No juvenile, adoption or guardianship records released. Will not fax results. Copy fee: $1.00 for first page, $.50 each add'l. No cert fee. Payee: Court Clerk. Personal checks accepted. Prepayment required. Mail requests: SASE required. Mail turnaround time can take 30 days or more. Record searching is a low priority.

Logan County

9th Judicial District Court 301 E. Harrison, Rm 201, Guthrie, OK 73044; 405-282-0123. Hours: 8:30AM-4:30PM (CST). *Felony, Misdemeanor, Civil, Eviction, Small Claims, Probate.*

Civil Records: Access: Mail, in person, online. Both court and visitors may perform in person searches. Search fee: $5.00 per name. Required to search: name, years to search. Civil cases indexed by defendant, plaintiff. Civil records on microfiche from 1907. Search records from 07/94 forward at www.odcr.com. There is no fee.

Criminal Records: Access: Mail, in person, online. Both court and visitors may perform in person searches. Search fee: $5.00 per name. Required to search: name, years to search; also helpful: SSN, DOB. Criminal records on microfiche from 1907. Search records from 07/94 forward at www.odcr.com. There is no fee.

General Information: No juvenile, mental health or adoption records released. Copy fee: $1.00 for first page, $.50 each add'l. Cert fee: $.50. Payee: Court Clerk. Personal checks accepted. Prepayment required. Mail requests: SASE requested. Turnaround time 7-10 days.

Love County

20th Judicial District Court 405 W. Main, Marietta, OK 73448; 580-276-2235. Hours: 8AM-4:30PM (CST). *Felony, Misdemeanor, Civil, Eviction, Small Claims, Probate.*

Civil Records: Access: Mail, in person. Both court and visitors may perform in person searches. Search fee: $5.00 per name. Required to search: name, years to search. Civil cases indexed by defendant, plaintiff. Civil records on docket books from 1907, computer records back to 1997.

Criminal Records: Access: Mail, in person. Both court and visitors may perform in person searches. Search fee: $5.00 per name. Required to search:

name, years to search; also helpful: DOB, SSN. Criminal records on docket books from 1907, computer records back to 1997.

General Information: Public Access terminal is available. No juvenile or adoptions records released. Copy fee: $1.00 for first page, $.50 each add'l. Cert fee: $.50. Payee: Court Clerk. Only cashiers checks and money orders accepted. Prepayment required. Mail requests: SASE required. Mail turnaround time 1-2 days.

Major County

4th Judicial District Court 500 E Broadway, Fairview, OK 73737; 580-227-4690. Hours: 8:30AM-4:30PM (CST). *Felony, Misdemeanor, Civil, Small Claims, Probate.*

Civil Records: Access: Phone, fax, mail, in person. Both court and visitors may perform in person searches. Search fee: $5.00 per name. Fee is per book. Required to search: name, years to search. Civil cases indexed by defendant, plaintiff. Civil records on docket books from 1907, on microfiche from 1970, on computer back to 1997.

Criminal Records: Access: Phone, fax, mail, in person. Both court and visitors may perform in person searches. Search fee: $5.00 per name. Fee is per book. Required to search: name, years to search, DOB; also helpful: SSN. Criminal records on docket books from 1907, on microfiche from 1970; on computer back to 1997.

General Information: Public Access terminal is available. No juvenile, adoptions or mental records released. Will fax results to local or toll free line. Copy fee: $1.00 for first page, $.50 each add'l. Cert fee: $.50. Payee: Court Clerk. Personal checks accepted. Prepayment required. Will bill attorneys or firms with previous credit paid. Mail requests: SASE required. Mail turnaround time 3 days.

Marshall County

20th Judicial District Court Box 58, Madill, OK 73446; 580-795-3278 X240. Hours: 8:30AM-5PM (CST). *Felony, Misdemeanor, Civil, Eviction, Small Claims, Probate.*

Civil Records: Access:
Mail, in person. Both court and visitors may perform in person searches. Search fee: $5.00. Required to search: name, years to search. Civil cases indexed by defendant, plaintiff. Civil records on docket books from 1907; computerized since 1997.

Criminal Records: Access: Mail, in person. Both court and visitors may perform in person searches. Search fee: $5.00. Required to search: name, years to search, DOB, SSN, signed release. Criminal records on docket books from 1907; computerized since 1997.

General Information: Public Access terminal is available. No juvenile, adoptions, mental health or guardianship records released. Copy fee: $1.00 for first page, $.50 each add'l. Cert fee: $3.00. Payee: Court Clerk. Personal checks accepted. Prepayment required. Mail requests: SASE required. Mail turnaround time 3 days.

Mayes County

12th Judicial District Court Box 867 (1st & Adair), Pryor, OK 74362; Civil phone: 918-825-2185; Criminal phone: 918-825-0133. Hours: 9AM-5PM (CST). *Felony, Misdemeanor, Civil, Eviction, Small Claims, Probate.*

Civil Records: Access: Phone, mail, in person, online. Both court and visitors may perform in person searches. Search fee: $1.00 per name per year. Search fee is payable to employee doing research after hours. Required to search: name, years to search. Civil cases indexed by defendant, plaintiff. Civil records archived from 1907 on microfilm, computerized since 1998.

Search records from 07/98 forward at www.odcr.com. There is no fee.

Criminal Records: Access: Phone, mail, in person, online. Both court and visitors may perform in person searches. Search fee: $1.00 per name per year. Search fee is payable to employee doing research after hours. Required to search: name, years to search; also helpful: DOB, SSN. Criminal records archived from 1907 on microfilm, computerized since 1998. Search records from 07/98 forward at www.odcr.com. There is no fee.

General Information: Public Access terminal is available. No mental, adoption, most juvenile, and some reports in guardianship records not released. Will not fax results. Copy fee: $1.00 for first page, $.50 each add'l. Cert fee: $.50. Payee: Clerk of Court. Personal checks accepted. Prepayment required. Mail requests: SASE required. Mail turnaround time 1 week.

McClain County

21st Judicial District Court 121 N. 2nd Rm 231, Purcell, OK 73080; 405-527-3221. Hours: 8AM-4:30PM (CST). *Felony, Misdemeanor, Civil, Eviction, Small Claims, Probate.*

Civil Records: Access: Mail, in person, online. Both court and visitors may perform in person searches. Search fee: $10.00 per name. Required to search: name, years to search. Civil cases indexed by defendant, plaintiff. Civil records on docket books and cards from 1907, computerized since 01/97. Search records from 01/97 forward at www.odcr.com. There is no fee.

Criminal Records: Access: Mail, in person, online. Both court and visitors may perform in person searches. Search fee: $10.00 per name. Required to search: name, years to search; also helpful: DOB, SSN. Criminal records kept in individual docket files. Search records from 01/97 forward at www.odcr.com. There is no fee.

General Information: Public Access terminal is available. No adoptions, mental health or juvenile records released. Will not fax results. Copy fee: $1.00 for first page, $.50 each add'l. Cert fee: $.50. Payee: Court Clerk. Personal checks accepted. Prepayment required. Mail requests: SASE required. Mail turnaround time 2 days.

McCurtain County

17th Judicial District Court Box 1378 (108 N Central Ave), Idabel, OK 74745; 580-286-3693; Fax: 580-286-7095. Hours: 8AM-4PM (CST). *Felony, Misdemeanor, Civil, Eviction, Small Claims, Probate.*

Civil Records: Access: Mail, in person, online. Both court and visitors may perform in person searches. Search fee: $5.00 per name. Required to search: name, years to search. Civil cases indexed by defendant, plaintiff. Civil records on docket books from 1907; on computer back to 1998. Online access to court records via the statewide OSCN system is pending.

Criminal Records: Access: Mail, in person, online. Both court and visitors may perform in person searches. Search fee: $5.00. Required to search: name, years to search; also helpful: SSN. Criminal records on docket books from 1907; on computer back to 1998. Online access to court records via the statewide OSCN system is pending.

General Information: Public Access terminal is available. No adoptions, guardianship or juvenile records released. Copy fee: $2.00 per page. Cert fee: $.50 per instrument. Payee: Court Clerk. Personal checks accepted. Prepayment required. Mail requests: SASE required. Mail turnaround time 1 day.

McIntosh County

18th Judicial District Court Box 426 (110 N First St), Eufaula, OK 74432; 918-689-2282. Hours: 8AM-4PM (CST). *Felony, Misdemeanor, Civil, Eviction, Small Claims, Probate.*

Civil Records: Access: Mail, in person. Both court and visitors may perform in person searches. Search fee: $5.00 per name. Required to search: name, years to search. Civil cases indexed by defendant, plaintiff. Civil records on microfilm since 1907; computerized back to 1996.

Criminal Records: Access: Mail, in person. Both court and visitors may perform in person searches. Search fee: $5.00 per name. Required to search: name, years to search; also helpful: SSN, DOB. Criminal records on microfilm since 1947; computerized back to 1996.

General Information: Public Access terminal is available. No adoptions, mental health, guardianship or juvenile records released. Will not fax results. Copy fee: $1.00 for first page, $.50 each add'l. Cert fee: $.50 per instrument. Payee: Court. No personal checks accepted; use cashier's check or money order. Prepayment required. Mail requests: SASE required. Mail turnaround time 3 days.

Murray County

20th Judicial District Court Box 578 (10th & Wyandotte St), Sulphur, OK 73086; 580-622-3223. Hours: 8AM-4:30PM, closed for lunch (CST). *Felony, Misdemeanor, Civil, Eviction, Small Claims, Probate.*

Civil Records: Access: Mail, in person. Both court and visitors may perform in person searches. Search fee: $5.00 per name. Required to search: name, years to search; also helpful: DOB. Civil cases indexed by defendant, plaintiff. Civil records on docket books from 1907, from 1973 back records are on microfilm; computerized back to 1997.

Criminal Records: Access: Mail, in person. Both court and visitors may perform in person searches. Search fee: $5.00 per name. Required to search: name, years to search; also helpful: SSN, DOB. Criminal records on docket books from 1907, from 1973 back records are on microfilm; computerized back to 1997.

General Information: Public Access terminal is available. (Has records since 1997.) No mental health, guardianship, juvenile or adoption records released. Will not fax results. Copy fee: $1.00 for first page, $.50 each add'l. Cert fee: $5.00. Payee: Murray County Court Clerk. Personal checks accepted. Prepayment required. Mail requests: SASE required. Mail turnaround time 2 days, immediate if easily accessible.

Muskogee County

15th Judicial District Court Box 1350 (200 State St), Muskogee, OK 74402; 918-682-7873. Hours: 8AM-4:30PM (CST). *Felony, Misdemeanor, Civil, Eviction, Small Claims, Probate.*

Civil Records: Access: Mail, in person, online. Both court and visitors may perform in person searches. Search fee: $10.00 per name. Required to search: name, years to search. Civil cases indexed by defendant, plaintiff. Civil records on docket books from 1907. Search records from 01/03/03 forward at www.odcr.com. There is no fee.

Criminal Records: Access: Mail, in person, online. Both court and visitors may perform in person searches. Search fee: $10.00 per name. Required to search: name, years to search, DOB; also helpful: SSN. Criminal records on docket books from 1907. Search records from 01/03/03 forward at www.odcr.com. There is no fee.

General Information: No adoptions, mental health, guardianship or juvenile records released. Copy fee: $1.00 for first page, $.50 each add'l. Cert fee: $.50. Payee: Court Clerk. Personal checks accepted. Prepayment required. Mail requests: SASE required. Mail turnaround time 2-3 days.

Noble County

8th Judicial District Court 300 Courthouse Dr, Box 14, Perry, OK 73077; 580-336-5187. Hours: 8AM-4:30PM (CST). *Felony, Misdemeanor, Civil, Eviction, Small Claims, Probate.*

Civil Records: Access: Mail, in person, online. Both court and visitors may perform in person searches. Search fee: $5.00 per name. Required to search: name, years to search. Civil cases indexed by defendant, plaintiff. Civil records on microfiche from 1893; computerized back to 1997. Search records from 01/01/97 forward at www.odcr.com. There is no fee.

Criminal Records: Access: Mail, in person, online. Both court and visitors may perform in person searches. Search fee: $5.00 per name. Required to search: name, years to search, DOB; also helpful: address, SSN. Criminal records on microfiche from 1893; computerized back to 1997. Search records from 01/01/97 forward at www.odcr.com. There is no fee.

General Information: Public Access terminal is available. No adoptions, mental health, guardianship or juvenile records released. Copy fee: $1.00 for first page, $.50 each add'l. Cert fee: $.50. Payee: Noble County Court Clerk. Personal checks accepted. Prepayment required. Mail requests: SASE appreciated. Turnaround time 1 day.

Nowata County

11th Judicial District Court 229 N. Maple, Nowata, OK 74048; 918-273-0127. Hours: 8AM-4:30PM (CST). *Felony, Misdemeanor, Civil, Eviction, Small Claims, Probate.*

Civil Records: Access: Mail, in person. Both court and visitors may perform in person searches. Search fee: $5.00 per name. Required to search: name, years to search. Civil cases indexed by defendant, plaintiff. Civil records on docket books from 1907; on computer since 1998.

Criminal Records: Access: Mail, in person. Both court and visitors may perform in person searches. Search fee: $5.00 per name. Required to search: name, years to search; also helpful: SSN. Criminal records on docket books from 1907; on computer since 1998.

General Information: Public Access terminal is available. No adoptions, mental health, guardianship or juvenile records released. Will fax results to local or toll free line. Copy fee: $1.00 for first page, $.50 each add'l. Cert fee: $.50 per page. Payee: Court Clerk. Personal checks accepted. Prepayment required. Mail requests: SASE requested. Turnaround time 1 day.

Okfuskee County

24th Judicial District Court Box 30 (Third & Atlanta St), Okemah, OK 74859; 918-623-0525; Fax: 918-623-2687. Hours: 8:30AM-4:30PM (CST). *Felony, Misdemeanor, Civil, Eviction, Small Claims, Probate.*

Civil Records: Access: Mail, in person. Both court and visitors may perform in person searches. Search fee: $5.00 per name. Required to search: name, years to search. Civil cases indexed by defendant, plaintiff. Civil records in files and docket books from 1907, computerized since 1996.

Criminal Records: Access: Mail, in person. Both court and visitors may perform in person searches. Search fee: $5.00 per name. Required to search:

name, years to search; also helpful: SSN. Criminal records in files and docket books from 1907, computerized since 1996.

General Information: Public Access terminal is available. No adoptions, mental health, guardianship or juvenile released. Will fax results to local or toll free line. Copy fee: $1.00 for first page, $.50 each add'l. Cert fee: $.50 per page. Payee: Court Clerk. Personal checks accepted. Prepayment required. Mail requests: SASE required. Mail turnaround time 3 days.

Oklahoma County

District Court 320 Robert S. Kerr St, Rm 409, Oklahoma City, OK 73102; 405-713-1705; Civil phone: 405-713-1725; Criminal phone: 405-713-1713; Probate phone: 405-713-1725. Hours: 8AM-5PM (CST). *Felony, Misdemeanor, Civil, Eviction, Small Claims, Probate.*

Note: 405-713-1738 Small Claims

Civil Records: Access: Mail, online, in person. Both court and visitors may perform in person searches. Search fee: Lengthy searches are $5.00 per half hour, otherwise no search fee. Required to search: name, years to search. Civil cases indexed by defendant, plaintiff. Civil records on microfiche from 1980, prior archived. Online access to court dockets is free at www.oscn.net/applications/oscn/casesearch.asp. Civil dockets go back to 12/1984.

Criminal Records: Access: Mail, online, in person. Both court and visitors may perform in person searches. Search fee: Lengthy searches $5.00 per half hour; commercial purpose searches: $25.00. Required to search: name, years to search, DOB; also helpful: SSN. Criminal records on microfiche from 1980, prior archived. Online access to criminal dockets is same as civil. Criminal dockets go back to 9/1988. The sheriff's current inmates and warrants list is free at www.oklahomacounty.org/cosheriff/.

General Information: Public Access terminal is available. No juvenile, sealed, or expunged records released. Copy fee: $1.00 for first page, $.50 each add'l. Cert fee: $.50. Payee: District Court Clerk. Personal checks accepted. Prepayment required. Mail requests: SASE required. Mail turnaround time 5-10 days.

Okmulgee County

24th Judicial District Court - Henryetta Branch 115 S 4th, Henryetta, OK 74437; 918-652-7142; Fax: 918-650-0287. Hours: 8:30AM-4:30PM (CST). *Felony, Misdemeanor, Civil, Eviction, Small Claims, Probate.*

Note: You must search both courts in this county, records are not co-mingled.

Civil Records: Access: Limited phone, mail, in person. Both court and visitors may perform in person searches. Search fee: $5.00 per name. Required to search: name, years to search. Civil cases indexed by defendant, plaintiff. Civil records on microfiche from 1970, computerized since 1997.

Criminal Records: Access: Limited phone, mail, in person. Both court and visitors may perform in person searches. Search fee: $5.00 per name. Required to search: name, years to search; also helpful: SSN. Criminal records on microfiche from 1970, books to 6-5-79, computerized since 1997.

General Information: No expunged or guardianship records released. Will fax results for $1.00 1st page; $.50 each page thereafter. Payment in advance. Copy fee: $1.00 for first page, $.50 each add'l. Cert fee: $.50. Payee: Court Clerk. Business checks accepted. Prepayment required. Mail requests: SASE required. Mail turnaround time 1-2 days; limited phone searching is immediate.

24th Judicial District Court - Okmulgee Branch 314 W 7th, Okmulgee, OK 74447; 918-756-3042. Hours: 8AM-4:30PM (CST). *Felony, Misdemeanor, Civil, Eviction, Small Claims, Probate.*

Civil Records: Access: Phone, mail, in person. Both court and visitors may perform in person searches. Search fee: $5.00 per name. Required to search: name, years to search. Civil cases indexed by defendant, plaintiff. Civil records on microfiche from 1986, archived from 1907, computerized since 1997.

Criminal Records: Access: Phone, mail, in person. Both court and visitors may perform in person searches. Search fee: $5.00 per name. Required to search: name, years to search; also helpful: SSN. Criminal records on microfiche from 1986, archived from 1907, computerized since 1997.

General Information: Public Access terminal is available. No juvenile, mental health, adoption or guardianship records released. Copy fee: $1.00 for first page, $.50 each add'l. Cert fee: $.50. Payee: Court Clerk. Business checks accepted. Prepayment required. Mail requests: SASE requested. Turnaround time 1-2 days.

Osage County

10th Judicial District Court County Courthouse, 600 Grandview, Pawhuska, OK 74056; 918-287-4104. Hours: 9AM-5PM (CST). *Felony, Misdemeanor, Civil, Eviction, Small Claims, Probate, Divorce.*

Civil Records: Access: Mail, in person, online. Both court and visitors may perform in person searches. Search fee: $5.00 per name. Required to search: name, years to search; also helpful: address. Civil cases indexed by defendant, plaintiff. Civil records archived from 1969. Search records from 01/96 forward at www.odcr.com. There is no fee.

Criminal Records: Access: Mail, in person, online. Both court and visitors may perform in person searches. Search fee: $5.00 per name. Required to search: name, years to search; also helpful: address. Criminal records archived from 1969. Search records from 01/96 forward at www.odcr.com. There is no fee.

General Information: Public Access terminal is available. No juvenile or adoption records released. Copy fee: $1.00 for first page, $.50 each add'l. Cert fee: $.50. Payee: Court Clerk. Only cashiers checks and money orders accepted. Prepayment required. Mail requests: SASE required. Mail turnaround time 2 days.

Ottawa County

13th Judicial District Court 102 E Central Ave, #300, Miami, OK 74354; 918-542-2801. Hours: 9:00AM-5:00PM (CST). *Felony, Misdemeanor, Civil, Eviction, Small Claims, Probate.*

Civil Records: Access: Phone, mail, in person, online. Both court and visitors may perform in person searches. Search fee: $5.00 per name. Required to search: name, years to search. Civil cases indexed by defendant, plaintiff. Civil records on docket books or cards from 1907, recent records computerized. Search records from 9/97 forward at www.odcr.com. There is no fee.

Criminal Records: Access: Mail, in person, online. Both court and visitors may perform in person searches. Search fee: $5.00. Required to search: name, years to search; also helpful: SSN. Criminal records on docket books or cards from 1907, recent records computerized. Search records from 9/97 forward at www.odcr.com. There is no fee.

General Information: Public Access terminal is available. No juvenile, mental health, adoption or guardianship records released. Copy fee: $1.00 for

first page, $.50 each add'l. Cert fee: $.50. Payee: Clerk of Court. Money orders accepted. Prepayment required. Mail requests: SASE required. Mail turnaround time 1-2 days.

Pawnee County

14th Judicial District Court Courthouse, 500 Harrison St, Pawnee, OK 74058; 918-762-2547. Hours: 8AM-4:30PM (CST). *Felony, Misdemeanor, Civil, Eviction, Small Claims, Probate.*

Civil Records: Access: Mail, in person, online. Both court and visitors may perform in person searches. Search fee: $5.00. Required to search: name, years to search. Civil cases indexed by defendant, plaintiff. Civil records on docket sheets to 1975, computerized from 1997. Search records from 01/97 forward at www.odcr.com. There is no fee.

Criminal Records: Access: Mail, in person, online. Both court and visitors may perform in person searches. Search fee: $5.00. Required to search: name, years to search; also helpful: SSN. Criminal records on docket sheets to 1975, computerized from 1997. Search records from 01/97 forward at www.odcr.com. There is no fee.

General Information: Public Access terminal is available. No sealed records released. Copy fee: $1.00 for first page, $.50 each add'l. Cert fee: $.50. Payee: Court Clerk. Personal checks accepted. Prepayment required. Mail requests: SASE required. Mail turnaround time 1-3 days.

Payne County

9th Judicial District Court 606 S. Husband Rm 308, Stillwater, OK 74074; 405-372-4774. Hours: 8AM-5PM (CST). *Felony, Misdemeanor, Civil, Eviction, Small Claims, Probate.*

Civil Records: Access: Mail, online, in person. Both court and visitors may perform in person searches. Search fee: $1.00 per name per year. Required to search: name, years to search. Civil cases indexed by defendant, plaintiff. Civil records on docket books from late 1800s, as of 1994 on computer. Online access to court dockets is free at www.oscn.net/applications/oscn/casesearch.asp. Dockets go back to 1/1994.

Criminal Records: Access: Mail, online, in person. Both court and visitors may perform in person searches. Search fee: $1.00 per name per year. Required to search: name, years to search, DOB, SSN, signed release. Criminal records on docket books from late 1800s, as of 1994 on computer. Online access to criminal dockets is same as civil.

General Information: Public Access terminal is available. No sealed records, juveniles or adoption records released. Copy fee: $1.00 for first page, $.50 each add'l. Cert fee: $.50 per page. Payee: Clerk of Court. Personal checks accepted. Prepayment required. Mail requests: SASE required. Mail turnaround time 2 days.

Pittsburg County

18th Judicial District Court Box 460 (115 E Carl Albert Parkway), McAlester, OK 74502; 918-423-4859. Hours: 8AM-5PM (CST). *Felony, Misdemeanor, Civil, Eviction, Small Claims, Probate.*

Civil Records: Access: Mail, in person. Both court and visitors may perform in person searches. Search fee: $5.00 per name. Required to search: name, years to search. Civil cases indexed by defendant, plaintiff. Civil records on microfiche since 1907; on computer since 1997.

Criminal Records: Access: Mail, in person. Both court and visitors may perform in person searches. Search fee: $5.00 per name. Required to search: name, years to search, DOB. Criminal records on microfiche since 1907; on computer since 1997.

General Information: Public Access terminal is available. No juvenile, adoptions, mental health or guardianship records released. Will not fax results. Copy fee: $1.00 for first page, $.50 each add'l. Cert fee: $.50. Payee: Court Clerk. Prepayment required. Mail requests: SASE required. Mail turnaround time 1-2 days.

Pontotoc County

22nd Judicial District Court Box 427 (120 W 13th), Ada, OK 74820; 580-332-5763. Hours: 8AM-5PM, closed noon to 1PM (CST). *Felony, Misdemeanor, Civil, Eviction, Small Claims, Probate.*

Civil Records: Access: Mail, in person. Both court and visitors may perform in person searches. Search fee: $5.00 per name. Required to search: name, years to search. Civil cases indexed by defendant, plaintiff. Civil records on card index from 1907; on computer back to 1997.

Criminal Records: Access: Mail, in person. Both court and visitors may perform in person searches. Search fee: $5.00 per name. Required to search: name, years to search; also helpful: DOB, SSN. Criminal records on card index from 1907; on computer back to 1990.

General Information: Public Access terminal is available. No juvenile, adoptions, mental health or guardianship records released. Copy fee: $1.00 for first page, $.50 each add'l. Cert fee: $.50. Payee: Clerk of Court. Personal checks accepted. Must prepay if out of state. Prepayment required. Mail requests: SASE required. Mail turnaround time 2 days.

Pottawatomie County

23rd Judicial District Court 325 N. Broadway, Shawnee, OK 74801; 405-273-3624. Hours: 8:30AM-Noon, 1-5 PM (CST). *Felony, Misdemeanor, Civil, Eviction, Small Claims, Probate.*

Civil Records: Access: Mail, in person, online. Both court and visitors may perform in person searches. Search fee: $5.00 per name. Required to search: name, years to search. Civil cases indexed by defendant, plaintiff. Civil records on computer from 07/97; prior records on book of names from 1906. Search records from 07/01/97 forward at www.odcr.com. There is no fee.

Criminal Records: Access: Mail, in person, online. Both court and visitors may perform in person searches. Search fee: $5.00 per name. Required to search: name, years to search; also helpful: SSN. Criminal records on computer from 07/97; prior records on book of names from 1960. Search records from 07/01/97 forward at www.odcr.com. There is no fee.

General Information: Public Access terminal is available. No juvenile, adoptions, mental health or guardianship records released. Copy fee: $1.00 for first page, $.50 each add'l. Cert fee: $.50. Payee: Court Clerk. Personal checks accepted. Prepayment required. Mail requests: SASE requested. Turnaround time 2 weeks or less.

Pushmataha County

17th Judicial District Court Pushmataha County Courthouse, 302 SW B, Antlers, OK 74523; 580-298-2274. Hours: 8AM-4:30PM (CST). *Felony, Misdemeanor, Civil, Eviction, Small Claims, Probate.*

Civil Records: Access: Mail, in person, online. Both court and visitors may perform in person searches. Search fee: $5.00 per name. Required to search: name, years to search. Civil cases indexed by defendant, plaintiff. Civil records on docket book from 1907. Online access to court dockets is free at www.oscn.net/applications/oscn/casesearch.asp.

Criminal Records: Access: Mail, in person, online. Both court and visitors may perform in person searches. Search fee: $5.00 per name. Required to search: name, years to search; also helpful: SSN. Criminal records on docket book from 1907. Online access to court dockets is free at www.oscn.net/applications/oscn/casesearch.asp.

General Information: No juvenile or adoption records released. Copy fee: $1.00 for first page, $.50 each add'l. Cert fee: $.50. Payee: Court Clerk. Personal checks accepted. Prepayment required. Mail requests: SASE required. Mail turnaround time 1 day.

Roger Mills County

2nd Judicial District Court Box 409 (LL Males Blvd & Broadway), Cheyenne, OK 73628; 580-497-3361. Hours: 8AM-4:30PM (CST). *Felony, Misdemeanor, Civil, Eviction, Small Claims, Probate.*

Civil Records: Access: Phone, mail, in person, online. Both court and visitors may perform in person searches. No search fee. Required to search: name, years to search. Civil cases indexed by defendant, plaintiff. Civil records on computer since 1992, in books since 1893. Online access to court dockets is free at www.oscn.net/applications/oscn/casesearch.asp.

Criminal Records: Access: Phone, mail, fax, in person, online. Both court and visitors may perform in person searches. No search fee. Required to search: name, years to search, DOB; also helpful: SSN. Criminal records on computer since 1992, in books since 1893.

General Information: Public Access terminal is available. No adoption, juvenile, mental health or guardianship records released. Will fax results for $1.00 per page. Copy fee: $1.00 for first page, $.50 each add'l. Cert fee: $.50. Payee: Court Clerk. Personal checks accepted. Prepayment required. Mail requests: SASE required. Mail turnaround time 1 day.

Rogers County

12th Judicial District Court Box 839 (219 S Missouri), Claremore, OK 74018; 918-341-5711. Hours: 8AM-4:30PM (CST). *Felony, Misdemeanor, Civil, Eviction, Small Claims, Probate.*

Civil Records: Access: Phone, mail, online, in person. Both court and visitors may perform in person searches. Search fee: None, but phone and mail requests require case number. Required to search: name, years to search. Civil cases indexed by defendant, plaintiff. Civil records in card index since 1907, some computerized. Online access to court dockets is free at www.oscn.net/applications/oscn/casesearch.asp. Dockets go back to 7/1997.

Criminal Records: Access: Phone, mail, online, in person. Both court and visitors may perform in person searches. Search fee: None, but phone and mail requests require case number. Required to search: name, years to search, DOB; also helpful: SSN. Criminal records on card index since 1907, some computerized. Online access to criminal dockets is the same as civil.

General Information: Public Access terminal is available. No juvenile or adoption records released. Copy fee: $1.00 for first page, $.50 each add'l. Cert fee: $.50. Payee: Court Clerk. Personal checks accepted. Prepayment required. Mail requests: SASE required. Mail turnaround time 1 day.

Seminole County

22nd Judicial District Court - Seminole Branch Box 1320, 401 Main St, Seminole, OK 74868; 405-382-3424. Hours: 8AM-Noon, 1-4PM (CST). *Civil, Small Claims, Probate.*

Note: Criminal records are now maintained at Seminole County Court Clerk, PO Box 130, Wewoka, OK, 405-257-6236.

Civil Records: Access: Phone, mail, in person. Only the court performs in person searches; visitors may not. Search fee: $5.00 per name. Required to search: name, years to search. Civil cases indexed by defendant, plaintiff. Civil records on index cards from 1931, probate from 1969; on computer back to 1996.

General Information: Copy fee: $1.00 for first page, $.50 each add'l. Cert fee: $.50. Payee: Court Clerk. Only cashiers checks and money orders accepted. Prepayment required. Mail requests: SASE required. Mail turnaround time 1 to 2 days.

22nd Judicial District Court - Wewoka Branch Box 130 (120 S Wewoka Ave), Wewoka, OK 74884; 405-257-6236. Hours: 8AM-4PM (CST). *Felony, Misdemeanor, Civil, Eviction, Small Claims, Probate.*

Civil Records: Access: Mail, in person, online. Both court and visitors may perform in person searches. Search fee: $5.00 per name. Required to search: name, years to search. Civil cases indexed by defendant, plaintiff. Civil records indexed on computer since 1995; prior records on books to 1907. Search records from 01/95 forward at www.odcr.com. There is no fee.

Criminal Records: Access: Mail, in person, online. Both court and visitors may perform in person searches. Search fee: $5.00 per name. Required to search: name, years to search; also helpful: SSN. Criminal records indexed on computer since 1995; prior records on books to 1908. Search records from 01/95 forward at www.odcr.com. There is no fee.

General Information: Public Access terminal is available. No juvenile or adoption records released. Will fax results to toll-free number only. Copy fee: $1.00 for first page, $.50 each add'l. Cert fee: $.50. Payee: Court Clerk. Personal checks accepted. Prepayment required. Mail requests: SASE required. Mail turnaround time 1 day.

Sequoyah County

15th Judicial District Court 120 E Chickasaw, Sallisaw, OK 74955; 918-775-4411. Hours: 8AM-4PM (CST). *Felony, Misdemeanor, Civil, Eviction, Small Claims, Probate.*

Civil Records: Access: Mail, in person. Both court and visitors may perform in person searches. Search fee: $5.00 per name. Required to search: name, years to search. Civil cases indexed by defendant, plaintiff. Civil records in files and dockets from 1907; on computer back to 1997.

Criminal Records: Access: Phone, mail, in person. Both court and visitors may perform in person searches. Search fee: $5.00 per name. Required to search: name, years to search; also helpful: SSN. Some criminal records on computer back to 1997, prior in files and dockets.

General Information: Public Access terminal is available. No juvenile, adoptions, mental health or guardianship records released. Will fax results to toll-free or local number. Copy fee: $1.00 for first page, $.50 each add'l. Cert fee: $2.50. Payee: Court Clerk. Personal checks accepted. Prepayment required. Will bill mail requests. Mail requests: SASE required. Mail turnaround time 1 week.

Stephens County

5th Judicial District Court 101 S 11th St, Rm 301, Duncan, OK 73533; 580-470-2000. Hours: 8:30AM-4:30PM (CST). *Felony, Misdemeanor, Civil, Eviction, Small Claims, Probate.*

Civil Records: Access: Mail, in person. Both court and visitors may perform in person searches. Search fee: $5.00 per name. Required to search: name, years to search. Civil cases indexed by defendant, plaintiff. Civil records on computer from 10/95; prior records on docket books from 1907.

Criminal Records: Access: Mail, in person. Both court and visitors may perform in person searches. Search fee: $5.00 per name. Required to search: name, years to search; also helpful: address, DOB, SSN. Criminal records on computer from 10/95; prior records on docket books from 1907.

General Information: Public Access terminal is available. No juvenile, adoptions, mental health or guardianship records released. Copy fee: $1.00 for first page, $.50 each add'l. Cert fee: $.50. Payee: Stephens County 5th Judicial Court. Personal checks not accepted. Prepayment required. Mail requests: SASE required. Mail turnaround time 1 day.

Texas County

1st Judicial District Court Box 1081 (319 N Main St), Guymon, OK 73942; 580-338-3003. Hours: 9AM-5PM (CST). *Felony, Misdemeanor, Civil, Eviction, Small Claims, Probate.*

Civil Records: Access: Mail, in person, online. Both court and visitors may perform in person searches. Search fee: $5.00 per name. Required to search: name, years to search. Civil cases indexed by defendant, plaintiff. Civil records on microfiche from 1976, archived prior, computerized since 03/95. Search records from 04/15/95 forward at www.odcr.com. There is no fee.

Criminal Records: Access: Mail, in person, online. Both court and visitors may perform in person searches. Search fee: $5.00 per name. Required to search: name, years to search; also helpful: SSN. Criminal records on microfiche from 1976, archived prior, computerized since 03/95. Search records from 04/15/95 forward at www.odcr.com. There is no fee.

General Information: Public Access terminal is available. No juvenile, adoptions, mental health or guardianship records released. Will fax results. Copy fee: $1.00 for first page, $.50 each add'l. Cert fee: $.50. Payee: Court Clerk. Personal checks accepted. Prepayment required. Mail requests: SASE required. Mail turnaround time 5 days; 1 day for phone.

Tillman County

3rd Judicial District Court Box 116 (Main & Gladstone), Frederick, OK 73542; 580-335-3023. Hours: 8AM-4PM (CST). *Felony, Misdemeanor, Civil, Eviction, Small Claims, Probate.*

Civil Records: Access: Mail, in person. Both court and visitors may perform in person searches. Search fee: $5.00 per name. Required to search: name, years to search. Civil cases indexed by defendant, plaintiff. Civil records on docket books from 1907; on computer back to 1998.

Criminal Records: Access: Mail, in person. Both court and visitors may perform in person searches. Search fee: $5.00 per name. Required to search: name, years to search, DOB; also helpful: SSN. Criminal records on docket books from 1907; on computer back to 1998.

General Information: Public Access terminal is available. No expunged records released. Copy fee: $1.00 for first page, $.50 each add'l. Copy charge is only if the person does their own search in person. Cert fee: $1.00. Payee: District Court. Business checks accepted. Prepayment required. Will bill law firms. Mail requests: SASE required. Mail turnaround time 1 day.

Tulsa County

14th Judicial District Court 500 S. Denver Ave, Tulsa, OK 74103-3832; 918-596-5000. Hours: 8:30AM-5PM (CST). *Felony, Misdemeanor, Civil, Eviction, Small Claims, Probate.*
Civil Records: Access: Mail, online, in person. Both court and visitors may perform in person searches. Search fee: $5.00 per name. Required to search: name, years to search. Civil cases indexed by defendant, plaintiff. Civil records on computer from 1984, on microfiche from 1907, archived from 1907. Online access to court dockets is free at www.oscn.net/applications/oscn/casesearch.asp. Civil dockets go back to 10/1984.
Criminal Records: Access: Mail, online, in person. Both court and visitors may perform in person searches. Search fee: $5.00 per name. Required to search: name, years to search; also helpful: SSN. Criminal records on computer from 1984, on microfiche from 1907, archived from 1907. Online access to criminal dockets is same as civil. Criminal dockets go back to 1/1988.
General Information: Public Access terminal is available. No juvenile, adoption or guardianship records released. Copy fee: $1.00 for first page, $.50 each add'l. Cert fee: $.50. Payee: Court Clerk. Will accept attorney personal checks. Prepayment required. Mail requests: SASE required. Mail turnaround time 1 week.

Wagoner County

15th Judicial District Court Box 249 (302 E Cherokee St), Wagoner, OK 74477; 918-485-4508. Hours: 8:00AM-4:30PM (CST). *Felony, Misdemeanor, Civil, Eviction, Small Claims, Probate.*
Civil Records: Access: Mail, in person, online. Both court and visitors may perform in person searches. Search fee: $5.00 per name. Required to search: name, years to search. Civil cases indexed by defendant, plaintiff. Civil records on docket books from 1980; on computer back to 1997. Search records from 01/90 forward at www.odcr.com. There is no fee.
Criminal Records: Access: Mail, in person, online. Both court and visitors may perform in person searches. Search fee: $5.00 per name if assisted. Required to search: name, years to search; also helpful: SSN. Criminal records are in files and dockets back to 1907; on computer back to 1997. Search records from 01/90 forward at www.odcr.com. There is no fee.
General Information: Public Access terminal is available. No juvenile, mental health, adoption or guardianship records released. Copy fee: $1.00 for first page, $.50 each add'l. Cert fee: $.50. Payee: Court Clerk. Personal checks accepted. Prepayment

required. Mail requests: SASE required. Mail turnaround time 1-2 days for civil, longer for criminal.

Washington County

11th Judicial District Court 420 S Johnstone, Rm 212, Bartlesville, OK 74003; 918-337-2880; Criminal phone: 918-337-2870; Fax: 918-337-2898. Hours: 8AM-5PM (CST). *Felony, Misdemeanor, Civil, Eviction, Small Claims, Probate.*
Civil Records: Access: Fax, mail, in person. Both court and visitors may perform in person searches. Search fee: $5.00 per name. Required to search: name, years to search. Civil cases indexed by defendant, plaintiff. Civil records on microfiche from 1988, on docket books from 1907; computerized records since 1995.
Criminal Records: Access: Fax, mail, in person. Both court and visitors may perform in person searches. Search fee: $5.00 per name. Required to search: name, years to search, signed release; also helpful: DOB, SSN. Criminal records on microfiche from 1988, on docket books from 1907; computerized records since 1997.
General Information: Public Access terminal is available. No juvenile, mental health, adoption or guardianship records released. Will fax results to local or toll free line. Copy fee: $1.00 for first page, $.50 each add'l. Cert fee: $.50. Payee: Court Clerk. Personal checks accepted. Prepayment required. Mail turnaround time 2-4 days.

Washita County

2nd Judicial District Court Box 397 (111 E Main St), Cordell, OK 73632; 580-832-3836. Hours: 8AM-4PM (CST). *Felony, Misdemeanor, Civil, Small Claims, Probate.*
Civil Records: Access: Mail, in person, online. Both court and visitors may perform in person searches. Search fee: $5.00 per name. Required to search: name, years to search. Civil cases indexed by defendant, plaintiff. Civil records on computer since 1998; prior records on microfiche from 1980s & on docket books from 1892. Search records from 10/97 forward at www.odcr.com. There is no fee.
Criminal Records: Access: Mail, in person, online. Both court and visitors may perform in person searches. Search fee: $5.00 per name. Required to search: name, years to search; also helpful: DOB, SSN, aliases. Criminal records on computer since 1998; prior records on microfiche from 1980s & on docket books from 1892. Search records from 10/97 forward at www.odcr.com. There is no fee.
General Information: Public Access terminal is available. No juvenile, mental health, adoption or guardianship records released. Will fax results for $1.00 per page. Copy fee: $1.00 for first page, $.50 each add'l. Cert fee: $.50. Payee: Court Clerk. Personal checks accepted. Prepayment required. Mail

requests: SASE required. Mail turnaround time same day.

Woods County

4th Judicial District Court Box 924 (407 Government St), Alva, OK 73717; 580-327-3119. Hours: 9AM-5PM (CST). *Felony, Misdemeanor, Civil, Eviction, Small Claims, Probate.*
Civil Records: Access: Mail, in person. Both court and visitors may perform in person searches. Search fee: $5.00 per name. Required to search: name, years to search. Civil cases indexed by defendant, plaintiff. Civil records on docket books from 1890.
Criminal Records: Access: Mail, in person. Both court and visitors may perform in person searches. Search fee: $5.00 per name. Required to search: name, years to search. Criminal records on computer since 1987, on dockets and cards from 1890s.
General Information: Public Access terminal is available. No juvenile, mental health, adoption or guardianship records released. Will not fax results. Copy fee: $1.00 for first page, $.50 each add'l. Cert fee: $.50. Payee: Clerk of Court. Personal checks accepted. Prepayment required. Mail requests: SASE required. Mail turnaround time 2 days.

Woodward County

4th Judicial District Court 1600 Main St, Woodward, OK 73801; 580-256-3413. Hours: 9AM-5PM (CST). *Felony, Misdemeanor, Civil, Eviction, Small Claims, Probate.*
Civil Records: Access: Mail, in person. Both court and visitors may perform in person searches. Search fee: $5.00 per name. Required to search: name, years to search. Civil cases indexed by defendant, plaintiff. Civil records on docket books from 1890, on microfiche from 1989; on computer from 1997.
Criminal Records: Access: Mail, in person. Both court and visitors may perform in person searches. Search fee: $5.00 per name. Required to search: name, years to search; also helpful: DOB, SSN. Criminal records on docket books from 1890, on microfiche from 1989; on computer from 1997.
General Information: Public Access terminal is available. No mental, juvenile, adoption, guardianship records released. Fee to fax results is 1.00 per document. Copy fee: $1.00 for first page, $.50 each add'l. Cert fee: $.50 per page. $5.00 for whole file. Payee: Court Clerk. Personal checks accepted. Prepayment required. Mail requests: SASE required. Mail turnaround time 1-2 days unless older cases found.

Oklahoma Recording Offices

ORGANIZATION: 77 counties, 77 recording offices. The recording officer is County Clerk. The entire state is in the Central Time Zone (CST).

REAL ESTATE RECORDS: Many counties will perform real estate searches by legal description. Copy fees are usually $1.00 per page. Certification usually costs $1.00 per document.

UCC RECORDS: Financing statements are filed centrally with the County Clerk of Oklahoma County. Prior to 7/2001, consumer goods, farm related, and real estate related collateral were dual filed with the local County Clerk as well as the County Clerk of Oklahoma County. Now only real estate related collateral is filed at the local level. All counties will perform UCC searches. Use search request form UCC-4. Search fees vary from usually $5.00 to $10.00 per debtor name for a written request and $3.00 per name by telephone. Copies usually cost $1.00 per page.

TAX LIEN RECORDS: Federal tax liens on personal property of businesses are filed with the County Clerk of Oklahoma County, which is the central filing office for the state. Other federal and all state tax liens are filed with the County Clerk. Usually state and federal tax liens on personal property are filed in separate indexes. Some counties will perform tax lien searches. Search fees vary.

OTHER LIENS: Judgment, mechanics, physicians, hospital.

ONLINE ACCESS: Very little is available online.

Adair County

County Clerk, PO Box 169, Stilwell, OK 74960. **Phone**-County Clerk, R/E & UCC Recording- 918-696-7198; fax-918-696-2603; hours 8AM-4:30PM
Will search UCC records. Search per debtor- $5.00. UCC search includes tax liens. Separate federal/state combined tax lien search- $5.00 per lien. Will search real estate records. RE record copy- $1.00 per page. UCC copy- 1.00 per page. Cert fee: $2.00 per page. Payee: Adair County Clerk. **Other phones:** Assessor-918-696-2012; Treasurer-918-696-7551; Elections-918-696-7221.

Alfalfa County

County Clerk, 300 S. Grand, Cherokee, OK 73728. **Phone**-580-596-3158; hours 8:30AM-4:30PM
Will search UCC records. Search per debtor- $10.00. UCC search includes tax liens. May search real estate records depending on situation. Record copy- $1.00 per page. Cert fee: $1.00 per page. Payee: Alfalfa County Clerk. **Other phones:** Assessor-580-596-2145; Treasurer-580-596-3148; Elections-580-596-2718.

Atoka County

County Clerk, 200 E. Court St, Atoka, OK 74525. **Phone**-580-889-5157; fax-580-889-5063; hours 8:30AM-4:30PM
Will search UCC records. Search per debtor- $10.00. Tax liens not included in UCC search. Tax lien search- $10.00 per debtor. Will not search real estate records. Record copy- $1.00 per page. Cert fee: $1.00 per cert. Payee: Atoka County Clerk. **Other phones:** Assessor-580-889-6036; Treasurer-580-889-5283.

Beaver County

County Clerk, PO Box 338, Beaver, OK 73932-0338. **Phone**-580-625-3141, R/E Recording-580-625-3418; fax-580-625-3430; hours 8AM-5PM
Will search UCC records. Search per debtor- $5.00. Will do tax lien search. Will search real estate records. Copy fee- $1.00 per page. Cert fee: $1.00 per inst. Payee: Beaver County Clerk. **Other phones:** Assessor-580-625-3116; Treasurer-580-625-3161.

Beckham County

County Clerk, PO Box 428, Sayre, OK 73662-0428. **Phone**-580-928-3383; fax-580-928-5220; hours 9AM-5PM
Will search UCC records. Search per debtor- $10.00. Will not search real estate or tax lien records. Record copy- $1.00 per page. Cert fee: $1.00 per instrument. Payee: Beckham County Clerk. **Other phones:** Assessor-580-928-3329; Treasurer-580-928-2589.

Blaine County

County Clerk, PO Box 138, Watonga, OK 73772. **Phone**-County Clerk, R/E & UCC Recording- 580-623-5890; fax-580-623-5009; hours 8AM-4PM
Will search limited UCC records. UCC search per debtor- $3.00. Will search limited tax liens. Will search limited real estate records. Copy fee- $1.00 per page. Cert fee: $1.00 per doc. Payee: County Clerk. **Other phones:** Assessor-580-623-5123; Treasurer-580-623-5007; Elections-580-623-5518; Vital Records-405-271-4040.

Bryan County

County Clerk, PO Box 1789, Durant, OK 74702. **Phone**-County Clerk, R/E & UCC Recording- 580-924-2202; fax-580-924-2289; hours 8AM-5PM
Will search UCC records. Search per debtor- $5.00. Federal/state combined tax lien search- $5.00 per debtor. Will search real estate records. RE record copy- $1.00 per copy. UCC copy- $1.00 per copy. Cert fee: $1.00 per impression. Payee: County Clerk. **Other phones:** Assessor-580-924-2166; Treasurer-580-924-0748; Appraiser/ Auditor-580-924-2166; Elections-580-924-3228.

Caddo County

County Clerk, PO Box 68, Anadarko, OK 73005. **Phone**-County Clerk, R/E & UCC Recording- 405-247-6609; fax-405-247-6510; hours 8:30AM-4:30PM
Will search UCC records. Search per debtor- $10.00. Will search tax liens. Will not search real estate records. Record copy fee- $1.00 per page. Cert fee: $1.00 per doc. Payee: Caddo County Clerk. **Other phones:** Assessor-405-247-2477; Treasurer-405-247-5151; Elections-405-247-5001; Vital Records-405-271-4040; Real Estate-405-247-6510.

Canadian County

County Clerk, PO Box 458, El Reno, OK 73036. **Phone**-405-262-1070 ext123; fax-405-422-2411. www.canadiancounty.org
Will search UCC records. Search per debtor- $10.00. Will not search real estate or tax lien records. UCC copy- $1.00 per page. Cert fee: $1.00 per doc. Payee: Canadian County Clerk. **Online Access to Land, Grantor/Grantee, Deed, Lien, Judgment records:** Access to recorders database is free http://landrecords.canadiancounty.org/coclerk/deeds/default.asp. Records go back to 1/2000. **Other phones:** Assessor-405-262-1070 x269; Treasurer-405-262-1070 x250.

Carter County

County Clerk, PO Box 1236, Ardmore, OK 73402. **Phone**-County Clerk, R/E & UCC Recording- 580-223-8162; hours 8AM-5PM www.brightok.net/chickasaw/ardmore/county/coclerk.html
Will search UCC records. Search per debtor- $5.00. Federal/state combined tax lien search- $5.00 per debtor. Will not search real estate records. Record copy- $1.00 per page. Cert fee: $1.00 per doc. Payee: Carter County Clerk. **Online Access to Assessor, Unsolved Case records:** The sheriff's unsolved mysteries page is free at www.brightok.net/cartercounty/UnsolvedMysteries.html. Search the county assessor database for free at www.cartercountyassessor.org/disclaim.htm. **Other phones:** Assessor-580-223-9594, 800-231-8668 x594 (in county); Treasurer-580-223-9467.

Cherokee County

County Clerk, 213 W. Delaware, Rm 200, Tahlequah, OK 74464. **Phone**-County Clerk, R/E & UCC Recording- 918-456-3171, UCC Recording-918-458-6512; fax-918-458-6508; hours 8AM-4:30PM (Recording hours 8AM-4PM)
Will search UCC records. Search per debtor- $5.00. Tax liens not included in UCC search. Separate federal/state combined tax lien search- $5.00 per debtor. Will search real estate records. Record copy- $1.00 per page. Cert fee: $1.50 per cert. Payee: Cherokee County Clerk. **Other phones:** Assessor-918-456-3201; Treasurer-918-456-3321; Elections-918-456-2261.

Choctaw County

County Clerk, 300 E, Duke, Courthouse, Hugo, OK 74743. **Phone-**County Clerk, R/E & UCC Recording-580-326-3778; fax-580-326-6787; hours 8AM-4PM Will search UCC records. Search per debtor- $10.00. Tax lien search- $5.00 per debtor. Will search real estate records. RE record copy- $1.00 per page. Cert fee: $1.00. Payee: County Clerk. **Other phones:** Assessor-580-326-2356; Treasurer-580-326-6142; Elections-580-326-5164; Vital Records-580-271-4040.

Cimarron County

County Clerk, PO Box 145, Boise City, OK 73933. **Phone-**County Clerk, R/E & UCC Recording- 580-544-2251; fax-580-544-2251; 8AM-Noon, 1-5PM Will search UCC records. Search per debtor- $10.00. UCC search includes tax liens. Separate federal/state combined tax lien search- $10.00 per debtor. Will search real estate records. Copy fee-$1.00 per page. Cert fee: $1.00 per doc. Payee: Cimarron County Clerk. **Other phones:** Assessor-580-544-2701; Treasurer-580-544-2261; Elections-580-544-3377.

Cleveland County

County Clerk, 641 E Robinson #300, Norman, OK 73071. **Phone-**County Clerk, R/E & UCC Recording-405-366-0240, UCC Recording-405-366-0234; fax-405-366-0229; hours 8:15AM-4:45PM www.okclev.cogov.net Will search UCC records. Search per debtor- $10.00 written, $10.00 verbal. Will search tax liens. Will not search real estate records. Copy fee- $1.00 per page. Cert fee: $1.00 per doc. Payee: County Clerk. **Online Access to Recording, Lien, Judgment, UCC, Fictitious Name, Military Discharge records:** Access to the Clerk Index is free at http://search.cogov.net/okclev/default.asp. For access to Tax Liens, Real Estate, UCC, Physician Liens and Mechanic Liens to to clevelandcountyclerk.net. **Other phones:** Assessor-405-366-0230; Treasurer-405-366-0217; Appraiser/ Auditor-405-366-0230; Elections-405-366-0210; Vital Records-405-271-4040.

Coal County

County Clerk, 4 N. Main, #1, Coalgate, OK 74538. **Phone-**County Clerk, R/E & UCC Recording- 580-927-2103; fax-580-927-4003; hours 8AM-4PM Will search UCC records. Search per debtor- $10.00. Will search tax liens. Will not search real estate records. Record copy- $1.00 per page. Cert fee: $1.00 per instrument. Payee: Coal County Clerk. **Other phones:** Assessor-580-927-3123; Treasurer-580-927-3121; Elections-580-927-3456; Vital Records-580-927-2281.

Comanche County

County Clerk, 315 SW 5th, Rm 304, Lawton, OK 73501-4347. **Phone-**County Clerk, R/E & UCC Recording- 580-355-5214; hours 8:30AM-5PM Will search UCC records. Search per debtor- $10.00. Will not search real estate or tax lien records. Record copy- $1.00 per page. Cert fee: $1.00 per doc. Payee: Comanche County Clerk. **Other phones:** Assessor-580-355-1052; Treasurer-580-355-5763; Elections-580-353-1880; Vital Records-405-271-4040.

Cotton County

County Clerk, 301 N. Broadway, Walters, OK 73572. **Phone-**County Clerk, R/E & UCC Recording- 580-875-3026; fax-580-875-3756; hours 8AM-4PM Will search UCC records. Search per debtor- $10.00. Will not search real estate or tax lien records. Copy fee- $1.00 per page. Cert fee: $1.00 per doc. Payee: Cotton County Clerk. **Other phones:**

Assessor-580-875-3289; Treasurer-580-875-3264; Elections-580-875-3403.

Craig County

County Clerk, PO Box 397, Vinita, OK 74301. **Phone-**918-256-2507; fax-918-256-3617; 8:30AM-4:30PM Will search UCC records. Search per debtor- $10.00. Will search tax liens. Will not search real estate records. Copy fee- $1.00 per page. **Other phones:** Assessor-918-256-8766; Treasurer-918-256-2286; Elections-918-256-7559.

Creek County

County Clerk, 317 E. Lee, 1st Fl, Sapulpa, OK 74066. **Phone-**918-227-6306, R/E Recording-918-227-4084; hours 8AM-5PM Will search UCC records. Search per debtor- $5.00. Will not search real estate or tax lien records. Record copy- $1.00 per page. Cert fee: $1.00 per cert. Payee: Creek County Clerk. **Other phones:** Assessor-918-224-4508; Treasurer-918-227-4501; Mapping-918-227-6357.

Custer County

County Clerk, PO Box 300, Arapaho, OK 73620. **Phone-**County Clerk, R/E & UCC Recording- 580-323-1221; fax-580-323-4421; hours 8AM-4PM Will search UCC records. Search per debtor- $5.00. Will search tax liens including federal tax liens. Federal/state combined tax lien search- $3.00 per debtor. Will not search real estate records. Copy fee-$1.00 per page. Cert fee: $1.00 per doc. Payee: County Clerk. **Other phones:** Assessor-580-323-3271; Treasurer-580-323-2292; Elections-580-323-2291; Vital Records-580-323-4040.

Delaware County

County Clerk, PO Box 309, Jay, OK 74346. **Phone-**918-253-4520; fax-918-253-8352; 8AM-4:30PM Will search UCC records. Search per debtor- $10.00. UCC search includes tax liens if requested. Will not search real estate records. UCC copy- $1.00 per page. Cert fee: $1.00 per cert. Payee: Delaware County Clerk. **Online Access to Real Estate, Deed records:** Access to land records is free at www.okcountyrecords.com. **Other phones:** Assessor-918-328-5561.

Dewey County

County Clerk, PO Box 368, Taloga, OK 73667. **Phone-**580-328-5361; fax-580-328-5652; hours 8AM-4PM Will search UCC records. Search per debtor- $10.00. Will not search real estate or tax lien records. Record copy- $1.00 per page. Cert fee: $1.00 per cert. Payee: Dewey County Clerk. **Other phones:** Assessor-580-328-5561; Treasurer-580-328-5501.

Ellis County

, PO Box 197, Arnett, OK 73832. **Phone-**, R/E & UCC Recording- 580-885-7301; fax-580-885-7258; hours 8:30AM-4:30PM Will search UCC records. Search per debtor- $10.00. Will search real estate records. Copy fee-$1.00 per instrument. Copy fee is $1.00 per page. Cert fee: $1.00 per page. Payee: Ellis County Clerk. **Other phones:** Assessor-580-885-7975; Treasurer-580-885-7670; Elections-580-885-7721; Vital Records-580-885-7301.

Garfield County

County Clerk, PO Box 1664, Enid, OK 73702-1664. **Phone-**County Clerk, R/E & UCC Recording- 580-237-0226; fax-580-249-5951; hours 8AM-4:30PM Will search UCC records. Search per debtor- $10.00. Will not search real estate or tax lien records. Copy fee- $1.00 per page. Cert fee: $1.00 per page. Payee: Garfield County Clerk. **Other phones:** Assessor-580-237-0220;

Appraiser/ Auditor-580-237-0220; Elections-580-237-6016; Court Clerk-580-237-0232.

Garvin County

County Clerk, PO Box 926, Pauls Valley, OK 73075. **Phone-**405-238-2772; fax-405-238-6283; hours 8:30-4:30PM Will search UCC records. Search per debtor- $5.00. Will not search real estate or tax lien records. UCC copy- $1.00 per page. Cert fee: $1.00. Payee: Garvin County Clerk. **Other phones:** Assessor-405-238-2409; Treasurer-405-238-7301.

Grady County

County Clerk, PO Box 1009, Chickasha, OK 73023. **Phone-**405-224-7388; fax-405-222-4506; hours 8AM-4:30PM www.gradycounty.net Will search UCC records. Search per debtor- $5.00. Will search tax liens. Will not search real estate records. Copy fee- $1.00 per page. Cert fee: $1.00 per doc. Payee: County Clerk. **Other phones:** Assessor-405-224-4361; Treasurer-405-224-5337; Elections-405-224-1430; Vital Records-405-271-4040.

Grant County

County Clerk, PO Box 167, Medford, OK 73759-0167. **Phone-**County Clerk, R/E & UCC Recording- 580-395-2274; fax-580-395-2086; hours 8AM-4:30PM Will search UCC records. Search per debtor- $5.00. UCC search includes tax liens if requested. Lien/UCC searches performed by phone only. Separate federal/state combined tax lien search- $5.00 per debtor. Will not search real estate records. Record copy- $1.00 per page. Cert fee: $1.00 per cert. Payee: Grant County Clerk. **Other phones:** Assessor-580-395-2844; Treasurer-580-395-2284; Elections-580-395-2862.

Greer County

County Clerk, PO Box 207, Mangum, OK 73554. **Phone-**County Clerk, R/E & UCC Recording- 580-782-3664; fax-580-782-3803; hours 8AM-4PM Will search UCC records. Search per debtor- $10.00. Tax liens not included in UCC search. Tax lien search- $5.00 per search. Will search real estate records. Copy fee- $1.00 per page. Cert fee: $1.00 per doc. Payee: Greer County Clerk. **Other phones:** Assessor-580-782-2740; Treasurer-580-782-5515; Appraiser/ Auditor-580-782-2454; Elections-580-782-2307; Vital Records-405-271-4040.

Harmon County

County Clerk, 14 W Hollis, Courthouse, Hollis, OK 73550. **Phone-**580-688-3658; hours 8-12;00-1-5PM Will search UCC records. Search per debtor- $5.00. Tax liens not included in UCC search. Tax lien search- $5.00 per debtor. Property transfer searches available. UCC copy- $1.00 per page. Cert fee: $2.00. Payee: Harmon County Clerk. **Other phones:** Assessor-580-882-2529; Treasurer-580-882-3566.

Harper County

County Clerk, PO Box 369, Buffalo, OK 73834. **Phone-**County Clerk, R/E & UCC Recording- 580-735-2012; fax-580-735-2612; hours 8AM-4PM Will search UCC records. Search per debtor- $10.00. UCC search includes tax liens if requested. Separate federal/state combined tax lien search- $10.00 per debtor. Will search real estate records. Copy fee-$1.00 per page. UCC copy- $1.00 per page. Cert fee: $1.00 per page. Payee: Harper County Clerk. **Other phones:** Assessor-580-735-2343; Treasurer-580-735-2442; Elections-580-735-2313.

Haskell County

County Clerk, 202 E. Main, Courthouse, Stigler, OK 74462. **Phone**-County Clerk, R/E & UCC Recording-918-967-2884; fax-918-967-2885; hours 8AM-4:30PM

Will search UCC records. Search per debtor- $10.00 written/$3.00 phone. Tax lien search- $10.00 per written/$3.00 by phone. Will not search real estate records. Copy fee- $1.00 per page. Cert fee: $1.00 per instrument. Payee: Haskell County Clerk. **Other phones:** Assessor-918-967-2611; Treasurer-918-967-2441; Elections-918-967-8792.

Hughes County

County Clerk, 200 N. Broadway ST. #5, Holdenville, OK 74848-3400. **Phone**-County Clerk, R/E & UCC Recording- 405-379-5487; fax-405-379-6890; hours 8AM-4:30PM

Will search UCC records. Search per debtor- $10.00. UCC search includes tax liens if requested. Separate federal/state combined tax lien search-$5.00 per debtor. Will not search real estate records. Record copy- $1.00 per page. Cert fee: $1.00 per seal. Payee: Hughes County Clerk. **Other phones:** Assessor-405-379-3862; Treasurer-405-379-5371; Elections-405-379-2174.

Jackson County

County Clerk, PO Box 515, Altus, OK 73522. **Phone**-County Clerk, R/E & UCC Recording- 580-482-4070; hours 8AM-4PM

Will search UCC records. Search per person- $10.00. Will not search tax liens. Real estate owner, mortgage, and property transfer searches available. Legal description required. Record copy- $1.00 per page. Cert fee: $1.00 per cert. Payee: Jackson County Clerk. **Other phones:** Assessor-580-482-0787; Treasurer-580-482-4371; Elections-580-482-2370; Vital Records-580-482-4070.

Jefferson County

County Clerk, 220 N. Main, Courthouse - Rm 103, Waurika, OK 73573. **Phone**-County Clerk, R/E & UCC Recording- 580-228-2029; fax-580-228-3418; hours 8AM-4PM

Will search UCC records. Search per debtor- $5.00. Will search tax liens including federal tax liens. Federal/state combined tax lien search- $1.00 per copy. Will not search real estate records. UCC copy-$1.00 per page. Cert fee: $1.00 per page. Payee: Jefferson County Clerk. **Other phones:** Assessor-580-228-2377; Treasurer-580-228-2967.

Johnston County

County Clerk, 414 W. Main, Rm 101, Tishomingo, OK 73460. **Phone**-County Clerk, R/E & UCC Recording-580-371-3184; fax-580-371-3662; 8:30AM-4:30PM

Will search UCC records. Search per debtor- $10.00. UCC search includes tax liens if requested. Tax lien search- $3.00 per debtor for uncertified verbal search. Federal/state combined Tax lien search-$10.00 per debtor. Real estate owner, mortgage, and property transfer searches available. UCC copy- $1.00 per page. Cert fee: $1.00 per instryment. Payee: Johnston County Clerk. **Other phones:** Assessor-580-371-3645; Treasurer-580-371-3082; Elections-580-371-3670; Vital Records-580-271-4040.

Kay County

County Clerk, PO Box 450, Newkirk, OK 74647-0450. **Phone**-County Clerk, R/E & UCC Recording- 580-362-2537; fax-580-362-3300; hours 8AM-4:30PM

Will search UCC records. Search per debtor- $10.00. Tax liens not included in UCC search. Tax lien search-no fee. Search real estate land records by mail or phone. Copy fee- $1.00 per page. Cert fee: $1.00 per page. Payee: Kay County Clerk. **Other phones:**

Assessor-580-362-2566; Treasurer-580-362-2523; Elections-580-362-2130.

Kingfisher County

County Clerk, 101 S. Main, Rm #3, Kingfisher, OK 73750. **Phone**-County Clerk, R/E & UCC Recording-405-375-3887; fax-405-375-6033; hours 8AM-4:30PM

Will search UCC records. Search per debtor- $10.00. Will not search real estate or tax lien records. Copy fee- $1.00 per page. Cert fee: $1.00 per doc. Payee: Judy Grellner, County Clerk. **Other phones:** Assessor-405-375-3884; Treasurer-405-375-3827; Appraiser/ Auditor-405-375-3884; Elections-405-375-3895.

Kiowa County

County Clerk, PO Box 73, Hobart, OK 73651-0073. **Phone**-County Clerk, R/E & UCC Recording- 580-726-5286; fax-580-726-6033; hours 9AM-5PM

Will search UCC records. Search per debtor- $10.00. Tax liens not included in UCC search. Tax lien search- $3.00 per debtor. Copy fee- $1.00 per page. Cert fee: $1.00 per doc. Payee: Kiowa County Clerk. **Other phones:** Assessor-580-726-2150; Treasurer-580-726-2362; Elections-580-726-2509.

Latimer County

County Clerk, 109 N Central, Rm 103, Wilburton, OK 74578. **Phone**-918-465-3543; fax-918-465-4001; hours 8AM-4:30PM

Will search UCC records. Search per debtor- $10.00. UCC search includes tax liens if requested. UCC copy- $1.00 per page. Cert fee: $1.00. Payee: Latimer County Clerk. **Other phones:** Assessor-918-465-3031; Treasurer-918-465-3450.

Le Flore County

County Clerk, PO Box 218, Poteau, OK 74953-0218. **Phone**-918-647-5738; fax-918-647-8930; hours 8AM-4:30PM

Will search UCC records. Search per debtor- $10.00. Will not search real estate records. Copy fee is $1.00 per page. Cert fee: None. Payee: Le Flore County Clerk. **Online Access to Real Estate, Deed records:** Access to land records is free at www.okcountyrecords.com. **Other phones:** Assessor-918-647-3652; Treasurer-918-647-3525; Elections-918-647-3701.

Lincoln County

County Clerk, PO Box 126, Chandler, OK 74834-0126. **Phone**-County Clerk, R/E & UCC Recording- 405-258-1264; hours 8:30AM-4:30PM

Will search UCC records. Search per debtor- $10.00. Tax liens not included in UCC search. Tax lien search- $3.00 per debtor. Property transfer searches available. Record copy- $1.00 per page. Cert fee: $1.00 per page. Payee: Lincoln County Clerk. **Online Access to Real Estate Recording records:** Land records are available at https://www.etitlesearch.com/services.asp. You can do a name search; choose from $25.00 monthly subscription or per click account. **Other phones:** Assessor-405-258-1209; Treasurer-405-258-1491; Elections-405-258-1349.

Logan County

County Clerk, 301 E. Harrison, #102, Guthrie, OK 73044-4999. **Phone**-County Clerk, R/E & UCC Recording- 405-282-0266; fax-405-282-0267; hours 8:30AM-4:30PM

Will search UCC records prior to 7/2001. Search per debtor- $10.00. Will not search tax liens. Offers only a very limited search of real estate records. Record copy- $1.00 per page. Cert fee: $1.00 per cert. Payee: Logan County Clerk. **Other phones:**

Assessor-405-282-3509; Treasurer-405-282-3154; Elections-405-282-1900; Vital Records-405-271-4040.

Love County

County Clerk, 405 W. Main, Rm 203, Marietta, OK 73448. **Phone**-580-276-3059; hours 8AM-Noon, 12:30-4:30PM

Will search UCC records. Search per debtor- $10.00. UCC search includes tax liens if requested. Separate federal/state combined tax lien search-no charge. Will not search real estate records. UCC copy-$1.00 per page. Cert fee: $1.00. Payee: Love County Clerk. **Other phones:** Assessor-580-276-3059; Treasurer-580-276-2360.

Major County

County Clerk, PO Box 379, Fairview, OK 73737-0379. **Phone**-580-227-4732, R/E Recording-580-227-3918, UCC Recording-580-227-3918; fax-580-227-2736; hours 8:30AM-4:30PM

Will search UCC records. Search per debtor- $10.00. Will not search real estate or tax lien records. UCC copy- $1.00 per page. Cert fee: $1.00. Payee: Major County Clerk. **Other phones:** Assessor-580-227-4821; Treasurer-580-227-4782.

Marshall County

County Clerk, Marshall County Courthouse, Rm 101, Madill, OK 73446. **Phone**-County Clerk, R/E & UCC Recording- 580-795-3220; fax-580-795-7596; hours 8:30AM-Noon, 12:30-5PM

Will search UCC records. Search per debtor- $10.00. UCC search includes tax liens if requested. Separate federal/state combined tax lien search-no charge. Real estate record owner searches available; legal description and name required. Record copy fee-$1.00 per page. Cert fee: $1.00 per cert. Payee: Marshall County Clerk. **Other phones:** Assessor-580-795-2398; Treasurer-580-795-2463; Appraiser/ Auditor-580-795-2398; Elections-580-795-5460.

Mayes County

County Clerk, 1 Court Place #120, Pryor, OK 74361. **Phone**-County Clerk, R/E & UCC Recording- 918-825-2426; fax-918-825-3803; hours 9AM-5PM

Will search UCC records. Search per debtor- $10.00 per search. Will not search real estate or tax lien records. Copy fee- $1.00 per page. Cert fee: $1.00 per doc. Payee: Mayes County Clerk. **Other phones:** Assessor-918-825-0625; Treasurer-918-825-0160; Appraiser/ Auditor-918-825-0625; Elections-918-825-1826.

McClain County

County Clerk, PO Box 629, Purcell, OK 73080-0629. **Phone**-County Clerk, R/E & UCC Recording- 405-527-3360; fax-405-5 27-5242; hours 8AM-4:30PM

Will search UCC records. Search per debtor- $3.00. Will search state/federal tax liens after 1994. Real estate owner, mortgage, and property transfer searches available. Record copy- $1.00 per page. Cert fee: $1.00 per cert. Payee: McClain County Clerk. **Other phones:** Assessor-405-527-3520; Treasurer-405-527-3261.

McCurtain County

County Clerk, PO Box 1078, Idabel, OK 74745. **Phone**-County Clerk, R/E & UCC Recording- 580-286-2370; fax-580-286-7040; hours 8AM-4PM

Will search UCC records. Search per debtor- $10.00. Tax liens not included in UCC search. Separate federal/state combined tax lien search- $5.00 per debtor. Will not search real estate records. UCC copy-$1.00 per page. Cert fee: $1.00 per cert. Payee: McCurtain County Clerk. **Other phones:** Assessor-580-286-5272; Treasurer-580-286-5128; Elections-580-286-7405; Vital Records-405-271-5600.

McIntosh County

County Clerk, PO Box 110, Eufaula, OK 74432-0110. **Phone**-918-689-5419; fax-918-689-3385; 8AM-4PM Will search UCC records. Search per debtor- $5.00. Will not search real estate records. UCC copy- $1.00 per page. Cert fee: $1.00. Payee: McIntosh County County Clerk. **Other phones:** Assessor-918-689-5419; Treasurer-918-689-2491.

Murray County

County Clerk, PO Box 442, Sulphur, OK 73086. **Phone**-County Clerk, R/E & UCC Recording- 580-622-3920; fax-580-622-6209; hours 8AM-4:30PM Will search UCC records. Search per debtor- $5.00. Will do tax lien search. Federal/state combined tax lien search- $10.00 per page. Will not search real estate records. Copy fee- $1.00 per page. Cert fee: $1.00 per cert. Payee: Murray County Clerk. **Other phones:** Assessor-580-622-3433; Treasurer-580-622-5622; Elections-580-622-3920.

Muskogee County

County Clerk, PO Box 1008, Muskogee, OK 74401. **Phone**-918-682-7781; hours 8AM-4:30PM Will search UCC records. Search per debtor- $10.00. Tax liens not included in UCC search. Separate federal/state combined tax lien search- $10.00 per debtor. Will not search real estate records. UCC copy- $1.00 per page. Cert fee: $1.00 per cert. Payee: Muskogee County Clerk. **Other phones:** Assessor-918-682-8781; Treasurer-918-682-0811.

Noble County

County Clerk, 300 Courthouse Dr, Box 11, Courthouse, Rm 201, Perry, OK 73077. **Phone**-County Clerk, R/E & UCC Recording- 580-336-2141; fax-580-336-2481; hours 8AM-4:30PM Will search UCC records. Search per debtor- $10.00. Will search tax liens including federal tax liens. Separate federal & state combined tax lien search- $5.00 per debtor. Will not search real estate records. Copy fee- $1.00 per page. Cert fee: $1.00 per page. Payee: Noble County Clerk. **Other phones:** Assessor-580-336-2185; Treasurer-580-336-2026; Elections-580-336-3527.

Nowata County

County Clerk, 229 N. Maple, Nowata, OK 74048. **Phone**-County Clerk, R/E & UCC Recording- 918-273-2480; fax-918-273-2481; hours 8AM-4:30PM Will search UCC records. Will not search real estate or tax lien records without book and page number. UCC copy- $1.00 per page. Cert fee: $1.00 per instrument. Payee: Nowata County Clerk. **Other phones:** Assessor-918-273-0581; Treasurer-918-273-3562; Elections-918-273-0710; Vital Records-918-273-0127.

Okfuskee County

County Clerk, PO Box 108, Okemah, OK 74859-0108. **Phone**-County Clerk, R/E & UCC Recording- 918-623-1724; fax-918-623-0739; hours 8AM-4PM Will search UCC records. Search per debtor- $10.00. Will search tax liens including federal tax liens. Federal/state combined tax lien search- $0.00. Copy fee- $1.00 per page. Cert fee: $1.00 per seal. Payee: County Clerk. **Other phones:** Assessor-918-623-1535; Treasurer-918-623-1494; Elections-918-623-0105; Vital Records-405-271-4040.

Oklahoma County

County Clerk, 320 Robert S. Kerr Ave, UCC Filing Ofc - Rm 107, Oklahoma City, OK 73102. **Phone**-405-713-1522, R/E Recording-405-713-1540; fax-405-713-1810; hours 8AM-5PM The OK UCC Central Filing Office is operated by the OK County Clerk's Office. Will search UCC records.

Search per debtor- $10.00. Will search federal tax liens. Will not search real estate records. UCC copy- $1.00 per page. Cert fee: 1.00 per page. Payee: Oklahoma County Clerk. **Online Access to Real Estate, Assessor, Grantor/Grantee, UCC, Property Tax, Inmate, Sex Offender, Most Wanted records:** Assessor and property information on the county assessor database are free at www.oklahomacounty.org/assessor/disclaim.htm. Real estate, UCC, grantor/grantee records on the county clerk database are free at www.oklahomacounty.org/coclerk. Also, search the treasurer's property info at www.oklahomacounty.org/Treasurer/searches/default2.asp. Also, search the sheriff lists of inmates, wanted, and sex offenders at www.oklahomacounty.org/sheriff/default.htm. **Other phones:** Assessor-405-278-3838; Treasurer-405-713-1300; Appraiser/Auditor-405-713-1200; Elections-405-713-1515.

Okmulgee County

County Clerk, PO Box 904, Okmulgee, OK 74447-0904. **Phone**-County Clerk, R/E & UCC Recording-918-756-0788; fax-918-758-1261; 8AM-4:30PM Will search UCC records. Search per debtor- $5.00 pr name. Tax lien search- $5.00 per debtor. Will search real estate records. Copy fee- $1.00 per page. **Other phones:** Assessor-918-758-0303; Treasurer-918-756-3848; Elections-918-756-2365; Vital Records-405-271-4040.

Osage County

County Clerk, PO Box 87, Pawhuska, OK 74056. **Phone**-918-287-3136; fax-918-287-4979; hours 8:30AM-5PM. Will search UCC records. Search per debtor- $10.00. Will not search real estate or tax lien records. Record copy- $1.00 per page. Cert fee: $1.00 per cert. Payee: Osage County Clerk. **Other phones:** Assessor-918-287-3448; Treasurer-918-287-3101; Appraiser/Auditor-918-287-3448; Elections-918-287-3036.

Ottawa County

County Clerk, 102 E. Central, #203, Miami, OK 74354-7043. **Phone**-County Clerk, R/E & UCC Recording-918-542-3332; fax-918-542-8260; hours 9AM-Noon,1-5PM; Recording until 4:00PM Will search UCC records. Search per debtor- $5.00. Will not search real estate or tax lien records. Record copy- $1.00 per page. Cert fee: $1.00 per cert. Payee: Ottawa County Clerk. **Other phones:** Assessor-918-542-9418; Treasurer-918-542-8232; Elections-918-542-2893; Vital Records-918-571-2600.

Pawnee County

County Clerk, 500 Harrison St., Courthouse, Rm 202, Pawnee, OK 74058. **Phone**-County Clerk, R/E & UCC Recording- 918-762-2732; fax-918-762-6404; hours 8AM-4:30PM Will search UCC records. Search per debtor- $10.00. Will not search real estate or tax lien records. Record copy- $1.00 per page. Cert fee: $1.00 per cert. Payee: Pawnee County Clerk. **Other phones:** Assessor-918-762-2402; Treasurer-918-762-2418; Elections-918-762-2125.

Payne County

County Clerk, 315 W 6th Ave #202, Stillwater, OK 74074. **Phone**-405-747-8310, R/E Recording-405-747-8345; hours 8AM-5PM Will search UCC records. Search per debtor- $5.00. Will not search real estate or tax lien records. Record copy- $1.00 per page. Cert fee: $1.00 per cert. Payee: Payne County Clerk. **Online Access to Real Estate, Deed records:** Access to land records is free at www.okcountyrecords.com. **Other phones:** Assessor-405-747-8300; Treasurer-405-747-9411; Appraiser/Auditor-405-747-8300; Vital Records-405-271-4040; 405-747-8344.

Pittsburg County

County Clerk, PO Box 3304, McAlester, OK 74502. **Phone**-918-423-6865; fax-918-423-7304; 8AM-5PM Will search UCC records. Search per debtor- $3.00 by phone, $10.00 in person. UCC search includes tax liens if requested. Tax lien search- $3.00 per debtor. Will search real estate records. Copy fee- $1.00 per page. Cert fee: $1.00 per page. Payee: Pittsburg County Clerk. **Other phones:** Assessor-918-423-4726; Treasurer-918-423-6895.

Pontotoc County

County Clerk, PO Box 1425, Ada, OK 74820. **Phone**-County Clerk, R/E & UCC Recording- 580-332-1425; fax-580-332-9509; hours-8AM-5PM www.pontotoccountyclerk.org Will search UCC records. Search per debtor- $10.00. Tax liens not included in UCC search. Will not search real estate records. Copy fee- $1.00 per page. **Online Access to Recording, Land, UCC, Judgment, Lien, Military records:** Access to the recorders records is free on the website. To search, login as guest and password a21b23. Password is case sensitive. **Other phones:** Assessor-580-332-0317; Treasurer-580-332-0183; Elections-580-332-4534; Vital Records-405-271-5600.

Pottawatomie County

County Clerk, PO Box 576, Shawnee, OK 74802. **Phone**-405-273-8222; fax-405-275-6898; 8:30AM-5PM. Will search UCC records. UCC search per debtor-$5.00 per search. Will search tax liens including federal tax liens. Tax lien search- No fee. Will search real estate records. Copy fee- $1.00 per page. Cert fee: $1.00 per doc. Payee: County Clerk. **Other phones:** Assessor-405-275-4740; Treasurer-405-273-0213; Elections-405-273-8367.

Pushmataha County

County Clerk, 302 SW 'B', Antlers, OK 74523. **Phone**-County Clerk, R/E & UCC Recording- 580-298-3626; fax-580-298-8452; hours 8AM-4:30PM Will search UCC records. Search per debtor- $5.00. Will not search real estate or tax lien records. Record copy- $1.00 per page. Cert fee: $2.00 per page. Payee: Pushmataha County Clerk. **Other phones:** Assessor-580-298-3504; Treasurer-580-298-2580; Appraiser/Auditor-580-298-3504; Elections-580-298-3292; County Clerk-580-298-2274.

Roger Mills County

County Clerk, PO Box 708, Cheyenne, OK 73628. **Phone**-580-497-3395, R/E Recording-580-497-3366 or 3395; fax-580-497-3488; hours 9AM-4:30PM Will not search records. UCC copy- $1.00 per page. Cert fee: $1.00. Payee: Roger Mills County Clerk. **Other phones:** Assessor-580-497-3350; Treasurer-580-497-3349; Elections-580-497-3330.

Rogers County

County Clerk, PO Box 1210, Claremore, OK 74018. **Phone**-County Clerk, R/E & UCC Recording- 918-341-2518; fax-918-341-4529; hours 8AM-5PM www.rogerscounty.org Will search UCC records. Search per debtor- $10.00. Will not search real estate or tax lien records. Record copy- $1.00 per page. Cert fee: $1.00 per cert. Payee: Rogers County Clerk. **Online Access to Assessor, Property Tax, Treasurer, Tax Roll, Real Estate Recording records:** Access to the assessor database is free at www.rogerscounty.org/search.html. Also, you may search the treasurers tax roll database free at www.rogerscounty.org/treasurer/search.html. Also, land records are at https://www.etitlesearch.com/services.asp. For registration and subscription information, call 870-856-3055. **Other phones:** Assessor-918-341-3290;

Treasurer-918-341-3159; Appraiser/ Auditor-918-341-0200; Elections-918-314-2965; Vital Records-405-271-4040.

Seminole County

County Clerk, PO Box 1180, Wewoka, OK 74884. **Phone**-405-257-2501; fax-405-257-6422; 8AM-4PM
Will search UCC records. Search per debtor- $5.00. Search request using non-standard form (per name)- $10.00. Tax liens not included in UCC search. Federal/state combined tax lien search- $10.00 Will not search real estate records. UCC copy- $1.00 per page. Cert fee: $1.00 per instrument. Payee: Seminole County Clerk. **Other phones:** Assessor-405-257-3371; Treasurer-405-257-6262.

Sequoyah County

County Clerk, 120 E. Chickasaw, Sallisaw, OK 74955. **Phone**-918-775-4516; fax-918-775-1218; hours 8-4
Will search UCC records. Search per debtor- $5.00. Will not search real estate or tax lien records. Copy fee- $1.00 per page. Cert fee: $1.00 per doc. Payee: Pay fees to Seg. Co Clerk. **Other phones:** Assessor-918-775-2062; Treasurer-918-775-9321; Elections-918-775-2614.

Stephens County

County Clerk, 101 S. 11th St, Rm 203, Duncan, OK 73533-4758. **Phone**-580-255-0977; fax-580-255-0991; hours 8:30AM-4:30PM
Will search UCC records. Search per debtor- $10.00. Will not search real estate records. UCC copy- $1.00 per page. Cert fee: $1.00. Payee: Stephens County Clerk. **Online Access to Real Estate, Deed records:** Access to land records is free at www.okcountyrecords.com. **Other phones:** Assessor-580-255-1542; Treasurer-580-255-0728.

Texas County

County Clerk, PO Box 197, Guymon, OK 73942-0197. **Phone**-County Clerk, R/E & UCC Recording- 580-338-3141; fax-580-338-4311; hours 9AM-5PM
Will search UCC records. Search per debtor- $5.00. Will not search real estate or tax lien records. Record copy- $1.00 per page. Cert fee: $1.00 per cert. Payee: Texas County Clerk. **Other phones:** Assessor-580-338-3060; Treasurer-580-338-7050; Elections-580-338-7644; Vital Records-405-271-4040.

Tillman County

County Clerk, PO Box 992, Frederick, OK 73542. **Phone**-County Clerk, R/E & UCC Recording- 580-335-3421; fax-580-335-3795; hours M-F 8AM-4PM www.oklahomacounty.org/countyclerk
Will search UCC records. Search per debtor- $10.00. Tax lien search- $10.00 per debtor. Will not search real estate records. RE record copy- $1.00 per page. All copies- $1.00 per page. Cert fee: $1.00 per page. Payee: County Clerk. **Other phones:** Assessor-580-335-3424; Treasurer-580-335-3425; Elections-580-335-2287; Vital Records-405-271-4040.

Tulsa County

County Clerk, 500 S. Denver Ave, County Admin. Bldg, Rm 112, Tulsa, OK 74103-3832. **Phone**-County Clerk, R/E & UCC Recording- 918-596-5801, UCC Recording-918-596-5864; fax-918-596-5867; hours 8:30AM-5PM www.tulsacounty.org
Will search UCC records. Search per debtor- $10.00. Will not search real estate or tax lien records. Copy fee is $1.00 per page. Cert fee: $1.00 per doc. Payee: County Clerk. **Online Access to Assessor, Treasurer, Recording, Deed, Property, Inmate records:** Access to Tulsa County's Land Records System requires an approved user agreement, username and password. Visit www.public.tulsacounty.org. Monthly access fee is $40.00 and 1st trial month is free. Records go back to 1979. For more information or signup, contact Dorise at 918-596-5206 or LRMIShelp@tulsacounty.org. Also, search inmate info on private company website at www.vinelink.com/index.jsp. **Other phones:** Assessor-918-596-5828; Treasurer-918-596-5030.

Wagoner County

County Clerk, PO Box 156, Wagoner, OK 74477. **Phone**-County Clerk, R/E & UCC Recording- 918-485-2216; fax-918-485-7709; hours 8AM-4:30PM
Will search UCC records. Search per debtor- $5.00. Will not search real estate or tax lien records. Copy fee- $1.00 per page. Cert fee: $1.00 per seal. Payee: Wagoner County Clerk. **Other phones:** Assessor-918-485-2367; Treasurer-918-485-2149; Elections-918-485-2142.

Washington County

County Clerk, 420 S Johnstone, #100, Bartlesville, OK 74003. **Phone**-918-337-2840, R/E Recording-918-337-2834, UCC Recording-918-337-2834; fax-918-337-2894; hours 8AM-5PM www.countycourthouse.org

Will search UCC records. Search per debtor- $5.00. Will not search real estate records. **Online Access to Land, Deed, Mortgage, Lien, Sex Offender records:** Access to the recorders database is free at www.countycourthouse.org/countyclerk/disclaimer.htm. Also, access to the sex offenders registry is free at www.countycourthouse.org/registry/index.htm. **Other phones:** Assessor-918-337-2830; Treasurer-918-337-2810; Elections-918-337-2850.

Washita County

County Clerk, PO Box 380, Cordell, OK 73632. **Phone**-County Clerk, R/E & UCC Recording- 580-832-3548; hours 8AM-4PM
Will search UCC records. Search per debtor- $10.00. Will search tax liens including federal tax liens. Will not search real estate records. Record copy- $1.00 per page. Cert fee: $1.00 per page. Payee: Washita County Clerk. **Other phones:** Assessor-580-832-2468; Treasurer-580-832-2667; Elections-580-832-3658.

Woods County

County Clerk, PO Box 386, Alva, OK 73717-0386. **Phone**-580-327-0998, R/E Recording-580-327-6229; fax-580-327-6222; hours 9AM-5PM
Will search UCC records. Search per debtor- $5.00. Separate federal/state combined tax lien search- $5.00 per debtor. Real estate owner, mortgage, and property transfer searches available. Record copy- $1.00 per page. Cert fee: $1.00 per instrument. Payee: Woods County Clerk. **Other phones:** Assessor-580-327-3118; Treasurer-580-327-0308; Elections-580-327-1452.

Woodward County

County Clerk, 1600 Main St, #8, Woodward, OK 73801-3051. **Phone**-580-254-6800, R/E Recording-580-256-3625, UCC Recording-580-256-3625; fax-580-254-6840; hours 9AM-5PM
Search per debtor- $5.00. Will not search real estate or tax lien records. Record copy- $1.00 per page. Cert fee: $1.00 per cert. Payee: Woodward County Clerk. **Other phones:** Assessor-580-254-5061; Treasurer-580-254-7404.

Oklahoma County Locator

You will usually be able to find the city name in the City/County Cross Reference below. In that case, it is a simple matter to determine the county from the cross reference. However, only the official US Postal Service city names are included in this index. There are an additional 40,000 place names that people use in their addresses. Therefore, we have also included a ZIP/City Cross Reference immediately following the City/County Cross Reference.

If you know the ZIP Code but the city name does not appear in the City/County Cross Reference index, look up the ZIP Code in the ZIP/City Cross Reference, find the city name, then look up the city name in the City/County Cross Reference. For example, you want to know the county for an address of Menands, NY 12204. There is no "Menands" in the City/County Cross Reference. The ZIP/City Cross Reference shows that ZIP Codes 12201-12288 are for the city of Albany. Looking back in the City/County Cross Reference, Albany is in Albany County.

Oklahoma - City/County Cross Reference

ACHILLE Bryan
ADA Pontotoc
ADAIR (74330) Mayes(97), Craig(2)
ADAMS Texas
ADDINGTON Jefferson
AFTON (74331) Delaware(62), Ottawa(35), Craig(1)
AGRA (74824) Lincoln(88), Payne(11)
ALBANY Bryan
ALBERT Caddo
ALBION Pushmataha
ALDERSON Pittsburg
ALEX (73002) Grady(82), McClain(17)
ALINE (73716) Alfalfa(62), Woods(30), Major(6)
ALLEN (74825) Pontotoc(78), Hughes(21)
ALTUS Jackson
ALTUS AFB Jackson
ALVA Woods
AMBER Grady
AMES (73718) Major(68), Garfield(29), Kingfisher(1)
AMORITA Alfalfa
ANADARKO Caddo
ANTLERS Pushmataha
APACHE (73006) Caddo(52), Comanche(47)
ARAPAHO Custer
ARCADIA (73007) Oklahoma(73), Logan(26)
ARDMORE Carter
ARKOMA Le Flore
ARNETT (73832) Ellis(91), Woodward(8)
ASHER Pottawatomie
ATOKA Atoka
ATWOOD Hughes
AVANT Osage
BACHE Pittsburg
BALKO Beaver
BARNSDALL Osage
BARTLESVILLE (74003) Washington(85), Osage(14)
BARTLESVILLE Washington
BATTIEST McCurtain
BEAVER Beaver
BEGGS Okmulgee
BENNINGTON Bryan
BESSIE Washita
BETHANY Oklahoma
BETHEL McCurtain
BIG CABIN (74332) Craig(87), Mayes(10), Rogers(1)
BILLINGS (74630) Noble(75), Garfield(22), Kay(1)
BINGER Caddo
BISON Garfield
BIXBY Tulsa
BLACKWELL Kay
BLAIR (73526) Jackson(90), Greer(9)
BLANCHARD (73010) McClain(62), Grady(37)
BLANCO Pittsburg
BLOCKER Pittsburg

BLUEJACKET (74333) Ottawa(90), Craig(9)
BOISE CITY Cimarron
BOKCHITO Bryan
BOKOSHE Le Flore
BOLEY Okfuskee
BOSWELL (74727) Choctaw(90), Bryan(9)
BOWLEGS Seminole
BOWRING Osage
BOYNTON (74422) Okmulgee(55), Muskogee(44)
BRADLEY (73011) Grady(98), Garvin(1)
BRAGGS Muskogee
BRAMAN Kay
BRAY Stephens
BRISTOW Creek
BROKEN ARROW Tulsa
BROKEN ARROW Wagoner
BROKEN BOW McCurtain
BROMIDE Johnston
BUFFALO Harper
BUNCH (74931) Cherokee(59), Adair(36), Sequoyah(3)
BURBANK Osage
BURLINGTON Alfalfa
BURNEYVILLE Love
BURNS FLAT Washita
BUTLER Custer
BYARS (74831) McClain(87), Pontotoc(9), Garvin(2)
BYRON Alfalfa
CACHE Comanche
CADDO (74729) Atoka(76), Bryan(23)
CALERA Bryan
CALUMET Canadian
CALVIN Hughes
CAMARGO Dewey
CAMERON Le Flore
CANADIAN Pittsburg
CANEY Atoka
CANTON (73724) Blaine(66), Dewey(33)
CANUTE Washita
CAPRON (73725) Woods(79), Alfalfa(20)
CARDIN Ottawa
CARMEN (73726) Alfalfa(82), Woods(17)
CARNEGIE (73015) Caddo(92), Washita(7)
CARNEY Lincoln
CARRIER Garfield
CARTER Beckham
CARTWRIGHT Bryan
CASHION (73016) Kingfisher(57), Logan(40), Canadian(1)
CASTLE Okfuskee
CATOOSA (74015) Rogers(71), Wagoner(26), Tulsa(1)
CEMENT (73017) Grady(66), Caddo(26), Comanche(6)
CENTRAHOMA Coal
CHANDLER Lincoln
CHATTANOOGA (73528) Comanche(62), Tillman(37)
CHECOTAH McIntosh
CHELSEA (74016) Rogers(93), Mayes(3), Nowata(1), Craig(1)

CHEROKEE Alfalfa
CHESTER (73838) Major(89), Woodward(10)
CHEYENNE Roger Mills
CHICKASHA Grady
CHOCTAW (73020) Oklahoma(97), Cleveland(2)
CHOUTEAU (74337) Mayes(94), Wagoner(5)
CLAREMORE (74019) Rogers(98), Mayes(1)
CLAREMORE Rogers
CLARITA Coal
CLAYTON (74536) Pushmataha(96), Pittsburg(2), Latimer(1)
CLEARVIEW Okfuskee
CLEO SPRINGS (73729) Major(88), Woods(9), Alfalfa(2)
CLEVELAND Pawnee
CLINTON (73601) Custer(97), Washita(2)
COALGATE Coal
COLBERT Bryan
COLCORD Delaware
COLEMAN (73432) Johnston(86), Atoka(13)
COLLINSVILLE (74021) Tulsa(77), Rogers(19), Washington(3)
COLONY (73021) Washita(63), Caddo(36)
COMANCHE Stephens
COMMERCE Ottawa
CONCHO Canadian
CONNERVILLE Johnston
COOKSON Cherokee
COPAN (74022) Washington(96), Osage(3)
CORDELL Washita
CORN Washita
COUNCIL HILL (74428) McIntosh(60), Muskogee(39)
COUNTYLINE Stephens
COVINGTON Garfield
COWETA Wagoner
COYLE (73027) Payne(53), Logan(46)
CRAWFORD Roger Mills
CRESCENT (73028) Logan(93), Kingfisher(6)
CROMWELL Seminole
CROWDER Pittsburg
CUSHING (74023) Payne(96), Lincoln(3)
CUSTER CITY Custer
CYRIL Caddo
DACOMA (73731) Woods(93), Alfalfa(6)
DAISY (74540) Atoka(75), Pushmataha(25)
DAVENPORT Lincoln
DAVIDSON Tillman
DAVIS (73030) Murray(97), Garvin(2)
DEER CREEK Grant
DELAWARE Nowata
DEPEW (74028) Creek(98), Lincoln(1)
DEVOL Cotton
DEWAR Okmulgee
DEWEY Washington
DIBBLE McClain
DILL CITY Washita
DISNEY Mayes

DOUGHERTY Murray
DOUGLAS Garfield
DOVER Kingfisher
DRUMMOND (73735) Garfield(98), Major(1)
DRUMRIGHT (74030) Creek(98), Payne(1)
DUKE (73532) Jackson(94), Greer(4)
DUNCAN Stephens
DURANT Bryan
DURHAM Roger Mills
DUSTIN (74839) Hughes(80), Okfuskee(14), McIntosh(4)
EAGLETOWN McCurtain
EAKLY Caddo
EARLSBORO (74840) Pottawatomie(80), Seminole(19)
EDMOND (73034) Oklahoma(77), Logan(22)
EDMOND Oklahoma
EL RENO Canadian
ELDORADO (73537) Jackson(95), Harmon(4)
ELGIN Comanche
ELK CITY Beckham
ELMER Jackson
ELMORE CITY Garvin
ENID Garfield
ERICK Beckham
EUCHA Delaware
EUFAULA (74432) McIntosh(92), Pittsburg(7)
FAIRFAX Osage
FAIRLAND Ottawa
FAIRMONT Garfield
FAIRVIEW Major
FANSHAWE Le Flore
FARGO (73840) Ellis(66), Woodward(33)
FAXON (73540) Comanche(97), Cotton(2)
FAY (73646) Blaine(44), Dewey(41), Custer(14)
FELT Cimarron
FINLEY Pushmataha
FITTSTOWN Johnston
FITTSTOWN Pontotoc
FITZHUGH Pontotoc
FLETCHER Comanche
FORGAN Beaver
FORT COBB Caddo
FORT GIBSON (74434) Muskogee(97), Wagoner(1)
FORT SILL Comanche
FORT SUPPLY (73841) Woodward(83), Ellis(13), Harper(3)
FORT TOWSON (74735) Choctaw(74), Pushmataha(25)
FOSS (73647) Washita(88), Custer(11)
FOSTER (73434) Stephens(59), Garvin(40)
FOX Carter
FOYIL Rogers
FRANCIS Pontotoc
FREDERICK Tillman
FREEDOM (73842) Woods(66), Woodward(24), Harper(9)
GAGE (73843) Ellis(95), Beaver(4)

GANS Sequoyah
GARBER Garfield
GARVIN McCurtain
GATE (73844) Beaver(51), Harper(48)
GEARY (73040) Blaine(69), Canadian(28), Adair(1)
GENE AUTRY Carter
GERONIMO (73543) Comanche(96), Cotton(3)
GLENCOE (74032) Payne(82), Pawnee(11), Noble(6)
GLENPOOL (74033) Tulsa(93), Creek(6)
GOLDEN McCurtain
GOLTRY (73739) Alfalfa(87), Garfield(12)
GOODWELL Texas
GORE (74435) Sequoyah(88), Muskogee(11)
GOTEBO (73041) Kiowa(79), Washita(20)
GOULD Harmon
GOWEN Latimer
GRACEMONT Caddo
GRAHAM Carter
GRANDFIELD Tillman
GRANITE Greer
GRANT Choctaw
GREENFIELD Blaine
GROVE Delaware
GUTHRIE Logan
GUYMON Texas
HAILEYVILLE Pittsburg
HALLETT Pawnee
HAMMON (73650) Roger Mills(74), Custer(25)
HANNA McIntosh
HARDESTY Texas
HARRAH (73045) Oklahoma(82), Lincoln(12), Pottawatomie(4)
HARTSHORNE (74547) Pittsburg(97), Latimer(2)
HASKELL (74436) Muskogee(59), Okmulgee(30), Wagoner(10)
HASTINGS (73548) Stephens(39), Jefferson(34), Cotton(25)
HAWORTH McCurtain
HAYWOOD Pittsburg
HEADRICK Jackson
HEALDTON Carter
HEAVENER Le Flore
HELENA Alfalfa
HENDRIX Bryan
HENNEPIN (73444) Carter(75), Garvin(12), Murray(12)
HENNESSEY (73742) Kingfisher(96), Garfield(3)
HENRYETTA (74437) Okmulgee(98), McIntosh(1)
HILLSDALE Garfield
HINTON (73047) Caddo(76), Canadian(23)
HITCHCOCK (73744) Blaine(92), Kingfisher(7)
HITCHITA McIntosh
HOBART Kiowa
HODGEN Le Flore
HOLDENVILLE Hughes
HOLLIS Harmon
HOLLISTER Tillman
HOMINY Osage
HONOBIA (74549) Le Flore(94), Pushmataha(5)
HOOKER Texas
HOPETON Woods
HOWE Le Flore
HOYT Haskell
HUGO Choctaw
HULBERT Cherokee
HUNTER (74640) Garfield(93), Grant(6)
HYDRO (73048) Caddo(44), Custer(36), Blaine(18)
IDABEL McCurtain
INDIAHOMA Comanche
INDIANOLA Pittsburg
INOLA (74036) Rogers(96), Mayes(3)

ISABELLA Major
JAY Delaware
JENKS Tulsa
JENNINGS (74038) Pawnee(63), Creek(36)
JET Alfalfa
JONES Oklahoma
KANSAS (74347) Delaware(97), Cherokee(2)
KAW CITY Kay
KELLYVILLE Creek
KEMP Bryan
KEMP CPO Bryan
KENEFIC (74748) Johnston(67), Bryan(18), Atoka(13)
KENTON Cimarron
KEOTA (74941) Haskell(85), Le Flore(14)
KETCHUM Mayes
KEYES Cimarron
KIAMICHI - HONOBIA CPO (74549) Le Flore(94), Pushmataha(5)
KIEFER Creek
KINGFISHER Kingfisher
KINGSTON Marshall
KINTA Haskell
KIOWA (74553) Pittsburg(71), Atoka(28)
KNOWLES Beaver
KONAWA (74849) Seminole(86), Pottawatomie(13)
KREBS Pittsburg
KREMLIN Garfield
LAHOMA (73754) Garfield(90), Major(9)
LAMAR Hughes
LAMONT (74643) Grant(92), Kay(7)
LANE Atoka
LANGLEY Mayes
LANGSTON Logan
LAVERNE (73848) Beaver(50), Harper(47), Ellis(2)
LAWTON Comanche
LEBANON Marshall
LEEDEY (73654) Dewey(62), Roger Mills(28), Custer(9)
LEFLORE Le Flore
LEHIGH (74556) Atoka(60), Coal(40)
LENAPAH Nowata
LEON Love
LEONARD Tulsa
LEQUIRE Haskell
LEXINGTON Cleveland
LINDSAY (73052) Garvin(63), McClain(31), Grady(4)
LOCO Stephens
LOCUST GROVE (74352) Mayes(82), Sequoyah(14), Wagoner(1)
LOGAN Beaver
LONE GROVE Carter
LONE WOLF (73655) Kiowa(97), Greer(2)
LONGDALE (73755) Blaine(62), Major(31), Dewey(6)
LOOKEBA Caddo
LOVELAND Tillman
LOYAL Kingfisher
LUCIEN (73757) Noble(84), Garfield(15)
LUCIEN CPO (73757) Noble(84), Garfield(15)
LUTHER (73054) Oklahoma(77), Lincoln(14), Logan(7)
MACOMB (74852) Pottawatomie(96), Cleveland(3)
MADILL (73446) Marshall(97), Carter(1)
MANCHESTER (73758) Grant(81), Alfalfa(18)
MANGUM (73554) Greer(98), Harmon(1)
MANITOU Tillman
MANNFORD (74044) Creek(69), Pawnee(30)
MANNSVILLE (73447) Johnston(97), Marshall(2)
MARAMEC (74045) Pawnee(98), Payne(1)
MARBLE CITY Sequoyah
MARIETTA Love

MARLAND Noble
MARLOW (73055) Stephens(87), Grady(10), Comanche(2)
MARSHALL (73056) Garfield(65), Logan(29), Kingfisher(4)
MARTHA Jackson
MAUD (74854) Pottawatomie(60), Seminole(39)
MAY (73851) Ellis(51), Harper(48)
MAYFIELD Beckham
MAYSVILLE (73057) Garvin(78), McClain(21)
MAZIE Mayes
MC LOUD (74851) Pottawatomie(74), Cleveland(15), Lincoln(10)
MCALESTER Pittsburg
MCCURTAIN (74944) Haskell(87), Le Flore(12)
MCLOUD (74851) Pottawatomie(74), Cleveland(15), Lincoln(10)
MEAD Bryan
MEDFORD Grant
MEDICINE PARK Comanche
MEEKER (74855) Lincoln(89), Pottawatomie(10)
MEERS Comanche
MENO Major
MERIDIAN Logan
MIAMI Ottawa
MILBURN Johnston
MILFAY Creek
MILL CREEK (74856) Johnston(91), Murray(8)
MILLERTON McCurtain
MINCO (73059) Grady(72), Canadian(14), Caddo(13)
MOFFETT Sequoyah
MONROE Le Flore
MOODYS Cherokee
MOORELAND Woodward
MORRIS Okmulgee
MORRISON Noble
MOUNDS (74047) Okmulgee(51), Creek(28), Tulsa(20)
MOUNTAIN PARK (73559) Kiowa(69), Comanche(30)
MOUNTAIN VIEW Kiowa
MOYERS Pushmataha
MULDROW Sequoyah
MULHALL (73063) Logan(83), Payne(16)
MUSE Le Flore
MUSKOGEE Muskogee
MUSTANG Canadian
MUTUAL Woodward
NARDIN (74646) Kay(89), Grant(10)
NASH (73761) Grant(93), Garfield(6)
NASHOBA Pushmataha
NEWALLA (74857) Cleveland(75), Oklahoma(23), Pottawatomie(1)
NEWCASTLE McClain
NEWKIRK Kay
NICOMA PARK Oklahoma
NINNEKAH Grady
NOBLE Cleveland
NORMAN (73072) Cleveland(95), McClain(4)
NORMAN Cleveland
NORTH MIAMI Ottawa
NOWATA Nowata
OAKHURST Tulsa
OAKS (74359) Delaware(63), Cherokee(36)
OAKWOOD (73658) Dewey(90), Blaine(9)
OCHELATA (74051) Washington(98), Osage(1)
OILTON Creek
OKARCHE (73762) Kingfisher(51), Canadian(48)
OKAY Wagoner
OKEENE (73763) Blaine(89), Major(7), Kingfisher(2)

OKEMAH (74859) Okfuskee(93), Seminole(6)
OKLAHOMA CITY (73128) Oklahoma(87), Canadian(12)
OKLAHOMA CITY (73169) Oklahoma(66), Cleveland(33)
OKLAHOMA CITY (73179) Oklahoma(86), Canadian(13)
OKLAHOMA CITY Cleveland
OKLAHOMA CITY Oklahoma
OKMULGEE Okmulgee
OKTAHA Muskogee
OLUSTEE Jackson
OMEGA (73764) Kingfisher(60), Blaine(39)
OOLOGAH Rogers
ORLANDO (73073) Logan(77), Garfield(19), Noble(2), Payne(1)
OSAGE Osage
OSCAR Jefferson
OVERBROOK (73453) Love(64), Carter(35)
OWASSO (74055) Tulsa(72), Rogers(27)
PADEN Okfuskee
PANAMA Le Flore
PANOLA Latimer
PAOLI (73074) Garvin(86), McClain(13)
PARK HILL Cherokee
PAULS VALLEY Garvin
PAWHUSKA Osage
PAWNEE Pawnee
PEGGS (74452) Cherokee(88), Mayes(11)
PERKINS (74059) Payne(96), Lincoln(3)
PERNELL Garvin
PERRY Noble
PHAROAH Okfuskee
PICHER Ottawa
PICKENS McCurtain
PIEDMONT (73078) Canadian(98), Oklahoma(1)
PITTSBURG Pittsburg
PLATTER Bryan
POCASSET (73079) Grady(91), Caddo(8)
POCOLA Le Flore
PONCA CITY (74604) Kay(70), Osage(29)
PONCA CITY Kay
POND CREEK Grant
PORTER Wagoner
PORUM (74455) Muskogee(80), McIntosh(19)
POTEAU Le Flore
PRAGUE (74864) Lincoln(74), Pottawatomie(25)
PRESTON Okmulgee
PROCTOR Adair
PRUE Osage
PRYOR Mayes
PURCELL McClain
PUTNAM (73659) Dewey(98), Custer(1)
QUAPAW Ottawa
QUINTON (74561) Pittsburg(78), Haskell(21)
RALSTON (74650) Pawnee(65), Osage(34)
RAMONA Washington
RANDLETT Cotton
RATLIFF CITY (73481) Carter(90), Stephens(6), Garvin(2)
RATLIFF CITY Carter
RATTAN Pushmataha
RAVIA Johnston
RED OAK Latimer
RED ROCK (74651) Noble(96), Pawnee(3)
REDBIRD Wagoner
RENTIESVILLE McIntosh
REYDON Roger Mills
RINGLING (73456) Jefferson(65), Carter(25), Love(8)
RINGOLD (74754) McCurtain(67), Pushmataha(30), Choctaw(2)
RINGWOOD Major
RIPLEY Payne
ROCKY (73661) Washita(97), Kiowa(2)

ROFF (74865) Pontotoc(91), Garvin(5), Murray(3)
ROLAND Sequoyah
ROOSEVELT (73564) Kiowa(97), Comanche(2)
ROSE (74364) Delaware(85), Mayes(12), Cherokee(1)
ROSSTON Harper
RUFE McCurtain
RUSH SPRINGS (73082) Grady(96), Comanche(3)
RYAN Jefferson
S COFFEYVILLE (74072) Nowata(97), Craig(2)
SAINT LOUIS Pottawatomie
SALINA (74365) Mayes(81), Delaware(18)
SALLISAW Sequoyah
SAND SPRINGS (74063) Tulsa(74), Osage(20), Creek(5)
SAPULPA (74066) Creek(98), Tulsa(1)
SAPULPA Creek
SASAKWA (74867) Seminole(95), Hughes(4)
SAVANNA Pittsburg
SAWYER Choctaw
SAYRE (73662) Beckham(97), Roger Mills(2)
SCHULTER Okmulgee
SEILING Dewey
SEMINOLE Seminole
SENTINEL Washita
SHADY POINT Le Flore
SHAMROCK Creek
SHARON Woodward
SHATTUCK Ellis
SHAWNEE Pottawatomie
SHIDLER (74652) Osage(96), Kay(3)
SKIATOOK (74070) Osage(60), Tulsa(30), Washington(9)
SLICK Creek
SMITHVILLE (74957) Le Flore(78), McCurtain(21)
SNOW Pushmataha
SNYDER (73566) Kiowa(88), Tillman(11)

SOPER Choctaw
SOUTHARD Blaine
SPARKS Lincoln
SPAVINAW (74366) Mayes(89), Delaware(10)
SPENCER Oklahoma
SPENCERVILLE (74760) Choctaw(65), Pushmataha(34)
SPERRY (74073) Tulsa(65), Osage(34)
SPIRO Le Flore
SPRINGER Carter
STERLING Comanche
STIDHAM McIntosh
STIDHAM COUNTRY CPU McIntosh
STIGLER (74462) Haskell(98), Pittsburg(1)
STILLWATER (74075) Payne(97), Noble(2)
STILLWATER Payne
STILWELL Adair
STONEWALL (74871) Pontotoc(93), Coal(2), Adair(2), Johnston(1)
STRANG Mayes
STRATFORD (74872) Garvin(58), Pontotoc(34), McClain(6)
STRINGTOWN Atoka
STROUD (74079) Lincoln(96), Creek(2)
STUART (74570) Hughes(56), Pittsburg(42), Coal(1)
SULPHUR Murray
SWEETWATER Roger Mills
SWINK Choctaw
TAFT Muskogee
TAHLEQUAH Cherokee
TALALA (74080) Rogers(82), Washington(17)
TALIHINA (74571) Le Flore(60), Latimer(33), Pushmataha(5)
TALOGA Dewey
TATUMS Carter
TECUMSEH Pottawatomie
TEMPLE Cotton
TERLTON (74081) Pawnee(94), Creek(5)
TERRAL Jefferson
TEXHOMA (73949) Cimarron(55), Texas(45)

TEXOLA Beckham
THACKERVILLE Love
THOMAS (73669) Custer(94), Blaine(3), Dewey(2)
TIPTON Tillman
TISHOMINGO Johnston
TONKAWA Kay
TRYON Lincoln
TULLAHASSEE Wagoner
TULSA (74106) Tulsa(94), Osage(5)
TULSA (74108) Tulsa(87), Wagoner(12)
TULSA (74116) Tulsa(62), Rogers(37)
TULSA (74127) Tulsa(60), Osage(39)
TULSA (74132) Tulsa(63), Creek(36)
TULSA Creek
TULSA Tulsa
TUPELO Coal
TURPIN (73950) Beaver(84), Texas(15)
TUSKAHOMA (74574) Pushmataha(51), Latimer(48)
TUSSY Carter
TUTTLE Grady
TWIN OAKS Delaware
TYRONE Texas
UNION CITY Canadian
VALLIANT (74764) McCurtain(90), Choctaw(9)
VELMA Stephens
VERA Washington
VERDEN (73092) Grady(75), Caddo(24)
VERNON McIntosh
VIAN Sequoyah
VICI (73859) Dewey(79), Woodward(17), Ellis(2)
VINITA Craig
VINSON (73571) Harmon(95), Greer(4)
WAGONER Wagoner
WAINWRIGHT Muskogee
WAKITA Grant
WALTERS (73572) Cotton(96), Comanche(3)
WANETTE (74878) Pottawatomie(88), Cleveland(11)
WANN (74083) Nowata(98), Washington(1)

WAPANUCKA (73461) Johnston(92), Atoka(7)
WARDVILLE (74576) Atoka(50), Pittsburg(50)
WARNER Muskogee
WASHINGTON McClain
WASHITA Caddo
WASHITA CPO Caddo
WATONGA Blaine
WATSON McCurtain
WATTS (74964) Adair(84), Delaware(15)
WAUKOMIS Garfield
WAURIKA Jefferson
WAYNE McClain
WAYNOKA (73860) Woods(91), Major(8)
WEATHERFORD (73096) Custer(97), Washita(2)
WEBBERS FALLS Muskogee
WELCH Craig
WELEETKA (74880) Okfuskee(97), Okmulgee(2)
WELLING Cherokee
WELLSTON (74881) Lincoln(90), Logan(9)
WELTY Okfuskee
WESTVILLE Adair
WETUMKA (74883) Hughes(98), Okfuskee(1)
WEWOKA Seminole
WHEATLAND Oklahoma
WHITEFIELD Haskell
WHITESBORO Le Flore
WILBURTON Latimer
WILLOW (73673) Greer(92), Beckham(7)
WILSON (73463) Carter(98), Love(1)
WISTER (74966) Le Flore(96), Latimer(3)
WOODWARD Woodward
WRIGHT CITY McCurtain
WYANDOTTE (74370) Ottawa(91), Delaware(8)
WYNNEWOOD Garvin
WYNONA Osage
YALE Payne
YUKON Canadian

Oklahoma - ZIP/City Cross Reference

73503-73503 FORT SILL	73669-73669 THOMAS	73945-73945 HOOKER	74344-74345 GROVE
73505-73507 LAWTON	73673-73673 WILLOW	73946-73946 KENTON	74346-74346 JAY
73520-73520 ADDINGTON	73701-73706 ENID	73947-73947 KEYES	74347-74347 KANSAS
73521-73522 ALTUS	73716-73716 ALINE	73949-73949 TEXHOMA	74349-74349 KETCHUM
73523-73523 ALTUS AFB	73717-73717 ALVA	73950-73950 TURPIN	74350-74350 LANGLEY
73526-73526 BLAIR	73718-73718 AMES	73951-73951 TYRONE	74352-74352 LOCUST GROVE
73527-73527 CACHE	73719-73719 AMORITA	74001-74001 AVANT	74353-74353 MAZIE
73528-73528 CHATTANOOGA	73720-73720 BISON	74002-74002 BARNSDALL	74354-74355 MIAMI
73529-73529 COMANCHE	73722-73722 BURLINGTON	74003-74006 BARTLESVILLE	74358-74358 NORTH MIAMI
73530-73530 DAVIDSON	73723-73723 BYRON	74008-74008 BIXBY	74359-74359 OAKS
73531-73531 DEVOL	73724-73724 CANTON	74009-74009 BOWRING	74360-74360 PICHER
73532-73532 DUKE	73725-73725 CAPRON	74010-74010 BRISTOW	74361-74362 PRYOR
73533-73536 DUNCAN	73726-73726 CARMEN	74011-74014 BROKEN ARROW	74363-74363 QUAPAW
73537-73537 ELDORADO	73727-73727 CARRIER	74015-74015 CATOOSA	74364-74364 ROSE
73538-73538 ELGIN	73728-73728 CHEROKEE	74016-74016 CHELSEA	74365-74365 SALINA
73539-73539 ELMER	73729-73729 CLEO SPRINGS	74017-74019 CLAREMORE	74366-74366 SPAVINAW
73540-73540 FAXON	73730-73730 COVINGTON	74020-74020 CLEVELAND	74367-74367 STRANG
73541-73541 FLETCHER	73731-73731 DACOMA	74021-74021 COLLINSVILLE	74368-74368 TWIN OAKS
73542-73542 FREDERICK	73733-73733 DOUGLAS	74022-74022 COPAN	74369-74369 WELCH
73543-73543 GERONIMO	73734-73734 DOVER	74023-74023 CUSHING	74370-74370 WYANDOTTE
73544-73544 GOULD	73735-73735 DRUMMOND	74026-74026 DAVENPORT	74401-74403 MUSKOGEE
73546-73546 GRANDFIELD	73736-73736 FAIRMONT	74027-74027 DELAWARE	74421-74421 BEGGS
73547-73547 GRANITE	73737-73737 FAIRVIEW	74028-74028 DEPEW	74422-74422 BOYNTON
73548-73548 HASTINGS	73738-73738 GARBER	74029-74029 DEWEY	74423-74423 BRAGGS
73549-73549 HEADRICK	73739-73739 GOLTRY	74030-74030 DRUMRIGHT	74425-74425 CANADIAN
73550-73550 HOLLIS	73741-73741 HELENA	74031-74031 FOYIL	74426-74426 CHECOTAH
73551-73551 HOLLISTER	73742-73742 HENNESSEY	74032-74032 GLENCOE	74427-74427 COOKSON
73552-73552 INDIAHOMA	73743-73743 HILLSDALE	74033-74033 GLENPOOL	74428-74428 COUNCIL HILL
73553-73553 LOVELAND	73744-73744 HITCHCOCK	74034-74034 HALLETT	74429-74429 COWETA
73554-73554 MANGUM	73746-73746 HOPETON	74035-74035 HOMINY	74430-74430 CROWDER
73555-73555 MANITOU	73747-73747 ISABELLA	74036-74036 INOLA	74431-74431 DEWAR
73556-73556 MARTHA	73749-73749 JET	74037-74037 JENKS	74432-74432 EUFAULA
73557-73557 MEDICINE PARK	73750-73750 KINGFISHER	74038-74038 JENNINGS	74434-74434 FORT GIBSON
73558-73558 MEERS	73753-73753 KREMLIN	74039-74039 KELLYVILLE	74435-74435 GORE
73559-73559 MOUNTAIN PARK	73754-73754 LAHOMA	74041-74041 KIEFER	74436-74436 HASKELL
73560-73560 OLUSTEE	73755-73755 LONGDALE	74042-74042 LENAPAH	74437-74437 HENRYETTA
73561-73561 OSCAR	73756-73756 LOYAL	74043-74043 LEONARD	74438-74438 HITCHITA
73562-73562 RANDLETT	73757-73757 LUCIEN	74044-74044 MANNFORD	74440-74440 HOYT
73564-73564 ROOSEVELT	73757-73757 LUCIEN CPO	74045-74045 MARAMEC	74441-74441 HULBERT
73565-73565 RYAN	73758-73758 MANCHESTER	74046-74046 MILFAY	74442-74442 INDIANOLA
73566-73566 SNYDER	73759-73759 MEDFORD	74047-74047 MOUNDS	74444-74444 MOODYS
73567-73567 STERLING	73760-73760 MENO	74048-74048 NOWATA	74445-74445 MORRIS
73568-73568 TEMPLE	73761-73761 NASH	74050-74050 OAKHURST	74446-74446 OKAY
73569-73569 TERRAL	73762-73762 OKARCHE	74051-74051 OCHELATA	74447-74447 OKMULGEE
73570-73570 TIPTON	73763-73763 OKEENE	74052-74052 OILTON	74450-74450 OKTAHA
73571-73571 VINSON	73764-73764 OMEGA	74053-74053 OOLOGAH	74451-74451 PARK HILL
73572-73572 WALTERS	73766-73766 POND CREEK	74054-74054 OSAGE	74452-74452 PEGGS
73573-73573 WAURIKA	73768-73768 RINGWOOD	74055-74055 OWASSO	74454-74454 PORTER
73575-73575 DUNCAN	73770-73770 SOUTHARD	74056-74056 PAWHUSKA	74455-74455 PORUM
73601-73601 CLINTON	73771-73771 WAKITA	74058-74058 PAWNEE	74456-74456 PRESTON
73620-73620 ARAPAHO	73772-73772 WATONGA	74059-74059 PERKINS	74457-74457 PROCTOR
73622-73622 BESSIE	73773-73773 WAUKOMIS	74060-74060 PRUE	74458-74458 REDBIRD
73624-73624 BURNS FLAT	73801-73802 WOODWARD	74061-74061 RAMONA	74459-74459 RENTIESVILLE
73625-73625 BUTLER	73832-73832 ARNETT	74062-74062 RIPLEY	74460-74460 SCHULTER
73626-73626 CANUTE	73834-73834 BUFFALO	74063-74063 SAND SPRINGS	74461-74461 STIDHAM
73627-73627 CARTER	73835-73835 CAMARGO	74066-74067 SAPULPA	74461-74461 STIDHAM COUNTRY CPU
73628-73628 CHEYENNE	73838-73838 CHESTER	74068-74068 SHAMROCK	74462-74462 STIGLER
73632-73632 CORDELL	73840-73840 FARGO	74070-74070 SKIATOOK	74463-74463 TAFT
73638-73638 CRAWFORD	73841-73841 FORT SUPPLY	74071-74071 SLICK	74464-74465 TAHLEQUAH
73639-73639 CUSTER CITY	73842-73842 FREEDOM	74072-74072 S COFFEYVILLE	74466-74466 TULLAHASSEE
73641-73641 DILL CITY	73843-73843 GAGE	74073-74073 SPERRY	74467-74467 WAGONER
73642-73642 DURHAM	73844-73844 GATE	74074-74078 STILLWATER	74468-74468 WAINWRIGHT
73644-73644 ELK CITY	73847-73847 KNOWLES	74079-74079 STROUD	74469-74469 WARNER
73645-73645 ERICK	73848-73848 LAVERNE	74080-74080 TALALA	74470-74470 WEBBERS FALLS
73646-73646 FAY	73849-73849 LOGAN	74081-74081 TERLTON	74471-74471 WELLING
73647-73647 FOSS	73851-73851 MAY	74082-74082 VERA	74472-74472 WHITEFIELD
73648-73648 ELK CITY	73852-73852 MOORELAND	74083-74083 WANN	74477-74477 WAGONER
73650-73650 HAMMON	73853-73853 MUTUAL	74084-74084 WYNONA	74501-74502 MCALESTER
73651-73651 HOBART	73855-73855 ROSSTON	74085-74085 YALE	74521-74521 ALBION
73654-73654 LEEDEY	73857-73857 SHARON	74100-74194 TULSA	74522-74522 ALDERSON
73655-73655 LONE WOLF	73858-73858 SHATTUCK	74301-74301 VINITA	74523-74523 ANTLERS
73656-73656 MAYFIELD	73859-73859 VICI	74330-74330 ADAIR	74525-74525 ATOKA
73658-73658 OAKWOOD	73860-73860 WAYNOKA	74331-74331 AFTON	74526-74526 BACHE
73659-73659 PUTNAM	73901-73901 ADAMS	74332-74332 BIG CABIN	74528-74528 BLANCO
73660-73660 REYDON	73931-73931 BALKO	74333-74333 BLUEJACKET	74529-74529 BLOCKER
73661-73661 ROCKY	73932-73932 BEAVER	74335-74335 CARDIN	74530-74530 BROMIDE
73662-73662 SAYRE	73933-73933 BOISE CITY	74337-74337 CHOUTEAU	74531-74531 CALVIN
73663-73663 SEILING	73937-73937 FELT	74338-74338 COLCORD	74533-74533 CANEY
73664-73664 SENTINEL	73938-73938 FORGAN	74339-74339 COMMERCE	74534-74534 CENTRAHOMA
73666-73666 SWEETWATER	73939-73939 GOODWELL	74340-74340 DISNEY	74535-74535 CLARITA
73667-73667 TALOGA	73942-73942 GUYMON	74342-74342 EUCHA	74536-74536 CLAYTON
73668-73668 TEXOLA	73944-73944 HARDESTY	74343-74343 FAIRLAND	74538-74538 COALGATE

74540-74540 DAISY	74543-74543 FINLEY	74546-74546 HAILEYVILLE	74548-74548 HAYWOOD
74542-74542 ATOKA	74545-74545 GOWEN	74547-74547 HARTSHORNE	74549-74549 HONOBIA
74549-74549 KIAMICHI - HONOBIA CPO	74720-74720 ACHILLE	74827-74827 ATWOOD	74877-74877 VERNON
74552-74552 KINTA	74721-74721 ALBANY	74829-74829 BOLEY	74878-74878 WANETTE
74553-74553 KIOWA	74722-74722 BATTIEST	74830-74830 BOWLEGS	74880-74880 WELEETKA
74554-74554 KREBS	74723-74723 BENNINGTON	74831-74831 BYARS	74881-74881 WELLSTON
74555-74555 LANE	74724-74724 BETHEL	74832-74832 CARNEY	74882-74882 WELTY
74556-74556 LEHIGH	74726-74726 BOKCHITO	74833-74833 CASTLE	74883-74883 WETUMKA
74557-74557 MOYERS	74727-74727 BOSWELL	74834-74834 CHANDLER	74884-74884 WEWOKA
74558-74558 NASHOBA	74728-74728 BROKEN BOW	74835-74835 CLEARVIEW	74901-74901 ARKOMA
74559-74559 PANOLA	74729-74729 CADDO	74836-74836 CONNERVILLE	74902-74902 POCOLA
74560-74560 PITTSBURG	74730-74730 CALERA	74837-74837 CROMWELL	74930-74930 BOKOSHE
74561-74561 QUINTON	74731-74731 CARTWRIGHT	74838-74838 SHAWNEE	74931-74931 BUNCH
74562-74562 RATTAN	74733-74733 COLBERT	74839-74839 DUSTIN	74932-74932 CAMERON
74563-74563 RED OAK	74734-74734 EAGLETOWN	74840-74840 EARLSBORO	74935-74935 FANSHAWE
74565-74565 SAVANNA	74735-74735 FORT TOWSON	74842-74842 FITTSTOWN	74936-74936 GANS
74567-74567 SNOW	74736-74736 GARVIN	74843-74843 FITZHUGH	74937-74937 HEAVENER
74569-74569 STRINGTOWN	74737-74737 GOLDEN	74844-74844 FRANCIS	74939-74939 HODGEN
74570-74570 STUART	74738-74738 GRANT	74845-74845 HANNA	74940-74940 HOWE
74571-74571 TALIHINA	74740-74740 HAWORTH	74848-74848 HOLDENVILLE	74941-74941 KEOTA
74572-74572 TUPELO	74741-74741 HENDRIX	74849-74849 KONAWA	74942-74942 LEFLORE
74574-74574 TUSKAHOMA	74743-74743 HUGO	74850-74850 LAMAR	74943-74943 LEQUIRE
74576-74576 WARDVILLE	74745-74745 IDABEL	74851-74851 MC LOUD	74944-74944 MCCURTAIN
74577-74577 WHITESBORO	74747-74747 KEMP	74851-74851 MCLOUD	74945-74945 MARBLE CITY
74578-74578 WILBURTON	74747-74747 KEMP CPO	74852-74852 MACOMB	74946-74946 MOFFETT
74601-74604 PONCA CITY	74748-74748 KENEFIC	74854-74854 MAUD	74947-74947 MONROE
74630-74630 BILLINGS	74750-74750 MILLERTON	74855-74855 MEEKER	74948-74948 MULDROW
74631-74631 BLACKWELL	74752-74752 PICKENS	74856-74856 MILL CREEK	74949-74949 MUSE
74632-74632 BRAMAN	74753-74753 PLATTER	74857-74857 NEWALLA	74951-74951 PANAMA
74633-74633 BURBANK	74754-74754 RINGOLD	74859-74859 OKEMAH	74953-74953 POTEAU
74636-74636 DEER CREEK	74755-74755 RUFE	74860-74860 PADEN	74954-74954 ROLAND
74637-74637 FAIRFAX	74756-74756 SAWYER	74862-74862 PHAROAH	74955-74955 SALLISAW
74640-74640 HUNTER	74759-74759 SOPER	74863-74863 FITTSTOWN	74956-74956 SHADY POINT
74641-74641 KAW CITY	74760-74760 SPENCERVILLE	74864-74864 PRAGUE	74957-74957 SMITHVILLE
74643-74643 LAMONT	74761-74761 SWINK	74865-74865 ROFF	74959-74959 SPIRO
74644-74644 MARLAND	74764-74764 VALLIANT	74866-74866 SAINT LOUIS	74960-74960 STILWELL
74646-74646 NARDIN	74766-74766 WRIGHT CITY	74867-74867 SASAKWA	74962-74962 VIAN
74647-74647 NEWKIRK	74801-74804 SHAWNEE	74868-74868 SEMINOLE	74963-74963 WATSON
74650-74650 RALSTON	74818-74818 SEMINOLE	74869-74869 SPARKS	74964-74964 WATTS
74651-74651 RED ROCK	74820-74821 ADA	74871-74871 STONEWALL	74965-74965 WESTVILLE
74652-74652 SHIDLER	74824-74824 AGRA	74872-74872 STRATFORD	74966-74966 WISTER
74653-74653 TONKAWA	74825-74825 ALLEN	74873-74873 TECUMSEH	
74701-74702 DURANT	74826-74826 ASHER	74875-74875 TRYON	

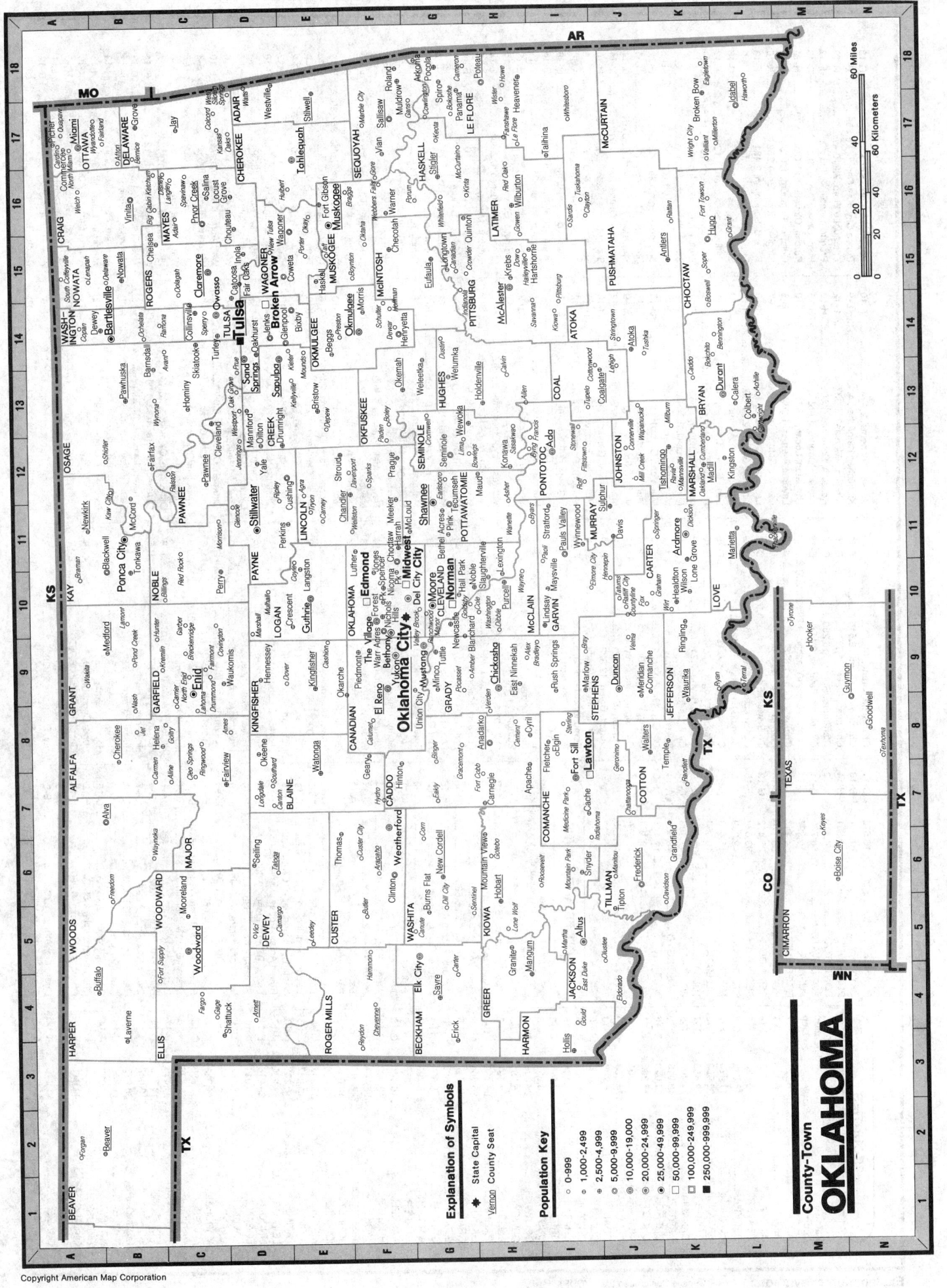

County-Town
OKLAHOMA

Explanation of Symbols

☀ State Capital

Vernon ⦿ County Seat

Population Key

o	0-999
⊙	1,000-2,499
⊕	2,500-4,999
⊚	5,000-9,999
⊛	10,000-19,000
⊜	20,000-24,999
⦿	25,000-49,999
□	50,000-99,999
▢	100,000-249,999
■	250,000-999,999

Copyright American Map Corporation

CITIES AND TOWNS

Note: The first name is that of the city or town, second, that of the county in which it is located, then the population and location on the map.

Explanation of symbols: •– Census Designated Place (CDP)

Oregon

General Help Numbers:

Governor's Office
State Capitol Bldg.   503-378-4582
900 Court St NE   Fax 503-378- 4863
Salem, OR 97301-4047   8AM-5PM
www.governor.state.or.us

Attorney General's Office
Department of Justice   503-378-4400
1162 Court St NE   Fax 503-378-4017
Salem, OR 97310   8AM-5PM
www.doj.state.or.us

Legislative Records
Oregon Legislative Assembly, Legislative Publications,
900 Court St, #49   503-986-1180
Salem, OR 97310   Fax 503-373-1527
www.leg.state.or.us   8AM-5PM

State Archives
Archives Division   503-373-0701
800 Summer St NE   Fax 503-373-0953
Salem, OR 97301   8AM-4:45PM
http://arcweb.sos.state.or.us

State Specifics:

Capital: Salem
                                        Marion County

Time Zone: PST

Number of Counties: 36

Population: 3,559,596

Web Site: www.oregon.gov

State Agencies

Criminal Records

Oregon State Police, Unit 11, Identification Services Section, PO Box 4395, Portland, OR 97208-4395 (Courier: 3772 Portland Rd NE, Bldg C, Salem, OR 97303); 503-378-3070, 503-378-2121 (Fax), 8AM-5PM.

www.osp.state.or.us

Indexing & Storage: Records are available from 1941 on and are computerized. It takes up to 8 days before new records are available for inquiry. Records are indexed on inhouse computer.

Records are normally destroyed after (records maintained indefinitely).

Searching: Three types of searches exist: open records search, own record search, and statutorily-required search. The latter can include an FBI fingerprint check for an additional $24.00 fee. Include the following in your request-name, date of birth, last known address. Submitting the SSN is helpful, but not required. Fingerprints are required only when subject submits the request. If record exists, person of record will be notified of the request and the record will not be released for 14 additional days.

Access by: mail, fax, online.

Fee & Payment: Open record search fee is $15.00 per individual name. If someone is submitting a search on oneself, the fee is $12.00 and fingerprints are required. Statutorily-required searches are $12.00 plus FBI fingerprint fee, if required. $5.00 fee to notarize. Fee payee: Oregon State Police. Prepayment required. Personal checks accepted. No credit cards accepted.

Mail search: Turnaround time: 5 days if clean. Records with hits can take as long as 3 weeks to return.

Fax search: Requesters must be pre-approved, however records are not returned by fax.

Online search: A web based site is available for requesting and receiving criminal records. website is ONLY for high-volume requesters who must be pre-approved. Results are posted as "No Record" or "In Process" ("In Process" means a record will be mailed in 14 days). Use the "open records" link to get into the proper site. Fee is $15.00 per record. Call 503-373-1808 x230 to receive the application, or visit the website.

Statewide Court Records

Court Administrator, Supreme Court Bldg, 1163 State St, Salem, OR 97301-2563; 503-986-5500, 503-986-5503 (Fax), 8AM-5PM.

www.ojd.state.or.us/osca

Note: The Appellate Courts office is located at 1163 State St.

Access by: online.

Online search: Appellate opinions are found at www.publications.ojd.state.or.us/. Online computer access is available through the Oregon Judicial Information Network (OJIN) which includes almost all cases filed in the Oregon state courts. There is a one-time setup fee of $295.00 plus usage fees of $10-13.00 per hour. The database contains criminal, civil, small claims, probate, and some but not all juvenile records. However, it does not contain any records from municipal nor county courts. For further information visit www.ojd.state.or.us/ojin, or call 800-858-9658 or 503-986-5588.

Sexual Offender Registry

Oregon State Police, SOR Unit, 255 Capitol St NE, 4th Fl, Salem, OR 97310; 503-378-3720, 503-363-5475 (Fax), 8AM-5PM.

www.osp.state.or.us

Indexing & Storage: It takes up to 8 days before new records are available for inquiry. Records are normally destroyed after 1 year after death of the offender.

Searching: Include the following in your request-name and DOB.

Access by: mail, phone, fax.

Fee & Payment: There is no fee.

Mail search: Turnaround time: up to 3 weeks.

Phone search: You can request a list or do a name check by phone.

Fax search: Requests accepted via fax.

Incarceration Records

Oregon Department of Corrections, Offender Information & Sentence Computation, PO Box 5670, Wilsonville, OR 97070-5670 (Courier: 24499 SW Grahams Ferry Rd, Bldg Z, Wilsonville, OR 97070); 503-570-6900, 503-570-6902 (Fax), 8AM-5PM.

www.doc.state.or.us/

Indexing & Storage: Records are available on current and former inmates. It takes up to 4 days before new records are available for inquiry. Records are normally destroyed after being microfilmed after final discharge.

Searching: Include the following in your request-full name; DOB and SID# helpful. Location, SID

number, physical identifiers, conviction and sentencing information, and release dates are provided.

Access by: mail, phone, fax, online.

Fee & Payment: Fees are charged for copies as follows: $.50 for paper, $1.25 from microfilm.

Mail search: Turnaround time: 2 to 4 weeks.

Phone search: Name searching permitted by phone.

Fax search: Same criteria as mail.

Online search: No online offender searching is available from this agency; there is a "Corrections Most Wanted" list in the pull down menu box. A private company offers free web access at www.vinelink.com/index.jsp; includes state, DOC, and most county jails. Also, you may email mary.l.solomon@doc.state.or.us for an inmate lookup.

Corporation, Limited Partnership, Limited Liability Company Records, Trademarks, Servicemarks, Fictitious Name, Assumed Name

Corporation Division, Public Service Building, 255 Capital St NE, #151, Salem, OR 97310-1327; 503-986-2317, 503-378-4381 (Fax), 8AM-5PM.

www.filinginoregon.com

Indexing & Storage: Records are available on the computer screen for 20 years after inactive. Assumed names are only available for 5 years after inactive. The records prior to 20 years ago are stored in the State Archives back to the 1800's for corporations only. New records are available for inquiry immediately. Records are indexed on microfilm, inhouse computer.

Searching: All information is public record. Include the following in your request-full name of business. In addition to the articles of incorporation, corporation records include the following information: last annual report, Prior (merged) names, Articles of Amendment.

Access by: mail, phone, fax, in person, online.

Fee & Payment: There is no search fee. Copies cost $5.00 per business name or $15.00 if certified, otherwise there is a $1.00 fee per business name for a computer printout. A Good Standing certificate is $10.00. Fee payee: Corporation Division. Prepayment required. Personal checks accepted. Credit cards accepted: MasterCard, Visa.

Mail search: Turnaround time: 7 to 10 days. A SASE is requested.

Phone search: There is a limit of 3 searches per phone call.

Fax search: Requesters must use a credit card, turnaround time is 5 days or less.

In person search: Turnaround time while you wait.

Online search: There is free, limited access at the website for business registry information.

Other access: A subscription service for new business lists on tapes and CDs of the database are available for $15.00 per month or $180.00 for an annual subscription. Call 503-986-2343 for more information.

Expedited service: Expedited service is available for phone and in person searches. Turnaround time: 1 day. They will ship overnight if you supply your shipper's account number. Fax requests are expedited only if phoned in first.

Uniform Commercial Code, Federal and State Tax Liens

UCC Division, Attn: Records, 255 Capitol St NE, Suite 151, Salem, OR 97310-1327; 503-986-2200 x6, 503-373-1166 (Fax), 8AM-5PM.

www.filinginoregon.com/ucc/index.htm

Note: State tax liens on personal property are filed here; state tax liens on real property are filed at the county level.

Indexing & Storage: Records are available on microfiche to 1963. It takes 2 to 4 days before new records are available for inquiry.

Searching: Use search request form UCC-11. The search includes tax liens filed here. Include the following in your request-debtor name.

Access by: mail, fax, in person, online.

Fee & Payment: The search fee is $10.00 per name, with copies is $15.00 per name. A document number request is $5.00. A state seal certificate is $15.00. CD service is $20.00 per CD. Special research projects are $20.00 per hour. Fee payee: Secretary of State. Prepayment required. Personal checks accepted. Credit cards accepted: MasterCard, Visa.

Mail search: Turnaround time: 1 to 4 days.

Fax search: A credit card is required. Results are mailed.

In person search: Searches done while you wait.

Online search: UCC index information can be obtained for free from the website. You can search by debtor name or by lien number. You can also download forms from here.

Other access: Monthly UCC information is released via e-mail, FTP or CD. Prices start at $15.00 per month or $150.00 annually for new filings, or $200 per month for all active filings. For more information, call Program Services at 503-986-2212.

Sales Tax Registrations
State does not impose sales tax.

Birth Certificates

Department of Human Services, Vital Records, PO Box 14050, Portland, OR 97293-0050 (Courier: 800 NE Oregon St, #205, Portland, OR 97232); 503-731-4095 (Recorded Message), 503-731-4108, 503-234-8417 (Fax), 8AM-4:30PM.

www.ohd.hr.state.or.us/chs/

Indexing & Storage: Records are available for 100 years to present. There are some delayed filed, unindexed records with DOBs from 1885 to 1904. Birth indexes prior to 100 years available at the State Archives. It takes 2 to 4 weeks before new records are available for inquiry.

Searching: Investigative searches must have a signed, notarized release from person of record or immediate family member, unless record over 100 years old. Records only available to legal guardians & legal representatives with proof of such Include the following in your request-full name, names of parents, mother's full maiden name, date of birth, place of birth, relationship to person of record. Must request "long form" if time of birth, hospital or physician's names is needed. The following data is not released: original records of adoption, except to adoptee over age of 21.

Access by: mail, phone, fax, in person, online.

Fee & Payment: The search fee is $20.00. Add $15.00 for each additional copy. Fee payee: DHS Vital Records Prepayment required. Personal checks accepted. Credit cards accepted: MasterCard, Visa, AmEx, Discover.

Mail search: Turnaround time: 2 to 3 weeks. Express mail requests are handled immediately. No SASE is required.

Phone search: See expedited service.

Fax search: See expedited service.

In person search: Turnaround time is under 20 minutes.

Online search: Order records online at www.vitalchek.com, a state designated vendor.

Expedited service: Fax and phone orders are billed to credit cards and processed the same day. There is an additional $12.50 service fee. Turnaround time: overnight delivery. Add fee for delivery service.

Death Records

Department of Human Services, Vital Records, PO Box 14050, Portland, OR 97293-0050 (Courier: 800 NE Oregon St, #205, Portland, OR 97232); 503-731-4095 (Recorded Message), 503-731-4108, 503-234-8417 (Fax), 8AM-4:30PM.

www.ohd.hr.state.or.us/chs/

Indexing & Storage: Records are available for 100 years to present. It takes 2 to 4 weeks before new records are available for inquiry.

Searching: Investigative searches must have a signed, notarized release from immediate family member or legal representative or person with a personal or operty right. After 50 years, a record becomes public record and there are no restrictions. Include the following in your request-full name, date of death, place of death, relationship to person of record, reason for information request. The name of the spouse is helpful. The date of birth is helpful for common names.

Access by: mail, phone, fax, in person, online.

Fee & Payment: The search fee is $20.00 and additional copies are $15.00 each. Fee payee: DHS Vital Records. Prepayment required. Personal checks accepted. Credit cards accepted: MasterCard, Visa, AmEx, Discover.

Mail search: Turnaround time: 2 to 3 weeks. Express mail requests are processed immediately. No SASE is required.

Phone search: See expedited service.

Fax search: See expedited service.

In person search: Turnaround time is within 20 minutes.

Online search: Records from 1903-1930 are available at www.heritagetrailpress.com/Death_Index/. You may order directly on Vital Chek's web page at www.VitalChek.com.

Other access: Indexes are available at many state libraries.

Expedited service: Phone and fax orders require use of a credit card and an additional $12.50 service fee. Turnaround time is generally in 24 hours. Turnaround time: overnight delivery. Carrier chosen to return documents determines fees.

Marriage Certificates

Department of Human Services, Vital Records, PO Box 14050, Portland, OR 97293-0050 (Courier: 800 NE Oregon St, #205, Portland, OR 97232); 503-731-4095 (Recorded Message), 503-731-4108, 503-234-8417 (Fax), 8AM-4:30PM.

www.ohd.hr.state.or.us/chs/

Indexing & Storage: Records are available from 1906 to present. Early records are in an abbreviated form called "Return of Marriage." It takes 4 to 8 weeks before new records are available for inquiry.

Searching: Records less than 50 years old are only available to family members, legal representatives or those with a personal or property right. Include the following in your request-names of husband and wife, date of marriage, place or county of marriage. Include daytime phone number and as many identifiers as possible.

Access by: mail, phone, fax, in person, online.

Fee & Payment: The search fee is $20.00, additional copies $15.00 per record. Fee payee: DHS Vital Records Prepayment required. Personal checks accepted. Credit cards accepted: MasterCard, Visa, AmEx, Discover.

Mail search: Turnaround time: 2 to 3 weeks. If request is expressed, it will be answered ASAP. No SASE is required.

Phone search: See expedited service.

Fax search: See expedited service.

In person search: Turnaround time is usually within 20 minutes.

Online search: Order online via www.vitalchek.com, a state approved vendor.

Other access: Many state libraries offer record indexes.

Expedited service: There is an additional $12.50 quick service search fee per telephone or fax order. Use of a credit card is required. Additional fees will be added, depending on carrier. For mail requests, enclose a prepaid, self-addressed envelope for overnight carrier.

Divorce Records

Department of Human Services, Vital Records, Suite 205, PO Box 14050, Portland, OR 97293-0050 (Courier: 800 NE Oregon St, #205, Portland, OR 97232); 503-731-4095 (Recorded Message), 502-731-4108, 503-234-8417 (Fax), 8AM-4:30PM.

www.ohd.hr.state.or.us/chs/

Indexing & Storage: Records are available from 1925 to present. It takes 4 to 8 weeks before new records are available for inquiry.

Searching: Records less than 50 years old are only available to family members, legal representatives or those with a personal or property right. Include the following in your request-date of divorce. Also include names of husband and wife, and reason for request.

Access by: mail, phone, fax, in person.

Fee & Payment: The search fee is $20.00, additional copies are $15.00 each. Fee payee: DHS Vital Records. Prepayment required. Using personal checks (with guarantee card) may delay processing by 2 weeks. For a mail request, enclose a prepaid, self-addressed envelope for overnight carrier. Personal checks accepted. Credit cards accepted: MasterCard, Visa, AmEx, Discover.

Mail search: Turnaround time: 2 to 3 weeks. Send request by overnight delivery and it will be processed ASAP. No SASE is required.

Phone search: See expedited service.

Fax search: See expedited services.

In person search: Turnaround time is usually within 20 minutes.

Other access: Indexes are available in many Oregon libraries.

Expedited service: There is an additional $10.50 service fee for ordering by fax or phone and you must use a credit card. Turnaround time: overnight delivery.

Workers' Compensation Records

Department of Consumer & Business Srvs, Workers Compensation Division, PO Box 14480, Salem, OR 97309-0405 (Courier: 350 Winter Street NE Rm 27, Salem, OR 97301-3879); 503-947-7818, 503-947-7993 (TTY), 503-945-7630 (Fax), 8AM-5PM M-F.

www.oregonwcd.org

Indexing & Storage: Records are available from 6 to 75 years back. It takes 4 days or less before new records are available for inquiry. Records are indexed on inhouse computer.

Searching: Per ORS 192.502(18), claims records are exempt from public disclosure. Access to records is at the discretion of the Director. In general, those with a legitimate business purpose are granted access. Include the following in your request-claimant name, Social Security Number, claim number, name and address of requester. A signed release by subject is honored. The website features rules, bulletins, forms, and publications.

Access by: mail, fax, in person, online.

Fee & Payment: The Department has the authority to charge for staff time and resources for any record request. Records releases only after disclosure requirements are met. Fee payee: DCBS. Prepayment required. Personal checks accepted. No credit cards accepted.

Mail search: Turnaround time: 14 days. No SASE is required.

Fax search: Fax requests are accepted if disclosure requirements are met. Completed report may be mailed back.

In person search: Completed report may need to be mailed back. Turnaround time: 1 to 14 days.

Online search: A search of employers that have coverage, and employers that have coverage ending soon is found at www.cbs.state.or.us/cgi-bin/wcd/employer.pl.

Other access: State is allowed to deliver data in other forms to parties that qualify under ORS 192.502(19).

Expedited service: Will expedite if requester agrees to payment.

Driver Records

Driver and Motor Vehicle Services, Record Services, 1905 Lana Ave, NE, Salem, OR 97314; 503-945-5000, 503-945-5425 (Fax), 8AM-5PM.

www.oregondmv.com

Note: Oregon differentiates between "employment" and "non-employment" records. Ongoing requesters with a permissible use and quailfy to receive personal information per state law may establish a Record Inquiry Account.

Indexing & Storage: Records are available for 3 or 5 years for minor convictions; 10 years for DUIs and major convictions; and 3 or 5 years after reinstatement for suspensions. It takes 2-3 weeks normally before new records are available for inquiry.

Searching: Permissible use requesters must open a Record Inquiry Account and are then approved to access via one of the automated systems. Casual requesters who do not present written consent may receive a "sanitized record." Include the following in your request-full name, date of birth, driver's license number. A driver's license report is available which lists the driver's name, address, date of birth, license number, issue and expiration dates, original business date, restrictions, status, and, if applicable, the ID card expiration date. The following data is not released: medical information, SSNs, photos.

Access by: mail, phone, fax.

Fee & Payment: Fee for a 3 year non-employment driving record is $1.50; $2.00 for a 3 year employment driving record; $3.00 for a "court print" record; $1.50 per record for a driver license information report. There is a charge of $1.50 for no record found. Fee payee: DMV Services. Prepayment required. Personal checks accepted. No credit cards accepted.

Mail search: Turnaround time: 1 day from receipt. A record request form and record fee list is available online. No SASE is required.

Phone search: Oregon offers "IVR" (DMV's Interactive Voice Response System) which reads information from computer files in a human sounding voice. A variety of records are available on IVR 24 hours a day. Call 503-945-7950 for more information.

Fax search: Records are available by fax, but only for approved account holders.

Other access: The agency offers an automated "flag program" that informs customers of activity on a name list. Call the Automated Reporting System at 503-945-5428/5427 for more information.

Vehicle Ownership, Vehicle Identification

Driver and Motor Vehicle Services, Record Services Unit, 1905 Lana Ave, NE, Salem, OR 97314; 503-945-5000, 503-945-5425 (Fax), 8AM-5PM.

www.oregondmv.com

Note: Ongoing requesters with a permissibile use and quality for personal information per state law may establish a Record Inquiry Account.

Indexing & Storage: Records are available from 1963 to present. Vehicle title and registration records are archived on microfilm and microfiche. It takes 2-3 weeks from issue before new records are available for inquiry.

Searching: Title and registration ownership records are open to the public, for a fee. By law, only certain entities may receive records with personal info. Casual requesters cannot obtain records with personal information without written consent of subject. Include the following in your request-name and DOB, or VIN or plate. The following data is not released: medical information, SSNs.

Access by: mail, phone, fax.

Fee & Payment: Vehicle record prints are $4.00, information given orally is $2.50 (to account holders). A complete vehicle title history is $22.50. An insurance information search is $10.00. Generally, $2.50 is charged if no record is found. Fee payee: Driver & Motor Services (DMV). Prepayment required. Personal checks accepted. No credit cards accepted.

Mail search: Turnaround time: 1 day. A SASE is helpful.

Phone search: The automated system called "IVR" is open 24 hours a day. An account is necessary. Call 503-945-7950 for more information.

Fax search: No searching by fax.

Accident Reports

Driver & Motor Vehicle Services Division, Accident Reports & Information, 1905 Lana Ave, NE, Salem, OR 97314; 503-945-5098, 503-945-5267 (Fax), 8AM-5PM.

www.oregondmv.com

Note: Police reports filed with the DMV are available. Copies of individual's reports are not, but information is provided in letter form to those involved or representing someone involved.

Indexing & Storage: Records are available for 5 years to present. It takes 2-4 weeks before new records are available for inquiry.

Searching: Qualified requesters include legal representatives, involved insurance companies and those involved with property damage or injury. Include the following in your request-full name, date of accident, location of accident. The police report is provided without personal information unless the requester qualifies for personal information under OR law.

Access by: mail, phone, fax, in person.

Fee & Payment: The fee is $8.50 for a police accident report. There is $1.50 charge for a "no record found." The letter described above is no charge to quailfied requesters; certification is $13.00 however. Information letters (from personal reports) are $12.50 each. Fee payee: DMV Services. Prepayment required. Personal checks accepted. No credit cards accepted.

Mail search: Turnaround time: 3 to 5 days. No SASE is required.

Phone search: This is only available for pre-approved accounts.

Fax search: This is only available for account holders. Same fees and turnaround time (3-5 days).

In person search: Turnaround time will vary, record may not be available same day.

Other access: Bulk release of police accident reports is available for sale to qualified requesters. Records are unsorted and include all counties.

Vessel Ownership, Vessel Registration

Oregon State Marine Board, Records, PO Box 14145, Salem, OR 97309 (Courier: 435 Commercial St NE, #400, Salem, OR 97301); 503-378-8587, 503-378-4597 (Fax), 8AM-5PM M-F.

www.boatoregon.com

Note: Lien information is shown on the title records.

Indexing & Storage: Records are available from 1997 to present for titles. Records are indexed on computer for the last 3 years. Records are on microfiche from the 1978 to the present. Titles and registrations are issued on all motorized boats and on sailboats 12 ft and over. It takes about one day before new records are available for inquiry.

Searching: Extremely large pleasure boats which move along the OR-WA-CA border for 60 days or more are sometimes documented with the US Coast Guard. Call 800-799-8362 for more information. To search, one of the following is required: name, Oregon #, or hull ID #. Requests can be made via e-mail, from the website,

Access by: mail, phone, fax, in person.

Fee & Payment: There is no fee for one search. Fees for lists are dependent on the time involved. Fee payee: State Marine Board. Prepayment required. Personal checks accepted. No credit cards accepted.

Mail search: Turnaround time: 7 to 10 days. No SASE is required.

Phone search: Limited registration information is released over the phone.

Fax search: Records are available by fax.

In person search: If the search is lengthy, the results will be returned by mail.

Other access: An opt out provision is in effect if mailing lists are requested. Records are available on CD or other electronic formats. For more information, call 503-378-8587, ext 232.

Voter Registration

Records not maintained by a state level agency.

Note: Records are maintained at the county level and cannot be purchased for commercial reasons. The agency plans on having a statewide voter registration database in place in 2006.

GED Certificates

Dept of Community Colleges/ Workforce Development, GED Program, 255 Capitol St NE, Salem, OR 97310; 503-378-8648 x369, 503-378-8434 (Fax), 8AM-5PM M-F.

www.odccwd.state.or.us

Note: A request form is available at the webpage. Use their search button and type in GED.

Searching: To verify, the following is a required: name, date/year of test, DOB, and SSN. If a copy of a transcript is requested, include the above plus a signed release.

Access by: mail, phone, fax, in person.

Fee & Payment: There is no fee for verification. Copies of transcripts are $5.00 each. Fee payee: State of Oregon Prepayment required. Money orders are accepted. Personal checks accepted. No credit cards accepted.

Mail search: Turnaround time: 7 to 10 days. No SASE is required.

Phone search: Will verify over phone.

Fax search: You may request a verification of transcript by fax.

In person search: Turnaround time is typically 5 minutes.

Hunting and Fishing License Information

Fish & Wildlife Department, Licensing Division, 3406 Cherry Ave NE, Salem, OR 97303; 503-947-6100, 503-947-6117 (Fax), 8AM-5PM.

www.dfw.state.or.us

Indexing & Storage: Records are available from 1996 on computer. It takes 24 hours before new records are available for inquiry. Records are normally destroyed after six years.

Searching: Include the following in your request-full name, DOB. Fishing licenses and hunting licenses are in the same building in different divisions. The following data is not released: phone numbers or Social Security Numbers.

Access by: mail, fax, in person.

Fee & Payment: The fee for a search is $5.00. The record is certified. Fee payee: O.D.F.W. Prepayment required. Personal checks accepted.

Credit cards accepted: MasterCard, Visa, Discover.

Mail search: Turnaround time: 1 to 3 days. No SASE is required.

Fax search: Same fees and turnaround time as mail requests.

In person search: Records are usually returned by mail.

Other access: This agency will release bulk lists for a fee. Call 503-947-6265

Oregon State Licensing Agencies

Licenses Searchable Online

Acupuncturist #29	www.bme.state.or.us/search.html
Aircraft Registration #3	www.aviation.state.or.us/registration/aircraftreg.shtml
Airport/Aircraft Landing Area #3	www.aviation.state.or.us/registration/airportlicense.shtml
Animal Feed/Food Processor #22	www.oda.state.or.us/index.html
Architect #6	www.architect-board.state.or.us/A-B.htm
Architectural Firm #6	www.architect-board.state.or.us/ARFirms.htm
Athletic Trainer #57	http://159.121.106.128/
Attorney #43	www.osbcle.org/members/start.asp
Audiologist #58	www.bspa.state.or.us//directory/default.htm
Bakery #23	www.oda.state.or.us/dbs/licenses/search.lasso?&division=fsd
Bank #26	http://dfcs.oregon.gov/banking.direct.htm
Bank Registered Agent #26	http://dfcs.oregon.gov/external/dfcs/banking/regagent/htm
Body Piercer #7	http://159.121.106.128/
Boiler Welder #19	www.oregonbcd.org/licensesearch.html
Boilermaker #19	www.oregonbcd.org/licensesearch.html
Brand / Brand Inspector #22	www.oda.state.or.us/index.html
Building Official #19	www.oregonbcd.org/licensesearch.html
Building Service Mechanic #19	www.oregonbcd.org/licensesearch.html
Check & Money Order Seller #26	http://dfcs.oregon.gov/transmitter/licensed.htm
Chiropractor/Chiropractic Assistant #8	www.obce.state.or.us
Christmas Tree Grower #25	www.oda.state.or.us/dbs/licenses/search.lasso?&division=nursery
Collection Agency #26	http://dfcs.oregon.gov/ca/cadirectory/pdf
Construction Contractor/Subcontractor #21	www.ccb.state.or.us/New_Web/new_search_bak.htm
Consumer Finance Company #26	http://dfcs.oregon.gov/cf/cfdatabase/search_main.htm
Cosmetologist #7	http://159.121.106.128/
Counselor, Licensed Professional #28	www.oblpct.state.or.us/
Credit Service Organization #26	http://dfcs.oregon.gov/cso/regietered.htm
Credit Union #26	http://dfcs.oregon.gov/cu/agents.htm
Dairy Establishment #23	www.oda.state.or.us/dbs/licenses/search.lasso?&division=fsd
Debt Consolidating Agency #26	http://dfcs.oregon.gov/dca/agents.htm
Dentist #55	www.oregondentistry.org/
Denture Technologist #57	http://159.121.106.128/
Diagnostic Radiologic Technologist #39	www.obrt.state.or.us
Diagnostic/Therapeutic Technologist #39	www.obrt.state.or.us
Dietitian #11	www.bld.state.or.us/directory/index.htm
Digital Signature Authority #26	http://dfcs.oregon.gov/digsig/licensed.htm
Dog Racing Occupation #42	http://lic.oregon.gov/cfmx/lic/index.cfm
Egg Handler/Breaker #23	www.oda.state.or.us/dbs/licenses/search.lasso?&division=fsd
Electrical Installation #19	www.oregonbcd.org/licensesearch.html
Electrician #19	www.oregonbcd.org/licensesearch.html
Elevator Journeyman, Limited #19	www.oregonbcd.org/licensesearch.html
Endowment Care #26	http://dfcs.oregon.gov/pdf/endowment_care_list.pdf
Energy Technician, Limited/Restricted #19	www.oregonbcd.org/licensesearch.html
Engineer #10	www.osbeels.org
Facial Technician/Technologist #7	http://159.121.106.128/
Fertilizer/Mineral/Lime Registrant #24	www.oda.state.or.us/dbs/search.lasso
Florist #25	www.oda.state.or.us/dbs/licenses/search.lasso?&division=nursery
Food Establishment, Retail #23	www.oda.state.or.us/dbs/licenses/search.lasso?&division=fsd
Food Exporter/Processing Facility #23	www.oda.state.or.us/dbs/licenses/search.lasso?&division=fsd
Food Producer/Distributor/Storage Facility #23	www.oda.state.or.us/dbs/licenses/search.lasso?&division=fsd
Frozen Desert-related Industry #23	www.oda.state.or.us/dbs/licenses/search.lasso?&division=fsd
Funeral Plan, Prearranged #26	http://dfcs.oregon.gov/pdf/preneeds_master_list.pdf
Geologist #12	www.open.org/~osbge/registrants.htm
Geologist, Engineering #12	www.open.org/~osbge/registrants.htm
Greenhouse Grower of Herbaceous Plants #25	www.oda.state.or.us/dbs/licenses/search.lasso?&division=nursery
Hair Stylist #7	http://159.121.106.128/
Heliport #3	www.aviation.state.or.us/registration/airportlicense.shtml
Horse Racing Occupation #42	http://lic.oregon.gov/cfmx/lic/index.cfm
Inspector, Building Code #19	www.oregonbcd.org/licensesearch.html

Inspector, Structural/Mechanical #19	www.oregonbcd.org/licensesearch.html
Insurance Adjuster #27	http://www4.cbs.state.or.us/ex/ins/inslic/agent/
Insurance Agency #27	www.cbs.state.or.us/external/imd/database/inslic/agency_main.htm
Insurance Agent #27	http://www4.cbs.state.or.us/ex/ins/inslic/agent/
Insurance Company #27	www.cbs.state.or.us/external/imd/database/inslic/comp_main.htm
Insurance Consultant #27	http://www4.cbs.state.or.us/ex/ins/inslic/agent/
Investment Advisor #26	http://dfcs.oregon.gov/external/imd/database/lear/adviser_search_main.htm
Landscape Business #21	https://orlsc.glsuite.us/renewal/glsweb/homeframe.aspx
Landscaper #25	www.oda.state.or.us/dbs/licenses/search.lasso?&division=nursery
Livestock-Related Business #22	www.oda.state.or.us/index.html
Manicurist/Nail Technician #7	http://159.121.106.128/
Manufactured Housing Construction #19	www.oregonbcd.org/licensesearch.html
Marriage & Family Therapist #28	www.oblpct.state.or.us/
Measuring Devices #20	http://oda.state.or.us/dbs/search.lasso#msd
Medical Doctor/Surgeon #29	www.bme.state.or.us/search.html
Midwife #57	http://159.121.106.128/
Milk Hauler/Milk Stabilization/Handler #23	www.oda.state.or.us/dbs/licenses/search.lasso?&division=fsd
Money Transmitter #26	http://dfcs.oregon.gov/transmitter/licensed.htm
Mortgage Banker/Broker/Lender #26	www.cbs.state.or.us/external/imd/database/lear/search_main.htm
Motor Fuel Quality #20	http://oda.state.or.us/dbs/search.lasso#msd
Non-Alcoholic Beverage Plant #23	www.oda.state.or.us/dbs/licenses/search.lasso?&division=fsd
Nurse / Nurse-LPN / Nursing Assistant #13	http://mscfprod1.iservices.state.or.us/nursinglu/LicenseLookup.cfm
Nursery Dealer #25	www.oda.state.or.us/dbs/licenses/search.lasso?&division=nursery
Nursery Stock/Native Plants Collector #25	www.oda.state.or.us/dbs/licenses/search.lasso?&division=nursery
Nursing Home Administrator #35	www.nhabd.state.or.us/directory/index.htm
Occupational Therapist/Therapist Assistant #36	www.otlb.state.or.us/directory/default.htm
Oil Module License #19	www.oregonbcd.org/licensesearch.html
Optometrist #14	www.oregono.org/doctorinfo.htm
Oregon Product #22	www.oda.state.or.us/index.html
Osteopathic Physician/Surgeon #29	www.bme.state.or.us/search.html
Pawnbroker #26	www.cbs.state.or.us/external/dfcs/pawn/shop/htm
Permanent Color Technician #7	http://159.121.106.128/
Pesticide Applicator/Trainee #24	www.oda.state.or.us/dbs/licenses/search.lasso?&division=pest
Pesticide Dealer/Company/Consultant #24	www.oda.state.or.us/dbs/licenses/search.lasso?&division=pest
Pesticide Product #24	www.oda.state.or.us/dbs/licenses/search.lasso?&division=pest
Physical Therapist/Assistant #45	www.ptboard.state.or.us
Physician / Physician Assistant #29	www.bme.state.or.us/search.html
Pilot #3	www.aviation.state.or.us/registration/pilotreg.shtml
Plans Examiner #19	www.oregonbcd.org/licensesearch.html
Plumber #19	www.oregonbcd.org/licensesearch.html
Podiatrist #29	www.bme.state.or.us/search.html
Pressure Vessel Installer #19	www.oregonbcd.org/licensesearch.html
Psychologist #16	www.obpe.state.or.us/licensee_applicant.htm
Psychologist Associate #16	www.obpe.state.or.us/licensee_applicant.htm
Public Accountant-CPA #5	www.boa.state.or.us
Pump Installation Contractor, Limited #21	www.cbs.state.or.us/external/imd/database/bcd/licensing/index.html
Radiologic Technologist Limited Permit #39	www.obrt.state.or.us
Radiologic Therapy Technologist #39	www.obrt.state.or.us
Real Estate Appraiser #4	http://oregonaclb.org/app_search.lasso
Refrigerated Plant #23	www.oda.state.or.us/dbs/licenses/search.lasso?&division=fsd
Respiratory Care Therapist #57	http://159.121.106.128/
Sanitarian/Sanitarian Trainee #57	http://159.121.106.128/
Shellfish-related Industry #23	www.oda.state.or.us/dbs/licenses/search.lasso?&division=fsd
Sign Contractor, Limited #21	www.cbs.state.or.us/external/imd/database/bcd/licensing/index.html
Sign Journeyman, Electrical #19	www.oregonbcd.org/licensesearch.html
Slaughterhouse #23	www.oda.state.or.us/dbs/licenses/search.lasso?&division=fsd
Special Qualifications Corporation #26	http://dfcs.oregon.gov/banking/specqual.htm
Speech Language Pathologist #58	www.bspa.state.or.us//directory/default.htm
Stage Journeyman, Electrical #19	www.oregonbcd.org/licensesearch.html
Steamfitter #19	www.oregonbcd.org/licensesearch.html
Surveyor, Land #10	www.osbeels.org
Tattoo Artist #57	http://159.121.106.128/
Teacher #53	www.tspc.state.or.us/lookup_query.asp
Transaction Verification #20	http://oda.state.or.us/dbs/search.lasso#msd
Travel Agent #26	http://dfcs.oregon.gov/sot/post.htm

Trust Company #26 .... http://dfcs.oregon.gov/banking/trust.htm
Veterinary Clinic/Product, Livestock #22 .... www.oda.state.or.us/index.html
Water Heater Installer, Limited #19 .... www.oregonbcd.org/licensesearch.html
Water Rights Examiner #10 .... www.osbeels.org
Water Treatment Installer #19 .... www.oregonbcd.org/licensesearch.html
Weighing Devices #20 .... http://oda.state.or.us/dbs/search.lasso#msd

Oregon Licensing Quick Finder

Acupuncturist #29 503-229-5770
Aircraft Registration #3 503-378-4880
Airport/Aircraft Landing Area #3 503-378-4880
Amusement Ride Inspector #19 503-378-4133
Animal Euthanasia Technician #54 503-731-4051
Animal Feed (Livestock) #22 503-986-4691
Animal Food Processor #22 503-986-4680
Animal Health Technician #54 503-731-4051
Architect #6 503-378-4270
Architectural Firm #6 503-378-4270
Athletic Trainer #57 503-378-8667
Attorney #43 503-620-0222
Audiologist #58 503-731-4050
Auditor, Municipal #5 503-378-4181
Bakery #23 503-986-4720
Bank #26 503-378-4140
Bank Registered Agent #26..................503-378-4140
Barber #7 503-378-8667
Body Piercer #7 503-378-8667
Boiler Welder #19 503-373-1268
Boilermaker #19 503-373-1268
Boxer #44 503-378-8739
Brand (Livestock) #22 503-986-4681
Brand Inspector #22 503-986-4681
Brewery #41 503-872-5124
Building Official #19 503-373-1248
Building Service Mechanic #19 503-373-1268
Cemetery #52 ....503-731-4040 x26
Check & Money Order Seller #26.........503-378-4140
Chiropractor/Chiropractic Assistant #8..503-378-5816
Christmas Tree Grower #25 503-986-4644
Collection Agency #26 503-378-4140
Construction Contractor/Subcontractor #21
................................503-378-4621 x4900
Consumer Finance Company #26........503-378-4140
Corrections Officer #18...........503-378-2100
Cosmetologist #7 503-378-8667
Counselor, Licensed Professional #28.503-378-5499
Court Reporter #59 503-986-5500
Credit Service Organization #26 503-378-4140
Credit Union #26 503-378-4140
Crematorium #52 ....503-731-4040 x26
Dairy Establishment #23 503-986-4720
Debt Consolidating Agency #26 503-378-4140
Dental Hygienist #55 503-229-5520
Dental Specialist #55 503-229-5520
Dentist #55 503-229-5520
Denture Technologist #57 503-378-8667
Denturist #9 503-378-8667
Diagnostic Radiologic Tech. #39..........503-731-4088
Diagnostic/Therapeutic Tech. #39........503-731-4088
Dietitian #11 503-731-4085
Digital Signature Authority #26 503-378-4140
Dog Racing Occupation #42.................503-731-4052
Drug Manufacturer/Whlse. #15 ....503-731-4032 x226
Drug Outlet, Over-Counter #15 ...503-731-4032 x231
Egg Handler/Breaker #23 503-986-4720
Electrical Installation #19 503-373-1268
Electrician #19 503-373-1268
Electrician, Maintenance #19 ...503-373-1268
Electrologist #7 503-378-8667
Electrology Instructor/School #7 503-378-8667
Elevator Journeyman, Limited #19.......503-373-1268
Embalmer/Embalmer Apprentice #52
................................503-731-4040 x26
EMD #18 503-378-2100

Endowment Care #26..........................503-378-4140
Energy Tech., Limited/Restricted #19..503-373-1268
Engineer #10 503-362-2666
Escrow Agent/Agency #46 503-378-4170
Facial Technician/Technologist #7 503-378-8667
Farm Labor Contractor #21 503-731-4200
Fertilizer/Mineral/Lime Registrant #24 .503-986-4600
Firefighter #18 503-378-2100
Florist #25 503-986-4644
Food Establishment, Retail #23 503-986-4720
Food Exporter/Processing Facility #23 503-986-4720
Food Producer/Distributor #23 503-986-4720
Food Storage Facility #23 503-986-4720
Forest Labor Contractor #21 503-731-4200
Frozen Desert-related Industry #23 503-986-4720
Funeral Establishment #52............ 503-731-4040 x26
Funeral Plan, Prearranged #26..........503-378-4140
Funeral Preneed Salesperson #52 503-731-4040 x26
Funeral Service Practitioner/Apprentice #52
................................503-731-4040 x26
Geologist #12 503-566-2837
Geologist, Engineering #12...............503-566-2837
Greenhouse Grower of Herbaceous Plants #25
................................503-986-4644
Hair Salon #7 503-378-8667
Hair Stylist #7 503-378-8667
Hairdresser #7 503-378-8667
Hearing Aid Dealer/Dispenser #2......503-378-8667
Heliport #3 503-378-4880
Home Inspector #21 ....503-378-4621 x4900
Horse Racing Occupation #42.......503-731-4052
Immediate Disposition Co. #52 ....503-731-4040 x26
Inspector, Building Code #19 503-373-1248
Inspector, Structural/Mechanical #19...503-373-1248
Insurance Adjuster #27 503-947-7980
Insurance Agency #27 503-947-7980
Insurance Agent #27 503-947-7980
Insurance Company #27 503-947-7980
Insurance Consultant #27 503-947-7980
Interpreter, Legal #59 503-986-5695
Investment Advisor #26............503-378-4140
Landscape Architect #50 503-589-0093
Landscape Business #21 503-378-4621
Landscaper #25 503-986-4644
Liquor Control #41 503-872-5000
Liquor Salesman/Agent #41 503-872-5123
Liquor, Wide Shipper #41.........503-872-5124
Livestock-Related Business #22 503-986-4680
Lobbyist #40 503-378-5105
Manicurist/Nail Technician #7 503-378-8667
Manufactured Housing Construct'n #19 503-373-1248
Marriage & Family Therapist #28 503-378-5499
Massage Therapist #38 503-365-8657
Measuring Devices #20 503-986-4670
Medical Doctor/Surgeon #29.............503-229-5770
Medical Examiner #51 503-280-6061
Midwife #57 503-378-8667
Milk Hauler/Milk Stabilization/Handler #23
................................503-986-4720
Money Transmitter #26 503-378-4140
Mortgage Banker/Broker/Lender #26...503-378-4140
Motor Fuel Quality #20 503-986-4670
Naturopathic Physician #34..............503-731-4045
Non-Alcoholic Beverage Plant #23 503-986-4720
Notary Public #37 503-986-2593
Nurse #13 503-731-3459

Nurse-LPN #13........................503-731-3459
Nursery Dealer #25 503-986-4644
Nursery Stock/Native Plants Collector #25...503-986-4644
Nursing Assistant #13 503-731-3459
Nursing Home Administrator #35.........503-731-4046
Occupational Therapist/Therapist Assistant #36
................................503-731-4048
Oil Module License #19 503-373-1268
Optometrist #14.......................503-373-7721
Oral Pathology Endorsement #9.........503-378-8667
Oregon Product #22.................503-986-4680
Osteopathic Physician/Surgeon #29....503-229-5770
Parole/Probation Officer #18.............503-378-2100
Pawnbroker #26 503-378-4140
Permanent Color Technician #7 503-378-8667
Pesticide Applicator/Trainee #24 503-986-4600
Pesticide Dealer/Company/Consultant #24
................................503-986-4600
Pesticide Product #24 503-986-4600
Pharmacist #15 ....503-731-4032 x227
Pharmacy #15 ....503-731-4032 x226
Physical Therapist/Assistant #45.........503-731-4047
Physician #29 503-229-5770
Physician Assistant #30 503-229-5770
Pilot #3...................................503-378-4880
Plans Examiner #19 503-373-1248
Plumber #19............................503-373-1268
Podiatrist #29 503-229-5770
Police Chief #18 503-378-2100
Police Officer #18.....................503-378-2100
Polygraph Examiner #18.............503-378-2100
Preneed Salesperson #52............ 503-731-4040 x26
Pressure Vessel Installer #19 503-373-1268
Private Security Officer #18 503-378-2100
Property Manager #46 503-378-4170
Psychologist #16 503-378-4154
Psychologist Associate #16 503-378-4154
Public Accountant-CPA #5.........503-378-4181
Public Accounting Firm #5 503-378-4181
Pump Installation Contr., Limited #21..503-731-4072
Radiologic Tech. Limited Permit #39...503-731-4088
Radiologic Therapy Technologist #39..503-731-4088
Real Estate Agent/Sales #46 503-378-4170
Real Estate Appraiser #4 503-485-2555
Real Estate Branch Office #46.............503-378-4170
Real Estate Broker #46 503-378-4170
Refrigerated Plant #23 503-986-4720
Respiratory Care Practitioner #32503-378-8667x4330
Respiratory Care Therapist #57 503-378-8667
Sanitarian #57 503-378-8667
Sanitarian/Sanitarian Trainee #57 503-378-8667
Savings & Loan Association #26 503-378-4140
School Counselor/Supervisor #53 503-378-6813
School Superintendent/Admin. #53 503-378-6813
Securities Broker/Dealer #26 503-378-4140
Securities Salesperson #26 503-378-4140
Shellfish-related Industry #23.............503-986-4720
Sign Contractor, Limited #21 ...503-731-4072
Sign Journeyman, Electrical #19 503-373-1268
Slaughterhouse #23 503-986-4720
Social Worker, Clinical #48 503-378-5735
Special Qualifications Corporation #26..503-378-4140
Speech Language Pathologist #58.......503-731-4050
Stage Journeyman, Electrical #19 503-373-1268
Steamfitter #19 503-373-1268

Surveyor, Land #10 503-362-2666	Trust Company #26 503-378-4140	Water Heater Installer, Limited #19 503-373-1268
Tattoo Artist #57 503-378-8667	Veterinarian #54 503-731-4051	Water Rights Examiner #10 503-362-2666
Tax Consultant/Preparer #17 503-378-4034	Veterinary Clinic, Livestock #22 503-986-4680	Water Treatment Installer #19 503-373-1268
Teacher #53 503-378-6813	Veterinary Product, Livestock #22 503-986-4680	Water Well Constructor #60 503-378-8455
Telecommunicator #18 503-378-2100	Veterinary Technician #54 503-731-4051	Weighing Devices #20 503-986-4670
Transaction Verification #20 503-986-4670	Waste Water Treatment System Operator #1	Winery #41 503-872-5124
Travel Agent #26 503-378-4140	 503-229-5622	Wrestler #44 503-378-8739

Oregon Licensing Agency Information

1 Department of Environmental Quality, Operator Certification Program, Water Quality Division, 811 SW 6th Ave, Portland, OR 97204; 503-229-5696, Fax: 503-229-6037.

2 Advisory Council on Hearing Aids, 700 Summer St, #320, Salem, OR 97301-1287; 503-378-8667, Fax: 503-370-9004.
www.hdlp.hr.state.or.us/hdhome.htm
Email: hdlp.mail@state.or.us

3 Department of Aviation, Aeronautics Section, 3040 25th S SE, Salem, OR 97302; 503-378-4880, Fax: 503-373-1688.
www.aviation.state.or.us

4 Appraiser Certification & Licensure Board, 1860 Hawthorne Avenue NE #200, Salem, OR 97303; 503-485-2555, Fax: 503-485-2559.
http://oregonaclb.org/
Email: jan@oregonaclb.org Search Database at
http://oregonaclb.org/app_search.lasso

5 Board of Accountancy, 3218 Pringle Rd SE, #110, Salem, OR 97302-6307; 503-378-4181, Fax: 503-378-3575.
www.boa.state.or.us
Email: david.r.hunter@state.or.us

6 Board of Architect Examiners, 750 Front St NE #260, Salem, OR 97301; 503-763-0662, Fax: 503-364-0510.
www.architect-board.state.or.us
Email: architect.board@state.or.us
Search Database at www.architect-board.state.or.us

7 Health Licensing Office, Board of Barbers & Hairdressers, 700 Summer St NE #320, Salem, OR 97301-1287; 503-378-8667, Fax: 503-370-9004.
www.hlo.state.or.us/welcome.htm
Email: hdlp.mail@state.or.us

8 Board of Chiropractic Examiners, 3218 Pringle Rd SE, #150, Salem, OR 97302-6311; 503-378-5816, Fax: 503-362-1260.
www.obce.state.or.us Email: oregon.obce@state.or.us

9 Board of Denture Technology, 700 Summer St, #320, Salem, OR 97301-1287; 503-378-8667, Fax: 503-585-2114.
www.hdlp.hr.state.or.us/dthome.htm
Email: hdlp.mail@state.or.us

10 Board of Examiners for Engineer & Land Surveyors, 728 Hawthorne Ave NE, Salem, OR 97301; 503-362-2666, Fax: 503-362-5454.
www.osbeels.org Email: osbeels@osbeels.org
Search Database at www.osbeels.org

11 Board of Examiners of Licensed Dietitians, 800 NE Oregon, #407, Portland, OR 97232; 503-731-4085, Fax: 503-731-4207.
www.bld.state.or.us
Email: doug.vanfleet@state.or.us
Search Database at
www.bld.state.or.us/directory/index.htm Note:
They do sell/provide lists.

12 Oregon State Board of Geologist Examiners, Sunset Center South, 1193 Royvonne Ave. SE #24, Salem, OR 97302;
503-566-2837, Fax: 503-485-2947.
www.osbge.org Email: osbge@open.org
Search Database at
www.open.org/~osbge/registrants.htm

13 Board of Nursing, 800 NE Oregon St, #465, Portland, OR 97232-2162; 503-731-4745, Fax: 503-731-4755. www.osbn.state.or.us
Email: oregon.bn.info@state.or.us
Search Database at http://mscfprod1.iserv ices.state.or.us/nursinglu/LicenseLookup.cfm

14 Board of Optometry, 3218 Pringle Rd SE, #270, Salem, OR 97310-6306;
503-373-7721, Fax: 503-378-3616.
www.oregonobo.org
Email: oregon.obo@state.or.us Search Database at
www.oregonobo.org/doctorinfo.htm

15 Board of Pharmacy, 800 NE Oregon St, State Office Bldg, #9, Rm 425, Portland, OR 97232; 503-731-4032, Fax: 503-731-4067.
www.pharmacy.state.or.us
Email: pharmacy.board@state.or.us Note: Verifications are free at this time. Lists are $80.00, contact Michael regarding lists at x227.

16 Board of Psychologist Examiners, 3218 Pringle Road, #130, Salem, OR 97301-6309; 503-378-4154, Fax: 503-378-3575.
www.obpe.state.or.us Search Database at
www.obpe.state.or.us/licensee_applicant.htm

17 Board of Tax Practitioners, 3218 Pringle Road, #120, Salem, OR 97302; 503-378-4034, Fax: 503-378-3575.
www.open.org/~ortaxbrd Email: tax.bd@state.or.us

18 Department of Public Safety Standards & Training, 550 N Monmouth Ave, Monmouth, OR 97361; 503-378-4600, Fax: 503-838-8907.
www.dpsst.state.or.us

19 Department of Consumer & Business Svcs, Building Codes Division, PO Box 14470, Salem, OR 97309-0404;
503-378-4100, Fax: 503-378-2322.
www.oregonbcd.org
Email: bcd.webmaster@state.or.us Search Database at
www.cbs.state.or.us/imd/database/bcd/licensing/in div/index.html

20 Department of Agriculture, Measurements Standards Division, 635 Capitol St NE, Salem, OR 97301-2532; 503-986-4670, Fax: 503-986-4784.
http://oda.state.or.us/msd
Email: msd-support@oda.state.or.us Search Database at http://oda.state.or.us/dbs/search.lasso#msd

21 Construction & Landscape Contractors Boards, 700 Summer St NE #300 PO Box 14140, Salem, OR 97309-5052; 503-378-4621 x4900, Fax: 503-373-2007.
www.ccb.state.or.us/New_Web/new_contact_us.htm

Email: ccbinfo@ccb.state.or.us Note: 24-hour Contractor Inquiry Line - 503-378-4610 or 888-366-5635.

22 Department of Agriculture, Animal Health & Identification Division (State Vet.), 635 Capitol St NE, Salem, OR 97310-0110; 503-986-4680, Fax: 503-986-4734.
www.oda.state.or.us/index.html
Email: tberg@oda.state.or.us
Search Database at
www.oda.state.or.us/index.html

23 Department of Agriculture, Food Safety Division, 635 Capitol St NE, Salem, OR 97301-2523; 503-986-4720, Fax: 503-986-4729.
www.oda.state.or.us/Food_Safety/FSDINFO.html
Email: rmckay@oda.state.or.us
Search Database at www.oda.state.or.us/dbs/li censes/search.lasso?&division=fsd Note: Updated weekly. Mailing labels available (database formatted ASCII files).

24 Department of Agriculture, Pesticides Division, 635 Capitol St NE, Salem, OR 97310-2523; 503-986-4635, Fax: 503-986-4735.
www.oda.state.or.us/pesticide/
Email: pestx@oda.state.or.us

25 Department of Agriculture, Plant Division, 635 Capitol St NE, Salem, OR 97310-0110; 503-986-4644, Fax: 503-986-4786.
www.oda.state.or.us
Search Database at
www.oda.state.or.us/dbs/licenses/search.lasso?&di vision=nursery

26 Department of Consumer & Business Svcs, Division of Finance and Corporate Securities, 350 Winter St, Labor & Industries Bldg, Rm 410, Salem, OR 97301-3881; 503-378-4140, Fax: 503-947-7862.
http://dfcs.oregon.gov

27 Department of Consumer and Business Svcs, Insurance Division, PO Box 14480 (350 Winter St NE, Rm 440), Salem, OR 97309-0405; 503-947-7980, Fax: 503-378-4351.
www.cbs.state.or.us/external/ins/
Email: dcbs.insmail@state.or.us
Search Database at
http://www4.cbs.state.or.us/ex/ins/inslic/agent/

28 Licensed Professional Counselors & Therapists, 3218 Pringle Rd SE, #250, Salem, OR 97302-6312; 503-378-5499.
www.oblpct.state.or.us Email: lpc.lmft@state.or.us
Search Database at www.oblpct.state.or.us/ Note: They provide downloadable labels and lists of professionals. They provide a $6.00 disk for labels or a $6.00 annual directory.

29 Board of Medical Examiners, 1500 SW 1st Ave #620, Portland, OR 97201; 503-229-5770, Fax: 503-229-6543.
www.bme.state.or.us/welcome.html
Email: bme.info@state.or.us Search Database at
www.bme.state.or.us/search.html

32 Respiratory Therapist Licensing Board, 700 Summer St NE #320, Salem, OR 97310-1287; 503-378-8667 x4330, Fax: 503-370-9004. www.hdlp.hr.state.or.us/rthome.htm Email: hdlp.mail@state.or.us

34 Naturopathic Board of Examiners, 800 NE Oregon, #407, Portland, OR 97232; 503-731-4045, Fax: 503-731-4207. www.obne.state.or.us Email: obne.info@state.or.us   Note: Mailing list form is at www.obne.state.or.us/forms.htm.

35 Nursing Home Board, 800 NE Oregon, #407, Portland, OR 97232; 503-731-4046, Fax: 503-731-4207. www.nhabd.state.or.us Email: janet.bartel@state.or.us Search Database at www.nhabd.state.or.us/directory/index.htm

36 Occupational Therapy Licensing, 800 NE Oregon, #407, Portland, OR 97232; 503-731-4048, Fax: 503-731-4207. www.otlb.state.or.us   Email: otlb.info@state.or.us Search Database at www.otlb.state.or.us/directory/default.htm

37 Office of Secretary of State, 255 Capitol St NE, #151, Salem, OR 97310-1327; 503-986-2593, Fax: 503-986-2300. www.filinginoregon.com/notary/index.htm Email: oregon.notary@state.or.us

38 Board of Massage Technicians, 748 Hawthorne Ave NE, Salem, OR 97301-4675; 503-365-8657, Fax: 503-385-4465. www.oregonmassage.org Email: shel@oregonmassage.org

39 Board of Radiologic Technology, 800 NE Oregon, #407, Portland, OR 97232; 503-731-4088, Fax: 503-872-6831. www.obrt.state.or.us Email: info.orbt@state.or.us

40 Government Standards & Pracrices Commission, 100 High St SE, #220, Salem, OR 97310; 503-378-5105, Fax: 503-373-1456. www.gspc.state.or.us Email: gspc.mail@state.or.us

41 Liquor Control Commission, 9079 SE McLoughlin Blvd, Portland, OR 97222-7355; 503-872-5000, Fax: 503-872-5018. www.olcc.state.or.us Email: Shannon.KILEY@state.or.us

42 Racing Commission, 800 NE Oregon, #11, Portland, OR 97232; 503-731-4052, Fax: 503-731-4053. www.dialoregon.net/~orc Email: sbarham@OregonVOS.net   Search Database at http://lic.oregon.gov/cfmx/lic/index.cfm

43 State Bar Association, 5200 SW Meadows Rd, Lake Oswego, OR 97035; 503-620-0222, Fax: 503-684-1366. www.osbar.org   Email: info@osbar.org Search Database at www.osbcle.org/members/start.asp

44 Boxing & Wrestling Commission, 3400 State St #G750, Salem, OR 97301; 503-378-8739, Fax: 503-304-9157. Email: jim.cassidy@state.or.us

45 Physical Therapist Licensing Board, 800 NE Oregon St, #407, Portland, OR 97232-2162; 503-731-4047, Fax: 503-731-4207. www.ptboard.state.or.us Email: ptboard.info@state.or.us Search Database at www.ptboard.state.or.us

46 Real Estate Agency, 1177 Center St NE, Salem, OR 97310-2503; 503-378-4170, Fax: 503-378-2491. www.rea.state.or.us

47 Sanitarians Registration Board, 700 Summer St NE, #320, Salem, OR 97301-1287; 503-378-8667, Fax: 503-370-9004. www.hdlp.hr.state.or.us/snhome.htm Email: hdlp.mail@state.or.us

48 Board of Clinical Social Workers, 3218 Pringle Rd SE, #240, Salem, OR 97302-6310; 503-378-5735, Fax: 503-373-1427. http://bcsw.state.or.us   Email: bcsw@state.or.us

50 Landscape Architect Board, 1193 Royvonne Ave SE #19, Salem, OR 97302; 503-589-0093, Fax: 503-589-0545. Email: oslab@uswest.net

52 Mortuary & Cemetery Board, 800 NE Oregon, #430, Portland, OR 97232-2195; 503-731-4040 X26, Fax: 503-731-4494. www.oregon.gov/MortCem/index.shtml Email: mortuary.board@state.or.us Search Database at http://lic.oregon.gov/cfmx/lic/index.cfm

53 Teacher Standards & Practices Commission, 465 Commercial St. NE, Salem, OR 97301; 503-378-6813, Fax: 503-378-4448. www.tspc.state.or.us Email: Matt.Garrett@state.or.us   Search Database at www.tspc.state.or.us/lookup_query.asp

54 Veterinary Medical Board, 800 NE Oregon, #407, Portland, OR 97232; 503-731-4051, Fax: 503-731-4207. Email: ovmeb@info@state.or.us

55 Board of Dentistry, 1515 SW 5th #602, Portland, OR 97201; 503-229-5520, Fax: 503-229-6606. www.oregondentistry.org Search Database at www.oregondentistry.org/

57 Health Licensing Office, Admin Svcs Division Manager, 700 Summer St NE #320, Salem, OR 97310-1287; 503-378-8667, Fax: 503-585-9114. www.hlo.state.or.us   Email: hlo.mail@state.or.us Search Database at http://159.121.106.128/

58 Board of Examiners for Speech-Language Pathology & Audiology, 800 NE Oregon St #21, State Office Bldg, Portland, OR 97232; 503-731-4050, Fax: 503-731-4207. www.bspa.state.or.us Email: brenda.felber@state.or.us   Search Database at http://bspa.ohd.hr.state.or.us/directory/default.htm

59 Judicial Department, Office of the State Court Administrator, 1163 State St, Salem, OR 97301-2563; 503-986-5500, Fax: 503-986-5503. www.ojd.state.or.us

60 Department of Water Resources, 725 Summer St. NE, Ste A, Salem, OR 97301-1271; 503-986-0900, Fax: 503-986-0903. www.wrd.state.or.us

Oregon Federal Courts

The following list indicates the district and division name for each county in the state. If the bankruptcy court location is different from the district court, then the location of the bankruptcy court appears in parentheses.

County/Court Cross Reference

County	Court	County	Court
Baker	Portland	Lake	Medford (Eugene)
Benton	Eugene	Lane	Eugene
Clackamas	Portland	Lincoln	Eugene
Clatsop	Portland	Linn	Eugene
Columbia	Portland	Malheur	Portland
Coos	Eugene	Marion	Eugene
Crook	Portland	Morrow	Portland
Curry	Medford (Eugene)	Multnomah	Portland
Deschutes	Eugene (Portland)	Polk	Portland (Eugene)
Douglas	Eugene	Sherman	Portland
Gilliam	Portland	Tillamook	Portland
Grant	Portland	Umatilla	Portland
Harney	Portland	Union	Portland
Hood River	Portland	Wallowa	Portland
Jackson	Medford (Eugene)	Wasco	Portland
Jefferson	Portland	Washington	Portland
Josephine	Medford (Eugene)	Wheeler	Portland
Klamath	Medford (Eugene)	Yamhill	Portland

Standards for Federal Courts: The search fee is $20.00 per item (one party name or case number). Certification fee is $7.00 per document. Copy fee is $.50 per page. All fees standard unless noted in profile. Mail Search: always enclose a stamped self addressed envelope unless otherwise noted. Most courts accept fax requests or will suggest a copying/search vendor. Before releasing records, all courts require prepayment unless noted in profile.

Open records are located at the court unless otherwise noted. District courts index by defendant and plaintiff as well as by case number. Bankruptcy courts usually index by debtor and case number. While most courts now have their indexes on computer, many still maintain index card files as well.

The universal PACER sign-up number is 800-676-6856. Find PACER and the Party/Case Index on the Web at http://pacer.psc.uscourts.gov. PACER dial-up access is $.60 per minute. Also, courts offering internet access via RACER, PACER, Web-PACER or the new CM-ECF charge $.07 per page fee unless noted as free.

US District Court

District of Oregon

Eugene Division 100 Federal Bldg, 211 E 7th Ave, Eugene, OR 97401 (courier address: Use mail address for courier delivery) 541-465-6423, Fax: 541-465-6344. www.ord.uscourts.gov

Counties: Benton, Coos, Deschutes, Douglas, Lane, Lincoln, Linn, Marion.

Indexing & Storage: New cases available in the index immediately after filing date. Records are also indexed on microfiche for criminal records older than 1986. District wide searches are available from this division.

Fee & Payment: Payment may be made by money order, cashier check, personal check, Visa, Mastercard. Payee: Clerk, U.S. District Court.

Phone Search: Only docket information available by phone.

Mail Search: A SASE not required.

In Person Search: Fee charged if court conducts your in person search for you.

PACER: PACER is available online at http://pacer.ord.uscourts.gov. Case records go back to September 1988. Records never purged. New records are online after 1 day.

Electronic Filing: Electronic filing information online at https://ecf.ord.uscourts.gov.

Medford Division 201 James A Redden U.S. Courthouse, 310 W 6th St, Medford, OR 97501 (courier address: Use mail address for courier delivery) 541-776-3926, Fax: 541-776-3925. www.ord.uscourts.gov

Counties: Curry, Jackson, Josephine, Klamath, Lake. Court set up in April 1994; Cases prior to that time were tried in Eugene.

Indexing & Storage: New cases available in the index 1 day after filing date.

Fee & Payment: Payment may be made by money order, cashier check, personal check, Visa, Mastercard. Payee: Clerk, USDC. Will fax docket listings no extra charge.

Phone Search: Only docket information available by phone. Will fax docket listings no extra charge.

Mail Search: A SASE not required.

In Person Search: Fee charged if court conducts your in person search for you.

PACER: PACER is available online at http://pacer.ord.uscourts.gov. Case records go back to September 1988. Records never purged. New records are online after 1 day.

Electronic Filing: Electronic filing information online at https://ecf.ord.uscourts.gov

Portland Division Clerk, 740 U.S. Courthouse, 1000 SW 3rd Ave, Portland, OR 97204-2902 (courier address: Use mail address for courier delivery) 503-326-8000, Fax: 503-326-8010. www.ord.uscourts.gov

Counties: Baker, Clackamas, Clatsop, Columbia, Crook, Gilliam, Grant, Harney, Hood River, Jefferson, Malheur, Morrow, Multnomah, Polk, Sherman, Tillamook, Umatilla, Union, Wallowa, Wasco, Washinton, Wheeler, Yamhill.

Indexing & Storage: New cases available in the index 24 hours after filing date. Records are also indexed on microfiche. District wide searches are available from this court. All civil cases after 8/88 and all criminal cases after 3/91 are maintained in this division for the other divisions.

Fee & Payment: Payment may be made by money order, cashier check, personal check. Payee: Clerk, USDC.

Phone Search: If the case number is known, docket information will be released over the phone.

Mail Search: A SASE not required.

In Person Search: Fee charged if court conducts your in person search for you.

PACER: PACER is available online at http://pacer.ord.uscourts.gov. Case records go back to September 1988. Records never purged. New records are online after 1 day.

Electronic Filing: Electronic filing information online at https://ecf.ord.uscourts.gov

U.S. Bankruptcy Court

District of Oregon

Eugene Division PO Box 1335, Eugene, OR 97440 (courier address: 151 W 7th St, #300, Eugene, OR 97440), 541-465-6448. www.orb.uscourts.gov

Counties: Benton, Coos, Curry, Deschutes, Douglas, Jackson, Josephine, Klamath, Lake, Lane, Lincoln, Linn, Marion.

Indexing & Storage: Cases indexed by debtor as well as by case number. New cases available in the index 1 day after filing date.

Fee & Payment: Payment may be made by money order, cashier check, personal check. Payee: Clerk, U.S. Bankruptcy Court.

Phone Search: Only docket information available by telephone. Automated voice case information service (VCIS) is available. Call VCIS at 800-726-2227 or 503-326-2249.

Mail Search: A SASE not required.

In Person Search: Fee charged if court conducts your in person search for you.

PACER: PACER is available online at http://pacer.orb.uscourts.gov. Records purged every six months. New civil records are online after 1 day.

Electronic Filing: Electronic filing information online at https://ecf.orb.uscourts.gov

Portland Division, 1001 SW 5th Ave, #700, Portland, OR 97204 (courier address: Use mail address for courier delivery) 503-326-2231. www.orb.uscourts.gov

Counties: Baker, Clackamas, Clatsop, Columbia, Crook, Gilliam, Grant, Harney, Hood River, Jefferson, Malheur, Morrow, Multnomah, Polk, Sherman, Tillamook, Umatilla, Union, Wallowa, Wasco, Washington, Wheeler, Yamhill.

Indexing & Storage: Cases indexed by debtor as well as by case number. New cases available in the index 1 day after filing date.

Fee & Payment: Payment may be made by money order, cashier check, personal check. Payee: Clerk, U.S. Bankruptcy Court.

Phone Search: Only docket information available by phone. Automated voice case information service (VCIS) is available. Call VCIS at 800-726-2227 or 503-326-2249.

In Person Search: Fee charged if court conducts your in person search for you.

PACER: PACER is available online at http://pacer.orb.uscourts.gov. Records purged every six months. New civil records are online after 1 day.

Electronic Filing: Electronic filing information online at https://ecf.orb.uscourts.gov

Oregon County Courts

Court	Jurisdiction	No. of Courts	How Organized
Circuit Courts*	General	38	27 Districts
County Courts*	Probate	6	6 Counties
Justice Courts	Municipal	35	
Municipal Courts	Municipal	112	
Tax Court	Special	1	

* Profiled in this Sourcebook.

	CIVIL								
Court	Tort	Contract	Real Estate	Min. Claim	Max. Claim	Small Claims	Estate	Eviction	Domestic Relations
Circuit Courts*	X	X	X	$0	No Max	$2500	X	X	X
County Courts*							X		X
Justice Courts	X	X	X	$200	$2500	$2500			
Municipal Courts									
Tax Court									

	CRIMINAL				
Court	Felony	Misdemeanor	DWI/DUI	Preliminary Hearing	Juvenile
Circuit Courts*	X	X	X	X	X
County Courts*					X
Justice Courts		X	X	X	
Municipal Courts		X	X		
Tax Court					

ADMINISTRATION   Court Administrator, Supreme Court Building, 1163 State St, Salem, OR, 97301-2563; 503-986-5500, Fax: 503-986-5503. www.ojd.state.or.us

COURT STRUCTURE   Effective January 15, 1998, the District and Circuit Courts were combined into "Circuit Courts." At the same time, 3 new judicial districts were created by splitting existing ones.

ONLINE ACCESS   Online computer access is available through the Oregon Judicial Information Network (OJIN). OJIN Online includes almost all cases filed in the Oregon state courts. Generally, the OJIN database contains criminal, civil, small claims, probate, and some but not all juvenile records. However, it does not contain any records from municipal nor county courts. There is a one-time setup fee of $295.00, plus a monthly usage charge (minimum $10.00) based on transaction type, type of job, shift, and number of units/pages (which averages $10-13 per hour). For further information and/or a registration packet, write to: Oregon Judicial System, Information Systems Division, ATTN: Technical Support, 1163 State Street, Salem OR 97310, or call 800-858-9658, or visit www.ojd.state.or.us/ojin

ADDITIONAL INFORMATION   Many Oregon courts indicated that in person searches would markedly improve request turnaround time as court offices are understaffed or spread very thin. Most Circuit Courts that have records on computer do have a public access terminal that will speed up in-person or retriever searches. Most records offices close from Noon to 1PM Oregon time for lunch. No staff is available during that period.

PROBATE COURTS   Probate is handled by the Circuit Court except in 6 counties (Gilliam, Grant, Harney, Malheur, Sherman, and Wheeler) where Probate in handled by County Courts.

Baker County

Circuit Court 1995 3rd St, #220, Baker City, OR 97814; 541-523-6305; Fax: 541-523-9738. Hours: 8AM-Noon, 1-5PM (PST). *Felony, Misdemeanor, Civil, Probate.*
www.ojd.state.or.us/baker
Civil Records: Access: Phone, fax, mail, in person. Both court and visitors may perform in person searches. Search fee: none. Required to search: name, years to search. Civil cases indexed by defendant, plaintiff. Civil records on computer from 1987, archives back to 1865. Index remotely online on the statewide OJIN system, call 800-858-9658 for information.
Criminal Records: Access: Phone, fax, mail, in person. Both court and visitors may perform in person searches. Search fee: none. Required to search: name, years to search. Criminal records on computer from 1987, archives back to 1865. Online access to criminal records is the same as civil.
General Information: Public Access terminal is available. No adoption, mental, juvenile or sealed records released. Fee to fax results is $2.00 1st page; $1.00 each add'l. Copy fee: $.25 per page. Cert fee: $5.00. Payee: State of Oregon. Personal checks accepted. Prepayment required. Mail requests: SASE required. Mail turnaround time 10 days.

Benton County

Circuit Court Box 1870 (120 NW Fourth St), Corvallis, OR 97339; 541-766-6828; Fax: 541-766-6028. Hours: 8AM-Noon, 1-5PM (PST). *Felony, Misdemeanor, Civil, Eviction, Small Claims, Probate.*
www.ojd.state.or.us/benton
Civil Records: Access: Phone, mail, online, in person. Both court and visitors may perform in person searches. Search fee: fee is court performs search. Required to search: name, years to search; also helpful: address. Civil cases indexed by defendant, plaintiff, case number. Civil records on computer from 1993, archives and microfiche back to the 1900s. Index remotely online on the statewide OJIN system, call 800-858-9658 for information.
Criminal Records: Access: Phone, mail, online, in person. Both court and visitors may perform in person searches. Search fee: fee if court performs search. Required to search: name, years to search, DOB, offense; also helpful: address, SSN, case number. Criminal records on computer from 1993, archives and microfiche back to the 1900s. Online access to criminal records is the same as civil.
General Information: Public Access terminal is available. No adoption, juvenile, sealed by judge, expunged, mental health records released. Will not fax results. Copy fee: $.25 per page. Cert fee: $5.00. Payee: State of Oregon. Personal checks accepted. Prepayment required. Mail requests: SASE required. Mail turnaround time up to 1 week.

Clackamas County

Circuit Court 807 Main St, Oregon City, OR 97045; 503-655-8447; Criminal phone: 503-655-8643. Hours: 10AM-5PM M-F (PST). *Felony, Misdemeanor, Civil, Eviction, Small Claims, Probate.*
Note: Records managemnet canbe reached at 503-650-3036.
Civil Records: Access: Mail, online, in person. Both court and visitors may perform in person searches. No search fee. Required to search: name, years to search. Civil cases indexed by defendant, plaintiff. Civil records on computer from 1986, index back to 1980. Index remotely online on the statewide OJIN system, call 800-858-9658 for information.

Criminal Records: Access: Mail, online, in person. Both court and visitors may perform in person searches. No search fee. Required to search: name, years to search, DOB. Criminal records on computer from 1986, index back to 1980. Online access to criminal records is the same as civil.
General Information: Public Access terminal is available. No adoption, juvenile, sealed by judge, expunged, mental health records released. Copy fee: $.25 per page. Cert fee: $5.00. Payee: State of Oregon. Personal checks accepted. Visa, MC accepted. Prepayment required. Mail requests: SASE required. Mail turnaround time 4-6 weeks.

Clatsop County

Circuit Court Box 835, Astoria, OR 97103; 503-325-8583; Civil phone: 503-325-8555; Fax: 503-325-9300. Hours: 8AM-Noon, 1-5PM (PST). *Felony, Misdemeanor, Civil, Eviction, Small Claims, Probate.*
www.ojd.state.or.us/clt/index.html
Civil Records: Access: Phone, mail, online, in person. Both court and visitors may perform in person searches. No search fee. Required to search: name, years to search. Civil cases indexed by defendant, plaintiff. Civil records on computer from 1987, archives back to 1900. Index remotely online on the statewide OJIN system, call 800-858-9658 for information.
Criminal Records: Access: Phone, mail, online, in person. Both court and visitors may perform in person searches. Search fee: None. Required to search: name, years to search, DOB. Criminal records on computer from 1987, archives back to 1900. Online access to criminal records is the same as civil.
General Information: Public Access terminal is available. No adoption, juvenile, sealed by judge, expunged, paternity or mental health records released. Will fax results to local or toll free line, otherwise $5.00. Copy fee: $.25 per page. Cert fee: $5.00. Payee: Clatsop County Circuit Court. Personal checks accepted. Prepayment required. Mail requests: SASE required. Mail turnaround time 2 weeks.

Columbia County

Circuit Court Columbia County Courthouse, 230 Strand St, St. Helens, OR 97051; 503-397-2327; Fax: 503-397-3226. Hours: 8AM-5PM (PST). *Felony, Misdemeanor, Civil, Eviction, Small Claims, Probate.*
Civil Records: Access: Mail, fax, online, in person. Both court and visitors may perform in person searches. No search fee. Required to search: name, years to search; also helpful: SSN, DOBaddress. Civil cases indexed by defendant, plaintiff. Civil records on computer from September, 1987, archives back to 1900. Index remotely online on the statewide OJIN system, call 800-858-9658 for information.
Criminal Records: Access: Mail, fax, online, in person. Both court and visitors may perform in person searches. No search fee. Required to search: name, years to search, DOB; also helpful: address, SSN, signed release. Criminal records on computer from September, 1987, archives back to 1900. Online access to criminal records is the same as civil.
General Information: Public Access terminal is available. No adoptions, juvenile, sealed by Judge, expunged, mental health records released. Will fax results for $2.00 1st page, $1.00 each add'l. Copy fee: $.25 per page. Cert fee: $5.00. Payee: State of Oregon. Personal checks accepted. Prepayment required. Mail requests: SASE required. Mail turnaround time 4-5 days.

Coos County

Circuit Court Courthouse, Coquille, OR 97423; 541-396-3121; Civil phone: X401; Criminal phone: X402; Fax: 541-396-3456. Hours: 8AM-Noon,1-5PM M-F (PST). *Felony, Misdemeanor, Civil, Eviction, Small Claims, Probate.*
http://cooscurrycourts.org
Note: Eviction, Small Claims and Probate records are available at 541-756-2020 ext 556. Circuit Court Annex at 1975 McPherson, North Bend OR 97459.
Civil Records: Access: Phone, mail, online, in person. Both court and visitors may perform in person searches. No search fee. Required to search: name, years to search; also helpful: address. Civil cases indexed by defendant, plaintiff. Civil records on computer from 1987, archives back to 1800. Index remotely online on the statewide OJIN system, call 800-858-9658 for information.
Criminal Records: Access: Phone, mail, online, in person. Both court and visitors may perform in person searches. No search fee. Required to search: name, years to search, DOB; also helpful: address, SSN. Criminal records on computer from 1987, archives back to 1800. Online access to criminal records is the same as civil.
General Information: Public Access terminal is available. No adoptions, sealed by Judge, expunged, paternity or mental health records released. Will fax results for a fee. Copy fee: $.25 per page. Cert fee: $5.00. Payee: State Courts. Personal checks accepted. Visa, MC accepted. Visa, MC. Not accepted for filing fees. Prepayment required. Mail requests: SASE required. Mail turnaround time 1-2 days.

Crook County

Circuit Court Crook County Courthouse, 300 NE Third St, Prineville, OR 97754; 541-447-6541. Hours: 8AM-5PM (PST). *Felony, Misdemeanor, Civil, Eviction, Small Claims, Probate.*
Civil Records: Access: Phone, mail, in person, online. Both court and visitors may perform in person searches. No search fee. Required to search: name, years to search; also helpful: address. Civil cases indexed by defendant, plaintiff. Civil records on computer from 1986, microfiche from 1907, archives from 1907. Index remotely online on the statewide OJIN system, call 800-858-9658 for information.
Criminal Records: Access: Phone, mail, in person, online. Both court and visitors may perform in person searches. No search fee. Required to search: name, years to search, DOB; also helpful: address, SSN. Criminal records on computer from 1986, microfiche from 1907, archives from 1907. Online access to criminal records is the same as civil.
General Information: No adoptions, juvenile, sealed by Judge, expunged, paternity or mental health records released. Copy fee: $.25 per page. Cert fee: $5.00. Payee: State of Oregon. Personal checks accepted. Prepayment required. Mail requests: SASE required. Mail turnaround time 2-4 days.

Curry County

Circuit Court Box 810, Gold Beach, OR 97444; 541-247-4511. Hours: 8-12 MTWF; 8-12 &1:30-5 Thurs (PST). *Felony, Misdemeanor, Civil, Eviction, Small Claims, Probate.*
www.cooscurrycourts.org
Civil Records: Access: Phone, mail, online, in person. Both court and visitors may perform in person searches. No search fee. Required to search: name, years to search; also helpful: address. Civil cases indexed by defendant, plaintiff. Civil records on computer from 1987, archives back to 1891. Index remotely online on the statewide OJIN system, call 800-858-9658 for information.

Criminal Records: Access: Phone, mail, online, in person. Both court and visitors may perform in person searches. No search fee. Required to search: name, years to search, DOB; also helpful: address, SSN. Criminal records on computer from 1987, archives back to 1891. Online access to criminal records is the same as civil.

General Information: Public Access terminal is available. No adoptions, sealed by Judge, expunged, paternity or mental health records released. Copy fee: $.25 per page. Add postage if SASE not enclosed. Cert fee: $5.00 for 1st page and $.25 for each add'l page. Payee: State Courts. Personal checks accepted. Visa, MC accepted. Prepayment required. Mail requests: SASE required. Mail turnaround time 1-2 days from receipt of payment.

Deschutes County

Deschutes County Courts 1100 NW Bond, Bend, OR 97701; 541-388-5300; Civil phone: X209; Criminal phone: X210; Probate phone: X208. Hours: 8AM-5PM (PST). *Felony, Misdemeanor, Civil, Eviction, Small Claims, Probate.*
www.deschutescircuitcourt.org
Civil Records: Access: Phone, mail, online, in person. Visitors must perform in person searches for themselves. No search fee. Required to search: name, years to search. Civil cases indexed by defendant, plaintiff. Civil records on computer from 9/87, books from 1976, archived from 1916 on microfiche. Index remotely online on the statewide OJIN system, call 800-858-9658 for information. Also, current calendars are free at www.ojd.state.or.us/des/calendar.nsf/.
Criminal Records: Access: Phone, mail, online, in person. Visitors must perform in person searches themselves. No search fee. Required to search: name, years to search, SSN. Criminal records on computer from 9/87, books from 1976, archived from 1916 on microfiche. Criminal Index available remotely online on the statewide OJIN system, call 800-858-9658. Records from 07/86 forward. Also, current calendars are free at www.ojd.state.or.us/des/calendar.nsf/.
General Information: Public Access terminal is available. No adoptions, juvenile, sealed by Judge, expunged, mental health records released. Copy fee: $.25 per page. Cert fee: $5.00. Payee: State of Oregon. Personal checks accepted. Prepayment required. Mail requests: SASE required. Mail turnaround time 3-5 days.

Douglas County

Circuit Court 1036 S E Douglas, Roseburg, OR 97470; 541-957-2471; Fax: 541-957-2462. Hours: 8AM-Noon, 1-5PM (PST). *Felony, Misdemeanor, Civil, Eviction, Small Claims, Probate.*
www.ojd.state.or.us/douglas
Civil Records: Access: Phone, mail, online, in person. Both court and visitors may perform in person searches. No search fee. Required to search: name, years to search. Civil cases indexed by defendant, plaintiff. Civil records on computer back to 10/1987, microfiche from 1974 (district) 1962 (circuit), archived from 1910. Index remotely online on the statewide OJIN system, call 800-858-9658 for information.
Criminal Records: Access: Phone, mail, online, in person. Both court and visitors may perform in person searches. No search fee. Required to search: name, years to search, DOB. Criminal records on computer back to 10/1987, microfiche from 1974 (district) 1962 (circuit), archived from 1910. Online access to criminal records is the same as civil.
General Information: Public Access terminal is available. No adoptions, juvenile, sealed by Judge, expunged or mental health records released. Will scan written documents and send in "PDF" format to an email address at no cost. Copy fee: $.25 per page. Cert

fee: $5.00. Payee: Oregon Judicial Department. Personal checks accepted. Prepayment required. Mail requests: SASE required. Mail turnaround time at least two weeks.

Gilliam County

Circuit Court Box 622, Condon, OR 97823; 541-384-3572; Fax: 541-384-2166. Hours: 1-5PM (PST). *Felony, Misdemeanor, Civil.*
http://seventhdistrict.ojd.state.or.us
Civil Records: Access: Phone, mail, online, in person. Only the court may perform in person searches. No search fee. Required to search: name, years to search. Civil cases indexed by defendant, plaintiff. Civil records on computer from 1989, index cards back to 1800s. Index remotely online on the statewide OJIN system, call 800-858-9658 for information.
Criminal Records: Access: Phone, mail, online, in person. Only the court may perform in person searches. No search fee. Required to search: name, years to search; also helpful: DOB. Criminal records on computer from 1989, index cards back to 1800s. Online access to criminal records is the same as civil.
General Information: No adoptions, juvenile, sealed by Judge, expunged, mental health records released. Will fax results for an add'l fee. Copy fee: $.25 per page. Cert fee: $5.00. Payee: Gilliam Circuit Court. Personal checks accepted. Prepayment required. Mail requests: SASE required. Mail turnaround time 1-2 days.

County Court 221 S Oregon, PO Box 427, Condon, OR 97823; 541-384-2311; Fax: 541-384-2166. Hours: 8:30AM-Noon, 1-5PM (PST). *Probate.*

Grant County

Circuit Court Box 159 (205 S. Humbolt St), Canyon City, OR 97820; 541-575-1438; Fax: 541-575-2165. Hours: 8AM-Noon, 1-5PM (PST). *Felony, Misdemeanor, Civil.*
www.ojd.state.or.us/grant
Civil Records: Access: Mail, online, in person. Only the court performs in person searches; visitors may not. No search fee. Required to search: name, years to search. Civil cases indexed by defendant, plaintiff. Civil records on computer from 1987, microfiche from 1950-1965, archives back to 1880. Index remotely online on the statewide OJIN system, call 800-858-9658 for information.
Criminal Records: Access: Mail, online, in person. Only the court performs in person searches; visitors may not. No search fee. Required to search: name, years to search. Criminal records on computer from 1987, microfiche from 1950-1965, archives back to 1880. Online access to criminal records is the same as civil.
General Information: No adoptions, juvenile, sealed by Judge, expunged, mental health records released. Copy fee: $.25 per page. Cert fee: $5.00. Payee: Grant County Circuit Court. Personal checks accepted. Prepayment required. Mail requests: SASE required. Mail turnaround time 3-5 days.

County Court 201 Humbolt St #290, Canyon City, OR 97820-6186; 541-575-1675; Fax: 541-575-2248. Hours: 8AM-5PM (PST). *Probate.*

Harney County

Circuit Court 450 N. Buena Vista, Burns, OR 97720; 541-573-5207; Fax: 541-573-5715. Hours: 8AM-12PM; 1PM-5PM (PST). *Felony, Misdemeanor, Civil.*
www.ojd.state.or.us/harney
Civil Records: Access: Phone, fax, mail, online, in person. Both court and visitors may perform in person searches. No search fee. Required to search: name,

years to search. Civil cases indexed by defendant, plaintiff. Civil records on computer from 1988, microfiche from 1970-1979, archives back to 1880. Index remotely online on the statewide OJIN system, call 800-858-9658 for information.
Criminal Records: Access: Phone, fax, mail, online, in person. Both court and visitors may perform in person searches. No search fee. Required to search: name, years to search. Criminal records on computer from 1988, microfiche from 1970-1979, archives back to 1880. Online access to criminal records is the same as civil.
General Information: Public Access terminal is available. No adoptions, juvenile, sealed by Judge, expunged, paternity or mental health records released. Will fax results $2.00 1st page, $1.00 each add'l. Copy fee: $.25 per page. Cert fee: $5.00. Payee: Harney Circuit Court. Personal checks accepted. Prepayment required. Mail requests: SASE required. Mail turnaround time 1-2 days.

County Court 450 N Buena Vista Ave, Burns, OR 97720-1518; 541-573-6641; Fax: 541-573-8370. Hours: 8:30AM-Noon, 1-5PM (PST). *Probate.*
www.co.harney.or.us

Hood River County

Circuit Court 309 State St., Hood River, OR 97031; 541-386-1862; Fax: 541-386-3465. Hours: 8AM-Noon, 1-5PM (PST). *Felony, Misdemeanor, Civil, Eviction, Small Claims, Probate.*
http://seventhdistrict.ojd.state.or.us
Civil Records: Access: Phone, fax, mail, online, in person. Both court and visitors may perform in person searches. No search fee. Required to search: name, years to search. Civil cases indexed by defendant, plaintiff. Civil records on computer from 1989, docket books from 1950. Index remotely online on the statewide OJIN system, call 800-858-9658 for information.
Criminal Records: Access: Phone, fax, mail, online, in person. Both court and visitors may perform in person searches. No search fee. Required to search: name, years to search, DOB. Criminal records on computer from 1989, docket books from 1950. Online access to criminal records is the same as civil.
General Information: Public Access terminal is available. No adoptions, juvenile, sealed by Judge, expunged, paternity or mental health records released. Copy fee: $.25 per page. Cert fee: $5.00. Payee: Hood River Trial Courts. Personal checks accepted. Credit cards accepted. Prepayment required. Mail requests: SASE required. Mail turnaround time 7 days.

Jackson County

Circuit Court 100 S. Oakdale, Medford, OR 97501; 541-776-7171; Fax: 541-776-7057. Hours: 8:30AM-5PM (PST). *Felony, Misdemeanor, Civil Actions, Eviction, Small Claims, Probate.*
http://jackson-court.ojd.state.or.us
Civil Records: Access: Mail, online, in person. Visitors must perform in person searches for themselves. No search fee. Required to search: name, years to search. Civil cases indexed by defendant, plaintiff. Civil records on computer from 1988, prior records on docket books and microfilm. Index remotely online on the statewide OJIN system, call 800-858-9658 for information.
Criminal Records: Access: Mail, online, in person. Visitors must perform in person searches for themselves. No search fee. Required to search: name, years to search, DOB. Criminal records on computer from 1988, prior records on docket books and microfilm. Online access to criminal records is the same as civil.
General Information: Public Access terminal is available. No adoptions, juvenile, sealed by Judge,

expunged, mental health records released. Copy fee: $.25 per page. Cert fee: $5.00. Payee: Jackson County Courts. Personal checks accepted. Credit cards accepted. Prepayment required. Mail requests: SASE required. Mail turnaround time 1 week.

Jefferson County

Circuit Court 75 SE C St., Ste "G", Madras, OR 97741-1750; 541-475-3317; Fax: 541-475-3421. Hours: 8AM-5PM (PST). *Felony, Misdemeanor, Civil, Eviction, Small Claims, Probate.*
Civil Records: Access: Mail, online, in person. Both court and visitors may perform in person searches. No search fee. Required to search: name, years to search. Civil cases indexed by defendant, plaintiff. Civil records on computer from Oct 1986, archives from 1916-1986. Index remotely online on the statewide OJIN system, call 800-858-9658 for information.
Criminal Records: Access: Mail, online, in person. Both court and visitors may perform in person searches. No search fee. Required to search: name, years to search, DOB. Criminal records on computer from Oct 1986, archives from 1916-1986. Online access to criminal records is the same as civil.
General Information: Public Access terminal is available. No adoptions, juvenile, sealed by Judge, expunged, mental health records released. Copy fee: $.25 per page. Cert fee: $5.00. Payee: State of Oregon. Personal checks accepted. Prepayment required. Mail requests: SASE required. Mail turnaround time 1-2 weeks.

Josephine County

Circuit Court Josephine County Courthouse, Rm 254, 500 NW 6th St, Grants Pass, OR 97526; 541-476-2309; Fax: 541-471-2079. Hours: 8AM-4PM (PST). *Felony, Misdemeanor, Civil, Eviction, Small Claims, Probate.*
Civil Records: Access: Fax, mail, online, in person. Both court and visitors may perform in person searches. No search fee. Required to search: name, years to search. Civil cases indexed by defendant, plaintiff. Civil records on computer from 1987, microfilm prior to 1980, archives from 1920, index books. Index remotely online on the statewide OJIN system, call 800-858-9658 for information.
Criminal Records: Access: Fax, mail, online, in person. Both court and visitors may perform in person searches. No search fee. Required to search: name, years to search, DOB. Criminal records on computer from 1987, microfilm prior to 1980, archives from 1920, index books. Online access to criminal records is the same as civil.
General Information: Public Access terminal is available. No adoptions, juvenile, sealed by Judge, expunged, mental health records released. No fee to fax results. Copy fee: $.25 per page. Cert fee: $5.00. Payee: Josephine County Court. Personal checks accepted. Visa, MC accepted. Prepayment required. Mail requests: SASE required. Mail turnaround time 10-15 working days.

Klamath County

Circuit Court 316 Main St, Klamath Falls, OR 97601; 541-883-5503; Civil phone: x222; Criminal phone: x232; Fax: 541-882-6109. Hours: 8AM-5PM (PST). *Felony, Misdemeanor, Civil, Eviction, Small Claims, Probate.*
http://klamath-court.ojd.state.or.us
Civil Records: Access: Mail, fax, online, in person. Both court and visitors may perform in person searches. Search fee: $7.50 if requested by mail. Required to search: name, years to search. Civil cases indexed by defendant, plaintiff. Civil records on computer from 1988, microfiche from 1940-1980. Index remotely online on the statewide OJIN system, call 800-858-9658 for information.

Criminal Records: Access: Mail, fax, online, in person. Both court and visitors may perform in person searches. Search fee: $7.50 if requested by mail. Required to search: name, years to search. Criminal records on computer from 1988, felony cases on microfiche from 1940-1980. Online access to criminal records is the same as civil.
General Information: Public Access terminal is available. No adoptions, juvenile, sealed by Judge, expunged, paternity or mental health records released. Fee to fax results is $2.00 1st page and $1.00 each add'l page. Copy fee: $.25 per page. Cert fee: $5.00. Payee: Klamath County Circuit Court. No Personal checks accepted. Visa, MC accepted. Prepayment required. Mail requests: SASE required. Mail turnaround time 2 weeks.

Lake County

Circuit Court 513 Center St., Lakeview, OR 97630; 541-947-6051; Fax: 541-947-3724. Hours: 8AM-Noon, 1-5PM (PST). *Felony, Misdemeanor, Civil, Eviction, Small Claims, Probate.*
Civil Records: Access: Mail, online, in person. Both court and visitors may perform in person searches. No search fee. Required to search: name, years to search. Civil cases indexed by defendant, plaintiff. Civil records on computer from 1988, index cards prior. Index remotely online on the statewide OJIN system, call 800-858-9658 for information.
Criminal Records: Access: Mail, online, in person. Both court and visitors may perform in person searches. Search fee: None,pre 1988 $7.50. Required to search: name, years to search. Criminal records on computer from 1988, index cards prior. Online access to criminal records is the same as civil.
General Information: Public Access terminal is available. No adoptions, juvenile, sealed by Judge, expunged or mental health records released. Will fax only if local and prepaid; $2.00 1st page, $1.00 each add'l. Copy fee: $.25 per page. Cert fee: $5.00. Payee: Lake County Circuit Court. Personal checks accepted. Prepayment required. Mail requests: SASE required. Mail turnaround time 2 weeks.

Lane County

Circuit Court 125 E. 8th Ave., Eugene, OR 97401; 541-682-4020. Hours: 8AM-5PM (PST). *Felony, Misdemeanor, Civil, Eviction, Small Claims, Probate.*
Civil Records: Access: Online, in person. Visitors must perform in person searches for themselves. No search fee. Required to search: name, years to search. Civil cases indexed by defendant, plaintiff. Civil records on computer from 1983, index books prior. Index remotely online on the statewide OJIN system, call 800-858-9658 for information.
Criminal Records: Access: Online, in person. Visitors must perform in person searches for themselves. No search fee. Required to search: name, years to search. Criminal records on computer from 1983, index books prior. Online access to criminal records is the same as civil.
General Information: Public Access terminal is available. No adoptions, juvenile, sealed by Judge, expunged, mental health records released. Copy fee: $.25 per page. Cert fee: $5.00 plus $.25 per page. Payee: Lane County Circuit Court or Lane County Courts. Personal checks accepted. Credit cards accepted. Accepted in person only. Prepayment required.

Lincoln County

Lincoln County Courts PO Box 100, Newport, OR 97365; 541-265-4236; Fax: 541-265-7561. Hours: 8AM-Noon, 1-5PM (PST). *Felony, Misdemeanor, Civil, Eviction, Small Claims, Probate.*

www.ojd.state.or.us/lincoln
Civil Records: Access: Mail, online, in person. Both court and visitors may perform in person searches. No search fee. Required to search: name. Civil cases indexed by defendant, plaintiff. Civil records on computer from 2/88, archives back to 1893, prior to 1988, years to search must be specified. Index remotely online on the statewide OJIN system, call 800-858-9658 for information.
Criminal Records: Access: Mail, online, in person. Both court and visitors may perform in person searches. No search fee. Required to search: name, years to search. Criminal records on computer from 2/88, archives back to 1893, prior to 1988, years to search must be specified. Online access to criminal records is the same as civil.
General Information: Public Access terminal is available. No adoptions, sealed by Judge, expunged, or mental health records released. Will fax results for $2.00 1st page and $1.00 each add'l. Copy fee: $.25 per page. Cert fee: $5.00 + $.25 per page. Payee: State of Oregon. Personal checks accepted. Visa, MC accepted. $1.00 minimum charge. Prepayment required. Mail requests: SASE required. Mail turnaround time 1 week.

Linn County

Circuit Court PO Box 1749, Albany, OR 97321; Civil phone: 541-967-3845; Criminal phone: 541-967-3841. Hours: 8AM-5PM (PST). *Felony, Misdemeanor, Civil, Eviction, Small Claims, Probate.*
www.ojd.state.or.us/linn-circuit
Civil Records: Access: Mail, online, in person. Both court and visitors may perform in person searches. No search fee. Required to search: name, years to search. Civil cases indexed by defendant, plaintiff. Civil records on computer from June 1987, archives back to 1863. Index remotely online on the statewide OJIN system, call 800-858-9658 for information.
Criminal Records: Access: Mail, online, in person. Both court and visitors may perform in person searches. No search fee. Required to search: name, years to search, DOB. Criminal records on computer from June 1987, archives back to 1863. Online access to criminal records is the same as civil.
General Information: Public Access terminal is available. No adoptions, juvenile, sealed by judge, expunged, paternity or mental health records released. Will not fax results. Copy fee: $.25 per page. Cert fee: $5.00. Payee: State of Oregon. Personal checks accepted. Visa, MC or debit card accepted. Prepayment required. Mail requests: SASE required. Mail turnaround time 5-10 days.

Malheur County

Circuit Court 251 B St West, Vale, OR 97918; 541-473-5171; Fax: 541-473-2213. Hours: 8AM-5PM (MST). *Felony, Misdemeanor, Civil, Eviction, Small Claims.*
www.ojd.state.or.us/malheur
Civil Records: Access: Mail, online, in person. Both court and visitors may perform in person searches. Search fee: No fee, unless access needed to archived records. Required to search: name, years to search. Civil cases indexed by defendant, plaintiff. Civil records on computer from July 1988, archived from 1887. Index remotely online on the statewide OJIN system, call 800-858-9658 for information.
Criminal Records: Access: Mail, online, in person. Both court and visitors may perform in person searches. Search fee: No fee unless archived records needed. Required to search: name, years to search, DOB. Criminal records on computer from July 1988, archived from 1887. Online access to criminal records is the same as civil.

General Information: Public Access terminal is available. No adoptions, juvenile, sealed by Judge, expunged, mental health records released. Fee to fax results is $2.50 1st page, $1.00 ea add'l. Incominf fax fee: $2.00 1st page, $1.00 2nd page. Copy fee: $.25 per page. Cert fee: $5.00. Payee: Trial Court Administrator. Personal checks accepted. Visa, MC accepted. Accepted for filing fees only. Prepayment required. Mail requests: SASE requested. Turnaround time 2 weeks minimum.

County Court 251 B St West, #4, Vale, OR 97918; 541-473-5123; Civil phone: 541-473-5151; Fax: 541-473-5523. Hours: 8:30AM-Noon, 1-5:00PM (MST). *Probate.*
www.sos.state.or.us

Marion County

Circuit Court PO Box 12869 (100 High St NE), Salem, OR 97309; 503-588-5101; Fax: 503-373-4360. Hours: 8AM-5PM (PST). *Felony, Misdemeanor, Civil, Eviction, Small Claims, Probate.*
http://marion-court.ojd.state.or.us
Civil Records: Access: Mail, online, in person. Both court and visitors may perform in person searches. No search fee. Required to search: name, years to search. Civil cases indexed by defendant, plaintiff. Civil records on computer from October 1986, prior to October 1986 on microfiche/microfilm. Index remotely online on the statewide OJIN system, call 800-858-9658 for information.
Criminal Records: Access: Mail, online, in person. Both court and visitors may perform in person searches. No search fee. Required to search: name, years to search, signed release; also helpful: DOB, SSN. Criminal records on computer from October 1986, prior to October 1986 on microfiche/microfilm. Online access to criminal records is the same as civil. Online access to the County sexual offenders registry is free at www.open.org/~msheriff/sexnotif.htm.
General Information: Public Access terminal is available. No adoptions, juvenile, sealed by Judge, expunged, paternity or mental health records released. Will fax results for $2.00 1st page; $1.00 each add'l page. Copy fee: $.50 per double-sided page. Cert fee: $5.00. Payee: State of Oregon. Personal checks accepted. Prepayment required. Mail requests: SASE required. Mail turnaround time minimum 5 days.

Morrow County

Circuit Court PO Box 609, Heppner, OR 97836; 541-676-5264; Fax: 541-676-9902. Hours: 8AM-Noon, 1-5PM (PST). *Felony, Misdemeanor, Civil, Eviction, Small Claims, Probate.*
www.ojd.state.or.us/morrow
Civil Records: Access: Phone, fax, mail, in person. Both court and visitors may perform in person searches. No search fee. Required to search: name, years to search. Civil cases indexed by defendant, plaintiff. Civil records on computer from 1987, archives back to 1940, index cards, docket books by case #. Index remotely online on the statewide OJIN system, call 800-858-9658 for information.
Criminal Records: Access: Phone, fax, mail, online, in person. Both court and visitors may perform in person searches. No search fee. Required to search: name, years to search, DOB. Criminal records on computer from 1987, archives back to 1940, index cards, docket books by case #. Online access to criminal records is the same as civil.
General Information: No adoptions, juvenile, sealed by Judge, expunged, paternity or mental health records released. No fee to fax results. Copy fee: $.25 per page. Cert fee: $5.00. Payee: Circuit Court. Personal checks accepted. Prepayment required. Mail

requests: SASE required. Mail turnaround time 1-3 days.

Multnomah County

Circuit Court 1021 SW 4th Ave, Rm 131, Portland, OR 97204; 503-988-3003. Hours: 8AM-4:30PM (Tele: 8:30-11AM; 1-3:30PM) (PST). *Felony, Misdemeanor, Civil Actions Over $10,000, Probate.*
Civil Records: Access: Mail, online, in person. Both court and visitors may perform in person searches. No search fee. Required to search: name, years to search. Civil cases indexed by defendant, plaintiff. Civil records on computer from 1988, microfiche, index books, docket books back to 1857. Index remotely online on the statewide OJIN system, call 800-858-9658 for information.
Criminal Records: Access: Mail, online, in person. Both court and visitors may perform in person searches. No search fee. Required to search: name, years to search; also helpful: DOB. Criminal records on computer from 1988, microfiche, index books, docket books back to 1857. Online access to criminal records is the same as civil.
General Information: Public Access terminal is available. No adoptions, juvenile, sealed by Judge, expunged or mental health records released. Copy fee: $.25 per page. Cert fee: $5.00. Payee: State of Oregon. Personal checks accepted. Prepayment required. Mail requests: SASE required. Mail turnaround time 4-5 days.

Circuit Court - Civil Division 1021 SW 4th Ave, Rm 210, Portland, OR 97204; 503-988-3022. Hours: 8:30AM-5PM (Tele: 8:30-5PM) (PST). *Civil Actions, Eviction, Small Claims.*
www.ojd.state.or.us/multnomah
Civil Records: Access: Phone, mail, online, in person. Both court and visitors may perform in person searches. Some limitations may apply. No search fee. Required to search: name, years to search. Civil cases indexed by defendant, plaintiff. Civil records on computer from 1988, microfiche 1984-1988, docket cards by case # and yr. Index remotely online on the statewide OJIN system, call 800-858-9658 for information.
General Information: Public Access terminal is available. No adoptions, juvenile, sealed by Judge, expunged, paternity or mental health records released. Copy fee: $.25 per page. Cert fee: $5.00 per document; exemplified-$10.00. Payee: State of Oregon. Personal checks accepted. Prepayment required. Mail requests: SASE required. Mail turnaround time 5 days.

Polk County

Circuit Court Polk County Courthouse, Rm 301, 850 Main St, Dallas, OR 97338; 503-623-3154; Civil phone: 503-623-3154; Criminal phone: 503-831-1778. Hours: 8AM-5PM (PST). *Felony, Misdemeanor, Civil, Eviction, Small Claims, Probate.*
www.ojd.state.or.us/plk/index.htm
Note: Fax for criminal is 503-831-1779; for civil is 503-623-6614.
Civil Records: Access: Phone, fax, mail, online, in person. Both court and visitors may perform in person searches. No search fee. Required to search: name, years to search. Civil cases indexed by defendant, plaintiff. Civil records on computer from 1985, microfilm, archives from 1969 (District) back to 1800s (Circuit). Index remotely online on the statewide OJIN system, call 800-858-9658 for information.
Criminal Records: Access: Phone, fax, mail, online, in person. Both court and visitors may perform in person searches. No search fee. Required to search:

name, years to search, DOB; also helpful: SSN. Criminal records on computer from 1985, microfilm, archives from 1969 (District) back to 1800s (Circuit). Online access to criminal records is the same as civil.
General Information: Public Access terminal is available. No adoptions, juvenile, sealed by Judge, expunged, mental health records released. No fee to fax results. Copy fee: $.25 per page. Cert fee: $5.00. Payee: Trial Court Administrator. Personal checks accepted. Visa, MC accepted. Credit cards accepted in person and for phone requests only. Prepayment required. Mail requests: SASE required. Mail turnaround time 2 weeks.

Sherman County

Circuit Court PO Box 402, Moro, OR 97039; 541-565-3650. Hours: 1-5PM (PST). *Felony, Misdemeanor, Civil.*
Civil Records: Access: Phone, mail, online, in person. Both court and visitors may perform in person searches. No search fee. Required to search: name, years to search. Civil cases indexed by defendant, plaintiff. Civil records on computer from 1992, microfiche up to 1987, index books, judgment docket books. Index remotely online on the statewide OJIN system, call 800-858-9658 for information.
Criminal Records: Access: Phone, mail, online, in person. Both court and visitors may perform in person searches. No search fee. Required to search: name, years to search, DOB. Criminal records on computer from 1992, microfiche up to 1987, index books, judgment docket books. Online access to criminal records is the same as civil.
General Information: Public Access terminal is available. No adoptions, juvenile, sealed by Judge, expunged, paternity or mental health records released. Will fax results for a fee of $2.00 1st.page, $1.00 per page. Copy fee: $.25 per page. Cert fee: $5.00. Payee: Sherman County Circuit Court. Personal checks accepted. Prepayment required. Mail requests: SASE required. Mail turnaround time 2-5 days.

County Court PO Box 365, Moro, OR 97039; 541-565-3606; Fax: 541-565-3312. Hours: 8AM-5PM (PST). *Probate.*

Tillamook County .

Circuit Court 201 Laurel Ave, Tillamook, OR 97141; 503-842-8014; Fax: 503-842-2597. Hours: 8AM-Noon; 1PM-5PM (PST). *Felony, Misdemeanor, Civil, Eviction, Small Claims, Probate.*
Civil Records: Access: Mail, fax, online, in person. Both court and visitors may perform in person searches. Search fee: None, unless massive searching needed. Required to search: name, years to search. Civil cases indexed by defendant, plaintiff. Civil records on computer from 1987, prior on case files. Index remotely online on the statewide OJIN system, call 800-858-9658 for information.
Criminal Records: Access: Mail, fax, online, in person. Both court and visitors may perform in person searches. Search fee: None, unless massive searching needed. Required to search: name, years to search. Criminal records on computer from 1987, prior on case files. Online access to criminal records is the same as civil.
General Information: Public Access terminal is available. No adoptions, juvenile, sealed by Judge, expunged, paternity or mental health records released. Will fax results for $1.00 1st page; $2.00 each add'l. Copy fee: $.25 per page. Cert fee: $5.00. Payee: Trial Court Administrator. Personal checks accepted, Visa, Mastercard accepted with minimum payment of $3.00. Prepayment required. Mail requests: SASE required. Mail turnaround time 2-3 days.

Umatilla County

Circuit Court PO Box 1307, Pendleton, OR 97801; 541-278-0341; Fax: 541-276-9030. Hours: 8AM-Noon; 1PM-5PM (PST). *Felony, Misdemeanor, Civil, Eviction, Small Claims, Probate.*

www.ojd.state.or.us/umatilla

Civil Records: Access: Mail, online, in person. Both court and visitors may perform in person searches. Search fee: $12.65 per hour. Required to search: name, years to search. Civil cases indexed by defendant, plaintiff. Civil records on computer from 11/86, microfiche, index card, docket books. Index remotely online on the statewide OJIN system, call 800-858-9658 for information.

Criminal Records: Access: Mail, online, in person. Both court and visitors may perform in person searches. Search fee: $12.65 per hour. Required to search: name, years to search. Criminal records on computer from 11/86, microfiche, index card, docket books. Online access to criminal records is the same as civil.

General Information: Public Access terminal is available. No adoptions, juvenile, sealed by Judge, expunged, paternity or mental health records released. Will not fax results. Copy fee: $.25 per page. Cert fee: $5.00. Payee: Trial Court Administrator. Personal checks accepted. Credit cards accepted. Prepayment required. Mail requests: SASE required. Mail turnaround time 1-3 weeks.

Union County

Circuit Court 1008 K Ave, La Grande, OR 97850; 541-962-9500; Fax: 541-963-0444. Hours: 8AM-Noon, 1-5PM (PST). *Felony, Misdemeanor, Civil, Eviction, Small Claims, Probate.*

www.ojd.state.or.us/union

Civil Records: Access: Mail, online, in person. Both court and visitors may perform in person searches. No search fee. Required to search: name, years to search. Civil cases indexed by defendant, plaintiff. Civil records on computer from 1986, archives back to 1800s, on ledger books/docket books. Index remotely online on the statewide OJIN system, call 800-858-9658 for information.

Criminal Records: Access: Mail, online, in person. Both court and visitors may perform in person searches. No search fee. Required to search: name, years to search, DOB. Criminal records on computer from 1986, archives back to 1800s, on ledger books/docket books. Online access to criminal records is the same as civil.

General Information: Public Access terminal is available. No adoptions, juvenile, sealed by Judge, expunged, paternity or mental health records released. Copy fee: $.25 per page. Cert fee: $5.00. Payee: Circuit Court. Personal checks accepted. Visa, MC accepted. Prepayment required. Mail requests: SASE required. Mail turnaround time 1-2 weeks.

Wallowa County

Circuit Court 101 S River St, Rm 204, Enterprise, OR 97828; 541-426-4991; Fax: 541-426-4992. Hours: 8AM-Noon; 1PM-5PM (PST). *Felony, Misdemeanor, Civil, Eviction, Small Claims, Probate.*

www.ojd.state.or.us/wallowa

Civil Records: Access: Phone, mail, online, in person. Both court and visitors may perform in person searches. No search fee. Required to search: name, years to search. Civil cases indexed by defendant, plaintiff. Civil records on computer from 1987, prior

on docket books. Index remotely online on the statewide OJIN system, call 800-858-9658 for information.

Criminal Records: Access: Phone, mail, online, in person. Both court and visitors may perform in person searches. No search fee. Required to search: name, years to search. Criminal records on computer from 1987, prior on docket books. Online access to criminal records is the same as civil.

General Information: Public Access terminal is available. No adoptions, juvenile, sealed by Judge, expunged, paternity or mental health records released. Will not fax results. Copy fee: $.25 per page. Cert fee: $5.00. Payee: Circuit Court. Personal checks accepted. Prepayment required. Copy fees may be billed. Mail requests: SASE required. Mail turnaround time 1-3 days.

Wasco County

Circuit Court PO Box 1400, The Dalles, OR 97058-1400; 541-296-3154; Civil phone: 541-506-2704; Criminal phone: 541-506-2708; Probate phone: 541-506-2704; Fax: 541-506-2711. Hours: 8AM-Noon,1-5PM (PST). *Felony, Misdemeanor, Civil, Eviction, Small Claims, Probate.*

http://seventhdistrict.ojd.state.or.us/html/wasco.html

Civil Records: Access: Phone, fax, mail, online, in person. Both court and visitors may perform in person searches. No search fee. Required to search: name, years to search. Civil cases indexed by defendant, plaintiff. Civil records on computer from 1989, prior records in docket books by case # and year back to 1900s. Index remotely online on the statewide OJIN system, call 800-858-9658 for information.

Criminal Records: Access: Phone, fax, mail, online, in person. Both court and visitors may perform in person searches. No search fee. Required to search: name, years to search, DOB. Criminal records on computer from 1989, prior records in docket books by case # and year back to 1900s. Online access to criminal records is the same as civil.

General Information: Public Access terminal is available. No adoptions, juvenile, sealed by Judge, expunged, paternity or mental health records released. Fee to fax results is $.25 per page. Copy fee: $.25 per page. Cert fee: $5.00. Payee: Trial Court Administrator. Personal checks accepted. Visa, MC accepted. Prepayment required. Mail requests: SASE required. Mail turnaround time 2-3 days.

Washington County

Circuit Court 150 N 1st, Hillsboro, OR 97124; 503-846-8888 x2302 (civ) x6060 (crim); Fax: 503-846-6087. Hours: 8-11:30AM, 12:30-3PM (PST). *Felony, Misdemeanor, Civil, Eviction, Small Claims, Probate.*

Civil Records: Access: Phone, mail, online, in person. Both court and visitors may perform in person searches. No search fee. Required to search: name, years to search. Civil cases indexed by defendant, plaintiff. Civil records on computer from 1982, prior on docket books. Index remotely online on the statewide OJIN system, call 800-858-9658 for information.

Criminal Records: Access: Phone, mail, online, in person. Both court and visitors may perform in person searches. No search fee. Required to search: name, years to search, DOB. Criminal records on computer from 1982, prior on docket books. Online access to criminal records is the same as civil.

General Information: Public Access terminal is available. No adoptions, juvenile, sealed by Judge, expunged, paternity or mental health records released.

Copy fee: $.25 per page. Cert fee: $5.00. Payee: State of Oregon. Personal checks accepted. Prepayment required. Mail turnaround time 2-5 days.

Wheeler County

Circuit Court PO Box 308, Fossil, OR 97830; 541-763-2541; Fax: 541-763-2026. Hours: 8:30AM-11:30AM (PST). *Felony, Misdemeanor, Civil.*

http://seventhdistrict.ojd.state.or.us

Civil Records: Access: Phone, mail, online, in person. Both court and visitors may perform in person searches. No search fee. Required to search: name, years to search. Civil cases indexed by defendant. Civil records on computer from 1989, docket books by case # and yr. Index remotely online on the statewide OJIN system, call 800-858-9658 for information.

Criminal Records: Access: Phone, mail, online, in person. Only the court performs in person searches; visitors may not. No search fee. Required to search: name, years to search, DOB. Criminal records on computer from 1989, docket books by case # and yr. Online access to criminal records is the same as civil.

General Information: No adoptions, juvenile, sealed by Judge, expunged, paternity or mental health records released. Will fax results to local or toll free line, otherwise extra fee incurred. Copy fee: $.25 per page. Cert fee: $5.00. Payee: Wheeler Circuit Court. Personal checks accepted. Prepayment required. Mail requests: SASE required. Mail turnaround time 1 week.

County Court PO Box 327 (701 Adams, Rm 204), Fossil, OR 97830; 541-763-2400; Fax: 541-763-2026. Hours: 8:30AM-4PM (PST). *Probate.*

Note: Probate index available remotely online on the statewide OJIN system, call 800-858-9658 for information.

Yamhill County

Circuit Court 535 NE Fifth, McMinnville, OR 97128; 503-434-7530; Fax: 503-472-5805. Hours: 9AM-Noon, 1-5PM (PST). *Felony, Misdemeanor, Civil, Eviction, Small Claims, Probate.*

http://yamhill-court.ojd.state.or.us

Civil Records: Access: Mail, online, in person. Both court and visitors may perform in person searches. No search fee. Required to search: name, years to search. Civil cases indexed by defendant, plaintiff. Civil records on computer from 1987, microfiche (10 yrs Dist, unlimited Circuit), archives back to 1900s, docket books by case # and yr. Index remotely online on the statewide OJIN system, call 800-858-9658 for information.

Criminal Records: Access: Mail, online, in person. Both court and visitors may perform in person searches. No search fee. Required to search: name, years to search, DOB. Criminal records on computer from 1987, microfiche (10 yrs Dist, unlimited Circuit), archives back to 1900s, docket books by case # and yr. Online access to criminal records is the same as civil.

General Information: Public Access terminal is available. No adoptions, juvenile, sealed by Judge, expunged or mental health records released. Copy fee: $.25 per page. Cert fee: $5.00. Payee: Trial Court. Two party, payroll checks not accepted. Visa, MC accepted. Prepayment required. Mail requests: SASE requested. Turnaround time 1-7 days.

Oregon Recording Offices

ORGANIZATION: 36 counties, 36 recording offices. The recording officer is County Clerk. 35 counties are in the Pacific Time Zone (PST) and one is in the Mountain Time Zone (MST).

REAL ESTATE RECORDS: Some counties will not perform real estate searches. Search fees vary. Many counties will search all liens together for $12.50 per name. Copy fees are usually $.25 per page. Certification usually costs $3.75 per document. The Assessor keeps tax and ownership records.

UCC RECORDS: Financing statements are filed at the state level, except for real estate related collateral. Many county clerks will perform UCC searches, fees vary from $3.50 to $13.50, we suggest to call first.

TAX LIEN RECORDS: All federal and state tax liens on personal property are filed with the Secretary of State. Other federal and state tax liens are filed with the County Clerk. Most counties will perform tax lien searches and include both with a UCC search for an extra $7.50 per name. Search fees vary widely.

OTHER LIENS: County tax, public utility, construction, judgment, hospital.

ONLINE ACCESS: A few counties offer Internet access to assessor records. There is no statewide system available.

Baker County

County Clerk, 1995 Third St, #150, Baker, OR 97814-3398. **Phone**-County Clerk, R/E & UCC Recording-541-523-8207; fax-541-523-8240; hours 8AM-5PM www.bakercounty.org
Will not search records. RE record copy- $.25 per page. Cert fee: $4.00 1st page. Payee: Baker County Clerk. **Online Access to Property, Assessor records:** Access to the assessor property database is free at www.bakercounty.org/Assessor/Assessor_Search.html. **Other phones:** Assessor-541-523-8203; Treasurer-541-523-8221; Elections-541-523-8207; Vital Records-541-731-4095.

Benton County

County Clerk, 120 NW 4th St, Rm 4, Corvallis, OR 97330. **Phone**-County Clerk, R/E & UCC Recording-541-766-6831; fax-541-766-6675; hours 8AM-5PM www.co.benton.or.us
UCC records search per debtor- $3.75. Federal/state combined tax lien search- $3.75 per debtor. Will search real estate records as time allows. RE record copy- $.25 per page. Copy fee is $.25 per page. Cert fee: $3.75 per record. Payee: Benton County Recorder. **Online Access to Real Estate, Assessor, Property, Inmate, 30-day Released Inmate, Most Wanted records:** The County is developing a Geographic Information System Internet site for viewing property information at www.co.benton.or.us/irm/gis/GISpage.htm. Search fee is $3.75 per record found. Also, assessment and taxation database download is free at www.co.benton.or.us/assessor/data_extract.html.
Search the sheriff's inmate list and 30-day release list as well as Most Wanted list at www.co.benton.or.us/sheriff/index.html. Also, sheriff's wanted "absconders" list at www.co.benton.or.us/sheriff/corrections/bccc/Absconders/. Also, a law enforcement case system may soon offer open case data. **Other phones:** Assessor-541-766-6855; Treasurer-541-766-6808; Elections-541-766-6756; Vital Records-503-731-4108.

Clackamas County

County Clerk, 2051 Kaen Rd, Oregon City, OR 97045. **Phone**-County Clerk, R/E & UCC Recording- 503-655-8551; hours 8:30AM-5PM M,T,Th,F; 9:30AM-5PM W www.co.clackamas.or.us/clerk
Will not search records. Copy fee- $.25 per page. Cert fee: $3.75 per doc. Payee: Clackamas County Clerk. **Online Access to Real Property, Most Wanted records:** Records on the County Metromap

database are free at http://topaz.metro-region.org/metromap/metromap.cfm. No name searching. Also, search the sheriff's most wanted list at www.co.clackamas.or.us/sheriff/mostwanted.htm.
Other phones: Assessor-503-655-8671; Treasurer-503-655-8915; Elections-503-655-8510; Vital Records-503-731-4095.

Clatsop County

County Clerk, PO Box 178, Astoria, OR 97103-0178. **Phone**-County Clerk, R/E & UCC Recording- 503-325-8511; fax-503-325-9307; hours 8:30AM-4:00PM www.co.clatsop.or.us
UCC records search per debtor- $3.75. Will not search tax liens. Will search real estate records. Copy fee- $.25 per page. **Other phones:** Assessor-503-325-8522; Treasurer-503-325-8565; Elections-503-325-8511; Vital Records-503-325-8511.

Columbia County

County Clerk, Courthouse, St. Helens, OR 97051-2041. **Phone**-County Clerk, R/E & UCC Recording- 503-397-3796; fax-503-397-7266; hours Recording hrs 9pm-4pm. Will not search records. RE record copy- $3.75 + $.25 per page. UCC copy- $3.75 + $.25 per page. Cert fee: $3.75 per doc. Payee: Columbia County Clerk. **Other phones:** Assessor-503-397-2240; Treasurer-503-397-7252; Elections-503-397-7214 & 3796; Vital Records-503-397-3796.

Coos County

County Clerk, 250 N Baxter, Courthouse, Coquille, OR 97423-1899. **Phone**-541-396-3121, R/E Recording-541-396-3121 x223, UCC Recording-541-396-3121 x223; fax-541-396-6551; hours 8AM-5PM (Closed to public: Noon-1PM) www.co.coos.or.us
UCC records search per debtor- $3.75. Search request using non-standard form (per name)- $12.50. Will not search real estate or tax lien records. RE record copy- $4.00 1st page, $.25 each add'l. UCC copy- $.25 per page. Cert fee: $3.75 per cert. Payee: Coos County Clerk. **Online Access to Assessor, Property, Sale records:** Access to the assessor property and sales data is free at http://coos.gtrsoft.com. **Other phones:** Assessor-541-396-3121 x274; Treasurer- x333; Elections- x301.

Crook County

County Clerk, 300 E. Third, Prineville, OR 97754. **Phone**-541-447-6553; fax-541-416-2145; 8AM-5PM
Will not search UCC records. Federal/state combined Tax lien search- $3.75 per debtor, paid in advance. Will search real estate records. RE record copy- $1.00

per page. Cert fee: $3.75 per cert. Payee: County Clerk. **Other phones:** Assessor-541-447-4133; Treasurer-541-447-6554; Elections-541-447-6553.

Curry County

County Clerk, PO Box 746, Gold Beach, OR 97444. **Phone**-County Clerk, R/E & UCC Recording- 541-247-3295; fax-541-247-6440; hours 8:30AM-4PM www.co.curry.or.us
Will not search UCC records. Tax lien search- $12.50 per debtor. Will search real estate records. Record copy- $.25 per page. Cert fee: $7.75 1st page, $.25 each add'l. Payee: Curry County Clerk. **Other phones:** Assessor-541-247-3294; Treasurer-541-247-3299; Elections-541-247-3297; Vital Records-503-731-4095.

Deschutes County

County Clerk, 1300 NW Wall St. #200, Bend, OR 97701. **Phone**-County Clerk, R/E & UCC Recording-541-388-6549; fax-541-389-6830; hours 8AM-4PM (recording hours) http://recordings.co.deschutes.or.us
Will not search records. RE record copy- $.25 per page + $3.75 location fee. UCC copy- $.25 per page + $3.75 location fee. Cert fee: $3.75 per doc. Payee: Deschutes County Clerk. **Online Access to Real Estate, Deed, Mortgage, Lien, Assessor, Property Tax records:** To access records on the Deschutes County "Assessor Inquiry System" website, go to www.co.deschutes.or.us/dial.cfm. Access tax information, assessment, appraisal details, ownership, sales information, transaction histories, account histories, land use records, and lot numbers for no fee. Also, search real estate, deeds, mortgages, liens on the clerk's recording system web inquiry for free at http://recordings.co.deschutes.or.us. Free registration for username and password is required. **Other phones:** Assessor-541-388-6508; Treasurer-541-388-6540; Elections-541-388-6546.

Douglas County

County Clerk, PO Box 10, Roseburg, OR 97470. **Phone**-541-440-4322, R/E Recording-541-440-4320; fax-541-440-4408; hours 8AM-4PM
Will not search UCC records. Tax lien search- $12.00 per debtor. Will search real estate records. Copy fee- $.50 per page; $2.50 min. Cert fee: $3.75 per doc. Payee: Douglas County Clerk. **Online Access to Assessor, Property records:** Access to the assessor property data is free at www.co.douglas.or.us/puboaa/cgi/oaasearch.pl. **Other phones:** Assessor-541-440-4222; Treasurer-541-440-3311; Elections-541-440-4252.

Gilliam County

County Clerk, PO Box 427, Condon, OR 97823. **Phone**-County Clerk, R/E & UCC Recording- 541-384-2311; fax-541-384-2166; 8:30AM-Noon, 1-5PM
UCC records search per debtor- $5.00. Tax lien search- $12.50 per debtor. Will not search real estate records. RE record copy- $.25 per page. UCC copy-$.25 per page. Cert fee: $3.75 per cert. Payee: Gilliam County Clerk. **Other phones:** Assessor-541-384-3781; Treasurer-541-384-6321; Elections-541-384-2311; Vital Records-541-384-2311.

Grant County

County Clerk, 201 S. Humbolt, #290, Canyon City, OR 97820. **Phone**-County Clerk, R/E & UCC Recording-541-575-1675; fax-541-575-2248.
UCC records search per debtor- $13.00. Will search real estate records. RE record copy- $3.75 per doc. UCC copy- $3.75 per doc. Cert fee: $3.75 per copy. Payee: County Clerk. **Other phones:** Assessor-541-575-0107; Treasurer-541-575-1798; Elections-541-575-1675.

Harney County

County Clerk, 450 N. Buena Vista, Burns, OR 97720. **Phone**-County Clerk, R/E & UCC Recording- 541-573-6641; fax-541-573-8370; hours 8:30AM-5PM (closed 1 hr for lunch) www.co.harney.or.us/
Will not search UCC or real estate records. Tax lien search- $12.50 per debtor. Cert fee: $3.75 per doc; $.50 per page. Payee: Harney County Clerk. **Other phones:** Assessor-541-573-8367; Treasurer-541-573-6541; Elections-541-573-6641.

Hood River County

County Clerk, 601 State St., Hood River, OR 97031-1871. **Phone**-541-386-1442/or/6849, R/E Recording-541-387-6849, UCC Recording-541-387-6849; fax-541-387-6864; hours 8AM-5PM. Will not search records. RE record copy- $3.75 1st page; $.25 each add'l. UCC copy- $3.75 1st page; $.25 each add'l. Cert fee: $7.75. Payee: Hood River County. **Other phones:** Assessor-541-386-4522; Treasurer-541-386-1301; Elections-541-386-1442.

Jackson County

County Clerk, 10 S. Oakdale, Rm 216A, Medford, OR 97501. **Phone**-541-774-6147, R/E Recording-541-774-6152; fax-541-774-6714; hours 8AM-4PM www.jacksoncounty.org
Will not search UCC or real estate records. Separate federal/state combined tax lien search- $4.00 per debtor Record copy- $4.00 1st page, $.25 each add'l. Cert fee: $3.75 per cert. Payee: County Clerk. **Other phones:** Assessor-541-774-6059; Treasurer-541-774-6541; Elections-541-774-6147.

Jefferson County

County Clerk, 66 S.E. D St, #C, Madras, OR 97741. **Phone**-County Clerk, R/E & UCC Recording- 541-475-4451; fax-541-325-5018.
Will search only UCC 1A and UCC 3A records. UCC search per debtor- $12.00. Federal/state combined tax lien search- $12.50 per debtor. Will not search real estate records. Copy fee-$.50 for microfilm copy; $.25 for scanned image. Cert fee: $3.75. Payee: Jefferson County. **Other phones:** Assessor-541-475-2443; Treasurer-541-475-4458; Elections-541-475-4451.

Josephine County

County Clerk, PO Box 69, Grants Pass, OR 97528. **Phone**-County Clerk, R/E & UCC Recording- 541-474-5240; fax-541-476-5246; hours 9AM-4PM
Will not search records. RE record copy- $4.00 per page. UCC copy- $4.00 per page. Cert fee: $3.75 per doc. Payee: Josephine-Co Clerk. **Other phones:**

Assessor-541-474-5260; Treasurer-541-474-5235; Elections-541-474-5243.

Klamath County

County Clerk, 305 Main St., Klamath Falls, OR 97601. **Phone**-800-377-6094, 541-883-5134, R/E Recording-541-883-5134, UCC Recording-541-883-5134; fax-541-885-6757; hours 8AM-5PM; Recording hours: 8AM-4PM www.co.klamath.or.us
Will not search records. Record copy- $1.00 per page. Cert fee: $7.75 per doc. Payee: Klamath County Clerk. **Other phones:** Assessor-541-883-5111; Treasurer-541-883-4297; Elections-541-883-5134.

Lake County

County Clerk, 513 Center St, Lakeview, OR 97630-1539. **Phone**-541-947-6006; fax-541-947-6015; hours 8:30AM-5PM
UCC records search per debtor- $10.00. Tax liens included in UCC search if requested for $12.50 total fee. Separate federal/state combined tax lien search- $7.50 per debtor. Real estate owner, mortgage, and property transfer searches available. RE record copy- $.25 per page. UCC copy- $4.00 1st.page per page.$.25 add'l. Cert fee: $3.75 per cert. Payee: Lake County Clerk. **Other phones:** Assessor-541-947-6000.

Lane County

County Clerk, 125 E. 8th Ave, Eugene, OR 97401. **Phone**-541-682-3654; fax-541-682-3330; hours 8AM-5PM; Recording 9AM-Noon, 1-4PM
Will not search UCC records. Federal/state combined tax lien search- $3.75 per doc by mail only. Will do real estate record searches by mail only. Copy fee-$.25 per page. Cert fee: $3.75 per cert. Payee: Lane County Clerk. **Online Access to Assessor, Real Estate, Property records:** Property records on the County Tax Map site are free at www.co.lane.or.us/taxmap/TaxMapSelect.asp. No name searching. Also, access to the Regional Land Information Database RLID is by subscription. Visit www.rlid.org or call Eric at 541-682-4338 for more information or signup. Initiation fee is $200; monthly access fee is $80.00. **Other phones:** Assessor-541-687-4321.

Lincoln County

County Clerk, 225 W. Olive St, Rm 201, Newport, OR 97365-3869. **Phone**-County Clerk, R/E & UCC Recording- 541-265-4131; fax-541-265-4950; hours 8:30AM-5PM
Will not search records. RE record copy- $3.75 + $.25 per page. UCC copy- $3.75 + $.25 per page. Cert fee: $7.50 per cert + $.25 per page. Payee: Lincoln County Clerk. **Other phones:** Assessor-541-265-4102; Treasurer-541-265-4139; Elections-541-265-4131.

Linn County

County Clerk, PO Box 100, Albany, OR 97321. **Phone**-541-967-3829; fax-541-926-5109; hours 8:30AM-5PM www.co.linn.or.us
UCC records search per debtor- $4.00. **Online Access to Assessor, Real Estate, Property Sale records:** Records on the County Property Records database are free at www.co.linn.or.us/assessor/NewPropSearch.asp. Also, property sale data is free at www.co.linn.or.us/assessorshomep/sale_web.htm. **Other phones:** Assessor-541-967-3808; Treasurer-541-967-3859; Elections-541-967-3831.

Malheur County

County Clerk, 251 B St West, #4, Vale, OR 97918. **Phone**-County Clerk, R/E & UCC Recording- 541-473-5151; fax-541-473-5523; hours 8:30AM-5PM MST www.malheurco.org

UCC records search per debtor- $3.75. Tax lien search- $2.75 per debtor. Will search real estate records. Copy fee-$.25 per page. Cert fee: $3.75 per name + $.25 per copy. Payee: County Clerk. **Other phones:** Assessor-541-473-5117; Treasurer-541-473-5165; Vital Records-541-889-7279.

Marion County

County Clerk, PO Box 14500, Salem, OR 97309. **Phone**-503-588-5225; fax-503-588-5237; hours 8:30AM-5PM http://clerk.co.marion.or.us/records
Will not search records. Copy fee- $.25 per page. Cert fee: $3.75. Payee: Marion County. **Online Access to Jail Inmate, Sex Offender records:** Access to the sheriff's database of inmates and sex offenders is free at http://sheriff.co.marion.or.us. **Other phones:** Assessor-503-588-5236; Elections-503-588-5041.

Morrow County

Chief Deputy Clerk, PO Box 338, Heppner, OR 97836. **Phone**-541-676-9061, R/E Recording-541-676-5604, UCC Recording-541-676-5604; fax-541-676-9876. www.rootsweb.com/~ormorrow/MorrowCountyCourthouse.htm
Will not search UCC or real estate records. UCC copy-$.25 per page. Cert fee: $3.75. **Other phones:** Assessor-541-676-5607; Treasurer-541-676-5630; Elections-541-676-5607; Vital Records-541-676-5603.

Multnomah County

County Clerk, PO Box 5007, Portland, OR 97208-5007. **Phone**-County Clerk, R/E & UCC Recording-503-988-3034; fax-503-988-3330; hours 8AM-5PM; Phone hours: 9AM-4:30PM
www.co.multnomah.or.us/dss/at/index.html
Will not search records. Records prior to 1850 are at Clackamas County. UCC copy- $.25 per page; $4.00 min. Cert fee: $3.00 per cert. Payee: Multnomah County Recorder. **Online Access to Real Property, Released Inmate, Restaurant Inspection records:** Records on the County Metromap database are free at http://topaz.metro-region.org/metromap/metromap.cfm. No name searching. The GIS-mapping site is very similar at http://gis.co.multnomah.or.us/sail/. Also, search the sheriff's release inmate list at www.inmatereleases.org/search.cfm. Search the Health Dept. restaurant inspections at www.mchealthinspect.org/inspections/index.html. **Other phones:** Assessor-503-988-3326; Elections-503-988-3720; Vital Records-503-731-4095 (State); Tax information line-503-988-3326.

Polk County

County Clerk, 850 Main St, Rm 201, Courthouse, Dallas, OR 97338-3179. **Phone**-County Clerk, R/E & UCC Recording- 503-623-9217; fax-503-623-0717; hours 8AM-5PM www.co.polk.or.us
Will not search records. Cert fee: $3.75. **Other phones:** Assessor-503-623-8391; Treasurer-503-623-9264; Elections-503-623-9217; Vital Records-503-623-8175.

Sherman County

Deputy Clerk, PO Box 365, Moro, OR 97039. **Phone**-Deputy Clerk, R/E & UCC Recording- 541-565-3606; fax-541-565-3312; hours 8AM-5PM
UCC records search per debtor- $13.00. Will search real estate records. UCC copy- $.25 per page. Cert fee: $3.75. Payee: Sherman County. **Other phones:** Assessor-541-565-3505; Treasurer-541-565-3553; Elections-541-565-3606.

Tillamook County

County Clerk, 201 Laurel Ave, Tillamook, OR 97141. **Phone**-County Clerk, R/E & UCC Recording- 503-842-3402; fax-503-842-1599; hours 8AM-Noon, 1PM-5PM
www.co.tillamook.or.us/gov/clerk/default.htm

Will not search UCC or tax liens records. Will do limited real estate searches. RE record copy- $4.00 1st page; $.25 each add'l. UCC copy- $4.00 1st page, $.25 per add'l. Cert fee: $7.75 + $.25 per add'l. Payee: Tillamook County Clerk. **Online Access to Assessor, Real Estate records:** Assessment and taxation records on the Property database are free at www.co.tillamook.or.us/Documents/Search/query.asp. Search by property ID number or by name in the general query. Also, search for property info on the GIS-mapping site at http://gisweb.co.tillamook.or.us. **Other phones:** Assessor-503-842-3400/3424; Treasurer-503-842-3425; Elections-503-842-3402; Vital Records-503-731-4095.

Umatilla County

County Clerk, PO Box 1227, Pendleton, OR 97801-1227. **Phone-**541-278-6236; fax-541-278-6345. Will not search UCC or real estate records. Cert fee: $3.75 per doc. Payee: Umatilla County Clerk. **Online Access to Jail records:** Access to the sheriff's current jail roster is free at www.co.umatilla.or.us/deptwebs/jail/inmates/ICURRENT.HTM. **Other phones:** Assessor-541-276-7111 x214.

Union County

County Clerk, 1001 4th St, #"D", La Grande, OR 97850. **Phone-**County Clerk, R/E & UCC Recording-541-963-1006; fax-541-963-1013; hours 8:30-5:00PM M-TH;9:00-4:00PM F Will not search records. UCC copy- $.25 per page. Cert fee: $3.75. Payee: Union County Clerk. **Other phones:** Assessor-541-963-1002; Treasurer-541-963-1018; Elections-541-963-1006; Vital Records-541-963-1006.

Wallowa County

County Clerk, 101 S. River, Rm 100 Door 16, Enterprise, OR 97828. **Phone-**County Clerk, R/E & UCC Recording- 541-426-4543 x15; fax-541-426-5901; hours 8:30AM-5PM UCC records search per debtor- $5.00. Will search tax liens. Will not search real estate records. UCC copy- $.25 per page, location fee $3.75. **Other phones:** Assessor-541-426-4543; Treasurer-541-426-4543 x14; Elections- x15; Vital Records- x15; State-503-731-4095.

Wasco County

County Clerk, 511 Washington St., Courthouse, The Dalles, OR 97058-2237. **Phone-**County Clerk, R/E & UCC Recording- 541-296-6159; fax-541-298-3607; hours 10AM-4PM Will not search records. Cert fee: $7.75. Payee: Wasco County Clerk. **Other phones:** Assessor-541-296-5477; Treasurer-541-296-3327; Elections-541-296-6159; Vital Records-503-731-4108.

Washington County

County Clerk, 155 N. 1st Ave, Mail Stop 9, Hillsboro, OR 97124. **Phone-**County Clerk, R/E & UCC Recording- 503-846-8752; hours 8:30AM-4:30PM www.co.washington.or.us UCC records search per debtor- $32.55 per hour. UCC search includes tax liens if requested. Tax lien search- $32.55 per hour. Will search real estate records. RE record copy- $4.00 1st page, $.25 each add'l. UCC copy- $4.00 1st page, $.25 each add'l of same doc. Cert fee: $3.75 per cert, only in addition to photocopy fee. Payee: Washington County Clerk. **Online Access to Real Estate**

records: Records on County GIS database are free at www.co.washington.or.us/gisaps/cfdocs/gisweb/par_2.htm. General Recording Office information is at www.co.washington.or.us/deptmts/at/recordng/record.htm. Also, records on the County Metromap database are free online at http://topaz.metro-region.org/metromap/metromap.cfm. No name searching. **Other phones:** Assessor-503-846-8741; Elections-503-846-8670; Vital Records-503-846-3538.

Wheeler County

County Clerk, PO Box 327, Fossil, OR 97830-0327. **Phone-**541-763-2400; fax-541-763-2026; hours 8:30AM-4PM UCC records search per debtor- $4.00. Will not search real estate or tax lien records. Copy fee- $.25 per page. Cert fee: $3.75 per cert. Payee: Wheeler County Clerk. **Other phones:** Assessor-541-763-4266; Treasurer-541-763-2078; Elections-541-763-2400; Vital Records-541-763-2400.

Yamhill County

County Clerk, 535 NE 5th St, Rm 119, McMinnville, OR 97128-4593. **Phone-**County Clerk, R/E & UCC Recording- 503-434-7518; fax-503-434-7520; hours 9AM-5PM www.co.yamhill.or.us/clerk Will not search records. UCC copy- $.25 per page. Cert fee: $3.75 per cert + $.25 per pg. Payee: Yamhill County Clerk. **Online Access to Property records:** Limited property information from the county surveyor is free at www.co.yamhill.or.us/surveyor/; no name searching. **Other phones:** Assessor-503-434-7521; Treasurer-503-434-7533; Elections-503-434-7518; Vital Records-503-434-7523.

Oregon County Locator

You will usually be able to find the city name in the City/County Cross Reference below. In that case, it is a simple matter to determine the county from the cross reference. However, only the official US Postal Service city names are included in this index. There are an additional 40,000 place names that people use in their addresses. Therefore, we have also included a ZIP/City Cross Reference immediately following the City/County Cross Reference.

If you know the ZIP Code but the city name does not appear in the City/County Cross Reference index, look up the ZIP Code in the ZIP/City Cross Reference, find the city name, then look up the city name in the City/County Cross Reference. For example, you want to know the county for an address of Menands, NY 12204. There is no "Menands" in the City/County Cross Reference. The ZIP/City Cross Reference shows that ZIP Codes 12201-12288 are for the city of Albany. Looking back in the City/County Cross Reference, Albany is in Albany County.

Oregon City/County Cross Reference

ADAMS Umatilla
ADEL Lake
ADRIAN Malheur
AGNESS Curry
ALBANY (97321) Linn(75), Benton(24)
ALBANY Linn
ALLEGANY Coos
ALSEA (97324) Benton(90), Lincoln(7), Lane(1)
ALVADORE Lane
AMITY (97101) Yamhill(84), Polk(15)
ANTELOPE Wasco
ARCH CAPE Clatsop
ARLINGTON Gilliam
AROCK Malheur
ASHLAND Jackson
ASHWOOD Jefferson
ASTORIA Clatsop
ATHENA Umatilla
AUMSVILLE Marion
AURORA (97002) Marion(76), Clackamas(23)
AZALEA Douglas
BAKER CITY (97814) Baker(95), Union(4)
BANDON Coos
BANKS Washington
BATES Grant
BAY CITY Tillamook
BEATTY Klamath
BEAVER Tillamook
BEAVERCREEK Clackamas
BEAVERTON Washington
BEND Deschutes
BLACHLY Lane
BLODGETT (97326) Lincoln(63), Benton(36)
BLUE RIVER Lane
BLY Klamath
BOARDMAN Morrow
BONANZA Klamath
BORING Clackamas
BRIDAL VEIL Multnomah
BRIDGEPORT Baker
BRIGHTWOOD Clackamas
BROADBENT Coos
BROGAN Malheur
BROOKINGS Curry
BROTHERS Deschutes
BROWNSVILLE Linn
BURNS Harney
BUTTE FALLS Jackson
BUXTON Washington
CAMAS VALLEY Douglas
CAMP SHERMAN Jefferson
CANBY Clackamas
CANNON BEACH Clatsop
CANYON CITY Grant
CANYONVILLE Douglas
CARLTON Yamhill
CASCADE LOCKS (97014) Multnomah(62), Hood River(37)
CASCADIA Linn
CAVE JUNCTION Josephine
CAYUSE Umatilla

CENTRAL POINT Jackson
CHEMULT (97731) Douglas(76), Klamath(23)
CHESHIRE Lane
CHILOQUIN Klamath
CHRISTMAS VALLEY Lake
CLACKAMAS Clackamas
CLATSKANIE (97016) Columbia(79), Clatsop(20)
CLOVERDALE Tillamook
COLTON Clackamas
COLUMBIA CITY Columbia
CONDON Gilliam
COOS BAY Coos
COQUILLE Coos
CORBETT (97019) Multnomah(95), Clackamas(4)
CORNELIUS Washington
CORVALLIS (97333) Benton(91), Linn(8)
CORVALLIS Benton
COTTAGE GROVE Lane
COVE Union
CRABTREE Linn
CRANE Harney
CRATER LAKE Klamath
CRAWFORDSVILLE Linn
CRESCENT Klamath
CRESCENT LAKE Klamath
CRESWELL Lane
CULP CREEK Lane
CULVER Jefferson
CURTIN Douglas
DAIRY Klamath
DALLAS Polk
DAYS CREEK Douglas
DAYTON Yamhill
DAYVILLE (97825) Grant(98), Wheeler(1)
DEADWOOD Lane
DEER ISLAND Columbia
DEPOE BAY Lincoln
DETROIT Marion
DEXTER Lane
DIAMOND Harney
DILLARD Douglas
DONALD Marion
DORENA Lane
DRAIN Douglas
DREWSEY Harney
DUFUR Wasco
DUNDEE Yamhill
DURKEE Baker
EAGLE CREEK Clackamas
EAGLE POINT Jackson
ECHO Umatilla
EDDYVILLE Lincoln
ELGIN Union
ELKTON Douglas
ELMIRA Lane
ENTERPRISE Wallowa
ESTACADA Clackamas
EUGENE Lane
FAIRVIEW Multnomah
FALL CREEK Lane
FALLS CITY Polk

FIELDS Harney
FLORENCE Lane
FOREST GROVE Washington
FORT KLAMATH Klamath
FORT ROCK Lake
FOSSIL Wheeler
FOSTER Linn
FOX Grant
FRENCHGLEN Harney
GALES CREEK Washington
GARDINER Douglas
GARIBALDI Tillamook
GASTON (97119) Washington(77), Yamhill(22)
GATES (97346) Marion(76), Linn(23)
GERVAIS Marion
GILCHRIST Klamath
GLADSTONE Clackamas
GLENDALE Douglas
GLENEDEN BEACH Lincoln
GLIDE Douglas
GOLD BEACH Curry
GOLD HILL Jackson
GOVERNMENT CAMP Clackamas
GRAND RONDE (97347) Polk(63), Yamhill(35), Tillamook(1)
GRANTS PASS (97527) Josephine(96), Jackson(3)
GRANTS PASS Josephine
GRASS VALLEY Sherman
GREENLEAF Lane
GRESHAM (97080) Multnomah(95), Clackamas(4)
GRESHAM Multnomah
HAINES Baker
HALFWAY Baker
HALSEY Linn
HAMMOND Clatsop
HARPER Malheur
HARRISBURG (97446) Linn(98), Lane(1)
HEBO Tillamook
HELIX Umatilla
HEPPNER Morrow
HEREFORD Baker
HERMISTON Umatilla
HILLSBORO (97123) Washington(96), Yamhill(3)
HILLSBORO Washington
HINES Harney
HOOD RIVER Hood River
HUBBARD (97032) Marion(84), Clackamas(15)
HUNTINGTON (97907) Malheur(66), Baker(33)
IDANHA (97350) Marion(75), Linn(25)
IDLEYLD PARK Douglas
IMBLER Union
IMNAHA Wallowa
INDEPENDENCE Polk
IONE Morrow
IRONSIDE Malheur
IRRIGON Morrow
JACKSONVILLE Jackson
JAMIESON Malheur

JEFFERSON (97352) Marion(97), Linn(2)
JOHN DAY Grant
JORDAN VALLEY Malheur
JOSEPH Wallowa
JUNCTION CITY (97448) Lane(98), Benton(1)
JUNTURA Malheur
KEIZER Marion
KENO Klamath
KENT Sherman
KERBY Josephine
KIMBERLY Grant
KLAMATH FALLS Klamath
LA GRANDE Union
LA PINE (97739) Deschutes(71), Klamath(27)
LAFAYETTE Yamhill
LAKE OSWEGO (97035) Clackamas(92), Multnomah(5), Washington(1)
LAKESIDE Coos
LAKEVIEW Lake
LANGLOIS Curry
LAWEN Harney
LEBANON Linn
LEXINGTON Morrow
LINCOLN CITY Lincoln
LOGSDEN Lincoln
LONG CREEK Grant
LORANE Lane
LOSTINE Wallowa
LOWELL Lane
LYONS (97358) Linn(68), Marion(31)
MADRAS Jefferson
MALIN Klamath
MANNING Washington
MANZANITA Tillamook
MAPLETON Lane
MARCOLA Lane
MARYLHURST Clackamas
MAUPIN Wasco
MCMINNVILLE Yamhill
MEACHAM Umatilla
MEDFORD Jackson
MEHAMA Marion
MERLIN Josephine
MERRILL Klamath
MIDLAND Klamath
MIKKALO Gilliam
MILL CITY (97360) Linn(71), Marion(28)
MILTON FREEWATER Umatilla
MITCHELL Wheeler
MOLALLA Clackamas
MONMOUTH (97361) Polk(97), Benton(2)
MONROE Benton
MONUMENT Grant
MORO Sherman
MOSIER Wasco
MOUNT ANGEL (97362) Marion(96), Clackamas(3)
MOUNT HOOD PARKDALE Hood River
MOUNT VERNON Grant
MULINO Clackamas
MURPHY Josephine
MYRTLE CREEK Douglas

MYRTLE POINT Coos
NEHALEM (97131) Tillamook(98),
  Clatsop(1)
NEOTSU Lincoln
NESKOWIN Tillamook
NETARTS Tillamook
NEW PINE CREEK (97635) Lake(71),
  Morrow(28)
NEWBERG (97132) Yamhill(98),
  Washington(1)
NEWPORT Lincoln
NORTH BEND Coos
NORTH PLAINS (97133) Washington(97),
  Multnomah(2)
NORTH POWDER (97867) Union(92),
  Baker(7)
NORWAY Coos
NOTI Lane
NYSSA Malheur
O BRIEN Josephine
OAKLAND Douglas
OAKRIDGE Lane
OCEANSIDE Tillamook
ODELL Hood River
ONTARIO Malheur
OPHIR Curry
OREGON CITY Clackamas
OTIS (97368) Lincoln(94), Tillamook(4),
  Baker(1)
OTTER ROCK Lincoln
OXBOW Baker
PACIFIC CITY Tillamook
PAULINA Crook
PENDLETON Umatilla
PHILOMATH Benton
PHOENIX Jackson
PILOT ROCK Umatilla
PLEASANT HILL Lane
PLUSH Lake
PORT ORFORD Curry
PORTLAND (97219) Multnomah(97),
  Clackamas(2)
PORTLAND (97231) Multnomah(90),
  Washington(6), Columbia(3)

PORTLAND (97266) Multnomah(74),
  Clackamas(25)
PORTLAND (97229) Washington(84),
  Multnomah(15)
PORTLAND Clackamas
PORTLAND Multnomah
PORTLAND Washington
POST Crook
POWELL BUTTE Crook
POWERS Coos
PRAIRIE CITY Grant
PRINCETON Harney
PRINEVILLE Crook
PROSPECT Jackson
RAINIER Columbia
REDMOND Deschutes
REEDSPORT Douglas
REMOTE Coos
RHODODENDRON Clackamas
RICHLAND Baker
RICKREALL Polk
RIDDLE Douglas
RILEY Harney
RITTER Grant
RIVERSIDE Malheur
ROCKAWAY BEACH Tillamook
ROGUE RIVER Jackson
ROSE LODGE Lincoln
ROSEBURG Douglas
RUFUS Sherman
SAGINAW Lane
SAINT BENEDICT Marion
SAINT HELENS Columbia
SAINT PAUL Marion
SALEM (97304) Polk(97), Yamhill(2)
SANDY Clackamas
SCAPPOOSE (97056) Columbia(98),
  Multnomah(1)
SCIO Linn
SCOTTS MILLS (97375) Marion(82),
  Clackamas(17)
SCOTTSBURG Douglas
SEAL ROCK Lincoln
SEASIDE Clatsop

SELMA Josephine
SENECA Grant
SHADY COVE Jackson
SHANIKO Wasco
SHEDD Linn
SHERIDAN (97378) Yamhill(84), Polk(15)
SHERWOOD (97140) Washington(89),
  Clackamas(8), Yamhill(1)
SILETZ Lincoln
SILVER LAKE Lake
SILVERTON Marion
SISTERS (97759) Deschutes(96),
  Jefferson(1), Linn(1)
SIXES Curry
SOUTH BEACH Lincoln
SPRAGUE RIVER Klamath
SPRAY Wheeler
SPRINGFIELD Lane
STANFIELD Umatilla
STAYTON (97383) Marion(96), Linn(3)
SUBLIMITY Marion
SUMMER LAKE Lake
SUMMERVILLE Union
SUMPTER (97877) Grant(82), Baker(18)
SUTHERLIN Douglas
SWEET HOME Linn
SWISSHOME Lane
TALENT Jackson
TANGENT Linn
TENMILE Douglas
TERREBONNE (97760) Jefferson(53),
  Deschutes(43), Crook(3)
THE DALLES Wasco
THURSTON Lane
TIDEWATER (97390) Lincoln(88), Lane(11)
TILLAMOOK Tillamook
TILLER Douglas
TIMBER Washington
TOLEDO Lincoln
TOLOVANA PARK Clatsop
TRAIL Jackson
TROUTDALE Multnomah
TUALATIN (97062) Washington(84),
  Clackamas(15)

TURNER Marion
TYGH VALLEY Wasco
UKIAH Umatilla
UMATILLA Umatilla
UMPQUA Douglas
UNITY Baker
VALE Malheur
VENETA Lane
VERNONIA Columbia
VIDA Lane
WALDPORT Lincoln
WALLOWA Wallowa
WALTERVILLE Lane
WALTON Lane
WARM SPRINGS Jefferson
WARREN Columbia
WARRENTON Clatsop
WASCO Sherman
WEDDERBURN Curry
WELCHES Clackamas
WEST LINN Clackamas
WESTFALL Malheur
WESTFIR Lane
WESTLAKE Lane
WESTON Umatilla
WHEELER Tillamook
WHITE CITY Jackson
WILBUR Douglas
WILDERVILLE Josephine
WILLAMINA (97396) Yamhill(53), Polk(46)
WILLIAMS Josephine
WILSONVILLE (97070) Clackamas(83),
  Washington(15)
WINCHESTER Douglas
WOLF CREEK Josephine
WOODBURN (97071) Marion(97),
  Clackamas(2)
YACHATS Lincoln
YAMHILL Yamhill
YONCALLA Douglas

Oregon ZIP/City Cross Reference

97001-97001 ANTELOPE
97002-97002 AURORA
97004-97004 BEAVERCREEK
97005-97008 BEAVERTON
97009-97009 BORING
97010-97010 BRIDAL VEIL
97011-97011 BRIGHTWOOD
97013-97013 CANBY
97014-97014 CASCADE LOCKS
97015-97015 CLACKAMAS
97016-97016 CLATSKANIE
97017-97017 COLTON
97018-97018 COLUMBIA CITY
97019-97019 CORBETT
97020-97020 DONALD
97021-97021 DUFUR
97022-97022 EAGLE CREEK
97023-97023 ESTACADA
97024-97024 FAIRVIEW
97026-97026 GERVAIS
97027-97027 GLADSTONE
97028-97028 GOVERNMENT CAMP
97029-97029 GRASS VALLEY
97030-97030 GRESHAM
97031-97031 HOOD RIVER
97032-97032 HUBBARD
97033-97033 KENT
97034-97035 LAKE OSWEGO
97036-97036 MARYLHURST
97037-97037 MAUPIN
97038-97038 MOLALLA
97039-97039 MORO
97040-97040 MOSIER

97041-97041 MOUNT HOOD PARKDALE
97042-97042 MULINO
97044-97044 ODELL
97045-97045 OREGON CITY
97048-97048 RAINIER
97049-97049 RHODODENDRON
97050-97050 RUFUS
97051-97051 SAINT HELENS
97053-97053 WARREN
97054-97054 DEER ISLAND
97055-97055 SANDY
97056-97056 SCAPPOOSE
97057-97057 SHANIKO
97058-97058 THE DALLES
97060-97060 TROUTDALE
97062-97062 TUALATIN
97063-97063 TYGH VALLEY
97064-97064 VERNONIA
97065-97065 WASCO
97067-97067 WELCHES
97068-97068 WEST LINN
97070-97070 WILSONVILLE
97071-97071 WOODBURN
97075-97075 BEAVERTON
97080-97080 GRESHAM
97101-97101 AMITY
97102-97102 ARCH CAPE
97103-97103 ASTORIA
97106-97106 BANKS
97107-97107 BAY CITY
97108-97108 BEAVER
97109-97109 BUXTON
97110-97110 CANNON BEACH

97111-97111 CARLTON
97112-97112 CLOVERDALE
97113-97113 CORNELIUS
97114-97114 DAYTON
97115-97115 DUNDEE
97116-97116 FOREST GROVE
97117-97117 GALES CREEK
97118-97118 GARIBALDI
97119-97119 GASTON
97121-97121 HAMMOND
97122-97122 HEBO
97123-97124 HILLSBORO
97125-97125 MANNING
97127-97127 LAFAYETTE
97128-97128 MCMINNVILLE
97130-97130 MANZANITA
97131-97131 NEHALEM
97132-97132 NEWBERG
97133-97133 NORTH PLAINS
97134-97134 OCEANSIDE
97135-97135 PACIFIC CITY
97136-97136 ROCKAWAY BEACH
97137-97137 SAINT PAUL
97138-97138 SEASIDE
97140-97140 SHERWOOD
97141-97141 TILLAMOOK
97143-97143 NETARTS
97144-97144 TIMBER
97145-97145 TOLOVANA PARK
97146-97146 WARRENTON
97147-97147 WHEELER
97148-97148 YAMHILL
97149-97149 NESKOWIN

97200-97299 PORTLAND
97301-97306 SALEM
97307-97307 KEIZER
97308-97314 SALEM
97321-97322 ALBANY
97324-97324 ALSEA
97325-97325 AUMSVILLE
97326-97326 BLODGETT
97327-97327 BROWNSVILLE
97329-97329 CASCADIA
97330-97333 CORVALLIS
97335-97335 CRABTREE
97336-97336 CRAWFORDSVILLE
97338-97338 DALLAS
97339-97339 CORVALLIS
97341-97341 DEPOE BAY
97342-97342 DETROIT
97343-97343 EDDYVILLE
97344-97344 FALLS CITY
97345-97345 FOSTER
97346-97346 GATES
97347-97347 GRAND RONDE
97348-97348 HALSEY
97350-97350 IDANHA
97351-97351 INDEPENDENCE
97352-97352 JEFFERSON
97355-97355 LEBANON
97357-97357 LOGSDEN
97358-97358 LYONS
97359-97359 MARION
97360-97360 MILL CITY
97361-97361 MONMOUTH
97362-97362 MOUNT ANGEL

97364-97364 NEOTSU	97446-97446 HARRISBURG	97537-97537 ROGUE RIVER	97820-97820 CANYON CITY
97365-97365 NEWPORT	97447-97447 IDLEYLD PARK	97538-97538 SELMA	97821-97821 CAYUSE
97366-97366 SOUTH BEACH	97448-97448 JUNCTION CITY	97539-97539 SHADY COVE	97823-97823 CONDON
97367-97367 LINCOLN CITY	97449-97449 LAKESIDE	97540-97540 TALENT	97824-97824 COVE
97368-97368 OTIS	97450-97450 LANGLOIS	97541-97541 TRAIL	97825-97825 DAYVILLE
97369-97369 OTTER ROCK	97451-97451 LORANE	97543-97543 WILDERVILLE	97826-97826 ECHO
97370-97370 PHILOMATH	97452-97452 LOWELL	97544-97544 WILLIAMS	97827-97827 ELGIN
97371-97371 RICKREALL	97453-97453 MAPLETON	97601-97603 KLAMATH FALLS	97828-97828 ENTERPRISE
97372-97372 ROSE LODGE	97454-97454 MARCOLA	97604-97604 CRATER LAKE	97830-97830 FOSSIL
97373-97373 SAINT BENEDICT	97455-97455 PLEASANT HILL	97620-97620 ADEL	97831-97831 FOX
97374-97374 SCIO	97456-97456 MONROE	97621-97621 BEATTY	97833-97833 HAINES
97375-97375 SCOTTS MILLS	97457-97457 MYRTLE CREEK	97622-97622 BLY	97834-97834 HALFWAY
97376-97376 SEAL ROCK	97458-97458 MYRTLE POINT	97623-97623 BONANZA	97835-97835 HELIX
97377-97377 SHEDD	97459-97459 NORTH BEND	97624-97624 CHILOQUIN	97836-97836 HEPPNER
97378-97378 SHERIDAN	97460-97460 NORWAY	97625-97625 DAIRY	97837-97837 HEREFORD
97380-97380 SILETZ	97461-97461 NOTI	97626-97626 FORT KLAMATH	97838-97838 HERMISTON
97381-97381 SILVERTON	97462-97462 OAKLAND	97627-97627 KENO	97839-97839 LEXINGTON
97383-97383 STAYTON	97463-97463 OAKRIDGE	97630-97630 LAKEVIEW	97840-97840 OXBOW
97384-97384 MEHAMA	97464-97464 OPHIR	97632-97632 MALIN	97841-97841 IMBLER
97385-97385 SUBLIMITY	97465-97465 PORT ORFORD	97633-97633 MERRILL	97842-97842 IMNAHA
97386-97386 SWEET HOME	97466-97466 POWERS	97634-97634 MIDLAND	97843-97843 IONE
97388-97388 GLENEDEN BEACH	97467-97467 REEDSPORT	97635-97635 NEW PINE CREEK	97844-97844 IRRIGON
97389-97389 TANGENT	97468-97468 REMOTE	97636-97636 PAISLEY	97845-97845 JOHN DAY
97390-97390 TIDEWATER	97469-97469 RIDDLE	97637-97637 PLUSH	97846-97846 JOSEPH
97391-97391 TOLEDO	97470-97470 ROSEBURG	97638-97638 SILVER LAKE	97848-97848 KIMBERLY
97392-97392 TURNER	97472-97472 SAGINAW	97639-97639 SPRAGUE RIVER	97850-97850 LA GRANDE
97394-97394 WALDPORT	97473-97473 SCOTTSBURG	97640-97640 SUMMER LAKE	97856-97856 LONG CREEK
97396-97396 WILLAMINA	97476-97476 SIXES	97641-97641 CHRISTMAS VALLEY	97857-97857 LOSTINE
97401-97405 EUGENE	97477-97478 SPRINGFIELD	97701-97709 BEND	97859-97859 MEACHAM
97406-97406 AGNESS	97479-97479 SUTHERLIN	97710-97710 FIELDS	97861-97861 MIKKALO
97407-97407 ALLEGANY	97480-97480 SWISSHOME	97711-97711 ASHWOOD	97862-97862 MILTON FREEWATER
97408-97408 EUGENE	97481-97481 TENMILE	97712-97712 BROTHERS	97864-97864 MONUMENT
97409-97409 ALVADORE	97482-97482 THURSTON	97720-97720 BURNS	97865-97865 MOUNT VERNON
97410-97410 AZALEA	97484-97484 TILLER	97721-97721 PRINCETON	97867-97867 NORTH POWDER
97411-97411 BANDON	97486-97486 UMPQUA	97722-97722 DIAMOND	97868-97868 PILOT ROCK
97412-97412 BLACHLY	97487-97487 VENETA	97730-97730 CAMP SHERMAN	97869-97869 PRAIRIE CITY
97413-97413 BLUE RIVER	97488-97488 VIDA	97731-97731 CHEMULT	97870-97870 RICHLAND
97414-97414 BROADBENT	97489-97489 WALTERVILLE	97732-97732 CRANE	97872-97872 RITTER
97415-97415 BROOKINGS	97490-97490 WALTON	97733-97733 CRESCENT	97873-97873 SENECA
97416-97416 CAMAS VALLEY	97491-97491 WEDDERBURN	97734-97734 CULVER	97874-97874 SPRAY
97417-97417 CANYONVILLE	97492-97492 WESTFIR	97735-97735 FORT ROCK	97875-97875 STANFIELD
97419-97419 CHESHIRE	97493-97493 WESTLAKE	97736-97736 FRENCHGLEN	97876-97876 SUMMERVILLE
97420-97420 COOS BAY	97494-97494 WILBUR	97737-97737 GILCHRIST	97877-97877 SUMPTER
97423-97423 COQUILLE	97495-97495 WINCHESTER	97738-97738 HINES	97880-97880 UKIAH
97424-97424 COTTAGE GROVE	97496-97496 WINSTON	97739-97739 LA PINE	97882-97882 UMATILLA
97425-97425 CRESCENT LAKE	97497-97497 WOLF CREEK	97740-97740 LAWEN	97883-97883 UNION
97426-97426 CRESWELL	97498-97498 YACHATS	97741-97741 MADRAS	97884-97884 UNITY
97427-97427 CULP CREEK	97499-97499 YONCALLA	97750-97750 MITCHELL	97885-97885 WALLOWA
97428-97428 CURTIN	97501-97501 MEDFORD	97751-97751 PAULINA	97886-97886 WESTON
97429-97429 DAYS CREEK	97502-97502 CENTRAL POINT	97752-97752 POST	97901-97901 ADRIAN
97430-97430 DEADWOOD	97503-97503 WHITE CITY	97753-97753 POWELL BUTTE	97902-97902 AROCK
97431-97431 DEXTER	97504-97504 MEDFORD	97754-97754 PRINEVILLE	97903-97903 BROGAN
97432-97432 DILLARD	97520-97520 ASHLAND	97756-97756 REDMOND	97904-97904 DREWSEY
97434-97434 DORENA	97522-97522 BUTTE FALLS	97758-97758 RILEY	97905-97905 DURKEE
97435-97435 DRAIN	97523-97523 CAVE JUNCTION	97759-97759 SISTERS	97906-97906 HARPER
97436-97436 ELKTON	97524-97524 EAGLE POINT	97760-97760 TERREBONNE	97907-97907 HUNTINGTON
97437-97437 ELMIRA	97525-97525 GOLD HILL	97761-97761 WARM SPRINGS	97908-97908 IRONSIDE
97438-97438 FALL CREEK	97526-97528 GRANTS PASS	97801-97801 PENDLETON	97909-97909 JAMIESON
97439-97439 FLORENCE	97530-97530 JACKSONVILLE	97810-97810 ADAMS	97910-97910 JORDAN VALLEY
97440-97440 EUGENE	97531-97531 KERBY	97812-97812 ARLINGTON	97911-97911 JUNTURA
97441-97441 GARDINER	97532-97532 MERLIN	97813-97813 ATHENA	97913-97913 NYSSA
97442-97442 GLENDALE	97533-97533 MURPHY	97814-97814 BAKER CITY	97914-97914 ONTARIO
97443-97443 GLIDE	97534-97534 O BRIEN	97817-97817 BATES	97917-97917 RIVERSIDE
97444-97444 GOLD BEACH	97535-97535 PHOENIX	97818-97818 BOARDMAN	97918-97918 VALE
97445-97445 GREENLEAF	97536-97536 PROSPECT	97819-97819 BRIDGEPORT	97920-97920 WESTFALL

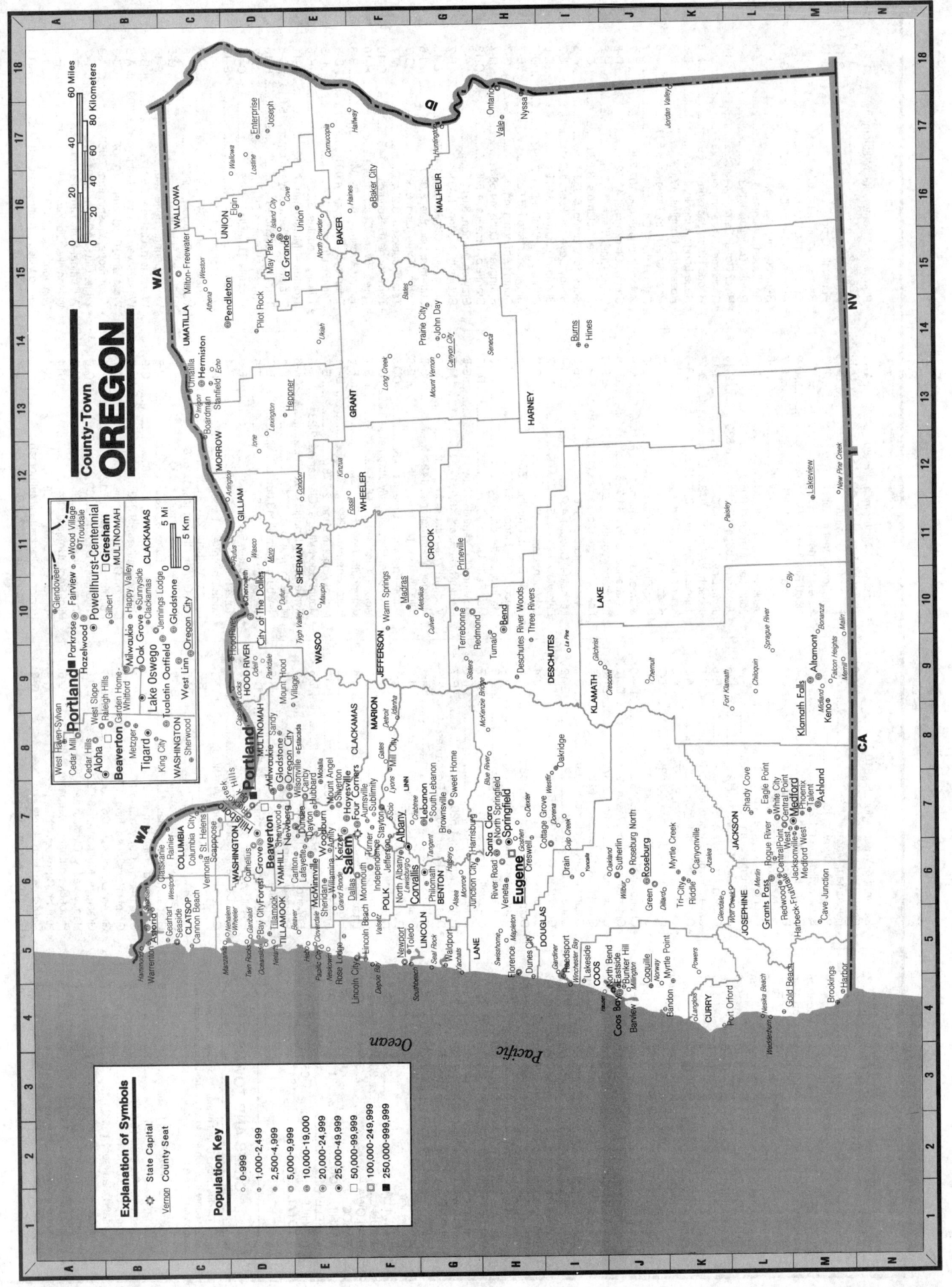

County-Town
OREGON

Explanation of Symbols

Vernon ○ County Seat

Population Key

- ○ 0-999
- ⊕ 1,000-2,499
- ⊕ 2,500-4,999
- ◉ 5,000-9,999
- ◎ 10,000-19,000
- ◉ 20,000-24,999
- ◉ 25,000-49,999
- ☐ 50,000-99,999
- ☐ 100,000-249,999
- ■ 250,000-999,999

COUNTIES

(36 Counties)

Name of County	Population	Location on Map
BAKER	15,317	E-15
BENTON	70,811	G-6
CLACKAMAS	278,850	F-8
CLATSOP	33,301	C-5
COLUMBIA	37,557	C-6
COOS	60,273	I-4
CROOK	14,111	G-11
CURRY	19,327	K-4
DESCHUTES	74,958	I-9
DOUGLAS	94,649	H-5
GILLIAM	1,717	D-11
GRANT	7,853	F-13
HARNEY	7,060	H-13
HOOD RIVER	16,903	D-9
JACKSON	146,389	L-6
JEFFERSON	13,676	F-9
JOSEPHINE	62,649	L-5
KLAMATH	57,702	I-8
LAKE	7,186	I-10
LANE	282,912	G-5
LINCOLN	38,889	G-5
LINN	91,227	F-7
MALHEUR	26,038	G-16
MARION	228,483	F-8
MORROW	7,625	C-12
MULTNOMAH	583,887	F-6
POLK	49,541	E-10
SHERMAN	1,918	D-5
TILLAMOOK	21,570	C-14
UMATILLA	59,249	D-15
UNION	23,598	C-16
WALLOWA	6,911	E-9
WASCO	21,683	D-6
WASHINGTON	311,554	D-6
WHEELER	1,396	F-11
YAMHILL	65,551	D-6
TOTAL	**2,842,321**	

CITIES AND TOWNS

Note: The first name is that of the city or town, second, that of the county in which it is located, then the population and location on the map.

City/Town, County, Population	Map
Albany, Benton/Linn, 29,462	F-6
Aloha, Washington, 34,284	B-8
Altamont, Klamath, 18,591	M-9
Amity, Yamhill, 1,175	E-6
Ashland, Jackson, 16,234	M-7
Astoria, Clatsop, 10,069	B-5
Aumsville, Marion, 1,650	F-7
Baker City, Baker, 9,140	F-16
Bandon, Coos, 2,215	J-4
Barview, Coos, 1,402	J-4
Bay City, Tillamook, 1,027	D-5
Beaverton, Washington, 53,310	D-7
Bend, Deschutes, 20,469	H-10
Boardman, Morrow, 1,387	C-13
Brookings, Curry, 4,400	M-4
Brownsville, Linn, 1,281	G-7
Bunker Hill, Coos, 1,242	J-4
Burns, Harney, 2,913	I-14
Canby, Clackamas, 8,983	E-7
Cannon Beach, Clatsop, 1,221	C-5
Canyon City, Grant, 648	G-14
Canyonville, Douglas, 1,219	K-6
Carlton, Yamhill, 1,289	E-6
Cave Junction, Josephine, 1,126	M-5
Cedar Hills, Washington, 9,294	A-8
Cedar Mill, Washington, 9,697	A-8
Central Point, Jackson, 7,509	L-7
Central Point West, Jackson	L-7
Chenoweth, Wasco, 3,246	D-10
City of the Dalles, Wasco, 11,060	D-10
Clackamas, Clackamas, 2,578	B-10
Clatskanie, Columbia, 1,629	B-6
Columbia City, Columbia, 1,003	C-7
Condon, Gilliam, 635	E-12
Coos Bay, Coos, 15,076	J-4
Coquille, Coos, 4,121	J-4
Cornelius, Washington, 6,148	D-6
Corvallis, Benton, 44,757	G-6
Cottage Grove, Lane, 7,402	I-6
Creswell, Lane, 2,431	H-7
Dallas, Polk, 9,422	F-6
Dayton, Yamhill, 1,526	E-7
Deschutes River Woods, Deschutes, 2,373	H-9
Drain, Douglas, 1,011	I-6
Dundee, Yamhill, 1,663	E-7
Dunes City, Lane, 1,081	H-5
Eagle Point, Jackson, 3,008	L-7
Eastside, Coos	J-4
Elgin, Union, 1,586	D-16
Enterprise, Wallowa, 1,905	D-17
Estacada, Clackamas, 2,016	E-8
Eugene, Lane, 112,669	H-6
Fairview, Multnomah, 2,391	A-11
Florence, Lane, 5,162	H-5
Fossil, Wheeler, 399	E-12
Four Corners, Marion, 12,156	F-7
Garden Home-Whitford, Washington, 6,652	B-8
Gearhart, Clatsop, 1,027	B-5
Gilbert, Multnomah	B-10
Gladstone, Clackamas, 10,152	D-7
Glendoveer, Multnomah	A-10
Gold Beach, Curry, 1,546	L-4
Grants Pass, Josephine, 17,488	L-6
Green, Douglas, 5,076	J-6
Gresham, Multnomah, 68,235	B-11
Happy Valley, Clackamas, 1,519	B-10
Harbeck-Fruitdale, Josephine, 3,982	L-6
Harbor, Curry, 2,143	M-4
Harrisburg, Linn, 1,939	G-6
Hayesville, Marion, 14,318	E-7
Hazelwood, Multnomah, 11,480	A-10
Heppner, Morrow, 1,412	D-13
Hermiston, Umatilla, 10,040	C-13
Hillsboro, Washington, 37,520	D-7
Hines, Harney, 1,452	I-14
Hood River, Hood River, 4,632	D-9
Hubbard, Marion, 1,881	E-7
Independence, Polk, 4,425	F-6
Jacksonville, Jackson, 1,896	M-7
Jefferson, Marion, 1,805	F-7
Jennings Lodge, Clackamas, 6,530	B-10
John Day, Grant, 1,836	G-14
Joseph, Wallowa, 1,073	D-17
Junction City, Lane, 3,670	G-6
Keizer, Marion, 21,884	E-7
Keno, Klamath	M-9
King City, Washington, 2,060	B-8
Klamath Falls, Klamath, 17,737	M-9
La Grande, Union, 11,766	D-15
Lafayette, Yamhill, 1,292	E-6
Lake Oswego, Clackamas/Multnomah/Washington, 30,576	B-9
Lakeside, Coos, 1,437	I-4
Lakeview, Lake, 2,526	M-12
Lebanon, Linn, 10,950	G-7
Lincoln Beach, Lincoln, 1,507	F-5
Lincoln City, Lincoln, 5,892	F-10
Madras, Jefferson, 3,443	D-15
May Park, Union	H-7
McMinnville, Yamhill, 17,894	E-6
Medford, Jackson, 46,951	M-7
Medford West, Jackson	M-7
Metzger, Washington, 3,149	B-8
Mill City, Linn/Marion, 1,555	F-8
Milton-Freewater, Umatilla, 5,533	C-15
Milwaukie, Clackamas/Multnomah, 18,692	D-7
Molalla, Clackamas, 3,651	E-7
Monmouth, Polk, 6,288	F-6
Moro, Sherman, 292	D-11
Mount Angel, Marion, 2,778	E-7
Mount Hood Village, Clackamas, 2,234	E-8
Myrtle Creek, Douglas, 3,063	K-6
Myrtle Point, Coos, 2,712	J-4
Newberg, Yamhill, 13,086	E-7
Newport, Lincoln, 8,437	F-5
North Albany, Benton, 4,325	F-6
North Bend, Coos, 9,614	J-4
North Springfield, Lane, 5,451	H-7
Nyssa, Malheur, 2,629	H-17
Oak Grove, Clackamas, 12,576	B-9
Oak Hills, Washington, 6,450	B-8
Oakridge, Lane, 3,063	I-8
Oatfield, Clackamas, 15,348	C-9
Ontario, Malheur, 9,392	H-18
Oregon City, Clackamas, 14,698	D-7
Pendleton, Umatilla, 15,126	D-14
Philomath, Benton, 2,983	G-6
Phoenix, Jackson, 3,239	M-7
Pilot Rock, Umatilla, 1,478	D-14
Port Orford, Curry, 1,025	K-4
Portland, Clackamas/Multnomah/Washington, 437,319	D-7
Powellhurst-Centennial, Multnomah, 28,756	B-10
Prairie City, Grant, 1,117	G-14
Prineville, Crook, 5,355	G-10
Rainier, Columbia, 1,674	C-7
Raleigh Hills, Washington, 6,066	B-8
Redmond, Deschutes, 7,163	G-10
Redwood, Josephine, 3,702	L-6
Reedsport, Douglas, 4,796	I-5
Riddle, Douglas, 1,143	K-6
River Road, Lane, 9,443	H-6
Rockcreek, Washington, 8,282	D-7
Rogue River, Jackson, 1,759	L-6
Rose Lodge, Lincoln, 1,257	E-5
Roseburg, Douglas, 17,032	J-6
Roseburg North, Douglas, 6,831	J-6
Saint Helens, Columbia, 7,535	C-7
Salem, Marion/Polk, 107,786	E-7
Sandy, Clackamas, 4,152	D-8
Santa Clara, Lane, 12,834	H-6
Scappoose, Columbia, 3,529	C-7
Seaside, Clatsop, 5,359	C-5
Shady Cove, Jackson, 1,351	L-7
Sheridan, Yamhill, 3,979	E-6
Sherwood, Washington, 3,093	D-7
Silverton, Marion, 5,635	E-7
South Lebanon, Linn, 1,203	G-7
Springfield, Lane, 44,683	H-7
Stanfield, Umatilla, 1,568	C-13
Stayton, Marion, 5,011	F-7
Sublimity, Marion, 1,491	F-7
Sunnyside, Clackamas, 4,423	B-10
Sutherlin, Douglas, 5,020	J-6
Sweet Home, Linn, 6,850	G-7
Talent, Jackson, 3,274	M-7
Terrebonne, Deschutes, 1,143	G-10
Three Rivers, Deschutes, 1,268	H-10
Tigard, Washington, 29,344	B-8
Tillamook, Tillamook, 4,001	D-5
Toledo, Lincoln, 3,174	F-5
Tri-City, Douglas, 3,585	K-6
Troutdale, Multnomah, 7,852	A-11
Tualatin, Clackamas/Washington, 15,013	C-8
Tumalo, Deschutes	H-10
Turner, Marion, 1,281	F-7
Umatilla, Umatilla, 3,046	C-13
Union, Union, 1,847	E-16
Vale, Malheur, 1,491	H-17
Veneta, Lane, 2,519	H-6
Vernonia, Columbia, 1,808	C-6
Waldport, Lincoln, 1,595	G-5
Warm Springs, Jefferson, 2,287	F-10
Warrenton, Clatsop, 2,681	B-5
West Haven-Sylvan, Washington, 6,009	A-8
West Linn, Clackamas, 16,367	C-9
West Slope, Washington, 7,959	A-8
White City, Jackson, 5,891	L-7
Willamina, Polk/Yamhill, 1,717	E-6
Wilsonville, Clackamas/Washington, 7,106	E-7
Winston, Douglas, 3,773	J-6
Wood Village, Multnomah, 2,814	A-11
Woodburn, Marion, 13,404	E-7

Explanation of symbols: ● – Census Designated Place (CDP)

Pennsylvania

General Help Numbers:

Governor's Office
225 Main Capitol Bldg
Harrisburg, PA 17120
http://www.governor.state.pa.us/

717-787-2500
Fax 717-772-8284
9AM-4:30PM

Attorney General's Office
Strawberry Square, 16th Floor
Harrisburg, PA 17120
www.attorneygeneral.gov

717-787-3391
Fax 717-787-1190
8AM-5PM

Legislative Records
General Assembly, Legislative Reference Bureau
Main Capitol Bldg, Room 641
Harrisburg, PA 17120
www.legis.state.pa.us

717-787-2342

8:30AM-5PM

State Archives
Bureau of Archives & History
350 North St
Harrisburg, PA 17120
www.phmc.state.pa.us

717-783-3281
Fax 717-787-4822
9AM-4PM TU-F

State Specifics:

Capital: Harrisburg
Dauphin County

Time Zone: EST

Number of Counties: 67

Population: 12,365,455

Web Site: www.state.pa.us

State Agencies

Criminal Records

State Police, Central Repository -164, 1800 Elmerton Ave, Harrisburg, PA 17110-9758; 717-783-5494, 717-783-9973, 8:15AM-4:15PM.

www.psp.state.pa.us/psp/site/default.asp

Indexing & Storage: Records are available from the 1920s. Records are available for all convictions. It takes 1 day before new records are available for inquiry. Records are indexed on fingerprint cards and inhouse computer. Records are normally destroyed after 3 years after individual is confirmed deceased by fingerprints.

Searching: Must make request on Request Form SP4-164 or the request will be returned. The form can be found on web page (help menu in PATCH section) or call for form. Include the following in your request-full name, date of birth, Social Security Number, sex, race, any aliases, all on proper form. A release is not required. The record database is 100% fingerprint-supported. Statutorily-required fingerprint searches include an FBI fingerprint search.

Access by: mail, online.

Fee & Payment: Fee is $10.00 per name search. Add $24.00 if for a statutorily-required FBI fingerprint check. Fee payee: Commonwealth of Pennsylvania. Prepayment required. No personal checks accepted. No credit cards accepted.

Mail search: Turnaround time: 2-3 weeks. Turnaround can be 6 weeks if a record has a hit. No self addressed stamped envelope is required.

Online search: Record checks are available for approved agencies through the Internet on the Pennsylvania Access to Criminal Histories (PATCH). This is a commercial system, the same $10.00 fee per name applies. PATCH accepts Visa, Discover, Master Card and American Express. Go to https://epatch.state.pa.us or call 717-705-1768 to register.

Expedited service: Will expedite one day turnaround if you provide prepaid overnight shipping envelope.

Statewide Court Records

Administrative Office of PA Courts, PO Box 229, Mechanicsburg, PA 17055; 717-795-2000, 717-795-2062 (Communications), 717-795-2050 (Fax), 9AM-5PM.

www.courts.state.pa.us

Note: The website offers links to a variety of translation, terminalogy, and code files that can be viewed or downloaded, along with a brief description.

Access by: mail, online.

Mail search: A Public Access Request Form is downloadable from the web page.

Online search: The Web Portal offers access to a variety of the Judiciary's Electronic Services (E-Services) such as Web Docket Sheets, DA Link, Superior Court's Web Docketing Statements, etc. Although the public has access to the Web Docket Sheets, the registration details for the other E-Services vary with each service. At present, name searching is not available. Go to http://ujsportal.pacourts.us for details. Also, search Appellate Court dockets at http://pacmsdocketsheet.aopc.org/.

Sexual Offender Registry

State Police Central Repository, Megan's Law Unit, 1800 Elmerton Ave, Harrisburg, PA 17110-9758; 717-783-4363, 717-783-9973, 717-705-8839 (Fax), 7AM-3PM.

www.psp.state.pa.us/psp/site/default.asp

Note: This office provides no searches except via email. The public may request information concerning sexually violent predators in a particular community by visiting the law enforcement office in that community, including local State Police offices.

Indexing & Storage: Records are available from July 8, 2000 forward.

Access by: online. No searching by mail.

Online search: On September 25, 2003 the Pennsylvania Supreme Court interpreted this provision of Megan's Law to require that a specific request be made before this information can be provided via electronic means. To make a specific request for information on Sexually Violent Predators, please email to ra-pspsvp@state.pa.us.

Incarceration Records

Pennsylvania Department of Corrections, Inmate Records Office, PO Box 598, Camp Hill, PA 17001-0598; 717-737-6538, 717-731-7159 (Fax), 8AM-4PM.

www.cor.state.pa.us

Indexing & Storage: Records are available on current and former inmates. It takes a minimum of 30 days before new records are available for inquiry. Records are normally destroyed after 10 years after maximum sentence date.

Searching: Include the following in your request-full name. DOB and SSN are helpful. Location, physical identifiers, conviction and sentencing information, and release dates are available.

Access by: mail, phone, fax, online.

Fee & Payment: There is no fee.

Mail search: Turnaround time: 1 to 2 weeks. Turnaround time on archived records may be longer than 2 weeks A SASE is requested.

Phone search: Includes historical information on released inmates.

Fax search: Can request via fax.

Online search: At the website, click on Inmate Locator for information about each inmate currently under the jurisdiction of the Department of Corrections. The site indicates where an inmate is housed, race, date of birth, marital status and other items. The Inmate Locator does not contain information on inmates not currently residing in a state correctional institution.

Corporation, Limited Partnership, Limited Liability Company, Limited Liability Partnerships Trademarks, Servicemarks, Fictitious Name, Assumed Name,

Corporation Bureau, Department of State, PO Box 8722, Harrisburg, PA 17105-8722 (Courier: 206 North Office Bldg, Harrisburg, PA 17120); 717-787-1057, 717-783-2244 (Fax), 8AM-5PM.

www.dos.state.pa.us/corps/site/default.asp

Indexing & Storage: Records are available from 1700's on. Records are indexed on computer since the 1800's.

Searching: Include the following in your request-full name of business. Corporation records include: Articles of Incorporation, Officers, Directors, DBAs, Prior (merged) names, Withdrawn and Reserved (120 days) names. Annual Reports on for-profit corporations are not required by the Department of State.

Access by: mail, phone, fax, in person, online.

Fee & Payment: The search fee is $15.00. Request for copies is $15.00 plus $3.00 per page. Certification is $40.00 plus $3.00 per copy. Printouts form computer or microfilm is $3.00 a page. A Good Standing is $40.00. Fee payee: Department of State. Prepayment required. Ongoing requesters should open a customer deposit account. Personal checks accepted. No credit cards accepted.

Mail search: Turnaround time: 3 to 5 days. No SASE is required.

Phone search: No fee for telephone request. They will provide basic information only.

Fax search: You must have an account to have materials returned by fax, same fees as above plus a $3.00 per page charge.

In person search: There are 2 computer terminals available for public use.

Online search: There is free general searching by entity name or number from the website. Searching by name provides a list of entities whose name starts with the search name entered. Users can click on any one entity in the list displayed to get more detailed information regarding that entity.

Other access: Business lists, UCC on microfilm, and financing statements are available in bulk for $.25 per name plus a $12.00 set-up fee.

Expedited service: Expedited service is available for mail and phone searches. Add $52.00 per transaction. If ordered before 1 PM, the record will be available by 5 PM.

Uniform Commercial Code

UCC Division, Department of State, PO Box 8721, Harrisburg, PA 17105-8721 (Courier: North Office Bldg, Rm 206, Harrisburg, PA 17120); 717-787-1057 x3, 717-783-2244 (Fax), 8AM-5PM.

www.dos.state.pa.us/DOS/site/default.asp

Indexing & Storage: Records are available from 1964 to present on microfiche and computer. It takes 2 to 3 days before new records are available for inquiry.

Searching: Use search request form UCC-11. All federal and state tax liens are filed at the Prothonotary of each county. Include the following in your request-debtor name. The agency will not expedite requests.

Access by: mail, fax, in person, online.

Fee & Payment: The search fee is $12.00 per debtor name, copies cost $3.00 per page. Certification is $28.00. Fee payee: Pennsylvania Department of State. Prepayment required. Deposit accounts are accepted. Personal checks accepted. No credit cards accepted.

Mail search: Turnaround time: 3 to 5 days. A SASE is requested.

Fax search: There is an additional $3.00 per page fee if returned by fax. A customer deposit account is required.

In person search: If the search is conducted by the customer, there is no $12.00 search fee.

Online search: The website allows a search of UCC-1 financing statements filed with the Corporation Bureau by debtor name or financing statement number; a list of financing statements is displayed. The site also allows a search of financing statement records filed with the Corporation Bureau by financing statement number.

Other access: Daily computer tapes and copies of microfilm are available. Call the number above for details.

Federal and State Tax Liens

Records not maintained by a state level agency.

Note: All federal and state tax liens are filed at the Prothonotary of each county.

Sales Tax Registrations

Revenue Department, Sales Tax Registration Division, Dept 280905, Harrisburg, PA 17128-0905; 717-783-9360, 717-787-3708 (Fax), 7:30AM-4:30PM.

www.revenue.state.pa.us

Note: Businesses can register online at www.pa100.state.pa.us/.

Indexing & Storage: Records are available from 1971 to present, easily searchable from 1995 to present. It takes 2 to 3 weeks before new records are available for inquiry.

Searching: This agency will only confirm that a business is registered. They will provide no other information unless a signed release is presented. Include the following in your request-EIN, tax permit number or business name. They will only search with a tax permit number.

Access by: mail, phone, fax.

Fee & Payment: There is no search fee.

Mail search: Turnaround time: 2 to 7 days. A SASE is requested.

Phone search: Records are available by phone.

Fax search: Same criteria as mail searches.

Birth Certificates

PA Department of Health, Division of Vital Records, PO Box 1528, New Castle, PA 16103-1528 (Courier: 101 S Mercer St, Room 401, New Castle, PA 16101); 724-656-3100 (Message Phone), 724-652-8951 (Fax), 8AM-4PM.

http://webserver.health.state.pa.us/health/cwp/view.asp?a=168&Q=229939

Indexing & Storage: Records are available from 1906 to present.

Searching: Must have a signed release from person of record or immediate family member. Include the following in your request-full name, names of parents, mother's maiden name, date of birth, place of birth, relationship to person of record, reason for information request. Must include daytime phone number.

Access by: mail, phone, fax, in person, online.

Fee & Payment: The fee is $10.00 per record. Fee payee: Vital Records. Prepayment required. Personal checks accepted. Credit cards accepted: MasterCard, Visa, AmEx, Discover.

Mail search: Turnaround time: 3 weeks. Credit cards not accepted for mail requests. A SASE is requested.

Phone search: Phone requests accepted with a credit card for an additional $7.00 fee. Turnaround time is 2-4 days.

Fax search: See expedited services

In person search: Turnaround time is 1 hour.

Online search: Expedited service is available at www.vitalchek.com, a state designated vendor.

Expedited service: Expedited service is available for fax requests. Use of the state form (downloadable from web site) is recommended. Turnaround time: 2 to 4 days. Add $7.00 for use of credit card, add fees for express delivery, if desired.

Death Records

Department of Health, Division of Vital Records, PO Box 1528, New Castle, PA 16103-1528 (Courier: 101 S Mercer St, Room 401, New Castle, PA 16101); 724-656-3100 (Message Phone), 724-652-8951 (Fax), 8AM-4:30PM.

www.dsf.health.state.pa.us/health/cwp/view.asp?a=168&Q=202275

Note: Statewide records are avilable from this office. Records from 1994 forward are available from these cities (only for that particular city): Erie, Harrisburg, Philadelphia, Pittsburgh, and Scranton. Visit the website for address information.

Indexing & Storage: Records are available from 1906 to present.

Searching: Must have a signed release from immediate family member, or give tangible evidence of need. Requester must be at least 18 years of age. Include the following in your

request-full name, date of death, place of death, relationship to person of record, reason for information request. SSN helpful, if known. Include daytime phone number.

Access by: mail, fax, in person, online.

Fee & Payment: The fee is $9.00 per record. Fee payee: Vital Records. Prepayment required. Personal checks accepted. Credit cards accepted: MasterCard, Visa, AmEx, Discover.

Mail search: Turnaround time: 3 to 4 weeks. A SASE is requested.

Fax search: See Expedited Service.

In person search: Turnaround time 1 hour.

Online search: Expedited service is available at www.vitalchek.com, a state designated vendor.

Expedited service: Expedited service is available for fax and online orders. Use of the state form (downloadable from web site) is recommended. Turnaround time: 2 to 4 days. Add $7.00 for use of credit card and cost of express delivery if desired.

Marriage Certificates, Divorce Records

Records not maintained by a state level agency.

Note: Marriage and divorce records are found at county level at Prothonotary of issue.

Workers' Compensation Records

Bureau of Workers' Compensation, Physical Records Section, 1171 S Cameron St, Rm 103, Harrisburg, PA 17104-2501; 717-772-4447, 7:30AM-4PM.

www.dli.state.pa.us/landi/site/default.asp

Indexing & Storage: Records are available for past 4 years. It takes 1 to 3 days before new records are available for inquiry. Records are indexed on inhouse computer. Records are normally destroyed after 4 years.

Searching: Only the party to the record is allowed full access without a subpoena or a signed release. The Agency will indicate if a record exists for a person, but will not give any other information to the public. Include the following in your request-claimant name, year, date of accident, Social Security Number. If not a party to claim, then include a signed release.

Access by: mail.

Fee & Payment: No fees involved for simple requests.

Mail search: Turnaround time: 14 days. No SASE is required.

Driver Records

Department of Transportation, Driver Record Services, PO Box 68695, Harrisburg, PA 17106-8695 (Courier: 1101 S Front Street, 3rd Fl, Harrisburg, PA 17104); 717-391-6190, 800-932-4600 (In-state only), 7:30AM-4:30PM.

www.dmv.state.pa.us

Note: Copies of tickets may be purchased from this location for a fee of $5.00 each.

Indexing & Storage: Records are available for minimum of 3 calendar years for moving violations or departmental actions, minimum of 7

yrs for DWIs, and indefinite for suspensions. Accidents are reported on record as involvement only. Driver's address appears on the record. It takes 15 days from receipt before new records are available for inquiry.

Searching: The agency must pre-authorize all customers of MVR vendor companies and of pre-employment screening firms. Include the following in your request-driver's license number, full name, date of birth. Casual requesters submit Form DL-503, which requires the signature of the subject or notarized signature of the requester. Large volume requesters must sign an agreement stating the individual authorizations are on file.

Access by: mail, in person, online.

Fee & Payment: The fee is $5.00 for each 3-year record or $10.00 for complete certified record. A 10 year employment record for commercial drivers is available for $5.00. Fee payee: Department of Transportation. Prepayment required. Personal checks accepted. No credit cards accepted.

Mail search: Turnaround time: 7 to 10 days. No SASE is required.

In person search: The state will process one record request while you wait, additional requests are mailed back to the requester.

Online search: The online system is available to high volume requesters. Fee is $5.00 per record. Call 717-787-7154 for more information. The resale of records over the Internet is strictly forbidden. Drivers may order their own record from the web page, using a PIN number.

Other access: Magnetic tape processing is available for batch reqeusters. There is a 500 record minimum order per day.

Vehicle Ownership, Vehicle Identification

Department of Transportation, Vehicle Record Services, PO Box 68691, Harrisburg, PA 17106-8691 (Courier: 1101 South Front St, Harrisburg, PA 17104); 717-391-6190, 800-932-6000 (In-state), 7:30AM-4:30PM.

www.dmv.state.pa.us

Note: This agency also holds records for unattached mobile homes. Encumbrance/lien information is not considered public information and is only released per DPPA guidelines.

Indexing & Storage: Records are normally destroyed after 10 years.

Searching: The requester must submit Form DL-135. The state does not authorize the bulk delivery or commercial use of ownership & vehicle information.

Access by: mail.

Fee & Payment: The fee is $5.00 per transaction. Title history may have more than one transaction per vehicle. You can call first to determine the number. There is an additional $5.00 for certification. Fee payee: Department of Transportation. Prepayment required. Personal checks accepted. No credit cards accepted.

Mail search: Turnaround time: 7 to 10 days. You can order a record in person, but results will be mailed. No SASE is required.

Other access: Bulk information is not sold for commercial purposes. Certain statistical type user requests will be honored.

Accident Reports

State Police Headquarters, Crash Reports Unit, 1800 Elmerton Ave, Harrisburg, PA 17110; 717-783-5516, 8AM-4PM.

www.psp.state.pa.us

Note: Order form is available at the website.

Indexing & Storage: Records are available for 10 years to present. It takes 60 days before new records are available for inquiry. Records are indexed on inhouse computer. Records are normally destroyed after 10 years.

Searching: Only those involved, their attorney or insurer may request a copy of the accident report. Include the following in your request-full name, date of accident, State Police incident number. The following data is not released: medical information or expunged records.

Access by: mail.

Fee & Payment: Reports are $8.00 per record. Fee payee: Commonwealth of Pennsylvania. Prepayment required. Personal checks accepted. No credit cards accepted.

Mail search: Turnaround time: 6 weeks or more.

Vessel Ownership, Vessel Registration

Access to Records is Restricted

Fish and Boat Commission, Licensing & Registration Section, PO Box 68900, Harrisburg, PA 17106-8900; 717-705-7940, 717-705-7931 (Fax), 8AM-4PM.

www.fish.state.pa.us

Note: Boat registration and ownership information is not open to the public. Liens are filed at UCC filing locations. As of 1998, this agency issues certificates of title.

Voter Registration

Records not maintained by a state level agency.

Note: The state is in the process of implementing a statewide database (SURE Project). 80% of the counties now participate. Until 100% participation is available, it is suggested to do record searches at the county level. Records cannot be sold or re-sold for commercial purposes.

GED Certificates

Commonwealth Diploma Program, GED Testing, 333 Market St 12th Fl, Harrisburg, PA 17126-0333; 717-787-6747, 8:30AM-4:30PM.

www.paadulted.org/able/site/default.asp

Searching: They will only honor written requests. No verbal or fax verifictaions are given. For all requests the following is required: a signed release, name, approximate year of test, date of birth, SSN, city of test, and a phone number where you can be reached.

Access by: mail, in person.

Fee & Payment: Verifications and copies of transcripts are $3.00 each. The fee is non-refundable. Fee payee: Commonwealth of PA. Prepayment required. Cashier's checks and money orders are accepted. No credit cards or personal checks accepted.

Mail search: Turnaround time: 3 to 4 weeks. No SASE is required.

In person search: Counter service is available.

Hunting License Information

Access to Records is Restricted

Game Commission, Hunting License Division, 2001 Elmerton Ave, Harrisburg, PA 17110-9797; 717-787-2084 (Hunting License Division), 717-787-2613 (Fax), 8AM-4PM.

www.theoutdoorshop.state.pa.us/fbg/

Note: Hunting license information is not released to the public.

Fishing License Information

Access to Records is Restricted

Fish & Boat Commission, Fishing License Division, PO Box 67000, Harrisburg, PA 17106 (Courier: 1601 Elmerton, Harrisburg, PA 17110); 717-705-7930 (Fishing License Division), 717-787-4250 (PA Game Division), 717-705-7931 (Fax), 8AM-4PM.

Pennsylvania State Licensing Agencies
Licenses Searchable Online

Acupuncturist #20	http://licensepa.state.pa.us/default.asp
Amphetamine Program #20	http://licensepa.state.pa.us/default.asp
Anesthesia Permit, Dental #18	www.mylicense.state.pa.us
Animal Health Technician #20	http://licensepa.state.pa.us/default.asp
Appraiser, Residential #20	http://licensepa.state.pa.us/default.asp
Appraiser/Broker #20	http://licensepa.state.pa.us/default.asp
Architect #20	http://licensepa.state.pa.us/default.asp
Architectural Firm #20	http://licensepa.state.pa.us/default.asp
Athletic Agent #22	www.licensepa.state.pa.us/default.asp
Athletic Trainer #20	http://licensepa.state.pa.us/default.asp
Attorney #1	http://padisciplinaryboard.org/attsearchdcd.php
Attorney, Disciplined #1	http://padisciplinaryboard.org/attsearchdcd.php
Auction House/Company #20	http://licensepa.state.pa.us/default.asp
Auctioneer #20	http://licensepa.state.pa.us/default.asp
Auctioneer, Real Estate #20	http://licensepa.state.pa.us/default.asp
Audiologist #20	http://licensepa.state.pa.us/default.asp
Bank #4	www.banking.state.pa.us/Banking/Banking/InstListQuery.asp
Barber/ Barber Shop/Manager #20	http://licensepa.state.pa.us/default.asp
Barber School/Teacher #20	http://licensepa.state.pa.us/default.asp
Boxer #22	www.dos.state.pa.us/sac/cwp/view.asp?a=1090&q=436810&sacNav=|
Builder/Owner, Real Estate #20	http://licensepa.state.pa.us/default.asp
Campground Membership Seller #20	http://licensepa.state.pa.us/default.asp
Cemetery Broker/Seller/Regis. #20	http://licensepa.state.pa.us/default.asp
Check Casher #4	www.banking.state.pa.us/Banking/Banking/InstListQuery.asp
Chiropractor #20	http://licensepa.state.pa.us/default.asp
Consumer Discount Company #4	www.banking.state.pa.us/Banking/Banking/InstListQuery.asp
Continuing Education Provider, Financial #4	www.banking.state.pa.us/Banking/Banking/InstListQuery.asp
Cosmetician Shop #20	http://licensepa.state.pa.us/default.asp
Cosmetologist/Cosmetician #20	http://licensepa.state.pa.us/default.asp
Cosmetology Teacher/School #20	http://licensepa.state.pa.us/default.asp
Cosmetology/Manicurist Shop #20	http://licensepa.state.pa.us/default.asp
Counselor, Professional #20	http://licensepa.state.pa.us/default.asp
Credit Services Loan Broker #4	www.banking.state.pa.us/Banking/Banking/InstListQuery.asp
Credit Union #4	www.banking.state.pa.us/Banking/Banking/InstListQuery.asp
Debt Collector #4	www.banking.state.pa.us/Banking/Banking/InstListQuery.asp
Dental Assistant, Expanded Function #18	www.mylicense.state.pa.us
Dental Hygienist #18	www.mylicense.state.pa.us
Dentist #18	www.mylicense.state.pa.us
Dietitian/Nutritionist LDN #20	http://licensepa.state.pa.us/default.asp
Engineer #20	http://licensepa.state.pa.us/default.asp
Evaluator, Appraisal #20	http://licensepa.state.pa.us/default.asp
Financial Holding Company #4	www.banking.state.pa.us/Banking/Banking/InstListQuery.asp
Funeral Director/Supervisor #20	http://licensepa.state.pa.us/default.asp
Funeral Establishment #20	http://licensepa.state.pa.us/default.asp
Geologist #20	http://licensepa.state.pa.us/default.asp
Hearing Examiners #20	http://licensepa.state.pa.us/default.asp
Installment Loan Seller #4	www.banking.state.pa.us/Banking/Banking/InstListQuery.asp
Insurance Company #11	www.insurance.state.pa.us
Landscape Architect #20	http://licensepa.state.pa.us/default.asp
Loan Correspondent #4	www.banking.state.pa.us/Banking/Banking/InstListQuery.asp
Lobbyist #17	www.ldrs.state.pa.us/webstat/query.asp
Manicurist #20	http://licensepa.state.pa.us/default.asp
Marriage & Family Therapist #20	http://licensepa.state.pa.us/default.asp
Medical Doctor #20	http://licensepa.state.pa.us/default.asp
Midwife #20	http://licensepa.state.pa.us/default.asp
Money Transmitter #4	www.banking.state.pa.us/Banking/Banking/InstListQuery.asp
Mortgage (1st) Banker/Broker #4	www.banking.state.pa.us/Banking/Banking/InstListQuery.asp
Mortgage (1st) Loan Correspondent #4	www.banking.state.pa.us/Banking/Banking/InstListQuery.asp
Mortgage (2nd) Lender/Loan Broker/Agent #4	www.banking.state.pa.us/Banking/Banking/InstListQuery.asp
Mortgage (Accelerated) Payment Provider #4	www.banking.state.pa.us/Banking/Banking/InstListQuery.asp

Nuclear Medicine Technologist #20	http://licensepa.state.pa.us/default.asp
Nurse #20	http://licensepa.state.pa.us/default.asp
Nursing Home Administrator #20	http://licensepa.state.pa.us/default.asp
Occupational Therapist/Assistant #20	http://licensepa.state.pa.us/default.asp
Optometrist #20	http://licensepa.state.pa.us/default.asp
Osteopathic Acupuncturist #20	http://licensepa.state.pa.us/default.asp
Osteopathic Physician Assistant #20	http://licensepa.state.pa.us/default.asp
Osteopathic Physician/Surgeon #20	http://licensepa.state.pa.us/default.asp
Osteopathic Respiratory Care #20	http://licensepa.state.pa.us/default.asp
Pawnbroker #4	www.banking.state.pa.us/Banking/Banking/InstListQuery.asp
Pharmacist/Pharmacy #20	http://licensepa.state.pa.us/default.asp
Physical Therapist/Assistant #20	http://licensepa.state.pa.us/default.asp
Physician Assistant #20	http://licensepa.state.pa.us/default.asp
Pilot, Navigational #20	http://licensepa.state.pa.us/default.asp
Podiatrist #20	http://licensepa.state.pa.us/default.asp
Psychologist #20	http://licensepa.state.pa.us/default.asp
Public Accountant-CPA, Individual/Corp. #20	http://licensepa.state.pa.us/default.asp
Public Accounting Partnership #20	http://licensepa.state.pa.us/default.asp
Radiation Therapy Technician #20	http://licensepa.state.pa.us/default.asp
Radiologic Auxilliary, Chiropractic #20	http://licensepa.state.pa.us/default.asp
Radiologic Technologist #20	http://licensepa.state.pa.us/default.asp
Real Estate Agent/Broker/Sales/School #20	http://licensepa.state.pa.us/default.asp
Real Estate Appraiser #20	http://licensepa.state.pa.us/default.asp
Rental Listing Referral Agent #20	http://licensepa.state.pa.us/default.asp
Reposessor #4	www.banking.state.pa.us/Banking/Banking/InstListQuery.asp
Respiratory Care Practitioner #20	http://licensepa.state.pa.us/default.asp
Sales Finance Company #4	www.banking.state.pa.us/Banking/Banking/InstListQuery.asp
Savings Association #4	www.banking.state.pa.us/Banking/Banking/InstListQuery.asp
Social Worker #20	http://licensepa.state.pa.us/default.asp
Speech-Language Pathologist #20	http://licensepa.state.pa.us/default.asp
Surveyor, Land #20	http://licensepa.state.pa.us/default.asp
Tablefunder, Wholesale #4	www.banking.state.pa.us/Banking/Banking/InstListQuery.asp
Teacher #6	https://www.tcs.ed.state.pa.us/validchk.asp
Therapist, Drugless #20	http://licensepa.state.pa.us/default.asp
Thrift Holding Company #4	www.banking.state.pa.us/Banking/Banking/InstListQuery.asp
Timeshare Salesperson #20	http://licensepa.state.pa.us/default.asp
Trust Company #4	www.banking.state.pa.us/Banking/Banking/InstListQuery.asp
Veterinarian / Veterinary Technician #20	http://licensepa.state.pa.us/default.asp

Pennsylvania Licensing Quick Finder

Acupuncturist #20 717-783-4858	Boxer #22 717-787-5720	Evaluator, Appraisal #20 717-783-4866
Ambulance Service #8 717-787-8740	Boxing Judge/Promoter/Second #22 ... 717-787-5720	Financial Holding Company #4 717-787-3717
Amphetamine Program #20 717-787-2568	Builder/Owner, Real Estate #20 717-783-3658	First Responder EMT #8 717-787-8740
Anesthesia Permit, Dental #18 717-783-7162	Campground Membership Seller #20 .. 717-783-3658	Funeral Director/Supervisor #20 717-783-3397
Animal Health Technician #20 717-783-7134	Cemetery Broker/Seller/Regis. #20 717-783-3658	Funeral Establishment #20 717-783-3397
Appraiser, Residential #20 717-783-4866	Check Casher #4 717-787-3717	Geologist #20 717-783-7049
Appraiser/Broker #20 717-783-4866	Child Day Care Facility #12 717-787-8691	Harness Racing #3 717-787-5789
Architect #20 717-783-3397	Chiropractor #20 717-783-7155	Hearing Aid Dealer #7 717-783-1389
Architectural Firm #20 717-783-3397	Consumer Discount Company #4 717-787-3717	Hearing Aid Fitter/Fitter Apprentice #7. 717-783-1389
Athletic Agent #22 717-787-5720	Continuing Education Provider, Financial #4	Hearing Examiners #20 717-783-1389
Athletic Event Manager #22 717-787-5720	 717-787-3717	Horse Racing #3 717-783-8726
Athletic Event Ring Announcer/Timekeeper #22	Cosmetician Shop #20 717-783-7130	Installment Loan Seller #4 717-787-3717
.... 717-787-5720	Cosmetologist/Cosmetician #20 717-783-7130	Insurance Agent #11 ....717-787-3840, 877-336-7479
Athletic Physician/Trainer #22 717-787-5720	Cosmetology Teacher/School #20 717-783-7130	Insurance Company #11 717-787-2735
Athletic Trainer #20 717-783-4858	Cosmetology/Manicurist Shop #20 717-783-7130	Investment Adviser #16 717-783-4211
Attorney #1 717-731-7073	Counselor, Professional #20 717-783-1389	Kickboxer #22 717-787-5720
Attorney, Disciplined #1 717-731-7073	Credit Services Loan Broker #4 717-787-3717	Laboratory, Medical #10 610-280-3464
Auction House/Company #20 717-783-3397	Credit Union #4 717-787-3717	Landscape Architect #20 717-772-8528
Auctioneer #20 717-783-3397	Debt Collector #4 717-787-3717	Liquor Distributor/Retailer/Whls #14 717-783-8250
Auctioneer, Real Estate #20 717-783-3658	Dental Assistant, expand'd Function #18717-783-7162	Loan Correspondent #4 717-787-3717
Audiologist #20 717-783-1389	Dental Hygienist #18 717-783-7162	Lobbyist #17 717-787-5920
Bank #4 717-787-3717	Dentist #18 717-783-7162	Manicurist #20 717-783-7130
Barber #20 717-783-3402	Dietitian/Nutritionist LDN #20 717-783-7142	Marriage & Family Therapist #20 717-783-1389
Barber School/Teacher #20 717-783-3402	Education Specialist #6 717-787-3356	Medical Doctor #20 717-787-2381
Barber Shop/Manager #20 717-783-3402	Emergency Health Professional #8 717-787-8740	Medical School #20 717-783-1400
Boat Registration #13 717-705-7940	Emergency Medical Technician #8 717-787-8740	Midwife #20 717-783-1400
Bondsman #11 .... 717-787-3840, 877-336-7479	Engineer #20 717-783-7049	Money Transmitter #4 717-787-3717

Mortgage (1st) Banker/Broker #4	717-787-3717
Mortgage (1st) Limited Broker #4	717-787-3717
Mortgage (1st) Loan Correspondent #4	717-787-3717
Mortgage (2nd) Lender/Loan Broker/Agent #4	717-787-3717
Mortgage (Accelerated) Payment Provider #4	717-787-3717
Notary Public #21	717-787-5280
Nuclear Medicine Technologist #20	717-787-4858
Nurse #20	717-783-7142
Nursing Home #9	610-594-8041
Nursing Home Administrator #20	717-783-7155
Occupational Therapist/Assistant #20	717-783-1389
Optometrist #20	717-783-7155
Osteopathic Acupuncturist #20	717-783-4858
Osteopathic Physician Assistant #20	717-783-4858
Osteopathic Physician/Surgeon #20	717-783-4858
Osteopathic Respiratory Care #20	717-783-4858
Paramedic #8	717-787-8740
Pawnbroker #4	717-787-3717
Pest Management Consultant #2	717-787-5231 x2
Pesticide Applicator/Technician #2	717-787-5231 x2
Pesticide Dealer #2	717-787-5231 x2
Pharmacist/Pharmacy #20	717-783-7156
Physical Therapist/Assistant #20	717-783-7134
Physician Assistant #20	717-787-2381
Pilot, Navigational #20	717-787-6802
Podiatrist #20	717-783-4858
Pre-Hospital RN #8	717-787-8740
Private Investigator #15	717-255-2692
Private School Staff #6	717-787-3356
Psychologist #20	717-783-7134
Public Accountant-CPA #20	717-783-1404
Public Accounting Partnership #20	717-783-1404
Public Adjuster/ Solicitor #11	717-787-3840, 877-336-7479
Radiation Therapy Technician #20	717-783-7155
Radiologic Auxilliary, Chiropractic #20	717-783-7155
Radiologic Technologist #20	717-783-4858
Real Estate Agent/Broker/Sales #20	717-783-3658
Real Estate Appraiser #20	717-783-4866
Real Estate School #20	717-783-3658
Referee #22	717-787-5720
Rental Listing Referral Agent #20	717-783-3658
Reposessor #4	717-787-3717
Respiratory Care Practitioner #20	717-783-4858
Sales Finance Company #4	717-787-3717
Savings Association #4	717-787-3717
School Administrator/Superintend't #6	717-787-3356
School Intermediate Unit Director #6	717-787-3356
School Supervisor #6	717-787-3356
Securities Agent #16	717-783-4212
Securities Broker/Dealer #16	717-783-4213
Social Worker #20	717-783-1389
Speech-Language Pathologist #20	717-783-1389
Surplus Lines Broker #11	717-787-3840, 877-336-7479
Surveyor, Land #20	717-783-7049
Tablefunder, Wholesale #4	717-787-3717
Teacher #5	717-787-2967
Teacher #6	717-787-3356
Therapist, Drugless #20	717-783-4858
Thrift Holding Company #4	717-787-3717
Timeshare Salesperson #20	717-783-3658
Title Insurance #11	717-787-3840, 877-336-7479
Trust Company #4	717-787-3717
Used Vehicle Lot #19	717-783-1697
Vehicle Auction #19	717-783-1697
Vehicle Dealer/Manufacturer/Dist. #19	717-783-1697
Vehicle Salesperson #19	717-783-1697
Veterinarian / Veterinary Tech. #20	717-783-7134
Viatical Settlement Broker #11	717-787-3840, 877-336-7479
Wrestling Promoter #22	717-787-5720

Pennsylvania Licensing Agency Information

1 Disciplinary Board of the Supreme Court, 2 Lemoyne Dr, First Fl, Lemoyne, PA 17055; 717-731-7073, Fax: 717-731-7080.
Search Database at www.padisciplinaryboard.org/disciplined_attorneys.html

2 Department of Agriculture, Bureau of Plant Industry, 2301 N Cameron St, Harrisburg, PA 17110-9408; 717-772-5231, Fax: 717-783-3275.
www.agriculture.state.pa.us
Email: dascott@state.pa.us

3 Department of Agriculture, Racing License Division, 2301 N Cameron St, Agriculture Office Bldg, Harrisburg, PA 17110-9408; 717-787-5196, Fax: 717-787-2271. www.pda.state.pa.us

4 Department of Banking, 333 Market St, 16th Fl, Harrisburg, PA 17111-2290; 717-787-2665, Fax: 717-787-8773.
www.banking.state.pa.us/
Email: pabanking@banking.state.pa.us

6 Department of Education, Teacher Certification, 333 Market St, 3rd Fl, Harrisburg, PA 17126-0333; 717-787-3356, Fax: 717-783-6736.
www.pde.state.pa.us
Email: na-teachercert@state.pa.us
Search Database at
https://www.tcs.ed.state.pa.us/validchk.asp Note: Use a teacher's SSN to verify certifications.

7 Bureau of Profession and Occupational Affairs, Board of Examiners in Speech-Language and Hearing, PO Box 2649, Harrisburg, PA 17105; 717-783-1389, Fax: 717-787-7769.
www.dos.state.pa.us/speech
Email: st-speech@state.pa.us Note: Direct list requests to Diane Miller at (717) 772-2244 or via e-mail: diamiller@state.pa.us.

8 Department of Health, Emergency Medical Services, PO Box 90 (7th & Forster), Harrisburg, PA 17108; 717-787-8740, Fax: 717-772-0910.
www.dsf.health.state.pa.us/health/site/

9 Department of Health, Long Term Care Division, 110 Pickering Way, Lionville, PA 19353; 610-594-8041, Fax: 610-436-3346.
www.health.state.pa.us/qa/ltc

10 Department of Health, Bureau of Labs, PO Box 500, Exton, PA 19341-0500; 610-280-3464, Fax: 610-436-3346.
www.health.state.pa.us/HPA/labinvst.htm

11 Department of Insurance, 1300 Strawberry Sq, Harrisburg, PA 17120;
717-787-2735, Fax: 717-787-8557.
www.insurance.state.pa.us
Search Database at www.insurance.state.pa.us

12 Department of Public Welfare, 1401 N 7th St., Harrisburg, PA 17105; 717-787-8691, Fax: 717-787-1529.
www.dpw.state.pa.us/ocyf/dpwocyf.asp

13 Fish & Boat Commission, 1601 Elmerton Ave, Harrisburg, PA 17110-9299;
717-705-7940, Fax: 717-705-7931.
www.fish.state.pa.us

14 Liquor Control Board, PO Box 8940 (Capitol & Forester St), Harrisburg, PA 17105-8940;
717-783-8250, Fax: 717-772-2165.
www.lcb.state.pa.us

16 Securities Commission, 1010 N 7th St, Eastgate-2nd Fl, Harrisburg, PA 17102-1410;
717-787-8061, Fax: 717-783-5122.
www.psc.state.pa.us

17 State Ethics Commission, 309 Finance Bldg, PO Box 11470, Harrisburg, PA 17108-1470;
717-783-1610, Fax: 717-783-0806.
www.ethics.state.pa.us Search Database at www.ldrs.state.pa.us/webstat/query.asp Note: The PA Online Lobbyist Network can be searched free at www.lobbyistnetwork.com.

18 Department of State, Board of Dentistry, PO Box 2649 (124 Pine St), Harrisburg, PA 17105-2649; 717-783-7162, Fax: 717-787-7769.
www.dos.state.pa.us/dent
Email: st-dentistry@state.pa.us
Search Database at www.mylicense.state.pa.us
Note: Direct list requests to Diane Miller at (717) 772-2244 or via e-mail: diamiller@state.pa.us.

19 Dept. of State, Professional & Occupational Affairs, Board of Vehicle Manufacturers, Dealers & Salespersons, Box 2649PO Box 2649 (2601 Northfield St), Harrisburg, PA 17110; 717-783-1697, Fax: 717-787-0250.
www.dos.state.pa.us/vehicle
Email: ra-st-vehicle@state.pa.us Note: For verifications you may contact the Board via e-mail at vehicle@pados.dos.state.pa.us. Direct list requests to Diane Miller at (717) 772-2244 or via e-mail: diamiller@state.pa.us.

20 Department of State, Professional & Occupational Affairs, P.O. Box 2649 (124 Pine St), Harrisburg, PA 17105;
717-787-8503, Fax: 717-787-7769.
www.dos.state.pa.us/bpoa/site/default.asp
Email: RA-BPOA@state.pa.us
Search Database at
http://licensepa.state.pa.us/default.asp Note: Direct list requests to Diane Miller at (717) 772-2244 or via e-mail: diamiller@state.pa.us.

21 Department of State, Elections & Legislation, 210 North Office Bldg, Rm 304, Harrisburg, PA 17120; 717-787-5280, Fax: 717-787-2854.
www.dos.state.pa.us/bcel/site/default.asp
Email: rcole@state.pa.us

22 Department of State, Athletic Commission, 2601 North 3rd Street, Harrisburg, PA 17110; 717-787-5720, Fax: 717-783-0824.
Email: sac@pados.dos.state.pa.us.

Pennsylvania Federal Courts

The following list indicates the district and division name for each county in the state. If the bankruptcy court location is different from the district court, then the location of the bankruptcy court appears in parentheses.

County/Court Cross Reference

County	District	Division
Adams	Middle	Harrisburg
Allegheny	Western	Pittsburgh
Armstrong	Western	Pittsburgh
Beaver	Western	Pittsburgh
Bedford	Western	Johnstown (Pittsburgh)
Berks	Eastern	Allentown/Reading (Reading)
Blair	Western	Johnstown (Pittsburgh)
Bradford	Middle	Scranton (Wilkes-Barre)
Bucks	Eastern	Philadelphia
Butler	Western	Pittsburgh
Cambria	Western	Johnstown (Pittsburgh)
Cameron	Middle	Williamsport (Wilkes-Barre)
Carbon	Middle	Scranton (Wilkes-Barre)
Centre	Middle	Williamsport (Harrisburg)
Chester	Eastern	Philadelphia
Clarion	Western	Pittsburgh (Erie)
Clearfield	Western	Johnstown (Pittsburgh)
Clinton	Middle	Williamsport (Wilkes-Barre)
Columbia	Middle	Williamsport (Wilkes-Barre)
Crawford	Western	Erie
Cumberland	Middle	Harrisburg
Dauphin	Middle	Harrisburg
Delaware	Eastern	Philadelphia
Elk	Western	Erie
Erie	Western	Erie
Fayette	Western	Pittsburgh
Forest	Western	Erie
Franklin	Middle	Harrisburg
Fulton	Middle	Harrisburg
Greene	Western	Pittsburgh
Huntingdon	Middle	Harrisburg
Indiana	Western	Pittsburgh
Jefferson	Western	Pittsburgh (Erie)
Juniata	Middle	Harrisburg
Lackawanna	Middle	Scranton (Wilkes-Barre)
Lancaster	Eastern	Allentown/Reading (Reading)
Lawrence	Western	Pittsburgh
Lebanon	Middle	Harrisburg
Lehigh	Eastern	Allentown/Reading (Reading)
Luzerne	Middle	Scranton (Wilkes-Barre)
Lycoming	Middle	Williamsport (Wilkes-Barre)
McKean	Western	Erie
Mercer	Western	Pittsburgh (Erie)
Mifflin	Middle	Harrisburg
Monroe	Middle	Scranton (Wilkes-Barre)
Montgomery	Eastern	Philadelphia
Montour	Middle	Williamsport (Harrisburg)
Northampton	Eastern	Allentown/Reading (Reading)
Northumberland	Middle	Williamsport (Harrisburg)
Perry	Middle	Williamsport (Harrisburg)
Philadelphia	Eastern	Philadelphia
Pike	Middle	Scranton (Wilkes-Barre)
Potter	Middle	Williamsport (Wilkes-Barre)
Schuylkill	Eastern	Allentown/Reading (Reading)
Snyder	Middle	Williamsport (Harrisburg)
Somerset	Western	Johnstown (Pittsburgh)
Sullivan	Middle	Williamsport (Wilkes-Barre)
Susquehanna	Middle	Scranton (Wilkes-Barre)
Tioga	Middle	Williamsport (Wilkes-Barre)
Union	Middle	Williamsport (Harrisburg)
Venango	Western	Erie
Warren	Western	Erie
Washington	Western	Pittsburgh
Wayne	Middle	Scranton (Wilkes-Barre)
Westmoreland	Western	Pittsburgh
Wyoming	Middle	Scranton (Wilkes-Barre)
York	Middle	Harrisburg

Standards for Federal Courts: The search fee is $20.00 per item (one party name or case number). Certification fee is $7.00 per document. Copy fee is $.50 per page. All fees standard unless noted in profile. Mail Search: always enclose a stamped self addressed envelope unless otherwise noted. Most courts accept fax requests or will suggest a copying/search vendor. Before releasing records, all courts require prepayment unless noted in profile. Open records are located at the court unless otherwise noted. District courts index by defendant and plaintiff as well as by case number. Bankruptcy courts usually index by debtor and case number. While most courts now have their indexes on computer, many still maintain index card files as well.

The universal PACER sign-up number is 800-676-6856. Find PACER and the Party/Case Index on the Web at http://pacer.psc.uscourts.gov. PACER dial-up access is $.60 per minute. Also, courts offering internet access via RACER, PACER, Web-PACER or the new CM-ECF charge $.07 per page fee unless noted as free.

US District Court

Eastern District of Pennsylvania

Allentown / Reading Division c/o Philadelphia Division, Room 2609, U.S. Courthouse, 601 Market St, Philadelphia, PA 19106-1797 (courier address: Use mail address for courier delivery) 215-597-7704, Fax: 215-597-6390. www.paed.uscourts.gov

Counties: Berks, Lancaster, Lehigh, Northampton, Schuylkill.

Indexing & Storage: Cases indexed by as well as by case number. New cases available in the index after filing date. Open records are located at the Philadelphia Division.

Fee & Payment: Payment may be made by money order, cashier check. Business checks are not accepted. Personal checks are not accepted.

Phone Search: No searching by telephone.

In Person Search: Permitted.

PACER: PACER is available online at http://pacer.paed.uscourts.gov. Case records go back to July 1, 1990. Records never purged. New records are online after 1 day.

Electronic Filing: Electronic filing information online at https://ecf.paed.uscourts.gov

Opinions Online: Court opinions are online at www.paed.uscourts.gov/contents.shtml

Other Online Access: Online access is available free at www.paed.uscourts.gov/us04000.asp?19. No fee to search; select document type and enter name as search string.

Philadelphia Division Room 2609, U.S. Courthouse, 601 Market St, Philadelphia, PA 19106-1797 (courier address: Use mail address for courier delivery) 215-597-7704, Fax: 215-597-6390. www.paed.uscourts.gov

Counties: Bucks, Chester, Delaware, Montgomery, Philadelphia.

Indexing & Storage: New cases available in the index immediately after filing date. The computer index is from 1990 on. Records are also indexed on microfiche. Indexes by judgment and by nature of suit are also available. District wide searches are available from this division.

Fee & Payment: Payment may be made by money order, cashier check, personal check, Visa, Mastercard. Payee: Clerk, U.S. District Court. Will fax docket listing $.50 per page.

Phone Search: Docket information available by phone if case number is known. Will fax docket listing $.50 per page.

In Person Search: Fee charged if court conducts your in person search for you.

PACER: PACER is available online at http://pacer.paed.uscourts.gov. Case records go back to July 1, 1990. Records never purged. New records are online after 1 day.

Electronic Filing: Electronic filing information online at https://ecf.paed.uscourts.gov

Opinions Online: Court opinions are online at www.paed.uscourts.gov/contents.shtml

Other Online Access: Online access is available free at www.paed.uscourts.gov/us04000.asp?19. No fee to search; select document type and enter name as search string.

U.S. Bankruptcy Court

Eastern District of Pennsylvania

Philadelphia Division 4th Floor, 900 Market St, Philadelphia, PA 19107 (courier address: Use mail address for courier delivery) 215-408-2800. www.paeb.uscourts.gov

Counties: Bucks, Chester, Delaware, Montgomery, Philadelphia.

Indexing & Storage: Cases indexed by debtor and creditors as well as by case number. New cases available in the index 1 day after filing date. A microfiche index is also maintained.

Fee & Payment: Payment may be made by money order, cashier check, business check, Visa or Mastercard. Personal checks are not accepted. Payee: Clerk, U.S. Bankruptcy Court.

Phone Search: Automated voice case information service (VCIS) is available. Call VCIS at 215-597-2244.

In Person Search: Fee charged if court conducts your in person search for you. In person searchers may not search the card index.

PACER: PACER is available online at http://pacer.paeb.uscourts.gov. Records purged every 6 months. New civil records are online after 1 day.

Electronic Filing: Electronic filing information online at https://ecf.paeb.uscourts.gov

Reading Division The Madison, 400 Washington St, Reading, PA 19601 (courier address: Use mail address for courier delivery) 610-320-5255. www.paeb.uscourts.gov

Counties: Berks, Lancaster, Lehigh, Northampton, Schuylkill.

Indexing & Storage: Cases indexed by debtor as well as by case number. New cases available in the index 1 day after filing date.

Fee & Payment: Payment may be made by money order, cashier check, business check, Visa or

Mastercard. Personal checks are not accepted. Payee: Clerk, U.S. Bankruptcy Court.

Phone Search: Only docket information available by phone. Automated voice case information service (VCIS) is available. VCIS- 215-597-2244.

In Person Search: Fee charged if court conducts your in person search for you.

PACER: PACER is available online at http://pacer.paeb.uscourts.gov. Records purged every 6 months. New civil records are online after 1 day.

Electronic Filing: Electronic filing information online at https://ecf.paeb.uscourts.gov

U.S. District Court

Middle District of Pennsylvania

Harrisburg Division PO Box 983, Harrisburg, PA 17108-0983 (courier address: U.S. Courthouse & Federal Bldg, 228 Walnut St, Harrisburg, PA 17108), 717-221-3920, Fax: 717-221-3959. www.pamd.uscourts.gov

Counties: Adams, Cumberland, Dauphin, Franklin, Fulton, Huntingdon, Juniata, Lebanon, Mifflin, York.

Indexing & Storage: New cases available in the index immediately after filing date.

Fee & Payment: Payment may be made by money order, cashier check, personal check, American Express, Visa, Mastercard. Payee: Clerk, U.S. District Court. Will fax results $1.00 per page.

Phone Search: No searching by telephone. Only accession numbers for a specific case are available by phone. Will fax results $1.00 per page.

Mail Search: A SASE not required.

In Person Search: Fee charged if court conducts your in person search for you.

PACER: PACER is available online at http://pacer.pamd.uscourts.gov. Document images available. Case records go back to May 1989. Records never purged. New records are online after 1 day.

Electronic Filing: Electronic filing information at https://ecf.pamd.uscourts.gov/cgi-bin/login.pl

Opinions Online: Court opinions are online at www.pamd.uscourts.gov/opinions.htm

Scranton Division Clerk's Office, William J Nealon Fedearl Bldg & U.S. Courthouse, PO Box 1148, Scranton, PA 18501 (courier address: 235 N Washington Ave, Room 101, Scranton, PA 18503), 570-207-5680, Fax: 717-207-5689. www.pamd.uscourts.gov

Counties: Bradford, Carbon, Lackawanna, Luzerne, Monroe, Pike, Susquehanna, Wayne, Wyoming.

Indexing & Storage: New cases available in the index 1 day after filing date. Records are also indexed on microfiche. Records are stored on an in-house computer from 1989. District wide searches are available for information from 1901 from this court.

Fee & Payment: Payment may be made by money order, cashier check, personal check, Visa, Mastercard. Payee: Clerk, U.S. District Court.

Phone Search: Only minimal docket information will be released over the phone.

Mail Search: A SASE not required.

In Person Search: Fee charged if court conducts your in person search for you.

PACER: PACER is available online at http://pacer.paeb.uscourts.gov. Records purged every 6 months. New civil records are online after 1 day.

Electronic Filing: Electronic filing information online at https://ecf.paeb.uscourts.gov

Williamsport Division PO Box 608, Williamsport, PA 17703 (courier address: Federal Bldg, ROom 218, 240 W 3rd St, Williamsport, PA 17701), 570-323-6380, Fax: 717-323-0636. www.pamd.uscourts.gov

Counties: Cameron, Centre, Clinton, Columbia, Lycoming, Montour, Northumberland, Perry, Potter, Snyder, Sullivan, Tioga, Union.

Indexing & Storage: New cases available in the index immediately after filing date.

Fee & Payment: Payment may be made by money order, cashier check, personal check, Visa, MC. Payee: Clerk, U.S. District Court.

Phone Search: Only docket information available.

In Person Search: Fee charged if court conducts your in person search for you.

PACER: PACER is available online at http://pacer.pamd.uscourts.gov. Document images available. Case records go back to May 1989. Records never purged. New records are online after 1 day.

Electronic Filing: Electronic filing information at https://ecf.pamd.uscourts.gov/cgi-bin/login.pl

Opinions Online: Court opinions are online at www.pamd.uscourts.gov/opinions.htm

U.S. Bankruptcy Court

Middle District of Pennsylvania

Harrisburg Division PO Box 908, Harrisburg, PA 17108 (courier address: 228 Walnut St, 3rd Floor, Harrisburg, PA 17101), 717-901-2800, Fax: 717-901-2822. www.pamb.uscourts.gov/

Counties: Adams, Centre, Cumberland, Dauphin, Franklin, Fulton, Huntingdon, Juniata, Lebanon, Mifflin, Montour, Northumberland, Perry, Schuylkill, Snyder, Union, York.

Indexing & Storage: Cases indexed by debtor as well as by case number. New cases available in the index 1 day after filing date.

Fee & Payment: Payment may be made by money order, cashier check, personal check. Debtor's checks are not accepted. Payee: Clerk, U.S. Bankruptcy Court.

Phone Search: Only docket information available by phone. Automated voice case information service (VCIS) is available. VCIS- 877-440-2699.

In Person Search: Fee charged if court conducts your in person search for you. Dukum's Copy Service 717-236-0179, available 9AM-1PM.

PACER: PACER is available online at http://pacer.pamb.uscourts.gov. Document images available. Case records go back to August 1986. Records never purged. New civil records are online after 1 day. **Electronic Filing:** Electronic filing information at https://ecf.pamb.uscourts.gov

Wilkes-Barre Division Clerk's Office, Max Rosen U.S. Courthouse, 197 S Main St, Wilkes-Barre, PA 18701 (courier address: Use mail address for courier delivery) 570-826-6450, Fax: 570-826-6694. www.pamb.uscourts.gov/

Counties: Bradford, Cameron, Carbon, Clinton, Columbia, Lackawanna, Luzerne, Lycoming, Monroe, Pike, Potter, Schuylkill, Sullivan, Susquehanna, Tioga, Wayne, Wyoming.

Indexing & Storage: Cases indexed by debtor as well as by case number. New cases available in the index 1-3 days after filing date.

Fee & Payment: Payment may be made by money order, cashier check, personal check. Debtor's checks are not accepted. Make checks payable to the Clerk for services other than copy services; for copies, make checks payable to Copy Service. Payee: Clerk, U.S. Bankruptcy Court.

Phone Search: Phone searches can be done if the name, social security number, or case number is provided. Only docket information will be released. Automated voice case information service (VCIS) is available. VCIS- 877-440-2699.

In Person Search: Permitted.

PACER: PACER is available online at http://pacer.pamb.uscourts.gov. Document images available. New civil records are online after 1 day.

Electronic Filing: Electronic filing information online at https://ecf.pamb.uscourts.gov

U.S. District Court

Western District of Pennsylvania

Erie Division PO Box 1820, Erie, PA 16507 (courier address: 102 U.S. Courthouse, 617 State St, Erie, PA 16501), Phone: 814-453-4829. www.pawd.uscourts.gov

Counties: Crawford, Elk, Erie, Forest, McKean, Venango, Warren.

Indexing & Storage: New cases available in the index 1 day after filing date. The court prefers that you perform searches at the Pittsburgh Division.

Fee & Payment: Payment may be made by money order, cashier check, personal check, Visa, Mastercard. Payee: Clerk, U.S. District Court.

Phone Search: Only the number, caption and attorneys' names will be released over the phone.

In Person Search: Fee charged if court conducts your in person search for you.

PACER: PACER is available online at http://pacer.pawd.uscourts.gov. Case records go back to 1994. Records never purged. New records are online after 1 day.

Johnstown Division Penn Traffic Bldg, Room 208, 319 Washington St, Johnstown, PA 15901 (Use mail address for courier delivery) 814-533-4504, Fax: 814-533-4519. www.pawd.uscourts.gov

Counties: Bedford, Blair, Cambria, Clearfield, Somerset.

Indexing & Storage: New cases available in the index 1 day after filing date. On computer since 1992. Card index from 1989 to 1992.

Fee & Payment: Payment may be made by money order, cashier check, personal check, Visa. Payee: Clerk, U.S. District Court.

Phone Search: Only the number, caption and attorneys' names will be released over the phone.

Mail Search: A SASE not required.

In Person Search: Fee charged if court conducts your in person search for you.

PACER: PACER is available online at http://pacer.pawd.uscourts.gov. Case records go back to 1994. Records never purged. New records are online after 1 day.

Pittsburgh Division U.S. Post Office & Courthouse, Room 829, 7th Ave & Grant St, Pittsburgh, PA 15219 (courier address: Use mail address for courier delivery) 412-208-7500. www.pawd.uscourts.gov

Counties: Allegheny, Armstrong, Beaver, Butler, Clarion, Fayette, Greene, Indiana, Jefferson, Lawrence, Mercer, Washington, Westmoreland.

Indexing & Storage: New cases available in the index 2 days after filing date. The Erie and Johnstown Divisions send complete paper copies of case records to Pittsburgh, so that all case records for the District are available here.

Fee & Payment: Payment may be made by money order, cashier check, personal check, Visa, Mastercard. Payee: Clerk, U.S. District Court.

Phone Search: Only docket information available.

In Person Search: Fee charged if court conducts your in person search for you.

PACER: PACER is available online at http://pacer.pawd.uscourts.gov. Case records go back to 1994. Records never purged. New records are online after 1 day.

U.S. Bankruptcy Court

Western District of Pennsylvania

Erie Division 717 State St, #501, Erie, PA 16501 (Use mail address for courier delivery) 814-453-7580, Fax: 814-453-3795. www.pawb.uscourts.gov

Counties: Clarion, Crawford, Elk, Erie, Forest, Jefferson, McKean, Mercer, Venango, Warren.

Indexing & Storage: Cases indexed by debtor as well as by case number. New cases available in the index 1 day after filing date.

Fee & Payment: Payment may be made by money order, cashier check, personal check. Payee: Clerk, U.S. Bankruptcy Court.

Phone Search: Docket information is available by phone. Automated voice case information service (VCIS) is available. Call VCIS at 412-355-3210.

In Person Search: Fee charged if court conducts your in person search for you.

PACER: PACER is available online at http://pacer.pawb.uscourts.gov. Records purged every six months. New civil records are online after 1 day.

Electronic Filing: Electronic filing information online at https://ecf.pawb.uscourts.gov

Pittsburgh Division 600 Grant St #5414, Pittsburgh, PA 15219-2801 (courier address: Use mail address for courier delivery) 412-644-2700. www.pawb.uscourts.gov

Counties: Allegheny, Armstrong, Beaver, Bedford, Blair, Butler, Cambria, Clearfield, Fayette, Greene, Indiana, Lawrence, Somerset, Washington, Westmoreland.

Indexing & Storage: Cases indexed by debtor as well as by case number. New cases available in the index 1 day after filing date. Records are also indexed on microfiche. District wide searches are available for information from 1986 from this division.

Fee & Payment: Payment may be made by money order, personal check. Debtor's checks are not accepted. Payee: Clerk, U.S. Bankruptcy Court.

Phone Search: Docket information is available by phone. Automated voice case information service (VCIS) is available. Call VCIS at 412-355-3210.

In Person Search: Fee charged if court conducts your in person search for you. Visa/MC only accepted for in person searches.

PACER: PACER is available online at http://pacer.pawb.uscourts.gov. Records purged every six months. New civil records are online after 1 day.

Electronic Filing: Electronic filing information online at https://ecf.pawb.uscourts.gov

Pennsylvania County Courts

Court	Jurisdiction	No. of Courts	How Organized
Court of Common Pleas*	General	103	60 Districts
Philadelphia Municipal Court*	Municipal	1	1st District
Philadelphia Traffic Court	Municipal	1	1st District
Pittsburgh Magistrates Court	Municipal	1	Pittsburgh
Register of Wills*	Probate	67	
District Justice Courts	Limited	556	60 Districts

* Profiled in this Sourcebook.

Court	CIVIL								
	Tort	Contract	Real Estate	Min. Claim	Max. Claim	Small Claims	Estate	Eviction	Domestic Relations
Court of Common Pleas*	X	X	X	$0	No Max			X	X
Philadelphia Municipal Court*	X	X	X	$0	$10,000	$5000		X	X
Philadelphia Traffic Court									
Pittsburgh City Magistrates Court			X	$0	No Max				
Register of Wills*							X		
District Justice Courts	X	X	X	$0	$8000	$8000			

Court	CRIMINAL				
	Felony	Misdemeanor	DWI/DUI	Preliminary Hearing	Juvenile
Court of Common Pleas*	X	X	X	X	X
Philadelphia Municipal Court*	X	X	X	X	
Philadelphia Traffic Court					
Pittsburgh City Magistrates Court		X	X	X	
Register of Wills*					
District Justice Courts		X	X	X	

ADMINISTRATION Administrative Office of Pennsylvania Courts, PO Box 229, Mechanicsburg, PA, 17055; 717-795-2000/2062, Fax: 717-795-2050. www.courts.state.pa.us

COURT STRUCTURE The Courts of Common Pleas are the general trial courts, with jurisdiction over both civil and criminal matters and appellate jurisdiction over matters disposed of by the special courts. The civil records clerk of the Court of Common Pleas is called the Prothonotary.

Small claims cases are, usually, handled by the District Justice Courts. These courts, which are designated as "special courts," also handle civil cases up to $8,000. However, all small claims and civil actions are recorded through the Prothonotary Section (civil) of the Court of Common Pleas, which then holds the records. It is not necessary to check with each Magisterial District Court, but rather to check with the Prothonotary for the county.

ONLINE ACCESS The state's 556 District Justice Courts are served by a statewide, automated case management system; online access to the case management system is not available.

Common Pleas criminal docket information if available from 20 counties by name or docket number for free at http://ujsportal.pacourts.us. Click on "E-Services." Name search under "Other Criteria." This site also provides access to appellate case information. Also, search Appellate Court dockets at http://pacmsdocketsheet.aopc.org/.

The Infocon County Access System provides direct dial-up access to court record information for 16 counties - Armstrong, Bedford, Blair, Butler, Clarion, Clinton, Erie, Franklin, Huntingdon, Juaniata, Lawrence, Mercer, Mifflin, Pike, Potter and Susquehanna. Set up entails a $50.00 base set-up fee plus $25.00 per county. The monthly usage fee minimum is $25.00, plus time charges. For Information, call Infocon at 814-472-6066.

ADDITIONAL INFORMATION

Fees vary widely among jurisdictions. Many courts will not conduct searches due to a lack of personnel or, if they do search, turnaround time may be excessively lengthy. Many courts have public access terminals for in-person searches.

PROBATE COURTS

Probate is handled by the Register of Wills.

Adams County

Court of Common Pleas - Civil 111-117 Baltimore St Rm 103, Gettysburg, PA 17325; 717-334-6781 X285; Fax: 717-334-0532. Hours: 8AM-4:30PM (EST). *Civil, Eviction.*
Civil Records: Access: In person. Visitors must perform in person searches for themselves. No search fee. Required to search: name, years to search. Civil cases indexed by defendant, plaintiff. Civil records on computer from 1988, some microfiche (dates unsure), on index from 1800s.
General Information: Public Access terminal is available. No mental health, sealed records released. Copy fee: $.25 per page. Cert fee: $8.00 per document. Payee: Prothonotary. Personal checks accepted. Prepayment required. Mail requests: SASE required. Mail turnaround time 1-2 days.

Court of Common Pleas - Criminal 111-117 Baltimore St, Gettysburg, PA 17325; 717-337-9806; Fax: 717-334-9333. Hours: 8AM-4:30PM (EST). *Felony, Misdemeanor.*
Criminal Records: Access: Mail, in person. Both court and visitors may perform in person searches. Search fee: $8.00 per name. Required to search: name, years to search, DOB. Criminal records on computer since 1986 on microfiche since 1974, previous records on microfilm to 1800s. The court may offer docket information at http://ujsportal.pacourts.us.
General Information: Public Access terminal is available. No juvenile records released. Will fax results for fee. Copy fee: $.25 per page. Cert fee: $8.00. Payee: Clerk of Courts. Personal checks accepted; no third party checks. Prepayment required. Mail requests: SASE required. Mail turnaround time 1 day.

Register of Wills 111-117 Baltimore St Rm 102, Gettysburg, PA 17325; 717-337-9826; Fax: 717-334-1758. Hours: 8AM-4:30PM (EST). *Probate.*

Allegheny County

Court of Common Pleas - Civil City County Bldg, 414 Grant St, 1st Fl, Pittsburgh, PA 15219; 412-350-4200. Hours: 8:30AM-4:30PM (EST). *Civil.*
www.county.allegheny.pa.us
Civil Records: Access: Mail, in person, online. Both court and visitors may perform in person searches. Search fee: $25.00 per name. Required to search: name, years to search. Civil cases indexed by defendant, plaintiff. Civil records archived from 1700s; on computer since 07/03/95. Online access to prothonotary civil records free at http://prothonotary.county.allegheny.pa.us/allegheny/welcome.htm. Registration required; search by case number. Also, the Techi provides court records services for those with PA Bar ID at www.techi.org/login.CFM.

General Information: Public Access terminal is available. No juvenile records released. Copy fee: $.50 per page. Cert fee: $8.00. Payee: Prothonotary of Allegheny County. Business checks accepted. Prepayment required. Businesses may set up a draw down account. Mail requests: SASE required. Mail turnaround time 10 days.

Court of Common Pleas - Criminal 220 Courthouse, 436 Grant St, Pittsburgh, PA 15219; 412-350-5322; Fax: 412-350-6154. Hours: 8:30AM-4:30PM (EST). *Felony, Misdemeanor.*
www.county.allegheny.pa.us/cofc/index.asp
Note: The Pittsburgh Magistrate Court can be reached at 412-255-2700.
Criminal Records: Access: Mail, in person, online. Both court and visitors may perform in person searches. Search fee: $15.00 per name. Required to search: name, years to search, DOB; also helpful: SSN. Criminal records on files, microfilm back to 1800s; on computer since. Online access to Common Pleas court records is free at http://prothonotary.county.allegheny.pa.us/allegheny/welcome.htm. Registration required; search by case number. Also, the Techi provides court records services for those with PA Bar ID at www.techi.org/login.CFM.
General Information: Public Access terminal is available. All records public. Will fax results locally only for the search fee. Copy fee: $.50 per page. Cert fee: $10.00. Payee: Clerk of Courts. Personal checks not accepted. Prepayment required. Mail requests: SASE required. Mail turnaround time 2 days.

Register of Wills 414 Grant St, City County Bldg, PIttsburgh, PA 15219; 412-350-4183; Fax: 412-350-3028. Hours: 8:30AM-4:30PM (EST). *Probate.*
www.county.allegheny.pa.us/regwills/index.asp

Armstrong County

Court of Common Pleas - Civil 500 E Market St, Kittanning, PA 16201; 724-548-3251; Probate phone: 724-548-3256; Fax: 724-548-3236. Hours: 8AM-4:30PM (EST). *Civil, Eviction.*
www.geocities.com/acprothonotary
Civil Records: Access: Online, in person. Both court and visitors may perform in person searches. Search fee: $10.00. Required to search: name, years to search. Civil cases indexed by defendant, plaintiff. Civil records on files, microfiche since 1930; on computer since 9/94. Internet access to court records is by subscription from a private company-Infocon at www.ic-access.com, 814-472-6066. See note at beginning of section.
General Information: Public Access terminal is available. No juvenile, civil commitment records released. Copy fee: $1.00 per page. Cert fee: $3.00. Payee: Prothonotary. Personal checks accepted. Prepayment required.

Court of Common Pleas - Criminal 500 Market St, Kittanning, PA 16201; 724-548-3252. Hours: 8AM-4:30PM (EST). *Felony, Misdemeanor.*
www.geocities.com/acprothonotary
Criminal Records: Access: Mail, online, in person. Both court and visitors may perform in person searches. Search fee: $10.00 per name. Required to search: name, years to search; also helpful: DOB, SSN. Criminal records in card file from early 1930; on computer since 1994. Search docket information by name or docket number for free at http://ujsportal.pacourts.us. Click on "E-Services." Name search under "Other Criteria." Also, see note at beginning of section.
General Information: Public Access terminal is available. No juvenile or mental health records released. Will not fax results. Copy fee: $1.00 per page. Cert fee: $5.00 first page; $1.00 each add'l. Payee: Clerk of Courts. Personal checks accepted. Prepayment required. Mail requests: SASE required. Mail turnaround time same day.

Register of Wills 500 Market St, Armstrong County Courthouse, Kittanning, PA 16201; 724-548-3256 X220; Fax: 724-548-3236. Hours: 8AM-4:30PM (EST). *Probate.*
Note: Internet access to records is available by subscription from a private company-Infocon at www.ic-access.com, 814-472-6066. See note at beginning of section.

Beaver County

Court of Common Pleas - Civil Beaver County Courthouse, 810 3rd St, Beaver, PA 15009; 724-728-5700. Hours: 8:30AM-4:30PM (EST). *Civil, Eviction.*
www.co.beaver.pa.us/prothonotary
Civil Records: Access: In person, mail. Both court and visitors may perform in person searches. No search fee. Required to search: name, years to search. Civil cases indexed by defendant, plaintiff. Civil records go back to 1800; on computer back to 1995.
General Information: Public Access terminal is available. No sealed records released. Copy fee: $.25 per page. Cert fee: $8.75. Payee: Prothonotary. Personal checks accepted. Prepayment required. Mail requests: SASE required. Mail turnaround time 1 week.

Court of Common Pleas - Criminal Beaver County Courthouse, 810 3rd St, Beaver, PA 15009; 724-728-5700; Fax: 724-728-8853. Hours: 8:30AM-4:30PM (EST). *Felony, Misdemeanor.*
www.co.beaver.pa.us
Criminal Records: Access: Fax, mail, in person, online. Both court and visitors may perform in person searches. Search fee: $17.50 per name. Required to search: name, years to search; also helpful: DOB, SSN. Criminal records on computer back to 1973, on microfiche since 1802. Search docket information by

name or docket number for free at http://ujsportal.pacourts.us. Click on "E-Services." Name search under "Other Criteria."

General Information: Public Access terminal is available. Records sealed by court order not released. Fee to fax results is $1.00 per page. Copy fee: $.25 per page. Cert fee: $8.75. Payee: Clerk of Courts Office. Personal checks accepted. Prepayment required. Mail requests: SASE required. Mail turnaround time 1 week.

Register of Wills Beaver County Courthouse, 810 3rd St, Beaver, PA 15009; 724-728-5700 X11265, X11274; Fax: 724-728-9810. Hours: 8:30AM-4:30PM (EST). *Probate.*

Bedford County

Court of Common Pleas - Criminal/Civil Bedford County Courthouse, Bedford, PA 15522; 814-623-4833; Fax: 814-623-4831. Hours: 8:30AM-4:30PM (EST). *Felony, Misdemeanor, Civil, Eviction.*

Civil Records: Access: Mail, in person, online. Both court and visitors may perform in person searches. Search fee: $18.00 per name. Required to search: name, years to search. Civil cases indexed by defendant, plaintiff. Civil records on file from late 1700s. Internet access to court records is by subscription from a private company-Infocon at www.ic-access.com, 814-472-6066. See note at beginning of section.

Criminal Records: Access: Mail, online, in person. Both court and visitors may perform in person searches. Search fee: $18.00 per name. Required to search: name, years to search, DOB. Criminal records on file from late 1700s. Online access to criminal records is the same as civil. Also, search docket information by name or docket number for free at http://ujsportal.pacourts.us. Click on "E-Services." Name search under "Other Criteria."

General Information: Public Access terminal is available. No sex related or juvenile records released. Will fax results to local or toll free line, if pre-paid. Copy fee: $.50 per page. Cert fee: $4.50. Payee: Prothonotary of Beford County. Personal checks not accepted. Prepayment required. Mail requests: SASE required. Mail turnaround time 2 weeks.

Register of Wills 200 S Juliana St, Bedford, PA 15522; 814-623-4836; Fax: 814-624-0488. Hours: 8:30AM-4:30PM (EST). *Probate.*

Note: Internet access to records is available by subscription from a private company-Infocon at www.ic-access.com, 814-472-6066. See note at beginning of section.

Berks County

Court of Common Pleas - Civil 2nd Fl, 633 Court St, Reading, PA 19601; 610-478-6970; Fax: 610-478-6969. Hours: 8AM-4PM (EST). *Civil, Eviction.*

Civil Records: Access: Mail, in person, online. Both court and visitors may perform in person searches. No search fee. Required to search: name, years to search. Civil cases indexed by defendant, plaintiff. Civil records partially on microfiche, on manual index files from 1750. Mail access limited to docket information only. The Registry of Wills has a free searchable website at www.berksregofwills.com/search_page.htm including marriage, estate, birth and death records for the county. The estate and marriage records are current. Also, the Prothontary has a remote dial-up system that allows users to access archived record indexes back to 1/1996. Fee is $300 per year. For information, call 610-478-6968.

General Information: Public Access terminal is available. No mental, sealed records released. Will fax results $5.00 1st page, $1.00 each add'l; for emergency only. Copy fee: $3.00 1st page; $1.00 each add'l page. In person copy fee is $.50 per page. Cert fee: $5.25. Payee: Prothonotary. Personal checks accepted. Prepayment required. Mail requests: SASE required. Mail turnaround time 1-2 days.

Court of Common Pleas - Criminal 4th Fl, 633 Court St, Reading, PA 19601; 610-478-6550; Fax: 610-478-6593. Hours: 8AM-5PM (EST). *Felony, Misdemeanor.*

Criminal Records: Access: Mail, in person. Visitors must perform in person searches for themselves. Search fee: none. Required to search: name, years to search; also helpful: DOB, SSN. Criminal records on computer from 1985 in files from 1992, prior archived. The court may offer docket information at http://ujsportal.pacourts.us. Will not do name lists by mail.

General Information: Public Access terminal is available. No juvenile records released. Copy fee: $.25 per page. Add $1.00 for each page after first 10. Cert fee: $8.00. Payee: Berks County Clerk of Courts. Only cashiers checks and money orders accepted. Credit cards accepted for payments on criminal cases only. Prepayment required. Mail requests: SASE required. Mail turnaround time 5 days.

Register of Wills 633 Court St 2nd Fl, Reading, PA 19601; 610-478-6600; Fax: 610-478-6251. Hours: 8AM-5PM (EST). *Probate.*
www.berksregofwills.com
Note: The Registry of Wills has a free searchable website at www.berksregofwills.com including records both for the county and the City of Reading. The estate and marriage records are current.

Blair County

Court of Common Pleas - Criminal/Civil 423 Allegheny St #144, Hollidaysburg, PA 16648; 814-693-3080; Criminal phone: 814-693-3084. Hours: 8AM-4PM (EST). *Felony, Misdemeanor, Civil, Eviction.*

Civil Records: Access: In person, online. Visitors must perform in person searches for themselves. No search fee. Required to search: name, years to search. Civil cases indexed by defendant, plaintiff. Civil records on computer from 1989, on index books from 1846 to 1989. Internet access to court records is by subscription from a private company-Infocon at www.ic-access.com, 814-472-6066. See note at beginning of section.

Criminal Records: Access: Mail, online, in person. Both court and visitors may perform in person searches. Search fee: $10.00 per name. Required to search: name, years to search, DOB; also helpful: SSN. Criminal records on computer from 1989, on index books from 1846 to 1989. Online access is the same as civil, see above.

General Information: Public Access terminal is available. No adoption records released. Copy fee: $.50 per page. Cert fee: $5.00. Payee: Blair County Prothonotary. Personal checks accepted. Prepayment required. Mail requests: SASE required. Mail turnaround time 2 days.

Register of Wills 423 Allegheny #145, Hollidaysburg, PA 16648-2022; 814-693-3095; Fax: 814-693-3093. Hours: 8AM-4PM (EST). *Probate.*

Note: Internet access to records is available by subscription from a private company-Infocon at www.ic-access.com, 814-472-6066. See note at beginning of section.

Bradford County

Court of Common Pleas - Criminal/Civil Courthouse, 301 Main St, Towanda, PA 18848; 570-265-1705; Fax: 570-265-1735. Hours: 9AM-5PM (EST). *Felony, Misdemeanor, Civil, Eviction.*

Civil Records: Access: Mail, in person. Both court and visitors may perform in person searches. Search fee: $8.00 per name. Required to search: name, years to search. Civil cases indexed by defendant, plaintiff. Civil records on computer from 1986, on microfiche from mid 1800s, archived from mid-1940s.

Criminal Records: Access: Mail, in person. Both court and visitors may perform in person searches. Search fee: $8.00 per name. Required to search: name, years to search, DOB. Criminal records on computer from 1986, on microfiche from mid 1800s, archived from mid-1940s. The court may offer docket information at http://ujsportal.pacourts.us.

General Information: Public Access terminal is available. Will fax results to local or toll free line. Copy fee: $.25 per page. Cert fee: $4.00. $8.00 for criminal records. Payee: Prothonotary. Personal checks accepted. Prepayment required. Mail requests: SASE required. Mail turnaround time 1-2 days.

Register of Wills 301 Main St., Towanda, PA 18848; 570-265-1702; Fax: 570-265-1721. Hours: 9AM-5PM (EST). *Probate.*

Bucks County

Court of Common Pleas - Civil 55 E Court St, Doylestown, PA 18901; 215-348-6191. Hours: 8:15AM-4:15PM (EST). *Civil, Eviction.*
www.buckscounty.org/courts

Civil Records: Access: Online, in person. Visitors must perform in person searches for themselves. No search fee. Required to search: name, years to search. Civil cases indexed by defendant, plaintiff. Civil records on computer back to 1980, prior on dockets. Access to civil online records is through a remote online system; contact Information Services Helpdesk 215-348-8080 for more information and signup. For a limited time, access is free at www.buckscounty.org/departments/public_access. Probate is also incldued.

General Information: Public Access terminal is available. No mental, sealed records released. Copy fee: $.25 per page. Cert fee: $4.50. Payee: Prothonotary. Personal checks accepted. Prepayment required.

Court of Common Pleas - Criminal Bucks County Courthouse, 55 E Court St, Doylestown, PA 18901; 215-348-6389; Civil phone: 215-348-6191; Probate phone: 215-348-6265; Fax: 215-348-6740. Hours: 8AM-4:30PM (EST). *Felony, Misdemeanor.*
www.buckscounty.org/courts

Criminal Records: Access: Mail, online, in person. Both court and visitors may perform in person searches. Search fee: $10.00 per name. Required to search: name, years to search, DOB. Criminal records on computer from 1980, some records on microfiche, on card index from 1932 to 1979. For a limited time, access is free at www.buckscounty.org/departments/public_access.

General Information: Public Access terminal is available. No sealed, juvenile or mental records released. Fee to fax results is $1.50 per page. No copy fee. Cert fee: $8.00. Payee: Clerk of Courts Criminal Division. Personal checks accepted. Prepayment required. Mail requests: SASE required. Mail turnaround time same day.

Register of Wills Bucks County Courthouse, 55 E. Court St., Doylestown, PA 18901; 215-348-6265; Fax: 215-348-6156. Hours: 8AM-4:30PM (EST). *Probate.*
www.buckscounty.org
Note: For a limited time, access is free at www.buckscounty.org/departments/public_access.

Butler County

Court of Common Pleas - Civil Butler County Courthouse, PO Box 1208, Butler, PA 16001-1208; 724-284-5214. Hours: 8:30AM-4:30PM (EST). *Civil, Eviction.*
Civil Records: Access: Phone, mail, online, in person. Visitors must perform in person searches for themselves. No search fee. Required to search: name, years to search. Civil cases indexed by defendant, plaintiff. Civil records on computer from 4/1/93, prior on docket books back to 1800. Internet access to court records is by subscription from a private company-Infocon at www.ic-access.com, 814-472-6066. See note at beginning of section.
General Information: Public Access terminal is available. No mental records released. Copy fee: $.25 per page. Cert fee: $4.00. Payee: Prothonotary. Personal checks accepted. Prepayment required.

Court of Common Pleas - Criminal PO Box 1208, Butler County Courthouse, 124 W Diamond St, Butler, PA 16003-1208; 724-284-5233; Civil phone: 724-284-5214; Probate phone: 724-284-5348; Fax: 724-284-5244. Hours: 8:30AM-4:30PM (EST). *Felony, Misdemeanor.*
www.co.butler.pa.us/CoC.htm
Criminal Records: Access: Mail, online, in person. Both court and visitors may perform in person searches. Search fee: $16.00 per name. Required to search: name, DOB; also helpful: years to search, SSN. Original records in office for 10 years. Computerized from 1988 to present, prior in Russell Index. Search docket information by name or docket number for free at http://ujsportal.pacourts.us. Click on "E-Services." Name search under "Other Criteria." See note at beginning of section.
General Information: Public Access terminal is available. No mental, sealed, juvenile (16 & under) victim records released. Will fax results only for government. Copy fee: $.50 per page. Cert fee: $8.00 per page. Payee: Clerk of Courts. Personal checks accepted. Prepayment required. Mail requests: SASE required. Mail turnaround time 1-2 days.

Register of Wills Butler County Courthouse, PO Box 1208, Butler, PA 16003-1208; 724-284-5348; Fax: 724-284-5278. Hours: 8:30AM-4:30PM (EST). *Probate.*
Note: Internet access to records is available by subscription from a private company-Infocon at www.ic-access.com, 814-472-6066. See note at beginning of section.

Cambria County

Court of Common Pleas - Civil 200 S Center St, Ebensburg, PA 15931; 814-472-1636; Fax: 814-472-5632. Hours: 9AM-4PM (EST). *Civil, Eviction.*
Civil Records: Access: Phone, mail, fax, in person. Both court and visitors may perform in person searches. No search fee. Required to search: name, years to search. Civil cases indexed by defendant, plaintiff. Civil records on computer from 1/1/94, prior on dockets from 1800s.
General Information: Public Access terminal is available. No divorce or mental records released. Fee to fax results is $1.00 per page. Copy fee: $.25 per page. Cert fee: $3.00. Payee: Prothonotary. Personal

checks accepted. Prepayment required. Mail requests: SASE requested. Turnaround time is usually 1 day.

Court of Common Pleas - Criminal Cambria County Courthouse S Center St, Ebensburg, PA 15931; 814-472-1540. Hours: 9AM-4PM (EST). *Felony, Misdemeanor.*
Criminal Records: Access: Mail, in person, online. Only the court performs in person searches; visitors may not. Search fee: $4.40 per name. Required to search: name, years to search, DOB; also helpful: SSN. Criminal conviction records are computerized, indexed from 1800s. Search docket information by name or docket number for free at http://ujsportal.pacourts.us. Click on "E-Services." Name search under "Other Criteria."
General Information: No sealed or child victim records released. Will fax results to a local or toll free number; search fee must be paid. Copy fee: $.50 per single page; $.75 two-sided page. Cert fee: $8.80. Payee: Clerk of Court. Third party checks not accepted. Prepayment required. Mail turnaround time 5-7 days.

Register of Wills 200 S Center St, Ebensburg, PA 15931; 814-472-5440 X1440; Probate phone: 814-472-1438; Fax: 814-472-0762. Hours: 9AM-4PM (EST). *Probate.*
www.co.cambria.pa.us

Cameron County

Court of Common Pleas - Civil Cameron County Courthouse, 20 E 5th St, Emporium, PA 15834; 814-486-9329; Fax: 814-468-0464. Hours: 8:30AM-4PM (EST). *Civil, Eviction.*
Civil Records: Access: Phone, fax, mail, in person. Both court and visitors may perform in person searches. No search fee. Required to search: name, years to search. Civil cases indexed by defendant, plaintiff. Civil records on computer from 1988, archived from 1860 to present.
General Information: Public Access terminal is available. No adoption, military discharge records released. Will not fax results. Copy fee: $.50 per page. Cert fee: $10.00. Payee: Prothonotary. Personal checks accepted. Credit cards not accepted. Prepayment required. Will bill fees with prior permission from clerk. Mail requests: SASE required. Mail turnaround time same day.

Court of Common Pleas - Criminal 20 E 5th St, Emporium, PA 15834; 814-486-9330; Fax: 814-486-0464. Hours: 8:30AM-4PM (EST). *Felony, Misdemeanor.*
Criminal Records: Access: Phone, fax, mail, in person, online. Both court and visitors may perform in person searches. No search fee. Required to search: name, years to search; also helpful: address, DOB, SSN. Criminal records archived from 1860. Search docket information by name or docket number for free at http://ujsportal.pacourts.us. Click on "E-Services." Name search under "Other Criteria."
General Information: Public Access terminal is available. No juvenile, mental health records released. Will not fax results. Copy fee: $.50 per page. Cert fee: $10.00. Payee: Clerk of Court. Personal checks accepted. Credit cards not accepted. Prepayment required. Mail requests: SASE required. Mail turnaround time same day.

Register of Wills Cameron County Courthouse, East 5th St., Emporium, PA 15834; 814-486-3355; Fax: 814-486-0464. Hours: 8:30AM-4PM (EST). *Probate.*

Carbon County

Court of Common Pleas - Civil PO Box 130, Courthouse, Jim Thorpe, PA 18229; 570-325-2481; Fax: 570-325-8047. Hours: 8:30AM-4:30PM (EST). *Civil, Eviction.*
www.carboncourts.com
Civil Records: Access: In person, online. Visitors must perform in person searches for themselves. No search fee. Required to search: name. Civil cases indexed by defendant, plaintiff. Civil records on computer from 1/84, financing statements from 1/87, on microfiche from 1/84, prior archived. Online access to the clerk of courts docket records is free at www.carboncourts.com/pubacc.htm. Registration required.
General Information: Public Access terminal is available. No abuse, mental health records released. Copy fee: $.25 per page. Cert fee: $8.15. Payee: Prothonotary of Carbon County. Personal checks accepted. Prepayment required.

Court of Common Pleas - Criminal County Courthouse, Jim Thorpe, PA 18229; 570-325-3637; Fax: 570-325-5705. Hours: 8:30AM-4PM (EST). *Felony, Misdemeanor.*
www.carboncourts.com
Criminal Records: Access: Phone, mail, in person, online. Only the court performs in person searches; visitors may not. No search fee. Required to search: name, years to search, DOB; also helpful: SSN. Criminal records on computer from 1973, on microfiche from 1800. Online access to the clerk of courts docket records is free at www.carboncourts.com/pubacc.htm. Registration required. The court may offer docket information at http://ujsportal.pacourts.us.
General Information: No juvenile, mental health records released. Cert fee: $5.00. Payee: Clerk of Courts Carbon County. Personal checks accepted. Prepayment required. Mail requests: SASE required. Mail turnaround time 1 day.

Register of Wills PO Box 286, Jim Thorpe, PA 18229; 570-325-2261; Fax: 570-325-5098. Hours: 8:30AM-4:30PM (EST). *Probate.*
Note: Docket information is available free online at www.carboncourts.com/pubacc.htm. Registration required.

Centre County

Court of Common Pleas - Criminal/Civil Centre County Courthouse, Bellefonte, PA 16823; 814-355-6796. Hours: 8:30AM-5PM (EST). *Felony, Misdemeanor, Civil, Eviction.*
www.co.centre.pa.us/courts.htm
Civil Records: Access: In person only. Visitors must perform in person searches for themselves. Search fee: $7.00 per name. Required to search: name, years to search, DOB. Civil cases indexed by defendant, plaintiff. Civil records on computer from 7-1-94, on docket books from 1986, on microfiche and archived from 1800 to 1986.
Criminal Records: Access: Mail, in person. Both court and visitors may perform in person searches. Search fee: $7.00 per name. Required to search: name, years to search, DOB. Criminal records on computer from 7-1-94, on card files and docket books from 1986, on microfiche and archived from 1800 to 1986. The court may offer docket information at http://ujsportal.pacourts.us.
General Information: Public Access terminal is available. No sex related, juvenile, mental records released. Will not fax results. Copy fee: $.50 per page. Cert fee: $4.00. Payee: Clerk of Court. Personal checks accepted. Prepayment required. Mail requests: SASE required. Mail turnaround time 3-5 days.

Register of Wills Willowbank Office Bldg, 414 Holmes Ave #2, Bellefonte, PA 16823; 814-355-6724, 355-6760; Fax: 814-355-8685. Hours: 8:30AM-5PM (EST). *Probate.* www.co.centre.pa.us/courts.htm

Chester County

Court of Common Pleas - Civil 2 N High St, #130, West Chester, PA 19380; 610-344-6300; Criminal phone: 610-344-6135. Hours: 8:30AM-4:30PM (EST). *Civil, Eviction.* www.chesco.org

Civil Records: Access: Online, in person. Visitors must perform in person searches for themselves. No search fee. Required to search: name, years to search. Civil cases indexed by defendant, plaintiff. Civil records on dockets from 1985 to present, on microfiche from 1981 to 1984, archived from 1700s. Internet access to county records including court records requires a sign-up and credit card payment. Application fee: $50. There is a $10.00 per month minimum (no charge for no activity); and $.10 each transaction beyond 100. Sign-up and/or logon at http://epin.chesco.org. Also, a miscellaneous court case list is free at www.chesco.org/judicial/misclist.html.

General Information: Public Access terminal is available. No sealed records released. Copy fee: $1.00 per page. Cert fee: $5.00. Payee: Prothonotary. Business checks accepted. Prepayment required. Mail requests: SASE helpful. Turnaround time is 1-2 days.

Court of Common Pleas - Criminal 2 N High St #160, West Chester, PA 19380; 610-344-6135. Hours: 8:30AM-4:30PM (EST). *Felony, Misdemeanor.* www.chesco.org

Criminal Records: Access: Mail, online, in person. Both court and visitors may perform in person searches. Search fee: $10.00 per name. Required to search: name, years to search; also helpful: DOB. Criminal records on computer and microfiche from mid-70s, archived from the 1700s. Internet access to county records including criminal records requires a sign-up and credit card payment. Application fee: $50. There is a $10.00 per month minimum (no charge for no activity); and $.10 each transaction beyond 100. Sign-up and/or logon at http://epin.chesco.org.

General Information: Public Access terminal is available. No juvenile records released. Copy fee: $1.00 per page. Cert fee: $5.00. Payee: Clerk of Courts. Business checks accepted. Prepayment required. Mail turnaround time 1 day.

Register of Wills 2 N High St, #109, West Chester, PA 19380-3073; 610-344-6335; Fax: 610-344-6218. Hours: 8:30AM-4:30PM (EST). *Probate.* Note: Internet access to probate records requires a sign-up and payment. Sign-up and/or logon at http://epin.chesco.org.

Clarion County

Court of Common Pleas - Civil Clarion County Courthouse,421 Main St, Clarion, PA 16214; 814-226-1119; Fax: 814-227-2501. Hours: 8AM-4:30PM (EST). *Civil, Eviction.*

Civil Records: Access: Phone, fax, mail, online, in person. Both court and visitors may perform in person searches. Search fee: $10.00 per name. Required to search: name, years to search. Civil cases indexed by defendant, plaintiff. Civil records on computer from mid-1990s, on dockets from 1800s. Internet access to court records is by subscription from a private company-Infocon at www.ic-access.com, 814-472-6066. See note at beginning of section.

General Information: Public Access terminal is available. No juvenile, mental health records released.

No fee to fax results. Copy fee: $.50 per page. Cert fee: $7.50. Payee: Prothonotary. Personal checks accepted. Prepayment required. Mail requests: SASE required. Mail turnaround time is 2-3 days.

Court of Common Pleas - Criminal Clarion County Courthouse, Main St, Clarion, PA 16214; 814-226-1119; Fax: 814-227-2501. Hours: 8AM-4:30PM (EST). *Felony, Misdemeanor.*

Criminal Records: Access: Phone, fax, mail, online, in person. Both court and visitors may perform in person searches. Search fee: $10.00 per name. Required to search: name, years to search, DOB. Criminal records on computer from 1990, microfiche 1976-1985, on docket books from 1800s. Internet access to court records is by subscription from a private company-Infocon at www.ic-access.com, 814-472-6066. See note at beginning of section. Also, search docket information by name or docket number for free at http://ujsportal.pacourts.us. Click on "E-Services."

General Information: Public Access terminal is available. No juvenile, mental health records released. No fee to fax results. Copy fee: $.50 per page. Cert fee: $7.50. Payee: Clerk of Court. Personal checks accepted. Prepayment required. Mail turnaround time same day.

Register of Wills Clarion County Courthouse, 421 Main St., Clarion, PA 16214; 814-226-4000 X2500; Fax: 814-226-1117. Hours: 8:30AM-4:30PM (EST). *Probate.* Note: Internet access to records is available by subscription from a private company-Infocon at www.ic-access.com, 814-472-6066. See note at beginning of section.

Clearfield County

Court of Common Pleas - Criminal/Civil PO Box 549 (1 N 2nd St), Clearfield, PA 16830; 814-765-2641; Civil phone: ext. 5988; Criminal phone: ext. 5980; Fax: 814-765-7659. Hours: 8:30AM-4PM (EST). *Felony, Misdemeanor, Civil, Eviction.* www.clearfieldco.org

Civil Records: Access: Mail, in person. Both court and visitors may perform in person searches. Search fee: $7.00 per name, 5-years search. Required to search: name, years to search; also helpful: address. Civil cases indexed by defendant, plaintiff. Civil records indexed (Russell System) on dockets from 1820s; on computer back to 11/00.

Criminal Records: Access: Mail, in person. Both court and visitors may perform in person searches. Search fee: $7.00 per name, 5-year search. Required to search: name, years to search, address, DOB, SSN, signed release. Criminal records indexed (Russell System) on dockets from 1820s; on computer back to 01/95. The court may offer docket information at http://ujsportal.pacourts.us.

General Information: Public Access terminal is available. No juvenile, sealed or mental health records released. Copy fee: $.25 per page. Cert fee: $1.50. Payee: Prothonotary. Personal checks accepted. Prepayment required. Mail requests: SASE required. Mail turnaround time 2 days.

Register of Wills & Clerk of Orphans Court PO Box 361, Clearfield, PA 16830; 814-765-2641 X1350/1; Fax: 814-765-6089. Hours: 8:30AM-4PM (EST). *Probate.*

Clinton County

Court of Common Pleas - Criminal/Civil 230 E Water St, Lock Haven, PA 17745; 570-893-4007. Hours: 8AM-5PM M, T, Th, F; 8AM-12:30PM Wed (EST). *Felony, Misdemeanor, Civil, Eviction.* www.clintoncountypa.com/courts.htm

Civil Records: Access: Online, in person. Visitors must perform in person searches for themselves. No search fee. Required to search: name, years to search. Civil cases indexed by defendant, plaintiff. Civil records on computer from 1992, on files from 1839. Internet access to court records is by subscription from a private company-Infocon at www.ic-access.com, 814-472-6066. See note at beginning of section.

Criminal Records: Access: Online, in person. Visitors must perform in person searches for themselves. No search fee. Required to search: name, years to search, DOB, SSN, signed release. Criminal records on computer from 1992, on files from 1839. Internet access to court records is by subscription from a private company-Infocon at www.ic-access.com, 814-472-6066. See note at beginning of section.

General Information: Public Access terminal is available. No sealed, mental health or minor victim abuse cases records released. Will not fax results. Copy fee: $.50 per page. Cert fee: $4.50. Payee: Clerk of Court or Prothonotary. Personal checks accepted. Prepayment required.

Register of Wills PO Box 943, Lock Haven, PA 17745; 570-893-4010; Fax: 570-893-4273. Hours: 8:30AM-5PM M,T,Th,F; 8AM-12:30PM Wed (EST). *Probate.* www.clintoncountypa.com Note: Internet access to records is available by subscription from a private company-Infocon at www.ic-access.com, 814-472-6066. See note at beginning of section.

Columbia County

Court of Common Pleas - Criminal/Civil PO Box 380, Bloomsburg, PA 17815; 570-389-5614. Hours: 8AM-4:30PM (EST). *Felony, Misdemeanor, Civil, Eviction.* http://columbiapa.org/county/courts/index.html Note: Opinions for civil and criminal cases are listed at the web site.

Civil Records: Access: In person only. Both court and visitors may perform in person searches. No search fee. Required to search: name, years to search. Civil cases indexed by defendant, plaintiff. Civil records on computer to 1992, on microfiche from 1814 to present, on dockets from 1814.

Criminal Records: Access: Mail, in person. Both court and visitors may perform in person searches. Search fee: $20.00 per name. Required to search: name, years to search; also helpful: DOB. Criminal records on computer to 1992, on microfiche from 1814 to present, on dockets from 1814. The court may offer docket information at http://ujsportal.pacourts.us.

General Information: Public Access terminal is available. No juvenile, adoption, mental health petition or OAPSA records released. Copy fee: $.50 per page. Cert fee: $4.00. Payee: Prothonotary or Clerk of Court. Personal checks accepted. Prepayment required. Mail requests: SASE required. Mail turnaround time same day.

Register of Wills 35 W Main St, PO Box 380, Bloomsburg, PA 17815; 570-389-5635/32; Fax: 570-389-5636. Hours: 8AM-4:30PM (EST). *Probate.*

Crawford County

Court of Common Pleas - Civil Crawford County Courthouse, 903 Diamond Park, Meadville, PA 16335; 814-333-7324; Criminal phone: 814-333-7442. Hours: 8:30AM-4:30PM (EST). *Civil, Eviction.*

Civil Records: Access: Mail, in person. Both court and visitors may perform in person searches. Search fee: $7.50 per name. Required to search: name, years

to search. Civil cases indexed by defendant, plaintiff. Civil records on dockets from 1800s.

General Information: Public Access terminal is available. No mental health, sealed records released. Copy fee: $.75 per page. Docket copy $1.50 per page. Cert fee: $1.50. Payee: Prothonotary Crawford County. Personal checks accepted with ID. Prepayment required. Mail requests: SASE required. Mail turnaround time 3 days.

Court of Common Pleas - Criminal
Crawford County Courthouse, 903 Diamond Park, Meadville, PA 16335; 814-333-7442; Fax: 814-337-7349. Hours: 8:30AM-4:30PM (EST). *Felony, Misdemeanor.*

http://co.crawford.pa.us/clerk_of_courts/clerk_of_courts_home.htm

Criminal Records: Access: Mail, in person, online. Both court and visitors may perform in person searches. Search fee: $10.00 to search, up to 5 names per $10.00. Required to search: name, years to search, signed release; also helpful: DOB & SSN. Criminal records computerized since 2000, on microfiche from 1974, on dockets from 1914, archived from 1880s. Search docket information by name or docket number for free at http://ujsportal.pacourts.us. Click on "E-Services." name search under "Other Criteria."

General Information: Public Access terminal is available. (Criminal records only.) No juvenile records released. Copy fee: $1.00 per page. Cert fee: $5.00 per document. Payee: Clerk of Courts. Personal checks accepted. Prepayment required. Mail requests: SASE required. Mail turnaround time 10-14 days.

Register of Wills 903 Diamond Park, Meadville, PA 16335; 814-373-2537, 814-333-7338; Fax: 814-337-5296. Hours: 8:30AM-4:30PM (EST). *Probate.*

Cumberland County

Court of Common Pleas - Civil
Cumberland County Courthouse, Rm 100, One Courthouse Sq, Carlisle, PA 17013-3387; 717-240-6195; Fax: 717-240-6573. Hours: 8AM-4:30PM (EST). *Civil, Eviction.*

www.ccpa.net

Civil Records: Access: In person only. Visitors must perform in person searches for themselves. No search fee. Required to search: name, years to search; also helpful: address. Civil cases indexed by defendant, plaintiff. Civil records on computer from 1994, on microfiche from 1966-1986, on dockets from 1800s. Judges opinions and court documents are free online, but searchable only by judge name, then year.

General Information: Public Access terminal is available. No mental health records released. Will not fax results. Copy fee: $.50 per page. No cert fee. Payee: Office of Prothonotary. No personal checks accepted. Prepayment required.

Court of Common Pleas - Criminal
Cumberland County Courthouse, East Wing, 1 Courthouse Sq, Carlisle, PA 17013-3387; 717-240-6250; Fax: 717-240-6571. Hours: 8AM-4:30PM (EST). *Felony, Misdemeanor.*

www.ccpa.net

Criminal Records: Access: Mail, in person, online. Both court and visitors may perform in person searches. Search fee: $17.00 per name. Required to search: name, years to search, DOB or SSN. Criminal records on computer from 1994, on files from 1976, archived from 1800s. Search docket information by name or docket number for free at http://ujsportal.pacourts.us. Click on "E-Services." Name search under "Other Criteria."

General Information: Public Access terminal is available. No juvenile records released (Including any case with a juvenile as the victim). Copy fee: $.50 per page. Payee: Clerk of Courts. Personal checks

accepted. Prepayment required. Mail requests: SASE required. Mail turnaround time same day.

Register of Wills Cumberland County Courthouse, Rm 102, 1 Courthouse Sq, Carlisle, PA 17013; 717-240-6345; Fax: 717-240-7797. Hours: 8AM-4:30PM (EST). *Probate.*

Dauphin County

Court of Common Pleas - Civil
PO Box 945, Harrisburg, PA 17108; 717-780-6520. Hours: 8AM-4:30PM (EST). *Civil, Eviction.*

http://dsf.pacounties.org/dauphin/site/default.asp

Civil Records: Access: Phone, mail, in person. Both court and visitors may perform in person searches. Search fee: $7.75 per name. Fee is per 5 years searched. Required to search: name, years to search. Civil cases indexed by defendant, plaintiff. Civil records on microfilm and dockets from 1970s, archived from 1700s; on computer back to 11/2001.

General Information: Public Access terminal is available. No mental health released. Copy fee: $.75 per page. Cert fee: $4.75 1st pg; $1.50 each add'l. Payee: Dauphin County Prothonotary. Business checks accepted. Prepayment required. Mail requests: SASE required. Mail turnaround time 1 day.

Court of Common Pleas - Criminal
Front & Market St, Harrisburg, PA 17101; 717-255-2692. Hours: 8:AM-4:30PM (EST). *Felony, Misdemeanor.*

http://dsf.pacounties.org/dauphin/site/default.asp

Criminal Records: Access: Mail, in person. Both court and visitors may perform in person searches. Search fee: $21.50 per name. Required to search: name, years to search; also helpful: DOB, SSN. Criminal records on dockets and computer from 1950, archived from 1700s. The court may offer docket information at http://ujsportal.pacourts.us.

General Information: Public Access terminal is available. No juvenile, mental records released. Copy fee: $.50 per page. Cert fee: $9.00. Payee: Clerk of Court. Business checks accepted. Prepayment required. Mail requests: SASE not required. Mail turnaround time 1 week.

Register of Wills Front& Market Sts. Rm 103, Harrisburg, PA 17101; 717-780-6500; Fax: 717-780-6474. Hours: 8AM-4:30PM (EST). *Probate.*

www.dauphinc.org

Delaware County

Court of Common Pleas - Criminal/Civil
201 W Front St, Media, PA 19063; 610-891-4370; Fax: 610-891-7257. Hours: 8:30AM-4:30PM (EST). *Felony, Misdemeanor, Civil, Eviction.*

www.co.delaware.pa.us

Civil Records: Access: Online, in person. Visitors must perform in person searches for themselves. No search fee. Required to search: name, years to search. Civil cases indexed by defendant, plaintiff. Civil records on computer from early 1990, on card file from 1920s, archived from 1800s. Online access to court civil records free (may begin charging at any time) at www2.co.delaware.pa.us/pa/default.htm. For more information, call 610-891-4675. Search online by document type, document number, etc.

Criminal Records: Access: Mail, in person. Both court and visitors may perform in person searches. No search fee. Required to search: name, years to search; also helpful: DOB, SSN. Criminal records on computer from late 1970s, prior on files. The court may offer docket information at http://ujsportal.pacourts.us.

General Information: Public Access terminal is available. No juvenile, mental health records released. Copy fee: $1.00 per page. Cert fee: $4.50 first page and $1.00 thereafter. Payee: Office of Judical Support. Business checks accepted. Prepayment required. Mail

requests: SASE required. Mail turnaround time 1-3 days.

Register of Wills Delaware County Courthouse, 201 W Front St, Media, PA 19063; 610-891-4400; Fax: 610-891-4812. Hours: 8:30AM-4:30PM (EST). *Probate.*

www.co.delaware.pa.us

Elk County

Court of Common Pleas - Criminal/Civil
PO Box 237, Ridgway, PA 15853; 814-776-5344; Fax: 814-776-5303. Hours: 8:30AM-4PM (EST). *Felony, Misdemeanor, Civil, Eviction.*

www.co.elk.pa.us/Courthouse.htm

Civil Records: Access: Phone, fax, mail, in person. Both court and visitors may perform in person searches. Search fee: $8.00 per name. Required to search: name, years to search. Civil cases indexed by defendant, plaintiff. Civil records on dockets from 1843, on comptuer back to 1998.

Criminal Records: Access: Phone, fax, mail, in person, online. Both court and visitors may perform in person searches. Search fee: $10.00 per name. Required to search: name, years to search, DOB. Criminal records on dockets from 1843, on computer back to 1998. Search docket information by name or docket number for free at http://ujsportal.pacourts.us. Click on "E-Services." Name search under "Other Criteria."

General Information: Public Access terminal is available. No mental health or juvenile records released. Copy fee: $.50 per page. Cert fee: $4.50 for civil; $8.50 for criminal. Payee: Elk County Prothonotary. Personal checks accepted. Prepayment required. Mail requests: SASE requested. Turnaround time 1 day.

Register of Wills PO Box 314, Ridgway, PA 15853; 814-776-5349; Fax: 814-776-5382. Hours: 8:30AM-4PM (EST). *Probate.*

Erie County

Court of Common Pleas - Civil
Erie County Courthouse, 140 W 6th St., Erie, PA 16501; 814-451-6250; Criminal phone: 814-451-6221; Probate phone: 814-451-6260. Hours: 8:30AM-4:30PM (EST). *Civil, Eviction.*

www.eriecounty.biz

Civil Records: Access: Mail, online, in person. Both court and visitors may perform in person searches. Search fee: $10.00. Required to search: name, years to search. Civil cases indexed by defendant, plaintiff. Civil records on computer from 1992, on dockets from 1971, on microfilm/microfiche from 1800s. Internet access to court records is by subscription from a private company-Infocon at www.ic-access.com, 814-472-6066. See note at beginning of section.

General Information: Public Access terminal is available. No sealed records released. Will fax results to local or toll free line. Copy fee: $.50 per page. Computer page $1.00 per page. Cert fee: $5.00. Payee: Prothonotary. Personal checks accepted. Prepayment required. Mail requests: SASE required. Mail turnaround time less than 1 week.

Court of Common Pleas - Criminal
Erie County Courthouse, 140 W 6th St, Erie, PA 16501; 814-451-6229; Fax: 814-451-6420. Hours: 8:30AM-4:30PM (EST). *Felony, Misdemeanor.*

www.eriecountygov.org/default.aspx?id=courts

Criminal Records: Access: Mail, online, in person. Both court and visitors may perform in person searches. Search fee: $10.00 per name. Required to search: name, years to search, DOB. Criminal records go back to 1960; records computerized back to 1992. Internet access to court records is by subscription from a private company-Infocon at www.ic-access.com, 814-472-6066. See note at beginning of section.

General Information: Public Access terminal is available. No juvenile or ARD records released. Will fax results to local or toll free line. Copy fee: $.10 per page. No cert fee. Payee: Clerk of Courts. Personal checks accepted. Prepayment required. Mail requests: SASE not required. Mail turnaround time 1 week.

Register of Wills Erie County Courthouse 140 W 6th St, Erie, PA 16501; 814-451-6260; Fax: 814-451-7010. Hours: 8:30AM-4:30PM (EST). *Probate.*
Note: Internet access to records is available by subscription from a private company-Infocon at www.ic-access.com, 814-472-6066. See note at beginning of section.

Fayette County

Court of Common Pleas - Civil 61 E Main St, Uniontown, PA 15401; 724-430-1272; Fax: 724-430-4555. Hours: 8AM-4:30PM (EST). *Civil, Eviction.*
Civil Records: Access: Mail, in person. Both court and visitors may perform in person searches. Search fee: $5.00 per name. Required to search: name, years to search. Civil cases indexed by defendant, plaintiff. Civil records on computer from 1999, archived from 1700s.
General Information: Public Access terminal is available. No mental records released. Copy fee: $.50 per page. Cert fee: $10.00. Payee: Prothonotary. Personal checks accepted. Prepayment required. Mail requests: SASE not required. Mail turnaround time 2 weeks.

Court of Common Pleas - Criminal 61 E Main St, Uniontown, PA 15401; 724-430-1253; Fax: 724-438-8410. Hours: 8AM-4:30PM (EST). *Felony, Misdemeanor.*
Criminal Records: Access: Fax, mail, in person, online. Both court and visitors may perform in person searches. Search fee: $15.00 for 5-year search; $30.00 for 5-yr. plus. Required to search: name, years to search, DOB; also helpful: SSN. Criminal records on computer from 1993, on files from 1800s. Search docket information by name or docket number for free at http://ujsportal.pacourts.us. Click on "E-Services." Name search under "Other Criteria."
General Information: Public Access terminal is available. No sex related or juvenile records released. Will fax results $3.00 per doc. Copy fee: $.50 per page. Cert fee: $16.50. Payee: Clerk of Courts. Personal checks accepted. Prepayment required. Mail requests: SASE not required. Mail turnaround time 3-5 days.

Register of Wills 61 E Main St, Uniontown, PA 15401; 724-430-1206; Fax: 724-430-1275. Hours: 8AM-4:30PM (EST). *Probate.*

Forest County

Court of Common Pleas 526 Elm St #2, Forest County Courthouse, Tionesta, PA 16353; 814-755-3526; Fax: 814-755-8837. Hours: 9AM-4PM (EST). *Felony, Misdemeanor, Civil, Eviction, Probate.*
http://users.penn.com/~wrncourt/
Note: Computerized records includes the Register of Wills.
Civil Records: Access: Mail, fax, in person. Both court and visitors may perform in person searches. No search fee. Required to search: name, years to search. Civil cases indexed by defendant, plaintiff. Computerized records from 2002, civil records on dockets since 1995, archived from 1857.
Criminal Records: Access: Mail, fax, in person, online. Both court and visitors may perform in person

searches. Search fee: $10.00 per name. Required to search: name, years to search; also helpful: DOB, SSN. Computerized records from 1995, archived from 1857. Search docket information by name or docket number for free at http://ujsportal.pacourts.us. Click on "E-Services." Name search under "Other Criteria."
General Information: Public Access terminal is available. No adoption records released. Fee to fax results is $4.00 per document. Copy fee: $3.00 per page. Cert fee: $2.00. Payee: Clerk of Courts. Personal checks accepted. Prepayment required. Mail requests: SASE required. Mail turnaround time same day.

Franklin County

Court of Common Pleas - Civil 157 Lincoln Way East, Chambersburg, PA 17201; 717-261-3858; Fax: 717-264-6772. Hours: 8:30AM-4:30PM (EST). *Civil, Eviction.*
Civil Records: Access: In person, online. Visitors must perform in person searches for themselves. Search fee: none. Required to search: name, years to search. Civil cases indexed by defendant, plaintiff. Civil records on file from 1985; on computer back to 4/1/1999. Internet access to court records is by subscription from a private company-Infocon at www.ic-access.com, 814-472-6066. See note at beginning of section.
General Information: Public Access terminal is available. No mental records released. Fee to fax results is $1.00 per page. Copy fee: $1.00 per page. Cert fee: $5.00 for 1st pg; $1.00 each add'l. Payee: Prothonotary. Personal checks accepted. Prepayment required.

Court of Common Pleas - Criminal 157 Lincoln Way East, Chambersburg, PA 17201; 717-261-3805; Fax: 717-261-3896. Hours: 8:30AM-4:30PM (EST). *Felony, Misdemeanor.*
Criminal Records: Access: Mail, in person. Both court and visitors may perform in person searches. Search fee: $10.00 per name. Required to search: name, years to search, DOB. Computerized back to 1995; criminal records on files for 50 years, archived from 1800s. The court may offer docket information at http://ujsportal.pacourts.us.
General Information: Public Access terminal is available. No juvenile records released. Copy fee: $.25 per page. Cert fee: $5.00. Payee: Clerk of Courts. Personal checks accepted. Prepayment required. Mail requests: SASE requested. Turnaround time same day.

Register of Wills 157 Lincoln Way East, Chambersburg, PA 17201; 717-261-3872; Fax: 717-263-5717. Hours: 8:30AM-4:30PM (EST). *Probate.*
Note: Internet access to records is available by subscription from a private company-Infocon at www.ic-access.com, 814-472-6066. See note at beginning of section.

Fulton County

Court of Common Pleas - Criminal/Civil Fulton County Courthouse, 201 N 2nd St, McConnellsburg, PA 17233; 717-485-4212; Fax: 717-485-5568 Attn: Court of Common Pleas. Hours: 8:30AM-4:30PM (EST). *Felony, Misdemeanor, Civil, Eviction.*
Civil Records: Access: In person only. Visitors must perform in person searches for themselves. No search fee. Required to search: name, years to search. Civil cases indexed by defendant, plaintiff. Civil records on docket index from 1850s; on computer back to 1999.
Criminal Records: Access: Mail, in person. Both court and visitors may perform in person searches. Search fee: $5.00 per name. Required to search:

name, years to search. Criminal records on docket index from 1850s; on computer back to 1994.
General Information: Public Access terminal is available. No juvenile, adoption records released. Will fax results $5.00 per doc. Copy fee: $.25 per page. Cert fee: $5.00. Payee: Prothonotary. Personal checks accepted. Prepayment required. Mail requests: SASE required. Mail turnaround time 3-5 days.

Register of Wills 201 N 2nd St, McConnellsburg, PA 17233; 717-485-4212; Fax: 717-485-5568. Hours: 8:30AM-4:30PM (EST). *Probate.*

Greene County

Court of Common Pleas - Civil Greene County Courthouse, Rm 105, Waynesburg, PA 15370; 724-852-5289. Hours: 8:30AM-4:30PM (EST). *Civil, Eviction.*
Civil Records: Access: Mail, in person. Visitors must perform in person searches for themselves. No search fee. Required to search: name, years to search. Civil cases indexed by defendant, plaintiff. Civil records go back to 1797; on computer back to 1996.
General Information: Public Access terminal is available. No mental health records released. Copy fee: $.50 per page. Cert fee: $8.00. Payee: Prothonotary. Personal checks accepted. Prepayment required. Mail requests: SASE required. Mail turnaround time 1 week.

Court of Common Pleas - Criminal Greene County Courthouse, 10 E High St, Waynesburg, PA 15370; 724-852-5281; Fax: 724-852-5316. Hours: 8:30AM-4:30PM (EST). *Felony, Misdemeanor.*
Criminal Records: Access: Mail, in person, free. Both court and visitors may perform in person searches. Search fee: $10.00 per name. Required to search: name, years to search, DOB, signed release; also helpful: SSN. Criminal records on index books from 1940s, on computer since 1996. Search docket information by name or docket number for free at http://ujsportal.pacourts.us. Click on "E-Services." Name search under "Other Criteria."
General Information: Public Access terminal is available. (Limited number of cases only.) No juvenile, adoption records released. Fee to fax results is $2.00 1st page; $1.00 each add'l page. Copy fee: $.50 per page. Cert fee: $8.00. Payee: Clerk of Courts. Personal checks accepted. Prepayment required. Mail requests: SASE required. Mail turnaround time same day.

Register of Wills Greene County Courthouse, 10 E High St, Waynesburg, PA 15370; 724-852-5283. Hours: 8:30AM-4PM (EST). *Probate.*

Huntingdon County

Court of Common Pleas - Criminal/Civil PO Box 39, Courthouse, Huntingdon, PA 16652; 814-643-1610; Fax: 814-643-4172. Hours: 8:30AM-4:30PM (EST). *Felony, Misdemeanor, Civil, Eviction.*
Civil Records: Access: In person, online. Visitors must perform in person searches for themselves. No search fee. Required to search: name, years to search; also helpful: address. Civil cases indexed by defendant, plaintiff. Civil records on computer from 08/03/92, on dockets from 1700s. Internet access to court records is by subscription from a private company-Infocon at www.ic-access.com, 814-472-6066. See note at beginning of section.
Criminal Records: Access: In person, online. Visitors must perform in person searches for themselves. No search fee. Required to search: name, years to search; also helpful: DOB, SSN. Criminal records on computer from 08/03/92, on dockets from 1700s. Internet access to court records is by

subscription from a private company-Infocon at www.ic-access.com, 814-472-6066. See note at beginning of section.

General Information: Public Access terminal is available. No juvenile records released. Copy fee: $.25 per page. Cert fee: $4.50. Payee: Prothonotary. Personal checks accepted. Prepayment required.

Register of Wills Courthouse, 223 Penn St, Huntingdon, PA 16652; 814-643-2740. Hours: 8:30AM-4:30PM (EST). *Probate.*

Note: Internet access to records is available by subscription from a private company-Infocon at www.ic-access.com, 814-472-6066. See note at beginning of section.

Indiana County

Court of Common Pleas - Criminal/Civil

County Courthouse, 825 Philadelphia St, Indiana, PA 15701; 724-465-3855/3858; Fax: 724-465-3968. Hours: 8AM-4PM (EST). *Felony, Misdemeanor, Civil, Eviction.*

Civil Records: Access: Mail, in person. Both court and visitors may perform in person searches. Search fee: $10.00 per name. Will not conduct judgment searches. Required to search: name, years to search. Civil cases indexed by defendant, plaintiff. Civil records on computer from 1994, prior on index files to1806.

Criminal Records: Access: Mail, in person, online. Both court and visitors may perform in person searches. Search fee: $10.00 per name. Required to search: name, years to search, DOB, signed release. Criminal records on computer from 1994, prior on index files to 1806. Search docket information by name or docket number for free at http://ujsportal.pacourts.us. Click on "E-Services." Name search under "Other Criteria."

General Information: Public Access terminal is available. No juvenile, commitment records released. Will fax results $.25 per page. Copy fee: $.25 per page. Cert fee: $3.00. Payee: Clerk of Court or Prothonotary. Personal checks accepted. Prepayment required. Mail turnaround time same day.

Register of Wills County Courthouse, 825 Philadelphia St, Indiana, PA 15701; 724-465-3860; Fax: 724-465-3863. Hours: 8AM-4:30PM (EST). *Probate.*

Jefferson County

Court of Common Pleas - Criminal/Civil

Courthouse, 200 Main St, Brookville, PA 15825; 814-849-1606 X225; Fax: 814-849-1625. Hours: 8:30AM-4:30PM (EST). *Felony, Misdemeanor, Civil, Eviction.*

Civil Records: Access: Mail, in person. Both court and visitors may perform in person searches. Search fee: $5.00 per name. Required to search: name, years to search. Civil cases indexed by defendant, plaintiff. Civil records on computer back to 1987; all incoming records microfilmed, records since 1823 on microfilm.

Criminal Records: Access: Mail, in person, online. Both court and visitors may perform in person searches. Search fee: $5.00 per name. Required to search: name, years to search, DOB; also helpful: SSN. Criminal records on computer back to 1987; all incoming records microfilmed, records since 1947 on microfilm. Search docket information by name or docket number for free at http://ujsportal.pacourts.us. Click on "E-Services." Name search under "Other Criteria."

General Information: Public Access terminal is available. No juvenile, mental health, records released, including criminal cases with a minor as a victim. Will fax results for $3.00 1st page; $1.00 for

every page thereafter. Copy fee: $.50 per page. Cert fee: $1.50. Payee: Clerk of Courts. Personal checks accepted. Prepayment required. Mail requests: SASE required. Mail turnaround time 2 days.

Register of Wills Jefferson County Courthouse, 200 Main St, Brookville, PA 15825; 814-849-1610; Fax: 814-849-1677. Hours: 8:30AM-4:30PM (EST). *Probate.*

Note: $5.00 search fee, $1.00 per copy.

Juniata County

Court of Common Pleas - Criminal/Civil

Juniata County Courthouse, Mifflintown, PA 17059; 717-436-7715; Fax: 717-436-7734. Hours: 8AM-4:30PM (EST). *Felony, Misdemeanor, Civil, Eviction.*

Civil Records: Access: Mail, in person. Both court and visitors may perform in person searches. Search fee: $5.00 per name. Required to search: name, years to search. Civil cases indexed by defendant, plaintiff. Civil records on computer go back to 1993, on dockets from 1836.

Criminal Records: Access: Phone, mail, in person. Both court and visitors may perform in person searches. Search fee: $5.00 per name. Required to search: name, years to search, DOB, SSN, signed release. Criminal records on computer go back to 1993, on dockets from 1894.

General Information: Public Access terminal is available. No juvenile records released. Copy fee: $.50 per page. Cert fee: $1.00 per page. Payee: Prothonotary or Clerk of Courts. Personal checks accepted. Prepayment required. Mail requests: SASE required. Mail turnaround time 1 week.

Register of Wills Juniata County Courthouse, PO Box 68, Mifflintown, PA 17059; 717-436-7709; Fax: 717-436-7756. Hours: 8AM-4:30PM M-F, 8AM-12PM Wed (June-Sept) (EST). *Probate.*

Note: Internet access to records is available by subscription from a private company-Infocon at www.ic-access.com, 814-472-6066. See note at beginning of section.

Lackawanna County

Court of Common Pleas - Civil

Clerk of Judicial Records, 200 N Washington Ave, Scranton, PA 18503-1551; 570-963-6724; Civil phone: 717-963-6723. Hours: 9AM-4PM (EST). *Civil, Eviction.*

Civil Records: Access: In person only. Visitors must perform in person searches for themselves. Search fee: No civil searches performed by court - but exceptions are made. Required to search: name, years to search. Civil cases indexed by defendant, plaintiff. Civil records computerized since 09/95, dockets from 1920s, archived from 1800s. Case number is required.

General Information: Public Access terminal is available. No juvenile records released. Copy fee: $.25 if self service; $.50 if done by Clerk; $1.00 for mail requesters first copy, $.50 each add'l. Cert fee: $4.50. Payee: Clerk of Judicial Records. Business checks accepted. Prepayment required.

Court of Common Pleas - Criminal

Lackawanna County Courthouse, Scranton, PA 18503; 570-963-6759; Fax: 570-963-6459. Hours: 9AM-4PM (EST). *Felony, Misdemeanor.*

Criminal Records: Access: Mail, fax, in person. Both court and visitors may perform in person searches. Search fee: $10.00 per name. Required to search: name, years to search, DOB, SSN. Criminal records computerized since 10/95, on dockets from 1983, archived from 1941, indexed by defendant only.

General Information: Public Access terminal is available. No juvenile records released. Will fax results to local or toll free line. Copy fee: $.50 per page. Cert fee: $8.00. Payee: Clerk of Judicial

Records. Business checks accepted. Prepayment required. Mail requests: SASE required. Mail turnaround time 1-2 days.

Register of Wills Register of Wills, County Courthouse, 200 N Washington Ave, Scranton, PA 18503; 570-963-6702; Fax: 570-963-6377. Hours: 9AM-4PM (EST). *Probate.*

Lancaster County

Court of Common Pleas - Civil

50 N Duke St, PO Box 83480, Lancaster, PA 17608-3480; 717-299-8282; Fax: 717-293-7210. Hours: 8:30AM-5PM (EST). *Civil, Eviction.*
www.co.lancaster.pa.us/courts/site/default.asp

Civil Records: Access: Online, in person. Visitors must perform in person searches for themselves. No search fee. Required to search: name, years to search; also helpful: address. Civil cases indexed by defendant, plaintiff. Civil records on computer from 7/87, in files from 1987, judgments on dockets from 1800s, others archived from 1800s. Access to the Prothonotary's civil court records is free at www.co.lancaster.pa.us/scripts/bannerweb.dll. Also, search the Prothonotary "Protection from Abuse" list for free at www.co.lancaster.pa.us/scripts/PFAWebQuery.exe. Also, historical court case schedules are free at www.co.lancaster.pa.us (click on "Court Schedules"). Also, access to remote online records requires a $25.00 monthly fee plus $.18 per minute. Includes Register, Treasurer, and other courthouse record data. Search by name or case number. Call Kathy Harris at 717-299-8252 for more information.

General Information: Public Access terminal is available. No naturalization records released. Will fax results $2.00 1st page, $1.00 each add'l. Fee higher for out of state faxing. Copy fee: $.50 per page. Cert fee: $5.00. Payee: Prothonotary. No personal or business checks accepted except from attorneys. Prepayment required. Mail requests: SASE required. Mail turnaround time 2-3 days.

Court of Common Pleas - Criminal

Clerk of Courts, 50 N Duke St, Lancaster, PA 17602; 717-299-8275. Hours: 8:30AM-5PM (EST). *Felony, Misdemeanor.*
www.co.lancaster.pa.us/courts/site/default.asp

Criminal Records: Access: Mail, in person. Both court and visitors may perform in person searches. Search fee: $20.00 per name. Required to search: name, years to search, SSN or DOB. Criminal records on computer from 1988, archived from 1901. Search the Prothonotary "Protection from Abuse" list for free at www.co.lancaster.pa.us/scripts/PFAWebQuery.exe.

General Information: Public Access terminal is available. No juvenile records released. Copy fee: $1.00 per copy or $1.00 for docket page including disposition; however, there is no copy fee if court does the search. Cert fee: $8.00. Payee: Clerk of Courts. Only cashiers checks and money orders accepted. Prepayment required. Mail requests: SASE required. Mail turnaround time 2 days.

Register of Wills 50 N. Duke St., Lancaster, PA 17602; 717-299-8243; Fax: 717-295-5914. Hours: 8:30AM-4:30PM (EST). *Probate.*
www.co.lancaster.pa.us

Lawrence County

Court of Common Pleas - Criminal/Civil

430 Court St, New Castle, PA 16101-3593; 724-656-2143; Civil phone: 724-656-1960; Criminal phone: 724-656-2188; Fax: 724-656-1988. Hours: 8AM-4PM (EST). *Felony, Misdemeanor, Civil, Eviction.*
www.co.lawrence.pa.us

Civil Records: Access: Fax, mail, online, in person. Both court and visitors may perform in person searches. Search fee: $10.00 per name. Required to search: name, years to search. Civil cases indexed by defendant, plaintiff. Civil records on computer from 1987, on Russell Index from 1885. Internet access to court records is by subscription from a private company-Infocon at www.ic-access.com, 814-472-6066. See note at beginning of section.

Criminal Records: Access: Fax, mail, online, in person. Both court and visitors may perform in person searches. Search fee: $16.00 per name. Required to search: name, years to search, signed release; also helpful: DOB, SSN. Criminal records on computer from 1994, on Russell Index from 1885. Internet access to court records is by subscription from a private company-Infocon at www.ic-access.com, 814-472-6066. See note at beginning of section. Also, search docket information by name or docket number for free at http://ujsportal.pacourts.us. Click on "E-Services." Name search under "Other Criteria."

General Information: Public Access terminal is available. No adoption, juvenile, impounded, or juvenile sex crime victim records released. Will fax results: local $1.00 plus $.50 per pg; long distance $3.00 plus $.50 per pg. Copy fee: $.50 per page. Cert fee: $1.50. Payee: Prothonotary. Business checks accepted. Prepayment required. Mail requests: SASE requested. Turnaround time ASAP.

Register of Wills 430 Court St, New Castle, PA 16101-3593; 724-656-2128/2159; Fax: 724-656-1966. Hours: 8AM-4PM (EST). *Probate.*

Note: Internet access to records is available by subscription from a private company-Infocon at www.ic-access.com, 814-472-6066. See note at beginning of section.

Lebanon County

Court of Common Pleas - Civil Municipal Bldg, Rm 104, 400 S 8th St, Lebanon, PA 17042; 717-274-2801 X2120. Hours: 8:30AM-4:30PM (EST). *Civil, Eviction.*

Civil Records: Access: Mail, in person. Visitors must perform in person searches for themselves. No search fee. Required to search: name, years to search; also helpful: address. Civil cases indexed by defendant, plaintiff. Civil records on computer from 1985, on files from 1883.

General Information: Public Access terminal is available. No mental health records released. Copy fee: $.50 per page. Cert fee: $9.00. Payee: Prothonotary. Personal checks accepted. Prepayment required. Mail requests: SASE required. Mail turnaround time is same day.

Court of Common Pleas - Criminal Municipal Bldg Rm 102, 400 S 8th St, Lebanon, PA 17042; 717-274-2801 X2118. Hours: 8:30AM-4:30PM (EST). *Felony, Misdemeanor.*

Criminal Records: Access: Phone, mail, in person. Both court and visitors may perform in person searches. Search fee: $18.00 per name. Required to search: name, years to search. Criminal records on computer from 1986, indexed from 1800s. Action number required for phone access.

General Information: Public Access terminal is available. No juvenile records released. Copy fee: $.50 per page. Cert fee: $9.00. Payee: Clerk of Court. Personal checks accepted. Prepayment required. Mail requests: SASE required. Mail turnaround time varies.

Register of Wills Municipal Bldg, Rm 105, 400 S 8th St, Lebanon, PA 17042; 717-274-2801 X2215; Probate phone: Ext 2217 & 2218; Fax: 717-274-8094. Hours: 8:30AM-4:30PM (EST). *Probate.*

Lehigh County

Court of Common Pleas - Civil 455 W Hamilton St, Allentown, PA 18101-1614; 610-782-3148; Civil phone: 610-782-3148; Probate: 610-782-3077; Probate phone: 610-782-3170; Fax: 610-770-3840. Hours: 8:30AM-4:30PM (EST). *Civil, Eviction.*

www.lccpa.org

Civil Records: Access: Mail, online, in person. Both the court and visitors may perform in person searches. No search fee. Required to search: name, years to search, DOB. Civil cases indexed by defendant, plaintiff. Civil records on computer since 1985, on microfilm from 1812, some in books. Access to the county online system requires monthly usage fee. Search by name or case number. Call Lehigh Cty Computer Svcs Dept at 610-782-3286 for more information.

General Information: Public Access terminal is available. No sealed, confidential, or impounded records released. Copy fee: $.50 per page; docket printout $3.00. Cert fee: $4.75. Payee: Clerk of Courts-Civil. Personal checks accepted. Prepayment required. Mail turnaround time is 2 days.

Court of Common Pleas - Criminal Clerk of courts, 455 W Hamilton St, Allentown, PA 18101-1614; 610-782-3077; Civil phone: 610-782-3148; Criminal phone: 610-782-3077; Fax: 610-770-6797. Hours: 8:30AM-4:30PM (EST). *Felony, Misdemeanor.*

www.lccpa.org

Criminal Records: Access: Mail, online, in person. Both court and visitors may perform in person searches. Search fee: $20.90 per name. Fee includes copy of certified docket. Required to search: name, years to search, DOB; SSN helpful. Criminal records on computer from 1990, on alpha index from 1962 to 1990, on microfilm from 1812. Access to the countywide online system requires monthly usage fee. Search by name or case number. Call Lehigh Cty Computer Svcs Dept at 610-782-3286 for more information. Also, free online access is under development; currently calendars and bench warrants are online at www.lehighcountycourt.org under "Calendars & Schedules."

General Information: Public Access terminal is available. No juvenile or impounded records released. No fee to fax results. Copy fee: $.50. Docket printout mailed $3.15. Cert fee: $8.45. Payee: Clerk of Courts-Criminal. Personal checks accepted. Prepayment required. Mail requests: SASE required. Mail turnaround time 1 week.

Register of Wills 455 W Hamilton, Allentown, PA 18101-1614; 610-782-3170; Fax: 610-782-3932. Hours: 8AM-4PM (EST). *Probate.*

Note: Access to the county online system to search Wills requires monthly usage fee. Call Lehigh Cty Computer Svcs Dept at 610-782-3286 for more information.

Luzerne County

Court of Common Pleas - Civil 200 N River St, Wilkes Barre, PA 18711-1001; 570-825-1745; Fax: 570-825-1757. Hours: 9AM-4:30PM (EST). *Civil, Eviction.*

Civil Records: Access: Phone, mail, in person. Both court and visitors may perform in person searches. Search fee: $16.75 per name for 5 years, $1.50 each add'l year, and $1.50 each reference cited. Required to search: name, years to search, address. Civil cases indexed by defendant, plaintiff. Civil records partially on microfiche and archives, on dockets from 1935.

General Information: No mental, sealed records released. Fee to fax results is $1.50 per page. Copy fee: $1.00 per page. Cert fee: $5.00. Payee:

Prothonotary. Personal checks accepted. Visa, MC, AmEx accepted but not accepted over the phone. Prepayment required. Mail requests: SASE required. Mail turnaround time 5 days.

Court of Common Pleas - Criminal 200 N River St, Wilkes Barre, PA 18711; 570-825-1585; Fax: 570-825-1843. Hours: 8AM-4:30PM (EST). *Felony, Misdemeanor.*

Criminal Records: Access: Fax, mail, in person. Only the court performs in person searches. Search fee: $15.00 per name. Required to search: name, years to search, DOB or SSN. Criminal records on computer, microfiche and archived from 1989, on files from 1972. Records from 1933 to 1959 destroyed in flood. Index starts in 1918. The court may offer docket information at http://ujsportal.pacourts.us.

General Information: No "M" number (confidential custody case) records released. No fee to fax results. Copy fee: $.35 per page. Cert fee: $7.00. Payee: Clerk of Courts. Personal checks accepted. Visa, MC, Discover accepted. Prepayment required. Mail requests: SASE not required. Mail turnaround time 1-2 days.

Register of Wills 200 N River St, Wilkes Barre, PA 18711; 570-825-1672, 570-825-1500 X670; Fax: 570-826-0869. Hours: 9AM-4:30PM (EST). *Probate.*

Lycoming County

Court of Common Pleas - Criminal/Civil 48 W 3rd St, Williamsport, PA 17701; 570-327-2251; Fax: 570-327-2505. Hours: 8:30AM-5PM (EST). *Felony, Misdemeanor, Civil, Eviction.*

Civil Records: Access: In person only. Visitors must perform in person searches for themselves. No search fee. Required to search: name, years to search; also helpful: address. Civil cases indexed by defendant, plaintiff. Civil records on computer from 1983, on dockets from 1795.

Criminal Records: Access: Mail, in person, online. Both court and visitors may perform in person searches. Search fee: $10.00 per name. Required to search: name, years to search, DOB; also helpful: address. Criminal records on computer from 1910. The court may offer docket information at http://ujsportal.pacourts.us.

General Information: Public Access terminal is available. No juvenile, cases involving minors, mental records released. Copy fee: $.50 per page. Cert fee: $5.00. Payee: Prothonotary. Personal checks accepted. Prepayment required. Mail requests: SASE required. Mail turnaround time same day.

Register of Wills Lycoming Co Courthouse, 48 W 3rd St, Williamsport, PA 17701; 570-327-2263, 327-2258; Fax: 570-327-6790. Hours: 8:30AM-5PM (EST). *Probate.*

McKean County

Court of Common Pleas - Criminal/Civil PO Box 273, Smethport, PA 16749; 814-887-3270; Fax: 814-887-3219. Hours: 8:30AM-4:30PM (EST). *Felony, Misdemeanor, Civil, Eviction.*

Civil Records: Access: Phone, fax, mail, in person. Both court and visitors may perform in person searches. Search fee: $15.00 per name. Required to search: name, years to search. Civil cases indexed by defendant, plaintiff. Civil records on computer since 1994, on microfiche from 1952 to 1962, on dockets from 1872.

Criminal Records: Access: Mail, in person, online. Both court and visitors may perform in person searches. Search fee: $15.00 per name. Required to search: name, years to search, DOB. Criminal records on computer since 1994, on dockets from 1872. Search docket information by name or docket number for free at http://ujsportal.pacourts.us. Click on "E-Services." Name search under "Other Criteria."

General Information: Public Access terminal is available. No sex related, juvenile, mental health records released. Will fax results for $2.00 per page. Copy fee: $.50 per page. Computer search copy fee: $1.00 per page. Cert fee: $10.00. Payee: Prothonotary or Clerk of Courts. Personal checks accepted. Prepayment required. Mail requests: SASE required. Mail turnaround time same day.

Register of Wills PO Box 202, Smethport, PA 16749-0202; 814-887-3263; Fax: 814-887-2242. Hours: 8:30AM-4:30PM (EST). *Probate.*

Mercer County

Court of Common Pleas - Civil 105 Mercer County Courthouse, Mercer, PA 16137; 724-662-3800. Hours: 8:30AM-4:30PM (EST). *Civil, Eviction.*
Civil Records: Access: In person, online. Visitors must perform in person searches for themselves. No search fee. Required to search: name, years to search. Civil cases indexed by defendant, plaintiff. Civil records on computer since 1994; prior records on dockets from 1930s, archived from 1700s. Include SSN and DOB in your search. Internet access to court records is by subscription from a private company-Infocon at www.ic-access.com, 814-472-6066. See note at beginning of section.
General Information: Public Access terminal is available. No mental, sealed records released. Copy fee: $2.00 per page. Cert fee: $4.50. Payee: Prothonotary or Clerk of Courts. Business checks accepted. Prepayment required. Mail requests: SASE required. Mail turnaround time 1-2 days.

Court of Common Pleas - Criminal 112 Mercer County Courthouse, Mercer, PA 16137; 724-662-3800 X2248. Hours: 8:30AM-4:30PM (EST). *Felony, Misdemeanor.*
www.mcc.co.mercer.pa.us/LOCRULES.htm
Criminal Records: Access: Mail, in person. Both court and visitors may perform in person searches. Search fee: $10.00 per name. Required to search: name, years to search; also helpful: DOB, SSN. Criminal records on computer since 1993, indexed since 1920, on files from 1980. The court may offer docket information at http://ujsportal.pacourts.us.
General Information: Public Access terminal is available. No juvenile records released. Fee to fax results is $1.00 per page. Copy fee: $.50 per page. Cert fee: $5.00. Payee: Clerk of Courts. Personal checks accepted. Prepayment required. Mail requests: SASE required. Mail turnaround time 1 day.

Register of Wills 112 Mercer County Courthouse, Mercer, PA 16137; 724-662-3800 X2248; Fax: 724-662-1604. Hours: 8:30AM-4:30PM (EST). *Probate.*

Mifflin County

Court of Common Pleas - Criminal/Civil 20 N Wayne St, Lewistown, PA 17044; 717-248-8146; Fax: 717-248-5275. Hours: 8AM-4:30PM (EST). *Felony, Misdemeanor, Civil, Eviction.*
www.co.mifflin.pa.us
Civil Records: Access: In person, online. Visitors must perform in person searches for themselves. No search fee. Required to search: name, years to search. Civil cases indexed by defendant, plaintiff. Civil records on computer from 1993, on microfiche from 1971-1990 prior on books. The court calendar is at the website. Internet access to court records is by subscription from a private company-Infocon at www.ic-access.com, 814-472-6066. See note at beginning of section.
Criminal Records: Access: In person, online. Visitors must perform in person searches for

themselves. No search fee. Required to search: name, years to search. Criminal records on computer from 1993, on microfiche from 1971-1990 prior on books. The court calendar is at the website. Internet access to court records is by subscription from a private company-Infocon at www.ic-access.com, 814-472-6066. See note at beginning of section. The court may offer docket information at http://ujsportal.pacourts.us.
General Information: Public Access terminal is available. No juvenile, mental health records released. Copy fee: $.50 per page. Cert fee: $4.50. Payee: Clerk of Courts. Personal checks accepted. Prepayment required.

Register of Wills 20 N. Wayne St., Lewistown, PA 17044; 717-242-1449; Fax: 717-248-2503. Hours: 8AM-4:30PM M-F (EST). *Probate.*
www.co.mifflin.pa.us/mifflin/site/default.asp
Note: Internet access to records is available by subscription from a private company-Infocon at www.ic-access.com, 814-472-6066.

Monroe County

Court of Common Pleas - Civil Monroe County Courthouse - Prothonotary, 7th & Monroe St, Stroudsburg, PA 18360; 570-517-3988; Fax: 570-420-3582. Hours: 8:30AM-4:30PM (EST). *Civil, Eviction.*
Note: Passport info 570-517-3370.
Civil Records: Access: Mail, in person. Both court and visitors may perform in person searches. Search fee: $5.00. Required to search: name, years to search; also helpful:DOB, SSN, signed release. Civil cases indexed by defendant, plaintiff. Civil records indexed on computer 1995 to present, prior in dockets.
General Information: Public Access terminal is available. No juvenile records released. Copy fee: $.50 per page. Cert fee: $3.00. Payee: Monroe County Prothonotary. Only cashiers checks and money orders accepted. Prepayment required. Mail requests: SASE not required. Mail turnaround time 1 day.

Court of Common Pleas - Criminal Monroe County Courthouse Rm 312, Stroudsburg, PA 18360-2190; 570-517-3385. Hours: 8:30AM-4:30PM (EST). *Felony, Misdemeanor.*
Criminal Records: Access: Mail, in person. Both court and visitors may perform in person searches. Search fee: $5.00 per name. Required to search: name, years to search; also helpful: address, DOB, SSN. Criminal records on computer since 1995; prior on dockets. The court may offer docket information at http://ujsportal.pacourts.us.
General Information: Public Access terminal is available. No sex related, juvenile, adoption records released. Copy fee: $1.00 per page. Cert fee: $5.00. Payee: Clerk of Court. Only cashiers checks and money orders accepted. Prepayment required. Mail requests: SASE required. Mail turnaround time 1 day.

Register of Wills Monroe County Courthouse, Stroudsburg, PA 18360; 570-517-3359; Fax: 570-420-3537. Hours: 8:30AM-4:30PM (EST). *Probate.*
Note: Online access to wills is available through a private company at www.landex.com/remote/. Fee is $.20 per minute and $.50 per fax page. Wills go back to 11/1836.

Montgomery County

Court of Common Pleas - Civil PO Box 311, Airy & Swede St, Norristown, PA 19404-0311; 610-278-3360; Fax: 610-278-5994. Hours: 8:30AM-4:15PM (EST). *Civil, Eviction.*
www.montcopa.org
Civil Records: Access: Mail, online, in person. Visitors must perform in person searches for

themselves. No search fee. Required to search: name, years to search. Civil cases indexed by defendant, plaintiff. Civil records on computer from 4/82, on microfilm from 1800s. Court and other records are free online at www.montcopa.org/mway/index.html. This includes active and purged civil cases, also active probate cases.
General Information: Public Access terminal is available. No mental health, divorce, sealed records released. Will fax results for $1.00 1st page, $.50 each add'l. Copy fee: $.25 per page. Cert fee: $4.50. Payee: Prothonotary. Personal checks accepted. Prepayment required. Mail requests: SASE required. Mail turnaround time is 2 days.

Court of Common Pleas - Criminal PO Box 311, Airy & Swede St, Norristown, PA 19404-0311; 610-278-3346; Fax: 610-278-5183. Hours: 8:30AM-4:15PM (EST). *Felony, Misdemeanor.*
www.montcopa.org
Criminal Records: Access: Mail, online, in person. Both court and visitors may perform in person searches. Search fee: $15.00 per name. Required to search: name, years to search, DOB, signed release. Criminal records on computer from 10/84, prior archived and on microfiche. Criminal court and other records are free online at www.montcopa.org/mway/index.html. Includes purged cases. This replaces the pay remote dial-up service. Online access to the county civil and probate active and purged records are also free.
General Information: Public Access terminal is available. No impounded, sealed records released. Copy fee: $1.00 per page. Cert fee: $7.00. Payee: Clerk of Courts. Business checks accepted. Visa, MC, Discover accepted. Accepted in person only. Prepayment required. Mail requests: SASE required. Mail turnaround time 5 days.

Register of Wills Airy & Swede St, PO Box 311, Norristown, PA 19404; 610-278-3400; Fax: 610-278-3240. Hours: 8:30AM-4:15PM (EST). *Probate.*
www.montcopa.org
Note: Search active probate cases at www.montcopa.org/mway/index.html.

Montour County

Court of Common Pleas - Criminal/Civil Montour County Courthouse, 29 Mill St, Danville, PA 17821; 570-271-3010; Fax: 570-271-3089. Hours: 9AM-4PM (EST). *Felony, Misdemeanor, Civil, Eviction.*
Civil Records: Access: Phone, fax, mail, in person, online. Both court and visitors may perform in person searches. Search fee: $10.00 per name. Required to search: name, years to search. Civil cases indexed by defendant, plaintiff. Civil records on books since 1991, on microfiche since 1939, on computer back to 1995. Actual files kept for 20 years. Internet access to court records is by subscription from a private company-Infocon at www.ic-access.com, 814-472-6066. See note at beginning of section.
Criminal Records: Access: Phone, fax, mail, in person, online. Both court and visitors may perform in person searches. Search fee: $10.00 per name. Required to search: name, years to search, DOB. Criminal records on books since 1991, on microfiche since 1939, on computer back to 1995. Actual files kept for 20 years. Internet access to court records is by subscription from a private company-Infocon at www.ic-access.com, 814-472-6066. See note at beginning of section.
General Information: Public Access terminal is available. No sex related, juvenile or adoption records released. Will fax results. Copy fee: $.50 per page. Cert fee: $4.00. Payee: Prothonotary. Personal checks accepted. Prepayment required. Mail requests: SASE required. Mail turnaround time 1-2 days.

Register of Wills 29 Mill St, Danville, PA 17821; 570-271-3012; Fax: 570-271-3071. Hours: 9AM-4PM (EST). *Probate.*

Note: Internet access to records is available by subscription from a private company-Infocon at www.ic-access.com, 814-472-6066. See note at beginning of section.

Northampton County

Court of Common Pleas - Civil Gov't Center, 669 Washington St Rm 207, Easton, PA 18042-7498; 610-559-3060. Hours: 8:30AM-4:30PM (EST). *Civil, Eviction.*
www.nccpa.org
Civil Records: Access: In person only. Visitors must perform in person searches for themselves. No search fee. Required to search: name, years to search; also helpful: address. Civil cases indexed by defendant, plaintiff. Civil records on computer since 1/85 (Civil) and 2/90 (Judgments). Search calendars and schedules for free online at www.nccpa.org/schedule.html.
General Information: Public Access terminal is available. No impounded or PFA abuse records released. Copy fee: $1.00 per page. Cert fee: $4.75. Payee: Clerk of Court-Civil or Prothonotary's Office. Business checks and certified check accepted; no personal checks. Prepayment required.

Court of Common Pleas - Criminal 669 Washington St, Easton, PA 18042-7494; 610-559-3000 X3046; Fax: 610-252-4391. Hours: 8:30AM-4:30PM (EST). *Felony, Misdemeanor.*
www.nccpa.org
Criminal Records: Access: Mail, in person. Both court and visitors may perform in person searches. Search fee: $10.00 per name. Required to search: name, years to search, DOB; also helpful: SSN. Criminal records on computer from 1984, on files from 1800s. Search calendars and schedules for free online at www.nccpa.org/schedule.html. The court may offer docket information at http://ujsportal.pacourts.us.
General Information: Public Access terminal is available. No juvenile, expunged records released. Will fax results ot local or toll free line. Copy fee: $.50 per page. Cert fee: $8.00. Payee: Criminal Division. Business checks accepted. Visa, MC accepted. Prepayment required. Mail requests: SASE not required. Mail turnaround time same day.

Register of Wills Government Center, 669 Washington St, Easton, PA 18042; 610-559-3094; Fax: 610-559-3735. Hours: 8:30AM-4:30PM (EST). *Probate.*

Northumberland County

Court of Common Pleas - Civil County Courthouse, 201 Market St, Rm #7, Sunbury, PA 17801-3468; 570-988-4151. Hours: 9AM-5PM M; 9AM-4:30PM T-F (EST). *Civil, Eviction.*
Civil Records: Access: Phone, mail, in person. Both court and visitors may perform in person searches. Search fee: $7.00 per name. Required to search: name, years to search. Civil cases indexed by defendant, plaintiff. Civil records on file from 1772; on computer back to 1998.
General Information: Public Access terminal is available. No adult abuse, involuntary treatment records released. Copy fee: $1.00 2st page; $.25. Each add'l. Cert fee: $4.00 plus $1.00 each add'l page. Payee: Northumberland Prothonotary. Business checks accepted. Prepayment required. Mail requests: SASE required. Mail turnaround time 1-2 days.

Court of Common Pleas - Criminal County Courthouse, 201 Market St, Rm 7, Sunbury, PA 17801-3468; 570-988-4148; Civil phone: 570-988-4151; Probate phone: 570-988-4143. Hours: 9AM-5PM M; 9AM-4:30PM T-F (EST). *Felony, Misdemeanor.*
Criminal Records: Access: Mail, in person. Both court and visitors may perform in person searches. Search fee: $10.00 per name. Required to search: name, years to search, DOB; also helpful: SSN. Criminal records indexed in office from 1945, on dockets from 1776, archived from 1776 to 1945, on computer back to 1998. The court may offer docket information at http://ujsportal.pacourts.us.
General Information: Public Access terminal is available. No juvenile records released. Will not fax results. Copy fee: $1.00 for first page, $.25 each add'l. First copy for in person requests is $.25. Cert fee: $4.00 plus $1.00 each additional page. Payee: Clerk of Courts Office. Personal checks accepted. Prepayment required. Mail requests: SASE required. Mail turnaround time 1-2 days.

Register of Wills 201 Market St, County Courthouse, Sunbury, PA 17801; 570-988-4143 and 570-988-4140; Fax: 570-988-4141. Hours: 9AM-4:30PM (EST). *Probate.*

Perry County

Court of Common Pleas - Criminal/Civil PO Box 223, (1 Courthouse Sq), New Bloomfield, PA 17068; 717-582-2131; Civil phone: 717-582-2131 X2240; Criminal phone: 717-582-2131 X2241. Hours: 8AM-4PM (EST). *Felony, Misdemeanor, Civil, Eviction.*
Civil Records: Access: In person only. Visitors must perform in person searches for themselves. No search fee. Required to search: name, years to search. Civil cases indexed by defendant, plaintiff. Civil records on dockets from 1800s.
Criminal Records: Access: Phone, fax, mail, in person. Both court and visitors may perform in person searches. Search fee: $10.00 per name. Required to search: name, years to search; also helpful: DOB, SSN. Criminal records on dockets from 1950.
General Information: Public Access terminal is available. No juvenile records released. No fee to fax results. Copy fee: $.40 per page. Cert fee: $5.00. Payee: Prothonotary or Clerk of Courts. Personal checks accepted. Prepayment required. Will bill to attorneys and abstract companies upon approval. Mail requests: SASE required. Mail turnaround time 1 week; phone turnaround is immediate.

Register of Wills PO Box 223, New Bloomfield, PA 17068; 717-582-2131; Fax: 717-582-5149. Hours: 8AM-4PM (EST). *Probate.*

Philadelphia County

Court of Common Pleas - Civil First Judicial District of PA, Rm 284, City Hall, Philadelphia, PA 19107; 215-686-6656; Fax: 215-567-7380. Hours: 9AM-5PM (EST). *Civil.*
http://courts.phila.gov
Civil Records: Access: Mail, online, in person. Both court and visitors may perform in person searches. Search fee: $35.00 per name. Required to search: name, years to search. Civil cases indexed by defendant, plaintiff. Civil records on computer from 1/82 to present, archived on files from 1700s to 1982. Access to 1st Judicial District Civil Trial records is free online at http://fjdwebserver.phila.gov. Search by name, judgment and docket information. There is also a civil docket access name search at http://courts.phila.gov.
General Information: Public Access terminal is available. No mental health, divorce, abuse, adoption

records released. Copy fee: $.50 per page. Cert fee: $30.00. Payee: Prothonotary. Business checks accepted. Prepayment required. Mail requests: SASE required. Mail turnaround time 1-5 days.

Clerk of Quarter Session 1301 Filbert St #310, Philadelphia, PA 19107; 215-683-7700 X01 & X02. Hours: 8AM-5PM (EST). *Felony, Misdemeanor.*
http://courts.phila.gov
Criminal Records: Access: Mail, in person. Both court and visitors may perform in person searches. Search fee: $10.00 per name. Required to search: name, years to search, DOB, signed release; also helpful: address, SSN, race, sex. Criminal records on computer and microfiche from 1969, archived from 1800s.
General Information: Public Access terminal is available. No sealed, grand jury, mental records released. Copy fee: $.25 per page. Cert fee: $12.50. Payee: Clerk of Quarter Sessions. Business checks accepted. Prepayment required. Mail requests: SASE required. Mail turnaround time 1-2 days.

Municipal Court 34 S 11th St, 5th Fl, Philadelphia, PA 19107; 215-686-7000; Fax: 215-569-9254. Hours: 9AM-5PM (EST). *Felony, Misdemeanor, Civil Actions Under $10,000, Eviction.*
http://fjd.phila.gov
Note: Court has jurisdiction over certain criminal offenses with jail terms up to five years.
Civil Records: Access: Mail, in person. Only the court performs in person searches; visitors may not. No search fee. Required to search: name, years to search, address. Civil cases indexed by defendant, plaintiff. Civil records on computer from 1969.
Criminal Records: Access: Mail, in person. Only the court performs in person searches; visitors may not. No search fee. Required to search: name, years to search, address, DOB, signed release. Criminal records on computer from 1969.
General Information: Copy fee: $.50 per page. Cert fee: $5.00. Payee: Prothonotary. Only cashiers checks and money orders accepted. Prepayment required. Mail requests: SASE required. Mail turnaround time 1-5 days.

Register of Wills City Hall Rm 180, Philadelphia, PA 19107; 215-686-6250/6282; Fax: 215-686-6293. Hours: 8:30AM-4:30PM (EST). *Probate.*

Pike County

Court of Common Pleas - Criminal/Civil 412 Broad St, Milford, PA 18337; 570-296-7231. Hours: 8:30AM-4:30PM (EST). *Felony, Misdemeanor, Civil, Eviction.*
Civil Records: Access: Phone, mail, online, in person. Both court and visitors may perform in person searches. No search fee. Required to search: name, years to search. Civil cases indexed by defendant, plaintiff. Civil records on files for 100 yrs, computerized since 1995. Internet access to court records is by subscription from a private company-Infocon at www.ic-access.com, 814-472-6066. See note at beginning of section. The court will only do searches from 01/95 forward.
Criminal Records: Access: Phone, mail, online, in person. Both court and visitors may perform in person searches. Search fee: $10.00 per name. Required to search: name, years to search. Criminal records on files for 100 yrs, computerized since 1995. Internet access to court records is by subscription from a private company-Infocon at www.ic-access.com, 814-472-6066. See note at beginning of section. The court will only do searches from 01/95 forward.

General Information: Public Access terminal is available. No juvenile, adoption, sealed records released. Copy fee: $.25 per page. Cert fee: $2.50 per page. Payee: Prothonotary. Personal checks not exceeding $25.00 accepted. Prepayment required. Mail requests: SASE required. Mail turnaround time varies.

Register of Wills 506 Broad St, Milford, PA 18337; 570-296-3508; Fax: 570-296-3514. Hours: 8:30AM-4:30PM (EST). *Probate.*

Note: Internet access to records is available by subscription from a private company-Infocon at www.ic-access.com, 814-472-6066. See note at beginning of section.

Potter County

Court of Common Pleas - Criminal/Civil

1 E 2nd St Rm 23, Coudersport, PA 16915; 814-274-9740; Fax: 814-274-3361. Hours: 8:30AM-4:30PM (EST). *Felony, Misdemeanor, Civil, Eviction.*

Civil Records: Access: Phone, fax, mail, in person, online. Both court and visitors may perform in person searches. No search fee. Required to search: name, years to search. Civil cases indexed by defendant, plaintiff. Civil records on dockets from early 1833 to 11/97; on computer since 11/97. Internet access to court records is by subscription from a private company-Infocon at www.ic-access.com, 814-472-6066. See note at beginning of section.

Criminal Records: Access: Phone, fax, mail, in person, online. Both court and visitors may perform in person searches. No search fee. Required to search: name, years to search, DOB. Criminal records on card index from 1983 to 6/27/97; on computer since 6/27/97; archived since 1839. Internet access to court records is by subscription from a private company-Infocon at www.ic-access.com, 814-472-6066. See note at beginning of section.

General Information: Public Access terminal is available. No juvenile records released. No fee to fax results if limited. Copy fee: $.25 per page. Cert fee: $5.00. Payee: Prothonotary & Clerk of Courts. Personal checks accepted. Prepayment required. Mail requests: SASE required. Mail turnaround time 2 weeks, phone turnaround immediate unless a lengthy search.

Register of Wills 1 E 2nd St. Courthouse Rm20, Coudersport, PA 16915; 814-274-8370. Hours: 8:30AM-4:30PM (EST). *Probate.*

Note: Internet access to records is available by subscription from a private company-Infocon at www.ic-access.com, 814-472-6066. See note at beginning of section.

Schuylkill County

Court of Common Pleas - Civil

401 N 2nd St, Pottsville, PA 17901-2528; 570-628-1270; Fax: 570-628-1261. Hours: 8:30AM-4:30PM (EST). *Civil, Eviction.*

www.co.schuylkill.pa.us

Civil Records: Access: Mail, in person. Both court and visitors may perform in person searches. Search fee: $5.00 per name. Required to search: name, years to search. Civil cases indexed by defendant, plaintiff. Civil records (suits) on computer from 1989, judgments on computer from 199 and on dockets from 1800s.

General Information: Public Access terminal is available. No master reports or sealed records released. Copy fee: $.25 per page. Cert fee: $4.00 per page. Payee: Prothonotary. Personal checks accepted. Prepayment required. Will bill copy fees. Mail requests: SASE requested. Turnaround time 1 day.

Court of Common Pleas - Criminal

410 N 2nd St, Pottsville, PA 17901; 570-622-5570 X1141; Civil phone: 570-628-1270; Probate phone: 570-628-1377; Fax: 570-628-1143. Hours: 8:30AM-4:30PM (EST). *Felony, Misdemeanor.*

www.co.schuylkill.pa.us

Criminal Records: Access: Fax, mail, in person. Both court and visitors may perform in person searches. Search fee: $15.00 plus $5.00 automation fee per name. Required to search: name, years to search, DOB; also helpful: SSN. Criminal records on computer from 4/88, on dockets from 1800s.

General Information: No juvenile records released. No fee to fax results. Copy fee: $.25 per page. Cert fee: $8.00. Payee: Clerk of Courts. Business checks accepted. Prepayment required. Mail requests: SASE not required. Mail turnaround time same day.

Register of Wills Courthouse 401 N 2nd St, Pottsville, PA 17901-2520; 570-628-1377; Fax: 570-628-1384. Hours: 8:30AM-4:30PM (EST). *Probate.*

Snyder County

Court of Common Pleas - Criminal/Civil

Snyder County Courthouse, PO Box 217, Middleburg, PA 17842; 570-837-4202. Hours: 8:30AM-4PM (EST). *Felony, Misdemeanor, Civil, Eviction.*

www.seda-cog.org/snyder/ical/calendar.asp

Civil Records: Access: Mail, in person. Both court and visitors may perform in person searches. Search fee: $10.00 per 5 years searched. Required to search: name, years to search. Civil cases indexed by defendant, plaintiff. Civil records on dockets from 1855, some on microfilm, computerized since 2001.

Criminal Records: Access: Mail, in person. Both court and visitors may perform in person searches. Search fee: $15.00 per name. Required to search: name, years to search. Criminal records on dockets from 1855, some on microfilm, computerized since 2001.

General Information: No juvenile records released. Copy fee: $.35 per page. Cert fee: $4.00. Payee: Prothonotary or Clerk of Courts. No personal checks. Prepayment required. Mail requests: SASE required. Mail turnaround time 2 days.

Register of Wills County Courthouse, 9 W Market St, PO Box 217, Middleburg, PA 17842; 570-837-4224; Fax: 570-837-4299. Hours: 8:30AM-4PM (EST). *Probate.*

www.seda-cog.org/snyder/ical/calendar.asp

Somerset County

Court of Common Pleas - Civil

111 E Union St #190, Somerset, PA 15501; 814-445-1428; Fax: 814-444-9270. Hours: 8:30AM-4PM (EST). *Civil, Eviction.*

www.co.somerset.pa.us

Civil Records: Access: Phone, fax, mail, in person. Both court and visitors may perform in person searches. Search fee: $12.00 per name. Required to search: name, years to search. Civil cases indexed by defendant, plaintiff. Civil records on computer from 1/92, on microfiche from 1920 to 1972, on dockets (Russell System for all other years prior to 1992). Hard copy must follow fax request.

General Information: Public Access terminal is available. No commitment records released. Will fax results $.50 per page. Copy fee: $.50 per page. Payee: Prothonotary of Somerset Co. Business checks accepted. Prepayment required. Mail requests: SASE required. Mail turnaround time 2-3 days.

Court of Common Pleas - Criminal

111 E Union St #180, Somerset, PA 15501; 814-445-1435; Civil phone: 814-445-1428; Probate phone: 814-445-1548. Hours: 8:30AM-4PM (EST). *Felony, Misdemeanor.*

www.co.somerset.pa.us

Criminal Records: Access: Phone, mail, in person. Both court and visitors may perform in person searches. Search fee: $5.00 per name. Required to search: name, years to search, DOB; also helpful: SSN. Criminal records on microfilm from 1920, archive dates uncertain, computerized since 1996.

General Information: Public Access terminal is available. No impounded records released. Copy fee: $.50 per copy. Cert fee: $1.00. Payee: Clerk of Courts. Personal checks accepted. Will bill copy fees. Mail requests: SASE not required. Mail turnaround time same day; phone turnaround is immediate.

Register of Wills 111 E Union St #170, Somerset, PA 15501-0586; 814-445-1548; Fax: 814-445-7991. Hours: 8:30AM-4PM (EST). *Probate.*

Sullivan County

Court of Common Pleas - Criminal/Civil

Main St, Laporte, PA 18626; 570-946-7351; Probate phone: 570-946-7351. Hours: 8:30AM-4PM (EST). *Felony, Misdemeanor, Civil, Eviction, Probate.*

Note: Includes the Register of Wills.

Civil Records: Access: In person. Visitors must perform in person searches for themselves. No search fee. Required to search: name, years to search. Civil cases indexed by defendant, plaintiff. Civil records on dockets from 1847 to present and on computer from August 2000.

Criminal Records: Access: In person. Visitors must perform in person searches for themselves. No search fee. Required to search: name, years to search; also helpful: SSN. Criminal records on dockets from 1847 to present and on computer from August 2000.

General Information: Public Access terminal is available. No juvenile records released. Copy fee: $2.00 per page. Cert fee: $3.00 per page. Payee: Prothonotary or Clerk of Courts. Personal checks accepted. Prepayment required.

Susquehanna County

Court of Common Pleas - Civil

Susquehanna Courthouse, PO Box 218, Montrose, PA 18801; 570-278-4600 X120. Hours: 9AM-4:30PM (EST). *Civil, Eviction.*

Civil Records: Access: Mail, in person, online. Both court and visitors may perform in person searches. Search fee: $7.50. Required to search: name, years to search. Civil cases indexed by defendant, plaintiff. Civil records on dockets from 1800s. Internet access to court records is by subscription from a private company-Infocon at www.ic-access.com, 814-472-6066. See note at beginning of section.

General Information: Public Access terminal is available. No juvenile records released. Copy fee: $1.00 per page. Cert fee: $4.50. Payee: Prothonotary. Personal checks accepted. Prepayment required. Mail requests: SASE required. Mail turnaround time usually same day.

Court of Common Pleas - Criminal

PO Box 218, Susquehanna Courthouse, 11 Maple St, Montrose, PA 18801; 570-278-4600 x321, x320, x323; Fax: 570-278-4191. Hours: 8:30AM-4:30PM (EST). *Felony, Misdemeanor.*

Criminal Records: Access: Mail, in person, online. Both court and visitors may perform in person searches. Search fee: $5.00 per name per 5 years. Required to search: name, years to search, DOB, SSN. Criminal records on dockets from 1800s, archived from 1971, computerized since 08/96.

Internet access to court records is by subscription from a private company-Infocon at www.ic-access.com, 814-472-6066. See note at beginning of section.

General Information: Public Access terminal is available. No juvenile records released. Will fax results. Copy fee: $1.00 per page. Cert fee: $3.00. Payee: Clerk of Courts. Personal checks accepted. Prepayment required. Mail requests: SASE required. Mail turnaround time same day.

Register of Wills Susquehanna County Courthouse, PO Box 218, Montrose, PA 18801; 570-278-4600 X113; Fax: 570-278-2963. Hours: 8:30AM-4:30PM (EST). *Probate.*

Tioga County

Court of Common Pleas - Criminal/Civil 116 Main St, Wellsboro, PA 16901; 570-724-9281. Hours: 9AM-4:30PM (EST). *Felony, Misdemeanor, Civil, Eviction.*

Civil Records: Access: In person only. Visitors must perform in person searches for themselves. No search fee. Required to search: name. Civil cases indexed by defendant. Civil records on dockets from 1827; computerized records since 1997.

Criminal Records: Access: Mail, in person. Both court and visitors may perform in person searches. Search fee: $5.00 per name per year. Required to search: name, years to search, signed release. Criminal records on dockets from 1827; computerized records since 1965.

General Information: Public Access terminal is available. No mental health, juvenile, abuse (14 or younger) records released. Copy fee: $.25 per page. Cert fee: $4.50. Payee: Tioga County Prothonotary. Personal checks accepted. Prepayment required. Mail requests: SASE required. Mail turnaround time same day when possible.

Register of Wills 116 Main St, Wellsboro, PA 16901; 570-724-9260. Hours: 9AM-4:30PM (EST). *Probate.*

Note: Online access to wills is available through a private company at www.landex.com/remote/. Fee is $.20 per minute and $.50 per fax page. Images and wills go back to 2/1999.

Union County

Court of Common Pleas - Criminal/Civil 103 S 2nd St, Lewisburg, PA 17837; 570-524-8751. Hours: 8:30AM-4:30PM (EST). *Felony, Misdemeanor, Civil, Eviction.*
www.unionco.org

Civil Records: Access: Phone, mail, in person, online. Both court and visitors may perform in person searches. No search fee. Required to search: name, years to search. Civil cases indexed by defendant, plaintiff. Civil records on computer from 1988, on microfiche (orphans court 1813 to 1988, marriage 1885 to 2001), on dockets from 1800s to 1988. Access judgment records for no fee at a private company site at www.courthouseonline.com/JudgSearch.asp?State=PA&County=Union&Abbrev=Un&Office=PO. Password required.

Criminal Records: Access: Phone, mail, in person, online. Both court and visitors may perform in person searches. No search fee. Required to search: name, years to search. Criminal records on computer from 1988, on microfiche (orphans court 1813 to 1988, marriage 1885 to 2001), on dockets from 1800s to 1988. Online access to judgments is the same as civil, see above.

General Information: Public Access terminal is available. No juvenile records released. Will not fax results. Copy fee: $.25 per page. Cert fee: $5.00.

Payee: Prothonotary or Clerk of Courts. Personal checks accepted. Prepayment required. Mail requests: SASE required. Mail turnaround time same day schedule permitting.

Register of Wills 103 S 2nd St, Lewisburg, PA 17837-1996; 570-524-8761. Hours: 8:30AM-4:30PM (EST). *Probate.*

Note: Search wills online at www.courthouseonline.com/WillsSearch.asp?State=PA&County=Union&Abbrev=Un&Office=RW

Venango County

Court of Common Pleas - Criminal/Civil Venango County Courthouse, 1168 Liberty St, Franklin, PA 16323; 814-432-9577; Fax: 814-432-9579. Hours: 8:30AM-4:30PM (EST). *Felony, Misdemeanor, Civil, Eviction.*
www.co.venango.pa.us

Civil Records: Access: Mail, in person. Both court and visitors may perform in person searches. Search fee: $7.00 per name. Required to search: name, years to search. Civil cases indexed by defendant, plaintiff. Civil records on computer from 1993, on dockets from 1800s.

Criminal Records: Access: Mail, in person, online. Both court and visitors may perform in person searches. Search fee: $7.00 per name. Required to search: name, years to search, DOB; also helpful: SSN. Criminal records on computer from 1993, on dockets from 1800s. Search docket information by name or docket number for free at http://ujsportal.pacourts.us. Click on "E-Services." Name search under "Other Criteria."

General Information: Public Access terminal is available. No juvenile records released. Fee to fax results is $1.00 per page. Copy fee: $.50 per page. Cert fee: $7.00. Payee: Clerk of Courts. Personal checks accepted. Prepayment required. Mail requests: SASE required. Mail turnaround time same day.

Register of Wills/Recorder of Deeds 1168 Liberty St, Franklin, PA 16323; 814-432-9534; Probate phone: 814-432-9539; Fax: 814-432-9569. Hours: 8:30AM-4:30PM (EST). *Probate.*

Warren County

Court of Common Pleas - Criminal/Civil 4th & Market St, Warren, PA 16365; 814-728-3440; Fax: 814-728-3459. Hours: 8:30AM-4:30PM (EST). *Felony, Misdemeanor, Civil, Eviction.*
http://users.penn.com/~wrncourt

Civil Records: Access: Fax, mail, in person. Both court and visitors may perform in person searches. Search fee: $20.00 per name. Required to search: name, years to search. Civil cases indexed by defendant, plaintiff. Civil records on computer from 2000, on dockets from 1800s.

Criminal Records: Access: Fax, mail, in person, online. Both court and visitors may perform in person searches. Search fee: $20.00 per name. Required to search: name, years to search; also helpful: DOB. Criminal records on computer from 2000, on dockets from 1800s. Search docket information by name or docket number for free at http://ujsportal.pacourts.us. Click on "E-Services." Name search under "Other Criteria."

General Information: Public Access terminal is available. No juvenile records released. No fee to fax results. Copy fee: $1.00 per page. Cert fee: $4.00. Payee: Prothonotary or Clerk of Courts. Business checks accepted. Prepayment required. Mail requests: SASE required. Mail turnaround time 2 days.

Register of Wills Courthouse, 204 4th Ave, Warren, PA 16365; 814-728-3430; Fax: 814-728-3476. Hours: 8:30AM-4:30PM (EST). *Probate.*

Washington County

Court of Common Pleas - Civil 1 S Main St #1001, Washington, PA 15301; 724-228-6770. Hours: 9AM-4:30PM (EST). *Civil, Eviction.*
www.co.washington.pa.us

Civil Records: Access: In person. Visitors must perform in person searches for themselves. No search fee. Required to search: name, years to search. Civil cases indexed by defendant, plaintiff. Civil records on computer from 1987, prior on dockets to 1800s.

General Information: Public Access terminal is available. Copy fee: $1.50 per page. Cert fee: $4.50. Payee: Prothonotary. Only cashiers checks and money orders accepted. Checks from attorneys accepted, otherwise prepayment required.

Court of Common Pleas - Criminal Courthouse #1005, 1 S Main St, Washington, PA 15301; 724-228-6787; Civil phone: 724-228-6770; Probate phone: 724-228-6775; Fax: 724-228-6890. Hours: 9AM-4:30PM (EST). *Felony, Misdemeanor.*
www.co.washington.pa.us

Criminal Records: Access: Mail, in person. Both court and visitors may perform in person searches. Search fee: $10.00 per name. Required to search: name, years to search, DOB; also helpful: address, SSN. Criminal records on computer since 10/87, prior on dockets, archived from 1785. The court may offer docket information at http://ujsportal.pacourts.us.

General Information: Public Access terminal is available. No juvenile records released. Will not fax results. Copy fee: $.25 per page. Cert fee: $8.00. Payee: Clerk of Courts. Personal checks accepted. Prepayment required. Mail requests: SASE required. Mail turnaround time over 1 week.

Register of Wills Courthouse, 1 S Main St #1002, Washington, PA 15301; 724-228-6775; Fax: 724-250-4820. Hours: 9AM-4:30PM (EST). *Probate.*

Wayne County

Court of Common Pleas - Criminal/Civil 925 Court St, Honesdale, PA 18431; 570-253-5970 X200; Fax: 570-253-0687. Hours: 8:30AM-4:30PM (EST). *Felony, Misdemeanor, Civil, Eviction.*

Civil Records: Access: In person only. Visitors must perform in person searches for themselves. No search fee. Required to search: name, years to search. Civil cases indexed by defendant, plaintiff. Civil records on daily docket entries, computerized since 1996.

Criminal Records: Access: In person. Visitors must perform in person searches for themselves. No search fee. Required to search: name, years to search. Criminal records on daily docket entries, computerized since 1996. The court may offer docket information at http://ujsportal.pacourts.us.

General Information: Public Access terminal is available. Juvenile records not released. Copy fee: $.50 per page. No cert fee. Personal checks accepted. Prepayment required.

Register of Wills 925 Court St, Honesdale, PA 18431; 570-253-5970 X212; Probate phone: ext. 213. Hours: 8:30AM-4:30PM (EST). *Probate.*
www.co-wayne-pa-us.org

Westmoreland County

Court of Common Pleas - Civil Courthouse Sq, Rm 501, PO Box 1630, Greensburg, PA 15601-1168; 724-830-3502; Fax: 724-830-3517. Hours: 8:30AM-4PM (EST). *Civil, Eviction.*

Civil Records: Access: Online, in person. Visitors must perform in person searches for themselves. No search fee. Required to search: name, years to search. Civil cases indexed by defendant, plaintiff. Civil records on computer from 9/85, on dockets from 1700s. Access to the remote online system requires

$100 setup (no set-up if accessed via Internet) plus $20 monthly minimum fee. System includes civil, criminal, prothonotary indexes, and recorder information. For information, call 724-830-3874.

General Information: Public Access terminal is available. No mental health records released. Copy fee: $.50 per page. Computer print out: $1.00 per page. Cert fee: $5.35. Payee: Prothonotary. Business checks accepted. Prepayment required.

Court of Common Pleas - Criminal

Criminal Division, 203 Courthouse Sq, Greensburg, PA 15601-1168; 724-830-3734; Fax: 724-830-3472/850-3979. Hours: 8:30AM-4PM (EST). *Felony, Misdemeanor.*

www.co.westmoreland.pa.us

Criminal Records: Access: Fax, mail, online, in person. Both court and visitors may perform in person searches. Search fee: $10.50 per. Required to search: name, years to search, signed release; also helpful: DOB, SSN. Criminal records on computer from 1941, on microfiche from 1793 to 1950, archived from 1773. Access to the commercial criminal online system requires $100 setup plus $20 monthly minimum fee. For information, call 724-830-3734. Also, search docket information by name or docket number for free at http://ujsportal.pacourts.us. Click on "E-Services." name search under "Other Criteria."

General Information: Public Access terminal is available. No juvenile records released. Will fax results $10.00 per doc. Copy fee: $.50 per page. Computer copy $.50 per page. Cert fee: $5.00. Payee: Clerk of Courts. Personal checks accepted. Attorney's checks accepted, otherwise prepayment required. Mail requests: SASE not required. Mail turnaround time 3 to 5 days.

Register of Wills 2 N Main St, #301, Greensburg, PA 15601; 724-830-3177; Fax: 724-850-3976. Hours: 8:30AM-4PM (EST). *Probate.*

Wyoming County

Court of Common Pleas - Criminal/Civil

Wyoming County Courthouse, Tunkhannock, PA 18657; 570-836-3200 X232-234; Fax: 570-836-4781. Hours: 8:30AM-4PM (EST). *Felony, Misdemeanor, Civil, Eviction.*

Civil Records: Access: In person only. Visitors must perform in person searches for themselves. No search fee. Required to search: name, years to search. Civil cases indexed by defendant, plaintiff. Civil records on dockets from 1800s.

Criminal Records: Access: In person. Visitors must perform in person searches for themselves. No search fee. Required to search: name, years to search; also helpful: DOB. Criminal records on dockets from 1800s.

General Information: Public Access terminal is available. No juvenile records released. Copy fee: $.25 per page. Cert fee: $7.00. Payee: Prothonotary or Clerk of Courts. Personal checks accepted. Prepayment required.

Register of Wills Wyoming County Courthouse, 1 Courthouse Sq, Tunkhannock, PA 18657; 570-836-3200 X2235; Fax: 570-996-5053. Hours: 8:30AM-4PM (EST). *Probate.*

York County

Court of Common Pleas - Civil

York County Courthouse, 45 N George St, York, PA 17401; 717-771-9611; Criminal phone: 717-771-9612; Probate phone: 717-771-9608. Hours: 8:30AM-4:30PM (EST). *Civil.*

www.york-county.org/departments/courts/crtf1.htm

Civil Records: Access: Online, in person, mail. Visitors must perform in person searches for themselves. No search fee. Required to search: name, years to search. Civil cases indexed by defendant, plaintiff. Civil records on computer from mid-1988, on dockets from 1800s, archived from mid-1700s. Access to the remote online system is set-up through Information Services. For more information, call 717-771-9235.

General Information: Public Access terminal is available. No mental health records released. Will not fax results. Copy fee: $1.00 per page. Cert fee: $5.25. Payee: Prothonotary. Only cashiers checks and money orders accepted. Prepayment required. Mail requests: SASE required. Mail turnaround time 1 day.

Court of Common Pleas - Criminal

45 N Goerge St, York County Courthouse, York, PA 17401; 717-771-9612; Fax: 717-771-9096. Hours: 8:30AM-4:30PM (EST). *Felony, Misdemeanor.*

www.york-county.org/departments/courts/crtf1.htm

Criminal Records: Access: Fax, mail, online, in person. Both court and visitors may perform in person searches. No search fee. Required to search: name. Criminal records on computer from 1987, on dockets from 1942, archived from 1700s. Access is at Information Service's remote online system for criminal records from mid-1988 forward. Usage fee is $.75 per minute plus a $200.00 setup fee. For more information, call 717-771-9321.

General Information: Public Access terminal is available. (Several terminals available.) No sex crime, juvenile records released. No fee to fax results. Copy fee: $.50 per page. Cert fee: $10.00. Payee: Clerk of Courts. Personal checks accepted. Prepayment required. Mail requests: SASE required. Mail turnaround time 1-2 weeks.

Register of Wills York County Courthouse 28 E Market St, York, PA 17401; 717-771-9263; Fax: 717-771-4678. Hours: 8:00AM-4:30PM (EST). *Probate.* Note: Online access to wills is available through a private company at www.landex.com/remote/. Fee is $.20 per minute and $.50 per fax page. Images and wills go back to 2/1999.

Pennsylvania Recording Offices

ORGANIZATION: 67 counties, 67 recording offices and 134 UCC filing offices. Each county has two different recording offices: the Prothonotary - their term for "Clerk" - accepted UCC and tax lien filings until 07/01/2001, and the Recorder of Deeds maintains real estate records. The entire state is in the Eastern Time Zone (EST).

REAL ESTATE RECORDS: County Recorders of Deeds will not perform real estate searches. Copy & certification fees vary.

UCC RECORDS: This was a dual filing state. Until 07/1/2001, Financing statements were filed both at the state level and with the Prothonotary, except for real estate related collateral, which were filed with the Recorder of Deeds. Now, only real estate related collateral is filed locally. Some county offices will not perform UCC searches. Use search request form UCC-11. Search fees are usually $59.00 per debtor name. Copies usually cost $.50-$2.00 per page. Counties also charge $5.00 per financing statement found on a search.

TAX LIEN RECORDS: All federal and state tax liens on personal property and on real property are filed with the Prothonotary. Usually, tax liens on personal property are filed in the judgment index of the Prothonotary. Some Prothonotaries will perform tax lien searches. Search fees are usually $5.00 per name.

OTHER LIENS: Judgment, municipal, mechanics.

ONLINE ACCESS: A number of counties provide web access to assessor data. The Infocon County Access System provides Internet and direct dial-up access to recorded record information for 15 Pennsylvania counties - Armstrong, Bedford, Blair, Butler, Clarion, Clinton, Erie, Franklin, Huntingdon, Juaniata, Lawrence, Mercer, Mifflin, Pike, and Potter. Fees are involved. Document images are available. For information, call Infocon at 814-472-6066 or visit www.ic-access.com

Adams County Prothonotary

County Prothonotary, 111-117 Baltimore St, Gettysburg, PA 17325. **Phone**-717-334-6781; fax-717-334-0532; hours 8AM-4:30PM. Will not search UCC or tax liens records. UCC copy- $.25 per page. Cert fee: $4.75. Payee: County Prothonotary. **Other phones:** Assessor-717-337-9837.

Adams County Recorder

County Recorder of Deeds, 111-117 Baltimore St, County Courthouse, Rm 102, Gettysburg, PA 17325. **Phone**-717-337-9826; fax-717-334-1758; hours 8AM-4:30PM. Will not any search UCC records.Will not search real estate records. RE record copy- $.25 per page. UCC copy- $2.00 per page. Cert fee: $2.00 per doc. Payee: Adams County Recorder of Deeds. **Other phones:** Assessor-717-334-6781 x216; Treasurer-717-334-6781 x221.

Allegheny County Prothonotary

County Prothonotary, 414 Grant St, City County Office Bldg, Pittsburgh, PA 15219. **Phone**-412-350-4200, R/E Recording-412-355-4226; fax-412-350-5260; hours 8:30AM-4:30PM
http://www2.county.allegheny.pa.us/realestate/
UCC records information or copy request (per debtor)- $59.00. UCC search includes tax liens if requested. Separate federal/state combined tax lien search- $25.00 per debtor. UCC copy- $2.00 per page. Payee: Allegheny County Prothonotary. **Online Access to Civil Court, UCC, Tax Lien, Real Estate, Assessor records:** Access to Common Pleas Civil records is free at http://prothonotary.county.allegheny.pa.us/allegheny/welcome.htm. Registration is required. UCC records are pre-7-1-2001. Online access to the certified values database is free at the website. Also, online access to Allegheny County real estate database is free at www2.county.allegheny.pa.us/realestate/Search.asp. **Other phones:** Assessor-412-350-4625.

Allegheny County Recorder

County Recorder of Deeds, 542 Forbes Ave, 101 County Office Bldg., Pittsburgh, PA 15219-2947.

Phone-412-350-4226; fax-412-350-6877; hours 8:30AM-4:30PM www.county.allegheny.pa.us
Will search UCC records, but only real estate related UCC filed here. Will search real estate records. Copy fee- $1.00 per page. Cert fee: $5.00 includes 1st 4 pages. Payee: Allegheny County Recorder of Deeds. **Online Access to Recorder, Deed, Mortgage, Real Estate records:** Access to the Recorder's Index search is at www.county.allegheny.pa.us/deeds/index.asp. Use username and password provided at website. Also, Land & A/R Inquiries found at www.county.allegheny.pa.us/dcs/dcsland.asp. **Other phones:** Assessor-412-355-4625; Treasurer-412-355-4100.

Armstrong County Prothonotary

County Prothonotary, 500 E Market St, County Courthouse, Kittanning, PA 16201. **Phone**-724-543-2500, R/E Recording-724-548-3280, UCC Recording-724-548-3251; fax-724-548-3351; hours 8:00AM-4:30PM www.geocities.com/acprothonotary
UCC records information or copy request (per debtor)- $59.00. $200.00 deposit required-will refund unused amount. $5.00 for each UCC Finding. Will not search tax liens. UCC copy- $2.00 per page. Cert fee: $5.00 + $1.00 add'l per page. Payee: Armstrong County Prothonotary. **Online Access to Tax Lien records:** Online search: see Register of Deeds. **Other phones:** Assessor-724-548-3487; Treasurer-724-548-3271; Elections-724-548-3222.

Armstrong County Recorder

County Recorder of Deeds, 500 Market St, County Courthouse, Kittanning, PA 16201-1495. **Phone**-724-548-3256, R/E Recording-724-548-3280, UCC Recording-724-548-3280; fax-724-548-3236; hours 8AM-4:30PM
Will not search UCC or real estate records. Will search the indexes on the computer. RE record copy- $1.00 per page. **Online Access to Real Estate, Marriage, Probate records:** Access is through a private company. For information, call Infocon at 814-472-6066 or www.ic-access.com. **Other phones:** Assessor-724-548-3489; Treasurer-724-548-3260; Appraiser/

Auditor-724-548-3489; Elections-724-548-3222; Vital Records-724-548-3100.

Beaver County Prothonotary

County Prothonotary, 810 Third St, County Courthouse, Beaver, PA 15009. **Phone**-724-728-3934 x11279; fax-724-728-3360; hours 8:30AM-4:30PM http://co.beaver.pa.us/prothonotary
Will not search UCC or tax liens records. Cert fee: $5.00 per request. Payee: Beaver County Prothonotary.

Beaver County Recorder

County Recorder of Deeds, 810 3rd St, County Courthouse, Beaver, PA 15009. **Phone**-County Recorder of Deeds, R/E & UCC Recording- 724-728-5700; fax-724-728-8479; hours 8:30AM-4:30PM www.co.beaver.pa.us
Will not any search UCC records.Will not search real estate records. Record copy- $1.00 per page. Cert fee: $1.50 per cert. Payee: Beaver County Recorder of Deeds. **Online Access to Real Estate, Deed, Mortgage, Assessor records:** Access to the Recorder's database is to be free at http://co.beaver.pa.us/Recorder/disclaimer.htm. This is a new system; the old system had Deed records go back to 1957; Mortgages to 7/1974; images to 6/1998. Also, search the assessor database for free at www.co.beaver.pa.us/RecorderofDeeds/. **Other phones:** Assessor-724-728-5700; Treasurer-724-728-5700; Elections-724-728-5700; 724-728-5700-Switchboard.

Bedford County Prothonotary

County Prothonotary, County Courthouse, Corner of Penn & Julliana, Bedford, PA 15522. **Phone**-814-623-4833; fax-814-623-4831; hours 8:30AM-4:30PM
UCC records information or copy request (per debtor)- $59.00. UCC search includes tax liens if requested. Tax lien search- $18.00 per debtor. UCC copy- $5.00 per page. Cert fee: $4.50 per cert. Payee: Bedford County Prothonotary.

Bedford County Recorder

County Recorder, 200 S. Juliana St, County Courthouse, Bedford, PA 15522. **Phone-**County Recorder, R/E & UCC Recording- 814-623-4836; fax-814-624-0488; hours 8:30AM-4:30PM www.bedford.net/regrec/home.html
Will not search UCC or real estate records. Copy fee-$.25 per page. Cert fee: $1.00 per doc. Payee: Recorder of Deeds. **Online Access to Real Estate, Assessor, Probate, Marriage records:** Access is through a private company. For information, call Infocon at 814-472-6066 or www.ic-access.com. **Other phones:** Assessor-814-623-4842; Treasurer-814-623-4846; Elections-814-623-4807; Vital Records-814-623-4833.

Berks County Prothonotary

County Prothonotary, 633 Court St., Reading, PA 19601. **Phone-**610-478-6980, R/E Recording-610-478-3380; fax-610-478-6969; hours 8AM-4PM www.berksprothy.com
Will not search UCC or tax liens records. **Online Access to Judgment, Lien, UCC, Civil Court records:** The Prothonotary has a remote dial-up system that allows users to access archived record indexes back to 1/1996 via the telephone. Fee is $300. For info, call 610-478-6968. Also, a website is being developed where you can access doc images. **Other phones:** Assessor-610-478-6262; Treasurer-610-478-6640; Elections-610-478-6490.

Berks County Recorder

Recorder of Deeds, 633 Court St, 3rd Fl, Reading, PA 19601. **Phone-**Recorder of Deeds, R/E & UCC Recording- 610-478-3380; fax-610-478-3359; hours 8AM-5PM www.berksrecofdeeds.com
Will search UCC records. UCC search per debtor-$12.00. Will not search real estate records. RE record copy- $1.00 per page. UCC copy- $2.00 per page. Cert fee: $28.00. **Online Access to Vital Statistic, Probate, DR Warrant records:** Access to the Registry of Wills' databases are free at www.berksregofwills.com/search_page.htm including county marriage, estate, birth and death records. Estate and marriage records are current. Also, search the domestic relations warrants list at www.drs.berks.pa.us/dro_warrant_list.htm. **Other phones:** Assessor-610-478-6262; Treasurer-610-478-6640; Elections-610-478-6490.

Blair County Prothonotary

County Prothonotary, 423 Allegheny St #144, Hollidaysburg, PA 16648. **Phone-**814-693-3080, R/E Recording-814-693-3095; hours 8AM-4PM
Will not search UCC or tax liens records. UCC copy-$1.00 per page. Cert fee: $5.00 per cert. Payee: Blair County Prothonotary. **Online Access to Tax Lien records:** Online search: see Register of Deeds.

Blair County Recorder

County Recorder of Deeds, 423 Allegheny St, #145, Hollidaysburg, PA 16648. **Phone-**County Recorder of Deeds, R/E & UCC Recording- 814-693-3095; fax-814-693-3093; hours 8AM-4PM
Will not any search UCC records.Will not search real estate or tax lien records. Record copy- $1.00 per page. Cert fee: $2.00 per doc. Payee: Blair County Recorder of Deeds. **Online Access to Real Estate, Marriage, Probate records:** Access is through a private company. For information, call Infocon at 814-472-6066 or www.ic-access.com. Indexes from 1998. **Other phones:** Assessor-814-695-5541 x223; Treasurer-814-693-3120; Appraiser/ Auditor-814-693-3110; Elections-814-693-3150.

Bradford County Prothonotary

County Prothonotary, 301 Main St, Courthouse, Towanda, PA 18848. **Phone-**570-265-1705, R/E Recording-570-265-1702; fax-570-265-1735; hours 9AM-5PM
Will search UCC records prior to 7/2001. Information or copy request (per debtor)- $59.00. Will not search tax liens. UCC copy- $.25 per page. Cert fee: $4.00 per doc. Payee: County Prothonotary. **Other phones:** Assessor-570-265-1714; Treasurer-570-265-1700; Elections-570-265-1717.

Bradford County Recorder

County Recorder of Deeds, 301 Main St, Courthouse, Towanda, PA 18848. **Phone-**County Recorder of Deeds, R/E & UCC Recording- 570-265-1702; fax-570-265-1721; hours 9AM-5PM
Will not search UCC or real estate records. Copy fee-$.50 per page. Cert fee: $2.00. Payee: Recorder of Deeds. **Online Access to Real Estate, Deed, Mortgage, Will records:** Access to Recorder of Deeds and Wills and Orphans Court is by subscription at www.landex.com/remote/. Fee is $.20 per minute, $.50 per fax page. Recorder data goes back to 1971. Images go back to 1997, also 1985-89. Wills and orphan court goes back to 1997. **Other phones:** Assessor-570-265-1714; Treasurer-570-265-1700.

Bucks County Prothonotary

County Prothonotary, 55 E. Court St., Courthouse, Doylestown, PA 18901. **Phone-**215-348-6191, R/E Recording-215-348-6209; fax-215-348-6184; hours 8:00AM-4:15PM www.buckscounty.org/courts/
Will not search UCC records. Will search tax liens; provide docket number. UCC copy- $1.50 per page. Cert fee: $4.50 per doc with a SASE. Payee: Bucks County Prothonotary. **Online Access to Recording, Judgment, Court, Voter Registration, Vital Statistic records:** Access to County records requires an ID number and password and payment of $25 monthly fee. Records go back to 1980. Lending agency, Register of Wills, liens, sheriff sales, voter registration, courts, prothonotary available. For information, contact Jack Morris at 215-348-6579 or visit www.buckscounty.org/departments/public_access/ Access to Vital Records at www.vitalchek.com. **Other phones:** Elections-215-348-6163.

Bucks County Recorder

County Recorder of Deeds, 55 E. Court St., Courthouse, Doylestown, PA 18901-4367. **Phone-**215-348-6209; hours 8:15AM-4:15PM (Recording Hours 8:15AM-4PM)
www.buckscounty.org/departments/registerofwills/index.html
Only real estate related UCC filed here; info or copy request (per debtor)- $59.00. Will not search real estate records. UCC copy- $1.00 per page. Cert fee: $1.50 per cert. Payee: Bucks County Recorder of Deeds. **Online Access to Assessor, Recorder, Real Estate, Tax Lien, Probate, Court, Will records:** Access to County records requires an ID number and password and payment of $25 monthly fee. Records go back to 1980. Lending agency, Register of Wills, liens, sheriff sales, voter registration, courts, prothonotary available. For information, contact Jack Morris at 215-348-6579 or visit www.buckscounty.org/departments/public_access/. **Other phones:** Assessor-215-348-6219; Treasurer-215-348-6244; Vital Records-724-656-3100.

Butler County Prothonotary

County Prothonotary, PO Box 1208, Butler, PA 16003-1208. **Phone-**724-284-5314; hours 8:30AM-4:30PM
Private company offers online access to most of the recorded records. Call Infocon at 814-472-6066. Will not search UCC or tax liens records. RE record copy-$.25 per page. Cert fee: $4.00 per cert. Payee: Butler County Prothonotary. **Other phones:** Treasurer-724-284-5149; Elections-724-284-5308.

Butler County Recorder

County Recorder of Deeds, PO Box 1208, Butler, PA 16003-1208. **Phone-**724-284-5340; fax-724-285-9099. www.co.butler.pa.us
Will not search UCC or real estate records. UCC copy-$1.00 per page. Cert fee: $1.50 per page. **Online Access to Marriage, Probate records:** Access marriage and probate records via a private company. For information, call Infocon at 814-472-6066. **Other phones:** Assessor-724-284-5316; Treasurer-724-284-5149; Elections-724-284-5310.

Cambria County Prothonotary

County Prothonotary, 200 S. Center St., Ebensburg, PA 15931. **Phone-**814-472-1637, R/E Recording-814-472-1473, UCC Recording-814-472-1636; fax-814-472-5632; hours 9AM-4PM
Will not search UCC or tax liens records. RE record copy- $.25 per page. UCC copy- $.25 per page. Cert fee: $3.00 per certification. Payee: Cambria County Prothonotary. **Other phones:** Assessor-814-472-1451; Treasurer-814-472-1643; Elections-814-472-1460.

Cambria County Recorder

Recorder of Deeds, 200 S. Center St., Cambria County Courthouse, Ebensburg, PA 15931. **Phone-**Recorder of Deeds, R/E & UCC Recording- 814-472-1473; fax-814-472-1412; hours-9AM-4PM
ttp://www.co.cambria.pa.us
UCC records information or copy request (per debtor)-$61.00. Will not search real estate records. Copy fee is $.75 per page. Payee: Recorder of Deeds. **Other phones:** Assessor-814-472-5440 x450; Treasurer-814-472-5440 x345; Elections-814-472-1464; Register of Wills-814-472-1440.

Cameron County Prothonotary

County Prothonotary, 20 E. 5th St, Emporium, PA 15834. **Phone-**814-486-3349; fax-814-486-0464; hours 8:30AM-4PM. UCC records information or copy request (per debtor)- $57.00. Will not search tax liens. UCC copy- $.50 per page. Cert fee: $5.00. Payee: Cameron County Prothonotary.

Cameron County Recorder

County Recorder of Deeds, 20 E. 5th St, Emporium, PA 15834. **Phone-**814-486-3349; fax-814-486-0464; hours 8:30AM-4PM
UCC records information or copy request (per debtor)-$57.00. Will not search real estate records. **Other phones:** Assessor-814-486-0723; Treasurer-814-486-3348.

Carbon County Prothonotary

County Prothonotary, PO Box 130, Jim Thorpe, PA 18229-0127. **Phone-**570-325-2481, R/E Recording-570-325-2651 (Recorder of Deeds), UCC Recording-570-325-2481 (Prothonotary); fax-570-325-8047; hours 8:30AM-4:30PM
Will not search UCC or tax liens records. UCC copy-$1.00 per page. Cert fee: $8.15 per cert. Payee: Carbon County Prothonotary. **Online Access to Tax Lien, UCC records:** Access to the county's remote public access dial-up database is free; 570-325-3288; instructions and registration are at www.carboncourts.com/pubacc. **Other phones:** Assessor-570-325-5254; Treasurer-570-325-2251; Elections-570-325-4801.

Carbon County Recorder

County Recorder of Deeds, PO Box 87, Jim Thorpe, PA 18229. **Phone-**570-325-2651; fax-570-325-2726; hours 8:30AM-4:30PM. Will not search UCC or real estate records. UCC copy- $1.00 per page. Cert fee: $1.50 per cert. Payee: Carbon County Recorder of Deeds. **Online Access to Real Estate, Probate, Grantor/Grantee records:** Access to docket information on the county's remote public access dial-up database is free; 570-325-3288; instructions and registration are at www.carboncourts.com/pubacc.htm. **Other phones:** Assessor-570-325-5254; Treasurer-570-325-2251; Elections-570-325-4801.

Centre County Prothonotary

County Prothonotary, Allegheny & High, County Courthouse, Bellefonte, PA 16823. **Phone-**814-355-6796, R/E Recording-814-355-6801; hours 8:30AM-5PM

UCC records information or copy request (per debtor)- $59.00. Will not search tax liens. UCC copy- $2.00 per page. Payee: Centre County Prothonotary. **Other phones:** Assessor-814-355-6721; Treasurer-814-355-6810; Elections-814-355-6703.

Centre County Recorder

County Recorder of Deeds, 414 Holmes Ave. #1, Bellefonte, PA 16823. **Phone-**814-355-6801, R/E and UCC Recording-814-355-6701; hours 8:30AM-5PM www.co.centre.pa.us/133.htm

Will not search UCC or real estate records. RE record copy- $.50 per page. Cert fee: $.150 per doc. Payee: Recorder of Deeds. **Online Access to Domestic Relations Warrants, Tax Assessment, Tax Claims, GIS records:** Access to the county list of outstanding bench warrants for child support non-payment is free at http://county.centreconnect.org/drs/default.asp. Web site for tax assessment, tax claims and GIS is www.webia.co.center.pa.us. **Other phones:** Assessor-814-355-6721; Treasurer-814-355-6810; Elections-814-355-6703.

Chester County Prothonotary

County Prothonotary, PO Box 2748, West Chester, PA 19380-0991. **Phone-**610-344-6111, R/E Recording-610-344-6330, UCC Recording-717-772-2149; fax-610-344-5903; hours 8:30AM-4:30PM www.chesco.org/prothy.html

Will search UCC records. Will not search tax liens. UCC copy- $1.00 1st page; $.50 each add'l. Payee: Prothonotary. **Online Access to Court Dockets, Property Tax, Warrant, Lien, Assessor records:** Access the prothonotary database at www.chesco.org/prothy.html. Click on "SEARCH:~." There is a $50 set up fee and $10 each month of use (if over 100 transacation per/mo, add $.10 per doc). Registration/password at 610-344-6884. Prothonotary records go back to 1990. **Other phones:** Assessor-610-344-6105; Treasurer-610-344-6370; Appraiser/Elections-610-344-6410; Vital Records-717-783-2548.

Chester County Recorder

County Recorder of Deeds, PO Box 2748, West Chester, PA 19380-0991. **Phone-**610-344-6330; fax-610-344-6408; hours 8:30AM-4:30PM, recording rm opens 7:30AM Monday. www.chesco.org/recorder

Will not search UCC or real estate records. RE record copy- $5.00 per page. UCC copy- $.50 per page self serve. $5.00 if by staff. Cert fee: $1.50. Fee to fax results is $5.00 per doc plus copy fee. Payee: Chester County Recorder of Deeds. **Online Access to Recording, Deed, Court, Vital Statistic, Archive records:** Searching countywide records including court records requires a sign-up and credit card payment. Application fee is $50. with $10.00 per month min. (no charge for no activity); and $.10 each transaction beyond 100. Sign-up and/or logon at http://epin.chesco.org. Also purchase county data as reports, labels, magnetic tape, and diskette. Also, genealogical and older vital statistics are free at

www.chesco.org/archives. Also, search Recorder of Deeds records for free at http://rod.chesco.org/icris/splash.jsp. **Other phones:** Assessor-610-344-6105; Treasurer-610-344-6370; BLR (Bureau of Land Records-for help with UPI #)-610-344-5968.

Clarion County Prothonotary

County Prothonotary, Main St, Courthouse, Clarion, PA 16214-1092. **Phone-**814-226-4000; fax-814-226-8069. Will not search UCC records. **Online Access to Tax Lien records:** Online search: see Register of Deeds.

Clarion County Recorder

County Recorder of Deeds, Courthouse, Corner of 5th Ave. & Main St., Clarion, PA 16214. **Phone-**814-226-4000 x2500, R/E Recording-814-226-4000 x2501, UCC Recording-814-226-4000 x2501; fax-814-226-1117. Will not search UCC or real estate records. **Online Access to Assessor, Real Estate, Voter Registration records:** Access is through a private company. For information, call Infocon at 814-472-6066 or www.ic-access.com. **Other phones:** Assessor-814-226-4000 x2301; Treasurer-814-226-4000 x2861.

Clearfield County Prothonotary

County Prothonotary, PO Box 549, Clearfield, PA 16830. **Phone-**814-765-2641, R/E Recording-814-765-2641 x1350, UCC Recording-814-765-2641 x1330; fax-814-765-7659; hours 8:30AM-4PM www.clearfieldco.org

UCC records information or copy request (per debtor)- $57.00. Will not search tax liens. UCC copy- $.25 per page. Cert fee: $1.50 per doc. Payee: Prothonotary. **Other phones:** Assessor-814-765-2641 x1128; Treasurer-814-765-2641 x1381; Appraiser/Auditor-814-765-2641 x1129; Elections-814-765-2641 x1140.

Clearfield County Recorder

County Recorder of Deeds, PO Box 361, Clearfield, PA 16830. **Phone-**County Recorder of Deeds, R/E & UCC Recording- 814-765-2641 x1350; fax-814-765-6089; hours 8:30AM-4PM www.clearfieldco.org

Will not search UCC records. Record copy- $.50 per page. **Online Access to Real Estate, Deed, Mortgage, Will records:** Access to Recorder of Deeds and Wills and Orphans Court is by subscription at www.landex.com/remote/. Fee is $.20 per minute, $.50 per fax page. Recorder data goes back to 1986. Images go back to 1997. Wills and orphan court records go back to 1990. Also, assessors county tax sale list is updated weekly at www.clearfieldco.org/tax_sale_list. **Other phones:** Assessor-814-765-2641 x5997; Treasurer-814-765-2641 x5985; Elections-814-765-2641 x5996; Vital Records-724-656-3100.

Clinton County Prothonotary

County Prothonotary, 230 E. Water St., Courthouse, Lock Haven, PA 17745. **Phone-**570-893-4007, R/E Recording-570-893-4010; fax-570-893-4288; hours 8AM-5PM M,T,Th,F; 8AM-12:30PM W www.clintoncountypa.com

UCC records information or copy request (per debtor)- $59.00. Will not search tax liens. UCC copy- $5.00 per page. Cert fee: $3.00 per cert. Payee: Clinton County Prothonotary. **Other phones:** Assessor-570-893-4033; Treasurer-570-893-4005; Appraiser/ Auditor-570-893-4030; Elections-570-893-4000; Vital Records-570-893-4010.

Clinton County Recorder

County Recorder of Deeds, PO Box 943, Lock Haven, PA 17745. **Phone-**County Recorder of Deeds, R/E & UCC Recording- 570-893-4010; fax-570-893-4273; hours 8:30AM-5PM. Will not any search UCC records.Will not search real estate records. Copy fee- $.50 per page. UCC copy- $.50 per page. Cert fee: $1.50 per cert. Payee: Clinton County Recorder of

Deeds. **Online Access to Real Estate, Probate, Property records:** Access to limited property data is free at www.clintoncountypa.com; click on "Parcel Query by Name." Site may be down. Also, access is available through a private company. For information, call Infocon at 814-472-6066 of www.ic-access.com. **Other phones:** Assessor-570-893-4034; Treasurer-570-893-4004.

Columbia County Prothonotary

County Prothonotary, PO Box 380, Bloomsburg, PA 17815. **Phone-**570-389-5614, R/E Recording-570-389-5635, UCC Recording-570-389-5617; hours 8AM-4:30PM

Will not search UCC or tax liens records. UCC copy- $1.00 per page. Cert fee: $4.00 per page. Payee: Columbia County Prothonotary. **Other phones:** Assessor-570-389-5646; Treasurer-570-389-5626; Elections-570-389-5640.

Columbia County Recorder

County Recorder of Deeds, PO Box 380, Bloomsburg, PA 17815. **Phone-**County Recorder of Deeds, R/E & UCC Recording- 570-389-5632; fax-570-389-5636; hours 8AM-4:30PM www.columbiapa.org/county/offices.html

Will not search UCC or real estate records. RE record copy- $.50 per page. UCC copy- $1.00 per page. Cert fee: $1.50 per cert. Payee: County Recorder of Deeds. **Other phones:** Assessor-570-389-5645; Treasurer-570-389-5626; Elections-570-389-5640.

Crawford County Prothonotary

County Prothonotary, 903 Diamond Park, County Courthouse, Meadville, PA 16335. **Phone-**814-333-7324, R/E Recording-814-373-2537; fax-814-337-5416; hours 8:30AM-4:30PM

UCC records information or copy request (per debtor)- $59.00. Will not search tax liens. UCC copy- $.75 per page. **Other phones:** Assessor-814-333-7302; Treasurer-814-333-7332; Elections-814-333-7307.

Crawford County Recorder

County Recorder of Deeds, 903 Diamond Park, Courthouse, Meadville, PA 16335. **Phone-**County Recorder of Deeds, R/E & UCC Recording- 814-373-2537; fax-814-337-5296; hours 8:30AM-4:30PM www.co.crawford.pa.us

Will not search UCC or real estate records. Record copy- $1.00 per page. Cert fee: $1.50 per doc. Payee: Crawford County Recorder of Deeds. **Other phones:** Assessor-814-333-7302; Treasurer-814-333-7332; Elections-814-333-7307.

Cumberland County Prothonotary

County Prothonotary, 1 Courthouse Sq, County Courthouse, Carlisle, PA 17013-3387. **Phone-**717-240-7832; hours 8AM-4:30PM

May or may not not search UCC records. Information or copy request (per debtor)- $59.00. Will not search tax liens. RE record copy- $.50 per copy. UCC copy- $.50 per page. Payee: Cumberland County Prothonotary.

Cumberland County Recorder

County Recorder of Deeds, 1 Courthouse Sq, County Courthouse, Carlisle, PA 17013. **Phone-**County Recorder of Deeds, R/E & UCC Recording- 717-240-6370, UCC Recording-717-240-5370; fax-717-240-6490; hours 8AM-4:30PM

Will not search UCC or real estate records. Copy fee- $.50 per page. Cert fee: $10.00 per cert by mail. Payee: Cumberland County Recorder of Deeds. **Online Access to Property Tax, Assessor, Cemetery records:** Access to property assessment data is free at www.ccpa.net/cumberland/cwp/view.asp?A=1137&Q=479825. No name searching. Also, search cemetery records for free on a private company site at www.rootsweb.com/~usgenweb/pa/cumberland/cemet. htm. **Other phones:** Assessor-717-240-6350; Treasurer-717-240-6380; Elections-717-240-6385.

Dauphin County Prothonotary

County Prothonotary, PO Box 945, Harrisburg, PA 17108. **Phone**-717-780-6520; hours 8AM-4:30PM www.dauphincounty.org
UCC records information or copy request (per debtor)-$57.50. Tax liens not included in UCC search. Separate federal/state combined tax lien search-$8.75 per 5 years. UCC copy- $.75 per page. Cert fee: $5.00 per case. Payee: County Prothonotary.

Dauphin County Recorder

County Recorder of Deeds, PO Box 12000, Harrisburg, PA 17108. **Phone**-717-780-6560; fax-717-780-6482; hours 8AM-4:30PM
Will not search UCC or real estate records. **Online Access to Property, Assessor, Property Sale records:** Access to county property data is free at www.dauphinpropertyinfo.org/propertymax/rover30.as p. To search free, create a limited guest account. Full access fee is $50.00 per month. If you wish to include property sales data, there is an add'l fee of $20.00. **Other phones:** Assessor-717-255-2735; Treasurer-717-255-2676.

Delaware County Prothonotary

County Prothonotary, 201 W. Front St, Rm 127, Delaware County Gov't Ctr Bldg, Media, PA 19063. **Phone**-610-891-5009; hours 8:30AM-4:30PM
Will not search UCC or tax liens records. UCC copy-$1.00 per page. Cert fee: $4.50 per cert. Payee: Office of Judicial Support. **Other phones:** Assessor-610-891-4891/4897.

Delaware County Recorder

County Recorder of Deeds, 201 W. Front St, Rm 107, Government Ctr. Bldg., Media, PA 19063. **Phone**-610-891-4260, R/E Recording-610-891-4144; hours 8:30AM-4:30PM
http://www2.co.delaware.pa.us/pa/default.htm
Will not any search UCC records. Will not search real estate records. UCC copy- $1.00 per page. Cert fee: $7.00 for 1st 4 pages; $1.00 each add'l. Payee: Delaware County Recorder of Deeds. **Online Access to Assessor, Deed, Real Estate, Judgment, Court records:** Access to the public access system is free - temporarily - at www2.co.delaware.pa.us/pa/publi caccess.asp. Records go back to 1982. No name searching. Also, property tax records are free on the Internet at http://taxrecords.com. **Other phones:** Assessor-610-891-4880; Treasurer-610-891-4272; Elections-610-891-4938.

Elk County Prothonotary

County Prothonotary, PO Box 237, Ridgway, PA 15853-0237. **Phone**-814-776-5344, R/E Recording-814-776-5349; fax-814-776-5303; hours 8:30AM-4PM
UCC records information or copy request (per debtor)-$57.00. Tax liens not included in UCC search. Federal/state combined tax lien search- $8.00 per debtor + $1.50 for each lien found. UCC copy-$.50 per page. Cert fee: $8.00 per search. Payee: Elk County Prothonotary. **Other phones:** Assessor-814-776-5340; Treasurer-814-776-5322; Elections-814-776-5337.

Elk County Recorder

County Recorder of Deeds, PO Box 314, Ridgway, PA 15853-0314. **Phone**-County Recorder of Deeds, R/E & UCC Recording- 814-776-5349; fax-814-776-5382; hours 8:30AM-4PM
Will not search UCC or tax liens records. Will search real estate records. RE record copy- $.50 per page. UCC copy- $1.00 per page. Cert fee: $1.50 per

instrument. Payee: Elk County Recorder of Deeds. **Other phones:** Assessor-814-776-5340; Treasurer-814-776-5322; Elections-814-776-5337.

Erie County Prothonotary

County Prothonotary, 140 W. 6th St, Rm 120, Erie, PA 16501-1080. **Phone**-814-451-6078; 8:30AM-4:30PM
UCC records information or copy request (per debtor)-$57.00. Will not search tax liens. UCC copy-$2.00 per page. Payee: Erie County Prothonotary. **Online Access to Tax Lien records:** Online search: see Register of Deeds.

Erie County Recorder

County Recorder of Deeds, PO Box 1849, Erie, PA 16507-0849. **Phone**-814-451-6246; fax-814-451-6213; hours 8:30AM-4:30PM
Will not search UCC or real estate records. Copy fee is $.50 per page. Cert fee: $1.00 per doc. Payee: Erie County Recorder of Deeds. **Online Access to Real Estate, Marriage, Probate records:** Access is through a private company. For information, call Infocon at 814-472-6066 or www.ic-access.com. Also, access to property records is free at www.mypropert yrecords.com/eriecountypa/. **Other phones:** Assessor-814-451-6225; Treasurer-814-451-6080.

Fayette County Prothonotary

County Prothonotary, 61 E. Main St, Courthouse, Uniontown, PA 15401. **Phone**-724-430-1272, R/E Recording-724-430-1238; hours 8AM-4:30PM
Will not search UCC or tax liens records. UCC copy-$.$50 per page. Payee: Fayette County Prothonotary. **Other phones:** Assessor-724-430-7350; Treasurer-724-430-1256; Appraiser/ Auditor-724-430-1350; Elections-724-430-1289; Vital Records-724-430-1206.

Fayette County Recorder

County Recorder of Deeds, 61 E. Main St, Courthouse, Uniontown, PA 15401-3389. **Phone**-County Recorder of Deeds, R/E Recording- 724-430-1238, UCC Recording-724-430-1272; fax-724-430-1238; hours 8AM-4:30PM
UCC records information or copy request (per debtor)-$61.00. Will not search real estate records. Copy fee-$1.00 per page. Cert fee: $3.00 per doc. Payee: County Recorder. **Online Access to Property, Assessor records:** Access to property assessments is free at www.fayetteproperty.org/assessor. **Other phones:** Assessor-724-430-1350; Treasurer-724-430-1256; Elections-724-430-1289; Vitals-724-430-1206.

Forest County Prothonotary

County Prothonotary, 526 Elm St #2, Tionesta, PA 16353. **Phone**-County Prothonotary, R/E & UCC Recording- 814-755-3526; fax-814-755-8837; hours 9AM-4PM www.co.forest.pa.us
Will not search UCC or tax liens records. Copy fee-$.25 per page. Cert fee: $2.00 per cert. Payee: Recorder of Deeds. **Other phones:** Assessor-814-755-3532; Treasurer-814-755-3536.

Forest County Recorder

County Recorder of Deeds, 526 Elm St #2, Tionesta, PA 16353. **Phone**-County Recorder of Deeds, R/E & UCC Recording- 814-755-3526; fax-814-755-8837; hours 9AM-4PM www.co.forest.pa.us
Will not search records. Copy fee- $.25 per page. Cert fee: $2.00 per cert. Copy fee is $25. per page. Payee: Recorder of Deeds. **Other phones:** Assessor-814-755-3532; Treasurer-814-755-3536.

Franklin County Prothonotary

County Prothonotary, 157 Lincoln Way East, County Court House, Chambersburg, PA 17201. **Phone**-717-261-3860, R/E Recording-717-261-3872; fax-717-264-6772; hours 8:30AM-5PM

Will not search UCC or tax liens records. UCC copy-$.50 per page. **Other phones:** Assessor-717-261-3801; Treasurer-717-261-3119; Elections-717-261-3886; UCC/Personal Property-717-261-3858.

Franklin County Recorder

County Recorder of Deeds, 157 Lincoln Way East, Chambersburg, PA 17201. **Phone**-717-264-4125; fax-717-263-5717; hours 8:30AM-4:30PM
Will not search UCC or real estate records. Cert fee: $1.50. Payee: County Recorder of Deeds. **Online Access to Real Estate, Probate records:** Access is through a private company. For information, call Infocon at 814-472-6066 or www.ic-access.com. **Other phones:** Assessor-717-261-3801; Treasurer-717-261-3120.

Fulton County Prothonotary

County Prothonotary, 201 N. Second St, Fulton County Courthouse, McConnellsburg, PA 17233-1198. **Phone**-County Prothonotary, R/E & UCC Recording- 717-485-4212; hours 8:30AM-4:30PM. Will not search UCC or tax liens records. RE record copy- $.50 per page. UCC copy- $1.00 per page. Cert fee: $5.00 per cert. Payee: Fulton County Prothonotary. **Other phones:** Assessor-717-485-3208; Treasurer-717-485-4454; Elections-717-485-3691.

Fulton County Recorder

County Recorder of Deeds, 201 N. Second St, Fulton County Courthouse, McConnellsburg, PA 17233-1198. **Phone**-County Recorder of Deeds, R/E & UCC Recording- 717-485-4212; hours 8:30AM-4:30PM
Public computer system in office. Will not search records. RE record copy- $.50 per page. UCC copy-$1.00 per page. Cert fee: $5.00 per doc, no page cost. Payee: Fulton County Recorder of Deeds. **Other phones:** Assessor-717-485-3208; Treasurer-717-485-4454; Elections-717-485-3691.

Greene County Prothonotary

County Prothonotary, 10 E. High St, Rm 105, Waynesburg, PA 15370. **Phone**-724-852-5289, R/E Recording-724-852-5283; hours 8:30AM-4:30PM
Will not search UCC or tax liens records. UCC copy-$1.00 per page. Cert fee: $6.00 per cert. Payee: Greene County Prothonotary.

Greene County Recorder

County Recorder of Deeds, 10 E High St, Courthouse, Waynesburg, PA 15370. **Phone**-County Recorder of Deeds, R/E & UCC Recording- 724-852-5283, UCC Recording-724-852-5289; hours 8:30AM-4:30PM
http://county.greenepa.net
Only real estate related UCC filed here; info or copy request (per debtor)- $63.00. Will not search real estate records. RE record copy- $.50 per page. UCC copy- $1.00 per page. Cert fee: $5.00 per cert. Payee: Greene County Recorder of Deeds. **Other phones:** Assessor-724-852-5211; Treasurer-724-852-5225; Elections-724-852-5230.

Huntingdon County Prothonotary

County Prothonotary, PO Box 39, Huntingdon, PA 16652-1486. **Phone**-814-643-1610, R/E Recording-814-643-2740; fax-814-643-4271; 8:30AM-4:30PM
Will not search UCC or tax liens records. Cert fee: $4.50 per page. Payee: Prothonotary. **Online Access to Tax Lien records:** Online search: see Register of Deeds. **Other phones:** Assessor-814-643-1000; Treasurer-814-643-3523; Elections-814-643-3091.

Huntingdon County Recorder

County Recorder of Deeds, 223 Penn St, Courthouse, Huntingdon, PA 16652. **Phone**-County Recorder of Deeds, R/E & UCC Recording- 814-643-2740; fax-814-643-8152; hours 8:30AM-4:30PM

Will not search UCC or real estate records. UCC copy-$2.00 per page. Cert fee: $1.50 per cert. Payee: Huntingdon County Recorder of Deeds. **Online Access to Real Estate, Marriage, Probate records:** Access is through a private company. For information, call Infocon at 814-472-6066 or www.ic-access.com. **Other phones:** Assessor-814-643-1000; Treasurer-814-643-3523; Elections-814-643-3091.

Indiana County Prothonotary

Prothonotary & Clerk of Courts, 825 Philadelphia St, Courthouse, 1st Fl, Indiana, PA 15701-3934. **Phone-**724-465-3855, R/E Recording-724-465-3860; fax-724-465-3968; hours 8AM-4PM. UCC records information or copy request (per debtor)- $59.00. Will not search tax liens. UCC copy- $.25 per page. **Other phones:** Assessor-724-465-3812; Treasurer-724-465-3845; Elections-724-465-3852; Vital Records-724-656-3100.

Indiana County Recorder

County Recorder of Deeds, 825 Philadelphia St, Courthouse, Indiana, PA 15701. **Phone-**County Recorder of Deeds, R/E & UCC Recording- 724-465-3860; fax-724-465-3863; hours 8AM-4PM
Will not search UCC or real estate records. Copy fee- $.25 per page. Cert fee: $3.00 for every 4 pages. Payee: Recorder of Deeds. **Other phones:** Assessor-724-465-3812; Treasurer-724-465-3845.

Jefferson County

Prothonotary & Clerk of Courts, 200 Main St, Court House, Rm 102, Brookville, PA 15825. **Phone-**814-849-1606, R/E Recording-814-849-1610; fax-814-849-1625; hours 8:30AM-4:30PM. Will not search UCC or tax liens records. UCC copy- $1.00 per page. Cert fee: $1.50 per page. Payee: County Prothonotary.

Jefferson County Recorder

County Recorder of Deeds, 200 Main St, Courthouse, Brookville, PA 15825. **Phone-**County Recorder of Deeds, R/E & UCC Recording- 814-849-1610; fax-814-849-1677; hours 8:30AM-4:30PM
Will not search UCC or real estate records. RE record copy- $1.00 per copy. Cert fee: $1.50 per certification. Payee: Recorder of Deeds. **Other phones:** Assessor-814-849-1637; Treasurer-814-849-1609; Elections-814-849-1603.

Juniata County Prothonotary

County Prothonotary, Courthouse, Mifflintown, PA 17059. **Phone-**717-436-7715, R/E Recording-717-436-7709; fax-717-436-7734; hours 8AM-4:30PM
UCC records information or copy request (per debtor)- $57.00. Will not search tax liens. UCC copy- $1.00 per page. Cert fee: $4.50 per doc. Payee: Juniata County Prothonotary. **Other phones:** Assessor-717-436-7740; Treasurer-717-436-7742; Elections-717-436-7706.

Juniata County Recorder

County Recorder of Deeds, PO Box 68, Mifflintown, PA 17059. **Phone-**County Recorder of Deeds, R/E & UCC Recording- 717-436-7709; fax-717-436-7756; hours 8AM-4:30PM
Will not search UCC or real estate records. UCC copy- $1.00 per page. Cert fee: $5.00 per doc. Payee: Juniata County Recorder of Deeds. **Online Access to Real Estate, Marriage, Probate records:** Access is through a private company. For information, call Infocon at 814-472-6066 or www.ic-access.com. **Other phones:** Assessor-717-436-7740; Treasurer-717-436-7742; Prothonotary-717-436-7715.

Lackawanna County Prothonotary

County Clerk of Judicial Records, 200 N. Washington Ave, Scranton, PA 18503. **Phone-**570-963-6723; fax-none; hours 9AM-4:00PM. Will not search UCC or tax liens records. Cert fee: $4.50. Payee:

Lackawanna County Clerk of Judicial Records. **Other phones:** Assessor-570-963-6728.

Lackawanna County Recorder

County Recorder of Deeds, 200 N. Washington, Courthouse, Scranton, PA 18503. **Phone-**County Recorder of Deeds, R/E & UCC Recording- 570-963-6775; hours 9AM-4PM. Will not any search UCC records.Will not search real estate records. UCC copy-$1.00 per page. Payee: Lackawanna County Recorder of Deeds. **Other phones:** Assessor-570-963-6728; Treasurer-570-963-6731.

Lancaster County Prothonotary

County Prothonotary, PO Box 83480, Lancaster, PA 17608-3480. **Phone-**717-299-8282, R/E Recording-717-299-8238; fax-717-293-7210; hours 8:30AM-5PM www.co.lancaster.pa.us
UCC records information or copy request (per debtor)-$57.00. Will not search tax liens. UCC copy- $.50 per page. Cert fee: $5.00 per page. Payee: Lancaster County Prothonotary. **Other phones:** Assessor-717-299-8381; Treasurer-717-299-8222; Elections-717-299-8293.

Lancaster County Recorder

County Recorder of Deeds, PO Box 83480, Lancaster, PA 17608. **Phone-**County Recorder of Deeds, R/E & UCC Recording- 717-299-8238; fax-717-299-8393; hours 8:30AM-4:30PM (recording); 8:30AM-5PM (for public) www.co.lancaster.pa.us
Will search UCC records, but only real estate related UCC filed here. Will not search real estate records. UCC copy- $1.00 per page. Cert fee: $1.50 per cert. Payee: Lancaster County Recorder of Deeds. **Online Access to Assessor, Real Estate, Recording, Tax Lien, UCC records:** Access to deeds, UCCs and other recordings is free at http://icris.lancasterdeeds.com/splash.jsp. Also, access to property data is free on the GIS-mapping site at www.co.lancaster.pa.us/gis/site/default.asp?. Click on GIS-Property Search, then choose Query to search by owner name. **Other phones:** Assessor-717-299-8381; Treasurer-717-299-8222.

Lawrence County Prothonotary

County Prothonotary, 430 Court St, Government Ctr, New Castle, PA 16101-3593. **Phone-**724-656-1943, R/E Recording-724-656-2128; fax-724-656-1988; hours 8AM-4PM
Will not search UCC or tax liens records. UCC copy-$2.00 per page. Payee: Lawrence County Prothonotary. **Online Access to Tax Lien records:** Online search: see Register of Deeds. **Other phones:** Assessor-724-656-2191; Treasurer-724-656-1978; Elections-724-656-2161; Vital Records-724-656-3100.

Lawrence County Recorder

County Recorder of Deeds, 430 Court St, Government Ctr, New Castle, PA 16101. **Phone-**724-656-2127; fax-724-656-1966; hours 8AM-4PM
Will not search UCC or real estate records. Copy fee- $.50 per page. Cert fee: $1.50 per doc. Payee: Recorder of Deeds. **Online Access to Real Estate, Assessor, Marriage, Probate records:** Access is through a private company. For information, call Infocon at 814-472-6066 or www.ic-access.com. **Other phones:** Assessor-724-656-2191; Treasurer-724-656-2183; Elections-724-656-2161.

Lebanon County

County Recorder of Deeds, 400 S. 8th St, Rm 107, Lebanon, PA 17042. **Phone-**717-274-2801, R/E Recording-717-274-2801 x2224, UCC Recording-717-274-2801 x2225; hours Recording Hours 8:30AM-4PM www.lebcounty.org
Will not search UCC or real estate records. RE record copy- $1.00 per page. UCC copy- $2.00 per page.

Cert fee: $2.00 per cert. Payee: Lebanon County Recorder of Deeds. **Other phones:** Assessor-717-274-2801 x2250; Treasurer-717-274-2801 x2229.

Lebanon County Prothonotary

County Prothonotary, 400 S. 8th St, Rm 104, Lebanon, PA 17042. **Phone-**County Prothonotary, R/E & UCC Recording- 717-274-2801; hours 8:30AM-4:30PM
May or may not search UCC records. Information or copy request (per debtor)- $57.00. Will not search tax liens. UCC copy- $2.00 per page. Payee: Lebanon County Prothonotary. **Other phones:** Assessor-717-274-2801; Treasurer-717-274-2801; Elections-717-274-2801; Vital Records-717-274-2801.

Lehigh County Prothonotary

County Prothonotary, 455 W. Hamilton St., Allentown, PA 18101-1614. **Phone-**610-782-3148, R/E Recording-610-782-3162; fax-610-770-3840; 8:30AM-4:30PM
The City of Bethlehem is in both Northampton and Lehigh counties. UCC records information or copy request (per debtor)- $59.00. Will not search real estate or tax lien records. UCC copy- $2.00 per page. Cert fee: $4.75 per doc. Payee: Lehigh County Clerk of Courts-Civil Division. **Online Access to Judgment, Deed, Lien, Voter Registration, Assessor, Occ License, Will, Civil/Criminal Court, Grantor/Grantee, Tax Sale records:** The county's full-access dial-up or internet pay system initial cost is approx. $300.00 for a yearly membership and a prepaid usage fee of $.05 per minute applies. For more info, call the Fiscal Office at 610- 782-3112 or visit www.lehighcounty.org/Fiscal/fiscal.cfm?doc=fiscal_dial-up.htm. Also, at www.lehighcounty.org, the new Grants database is searched free; free registration required. You may also search assessments but no name searching. Tax sales search is free. **Other phones:** Assessor-610-782-3038; Treasurer-610-782-3115; Elections-610-782-3194.

Lehigh County Recorder

County Recorder of Deeds, 17 S 7th St, Rm 350, Allentown, PA 18101. **Phone-**610-782-3162, R/E Recording-610-820-3162; fax-610-782-3116; hours 8am-4pm. Will not search UCC or real estate records. Copy fee- $1.00 per page. Cert fee: $1.50 per doc. Payee: Recorder of Deeds. **Online Access to Assessor, Real Estate, Tax Lien, Marriage records:** A dial-up system is available 24 hours daily; there are set-up and usage fees. Records go back to 1984. Lending agency information and court records included. Call Lehigh County Computer Svcs Dept at 610-782-3286 for more information. **Other phones:** Assessor-610-820-3038; Treasurer-610-820-3113; Elections-610-820-3194; Clerk of Courts-610-782-3148.

Luzerne County Prothonotary

County Prothonotary, 200 N. River St, County Court House, Wilkes-Barre, PA 18711-1001. **Phone-**570-825-1745, UCC Recording-570-825-1749; fax-570-825-1757. Will not search UCC or tax liens records. Cert fee: $5.00 per doc, add'l $1.50 for each page of same doc. Payee: Prothonotary.

Luzerne County Recorder

County Recorder of Deeds, 200 N. River St, Courthouse, Wilkes-Barre, PA 18711. **Phone-**County Recorder of Deeds, R/E & UCC Recording- 570-825-1641; fax-570-970-4580; hours 9AM-4:30PM
Mortgages & Real Estate related UCCs only found in this office. Will not search UCC or real estate records. Record copy- $1.00 per page. Cert fee: $1.00 per page, $1.00 per certification. Payee: Luzerne County Recorder of Deeds. **Online Access to Recorder, Deed records:** Access is through a private company at www.landex.com/remote/. Fee is $.20 per minute and $.50 per fax page. Index goes back to 1/1993; images go back to 9/1993. **Other phones:**

Assessor-570-825-1540; Treasurer-570-825-1786; Elections-570-825-1716.

Lycoming County Prothonotary

County Prothonotary, 48 W. Third St, Williamsport, PA 17701. **Phone**-570-327-2251, R/E Recording-570-327-2263; hours 8:30AM-5PM. Will not search UCC or tax liens records. UCC copy- $1.00 per page. Cert fee: $5.00 per doc. Payee: County Prothonotary. **Other phones:** Assessor-570-327-2301; Treasurer-570-327-2248; Elections-570-327-2267.

Lycoming County Recorder

County Recorder of Deeds, 48 W. Third St, Williamsport, PA 17701. **Phone**-County Recorder of Deeds, R/E & UCC Recording- 570-327-2263; fax-570-327-2511; hours 8:30AM-5PM
Will not search UCC or real estate records. RE record copy- $.50 per page. UCC copy- $1.00 per page. Cert fee: $1.50 per cert. Payee: Lycoming County Recorder of Deeds. **Other phones:** Assessor-570-327-2302; Treasurer-570-327-2249.

McKean County Prothonotary

County Prothonotary, PO Box 273, Smethport, PA 16749. **Phone**-814-887-3271, R/E Recording-814-887-3253; fax-814-887-3219; hours 8:30AM-4:30PM
UCC records information or copy request (per debtor)- $59.00. Tax liens not included in UCC search. Tax lien search- $15.00 per debtor. UCC copy- $.50 per page. Cert fee: $10.00. **Other phones:** Assessor-814-887-3214; Treasurer-814-887-3220; Elections-814-887-3203.

McKean County Recorder

Recorder of Deeds, 500 W. Main St., Smethport, PA 16749. **Phone**-814-887-3253, R/E Recording-814-887-3250, UCC Recording-814-887-3250; fax-814-887-3255; hours 8:30AM-4:30PM
Will not search UCC or real estate records. Copy fee- $1.00 per page. Cert fee: $1.50 per doc. Payee: Anne Bosworth-Recorder of Deeds. **Other phones:** Assessor-814-887-3215; Treasurer-814-887-3220; Elections-814-887-3203; Vital Records-814-887-3260.

Mercer County Prothonotary

County Prothonotary, 105 Mercer County Courthouse, Mercer, PA 16137-0066. **Phone**-724-662-3800 x2261; fax-none; hours 8:30AM-4:30PM. Will not search UCC or tax liens records. Copy fee- $1.00 per page. Payee: Mercer County Prothonotary. **Online Access to Tax Lien records:** Online search: see Register of Deeds. **Other phones:** Assessor-724-662-3800.

Mercer County Recorder

County Recorder of Deeds, 109 Courthouse, Mercer, PA 16137-1293. **Phone**-724-662-3800, R/E Recording-724-662-3800 x2277; fax-724-662-2096; hours 8:30AM-4:30PM. Will not search UCC or real estate records. RE record copy fee- $1.00 per page. UCC copy- $1.00 per page. Cert fee: $2.00 per instument. Payee: Recorder. **Online Access to Real Estate, Assessor records:** Access is through a private company. For information, call Infocon at 814-472-6066 or www.ic-access.com. **Other phones:** Assessor-724-662-3800 x505; Treasurer-724-662-3800 x257.

Mifflin County Prothonotary

County Prothonotary, 20 N. Wayne St, Lewistown, PA 17044. **Phone**-717-248-8146; fax-717-248-5275; hours 8AM-4:30PM. Will not search UCC or tax liens records. **Online Access to Tax Lien records:** Online search: see Register of Deeds.

Mifflin County Recorder

County Recorder of Deeds, 20 N. Wayne St, Lewistown, PA 17044. **Phone**-717-242-1449, R/E

Recording-717-248-6733; fax-717-248-2503; hours 8AM-4:30PM www.co.mifflin.pa.us
Will not search UCC or real estate records. Copy fee- $.50 per page. Cert fee: $1.50 per cert. Payee: Mifflin County Recorder of Deeds. **Online Access to Real Estate, Assessor, Probate, GIS Mapping records:** Access is through a private company. For information, call Infocon at 814-472-6066 or www.ic-access.com. You may sign up online. Also, property data is free at www.co.mifflin.pa.us. Use the new free Web Mapping Parcel Application to name search for property data. **Other phones:** Assessor-717-248-5783; Treasurer-717-248-8439.

Monroe County Prothonotary

County Prothonotary, N. 7th & Monroe St, Courthouse, Rm 303, Stroudsburg, PA 18360-2190. **Phone**-570-420-3570; fax-570-420-3582; hours 8:30AM-4:30PM
Will search UCC records. UCC search per debtor- $5.00 per name. Separate federal/state combined tax lien search- $5.00 per debtor UCC copy- $1.00 per page. Cert fee: $3.00 per packet. Payee: Monroe County Prothonotary. **Other phones:** Assessor-570-420-3412; Treasurer-570-420-3410; Elections-570-420-3468.

Monroe County Recorder

County Recorder of Deeds, 7th & Monroe St, Courthouse, Stroudsburg, PA 18360-2185. **Phone**-570-420-3530, R/E Recording-570-420-3400; fax-570-420-3537; hours 8:30AM-4:30PM
Will search UCC records. Will not search real estate records. **Online Access to Real Estate, Deed, Will, Mortgage records:** Access is through a private company at www.landex.com/remote/. Fee is $.20 per minute and $.50 per fax page. Land Index goes back to 1/1979; wills go back to 11/1836; images go back to 8/1997. **Other phones:** Assessor-570-420-3412; Treasurer-570-420-3510.

Montgomery County Prothonotary

County Prothonotary, PO Box 311, Norristown, PA 19404. **Phone**-610-278-3360; fax-610-278-5994; hours 8:30AM-4:15PM. UCC records information or copy request (per debtor)- $59.00. Will not search tax liens. UCC copy- $5.00 per page. Payee: Montgomery County Prothonotary. **Other phones:** Assessor-610-278-3761.

Montgomery County Recorder

County Recorder of Deeds, PO Box 311, Norristown, PA 19404-0311. **Phone**-610-278-3289, R/E Recording-610-278-3868; fax-610-278-3869; hours 8:30AM-4:15PM www.montcopa.org
Only real estate related UCC filed here; info or copy request (per debtor)- $59.00. Will not search real estate records. UCC copy- $1.00 per page. Cert fee: $1.50 per cert. Payee: Montgomery County Recorder of Deeds. **Online Access to Assessor, Real Estate, Recording, Deed, Tax Lien, Owner Name, Estate, Tax Claim Property records:** Register of Deeds records are free at www.montcopa.org/MWAY/index.html. There are several search options. Records on the County PIR database are free at www.montcopa.org/reassessment/boahome0.htm.
Records date back to 1990. Lending agency and prothonotary information are on the system. Also, search estate names for free at www.montcopa.org/MWAY/estate.html. Search BOA owner names at www.montcopa.org/MWAY/owner.html Also, search tax claim properties list at www.montcopa.org/taxclaim/repoproperties.asp. **Other phones:** Assessor-610-278-3761; Treasurer-610-278-3066; Elections-610-278-3075.

Montour County Prothonotary

County Prothonotary, 29 Mill St, Courthouse, Danville, PA 17821. **Phone**-570-271-3010, R/E UCC Recording-

570-271-3012, fax-570-271-3089; hours-9AM-4PM www.montourco.org/montour/site/default.asp
UCC records information or copy request (per debtor)- $57.00. Tax liens not included in UCC search. Separate federal/state combined tax lien search- $10.00 per debtor. UCC copy- $1.00 per page. Payee: Montour County Prothonotary. **Online Access to Will records:** A register of wills from 1850 to present is at www.montourco.org/montour/cwp/view.asp?a=770&Q=417826&montourNav=|8473|. **Other phones:** Assessor-570-271-3006; Treasurer-570-271-3016; Elections-570-271-3000; Vital Records-570-271-3010.

Montour County Recorder

Register & Recorder, 29 Mill St, Courthouse, Danville, PA 17821. **Phone**-570-271-3012; fax-570-271-3071. www.montourco.org
UCC records information or copy request (per debtor)- $57.00. Tax lien search- $5.00 per debtor. Will search real estate records. Copy fee- $.50 per page. Cert fee: $.50 per page + $1.50. Payee: Register & Recorder. **Online Access to Deed, Will, Marriage records:** Access to Register of Deeds data is by subscription from a private company, visit www.ic-access.com. Also includes Prothonotary, Marriages, Clerk of Courts. Will index is also free at the county website. At www.montour.org, click on Register & Recorder, then Will Index. **Other phones:** Assessor-570-271-3006; Treasurer-570-271-3016; Elections-570-271-3000.

Northampton County Prothonotary

County Prothonotary, 669 Washington St., 2nd Fl, Rm 207, Easton, PA 18042-7498. **Phone**-610-559-3060; hours 8:30AM-4:30PM
The City of Bethlehem is in both Northampton and Lehigh counties. UCC records information or copy request (per debtor)- $59.00. UCC certification- $28.00 per page; $5.00 each reference found. Will not search tax liens. UCC copy- $2.00 per page. Cert fee: $4.75 per page. Payee: Northampton County Prothonotary. **Other phones:** Assessor-610-559-3000; Treasurer-610-559-3000; Elections-610-559-3000.

Northampton County Recorder

County Recorder of Deeds, 669 Washington St, Government Ctr, Easton, PA 18042. **Phone**-610-559-3077; fax-610-559-3103; hours 8:30AM-4:30PM
The City of Bethlehem is in both Northampton and Lehigh counties. Will not any search UCC records.Will not search real estate records. UCC copy- $1.00 per page. Payee: Northampton County Recorder of Deeds. **Online Access to Real Estate, Deed, Mortgage, Misc. Recording, Property, Assessor records:** Two sources are available. One is a private company at www.landex.com/remote/. Fee is $.20 per minute and $.50 per fax page. Deeds data goes back to 11/85; mortgages to 2/88; faxable images go back to 5/94. Also, online access to assessor's property records data is free at www.ncpub.org. **Other phones:** Assessor-610-559-3160.

Northumberland County Prothonotary

County Prothonotary, 201 Market St, Courthouse, Rm 7, Sunbury, PA 17801-3468. **Phone**-570-988-4151, R/E Recording-570-988-4143; hours 9AM-4:30PM (M-open until 5PM)
UCC records or copy request (per debtor)- $59.00. Will not search tax liens. UCC copy- $2.00 per page. Cert fee: $4.00 per 1st page, $1.00 each add'l. Payee: County Prothonotary. **Other phones:** Assessor-570-988-4112; Treasurer-570-988-4161; Elections-570-988-4211.

Northumberland County Recorder

County Recorder of Deeds, 201 Market St, Court House, Sunbury, PA 17801. **Phone**-570-988-4140; hours 9AM-4:30PM. Will not search UCC or real estate records. UCC copy- $5.00 per page. Cert fee: None. Payee: Northumberland County Recorder of Deeds. **Other phones:** Assessor-570-988-4312; Treasurer-570-988-4160.

Perry County Prothonotary

County Prothonotary, PO Box 325, New Bloomfield, PA 17068-0325. **Phone**-717-582-2131; 8AM-4PM Will not search UCC or tax liens records. RE record copy- $.40 per page. Cert fee: $5.00 per cert. Payee: Perry County Prothonotary.

Perry County Recorder

County Recorder of Deeds, PO Box 223, New Bloomfield, PA 17068. **Phone**-717-582-2131; hours 8AM-4PM

Will not search UCC or real estate records. Copy fee- $.50 per page. Cert fee: $2.00 per cert. Payee: Perry County Recorder of Deeds. **Online Access to Real Estate, Deed records:** Access to Recorder of Deeds is by subscription at www.landex.com/remote/. Fee is $.20 per minute, $.50 per fax page. Recorder data goes back to 1973; images to 1820. **Other phones:** Assessor-717-582-8984x3; Treasurer-717-582-8984 x4.

Philadelphia County Prothonotary

County Prothonotary, Broad & Market Sts, City Hall, Rm 271, Philadelphia, PA 19107. **Phone**-215-686-6664; hours 9AM-3PM

UCC records information or copy request (per debtor)- $59.00. Tax liens not included in UCC search. Tax lien search- $30.00 per debtor. UCC copy- $1.00 per page. Payee: Philadelphia County Prothonotary. **Online Access to Judgment, Lien, Civil Court records:** Assess to Prothonotary records is free at http://fjdwebserver.phila.gov/fjd/repl 1/zk_fjd_public_qry_02.zp_judgment_setup_idx.html. Judgments and liens on behalf of governmental entites only. **Other phones:** Assessor-215-686-4334.

Philadelphia County Recorder

County Recorder of Deeds, Broad & Market Sts, City Hall, Rm 153, Philadelphia, PA 19107. **Phone**-215-686-2260, R/E Recording-215-686-2291; 8AM-2PM Only real estate related UCC filed here; info or copy request (per debtor)-. Will not search real estate records. UCC copy- $2.00 per page. Payee: Philadelphia County Recorder of Deeds. **Online Access to Property, Assessor, Death records:** Search property assessment data for free at http://brtweb.phila.gov/index.aspx. No name searching. Also, deeper data and name searching is by subscription at http://currentstatus.com, a private company. Also, search the Philadelphia area obituaries for free at www.legacy.com/philly/LegacyHome.asp. **Other phones:** Assessor-215-686-4334; Treasurer-215-686-2312.

Pike County Prothonotary

County Prothonotary, 412 Broad St, Milford, PA 18337. **Phone**-570-296-7231; fax-none; hours 8:30AM-4:30PM

Will not search UCC or tax liens records. Cert fee: $5.00 per doc, no copy cost. Payee: Pike County Prothonotary. **Online Access to Tax Lien records:** Online search: see Register of Deeds. **Other phones:** Assessor-570-296-3417; Elections-570-296-3426.

Pike County Recorder

County Recorder of Deeds, 506 Broad St, Milford, PA 18337. **Phone**-570-296-3508; fax-570-296-3514; hours 8:30AM-4:30PM

Only real estate related UCC filed here; info or copy request (per debtor)- $100.00. Will not search real estate records. RE record copy- $.50 per page. Cert fee: $5.00 up to 4 pg, $.50 addl pg. Payee: Pike County Recorder of Deeds. **Online Access to Probate records:** Access is through a private company. For information, call Infocon at 814-472-6066 or www.ic-access.com. **Other phones:** Assessor-570-296-3417; Treasurer-570-296-3441.

Potter County Prothonotary

County Prothonotary, 1 E. 2nd St, Rm 23, Courthouse, Coudersport, PA 16915. **Phone**-814-274-9740, R/E Recording-814-274-8370; fax-814-274-3361; hours 8:30AM-4:30PM

UCC records information or copy request (per debtor)- $59.00. Will not search tax liens. UCC copy- $.25 per page. **Online Access to Tax Lien records:** Online search: see Register of Deeds. **Other phones:** Assessor-814-274-0488; Treasurer-814-274-9775; Elections-814-274-8467; Vital Records-814-274-9740.

Potter County Recorder

County Recorder of Deeds, Courthouse, Rm 20, Coudersport, PA 16915. **Phone**-814-274-8370; fax-814-274-3360; hours 8:30AM-4:30PM

Will not name search UCC records. Information or copy request (per debtor)- $57.00. Will not search real estate records. UCC copy- $1.00 per page. Cert fee: $1.50 per cert. Payee: Potter County Recorder of Deeds. **Online Access to Real Estate, Assessor, Probate records:** Access is through a private company. For information, call Infocon at 814-472-6066 or www.ic-access.com. **Other phones:** Assessor-814-247-0488; Treasurer-814-274-9775.

Schuylkill County Prothonotary

County Prothonotary, 401 N. Second St., Pottsville, PA 17901-2520. **Phone**-570-628-1270, R/E Recording-570-628-1480; fax-570-628-1261; 8:30AM-4:30PM

UCC records information or copy request (per debtor)- $57.00. Tax liens not included in UCC search. Tax lien search- $5.00 per 5 years. UCC copy- $.25 per page. Cert fee: $4.00. Payee: Schuylkill County Prothonotary. **Other phones:** Assessor-570-628-1025; Treasurer-570-628-1433; Elections-570-628-3040.

Schuylkill County Recorder

County Recorder of Deeds, 401 N. Second St., Pottsville, PA 17901. **Phone**-County Recorder of Deeds, R/E & UCC Recording- 570-628-1480; hours 8:30AM-4:30PM. Will not search UCC or real estate records. UCC copy- $8.00 per doc. Cert fee: $1.50 per cert. Payee: Schuylkill County Recorder of Deeds. **Other phones:** Assessor-570-628-1024; Treasurer-570-628-1433.

Snyder County Prothonotary

County Prothonotary, PO Box 217, Middleburg, PA 17842-0217. **Phone**-570-837-4202; fax-570-837-4275; hours 8:30AM-4PM. Will not search UCC or tax liens records. UCC copy- $.35 per page. Cert fee: $4.50. Payee: Snyder County Prothonotary. **Other phones:** Assessor-570-837-4216.

Snyder County Recorder

County Recorder of Deeds, PO Box 217, Middleburg, PA 17842-0217. **Phone**-County Recorder of Deeds, R/E & UCC Recording- 570-837-4225; fax-570-837-4299; hours 8:30AM-4PM

Will not search UCC or real estate records. RE record copy- $1.00 per page. Cert fee: $1.50 per cert. Payee: Snyder County Recorder of Deeds. **Other phones:** Assessor-570-837-4218; Treasurer-570-837-4221.

Somerset County Prothonotary

County Prothonotary, 111 E. Union St, #190, Somerset, PA 15501. **Phone**-814-445-1428, R/E Recording-814-445-1547; fax-814-444-9270; hours 8:30AM-4PM UCC records information or copy request (per debtor)- $59.00. Will not search tax liens. RE record copy- $.50 per copy. UCC copy- $.50 per page. Payee: Somerset County Prothonotary. **Other phones:** Assessor-814-445-1536; Treasurer-814-445-1482; Elections-814-445-1549.

Somerset County Recorder

County Recorder of Deeds, 300 N Center Ave, #400, #140, Somerset, PA 15501. **Phone**-County Recorder of Deeds, R/E & UCC Recording- 814-445-1547; fax-814-445-1563; hours 8:30AM-4PM

Will search UCC records. Will not search real estate records. RE record copy- $.50 per page. UCC copy- $2.00 per page. Cert fee: $2.00 per page. Payee: Somerset County Recorder of Deeds. **Other phones:** Assessor-814-445-1536; Treasurer-814-445-1482.

Sullivan County Prothonotary

County Prothonotary, Main St, Courthouse, Laporte, PA 18626. **Phone**-County Prothonotary, R/E & UCC Recording- 570-946-7351; fax-570-946-7105; hours 8:30AM-4PM. Will not search UCC or tax liens records. UCC copy- $.25 per page. Cert fee: $3.00. Payee: Sullivan County Prothonotary. **Other phones:** Assessor-570-946-5061; Treasurer-570-946-7331; Elections-570-946-5201.

Sullivan County Recorder

County Recorder of Deeds, Main St, Courthouse, Laporte, PA 18626. **Phone**-County Recorder of Deeds, R/E & UCC Recording- 570-946-7351; fax-570-946-7105; hours 8:30AM-4PM

Will not any search UCC records.Will not search real estate records. RE record copy- $.25 per page. UCC copy- $1.00 per financing statement. Cert fee: $3.00 per cert. Payee: Sullivan County Recorder of Deeds. **Other phones:** Assessor-570-946-5061; Treasurer-570-946-7331; Elections-570-946-5201.

Susquehanna County Prothonotary

County Prothonotary, PO Box 218, Montrose, PA 18801-0218. **Phone**-570-278-4600 x121, R/E Recording-570-278-4600 x112, UCC Recording-570-278-4600 x120; fax-570-278-4191; hours 9AM-4:30PM

Will search UCC records. UCC search per debtor- $59.00 per name. Will not search tax liens. UCC copy- $.25 per page. Cert fee: $7.50 per name. Payee: Prothonotary. **Online Access to Prothonotary records:** Access is through a private company. For information, call Infocon at 814-472-6066 or www.ic-access.com. **Other phones:** Assessor-570-278-4600 x151; Treasurer-570-278-4600 x130; Elections-570-278-4600 x220.

Susquehanna County Recorder

Recorder of Deeds, PO Box 218, Montrose, PA 18801. **Phone**-570-278-4600 x112/3, R/E Recording-570-278-4600 x112, UCC Recording-570-278-4600 x112; fax-570-278-2963; hours 8:30AM-4:30PM

Will not search UCC or real estate records. RE record copy- $2.00 per deed. UCC copy- $1.00 per page. Cert fee: $1.50 per doc. Payee: Recorder of Deeds. **Other phones:** Assessor-570-278-4600 x150; Treasurer-570-278-4600 x130; Vital Records-570-278-4600 x112.

Tioga County Prothonotary

County Prothonotary, 116 Main St, Courthouse, Wellsboro, PA 16901. **Phone**-570-724-9281, R/E Recording-570-724-9260; hours 9AM-4:30PM

Will not search UCC or tax liens records. Cert fee: $4.50 per cert. Payee: Tioga County Prothonotary. **Other phones:** Assessor-570-724-9117; Treasurer-570-724-9213; Elections-570-723-8230.

Tioga County Recorder

County Recorder of Deeds, 116 Main St, Courthouse, Wellsboro, PA 16901. **Phone**-570-724-9260, R/E Recording-570-724-1906; hours 9AM-4:30PM

Will not search UCC or real estate records. Record copy- $1.00 per page. Cert fee: $1.50 per cert. Payee: Tioga County Recorder of Deeds. **Online Access to Real Estate, Deed, Will records:** Access is through a private company at www.landex.com/remote/. Fee is $.20 per minute and $.50 per fax page. Recorders data goes back to 1977; images and wills go back to 2/1999. **Other phones:** Assessor-570-724-9117; Treasurer-570-723-9213.

Union County Prothonotary

County Prothonotary, 103 S. 2nd St, Courthouse, Lewisburg, PA 17837. **Phone**-570-524-8751, R/E Recording-570-524-8761, UCC Recording-570-524-8761; fax-570-524-1628; hours 8:30AM-4:30PM www.unionco.org

Will not search UCC or tax liens records. UCC copy-$2.00 per page. Cert fee: $5.00 per doc. Payee: Union County Prothonotary. **Other phones:** Assessor-570-524-8611; Treasurer-570-524-8781; Elections-570-524-8681.

Union County Recorder

County Recorder of Deeds, 103 S. 2nd St, Courthouse, Lewisburg, PA 17837-1996. **Phone**-570-524-8761; hours 8:30AM-4:15PM www.unionco.org

Will not any search UCC records.Will not search real estate records. RE record copy- $1.00 per page. Xerox copy only, payment required in advance using SASE. UCC copy- $1.00 per page. Cert fee: $1.50 per cert and $.25 per page. Payee: Union County Recorder of Deeds. **Other phones:** Assessor-570-524-8611; Treasurer-570-524-8781; Elections-570-524-8603.

Venango County Prothonotary

County Prothonotary, Courthouse, Franklin, PA 16323. **Phone**-814-432-9577, R/E Recording-814-432-9534, UCC Recording-814-432-9534; fax-814-432-9579; hours 8:30AM-4:30PM

UCC records information or copy request (per debtor)-$59.00. UCC search includes tax liens if requested. Separate federal/state combined tax lien search-$7.00 per debtor. Copy fee-$1.00 per page. UCC copy- $1.00 per page. Cert fee: $7.00 per name. Payee: Venango County Prothonotary. **Other phones:** Assessor-814-432-9515; Treasurer-814-432-9525; Elections-814-432-9514.

Venango County Recorder

County Recorder of Deeds, PO Box 831, Franklin, PA 16323. **Phone**-814-432-9539, R/E Recording-814-432-9535, UCC Recording-814-432-9535; fax-814-432-9569; hours-8:30AM-4:30PM www.co.venango.pa.us/Directory/index.htm

Will not search UCC or real estate records. Copy fee-$1.00 per page. Cert fee: $1.50 per page. Payee: Recorder of Deeds. **Other phones:** Assessor-814-432-9516; Treasurer-814-432-9525; Elections-814-432-9514; Vital Records-814-432-9535/1893/1905.

Warren County Prothonotary

County Prothonotary, 4th & Market Sts, Courthouse, Warren, PA 16365. **Phone**-814-723-7550, UCC Recording-814-723-7550 x4; fax-814-728-3459; hours 8:30AM-4:30PM. Will search UCC records. UCC

search per debtor- $5.00. Will not search tax liens. UCC copy- $.25 per page. Cert fee: $5.00. Payee: Warren County Prothonotary. **Other phones:** Treasurer-814-723-7550 x3.

Warren County Recorder

County Recorder of Deeds, 204 Fourth Ave, Courthouse, Warren, PA 16365. **Phone**-814-723-7550; hours 8:30AM-3:30PM

Will not search UCC or real estate records. RE record copy- $5.00 per doc by mail. UCC copy- $1.00 per page. Cert fee: $5.00 per cert. Payee: Warren County Recorder of Deeds. **Other phones:** Assessor-814-723-7550; Treasurer-814-723-7550.

Washington County Prothonotary

County Prothonotary, 1 S. Main St, #1001, Courthouse, Washington, PA 15301. **Phone**-724-228-6770, R/E Recording-724-228-6806; fax-724-229-5913; hours 9AM-4:30PM. UCC records information or copy request (per debtor)- $59.00. Will not search tax liens. UCC copy- $1.50 per page. Cert fee: $4.50 per seal. Payee: Washington County Prothonotary. **Other phones:** Assessor-724-228-6850; Treasurer-724-228-6780; Elections-724-228-6750.

Washington County Recorder

Recorder of Deeds, 1 S. Main St, Rm 1006, Washington County Courthouse, Washington, PA 15301. **Phone**-Recorder of Deeds, R/E & UCC Recording- 724-228-6806, UCC Recording-724-228-6770; fax-724-228-6737; hours 9AM-4:30PM www.co.washington.pa.us

Will not search UCC or real estate records. RE record copy- $10.00 per doc. UCC copy- $.50 per page. Cert fee: $10.00 and copies included. Payee: Recorder of Deeds. **Online Access to Assessor, Real Estate records:** Records are on the county online system. Records date back to 1952. Register of Wills information and lending agency information is also available. For information, call 724-228-6766. **Other phones:** Assessor-724-228-6850; Treasurer-724-228-6780; Elections-724-228-6750.

Wayne County Prothonotary

County Prothonotary, 925 Court St, Courthouse, Honesdale, PA 18431-1996. **Phone**-570-253-5970 x200/3, R/E Recording-570-253-5970 x212, UCC Recording-570-253-5970 x200; fax-570-253-0687; hours 8:30AM-4:30PM

UCC records information or copy request (per debtor)-$59.00. Will not search tax liens. UCC copy- $.50 per page. Payee: Wayne County Prothonotary. **Other phones:** Assessor-570-253-5970 x216; Treasurer-570-253-5970 x125; Elections-570-253-5970 x165; Vital Records-570-253-5970 x200.

Wayne County Recorder

County Recorder of Deeds, 925 Court St, Honesdale, PA 18431-1996. **Phone**-County Recorder of Deeds, R/E & UCC Recording- 570-253-5970 x212; hours 8:30AM-4:30PM www.co.wayne.pa.us/recorder.asp

Will not search UCC or real estate records. Copy fee-$.50 per page. Cert fee: $1.50 per doc. Payee: Wayne County Recorder of Deeds. **Other phones:** Assessor-570-253-5970 x216; Treasurer-570-253-5970 x125; Elections-570-253-5970 x165.

Westmoreland County Prothonotary

County Prothonotary, PO Box 1630, Greensburg, PA 15601. **Phone**-724-830-3516; hours 8:30AM-4PM Will not search UCC records. UCC copy- $1.00 per page. Cert fee: $5.35 per cert. Payee: Westmoreland County Prothonotary.

Westmoreland County Recorder

2 N Main St #203, Greensburg, PA 15601. **Phone**-724-830-3734, R/E Recording-724-830-3518, UCC Recording-724-830-3518; fax-724-850-3979. www.co.westmoreland.pa.us

UCC records information or copy request (per debtor)-$97.00. Will not search real estate records. **Online Access to Real Estate, Tax Lien, Mortgage, UCC, Deed records:** The Register's fee-based system has been replaced by a free, searchable site at www.wcdeeds.us/dts/default.asp. Choose simple, advanced, or instrument search. **Other phones:** Assessor-724-830-3490; Treasurer-724-830-3173; Elections-724-830-3150.

Wyoming County Prothonotary

County Prothonotary, 1 Courthouse Sq, Wyoming County Courthouse, Tunkhannock, PA 18657-1219. **Phone**-717-836-3200, R/E Recording-717-836-3200 x235; hours 8:30AM-4PM

Will not search UCC or tax liens records. UCC copy- $.25 per copy. Cert fee: $7.00 per cert. Payee: Wyoming County Prothonotary. **Other phones:** Assessor-717-836-3200; Treasurer-717-836-3200; Elections-717-836-3200; Vital Records-717-836-3200.

Wyoming County Recorder

County Recorder of Deeds, 1 Courthouse Sq, Tunkhannock, PA 18657. **Phone**-570-996-2361, R/E Recording-717-836-3200; hours 8:30AM-4PM

Will not search UCC or real estate records. UCC copy- $.25 per page. Cert fee: $5.00 per cert. Payee: Wyoming County Recorder of Deeds. **Other phones:** Assessor-717-836-3200 x261; Treasurer-717-836-3200 x287.

York County Prothonotary

County Prothonotary, 28 E. Market St, York, PA 17401. **Phone**-717-771-9611, R/E Recording-717-771-9806, UCC Recording-717-771-9608; fax-717-771-4629; hours 8AM-5PM www.york-county.org

Will not search UCC or tax liens records. Copy fee-$1.00 per page. Cert fee: $5.25 per 1st page, $1.75 each add'l. **Other phones:** Assessor-717-771-9232; Treasurer-717-771-9603; Elections-717-771-9604.

York County Recorder

Recorder of Deeds, 28 E. Market St, York, PA 17401. **Phone**-717-771-9295; fax-717-771-9582; hours 8AM-4:30PM

www.york-county.org/departments/deeds/deeds.htm

Will not search UCC records. Will search real estate records. Record copy- $.50 per page. **Online Access to Assessor, Real Estate, Deed, Death, Inmate, Naturalization records:** Two sources are available. Online access to the assessors database is free through the GIS data at http://207.140.67.68/york. Also, access is by subscription from Landex at www.landex.com/remote. Base fee is $.20 per minute, $.50 per fax page. Records go back to 1990; images to 1990. Search inmate list at www.york-county.org/departments/prison/prison.htm. Search most wanted list at www.york-county.org/departments/sheriff/Sheriff_home.htm. Also, search parcel numbers at www.york-county.org/departments/assessment/tx_asmnt.htm. Search the death index prior to 1959 at www.york-county.org/cgi-bin/Affdeath.cgi; naturalizations at www.york-county.org/cgi-bin/natural.cgi. **Other phones:** Assessor-717-771-9220; Treasurer-717-771-9603.

Pennsylvania County Locator

You will usually be able to find the city name in the City/County Cross Reference below. In that case, it is a simple matter to determine the county from the cross reference. However, only the official US Postal Service city names are included in this index. There are an additional 40,000 place names that people use in their addresses. Therefore, we have also included a ZIP/City Cross Reference immediately following the City/County Cross Reference.

If you know the ZIP Code but the city name does not appear in the City/County Cross Reference index, look up the ZIP Code in the ZIP/City Cross Reference, find the city name, then look up the city name in the City/County Cross Reference. For example, you want to know the county for an address of Menands, NY 12204. There is no "Menands" in the City/County Cross Reference. The ZIP/City Cross Reference shows that ZIP Codes 12201-12288 are for the city of Albany. Looking back in the City/County Cross Reference, Albany is in Albany County.

Pennsylvania City/County Cross Reference

AARONSBURG Centre
ABBOTTSTOWN (17301) Adams(97), York(2)
ABINGTON Montgomery
ACKERMANVILLE Northampton
ACME (15610) Westmoreland(96), Fayette(3)
ACOSTA Somerset
ADAH Fayette
ADAMSBURG Westmoreland
ADAMSTOWN Lancaster
ADAMSVILLE (16110) Crawford(90), Mercer(9)
ADDISON Somerset
ADRIAN Armstrong
AIRVILLE York
AKRON Lancaster
ALBA Bradford
ALBION (16401) Erie(91), Crawford(8)
ALBION Erie
ALBRIGHTSVILLE (18210) Carbon(90), Monroe(9)
ALBURTIS (18011) Berks(61), Lehigh(38)
ALDENVILLE Wayne
ALEPPO Greene
ALEXANDRIA Huntingdon
ALIQUIPPA Beaver
ALLENPORT Washington
ALLENSVILLE (17002) Mifflin(87), Huntingdon(12)
ALLENTOWN (18109) Lehigh(97), Northampton(2)
ALLENTOWN Lehigh
ALLENWOOD (17810) Lycoming(63), Union(36)
ALLISON Fayette
ALLISON PARK Allegheny
ALLPORT Clearfield
ALTOONA Blair
ALUM BANK Bedford
ALVERDA Indiana
ALVERTON Westmoreland
AMBERSON Franklin
AMBLER Montgomery
AMBRIDGE (15003) Beaver(95), Allegheny(4)
AMITY Washington
ANALOMINK Monroe
ANDREAS (18211) Schuylkill(84), Carbon(15)
ANITA Jefferson
ANNVILLE Lebanon
ANTES FORT Lycoming
APOLLO (15613) Westmoreland(50), Armstrong(49)
AQUASHICOLA Carbon
ARCADIA Indiana
ARCHBALD Lackawanna
ARCOLA Montgomery
ARDARA Westmoreland
ARDMORE (19003) Montgomery(62), Delaware(37)
ARENDTSVILLE Adams

ARISTES Columbia
ARMAGH Indiana
ARMBRUST Westmoreland
ARNOT Tioga
ARONA Westmoreland
ARTEMAS Bedford
ASHFIELD Carbon
ASHLAND Schuylkill
ASHVILLE (16613) Cambria(98), Blair(1)
ASPERS Adams
ASTON Delaware
ATGLEN (19310) Chester(98), Lancaster(1)
ATHENS Bradford
ATLANTIC Crawford
ATLASBURG Washington
AUBURN Schuylkill
AUDUBON Montgomery
AULTMAN Indiana
AUSTIN (16720) Potter(58), Cameron(36), McKean(5)
AVELLA Washington
AVIS Clinton
AVONDALE Chester
AVONMORE Westmoreland
BADEN (15005) Beaver(87), Allegheny(12)
BAINBRIDGE Lancaster
BAIRDFORD Allegheny
BAKERS SUMMIT Bedford
BAKERSTOWN Allegheny
BALA CYNWYD Montgomery
BALLY Berks
BANGOR Northampton
BARNESBORO (15714) Cambria(79), Indiana(20)
BARNESVILLE Schuylkill
BART Lancaster
BARTO (19504) Berks(67), Montgomery(32)
BARTONSVILLE Monroe
BATH Northampton
BAUSMAN Lancaster
BEACH HAVEN Luzerne
BEACH LAKE (18405) Wayne(96), Pike(3)
BEALLSVILLE Washington
BEAR CREEK Luzerne
BEAR LAKE Warren
BEAVER FALLS Beaver
BEAVER MEADOWS (18216) Luzerne(69), Carbon(30)
BEAVER SPRINGS Snyder
BEAVERDALE Cambria
BEAVERTOWN Snyder
BECCARIA Clearfield
BECHTELSVILLE (19505) Berks(94), Montgomery(5)
BEDFORD Bedford
BEDMINSTER Bucks
BEECH CREEK (16822) Clinton(91), Centre(8)
BELLE VERNON (15012) Fayette(56), Westmoreland(41), Washington(1)
BELLEFONTE Centre

BELLEVILLE Mifflin
BELLWOOD Blair
BELSANO Cambria
BENDERSVILLE Adams
BENEZETT Elk
BENSALEM Bucks
BENTLEYVILLE Washington
BENTON (17814) Columbia(62), Luzerne(29), Lycoming(4), Sullivan(3)
BERLIN Somerset
BERNVILLE Berks
BERRYSBURG Dauphin
BERWICK (18603) Columbia(79), Luzerne(20)
BERWYN Chester
BESSEMER Lawrence
BETHEL Berks
BETHEL PARK Allegheny
BETHLEHEM (18018) Lehigh(52), Northampton(47)
BETHLEHEM (18017) Northampton(94), Lehigh(5)
BETHLEHEM Lehigh
BETHLEHEM Northampton
BEYER Indiana
BIG COVE TANNERY Fulton
BIG RUN Jefferson
BIGLER Clearfield
BIGLERVILLE (17307) Adams(98), Cumberland(1)
BIRCHRUNVILLE Chester
BIRD IN HAND Lancaster
BIRDSBORO Berks
BLACK LICK Indiana
BLAIN Perry
BLAIRS MILLS Huntingdon
BLAIRSVILLE (15717) Indiana(88), Westmoreland(11)
BLAKESLEE (18610) Monroe(98), Luzerne(1)
BLANCHARD Centre
BLANDBURG Cambria
BLANDON Berks
BLOOMING GLEN Bucks
BLOOMSBURG Columbia
BLOSSBURG Tioga
BLUE BALL Lancaster
BLUE BELL Montgomery
BLUE RIDGE SUMMIT Franklin
BOALSBURG Centre
BOBTOWN Greene
BODINES Lycoming
BOILING SPRINGS Cumberland
BOLIVAR Westmoreland
BOSWELL Somerset
BOVARD Westmoreland
BOWERS Berks
BOWMANSDALE Cumberland
BOWMANSTOWN Carbon
BOWMANSVILLE Lancaster
BOYERS Butler
BOYERTOWN (19512) Berks(95), Montgomery(4)

BOYNTON Somerset
BRACKENRIDGE Allegheny
BRACKNEY Susquehanna
BRADDOCK Allegheny
BRADENVILLE Westmoreland
BRADFORD McKean
BRADFORDWOODS Allegheny
BRANCHDALE Schuylkill
BRANCHTON Butler
BRANDAMORE Chester
BRANDY CAMP Elk
BRAVE Greene
BREEZEWOOD (15533) Bedford(94), Fulton(5)
BREINIGSVILLE Lehigh
BRIDGEPORT Montgomery
BRIDGEVILLE (15017) Allegheny(97), Washington(2)
BRIER HILL Fayette
BRISBIN Clearfield
BRISTOL Bucks
BROAD TOP Huntingdon
BROCKPORT (15823) Elk(81), Jefferson(18)
BROCKTON Schuylkill
BROCKWAY (15824) Jefferson(97), Clearfield(2)
BRODHEADSVILLE Monroe
BROGUE York
BROOKHAVEN Delaware
BROOKLYN Susquehanna
BROOKVILLE Jefferson
BROOMALL Delaware
BROWNFIELD Fayette
BROWNSTOWN Lancaster
BROWNSVILLE (15417) Fayette(62), Washington(37)
BRUIN Butler
BRUSH VALLEY Indiana
BRYN ATHYN Montgomery
BRYN MAWR (19010) Delaware(53), Montgomery(46)
BUCK HILL FALLS Monroe
BUCKINGHAM Bucks
BUENA VISTA Allegheny
BUFFALO MILLS (15534) Bedford(98), Somerset(1)
BULGER Washington
BUNOLA Allegheny
BURGETTSTOWN Washington
BURLINGTON Bradford
BURNHAM Mifflin
BURNSIDE Clearfield
BURNT CABINS (17215) Fulton(82), Huntingdon(17)
BUSHKILL Pike
BUTLER Butler
BYRNEDALE Elk
CABOT Butler
CADOGAN Armstrong
CAIRNBROOK Somerset
CALIFORNIA Washington
CALLENSBURG Clarion

CALLERY Butler
CALUMET Westmoreland
CALVIN Huntingdon
CAMBRA Luzerne
CAMBRIDGE SPRINGS (16403) Crawford(93), Erie(6)
CAMP HILL (17011) Cumberland(98), York(1)
CAMP HILL Cumberland
CAMP HILL Lebanon
CAMPBELLTOWN Lebanon
CAMPTOWN Bradford
CANADENSIS (18325) Monroe(63), Pike(36)
CANONSBURG Washington
CANTON (17724) Bradford(82), Tioga(7), Sullivan(7), Lycoming(3)
CARBONDALE Lackawanna
CARDALE Fayette
CARLISLE Cumberland
CARLTON (16311) Mercer(87), Venango(12)
CARMICHAELS Greene
CARNEGIE Allegheny
CARROLLTOWN Cambria
CARVERSVILLE Bucks
CASHTOWN Adams
CASSANDRA Cambria
CASSVILLE Huntingdon
CASTANEA Clinton
CATASAUQUA (18032) Lehigh(68), Northampton(31)
CATAWISSA (17820) Columbia(96), Montour(3)
CECIL Washington
CEDAR RUN Lycoming
CEDARS Montgomery
CENTER VALLEY Lehigh
CENTERPORT Berks
CENTERVILLE Crawford
CENTRAL CITY Somerset
CENTRALIA Columbia
CENTRE HALL Centre
CHADDS FORD (19317) Delaware(63), Chester(36)
CHALFONT Bucks
CHALK HILL Fayette
CHALKHILL Fayette
CHAMBERSBURG Franklin
CHAMBERSVILLE Indiana
CHAMPION (15622) Westmoreland(84), Fayette(8), Somerset(7)
CHANDLERS VALLEY Warren
CHARLEROI Washington
CHATHAM Chester
CHELTENHAM Montgomery
CHERRY TREE (15724) Indiana(66), Clearfield(26), Cambria(7)
CHERRYVILLE Northampton
CHEST SPRINGS Cambria
CHESTER Delaware
CHESTER HEIGHTS Delaware
CHESTER SPRINGS Chester
CHESTNUT RIDGE Fayette
CHESWICK Allegheny
CHEYNEY (19319) Delaware(97), Chester(2)
CHICORA (16025) Butler(81), Armstrong(18)
CHINCHILLA Lackawanna
CHRISTIANA Lancaster
CLAIRTON Allegheny
CLARENCE Centre
CLARENDON Warren
CLARIDGE Westmoreland
CLARINGTON (15828) Jefferson(92), Forest(5), Elk(2)
CLARION Clarion
CLARK Mercer
CLARKS MILLS Mercer
CLARKS SUMMIT Lackawanna
CLARKSBURG Indiana

CLARKSVILLE (15322) Washington(56), Greene(43)
CLAYSBURG (16625) Bedford(75), Blair(24)
CLAYSVILLE Washington
CLEARFIELD Clearfield
CLEARVILLE Bedford
CLIFFORD Susquehanna
CLIFTON HEIGHTS Delaware
CLIMAX Armstrong
CLINTON (15026) Beaver(78), Allegheny(15), Washington(6)
CLINTONVILLE Venango
CLUNE Indiana
CLYMER Indiana
COAL CENTER Washington
COAL TOWNSHIP Northumberland
COALDALE Schuylkill
COALPORT (16627) Clearfield(93), Cambria(6)
COATESVILLE Chester
COBURN Centre
COCHRANTON (16314) Crawford(90), Mercer(6), Venango(3)
COCHRANVILLE Chester
COCOLAMUS Juniata
CODORUS York
COGAN STATION Lycoming
COKEBURG Washington
COLEBROOK Lebanon
COLLEGEVILLE Montgomery
COLMAR Montgomery
COLUMBIA Lancaster
COLUMBIA CROSS ROADS (16914) Bradford(93), Tioga(6)
COLUMBUS Warren
COLVER Cambria
COMMODORE Indiana
CONCORD Franklin
CONCORDVILLE Delaware
CONESTOGA Lancaster
CONFLUENCE (15424) Somerset(77), Fayette(22)
CONNEAUT LAKE Crawford
CONNEAUTVILLE Crawford
CONNELLSVILLE Fayette
CONNOQUENESSING Butler
CONSHOHOCKEN Montgomery
CONWAY Beaver
CONYNGHAM Luzerne
COOKSBURG (16217) Clarion(91), Forest(8)
COOLSPRING Jefferson
COOPERSBURG (18036) Lehigh(88), Bucks(11)
COOPERSTOWN (16317) Venango(93), Crawford(6)
COPLAY Lehigh
CORAL Indiana
CORAOPOLIS Allegheny
CORNWALL Lebanon
CORRY (16407) Erie(87), Warren(7), Crawford(5)
CORSICA (15829) Jefferson(74), Clarion(25)
COUDERSPORT Potter
COULTERS Allegheny
COUPON Cambria
COURTNEY Washington
COVINGTON Tioga
COWANESQUE Tioga
COWANSVILLE Armstrong
CRABTREE Westmoreland
CRALEY York
CRANBERRY (16319) Venango(60), Clarion(39)
CRANBERRY TWP Butler
CRANESVILLE Erie
CREAMERY Montgomery
CREEKSIDE (15732) Indiana(92), Armstrong(4), Allegheny(2)
CREIGHTON Allegheny
CRESCENT Allegheny

CRESCO (18326) Monroe(98), Pike(1)
CRESSON Cambria
CRESSONA Schuylkill
CROSBY McKean
CROSS FORK (17729) Clinton(59), Potter(40)
CROWN Clarion
CROYDON Bucks
CRUCIBLE Greene
CRUM LYNNE Delaware
CRYSTAL SPRING Fulton
CUDDY Allegheny
CUMBOLA Schuylkill
CURLLSVILLE Clarion
CURRYVILLE Blair
CURTISVILLE Allegheny
CURWENSVILLE Clearfield
CUSTER CITY McKean
CYCLONE McKean
DAGUS MINES Elk
DAISYTOWN Washington
DALLAS (18612) Luzerne(97), Wyoming(2)
DALLAS Luzerne
DALLASTOWN York
DALMATIA (17017) Northumberland(64), Dauphin(35)
DALTON (18414) Lackawanna(78), Wyoming(21)
DAMASCUS Wayne
DANBORO Bucks
DANIELSVILLE Northampton
DANVILLE (17821) Montour(82), Northumberland(16), Columbia(1)
DANVILLE Montour
DARBY Delaware
DARLINGTON Beaver
DARRAGH Westmoreland
DAUBERVILLE Berks
DAUPHIN Dauphin
DAVIDSVILLE Somerset
DAWSON Fayette
DAYTON (16222) Armstrong(66), Jefferson(16), Indiana(16)
DE LANCEY Jefferson
DE YOUNG Elk
DEFIANCE Bedford
DELANO Schuylkill
DELAWARE WATER GAP Monroe
DELMONT Westmoreland
DELTA York
DENBO Washington
DENVER Lancaster
DERRICK CITY McKean
DERRY Westmoreland
DEVAULT Chester
DEVON Chester
DEWART Northumberland
DICKERSON RUN Fayette
DICKINSON Cumberland
DICKSON CITY Lackawanna
DILLINER Greene
DILLSBURG York
DILLTOWN Indiana
DIMOCK Susquehanna
DINGMANS FERRY Pike
DISTANT Armstrong
DIXONVILLE Indiana
DONEGAL Westmoreland
DONORA Washington
DORNSIFE (17823) Northumberland(98), Schuylkill(1)
DOUGLASSVILLE Berks
DOVER York
DOWNINGTOWN Chester
DOYLESBURG Franklin
DOYLESTOWN Bucks
DRAVOSBURG Allegheny
DRESHER Montgomery
DREXEL HILL Delaware
DRIFTING Clearfield
DRIFTON Luzerne
DRIFTWOOD (15832) Cameron(85), Elk(14)

DRUMORE Lancaster
DRUMS Luzerne
DRY RUN Franklin
DU BOIS Clearfield
DUBLIN Bucks
DUDLEY Huntingdon
DUKE CENTER McKean
DUNBAR Fayette
DUNCANNON Perry
DUNCANSVILLE Blair
DUNLEVY Washington
DUNLO Cambria
DUQUESNE Allegheny
DURHAM Bucks
DURYEA Luzerne
DUSHORE (18614) Sullivan(94), Wyoming(3), Bradford(1)
DYSART (16636) Cambria(90), Blair(9)
EAGLES MERE Sullivan
EAGLEVILLE Montgomery
EARLINGTON Montgomery
EARLVILLE Berks
EAST BERLIN (17316) Adams(81), York(18)
EAST BRADY (16028) Clarion(84), Armstrong(15)
EAST BUTLER Butler
EAST EARL Lancaster
EAST FREEDOM Blair
EAST GREENVILLE (18041) Montgomery(70), Lehigh(23), Bucks(3), Berks(2)
EAST HICKORY Forest
EAST MC KEESPORT Allegheny
EAST MILLSBORO Fayette
EAST PETERSBURG Lancaster
EAST PITTSBURGH Allegheny
EAST PROSPECT York
EAST SMETHPORT McKean
EAST SMITHFIELD Bradford
EAST SPRINGFIELD Erie
EAST STROUDSBURG Monroe
EAST TEXAS Lehigh
EAST VANDERGRIFT Westmoreland
EAST WATERFORD (17021) Juniata(87), Huntingdon(6), Franklin(3), Perry(2)
EASTON Northampton
EAU CLAIRE Butler
EBENSBURG Cambria
EBERVALE Luzerne
EDGEMONT Delaware
EDINBORO (16412) Erie(76), Crawford(23)
EDINBORO Erie
EDINBURG Lawrence
EDMON Armstrong
EFFORT Monroe
EIGHTY FOUR Washington
ELCO Washington
ELDERSVILLE Washington
ELDERTON Armstrong
ELDRED McKean
ELGIN Erie
ELIZABETH Allegheny
ELIZABETHTOWN (17022) Lancaster(90), Dauphin(9)
ELIZABETHVILLE Dauphin
ELKINS PARK Montgomery
ELKLAND Tioga
ELLIOTTSBURG Perry
ELLSWORTH Washington
ELLWOOD CITY (16117) Lawrence(67), Beaver(32)
ELM Lancaster
ELMHURST Lackawanna
ELMORA Cambria
ELRAMA Washington
ELTON Cambria
ELVERSON (19520) Chester(69), Berks(30)
ELYSBURG (17824) Northumberland(81), Columbia(17), Montour(1)
EMEIGH Cambria
EMIGSVILLE York

EMLENTON (16373) Venango(49), Clarion(47), Butler(3)
EMMAUS Lehigh
EMPORIUM (15834) Cameron(97), Elk(1)
ENDEAVOR Forest
ENOLA Cumberland
ENON VALLEY (16120) Lawrence(94), Beaver(5)
ENTRIKEN Huntingdon
EPHRATA Lancaster
EQUINUNK Wayne
ERIE Erie
ERNEST Indiana
ERWINNA Bucks
ESSINGTON Delaware
ETTERS York
EVANS CITY Butler
EVERETT Bedford
EVERSON Fayette
EXCELSIOR Northumberland
EXPORT Westmoreland
EXTON Chester
FACTORYVILLE (18419) Wyoming(79), Lackawanna(20)
FAIRBANK Fayette
FAIRCHANCE Fayette
FAIRFIELD Adams
FAIRHOPE Somerset
FAIRLESS HILLS Bucks
FAIRMOUNT CITY Clarion
FAIRVIEW Erie
FAIRVIEW VILLAGE Montgomery
FALLENTIMBER (16639) Cambria(83), Clearfield(16)
FALLS (18615) Wyoming(90), Luzerne(7), Lackawanna(2)
FALLS CREEK (15840) Jefferson(96), Clearfield(3)
FANNETTSBURG Franklin
FARMINGTON Fayette
FARRANDSVILLE Clinton
FARRELL Mercer
FAWN GROVE York
FAYETTE CITY Fayette
FAYETTEVILLE (17222) Franklin(94), Adams(5)
FEASTERVILLE TREVOSE Bucks
FELTON York
FENELTON Butler
FERNDALE Bucks
FINLEYVILLE (15332) Washington(92), Allegheny(7)
FIRST NAT BANK Erie
FISHER Clarion
FISHERTOWN Bedford
FLEETVILLE Lackawanna
FLEETWOOD Berks
FLEMING Centre
FLICKSVILLE Northampton
FLINTON Cambria
FLOURTOWN Montgomery
FOGELSVILLE Lehigh
FOLCROFT Delaware
FOLSOM Delaware
FOMBELL (16123) Beaver(69), Lawrence(30)
FORBES ROAD Westmoreland
FORCE Elk
FORD CITY Armstrong
FORD CLIFF Armstrong
FOREST CITY (18421) Susquehanna(47), Wayne(31), Lackawanna(20)
FOREST GROVE Bucks
FORESTVILLE Butler
FORKSVILLE Sullivan
FORT HILL Somerset
FORT LITTLETON Fulton
FORT LOUDON Franklin
FORT WASHINGTON Bucks
FORT WASHINGTON Montgomery
FOUNTAINVILLE Bucks
FOXBURG Clarion
FRACKVILLE Schuylkill

FRANCONIA Montgomery
FRANKLIN Venango
FRANKLINTOWN York
FREDERICK Montgomery
FREDERICKSBURG (17026) Lebanon(90), Berks(9)
FREDERICKTOWN Washington
FREDONIA Mercer
FREEBURG Snyder
FREEDOM Beaver
FREELAND Luzerne
FREEPORT (16229) Armstrong(64), Butler(23), Westmoreland(10), Allegheny(1)
FRENCHVILLE Clearfield
FRIEDENS Somerset
FRIEDENSBURG Schuylkill
FRIENDSVILLE Susquehanna
FROSTBURG Jefferson
FRYBURG Clarion
FURLONG Bucks
GAINES (16921) Tioga(96), Potter(3)
GALETON Potter
GALLITZIN (16641) Cambria(96), Blair(3)
GANS Fayette
GAP (17527) Lancaster(91), Chester(8)
GARARDS FORT Greene
GARDENVILLE Bucks
GARDNERS (17324) Adams(66), Cumberland(33)
GARLAND Warren
GARRETT Somerset
GASTONVILLE Washington
GEIGERTOWN Berks
GENESEE Potter
GEORGETOWN Beaver
GERMANSVILLE Lehigh
GETTYSBURG Adams
GIBBON GLADE Fayette
GIBSON Susquehanna
GIBSONIA (15044) Allegheny(95), Butler(4)
GIFFORD McKean
GILBERT Monroe
GILBERTON Schuylkill
GILBERTSVILLE Montgomery
GILLETT Bradford
GIPSY Indiana
GIRARD Erie
GIRARDVILLE Schuylkill
GLADWYNE Montgomery
GLASGOW Cambria
GLASSPORT Allegheny
GLEN CAMPBELL (15742) Indiana(91), Clearfield(8)
GLEN HOPE Clearfield
GLEN LYON Luzerne
GLEN MILLS (19342) Delaware(98), Chester(1)
GLEN RICHEY Clearfield
GLEN RIDDLE LIMA Delaware
GLEN ROCK York
GLENMOORE Chester
GLENOLDEN Delaware
GLENSHAW Allegheny
GLENSIDE Montgomery
GLENVILLE York
GLENWILLARD Allegheny
GOODVILLE Lancaster
GORDON Schuylkill
GORDONVILLE Lancaster
GOULDSBORO (18424) Wayne(54), Lackawanna(38), Luzerne(3), Monroe(2)
GOWEN CITY Northumberland
GRADYVILLE Delaware
GRAMPIAN Clearfield
GRAND VALLEY (16420) Warren(81), Crawford(17), Jefferson(1)
GRANTHAM Cumberland
GRANTVILLE (17028) Dauphin(80), Lebanon(19)
GRANVILLE Mifflin
GRANVILLE SUMMIT Bradford
GRAPEVILLE Westmoreland

GRASSFLAT Clearfield
GRATZ Dauphin
GRAY Somerset
GRAYSVILLE Greene
GREAT BEND Susquehanna
GREELEY Pike
GREEN LANE (18054) Montgomery(83), Bucks(16)
GREEN PARK Perry
GREENCASTLE Franklin
GREENOCK Allegheny
GREENSBURG Westmoreland
GREENTOWN Pike
GREENVILLE (16125) Mercer(95), Crawford(4)
GRINDSTONE Fayette
GROVE CITY (16127) Mercer(93), Venango(5)
GROVER Bradford
GUYS MILLS Crawford
GWYNEDD Montgomery
GWYNEDD VALLEY Montgomery
HADLEY Mercer
HALIFAX Dauphin
HALLSTEAD Susquehanna
HAMBURG Berks
HAMILTON Jefferson
HAMLIN Wayne
HANNASTOWN Westmoreland
HANOVER (17331) York(83), Adams(16)
HANOVER York
HARBORCREEK Erie
HARFORD Susquehanna
HARLEIGH Luzerne
HARLEYSVILLE Montgomery
HARMONSBURG Crawford
HARMONY (16037) Butler(82), Lawrence(13), Beaver(3)
HARRISBURG Dauphin
HARRISON CITY Westmoreland
HARRISON VALLEY Potter
HARRISONVILLE Fulton
HARRISVILLE (16038) Venango(53), Butler(46)
HARTLETON Union
HARTSTOWN Crawford
HARVEYS LAKE (18618) Luzerne(86), Wyoming(13)
HARWICK Allegheny
HASTINGS (16646) Cambria(95), Clearfield(4)
HATBORO (19040) Montgomery(96), Bucks(3)
HATFIELD (19440) Montgomery(91), Bucks(8)
HAVERFORD (19041) Montgomery(73), Delaware(26)
HAVERTOWN Delaware
HAWK RUN Clearfield
HAWLEY (18428) Wayne(64), Pike(35)
HAWTHORN Clarion
HAZEL HURST McKean
HAZLETON Luzerne
HEGINS Schuylkill
HEILWOOD Indiana
HELFENSTEIN Schuylkill
HELLERTOWN (18055) Northampton(97), Bucks(2)
HENDERSONVILLE Washington
HENRYVILLE Monroe
HEREFORD Berks
HERMAN Butler
HERMINIE Westmoreland
HERMITAGE Mercer
HERNDON (17830) Northumberland(98), Dauphin(1)
HERRICK CENTER Susquehanna
HERSHEY (17033) Dauphin(96), Lebanon(3)
HESSTON Huntingdon
HIBBS Fayette
HICKORY Washington
HIDDEN VALLEY Somerset

HIGHSPIRE Dauphin
HILLER Fayette
HILLIARDS Butler
HILLSDALE Indiana
HILLSGROVE (18619) Sullivan(81), Lycoming(18)
HILLSVILLE Lawrence
HILLTOWN Bucks
HOLBROOK Greene
HOLICONG Bucks
HOLLIDAYSBURG Blair
HOLLSOPPLE Somerset
HOLMES Delaware
HOLTWOOD Lancaster
HOME Indiana
HOMER CITY Indiana
HOMESTEAD Allegheny
HONEY BROOK (19344) Chester(89), Lancaster(10)
HONEY GROVE (17035) Juniata(98), Perry(1)
HOOKSTOWN Beaver
HOOVERSVILLE Somerset
HOP BOTTOM Susquehanna
HOPELAND Lancaster
HOPEWELL Bedford
HOPWOOD Fayette
HORSHAM Montgomery
HOSTETTER Westmoreland
HOUSTON Washington
HOUTZDALE Clearfield
HOWARD Centre
HUGHESVILLE Lycoming
HUMMELS WHARF Snyder
HUMMELSTOWN Dauphin
HUNKER Westmoreland
HUNLOCK CREEK Luzerne
HUNTINGDON Huntingdon
HUNTINGDON VALLEY (19006) Montgomery(91), Bucks(8)
HUNTINGTON MILLS Luzerne
HUSTONTOWN (17229) Fulton(93), Huntingdon(6)
HUTCHINSON Westmoreland
HYDE Clearfield
HYDE PARK Westmoreland
HYDETOWN Crawford
HYNDMAN (15545) Bedford(77), Somerset(22)
HYNER Clinton
ICKESBURG Perry
IDAVILLE Adams
IMLER (16655) Bedford(98), Blair(1)
IMMACULATA Chester
IMPERIAL Allegheny
INDIAN HEAD Fayette
INDIANA Indiana
INDIANOLA Allegheny
INDUSTRY Beaver
INGOMAR Allegheny
INTERCOURSE Lancaster
IRVINE Warren
IRVONA Clearfield
IRWIN Westmoreland
ISABELLA Fayette
JACKSON Susquehanna
JACKSON CENTER Mercer
JACOBS CREEK Westmoreland
JAMES CITY Elk
JAMES CREEK (16657) Huntingdon(98), Bedford(1)
JAMESTOWN (16134) Crawford(90), Mercer(9)
JAMISON Bucks
JEANNETTE Westmoreland
JENKINTOWN Montgomery
JENNERS Somerset
JENNERSTOWN Somerset
JERMYN Lackawanna
JEROME Somerset
JERSEY MILLS Lycoming

JERSEY SHORE (17740) Lycoming(86), Clinton(13)
JERSEY SHORE Lycoming
JESSUP Lackawanna
JIM THORPE Carbon
JOFFRE Washington
JOHNSONBURG Elk
JOHNSTOWN (15905) Cambria(89), Somerset(10)
JOHNSTOWN Cambria
JONES MILLS Westmoreland
JONESTOWN Lebanon
JOSEPHINE Indiana
JULIAN Centre
JUNEAU Indiana
JUNEDALE Carbon
KANE (16735) McKean(71), Elk(28)
KANTNER Somerset
KARNS CITY (16041) Butler(54), Armstrong(45)
KARTHAUS (16845) Clearfield(70), Centre(29)
KEISTERVILLE Fayette
KELAYRES Schuylkill
KELTON Chester
KEMBLESVILLE Chester
KEMPTON (19529) Berks(51), Lehigh(48)
KENNERDELL Venango
KENNETT SQUARE Chester
KENT Indiana
KERSEY Elk
KIMBERTON Chester
KING OF PRUSSIA Chester
KING OF PRUSSIA Montgomery
KINGSLEY Susquehanna
KINGSTON Luzerne
KINTNERSVILLE Bucks
KINZERS Lancaster
KIRKWOOD Lancaster
KITTANNING Armstrong
KLEINFELTERSVILLE Lebanon
KLINGERSTOWN (17941) Schuylkill(84), Northumberland(15)
KNOX Clarion
KNOX DALE Jefferson
KNOXVILLE Tioga
KOPPEL Beaver
KOSSUTH Clarion
KREAMER Snyder
KRESGEVILLE Monroe
KULPMONT Northumberland
KULPSVILLE Montgomery
KUNKLETOWN (18058) Monroe(70), Carbon(29)
KUTZTOWN (19530) Berks(90), Lehigh(9)
KYLERTOWN Clearfield
LA BELLE Fayette
LA JOSE Clearfield
LA PLUME Lackawanna
LACEYVILLE (18623) Wyoming(46), Bradford(38), Susquehanna(15)
LACKAWAXEN Pike
LAFAYETTE HILL Montgomery
LAHASKA Bucks
LAIRDSVILLE Lycoming
LAKE ARIEL (18436) Wayne(67), Lackawanna(32)
LAKE CITY Erie
LAKE COMO Wayne
LAKE HARMONY Carbon
LAKE LYNN Fayette
LAKE WINOLA Wyoming
LAKEVILLE Wayne
LAKEWOOD Wayne
LAMAR Clinton
LAMARTINE Clarion
LAMPETER Lancaster
LANCASTER Lancaster
LANDENBERG Chester
LANDINGVILLE Schuylkill
LANDISBURG Perry
LANDISVILLE Lancaster
LANESBORO Susquehanna

LANGELOTH Washington
LANGHORNE Bucks
LANSDALE Montgomery
LANSDOWNE Delaware
LANSE Clearfield
LANSFORD Carbon
LAPORTE Sullivan
LARIMER Westmoreland
LATROBE Westmoreland
LATTIMER MINES Luzerne
LAUGHLINTOWN Westmoreland
LAURELTON Union
LAURYS STATION Lehigh
LAVELLE Schuylkill
LAWN Lebanon
LAWRENCE Washington
LAWRENCEVILLE Tioga
LAWTON Susquehanna
LE RAYSVILLE (18829) Bradford(95), Susquehanna(4)
LEBANON Lebanon
LECK KILL (17836) Northumberland(78), Schuylkill(21)
LECKRONE Fayette
LECONTES MILLS Clearfield
LEDERACH Montgomery
LEECHBURG (15656) Armstrong(51), Westmoreland(48)
LEEPER Clarion
LEESPORT Berks
LEETSDALE Allegheny
LEHIGH VALLEY Northampton
LEHIGHTON Carbon
LEHMAN Luzerne
LEISENRING Fayette
LEMASTERS Franklin
LEMONT Centre
LEMONT FURNACE Fayette
LEMOYNE Cumberland
LENHARTSVILLE Berks
LENNI Delaware
LENOXVILLE Susquehanna
LEOLA Lancaster
LEROY Bradford
LEVITTOWN Bucks
LEWIS RUN McKean
LEWISBERRY York
LEWISBURG Union
LEWISTOWN Mifflin
LEWISVILLE Chester
LIBERTY (16930) Tioga(73), Lycoming(26)
LIBRARY Allegheny
LICKINGVILLE Clarion
LIGHT STREET Columbia
LIGONIER Westmoreland
LILLY Cambria
LIMEKILN Berks
LIMEPORT Lehigh
LIMESTONE Clarion
LINCOLN UNIVERSITY Chester
LINDEN Lycoming
LINE LEXINGTON (18932) Bucks(93), Montgomery(6)
LINESVILLE Crawford
LIONVILLE Chester
LISTIE Somerset
LITITZ Lancaster
LITTLE MEADOWS (18830) Susquehanna(91), Bradford(8)
LITTLESTOWN Adams
LIVERPOOL (17045) Perry(71), Juniata(23), Snyder(4)
LLEWELLYN Schuylkill
LOCK HAVEN (17745) Clinton(98), Lycoming(1)
LOCUST GAP Northumberland
LOCUSTDALE Schuylkill
LOGANTON Clinton
LOGANVILLE York
LONG POND Monroe
LOPEZ Sullivan
LORETTO Cambria
LOST CREEK Schuylkill

LOWBER Westmoreland
LOYALHANNA Westmoreland
LOYSBURG Bedford
LOYSVILLE Perry
LUCERNEMINES Indiana
LUCINDA Clarion
LUDLOW McKean
LUMBERVILLE Bucks
LURGAN Franklin
LUTHERSBURG Clearfield
LUXOR Westmoreland
LUZERNE Luzerne
LYKENS Dauphin
LYNDELL Chester
LYNDORA Butler
LYON STATION Berks
MACKEYVILLE Clinton
MACUNGIE (18062) Lehigh(89), Berks(10)
MADERA Clearfield
MADISON Westmoreland
MADISONBURG Centre
MAHAFFEY (15757) Clearfield(98), Indiana(1)
MAHANOY CITY Schuylkill
MAHANOY PLANE Schuylkill
MAINESBURG (16932) Tioga(98), Bradford(1)
MAINLAND Montgomery
MALVERN Chester
MAMMOTH Westmoreland
MANCHESTER York
MANHEIM (17545) Lancaster(98), Lebanon(1)
MANNS CHOICE Bedford
MANOR Westmoreland
MANORVILLE Armstrong
MANSFIELD Tioga
MAPLETON DEPOT Huntingdon
MAR LIN Schuylkill
MARBLE Clarion
MARCHAND Indiana
MARCUS HOOK Delaware
MARIANNA Washington
MARIENVILLE (16239) Forest(62), Clarion(37)
MARIETTA Lancaster
MARION Franklin
MARION CENTER Indiana
MARION HEIGHTS Northumberland
MARKLETON Somerset
MARKLEYSBURG Fayette
MARS (16046) Butler(86), Allegheny(13)
MARSHALLS CREEK Monroe
MARSTELLER Cambria
MARTIN Fayette
MARTINDALE Lancaster
MARTINS CREEK Northampton
MARTINSBURG (16662) Blair(69), Bedford(30)
MARY D Schuylkill
MARYSVILLE (17053) Perry(97), Cumberland(2)
MASONTOWN Fayette
MATAMORAS Pike
MATHER Greene
MATTAWANA Mifflin
MAXATAWNY Berks
MAYPORT (16240) Jefferson(55), Clarion(40), Armstrong(3)
MAYTOWN Lancaster
MC ALISTERVILLE Juniata
MC CLELLANDTOWN Fayette
MC CLURE (17841) Mifflin(85), Snyder(14)
MC CONNELLSBURG Fulton
MC CONNELLSTOWN Huntingdon
MC DONALD (15057) Washington(81), Allegheny(18)
MC ELHATTAN Clinton
MC EWENSVILLE Northumberland
MC GRANN Armstrong
MC INTYRE Indiana
MC KEAN Erie
MC KEES ROCKS Allegheny

MC KEESPORT (15131) Allegheny(95), Westmoreland(4)
MC KEESPORT Allegheny
MC KNIGHTSTOWN Adams
MC SHERRYSTOWN Adams
MC VEYTOWN Mifflin
MCADOO (18237) Schuylkill(98), Carbon(1)
MEADOW LANDS Washington
MEADVILLE Crawford
MECHANICSBURG (17055) Cumberland(98), York(1)
MECHANICSBURG Cumberland
MECHANICSVILLE Bucks
MEDIA Delaware
MEHOOPANY Wyoming
MELCROFT Fayette
MENDENHALL Chester
MENGES MILLS York
MENTCLE Indiana
MERCERSBURG (17236) Franklin(92), Fulton(7)
MERION STATION Montgomery
MERRITTSTOWN Fayette
MERTZTOWN (19539) Berks(87), Lehigh(12)
MESHOPPEN (18630) Susquehanna(50), Wyoming(50)
MEXICO Juniata
MEYERSDALE Somerset
MIDDLEBURG Snyder
MIDDLEBURY CENTER Tioga
MIDDLEPORT Schuylkill
MIDDLETOWN Dauphin
MIDLAND Beaver
MIDWAY Washington
MIFFLIN Juniata
MIFFLINBURG Union
MIFFLINTOWN Juniata
MIFFLINVILLE Columbia
MILAN Bradford
MILANVILLE Wayne
MILDRED Sullivan
MILESBURG Centre
MILFORD Pike
MILFORD SQUARE Bucks
MILL CREEK (17060) Huntingdon(88), Mifflin(11)
MILL HALL Clinton
MILL RUN Fayette
MILL VILLAGE Erie
MILLERSBURG Dauphin
MILLERSTOWN (17062) Perry(90), Juniata(9)
MILLERSVILLE Lancaster
MILLERTON (16936) Tioga(87), Bradford(12)
MILLHEIM Centre
MILLMONT Union
MILLRIFT Pike
MILLS Potter
MILLSBORO Washington
MILLVILLE Columbia
MILNESVILLE Luzerne
MILROY Mifflin
MILTON (17847) Northumberland(94), Montour(5)
MINERAL POINT Cambria
MINERAL SPRINGS Clearfield
MINERSVILLE Schuylkill
MINGOVILLE Centre
MINISINK HILLS Monroe
MIQUON Montgomery
MODENA Chester
MOHNTON (19540) Berks(94), Lancaster(5)
MOHRSVILLE Berks
MONACA Beaver
MONESSEN Westmoreland
MONOCACY STATION Berks
MONONGAHELA (15063) Washington(95), Allegheny(3)
MONROETON Bradford

MONROEVILLE Allegheny
MONT ALTO Franklin
MONT CLARE Montgomery
MONTANDON Northumberland
MONTGOMERY Lycoming
MONTGOMERYVILLE Montgomery
MONTOURSVILLE Lycoming
MONTROSE Susquehanna
MOOSIC (18507) Lackawanna(98),
    Luzerne(1)
MORANN Clearfield
MORGAN Allegheny
MORGANTOWN (19543) Berks(78),
    Lancaster(17), Chester(3)
MORRIS (16938) Tioga(67), Lycoming(32)
MORRIS RUN Tioga
MORRISDALE Clearfield
MORRISVILLE Bucks
MORTON Delaware
MOSCOW (18444) Lackawanna(93),
    Wayne(6)
MOSHANNON Centre
MOUNT AETNA Berks
MOUNT BETHEL Northampton
MOUNT BRADDOCK Fayette
MOUNT CARMEL Northumberland
MOUNT GRETNA Lebanon
MOUNT HOLLY SPRINGS Cumberland
MOUNT JEWETT McKean
MOUNT JOY Lancaster
MOUNT MORRIS Greene
MOUNT PLEASANT (15666)
    Westmoreland(83), Fayette(16)
MOUNT PLEASANT MILLS (17853)
    Snyder(86), Juniata(13)
MOUNT POCONO Monroe
MOUNT UNION (17066) Huntingdon(70),
    Mifflin(29)
MOUNT WOLF York
MOUNTAIN TOP Luzerne
MOUNTAINHOME Monroe
MOUNTVILLE Lancaster
MUIR Schuylkill
MUNCY (17756) Lycoming(89),
    Northumberland(8), Montour(1)
MUNCY VALLEY (17758) Sullivan(65),
    Lycoming(34)
MUNSON (16860) Clearfield(76),
    Centre(23)
MURRYSVILLE (15668)
    Westmoreland(97), Allegheny(2)
MUSE Washington
MYERSTOWN (17067) Lebanon(81),
    Berks(18)
NANTICOKE Luzerne
NANTY GLO Cambria
NARBERTH Montgomery
NARVON (17555) Lancaster(96), Berks(2),
    Chester(1)
NATRONA HEIGHTS Allegheny
NAZARETH Northampton
NEEDMORE Fulton
NEELYTON Huntingdon
NEFFS Lehigh
NELSON Tioga
NEMACOLIN Greene
NESCOPECK (18635) Luzerne(74),
    Columbia(25)
NESQUEHONING (18240) Carbon(85),
    Schuylkill(14)
NEW ALBANY (18833) Bradford(89),
    Sullivan(10)
NEW ALEXANDRIA Westmoreland
NEW BALTIMORE Somerset
NEW BEDFORD Lawrence
NEW BERLIN Union
NEW BERLINVILLE Berks
NEW BETHLEHEM (16242) Clarion(92),
    Armstrong(7)
NEW BLOOMFIELD Perry
NEW BRIGHTON Beaver
NEW BUFFALO Perry
NEW CASTLE Lawrence

NEW COLUMBIA Union
NEW CUMBERLAND (17070)
    Cumberland(55), York(44)
NEW DERRY Westmoreland
NEW EAGLE Washington
NEW ENTERPRISE Bedford
NEW FLORENCE (15944) Indiana(63),
    Westmoreland(36)
NEW FREEDOM York
NEW FREEPORT Greene
NEW GALILEE (16141) Lawrence(70),
    Beaver(29)
NEW GENEVA Fayette
NEW GERMANTOWN Perry
NEW HOLLAND Lancaster
NEW HOPE Bucks
NEW KENSINGTON (15068)
    Westmoreland(91), Allegheny(8)
NEW KENSINGTON Westmoreland
NEW KINGSTOWN Cumberland
NEW LONDON Chester
NEW MILFORD Susquehanna
NEW MILLPORT Clearfield
NEW OXFORD Adams
NEW PARIS Bedford
NEW PARK York
NEW PHILADELPHIA Schuylkill
NEW PROVIDENCE Lancaster
NEW RINGGOLD Schuylkill
NEW SALEM Fayette
NEW STANTON Westmoreland
NEW TRIPOLI Lehigh
NEW WILMINGTON (16142)
    Lawrence(69), Mercer(30)
NEW WILMINGTON Lawrence
NEWBURG (17240) Cumberland(68),
    Franklin(31)
NEWELL Fayette
NEWFOUNDLAND (18445) Wayne(81),
    Pike(18)
NEWMANSTOWN (17073) Lebanon(93),
    Lancaster(6)
NEWPORT Perry
NEWRY Blair
NEWTON HAMILTON Mifflin
NEWTOWN Bucks
NEWTOWN SQUARE (19073)
    Delaware(97), Chester(2)
NEWVILLE Cumberland
NICHOLSON (18446) Wyoming(54),
    Susquehanna(42), Lackawanna(2)
NICKTOWN Cambria
NINEVEH Greene
NISBET Lycoming
NORMALVILLE Fayette
NORRISTOWN Chester
NORRISTOWN Montgomery
NORTH APOLLO Armstrong
NORTH BEND Clinton
NORTH EAST Erie
NORTH SPRINGFIELD Erie
NORTH VERSAILLES Allegheny
NORTH WALES (19454) Montgomery(81),
    Bucks(18)
NORTH WALES Montgomery
NORTH WASHINGTON Butler
NORTHAMPTON Northampton
NORTHPOINT Indiana
NORTHUMBERLAND Northumberland
NORVELT Westmoreland
NORWOOD Delaware
NOTTINGHAM (19362) Chester(98),
    Lancaster(1)
NOXEN (18636) Wyoming(84),
    Luzerne(15)
NU MINE Armstrong
NUANGOLA Luzerne
NUMIDIA Columbia
NUREMBERG (18241) Luzerne(56),
    Schuylkill(43)
OAK RIDGE Armstrong
OAKDALE Allegheny
OAKLAND MILLS Juniata

OAKMONT Allegheny
OAKS Montgomery
OHIOPYLE Fayette
OIL CITY Venango
OLANTA Clearfield
OLD FORGE Lackawanna
OLD ZIONSVILLE Lehigh
OLEY Berks
OLIVEBURG Jefferson
OLIVER Fayette
OLYPHANT Lackawanna
ONEIDA Schuylkill
ONO Lebanon
ORANGEVILLE Columbia
ORBISONIA (17243) Huntingdon(98),
    Juniata(1)
OREFIELD Lehigh
ORELAND Montgomery
ORRSTOWN Franklin
ORRTANNA Adams
ORSON Wayne
ORVISTON Centre
ORWIGSBURG Schuylkill
OSCEOLA Tioga
OSCEOLA MILLS (16666) Clearfield(91),
    Centre(7), Blair(1)
OSTERBURG Bedford
OTTSVILLE Bucks
OXFORD (19363) Chester(93),
    Lancaster(6)
PALM (18070) Berks(54), Montgomery(45)
PALMERTON (18071) Carbon(98),
    Monroe(1)
PALMYRA (17078) Lebanon(94),
    Dauphin(5)
PAOLI Chester
PARADISE Lancaster
PARDEESVILLE Luzerne
PARKER (16049) Clarion(75), Butler(12),
    Armstrong(11)
PARKER FORD Chester
PARKESBURG Chester
PARKHILL Cambria
PARRYVILLE Carbon
PATTON Cambria
PAUPACK Pike
PAXINOS Northumberland
PAXTONVILLE Snyder
PEACH BOTTOM Lancaster
PEACH GLEN Adams
PECKVILLE Lackawanna
PEN ARGYL Northampton
PENFIELD Clearfield
PENN Westmoreland
PENN RUN Indiana
PENNS CREEK Snyder
PENNS PARK Bucks
PENNSBURG (18073) Montgomery(91),
    Bucks(8)
PENNSYLVANIA FURNACE (16865)
    Centre(88), Huntingdon(11)
PENRYN Lancaster
PEQUEA Lancaster
PERKASIE Bucks
PERKIOMENVILLE Montgomery
PERRYOPOLIS Fayette
PETERSBURG Huntingdon
PETROLIA Butler
PHILADELPHIA Bucks
PHILADELPHIA Delaware
PHILADELPHIA Montgomery
PHILADELPHIA Philadelphia
PHILIPSBURG (16866) Centre(60),
    Clearfield(39)
PHOENIXVILLE (19460) Chester(98),
    Montgomery(1)
PICTURE ROCKS Lycoming
PILLOW Dauphin
PINE BANK Greene
PINE FORGE Berks
PINE GROVE Schuylkill
PINE GROVE MILLS Centre
PINEVILLE Bucks

PIPERSVILLE Bucks
PITCAIRN Allegheny
PITMAN (17964) Schuylkill(94),
    Northumberland(5)
PITTSBURGH (15241) Allegheny(98),
    Washington(1)
PITTSBURGH Allegheny
PITTSFIELD Warren
PITTSTON (18641) Luzerne(93),
    Lackawanna(6)
PITTSTON Luzerne
PLAINFIELD Cumberland
PLEASANT HALL Franklin
PLEASANT MOUNT Wayne
PLEASANT UNITY Westmoreland
PLEASANTVILLE (16341) Venango(92),
    Forest(7)
PLUMSTEADVILLE Bucks
PLUMVILLE Indiana
PLYMOUTH Luzerne
PLYMOUTH MEETING Montgomery
POCONO LAKE Monroe
POCONO LAKE PRESERVE Monroe
POCONO MANOR Monroe
POCONO PINES Monroe
POCONO SUMMIT Monroe
POCOPSON Chester
POINT MARION Fayette
POINT PLEASANT Bucks
POLK (16342) Venango(97), Mercer(2)
POMEROY Chester
PORT ALLEGANY (16743) McKean(95),
    Potter(4)
PORT CARBON Schuylkill
PORT CLINTON Schuylkill
PORT MATILDA Centre
PORT ROYAL Juniata
PORT TREVORTON Snyder
PORTAGE (15946) Cambria(94), Blair(2),
    Bedford(2)
PORTERS SIDELING York
PORTERSVILLE (16051) Butler(81),
    Lawrence(18)
PORTLAND Northampton
POTTERSDALE (16871) Clearfield(87),
    Clinton(12)
POTTS GROVE Northumberland
POTTSTOWN Chester
POTTSTOWN Montgomery
POTTSVILLE Schuylkill
POYNTELLE Wayne
PRESTO Allegheny
PRESTON PARK Wayne
PRICEDALE Westmoreland
PROMPTON Wayne
PROSPECT Butler
PROSPECT PARK Delaware
PROSPERITY (15329) Washington(88),
    Greene(11)
PULASKI (16143) Lawrence(89),
    Mercer(10)
PUNXSUTAWNEY (15767) Jefferson(91),
    Indiana(7), Clearfield(1)
QUAKAKE Schuylkill
QUAKERTOWN Bucks
QUARRYVILLE Lancaster
QUECREEK Somerset
QUEEN Bedford
QUENTIN Lebanon
QUINCY Franklin
RAILROAD York
RALSTON Lycoming
RAMEY Clearfield
RANSOM Lackawanna
RAVINE Schuylkill
REA Washington
READING Berks
REAMSTOWN Lancaster
REBERSBURG Centre
REBUCK Northumberland
RECTOR Westmoreland
RED HILL Montgomery
RED LION York

REEDERS Monroe
REEDSVILLE Mifflin
REFTON Lancaster
REHRERSBURG Berks
REINHOLDS (17569) Lancaster(80),
   Berks(19)
RENFREW Butler
RENO Venango
RENOVO Clinton
REPUBLIC Fayette
REVERE Bucks
REVLOC Cambria
REW McKean
REXMONT Lebanon
REYNOLDSVILLE Jefferson
RHEEMS Lancaster
RICES LANDING Greene
RICEVILLE Crawford
RICHBORO Bucks
RICHEYVILLE Washington
RICHFIELD (17086) Juniata(60),
   Snyder(39)
RICHLAND (17087) Lebanon(54),
   Berks(45)
RICHLANDTOWN Bucks
RIDDLESBURG Bedford
RIDGWAY (15853) Elk(96), Jefferson(3)
RIDLEY PARK Delaware
RIEGELSVILLE (18077) Bucks(90),
   Northampton(9)
RILLTON Westmoreland
RIMERSBURG Clarion
RINGGOLD Jefferson
RINGTOWN Schuylkill
RIVERSIDE Northumberland
RIXFORD McKean
ROARING BRANCH (17765) Tioga(57),
   Lycoming(41)
ROARING SPRING (16673) Blair(68),
   Bedford(31)
ROBERTSDALE (16674) Huntingdon(98),
   Fulton(1)
ROBESONIA (19551) Berks(93),
   Lebanon(4), Lancaster(2)
ROBINSON Indiana
ROCHESTER Beaver
ROCHESTER MILLS Indiana
ROCK GLEN Luzerne
ROCKHILL FURNACE Huntingdon
ROCKTON Clearfield
ROCKWOOD Somerset
ROGERSVILLE Greene
ROME Bradford
RONCO Fayette
RONKS Lancaster
ROSCOE Washington
ROSSITER (15772) Indiana(98),
   Jefferson(1)
ROSSVILLE York
ROULETTE Potter
ROUSEVILLE Venango
ROUZERVILLE Franklin
ROWLAND Pike
ROXBURY Franklin
ROYERSFORD Montgomery
RUFFS DALE Westmoreland
RURAL RIDGE Allegheny
RURAL VALLEY Armstrong
RUSHLAND Bucks
RUSHVILLE Susquehanna
RUSSELL Warren
RUSSELLTON Allegheny
SABINSVILLE (16943) Potter(56),
   Tioga(43)
SACRAMENTO Schuylkill
SADSBURYVILLE Chester
SAEGERTOWN Crawford
SAGAMORE Armstrong
SAINT BENEDICT Cambria
SAINT BONIFACE Cambria
SAINT CLAIR Schuylkill
SAINT JOHNS Luzerne
SAINT MARYS Elk

SAINT MICHAEL Cambria
SAINT PETERS Chester
SAINT PETERSBURG Clarion
SAINT THOMAS Franklin
SALFORD Montgomery
SALFORDVILLE Montgomery
SALINA Westmoreland
SALISBURY Somerset
SALIX Cambria
SALONA Clinton
SALTILLO Huntingdon
SALTSBURG (15681) Indiana(70),
   Westmoreland(29)
SANDY LAKE Mercer
SANDY RIDGE Centre
SARVER (16055) Butler(94), Armstrong(4)
SASSAMANSVILLE Montgomery
SAXONBURG Butler
SAXTON (16678) Bedford(94),
   Huntingdon(5)
SAYLORSBURG Monroe
SAYRE Bradford
SCENERY HILL Washington
SCHAEFFERSTOWN Lebanon
SCHELLSBURG Bedford
SCHENLEY Armstrong
SCHNECKSVILLE Lehigh
SCHUYLKILL HAVEN Schuylkill
SCHWENKSVILLE Montgomery
SCIOTA Monroe
SCOTLAND Franklin
SCOTRUN Monroe
SCOTTDALE (15683) Westmoreland(88),
   Fayette(11)
SCRANTON Lackawanna
SEANOR Somerset
SELINSGROVE (17870) Snyder(97),
   Union(2)
SELLERSVILLE Bucks
SELTZER Schuylkill
SEMINOLE Armstrong
SENECA Venango
SEVEN VALLEYS York
SEWARD (15954) Indiana(72),
   Westmoreland(27)
SEWICKLEY (15143) Allegheny(94),
   Beaver(5)
SEWICKLEY Allegheny
SHADE GAP Huntingdon
SHADY GROVE Franklin
SHAMOKIN Northumberland
SHAMOKIN DAM Snyder
SHANKSVILLE Somerset
SHARON Mercer
SHARON HILL Delaware
SHARPSVILLE Mercer
SHARTLESVILLE Berks
SHAVERTOWN Luzerne
SHAWANESE Luzerne
SHAWNEE ON DELAWARE Monroe
SHAWVILLE Clearfield
SHEAKLEYVILLE Mercer
SHEFFIELD (16347) Warren(84),
   Forest(15)
SHELOCTA (15774) Indiana(51),
   Armstrong(48)
SHENANDOAH Schuylkill
SHEPPTON Schuylkill
SHERMANS DALE (17090) Perry(98),
   Cumberland(1)
SHICKSHINNY (18655) Luzerne(92),
   Columbia(7)
SHINGLEHOUSE (16748) McKean(56),
   Potter(43)
SHIPPENSBURG (17257)
   Cumberland(62), Franklin(37)
SHIPPENVILLE Clarion
SHIPPINGPORT Beaver
SHIRLEYSBURG Huntingdon
SHOEMAKERSVILLE Berks
SHOHOLA Pike
SHREWSBURY York
SHUNK Sullivan

SIDMAN Cambria
SIGEL (15860) Jefferson(65), Elk(30),
   Clarion(3)
SILVER SPRING Lancaster
SILVERDALE Bucks
SINNAMAHONING Cameron
SIPESVILLE Somerset
SIX MILE RUN Bedford
SKIPPACK Montgomery
SKYTOP Monroe
SLATE RUN Lycoming
SLATEDALE Lehigh
SLATINGTON Lehigh
SLICKVILLE Westmoreland
SLIGO Clarion
SLIPPERY ROCK (16057) Butler(78),
   Lawrence(19), Mercer(2)
SLOVAN Washington
SMETHPORT McKean
SMICKSBURG (16256) Indiana(98),
   Jefferson(1)
SMITHFIELD Fayette
SMITHMILL Clearfield
SMITHTON Westmoreland
SMOCK Fayette
SMOKERUN Clearfield
SMOKETOWN Lancaster
SNOW SHOE Centre
SNYDERSBURG Clarion
SNYDERTOWN Northumberland
SOLEBURY Bucks
SONESTOWN Sullivan
SOUDERSBURG Lancaster
SOUDERTON (18964) Montgomery(95),
   Bucks(4)
SOUTH CANAAN Wayne
SOUTH FORK Cambria
SOUTH GIBSON Susquehanna
SOUTH HEIGHTS Beaver
SOUTH MONTROSE Susquehanna
SOUTH MOUNTAIN Franklin
SOUTH PARK Allegheny
SOUTH STERLING Wayne
SOUTHAMPTON Bucks
SOUTHEASTERN Chester
SOUTHVIEW Washington
SOUTHWEST Westmoreland
SPANGLER Cambria
SPARTANSBURG (16434) Crawford(96),
   Warren(3)
SPINNERSTOWN Bucks
SPRAGGS Greene
SPRANKLE MILLS Jefferson
SPRING CHURCH Armstrong
SPRING CITY Chester
SPRING CREEK Warren
SPRING GLEN (17978) Schuylkill(98),
   Dauphin(1)
SPRING GROVE York
SPRING HOUSE Montgomery
SPRING MILLS Centre
SPRING MOUNT Montgomery
SPRING RUN Franklin
SPRINGBORO Crawford
SPRINGDALE Allegheny
SPRINGFIELD Delaware
SPRINGS Somerset
SPRINGTOWN Bucks
SPRINGVILLE (18844) Susquehanna(98),
   Wyoming(1)
SPROUL Blair
SPRUCE CREEK Huntingdon
STAHLSTOWN Westmoreland
STAR JUNCTION Fayette
STARFORD Indiana
STARLIGHT Wayne
STARRUCCA (18462) Wayne(97),
   Susquehanna(2)
STATE COLLEGE Centre
STATE LINE Franklin
STEELVILLE Chester
STERLING (18463) Pike(63), Wayne(36)
STEVENS Lancaster

STEVENSVILLE Bradford
STEWARTSTOWN York
STILLWATER (17878) Columbia(74),
   Luzerne(25)
STOCKDALE Washington
STOCKERTOWN Northampton
STONEBORO (16153) Mercer(88),
   Venango(11)
STONY RUN Berks
STOYSTOWN Somerset
STRABANE Washington
STRASBURG Lancaster
STRATTANVILLE Clarion
STRAUSSTOWN Berks
STRONGSTOWN (15957) Indiana(60),
   Cambria(40)
STROUDSBURG Monroe
STUMP CREEK Jefferson
STURGEON Allegheny
SUGAR GROVE Warren
SUGAR RUN Bradford
SUGARLOAF Luzerne
SUMMERDALE Cumberland
SUMMERHILL Cambria
SUMMERVILLE (15864) Jefferson(64),
   Clarion(35)
SUMMIT HILL Carbon
SUMMIT STATION Schuylkill
SUMNEYTOWN Montgomery
SUNBURY Northumberland
SUPLEE Chester
SUSQUEHANNA (18847)
   Susquehanna(97), Wayne(2)
SUTERSVILLE Westmoreland
SWARTHMORE Delaware
SWEET VALLEY Luzerne
SWENGEL Union
SWIFTWATER Monroe
SYBERTSVILLE Luzerne
SYCAMORE Greene
SYKESVILLE (15865) Jefferson(94),
   Clearfield(5)
SYLVANIA Bradford
TAFTON Pike
TALMAGE Lancaster
TAMAQUA Schuylkill
TAMIMENT Pike
TANNERSVILLE Monroe
TARENTUM Allegheny
TARRS Westmoreland
TATAMY Northampton
TAYLOR Lackawanna
TAYLORSTOWN Washington
TELFORD (18969) Montgomery(60),
   Bucks(39)
TEMPLE Berks
TEMPLETON Armstrong
TERRE HILL Lancaster
THOMASVILLE York
THOMPSON (18465) Susquehanna(86),
   Wayne(13)
THOMPSONTOWN Juniata
THORNDALE Chester
THORNTON Delaware
THREE SPRINGS (17264) Huntingdon(96),
   Fulton(3)
TIDIOUTE (16351) Warren(95), Forest(4)
TIMBLIN Jefferson
TIOGA Tioga
TIONA Warren
TIONESTA (16353) Clarion(72), Forest(15),
   Venango(11)
TIPTON Blair
TIRE HILL Somerset
TITUSVILLE (16354) Crawford(64),
   Venango(34)
TOBYHANNA Monroe
TODD Huntingdon
TOPTON Berks
TORRANCE Westmoreland
TOUGHKENAMON Chester
TOWANDA Bradford
TOWER CITY Schuylkill

TOWNVILLE Crawford
TRAFFORD (15085) Westmoreland(98),
   Allegheny(1)
TRANSFER Mercer
TREICHLERS Northampton
TREMONT Schuylkill
TRESCKOW Carbon
TREVORTON Northumberland
TREXLERTOWN Lehigh
TROUT RUN Lycoming
TROUTVILLE Clearfield
TROXELVILLE Snyder
TROY (16947) Bradford(92), Tioga(7)
TRUMBAUERSVILLE Bucks
TUNKHANNOCK Wyoming
TURBOTVILLE (17772)
   Northumberland(55), Montour(44)
TURKEY CITY Clarion
TURTLE CREEK Allegheny
TURTLEPOINT McKean
TUSCARORA Schuylkill
TWIN ROCKS Cambria
TYLER HILL Wayne
TYLERSBURG Clarion
TYLERSPORT Montgomery
TYLERSVILLE Clinton
TYRONE (16686) Blair(73),
   Huntingdon(20), Centre(6)
ULEDI Fayette
ULSTER Bradford
ULYSSES Potter
UNION CITY (16438) Crawford(55),
   Erie(44)
UNION DALE (18470) Susquehanna(92),
   Wayne(7)
UNIONTOWN Fayette
UNIONVILLE Chester
UNITED Westmoreland
UNITY HOUSE Pike
UNITYVILLE (17774) Lycoming(98),
   Columbia(1)
UNIVERSITY PARK Centre
UPPER BLACK EDDY Bucks
UPPER DARBY Delaware
UPPERSTRASBURG Franklin
URSINA Somerset
UTICA (16362) Venango(86), Mercer(11),
   Crawford(1)
UWCHLAND Chester
VALENCIA (16059) Butler(92),
   Allegheny(7)
VALIER Jefferson
VALLEY FORGE Chester
VALLEY FORGE Montgomery
VALLEY VIEW Schuylkill
VAN VOORHIS Washington

VANDERBILT Fayette
VANDERGRIFT (15690)
   Westmoreland(55), Armstrong(44)
VENANGO Crawford
VENETIA Washington
VENUS (16364) Venango(69), Clarion(30)
VERONA Allegheny
VESTABURG Washington
VICKSBURG Union
VILLA MARIA Lawrence
VILLANOVA (19085) Delaware(56),
   Montgomery(43)
VINTONDALE (15961) Indiana(90),
   Cambria(9)
VIRGINVILLE Berks
VOLANT (16156) Lawrence(88),
   Mercer(11)
VOWINCKEL (16260) Clarion(95),
   Forest(4)
WAGONTOWN Chester
WALLACETON Clearfield
WALLINGFORD Delaware
WALNUT BOTTOM Cumberland
WALNUTPORT Northampton
WALSTON Jefferson
WALTERSBURG Fayette
WAMPUM (16157) Lawrence(92),
   Beaver(7)
WAPWALLOPEN Luzerne
WARFORDSBURG Fulton
WARMINSTER Bucks
WARREN Warren
WARREN CENTER Bradford
WARRENDALE Allegheny
WARRINGTON Bucks
WARRIORS MARK (16877)
   Huntingdon(50), Centre(49)
WASHINGTON BORO Lancaster
WASHINGTON CROSSING Bucks
WASHINGTONVILLE Montour
WATERFALL Fulton
WATERFORD (16441) Erie(95),
   Crawford(4)
WATERVILLE Lycoming
WATSONTOWN (17777)
   Northumberland(98), Montour(1)
WATTSBURG Erie
WAVERLY Lackawanna
WAYMART Wayne
WAYNE (19087) Delaware(49),
   Chester(40), Montgomery(9)
WAYNE Delaware
WAYNESBORO Franklin
WAYNESBURG Greene
WEATHERLY (18255) Carbon(96),
   Luzerne(3)

WEBSTER Westmoreland
WEEDVILLE Elk
WEIKERT Union
WELLERSBURG Somerset
WELLS TANNERY Fulton
WELLSBORO Tioga
WELLSVILLE York
WENDEL Westmoreland
WERNERSVILLE Berks
WEST ALEXANDER Washington
WEST CHESTER Chester
WEST DECATUR Clearfield
WEST ELIZABETH Allegheny
WEST FINLEY (15377) Washington(90),
   Greene(9)
WEST GROVE Chester
WEST HICKORY Forest
WEST LEBANON Indiana
WEST LEISENRING Fayette
WEST MIDDLESEX (16159) Mercer(80),
   Lawrence(19)
WEST MIDDLETOWN Washington
WEST MIFFLIN Allegheny
WEST MILTON Union
WEST NEWTON (15089)
   Westmoreland(97), Allegheny(2)
WEST PITTSBURG Lawrence
WEST POINT Montgomery
WEST SALISBURY Somerset
WEST SPRINGFIELD Erie
WEST SUNBURY Butler
WEST WILLOW Lancaster
WESTFIELD Tioga
WESTLAND Washington
WESTLINE McKean
WESTMORELAND CITY Westmoreland
WESTON Luzerne
WESTOVER Clearfield
WESTPORT Clinton
WESTTOWN Chester
WEXFORD Allegheny
WHEATLAND Mercer
WHITE Fayette
WHITE DEER Union
WHITE HAVEN (18661) Luzerne(91),
   Carbon(8)
WHITE MILLS Wayne
WHITEHALL Lehigh
WHITNEY Westmoreland
WICKHAVEN Fayette
WICONISCO Dauphin
WIDNOON Armstrong
WILBURTON Columbia
WILCOX (15870) Elk(94), McKean(5)
WILDWOOD Allegheny
WILKES BARRE Luzerne

WILLIAMSBURG (16693) Blair(93),
   Huntingdon(6)
WILLIAMSON Franklin
WILLIAMSPORT Lycoming
WILLIAMSTOWN Dauphin
WILLOW GROVE Montgomery
WILLOW HILL Franklin
WILLOW STREET Lancaster
WILMERDING Allegheny
WILMORE Cambria
WINBURNE Clearfield
WIND GAP Northampton
WIND RIDGE Greene
WINDBER (15963) Somerset(85),
   Cambria(14)
WINDSOR York
WINFIELD (17889) Union(82), Snyder(17)
WITMER Lancaster
WOMELSDORF Berks
WOOD Bedford
WOODBURY Bedford
WOODLAND Clearfield
WOODLYN Delaware
WOODWARD Centre
WOOLRICH Clinton
WORCESTER Montgomery
WORTHINGTON Armstrong
WORTHVILLE Jefferson
WOXALL Montgomery
WRIGHTSVILLE York
WYALUSING Bradford
WYANO Westmoreland
WYCOMBE Bucks
WYNCOTE Montgomery
WYNNEWOOD (19096) Montgomery(95),
   Delaware(4)
WYOMING Luzerne
WYSOX Bradford
YATESBORO Armstrong
YEAGERTOWN Mifflin
YORK HAVEN York
YORK NEW SALEM York
YORK SPRINGS (17372) Adams(96),
   York(2)
YOUNGSTOWN Westmoreland
YOUNGSVILLE Warren
YOUNGWOOD Westmoreland
YUKON Westmoreland
ZELIENOPLE (16063) Butler(83),
   Beaver(16)
ZIEGLERVILLE Montgomery
ZION GROVE (17985) Schuylkill(97),
   Columbia(2)
ZIONHILL Bucks
ZIONSVILLE (18092) Lehigh(94), Berks(5)
ZULLINGER Franklin

Pennsylvania ZIP/City Cross Reference

15001-15001	ALIQUIPPA	15104-15104	BRADDOCK	15370-15370	WAYNESBURG	15492-15492	WICKHAVEN
15003-15003	AMBRIDGE	15106-15106	CARNEGIE	15376-15376	WEST ALEXANDER	15501-15501	SOMERSET
15004-15004	ATLASBURG	15108-15108	CORAOPOLIS	15377-15377	WEST FINLEY	15502-15502	HIDDEN VALLEY
15005-15005	BADEN	15110-15110	DUQUESNE	15378-15378	WESTLAND	15510-15510	SOMERSET
15006-15006	BAIRDFORD	15112-15112	EAST PITTSBURGH	15379-15379	WEST MIDDLETOWN	15520-15520	ACOSTA
15007-15007	BAKERSTOWN	15116-15116	GLENSHAW	15380-15380	WIND RIDGE	15521-15521	ALUM BANK
15009-15009	BEAVER	15120-15120	HOMESTEAD	15401-15401	UNIONTOWN	15522-15522	BEDFORD
15010-15010	BEAVER FALLS	15122-15123	WEST MIFFLIN	15410-15410	ADAH	15530-15530	BERLIN
15012-15012	BELLE VERNON	15126-15126	IMPERIAL	15411-15411	ADDISON	15531-15531	BOSWELL
15014-15014	BRACKENRIDGE	15127-15127	INGOMAR	15412-15412	ALLENPORT	15532-15532	BOYNTON
15015-15015	BRADFORDWOODS	15129-15129	LIBRARY	15413-15413	ALLISON	15533-15533	BREEZEWOOD
15017-15017	BRIDGEVILLE	15129-15129	SOUTH PARK	15415-15415	BRIER HILL	15534-15534	BUFFALO MILLS
15018-15018	BUENA VISTA	15130-15135	MC KEESPORT	15416-15416	BROWNFIELD	15535-15535	CLEARVILLE
15019-15019	BULGER	15136-15136	MC KEES ROCKS	15417-15417	BROWNSVILLE	15536-15536	CRYSTAL SPRING
15020-15020	BUNOLA	15137-15137	NORTH VERSAILLES	15419-15419	CALIFORNIA	15537-15537	EVERETT
15021-15021	BURGETTSTOWN	15139-15139	OAKMONT	15420-15420	CARDALE	15538-15538	FAIRHOPE
15022-15022	CHARLEROI	15140-15140	PITCAIRN	15421-15421	CHALKHILL	15539-15539	FISHERTOWN
15024-15024	CHESWICK	15142-15142	PRESTO	15421-15421	CHALK HILL	15540-15540	FORT HILL
15025-15025	CLAIRTON	15143-15143	SEWICKLEY	15422-15422	CHESTNUT RIDGE	15541-15541	FRIEDENS
15026-15026	CLINTON	15144-15144	SPRINGDALE	15423-15423	COAL CENTER	15542-15542	GARRETT
15027-15027	CONWAY	15145-15145	TURTLE CREEK	15424-15424	CONFLUENCE	15544-15544	GRAY
15028-15028	COULTERS	15146-15146	MONROEVILLE	15425-15425	CONNELLSVILLE	15545-15545	HYNDMAN
15029-15029	COURTNEY	15147-15147	VERONA	15427-15427	DAISYTOWN	15546-15546	JENNERS
15030-15030	CREIGHTON	15148-15148	WILMERDING	15428-15428	DAWSON	15547-15547	JENNERSTOWN
15031-15031	CUDDY	15189-15189	SEWICKLEY	15429-15429	DENBO	15548-15548	KANTNER
15032-15032	CURTISVILLE	15200-15295	PITTSBURGH	15430-15430	DICKERSON RUN	15549-15549	LISTIE
15033-15033	DONORA	15301-15301	WASHINGTON	15431-15431	DUNBAR	15550-15550	MANNS CHOICE
15034-15034	DRAVOSBURG	15310-15310	ALEPPO	15432-15432	DUNLEVY	15551-15551	MARKLETON
15035-15035	EAST MC KEESPORT	15311-15311	AMITY	15433-15433	EAST MILLSBORO	15552-15552	MEYERSDALE
15036-15036	ELDERSVILLE	15312-15312	AVELLA	15434-15434	ELCO	15553-15553	NEW BALTIMORE
15037-15037	ELIZABETH	15313-15313	BEALLSVILLE	15435-15435	FAIRBANK	15554-15554	NEW PARIS
15038-15038	ELRAMA	15314-15314	BENTLEYVILLE	15436-15436	FAIRCHANCE	15555-15555	QUECREEK
15042-15042	FREEDOM	15315-15315	BOBTOWN	15437-15437	FARMINGTON	15557-15557	ROCKWOOD
15043-15043	GEORGETOWN	15316-15316	BRAVE	15438-15438	FAYETTE CITY	15558-15558	SALISBURY
15044-15044	GIBSONIA	15317-15317	CANONSBURG	15439-15439	GANS	15559-15559	SCHELLSBURG
15045-15045	GLASSPORT	15320-15320	CARMICHAELS	15440-15440	GIBBON GLADE	15560-15560	SHANKSVILLE
15046-15046	GLENWILLARD	15321-15321	CECIL	15442-15442	GRINDSTONE	15561-15561	SIPESVILLE
15046-15046	CRESCENT	15322-15322	CLARKSVILLE	15443-15443	HIBBS	15562-15562	SPRINGS
15047-15047	GREENOCK	15323-15323	CLAYSVILLE	15444-15444	HILLER	15563-15563	STOYSTOWN
15049-15049	HARWICK	15324-15324	COKEBURG	15445-15445	HOPWOOD	15564-15564	WELLERSBURG
15050-15050	HOOKSTOWN	15325-15325	CRUCIBLE	15446-15446	INDIAN HEAD	15565-15565	WEST SALISBURY
15051-15051	INDIANOLA	15327-15327	DILLINER	15447-15447	ISABELLA	15601-15606	GREENSBURG
15052-15052	INDUSTRY	15329-15329	PROSPERITY	15448-15448	JACOBS CREEK	15610-15610	ACME
15053-15053	JOFFRE	15330-15330	EIGHTY FOUR	15449-15449	KEISTERVILLE	15611-15611	ADAMSBURG
15054-15054	LANGELOTH	15331-15331	ELLSWORTH	15450-15450	LA BELLE	15612-15612	ALVERTON
15055-15055	LAWRENCE	15332-15332	FINLEYVILLE	15451-15451	LAKE LYNN	15613-15613	APOLLO
15056-15056	LEETSDALE	15333-15333	FREDERICKTOWN	15454-15454	LECKRONE	15615-15615	ARDARA
15057-15057	MC DONALD	15334-15334	GARARDS FORT	15455-15455	LEISENRING	15616-15616	ARMBRUST
15059-15059	MIDLAND	15336-15336	GASTONVILLE	15456-15456	LEMONT FURNACE	15617-15617	ARONA
15060-15060	MIDWAY	15337-15337	GRAYSVILLE	15458-15458	MC CLELLANDTOWN	15618-15618	AVONMORE
15061-15061	MONACA	15338-15338	GREENSBORO	15459-15459	MARKLEYSBURG	15619-15619	BOVARD
15062-15062	MONESSEN	15339-15339	HENDERSONVILLE	15460-15460	MARTIN	15620-15620	BRADENVILLE
15063-15063	MONONGAHELA	15340-15340	HICKORY	15461-15461	MASONTOWN	15621-15621	CALUMET
15064-15064	MORGAN	15341-15341	HOLBROOK	15462-15462	MELCROFT	15622-15622	CHAMPION
15065-15065	NATRONA HEIGHTS	15342-15342	HOUSTON	15463-15463	MERRITTSTOWN	15623-15623	CLARIDGE
15066-15066	NEW BRIGHTON	15344-15344	JEFFERSON	15464-15464	MILL RUN	15624-15624	CRABTREE
15067-15067	NEW EAGLE	15345-15345	MARIANNA	15465-15465	MOUNT BRADDOCK	15625-15625	DARRAGH
15068-15069	NEW KENSINGTON	15346-15346	MATHER	15466-15466	NEWELL	15626-15626	DELMONT
15071-15071	OAKDALE	15347-15347	MEADOW LANDS	15467-15467	NEW GENEVA	15627-15627	DERRY
15072-15072	PRICEDALE	15348-15348	MILLSBORO	15468-15468	NEW SALEM	15628-15628	DONEGAL
15074-15074	ROCHESTER	15349-15349	MOUNT MORRIS	15469-15469	NORMALVILLE	15629-15629	EAST VANDERGRIFT
15075-15075	RURAL RIDGE	15350-15350	MUSE	15470-15470	OHIOPYLE	15630-15630	EDMON
15076-15076	RUSSELLTON	15351-15351	NEMACOLIN	15472-15472	OLIVER	15631-15631	EVERSON
15077-15077	SHIPPINGPORT	15352-15352	NEW FREEPORT	15473-15473	PERRYOPOLIS	15632-15632	EXPORT
15078-15078	SLOVAN	15353-15353	NINEVEH	15474-15474	POINT MARION	15633-15633	FORBES ROAD
15081-15081	SOUTH HEIGHTS	15354-15354	PINE BANK	15475-15475	REPUBLIC	15634-15634	GRAPEVILLE
15082-15082	STURGEON	15356-15356	REA	15476-15476	RONCO	15635-15635	HANNASTOWN
15083-15083	SUTERSVILLE	15357-15357	RICES LANDING	15477-15477	ROSCOE	15636-15636	HARRISON CITY
15084-15084	TARENTUM	15358-15358	RICHEYVILLE	15478-15478	SMITHFIELD	15637-15637	HERMINIE
15085-15085	TRAFFORD	15359-15359	ROGERSVILLE	15479-15479	SMITHTON	15638-15638	HOSTETTER
15086-15086	WARRENDALE	15360-15360	SCENERY HILL	15480-15480	SMOCK	15639-15639	HUNKER
15087-15087	WEBSTER	15361-15361	SOUTHVIEW	15482-15482	STAR JUNCTION	15640-15640	HUTCHINSON
15088-15088	WEST ELIZABETH	15362-15362	SPRAGGS	15483-15483	STOCKDALE	15641-15641	HYDE PARK
15089-15089	WEST NEWTON	15363-15363	STRABANE	15484-15484	ULEDI	15642-15642	IRWIN
15090-15090	WEXFORD	15364-15364	SYCAMORE	15485-15485	URSINA	15644-15644	JEANNETTE
15091-15091	WILDWOOD	15365-15365	TAYLORSTOWN	15486-15486	VANDERBILT	15646-15646	JONES MILLS
15095-15096	WARRENDALE	15366-15366	VAN VOORHIS	15488-15488	WALTERSBURG	15647-15647	LARIMER
15101-15101	ALLISON PARK	15367-15367	VENETIA	15489-15489	WEST LEISENRING	15650-15650	LATROBE
15102-15102	BETHEL PARK	15368-15368	VESTABURG	15490-15490	WHITE	15655-15655	LAUGHLINTOWN

15656-15656 LEECHBURG	15761-15761 MENTCLE	15957-15957 STRONGSTOWN	16172-16172 NEW WILMINGTON
15658-15658 LIGONIER	15762-15762 NICKTOWN	15958-15958 SUMMERHILL	16201-16201 KITTANNING
15660-15660 LOWBER	15763-15763 NORTHPOINT	15959-15959 TIRE HILL	16210-16210 ADRIAN
15661-15661 LOYALHANNA	15764-15764 OLIVEBURG	15960-15960 TWIN ROCKS	16211-16211 BEYER
15662-15662 LUXOR	15765-15765 PENN RUN	15961-15961 VINTONDALE	16212-16212 CADOGAN
15663-15663 MADISON	15767-15767 PUNXSUTAWNEY	15962-15962 WILMORE	16213-16213 CALLENSBURG
15664-15664 MAMMOTH	15770-15770 RINGGOLD	15963-15963 WINDBER	16214-16214 CLARION
15665-15665 MANOR	15771-15771 ROCHESTER MILLS	16001-16003 BUTLER	16215-16215 KITTANNING
15666-15666 MOUNT PLEASANT	15772-15772 ROSSITER	16016-16020 BOYERS	16216-16216 CLIMAX
15668-15668 MURRYSVILLE	15773-15773 SAINT BENEDICT	16021-16021 BRANCHTON	16217-16217 COOKSBURG
15670-15670 NEW ALEXANDRIA	15774-15774 SHELOCTA	16022-16022 BRUIN	16218-16218 COWANSVILLE
15671-15671 NEW DERRY	15775-15775 SPANGLER	16023-16023 CABOT	16220-16220 CROWN
15672-15672 NEW STANTON	15776-15776 SPRANKLE MILLS	16024-16024 CALLERY	16221-16221 CURLLSVILLE
15673-15673 NORTH APOLLO	15777-15777 STARFORD	16025-16025 CHICORA	16222-16222 DAYTON
15674-15674 NORVELT	15778-15778 TIMBLIN	16027-16027 CONNOQUENESSING	16223-16223 DISTANT
15675-15675 PENN	15779-15779 TORRANCE	16028-16028 EAST BRADY	16224-16224 FAIRMOUNT CITY
15676-15676 PLEASANT UNITY	15780-15780 VALIER	16029-16029 EAST BUTLER	16225-16225 FISHER
15677-15677 RECTOR	15781-15781 WALSTON	16030-16030 EAU CLAIRE	16226-16226 FORD CITY
15678-15678 RILLTON	15783-15783 WEST LEBANON	16033-16033 EVANS CITY	16228-16228 FORD CLIFF
15679-15679 RUFFS DALE	15784-15784 WORTHVILLE	16034-16034 FENELTON	16229-16229 FREEPORT
15680-15680 SALINA	15801-15801 DU BOIS	16035-16035 FORESTVILLE	16230-16230 HAWTHORN
15681-15681 SALTSBURG	15821-15821 BENEZETT	16036-16036 FOXBURG	16232-16232 KNOX
15682-15682 SCHENLEY	15822-15822 BRANDY CAMP	16037-16037 HARMONY	16233-16233 LEEPER
15683-15683 SCOTTDALE	15823-15823 BROCKPORT	16038-16038 HARRISVILLE	16234-16234 LIMESTONE
15684-15684 SLICKVILLE	15824-15824 BROCKWAY	16039-16039 HERMAN	16235-16235 LUCINDA
15685-15685 SOUTHWEST	15825-15825 BROOKVILLE	16040-16040 HILLIARDS	16236-16236 MC GRANN
15686-15686 SPRING CHURCH	15827-15827 BYRNEDALE	16041-16041 KARNS CITY	16238-16238 MANORVILLE
15687-15687 STAHLSTOWN	15828-15828 CLARINGTON	16045-16045 LYNDORA	16239-16239 MARIENVILLE
15688-15688 TARRS	15829-15829 CORSICA	16046-16046 MARS	16240-16240 MAYPORT
15689-15689 UNITED	15831-15831 DAGUS MINES	16048-16048 NORTH WASHINGTON	16242-16242 NEW BETHLEHEM
15690-15690 VANDERGRIFT	15832-15832 DRIFTWOOD	16049-16049 PARKER	16244-16244 NU MINE
15691-15691 WENDEL	15834-15834 EMPORIUM	16050-16050 PETROLIA	16245-16245 OAK RIDGE
15692-15692 WESTMORELAND CITY	15840-15840 FALLS CREEK	16051-16051 PORTERSVILLE	16246-16246 PLUMVILLE
15693-15693 WHITNEY	15841-15841 FORCE	16052-16052 PROSPECT	16248-16248 RIMERSBURG
15695-15695 WYANO	15845-15845 JOHNSONBURG	16053-16053 RENFREW	16249-16249 RURAL VALLEY
15696-15696 YOUNGSTOWN	15846-15846 KERSEY	16054-16054 SAINT PETERSBURG	16250-16250 SAGAMORE
15697-15697 YOUNGWOOD	15847-15847 KNOX DALE	16055-16055 SARVER	16253-16253 SEMINOLE
15698-15698 YUKON	15848-15848 LUTHERSBURG	16056-16056 SAXONBURG	16254-16254 SHIPPENVILLE
15701-15705 INDIANA	15849-15849 PENFIELD	16057-16057 SLIPPERY ROCK	16255-16255 SLIGO
15710-15710 ALVERDA	15851-15851 REYNOLDSVILLE	16058-16058 TURKEY CITY	16256-16256 SMICKSBURG
15711-15711 ANITA	15853-15853 RIDGWAY	16059-16059 VALENCIA	16257-16257 SNYDERSBURG
15712-15712 ARCADIA	15856-15856 ROCKTON	16061-16061 WEST SUNBURY	16258-16258 STRATTANVILLE
15713-15713 AULTMAN	15857-15857 SAINT MARYS	16063-16063 ZELIENOPLE	16259-16259 TEMPLETON
15714-15714 BARNESBORO	15860-15860 SIGEL	16066-16066 CRANBERRY TWP	16260-16260 VOWINCKEL
15715-15715 BIG RUN	15861-15861 SINNAMAHONING	16101-16108 NEW CASTLE	16261-16261 WIDNOON
15716-15716 BLACK LICK	15863-15863 STUMP CREEK	16110-16110 ADAMSVILLE	16262-16262 WORTHINGTON
15717-15717 BLAIRSVILLE	15864-15864 SUMMERVILLE	16111-16111 ATLANTIC	16263-16263 YATESBORO
15720-15720 BRUSH VALLEY	15865-15865 SYKESVILLE	16112-16112 BESSEMER	16301-16301 OIL CITY
15721-15721 BURNSIDE	15866-15866 TROUTVILLE	16113-16113 CLARK	16311-16311 CARLTON
15722-15722 CARROLLTOWN	15868-15868 WEEDVILLE	16114-16114 CLARKS MILLS	16312-16312 CHANDLERS VALLEY
15723-15723 CHAMBERSVILLE	15870-15870 WILCOX	16115-16115 DARLINGTON	16313-16313 CLARENDON
15724-15724 CHERRY TREE	15901-15915 JOHNSTOWN	16116-16116 EDINBURG	16314-16314 COCHRANTON
15725-15725 CLARKSBURG	15920-15920 ARMAGH	16117-16117 ELLWOOD CITY	16316-16316 CONNEAUT LAKE
15727-15727 CLUNE	15921-15921 BEAVERDALE	16120-16120 ENON VALLEY	16317-16317 COOPERSTOWN
15728-15728 CLYMER	15922-15922 BELSANO	16121-16121 FARRELL	16319-16319 CRANBERRY
15729-15729 COMMODORE	15923-15923 BOLIVAR	16123-16123 FOMBELL	16321-16321 EAST HICKORY
15730-15730 COOLSPRING	15924-15924 CAIRNBROOK	16124-16124 FREDONIA	16322-16322 ENDEAVOR
15731-15731 CORAL	15925-15925 CASSANDRA	16125-16125 GREENVILLE	16323-16323 FRANKLIN
15732-15732 CREEKSIDE	15926-15926 CENTRAL CITY	16127-16127 GROVE CITY	16326-16326 FRYBURG
15733-15733 DE LANCEY	15927-15927 COLVER	16130-16130 HADLEY	16327-16327 GUYS MILLS
15734-15734 DIXONVILLE	15928-15928 DAVIDSVILLE	16131-16131 HARTSTOWN	16328-16328 HYDETOWN
15736-15736 ELDERTON	15929-15929 DILLTOWN	16132-16132 HILLSVILLE	16329-16329 IRVINE
15737-15737 ELMORA	15930-15930 DUNLO	16133-16133 JACKSON CENTER	16331-16331 KOSSUTH
15738-15738 EMEIGH	15931-15931 EBENSBURG	16134-16134 JAMESTOWN	16332-16332 LICKINGVILLE
15739-15739 ERNEST	15934-15934 ELTON	16136-16136 KOPPEL	16333-16333 LUDLOW
15740-15740 FROSTBURG	15935-15935 HOLLSOPPLE	16137-16137 MERCER	16334-16334 MARBLE
15741-15741 GIPSY	15936-15936 HOOVERSVILLE	16140-16140 NEW BEDFORD	16335-16335 MEADVILLE
15742-15742 GLEN CAMPBELL	15937-15937 JEROME	16141-16141 NEW GALILEE	16340-16340 PITTSFIELD
15744-15744 HAMILTON	15938-15938 LILLY	16142-16142 NEW WILMINGTON	16341-16341 PLEASANTVILLE
15745-15745 HEILWOOD	15940-15940 LORETTO	16143-16143 PULASKI	16342-16342 POLK
15746-15746 HILLSDALE	15942-15942 MINERAL POINT	16145-16145 SANDY LAKE	16343-16343 RENO
15747-15747 HOME	15943-15943 NANTY GLO	16146-16146 SHARON	16344-16344 ROUSEVILLE
15748-15748 HOMER CITY	15944-15944 NEW FLORENCE	16148-16148 HERMITAGE	16345-16345 RUSSELL
15750-15750 JOSEPHINE	15945-15945 PARKHILL	16150-16150 SHARPSVILLE	16346-16346 SENECA
15751-15751 JUNEAU	15946-15946 PORTAGE	16151-16151 SHEAKLEYVILLE	16347-16347 SHEFFIELD
15752-15752 KENT	15948-15948 REVLOC	16153-16153 STONEBORO	16350-16350 SUGAR GROVE
15753-15753 LA JOSE	15949-15949 ROBINSON	16154-16154 TRANSFER	16351-16351 TIDIOUTE
15754-15754 LUCERNEMINES	15951-15951 SAINT MICHAEL	16155-16155 VILLA MARIA	16352-16352 TIONA
15756-15756 MC INTYRE	15952-15952 SALIX	16156-16156 VOLANT	16353-16353 TIONESTA
15757-15757 MAHAFFEY	15953-15953 SEANOR	16157-16157 WAMPUM	16354-16354 TITUSVILLE
15758-15758 MARCHAND	15954-15954 SEWARD	16159-16159 WEST MIDDLESEX	16360-16360 TOWNVILLE
15759-15759 MARION CENTER	15955-15955 SIDMAN	16160-16160 WEST PITTSBURG	16361-16361 TYLERSBURG
15760-15760 MARSTELLER	15956-15956 SOUTH FORK	16161-16161 WHEATLAND	16362-16362 UTICA

16364-16364 VENUS	16652-16654 HUNTINGDON	16839-16839 GRASSFLAT	17013-17013 CARLISLE
16365-16367 WARREN	16655-16655 IMLER	16840-16840 HAWK RUN	17014-17014 COCOLAMUS
16368-16368 IRVINE	16656-16656 IRVONA	16841-16841 HOWARD	17015-17015 COLEBROOK
16368-16368 WARREN	16657-16657 JAMES CREEK	16843-16843 HYDE	17016-17016 CORNWALL
16369-16369 IRVINE	16659-16659 LOYSBURG	16844-16844 JULIAN	17017-17017 DALMATIA
16369-16369 WARREN	16660-16660 MC CONNELLSTOWN	16845-16845 KARTHAUS	17018-17018 DAUPHIN
16370-16370 WEST HICKORY	16661-16661 MADERA	16847-16847 KYLERTOWN	17019-17019 DILLSBURG
16371-16371 YOUNGSVILLE	16662-16662 MARTINSBURG	16848-16848 LAMAR	17020-17020 DUNCANNON
16372-16372 CLINTONVILLE	16663-16663 MORANN	16849-16849 LANSE	17021-17021 EAST WATERFORD
16373-16373 EMLENTON	16664-16664 NEW ENTERPRISE	16850-16850 LECONTES MILLS	17022-17022 ELIZABETHTOWN
16374-16374 KENNERDELL	16665-16665 NEWRY	16851-16851 LEMONT	17023-17023 ELIZABETHVILLE
16375-16375 LAMARTINE	16666-16666 OSCEOLA MILLS	16852-16852 MADISONBURG	17024-17024 ELLIOTTSBURG
16388-16388 MEADVILLE	16667-16667 OSTERBURG	16853-16853 MILESBURG	17025-17025 ENOLA
16401-16401 ALBION	16668-16668 PATTON	16854-16854 MILLHEIM	17026-17026 FREDERICKSBURG
16402-16402 BEAR LAKE	16669-16669 PETERSBURG	16855-16855 MINERAL SPRINGS	17027-17027 GRANTHAM
16403-16403 CAMBRIDGE SPRINGS	16670-16670 QUEEN	16856-16856 MINGOVILLE	17028-17028 GRANTVILLE
16404-16404 CENTERVILLE	16671-16671 RAMEY	16858-16858 MORRISDALE	17029-17029 GRANVILLE
16405-16405 COLUMBUS	16672-16672 RIDDLESBURG	16859-16859 MOSHANNON	17030-17030 GRATZ
16406-16406 CONNEAUTVILLE	16673-16673 ROARING SPRING	16860-16860 MUNSON	17031-17031 GREEN PARK
16407-16407 CORRY	16674-16674 ROBERTSDALE	16861-16861 NEW MILLPORT	17032-17032 HALIFAX
16410-16410 CRANESVILLE	16675-16675 SAINT BONIFACE	16863-16863 OLANTA	17033-17033 HERSHEY
16411-16411 EAST SPRINGFIELD	16677-16677 SANDY RIDGE	16864-16864 ORVISTON	17034-17034 HIGHSPIRE
16412-16412 EDINBORO	16678-16678 SAXTON	16865-16865 PENNSYLVANIA FURNACE	17035-17035 HONEY GROVE
16413-16413 ELGIN	16679-16679 SIX MILE RUN	16866-16866 PHILIPSBURG	17036-17036 HUMMELSTOWN
16415-16415 FAIRVIEW	16680-16680 SMITHMILL	16868-16868 PINE GROVE MILLS	17037-17037 ICKESBURG
16416-16416 GARLAND	16681-16681 SMOKERUN	16870-16870 PORT MATILDA	17038-17038 JONESTOWN
16417-16417 GIRARD	16682-16682 SPROUL	16871-16871 POTTERSDALE	17039-17039 KLEINFELTERSVILLE
16420-16420 GRAND VALLEY	16683-16683 SPRUCE CREEK	16872-16872 REBERSBURG	17040-17040 LANDISBURG
16421-16421 HARBORCREEK	16684-16684 TIPTON	16873-16873 SHAWVILLE	17041-17041 LAWN
16422-16422 HARMONSBURG	16685-16685 TODD	16874-16874 SNOW SHOE	17042-17042 LEBANON
16423-16423 LAKE CITY	16686-16686 TYRONE	16875-16875 SPRING MILLS	17043-17043 LEMOYNE
16424-16424 LINESVILLE	16689-16689 WATERFALL	16876-16876 WALLACETON	17044-17044 LEWISTOWN
16426-16426 MC KEAN	16691-16691 WELLS TANNERY	16877-16877 WARRIORS MARK	17045-17045 LIVERPOOL
16427-16427 MILL VILLAGE	16692-16692 WESTOVER	16878-16878 WEST DECATUR	17046-17046 LEBANON
16428-16428 NORTH EAST	16693-16693 WILLIAMSBURG	16879-16879 WINBURNE	17047-17047 LOYSVILLE
16430-16430 NORTH SPRINGFIELD	16694-16694 WOOD	16880-16880 BELLEFONTE	17048-17048 LYKENS
16432-16432 RICEVILLE	16695-16695 WOODBURY	16881-16881 WOODLAND	17049-17049 MC ALISTERVILLE
16433-16433 SAEGERTOWN	16698-16698 HOUTZDALE	16882-16882 WOODWARD	17050-17050 MECHANICSBURG
16434-16434 SPARTANSBURG	16699-16699 CRESSON	16901-16901 WELLSBORO	17051-17051 MC VEYTOWN
16435-16435 SPRINGBORO	16701-16701 BRADFORD	16910-16910 ALBA	17052-17052 MAPLETON DEPOT
16436-16436 SPRING CREEK	16720-16720 AUSTIN	16911-16911 ARNOT	17053-17053 MARYSVILLE
16438-16438 UNION CITY	16724-16724 CROSBY	16912-16912 BLOSSBURG	17054-17054 MATTAWANA
16440-16440 VENANGO	16725-16725 CUSTER CITY	16914-16914 COLUMBIA CROSS ROADS	17055-17055 MECHANICSBURG
16441-16441 WATERFORD	16726-16726 CYCLONE	16915-16915 COUDERSPORT	17056-17056 MEXICO
16442-16442 WATTSBURG	16727-16727 DERRICK CITY	16917-16917 COVINGTON	17057-17057 MIDDLETOWN
16443-16443 WEST SPRINGFIELD	16728-16728 DE YOUNG	16918-16918 COWANESQUE	17058-17058 MIFFLIN
16444-16444 EDINBORO	16729-16729 DUKE CENTER	16920-16920 ELKLAND	17059-17059 MIFFLINTOWN
16475-16475 ALBION	16730-16730 EAST SMETHPORT	16921-16921 GAINES	17060-17060 MILL CREEK
16500-16565 ERIE	16731-16731 ELDRED	16922-16922 GALETON	17061-17061 MILLERSBURG
16566-16566 FIRST NAT BANK	16732-16732 GIFFORD	16923-16923 GENESEE	17062-17062 MILLERSTOWN
16601-16603 ALTOONA	16733-16733 HAZEL HURST	16925-16925 GILLETT	17063-17063 MILROY
16611-16611 ALEXANDRIA	16734-16734 JAMES CITY	16926-16926 GRANVILLE SUMMIT	17064-17064 MOUNT GRETNA
16613-16613 ASHVILLE	16735-16735 KANE	16927-16927 HARRISON VALLEY	17065-17065 MOUNT HOLLY SPRINGS
16614-16614 BAKERS SUMMIT	16738-16738 LEWIS RUN	16928-16928 KNOXVILLE	17066-17066 MOUNT UNION
16616-16616 BECCARIA	16740-16740 MOUNT JEWETT	16929-16929 LAWRENCEVILLE	17067-17067 MYERSTOWN
16617-16617 BELLWOOD	16743-16743 PORT ALLEGANY	16930-16930 LIBERTY	17068-17068 NEW BLOOMFIELD
16619-16619 BLANDBURG	16744-16744 REW	16932-16932 MAINESBURG	17069-17069 NEW BUFFALO
16620-16620 BRISBIN	16745-16745 RIXFORD	16933-16933 MANSFIELD	17070-17070 NEW CUMBERLAND
16621-16621 BROAD TOP	16746-16746 ROULETTE	16935-16935 MIDDLEBURY CENTER	17071-17071 NEW GERMANTOWN
16622-16622 CALVIN	16748-16748 SHINGLEHOUSE	16936-16936 MILLERTON	17072-17072 NEW KINGSTOWN
16623-16623 CASSVILLE	16749-16749 SMETHPORT	16937-16937 MILLS	17073-17073 NEWMANSTOWN
16624-16624 CHEST SPRINGS	16750-16750 TURTLEPOINT	16938-16938 MORRIS	17074-17074 NEWPORT
16625-16625 CLAYSBURG	16751-16751 WESTLINE	16939-16939 MORRIS RUN	17075-17075 NEWTON HAMILTON
16627-16627 COALPORT	16801-16801 STATE COLLEGE	16940-16940 NELSON	17076-17076 OAKLAND MILLS
16629-16629 COUPON	16802-16802 UNIVERSITY PARK	16941-16941 GENESEE	17077-17077 ONO
16630-16630 CRESSON	16803-16805 STATE COLLEGE	16942-16942 OSCEOLA	17078-17078 PALMYRA
16631-16631 CURRYVILLE	16820-16820 AARONSBURG	16943-16943 SABINSVILLE	17080-17080 PILLOW
16633-16633 DEFIANCE	16821-16821 ALLPORT	16945-16945 SYLVANIA	17081-17081 PLAINFIELD
16634-16634 DUDLEY	16822-16822 BEECH CREEK	16946-16946 TIOGA	17082-17082 PORT ROYAL
16635-16635 DUNCANSVILLE	16823-16823 BELLEFONTE	16947-16947 TROY	17083-17083 QUENTIN
16636-16636 DYSART	16825-16825 BIGLER	16948-16948 ULYSSES	17084-17084 REEDSVILLE
16637-16637 EAST FREEDOM	16826-16826 BLANCHARD	16950-16950 WESTFIELD	17085-17085 REXMONT
16638-16638 ENTRIKEN	16827-16827 BOALSBURG	17001-17001 CAMP HILL	17086-17086 RICHFIELD
16639-16639 FALLENTIMBER	16828-16828 CENTRE HALL	17002-17002 ALLENSVILLE	17087-17087 RICHLAND
16640-16640 FLINTON	16829-16829 CLARENCE	17003-17003 ANNVILLE	17088-17088 SCHAEFFERSTOWN
16641-16641 GALLITZIN	16830-16830 CLEARFIELD	17004-17004 BELLEVILLE	17089-17089 CAMP HILL
16644-16644 GLASGOW	16832-16832 COBURN	17005-17005 BERRYSBURG	17090-17090 SHERMANS DALE
16645-16645 GLEN HOPE	16833-16833 CURWENSVILLE	17006-17006 BLAIN	17091-17091 CAMP HILL
16646-16646 HASTINGS	16834-16834 DRIFTING	17007-17007 BOILING SPRINGS	17091-17091 LEBANON
16647-16647 HESSTON	16835-16835 FLEMING	17008-17008 BOWMANSDALE	17093-17093 SUMMERDALE
16648-16648 HOLLIDAYSBURG	16836-16836 FRENCHVILLE	17009-17009 BURNHAM	17094-17094 THOMPSONTOWN
16650-16650 HOPEWELL	16837-16837 GLEN RICHEY	17010-17010 CAMPBELLTOWN	17097-17097 WICONISCO
16651-16651 HOUTZDALE	16838-16838 GRAMPIAN	17011-17012 CAMP HILL	17098-17098 WILLIAMSTOWN

17099-17099 YEAGERTOWN	17339-17339 LEWISBERRY	17580-17580 TALMAGE	17844-17844 MIFFLINBURG
17100-17177 HARRISBURG	17340-17340 LITTLESTOWN	17581-17581 TERRE HILL	17845-17845 MILLMONT
17201-17201 CHAMBERSBURG	17342-17342 LOGANVILLE	17582-17582 WASHINGTON BORO	17846-17846 MILLVILLE
17210-17210 AMBERSON	17343-17343 MC KNIGHTSTOWN	17583-17583 WEST WILLOW	17847-17847 MILTON
17211-17211 ARTEMAS	17344-17344 MC SHERRYSTOWN	17584-17584 WILLOW STREET	17850-17850 MONTANDON
17212-17212 BIG COVE TANNERY	17345-17345 MANCHESTER	17585-17585 WITMER	17851-17851 MOUNT CARMEL
17213-17213 BLAIRS MILLS	17346-17346 MENGES MILLS	17600-17699 LANCASTER	17853-17853 MOUNT PLEASANT MILLS
17214-17214 BLUE RIDGE SUMMIT	17347-17347 MOUNT WOLF	17701-17705 WILLIAMSPORT	17855-17855 NEW BERLIN
17215-17215 BURNT CABINS	17349-17349 NEW FREEDOM	17720-17720 ANTES FORT	17856-17856 NEW COLUMBIA
17217-17217 CONCORD	17350-17350 NEW OXFORD	17721-17721 AVIS	17857-17857 NORTHUMBERLAND
17218-17218 DICKINSON	17352-17352 NEW PARK	17722-17722 BODINES	17858-17858 NUMIDIA
17219-17219 DOYLESBURG	17353-17353 ORRTANNA	17723-17723 JERSEY SHORE	17859-17859 ORANGEVILLE
17220-17220 DRY RUN	17354-17354 PORTERS SIDELING	17724-17724 CANTON	17860-17860 PAXINOS
17221-17221 FANNETTSBURG	17355-17355 RAILROAD	17726-17726 CASTANEA	17861-17861 PAXTONVILLE
17222-17222 FAYETTEVILLE	17356-17356 RED LION	17727-17727 CEDAR RUN	17862-17862 PENNS CREEK
17223-17223 FORT LITTLETON	17358-17358 ROSSVILLE	17728-17728 COGAN STATION	17864-17864 PORT TREVORTON
17224-17224 FORT LOUDON	17360-17360 SEVEN VALLEYS	17729-17729 CROSS FORK	17865-17865 POTTS GROVE
17225-17225 GREENCASTLE	17361-17361 SHREWSBURY	17730-17730 DEWART	17866-17866 COAL TOWNSHIP
17228-17228 HARRISONVILLE	17362-17362 SPRING GROVE	17731-17731 EAGLES MERE	17867-17867 REBUCK
17229-17229 HUSTONTOWN	17363-17363 STEWARTSTOWN	17734-17734 FARRANDSVILLE	17868-17868 RIVERSIDE
17231-17231 LEMASTERS	17364-17364 THOMASVILLE	17735-17735 GROVER	17870-17870 SELINSGROVE
17232-17232 LURGAN	17365-17365 WELLSVILLE	17737-17737 HUGHESVILLE	17872-17872 SHAMOKIN
17233-17233 MC CONNELLSBURG	17366-17366 WINDSOR	17738-17738 HYNER	17876-17876 SHAMOKIN DAM
17235-17235 MARION	17368-17368 WRIGHTSVILLE	17739-17739 JERSEY MILLS	17877-17877 SNYDERTOWN
17236-17236 MERCERSBURG	17370-17370 YORK HAVEN	17740-17740 JERSEY SHORE	17878-17878 STILLWATER
17237-17237 MONT ALTO	17371-17371 YORK NEW SALEM	17742-17742 LAIRDSVILLE	17880-17880 SWENGEL
17238-17238 NEEDMORE	17372-17372 YORK SPRINGS	17743-17743 LEROY	17881-17881 TREVORTON
17239-17239 NEELYTON	17375-17375 PEACH GLEN	17744-17744 LINDEN	17882-17882 TROXELVILLE
17240-17240 NEWBURG	17400-17415 YORK	17745-17745 LOCK HAVEN	17883-17883 VICKSBURG
17241-17241 NEWVILLE	17501-17501 AKRON	17747-17747 LOGANTON	17884-17884 WASHINGTONVILLE
17243-17243 ORBISONIA	17502-17502 BAINBRIDGE	17748-17748 MC ELHATTAN	17885-17885 WEIKERT
17244-17244 ORRSTOWN	17503-17503 BART	17749-17749 MC EWENSVILLE	17886-17886 WEST MILTON
17246-17246 PLEASANT HALL	17504-17504 BAUSMAN	17750-17750 MACKEYVILLE	17887-17887 WHITE DEER
17247-17247 QUINCY	17505-17505 BIRD IN HAND	17751-17751 MILL HALL	17888-17888 WILBURTON
17249-17249 ROCKHILL FURNACE	17506-17506 BLUE BALL	17752-17752 MONTGOMERY	17889-17889 WINFIELD
17250-17250 ROUZERVILLE	17507-17507 BOWMANSVILLE	17754-17754 MONTOURSVILLE	17901-17901 POTTSVILLE
17251-17251 ROXBURY	17508-17508 BROWNSTOWN	17756-17756 MUNCY	17920-17920 ARISTES
17252-17252 SAINT THOMAS	17509-17509 CHRISTIANA	17758-17758 MUNCY VALLEY	17921-17921 ASHLAND
17253-17253 SALTILLO	17512-17512 COLUMBIA	17759-17759 NISBET	17922-17922 AUBURN
17254-17254 SCOTLAND	17516-17516 CONESTOGA	17760-17760 NORTH BEND	17923-17923 BRANCHDALE
17255-17255 SHADE GAP	17517-17517 DENVER	17762-17762 PICTURE ROCKS	17925-17925 BROCKTON
17256-17256 SHADY GROVE	17518-17518 DRUMORE	17763-17763 RALSTON	17927-17927 CENTRALIA
17257-17257 SHIPPENSBURG	17519-17519 EAST EARL	17764-17764 RENOVO	17929-17929 CRESSONA
17260-17260 SHIRLEYSBURG	17520-17520 EAST PETERSBURG	17765-17765 ROARING BRANCH	17930-17930 CUMBOLA
17261-17261 SOUTH MOUNTAIN	17521-17521 ELM	17767-17767 SALONA	17931-17932 FRACKVILLE
17262-17262 SPRING RUN	17522-17522 EPHRATA	17768-17768 SHUNK	17933-17933 FRIEDENSBURG
17263-17263 STATE LINE	17527-17527 GAP	17769-17769 SLATE RUN	17934-17934 GILBERTON
17264-17264 THREE SPRINGS	17528-17528 GOODVILLE	17770-17770 SONESTOWN	17935-17935 GIRARDVILLE
17265-17265 UPPERSTRASBURG	17529-17529 GORDONVILLE	17771-17771 TROUT RUN	17936-17936 GORDON
17266-17266 WALNUT BOTTOM	17532-17532 HOLTWOOD	17772-17772 TURBOTVILLE	17938-17938 HEGINS
17267-17267 WARFORDSBURG	17533-17533 HOPELAND	17773-17773 TYLERSVILLE	17939-17939 HELFENSTEIN
17268-17268 WAYNESBORO	17534-17534 INTERCOURSE	17774-17774 UNITYVILLE	17941-17941 KLINGERSTOWN
17270-17270 WILLIAMSON	17535-17535 KINZERS	17776-17776 WATERVILLE	17942-17942 LANDINGVILLE
17271-17271 WILLOW HILL	17536-17536 KIRKWOOD	17777-17777 WATSONTOWN	17943-17943 LAVELLE
17272-17272 ZULLINGER	17537-17537 LAMPETER	17778-17778 WESTPORT	17944-17944 LLEWELLYN
17294-17294 BLUE RIDGE SUMMIT	17538-17538 LANDISVILLE	17779-17779 WOOLRICH	17945-17945 LOCUSTDALE
17301-17301 ABBOTTSTOWN	17540-17540 LEOLA	17801-17801 SUNBURY	17946-17946 LOST CREEK
17302-17302 AIRVILLE	17543-17543 LITITZ	17810-17810 ALLENWOOD	17948-17948 MAHANOY CITY
17303-17303 ARENDTSVILLE	17545-17545 MANHEIM	17812-17812 BEAVER SPRINGS	17949-17949 MAHANOY PLANE
17304-17304 ASPERS	17547-17547 MARIETTA	17813-17813 BEAVERTOWN	17951-17951 MAR LIN
17306-17306 BENDERSVILLE	17549-17549 MARTINDALE	17814-17814 BENTON	17952-17952 MARY D
17307-17307 BIGLERVILLE	17550-17550 MAYTOWN	17815-17815 BLOOMSBURG	17953-17953 MIDDLEPORT
17309-17309 BROGUE	17551-17551 MILLERSVILLE	17820-17820 CATAWISSA	17954-17954 MINERSVILLE
17310-17310 CASHTOWN	17552-17552 MOUNT JOY	17821-17822 DANVILLE	17957-17957 MUIR
17311-17311 CODORUS	17554-17554 MOUNTVILLE	17823-17823 DORNSIFE	17959-17959 NEW PHILADELPHIA
17312-17312 CRALEY	17555-17555 NARVON	17824-17824 ELYSBURG	17960-17960 NEW RINGGOLD
17313-17313 DALLASTOWN	17557-17557 NEW HOLLAND	17825-17825 EXCELSIOR	17961-17961 ORWIGSBURG
17314-17314 DELTA	17560-17560 NEW PROVIDENCE	17827-17827 FREEBURG	17963-17963 PINE GROVE
17315-17315 DOVER	17562-17562 PARADISE	17828-17828 GOWEN CITY	17964-17964 PITMAN
17316-17316 EAST BERLIN	17563-17563 PEACH BOTTOM	17829-17829 HARTLETON	17965-17965 PORT CARBON
17317-17317 EAST PROSPECT	17564-17564 PENRYN	17830-17830 HERNDON	17966-17966 RAVINE
17318-17318 EMIGSVILLE	17565-17565 PEQUEA	17831-17831 HUMMELS WHARF	17967-17967 RINGTOWN
17319-17319 ETTERS	17566-17566 QUARRYVILLE	17832-17832 MARION HEIGHTS	17968-17968 SACRAMENTO
17320-17320 FAIRFIELD	17567-17567 REAMSTOWN	17833-17833 KREAMER	17970-17970 SAINT CLAIR
17321-17321 FAWN GROVE	17568-17568 REFTON	17834-17834 KULPMONT	17972-17972 SCHUYLKILL HAVEN
17322-17322 FELTON	17569-17569 REINHOLDS	17835-17835 LAURELTON	17974-17974 SELTZER
17323-17323 FRANKLINTOWN	17570-17570 RHEEMS	17836-17836 LECK KILL	17976-17976 SHENANDOAH
17324-17324 GARDNERS	17572-17573 RONKS	17837-17837 LEWISBURG	17978-17978 SPRING GLEN
17325-17326 GETTYSBURG	17575-17575 SILVER SPRING	17839-17839 LIGHT STREET	17979-17979 SUMMIT STATION
17327-17327 GLEN ROCK	17576-17576 SMOKETOWN	17840-17840 LOCUST GAP	17980-17980 TOWER CITY
17329-17329 GLENVILLE	17577-17577 SOUDERSBURG	17841-17841 MC CLURE	17981-17981 TREMONT
17331-17334 HANOVER	17578-17578 STEVENS	17842-17842 MIDDLEBURG	17982-17982 TUSCARORA
17337-17337 IDAVILLE	17579-17579 STRASBURG	17843-17843 BEAVER SPRINGS	17983-17983 VALLEY VIEW

17985-17985	ZION GROVE
18001-18003	LEHIGH VALLEY
18010-18010	ACKERMANVILLE
18011-18011	ALBURTIS
18012-18012	AQUASHICOLA
18013-18013	BANGOR
18014-18014	BATH
18015-18025	BETHLEHEM
18030-18030	BOWMANSTOWN
18031-18031	BREINIGSVILLE
18032-18032	CATASAUQUA
18034-18034	CENTER VALLEY
18035-18035	CHERRYVILLE
18036-18036	COOPERSBURG
18037-18037	COPLAY
18038-18038	DANIELSVILLE
18039-18039	DURHAM
18040-18040	EASTON
18041-18041	EAST GREENVILLE
18042-18045	EASTON
18046-18046	EAST TEXAS
18049-18049	EMMAUS
18050-18050	FLICKSVILLE
18051-18051	FOGELSVILLE
18052-18052	WHITEHALL
18053-18053	GERMANSVILLE
18054-18054	GREEN LANE
18055-18055	HELLERTOWN
18056-18056	HEREFORD
18058-18058	KUNKLETOWN
18059-18059	LAURYS STATION
18060-18060	LIMEPORT
18062-18062	MACUNGIE
18063-18063	MARTINS CREEK
18064-18064	NAZARETH
18065-18065	NEFFS
18066-18066	NEW TRIPOLI
18067-18067	NORTHAMPTON
18068-18068	OLD ZIONSVILLE
18069-18069	OREFIELD
18070-18070	PALM
18071-18071	PALMERTON
18072-18072	PEN ARGYL
18073-18073	PENNSBURG
18074-18074	PERKIOMENVILLE
18076-18076	RED HILL
18077-18077	RIEGELSVILLE
18078-18078	SCHNECKSVILLE
18079-18079	SLATEDALE
18080-18080	SLATINGTON
18081-18081	SPRINGTOWN
18083-18083	STOCKERTOWN
18084-18084	SUMNEYTOWN
18085-18085	TATAMY
18086-18086	TREICHLERS
18087-18087	TREXLERTOWN
18088-18088	WALNUTPORT
18091-18091	WIND GAP
18092-18092	ZIONSVILLE
18098-18099	EMMAUS
18100-18195	ALLENTOWN
18201-18202	HAZLETON
18210-18210	ALBRIGHTSVILLE
18211-18211	ANDREAS
18212-18212	ASHFIELD
18214-18214	BARNESVILLE
18216-18216	BEAVER MEADOWS
18218-18218	COALDALE
18219-18219	CONYNGHAM
18220-18220	DELANO
18221-18221	DRIFTON
18222-18222	DRUMS
18223-18223	EBERVALE
18224-18224	FREELAND
18225-18225	HARLEIGH
18229-18229	JIM THORPE
18230-18230	JUNEDALE
18231-18231	KELAYRES
18232-18232	LANSFORD
18234-18234	LATTIMER MINES
18235-18235	LEHIGHTON
18237-18237	MCADOO
18239-18239	MILNESVILLE
18240-18240	NESQUEHONING
18241-18241	NUREMBERG
18242-18242	ONEIDA
18243-18243	PARDEESVILLE
18244-18244	PARRYVILLE
18245-18245	QUAKAKE
18246-18246	ROCK GLEN
18247-18247	SAINT JOHNS
18248-18248	SHEPPTON
18249-18249	SUGARLOAF
18250-18250	SUMMIT HILL
18251-18251	SYBERTSVILLE
18252-18252	TAMAQUA
18254-18254	TRESCKOW
18255-18255	WEATHERLY
18256-18256	WESTON
18301-18301	EAST STROUDSBURG
18320-18320	ANALOMINK
18321-18321	BARTONSVILLE
18322-18322	BRODHEADSVILLE
18323-18323	BUCK HILL FALLS
18324-18324	BUSHKILL
18325-18325	CANADENSIS
18326-18326	CRESCO
18327-18327	DELAWARE WATER GAP
18328-18328	DINGMANS FERRY
18330-18330	EFFORT
18331-18331	GILBERT
18332-18332	HENRYVILLE
18333-18333	KRESGEVILLE
18334-18334	LONG POND
18335-18335	MARSHALLS CREEK
18336-18336	MATAMORAS
18337-18337	MILFORD
18340-18340	MILLRIFT
18341-18341	MINISINK HILLS
18342-18342	MOUNTAINHOME
18343-18343	MOUNT BETHEL
18344-18344	MOUNT POCONO
18346-18346	POCONO SUMMIT
18347-18347	POCONO LAKE
18348-18348	POCONO LAKE PRESERVE
18349-18349	POCONO MANOR
18350-18350	POCONO PINES
18351-18351	PORTLAND
18352-18352	REEDERS
18353-18353	SAYLORSBURG
18354-18354	SCIOTA
18355-18355	SCOTRUN
18356-18356	SHAWNEE ON DELAWARE
18357-18357	SKYTOP
18360-18360	STROUDSBURG
18370-18370	SWIFTWATER
18371-18371	TAMIMENT
18372-18372	TANNERSVILLE
18373-18373	UNITY HOUSE
18401-18401	ALDENVILLE
18403-18403	ARCHBALD
18405-18405	BEACH LAKE
18407-18407	CARBONDALE
18410-18410	CHINCHILLA
18411-18411	CLARKS SUMMIT
18413-18413	CLIFFORD
18414-18414	DALTON
18415-18415	DAMASCUS
18416-18416	ELMHURST
18417-18417	EQUINUNK
18419-18419	FACTORYVILLE
18420-18420	FLEETVILLE
18421-18421	FOREST CITY
18424-18424	GOULDSBORO
18425-18425	GREELEY
18426-18426	GREENTOWN
18427-18427	HAMLIN
18428-18428	HAWLEY
18430-18430	HERRICK CENTER
18431-18431	HONESDALE
18433-18433	JERMYN
18434-18434	JESSUP
18435-18435	LACKAWAXEN
18436-18436	LAKE ARIEL
18437-18437	LAKE COMO
18438-18438	LAKEVILLE
18439-18439	LAKEWOOD
18440-18440	LA PLUME
18441-18441	LENOXVILLE
18443-18443	MILANVILLE
18444-18444	MOSCOW
18445-18445	NEWFOUNDLAND
18446-18446	NICHOLSON
18447-18448	OLYPHANT
18449-18449	ORSON
18451-18451	PAUPACK
18452-18452	PECKVILLE
18453-18453	PLEASANT MOUNT
18454-18454	POYNTELLE
18455-18455	PRESTON PARK
18456-18456	PROMPTON
18457-18457	ROWLAND
18458-18458	SHOHOLA
18459-18459	SOUTH CANAAN
18460-18460	SOUTH STERLING
18461-18461	STARLIGHT
18462-18462	STARRUCCA
18463-18463	STERLING
18464-18464	TAFTON
18465-18465	THOMPSON
18466-18466	TOBYHANNA
18469-18469	TYLER HILL
18470-18470	UNION DALE
18471-18471	WAVERLY
18472-18472	WAYMART
18473-18473	WHITE MILLS
18500-18505	SCRANTON
18507-18507	MOOSIC
18508-18515	SCRANTON
18517-18517	TAYLOR
18518-18518	OLD FORGE
18519-18519	DICKSON CITY
18522-18577	SCRANTON
18601-18601	BEACH HAVEN
18602-18602	BEAR CREEK
18603-18603	BERWICK
18610-18610	BLAKESLEE
18611-18611	CAMBRA
18612-18612	DALLAS
18614-18614	DUSHORE
18615-18615	FALLS
18616-18616	FORKSVILLE
18617-18617	GLEN LYON
18618-18618	HARVEYS LAKE
18619-18619	HILLSGROVE
18621-18621	HUNLOCK CREEK
18622-18622	HUNTINGTON MILLS
18623-18623	LACEYVILLE
18624-18624	LAKE HARMONY
18625-18625	LAKE WINOLA
18626-18626	LAPORTE
18627-18627	LEHMAN
18628-18628	LOPEZ
18629-18629	MEHOOPANY
18630-18630	MESHOPPEN
18631-18631	MIFFLINVILLE
18632-18632	MILDRED
18634-18634	NANTICOKE
18635-18635	NESCOPECK
18636-18636	NOXEN
18637-18637	NUANGOLA
18640-18641	PITTSTON
18642-18642	DURYEA
18643-18643	PITTSTON
18644-18644	WYOMING
18651-18651	PLYMOUTH
18653-18653	RANSOM
18654-18654	SHAWANESE
18655-18655	SHICKSHINNY
18656-18656	SWEET VALLEY
18657-18657	TUNKHANNOCK
18660-18660	WAPWALLOPEN
18661-18661	WHITE HAVEN
18690-18690	DALLAS
18700-18703	WILKES BARRE
18704-18704	KINGSTON
18705-18706	WILKES BARRE
18707-18707	MOUNTAIN TOP
18708-18708	SHAVERTOWN
18709-18709	LUZERNE
18710-18774	WILKES BARRE
18801-18801	MONTROSE
18810-18810	ATHENS
18812-18812	BRACKNEY
18813-18813	BROOKLYN
18814-18814	BURLINGTON
18815-18815	CAMPTOWN
18816-18816	DIMOCK
18817-18817	EAST SMITHFIELD
18818-18818	FRIENDSVILLE
18820-18820	GIBSON
18821-18821	GREAT BEND
18822-18822	HALLSTEAD
18823-18823	HARFORD
18824-18824	HOP BOTTOM
18825-18825	JACKSON
18826-18826	KINGSLEY
18827-18827	LANESBORO
18828-18828	LAWTON
18829-18829	LE RAYSVILLE
18830-18830	LITTLE MEADOWS
18831-18831	MILAN
18832-18832	MONROETON
18833-18833	NEW ALBANY
18834-18834	NEW MILFORD
18837-18837	ROME
18839-18839	RUSHVILLE
18840-18840	SAYRE
18842-18842	SOUTH GIBSON
18843-18843	SOUTH MONTROSE
18844-18844	SPRINGVILLE
18845-18845	STEVENSVILLE
18846-18846	SUGAR RUN
18847-18847	SUSQUEHANNA
18848-18848	TOWANDA
18850-18850	ULSTER
18851-18851	WARREN CENTER
18853-18853	WYALUSING
18854-18854	WYSOX
18901-18901	DOYLESTOWN
18910-18910	BEDMINSTER
18911-18911	BLOOMING GLEN
18912-18912	BUCKINGHAM
18913-18913	CARVERSVILLE
18914-18914	CHALFONT
18915-18915	COLMAR
18916-18916	DANBORO
18917-18917	DUBLIN
18918-18918	EARLINGTON
18920-18920	ERWINNA
18921-18921	FERNDALE
18922-18922	FOREST GROVE
18923-18923	FOUNTAINVILLE
18924-18924	FRANCONIA
18925-18925	FURLONG
18926-18926	GARDENVILLE
18927-18927	HILLTOWN
18928-18928	HOLICONG
18929-18929	JAMISON
18930-18930	KINTNERSVILLE
18931-18931	LAHASKA
18932-18932	LINE LEXINGTON
18933-18933	LUMBERVILLE
18934-18934	MECHANICSVILLE
18935-18935	MILFORD SQUARE
18936-18936	MONTGOMERYVILLE
18938-18938	NEW HOPE
18940-18940	NEWTOWN
18942-18942	OTTSVILLE
18943-18943	PENNS PARK
18944-18944	PERKASIE
18946-18946	PINEVILLE
18947-18947	PIPERSVILLE
18949-18949	PLUMSTEADVILLE
18950-18950	POINT PLEASANT
18951-18951	QUAKERTOWN
18953-18953	REVERE
18954-18954	RICHBORO
18955-18955	RICHLANDTOWN
18956-18956	RUSHLAND
18957-18957	SALFORD
18958-18958	SALFORDVILLE

ZIP Range	Place		ZIP Range	Place		ZIP Range	Place		ZIP Range	Place
18960-18960	SELLERSVILLE		19050-19050	LANSDOWNE		19357-19357	MENDENHALL		19475-19475	SPRING CITY
18962-18962	SILVERDALE		19052-19052	LENNI		19358-19358	MODENA		19477-19477	SPRING HOUSE
18963-18963	SOLEBURY		19053-19053	FEASTERVILLE TREVOSE		19360-19360	NEW LONDON		19478-19478	SPRING MOUNT
18964-18964	SOUDERTON		19054-19059	LEVITTOWN		19362-19362	NOTTINGHAM		19480-19480	UWCHLAND
18966-18966	SOUTHAMPTON		19059-19059	PHILADELPHIA		19363-19363	OXFORD		19481-19485	VALLEY FORGE
18968-18968	SPINNERSTOWN		19061-19061	MARCUS HOOK		19365-19365	PARKESBURG		19486-19486	WEST POINT
18969-18969	TELFORD		19063-19063	MEDIA		19366-19366	POCOPSON		19487-19487	KING OF PRUSSIA
18970-18970	TRUMBAUERSVILLE		19064-19064	SPRINGFIELD		19367-19367	POMEROY		19488-19489	NORRISTOWN
18971-18971	TYLERSPORT		19065-19065	MEDIA		19369-19369	SADSBURYVILLE		19490-19490	WORCESTER
18972-18972	UPPER BLACK EDDY		19066-19066	MERION STATION		19370-19370	STEELVILLE		19492-19492	ZIEGLERVILLE
18974-18974	WARMINSTER		19067-19067	MORRISVILLE		19371-19371	SUPLEE		19493-19496	VALLEY FORGE
18976-18976	WARRINGTON		19070-19070	MORTON		19372-19372	THORNDALE		19501-19501	ADAMSTOWN
18977-18977	WASHINGTON CROSSING		19072-19072	NARBERTH		19373-19373	THORNTON		19503-19503	BALLY
18979-18979	WOXALL		19073-19073	NEWTOWN SQUARE		19374-19374	TOUGHKENAMON		19504-19504	BARTO
18980-18980	WYCOMBE		19074-19074	NORWOOD		19375-19375	UNIONVILLE		19505-19505	BECHTELSVILLE
18981-18981	ZIONHILL		19075-19075	ORELAND		19376-19376	WAGONTOWN		19506-19506	BERNVILLE
18991-18991	WARMINSTER		19076-19076	PROSPECT PARK		19380-19383	WEST CHESTER		19507-19507	BETHEL
19001-19001	ABINGTON		19078-19078	RIDLEY PARK		19390-19390	WEST GROVE		19508-19508	BIRDSBORO
19002-19002	AMBLER		19079-19079	SHARON HILL		19395-19395	WESTTOWN		19510-19510	BLANDON
19003-19003	ARDMORE		19080-19080	WAYNE		19397-19399	SOUTHEASTERN		19511-19511	BOWERS
19004-19004	BALA CYNWYD		19081-19081	SWARTHMORE		19401-19404	NORRISTOWN		19512-19512	BOYERTOWN
19006-19006	HUNTINGDON VALLEY		19082-19082	UPPER DARBY		19405-19405	BRIDGEPORT		19516-19516	CENTERPORT
19007-19007	BRISTOL		19083-19083	HAVERTOWN		19406-19406	KING OF PRUSSIA		19517-19517	DAUBERVILLE
19008-19008	BROOMALL		19085-19085	VILLANOVA		19407-19407	AUDUBON		19518-19518	DOUGLASSVILLE
19009-19009	BRYN ATHYN		19086-19086	WALLINGFORD		19408-19408	EAGLEVILLE		19519-19519	EARLVILLE
19010-19010	BRYN MAWR		19087-19089	WAYNE		19409-19409	FAIRVIEW VILLAGE		19520-19520	ELVERSON
19012-19012	CHELTENHAM		19090-19090	WILLOW GROVE		19415-19415	EAGLEVILLE		19522-19522	FLEETWOOD
19013-19013	CHESTER		19091-19091	MEDIA		19420-19420	ARCOLA		19523-19523	GEIGERTOWN
19014-19014	ASTON		19092-19093	PHILADELPHIA		19421-19421	BIRCHRUNVILLE		19525-19525	GILBERTSVILLE
19015-19015	BROOKHAVEN		19094-19094	WOODLYN		19422-19422	BLUE BELL		19526-19526	HAMBURG
19016-19016	CHESTER		19095-19095	WYNCOTE		19423-19423	CEDARS		19529-19529	KEMPTON
19017-19017	CHESTER HEIGHTS		19096-19096	WYNNEWOOD		19424-19424	BLUE BELL		19530-19530	KUTZTOWN
19018-19018	CLIFTON HEIGHTS		19098-19098	HOLMES		19425-19425	CHESTER SPRINGS		19533-19533	LEESPORT
19019-19019	PHILADELPHIA		19099-19255	PHILADELPHIA		19426-19426	COLLEGEVILLE		19534-19534	LENHARTSVILLE
19020-19020	BENSALEM		19301-19301	PAOLI		19428-19429	CONSHOHOCKEN		19535-19535	LIMEKILN
19021-19021	CROYDON		19310-19310	ATGLEN		19430-19430	CREAMERY		19536-19536	LYON STATION
19022-19022	CRUM LYNNE		19311-19311	AVONDALE		19432-19432	DEVAULT		19538-19538	MAXATAWNY
19023-19023	DARBY		19312-19312	BERWYN		19435-19435	FREDERICK		19539-19539	MERTZTOWN
19025-19025	DRESHER		19316-19316	BRANDAMORE		19436-19436	GWYNEDD		19540-19540	MOHNTON
19026-19026	DREXEL HILL		19317-19317	CHADDS FORD		19437-19437	GWYNEDD VALLEY		19541-19541	MOHRSVILLE
19027-19027	ELKINS PARK		19318-19318	CHATHAM		19438-19438	HARLEYSVILLE		19542-19542	MONOCACY STATION
19028-19028	EDGEMONT		19319-19319	CHEYNEY		19440-19440	HATFIELD		19543-19543	MORGANTOWN
19029-19029	ESSINGTON		19320-19320	COATESVILLE		19441-19441	HARLEYSVILLE		19544-19544	MOUNT AETNA
19030-19030	FAIRLESS HILLS		19330-19330	COCHRANVILLE		19442-19442	KIMBERTON		19545-19545	NEW BERLINVILLE
19031-19031	FLOURTOWN		19331-19331	CONCORDVILLE		19443-19443	KULPSVILLE		19547-19547	OLEY
19032-19032	FOLCROFT		19333-19333	DEVON		19444-19444	LAFAYETTE HILL		19548-19548	PINE FORGE
19033-19033	FOLSOM		19335-19335	DOWNINGTOWN		19446-19446	LANSDALE		19549-19549	PORT CLINTON
19034-19034	FORT WASHINGTON		19339-19340	CONCORDVILLE		19450-19450	LEDERACH		19550-19550	REHRERSBURG
19035-19035	GLADWYNE		19341-19341	EXTON		19451-19451	MAINLAND		19551-19551	ROBESONIA
19036-19036	GLENOLDEN		19342-19342	GLEN MILLS		19452-19452	MIQUON		19554-19554	SHARTLESVILLE
19037-19037	GLEN RIDDLE LIMA		19343-19343	GLENMOORE		19453-19453	MONT CLARE		19555-19555	SHOEMAKERSVILLE
19038-19038	GLENSIDE		19344-19344	HONEY BROOK		19454-19455	NORTH WALES		19557-19557	STONY RUN
19039-19039	GRADYVILLE		19345-19345	IMMACULATA		19456-19456	OAKS		19559-19559	STRAUSSTOWN
19040-19040	HATBORO		19346-19346	KELTON		19457-19457	PARKER FORD		19560-19560	TEMPLE
19041-19041	HAVERFORD		19347-19347	KEMBLESVILLE		19460-19460	PHOENIXVILLE		19562-19562	TOPTON
19043-19043	HOLMES		19348-19348	KENNETT SQUARE		19462-19462	PLYMOUTH MEETING		19564-19564	VIRGINVILLE
19044-19044	HORSHAM		19350-19350	LANDENBERG		19464-19465	POTTSTOWN		19565-19565	WERNERSVILLE
19046-19046	JENKINTOWN		19351-19351	LEWISVILLE		19468-19468	ROYERSFORD		19567-19567	WOMELSDORF
19047-19048	LANGHORNE		19352-19352	LINCOLN UNIVERSITY		19470-19470	SAINT PETERS		19600-19640	READING
19048-19048	FORT WASHINGTON		19353-19353	LIONVILLE		19472-19472	SASSAMANSVILLE			
19049-19049	LANGHORNE		19354-19354	LYNDELL		19473-19473	SCHWENKSVILLE			
19049-19049	FORT WASHINGTON		19355-19355	MALVERN		19474-19474	SKIPPACK			

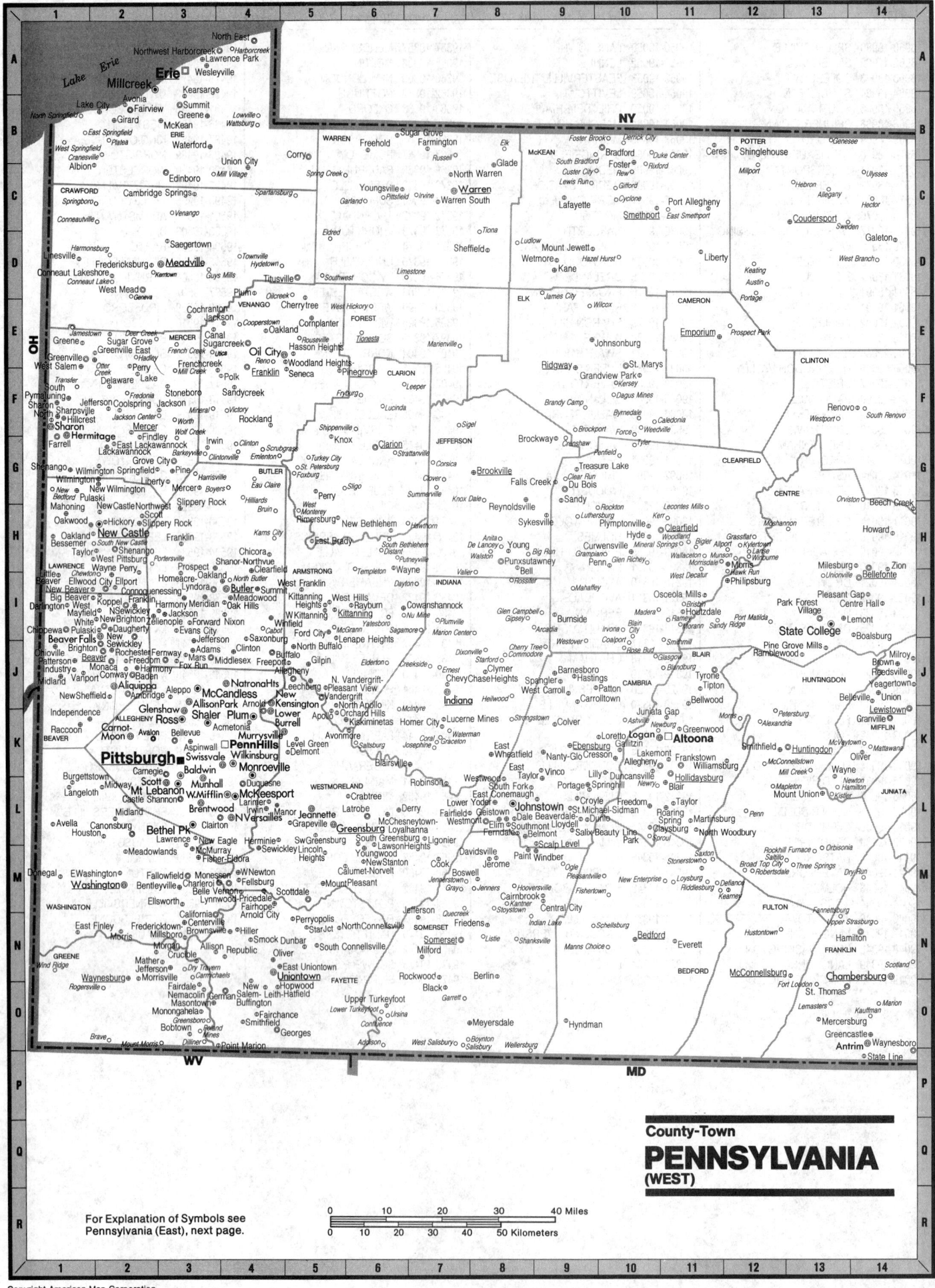

County-Town
PENNSYLVANIA
(WEST)

For Explanation of Symbols see
Pennsylvania (East), next page.

0   10   20   30   40 Miles

0 10 20 30 40 50 Kilometers

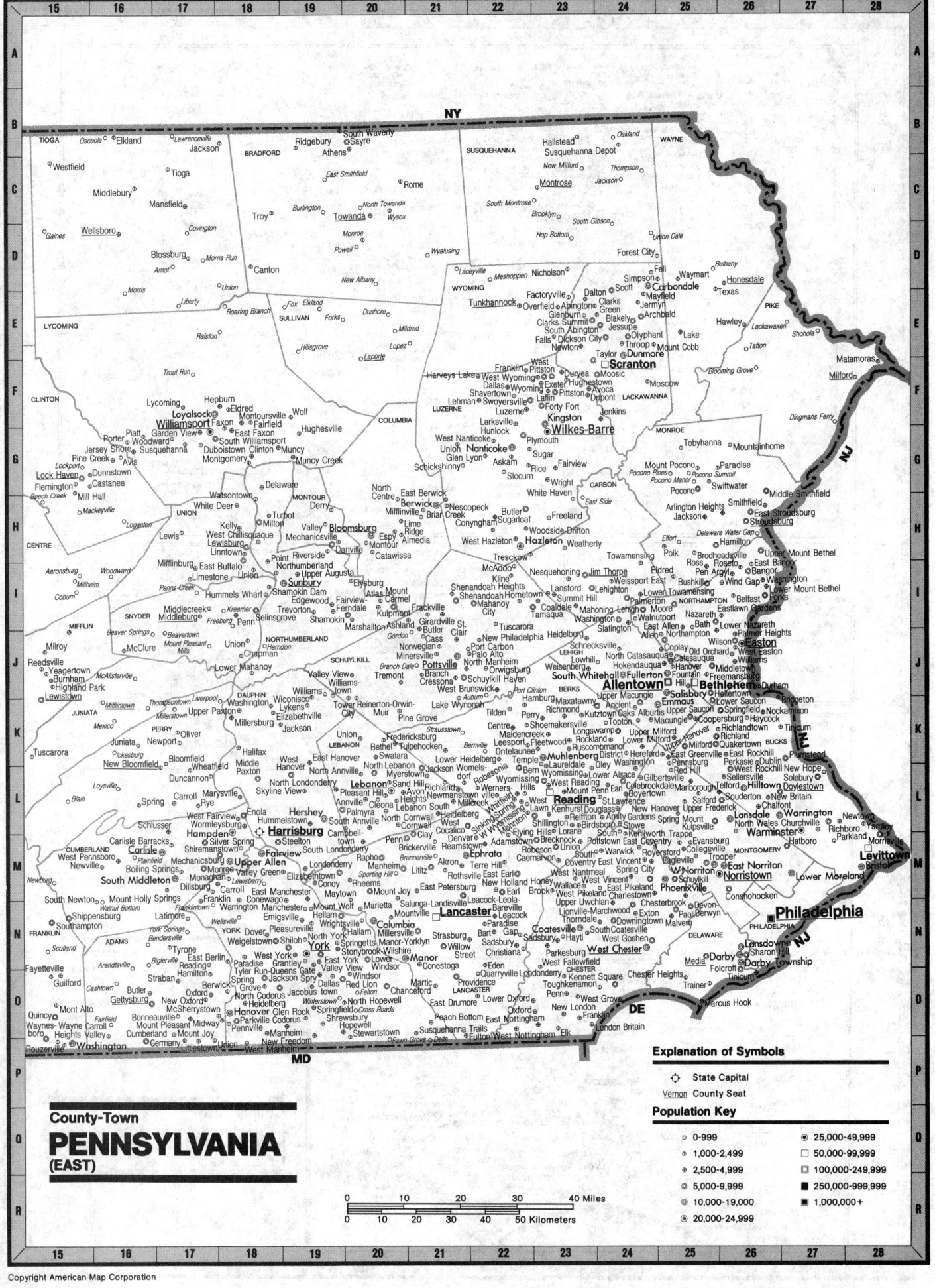

County-Town

PENNSYLVANIA
(EAST)

Explanation of Symbols

◇ State Capital
Vernon County Seat

Population Key

○	0-999	◉	25,000-49,999
◔	1,000-2,499	□	50,000-99,999
⊕	2,500-4,999	☐	100,000-249,999
◍	5,000-9,999	■	250,000-999,999
◉	10,000-19,000	■	1,000,000+
◉	20,000-24,999		

0   10   20   30   40 Miles
0   10   20   30   40   50 Kilometers

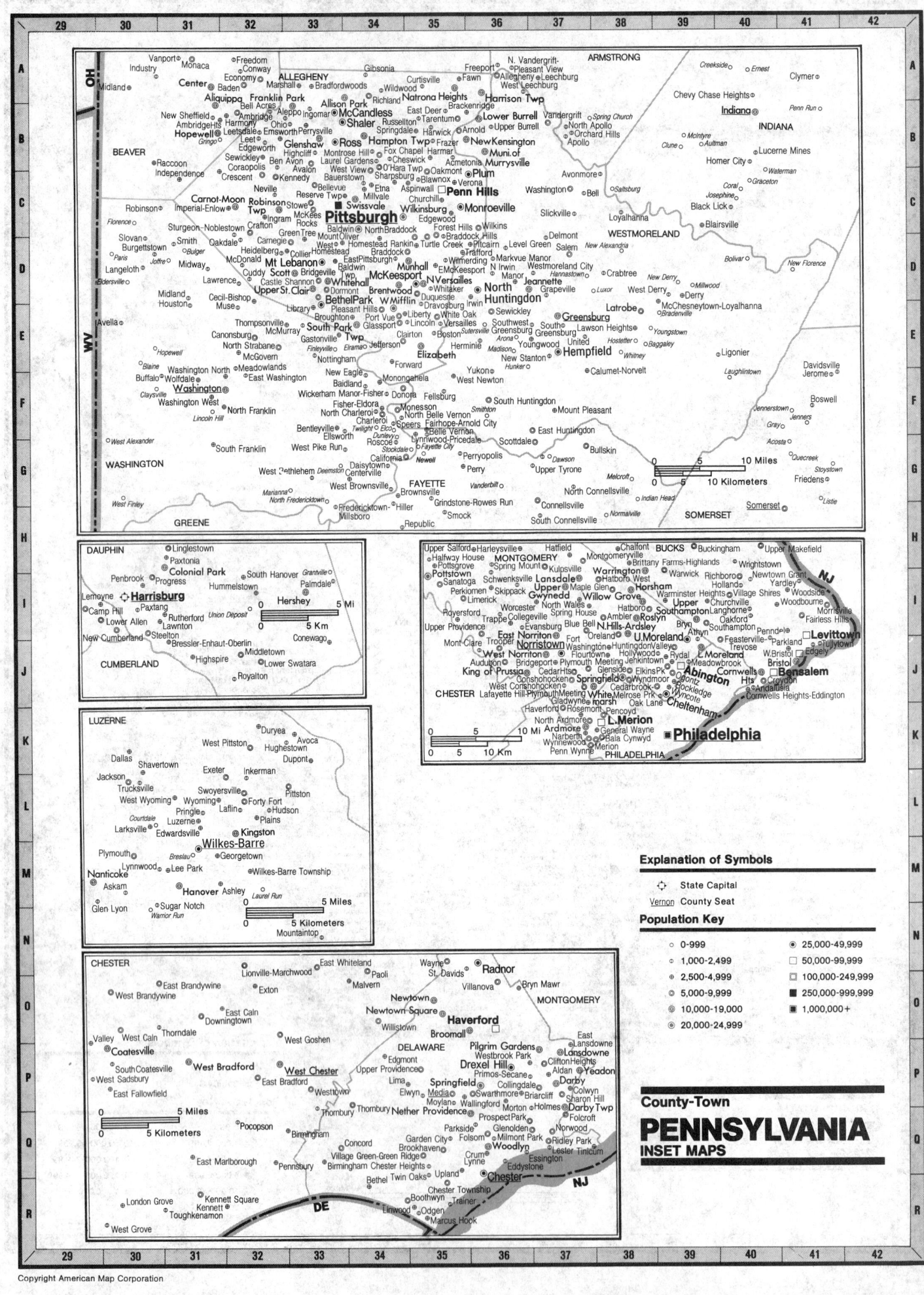

County-Town
PENNSYLVANIA
INSET MAPS

Explanation of Symbols

◇	State Capital
Vernon	County Seat

Population Key

○ 0-999		⊗ 25,000-49,999
○ 1,000-2,499		□ 50,000-99,999
⊙ 2,500-4,999		▣ 100,000-249,999
⊙ 5,000-9,999		■ 250,000-999,999
⊙ 10,000-19,000		▪ 1,000,000+
⊙ 20,000-24,999		

CITIES AND TOWNS

Note: The first name is that of the city or town, second, that of the county in which it is located, then the population and location on the map.

Great Bend, Susquehanna, 1,817 .... B-23
Green, Indiana, 4,095 .... J-8
Green Tree, Allegheny, 4,905 .... G-5
Greencastle, Franklin, 3,600 .... O-14
Greene, Beaver, 2,573 .... J-1
Greene, Clinton, 1,153 .... H-16
▲ *Greene, Erie, 4,959* B-3
Greene, Franklin, 11,930 .... N-15
Greene, Mercer, 1,247 .... E-1
Greene, Pike, 2,097 .... F-26
Greenfield, Blair, 3,802 .... J-9
Greenfield, Erie, 1,770 .... A-4
Greenfield, Lackawanna, 1,743 .... D-24
Greensburg, Westmoreland, 16,318 .... L-5
Greenville, Mercer, 6,734 .... E-1
• Greenville East, Mercer, 1,419 .... E-2
Greenwich, Berks, 2,977 .... K-23
Greenwood, Blair K-11
Greenwood, Columbia, 1,972 .... G-20
Greenwood, Crawford, 1,361 .... D-2
Gregg, Centre, 1,805 .... I-15
Gregg, Union, 1,114 .... G-18
• Grindstone-Rowes Run, Fayette, 1,041 .... G-35
Grove City, Mercer, 8,240 .... G-3
Guilford, Franklin, 11,893 .... O-15
• Guilford, Franklin, 1,618 .... O-15
Gulich, Clearfield, 1,192 .... I-11
Haines, Centre, 1,315 .... I-16
Halfmoon, Centre, 1,469 .... J-12
• Halfway House, Montgomery, 1,415 .... L-24
Halifax, Dauphin, 3,449 .... K-18
Hallam, York, 1,375 .... N-19
Hallstead, Susquehanna, 1,274 .... B-23
Hamburg, Berks, 3,987 .... K-22
▲ *Hamilton, Adams, 1,760* O-16
▲ *Hamilton, Franklin, 7,745* N-14
▲ *Hamilton, Monroe, 6,681* H-25
Hamiltonban, Adams, 1,872 .... O-16
▲ *Hampden, Cumberland, 20,384* M-18
• *Hampton, Allegheny, 15,568* J-3
Hanover, Beaver, 3,470 .... K-1
▲ *Hanover, Lehigh, 2,243* J-25
▲ *Hanover, Luzerne, 12,050* G-22
▲ *Hanover, Northampton, 7,176* J-25
Hanover, Washington, 2,883 .... L-1
Hanover, York, 14,399 .... O-18
Harborcreek, Erie, 15,108 .... A-4
Harford, Susquehanna, 1,100 .... G-23
• Harleysville, Montgomery, 7,405 .... L-25
▲ *Harmar, Allegheny, 3,144* B-35
• *Harmony, Beaver, 3,694* J-2
Harmony, Butler, 1,054 .... I-3
Harris, Centre, 4,167 .... I-14
Harrisburg, Dauphin, 52,376 .... L-18
• *Harrison, Allegheny, 11,763* J-4
Harrison, Potter, 1,129 .... B-14
Hartley, Union, 1,896 .... I-16
Harveys Lake, Luzerne, 2,746 .... F-22
Harwick, Allegheny B-35
• Hasson Heights, Venango, 1,610 .... E-5
Hastings, Cambria, 1,431 .... J-9
Hatboro, Montgomery, 7,382 .... M-27
Hatboro West, Montgomery I-38
Hatfield, Montgomery, 2,650 .... L-26
Hatfield, Montgomery, 15,357 .... L-26
Haverford, Delaware, 49,848 .... D-36
Haverford, Montgomery J-37
Hawley, Wayne, 1,244 .... E-26
▲ *Haycock, Bucks, 2,165* K-26
Hayfield, Crawford, 2,937 .... C-2
Hayti, Chester N-23
Hazle, Luzerne, 9,323 .... H-22
Hazleton, Luzerne, 24,730 .... H-22
Hegins, Schuylkill, 3,561 .... J-20
Heidelberg, Allegheny, 1,238 .... D-32
▲ *Heidelberg, Berks, 1,513* L-22
▲ *Heidelberg, Lebanon, 3,797* L-21
▲ *Heidelberg, Lehigh, 3,250* J-23
▲ *Heidelberg, York, 2,622* O-18
▲ *Hellam, York, 5,123* N-20
Hellertown, Northampton, 5,662 .... J-25
Hemlock, Columbia, 1,546 .... H-20
Hempfield, Mercer, 3,826 .... E-2
▲ *Hempfield, Westmoreland, 42,609* E-36
Henderson, Jefferson, 1,376 .... H-8
Henry Clay, Fayette, 1,860 .... O-6
▲ *Hepburn, Lycoming, 2,834* F-18
▲ *Hereford, Berks, 3,026* K-24
Herminie, Westmoreland L-4
Hermitage, Mercer, 15,300 .... F-1
• Hershey, Dauphin, 11,860 .... L-19
▲ *Hickory, Lawrence, 2,317* H-2
Highcliff, Allegheny B-33
Highland, Chester, 1,199 .... O-23
• Highland Park, Mifflin, 1,583 .... J-15
Highspire, Dauphin, 2,668 .... J-31
• Hiller, Fayette, 1,401 .... N-4
▲ *Hilltown, Bucks, 10,582* L-26
• Hokendauqua, Lehigh, 3,413 .... J-25
Holland, Bucks I-40
Hollenback, Luzerne, 1,198 .... H-22
Hollidaysburg, Blair, 5,624 .... L-11
Hollywood, Montgomery J-39
Holmes, Delaware P-37
• Homeacre-Lyndora, Butler, 7,511 .... I-3
Homer City, Indiana, 1,809 .... K-7
Homestead, Allegheny, 4,179 .... C-34
• Hometown, Schuylkill, 1,545 .... I-22
Honesdale, Wayne, 4,972 .... D-25
Honey Brook, Chester, 1,184 .... M-23
Honey Brook, Chester, 5,449 .... M-23
▲ *Hopewell, Beaver, 13,274* J-2
Hopewell, Bedford, 1,928 .... M-11
Hopewell, Cumberland, 1,913 .... M-15
▲ *Hopewell, York, 3,177* O-20
• Hopwood, Fayette, 2,021 .... O-4
• Horsham, Montgomery, 15,051 .... I-38
Horsham, Montgomery, 21,896 .... I-38
Horton, Elk, 1,655 .... F-9
Houston, Washington, 1,445 .... L-2
Houtzdale, Clearfield, 1,204 .... I-11
Howard, Centre, 1,004 .... H-14
Hudson, Luzerne L-32
Hughestown, Luzerne, 1,734 .... F-23
Hughesville, Lycoming, 2,049 .... G-19
• Hummels Wharf, Snyder, 1,069 .... I-18
Hummelstown, Dauphin, 3,981 .... L-19
▲ *Hunlock, Luzerne, 2,496* G-22
Huntingdon, Huntingdon, 6,843 .... K-13
Huntingdon Valley, Montgomery J-39
Huntington, Adams, 1,989 .... N-17
Huntington, Luzerne, 1,905 .... G-21
Huston, Blair, 1,189 .... L-11
Huston, Centre, 1,282 .... I-13
Huston, Clearfield, 1,352 .... G-10
• Hyde, Clearfield, 1,643 .... H-16
Hyndman, Bedford, 1,019 .... O-9
• Imperial-Enlow, Allegheny, 3,449 .... C-32
▲ *Independence, Beaver, 2,563* K-1
Independence, Washington, 1,868 .... L-1
▲ *Indiana, Allegheny, 6,024* B-35
Indiana, Indiana, 15,174 .... J-7
Industry, Beaver, 2,124 .... J-1
Ingomar, Allegheny A-33
Ingram, Allegheny, 3,901 .... C-32
Inkerman, Luzerne K-32
Irwin, Venango, 1,182 .... G-3
Irwin, Westmoreland, 4,604 .... L-4
▲ *Jackson, Butler, 3,078* I-3
Jackson, Cambria, 5,213 .... K-8
Jackson, Dauphin, 1,797 .... K-19
▲ *Jackson, Lebanon, 5,732* L-21
▲ *Jackson, Luzerne, 5,336* F-22
Jackson, Mercer, 1,089 .... F-3
▲ *Jackson, Monroe, 3,757* H-25
Jackson, Snyder, 1,383 .... I-18
Jackson, Tioga, 2,072 .... B-18
Jackson, Venango, 1,089 .... E-4
▲ *Jackson, York, 6,244* O-18
Jacobus, York, 1,370 .... O-19
Jay, Elk, 2,087 .... F-9
Jeannette, Westmoreland, 11,221 .... L-5
Jefferson, Allegheny, 9,533 .... E-34
Jefferson, Berks, 1,410 .... K-22
▲ *Jefferson, Butler, 4,812* J-3
Jefferson, Fayette, 2,047 .... N-4
Jefferson, Greene, 2,536 .... N-3
Jefferson, Lackawanna, 3,438 .... E-24
Jefferson, Mercer, 1,998 .... F-2
Jefferson, Somerset, 1,462 .... N-7
Jefferson, Washington, 1,212 .... L-1
▲ *Jenkins, Luzerne, 4,740* F-24
Jenkintown, Montgomery, 4,574 .... J-39
Jenks, Forest, 1,321 .... E-8
Jenner, Somerset, 4,147 .... M-8
Jermyn, Lackawanna, 2,263 .... E-24
• Jerome, Somerset, 1,074 .... M-8
Jersey Shore, Lycoming, 4,353 .... G-16
Jessup, Lackawanna, 4,605 .... E-24
Jim Thorpe, Carbon, 5,048 .... I-23
Johnsonburg, Elk, 3,350 .... F-9
Johnstown, Cambria, 28,134 .... L-8
Jones, Elk, 1,870 .... F-9
Juniata, Blair, 1,116 .... L-10
Juniata, Perry, 1,278 .... K-16
Kane, Mc Kean, 4,590 .... D-9
Kearsarge, Erie B-3
Keating, Mc Kean, 3,070 .... C-10
▲ *Kelly, Union, 4,561* H-18
Kenhorst, Berks, 2,918 .... L-23
• Kenilworth, Chester, 1,890 .... M-24
Kennedy, Allegheny, 7,265 .... C-32
• Kennedy Township, Allegheny, 7,152 .... C-32
▲ *Kennett, Chester, 4,624* R-32
Kennett Square, Chester, 5,218 .... O-24
Kidder, Carbon, 1,319 .... G-23
Kimmel, Bedford, 1,605 .... M-10
King, Bedford, 1,226 .... M-10
• King of Prussia, Montgomery, 18,406 .... J-36
Kingston, Luzerne, 14,507 .... F-23
Kingston, Luzerne, 6,763 .... F-23
Kiskiminetas, Armstrong, 5,456 .... K-6
Kittanning, Armstrong, 2,310 .... K-5
Kittanning, Armstrong, 5,120 .... K-5
Kittanning Heights, Armstrong I-5
▲ *Kline, Schuylkill, 1,722* I-22
Knox, Clarion, 1,182 .... G-5
Knox, Clarion, 1,281 .... G-5
Knox, Jefferson, 1,014 .... G-8
Koppel, Beaver, 1,024 .... I-2
Kulpmont, Northumberland, 3,233 .... I-20
• Kulpsville, Montgomery, 5,183 .... L-25
Kutztown, Berks, 4,704 .... K-23
▲ *Lackawannock, Mercer, 2,677* G-2
Lackawaxen, Pike, 2,832 .... E-27
Lafayette, Mc Kean, 2,106 .... C-9
Lafayette Hill-Plymouth Meeting, Montgomery J-37
Laflin, Luzerne, 1,498 .... F-23
Lake, Luzerne, 1,924 .... F-21
▲ *Lake, Wayne, 3,287* G-25
Lake City, Erie, 2,519 .... B-2
• Lake Wynonah, Schuylkill, 1,055 .... J-21
Lakemont, Blair K-11
Lamar, Clinton, 2,345 .... H-15
Lancaster, Butler, 2,268 .... I-2
Lancaster, Lancaster, 13,187 .... N-21
Lancaster, Lancaster, 55,551 .... N-21
Langhorne, Bucks, 1,361 .... I-40
Lansdale, Montgomery, 16,362 .... L-26
Lansdowne, Delaware, 11,712 .... N-26
Lansford, Carbon, 4,583 .... I-23
Laporte, Sullivan, 328 .... F-20
Larimer, Westmoreland L-4
Larksville, Luzerne, 4,700 .... F-22
▲ *Latimore, Adams, 2,209* N-17
Latrobe, Westmoreland, 9,265 .... L-6
Laurel Gardens, Allegheny B-34
Laureldale, Berks, 3,726 .... K-23
• Lawnton, Dauphin, 3,221 .... H-30
Lawrence, Clearfield, 8,000 .... G-10
Lawrence, Tioga, 1,519 .... B-3
Lawrence, Washington L-3
• *Lawrence Park, Erie, 4,310* A-3
• Lawson Heights, Westmoreland, 2,464 .... M-6
Le Boeuf, Erie, 1,521 .... C-4
▲ *Leacock, Lancaster, 4,668* M-21
• Leacock-Leola-Bareville, Lancaster, 5,685 .... M-21
Lebanon, Lebanon, 24,800 .... L-20
• Lebanon South, Lebanon, 1,764 .... L-20
Lee Park, Luzerne M-31
Leechburg, Armstrong, 2,504 .... J-5
Leesport, Berks, 1,270 .... K-22
▲ *Leet, Allegheny, 1,731* B-32
Leetsdale, Allegheny, 1,387 .... B-32
▲ *Lehigh, Northampton, 9,296* I-24
Lehigh, Wayne, 1,178 .... F-25
Lehighton, Carbon, 5,914 .... I-23
▲ *Lehman, Luzerne, 3,076* F-22
Lehman, Pike, 3,055 .... G-27
• Leith-Hatfield, Fayette, 2,437 .... O-4
Lemon, Wyoming, 1,264 .... D-22
Lemoyne, Cumberland, 3,959 .... M-18
• Lenape Heights, Armstrong, 1,355 .... J-5
Lenox, Susquehanna, 1,581 .... D-24
Lester, Delaware Q-37
Letterkenny, Franklin, 2,251 .... N-14
Level Green, Westmoreland K-5
• Levittown, Bucks, 55,362 .... M-28
Lewis, Lycoming, 1,194 .... F-17
Lewis, Northumberland, 1,881 .... G-18
Lewis, Union, 1,222 .... H-17
Lewisburg, Union, 5,785 .... H-18
Lewistown, Mifflin, 9,341 .... K-15
Liberty, Allegheny, 2,744 .... E-34
Liberty, Bedford, 1,478 .... M-11
Liberty, Centre, 1,747 .... H-14
Liberty, Mc Kean, 1,764 .... D-11
Liberty, Mercer, 1,223 .... G-3
Liberty, Montour, 1,309 .... H-19
Liberty, Susquehanna, 1,353 .... B-23
Library, Allegheny D-33
Licking Creek, Fulton, 1,410 .... N-12
Ligonier, Westmoreland, 1,638 .... L-7
Ligonier, Westmoreland, 6,979 .... L-7
Lilly, Cambria, 1,162 .... K-10
• Lima, Delaware, 2,670 .... P-35
• Lime Ridge, Columbia, 1,051 .... H-20
▲ *Limerick, Montgomery, 6,691* H-36
Limestone, Clarion, 1,686 .... G-6
Limestone, Lycoming, 1,893 .... G-17
Limestone, Union, 1,346 .... I-17
Lincoln, Allegheny, 1,187 .... E-7
Lincoln, Somerset, 1,655 .... M-7
Lincoln Heights, Westmoreland M-5
Linesville, Crawford, 1,166 .... D-1
• Linglestown, Dauphin, 5,862 .... L-18
• Linntown, Union, 1,640 .... H-18
• Linwood, Delaware, 3,425 .... R-35
• Lionville-Marchwood, Chester, 6,468 .... N-32
Litchfield, Bradford, 1,296 .... B-20
Lititz, Lancaster, 8,280 .... M-21
Little Beaver, Lawrence, 1,251 .... I-1
Little Britain, Lancaster, 2,701 .... O-22
Littlestown, Adams, 2,974 .... P-17
Lock Haven, Clinton, 9,230 .... G-15
Locust, Columbia, 1,308 .... I-20
▲ *Logan, Blair, 12,381* K-11
▲ *London Britain, Chester, 2,671* O-23
▲ *London Grove, Chester, 3,922* R-30
Londonderry, Bedford, 1,893 .... O-9
▲ *Londonderry, Chester, 1,243* O-23
▲ *Londonderry, Dauphin, 4,926* M-19
▲ *Longswamp, Berks, 5,387* K-24
• Lorane, Berks, 2,580 .... L-9
Loretto, Cambria, 1,072 .... K-10
• Lower Allen, Cumberland, 6,329 .... I-29
Lower Allen, Cumberland, 15,254 .... M-18
▲ *Lower Alsace, Berks, 4,627* L-23
Lower Augusta, Northumberland, 1,024 .... I-18
Lower Burrell, Westmoreland, 12,251 .... K-4
Lower Chanceford, York, 2,454 .... O-20
Lower Chichester, Delaware, 3,660 .... O-25
Lower Frankford, Cumberland, 1,491 .... L-16
Lower Frederick, Montgomery, 3,396 .... L-25
Lower Gwynedd, Montgomery, 9,958 .... M-26
▲ *Lower Heidelberg, Berks, 2,209* L-22
Lower Macungie, Lehigh, 16,871 .... K-24
Lower Mahanoy, Northumberland, 1,669 .... J-18
Lower Makefield, Bucks, 25,083 .... L-28
Lower Merion, Montgomery, 58,003 .... K-38
Lower Mifflin, Cumberland, 1,700 .... M-15
▲ *Lower Milford, Lehigh, 3,269* K-25
▲ *Lower Moreland, Montgomery, 11,768* M-27
▲ *Lower Mount Bethel, Northampton, 3,187* I-26
▲ *Lower Nazareth, Northampton, 4,483* J-26
▲ *Lower Oxford, Chester, 3,264* O-22
Lower Paxton, Dauphin, 39,162 .... H-31
Lower Pottsgrove, Montgomery, 8,808 .... L-24
Lower Providence, Montgomery, 19,351 .... M-25
Lower Salford, Montgomery, 10,735 .... L-25
▲ *Lower Saucon, Northampton, 8,448* J-26
Lower Southampton, Bucks, 19,860 .... J-39
▲ *Lower Swatara, Dauphin, 7,072* J-32
▲ *Lower Towamensing, Carbon, 2,948* I-24
Lower Tyrone, Fayette, 1,138 .... N-4
▲ *Lower Windsor, York, 7,051* N-20
▲ *Lower Yoder, Cambria, 3,342* L-8
▲ *Lowhill, Lehigh, 1,602* J-24
▲ *Loyalhanna, Westmoreland, 2,171* C-38
▲ *Loyalsock, Lycoming, 10,644* F-18
• Lucerne Mines, Indiana, 1,074 .... K-7
Lurgan, Franklin, 2,026 .... M-15
Luzerne, Fayette, 4,904 .... N-4
Luzerne, Luzerne, 3,206 .... F-22
▲ *Lycoming, Lycoming, 1,748* F-17
Lykens, Dauphin, 1,238 .... K-19
Lykens, Dauphin, 1,986 .... K-19
Lynn, Lehigh, 3,220 .... J-23
Lynnwood, Luzerne M-30
• Lynnwood-Pricedale, Fayette/ Westmoreland, 2,664 .... M-4
Macungie, Lehigh, 2,597 .... K-24
Madison, Clarion, 1,423 .... H-5
Madison, Columbia, 1,565 .... G-20
Madison, Lackawanna, 2,207 .... F-25
Mahanoy, Schuylkill, 1,273 .... I-22
Mahanoy City, Schuylkill, 5,209 .... I-22
Mahoning, Armstrong, 1,504 .... J-5
▲ *Mahoning, Carbon, 4,198* I-24
▲ *Mahoning, Lawrence, 3,560* M-1
Mahoning, Montour, 4,134 .... H-19
▲ *Maidencreek, Berks, 3,397* K-23
Main, Columbia, 1,241 .... H-21
Malvern, Chester, 2,944 .... N-25
Manchester, York, 1,830 .... N-19
Manchester, York, 7,517 .... N-19
Manheim, Lancaster, 28,880 .... M-20
Manheim, Lancaster, 5,011 .... M-20
▲ *Manheim, York, 2,692* O-19
Manor, Armstrong, 4,482 .... H-6
▲ *Manor, Lancaster, 14,130* N-20
Manor, Westmoreland, 2,627 .... L-4
Mansfield, Tioga, 3,538 .... C-17
• Maple Glen, Montgomery, 5,881 .... I-38
Marcus Hook, Delaware, 2,546 .... O-25
Marietta, Lancaster, 2,778 .... N-20
Marion, Berks, 1,415 .... L-21
Marion, Butler, 1,113 .... G-3
Markvue Manor, Westmoreland D-36
▲ *Marlborough, Montgomery, 3,116* L-25
Marple, Delaware, 23,123 .... O-32
Mars, Butler, 1,713 .... J-3
▲ *Marshall, Allegheny, 4,010* A-33
• Marshallton, Northumberland, 1,482 .... I-20
▲ *Martic, Lancaster, 4,362* O-21
Martinsburg, Blair, 2,119 .... L-11
Marysville, Perry, 2,425 .... L-18
Masontown, Fayette, 3,759 .... O-3
Matamoras, Pike, 1,934 .... F-28
Mather, Greene N-3
▲ *Maxatawny, Berks, 5,724* K-23
Mayfield, Lackawanna, 1,890 .... E-24
• Maytown, Lancaster, 1,720 .... N-20
McAdoo, Schuylkill, 2,459 .... I-22
McCalmont, Jefferson, 1,006 .... H-8
• *McCandless, Allegheny, 28,781* J-33
• McChesneytown-Loyalhanna, Westmoreland, 3,708 .... L-6
McClure, Snyder, 1,070 .... J-16
McConnellsburg, Fulton, 1,106 .... N-12
McDonald, Allegheny/ Washington, 2,252 .... D-32
• McGovern, Washington, 2,504 .... E-32
▲ *McKean, Erie, 4,503* B-3
McKees Rocks, Allegheny, 7,691 .... C-33
McKeesport, Allegheny, 26,016 .... L-32
• McMurray, Washington, 4,082 .... M-3
McSherrystown, Adams, 2,769 .... O-17
Mead, Warren, 1,579 .... C-8
Meadowbrook, Montgomery J-39
Meadowlands, Washington M-2
• Meadowood, Butler, 3,011 .... I-4
Meadville, Crawford, 14,318 .... D-3
Mechanicsburg, Cumberland, 9,452 .... M-18
• Mechanicsville, Montour, 2,803 .... H-19
Media, Delaware, 5,957 .... N-25
Menallen, Adams, 2,700 .... N-16
Menallen, Fayette, 4,739 .... N-4
Menno, Mifflin, 1,637 .... K-13
Mercer, Butler, 1,110 .... G-3
Mercer, Mercer, 2,444 .... G-2
Mercersburg, Franklin, 1,640 .... D-13
• Meridian, Butler, 3,473 .... I-3
Merion, Montgomery K-37
Metal, Franklin, 1,612 .... N-13
Meyersdale, Somerset, 2,518 .... O-8
Middle Paxton, Dauphin, 5,129 .... L-19
▲ *Middle Smithfield, Monroe, 6,382* G-26
Middleburg, Snyder, 1,422 .... I-17
Middlebury, Tioga, 1,244 .... C-16
Middlecreek, Snyder, 1,791 .... I-17
▲ *Middlesex, Butler, 5,578* J-3
Middlesex, Cumberland, 5,780 .... L-17
Middletown, Bucks, 43,063 .... L-28
Middletown, Dauphin, 9,254 .... M-19
Middletown, Delaware, 14,130 .... P-31
• Middletown, Northampton, 6,866 .... J-25
Midland, Beaver, 3,321 .... J-1
Midland, Washington L-2
• Midway, Adams, 2,254 .... O-18
Midway, Washington, 1,043 .... L-2
Mifflin, Columbia, 2,305 .... H-21
Mifflin, Lycoming, 1,110 .... F-16
Mifflinburg, Union, 3,480 .... I-17
Mifflintown, Juniata, 866 .... K-16
• Mifflinville, Columbia, 1,329 .... H-21
Miles, Centre, 1,494 .... I-14
Milesburg, Centre, 1,144 .... H-14
▲ *Milford, Bucks, 7,360* K-25
Milford, Juniata, 1,429 .... K-15
Milford, Pike, 1,013 .... F-28
Milford, Pike, 1,064 .... F-28
Milford, Somerset, 1,544 .... N-7
Mill Hall, Clinton, 1,702 .... G-15
▲ *Millcreek, Erie, 46,820* A-3
Millcreek, Lebanon, 2,687 .... C-21
Millersburg, Dauphin, 2,729 .... K-18
Millersville, Lancaster, 8,099 .... N-20
Millvale, Allegheny, 4,341 .... C-34
Milmont Park, Delaware Q-35
• Milroy, Mifflin, 1,456 .... J-15
Milton, Northumberland, 6,746 .... H-18
Minersville, Schuylkill, 4,877 .... J-21
Mohnton, Berks, 2,484 .... L-22
Monaca, Beaver, 6,739 .... J-2
▲ *Monaghan, York, 2,009* M-18
Monessen, Westmoreland, 9,901 .... F-34
▲ *Monongahela, Greene, 1,858* O-3
Monongahela, Washington, 4,928 .... F-34
Monroe, Bedford, 1,305 .... O-11
Monroe, Bradford, 1,235 .... D-23
Monroe, Clarion, 1,314 .... G-6
▲ *Monroe, Cumberland, 5,468* M-17
Monroe, Juniata, 1,800 .... J-17
Monroe, Snyder, 3,881 .... I-19
Monroe, Wyoming, 1,802 .... F-22
Monroeville, Allegheny, 29,169 .... K-4
Mont Alto, Franklin, 1,395 .... O-15
Mont Clare, Montgomery J-36
Montgomery, Franklin, 4,558 .... O-13
Montgomery, Indiana, 1,729 .... I-9
Montgomery, Lycoming, 1,631 .... G-18
Montgomery, Montgomery, 12,179 .... M-26
• Montgomeryville, Montgomery, 9,114 .... H-37
▲ *Montour, Columbia, 1,419* H-20
Montoursville, Lycoming, 4,983 .... F-18
Montrose, Susquehanna, 1,982 .... C-23
Montrose Hill, Allegheny B-34
Moon, Allegheny, 19,631 .... K-3
▲ *Moore, Northampton, 8,418* I-25
Moosic, Lackawanna, 5,339 .... F-23
▲ *Morgan, Greene, 2,887* N-3
▲ *Morris, Clearfield, 2,680* I-11
Morris, Washington, 1,145 .... N-2
Morrisville, Bucks, 9,765 .... M-28
• Morrisville, Greene, 1,365 .... N-2
Morton, Delaware, 2,851 .... P-36
Moscow, Lackawanna, 1,527 .... F-24
Mount Carmel, Northumberland, 2,679 .... I-20
Mount Carmel, Northumberland, 7,196 .... I-20
• Mount Cobb, Lackawanna, 2,043 .... E-24
Mount Holly Springs, Cumberland, 1,925 .... M-17
Mount Jewett, Mc Kean, 1,029 .... D-9
▲ *Mount Joy, Adams, 2,848* O-16
Mount Joy, Lancaster, 6,227 .... M-20
Mount Joy, Lancaster, 6,398 .... M-20
• *Mount Lebanon, Allegheny, 33,362* L-3
Mount Oliver, Allegheny, 4,160 .... D-33
Mount Penn, Berks, 2,883 .... L-23
▲ *Mount Pleasant, Adams, 4,076* O-18
Mount Pleasant, Columbia, 1,383 .... H-20
Mount Pleasant, Washington, 3,555 .... M-3
Mount Pleasant, Wayne, 1,271 .... C-25
Mount Pleasant, Westmoreland, 11,341 .... M-5
Mount Pleasant, Westmoreland, 4,787 .... M-5
Mount Pocono, Monroe, 1,795 .... G-25
Mount Union, Huntingdon, 2,878 .... L-13
Mount Wolf, York, 1,365 .... N-19
• Mountainhome, Monroe, 1,042 .... G-25
Mountaintop, Luzerne N-33
Mountville, Lancaster, 1,977 .... N-20
Moylan, Delaware P-35
Muddy Creek, Butler, 2,139 .... H-3
▲ *Muhlenberg, Berks, 12,636* K-23
Muncy, Lycoming, 1,036 .... G-18
Muncy, Lycoming, 2,702 .... G-18
▲ *Muncy Creek, Lycoming, 3,401* G-19
Munhall, Allegheny, 13,158 .... L-3
Municipality of Murrysville, Westmoreland, 17,240 .... B-36
Muse, Washington D-32
Myerstown, Lebanon, 3,236 .... L-21
Nanticoke, Luzerne, 12,267 .... G-22
Nanty-Glo, Cambria, 3,190 .... K-9
Napier, Bedford, 2,054 .... N-9
Narberth, Montgomery, 4,278 .... K-37
Natrona Heights, Allegheny J-4
Nazareth, Northampton, 5,713 .... I-25
• Nemacolin, Greene, 1,097 .... O-3
Nescopeck, Luzerne, 1,072 .... H-21
Nescopeck, Luzerne, 1,651 .... H-21
Neshannock, Lawrence, 8,373 .... H-2
Nesquehoning, Carbon, 3,364 .... I-23
• *Nether Providence, Delaware, 13,229* Q-35
▲ *Neville, Allegheny, 1,273* C-32
New Beaver, Lawrence, 1,736 .... I-1
New Bethlehem, Clarion, 1,151 .... H-6
New Bloomfield, Perry L-17
New Brighton, Beaver, 6,854 .... A-31
New Britain, Bucks, 2,174 .... L-26
New Britain, Bucks, 9,099 .... L-26
New Castle, Lawrence, 28,334 .... H-2
• New Castle Northwest, Lawrence, 1,515 .... H-2
New Cumberland, Cumberland, 7,665 .... M-18
New Eagle, Washington, 2,172 .... L-3
New Freedom, York, 2,920 .... O-19
New Garden, Chester, 5,430 .... O-24
▲ *New Hanover, Montgomery, 5,956* I-35
New Holland, Lancaster, 4,484 .... M-22
New Hope, Bucks, 1,400 .... L-27
New Kensington, Westmoreland, 15,894 .... J-4
▲ *New London, Chester, 2,721* O-23
New Milford, Susquehanna, 1,731 .... C-23
New Oxford, Adams, 1,617 .... O-17
New Philadelphia, Schuylkill, 1,283 .... J-22
• New Salem-Buffington, Fayette, 1,169 .... O-4
▲ *New Sewickley, Beaver, 6,861* I-2
New Sheffield, Beaver B-31
New Stanton, Westmoreland, 2,081 .... M-6
New Wilmington, Lawrence, 2,706 .... G-2
Newberry, York, 12,003 .... M-19
Newlin, Chester, 1,092 .... N-24
• Newmanstown, Lebanon, 1,410 .... L-21
Newport, Luzerne, 4,593 .... G-22
Newport, Perry, 1,568 .... K-17
▲ *Newton, Lackawanna, 2,843* E-23
Newtown, Bucks, 2,565 .... L-27
Newtown, Bucks, 13,685 .... L-27
▲ *Newtown, Delaware, 11,366* N-25
• Newtown Grant, Bucks, 2,141 .... I-40
Newtown Square, Delaware O-35
Newville, Cumberland, 1,349 .... M-16
Nicholson, Fayette, 1,995 .... O-4
Nicholson, Wyoming, 1,287 .... D-23
• Nixon, Butler, 1,342 .... I-4
▲ *Nockamixon, Bucks, 3,329* K-27
Norristown, Montgomery, 30,749 .... M-25
▲ *North Annville, Lebanon, 2,441* L-20
North Apollo, Armstrong, 1,391 .... J-5
North Ardmore, Montgomery K-37
North Beaver, Lawrence, 3,982 .... I-1
North Belle Vernon, Westmoreland, 2,112 .... F-34
North Bethlehem, Washington, 1,864 .... N-3
North Braddock, Allegheny, 7,036 .... C-34
▲ *North Buffalo, Armstrong, 2,897* J-5
No.th Catasauqua, Northampton, 2,867 .... J-25
▲ *North Centre, Columbia, 1,860* H-20
North Charleroi, Washington, 1,562 .... F-34
▲ *North Codorus, York, 7,565* O-18
North Cornwall, Lebanon, 4,886 .... L-20
North Coventry, Chester, 7,506 .... L-24
North East, Erie, 4,617 .... A-4
North East, Erie, 6,283 .... A-4
North Fayette, Allegheny, 9,537 .... C-32
▲ *North Franklin, Washington, 4,997* F-31
North Heidelberg, Berks, 1,288 .... L-22
North Hills-Ardsley, Montgomery I-38
▲ *North Hopewell, York, 2,205* O-19
▲ *North Huntingdon, Westmoreland, 28,158* E-36
North Lebanon, Lebanon, 9,741 .... L-20
▲ *North Londonderry, Lebanon, 5,630* L-19
North Mahoning, Indiana, 1,254 .... I-8
▲ *North Manheim, Schuylkill, 3,404* J-22
North Middleton, Cumberland, 9,833 .... M-17
North Newton, Cumberland, 1,779 .... M-16
▲ *North Sewickley, Beaver, 6,178* I-2
▲ *North Strabane, Washington, 8,157* E-33
North Union, Fayette, 13,910 .... N-5
North Union, Schuylkill, 1,143 .... I-21
• North Vandergrift-Pleasant View, Armstrong, 1,431 .... J-5
• *North Versailles, Allegheny, 12,302* L-32
North Wales, Montgomery, 3,802 .... M-26
North Whitehall, Lehigh, 10,827 .... J-24
▲ *North Woodbury, Blair, 2,219* K-11
North York, York, 1,689 .... N-19
Northampton, Bucks, 35,406 .... L-27
Northampton, Northampton, 8,717 .... J-25
Northmoreland, Wyoming, 1,462 .... E-22
Northumberland, Northumberland, 3,860 .... I-18
• Northwest Harborcreek, Erie, 6,662 .... A-4
▲ *Norwegian, Schuylkill, 1,938* J-22
Norwood, Delaware, 6,162 .... Q-37
▲ *Nottingham, Washington, 2,303* E-33
• Oak Hills, Butler, 2,245 .... I-4
Oak Lane, Montgomery J-39
Oakdale, Allegheny, 1,752 .... C-32
Oakford, Bucks I-40
▲ *Oakland, Butler, 2,820* I-4
• Oakland, Lawrence, 1,766 .... H-1
Oakland, Venango, 1,527 .... E-4
Oakmont, Allegheny, 6,961 .... B-35
• Oakwood, Lawrence, 2,541 .... H-1
Ogden, Delaware R-35
• *O'Hara Township, Allegheny, 9,096* C-35
▲ *Ohio, Allegheny, 2,459* B-33
Ohioville, Beaver, 3,865 .... J-1
Oil City, Venango, 11,949 .... E-5
Oil Creek, Crawford, 2,069 .... D-5
Old Forge, Lackawanna, 8,834 .... F-23
Old Lycoming, Lycoming, 5,526 .... F-17
• Old Orchard, Northampton, 2,598 .... I-26
▲ *Oley, Berks, 3,362* L-23
• Oliver, Fayette, 3,271 .... N-4
Oliver, Jefferson, 1,119 .... H-7
Oliver, Mifflin, 1,822 .... K-14
▲ *Oliver, Perry, 2,039* K-17
Olyphant, Lackawanna, 5,222 .... E-24
Oneida, Huntingdon, 1,085 .... K-13
▲ *Ontelaunee, Berks, 1,359* K-23
Orange, Columbia, 1,043 .... G-20
• Orchard Hills, Armstrong, 2,019 .... K-6
• Oreland, Montgomery, 5,695 .... I-38
Orwell, Bradford, 1,107 .... C-21
Orwigsburg, Schuylkill, 2,780 .... J-22
Osceola Mills, Clearfield, 1,310 .... I-11
Otto, Mc Kean, 1,820 .... B-10
▲ *Overfield, Wyoming, 1,466* E-23
▲ *Oxford, Adams, 3,437* O-17
Oxford, Chester, 3,769 .... O-23
Paint, Clarion, 1,730 .... F-6
Paint, Somerset, 1,091 .... M-8
Paint, Somerset, 3,491 .... M-8
Palmdale, Dauphin I-33
Palmer, Northampton, 14,965 .... J-25
• Palmer Heights, Northampton, 3,960 .... I-26
Palmerton, Carbon, 5,394 .... I-24
Palmyra, Lebanon, 6,910 .... L-19
Palmyra, Pike, 1,976 .... E-26
Palo Alto, Schuylkill, 1,192 .... J-22
• Paoli, Chester, 5,603 .... N-25
• Paradise, Lancaster, 1,043 .... N-22
Paradise, Lancaster, 4,430 .... N-22
▲ *Paradise, Monroe, 2,251* G-25
▲ *Paradise, York, 3,180* O-18
• Park Forest Village, Centre, 6,703 .... I-13
Parkesburg, Chester, 2,981 .... N-23
Parkland, Bucks M-27
Parks, Armstrong, 2,739 .... J-5
Parkside, Delaware, 2,369 .... Q-35
• Parkville, York, 6,014 .... O-18
• *Patterson, Beaver, 3,074* J-1
Patton, Cambria, 2,206 .... J-9
Patton, Centre, 9,971 .... I-13
Paupack, Wayne, 1,696 .... E-26
Paxtang, Dauphin, 1,599 .... I-30
• Paxtonia, Dauphin, 4,862 .... H-30
Peach Bottom, York, 3,444 .... O-21
Pen Argyl, Northampton, 3,492 .... I-26
Penbrook, Dauphin, 2,791 .... I-30
Pencoyd, Montgomery K-38
Penn, Berks, 1,831 .... K-23
Penn, Butler, 5,080 .... I-4
▲ *Penn, Chester, 2,257* O-23
Penn, Clearfield, 1,372 .... H-10
Penn, Cumberland, 2,425 .... M-16
▲ *Penn, Lancaster, 6,760* M-21
▲ *Penn, Perry, 3,283* L-17
▲ *Penn, Snyder, 3,208* I-18
Penn, Westmoreland, 15,945 .... K-6
Penn, York, 11,658 .... O-18
Penn Forest, Carbon, 2,895 .... H-24
• Penn Hills, Allegheny, 51,430 .... K-4
Penn Hills, Allegheny, 51,479 .... K-4
• Penn Wynne, Montgomery, 5,807 .... K-37
Penndel, Bucks, 2,703 .... I-41
Pennsburg, Montgomery, 2,460 .... K-25
▲ *Pennsbury, Chester, 3,326* Q-32
• Pennville, York, 1,559 .... O-18
Pequea, Lancaster, 4,512 .... N-21
Perkasie, Bucks, 7,878 .... L-26
▲ *Perkiomen, Montgomery, 3,200* I-36
▲ *Perry, Berks, 2,516* K-23
Perry, Clarion, 1,076 .... G-5
▲ *Perry, Fayette, 2,817* G-35
Perry, Greene, 1,719 .... O-2
Perry, Jefferson, 1,293 .... H-8
▲ *Perry, Lawrence, 1,841* H-2
Perry, Mercer, 1,468 .... E-2

Explanation of symbols: • – Census Designated Place (CDP) ▲ *italics* – Townships (shown on the map) • *italics* – Township shown which is also a CDP *italics* – Townships (not shown on the map)

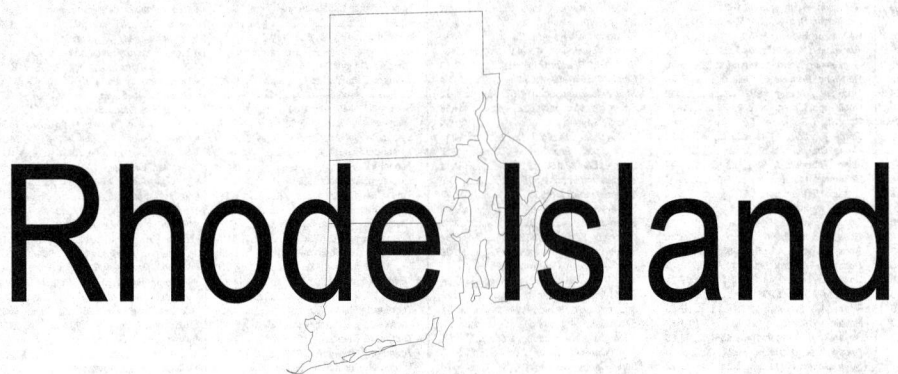

Rhode Island

General Help Numbers:

Governor's Office
222 State House   401-222-2080
Providence, RI 02903   Fax 401-222-5894
www.governor.state.ri.us   8:30AM-4:30PM

Attorney General's Office
150 S Main St   401-274-4400
Providence, RI 02903   Fax 401-222-1331
www.riag.state.ri.us   8:30AM-4:30PM

Legislative Records
Secretary of State
Public Information Center   401-222-3983
State House, Room 38   Fax 401-222-1404
Providence, RI 02903   8:30AM-4:30PM
www.rilin.state.ri.us

State Archives
State Archives & Public Records Admin.   401-222-2353
337 Westminster St   Fax 401-222-3199
Providence, RI 02903   8:30AM-4:30PM M-SA
www.state.ri.us/archives

State Specifics:

Capital: Providence
                                              Providence County

Time Zone: EST

Number of Counties: 5

Population: 1,076,164

Web Site: www.state.ri.us

State Agencies

Criminal Records

Department of Attorney General, Bureau of Criminal Identification, 150 S Main Street, Providence, RI 02903; 401-274-4400 x2353, 401-222-1331 (Fax), 8:30AM-4:30PM.

www.riag.ri.gov

Indexing & Storage: It takes 1-7 days before new records are available for inquiry. Records are normally destroyed after court order or expungment.

Searching: Criminal records are only released to law enforcement agencies, the subject, or, rarely, to those with a signed notarized authorization from

the subject. Records may be obtained at the county level. Include the following in your request-signed notarized release from subject, DOB, picture ID and DOB of the requester. Fingerprints and SSN are optional. They will call the Notary on the authorization for verification. 100% of the records are fingerprint-supported.

Access by: mail, in person.

Fee & Payment: The fee is $5.00 per name. If required, the FBI fingerprint search is an additional $24.00. Fee payee: Department of Attorney General. Prepayment required. Personal checks accepted. No credit cards or cash accepted.

Mail search: Turnaround time: up to 2 weeks. A SASE is required.

In person search: Turnaround time is while you wait.

Other access: This agency does not offer online access, but the state court system does. See that profile for details.

Statewide Court Records

Court Administrator, Supreme Court, 250 Benefit St, Providence, RI 02903; 401-222-3272, 401-222-3599 (Fax), 8:30AM-4:30PM.

www.courts.state.ri.us

Note: For questions regarding the Superior Courts, call 401-222-2622. For questions regarding the District Courts, call 401-458-3156.

Indexing & Storage: It takes 24 hours before new records are available for inquiry. Records are normally destroyed after 3 to 50 years, depending on case.

Searching: Include the following in your request-names involved or case number.

Access by: mail, in person, online.

Mail search: Requests are accepted by mail. A SASE is required.

In person search: Limted in-person searching of District, Superior, and Family court cases are available. Most records are in the period from the mid 1980's through the mid 1990's.

Online search: The Rhode Island Judiciary offers free Internet access to court criminal records statewide at http://courtconnect.courts.state.ri.us. A word of caution, this website is provided as an informational service only and should not be relied upon as an official record of the court. Supreme Court opinions are available from the website.

Other access: Bulk data is available, call for details.

Sexual Offender Registry

Access to Records is Restricted

Department of Attorney General, BCI Unit, 150 S Main Street, Providence, RI 02903; 401-274-4400, 8:30AM-4:30PM.

www.riag.state.ri.us

Note: The state's Sexual Offender Registry is not available to the public. Searching must be done at the local level.

Incarceration Records

Rhode Island Department of Corrections, Assistant to the Director, 40 Howard Avenue, Cranston, RI 02920; 401-462-3900, 401-464-2630 (Fax), 8AM-4:30PM.

www.doc.state.ri.us

Indexing & Storage: Records are available on current and former inmates. It takes 1 to 3 days before new records are available for inquiry.

Searching: Include the following in your request-full name; DOB helpful. Location, physical identifiers, conviction and sentencing information, and release dates are provided.

Access by: mail, phone, fax, online.

Fee & Payment: There is no fee.

Mail search: Turnaround time: 30 days. No SASE is required.

Phone search: Limited name searching available by phone.

Fax search: Records are available by fax.

Online search: There is no access to inmate records through the agency, however a private company offers free web access to DOC records at www.vinelink.com/index.jsp.

Corporation, Fictitious Name, Limited Partnerships, Limited Liability Company, Limited Liability

Partnerships, Not For Profit Entities

Secretary of State, Corporations Division, 100 N Main St, Providence, RI 02903-1335; 401-222-3040, 401-222-1309 (Fax), 8:30AM-4:30PM.

http://155.212.254.78/corporations.htm

Indexing & Storage: Records are available from the beginning of the Division. Records are computerized since 1984. It takes 5 days before new records are available for inquiry. Records are indexed on an inhouse computer.

Searching: Include the following in your request-full name of business.

Access by: mail, phone, in person, online.

Fee & Payment: The copy fee is $.15 per page. Certification costs $5.00 per document plus copy fees. There is no search fee. Fee payee: Secretary of State. Personal checks accepted. No credit cards accepted.

Mail search: Turnaround time: variable. A SASE helpful.

Phone search: They will give date of incorporation, registered agent, one officer, status, and whether domestic or foreign. Certified copies and documents can be ordered, but must be picked up in person, takes 48 hours.

In person search: Certified copies and certifications may not be available same day.

Online search: At the web, search filings for active and inactive Rhode Island and foreign business corporations, non-profit corporations, limited partnerships, limited liability companies, and limited liability partnerships. Weekly lisiting of new corporations are also available. There is no fee.

Other access: The corporation database may be purchased on CD.

Trademarks/Servicemarks

Secretary of State, Trademark Section, 100 N Main St, Providence, RI 02903-1335; 401-222-1487, 401-222-3879 (Fax), 8:30AM-4:30PM.

www.corps.state.ri.us/trademarks.htm

Indexing & Storage: Records are available from the beginning of the Division. It takes less than one week before new records are available for inquiry.

Searching: All records are open to the public. Include the following in your request-trademark/servicemark name, registration number and applicant name, if known.

Access by: mail, phone, in person.

Fee & Payment: There is no search fee. The copy fee is $.15 per page. Fee payee: Secretary of State

Mail search: Turnaround time: 3 to 5 days. No SASE is required.

Phone search: Limited verification information available.

In person search: Counter service is available.

Uniform Commercial Code

UCC Section, Secretary of State, 100 North Main St, Providence, RI 02903; 401-222-3040, 401-222-3879 (Fax), 8:30AM-4:30PM.

http://155.212.254.78/corporations.htm

Note: The agency is working towards having online access to records within the year.

Indexing & Storage: It takes 24 hours before new records are available for inquiry. Records are indexed on hard copy.

Searching: Use search request form UCC-11. All tax liens are filed at the city/town level. Include the following in your request-debtor name.

Access by: mail, in person.

Fee & Payment: The search fee is $5.00 per name, copies are $.15 each. Add $5.00 for certification. Fee payee: Secretary of State. Prepayment required. Personal checks accepted. No credit cards accepted.

Mail search: Turnaround time: 1 to 2 working days. SASE recommended.

In person search: If you do the search yourself, there is no search fee. Records may be viewed only.

Federal Tax Liens, State Tax Liens

Records not maintained by a state level agency.

Note: All records are located at the county level.

Sales Tax Registrations

Taxation Division, Sales & Use Tax Office, One Capitol Hill, Providence, RI 02908-5800; 401-222-2937, 401-222-6288 (Fax), 8:30AM-4PM.

www.tax.state.ri.us

Indexing & Storage: Records are available from the 1960's. All current permits are on the computer, all inactive records are kept on microfiche. New records are available for inquiry immediately. Records are normally destroyed after 7 years.

Searching: This agency will only confirm that a business is registered. They will provide no other information. Include the following in your request-business name. They will also search by tax permit number.

Access by: mail, phone, fax, in person.

Fee & Payment: There is no search fee nor a copy fee, unless extensive documents are requested.

Mail search: Turnaround time: 7 to 10 days. A SASE is requested.

Phone search: It will take 24 hours for a response.

Fax search: Same criteria as mail searching.

In person search: It will take 24 hours for a response.

Expedited service: Will try to expedite search, if requested.

Birth Certificates

State Department of Health, Division of Vital Records, 3 Capitol Hill, Room 101, Providence, RI 02908-5097; 401-222-2812, 401-222-2811, 8:30AM-4:30PM.

www.healthri.org/

Note: If the record is less than 100 years old, it can also be obtained from the city or town where birth occurred.

Indexing & Storage: Records are available from 1902 to present. New records are available for inquiry immediately. Records are indexed on microfiche, inhouse computer.

Searching: Investigative searches must have a signed release from person of record or immediate family member. Include the following in your request-full name, names of parents, mother's maiden name, date of birth, place of birth.

Access by: mail, phone, in person.

Fee & Payment: The fee is $15.00 for 2 years searched and $.50 for each additional year. Fee payee: General Treasurer, State of Rhode Island. Prepayment required. Credit cards for emergencies only. Personal checks accepted. Credit cards accepted: MasterCard, Visa, AmEx, Discover.

Mail search: Turnaround time: 6 to 8 weeks. A SASE is requested. Include photo copy of requester's ID (DL, passport, etc).

Phone search: This is for emergency, expedited needs only.

In person search: Turnaround time while you wait.

Expedited service: Expedited service is available for mail and phone searches. Turnaround time: 3 to 5 days. Add $23.00 for courier service and use of a credit card.

Death Records

State Department of Health, Division of Vital Records, 3 Capitol Hill, Room 101, Providence, RI 02908-5097; 401-222-2812, 401-222-2811, 8:30AM-4:30PM.

www.healthri.org/

Note: Records less than 50 years old can be obtained at the town or city where death took place.

Indexing & Storage: Records are available from 1952 to present. For records from 1853 to 1951, contact RI Archives at 401-222-2353. New records are available for inquiry immediately. Records are indexed on microfiche, inhouse computer.

Searching: Investigative searches must have a signed release from immediate family member. Include the following in your request-full name, date of death, place of death, names of parents, mother's maiden name. Any other identifying information is helpful.

Access by: mail, phone, in person.

Fee & Payment: The fee is $15.00 for 2 years searched and $.50 for each additional year. Fee payee: General Treasurer, State of Rhode Island. Prepayment required. Credit cards are for emergency use only. Personal checks accepted. Credit cards accepted: MasterCard, Visa, AmEx, Discover.

Mail search: Turnaround time: 6 to 8 weeks. A SASE is requested. Include photo copy of requester's ID (DL, passport, etc).

Phone search: See expedited services.

In person search: Simple requests may be processed while you wait.

Expedited service: Expedited service is available for mail and phone searches. Turnaround time: 3 to 5 days. Add $23.00 for courier service and use of a credit card.

Marriage Certificates

State Department of Health, Division of Vital Records, 3 Capitol Hill, Room 101, Providence, RI 02908-5097; 401-222-2812, 401-222-2811, 8:30AM-4:30PM M-F.

www.healthri.org/

Note: The record may be obtained from the town or city where the marriage took place, if the record is less than 100 years old.

Indexing & Storage: Records are available from 1902 to present. New records are available for inquiry immediately. Records are indexed on microfiche, inhouse computer.

Searching: Investigative searches must have a signed release from persons of record or immediate family member. Include the following in your request-names of husband and wife, date of marriage, place or county of marriage, wife's maiden name.

Access by: mail, phone, in person.

Fee & Payment: The search fee is $15.00 for 2 years searched and $.50 for each additional year. Fee payee: General Treasurer, State of Rhode Island. Prepayment required. Credit card use is for expedited service only. Personal checks accepted. Credit cards accepted: MasterCard, Visa, AmEx, Discover.

Mail search: Turnaround time: 6 to 8 weeks. A SASE is requested. Include photo copy of requester's ID (DL, passport, etc).

Phone search: See expedited services.

In person search: Simple requests may be processed while you wait.

Expedited service: Expedited service is available for mail and phone searches. Turnaround time: 3 to 5 days. Add $23.00 for courier service and use of a credit card.

Divorce Records

Records not maintained by a state level agency.

Note: Divorce records are found at one of the 4 county Family Courts.

Workers' Compensation Records

Department of Labor & Training, Division of Workers' Compensation, PO Box 20190, Cranston, RI 02920 (Courier: 1511 Pontiac Ave, Cranston, RI 02920); 401-462-8100, 401-462-8105 (Fax), 8:30AM-4PM.

www.dlt.state.ri.us

Indexing & Storage: Records are available from 1970s. New records are available for inquiry immediately. Records are indexed on inhouse computer. Records are normally destroyed after 30 years.

Searching: Records are not available for employment screening. A first report of injury is not public, by law. Records are released to claimant, attorneys, employer and insurer only if connected to case. Include the following in your request-claimant name, Social Security Number, file number (if known), reason for information request, specific records that you need copies of. Records of insurance carrier coverage only are available for no charge by phone or mail. The following data is not released: medical records.

Access by: mail, fax, in person.

Fee & Payment: The search fee is $15.00 per hour. Copies are $.15 per page. There is a $.40 per page fee for return by fax. Fee payee: Department of Labor & Training. Prepayment is required for

first time requesters. Personal checks accepted. No credit cards accepted.

Mail search: Turnaround time: 1 to 2 weeks. A SASE is requested.

Fax search: You may request records by fax.

In person search: Proof of identity is required.

Driver Records

Division of Motor Vehicles, Driving Record Clerk, Operator Control, 286 Main Street, Pawtucket, RI 02860; 401-721-2650, 8:30AM-4:30PM.

www.dmv.state.ri.us

Note: Copies of tickets may be obtained without fee by writing to the Traffic Tribunal at 345 Harris Ave, Providence 02908.

Indexing & Storage: Records are available for 3 years for accidents and moving violations, 5 years for alcohol-related violations or suspensions, 3 years after reinstatement for suspensions. Surrendered licenses are purged 3 years after expiration. It takes 20 days after received from courts before new records are available for inquiry.

Searching: Information is not made available for the purpose of commercial solicitation or trade. A description of proposed use must be submitted in advance for departmental approval of high volume requesters. Include the following in your request-driver's license number, full name, date of birth. Casual requesters must have consent of subject. The following data is not released: Social Security Numbers.

Access by: mail, in person, online.

Fee & Payment: The fee is $16.00 per record request, $18.00 if online. This is the highest fee in the nation for an online driving record. Fee payee: Division of Motor Vehicles. Prepayment required. Personal checks accepted. No credit cards accepted.

Mail search: Turnaround time: 1 week. A SASE is requested.

In person search: Although you may request a record in person, results must be picked up the next day or mailed back.

Online search: Driving records are available online for permissible users from the state's web portal. The fee is $18.00 per record. All users must be approved by the DMV's Administrator's Office. For details, please call Ms. Elaine Phillips.

Vehicle Ownership, Vehicle Identification

Registry of Motor Vehicles, Vehicle Records, 100 Main Street, Pawtucket, RI 02860; 401-588-3020 x2552 (Registration), 401-588-3018 (Title Section), 401-721-2697 (Fax), 8:30AM-3:30PM.

www.dmv.state.ri.us

Note: For title information, contact the Title Section in Rm 108.

Indexing & Storage: Records are available for 3 years for title information, for 10 years for registration information. It takes 1 week before new records are available for inquiry. Records are normally destroyed after 3 years after titled vehicle is 10 years old (title records). Registarion records available for 10 years.

Searching: Request must be in writing and the purpose stated. Records will not be released for commercial or solicitation purposes. Casual requesters cannot obtain records unless written consent of subject is given. Include the following in your request-for title: reason for request, VIN, year, make, owner name/address, your signature. For registration: VIN, plate, owner name/address, your name/adr. For DR: DR#, name, address. In all record requests, the agency would like to know the reason for request.

Access by: mail, in person.

Fee & Payment: The fee is $10.00 per record request for registration and license data, and $25.00 for title information. The state will release lien information. There is a full charge for a no record found request. Fee payee: Registry of Motor Vehicles. Prepayment required. Personal checks accepted. No credit cards accepted.

Mail search: Turnaround time: 1 week. A self addressed stamped envelope is requested.Title information turnaround is 4-6 weeks.

In person search: Title information can be obtained in person. Registation records are not released in person, but are mailed.

Other access: Bulk retrieval of vehicle and ownership information is limited to statistical purposes.

Accident Reports

Rhode Island State Police, Accident Record Division, 311 Danielson Pike, North Scituate, RI 02857; 401-444-1143, 401-444-1133 (Fax), 10AM-4PM M,T,F; till 6:30PM on Wed.

www.risp.state.ri.us

Indexing & Storage: Records are available for the past 2 years plus the current year. Accidents before that are stored in archives. Hard copy files are indexed. It takes 7-14 days before new records are available for inquiry. Records are normally destroyed after 5 years.

Searching: Include the following in your request-reason for information request, full name, date of accident, location of accident.

Access by: mail, phone, in person.

Fee & Payment: The fee is $10.00 per record. Fee payee: Treasurer - State of Rhode Island. Prepayment required. Personal checks accepted. No credit cards accepted.

Mail search: Turnaround time: 1 week. A SASE is requested.

Phone search: No fee for telephone request. The office will let a requester know if a report is available, but information will not be given over the phone.

In person search: Same day processing is available, provided report has been received.

Vessel Ownership, Vessel Registration

Dept of Environmental Management, Boat Registration & Licensing, 235 Promenade, Rm 360, Providence, RI 02908; 401-222-6647, 401-222-1181 (Fax), 8:30AM-3:30PM M-F.

www.state.ri.us/dem

Indexing & Storage: Records are available from the late 1970s to the present. Records are computer indexed for the last 3 years. This is a title state, lien information shows on the title record. All boats over 14 ft must be titled and registered.

Searching: All requests must be in writing on the agency's request form. Call or write for the form. Records cannot be purchased for solicitation or commercial purposes. This agency complies with DPPA. Include the following in your request-name or registration number or RI number.

Access by: mail, in person.

Fee & Payment: There is no fee, unless extensive searching is involved which is a $15.00 per hour charge.

Mail search: Turnaround time: 1 to 2 weeks. No SASE is required.

In person search: Turnaround time depending on staff availability.

Voter Registration

Records not maintained by a state level agency.

Note: The Local Board of Canvassers keeps records at the town and city level. Although records are open, they may not be purchased for commercial purposes. At present there is no central state database of votors, however this will be in place in 2006.

GED Certificates

Department of Education, GED Testing, 255 Westminster, Providence, RI 02908; 401-222-4600 x2181, 7:30AM-4PM.

Searching: Include the following in your request-Social Security Number, date of birth, year of testingn name at time of test. A signed release is also required for a verification or transcript copy.

Access by: mail, phone, in person.

Fee & Payment: The fee for a transcript is $5.00 or duplicate diploma. There is no fee for a verification. Fee payee: General Treasurer, State of Rhode Island. Prepayment required. Personal checks accepted. No credit cards accepted.

Mail search: Turnaround time: 1 week. No SASE is required.

Phone search: Limited data is available.

In person search: Simple requests may be processed while you wait.

Hunting and Fishing License Information

Boat Registration & Licensing, Licensing, 235 Promenade St, Rm 360, Providence, RI 02908; 401-222-3576, 401-222-1181 (Fax), 8:30AM-3:30PM.

www.state.ri.us/dem

Note: Recreational license information is kept on paper (forwarded to this office by vendors), and is not computerized.

Indexing & Storage: Records are available for several years.

Searching: Although all records are considered open, commercial use of the records is not permitted. Include the following in your request-date of application, date of birth, address. Also, include where purchased. Requests must be in writing.

Access by: mail, phone, fax, in person.

Fee & Payment: There is no fee for a short search or confirmation. Otherwise, for extensive searches the rate $15.00 per hour. Fee payee: RI DEM. Prepayment required. Personal checks accepted. No credit cards accepted.

Mail search: Turnaround time: 1 week to 10 days.

Phone search: They will confirm only.

Fax search: Same criteria as mail searches.

In person search: They will return by mail.

Rhode Island State Licensing Agencies

Licenses Searchable Online

Acupuncturist #13	http://health.ri.mylicense.com
Ambulatory Care Facility #13	http://health.ri.mylicense.com
Asbestos Abatement Worker #13	http://health.ri.mylicense.com
Assisted Living Facility #13	http://health.ri.mylicense.com
Athletic Trainer #13	http://health.ri.mylicense.com
Audiologist #13	http://health.ri.mylicense.com
Automobile Body Shop #11	www.dbr.state.ri.us/pdf_forms/clr/Auto%20Body%20Shop%20-%20Licensee%20List.pdf
Automobile Glass Installer #11	www.dbr.state.ri.us/pdf_forms/clr/Auto%20Glass%20-%20Licensee%20List.pdf
Automobile Wrecker #11	www.dbr.state.ri.us/pdf_forms/clr/Auto%20Wrecking%20-%20Licensee%20List.pdf
Barber Shop #13	http://health.ri.mylicense.com
Barber/Barber Instructor #13	http://health.ri.mylicense.com
Birth Center #13	http://health.ri.mylicense.com
Blood Test Screener #13	http://health.ri.mylicense.com
Cable Installer #4	www.crb.state.ri.us/search.php
Charter School #16	www.ridoe.net/charterschools/list.htm
Check Casher #5	www.dbr.state.ri.us/pdf_forms/bank/List%20of%20Licensees%2001-28-04.pdf
Chimney Sweep #4	www.crb.state.ri.us/search.php
Chiropractor #13	http://health.ri.mylicense.com
Clinical Lab Scientist #7	http://12.153.47.221/
Contractor, Residential Building #4	www.crb.state.ri.us/search.php
Contractor, Watch List #4	www.crb.state.ri.us/watchlist.php
Cosmetologist/Cosmetology Instructor #13	http://health.ri.mylicense.com
CPA #1	www.dbr.state.ri.us/pdf_forms/ba/Licensed%20CPAs%20and%20PAs.pdf
Cytotechnologist #7	http://12.153.47.221/
Debt Pooler #5	www.dbr.state.ri.us/pdf_forms/bank/List%20of%20Licensees%2001-28-04.pdf
Dental Hygienist #13	http://health.ri.mylicense.com
Dentist #13	http://health.ri.mylicense.com
Dietitian/Nutritionist #13	http://health.ri.mylicense.com
Electrologist #13	http://health.ri.mylicense.com
Electron Microscopy, Clinical Lab Scientist #7	http://12.153.47.221/
Embalmer #13	http://health.ri.mylicense.com
Emergency Care Facility #13	http://health.ri.mylicense.com
Emergency Medical Technician/Services #13	http://health.ri.mylicense.com
Esthetician #13	http://health.ri.mylicense.com
Financial Institution #5	www.dbr.state.ri.us/pdf_forms/bank/List%20of%20Licensees%2001-28-04.pdf
Funeral Director #13	http://health.ri.mylicense.com
Group Home #13	http://health.ri.mylicense.com
Hairdresser/Hairdresser Instructor #13	http://health.ri.mylicense.com
Hazardous Waste Transporter #9	www.state.ri.us/dem/programs/benviron/waste/transpor/index.htm
Hearing Aid Dispenser #13	http://health.ri.mylicense.com
Histologic Technician, Clinical #7	http://12.153.47.221/
Home Care Provider #13	http://health.ri.mylicense.com
Home Nursing Care #13	http://health.ri.mylicense.com
Hospice Provider #13	http://health.ri.mylicense.com
Hospital #13	http://health.ri.mylicense.com
Insurance Broker/Producer/Agent #5	www.dbr.state.ri.us/lic_search.php
Interpreter for the Deaf #13	http://health.ri.mylicense.com
Laboratory, Medical #13	http://health.ri.mylicense.com
Lender/Loan Broker #5	www.dbr.state.ri.us/pdf_forms/bank/List%20of%20Licensees%2001-28-04.pdf
Lobbyist #25	www.corps.state.ri.us/lobby/default.asp
Manicurist / Manicurist Shop #13	http://health.ri.mylicense.com
Marriage & Family Therapist #13	http://health.ri.mylicense.com
Massage Therapist #13	http://health.ri.mylicense.com
Medical Doctor #13	http://health.ri.mylicense.com
Medical Waste Transporter #9	www.state.ri.us/dem/programs/benviron/waste/transpor/index.htm
Mental Health Counselor #13	http://health.ri.mylicense.com
Midwife #13	http://health.ri.mylicense.com
Money Broker / Transferer #5	www.dbr.state.ri.us/pdf_forms/bank/List%20of%20Licensees%2001-28-04.pdf
Mortgage Broker #5	www.dbr.state.ri.us/pdf_forms/bank/List%20of%20Licensees%2001-28-04.pdf
Notary Public #15	www.corps.state.ri.us/notaries/notaries.htm

Nuclear Medicine Technologist #13...................http://health.ri.mylicense.com
Nurse / Nurse-LPN #13 ....http://health.ri.mylicense.com
Nursing Assistant /Nursing Service #13 ....http://health.ri.mylicense.com
Nursing Home Administrator #13.......................http://health.ri.mylicense.com
Occupational Therapist #13...............................http://health.ri.mylicense.com
Office Operatories (Medical) #13.......................http://health.ri.mylicense.com
Optician #13..http://health.ri.mylicense.com
Optometrist #13 ....http://health.ri.mylicense.com
Osteopathic Physician #13 ....www.docboard.org/ri/df/search.htm
Outpatient Rehabilitation #13 ....http://health.ri.mylicense.com
Pharmacist/Pharmacy Tech./Pharmacy #3 ....http://12.153.47.221/
Phlebotomy Station #13....................................http://health.ri.mylicense.com
Physical Therapist / Therapist Assistant #13......http://health.ri.mylicense.com
Physician / Physician Assistant #13 ....http://health.ri.mylicense.com
Podiatrist #13 ....http://health.ri.mylicense.com
Prosthetist #13 ....http://health.ri.mylicense.com
Psychologist #13...http://health.ri.mylicense.com
Public Accountant-CPA #1 ....www.dbr.state.ri.us/pdf_forms/ba/Licensed%20CPAs%20and%20PAs.pdf
Public Accounting Firm #1 ....www.dbr.state.ri.us/pdf_forms/ba/Licensed%20Public%20Accounting%20Firms.pdf
Radiation Therapist #13....................................http://health.ri.mylicense.com
Radiographer #13 ....http://health.ri.mylicense.com
Real Estate Agent/Sales #5..............................www.dbr.state.ri.us/pdf_forms/RE-Real%20Estate%20Salespersons.pdf
Real Estate Appraiser #5..................................www.dbr.state.ri.us/pdf_forms/RE-Real%20Estate%20Appraisers.pdf
Real Estate Broker #5.......................................www.dbr.state.ri.us/pdf_forms/RE-Real%20Estate%20Brokers.pdf
Residential Care Facility #13 ....http://health.ri.mylicense.com
Residential Facility #22....................................www.dcyf.ri.gov
Respiratory Care Practitioner #13 ....http://health.ri.mylicense.com
Roofer, Commercial #4.....................................www.crb.state.ri.us/search.php
Salvage Yard #11 ....www.dbr.state.ri.us/pdf_forms/clr/Auto%20Salvage%20-%20Licensee%20List.pdf
Sanitarian #13...http://health.ri.mylicense.com
Security Alarm Installer #4...............................www.crb.state.ri.us/search.php
Septic Transporter #9 ....www.state.ri.us/dem/programs/benviron/waste/transpor/index.htm
Social Worker #13 ....http://health.ri.mylicense.com
Speech/Language Pathologist #13.....................http://health.ri.mylicense.com
Surgery Center, Freestanding #13 ....http://health.ri.mylicense.com
Tanning Facility #13...http://health.ri.mylicense.com
Tattoo Artist #13 ....http://health.ri.mylicense.com
Underground Sprinkler Installer #4....................www.crb.state.ri.us/search.php
Veterinarian #13 ....http://health.ri.mylicense.com
X-ray Facility / X-ray, Portable #13....................http://health.ri.mylicense.com

Rhode Island Licensing Quick Finder

Acupuncturist #13...................................401-222-2827
Alarm Agent/Company #11 401-222-3857
Ambulatory Care Facility #13 401-222-2827
Arborist #10 401-647-3367
Architect #5..401-222-2565
Asbestos Abatement Worker #13...........401-222-3601
Assisted Living Facility #13 401-222-2827
Athletic Trainer #13................................401-222-5888
Attorney #21 401-222-4233
Auctioneer #11.......................................401-222-3857
Audiologist #13 401-222-2827
Automobile Body Shop #11 401-222-3857
Automobile Glass Installer #11...............401-222-3857
Automobile Wrecker #11 401-222-3857
Bank #5..401-222-2405
Bank Holding Company #5......................401-222-2405
Barber Shop #13.....................................401-222-2827
Barber/Barber Instructor #13.................401-222-2827
Beekeeper #9 ....401-222-2781 x4519
Birth Center #13......................................401-222-2827
Blaster #19...401-294-0861
Blood Test Screener #13.........................401-222-2827
Bondsman #18..401-222-3212
Boxer #5...401-222-6541
Cable Installer #4...................................401-222-1268
Cattle Dealer #9..........................401-222-2781 x4503

Charter School #16..................................401-222-4600
Check Casher #5.....................................401-222-2405
Chem'l Dependency Clinical Supv'r #6.401-233-2215
Chemical Dependency Prof./Advn'd #6.401-233-2215
Chimney Sweep #4 401-222-1268
Chiropractor #13.....................................401-222-2827
Clinical Lab Scientist, Cytogenetic #7..401-222-2827
Clinical Lab Scientist/Technician #7......401-222-2877
Clinical Supervisor, Recognized #6 401-233-2215
Contractor, Resid'l Building #4 401-222-1268
Contractor, Watch List #4 401-222-1268
Controlled Substance Wholesaler #3....401-222-2837
Cosmetologist/Cosmetology Instr. #13 .401-222-2827
Court Reporter #26.................................401-222-3215
CPA #1 401-222-3185
Credit Union #5.......................................401-222-2405
Cytotechnologist #7...............................401-222-2827
Day Care, Children #22 401-528-3624
Debt Pooler #5..401-222-2405
Dentist/Dental Hygienist #13.................401-222-2151
Dietitian/Nutritionist #13 401-222-5888
Electrician #8 401-462-8571
Electrologist #13 401-222-2827
Electron Microscopy, Lab Scientist #7.401-222-2827
Elevator Inspector/Mechanic #8...........401-462-8579
Embalmer #13 401-222-2827

Emergency Care Facility #13 401-222-2827
Emergency Medical Tech./Svcs #13.....401-222-2401
Engineer #2 401-222-2038
Esthetician #13.......................................401-222-2827
Family/Group Day Care Home Provider #22
....401-528-3624
Financial Institution #5 401-222-2405
Fire Alarm Installer #19 401-294-0861
Fire Extinguisher Installer/Svc. #19 401-294-0861
Fireworks Shooter #19 401-294-0861
Fisher, Commercial #9............................401-222-6647
Foster Care/Home #22............................401-528-3606
Funeral Director #13 401-222-2827
Fur Buyer #9...401-222-6647
Group Home #13 401-222-2827
Hairdresser/Hairdresser Instructor #13. 401-222-2827
Haz. Waste Transporter #9.......401-222-4700 x7517
Health Club #11......................................401-222-3857
Hearing Aid Dispenser #13 401-222-2827
Histologic Technician, Clinical #7 401-222-2827
Hoisting Engineer #8 401-462-8554
Home Care Provider #13.........................401-222-2827
Home Nursing Care #13 401-222-2827
Hospice Provider #13..............................401-222-2827
Hospital #13 401-222-2827
Hypodermic Dispenser #3......................401-222-2837

Insurance Adjuster / Appraiser #5 401-222-2223	Office Operatories (Medical) #13 401-222-2827	Sanitarian #13 401-222-2827
Insurance Broker/Producer/Agent #5 ... 401-222-2223	Optician #13 401-222-2827	School Coach #16 401-222-2675
Insurance Solicitor #5 401-222-2223	Optometrist #13 401-222-2827	School Guidance Counselor #16 401-222-2675
Interpreter for the Deaf #13 401-222-2827	Osteopathic Physician #13 401-222-3855	School Principal/Superin't/Supv'r #16.. 401-222-2675
Investment Advisor #5 401-222-3048	Outpatient Rehabilitation #13 401-222-2827	School Psychologist/Social Worker #16 401-222-2675
Laboratory, Medical #13 401-222-2827	Park Ranger #12 401-222-2632	Securities Broker/Dealer #5 401-222-3048
Land Surveyor Firm #2 401-222-2038	Pesticide Applicator #9 .... 401-222-2781 x4510	Securities Broker/Dealer Sales Rep. #5 401-222-3048
Landscape Architect #2 401-222-2038	Pharmacist/Pharmacy Technician #3... 401-222-2837	Security Alarm Installer #4 401-222-1268
Landscaper #5 401-222-2565	Pharmacy #3 401-222-2837	Septic Transporter #9 .... 401-222-4700 x7517
Lender/Loan Broker #5 401-222-2405	Phlebotomy Station #13 401-222-2827	Sewage Disposal System Installer #9.. 401-222-6820
Lifeguard #12 401-222-2632	Physical Therapist /Assistant #13 401-222-2827	Sheet Metal Technician/Worker #8...... 401-462-8535
Liquor Control #5 401-222-2562	Physician / Physician Assistant #13.... 401-222-2827	Social Worker #13 401-222-2827
Lobbyist #25 401-222-6616	Physicians Controlled Substance #3.... 401-222-2837	Speech/Language Pathologist #13 401-222-2827
Manicurist / Manicurist Shop #13 401-222-2827	Pilot, Ship #20 401-783-5551	Surgery Center, Freestanding #13....... 401-222-2827
Marriage & Family Therapist #13 401-222-2827	Pipefitter #8 401-462-8535	Surveyor, Land #5 401-222-2565
Massage Therapist #13 401-222-2827	Plumber/Master Plumber/Journey'n #8. 401-462-8525	Tanning Facility #13 401-222-2827
Medical Doctor #13 401-222-2827	Podiatrist #13 401-222-2827	Tattoo Artist #13 401-222-2827
Medical Waste Transporter #9 .. 401-222-4700 x7517	Prevention Specialist/Spvr./Advanced #6 401-233-2215	Teacher #16 401-222-2675
Mental Health Counselor #13 401-222-2827	Prosthetist #13 401-222-2827	Telecommunications Technician #8..... 401-462-8533
Midwife #13 401-222-5700	Psychologist #13 401-222-2827	Trapper #9 401-222-6647
Mobile Home Park #11 401-222-3857	Public Accountant-CPA/Firm #1 401-222-3185	Travel Agent #11 401-222-3857
Mobile/Mfg'd Home Mfg./Dealer #11 401-222-3857	Pyrotechnic Operator #19 401-294-0861	Underground Sprinkler Installer #4 401-222-1268
Money Broker #5 401-222-2405	Radiation Therapist #13 401-222-2827	Upholstery/Bedding Mfg. #11................ 401-222-3857
Money Transferer #5 401-222-2405	Radiographer #13................................. 401-222-2827	Vendor Employee #5............................ 401-222-2405
Mortgage Broker #5 401-222-2405	Reading Specialist #16......................... 401-222-2675	Veterinarian #13 401-222-2827
Notary Public #15 401-222-1487	Real Estate Agent/Broker/Sales #5..... 401-222-2255	Waste Water Treatment Plant Operator #9
Nuclear Medicine Technologist #13 401-222-5700	Real Estate Appraiser #5 401-222-2255	 401-222-6820
Nurse / Nurse-LPN #13 401-222-5700	Refrigeration Technician #8 401-462-8535	Wildlife Propagator #9.......................... 401-222-6647
Nurseryman #9 .... 401-222-2781 x4516	Residential Care Facility #13................ 401-222-2827	Wildlife Rehabilitator #23 401-789-0281
Nursing Assistant/Service #13 401-222-5888	Residential Facility #22 401-528-3623	Woods Operator #10............................ 401-647-3367
Nursing Home Administrator #13 401-222-5888	Respiratory Care Practitioner #13......... 401-222-2827	Wrestler #5 401-222-6541
Nursing Service #13 401-222-2827	Roofer, Commercial #4 401-222-1268	X-ray Facility /Portable #13.................. 401-222-2827
Occupational Therapist #13.................. 401-222-2827	Salvage Yard #11 401-222-3857	

Rhode Island Licensing Agency Information

1 Department of Business Regulation, Board of Accountancy, 233 Richmond St, Providence, RI 02903-4236; 401-222-3185, Fax: 401-222-6654. www.dbr.state.ri.us/account.html Search Database at www.dbr.state.ri.us/pdf_forms/ba/Licensed%20CPAs%20and%20PAs.pdf

3 Board of Pharmacy, 3 Capitol Hill, Rm 205, Providence, RI 02908; 401-222-2837, Fax: 401-222-2158. www.health.state.ri.us Search Database at http://12.153.47.221/

4 Contractors' Registration Board, 1 Capitol Hill, 2nd Fl, Providence, RI 02908; 401-222-1268, Fax: 401-222-2599. www.crb.state.ri.us Email: gwhalen@doa.state.ri.us Search Database at www.crb.state.ri.us/search.php

5 Business Regulation Department, Division of Commercial Licensing & Regulation, 233 Richmond St, Providence, RI 02903-4232; 401-222-2246. www.dbr.state.ri.us

6 Certification of Chemical Dependency Professionals, 345 Waterman Ave, Smithfield, RI 02917; 401-233-2215, Fax: 401-233-0690. Email: ricert@msn.com

7 Clinical Laboratory Advisory Board, 3 Capitol Hill, Rm 104, Providence, RI 02908; 401-222-2827, Fax: 401-222-1272. www.health.state.ri.us Search Database at http://12.153.47.221/

8 Dept. of Labor & Training, Div. of Professional Regulation - Bldg #70, PO Box 20247 (1511 Pontiac Av), Providence, RI 02920-0943; 401-462-8527, Fax: 401-462-8528. www.dlt.state.ri.us

9 Dept. of Environmental Mgmt, Bureau of Natural Resources, 235 Promenade St, #260, Prov-

idence, RI 02908-5767; 401-222-4700, Fax: 401-222-6802. www.state.ri.us/dem/programs/index.htm

10 Department of Environmental Management, Division of Forest Environment, 1037 Hartford Pike, North Scituate, RI 02857; 401-647-3367, Fax: 401-647-3590. www.state.ri.us/dem/programs/bnatres/forest/index.htm Email: riforestry@edgenet.net

11 Division of Licensing & Consumer Protection, Commercial Licensing, 233 Richmond St, Providence, RI 02903; 401-222-3857, Fax: 401-222-6654. www.dbr.state.ri.us

12 Division of Parks & Recreation, 2321 Hartford Ave, Johnston, RI 02919; 401-222-2632, Fax: 401-934-0610. www.riparks.com/index.htm Email: riparks@earthlink.net

13 Health Department, Professional Regulation Division, 3 Capitol Hill, Rm 205, Providence, RI 02908-5097; 401-222-2827, Fax: 401-222-1272. www.health.state.ri.us email: library@health.state.ri.us Search Database at http://health.ri.mylicense.com Note: Also, search medical doctors and osteopaths at www.docboard.org/ri/df/search.htm.

15 Office of Secretary of State, Notary Public Section, 100 N Main St, Providence, RI 02903; 401-222-1487, Fax: 401-222-3879. www.state.ri.us Email: notaries@sec.state.ri.us Search Database at www.state.ri.us/ Note: To search, there are separate buttons for the Notary Public Section or Lobbyist.

16 Department of Education, Office of Teacher Certification, 255 Westminster St, Providence, RI 02903; 401-222-4600, Fax: 401-222-2048. www.ridoe.net

18 Superior Court, Bondsman Registration, 250 Benefit St, Rm 533, Providence, RI 02903; 401-222-3212, Fax: 401-272-4645. Note: Direct written requests to Judge Jos. F. Rodgers, Jr.

19 State Fire Marshall's Office, 24 Conway Ave, Quansit-Davisville Industrial Park, Davisville/North Kingston, RI 02852; 401-294-0861, Fax: 401-295-9092.

20 Pilotage Commission, 301 Great Island Rd, Galilee, RI 02882; 401-783-5551, Fax: 401-783-7285.

21 Supreme Court, Board of Bar Examiners, 250 Benefit St, Providence, RI 02903; 401-222-4233, Fax: 401-222-3599. www.courts.state.ri.us/supreme/bar/barexaminers.htm Email: kcacchiotti@courts.state.ri.us

22 Department of Children, Youth & Famillies, 101 Friendship St #101, Providence, RI 02903; 401-528-3624. www.dcyf.state.ri.us Search at www.dcyf.state.ri.us/cgi-bin/dcyf.cgi

23 Department of Environmental Management, Division of Fish & Wildlife, Box 218, West Kingston, RI 02892; 401-789-0281, Fax: 401-783-7490. www.state.ri.us/dem Email: lgibson@

25 Office of Secretary of State, Lobbyist Registration, State House, Smith St, Rm 38, Providence, RI 02903; 401-222-6616, Fax: 401-222-1404. www.state.ri.us/ To search, there are separate buttons for the Notary Public Section or Lobbyist.

26 Court Administrator Office, 250 Benefit St, #506, Providence, RI 02903; 401-222-3215.

Rhode Island Federal Courts

The following list indicates the district and division name for each county in the state.

County/Court Cross Reference

Bristol...Providence

Kent..Providence

Newport..Providence

Providence...Providence

Washington...Providence

US District Court

District of Rhode Island

Providence Division Clerk's Office, One Exchange Terrace, Federal Bldg, Providence, RI 02903 (Use mail address for courier delivery) 401-752-7200, Fax: 401-752-7247. www.rid.uscourts.gov

Counties: All counties in Rhode Island.

Indexing & Storage: New cases available in the index 1-2 days after filing date. Computer indexing is since 1991. Anything prior to that is maintained on card index. District wide searches are available from this court. Naturalization records are at Federal Records Center in Waltham, Mass.

Fee & Payment: Payment may be made by money order, cashier check, personal check. Payee: Clerk, U.S. District Court.

Phone Search: Only the case number or name will be released over the phone.

In Person Search: Fee charged if court conducts your in person search for you.

PACER: PACER is available online at http://pacer.rid.uscourts.gov. Case records go back to December 1988. Records never purged. New records are online after 2 days.

U.S. Bankruptcy Court

District of Rhode Island

Providence Division 6th Floor, 380 Westminster St, Providence, RI 02903 (courier address: Use mail address for courier delivery) 401-528-4477, Fax: 401-528-4470. www.rib.uscourts.gov

Counties: All counties in Rhode Island.

Indexing & Storage: Cases indexed by debtor and creditors as well as by case number. New cases available in the index 1 day after filing date.

Fee & Payment: Payment may be made by money order, cashier check, personal check, Visa or Mastercard. Debtors checks are not accepted. Payee: Clerk, U.S. Bankruptcy Court. Will fax results $15.00 per item.

Phone Search: Only docket information available by phone. Automated voice case information service (VCIS) is available. Call VCIS at 800-843-2841 or 401-528-4476.

In Person Search: Fee charged if court conducts your in person search for you.

PACER: PACER is available online at http://pacer.rib.uscourts.gov. Document images available. Records purged every three years. New civil records are online after 1 day.

Electronic Filing: Electronic filing information online at https://ecf.rib.uscourts.gov

Standards for Federal Courts: The search fee is $20.00 per item (one party name or case number). Certification fee is $7.00 per document. Copy fee is $.50 per page. All fees standard unless noted in profile. Mail Search: always enclose a stamped self addressed envelope unless otherwise noted. Most courts accept fax requests or will suggest a copying/search vendor. Before releasing records, all courts require prepayment unless noted in profile.

Open records are located at the court unless otherwise noted. District courts index by defendant and plaintiff as well as by case number. Bankruptcy courts usually index by debtor and case number. While most courts now have their indexes on computer, many still maintain index card files as well.

The universal PACER sign-up number is 800-676-6856. Find PACER and the Party/Case Index on the Web at http://pacer.psc.uscourts.gov. PACER dial-up access is $.60 per minute. Also, courts offering internet access via RACER, PACER, Web-PACER or the new CM-ECF charge $.07 per page fee unless noted as free.

Rhode Island County Courts

Court	Jurisdiction	No. of Courts	How Organized
Superior Courts*	General	4	4 Divisions
District Courts*	Limited	4	6 Divisions
Municipal Courts	Municipal	16	
Probate Courts*	Probate	39	39 Cities/ Towns
Family Courts	Special	4	4 Divisions
Workers' Compensation Court	Special	1	

* Profiled in this Sourcebook.

Court	CIVIL								
	Tort	Contract	Real Estate	Min. Claim	Max. Claim	Small Claims	Estate	Eviction	Domestic Relations
Superior Courts*	X	X	X	$5000	No Max				
District Courts*	X	X	X	$1500	$10,000	$1500		X	
Municipal Courts									
Probate Courts*							X		
Family Courts									X
Workers' CompCourt									

Court	CRIMINAL				
	Felony	Misdemeanor	DWI/DUI	Preliminary Hearing	Juvenile
Superior Courts*	X				
District Courts*		X	X	X	
Municipal Courts					
Probate Courts*					
Family Courts					X
Workers' Comp Court					

ADMINISTRATION   Court Administrator, Supreme Court, 250 Benefit St, Providence, RI, 02903; 401-222-3272, Fax: 401-222-3599. www.courts.state.ri.us

COURT STRUCTURE   Rhode Island has five counties, but only four Superior/District Court Locations (2nd-Newport, 3rd-Kent, 4th-Washignton, and 6th-Prividence/Bristol Districts). Bristol and Providence counties are completely merged at the Providence location. Civil claims between $5000 and $10,000 may be filed in either Superior or District Court at the discretion of the filer. For questions regarding the Superior Courts, call 401-222-2622. For questions regarding the District Courts, call 401-458-3156.

ONLINE ACCESS   The Rhode Island Judiciary offers free Internet access to court criminal records statewide at http://courtconnect.courts.state.ri.us. A word of caution, this website is provided as an informational service only and should not be relied upon as an official record of the court. Superior (civil, family) and Appellate courts are online internally for court personnel only.

PROBATE COURTS   Probate is handled by the Town Clerk at the 39 cities and towns across Rhode Island.

Bristol County

Superior & District Courts c/o Bristol Town Hall, 10 Court St, Bristol, RI 02809; 401-253-7000. Hours: 8:30-4PM (EST). *Probate Only.*
Note: Do not send criminal or civil (except probate) record requests here. All civil and criminal cases are handled by the Providence County courts.

Barrington Town Hall 283 County Road, Barrington, RI 02806; 401-247-1900 x4; Fax: 401-245-5003. Hours: 8:30AM-4:30PM (EST). *Probate.*

Bristol Town Hall 10 Court St, Bristol, RI 02809; 401-253-7000 x21; Fax: 401-253-1570. Hours: 8:30AM-4PM (EST). *Probate.*

Warren Town Hall 514 Main St, Warren, RI 02885; 401-245-7340; Fax: 401-245-7421. Hours: 9AM-4PM (EST). *Probate.*

Kent County

Superior Court 222 Quaker Lane, Warwick, RI 02886; 401-822-1311. Hours: 8:30AM-4:00PM (EST). *Felony, Civil Actions Over $10,000.*
www.courts.state.ri.us
Civil Records: Access: In person only. Visitors must perform in person searches for themselves. No search fee. Required to search: name, years to search. Civil cases indexed by defendant, plaintiff. Civil records on computer from 1987.
Criminal Records: Access: In person, online. Visitors must perform in person searches for themselves. No search fee. Required to search: name, years to search, signed release; also helpful: DOB. Criminal records on computer from 1987. Free Internet access is at http://courtconnect.courts.state.ri.us. This website is provided as an informational service only and should not be relied upon as an official record of the court.
General Information: Public Access terminal is available. (Records go back to 1997.) No adoption, confidential or sealed records released. Copy fee: $.15 per page. Cert fee: $3.00 per page. Exemplified copies: $9.00 each plus $3.00 per page. Payee: Clerk of Superior Court. Personal checks accepted. Prepayment required.

3rd Division District Court 222 Quaker Lane, Warwick, RI 02886-0107; 401-822-1771. Hours: 8:30AM-4:30PM (EST). *Misdemeanor, Civil Actions Under $10,000, Eviction, Small Claims.*
Civil Records: Access: In person only. Visitors must perform in person searches for themselves. No search fee. Required to search: name, years to search. Civil cases indexed by defendant, plaintiff. Civil records for 1995-1997 on index cards. Archives stored at Rhode Island Judicial Records Center, 1 Hill St, Pawtucket, RI 02860, 401-277-3249. Records destroyed after 10 years, but remain in docket books.
Criminal Records: Access: In person, online. Visitors must perform in person searches for themselves. No search fee. Required to search: name, years to search, DOB, signed release. Criminal records for 1995-1997 on index cards. Archives stored at Rhode Island Judicial Records Center. Records destroyed after 10 years, but remain in docket books. Free Internet access at http://courtconnect.courts.state.ri.us. This website is provided as an informational service only and should not be relied upon as an official record of the court.
General Information: No mental or sealed records released. Copy fee: $1.00 per page. Cert fee: $1.00 per page. Payee: 3rd District Court. Personal checks accepted. Visa, AmEx accepted. Prepayment required.

Coventry Town Hall 1670 Flat River Road, Coventry, RI 02816; 401-822-9174; Fax: 401-822-9132. Hours: 8:30AM-4:30PM (EST). *Probate.*

East Greenwich Town Hall 125 Main St (PO Box 111), East Greenwich, RI 02818; 401-886-8607; 8604; Fax: 401-886-8625. Hours: 8:30AM-4:30PM (EST). *Probate.*

Warwick City Hall 3275 Post Road, Warwick, RI 02886; 401-738-2000 (x6213); Fax: 401-738-6639. Hours: 8:30AM-4:30PM (EST). *Probate.*

West Greenwich Town Hall 280 Victory Highway, West Greenwich, RI 02817; 401-392-3800; Fax: 401-392-3805. Hours: 9AM-4PM M,T,Th,F; 9AM-4PM, 7-9PM W (EST). *Probate.*

West Warwick Town Hall 1170 Main St, West Warwick, RI 02893-4829; 401-822-9201; Fax: 401-822-9266. Hours: 8:30AM-4:30PM; 8:30AM-4PM June 1st-Labor Day (EST). *Probate.*

Newport County

Superior Court Florence K Murray Judicial Complex, 45 Washington Sq, Newport, RI 02840; 401-841-8330; Fax: 401-846-1673. Hours: 8:30AM-4:30PM (July and August till 4PM) (EST). *Felony, Civil Actions Over $10,000.*
Civil Records: Access: Mail, fax, in person. Both court and visitors may perform in person searches. Search fee: $15.00 per hour for search and review. Required to search: name, years to search. Civil cases indexed by defendant, plaintiff. Civil records on computer from 1989. Prior records archived at Rhode Island Records Center.
Criminal Records: Access: Mail, fax, in person, online. Both court and visitors may perform in person searches. Search fee: $15.00 per hour for search and review. Required to search: name, years to search, DOB. Criminal records on computer from 1983, index from 1968. Prior records archived at Records Center. Free Internet access is at http://courtconnect.courts.state.ri.us. This website is provided as an informational service only and should not be relied upon as an official record of the court.
General Information: Public Access terminal is available. No child molestation or sexual assault records released. Copy fee: $.50 per page. Cert fee: $3.00 per page. Payee: Clerk Superior Court. Personal checks accepted. Prepayment required. Mail requests: SASE required. Mail turnaround time 1 day.

2nd District Court 45 Washington Sq, Newport, RI 02840; 401-841-8350. Hours: 8:30AM-4:30PM (4PM-summer months) (EST). *Misdemeanor, Civil Actions Under $10,000, Eviction, Small Claims.*
Civil Records: Access: In person only. Visitors must perform in person searches for themselves. No search fee. Required to search: name, years to search. Civil cases indexed by defendant, plaintiff. Civil records on index cards for past 3 years, prior archived at Pawtucket Judicial Records Center.
Criminal Records: Access: In person, online. Visitors must perform in person searches for themselves. No search fee. Required to search: name. Overall records from 1999-2002. Computerized records from 1999-2004. Free Internet access at http://courtconnect.courts.state.ri.us. This website is provided as an informational service only and should not be relied upon as an official record of the court.
General Information: Public Access terminal is available. No juvenile, family court, sealed, expunged or ordered by judge or adoption records released. Copy fee: $.15 per page. Cert fee: $1.00. Payee: 2nd District Court. No personal checks accepted. Prepayment required.

Jamestown Town Hall 93 Narragansett Ave, Jamestown, RI 02835; 401-423-7200; Fax: 401-423-7230. Hours: 8AM-4:30PM (EST). *Probate.*

Little Compton Town Hall 40 Commons, PO Box 226, Little Compton, RI 02837; 401-635-4400; Fax: 401-635-2470. Hours: 8AM-4PM (EST). *Probate.*

Middletown Town Hall 350 E Main Road, Middletown, RI 02842; 401-847-0009; Fax: 401-845-0406. Hours: 8AM-5PM (EST). *Probate.*

Newport City Hall 43 Broadway, Newport, RI 02840; 401-846-9600; Fax: 401-849-8757/848-5750. Hours: 8:30AM-4:30PM (EST). *Probate.*

Portsmouth Town Hall 2200 E Main Road, Portsmouth, RI 02871; 401-683-2101. Hours: 9AM-4PM (EST). *Probate.*

Tiverton Town Hall 343 Highland Road, Tiverton, RI 02878; 401-625-6700; Fax: 401-625-6705. Hours: 8:30AM-4PM (EST). *Probate.*

Providence County

Providence/Bristol Superior Court 250 Benefit St, Providence, RI 02903; 401-222-3250. Hours: 8:30AM-4PM (EST). *Felony, Civil Actions Over $10,000.*
www.courts.state.ri.us
Note: All civil and criminal cases for Bristol are handled by the Providence County courts.
Civil Records: Access: Phone, mail, in person. Visitors must perform in person searches for themselves. No search fee. Required to search: name, years to search. Civil cases indexed by defendant, plaintiff. Civil records on computer since 1983.
Criminal Records: Access: In person, online. Visitors must perform in person searches for themselves. No search fee. Required to search: name, years to search, DOB. Criminal records on computer since 1983. Free Internet access to criminal records is at http://courtconnect.courts.state.ri.us. This website is provided as an informational service only and should not be relied upon as an official record of the court.
General Information: Public Access terminal is available. No adoption, confidential or sealed records released. Copy fee: $.15 per page. Cert fee: $3.00. Payee: Providence Superior Court. Personal checks accepted. Prepayment required.

6th Division District Court 1 Dorrance Plaza 2nd Fl, Providence, RI 02903; 401-458-5400. Hours: 8:30AM-4PM (EST). *Misdemeanor, Civil Actions Under $10,000, Eviction, Small Claims.*
Note: All civil and criminal cases are handled by the Providence County courts.
Civil Records: Access: Mail, phone, in person. Both court and visitors may perform in person searches. No search fee. Required to search: name, years to search. Civil cases indexed by defendant, plaintiff. Civil records on card files to present. Phone access limited to one name.
Criminal Records: Access: Mail, phone, in person, online. Both court and visitors may perform in person searches. No search fee. Required to search: name, years to search. Criminal records for misdemeanor on computer from 1989. Free Internet access to criminal records is at http://courtconnect.courts.state.ri.us. This website is provided as an informational service only and should not be relied upon as an official record of the court. Phone requests limited to one name.
General Information: No adoption, confidential or sealed records released. Copy fee: $.50 per page. Cert fee: $1.00. Payee: 6th Division District Court. Personal checks accepted. Prepayment required. Mail requests: SASE required. Mail turnaround time varies.

Burrillville Town Hall 105 Harrisville Main St, Harrisville, RI 02830; 401-568-4300 x114 or x110; Fax: 401-568-0490. Hours: 8:30AM-4:30PM M-W; 8:30AM-7:00PM Th.; 8:30AM-12:30PM F. (EST). *Probate.*
www.burrillville.org/Public_Documents/BurrillvilleR I_Clerk/probate

Central Falls City Hall City Clerk's Office, 580 Broad St, Central Falls, RI 02863; 401-727-7400; Fax: 401-727-7406. Hours: 8:30AM-4:30PM (EST). *Probate.*
www.centralfallsri.us

Cranston City Hall 869 Park Ave, Cranston, RI 02910; 401-461-1000 X3197; Fax: 401-780-3150. Hours: 8:30AM-4:30PM (EST). *Probate.*

Cumberland Town Hall 45 Broad St, PO Box 7, Cumberland, RI 02864; 401-728-2400; Fax: 401-724-1103. Hours: 8:30AM-4:30PM (EST). *Probate.*

East Providence City Hall 145 Taunton Ave, East Providence, RI 02914; 401-435-7500; Fax: 401-435-4630. Hours: 8AM-4PM (EST). *Probate.*

Foster Town Hall 181 Howard Hill Rd, Foster, RI 02825; 401-392-9200; Fax: 401-392-9201. Hours: 9AM-4PM (EST). *Probate.*

Glocester Town Hall 1145 Putnam Pike, Glocester/ Chepachet, RI 02814; 401-568-6206; Fax: 401-568-5850. Hours: 8AM-4:30PM (EST). *Probate.*

Johnston Town Hall 1385 Hartford Ave, Johnston, RI 02919; 401-351-6618/401-553-8830 (Direct Phone); Fax: 401-553-8835/331-4271. Hours: 8:30AM-4:30PM (EST). *Probate.*
Note: Online access to probate court records is available at http://johnston-ri.com/probate.asp. Search by last name.

Lincoln Town Hall PO Box 100, 100 Old River Rd, Lincoln, RI 02865; 401-333-8450, 333-8451; Fax: 401-333-3648. Hours: 9AM-4:30PM (EST). *Probate.*
www.lincolnri.org/clerksoffice.shtml
Note: Court meets fourth Monday at 9 AM.

North Providence Town Hall 2000 Smith St, North Providence, RI 02911; 401-232-0900; Fax: 401-233-1409. Hours: 8:30AM-4:30PM (EST). *Probate.*

North Smithfield Town Hall Municipal Annex, 575 Smithfield Rd, North Smithfield, RI 02896; 401-767-2200 x216; Probate phone: 401-767-2200 x220, 221; Fax: 401-356-4057. Hours: 8AM-4PM M, T, W; 8AM-7PM Th; 8AM-noon F (EST). *Probate.*

Pawtucket City Hall 137 Roosevelt Ave, Pawtucket, RI 02860; 401-728-0500 x259 or x223; Fax: 401-728-8932. Hours: 8:30AM-4:30PM (EST). *Probate.*

Providence City Hall 25 Dorrance St, Providence, RI 02903; 401-421-7740; Fax: 401-861-6208. Hours: 8:30AM-4:00PM (EST). *Probate.*
Note: All civil and criminal cases are handled by the Providence County courts.

Scituate Town Hall 195 Danielson Pike, PO Box 328, North Scituate, RI 02857; 401-647-2822; Fax: 401-647-7220. Hours: 8:30AM-4PM (EST). *Probate.*

Smithfield Town Hall 64 Farnum Pike, Smithfield, RI 02917; 401-233-1000 X111; Probate phone: 401-233-1000 X114; Fax: 401-232-7244. Hours: 9AM-4:30PM (EST). *Probate.*

Woonsocket City Hall 169 Main St, Woonsocket, RI 02895; 401-762-6400; Probate phone: 401-767-9248; Fax: 401-765-0022. Hours: 8:30AM-4PM (EST). *Probate.*

Washington County

Superior Court 4800 Towerhill Rd, Wakefield, RI 02879; 401-782-4121. Hours: 8:30AM-4:30PM (Sept-June) 8:30AM-4PM (July & Aug) (EST). *Felony, Civil Actions Over $10,000.*
Civil Records: Access: Phone, mail, in person. Both court and visitors may perform in person searches. No search fee. Required to search: name, years to search. Civil cases indexed by defendant, plaintiff. Civil records on computer from 1984, on index prior to 1984. Archived at Record Center, 401-277-3249. Phone requests taken only after 3PM.
Criminal Records: Access: Mail, in person, online. Both court and visitors may perform in person searches. No search fee. Required to search: name, years to search; also helpful: DOB. Criminal records on computer from 1984, on index prior to 1984. Archived at Record Center, 401-277-3249. Free Internet access is at http://courtconnect.courts.state.ri.us. This website is provided as an informational service only and should not be relied upon as an official record of the court.
General Information: Public Access terminal is available. No confidential or sealed records released. Will fax results to local or toll free line. Copy fee: $.15 per page. Cert fee: $3.00. Payee: Washington Superior Court. Personal checks accepted. Prepayment required. Mail requests: SASE required. Mail turnaround time 1 week.

4th District Court 4800 Towerhill Rd, Wakefield, RI 02879; 401-782-4131. Hours: 8:30AM-4:30PM (EST). *Misdemeanor, Civil Actions Under $10,000, Eviction, Small Claims.*
Civil Records: Access: In person only. Visitors must perform in person searches for themselves. No search fee. Required to search: name, years to search. Civil cases indexed by defendant, plaintiff. Civil records on index cards, small claims indexed by plaintiff only.
Criminal Records: Access: In person, online. Visitors must perform in person searches for themselves. No search fee. Required to search: name, years to search, DOB. Criminal records available on computer beginning in 1996. Free Internet access at http://courtconnect.courts.state.ri.us. This website is provided as an informational service only and should not be relied upon as an official record of the court.
General Information: Public Access terminal is available. (Terminal is for criminal records only.) No family court records released. Copy fee: $.15 per page. Cert fee: $3.00. Payee: Court Clerk. Visa/MC,

money orders accepted. Personal checks not accepted. Prepayment required.

Charlestown Town Hall 4540 S County Tr, Charlestown, RI 02813; 401-364-1200; Fax: 401-364-1238. Hours: 8:30AM-4:30PM (EST). *Probate.*
Note: Nothing done on county level. Each city/town has their own Probate Court. Court first Tuesday of the month at 9:30AM.

Exeter Town Hall 675 Ten Rod Rd, Exeter, RI 02822; 401-294-3891 (295-7500); Fax: 401-295-1248. Hours: 9AM-4PM (EST). *Probate.*
Note: Probate Court held fourth Monday monthly at 2:00 PM.

Hopkinton Town Hall 1 Town House Rd, Hopkinton, RI 02833; 401-377-7777; Fax: 401-377-7788. Hours: 8:30AM-4:30PM or by appointment (EST). *Probate.*
Note: Civil cases etc heard in County Courthouse, not Town

Narragansett Town Hall 25 5th Ave, Narragansett, RI 02882; 401-789-1044 X621; Fax: 401-783-9637. Hours: 8:30AM-4:30PM (EST). *Probate.*

New Shoreham Town Hall Old Town Road, PO Drawer 220, Block Island, RI 02807; 401-466-3200; Fax: 401-466-3219. Hours: 9AM-3PM,F-9-5PM (EST). *Probate.*

North Kingstown Town Hall 80 Boston Neck Rd, North Kingstown, RI 02852-5762; 401-294-3331; Probate phone: 401-294-3331 x122; Fax: 401-294-2437. Hours: 8:30AM-4:30PM (EST). *Probate.*
www.northkingstown.org

Richmond Town Hall 5 Richmond Townhouse Rd., Wyoming, RI 02898; 401-539-2497; Fax: 401-539-1089. Hours: 9AM-4PM; 8:30 AM on second Tuesday (EST). *Probate.*

South Kingstown Town Hall 180 High St, Wakefield, RI 02879; 401-789-9331; Fax: 401-789-5280. Hours: 8:30AM-4:30PM (EST). *Probate.*

Westerly Town Hall 45 Broad St, Westerly, RI 02891; 401-348-2500; Fax: 401-348-2571. Hours: 8:30AM-4:30PM (EST). *Probate.*
Note: This court also handles ordinance violations.

Rhode Island Recording Offices

ORGANIZATION:

5 counties and 39 towns, 39 recording offices. The recording officer is Town/City Clerk (Recorder of Deeds). The Town/City Clerk usually also serves as the Recorder of Deeds. There is no county administration in Rhode Island that handles recording. The entire state is in the Eastern Time Zone (EST). Be aware that the recordings in the counties of Bristol, Newport, and Providence can relate to property located in other cities/ towns even though each of these three cities bears the same name as the county.

Towns will not perform real estate searches. Copy fees are usually $1.50 per page. Certification usually costs $3.00 per document.

REAL ESTATE RECORDS:

Towns will not perform real estate searches. Copy fees are usually $1.50 per page. Certification usually costs $3.00 per document.

UCC RECORDS:

Financing statements are filed at the state level, except for farm related and real estate related collateral, which are filed with the Town/City Clerk. Most recording offices will not perform UCC searches. Use search request form UCC-11. Copy fees are usually $1.50 per page. Certification usually costs $3.00 per document.

TAX LIEN RECORDS:

All federal and state tax liens on personal property and on real property are filed with the Recorder of Deeds. Towns will not perform tax lien searches.

OTHER LIENS:

Mechanics, municipal, lis pendens.

ONLINE ACCESS:

A private vendor has placed on the Internet the assessor records from a number of towns. Visit http://data.visionappraisal.com

Barrington Town

Town Clerk, 283 County Rd, Town Hall, Barrington, RI 02806. **Phone-**Town Clerk, R/E & UCC Recording-401-247-1900; fax-401-245-5003; hours 8:30AM-4:30PM
Will not search records. Copy fee- $1.50 per page. Cert fee: $3.00 per cert. Payee: Town of Barrington. **Other phones:** Assessor-401-247-1900; Treasurer-401-247-1900; Appraiser/ Auditor-401-247-1900; Elections-401-247-1900; Vital Records-401-247-1900.

Bristol Town

Town Clerk, 10 Court St, Town Hall, Bristol, RI 02809. **Phone-**401-253-7000, R/E Recording-401-253-7000 x36; fax-401-253-3080; hours 8:30AM-4PM www.onlinebristol.com
Will search UCC records. Search per debtor- $5.00. Will not search real estate or tax lien records. UCC copy- $2.00 per page. Cert fee: $3.00 per cert. Payee: Town of Bristol. **Online Access to Real Estate records:** Search free at http://69.95.33.2/NewDatabases.html. **Other phones:** Assessor-401-253-7000 x38; Treasurer-401-253-7000 x16; Elections-401-253-7000 x35; Vital Records-401-253-7000 x21.

Burrillville Town

Town Clerk, 105 Harrisville Main St, Town Hall, Harrisville, RI 02830-1499. **Phone-**401-568-4300, R/E Recording-401-568-4300 x113, UCC Recording-401-568-4300 x113; fax-401-568-0490; hours 8:30AM-4:30PM M-W; 8:30AM-7PM Th; 8:30AM-12:30PM F www.burrillville.org
Will not search records. Copy fee- $1.50 per page. Cert fee: $3.00 per cert. Payee: Burrillville Town Clerk. **Online Access to Property, Tax Assessor records:** Access to property records is free at www.opaldata.com/crcdb/burrillville.htm. **Other phones:** Assessor-401-568-4300; Treasurer-401-568-4300; Appraiser/ Auditor-401-568-4300; Elections-401-568-4300; Vital Records-401-568-4300 x111.

Central Falls City

City Clerk, 580 Broad St, City Hall, Central Falls, RI 02863. **Phone-**City Clerk, R/E & UCC Recording-401-727-7400; fax-401-727-7406; hours 8:30AM-4:30PM www.centralfallsri.us
Will not search records. UCC copy- $1.00 per page. Payee: City of Central Falls. **Online Access to Property, Assessor records:** Access to city property data is free at http://data.visionappraisal.com/CentralFallsRI/. **Other phones:** Assessor-401-727-7430; Treasurer-401-727-7470; Elections-401-727-7450; Vital Records-401-727-7400.

Charlestown Town

Town Clerk, 4540 South County Trail, Charlestown, RI 02813. **Phone-**Town Clerk, R/E & UCC Recording-401-364-1200; fax-401-364-1238; hours 8:30AM-4:30PM www.charlestownri.org
Will not search records. Copy fee- $1.50 per page. Cert fee: $3.00 per cert. Payee: Town of Charlestown. **Other phones:** Assessor-401-364-1233; Treasurer-401-364-1235; Elections-401-364-1200; Vital Records-401-364-1200.

Coventry Town

Town Clerk, 1670 Flat River Rd, Town Hall, Coventry, RI 02816-8911. **Phone-**401-822-9174; fax-401-822-9132.
Will not search records. UCC copy- $1.00 per page. Cert fee: $3.00 per doc + $1.50 per page. **Online Access to Assessor, Property records:** Access to 2003 property indexes is free at http://69.95.33.2/NewDatabases.html. **Other phones:** Assessor-401-822-9163.

Cranston City

City Clerk, 869 Park Ave, City Hall, Cranston, RI 02910. **Phone-**401-461-1000 x3130; hours 8:30AM-4:30PM
Will search UCC records. Search per debtor- $5.00. Will not search real estate or tax lien records. Copy fee- $1.50 per page. Cert fee: $3.00 per cert. Payee: City of Cranston. **Online Access to Assessor,**

Property records: Records on the city assessor database are at http://data.visionappraisal.com/CranstonRI/. Free registration is required for full data. **Other phones:** Assessor-401-461-1000 x3181.

Cumberland Town

Town Clerk, PO Box 7, Cumberland, RI 02864-0808. **Phone-**401-728-2400, R/E Recording-401-728-2400 x35, UCC Recording-401-728-2400 x35; fax-401-724-1103; hours 8:30AM-4:30PM www.cumberlandri.org
Will not search records. Record copy- $1.00 per page. Cert fee: $3.00 per cert. Payee: Town of Cumberland. **Online Access to Property, Assessor records:** Access to property data is free at www.opaldata.com/crcdb/cumberland.htm. **Other phones:** Assessor-401-728-2400 x13; Treasurer-401-728-2400 x20; Appraiser/ Auditor-401-728-2400 x15; Elections-401-728-2400 x31; Vital Records-401-728-2400 x33.

East Greenwich Town

Town Clerk, PO Box 111, East Greenwich, RI 02818. **Phone-**401-886-8603, R/E Recording-401-886-8602, UCC Recording-401-886-8602; fax-401-886-8625; hours 8:30AM-4:30PM www.eastgreenwichri.com
Will search UCC records. Will not search real estate records. **Online Access to Property records:** Limited Finance Dept. property sales information is listed at www.eastgreenwichri.com/finance.htm. See bottom of web page. Also, access to 2003 property indexes is free at http://69.95.33.2/NewDatabases.html. **Other phones:** Assessor-401-886-8614; Treasurer-401-886-8608; Elections-401-886-8603; Vital Records-401-886-8602.

East Providence City

Town Clerk, 145 Taunton Ave, City Hall, East Providence, RI 02914. **Phone-**401-435-7500, R/E Recording-401-435-7594, UCC Recording-401-435-7594; fax-401-435-4630; hours 8AM-3:30PM www.eastprovidence.com
Will not search records. Cert fee: $3.00 per doc. Payee: City of East Providence. **Online Access to Assessor, Property records:** Assess to Town property

data is free at http://data.visionappraisal.com/EastProvidenceRI/. **Other phones:** Assessor-401-435-7574; Treasurer-401-435-7560; Elections-401-435-7503; Vital Records-401-435-7596.

Exeter Town

Deputy Town Clerk, 675 Ten Rod Rd, Town Hall, Exeter, RI 02822. **Phone-**Deputy Town Clerk, R/E & UCC Recording- 401-294-3891; fax-401-295-1248; hours 9AM-4PM www.town.exeter.ri.us
Will not search records. **Online Access to Assessor, Property records:** Access may be available from a private company at www.opaldata.com/crcdb/exeter.htm. **Other phones:** Assessor-401-294-5734; Treasurer-401-267-1024; Appraiser/ Auditor-401-294-2287; Elections-401-294-2287; Vital Records-401-294-3891.

Foster Town

Town Clerk, 181 Howard Hill Rd, Town Hall, Foster, RI 02825-1227. **Phone-**Town Clerk, R/E & UCC Recording- 401-392-9200; fax-401-392-9201; hours 9AM-3:30PM
Will not search records. RE record copy- $1.50 per page. UCC copy- $2.00 per page. Cert fee: $3.00 per cert. Payee: Town of Foster. **Other phones:** Assessor-401-392-9202; Treasurer-401-392-9207; Elections-401-392-9200; Vital Records-401-392-9200.

Glocester Town

Town Clerk, PO Drawer B, Glocester/ Chepachet, RI 02814-0702. **Phone-**Town Clerk, R/E & UCC Recording- 401-568-6206; fax-401-568-5850; hours 8AM-4:30PM www.glocesterri.org/townclerk.htm
Will not search records. Copy fee- $1.50 per page. Cert fee: $3.00 per doc. Payee: Town of Glocester. **Other phones:** Assessor-401-568-3329; Treasurer-401-568-3342; Elections-401-568-6206; Vital Records-401-568-6206; Tax Collector-401-568-5510.

Hopkinton Town

Town Clerk, 1 Town House Rd, Town Hall, Hopkinton, RI 02833. **Phone-**Town Clerk, R/E & UCC Recording- 401-377-7777; fax-401-377-7788; hours 8:30AM-4:30PM
Will not search records. Copy fee- $1.50 per page. Cert fee: $3.00 per cert + $1.50 per page. Payee: Town of Hopkinton. **Online Access to Property, Assessor records:** Access to town property data is free at www.opaldata.com/crcdb/hopkinton.htm. **Other phones:** Assessor-401-377-7780; Treasurer-401-377-7766; Elections-401-377-7777; Vital Records-401-377-7777.

Jamestown Town

Town Clerk, 93 Narragansett Ave, Town Hall, Jamestown, RI 02835. **Phone-**Town Clerk, R/E & UCC Recording- 401-423-7200; fax-401-423-7230; hours 8AM-4:30PM www.jamestownri.net
Will not search records. **Online Access to Real Estate records:** Search free at http://69.95.33.2/NewDatabases.html. **Other phones:** Assessor-401-423-7200; Treasurer-401-423-7200; Appraiser/ Auditor-401-423-7200; Elections-401-423-7200; Vital Records-401-423-7200.

Johnston Town

Town Clerk, 1385 Hartford Ave, Town Hall, Johnston, RI 02919. **Phone-**Town Clerk, R/E & UCC Recording-401-351-6618; fax-401-331-4271; hours 8:30AM-4:30PM www.johnston-ri.com
Will search UCC records. Will not search real estate records. Copy fee- $1.00 per page. Cert fee: $4.00 per doc. Payee: Town of Johnston. **Online Access to Assessor, Property records:** Assess to Town property data is free at http://data.visionappraisal.com/JohnstonRI/. Free registration is required. **Other phones:** Assessor-401-

351-6618; Treasurer-401-351-6618; Appraiser/ Auditor-401-351-6618; Elections-401-351-6618; Vital Records-401-351-6618.

Lincoln Town

Town Clerk, PO Box 100, Lincoln, RI 02865. **Phone-**Town Clerk, R/E & UCC Recording- 401-333-1100; fax-401-333-3648. www.lincolnri.net
Will not search real estate records. **Online Access to Property, Assessor records:** Access to town property data is avaailable free at www.opaldata.com/crcdb/lincoln.htm. **Other phones:** Assessor-401-333-1100; Treasurer-401-333-1100; Appraiser/ Auditor-401-333-1100; Elections-401-333-1100; Vital Records-401-333-1100.

Little Compton Town

Town Clerk, PO Box 226, Little Compton, RI 02837-0226. **Phone-**Town Clerk, R/E & UCC Recording-401-635-4400; fax-401-635-2470; hours 8AM-4PM
Will not search records. Copy fee- $1.50 per page. Cert fee: $3.00 per instrument. Payee: Town of Little Compton. **Other phones:** Assessor-401-635-4509; Treasurer-401-635-4219; Elections-401-635-4400; Vital Records-401-635-4400.

Middletown Town

Town Clerk, 350 E. Main Rd, Town Hall, Middletown, RI 02842. **Phone-**Town Clerk, R/E & UCC Recording-401-847-0009; fax-401-848-0500; hours 8AM-5PM www.ci.middletown.ri.us
Will search UCC records. Search per debtor- $5.00. Will not search real estate or tax lien records. Copy fee- $1.50 per page. Cert fee: $3.00 per doc + $1.50 per pages of doc. Payee: Town of Middletown. **Online Access to Assessor, Property records:** Records on the town assessor database are at http://data.visionappraisal.com/MiddletownRI/. Free registration is required for full data. **Other phones:** Assessor-401-847-7300; Treasurer-401-846-4473; Elections-401-849-5540; Vital Records-401-847-0009.

Narragansett Town

Town Clerk, 25 Fifth Ave, Town Hall, Narragansett, RI 02882. **Phone-**401-789-1044, R/E Recording-401-789-1044 x623; fax-401-783-9637; 8:30AM-4:30PM
Will not search records. RE record copy- $1.50 per page. UCC copy- $1.00 per page. Cert fee: $3.00 per cert. Payee: Town of Narragansett. **Online Access to Assessor, Property records:** Records on the town assessor database are online at http://data.visionappraisal.com/NarragansettRI/. Free registration is required for full data. **Other phones:** Assessor-401-789-1044 x236.

New Shoreham Town

Town Clerk, PO Drawer 220, Block Island, RI 02807. **Phone-**Town Clerk, R/E & UCC Recording- 401-466-3200; fax-401-466-3219; hours 9AM-3PM
Will not search records. Copy fee- $1.50 per page. Cert fee: $3.00 + $1.50 per page. Payee: Town of New Shoreham. **Online Access to Assessor, Property records:** Assess to Town property data is at http://data.visionappraisal.com/NewShorehamRI/. **Other phones:** Assessor-401-466-3217; Treasurer-401-466-3208; Appraiser/ Auditor-401-466-3208; Elections-401-466-3200; Vital Records-401-466-3200.

Newport City

Recorder of Deeds, 43 Broadway, Town Hall, Newport, RI 02840-2798. **Phone-**401-846-9600 x209, R/E Recording-401-846-9600 x209, UCC Recording-401-846-9600 x209; fax-401-849-8757; hours 8:30AM-5PM (Recording Hours-8:30AM-4PM) www.cityofnewport.com
Will not search records. Copy fee- $1.50 per page. Cert fee: $3.00 per cert. Payee: City of Newport. **Online Access to Assessor, Property records:**

Access is via a private company at http://data.visionappraisal.com/NewportRI/. Free registration is required for full data. **Other phones:** Assessor-401-846-9600 x229 or 228 or 313; Elections-401-846-9600 x319 or 320 or 318; Vital Records-401-846-9600 x327 or 328 or 329 or 326; Timeshare Request:-401-846-9600 x530.

North Kingstown Town

Town Clerk, 80 Boston Neck Rd, Town Hall, North Kingstown, RI 02852. **Phone-**401-294-3331, R/E Recording-401-294-3331 x125, UCC Recording-401-294-3331 x125; www.northkingstown.org
Will not search records. RE record copy- $1.50 per page ($3.00 credit card fee). Must include book & AG #'s. Cert fee: $3.00 per doc. Payee: Town of N Kingstown. **Online Access to Assessor, Property records:** Access is via a private company at http://data.visionappraisal.com/NorthkingstownRI/. Free registration is required for full data. **Other phones:** Assessor-401-294-3331 x110; Treasurer-401-294-3331 x148; Elections-401-294-3331 x129; Vital Records-401-294-3331 x122.

North Providence Town

Town Clerk, 2000 Smith St, Town Hall, North Providence, RI 02911. **Phone-**401-232-0900, R/E Recording-401-232-0900 x213-214, UCC Recording-401-232-0900 x213-214; fax-401-233-1409; hours 8:30AM-4:30PM (Summer hours 8:30 AM-4PM)
Will not search records. RE record copy- $1.00 per page. UCC copy- $2.00 per page. Cert fee: $3.00 per cert. Payee: Town of North Providence. **Other phones:** Assessor-401-232-0900 x209; Treasurer-401-232-0900 x218; Elections-401-232-0900 x241-235; Vital Records-401-232-0900 x213-214.

North Smithfield Town

Town Clerk, 575 Smithfield Rd, Town Hall, North Smithfield, RI 02896. **Phone-**401-767-2200, R/E Recording-401-767-2200 x1, UCC Recording-401-767-2200 x1; fax-401-356-4057; hours 8AM-4PM M-W; 8AM-7PM Th; 8AM-Noon F
Will not search records. Copy fee- $1.50 per page. Cert fee: $3.00 per doc. Payee: Town of North Smithfield. **Online Access to Assessor, Property records:** Access is via a private company at http://data.visionappraisal.com/NorthsmithfieldRI/. Free registration is required to view full data. **Other phones:** Assessor-401-767-2200; Treasurer-401-767-2202; Elections-401-767-2200 x216; Vital Records-401-767-2200 x216.

Pawtucket City

City Clerk, 137 Roosevelt Ave, City Hall, Pawtucket, RI 02860. **Phone-**401-728-0500, R/E Recording-401-728-0500 x262, UCC Recording-401-728-0500 x262; fax-401-728-8932; hours-8:30AM-3:30PM www.pawtucketri.com
Will not search records. Record copy fee- $1.50 per page. Cert fee: $3.00 per doc. Payee: City of Pawtucket. **Online Access to Recording, Deed, Real Estate records:.** **Other phones:** Assessor-401-728-0500 x338; Treasurer-401-728-0500 x244; Elections-401-728-0500 x207; Vital Records-401-728-0500 x224.

Portsmouth Town

Town Clerk, PO Box 155, Portsmouth, RI 02871. **Phone-**Town Clerk, R/E & UCC Recording- 401-683-2101; hours Recording Hours 9AM-3:45PM www.portsmouthri.com/frames.htm
Will not search records. Copy fee- $1.50 per page. Cert fee: $3.00 per certification + $1.50 per page. Payee: Town of Portsmouth. **Online Access to Assessor, Property records:** Records on the Town of Portsmouth assessor database are online at http://data.visionappraisal.com/PortsmouthRI/. Free

registration is required to view full data. **Other phones:** Assessor-401-683-1536; Treasurer-401-683-9118; Appraiser/ Auditor-401-683-1536; Elections-401-683-3157; Vital Records-401-683-2101.

Providence City

City Clerk, 25 Dorrance St, City Hall, Providence, RI 02903. **Phone**-401-421-7740 x312; hours 8:30AM-4:30PM (Recording Hours 8:30AM-4PM)
Will not search records. RE record copy- $1.50 per page. UCC copy- $2.00 per page. Cert fee: $3.00 per cert. Payee: Providence City Recorder of Deeds. **Other phones:** Assessor-401-421-5900.

Richmond Town

Town Clerk, 5 Richmond Townhouse Rd., Town Hall, Wyoming, RI 02898. **Phone**-Town Clerk, R/E & UCC Recording- 401-539-2497; fax-401-539-1089; hours 9AM-4PM www.richmondri.com
Will not search records. Copy fee- $1.50 per page. Cert fee: $3.00 per doc. Payee: Town of Richmond. **Other phones:** Assessor-401-539-2130; Treasurer-401-539-2498; Elections-401-539-2497; Vital Records-401-539-2497.

Scituate Town

Town Clerk, PO Box 328, North Scituate, RI 02857-0328. **Phone**-Town Clerk, R/E & UCC Recording-401-647-2822; fax-401-647-7220; hours 8:30AM-4PM www.scituateri.org/townhall.htm
Will not search records. UCC copy- $1.50 per page. Cert fee: $3.00 1st pg, $1.50 each add'l. Payee: Town of Scituate. **Online Access to Property, Assessor records:** Access to town property data is free at www.opaldata.com/crcdb/scituate.htm. **Other phones:** Assessor-401-647-2919; Treasurer-401-647-2547.

Smithfield Town

Town Clerk, 64 Farnum Pike, Town Hall, Esmond, RI 02917. **Phone**-Town Clerk, R/E & UCC Recording-401-233-1000; fax-401-232-7244; hours M-F 8:30-4:30PM www.smithfieldri.com
Will not search records. UCC copy- $1.50 per page. Cert fee: $3.00 per instrument. Payee: Town of Smithfield. **Online Access to Property, Assessor records:** Access to town property data is free at http://data.visionappraisal.com/SmithfieldRI/. Free registration is required. **Other phones:** Assessor-401-233-1014; Treasurer-401-233-1005; Elections-401-233-1000; Vital Records-401-233-1000.

South Kingstown Town

Town Clerk, PO Box 31, Wakefield, RI 02880. **Phone**-401-789-9331, R/E Recording-401-789-9331 x234, UCC Recording-401-789-9331 x234; fax-401-788-9792; hours 8:30AM-4:30PM, recording stops at 4PM. www.southkingstownri.com
Will not search records. Copy fee- $1.50 per page. Cert fee: $3.00 per cert. Payee: Town of South Kingstown. **Online Access to Real Estate, Assessor records:** Access to the property values database is at www.southkingstownri.com/code/propvalues_search.cfm. Also, assess to Town property data is free at http://data.visionappraisal.com/SouthKingstownRI/.
Other phones: Assessor-401-789-9331 x220; Treasurer-401-789-9331 x209; Elections-401-789-9331 x231; Vital Records-401-789-9331 x230.

Tiverton Town

Town Clerk, 343 Highland Rd, Town Hall, Tiverton, RI 02878. **Phone**-401-625-6700; fax-401-625-6705; hours 8:30AM-4PM
Will not search records. UCC copy- $1.50 per page. Cert fee: $3.00 per cert. Payee: Town of Tiverton. **Online Access to Assessor, Property records:** Records on the town assessor database are online at http://data.visionappraisal.com/TivertonRI/. Free

registration is required for full data. **Other phones:** Assessor-401-625-5609.

Warren Town

Town Clerk, 514 Main St, Town Hall, Warren, RI 02885. **Phone**-Town Clerk, R/E & UCC Recording-401-245-7340; fax-401-245-7421; hours 9AM-4PM
Will not search records. RE record copy- $1.50 per page. UCC copy- $.15 per page. Cert fee: $5.00 per doc. Payee: Town of Warren. **Online Access to Property records:** Access to 2003 property indexes is free at http://69.95.33.2/NewDatabases.html. **Other phones:** Assessor-401-245-7342; Treasurer-401-245-7341; Appraiser/ Auditor-401-245-7342; Elections-401-245-7340; Vital Records-401-245-7340; Town Manager-401-245-7554.

Warwick City

City Clerk, 3275 Post Rd, Warwick, RI 02886. **Phone**-401-738-2000, R/E Recording-401-738-2000 x6218, UCC Recording-401-738-2000 x6218; fax-401-738-6639; hours 8:30AM-4:30PM www.warwickri.com
Will search UCC records. Search per debtor- $5.00 per request. Will not search real estate or tax lien records. Copy fee- $1.50 per page. Cert fee: $3.00 per cert + $1.50 per page. **Online Access to Tax Assessor records:** Access found at www.warwickri.gov. **Other phones:** Assessor-401-738-2000 x6016; Treasurer-401-738-2000 x6228; Elections-401-738-2000 x6223; Vital Records-401-738-2000 x6215.

West Greenwich Town

Town Clerk, 280 Victory Highway, Town Hall, West Greenwich, RI 02817. **Phone**-401-397-5016; fax-401-392-3805; hours 9AM-4PM M-F; 7-9PM W
Will not search records. Cert fee: $4.50. Payee: West Greenwich Town Clerk. **Other phones:** Assessor-401-397-5016 x3.

West Warwick Town

Town Clerk, 1170 Main St, Town Hall, West Warwick, RI 02893-4829. **Phone**-Town Clerk, R/E & UCC Recording- 401-822-9201; fax-401-822-9266; hours 8:30AM-4:30PM
Will search UCC records. Search per debtor- $5.00. Will not search real estate or tax lien records. RE record copy- $1.50 per page. UCC copy- $.15 per page. Cert fee: $3.00 per doc. Payee: Town of West Warwick. **Other phones:** Assessor-401-822-9208; Treasurer-401-822-9216; Elections-401-822-9201; Vital Records-401-822-9201.

Westerly Town

Town Clerk, 45 Broad St, Town Hall, Westerly, RI 02891. **Phone**-Town Clerk, R/E & UCC Recording-401-348-2500; fax-401-348-2571; hours 8:30AM-4:30PM M-F
Will not search records. Copy fee- $1.50 per page. Cert fee: $3.00 per doc. Payee: Westerly Town Clerk. **Other phones:** Assessor-401-348-2500; Treasurer-401-348-2500; Appraiser/ Auditor-401-348-2500; Elections-401-348-2500; Vital Records-401-348-2500.

Woonsocket City

Town Clerk, 169 Main St, City Hall, Woonsocket, RI 02895. **Phone**-401-762-6400, R/E Recording-401-767-9248, UCC Recording-401-767-9248; fax-401-765-4569.
Will not search records. Copy fee- $1.50 per page. Cert fee: $3.00 per doc. Payee: City Clerks Office. **Other phones:** Assessor-401-762-6400 x109; Treasurer-401-767-9280; Elections-401-767-9224; Vital Records-401-767-8875.

Rhode Island County Locator

You will usually be able to find the city name in the City/County Cross Reference below. In that case, it is a simple matter to determine the county from the cross reference. However, only the official US Postal Service city names are included in this index. There are an additional 40,000 place names that people use in their addresses. Therefore, we have also included a ZIP/City Cross Reference immediately following the City/County Cross Reference.

If you know the ZIP Code but the city name does not appear in the City/County Cross Reference index, look up the ZIP Code in the ZIP/City Cross Reference, find the city name, then look up the city name in the City/County Cross Reference. For example, you want to know the county for an address of Menands, NY 12204. There is no "Menands" in the City/County Cross Reference. The ZIP/City Cross Reference shows that ZIP Codes 12201-12288 are for the city of Albany. Looking back in the City/County Cross Reference, Albany is in Albany County.

Rhode Island City/County Cross Reference

ADAMSVILLE Newport	EXETER Washington	MANVILLE Providence	RUMFORD Providence
ALBION Providence	FISKEVILLE Providence	MAPLEVILLE Providence	SAUNDERSTOWN Washington
ASHAWAY Washington	FORESTDALE Providence	MIDDLETOWN Newport	SHANNOCK Washington
BARRINGTON Bristol	FOSTER Providence	NARRAGANSETT Washington	SLATERSVILLE Providence
BLOCK ISLAND Washington	GLENDALE Providence	NEWPORT Newport	SLOCUM Washington
BRADFORD Washington	GREENE Kent	NORTH KINGSTOWN Washington	SMITHFIELD Providence
BRISTOL Bristol	GREENVILLE Providence	NORTH PROVIDENCE Providence	TIVERTON Newport
CAROLINA Washington	HARMONY Providence	NORTH SCITUATE Providence	WAKEFIELD Washington
CENTRAL FALLS Providence	HARRISVILLE Providence	NORTH SMITHFIELD Providence	WARREN Bristol
CHARLESTOWN Washington	HOPE Providence	OAKLAND Providence	WARWICK Kent
CHEPACHET Providence	HOPE VALLEY Washington	PASCOAG Providence	WEST GREENWICH Kent
CLAYVILLE Providence	HOPKINTON Washington	PAWTUCKET Providence	WEST KINGSTON Washington
COVENTRY Kent	JAMESTOWN Newport	PEACE DALE Washington	WEST WARWICK Kent
CRANSTON Providence	JOHNSTON Providence	PORTSMOUTH Newport	WESTERLY Washington
CUMBERLAND Providence	KENYON Washington	PROVIDENCE Providence	WOOD RIVER JUNCTION Washington
EAST GREENWICH Kent	KINGSTON Washington	PRUDENCE ISLAND Bristol	WOONSOCKET Providence
EAST PROVIDENCE Providence	LINCOLN Providence	RIVERSIDE Providence	WYOMING Washington
ESCOHEAG Washington	LITTLE COMPTON Newport	ROCKVILLE Washington	

Rhode Island ZIP/City Cross Reference

02801-02801 ADAMSVILLE	02860-02862 PAWTUCKET	
02802-02802 ALBION	02863-02863 CENTRAL FALLS	
02804-02804 ASHAWAY	02864-02864 CUMBERLAND	
02806-02806 BARRINGTON	02865-02865 LINCOLN	
02807-02807 BLOCK ISLAND	02871-02871 PORTSMOUTH	
02808-02808 BRADFORD	02872-02872 PRUDENCE ISLAND	
02809-02809 BRISTOL	02873-02873 ROCKVILLE	
02812-02812 CAROLINA	02874-02874 SAUNDERSTOWN	
02813-02813 CHARLESTOWN	02875-02875 SHANNOCK	
02814-02814 CHEPACHET	02876-02876 SLATERSVILLE	
02815-02815 CLAYVILLE	02877-02877 SLOCUM	
02816-02816 COVENTRY	02878-02878 TIVERTON	
02817-02817 WEST GREENWICH	02879-02880 WAKEFIELD	
02818-02818 EAST GREENWICH	02881-02881 KINGSTON	
02821-02821 ESCOHEAG	02882-02882 NARRAGANSETT	
02822-02822 EXETER	02883-02883 PEACE DALE	
02823-02823 FISKEVILLE	02885-02885 WARREN	
02824-02824 FORESTDALE	02886-02889 WARWICK	
02825-02825 FOSTER	02891-02891 WESTERLY	
02826-02826 GLENDALE	02892-02892 WEST KINGSTON	
02827-02827 GREENE	02893-02893 WEST WARWICK	
02828-02828 GREENVILLE	02894-02894 WOOD RIVER JUNCTION	
02829-02829 HARMONY	02895-02895 WOONSOCKET	
02830-02830 HARRISVILLE	02896-02896 NORTH SMITHFIELD	
02831-02831 HOPE	02898-02898 WYOMING	
02832-02832 HOPE VALLEY	02900-02909 PROVIDENCE	
02833-02833 HOPKINTON	02910-02910 CRANSTON	
02835-02835 JAMESTOWN	02911-02911 NORTH PROVIDENCE	
02836-02836 KENYON	02912-02912 PROVIDENCE	
02837-02837 LITTLE COMPTON	02914-02914 EAST PROVIDENCE	
02838-02838 MANVILLE	02915-02915 RIVERSIDE	
02839-02839 MAPLEVILLE	02916-02916 RUMFORD	
02840-02841 NEWPORT	02917-02917 SMITHFIELD	
02842-02842 MIDDLETOWN	02918-02918 PROVIDENCE	
02852-02854 NORTH KINGSTOWN	02919-02919 JOHNSTON	
02857-02857 NORTH SCITUATE	02920-02921 CRANSTON	
02858-02858 OAKLAND	02940-02940 PROVIDENCE	
02859-02859 PASCOAG		

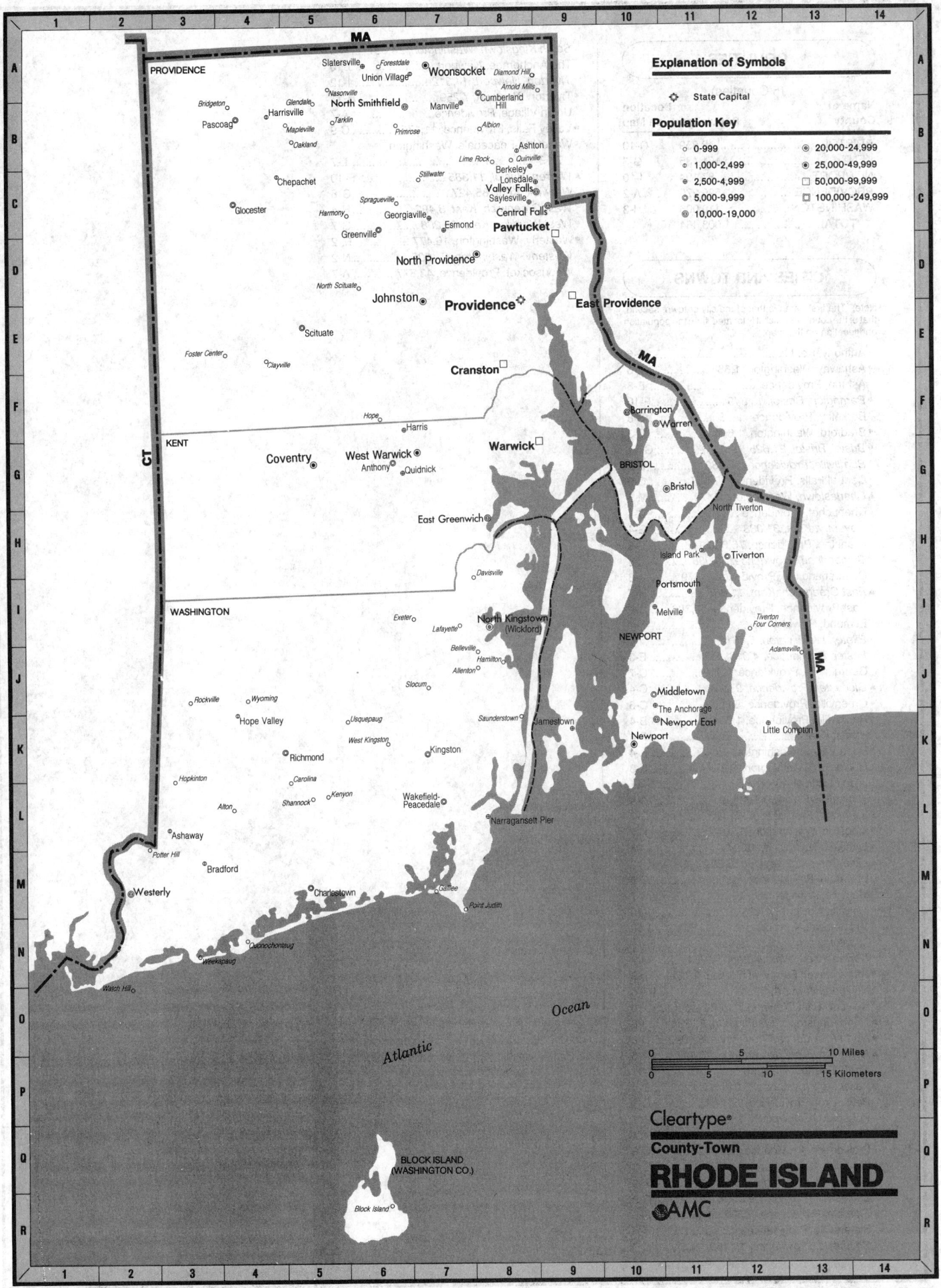

RHODE ISLAND

COUNTIES

(5 Counties)

Name of County	Population	Location on Map
BRISTOL	48,859	G-10
KENT	161,135	G-3
NEWPORT	87,194	I-10
PROVIDENCE	596,270	A-2
WASHINGTON	110,006	I-3
TOTAL	1,003,464	

CITIES AND TOWNS

Note: The first name is that of the city or town, second, that of the county in which it is located, then the population and location on the map.

Anthony, Kent G-6
• Ashaway, Washington, 1,584 .... L-3
Ashton, Providence B-8
• Barrington, Bristol, 15,849 .... F-10
Berkeley, Providence B-8
• Bradford, Washington, 1,604 .... M-3
• Bristol, Bristol, 21,625 .... G-11
Burrillville, Providence, 16,230 .... B-5
Central Falls, Providence, 17,637 .... C-9
▲ Charlestown, Washington, 6,478 .... M-5
Chepachet, Providence C-4
▲ Coventry, Kent, 31,083 .... G-4
Cranston, Providence, 76,060 .... E-8
Cumberland, Providence, 29,038 .... A-8
• Cumberland Hill, Providence, 6,379 ... A-8
▲ East Greenwich, Kent, 11,865 .... H-7
East Providence, Providence, 50,380 ..... D-9
Esmond, Providence C-7
Exeter, Washington, 5,461 .... I-6
Foster, Providence, 4,316 .... E-3
Georgiaville, Providence C-7
▲ Glocester, Providence, 9,227 .... C-4
• Greenville, Providence, 8,303 .... C-6
• Harrisville, Providence, 1,654 .... B-4
Harris, Kent F-6
• Hope Valley, Washington, 1,446 .... K-4
Hopkinton, Washington, 6,873 .... K-3
Island Park, Newport H-11
▲ Jamestown, Newport, 4,999 .... J-9
▲ Johnston, Providence, 26,542 .... D-7
• Kingston, Washington, 6,504 .... K-7
▲ Lincoln, Providence, 18,045 .... C-8
▲ Little Compton, Newport, 3,339 .... K-12
Lonsdale, Providence C-8
Manville, Providence B-7
• Melville, Newport, 4,426 .... I-10
Middletown, Newport J-10
Middletown, Newport, 19,460 .... K-11
Narragansett, Washington, 14,985 .... M-7
• Narragansett Pier, Washington, 3,721 ..... L-8
Newport, Newport, 28,227 .... K-10
• Newport East, Newport, 11,080 .... K-10
▲ North Kingstown, Washington, 23,786 ...... I-8
• North Providence, Providence, 32,090 ... D-8
▲ North Smithfield, Providence, 10,497 ...... A-6
North Tiverton, Newport H-11
• Pascoag, Providence, 5,011 .... B-4
Pawtucket, Providence, 72,644 .... C-9
Portsmouth, Newport I-11
Portsmouth, Newport, 16,857 .... I-11
Providence, Providence, 160,728 .... D-8
Quidnick, Kent G-6
▲ Richmond, Washington, 5,351 .... K-5
Saylesville, Providence C-8
▲ Scituate, Providence, 9,796 .... E-6
Slatersville, Providence A-6
Smithfield, Providence, 19,163 .... C-7

South Kingstown, Washington, 24,631 .... K-6
The Anchorage, Newport J-10
Tiverton, Newport, 14,312 .... I-12
• Tiverton, Newport, 7,259 .... H-12
Union Village, Providence A-7
• Valley Falls, Providence, 11,175 .... C-9
• Wakefield-Peacedale, Washington,
   7,134 .... L-7
▲ Warren, Bristol, 11,385 .... F-10
Warwick, Kent, 85,427 .... G-8
West Greenwich, Kent, 3,492 .... H-4
• West Warwick, Kent, 29,268 .... G-7
• Westerly, Washington, 16,477 .... M-2
Westerly, Washington, 21,605 .... N-2
Woonsocket, Providence, 43,877 .... A-7

Explanation of symbols: • – Census Designated Place (CDP)   • *italics* – Township shown which is also a CDP   *italics* – Townships (not shown on the map)
▲ *italics* – Townships (shown on the map)

South Carolina

General Help Numbers:

Governor's Office
PO Box 11829
Columbia, SC 29211
www.state.sc.us/governor

803-734-9400
Fax 803-734-9413
8AM-6PM

Attorney General's Office
PO Box 11549
Columbia, SC 29211
www.scattorneygeneral.org

803-734-3970
Fax 803-734-4323
8:30AM-5:30PM

Legislative Records
937 Assembly Street, Rm 220
Columbia, SC 29201
www.scstatehouse.net

803-734-2060

9AM-5PM M-F

State Archives
8301 Parklane Rd
Columbia, SC 29223
www.state.sc.us/scdah

803-896-6100
Fax 803-896-6198
8:30AM-5PM M-F

State Specifics:

Capital:	Columbia
	Richland County
Time Zone:	EST
Number of Counties:	46
Population:	4,147,152
Web Site:	

www.myscgov.com

State Agencies

Criminal Records

South Carolina Law Enforcement Division (SLED), Criminal Records Section, PO Box 21398, Columbia, SC 29221 (Courier: 4400 Broad River Rd, Columbia, SC 29210); 803-896-7043, 803-896-7022 (Fax), 8:30AM-5PM.

www.sled.state.sc.us

Indexing & Storage: Records are available from the 1960s. It takes 1 to 12 days before new records are available for inquiry. Records are indexed on inhouse computer. Records are maintained indefinitely unless expunged.

Searching: Criminal records are open without restrictions. Include the following in your request- full name, any aliases, sex, race, and DOB. The SSN is helpful. 100% of the records are fingerprint supported. However, this agency will not do fingerprint searches.

Access by: mail, in person, online.

Fee & Payment: The search fee is $25.00 per individual. The fee is $8.00 for non-profit organizations, pre-approval is required. Fee payee: SLED. Prepayment required. Business and company checks are accepted, personal checks are not. No credit cards accepted, except online.

Mail search: Turnaround time: 5 to 7 days. They will return by overnight delivery service if prepaid and materials provided. A SASE is requested.

In person search: Turnaround time is within minutes for three names or less.

Online search: SLED offers commercial access to criminal record history from 1960 forward on the website. Fees are $25.00 per screening or $8.00 if for a charitable organization. Credit card ordering accepted. Visit the website or call 803-896-7219 for details.

Statewide Court Records

Court Administration, 1015 Sumter St, 2nd Floor, Columbia, SC 29201; 803-734-1800, 803-734-1355 (Fax), 8:30AM-5PM M-F.

www.sccourts.org/

Note: Except for certain online research capabilities, all court record access must be done at the local level.

Access by: online.

Online search: Appellate and Supreme Court opinions and calendars are available from the website. There is no online access to statewide trial court records.

Sexual Offender Registry

Sex Offender Registry, c/o SLED, PO Box 21398, Columbia, SC 29221 (Courier: 4400 Broad River Rd, Columbia, SC 29210); 803-896-7043, 803-896-7022 (Fax), 8:30AM-5PM.

www.sled.state.sc.us

Indexing & Storage: Records are available from 1994 to present. Records are normally destroyed after court order.

Searching: Include the following in your request-proper form. All requests are screened as to the age of the offender. Therefore, all requests must be on a state form, which can be downloaded from the Internet. The following data is not released: registrants under 17 unless as required by law.

Access by: mail, phone, online.

Fee & Payment: There is no fee unless ordered by a business then fee is $17.00.

Mail search: Turnaround time: 5 to 7 days. They will return by overnight delivery service if prepaid and materials provided. A SASE is requested.

Phone search: Searching by telephone available.

Online search: Access is available from the website. Click on Sexual Offender Registry. Search by name or ZIP Code, county or city.

Incarceration Records

Department of Corrections, Inmate Records Branch, 4444 Broad River Rd, Columbia, SC 29221-1787; 803-896-8531, 877-846-3472 (Automated Information), 803-896-1217 (Fax), 8AM-5PM.

www.state.sc.us/scdc/

Indexing & Storage: Records are available on current and former inmates. It takes 1 to 2 days before new records are available for inquiry.

Searching: Include the following in your request-provide full name, DOB, SSN. The SCDC number is helpful. Location, SCDC number, physical identifiers, conviction and sentencing information, FBI number, and release dates are provided.

Access by: mail, phone, online.

Fee & Payment: There is no search fee, but there is a copy fee of $.25 per page.

Mail search: Turnaround time: 1-2 weeks. A SASE is requested.

Phone search: Name searching available by phone.

Online search: The Inmate Search on the Internet is found at http://sword.doc.state.sc.us/incarceratedInmateSearch/index.jsp or click on Inmate search at the main website.

Corporation, Trademarks, Servicemarks, Limited Partnerships, Limited

Liability Companys, Limited Liability Partnerships

Corporation Division, Capitol Complex, PO Box 11350, Columbia, SC 29211 (Courier: Edgar A. Brown Bldg, Room 525, 1205 Pendleton Street, Columbia, SC 29201); 803-734-2158, 803-734-1614 (Fax), 8:30PM-5PM.

www.scsos.com/

Note: This office also handles not-for-profit entity records. Trademarks and service marks are not on the computer but are in this department.

Indexing & Storage: Records are available from 1800's on. In house computer records are from 1985 on. Older records are stored at the State Archives. New records are available for inquiry immediately. Records are indexed on microfilm, inhouse computer.

Searching: This office will not release company's officer's names and addresses. For that information, call the Dept of Revenue at 803-898-5751. Include the following in your request-full name of business. In addition to the articles of incorporation, corporation records include the following information: Prior (merged) names, Inactive and Reserved names.

Access by: mail, phone, in person, online.

Fee & Payment: No search fee, copy fee is $1.00 per page for the first page and $.50 per page for each additional. If record is to be certified, the fee is an additional $2.00. Fee payee: Secretary of State. Prepayment required. Personal checks accepted. No credit cards accepted.

Mail search: Turnaround time: 1 to 2 days. A SASE is requested.

Phone search: No fee for telephone request. They will provide basic information only.

In person search: Information requests are available.

Online search: This free web-based program is called the Online Business Filings, search page at www.scsos.com/corp_search.htm. Search by filing name or registered agent. The database provides access to basic filing information about any entity filed with the office. Registered agents' names and addresses, dates of business filings and types of filings are all available. The database is updated every 48 hours.

Fictitious Name, Assumed Name, Trade Names

Records not maintained by a state level agency.

Note: Records are found at the county level.

Annual Reports, Directors and Officers

Department of Revenue, Office Services/Records, Photocopy Section, Columbia, SC 29214; 803-898-5751, 803-898-5888 (Fax), 8:30AM-5PM.

www.sctax.org/DOR/default.htm

Indexing & Storage: Records are available from 1990 on. Records are indexed on inhouse computer, hard copy.

Searching: Information on partnerships and on taxes is not public. Include the following in your request-full name of business. They will give officers and registered agent information only if it

appears on the annual report. Request forms can be downloaded from the website.

Access by: mail, fax, in person.

Fee & Payment: The fee is $2.63 which is on a per year basis for the annual reports. Fee payee: South Carolina Department of Revenue. Prepayment required. Personal checks accepted. No credit cards accepted.

Mail search: Turnaround time: 1 week. A SASE is requested.

Fax search: Turnaround is usually in 1 day.

In person search: You may request information in person, but will not receive copies the same day.

Uniform Commercial Code

UCC Division, Secretary of State, PO Box 11350, Columbia, SC 29211 (Courier: Edgar Brown Bldg, 1205 Pendelton St #525, Columbia, SC 29201); 803-734-1961, 803-734-2164 (Fax), 8:30AM-5PM.

www.scsos.com/Uniform_Commercial_Code.htm

Indexing & Storage: Records are available from 1968. Records are computerized since 1985.

Searching: The agency prefers UCC-11 forms, but will still accept UCC-4 for in-state requests. All tax liens are filed at the county level. Include the following in your request-debtor name.

Access by: mail, fax, in person, online.

Fee & Payment: The search fee is $5.00, there is no search fee if file number given. Copies are $2.00 for the first page, plus $1.00 for each page of attachments. Certification is $2.00 per copy. Fee payee: Secretary of State. Prepayment required. Personal checks accepted. No credit cards accepted.

Mail search: Turnaround time: 3 to 5 days. A SASE is requested.

Fax search: There is an additional $5.00 fee for faxing in and $10.00 fee for faxing back.

In person search: You can use their PC to look up records, but copies requested are still mailed days later.

Online search: Free access to index at www.scsos.com/uccsearch.htm. Search by debtor name or number. Information on filings after that date must be obtained by mail or email (SCUCC@INFOAVE.NET).

Federal Tax Liens, State Tax Liens

Records not maintained by a state level agency.

Note: Tax lien data is found at the county level.

Sales Tax Registrations

Revenue Dept, Sales Tax Registration Records, PO Box 125, Columbia, SC 29214 (Courier: 301 Gervais St, Columbia, SC 29214); 803-898-5872, 803-898-5888 (Fax), 8:30AM-4:45PM.

www.sctax.org/default.htm

Indexing & Storage: Records are available for 4 to 5 years, then are archived on hard copy. Records are indexed on inhouse computer.

Searching: This agency will only confirm that a business is registered. They will provide no other information. Include the following in your request-business name. They can also search by tax permit number, owner name, business name, or federal ID.

Access by: mail, phone, fax, in person.

Mail search: Turnaround time: 7 days. A SASE is requested. No fee for mail request.

Phone search: No fee for telephone request.

Fax search: Fax searching available.

In person search: No fee for request.

Birth Certificates

South Carolina DHEC, Vital Records, 2600 Bull St, Columbia, SC 29201-1797; 803-898-3630, 803-898-3631 (Order Line), 877-284-1008 (Expedite), 803-898-3761 (Fax), 8:30AM-4:30PM.

www.scdhec.net/vr/index.htm

Note: A "short form" wallet size birth certificate can be obtained from any SC county. This form will not show parent names.

Indexing & Storage: Records are available from January 1, 1915 to present. It takes 2 months before new records are available for inquiry. Records are indexed on microfiche, inhouse computer.

Searching: Records will only be released to the registrant (if 18 or older), parents named on certificate, guardian or legal representative. Include the following in your request-full name, full names of father, mother's full maiden name, date of birth, place of birth. Two types of certificates are issued: wallet-size; photocopy certification (actual birth certificate).

Access by: mail, phone, fax, in person.

Fee & Payment: The fee is $12.00 per name. Add $3.00 per copy for additional copies of same certificate. Add $9.95 for use of credit card. Fee payee: DHEC. Prepayment required. Credit cards accepted for phone and fax requests only. Personal checks not accepted. Credit cards accepted: MasterCard, Visa, Discover.

Mail search: Turnaround time: 7 to 8 weeks. No SASE is required.

Phone search: Phone requests are accepted, using a credit card. See expedited service from Vitalchek.

Fax search: Same criteria as phone searches. Is considered expedited.

In person search: Turnaround time is within 1 hour.

Expedited service: Expedited service is available for mail requests for an additional $5.00 from this agency. To have search "expedited" by phone, online or fax from www.vitalchek.com, add $12.95; add $13.50 for FedEx delivery.

Death Records

South Carolina DHEC, Vital Records, 2600 Bull St, Columbia, SC 29201-1797; 803-898-3630, 803-898-3631 (Order Line), 803-799-0301 (Fax), 8:30AM-4:30PM.

www.scdhec.net/vr/index.htm

Indexing & Storage: Records are available from January 1, 1915 to date. New records are available for inquiry immediately. Records are indexed on microfiche, inhouse computer.

Searching: Copies are available to those who show a direct, tangible interest in a determination of a personal or property right. If less than 5 years,

records are at county also. Include the following in your request-full name, date of death, place of death.

Access by: mail, phone, fax, in person.

Fee & Payment: The search fee is $12.00 per name. Add $3.00 per copy for additional copies. Add $9.95 for use of credit card. Fee payee: DHEC. Prepayment required. Credit cards accepted for phone and fax requests only. Personal checks accepted. Credit cards accepted: MasterCard, Visa, AmEx, Discover.

Mail search: Turnaround time: 7 to 8 weeks. No SASE is required.

Phone search: Phone requests are accepted, using a credit card. See expedited service from Vitalchek.

Fax search: See expedited service.

In person search: Turnaround time within 1 hour.

Expedited service: Expedited service is available for mail requests for an additional $5.00 from this agency. To have search "expedited" by phone, online or fax from www.vitalchek.com, add $12.95; add $13.50 for FedEx delivery.

Marriage Certificates

South Carolina DHEC, Vital Records, 2600 Bull St, Columbia, SC 29201-1797; 803-898-3630, 803-898-3631 (Order Line), 803-799-0301 (Fax), 8:30AM-4:30PM.

www.scdhec.net/vr/index.htm

Note: Copies may also be obtained from the Probate Judge in the county where license was issued.

Indexing & Storage: Records are available from July 1, 1950 to present. New records are available for inquiry immediately. Records are indexed on microfiche, inhouse computer.

Searching: Records are released only to the subjects, their adult children, former or present spouses and legal representatives. Others may obtain a statement of marriage date and place. Include the following in your request-names of husband and wife, date of marriage, place or county where marriage license issued.

Access by: mail, phone, fax, in person.

Fee & Payment: The search fee is $12.00 per name, add $3.00 for each additional copy. Use of credit card is additional $9.95. Fee payee: DHEC. Prepayment required. Credit cards accepted for phone and fax searches only. Personal checks accepted. Credit cards accepted: MasterCard, Visa, AmEx, Discover.

Mail search: Turnaround time: 7 weeks. No SASE is required.

Phone search: Phone requests are accepted, using a credit card. See expedited service from Vitalchek.

Fax search: See expedited service.

In person search: Turnaround time within 1 hour.

Expedited service: Expedited service is available for mail requests for an additional $5.00 from this agency. To have search "expedited" by phone, online or fax from www.vitalchek.com, add $12.95; add $13.50 for FedEx delivery.

Divorce Records

South Carolina DHEC, Vital Records, 2600 Bull St, Columbia, SC 29201-1797; 803-898-3630,

803-898-3631 (Order Line), 803-799-0301 (Fax), 8:30AM-4:30PM.

www.scdhec.net/vr/index.htm

Indexing & Storage: Records are available from July 1, 1962 to present. New records are available for inquiry immediately. Records are indexed on microfiche, inhouse computer.

Searching: Records are available only to the parties, their adult children, a present or former spouse, and their legal representatives. Others may obtain a statement of the date and county of the event. Include the following in your request-names of husband and wife, date of divorce, place of divorce.

Access by: mail, phone, fax, in person.

Fee & Payment: The fee is $12.00 per name. Add $3.00 per copy for additional copies. Use of credit card is $9.95. Fee payee: DHEC. Prepayment required. Credit cards accepted for phone and fax requests only. Personal checks accepted. Credit cards accepted: MasterCard, Visa, AmEx, Discover.

Mail search: Turnaround time: 7 weeks. No SASE is required.

Phone search: Phone requests are accepted, using a credit card. See expedited service from Vitalchek.

Fax search: See expedited service.

In person search: Turnaround time within 1 hour.

Expedited service: Expedited service is available for mail requests for an additional $5.00 from this agency. To have search "expedited" by phone, online or fax from www.vitalchek.com, add $12.95; add $13.50 for FedEx delivery.

Workers' Compensation Records

Workers Compensation Commission, PO Box 1715, Columbia, SC 29202 (Courier: 1612 Marion St, Columbia, SC 29201); 803-737-5700, 803-737-5768 (Fax), 8:30AM-5PM.

www.wcc.state.sc.us

Indexing & Storage: Records are available from 1983 on the computer. Some of the older records are at this office and the rest are at the State Archives. Call office first for location of records. New records are available for inquiry immediately. Records are indexed on inhouse computer, books (volumes). Records are normally destroyed after 5 years after closing.

Searching: Must have a signed release from claimant and you must specify what records you want. Include the following in your request-claimant name, Social Security Number, date of accident.

Access by: mail, fax, in person.

Fee & Payment: The search fee is $10.00 per record and includes a computer printout. File copies cost $20.00 for the first up to 20 pages and $.50 for each additional page. Fee payee: SC Workers Compensation Commission. Prepayment required. Personal checks accepted. No credit cards accepted.

Mail search: Turnaround time: 1 week. A SASE is requested.

Fax search: You can request by fax, but reply is sent by mail, same turnaround time.

In person search: Records are still returned by mail.

Driver License Information, Driver Records

Department of Motor Vehicles, Driver Records Section, PO Box 1498, Columbia, SC 29216-0035 (Courier: 10311 Wilson Blvd, Blythewood, SC 29216); 803-737-4000, 803-737-1077 (Fax), 8:30AM-5PM.

www.scdmvonline.com/

Note: Copies of tickets are available from this department for a fee of $6.00 per record.

Indexing & Storage: Records are available for up to 10 years for moving violations, DWIs and suspensions. Records provided to the public are limited to 3 or 10 years. The state will show moving violations regardless of whether the fine was not paid and license suspended. It takes 1 to 4 weeks before new records are available for inquiry. Records are normally destroyed after 10 years.

Searching: Driving records and Identification card information is confidential by statute. Requests must fall within the guidelines of DPPA. Casual requesters must submit consent of subject if personal information is to be released. Include the following in your request-Form MV-70 which requires driver's license number or full name and DOB. Consent of driver needed if requester not DPPA approved. The following data is not released: Social Security Numbers or personal information (height, weight, sex, eye color, etc.).

Access by: mail, phone, fax, in person, online.

Fee & Payment: The fee is $6.00 per record request. Fee payee: Department of Motor Vehicles Prepayment required. Personal checks accepted. Credit cards only accepted for call center and online.

Mail search: Turnaround time: 5 days. Fee and return address must be submitted with each request. No SASE is required.

Phone search: Phone searching is only available for account holders.

Fax search: Fax requesting is only available for account holders.

In person search: Most DMV Branch offices in the state will process up to 10 records while you wait.

Online search: The online system offers basic driver data, for a 3 year or a 10 year record. This is a single inquiry process. Network charges will be incurred as well as initial set-up and a security deposit. The system is up between 8 AM and 7 PM. Fee is $6.00 per record. Access is through the AAMVAnet (IBMIN), which requesters much "join." Call Wanda DeLeon at 803-737-0975 for further information.

Other access: Magnetic tape and cassette batch processing is available.

Vehicle Ownership, Vehicle Identification

Division of Motor Vehicles, Title and Registration Records Section, PO Box 1498, Columbia, SC 29216 (Courier: 955 Park St, Columbia, SC 29201); 803-737-4000, 803-737-1112 (Fax), 8:30AM-5PM.

www.state.sc.us/dps/dmv

Note: For Registration, use PO Box address with ZIP 29216-0022; use ZIP 29216-0024 for Titles.

Indexing & Storage: Records are available for 10 years for titles, 3 years for registration. The index to the records is computerized since 1984. It takes one day before new records are available for inquiry.

Searching: Information regarding the name, address and telephone number will not be released to the public, unless the requester completes form provided by department. Information is not provided to casual requesters. Requesters must be in compliance with DPPA.

Access by: mail, phone, fax, in person.

Fee & Payment: The fee is $6.00 per record request for all records, including lien information. Fee payee: SC Department of Motor Vehicles. Prepayment required. A deposit account is available for ongoing requesters by mail or phone. Personal checks accepted. No credit cards accepted.

Mail search: Turnaround time: 3 days. No SASE is required.

Phone search: Telephone searching is available for pre-approved, ongoing requesters. A deposit is required.

Fax search: See expedited service. This is only available to pre-approved, ongoing requesters. A deposit is required.

In person search: You may search in person.

Other access: South Carolina offers a variety of bulk retrieval programs where permitted by law. There is a minimum charge of $1,000.00. For more information, call customer service department for automated searches.

Expedited service: Expedited service is available for fax searches. Turnaround time: 1 to 2 days. Must have a deposit account. The fax number is 803-737-2299.

Accident Reports

Accident Reports, Financial Responsibilty Office, PO Box 1498, Columbia, SC 29216-0040 (Courier: 955 Park St, Columbia, SC 29201); 803-737-4000, 803-737-4483 (Fax), 8:30AM-5PM.

Indexing & Storage: Records are available for 10 years to present. The records are indexed on computer. It takes one week after receipt from enforcement agency before new records are available for inquiry. Records are indexed on inhouse computer.

Searching: Must have full name of all the drivers involved in the accident. Include the following in your request-full name, date of accident, driver's license number, county.

Access by: mail, in person.

Fee & Payment: The fee is $6.00 for an accident research or insurance research. You may call to find out if record is on file. Fee payee: Department of Motor Vehicles Ongoing requesters may open an account with a $100.00 deposit and then will be billed monthly. Personal checks accepted. No credit cards accepted now, but may the near future.

Mail search: Turnaround time: 7 to 10 days. Information requests are available. A SASE is requested.

In person search: Records will be processed while you wait, but only at field office on Shep Road.

Expedited service: Expedited service is available for $20.00 per report. Turnaround time: 3 days or less.

Vessel Ownership, Vessel Registration

Dept of Natural Resources, Registration & Titles, PO Box 167, Columbia, SC 29202 (Courier: 1000 Assembly St, Room 104, Columbia, SC 29201); 803-734-3857, 803-734-4138 (Fax), 8:30AM-5PM.

www.dnr.state.sc.us

Note: Boats can be registered and titled. Motors are titled. Thus, to search for a boat with a motor, two record schecks are required.

Indexing & Storage: Records are available from mid 80's to present. Inactive records are put on microfiche seven years after becoming inactive. It takes 30 days before new records are available for inquiry. Records are indexed on computer, older records on microfiche.

Searching: State law prohibits the release of records for commercial solicitation. All motorized boats must be titled and registered. All sailboats must be titled, and if used with propulsion then registered. To search, one of the following is required: name and address, hull ID #, title #, or SC (serial) #. The following data is not released: Social Security Numbers.

Access by: mail, in person.

Fee & Payment: The search fee for all types of searches is $10.00 per record request. If search both if no motor, and $20.00 per record for the motor registration. Fee payee: SC Dept of Natural Resources. Prepayment required. Personal checks accepted. No credit cards accepted.

Mail search: Turnaround time: 7 to 20 days. No SASE is required.

In person search: Turnaround time is usually same day.

Voter Registration

State Election Commission, Records, PO Box 5987, Columbia, SC 29250; 803-734-9060, 803-734-9366 (Fax), 8:30AM-5PM.

www.state.sc.us/scsec

Indexing & Storage: Records are available for all active records. It takes one day or less before new records are available for inquiry.

Searching: Records are open to the public. To search, provide the name with the county or DOB. The following data is not released: Social Security Numbers.

Access by: mail, phone, fax, in person.

Fee & Payment: There is no search fee unless extensive time involved. Copies are $.20 each. Requester must pre-pay if courier service desired. Fee payee: State Election Commission. Prepayment required. Personal checks accepted. No credit cards accepted.

Mail search: Turnaround time: 1 to 2 days.

Phone search: Records are available by phone.

Fax search: Same criteria as mail searching. There is a $.20 fee per page to return by fax.

In person search: Simple requests may be processed while you wait.

Other access: Lists, labels, diskettes, and magnetic tapes are available with a variety of sort features. The minimum charge varies from $75 to $160 depending on the media.

GED Certificates

GED Testing Office, 1429 Senate St, #402, Columbia, SC 29201; 803-734-8347 x5, 803-734-8336 (Fax), 8:30AM-5PM M-F.

www.sde.state.sc.us/

Indexing & Storage: It takes 6 weeks before new records are available for inquiry.

Searching: To search, all of the following is required: a signed release, name, SSN, and approximate date and city. Specify if for civilian or military use.

Access by: mail, fax, in person.

Fee & Payment: There is no fee for a verification. There is a $5.00 fee for a copy of a transcript by mail, $3.00 if by fax. Fee payee: SC Dept of Education. Prepayment required. Cash and money orders are accepted. No credit cards accepted.

Mail search: Turnaround time is 3-5 days. No SASE is required.

Fax search: After sending fax, call back in 15 minutes for verification.

In person search: Records may be requested in person. Requester must present state-issued ID.

Hunting and Fishing License Information

Records not maintained by a state level agency.

Note: They do not have a central database. Licenses are kept on file within the License Division by the county and agent where the license was sold, however the records are not open to the public.

South Carolina State Licensing Agencies

Licenses Searchable Online

Accounting Practitioner-AP #2	http://lookup.llronline.com/index.asp
Acupuncturist #39	http://lookup.llronline.com/Lookup/Medical.asp
Airport Contact #35	www.scaeronautics.com/directorySearch.asp
Animal Health Technician #43	http://lookup.llronline.com/Lookup/Mh.asp
Architect #3	http://lookup.llronline.com/index.asp
Architectural Partnership/Corp #3	http://lookup.llronline.com/index.asp
Attorney #48	www.scbar.org/member/directory.asp
Auction Company/Auctioneer/Auctioneer Apprentice #50	http://lookup.llronline.com/Lookup/Auctioneers.asp
Audiologist #22	http://lookup.llronline.com/Lookup/Speech/Speech_01.asp
Aviation Facility #35	www.scaeronautics.com/AirportSearch.asp
Barber Instructor/School #47	http://lookup.llronline.com/lookup/barbers.asp
Barber/Barber Apprentice #47	http://lookup.llronline.com/lookup/barbers.asp
Bodywork Therapist #47	http://lookup.llronline.com/Lookup/Massage.asp
Building Inspector/Official #21	http://lookup.llronline.com/Lookup/Bcc/Bcc_01.asp
Burglar Alarm Contractor #24	http://lookup.llronline.com/index.asp
Chiropractor #4	http://lookup.llronline.com/lookup/Chiro/Chiro_01.asp
Contractor, General & Mechanical #24	http://lookup.llronline.com/Lookup/Contractors.asp
Contractor, Specialty Residential #45	http://lookup.llronline.com/Lookup/Resbu/Resbu_01.asp
Cosmetologist/Cosmetology Instructor/School #5	http://lookup.llronline.com/lookup/Cosmetology/Cosmetology_01.asp
Counselor, Professional #8	http://lookup.llronline.com/lookup/Counselors.asp
Dentist/Dental Hygienist #6	http://lookup.llronline.com/Lookup/Dentistry.asp
Dental Specialist/Technician #6	http://lookup.llronline.com/Lookup/Dentistry.asp
Embalmer #11	http://lookup.llronline.com/Lookup/Funeral.asp
Emergency Medical Svc. (Ambulance Co) #27	www.scems.com/emsassn/members.html
Engineer #7	http://lookup.llronline.com/lookup/Engineers.asp
Esthetician #5	http://lookup.llronline.com/lookup/Cosmetology/Cosmetology_01.asp
Ethics Debtors #37	www.state.sc.us/ethics/Debtors%20page%20Lead.htm
Forester #38	http://lookup.llronline.com/Lookup/Foresters.asp
Funeral Director/Funeral Home #11	http://lookup.llronline.com/Lookup/Funeral.asp
Geologist #20	http://lookup.llronline.com/Lookup/Geologists.asp
Hair Care Master Specialist #47	http://lookup.llronline.com/lookup/barbers.asp
Home Builder, Residential #45	http://lookup.llronline.com/Lookup/Resbu/Resbu_01.asp
Housing Inspector #21	http://lookup.llronline.com/Lookup/Bcc/Bcc_01.asp
Inspector, Mech./Elec./Plumb./Prov. #21	http://lookup.llronline.com/Lookup/Bcc/Bcc_01.asp
Insurance Agency/Company/Filing #31	https://www.doi.state.sc.us/Eng/Public/Static/DBSearch.aspx
Insurance Agent #31	https://www.doi.state.sc.us/Eng/Public/Static/DBSearch.aspx
Landscape Architect #40	www.dnr.state.sc.us/water/envaff/prolicense/prolicense.html
Lobbyist #37	www.scstatehouse.net/reports/lobby1.doc
Lobbyist Principal #37	www.scstatehouse.net/reports/lobby2.doc
Manicure Assistant #47	http://lookup.llronline.com/lookup/barbers.asp
Manicurist #5	http://lookup.llronline.com/lookup/Cosmetology/Cosmetology_01.asp
Manufactured House Mfg/Dealer/Rep #41	http://lookup.llronline.com/Lookup/Mh.asp
Manufactured House Sales/Install/Repair #41	http://lookup.llronline.com/Lookup/Mh.asp
Marriage & Family Therapist #8	http://lookup.llronline.com/lookup/Counselors.asp
Massage Therapist #47	http://lookup.llronline.com/Lookup/Massage.asp
Medical Doctor #39	http://lookup.llronline.com/Lookup/Medical.asp
Nail Technician #5	http://lookup.llronline.com/lookup/Cosmetology/Cosmetology_01.asp
Nurses (RN / LPN) #12	http://lookup.llronline.com/lookup/Nursing/Nurse_01.asp
Nursing Home Administrator #32	http://lookup.llronline.com/Lookup/LTC.asp
Occupational Therapist/Assistant #13	http://lookup.llronline.com/Lookup/OT/OT_01.asp
Optician #14	http://lookup.llronline.com/Lookup/Opticians.asp
Optometrist #9	http://lookup.llronline.com/Lookup/Optometry.asp
Osteopathic Physician #39	http://lookup.llronline.com/Lookup/Medical.asp
Percolation Test Technician #36	http://lookup.llronline.com/Lookup/Environmental.asp
Pharmacist/Pharmacy Technician #15	http://lookup.llronline.com/lookup/pharmacy.asp
Pharmacy/Drug Outlet #15	http://lookup.llronline.com/lookup/pharmacy.asp
Physical Therapist/Therapist Asst #16	http://lookup.llronline.com/Lookup/PT/PT_01.asp
Physician Assistant #39	http://lookup.llronline.com/Lookup/Medical.asp
Pilot #35	www.scaeronautics.com/AirportSearch.asp
Plans Examiner #21	http://lookup.llronline.com/Lookup/Bcc/Bcc_01.asp

Podiatrist #17 .... http://lookup.llronline.com/Lookup/Podiatry.asp
Produce Whlse Dealer #25 .... www.scda.state.sc.us/buyscproducts/wholesalers/wholesalers.htm
Psycho-Educational Specialist #8 .... http://lookup.llronline.com/lookup/Counselors.asp
Psychologist #18 .... http://lookup.llronline.com/Lookup/Psychology.asp
Public Accountant-CPA #2 .... http://lookup.llronline.com/index.asp
Real Estate Appraiser #44 .... www.asc.gov/content/category1/appr_by_state.asp
Residential Care, Community #32 .... http://lookup.llronline.com/Lookup/LTC.asp
Respiratory Care Practitioner #39 .... http://lookup.llronline.com/Lookup/Medical.asp
Shampoo Assistant #47 .... http://lookup.llronline.com/lookup/barbers.asp
Social Worker #18 .... http://lookup.llronline.com/Lookup/SW.asp
Soil Classifier #40 .... www.dnr.state.sc.us/water/envaff/prolicense/prolicense.html
Solid Waste Landfill #30 .... www.scdhec.net/lwm/html/min.html
Speech-Language Pathologist #22 .... http://lookup.llronline.com/Lookup/Speech/Speech_01.asp
Sprinkler Systems Contractor #24 .... http://lookup.llronline.com/index.asp
Surveyor, Land #7 .... http://lookup.llronline.com/lookup/Engineers.asp
Swimming Pool/Spa Operator #36 .... http://lookup.llronline.com/Lookup/Environmental.asp
Veterinarian #43 .... http://lookup.llronline.com/Lookup/Mh.asp
Waste Water Treatment Plant Operator #36 ... http://lookup.llronline.com/Lookup/Environmental.asp
Water Treatment Registration #36 .... http://lookup.llronline.com/Lookup/Environmental.asp
Well Driller #36 .... http://lookup.llronline.com/Lookup/Environmental.asp
Wholesaler/Shipper (Food) #25 .... www.scda.state.sc.us/buyscproducts/shippers/shippers.htm

South Carolina Licensing Quick Finder

Accounting Practitioner-AP #2 803-896-4770
Acupuncturist #39 803-896-4500
Agricultural Dealer/Handler #25 803-734-2182
Airport Contact #35 803-896-6260
Alcoholic Beverage Sunday Sales #34 . 803-898-5880
Alcoholic Beverage Vendor/Mfg./Whlse. #34
                                          803-898-5864
Amusement Ride #46 803-734-9711
Animal Health Technician #43 803-896-4598
Architect #3 803-896-4408
Architectural Partners/Corp #3 803-896-4408
Athletic Contest #49 803-896-4571
Athletic Trainer #49 803-896-4571
Attorney #48 803-799-6653
Auction Company #50 803-896-4853
Auctioneer/Auctioneer Apprentice #50.. 803-896-4853
Audiologist #22 803-896-4650
Aviation Facility #35 803-896-6260
Bank #10 803-734-2001
Barber Instructor/School #47 803-896-4588
Barber Shop #47 803-896-4588
Barber/Barber Apprentice #47 803-896-4588
Bodywork Therapist #47 803-896-4498
Boxer/Boxing Professional #49 803-896-4571
Building Inspector/Official #21 803-896-4688
Burglar Alarm Contractor #24 803-896-4686
Butterfat Tester #25 803-737-9700
Chiropractor #4 803-896-4587
Constable #51 803-896-7014
Contact Lens License #14 803-896-4681
Contractor, General & Mechanical #24 . 803-896-4686
Contractor, Specialty Resid'l #45 803-896-4696
Cosmetologist #5 803-896-4494
Cosmetology Instructor/School #5 803-896-4494
Counselor, Professional #8 803-896-4658
Dental Hygienist #6 803-896-4599
Dental Specialist/Technician #6 803-896-4599
Dentist #6 803-896-4599
Electrician #42 803-933-1209
Elevator Service #46 803-734-9711
Embalmer #11 803-896-4497
Emergency Medical Svc. (Ambulance Co) #27
                                        803-545-4202
Emergency Medical Technician #27 803-545-4204
Engineer #7 803-896-4422
Esthetician #5 803-896-4494
Ethics Debtors #37 803-253-4192

Feed Manufacturer/Product #25 803-737-9700
Financial Institution #10 803-734-2001
Forester #38 803-896-4675
Funeral Director / Funeral Home #11.. 803-896-4497
Geologist #20 803-896-4498
Hair Care Master Specialist #47 803-896-4588
Hearing Aid Dispenser/Fitter #22 803-896-4650
Heating & Air/Gas Fitting #42 803-933-1209
Home Builder, Residential #45 803-896-4696
Housing Inspector #21 803-896-4688
Inspector, Mech./Elec./Plmb./Prov. #21 803-896-4688
Insurance Agency/Company/Filing #31 803-737-6221
Insurance Agent #31 803-737-6095
Investment Advisor #1 803-734-9916
Landscape Architect #40 803-734-9131
Liquor Permit, Special Event #34 803-898-5864
Lobbyist #37 803-253-4192
Lobbyist Principal #37 803-253-4192
Manicure Assistant #47 803-896-4588
Manicurist #5 803-896-4494
Manufactured House Mfg/Dealer/Rep #41
                                        803-896-4682
Manufactured House Sales/Install/Repair #41
                                        803-896-4682
Marriage & Family Therapist #8 803-896-4658
Massage Therapist #47 803-896-4498
Medical Doctor #39 803-896-4500
Mine Site #30 803-896-4000
Nail Technician #5 803-896-4494
Notary Public #23 803-734-2512
Nurses (RN + LPN) #12 803-896-4550
Nursing Home Administrator #32 803-896-4544
Occupational Therapist/Assistant #13.. 803-896-4683
Optician #14 803-896-4681
Optician Apprentice #14 803-896-4681
Optometrist #9 803-869-4679
Osteopathic Physician #39 803-896-4500
Percolation Test Technician #36 803-896-4430
Pesticide Applicator #33 803-646-2155
Pesticide Dealer #33 803-646-2155
Pharmacist/Pharmacy Technician #15.. 803-896-4700
Pharmacy/Drug Outlet #15 803-896-4700
Physical Therapist/Therapist Asst #16.. 803-896-4655
Physician Assistant #39 803-896-4500
Pilot #35 803-896-6260
Pipefitter #42 803-933-1209
Plans Examiner #21 803-896-4688

Plumbing #42 803-933-1209
Podiatrist #17 803-896-4685
Polygraph Examiner #51 803-896-7292
Private Detective #51 803-896-7014
Produce Whlse Dealer #25 803-737-9700
Property Manager #44 803-896-4400
Psycho-Educational Specialist #8 803-896-4658
Psychologist #18 803-896-4664
Public Accountant-CPA #2 803-896-4770
Pyrotechnic Technician #19 803-896-9807
Pyrotechnic Whsle./Facility/Jobber #19 803-896-4420
Real Estate Appraiser #44 803-896-4400
Real Estate Broker #44 803-896-4400
Residential Care, Community #32 803-896-4544
Respiratory Care Practitioner #39 803-896-4500
Sanitarian #28 803-896-0646
School Guidance Counselor #26 803-734-8466
School Media Communications Spec. #26
                                        803-734-8466
School Principal/Supv'r/Super't #26..... 803-734-8466
Securities Agent #1 803-734-9916
Securities Broker/Dealer #1 803-734-9916
Security Guard/Security Company #51. 803-896-7014
Seed Salesperson #25 803-737-9690
Shampoo Assistant #47 803-896-4588
Sheet Metal #42 803-933-1209
Social Worker #18 803-896-4665
Soil Classifier #40 803-734-9131
Solid Waste Landfill #30 803-896-4148
Solid Waste Landfill Operator #30 803-896-4148
Speech-Language Pathologist #22.........803-896-4650
Sprinkler Systems Contr. #24 803-896-4686
Surveyor, Land #7 803-896-4422
Swimming Pool/Spa Operator #36 803-896-4430
Teacher #26 803-734-8466
Timeshare/Land Salesperson #44 803-896-4400
Veterinarian #43 803-896-4598
Waste Water Treatment Plant Operator #36
                                        803-896-4430
Water Treatment Registration #36 803-896-4430
Weighman #25 803-737-9700
Weighmaster #25 803-737-9696
Well Driller #36 803-896-4430
Wholesaler/Shipper (Food) #25 803-737-9700
Wrestler/Wrestling Professional #49.... 803-896-4571

South Carolina Licensing Agency Information

1 Attorney Generals Office, Securities Division, PO Box 11549 (1000 Assembly St, Rembert C. Dennis Building), Columbia, SC 29211-1549; 803-734-9916, Fax: 803-734-0032. www.scsecurities.org/index.html

2 Department of Labor, Licensing & Regulation, Board of Accountancy, PO Box 11329 (110 Centerview Dr.), Columbia, SC 29211; 803-896-4770, Fax: 803-896-4554. www.llr.state.sc.us/pol.asp Email: mcwhortm@mail.llr.state.sc Search Database at http://lookup.llronline.com/index.asp

3 Department of Labor, Licensing & Regulation, Board of Architectural Examiners, PO Box 11419 (110 Centerview Dr, #201), Columbia, SC 29211; 803-896-4408, Fax: 803-734-4410. www.llr.state.sc.us/pol.asp   Search Database at http://lookup.llronline.com/index.asp

4 Department of Labor, Licensing & Regulation, Division\Chiropractic Examiners, PO Box 11329 (110 Centerview Dr, #306), Columbia, SC 29211-1329; 803-896-4587, Fax: 803-896-4719. www.llr.state.sc.us/pol.asp Email: denninsonp@ur.sc.gov   Search Database at http://lookup.llronline.com/index.asp

5 Department of Labor, Licensing & Regulation, Board of Cosmetology, PO Box 11329 (110 Centerview Dr), Columbia, SC 29211-1329; 803-896-4494, Fax: 803-896-4484. www.llr.state.sc.us/pol.asp Search Database at http://lookup.llronline.com/index.asp   Note: See also Board of Barber examiners for Shampoo Assistant and Master Hair Care Specialist.

6 Department of Labor, Licensing & Regulation, Board of Dentistry, PO Box 11329 (110 Centerview Dr, Ste 306), Columbia, SC 29211-1329; 803-896-4599, Fax: 803-896-4596. www.llr.state.sc.us/pol.asp Email: joness@mail.llr.state.sc.us   Search Database at http://lookup.llronline.com/Lookup/Dentistry.asp

7 Department of Labor, Licensing & Regulation, Board of Prof. Engineers & Land Surveyors, PO Box 11597 (110 Centerview Dr, #201), Columbia, SC 29211-1597; 803-896-4422, Fax: 803-896-4427. www.llr.state.sc.us/pol.asp   Search Database at http://lookup.llronline.com/index.asp

8 Department of Labor, Licensing & Regulation, Board of Examiners of Prof. Counselors / Family Therapists, PO Box 11329 (110 Centerview, #306), Columbia, SC 29211; 803-896-4658, Fax: 803-896-4719. www.llr.state.sc.us/pol.asp Email: harringtons@mail.llr.state.sc.us   Search Database at http://lookup.llronline.com/index.asp   Note: List are availibe through email or on diskette of $30.00.

9 Department of Labor, Licensing & Regulation, Board of Examiners in Optometry, PO Box 11329 (110 Centerview Dr.), Columbia, SC 29211-1329; 803-896-4679, Fax: 803-896-4719. www.llr.state.sc.us/pol.asp Email: combsa@mail.llr.state.sc.us Search Database at http://lookup.llronline.com/index.asp   Note: Online disciplinary records only go back to 1994.

10 Board of Financial Institutions, PO Box 12549 (1015 Sumter St, Rm 309), Columbia, SC 29201; 803-734-2001, Fax: 803-734-2013.

11 Department of Labor, Licensing & Regulation, Board of Funeral Service, PO Box 11329 (110 Centerview Dr, #104), Columbia, SC 29211-1329; 803-896-4497, Fax: 803-896-4484/4554. www.llr.state.sc.us/pol.asp Search Database at http://lookup.llronline.com/index.asp

12 Department of Labor, Licensing & Regulation, Board of Nursing, PO Box 12367 (110 Centerview Dr, #202), Columbia, SC 29211-2367; 803-896-4550, Fax: 803-896-4525. www.llr.state.sc.us/pol/nursing/ Email: hurseboard@llr.sc.gov   Search Database at http://lookup.llronline.com/index.asp

13 Department of Labor, Licensing & Regulation, Board of Occupational Therapy, PO Box 11329 (110 Centerview Dr, #306), Columbia, SC 29211; 803-896-4683, Fax: 803-896-4719. www.llr.state.sc.us/pol.asp Email: cokk@mail.llr.state.sc.us   Search Database at http://lookup.llronline.com/index.asp   Note: Online records only go back to 1994.

14 Department of Labor, Licensing & Regulation, Board of Examiners in Optometry, PO Box 11329 (110 Centerview Dr.), Columbia, SC 29211-1329; 803-896-4681, Fax: 803-896-4719. www.llr.state.sc.us/pol.asp Email: combsa@mail.llr.state.sc.us   Search Database at http://lookup.llronline.com/index.asp   Note: Online records only go back to 1994.

15 Department of Labor, Licensing & Regulation, Board of Pharmacy, 110 Centerview Dr, Kingstree Bldg, #306, Columbia, SC 29211-1927; 803-896-4700, Fax: 803-896-4596. www.llr.state.sc.us/pol.asp Email: funderbm@mail.llr.state.sc.us Search Database at http://lookup.llronline.com/index.asp

16 Department of Labor, Licensing & Regulation, Board of Physical Therapy Examiners, PO Box 11329 (110 Centerview Dr,), Columbia, SC 29211; 803-896-4655, Fax: 803-896-4719. www.llr.state.sc.us/pol.asp Email: reynoldsv@llr.sc.gov Search Database at http://lookup.llronline.com/index.asp

17 Department of Labor, Licensing & Regulation, Board of Podiatry Examiners, PO Box 11289 (110 Centerview Dr, #202), Columbia, SC 29211-1289; 803-896-4685, Fax: 803-896-4515. www.llr.state.sc.us/pol/podiatry Email: podiatry@mail.llr.state.sc.us Search Database at http://lookup.llronline.com/index.asp

18 Department of Labor, Licensing & Regulation, Board of Examiners in Psychology/Social Work Examiners, PO Box 11329 (110 Centerview Dr), Columbia, SC 29211-1329; 803-896-4664, Fax: 803-896-4687. www.llr.state.sc.us/pol.asp Email: glennp@llk.sc.gov Search Database at http://lookup.llronline.com/index.asp   Note: Online psychologist records only go bck to 1994.

19 Department of Labor, Licensing & Regulation, Board of Pyrotechnic Safety, PO Box 11847 (110 Centerview Dr, #201), Columbia, SC 29211-1329; 803-896-4400, Fax: 803-896-4404. www.llr.state.sc.us/POL/Pyrotechnic

20 Department of Labor, Licensing & Regulation, Board of Registration for Geologists, PO Box 11329 (110 Centerview Dr, #104), Columbia, SC 29211-1329; 803-896-4498, Fax: 803-896-4484. www.llr.state.sc.us/pol.asp Email: pyattl@mail.llr.state.sc.us   Search Database at http://lookup.llronline.com/index.asp

21 Department of Labor, Licensing & Regulation, Building Codes Council, PO Box 11329 (110 Centerview Dr, #102), Columbia, SC 29211-1329; 803-896-4636, Fax: 803-896-4814. www.llr.state.sc.us/pol.asp Email: reynoldsv@mail.llr.state.sc.us   Search Database at http://lookup.llronline.com/index.asp

22 Department of Labor, Licensing & Regulation, Board of Examiners for Speech-Language Pathology & Audiology, PO Box 11329 (110 Centerview Dr, #306), Columbia, SC 29211-1329; 803-896-4650, Fax: 803-896-4719. www.llr.state.sc.us/pol.asp Email: reynoldsv@mail.llr.state.sc.us   Search Database at http://lookup.llronline.com/index.asp

23 Secretary of State, Notaries & Apostilles Office, PO Box 11350 (1205 Pendleton St #525), Columbia, SC 29211; 803-734-2512. www.scsos.com/notariesbc.htm Email: pathamby@infoave.net

24 Department of Labor, Licensing & Regulation, Contractor's Licensing Board, PO Box 11329 (110 Centerview Dr, #201), Columbia, SC 29211-1329; 803-896-4686, Fax: 803-896-4364. www.llr.state.sc.us/pol.asp   Search Database at http://lookup.llronline.com/index.asp

25 Department of Agriculture, PO Box 11280, Columbia, SC 29211; 803-734-2210, Fax: 803-734-2192. www.scda.state.sc.us Email: bwalton@scda.sc.gov Search Database at www.scda.state.sc.us/

26 Department of Education, Office of Teacher Certification, 1429 Senate St, Columbia, SC 29201; 803-734-8466, Fax: 803-734-2873. www.scteachers.org Email: certification@scteachers.org

27 Department of Health & Environmental Control, EMS Department, 2600 Bull St, Columbia, SC 29201; 803-545-4204, Fax: 803-545-4212.   www.scemsa.com

28 Department of Health & Environmental Control, Department of Licensing - Sanitarians, 2600 Bull St, Columbia, SC 29201; 803-896-0646, Fax: 803-896-0645. www.scdhec.net Email: macphadt@dhec.sc.gov

30 Department of Health & Environmental Control, Bureau of Land and Waste Management, 2600 Bull St, Columbia, SC 29201; 803-896-4000, Fax: 803-896-4001. www.scdhec.net   Search Database at www.scdhec.net/lwm/html/min.html   Note: For Landfill Operators, search by county.

31 Department of Insurance, PO Box 100105 (300 Arbor Lake Dr., #1200), Columbia, SC 29202-3105; 803-737-6095, Fax: 803-737-6100. www.doi.state.sc.us
Email: AgntMail@doi.state.sc.us   Search Database at https://www.doi.state.sc.us/Eng/Public/Static/DBS earch.aspx

32 Department of Labor, Licensing & Regulation, Board of Long Term Care Administrators, PO Box 11329, Columbia, SC 29211; 803-896-4544, Fax: 803-896-4555.
www.llr.state.sc.us/pol.asp
Email: welbornd@mail.llr.state.sc.us   Search Database at http://lookup.llronline.com/index.asp

33 Department of Pesticide Regulation, 511 Winghouse Rd, Pendelton, SC 29670; 864-646-2150, Fax: 864-646-2179.
http://dpr.clemson.edu

34 Department of Revenue & Taxation, Alcoholic Beverage Section, PO Box 125, Columbia, SC 29214; 803-898-5864, Fax: 803-898-5899. Note: The state list of Sunday Sales permits for alcoholic beverages is temporarily unavailable.

35 Division of Aeronautics, PO Box 280068 (2553 Airport Blvd, West Columbia), Columbia, SC 29228-0068;
803-896-6260, Fax: 803-896-6277.
www.scaeronautics.com
Email: pwerts@aeronautics.state.sc.us

36 Department of Labor, Licensing & Regulation, Environmental Certification Board, PO Box 11409, Columbia, SC 29211;
803-896-4430, Fax: 803-896-4424.
www.llr.state.sc.us/pol.asp
Search Database at http://lookup.llronline.com/Lo okup/Environmental.asp

37 Ethics Commission, 5000 Thurmond Mall #250, Columbia, SC 29201;
803-253-4192, Fax: 803-253-7539.
www.state.sc.us/ethics/   Search Database at www.scstatehouse.net/reports/ethrpt.htm

38 Department of Labor, Licensing & Regulation, Board of Registration for Foresters, PO Box 11419, Columbia, SC 29211-1329; 803-896-4675, Fax: 803-896-4595.
www.llr.state.sc.us/pol.asp
Email: pyattl@mail.llr.state.sc.us
Search Database at http://lookup.llronline.com/Lookup/Foresters.asp

39 Department of Labor, Licensing & Regulation, Board of Medical Examiners, PO Box 11289 (110 Centerview Dr, #202), Columbia, SC 29211-1289; 803-896-4500, Fax: 803-896-4515.
www.llr.state.sc.us/POL/Medical/
Email: medboard@mail.llr.state.sc.us
Search Database at http://lookup.llronline.com/Lookup/Medical.asp

40 Department of Natural Resources, Land, Water & Conservation Div., Licensing Program, 1000 Assembly St. (PO Box 167), Columbia, SC 29201; 803-734-9131, Fax: 803-734-9200.
www.dnr.state.sc.us   Email: moorer@dnr.
Search Database at www.dnr.state.sc.us/water/ envaff/prolicense/prolicense.html

41 Department of Labor, Licensing & Regulation, Manufactured Housing Board, PO Box 11329 (110 Centerview Dr, #102), Columbia, SC 29211-1329; 803-896-4682, Fax: 803-896-4814.
www.llr.state.sc.us/pol.asp
Email: bennettd@mail.llr.state.sc.us
Search Database at http://lookup.llronline.com/index.asp

42 Municipal Association of South Carolina, Trades Certification Program, PO Box 12109 (1411 Gervais St), Columbia, SC 29211; 803-779-9574, Fax: 803-933-1299.
www.masc.sc/trades/trades.htm Note: Will verify by phone.

43 Department of Labor, Licensing & Regulation, Board of Veterinary Medical Examiners, PO Box 11329, Columbia, SC 29211-1329; 803-896-4598, Fax: 803-896-4719.
www.llr.state.sc.us/pol.asp
Email: motonm@llr.sc.gov
Search Database at http://lookup.llronline.com/index.asp

44 Real Estate Commission, PO Box 11847 (110 Centerview Dr #201), Columbia, SC 29211-1847; 803-896-4400, Fax: 803-896-4404.
www.llr.state.sc.us/pol.asp
Email: selmanr@mail.llr.state.sc.us

45 Department of Labor, Licensing & Regulation, Residential Home Builders Commission, PO Box 11329 (110 Centerview Dr, #201), Columbia, SC 29211-1329; 803-896-4696, Fax: 803-896-4656.
www.llr.state.sc.us/pol.asp
Email: driverc@mail.llr.state.sc.us
Search Database at http://lookup.llronline.com/index.asp

46 Department of Labor, Licensing & Regulation, Office of Elevators & Amusement Rides, PO Box 11329, Columbia, SC 29211-1329; 803-734-9711, Fax: 803-737-9119.
www.llr.state.sc.us

47 Department of Labor, Licensing & Regulation, Board of Barber Examiners, Massage/Bodywork Therapy, PO Box 11329 (110 Centerview Dr, #104), Columbia, SC 29211-1329; 803-896-4491, Fax: 803-896-4484.
www.llr.state.sc.us/POL/Barber/
Email: jonese@mail.llr.state.sc.us
Search Database at http://lookup.llronline.com/index.asp

48 Supreme Court, 950 Taylor St, Columbia, SC 29202; 803-799-6653, Fax: 803-799-4118.
www.scbar.org
Email: scbar-info@scbar.org
Search Database at www.scbar.org/member/directory.asp

49 Department of Labor, Licensing & Regulation, Athletic Commission, PO Box 11329 (110 Centerview Dr), Columbia, SC 29211; 803-896-4571, Fax: 803-896-4595.
www.llr.state.sc.us/pol.asp
Email: halll@mail.llr.state.sc.us

50 Department of Labor, Licensing & Regulation, Auctioneer's Commission, PO Box 11329 (110 Centerview Dr, #104), Columbia, SC 29211-1329; 803-896-4853, Fax: 803-896-4484.
www.llr.state.sc.us/pol.asp
Email: pyatt@mail.llr.state.sc.us
Search Database at http://lookup.llronline.com/index.asp

51 Law Enforcement Division, Regulatory Department, 4400 Broad River Rd, Columbia, SC 29210; 803-737-9000, Fax: 803-896-7041.
www.sled.state.sc.us

South Carolina Federal Courts

The following list indicates the district and division name for each county in the state. If the bankruptcy court location is different from the district court, then the location of the bankruptcy court appears in parentheses.

County/Court Cross Reference

Abbeville	Greenwood (Columbia)	Greenwood	Greenwood (Columbia)
Aiken	Greenwood (Columbia)	Hampton	Beaufort (Columbia)
Allendale	Greenwood (Columbia)	Horry	Florence (Columbia)
Anderson	Anderson (Columbia)	Jasper	Beaufort (Columbia)
Bamberg	Greenwood (Columbia)	Kershaw	Columbia
Barnwell	Greenwood (Columbia)	Lancaster	Greenwood (Columbia)
Beaufort	Beaufort (Columbia)	Laurens	Greenville (Columbia)
Berkeley	Charleston (Columbia)	Lee	Columbia
Calhoun	Greenwood (Columbia)	Lexington	Columbia
Charleston	Charleston (Columbia)	Marion	Florence (Columbia)
Cherokee	Spartanburg (Columbia)	Marlboro	Florence (Columbia)
Chester	Spartanburg (Columbia)	McCormick	Greenwood (Columbia)
Chesterfield	Florence (Columbia)	Newberry	Greenwood (Columbia)
Clarendon	Charleston (Columbia)	Oconee	Anderson (Columbia)
Colleton	Charleston (Columbia)	Orangeburg	Greenwood (Columbia)
Darlington	Florence (Columbia)	Pickens	Anderson (Columbia)
Dillon	Florence (Columbia)	Richland	Columbia
Dorchester	Charleston (Columbia)	Saluda	Greenwood (Columbia)
Edgefield	Greenwood (Columbia)	Spartanburg	Spartanburg (Columbia)
Fairfield	Greenwood (Columbia)	Sumter	Columbia
Florence	Florence (Columbia)	Union	Spartanburg (Columbia)
Georgetown	Charleston (Columbia)	Williamsburg	Florence (Columbia)
Greenville	Greenville (Columbia)	York	Spartanburg (Columbia)

Standards for Federal Courts: The search fee is $20.00 per item (one party name or case number). Certification fee is $7.00 per document. Copy fee is $.50 per page. All fees standard unless noted in profile. Mail Search: always enclose a stamped self addressed envelope unless otherwise noted. Most courts accept fax requests or will suggest a copying/search vendor. Before releasing records, all courts require prepayment unless noted in profile.

Open records are located at the court unless otherwise noted. District courts index by defendant and plaintiff as well as by case number. Bankruptcy courts usually index by debtor and case number. While most courts now have their indexes on computer, many still maintain index card files as well.

The universal PACER sign-up number is 800-676-6856. Find PACER and the Party/Case Index on the Web at http://pacer.psc.uscourts.gov. PACER dial-up access is $.60 per minute. Also, courts offering internet access via RACER, PACER, Web-PACER or the new CM-ECF charge $.07 per page fee unless noted as free.

US District Court

District of South Carolina

Anderson Division c/o Greenville Division, PO Box 10768, Greenville, SC 29603 (courier address: 300 E Washington St, Greenville, SC 29601), 864-241-2700. www.scd.uscourts.gov

Counties: Anderson, Oconee, Pickens.

Indexing & Storage: Cases indexed by as well as by case number. New cases available in the index after filing date. Open records are located at the Greenville Division.

Fee & Payment: Payment may be made by money order, cashier check. Business checks are not accepted. Personal checks are not accepted.

Phone Search: No searching by telephone.

Mail Search: A SASE not required.

In Person Search: Permitted.

PACER: PACER is available online at http://pacer.scd.uscourts.gov. Document images available. Case records go back to January 1990. Records never purged. New records are online after 1 day.

Opinions Online: Court opinions are online at www.law.sc.edu/dsc/dsc.htm

Beaufort Division c/o Charleston Division, PO Box 835, Charleston, SC 29402 (courier address: 85 Broad St, Hollings Judicial Center, Charleston, SC 29401), 843-579-1401, Fax: 803-579-1402. www.scd.uscourts.gov

Counties: Beaufort, Hampton, Jasper.

Indexing & Storage: Cases indexed by as well as by case number. New cases available in the index after filing date. Open records are located at the Charleston Division. Civil records are sent to Federal Records Center 1 year after case close. Criminal records are sent 5 years after case close.

Fee & Payment: Payment may be made by money order, cashier check. Business checks are not accepted. Personal checks are not accepted.

Phone Search: No searching by telephone.

In Person Search: Permitted.

PACER: PACER is available online at http://pacer.scd.uscourts.gov. Document images available. Case records go back to January 1990. Records never purged. New records are online after 1 day.

Opinions Online: Court opinions are online at www.law.sc.edu/dsc/dsc.htm

Charleston Division
PO Box 835, Charleston, SC 29402 (courier address: 85 Broad St, Hollings Judicial Center, Charleston, SC 29401), 843-579-1401, Fax: 803-579-1402. www.scd.uscourts.gov

Counties: Berkeley, Charleston, Clarendon, Colleton, Dorchester, Georgetown.

Indexing & Storage: New cases available in the index 1-2 days after filing date. Older records are indexed on cards and microfiche. District wide searches are available for information from 1980 from this court.

Fee & Payment: Payment may be made by money order, cashier check, personal check. Payee: U.S. District Court.

Phone Search: Only docket information available.

In Person Search: Fee charged if court conducts your in person search for you.

PACER: PACER is available online at http://pacer.scd.uscourts.gov. Document images available. Case records go back to January 1990. Records never purged. New records are online after 1 day.

Opinions Online: Court opinions are online at www.law.sc.edu/dsc/dsc.htm

Columbia Division
1845 Assembly St, Columbia, SC 29201 (courier address: Use mail address for courier delivery) 803-765-5816. www.scd.uscourts.gov

Counties: Kershaw, Lee, Lexington, Richland, Sumter.

Indexing & Storage: New cases available in the index 1 month after filing date. Older records are also indexed on microfiche. District wide searches are available from this court.

Fee & Payment: Payment may be made by money order, cashier check, personal check. Payee: Clerk, U.S. District Court.

Phone Search: No searching by telephone. If a case number, caption and judge are provided, docket information is given. The court will not search case numbers or captions on the phone.

Mail Search: A SASE not required.

In Person Search: Fee charged if court conducts your in person search for you.

PACER: PACER is available online at http://pacer.scd.uscourts.gov. Document images available. Case records go back to January 1990. Records never purged. New records are online after 1 day.

Opinions Online: Court opinions are online at www.law.sc.edu/dsc/dsc.htm

Florence Division
PO Box 2317, Florence, SC 29503 (courier address: 401 W Evans St, McMillan Federal Bldg., Room 361, Florence, SC 29501), 843-676-3820, Fax: 843-676-3831. www.scd.uscourts.gov

Counties: Chesterfield, Darlington, Dillon, Florence, Horry, Marion, Marlboro, Williamsburg.

Indexing & Storage: New cases available in the index 24-48 hours after filing date. District wide searches are available from this court.

Fee & Payment: Payment may be made by money order, cashier check, personal check. Payee: Clerk, U.S. District Court.

Phone Search: No searching by telephone.

In Person Search: Fee charged if court conducts your in person search for you.

PACER: PACER is available online at http://pacer.scd.uscourts.gov. Document images available. Case records go back to January 1990. Records never purged. New records are online after 1 day.

Opinions Online: Court opinions are online at www.law.sc.edu/dsc/dsc.htm

Greenville Division
PO Box 10768, Greenville, SC 29603 (courier address: 300 E Washington St, Greenville, SC 29601), 864-241-2700, Fax: 864-241-2711. www.scd.uscourts.gov

Counties: Greenville, Laurens.

Indexing & Storage: New cases available in the index 24 hours after filing date. The computer index is from 1991 on. Older records are indexed on microfiche.

Fee & Payment: Payment may be made by money order, cashier check, personal check. Payee: Clerk, U.S. District Court.

Phone Search: Only the case number, parties and attorneys' names will be released over the phone.

Mail Search: A SASE not required.

In Person Search: Fee charged if court conducts your in person search for you.

PACER: PACER is available online at http://pacer.scd.uscourts.gov. Document images available. Case records go back to January 1990. Records never purged. New records are online after 1 day.

Opinions Online: Court opinions are online at www.law.sc.edu/dsc/dsc.htm

Greenwood Division
c/o Greenville Division, PO Box 10768, Greenville, SC 29603 (courier address: 300 E Washington St, Greenville, SC 29601), 864-241-2700, Fax: 864-241-2711. www.scd.uscourts.gov

Counties: Abbeville, Aiken, Allendale, Bamberg, Barnwell, Calhoun, Edgefield, Fairfield, Greenwood, Lancaster, McCormick, Newberry, Orangeburg, Saluda.

Indexing & Storage: Cases indexed by as well as by case number. New cases available in the index after filing date. Open records are located at the Greenville Division.

Fee & Payment: Payment may be made by money order, cashier check. Business checks are not accepted. Personal checks are not accepted.

Phone Search: No searching by telephone.

Mail Search: A SASE not required.

In Person Search: Permitted.

PACER: PACER is available online at http://pacer.scd.uscourts.gov. Document images available. Case records go back to January 1990. Records never purged. New records are online after 1 day.

Opinions Online: Court opinions are online at www.law.sc.edu/dsc/dsc.htm

Spartanburg Division
c/o Greenville Division, PO Box 10768, Greenville, SC 29603 (courier address: 300 E Washington St, Greenville, SC 29601), 864-241-2700, Fax: 864-241-2711. www.scd.uscourts.gov

Counties: Cherokee, Chester, Spartanburg, Union, York.

Indexing & Storage: Cases indexed by as well as by case number. New cases available in the index after filing date. Open records are located at the Greenville Division.

Fee & Payment: Payment may be made by money order, cashier check. Business checks are not accepted. Personal checks are not accepted.

Phone Search: No searching by telephone.

Mail Search: A SASE not required.

In Person Search: Permitted.

PACER: PACER is available online at http://pacer.scd.uscourts.gov. Document images available. Case records go back to January 1990. Records never purged. New records are online after 1 day.

Opinions Online: Court opinions are online at www.law.sc.edu/dsc/dsc.htm

U.S. Bankruptcy Court
District of South Carolina

Columbia Division
PO Box 1448, Columbia, SC 29202 (courier address: 1100 Laurel St, Columbia, SC 29201), 803-765-5436. www.scb.uscourts.gov

Counties: All counties in South Carolina.

Indexing & Storage: Cases indexed by debtor as well as by case number. New cases available in the index 1-2 days after filing date. Creditor lists are available through PACER. The bankruptcy information maintained at the U.S. Bankruptcy Court, Columbia Division encompasses all bankruptcy information available for the District of South Carolina.

Fee & Payment: Payment may be made by money order, cashier check, personal check. Debtor's checks are not accepted. Payee: Clerk, U.S. Bankruptcy Court.

Phone Search: Automated voice case information service (VCIS) is available. Call VCIS at 800-669-8767 or 803-765-5211.

In Person Search: Fee charged if court conducts your in person search for you. Copying and searching available for fee via the court's copy service, West Coast Copy, 803-255-0166.

PACER: PACER is available online at http://pacer.scb.uscourts.gov. Document images available. Case records go back to November 1988. Records never purged. New civil records are online after 1 day.

Electronic Filing: Electronic filing information online at https://ecf.scb.uscourts.gov

South Carolina County Courts

Court	Jurisdiction	No. of Courts	How Organized
Circuit Courts*	General	46	16 Circuits
Magistrate Courts*	Limited	182	
Municipal Courts	Municipal	160	
Probate Courts*	Probate	46	
Family Courts	Special	46	16 Circuits

* Profiled in this Sourcebook.

Court	CIVIL								
	Tort	Contract	Real Estate	Min. Claim	Max. Claim	Small Claims	Estate	Eviction	Domestic Relations
Circuit Courts*	X	X	X	$5000	No Max	$7500			
Magistrate Courts	X		X	$0	$7500	$7500		X	
Municipal Courts									
Probate Courts*							X		
Family Courts									X

Court	CRIMINAL				
	Felony	Misdemeanor	DWI/DUI	Preliminary Hearing	Juvenile
Circuit Courts*	X	X	X		
Magistrate Courts*		X	X	X	
Municipal Courts		X	X	X	
Probate Courts*					
Family Courts					X

ADMINISTRATION   Court Administration, 1015 Sumter St, 2nd Floor, Columbia, SC, 29201; 803-734-1800, Fax: 803-734-1355. www.sccourts.org

COURT STRUCTURE   The 46 SC counties are divided among sixteen judicial circuits. The circuit courts are in operation at the county level and consist of a court of general sessions (criminal) and a court of common pleas (civil). A family court is also in operation at the county level. The over 300 Magistrate and Municipal Courts (often referred to as "Summary Courts") only handle misdemeanor cases involving a $500.00 fine and/or 30 days or less jail time.

The maximum civil claim monetary amount for the Magistrate Courts increased from $2,500 to $5,000 as of January 1, 1996. In 2001, this civil limit was raised to $7,500.

ONLINE ACCESS   Appellate and Supreme Court opinions are available from the web site. There is no access to statewide trial court records, but several counties offer online access.

ADDITIONAL INFORMATION   If requesting a record in writing, it is recommended that the words "request that General Session, Common Pleas, and Family Court records be searched" be included in the request.

Most South Carolina courts will not conduct searches. However, if a name and case number are provided, many will pull and copy the record. Search fees vary widely as they are set by each county individually.

Abbeville County

Circuit Court PO Box 99, 103 Court Sq, Rm 102, Abbeville, SC 29620; 864-366-5074; Fax: 864-459-9188. Hours: 8AM-5PM (EST). *Felony, Misdemeanor, Civil Actions Over $7,500.*
Civil Records: Access: In person only. Visitors must perform in person searches for themselves. No search fee. Required to search: name, years to search. Civil cases indexed by defendant, plaintiff. Civil records on card index from 1870.
Criminal Records: Access: In person only. Visitors must perform in person searches for themselves. No search fee. Required to search: name, years to search; also helpful: SSN. Criminal records on card index from 1870.
General Information: No adoption, juvenile, sealed or expunged records released. Copy fee: $.50 per page. Cert fee: $1.00 per page. Payee: Clerk of Court. Personal checks accepted. Prepayment required.

Probate Court PO Box 70, Abbeville, SC 29620; 864-459-4626; Fax: 864-459-4023. Hours: 9AM-5PM (EST). *Probate.*

Aiken County

Circuit Court PO Box 583, Aiken, SC 29802; 803-642-1715. Hours: 8:30AM-5PM (EST). *Felony, Misdemeanor, Civil Actions Over $7,500.*
http:www.aikencountysc.gov
Civil Records: Access: In person only. Both court and visitors may perform in person searches. No search fee. Required to search: name, years to search. Civil cases indexed by defendant, plaintiff. Civil records on computer from 1988; on microfiche, archives and card index from 1800s.
Criminal Records: Access: In person only. Both court and visitors may perform in person searches. Search fee: $10.00 per hour. Required to search: name, years to search, DOB; also helpful: SSN. Criminal records on computer from 1990; on microfiche, archives and card index from 1800s.
General Information: Public Access terminal is available. No adoption, juvenile, sealed or expunged records released. Will not fax results. Copy fee: $.25 per page. Cert fee: $1.00. Payee: Clerk of Court. Only cashiers checks and money orders accepted. Prepayment required.

Aiken Magistrate Court 1680 Richland Ave W, #70, Aiken, SC 29801; 803-642-1744/1747; Fax: 803-642-1749. Hours: 9AM-5PM (EST). *Misdemeanor, Civil Actions Under $7,500, Eviction, Small Claims.*

Graniteville Magistrate Court 50 Canal St, #14, Graniteville, SC 29829; 803-663-6634/6635; Fax: 803-663-6635. Hours: 9AM-5PM (EST). *Civil Actions Under $7,500, Misdemeanor, Eviction, Small Claims.*
Note: Misdemeanor records accessed same as civil.

Langley Magistrate Court PO Box 769, Langley, SC 29834; 803-593-5171/5172; Fax: 803-593-8402. Hours: 9AM-5PM (EST). *Misdemeanor, Civil Actions Under $7,500, Eviction, Small Claims.*

Monetta Magistrate Court 5697 Columbia Hwy N, PO Box 190, Monetta, SC 29105; 803-685-7125; Fax: 803-685-7988. Hours: 8:30-12:30;1:30-4:30 (EST). *Misdemeanor, Civil Actions Under $7,500, Eviction, Small Claims.*

New Ellenton Magistrate Court PO Box 40, New Ellenton, SC 29809; 803-652-3609; Fax: 803-652-2653. Hours: 9-5:00PM (EST). *Misdemeanor, Civil Actions Under $7,500, Eviction, Small Claims.*

North Augusta Magistrate Court PO Box 6493, North Augusta, SC 29861; 803-202-3580/3581; Fax: 803-202-3583. Hours: 9AM-5PM (EST). *Misdemeanor, Civil Actions Under $7,500, Eviction, Small Claims.*

Probate Court PO Box 1576 (109 Park Ave), Aiken, SC 29802; 803-642-2000; Fax: 803-642-2007. Hours: 8:30AM-5PM (EST). *Probate.*

Allendale County

Circuit Court PO Box 126, 611 A W. Mulberry St, Allendale, SC 29810; 803-584-2737; Fax: 803-584-7058. Hours: 9AM-5PM (EST). *Felony, Misdemeanor, Civil Actions Over $7,500.*
Civil Records: Access: Phone, mail, in person. Both court and visitors may perform in person searches. Search fee: $5.00 per name. Required to search: name, years to search. Civil cases indexed by defendant, plaintiff. Civil records on computer 1988, card index from 1919.
Criminal Records: Access: Phone, mail, in person. Both court and visitors may perform in person searches. Search fee: $5.00 per name. Required to search: name, years to search, DOB, signed release; also helpful: SSN. Criminal records kept on computer for 3 years.
General Information: Public Access terminal is available. No adoption, juvenile, sealed or expunged records released. Copy fee: $.50 per page. Cert fee: $2.00. Payee: Clerk of Court. Personal checks accepted. Prepayment required. Mail requests: SASE required. Mail turnaround time 2 days.

Allendale Magistrate Court 160 Law Enforcement Court, Fairfax, SC 29827; 803-584-3755; Fax: 803-584-7980. Hours: 9AM-5PM (EST). *Misdemeanor, Civil Actions Under $7,500, Eviction, Small Claims.*
Note: Now combined with Fairfax Court; address and phone given above.

Fairfax Magistrate Court 160 Law Enforcement Court, PO Box 516, Fairfax, SC 29827; 803-584-3755; Fax: 803-584-7980. Hours: 9-5PM (EST). *Misdemeanor, Civil Actions Under $7,500, Eviction, Small Claims.*

Probate Court PO Box 603, Courthouse Complex, Allendale, SC 29810; 803-584-3157; Fax: 803-584-7053. Hours: 9AM-5PM (EST). *Probate.*

Anderson County

Circuit Court PO Box 8002, Anderson, SC 29622; 864-260-4053; Fax: 864-260-4715. Hours: 8:30AM-5PM (EST). *Felony, Misdemeanor, Civil Actions Over $7,500.*
Civil Records: Access: In person, online. Visitors must perform in person searches for themselves. No search fee. Required to search: name, years to search. Civil cases indexed by defendant, plaintiff. Civil records on computer back to 1994, prior on cards. Access to Cricuit Court records is free at http://acpass.andersoncountysc.org/coc_main.htm. Includes Family Court records. Mail searches available to state agencies only.
Criminal Records: Access: In person, online. Visitors must perform in person searches for themselves. No search fee. Required to search: name, years to search, DOB, SSN, signed release. Criminal records on computer back to 1994, prior on cards. Access to criminal records is the same as civil.
General Information: Public Access terminal is available. No adoption, juvenile, sealed or expunged records released. Copy fee: $.50 per page. No cert fee. Payee: Clerk of Court. Personal checks accepted. Prepayment required.

Anderson Magistrate Court PO Box 8002, Anderson, SC 29622; 864-260-4156/4055; Fax: 864-260-4144. Hours: 8:30AM-5PM (EST). *Misdemeanor, Civil Actions Under $7,500, Eviction, Small Claims.*
www.andersoncountysc.org

Honea Path Magistrate Court PO Box 505, Honea Path, SC 29654; 864-369-0015; Fax: 864-369-0015. Hours: 8:30AM-2PM M, T, TH; 8:30AM-Noon W (EST). *Misdemeanor, Civil Actions Under $7,500, Eviction, Small Claims.*

Iva Magistrate Court, PO Box 118, Iva, SC 29655; 864-348-6192; Fax: 864-348-7562. *Misdemeanor, Civil Actions Under $7,500, Eviction, Small Claims.*
Note: The court holds warrants and criminal actions with sentences of 30 days and/or $500 fine.

Pelzer Magistrate Court PO Box 824, Pelzer, SC 29669; 864-947-5225; Fax: 864-947-5225. Hours: 8AM-5PM (EST). *Civil Actions Under $7,500, Eviction, Small Claims, Misdemeanor.*

Pendleton Magistrate Court 100 E Queen, Pendleton, SC 29670; 864-646-6701; Fax: 864-646-6704. Hours: 8-4pm;T,W; 8-2PM TH (EST). *Misdemeanor, Civil Actions Under $7,500, Eviction, Small Claims.*

Piedmont Magistrate Court PO Box 51312, Piedmont, SC 296; 864-295-2651; Fax: 864-295-5962. Hours: 9AM-5PM (EST). *Misdemeanor, Civil Actions Under $7,500, Eviction, Small Claims.*
Note: Physical address is 104 Annex Way, Easley SC 29642.

Starr Magistrate Court 7626 Hwy 81 S, PO Box 247, Starr, SC 29684; 864-352-3157; Fax: 864-352-3157. *Misdemeanor, Civil Actions Under $7,500, Eviction, Small Claims.*

Williamston Magistrate Court 12 W Main St, PO Box 125, Williamston, SC 29697; 864-847-8580; Fax: 864-847-8580. Hours: 9AM-Noon; 1PM-5PM T, W, TH (EST). *Misdemeanor, Civil Actions Under $7,500, Eviction, Small Claims.*

Probate Court PO Box 8002, Anderson, SC 29622; 864-260-4049; Fax: 864-260-4811. Hours: 8:30AM-5PM (EST). *Probate.*
Note: Access to the county probate court, marriage, estate, and guardian/conservatorship records is available free at http://acpass.andersoncountysc.org/Probate_Main.htm

Bamberg County

Circuit Court PO Box 150, Bamberg, SC 29003; 803-245-3025; Fax: 803-245-3088. Hours: 9AM-5PM (EST). *Felony, Misdemeanor, Civil Actions Over $7,500.*
Civil Records: Access: Mail, in person fax. Both court and visitors may perform in person searches. Search fee: $5.00 per name. Required to search: name, years to search. Civil cases indexed by defendant, plaintiff. Civil records on index books, files back to 1890.
Criminal Records: Access: Mail, in person,fax. Both court and visitors may perform in person searches. Search fee: $5.00 per name. Required to search: name, years to search, DOB; also helpful: SSN. Criminal records on index books, files back to 1890.
General Information: No adoption, juvenile, sealed or expunged records released. Copy fee: $.25 per page. Cert fee: $1.00. Payee: Clerk of Court. Personal checks accepted. Prepayment required. Mail requests: SASE required. Mail turnaround time 1-2 days.

Bamberg Magistrate Court PO Box 187, Bamberg, SC 29003; 803-245-3016; Fax: 803-245-3085. Hours: 9AM-5PM M-F (EST). *Misdemeanor, Civil Actions Under $7,500, Eviction, Small Claims.*

Probate Court PO Box 180, Bamberg, SC 29003; 803-245-3008; Fax: 803-245-3008. Hours: 9AM-5PM (EST). *Probate.*

Barnwell County

Circuit Court PO Box 723, Barnwell, SC 29812; 803-541-1020; Fax: 803-541-1025. Hours: 9AM-5PM (EST). *Felony, Misdemeanor, Civil Actions Over $7,500.*

Note: Records location is; 141 Main St, Barnwell, SC, 29812

Civil Records: Access: In person only. Visitors must perform in person searches for themselves. No search fee. Required to search: name, years to search. Civil cases indexed by defendant. Civil records on computer from 1988.

Criminal Records: Access: In person only. Visitors must perform in person searches for themselves. No search fee. Required to search: name, years to search, DOB, SSN. Criminal records on computer from 1988.

General Information: No adoption, juvenile, sealed or expunged records released. Copy fee: $.50 per page. Cert fee: $1.00. Payee: Clerk of Court. Personal checks accepted. Prepayment required.

Barnwell Magistrate Court PO Box 1205, Barnwell, SC 29812; 803-541-1035; Fax: 83-541-1055. Hours: 9AM-Noon, 1-5PM (EST). *Misdemeanor, Civil Actions Under $7,500, Eviction, Small Claims.*

Blackville Magistrate Court 5997 Lartique St, Blackville, SC 29817; 803-284-2765; Fax: 803-284-9107. Hours: 8AM-5PM M, T, TH, F; 8AM-Noon W (EST). *Misdemeanor, Civil Actions Under $7,500, Eviction, Small Claims.*

Williston Magistrate Court PO Box 485, Williston, SC 29853; 803-266-3700; Fax: 803-266-5496. Hours: 9AM-5PM (EST). *Misdemeanor, Civil Actions Under $7,500, Eviction, Small Claims.*

Probate Court Rm 108, County Courthouse, Barnwell, SC 29812; 803-541-1032; Fax: 803-541-1012. Hours: 9AM-5PM (EST). *Probate.*

Beaufort County

Circuit Court PO Drawer 1128 (128 Ribaut Rd, Rm 208), Beaufort, SC 29901; 843-470-5218; Fax: 843-470-5248. Hours: 8AM-5PM (EST). *Felony, Misdemeanor, Civil Actions Over $7,500.*

www.bcgov.org/Clerk_Court/clerk_court.htm

Civil Records: Access: Mail, in person. Both court and visitors may perform in person searches. Search fee: $10.00 per name. Required to search: name, years to search. Civil cases indexed by defendant, plaintiff. Civil records on computer back to 1985; prior in index books.

Criminal Records: Access: In person only. Both court and visitors may perform in person searches. Search fee: $10.00 per name. Required to search: name, years to search, DOB; also helpful: SSN. Criminal records on computer back to 1985; prior in index books.

General Information: Public Access terminal is available. No adoption, juvenile, sealed or expunged records released. Copy fee: $.25 per page. Cert fee: $1.00. Payee: Clerk of Court. Personal checks accepted. Prepayment required.

Beaufort Magistrate Court PO Box 2207, Beaufort, SC 29901-2207; 843-470-5202 (470-5204); Fax: 843-470-5206. Hours: 8AM-4PM M-TH, 8Am-1200 F

8AM-4PM M-Th. (EST). *Misdemeanor, Civil Actions Under $7,500, Eviction, Small Claims, Traffic.*

Bluffton Magistrate Court PO Box 840, Bluffton, SC 29910; 843-757-1500; Fax: 843-757-1527. Hours: 8AM-5PM (EST). *Misdemeanor, Civil Actions Under $7,500, Eviction, Small Claims.*

Hilton Head Magistrate Court PO Box 22895, Hilton Head, SC 29925; 843-842-4260; Fax: 843-842-4261. *Misdemeanor, Civil Actions Under $7,500, Eviction, Small Claims.*

Lobeco Magistrate Court PO Box 845, Lobeco, SC 29931-0845; 843-846-3902; Fax: 843-846-0823. Hours: 5:30PM-7:30P M, W (EST). *Misdemeanor, Civil Actions Under $7,500, Eviction, Small Claims.*

St Helena Island Magistrate Court PO Box 1271, St Helena Island, SC 29920; 843-838-3212; Fax: 843-838-3212. Hours: 1PM-5PM (EST). *Misdemeanor, Civil Actions Under $7,500, Eviction, Small Claims.*

Probate Court PO Box 1083, Beaufort, SC 29901-1083; 843-470-5319; Fax: 843-470-5324. Hours: 8AM-5PM (EST). *Probate.*

Berkeley County

Circuit Court PO Box 219, Moncks Corner, SC 29461; 843-719-4400. Hours: 9AM-5PM (EST). *Felony, Misdemeanor, Civil Actions Over $7,500.*

Civil Records: Access: In person only. Visitors must perform in person searches for themselves. No search fee. Required to search: name, years to search. Civil cases indexed by defendant, plaintiff. Civil records on computer from early 1980s, prior on books.

Criminal Records: Access: In person only. Visitors must perform in person searches for themselves. No search fee. Required to search: name, years to search, DOB, SSN. Criminal records on computer from early 1980s, prior on books. Court personnel will not perform name searches for criminal record information.

General Information: Public Access terminal is available. No adoption, juvenile, sealed or expunged records released. No cert fee.

Central Summary Court 103 Gulledge St, Moncks Corner, SC 29461; 843-719-4050 or 723-3800 X4050; Fax: 843-719-4534. Hours: 9AM-5PM (EST). *Misdemeanor, Civil Actions Under $7,500, Eviction, Small Claims.*

www.co.berkeley.sc.us

Note: Formerly Moncks Corner Magistrate Court.

Goose Creek Magistrate Court 538 Redbank Rd, Goose Creek, SC 29445; 843-553-7080; Fax: 843-553-7074. Hours: 9AM-5PM (EST). *Misdemeanor, Civil Actions Under $7,500, Eviction, Small Claims.*

Note: The former Summervile Magistrate Court merged with this court. Note there is also a Summerville Magsitrate Court in Dorchester county.

St Stephen Magistrate Court PO Box 1433, St Stephen, SC 29479; 843-567-7400; Fax: 843-567-3102. Hours: 9AM-5PM (EST). *Misdemeanor, Civil Actions Under $7,500, Eviction, Small Claims.*

Probate Court 300 B California Ave, Moncks Corner, SC 29461; 843-719-4519; Fax: 843-719-4527. Hours: 9AM-5PM (EST). *Probate.*

Calhoun County

Circuit Court PO Box 709, St Matthews, SC 29135-0709; 803-874-3524; Fax: 803-874-1942. Hours: 9AM-5PM (EST). *Felony, Misdemeanor, Civil Actions Over $7,500.*

Civil Records: Access: In person only. Visitors must perform in person searches for themselves. No search fee. Required to search: name, years to search. Civil cases indexed by defendant, plaintiff. Civil records on computer from 1982, prior on index books from 1908.

Criminal Records: Access: In person only. Both court and visitors may perform in person searches. No search fee. Required to search: name, years to search, DOB. Criminal records on computer from 1982, prior on index books from 1908.

General Information: Public Access terminal is available. No adoption, juvenile, sealed or expunged records released. Copy fee: $.25 per page. No cert fee. Payee: Clerk of Court. Personal checks accepted. Prepayment required.

Cameron Magistrate Court Cameron Town Hall, PO Box 663, Cameron, SC 29030; 803-823-2266; Fax: 803-823-2288. Hours: 1PM-5PM T, TH (EST). *Misdemeanor, Civil Actions Under $7,500, Eviction, Small Claims.*

Note: This court is also a Municipal Court.

Cameron/Lone Starr Magistrate Court PO Box 663, Cameron, SC 29030; 803-823-2266. Hours: 1-5PM T & TH (EST). *Misdemeanor, Civil Actions Under $7,500, Eviction, Small Claims.*

St Matthews Magistrate Court 1623 Bridge St W, PO Box 191, St Matthews, SC 29135; 803-874-1112; Fax: 803-874-1111. Hours: 9AM-5PM (EST). *Misdemeanor, Civil Actions Under $7,500, Eviction, Small Claims.*

Probate Court 902 Huff Dr., St Matthews, SC 29135; 803-874-3514; Fax: 803-874-1942. Hours: 9AM-5PM (EST). *Probate.*

Charleston County

Circuit Court 100 Broad St, #106, Charleston, SC 29401-2210; 843-958-5000; Fax: 843-958-5020. Hours: 8:30AM-5PM (EST). *Felony, Misdemeanor, Civil Actions Over $7,500.*

http://www3.charlestoncounty.org

Civil Records: Access: Online, in person. Visitors must perform in person searches for themselves. No search fee. Required to search: name, years to search. Civil cases indexed by defendant, plaintiff. Civil records on computer from 1988, microfiche and archives from mid 1853. Access to civil records (1988 forward), judgments and lis pendens are free online at www3.charlestoncounty.org/connect. Online document images go back to 1/1/1999.

Criminal Records: Access: Mail, online, in person. Both court and visitors may perform in person searches. Search fee: $10.00 per name. Required to search: name, years to search, DOB; also helpful: SSN. Criminal records on computer from 4/92, prior on books and microfilm from 1918. The Internet offers access to criminal records from 04/92 forward. Search by name or case number. There is no fee.

General Information: Public Access terminal is available. No adoption, juvenile, sealed or expunged records released. No fee to fax results. Copy fee: $.25 per page. Cert fee: $1.00. Payee: Clerk of Court. Business checks accepted. Prepayment required. Mail requests: SASE required. Mail turnaround time 3 days.

Charleston Magistrate Court 4045 Bridgeview Dr, PO Box 60037, Charleston, SC 29419; 843-202-6600; Criminal phone: 843-554-2462; Fax: 843-202-6620. Hours: 8:30AM-4:30PM (EST). *Civil Actions Under $7,500, Misdemeanor, Eviction, Small Claims.*

www.charlestoncounty.org

Note: County magistrate requests for background checks are forwarded to the Sheriff's Office (843-202-6610).

Civil Records: Access: In person, online. Search fee: $17.50. Civil records from 1998 forward can be access via www3.charlestoncounty.org/connect?ref=Magistrates.

Criminal Records: Access: In person,online. No search fee. Criminal and traffic records from 1993 forward can be searched free at www3.charlestoncounty.org/connect?ref=Magistrates. Requests for background checks are forwarded to the Sheriff's Office, except for military personnel.

General information: Payee: County Treasurer. Prepayment required.

Charleston Magistrate Court 995 Morrison Dr, PO Box 941, Charleston, SC 29402; 843-724-6719; Fax: 843-745-6785. Hours: 8:30-5PM M-TH.; 8AM-1PM F (EST). *Misdemeanor, Civil Actions Under $7,500, Eviction.*

Note: County magistrate courts records from 1998 forward can be searched free at www3.charlestoncounty.org/connect?ref=Magistrates.

Charleston Magistrate Court 995 Morrison Dr, PO Box 941, Charleston, SC 29402; 843-724-6720; Fax: 843-724-6785. Hours: 8:00AM-5PM M-TH; 8:30AM-1PM F (EST). *Small Claims.*

Note: County magistrate courts records from 1998 forward can be searched free at www3.charlestoncounty.org/connect?ref=Magistrates.

East Cooper Magistrate Court 1189 Iron Bridge Rd, #300, PO Box 584, Mt Pleasant, SC 29466; 843-856-1205; Fax: 843-856-1188. Hours: 8AM-5PM (EST). *Misdemeanor, Civil Actions Under $7,500, Eviction.*

http://www3.charlestoncounty.org/docs/CoC/index.html

Note: County magistrate courts records from 1998 forward can be searched free at www3.charlestoncounty.org/connect?ref=Magistrates.

Edisto Island Magistrate Court 8070 Indigo Hill Rd, PO Box 216, Edisto Island, SC 29438; 843-869-2909; Fax: 843-869-4460. Hours: 4:00PM-6PM M, W (EST). *Misdemeanor, Civil Actions Under $7,500, Eviction, Traffic.*

Note: County magistrate courts records from 1998 forward can be searched free at www3.charlestoncounty.org/connect?ref=Magistrates.

James Island Magistrate Court PO Box 12226, James Island, SC 29422; 843-795-1140; Fax: 843-406-2753. Hours: 8:30AM-5PM M-TH.; 8AM-Noon F (EST). *Misdemeanor, Civil Actions Under $7,500, Eviction, Small Claims.*

Note: County magistrate courts records from 1998 forward can be searched free at www3.charlestoncounty.org/connect?ref=Magistrates.

Johns Island Magistrate Court 1521 Main Rd, Johns Island, SC 29455; 843-559-1218; Fax: 843-559-2378. Hours: 8:30AM-5PM T, TH; 9AM-7PM M, W, F (EST). *Misdemeanor, Civil Actions Under $7,500, Eviction, Small Claims.*

Note: County magistrate courts records from 1998 forward can be searched free at www3.charlestoncounty.org/connect?ref=Magistrates.

McClellanville Magistrate Court 9888 Randall Rd, PO Box 7, McClellanville, SC 29458; 843-887-3334; Fax: 843-887-3901. Hours: 9AM-Noon, 1-4PM M-TH (EST). *Misdemeanor, Civil Actions Under $7,500, Eviction, Small Claims.*

Note: County magistrate courts records from 1998 forward can be searched free at www3.charlestoncounty.org/connect?ref=Magistrates.

North Charleston Magistrate Court 7272 Cross County Rd, North Charleston, SC 29419; 843-767-2743; Fax: 843-760-6887. Hours: 8:30AM-4:30PM (EST). *Misdemeanor, Civil Actions Under $7,500, Eviction, Small Claims.*

Note: County magistrate courts records from 1998 forward can be searched free at www3.charlestoncounty.org/connect?ref=Magistrates.

North Charleston Magistrate Court 2036 Cherokee St, PO Box 71316, North Charleston, SC 29416; 843-745-2215; Fax: 843-745-2334. Hours: 8AM-4:30PM (EST). *Misdemeanor, Civil Actions Under $7,500, Eviction, Small Claims.*

Note: County magistrate courts records from 1998 forward can be searched free at www3.charlestoncounty.org/connect?ref=Magistrates.

North Charleston Magistrate Court 4045 Bridge View Dr, #B146, PO Box 70235, North Charleston, SC 29405; 843-202-6650; Fax: 843-202-6652. Hours: 8:30AM-4:30PM (EST). *Misdemeanor, Civil Actions Under $7,500, Small Claims.*

Note: County magistrate courts records from 1998 forward can be searched free at www3.charlestoncounty.org/connect?ref=Magistrates.

Ravenel Magistrate Court 5962 Hwy 165, #200, Ravenel, SC 29470; 843-889-8332; Fax: 843-889-9202. Hours: 8:30AM-4:30PM (EST). *Misdemeanor, Civil Actions Under $7,500, Eviction, Small Claims.*

Note: County magistrate courts records from 1998 forward can be searched free at www3.charlestoncounty.org/connect?ref=Magistrates.

West Ashley Magistrate Court 1720 Sam Rittenberg Blvd, Unit 11, PO Box 31861, Charleston, SC 29417; 843-766-6531; Fax: 843-571-4751. Hours: 8:30AM-4:30 PM M-TH.; 8AM-1PM F (EST). *Civil Actions Under $7,500, Eviction.*

www.charlestoncounty.org

Note: County magistrate courts records from 1998 forward can be searched free at www3.charlestoncounty.org/connect?ref=Magistrates.

Probate Court 84 Broad St., North Charleston, SC 29401-2284; 843-958-5030; Fax: 843-958-5044. Hours: 8:30AM-5PM (EST). *Probate.*

Note: Access to Estate and Wills records is available free at http://www3.charlestoncounty.org/connect/LU_GROUP_2?ref=Conserv.

Cherokee County

Circuit Court PO Drawer 2289, Gaffney, SC 29342; 864-487-2571; Civil phone: 864-487-2533; Probate phone: 864-487-2588; Fax: 864-487-2754. Hours: 8:30AM-5PM (EST). *Felony, Misdemeanor, Civil Actions Over $7,500.*

Civil Records: Access: In person only. Visitors must perform in person searches for themselves. No search fee. Required to search: name, years to search. Civil cases indexed by defendant, plaintiff. Civil records go back to 1897; computerized records go back to 1994.

Criminal Records: Access: In person only. Visitors must perform in person searches for themselves. No search fee. Required to search: name, years to search.

Criminal records on computer from 1994, prior on books.

General Information: Public Access terminal is available. No adoption, juvenile, sealed or expunged records released. Copy fee: $.50 per page. Cert fee: $1.00. Payee: Clerk of Court. Business checks accepted. Prepayment required.

Blacksburg Magistrate Court 101 S Shelby St, PO Box 427, Blacksburg, SC 29702; 864-839-2492; Fax: 864-839-3415. Hours: 8:30AM-5PM (EST). *Misdemeanor, Civil Actions Under $7,500, Eviction, Small Claims.*

Cherokee County Magistrate Court 312 E Frederick St, PO Box 336, Gaffney, SC 29342-0336; 864-487-2533/2501; Fax: 864-902-8425. Hours: 8:30AM-5PM (EST). *Misdemeanors, Civil Actions Under $7,500, Eviction, Small Claims.*

www.cherokeemagistrate.com

Note: Civil Action minimum was increased to $7,500 on January 1, 2001.

Probate Court 1434 N Limestone St, Peachtree Ctr, Gaffney, SC 29340; 864-487-2583; Fax: 864-902-8426. Hours: 9AM-4:30PM (EST). *Probate.*

Chester County

Circuit Court PO Drawer 580, Chester, SC 29706; 803-385-2605; Fax: 803-581-7975. Hours: 8:30AM-5PM (EST). *Felony, Misdemeanor, Civil Actions Over $7,500.*

Civil Records: Access: In person. Visitors must perform in person searches for themselves. No search fee. Required to search: name, years to search, address. Civil cases indexed by defendant, plaintiff. Civil records on computer from 1989, microfiche from 1927.

Criminal Records: Access: In person. Visitors must perform in person searches for themselves. No search fee. Required to search: name, years to search, DOB, signed release; also helpful: SSN. Criminal records on computer from 1994, docket books prior.

General Information: Public Access terminal is available. (Public access for civil only.) No adoption, juvenile, sealed or expunged records released. Copy fee: $.50 per page. Cert fee: $1.00. Payee: Clerk of Court. Personal checks accepted. Prepayment required.

Chester Magistrate Court 2740 Dawson Dr, PO Box 727, Chester, SC 29706; 803-581-5136; 581-3040; Fax: 803-581-3033. Hours: 9AM-5PM (EST). *Misdemeanor, Civil Actions Under $7,500, Eviction, Small Claims.*

Probate Court PO Drawer 580, Chester, SC 29706; 803-385-2604; Fax: 803-581-5180. Hours: 8:30AM-5PM (EST). *Probate.*

Note: Records go back to late 1780s.

Chesterfield County

Circuit Court PO Box 529, Chesterfield, SC 29709; 843-623-2574; Probate phone: 843-623-2376; Fax: 843-623-6944. Hours: 8:30AM-5PM (EST). *Felony, Misdemeanor, Civil Actions Over $7,500.*

Civil Records: Access: Mail, in person. Both court and visitors may perform in person searches. Search fee: $5.00 per name. Required to search: name, years to search. Civil cases indexed by defendant, plaintiff. Civil records on computer back to 1986, prior on docket books.

Criminal Records: Access: Mail, in person. Both court and visitors may perform in person searches. Search fee: $5.00 per name. Required to search: name, years to search, DOB, SSN. Criminal records on computer back to 1986, prior on docket books.

General Information: No adoption, juvenile, sealed or expunged records released. Will fax results free to toll-free number; $5.00 fee if to non-toll-free number. Copy fee: $2.00 per document and $.25 per page after 1st 4 pages. No cert fee. Payee: Clerk of Court. Personal checks accepted. Prepayment required. Mail requests: SASE required. Mail turnaround time 3 days.

Cheraw Magistrate Court 563 Hwy 52 N, PO Box 364, Cheraw, SC 29520; 843-537-3323; Fax: 843-537-3883. Hours: 6AM-6PM (EST). *Misdemeanor, Civil Actions Under $7,500, Eviction, Small Claims.*

Cheraw Magistrate Court 1486 Hinson Hill Rd, Cheraw, SC 29520; 843-623-2955; Fax: 843-623-2955. Hours: 11AM-5PM M,T,W; 12-3PM Thur. (EST). *Misdemeanor, Civil Actions Under $7,500, Eviction, Small Claims.*

Cheraw Magistrate Court 639 CC Chapman Rd, Cheraw, SC 29520; 843-537-8411,843-537-7139; Fax: 843-537-8404. Hours: 8:30AM-5PM (EST). *Misdemeanor, Civil Actions Under $7,500, Eviction, Small Claims.*

Chesterfield Magistrate Court 1515 E Jackson Rd, Chesterfield, SC 29709; 843-623-7929; Fax: 843-623-7929. Hours: 9AM-4PM,M-TH (EST). *Misdemeanor, Civil Actions Under $7,500, Eviction, Small Claims.*

McBee Magistrate Court Box 576, McBee, SC 29101; 843-335-6464. *Misdemeanor, Civil Actions Under $7,500, Eviction, Small Claims.*

Pageland Magistrate Court 310 W McGregor St, PO Box 133, Pageland, SC 29728; 843-672-5685. Hours: 10AM-3PM (EST). *Misdemeanor, Civil Actions Under $7,500, Eviction, Small Claims.*

Patrick Magistrate Court 10292 Hwy 102, Patrick, SC 29584; 843-498-6398. Hours: 1PM-5PM M-TH (EST). *Misdemeanor, Civil Actions Under $7,500, Eviction, Small Claims.*

Ruby Magistrate Court 408 Deaton St, PO Box 131, Ruby, SC 29741; 843-634-6597. Hours: 10AM-3PM M,T,TH,F (EST). *Misdemeanor, Civil Actions Under $7,500, Eviction, Small Claims.*

Probate Court County Courthouse, 200 W Main St, Chesterfield, SC 29709; 843-623-2376; Fax: 843-623-9886. Hours: 8:30AM-5PM (EST). *Probate.*

Clarendon County

Circuit Court PO Box 136, Manning, SC 29102; 803-435-4444; Civil phone: 803-435-4443; Criminal phone: 803-435-4210x309. Hours: 8:30AM-5PM (EST). *Felony, Misdemeanor, Civil Actions Over $7,500.*
Civil Records: Access: Mail, in person. Both court and visitors may perform in person searches. Search fee: $27.00. Includes all copy fees. Required to search: name, years to search. Civil cases indexed by defendant, plaintiff. Civil records on computer from 1988, index books from 1865.
Criminal Records: Access: Mail, in person. Both court and visitors may perform in person searches. Search fee: $27.50. Includes copy fees. Required to search: name, years to search. Criminal records on computer from 1983, index books from 1865.
General Information: Public Access terminal is available. No adoption, juvenile, sealed or expunged records released. Copy fee: $.25 per page. Cert fee: $2.00. Payee: Clerk of Court. Personal checks accepted. Prepayment required. Mail requests: SASE required. Mail turnaround time 5 days.

Manning Magistrate Court 10 Keitt St, PO Box 371, Manning, SC 29102; 803-435-2670/8925; Fax: 803-435-0885. Hours: 8:30AM-5PM (EST). *Misdemeanor, Civil Actions Under $7,500, Eviction, Small Claims.*

Summerton Magistrate Court 216 Main St, PO Box 386, Summerton, SC 29148; 803-485-8228. Hours: 9AM-Noon T, W, TH (EST). *Misdemeanor, Civil Actions Under $7,500, Eviction, Small Claims.*

Probate Court PO Box 307, Manning, SC 29102; 803-435-8774; Fax: 803-435-8698. Hours: 8:30AM-5PM (EST). *Probate.*

Colleton County

Circuit Court PO Box 620, Walterboro, SC 29488; 843-549-5791; Fax: 843-549-2875. Hours: 8:00AM-5PM (EST). *Felony, Misdemeanor, Civil Actions Over $7,500.*
www.colletoncounty.org/legalcourt/index.html
Civil Records: Access: Phone, fax, mail, in person. Both court and visitors may perform in person searches. Search fee: $10.00 per name. Required to search: name, years to search. Civil cases indexed by defendant, plaintiff. Civil records on computer from 1986, on index books from 1865.
Criminal Records: Access: Phone, fax, mail, in person. Both court and visitors may perform in person searches. Search fee: $10.00 per name. Required to search: name, years to search; also helpful: SSN, DOB. Criminal records on computer from 1986, on index books from 1865.
General Information: No adoption, juvenile, PTI, sealed or expunged records released. Extra $2.00 fee to receive and fax results. Copy fee: $.50 per page. Cert fee: $1.00. Payee: Clerk of Court. Business checks accepted. Prepayment required. Mail requests: SASE required. Mail turnaround time 2 days.

Green Pond Magistrate Court 8464 Ace Basin Pky, Green Pond, SC 29446; 843-844-8486; Fax: 843-844-8835. Hours: 9AM-4:30PM (EST). *Misdemeanor, Civil Actions Under $7,500, Eviction, Small Claims.*

Walterboro Magistrate Court 40-B Klein St, PO Box 1732, Walterboro, SC 29488; 843-549-1122; Fax: 843-549-9010. Hours: 8AM-5PM (EST). *Misdemeanor, Civil Actions Under $7,500, Eviction, Small Claims.*

Walterboro Magistrate Court 149 Magistrate Ln, Walterboro, SC 29488; 843-538-3637/3903; Fax: 843-538-5173. Hours: 8AM-5PM (EST). *Misdemeanor, Civil Actions Under $7,500, Eviction, Small Claims.*

Probate Court PO Box 1036, Walterboro, SC 29488-0031; 843-549-7216; Fax: 843-549-5571. Hours: 8:00AM-5PM (EST). *Probate.*

Darlington County

Circuit Court PO Box 1177, Darlington, SC 29540; 843-398-4339; Fax: 843-398-4172. Hours: 8:30AM-5PM (EST). *Felony, Misdemeanor, Civil Actions Over $7,500.*
Civil Records: Access: In person, mail, fax. Visitors must perform in person searches for themselves. No search fee. Required to search: name, years to search. Civil cases indexed by defendant, plaintiff. Civil records on computer from 1989, on index books from 1805.
Criminal Records: Access: In person, mail, fax. Visitors must perform in person searches for themselves. No search fee. Required to search: name, years to search; also helpful: DOB, SSN. Criminal records on computer from 1989, on index books from

1805. Will give disposition & sentence over phone if case number given.
General Information: No adoption, juvenile, sealed or expunged records released. Will fax results to local or toll free line. Copy fee: $.10 per page. No cert fee. Payee: Clerk of Court. Business checks accepted. Prepayment required.

Darlington Magistrate Court PO Box 782 (115 Camp Rd), Darlington, SC 29540; 843-398-4340; Fax: 843-398-4458. Hours: 8:30AM-5PM (EST). *Misdemeanor, Civil Actions Under $7,500, Eviction, Small Claims.*

Hartsville Magistrate Court 404 S 4th St, PO Box 1765, Hartsville, SC 29550; 843-332-9661; Fax: 843-332-7212. Hours: 8:30AM-5PM (EST). *Misdemeanor, Civil Actions Under $7,500, Eviction, Small Claims.*

Lamar Magistrate Court 103 Warren Ave, PO Box 38, Lamar, SC 29069; 843-326-5441; Fax: 843-326-1543. Hours: 8AM-6PM T, W, TH (EST). *Misdemeanor, Civil Actions Under $7,500, Eviction, Small Claims.*

Probate Court #1 Public Sq – Courthouse, Rm 208, Darlington, SC 29532; 843-398-4310; Fax: 843-398-4076. Hours: 8:30AM-5PM (EST). *Probate.*

Dillon County

Circuit Court PO Drawer 1220, Dillon, SC 29536; 843-774-1425. Hours: 8:30AM-5PM (EST). *Felony, Misdemeanor, Civil Actions Over $7,500.*
Civil Records: Access: Mail, in person. Both court and visitors may perform in person searches. Search fee: $10.00 per name. Required to search: name, years to search. Civil cases indexed by defendant, plaintiff. Civil records on computer from 1990, on docket books prior.
Criminal Records: Access: Mail, in person. Both court and visitors may perform in person searches. Search fee: $10.00 per name. Required to search: name, years to search; also helpful: DOB, SSN. Criminal records on computer from 1990, on docket books prior.
General Information: No adoption, juvenile, sealed or expunged records released. Will fax results to local or toll free line. Copy fee: $.50 per page. No cert fee. Payee: Clerk of Court. Personal checks accepted. Prepayment required. Mail requests: SASE required. Mail turnaround time 1 day.

Dillon Magistrate Court 200 S 5th Ave, PO Box 1016, Dillon, SC 29536; 843-774-1407; Fax: 843-774-1453. Hours: 8:30AM-5PM (EST). *Misdemeanor, Civil Actions Under $7,500, Eviction, Small Claims.*

Dillon Magistrate Court 200 S 5th Ave, PO Box 1016, Dillon, SC 29536; 843-774-1406. Hours: 8:30AM-5PM (EST). *Misdemeanor, Civil Actions Under $7,500, Eviction, Small Claims.*

Lake View Magistrate Court PO Box 824, Lake View, SC 29563; 843-759-2861; Fax: 843-759-0177. *Misdemeanor, Civil Actions Under $7,500, Eviction, Small Claims.*

Probate Court PO Box 189, Dillon, SC 29536; 843-774-1423; Fax: 843-841-3732. Hours: 8:30AM-5PM (EST). *Probate.*

Dorchester County

Circuit Court 101 Ridge St, St George, SC 29477; 843-563-0160; Civil phone: 843-563-0113; Criminal phone: 843-563-; Fax: 843-563-0178. Hours: 8:30AM-5PM (EST). *Felony, Misdemeanor, Civil Actions Over $7,500.*

Civil Records: Access: In person only. Visitors must perform in person searches for themselves. No search fee. Required to search: name, years to search. Civil cases indexed by defendant, plaintiff. Civil records on index books back to 1950s, on computer since 1994.

Criminal Records: Access: In person only. Visitors must perform in person searches for themselves. No search fee. Required to search: name, years to search, DOB, signed release; also helpful: SSN. Criminal records on index books back to 1950s, on computer since 1994.

General Information: No adoption, juvenile, sealed or expunged records released. Copy fee: $.50 per page. No cert fee. Payee: Clerk of Court. Personal checks accepted. Prepayment required.

Dorchester County Court 101 Ridge St, St George, SC 29477; Civil phone: 843-563-0164; Criminal phone: 843-563-0130; Fax: 843-563-0123. Hours: 8AM-5PM (EST). *Civil Actions Under $7,500, Eviction, Small Claims.*

Civil Records: Access: Mail. No search fee.

General Information: Public Access terminal is available. Turnaround time 5-7 days.

St George Magistrate Court 101 Ridge St, St George, SC 29477; 843-832-0130; Fax: 843-563-0123. Hours: 8:30AM-5PM (EST). *Misdemeanor, Civil Actions Under $7,500, Eviction, Small Claims.*

Summerville Magistrate Court 212 Deming Way, Box 10, Summerville, SC 29483; 843-832-0370; Fax: 843-832-0371. Hours: 8:30AM-5PM (EST). *Misdemeanor, Civil Actions Under $7,500, Eviction, Small Claims.*

Probate Court 101 Ridge St, County Courthouse, St George, SC 29477; 843-563-0105; Fax: 843-563-0245. Hours: 8:30AM-5PM (EST). *Probate.*

Edgefield County

Circuit Court PO Box 34, Edgefield, SC 29824; 803-637-4082; Fax: 803-637-4117. Hours: 8:30AM-5PM (EST). *Felony, Misdemeanor, Civil Actions Over $7,500.*

Civil Records: Access: Mail, in person. Both court and visitors may perform in person searches. Search fee: $5.00 per name. Required to search: name, years to search. Civil cases indexed by defendant, plaintiff. Civil records archived from 1839; on computer back to 1987.

Criminal Records: Access: Mail, in person. Both court and visitors may perform in person searches. Search fee: $5.00 per name. Required to search: name, years to search, DOB; also helpful: SSN. Criminal records archived from 1839; on computer back to 1987.

General Information: Public Access terminal is available. No adoption, juvenile, sealed or expunged records released. Copy fee: $.50 per page. Cert fee: $1.00. Payee: Clerk of Court. Business checks accepted. Prepayment required. Mail requests: SASE required. Mail turnaround time 1 day.

Edgefield Magistrate Court 129 Courthouse Sq, #212, PO Box 664, Edgefield, SC 29824; 803-637-4090; Fax: 803-637-4101. Hours: 8:30AM-4:30PM (EST). *Misdemeanor, Civil Actions Under $7,500, Eviction, Small Claims.*

Probate Court 124 Courthouse Sq, Edgefield, SC 29824; 803-637-4076; Fax: 803-637-7157. Hours: 8:30AM-5PM (EST). *Probate.*

Fairfield County

Circuit Court PO Drawer 299, Winnsboro, SC 29180; 803-712-6526. Hours: 9AM-5PM (EST). *Felony, Misdemeanor, Civil Actions Over $7,500.*

Civil Records: Access: In person only. Visitors must perform in person searches for themselves. No search fee. Required to search: name, years to search. Civil cases indexed by defendant, plaintiff. Civil records on docket books. The court provides an index, but will not do record searching.

Criminal Records: Access: In person only. Visitors must perform in person searches for themselves. No search fee. Required to search: name, years to search, DOB; also helpful: SSN. Criminal records on docket books.

General Information: No adoption, juvenile, sealed or expunged records released. Copy fee: $.25 per page. Cert fee: $1.00. Payee: Clerk of Court. No personal checks accepted. Prepayment required.

Winnsboro Magistrate Court 115-B S Congress St, Winnsboro, SC 29180; 803-635-4525; Fax: 803-635-5717. Hours: 9AM-5PM (EST). *Misdemeanor, Civil Actions Under $7,500, Eviction, Small Claims.*

Probate Court PO Box 385, Winnsboro, SC 29180; 803-712-6519; Fax: 803-712-6939. Hours: 9AM-5PM (EST). *Probate.*

Florence County

Circuit Court Drawer E, City County Complex (180 N Irby St), Florence, SC 29501; 843-665-3031. Hours: 8:30AM-5PM (EST). *Felony, Misdemeanor, Civil Actions Over $7,500.*
www.florenceco.org/index.html

Civil Records: Access: Mail, in person, online. Both court and visitors may perform in person searches. Search fee: $5.00 per name. Required to search: name, years to search. Civil cases indexed by defendant, plaintiff. Civil records on computer from 1984, on microfiche and docket books from 1900s. Search liens, deeds, recorded documents from 1994 at http://web.florenceco.org/cgi-bin/coc/coc.cgi. Can search by name or business name.

Criminal Records: Access: Online, in person. Visitors must perform in person searches for themselves. No search fee. Required to search: name, years to search, DOB; also helpful: SSN. Criminal records on computer from 1984, on microfiche and docket books from 1898. Criminal record from 1995 forward are at http://web.florenceco.org/cgi-bin/warrants/war.cgi.

General Information: Public Access terminal is available. No adoption, juvenile, sealed or expunged records released. Copy fee: $.50. Cert fee: $1.00. Payee: Clerk of Court. Personal checks accepted. Prepayment required. Mail requests: SASE required. Mail turnaround time 10-14 days.

Florence Magistrate Court 180 N Irby St (MSC-W), Florence, SC 29501; 843-665-0031; Fax: 843-661-7800. Hours: 8:30AM-4:00PM M-TH; 8:30AM-4:30PM F (EST). *Misdemeanor, Civil Actions Under $7,500, Eviction, Small Claims.*

Johnsonville Magistrate Court 117 W Broadway, Johnsonville, SC 29555; 843-380-9211. Hours: 8:30AM-5PM M,T,W (EST). *Misdemeanor, Civil Actions Under $7,500, Eviction, Small Claims.*
www.florenceco.org

Lake City Magistrate Court PO Box 39, Lake City, SC 29560; 843-394-5461; Fax: 843-394-3865. Hours: 8:30AM-5PM (EST). *Misdemeanor, Civil Actions Under $7,500, Eviction, Small Claims.*

Olanta Magistrate Court PO Box 362, Olanta, SC 29114; 843-396-9056. Hours: 8:30AM-5PM (EST). *Misdemeanor, Civil Actions Under $7,500, Eviction, Small Claims.*

Pamplico Magistrate Court 124 3rd Ave E, PO Box 367, Pamplico, SC 29583; 843-493-0072;

Fax: 843-493-5391. Hours: 8:30AM-4:30PM T, W, TH; 8:30AM-2:30PM M (EST). *Civil Actions Under $7,500, Misdemeanor, Eviction, Small Claims, Traffic.*

Timmonsville Magistrate Court 307 Smith St, PO Box 190, Timmonsville, SC 29161; 843-346-7472; Fax: 843-346-0660. Hours: 8:30-5PM (EST). *Misdemeanor, Civil Actions Under $7,500, Eviction, Small Claims.*

Probate Court 180 N Irby, MSC-L, Florence, SC 29501; 843-665-3085; Fax: 843-665-3068. Hours: 8:30AM-5PM (EST). *Probate.*

Georgetown County

Circuit Court PO Box 421270, Georgetown, SC 29442; 843-546-3215; Civil phone: 843-545-3041; Criminal phone: 843-545-3053; Fax: 843-546-3281. Hours: 8:30AM-5PM (EST). *Felony, Misdemeanor, Civil Actions Over $7,500.*

Civil Records: Access: In person only. Visitors must perform in person searches for themselves. No search fee. Required to search: name, years to search. Civil cases indexed by defendant, plaintiff. Civil records on index from 1926.

Criminal Records: Access: In person only. Visitors must perform in person searches for themselves. No search fee. Required to search: name, years to search, DOB; also helpful: SSN. Criminal records on index from 1926, computerized since 2001.

General Information: Public Access terminal is available. No adoption, juvenile, sealed or expunged records released. Copy fee: $.50 per page. Cert fee: $1.00 per page. Payee: Clerk of Court. Business checks accepted. Prepayment required.

Andrews Magistrate Court 110 N Morgan Ave, Andrews, SC 29510; 843-264-8811; Fax: 843-264-5177. Hours: 8:30AM-4:30PM (EST). *Misdemeanor, Civil Actions Under $7,500, Eviction, Small Claims.*

Georgetown Magistrate Court 333 Cleveland St, PO Box 807, Georgetown, SC 29442; 843-545-3381; Fax: 843-545-3394. Hours: 8:30AM-5PM (EST). *Misdemeanor, Civil Actions Under $7,500, Eviction, Small Claims.*

Georgetown Magistrate Court 1277 N Frasier St, PO Box 1838, Georgetown, SC 29442; 843-545-8140; Fax: 843-545-8142. *Traffic Only.* Note: This court now handles only traffic offenses.

Murrells Inlet Magistrate Court 4450 Murrells Inlet Rd, PO Box 859, Murrells Inlet, SC 29576; 843-651-6292; Fax: 843-651-6685. Hours: 8AM-4:30PM (EST). *Misdemeanor, Civil Actions Under $7,500, Eviction, Small Claims.*

Pawleys Island Magistrate Court 291 Parkersville Rd, PO Box 1830, Pawleys Island, SC 29585; 843-237-8995; Fax: 843-237-3244. Hours: 8AM-4:30PM (EST). *Misdemeanor, Civil Actions Under $7,500, Eviction, Small Claims.*

Plesant Hill Magistrate Court 9174 Pleasant Hill Dr, Hemingway, SC 29554; 843-558-9711; Fax: 843-558-5827. Hours: 8:30AM-1200,1PM-4:30 (EST). *Misdemeanor, Civil Actions Under $7,500, Eviction, Small Claims.*

Probate Court PO Box 421270, Georgetown, SC 29442; 843-545-3274; Fax: 843-545-3292. Hours: 8:30AM-5PM (EST). *Probate.*

Greenville County

Circuit Court 305 E North St, Rm 227, Greenville, SC 29601; 864-467-8551; Fax: 864-467-8513. Hours: 8:30AM-5PM (EST). *Felony, Misdemeanor, Civil Actions Over $7,500.*

www.greenvillecounty.org

Civil Records: Access: In person only. Visitors must perform in person searches for themselves. No search fee. Required to search: name, years to search. Civil cases indexed by defendant, plaintiff. Civil records on computer from 1985, on docket books from 1900s.

Criminal Records: Access: In person only. Visitors must perform in person searches for themselves. No search fee. Required to search: name, years to search, DOB, SSN, signed release. Criminal records on computer from 1985, on docket books from 1900s.

General Information: Public Access terminal is available. No adoption, juvenile, sealed or expunged records released. Copy fee: $.25 per page. Cert fee: $1.00. Payee: Clerk of Court. Only cashiers checks and money orders accepted. Prepayment required.

Gantt Magistrate Court 1103 White Horse Rd, Greenville, SC 29605; Civil phone: 864-277-0856; Criminal phone: 864-277-4429; Fax: 864-277-4376. Hours: 8:30AM-5PM (EST). *Misdemeanor, Civil Actions Under $7,500, Eviction, Small Claims.* www.greenvillecounty.org/Magistrate_Courts

Greenville Magistrate Courts #1 & #2 4 McGhee St, LEC Rm 116A, Greenville, SC 29601; 864-467-5312 (City #1), 864-467-5302 (City #2); Fax: 864-467-5105. Hours: 8:30AM-5PM (EST). *Misdemeanor, Civil Actions Under $7,500, Eviction, Small Claims.* www.greenvillecounty.org/Magistrate_Courts

Piedmont Magistrate Court 8150 Augusta Rd, Piedmont, SC 29673; 864-277-9555; Fax: 864-277-8345. Hours: 8:30AM-5PM (EST). *Misdemeanor, Civil Actions Under $7,500, Eviction, Small Claims.* www.greenvillecounty.org/Magistrate_Courts

Simpsonville Magistrate Court 3725 Grandview Dr, #5, Simpsonville, SC 296180; 864-963-3457; Fax: 864-963-0029. Hours: 8:30AM-5:00PM (EST). *Misdemeanor, Civil Actions Under $7,500, Eviction, Small Claims.* www.greenvillecounty.org/Magistrate_Courts

Taylors Magistrate Court 2801 Wade Hampton Blvd, Taylors, SC 29687; 864-244-2922; Fax: 864-268-1333. Hours: 8:30AM-5PM (EST). *Misdemeanor, Civil Actions Under $7,500, Eviction, Small Claims.* www.greenvillecounty.org/Magistrate_Courts

Travelers Rest Magistrate Court 114 N Poinsett Hwy, Travelers Rest, SC 29690; 864-834-6910; Fax: 864-834-6911. Hours: 9AM-4PM (EST). *Misdemeanor, Civil Actions Under $7,500, Eviction, Small Claims.* www.greenvillecounty.org/Magistrate_Courts

West Greenville Magistrate Court 6247 White Horse Rd, Greenville, SC 29611; 864-294-4810; Fax: 864-294-4801. Hours: 8:30AM-5PM (EST). *Misdemeanor, Civil Actions Under $7,500, Eviction, Small Claims.* www.greenvillecounty.org/Magistrate_Courts

Probate Court 301 University Ridge, #1200, Greenville, SC 29601; 864-467-7170; Fax: 864-467-7198. Hours: 8:30AM-5PM (EST). *Probate.* www.greenvillecounty.org/probate/index.htm

Greenwood County

Circuit Court Courthouse, Rm 114, 528 Monument St, Greenwood, SC 29646; 864-942-8547; Fax: 864-942-8693. Hours: 8:30AM-5PM (EST). *Felony, Misdemeanor, Civil Actions Over $7,500.*
Civil Records: Access: Mail, in person. Visitors must perform in person searches for themselves. Search fee: $2.00 per name. Required to search: name, years

to search. Civil cases indexed by defendant, plaintiff. Civil records on docket books from 1897; on computer back to 2000.

Criminal Records: Access: Mail, in person. Visitors must perform in person searches for themselves. Search fee: $2.00 per name. Required to search: name, years to search, DOB; also helpful: SSN. Criminal records on alpha index from 1897; on computer back to 2000. The court will not perform party name searches for in-person requesters.

General Information: Public Access terminal is available. (Only civil searching available.) No adoption, juvenile, sealed or expunged records released. Copy fee: $.25 per page. Cert fee: $2.00. Payee: Clerk of Court. Business checks accepted. Prepayment required. Mail requests: SASE required. Mail turnaround time 1-2 days.

Greenwood Magistrate Court Greenood County Courthouse, Rm 100, 528 Monument St., Greenwood, SC 29646; 864-942-8655; Fax: 864-942-8663. Hours: 8:30AM-5PM (EST). *Misdemeanor, Civil Actions Under $7,500, Eviction, Small Claims.*

Probate Court PO Box 1210, Greenwood, SC 29648; 864-942-8625; Fax: 864-942-8620. Hours: 8:30AM-5PM (EST). *Probate.*

Hampton County

Circuit Court PO Box 7, Hampton, SC 29924; 803-943-7510. Hours: 8AM-5PM (EST). *Felony, Civil Actions Over $7,500.* www.hcroster.com
Civil Records: Access: In person only. Visitors must perform in person searches for themselves. No search fee. Required to search: name, years to search. Civil cases indexed by defendant, plaintiff. Civil records on docket books, archived from 1878.

Criminal Records: Access: In person only. Visitors must perform in person searches for themselves. No search fee. Required to search: name, years to search, DOB; also helpful: SSN. Criminal records on docket books, archived from 1878.

General Information: No adoption, juvenile, sealed or expunged records released. Copy fee: $.50 per page. Cert fee: $1.00. Payee: Clerk of Court. Personal checks accepted. Prepayment required.

Estill Magistrate Court 125 Railroad St. SE, PO Box 969, Estill, SC 29918; 803-625-3232; Fax: 803-625-2148. Hours: 2PM-5PM (EST). *Misdemeanor, Civil Actions Under $7,500, Eviction, Small Claims.*

Varnville Magistrate Court Law Enforcement Ctr, 411 Cemetery Rd, PO Box 1299, Varnville, SC 29944; 803-943-7511; Fax: 843-943-7557. Hours: 8:30AM-4:30PM (EST). *Misdemeanor, Civil Actions Under $7,500, Eviction, Small Claims.*

Probate Court PO Box 601, Hampton, SC 29924; 803-943-7512; Fax: 803-943-7596, 803-943-7540. Hours: 8AM-5PM (EST). *Probate.*

Horry County

Circuit Court PO Box 677, Conway, SC 29526; 843-915-5080; Fax: 843-915-6018. Hours: 8AM-5PM (EST). *Felony, Misdemeanor, Civil Actions Over $7,500.*
Civil Records: Access: Phone, mail, in person. Both court and visitors may perform in person searches. Search fee: $3.00 per name. Required to search: name, years to search. Civil cases indexed by defendant, plaintiff. Civil records on computer from 1987, on alpha index from 1920s.

Criminal Records: Access: Phone, mail, in person. Both court and visitors may perform in person searches. Search fee: $3.00 per name. Required to search: name, years to search, DOB, SSN, signed

release. Criminal records on computer from 1987, on alpha index from 1920s.

General Information: No adoptions, juvenile, sealed or expunged records released. Copy fee: $.50 per page. Cert fee: $1.00. Payee: Clerk of Court. Business checks accepted. Prepayment required. Mail requests: SASE helpful. Turnaround time 2 days.

Little River Summary Court 107 Highway 57 N, Little River, SC 29566; 843-399-5543; Fax: 843-399-6792. Hours: 8AM-5PM (EST). *Civil Actions Under $7,500, Eviction, Small Claims.*
Note: This is a Magistrate Court

Aynor Magistrate Court PO Box 115, Aynor, SC 29511; 843-358-5508; Fax: 843-358-0704. Hours: 8AM-5PM (EST). *Misdemeanor, Civil Actions Under $7,500, Eviction, Small Claims.*

Conway Magistrate Court 1201 3rd Ave., PO Box 1236, Conway, SC 29528; 843-915-5290; Fax: 843-915-7683. Hours: 8AM-5PM (EST). *Misdemeanor, Civil Actions Under $7,500, Eviction, Small Claims.*

Conway Magistrate Court 1201 3rd Av, 2nd Fl, Conway, SC 29526; 843-915-6290; Fax: 843-915-5290. Hours: 8AM-5PM (EST). *Misdemeanor, Civil Actions Under $7,500, Eviction, Small Claims.*

Green Sea Magistrate Court 5527 Hwy #9, PO Box 153, Green Sea, SC 29545; 843-392-1219; Fax: 843-392-1834. Hours: 8AM-5PM (EST). *Misdemeanor, Civil Actions Under $7,500, Eviction, Small Claims.*

Loris Magistrate Court 3817 Walnut St, Loris, SC 29569; 843-756-7918/6674; Fax: 843-756-1355. Hours: 8AM-5PM (EST). *Misdemeanor, Civil Actions Under $7,500, Eviction, Small Claims.*

Myrtle Beach Magistrate Court 1201 21st Ave N, Myrtle Beach, SC 29577; 843-444-6127; Fax: 843-444-6131. Hours: 8AM-5PM (EST). *Misdemeanor, Civil Actions Under $7,500, Eviction, Small Claims.*

South Strand Magistrate Court 9630 Scipio Lane, Myrtle Beach, SC 29588-7568; 843-238-3277/3677; Fax: 843-238-3591. Hours: 8AM-5PM (EST). *Misdemeanor, Civil Actions Under $7,500, Eviction, Small Claims.*

Probate Court PO Box 288, Conway, SC 29528; 843-915-5370; Fax: 843-915-6370/71. Hours: 8AM-5PM (EST). *Probate.* www.horrycounty.org

Jasper County

Circuit Court PO Box 248, Ridgeland, SC 29936; 843-726-7710. Hours: 8:30AM-5PM (EST). *Felony, Misdemeanor, Civil Actions Over $7,500.*
Civil Records: Access: In person only. Visitors must perform in person searches for themselves. No search fee. Required to search: name, years to search. Civil cases indexed by defendant, plaintiff. Civil records on computer back to 1999; prior on books to 1912.

Criminal Records: Access: In person only. Both court and visitors may perform in person searches. Search fee: $5.00 per name. Required to search: name, years to search, DOB; also helpful: SSN, signed release. Criminal records on computer back to 1999; prior on books to 1912.

General Information: Public Access terminal is available. No adoption, juvenile, sealed or expunged records released. Fee to fax results is $2.00 per document. Copy fee: $1.00 per page. Cert fee: $1.00. Payee: Clerk of Court. Personal checks not accepted. Prepayment required.

Hardeeville Magistrate Court 21 Martin St, PO Box 1169, Hardeeville, SC 29927; 843-784-2628; Fax: 843-784-3245. Hours: 9AM-5Pm (EST). *Misdemeanor, Civil Actions Under $7,500, Eviction, Small Claims.*

Ridgeland Magistrate Court Rte 2, Box 73, Pineland, SC 29936; 843-726-8590; 843-625-5743; Fax: 843-726-7745. *Misdemeanor, Civil Actions Under $7,500, Eviction, Small Claims.*

Ridgeland Magistrate Court 111 W Adams St, PO Box 665, Ridgeland, SC 29936; 843-726-7737; Fax: 843-726-7745. Hours: 9AM-Noon; 1PM-5PM (EST). *Misdemeanor, Civil Actions Under $7,500, Eviction, Small Claims.*

Probate Court PO Box 1028, Ridgeland, SC 29936; 843-726-7719; Fax: 843-726-5137. Hours: 9AM-5PM (EST). *Probate.*

Kershaw County

Circuit Court County Courthouse, Rm 313, PO Box 1557, Camden, SC 29020; 803-425-1500 x5623; Probate phone: 803-425-1500 x5351; Fax: 803-425-1505. Hours: 8:30AM-5PM (EST). *Felony, Misdemeanor, Civil Actions Over $7,500.*
Civil Records: Access: Mail, in person. Visitors must perform in person searches for themselves. Search fee: $20.00. Required to search: name, years to search. Civil cases indexed by defendant, plaintiff. Civil records archived from 1797, computerized records from 1994.
Criminal Records: Access: Mail, in person. Visitors must perform in person searches for themselves. Search fee: $20.00. Required to search: name, years to search, DOB; also helpful: SSN. Criminal records archived from 1890, computerized records from 1994.
General Information: Public Access terminal is available. No adoption, juvenile, sealed or expunged records released. Will not fax results. Copy fee: $.50 per page. Cert fee: $1.00. Payee: Clerk of Court. Personal checks accepted. Prepayment required. Mail turnaround time 1 day.

Bethune Magistrate Court 202 N Main St, PO Box 215, Bethune, SC 29009; 843-334-8460; Fax: 843-334-8450. Hours: 9AM-5PM (EST). *Misdemeanor, Civil Actions Under $7,500, Eviction, Small Claims.*

Camden Magistrate Court County Courthouse, #202, 1121 Broad St, PO Box 1528, Camden, SC 29020; 803-425-1500 X386; Fax: 803-425-6044. Hours: 8AM-5PM (EST). *Misdemeanor, Civil Actions Under $7,500, Eviction, Small Claims.*

Probate Court 1121 Broad St, Rm 302, Camden, SC 29020; 803-425-1500; Fax: 803-425-7673. Hours: 8:30AM-5PM (EST). *Probate.*

Lancaster County

Circuit Court PO Box 1809, Lancaster, SC 29721; 803-285-1581; Fax: 803-416-9388. Hours: 8:30AM-5PM (EST). *Felony, Misdemeanor, Civil Actions Over $7,500.*
Civil Records: Access: In person only. Both court and visitors may perform in person searches. Search fee: none. Required to search: name, years to search. Civil cases indexed by defendant, plaintiff. Civil records on computer from 1987, microfiche from 1937, alpha index from 1764.
Criminal Records: Access: In person only. Both court and visitors may perform in person searches. Search fee: none. Required to search: name, years to search, DOB; also helpful: SSN. Criminal records on computer from 1987, microfiche from 1937, alpha index from 1764.

General Information: No adoption, juvenile, sealed or expunged records released. Copy fee: $.25 per page. Cert fee: $2.50. Payee: Clerk of Court. Personal checks accepted. Prepayment required.

Lancaster Magistrate Court 101 S Wylie St, Lancaster, SC 29720; 803-283-3983; Fax: 803-416-9407. Hours: 8:30AM-5PM (EST). *Misdemeanor, Civil Actions Under $7,500, Eviction, Small Claims.*

Probate Court PO Box 1809, Lancaster, SC 29721; 803-283-3379; Fax: 803-283-3370. Hours: 8:30AM-5PM (EST). *Probate.*
www.lancastercountysc.net/ProbateCourt

Laurens County

Circuit Court PO Box 287, Laurens, SC 29360; 864-984-3538; Fax: 864-984-7023. Hours: 9AM-5PM (EST). *Felony, Misdemeanor, Civil Actions Over $7,500.*
Civil Records: Access: Mail, in person. Both court and visitors may perform in person searches. Search fee: $5.00 per name. Required to search: name, years to search. Civil cases indexed by defendant, plaintiff. Civil records on index books back to 1800s; on computer back to 1980.
Criminal Records: Access: Mail, in person. Both court and visitors may perform in person searches. Search fee: $5.00 per name. Required to search: name, years to search, DOB; also helpful: SSN. Criminal records on index books back to 1950s; on computer back to 1980.
General Information: No adoption, juvenile, sealed or expunged records released. Copy fee: $.50 per page. Cert fee: $1.00 per page. Payee: Clerk of Court. Personal checks accepted. Prepayment required. Mail requests: SASE required. Mail turnaround time 2-3 days.

Clinton Magistrate Court 203 W Pitts St, Clinton, SC 29325; 864-833-5879; Fax: 864-833-7502. Hours: 8AM-5PM M, T; 8AM-Noon W; 8AM-10AM F (EST). *Misdemeanor, Civil Actions Under $7,500, Eviction, Small Claims.*

Gray Court Magistrate Court 329 Main St, Town Hall, PO Box 438, Gray Court, SC 29645; 864-876-4390. Hours: 9AM-5PM,M,T,W; 9AM-2PM Th (EST). *Misdemeanor, Civil Actions Under $7,500, Eviction, Small Claims.*

Laurens Magistrate Court PO Box 925, Laurens, SC 29360; 864-683-4485. Hours: 9AM-5PM (EST). *Misdemeanor, Civil Actions Under $7,500, Eviction, Small Claims.*

Probate Court PO Box 194, (100 Hillcrest Sq, #A), Laurens, SC 29360; 864-984-7315; Probate phone: 864-984-7731; Fax: 864-984-3779. Hours: 9AM-5PM (EST). *Probate.*

Lee County

Circuit Court PO Box 387, Bishopville, SC 29010; 803-484-5341; Fax: 803-484-1632. Hours: 9AM-5PM (EST). *Felony, Misdemeanor, Civil Actions Over $7,500.*
Civil Records: Access: Mail, in person. Both court and visitors may perform in person searches. Search fee: $5.00 per name. Required to search: name, years to search. Civil cases indexed by defendant, plaintiff. Civil records on computer from 1991, on archives from 1900s.
Criminal Records: Access: Mail, in person. Both court and visitors may perform in person searches. Search fee: $2.00 per name. Required to search: name, years to search, DOB; also helpful: SSN. Criminal records on computer from 1991, on archives from 1900s.

General Information: Public Access terminal is available. No adoption, juvenile, sealed or expunged records released. Will not fax results. Copy fee: $.25 per page. $1.00 minimum. Cert fee: $1.00. Payee: Clerk of Court. Business checks accepted. Prepayment required. Mail requests: SASE required. Mail turnaround time 2 days.

Bishopville Magistrate Court 115 Gregg St, PO Box 2, Bishopsville, SC 29010; 803-484-6463, 484-9184; Fax: 803-484-5163. Hours: 9AM-5-PM (EST). *Misdemeanor, Civil Actions Under $7,500, Eviction, Small Claims.*

Probate Court PO Box 24, Bishopville, SC 29010; 803-484-5341 X338, X339, X361; Fax: 803-484-6881. Hours: 9AM-5PM (EST). *Probate.*

Lexington County

Circuit Court Lexington County Courthouse, Rm 107, 205 E Main St, Lexington, SC 29072; 803-359-8212; Civil phone: 803-359-8252; Criminal phone: 803-359-8553; Probate phone: 803-359-8324; Fax: 803-359-8314. Hours: 8AM-5PM (EST). *Felony, Misdemeanor, Civil Actions Over $7,500.*
Civil Records: Access: Mail, in person. Both court and visitors may perform in person searches. Search fee: $3.00 per name. Required to search: name, years to search. Civil cases indexed by defendant, plaintiff. Civil records on index from 1936.
Criminal Records: Access: Fax, mail, in person. Both court and visitors may perform in person searches. Search fee: $3.00 per name. Required to search: name, years to search, DOB, SSN. Criminal records on computer since 1983.
General Information: Public Access terminal is available. No adoption, juvenile, sealed or expunged records released. Copy fee: $.25 per page. Cert fee: $1.00. Payee: County of Lexington. Personal checks accepted. Prepayment required. Mail requests: SASE required. Mail turnaround time 3 days.

Batesburg Leesville Magistrate Court 231 W Church St, Batesburg, SC 29006; 803-359-8330/532-9204/9205; Fax: 803-532-0357. Hours: 8:AM-4:30PM (EST). *Misdemeanor, Civil Actions Under $7,500, Eviction, Small Claims.*

Cayce Magistrate Court 650 Knox Abbott Dr, Cayce, SC 29033; 803-796-7100; Fax: 803-796-7635. Hours: 8AM-4:30PM (EST). *Misdemeanor, Civil Actions Under $7,500, Eviction, Small Claims.*

Columbia Magistrate Court 111 Lin Creek, Columbia, SC 29212; 803-781-7584/7585; Fax: 803-749-4050. *Misdemeanor, Civil Actions Under $7,500, Eviction, Small Claims.*

Lexington Magistrate Court 605 W Main St #100, Magistrate's Office, Lexington, SC 29072; 803-359-8221; Fax: 803-359-8155. Hours: 8:30AM-4:30PM (EST). *Misdemeanor, Civil Actions Under $7,500, Eviction, Small Claims.*

Swansea Magistrate Court 500 Charlie Rast Rd, PO Box 457, Swansea, SC 29160; 803-568-3616; Fax: 803-568-4078. Hours: 8:30AM-4:30PM (EST). *Misdemeanor, Civil Actions Under $7,500, Eviction, Small Claims.*

Probate Court County Courthouse, Rm 110, 139 E Main St, Lexington, SC 29072-3488; 803-359-8324; Fax: 803-359-8199. Hours: 8AM-5PM (EST). *Probate.*

Marion County

Circuit Court PO Box 295, Marion, SC 29571; 843-423-8240. Hours: 8:30AM-5PM (EST). *Felony, Misdemeanor, Civil Actions Over $7,500.*
Civil Records: Access: In person only. Visitors must perform in person searches for themselves. No search fee. Required to search: name, years to search. Civil cases indexed by defendant, plaintiff. Civil records on computer since 1988; prior records on index cards from 1800s.
Criminal Records: Access: In person only. Visitors must perform in person searches for themselves. No search fee. Required to search: name, years to search, DOB; also helpful: SSN. Criminal records on computer since 1988; prior records on index cards from 1800s.
General Information: No adoption, juvenile, sealed or expunged records released. Copy fee: $.25 per page. Cert fee: $1.00.

Gresham Magistrate Court 2715 Hwy 76 E, #B, Mullins, SC 25974, 843-423-8208. Hours: 8:30AM-5PM (EST). *Misdemeanor, Civil Actions Under $7,500, Eviction, Small Claims.*

Marion Magistrate Court 2715 W Hwy 76, #B, Mullins, SC 29574-6015; 843-423-8208; Fax: 843-423-8394. Hours: 8:30AM-5PM (EST). *Misdemeanor, Civil Actions Under $7,500, Eviction, Small Claims.*

Mullins Magistrate Court 2715 US Hwy 76, #B, Mullins, SC 29574; 843-423-8208 X231; Fax: 843-423-8394. Hours: 8:30AM-5PM (EST). *Misdemeanor, Civil Actions Under $7,500, Eviction, Small Claims.*

Probate Court PO Box 583, Marion, SC 29571; 843-423-8244; Fax: 843-431-5026. Hours: 8:30AM-5PM (EST). *Probate.*

Marlboro County

Circuit Court PO Drawer 996, Bennettsville, SC 29512; 843-479-5613; Fax: 843-479-5640. Hours: 8:30AM-5PM (EST). *Felony, Misdemeanor, Civil Actions Over $7,500.*
Civil Records: Access: Mail, in person. Visitors must perform in person searches for themselves. Search fee: $5.00 per name. Required to search: name, years to search. Civil cases indexed by defendant, plaintiff. Civil records on computer from 1985, on index from 1786.
Criminal Records: Access: Mail, in person. Visitors must perform in person searches for themselves. Search fee: $5.00 per name. Required to search: name, years to search, DOB; also helpful: SSN. Criminal records on computer from 1985, on index from 1786.
General Information: No adoption, juvenile, sealed or expunged records released. Copy fee: $.25 per page. Cert fee: $2.00. Payee: Clerk of Court. Personal checks accepted. Prepayment required. Mail requests: SASE required. Mail turnaround time 1 day.

Marlboro County Summary Court PO Box 418, Bennettsville, SC 29512; 843-479-5620/5621; Fax: 843-479-5646. Hours: 8:30AM-4:30PM (EST). *Civil Actions Under $7,500, Eviction, Small Claims.*
Civil Records: Access: Mail. No search fee.
General information: Turnaround time 5-7 days.

Bennettsville Magistrate Court 211 N Marlboro St, PO Box 418, Bennettsville, SC 29512; 843-479-5620; Fax: 843-479-5646. Hours: 8:30AM-4:30PM M-Th; Civil 4-5PM (EST). *Misdemeanor, Civil Actions Under $7,500, Eviction, Small Claims.*
Note: Court is again active.

Probate Court PO Box 455, Bennettsville, SC 29512; 843-479-5610; Fax: 843-479-5668. Hours: 8:30AM-5PM (EST). *Probate.*

McCormick County

Circuit Court 133 S Mine St, McCormick, SC 29835; 864-465-2195; Probate phone: 864-465-2428; Fax: 864-465-0071. Hours: 9AM-5PM (EST). *Felony, Misdemeanor, Civil Actions Over $7,500.*
Civil Records: Access: In person. Visitors must perform in person searches for themselves. No search fee. Required to search: name, years to search. Civil cases indexed by defendant, plaintiff. Civil records on index books from 1916.
Criminal Records: Access: In person. Visitors must perform in person searches for themselves. No search fee. Required to search: name, years to search, DOB; also helpful: SSN. Criminal records on index books from 1916.
General Information: No adoption, juvenile, sealed or expunged records released. Copy fee: $.35 per page. Cert fee: $1.00. Payee: Clerk of Court. Prepayment required.

McCormick Magistrate Court 211 Augusta Ext., PO Box 1116, McCormick, SC 29835; 864-465-2316; Fax: 864-465-2582. Hours: 9AM-5PM (EST). *Misdemeanor, Civil Actions Under $7,500, Eviction, Small Claims.*

Probate Court 133 S Mine St, #101, McCormick, SC 29835; 864-465-2630; Fax: 864-465-0071. Hours: 9AM-5PM (EST). *Probate.*

Newberry County

Circuit Court PO Box 278, Newberry, SC 29108; 803-321-2110; Fax: 803-321-2111. Hours: 8:30AM-5PM (EST). *Felony, Misdemeanor, Civil Actions Over $7,500.*
www.newberrycounty.net
Civil Records: Access: Mail, in person. Both court and visitors may perform in person searches. No search fee. Required to search: name, years to search. Civil cases indexed by defendant, plaintiff. Civil records on computer from 1983, docket books from 1776.
Criminal Records: Access: In person only. Visitors must perform in person searches for themselves. No search fee. Required to search: name, years to search, DOB; also helpful: SSN. Criminal records on computer from 1983, docket books from 1776.
General Information: Public Access terminal is available. No adoption, juvenile, sealed, PTI or expunged records released. Copy fee: $.20 per page. Cert fee: $1.00. Payee: Clerk of Court. Only cashiers checks and money orders accepted. Prepayment required. Mail turnaround time 1 week.

Little Mountain Magistrate Court 824 Main St, PO Box 95, Little Mountain, SC 29075; 803-345-1040; Fax: 803-945-7222. Hours: 2PM-5PM T, W (EST). *Misdemeanor, Civil Actions Under $7,500, Eviction, Small Claims.*

Newberry Magistrate Court 3239 Louis Rich Rd, Newberry, SC 29108; 803-321-2144/2145; Fax: 803-321-2172. Hours: 8:30-5PM (EST). *Misdemeanor, Civil Actions Under $7,500, Eviction, Small Claims, Traffic.*

Whitmire Magistrate Court 313 Main St, PO Box 62, Whitmire, SC 29178; 803-694-5756; Fax: 803-694-5756. Hours: M 1:30-6PM; W 1:30-6PM (EST). *Misdemeanor, Civil Actions Under $7,500, Eviction, Small Claims.*

Probate Court PO Box 442, Newberry, SC 29108; 803-321-2118; Fax: 803-321-2119. Hours: 8:30AM-5PM (EST). *Probate.*

Oconee County

Circuit Court PO Box 678, Walhalla, SC 29691; 864-638-4280; Fax: 864-638-4282. Hours: 8:30AM-5PM (EST). *Felony, Misdemeanor, Civil Actions Over $7,500.*
Civil Records: Access: In person only. Visitors must perform in person searches for themselves. No search fee. Required to search: name, years to search. Civil cases indexed by defendant, plaintiff. Civil records on index cards from 1868; on computer back to 1994.
Criminal Records: Access: In person only. Visitors must perform in person searches for themselves. No search fee. Required to search: name, years to search; also helpful: DOB, SSN, signed release. Criminal records on index cards from 1868; on computer back to 1994.
General Information: Public Access terminal is available. No adoption, juvenile, sealed or expunged records released. Copy fee: $1.00 for first page, $.50 each add'l. No cert fee. Payee: Clerk of Court. Personal checks accepted. Prepayment required.

County Summary Court 208 Booker Dr, Walhalla, SC 29691; 864-638-4127; Fax: 864-638-4229. Hours: 8:30AM-5PM (EST). *Civil Actions Under $7,500, Eviction, Small Claims.*
Civil Records: Access: Mail only. Only the court performs searches; visitors may not. No search fee. Required to search: name.
General Information: Will not fax results. Copy fee: $.50 per page. Payee: County Treasurer. Prepayment required. Mail turnaround time 5-7 days.

Walhalla Magistrate Court 208 Booker Dr, Walhalla, SC 29691; 864-638-4127; Fax: 864-638-4229. Hours: 8:30AM-5PM (EST). *Misdemeanor, Civil Actions Under $7,500, Eviction, Small Claims.*

Probate Court PO Box 471, Walhalla, SC 29691; 864-638-4275; Fax: 864-638-4278. Hours: 8:30AM-5PM (EST). *Probate.*

Orangeburg County

Circuit Court PO Box 9000, Orangeburg, SC 29116; 803-533-6260; Fax: 803-534-3848. Hours: 8:30AM-5PM (EST). *Felony, Misdemeanor, Civil Actions Over $7,500.*
Civil Records: Access: In person only. Visitors must perform in person searches for themselves. No search fee. Required to search: name, years to search. Civil cases indexed by defendant, plaintiff. Civil records on index cards from 1924.
Criminal Records: Access: In person only. Visitors must perform in person searches for themselves. No search fee. Required to search: name, years to search, DOB; also helpful: SSN. Criminal records on index cards from 1924.
General Information: No adoption, juvenile, sealed or expunged records released. Copy fee: $.50 per page. Cert fee: $1.00. Payee: Clerk of Court. Personal checks accepted. Prepayment required.

Bowman Magistrate Court 6803 Charleston Hwy, PO Box 365, Bowman, SC 29018; 803-829-2831. *Misdemeanor, Civil Actions Under $7,500, Eviction, Small Claims.*

Branchville Magistrate Court 7644 Freedom Rd, PO Box 85, Branchville, SC 29432; 803-274-8820; Fax: 803-274-8760. Hours: 4PM-7PM M & W (EST). *Misdemeanor, Civil Actions Under $7,500, Eviction, Small Claims.*

Elloree Magistrate Court 2614 Cleveland St, PO Box 436, Elloree, SC 29047; 803-897-4626; Fax: 803-897-2165. *Misdemeanor, Civil Actions Under $7,500, Eviction, Small Claims.*
www.orangeburgcounty.org

Eutawville Magistrate Court 300 Porcher Ave, PO Box 188, Eutawville, SC 29048; 803-492-3374; Fax: 803-496-5850. *Misdemeanor, Civil Actions Under $7,500, Eviction, Small Claims.*

Holly Hill Magistrate Court 7324 Old State Rd, Hwy 176, PO Box 154, Holly Hill, SC 29059; 803-496-9533; Fax: 803-496-9533. Hours: 11AM-4PM T & TH (EST). *Misdemeanor, Civil Actions Under $7,500, Eviction, Small Claims.*

North Magistrate Court 9305 North Rd, PO Box 399, North, SC 29112; 803-247-2101; Fax: 803-247-3045. Hours: 8:30AM-4:30PM M-TH; 8:30AM-3PM F (EST). *Misdemeanor, Civil Actions Under $7,500, Eviction, Small Claims.*

Norway Magistrate Court 8413 Savannah Hwy, PO Box 67, Norway, SC 29113; 803-263-4100; Fax: 803-263-4292. Hours: 9-Noon; M,W (EST). *Misdemeanor, Civil Actions Under $7,500, Eviction, Small Claims.*

Orangeburg County Magistrate Court 1540 Ellis Ave NE, PO Box 9000, Orangeburg, SC 29116; 803-533-5880/5879; Fax: 803-516-4011. Hours: 8:30AM-5PM (EST). *Misdemeanor, Civil Actions Under $7,500, Eviction, Small Claims.*

Orangeburg Magistrate Court PO Box 9000, Orangeburg, SC 29115; 803-533-5843; Fax: 803-533-5929. Hours: 8:30-5PM (EST). *Misdemeanor, Civil Actions Under $7,500, Eviction, Small Claims.*

Springfield Magistrate Court 7304 Festival Trail Rd, PO Box 125, Springfield, SC 29146; 803-258-1002; Fax: 803-258-1006. Hours: 9AM-5PM (EST). *Misdemeanor, Civil Actions Under $7,500, Eviction, Small Claims.*

Probate Court PO Drawer 9000, Orangeburg, SC 29116-9000; 803-533-6280; Fax: 803-533-6279. Hours: 8:30AM-5PM (EST). *Probate.*

Pickens County

Circuit Court PO Box 215, Pickens, SC 29671; 864-898-5857; Fax: 864-898-5863. Hours: 8:30AM-5PM (EST). *Felony, Misdemeanor, Civil Actions Over $7,500.*
www.co.pickens.sc.us
Civil Records: Access: In person only. Both court and visitors may perform in person searches. No search fee. Required to search: name, years to search. Civil cases indexed by defendant, plaintiff. Civil records on computer from 1990, on index from 1970.
Criminal Records: Access: In person only. Both court and visitors may perform in person searches. No search fee. Required to search: name, years to search, DOB; also helpful: SSN. Criminal records on computer from 1990, on index from 1970.
General Information: Public Access terminal is available. No adoption, juvenile, sealed or expunged records released. Copy fee: $.50 per page. Cert fee: $1.00. Payee: Clerk of Court. Personal checks accepted. Prepayment required.

Clemson Magistrate Court 115-B Commons Way, Central, SC 29630; 864-639-8084; Fax: 864-639-0701. Hours: 8:30AM-4:30PM (EST). *Misdemeanor, Civil Actions Under $7,500, Eviction, Small Claims.*

Easley Magistrate Court 110 W 1st Ave, Easley, SC 29640; 864-850-7076; Fax: 864-850-7075. Hours: 8:30AM-4:30PM (EST). *Misdemeanor, Civil Actions Under $7,500, Eviction, Small Claims.*

Liberty Magistrate Court #147-B Kay Holcombe Rd, Liberty, SC 29657; 864-843-5821; Fax: 864-843-5824. Hours: 8:30AM-5PM (EST).

Misdemeanor, Civil Actions Under $7,500, Eviction, Small Claims.

Pickens Magistrate Court 216-A, Law Enforcement Ctr Rd, Pickens, SC 29671; 864-898-5551/5552; Fax: 864-898-5546. Hours: 8:30AM-5PM (EST). *Misdemeanor, Civil Actions Under $7,500, Eviction, Small Claims.*

Probate Court 222 McDaniel Ave, #B-16, Pickens, SC 29671; 864-898-5903; Fax: 864-898-5924. Hours: 8:00AM-5PM (EST). *Probate.*

Richland County

Circuit Court PO Box 2766, Columbia, SC 29202; 803-576-1999; Fax: 803-748-5039 civ; 576-1925 crim. Hours: 8:30AM-5PM (EST). *Felony, Misdemeanor, Civil Actions Over $7,500.*
Civil Records: Access: Mail, in person. Both court and visitors may perform in person searches. Search fee: $2.00 per name. Required to search: name, years to search. Civil cases indexed by defendant, plaintiff. Civil records on computer from 1987. Many prior records indexed to 1920s.
Criminal Records: Access: In person only. Visitors must perform in person searches themselves. No search fee. Required to search: name, years to search; also helpful: DOB, SSN. Criminal records on index to 1920s, computerized since 1987.
General Information: Public Access terminal is available. No adoption, juvenile, sealed or expunged records released. Will fax to gov't agencies only. Copy fee: $.50 for first page, $.15 each add'l. No cert fee. Payee: Richland County Clerk. Personal checks accepted. Prepayment required. Mail requests: SASE required. Mail turnaround time 1 day.

Central Magistrate Court Richland Central Court, 1400 Huger St, PO Box 192, Columbia, SC 29202; 803-576-2300; Fax: 803-7576-2325. Hours: 8:30AM-5PM M-F (EST). *Misdemeanor (Criminal Domestic Violence), Civil Actions Under 7,500, Traffic.*

Columbia Magistrate Court 1731 Laurel St, PO Box 192, Columbia, SC 29202; 803-576-2510; Fax: 803-576-2519. Hours: 8:30AM-5PM (EST). *Misdemeanor, Civil Actions Under $7,500, Eviction, Small Claims.*

Dentsville Magistrate Court 2500 Decker Blvd, #B-1, Columbia, SC 29206; 803-576-2560; Fax: 803-576-2569. Hours: 8:30AM-5PM (EST). *Misdemeanor, Civil Actions Under $7,500, Eviction, Small Claims.*

Dutch Fork Magistrate Court 1223 St Andrews Rd, Columbia, SC 29210; 803-576-2540; Fax: 803-576-2545. Hours: 8.:30AM-4:30PM (EST). *Misdemeanor, Civil Actions Under $7,500, Eviction, Small Claims.*

Hopkins Magistrate Court 6108 Cabin Creek Rd, PO Box 70, Hopkins, SC 29061; 803-576-2530; Fax: 803-576-2535. Hours: 8:30AM-5PM (EST). *Misdemeanor, Civil Actions Under $7,500, Eviction, Small Claims.*

Lykesland Magistrate Court 1403 Caroline Rd, PO Box 9523, Columbia, SC 29290; 803-576-2500; Fax: 803-576-2504. Hours: 8:30AM-5PM (EST). *Misdemeanor, Civil Actions Under $7,500, Eviction, Small Claims.*

Olympia Magistrate Court 1601 B Shop Rd, PO Box 9305, Columbia, SC 29201; 803-576-2550; Fax: 803-576-2555. Hours: 8:30AM-5PM (EST). *Misdemeanor, Civil Actions Under $7,500, Eviction, Small Claims.*

Pontiac Magistrate Court 10509 Two Notch Rd, #D, Elgin, SC 29045; 803-576-2520; Fax: 803-576-2522. Hours: 8:30AM-5PM (EST). *Misdemeanor, Civil Actions Under $7,500, Eviction, Small Claims.*

Upper Township Magistrate Court 4919 Rhett St, Columbia, SC 29203; 803-576-2570; Fax: 803-576-2579. Hours: 8:30-Noon; 1:15PM-5PM (EST). *Misdemeanor, Civil Actions Under $7,500, Eviction, Small Claims.*

Waverly Magistrate Court 2712 Middleburg Dr, #106, Columbia, SC 29204; 803-576-2590; Fax: 803-576-2599. Hours: 8:30AM-5PM (EST). *Misdemeanor, Civil Actions Under $7,500, Eviction, Small Claims.*

Probate Court PO Box 192 (1701 Main St, #207), Columbia, SC 29202; 803-576-1961; Fax: 803-576-1993. Hours: 8:30AM-5PM (EST). *Probate.*
www.richlandonline.com/probate.htm

Saluda County

Circuit Court County Courthouse, 100 E Church St, #6, Saluda, SC 29138; 864-445-3303/2168; Fax: 864-445-3772. Hours: 8:30AM-5PM (EST). *Felony, Misdemeanor, Civil Actions Over $7,500.*
Civil Records: Access: In person. Both court and visitors may perform in person searches. No search fee. Required to search: name, years to search, address. Civil cases indexed by defendant, plaintiff. Civil records on computer from 1995, on index from 1897.
Criminal Records: Access: In person. Both court and visitors may perform in person searches. No search fee. Required to search: name, years to search, address, DOB, signed release; also helpful: SSN. Criminal records on computer from 1995, on index from 1897. Request must be in writing.
General Information: Public Access terminal is available. No adoption, juvenile, sealed or expunged records released. Copy fee: $.25 per page. Cert fee: $1.00. Payee: Clerk of Court. Personal checks accepted. Prepayment required.

Saluda Magistrate Court 120 S Main St, Courthouse Annex, Saluda, SC 29138; 864-445-2846; Civil phone: 864-445-2863; Fax: 864-445-3684. Hours: 8AM-4:30PM (EST). *Misdemeanor, Civil Actions Under $7,500, Eviction, Small Claims.*

Probate Court 100 E Church St, Saluda, SC 29138; 864-445-7110; Fax: 864-445-9726. Hours: 8:30AM-5PM (EST). *Probate.*

Spartanburg County

Circuit Court County Courthouse, 180 Magnolia St, Spartanburg, SC 29306; 864-596-2591; Fax: 864-596-2239. Hours: 8:30AM-5PM (EST). *Felony, Misdemeanor, Civil Actions Over $7,500.*
www.spartanburgcounty.org/govt/depts/coc/index.htm
Civil Records: Access: In person only. Visitors must perform in person searches for themselves. No search fee. Required to search: name, years to search. Civil cases indexed by defendant, plaintiff. Civil records on computer from 1975, on microfiche from 1960, on alpha index from 1800s.
Criminal Records: Access: In person only. Visitors must perform in person searches for themselves. No search fee. Required to search: name, years to search, DOB, SSN, signed release. Criminal records on computer from 1975, on microfiche from 1960, on alpha index from 1800s. The public may search the index.
General Information: Public Access terminal is available. (Civil only.) No adoption, juvenile, sealed or expunged records released. Copy fee: $1.00 per

page. Cert fee: $1.00. Payee: Clerk of Court. Personal checks accepted. Prepayment required.

Chesnee Magistrate Court
201 Cherokee St, Chesnee, SC 29323; 864-461-3402; Fax: 864-596-3622. *Misdemeanor, Civil Actions Under $7,500, Eviction, Small Claims.*

Inman Magistrate Court
7 Mill St, Inman, SC 29349; 864-472-4447/6247; Fax: 864-596-3622. Hours: 9AM-8PM M; 8AM-Noon T (EST). *Misdemeanor, Civil Actions Under $7,500, Eviction, Small Claims.*

Landrum Magistrate Court
137-B N Howard Ave, PO Box 744, Landrum, SC 29356; 864-457-7245; Fax: 864-596-3622. Hours: Open Tues (EST). *Misdemeanor, Civil Actions Under $7,500, Eviction, Small Claims.*

Pacolet Magistrate Court
980 Sunny Acres Rd, PO Box 416, Pacolet Mills, SC 29373; 864-474-0344/3391; Fax: 864-503-2417. Hours: 6PM-10PM M & W, 6PM-9PM TH (EST). *Misdemeanor, Civil Actions Under $7,500, Eviction, Small Claims.*

Reidville Magistrate Court
7450 Reidville Rd, PO Box 124, Reidville, SC 29375; 864-433-9223. Hours: 10AM-5:30PM Tues.; 9AM-2PM TH (EST). *Misdemeanor, Civil Actions Under $7,500, Eviction, Small Claims.*

Spartanburg Magistrate Court
County Courthouse, Rm 105, 180 Magnolia St, Spartanburg, SC 29306; 864-596-2564; Fax: 864-596-3622. Hours: 8AM-5PM (EST). *Misdemeanor, Civil Actions Under $7,500, Eviction, Small Claims.*

Probate Court
180 Magnolia St, Rm 302, Spartanburg, SC 29306-2392; 864-596-2556; Fax: 864-596-2011. Hours: 8:30AM-5PM (EST). *Probate.*

Sumter County

Circuit Court
141 N Main, Sumter, SC 29150; 803-436-2227; Civil phone: 803-436-2231; Criminal phone: 803-436-2264/65; Fax: 803-436-2223. Hours: 8:30AM-5PM (EST). *Felony, Misdemeanor, Civil Actions Over $7,500.*
www.sumtercountysc.org
Civil Records: Access: Mail, in person, online. Both court and visitors may perform in person searches. Search fee: $10.00 per name. Required to search: name, years to search; also helpful: address. Civil cases indexed by defendant, plaintiff. Civil records on computer from 1987, microfiche and books from 1900s. Family court records are online at the website.
Criminal Records: Access: Mail, in person. Both court and visitors may perform in person searches. Search fee: $5.00 per name. Required to search: name, years to search, DOB, SSN, signed release; also helpful: address. Criminal records in books.
General Information: No adoption, juvenile, sealed or expunged records released. Will not fax results. Copy fee: $1.00 1st page; $.25 each add'l page. Cert fee: $5.00. Payee: Sumter County Treasurer. Business checks accepted. Prepayment required. Mail requests: SASE required. Mail turnaround time 2 days.

Mayesville Magistrate Court
PO Box 236, Town Hall, Mayesville, SC 29104; 803-436-9372. *Misdemeanor, Civil Actions Under $7,500, Eviction, Small Claims.*

Sumter Magistrate Court
115 N Harvin St, PO Box 1428, Sumter, SC 29151; 803-436-2280; Fax: 803-436-2789. *Misdemeanor, Civil Actions Under $7,500, Eviction, Small Claims.*

Probate Court
141 N Main, Rm 111, Sumter, SC 29150; 803-436-2166; Fax: 803-436-2407. Hours: 8:30AM-5PM (EST). *Probate.*

Union County

Circuit Court
PO Box 703 (210 W Main St), Union, SC 29379; 864-429-1630; Fax: 864-429-1715. Hours: 9AM-5PM (EST). *Felony, Misdemeanor, Civil Actions Over $7,500.*
www.countyofunion.com/Clerk.html
Note: The court will mail or fax specific case documents, if case number provided. Fees involved.
Civil Records: Access: In person only. Visitors must perform in person searches for themselves. No search fee. Required to search: name, years to search. Civil cases indexed by defendant, plaintiff. All records on computer.
Criminal Records: Access: In person only. Visitors must perform in person searches for themselves. No search fee. Required to search: name, years to search; also helpful: SSN, DOB. Criminal records on computer.
General Information: Public Access terminal is available. No adoption, juvenile, sealed or expunged records released. Copy fee: $.50 per page. Cert fee: $2.00. Payee: Clerk of Court. Personal checks accepted. Prepayment required.

Union Magistrate Court
210 W Main St, Union, SC 29379; 864-429-1648. *Misdemeanor, Civil Actions Under $7,500, Eviction, Small Claims.*
Note: This is the only magistrate court bldg in county. There are 3 part-time Magistrates who work out of jails or other county offcies at night when required.

Probate Court
PO Box 447, Union, SC 29379; 864-429-1625; Fax: 864-427-1198. Hours: 9AM-5PM (EST). *Probate.*

Williamsburg County

Circuit Court
125 W Main St, Kingstree, SC 29556; 843-355-9321 X552; Fax: 843-354-7821. Hours: 8:30AM-5PM (EST). *Felony, Misdemeanor, Civil Actions Over $7,500.*
Civil Records: Access: In person. Both court and visitors may perform in person searches. Search fee: $5.00 per name. Required to search: name, years to search. Civil cases indexed by defendant, plaintiff. Civil records on books, archived from 1980-1989, indexed from 1806; computerized records since 1993.
Criminal Records: Access: In person. Both court and visitors may perform in person searches. No search fee. Required to search: name, years to search, DOB; also helpful: SSN. Criminal records on books, archived from 1980-1989, indexed from 1806; computerized records since 1993.
General Information: Public Access terminal is available. No adoption, juvenile, sealed or expunged records released. Copy fee: $.25 per page. No cert fee. Payee: Clerk of Court. Personal checks accepted. Prepayment required.

Hemingway Magistrate Court
206 E Broad St, PO Box 416, Hemingway, SC 29554; 843-558-2116; Fax: 843-5578-5314. *Misdemeanor, Civil Actions Under $7,500, Eviction, Small Claims.*

Kingstree Magistrate Court
10 Courthouse Sq, Kingstree, SC 29556; 843-355-9321 x179. Hours: 8:00AM-5PM (EST). *Misdemeanor, Civil Actions Under $7,500, Eviction, Small Claims.*

Nesmith Magistrate Court
10 Courthouse Sq, Kingstree, SC 29556; 843-355-9321 ext 179; Fax: 843-355-6444. *Misdemeanor, Civil Actions Under $7,500, Eviction, Small Claims.*

Probate Court
PO Box 1005, Kingstree, SC 29556; 843-355-9321 x558; Fax: 843-355-9305. Hours: 8:00AM-5PM (EST). *Probate.*

York County

Circuit Court
PO Box 649, York, SC 29745; 803-684-8506; Civil phone: 803-684-8507; Criminal phone: 803-628-3036; Probate phone: 803-684-8513. Hours: 8AM-5PM (EST). *Felony, Misdemeanor, Civil Actions Over $7,500.*
Civil Records: Access: Mail, in person. Both court and visitors may perform in person searches. Search fee: $5.00 per name. Required to search: name, years to search. Civil cases indexed by defendant, plaintiff. Civil records on computer from 1982, in books from 1932.
Criminal Records: Access: Fax, mail, in person. Both court and visitors may perform in person searches. Search fee: $5.00 per name. Required to search: name, years to search, DOB; also helpful: SSN. Criminal records on computer from 1982, in books from 1932.
General Information: No adoption, juvenile, sealed or expunged records released. Will fax results $5.00 per doc. Copy fee: $.40 per page. Cert fee: $1.00. Payee: Clerk of Court. Personal checks accepted. Prepayment required. Mail requests: SASE required. Mail turnaround time 1 day.

Clover Magistrate Court
201 S Main St, Clover, SC 29710; 803-222-9404; Fax: 803-222-4081. Hours: 8AM-5PM (EST). *Misdemeanor, Civil Actions Under $7,500, Eviction, Small Claims.*

Fort Mill Magistrate Court
114 Springs St, Fort Mill, SC 29715; 803-547-5572/5573; Fax: 803-547-6344. Hours: 8AM-5PM (EST). *Misdemeanor, Civil Actions Under $7,500, Eviction, Small Claims.*

Hickory Grove Magistrate Court
PO Box 37, Hickory Grove, SC 29717; 803-925-2815. *Misdemeanor, Civil Actions Under $7,500, Eviction, Small Claims.*

Rock Hill Magistrate Court
529 S Cherry, Rock Hill, SC 29730; 803-909-7600; Fax: 803-909-7606. *Misdemeanor, Civil Actions Under $7,500, Eviction, Small Claims.*

York Magistrate Court
1675 York Hwy, York, SC 29745; 803-628-3029; Fax: 803-328-8353. Hours: 8AM-5PM (EST). *Misdemeanor, Civil Actions Under $7,500, Eviction, Small Claims.*

Probate Court
PO Box 219, York, SC 29745; 803-684-8513 X8630; Fax: 803-684-8536. Hours: 8AM-5PM (EST). *Probate.*

South Carolina Recording Offices

ORGANIZATION: 46 counties, 46 recording offices. The recording officer is. Register of Mesne Conveyances or Clerk of Court (This varies by county). The entire state is in the Eastern Time Zone (EST).

REAL ESTATE RECORDS: Most counties will not perform real estate searches. Copy and certification fees vary. The Assessor keeps tax records.

UCC RECORDS: Financing statements are filed at the state level, except for real estate related collateral, which are filed with the Register. However, prior to 07/2001, consumer goods and farm collateral were also filed at the Register and these older records can be searched there. As a general rule, all recording offices will perform UCC searches. Search fees are usually $5.00 per debtor name. Copy fees are usually $1.00 per page.

TAX LIEN RECORDS: All federal and state tax liens on personal property and on real property are filed with the Register of Mesne Conveyances (Clerk of Court). Some counties will perform tax lien searches. Search fees and copy fees vary.

ONLINE ACCESS: There is no statewide system, buy several counties have placed free record data on their web sites.

Abbeville County

Clerk of Court, PO Box 99, Abbeville, SC 29620. **Phone**-864-459-5074, R/E Recording-864-459-4944, UCC Recording-864-459-4944; fax-864-459-9188; hours 9AM-5PM
Will search UCC records. Search per debtor- $5.00. Will not search real estate or tax lien records. UCC copy- $1.00 per page. Payee: Abbeville Clerk of Court. **Other phones:** Assessor-864-459-4921; Treasurer-864-459-2539; Appraiser/ Auditor-864-459-4921; Elections-864-459-5083.

Aiken County

County Register of Mesne Conveyances, PO Box 537, Aiken, SC 29802-0537. **Phone**-County Register of Mesne Conveyances, R/E & UCC Recording- 803-642-2072, UCC Recording-803-642-2075; 8:30AM-5PM
Will not search UCC records. Tax lien search- $5.00 per debtor. Real estate record owner and mortgage searches available. Available for walk-ins only. Record copy- $.50 per page. Cert fee: $1.00 per cert. Payee: Aiken County Register of Mesne Conveyances. **Other phones:** Assessor-803-642-1576; Treasurer-803-642-2055; Appraiser/ Auditor-803-642-1576; Elections-803-642-2028.

Allendale County

Clerk of Court, PO Box 126, Allendale, SC 29810. **Phone**-803-584-2737; fax-803-584-7058; 9AM-5PM
Will search UCC records. Search per debtor- $5.00. Will not search real estate or tax lien records. RE record copy- $.25 per page. UCC copy- $1.00 per page. Cert fee: $2.00 per page. Payee: Allendale Clerk of Court. **Other phones:** Assessor-803-584-2572; Treasurer-803-584-3876.

Anderson County

Register of Deeds, PO Box 8002, Anderson, SC 29622. **Phone**-Register of Deeds, R/E & UCC Recording- 864-260-4054; fax-864-260-4443; hours 8:30AM-5PM www.andersoncountysc.org
Will not search records. Cert fee: $1.00 per doc. **Online Access to Real Estate, Property Tax, Sale, Assessor, Marriage, Estate, Guardianship, Vehicle, Permit, Court records:** Access to the county ACPASS super search site is free at http://acpass.andersoncountysc.org/courts.htm. **Other phones:** Assessor-864-260-4028; Treasurer-864-260-4033; Anderson County Operator-864-260-4444.

Bamberg County

Clerk of Court, PO Box 150, Bamberg, SC 29003. **Phone**-Clerk of Court, R/E & UCC Recording- 803-245-3025; fax-803-245-3088; hours 9AM-5PM

Will not search UCC or real estate records. Cert fee: $5.00 per doc. **Other phones:** Assessor-803-245-3010; Treasurer-803-245-3003; Appraiser/ Auditor-803-245-3010; Elections-803-245-3028; Probate Court-803-245-3008; Auditor-803-245-3006.

Barnwell County

Clerk of Court, PO Box 723, Barnwell, SC 29812-0723. **Phone**-803-541-1020; fax-803-541-1025.
Will search UCC records. Search per debtor- $5.00. Will not search real estate records. **Other phones:** Assessor-803-541-1011; Treasurer-803-541-1050.

Beaufort County

Clerk of Court, PO Box 1128, Beaufort, SC 29901. **Phone**-843-470-5218, R/E Recording-843-470-2700, UCC Recording-843-470-2715; fax-843-470-5248. www.co.beaufort.sc.us
Will search UCC records. Search per debtor- $5.00. Search request using non-standard form (per name)- $8.00. **Online Access to Assessor, Property records:** Access to the public records search database is free online at http://rodweb.co.beaufort.sc.us. Also, search assessor data at www.co.beaufort.sc.us/assessor/frameset.asp. A fuller records subscription service requiring registration, fees, and logon is under development. **Other phones:** Assessor-843-470-2513; Treasurer-843-470-2766; Elections-843-470-3753.

Berkeley County

Clerk of Court, 223 N. Live Oak Drive, Moncks Corner, SC 29461. **Phone**-843-719-4084; fax-843-719-4851; hours 8AM-5PM www.co.berkeley.sc.us
Will not search records. UCC copy- $.35 per page. Cert fee: $2.00. Payee: Berkeley County Clerk of Court. **Online Access to Property, Assessor, Personal Property, Vehicle Tax, Property Sale, Real Estate, Recording, UCC records:** Access real estate data is at www.co.berkeley.sc.us/e_services/index.php. Also, search the clerks document database for free at www.landaccess.com. Click on SC-Berkeley. Records go back to 1/2/1997. **Other phones:** Assessor-843-761-6900 x4061; Treasurer-843-761-3800.

Calhoun County

Clerk of Court, 902 F.R. Huff Drive, St. Matthews, SC 29135. **Phone**-803-874-3524; fax-803-874-1942; hours 9AM-5PM. Will not search records. Copy fee is $.25 per page. Cert fee: $.25 per page. Payee: Calhoun County Treasurer. **Other phones:** Assessor-803-874-3613; Treasurer-803-874-3519.

Charleston County

Clerk of Court, PO Box 726, Charleston, SC 29402. **Phone**-Clerk of Court, R/E & UCC Recording- 843-

958-4800; fax-843-958-4803. www.charlestoncounty.org
Will not search records. Copy fee-$.25 per page. Cert fee: $5.00. **Online Access to Real Estate, Deed, Mortgage, Property Tax, Judgment, Marriage, Will/Estate, Guardianship, Conservatorship records:** Access to the county's GIS mapping database of property records is free at http://gisweb.charlestoncounty.org. Also, online access the auditor & treasurer's tax system database is free at http://taxweb.charlestoncounty.org. Also, search the court records for judgments at www3.charlestoncounty.org/connect?ref=MIE. Also, search all records including marriages, estates/wills, and guardianships at www.charlestoncounty.org/index2.asp?p=/publicrecords.htm. **Other phones:** Assessor-843-958-4100; Treasurer-843-958-4360; Elections-843-745-2226; Vital Records-843-740-0801.

Cherokee County

Clerk of Court, PO Drawer 2289, Gaffney, SC 29342. **Phone**-Clerk of Court, R/E & UCC Recording- 864-487-2571; fax-864-487-2754; hours 8:30AM-5PM
Will not search records. Copy fee- $.50 per page. Cert fee: $1.00 per cert. Payee: Cherokee Clerk of Court. **Other phones:** Assessor-864-487-2552; Treasurer-864-487-2551; Elections-864-487-2563; Vital Records-864-487-2571.

Chester County

Clerk of Court, PO Drawer 580, Chester, SC 29706. **Phone**-803-385-2605; fax-803-581-7975.
Will search UCC records. Search per debtor- $5.00. Will not search real estate or tax lien records. UCC copy- $.25 per page. **Other phones:** Assessor-803-377-4177; Treasurer-803-385-2608.

Chesterfield County

Clerk of Court, PO Box 529, Chesterfield, SC 29709. **Phone**-Clerk of Court, R/E & UCC Recording- 843-623-2574, UCC Recording-843-623-7853; fax-843-623-6944; hours 8:30AM-5PM
Will search UCC records. Search per debtor- $5.00. Will only do an in-person tax lien search. Will not search real estate records. RE record copy- $2.00 1st 4 pages;$.25 each add'l. UCC copy- $2.00 per name. Cert fee: $1.00 per instrument. Payee: Clerk of Court. **Other phones:** Assessor-843-623-7362; Treasurer-843-623-2563; Appraiser/ Auditor-843-623-7362; Elections-843-623-2265; Vital Records-843-623-2117.

Clarendon County

Clerk of Court-Register of Deeds, PO Box 136, Manning, SC 29102. **Phone**-803-435-4443, R/E

Recording-803-435-4444, UCC Recording-803-435-4444; fax-803-435-8258; hours 8:30AM-5PM Will not search records. Copy fee- $.25 per page. Cert fee: $2.00 per 4 pages; $.25 each add'l. **Other phones:** Assessor-803-435-4423.

Colleton County

Register of Deeds, PO Box 620, Walterboro, SC 29488-0028. **Phone**-Register of Deeds, R/E & UCC Recording- 843-542-2745; fax-843-542-2749; hours 8AM-5PM. Will not search records. RE record copy-$1.50 1st page, $.50 each add'l. UCC copy- $1.50 1st page, $.50 each add'l. Cert fee: $1.00 per doc. Payee: Clerk of Court. **Other phones:** Assessor-843-549-1213; Treasurer-843-549-2233; Elections-843-549-2842; Vital Records-843-549-1516.

Darlington County

Clerk of Court, PO Box 1177, Darlington, SC 29540. **Phone**-Clerk of Court, R/E & UCC Recording- 843-398-4330; fax-843-393-6871; hours 8:30AM-5PM Will not search UCC or real estate records. **Other phones:** Assessor-843-398-4180; Treasurer-843-398-4160.

Dillon County

Clerk of Court, PO Drawer 1220, Dillon, SC 29536. **Phone**-Clerk of Court, R/E & UCC Recording- 843-774-1425; fax-843-841-3706; hours 8:30AM-5PM Will search UCC records. Search per debtor- $10.00. UCC search includes tax liens if requested. Separate federal/state combined tax lien search-$10.00 per debtor. Will not search real estate records. RE record copy- $.25 per page. UCC copy- $.50 per page. Cert fee: None. Payee: Dillon Clerk of Court. **Other phones:** Assessor-843-774-1412; Treasurer-843-774-1416; Appraiser/ Auditor-843-774-1412; Elections-843-774-1403; Vital Records-843-774-5611; Auditor-843-774-1418; Probate-8437741423.

Dorchester County

Clerk of Court, PO Box 38, St. George, SC 29477. **Phone**-843-563-0106, R/E Recording-843-832-0153, UCC Recording-843-832-0153; fax-843-563-0182; hours 8:30AM-5PM. Will not search records. UCC copy- $.50 per page. Cert fee: $2.00. Payee: Dorchester County Clerk of Court. **Other phones:** Assessor-843-563-0156; Treasurer-843-563-0165; Appraiser/ Auditor-843-563-0156; Elections-843-563-0132; Vital Records-843-563-0107.

Edgefield County

Clerk of Court, PO Box 34, Edgefield, SC 29824. **Phone**-803-637-4080, R/E Recording-803-637-4049, UCC Recording-803-637-4049; fax-803-637-4117; hours 8:30AM-5PM Will not search records. UCC copy- $1.00 per page. Cert fee: $1.00 per doc. Payee: Registrar of Deeds. **Other phones:** Assessor-803-637-4066; Treasurer-803-637-4069; Appraiser/ Auditor-803-637-4057; Elections-803-637-4072.

Fairfield County

Clerk of Court, PO Drawer 299, Winnsboro, SC 29180. **Phone**-803-712-6526; hours 9AM-5PM Will not search records. RE record copy- $.25 per page. UCC copy- $.25 per page. Cert fee: $1.00 per cert. Payee: Fairfield Clerk of Court. **Other phones:** Assessor-803-635-1411; Treasurer-803-635-1411.

Florence County

Clerk of Court, MSC-E City/County Complex, Florence, SC 29501. **Phone**-Clerk of Court, R/E & UCC Recording- 843-665-3031; fax-843-665-3097; hours 8:30AM-5PM. Will not search records. UCC copy- $1.00 per page. Cert fee: None. Payee:

Florence County. **Other phones:** Assessor-843-665-3056; Treasurer-843-665-3041.

Georgetown County

Register of Deeds, PO Box 421270, Georgetown, SC 29442. **Phone**-Register of Deeds, R/E & UCC Recording- 843-545-3088; hours 8:30AM-5PM www.georgetowncountysc.org Will not search records. RE record copy- $.50 per page. UCC copy- $1.00 per page. Cert fee: $1.00 per cert. Payee: Georgetown County Register of Deeds. **Online Access to Property, GIS, Recording, Real Estate, Deed, UCC records:** Access to porperty data on the GIS-mappign site is free at http://gismap.georgetowncountysc.org/main.asp. Use "Type of Search" to select name searching. Also, access the clerks database free at www.landaccess.com. Click on SC-Georgetown. Index goes back to 1/1977. **Other phones:** Assessor-843-545-3014; Treasurer-843-545-3098; Elections-843-545-3339; Vital Records-843-546-0174.

Greenville County

Register of Deeds, 301 University Ridge, #1300, County Sq #1300, Greenville, SC 29601-3655. **Phone**-Register of Deeds, R/E & UCC Recording- 864-467-7240, UCC Recording-864-467-7180; fax-864-467-7107; hours 8:30AM-5PM www.greenvillecounty.org Will not search records. Copy fee- $.25 per page. Cert fee: $1.00 per doc. Payee: Register of Deeds. **Online Access to Real Property, Deed, Vehicle, Property Tax, Most Wanted, Missing Person records:** Search the Register of Deeds database free online at www.greenvillecounty.org. Click on Register of Deeds Search. Also, search the property tax and vehicles data at www.greenvillecounty.org/voTaxQry/wcmain.asp. Also, search the real estate data at www.greenvillecounty.org/vrealpr24/clrealprop.asp. No name searching. Also, search the sheriff's most wanted and missing persons lists at www.gcso.org. **Other phones:** Assessor-864-467-7300; Treasurer-864-467-7210.

Greenwood County

Clerk of Court, 528 Monument St., Courthouse, Greenwood, SC 29646. **Phone**-Clerk of Court, R/E & UCC Recording- 864-942-8551, UCC Recording-864-942-8613; fax-864-942-8693; hours 8:30AM-5PM www.co.greenwood.sc.us Will not search records. UCC copy- $1.00 per page. Cert fee: $1.00 per cert. Payee: Greenwood Clerk of Court. **Online Access to Assessor, Property records:** Records on the County Parcel Search database are free at http://165.166.39.5/website/gis/viewer.htm. Click on search and choose to search by owner name. An interactive map is included. **Other phones:** Assessor-864-942-8536; Treasurer-864-942-8528; Appraiser/Auditor-864-942-8534; Elections-864-942-8521.

Hampton County

Clerk of Court, PO Box 7, Hampton, SC 29924. **Phone**-Clerk of Court, R/E & UCC Recording- 803-943-7510; fax-803-943-7596; hours 8AM-5PM Will not search records. UCC copy- $5.00 per instrument. Cert fee: $1.00 per instrument. Payee: Clerk of Court. **Other phones:** Assessor-803-943-7507; Treasurer-803-943-7509; Appraiser/ Auditor-803-943-7507; Vital Records-803-943-3878.

Horry County

Register of Deeds, PO Box 470, Conway, SC 29528. **Phone**-Register of Deeds, R/E & UCC Recording- 843-915-5000, UCC Recording-843-915-5430; fax-843-915-6430; hours 8AM-5PM www.horrycounty.org Will not search records. Copy fee-$1.50 per page self serve; $1.00 per page otherwise. UCC copy- $8.00 for 1-4 pages, $1.00 each add'l. Cert fee: $2.00.

Payee: Register of Deeds. **Online Access to Recorder, Deed, Lien, Real Property records:** Access to the recorders database is free at www.horrycounty.org/gateway/disclaimer/idx_rod.html . Also, search the real property database at www.horrycounty.org/gateway/disclaimer/idx_real.html. **Other phones:** Assessor-843-915-5000; Treasurer-843-915-5430; Appraiser/ Auditor-843-915-5050; Elections-843-915-5440; Vital Records-843-248-3958; Register of Deeds Main Switchboard-843-915-5430.

Jasper County

Clerk of Court, PO Box 248, Ridgeland, SC 29936. **Phone**-Clerk of Court, R/E & UCC Recording- 843-726-7710; fax-843-726-7782; hours 9AM-5PM Will not search records. Copy fee- $1.00 per page. **Other phones:** Assessor-843-726-7725; Treasurer-843-726-7722; Appraiser/ Auditor-843-726-7725; Elections-843-726-7709; Vital Records-843-726-7790.

Kershaw County

Register of Deeds, 515 Walnut St #180, Camden, SC 29020. **Phone**-803-425-1500, R/E Recording-803-425-1500 x5368/5367/5365, UCC Recording-803-425-1500 x5367; fax-803-425-7673; hours 8:30AM-5PM Will not search records. RE record copy- $.50 per page. UCC copy- $1.00 per page. Cert fee: $1.00 per cert. Payee: Kershaw Register of Deeds. **Other phones:** Assessor-803-425-1500 x5332; Treasurer-803-425-1500 x5314; Appraiser/ Auditor-803-425-1500 x5327; Elections-803-424-4016/ 424-4017; Vital Records-803-425-6012.

Lancaster County

Clerk of Court, 101 N Main St, Lancaster, SC 29720. **Phone**-Clerk of Court, R/E & UCC Recording- 803-285-1581; fax-803-416-9388. Will search UCC records. Search per debtor- $5.00. **Other phones:** Assessor-803-285-6964; Treasurer-803-285-7939; Appraiser/ Auditor-803-285-6964; Elections-803-285-2969; Vital Records-803-286-9948.

Laurens County

Clerk of Court, PO Box 287, Laurens, SC 29360. **Phone**-864-984-3538; fax-864-984-7023; 9AM-5PM Will not search records. RE record copy- $.50 per page. UCC copy- $1.00 per page. Cert fee: $1.00 per cert. Payee: Laurens Clerk of Court. **Other phones:** Assessor-864-984-6546.

Lee County

Register of Deeds, PO Box 387, Bishopville, SC 29010. **Phone**-803-484-5341, R/E Recording-803-484-5341 x333, UCC Recording-803-484-5341 x378; fax-803-484-1632; hours 9AM-5PM Will search UCC records. Search per debtor- $5.00. Will not search real estate or tax lien records. UCC copy- $.25 per page. **Other phones:** Assessor-803-484-5341 x362; Treasurer-803-484-5341 x327.

Lexington County

Register of Deeds, 212 S Lake Drive, Lexington, SC 29072. **Phone**-Register of Deeds, R/E & UCC Recording- 803-359-8168, UCC Recording-803-359-8470; fax-803-359-8189; hours 8AM-5PM www.lex-co.com/my_lex.html Will not search records. RE record copy- $.35 per page. UCC copy- $.35 per page. Cert fee: $1.00 per doc. Payee: County of Lexington. **Online Access to Assessor, Property records:** Access to county Reassessment Information is free at www.lex-co.com/my_lex.html. Click on "Assessment Information.". **Other phones:** Assessor-803-359-8190; Treasurer-803-359-8217.

Marion County

Clerk of Court, PO Box 295, Marion, SC 29571. **Phone**-Clerk of Court, R/E & UCC Recording- 843-423-8240; fax-843-423-8306; hours 8:30AM-5PM
Will not search records. RE record copy- $3.00 1st 4 pages, $.25 each add'l. UCC copy- $1.00 per page. Cert fee: $1.00 per page. Payee: Marion Clerk of Court. **Other phones:** Assessor-843-423-8225; Treasurer-843-423-8230.

Marlboro County

Clerk of Court, PO Drawer 996, Bennettsville, SC 29512. **Phone**-843-479-5613; fax-843-479-5640; hours 8:30AM-5PM
Will not search records. RE record copy- $.20 per page. UCC copy- $1.00 per page. Cert fee: $2.00 per cert. Payee: Marlboro Clerk of Court.

McCormick County

Clerk of Court, 133 S. Mine St Rm102, Courthouse, Rm 102, McCormick, SC 29835. **Phone**-Clerk of Court, R/E & UCC Recording- 864-465-2195; fax-864-465-0071; hours 9AM-5PM
Will not search records. RE record copy- $.35 per page. UCC copy- $.35 per page. Cert fee: $1.00 per cert. Payee: Clerk of Court. **Other phones:** Assessor-864-465-2931; Treasurer-864-465-2332; Appraiser/ Auditor-864-465-2431; Elections-864-465-2089.

Newberry County

Court Clerk, PO Drawer 10, Newberry, SC 29108. **Phone**-Court Clerk, R/E & UCC Recording- 803-321-2110; fax-803-321-2111; hours 8:30AM-5PM
Will search UCC records. Search per debtor- $5.00. Will not search real estate or tax lien records. UCC copy- $1.35 per page. Cert fee: $1.20. Payee: Newberry County Clerk. **Online Access to Assessor, Real Estate, Auditor, Property Tax, Treasurer records:** Access to databases for the assessor is free at http://209.213.28.38/vpn/assessor2.htm Access to property tax data is at www.newberrycounty.net/auditor/Index.html. Also, the treasurer database is free at http://209.213.28.38/vpn/treasurer.htm. **Other phones:** Assessor-803-321-2125; Treasurer-803-321-2130.

Oconee County

Register of Deeds, 415 S Pine St, Walhalla, SC 29691. **Phone**-Register of Deeds, R/E & UCC Recording- 864-638-4285; hours 8:30AM-5PM www.oconeesc.com
Will not search records. RE record copy- $.50 per page. UCC copy- $5.00 for 4 pages. Cert fee: $1.00. Payee: Register of Deeds. **Online Access to Land, Deed, Mortgage, Plat records:** Access to county land records is free at www.oconeesc.com/idxweb/indexing/idx_name_search.asp. **Other phones:** Assessor-864-638-4150; Treasurer-864-638-4162.

Orangeburg County

Register of Deeds, Box 9000, Orangeburg, SC 29116-9000. **Phone**-Register of Deeds, R/E & UCC Recording- 803-533-6236; fax-803-535-2354; hours 8:30AM-5PM
Will not search records. Copy fee- $.50 per page. Payee: Register of Deeds. **Online Access to Assessor, Property records:** Access to county property tax records is free at www.orangeburgcounty.org/Assessor/main.asp. **Other phones:** Assessor-803-533-6220; Treasurer-803-533-6130; Appraiser/ Auditor-803-533-6229; Elections-803-533-6213; Vital Records-803-533-6239.

Pickens County

Register of Deeds, 222 McDaniel Ave. B-5, Pickens, SC 29671. **Phone**-Register of Deeds, R/E & UCC Recording- 864-898-5868; fax-864-898-5924; hours 8AM-5PM www.co.pickens.sc.us
Will not search records. UCC copy- $2.00 per page. Cert fee: $1.00 per doc. Payee: Register of Deeds. **Online Access to Assessor, Property, Voter Registration, Most Wanted, Property Tax records:** Access to the assessors property database is free at http://207.232.162.146/assessor/disclaim.asp. Search property tax records at www.co.pickens.sc.us/onlinetaxes/. Also, access voter registration records at www.co.pickens.sc.us/Voter.ASP and click on "Lookup your registration information." View the sheriff's most wanted list at www.pickenscosheriff.org/most_wanted.htm. **Other phones:** Assessor-864-898-5871; Treasurer-864-898-5883; Appraiser/ Auditor-864-898-5878; Elections-864-898-5848; Vital Records-864-898-5965.

Richland County

Register of Deeds, PO Box 192, Columbia, SC 29202. **Phone**-803-576-1910; fax-803-576-1922; hours 8:30AM-5PM
Will search UCC records. Search per debtor- $5.00. Will not search real estate records. Payee: Richland County Register of Deeds. **Online Access to Assessor, Property records:** Access to county property information is free at www.richlandmaps.com. Click on "Property Info" however, there is no name searching. **Other phones:** Assessor-803-748-5038.

Saluda County

Clerk of Court, Courthouse, Saluda, SC 29138. **Phone**-Clerk of Court, R/E & UCC Recording- 864-445-3303; fax-864-445-3772; hours 8:30AM-5PM
Will not search records. Copy fee is $1.00 per page. Cert fee: $1.00. Payee: Saluda County Clerk of Court. **Other phones:** Assessor-864-445-8121; Treasurer-864-445-2875.

Spartanburg County

County Register of Mesne Conveyances, 366 N. Church St, County Admin. Offices, Spartanburg, SC 29303. **Phone**-864-596-2514; hours 8:30AM-5PM
Will not search records. RE record copy- $10.00 for deeds and mortgages; $6.00 or less for other docs. UCC copy- $.50 per page. Cert fee: $2.00 per cert. Payee: Spartanburg County Register of Mesne Conveyances. **Other phones:** Assessor-864-596-2544; Treasurer-864-596-2603.

Sumter County

Register of Deeds, 141 N. Main St., Courthouse, Rm 202, Sumter, SC 29150. **Phone**-Register of Deeds, R/E & UCC Recording- 803-436-2177, UCC Recording-803-436-2179;   hours-8:30AM-5PM www.sumtercountysc.org
Will not search records. Copy fee- $.50 per page. Cert fee: $2.00 1st pg, $.50 each. Payee: Sumter County Register of Deeds. **Online Access to Real Estate, Recording, Deed, Property Tax records:** Search county e-gov data free at www.sumtercountysc.org/disclaim.htm. **Other phones:** Assessor-803-436-2112; Treasurer-803-436-2213; Appraiser/ Auditor-803-436-2112; Elections-803-436-2310.

Union County

Clerk of Court, PO Box 703, Union, SC 29379. **Phone**-Clerk of Court, R/E & UCC Recording- 864-429-1630; fax-864-429-1715;   hours-9AM-5PM www.judicial.state.sc.us/clerks/union
Will search UCC records. Search per debtor- $5.00. Will not search real estate or tax lien records. RE record copy- $.50 per page. UCC copy- $1.00 per page. Cert fee: $1.00 per UCC. Payee: Union Clerk of Court. **Other phones:** Assessor-864-429-1650; Treasurer-864-429-1606; Elections-864-429-1616; Vital Records-864-429-1690.

Williamsburg County

Clerk of Court, 125 W. Main St, Kingstree, SC 29556. **Phone**-843-355-9321 ext552; fax-843-355-7821; hours 8AM-5PM. Will not search records. UCC copy- $1.00 per page. Cert fee: $3.00. Payee: Williamsburg County Clerk of Court. **Other phones:** Assessor-843-354-7059.

York County

Clerk of Court, PO Box 649, York, SC 29745. **Phone**-803-684-8510; hours 8AM-5PM
Will not search UCC or real estate records. Federal/state combined tax lien search- $5.00 per debtor. RE record copy- $.40 per page. UCC copy- $1.00 per page. Cert fee: $1.00 per doc. Payee: York Clerk of Court. **Online Access to Property, GIS, Recorder, Real Estate, Deed, UCC records:** Access to the county GIS and property data is free at http://maps.yorkcountygov.com/gisonline/. Click on "GIS Online" and name search at the main map page. Also, access to the clerk's records database is free at www.landaccess.com. Click on SC-York. Index goes back to 7/1982. **Other phones:** Assessor-803-684-8526; Treasurer-803-684-8528; Elections-803-684-1242; Vital Records-803-909-7300.

South Carolina County Locator

You will usually be able to find the city name in the City/County Cross Reference below. We have also included a ZIP/City Cross Reference following the City/County Cross Reference. If you know the ZIP Code but the city name does not appear in the City/County Cross Reference, look up the ZIP Code in the ZIP/City Cross Reference, find the city name, then look up the city name in the City/County Cross Reference.

South Carolina City/County Cross Reference

ABBEVILLE Abbeville
ADAMS RUN (29426) Charleston(78), Dorchester(21)
AIKEN Aiken
ALCOLU (29001) Clarendon(93), Sumter(6)
ALLENDALE Allendale
ANDERSON Anderson
ANDREWS (29510) Georgetown(58), Williamsburg(41)
ARCADIA Spartanburg
AWENDAW Charleston
AYNOR Horry
BALLENTINE Richland
BAMBERG Bamberg
BARNWELL Barnwell
BATESBURG (29006) Lexington(51), Saluda(30), Aiken(17)
BATH Aiken
BEAUFORT Beaufort
BEECH ISLAND Aiken
BELTON (29627) Anderson(93), Greenville(5)
BENNETTSVILLE Marlboro
BETHERA Berkeley
BETHUNE (29009) Kershaw(83), Chesterfield(9), Lee(7)
BISHOPVILLE Lee
BLACKSBURG (29702) Cherokee(96), York(3)
BLACKSTOCK (29014) Chester(58), Fairfield(41)
BLACKVILLE (29817) Barnwell(79), Bamberg(20)
BLAIR Fairfield
BLENHEIM Marlboro
BLUFFTON Beaufort
BLYTHEWOOD (29016) Richland(91), Fairfield(8)
BONNEAU Berkeley
BORDEN Sumter
BOWLING GREEN York
BOWMAN (29018) Orangeburg(93), Dorchester(6)
BRADLEY (29819) Greenwood(80), Abbeville(17), McCormick(1)
BRANCHVILLE (29432) Orangeburg(72), Bamberg(23), Dorchester(4)
BRUNSON Hampton
BUFFALO Union
CADES (29518) Williamsburg(96), Clarendon(3)
CALHOUN FALLS (29628) Abbeville(97), McCormick(2)
CAMDEN (29020) Kershaw(94), Lee(5)
CAMERON (29030) Calhoun(72), Orangeburg(27)
CAMPOBELLO (29322) Spartanburg(98), Greenville(1)
CANADYS Colleton
CARLISLE (29031) Union(47), Chester(34), Fairfield(18)
CASSATT (29032) Kershaw(72), Lee(27)
CATAWBA York
CAYCE Lexington
CENTENARY Marion
CENTRAL (29630) Pickens(93), Anderson(6)
CHAPIN (29036) Lexington(72), Richland(21), Newberry(6)
CHAPPELLS (29037) Newberry(68), Saluda(28), Laurens(3)
CHARLESTON (29406) Charleston(76), Berkeley(23)

CHARLESTON (29418) Charleston(78), Dorchester(21)
CHARLESTON (29420) Dorchester(63), Charleston(36)
CHARLESTON Berkeley
CHARLESTON Charleston
CHARLESTON AFB Charleston
CHERAW Chesterfield
CHEROKEE FALLS Cherokee
CHESNEE (29323) Spartanburg(87), Cherokee(12)
CHESTER Chester
CHESTERFIELD Chesterfield
CLARKS HILL (29821) Edgefield(51), McCormick(48)
CLEARWATER Aiken
CLEMSON Pickens
CLEVELAND (29635) Greenville(73), Pickens(26)
CLIFTON Spartanburg
CLINTON Laurens
CLIO (29525) Marlboro(97), Dillon(2)
CLOVER York
COLUMBIA (29212) Lexington(78), Richland(21)
COLUMBIA (29210) Richland(69), Lexington(30)
COLUMBIA Lexington
COLUMBIA Richland
CONESTEE Greenville
CONVERSE Spartanburg
CONWAY Horry
COOSAWATCHIE Jasper
COPE Orangeburg
CORDESVILLE Berkeley
CORDOVA Orangeburg
COTTAGEVILLE Colleton
COWARD Florence
COWPENS (29330) Spartanburg(64), Cherokee(35)
CROCKETVILLE Hampton
CROSS (29436) Berkeley(94), Orangeburg(5)
CROSS ANCHOR Spartanburg
CROSS HILL (29332) Laurens(90), Newberry(9)
DALE Beaufort
DALZELL (29040) Sumter(81), Lee(18)
DARLINGTON Darlington
DAUFUSKIE ISLAND Beaufort
DAVIS STATION Clarendon
DENMARK Bamberg
DILLON Dillon
DONALDS (29638) Abbeville(86), Greenwood(13)
DORCHESTER Dorchester
DRAYTON Spartanburg
DUE WEST Abbeville
DUNCAN Spartanburg
EARLY BRANCH (29916) Hampton(57), Jasper(42)
EASLEY (29642) Pickens(69), Anderson(30)
EASLEY Pickens
EASTOVER Richland
EDGEFIELD Edgefield
EDGEMOOR Chester
EDISTO ISLAND (29438) Colleton(58), Charleston(41)
EFFINGHAM Florence
EHRHARDT (29081) Bamberg(92), Colleton(7)

ELGIN (29045) Kershaw(56), Richland(39), Fairfield(3)
ELKO Barnwell
ELLIOTT Lee
ELLOREE (29047) Orangeburg(50), Calhoun(49)
ENOREE (29335) Spartanburg(70), Laurens(25), Union(4)
ESTILL Hampton
EUTAWVILLE Orangeburg
FAIR PLAY (29643) Oconee(80), Anderson(19)
FAIRFAX (29827) Allendale(98), Hampton(1)
FAIRFOREST Spartanburg
FINGERVILLE Spartanburg
FLORENCE (29501) Florence(92), Darlington(7)
FLORENCE Florence
FLOYD DALE Dillon
FOLLY BEACH Charleston
FORK Dillon
FORT LAWN Chester
FORT MILL (29715) York(69), Lancaster(30)
FORT MILL York
FOUNTAIN INN (29644) Laurens(60), Greenville(39)
FURMAN Hampton
GABLE (29051) Clarendon(53), Sumter(46)
GADSDEN Richland
GAFFNEY Cherokee
GALIVANTS FERRY Horry
GARNETT (29922) Hampton(69), Jasper(30)
GASTON (29053) Lexington(81), Calhoun(18)
GEORGETOWN Georgetown
GIFFORD Hampton
GILBERT Lexington
GLENDALE Spartanburg
GLOVERVILLE Aiken
GOOSE CREEK Berkeley
GRAMLING Spartanburg
GRANITEVILLE Aiken
GRAY COURT Laurens
GREAT FALLS (29055) Chester(65), Fairfield(34)
GREELEYVILLE (29056) Williamsburg(88), Clarendon(11)
GREEN POND Colleton
GREEN SEA Horry
GREENVILLE (29611) Greenville(93), Anderson(3), Pickens(2)
GREENVILLE Greenville
GREENWOOD Greenwood
GREER (29651) Greenville(54), Spartanburg(45)
GREER Greenville
GRESHAM Marion
GROVER Dorchester
HAMER Dillon
HAMPTON Hampton
HARDEEVILLE Jasper
HARLEYVILLE Dorchester
HARTSVILLE (29550) Darlington(84), Chesterfield(13), Lee(1)
HARTSVILLE Darlington
HEATH SPRINGS (29058) Lancaster(94), Kershaw(6)
HEMINGWAY (29554) Georgetown(52), Williamsburg(44), Florence(2)
HICKORY GROVE York

HILDA Barnwell
HILTON HEAD ISLAND Beaufort
HODGES (29653) Greenwood(93), Abbeville(6)
HODGES Greenwood
HOLLY HILL (29059) Orangeburg(96), Berkeley(3)
HOLLYWOOD Charleston
HONEA PATH (29654) Anderson(59), Abbeville(21), Laurens(11), Greenville(7)
HOPKINS Richland
HORATIO Sumter
HUGER (29450) Berkeley(98), Charleston(1)
INMAN Spartanburg
IRMO (29063) Richland(91), Lexington(8)
ISLANDTON Colleton
ISLE OF PALMS Charleston
IVA (29655) Anderson(58), Abbeville(41)
JACKSON Aiken
JACKSONBORO Colleton
JAMESTOWN Berkeley
JEFFERSON Chesterfield
JENKINSVILLE Fairfield
JOANNA Laurens
JOHNS ISLAND Charleston
JOHNSONVILLE (29555) Florence(93), Williamsburg(6)
JOHNSTON (29832) Edgefield(72), Saluda(27)
JONESVILLE Union
KERSHAW (29067) Lancaster(73), Kershaw(26)
KINARDS (29355) Newberry(54), Laurens(45)
KINGS CREEK Cherokee
KINGSTREE Williamsburg
KLINE Barnwell
LA FRANCE Anderson
LADSON (29456) Dorchester(41), Berkeley(40), Charleston(18)
LADYS ISLAND Beaufort
LAKE CITY (29560) Florence(73), Williamsburg(14), Clarendon(12)
LAKE VIEW Dillon
LAMAR (29069) Darlington(87), Lee(12)
LANDO Chester
LANDRUM (29356) Spartanburg(58), Greenville(41)
LANE Williamsburg
LANGLEY Aiken
LATTA (29565) Dillon(87), Marion(10), Marlboro(2)
LAURENS Laurens
LEESVILLE (29070) Lexington(74), Saluda(25)
LEXINGTON Lexington
LIBERTY (29657) Pickens(86), Anderson(13)
LIBERTY HILL Kershaw
LITTLE MOUNTAIN (29075) Newberry(81), Richland(13), Lexington(5)
LITTLE RIVER Horry
LITTLE ROCK Dillon
LIVINGSTON Orangeburg
LOBECO Beaufort
LOCKHART Union
LODGE (29082) Colleton(92), Bamberg(7)
LONE STAR Calhoun
LONG CREEK Oconee
LONGS Horry
LORIS Horry
LOWNDESVILLE Abbeville

LUGOFF (29078) Kershaw(96), Richland(3)
LURAY (29932) Allendale(56),
   Hampton(43)
LYDIA Darlington
LYMAN Spartanburg
LYNCHBURG (29080) Lee(50), Sumter(49)
MANNING Clarendon
MARIETTA (29661) Greenville(76),
   Pickens(23)
MARTIN (29836) Allendale(94), Barnwell(5)
MAULDIN Greenville
MAYESVILLE (29104) Lee(50), Sumter(49)
MAYO Spartanburg
MC BEE (29101) Chesterfield(83),
   Darlington(16)
MC CLELLANVILLE Charleston
MC COLL Marlboro
MC CONNELLS York
MC CORMICK (29835) McCormick(93),
   Edgefield(6)
MC CORMICK McCormick
MILEY Hampton
MINTURN Dillon
MODOC (29838) Edgefield(62),
   McCormick(36), Fairfield(1)
MONCKS CORNER Berkeley
MONETTA (29105) Aiken(66), Saluda(33)
MONTICELLO Fairfield
MONTMORENCI Aiken
MOORE Spartanburg
MOUNT CARMEL McCormick
MOUNT CROGHAN Chesterfield
MOUNT PLEASANT Charleston
MOUNTAIN REST Oconee
MOUNTVILLE Laurens
MULLINS Marion
MURRELLS INLET (29576) Horry(56),
   Georgetown(43)
MYRTLE BEACH Horry
NEESES Orangeburg
NESMITH Williamsburg
NEW ELLENTON Aiken
NEW ZION (29111) Clarendon(92),
   Williamsburg(7)
NEWBERRY Newberry
NEWRY Oconee
NICHOLS (29581) Horry(81), Marion(10),
   Dillon(8)
NINETY SIX (29666) Greenwood(95),
   Saluda(4)
NORRIS Pickens
NORTH (29112) Orangeburg(91),
   Calhoun(6), Lexington(2)
NORTH AUGUSTA (29841) Aiken(98),
   Edgefield(1)
NORTH AUGUSTA (29860) Edgefield(65),
   Aiken(34)
NORTH AUGUSTA Aiken
NORTH CHARLESTON Berkeley

NORTH CHARLESTON Charleston
NORTH MYRTLE BEACH Horry
NORWAY Orangeburg
OKATIE Beaufort
OLANTA (29114) Florence(59), Sumter(39)
OLAR (29843) Bamberg(90), Barnwell(9)
ORANGEBURG (29118) Orangeburg(94),
   Calhoun(5)
ORANGEBURG Orangeburg
PACOLET (29372) Spartanburg(69),
   Union(15), Cherokee(14)
PACOLET MILLS Spartanburg
PAGELAND Chesterfield
PAMPLICO Florence
PARKSVILLE McCormick
PATRICK Chesterfield
PAULINE (29374) Spartanburg(94),
   Union(6)
PAWLEYS ISLAND Georgetown
PEAK Newberry
PELION Lexington
PELZER (29669) Anderson(65),
   Greenville(34)
PENDLETON (29670) Anderson(98),
   Pickens(1)
PERRY Aiken
PICKENS Pickens
PIEDMONT (29673) Anderson(50),
   Greenville(49)
PINELAND (29934) Jasper(83),
   Hampton(16)
PINEVILLE Berkeley
PINEWOOD (29125) Clarendon(54),
   Sumter(45)
PINOPOLIS Berkeley
PLUM BRANCH (29845) McCormick(94),
   Edgefield(5)
POMARIA Newberry
PORT ROYAL Beaufort
POSTON Horry
PROSPERITY (29127) Newberry(95),
   Saluda(4)
RAINS Marion
RAVENEL (29470) Charleston(87),
   Dorchester(12)
REEVESVILLE (29471) Dorchester(96),
   Orangeburg(3)
REIDVILLE Spartanburg
REMBERT (29128) Sumter(77), Lee(15),
   Kershaw(7)
RICHBURG Chester
RICHLAND Oconee
RIDGE SPRING (29129) Aiken(47),
   Saluda(44), Edgefield(8)
RIDGELAND (29936) Jasper(97),
   Beaufort(2)
RIDGEVILLE (29472) Dorchester(62),
   Colleton(20), Berkeley(16)

RIDGEWAY (29130) Fairfield(86),
   Kershaw(11), Richland(1)
RIMINI (29131) Sumter(65), Clarendon(34)
RION Fairfield
ROCK HILL York
ROEBUCK Spartanburg
ROUND O Colleton
ROWESVILLE Orangeburg
RUBY Chesterfield
RUFFIN Colleton
RUSSELLVILLE Berkeley
SAINT GEORGE Dorchester
SAINT HELENA ISLAND Beaufort
SAINT MATTHEWS (29135) Calhoun(97),
   Orangeburg(2)
SAINT STEPHEN Berkeley
SALEM Oconee
SALLEY (29137) Aiken(85),
   Orangeburg(14)
SALTERS Williamsburg
SALUDA (29138) Saluda(97),
   Greenwood(2)
SANDY SPRINGS Anderson
SANTEE Orangeburg
SARDINIA Clarendon
SCOTIA Hampton
SCRANTON Florence
SEABROOK Beaufort
SELLERS (29592) Dillon(70), Marion(29)
SENECA Oconee
SHARON York
SHAW A F B Sumter
SHELDON Beaufort
SILVERSTREET Newberry
SIMPSONVILLE Greenville
SIX MILE Pickens
SLATER Greenville
SMOAKS (29481) Colleton(85),
   Bamberg(14)
SMYRNA York
SOCIETY HILL (29593) Darlington(53),
   Chesterfield(46)
SPARTANBURG (29307) Spartanburg(97),
   Cherokee(2)
SPARTANBURG Spartanburg
SPRINGFIELD (29146) Orangeburg(73),
   Aiken(26)
STARR Anderson
STARTEX Spartanburg
STATE PARK Richland
SULLIVANS ISLAND Charleston
SUMMERTON Clarendon
SUMMERVILLE (29483) Dorchester(70),
   Berkeley(29)
SUMMERVILLE (29485) Dorchester(89),
   Charleston(10)
SUMMERVILLE Dorchester
SUMTER Sumter
SUNSET Pickens

SWANSEA (29160) Lexington(52),
   Calhoun(47)
SYCAMORE Allendale
TAMASSEE Oconee
TATUM Marlboro
TAYLORS Greenville
TIGERVILLE Greenville
TILLMAN Jasper
TIMMONSVILLE (29161) Florence(80),
   Darlington(19)
TOWNVILLE (29689) Anderson(89),
   Oconee(10)
TRAVELERS REST Greenville
TRENTON (29847) Edgefield(65),
   Aiken(34)
TRIO Williamsburg
TROY (29848) Greenwood(85),
   McCormick(10), Saluda(2), Edgefield(1)
TURBEVILLE (29162) Clarendon(97),
   Sumter(2)
ULMER Allendale
UNA Spartanburg
VAN WYCK Lancaster
VANCE Orangeburg
VARNVILLE (29944) Hampton(89),
   Jasper(10)
VAUCLUSE Aiken
WADMALAW ISLAND Charleston
WAGENER Aiken
WALHALLA Oconee
WALLACE Marlboro
WALTERBORO Colleton
WARD Saluda
WARE SHOALS (29692) Laurens(66),
   Greenwood(24), Abbeville(9)
WARRENVILLE Aiken
WATERLOO Laurens
WEDGEFIELD Sumter
WELLFORD Spartanburg
WEST COLUMBIA Lexington
WEST UNION Oconee
WESTMINSTER Oconee
WESTVILLE Kershaw
WHITE OAK Fairfield
WHITE ROCK Richland
WHITE STONE Spartanburg
WHITMIRE (29178) Newberry(78),
   Union(16), Laurens(5)
WILLIAMS Colleton
WILLIAMSTON Anderson
WILLISTON (29853) Barnwell(65), Aiken(34)
WINDSOR Aiken
WINNSBORO (29180) Fairfield(97),
   Richland(2)
WISACKY Lee
WOODRUFF (29388) Spartanburg(93),
   Laurens(6)
YEMASSEE (29945) Colleton(30),
   Hampton(29), Jasper(28), Beaufort(11)

South Carolina ZIP/City Cross Reference

29001-29001	ALCOLU	29041-29041	DAVIS STATION	29070-29070	LEESVILLE	29114-29114	OLANTA
29002-29002	BALLENTINE	29042-29042	DENMARK	29071-29073	LEXINGTON	29115-29118	ORANGEBURG
29003-29003	BAMBERG	29044-29044	EASTOVER	29074-29074	LIBERTY HILL	29122-29122	PEAK
29006-29006	BATESBURG	29045-29045	ELGIN	29075-29075	LITTLE MOUNTAIN	29123-29123	PELION
29009-29009	BETHUNE	29046-29046	ELLIOTT	29076-29076	LIVINGSTON	29124-29124	PERRY
29010-29010	BISHOPVILLE	29047-29047	ELLOREE	29077-29077	LONE STAR	29125-29125	PINEWOOD
29014-29014	BLACKSTOCK	29048-29048	EUTAWVILLE	29078-29078	LUGOFF	29126-29126	POMARIA
29015-29015	BLAIR	29051-29051	GABLE	29079-29079	LYDIA	29127-29127	PROSPERITY
29016-29016	BLYTHEWOOD	29052-29052	GADSDEN	29080-29080	LYNCHBURG	29128-29128	REMBERT
29017-29017	BORDEN	29053-29053	GASTON	29081-29081	EHRHARDT	29129-29129	RIDGE SPRING
29018-29018	BOWMAN	29054-29054	GILBERT	29082-29082	LODGE	29130-29130	RIDGEWAY
29020-29020	CAMDEN	29055-29055	GREAT FALLS	29101-29101	MC BEE	29131-29131	RIMINI
29030-29030	CAMERON	29056-29056	GREELEYVILLE	29102-29102	MANNING	29132-29132	RION
29031-29031	CARLISLE	29058-29058	HEATH SPRINGS	29104-29104	MAYESVILLE	29133-29133	ROWESVILLE
29032-29032	CASSATT	29059-29059	HOLLY HILL	29105-29105	MONETTA	29135-29135	SAINT MATTHEWS
29033-29033	CAYCE	29061-29061	HOPKINS	29106-29106	MONTICELLO	29137-29137	SALLEY
29036-29036	CHAPIN	29062-29062	HORATIO	29107-29107	NEESES	29138-29138	SALUDA
29037-29037	CHAPPELLS	29063-29063	IRMO	29108-29108	NEWBERRY	29142-29142	SANTEE
29038-29038	COPE	29065-29065	JENKINSVILLE	29111-29111	NEW ZION	29143-29143	SARDINIA
29039-29039	CORDOVA	29067-29067	KERSHAW	29112-29112	NORTH	29145-29145	SILVERSTREET
29040-29040	DALZELL	29069-29069	LAMAR	29113-29113	NORWAY	29146-29146	SPRINGFIELD

29147-29147 STATE PARK	29440-29442 GEORGETOWN	29589-29589 RAINS	29728-29728 PAGELAND
29148-29148 SUMMERTON	29445-29445 GOOSE CREEK	29590-29590 SALTERS	29729-29729 RICHBURG
29150-29151 SUMTER	29446-29446 GREEN POND	29591-29591 SCRANTON	29730-29734 ROCK HILL
29152-29152 SHAW A F B	29447-29447 GROVER	29592-29592 SELLERS	29741-29741 RUBY
29153-29154 SUMTER	29448-29448 HARLEYVILLE	29593-29593 SOCIETY HILL	29742-29742 SHARON
29160-29160 SWANSEA	29449-29449 HOLLYWOOD	29594-29594 TATUM	29743-29743 SMYRNA
29161-29161 TIMMONSVILLE	29450-29450 HUGER	29595-29595 TRIO	29744-29744 VAN WYCK
29162-29162 TURBEVILLE	29451-29451 ISLE OF PALMS	29596-29596 WALLACE	29745-29745 YORK
29163-29163 VANCE	29452-29452 JACKSONBORO	29597-29598 NORTH MYRTLE BEACH	29801-29808 AIKEN
29164-29164 WAGENER	29453-29453 JAMESTOWN	29601-29617 GREENVILLE	29809-29809 NEW ELLENTON
29166-29166 WARD	29455-29455 JOHNS ISLAND	29620-29620 ABBEVILLE	29810-29810 ALLENDALE
29168-29168 WEDGEFIELD	29456-29456 LADSON	29621-29626 ANDERSON	29812-29812 BARNWELL
29169-29172 WEST COLUMBIA	29457-29457 JOHNS ISLAND	29627-29627 BELTON	29813-29813 HILDA
29175-29175 WESTVILLE	29458-29458 MC CLELLANVILLE	29628-29628 CALHOUN FALLS	29814-29814 KLINE
29176-29176 WHITE OAK	29461-29461 MONCKS CORNER	29630-29630 CENTRAL	29816-29816 BATH
29177-29177 WHITE ROCK	29464-29466 MOUNT PLEASANT	29631-29634 CLEMSON	29817-29817 BLACKVILLE
29178-29178 WHITMIRE	29468-29468 PINEVILLE	29635-29635 CLEVELAND	29819-29819 BRADLEY
29180-29180 WINNSBORO	29469-29469 PINOPOLIS	29636-29636 CONESTEE	29821-29821 CLARKS HILL
29183-29183 WISACKY	29470-29470 RAVENEL	29638-29638 DONALDS	29822-29822 CLEARWATER
29200-29292 COLUMBIA	29471-29471 REEVESVILLE	29639-29639 DUE WEST	29824-29824 EDGEFIELD
29301-29319 SPARTANBURG	29472-29472 RIDGEVILLE	29640-29642 EASLEY	29826-29826 ELKO
29320-29320 ARCADIA	29474-29474 ROUND O	29643-29643 FAIR PLAY	29827-29827 FAIRFAX
29321-29321 BUFFALO	29475-29475 RUFFIN	29644-29644 FOUNTAIN INN	29828-29828 GLOVERVILLE
29322-29322 CAMPOBELLO	29476-29476 RUSSELLVILLE	29645-29645 GRAY COURT	29829-29829 GRANITEVILLE
29323-29323 CHESNEE	29477-29477 SAINT GEORGE	29646-29649 GREENWOOD	29831-29831 JACKSON
29324-29324 CLIFTON	29479-29479 SAINT STEPHEN	29650-29652 GREER	29832-29832 JOHNSTON
29325-29325 CLINTON	29481-29481 SMOAKS	29653-29653 HODGES	29834-29834 LANGLEY
29329-29329 CONVERSE	29482-29482 SULLIVANS ISLAND	29654-29654 HONEA PATH	29835-29835 MC CORMICK
29330-29330 COWPENS	29483-29485 SUMMERVILLE	29655-29655 IVA	29836-29836 MARTIN
29331-29331 CROSS ANCHOR	29487-29487 WADMALAW ISLAND	29656-29656 LA FRANCE	29838-29838 MODOC
29332-29332 CROSS HILL	29488-29488 WALTERBORO	29657-29657 LIBERTY	29839-29839 MONTMORENCI
29333-29333 DRAYTON	29492-29492 CHARLESTON	29658-29658 LONG CREEK	29840-29840 MOUNT CARMEL
29334-29334 DUNCAN	29493-29493 WILLIAMS	29659-29659 LOWNDESVILLE	29841-29841 NORTH AUGUSTA
29335-29335 ENOREE	29501-29506 FLORENCE	29661-29661 MARIETTA	29842-29842 BEECH ISLAND
29336-29336 FAIRFOREST	29510-29510 ANDREWS	29662-29662 MAULDIN	29843-29843 OLAR
29338-29338 FINGERVILLE	29511-29511 AYNOR	29664-29664 MOUNTAIN REST	29844-29844 PARKSVILLE
29340-29342 GAFFNEY	29512-29512 BENNETTSVILLE	29665-29665 NEWRY	29845-29845 PLUM BRANCH
29346-29346 GLENDALE	29516-29516 BLENHEIM	29666-29666 NINETY SIX	29846-29846 SYCAMORE
29348-29348 GRAMLING	29518-29518 CADES	29667-29667 NORRIS	29847-29847 TRENTON
29349-29349 INMAN	29519-29519 CENTENARY	29669-29669 PELZER	29848-29848 TROY
29351-29351 JOANNA	29520-29520 CHERAW	29670-29670 PENDLETON	29849-29849 ULMER
29353-29353 JONESVILLE	29525-29525 CLIO	29671-29671 PICKENS	29850-29850 VAUCLUSE
29355-29355 KINARDS	29526-29528 CONWAY	29672-29672 SENECA	29851-29851 WARRENVILLE
29356-29356 LANDRUM	29530-29530 COWARD	29673-29673 PIEDMONT	29853-29853 WILLISTON
29360-29360 LAURENS	29532-29532 DARLINGTON	29675-29675 RICHLAND	29856-29856 WINDSOR
29364-29364 LOCKHART	29536-29536 DILLON	29676-29676 SALEM	29860-29861 NORTH AUGUSTA
29365-29365 LYMAN	29540-29540 DARLINGTON	29677-29677 SANDY SPRINGS	29899-29899 MC CORMICK
29368-29368 MAYO	29541-29541 EFFINGHAM	29678-29679 SENECA	29901-29906 BEAUFORT
29369-29369 MOORE	29542-29542 FLOYD DALE	29680-29681 SIMPSONVILLE	29907-29907 LADYS ISLAND
29370-29370 MOUNTVILLE	29543-29543 FORK	29682-29682 SIX MILE	29909-29909 OKATIE
29372-29372 PACOLET	29544-29544 GALIVANTS FERRY	29683-29683 SLATER	29910-29910 BLUFFTON
29373-29373 PACOLET MILLS	29545-29545 GREEN SEA	29684-29684 STARR	29911-29911 BRUNSON
29374-29374 PAULINE	29546-29546 GRESHAM	29685-29685 SUNSET	29912-29912 COOSAWATCHIE
29375-29375 REIDVILLE	29547-29547 HAMER	29686-29686 TAMASSEE	29913-29913 CROCKETVILLE
29376-29376 ROEBUCK	29550-29551 HARTSVILLE	29687-29687 TAYLORS	29914-29914 DALE
29377-29377 STARTEX	29554-29554 HEMINGWAY	29688-29688 TIGERVILLE	29915-29915 DAUFUSKIE ISLAND
29378-29378 UNA	29555-29555 JOHNSONVILLE	29689-29689 TOWNVILLE	29916-29916 EARLY BRANCH
29379-29379 UNION	29556-29556 KINGSTREE	29690-29690 TRAVELERS REST	29918-29918 ESTILL
29384-29384 WATERLOO	29560-29560 LAKE CITY	29691-29691 WALHALLA	29920-29920 SAINT HELENA ISLAND
29385-29385 WELLFORD	29563-29563 LAKE VIEW	29692-29692 WARE SHOALS	29921-29921 FURMAN
29386-29386 WHITE STONE	29564-29564 LANE	29693-29693 WESTMINSTER	29922-29922 GARNETT
29388-29388 WOODRUFF	29565-29565 LATTA	29695-29695 HODGES	29923-29923 GIFFORD
29390-29391 DUNCAN	29566-29566 LITTLE RIVER	29696-29696 WEST UNION	29924-29924 HAMPTON
29395-29395 JONESVILLE	29567-29567 LITTLE ROCK	29697-29697 WILLIAMSTON	29925-29926 HILTON HEAD ISLAND
29401-29403 CHARLESTON	29568-29568 LONGS	29698-29698 GREENVILLE	29927-29927 HARDEEVILLE
29404-29404 CHARLESTON AFB	29569-29569 LORIS	29702-29702 BLACKSBURG	29928-29928 HILTON HEAD ISLAND
29405-29410 CHARLESTON	29570-29570 MC COLL	29703-29703 BOWLING GREEN	29929-29929 ISLANDTON
29410-29410 NORTH CHARLESTON	29571-29571 MARION	29704-29704 CATAWBA	29931-29931 LOBECO
29411-29415 CHARLESTON	29572-29572 MYRTLE BEACH	29705-29705 CHEROKEE FALLS	29932-29932 LURAY
29415-29415 NORTH CHARLESTON	29573-29573 MINTURN	29706-29706 CHESTER	29933-29933 MILEY
29416-29425 CHARLESTON	29574-29574 MULLINS	29708-29708 FORT MILL	29934-29934 PINELAND
29426-29426 ADAMS RUN	29575-29575 MYRTLE BEACH	29709-29709 CHESTERFIELD	29935-29935 PORT ROYAL
29429-29429 AWENDAW	29576-29576 MURRELLS INLET	29710-29710 CLOVER	29936-29936 RIDGELAND
29430-29430 BETHERA	29577-29579 MYRTLE BEACH	29712-29712 EDGEMOOR	29938-29938 HILTON HEAD ISLAND
29431-29431 BONNEAU	29580-29580 NESMITH	29714-29714 FORT LAWN	29939-29939 SCOTIA
29432-29432 BRANCHVILLE	29581-29581 NICHOLS	29715-29716 FORT MILL	29940-29940 SEABROOK
29433-29433 CANADYS	29582-29582 NORTH MYRTLE BEACH	29717-29717 HICKORY GROVE	29941-29941 SHELDON
29434-29434 CORDESVILLE	29583-29583 PAMPLICO	29718-29718 JEFFERSON	29943-29943 TILLMAN
29435-29435 COTTAGEVILLE	29584-29584 PATRICK	29719-29719 KINGS CREEK	29944-29944 VARNVILLE
29436-29436 CROSS	29585-29585 PAWLEYS ISLAND	29720-29722 LANCASTER	29945-29945 YEMASSEE
29437-29437 DORCHESTER	29587-29587 MYRTLE BEACH	29724-29724 LANDO	29948-29948 HILTON HEAD ISLAND
29438-29438 EDISTO ISLAND	29588-29588 POSTON	29726-29726 MC CONNELLS	
29439-29439 FOLLY BEACH	29588-29588 MYRTLE BEACH	29727-29727 MOUNT CROGHAN	

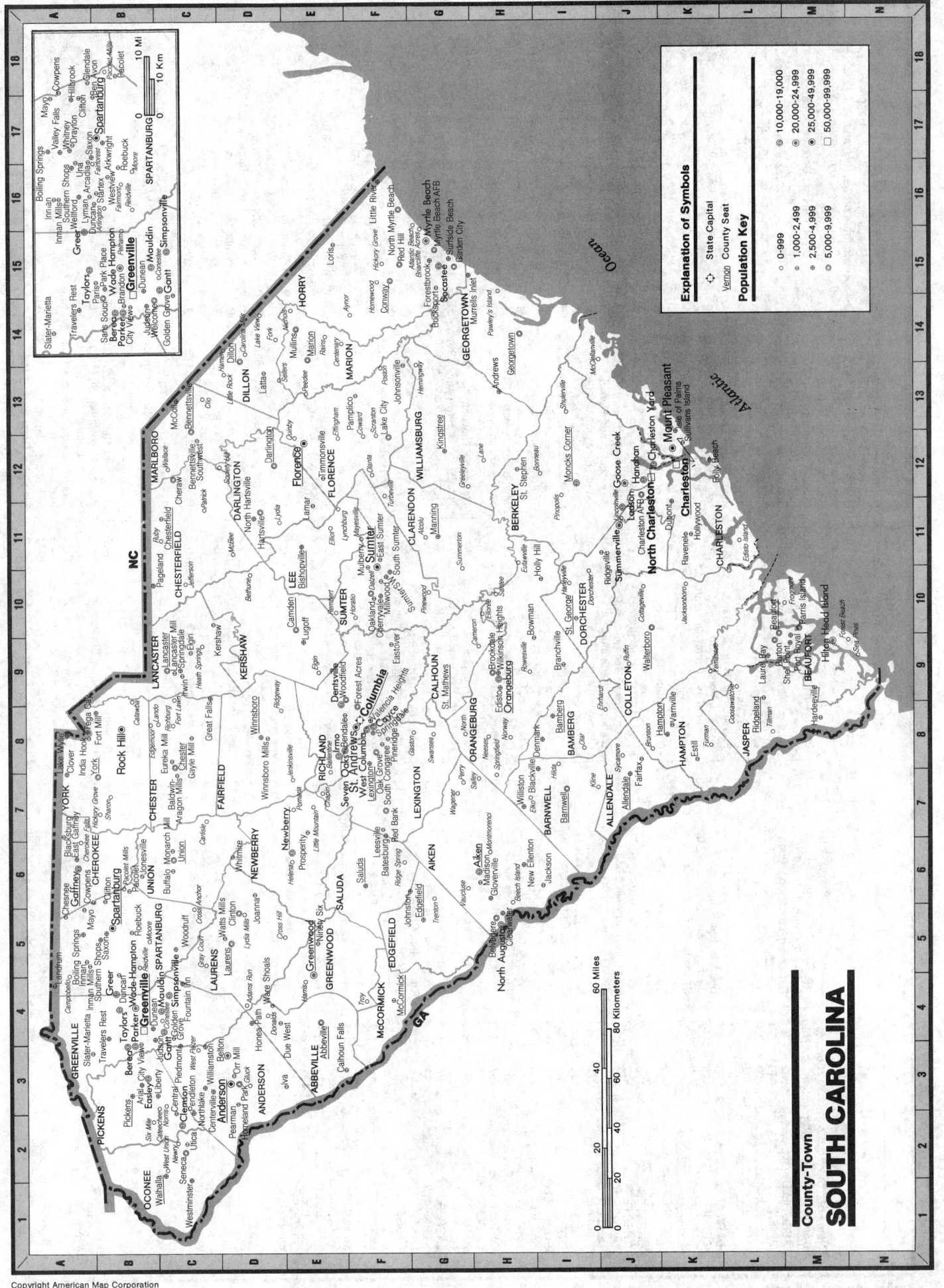

County-Town
SOUTH CAROLINA

Explanation of Symbols

◇ State Capital
<u>Vernon</u> County Seat

Population Key

○ 0-999
○ 1,000-2,499
⊚ 2,500-4,999
⊚ 5,000-9,999

◉ 10,000-19,000
◎ 20,000-24,999
◉ 25,000-49,999
□ 50,000-99,999

COUNTIES

(46 Counties)

Name of County	Population	Location on Map
ABBEVILLE	23,862	E-3
AIKEN	120,940	G-6
ALLENDALE	11,722	J-7
ANDERSON	145,196	C-2
BAMBERG	16,902	I-8
BARNWELL	20,293	I-7
BEAUFORT	86,425	M-9
BERKELEY	128,776	H-11
CALHOUN	12,753	G-9
CHARLESTON	295,039	K-11
CHEROKEE	44,506	B-6
CHESTER	32,170	B-7
CHESTERFIELD	38,577	C-10
CLARENDON	28,450	G-11
COLLETON	34,377	J-8
DARLINGTON	61,851	D-11
DILLON	29,114	D-13
DORCHESTER	83,060	I-9
EDGEFIELD	18,375	F-5
FAIRFIELD	22,295	D-7
FLORENCE	114,344	E-12
GEORGETOWN	46,302	G-14
GREENVILLE	320,167	A-3
GREENWOOD	59,567	E-4
HAMPTON	18,191	K-8
HORRY	144,053	E-14
JASPER	15,487	L-8
KERSHAW	43,599	D-9
LANCASTER	54,516	C-9
LAURENS	58,092	C-4
LEE	18,437	E-10
LEXINGTON	167,611	F-7
MARION	33,899	F-13
MARLBORO	29,361	C-12
MCCORMICK	8,868	F-4
NEWBERRY	33,172	D-6
OCONEE	57,494	B-1
ORANGEBURG	84,803	H-8
PICKENS	93,894	B-2
RICHLAND	285,720	F-7
SALUDA	16,357	E-6
SPARTANBURG	226,800	C-5
SUMTER	102,637	E-10
UNION	30,337	B-6
WILLIAMSBURG	36,815	G-12
YORK	131,497	A-7
TOTAL	**3,486,703**	

CITIES AND TOWNS

Note: The first name is that of the city or town, second, that of the county in which it is located, then the population and location on the map.

- Abbeville, Abbeville, 5,778 — E-4
- Aiken, Aiken, 19,872 — H-6
- Allendale, Allendale, 4,410 — J-7
- Anderson, Anderson, 26,184 — D-3
- •Andrews, Georgetown/Williamsburg, 3,050 — G-13
- •Arial, Pickens, 2,604 — B-3
- Baldwin-Aragon Mills, Chester, 3,843 — C-7
- Bamberg, Bamberg, 3,843 — I-8
- Barnwell, Barnwell, 5,255 — I-7
- Batesburg, Lexington/Saluda, 4,082 — F-7
- Beaufort, Beaufort, 9,576 — L-10
- •Belton, Anderson, 4,646 — D-3
- •Belvedere, Aiken, 6,133 — H-5
- Bendale, Barnwell — I-7
- Bennettsville, Marlboro, 9,345 — C-13
- •Bennettsville Southwest, Marlboro, 4,388 — C-13
- •Berea, Greenville, 13,535 — A-3
- Bishopville, Lee, 3,560 — E-10
- Blacksburg, Cherokee, 1,907 — A-6
- Blackville, Barnwell, 2,688 — I-7
- •Boiling Springs, Spartanburg, 3,522 — B-5
- Bowman, Orangeburg, 1,063 — H-8
- Branchville, Orangeburg, 1,107 — H-8
- Brandon, Greenville — A-3
- •Brookdale, Orangeburg, 5,339 — H-9
- •Bucksport, Horry, 1,022 — F-14
- •Buffalo, Union, 1,569 — C-6
- •Burton, Beaufort, 6,917 — L-10
- Calhoun Falls, Abbeville, 2,328 — E-3
- Camden, Kershaw, 6,696 — D-9
- Cayce, Lexington, 11,163 — F-8
- •Centerville, Anderson, 4,866 — D-3
- Central, Pickens, 2,438 — B-3
- Charleston, Charleston, 80,414 — K-11
- Charleston Base, Charleston — K-11
- Charleston Yard, Charleston — K-11
- Cheraw, Chesterfield, 5,505 — C-12
- •Cherryvale, Sumter, 3,061 — E-10
- Chesnee, Cherokee/Spartanburg, 1,280 — B-5
- Chester, Chester, 7,158 — B-7
- Chesterfield, Chesterfield, 1,373 — C-11
- City View, Greenville, 1,490 — B-3
- •Clearwater, Aiken, 4,731 — H-5
- Clemson, Anderson/Pickens, 11,096 — C-3
- Clifton, Spartanburg — B-3
- Clinton, Laurens, 7,987 — C-5
- Clover, York, 3,422 — A-7
- Columbia, Richland, 98,052 — F-8
- Conway, Horry, 9,819 — E-15
- Cowpens, Spartanburg, 2,176 — B-5
- Darlington, Darlington, 7,311 — D-12
- Denmark, Bamberg, 3,762 — I-8
- •Dentsville, Richland, 11,839 — F-8
- Dillon, Dillon, 6,829 — D-14
- Due West, Abbeville, 1,220 — E-3
- •Duncan, Spartanburg, 2,152 — B-5
- •Dupont, Charleston — K-11
- Easley, Pickens, 15,195 — B-3
- •East Gaffney, Cherokee, 3,278 — A-6
- •East Sumter, Sumter, 1,590 — F-11
- Eastover, Richland, 1,044 — F-9
- Edgefield, Edgefield, 2,563 — G-5
- •Edisto, Orangeburg, 2,815 — H-9
- •Elgin, Lancaster, 2,196 — C-9
- Estill, Hampton, 2,387 — K-8
- •Eureka Mill, Chester, 1,738 — C-8
- Fairfax, Allendale/Hampton, 2,317 — J-8
- Florence, Florence, 29,813 — E-12
- Folly Beach, Charleston, 1,398 — K-12
- Forest Acres, Richland, 7,197 — F-8
- •Forestbrook, Horry, 2,502 — G-15
- Fort Mill, York, 4,930 — B-8
- Fountain Inn, Greenville/Laurens, 4,388 — C-4
- Gaffney, Cherokee, 13,145 — A-6
- Gantt, Greenville, 13,891 — C-4
- Garden City, Horry, 6,305 — G-15
- Gayle Mill, Chester, 1,037 — C-8
- Georgetown, Georgetown, 9,517 — H-14
- Glendale, Spartanburg, 3,522 — B-5
- •Gloverville, Aiken, 2,753 — H-6
- •Golden Grove, Greenville, 2,055 — C-4
- Goose Creek, Berkeley/Charleston, 24,692 — J-12
- Great Falls, Chester, 2,307 — C-9
- Greenville, Greenville, 58,282 — B-4
- Greenwood, Greenwood, 20,807 — E-5
- Greer, Greenville/Spartanburg, 10,322 — B-4
- Hampton, Hampton, 2,997 — K-8
- Hanahan, Berkeley, 13,176 — J-12
- Hardeeville, Jasper, 1,583 — M-8
- Hartsville, Darlington, 8,372 — D-11
- •Hillbrook, Spartanburg — A-17
- Hilton Head Island, Beaufort, 23,694 — M-9
- Holly Hill, Orangeburg, 1,478 — I-10
- Hollywood, Charleston, 2,094 — K-11
- Homeland Park, Anderson, 6,569 — D-3
- Honea Path, Abbeville/Anderson, 3,841 — D-4
- India Hook, York, 1,506 — A-8
- Inman, Spartanburg, 1,742 — A-5
- Inman Mills, Spartanburg, 1,571 — A-5
- Irmo, Lexington/Richland, 11,280 — E-8
- Irwin, Lancaster, 1,296 — C-9
- Isle of Palms, Charleston, 3,680 — K-13
- Iva, Anderson, 1,174 — D-5
- Jackson, Aiken, 1,681 — I-6
- Joanna, Laurens, 1,735 — D-6
- Johnsonville, Florence, 1,415 — F-13
- Johnston, Edgefield, 2,688 — G-6
- Jonesville, Union, 1,205 — B-6
- Judson, Greenville, 2,859 — B-4
- Kershaw, Lancaster, 1,814 — D-10
- Kingstree, Williamsburg, 3,858 — G-12
- •Ladson, Berkeley/Charleston, 13,540 — J-11
- Lake City, Florence, 7,153 — F-12
- •Lake Wylie, York, 2,599 — A-8
- Lamar, Darlington, 1,125 — E-11
- Lancaster, Lancaster, 8,914 — C-9
- •Lancaster Mill, Lancaster, 2,373 — C-9
- Landrum, Spartanburg, 2,347 — A-4
- Latta, Dillon, 1,565 — D-13
- •Laurel Bay, Beaufort, 4,972 — L-9
- Laurens, Laurens, 9,694 — D-5
- Leesville, Lexington, 2,025 — F-7
- Lexington, Lexington, 3,289 — F-8
- •Liberty, Pickens, 3,228 — B-3
- •Little River, Horry, 3,470 — F-16
- Loris, Horry, 2,067 — E-15
- Lugoff, Kershaw, 3,211 — E-10
- Lyman, Spartanburg, 2,271 — A-16
- Manning, Clarendon, 4,428 — G-11
- Marion, Marion, 7,658 — E-14
- Mauldin, Greenville, 11,587 — C-4
- •Mayo, Spartanburg, 1,569 — B-5
- McColl, Marlboro, 2,685 — C-13
- McCormick, McCormick, 1,659 — F-4
- Millwood, Sumter, 1,070 — F-10
- •Monarch Mill, Union, 2,214 — C-6
- Moncks Corner, Berkeley, 5,607 — I-12
- Mount Pleasant, Charleston, 30,108 — K-12
- •Mulberry, Sumter, 1,097 — F-11
- Mullins, Marion, 5,910 — E-14
- •Murrells Inlet, Georgetown, 3,334 — G-15
- Myrtle Beach, Horry, 24,848 — G-15
- Myrtle Beach Base, Horry — G-15
- New Ellenton, Aiken, 2,515 — H-6
- Newberry, Newberry, 10,542 — E-6
- Ninety Six, Greenwood, 2,099 — E-5
- North Augusta, Aiken/Edgefield, 15,351 — H-5
- North Charleston, Berkeley/Charleston/Dorchester, 70,218 — J-12
- •North Hartsville, Darlington, 2,906 — D-11
- North Myrtle Beach, Horry, 8,636 — F-16
- •Northlake, Anderson, 3,162 — C-3
- Oak Grove, Lexington, 7,173 — F-10
- •Oakland, Sumter, 1,298 — B-4
- Orangeburg, Orangeburg, 13,739 — H-9
- Pacolet, Spartanburg, 1,736 — B-6
- Pageland, Chesterfield, 2,666 — B-10
- Pamplico, Florence, 1,314 — F-13
- Park Place, Greenville — B-15
- •Parker, Greenville, 11,072 — B-15
- •Parris Island, Beaufort, 7,172 — M-10
- Pendleton, Anderson, 3,314 — C-3
- •Piedmont, Anderson/Greenville, 4,143 — C-3
- Pineridge, Lexington, 1,731 — F-8
- Port Royal, Beaufort, 2,985 — M-9
- Prosperity, Newberry, 1,116 — E-7
- Ravenel, Charleston, 2,165 — K-11
- Red Bank, Lexington, 5,950 — F-7
- •Red Hill, Horry, 6,112 — F-15
- Ridgeland, Jasper, 1,071 — L-8
- Ridgeville, Dorchester, 1,625 — I-11
- •Rock Hill, York, 41,643 — B-8
- •Roebuck, Spartanburg, 1,966 — B-5
- Saint Andrews, Richland, 25,692 — F-8
- Saint George, Dorchester, 2,077 — I-10
- Saint Matthews, Calhoun, 2,345 — G-9
- Saint Stephen, Berkeley, 1,697 — H-12
- Saluda, Saluda, 2,798 — F-6
- •Sans Souci, Greenville, 7,612 — B-14
- •Saxon, Spartanburg, 4,002 — B-5
- Seneca, Oconee, 7,726 — C-2
- Seven Oaks, Lexington, 15,722 — E-8
- Shannontown, Sumter — F-11
- Shell Point, Beaufort, 2,885 — M-9
- Simpsonville, Greenville, 11,708 — C-4
- Slater-Marietta, Greenville, 2,245 — A-3
- Socastee, Horry, 10,426 — G-15
- South Congaree, Lexington, 2,406 — F-8
- South Sumter, Sumter, 4,371 — F-10
- •Southern Shops, Spartanburg, 3,378 — B-5
- Spartanburg, Spartanburg, 43,467 — B-5
- Springdale, Lancaster, 2,643 — C-9
- Springdale, Lexington, 3,226 — F-8
- Startex, Spartanburg, 1,162 — B-16
- •Sullivan's Island, Charleston, 1,623 — K-12
- Summerville, Berkeley/Charleston/Dorchester, 22,519 — J-11
- Sumter, Sumter, 41,943 — F-11
- Surfside Beach, Horry, 3,845 — G-15
- •Taylors, Greenville, 19,619 — B-4
- Tega Cay, York, 3,016 — A-8
- Timmonsville, Florence, 2,182 — E-12
- Travelers Rest, Greenville, 3,069 — B-4
- Union, Union, 9,836 — C-6
- •Utica, Oconee, 1,478 — C-2
- •Valencia Heights, Richland, 4,122 — D-11
- Valley Falls, Spartanburg, 3,504 — F-16
- •Varnville, Hampton, 1,970 — K-8
- •Wade Hampton, Greenville, 20,014 — B-4
- Walhalla, Oconee, 3,755 — C-2
- Walterboro, Colleton, 5,492 — J-10
- Ware Shoals, Abbeville/Greenwood/Laurens, 2,497 — D-4
- Watts Mills, Laurens, 1,535 — D-5
- •Welcome, Greenville, 6,560 — B-14
- Wellford, Spartanburg, 2,511 — A-16
- West Columbia, Lexington, 10,588 — F-8
- Westminster, Oconee, 3,120 — C-1
- Whitmire, Newberry, 1,702 — D-6
- •Wilkinson Heights, Orangeburg, 3,394 — H-9
- Williamston, Anderson, 3,876 — M-9
- Williston, Barnwell, 3,099 — E-7
- Winnsboro, Fairfield, 3,475 — D-8
- Winnsboro Mills, Fairfield, 2,275 — F-9
- •Woodfield, Richland, 8,862 — F-9
- Woodruff, Spartanburg, 4,365 — C-5
- York, York, 6,709 — B-7

Explanation of symbols: • – Census Designated Place (CDP)

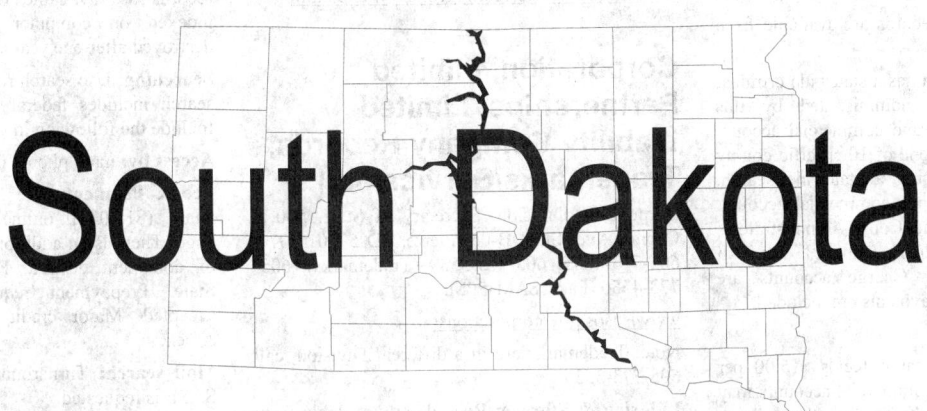

South Dakota

General Help Numbers:

Governor's Office
State Capitol, 500 E Capitol Ave
Pierre, SD 57501-5070
www.state.sd.us/governor/

605-773-3212
Fax 605-773-4711
8AM-5PM

Attorney General's Office
State Capitol, 500 E Capitol Ave
Pierre, SD 57501-5070
www.state.sd.us/attorney/index.htm

605-773-3215
Fax 605-773-4106
8AM-5PM

Legislative Records
South Dakota Legislature, Capitol Bldg
Legislative Research Council
500 E Capitol Ave
Pierre, SD 57501
http://legis.state.sd.us

605-773-3251
Fax 605-773-4576
8AM-5PM

State Archives
Cultural Heritage Center/State Archives
900 Governors Dr
Pierre, SD 57501-2217
http://www.sdhistory.org/

605-773-3804
Fax 605-773-6041
9AM-4:30PM

State Specifics:

Capital:
Pierre
Hughes County

Time Zone:
CST*
* South Dakota's eighteen western-most counties are MST: They are: Bennett, Butte, Corson, Custer, Dewey, Fall River, Haakon, Harding, Jackson, Lawrence, Meade, Mellette, Pennington, Perkins, Shannon, Stanley, Todd, Ziebach,

Number of Counties:
66

Population:
764,309

Web Site:
www.state.sd.us

State Agencies

Criminal Records
Division of Criminal Investigation, Identification Section, 500 E Capitol, Pierre, SD 57501-5070; 605-773-3331, 605-773-4629 (Fax), 8AM-5PM.

http://dci.sd.gov/

Indexing & Storage: Records are available for 10 years for misdemeanors and lifetime for felonies. It takes 1 day before new records are available for inquiry. Records are indexed on inhouse computer (90+%); only older records not computerized. Records are normally destroyed after 10 years if a misdemeanor, generally.

Searching: Include the following in your request-date of birth, full name, set of fingerprints, signed release form. The form requires identifying information: color of hair and eyes, height, weight, date of birth, SSN. The following data is not released: juvenile records, minor traffic violations or out-of-state or federal charges.

Access by: mail.

Fee & Payment: The fee is $15.00 per name. Statutorily-required fingerprint checks will include an FBI fingerprint check for an additional $24.00. Fee payee: Division of Criminal Investigation. Prepayment required. Personal checks accepted. No credit cards accepted.

Mail search: Turnaround time: 5 to 10 working days. Upon receipt of those requirements, they will

conduct a search of their files and supply a copy of any criminal history that is found or a statement that there is no criminal history. A SASE is requested.

Other access: The State Court Administrator's Office has a statewide database of criminal record information from the state's circuit courts. For more information about setting up a commercial account, contact Jill Gusso at 605-773-3474.

Statewide Court Records
State Court Administrator, State Capitol Bldg, 500 E Capitol Ave, Pierre, SD 57501-5059; 605-773-3474, 605-773-5627 (Fax), 8AM-5PM.

www.sdjudicial.com

Note: The Supreme Court calendar, opinions, and 2nd oral arguments may be searched from the website.

Indexing & Storage: Records are available from July 1, 1989 forward.

Searching: South Dakota has a statewide criminal record search database administrated by this office. All mail requests and commercial account requests are assigned to one of 10 specific county court clerks for processing a statewide search. Requesters may to set up a commercial account. Contact Jill Gusso at the Court Administrator's Office at the address above, or at jill.gusso@ujs.state.sd.us. Charge accounts are available, if guaranteed payments are included.

Access by: mail, fax.

Fee & Payment: The search fee is $15.00 per record. State authorized commercial accounts may order and receive records by fax, there is an additional $5.00 fee unless a non-toll free line is used.

Mail search: Turnaround time: is usually 1-4 days. No searching by mail.

Fax search: If authorized.

Sexual Offender Registry

Division of Criminal Investigation, Identification Section - SOR Unit, 500 E Capitol, Pierre, SD 57501-5070 (Courier: 3444 East Highway 34, Pierre, SD 57501); 605-773-3331, 605-773-4614, 605-773-2596 (Fax), 8AM-5PM.

http://dci.sd.gov/administration/id/sexoffender/index.asp

Note: Online access (see below) is only by county. This agency urges the public to visit local law enforcement offices for access to lists.

Indexing & Storage: Records are available from 1994. It takes over 30 days before new records are available for inquiry. Records are normally destroyed after court order, moved, or deceased.

Access by: online. No searching by mail.

Online search: Searching is available from the website. Note that there is no statewide search, all searches are done on a county basis.

Incarceration Records

SD Department of Corrections, Central Records Office, 3200 E. Highway 34, 500 E. Capitol Avenue, Pierre, SD 57501-5070 (Courier: 1600 North Dr, Pierre, SD 57504); 605-773-3478, 605-367-5190 (Sioux Falls Central Records), 605-773-3194 (Fax), 8AM-4PM.

www.state.sd.us/corrections/corrections.html

Indexing & Storage: Records are available on current and former inmates. It takes up to 3 days before new records are available for inquiry. Records are normally destroyed after one year from final discharge.

Searching: The computerized records system does not track records back further than those inmates who were discharged in 1985. Include the following in your request-name and DOB or SSN. Location, conviction and sentencing information are available. The following data is not released: medical, treatment, and disciplinary records.

Access by: phone. No searching by mail.

Phone search: For phone search, call the Department's Office of Community Relations at 302-739-5601 x246.

Other access: A department most wanted list is available at www.state.sd.us/corrections/most_wanted.htm.

Corporation, Limited Partnerships, Limited Liability Company Records, Trademarks/Servicemarks

Corporation Division, Secretary of State, 500 E Capitol Ave, Suite B-05, Pierre, SD 57501-5070; 605-773-4845, 605-773-3539 (Trademarks), 605-773-4550 (Fax), 8AM-5PM.

www.sdsos.gov/corporations/

Note: Trademarks are in a different Division, call 605-773-3539.

Indexing & Storage: Records are available from the founding of the state. New records are available for inquiry immediately. Records are indexed on microfiche, inhouse computer.

Searching: Include the following in your request-full name of business. In addition to the articles of incorporation, corporation records include the following information: Annual Reports, Officers, Directors, Registered Agent, Prior (merged) names, Inactive and Reserved names.

Access by: mail, phone, fax, in person, online.

Fee & Payment: There is no fee for a general search. A Certificate of Good Standing is available for a fee of $15.00. Copies are $1.00 per page, add $10.00 for certification. Fee payee: Secretary of State. Prepayment required. Personal checks accepted. Major credit cards accepted.

Mail search: Turnaround time: 1 to 3 days. A SASE is requested.

Phone search: They will provide basic information only.

Fax search: Records can be returned by fax for $1.00 per page plus a $5.00 fax fee.

In person search: Turnaround time is immediate.

Online search: Search the Secretary of State Corporations Div. Database free at www.state.sd.us/applications/st02corplook/corpfile.asp. Trademark searches may be requested via e-mail at anissa.grambihler@state.sd.us.

Other access: The corporate database may be purchased on CD for $1,000 with $500 monthly updates.

Expedited service: Expedited service is available for an additional $20.00 per request.

Fictitious Name, Assumed Name

Records not maintained by a state level agency.

Note: Records are located at the county level.

Uniform Commercial Code, Federal Tax Liens

UCC Division, Secretary of State, 500 East Capitol, Pierre, SD 57501-5077; 605-773-4422, 605-773-4550 (Fax), 8AM-5PM.

www.sdsos.gov/ucc

Note: Federal tax liens on business filed here, if on individuals then filed at county level.

Indexing & Storage: Records are available for all active records. It takes less than 1 day before new records are available for inquiry. Records are indexed on computer. Records are normally destroyed after one year after lapse.

Searching: Use search request form UCC-11. The search includes federal tax liens on businesses. Include the following in your request-debtor name.

Access by: mail, phone, fax, in person, online.

Fee & Payment: The fee is $20.00 per debtor name, ($15.00 if online). Copies are $1.00 per page. There is an additional $10.00 if certification of document desired. Fee payee: Secretary of State. Prepayment required. Personal checks accepted. Major credit cards accepted, except Amex.

Mail search: Turnaround time: 1 to 2 days. A SASE is requested.

Phone search: Limited information is given over the phone. Reports can be ordered.

Fax search: Use of a credit card is required or prepay. Fee is additional $5.00 to fax back.

In person search: Simple requests may be processed while you wait.

Online search: Dakota Fast File is the filing and searching service available from the website. This is a commercial service that requires registration and a $120-360 fee per year. A certified search is also available.

Other access: FTP downloads are availbale for purchase.

Expedited service: Expedited service is available for mail, phone and fax searches. Turnaround time: 1 day. Add $20.00 per debtor name.

State Tax Liens, Federal Tax Liens

Records not maintained by a state level agency.

Note: All state tax liens and federal tax liens on individuals are filed at the county level.

Sales Tax Registrations

Department of Revenue and Regulation, Business Tax Division, 445 E Capitol, Pierre, SD 57501-3100; 605-773-3311, 605-773-6729 (Fax), 8AM-5PM.

www.state.sd.us/drr2/revenue.html

Indexing & Storage: Records are available from 1992 on computer. Records have been placed on microfilm from 1970 to 1996.

Searching: This agency will only confirm if a business is registered and licensed. They will provide no other information. Include the following in your request-business name. Also search by tax permit number or owner name.

Access by: mail, phone, fax, in person.

Mail search: Turnaround time: 2 to 3 weeks. A SASE is requested. No fee for mail request.

Phone search: No fee for telephone request.

Fax search: There is no fee, turnaround time is 2-3 weeks.

In person search: No fee for request. Usually requests can be processed while you wait.

Birth Certificates

South Dakota Department of Health, Vital Records, 600 E Capitol, Pierre, SD 57501-2536; 605-773-4961, 605-773-5683 (Fax), 8AM-5PM.

www.state.sd.us/doh/VitalRec/index.htm

Indexing & Storage: Records are available from 1906 to present. New records are available for inquiry immediately.

Searching: Include the following in your request-full name, names of parents, mother's maiden name, date of birth, place of birth. Any county Register of Deeds can provide a computer generated birth certificate for the same fee. The following data is not released: sealed records.

Access by: mail, phone, in person, online.

Fee & Payment: The fee is $10.00. Use of a credit card is an additional $10.00 expedited fee. Fee payee: South Dakota Department of Health. Prepayment required. Personal checks accepted. Credit cards accepted: MasterCard, Visa, AmEx, Discover.

Mail search: Turnaround time: 4 to 5 days. No SASE is required.

Phone search: You must use a credit card, considered expedited service.

In person search: Turnaround time 30 minutes.

Online search: You can search free at the website for birth records over 100 years old. You can order recent (less than 100 years) birth records at the website, for a fee.

Expedited service: Expedited service is available for web and phone searches. Turnaround time: overnight delivery. Add delivery fee and use of credit card fee.

Death Records

South Dakota Department of Health, Vital Records, 600 E Capitol, Pierre, SD 57501-2536; 605-773-4961, 605-773-5683 (Fax), 8AM-5PM.

www.state.sd.us/doh/VitalRec/index.htm

Indexing & Storage: Records are available from 1905 to present. New records are available for inquiry immediately.

Searching: Include the following in your request-full name, date of death, place of death. The following data is not released: sealed records.

Access by: mail, phone, in person, online.

Fee & Payment: The fee is $10.00 per record. There is an additional $10.00 fee if a credit card is used. Fee payee: South Dakota Department of Health. Prepayment required. Personal checks accepted. Credit cards accepted: MasterCard, Visa, AmEx, Discover.

Mail search: Turnaround time: 4 to 5 days. No SASE is required.

Phone search: You must use a credit card.

In person search: Turnaround time is 30 minutes.

Online search: Records may be ordered online at the web site.

Expedited service: Expedited service is available for Internet and phone searches. Turnaround time: overnight delivery. Add delivery fee and use of credit card fee.

Marriage Certificates

South Dakota Department of Health, Vital Records, 600 E Capitol, Pierre, SD 57501-2536; 605-773-4961, 605-773-5683 (Fax), 8AM-5PM.

www.state.sd.us/doh/VitalRec/index.htm

Indexing & Storage: Records are available from 1905 to present. New records are available for inquiry immediately.

Searching: Include the following in your request-names of husband and wife, date of marriage, place or county of marriage. Also include wife's maiden name.

Access by: mail, phone, in person, online.

Fee & Payment: The fee is $7.00 per record. There is an additional $10.00 expedited fee if a credit card is used. Fee payee: South Dakota Department of Health. Prepayment required. Personal checks accepted. Credit cards accepted: MasterCard, Visa, AmEx, Discover.

Mail search: Turnaround time: 4 to 5 days. No SASE is required.

Phone search: You must use a credit card.

In person search: Turnaround time is 30 minutes.

Online search: Records may be ordered online at the web site.

Expedited service: Expedited service is available for Internet and phone searches. Turnaround time: overnight delivery. Add delivery fee and use of credit card fee.

Divorce Records

South Dakota Department of Health, Vital Records, 600 E Capitol, Pierre, SD 57501-2536; 605-773-4961, 605-773-5683 (Fax), 8AM-5PM.

www.state.sd.us/doh/VitalRec/index.htm

Indexing & Storage: Records are available from 1905 to present. New records are available for inquiry immediately.

Searching: Include the following in your request-names of husband and wife, date of divorce, place of divorce. The following data is not released: sealed records.

Access by: mail, phone, in person, online.

Fee & Payment: The fee is $7.00 per record. There is an additional $10.00 expedited fee if a credit card is used. Fee payee: South Dakota Department of Health. Prepayment required. Personal checks accepted. Credit cards accepted: MasterCard, Visa, AmEx, Discover.

Mail search: Turnaround time: 4 to 5 days. No SASE is required.

Phone search: You must use a credit card.

In person search: Turnaround time 30 minutes.

Online search: Records may be ordered at the web site.

Expedited service: Expedited service is available for Internet and phone searches. Turnaround time: overnight delivery. Add delivery fee and use of credit card fee.

Workers' Compensation Records

Labor Department, Workers Compensation Division, 700 Governors Dr, Pierre, SD 57501; 605-773-3681, 605-773-4211 (Fax), 8AM-5PM.

www.state.sd.us/dol/dlm/dlm-home.htm

Indexing & Storage: Records are available from 1973. New records are available for inquiry immediately. Records are indexed on inhouse computer.

Searching: Must have a signed release from the claimant. Must also specify which records you are requesting. A computer search will only go back to July 1989. Fraud reports and sealed files are not released. Include the following in your request-claimant name, Social Security Number, date of accident, body part injured.

Access by: mail.

Fee & Payment: Search fee is $20.00 per file or date of injury, copies are included. Fee payee: Division of Labor Management. Prepayment required. Personal checks accepted. No credit cards accepted.

Mail search: Turnaround time: 1 week.

Driver Records

Dept of Public Safety, Office of Driver Licensing, 118 W Capitol, Pierre, SD 57501; 605-773-6883, 605-773-3018 (Fax), 8AM-5PM.

www.state.sd.us/dps/dl/sddriver.htm

Note: Ticket information is maintained at the local courts, not at the state.

Indexing & Storage: Records are available for 3 years for moving violations and DWIs. Speeding violations less than 10 mph over and out-of-state speeding violations (except for commercial drivers), suspensions and revocations are not listed on the record. It takes 1 to 3 weeks before new records are available for inquiry.

Searching: Casual requesters can only obtain records with the written permission of the subject. All other requesters must certify for what reason they are obtaining the information and comply with DPPA policies. Request forms can be downloaded from website. Include the following in your request-full name, date of birth. If for a non-permissible (DPPA) use, then notarized signature of driver needed. A secondary search will be done with the license number if no record is found on the name search. Suggest employers and insurance companies use MVR Request Form 2. The following data is not released: Social Security Numbers.

Access by: mail, phone, in person, online.

Fee & Payment: The fee is $4.00 per record. The agency charges sales tax, if record request comes from a South Dakota address. Fee payee: Dept of Public Safety Prepayment required. Personal checks accepted. No credit cards accepted.

Mail search: Turnaround time: 48 hours. The DL#, name, and DOB are all needed when requesting records via mail.

Phone search: Pre-approved accounts may order via the telephone. This is a very limited access.

In person search: Turnaround time while you wait at this location and at the Sioux Falls Driver Exam Station.

Online search: The system is open for batch requests 24 hours a day. There is a minimum of 250 requests daily. It generally takes 10 minutes to process a batch. The current fee is $4.00 per record and there are some start-up costs. For more information, call 605-773-6883.

Other access: Lists are available to the insurance industry.

Vehicle Ownership, Vehicle Identification, Vessel Ownership, Vessel Registration

Division of Motor Vehicles, Information Section, 445 E Capitol Ave, Pierre, SD 57501-3185; 605-773-3541, 605-773-2550 (Fax), 8AM-5PM.

www.state.sd.us/drr2/motorvcl.htm

Note: The DMV took over the registration and title process for boats in 1992. All boats (except canoes, inflatables, kayaks, sailboards) over 12 ft in length, and motorized boats must be titled and registered.

Indexing & Storage: Records are available for 20 years to present. It takes 2 weeks before new records are available for inquiry.

Searching: The agency requires all requests for vehicle related records be on the Division DPPA Form. Casual requesters (individuals) can only obtain information with written permission of the subject. Include the following in your request-DPPA Form. All requests must be in writing.

Access by: mail, in person.

Fee & Payment: The fee for VIN, plate, owner, title, or lien searches is $2.00 per record. A complete title history from microfilm is $5.00. Fee payee: Division of Motor Vehicles. Prepayment required. Personal checks accepted. No credit cards accepted.

Mail search: Turnaround time: 1 day to 1 week. Must provide DPPA request form. A SASE is requested.

In person search: You may request records in person, but the request must be in writing on the Division DPPA Form.

Accident Reports

Department of Public Safety, Accident Records, 118 W Capitol Ave, Pierre, SD 57501-2000; 605-773-3868, 605-773-6893 (Fax), 8AM-5PM.

Indexing & Storage: Records are available for 10 years to present. It takes 2 weeks from receipt from law enforcement agency before new records are available for inquiry.

Searching: Include the following in your request-full name, date of accident, location of accident.

Access by: mail, in person.

Fee & Payment: The fee is $4.00 per record. Fee payee: Accident Records. Prepayment required. Personal checks accepted. No credit cards accepted.

Mail search: Turnaround time: 5 days. A self addressed envelope is requested.

In person search: Normal turnaround time is immediate if the record is on file.

Expedited service: Will return report via fax once record fee is paid.

Voter Registration

Records not maintained by a state level agency.

Note: The Secretary of State and County Auditors throughout the state have compiled a statewide voter registration file of the official voter registration files in each county auditor's office. County auditors update the statewide file on a daily basis. Name searching should be done at the county level.

GED Certificates

SD Department of Labor, AEL/GED/Literacy, 700 Governors Drive, Pierre, SD 57501-2291; 605-773-3101, 605-773-6184 (Fax), 8AM-5PM.

www.state.sd.us/dol/GED/index.html

Note: You may e-mail requests to marcia.hess@state.sd.us.

Indexing & Storage: Records are available from 1942 to present. It takes 3-4 weeks before new records are available for inquiry. Records are normally destroyed after 2 years for partial test scores.

Searching: Include the following in your request-name at time of test, DOB, SSN and a signed release is required for either a verification or a copy of a transcript.

Access by: mail, fax, in person.

Fee & Payment: The fee for verifications or for a copy of a transcript is $5.00. Fee payee: SD Dept of Labor Prepayment required. Personal checks not accepted.

Mail search: Turnaround time: 1 to 3 days. No SASE is required. No fee for mail request.

Fax search: Results will available in 1 day, but will only send transcript after $5.00 fee received.

In person search: You can wait for results.

Hunting and Fishing License Information

Game, Fish & Parks Department, License Division, 412 W Missouri, Pierre, SD 57501; 605-773-3926, 605-773-5842 (Fax), 8AM-5PM.

www.state.sd.us/gfp

Indexing & Storage: Records are available for current and previous years only.

Searching: Requests must be in writing. They will release address data. The DOB and address are helpful.

Access by: in person.

Fee & Payment: The fee depends on the extent of the names and the search. The state refuses to quote a price at this time.

In person search: There is no fee, if the search request is simple.

Other access: Mailing lists are available, list is $100.00 per 1000 names. They have records for big game licensees.

South Dakota State Licensing Agencies

Licenses Searchable Online

Abstractor Business #1	www.state.sd.us/drr/reg/abstracters/roster.htm
Ambulance Service #20	www.state.sd.us/dps/ems/
Animal Remedy (medicine/drug for animals) #19	www.state.sd.us/doa/das/hp-af-ar.htm
Architect #23	www.state.sd.us/dol/boards/engineer/Roster/roster.htm
Asbestos Service Company #36	www.state.sd.us/denr/ENVIRO/SOLID/Certified%20Asbestos%20Services2.pdf
Athletic Trainer #10	www.state.sd.us/doh/medical/
Auctioneer #28	www.state.sd.us/drr2/reg/realestate/roster_licensees/roster.htm
Audiologist #30	www.state.sd.us/doh/audiology/roster.htm
Bail Bond Agent #37	www.state.sd.us/drr2/reg/insurance/producers/bailbonds.xls
Bank #2	www.state.sd.us/banking
Barber #4	www.state.sd.us/dol/boards/barber/barbers.htm
Barber Shop #4	www.state.sd.us/dol/boards/barber/shops.htm
Counselor #6	www.state.sd.us/dhs/boards/counselor/roster.htm
Crematory #29	www.state.sd.us/doh/funeral/roster.htm
Dietitian/Nutritionist #10	www.state.sd.us/doh/medical/
Driller, Oil and Gas #17	www.state.sd.us/denr/DES/Mining/Oil&Gas/NewPermit.htm
Embalmer #29	www.state.sd.us/doh/funeral/roster.htm
Engineer #23	www.state.sd.us/dol/boards/engineer/Roster/roster.htm
Engineer, Petroleum Environmental #23	www.state.sd.us/dol/boards/engineer/Roster/roster.htm
Environmental Site Assessor #36	www.state.sd.us/denr/DES/ground/tanks/contractorlist.htm
Fertilizer #19	www.state.sd.us/doa/das/hp-fert.htm
Funeral Director/Embalmer/Establishment #29	www.state.sd.us/doh/funeral/roster.htm
Funeral Service #29	www.state.sd.us/doh/funeral/roster.htm
Hazardous Waste #36	www.state.sd.us/denr/des/WasteMgn/HWaste/contractors.htm
Hearing Aid Dispenser #30	www.state.sd.us/doh/audiology/roster.htm
Home Inspector #28	www.state.sd.us/drr2/reg/realestate/roster_licensees/roster.htm
Insurance Company #37	www.state.sd.us/drr2/reg/insurance/CompareStatmt/Address.htm
Landfill #36	www.state.sd.us/denr/des/wastemgn/landfillmaps/statemap.htm
Landscape Architect #23	www.state.sd.us/dol/boards/engineer/landsurveynumbers.htm
Lobbyist #27	www.sdsos.gov/lobbyist/
Marriage & Family Therapist #6	www.state.sd.us/dhs/boards/counselor/roster.htm
Medical Assistant #10	www.state.sd.us/doh/medical/
Medical Doctor #10	www.state.sd.us/doh/medical/
Money Lending License #2	www.state.sd.us/banking
Money Order Business #2	www.state.sd.us/banking
Mortgage Broker/Lender #2	www.state.sd.us/banking
Notary Public #27	www.sdsos.gov/notaries/
Nursing Home Administrator #8	www.state.sd.us/doh/nursingfacility/roster.htm
Occupational Therapist/Assistant #10	www.state.sd.us/doh/medical/
Oil & Gas Driller #17	www.state.sd.us/denr/DES/Mining/Oil&Gas/NewPermit.htm
Optometrist #9	www.arbo.org/odfinder/LicSearch.asp
Osteopathic Physician #10	www.state.sd.us/doh/medical/
Pesticide Applicator/Dealer #19	www.state.sd.us/doa/das/
Pet Health Insurer #37	www.state.sd.us/drr2/reg/insurance/CompareStatmt/PetInsurers.htm
Petroleum Release Assessor/Remediator #23	www.state.sd.us/dol/boards/engineer/Roster/roster.htm
Physical Therapist/Assistant #10	www.state.sd.us/doh/medical/
Physician/Medical Assistant #10	www.state.sd.us/doh/medical/
Podiatrist #14	www.state.sd.us/doh/podiatry/roster.htm
Property Manager #28	www.state.sd.us/drr2/reg/realestate/roster_licensees/roster.htm
Psychologist #15	www.state.sd.us/dhs/boards/psychologists/roster.htm
Public Accountant-CPA #3	www.state.sd.us/dol/boards/accountancy/annreg.pdf
Real Estate Agent/Sales #28	www.state.sd.us/drr2/reg/realestate/roster_licensees/roster.htm
Real Estate Broker #28	www.state.sd.us/drr2/reg/realestate/roster_licensees/roster.htm
Recycler #36	www.state.sd.us/denr/des/wastemgn/Recycling/recycgu.htm
Recycler, Specialty #36	www.state.sd.us/denr/des/wastemgn/wasteprg.htm
Re-insurer, Accredited/Qualified #37	www.state.sd.us/drr2/reg/insurance/Financial/AQReinsurers.pdf
Respiratory Care Practitioner #10	www.state.sd.us/doh/medical/
Scrap Tire Company #36	www.state.sd.us/denr/des/WasteMgn/Recycling/rectires.htm
Social Worker #15	www.state.sd.us/dhs/boards/socialwork/roster.htm
Spill Clean-up Company #36	www.state.sd.us/denr/DES/ground/tanks/contractorlist.htm

Storage Tank, Above/Below Ground #36 .... www.state.sd.us/denr/DES/Ground/tanks/search/Index.asp
Surveyor, Land #23 .... www.state.sd.us/dol/boards/engineer/Roster/roster.htm
Tank Remover #36 .... www.state.sd.us/denr/DES/ground/tanks/contractorlist.htm
Testing Lab, Environmental #36 .... www.state.sd.us/denr/des/WasteMgn/Recycling/Recpage1.htm
Timeshare Real Estate #28 .... www.state.sd.us/drr2/reg/realestate/roster_licensees/roster.htm
Waste Water Collection System Operator #12 .... www.state.sd.us/denr/databases/operator/index.cfm
Waste Water Treatment Plant Operator #12 .... www.state.sd.us/denr/databases/operator/index.cfm
Water Distributor #12 .... www.state.sd.us/denr/databases/operator/index.cfm
Water Treatment Operator #39 .... www.state.sd.us/denr/databases/operator/index.cfm
Water Treatment Plant Operator #12 .... www.state.sd.us/denr/databases/operator/index.cfm
Weapon, Concealed #27 .... www.sdsos.gov/firearms/
Well Driller #36 .... www.state.sd.us/denr/des/waterrights/drillers.htm

South Dakota Licensing Quick Finder

9-1-1 Telecommunicator #25 605-773-3584
Abstractor #1 605-869-2269
Abstractor Business #1 605-869-2269
Acupuncturist #5 605-668-9017
Alcoholic Beverage Distributor #21 605-773-3311
Ambulance Service #20 605-773-4031
Animal Feed Seller/Producer #19 605-773-4432
Animal Remedy (medicine/drug for animals) #19
.... 605-773-4432
Appliance Contr./Journeyman/Apprentice #34
.... 605-773-3429
Architect #23 605-394-2510
Asbestos Abatement Worker/Co. #36 .. 605-773-3153
Athletic Trainer #10 605-334-8343
Attorney #32 605-224-7554
Auctioneer #28 605-773-3600
Audiologist #30 605-642-1600
Bail Bond Agent #37 605-773-3513
Bank #2 605-773-3421
Barber #4 605-642-1600
Barber Shop #4 605-642-1600
Beauty Shop/Salon #18 605-773-6193
Brokerage Firm #31 605-773-4823
Business Opportunities Broker #31 605-773-4823
Canine Team #25 605-773-3584
Chiropractor #5 605-668-9017
Cigarette Wholesaler #21 605-773-3311
Clinical Nurse Specialist #11 605-362-2760
Cosmetologist #18 605-773-6193
Cosmetology Instructor/Salon #18 605-773-6193
Counselor #6 605-331-2927
Court/Shorthand Reporter #38 605-773-3474
Crematory #29 605-642-1600
Dental Assistant/Hygienist #7 605-224-1282
Dentist #7 605-224-1282
Dietitian/Nutritionist #10 605-334-8343
Driller, Oil and Gas #17 605-394-2229
Drug Wholesaler #13 605-362-2737
Electrical Inspector #33 605-773-3573
Electrician #33 605-773-3573
Embalmer #29 605-642-1600
Emergency Medical Technician #20 605-773-4031
Engineer #23 605-394-2510
Engineer, Petroleum Environm'l #23 605-394-2510
Environmental Site Assessor #36 605-773-3296
Esthetician #18 605-773-6193
Fertilizer #19 605-773-4432
Franchise Sales #31 605-773-4823

Funeral Director/Embalmer #29 605-642-1600
Funeral Establishment #29 605-642-1600
Funeral Service #29 605-642-1600
Gaming #24 605-773-6050
Hazardous Waste #36 605-773-3153
Hearing Aid Dispenser #30 605-642-1600
Home Inspector #28 605-773-3600
Insurance Agent #37 605-773-3513
Insurance Company #37 605-773-3563
Investment Advisor #31 605-773-4823
Landfill #36 605-773-3153
Landscape Architect #23 605-394-2510
Laundromat #21 605-773-3311
Law Enforcement Officer #25 605-773-3584
Livestock Dealer #16 605-773-3321
Loan Production #2 605-773-3421
Lobbyist #27 605-773-3539
Manicurist/Nail Technician #18 605-773-6193
Marriage & Family Therapist #6 605-331-2927
Medical Assistant #10 605-334-8343
Medical Doctor #10 605-334-8343
Midwife Nurse #11 605-362-2760
Milk Grader/Hauler #19 605-773-4294
Milk Tester/Sampler #19 605-773-4294
Mobile Home Contractor #34 605-773-3429
Money Lending License #2 605-773-3421
Money Order Business #2 605-773-3421
Mortgage Broker/Lender #2 605-773-3421
Nail Salon #18 605-773-6193
Notary Public #27 605-773-3539
Nurse #11 605-362-2760
Nurse Aide Certified #11 605-362-2760
Nurse Anesthetist #11 605-362-2760
Nurse Practitioner, Certified #11 605-362-2760
Nurse-RN #11 605-362-2760
Nurses Aide #35 605-362-2762
Nurses Aide Applicant #35 605-362-2762
Nursing Home Administrator #8 605-331-5040
Occupational Therapist/Assistant #10... 605-334-8343
Oil & Gas Driller #17 605-394-2229
Optometrist #9 605-347-2136
Osteopathic Physician #10 605-334-8343
Paramedic #20 605-773-4031
Pesticide Applicator/Dealer #19 605-773-4432
Pet Health Insurer #37 605-773-3563
Petroleum Release Assessor #23 605-394-2510
Petroleum Release Assessor/Remediator #23
.... 605-394-2510

Pharmacist/Pharmacy #13 605-362-2737
Physical Therapist/Assistant #10 605-334-8343
Physician/Medical Assistant #10 605-334-8343
Plumber #34 605-773-3429
Podiatrist #14 605-642-1600
Polygraph Examiner #25 605-773-3584
Property Manager #28 605-773-3600
Psychologist #15 605-642-1600
Public Accountant-CPA #3 605-367-5770
Racing #24 605-773-6050
Radiologist (Chiropractic) #5 605-668-9017
Radiology (Dental) #7 605-224-1282
Real Estate Agent/Sales #28 605-773-3600
Real Estate Broker #28 605-773-3600
Recycler #36 605-773-3153
Recycler, Specialty #36 605-773-3153
Re-insurer, Accredited/Qualified #37 ... 605-773-3563
Respiratory Care Practitioner #10........ 605-334-8343
School Counselor #22 605-773-3553
School Principal/Superintendent #22... 605-773-3553
Scrap Tire Company #36 605-773-3153
Securities Agent/Broker/Dealer #31... 605-773-4823
Sewage/Water Installation Contr./Instal. #34
.... 605-773-3429
Social Worker #15 605-642-1600
Spill Clean-up Company #36 605-773-3296
Storage Tank, Above/Below Gr'nd #36. 605-773-3296
Surveyor, Land #23 605-394-2510
Tank Remover #36 605-773-3296
Teacher #22 605-773-3553
Testing Lab, Environmental #36 605-773-3296
Timeshare Real Estate #28 605-773-3600
Veterinarian/Veterinary Tech. #16 605-773-3321
Veterinary Corporation #16 605-773-3321
Waste Water Collection System Operator #12
.... 605-773-3151
Waste Water Treatment Plant Operator #12
.... 605-773-3151
Water Conditioning Plumb'g Instal. #34 605-773-3429
Water Distributor #12 605-773-3151
Water Treatment Operator #39 605-773-4208
Water Treatment Plant Operator #12... 605-773-3151
Weapon, Concealed #27 605-773-3537
Well Driller #36 605-773-3352

South Dakota Licensing Agency Information

1 Abstractors Board of Examiners, PO Box 187, Kennebec, SD 57544-0187; 605-869-2269, Fax: 605-869-2269. www.state.sd.us/drr/reg/abstracters/abst-hom.htm Email: lctc@wcenet.com   Search Database at www.state.sd.us/drr/reg/abstracters/abst-hom.htm

2 Department of Revenue & Regulation, Division of Banking, 217 1/2 W Missouri, Pierre, SD 57501-4590; 605-773-3421, Fax: 605-773-5367. www.state.sd.us/banking Email: cassandra.nagel@state.sd.us Search Database at www.state.sd.us/banking

3 Board of Accountancy, 301 E 14th St, #200, Sioux Falls, SD 57104-5022; 605-367-5770, Fax: 605-367-5773. www.state.sd.us/dcr/accountancy Email: sdbdact@dtgnet.com   Search Database at www.state.sd.us/dol/boards/accountancy/annreg.pdf Note: To search, scroll down through the alphabetical listings.

4 Board of Barber Examiners, c/o Carol Tellinghuisen, Executive Secretary, 135 E Illinois #214, Spearfish, SD 57783; 605-642-1600, Fax: 605-642-1756. www.state.sd.us/dol/boards/barber/ Email: proflic@rushmore.com Search Database at www.state.sd.us/dol/boards/barber/roster.htm

5 Board of Chiropractic Examiners, 2603 Ella Lane, Yankton, SD 57078; 605-668-9017, Fax: 605-668-9017. www.state.sd.us/doh/chiropractic/ Email: sdbce@mchsi.com

6 Board of Counselor Examiners, PO Box 1822, Sioux Falls, SD 57101-1822; 605-331-2927, Fax: 605-331-2043.   www.state.sd.us Email: sdbce.msp@midconetwork.com Search at www.state.sd.us/dhs/boards/counselor/roster.htm

7 Board of Dentistry, PO Box 1037, Pierre, SD 57501-1037; 605-224-1282, Fax: 605-224-7426. www.state.sd.us/doh/dentistry/

8 Board of Examiners for Nursing Home Administrators, PO Box 632, Sioux Falls, SD 57101-0632; 605-331-5040, Fax: 605-331-2043. www.state.sd.us/doh/nursingfacility/roster.htm

9 Board of Examiners in Optometry, PO Box 370, Sturgis, SD 57785-0370; 605-347-2136, Fax: 605-347-5823. www.state.sd.us/doh/optometry/ Email: sdoptbd_99@yahoo.com   Search Database at www.arbo.org/odfinder/LicSearch.asp

10 Board of Medical & Osteopathic Examiners, 1323 S Minnesota Ave, Sioux Falls, SD 57105-0685; 605-334-8343, Fax: 605-336-0270. www.state.sd.us/doh/medical/ Email: jphalen@sdsma.org

11 Board of Nursing, 4305 S Louise Ave, #201, Sioux Falls, SD 57106-3124; 605-362-2760, Fax: 605-362-2768. www.state.sd.us/doh/nursing/ Email: jean.mcguire@state.sd.us Note: Online searching/verification system is being updated; check main website.

12 Board of Operator Certification, 523 E Capitol Ave, Foss Bldg, Pierre, SD 57501; 605-773-3151, Fax: 605-773-6035. www.state.sd.us/denr/denr.html Email: rob.kittay@state.sd.us   Search Database at www.state.sd.us/denr/databases/operator/index.cfm

13 Board of Pharmacy, 4305 S Louise Ave, #104, Sioux Falls, SD 57106-3115; 605-362-2737, Fax: 605-362-2738. www.state.sd.us/doh/pharmacy/index.htm Email: dennis.jones@state.sd.us

14 Board of Podiatry Examiners, 135 E Illinois, #214, Spearfish, SD 57783; 605-642-1600, Fax: 605-642-1756. www.state.sd.us/doh/podiatry/index.htm Email: proflic@rushmore.com   Search Database at www.state.sd.us/doh/podiatry/roster.htm

15 Board of Social Work Examiners/Psychologist Examiners, 135 E Illinois, #214, Spearfish, SD 57783; 605-642-1600, Fax: 605-642-1756. www.state.sd.us/dhs/boards/socialwork/soc-hom.htm   Email: proflic@rushmore.com Search Database at www.state.sd.us/dhs/boards/socialwork/roster.htm

16 Board of Veterinary Medical Examiners, 411 S Fort St, Pierre, SD 57501-4503; 605-773-3321, Fax: 605-773-5459. www.state.sd.us/aib/   Email: dr.holland@state.sd.us

17 Department of Environment & Natural Resources, Oil & Gas Section, Minerals & Mining Program, 2050 W. Main, #1, Rapid City, SD 57701; 605-394-2229. www.state.sd.us/denr/DES/Mining/Oil&Gas/O&Ghome.htm Search Database at www.state.sd.us/denr/DES/Mining/Oil&Gas/NewPermit.htm Note: Permit records go back five years.

18 Cosmetology Commission, 500 E Capitol, Pierre, SD 57501-5070; 605-773-6193, Fax: 605-773-7175.   Email: sdcosmo@sd.cybernex.net

19 Department of Agriculture, Division of Ag Services, 523 E Capitol, Foss Bldg, Pierre, SD 57501-3182; 605-773-3724, Fax: 605-773-3481. www.state.sd.us/doa/das/

20 Department Public Safety, Emergency Medical Services, 118 W. Capitol, Pierre, SD 57501; 605-773-4031, Fax: 605-773-6631. www.state.sd.us/dps/ems Email: bob.graff@state.sd.us Note: Search license lists for air ambulance and instate/out-of-state ground ambulance services.

21 Department of Revenue & Regulation, Property & Special Taxes - Special Tax Division, 445 E Capitol Ave, Pierre, SD 57501-3185; 605-773-3311, Fax: 605-773-5129. www.state.sd.us/revenue Email: specialT@rev.state.sd.us

22 Education & Cultural Affairs Department, Office of Policy & Accountability, 700 Governors Dr, Pierre, SD 57501-2291; 605-773-3553, Fax: 605-773-6139.   www.state.sd.us/deca/ Email: janelle.toman@state.sd.us

23 Department of Labor, Board of Technical Professions, 2040 W Main St, #304, Rapid City, SD 57702-2447; 605-394-2510, Fax: 605-395-2509.   www.state.sd.us/dcr/engineer Email: ann.whipple@state.sd.us Search Database at www.state.sd.us/dol/boards/engineer/Roster/index.cfm Note: Roster available for $25.00 by print, disk, or email.

24 Gaming Commission, 118 W Capitol Ave, Pierre, SD 57501-5070; 605-773-6050, Fax: 605-773-6053. www.state.sd.us/dcr/gaming/gam-hom.htm

25 Law Enforcement Standards & Training Commission, Division of Criminal Justice Training Center, Pierre, SD 57501; 605-773-3584, Fax: 605-773-7203.   www.state.sd.us Email: bryan.gortmaker@state.sd.us

27 Office of Secretary of State, Lobbyist Coordinator, Notaries, 500 E Capitol Ave, State Capitol Bldg, #204, Pierre, SD 57501-5070; 605-773-3537, Fax: 605-773-6580. http://sdsos.gov/   Email: anissa.grambihler@state.sd.us Search Database at http://sdsos.gov/

28 Real Estate Com., 118 W Capitol, Pierre, SD 57501;   605-773-3600, Fax: 605-773-4356. www.state.sd.us/drr/reg/realestate/index.htm Email: norma.schilling@state.sd.us   Search Database at www.state.sd.us/drr2/reg/realestate/roster_licensees/roster.htm

29 Board of Funeral Svcs, 135 E Illinois, #214, Spearfish, SD 57783; 605-642-1600, Fax: 605-642-1756. www.state.sd.us/doh/funeral/ Email: proflic@rushmore.com Search Database at www.state.sd.us/doh/funeral/roster.htm

30 Board of Hearing Aid Dispensers and Audiologists, 135 E Illinois # 214, Spearfish, SD 57783-0654; 605-642-1600, Fax: 605-642-1756. www.state.sd.us/doh/audiology/ Email: proflic@rushmore.com   Search Database at www.state.sd.us/doh/audiology/roster.htm

31 Dept of Revenue & Regulation, Division of Securities, 445 E Capitol Ave, Pierre, SD 57501-3185; 605-773-4823, Fax: 605-773-5953. www.state.sd.us/drr2/reg/securities/broker.htm Email: melita.hauge@state.sd.us

32 State Bar, 222 E Capitol Ave, Pierre, SD 57501-2596; 605-224-7554, Fax: 605-224-0282. www.sdbar.org   Email: tbarnett@sdbar.org

33 Electrical Commission, 118 W Capitol, Pierre, SD 57501-5070; 605-773-3573, Fax: 605-773-6213. www.state.sd.us/dcr/electrical/ELEC_HOM.htm

34 Plumbing Commission, 308 S. Pierce St., Pierre, SD 57501; 605-773-3429, Fax: 605-773-5405.   www.state.sd.us/dcr/plumbing Email: mike.richards@state.sd.us

35 Healthcare Administration, Nurses Aide Testing, 804 N Western Av, Souix Falls, SD 57104-2098; 605-362-2762, Fax: 605-339-1354. www.sdhca.org   Email: sdhca@worldnet.att.net

36 Department of Environment & Natural Resources, Division of Environmental Svcs, 523 E Capitol Ave, Pierre, SD 57501-3182; 605-773-3153.   www.state.sd.us

37 Department of Commerce & Regulation, Division of Insurance, 445 E Capitol, Pierre, SD 57501; 605-773-3563, Fax: 605-773-5369. www.state.sd.us/dcr/insurance

38 Supreme Court, Unified Judicial Court Administrators Office, Capitol Bldg, 500 E Capitol, Pierre, SD 57501; 605-773-3474, Fax: 605-773-5627. www.sdjudicial.com Email: jill.gusso@ujs.state.sd.us

39 Department of Environment & Natural Resources, Division of Environmental Svcs, Drinking Water Program, 523 E Capitol Ave, Pierre, SD 57501; 605-773-4208. www.state.sd.us/denr/enviro

South Dakota Federal Courts

The following list indicates the district and division name for each county in the state. If the bankruptcy court location is different from the district court, then the location of the bankruptcy court appears in parentheses.

County/Court Cross Reference

Aurora	Sioux Falls	Hyde	Pierre
Beadle	Sioux Falls	Jackson	Pierre
Bennett	Rapid City (Pierre)	Jerauld	Pierre
Bon Homme	Sioux Falls	Jones	Pierre
Brookings	Sioux Falls	Kingsbury	Sioux Falls
Brown	Aberdeen (Pierre)	Lake	Sioux Falls
Brule	Sioux Falls	Lawrence	Rapid City (Pierre)
Buffalo	Pierre	Lincoln	Sioux Falls
Butte	Aberdeen (Pierre)	Lyman	Pierre
Campbell	Aberdeen (Pierre)	Marshall	Aberdeen (Pierre)
Charles Mix	Sioux Falls	McCook	Sioux Falls
Clark	Aberdeen (Pierre)	McPherson	Aberdeen (Pierre)
Clay	Sioux Falls	Meade	Rapid City (Pierre)
Codington	Aberdeen (Pierre)	Mellette	Pierre
Corson	Aberdeen (Pierre)	Miner	Sioux Falls
Custer	Rapid City (Pierre)	Minnehaha	Sioux Falls
Davison	Sioux Falls	Moody	Sioux Falls
Day	Aberdeen (Pierre)	Pennington	Rapid City (Pierre)
Deuel	Aberdeen (Pierre)	Perkins	Rapid City (Pierre)
Dewey	Pierre	Potter	Pierre
Douglas	Sioux Falls	Roberts	Aberdeen (Pierre)
Edmunds	Aberdeen (Pierre)	Sanborn	Sioux Falls
Fall River	Rapid City (Pierre)	Shannon	Rapid City (Pierre)
Faulk	Pierre	Spink	Aberdeen (Pierre)
Grant	Aberdeen (Pierre)	Stanley	Pierre
Gregory	Pierre	Sully	Pierre
Haakon	Pierre	Todd	Pierre
Hamlin	Aberdeen (Pierre)	Tripp	Pierre
Hand	Pierre	Turner	Sioux Falls
Hanson	Sioux Falls	Union	Sioux Falls
Harding	Rapid City (Pierre)	Walworth	Aberdeen (Pierre)
Hughes	Pierre	Yankton	Sioux Falls
Hutchinson	Sioux Falls	Ziebach	Pierre

Standards for Federal Courts: The search fee is $20.00 per item (one party name or case number). Certification fee is $7.00 per document. Copy fee is $.50 per page. All fees standard unless noted in profile. Mail Search: always enclose a stamped self addressed envelope unless otherwise noted. Most courts accept fax requests or will suggest a copying/search vendor. Before releasing records, all courts require prepayment unless noted in profile.

Open records are located at the court unless otherwise noted. District courts index by defendant and plaintiff as well as by case number. Bankruptcy courts usually index by debtor and case number. While most courts now have their indexes on computer, many still maintain index card files as well.

The universal PACER sign-up number is 800-676-6856. Find PACER and the Party/Case Index on the Web at http://pacer.psc.uscourts.gov. PACER dial-up access is $.60 per minute. Also, courts offering internet access via RACER, PACER, Web-PACER or the new CM-ECF charge $.07 per page fee unless noted as free.

US District Court

District of South Dakota

Aberdeen Division c/o Pierre Division, Federal Bldg & Courthouse, 225 S Pierre St, Room 405, Pierre, SD 57501 (courier address: Use mail address for courier delivery) 605-224-5849, Fax: 605-224-0806. www.sdd.uscourts.gov

Counties: Brown, Campbell, Clark, Codington, Corson, Day, Deuel, Edmunds, Grant, Hamlin, McPherson, Marshall, Roberts, Spink, Walworth. Judge Battey's closed case records are located at the Rapid City Division.

Indexing & Storage: Cases indexed by as well as by case number. New cases available in the index after filing date. Open records are located at the Pierre Division.

Fee & Payment: Payment may be made by money order, cashier check. Business checks are not accepted. Personal checks are not accepted.

Phone Search: No searching by telephone.

In Person Search: Permitted.

PACER: PACER is available online at http://pacer.sdd.uscourts.gov. Court does not allow electronic access to criminal cases. Civil document images available. Records purged every six months. New records are online after 1 day.

Electronic Filing: Currently in the process of implementing CM/ECF.

Pierre Division Federal Bldg & Courthouse, Room 405, 225 S Pierre St, Pierre, SD 57501 (Use mail address for courier delivery) 605-224-5849, Fax: 605-224-0806. www.sdd.uscourts.gov

Counties: Buffalo, Dewey, Faulk, Gregory, Haakon, Hand, Hughes, Hyde, Jackson, Jerauld, Jones, Lyman, Mellette, Potter, Stanley, Sully, Todd, Tripp, Ziebach.

Indexing & Storage: New cases available in the index 1 day after filing date.

Fee & Payment: Payment may be made by money order, cashier check, personal check. Payee: Clerk, U.S. District Court.

Phone Search: Only docket information available.

In Person Search: Fee charged if court conducts your in person search for you.

PACER: PACER is available online at http://pacer.sdd.uscourts.gov. Court does not allow electronic access to criminal cases. Civil document images available. Records purged every six months. New records are online after 1 day.

Electronic Filing: Electronic filing information online at https://ecf.sdd.uscourts.gov

Rapid City Division Clerk's Office, Room 302, 515 9th St, Rapid City, SD 57701 (courier address: Use mail address for courier delivery) 605-343-3744, Fax: 605-343-4367. www.sdd.uscourts.gov

Counties: Bennett, Butte, Custer, Fall River, Harding, Lawrence, Meade, Pennington, Perkins, Shannon.

Judge Battey's closed cases are located here.

Indexing & Storage: New cases available in the index 24 hours after filing date.

Fee & Payment: Payment may be made by money order, cashier check, business check. Personal checks are not accepted. Payee: Clerk, U.S. District Court. Will fax results $1.50 per page, prepaid.

Phone Search: Only docket information available by telephone. Will fax results $1.50 per page, prepaid.

Mail Search: A SASE not required.

In Person Search: Fee charged if court conducts your in person search for you.

PACER: PACER is available online at http://pacer.sdd.uscourts.gov. Court does not allow electronic access to criminal cases. Civil document images available. Records purged every six months. New records are online after 1 day.

Electronic Filing: Electronic filing information online at https://ecf.sdd.uscourts.gov

Sioux Falls Division P.O. Box 5060, Sioux Falls, SD 57117-5060 (courier address: Room 128, U.S. Courthouse, 400 S Phillips Ave, Sioux Falls, SD 57104-6851), 605-330-4447, Fax: 605-330-4312. www.sdd.uscourts.gov

Counties: Aurora, Beadle, Bon Homme, Brookings, Brule, Charles Mix, Clay, Davison,

Douglas, Hanson, Hutchinson, Kingsbury, Lake, Lincoln, McCook, Miner, Minnehaha, Moody, Sanborn, Turner, Union, Yankton.

Indexing & Storage: New cases available in the index 1 day after filing date.

Fee & Payment: Payment may be made by money order, cashier check, personal check. Payee: Clerk, U.S. District Court. Wil fax results $1.50 per page.

Phone Search: Only docket information for civil cases will be released over the phone. Wil fax results $1.50 per page.

In Person Search: Fee charged if court conducts your in person search for you.

PACER: PACER is available online at http://pacer.sdd.uscourts.gov. Court does not allow electronic access to criminal cases. Civil document images available. Records purged every six months. New records are online after 1 day.

Electronic Filing: Electronic filing information online at https://ecf.sdd.uscourts.gov

U.S. Bankruptcy Court

District of South Dakota ·

Pierre Division Clerk, Room 203, Federal Bldg, 225 S Pierre St, Pierre, SD 57501 (Use mail address for courier delivery) 605-224-0560, Fax: 605-224-9020. www.sdb.uscourts.gov

Counties: Bennett, Brown, Buffalo, Butte, Campbell, Clark, Codington, Corson, Custer, Day, Deuel, Dewey, Edmunds, Fall River, Faulk, Grant, Gregory, Haakon, Hamlin, Hand, Harding, Hughes, Hyde, Jackson, Jerauld, Jones, Lawrence, Lyman, Marshall, McPherson, Meade,Mellette, Pennington, Perkins, Potter, Roberts, Shannon, Spink, Stanley, Sully, Todd, Tripp, Walworth, Ziebach.

Indexing & Storage: Cases indexed by debtor and creditors as well as by case number, New cases available in the index immediately after filing date. District wide searches are available for information from 10/1/91 from this court.

Fee & Payment: Payment may be made by money order, cashier check, in-state business check. Personal checks are not accepted. Payee: Clerk, U.S. Bankruptcy Court. Will fax docket listings no extra charge.

Phone Search: Only docket information available by phone. Automated voice case information service (VCIS) is available. Call VCIS at 800-768-6218 or 605-330-4559. Will fax docket listings no extra charge.

In Person Search: Permitted.

PACER: PACER is available online at http://pacer.sdb.uscourts.gov. Document images available. Case records go back to October 1, 1991. Records never purged. New civil records are online after 1 day.

Electronic Filing: Electronic filing information online at https://ecf.sdb.uscourts.gov

Sioux Falls Division PO Box 5060, Sioux Falls, SD 57117-5060 (courier address: Room 117, 400 S Phillips Ave, Sioux Falls, SD 57102), 605-330-4544, Fax: 605-330-4560. www.sdb.uscourts.gov

Counties: Aurora, Beadle, Bon Homme, Brookings, Brule, Charles Mix, Clay, Davison, Douglas, Hanson, Hutchinson, Kingsbury, Lake, Lincoln, McCook, Miner, Minnehaha, Moody, Sanborn, Turner, Union, Yankton.

Indexing & Storage: Cases indexed by debtor and creditors as well as by case number. New cases available in the index 1 day after filing date. District wide searches are available for information from 10/1/91 from this court.

Fee & Payment: Payment may be made by money order, cashier check, in-state business check. Personal checks are not accepted. Payee: Clerk, U.S. Bankruptcy Court. Will fax back docket listing no extra charge.

Phone Search: Only docket information available by phone. Automated voice case information service (VCIS) is available. Call VCIS at 800-768-6218 or 605-330-4559. Will fax back docket listing no extra charge.

In Person Search: Permitted.

PACER: PACER is available online at http://pacer.sdb.uscourts.gov. Document images available. Case records go back to October 1, 1991. Records never purged. New civil records are online after 1 day.

Electronic Filing: Electronic filing information online at https://ecf.sdb.uscourts.gov

South Dakota County Courts

Court	Jurisdiction	No. of Courts	How Organized
Circuit Courts*	General	66	7 Circuits
Magistrate Courts		66	

* Profiled in this Sourcebook.

Court	CIVIL								
	Tort	Contract	Real Estate	Min. Claim	Max. Claim	Small Claims	Estate	Eviction	Domestic Relations
Circuit Courts*	X	X	X	$0	No Max	$8000	X	X	X
Magistrate Courts				$0	$10,000	$8000	X	X	X

Court	CRIMINAL				
	Felony	Misdemeanor	DWI/DUI	Preliminary Hearing	Juvenile
Circuit Courts*	X	X	X	X	X
Magistrate Courts		X	X	X	

ADMINISTRATION

State Court Administrator, State Capitol Building, 500 E Capitol Av, Pierre, SD, 57501; 605-773-3474, Fax: 605-773-5627. www.sdjudicial.com

COURT STRUCTURE

The state re-aligned their circuits from 8 to 7 effective June, 2000.

South Dakota has a statewide criminal record search database, administered by the State Court Administrator's Office in Pierre. All criminal record information from July 1, 1989 forward, statewide, is contained in the database. To facilitate quicker access for the public, the state has designated 10 county record centers to process all mail or ongoing commercial accounts' criminal record requests. All mail requests are forwarded to, and commercial account requests are assigned to one of 10 specific county court clerks for processing a statewide search. For faster service on mail requests, use Hanson or Miner Counties. Note that walk-in requesters seeking a single or minimum of requests may still obtain a record from their local county court. Five counties (Buffalo, Campbell, Dewey, McPherson, and Ziebach) do not have computer terminals in-house. The criminal records from these counties are entered into the database by court personnel from another location.

The search fee is $15.00 per record. State authorized commercial accounts may order and receive records by fax, there is an additional $5.00 fee unless a non-toll free line is used.

Requesters who wish to set up a commercial account are directed to contact Jill Gusso at the Court Administrator's Office in Pierre at the address mentioned above, or at jill.gusso@ujs.state.sd.us

ONLINE ACCESS

There is no statewide online access computer system currently available. Larger courts are being placed on computer systems at a rate of 4 to 5 courts per year. Access is intended for internal use only. Smaller courts place their information on computer cards that are later sent to Pierre for input by the state office.

ADDITIONAL INFORMATION

Most South Dakota courts do not allow the public to perform searches, but rather require the court clerk to do them for a fee of $15.00 per name. A special Record Search Request Form must be used. Searches will be returned with a disclaimer stating that the clerk is not responsible for the completeness of the search. Clerks are not required to respond to telephone or fax requests, but many courts will return records via fax to ongoing commercial accounts. Many courts are not open all day so they prefer written requests.

Aurora County

Circuit Court PO Box 366, 401 N Main St., Plankinton, SD 57368-0366; 605-942-7165; Fax: 605-942-7170. Hours: 8AM-Noon, 1-5PM (CST). *Felony, Misdemeanor, Civil, Eviction, Small Claims, Probate.*

Civil Records: Access: Fax, mail, in person. Both court and visitors may perform in person searches. Search fee: $15.00 per name. Required to search: name, years to search; also helpful: address. Civil cases indexed by defendant, plaintiff. Civil records on manual index since 1879, some computerized since 1988.

Criminal Records: Access: Fax, mail, in person. Only the court performs in person searches; visitors may not. Search fee: $15.00 per name. Required to search: name, years to search, signed release; also helpful: address, DOB, SSN. Criminal records are computerized since 07/89 on a statewide system.

General Information: No juvenile, sealed, dismissed, adoption or mental health records released. Will fax results for $1.00 per page; $5.00 minimum. Copy fee: $.20 per page. Cert fee: $2.00. Payee: Aurora County Clerk of Court. Business checks accepted. Prepayment required. Mail requests: SASE required. Mail turnaround time 1 day.

Beadle County

Circuit Court PO Box 1358, Huron, SD 57350-1358; 605-353-7165; Fax: 605-353-0118. Hours: 8AM-5PM (CST). *Felony, Misdemeanor, Civil, Eviction, Small Claims, Probate.*

Civil Records: Access: Mail, in person. Only the court performs in person searches; visitors may not. Search fee: $15.00 per name. Required to search: name, years to search. Civil cases indexed by defendant, plaintiff. Civil records on computer from 1990 (limited), cards from 1900. Not for public use.

Criminal Records: Access: Mail, in person. Only the court performs in person searches; visitors may not. Search fee: $15.00 per name. Required to search: name, years to search, DOB; also helpful: SSN. Criminal records are computerized since 07/89 on a statewide system. Mail requests are forwarded to Hand County for processing.

General Information: No juvenile, sealed, dismissed, adoption, or mental health records released. Copy fee: $.20 per page. Cert fee: $2.00. Payee: Beadle County Clerk of Court. Personal checks accepted. Out of state checks not accepted. Prepayment required. Mail turnaround time up to 2 weeks.

Bennett County

Circuit Court PO Box 281, Martin, SD 57551-0281; 605-685-6969; Fax: 605-685-1075. Hours: 8AM-4:30PM (MST). *Felony, Misdemeanor, Civil, Eviction, Small Claims, Probate.*

Civil Records: Access: Mail, in person. Only the court performs in person searches; visitors may not. Search fee: $15.00 per name. Required to search: name, years to search; also helpful: address. Civil cases indexed by defendant, plaintiff. Civil records on index from 1912.

Criminal Records: Access: Mail, in person. Only the court performs in person searches; visitors may not. Search fee: $15.00 per name. Required to search: name, years to search, DOB; also helpful: address. Request form available. Criminal records are computerized since 07/89 on a statewide system. All mail requests are forwarded to Potter County for processing.

General Information: No juvenile, sealed, dismissed, or mental health records released. Copy fee: $.20 per page. Cert fee: $2.00. Payee: Bennett County Clerk of Courts. Business checks accepted.

Prepayment required. Mail requests: SASE required. Mail turnaround time 48 hours.

Bon Homme County

Circuit Court PO Box 6, Tyndall, SD 57066; 605-589-4215; Fax: 605-589-4245. Hours: 8AM-4:30PM (CST). *Felony, Misdemeanor, Civil, Eviction, Small Claims, Probate.*

Civil Records: Access: Fax, mail, in person. Both court and visitors may perform in person searches. Search fee: $15.00 per name. Required to search: name, years to search; also helpful: address. Civil cases indexed by defendant, plaintiff. Civil records on alpha index books from 1877. Requests should be in writing.

Criminal Records: Access: Mail, in person. Only the court performs in person searches; visitors may not. Search fee: $15.00 per name. Required to search: name, years to search, DOB, signed release; also helpful: address, SSN. Criminal records are computerized since 07/89 on a statewide system. All mail requests are forwarded to Douglas County for processing.

General Information: No juvenile, sealed, dismissed, or mental health records released. Will fax results $1.00 per page, $5.00 minimum, no fee if local or toll free. Copy fee: $.25 per page. Cert fee: $2.00. Payee: Bon Homme County Clerk of Court. Personal checks accepted. Prepayment required. Mail requests: SASE required. Mail turnaround time 3 days to 1 week.

Brookings County

Circuit Court 314 6th Ave, Brookings, SD 57006; 605-688-4200; Fax: 605-688-4952. Hours: 8AM-5PM (CST). *Felony, Misdemeanor, Civil, Eviction, Small Claims, Probate.*

Civil Records: Access: Mail, in person. Only the court performs in person searches; visitors may not. Search fee: $15.00 per name. Required to search: name, years to search; also helpful: address. Civil cases indexed by defendant, plaintiff. Civil records on alpha index books from 1900s.

Criminal Records: Access: Mail, in person. Only the court performs in person searches; visitors may not. Search fee: $15.00 per name. Required to search: name, years to search, DOB; also helpful: address, SSN. Criminal records on computer since July 1989 on a statewide system. All mail requests are forwarded to Hand County for processing.

General Information: No juvenile, sealed, dismissed, or mental health records released. Fee to fax results is $1.00 per page; $5.00 minimum. Copy fee: $.20 per page. Cert fee: $2.00. Payee: Brookings County Clerk of Court. Only cashiers checks and money orders accepted. Prepayment required. Mail requests: SASE required. Mail turnaround time 3 days.

Brown County

Circuit Court 101 1st Ave SE, Aberdeen, SD 57401; 605-626-2451; Fax: 605-626-2491. Hours: 8AM-5PM (CST). *Felony, Misdemeanor, Civil, Eviction, Small Claims, Probate.*

Civil Records: Access: Mail, in person. Both court and visitors may perform in person searches. Search fee: $15.00 per name. Required to search: name, years to search; also helpful: address. Civil cases indexed by defendant, plaintiff. Civil records on registers from 1975 (misdemeanor), registers from 1900s (civil).

Criminal Records: Access: Mail, in person. Only the court performs in person searches; visitors may not. Search fee: $15.00 per name. Required to search: name, years to search, DOB; also helpful: address, signed release, SSN. Criminal records on computer since 07/89 on a statewide system. All mail requests are forwarded to Edmunds County for processing.

General Information: No juvenile, sealed, dismissed, or mental health records released. Will fax results to local or toll free line. Copy fee: $.20 per page. Cert fee: $2.00. Payee: Brown County Clerk of Court. Personal checks accepted. Prepayment required. Mail requests: SASE required. Mail turnaround time 1-3 days.

Brule County

Circuit Court 300 S Courtland, #111, Chamberlain, SD 57325-1599; 605-734-4580; Fax: 605-734-4582. Hours: 8AM-Noon, 1-5PM (CST). *Felony, Misdemeanor, Civil, Eviction, Small Claims, Probate.*

Civil Records: Access: Fax, mail, in person. Both court and visitors may perform in person searches. Search fee: $15.00 per name. Required to search: name, years to search; also helpful: address. Civil cases indexed by defendant, plaintiff. Civil records on index books or docket books from 1875.

Criminal Records: Access: Fax, mail, in person. Only the court performs in person searches; visitors may not. Search fee: $15.00 per name. Required to search: name, years to search, DOB; also helpful: address, SSN. Criminal records on computer since July 1989 on a statewide system. All mail requests are forwarded to Miner County for processing. Fax requests accepted for commercial accounts only and are forwarded as well.

General Information: No juvenile, sealed, dismissed, or mental health records released. Will fax results $1.00 per page, $5.00 minimum. Copy fee: $.20 per page. Cert fee: $2.00. Payee: Brule County Clerk of Court. Personal checks accepted. Prepayment required. Mail requests: SASE required. Mail turnaround time 3-5 days.

Buffalo County

Circuit Court PO Box 148, Gann Valley, SD 57341; 605-293-3234; Fax: 605-293-3240. Hours: 9AM-Noon (CST). *Felony, Misdemeanor, Civil, Eviction, Small Claims, Probate.*

Note: Only records prior to 2000 are at Gann Valley. Records after 2000 are at the Brule Circuit Court Clerk, 300 S. Courtland, #111, Chamberlin SD 57325, 605-734-4586. Records -605-734-4580

Civil Records: Access: Mail, in person. Only the court performs in person searches; visitors may not. Search fee: $15.00 per name. Required to search: name, years to search; also helpful: address. Civil cases indexed by defendant, plaintiff. All data on alpha index from 1915 to 2000 only.

Criminal Records: Access: Mail, in person. Only the court performs in person searches; visitors may not. Search fee: $15.00 per name. Required to search: name, years to search, DOB; also helpful: address, SSN. Criminal records are on books to 2000, but computerized on the statewide computer system since 07/89. All mail requests are forwarded to Miner County for processing.

General Information: No juvenile, sealed, dismissed, or mental health records released. Copy fee: $.25 per page. Cert fee: $2.00. Payee: Buffalo County Clerk of Court. Personal checks accepted. Prepayment required. Mail requests: SASE required. Mail turnaround time 1 week.

Butte County

Circuit Court PO Box 250, Belle Fourche, SD 57717-0250; 605-892-2516; Fax: 605-892-2836. Hours: 8AM-Noon, 1-5PM (MST). *Felony, Misdemeanor, Civil, Eviction, Small Claims, Probate.*

Civil Records: Access: Mail, in person. Only the court performs in person searches; visitors may not. Search fee: $15.00 per name. Required to search:

name, years to search; also helpful: DOB, address. Civil cases indexed by defendant, plaintiff. All data on alpha index from 1900s.

Criminal Records: Access: Mail, in person. Only the court performs in person searches; visitors may not. Search fee: $15.00 per name. Required to search: name, years to search; also helpful: DOB, address. Criminal records on computer since 07/89 on a statewide system.

General Information: No juvenile, sealed, dismissed, or mental health records released. Will fax results to local or toll free line. Copy fee: $.20 per page. Cert fee: $2.00. Payee: Butte County Clerk of Court. Personal checks accepted. Prepayment required. Mail requests: SASE required. Mail turnaround time varies.

Campbell County

Circuit Court PO Box 146, Mound City, SD 57646; 605-955-3536; Fax: 605-955-3308. Hours: 8AM-Noon T-W-F (CST). *Felony, Misdemeanor, Civil, Small Claims, Probate.*

Civil Records: Access: Mail, in person. Both court and visitors may perform in person searches. Search fee: $15.00 per name. Required to search: name, years to search; also helpful: address. Civil cases indexed by defendant, plaintiff. All data on alpha index from 1800s.

Criminal Records: Access: Mail, in person. Only the court performs in person searches; visitors may not. Search fee: $15.00 per name. Required to search: name, years to search, DOB; also helpful: address, SSN. Although records are computerized at the state level, this office has records and indices on paper. All mail requests are forwarded to Edmunds County for processing.

General Information: No juvenile, sealed, dismissed, or mental health records released. Will fax results to local or toll free line. Copy fee: $.20 per page. Cert fee: $2.00. Payee: Campbell County Clerk of Court. Only cashiers checks and money orders accepted. Prepayment required. Mail requests: SASE required. Mail turnaround time varies.

Charles Mix County

Circuit Court PO Box 640, Lake Andes, SD 57356; 605-487-7511; Fax: 605-487-7547. Hours: 8AM-4:30PM (CST). *Felony, Misdemeanor, Civil, Eviction, Small Claims, Probate.*

Civil Records: Access: Fax, mail, in person. Both court and visitors may perform in person searches. Search fee: $15.00 per name. Required to search: name, years to search; also helpful: address. Civil cases indexed by defendant, plaintiff. Civil records on alpha index books from 1917.

Criminal Records: Access: Fax, mail, in person. Only the court performs in person searches; visitors may not. Search fee: $15.00 per name. Required to search: name, years to search, DOB; also helpful: address, SSN. Criminal records on computer since 07/89 on a statewide system located in Douglas County. All mail and fax requests are forwarded to Douglas County for processing.

General Information: No juvenile, sealed, dismissed, or mental health records released. Will fax results $1.00 per page, $5.00 minimum. Copy fee: $.20 per page. Cert fee: $2.00. Payee: Charles Mix County Clerk of Court. Personal check accepted with SSN or DL#. Prepayment required. Mail requests: SASE required. Mail turnaround time 2-5 days.

Clark County

Circuit Court PO Box 294, Clark, SD 57225; 605-532-5851. Hours: 8AM-Noon, 1-5PM (CST). *Felony, Misdemeanor, Civil, Eviction, Small Claims, Probate.*

Civil Records: Access: Mail, in person. Only the court performs in person searches; visitors may not. Search fee: $15.00 per name. Required to search: name, years to search; also helpful: address. Civil cases indexed by defendant, plaintiff. Civil records on alpha index cards from 1969.

Criminal Records: Access: Mail, in person. Only the court performs in person searches; visitors may not. Search fee: $15.00 per name. Required to search: name, years to search, DOB; also helpful: address, SSN. Criminal records on computer since 1986 on a statewide system. All mail requests are forwarded to Hand County for processing, PO Box 122, Miller, SD 57362-0122.

General Information: No juvenile, sealed, dismissed, or mental health records released. Copy fee: $.20 per page. Cert fee: $2.00. Payee: Clark County Clerk of Court. Personal checks accepted. Prepayment required. Mail requests: SASE required. Mail turnaround time 1-4 days.

Clay County

Circuit Court PO Box 377, Vermillion, SD 57069; 605-677-6755/6; Fax: 605-677-8885. Hours: 8AM-5PM (CST). *Felony, Misdemeanor, Civil, Eviction, Small Claims, Probate.*

Civil Records: Access: Mail, in person. Both court and visitors may perform in person searches. Search fee: $15.00 per name. Required to search: name, years to search; also helpful: address. Civil cases indexed by defendant, plaintiff. Civil records on computer from 1993, in books to 1920, and archived from 1800s.

Criminal Records: Access: Mail, in person. Only the court performs in person searches; visitors may not. Search fee: $15.00 per name. Required to search: name, years to search, DOB; also helpful: address, SSN. Criminal records on computer from 1989, in books to 1920, and archived from 1800s. All mail requests are forwarded to Aurora or Hanson County for processing.

General Information: No juvenile, sealed, dismissed, or mental health records released. Will fax results to local or toll free line. Copy fee: $.20 per page. Cert fee: $2.00. Payee: Clay County Clerk of Court. Personal checks accepted. Prepayment required. Mail requests: SASE required. Mail turnaround time 2-4 days.

Codington County

Circuit Court PO Box 1054, Watertown, SD 57201; 605-882-5095. Hours: 8AM-5PM (CST). *Felony, Misdemeanor, Civil, Eviction, Small Claims, Probate.*

Civil Records: Access: Mail, in person. Only the court performs in person searches; visitors may not. Search fee: $15.00 per name. Required to search: name, years to search. Civil cases indexed by defendant, plaintiff. Civil records on computer from 1991 and alpha index cards back to 1890.

Criminal Records: Access: Mail, in person. Only the court performs in person searches; visitors may not. Search fee: $15.00 per name. Required to search: name, years to search, DOB. Criminal records on computer since 07/89 on a statewide system. Mail requests for dates 1989 to present are forwarded to Hand County for processing. Prior to 1989 processed in Codington County.

General Information: No juvenile, sealed, dismissed, or mental health records released. Copy fee: $.20 per page. Cert fee: $2.00. Payee: Codington County Clerk of Court. Business checks accepted.

Prepayment required. Mail requests: SASE required. Mail turnaround time 2 days.

Corson County

Circuit Court PO Box 175, McIntosh, SD 57641; 605-273-4201; Fax: 605-273-4597. Hours: 9:30AM-2:30PM (MST). *Felony, Misdemeanor, Civil, Eviction, Small Claims, Probate.*

Civil Records: Access: Mail, fax, in person. Both court and visitors may perform in person searches. Search fee: $15.00 per name. Required to search: name, years to search; also helpful: address. Civil cases indexed by defendant, plaintiff. All data on alpha index from 1940s.

Criminal Records: Access: Mail, in person. Only the court performs in person searches; visitors may not. Search fee: $15.00 per name. Required to search: name, years to search, DOB; also helpful: address, SSN. Criminal records on computer back to 1989. All phone requests are forwarded to Lawrence County for processing.

General Information: No juvenile, sealed, dismissed, adoption or mental health records released. Copy fee: $.20 per page. Cert fee: $2.00. Payee: Corson County Clerk of Court. Personal checks accepted. Prepayment required. Mail requests: SASE not required. Mail turnaround time 1 day.

Custer County

Circuit Court 420 Mt Rushmore Rd, Custer, SD 57730; 605-673-4816; Fax: 605-673-3416. Hours: 8AM-5PM (MST). *Felony, Misdemeanor, Civil, Eviction, Small Claims, Probate.*

Civil Records: Access: Mail, in person. Only the court performs in person searches; visitors may not. Search fee: $15.00 per name. Required to search: name, years to search, SSN; also helpful: address. Civil cases indexed by defendant, plaintiff. Probate on microfiche from 1915, all other data on docket books and index cards from 1960s.

Criminal Records: Access: Mail, in person. Only the court performs in person searches; visitors may not. Search fee: $15.00 per name. Required to search: name, years to search, DOB, SSN, signed release; also helpful: address. Criminal records on computer since 07/89 on a statewide system. Criminal searches are performed through the Search Center at Harding County Clerk, PO Box 534, Buffalo, SD 57720.

General Information: No juvenile, sealed, dismissed, or mental health records released. Copy fee: $.25 per page. Cert fee: $2.00. Payee: Custer County Clerk of Court. Personal checks accepted. Prepayment required. Mail requests: SASE required. Mail turnaround time 2 days.

Davison County

Circuit Court PO Box 927, Mitchell, SD 57301; 605-995-8105; Fax: 605-995-8105. Hours: 8AM-5PM (CST). *Felony, Misdemeanor, Civil, Eviction, Small Claims, Probate.*

Civil Records: Access: Mail, in person. Both court and visitors may perform in person searches. Search fee: $15.00 per name. Required to search: name, years to search; also helpful: address. Civil cases indexed by defendant. All data on alpha index from 1900s.

Criminal Records: Access: Mail, in person. Only the court performs in person searches; visitors may not. Search fee: $15.00 per name. Required to search: name, years to search, DOB; also helpful: address, SSN. Criminal records are computerized since 07/89 on a statewide system. All mail requests are forwarded to Miner County for processing.

General Information: No juvenile, sealed, dismissed, or mental health records released. Copy fee: $.20 per page. Cert fee: $2.00. Payee: Davison County Clerk of Court. Personal checks accepted. Out of state checks not accepted. Prepayment required.

Mail requests: SASE required. Mail turnaround time 1 week.

Day County

Circuit Court 711 W 1st St, Webster, SD 57274; 605-345-3771; Fax: 605-345-3818. Hours: 8AM-5PM (CST). *Felony, Misdemeanor, Civil, Small Claims, Probate.*

Civil Records: Access: Mail, in person. Only the court performs in person searches; visitors may not. Search fee: $15.00 per name. Required to search: name, years to search; also helpful: address. Civil cases indexed by defendant. Civil records on docket books from 1800s.

Criminal Records: Access: Mail, in person. Only the court performs in person searches; visitors may not. Search fee: $15.00 per name. Required to search: name, years to search, DOB; also helpful: address, SSN. Criminal records on computer since 1982 on a statewide system. All mail requests are forwarded to Edmunds County for processing.

General Information: No juvenile, sealed, dismissed, or mental health records released. Copy fee: $.20 per page. Cert fee: $2.00. Payee: Day County Clerk of Court. Prepayment required. Mail requests: SASE required. Mail turnaround time 1 week.

Deuel County

Circuit Court PO Box 308, Clear Lake, SD 57226; 605-874-2120. Hours: 8AM-5PM (CST). *Felony, Misdemeanor, Civil, Eviction, Small Claims, Probate.*

Civil Records: Access: Mail, in person. Only the court performs in person searches; visitors may not. Search fee: $15.00 per name. Required to search: name, years to search; also helpful: address. Civil cases indexed by defendant, plaintiff. Civil records on docket books.

Criminal Records: Access: Mail, in person. Only the court performs in person searches; visitors may not. Search fee: $15.00 per name. Required to search: name, years to search, DOB, signed release; also helpful: address, SSN. Criminal records on computer since 07/89 on a statewide system. Best to forward criminal record searches to the Criminal Search Center in Hand County.

General Information: No juvenile, sealed, dismissed, or mental health records released. Will not fax results. Copy fee: $.20 per page. Cert fee: $2.00. Payee: Deuel County Clerk of Court. Personal checks accepted. Prepayment required. Mail requests: SASE required. Mail turnaround time 1-2 days.

Dewey County

Circuit Court PO Box 96, Timber Lake, SD 57656; 605-865-3566. Hours: 9:30AM-Noon, 1-2:30PM (MST). *Felony, Misdemeanor, Civil, Eviction, Small Claims, Probate.*

Civil Records: Access: Mail, in person. Both court and visitors may perform in person searches. Search fee: $15.00 per name. Required to search: name, years to search; also helpful: address. Civil cases indexed by defendant, plaintiff. All data on alpha index and docket books from 1900s; computerized back to 1999.

Criminal Records: Access: Mail, in person. Only the court performs in person searches; visitors may not. Search fee: $15.00 per name. Required to search: name, years to search, DOB; also helpful: address, SSN, signed release. Criminal records data on alpha index and docket books from 1900s; computerized back to 1999. All mail requests are forwarded to Lawrence County for processing.

General Information: No juvenile, adoption, sealed, dismissed, or mental health records released. Fee to fax results is $1.00 per page; $5.00 per document. Copy fee: $.25 per page. Cert fee: $2.00. Payee:

Dewey County Clerk of Court. Personal checks accepted. Prepayment required. Mail requests: SASE required. Mail turnaround time 2 days to 1 week.

Douglas County

Circuit Court PO Box 36, Armour, SD 57313; 605-724-2585. Hours: 8:30AM-1:30PM M-Th (CST). *Felony, Misdemeanor, Civil, Eviction, Small Claims, Probate.*

Civil Records: Access: Mail, in person. Both court and visitors may perform in person searches. Search fee: $15.00 per name. Required to search: name, years to search; also helpful: address. Civil cases indexed by defendant. Civil records on docket books from late 1800s.

Criminal Records: Access: Fax, mail, in person. Only the court performs in person searches; visitors may not. Search fee: $15.00 per name. Required to search: name, years to search, DOB, signed release; also helpful: address, SSN. Criminal records are computerized since 07/89 on a statewide system.

General Information: No juvenile, sealed, dismissed, or mental health records released. Will fax results to local or toll free line. Copy fee: $.20 per page. Cert fee: $2.00. Payee: Douglas County Clerk of Court. Personal checks accepted. Prepayment required. Mail requests: SASE required. Mail turnaround time 1-2 weeks; will release limited civil data over phone.

Edmunds County

Circuit Court PO Box 384, Ipswich, SD 57451; 605-426-6671; Fax: 605-426-6323. Hours: 8AM-Noon, 1-5PM (CST). *Felony, Misdemeanor, Civil, Eviction, Small Claims, Probate.*

Civil Records: Access: Fax, mail, in person. Both court and visitors may perform in person searches. Search fee: $15.00 per name. Required to search: name, years to search; also helpful: address. Civil cases indexed by defendant, plaintiff. Civil records on docket books from late 1800s.

Criminal Records: Access: Fax, mail, in person. Only the court performs in person searches; visitors may not. Search fee: $15.00 per name. Required to search: name, years to search, DOB; also helpful: SSN, signed release. Criminal records on computer since 07/89; prior records on docket books. Fax requests are for commercial accounts only. Results are statewide.

General Information: No juvenile, sealed or mental health records released. Will fax results to local or toll free line. Copy fee: $.25 per page. Cert fee: $2.00. Payee: Edmunds County Clerk of Court. Personal checks accepted. Prepayment required. Mail requests: SASE required. Mail turnaround time 1 day to 1 week.

Fall River County

Circuit Court 906 N River St, Hot Springs, SD 57747; 605-745-5131. Hours: 8AM-5PM (MST). *Felony, Misdemeanor, Civil, Eviction, Small Claims, Probate.*

Note: Also handles cases for Shannon County. Specify which county in any search request.

Civil Records: Access: Mail, in person. Only the court performs in person searches; visitors may not. Search fee: $15.00 per name. Required to search: name, years to search; also helpful: DOB. Civil cases indexed by defendant, plaintiff. Civil records on computer from 1992, files from 1889 archived off site.

Criminal Records: Access: Mail, in person. Only the court performs in person searches; visitors may not. Search fee: $15.00 per name. Required to search: name, years to search, DOB; also helpful: address,

SSN. Criminal records on computer since 07/89 on a statewide system.

General Information: No juvenile, sealed, adoption, or mental health records released. Will fax results to local or toll free line. Copy fee: $.25 per page. Cert fee: $2.00 per document. Payee: Clerk of Court. Personal checks accepted. Prepayment required. Mail requests: SASE required. Mail turnaround time 1 week.

Faulk County

Circuit Court PO Box 357, Faulkton, SD 57438; 605-598-6223; Fax: 605-598-6252. Hours: 1:00PM-5:00PM (CST). *Felony, Misdemeanor, Civil, Eviction, Small Claims, Probate.*

Civil Records: Access: Mail, in person. Both court and visitors may perform in person searches. Search fee: $15.00 per name. Required to search: name, years to search; also helpful: address. Civil cases indexed by defendant. Civil records on docket books from 1900s.

Criminal Records: Access: Mail, in person. Only the court performs in person searches; visitors may not. Search fee: $15.00 per name. Required to search: name, years to search, DOB; also helpful: address, SSN. Criminal records are computerized since 07/89 on a statewide system. All mail requests are forwarded to Edmunds County for processing.

General Information: Public Access terminal is available. No juvenile, sealed, dismissed, adoption, or mental health records released. Will fax results for $1.00 per page with $5.00 minimum. Copy fee: $.20 per page. Cert fee: $2.00. Payee: Faulk County Clerk of Court. Personal checks accepted. Prepayment required. Mail requests: SASE required. Mail turnaround time 1-2 days.

Grant County

Circuit Court PO Box 509, Milbank, SD 57252; 605-432-5482. Hours: 8AM-Noon, 1-5PM (CST). *Felony, Misdemeanor, Civil, Eviction, Small Claims, Probate.*

Civil Records: Access: Mail, in person. Only the court performs in person searches; visitors may not. Search fee: $15.00 per name. Required to search: name, years to search; also helpful: address. Civil cases indexed by defendant, plaintiff. Civil records on computer from 1995, docket books from 1800s.

Criminal Records: Access: Mail, in person. Only the court performs in person searches; visitors may not. Search fee: $15.00 per name. Required to search: name, years to search, DOB; also helpful: address, SSN. Criminal records on computer since 07/89 on a statewide system. All mail requests are forwarded to and processed by Hand County.

General Information: No juvenile, sealed, dismissed, adoption or mental health records released. Copy fee: $.25 per page. Cert fee: $2.00. Payee: Grant County Clerk of Court. Prepayment required. Mail requests: SASE required. Mail turnaround time 1 week by mail; immediate by phone if on computer.

Gregory County

Circuit Court PO Box 430, Burke, SD 57523; 605-775-2665. Hours: 8AM-Noon, 1-5PM (CST). *Felony, Misdemeanor, Civil, Eviction, Small Claims, Probate.*

Civil Records: Access: Mail, in person. Only the court performs in person searches; visitors may not. Search fee: $15.00 per name. Required to search: name, years to search; also helpful: address. Civil cases indexed by defendant, plaintiff. Civil records on docket books from late 1800s, computerized since 1999.

Criminal Records: Access: Mail, in person. Only the court performs in person searches; visitors may not. Search fee: $15.00 per name. Required to search: name, years to search, DOB, signed release; also helpful: address, SSN. Criminal records on computer back to 07/89 on a statewide system. All mail requests are forwarded to Potter County for processing.

General Information: No juvenile, sealed, dismissed, or mental health records released. Will fax results for a fee. Copy fee: $.20 per page. Cert fee: $2.00. Payee: Gregory County Clerk of Court. Only cashiers checks and money orders accepted. Prepayment required. Mail requests: SASE required. Mail turnaround time 1 week.

Haakon County

Circuit Court PO Box 70, Philip, SD 57567; 605-859-2627. Hours: 8AM-Noon (MST). *Felony, Misdemeanor, Civil, Eviction, Small Claims, Probate.*

Civil Records: Access: Mail, in person. Only the court performs in person searches; visitors may not. Search fee: $15.00 per name. Required to search: name, years to search; also helpful: address. Civil cases indexed by defendant, plaintiff. Civil records on register from 1915.

Criminal Records: Access: Mail, in person. Only the court performs in person searches; visitors may not. Search fee: $15.00 per name. Required to search: name, years to search, DOB; also helpful: address, SSN. Criminal records are computerized since 07/89 on a statewide system. All mail requests are forwarded to Potter County for processing.

General Information: No juvenile, sealed, dismissed, or mental health records released. Fee to fax results is $1.00 per page; $5.00 minimum. Copy fee: $.20 per page. Cert fee: $2.00. Payee: Haakon County Clerk of Court. Local checks accepted only. Prepayment required. Mail requests: SASE required. Mail turnaround time 1 day.

Hamlin County

Circuit Court PO Box 256, Hayti, SD 57241; 605-783-3751; Fax: 605-783-2157. Hours: 8:30AM-Noon, 12:30-4:30PM (CST). *Felony, Misdemeanor, Civil, Eviction, Small Claims, Probate.*

Civil Records: Access: Mail, in person. Only the court performs in person searches; visitors may not. Search fee: $15.00 per name. Required to search: name, years to search; also helpful: address. Civil cases indexed by defendant, plaintiff. Civil records on docket books from 1800s.

Criminal Records: Access: Mail, in person. Only the court performs in person searches; visitors may not. Search fee: $15.00 per name. Required to search: name, years to search, DOB; also helpful: address, SSN. Criminal records on computer since 07/89 on a statewide system.

General Information: No juvenile, sealed, dismissed, or mental health records released. Will fax results for $5.00. Copy fee: $.20 per page. Cert fee: $2.00. Payee: Hamlin County Clerk of Court. Personal checks accepted. Prepayment required. Mail requests: SASE required. Mail turnaround time 1 day.

Hand County

Circuit Court PO Box 122, Miller, SD 57362; 605-853-3337; Fax: 605-853-3779. Hours: 8AM-5PM (CST). *Felony, Misdemeanor, Civil, Small Claims, Probate.*

Civil Records: Access: Mail, in person. Only the court performs in person searches; visitors may not. Search fee: $15.00 per name. Required to search: name, years to search; also helpful: address. Civil cases indexed by defendant. All data on alpha index and docket books from late 1800s.

Criminal Records: Access: Fax, mail, in person. Only the court performs in person searches; visitors may not. Search fee: $15.00 per name. Required to search: name, years to search, DOB; also helpful: address, SSN. Criminal records on computer since

07/89 on a statewide system. Fax requesting for commercial accounts only.

General Information: No juvenile, sealed, dismissed, or mental health records released. Will fax results; fee is $5.00 per doc if non-toll free number; no charge if to toll-free number. Copy fee: $.20 per page. Cert fee: $2.00. Payee: Hand County Clerk of Court. Business checks accepted. Prepayment required. Mail requests: SASE required. Mail turnaround time 1 day.

Hanson County

Circuit Court PO Box 127, Alexandria, SD 57311; 605-239-4446; Fax: 605-239-9446. Hours: 8AM-5PM; Closed from 12:00-1:00 (CST). *Felony, Misdemeanor, Civil, Small Claims, Probate.*

Civil Records: Access: Fax, mail, in person. Only the court performs in person searches; visitors may not. Search fee: $15.00 per name. Required to search: name, years to search; also helpful: address. Civil cases indexed by defendant, plaintiff. Civil records on docket books from 1902; on computer back to 2000.

Criminal Records: Access: Mail, in person. Only the court performs in person searches; visitors may not. Search fee: $15.00 per name. Required to search: name, years to search, DOB; also helpful: address, SSN. Criminal records computerized since 07/89 on a statewide system.

General Information: No juvenile, sealed, dismissed, adoption or mental health records released. Will fax results for $5.00 per document. $1.00 per page after 5 pages. Copy fee: $.20 per page. Cert fee: $2.00. Payee: Hanson County Clerk of Court. Personal checks accepted. Prepayment required. Mail requests: SASE required. Mail turnaround time varies.

Harding County

Circuit Court PO Box 534, Buffalo, SD 57720; 605-375-3351. Hours: 9:30AM-Noon, 1-2:30PM (MST). *Felony, Misdemeanor, Civil, Eviction, Small Claims, Probate.*

Note: This court is the designated search center of Harding and Pennington County criminal records. For eviction information the court says to contact Harding County Sheriff, PO Box 207, Buffalo SD 57720.

Civil Records: Access: Mail, in person. Both court and visitors may perform in person searches. Search fee: $15.00 per name. Required to search: name, years to search, DOB; also helpful: address. Civil cases indexed by defendant. Civil records in archives from 1909 to 1920, index books from 1920.

Criminal Records: Access: Fax, mail, in person. Only the court performs in person searches; visitors may not. Search fee: $15.00 per name. Required to search: name, years to search, DOB; also helpful: address, SSN. Criminal records are computerized since 07/89 on a statewide system. Fax requests for commercial accounts only.

General Information: No juvenile, sealed, dismissed, or mental health records released. Will fax results $1.00 per page, $5.00 minimum, no fee if local or toll free. Copy fee: $.20 per page. Cert fee: $2.00. Payee: Harding County Clerk of Court. Personal checks accepted. Prepayment required. Mail requests: SASE required. Mail turnaround time 1 week.

Hughes County

Circuit Court 104 E Capital, Pierre, SD 57501; 605-773-3713. Hours: 8AM-5PM (CST). *Felony, Misdemeanor, Civil, Eviction, Small Claims, Probate.*

Civil Records: Access: Mail, in person. Only the court performs in person searches; visitors may not. Search fee: $15.00 per name. Required to search: name, years to search; also helpful: address. Civil cases indexed by defendant, plaintiff. Civil records on microfiche from 1948 to 1973. From 1974 forward

have hard copy file, starting 1991 index and docketing on computer.

Criminal Records: Access: Mail, in person. Only the court performs in person searches; visitors may not. Search fee: $15.00 per name. Required to search: name, years to search, DOB; also helpful: address. Criminal records on computer since 1988 on a statewide system. All mail requests are forwarded to Potter County for processing.

General Information: No juvenile, adoption, any record sealed by the Court or mental health records released. Copy fee: $.20 per page. Cert fee: $2.00. Payee: Hughes County Clerk of Court. Personal checks accepted. Prepayment required. Mail requests: SASE required. Mail turnaround time approx. 2 days.

Hutchinson County

Circuit Court 140 Euclid, Rm 36, Olivet, SD 57052-2103; 605-387-4215; Fax: 605-387-4208. Hours: 8AM-Noon, 1-5PM (CST). *Felony, Misdemeanor, Civil, Eviction, Small Claims, Probate.*

Civil Records: Access: Fax, mail, in person. Only the court performs in person searches; visitors may not. Search fee: $15.00 per name. Required to search: name, years to search; also helpful: address. Civil cases indexed by defendant, plaintiff. Civil records on docket books and index cards from 1800s, on computer since 1994.

Criminal Records: Access: Fax, mail, in person. Only the court performs in person searches; visitors may not. Search fee: $15.00 per name. Required to search: name, years to search, DOB; also helpful: address, SSN. Older records on docket books and index cards, records since 07/89 are computerized on a statewide system. All fax and mail requests are forwarded to Douglas County for processing.

General Information: No juvenile, sealed, dismissed, adoption or mental health records released. Will fax results $5.00 per doc; no fee to toll free number; must be a commercial account. Copy fee: $.10 per page. Cert fee: $2.00. Payee: Hutchinson County Clerk of Court. Business checks accepted. Prepayment required. Mail requests: SASE required. Mail turnaround time 1 day.

Hyde County

Circuit Court PO Box 306, Highmore, SD 57345; 605-852-2512; Fax: 605-852-2767. Hours: 8AM-12PM (CST). *Felony, Misdemeanor, Civil, Eviction, Small Claims, Probate.*

Civil Records: Access: Fax, mail, in person. Only the court performs in person searches; visitors may not. Search fee: $15.00 per name. Required to search: name, years to search; also helpful: address. Civil cases indexed by defendant, plaintiff. Civil records on docket books from 1920s, computerized from 2000.

Criminal Records: Access: Fax, mail, in person. Only the court performs in person searches; visitors may not. Search fee: $15.00 per name. Required to search: name, years to search, DOB, signed release; also helpful: address, SSN. Criminal records are computerized since 07/89 on a statewide system. All fax and mail requests are forwarded to Potter County for processing.

General Information: No juvenile, sealed, dismissed, or mental health records released. Will fax results $5.00 per doc; no fee to local or toll free number. Copy fee: $.25 per page. Cert fee: $2.00. Payee: Hyde County Clerk of Courts. Personal checks accepted. Prepayment required. Mail requests: SASE required. Mail turnaround time 1-3 days.

Jackson County

Circuit Court PO Box 128, Kadoka, SD 57543; 605-837-2122. Hours: 8AM-Noon, 1-5PM (MST). *Felony, Misdemeanor, Civil, Eviction, Small Claims, Probate.*

Civil Records: Access: Mail, in person. Only the court performs in person searches; visitors may not. Search fee: $15.00 per name. Required to search: name, years to search; also helpful: address. Civil cases indexed by defendant. Civil records on "Register of Action" from 1915; on comptuer back to 1993.

Criminal Records: Access: Mail, in person. Only the court performs in person searches; visitors may not. Search fee: $15.00 per name. Required to search: name, years to search, DOB; also helpful: address, SSN. Criminal records on computer back to 07/89 on a statewide system; other records go back to 1920. All mail requests are forwarded to Potter County for processing.

General Information: No juvenile, sealed, dismissed, or mental health records released. Will fax results to local or toll free line. Copy fee: $.20 per page. Cert fee: $2.00. Payee: Jackson County Clerk of Court. Personal checks accepted. Prepayment required. Mail requests: SASE required. Mail turnaround time 1-2 days.

Jerauld County

Circuit Court PO Box 435, Wessington Springs, SD 57382; 605-539-1202; Fax: 605-539-1203. Hours: 8AM-5PM (CST). *Felony, Misdemeanor, Civil, Eviction, Small Claims, Probate.*

Civil Records: Access: Mail, in person. Only the court performs in person searches; visitors may not. Search fee: $15.00 per name. Required to search: name, years to search; also helpful: address. Civil cases indexed by defendant. Civil records on docket books from 1900s.

Criminal Records: Access: Mail, in person. Only the court performs in person searches; visitors may not. Search fee: $15.00 per name. Required to search: name, years to search, DOB; also helpful: address, SSN. Criminal records are computerized since 1989 on a statewide system. Fax requesting for commercial accounts only.

General Information: No juvenile, sealed, dismissed, or mental health records released. Will fax results $5.00 per page. Copy fee: $.25 per page. Cert fee: $2.00. Payee: Jerauld County Clerk of Court. Personal checks accepted. Prepayment required. Mail requests: SASE required. Mail turnaround time 2 days.

Jones County

Circuit Court PO Box 448, Murdo, SD 57559; 605-669-2361; Fax: 605-669-2641. Hours: 8AM-Noon, 1-5PM (CST). *Felony, Misdemeanor, Civil, Eviction, Small Claims, Probate.*

Note: Criminal cases and records at Potter County.

Civil Records: Access: Mail, in person. Only the court performs in person searches; visitors may not. Search fee: $15.00 per name. Required to search: name, years to search; also helpful: address. Civil cases indexed by defendant, plaintiff. Civil records on docket books from 1900s.

Criminal Records: Access: Mail, in person. Only the court performs in person searches; visitors may not. Search fee: $15.00 per name. Required to search: name, years to search, DOB, SSN; also helpful: address. Criminal records are computerized since 07/89 on a statewide system. Records on books go back to 1917. All requests are forwarded to Potter County for processing.

General Information: No juvenile, sealed, dismissed, or mental health records released. Fee to

fax results is $1.00 per page; minimum $5.00. Copy fee: $.20 per page. Cert fee: $2.00. Payee: Jones County Clerk of Court (civil cases). Potter County Clerk of Court (criminal cases). Business checks accepted. Prepayment required. Mail requests: SASE required. Mail turnaround time 3 days to 1 week.

Kingsbury County

Circuit Court PO Box 176, De Smet, SD 57231-0176; 605-854-3811; Fax: 605-854-9080. Hours: 8AM-Noon, 1-5PM (CST). *Felony, Misdemeanor, Civil, Eviction, Small Claims, Probate.*

Civil Records: Access: Mail, in person. Both court and visitors may perform in person searches. Search fee: $15.00 per name. Required to search: name, years to search; also helpful: address plus DOB. Civil cases indexed by defendant, plaintiff. Civil records on computer printed index from 1978 and bound books from 1890.

Criminal Records: Access: Mail, in person. Only the court performs in person searches; visitors may not. Search fee: $15.00 per name. Required to search: name, years to search, DOB; also helpful: address, SSN. Criminal records on computer since 07/89 on a statewide system. All mail requests are forwarded to Hand County for processing.

General Information: No juvenile, sealed, dismissed, adoption or mental health records released. Copy fee: $.20 per page. Cert fee: $2.00. Payee: Kingsbury County Clerk of Court. Personal checks accepted. Prepayment required. Mail requests: SASE required. Mail turnaround time same day.

Lake County

Circuit Court 200 E Center St, Madison, SD 57042; 605-256-5644. Hours: 8AM-Noon, 1-5PM (CST). *Felony, Misdemeanor, Civil, Eviction, Small Claims, Probate.*

Civil Records: Access: Mail, in person. Only the court performs in person searches; visitors may not. Search fee: $15.00 per name. Required to search: name, years to search; also helpful: address. Civil cases indexed by defendant. Civil records on computer from 1985, docket books from 1800s.

Criminal Records: Access: Mail, in person. Only the court performs in person searches; visitors may not. Search fee: $15.00 per name. Required to search: name, years to search, DOB, signed release; also helpful: address, SSN. Criminal records on computer since 1989 on a statewide system; prior records on docket books since 1800s. All mail requests are forwarded to Miner County for processing.

General Information: No juvenile, sealed, dismissed, or mental health records released. Copy fee: $.20 per page. Cert fee: $2.00. Payee: Lake County Clerk of Court. Personal checks accepted. Prepayment required. Mail requests: SASE required. Mail turnaround time 1 day.

Lawrence County

Circuit Court PO Box 626, Deadwood, SD 57732; 605-578-2040. Hours: 8AM-5PM (MST). *Felony, Misdemeanor, Civil, Eviction, Small Claims, Probate.*

Civil Records: Access: Mail, in person. Only the court performs in person searches; visitors may not. Search fee: $15.00 per name. Required to search: name, years to search; also helpful: address. Civil cases indexed by defendant, plaintiff. Civil records on computer from 1989 and index books from 1800s.

Criminal Records: Access: Fax, mail, in person. Only the court performs in person searches; visitors may not. Search fee: $15.00 per name. Required to search: name, years to search, DOB; also helpful: address, SSN. Criminal records on computer since 07/89 on a statewide system. Fax requesting only for commercial accounts.

General Information: No juvenile, sealed, dismissed, or mental health records released. Will fax results $5.00 per doc; no fee to local or toll free number. Copy fee: $.20 per page. Cert fee: $2.00. Payee: Lawrence County Clerk of Court. Personal checks accepted. Prepayment required. Mail requests: SASE required. Mail turnaround time 2 weeks.

Lincoln County

Circuit Court Clerk of Courts, 100 E 5th St, Canton, SD 57013; 605-987-5891. Hours: 8AM-5PM (CST). *Felony, Misdemeanor, Civil, Eviction, Small Claims, Probate.*

Civil Records: Access: Mail, in person. Only the court performs in person searches; visitors may not. Search fee: $15.00 per name. Required to search: name, years to search; also helpful: address. Civil cases indexed by defendant, plaintiff. Civil records on docket books from 1900s. Visitor may search written index pre-1993; only the court searches computer records 1994 forward.

Criminal Records: Access: Mail, in person. Only the court performs in person searches; visitors may not. Search fee: $15.00 per name. Required to search: name, years to search, DOB; also helpful: address, SSN. Criminal records on computer since 07/89 on a statewide system. All mail requests are forwarded to Douglas County.

General Information: No juvenile, sealed, dismissed, adoption or mental health records released. Copy fee: $.20 per page. Cert fee: $2.00. Payee: Lincoln County Clerk of Court. Personal checks accepted. Prepayment required. Mail requests: SASE required. Mail turnaround time 3 days, longer for probate.

Lyman County

Circuit Court PO Box 235, Kennebec, SD 57544; 605-869-2277. Hours: 8AM-5PM (CST). *Felony, Misdemeanor, Civil, Eviction, Small Claims, Probate.*

Civil Records: Access: Mail, in person. Both court and visitors may perform in person searches. Search fee: $15.00 per name. Required to search: name, years to search; also helpful: address. Civil cases indexed by defendant, plaintiff. Civil records on docket books from 1900s; on computer back one year.

Criminal Records: Access: Mail, in person. Only the court performs in person searches; visitors may not. Search fee: $15.00 per name. Required to search: name, years to search, DOB; also helpful: address, SSN. Criminal records on computer since 07/89 on a statewide system. All mail requests forwarded to Potter county for processing.

General Information: No juvenile, sealed, dismissed, or mental health records released. Fee to fax results is $1.00 per page. Copy fee: $.25 per page. Cert fee: $2.00. Payee: Lyman County Clerk of Court. Personal checks accepted. Prepayment required. Mail requests: SASE required. Mail turnaround time 1 week.

Marshall County

Circuit Court PO Box 130, Britton, SD 57430; 605-448-5213. Hours: 8AM-Noon, 1-5PM M-TH (CST). *Felony, Misdemeanor, Civil, Eviction, Small Claims, Probate.*

Civil Records: Access: Mail, in person. Only the court performs in person searches; visitors may not. Search fee: $15.00 per name. Required to search: name, years to search; also helpful: address. Civil cases indexed by defendant, plaintiff. Civil records on docket books from 1800s.

Criminal Records: Access: Phone, mail, in person. Only the court performs in person searches; visitors may not. Search fee: $15.00 per name. Required to search: name, years to search, DOB; also helpful:

address, SSN. Criminal records are computerized since 07/89 on a statewide system. All mail requests forwarded to Edmunds County Search Center for processing. (605-426-6671).

General Information: No juvenile, sealed, dismissed, or mental health records released. Will fax results to local or toll free line. Copy fee: $.20 per page. Cert fee: $2.00. Payee: Marshall County Clerk of Court. Personal checks accepted. Prepayment required. Mail requests: SASE required. Mail turnaround time 1 week.

McCook County

Circuit Court PO Box 504, Salem, SD 57058; 605-425-2781; Fax: 605-425-3144. Hours: 8AM-12:30-1-4:30PM (CST). *Felony, Misdemeanor, Civil, Eviction, Small Claims, Probate.*

Civil Records: Access: Mail, in person. Both court and visitors may perform in person searches. Search fee: $15.00 per name. Required to search: name, years to search; also helpful: address. Civil cases indexed by defendant, plaintiff. Civil records in index and docket books from late 1800s.

Criminal Records: Access: Mail, in person. Only the court performs in person searches; visitors may not. Search fee: $15.00 per name. Required to search: name, years to search, DOB, signed release; also helpful: address, SSN. Criminal records are computerized since 07/89 on a statewide system. All mail requests are forwarded to Miner County for processing. In person requests must be written.

General Information: No juvenile, sealed, dismissed, or mental health records released. Copy fee: $.20 per page. Cert fee: $2.00. Payee: McCook County Clerk of Court. Personal checks accepted. Prepayment required. Mail requests: SASE required. Mail turnaround time 1 day.

McPherson County

Circuit Court PO Box 248, Leola, SD 57456; 605-439-3361; Fax: 605-439-3394. Hours: 8AM-Noon (CST). *Felony, Misdemeanor, Civil, Eviction, Small Claims, Probate.*

Civil Records: Access: Mail, in person. Both court and visitors may perform in person searches. Search fee: $15.00 per name. Required to search: name, years to search; also helpful: address. Civil cases indexed by defendant, plaintiff. Civil records on register of action from 1910, records are not computerized. There is no fee if case number is known for in person searchers.

Criminal Records: Access: Mail, in person. Only the court performs in person searches; visitors may not. Search fee: $15.00 per name. Required to search: name, years to search, DOB, signed release; also helpful: address, SSN. Criminal records on register of action from 1910, records are not computerized. All mail requests are forwarded to Edmunds County for processing. Ph#-605-426-6671.

General Information: No juvenile, sealed, dismissed, adoption or mental health records released. Will fax results to local or toll free line. Copy fee: $.25 per page. Cert fee: $2.00. Payee: McPherson County Clerk of Court. Personal checks accepted. Prepayment required. Mail requests: SASE required. Mail turnaround time 1 day to 1 week.

Meade County

Circuit Court PO Box 939, Sturgis, SD 57785; 605-347-4411; Fax: 605-347-3526. Hours: 8AM-Noon, 1-5PM (MST). *Felony, Misdemeanor, Civil, Eviction, Small Claims, Probate.*

Civil Records: Access: Mail, in person. Both court and visitors may perform in person searches. Search fee: $15.00 per name. Required to search: name, years to search; also helpful: address. Civil cases indexed by defendant, plaintiff. Civil records on index cards and docket books from 1800s.

Criminal Records: Access: Mail, in person. Only the court performs in person searches; visitors may not. Search fee: $15.00 per name. Required to search: name, years to search, DOB, signed release; also helpful: address, SSN. Criminal records on computer since 07/89 on a statewide system. All mail requests are forwarded to Lawrence County for processing.

General Information: No juvenile, sealed, dismissed, or mental health records released. Copy fee: $.20 per page. Cert fee: $2.00. Payee: Meade County Clerk of Courts. Personal checks accepted. Prepayment required. Mail requests: SASE required. Mail turnaround time 1 day to 2 weeks.

Mellette County

Circuit Court PO Box 257, White River, SD 57579; 605-259-3230; Fax: 605-259-3194. Hours: 8AM-Noon (CST). *Felony, Misdemeanor, Civil, Eviction, Small Claims, Probate.*

Civil Records: Access: Phone, mail, in person. Both court and visitors may perform in person searches. Search fee: $15.00 per name. Required to search: name, years to search; also helpful: address. Civil cases indexed by defendant. Civil records on index cards and docket books from 1900s.

Criminal Records: Access: Mail, in person. Only the court performs in person searches; visitors may not. Search fee: $15.00 per name. Required to search: name, years to search, DOB, signed release; also helpful: address, SSN. Criminal records are computerized since 07/89 on a statewide system. All mail requests are forwarded to Potter County for processing.

General Information: No juvenile, sealed, dismissed, or mental health records released. Will fax results to local or toll free line. Copy fee: $.20 per page. Cert fee: $2.00. Payee: Mellette County Clerk of Court. Personal checks accepted. Prepayment required. Mail requests: SASE required. Mail turnaround time 3 days; probate up to 1 month.

Miner County

Circuit Court PO Box 265, Howard, SD 57349; 605-772-4612; Fax: 605-772-4412. Hours: 8AM-noon; 1-5PM (CST). *Felony, Misdemeanor, Civil, Eviction, Small Claims, Probate.*

Civil Records: Access: Mail, in person. Both court and visitors may perform in person searches. Search fee: $15.00 per name. Required to search: name, years to search. Civil cases indexed by defendant, plaintiff. Civil records on docket books from 1900s.

Criminal Records: Access: Fax, mail, in person. Only the court performs in person searches; visitors may not. Search fee: $15.00 per name. Required to search: name, years to search, DOB; also helpful: SSN. Criminal records are computerized since 1989. This is a statewide search.

General Information: No juvenile, sealed, dismissed or mental health records released. Will fax results $5.00 per doc; no fee to local or toll free number. Copy fee: $.25 per page. Cert fee: $2.00 per page. Payee: Miner County Clerk of Court. Personal checks accepted. Prepayment required. Mail requests: SASE required. Mail turnaround time 2 days.

Minnehaha County

Circuit Court 425 N Dakota Ave, Sioux Falls, SD 57104; 605-367-5900; Fax: 605-367-5916. Hours: 8AM-5PM (CST). *Felony, Misdemeanor, Civil, Eviction, Small Claims, Probate.*

Civil Records: Access: Mail, in person. Only the court performs in person searches; visitors may not. Search fee: $15.00 per name. Required to search: name, years to search; also helpful: address. Civil cases indexed by defendant, plaintiff. Civil records on computer from 1989, docket books from 1800s.

Criminal Records: Access: Mail, in person. Only the court performs in person searches; visitors may not. Search fee: $15.00 per name. Required to search: name, years to search, DOB, signed release; also helpful: address, SSN. Criminal records on computer since 07/89. All mail requests are forwarded to either Jerauld or Sanborn counties for processing. This is a statewide system.

General Information: No juvenile, sealed, dismissed or mental health records released. Copy fee: $.20 per page. Cert fee: $2.00. Payee: Minnehaha County Clerk of Court. Personal checks accepted. Prepayment required. Mail requests: SASE required. Mail turnaround time 2 weeks.

Moody County

Circuit Court 101 E Pipestone, Flandreau, SD 57028; 605-997-3181; Fax: 605-997-3861. Hours: 8AM-5PM (CST). *Felony, Misdemeanor, Civil, Eviction, Small Claims, Probate.*

Civil Records: Access: Mail, in person. Only the court performs in person searches; visitors may not. Search fee: $15.00 per name. Required to search: name, years to search; also helpful: address. Civil cases indexed by defendant, plaintiff. Civil records on computer from 1992 and docket books from 1800s.

Criminal Records: Access: Mail, in person. Only the court performs in person searches; visitors may not. Search fee: $15.00 per name. Required to search: name, years to search, DOB; also helpful: address, SSN. Criminal records on computer since 07/89 on a statewide index. All mail requests are forwarded to Miner County of processing.

General Information: No juvenile, sealed, dismissed, adoption or mental health records released. Copy fee: $.25 per page. Cert fee: $2.00. Payee: Moody County Clerk of Court. Personal checks accepted. Prepayment required. Mail requests: SASE required. Mail turnaround time 2-3 days.

Pennington County

Circuit Court PO Box 230, Rapid City, SD 57709; 605-394-2575. Hours: 8AM-5PM (MST). *Felony, Misdemeanor, Civil, Eviction, Small Claims, Probate.*

Note: Direct all record search requests to Harding County, PO Box 534, Buffalo SD 57720; phone 605-375-3351.

Civil Records: Access: Mail, in person. Only the court performs in person searches; visitors may not. No search fee. Required to search: name, years to search; also helpful: address. Civil records on computer from 1991, cards and docket books from 1800s.

Criminal Records: Access: None at this location. No search fee. Required to search: name, years to search, DOB; also helpful: address, SSN. Criminal records are computerized since 1989 on a statewide system. If prior to 1989, mail requests should be sent to Pennington County Clerk - arrest date and charge is required to conduct search. If 1989 to present, mail to Harding County Clerk, POB 534, Buffalo, SD 57720, 605-375-3351.

General Information: No juvenile, sealed, dismissed, or mental health records released. Cert fee: $2.00. Prepayment required. Mail requests: SASE required. Mail turnaround time 2 weeks.

Perkins County

Circuit Court PO Box 426, Bison, SD 57620-0426; 605-244-5626; Fax: 605-244-7110. Hours: 8AM-Noon, 1-5PM (MST). *Felony, Misdemeanor, Civil, Eviction, Small Claims, Probate.*

Civil Records: Access: Fax, mail, in person. Both court and visitors may perform in person searches. Search fee: $15.00 per name. Required to search:

name, years to search. Civil cases indexed by defendant, plaintiff. Civil records on docket books from 1908; on computer back to 1999.

Criminal Records: Access: Fax, mail, in person. Only the court performs in person searches; visitors may not. Search fee: $15.00 per name. Required to search: name, years to search, DOB, signed release. Criminal records are computerized back to 07/89 on a statewide system. All fax and mail requests are forwarded to Lawrence County for processing.

General Information: No juvenile, sealed or mental health records released. Will fax results $1.00 per page, $5.00 minimum; no fee if toll free call. Copy fee: $.25 per page. Cert fee: $2.00. Payee: Perkins County Clerk of Courts. Only cashiers checks and money orders accepted. Prepayment required. Mail requests: SASE requested. Turnaround time varies.

Potter County

Circuit Court 201 S Exene, Gettysburg, SD 57442; 605-765-9472; Fax: 605-765-9670. Hours: 8AM-Noon, 1-5PM (CST). *Felony, Misdemeanor, Civil, Eviction, Small Claims, Probate.*

Civil Records: Access: Mail, in person. Only the court performs in person searches; visitors may not. Search fee: $15.00 per name. Required to search: name, years to search; also helpful: address. Civil cases indexed by defendant, plaintiff. Civil records on index cards and docket books from 1889. Request must be in writing.

Criminal Records: Access: Fax, mail, in person. Only the court performs in person searches; visitors may not. Search fee: $15.00 per name. Required to search: name, years to search, DOB, signed release; also helpful: address, SSN. Criminal records are indexed on computer since 07/89 on a statewide system. Requests must be in writing.

General Information: No juvenile, sealed, dismissed, adoption or mental health records released. Will fax results $5.00 per doc; no fee to toll free number; must be a commercial account. Copy fee: $.20 per page. Cert fee: $2.00. Payee: Potter County Clerk of Court. Personal checks accepted. Prepayment required. Mail requests: SASE required. Mail turnaround time 1-2 days.

Roberts County

Circuit Court 411 2nd Ave E, Sisseton, SD 57262; 605-698-3395; Fax: 605-698-7894. Hours: 8AM-5PM (CST). *Felony, Misdemeanor, Civil, Eviction, Small Claims, Probate.*

Civil Records: Access: Mail, in person. Only the court performs in person searches; visitors may not. Search fee: $15.00 per name. Required to search: name, years to search; also helpful: address. Civil cases indexed by defendant, plaintiff. Civil records on computer from 1992, microfilm from 1920 to 1975 and original files from 1986.

Criminal Records: Access: Mail, in person. Only the court performs in person searches; visitors may not. Search fee: $15.00 per name. Required to search: name, years to search, DOB; also helpful: address, SSN. Criminal records on computer since 1988 on a state wide system. Criminal search requests should be sent to Edmunds County (PO Box 384, Ipswich SD 57451; 605-426-6323 fax) for processing.

General Information: Public Access terminal is available. No juvenile, sealed, dismissed, adoption or mental health records released. Will fax results to local or toll free line. Copy fee: $.20 per page. Cert fee: $2.00. Payee: Roberts County Clerk of Court (or, Edmunds City Clerk, if a criminal search. Personal checks accepted. Prepayment required. Mail requests: SASE required. Mail turnaround time 2-3 days.

Sanborn County

Circuit Court PO Box 56, Woonsocket, SD 57385; 605-796-4515; Fax: 605-796-4502. Hours: 8AM-5PM (CST). *Felony, Misdemeanor, Civil, Eviction, Small Claims, Probate.*

Civil Records: Access: Mail, in person. Only the court performs in person searches; visitors may not. Search fee: $15.00 per name. Required to search: name, years to search; also helpful: address. Civil cases indexed by defendant, plaintiff. Civil records on docket books from 1890s.

Criminal Records: Access: Fax, mail, in person. Only the court performs in person searches; visitors may not. Search fee: $15.00 per name. Required to search: name, years to search, DOB; also helpful: address, SSN. Criminal records are computerized since 1989 on a statewide system.

General Information: No juvenile, sealed, dismissed, or mental health records released. Will fax results $1.00 per page, $5.00 minimum; no fee if toll free call. Copy fee: $.25 per page. Cert fee: $2.00. Payee: Sanborn County Clerk of Courts. Personal checks accepted; no two party checks. Prepayment required. Mail requests: SASE required. Mail turnaround time 1 week.

Shannon County

Circuit Court 906 N River St, Hot Springs, SD 57747; 605-745-5131. Hours: 8AM-5PM (MST). *Felony, Misdemeanor, Civil, Eviction, Small Claims, Probate.*

Note: Also handles cases for Fall River County. Specify which county in your search request.

Civil Records: Access: Mail, in person. Only the court performs in person searches; visitors may not. Search fee: $15.00 per name. Required to search: name, years to search; also helpful: address, DOB, SSN. Civil cases indexed by defendant, plaintiff. Civil records on computer from 1992, older files archived off site to 1889.

Criminal Records: Access: Mail, in person. Only the court performs in person searches; visitors may not. Search fee: $15.00 per name. Required to search: name, years to search, DOB; also helpful: address, SSN. Criminal records on computer since 07/89 on a statewide system.

General Information: No juvenile, sealed, adoption, or mental health records released. Will fax results to local or toll free line. Copy fee: $.25 per page. Cert fee: $2.00. Payee: Shannon County Clerk of Court. Personal checks accepted. Prepayment required. Mail requests: SASE required. Mail turnaround time 1 week.

Spink County

Circuit Court 210 E 7th Ave, Redfield, SD 57469; 605-472-4535; Fax: 605-472-4352. Hours: 8AM-5PM (CST). *Felony, Misdemeanor, Civil, Eviction, Small Claims, Probate.*

Civil Records: Access: Phone, fax, mail, in person. Only the court performs in person searches; visitors may not. Search fee: $15.00 per name. Required to search: name, years to search; also helpful: address. Civil cases indexed by defendant, plaintiff. Civil records on docket books from 1882.

Criminal Records: Access: Phone, fax, mail, in person. Only the court performs in person searches; visitors may not. Search fee: $15.00 per name. Required to search: name, years to search, DOB; also helpful: address, SSN. Criminal records on computer since 1988 on a statewide system. All fax and mail requests are forwarded to Edmunds County for processing.

General Information: No juvenile, sealed, dismissed, or mental health records released. Will fax results $5.00 per doc; no fee to toll free number; must

be a commercial account. Copy fee: $.20 per page. Cert fee: $2.00. Payee: Spink County Clerk of Court. Personal checks accepted. Prepayment required. Mail requests: SASE required. Mail turnaround time 1 day.

Stanley County

Circuit Court PO Box 758, Fort Pierre, SD 57532; 605-223-7735; Fax: 605-223-7738. Hours: 8AM-5PM (CST). *Felony, Misdemeanor, Civil, Eviction, Small Claims, Probate.*

Civil Records: Access: Fax, mail, in person. Both court and visitors may perform in person searches. Search fee: $15.00 per name. Required to search: name, years to search; also helpful: address. Civil cases indexed by defendant, plaintiff. Civil records on docket books from 1973. Requests must be in writing.

Criminal Records: Access: Fax, mail, in person. Only the court performs in person searches; visitors may not. Search fee: $15.00 per name. Required to search: name, years to search, DOB; also helpful: address, SSN. Criminal records on computer since 1989 on a statewide system. All mail requests are forwarded to Potter County for processing.

General Information: No juvenile, sealed, dismissed, or mental health records released. Copy fee: $.20 per page. Cert fee: $2.00. Payee: Stanley County Clerk of Court. Personal checks accepted. Prepayment required. Mail requests: SASE required. Mail turnaround time 1-2 days.

Sully County

Circuit Court PO Box 188, Onida, SD 57564; 605-258-2535; Fax: 605-258-2270. Hours: 8AM-Noon (CST). *Felony, Misdemeanor, Civil, Eviction, Small Claims, Probate.*

Civil Records: Access: Mail, in person. Only the court performs in person searches; visitors may not. Search fee: $15.00 per name. Required to search: name, years to search; also helpful: address. Civil cases indexed by defendant, plaintiff. Civil records on docket books from 1900s.

Criminal Records: Access: Mail, in person. Only the court performs in person searches; visitors may not. Search fee: $15.00 per name. Required to search: name, years to search; also helpful: address. Criminal records on computer since 07/89 on statewide system; local computer back to 2000. All mail requests are forwarded to Potter County for processing.

General Information: No juvenile, sealed, dismissed, or mental health records released. Will fax results for fee. Copy fee: $.25 per page. Cert fee: $2.00. Payee: Sully County Clerk of Court. No personal checks accepted. Prepayment required. Mail requests: SASE required. Mail turnaround time 1-2 days.

Todd County

Circuit Court 200 E 3rd St, PO Box 311, Winner, SD 57580; 605-842-2266; Fax: 605-842-2267. Hours: 8AM-5PM (MST). *Felony, Misdemeanor, Civil, Eviction, Small Claims, Probate.*

Civil Records: Access: Mail, in person. Only the court performs in person searches; visitors may not. Search fee: $15.00 per name. Required to search: name, years to search; also helpful: address. Civil cases indexed by defendant, plaintiff. Civil records on docket books from 1920s.

Criminal Records: Access: Mail, in person. Only the court performs in person searches; visitors may not. Search fee: $15.00 per name. Required to search: name, years to search, DOB, signed release; also helpful: address, SSN. Criminal records on computer since 07/89 on statewide system. All mail requests are forwarded to Potter County for processing.

General Information: No juvenile, sealed, dismissed, or mental health records released. Copy fee: $.20 per page. Cert fee: $2.00. Payee: Todd

County Clerk of Court. Personal checks accepted. Prepayment required. Mail requests: SASE required. Mail turnaround time 2 days.

Tripp County

Circuit Court PO Box 311, 200 E 3rd St, Winner, SD 57580; 605-842-2266; Fax: 605-842-2267. Hours: 8AM-5PM (CST). *Felony, Misdemeanor, Civil, Eviction, Small Claims, Probate.*

Civil Records: Access: Mail, in person. Only the court performs in person searches; visitors may not. Search fee: $15.00 per name. Required to search: name, years to search; also helpful: address. Civil cases indexed by defendant, plaintiff. Civil records on docket books from 1920s. All requests must be in writing.

Criminal Records: Access: Mail, in person. Only the court performs in person searches; visitors may not. Search fee: $15.00 per name. Required to search: name, years to search, DOB, signed release; also helpful: address, SSN. Criminal records on computer since 1989 on statewide system. All mail requests are forwarded to Potter County for processing.

General Information: No juvenile, sealed, dismissed, or mental health records released. Copy fee: $.20 per page. Cert fee: $2.00. Payee: Tripp County Clerk of Court. Personal checks accepted. Prepayment required. Mail requests: SASE required. Mail turnaround time 2 days.

Turner County

Circuit Court PO Box 446, Parker, SD 57053; 605-297-3115; Fax: 605-297-2115. Hours: 8AM-5PM (CST). *Felony, Misdemeanor, Civil, Eviction, Small Claims, Probate.*

Civil Records: Access: Mail, in person. Only the court performs in person searches; visitors may not. Search fee: $15.00 per name. Required to search: name, years to search; also helpful: address, DOB, and drivers license number. Civil cases indexed by defendant, plaintiff. Civil records on index cards and docket books from 1900s.

Criminal Records: Access: Mail, in person. Only the court performs in person searches; visitors may not. Search fee: $15.00 per name. Required to search: name, years to search, DOB, signed release; also helpful: address, SSN, drivers license number. Criminal records on computer since 07/89 on a statewide system. All mail requests are forwarded to Douglas County for processing.

General Information: No juvenile, sealed, dismissed, or mental health records released. Fee to fax results is $1.00 per page; $5.00 minimum. Copy fee: $.25 per page. Cert fee: $2.00. Payee: Turner County Clerk of Courts. Prepayment required. Mail requests: SASE required. Mail turnaround time 2 days.

Union County

Circuit Court PO Box 757, Elk Point, SD 57025; 605-356-2132; Fax: 605-356-3687. Hours: 8:30AM-5PM (CST). *Felony, Misdemeanor, Civil, Eviction, Small Claims, Probate.*

Civil Records: Access: Fax, mail, in person. Only the court performs in person searches; visitors may not. Search fee: $15.00 per name. Required to search: name, years to search; also helpful: address. Civil cases indexed by defendant, plaintiff. Civil records on computer from 1990, docket books from 1900s.

Criminal Records: Access: Fax, mail, in person. Only the court performs in person searches; visitors may not. Search fee: $15.00 per name. Required to search: name, years to search, DOB; also helpful: address, SSN. Criminal records on computer since 1988 on a statewide system, on docket books from 1900s. All mail requests for years 1988 to present are forwarded to Douglas County for processing.

General Information: No juvenile, sealed, dismissed, or mental health records released. Fee to fax results is $5.00 or $1.00 per page, whichever is greater. Copy fee: $.20 per page. Cert fee: $2.00. Payee: Union County Clerk of Court. Personal checks accepted. Prepayment required. Mail requests: SASE required. Mail turnaround time 1-2 days.

Walworth County

Circuit Court PO Box 328, Selby, SD 57472; 605-649-7311; Fax: 605-649-7624. Hours: 8AM-5PM (CST). *Felony, Misdemeanor, Civil, Eviction, Small Claims, Probate.*

Civil Records: Access: Mail, in person. Only the court performs in person searches; visitors may not. Search fee: $15.00 per name. Required to search: name, years to search; also helpful: address. Civil cases indexed by defendant, plaintiff. Civil records on index cards and docket books from 1900s.

Criminal Records: Access: Mail, in person. Only the court performs in person searches; visitors may not. Search fee: $15.00 per name. Required to search: name, years to search, DOB, signed release; also helpful: address, SSN. Criminal records on computer since 07/89 in a statewide system. All mail requests are forwarded to Edmunds County for processing.

General Information: No juvenile, sealed, dismissed, or mental health records released. Copy fee: $.20 per page. Cert fee: $2.00. Payee: Walworth County Clerk of Court. Personal checks accepted. Prepayment required. Mail requests: SASE required. Mail turnaround time 1-2 days.

Yankton County

Circuit Court Clerk of Courts, PO Box 155, Yankton, SD 57078; 605-668-3080; Fax: 605-668-5411. Hours: 8AM-5PM (CST). *Felony, Misdemeanor, Civil, Small Claims (and Eviction), Probate.*

Civil Records: Access: Mail, in person. Both court and visitors may perform in person searches. Search fee: $15.00 per name. Required to search: name, years to search; also helpful: address, DOB, SSN. Civil cases indexed by defendant, plaintiff. Civil records on computer from 1991, docket books from 1900s. Visitors only have access to the book index.

Criminal Records: Access: Mail, in person. Both court and visitors may perform in person searches. Search fee: $15.00 per name. Must be a state authorized account. Required to search: name, years to search, DOB; also helpful: address, SSN. Criminal records on computer since 07/89 on a statewide system, Class II offenses not accessible on computer to public. Visitors only have access to the book index. All mail requests are forwarded to Douglas County for processing.

General Information: No juvenile, sealed, dismissed, or mental health records released. Will fax results to toll-free number for $1 per page, $5 minimum. Copy fee: $.20 per page. Cert fee: $2.00. Payee: Yankton County Clerk of Court. Personal checks accepted. Prepayment required. Mail requests: SASE required. Mail turnaround time 1 week.

Ziebach County

Circuit Court PO Box 306, Dupree, SD 57623; 605-365-5159. Hours: 9:30AM-Noon, 1-2:30PM (MST). *Felony, Misdemeanor, Civil, Eviction, Small Claims, Probate.*

Civil Records: Access: Mail, in person. Only the court performs in person searches; visitors may not. Search fee: $15.00 per name. Required to search: name, years to search; also helpful: address. Civil cases indexed by defendant. Civil records on index books from 1900s.

Criminal Records: Access: Mail, in person. Only the court performs in person searches; visitors may not. Search fee: $15.00 per name. Required to search: name, years to search, DOB; also helpful: address, SSN. Criminal records on index books from 1900s. All mail requests are forwarded to Lawrence County for processing.

General Information: No juvenile, sealed, dismissed, adoption or mental health records released. Will fax results to local or toll free line, otherwise $1.00 per page, $5.00 minimum. Copy fee: $.10 per page. Cert fee: $2.00. Payee: Ziebach County Clerk of Court. Personal checks accepted. Prepayment required. Mail requests: SASE required. Mail turnaround time

South Dakota Recording Offices

ORGANIZATION: 66 counties, 66 recording offices. The recording officer is. Register of Deeds. 48 counties are in the Central Time Zone (CST) and 18 are in the Mountain Time Zone (MST).

REAL ESTATE RECORDS: Many counties will perform real estate searches. Search fees and copy fees vary. Certification usually costs $1.00 per document.

UCC RECORDS: Financing statements are filed at the state level, except for real estate related collateral, which are filed with the Register of Deeds. All recording offices will perform UCC searches. All counties have access to a statewide database of UCC filings. Use search request form UCC-11. Searches fees are usually $12.00 to $20.00 per debtor name, $10.00 if online. Copy fees are usually $1.00 per page. Certification is $2.00 or $5.00.

TAX LIEN RECORDS: Federal and state tax liens on personal property of businesses are filed with the Secretary of State. Other federal and state tax liens are filed with the county Register of Deeds. Most counties will perform tax lien searches. Search fees and copy fees vary.

OTHER LIENS: Mechanics, motor vehicle, materials.

ONLINE ACCESS: Access to UCC records are available online through the SOS's Fast File Internet Access System at www.state.sd.us/sos/ucc.htm. Registration and annual fee is required. A certified search is also available. A new system named "Expa" is soon to be available for the occasional user.

Aurora County

Register of Deeds, PO Box 397, Plankinton, SD 57368. **Phone**-Register of Deeds, R/E & UCC Recording- 605-942-7161; fax-605-942-7751; hours 8AM-N, 1-5PM UCC records search per debtor- $12.00. UCC search includes tax liens. Separate federal/state combined tax lien search- $1.00 per doc. Will not search real estate records. RE record copy- $1.00 per doc. Cert fee: $2.00 per doc. Payee: Register of Deeds. **Other phones:** Assessor-605-942-7164; Treasurer-605-942-7162; Vital Records-605-942-7161.

Beadle County

Register of Deeds, PO Box 55, Huron, SD 57350-0055. **Phone**-Register of Deeds, R/E & UCC Recording- 605-353-8412; fax-605-353-8402; hours 8AM-5PM UCC records search per debtor- $10.00. Federal/state combined tax lien search- $5.00 per debtor. Will not search real estate records. RE record copy- $1.00 for 5 pages; $.20 each after 1st 5. UCC copy-$1.00 per page. Cert fee: $2.00 per doc. Payee: Register of Deeds. **Other phones:** Assessor-605-353-8408; Treasurer-605-353-8405; Appraiser/ Auditor-605-353-8408; Elections-605-353-8400; Vital Records-605-353-8412.

Bennett County

Register of Deeds, PO Box 433, Martin, SD 57551-0433. **Phone**-605-685-6054; fax-605-685-6311; hours 8AM-N, 12:30-4:30AM UCC records search per debtor- $10.00 per person. Federal/state combined tax lien search- $5.00 per debtor Will not search real estate records. UCC copy-$1.00 per doc. Cert fee: $2.00 per doc. Payee: Register of Deeds. **Other phones:** Assessor-605-685-6991; Treasurer-605-685-6092.

Bon Homme County

C, PO Box 3, Tyndall, SD 57066. **Phone**-605-589-4217, R/E Recording-605-589-3302; 8AM-4:30PM UCC records search per debtor- $10.00. UCC search includes tax liens if requested. Separate federal/state combined tax lien search- $15.00 per debtor. Will not search real estate records. UCC copy-$1.00 per page. Cert fee: $2.00 per cert. Payee: Bon Homme County Register of Deeds. **Other phones:** Assessor-605-589-3462.

Brookings County

Register of Deeds, 314 6th Ave, Courthouse, Brookings, SD 57006-2084. **Phone**-605-696-8240, R/E Recording-605-692-2724; fax-605-696-8245; hours 8AM-5PM UCC records search per debtor- $20.00. UCC search includes tax liens if requested. Separate federal/state combined tax lien search- $5.00 per debtor. Will not search real estate records. Record copy- $1.00 per page. Cert fee: $2.00 per cert. Payee: Brookings County Register of Deeds. **Other phones:** Assessor-605-696-8220; Treasurer-605-696-8250; Appraiser/ Auditor-605-696-8301; Elections-605-696-8220; Vital Records-605-696-8240.

Brown County

Register of Deeds, PO Box 1307, Aberdeen, SD 57402-1307. **Phone**-605-626-7140, R/E Recording-605-622-7140; fax-605-626-4010. UCC records search per debtor- $12.00. Will search tax liens including federal tax liens. Tax lien search- $5.00. Will not search real estate records. Copy fee is $1.00 per page. Cert fee: $5.00. **Other phones:** Assessor-605-622-7133.

Brule County

Register of Deeds, 300 S. Courtland, #110, Chamberlain, SD 57325. **Phone**-605-734-4434; fax-605-234-4434; hours 8AM-Noon,1-5PM UCC records search per debtor- $12.00. Separate federal/state combined tax lien search- $4.00 per debtor. Will not search real estate records. UCC copy-$1.00 per page. Cert fee: $5.00 per doc. Payee: Brule County Register of Deeds. **Other phones:** Assessor-605-734-4432; Treasurer-605-734-4436; Elections-605-734-4430; Vital Records-605-734-4434.

Buffalo County

Register of Deeds, PO Box 174, Gannvalley, SD 57341. **Phone**-605-293-3239; fax-605-293-3240; hours 9AM-5PM UCC records search per debtor- $12.00. Search request using non-standard form (per name)-$13.00. Separate federal & state combined tax lien search- $10.00 Will not search real estate records. UCC copy- $.25 per page. Cert fee: $1.00. Payee: Register of Deeds. **Other phones:** Assessor-605-293-3236; Treasurer-605-293-3236.

Butte County

Register of Deeds, 839 Fifth Ave, Belle Fourche, SD 57717. **Phone**-605-892-2912; fax-605-829-4525; hours 8AM-5PM UCC records search per debtor- $20.00. Tax lien search- $5.00 per debtor. Will not search real estate records. RE record copy- $1.00 per doc. UCC copy-$1.00 per page. Cert fee: $2.00 per doc. Payee: Butte County Register of Deeds. **Other phones:** Assessor-605-892-3950; Treasurer-605-892-4456; Appraiser/ Auditor-605-892-3950; Elections-605-892-4485; Vital Records-605-892-2912.

Campbell County

Register of Deeds, PO Box 148, Mound City, SD 57646-0148. **Phone**-Register of Deeds, R/E & UCC Recording- 605-955-3505; fax-605-955-3308; hours 8AM-Noon; 1-5PM. UCC records search per debtor-$20.00. Will not search real estate records. RE record copy- $1.00 1st 5 pages; $.20 per page thereafter. Cert fee: $2.00 per instrument. Payee: Campbell County Register of Deeds. **Other phones:** Assessor-605-955-3577; Treasurer-605-955-3388; Appraiser/ Auditor-605-955-3577; Elections-605-955-3366; Vital Records-605-955-3505.

Charles Mix County

Register of Deeds, PO Box 206, Lake Andes, SD 57356-0206. **Phone**-Register of Deeds, R/E & UCC Recording- 605-487-7141; fax-605-487-7221; hours 8AM-4:30PM, UCC records search per debtor-$10.00. Tax liens not included in UCC search. Tax lien search- $10.00 per search. Will not search real estate records. Record copy- $1.00 per instrument. Cert fee: $2.00. Payee: Charles Mix County Register of Deeds. **Other phones:** Assessor-605-487-7382; Treasurer-605-487-7542; Elections-605-487-7131; Vital Records-605-487-7141.

Clark County

Register of Deeds, PO Box 294, Clark, SD 57225-0294. **Phone**-605-532-5363, R/E Recording-605-632-5363, UCC Recording-605-632-5363; fax-605-532-5931; hours 8AM-5PM UCC records search per debtor- $10.00. Tax liens included in UCC search. Separate federal & state combined tax lien search- no fee. Will search real estate records. RE record copy- $1.00 per page.

UCC copy- $1.00 per instrument. Cert fee: $2.00 per cert. Payee: Register of Deeds. **Other phones:** Assessor-605-532-3751; Treasurer-605-532-5911; Elections-605-532-5921; Vital Records-605-632-5363.

Clay County

Register of Deeds, 211 W. Main St, #202, Vermillion, SD 57069. **Phone-**Register of Deeds, R/E & UCC Recording- 605-677-7130; hours 8AM-5PM

UCC records search per debtor- $20.00. Tax liens not included in UCC search. Separate federal/state combined tax lien search- $5.00 per page. Will not search real estate records. RE record copy- $1.00 per doc up to 5 pages. UCC copy- $1.00 per page. Cert fee: $2.00 per cert. Payee: Clay County Register of Deeds. **Other phones:** Assessor-605-677-7140; Treasurer-605-677-7123; Elections-605-677-7120; Vital Records-605-677-7130.

Codington County

Register of Deeds, 14 1st Ave S.E., Watertown, SD 57201-3695. **Phone-**605-882-6278; fax-602-882-5230; hours 8AM-5PM. UCC records search per debtor-$20.00. Tax lien search- $12.00 UCC Standard/$13.00 Non-Standard form. Will not search real estate records. Copy fee- $1.00 per doc. Cert fee: $2.00 per doc. Payee: Register of Deeds. **Other phones:** Assessor-605-886-6274; Treasurer-605-886-6285; Appraiser/ Auditor-605-886-6274; Elections-605-882-6297; Vital Records-605-882-6278.

Corson County

Register of Deeds, PO Box 256, McIntosh, SD 57641-0256. **Phone-**605-273-4395; fax-605-273-4233; hours 8-12:00-1-5PM. UCC records search per debtor-$10.00. Will not search real estate records. UCC copy- $1.00 per page. Cert fee: $2.00. Payee: Register of Deeds. **Other phones:** Assessor-605-273-4354; Treasurer-605-273-4552.

Custer County

Register of Deeds, 420 Mount Rushmore Rd, Custer, SD 57730-1934. **Phone-**605-673-8171; fax-605-673-8148; hours 8AM-5PM M-Th.

Will not search UCC or real estate records. **Other phones:** Assessor-605-673-8170; Treasurer-605-673-8172; Appraiser/ Auditor-605-673-8970; Elections-605-673-8173; Vital Records-605-673-8171.

Davison County

Register of Deeds, 200 E. 4th, Courthouse, Mitchell, SD 57301-2692. **Phone-**Register of Deeds, R/E & UCC Recording- 605-995-8616; fax-605-995-8648; hours 8AM-5PM

www.davisoncounty.org/registerofdeeds.html

UCC records search per debtor- $20.00. Tax lien search available. Tax lien search- $5.00 per debtor. Will not search real estate records. RE record copy- $1.00 per doc. UCC copy- $1.00 per page. **Other phones:** Assessor-605-995-8613; Treasurer-605-995-8617; Appraiser/ Auditor-605-995-8613; Elections-605-995-8608; Vital Records-605-995-8616; Court Clerk-605-995-8105.

Day County

Register of Deeds, 711 W. 1st St, Webster, SD 57274-1396. **Phone-**Register of Deeds, R/E & UCC Recording- 605-345-9506; fax-605-345-9507; hours 8AM-Noon 1PM-5PM. UCC records search per debtor- $12.00. UCC search includes tax liens if requested. Separate federal/state combined tax lien search- $5.00 per debtor. Will not search real estate records. UCC copy- $1.00 per page. Cert fee: $2.00 per cert. Payee: Day County Register of Deeds. **Other phones:** Assessor-605-345-9502; Treasurer-605-345-9510; Elections-605-345-9500; Vital Records-605-345-9506.

Deuel County

Register of Deeds, PO Box 307, Clear Lake, SD 57226. **Phone-**Register of Deeds, R/E & UCC Recording- 605-874-2268; fax-605-874-1306; hours 8AM-5PM

UCC records search per debtor- $12.00. Will search tax liens including federal tax liens. Federal/state combined tax lien search- $5.00 per debtor. Will not search real estate records. RE record copy- $1.00 per recorded instrument. UCC copy- $1.00 per page. Cert fee: $2.00 per recorded instrument. Payee: Register of Deeds. **Other phones:** Assessor-605-874-2229; Treasurer-605-874-2483; Elections-605-874-2312; Vital Records-605-874-2268.

Dewey County

Register of Deeds, PO Box 117, Timber Lake, SD 57656-0117. **Phone-**Register of Deeds, R/E & UCC Recording- 605-865-3661; fax-605-865-3691; hours 8AM-12:00-1-5PM. UCC records search per debtor-$10.00. Separate federal & state combined tax lien search- $8.00 Will search real estate records. UCC copy- $1.00 per page. Cert fee: $2.00. Payee: Dewey County Clerk. **Other phones:** Assessor-605-865-3573; Treasurer-605-865-3501; Appraiser/ Auditor-605-865-3730; Elections-605-865-3672; Vital Records-605-865-3661.

Douglas County

Register of Deeds, PO Box 267, Armour, SD 57313-0267. **Phone-**Register of Deeds, R/E & UCC Recording- 605-724-2204; fax-605-724-2204; hours 8AM-12, 1PM-5PM

UCC records search per debtor- $10.00. Will search tax liens. Will search real estate records. RE record copy- $1.00 for 5 pages. UCC copy- $1.00 per page. Cert fee: $2.00 per doc. Payee: Register of Deeds. **Other phones:** Assessor-605-724-2688; Treasurer-605-724-2318; Appraiser/ Auditor-605-724-2688; Elections-605-724-2423; Vital Records-605-724-2204.

Edmunds County

Register of Deeds, PO Box 386, Ipswich, SD 57451-0386. **Phone-**Register of Deeds, R/E & UCC Recording- 605-426-6431; fax-605-426-6257; hours 8AM-Noon,1-5PM

UCC records search per debtor- $10.00. Will not search real estate records. Record copy- $1.00 per page. Cert fee: $2.00 per cert. Payee: Edmunds County Register of Deeds. **Other phones:** Assessor-605-426-6841; Treasurer-605-426-6801; Appraiser/ Auditor-605-426-6841; Elections-605-426-6762; Vital Records-605-426-6431.

Fall River County

Register of Deeds, 906 N. River St, Hot Springs, SD 57747. **Phone-**605-745-5139; fax-605-745-6835. Will not search records. **Other phones:** Assessor-605-745-5136; Treasurer-605-745-5145.

Faulk County

Register of Deeds, PO Box 309, Faulkton, SD 57438. **Phone-**605-598-6228; fax-605-598-6680; hours 8AM-Noon,1-5PM

UCC records search per debtor- $10.00. Will not search tax liens. Real estate owner and property transfer searches available. RE record copy- $1.00 per doc. UCC copy- $1.00 per page. Cert fee: $2.00 per cert. Payee: Faulk County Register of Deeds. **Other phones:** Assessor-605-598-6225; Treasurer-605-598-6232; Vital Records-605-598-6228.

Grant County

Register of Deeds, PO Box 587, Milbank, SD 57252. **Phone-**Register of Deeds, R/E & UCC Recording- 605-432-4752; fax-605-432-9004; hours 8AM-5PM

UCC records search per debtor- $20.00. UCC search includes tax liens if requested. Separate federal/state combined tax lien search- $5.00 per debtor. Will not search real estate records. RE record copy- $1.00 per doc. UCC copy- $1.00 per page. Cert fee: $2.00 per cert. Payee: Grant County Register of Deeds. **Other phones:** Assessor-605-432-6532; Treasurer-605-432-5651; Appraiser/ Auditor-605-432-6532; Elections-605-432-6711; Vital Records-605-432-4752.

Gregory County

Register of Deeds, PO Box 437, Burke, SD 57523. **Phone-**605-775-2624; fax-605-775-9116; hours 8AM-12:00,1-5PM

UCC records search per debtor- $10.00. Will not search real estate or tax lien records. UCC copy- $1.00 per page. Cert fee: $3.00. Payee: Gregory County Register of Deeds. **Other phones:** Assessor-605-775-2673; Treasurer-605-775-2605.

Haakon County

Register of Deeds, PO Box 100, Philip, SD 57567-0100. **Phone-**605-859-2785; 8AM-Noon,1-5PM

UCC records search per debtor- $10.00. Will not search real estate or tax lien records. Record copy- $1.00 per page. Cert fee: $2.00 per cert. Payee: Haakon County Register of Deeds. **Other phones:** Assessor-605-859-2824; Treasurer-605-859-2612.

Hamlin County

Register of Deeds, PO Box 56, Hayti, SD 57241. **Phone-**605-783-3206; hours 8AM-Noon, 1-5PM

Will not search records. UCC copy- $1.00 per page. Payee: Hamlin County Register of Deeds. **Other phones:** Assessor-605-783-3331; Treasurer-605-783-3441.

Hand County

Register of Deeds, 415 W. 1st Ave, Miller, SD 57362-1346. **Phone-**Register of Deeds, R/E & UCC Recording- 605-853-3512; fax-605-853-2769; hours 8AM-5PM

UCC records search per debtor- $10.00. Will do a separate tax lien search. Tax lien search- $5.00 per debtor. Will not search real estate records. RE record copy- $1.00 per doc. UCC copy- $1.00 per page. Cert fee: $2.00 per copy. Payee: Register of Deeds. **Other phones:** Assessor-605-853-2115; Treasurer-605-853-2136; Appraiser/ Auditor-605-853-2182; Vital Records-605-853-3512.

Hanson County

Register of Deeds, PO Box 500, Alexandria, SD 57311-0500. **Phone-**Register of Deeds, R/E & UCC Recording- 605-239-4512; fax-605-239-4296; hours 8AM-Noon; 1-5PM

UCC records search per debtor- $12.00. Will search real estate records. RE record copy- $1.00 per doc. UCC copy- $1.00 per page. Cert fee: $2.00 per doc; $.20 each page after 5 pages. Payee: Register of Deeds. **Other phones:** Assessor-605-239-4445; Treasurer-605-239-4723; Appraiser/ Auditor-605-239-4445; Elections-605-239-4714; Vital Records-605-239-4512.

Harding County

Register of Deeds, PO Box 101, Buffalo, SD 57720. **Phone-**605-375-3321; fax-605-375-3318; hours 8AM-Noon, 1-5PM

UCC records search per debtor- $15.00. Tax liens not included in UCC search. Tax lien search- $4.00 per debtor. Real estate record owner and mortgage searches available. Record copy- $1.00 per page. Cert fee: $5.00. Payee: Harding County Register of Deeds. **Other phones:** Assessor-605-375-3234; Treasurer-605-375-3542.

Hughes County

Register of Deeds, 104 E. Capital, Pierre, SD 57501. **Phone**-Register of Deeds, R/E & UCC Recording- 605-773-7495; fax-605-773-7479; hours 8AM-5PM www.sdcounties.org
UCC records search per debtor- $12.00. Federal/state combined tax lien search- $5.00 per debtor. Will search real estate records. Copies are $1.00 for a recorded doc. Fax fee: $3.00 for 1st doc; $1.00 each add'l doc. UCC copy- $1.00 per page. Cert fee: $2.00 for 1st 5 pages, $.20 extra thereafter. Payee: Hughes County. **Other phones:** Assessor-605-773-7483; Treasurer-605-773-7491; Appraiser/ Auditor-605-773-7483; Elections-605-773-7451; Vital Records-605-773-7495.

Hutchinson County

Register of Deeds, 140 Euclid St, Rm 37, Olivet, SD 57052-2103. **Phone**-605-387-4217, R/E Recording-605-387-2838; fax-605-387-4209; hours 8AM-Noon 1-5PM
UCC records search per debtor- $20.00. Will not search real estate records. UCC copy- $1.00 per page. Cert fee: $10.00. **Other phones:** Assessor-605-387-4210; Treasurer-605-387-4213; Appraiser/ Auditor-605-387-4210; Elections-605-387-4217.

Hyde County

Register of Deeds, PO Box 342, Highmore, SD 57345. **Phone**-605-852-2517; hours 8-12:00-1-5PM
UCC records search per debtor- $10.00. UCC search includes tax liens if requested. Separate federal/state combined tax lien search-no charge. Will not search real estate records. UCC copy- $1.00 per page. Cert fee: $2.00 per Doc. Payee: Hyde County Register of Deeds. **Other phones:** Assessor-605-852-2570; Treasurer-605-852-2510.

Jackson County

Register of Deeds, PO Box 248, Kadoka, SD 57453. **Phone**-605-837-2420; hours 8AM-5PM
UCC records search per debtor- $10.00. UCC search includes tax liens if requested. Will not search real estate records. Record copy- $1.00 per page. Cert fee: $2.00 per cert. Payee: Jackson County Register of Deeds. **Other phones:** Assessor-605-837-2424; Treasurer-605-837-2423.

Jerauld County

Register of Deeds, PO Box 452, Wessington Springs, SD 57382-0452. **Phone**-605-539-1221; hours 8AM-12, 1PM-5PM
UCC records search per debtor- $10.00. UCC search includes tax liens if requested. Real estate owner, mortgage, and property transfer searches available. UCC copy- $1.00 per page. Cert fee: $2.00 per cert. Payee: Jerauld County Register of Deeds. **Other phones:** Assessor-605-539-9701; Treasurer-605-539-1241.

Jones County

Register of Deeds, PO Box 446, Murdo, SD 57559. **Phone**-605-669-7104; hours 8AM-5PM
UCC records search per debtor- $10.00. UCC search includes tax liens if requested. Separate federal/state combined tax lien search-no charge. Will not search real estate records. UCC copy- $1.00 per page. Cert fee: $2.00 1st 5 pg, $.20 each addl. Payee: Jones County Register of Deeds. **Other phones:** Assessor-605-669-2122; Treasurer-605-669-2122.

Kingsbury County

Register of Deeds, PO Box 146, De Smet, SD 57231-0146. **Phone**-605-854-3591; fax-605-854-3833; hours 8AM-Noon, 1PM-5PM

UCC records search per debtor- $20.00. Will not search real estate records. Copy fee is $1.00 per page. Cert fee: $2.00. Payee: Kingsbury County Register of Deeds. **Other phones:** Assessor-605-854-3593; Treasurer-605-854-3411; Elections-605-854-3832.

Lake County

Register of Deeds, PO Box 266, Madison, SD 57042. **Phone**-Register of Deeds, R/E & UCC Recording- 605-256-7614; fax-605-256-7622; hours 8AM-5PM
UCC records search per debtor- $10.00. Will search tax liens. Will search real estate records. RE record copy- $1.00 per page. Cert fee: $2.00 per instrument. Payee: Register of Deeds. **Other phones:** Assessor-605-256-7605; Treasurer-605-256-7618; Vital Records-605-256-7614.

Lawrence County

Register of Deeds, PO Box 565, Deadwood, SD 57732. **Phone**-605-578-3930; hours 8AM-5PM
UCC records search per debtor- $20.00. Tax liens not included in UCC search. Separate federal tax lien search- $5.00 per debtor. Real estate record owner searches available. UCC copy- $1.00 per page. Cert fee: $2.00 1st 5 pg, $.20 each addl. Payee: Lawrence County Register of Deeds. **Other phones:** Assessor-605-578-3680.

Lincoln County

Register of Deeds, 100 E. 5th, Canton, SD 57013-1789. **Phone**-Register of Deeds, R/E & UCC Recording- 605-764-5661; fax-605-764-5932; hours 8AM-5PM
UCC records search per debtor- $10.00. UCC search includes tax liens if requested. Real estate owner, mortgage, and property transfer searches available. UCC copy- $1.00 per page. Cert fee: $2.00 per cert. Payee: Lincoln County Register of Deeds. **Other phones:** Assessor-605-764-2571; Treasurer-605-764-5701; Elections-605-764-2581; Vital Records-605-764-5661.

Lyman County

Register of Deeds, PO Box 98, Kennebec, SD 57544-0098. **Phone**-Register of Deeds, R/E & UCC Recording- 605-869-2297; fax-605-869-2203; hours 8AM-Noon;1-5PM
Will not search UCC records. Tax lien search- $5.00 per debtor. Record copy- $1.00 per page. Cert fee: $2.00 per page. Payee: Lyman Co. Registrar of Deeds. **Other phones:** Assessor-605-869-2206; Treasurer-605-869-2295; Appraiser/ Auditor-605-869-2206; Elections-605-869-2247; Vital Records-605-869-2297.

Marshall County

Register of Deeds, PO Box 130, Britton, SD 57430. **Phone**-Register of Deeds, R/E & UCC Recording- 605-448-2352; fax-605-448-2116; hours 8AM-5PM
UCC records search per debtor- $20.00. Will not search real estate or tax lien records unless provided with legal description. Copies are $1.00 each. UCC copy- $1.00 per page. Cert fee: $2.00. Payee: Marshall County Register of Deeds. **Other phones:** Assessor-605-448-5291; Treasurer-605-448-2451; Appraiser/ Auditor-605-448-2822; Elections-605-448-2401; Vital Records-605-448-2352.

McCook County

Register of Deeds, PO Box 338, Salem, SD 57058-0338. **Phone**-Register of Deeds, R/E & UCC Recording- 605-425-2701; fax-605-425-2534; hours 8:30AM-4:30PM
UCC records search per debtor- $12.00. Tax liens not included in UCC search. Separate federal tax lien search- $5.00 per debtor. Real estate record owner searches available. RE record copy- $1.00 per page up to 10 pages. UCC copy- $1.00 per page. Cert fee: $2.00 per cert. Payee: McCook County

Register of Deeds. **Other phones:** Assessor-605-425-2681; Treasurer-605-425-2721; Elections-605-425-2791; Vital Records-605-425-2701.

McPherson County

Register of Deeds, PO Box 129, Leola, SD 57456. **Phone**-605-439-3151; fax-605-439-3394.
UCC records search per debtor- $20.00. Tax liens not included in UCC search. Federal/state combined tax lien -no charge Will not search real estate records. UCC copy- $1.00 per page. Cert fee: $2.00. Payee: Register of Deeds. **Other phones:** Assessor-605-439-3663; Treasurer-605-439-3544.

Meade County

Register of Deeds, 1425 Sherman St, Sturgis, SD 57785. **Phone**-605-347-2356; fax-605-347-5925; hours 8AM-5PM
UCC records search per debtor- $10.00. UCC search includes tax liens. Will not search real estate records. RE record copy- $1.00 per doc. UCC copy- $1.00 per page. Cert fee: $10.00 per doc. **Other phones:** Assessor-605-347-3818; Treasurer-605-347-5871.

Mellette County

Register of Deeds, PO Box 183, White River, SD 57579-0183. **Phone**-605-259-3371; fax-605-259-3194; hours 8AM-Noon,1-5PM
UCC records search per debtor- $10.00. UCC search includes tax liens if requested. Separate federal & state combined tax lien search- $10.00 per search. Real estate record owner and mortgage searches available. Record copy- $1.00 per page. Cert fee: $2.00 per cert. Payee: Mellette County Register of Deeds. **Other phones:** Assessor-605-259-3150; Treasurer-605-259-3151.

Miner County

Register of Deeds, PO Box 546, Howard, SD 57349. **Phone**-Register of Deeds, R/E & UCC Recording- 605-772-5621; fax-605-772-4148; hours 8AM-N, 1-5PM
UCC records search per debtor- $10.00. Will not search tax liens. RE record copy- $1.00 per instrument up to 5 pages. Cert fee: $1.00 per instrument. Payee: Miner County Register of Deeds. **Other phones:** Assessor-605-772-4241; Treasurer-605-772-4652; Appraiser/ Auditor-605-772-4671.

Minnehaha County

Register of Deeds, 415 N Dakota Ave, Sioux Falls, SD 57104-2465. **Phone**-Register of Deeds, R/E & UCC Recording- 605-367-4223; fax-605-367-8314; hours 8AM-5PM
www.minnehahacounty.org/depts/register_deeds/register_deeds.asp
UCC records search per debtor- $20.00. UCC search includes federal tax liens only. Separate federal/state combined tax lien search- $4.00 per debtor. Will not search real estate records. UCC copy- $1.00 per page. Cert fee: $2.00 1st 5 pg, $.20 each addl. Payee: Minnehaha County Register of Deeds. **Online Access to Property Tax records:** Access to the county property tax database is free at www.minnehahacounty.org/property_tax/Index.asp. No name searching at this time. **Other phones:** Assessor-605-367-4228; Treasurer-605-367-4212; Appraiser/ Auditor-605-367-4228; Elections-605-367-4220; Vital Records-605-367-4223.

Moody County

Register of Deeds, PO Box 247, Flandreau, SD 57028-0247. **Phone**-Register of Deeds, R/E & UCC Recording- 605-997-3151; fax-605-997-9996; hours 8AM-5PM
UCC records search per debtor- $20.00. Tax lien search- $5.00 per debtor. Will not search real estate records. UCC copy- $1.00 per page. Cert fee: $2.00

per cert; $.20 per page after 5 pages. Payee: Moody County Register of Deeds. **Other phones:** Assessor-605-997-3101; Treasurer-605-997-3171; Vital Records-605-997-3151.

Pennington County

Register of Deeds, 315 St. Joe St, Rapid City, SD 57701. **Phone-**Register of Deeds, R/E & UCC Recording- 605-394-2177; hours 8AM-5PM

UCC records search per debtor- $12.00. Tax liens not included in UCC search. Separate federal tax lien search- $5.00 per debtor. Will not search real estate records. RE record copy- $1.00 1st 5 pages; $.20 each add'l. UCC copy- $1.00 per page. Cert fee: $2.00 1st 5 pg, $.20 each addl. Payee: Pennington County Register of Deeds. **Online Access to Property Tax, Assessor records:** Access to the county property tax database is free at www.co.pennington.sd.us/doe/look%20up%20options. htm. **Other phones:** Assessor-605-394-2175; Treasurer-605-394-2161; Elections-605-394-2153; Vital Records-605-394-2177.

Perkins County

Register of Deeds, PO Box 127, Bison, SD 57620. **Phone-**Register of Deeds, R/E & UCC Recording- 605-244-5620; fax-605-244-7289; hours 8AM-5PM

UCC records search per debtor- $12.00. Tax liens not included in UCC search. Federal/state combined tax lien search- $5.00 per lien. Will not search real estate records. RE record copy- $1.00 per instrument. UCC copy- $1.00 per page. Cert fee: $2.00 per instrument. Payee: Perkins Co. Registrar of Deeds. **Other phones:** Assessor-605-244-5623; Treasurer-605-244-5613; Vital Records-605-773-4961.

Potter County

Register of Deeds, 201 S. Exene, Gettysburg, SD 57442. **Phone-**605-765-9467; fax-605-765-2836; hours 8AM-5PM

UCC records search per debtor- $10.00. Will not search real estate or tax lien records. UCC copy- $1.00 per page. Cert fee: $2.00. Payee: Potter County Register of Deeds. **Other phones:** Assessor-605-765-2481; Treasurer-605-765-9403; Elections-605-765-9408; Vital Records-605-765-9467.

Roberts County

Register of Deeds, 411 E. 2nd Ave, Sisseton, SD 57262. **Phone-**605-698-7152; hours 8AM-5PM

UCC records search per debtor- $20.00. UCC search includes tax liens if requested. Separate federal/state combined tax lien search-no charge. Mortgage searches available. Record copy- $1.00 per page. Cert fee: $10.00 per cert. Payee: Roberts County Register of Deeds. **Other phones:** Assessor-605-698-3205; Treasurer-605-698-7245.

Sanborn County

Register of Deeds, PO Box 295, Woonsocket, SD 57385. **Phone-**Register of Deeds, R/E & UCC Recording- 605-796-4516; fax-605-796-4509; hours 8AM-5PM

UCC records search per debtor- $12.00 (using standard form). Tax lien search- $5.00 per debtor. Will not search real estate records. RE record copy- $1.00 per doc. UCC copy- $1.00 per page. Cert fee: $2.00 per doc. Payee: Register of Deeds. **Other phones:** Assessor-605-796-4514; Treasurer-605-796-4512; Vital Records-605-796-4516.

Shannon County

Register of Deeds, 906 N. River St, Hot Springs, SD 57747. **Phone-**605-745-5139; hours 8AM-5PM

Will not search records. UCC copy- $1.00 per page. Cert fee: $2.00 1st 5 pg, $.20 each addl. Payee: Shannon County Register of Deeds. **Other phones:** Assessor-605-745-5141; Treasurer-605-745-5145.

Spink County

Register of Deeds, 210 E. 7th Ave, Redfield, SD 57469-0266. **Phone-**Register of Deeds, R/E & UCC Recording- 605-472-0150; fax-605-472-2410; hours 8AM-5PM

UCC records search per debtor- $12.00 1st name, $13.00 2 names. Tax lien search- $5.00. Will not search real estate records. UCC copy- $1.00 per page. **Other phones:** Assessor-605-472-2891; Treasurer-605-472-0880; Elections-605-472-1825; Vital Records-605-472-0150.

Stanley County

Register of Deeds, PO Box 596, Fort Pierre, SD 57532. **Phone-**605-223-7786, R/E Recording-605-223-2610, UCC Recording-605-223-2610; fax-605-223-7788; hours 8AM-Noon,1-5PM

UCC records search per debtor- $10.00. UCC search includes tax liens if requested. Real estate owner, mortgage, and property transfer searches available. UCC copy- $1.00 per page. Cert fee: $2.00 1st 5 pg, $.20 each addl. Payee: Stanley County Register of Deeds. **Other phones:** Assessor-605-223-2746; Treasurer-605-223-2648; Elections-605-223-2673; Vital Records-605-223-2610.

Sully County

Register of Deeds, PO Box 265, Onida, SD 57564. **Phone-**Register of Deeds, R/E & UCC Recording- 605-258-2331; fax-605-258-2884.

UCC records search per debtor- $10.00. Will not search real estate records. **Other phones:** Assessor-605-258-2522; Treasurer-605-258-2444; Appraiser/ Auditor-605-258-2522; Elections-605-258-2541; Vital Records-605-258-2331.

Todd County

Register of Deeds, 200 E 3rd St, Winner, SD 57580-1806. **Phone-**Register of Deeds, R/E & UCC Recording- 605-842-2208; fax-605-842-1116; hours 8AM-5PM

UCC records search per debtor- $20.00. Tax liens not included in UCC search. Tax lien search- $5.00 per debtor. RE record copy- $1.00 per instrument; add'l $.20 per page after 5 pages. UCC copy- $1.00 per page. Cert fee: $5.00. Payee: Todd County Registrar of Deeds. **Other phones:** Assessor-605-856-4633; Treasurer-605-842-1700.

Tripp County

Register of Deeds, 200 E 3rd St, Courthouse, Winner, SD 57580-1806. **Phone-**Register of Deeds, R/E & UCC Recording- 605-842-2208; fax-605-842-3621; hours 8AM-5PM

UCC records search per debtor- $20.00. Tax liens not included in UCC search. Tax lien search- $5.00 per debtor. Property transfer searches available. RE record copy- $1.00 per instrument; add'l $.20 per page after 5 pages. UCC copy- $1.00 per page. Cert fee: $5.00 per cert. Payee: Tripp County Register of Deeds. **Other phones:** Assessor-605-842-2300; Treasurer-605-842-1700.

Turner County

Register of Deeds, PO Box 485, Parker, SD 57053-0485. **Phone-**605-297-3443; fax-605-297-5556.

UCC records search per debtor- $10.00. Tax liens not included in UCC search. Tax lien search- $5.00 per debtor. Will not search real estate records. **Other phones:** Assessor-605-297-4420; Treasurer-605-297-4425.

Union County

Register of Deeds, PO Box 490, Elk Point, SD 57025-0490. **Phone-**605-356-2191, R/E Recording-605-356-2041; fax-605-356-3047; hours 8:30AM-5PM

UCC records search per debtor- $10.00. UCC search includes tax liens if requested. Will not search real estate records. RE record copy- $1.00 per 4-page microfilm card. UCC copy- $1.00 per page. Cert fee: $2.00 5 pages, $.20 per add'l. Payee: Register of Deeds. **Online Access to Property records:** Access to data is from a private company at www.publicbuzz.com; registration is required and free for one county only. Register and select Union, SD as your free county. You may purchase more counties for $5 per month. **Other phones:** Assessor-605-356-2252; Treasurer-605-356-2391; Elections-605-356-2101; Vital Records-605-356-2191.

Walworth County

Register of Deeds, PO Box 159, Selby, SD 57472-0159. **Phone-**605-649-7057, R/E Recording-605-649-7311; fax-605-649-7867; hours 8AM-Noon,1-5PM

UCC records search per debtor- $12.00. Search request using non-standard form (per name)- $13.00. Tax liens not included in UCC search. Tax lien search- $5.00 per debtor. Real estate record owner and mortgage searches available. UCC copy- $1.00 per page. Cert fee: $2.00 1st 5 pg, $.20 each addl. Payee: Walworth County Register of Deeds. **Other phones:** Assessor-605-649-7737; Treasurer-605-649-7737.

Yankton County

Register of Deeds, PO Box 694, Yankton, SD 57078. **Phone-**605-260-4400 x5; fax-605-668-9682; hours 9AM-5PM

UCC records search per debtor- $10.00. Tax liens not included in UCC search. Separate federal/state combined tax lien search-no charge. Will not search real estate records for last deed of record only. UCC copy- $1.00 per page. Cert fee: $2.00 per cert. Payee: Yankton County Register of Deeds. **Other phones:** Assessor-605-260-4400 x3; Treasurer-605-260-4400 x7.

Ziebach County

Register of Deeds, PO Box 68, Dupree, SD 57623. **Phone-**605-365-5165; fax-605-365-5204; 8AM-5PM

UCC records search per debtor- $10.00. Will not search real estate or tax lien records. UCC copy- $1.00 per page. Cert fee: $2.00 per cert. Payee: Ziebach County Register of Deeds. **Other phones:** Assessor-605-365-5129; Treasurer-605-365-5173.

South Dakota County Locator

You will usually be able to find the city name in the City/County Cross Reference below. In that case, it is a simple matter to determine the county from the cross reference. However, only the official US Postal Service city names are included in this index. We have also included a ZIP/City Cross Reference immediately following the City/County Cross Reference. If you know the ZIP Code but the city name does not appear in the City/County Cross Reference index, look up the ZIP Code in the ZIP/City Cross Reference, find the city name, then look up the city name in the City/County Cross Reference.

South Dakota City/County Cross Reference

ABERDEEN Brown
AGAR Sully
AKASKA Walworth
ALCESTER (57001) Union(94), Lincoln(5)
ALEXANDRIA (57311) Hanson(97), Hutchinson(1)
ALLEN (57714) Bennett(93), Jackson(6)
ALPENA (57312) Jerauld(58), Beadle(39), Sanborn(1)
AMHERST (57421) Marshall(91), Brown(8)
ANDOVER (57422) Day(95), Brown(4)
ARDMORE Fall River
ARLINGTON (57212) Kingsbury(70), Brookings(22), Hamlin(6)
ARMOUR (57313) Douglas(80), Charles Mix(19)
ARTESIAN Sanborn
ASHTON (57424) Spink(93), Faulk(6)
ASTORIA (57213) Deuel(75), Brookings(24)
AURORA (57002) Brookings(97), Moody(2)
AVON (57315) Bon Homme(98), Charles Mix(1)
BADGER Kingsbury
BALTIC Minnehaha
BANCROFT Kingsbury
BARNARD Brown
BATESLAND (57716) Shannon(86), Bennett(13)
BATH Brown
BEAVER CREEK Tripp
BELLE FOURCHE (57717) Butte(96), Lawrence(2)
BELVIDERE (57521) Jackson(78), Mellette(21)
BERESFORD (57004) Union(62), Lincoln(29), Clay(8)
BETHLEHEM Meade
BIG STONE CITY (57216) Grant(76), Roberts(23)
BISON Perkins
BLACK HAWK (57718) Meade(98), Pennington(1)
BLUNT (57522) Hughes(90), Sully(9)
BONESTEEL Gregory
BOWDLE (57428) Edmunds(79), Walworth(19)
BOX ELDER (57719) Pennington(89), Meade(10)
BRADLEY Clark
BRANDON Minnehaha
BRANDT Deuel
BRENTFORD Spink
BRIDGEWATER (57319) McCook(72), Turner(13), Hutchinson(13)
BRISTOL Day
BRITTON Marshall
BROOKINGS (57006) Brookings(97), Moody(2)
BROOKINGS Brookings
BRUCE Brookings
BRYANT (57221) Hamlin(86), Clark(10), Kingsbury(2)
BUFFALO Harding
BUFFALO GAP (57722) Custer(69), Fall River(22), Shannon(7)
BUFFALO RIDGE Minnehaha
BULLHEAD Corson
BURBANK (57010) Clay(73), Union(26)
BURKE Gregory

CAMP CROOK Harding
CANISTOTA McCook
CANOVA (57321) Hanson(46), Miner(43), McCook(9)
CANTON Lincoln
CAPUTA Pennington
CARPENTER (57322) Beadle(41), Clark(39), Spink(19)
CARTER (57526) Tripp(75), Todd(18), Mellette(5)
CARTHAGE (57323) Miner(90), Kingsbury(8)
CASTLEWOOD (57223) Hamlin(97), Deuel(2)
CAVOUR Beadle
CEDARBUTTE Mellette
CENTERVILLE (57014) Turner(72), Clay(13), Lincoln(13)
CHAMBERLAIN (57325) Brule(98), Buffalo(1)
CHAMBERLAIN Brule
CHANCELLOR (57015) Turner(96), Minnehaha(3)
CHERRY CREEK Ziebach
CHESTER (57016) Lake(89), Minnehaha(10)
CLAIRE CITY Roberts
CLAREMONT (57432) Brown(83), Marshall(16)
CLARK (57225) Clark(90), Deuel(9)
CLEAR LAKE (57226) Deuel(97), Hamlin(2)
COLMAN (57017) Moody(95), Lake(4)
COLOME Tripp
COLTON (57018) Minnehaha(96), Lake(2)
COLUMBIA Brown
CONDE (57434) Spink(67), Brown(16), Day(8), Clark(6)
CORONA (57227) Roberts(97), Grant(2)
CORSICA Douglas
CORSON Minnehaha
CREIGHTON Pennington
CRESBARD (57435) Faulk(90), Edmunds(9)
CROCKER Clark
CROOKS Minnehaha
CUSTER (57730) Custer(97), Pennington(2)
DALLAS (57529) Gregory(69), Tripp(30)
DANTE Charles Mix
DAVIS (57021) Turner(98), Lincoln(1)
DE SMET Kingsbury
DEADWOOD Lawrence
DELL RAPIDS (57022) Minnehaha(88), Moody(11)
DELMONT (57330) Douglas(73), Charles Mix(18), Hutchinson(8)
DIMOCK (57331) Hutchinson(67), Douglas(17), Davison(14)
DOLAND Spink
DRAPER (57531) Jones(98), Lyman(1)
DUPREE (57623) Ziebach(91), Dewey(8)
EAGLE BUTTE Dewey
EDEN (57232) Marshall(97), Day(2)
EDGEMONT (57735) Custer(62), Fall River(37)
EGAN Moody
ELK POINT Union
ELKTON (57026) Brookings(82), Moody(17)

ELLSWORTH AFB Meade
ELM SPRINGS Meade
EMERY (57332) Hutchinson(48), Hanson(38), McCook(12)
ENNING Meade
ERWIN (57233) Kingsbury(96), Hamlin(3)
ESTELLINE (57234) Hamlin(67), Deuel(30), Brookings(2)
ETHAN (57334) Davison(65), Hanson(25), Hutchinson(9)
EUREKA (57437) McPherson(75), Campbell(24)
FAIRBURN Custer
FAIRFAX Gregory
FAIRVIEW Lincoln
FAITH (57626) Meade(52), Perkins(42), Ziebach(5)
FAULKTON Faulk
FEDORA (57337) Miner(94), Sanborn(5)
FERNEY Brown
FIRESTEEL (57628) Corson(50), Dewey(50)
FLANDREAU Moody
FLORENCE (57235) Codington(93), Day(6)
FORT MEADE Meade
FORT PIERRE (57532) Stanley(98), Lyman(1)
FORT THOMPSON Buffalo
FRANKFORT Spink
FREDERICK Brown
FREEMAN (57029) Hutchinson(76), Turner(23)
FRUITDALE Butte
FULTON (57340) Hanson(90), Miner(9)
GANN VALLEY (57341) Buffalo(96), Brule(3)
GARDEN CITY Clark
GARRETSON Minnehaha
GARY Deuel
GAYVILLE (57031) Yankton(81), Clay(18)
GEDDES (57342) Charles Mix(98), Douglas(1)
GETTYSBURG (57442) Potter(96), Dewey(2), Sully(1)
GLAD VALLEY Ziebach
GLENCROSS (57630) Dewey(91), Corson(8)
GLENHAM (57631) Walworth(91), Campbell(9)
GOODWIN (57238) Deuel(72), Codington(23), Hamlin(3), Grant(1)
GREGORY (57533) Gregory(88), Lyman(6), Tripp(5)
GRENVILLE Day
GROTON Brown
HAMILL (57534) Tripp(85), Lyman(14)
HARRISBURG Lincoln
HARRISON Douglas
HARROLD (57536) Hughes(84), Sully(11), Hyde(3)
HARTFORD Minnehaha
HAYES (57537) Stanley(88), Haakon(12)
HAYTI Hamlin
HAZEL (57242) Hamlin(78), Codington(21)
HECLA Brown
HENRY (57243) Codington(95), Clark(4)
HERMOSA (57744) Custer(53), Pennington(45), Shannon(1)
HERREID Campbell
HERRICK Gregory

HETLAND Kingsbury
HIGHMORE (57345) Hyde(90), Faulk(9)
HILL CITY Pennington
HITCHCOCK (57348) Beadle(65), Spink(34)
HOLABIRD Hyde
HOSMER (57448) Edmunds(77), McPherson(22)
HOT SPRINGS (57747) Fall River(97), Custer(2)
HOUGHTON Brown
HOVEN (57450) Potter(61), Walworth(38)
HOWARD Miner
HOWES (57748) Meade(98), Buffalo(1)
HUDSON (57034) Lincoln(93), Union(6)
HUMBOLDT (57035) Minnehaha(97), McCook(2)
HURLEY Turner
HURON Beadle
IDEAL Tripp
INTERIOR (57750) Jackson(96), Pennington(3)
IONA (57542) Lyman(98), Gregory(1)
IPSWICH (57451) Edmunds(95), Brown(4)
IRENE (57037) Yankton(63), Clay(19), Turner(17)
IROQUOIS (57353) Kingsbury(65), Beadle(32), Clark(1)
ISABEL (57633) Dewey(62), Corson(32), Ziebach(5)
JAVA (57452) Walworth(74), Campbell(26)
JEFFERSON Union
KADOKA (57543) Jackson(98), Haakon(1)
KAYLOR Hutchinson
KELDRON Corson
KENNEBEC (57544) Lyman(98), Tripp(1)
KEYSTONE Pennington
KIMBALL (57355) Jerauld(55), Brule(42), Buffalo(2)
KRANZBURG Codington
KYLE (57752) Shannon(80), Jackson(20)
LABOLT Grant
LAKE ANDES Charles Mix
LAKE CITY Marshall
LAKE NORDEN (57248) Hamlin(86), Kingsbury(13)
LAKE PRESTON Kingsbury
LANE Jerauld
LANGFORD (57454) Marshall(79), Day(20)
LANTRY Dewey
LEAD Lawrence
LEBANON Potter
LEMMON (57638) Perkins(96), Corson(3)
LENNOX (57039) Lincoln(94), Turner(5)
LEOLA (57456) McPherson(98), Edmunds(1)
LESTERVILLE (57040) Yankton(95), Bon Homme(4)
LETCHER (57359) Sanborn(76), Aurora(11), Davison(10), Jerauld(1)
LINN (57483) Hand(48), Faulk(35), Spink(16)
LITTLE EAGLE Corson
LODGEPOLE Perkins
LONG VALLEY Jackson
LONGLAKE McPherson
LOWER BRULE Lyman
LUDLOW Harding
LYONS Minnehaha
MAHTO Corson

MANDERSON Shannon
MANSFIELD (57460) Brown(62), Spink(18), Faulk(9), Edmunds(9)
MARCUS Meade
MARION (57043) Turner(94), McCook(3), Hutchinson(1)
MARTIN Bennett
MARTY Charles Mix
MARVIN (57251) Grant(91), Roberts(8)
MC INTOSH Corson
MC LAUGHLIN Corson
MEADOW (57644) Perkins(75), Corson(14), Ziebach(10)
MECKLING Clay
MELLETTE (57461) Spink(98), Brown(1)
MENNO (57045) Hutchinson(86), Yankton(12), Turner(1)
MIDLAND (57552) Haakon(52), Stanley(32), Jackson(9), Mellette(3)
MILBANK (57252) Grant(98), Roberts(1)
MILBANK Grant
MILESVILLE Haakon
MILLER (57362) Hand(98), Buffalo(1)
MINA (57462) Edmunds(86), Brown(13)
MISSION Todd
MISSION HILL Yankton
MISSION RIDGE Stanley
MITCHELL (57301) Davison(98), Hanson(1)
MOBRIDGE Walworth
MONROE (57047) McCook(61), Turner(38)
MONTROSE (57048) McCook(90), Minnehaha(8)
MORRISTOWN Corson
MOUND CITY Campbell
MOUNT VERNON (57363) Davison(91), Aurora(4), Sanborn(3)
MUD BUTTE (57758) Meade(78), Perkins(17), Butte(3)
MURDO (57559) Jones(95), Mellette(4)
NEMO Lawrence
NEW EFFINGTON Roberts
NEW HOLLAND Douglas
NEW UNDERWOOD (57761) Pennington(62), Meade(37)
NEWELL (57760) Butte(80), Meade(17), Harding(1)
NISLAND Butte
NORRIS (57560) Mellette(53), Bennett(28), Jackson(18)
NORTH SIOUX CITY Union
NORTHVILLE (57465) Spink(62), Faulk(38)
NUNDA Lake
OACOMA Lyman
OELRICHS Fall River
OGLALA Shannon
OKATON Jones
OKREEK Todd
OLDHAM (57051) Kingsbury(92), Miner(5), Lake(1)

OLIVET Hutchinson
ONAKA (57466) Faulk(78), Edmunds(19), Potter(1)
ONIDA (57564) Sully(97), Hyde(2)
OPAL Meade
ORAL Fall River
ORIENT (57467) Hand(69), Faulk(30)
ORTLEY (57256) Grant(55), Roberts(33), Day(6), Codington(5)
OWANKA (57767) Pennington(64), Meade(36)
PARADE Dewey
PARKER (57053) Turner(95), McCook(3), Minnehaha(1)
PARKSTON (57366) Hutchinson(94), Douglas(4)
PARMELEE (57566) Todd(82), Mellette(17)
PEEVER Roberts
PHILIP (57567) Haakon(79), Jackson(12), Gregory(7)
PICKSTOWN Charles Mix
PIEDMONT Meade
PIERPONT Day
PIERRE (57501) Hughes(97), Sully(2)
PINE RIDGE Shannon
PLANKINTON Aurora
PLATTE (57369) Charles Mix(95), Aurora(2), Douglas(1)
POLLOCK Campbell
PORCUPINE Shannon
PRAIRIE CITY (57649) Perkins(89), Harding(10)
PRESHO Lyman
PRINGLE Custer
PROVO Fall River
PUKWANA (57370) Brule(83), Buffalo(16)
QUINN (57775) Pennington(56), Haakon(25), Jackson(18)
RALPH Harding
RAMONA (57054) Lake(97), Kingsbury(1), Miner(1)
RAPID CITY (57702) Pennington(98), Meade(1)
RAPID CITY Pennington
RAVINIA Charles Mix
RAYMOND (57258) Clark(87), Spink(12)
RED OWL Meade
REDFIELD (57469) Spink(96), Hand(3)
REDIG Harding
REE HEIGHTS (57371) Hand(96), Hyde(2), Buffalo(1)
RELIANCE Lyman
RENNER Minnehaha
REVA (57651) Harding(66), Perkins(33)
REVILLO (57259) Grant(68), Deuel(31)
RIDGEVIEW Dewey
ROCHFORD Pennington
ROCKHAM (57470) Faulk(54), Hand(45)
ROSCOE Edmunds
ROSEBUD Todd

ROSHOLT Roberts
ROSLYN (57261) Day(98), Marshall(1)
ROWENA Minnehaha
RUTLAND (57057) Lake(97), Moody(2)
SAINT CHARLES Gregory
SAINT FRANCIS Todd
SAINT LAWRENCE Hand
SAINT ONGE (57779) Lawrence(93), Butte(6)
SALEM (57058) McCook(93), Miner(6)
SCENIC (57780) Pennington(94), Shannon(5)
SCOTLAND (57059) Bon Homme(89), Hutchinson(10)
SELBY Walworth
SENECA (57473) Faulk(80), Potter(19)
SHADEHILL Perkins
SHERMAN Minnehaha
SINAI Brookings
SIOUX FALLS (57108) Lincoln(76), Minnehaha(23)
SIOUX FALLS (57106) Minnehaha(92), Lincoln(7)
SIOUX FALLS Minnehaha
SISSETON (57262) Roberts(96), Marshall(3)
SMITHWICK Fall River
SOUTH SHORE (57263) Codington(81), Grant(18)
SPEARFISH Lawrence
SPENCER (57374) Hanson(53), McCook(46)
SPRINGFIELD Bon Homme
STEPHAN Hyde
STICKNEY (57375) Aurora(97), Davison(2)
STOCKHOLM (57264) Grant(98), Codington(1)
STRANDBURG (57265) Grant(70), Deuel(25), Codington(3)
STRATFORD (57474) Brown(94), Spink(5)
STURGIS (57785) Meade(98), Lawrence(1)
SUMMIT (57266) Roberts(55), Grant(44)
TABOR (57063) Bon Homme(84), Yankton(15)
TEA (57064) Lincoln(94), Turner(5)
TIMBER LAKE Dewey
TOLSTOY (57475) Potter(59), Edmunds(38), Walworth(1)
TORONTO (57268) Deuel(76), Brookings(23)
TRAIL CITY (57657) Corson(90), Dewey(9)
TRENT Moody
TRIPP (57376) Hutchinson(86), Bon Homme(12), Charles Mix(1)
TULARE (57476) Spink(86), Hand(13)
TURTON Spink
TUTHILL Bennett
TWIN BROOKS Grant
TYNDALL Bon Homme
UNION CENTER Meade

UTICA Yankton
VALE (57788) Meade(52), Butte(47)
VALLEY SPRINGS Minnehaha
VEBLEN (57270) Marshall(86), Roberts(13)
VERMILLION Clay
VIBORG (57070) Turner(93), Yankton(6)
VIENNA (57271) Clark(76), Hamlin(23)
VIRGIL (57379) Beadle(80), Jerauld(19)
VIVIAN (57576) Lyman(92), Jones(8)
VOLGA (57071) Brookings(95), Lake(3), Moody(1)
VOLIN (57072) Yankton(78), Clay(21)
WAGNER Charles Mix
WAKONDA (57073) Clay(94), Turner(5)
WAKPALA Corson
WALKER Corson
WALL Pennington
WALLACE (57272) Codington(87), Clark(10), Day(2)
WANBLEE (57577) Jackson(98), Bennett(1)
WARD Moody
WARNER Brown
WASTA (57791) Pennington(50), Meade(49)
WATAUGA Corson
WATERTOWN Codington
WAUBAY (57273) Day(88), Roberts(11)
WAVERLY Codington
WEBSTER (57274) Day(98), Clark(1)
WENTWORTH (57075) Lake(98), Moody(1)
WESSINGTON (57381) Beadle(59), Hand(40)
WESSINGTON SPRINGS (57382) Jerauld(94), Aurora(3), Beadle(1)
WESTPORT (57481) Brown(59), McPherson(30), Edmunds(10)
WEWELA Tripp
WHITE Brookings
WHITE LAKE (57383) Aurora(98), Brule(1)
WHITE OWL Meade
WHITE RIVER Mellette
WHITEHORSE Dewey
WHITEWOOD (57793) Lawrence(84), Meade(13), Butte(2)
WILLOW LAKE Clark
WILMOT Roberts
WINFRED (57076) Miner(53), Lake(46)
WINNER (57580) Tripp(98), Todd(1)
WITTEN Tripp
WOLSEY Beadle
WOOD Mellette
WOONSOCKET (57385) Sanborn(83), Jerauld(14), Aurora(1)
WORTHING Lincoln
WOUNDED KNEE Shannon
YALE Beadle
YANKTON Yankton
ZEONA (57795) Perkins(66), Butte(33)

South Dakota ZIP/City Cross Reference

57001-57001	ALCESTER
57002-57002	AURORA
57003-57003	BALTIC
57004-57004	BERESFORD
57005-57005	BRANDON
57006-57007	BROOKINGS
57010-57010	BURBANK
57012-57012	CANISTOTA
57013-57013	CANTON
57014-57014	CENTERVILLE
57015-57015	CHANCELLOR
57016-57016	CHESTER
57017-57017	COLMAN
57018-57018	COLTON
57019-57019	CORSON
57020-57020	CROOKS
57021-57021	DAVIS
57022-57022	DELL RAPIDS
57024-57024	EGAN
57025-57025	ELK POINT
57026-57026	ELKTON
57027-57027	FAIRVIEW
57028-57028	FLANDREAU
57029-57029	FREEMAN
57030-57030	GARRETSON
57031-57031	GAYVILLE
57032-57032	HARRISBURG
57033-57033	HARTFORD
57034-57034	HUDSON
57035-57035	HUMBOLDT
57036-57036	HURLEY
57037-57037	IRENE
57038-57038	JEFFERSON
57039-57039	LENNOX
57040-57040	LESTERVILLE
57041-57041	LYONS
57042-57042	MADISON
57043-57043	MARION
57044-57044	MECKLING
57045-57045	MENNO
57046-57046	MISSION HILL
57047-57047	MONROE
57048-57048	MONTROSE
57049-57049	NORTH SIOUX CITY
57050-57050	NUNDA
57051-57051	OLDHAM
57052-57052	OLIVET
57053-57053	PARKER
57054-57054	RAMONA
57055-57055	RENNER
57056-57056	ROWENA
57057-57057	RUTLAND
57058-57058	SALEM
57059-57059	SCOTLAND
57060-57060	SHERMAN
57061-57061	SINAI
57062-57062	SPRINGFIELD
57063-57063	TABOR
57064-57064	TEA
57065-57065	TRENT
57066-57066	TYNDALL
57067-57067	UTICA
57068-57068	VALLEY SPRINGS
57069-57069	VERMILLION
57070-57070	VIBORG
57071-57071	VOLGA
57072-57072	VOLIN
57073-57073	WAKONDA
57074-57074	WARD
57075-57075	WENTWORTH
57076-57076	WINFRED
57077-57077	WORTHING
57078-57079	YANKTON
57100-57110	SIOUX FALLS
57115-57115	BUFFALO RIDGE
57116-57198	SIOUX FALLS

57201-57201 WATERTOWN	57341-57341 GANN VALLEY	57474-57474 STRATFORD	57650-57650 RALPH
57202-57202 WAVERLY	57342-57342 GEDDES	57475-57475 TOLSTOY	57651-57651 REVA
57212-57212 ARLINGTON	57344-57344 HARRISON	57476-57476 TULARE	57652-57652 RIDGEVIEW
57213-57213 ASTORIA	57345-57345 HIGHMORE	57477-57477 TURTON	57653-57653 SHADEHILL
57214-57214 BADGER	57346-57346 STEPHAN	57479-57479 WARNER	57656-57656 TIMBER LAKE
57216-57216 BIG STONE CITY	57348-57348 HITCHCOCK	57481-57481 WESTPORT	57657-57657 TRAIL CITY
57217-57217 BRADLEY	57349-57349 HOWARD	57483-57483 LINN	57658-57658 WAKPALA
57218-57218 BRANDT	57350-57350 HURON	57501-57501 PIERRE	57659-57659 WALKER
57219-57219 BRISTOL	57353-57353 IROQUOIS	57520-57520 AGAR	57660-57660 WATAUGA
57220-57220 BRUCE	57354-57354 KAYLOR	57521-57521 BELVIDERE	57661-57661 WHITEHORSE
57221-57221 BRYANT	57355-57355 KIMBALL	57522-57522 BLUNT	57701-57703 RAPID CITY
57223-57223 CASTLEWOOD	57356-57356 LAKE ANDES	57523-57523 BURKE	57706-57706 ELLSWORTH AFB
57224-57224 CLAIRE CITY	57357-57357 RAVINIA	57526-57526 CARTER	57708-57708 BETHLEHEM
57225-57225 CLARK	57358-57358 LANE	57527-57527 CEDARBUTTE	57709-57709 RAPID CITY
57226-57226 CLEAR LAKE	57359-57359 LETCHER	57528-57528 COLOME	57714-57714 ALLEN
57227-57227 CORONA	57361-57361 MARTY	57529-57529 DALLAS	57715-57715 ARDMORE
57229-57229 CROCKER	57362-57362 MILLER	57531-57531 DRAPER	57716-57716 BATESLAND
57231-57231 DE SMET	57363-57363 MOUNT VERNON	57532-57532 FORT PIERRE	57717-57717 BELLE FOURCHE
57232-57232 EDEN	57364-57364 NEW HOLLAND	57533-57533 GREGORY	57718-57718 BLACK HAWK
57233-57233 ERWIN	57365-57365 OACOMA	57534-57534 HAMILL	57719-57719 BOX ELDER
57234-57234 ESTELLINE	57366-57366 PARKSTON	57536-57536 HARROLD	57720-57720 BUFFALO
57235-57235 FLORENCE	57367-57367 PICKSTOWN	57537-57537 HAYES	57722-57722 BUFFALO GAP
57236-57236 GARDEN CITY	57368-57368 PLANKINTON	57538-57538 HERRICK	57724-57724 CAMP CROOK
57237-57237 GARY	57369-57369 PLATTE	57540-57540 HOLABIRD	57725-57725 CAPUTA
57238-57238 GOODWIN	57370-57370 PUKWANA	57541-57541 IDEAL	57729-57729 CREIGHTON
57239-57239 GRENVILLE	57371-57371 REE HEIGHTS	57542-57542 IONA	57730-57730 CUSTER
57241-57241 HAYTI	57373-57373 SAINT LAWRENCE	57543-57543 KADOKA	57732-57732 DEADWOOD
57242-57242 HAZEL	57374-57374 SPENCER	57544-57544 KENNEBEC	57735-57735 EDGEMONT
57243-57243 HENRY	57375-57375 STICKNEY	57545-57545 BEAVER CREEK	57736-57736 ELM SPRINGS
57244-57244 HETLAND	57376-57376 TRIPP	57547-57547 LONG VALLEY	57737-57737 ENNING
57245-57245 KRANZBURG	57379-57379 VIRGIL	57548-57548 LOWER BRULE	57738-57738 FAIRBURN
57246-57246 LABOLT	57380-57380 WAGNER	57551-57551 MARTIN	57741-57741 FORT MEADE
57247-57247 LAKE CITY	57381-57381 WESSINGTON	57552-57552 MIDLAND	57742-57742 FRUITDALE
57248-57248 LAKE NORDEN	57382-57382 WESSINGTON SPRINGS	57553-57553 MILESVILLE	57744-57744 HERMOSA
57249-57249 LAKE PRESTON	57383-57383 WHITE LAKE	57555-57555 MISSION	57745-57745 HILL CITY
57251-57251 MARVIN	57384-57384 WOLSEY	57557-57557 MISSION RIDGE	57747-57747 HOT SPRINGS
57252-57253 MILBANK	57385-57385 WOONSOCKET	57559-57559 MURDO	57748-57748 HOWES
57255-57255 NEW EFFINGTON	57386-57386 YALE	57560-57560 NORRIS	57750-57750 INTERIOR
57256-57256 ORTLEY	57399-57399 HURON	57562-57562 OKATON	57751-57751 KEYSTONE
57257-57257 PEEVER	57401-57402 ABERDEEN	57563-57563 OKREEK	57752-57752 KYLE
57258-57258 RAYMOND	57420-57420 AKASKA	57564-57564 ONIDA	57754-57754 LEAD
57259-57259 REVILLO	57421-57421 AMHERST	57566-57566 PARMELEE	57755-57755 LUDLOW
57260-57260 ROSHOLT	57422-57422 ANDOVER	57567-57567 PHILIP	57756-57756 MANDERSON
57261-57261 ROSLYN	57424-57424 ASHTON	57568-57568 PRESHO	57757-57757 MARCUS
57262-57262 SISSETON	57426-57426 BARNARD	57569-57569 RELIANCE	57758-57758 MUD BUTTE
57263-57263 SOUTH SHORE	57427-57427 BATH	57570-57570 ROSEBUD	57759-57759 NEMO
57264-57264 STOCKHOLM	57428-57428 BOWDLE	57571-57571 SAINT CHARLES	57760-57760 NEWELL
57265-57265 STRANDBURG	57429-57429 BRENTFORD	57572-57572 SAINT FRANCIS	57761-57761 NEW UNDERWOOD
57266-57266 SUMMIT	57430-57430 BRITTON	57574-57574 TUTHILL	57762-57762 NISLAND
57268-57268 TORONTO	57432-57432 CLAREMONT	57576-57576 VIVIAN	57763-57763 OELRICHS
57269-57269 TWIN BROOKS	57433-57433 COLUMBIA	57577-57577 WANBLEE	57764-57764 OGLALA
57270-57270 VEBLEN	57434-57434 CONDE	57578-57578 WEWELA	57765-57765 OPAL
57271-57271 VIENNA	57435-57435 CRESBARD	57579-57579 WHITE RIVER	57766-57766 ORAL
57272-57272 WALLACE	57436-57436 DOLAND	57580-57580 WINNER	57767-57767 OWANKA
57273-57273 WAUBAY	57437-57437 EUREKA	57584-57584 WITTEN	57769-57769 PIEDMONT
57274-57274 WEBSTER	57438-57438 FAULKTON	57585-57585 WOOD	57770-57770 PINE RIDGE
57276-57276 WHITE	57439-57439 FERNEY	57601-57601 MOBRIDGE	57772-57772 PORCUPINE
57278-57278 WILLOW LAKE	57440-57440 FRANKFORT	57620-57620 BISON	57773-57773 PRINGLE
57279-57279 WILMOT	57441-57441 FREDERICK	57621-57621 BULLHEAD	57774-57774 PROVO
57301-57301 MITCHELL	57442-57442 GETTYSBURG	57622-57622 CHERRY CREEK	57775-57775 QUINN
57311-57311 ALEXANDRIA	57445-57445 GROTON	57623-57623 DUPREE	57776-57776 REDIG
57312-57312 ALPENA	57446-57446 HECLA	57625-57625 EAGLE BUTTE	57777-57777 RED OWL
57313-57313 ARMOUR	57448-57448 HOSMER	57626-57626 FAITH	57778-57778 ROCHFORD
57314-57314 ARTESIAN	57449-57449 HOUGHTON	57628-57628 FIRESTEEL	57779-57779 SAINT ONGE
57315-57315 AVON	57450-57450 HOVEN	57629-57629 GLAD VALLEY	57780-57780 SCENIC
57316-57316 BANCROFT	57451-57451 IPSWICH	57630-57630 GLENCROSS	57782-57782 SMITHWICK
57317-57317 BONESTEEL	57452-57452 JAVA	57631-57631 GLENHAM	57783-57783 SPEARFISH
57319-57319 BRIDGEWATER	57454-57454 LANGFORD	57632-57632 HERREID	57785-57785 STURGIS
57321-57321 CANOVA	57455-57455 LEBANON	57633-57633 ISABEL	57787-57787 UNION CENTER
57322-57322 CARPENTER	57456-57456 LEOLA	57634-57634 KELDRON	57788-57788 VALE
57323-57323 CARTHAGE	57457-57457 LONGLAKE	57636-57636 LANTRY	57790-57790 WALL
57324-57324 CAVOUR	57460-57460 MANSFIELD	57638-57638 LEMMON	57791-57791 WASTA
57325-57326 CHAMBERLAIN	57461-57461 MELLETTE	57639-57639 LITTLE EAGLE	57792-57792 WHITE OWL
57328-57328 CORSICA	57462-57462 MINA	57640-57640 LODGEPOLE	57793-57793 WHITEWOOD
57329-57329 DANTE	57465-57465 NORTHVILLE	57641-57641 MC INTOSH	57794-57794 WOUNDED KNEE
57330-57330 DELMONT	57466-57466 ONAKA	57642-57642 MC LAUGHLIN	57795-57795 ZEONA
57331-57331 DIMOCK	57467-57467 ORIENT	57643-57643 MAHTO	57799-57799 SPEARFISH
57332-57332 EMERY	57468-57468 PIERPONT	57644-57644 MEADOW	
57334-57334 ETHAN	57469-57469 REDFIELD	57645-57645 MORRISTOWN	
57335-57335 FAIRFAX	57470-57470 ROCKHAM	57646-57646 MOUND CITY	
57337-57337 FEDORA	57471-57471 ROSCOE	57647-57647 PARADE	
57339-57339 FORT THOMPSON	57472-57472 SELBY	57648-57648 POLLOCK	
57340-57340 FULTON	57473-57473 SENECA	57649-57649 PRAIRIE CITY	

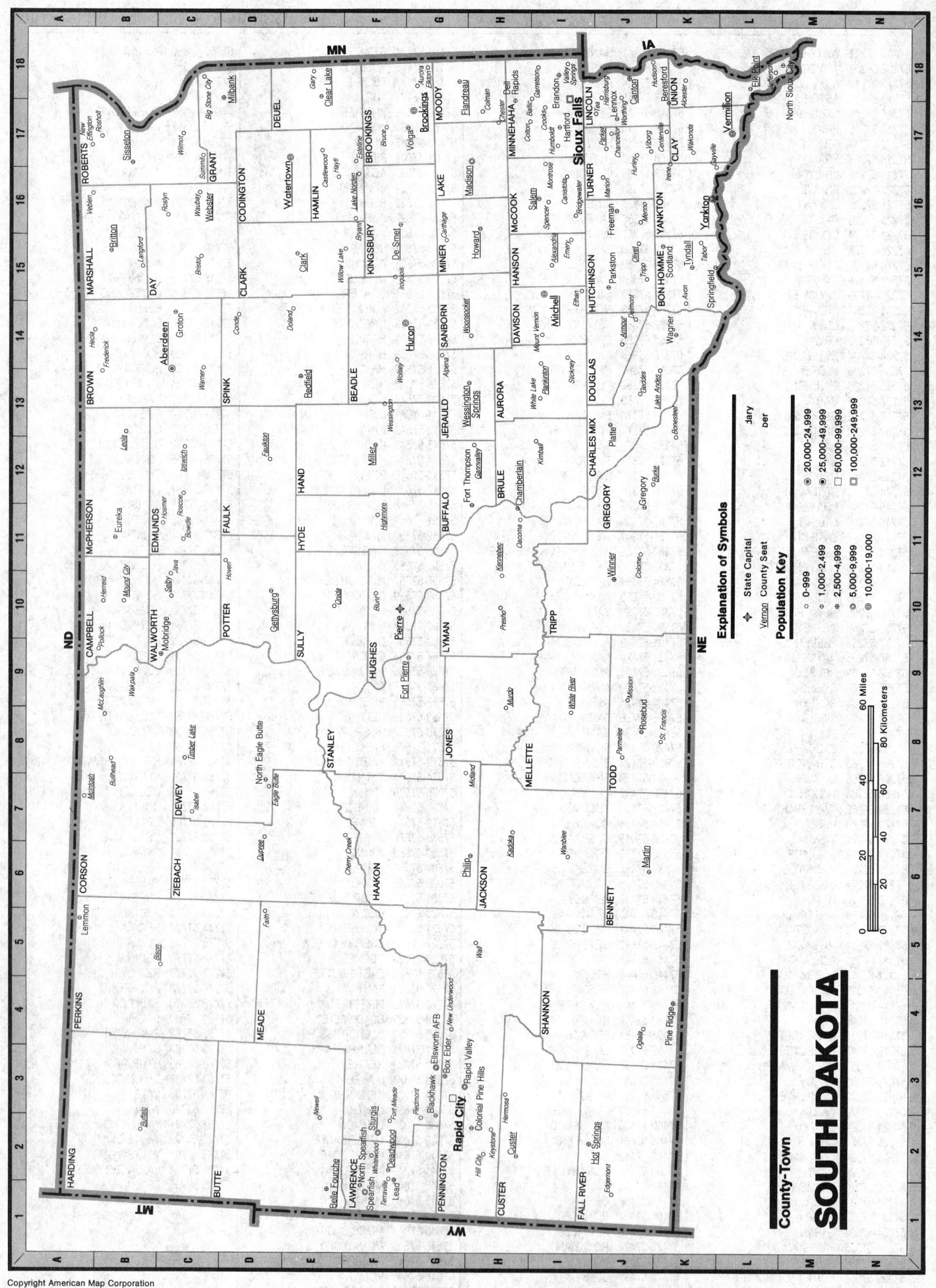

SOUTH DAKOTA

County-Town

Explanation of Symbols

⬥ State Capital
Vernon ◉ County Seat

Population Key

○ 0-999
◎ 1,000-2,499
◉ 2,500-4,999
⊙ 5,000-9,999
◉ 10,000-19,000
◉ 20,000-24,999
◉ 25,000-49,999
□ 50,000-99,999
▣ 100,000-249,999

MN
IA
ND
NE
MT
SD

0   20   40   60 Miles
0   20   40   60   80 Kilometers

COUNTIES

(66 Counties)

Name of County	Population	Location on Map
AURORA	3,135	H-13
BEADLE	18,253	F-13
BENNETT	3,206	J-5
BON HOMME	7,089	J-14
BROOKINGS	25,207	F-17
BROWN	35,580	A-13
BRULE	5,485	H-12
BUFFALO	1,759	G-11
BUTTE	7,914	C-1
CAMPBELL	1,965	A-9
CHARLES MIX	9,131	I-12
CLARK	4,403	D-15
CLAY	13,186	K-17
CODINGTON	22,698	D-16
CORSON	4,195	A-6
CUSTER	6,179	H-1
DAVISON	17,503	H-14
DAY	6,978	B-15
DEUEL	4,522	D-17
DEWEY	5,523	C-7
DOUGLAS	3,746	I-13
EDMUNDS	4,356	B-11
FALL RIVER	7,353	I-1
FAULK	2,744	C-11
GRANT	8,372	C-16
GREGORY	5,359	J-11
HAAKON	2,624	F-6
HAMLIN	4,974	E-16
HAND	4,272	E-12
HANSON	2,994	H-15
HARDING	1,669	A-1
HUGHES	14,817	F-9
HUTCHINSON	8,262	I-14
HYDE	1,696	E-11
JACKSON	2,811	H-6
JERAULD	2,425	G-13
JONES	1,324	G-8
KINGSBURY	5,925	F-15
LAKE	10,550	G-16
LAWRENCE	20,655	F-1
LINCOLN	15,427	I-17
LYMAN	3,638	G-9
MARSHALL	4,844	A-15
MCCOOK	5,688	H-16
MCPHERSON	3,228	A-11
MEADE	21,878	D-4
MELLETTE	2,137	H-7
MINER	3,272	G-15
MINNEHAHA	123,809	H-17
MOODY	6,507	G-17
PENNINGTON	81,343	G-1
PERKINS	3,932	A-4
POTTER	3,190	C-10
ROBERTS	9,914	A-16
SANBORN	2,833	G-14
SHANNON	9,902	I-4
SPINK	7,981	C-13
STANLEY	2,453	E-8
SULLY	1,589	E-9
TODD	8,352	J-7
TRIPP	6,924	I-10
TURNER	8,576	I-16
UNION	10,189	K-17
WALWORTH	6,087	B-9
YANKTON	19,252	J-16
ZIEBACH	2,220	C-6
TOTAL	**696,004**	

CITIES AND TOWNS

Note: The first name is that of the city or town, second, that of the county in which it is located, then the population and location on the map.

Aberdeen, Brown, 24,927 ... C-14
Alexandria, Hanson, 518 ... I-15
Armour, Douglas, 854 ... J-14
Belle Fourche, Butte, 4,335 ... E-1
Beresford, Lincoln/Union, 1,849 ... K-17
Bison, Perkins, 451 ... B-5
● Blackhawk, Meade, 1,995 ... G-2
Box Elder, Pennington, 2,680 ... G-3
Brandon, Minnehaha, 3,543 ... I-18
Britton, Marshall, 1,394 ... B-15
Brookings, Brookings, 16,270 ... F-17
Buffalo, Harding, 488 ... B-2
Burke, Gregory, 756 ... J-12
Canton, Lincoln, 2,787 ... C-14
Chamberlain, Brule, 2,347 ... H-11
Clark, Clark, 1,292 ... E-15
Clear Lake, Deuel, 1,247 ... E-17
● Colonial Pine Hills, Pennington, 1,553 ... H-2
Custer, Custer, 1,741 ... H-2
De Smet, Kingsbury, 1,172 ... F-16
Deadwood, Lawrence, 1,830 ... F-2
Dell Rapids, Minnehaha, 2,484 ... H-18
Dupree, Ziebach, 484 ... D-7
Elk Point, Union, 1,423 ... L-18
● Ellsworth AFB, Meade/Pennington, 7,017 ... G-3
Eureka, McPherson, 1,197 ... B-11
Faulkton, Faulk, 809 ... D-12
Flandreau, Moody, 2,311 ... G-18
Fort Pierre, Stanley, 1,854 ... F-9
● Fort Thompson, Buffalo, 1,088 ... G-11
Freeman, Hutchinson, 1,293 ... I-16
Gannvalley, Buffalo ... G-12
Gettysburg, Potter, 1,510 ... D-10
Gregory, Gregory, 1,384 ... J-11
Groton, Brown, 1,196 ... C-14
Hartford, Minnehaha, 1,262 ... I-17
Highmore, Hyde, 835 ... F-11
Hot Springs, Fall River, 4,325 ... I-2
Howard, Miner, 1,156 ... H-16
Huron, Beadle, 12,448 ... F-14
Ipswich, Edmunds, 965 ... C-12
Kadoka, Jackson, 736 ... H-7
Kennebec, Lyman, 284 ... H-10
Lake Andes, Charles Mix, 846 ... J-13
Lake Norden, Hamlin, 427 ... E-16
Lead, Lawrence, 3,632 ... F-2
Lemmon, Perkins, 1,614 ... A-5
Lennox, Lincoln, 1,767 ... J-17
Leola, McPherson, 521 ... B-13
Madison, Lake, 6,257 ... G-17
Martin, Bennett, 1,151 ... J-6
McIntosh, Corson, 302 ... A-7
Milbank, Grant, 3,879 ... C-18
Miller, Hand, 1,678 ... F-12
Mitchell, Davison, 13,798 ... I-15
Mobridge, Walworth, 3,768 ... B-9
Mound City, Campbell, 89 ... B-10
Murdo, Jones, 679 ... H-9
● North Eagle Butte, Dewey, 1,423 ... D-7
North Sioux City, Union, 2,019 ... L-18
● North Spearfish, Lawrence, 2,274 ... F-2
Olivet, Hutchinson, 74 ... J-15
Onida, Sully, 761 ... E-10
Parker, Turner, 984 ... J-17
Parkston, Hutchinson, 1,572 ... J-15
Philip, Haakon, 1,077 ... G-6
Pierre, Hughes, 12,906 ... F-9
● Pine Ridge, Shannon, 2,596 ... K-4
Plankinton, Aurora, 604 ... I-14
Platte, Charles Mix, 1,311 ... J-13
Rapid City, Pennington, 54,523 ... G-3
Rapid Valley, Pennington, 5,968 ... G-3
Redfield, Spink, 2,770 ... E-13
● Rosebud, Todd, 1,538 ... J-8
Salem, McCook, 1,289 ... H-16
Selby, Walworth, 707 ... C-10
Sioux Falls, Lincoln/Minnehaha, 100,814 ... I-17
Sisseton, Roberts, 2,181 ... B-17
Spearfish, Lawrence, 6,966 ... F-1
Sturgis, Meade, 5,330 ... F-2
Timber Lake, Dewey, 517 ... C-8
Tyndall, Bon Homme, 1,201 ... K-15
Vermillion, Clay, 10,034 ... L-17
Volga, Brookings, 1,263 ... F-17
Wagner, Charles Mix, 1,462 ... K-14
Watertown, Codington, 17,592 ... D-17
Webster, Day, 2,017 ... C-16
Wessington Springs, Jerauld, 1,083 ... G-13
White River, Mellette, 595 ... I-8
Winner, Tripp, 3,354 ... J-10
Woonsocket, Sanborn, 766 ... G-14
Yankton, Yankton, 12,703 ... K-16

Explanation of symbols: ● – Census Designated Place (CDP)

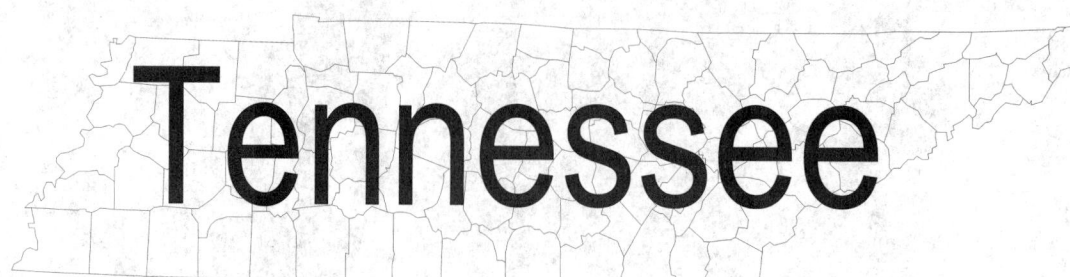

General Help Numbers:

Governor's Office

State Capitol, 1st Floor   615-741-2001
Nashville, TN 37243-0001   Fax 615-532-9711
www.state.tn.us/governor   8AM-5PM

Attorney General's Office

PO Box 20207   615-741-3491
Nashville, TN 37202-0207   Fax 615-741-2009
www.attorneygeneral.state.tn.us   8AM-4:30PM

Legislative Records

Office of Legislative Information Services   615-741-3511
Rachel Jackson Bldg, 1st Floor   615-741-0927
Nashville, TN 37243   8AM-4:30PM
www.legislature.state.tn.us

State Archives

State Library & Archives Division   615-741-7996
403 7th Ave N   Fax 615-532-9293
Nashville, TN 37243-0312   8AM-6PM M-SA
www.state.tn.us/sos/statelib/tslahome.htm

State Specifics:

Capital:

Nashville
Davidson County

Time Zone:

CST*

* Tennessee's twenty-nine eastern-most counties are EST: They are: Anderson, Blount, Bradley, Campbell, Carter, Claiborne, Cocke, Grainger, Greene, Hamilton, Hancock, Hawkins, Jefferson, Johnson, Knox, Loudon, McMinn, Meigs, Monroe, Morgan, Polk, Rhea, Roane, Scott, Sevier, Sullivan, Unicoi, Union, Washington.

Number of Counties:

95

Population:

5,841,748

Web Site:

www.state.tn.us

State Agencies

Criminal Records

Tennessee Bureau of Investigation, Records and Identification Unit, 901 R S Gass Blvd, Nashville, TN 37216; 615-744-4000 x1, 615-744-4651 (Fax), 24 hours daily.

www.tbi.state.tn.us

Note: Records available to general public. Per statute, fingerprint-based background checks be conducted for paid or volunteer employment or licensing such as such as child care, teachers, security and armed guards, security system contractors, etc. The agency maintains a website at www.ticic.state.tn.us for searching of sexual offenders, missing children, and people placed on parole who reside in TN.

Indexing & Storage: Records stored on inhouse computer and fingerprint cards. Records maintained indefinitely. All records are fingerprint

based, as submitted by the arresting agencies. All records are released to those entitled, including those without dispositions.

Searching: Include the following in your request-name, DOB, AKA's. Sex, race and current address are helpful. The agency maintains a website at www.ticic.state.tn.us for searching of sexual offenders, missing children, and people placed on parole who reside in TN. The search system is called TORIS (Tennessee Open Records Information Service). A request form can be downloaded from the webpage.

Access by: mail, fax

Fee & Payment: The fee is $29.00 per record for a name check. Statutorily-required fingerprint checks will include an FBI fingerprint check for an additional $24.00. Fee payee: Tennessee Bureau of Investigation. Prepayment required. Business and

personal checks not accepted. Major credit cards accepted.

Mail search: Turnaround time: 2 to 5 working days. A SASE is requested.

Fax search: Use of credit card required.

Statewide Court Records

Administrative Office of the Courts, Nashville City Center, 511 Union St, Suite 600, Nashville, TN 37219; 615-741-2687, 615-741-6285 (Fax), 8AM-4:30PM.

www.tsc.state.tn.us

Note: Except for certain online research capabilities, all court record access must be done at the local level.

Access by: online. No searching by mail.

Online search: The Administrative Office of Courts provides access to Appellate Court opinions at www.tsc.state.tn.us/geninfo/Courts/AppellateCourts.htm. Several counties offer online access to court records, but there is no statewide access system.

Sexual Offender Registry

Tennessee Bureau of Investigation, Sexual Offender Registry, 901 R S Gass Blvd., Nashville, TN 37216; 888-837-4170, 615-744-4655 (Fax), 24 hours daily.

www.ticic.state.tn.us/

Note: Other than the website, records are not open to the public for viewing. While this agency will do a limited phone verification, it is suggested to go to local law enforcement for extensive checks.

Indexing & Storage: Records are available from 07/01/97 forward. Records are normally destroyed after death of the offender.

Searching: Include the following in your request-name, DOB; SSN is helpful. The following data is not released: expunged records

Access by: phone, online.

Phone search: Records are available by phone.

Online search: Search sexual offenders at website by name, county or ZIP Code. One may also search for missing children, and people placed on parole who reside in Tennessee.

Incarceration Records

Tennessee Department of Corrections, Rachel Jackson Building, 2nd Fl, 320 6th Avenue, N., Nashville, TN 37243-0465; 615-741-1000, 615-532-1497 (Fax), 8AM-5PM.

www.state.tn.us/correction/

Indexing & Storage: Records are available on current and former inmates. It takes 7 days before new records are available for inquiry. Records are normally destroyed after 100 years.

Searching: Location, conviction and sentencing information are provided. Include the following in your request-first and last name. The SSN and DOB are helpful. The following data is not released: medical information and SSNs.

Access by: mail, phone, fax, online.

Fee & Payment: Fees apply when hard copies are needed: $10.00 for search, $.20 per page Fee payee: State of Tennessee

Mail search: Turnaround time: 10 - 15 working days. Also, historical archived inmate information is available from Operational Support Services; generally, there is a $10.00 archive search fee and $.20 per page copy fee. No SASE is required.

Phone search: Limited phone searching is available.

Fax search: Fax requesting available.

Online search: Extensive search capabilities are offered from the website. Click on FOIL - Inmate Search.

Other access: A CD-Rom is available with only public information from current offender database; nominal fee; contact the Planning & Research Division.

Expedited service: Will expedite for law enforcement or emergency (3 days), but only if shipping is paid in advance.

Corporation, Limited Partnership, Fictitious Name, Assumed Name, Limited Liability Company

TN Sec of State: Corporations, William R Snodgrass Tower, 312 Eighth Ave. N, 6th Fl, Nashville, TN 37243; 615-741-2286, 615-741-6488 (Copies), 615-741-7310 (Fax), 8AM-4:30PM.

www.state.tn.us/sos/service.htm

Indexing & Storage: Records are available from 1875 to present. Records are computerized and are on microfilm from 1979. It takes 2 to 3 days before new records are available for inquiry. Records are indexed on inhouse computer.

Searching: All information is considered public record. Include the following in your request-full name of business. In addition to the articles of incorporation, corporation records include the following information: Annual Reports, Officers, Directors, DBAs (assumed names only), Prior (merged) names, Inactive and Reserved names.

Access by: mail, phone, in person, online.

Fee & Payment: Certification costs $20.00. Corp., LLC, LP, and LLP records cost $20.00 per entity, which includes certification. Fee payee: Secretary of State. Prepayment required. Personal checks accepted. No credit cards accepted.

Mail search: Turnaround time: 1 to 3 days. Certificates are usually processed in 1 day.

Phone search: Limited information is given over the phone. Requests for certificates must be in writing.

In person search: Turnaround time is immediate unless certified documents are ordered which are ready the next day.

Online search: There is a free online search at www.tennesseeanytime.org/sosname/ for name availability and at www.tennesseeanytime.org/soscorp/ for business records. This gives access to over 4,000,000 records relating to corporations, limited liability companies, limited partnerships and limited liability partnerships formed or registered in Tennessee.

Other access: Some data can be purchased in bulk or list format. Call 615-532-9007 for more details.

Trademarks/Servicemarks, Trade Names

Secretary of State, Trademarks/Tradenames Division, 312 8th Ave North, 6th Fl, Nashville, TN 37243-0306; 615-741-0531, 615-741-7310 (Fax), 8AM-4:30PM.

www.state.tn.us/sos/service.htm

Indexing & Storage: Records are available from the 1950s to present. It takes 2 to 3 days before new records are available for inquiry. Records are indexed on microfilm.

Searching: Include the following in your request-trademark/servicemark name, name of owner, date of application.

Access by: mail, phone, in person, online.

Fee & Payment: There is a $20.00 search fee, add $2.00 for certification. Fee payee: Secretary of State. Personal checks accepted. No credit cards accepted.

Mail search: Turnaround time: 1 to 3 days. A SASE is requested.

Phone search: No fee for telephone request.

In person search: Turnaround time is while you wait.

Online search: The Internet provides a record search of TN Trademarks, newest records are 3 days old.

Other access: The agency will provide a file update every three months for $1.00 per page. Requests must be in writing.

Uniform Commercial Code

TN Sec of State - UCC Records, William R Snodgrass Tower, 312 Eighth Ave N, 6th Fl, Nashville, TN 37243; 615-741-3276, 615-741-7310 (Fax), 8AM-4:30PM.

www.state.tn.us/sos

Note: State and federal tax liens are filed at the county level with the Register of Deeds where the lienee or its property is located.

Indexing & Storage: Records are available from 1964. Records are computerized from 03/01/96. It takes 2-3 days before new records are available for inquiry.

Searching: Use search request form UCC-11. Include the following in your request-debtor name.

Access by: mail, in person, online.

Fee & Payment: The fee is $15.00 per debtor or debtor address, copies are $1.00 per page. Fee payee: Secretary of State. Prepayment required. Personal checks accepted. No credit cards accepted.

Mail search: Turnaround time: 2-3 days.

In person search: The results are mailed in 2-3 days.

Online search: Free access to general information at www.ja.state.tn.us/sos/iets3/ieuc/PgUCCSearch.jsp. Search by debtor name or file number. Images are not available.

Federal and State Tax Liens

Records not maintained by a state level agency.

Note: State and federal tax liens are filed at the county level with the Register of Deeds where the liened property is located.

Sales Tax Registrations

Access to Records is Restricted

Revenue Department, Sales Tax Registration, Andrew Jackson Bldg, 500 Deaderick St, Nashville, TN 37242-0100; 615-741-3580, 615-253-0600, 615-253-6299 (Fax), 8AM-4:30PM.

www.state.tn.us/revenue/

Note: This agency refuses to make any information about registrants available.

Birth Certificates

Tennessee Department of Health, Office of Vital Records, 421 5th Ave North, 1st floor, Nashville, TN 37247; 615-741-1763, 615-741-0778 (Credit card order), 615-726-2559 (Fax), 8AM-4PM.

http://www2.state.tn.us/health/vr/index.htm

Note: The fax number above is for expedited orders only.

Indexing & Storage: Records are available for 100 years to present. For birth records prior, contact the State Library and Archives at 615-741-2764. Short forms are only available since 1949. New records are available for inquiry immediately. Records are indexed on inhouse computer.

Searching: Must have a signed release from person of record or immediate family member for certified copy. Medical and health information is not released. Include the following in your request-full name, names of parents, mother's maiden name, date of birth, place of birth, relationship to person of record. Daytime phone helpful.

Access by: mail, phone, fax, in person, online.

Fee & Payment: $12.00 for the long (copy of actual certificate) form; $7.00 for the short computerized form. Add $4.00 per name per copy for additional copies. Fee payee: Tennessee Vital Records. Prepayment required. Personal checks accepted. Credit cards accepted: MasterCard, Visa, AmEx, Discover.

Mail search: Turnaround time: 2 to 3 weeks. No SASE is required.

Phone search: You must use credit cards with fax or phone requests. There is an additional $10.00 fee. Phone service is available from 8AM to 4PM.

Fax search: Fax requests are handled like phone requests.

In person search: Wait time is 15 minutes.

Online search: Records may be ordered from the web site, but are returned by mail. Go to https://www2.state.tn.us/health/vital/index.asp.

Expedited service: Expedited service is available for phone, fax or online searches. Turnaround time: 2 to 3 days. Phone and fax records ordered by credit card, for $10.00 extra, can be returned overnight for an additional fee of $13.25.

Death Records

Tennessee Department of Health, Office of Vital Records, 421 5th Ave North, 1st floor, Nashville, TN 37247; 615-741-1763, 615-741-0778 (Credit card order), 615-726-2559 (Fax), 8AM-4PM.

http://www2.state.tn.us/health/vr/index.htm

Indexing & Storage: Records are available for 50 years. Previous records are at the State Archives at 615-726-2559. It takes 3 months or less before new records are available for inquiry. Records are indexed on inhouse computer.

Searching: Must have a signed release from immediate family member. Cause of death is restricted to immediate family members or their representatives and must be specifically requested. Include the following in your request-full name, names of parents, mother's maiden name, date of death, place of death, reason for information request, relationship to person of record. Daytime phone helpful.

Access by: mail, phone, fax, in person, online.

Fee & Payment: The fee is $7.00 per name. Fee payee: Tennessee Vital Records. Prepayment required. Personal checks accepted. Credit cards accepted: MasterCard, Visa, AmEx, Discover.

Mail search: Turnaround time: 2 to 3 weeks. No SASE is required.

Phone search: You must use a credit card for an additional fee of $10.00. Turnaround time is one day.

Fax search: Same criteria as phone requests.

In person search: Wait is 15 minutes.

Online search: Records may be ordered online at the web site, but are returned by mail. The Cleveland (Tennessee) Public Library staff and volunteers have published the 1914-1925 death records of thirty-three counties at www.state.tn.us/sos/statelib/pubsvs/death.htm#index. It should be noted that the records of children under two years of age have been omitted from this project.

Expedited service: Expedited service is available for phone, fax or online searches. Turnaround time: 2 to 3 days. Phone and fax records ordered by credit card, for $10.00 extra, can be returned overnight for an additional fee of $13.25.

Marriage Certificates

Tennessee Department of Health, Office of Vital Records, 421 5th Ave North, 1st floor, Nashville, TN 37247; 615-741-1763, 615-741-0778 (Credit card order), 615-726-2559 (Fax), 8AM-4PM.

http://www2.state.tn.us/health/vr/index.htm

Indexing & Storage: Records are available for 50 years. Older records are at the state archives. It takes 1 month before new records are available for inquiry. Records are indexed on inhouse computer.

Searching: Must have a signed release from persons of record or immediate family member for certified copy. Information on race or previous marriages is only released for statistical purposes. Include the following in your request-names of husband and wife, date of marriage, place or county of marriage.

Access by: mail, phone, fax, in person, online.

Fee & Payment: The search fee is $12.00. Add $4.00 for each additional copy. Fee payee: Tennessee Vital Records. Prepayment required. Personal checks accepted. Credit cards accepted: MasterCard, Visa, AmEx, Discover.

Mail search: Turnaround time: 2 to 3 weeks. No SASE is required.

Phone search: You must use a credit card for an additional $10.00 fee. Records are processed in 24 hours.

Fax search: Same criteria as phone searching.

In person search: Wait time is about 15 minutes.

Online search: Records may be ordered from the web site, but are returned by mail.

Expedited service: Expedited service is available for phone, fax or online searches. Turnaround time: 2 to 3 days. Phone and fax records ordered by credit card, for $10.00 extra, can be returned overnight for an additional fee of $13.25.

Divorce Records

Tennessee Department of Health, Office of Vital Records, 421 5th Ave North, 1st floor, Nashville, TN 37247; 615-741-1763, 615-741-0778 (Credit card order), 615-726-2559 (Fax), 8AM-4PM.

http://www2.state.tn.us/health/vr/index.htm

Indexing & Storage: Records are available for 50 years. Older records are at the state archives. It takes 2 weeks to 2 months before new records are available for inquiry. Records are indexed on inhouse computer.

Searching: Must have a signed release from person of record or immediate family member. Information on previous marriages and education

is released for statistical use only. Include the following in your request-names of husband and wife, date of divorce, place of divorce.

Access by: mail, phone, fax, in person, online.

Fee & Payment: The search fee is $12.00. There is an additional $4.00 charge for an extra copy. Fee payee: Tennessee Vital Records. Prepayment required. Personal checks accepted. Credit cards accepted: MasterCard, Visa, AmEx, Discover.

Mail search: Turnaround time: 2 to 3 weeks. No SASE is required.

Phone search: You must use a credit card and there is an additional fee of $10.00. Records are processed in one day.

Fax search: Same criteria as phone searching.

In person search: Wait time is about 15 minutes.

Online search: Records may be ordered online, but are returned by mail.

Expedited service: Expedited service is available for phone, fax or online searches. Turnaround time: 2 to 3 days. Phone and fax records ordered by credit card, for $10.00 extra, can be returned overnight for an additional fee of $13.25.

Workers' Compensation Records

Tennessee Department of Labor, Workers Compensation Division, 710 James Robertson Pkwy, 2nd Floor, Nashville, TN 37243-0661; 615-253-1842, 615-532-1942 (Fax), 8AM-4:30PM.

www.state.tn.us/labor-wfd/wcomp.html

Indexing & Storage: Records are available from 09/91 on computer, from 1987 to present on microfiche. Prior records are maintained on index cards. It takes 90 days before new records are available for inquiry.

Searching: Unless you have a signed authorization from the injured party or are an attorney representing the injured party, a court order is required to obtain records. This information is not considered public record; however, they'll tell if a claim is on file. The SSN, company name, date of injury, and claim # is required for searching records after 1987, prior record searching requires the name of the company involved.

Access by: mail, fax, in person.

Fee & Payment: The search fee is $10.00, copy fee is $.25 per page, add cost of postage also. Fee payee: State of Tennessee Treasurer. Personal checks accepted. No credit cards accepted.

Mail search: Turnaround time: 1 week. They will invoice you for copies and postage. No SASE is required.

Fax search: This will not effect turnaround time.

In person search: Records are still returned in 2 weeks, but you can pick them up.

Driver Records

Dept. of Safety, Financial Responsibility Section, Attn: Driving Records, 1150 Foster Ave, Nashville, TN 37210; 615-741-3954, 615-253-2093 (Fax), 8AM-4:30PM.

www.tennessee.gov/safety/

Note: Tickets are available from this office for a $5.00 fee per record.

Indexing & Storage: Records are available for past 3 years for convictions, if valid; 7 years if the license is suspended, restricted, or revoked. It takes 30 days or more before new records are available for inquiry. Records are normally destroyed after when records are destroyed depends on the type of violation.

Searching: Tennessee passed legislation similar to DPPA. Casual requesters must have written notarized authorization to receive record information with address data. Include the following in your request-license number and last name or DOB.

Access by: mail, in person, online.

Fee & Payment: The fee is $5.00 per record. Fee payee: Tennessee Department of Safety. Prepayment required. Certified checks or money orders are preferred. No personal checks accepted. MasterCard & Visa accepted in person only.

Mail search: Turnaround time: 2 weeks.

In person search: Up to 10 requests will be processed while you wait at this location or at offices in Nashville, Memphis, Knoxville, Chattanooga, and various Driver License Testing Centers.

Online search: Driving records are available to subscribers, signup at www.tennesseeanytime.org. There is a $75 registration fee. Records are available 24 hours daily on an interactive basis. Records are $5.00 each. Suggested only for ongoing users. Call 1-866-886-3468 for more information.

Other access: Magnetic tape retrieval is available for high volume users. Purchase of the DL file is available for approved requesters.

Vehicle Ownership, Vehicle Identification

Title and Registration Division, Information Unit, 44 Vantage Way #160, Nashville, TN 37243-8050; 615-741-3101 (Titles), 888-871-3171, 615-253-4259 (Fax), 8AM-4:30PM.

www.tennessee.gov/safety/nav2.html

Indexing & Storage: Records are available for 5 years to present. Microfilm records go back to 1964. It takes 12 weeks before new records are available for inquiry.

Searching: The agency follows the DPPA guidelines for permissible requesters. Records are not released to casual requesters without consent. The state recommends use of their form-SF1255. Include the following in your request-purpose of request, copy of requester's photo ID, and requester's signature.

Access by: mail, in person, online.

Fee & Payment: The fee is $1.00 for general inquiry, $5.00 for current title data, and $15.00 for a complete title history. Fee payee: Titling and Registration. Prepayment required. Personal checks accepted. No credit cards accepted.

Mail search: Turnaround time: 2 to 4 weeks. A SASE is requested.

In person search: Turnaround time is while you wait, unless photocopy of actual document is required. The office closes at 4PM for walk-in customers. Photo ID required.

Online search: Onlines access is available for approved subscribers from Interactive Vehicle,

Title, and Registration (ITVR) at www.tennesseeanytime.org/online/mvr.html. IVTR allows subscribers to retrieve vehicle, title, and registration information for vehicles registered in Tennessee. Search with license plate or VIN. Subscriptions to access IVTR can take up to 3-4 weeks for processing pending approval and verification of subscribers.

Accident Reports

Financial Responsibility Section, Records Unit, 1150 Foster Avenue, Nashville, TN 37210; 615-741-3954, 615-253-2093 (Fax), 8AM-4:30PM.

www.tennessee.gov/safety/

Note: Also, you can obtain accident reports from the investigating agency.

Indexing & Storage: Records are available from 1992 to present. It takes 30 days before new records are available for inquiry. Records are normally destroyed after 10 years.

Searching: Include the following in your request-full name, date of accident, location of accident. Also, include the county of the accident and DL of driver(s).

Access by: mail, in person.

Fee & Payment: The fee is $4.00 per record copy. Fee payee: Tennessee Department of Safety. Prepayment required. Agency prefers money orders and certified checks. Personal checks not accepted. MasterCard & Visa accepted for in person only.

Mail search: Turnaround time: 2 weeks.

In person search: Turnaround time is immediate.

Vessel Ownership, Vessel Registration

Wildlife Resources Agency, Boating Division, PO Box 40747, Nashville, TN 37204; 615-781-6585, 615-741-4606 (Fax), 8AM-4:30PM.

www.state.tn.us/twra

Note: All liens are filed with the Secretary of State.

Indexing & Storage: Records are available for the past 3 years. Records are indexed on computer. The state does not issue titles. All motorized boats and all sailboats must be registered. It takes 30 days before new records are available for inquiry. Records are normally destroyed after 5 years.

Searching: Search via email to darren.rider@state.tn.us To search, one of the following is required: Tennessee ID #, hull ID #, name, or SSN.

Access by: mail, phone, fax, in person.

Fee & Payment: There is no fee to do 1 or 2 searches; however, large lists may incur a charge.

Mail search: Turnaround time: 2 days.

Phone search: Whether a phone search will be performed depends on how busy the personnel is at the time of the call. Phone searches are only verbal verifications and require a Tennessee ID # to search.

Fax search: Turnaround time is 2 days. Results will be sent by mail.

In person search: Turnaround time is usually immediate, when staff available.

Voter Registration

Access to Records is Restricted

Secretary of State, Division of Elections, 312 Eighth Avenue North, 9th Fl, Nashville, TN 37243; 615-741-7956, 615-741-1278 (Fax), 8AM-4:30PM.

www.state.tn.us/sos/election.htm

Note: The statewide database cannot be accessed. However, records are held by the Administrator of Elections at the county level. Records can only be purchased for politically-related purposes.

GED Certificates

Department of Labor & Workforce Development, GED Records - Davy Crockett Tower, 500 James Robertson Parkway, 11th Fl, Nashville, TN 37245; 615-741-7054, 615-532-4899 (Fax), 8AM-4:30PM.

www.state.tn.us/labor-wfd/AE/aeged.htm

Indexing & Storage: It takes 2 weeks before new records are available for inquiry. Records are normally destroyed after never.

Searching: Include the following in your request-date of birth, Social Security Number, signed release. Include your daytime telephone number. Year diploma issued also helpful.

Access by: mail, fax, in person.

Fee & Payment: There is no fee for a verification.

Mail search: Turnaround time is 7 to 10 days.

Fax search: Turnaround time is 3 days.

In person search: Simple requests may be processed while you wait.

Hunting and Fishing License Information

Wildlife Resources Agency, Sportsman License Division, PO Box 40747, Nashville, TN 37204; 615-781-6585, 615-781-5277 (Fax), 8AM-4:30PM.

www.state.tn.us/twra/

Indexing & Storage: Records are available since 1999.

Searching: Include the following in your request-reason for request.

Access by: mail, phone, fax, in person.

Fee & Payment: There is no search fee, the copy fee is $.10.

Mail search: Turnaround time: 1 week.

Phone search: Verification only.

Fax search: Search requests accepted by fax.

In person search: Turnaround time while you wait, time permitting.

Other access: They do have mailing lists available for $300.00, call number above for information.

Tennessee State Licensing Agencies
Licenses Searchable Online

Accounting Firm #3	www.state.tn.us/cgi-bin/commerce/roster2.pl
Alarm Contractor #3	www.state.tn.us/cgi-bin/commerce/roster2.pl
Animal Euthanasia Technician #7	http://www2.state.tn.us/health/licensure/index.htm
Architect #3	www.state.tn.us/cgi-bin/commerce/roster2.pl
Athletic Trainer #7	http://www2.state.tn.us/health/licensure/index.htm
Auctioneer / Auction Company #3	www.state.tn.us/cgi-bin/commerce/roster2.pl
Audiologist #7	http://www2.state.tn.us/health/licensure/index.htm
Barber School/Barber Shop #3	www.state.tn.us/cgi-bin/commerce/roster2.pl
Barber/Barber Technician #3	www.state.tn.us/cgi-bin/commerce/roster2.pl
Boxing/Racing Personnel #3	www.state.tn.us/cgi-bin/commerce/roster2.pl
Chiropractor/Chiropractic Therapy Assist. #7	http://www2.state.tn.us/health/licensure/index.htm
Clinical Lab Technician/Personnel #6	http://www2.state.tn.us/health/licensure/index.htm
Collection Agent/Manager #3	www.state.tn.us/cgi-bin/commerce/roster2.pl
Contractor #3	www.state.tn.us/cgi-bin/commerce/roster2.pl
Cosmetologist #3	www.state.tn.us/cgi-bin/commerce/roster2.pl
Cosmetology Shop/School #3	www.state.tn.us/cgi-bin/commerce/roster2.pl
Counselor, Alcohol & Drug Abuse #7	http://www2.state.tn.us/health/licensure/index.htm
Counselor, Associate/Professional #7	http://www2.state.tn.us/health/licensure/index.htm
Dental Hygienist #7	http://www2.state.tn.us/health/licensure/index.htm
Dentist/Dental Assistant #7	http://www2.state.tn.us/health/licensure/index.htm
Dietitian/Nutritionist #7	http://www2.state.tn.us/health/licensure/index.htm
Electrologist / Electrology Instructor/School #7	http://www2.state.tn.us/health/licensure/index.htm
Embalmer #3	www.state.tn.us/cgi-bin/commerce/roster2.pl
Emergency Medical Personnel/Dispatcher #7	http://www2.state.tn.us/health/licensure/index.htm
Emergency Medical Service #7	http://www2.state.tn.us/health/licensure/index.htm
Engineer #3	www.state.tn.us/cgi-bin/commerce/roster2.pl
First Responder EMS #7	http://www2.state.tn.us/health/licensure/index.htm
Funeral & Burial Director/Apprentice #3	www.state.tn.us/cgi-bin/commerce/roster2.pl
Funeral & Burial Establishment/Cemetery #3	www.state.tn.us/cgi-bin/commerce/roster2.pl
Geologist #3	www.state.tn.us/cgi-bin/commerce/roster2.pl
Hearing Aid Dispenser #7	http://www2.state.tn.us/health/licensure/index.htm
Home Improvement #3	www.state.tn.us/cgi-bin/commerce/roster2.pl
Insurance Agent / Insurance Firm #3	www.state.tn.us/cgi-bin/commerce/roster2.pl
Interior Designer #3	www.state.tn.us/cgi-bin/commerce/roster2.pl
Laboratory Personnel, Medical #6	http://www2.state.tn.us/health/licensure/index.htm
Landscape Architect/Architect Firm #3	www.state.tn.us/cgi-bin/commerce/roster2.pl
Lobbyist #10	www.state.tn.us/tref/lobbyists/lobbyists.htm
Marriage & Family Therapist #7	http://www2.state.tn.us/health/licensure/index.htm
Massage Therapist/Establishment #7	http://www2.state.tn.us/health/licensure/index.htm
Medical Disciplinary Tracking #6	http://www2.state.tn.us/health/abuseregistry/index.html
Medical Doctor #6	http://www2.state.tn.us/health/licensure/index.htm
Midwife #7	http://www2.state.tn.us/health/licensure/index.htm
Motor Vehicle Auction #3	www.state.tn.us/cgi-bin/commerce/roster2.pl
Motor Vehicle Dealer/Salesperson #3	www.state.tn.us/cgi-bin/commerce/roster2.pl
Nurse-RN/LPN #6	http://www2.state.tn.us/health/licensure/index.htm
Nurses' Aide #6	http://www2.state.tn.us/health/licensure/index.htm
Nursing Home Administrator #7	http://www2.state.tn.us/health/licensure/index.htm
Occupational Therapist/Assistant #7	http://www2.state.tn.us/health/licensure/index.htm
Optician, Dispensing #7	http://www2.state.tn.us/health/licensure/index.htm
Optometrist #7	http://www2.state.tn.us/health/licensure/index.htm
Orthopedic Physician Assistant #6	http://www2.state.tn.us/health/licensure/index.htm
Osteopathic Physician #6	http://www2.state.tn.us/health/licensure/index.htm
Pastoral Therapist, Clinical #7	http://www2.state.tn.us/health/licensure/index.htm
Personnel Leasing #3	www.state.tn.us/cgi-bin/commerce/roster2.pl
Pest Control Operator #11	http://www2.state.tn.us/agriculture/onlineinfo/
Pharmacist/Pharmacy/Pharmacy Researcher #3	www.state.tn.us/cgi-bin/commerce/roster2.pl
Physical Therapist/Assistant #6	http://www2.state.tn.us/health/licensure/index.htm
Physician Assistant #6	http://www2.state.tn.us/health/licensure/index.htm
Podiatrist #7	http://www2.state.tn.us/health/licensure/index.htm
Polygraph Examiner #3	www.state.tn.us/cgi-bin/commerce/roster2.pl

Private Investigator/Inv. Company #3 .... www.state.tn.us/cgi-bin/commerce/roster2.pl
Psychological Examiner #7 .... http://www2.state.tn.us/health/licensure/index.htm
Psychologist #7 .... http://www2.state.tn.us/health/licensure/index.htm
Public Accountant-CPA #3 .... www.state.tn.us/cgi-bin/commerce/roster2.pl
Racetrack #3 .... www.state.tn.us/cgi-bin/commerce/roster2.pl
Radiologic Technologist #6 .... http://www2.state.tn.us/health/licensure/index.htm
Real Estate Agent/Broker/Sales #3 .... www.state.tn.us/cgi-bin/commerce/roster2.pl
Real Estate Appraiser #3 .... www.state.tn.us/cgi-bin/commerce/roster2.pl
Real Estate Firm #3 .... www.state.tn.us/cgi-bin/commerce/roster2.pl
Respiratory Care Therapist/Tech./Assist. #6 .... http://www2.state.tn.us/health/licensure/index.htm
School Administrative Adminstrator #5 .... www.k-12.state.tn.us/tcertinf
School Counselor #5 .... www.k-12.state.tn.us/tcertinf
School Food Service Supervisor #5 .... www.k-12.state.tn.us/tcertinf
School Librarian/Psychologist/Reading Specialist #5 .... www.k-12.state.tn.us/tcertinf
School Vocational Endorsement #5 .... www.k-12.state.tn.us/tcertinf
Security Company #3 .... www.state.tn.us/cgi-bin/commerce/roster2.pl
Security Guard/Security Trainer #3 .... www.state.tn.us/cgi-bin/commerce/roster2.pl
Social Worker, Master/Clinical #7 .... http://www2.state.tn.us/health/licensure/index.htm
Speech Pathologist #7 .... http://www2.state.tn.us/health/licensure/index.htm
Teacher #5 .... www.k-12.state.tn.us/tcertinf
Timeshare Agent #3 .... www.state.tn.us/cgi-bin/commerce/roster2.pl
Veterinarian #7 .... http://www2.state.tn.us/health/licensure/index.htm
X-ray Operator #6 .... http://www2.state.tn.us/health/licensure/index.htm
X-ray Technologist, Podiatry #6 .... http://www2.state.tn.us/health/licensure/index.htm

Tennessee Licensing Quick Finder

Accounting Firm #3 615-741-2550
Alarm Contractor #3 615-741-9771
Alcohol Package Store #1 615-741-1602
Alcohol Server #1 615-741-1602
American Reg. Rad. Tech. #6 615-687-0048
Animal Euthanasia Technician #7 615-532-3202
Animal/Livestock Dealer #11 615-837-5241
Architect #3 615-741-3221
Athletic Trainer #7 615-532-3202
Attorney #12 .... 615-361-7500, 800-486-5714
Auction Company #3 615-741-3600
Auctioneer #3 615-741-3600
Audiologist #7 615-532-3202
Barber School/Barber Shop #3 615-741-2294
Barber/Barber Technician #3 615-741-2294
Bed & Breakfast #14 615-741-7206
Boiler Operator #8 901-379-4200
Boxing/Racing Personnel #3 615-741-6837
Camp #14 615-741-7206
Chiropractor/Chiropractic Therapy Assist. #7
.... 615-532-3202
Clinical Lab Technician/Personnel #6 .. 615-532-5128
Collection Agent/Manager #3 615-741-1741
Contractor #3 615-741-8307
Cosmetologist #3 615-741-2515
Cosmetology Shop/School #3 615-741-2515
Counselor, Alcohol & Drug Abuse #7 615-532-5097
Counselor, Associate/Prof'l #7 615-532-3202
Court Reporter/Stenographer #2 423-756-0221
Dental Hygienist #7 615-532-3202
Dentist/Dental Assistant #7 615-532-3202
Dietitian/Nutritionist #7 615-532-3202
Electrologist #7 615-532-3202
Electrology Instructor/School #7 615-532-3202
Elevator Inspector #15 615-741-2123
Embalmer #3 615-741-5062
Emergency Medical Personnel/Dispatcher #7
.... 615-532-3202
Emergency Medical Service #7 615-532-3202
Engineer #3 615-741-3221
Environmentalist #7 615-532-3202
Fire Protection Sprinkler System Contractor #3
.... 615-741-1322
First Responder EMS #7 615-532-3202
Food Service Establishment #14 615-741-7206

Funeral & Burial Director/Apprent. #3 ... 615-741-5062
Funeral & Burial Est./Cemetery #3 615-741-5062
Geologist #3 615-741-3611
Health Care Facility #6 615-741-7221
Hearing Aid Dispenser #7 615-532-3202
Home Improvement #3 615-741-8307
Hotel #14 615-741-7206
Insurance Agent/Ins. Firm #3 615-741-2693
Insurance Education Provider #3 615-741-2693
Interior Designer #3 615-741-3221
Investment Advisor #3 615-741-2947
Laboratory Personnel, Medical #6 615-532-5128
Landscape Architect/Architect Firm #3 . 615-741-3221
Liquor Sale/Permit #1 615-741-1602
Livestock Brand #11 615-837-5241
Lobbyist #10 615-741-7959
Manicurist #3 615-741-2515
Marriage & Family Therapist #7 615-532-3202
Massage Therapist/Establishment #7 .. 615-532-5083
Medical Disciplinary Tracking #6 615-532-3421
Medical Doctor #6 615-532-4384
Midwife #7 615-532-3202
Milk Tester/Sampler #11 615-837-5151
Motor Vehicle Auction #3 615-741-2711
Motor Vehicle Dealer/Salesperson #3 .. 615-741-2711
Notary Public #9 615-741-3699
Nurse-RN/LPN #6 615-532-5166
Nursery #11 615-837-5512
Nursery Plant Dealer #11 615-837-5512
Nurses' Aide #6 615-741-7670
Nursing Home Administrator #7 615-532-3202
Occupational Therapist/Assistant #7 615-532-3202
Optician, Dispensing #7 615-532-3202
Optometrist #7 615-532-3202
Orthopedic Physician Assistant #6 615-532-4384
Osteopathic Physician #6 615-532-4384
Pastoral Therapist, Clinical #7 615-532-3202
Personnel Leasing #3 615-741-3449
Pest Control Operator #11 615-837-5138
Pharmacist #3 615-741-2718
Pharmacy #3 615-741-2718
Pharmacy Researcher #3 615-741-2718
Physical Therapist/Assistant #6 615-532-5135
Physician Assistant #6 615-532-4384
Plumber/Plumbing Company #8 901-379-4200

Podiatrist #7 615-532-3202
Polygraph Examiner #3 615-741-4827
Private Investigative Company #3 615-741-4827
Private Investigator #3 615-741-4827
Private Security Guard #3 615-741-6382
Psychological Examiner #7 615-532-3202
Psychologist #7 615-532-3202
Public Accountant-CPA #3 615-741-2550
Racetrack #3 615-741-2384
Radiologic Technologist #6 615-532-3202
Real Estate Agent/Broker/Sales #3 615-741-2273
Real Estate Appraiser #3 615-741-1831
Real Estate Firm #3 615-741-2273
Refrigeration Installer/Contractor #8 901-379-4200
Respir'y Care Therapist/Tech./Assist. #6
.... 615-532-5096
School Administrative Adminstrator #5 . 615-532-4885
School Counselor #5 615-532-4885
School Food Service Supervisor #5 615-532-4885
School Librarian #5 615-532-4885
School Psychologist #5 615-532-4885
School Reading Specialist #5 615-532-4885
School Vocational Endorsement #5 615-532-4885
Securities Agent/Broker/Dealer #3 615-741-2947
Security Company #3 615-741-9771
Security Guard #3 615-741-9771
Security Trainer #3 615-741-9771
Shampoo Technician #3 615-741-2515
Shorthand Reporter #2 423-756-0221
Social Worker, Master/Clinical #7 615-532-3202
Speech Pathologist #7 615-532-3202
Surveyor, Land #3 615-741-3611
Swimming Pool #14 615-741-7206
Tattoo Artist/Apprentice #14 615-741-7206
Teacher #5 615-532-4885
Timeshare Agent #3 615-741-2273
Veterinarian #7 615-532-3202
Water Treatment Plant Operator #13 .. 615-898-8090
Weigher, Public (Bulk Products, Aggregates) #11
.... 615-837-5109
Weighmaster #11 615-837-5109
Weigh Scales Service Technician #11 .. 615-837-5109
Wine Production/Sale/Transport #1 615-741-1602
X-ray Operator #6 615-532-4384
X-ray Technologist, Podiatry #6 615-532-5157

Tennessee Licensing Agency Information

1 Alcoholic Beverage Commission, 226 Capitol Blvd Bldg, #300, Nashville, TN 37243-0755; 615-741-1602, Fax: 615-741-0847.
www.state.tn.us/abc/
Email: stallman@mail.state.tn.us

3 Department of Commerce & Insurance, 500 James Robertson Pky, 2nd Fl, Nashville, TN 37243; 615-741-2241, Fax: 615-532-2965.
www.state.tn.us/commerce/index.html
Email: dci@mail.state.tn.us
Search Database at www.state.tn.us/cgi-bin/commerce/roster2.pl Note: Additional toll-free phone number for insurance-related professional licensing is 888-416-0868.

5 Department of Education, Office of Teacher Licensing, 710 James Robertson Pky, Andrew Johnson Tower, 5th Fl, Nashville, TN 37243-0377; 615-532-4885, Fax: 615-532-1448.
www.state.tn.us/education/lic_home.htm
Email: Sandy.willis@state.tn.us
Search Database at www.k-12.state.tn.us/tcertinf
Note: Teacher certification search may be available at the website.

6 Department of Health, Medical Professions, 425 5th Ave N, Cordell Hull Bldg, 1st Fl, Nashville, TN 37247-1010; 615-532-3202.
http://www2.state.tn.us/health
Search Database at
http://www2.state.tn.us/health/licensure/index.htm

7 Department of Health, Allied Health Professions - Licensing, 425 5th Ave N, Cordell Hull Bldg, 1st Fl, Nashville, TN 37247-1010; 615-532-3202.
http://www2.state.tn.us/health
Search Database at
http://www2.state.tn.us/health/licensure/index.htm

8 Mechanical Licensing Board, (Shelby County/Western Tennesee), 6465 Mullins Station Rd, Memphis, TN 38134; 901-379-4200, Fax: 901-379-4202.

9 Office of Secretary of State, 312 8th Av N, 6th Fl, W R Snodgrass Tower, Nashville, TN 37243-0306; 615-741-3699, Fax: 615-741-7310.
www.state.tn.us/sos/service.htm

10 Registry of Election Finance, 404 James Robertson Pky, #1614, Nashville, TN 37243; 615-741-7959, Fax: 615-532-8902/8905.
www.state.tn.us/tref
Email: registry.info@state.tn.us
Search Database at
www.state.tn.us/tref/lobbyists/lobbyists.htm

11 Department of Agriculture, Melrose Station, Nashville, TN 37204; 615-837-5120, Fax: 615-837-5335.
www.state.tn.us/agriculture

12 Supreme Court of Tennessee, Board of Professional Responsibility, 1101 Kermit Dr., #730, Nashville, TN 37217; 615-361-7500, 800-486-5714, Fax: 615-367-2480.
Email: ethics@tbpr.org

13 Water & Wastewater Certification Program, 2022 Blanton Dr, Fleming Training Ctr, Murfreesboro, TN 37129; 615-898-8090, Fax: 615-818-8064.

14 Department of Health, Division of General Environmental Health, 415 5th Ave N, Cordell Hull Bldg 6th Fl, Nashville, TN 37247-3901; 615-741-7206, Fax: 615-741-8510.
www.state.tn.us/health

15 Department of Labor, Boiler & Elevator Division, Board of Boiler Rules, 710 James Robertson Pky, Andrew Johnson Tower 4th Fl, Nashville, TN 37243; 615-741-2123.
www.state.tn.us/labor-wfd/bediv.html

Tennessee Federal Courts

The following list indicates the district and division name for each county in the state. If the bankruptcy court location is different from the district court, then the location of the bankruptcy court appears in parentheses.

County/Court Cross Reference

County	District	Division
Anderson	Eastern	Knoxville
Bedford	Eastern	Winchester (Chattanooga)
Benton	Western	Jackson
Bledsoe	Eastern	Chattanooga
Blount	Eastern	Knoxville
Bradley	Eastern	Chattanooga
Campbell	Eastern	Knoxville
Cannon	Middle	Nashville
Carroll	Western	Jackson
Carter	Eastern	Greeneville (Knoxville)
Cheatham	Middle	Nashville
Chester	Western	Jackson
Claiborne	Eastern	Knoxville
Clay	Middle	Cookeville (Nashville)
Cocke	Eastern	Greeneville (Knoxville)
Coffee	Eastern	Winchester (Chattanooga)
Crockett	Western	Jackson
Cumberland	Middle	Cookeville (Nashville)
Davidson	Middle	Nashville
De Kalb	Middle	Cookeville (Nashville)
Decatur	Western	Jackson
Dickson	Middle	Nashville
Dyer	Western	Memphis
Fayette	Western	Memphis
Fentress	Middle	Cookeville (Nashville)
Franklin	Eastern	Winchester (Chattanooga)
Gibson	Western	Jackson
Giles	Middle	Columbia (Nashville)
Grainger	Eastern	Knoxville
Greene	Eastern	Greeneville (Knoxville)
Grundy	Eastern	Winchester (Chattanooga)
Hamblen	Eastern	Greeneville (Knoxville)
Hamilton	Eastern	Chattanooga
Hancock	Eastern	Greeneville (Knoxville)
Hardeman	Western	Jackson
Hardin	Western	Jackson
Hawkins	Eastern	Greeneville (Knoxville)
Haywood	Western	Jackson
Henderson	Western	Jackson
Henry	Western	Jackson
Hickman	Middle	Columbia (Nashville)
Houston	Middle	Nashville
Humphreys	Middle	Nashville
Jackson	Middle	Cookeville (Nashville)
Jefferson	Eastern	Knoxville
Johnson	Eastern	Greeneville (Knoxville)
Knox	Eastern	Knoxville
Lake	Western	Jackson
Lauderdale	Western	Memphis
Lawrence	Middle	Columbia (Nashville)
Lewis	Middle	Columbia (Nashville)
Lincoln	Eastern	Winchester (Chattanooga)
Loudon	Eastern	Knoxville
Macon	Middle	Cookeville (Nashville)
Madison	Western	Jackson
Marion	Eastern	Chattanooga
Marshall	Middle	Columbia (Nashville)
Maury	Middle	Columbia (Nashville)
McMinn	Eastern	Chattanooga
McNairy	Western	Jackson
Meigs	Eastern	Chattanooga
Monroe	Eastern	Knoxville
Montgomery	Middle	Nashville
Moore	Eastern	Winchester (Chattanooga)
Morgan	Eastern	Knoxville
Obion	Western	Jackson
Overton	Middle	Cookeville (Nashville)
Perry	Western	Jackson
Pickett	Middle	Cookeville (Nashville)
Polk	Eastern	Chattanooga
Putnam	Middle	Cookeville (Nashville)
Rhea	Eastern	Chattanooga
Roane	Eastern	Knoxville
Robertson	Middle	Nashville
Rutherford	Middle	Nashville
Scott	Eastern	Knoxville
Sequatchie	Eastern	Chattanooga
Sevier	Eastern	Knoxville
Shelby	Western	Memphis
Smith	Middle	Cookeville (Nashville)
Stewart	Middle	Nashville
Sullivan	Eastern	Greeneville (Knoxville)
Sumner	Middle	Nashville
Tipton	Western	Memphis
Trousdale	Middle	Nashville
Unicoi	Eastern	Greeneville (Knoxville)
Union	Eastern	Knoxville
Van Buren	Eastern	Winchester (Chattanooga)
Warren	Eastern	Winchester (Chattanooga)
Washington	Eastern	Greeneville (Knoxville)
Wayne	Middle	Columbia (Nashville)
Weakley	Western	Jackson
White	Middle	Cookeville (Nashville)
Williamson	Middle	Nashville
Wilson	Middle	Nashville

Standards for Federal Courts: The search fee is $20.00 per item (one party name or case number). Certification fee is $7.00 per document. Copy fee is $.50 per page. All fees standard unless noted in profile. Mail Search: always enclose a stamped self addressed envelope unless otherwise noted. Most courts accept fax requests or will suggest a copying/search vendor. Before releasing records, all courts require prepayment unless noted in profile. Open records are located at the court unless otherwise noted. District courts index by defendant and plaintiff as well as by case number. Bankruptcy courts usually index by debtor and case number. While most courts now have their indexes on computer, many still maintain index card files as well.

PACER - The universal PACER sign-up number is 800-676-6856. Find PACER and the Party/Case Index on the Web at http://pacer.psc.uscourts.gov. PACER dial-up access is $.60 per minute. Also, courts offering internet access via RACER, PACER, Web-PACER or the new CM-ECF charge $.07 per page fee unless noted as free.

US District Court

Eastern District of Tennessee

Chattanooga Division Clerk's Office, PO Box 591, Chattanooga, TN 37401 (courier address: Room 309, 900 Georgia Ave, Chattanooga, TN 37402), 423-752-5200, Fax: 423-752-5205. www.tned.uscourts.gov

Counties: Bledsoe, Bradley, Hamilton, McMinn, Marion, Meigs, Polk, Rhea, Sequatchie.

Indexing & Storage: New cases available in the index 1-2 days after filing date.

Fee & Payment: Payment may be made by money order, cashier check, personal check. Payee: Clerk, U.S. District Court.

Phone Search: Only docket information available.

In Person Search: Fee charged if court conducts your in person search for you. Obtain copying from an independent copy service, Legal Impressions.

PACER: PACER is available online at http://pacer.tned.uscourts.gov. Case records go back to 1994. Records never purged. New records are online after 1 day.

Electronic Filing: Electronic filing information online at https://ecf.tned.uscourts.gov

Greeneville Division U.S. District Court, 220 West Depot Street, Ste 200, Greeneville, TN 37743 (Use mail address for courier delivery) 423-639-3105, Fax: 423-639-7134. www.tned.uscourts.gov

Counties: Carter, Cocke, Greene, Hamblen, Hancock, Hawkins, Johnson, Sullivan, Unicoi, Washington.

Indexing & Storage: New cases available in the index immediately after filing date.

Fee & Payment: Payment may be made by money order, cashier check, personal check. Payee: Clerk, U.S. District Court.

Phone Search: Only docket information available by phone.

Mail Search: A SASE not required.

In Person Search: Fee charged if court conducts your in person search for you. Only use the computer terminal to search cases from 1994 on.

PACER: PACER is available online at http://pacer.tned.uscourts.gov. Case records go back to 1994. Records never purged. New records are online after 1 day.

Electronic Filing: Electronic filing information online at https://ecf.tned.uscourts.gov

Knoxville Division Clerk's Office, 800 Market St Ste 130, Knoxville, TN 37902 (Use mail address for courier delivery) 865-545-4228, Fax: 865-545-4247. www.tned.uscourts.gov

Counties: Anderson, Blount, Campbell, Claiborne, Grainger, Jefferson, Knox, Loudon, Monroe, Morgan, Roane, Scott, Sevier, Union.

Indexing & Storage: New cases available in the index 1-2 days after filing date. Computerized index as of June 1, 1992. Index cards prior to June 1, 1992.

Fee & Payment: Payment may be made by money order, cashier check, personal check. Payee: Clerk, U.S. District Court.

Phone Search: Only docket information available.

Mail Search: A SASE not required.

In Person Search: Fee charged if court conducts your in person search for you.

PACER: PACER is available online at http://pacer.ohsd.uscourts.gov. Case records go back to 1994. Records never purged. New records are online after 1 day.

Electronic Filing: Electronic filing information online at https://ecf.tned.uscourts.gov

Winchester Division PO Box 459, Winchester, TN 37398 (courier: 200 S Jefferson St, Room 201, Winchester, TN 37397), 931-967-1444, Fax: 931-967-9693. www.tned.uscourts.gov

Counties: Bedford, Coffee, Franklin, Grundy, Lincoln, Moore, Van Buren, Warren.

Indexing & Storage: New cases available in the index 1-2 days after filing date. Office has just begun maintaining records in 1997.

Fee & Payment: Payment may be made by money order, cashier check, personal check. Payee: Clerk, U.S. District Court.

Phone Search: Only docket information available.

In Person Search: Fee charged if court conducts your in person search for you.

PACER: PACER is available online at http://pacer.tned.uscourts.gov. Case records go back to 1994. Records never purged. New records are online after 1 day.

Electronic Filing: Electronic filing information online at https://ecf.tned.uscourts.gov

U.S. Bankruptcy Court

Eastern District of Tennessee

Northern Division 800 Market St #330, Howard H Baker Jr U.S. Courthouse, Knoxville, TN 37902 (Use mail address for courier delivery) 865-545-4279. www.tneb.uscourts.gov

Counties: Anderson, Blount, Campbell, Carter, Claiborne, Cocke, Grainger, Greene, Hamblen, Hancock, Hawkins, Jefferson, Johnson, Knox, Loudon, Monroe, Morgan, Roane, Scott, Sevier, Sullivan, Unicoi, Union, Washington.

Indexing & Storage: Cases indexed by debtor as well as by case number. New cases available in the index 2-3 days after filing date. District wide searches are possible for limited information from 1/86 from this court.

Fee & Payment: Payment may be made by money order, cashier check, personal check. Payee: Clerk, U.S. Bankruptcy Court.

Phone Search: The court will only confirm debtor names, SSN, address, attorney, trustee, chapter filed, date of filing, date of discharge/dismissal, date case closed, in addition to limited information regarding motions, hearings, etc. Automated voice case information service (VCIS) is available. Call VCIS at 800-767-1512 or 423-752-5272.

In Person Search: Fee charged if court conducts your in person search for you.

PACER: PACER is available online at http://pacer.tneb.uscourts.gov. Records purged as deemed necessary. New civil records are online after 1 day.

Electronic Filing: Currently in the process of implementing CM/ECF.

Southern Division Historic U.S. Courthouse, 31 E 11th St, Chattanooga, TN 37402 (courier address: Use mail address for courier delivery) 423-752-5163. www.tneb.uscourts.gov

Counties: Bedford, Bledsoe, Bradley, Coffee, Franklin, Grundy, Hamilton, Lincoln, Marion, McMinn, Meigs, Moore, Polk, Rhea, Sequatchie, Van Buren, Warren.

Indexing & Storage: Cases indexed by debtor and creditors as well as by case number. New cases available in the index 2 days after filing date. The court needs the name of the debtor and to obtain positive identification, a social security number or address is needed.

Fee & Payment: Payment may be made by money order, cashier check, business check. Personal checks are not accepted. Will invoice for copy fees only. Payee: U.S. Bankruptcy Court.

Phone Search: The court will only confirm bankruptcy filings over the phone and will only honor up to three requests per phone call per day. Automated voice case information service (VCIS) available. VCIS: 800-767-1512 or 423-752-5272.

Mail Search: A SASE not required.

In Person Search: Fee charged if court conducts your in person search for you.

PACER: PACER is available online at http://pacer.tneb.uscourts.gov. Records purged as deemed necessary. New civil records are online after 1 day.

Electronic Filing: Currently in the process of implementing CM/ECF.

U.S. District Court

Middle District of Tennessee

Columbia Division c/o Nashville Division, 800 U.S. Courthouse, 801 Broadway, Nashville, TN 37203 (Use mail address for courier delivery) 615-736-5498. www.tnmd.uscourts.gov

Counties: Giles, Hickman, Lawrence, Lewis, Marshall, Maury, Wayne.

Indexing & Storage: Cases indexed by as well as by case number. New cases available in the index after filing date. Open records are located at the Nashville Division.

Fee & Payment: Payment may be made by money order, cashier check. Business checks are not accepted. Personal checks are not accepted.

Phone Search: No searching by telephone.

Mail Search: A SASE not required.

In Person Search: Permitted.

PACER: PACER is available online at http://pacer.tnmd.uscourts.gov. Records purged every year. New records are online after 1 day.

Electronic Filing: Currently in the process of implementing CM/ECF.

Cookeville Division c/o Nashville Division, 800 U.S. Courthouse, 801 Broadway, Nashville, TN 37203 (courier address: Use mail address for courier delivery) 615-736-5498, Fax: 615-736-7488. www.tnmd.uscourts.gov

Counties: Clay, Cumberland, De Kalb, Fentress, Jackson, Macon, Overton, Pickett, Putnam, Smith, White.

Indexing & Storage: New cases available in the index 1 month after filing date. Records are also indexed on microfiche. Open records are located at the Nashville Division.

Fee & Payment: Payment may be made by money order, cashier check, business check. Personal checks are not accepted. Payee: Clerk, U.S. District Court.

Phone Search: Only docket information available.

In Person Search: Fee charged if court conducts your in person search for you.

PACER: PACER is available online at http://pacer.tnmd.uscourts.gov. Records purged every year. New records are online after 1 day.

Electronic Filing: Currently in the process of implementing CM/ECF.

Nashville Division 800 U.S. Courthouse, 801 Broadway, Nashville, TN 37203 (courier address: Use mail address for courier delivery) 615-736-5498, Fax: 615-736-7488. www.tnmd.uscourts.gov

Counties: Cannon, Cheatham, Davidson, Dickson, Houston, Humphreys, Montgomery, Robertson, Rutherford, Stewart, Sumner, Trousdale, Williamson, Wilson.

Indexing & Storage: New cases available in the index immediately after filing date. Records are also indexed on microfiche.

Fee & Payment: Payment may be made by money order, cashier check, personal check. Payee: Clerk, U.S. District Court.

Phone Search: Only docket information available.

Mail Search: A SASE not required.

In Person Search: Fee charged if court conducts your in person search for you.

PACER: PACER is available online at http://pacer.tnmd.uscourts.gov. Records purged every year. New records are online after 1 day.

Electronic Filing: Currently in the process of implementing CM/ECF.

U.S. Bankruptcy Court

Middle District of Tennessee

Nashville Division PO Box 24890, Nashville, TN 37202-4890 (courier address: Customs House, Room 200, 701 Broadway, Nashville, TN 37203), 615-736-5584. www.tnmb.uscourts.gov

Counties: Cannon, Cheatham, Clay, Cumberland, Davidson, De Kalb, Dickson, Fentress, Giles, Hickman, Houston, Humphreys, Jackson, Lawrence, Lewis, Macon, Marshall, Maury, Montgomery, Overton, Pickett, Putnam, Robertson, Rutherford, Smith, Stewart, Sumner, Trousdale, Wayne, White, Williamson, Wilson.

Indexing & Storage: Cases indexed by debtor as well as by case number. New cases available in the index 24 hours after filing date.

Fee & Payment: Payment may be made by money order, cashier check, business check. Personal checks are not accepted. Payee: Clerk, U.S. Bankruptcy Court.

Phone Search: Only docket information available.

In Person Search: Fee charged if court conducts your in person search for you. Forms are available to obtain access to the files.

PACER: PACER is available online at http://pacer.tnmb.uscourts.gov. To search without paying a registration fee you may request an exemption by downloading a registration form from: http://pacer.psc.uscourts.gov/faxform.html. Fax the form to 210-301-6441. Case records go back to September 1989. Records never purged. New civil records are online after 1 day.

Electronic Filing: Currently in the process of implementing CM/ECF.

Other Online Access: Court does not participate in the U.S. party case index.

U.S. District Court

Western District of Tennessee

Jackson Division Rm 26, U.S. Courthouse 262, 111 S Highland, Jackson, TN 38301 (courier address: Use mail address for courier delivery) 731-421-9200, Fax: 731-421-9210. www.tnwd.uscourts.gov

Counties: Benton, Carroll, Chester, Crockett, Decatur, Gibson, Hardeman, Hardin, Haywood, Henderson, Henry, Lake, McNairy, Madison, Obion, Perry, Weakley.

Indexing & Storage: New cases available in the index 1-2 days after filing date.

Fee & Payment: Payment may be made by money order, cashier check, personal check, Visa, Mastercard. Payee: Clerk, U.S. District Court.

Phone Search: Only docket information available.

In Person Search: Fee charged if court conducts your in person search for you.

PACER: PACER is available online at http://pacer.tnwd.uscourts.gov. Document images available. Records purged as deemed necessary. New records are online after 2 days.

Electronic Filing: Electronic filing information online at https://ecf.tnwd.uscourts.gov

Memphis Division Federal Bldg, Room 242, 167 N Main, Memphis, TN 38103 (Use mail address for courier delivery) 901-495-1200, Fax: 901-495-1250. www.tnwd.uscourts.gov

Counties: Dyer, Fayette, Lauderdale, Shelby, Tipton.

Indexing & Storage: New cases available in the index 1-2 days after filing date.

Fee & Payment: Payment may be made by money order, cashier check, personal check, Visa, Mastercard. Payee: Clerk, U.S. District Court. Will fax docket listings $.50 per page.

Phone Search: Only docket information available by phone. Will fax docket listings $.50 per page.

In Person Search: Fee charged if court conducts your in person search for you.

PACER: PACER is available online at http://pacer.tnwd.uscourts.gov. Document images available. Records purged as deemed necessary. New records are online after 2 days.

Electronic Filing: Electronic filing information online at https://ecf.tnwd.uscourts.gov

U.S. Bankruptcy Court

Western District of Tennessee

Eastern Division Room 107, 111 S Highland Ave, Jackson, TN 38301 (courier address: Use mail address for courier delivery) 731-421-9300. www.tnwb.uscourts.gov

Counties: Benton, Carroll, Chester, Crockett, Decatur, Gibson, Hardeman, Hardin, Haywood, Henderson, Henry, Lake, Madison, McNairy, Obion, Perry, Weakley.

Indexing & Storage: Cases indexed by debtor as well as by case number. New cases available in the index 1-2 days after filing date.

Fee & Payment: Payment may be made by money order, cashier check, business check. Personal checks are not accepted. A search fee is charged only when certification of the search is issued. Payee: U.S. Bankruptcy Court.

Phone Search: Only docket information available by phone. Automated voice case information service (VCIS) is available. Call VCIS at 888-381-4961.

Mail Search: A SASE not required.

In Person Search: Fee charged if court conducts your in person search for you.

PACER: PACER is available online at http://pacer.tnwb.uscourts.gov. Case records go back to 1994. Records never purged. New civil records are online after 2 days.

Electronic Filing: Electronic filing information online at https://ecf.tnwb.uscourts.gov

Western Division Suite 413, 200 Jefferson Ave, Memphis, TN 38103 (courier address: Use mail address for courier delivery) 901-328-3500, Fax: 901-328-3500. www.tnwb.uscourts.gov

Counties: Dyer, Fayette, Lauderdale, Shelby, Tipton.

Indexing & Storage: Cases indexed by debtor as well as by case number. New cases available in the index 2 days after filing date.

Fee & Payment: Payment may be made by money order, cashier check, business check. Personal checks are not accepted. In general, if the cost of copies exceeds the amount of the check, the court will bill for the excess by mail. Payee: Clerk, U.S. Bankruptcy Court.

Phone Search: Only docket information available by phone. Automated voice case information service (VCIS) is available. Call VCIS at 888-381-4961.

Mail Search: A SASE not required.

In Person Search: Permitted.

PACER: PACER is available online at http://pacer.tnwb.uscourts.gov. Case records go back to 1994. Records never purged. New civil records are online after 2 days.

Electronic Filing: Electronic filing information online at https://ecf.tnwb.uscourts.gov

Tennessee County Courts

Court	Jurisdiction	No. of Courts	How Organized
Circuit Courts*	General	15	31 Districts
Chancery Courts*	General	87	31 Districts
General Sessions Courts*	Limited	16	By County
Combined Circuit/ General Sessions*		87	By County
Municipal Courts	Municipal	300	
Probate/County Courts*	Probate	25	By County
Juvenile Courts	Special	17	By County

* Profiled in this Sourcebook.

CIVIL									
Court	Tort	Contract	Real Estate	Min. Claim	Max. Claim	Small Claims	Estate	Eviction	Domestic Relations
Circuit Courts*	X	X	X	$0	No Max				X
Chancery Court*	X	X	X	$0	No Max		X		X
General Sessions *	X	X	X	$0	$15,000	X	X		X
Municipal Courts									
Probate/County Courts*							X		
Juvenile Courts									X

CRIMINAL					
Court	Felony	Misdemeanor	DWI/DUI	Preliminary Hearing	Juvenile
Circuit Courts*	X	X	X		
Criminal Courts*	X	X	X		
Chancery Court*					
General Sessions *		X	X	X	X
Municipal Courts		X	X		
Probate Courts*					
Juvenile Courts					X

ADMINISTRATION   Administrative Office of the Courts, 511 Union St (Nashville City Center) #600, Nashville, TN, 37219; 615-741-2687, Fax: 615-741-6285. www.tsc.state.tn.us

COURT STRUCTURE   Criminal cases are handled by the Circuit Courts and General Sessions Courts. Generally, misdemeanor cases are heard by General Sessions, but in Circuit Court if connected to a felony. All General Sessions Courts have raised the maximum civil case limit to $15,000 from $10,000. The Chancery Courts, in addition to handling probate, also hear certain types of equitable civil cases. Combined courts vary by county, and the counties of Davidson, Hamilton, Knox, and Shelby have separate Criminal Courts.

ONLINE ACCESS   The Administrative Office of Courts provides access to Appellate Court opinions at the web site www.tsc.state.tn.us. Several counties offer online access to court records.

PROBATE COURTS   Probate is handled in the Chancery or County Courts, except in several counties where it is handled by the Probate Court.

Anderson County

7th District Circuit & General Sessions

Court 100 N. Main St, Clinton, TN 37716; 865-457-5400; Fax: 865-259-2345. Hours: 8AM-4:30PM (EST). *Felony, Misdemeanor, Civil, Eviction, Small Claims.*

Civil Records: Access: In person only. Visitors must perform in person searches for themselves. No search fee. Required to search: name, years to search. Civil cases indexed by defendant, plaintiff. Civil records on computer from 1988, archived from 1947.

Criminal Records: Access: In person only. Visitors must perform in person searches for themselves. No search fee. Required to search: name, years to search, DOB, SSN. Criminal records on computer from 1988, archived from 1947.

General Information: Public Access terminal is available. No juvenile records released. Copy fee: $1.00 per page. Cert fee: $2.00 per page. Payee: Circuit Court Clerk or General Sessions Clerk. Personal checks accepted. Prepayment required.

Chancery Court Anderson County Courthouse, PO Box 501, Clinton, TN 37717; 865-457-5400; Probate phone: 865-457-6207; Fax: 865-457-6267. Hours: 8:30AM-4:30PM (EST). *Civil, Probate.*

Civil Records: Access: Phone, mail, in person. Both court and visitors may perform in person searches. No search fee. Required to search: name, years to search. Civil cases indexed by defendant, plaintiff. Civil records on computer 1992 to present, prior records on another system.

General Information: No adoption or mental health records released. Copy fee: $2.00 for first page, $1.00 each add'l. Cert fee: $4.00. Payee: Clerk and Master. Personal checks accepted. Prepayment required. Mail turnaround time is 2 days.

Bedford County

17th District Circuit & General Sessions

Court 1 Public Sq, #200, Shelbyville, TN 37160; 931-684-3223. Hours: 8AM-4PM (CST). *Felony, Misdemeanor, Civil, Eviction, Small Claims.*

Civil Records: Access: In person only. Visitors must perform in person searches for themselves. No search fee. Required to search: name, years to search. Civil cases indexed by defendant, plaintiff. Civil records on archives and books from 1934; computerized records since 1994.

Criminal Records: Access: In person only. Visitors must perform in person searches for themselves. No search fee. Required to search: name, years to search, DOB; also helpful: SSN. Criminal records on archives and books from 1934; computerized records since 1994.

General Information: Public Access terminal is available. No juvenile, adoptions, mental health, expunged or sealed records released. Copy fee: $1.00 per page. Cert fee: $ 2.00. Payee: Thomas Smith, Clerk. Personal checks accepted. Prepayment required.

Chancery Court Chancery Court, 1 Public Sq, #302, Shelbyville, TN 37160; 931-684-1672. Hours: 8AM-4PM M-Th, 8AM-5PM Fri (CST). *Civil, Probate.*

Civil Records: Access: In person only. Visitors must perform in person searches for themselves. No search fee. Required to search: name, years to search. Civil cases indexed by defendant, plaintiff. Civil records on books from 9/82 (probate), prior records back to 1800s filed in county clerk's office.

General Information: No adoption records released. Copy fee: $.50 per page. Cert fee: $5.00. Payee: Clerk and Master. Personal checks accepted. Prepayment required.

Benton County

24th District Circuit & General Sessions

Court 1 E Court Sq, Rm 207, Camden, TN 38320; 731-584-6711; Fax: 731-584-2081. Hours: 8AM-4PM M-Th; 8AM-5PM F (CST). *Felony, Misdemeanor, Civil, Eviction, Small Claims.*

Civil Records: Access: In person only. Both court and visitors may perform in person searches. No search fee. Required to search: name, years to search. Civil cases indexed by defendant, plaintiff. Civil records computerized since 1995. Public can only use docket books to search, older records archived to 1800s.

Criminal Records: Access: In person only. Both court and visitors may perform in person searches. No search fee. Required to search: name, years to search. Criminal records computerized since 1995. Public can only use docket books to search, older records archived to 1800s.

General Information: No juvenile records released without judge approval. Will not fax results. Copy fee: $1.00 per page. Cert fee: $5.00. Payee: Circuit Court Clerk or General Session. Business checks accepted. Prepayment required.

Chancery Court 1 E Court Sq, Courthouse Rm 206, Camden, TN 38320; 731-584-4435; Fax: 731-584-1407. Hours: 8AM-4PM M-Th; 8AM-5PM F (CST). *Civil, Probate.*

Civil Records: Access: In person only. Visitors must perform in person searches for themselves. No search fee. Required to search: name, years to search. Civil cases indexed by defendant, plaintiff. Civil records in books since 1880.

General Information: Public Access terminal is available. No adoption or sealed records released. Cert fee: $6.00. Payee: Clerk & Master. No personal checks accepted. Prepayment required.

Bledsoe County

12th District Circuit & General Sessions

Court PO Box 455, Pikeville, TN 37367; 423-447-6488; Fax: 423-447-2534. Hours: 8AM-4PM (CST). *Felony, Misdemeanor, Civil, Eviction, Small Claims.*

Civil Records: Access: In person only. Visitors must perform in person searches for themselves. No search fee. Required to search: name, years to search. Civil cases indexed by plaintiff. Civil records archived from 1920 in books.

Criminal Records: Access: In person only. Visitors must perform in person searches for themselves. Search fee: none. Required to search: name, years to search, DOB. Criminal records archived from 1920 in books.

General Information: Public Access terminal is available. (Only criminal records available.) No juvenile records released. Copy fee: $.25 per page. Cert fee: $3.00. Prepayment required.

Chancery Court PO Box 389, Pikeville, TN 37367; 423-447-2484; Fax: 423-447-6856. Hours: 8AM-4PM M,T,W,F; 8AM-Noon Sat (CST). *Civil, Probate.*

Civil Records: Access: Fax, mail, in person. Both court and visitors may perform in person searches. No search fee. Required to search: name, years to search. Civil cases indexed by defendant, plaintiff. Civil records on books since 1856.

General Information: No juvenile or adoption records released. Will fax results for $2.00 per page. Copy fee: $1.00 per page. Cert fee: $2.00 per page. Payee: Bledsoe County Clerk and Master. Personal checks accepted. Prepayment required. Mail turnaround time 3 days.

Blount County

5th District General Sessions Court 926

E Lamar Alexander Pky, Maryville, TN 37804-6201; 865-273-5450; Fax: 865-273-5411. Hours: 8AM-4:30PM (EST). *Misdemeanor, Civil, Eviction, Small Claims.*

www.blounttn.org/circuit

Civil Records: Access: Mail, in person. Both court and visitors may perform in person searches. Search fee: $15.00 per name. Required to search: name, years to search. Civil cases indexed by defendant, plaintiff. Civil records archived in books back to 1991; on computer back to 1996.

Criminal Records: Access: Mail, in person. Both court and visitors may perform in person searches. Search fee: $15.00 per name. Required to search: name, years to search. Criminal records archived in books back to 1991; on computer back to 1996.

General Information: Public Access terminal is available. No juvenile records released. Will fax results. Copy fee: $1.00 per page. Cert fee: $5.00. Payee: Circuit Court Clerk or General Session. Business checks accepted. Prepayment required. Mail turnaround time 6-10 days.

Circuit Court 926 E Lamar Alexander Pky, 1st Fl, Maryville, TN 37804; 865-273-5400; Probate phone: 865-273-5800; Fax: 865-273-5411. Hours: 8AM-4:30PM (EST). *Felony, Misdemeanor, Civil.*

Civil Records: Access: Mail, in person. Both court and visitors may perform in person searches. Search fee: $15.00 per name. Required to search: name, years to search. Civil cases indexed by defendant. Civil records on books.

Criminal Records: Access: Mail, in person. Visitors must perform in person searches for themselves. No search fee. Required to search: name, years to search. Criminal records on books.

General Information: Public Access terminal is available. No juvenile records released. Copy fee: $1.00 per page. Cert fee: $5.00. Payee: Circuit Court Clerk. Only cashiers checks and money orders accepted. Prepayment required.

County Clerk 345 Court St, Old Courthouse, Maryville, TN 37804; 865-273-5800; Fax: 865-273-5815. Hours: 8AM-4:30PM (EST). *Probate.*

Bradley County

10th District Circuit & General Sessions

Court Courthouse, Rm 205, 155 N Ocoee St, Cleveland, TN 37311-5068; 423-476-0692; Fax: 423-476-0488. Hours: 8:30AM-4:30PM M-Th, 8:30AM-5PM Fri (EST). *Felony, Misdemeanor, Civil, Eviction, Small Claims.*

Civil Records: Access: Mail, in person. Both court and visitors may perform in person searches. Search fee: $25.00 per name. Required to search: name, years to search. Civil cases indexed by defendant, plaintiff. Civil records archived from 1990, on computer from 1990.

Criminal Records: Access: Mail, in person. Both court and visitors may perform in person searches. Search fee: $25.00 per name plus $2.00 data charge. Required to search: name, years to search, signed release. Criminal records archived from 1990, on computer from 1990.

General Information: No juvenile records released. Fee to fax results is $1.00 per page. Copy fee: $.30 per page. Cert fee: $10.00. Payee: Circuit Court Clerk or General Session. Personal checks accepted. Prepayment required. Mail turnaround time 10 days.

Chancery Court 55 N Ocoee St, Rm 203, Cleveland, TN 37311; 423-476-0526. Hours: 8:30AM-4:30PM M-Th, 8:30AM-5PM Fri (EST). *Civil, Probate.*

Civil Records: Access: Phone, in person. Both court and visitors may perform in person searches. Search fee: Search fee based on request submitted. Required to search: name, years to search. Civil cases indexed by defendant, plaintiff. Civil records filed in books back to 1861.

General Information: No adoption records released. Will fax results if requested. Copy fee: $1.00 per page. Cert fee: $10.00. Payee: Clerk and Master. Personal checks accepted. Prepayment required. Mail turnaround time same day.

Campbell County

8th District Circuit & General Sessions

Court PO Box 26, Jacksboro, TN 37757; 423-562-2624. Hours: 8AM-4:30PM (EST). *Felony, Misdemeanor, Civil, Eviction, Small Claims.*

Civil Records: Access: Mail, in person. Both court and visitors may perform in person searches. No search fee. Required to search: name, years to search. Civil cases indexed by defendant, plaintiff. Civil records on computer since 1991. On microfiche from 1987 and archived since court started located at La Follette Library, La Follette, TN 37766.

Criminal Records: Access: Mail, in person. Both court and visitors may perform in person searches. No search fee. Required to search: name, years to search, DOB, SSN. Criminal records on computer since 1991. On microfiche from 1987 and archived since court started located at La Follette Library, La Follette, TN 37766.

General Information: Public Access terminal is available. No juvenile, adoption and judicial hospitalization records released. Copy fee: $1.00 per page. Cert fee: $3.00. Payee: Circuit Court Clerk or General Session. Business checks accepted. Prepayment required. Mail turnaround time depends on type of search.

Chancery Court PO Box 182 (570 Main St, #110), Jacksboro, TN 37757; 423-562-3496. Hours: 8AM-4:30PM (EST). *Civil, Probate.*

Civil Records: Access: In person, mail. Visitors must perform in person searches for themselves. No search fee. Required to search: name, years to search. Civil cases indexed by defendant, plaintiff. Civil records filed in books, microfiche available at LaFollette Library since 1842.

General Information: No adoption records released. Fee to fax results is $1.00 per page and $.50 per document. Copy fee: $1.00 per page. Cert fee: $4.00. Payee: Clerk and Master. Business checks accepted. Prepayment required. Mail requests: SASE preferred. Turnaround time 1-2 days.

Cannon County

16th District Circuit & General Sessions

Court County Courthouse Public Sq, Woodbury, TN 37190; 615-563-4461; Fax: 615-563-6391. Hours: 8AM-4PM M,T,TH,F; 8AM-Noon Wed (CST). *Felony, Misdemeanor, Civil, Eviction, Small Claims.*
Civil Records: Access: In person only. Visitors must perform in person searches for themselves. No search fee. Required to search: name, years to search. Civil cases indexed by defendant, plaintiff. Civil records archived on books from 1980s.

Criminal Records: Access: In person only. Visitors must perform in person searches for themselves. No search fee. Required to search: name, years to search, DOB. Criminal records archived on books from 1980s.

General Information: Public Access terminal is available. No juvenile records released. Copy fee: $1.00 per page. Cert fee: $4.00. Payee: Circuit Court Clerk or General Session. Personal checks accepted. Prepayment required.

County Court County Courthouse Public Sq, Woodbury, TN 37190; 615-563-4278/5936; Fax: 615-563-1289. Hours: 8AM-4PM M,T,TH,F; 8AM-Noon Sat (CST). *Probate.*

Carroll County

24th District Circuit & General Sessions

Court 99 Court Sq, #103, Huntingdon, TN 38344; Civil phone: 731-986-1929 (Circuit; 731-986-1926 (Gen Sess). Hours: 8AM-4PM (CST). *Felony, Misdemeanor, Civil, Eviction, Small Claims.*
Civil Records: Access: In person only. Only the court may perform searches. Search fee: $5.00 per name. Required to search: name, years to search. Civil cases indexed by defendant, plaintiff. Civil records archived from 1924; on computer from 1989.

Criminal Records: Access: In person only. Only the court performs in person searches; visitors may not. Search fee: $5.00 per name. Required to search: name, years to search, DOB. Criminal records archived from 1925; on computer from 1989.

General Information: Copy fee: $.50 per page. No copies by mail. Cert fee: $6.00. Payee: Circuit Court Clerk or General Session. Only cashiers checks and money orders accepted. Prepayment required.

Chancery Court 99 Court Sq, #105, Huntingdon, TN 38344; 731-986-1920. Hours: 8AM-4PM M-F (CST). *Civil, Probate.*

Civil Records: Access: Mail, in person. Both court and visitors may perform in person searches. Search fee: $10.00. Required to search: name, years to search. Civil cases indexed by defendant, plaintiff. Civil records on computer since 6/88, sotred since 1822.

General Information: No adoption or sealed documents released. Will fax results for $2.00 per page. Copy fee: $1.00 per page and $3.00 per document. Cert fee: $6.00 per document. Payee: Clerk and Master. Checks, money orders and cashiers checks accepted. Prepayment required. Mail requests: SASE required ($.52 postage). Turnaround time 5-10 days.

Carter County

1st District Circuit & General Sessions

Court Carter County Justice Center, 900 E Elk Ave, Elizabethton, TN 37643; 423-542-1835; Civil phone: 423-542-1825; Fax: 423-542-3742. Hours: 8AM-5PM (EST). *Felony, Misdemeanor, Civil, Eviction, Small Claims.*
Civil Records: Access: In person only. Visitors perform in person searches for themselves. No search fee. Required to search: name, years to search. Civil cases indexed by defendant, plaintiff. Civil records archived from 1800s (partial lost in fire), on computer from 02/92.

Criminal Records: Access: In person only. Visitors must perform in person searches for themselves. No search fee. Required to search: name, years to search. Criminal records archived from 1800s (partial lost in fire), on computer from 4-92.

General Information: Public Access terminal is available. No juvenile, psychiatric or expunged records released. Cert fee: $7.00 plus $1.00 each add'l page. Payee: Circuit Court Clerk or General Session. Personal checks accepted. Prepayment required.

County Court 801 E Elk Ave., Elizabethton, TN 37643; 423-542-1814; Fax: 423-547-1502. Hours: 8AM-4:30PM (EST). *Probate.*

Cheatham County

23rd District Circuit Court 100 Public Sq, Rm 225, Ashland City, TN 37015; 615-792-3272; Fax: 615-792-3203. Hours: 8AM-4PM (CST). *Felony, Civil Actions over $15,000, Misdemeanors.*
Note: Circuit Court is Rm 225, General Sessions is Rm 223 (615-792-4866); they must be searched separately. Circuit court handles felony, civil actions over $15,000, some misdemeanors; General Sessions handles misdemeanors, small claims, civil under $15,000.

Civil Records: Access: Mail, in person. Both court and visitors may perform in person searches. Search fee: $5.00 per name. Required to search: name, years to search. Civil cases indexed by defendant, plaintiff. Civil records archived on books from 1946 in office, since court started in storage and on computer from 1990.

Criminal Records: Access: Mail, in person. Both court and visitors may perform in person searches. Search fee: $5.00 per name. Required to search: name, years to search. Criminal records archived on books from 1946 in office, since court started in storage and on computer from 1990.

General Information: No juvenile records released. Copy fee: $2.50 per document (or $1.00 per page). Cert fee: $5.00. Payee: Circuit Court Clerk. Prepayment required. Mail requests: SASE required. Mail turnaround time 2-3 days.

General Sessions 100 Public Sq, Rm 223, Ashland City, TN 37015; 615-792-4866; Fax: 615-792-3203. Hours: 8AM-4PM (CST). *Misdemeanor, Civil under $15,000, Eviction, Small Claims.*

Civil Records: Access: Mail, in person. Both court and visitors may perform in person searches. Search fee: $5.00 per name. Required to search: name, years to search. Civil cases indexed by defendant, plaintiff. Civil records archived on books from 1946 in office, since court started in storage and on computer from 1990.

Criminal Records: Access: Mail, in person. Both court and visitors may perform in person searches. Search fee: $5.00 per name. Required to search: name, years to search. Criminal records archived on books from 1946 in office, since court started in storage and on computer from 1990.

General Information: No juvenile records released. Copy fee: $2.50 per document (or $1.00 per page). Cert fee: $5.00. Payee: General Sessions Clerk. Prepayment required. Mail requests: SASE required. Mail turnaround time 2-3 days.

Chancery Court Clerk & Master, #106, Ashland City, TN 37015; 615-792-4620. Hours: 8AM-4PM (CST). *Civil, Probate.*

Civil Records: Access: In person only. Visitors must perform in person searches for themselves. No search fee. Required to search: name, years to search. Civil cases indexed by defendant, plaintiff. Civil records on computer.

General Information: No adoption records released. Copy fee: $1.00 per page. Cert fee: $2.00. Payee: Chancery Court. Personal checks accepted. Prepayment required. Mail requests: SASE required. Mail turnaround time same day.

Chester County

26th District Circuit & General Sessions

Court PO Box 133, Henderson, TN 38340; 731-989-2454; Fax: 731-989-9184. Hours: 8AM-4PM (CST). *Felony, Misdemeanor, Civil, Eviction, Small Claims.*
Civil Records: Access: Mail, in person. Both court and visitors may perform in person searches. Search fee: $20.00. Required to search: name, years to search. Civil cases indexed by defendant, plaintiff. Civil records in books and archived from 1892.

Criminal Records: Access: Mail, in person. Both court and visitors may perform in person searches. Search fee: $20.00 per name. Required to search: name, years to search, DOB. Criminal records in books and archived from 1892.

General Information: No juvenile records released. Copy fee: $1.00 per page. Cert fee: $5.00. Payee: Circuit Court, or General Sessions Clerk. Prepayment required. Mail turnaround time 2 days.

Chancery Court Clerk & Master, PO Box 262, Henderson, TN 38340; 731-989-7171; Fax: 731-989-7176. Hours: 8AM-4PM (CST). *Civil, Probate.*

Civil Records: Access: Mail, in person. Visitors must perform in person searches for themselves. Search fee: $5.00. Required to search: name, years to search. Civil cases indexed by defendant, plaintiff. Civil records on books.

General Information: No adoption or sealed records released. Will fax for fee of $5.00 per certified copy. Copy fee: $1.00 per page. Cert fee: $3.00. Payee: Clerk and Master. Personal checks accepted. Prepayment required. Mail turnaround time 2 days.

Claiborne County

8th District Criminal, Circuit & General Sessions Court 1740 Main St, #201, Tazewell, TN 37879; 423-626-8181; Fax: 423-626-5631. Hours: 8:30AM-4PM M-F, 9AM-Noon Sat (EST). *Felony, Misdemeanor, Civil, Eviction, Small Claims.*

Civil Records: Access: Mail, fax, in person. Both court and visitors may perform in person searches. Search fee: $10.00 per name. Required to search: name, years to search. Civil cases indexed by defendant, plaintiff. Civil records archived since 1932; on computer back to 1986.

Criminal Records: Access: Mail, fax, in person. Both court and visitors may perform in person searches. Search fee: $10.00 per name. Required to search: name, years to search. Criminal records archived since 1932; on computer back to 1986.

General Information: Public Access terminal is available. No adoption records released. Fee to fax results is $.25 per page. Copy fee: $.25 per page. Cert fee: $5.00. Payee: Circuit Court Clerk or General Sessions. Business checks accepted. In state personal checks accepted. Prepayment required. Mail requests: SASE required. Mail turnaround time 2-3 days.

Chancery Court PO Box 180, Tazewell, TN 37879; 423-626-3284; Fax: 423-626-3604. Hours: 8:30AM-Noon, 1-4PM (EST). *Civil, Probate.*

Civil Records: Access: Mail, in person. Both court and visitors may perform in person searches. No search fee. Required to search: name, years to search. Civil cases indexed by defendant, plaintiff. Civil records kept on books back to 1932; recent on computer.

General Information: No adoption records released. Copy fee: $.25 per page. Cert fee: $5.00. Payee: Clerk and Master. Personal checks accepted. Prepayment required. Mail turnaround time 1-2 days.

Clay County

13th District Circuit & General Sessions Court PO Box 749, Celina, TN 38551; 931-243-2557. Hours: 8AM-5PM (CST). *Felony, Misdemeanor, Civil, Eviction, Small Claims.*

Civil Records: Access: In person only. Visitors must perform in person searches for themselves. No search fee. Required to search: name, years to search. Civil cases indexed by plaintiff, defendant. Civil records archived from early 1900s, on microfiche from 1986.

Criminal Records: Access: In person only. Visitors must perform in person searches for themselves. Search fee: No chg. Required to search: name, years to search; also helpful: SSN. Criminal records archived from early 1900s, on microfiche from 1986.

General Information: Public Access terminal is available. No juvenile records released. Copy fee: $.25 per page. No cert fee. Payee: Circuit Court, or

General Sessions Clerk. Personal checks accepted. Prepayment required.

Chancery Court PO Box 332, Celina, TN 38551; 931-243-3145. Hours: 8AM-4PM M,T,TH,F; 8AM-Noon W (CST). *Civil, Probate.*

Civil Records: Access: Mail, in person. Both court and visitors may perform in person searches. No search fee. Required to search: name, years to search. Civil cases indexed by defendant, plaintiff. Civil records on books.

General Information: No juvenile records released. No copy fee. No cert fee. Turnaround time 1 week.

Cocke County

4th District Circuit Court 111 Court Ave, Rm 201, Newport, TN 37821; 423-623-6124; Fax: 423-625-3889. Hours: 8:30AM-5PM (EST). *Felony, Misdemeanor, Civil Actions Over $15,000.*

Civil Records: Access: Mail, in person. Both court and visitors may perform in person searches. Search fee: $3.00 per name. Required to search: name, years to search. Civil cases indexed by defendant, plaintiff. Civil records archived from late 1800s.

Criminal Records: Access: Mail, in person. Both court and visitors may perform in person searches. Search fee: $3.00 per name. Required to search: name, years to search, DOB. Criminal records archived from late 1800s.

General Information: No divorce or sealed records released. Will fax results to local or toll free line. Copy fee: $.25 per page. Cert fee: $5.00. Payee: Circuit Court. Personal checks accepted. Prepayment required. Mail requests: SASE required. Mail turnaround time ASAP.

General Sessions Court 111 Court Ave, Newport, TN 37821; 423-623-8619; Fax: 423-623-9808. Hours: 8AM-4PM (EST). *Misdemeanor, Civil Actions Under $15,000, Eviction, Small Claims.*

Civil Records: Access: Phone, mail, in person. Both court and visitors may perform in person searches. Search fee: $3.00 per name. Required to search: name, years to search. Civil cases indexed by defendant, plaintiff. Civil records on books at least 10 years.

Criminal Records: Access: Phone, mail, in person. Both court and visitors may perform in person searches. Search fee: $3.00 per name. Required to search: name, years to search. DOB, SSN. Criminal records on books at least 10 years.

General Information: Public Access terminal is available. Will fax results, if prepaid. Copy fee: $3.00 per document. Cert fee: $3.00. Payee: General Sessions Court. Business checks accepted. Prepayment required. Mail requests: SASE required. Mail turnaround time varies.

Chancery Court Courthouse Annex, 360 E Main St, #103, Newport, TN 37821; 423-623-3321; Criminal phone: 423-623-6124; Fax: 423-625-3642. Hours: 8AM-4:30PM (EST). *Civil, Probate.*

Civil Records: Access: Phone, mail, in person. Only the court performs in person searches; visitors may not. No search fee. Required to search: name, years to search. Civil cases indexed by defendant, plaintiff. Civil records on computer since 1984, on books from 1930.

General Information: No sealed records released. Will fax results to local or toll free line. Copy fee: $.25 per page. Cert fee: $3.00. Payee: Chancery Court, Clerk and Master. Personal checks accepted. Prepayment required. Mail requests: SASE required. Mail turnaround time 1 week.

Coffee County

14th District Circuit & General Sessions Court PO Box 629, Manchester, TN 37349; 931-723-5110. Hours: 8AM-4:30PM (CST). *Felony, Misdemeanor, Civil, Eviction, Small Claims.*

Civil Records: Access: Mail, in person. Both court and visitors may perform in person searches. Search fee: $25.00 per case/defendant form 1991 to present; $50.00 if prior. Required to search: name, years to search. Civil cases indexed by defendant, plaintiff. Civil records archived from late 1800s, indexed chronologically by court date.

Criminal Records: Access: Mail, in person. Both court and visitors may perform in person searches. Search fee: Same fees as civil. Required to search: name, years to search, DOB; also helpful: SSN. Criminal records archived from late 1800s, indexed chronologically by court date.

General Information: Public Access terminal is available. No juvenile record released. Copy fee: $.50 per page add'l $.25. Cert fee: $3.50. Payee: General Sessions Clerk. Personal checks accepted. Prepayment required. Mail requests: SASE required. Mail turnaround time 1 week.

Chancery Court 300 Hillsboro Blvd, Rm 102, Manchester, TN 37355; 931-723-5132; Criminal phone: 931-723-5110. Hours: 8AM-4:30PM (CST). *Civil, Probate.*

Civil Records: Access: Mail, in person. Both court and visitors may perform in person searches. No search fee. Required to search: name, years to search. Civil cases indexed by defendant, plaintiff. Civil records on books after 1980, before 1980 filed in County Clerk's Office.

General Information: Public Access terminal is available. No juvenile or adoption records released. Copy fee: $.50 per page. Cert fee: $3.50. Payee: Chancery Court. Personal checks accepted. Prepayment required. Mail requests: SASE helpful. Turnaround time is 1-2 days.

Crockett County

Circuit & General Sessions Court 1 S Bell St, #6 Courthouse, Alamo, TN 38001; 731-696-5462; Fax: 731-696-2605. Hours: 8AM-4PM (CST). *Felony, Misdemeanor, Civil, Eviction, Small Claims.*

Civil Records: Access: Mail, fax, in person. Both court and visitors may perform in person searches. Search fee: $10.00 per name. Required to search: name, years to search. Civil cases indexed by defendant, plaintiff. Civil records archived since court started, records prior to 1986 on docket books. All requests must be in writing.

Criminal Records: Access: Mail, fax, in person. Both court and visitors may perform in person searches. Search fee: $10.00 per name. Required to search: name, years to search, DOB; also helpful: SSN, sex. Criminal records on docket books, on computer from 1993. All requests must be in writing.

General Information: Public Access terminal is available. No adoption or mental records released. Copy fee: $1.00 per page. Cert fee: $6.00. Payee: Circuit Court, or General Sessions Clerk. Business checks accepted. Prepayment required. Mail requests: SASE requested. Turnaround time 1-2 days.

Chancery Court 1 S Bells St, #5, Alamo, TN 38001; 731-696-5458; Fax: 731-696-3028. Hours: 8AM-4PM (CST). *Civil, Probate.*

Civil Records: Access: Mail, in person. Both court and visitors may perform in person searches. No search fee. Required to search: name, years to search. Civil cases indexed by defendant, plaintiff. Civil records on books bacl to 1872.

General Information: No adoption records released. Will fax results for $1.00 per page. Copy fee: $1.00

per page. Cert fee: $6.00 for cert & seal plus $1.00 per page. Payee: Chancery Court Clerk. Personal checks accepted. Prepayment required. Mail requests: SASE required. Mail turnaround time 1-3 days.

Cumberland County

13th District Circuit & General Sessions Court 2 N Main St, #302, Crossville, TN 38555; 931-484-6647; Fax: 931-456-5013. Hours: 8AM-4PM (CST). *Felony, Misdemeanor, Civil, Eviction, Small Claims.*
Note: Above phone number is for General Sessions; Circuit can be reached at 931-484-5852.
Civil Records: Access: In person only. Visitors must perform in person searches for themselves. No search fee. Required to search: name, years to search. Civil cases indexed by defendant, plaintiff. Civil records archived on books from 1940s approx.; on computer back to 1996.
Criminal Records: Access: In person only. Visitors must perform in person searches for themselves. No search fee. Required to search: name, years to search, DOB; also helpful: SSN. Criminal records archived on books from 1940s approx.; on computer back to 1996.
General Information: Public Access terminal is available. No sealed records released. No cert fee. Prepayment required.

Chancery Court 2 N Main St, #101, Crossville, TN 38555-4583; 931-484-4731; Criminal phone: 931-484-5852. Hours: 8AM-4PM (CST). *Civil, Probate.*
Civil Records: Access: Mail, in person. Both court and visitors may perform in person searches. No search fee. Required to search: name, years to search. Civil cases indexed by defendant, plaintiff. Civil records on computer since 1991, on books since 1900s.
General Information: Public Access terminal is available. No juvenile, adoption records released. Copy fee: $.50 per page. No cert fee. Payee: Clerk and Master. Only cashiers checks and money orders accepted. Prepayment required. Mail requests: SASE requested. Turnaround time 2 days.

Davidson County

20th District Criminal Court Metro Courthouse, Rm 309, 601 Mainstream Dr., Nashville, TN 37201; 615-862-5601; Fax: 615-862-5676. Hours: 8AM-4PM (CST). *Felony, Misdemeanor.*
www.nashville.org/ccrt
Criminal Records: Access: Mail, online, in person. Both court and visitors may perform in person searches. Search fee: $15.00 per name. Required to search: name, years to search, DOB, signed release; also helpful: SSN, race. Records from Metropolitan Nashville and Davidson County Criminal Court database are free online at www.nashville.org/ccrt. Search the criminal court dockets by date. Also, the City of Nashville sponsors an Internet site at www.police.nashville.org/justice/default.asp.
General Information: No records unauthorized by statutes released. Copy fee: $.25 per page. Cert fee: $6.00. Payee: Circuit Court Clerk. Personal checks accepted. Visa, MC, Discover. Prepayment required. Mail requests: SASE required. Mail turnaround time 2-3 days.

Circuit Court 506 Metro Courthouse, Nashville, TN 37201; 615-862-5181. Hours: 8AM-4:30PM (CST). *Civil.*
www.nashville.gov/circuit
Note: Physical address is 523 Mainstream Dr, Rm 200, Nashville.
Civil Records: Access: Mail, in person. Both court and visitors may perform in person searches. No

search fee. Required to search: name, years to search. Civil cases indexed by defendant, plaintiff. Civil records archived on books from 1800s, on computer from 1974.
General Information: Public Access terminal is available. No juvenile or adoption records released. Will not fax results. Copy fee: $.50 per page. Cert fee: $2.00 per page. Payee: Circuit Court Clerk. Prepayment required. Mail turnaround time 2-3 days.

General Sessions Court 501 Great Circle Rd., Nashville, TN 37228; 615-862-5195; Fax: 615-862-5924. Hours: 8AM-4:30PM (CST). *Civil Actions Under $15,000, Eviction, Small Claims.*
www.nashville.gov/circuit/sessions
Civil Records: Access: Mail, in person. Visitors must perform in person searches for themselves. Search fee: $6.00 for an abstract of judgment. Required to search: name, years to search.
General Information: Public Access terminal is available. No juvenile records released. Copy fee: $1.00 per page. Cert fee: $3.00 per page. Payee: General Sessions Court Clerk. Prepayment required.

Probate Court 105 Metro Courthouse, Nashville, TN 37201; 615-862-5980; Fax: 615-862-5987. Hours: 8AM-4:30 (CST). *Probate.*

De Kalb County

13th District Circuit & General Sessions Court 1 Public Sq, Rm 303, Smithville, TN 37166; 615-597-5711. Hours: 8AM-4:30PM M,T,W,Th; 8AM-5PM Fri (CST). *Felony, Misdemeanor, Civil, Eviction, Small Claims.*
Civil Records: Access: In person only. Both court and visitors may perform in person searches. No search fee. Required to search: name, years to search. Civil cases indexed by defendant, plaintiff. Civil records archived in office last 10 years. Prior to 1982, records are not very accurate because of fire. Dist Court records on computer back to 2001; General Sessions to mid-2000.
Criminal Records: Access: In person only. Visitors must perform in person searches for themselves. No search fee. Required to search: name, years to search, DOB; also helpful: SSN. Criminal records archived in office last 10 years. Prior to 1982, records are not very accurate because of fire. Dist Court records on computer back to 2001; General Sessions to mid-2000.
General Information: Public Access terminal is available. No juvenile records released. Will fax results for $1.00 per page. Copy fee: $1.00 per page. Cert fee: $6.00. Payee: Circuit Court, or General Sessions Clerk. Personal checks accepted. Prepayment required.

Chancery Court 1 Public Sq, Rm 302, Smithville, TN 37166; 615-597-4360. Hours: 8AM-4PM (CST). *Civil, Probate.*
Civil Records: Access: In person only. Visitors must perform in person searches for themselves. No search fee. Required to search: name, years to search. Civil cases indexed by defendant, plaintiff. Civil records on books, computerized as of 6/00.
General Information: Public Access terminal is available. No adoption, juvenile records released. Copy fee: $1.00 per page. Cert fee: $6.00. Payee: Clerk and Master. Personal checks accepted. Prepayment required.

Decatur County

24th District Circuit & General Sessions Court PO Box 488, Decaturville, TN 38329; 731-852-3125; Fax: 731-852-2130. Hours: 8AM-4PM M,T,TH,F; 8AM-Noon W & Sat (CST). *Felony, Misdemeanor, Civil, Eviction, Small Claims.*
Civil Records: Access: In person only. Visitors must perform in person searches for themselves. No search fee. Required to search: name, years to search. Civil cases indexed by defendant, plaintiff. Civil records archived on books from 1927; computerized records since 1996.
Criminal Records: Access: In person only. Visitors must perform in person searches for themselves. No search fee. Required to search: name, years to search, DOB, SSN, signed release. Criminal records archived on books from 1927; computerized records since 1996.
General Information: No adoption records released. Copy fee: $1.00 per page. Cert fee: $2.00 per page. Payee: Circuit Court. Business checks accepted. Prepayment required.

Chancery Court Clerk & Master, Decaturville, TN 38329; 731-852-3422; Fax: 731-852-2130. Hours: 9M-4PM M,T,TH,F; 9AM-Noon W (CST). *Civil, Probate.*
Civil Records: Access: In person only. Visitors must perform in person searches for themselves. No search fee. Required to search: name, years to search. Civil cases indexed by plaintiff. Probate records in books since 1869 for probate, civil records in books since 1958.
General Information: No adoption records released. Copy fee: $.25 per page. Cert fee: $2.00. Payee: Elizabeth Carpenter, Clerk and Master. Personal checks accepted. Prepayment required.

Dickson County

23rd District Circuit Court Court Sq, PO Box 70, Charlotte, TN 37036; 615-789-7010; Fax: 615-789-7018. Hours: 8AM-4PM (CST). *Felony, Misdemeanor, Civil Actions Over $15,000.*
Civil Records: Access: Phone, fax, mail, in person. Both court and visitors may perform in person searches. Search fee: $6.00 per name. Required to search: name, years to search. Civil cases indexed by defendant, plaintiff. Civil records archived from 1800s, on computer from 1986, some records back to 1974.
Criminal Records: Access: Phone, fax, mail, in person. Both court and visitors may perform in person searches. Search fee: $6.00 per name. Required to search: name, years to search; also helpful: DOB. Criminal records archived from 1800s, on computer from 1986, some records back to 1974.
General Information: No adoption records released. Will fax results $6.00 per document. Copy fee: $.50 per page. Cert fee: $2.00. Payee: Circuit Court Clerk. Personal checks accepted. Prepayment required. Mail requests: SASE required. Mail turnaround time 1 day.

General Sessions PO Box 217, Charlotte, TN 37036; 615-789-5414; Fax: 615-789-3456. Hours: 8AM-4PM (CST). *Civil Actions Under $15,000, Eviction, Small Claims.*
Civil Records: Access: Phone, mail, in person. Both court and visitors may perform in person searches. Search fee: $6.00. Required to search: name, years to search. Civil cases indexed by defendant. Civil records archived since court began, on computer from Aug 1991.
General Information: No sealed or expunged records released. Copy fee: $.50 per page. Cert fee: $3.00. Payee: General Sessions. Personal checks accepted. Prepayment required. Mail requests: SASE required. Mail turnaround time 2-3 days.

County Court Court Sq, 4000 Hwy 48 N, #1, Charlotte, TN 37036; 615-789-0250. Hours: 8AM-4PM (CST). *Probate.*

Dyer County

29th District Circuit & General Sessions Court
PO Box 1360, Dyersburg, TN 38025; 731-286-7809; Fax: 731-288-7728. Hours: 8:30AM-4:30PM (CST). *Felony, Misdemeanor, Civil, Eviction, Small Claims.*

Note: Public access terminal is available, and public may also search books.

Civil Records: Access: Mail, in person. Both court and visitors may perform in person searches. Search fee: $25.00 per name. Required to search: name, years to search. Civil cases indexed by defendant, plaintiff. Civil records archived since 1992.

Criminal Records: Access: Mail, in person. Both court and visitors may perform in person searches. Search fee: $25.00 per name. Required to search: name, years to search, DOB, SSN. Criminal records archived since 1992.

General Information: Public Access terminal is available. No juvenile records released. Copy fee: $1.00 per page. No cert fee. Payee: Circuit Court, or General Sessions Clerk. Personal checks not accepted. Prepayment required. Mail requests: SASE required. Mail turnaround time 2 weeks.

Chancery Court
PO Box 1360, Dyersburg, TN 38024; 731-286-7818; Fax: 731-288-7706. Hours: 8:30AM-4:30PM M-F (CST). *Civil, Probate.*

Civil Records: Access: Mail, in person. Both court and visitors may perform in person searches. No search fee. Required to search: name, years to search. Civil cases indexed by defendant, plaintiff. Civil records on books.

General Information: No adoption, juvenile records released. Copy fee: $.50 per page. Cert fee: $1.00. Payee: Chancery Court Clerk. Personal checks accepted. Prepayment required. Mail requests: SASE requested. Turnaround time 1 week.

Fayette County

25th District Circuit & General Sessions Court
PO Box 670, Somerville, TN 38068; 901-465-5205; Fax: 901-465-5215. Hours: 9AM-5PM (CST). *Felony, Misdemeanor, Civil, Eviction, Small Claims.*

Civil Records: Access: In person only. Visitors must perform in person searches for themselves. No search fee. Required to search: name, years to search. Civil cases indexed by defendant, plaintiff. Civil records on computer since 1991, prior records archived since court began, some older records destroyed by fire.

Criminal Records: Access: In person only. Visitors must perform in person searches for themselves. No search fee. Required to search: name, years to search, DOB, SSN. Criminal records on computer since 1991, prior records archived since court began, some older records destroyed by fire.

General Information: Public Access terminal is available. No adoption or sealed records released. Copy fee: $.25 per page. Cert fee: $6.00. Payee: Circuit Court, or General Sessions Clerk. Personal checks accepted. Prepayment required.

Chancery Court
PO Drawer 220, Somerville, TN 38068; 901-465-5220; Fax: 901-465-5217. Hours: 9AM-5PM (CST). *Civil, Probate.*

Civil Records: Access: In person only. Visitors must perform in person searches for themselves. No search fee. Required to search: name, years to search. Civil cases indexed by defendant, plaintiff. Civil records on computer since 10/92; on books.

General Information: Public Access terminal is available. No adoption records released. Will fax

specific case file copies. Copy fee: $1.00 per page. Cert fee: $4.00 for 1st page, $2.00 each add'l page. Payee: Clerk and Master. Personal checks accepted. Prepayment required.

Fentress County

8th District Circuit & General Sessions Court
PO Box 699, Jamestown, TN 38556; 931-879-7919; Fax: 931-879-3014. Hours: 8AM-4PM M-F; 8AM-Noon Sat (CST). *Felony, Misdemeanor, Civil, Eviction, Small Claims.*

Civil Records: Access: Mail, in person. Both court and visitors may perform in person searches. Search fee: $25.00 per name. Required to search: name, years to search. Civil cases indexed by defendant, plaintiff. Civil records archived from 1800s, readily available for 20 years.

Criminal Records: Access: Mail, in person, fax. Both court and visitors may perform in person searches. Search fee: $25.00 per name. Required to search: name, years to search, DOB, SSN. Criminal records archived from 1800s, readily available for 20 years.

General Information: No juvenile records released. Copy fee: $.25 per page. Cert fee: $2.00. Payee: Circuit Court Clerk or General Session. Personal checks accepted. Prepayment required. Mail requests: SASE required. Mail turnaround time 5 days.

Chancery Court
PO Box 66, Jamestown, TN 38556; 931-879-8615; Fax: 931-879-4236. Hours: 9AM-5PM M,T,TH,F; 9AM-Noon W (CST). *Civil, Probate.*

Civil Records: Access: Mail, in person. Both court and visitors may perform in person searches. No search fee. Required to search: name, years to search. Civil cases indexed by defendant, plaintiff. Civil records in books.

General Information: No sealed or adoption records released. Copy fee: $.25 per page. Cert fee: $4.00. Payee: Clerk and Master. Personal checks accepted. Prepayment required. Mail turnaround time 1-5 days.

Franklin County

12th District Circuit Court & General Sessions
1 S Jefferson St, Winchester, TN 37398; 931-967-2923; Fax: 931-962-1479. Hours: 8AM-4:30PM (CST). *Felony, Misdemeanor, Civil, Eviction, Small Claims.*

Civil Records: Access: Mail, in person. Both court and visitors may perform in person searches. Search fee: $10.00 per name. Required to search: name, years to search. Civil cases indexed by defendant, plaintiff. Civil records archived on docket books from 1940s, on computer since mid 1991.

Criminal Records: Access: Mail, in person. Both court and visitors may perform in person searches. Search fee: $10.00 per name. Required to search: name, years to search, DOB; also helpful: SSN. Criminal records archived on docket books from 1940s, on computer since mid 1991.

General Information: Public Access terminal is available. No juvenile records released. Will fax results. Copy fee: $.25 per page. Cert fee: $4.00. Payee: Circuit Court Clerk or General Session. Business checks accepted. Prepayment required. Mail turnaround time 1 week.

County Court
1 S Jefferson St, Winchester, TN 37398; 931-962-1485; Fax: 931-962-3394. Hours: 8AM-4:30PM (CST). *Probate.*

Gibson County

28th District Circuit & General Sessions Court
295 N College, PO Box 147, Trenton, TN 38382; 731-855-7615; Fax: 731-855-7676. Hours: 8AM-4:30PM (CST). *Felony, Misdemeanor, Civil,*

Eviction, Small Claims.

Civil Records: Access: Fax, mail, in person. Both court and visitors may perform in person searches. Search fee: $5.00 per name. Required to search: name, years to search; also helpful: address. Civil cases indexed by defendant, plaintiff. Civil records archived in vault mid 1800s, in office since 1982. On computer since 1990.

Criminal Records: Access: Fax, mail, in person. Both court and visitors may perform in person searches. Search fee: $5.00 per name. Required to search: name, years to search; also helpful: address, DOB, SSN. Criminal records archived in vault mid 1800s, in office since 1982. On computer since 1990.

General Information: Public Access terminal is available. No adoption or expunged records released. No fee to fax results. Copy fee: $.25 per page. $3.00 maximum fee. Cert fee: $5.00. Payee: Circuit Court Clerk. Business checks accepted. In-state checks accepted. Prepayment required. Mail requests: SASE requested. Turnaround time 1-3 days.

Chancery Court
Clerk & Master, PO Box 290, Trenton, TN 38382; 731-855-7639; Fax: 731-855-7655. Hours: 8AM-4:30PM (CST). *Civil, Probate.*

Civil Records: Access: In person only. Visitors must perform in person searches for themselves. No search fee. Required to search: name, years to search. Civil cases indexed by defendant, plaintiff. Probate records in this office since 9/82, prior records filed in County Clerk's office, computerized records go back to 1967.

General Information: Public Access terminal is available. No adoption, commitment records released. Will fax results $10.00 per doc. Copy fee: $1.00 per page. Cert fee: $6.00. Payee: Clerk & Master. Money orders or certified checks accepted. No personal checks. Prepayment required.

Giles County

22nd District Circuit & General Sessions Court
PO Box 678, Pulaski, TN 38478; 931-363-5311; Fax: 931-424-4790. Hours: 8AM-4PM (CST). *Felony, Misdemeanor, Civil, Eviction, Small Claims.*

Civil Records: Access: mail, fax, in-person. Both court and visitors may perform in person searches. Search fee: $20.00 per name. Required to search: name, years to search. Civil cases indexed by defendant, plaintiff. Civil records on computer from 1/90, remaining records filed in docket books.

Criminal Records: Access: Phone, mail, fax, in person. Both court and visitors may perform in person searches. Search fee: $20.00 per name. Required to search: name, years to search, DOB; also helpful: SSN. Criminal records on computer from 1/90, remaining records filed in docket books.

General Information: Public Access terminal is available. No juvenile records released without signed release. Copy fee: $.25 per page. Cert fee: $6.00. Payee: Circuit Court Clerk. Prepayment required. Mail requests: SASE required. Mail turnaround time 1 week.

County Court
PO Box 678, Pulaski, TN 38478; 931-363-1509; Fax: 931-424-4795. Hours: 8AM-4PM M-F (CST). *Probate.*

Grainger County

4th District Circuit & General Sessions Court
PO Box 157, Rutledge, TN 37861; 865-828-3605. Hours: 8:30AM-4:30PM (EST). *Felony, Misdemeanor, Civil, Eviction, Small Claims.*

Civil Records: Access: In person only. Visitors must perform in person searches for themselves. No search fee. Required to search: name, years to search. Civil cases indexed by defendant, plaintiff. Civil records archived from 1977 in office.

Criminal Records: Access: In person only. Visitors must perform in person searches for themselves. No search fee. Required to search: name, years to search, DOB, SSN. Criminal records archived from 1977 in office.

General Information: Public Access terminal is available. No sealed records released. Copy fee: $1.00 per page. Cert fee: $4.00. Payee: Circuit Court Clerk. Business checks accepted. Prepayment required.

Chancery Court Clerk & Master, PO Box 160, Rutledge, TN 37861; 865-828-4436; Fax: 865-828-8714. Hours: 8:30AM-4:30PM M,T,Th,F, 8:30AM-Noon Wed (EST). *Civil, Probate.*

Civil Records: Access: Phone, fax, mail, in person. Both court and visitors may perform in person searches. No search fee. Required to search: name, years to search. Civil cases indexed by defendant, plaintiff. Civil records on books.

General Information: No adoption records released. Will fax results to local or toll free line. Copy fee: $1.00 per page. Cert fee: $4.00. Payee: Clerk & Master. Personal checks accepted. Prepayment required. Mail requests: SASE requested. Turnaround time varies.

Greene County

3rd District Circuit & General Sessions
Court 101 S Main, Geene County Courthouse, Greeneville, TN 37743; 423-798-1760; Fax: 423-798-1763. Hours: 8AM-4:30PM (EST). *Felony, Misdemeanor, Civil, Eviction, Small Claims.*

Civil Records: Access: In person only. Visitors must perform in person searches for themselves. No search fee. Required to search: name, years to search. Civil cases indexed by defendant, plaintiff. Civil records archived since court started, on computer from end of 1990.

Criminal Records: Access: In person only. Visitors must perform in person searches for themselves. No search fee. Required to search: name, years to search. Criminal records archived since court started, on computer from end of 1990.

General Information: Public Access terminal is available. No adoption records released. Copy fee: $1.00 per page. Cert fee: $3.00. Payee: Circuit Court Clerk. Personal checks accepted. Prepayment required.

County Court 204 N Cutler St, #200, County Courthouse Annex, Greeneville, TN 37745; 423-798-1708, 798-1709; Fax: 423-798-1822. Hours: 8AM-4:30PM (EST). *Probate.*

Grundy County

12th District Circuit & General Sessions
Court PO Box 161, Altamont, TN 37301; 931-692-3368; Fax: 931-692-2414. Hours: 8AM-4PM M-Th; 8AM-5PM F (CST). *Felony, Misdemeanor, Civil, Eviction, Small Claims.*

Civil Records: Access: Mail, fax, in person. Both court and visitors may perform in person searches. Search fee: $10.00 per name. Fee is per court. Required to search: name, years to search. Civil cases indexed by defendant, plaintiff. Civil records on computer since 1993, prior records in books to 1990. Before 1990 on microfiche since 1868.

Criminal Records: Access: Mail, fax, in person. Both court and visitors may perform in person searches. Search fee: $10.00 per name. Fee is per court. Required to search: name, years to search, DOB; also helpful: SSN. Criminal records on computer since 1993, prior records in books to 1990. Before 1990 on microfiche since 1868.

General Information: No juvenile records released. Fee to fax results is $4.00 per document. Copy fee: $1.00 per page. Cert fee: $5.00. Payee: Circuit Court

Clerk. Prepayment required. Mail turnaround time 5 days.

Chancery Court PO Box 174, Altamont, TN 37301; 931-692-3455; Fax: 931-692-4125. Hours: 8AM-4PM M-Th; 8AM-5pm F (CST). *Civil, Probate.*

Civil Records: Access: Phone, mail, in person. Both court and visitors may perform in person searches. Search fee: $5.00 per name. Required to search: name, years to search. Civil cases indexed by defendant, plaintiff. Civil records on computer since 1993, on books back to 1990.

General Information: No adoption records released. Will fax results to local or toll free line. Copy fee: $.25 per page. Cert fee: $2.00. Payee: Clerk & Master. Personal checks accepted. Prepayment required. Mail requests: SASE requested. Turnaround time 5 days.

Hamblen County

3rd District Circuit & General Sessions
Court 510 Allison St, Morristown, TN 37814; 423-586-5640; Fax: 423-585-2764. Hours: 8AM-4PM M-Th, 8AM-5PM Fri, 9-11:30AM Sat (CST). *Felony, Misdemeanor, Civil, Eviction, Small Claims.*

Civil Records: Access: Mail, in person. Both court and visitors may perform in person searches. Search fee: $5.00 per name. Required to search: name, years to search. Civil cases indexed by defendant, plaintiff. Civil records archived from early 1900s, on computer from 1989.

Criminal Records: Access: Mail, in person. Both court and visitors may perform in person searches. Search fee: $5.00 per name. Required to search: name, years to search, DOB; also helpful: SSN. Criminal records archived from early 1900s, on computer from 1989.

General Information: Public Access terminal is available. No adoption records released. Copy fee: $.25 per page. Cert fee: $4.00. Payee: Circuit Court Clerk or General Sessions. Personal checks accepted. Prepayment required. Mail requests: SASE required. Mail turnaround time 1 day.

Chancery Court 511 W 2nd North St, Morristown, TN 37814; 423-586-9112; Fax: 423-318-2510. Hours: 8AM-4PM M-Th; 8AM-4:30PM F (EST). *Civil.*

Civil Records: Access: Phone, fax, mail, in person. Both court and visitors may perform in person searches. No search fee. Required to search: name, years to search. Civil cases indexed by defendant, plaintiff. Civil records on computer from 1979; prior on books back to 1870s.

General Information: Public Access terminal is available. (Public terminal for civil in person searches.) No adoption records released. Will fax results $1.00 per page. Copy fee: $.50 per page. Cert fee: $2.00 plus $1.00 per page. Payee: Clerk & Master. Personal checks accepted. Prepayment required. Mail turnaround time 3-5 days.

Hamilton County

11th District Civil Court
Rm 500 Courthouse, 625 Georgia Ave, Chattanooga, TN 37402; 423-209-6700; Fax: 423-209-6701. Hours: 8AM-4PM (EST). *Civil Actions Over $15,000.*
www.hamiltontn.gov/courts

Civil Records: Access: Phone, fax, mail, in person, online. Both court and visitors may perform in person searches. No search fee. Required to search: name, years to search. Civil cases indexed by defendant, plaintiff. Civil records archived from 1921, on computer back to 7/89. Court minutes are on microfiche. Online access to current court dockets are free   at

www.hamiltontn.gov/courts/CircuitClerk/dockets/default.htm.

General Information: Public Access terminal is available. No adoptions or judicial hospitalization records released. Will fax results to local numbers only. Copy fee: $2.00 per page. Cert fee: $4.00. Payee: Circuit Court Clerk. Personal checks accepted. Prepayment required. Mail turnaround time 1 week.

11th District General Sessions Court
Civil Division, 600 Market St, Rm 111, Chattanooga, TN 37402; 423-209-7630; Fax: 423-209-7631. Hours: 8AM-4PM (EST). *Civil Actions Under $15,000, Eviction, Small Claims.*
www.hamiltontn.gov/courts/sessions/default.htm

Civil Records: Access: Phone, mail, in person, online. Both court and visitors may perform in person searches. No search fee. Required to search: name, years to search. Civil cases indexed by defendant, plaintiff. Civil records archived on docket books, on computer from 6/1985. Online access to current court dockets is free at www.hamiltontn.gov/Courts/Sessions/dockets/default.htm.

General Information: Public Access terminal is available. No mental health records released. Copy fee: $1.00 per page. Cert fee: $4.00. Payee: Sessions Court Clerk. Personal checks accepted. Prepayment required. Mail turnaround time 3-4 days.

11th District Criminal Court
600 Market St, Rm 102, Chattanooga, TN 37402; 423-209-7500; Fax: 423-209-7501. Hours: 8AM-4PM (EST). *Felony, Misdemeanor.*
www.hamiltontn.gov/courts

Criminal Records: Access: Mail, in person, online. Both court and visitors may perform in person searches. Search fee: $10.00 per name. Required to search: name, years to search, DOB, signed release; also helpful: SSN. Criminal records on computer since 1990, prior records in books. Online access to current court dockets is free at www.hamiltontn.gov/Courts/CriminalClerk/dockets/default.htm.

General Information: Public Access terminal is available. No juvenile records released. Copy fee: $1.00 per page. No cert fee. Payee: Criminal Court Clerk. Only cashiers checks and money orders accepted. Prepayment required. Mail requests: SASE helpful. Turnaround time 1 week.

Chancery Court Chancery Court, Clerk & Master, 201 E 7th St, Rm 300, Chattanooga, TN 37402; 423-209-6600; Fax: 423-209-6601. Hours: 8AM-4PM (EST). *Civil, Probate.*
www.hamiltontn.gov/Courts/ClerkMaster/default.htm

Civil Records: Access: Phone, mail, in person, online. Both court and visitors may perform in person searches. No search fee. Required to search: name, years to search. Civil cases indexed by defendant, plaintiff. Civil records on index cards from 1919, on dockets from 6/56, microfilm: wills since 1862, inventories since 1911, settlements since 1869, bonds and letters since 1878. Chancery dockets are online at www.hamiltontn.gov/Courts/Chancery/dockets/default.htm.

General Information: Public Access terminal is available. No mental health, adoption records released. Will fax results $1.00 per page. Copy fee: $1.00 per page 1-5 pages; $2.00 each 5-10 pages; $.25 over 10. Cert fee: $4.00 ($10 if Act of Congress) plus $2.00 per page. Payee: Hamilton County Clerk and Master. Personal checks accepted. Prepayment required. Mail requests: SASE required. Mail turnaround time 2-3 days.

Hancock County

3rd District Circuit & General Sessions

Court PO Box 347, Sneedville, TN 37869; 423-733-2954; Fax: 423-733-2119. Hours: 8AM-4PM, W S 8-12:00 (EST). *Felony, Misdemeanor, Civil, Eviction, Small Claims.*

Civil Records: Access: Mail, in person. Both court and visitors may perform in person searches. Search fee: $4.00 per name. Required to search: name, years to search. Civil cases indexed by plaintiff. Civil records archived on books from 1934.

Criminal Records: Access: Mail, in person. Both court and visitors may perform in person searches. Search fee: $4.00 per name. Required to search: name, years to search, DOB; also helpful: SSN. Criminal records archived on books from 1934.

General Information: No juvenile records released. Will fax results. Copy fee: $.50 per page. No cert fee. Payee: Circuit Court Clerk. Personal checks accepted. Prepayment required. Mail turnaround time 3-4 days.

Chancery Court PO Box 277, Sneedville, TN 37869; 423-733-4524; Fax: 423-733-2762. Hours: 8AM-4PM (EST). *Civil, Probate.*

Civil Records: Access: Mail, in person. Both court and visitors may perform in person searches. No search fee. Required to search: name, years to search. Civil cases indexed by defendant, plaintiff. Civil records on books.

General Information: Public Access terminal is available. No adoption records released. Copy fee: $.50 per page. Cert fee: $1.00. Payee: Clerk & Master. Personal checks accepted. Prepayment required. Mail requests: SASE requested. Turnaround time 2 days.

Hardeman County

25th District Circuit & General Sessions

Court Courthouse, 100 N Main, Bolivar, TN 38008; 731-658-6524; Fax: 731-658-4584. Hours: 8:30AM-4:30PM M-Th, 8AM-5PM Fri (CST). *Felony, Misdemeanor, Civil, Eviction, Small Claims.*

Civil Records: Access: In person only. Visitors must perform in person searches for themselves. No search fee. Required to search: name, years to search. Civil cases indexed by defendant, plaintiff. Civil records on computer since 12/92, archived General Sessions from 1960 and Circuit from 1800s.

Criminal Records: Access: In person only. Visitors must perform in person searches for themselves. No search fee. Required to search: name, years to search, DOB, SSN, signed release. Criminal records on computer since 12/92, archived General Sessions from 1960 and Circuit from 1800s.

General Information: No juvenile records released. Copy fee: $1.00 per page. Cert fee: $4.00 per document. Payee: Circuit Court Clerk. Only cashiers checks and money orders accepted. Hardeman county personal checks accepted. Prepayment required.

Chancery Court PO Box 45, Bolivar, TN 38008; 731-658-3142; Fax: 731-658-4580. Hours: 8:30AM-4:30PM M-TH, 8:30AM-5PM F (CST). *Civil, Probate.*

Civil Records: Access: Phone, mail, fax, in person. Both court and visitors may perform in person searches. No search fee. Required to search: name, years to search. Civil cases indexed by defendant, plaintiff. Civil records on books back to 1825; computerized back to 1975.

General Information: Public Access terminal is available. No mental health, adoption records released. Fee to fax results is $1.00 per page. Copy fee: $.50 per page. Additional fee for postage. Cert fee: $2.00 per page. Payee: Chancery Court Clerk. Business checks accepted. Prepayment required. Mail requests: SASE requested. Turnaround time 1 day.

Hardin County

24th District Circuit & General Sessions

Court 601 Main St, Savannah, TN 38372; 731-925-3583; Fax: 731-926-2955. Hours: 8AM-4:30PM M,T,TH,F, 8AM-Noon W (CST). *Felony, Misdemeanor, Civil, Eviction, Small Claims.*

Civil Records: Access: In person only. Visitors must perform in person searches for themselves. No search fee. Required to search: name, years to search. Civil cases indexed by defendant, plaintiff. Civil records archived on books and on microfiche from 1800s, on computer from 1996.

Criminal Records: Access: In person only. Visitors must perform in person searches for themselves. No search fee. Required to search: name, years to search. Criminal records archived on books and on microfiche from 1800s, on computer from 1996.

General Information: No juvenile records released. Copy fee: $.50 per page. Cert fee: $5.00. Payee: Circuit Court Clerk. Hardin county personal checks accepted. Prepayment required.

County Court 601 Main St, Savannah, TN 38372; 731-925-3921; Fax: 731-926-4313. Hours: 8AM-4:30PM M,T,TH,F, 8AM-12PM W & Sat (CST). *Probate.*

Hawkins County

3rd District Circuit & General Sessions

Court 100 E Main St, Rogersville, TN 37857; 423-272-3397; Fax: 423-272-9646. Hours: 8AM-4PM (EST). *Felony, Misdemeanor, Civil, Eviction, Small Claims.*

Civil Records: Access: In person only. Visitors must perform in person searches for themselves. No search fee. Required to search: name, years to search. Civil cases indexed by defendant, plaintiff. Civil records archived on books from 1800s.

Criminal Records: Access: In person only. Visitors must perform in person searches for themselves. No search fee. Required to search: name, years to search. Criminal records archived on books from 1800s.

General Information: Public Access terminal is available. No juvenile records released. Copy fee: $1.00 per page. Cert fee: $4.00 ($6 if Acts of Congress) plus $2.00 per page. Payee: Circuit Court Clerk. No personal checks accepted.

Chancery Court PO Box 908, Rogersville, TN 37857; 423-272-8150. Hours: 8AM-4PM (EST). *Civil, Probate.*

Civil Records: Access: In person, mail. Visitors must perform in person searches for themselves. Search fee: no fee, except for genealogy. Required to search: name, years to search. Civil cases indexed by defendant, plaintiff. Civil records on index books from 1927 to present.

General Information: No adoption records released. Copy fee: $1.00 per page. Cert fee: $2.00. Payee: Hawkins County Clerk and Master. Personal checks accepted. Prepayment required.

Haywood County

28th District Circuit & General Sessions

Court 1 N Washington Ave, Brownsville, TN 38012; 731-772-1112; Fax: 731-772-8139. Hours: 8:30AM-5PM (CST). *Felony, Misdemeanor, Civil, Eviction, Small Claims.*

Civil Records: Access: Phone, mail, fax, in person. Both court and visitors may perform in person searches. No search fee. Required to search: name, years to search. Civil cases indexed by defendant, plaintiff. Civil records on computer since 8/1991, prior archived since the 1800s.

Criminal Records: Access: Phone, mail, fax, in person. Both court and visitors may perform in person

searches. No search fee. Required to search: name, years to search, DOB; also helpful: SSN. Criminal records on computer since 8/1991, prior archived since the 1800s.

General Information: No juvenile records released. Copy fee: $1.00 per page. Cert fee: $3.50. Payee: Circuit Court Clerk. No personal checks accepted. Prepayment required. Mail turnaround time dependent upon search.

Chancery Court 1 N Washington, PO Box 356, Brownsville, TN 38012; 731-772-0122; Fax: 731-772-7802. Hours: 8:30AM-5PM (CST). *Civil, Probate.*

Civil Records: Access: In person only. Visitors must perform in person searches for themselves. No search fee. Required to search: name, years to search. Civil cases indexed by defendant, plaintiff. Probate records on books since 9/82; other records go back to 1800s.

General Information: No adoption or sealed records released. Copy fee: $1.00 per page. Cert fee: $5.00. Payee: Chancery Court. Personal checks accepted. Prepayment required. Mail turnaround time 2 days.

Henderson County

26th District Circuit & General Sessions

Court 17 Monroe Ave, #9, Henderson County Courthouse, Lexington, TN 38351; 731-968-2031; Fax: 731-967-9441 (criminal). Hours: 8AM-4:30PM M,T,TH,F (CST). *Felony, Misdemeanor, Civil, Eviction, Small Claims.*

Civil Records: Access: Mail, in person. Both court and visitors may perform in person searches. Search fee: $6.00 per name. Required to search: name, years to search. Civil cases indexed by defendant, plaintiff. Civil records on cards or books, archived from 1800s; on computer back 5 years.

Criminal Records: Access: Mail, in person. Both court and visitors may perform in person searches. Search fee: $6.00 per name. Required to search: name, years to search, DOB; also helpful- SSN. Criminal records on cards or books, archived from 1800s; on computer back 5 years.

General Information: Public Access terminal is available. No sealed indictment records released. Will fax results for $10.00 per document. Copy fee: $3.00 per page. Cert fee: $6.00. Payee: Circuit Court Clerk. No personal checks accepted. Prepayment required. Mail requests: SASE required. Mail turnaround time 1-2 weeks.

Chancery Court 17 Monroe, Rm 2, 2nd Fl, Lexington, TN 38351; 731-968-2801; Fax: 731-967-5380. Hours: 8AM-4:30PM (CST). *Civil, Probate.*

Civil Records: Access: Phone, mail, fax, in person. Both court and visitors may perform in person searches. Court will only do recent searches that may be found on computer. Search fee: none. Required to search: name, years to search. Civil cases indexed by defendant, plaintiff. Civil records on computer back to 6/2000; prior in books to 1895.

General Information: No confidential adoption records released. Fee to fax results is $2.00 per page. Copy fee: $2.00 per page. Cert fee: $2.00. Payee: Chancery Court. Only cashiers checks and money orders accepted. Prepayment required. Mail requests: SASE required. Mail turnaround time dependent on search length.

Henry County

24th District Circuit & General Sessions

Court PO Box 429, Paris, TN 38242; 731-642-0461; Fax: 731-642-1244. Hours: 8AM-4:30PM (CST). *Felony, Misdemeanor, Civil, Eviction, Small Claims.*

Note: The General Sessions Court records date to 1962, when court was created.

Civil Records: Access: Fax, mail, in person. Both court and visitors may perform in person searches. Search fee: $5.00. Required to search: name, years to search. Civil cases indexed by defendant, plaintiff. Civil records archived from 1820s (you search) or 1900s (they search); General Sessions on computer from 1991.

Criminal Records: Access: Fax, mail, in person. Both court and visitors may perform in person searches. Search fee: $5.00. Required to search: name, years to search; also helpful: SSN, DOB. Criminal records archived from 1820s to 1939, (you search) or 1940 present (they search); General Sessions on computer from 1991.

General Information: Public Access terminal is available. No juvenile records released. Will fax results only of account is set up before hand. Copy fee: $.25 per page. Cert fee: $2.00. Payee: Circuit Court Clerk or General Sessions Court Clerk. Personal checks accepted. Prepayment required. Mail turnaround time 1-2 weeks.

County Court PO Box 24, Paris, TN 38242; 731-642-2412; Fax: 731-644-0947. Hours: 8AM-4:30PM (CST). *Probate.*

Hickman County

21st District Circuit & General Sessions
Court 104 College Ave, #204, Centerville, TN 37033; 931-729-2211; Probate phone: 931-729-2522; Fax: 931-729-6141. Hours: 8AM-4PM (CST). *Felony, Misdemeanor, Civil, Eviction, Small Claims.*
Civil Records: Access: Mail, fax, in person. Both court and visitors may perform in person searches. Search fee: $10.00. Required to search: name, years to search. Civil cases indexed by defendant, plaintiff. Civil records on computer since 1993, prior records on books to 1849.
Criminal Records: Access: Mail, fax, in person. Both court and visitors may perform in person searches. Search fee: $10.00. Required to search: name, years to search. Criminal records on computer since 1993, prior records on books to 1849.
General Information: No juvenile records released. Will fax results if copy of check also faxed. Copy fee: $1.00 per page. Cert fee: $5.00. Payee: Circuit Court Clerk. No personal checks accepted. Prepayment required.

Chancery Court 104 College Ave, #202, Centerville, TN 37033; 931-729-2522; Fax: 931-729-3726. Hours: 8AM-4PM (CST). *Civil, Probate.*
Civil Records: Access: Mail, in person. Both court and visitors may perform in person searches. No search fee. Required to search: name, years to search. Civil cases indexed by defendant, plaintiff. Civil records on books since 1965; computerized records since 1984.
General Information: No confidential or adoption records released. Will fax results for $2.00 per page. Copy fee: $1.00 per page. Cert fee: $3.00. Payee: Clerk & Master. Personal checks accepted. Prepayment required. Mail requests: SASE requested. Turnaround time 1 week.

Houston County

23rd District Circuit & General Sessions
Court PO Box 403, Erin, TN 37061; 931-289-4673; Fax: 931-289-5182. Hours: 8AM-4:30PM (CST). *Felony, Misdemeanor, Civil, Eviction, Small Claims.*
Civil Records: Access: In person only. Visitors must perform in person searches for themselves. No search fee. Required to search: name, years to search. Civil cases indexed by defendant, plaintiff. Civil records archived from 1930s in books. This office does not do record searches anymore.

Criminal Records: Access: In person only. Visitors must perform in person searches for themselves. No search fee. Required to search: name, years to search, DOB; also helpful: SSN. Criminal records archived from 1930s in books. This office does not do record searches anymore.
General Information: No juvenile records released. Copy fee: $.25 per page. Cert fee: $3.50. Payee: Circuit Court Clerk. Personal checks accepted. Prepayment required.

Chancery Court PO Box 332, Erin, TN 37061; 931-289-3870; Fax: 931-289-5679. Hours: 8AM-4PM (CST). *Civil, Probate.*
Civil Records: Access: Mail, in person. Both court and visitors may perform in person searches. No search fee. Required to search: name, years to search. Civil cases indexed by defendant, plaintiff. Civil records on books. All requests must be in writing.
General Information: No adoption records released. Copy fee: $.25 per page. Cert fee: $3.50. Payee: Clerk & Master. Personal checks accepted. Prepayment required. Mail turnaround time 2 days.

Humphreys County

23rd District Circuit & General Sessions
Court Rm 106, Waverly, TN 37185; 931-296-2461; Fax: 931-296-1651. Hours: 8AM-4:30PM (CST). *Felony, Misdemeanor, Civil, Eviction, Small Claims.*
Civil Records: Access: Phone, fax, mail, in person. Both court and visitors may perform in person searches. Search fee: $1.00 per name per year. If more than 15 years, the fee is a flat $25.00. Required to search: name, years to search. Civil cases indexed by defendant, plaintiff. Civil records archived from early 1900s, on computer back to 1989.
Criminal Records: Access: Phone, fax, mail, in person. Both court and visitors may perform in person searches. Search fee: $1.00 per name per year. If more than 15 years, the fee is a flat $25.00. Required to search: name, years to search, DOB, SSN, signed release. Criminal records archived from early 1900s, on computer back to 1989.
General Information: No expunged records released. Copy fee: $.25 per page. Cert fee: $2.00 for the document seal plus $2.00 per page. Payee: Donna McLeod, Rm 106, Courthouse, Waverly TN. Business checks accepted. Prepayment required. Mail requests: SASE required. Mail turnaround time same day.

County Court Clerk, Rm 2, Courthouse Annex, Waverly, TN 37185; 931-296-7671, 931-296-6503; Fax: 931-296-0823. Hours: 8AM-4:30PM (CST). *Probate.*

Jackson County

15th District Circuit & General Sessions
Court PO Box 205, Gainesboro, TN 38562; 931-268-9314; Fax: 931-268-4555. Hours: 8AM-4PM M,T,TH,F; 8AM-3PM W; 8AM-Noon Sat (CST). *Felony, Misdemeanor, Civil, Eviction, Small Claims.*
Civil Records: Access: Fax, mail, in person. Both court and visitors may perform in person searches. Search fee: $5.00 per name. Required to search: name, years to search. Civil cases indexed by defendant, plaintiff. Civil records archived from 1900s in books, computerized since 2000.
Criminal Records: Access: Fax, mail, in person. Both court and visitors may perform in person searches. Search fee: $5.00 per name. Required to search: name, years to search, DOB; also helpful: SSN. Criminal records archived from 1900s in books, computerized since 2000.
General Information: No juvenile records released. Copy fee: $.50 per page (first 24 are free). Cert fee: $5.00. Payee: Circuit Court Clerk. Business checks

accepted. Prepayment required. Mail requests: SASE required. Mail turnaround time 1 week.

Chancery Court PO Box 733, Gainesboro, TN 38562-0733; 931-268-9516; Fax: 931-268-9512. Hours: 8AM-4PM M,T,TH,F; 8AM-3PM W (CST). *Probate.*
www.jacksonco.com

Jefferson County

4th District Circuit & General Sessions
Court PO Box 671, Dandridge, TN 37725; 865-397-2786; Fax: 865-397-4894. Hours: 8AM-4PM M-F (EST). *Felony, Misdemeanor, Civil, Eviction, Small Claims.*
Civil Records: Access: Mail, in person. Both court and visitors may perform in person searches. No search fee. Required to search: name, years to search. Civil cases indexed by defendant, plaintiff. Civil records archived from early 1900s on books.
Criminal Records: Access: Mail, in person. Both court and visitors may perform in person searches. No search fee. Required to search: name, years to search, DOB, SSN, signed release. Criminal records archived from early 1900s on books. Searches done by the court are for only 5 years of records.
General Information: No adoption or juvenile records released. Copy fee: $.25 per page. Cert fee: $3.00. Copy fee included in cert fee. Payee: Circuit Court Clerk. Only cashiers checks and money orders accepted. Prepayment required. Mail requests: SASE required. Mail turnaround time 1 week.

County Court PO Box 710, Dandridge, TN 37725; 865-397-2935; Fax: 865-397-3839. Hours: 8AM-4PM M-F, 8AM-11PM Sat (EST). *Probate.*

Johnson County

1st District Circuit & General Sessions
Court PO Box 73, Mountain City, TN 37683; 423-727-9012; Fax: 423-727-7047. Hours: 8:30AM-5PM (EST). *Felony, Misdemeanor, Civil, Eviction, Small Claims.*
Civil Records: Access: Phone, mail, in person. Both court and visitors may perform in person searches. Search fee: $5.00 per name. Required to search: name, years to search. Civil cases indexed by defendant, plaintiff. Civil records in docket books, sessions 1976, criminal & circuit 1800s.
Criminal Records: Access: Phone, mail, in person. Both court and visitors may perform in person searches. Search fee: $5.00 per name. Required to search: name, years to search, DOB. Criminal records in docket books, sessions 1976, criminal & circuit 1800s.
General Information: No adoption, expunged or juvenile records released. Copy fee: $2.00 per page. Cert fee: $2.00. Payee: Circuit Court Clerk. Only cashiers checks and money orders accepted. Prepayment required. Mail requests: SASE required. Mail turnaround time 2-3 days.

Chancery Court PO Box 196, Mountain City, TN 37683; 423-727-7853; Fax: 423-727-7047. Hours: 8:30AM-12:00,1-5PM (EST). *Civil, Probate.*
Civil Records: Access: Mail, in person. Both court and visitors may perform in person searches. No search fee. Required to search: name, years to search. Civil cases indexed by defendant, plaintiff. Civil records on books and files.
General Information: No adoption records released. Copy fee: $1.00 per page. Cert fee: $2.00 plus $2.00 per page. Payee: Clerk & Master. Only cashiers checks and money orders accepted. Prepayment required. Mail requests: SASE required. Mail turnaround time same day.

Knox County

6th District Criminal Court 400 Main Ave, Rm 149, Knoxville, TN 37902; 865-215-2492; Fax: 865-215-4291. Hours: 8AM-4:30PM (EST). *Felony, Misdemeanor.*

www.knoxcounty.org

Criminal Records: Access: Fax, mail, in person. Only the court performs in person searches; visitors may not. Search fee: $5.00 per name. Required to search: name, years to search, DOB; also helpful: address, SSN, signed release. Criminal records on computer back to 1980; on books from 1962.

General Information: Public Access terminal is available. No sealed records released. Copy fee: $2.00 per page. Cert fee: $2.00. Payee: Criminal Court Clerk. Personal checks accepted. Prepayment required. Mail requests: SASE not required. Mail turnaround time 48 hours.

Circuit Court 400 Main Ave, Rm M-30, PO Box 379, Knoxville, TN 37901; 865-215-2400; Fax: 865-215-4251. Hours: 8AM-5PM; 4:30 PM Fri. (EST). *Civil Actions Over $15,000.*

www.knoxcounty.org

Civil Records: Access: Phone, fax, mail, in person. Both court and visitors may perform in person searches. Search fee: $5.00. Required to search: name, years to search. Civil cases indexed by defendant, plaintiff. Civil records on computer from 1986, prior records archived and on microfilm.

General Information: Public Access terminal is available. No adoption or sealed records released. Copy fee: $1.00 per page. Cert fee: $3.50. Payee: Circuit Court Clerk. Personal checks accepted. Visa, MC accepted. Prepayment required. Mail turnaround time 2-3 days.

General Sessions Court 300 Main Ave, Rm 318, PO Box 379, Knoxville, TN 37901; 865-215-2518. Hours: 8AM-4:30PM (EST). *Civil Actions Under $15,000, Eviction, Small Claims.*

www.knoxcounty.org

Civil Records: Access: Mail, in person. Both court and visitors may perform in person searches. Search fee: $5.00. Required to search: name, years to search. Civil cases indexed by defendant, plaintiff. Civil records on books and computer.

General Information: Public Access terminal is available. No juvenile or adoption records released. Copy fee: $1.50 per page. Cert fee: $3.50. Payee: General Sessions Court. Personal checks accepted. Visa, MC accepted. Prepayment required. Mail turnaround time 1 week.

Chancery Court 400 Main Ave, Rm #215, Knoxville, TN 37902; 865-215-2555 (Chancery); Criminal phone: 865-215-2492; Probate phone: 865-215-2389; Fax: 865-215-2920. Hours: 8AM-4:30PM (EST). *Civil, Probate.*

www.knoxcounty.org

Civil Records: Access: Phone, fax, mail, in person. Visitors must perform in person searches for themselves. Search fee: $5.00. Required to search: name, years to search. Civil cases indexed by defendant, plaintiff. Civil records on computer since 1978, prior records on books.

General Information: Public Access terminal is available. No commitment or adoption records released. Will fax results $1.00 per page. Copy fee: $2.00 per page. Cert fee: $4.00. Payee: Chancery or Probate Court. Personal checks accepted. Prepayment required. Mail requests: SASE requested. Turnaround time 1-2 days.

Lake County

29th District Circuit & General Sessions Court 229 Church St, PO Box 11, Tiptonville, TN 38079; 731-253-7137; Fax: 731-253-8930. Hours: 8AM-4PM (CST). *Felony, Misdemeanor, Civil, Eviction, Small Claims.*

Civil Records: Access: In person only. Visitors must perform in person searches for themselves. Search fee: none. Required to search: name, years to search. Civil cases indexed by defendant, plaintiff. Civil records archived on books in office up to 30 yrs, vault records before 1960; General Sessions computerized records go back to 1997.

Criminal Records: Access: In person only. Visitors must perform in person searches for themselves. Search fee: none. Required to search: name, years to search, DOB; also helpful: SSN. Criminal records archived on books in office up to 30 yrs, vault records before 1960.

General Information: No sealed records released. Copy fee: $1.00 per page. Cert fee: $3.00. Payee: Circuit Court Clerk. Personal checks accepted. Prepayment required.

Chancery Court 229 Church Lake County Courthouse, Box 12, Tiptonville, TN 38079; 731-253-8926. Hours: 9AM-4PM (CST). *Probate.*

Civil Records: Access: Mail, in person. Both court and visitors may perform in person searches. No search fee. Required to search: name, years to search. Civil cases indexed by defendant. Civil records on books and files from 1984, prior records filed in county clerks office.

General Information: Copy fee: $.50 per page. Cert fee: $6.00. Payee: Clerk and Master. Personal checks accepted. Prepayment required. Mail turnaround time 3-5 days.

Lauderdale County

25th District Circuit Court Lauderdale County Justice Center, 675 Hwy 51 S, PO Box 509, Ripley, TN 38063; 731-635-0101; Fax: 731-221-8663. Hours: 8AM-4:30PM (CST). *Felony, Misdemeanor, Civil Actions Over $15,000.*

Civil Records: Access: Phone, mail, in person. Both court and visitors may perform in person searches. Search fee: $10.00 per name. Required to search: name, years to search. Civil cases indexed by defendant, plaintiff. Civil records archived on books from 1800s; on computer back to 1992.

Criminal Records: Access: Mail, in person. Both court and visitors may perform in person searches. Search fee: $10.00 per name. Required to search: name, years to search; also helpful: DOB, SSN. Criminal records archived on books from 1800s; on computer back to 1992.

General Information: Public Access terminal is available. No sealed or adoption records released. Copy fee: $1.00 per page. Cert fee: $10.00. Payee: Circuit Court Clerk. Personal checks accepted in county. Prepayment required. Mail requests: SASE required. Mail turnaround time 2-3 days.

General Sessions Court PO Box 509, Ripley, TN 38063; 731-635-2572; Fax: 731-221-8663. Hours: 8AM-4:30PM (till noon on Wed) (CST). *Civil Actions Under $15,000, Eviction, Small Claims.*

Civil Records: Access: Mail, in person. Both court and visitors may perform in person searches. Search fee: $10.00 per name. Required to search: name, years to search. Civil cases indexed by defendant, plaintiff. Civil records on computer since 1992, records prior to 1984 on docket books.

General Information: Public Access terminal is available. No confidential records released. Copy fee: $1.00 per page. Cert fee: $10.00. Payee: General Sessions. Business checks accepted. Prepayment

required. Mail requests: SASE required. Mail turnaround time 2-3 days.

County Court Courthouse, 100 Court Sq, Ripley, TN 38063; 731-635-2561; Fax: 731-635-9682. Hours: 8AM-4:30PM M,T,TH,F; 8AM-Noon W (CST). *Probate.*

Lawrence County

22nd District Circuit & General Sessions Court NBU #12, 240 W Gaines, Lawrenceburg, TN 38464; 931-762-4398; Fax: 931-766-4471. Hours: 8AM-4:30PM (CST). *Felony, Misdemeanor, Civil, Eviction, Small Claims.*

Civil Records: Access: In person only. Visitors must perform in person searches for themselves. No search fee. Required to search: name, years to search. Civil cases indexed by defendant, plaintiff. Civil records archived on books since court started in 1940s.

Criminal Records: Access: In person only. Visitors must perform in person searches for themselves. No search fee. Required to search: name, years to search, DOB, SSN. Criminal records archived on books since court started in 1940s.

General Information: Public Access terminal is available. No expunged records released. Copy fee: $1.00 per page. Cert fee: $5.00. Payee: Circuit Court Clerk. Only cashiers checks and money orders accepted. Prepayment required.

County Clerk 240 W Gaines St, NBU #2, Lawrenceburg, TN 38464; 931-762-7700; ext 116; Fax: 931-766-4146. Hours: 8AM-4:30PM (CST). *Probate.*

Note: Leon Clanton Ext 177

Lewis County

21st District Circuit & General Sessions Court Courthouse, 110 Park Ave N, Rm 201, Hohenwald, TN 38462; 931-796-3724; Fax: 931-796-6021. Hours: 8AM-4:30PM (CST). *Felony, Misdemeanor, Civil, Eviction, Small Claims.*

Civil Records: Access: In person only. Visitors must perform in person searches for themselves. No search fee. Required to search: name, years to search. Civil cases indexed by defendant, plaintiff. Civil records archived 15 years in office, 1800s in vault.

Criminal Records: Access: In person only. Visitors must perform in person searches for themselves. No search fee. Required to search: name, years to search; also helpful: SSN. Criminal records archived 15 years in office, 1800s in vault.

General Information: No juvenile, adoption records released. Copy fee: $1.00 per page. Cert fee: $2.00 per document plus $2.00 per page. Payee: Circuit Court Clerk. Personal checks accepted. Prepayment required.

Chancery Court Lewis County Courthouse, 110 Park Ave N, Rm 208, Hohenwald, TN 38462; 931-796-3734; Fax: 931-796-6017. Hours: 8AM-4:30PM (CST). *Civil, Probate.*

Civil Records: Access: In person only. Visitors must perform in person searches for themselves. No search fee. Required to search: name, years to search. Civil cases indexed by defendant, plaintiff. Civil records on computer since 10/94, prior records indexed on computer by name or case number.

General Information: No adoption records released. Copy fee: $1.00 per page. Cert fee: $2.00. Payee: Clerk & Master. Personal checks accepted. Prepayment required.

Lincoln County

17th District Circuit & General Sessions Court
112 Main Ave S, Rm 203, Fayetteville, TN 37334; 931-433-2334; Fax: 931-438-1577. Hours: 8AM-4PM (CST). *Felony, Misdemeanor, Civil, Eviction, Small Claims.*

Civil Records: Access: Phone, fax, mail, in person. Both court and visitors may perform in person searches. Search fee: $10.00 per name. Fee is for 5 years. Add $1.00 for each add'l year. Required to search: name, years to search. Civil cases indexed by defendant, plaintiff. Civil records archived on books since court started; files go back 10 years; on computer back to 1995.

Criminal Records: Access: Phone, fax, mail, in person. Both court and visitors may perform in person searches. Search fee: $10.00 per name. Fee is for 5 years. Add $1.00 for each add'l year. Required to search: name, years to search, DOB, SSN, signed release. Criminal records archived on books since court started; files go back 10 years; on computer back to 1995.

General Information: No probation records released. Will fax results $2.00 per page. Copy fee: $1.00 per page. Cert fee: $4.00. Payee: Circuit Court Clerk. Business checks accepted. Prepayment required. Mail requests: SASE required. Mail turnaround time 1-2 days.

Chancery Court
112 Main Ave, Rm B109, Fayetteville, TN 37334; 931-433-1482; Fax: 931-433-9313. Hours: 8AM-4PM (CST). *Civil, Probate.*

Civil Records: Access: In person only. Visitors must perform in person searches for themselves. No search fee. Required to search: name, years to search. Civil cases indexed by defendant, plaintiff. Civil records archived on books.

General Information: No adoption, divorce records released. Fee to fax results is $1.00 per page. Copy fee: $1.00 per page. Cert fee: $4.00 plus $2.00 per page. Payee: Clerk & Master. Personal checks accepted. Prepayment required.

Loudon County

9th District Criminal & Circuit Court
PO Box 280, Loudon, TN 37774; 865-458-2042; Fax: 865-458-2043. Hours: 8AM-4:30PM (EST). *Felony, Civil.*

www.loudoncounty.com/ccc.htm

Civil Records: Access: Phone, fax, mail, in person. Both court and visitors may perform in person searches. Search fee: $5.00 per name. Required to search: name, years to search. Civil cases indexed by defendant, plaintiff. Civil records archived from 1870 on books, on computer from 8/1990.

Criminal Records: Access: Phone, fax, mail, in person. Both court and visitors may perform in person searches. Search fee: $5.00 per name. Required to search: name, years to search. Criminal records archived from 1800s on books, on computer from 8/1990.

General Information: No juvenile, adoption records released. Copy fee: $1.00 per page. Cert fee: $2.00. Payee: Circuit Court. Personal checks accepted. Prepayment required. Mail requests: SASE requested. Turnaround time 2-4 days.

General Sessions Court
PO Box 280, Loudon, TN 37774; 865-986-3505; Fax: 865-986-2535. Hours: 8AM-5PM (EST). *Misdemeanorl, Eviction, Small Claims.*

www.loudoncounty.com/ccc.htm

Note: General Sessions (Eviction, small claims, some misdemeanor, and juvenile court) located at 12680 Hwy 11 W, #3, Lenoir City, TN 37771, 423-986-3505.

Civil Records: Access: Phone, fax, mail, in person. Both court and visitors may perform in person searches. Search fee: $5.00 per name. Required to search: name, years to search. Civil cases indexed by defendant, plaintiff. Civil records archived from 1870 on books, on computer from 1995.

Criminal Records: Access: Phone, fax, mail, in person. Both court and visitors may perform in person searches. Search fee: $5.00 per name. Required to search: name, years to search. Criminal records archived from 1800s on books, on computer from 1995.

General Information: No juvenile, adoption records released. Copy fee: $1.00 per page. Cert fee: $2.00. Payee: General Sessions Court. Personal checks accepted. Prepayment required. Mail requests: SASE requested. Turnaround time 2-4 days.

County Court
101 Mulberry St, #200, Loudon, TN 37774; 865-458-2726; Fax: 865-458-9891. Hours: 8AM-4:30PM (EST). *Probate.*

Macon County

15th District Circuit & General Sessions Court
Court Clerk, 904 Hwy 52 Bypass, Lafayette, TN 37083; 615-666-2354; Probate phone: 615-666-2000; Fax: 615-666-3001. Hours: 8AM-4:30PM M-TH; 8AM-5PM F (CST). *Felony, Misdemeanor, Civil, Eviction, Small Claims, Probate.*

Note: Probate hours are 8AM-4PM.

Civil Records: Access: In person only. Visitors must perform in person searches for themselves. Search fee: $1.00 per copy. Required to search: name, years to search. Civil cases indexed by defendant, plaintiff. Civil records archived in office from 1975, rest in records room from 1960; on computer since 1997.

Criminal Records: Access: In person only. Visitors must perform in person searches for themselves. Search fee: $1.00 per copy. Required to search: name, years to search, DOB; also helpful: SSN. Criminal records archived in office from 1975, rest in records room from 1960, on computer since1997.

General Information: Public Access terminal is available. No juvenile or adoption records released. Copy fee: $1.00 per page. Cert fee: $5.00. Payee: Circuit Court Clerk. Personal checks accepted only if from this county. Prepayment required.

Madison County

26th District Circuit Court
515 S Liberty St, Jackson, TN 38301; 731-423-6035 x1049. Hours: 8AM-4PM (CST). *Felony, Misdemeanor, Civil Actions Over $15,000.*

www.co.madison.tn.us

Note: Misdemeanor cases here are usually accompanied by felonies.

Civil Records: Access: In person only. Visitors must perform in person searches for themselves. No search fee. Required to search: name, years to search. Civil cases indexed by defendant, plaintiff. Civil records archived on books in office from 1963; on computer back to 1995.

Criminal Records: Access: In person only. Visitors must perform in person searches for themselves. No search fee. Required to search: name, years to search; also helpful: DOB, SSN. Criminal records computerized since 1995, on books from 1965.

General Information: Public Access terminal is available. No sealed records released. Will not fax results. Copy fee: $.25 per page. Searcher can bring own paper then $.10 charges for copies. Cert fee: $5.00. Payee: Circuit Court Clerk. Cashiers checks and money orders accepted. Prepayment required.

General Sessions Court
515 S Liberty St, Jackson, TN 38301; Civil phone: 731-423-6018; Criminal phone: 731-423-6128. Hours: 8AM-4PM (CST). *Misdemeanor, Civil Actions Under $15,000, Eviction, Small Claims.*

Civil Records: Access: Mail, in person. Visitors must perform in person searches for themselves. Search fee: none. Required to search: name, years to search. Civil cases indexed by defendant, plaintiff. Civil records computerized since 01/98, archived on books in office from 1982, rest stored elsewhere from 1950s.

Criminal Records: Access: In person only. Visitors must perform in person searches for themselves. Search fee: none. Required to search: name. Records stored since 1950s, computerized since 01/98.

General Information: Public Access terminal is available. Copy fee: $1.50 per page. Cert fee: $4.00 for civil, $5.00 for criminal. Payee: General Sessions Court. Only cashiers checks and money orders accepted. Prepayment required. Mail turnaround time 1 week.

Probate Division - General Sessions Division II
110 Irby St, #102, Jackson, TN 38302; 731-988-3025; Fax: 731-988-3807. Hours: 8:30-12, 1-4:30PM (CST). *Probate.*

Marion County

12th District Circuit & General Sessions Court
PO Box 789, Courthouse Sq, Jasper, TN 37347; 423-942-2134; Fax: 423-942-4160. Hours: 8AM-4PM (CST). *Felony, Misdemeanor, Civil, Eviction, Small Claims.*

Civil Records: Access: Phone, mail, in person. Both court and visitors may perform in person searches. Search fee: $3.00 per name. Required to search: name, years to search. Civil cases indexed by defendant, plaintiff. Civil records on computer from 1988, prior records archived on books and microfiche since 1922.

Criminal Records: Access: Phone, mail, in person. Both court and visitors may perform in person searches. Search fee: $3.00 per name. Required to search: name, years to search, DOB; also helpful: SSN. Criminal records on computer from 1988, prior records archived on books and microfiche since 1922.

General Information: No adoption records released. Will fax results to local or toll free line. Copy fee: $.50 per page. Cert fee: $3.00. Payee: Circuit Court Clerk. Personal checks accepted. Prepayment required. Mail turnaround time 1 week.

Chancery Court
PO Box 789, Jasper, TN 37347; 423-942-2601; Fax: 423-942-0291. Hours: 8AM-4PM (CST). *Civil, Probate.*

Civil Records: Access: Mail, in person. Both court and visitors may perform in person searches. No search fee. Required to search: name, years to search. Civil cases indexed by defendant, plaintiff. Civil records on computer since 03/94, prior records on books.

General Information: Public Access terminal is available. No adoption records released. Will not fax results. Copy fee: $.50 per page. Cert fee: $3.00. Payee: Clerk and Master. Personal checks accepted. Prepayment required. Mail requests: SASE requested. Turnaround time 1 day.

Marshall County

17th District Circuit & General Sessions Court
Courthouse, Lewisburg, TN 37091; 931-359-0536; Fax: 931-359-0543. Hours: 8AM-4PM (CST). *Felony, Misdemeanor, Civil, Eviction, Small Claims.*

Civil Records: Access: In person only. Visitors must perform in person searches for themselves. No search fee. Required to search: name, years to search. Civil

cases indexed by plaintiff. Civil records archived on books; also on computer back to 2000.
Criminal Records: Access: In person only. Visitors must perform in person searches for themselves. No search fee. Required to search: name, years to search; also helpful: DOB, SSN. Criminal records in docket books back to 1987; on comptuer back to 2000.
General Information: Public Access terminal is available. No adoption records released. Will fax specific document to local or toll-free number. Copy fee: $1.00 per page. Cert fee: $5.00. Payee: Circuit Court Clerk. No personal checks accepted. Prepayment required.

Chancery Court 201 Marshall County Courthouse, Lewisburg, TN 37091; 931-359-2181; Fax: 931-359-0524. Hours: 8AM-4PM (CST). *Probate.*
Note: Probate is handled by the Clerk & Master.

Maury County

Circuit & General Sessions Court Maury County Courthouse, 41 Public Sq, Columbia, TN 38401; 931-381-3690; Criminal phone: 931-375-1100; Fax: 931-381-3985. Hours: 8AM-4PM (CST). *Felony, Misdemeanor, Civil, Eviction, Small Claims.*
Civil Records: Access: Fax, mail, in person. Visitors must perform in person searches for themselves. No search fee. Required to search: name, years to search. Civil cases indexed by defendant, plaintiff. Civil records on books since 1984; on computer back to 1989.
Criminal Records: Access: In person only. Visitors must perform in person searches for themselves. No search fee. Required to search: name, years to search; also helpful: DOB, SSN. Criminal records on computer back to 1989; others go back to early 1900s.
General Information: Public Access terminal is available. No juvenile records released. Will fax results for $1.00 per page. Copy fee: $1.00 per page. Cert fee: $6.00. Payee: Circuit Court Clerk. No personal checks accepted; use money order or cashiers check. Prepayment required.

Probate Court Maury County Courthouse, Clerk & Masters Office, 41 Public Sq, Columbia, TN 38401; 931-381-3690 x515; Fax: 931-308-5614. Hours: 8AM-4PM (CST). *Probate.*
Note: Records on computer go back to 1991.

McMinn County

10th District Circuit & General Sessions Court PO Box 506, Athens, TN 37303; 423-745-1923; Fax: 423-744-1642. Hours: 8:30AM-4PM (EST). *Felony, Misdemeanor, Civil, Eviction, Small Claims, Probate.*
Civil Records: Access: Phone, fax, mail, in person. Both court and visitors may perform in person searches. Search fee: $3.00 per name. Required to search: name, years to search; also helpful: address. Civil cases indexed by defendant, plaintiff. Civil records archived approximately 20 years; computerized back to 1996. Phone access is limited to three names.
Criminal Records: Access: Phone, fax, mail, in person. Both court and visitors may perform in person searches. Search fee: $3.00. Required to search: name, years to search, DOB, SSN; also helpful: address. Criminal records archived approximately 20 years; computerized back to 1996. Phone access is limited to three names.
General Information: No juvenile, adoption records released. Fee to fax results is $2.00 per page. Copy fee: $2.00 per page. Cert fee: $4.00. Payee: Circuit Court Clerk. Business checks accepted. Prepayment required. Mail turnaround time 5-10 days.

McNairy County

25th District Circuit & General Sessions Court 300 Industrial Dr, Selmer, TN 38375; 731-645-1015; Fax: 731-645-1003. Hours: 8AM-4:30PM M-F; 8AM-Noon Sat (CST). *Felony, Misdemeanor, Civil, Eviction, Small Claims.*
Civil Records: Access: Mail, in person. Both court and visitors may perform in person searches. Search fee: $20.00 per name. Required to search: name, years to search. Civil cases indexed by defendant, plaintiff. Civil records archived on docket books since 1966; computerized records since 2/95.
Criminal Records: Access: Mail, in person. Both court and visitors may perform in person searches. Search fee: $20.00 per name. Required to search: name, years to search, DOB, SSN. Criminal records archived on docket books since 1966; computerized records since 2/95.
General Information: Public Access terminal is available. No juvenile records released. Copy fee: $.25 per page. Cert fee: $6.00. Payee: Circuit Court Clerk. Personal checks accepted. Prepayment required. Mail turnaround time 1-2 days.

Chancery Court Chancery Court, Clerk & Master, Courthouse, Rm 205, Selmer, TN 38375; 731-645-5446; Fax: 731-646-1165. Hours: 8AM-4PM M,T,Th,F; Closed W (CST). *Civil, Probate.*
Civil Records: Access: In person only. Visitors must perform in person searches for themselves. No search fee. Required to search: name, years to search. Civil cases indexed by defendant, plaintiff. Civil records on books.
General Information: No adoption records released. Will not fax results. Copy fee: $.50. Cert fee: $5.00. Payee: Clerk & Master. Personal checks accepted. Prepayment required.

Meigs County

9th District Circuit & General Sessions Court PO Box 205, Decatur, TN 37322; 423-334-5821; Fax: 423-334-4819. Hours: 8:30AM-4:30PM till noon on Wed (EST). *Felony, Misdemeanor, Civil, Eviction, Small Claims.*
Civil Records: Access: Mail, in person. Both court and visitors may perform in person searches. No search fee. Required to search: name, years to search. Civil cases indexed by defendant, plaintiff. Civil records archived in office from 1930s, records in storage go further. They refer all name searches to an outside agency.
Criminal Records: Access: In person only. Both court and visitors may perform in person searches. No search fee. Required to search: name, years to search. Criminal records archived in office from 1930s, records in storage go further. They refer all name searches to an outside agency.
General Information: No juvenile records released. Copy fee: $.25 per page. Cert fee: $10.00. Payee: Circuit Court Clerk. Personal checks accepted. Prepayment required.

Chancery Court PO Box 5, Decatur, TN 37322; 423-334-5243. Hours: 8AM-5PM M,T,TH,F; 8:30AM-Noon Wed (EST). *Civil, Probate.*
Civil Records: Access: In person only. Visitors must perform in person searches for themselves. No search fee. Required to search: name, years to search. Civil cases indexed by defendant, plaintiff. Civil records on dockets since 1940.
General Information: No adoption records released. Will fax results for $.25 per page for 3 pages or less. Copy fee: $.25 per page. Cert fee: $5.50. Payee: Meigs County Chancery Court. Personal checks accepted. Prepayment required.

Monroe County

10th District Circuit I Courts 105 College St, Madisonville, TN 37354; 423-442-2396; Fax: 423-442-9538. Hours: 8AM-4:30PM (EST). *Felony, Misdemeanor, Civil over $10,000.*
Civil Records: Access: Mail, in person. Both court and visitors may perform in person searches. Search fee: $10.00 per name. Required to search: name, years to search. Civil cases indexed by defendant, plaintiff. Civil records on computer since 1991, records on books in office for 10 years, unspecified prior to then.
Criminal Records: Access: Mail, in person. Both court and visitors may perform in person searches. Search fee: $10.00 per name. Required to search: name, years to search. Criminal records on computer since 1991, records on books in office for 10 years, unspecified prior to then.
General Information: Public Access terminal is available. No juvenile records released. Will fax results for $2.00 per page. Copy fee: $1.00 per page. Cert fee: $4.00. Payee: Circuit Court Clerk. Personal checks accepted. Prepayment required. Mail turnaround time 2 days.

General Sessions Court 300 Tellico St, Madisonville, TN 37354; 423-442-9537; Fax: 423-420-9091. Hours: 8AM-4:30PM (EST). *Civil under $15,000, Eviction, Small Claims.*
Civil Records: Access: Mail, in person. Both court and visitors may perform in person searches. Search fee: $10.00 per name. Required to search: name, years to search. Civil cases indexed by defendant, plaintiff. Civil records on computer since 1991, records on books in office for 10 years, unspecified prior to then.
General Information: Public Access terminal is available. No juvenile records released. Will fax results for $2.00 per page. Copy fee: $1.00 per page. Cert fee: $5.00. Payee: Circuit Court Clerk. Personal checks accepted. Prepayment required. Mail turnaround time 2 days.

Chancery Court 105 College St, #2, Madisonville, TN 37354; 423-442-2644; Probate phone: 423-442-4573; Fax: 423-420-0048. Hours: 8:30AM-4:30PM (4PM on W) (EST). *Civil, Probate.*
Civil Records: Access: Mail, in person. Both court and visitors may perform in person searches. No search fee. Required to search: name, years to search. Civil cases indexed by plantiff and defendant. Civil records on computer since 1993, prior records on books.
General Information: No adoption, sealed records released. Will fax results to local or toll free line. Copy fee: $2.00 per page. Cert fee: $4.00. Payee: Chancery Court. Personal checks accepted. Prepayment required. Mail requests: SASE requested. Turnaround time 2-3 days.

Montgomery County

Montgomery County Circuit & General Sessions Court 2 Millennium Plaza, #115, Clarksville, TN 37040; 931-648-5700; Fax: 931-648-5731. Hours: 8AM-4:30PM (CST). *Felony, Misdemeanor, Civil, Evictions, Small Claims.*
Civil Records: Access: Mail, in person. Both court and visitors may perform in person searches. Search fee: $10.00 per name. Required to search: name, years to search. Civil cases indexed by defendant, plaintiff. Civil records on computer back to 11/1999, archived on books in office from 1970s, on microfiche from 1950s.
Criminal Records: Access: Mail, in person. Both court and visitors may perform in person searches. Search fee: $10.00 per name. Required to search: name, years to search, DOB; also helpful-signed release, SSN. Criminal records on computer back to

1985; prior records archived on books from 1970s, on microfiche from 1950s.

General Information: Public Access terminal is available. No juvenile records released. Will fax results to local or toll free line. Copy fee: $.50 per page. Cert fee: $6.00. Payee: Circuit Court (Criminal or General Sessions Court (civil). Business checks accepted. Prepayment required. Mail requests: SASE required.

Chancery Court Chancery Court, Clerk & Master, County Court Center, 2 Millenium Plaza, #101, Clarksville, TN 37040; 931-648-5703. Hours: 8AM-4:15PM (CST). *Civil, Probate.*

Civil Records: Access: In person only. Visitors must perform in person searches for themselves. No search fee. Required to search: name, years to search. Civil cases indexed by defendant, plaintiff. Civil records on books and microfilm.

General Information: Public Access terminal is available. No adoption or sealed records released. Copy fee: $1.00 per page. Cert fee: $2.00 per page. Payee: Clerk & Master. Business checks accepted. Prepayment required.

Moore County

17th District Circuit & General Sessions

Court Courthouse, PO Box 206, Lynchburg, TN 37352; 931-759-7208; Fax: 931-759-5673. Hours: 8AM-4:30PM MTWF; 8AM-Noon Sat (CST). *Felony, Misdemeanor, Civil, Eviction, Small Claims.*

Civil Records: Access: Mail, in person. Both court and visitors may perform in person searches. Search fee: $5.00 per name. Required to search: name, years to search. Civil cases indexed by defendant, plaintiff. Civil records archived to 1862, on docket books and microfiche from 1862 to 1980s.

Criminal Records: Access: Mail, in person. Both court and visitors may perform in person searches. Search fee: $5.00 per name. Required to search: name, years to search. Criminal records archived to 1862, on docket books and microfiche from 1862 to 1980s.

General Information: No juvenile records released. Copy fee: $2.00 per page. Cert fee: $2.00. Payee: Circuit Court Clerk. Only cashiers checks and money orders accepted. Prepayment required. Mail requests: SASE required. Mail turnaround time 7-10 days.

Chancery Court PO Box 206, Lynchburg, TN 37352; 931-759-7028; Fax: 931-759-5610. Hours: 8AM-4:30PM M-W,F; 8AM-Noon Sat (CST). *Civil, Probate.*

Civil Records: Access: In person only. Visitors must perform in person searches for themselves. No search fee. Required to search: name, years to search. Civil cases indexed by plaintiff. Civil records on books.

General Information: No adoption or sealed records released. Will not fax results. Copy fee: $1.00 per page. Cert fee: $5.00. Payee: Clerk and Master. Only cashiers checks and money orders accepted. Prepayment required.

Morgan County

9th District Circuit & General Sessions

Court PO Box 163, Wartburg, TN 37887; 423-346-3503. Hours: 8AM-4PM (EST). *Felony, Misdemeanor, Civil, Eviction, Small Claims.*

Civil Records: Access: In person only. Visitors must perform in person searches for themselves. No search fee. Required to search: name, years to search. Civil cases indexed by defendant, plaintiff. Civil records archived on books from 1855.

Criminal Records: Access: In person only. Visitors must perform in person searches for themselves. No search fee. Required to search: name, years to search;

also helpful: DOB, SSN. Criminal records archived on books from 1855; computerized since 2/01.

General Information: No sealed records released. Copy fee: $2.00 first page, $.50 each add'l. Cert fee: $6.00. Payee: Circuit Court Clerk. Only cashiers checks and money orders accepted. Prepayment required.

Chancery Court PO Box 789, Wartburg, TN 37887; 423-346-3881. Hours: 8AM-4PM (EST). *Civil, Probate.*

Civil Records: Access: Phone, mail, in person. Both court and visitors may perform in person searches. No search fee. Required to search: name, years to search. Civil cases indexed by defendant, plaintiff. Civil records in books since 1883, on microfiche since 1939 at state archives.

General Information: No adoption or conservatorship records released. Will fax results to local or toll free line. Copy fee: $.50 per page. Cert fee: $10.00. Payee: Clerk & Master. Personal checks accepted. Prepayment required. Mail requests: SASE required. Mail turnaround time 1-8 days.

Obion County

27th District Circuit Court 7 Bill Burnett

Circle, Union City, TN 38261; 731-885-1372; Fax: 731-885-7515. Hours: 8:30AM-4:30PM (CST). *Felony, Misdemeanor, Civil Actions Over $10,000.*

Civil Records: Access: Mail, in person. Both court and visitors may perform in person searches. Search fee: $5.00 per name. Required to search: name, years to search. Civil cases indexed by defendant, plaintiff. Civil records for criminal archived on books from 1969, civil on books from 1974, rest are located elsewhere.

Criminal Records: Access: Mail, in person. Both court and visitors may perform in person searches. Search fee: $5.00. Misdemeanor records are $5.00 per year. Required to search: name, years to search, DOB, SSN. Criminal records for criminal archived on books from 1969, civil on books from 1974, rest are located elsewhere.

General Information: No adoption records released. Copy fee: $1.00 per page. Cert fee: $3.00. Payee: Circuit Court. Business checks accepted. Prepayment required. Mail requests: SASE required. Mail turnaround time 2 days.

General Sessions Court 9 Bill Burnett Circle, Union City, TN 38281-0236; 731-885-1811; Fax: 731-885-7515. Hours: 8:30AM-4:30PM (CST). *Civil Actions Under $15,000, Eviction, Small Claims.*

Civil Records: Access: Mail, in person. Both court and visitors may perform in person searches. Search fee: $5.00 5 years & under; $10.00 over 5 years. Required to search: name. Civil cases indexed by defendant, plaintiff. Civil records kept in office for last 10 years, computerized since 1994.

General Information: Public Access terminal is available. No juvenile or adoption records released. Copy fee: $1.00 per page. Cert fee: $3.00. Payee: Circuit Court Clerk. Personal checks accepted. Prepayment required. Mail requests: SASE required. Mail turnaround time 2 days.

Chancery Court PO Box 187, Union City, TN 38281; 731-885-2562; Fax: 731-885-7515. Hours: 8:30AM-4:30PM (CST). *Civil, Probate.*

Civil Records: Access: Phone, mail, in person. Both court and visitors may perform in person searches. No search fee. Required to search: name, years to search. Civil cases indexed by defendant, plaintiff. Civil records (probate) from 9/82 on books in Chancery office, prior records on index books in County Clerk's office.

General Information: No adoption or sealed records released. Will fax results for $3.00 per document.

Copy fee: $1.00 per page. Cert fee: $4.00. Payee: Clerk and Master. Personal checks accepted. Prepayment required. Mail turnaround time 2 days.

Overton County

13th District Circuit & General Sessions

Court Overton County Courthouse, 100 Joan Tom Poindexter Dr, Livingston, TN 38570; 931-823-2312; Fax: 931-823-9728. Hours: 8AM-4:30PM M,T,TH,F, 8AM-Noon W & Sat (CST). *Felony, Misdemeanor, Civil, Eviction, Small Claims.*

Civil Records: Access: Mail, in person. Both court and visitors may perform in person searches. No search fee. Required to search: name, years to search. Civil cases indexed by defendant, plaintiff. Civil records archived on books from late 1800s; computerized records since 1996.

Criminal Records: Access: Mail, in person. Both court and visitors may perform in person searches. No search fee. Required to search: name, years to search, DOB, SSN, signed release. Criminal records archived on books from late 1800s; computerized records since 1996.

General Information: No juvenile records released. Copy fee: $.50 per page. Cert fee: $5.00 per page. Payee: Circuit Court Clerk. Business checks accepted. Prepayment required. Mail requests: SASE required. Mail turnaround time 3-5 days.

County Court Courthouse Annex, University St, PO Box 127, Livingston, TN 38570; 931-823-2536; Fax: 931-823-7631. Hours: 8AM-4PM (CST). *Probate.*

Perry County

21st District Circuit & General Sessions

Court PO Box 91, Linden, TN 37096; 931-589-2218; Fax: 931-589-2350. Hours: 8AM-4PM (CST). *Felony, Misdemeanor, Civil, Eviction, Small Claims.*

Civil Records: Access: Mail, in person, phone. Both court and visitors may perform in person searches. No search fee. Required to search: name, years to search. Civil cases indexed by defendant, plaintiff. Civil records archived on books from 1941, on microfiche (limited) at library.

Criminal Records: Access: Mail, in person, phone. Both court and visitors may perform in person searches. No search fee. Required to search: name, years to search, DOB, SSN. Criminal records archived on books from 1941, on microfiche (limited) at library.

General Information: No adoption records released. No copy fee. No cert fee. Payee: Circuit Court Clerk. Personal checks accepted. Prepayment required. Mail requests: SASE required. Mail turnaround time 2-3 days.

Chancery Court PO Box 251, Linden, TN 37096; 931-589-2217; Fax: 931-589-2350. Hours: 8AM-4PM (CST). *Civil, Probate.*

Civil Records: Access: In person only. Visitors must perform in person searches for themselves. No search fee. Required to search: name, years to search. Civil cases indexed by defendant, plaintiff. Civil records (probate) on books from 1982, prior records in County Clerks office.

General Information: No adoption records released. Copy fee: $1.50 per page. Cert fee: $5.00. Payee: Clerk and Master. Local checks accepted. Prepayment required.

Pickett County

13th District Circuit & General Sessions

Court PO Box 188, Byrdstown, TN 38549; 931-864-3958; Fax: 931-864-6885. Hours: 8AM-4PM (CST). *Felony, Misdemeanor, Civil, Eviction, Small Claims.*

Civil Records: Access: Mail, in person. Both court and visitors may perform in person searches. Search fee: $10.00 per name. Required to search: name, years to search. Civil cases indexed by defendant. Civil records archived on books but not specific.

Criminal Records: Access: Mail, in person. Both court and visitors may perform in person searches. Search fee: $10.00 per name. Required to search: name, years to search; also helpful: SSN. Criminal records not computerized, all on books.

General Information: No adoption or juvenile records released. No copy fee. No cert fee. Payee: Circuit Court Clerk. Personal checks accepted. Prepayment required. Mail turnaround time 3-4 days.

County Court PO Box 5, Courthoue Sq, Byrdstown, TN 38549; 931-864-3879; Fax: 931-864-7087. Hours: 8AM-4PM M,T,Th,F, 8-11AM W & Sat (CST). *Probate.*

Polk County

10th District Circuit & General Sessions Court
PO Box 256, Benton, TN 37307; 423-338-4524; Fax: 423-338-8611. Hours: 8:30AM-4:30PM M-F (EST). *Felony, Misdemeanor, Civil, Eviction, Small Claims.*

Civil Records: Access: Mail, in person. Both court and visitors may perform in person searches. Search fee: $5.00 per name. Required to search: name, years to search. Civil cases indexed by defendant, plaintiff. Civil records archived from 1936, computerized since 2000.

Criminal Records: Access: Mail, in person. Both court and visitors may perform in person searches. Search fee: $5.00 per name. Required to search: name, years to search, DOB, SSN. Criminal records archived from 1936, computerized since 2000.

General Information: Public Access terminal is available. No juvenile records released. Will fax results for $5.00 per name. Copy fee: $5.00 per document. Cert fee: varies according to document size. Payee: Circuit Court Clerk. Personal checks accepted. Prepayment required. Mail requests: SASE requested. Turnaround time 3 days.

Chancery Court PO Drawer L, Benton, TN 37307; 423-338-4522; Fax: 423-338-4553. Hours: 8:30AM-4:30PM (EST). *Civil, Probate.*

Civil Records: Access: Mail, in person. Both court and visitors may perform in person searches. Search fee: $5.00 per name. Fee varies by document. Required to search: name, years to search. Civil cases indexed by defendant, plaintiff. Civil records on books up to 1800s, computerized since 10/2000.

General Information: No adoption records released. Will fax results to local or toll free line. Copy fee: $1.00 per page. Cert fee: $2.00 per page; $2.00 per certificate. Payee: Chancery Court. Personal checks accepted. Prepayment required. Mail turnaround time is 3 days.

Putnam County

13th District Circuit & General Sessions Court
421 E Spring St, 1C-49A, Cookeville, TN 38501; 931-528-1508. Hours: 8AM-4PM (CST). *Felony, Misdemeanor, Civil, Eviction, Small Claims.* www.dockets.putnamco.org/

Note: Current docket information is available at the web site.

Civil Records: Access: In person. Visitors must perform in person searches for themselves. No search fee. Required to search: name, years to search. Civil cases indexed by defendant, plaintiff. Civil records archived in office from 1980s, unknown before then; computerized records since 1995.

Criminal Records: Access: In person. Visitors must perform in person searches for themselves. No search

fee. Required to search: name, years to search; also helpful: SSN. Criminal records computerized since 1995.

General Information: Public Access terminal is available. No juvenile or adoption records released. Copy fee: $.25 per page. Cert fee: $4.50. Payee: Circuit Court Clerk. Business checks accepted. Prepayment required.

Probate & Juvenile Court PO Box 220, Cookeville, TN 38503-0220; 931-526-7106; Fax: 931-372-8201. Hours: 8AM-4:00PM (CST). *Probate, Juvenile.*

Rhea County

12th District Circuit & General Sessions Court
1475 Market St, Rm 200, Dayton, TN 37321; 423-775-7805; Civil phone: 423-775-7805; Criminal phone: 423-775-7818; Probate phone: 423-775-7806; Fax: 423-775-7895. Hours: 8AM-4:30PM (EST). *Felony, Misdemeanor, Civil, Eviction, Small Claims, Probate.*

Note: Probate located at the Rhea County Clerk and Master's Office. Fax # 423-775-4046.

Civil Records: Access: In person only. Visitors must perform in person searches for themselves. No search fee. Required to search: name, years to search. Civil cases indexed by defendant, plaintiff. Civil records in docket books.

Criminal Records: Access: Mail, fax, in person. Both court and visitors may perform in person searches. However, court will only do name searches if current or within past year. No search fee. Required to search: name, years to search; also helpful: DOB, SSN. Criminal records in docket books.

General Information: Public Access terminal is available. (Very limited, recent civil cases only.) No adoption records released. Copy fee: $.25 per page. Cert fee: $4.50. Payee: Circuit Court Clerk. Local personal checks accepted; no out of state. Prepayment required.

Roane County

9th District Circuit & General Sessions Court
PO Box 73, Kingston, TN 37763; 865-376-2390; Fax: 865-717-4141. Hours: 8:30AM-6PM Mon; 8:30AM-4:30PM T-F (EST). *Felony, Misdemeanor, Civil, Eviction, Small Claims.*

Note: General Sessions phone is 865-376-5584, their records are separate from Circuit Court records.

Civil Records: Access: Mail, fax, in person. Both court and visitors may perform in person searches. Search fee: $5.00 per name. Required to search: name, years to search. Civil cases indexed by defendant, plaintiff. Civil records archived since court started, General Sessions and Circuit are on computer since 1991.

Criminal Records: Access: Mail, fax, in person. Both court and visitors may perform in person searches. Search fee: $5.00 per name. Required to search: name, years to search, DOB; also helpful, SSN, signed release. Criminal records archived since court started, General Sessions and Circuit are on computer since 1991.

General Information: Public Access terminal is available. No adoption, expunged records released. Will fax results. Copy fee: $.50 per page. Cert fee: $5.00. Payee: Circuit Court Clerk. Business checks accepted. Prepayment required. Mail requests: SASE required. Mail turnaround time 2-3 days.

Chancery Court PO Box 402, Kingston, TN 37763; 865-376-2487; Fax: 865-376-1228. Hours: 8:30AM-6PM M, 8:30AM-4:30PM T-F (EST). *Civil, Probate.*

Civil Records: Access: Phone, mail, in person. Both court and visitors may perform in person searches.

Search fee: $5.00. Required to search: name, years to search. Civil cases indexed by defendant, plaintiff. Civil records on books; on computer since 7/95. Tax records on computer since 1982.

General Information: No adoption records released. Fee to fax results is $1.00 per page. Copy fee: $.50 per page. Cert fee: $2.00. Payee: Clerk and Master. Personal checks accepted. Prepayment required. Mail requests: SASE not required. Mail turnaround time same day.

Robertson County

19th District Circuit Court
Robertson County Courthouse, Rm 200, Springfield, TN 37172; 615-384-7864; Fax: 615-384-0246. Hours: 8AM-4:30PM (CST). *Felony, Misdemeanor.*

Civil Records: Access: Phone, fax, mail, in person. Both court and visitors may perform in person searches. Search fee: $5.00 per name. Required to search: name, years to search. Civil cases indexed by defendant, plaintiff. Civil records archived in office from 1980s, archived from 1800s located elsewhere.

Criminal Records: Access: Phone, fax, mail, in person. Both court and visitors may perform in person searches. Search fee: $5.00 per name. Required to search: name, years to search; also helpful: DOB, SSN. Criminal records archived in office from 1980s, archived from 1800s located elsewhere. No long distance outgoing faxing.

General Information: Public Access terminal is available. No sealed records released. Copy fee: $.25 per page. Cert fee: $5.00. Payee: Circuit Court Clerk. Personal checks accepted. Prepayment required. Mail requests: SASE required. Mail turnaround time 15 days.

General Sessions Court 529 S Brown St, Springfield, TN 37172-2941; 615-382-2324; Fax: 615-382-3113. Hours: 8AM-4:30PM (CST). *Misdemeanor, Civil Actions under $15,000, Eviction, Small Claims, Traffic.*

Civil Records: Access: Fax, mail, in person. Both court and visitors may perform in person searches. Search fee: $5.00 per name. Required to search: name, years to search. Civil cases indexed by defendant, plaintiff. Civil records archived in office from 1994, archived from 1800s located elsewhere.

Criminal Records: Access: Fax, mail, in person. Both court and visitors may perform in person searches. Search fee: $5.00 per name. Required to search: name, years to search; also helpful: DOB, SSN. Criminal records archived in office from 1994, archived from 1800s located elsewhere. No long distance outgoing faxing.

General Information: Public Access terminal is available. No sealed records released. Copy fee: $.50 per page. Cert fee: $2.00 plus $1.00 per page. Payee: Circuit Court Clerk. Personal checks not accepted. Prepayment required. Mail requests: SASE required. Mail turnaround time 7 days.

Chancery Court 501 Main St - 101 Robertson, County Courthouse, Springfield, TN 37172; 615-384-5650. Hours: 8AM-4:30PM (CST). *Civil, Probate.*

Civil Records: Access: Mail, in person. Both court and visitors may perform in person searches. Search fee: $2.00. Required to search: name, years to search. Civil cases indexed by defendant, plaintiff. Civil records in books since 1982, computerized from 09/94 to present, all chancery records on books.

General Information: No adoption records released. Will fax results for $2.00 per name. Copy fee: $1.00 per page. Cert fee: $2.00. Payee: Clerk & Master. Personal checks accepted. Prepayment required. Mail requests: SASE required. Mail turnaround time 1-2 days.

Rutherford County

16th District Circuit Court Judicial Bldg, Rm 201, Murfreesboro, TN 37130; Civil phone: 615-898-7820; Criminal phone: 615-898-7812; Fax: 615-217-7118. Hours: 8AM-4:15PM (CST). *Felony, Misdemeanor, Civil Actions Over $15,000.*
Civil Records: Access: In person only. Visitors must perform in person searches for themselves. No search fee. Required to search: name, years to search. Civil cases indexed by defendant, plaintiff. Civil records archived since court started, criminal on computer since 1986.
Criminal Records: Access: In person only. Visitors must perform in person searches for themselves. No search fee. Required to search: name, years to search, DOB, signed release; also helpful: SSN. Criminal records archived since court started, criminal on computer since 1990.
General Information: Public Access terminal is available. No expunged, sealed criminal records released. Copy fee: $1.00 per page. Cert fee: $2.00 per page. Payee: Circuit Court Clerk. Personal checks accepted.

General Sessions Court Judicial Bldg, Rm 101, Murfreesboro, TN 37130; 615-898-7831; Fax: 615-898-7835. Hours: 8AM-4:15PM (CST). *Civil Actions Under $15,000, Eviction, Small Claims.*
Civil Records: Access: In person only. Visitors must perform in person searches for themselves. No search fee. Required to search: name, years to search, DOB, SSN. Civil cases indexed by defendant, plaintiff. Civil records go back to 1948; on computer from 1986.
General Information: Public Access terminal is available. No juvenile records released. Copy fee: $1.00 per page. Cert fee: $4.00 plus copy fee. Payee: General Sessions Court. No personal checks accepted. Prepayment required.

County Court 319 N Maple St, Murfreesboro, TN 37130; 615-898-7798; Fax: 615-898-7830. Hours: 8AM-4PM M-Th; 8AM-5PM F (CST). *Probate.*

Scott County

8th District Circuit & General Sessions Court PO Box 330, Huntsville, TN 37756; 423-663-2440; Fax: 423-663-2595. Hours: 8AM-4:30PM (EST). *Felony, Misdemeanor, Civil, Eviction, Small Claims, Probate.*
Civil Records: Access: Phone, mail, in person. Both court and visitors may perform in person searches. Search fee: $10.00 per name per year. Required to search: name, years to search. Civil cases indexed by defendant, plaintiff. Civil records archived in docket books but not specified, on computer from 1991.
Criminal Records: Access: Phone, mail, in person. Both court and visitors may perform in person searches. Search fee: $10.00 per name per year. Fee varies according to info requested. Required to search: name, years to search, DOB; also helpful: SSN. Criminal records archived in docket books but not specified, on computer from 1991.
General Information: No juvenile records released. Will fax results to local or toll free line. Copy fee: $.50 per page. Cert fee: $2.00. Payee: Circuit Court Clerk. Personal checks accepted. Prepayment required. Mail requests: SASE required. Mail turnaround time same week.

Sequatchie County

12th District Circuit & General Sessions Court PO Box 551, Dunlap, TN 37327; 423-949-2618; Fax: 423-949-2902. Hours: 8AM-4PM (CST). *Felony, Misdemeanor, Civil, Eviction, Small Claims.*
Civil Records: Access: Phone, fax, mail, in person. Both court and visitors may perform in person searches. No search fee. Required to search: name, years to search. Civil cases indexed by defendant, plaintiff. Civil records archived on books but not specified.
Criminal Records: Access: Phone, fax, mail, in person. Both court and visitors may perform in person searches. No search fee. Required to search: name, years to search, DOB; also helpful: SSN. Criminal records not computerized.
General Information: No adoption records released. Will fax results for $1.00 per page. Copy fee: $1.00 per page. Cert fee: $4.00. Payee: Circuit Court Clerk. Personal checks accepted. Prepayment required. Mail turnaround time 1 week.

Chancery Court PO Box 1651, Dunlap, TN 37327; 423-949-3670; Fax: 423-949-2579. Hours: 8AM-4PM (CST). *Civil, Probate.*
Civil Records: Access: Fax, mail, in person. Both court and visitors may perform in person searches. No search fee. Required to search: name, years to search. Civil cases indexed by defendant, plaintiff. Civil records on books.
General Information: No sealed or adoption records released. Will fax results $1.00 per page. Copy fee: $1.00 per page. Cert fee: $2.00. Payee: Clerk and Master. Personal checks accepted. Prepayment required. Mail turnaround time 1 week.

Sevier County

4th District Circuit Court 125 Court Ave, #204E, Sevierville, TN 37862; 865-453-5536; Criminal phone: 865-774-3731; Fax: 865-774-9792. Hours: 8AM-4:30PM M-TH, 8AM-6PM F (EST). *Felony, Misdemeanor, Civil Actions over $15,000.*
Civil Records: Access: Fax, mail, in person. Both court and visitors may perform in person searches. Search fee: $10.00. Required to search: name, years to search. Civil cases indexed by defendant, plaintiff. Civil records computerized back to 1993. Records before 1980s difficult to locate.
Criminal Records: Access: Fax, mail, in person. Both court and visitors may perform in person searches. Search fee: $10.00. Required to search: name, years to search; also helpful: SSN. Criminal records computerized back to 1993.
General Information: Public Access terminal is available. No expunged records released. Will fax results $1.00 per page. Copy fee: $1.00 per page. Cert fee: $4.00. Payee: Circuit Court or General Sessions Clerk. Personal checks accepted. Prepayment required. Mail requests: SASE required. Mail turnaround time 1 week.

General Sessions Court 125 Court Ave, #107E, Sevierville, TN 37862; 865-453-6116; Civil phone: 865-429-5671; Criminal phone: 865-453-6116; Fax: 865-774-3842. Hours: 8AM-4:30PM M-TH, 8AM-6PM F (EST). *Misdemeanor, Civil Actions Under $25,000, Eviction, Small Claims.*
Civil Records: Access: Phone, fax, mail, in person. Only the court performs in person searches; visitors may not. Search fee: $15.00 per name. Required to search: name, years to search. Civil cases indexed by defendant, plaintiff. Civil records computerized back to 1995. Records before 1980s difficult to locate.
Criminal Records: Access: Fax, mail, in person. Only the court performs in person searches; visitors may not. Search fee: $15.00 per name. Required to search: name, years to search; also helpful: SSN, date of arrest. Criminal records computerized back to 1995; index back to 1973.
General Information: No expunged records released. Will fax results $1.00 per page. Copy fee: $1.00 per page. Cert fee: $5.00. Payee: Circuit Court or General Sessions Clerk. Personal checks not accepted. Prepayment required. Mail requests: SASE not required. Mail turnaround time 1 week.

County Court

County Court 125 Court Ave, #202, Sevierville, TN 37862; 865-453-5502; Fax: 865-453-6830. Hours: 8AM-4:30PM (EST). *Probate.*

Shelby County

Circuit Court 140 Adams Ave, Rm 224, Memphis, TN 38103; 901-545-4006; Fax: 901-545-3952. Hours: 8AM-4:30PM (CST). *Civil Actions Over $25,000.*
www.circuitcourt.co.shelby.tn.us/
Note: A second office is located at 942 Mt. Moriah, phone 901-685-9992.
Civil Records: Access: Fax, mail, in person, online. Both court and visitors may perform in person searches. Search fee: $5.00 per name. Required to search: name; also helpful: years to search. Civil cases indexed by defendant, plaintiff. Civil records archived from early 1900s, on computer from 1991, on microfiche from 1980. Search the clerk's circuit court records for free at the website or at http://circuitdata.co.shelby.tn.us/crwebplsql/ck_public_qry_main.cp_main_idx%20.
General Information: Public Access terminal is available. No juvenile or adoption records released. Will fax results $1.00 per page. Copy fee: $.50 per page. Cert fee: $5.00 instate, $8.00 out-of-state. Payee: Circuit Court Clerk. Personal checks accepted. Prepayment required. Mail turnaround time 5-8 days.

30th District Criminal Court Office of the Criminal Court, 201 Poplar, Rm 4-01, Memphis, TN 38103; 901-545-5001; Fax: 901-545-3679. Hours: 8AM-4:30PM (CST). *Felony.*
www.co.shelby.tn.us/county_gov/court_clerks/criminal_court/index.html
Criminal Records: Access: Fax, mail, in person, online. Both court and visitors may perform in person searches. Search fee: $5.00 per name. There is no fee if you do the search yourself. Required to search: name, years to search, DOB, SSN. Criminal records on computer for approximately 15 years, prior records archived since court started. Search the criminal court records for free at http://jssi.co.shelby.tn.us/.
General Information: Public Access terminal is available. No expunged or sealed records released. Fee to fax results is $4.00 per document if out of town, $3.00 is in-town. Copy fee: $2.00 per page. Cert fee: $6.00. Payee: Criminal Court Clerk. Business checks accepted. Visa, MC accepted in person only. Prepayment required. Mail turnaround time 3 days.

Chancery Court 140 Adams, Rm 308, Memphis, TN 38103; 901-545-4002; Fax: 901-545-3309. Hours: 8AM-4:30PM (CST). *Civil Actions Under $25,000, Equity Cases (also, lower Circuit Court Civil issues).*
www.co.shelby.tn.us/county_gov/court_clerks/chancery_court/index.htm
Civil Records: Access: Mail, fax, in person, online. Only the court performs in person searches; visitors may not. Search fee: $5.00 per name. Required to search: name, years to search. Civil cases indexed by defendant, plaintiff. Search court records for free at http://chancerydata.co.shelby.tn.us/chwebplsql/ck_public_qry_main.cp_main_idx.
General Information: No juvenile or adoption records released. Copy fee: $1.00 per page. Cert fee: $10.00 per document. Payee: Chancery Court Clerk. Prepayment required. Mail requests: SASE requested. Turnaround time 1 week.

General Sessions - Civil 140 Adams, Rm 106, Memphis, TN 38103; 901-576-4031; Fax: 901-545-4515. Hours: 8AM-4:30PM (CST). *Civil Actions Under $25,000, Eviction, Small Claims.*
http://generalsessionscourt.co.shelby.tn.us
Note: There is a East Divison office at 942-A Mt. Moriah Rd., ph 901-685-9992, fax 901-685-9856.

Civil Records: Access: In person, online. Visitors must perform in person searches for themselves. No search fee. Required to search: name, years to search. Civil cases indexed by defendant, plaintiff. Civil records archived 10 years in office, (prior records unsure), some microfiche and on computer from 1982. Search the court records for free at http://circuitdata.co.shelby.tn.us/gnwebplsql/ck_public_qry_main.cp_main_idx.

General Information: Public Access terminal is available. No mental commitment records released. Copy fee: $1.50 per page. Cert fee: $6.00. Payee: General Sessions Court Clerk. Personal checks accepted. Prepayment required.

General Sessions - Criminal 201 Poplar, Rm 81, Memphis, TN 38103; 901-545-5100; Fax: 901-545-3655. Hours: 8AM-4:30PM (CST). *Misdemeanor.*

http://generalsessionscourt.co.shelby.tn.us

Criminal Records: Access: Mail, in person, online. Both court and visitors may perform in person searches. Search fee: $10.00 per name. Use of terminal is $10.00 each 20 minutes. Required to search: name, years to search, DOB; also helpful: SSN. Criminal records on computer since 1982, prior records archived since court started. Search the criminal court records for free at http://jssi.co.shelby.tn.us/.

General Information: Public Access terminal is available. No mental records released. Copy fee: $1.50 per page. No cert fee. Payee: General Sessions Court. Personal checks accepted. Prepayment required. Mail requests: SASE not required. Mail turnaround time 2-5 days.

Probate Court 140 Adams, Rm 124, Memphis, TN 38103; 901-545-4040; Fax: 901-545-4746. Hours: 8AM-4:30PM (CST). *Probate.*

www.probate.co.shelby.tn.us

Note: Probate court records are available fee online at www.probatedata.co.shelby.tn.us.

Smith County

15th District Circuit & General Sessions Court 211 Main St, Carthage, TN 37030; 615-735-0500 (Gen Sess.); 615-735-8260 (Circuit Ct); Fax: 615-735-8261. Hours: 8AM-4PM M-F (CST). *Felony, Misdemeanor, Civil, Eviction, Small Claims.*

Civil Records: Access: Mail, in person. Visitors must perform in person searches for themselves. No search fee. Required to search: name, years to search. Civil cases indexed by defendant, plaintiff. Civil records on computer from 3/92, prior records archived on books, questionable to dates.

Criminal Records: Access: Phone, mail, in person. Visitors must perform in person searches for themselves. No search fee. Required to search: name, years to search. Criminal records on computer from 3/92, prior records archived on books, questionable to dates.

General Information: No juvenile records released. Will not fax results. Copy fee: $.25 per page. Cert fee: $6.00. Payee: Circuit Court Clerk. Only cashiers checks and money orders accepted. Prepayment required. Mail turnaround time 1-2 days.

Chancery Court 211 N Main St, Carthage, TN 37030; 615-735-2092; Fax: 615-735-8261. Hours: 8AM-4PM (CST). *Civil, Probate.*

Civil Records: Access: Fax, mail, in person. Only the court performs in person searches; visitors may not. No search fee. Required to search: name, years to search. Civil cases indexed by defendant, plaintiff. Civil records on books back to 1825.

General Information: No adoption records released. Fee to fax results is $1.00 per page. Copy fee: $.50 per page. Cert fee: $4.00. Payee: Clerk and Master.

Personal checks accepted. Prepayment required. Mail requests: SASE requested. Turnaround time 1 day.

Stewart County

23rd District Circuit & General Sessions Court PO Box 193, Dover, TN 37058; 931-232-7042; Fax: 931-232-3111. Hours: 8AM-4:30PM (CST). *Felony, Misdemeanor, Civil, Eviction, Small Claims.*

Civil Records: Access: Mail, in person. Visitors must perform in person searches for themselves. No search fee. Required to search: name, years to search. Civil cases indexed by plaintiff. Civil records archived on books from 1800s, on computer through 8/1993.

Criminal Records: Access: Mail, in person. Visitors must perform in person searches for themselves. No search fee. Required to search: name, years to search. Criminal records archived on books from 1800s, on computer through 8/1993.

General Information: No expunged records released. Will fax results to local or toll free line. No cert fee. Turnaround time 1-10 days.

Chancery Court PO Box 102, Dover, TN 37058; 931-232-5665; Fax: 931-232-3111. Hours: 8AM-4:30PM (CST). *Civil, Probate.*

Civil Records: Access: Mail, in person. Only the court performs in person searches; visitors may not. No search fee. Required to search: name, years to search. Civil cases indexed by defendant, plaintiff. Civil records on books to 1865; computerized since 1994.

General Information: No adoption records released. Copy fee: $.50 per page. Cert fee: $4.00. Payee: Clerk and Master. Personal checks accepted. Prepayment required. Mail requests: SASE required. Mail turnaround time 1 week.

Sullivan County

Bristol Circuit Court - Civil Division Courthouse, Rm 131, 801 Anderson St, Bristol, TN 37620; 423-989-4354. Hours: 8AM-5PM (EST). *Civil.*

www.bridgeweb.org

Civil Records: Access: In person. Visitors may perform in person searches. No search fee. Civil cases indexed by defendant, plaintiff. Civil records archived from 1930s (minute books, unsure of docket books), on computer from 1986.

General Information: Public Access terminal is available. No adoption or sealed records released. Will not fax results. Copy fee: $1.00 per page. Cert fee: $5.00 for the seal and $1.00 per page. Payee: Circuit Court Clerk. Personal checks accepted.

Kingsport Circuit Court - Civil Division 225 W Center St, Kingsport, TN 37660; 423-224-1724. Hours: 8AM-5PM (EST). *Civil Actions Over $15,000.*

Civil Records: Access: Phone, mail, in person. Both court and visitors may perform in person searches. No search fee. Required to search: name, years to search. Civil cases indexed by defendant, plaintiff. Civil records archived from 1920s, on computer from 1985.

General Information: Public Access terminal is available. No juvenile, adoption records released. Will not fax results. Copy fee: $1.00 per page. Cert fee: $5.00. Payee: Circuit Court Clerk. Personal checks accepted. Prepayment required. Mail requests: SASE requested. Turnaround time 2-3 days.

2nd District Circuit Court 140 Blockville ByPass, PO Box 585, Blountville, TN 37617; 423-323-5158. Hours: 8AM-5PM (EST). *Felony, Misdemeanor.*

Criminal Records: Access: In person only. Visitors must perform in person searches for themselves. No search fee. Required to search: name, years to search,

DOB; also helpful: SSN. Criminal records on computer since 12/83; prior records archived since the 1800s.

General Information: Public Access terminal is available. No juvenile records released. Copy fee: $1.00 per page. Cert fee: $7.00 per page. Payee: Circuit Court Clerk. Personal checks accepted.

Bristol General Sessions Court Courthouse, 801 Anderson St, Rm 131, Bristol, TN 37620; 423-989-4352. Hours: 8AM-5PM (EST). *Misdemeanor, Civil Actions Under $15,000, Eviction, Small Claims.*

www.bridgeweb.org/docketts.htm

Civil Records: Access: In person only. Visitors must perform in person searches for themselves. No search fee. Required to search: name, years to search. Civil cases indexed by defendant, plaintiff. Civil records archived since court started (stored in Blountville), on computer from 1986. Access to dockets and rules is free online at www.bridgeweb.org/docketts.htm.

Criminal Records: Access: In person only. Visitors must perform in person searches for themselves. No search fee. Required to search: name, years to search. Criminal records archived since court started (stored in Blountville), on computer from 1986. Access to dockets and rules is free online at www.bridgeweb.org/docketts.htm.

General Information: Public Access terminal is available. No juvenile records released. Cert fee: $5.00. Payee: Circuit Court Clerk. Personal checks accepted. Prepayment required.

Chancery Court PO Box 327, Blountville, TN 37617; 423-323-6483; Fax: 423-279-3280. Hours: 8AM-5PM (EST). *Civil, Probate.*

Civil Records: Access: Mail, in person. Both court and visitors may perform in person searches. No search fee. Required to search: name, years to search. Civil cases indexed by defendant, plaintiff. Civil records on books back to 1867; computerized records go back to 1996.

General Information: Public Access terminal is available. No adoption records released. Copy fee: Varies by length of document. Cert fee: $5.00. Payee: Chancery Court. Personal checks accepted. Prepayment required.

Kingsport General Sessions 200 Shelby St, Kingsport, TN 37660; 423-224-1711. Hours: 8AM-5PM (EST). *Misdemeanor, Civil Actions Under $15,000, Eviction, Small Claims.*

Civil Records: Access: In person only. Visitors must perform in person searches for themselves. No search fee. Required to search: name, years to search. Civil cases indexed by defendant, plaintiff. Civil records archived in office from 1973, on computer from 1981.

Criminal Records: Access: In person only. Visitors must perform in person searches for themselves. No search fee. Required to search: name, years to search; also helpful: SSN. Criminal records archived in office from 1973, on computer from 1981.

General Information: Public Access terminal is available. No juvenile records released. Copy fee: $1.00 per page. Cert fee: $7.00 per page. Payee: General Sessions Clerk. Personal checks accepted. Prepayment required.

Sumner County

18th District Circuit & General Sessions Court Public Sq, PO Box 549, Gallatin, TN 37066; 615-452-4367; Fax: 615-451-6027. Hours: 8AM-4:30PM (CST). *Felony, Misdemeanor, Civil, Eviction, Small Claims.*

Civil Records: Access: In person only. Visitors must perform in person searches for themselves. No search fee. Required to search: name, years to search. Civil

cases indexed by defendant, plaintiff. Civil records archived on books in office from 1981.

Criminal Records: Access: In person only. Visitors must perform in person searches for themselves. No search fee. Required to search: name, years to search. Criminal records archived on books in office from 1958, computerized back to 1997.

General Information: Public Access terminal is available. No juvenile, adoption records released. Copy fee: $1.00 per page. Cert fee: $4.00. Payee: Circuit Court Clerk. Only cashiers checks and money orders accepted. Prepayment required.

Chancery Court Rm 300, Sumner County Courthouse, Gallatin, TN 37066; 615-452-4282; Fax: 615-451-6031. Hours: 8AM-4:30PM (CST). *Civil, Probate.*

Civil Records: Access: Phone, fax, mail, in person. Both court and visitors may perform in person searches. Search fee: $5.00. Required to search: name, years to search. Civil cases indexed by defendant, plaintiff. Civil records go back to 1981.

General Information: No juvenile or adoption records released. Will fax results for $1.00 per page. Copy fee: $1.00 per page. Cert fee: $4.00 plus $2.00 per page. Payee: Clerk and Master. Only money orders, cash, or business checks accepted. Prepayment required. Mail turnaround time 1-2 days.

Tipton County

25th District Circuit & General Sessions Court 1801 S College, Rm 102, Covington, TN 38019; 901-475-3310. Hours: 8AM-5PM (CST). *Felony, Misdemeanor, Civil, Eviction, Small Claims.*
Civil Records: Access: Mail, in person. Both court and visitors may perform in person searches. Search fee: $10.00 per name per court. $25.00 for computer info before 07/91. Required to search: name, years to search. Civil cases indexed by defendant, plaintiff. Civil records on computer from July 1991, prior records on docket books.

Criminal Records: Access: Mail, in person. Both court and visitors may perform in person searches. Search fee: $10.00 per name per court. Required to search: name, years to search, DOB; also helpful: SSN. Criminal records on computer from July 1992, prior records on docket books.

General Information: Public Access terminal is available. No juvenile or adoption records released. Copy fee: $.50 per page. Cert fee: $5.00. Payee: Circuit Court Clerk or General Sessions. Personal checks accepted. Prepayment required. Mail requests: SASE requested. Turnaround time 1 week.

Chancery Court Tipton County Justice Ctr, 1801 S College, #110, Covington, TN 38019; 901-476-0209; Fax: 901-476-0246. Hours: 8AM-5PM (CST). *Civil, Probate.*
Civil Records: Access: Phone, fax, mail, in person. Both court and visitors may perform in person searches. No search fee. Required to search: name, years to search. Civil cases indexed by defendant, plaintiff. Civil records on books since 1800s, on computer since 1991.

General Information: Public Access terminal is available. (Public terminal for civil in person searchers.) No adoption records released. Copy fee: $.50 per page. Cert fee: $4.00 plus $2.00 per page. Payee: Tipton County Chancery Court. Personal checks accepted. Prepayment required. Mail requests: SASE required. Mail turnaround time ASAP.

Trousdale County

15th District Circuit & General Sessions Court 200 E Main St, Rm 5, Hartsville, TN 37074; 615-374-3411; Fax: 615-374-1100. Hours: 8AM-4:30PM (CST). *Felony, Misdemeanor, Civil, Eviction, Small Claims.*
Civil Records: Access: In person only. Visitors must perform in person searches for themselves. No search fee. Required to search: name, years to search. Civil cases indexed by defendant, plaintiff. Civil records archived on books since 1927.

Criminal Records: Access: In person only. Visitors must perform in person searches for themselves. No search fee. Required to search: name, years to search. Criminal records archived on books since 1927.

General Information: No juvenile or adoption records released. Will fax results for fee. Copy fee: $1.00 per page. Cert fee: $3.00. Payee: Circuit Court Clerk. Only cashiers checks and money orders accepted. Prepayment required.

Chancery Court Courthouse Rm 1, 200 E Main St, Hartsville, TN 37074; 615-374-2996; Fax: 615-374-1100. Hours: 8AM-4:30PM (CST). *Civil, Probate.*
Civil Records: Access: In person only. Visitors must perform in person searches for themselves. No search fee. Required to search: name, years to search. Civil cases indexed by defendant, plaintiff. Civil records on book since 9/80, prior records in County Clerks office.
General Information: No adoption or sealed records released. Will fax results. Copy fee: $1.00 per page. Cert fee: $3.00 plus $.50 per page. Payee: Clerk and Master. Personal checks accepted. Prepayment required.

Unicoi County

1st District Circuit & General Sessions Court PO Box 2000, Erwin, TN 37650; 423-743-3541. Hours: 9AM-5PM (EST). *Felony, Misdemeanor, Civil, Eviction, Small Claims.*
Civil Records: Access: Mail, in person. Both court and visitors may perform in person searches. Search fee: $10.00 per name. Required to search: name, years to search. Civil cases indexed by defendant, plaintiff. Civil records archived on books from 1932 (felonies) and 1961 (misdemeanors); only general sessions is on computer back to late 1996.
Criminal Records: Access: Mail, in person. Both court and visitors may perform in person searches. Search fee: $10.00 per name. Required to search: name, years to search, DOB. Criminal records archived on books from 1932 (felonies) and 1961 (misdemeanors); only general sessions is on computer back to late 1996.
General Information: Public Access terminal is available. No adoption records released. Will fax results to local or toll free line. Copy fee: $.25 per page. Cert fee: $4.50 per document plus $.50 per page. Payee: Circuit Court Clerk. Personal checks accepted. Prepayment required. Mail turnaround time 2 days.

Probate Court PO Box 340, Erwin, TN 37650; 423-743-3381; Fax: 423-743-5430. Hours: 9AM-5PM M-F, 9AM-Noon Sat (EST). *Probate.*

Union County

8th District Circuit & General Sessions Court 901 E Main St, #220, Maynardville, TN 37807; 865-992-5493. Hours: 8AM-4PM Mon-Fri; 8AM-Noon Sat. (EST). *Felony, Misdemeanor, Civil, Eviction, Small Claims.*
Civil Records: Access: Mail, in person. Both court and visitors may perform in person searches. Search fee: $10.00 per name. Required to search: name, years

to search. Civil cases indexed by defendant, plaintiff. Civil records archived on books from 1969.

Criminal Records: Access: Mail, in person. Both court and visitors may perform in person searches. Search fee: $10.00 per name. Required to search: name, years to search, DOB, SSN. Criminal records archived on books from 1969.

General Information: Public Access terminal is available. No sealed records released. Will fax results. Copy fee: $.25 per page. Cert fee: $4.00. Payee: Circuit Court Clerk. Personal checks accepted. Prepayment required. Mail turnaround time 1 week.

Chancery Court 901 Main St, #215, Maynardville, TN 37807-3510; 865-992-5942. Hours: 8AM-4PM (6PM F) (EST). *Civil, Probate.*
Civil Records: Access: Phone, mail, in person. Both court and visitors may perform in person searches. No search fee. Required to search: name, years to search. Civil cases indexed by plaintiff. Civil records on books back to 1969.
General Information: No adoption records released. Fee to fax results is $1.00 per page. Copy fee: $.25 per page. Cert fee: $4.00. Payee: Union County Clerk and Master. Personal checks accepted. Prepayment required. Mail turnaround time 1 week.

Van Buren County

31st District Circuit & General Sessions Court PO Box 126, Spencer, TN 38585; 931-946-2153; Fax: 931-946-7572. Hours: 8AM-5PM (CST). *Felony, Misdemeanor, Civil, Eviction, Small Claims.*
Civil Records: Access: Mail, in person. Both court and visitors may perform in person searches. Search fee: $10.00 per name. Required to search: name, years to search. Civil cases indexed by defendant. Civil records archived on books, date unspecified.
Criminal Records: Access: Mail, in person. Both court and visitors may perform in person searches. Search fee: $10.00 per name. Required to search: name, years to search, DOB; also helpful: SSN. Criminal records archived on books, date unspecified.
General Information: No juvenile records released. Will fax results ot local or toll free line. Copy fee: $.25 per page. Cert fee: $3.00. Payee: Circuit Court Clerk. Only cashiers checks and money orders accepted. Prepayment required. Mail turnaround time 2 weeks.

County Court PO Box 153, Spencer, TN 38585; 931-946-7175; Fax: 931-946-7572. Hours: 8AM-4PM M-TH.; 8AM-5PM F (CST). *Probate.*

Warren County

31st District Circuit & General Sessions Court 111 Court Sq, PO Box 639, McMinnville, TN 37111; 931-473-2373; Probate phone: 931-473-2364; Fax: 931-473-3726. Hours: 8AM-4:30PM M-TH; 8AM-5PM F (CST). *Felony, Misdemeanor, Civil, Eviction, Small Claims.*
Civil Records: Access: Mail, in person. Both court and visitors may perform in person searches. Search fee: $5.00 per name. Required to search: name, years to search. Civil cases indexed by defendant, plaintiff. Civil records on computer since 1988 (General Sessions), archived in office from 1939 (Circuit).
Criminal Records: Access: Mail, in person. Both court and visitors may perform in person searches. Search fee: $5.00 per name. Required to search: name, years to search, DOB, SSN, offense, date of offense. Criminal records on computer since 1988 (General Sessions), archived in office from 1939 (Circuit).
General Information: Public Access terminal is available. No adoption or juvenile records released. Will fax results for an add'l $5.00 fee. Copy fee: $1.00 per page. Cert fee: $2.00. Payee: Circuit Court

Clerk. Personal checks accepted. Prepayment required. Mail turnaround time 1-2 days.

Chancery Court PO Box 639, McMinnville, TN 37111; 931-473-2364; Fax: 931-473-3232. Hours: 8AM-4:30PM M-TH, 8AM-5PM F (CST). *Civil, Probate.*

Civil Records: Access: Mail, in person. Both court and visitors may perform in person searches. No search fee. Required to search: name, years to search. Civil cases indexed by defendant, plaintiff. Civil records on books.

General Information: No adoption records released. Copy fee: $2.00 per page. Cert fee: $4.00 for first page, $2.00 each add'l. Payee: Clerk and Master. Personal checks accepted. Prepayment required. Mail requests: SASE required. Mail turnaround time 1 week.

Washington County

1st District Circuit & General Sessions Court PO Box 356, Jonesborough, TN 37659; 423-753-1611; Fax: 423-753-1809. Hours: 8AM-5PM (EST). *Felony, Misdemeanor, Civil, Eviction, Small Claims.*

Note: Access to all public records is available in Johnson County.

Civil Records: Access: In person only. Both court and visitors may perform in person searches. Search fee: $5.00 per name. Required to search: name, years to search. Civil cases indexed by defendant, plaintiff. Civil records archived from 1800s, on computer from 1989.

Criminal Records: Access: In person only. Both court and visitors may perform in person searches. Search fee: $5.00 per name. Required to search: name, years to search, DOB, SSN. Criminal records archived from 1800s, on computer from 1989.

General Information: Public Access terminal is available. No sealed, juvenile, adoption records released. Copy fee: $2.00 per page. Cert fee: $4.00. Payee: Circuit Court Clerk. Personal checks accepted. Prepayment required.

General Sessions 101 E Market St, Johnson City, TN 37604; 423-461-1412; Fax: 423-926-4862. Hours: 8AM-5PM (EST). *Civil Actions Under $15,000, Eviction, Small Claims.*

Civil Records: Access: Mail, in person. Both court and visitors may perform in person searches. Search fee: $5.00 per name. Required to search: name, years to search. Civil cases indexed by defendant, plaintiff. Civil records archived since court started, computerized since 1990.

General Information: Public Access terminal is available. No sealed records released. Copy fee: $2.00 per page. Cert fee: $8.00. Payee: Circuit Court Clerk. In state checks accepted. Prepayment required. Mail requests: SASE requested. Turnaround time 1-2 weeks.

Johnson City Law Court - Civil 101 E Market St, Johnson City, TN 37604; 423-461-1475; Fax: 423-926-4862. Hours: 8AM-5PM (EST). *Civil Actions Over $15,000.*

Civil Records: Access: Mail, in person. Both court and visitors may perform in person searches. Search fee: $5.00 per name. Required to search: name, years to search. Civil cases indexed by defendant, plaintiff. Civil records on computer from 1988.

General Information: Public Access terminal is available. No sealed records released. Copy fee: $2.00 per page. Cert fee: $4.00. Payee: Circuit Court Clerk. Personal checks accepted. Out of state checks not accepted. Prepayment required. Mail requests: SASE requested. Turnaround time 1 week.

Probate Court PO Box 218, Jonesborough, TN 37659; 423-753-1623; Fax: 423-753-4716. Hours: 8AM-5PM (EST). *Probate.*

Wayne County

22nd District Circuit & General Sessions Court PO Box 869, Waynesboro, TN 38485; 931-722-5519; Fax: 931-722-5994. Hours: 8AM-4PM M,T,TH,F, 8AM-Noon W & Sat (CST). *Felony, Misdemeanor, Civil, Eviction, Small Claims.*

Civil Records: Access: Phone, mail, in person. Both court and visitors may perform in person searches. Search fee: $5.00 per name. Required to search: name, years to search. Civil cases indexed by defendant, plaintiff. Civil records archived on books from 1800s.

Criminal Records: Access: Phone, mail, in person. Both court and visitors may perform in person searches. Search fee: $5.00 per name. Required to search: name, years to search, DOB, SSN. Criminal records archived on books from 1800s.

General Information: No juvenile or adoption records released. Cert fee: Same as copy fee. Payee: Circuit Court Clerk. Personal checks accepted. Prepayment required. Mail turnaround time 7-10 days.

Chancery Court PO Box 101, Waynesboro, TN 38485; 931-722-5517; Fax: 931-722-5517. Hours: 8AM-4PM (CST). *Civil, Probate.*

Civil Records: Access: Mail, in person. Both court and visitors may perform in person searches. No search fee. Required to search: name, years to search. Civil cases indexed by defendant, plaintiff. Civil records on books; computerized since 12/92.

General Information: No adoption records released. Will fax results to local or toll free line. No copy fee. Cert fee: $3.00 minimum or $1.00 per page. Payee: Clerk and Master. Personal checks accepted. Prepayment required. Mail requests: SASE requested. Turnaround time 2 days.

Weakley County

27th District Circuit & General Sessions Court PO Box 28, Dresden, TN 38225; 731-364-3455; Fax: 731-364-6765. Hours: 8AM-4:30PM (CST). *Felony, Misdemeanor, Civil, Eviction, Small Claims.*

Civil Records: Access: In person only. Visitors must perform in person searches for themselves. No search fee. Required to search: name, years to search. Civil cases indexed by defendant, plaintiff. Civil records archived on since court started, on books; computerized since 1997.

Criminal Records: Access: In person only. Visitors must perform in person searches for themselves. No search fee. Required to search: name, years to search, DOB; also helpful: SSN. Criminal records archived on since court started, on books; computerized since 1997.

General Information: Public Access terminal is available. No adoption or sealed records released. Copy fee: $1.00 per page. Cert fee: $6.00. Payee: Circuit Court Clerk. No personal checks accepted. Prepayment required.

Chancery Court PO Box 197, Dresden, TN 38225; 731-364-3454; Fax: 731-364-5247. Hours: 8AM-4:30PM (CST). *Civil, Probate.*

Note: Court will not do searches for geneaology.

Civil Records: Access: Mail, in person. Both court and visitors may perform in person searches. No search fee. Required to search: name, years to search. Civil cases indexed by defendant, plaintiff. Civil records on computer since 1982, prior records indexed from 1927; Probate to 1800s.

General Information: No adoption or sealed records released. Will fax results for $1.00 per page. Fee must be prepaid. Copy fee: $1.00 per page. Cert fee: $5.00. Payee: Clerk and Master. Personal checks accepted. Prepayment required. Mail turnaround time 1 week.

White County

13th District Circuit & General Sessions Court 111 Depot St #1, Sparta, TN 38583; 931-836-3205; Fax: 931-836-3526. Hours: 8AM-5PM (CST). *Felony, Misdemeanor, Civil, Eviction, Small Claims.*

Civil Records: Access: In person only. Visitors must perform in person searches for themselves. No search fee. Required to search: name, years to search. Civil cases indexed by defendant, plaintiff. Civil records archived since court started, computerized since 1996.

Criminal Records: Access: In person only. Visitors must perform in person searches for themselves. No search fee. Required to search: name, years to search, DOB; also helpful: SSN. Criminal records archived since court started; computerized records since 19996.

General Information: No juvenile, adoption records released. Copy fee: $.50. Cert fee: $3.50. Payee: Circuit Court Clerk. Personal checks accepted. Prepayment required.

Chancery Court White County Courthouse, Rm 303, Sparta, TN 38583; 931-836-3787. Hours: 8AM-4PMn (CST). *Civil, Probate.*

Civil Records: Access: Phone, in person. Visitors must perform in person searches for themselves. No search fee. Required to search: name, years to search. Civil cases indexed by defendant, plaintiff. Overall records go back to 1842.

General Information: No adoption records released. Will not fax results. Copy fee: $1.00 per page. Cert fee: $2.00. Payee: Clerk and Master. Personal checks accepted. Prepayment required.

Williamson County

21st District Circuit & General Sessions Court 135 4th Ave Rm 203, Franklin, TN 37064; 615-790-5454; Fax: 615-790-5411. Hours: 8AM-4:30PM (CST). *Felony, Misdemeanor, Civil, Eviction, Small Claims.*

Civil Records: Access: Mail, in person. Both court and visitors may perform in person searches. Search fee: $15.00 per name. Required to search: name, years to search. Civil cases indexed by defendant, plaintiff. Civil records archived on books from 1810, on computer from 1992.

Criminal Records: Access: Mail, in person. Both court and visitors may perform in person searches. Search fee: $12.00 per name. Misdemeanor search is $30.00. Required to search: name, years to search, DOB; also helpful: SSN. Criminal records archived on books from 1810, on computer from 1992.

General Information: Public Access terminal is available. Cert fee: $4.00. Payee: Circuit Court Clerk. Personal checks accepted. Prepayment required. Mail requests: SASE not required. Mail turnaround time 3 days.

Chancery Court Clerk & Master, PO Box 1666, Franklin, TN 37064; 615-790-5428; Fax: 615-790-5626. Hours: 8AM-4:30PM (CST). *Civil, Probate.*

Civil Records: Access: Phone, mail, in person. Both court and visitors may perform in person searches. No search fee. Required to search: name, years to search. Civil cases indexed by defendant, plaintiff. Civil records on computer since 1991, prior records on books since 1800s (no probate on computer).

General Information: No adoption, sealed records released. Copy fee: $1.00 per page. Cert fee: $2.00 per document. Payee: Clerk and Master. Local checks accepted. Prepayment required. Mail requests: SASE requested.

Wilson County

15th District Circuit & General Sessions

Court PO Box 518, Lebanon, TN 37088-0518; 615-444-2042; Fax: 615-449-3420. Hours: 8AM-4PM M-Th, 8AM-5PM F (CST). *Felony, Misdemeanor, Civil, Eviction, Small Claims.*

Civil Records: Access: In person only. Visitors must perform in person searches for themselves. No search fee. Required to search: name, years to search. Civil cases indexed by defendant, plaintiff. Civil records archived in office from 1982, from 1800s located elsewhere, on computer from 1990, on microfiche from 1940s.

Criminal Records: Access: In person only. Visitors must perform in person searches for themselves. No search fee. Required to search: name, years to search, DOB, SSN. Criminal records archived in office from 1982, from 1800s located elsewhere, on computer from 1190, on microfiche from 1940s.

General Information: Public Access terminal is available. No adoption, juvenile records released. Copy fee: $1.00 per page. Cert fee: $6.00. Plus $2.00 each additional page. Payee: Circuit Court Clerk. Business checks accepted. Prepayment required.

Probate Court PO Box 950, Lebanon, TN 37088-0950; 615-443-2627; Probate phone: 615-444-2835; Fax: 615-443-2628. Hours: 8AM-4:30PM M-Th, 8AM-5PM Fri (CST). *Probate.*

Note: Probate is now Clerk & Master.

Tennessee Recording Offices

ORGANIZATION: 95 counties, 96 recording offices. The recording officer is. Register of Deeds. Sullivan County has two offices. 66 counties are in the Central Time Zone (CST) and 29 are in the Eastern Time Zone (EST).

REAL ESTATE RECORDS: Counties will not perform real estate searches. Certified copies usually cost $1.00 per page. Tax records are kept at the Assessor's Office.

UCC RECORDS: Financing statements are filed at the state level, except for real estate related collateral, which are filed with the Register of Deeds. However, prior to 07/2001, consumer goods and farm collateral were also filed at the Register of Deeds and these older records can be searched there. Many recording offices will not perform UCC searches. Use search request form UCC-11. Search fee is usually $12-15, the copy fee is $1.00.

TAX LIEN RECORDS: All federal tax liens are filed with the county Register of Deeds. State tax liens are filed with the Secretary of State or the Register of Deeds. Counties will not perform tax lien searches.

OTHER LIENS: Judgment, materialman, mechanics, trustee.

ONLINE ACCESS: The State Comptroller of the Treasury Real Estate Assessment Database can be searched free at http://170.142.31.248/. Select a county then search by name for real property information. Counties not on the system are Davidson, Hamilton, Knox, Shelby, and Unicoi.

Online access to forty counties' property and deeds indexes and images is available via a private company at http://auth.titlesearcher.com/ts/ts.asp or email support@TitleSearcher.com. Registration, login, and monthly $35 fee per county required, plus $20. set up. A $5 per day plan is also available.

Also, online access to 22 counties' property, deeds, judgment, liens, and UCCs is available via a private company at www.ustitlesearch.com or call 615-223-5420. Registration, login, and monthly $25 fee required, plus $50 set up. Use DEMO username to try system.

Finally, www.tnrealestate.com offers free and fee services for real estate information from all counties.

Anderson County

Register of Deeds, 100 N Main St, Courthouse, Rm 205, Clinton, TN 37716-3688. **Phone-**865-457-5400; fax-865-457-1638; hours 8:30AM-4:30PM
Will not search records. UCC copy- None. Cert fee: $1.00. Payee: Anderson County Register of Deeds. **Online Access to Land, Property Assessor, Recorder, Deed records:** Access assessment data via the state system, see section introduction.. Access to property and deeds indexes and images is via a private company at www.titlesearcher.com. Fee/registration required; see state introduction. **Other phones:** Assessor-865-457-5400 x225.

Bedford County

Register of Deeds, 108 Northside Sq, Shelbyville, TN 37160. **Phone-**Register of Deeds, R/E & UCC Recording- 931-684-5719; fax-931-685-2086. http://titlesearcher.com
Will not search records. Copy fee- $.25 per page. Cert fee: $1.00 per page. Payee: Bedford County Register of Deeds. **Online Access to Land, Property Assessor, Recorder, Deed records:** Access assessment data via the state system, see section introduction.. Access to property and deeds indexes and images is via a private company at www.titlesearcher.com. Fee/registration required; see state introduction. **Other phones:** Assessor-931-684-6390; Treasurer-931-684-4303; Appraiser-931-684-4303; Elections-931-684-0531.

Benton County

Register of Deeds, 1 E. Court Sq, #105, Camden, TN 38320-2070. **Phone-**731-584-6661; hours 8AM-4PM; 8AM-5PM F
Will search UCC records prior to 7/2001 and current fixture (land) files. Search per debtor- $15.00. Will not search real estate or tax lien records. RE record copy- $.75 per page. UCC copy- $1.00 per page. Cert fee: $1.00 per cert. Payee: Benton County

Register of Deeds. **Online Access to Real Estate, Deed, Judgment, Lien, UCC, Property Assessor records:** Access assessment data via the state system, see section introduction.. Access to indexes and images is via a private company at www.ustitlesearch.com. Registration and monthly fee required; see state introduction. **Other phones:** Assessor-731-584-7615.

Bledsoe County

Register of Deeds, PO Box 385, Pikeville, TN 37367. **Phone-**Register of Deeds, R/E & UCC Recording- 423-447-2020; fax-423-447-6856; hours 8AM-4PM
Will not search records. Copy fee- $.25 per page. Cert fee: $1.00 per page. Payee: Register of Deeds. **Online Access to Land, Property Assessor, Deed, Recording records:** Access assessment data via the state system, see section introduction.. Access to property and deeds indexes and images is via a private company at www.titlesearcher.com. Fee/registration required; see state introduction. **Other phones:** Assessor-423-447-6548; Treasurer-423-447-2369; Appraiser-423-447-6548; Elections-423-447-2776.

Blount County

Register of Deeds, 349 Court St, Maryville, TN 37804-5906. **Phone-**865-273-5880; fax-865-273-5890; hours 8AM-4:30PM. Will not search records. UCC copy- $.50 per page. Cert fee: $1.00. Payee: Blount County Register of Deeds. **Online Access to Property Assessor records:** Access assessment data via the state system, see section introduction.. **Other phones:** Assessor-865-982-5130.

Bradley County

Register of Deeds, PO Box 579, Cleveland, TN 37364-0579. **Phone-**423-476-0513; fax-423-478-8888; hours 8:30AM-4:30PM
Will not search records. **Online Access to Land, Property Assessor, Deed, Recording records:** Access assessment data via the state system, see section introduction.. Access to property and deeds indexes and

images is via a private company at www.titlesearcher.com. Fee/registration required; see state introduction. **Other phones:** Assessor-423-476-0505.

Campbell County

Register of Deeds, PO Box 85, Jacksboro, TN 37757. **Phone-**Register of Deeds, R/E & UCC Recording- 423-562-3864, UCC Recording-423-562-8195; fax-423-562-9833; hours 8AM-4:30PM
Will search UCC records prior to 7/2001 and current fixture (land) files. Search per debtor- $12.00. Tax liens not included in UCC search. Separate federal/state combined tax lien search- $8.00 per debtor. Will not search real estate records. RE record copy- $.25 per copy. UCC copy- $1.00 per page. Cert fee: $1.00 per page. Payee: Campbell County Register of Deeds. **Online Access to Land, Deed, Property Assessor, Deed, Recording records:** Access assessment data via the state system, see section introduction.. Access to property and deeds indexes and images is via a private company at www.titlesearcher.com. Fee/registration required; see state introduction. Images go back to 6/2003. **Other phones:** Assessor-423-562-3201; Treasurer-423-562-5185; Appraiser-423-562-3201.

Cannon County

Register of Deeds, Courthouse, Woodbury, TN 37190. **Phone-**615-563-2041; fax-615-563-5696; 8AM-4PM
Will search UCC records prior to 7/2001 and current fixture (land) files. Search per debtor- $15.00. Will not search real estate or tax lien records. Copy fee- $.50 per page. Cert fee: $1.00 per page. **Online Access to Real Estate, Deed, Judgment, Lien, UCC, Property Assessor records:** Access assessment data via the state system, see section introduction.. Access to real estate records is at www.ustitlesearch.com. Registration and fee required; information at website; also see state introduction. **Other phones:** Assessor-615-563-5437.

Carroll County

Register of Deeds, 625 High St, #104, Carroll County Office Complex, Huntingdon, TN 38344. **Phone-**731-986-1952; fax-731-986-1955; hours 8AM-4PM Will not search records. Cert fee: $1.50. Payee: Carroll County Register of Deeds. **Online Access to Real Estate, Deed, Judgment, Lien, UCC, Property Assessor records:** Access assessment data via the state system, see section introduction.. Access to indexes and images is via a private company at www.ustitlesearch.com. Registration and monthly fee required; see state introduction. **Other phones:** Assessor-731-986-1975.

Carter County

Register of Deeds, 801 E. Elk Ave, Elizabethton, TN 37643. **Phone-**423-542-1830; hours 8:30AM-5PM Will not search records. UCC copy- $1.00 per page. Payee: Carter County Register of Deeds. **Online Access to Land, Property Assessor, Deed, Recording records:** Access assessment data via the state system, see section introduction.. Access to property and deeds indexes and images is via a private company at www.titlesearcher.com. Fee/registration required; see state introduction. **Other phones:** Assessor-423-542-1806.

Cheatham County

Register of Deeds, PO Box 453, Ashland City, TN 37015. **Phone-**615-792-4317; fax-615-792-2039; hours 8AM-4PM Will not search records. UCC copy- $.25 per page. Cert fee: $1.00. Payee: Register of Deeds. **Online Access to Real Estate, Deed, Judgment, Lien, UCC, Property Assessor records:** Access assessment data via the state system, see section introduction.. Access to indexes and images is via a private company at www.ustitlesearch.com. Registration and monthly fee required; see state introduction. **Other phones:** Assessor-615-792-5371; Treasurer-615-792-4298.

Chester County

Register of Deeds, PO Box 292, Henderson, TN 38340. **Phone-**Register of Deeds, R/E & UCC Recording- 731-989-4991; hours 8AM-4PM Will not search records. Cert fee: $1.00 per page. Payee: Chester County Register of Deeds. **Online Access to Real Estate, Deed, Judgment, Lien, UCC, Property Assessor records:** Access assessment data via the state system, see section introduction.. Access to indexes and images is via a private company at www.ustitlesearch.com. Registration and monthly fee required; see state introduction. **Other phones:** Assessor-731-989-4882; Treasurer-731-989-3993.

Claiborne County

Register of Deeds, PO Box 117, Tazewell, TN 37879. **Phone-**423-626-3325; hours 8:30AM-4PM Will not search UCC or tax liens records. Real estate record owner and property searches available. UCC copy- $.25 per page. Cert fee: $4.00 per cert. Payee: Claiborne County Register of Deeds. **Online Access to Land, Property Assessor, Deed, Recording records:** Access assessment data via the state system, see section introduction.. Access to property and deeds indexes and images is via a private company at www.titlesearcher.com. Fee/registration required; see state introduction. **Other phones:** Assessor-423-626-3276; Treasurer-423-626-3275.

Clay County

Register of Deeds, PO Box 430, Celina, TN 38551. **Phone-**931-243-3298; fax-931-243-6723; hours 8AM-4PM M,T,Th,F; 8AM-Noon Sat Will not search records. RE record copy- $.25 per page. Payee: Clay County Register of Deeds. **Online Access to Land, Property Assessor, Deed,**

Recording records: Access assessment data via the state system, see section introduction.. Access to property and deeds indexes and images is via a private company at www.titlesearcher.com. Fee/registration required; see state introduction. **Other phones:** Assessor-931-243-2599; Treasurer-931-243-2310.

Cocke County

Register of Deeds, 111 Court Ave, Rm 102, Courthouse, Newport, TN 37821-3102. **Phone-**423-623-7540; hours 8AM-4:30PM M,T,Th,F; 8AM-Noon W,Sat Will not search records. UCC copy- $.25 per page. Cert fee: None. Payee: Cocke County Register of Deeds. **Online Access to Land, Property Assessor, Deed, Recording records:** Access assessment data via the state system, see section introduction.. Access to property and deeds indexes and images is via a private company at www.titlesearcher.com. Fee/registration required; see state introduction. **Other phones:** Assessor-423-623-7024; Trustee-423-623-3037.

Coffee County

Register of Deeds, PO Box 178, Manchester, TN 37349. **Phone-**Register of Deeds, R/E & UCC Recording- 931-723-5130; fax-931-723-8232. Will not search records. RE record copy- $.50 per page. UCC copy- $1.00 per page. Cert fee: $1.00 per page. Payee: Register of Deeds. **Online Access to Land, Property Assessor, Deed, Recording records:** Access assessment data via the state system, see section introduction.. Access to property and deeds indexes and images is via a private company at www.titlesearcher.com. Fee/registration required; see state introduction. **Other phones:** Assessor-931-723-5126.

Crockett County

Register of Deeds, 1 S Bells St #2, County Courthouse, Alamo, TN 38001. **Phone-**731-696-5455; fax-731-696-3028; hours 8AM-4PM Will not search UCC or real estate records. Copy fee- $.25 per page. Cert fee: $1.00 per page. Payee: Crockett County Register of Deeds. **Online Access to Real Estate, Deed, Judgment, Lien, UCC, Property Assessor records:** Access assessment data via the state system, see section introduction.. Access to indexes and images is via a private company at www.ustitlesearch.com. Registration and monthly fee required; see state introduction. **Other phones:** Assessor-731-696-5456; Treasurer-731-696-5454.

Cumberland County

Register of Deeds, 2 N. Main St, #204, Crossville, TN 38555-4583. **Phone-**931-484-5559; hours 8AM-4PM Will not search records. RE record copy- $5.00 up to 10 pages; $.50 each add'l. UCC copy- $1.00 per page. Cert fee: $2.00 1st pg, $1.00 each add'l. Payee: Cumberland County Register of Deeds. **Online Access to Land, Property Assessor, Deed, Recording records:** Access assessment data via the state system, see section introduction.. Access to property and deeds indexes and images is via a private company at www.titlesearcher.com. Fee/registration required; see state introduction. **Other phones:** Assessor-931-484-5745;   Elections-931-484-4919; Trustee-931-484-5730.

Davidson County

Register of Deeds, 103 Metro Courthouse, Nashville, TN 37201-5028. **Phone-**Register of Deeds, R/E & UCC Recording- 615-862-6790; fax-615-880-2039; 8AM-4:25PM www.registerofdeeds.nashville.org Will not search records. Copy fee- $.50 per page. Cert fee: $1.00 per page. Payee: Register of Deeds. **Online Access to Property, Inmate records:** Property records on the Metropolitan Planning Commission City of Nashville database are free at

www3.nashville.org. Click on "name search." There is also a commercial online service that allows subscribers to download information via an FTP site. To subscribe fill out application and send with check for $25.00. Also, search inmate info on private company website at www.vinelink.com/index.jsp. **Other phones:** Assessor-615-862-6080.

De Kalb County

Register of Deeds, One Public Sq, Rm 201, Smithville, TN 37166. **Phone-**615-597-4153; fax-615-597-7420; hours 8AM-4:30PM Will not search records. UCC copy- $.25 per page. Cert fee: $1.00. Payee: De Kalb County Register of Deeds. **Online Access to Property Assessor records:** Access assessment data via the state system, see section introduction.. **Other phones:** Assessor-615-597-5925; Trustee-615-597-5176.

Decatur County

Register of Deeds, PO Box 488, Decaturville, TN 38329. **Phone-**731-852-3712; hours 8AM-4PM M, T, Th, F; 8AM-Noon W, Sat www.titlesearcher.com Will not search records. Record copy- $1.00 per page. Cert fee: $1.00 per page. Payee: Decatur County Register of Deeds. **Online Access to Land, Property Assessor, Deed, Recording records:** Access assessment data via the state system, see section introduction.. Access to property and deeds indexes and images is via a private company at www.titlesearcher.com. Fee/registration required; see state introduction. **Other phones:** Assessor-731-852-3117; Treasurer-731-852-3723.

Dickson County

Register of Deeds, PO Box 130, Charlotte, TN 37036. **Phone-**615-789-5123; fax-615-789-3893; 8AM-4PM Will search UCC records prior to 7/2001 and current fixture (land) files. UCC search per debtor- $15.00. Will not search real estate or tax lien records. UCC copy- $1.00 per page. Cert fee: $1.00. Payee: Dickson County Register of Deeds. **Online Access to Real Estate, Deed, Judgment, Lien, UCC, Property Assessor records:** Access assessment data via the state system, see section introduction.. Also, access to indexes and images is via a private company at www.ustitlesearch.com. Registration and monthly fee required; see state introduction. Also, a second private company offers access to online access to property and deeds indexes and images at www.titlesearcher.com. Fee/registration required; see state introduction. **Other phones:** Assessor-615-789-4171.

Dyer County

Register of Deeds, PO Box 1360, Dyersburg, TN 38025-1360. **Phone-**Register of Deeds, R/E & UCC Recording- 731-286-7806; fax-731-288-7724; hours 8:30AM-4:30PM www.co.dyer.tn.us Will not search records. Copy fee- $.50 per page. Cert fee: $1.00 per instrument. Payee: Dyer County Register. **Online Access to Real Estate, Deed, Judgment, Lien, UCC, Property Tax records:** Access to indexes and images is via a private company at www.ustitlesearch.com. Registration and monthly fee required; see state introduction. Access assessment data via the state system, see section introduction.. Also, property tax information is free online at https://dyer.tn.ezgov.com/property/review_search.jsp however, no name searching. **Other phones:** Assessor-731-286-7805; Treasurer-731-286-7802; Elections-731-286-4268; Vital Records-731-286-7814.

Fayette County

Register of Deeds, PO Box 99, Somerville, TN 38068-0099. **Phone-**901-465-5251; hours 9AM-5PM Will search UCC records prior to 7/2001 and current fixture (land) files. Will not search real estate or tax lien records. Copy fee- $1.00 per page. Cert fee: $1.00 per cert + $1.00 per page. Payee: Fayette County Register of Deeds. **Online Access to Land, Property Assessor, Deed, Recording records:** Access assessment data via the state system, see section introduction.. Access to property and deeds indexes and images is via a private company at www.titlesearcher.com. Fee/registration required; see state introduction. **Other phones:** Assessor-901-465-5226; Treasurer-901-465-5224; Elections-901-465-5223.

Fentress County

Register of Deeds, PO Box 341, Jamestown, TN 38556. **Phone-**Register of Deeds, R/E & UCC Recording- 931-879-7818; fax-931-879-4502; hours 8AM-4PM
Will not search records. RE record copy- $.25 per page. UCC copy- $1.00 per page. Cert fee: $1.00 per page. Payee: Register of Deeds. **Online Access to Land, Property Assessor, Deed, Recording records:** Access assessment data via the state system, see section introduction.. Access to property and deeds indexes and images is via a private company at www.titlesearcher.com. Fee/registration required; see state introduction. **Other phones:** Assessor-931-879-9194; Treasurer-931-879-7717; Appraiser-931-879-8294; Elections-931-879-7162; Vital Records-931-879-8014; County Executive-931-879-7713.

Franklin County

Register of Deeds, 1 S Jefferson St, Rm #6, Franklin County Courthouse, Winchester, TN 37398-0101. **Phone-**Register of Deeds, R/E & UCC Recording- 931-967-2840; hours 8AM-4:30PM; 8AM-Noon Sat www.titlesearcher.com
Will not search records. RE record copy- $.50 1st page, $.50 each add'l. UCC copy- $1.00 per page. Cert fee: $1.00 per page. Payee: Franklin County Register of Deeds. **Online Access to Land, Property Assessor, Deed, Recorder records:** Access assessment data via the state system, see section introduction.. Access to property and deeds indexes and images is via a private company at www.titlesearcher.com. Registration and password required; signup at website. **Other phones:** Assessor-931-967-3869; Treasurer-931-967-2962.

Gibson County

Register of Deeds, 1 Court Sq, Courthouse, Trenton, TN 38382. **Phone-**731-855-7628; fax-731-855-7650; hours 8AM-4:30PM M-F; 8AM-Noon Sat.
Will not search UCC or real estate records. Copy fee- $.50 per page. **Online Access to Real Estate, Deed, Judgment, Lien, UCC, Property Assessor records:** Access assessment data via the state system, see section introduction.. Access to indexes and images is via a private company at www.ustitlesearch.com. Registration and monthly fee required; see state introduction. **Other phones:** Assessor-731-855-7634; Elections-731-855-7669.

Giles County

Register of Deeds, PO Box 678, Pulaski, TN 38478. **Phone-**Register of Deeds, R/E & UCC Recording- 931-363-5137; fax-931-424-6101; hours 8AM-4PM www.usit.net/giles/Government/register.htm
Will not search records. RE record copy- $.25 per page. UCC copy- $1.00 per page. Cert fee: $1.00 per page. Payee: Giles County Register of Deeds. **Online Access to Land, Property Assessor, Deed, Recording records:** Access assessment data via the state system, see section introduction.. Access to property and deeds indexes and images is via a private company at www.titlesearcher.com. Fee/registration required; see state introduction. **Other phones:** Assessor-931-363-2166; Treasurer-931-363-1676; Appraiser-931-363-2166; Elections-931-363-2424; Trustee-931-363-1676.

Grainger County

Register of Deeds, PO Box 174, Rutledge, TN 37861. **Phone-**865-828-3511; fax-865-828-4300; hours 8:30-4:30PM
Will search UCC records prior to 7/2001 and current fixture (land) files. Search per debtor- $15.00. Will not search real estate or tax lien records. UCC copy- $1.00 per page. Cert fee: $5.00. Payee: Grainger County Register of Deeds. **Online Access to Land, Property Assessor, Deed, Recording records:** Access assessment data via the state system, see section introduction.. Access to property and deeds indexes and images is via a private company at www.titlesearcher.com. Fee/registration required; see state introduction. **Other phones:** Assessor-865-828-5858; Vital Records-615-741-1763; Trustee-865-828-3514.

Greene County

Register of Deeds, 101 S. Main St. #201, Courthouse, Greeneville, TN 37743. **Phone-**423-798-1726, R/E Recording-423-639-1726, UCC Recording-423-639-1726; hours 8AM-4:30PM
Will not search records. UCC copy- $1.00 per page. Cert fee: $1.00 per page. Payee: Greene County Register of Deeds. **Online Access to Land, Property Assessor, Deed, Recording records:** Access assessment data via the state system, see section introduction.. Access to property and deeds indexes and images is via a private company at www.titlesearcher.com. Fee/registration required; see state introduction. **Other phones:** Assessor-423-638-1738; Treasurer-423-639-1705.

Grundy County

Register of Deeds, PO Box 35, Altamont, TN 37301-0035. **Phone-**931-692-3621; fax-931-692-3627. www.tngenweb.org/grundy/
Will search UCC records prior to 7/2001 and current fixture (land) files. Will not search real estate records. **Online Access to Real Estate, Deed, Judgment, Lien, UCC, Property Assessor records:** Access assessment data via the state system, see section introduction.. Access to property and deeds indexes and images is via a private company at www.titlesearcher.com. Fee/registration required; see state introduction. Also, access to indexes and images is via a private company at www.ustitlesearch.com. Registration and monthly fee required; see state introduction. **Other phones:** Assessor-931-692-3596.

Hamblen County

Register of Deeds, 511 W. 2nd North St, Morristown, TN 37814. **Phone-**423-586-6551; fax-423-587-9798; hours 8:00AM-4:00PM M-F
Will search UCC records prior to 7/2001 and current fixture (land) files. Search per debtor- $15.00. Federal/state combined tax lien search- $1.00 per doc + $.25 per page to mail. Will not search real estate records. Copy fee- $1.00 per doc + $.25 per page to mail. Cert fee: $1.00 per page. Payee: Register of Deeds. **Online Access to Land, Property Assessor, Deed, Recording records:** Access assessment data via the state system, see section introduction.. Access to property and deeds indexes and images is via a private company at www.titlesearcher.com. Fee/registration required; see state introduction.

Hamilton County

Register of Deeds, PO Box 1639, Chattanooga, TN 37401-1639. **Phone-**423-209-6560; fax-423-209-6561; hours 7:30AM-5PM www.hamiltontn.gov/register
Will Search UCC records prior to 7/2001 and current fixture (land) files. Will not search real estate or tax lien records. UCC copy- $1.00 per page. Cert fee: $1.00 per page. Payee: Hamilton County Register

of Deeds. **Online Access to Real Estate, Recording, Deed, Property Assessor, Delinquent Tax records:** The County Register of Deeds subscription service is $50 per month and $1.00 per fax page. Search by name, address, or book & page. For info, call 423-209-6560; or visit www.hamiltontn.gov/Register/default.htm. Credit cards accepted. Also, property assessor and register of deeds records are free at www.hamiltontn.gov/DataServices/default.htm. Click on "Assessor of Property Inquiry." Also, search here for court records. Also, search back tax lists are at www.hamiltontn.gov/Trustee/delinquent%20taxes.htm. Also, search City of Chattanooga property tax database at http://propertytax.chattanooga.gov. **Other phones:** Assessor-423-209-7300; Treasurer-423-209-7270.

Hancock County

Register of Deeds, PO Box 347, Sneedville, TN 37869. **Phone-**423-733-4545; hours 8:30AM-4PM; 8:30AM-Noon W,Sat
Will search UCC records prior to 7/2001 and current fixture (land) files. Search per debtor- $12.00. Will not search real estate or tax lien records. UCC copy- $1.00 per page. Cert fee: $5.00. Payee: Hancock County Register of Deeds. **Online Access to Real Estate, Deed, Judgment, Lien, UCC, Property Assessor records:** Access assessment data via the state system, see section introduction.. Access to real estate records is at www.ustitlesearch.com. Registration and fee required; information at website; also see state introduction. **Other phones:** Assessor-423-733-2332; Treasurer-423-733-2939; Elections-423-733-4549.

Hardeman County

Register of Deeds, Courthouse, 100 N Main St., Bolivar, TN 38008. **Phone-**Register of Deeds, R/E & UCC Recording- 731-658-3476; fax-731-658-3075; hours 8:30AM-4:30PM; 8:30AM-5PM F
Will not search records. RE record copy- $.50 per page. UCC copy- $1.00 per page. Cert fee: $1.00 per page. Payee: Hardeman County Register of Deeds. **Online Access to Real Estate, Deed, Judgment, Lien, UCC, Property Assessor records:** Access assessment data via the state system, see section introduction.. Access to indexes and images is via a private company at www.ustitlesearch.com. Registration and monthly fee required; see state introduction. **Other phones:** Assessor-731-658-6522; Treasurer-731-658-5541; Appraiser-731-658-6522; Elections-731-658-4751.

Hardin County

Register of Deeds, Courthouse, Savannah, TN 38372. **Phone-**731-925-4936; hours 8AM-4:30PM M,T,Th,F; 8AM-Noon W
Will search UCC records prior to 7/2001 and current fixture (land) files. Will not search real estate or tax lien records. UCC copy- $1.00 per page. Cert fee: $1.00 per cert. Payee: Hardin County Register of Deeds. **Online Access to Real Estate, Deed, Judgment, Lien, UCC, Property Assessor records:** Access assessment data via the state system, see section introduction.. Access to indexes and images is via a private company at www.ustitlesearch.com. Registration and monthly fee required; see state introduction. **Other phones:** Assessor-731-925-9031; Treasurer-731-925-8180.

Hawkins County

Register of Deeds, PO Box 235, Rogersville, TN 37857. **Phone-**Register of Deeds, R/E & UCC Recording- 423-272-8304; fax-423-921-3170; hours 8AM-4PM; W & Sat 8AM-N
Will not search records. UCC copy- $1.00 per page. Cert fee: $1.00 per page. Payee: Register of Deeds. **Online Access to Land, Property Assessor, Deed, Recording records:** Access assessment data via the

state system, see section introduction.. Access to property and deeds indexes and images is via a private company at www.titlesearcher.com. Fee/registration required; see state introduction. **Other phones:** Assessor-423-272-8505; Treasurer-423-272-7022 Trustee; Elections-423-272-8061.

Haywood County

Register of Deeds, 1 N. Washington, Courthouse, Brownsville, TN 38012. **Phone**-731-772-1432; hours 8:30AM-5PM

Will search UCC records prior to 7/2001 and current fixture (land) files. Search per debtor- $12.00. Will not search real estate or tax lien records. UCC copy- $1.00 per page. Payee: Haywood County Register of Deeds. **Online Access to Property Assessor records:** Access assessment data via the state system, see section introduction.. **Other phones:** Assessor-731-772-0432; Treasurer-731-772-1722.

Henderson County

Register of Deeds, Courthouse, Lexington, TN 38351. **Phone**-Register of Deeds, R/E & UCC Recording- 731-968-2941; hours 8AM-4:30PM; closed on Sat.
Will not search records. Copy fee- $.25 per page. Cert fee: $1.00 per page. Payee: Henderson County Register of Deeds. **Online Access to Real Estate, Deed, Judgment, Lien, UCC, Property Assessor records:** Access assessment data via the state system, see section introduction.. Access to indexes and images is via a private company at www.ustitlesearch.com. Registration and monthly fee required; see state introduction. **Other phones:** Assessor-731-968-6881; Treasurer-731-968-2246.

Henry County

Register of Deeds, PO Box 44, Paris, TN 38242. **Phone**-Register of Deeds, R/E & UCC Recording- 731-642-4081; fax-731-642-2123; hours 8:30AM-4:30PM
Will not search records. Cert fee: $1.00 per page. **Online Access to Real Estate, Deed, Judgment, Lien, UCC, Property Assessor records:** Access assessment data via the state system, see section introduction.. Access to indexes and images is via a private company at www.ustitlesearch.com. Registration and monthly fee required; see state introduction. **Other phones:** Assessor-731-642-0162; Elections-731-642-0411; Trustee-731-642-6633.

Hickman County

Register of Deeds, #1 Courthouse, Centerville, TN 37033-1639. **Phone**-Register of Deeds, R/E & UCC Recording- 931-729-4882; hours 7:30AM-4PM
Will search UCC records prior to 7/2001 and current fixture (land) files. Search per debtor- $15.00. Will not search real estate or tax lien records. Record copy- $1.00 per page. Cert fee: $1.00 per page. Payee: Hickman County Register of Deeds. **Online Access to Land, Property Assessor, Deed, Recording records:** Access assessment data via the state system, see section introduction.. Access to property and deeds indexes and images is via a private company at www.titlesearcher.com. Fee/registration required; see state introduction. **Other phones:** Assessor-931-729-2169.

Houston County

Register of Deeds, PO Box 388, Erin, TN 37061. **Phone**-931-289-3141; fax-931-289-4240.
Will search UCC records prior to 7/2001 and current fixture (land) files. Will not search real estate records. **Online Access to Real Estate, Deed, Judgment, Lien, UCC, Property Assessor records:** Access assessment data via the state system, see section introduction.. Also, access to indexes and images is via a private company at www.ustitlesearch.com. Registration and monthly fee required; see state introduction. **Other phones:** Assessor-931-289-3929; Vital Records-615-726-2559.

Humphreys County

Register of Deeds, 102 Thompson St, Courthouse Annex, Rm 3, Waverly, TN 37185. **Phone**-Register of Deeds, R/E & UCC Recording- 931-296-7681; hours 8AM-4:30PM

Will not search records. Record copy- $1.00 per page. Cert fee: $1.00 per page. Payee: Humphreys County Register of Deeds. **Online Access to Land, Property Assessor, Deed, Recording records:** Access assessment data via the state system, see section introduction.. Access to property and deeds indexes and images is via a private company at www.titlesearcher.com. Fee/registration required; see state introduction. **Other phones:** Assessor-931-296-2919; Treasurer-931-296-2414.

Jackson County

Register of Deeds, PO Box 301, Gainesboro, TN 38562. **Phone**-Register of Deeds, R/E & UCC Recording- 931-268-9012; hours 8AM-4PM M,T,Th,F; 8AM-2PM W; 8AM-Noon Sat
Will not search records. RE record copy- $.25 per page. UCC copy- $1.00 per page. Cert fee: $1.00 per doc. Payee: Jackson County Register of Deeds. **Online Access to Land, Property Assessor, Deed, Recording records:** Access assessment data via the state system, see section introduction.. Access to property and deeds indexes and images is via a private company at www.titlesearcher.com. Fee/registration required; see state introduction. **Other phones:** Assessor-931-268-0246; Treasurer-931-268-9417; Elections-931-268-9284.

Jefferson County

Register of Deeds, PO Box 58, Dandridge, TN 37725. **Phone**-865-397-2918; 8AM-4PM; 8-11AM Sat
Will not search UCC records but will do an index name search back 3 years only. Will not search real estate or tax lien records. UCC copy- $1.00 per page. Cert fee: $1.00 per page. Payee: Jefferson County Register of Deeds. **Online Access to Land, Property Assessor, Deed, Recording records:** Access assessment data via the state system, see section introduction.. Access to property and deeds indexes and images is via a private company at www.titlesearcher.com. Fee/registration required; see state introduction. **Other phones:** Assessor-865-397-3326; Treasurer-865-397-2101.

Johnson County

Register of Deeds, 222 W Main St, Mountain City, TN 37683. **Phone**-Register of Deeds, R/E & UCC Recording- 423-727-7841; fax-423-727-7047; hours 8:30AM-5PM
Will not search UCC or tax liens records. Will search real estate records if book and page number is provided. Copy fee- $1.00 per page. Cert fee: $1.00 per page. Payee: Register of Deeds. **Online Access to Land, Property Assessor, Deed, Recording records:** Access assessment data via the state system, see section introduction.. Access to property and deeds indexes and images is via a private company at www.titlesearcher.com. Images go back to 4/2003. Fee/registration required; see state introduction. **Other phones:** Assessor-423-727-7692; Treasurer-423-727-9062; Elections-423-727-8592.

Knox County

Register of Deeds, 400 W. Main Ave, Rm 225, Knoxville, TN 37902. **Phone**-865-215-2330; fax-865-215-2332; hours-8AM-4:30PM www.knoxcounty.org/register/index.html
Will search UCC records prior to 7/2001 and current fixture (land) files to let you know if documents exist. Will not search real estate or tax lien records. RE record copy- $.50 per page. UCC copy- $1.00 per page. Cert fee: $1.00 per page. Payee: Knox

County Register of Deeds. **Online Access to Real Estate, Property Tax records:** Search the property tax rolls for free at www.knoxcounty.org/tax_search. Also, the GIS Dept offers a property map and details report at www.kgis.org/PropertyMapByAddress.asp. Address searching only. **Other phones:** Assessor-865-521-2360; Treasurer-865-521-2305.

Lake County

Register of Deeds, 229 Church St, Box 5, Courthouse, Tiptonville, TN 38079. **Phone**-Register of Deeds, R/E & UCC Recording- 731-253-7462; fax-731-253-6815; hours 8AM-4PM
Will not search records. Copy fee- $.50 per page. Cert fee: $1.00 per page. Payee: Register of Deeds. **Online Access to Real Estate, Deed, Judgment, Lien, UCC, Property Assessor records:** Access assessment data via the state system, see section introduction.. Access to indexes and images is via a private company at www.ustitlesearch.com. Registration and monthly fee required; see state introduction. **Other phones:** Assessor-731-253-7200.

Lauderdale County

Register of Deeds, Courthouse, Ripley, TN 38063. **Phone**-731-635-2171; fax-731-635-9682.
Will search UCC records prior to 7/2001 and current fixture (land) files. Search per debtor- $12.00. Will not search real estate records. **Online Access to Real Estate, Deed, Judgment, Lien, UCC, Property Assessor records:** Access assessment data via the state system, see section introduction.. Access to indexes and images is via a private company at www.ustitlesearch.com. Registration and monthly fee required; see state introduction. **Other phones:** Assessor-731-635-9561; Treasurer-731-635-0712; Elections-615-741-7956.

Lawrence County

Register of Deeds, 240 W. Gaines St, N.B.U. #18, Lawrenceburg, TN 38464. **Phone**-Register of Deeds, R/E & UCC Recording- 931-766-4100; fax-931-766-5602; hours 8:00AM-4:30PM www.titlesearcher.com
Will not search records. Copy fee- $.25 per page. Cert fee: $1.00 per page. Payee: Teresa Dunkin, Register of Deeds. **Online Access to Land, Property Assessor, Deed, Recording records:** Access assessment data via the state system, see section introduction.. Access to property and deeds indexes and images is via a private company at www.titlesearcher.com. Fee/registration required; see state introduction. **Other phones:** Assessor-931-766-4104; Treasurer-931-766-4110; Appraiser-931-766-4104; Elections-931-766-4130; Vital Records-615-741-1763.

Lewis County

Register of Deeds, 110 N Park Ave, Courthouse, Rm 104, Hohenwald, TN 38462. **Phone**-Register of Deeds, R/E & UCC Recording- 931-796-2255; hours 8AM-4:30PM
Will search UCC records. Search per debtor- $15.00. Will not search real estate or tax lien records. RE record copy- $.25 per page. UCC copy- $1.00 per page. Cert fee: $1.00 per doc. Payee: Lewis County Register of Deeds. **Online Access to Real Estate, Deed, Judgment, Lien, UCC, Property Assessor records:** Access assessment data via the state system, see section introduction.. Access to indexes and images is via a private company at www.ustitlesearch.com. Registration and monthly fee required; see state introduction. **Other phones:** Assessor-931-796-5848; Treasurer-931-796-2226; Elections-931-796-3662.

Lincoln County

Register of Deeds, 112 Main Ave S, Rm 104, Fayetteville, TN 37334. **Phone**-Register of Deeds, R/E

& UCC Recording- 931-433-5366; fax-931-433-9312; hours 8AM-4PM

Will not search records. RE record copy- $.25 per sheet. Cert fee: $1.00 per sheet. Payee: Lincoln County Register of Deeds. **Online Access to Land, Property Assessor, Deed, Recording records:** Access assessment data via the state system, see section introduction.. Access to property and deeds indexes and images is via a private company at www.titlesearcher.com. Fee/registration required; see state introduction. **Other phones:** Assessor-931-433-5409; Treasurer-931-433-1371; Elections-931-433-6220.

Loudon County

Register of Deeds, PO Box 395, Loudon, TN 37774. **Phone**-865-458-2605; fax-865-458-9028; hours 8AM-4:30PM

Will not search records. UCC copy- $.25 per page. Cert fee: $1.00. Payee: Loudon County Register of Deeds. **Online Access to Land, Property Assessor, Deed, Recording records:** Access assessment data via the state system, see section introduction.. Access to property and deeds indexes and images is via a private company at www.titlesearcher.com. Images go back to 4/2003. Fee/registration required; see state introduction. **Other phones:** Assessor-865-458-2050; Elections-865-458-2560.

Macon County

Register of Deeds, Courthouse, Rm 102, Lafayette, TN 37083. **Phone**-615-666-2353; fax-615-666-2691; hours 8AM-4:30PM M,T,W,F; 8AM-4PM TH www.maconcountytn.com/register_of_deeds.htm

Will search UCC records prior to 7/2001 and current fixture (land) files. Search per debtor- $12.00. Will not search real estate records. **Online Access to Land, Property Assessor, Deed, Recording records:** Access assessment data via the state system, see section introduction.. Access to property and deeds indexes and images is via a private company at www.titlesearcher.com. Fee/registration required; see state introduction. **Other phones:** Assessor-615-666-3688; Elections-615-666-2199; Trustee-615-666-3624.

Madison County

Register of Deeds, 100 Main St, Courthouse, Rm 109, Jackson, TN 38301. **Phone**-Register of Deeds, R/E & UCC Recording- 731-423-6028; fax-731-422-1171. Will not search records. UCC copy- $1.00 per page if mailed. Cert fee: $1.00 per page. Payee: Register of Deeds. **Online Access to Land, Property Assessor, Deed, Recording records:** Access assessment data via the state system, see section introduction.. Access to property and deeds indexes and images is via a private company at www.titlesearcher.com. Fee/registration required; see state introduction. **Other phones:** Assessor-731-423-6100; Treasurer-731-423-6027.

Marion County

Register of Deeds, PO Box 789, Jasper, TN 37347. **Phone**-423-942-2573; hours 8AM-4PM M-F

Will not search records. Copy fee- $.50 per page. Cert fee: $1.00 per page. Payee: Marion County Register of Deeds. **Online Access to Land, Property Assessor, Deed, Recording records:** Access assessment data via the state system, see section introduction.. Access to property and deeds indexes and images is via a private company at www.titlesearcher.com. Fee/registration required; see state introduction. **Other phones:** Assessor-423-942-3494.

Marshall County

Register of Deeds, 1103 Courthouse Annex, Lewisburg, TN 37091. **Phone**-931-359-4933; hours 8AM-4PM

Will not search records. Copy fee- $1.00 per page. Cert fee: $1.00 per page. Payee: Marshall County Register of Deeds. **Online Access to Real Estate, Deed, Judgment, Lien, UCC, Property Assessor records:** Access assessment data via the state system, see section introduction.. Access to property and deeds indexes and images is via a private company at www.titlesearcher.com. Fee/registration required; see state introduction. Also, access to indexes and images is via a private company at www.ustitlesearch.com. Registration and monthly fee required; see state introduction. **Other phones:** Assessor-931-359-3238.

Maury County

Register of Deeds, PO Box 769, Columbia, TN 38402-0769. **Phone**-Register of Deeds, R/E & UCC Recording- 931-381-3690 x358; hours 8AM-4PM www.titlesearcher.com

Will not search records. Copy fee- $.50 per page. Cert fee: $1.00 per cert. Payee: Maury County Register of Deeds. **Online Access to Land, Property Assessor, Deed, Recording, Sexual Offender Registry records:** Access assessment data via the state system, see section introduction.. Access to property and deeds indexes and images is via a private company at www.titlesearcher.com. Fee/registration required; see state introduction. Also, Sexual offender registry found at www.ticic.state.tn.us/SEX_ofndr/search_short.asp. **Other phones:** Assessor-931-381-3690 x253; Elections-931-381-4691.

McMinn County

Register of Deeds, PO Box 1074, Athens, TN 37371-1074. **Phone**-Register of Deeds, R/E & UCC Recording- 423-745-1232; fax-423-745-0095; hours 8:30-4:00 M-F

Will search UCC records prior to 7/2001 and current fixture (land) files. Search per debtor- $15.00. Will not search real estate or tax lien records. Copy fee- $.25 per page. Cert fee: $1.00 per page. Payee: Register of Deeds. **Online Access to Real Estate, Deed, Judgment, Lien, UCC, Property Assessor records:** Access assessment data via the state system, see section introduction.. Access to indexes and images is via a private company at www.ustitlesearch.com. Registration and monthly fee required; see state introduction. Records go back to 9-1-99. **Other phones:** Assessor-423-745-2743; Treasurer-423-745-4103; Elections-423-745-0843; Trustee-423-745-1291; Circuit Court Clerk-423-745-1923.

McNairy County

Register of Deeds, PO Box 158, Selmer, TN 38375. **Phone**-731-645-3656; fax-731-645-3656; hours 8AM-4:30PM M,T,Th,F; 8AM-Noon Sat

Will search UCC records prior to 7/2001 and current fixture (land) files. Search per debtor- $12.00. Tax liens not included in UCC search. Separate federal/state combined tax lien search- $25.00 per debtor. Real estate record owner and mortgage searches available. Cert fee: $2.00 per doc. Payee: McNairy County Register of Deeds. **Online Access to Real Estate, Deed, Judgment, Lien, UCC, Property Assessor records:** Access assessment data via the state system, see section introduction.. Access to indexes and images is via a private company at www.ustitlesearch.com. Registration and monthly fee required; see state introduction. **Other phones:** Assessor-731-645-5146; Vital Records-731-645-3511.

Meigs County

Register of Deeds, PO Box 245, Decatur, TN 37322. **Phone**-423-334-5228; fax-423-334-5228; hours 8AM-5PM M,T,Th,F; 8AM-Noon Sat

Will not search records. Cert fee: $2.00 per page. Payee: Meigs County Register of Deeds. **Online Access to Property Assessor records:** Access assessment data via the state system, see section

introduction.. **Other phones:** Assessor-423-334-5231; Trustee-423-334-5119.

Monroe County

Register of Deeds, 103 College St - #4, Madisonville, TN 37354. **Phone**-423-442-2440; hours 8:30AM-4:30PM M,T,Th,F; 8:30AM-Noon W & Sat

Will not search UCC records prior to 1-98. Will not search real estate or tax lien records. UCC copy- $1.00 per page. Cert fee: $1.00 per page. Payee: Monroe County Register of Deeds. **Online Access to Land, Property Assessor, Deed, Recording records:** Access assessment data via the state system, see section introduction.. Access to property and deeds indexes and images is via a private company at www.titlesearcher.com. Fee/registration required; see state introduction. **Other phones:** Assessor-423-442-3637; Treasurer-423-442-2920; Appraiser-423-442-3637.

Montgomery County

Register of Deeds, PO Box 1124, Clarksville, TN 37041. **Phone**-931-648-5713; fax-931-553-5157; hours 8AM-4:30PM

Will not search records. UCC copy- $.25 per page. Cert fee: $1.00. Payee: Register of Deeds. **Online Access to Real Estate, Deed, Judgment, Lien, UCC, Property Assessor records:** Access assessment data via the state system, see section introduction.. Access to property and deeds indexes and images is via a private company at www.titlesearcher.com. Fee/registration required; see state introduction. Also, access to indexes and images is via a private company at www.ustitlesearch.com. Registration and monthly fee required; see state introduction. **Other phones:** Assessor-931-648-5709; Trustee-931-648-5710.

Moore County

Register of Deeds, PO Box 206, Lynchburg, TN 37352. **Phone**-931-759-7913; fax-931-759-6394; hours 8AM-4:30PM; Closed Th; 8AM-Noon Sat

Will not search records. RE record copy- $.50 per page. UCC copy- $1.00 per page. Cert fee: $1.00 per cert. Payee: Moore County Register of Deeds. **Online Access to Property Assessor records:** Access assessment data via the state system, see section introduction.. **Other phones:** Assessor-931-759-7044.

Morgan County

Register of Deeds, PO Box 311, Wartburg, TN 37887. **Phone**-423-346-3105; hours 8AM-4PM

Will search UCC records prior to 7/2001 and current fixture (land) files. Search per debtor- $15.00. Will not search real estate or tax lien records. UCC copy- $1.00 per page. Cert fee: $1.00 per page. Payee: Morgan County Register of Deeds. **Online Access to Real Estate, Deed, Judgment, Lien, UCC, Property Assessor records:** Access assessment data via the state system, see section introduction.. Also, access to indexes and images is via a private company at www.ustitlesearch.com. Registration and monthly fee required; see state introduction. **Other phones:** Assessor-423-346-3130; Appraiser-423-346-3130.

Obion County

Register of Deeds, PO Box 514, Union City, TN 38261. **Phone**-Register of Deeds, R/E & UCC Recording- 731-885-9351; fax-731-885-7515; hours 8:AM-4:30PM

Will not search records. Copy fee- $.50 per page. Cert fee: $1.00 per page. Payee: Register of Deeds. **Online Access to Property Assessor records:** Access assessment data via the state system, see section introduction.. **Other phones:** Assessor-731-885-2931; Elections-731-885-1901.

Overton County

Register of Deeds, 317 E. University St, Rm 150, Livingston, TN 38570. **Phone**-931-823-4011; hours

8AM-4:30PM. Will not search records. RE record copy- $.25 per page. UCC copy- $1.00 per page. Cert fee: $1.00 per page. Payee: Overton County Register of Deeds. **Online Access to Property Assessor records:** Access assessment data via the state system, see section introduction..

Perry County

Register of Deeds, PO Box 62, Linden, TN 37096-0062. **Phone-**Register of Deeds, R/E & UCC Recording- 931-589-2210; fax-931-589-2215; hours 8AM-4PM

Will search UCC records prior to 7/2001 and current fixture (land) files. Search per debtor- $12.00. UCC search includes tax liens if requested. Separate federal/state combined tax lien search-no charge. Will not search real estate records. UCC copy- $1.00 per page. Cert fee: $5.00 per doc. Payee: Perry County Register of Deeds. **Online Access to Land, Property Assessor, Deed, Recording records:** Access assessment data via the state system, see section introduction.. Access to property and deeds indexes and images is via a private company at www.titlesearcher.com. Fee/registration required; see state introduction. **Other phones:** Assessor-931-589-2277; Treasurer-931-589-2313.

Pickett County

Register of Deeds, PO Box 5, Byrdstown, TN 38549. **Phone-**931-864-3316; fax-931-864-6615; hours 8AM-11:00-12:00-4PM

Will not search records. UCC copy- $.25 per page. Cert fee: $3.00. Payee: Register of Deeds. **Online Access to Property Assessor records:** Access assessment data via the state system, see section introduction.. **Other phones:** Assessor-931-864-3114.

Polk County

Register of Deeds, PO Box 293, Benton, TN 37307. **Phone-**423-338-4537; hours 8:30AM-4:30PM Will not search records. UCC copy- $1.00 per page. Cert fee: $1.00 per page. Payee: Polk County Register of Deeds. **Online Access to land, Property Assessor, Deed, Recording records:** Access assessment data via the state system, see section introduction.. Access to property and deeds indexes and images is via a private company at www.titlesearcher.com. Fee/registration required; see state introduction. **Other phones:** Assessor-423-338-4505; Trustee-423-338-4545.

Putnam County

Register of Deeds, PO Box 487, Cookeville, TN 38503-0487. **Phone-**931-526-7101; hours 8AM-4PM Will search UCC records prior to 7/2001 and current fixture (land) files. Search per debtor- $15.00. Will not search real estate or tax lien records. UCC copy- $1.00 per page. Cert fee: $1.00 per page. Payee: Putnam County Register of Deeds. **Online Access to Real Estate, Deed, Judgment, Lien, UCC, Property Assessor records:** Access assessment data via the state system, see section introduction.. Also, access to indexes and images is via a private company at www.ustitlesearch.com. Registration and monthly fee required; see state introduction. **Other phones:** Assessor-931-528-8428; Treasurer-931-528-8845.

Rhea County

Register of Deeds, 375 Church St #106, Dayton, TN 37321. **Phone-**Register of Deeds, R/E & UCC Recording- 423-775-7841; hours 8AM-4:30PM Will not search records. UCC copy- $.25 per page. Cert fee: $1.00 per page. Payee: Rhea County Register of Deeds. **Online Access to Land, Property Assessor records:** Access assessment data via the state system, see section introduction.. Access to property and deeds indexes and images is via a private company at www.titlesearcher.com. Fee/registration required; see

state introduction. Images go back to May 28, 2003. **Other phones:** Assessor-423-775-7840; Treasurer-423-775-7810.

Roane County

Register of Deeds, PO Box 181, Kingston, TN 37763. **Phone-**865-376-4673; hours 8:30AM-6PM M; 8:30AM-4:30PM T-F

Will not search records. Record copy- $1.00 per page. Cert fee: $1.00 per page. Payee: Roane County Register of Deeds. **Online Access to Land, Property Assessor, Deed, Recording records:** Access assessment data via the state system, see section introduction.. Access to property and deeds indexes and images is via a private company at www.titlesearcher.com. Fee/registration required; see state introduction. Images go back to June 5, 2003. **Other phones:** Assessor-865-376-4362; Trustee-865-376-4938.

Robertson County

Register of Deeds, 525 S. Brown St., Springfield, TN 37172. **Phone-**Register of Deeds, R/E & UCC Recording- 615-384-3772; hours 8AM-4:30PM Will not search records. Cert fee: $1.00 per page. Payee: Robertson County Register of Deeds. **Online Access to Real Estate, Deed, Judgment, Lien, UCC, Property Assessor records:** Access assessment data via the state system, see section introduction.. Access to indexes and images is via a private company at www.ustitlesearch.com. Registration and monthly fee required; see state introduction. **Other phones:** Assessor-615-384-4311; Elections-615-384-5592.

Rutherford County

Register of Deeds, PO Box 5050, Murfreesboro, TN 37133-5050. **Phone-**615-898-7870; fax-615-898-7987; hours 8AM-4PM

Will not search records. UCC copy- $.50 per page. Cert fee: $1.00. Payee: Rutherford County Register of Deeds. **Online Access to Real Estate, Deed, Judgment, Lien, UCC, Property Assessor records:** Access assessment data via the state system, see section introduction.. Also, access to indexes and images is via a private company at www.ustitlesearch.com. Registration and monthly fee required; see state introduction. **Other phones:** Assessor-615-898-7750.

Scott County

Register of Deeds, PO Box 61, Huntsville, TN 37756. **Phone-**423-663-2417; hours 8AM-4:30PM Will not search records. UCC copy- $1.00 per page. Cert fee: $1.00 per page. Payee: Scott County Register of Deeds. **Online Access to Property Assessor records:** Access assessment data via the state system, see section introduction.. **Other phones:** Assessor-423-663-2420; Treasurer-423-663-2598.

Sequatchie County

Register of Deeds, PO Box 174, Dunlap, TN 37327. **Phone-**Register of Deeds, R/E & UCC Recording- 423-949-2512; fax-423-949-6554; hours 8AM-5PM Will not search records. UCC copy- $1.00 per page. Cert fee: $1.00. Payee: Sequatchie County Register of Deeds. **Online Access to Land, Property Assessor, Deed, Recording records:** Access assessment data via the state system, see section introduction.. Access to property and deeds indexes and images is via a private company at www.titlesearcher.com. Fee/registration required; see state introduction. **Other phones:** Assessor-423-949-3534.

Sevier County

Register of Deeds, 125 Court Ave, Courthouse #209W, Sevierville, TN 37862. **Phone-**Register of Deeds, R/E

& UCC Recording- 865-453-2758; hours 8AM-4:30PM M-Th; 8AM-6PM F www.titlesearcher.com Will not search records. RE record copy- $1.00 up to 4 pages. UCC copy- $1.00 per page. Cert fee: $1.00 per page. Payee: Sevier County Register of Deeds. **Online Access to Land, Property Assessor, Deed, Recording records:** Access assessment data via the state system, see section introduction.. Access to property and deeds indexes and images is via a private company at www.titlesearcher.com. Fee/registration required; see state introduction. **Other phones:** Assessor-865-453-3242; Appraiser-865-453-3242; Elections-865-453-6985; Trustee-865-453-2767.

Shelby County

Register of Deeds, 160 N. Main St, Rm 519, Memphis, TN 38173-0823. **Phone-**901-545-4366; fax-901-545-3837; hours 8AM-4:30PM http://register.shelby.tn.us Will not search records. Copy fee- $.10 per page. Cert fee: $1.00 per doc. Payee: Shelby County Retister. **Online Access to Real Estate, Lien, Recording, Judgment, Lien records:** Free access to the register database is online at http://register.shelby.tn.us/menu.php. Partial indexes and images go back to 1986; full to 12/2001. Access to property and deeds indexes and images is via a private company at www.titlesearcher.com. Fee/registration required; see state introduction.

Smith County

Register of Deeds, 122 Turner High Circle, #113, Carthage, TN 37030. **Phone-**615-735-1760; fax-615-735-8263; hours 8AM-4PM

Will not search records. UCC copy- $.25 per page. Cert fee: $1.00 + $2.00 processing. Payee: Smith County Register of Deeds. **Online Access to Land, Property Assessor, Deed, Recording records:** Access assessment data via the state system, see section introduction.. Access to property and deeds indexes and images is via a private company at www.titlesearcher.com. Fee/registration required; see state introduction. **Other phones:** Assessor-615-735-1750.

Stewart County

Register of Deeds, PO Box 57, Dover, TN 37058. **Phone-**931-232-5990; hours 8AM-4:30PM Will not search records. UCC copy- $.25 per page. Cert fee: $1.00 per page. Payee: Stewart County Register of Deeds. **Online Access to Real Estate, Deed, Judgment, Lien, UCC, Property Assessor records:** Access assessment data via the state system, see section introduction.. Access to real estate records is at www.ustitlesearch.com. Registration and fee required; information at website; also see state introduction. **Other phones:** Assessor-931-232-5252; Trustee-931-232-7026.

Sullivan County Blountville Office

Register of Deeds, 3411 Hwy 126, #101, Blountville, TN 37617. **Phone-**Register of Deeds, R/E & UCC Recording- 423-323-6420; fax-423-279-2771; hours 8AM-5PM

Will not search records. UCC copy- $2.00 per page. Cert fee: $1.00. Payee: Sullivan County Register of Deeds. **Online Access to Property Assessor records:** Access assessment data via the state system, see section introduction.. **Other phones:** Assessor-423-323-6455; Appraiser-423-323-6455; Elections-423-323-6444; Vital Records-423-279-2777; Trustee-423-323-6464.

Sullivan County Bristol Office

Register of Deeds, 801 Anderson St., Bristol, TN 37620. **Phone-**Register of Deeds, R/E & UCC Recording- 423-989-4370; hours 8AM-5PM Will not search records. Copy fee- $2.00 per page. Cert fee: $1.00 per page. Payee: Sullivan County

Register of Deeds. **Online Access to Property Assessor records:** Access assessment data via the state system, see section introduction.. **Other phones:** Assessor-423-323-6455; Treasurer-423-323-6464; Appraiser-423-323-6455; Elections-423-323-6444; Vital Records-423-279-2777.

Sumner County

Register of Deeds, PO Box 299, Gallatin, TN 37066-0299. **Phone-**Register of Deeds, R/E & UCC Recording- 615-452-3892; hours 8AM-4:30PM www.deeds.sumnertn.org
Will not search records. UCC copy- $1.00 per page. Cert fee: $1.50 per page. Payee: Sumner County Register of Deeds. **Online Access to Real Estate, Recording, Deed, Property Tax records:** Access to the Register of Deeds website requires a $25.00 set-up fee and $50.00 monthly user fee. For information, call the Register at 615-452-3892 or download the User Agreement from the website at www.deeds.sumnertn.org Also, Access assessment data via the state system, see section introduction.. **Other phones:** Assessor-615-452-2412; Trustee-615-452-1260.

Tipton County

Register of Deeds, PO Box 644, Covington, TN 38019-0644. **Phone-**Register of Deeds, R/E & UCC Recording- 901-476-0204; fax-901-476-0227; hours 8AM-5PM
Will not search records. UCC copy- $1.00 per page. Cert fee: $1.00 per page. Payee: Tipton County Register of Deeds. **Online Access to Real Estate, Deed, Judgment, Lien, UCC, Property Assessor records:** Access assessment data via the state system, see section introduction.. Access to indexes and images is via a private company at www.ustitlesearch.com. Registration and monthly fee required; see state introduction. **Other phones:** Assessor-901-476-0213; Treasurer-901-476-0211; Elections-901-476-0223.

Trousdale County

Register of Deeds, 200 E. Main St. #8, Hartsville, TN 37074-1706. **Phone-**615-374-2921; fax-615-374-1100; hours 8AM-4:30PM
Will not search records. UCC copy- $.25 per page. Cert fee: $3.00. Payee: Trousdale County Register of Deeds. **Online Access to Real Estate, Deed, Judgment, Lien, UCC, Property Assessor records:** Access assessment data via the state system, see section introduction.. Also, access to indexes and images is via a private company at www.ustitlesearch.com. Registration and monthly fee required; see state introduction. **Other phones:** Assessor-615-374-2553.

Unicoi County

Register of Deeds, PO Box 305, Erwin, TN 37650-0305. **Phone-**423-743-6104; fax-423-743-6278; hours 9AM-5PM; 9AM-Noon Sat www.titlesearcher.com
Will not search records. Record copy- $1.00 per page. Cert fee: $1.00 per page. Payee: Unicoi County Register of Deeds. **Online Access to Land, Deed, Recording records:** Access to property and deeds indexes and images is via a private company at www.titlesearcher.com. Fee/registration required; see state introduction. Images go back to 1/1997. **Other phones:** Assessor-423-743-3801; Treasurer-423-743-3011; Elections-423-743-6521.

Union County

Register of Deeds, 901 Main St #108, Maynardville, TN 37807. **Phone-**865-992-8024; hours 8AM-4PMM,T,Th.F; 8AM-Noon W,Sat

Will not search records. UCC copy- $1.00 per page. Cert fee: $1.00 per page. Payee: Union County Register of Deeds. **Online Access to Land, Lien, Will, Deed, Judgment, Recorder, Property Assessor records:** Search the Recorder's database for free at www.courthouseonline.com/DeedSearch.asp?State=PA&County=Union&Abbrev=Un&Office=RD. Also, Access assessment data via the state system, see section introduction.. Also, access to property and deeds indexes and images is via a private company at www.titlesearcher.com. Fee/registration required; see state introduction. **Other phones:** Assessor-865-992-3211; Trustee-865-992-5943.

Van Buren County

Register of Deeds, PO Box 9, Spencer, TN 38585. **Phone-**931-946-7363; fax-931-946-7363; hours 8AM-4PM M-Th, 8AM-5PM F www.titlesearcher.com
Will not search UCC or real estate records. UCC copy- $.50 per page. **Online Access to Land, Property Assessor, Deed, Recording records:** Access assessment data via the state system, see section introduction.. Access to property and deeds indexes and images is via a private company at www.titlesearcher.com. Fee/registration required; see state introduction. **Other phones:** Assessor-931-946-2451.

Warren County

Register of Deeds, PO Box 128, McMinnville, TN 37111. **Phone-**Register of Deeds, R/E & UCC Recording- 931-473-2926, UCC Recording-931-473-8663; fax-931-474-2114; hours 8AM-4:30PM M-Th; 8AM-5PM F. Will not search records. Record copy- $1.00 per page. Cert fee: $2.00 per page. Payee: Warren County Register of Deeds. **Online Access to Real Estate, Deed, Judgment, Lien, UCC, Property Assessor records:** Access assessment data via the state system, see section introduction.. Access to indexes and images is via a private company at www.ustitlesearch.com. Registration and monthly fee required; see state introduction. **Other phones:** Assessor-931-473-3450.

Washington County

Register of Deeds, PO Box 69, Jonesboro, TN 37659. **Phone-**423-753-1644, R/E Recording-423-753-1645, UCC Recording-423-753-1648; fax-423-753-1743; hours 8AM-5PM. Will not search records. UCC copy- $.50 per page. Cert fee: None. Payee: Washington County Register of Deeds. **Online Access to Real Estate, Deed, Judgment, Lien, UCC, Property Assessor records:** Access assessment data via the state system, see section introduction.. Access to indexes and images is via a private company at www.ustitlesearch.com. Registration and monthly fee required; see state introduction. Also, access to property and deeds indexes and images is via a private company at www.titlesearcher.com. Fee/registration required; see state introduction. **Other phones:** Assessor-423-753-1670; Treasurer-423-753-1610; Elections-423-753-1688; Vital Records-423-753-1621.

Wayne County

Register of Deeds, PO Box 465, Waynesboro, TN 38485. **Phone-**931-722-5518; fax-931-722-5518; hours 8AM-4PM M T TH F; 8AM-Noon W & Sat
Will search UCC records. Will not search real estate or tax lien records. Copy fee- $.50 per page. Cert fee: $1.00 per cert + $.25 per page. Payee: Wayne County Register. **Online Access to Land, Property Assessor, Deed, Recording records:** Access assessment data via the state system, see section introduction.. Access to property and deeds indexes and

images is via a private company at www.titlesearcher.com. Fee/registration required; see state introduction. **Other phones:** Assessor-931-722-5282; Treasurer-931-722-3269; Appraiser-931-722-5282; Elections-931-722-3517.

Weakley County

Register of Deeds, PO Box 45, Dresden, TN 38225-0045. **Phone-**731-364-3646; fax-731-364-5284; hours 8:30AM-4:30PM
Will not search records. UCC copy- $.25 per page. Cert fee: $1.00. Payee: Register of Deeds. **Online Access to Land, Property Assessor, Deed, Judgment records:** Access assessment data via the state system, see section introduction.. Access to property and deeds indexes and images is via a private company at www.titlesearcher.com. Fee/registration required; see state introduction. **Other phones:** Assessor-731-364-3677; Trustee-731-364-3643.

White County

Register of Deeds, PO Box 86, Sparta, TN 38583-0086. **Phone-**931-836-2817; fax-931-836-8418. www.tennesseeanytime.org/local/white.html
Will search UCC records prior to 7/2001 and current fixture (land) files. Will not search real estate records. **Online Access to Land, Property Assessor, Deed, Recording records:** Access assessment data via the state system, see section introduction.. Access to property and deeds indexes and images is via a private company at www.titlesearcher.com. Fee/registration required; see state introduction. **Other phones:** Assessor-931-836-3480; Elections-615-741-7956.

Williamson County

Register of Deeds, PO Box 808, Franklin, TN 37065-0808. **Phone-**Register of Deeds, R/E & UCC Recording- 615-790-5706; hours 8AM-4:30PM
Will not search records. UCC copy- $1.00 per page. Cert fee: $1.00 per page. Payee: Williamson County Register of Deeds. **Online Access to Deed, Property, Tax Assessor, Recording records:** Access to the Professional Access database by subscription is a $50 per month fee. Information and sign-up at http://williamson-tn.org/co_gov/profacc.htm. Also, Access assessment data via the state system, see section introduction.. Also, access to property and deeds indexes and images is via a private company at www.titlesearcher.com. Images go back to 11/1992; registration and user fee required. **Other phones:** Assessor-615-790-5708; Treasurer-615-790-5709; Appraiser-615-790-5708; Elections-615-790-5712.

Wilson County

Register of Deeds, PO Box 176, Lebanon, TN 37087-0176. **Phone-**Register of Deeds, R/E & UCC Recording- 615-443-2611; fax-615-443-3288; hours 8AM-4PM www.wilsondeeds.com
Will not search records. RE record copy- $.25 per page. Cert fee: $1.00 per page. Payee: Wilson Register. **Online Access to Real Estate, Lien, Recording, Property Assessor records:** Access to the Register of Deeds database requires a $10 registration fee then $25.00 per month usage fee. Includes indexes 1993; images back to 1996. Also, Access assessment data via the state system, see section introduction.. Also, Online access to property and deeds indexes and images is via a private company at www.titlesearcher.com. A per day only fee/registration required; see state introduction. **Other phones:** Assessor-615-444-8661; Treasurer-615-444-0894; Appraiser-615-444-8661; Elections-615-444-0216

Tennessee County Locator

You will usually be able to find the city name in the City/County Cross Reference below. In that case, it is a simple matter to determine the county from the cross reference. However, only the official US Postal Service city names are included in this index. There are an additional 40,000 place names that people use in their addresses. Therefore, we have also included a ZIP/City Cross Reference immediately following the City/County Cross Reference.

If you know the ZIP Code but the city name does not appear in the City/County Cross Reference index, look up the ZIP Code in the ZIP/City Cross Reference, find the city name, then look up the city name in the City/County Cross Reference. For example, you want to know the county for an address of Menands, NY 12204. There is no "Menands" in the City/County Cross Reference. The ZIP/City Cross Reference shows that ZIP Codes 12201-12288 are for the city of Albany. Looking back in the City/County Cross Reference, Albany is in Albany County.

Tennessee City/County Cross Reference

ADAMS (37010) Robertson(58), Montgomery(41)
ADAMSVILLE (38310) McNairy(56), Hardin(43)
AFTON Greene
ALAMO Crockett
ALCOA Blount
ALEXANDRIA (37012) De Kalb(78), Wilson(11), Smith(10)
ALLARDT Fentress
ALLONS (38541) Overton(66), Clay(33)
ALLRED Overton
ALPINE (38543) Overton(81), Pickett(18)
ALTAMONT Grundy
ANDERSONVILLE (37705) Anderson(68), Union(31)
ANTIOCH Davidson
APISON Hamilton
ARDMORE (38449) Giles(68), Lincoln(31)
ARLINGTON (38002) Shelby(90), Fayette(9)
ARNOLD AFB Coffee
ARRINGTON (37014) Williamson(58), Rutherford(41)
ARTHUR Claiborne
ASHLAND CITY (37015) Cheatham(95), Davidson(3)
ATHENS McMinn
ATOKA (38004) Tipton(94), Shelby(5)
ATWOOD (38220) Carroll(94), Gibson(5)
AUBURNTOWN (37016) Cannon(73), Wilson(26)
BAKEWELL Hamilton
BATH SPRINGS Decatur
BAXTER (38544) Putnam(91), De Kalb(8)
BEAN STATION Grainger
BEECH BLUFF (38313) Madison(51), Henderson(25), Chester(23)
BEECHGROVE (37018) Coffee(97), Bedford(2)
BEERSHEBA SPRINGS Grundy
BELFAST Marshall
BELL BUCKLE (37020) Bedford(79), Rutherford(20)
BELLS (38006) Crockett(78), Haywood(15), Madison(5)
BELVIDERE Franklin
BENTON Polk
BETHEL SPRINGS (38315) McNairy(84), Chester(15)
BETHPAGE (37022) Sumner(73), Trousdale(24), Macon(1)
BIG ROCK Stewart
BIG SANDY Benton
BIRCHWOOD (37308) Hamilton(65), Meigs(34)
BLAINE (37709) Grainger(83), Union(14), Knox(2)
BLOOMINGTON SPRINGS (38545) Jackson(61), Putnam(38)
BLOUNTVILLE Sullivan
BLUFF CITY Sullivan
BOGOTA Dyer
BOLIVAR Hardeman

BON AQUA (37025) Hickman(80), Dickson(17), Williamson(2)
BRADEN Fayette
BRADFORD Gibson
BRADYVILLE (37026) Cannon(90), Coffee(9)
BRENTWOOD (37027) Williamson(82), Davidson(17)
BRENTWOOD Williamson
BRICEVILLE Anderson
BRIGHTON (38011) Tipton(97), Shelby(2)
BRISTOL Sullivan
BROWNSVILLE Haywood
BRUCETON (38317) Carroll(94), Benton(5)
BRUNSWICK Shelby
BRUSH CREEK Smith
BUCHANAN Henry
BUENA VISTA (38318) Carroll(97), Benton(2)
BUFFALO VALLEY (38548) Putnam(76), Smith(23)
BULLS GAP (37711) Greene(60), Hawkins(35), Hamblen(3)
BUMPUS MILLS Stewart
BURLISON Tipton
BURNS Dickson
BUTLER (37640) Johnson(66), Carter(33)
BYBEE Cocke
BYRDSTOWN (38549) Pickett(98), Fentress(1)
CALHOUN (37309) McMinn(87), Polk(12)
CAMDEN Benton
CAMPAIGN Warren
CARTHAGE Smith
CARYVILLE Campbell
CASTALIAN SPRINGS (37031) Sumner(59), Trousdale(40)
CEDAR GROVE Carroll
CEDAR HILL (37032) Robertson(94), Cheatham(4)
CELINA (38551) Clay(98), Jackson(1)
CENTERVILLE Hickman
CHAPEL HILL (37034) Marshall(83), Bedford(16)
CHAPMANSBORO (37035) Cheatham(98), Montgomery(1)
CHARLESTON Bradley
CHARLOTTE (37036) Dickson(93), Cheatham(6)
CHATTANOOGA (37419) Hamilton(87), Marion(12)
CHATTANOOGA Hamilton
CHESTNUT MOUND Smith
CHEWALLA McNairy
CHRISTIANA Rutherford
CHUCKEY (37641) Greene(89), Washington(10)
CHURCH HILL Hawkins
CLAIRFIELD (37715) Claiborne(83), Campbell(16)
CLARKRANGE Fentress
CLARKSBURG Carroll
CLARKSVILLE Montgomery
CLEVELAND Bradley

CLIFTON (38425) Wayne(94), Perry(5)
CLINTON Anderson
COALFIELD Morgan
COALMONT Grundy
COKERCREEK Monroe
COLLEGE GROVE (37046) Williamson(85), Rutherford(12), Marshall(1)
COLLEGEDALE Hamilton
COLLIERVILLE (38017) Shelby(82), Fayette(17)
COLLIERVILLE Shelby
COLLINWOOD Wayne
COLUMBIA Maury
COMO Henry
CONASAUGA Polk
COOKEVILLE (38501) Putnam(92), Jackson(6)
COOKEVILLE (38506) Putnam(82), Overton(12), White(5)
COOKEVILLE Putnam
COPPERHILL Polk
CORDOVA Shelby
CORNERSVILLE (37047) Marshall(79), Giles(19), Lincoln(1)
CORRYTON (37721) Knox(79), Union(20)
COSBY (37722) Cocke(82), Sevier(17)
COTTAGE GROVE (38224) Henry(94), Weakley(5)
COTTONTOWN (37048) Sumner(91), Robertson(8)
COUNCE Hardin
COVINGTON Tipton
COWAN Franklin
CRAB ORCHARD Cumberland
CRAWFORD Overton
CROCKETT MILLS Crockett
CROSS PLAINS Robertson
CROSSVILLE Cumberland
CRUMP Hardin
CULLEOKA (38451) Maury(87), Marshall(12)
CUMBERLAND CITY (37050) Stewart(80), Montgomery(13), Houston(6)
CUMBERLAND FURNACE (37051) Dickson(66), Montgomery(33)
CUMBERLAND GAP Claiborne
CUNNINGHAM (37052) Montgomery(97), Dickson(2)
CYPRESS INN Wayne
DANDRIDGE (37725) Jefferson(98), Sevier(1)
DARDEN (38328) Henderson(76), Decatur(23)
DAYTON (37321) Rhea(98), Bledsoe(1)
DECATUR (37322) Meigs(96), McMinn(3)
DECATURVILLE (38329) Decatur(94), Henderson(5)
DECHERD (37324) Franklin(97), Grundy(2)
DEER LODGE (37726) Morgan(85), Fentress(14)
DEL RIO Cocke
DELANO (37325) Polk(79), McMinn(20)
DELLROSE Lincoln

DENMARK Madison
DENVER Humphreys
DICKSON (37055) Dickson(98), Hickman(1)
DICKSON Dickson
DIXON SPRINGS (37057) Trousdale(48), Macon(29), Smith(21)
DOVER Stewart
DOWELLTOWN De Kalb
DOYLE (38559) White(74), Van Buren(25)
DRESDEN Weakley
DRUMMONDS Tipton
DUCK RIVER Hickman
DUCKTOWN Polk
DUFF Campbell
DUKEDOM Weakley
DUNLAP (37327) Sequatchie(90), Bledsoe(9)
DYER Gibson
DYERSBURG Dyer
EADS (38028) Fayette(56), Shelby(43)
EAGAN Claiborne
EAGLEVILLE (37060) Rutherford(85), Bedford(9), Williamson(4)
EATON Gibson
EIDSON (37731) Hawkins(65), Hancock(34)
ELBRIDGE Obion
ELGIN Scott
ELIZABETHTON Carter
ELKTON Giles
ELLENDALE Shelby
ELMWOOD Smith
ELORA (37328) Lincoln(80), Franklin(19)
ENGLEWOOD (37329) McMinn(93), Monroe(6)
ENVILLE (38332) Chester(89), McNairy(10)
ERIN (37061) Houston(96), Humphreys(3)
ERWIN (37650) Unicoi(95), Washington(4)
ESTILL SPRINGS (37330) Franklin(94), Coffee(5)
ETHRIDGE (38456) Lawrence(77), Giles(22)
ETOWAH McMinn
EVA Benton
EVENSVILLE (37332) Rhea(98), Bledsoe(1)
FAIRVIEW (37062) Williamson(98), Dickson(1)
FALL BRANCH (37656) Greene(49), Washington(43), Sullivan(7)
FARNER Polk
FAYETTEVILLE Lincoln
FINGER (38334) McNairy(80), Chester(19)
FINLEY Dyer
FIVE POINTS Lawrence
FLAG POND Unicoi
FLINTVILLE (37335) Lincoln(96), Franklin(3)
FOSTERVILLE Rutherford
FOWLKES Dyer
FRANKEWING (38459) Giles(56), Lincoln(43)
FRANKLIN Williamson

FRIENDSHIP (38034) Crockett(80), Dyer(19)
FRIENDSVILLE (37737) Blount(92), Loudon(7)
FRUITVALE Crockett
GADSDEN Crockett
GAINESBORO Jackson
GALLATIN Sumner
GALLAWAY Fayette
GATES (38037) Lauderdale(68), Haywood(31)
GATLINBURG Sevier
GEORGETOWN (37336) Meigs(40), Bradley(40), Hamilton(19)
GERMANTOWN Shelby
GIBSON Gibson
GLADEVILLE Wilson
GLEASON (38229) Weakley(98), Henry(1)
GOODLETTSVILLE (37072) Davidson(59), Sumner(32), Robertson(8)
GOODLETTSVILLE Davidson
GOODSPRING Giles
GORDONSVILLE Smith
GRAND JUNCTION (38039) Hardeman(72), Fayette(27)
GRANDVIEW (37337) Cumberland(52), Rhea(47)
GRANVILLE (38564) Jackson(90), Putnam(9)
GRAYSVILLE (37338) Rhea(63), Bledsoe(23), Sequatchie(11), Hamilton(1)
GREENBACK (37742) Loudon(73), Blount(26)
GREENBRIER Robertson
GREENEVILLE Greene
GREENFIELD Weakley
GRIMSLEY Fentress
GRUETLI LAAGER Grundy
GUILD Marion
GUYS McNairy
HALLS (38040) Lauderdale(83), Crockett(11), Dyer(4)
HAMPSHIRE (38461) Maury(93), Lewis(6)
HAMPTON Carter
HARRIMAN (37748) Roane(89), Morgan(10)
HARROGATE Claiborne
HARTFORD Cocke
HARTSVILLE (37074) Trousdale(86), Macon(13)
HEISKELL (37754) Anderson(53), Knox(40), Union(5)
HELENWOOD Scott
HENDERSON (38340) Chester(91), Hardeman(8)
HENDERSONVILLE Sumner
HENNING Lauderdale
HENRY Henry
HERMITAGE (37076) Davidson(95), Wilson(4)
HICKMAN (38567) Smith(95), De Kalb(4)
HICKORY VALLEY (38042) Hardeman(98), Fayette(1)
HICKORY WITHE Fayette
HILHAM (38568) Overton(58), Clay(26), Jackson(14)
HILLSBORO Coffee
HIXSON Hamilton
HOHENWALD Lewis
HOLLADAY (38341) Benton(82), Decatur(13), Henderson(3)
HOLLOW ROCK Carroll
HORNBEAK Obion
HORNSBY (38044) Hardeman(91), McNairy(5), Chester(3)
HUMBOLDT (38343) Gibson(76), Crockett(15), Madison(7)
HUNTINGDON Carroll
HUNTLAND Franklin
HUNTSVILLE Scott
HURON Henderson
HURRICANE MILLS Humphreys

IDLEWILD Gibson
INDIAN MOUND (37079) Stewart(80), Montgomery(19)
IRON CITY (38463) Lawrence(63), Wayne(36)
ISABELLA Polk
JACKS CREEK Chester
JACKSBORO Campbell
JACKSON Madison
JAMESTOWN Fentress
JASPER Marion
JELLICO Campbell
JOELTON (37080) Davidson(51), Cheatham(48)
JOHNSON CITY (37601) Washington(76), Carter(22), Unicoi(1)
JOHNSON CITY Washington
JONESBOROUGH Washington
KELSO Lincoln
KENTON (38233) Gibson(68), Obion(31)
KINGSPORT (37660) Sullivan(95), Hawkins(4)
KINGSPORT (37663) Sullivan(97), Washington(2)
KINGSPORT Sullivan
KINGSTON Roane
KINGSTON SPRINGS Cheatham
KNOXVILLE (37931) Knox(98), Anderson(1)
KODAK (37764) Sevier(89), Knox(9)
KYLES FORD Hancock
LA FOLLETTE Campbell
LA GRANGE Fayette
LA VERGNE (37086) Rutherford(98), Davidson(1)
LA VERGNE Rutherford
LACONIA Fayette
LAFAYETTE Macon
LAKE CITY (37769) Anderson(78), Campbell(21)
LANCASTER (38569) Smith(77), De Kalb(22)
LANCING Morgan
LASCASSAS (37085) Rutherford(79), Wilson(20)
LAUREL BLOOMERY Johnson
LAVINIA Carroll
LAWRENCEBURG (38464) Lawrence(94), Giles(3), Wayne(2)
LEBANON (37087) Wilson(96), Trousdale(2)
LEBANON (37090) Wilson(97), Smith(2)
LEBANON Wilson
LENOIR CITY (37771) Loudon(92), Roane(7)
LENOIR CITY Loudon
LENOX Dyer
LEOMA (38468) Lawrence(90), Giles(9)
LEWISBURG (37091) Marshall(96), Bedford(3)
LEXINGTON Henderson
LIBERTY (37095) De Kalb(76), Cannon(19), Wilson(3)
LIMESTONE (37681) Greene(55), Washington(44)
LINDEN (37096) Perry(88), Wayne(10)
LIVINGSTON Overton
LOBELVILLE (37097) Perry(98), Humphreys(1)
LONE MOUNTAIN Claiborne
LOOKOUT MOUNTAIN Hamilton
LORETTO Lawrence
LOUDON (37774) Loudon(94), Roane(4)
LOUISVILLE Blount
LOWLAND Hamblen
LUPTON CITY Hamilton
LURAY Chester
LUTTRELL (37779) Union(92), Knox(5), Grainger(1)
LUTTS Wayne
LYLES Hickman
LYNCHBURG Moore
LYNNVILLE (38472) Giles(92), Marshall(7)

MACON Fayette
MADISON Davidson
MADISONVILLE (37354) Monroe(98), McMinn(1)
MANCHESTER Coffee
MANSFIELD Henry
MARTIN Weakley
MARYVILLE (37801) Blount(94), Monroe(5)
MARYVILLE Blount
MASCOT (37806) Knox(91), Grainger(8)
MASON (38049) Fayette(78), Tipton(21)
MAURY CITY Crockett
MAYNARDVILLE (37807) Union(98), Knox(1)
MC DONALD (37353) Bradley(88), Hamilton(11)
MC EWEN (37101) Humphreys(89), Houston(5), Hickman(5)
MC KENZIE (38201) Carroll(75), Weakley(14), Henry(10)
MC LEMORESVILLE Carroll
MC MINNVILLE (37110) Warren(97), Grundy(1), Cannon(1)
MC MINNVILLE Warren
MEDINA (38355) Gibson(57), Madison(42)
MEDON (38356) Madison(54), Hardeman(33), Chester(11)
MEMPHIS Shelby
MERCER (38392) Madison(66), Hardeman(33)
MICHIE (38357) McNairy(80), Hardin(19)
MIDDLETON Hardeman
MIDWAY Greene
MILAN Gibson
MILLEDGEVILLE (38359) Chester(77), McNairy(19), Hardin(2)
MILLIGAN COLLEGE Carter
MILLINGTON (38053) Shelby(83), Tipton(16)
MILLINGTON Shelby
MILTON (37118) Rutherford(66), Wilson(24), Cannon(9)
MINOR HILL Giles
MISTON Dyer
MITCHELLVILLE Sumner
MOHAWK Greene
MONROE (38573) Overton(64), Pickett(35)
MONTEAGLE (37356) Marion(83), Grundy(16)
MONTEREY (38574) Putnam(65), Overton(15), Cumberland(14), Fentress(4)
MOORESBURG (37811) Hawkins(95), Grainger(4)
MORLEY Campbell
MORRIS CHAPEL (38361) Hardin(89), McNairy(10)
MORRISON (37357) Warren(58), Coffee(30), Cannon(9), Grundy(1)
MORRISTOWN Hamblen
MOSCOW Fayette
MOSHEIM Greene
MOSS Clay
MOUNT CARMEL Hawkins
MOUNT JULIET (37122) Wilson(96), Rutherford(3)
MOUNT JULIET Wilson
MOUNT PLEASANT (38474) Maury(94), Lewis(3), Giles(1), Lawrence(1)
MOUNT VERNON Monroe
MOUNTAIN CITY Johnson
MOUNTAIN HOME Washington
MULBERRY (37359) Moore(53), Lincoln(46)
MUNFORD Tipton
MURFREESBORO Rutherford
NASHVILLE (37221) Davidson(96), Williamson(3)
NASHVILLE Davidson
NEW JOHNSONVILLE Humphreys
NEW MARKET Jefferson
NEW TAZEWELL (37825) Claiborne(96), Union(3)

NEW TAZEWELL Claiborne
NEWBERN Dyer
NEWCOMB Campbell
NEWPORT Cocke
NIOTA (37826) McMinn(94), Meigs(6)
NOLENSVILLE (37135) Williamson(78), Rutherford(15), Davidson(6)
NORENE Wilson
NORMANDY (37360) Coffee(46), Bedford(38), Moore(14)
NORRIS Anderson
NUNNELLY Hickman
OAK RIDGE (37830) Anderson(93), Roane(5), Knox(1)
OAK RIDGE Anderson
OAKDALE Morgan
OAKFIELD Madison
OAKLAND Fayette
OBION (38240) Obion(93), Dyer(6)
OCOEE Polk
OLD HICKORY (37138) Davidson(68), Wilson(31)
OLDFORT (37362) Bradley(87), Polk(12)
OLIVEHILL (38475) Hardin(86), Wayne(13)
OLIVER SPRINGS (37840) Roane(35), Morgan(32), Anderson(32)
ONEIDA Scott
ONLY Hickman
OOLTEWAH Hamilton
ORLINDA Robertson
OZONE Cumberland
PALL MALL (38577) Fentress(50), Pickett(49)
PALMER (37365) Grundy(90), Sequatchie(7), Marion(1)
PALMERSVILLE Weakley
PALMYRA Montgomery
PARIS (38242) Henry(98), Weakley(1)
PARROTTSVILLE Cocke
PARSONS Decatur
PEGRAM (37143) Cheatham(86), Davidson(13)
PELHAM Grundy
PETERSBURG (37144) Lincoln(56), Marshall(32), Bedford(7), Moore(1)
PETROS Morgan
PHILADELPHIA (37846) Loudon(59), Roane(23), Monroe(15), McMinn(1)
PICKWICK DAM Hardin
PIGEON FORGE Sevier
PIKEVILLE (37367) Bledsoe(84), Cumberland(9), Van Buren(6)
PINEY FLATS Sullivan
PINSON (38366) Chester(52), Madison(47)
PIONEER (37847) Scott(63), Campbell(36)
PLEASANT HILL Cumberland
PLEASANT SHADE (37145) Smith(73), Macon(15), Jackson(11)
PLEASANT VIEW (37146) Cheatham(71), Robertson(28)
PLEASANTVILLE Hickman
POCAHONTAS (38061) Hardeman(63), McNairy(36)
PORTLAND (37148) Sumner(94), Robertson(5)
POWDER SPRINGS (37848) Union(66), Grainger(33)
POWELL (37849) Knox(82), Anderson(17)
PRIMM SPRINGS (38476) Williamson(36), Hickman(35), Maury(27)
PROSPECT Giles
PRUDEN Claiborne
PULASKI Giles
PURYEAR Henry
QUEBECK White
RAMER McNairy
READYVILLE (37149) Rutherford(64), Cannon(35)
REAGAN (38368) Henderson(76), Chester(23)
RED BOILING SPRINGS (37150) Macon(75), Clay(23)
RELIANCE (37369) Polk(81), Monroe(18)

RICEVILLE McMinn
RICKMAN Overton
RIDDLETON Smith
RIDGELY (38080) Lake(62), Dyer(33), Obion(3)
RIDGETOP Robertson
RIPLEY (38063) Lauderdale(94), Haywood(5)
RIVES Obion
ROAN MOUNTAIN Carter
ROBBINS (37852) Scott(90), Morgan(9)
ROCK ISLAND (38581) Warren(77), Van Buren(21)
ROCKFORD (37853) Blount(94), Knox(5)
ROCKVALE (37153) Rutherford(91), Bedford(8)
ROCKWOOD (37854) Roane(76), Cumberland(15), Morgan(7)
ROGERSVILLE Hawkins
ROSSVILLE Fayette
RUGBY Morgan
RUSSELLVILLE Hamblen
RUTHERFORD Gibson
RUTLEDGE Grainger
SAINT ANDREWS Franklin
SAINT BETHLEHEM Montgomery
SAINT JOSEPH Lawrence
SALE CREEK Hamilton
SALTILLO (38370) Hardin(96), Henderson(3)
SAMBURG Obion
SANTA FE Maury
SARDIS (38371) Hardin(59), Henderson(40)
SAULSBURY Hardeman
SAVANNAH Hardin
SCOTTS HILL (38374) Decatur(98), Henderson(1)
SELMER McNairy
SEQUATCHIE Marion
SEVIERVILLE (37876) Sevier(97), Jefferson(2)
SEVIERVILLE Sevier
SEWANEE Franklin
SEYMOUR (37865) Sevier(80), Blount(19)
SHADY VALLEY Johnson
SHARON Weakley
SHARPS CHAPEL Union
SHAWANEE Claiborne

SHELBYVILLE (37160) Bedford(97), Moore(2)
SHELBYVILLE Bedford
SHERWOOD Franklin
SHILOH (38376) Hardin(80), McNairy(19)
SIGNAL MOUNTAIN (37377) Hamilton(88), Sequatchie(11)
SILERTON Hardeman
SILVER POINT (38582) Putnam(71), De Kalb(28)
SLAYDEN Dickson
SMARTT Warren
SMITHVILLE (37166) De Kalb(89), Warren(9), Cannon(1)
SMYRNA Rutherford
SNEEDVILLE (37869) Hancock(65), Hawkins(27), Claiborne(7)
SODDY DAISY (37379) Hamilton(94), Sequatchie(4)
SODDY DAISY Hamilton
SOMERVILLE Fayette
SOUTH FULTON (38257) Obion(94), Weakley(5)
SOUTH PITTSBURG Marion
SOUTHSIDE Montgomery
SPARTA (38583) White(86), De Kalb(6), Cumberland(3), Putnam(2)
SPEEDWELL (37870) Claiborne(76), Campbell(12), Union(10)
SPENCER Van Buren
SPRING CITY (37381) Rhea(95), Bledsoe(4)
SPRING CREEK Madison
SPRING HILL (37174) Maury(56), Williamson(42)
SPRINGFIELD Robertson
SPRINGVILLE Henry
STANTON (38069) Haywood(83), Tipton(8), Fayette(8)
STANTONVILLE McNairy
STEWART (37175) Houston(79), Stewart(20)
STRAWBERRY PLAINS (37871) Knox(44), Jefferson(40), Sevier(15)
SUGAR TREE (38380) Decatur(67), Benton(32)
SUMMERTOWN (38483) Lawrence(76), Lewis(19), Giles(2), Maury(1)
SUMMITVILLE Coffee

SUNBRIGHT (37872) Morgan(95), Scott(4)
SURGOINSVILLE Hawkins
SWEETWATER (37874) Monroe(87), McMinn(6), Loudon(5)
TAFT Lincoln
TALBOTT (37877) Hamblen(61), Jefferson(38)
TALLASSEE Blount
TAZEWELL (37879) Claiborne(95), Hancock(4)
TELFORD Washington
TELLICO PLAINS Monroe
TEN MILE (37880) Roane(58), Meigs(40)
TENNESSEE RIDGE (37178) Houston(86), Stewart(13)
THOMPSONS STATION Williamson
THORN HILL (37881) Grainger(64), Hancock(34)
TIGRETT Dyer
TIPTONVILLE Lake
TOONE Hardeman
TOWNSEND Blount
TRACY CITY (37387) Marion(66), Grundy(33)
TRADE Johnson
TREADWAY Hancock
TRENTON Gibson
TREZEVANT Carroll
TRIMBLE (38259) Dyer(86), Obion(8), Gibson(4)
TROY Obion
TULLAHOMA (37388) Coffee(72), Franklin(18), Moore(8)
TURTLETOWN Polk
UNICOI Unicoi
UNION CITY Obion
UNIONVILLE (37180) Bedford(94), Rutherford(5)
VANLEER (37181) Dickson(98), Houston(1)
VIOLA Warren
VONORE (37885) Monroe(97), Loudon(2)
WALLAND Blount
WALLING White
WARTBURG Morgan
WARTRACE (37183) Bedford(72), Coffee(18), Moore(8)
WASHBURN (37888) Grainger(90), Union(9)

WATAUGA (37694) Carter(76), Sullivan(18), Washington(5)
WATERTOWN (37184) Wilson(96), Smith(3)
WATTS BAR DAM Rhea
WAVERLY Humphreys
WAYNESBORO (38485) Wayne(98), Lewis(1)
WESTMORELAND (37186) Sumner(58), Macon(41)
WESTPOINT (38486) Lawrence(84), Wayne(15)
WESTPORT (38387) Carroll(90), Benton(9)
WHITE BLUFF (37187) Dickson(93), Cheatham(6)
WHITE HOUSE (37188) Robertson(60), Sumner(39)
WHITE PINE (37890) Jefferson(93), Hamblen(6)
WHITES CREEK Davidson
WHITESBURG (37891) Hamblen(68), Hawkins(31)
WHITESIDE Marion
WHITEVILLE (38075) Hardeman(70), Fayette(15), Haywood(14)
WHITLEYVILLE (38588) Jackson(75), Clay(19), Macon(5)
WHITWELL (37397) Marion(95), Sequatchie(4)
WILDER (38589) Overton(54), Fentress(45)
WILDERSVILLE Henderson
WILLIAMSPORT (38487) Maury(94), Hickman(5)
WILLISTON Fayette
WINCHESTER (37398) Franklin(98), Moore(1)
WINFIELD Scott
WINONA Scott
WOODBURY (37190) Cannon(98), Warren(1)
WOODLAND MILLS Obion
WOODLAWN Montgomery
WYNNBURG Lake
YORKVILLE Gibson
YUMA (38390) Carroll(80), Henderson(19)

Tennessee ZIP/City Cross Reference

37010-37010	ADAMS
37011-37011	ANTIOCH
37012-37012	ALEXANDRIA
37013-37013	ANTIOCH
37014-37014	ARRINGTON
37015-37015	ASHLAND CITY
37016-37016	AUBURNTOWN
37018-37018	BEECHGROVE
37019-37019	BELFAST
37020-37020	BELL BUCKLE
37022-37022	BETHPAGE
37023-37023	BIG ROCK
37024-37024	BRENTWOOD
37025-37025	BON AQUA
37026-37026	BRADYVILLE
37027-37027	BRENTWOOD
37028-37028	BUMPUS MILLS
37029-37029	BURNS
37030-37030	CARTHAGE
37031-37031	CASTALIAN SPRINGS
37032-37032	CEDAR HILL
37033-37033	CENTERVILLE
37034-37034	CHAPEL HILL
37035-37035	CHAPMANSBORO
37036-37036	CHARLOTTE
37037-37037	CHRISTIANA
37040-37044	CLARKSVILLE
37046-37046	COLLEGE GROVE

37047-37047	CORNERSVILLE
37048-37048	COTTONTOWN
37049-37049	CROSS PLAINS
37050-37050	CUMBERLAND CITY
37051-37051	CUMBERLAND FURNACE
37052-37052	CUNNINGHAM
37054-37054	DENVER
37055-37056	DICKSON
37057-37057	DIXON SPRINGS
37058-37058	DOVER
37059-37059	DOWELLTOWN
37060-37060	EAGLEVILLE
37061-37061	ERIN
37062-37062	FAIRVIEW
37063-37063	FOSTERVILLE
37064-37065	FRANKLIN
37066-37066	GALLATIN
37067-37069	FRANKLIN
37070-37070	GOODLETTSVILLE
37071-37071	GLADEVILLE
37072-37072	GOODLETTSVILLE
37073-37073	GREENBRIER
37074-37074	HARTSVILLE
37075-37075	HENDERSONVILLE
37076-37076	HERMITAGE
37077-37077	HENDERSONVILLE
37078-37078	HURRICANE MILLS
37079-37079	INDIAN MOUND

37080-37080	JOELTON
37082-37082	KINGSTON SPRINGS
37083-37083	LAFAYETTE
37085-37085	LASCASSAS
37086-37086	LA VERGNE
37087-37088	LEBANON
37089-37089	LA VERGNE
37090-37090	LEBANON
37091-37091	LEWISBURG
37095-37095	LIBERTY
37096-37096	LINDEN
37097-37097	LOBELVILLE
37098-37098	LYLES
37101-37101	MC EWEN
37110-37111	MC MINNVILLE
37115-37116	MADISON
37118-37118	MILTON
37119-37119	MITCHELLVILLE
37121-37122	MOUNT JULIET
37127-37133	MURFREESBORO
37134-37134	NEW JOHNSONVILLE
37135-37135	NOLENSVILLE
37136-37136	NORENE
37137-37137	NUNNELLY
37138-37138	OLD HICKORY
37140-37140	ONLY
37141-37141	ORLINDA
37142-37142	PALMYRA

37143-37143	PEGRAM
37144-37144	PETERSBURG
37145-37145	PLEASANT SHADE
37146-37146	PLEASANT VIEW
37147-37147	PLEASANTVILLE
37148-37148	PORTLAND
37149-37149	READYVILLE
37150-37150	RED BOILING SPRINGS
37151-37151	RIDDLETON
37152-37152	RIDGETOP
37153-37153	ROCKVALE
37155-37155	SAINT BETHLEHEM
37160-37162	SHELBYVILLE
37165-37165	SLAYDEN
37166-37166	SMITHVILLE
37167-37167	SMYRNA
37171-37171	SOUTHSIDE
37172-37172	SPRINGFIELD
37174-37174	SPRING HILL
37175-37175	STEWART
37178-37178	TENNESSEE RIDGE
37179-37179	THOMPSONS STATION
37180-37180	UNIONVILLE
37181-37181	VANLEER
37183-37183	WARTRACE
37184-37184	WATERTOWN
37185-37185	WAVERLY
37186-37186	WESTMORELAND

37187-37187 WHITE BLUFF	37382-37382 SUMMITVILLE	37765-37765 KYLES FORD	38015-38015 BURLISON
37188-37188 WHITE HOUSE	37383-37383 SEWANEE	37766-37766 LA FOLLETTE	38016-38016 CORDOVA
37189-37189 WHITES CREEK	37384-37384 SODDY DAISY	37769-37769 LAKE CITY	38017-38017 COLLIERVILLE
37190-37190 WOODBURY	37385-37385 TELLICO PLAINS	37770-37770 LANCING	38018-38018 CORDOVA
37191-37191 WOODLAWN	37387-37387 TRACY CITY	37771-37772 LENOIR CITY	38019-38019 COVINGTON
37200-37250 NASHVILLE	37388-37388 TULLAHOMA	37773-37773 LONE MOUNTAIN	38021-38021 CROCKETT MILLS
37301-37301 ALTAMONT	37389-37389 ARNOLD AFB	37774-37774 LOUDON	38023-38023 DRUMMONDS
37302-37302 APISON	37391-37391 TURTLETOWN	37777-37777 LOUISVILLE	38024-38025 DYERSBURG
37303-37303 ATHENS	37394-37394 VIOLA	37778-37778 LOWLAND	38027-38027 COLLIERVILLE
37304-37304 BAKEWELL	37395-37395 WATTS BAR DAM	37779-37779 LUTTRELL	38028-38028 EADS
37305-37305 BEERSHEBA SPRINGS	37396-37396 WHITESIDE	37801-37804 MARYVILLE	38029-38029 ELLENDALE
37306-37306 BELVIDERE	37397-37397 WHITWELL	37806-37806 MASCOT	38030-38030 FINLEY
37307-37307 BENTON	37398-37398 WINCHESTER	37807-37807 MAYNARDVILLE	38033-38033 FOWLKES
37308-37308 BIRCHWOOD	37400-37499 CHATTANOOGA	37809-37809 MIDWAY	38034-38034 FRIENDSHIP
37309-37309 CALHOUN	37501-37544 MEMPHIS	37810-37810 MOHAWK	38036-38036 GALLAWAY
37310-37310 CHARLESTON	37601-37615 JOHNSON CITY	37811-37811 MOORESBURG	38037-38037 GATES
37311-37312 CLEVELAND	37616-37616 AFTON	37812-37812 MORLEY	38039-38039 GRAND JUNCTION
37313-37313 COALMONT	37617-37617 BLOUNTVILLE	37813-37816 MORRISTOWN	38040-38040 HALLS
37314-37314 COKERCREEK	37618-37618 BLUFF CITY	37818-37818 MOSHEIM	38041-38041 HENNING
37315-37315 COLLEGEDALE	37620-37625 BRISTOL	37819-37819 NEWCOMB	38042-38042 HICKORY VALLEY
37316-37316 CONASAUGA	37640-37640 BUTLER	37820-37820 NEW MARKET	38043-38043 HICKORY WITHE
37317-37317 COPPERHILL	37641-37641 CHUCKEY	37821-37822 NEWPORT	38044-38044 HORNSBY
37318-37318 COWAN	37642-37642 CHURCH HILL	37824-37825 NEW TAZEWELL	38045-38045 LACONIA
37320-37320 CLEVELAND	37643-37644 ELIZABETHTON	37826-37826 NIOTA	38046-38046 LA GRANGE
37321-37321 DAYTON	37645-37645 MOUNT CARMEL	37828-37828 NORRIS	38047-38047 LENOX
37322-37322 DECATUR	37650-37650 ERWIN	37829-37829 OAKDALE	38048-38048 MACON
37323-37323 CLEVELAND	37656-37656 FALL BRANCH	37830-37831 OAK RIDGE	38049-38049 MASON
37324-37324 DECHERD	37657-37657 FLAG POND	37840-37840 OLIVER SPRINGS	38050-38050 MAURY CITY
37325-37325 DELANO	37658-37658 HAMPTON	37841-37841 ONEIDA	38052-38052 MIDDLETON
37326-37326 DUCKTOWN	37659-37659 JONESBOROUGH	37842-37842 OZONE	38053-38055 MILLINGTON
37327-37327 DUNLAP	37660-37669 KINGSPORT	37843-37843 PARROTTSVILLE	38056-38056 MISTON
37328-37328 ELORA	37680-37680 LAUREL BLOOMERY	37845-37845 PETROS	38057-38057 MOSCOW
37329-37329 ENGLEWOOD	37681-37681 LIMESTONE	37846-37846 PHILADELPHIA	38058-38058 MUNFORD
37330-37330 ESTILL SPRINGS	37682-37682 MILLIGAN COLLEGE	37847-37847 PIONEER	38059-38059 NEWBERN
37331-37331 ETOWAH	37683-37683 MOUNTAIN CITY	37848-37848 POWDER SPRINGS	38060-38060 OAKLAND
37332-37332 EVENSVILLE	37684-37684 MOUNTAIN HOME	37849-37849 POWELL	38061-38061 POCAHONTAS
37333-37333 FARNER	37686-37686 PINEY FLATS	37851-37851 PRUDEN	38063-38063 RIPLEY
37334-37334 FAYETTEVILLE	37687-37687 ROAN MOUNTAIN	37852-37852 ROBBINS	38066-38066 ROSSVILLE
37335-37335 FLINTVILLE	37688-37688 SHADY VALLEY	37853-37853 ROCKFORD	38067-38067 SAULSBURY
37336-37336 GEORGETOWN	37690-37690 TELFORD	37854-37854 ROCKWOOD	38068-38068 SOMERVILLE
37337-37337 GRANDVIEW	37691-37691 TRADE	37857-37857 ROGERSVILLE	38069-38069 STANTON
37338-37338 GRAYSVILLE	37692-37692 UNICOI	37860-37860 RUSSELLVILLE	38070-38070 TIGRETT
37339-37339 GRUETLI LAAGER	37694-37694 WATAUGA	37861-37861 RUTLEDGE	38071-38071 TIPTON
37340-37340 GUILD	37699-37699 PINEY FLATS	37862-37862 SEVIERVILLE	38074-38074 BOLIVAR
37341-37341 HARRISON	37701-37701 ALCOA	37863-37863 PIGEON FORGE	38075-38075 WHITEVILLE
37342-37342 HILLSBORO	37705-37705 ANDERSONVILLE	37864-37864 SEVIERVILLE	38076-38076 WILLISTON
37343-37343 HIXSON	37707-37707 ARTHUR	37865-37865 SEYMOUR	38077-38077 WYNNBURG
37345-37345 HUNTLAND	37708-37708 BEAN STATION	37866-37866 SHARPS CHAPEL	38079-38079 TIPTONVILLE
37346-37346 ISABELLA	37709-37709 BLAINE	37867-37867 SHAWANEE	38080-38080 RIDGELY
37347-37347 JASPER	37710-37710 BRICEVILLE	37868-37868 PIGEON FORGE	38083-38083 MILLINGTON
37348-37348 KELSO	37711-37711 BULLS GAP	37869-37869 SNEEDVILLE	38088-38088 CORDOVA
37349-37349 MANCHESTER	37713-37713 BYBEE	37870-37870 SPEEDWELL	38100-38137 MEMPHIS
37350-37350 LOOKOUT MOUNTAIN	37714-37714 CARYVILLE	37871-37871 STRAWBERRY PLAINS	38138-38139 GERMANTOWN
37351-37351 LUPTON CITY	37715-37715 CLAIRFIELD	37872-37872 SUNBRIGHT	38140-38182 MEMPHIS
37352-37352 LYNCHBURG	37716-37717 CLINTON	37873-37873 SURGOINSVILLE	38183-38183 GERMANTOWN
37353-37353 MC DONALD	37719-37719 COALFIELD	37874-37874 SWEETWATER	38184-38197 MEMPHIS
37354-37354 MADISONVILLE	37721-37721 CORRYTON	37876-37876 SEVIERVILLE	38201-38201 MC KENZIE
37355-37355 MANCHESTER	37722-37722 COSBY	37877-37877 TALBOTT	38220-38220 ATWOOD
37356-37356 MONTEAGLE	37723-37723 CRAB ORCHARD	37878-37878 TALLASSEE	38221-38221 BIG SANDY
37357-37357 MORRISON	37724-37724 CUMBERLAND GAP	37879-37879 TAZEWELL	38222-38222 BUCHANAN
37358-37358 MOUNT VERNON	37725-37725 DANDRIDGE	37880-37880 TEN MILE	38223-38223 COMO
37359-37359 MULBERRY	37726-37726 DEER LODGE	37881-37881 THORN HILL	38224-38224 COTTAGE GROVE
37360-37360 NORMANDY	37727-37727 DEL RIO	37882-37882 TOWNSEND	38225-38225 DRESDEN
37361-37361 OCOEE	37729-37729 DUFF	37883-37883 TREADWAY	38226-38226 DUKEDOM
37362-37362 OLDFORT	37730-37730 EAGAN	37885-37885 VONORE	38227-38227 ELBRIDGE
37363-37363 OOLTEWAH	37731-37731 EIDSON	37886-37886 WALLAND	38229-38229 GLEASON
37364-37364 CLEVELAND	37732-37732 ELGIN	37887-37887 WARTBURG	38230-38230 GREENFIELD
37365-37365 PALMER	37733-37733 RUGBY	37888-37888 WASHBURN	38231-38231 HENRY
37366-37366 PELHAM	37737-37737 FRIENDSVILLE	37890-37890 WHITE PINE	38232-38232 HORNBEAK
37367-37367 PIKEVILLE	37738-37738 GATLINBURG	37891-37891 WHITESBURG	38233-38233 KENTON
37369-37369 RELIANCE	37742-37742 GREENBACK	37892-37892 WINFIELD	38235-38235 MC LEMORESVILLE
37370-37370 RICEVILLE	37743-37745 GREENEVILLE	37893-37893 WINONA	38236-38236 MANSFIELD
37371-37371 ATHENS	37748-37748 HARRIMAN	37900-37999 KNOXVILLE	38237-38238 MARTIN
37372-37372 SAINT ANDREWS	37752-37752 HARROGATE	38001-38001 ALAMO	38240-38240 OBION
37373-37373 SALE CREEK	37753-37753 HARTFORD	38002-38002 ARLINGTON	38241-38241 PALMERSVILLE
37374-37374 SEQUATCHIE	37754-37754 HEISKELL	38004-38004 ATOKA	38242-38242 PARIS
37375-37375 SEWANEE	37755-37755 HELENWOOD	38006-38006 BELLS	38251-38251 PURYEAR
37376-37376 SHERWOOD	37756-37756 HUNTSVILLE	38007-38007 BOGOTA	38253-38253 RIVES
37377-37377 SIGNAL MOUNTAIN	37757-37757 JACKSBORO	38008-38008 BOLIVAR	38254-38254 SAMBURG
37378-37378 SMARTT	37760-37760 JEFFERSON CITY	38010-38010 BRADEN	38255-38255 SHARON
37379-37379 SODDY DAISY	37762-37762 JELLICO	38011-38011 BRIGHTON	38256-38256 SPRINGVILLE
37380-37380 SOUTH PITTSBURG	37763-37763 KINGSTON	38012-38012 BROWNSVILLE	38257-38257 SOUTH FULTON
37381-37381 SPRING CITY	37764-37764 KODAK	38014-38014 BRUNSWICK	38258-38258 TREZEVANT

38259-38259 TRIMBLE	38348-38348 LAVINIA	38450-38450 COLLINWOOD	38545-38545 BLOOMINGTON SPRINGS
38260-38260 TROY	38351-38351 LEXINGTON	38451-38451 CULLEOKA	38547-38547 BRUSH CREEK
38261-38261 UNION CITY	38352-38352 LURAY	38452-38452 CYPRESS INN	38548-38548 BUFFALO VALLEY
38271-38271 WOODLAND MILLS	38355-38355 MEDINA	38453-38453 DELLROSE	38549-38549 BYRDSTOWN
38281-38281 UNION CITY	38356-38356 MEDON	38454-38454 DUCK RIVER	38550-38550 CAMPAIGN
38301-38308 JACKSON	38357-38357 MICHIE	38455-38455 ELKTON	38551-38551 CELINA
38310-38310 ADAMSVILLE	38358-38358 MILAN	38456-38456 ETHRIDGE	38552-38552 CHESTNUT MOUND
38311-38311 BATH SPRINGS	38359-38359 MILLEDGEVILLE	38457-38457 FIVE POINTS	38553-38553 CLARKRANGE
38313-38313 BEECH BLUFF	38361-38361 MORRIS CHAPEL	38459-38459 FRANKEWING	38554-38554 CRAWFORD
38314-38314 JACKSON	38362-38362 OAKFIELD	38460-38460 GOODSPRING	38555-38555 CROSSVILLE
38315-38315 BETHEL SPRINGS	38363-38363 PARSONS	38461-38461 HAMPSHIRE	38556-38556 JAMESTOWN
38316-38316 BRADFORD	38365-38365 PICKWICK DAM	38462-38462 HOHENWALD	38557-38557 CROSSVILLE
38317-38317 BRUCETON	38366-38366 PINSON	38463-38463 IRON CITY	38559-38559 DOYLE
38318-38318 BUENA VISTA	38367-38367 RAMER	38464-38464 LAWRENCEBURG	38560-38560 ELMWOOD
38320-38320 CAMDEN	38368-38368 REAGAN	38468-38468 LEOMA	38562-38562 GAINESBORO
38321-38321 CEDAR GROVE	38369-38369 RUTHERFORD	38469-38469 LORETTO	38563-38563 GORDONSVILLE
38324-38324 CLARKSBURG	38370-38370 SALTILLO	38471-38471 LUTTS	38564-38564 GRANVILLE
38326-38326 COUNCE	38371-38371 SARDIS	38472-38472 LYNNVILLE	38565-38565 GRIMSLEY
38327-38327 CRUMP	38372-38372 SAVANNAH	38473-38473 MINOR HILL	38567-38567 HICKMAN
38328-38328 DARDEN	38374-38374 SCOTTS HILL	38474-38474 MOUNT PLEASANT	38568-38568 HILHAM
38329-38329 DECATURVILLE	38375-38375 SELMER	38475-38475 OLIVEHILL	38569-38569 LANCASTER
38330-38330 DYER	38376-38376 SHILOH	38476-38476 PRIMM SPRINGS	38570-38570 LIVINGSTON
38331-38331 EATON	38377-38377 SILERTON	38477-38477 PROSPECT	38571-38572 CROSSVILLE
38332-38332 ENVILLE	38378-38378 SPRING CREEK	38478-38478 PULASKI	38573-38573 MONROE
38333-38333 EVA	38379-38379 STANTONVILLE	38481-38481 SAINT JOSEPH	38574-38574 MONTEREY
38334-38334 FINGER	38380-38380 SUGAR TREE	38482-38482 SANTA FE	38575-38575 MOSS
38336-38336 FRUITVALE	38381-38381 TOONE	38483-38483 SUMMERTOWN	38577-38577 PALL MALL
38337-38337 GADSDEN	38382-38382 TRENTON	38485-38485 WAYNESBORO	38578-38578 PLEASANT HILL
38338-38338 GIBSON	38387-38387 WESTPORT	38486-38486 WESTPOINT	38579-38579 QUEBECK
38339-38339 GUYS	38388-38388 WILDERSVILLE	38487-38487 WILLIAMSPORT	38580-38580 RICKMAN
38340-38340 HENDERSON	38389-38389 YORKVILLE	38488-38488 TAFT	38581-38581 ROCK ISLAND
38341-38341 HOLLADAY	38390-38390 YUMA	38501-38503 COOKEVILLE	38582-38582 SILVER POINT
38342-38342 HOLLOW ROCK	38391-38391 DENMARK	38504-38504 ALLARDT	38583-38583 SPARTA
38343-38343 HUMBOLDT	38392-38392 MERCER	38505-38506 COOKEVILLE	38585-38585 SPENCER
38344-38344 HUNTINGDON	38393-38393 CHEWALLA	38541-38541 ALLONS	38587-38587 WALLING
38345-38345 HURON	38401-38402 COLUMBIA	38542-38542 ALLRED	38588-38588 WHITLEYVILLE
38346-38346 IDLEWILD	38425-38425 CLIFTON	38543-38543 ALPINE	38589-38589 WILDER
38347-38347 JACKS CREEK	38449-38449 ARDMORE	38544-38544 BAXTER	

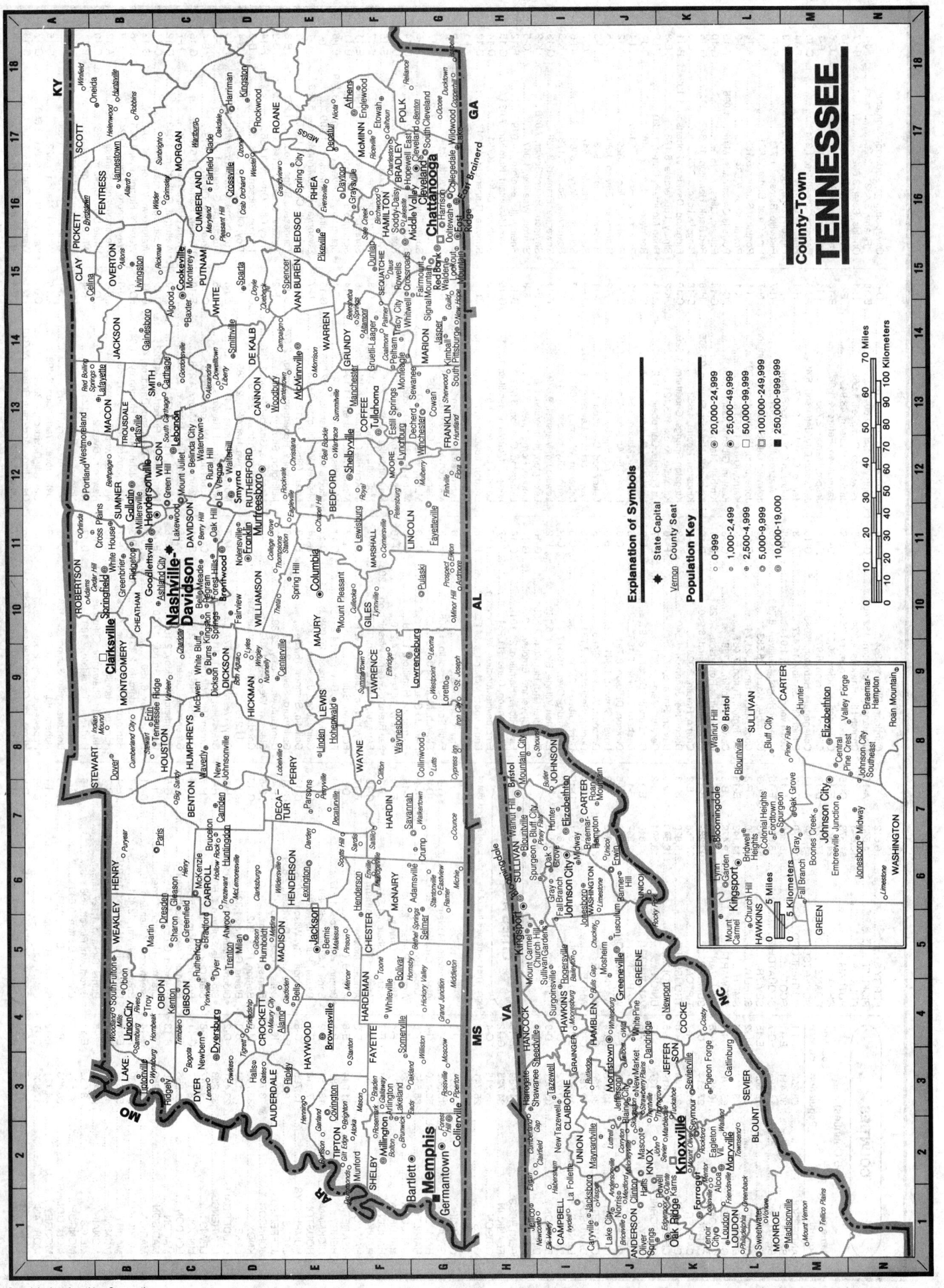

TENNESSEE

County-Town

Explanation of Symbols

★ State Capital

Vernon ◉ County Seat

Population Key

○	0-999
⊙	1,000-2,499
⊕	2,500-4,999
◉	5,000-9,999
⊛	10,000-19,000
●	20,000-24,999
◉	25,000-49,999
□	50,000-99,999
⊡	100,000-249,999
■	250,000-999,999

COUNTIES

(95 Counties)

Name of County	Population	Location on Map
ANDERSON	68,250	J-1
BEDFORD	30,411	E-11
BENTON	14,524	C-7
BLEDSOE	9,669	E-15
BLOUNT	85,969	L-2
BRADLEY	73,712	F-16
CAMPBELL	35,079	I-1
CANNON	10,467	D-13
CARROLL	27,514	C-6
CARTER	51,505	I-7
CHEATHAM	27,140	B-10
CHESTER	12,819	F-5
CLAIBORNE	26,137	I-2
CLAY	7,238	A-15
COCKE	29,141	K-4
COFFEE	40,339	F-13
CROCKETT	13,378	D-4
CUMBERLAND	34,736	C-16
DAVIDSON	510,784	C-11
DEKALB	14,360	D-14
DECATUR	10,472	D-7
DICKSON	35,061	D-9
DYER	34,854	C-3
FAYETTE	25,559	F-3
FENTRESS	14,669	B-16
FRANKLIN	34,725	G-12
GIBSON	46,315	C-4
GILES	25,741	F-10
GRAINGER	17,095	I-3
GREENE	55,853	J-5
GRUNDY	13,362	F-14
HAMBLEN	50,480	I-4
HAMILTON	285,536	F-16
HANCOCK	6,739	H-4
HARDEMAN	23,377	F-4
HARDIN	22,633	F-7
HAWKINS	44,565	I-4
HAYWOOD	19,437	E-3
HENDERSON	21,844	E-6
HENRY	27,888	B-6
HICKMAN	16,754	D-9
HOUSTON	7,018	C-8
HUMPHREYS	15,795	C-8
JACKSON	9,297	B-14
JEFFERSON	33,016	K-3
JOHNSON	13,766	I-8
KNOX	335,749	J-2
LAKE	7,129	B-3
LAUDERDALE	23,491	D-2
LAWRENCE	35,303	F-9
LEWIS	9,247	E-8
LINCOLN	28,157	G-11
LOUDON	31,255	L-1
MACON	15,906	B-13
MADISON	77,982	D-5
MARION	24,860	G-14
MARSHALL	21,539	F-11
MAURY	54,812	E-10
MCMINN	42,383	F-17
MCNAIRY	22,422	F-6
MEIGS	8,033	E-17
MONROE	30,541	L-1
MONTGOMERY	100,498	B-9
MOORE	4,721	F-12
MORGAN	17,300	C-17
OBION	31,717	C-4
OVERTON	17,636	B-15
PERRY	6,612	E-7
PICKETT	4,548	A-15
POLK	13,643	F-17
PUTNAM	51,373	C-15
RHEA	24,344	E-16
ROANE	47,227	D-17
ROBERTSON	41,494	A-10
RUTHERFORD	118,570	D-12
SCOTT	18,358	A-17
SEQUATCHIE	8,863	F-15
SEVIER	51,043	L-3
SHELBY	826,330	F-2
SMITH	14,143	B-13
STEWART	9,479	B-8
SULLIVAN	143,596	H-6
SUMNER	103,281	B-11
TIPTON	37,568	E-2
TROUSDALE	5,920	B-13
UNICOI	16,549	J-6
UNION	13,694	I-2
VAN BUREN	4,846	E-15
WARREN	32,992	E-14
WASHINGTON	92,315	I-6
WAYNE	13,935	F-8
WEAKLEY	31,972	B-5
WHITE	20,090	C-14
WILLIAMSON	81,021	D-10
WILSON	67,675	C-12
TOTAL	4,877,185	

CITIES AND TOWNS

Note: The first name is that of the city or town, second, that of the county in which it is located, then the population and location on the map.

Adamsville, McNairy, 1,745 ... G-6
Alamo, Crockett, 2,426 ... D-4
Alcoa, Blount, 6,400 ... K-2
Algood, Putnam, 2,399 ... C-15
Altamont, Grundy, 679 ... F-14
Arlington, Shelby, 1,541 ... F-3
Ashland City, Cheatham, 2,552 ... C-10
Athens, McMinn, 12,054 ... F-17
Atwood, Carroll, 1,066 ... D-5
•Banner Hill, Unicoi, 1,717 ... J-6
Bartlett, Shelby, 26,989 ... F-2
Baxter, Putnam, 1,289 ... C-14
•Belinda City, Wilson, 2,098 ... C-12
Belle Meade, Davidson, 2,839 ... C-11
Bells, Crockett, 1,643 ... E-4
Bemis, Madison ... E-5
Benton, Polk, 992 ... G-17
Blaine, Grainger, 1,326 ... J-3
•Bloomingdale, Sullivan, 10,953 ... H-6
•Blountville, Sullivan, 2,605 ... H-6
Bluff City, Sullivan, 1,390 ... H-7
Bolivar, Hardeman, 5,969 ... F-4
Boones Creek, Washington ... M-7
Bradford, Gibson, 1,154 ... C-5
Braemar-Hampton, Carter ... I-7
Brentwood, Williamson, 16,392 ... D-11
Bristol, Sullivan, 23,421 ... H-7
Brownsville, Haywood, 10,019 ... E-4
Bruceton, Carroll, 1,586 ... C-7
Burns, Dickson, 1,127 ... D-9
Byrdstown, Pickett, 998 ... A-16
Camden, Benton, 3,643 ... C-7
Carthage, Smith, 2,386 ... C-13
Caryville, Campbell, 1,751 ... I-1
Celina, Clay, 1,493 ... B-15
Centerville, Hickman, 3,616 ... D-9
•Central, Carter, 2,635 ... M-8
Charlotte, Dickson, 854 ... D-9
Chattanooga, Hamilton, 152,466 ... G-15
Church Hill, Hawkins, 4,834 ... H-5
Clarksville, Montgomery, 75,494 ... B-9
Cleveland, Bradley, 30,354 ... G-17
Clinton, Anderson, 8,972 ... J-1
Collegedale, Hamilton, 5,048 ... G-16
Collierville, Shelby, 14,427 ... G-3
Collinwood, Wayne, 1,014 ... G-8
•Colonial Heights, Sullivan, 6,716 ... L-6
Columbia, Maury, 28,583 ... E-10
Cookeville, Putnam, 21,744 ... C-15
Covington, Tipton, 7,487 ... E-3
Cowan, Franklin, 1,738 ... G-13
Cross Plains, Robertson, 1,025 ... B-11
Crossville, Cumberland, 6,930 ... D-16
Crump, Hardin, 2,028 ... G-7
Dandridge, Jefferson, 1,540 ... J-3
Dayton, Rhea, 5,671 ... F-16
Decatur, Meigs, 1,361 ... E-17
Decaturville, Decatur, 879 ... E-7
Decherd, Franklin, 2,196 ... G-13
Dickson, Dickson, 8,791 ... C-9
Dover, Stewart, 1,341 ... B-8
Dresden, Weakley, 2,488 ... C-5
Dunlap, Sequatchie, 3,731 ... F-15
Dyer, Gibson, 2,204 ... C-5
Dyersburg, Dyer, 16,317 ... C-3
•Eagleton Village, Blount, 5,169 ... K-2
•East Brainerd, Hamilton, 11,594 ... G-16
•East Cleveland, Bradley, 1,249 ... G-17
East Ridge, Hamilton, 21,101 ... G-16
Elizabethton, Carter, 11,931 ... I-7
Embreeville Junction, Washington ... M-7
Englewood, McMinn, 1,611 ... F-18
Erin, Houston, 1,586 ... B-8
Erwin, Unicoi, 5,015 ... J-6
Estill Springs, Franklin, 1,408 ... F-13
Etowah, McMinn, 3,815 ... F-18
•Fairfield Glade, Cumberland, 2,209 ... C-16
•Fairmount, Hamilton, 1,578 ... G-15
Fairview, Williamson, 4,210 ... D-10
•Fall Branch, Greene/Washington, 1,203 ... M-6
Farragut, Knox/Loudon, 12,793 ... K-1
Fayetteville, Lincoln, 6,921 ... G-12
Fordtown, Sullivan ... L-7
Forest Hills, Davidson, 4,231 ... C-11
Franklin, Williamson, 20,098 ... D-11
Gainesboro, Jackson, 1,002 ... B-14
Gallatin, Sumner, 18,794 ... B-12
Gatlinburg, Sevier, 3,417 ... L-3
Germantown, Shelby, 32,893 ... G-2
Gleason, Weakley, 1,402 ... C-6
Goodlettsville, Davidson/Sumner, 11,219 ... B-11
•Gray, Washington, 1,071 ... M-7
Graysville, Rhea, 1,301 ... F-16
•Green Hill, Wilson, 6,763 ... C-11
Greenbrier, Robertson, 2,873 ... B-11
Greeneville, Greene, 13,532 ... J-5
Greenfield, Weakley, 2,105 ... C-5
Gruetli-Laager, Grundy, 1,810 ... F-14
•Halls, Knox, 6,450 ... J-2
Halls, Lauderdale, 2,431 ... D-3
Harriman, Morgan/Roane, 7,119 ... D-17
•Harrison, Hamilton, 7,191 ... G-16
•Harrogate-Shawanee, Claiborne, 2,657 ... H-3
Hartsville, Trousdale, 2,188 ... B-13
Henderson, Chester, 4,760 ... F-5
Hendersonville, Sumner, 32,188 ... C-11
Hohenwald, Lewis, 3,760 ... E-9
•Hopewell, Bradley, 2,569 ... G-16
Humboldt, Gibson/Madison, 9,651 ... D-5
•Hunter, Carter, 1,250 ... I-7
Huntingdon, Carroll, 4,180 ... D-6
Huntsville, Scott, 660 ... B-18
Jacksboro, Campbell, 1,568 ... I-1
Jackson, Madison, 48,949 ... E-5
Jamestown, Fentress, 1,862 ... B-16
Jasper, Marion, 2,780 ... G-14
Jefferson City, Jefferson, 5,494 ... J-3
Jellico, Campbell, 2,447 ... H-1
Johnson City, Carter/Sullivan/Washington, 49,381 ... N-7
Johnson City Southeast, Washington ... N-7
Jonesboro, Washington, 3,091 ... I-6
•Karns, Knox, 1,458 ... K-1
Kenton, Gibson/Obion, 1,366 ... C-4
Kimball, Marion, 1,243 ... G-14
Kingsport, Hawkins/Sullivan, 36,365 ... H-6
Kingston, Roane, 4,552 ... D-18
Kingston Springs, Cheatham, 1,529 ... C-10
Knoxville, Knox, 165,121 ... K-2
La Follette, Campbell, 7,192 ... I-1
La Vergne, Rutherford, 7,499 ... D-12
Lafayette, Macon, 3,641 ... B-13
Lake City, Anderson/Campbell, 2,166 ... J-1
Lakeland, Shelby, 1,204 ... F-2
Lakewood, Davidson, 2,009 ... C-11
Lawrenceburg, Lawrence, 10,412 ... G-9
Lebanon, Wilson, 15,208 ... C-12
Lenoir City, Loudon, 6,147 ... K-1
Lewisburg, Marshall, 9,879 ... F-11
Lexington, Henderson, 5,810 ... E-6
Linden, Perry, 1,099 ... E-8
Livingston, Overton, 3,809 ... B-15
Lookout Mountain, Hamilton, 1,901 ... G-15
Loretto, Lawrence, 1,515 ... G-9
Loudon, Loudon, 4,026 ... L-1
Lynchburg, Moore, 4,721 ... F-12
Lynn Garden, Sullivan ... L-6
Madisonville, Monroe, 3,033 ... M-1
Manchester, Coffee, 7,709 ... F-13
Martin, Weakley, 8,600 ... B-5
Maryville, Blount, 19,208 ... K-2
•Mascot, Knox, 2,138 ... J-2
Maynardville, Union, 1,298 ... J-2
McEwen, Humphreys, 1,442 ... C-8
McKenzie, Carroll/Henry/Weakley, 5,168 ... C-6
McMinnville, Warren, 11,194 ... E-14
Memphis, Shelby, 610,337 ... G-1
•Middle Valley, Hamilton, 12,255 ... G-15
•Midway, Washington, 2,953 ... N-7
Milan, Gibson, 7,512 ... D-5
Millersville, Robertson/Sumner, 2,575 ... B-11
Millington, Shelby, 17,866 ... F-2
Monteagle, Grundy/Marion, 1,138 ... G-14
Monterey, Putnam, 2,559 ... C-15
Morristown, Hamblen, 21,385 ... J-4
Mosheim, Greene, 1,451 ... J-5
Mount Carmel, Hawkins, 4,082 ... H-5
Mount Juliet, Wilson, 5,389 ... C-12
Mount Pleasant, Maury, 4,278 ... E-10
Mountain City, Johnson, 2,169 ... H-8
Munford, Tipton, 2,326 ... F-2
Murfreesboro, Rutherford, 44,922 ... D-12
Nashville-Davidson, Davidson, 488,374 ... C-11
New Johnsonville, Humphreys, 1,643 ... D-7
New Market, Jefferson, 1,086 ... J-3
New Tazewell, Claiborne, 1,864 ... I-3
Newbern, Dyer, 2,515 ... C-4
Newport, Cocke, 7,123 ... K-4
•Nolensville, Williamson, 1,570 ... D-11
Norris, Anderson, 1,303 ... J-1
•Oak Grove, Washington, 3,498 ... I-6
Oak Hill, Davidson, 4,301 ... C-11
Oak Ridge, Anderson/Roane, 27,310 ... K-1
Obion, Obion, 1,241 ... B-4
Oliver Springs, Anderson/Morgan/Roane, 3,433 ... J-1
Oneida, Scott, 3,502 ... B-17
•Ooltewah, Hamilton, 4,903 ... G-16
Paris, Henry, 9,332 ... C-6
Parsons, Decatur, 2,033 ... E-7
Pegram, Cheatham, 1,371 ... C-10
Pelham, Grundy ... F-14
Pigeon Forge, Sevier, 3,027 ... K-3
Pikeville, Bledsoe, 1,771 ... E-16
•Pine Crest, Carter, 3,821 ... N-8
Portland, Sumner, 5,165 ... A-12
•Powell, Knox, 7,534 ... J-2
Powells Crossroads, Marion, 1,098 ... F-15
Pulaski, Giles, 7,895 ... G-10
Red Bank, Hamilton, 12,322 ... G-15
Ridgely, Lake, 1,775 ... C-3
Ridgetop, Davidson/Robertson, 1,132 ... B-11
Ripley, Lauderdale, 6,188 ... E-3
•Roan Mountain, Carter, 1,220 ... N-9
Rockwood, Roane, 5,348 ... D-17
Rogersville, Hawkins, 4,149 ... I-4
•Rural Hill, Wilson, 1,329 ... C-12
Rutherford, Gibson, 1,303 ... C-5
Rutledge, Grainger, 903 ... I-3
Savannah, Hardin, 6,547 ... G-7
Selmer, McNairy, 3,838 ... G-6
Sevierville, Sevier, 7,178 ... K-3
•Sewanee, Franklin, 2,128 ... G-13
•Seymour, Blount/Sevier, 7,026 ... K-2
Sharon, Weakley, 1,047 ... C-5
Shelbyville, Bedford, 14,049 ... F-12
Signal Mountain, Hamilton, 7,034 ... G-15
Smithville, DeKalb, 3,791 ... D-14
Smyrna, Rutherford, 13,647 ... D-12
Sneedville, Hancock, 1,446 ... I-4
Soddy-Daisy, Hamilton, 8,240 ... F-16
Somerville, Fayette, 2,047 ... F-3
•South Cleveland, Bradley, 5,372 ... G-17
South Fulton, Obion, 2,688 ... B-5
South Pittsburg, Marion, 3,295 ... G-14
Sparta, White, 4,681 ... D-15
Spencer, Van Buren, 1,125 ... E-15
Spring City, Rhea, 2,199 ... E-17
Spring Hill, Maury/Williamson, 1,464 ... E-11
Springfield, Robertson, 11,227 ... B-11
•Spurgeon, Sullivan/Washington, 3,149 ... I-6
Surgoinsville, Hawkins, 1,499 ... I-4
Sweetwater, McMinn/Monroe, 5,066 ... L-1
Tazewell, Claiborne, 2,150 ... I-3
Tennessee Ridge, Houston, 1,271 ... B-8
Tiptonville, Lake, 2,149 ... B-3
Tracy City, Grundy, 1,556 ... F-14
Trenton, Gibson, 4,836 ... D-5
Troy, Obion, 1,047 ... B-4
Tullahoma, Coffee/Franklin, 16,761 ... F-13
Tusculum, Greene, 1,918 ... J-5
Union City, Obion, 10,513 ... B-4
Walden, Hamilton, 1,523 ... G-15
•Walnut Hill, Sullivan, 3,332 ... H-7
•Walterhill, Rutherford, 1,043 ... D-12
Wartburg, Morgan, 932 ... C-17
Watertown, Wilson, 1,250 ... C-13
Waverly, Humphreys, 3,925 ... C-8
Waynesboro, Wayne, 1,824 ... F-8
Westmoreland, Sumner, 1,726 ... A-12
White Bluff, Dickson, 1,988 ... C-10
White House, Robertson/Sumner, 2,987 ... B-11
White Pine, Jefferson, 1,771 ... J-4
Whiteville, Hardeman, 1,050 ... F-4
Whitwell, Marion, 1,622 ... G-15
•Wildwood Lake, Bradley, 2,680 ... G-17
Winchester, Franklin, 6,305 ... G-13
Woodbury, Cannon, 2,287 ... D-13

Explanation of symbols: •– Census Designated Place (CDP)

General Help Numbers:

Governor's Office
PO Box 12428
Austin, TX 78711-2428
www.governor.state.tx.us

512-463-2000
Fax 512-463-1849
7:30AM-5:30PM

Attorney General's Office
PO Box 12548
Austin, TX 78711-2548
www.oag.state.tx.us

512-463-2100
Fax 512-463-2063
7:30AM-5:30PM

Legislative Records
Legislative Reference Library
PO Box 12488
Austin, TX 78711-2488
www.lrl.state.tx.us

512-463-1252
Fax 512-475-4626
8AM-5PM

State Archives
PO Box 12927
Austin, TX 78711-2927
www.tsl.state.tx.us

512-463-5455
Fax 512-463-5436
8AM-5PM
Genealogy 8-5 TU-SA

State Specifics:

Capital:

Austin
Travis County

Time Zone:

CST*

* Texas' two western-most counties are MST:
They are: El Paso and Hudspeth,

Number of Counties:

254

Population:

22,118,509

Web Site:

www.state.tx.us

State Agencies

Criminal Records

Dept of Public Safety, Correspondence Section, Crime Records Service, PO Box 15999, Austin, TX 78761-5999 (Courier: 5805 N Lamar, Bldg G, Austin, TX 78752); 512-424-2474, 512-424-5011 (Fax), 8AM-5PM.

http://records.txdps.state.tx.us

Indexing & Storage: Records are available from 1930 to present. It takes 1 day before new records are available for inquiry. Records are indexed on inhouse computer. Records are normally destroyed after a court order, otherwise they are not destroyed.

Searching: To obtain ALL arrest information (conviction and non-conviction), must have a signed release and full set of fingerprints from the person of record. To obtain conviction and deferred adjudication data only, submit full name, sex, race, and DOB. The SSN is helpful, but not required. No letter of authorization is needed for the conviction only report. The following data is not released: juvenile records.

Access by: mail, in person, online.

Fee & Payment: The fee is $15.00 for the full search using fingerprints, and $10.00 for a name-based search. If required, the FBI fingerprint check is an additional $24.00. Fee payee: Texas Department of Public Safety. Prepayment

required. Credit cards are accepted for online searches only. Personal checks accepted. Credit cards accepted: MasterCard, Visa.

Mail search: Turnaround time: 2 weeks. No SASE is required.

In person search: Records requested at the Dept. of Public Safety Crime Records Service in Austin usually takes 1-2 business days.

Online search: Records can be pulled from the website. Requesters may use a credit card or establish an account and pre-purchse credits. The fee established by the Department (Sec. 411.135(b)) is $3.15 per request plus a $.57 handling fee. These checks are instantaneous and provide convictions and deferred adjudications only.

Statewide Court Records

Office of Court Administration, PO Box 12066, Austin, TX 78711-2066 (Courier: 205 W 14th St, Ste. 600, Austin, TX 78711); 512-463-1625, 512-463-1648 (Fax), 8AM-5PM.

www.courts.state.tx.us/oca

Note: Except for certain online research capabilities, all court record access must be done at the local level.

Searching: Trial court records are maintained by each county.

Access by: online. No searching by mail.

Online search: Case records of the Supreme Court can be searched at www.supreme.courts.state.tx.us. Court of Criminal Appeals opinions at www.cca.courts.state.tx.us. All Appellate Court case records at www.courts.state.tx.us/appcourt.asp.

Sexual Offender Registry

Dept of Public Safety, Sex Offender Registration, PO Box 4143, Austin, TX 78765-4143; 512-424-2478, 8AM-5PM.

http://records.txdps.state.tx.us

Indexing & Storage: It takes 1 day before new records are available for inquiry.

Searching: A sex offender's home telephone number, SSN, drivers license number will not be released.

Access by: mail, online.

Fee & Payment: A $10.00 fee is charged for mail searches only. Fee payee: Texas Department of Public Safety. Prepayment required. Personal checks accepted.

Mail search: Turnaround time: 1-2 weeks. There is a $10.00 fee. No SASE is required.

Online search: Sex offender data is available online at http://records.txdps.state.tx.us/soSearch/soSearch.cfm. There is no charge for a sex offender search. To see which organizations have purchased the sexual offender database, go to http://records.txdps.state.tx.us/forsale.cfm.

Incarceration Records

Texas Department of Criminal Justice, Bureau of Classification and Records, PO Box 99, Huntsville, TX 77342-5099; 936-295-6371, 800-535-0283 (In State Parole Status line), 8AM-5PM.

www.tdcj.state.tx.us

Note: Previous convictions and sex offender registration inquiries should be directed to the Dept. of Public Safety, 5805 N Lamar, Austin, TX 78752, 512-424-2000 or www.txdps.state.tx.us.

Indexing & Storage: Records are available on current and former inmates. It takes 1-3 days before new records are available for inquiry. Records are stored in microfiche archive.

Searching: Include the following in your request-name and 7-digit TDCJ number or their full name, date of birth or Social Security Number, and county of conviction. Location, conviction and sentencing information are provided.

Access by: mail, phone, online.

Fee & Payment: No fee for information.

Mail search: Turnaround time: 7 to 10 days. Requests in writing must be on letterhead paper.

Phone search: Name searching is permitted by phone. An Offender Information Line at 800-535-0283 allows you to check a paroled or incarcerated offender's status. Offender's name and 7-digit TDCJ number or their full name, date of birth or Social Security Number, and county of conviction required.

Online search: No online searching is available direct from this agency, but you may send an email search request to classify@tdcj.state.tx.us. Also, a private company offers free web access at www.vinelink.com/index.jsp.

Corporation, Fictitious Name, Limited Partnership, Limited Liability Company Records, Assumed Name, Trademarks/Servicemarks

Secretary of State, Corporation Section, PO Box 13697, Austin, TX 78711-3697 (Courier: J Earl Rudder Bldg, 1019 Brazos, B-13, Austin, TX 78701); 512-463-5555 (Information), 512-463-5578 (Copies), 512-463-5643 (Fax), 8AM-5PM.

www.sos.state.tx.us

Note: Ongoing requesters are encourged to set-up a Client Account.

Indexing & Storage: Records are available from the 1800s. Records are indexed on inhouse computer, online.

Searching: New records are available immediately on the computer, but it takes 12 days before new records are available to be copied. Requests may be ordered via e-mail from the website. Include the following in your request-full name of business, corporation file number. In addition to the articles of incorporation, corporation records include the following information: Public Information Reports (extracted information from the database only), Officers, Directors, DBAs, Prior (merged) names, Inactive and Reserved names.

Access by: mail, phone, fax, in person, online.

Fee & Payment: Certification is $10.00 plus $1.00 per document page. Long form is $25.00. Uncertified copies are $.10 per page, if over 50 copies then $.15 per page. If credit card used, add 2.1%. Fee payee: Secretary of State. Frequent requesters may set up a pre-paid billing account. Personal checks accepted. Credit cards accepted: MasterCard, Visa, Discover.

Mail search: Turnaround time: 3 to 5 days. No SASE is required.

Phone search: No fee for telephone request.

Fax search: Fax requests cost an additional $2.00 per page plus expedited fees.

In person search: Public access terminals are available for walk-in requesters.

Online search: There are several online methods available. Web access is available 24 hours daily. There is a $1.00 fee for each record searched. Filing procedures and forms are available from the website or from 900-263-0060 ($1.00 per minute). Also, Corporate and other TX Sec of State data is available via SOSDirect on the Web; visit www.sos.state.tx.us/corp/sosda/index.shtml. SOSDA accounts are converted to SOSDirect.

Printing and certifying capabilities. Also, general corporation information is available at no fee at http://ecpa.cpa.state.tx.us/coa/Index.html from the State Comptroller office.

Other access: The agency makes portions of its database available for purchase. Call 512-475-2755 for more information.

Expedited service: Expedited service is available for mail, phone and in person searches. Add $10.00 per document.

Uniform Commercial Code, Federal Tax Liens

UCC Section, Secretary of State, PO Box 13193, Austin, TX 78711-3193 (Courier: 1019 Brazos St, Rm B-13, Austin, TX 78701); 512-475-2705, 512-475-2812 (Fax), 8AM-5PM.

www.sos.state.tx.us/ucc/index.shtml

Indexing & Storage: Records are available from 1966; imaged and stored in the BEST System. It takes 3 to 5 days before new records are available for inquiry. Records are indexed on microfilm, imicrofiche and inhouse computer. Records are normally destroyed after (purged) 1 years past lapse date.

Searching: Use search request form UCC-11. The search includes all federal liens on businesses. Federal liens on individuals and all state tax liens are filed at the county level. Include the following in your request-debtor name.

Access by: mail, phone, fax, in person, online.

Fee & Payment: Using the approved form - $15.00 per name; other forms - $30.00 per name; copies - $1.00 per page. Effective 5/9/01, a version of the UCC-11 was designated as the standard form. Fee payee: Secretary of State. Prepayment required. Personal checks accepted. MC, Visa, Discover and LegalEase cards accepted.

Mail search: Turnaround time: 1 to 2 weeks. No SASE is required.

Phone search: Debtor names will be released. Collateral is listed on imaged documents only.

Fax search: There is an additional fee of $15.00.

In person search: You may request information in person.

Online search: UCC and other Texas Secretary of State data is available via SOSDirect on the Web at www.sos.state.tx.us/corp/sosda/index.shtml. UCC records are $1.00 per search, with printing ($1.00 per page) and certifying ($10.00), also. General information and forms can also be found at the website.

Other access: This agency offers the database for sale, contact the Information Services Dept at 512-463-5609 for further details.

Expedited service: Expedited service is available for mail, in-person and phone searches. Turnaround time: 24 hours. Add $15.00 per form. Expedited mail service is offered. Also, you can include your delivery service account number for fastest return.

State Tax Liens

Records not maintained by a state level agency.

Note: Records are located at the county level.

Sales Tax Registrations

Comptroller of Public Accounts, Sax Tax Permits, PO Box 13528, Austin, TX 78711-3528 (Courier: LBJ Office Bldg, 111 E 17th St, Austin, TX 78774); 800-531-5441 x66013, 800-252-1386 (Other Business Searches), 512-475-1610 (Fax), 8AM-5PM.

www.window.state.tx.us/taxinfo/sales/

Indexing & Storage: Records are available from 1980 to present. It takes 6 weeks before new records are available for inquiry. Records are normally destroyed after 20 years.

Searching: This agency will provide the following business information: business name, address, phone number, tax permit number, a list of officers & directors, and the registered agent for a corporation. Audit results are not released. Include the following in your request-business name. They will also search by tax permit number.

Access by: mail, phone, fax, in person, online.

Fee & Payment: There is no search fee. Fee payee: Comptroller of Public Accounts. Prepayment required. Personal checks accepted. No credit cards accepted.

Mail search: Turnaround time: 10 working days. If more than 3 businesses are requested, the agency prefers that you request by mail. No SASE is required. No fee for mail request.

Phone search: No fee for telephone request. The agency will provide responses to 3 business names or less over the phone.

Fax search: Fax search requests accepted.

In person search: No fee for request. They will verify information or will mail a letter.

Online search: This office makes general corporation information available at http://ecpa.cpa.state.tx.us/vendor/tpsearch1.html. There is no fee. Go to http://aixtcp.cpa.state.tx.us/star/ to search 16,000+ documents by index or collection. Send email requests, send to open.records@cpa.state.tx.us.

Other access: Sales tax registration lists are available to download as ftp files.

Expedited service: Will expedite at customer expense.

Birth Certificates

Texas Department of Health, Bureau of Vital Statistics, PO Box 12040, Austin, TX 78711-2040 (Courier: 1100 W 49th St, Austin, TX 78756-3191); 512-758-7366, 512-758-7711 (Fax), 8AM-5PM.

www.tdh.state.tx.us/bvs

Indexing & Storage: Records are available from 1903 to present. It takes receipt from local registration officials before new records are available for inquiry. Records are indexed on microfiche, index cards, inhouse computer.

Searching: Must have a signed, notarized release from person of record or immediate family member and name and address of requester for records less than 75 years old. Otherwise a Verification of Birth is issued. Include the following in your request-full name, names of parents, mother's maiden name, date of birth, place of birth, relationship to person of record, reason for information request. Must send a copy of requester's photo ID or show a photo ID for in-person searches. The following data is not released: Social Security Numbers.

Access by: mail, fax, in person.

Fee & Payment: The search fee is $11.00 per name. Fee payee: Bureau of Vital Statistics. Prepayment required. Credit cards accepted for fax requests only. Personal checks accepted. Credit cards accepted: MasterCard, Visa.

Mail search: Turnaround time: 6 to 8 weeks. No SASE is required.

Fax search: See expedited service.

In person search: Turnaround time 1-2 hours.

Other access: Birth Indexes from 1926-1995 are available on CD-Rom and microfiche.

Expedited service: Expedited service is available for fax searches at 512-458-7711. Turnaround time: 48 to 96 hours. Add $5.00 expedited service fee, and either $8.00 for UPS ground or $13.65 for US Express mail.

Death Records

Texas Department of Health, Bureau of Vital Statistics, PO Box 12040, Austin, TX 78711-2040 (Courier: 1100 W 49th St, Austin, TX 78756-3191); 512-758-7366, 512-758-7711 (Fax), 8AM-5PM.

www.tdh.state.tx.us/bvs

Indexing & Storage: Records are available from 1903 to present. It takes receipt from local registration officials before new records are available for inquiry. Records are indexed on microfiche, index cards, inhouse computer.

Searching: Must have a signed release from immediate family member and requester's name and current address for records less than 25 years old. Otherwise a Verification of Death is issued. Include the following in your request-full name, date of death, place of death, Social Security Number, relationship to person of record, reason for information request. You must include a copy of requesters' photo ID or show a photo ID for in person requests. The following data is not released: Social Security Numbers.

Access by: mail, fax, in person.

Fee & Payment: The search fee is $9.00 per name. Add $3.00 per name per copy for each additional copy. Fee payee: Bureau of Vital Statistics. Prepayment required. Credit cards accepted for fax requests only. Personal checks accepted. Credit cards accepted: MasterCard, Visa.

Mail search: Turnaround time: 6 to 8 weeks. No SASE is required.

Fax search: See expedited service.

In person search: Turnaround time 1-2 hours.

Other access: Death Indexes from 1964-1998 are available on CD-Rom and microfiche.

Expedited service: Expedited service is available for fax searches at 512-458-7711. Turnaround time: 48 to 96 hours. Add $5.00 expedited service fee, and either $8.00 for UPS ground or $13.65 for US Express mail.

Marriage Certificates

Texas Department of Health, Bureau of Vital Statistics, 1100 W 49th St, Austin, TX 78756 (Courier: 1100 W 49th St, Austin, TX 78756-3191); 512-758-7366, 512-758-7711 (Fax), 8AM-5PM.

www.tdh.state.tx.us/bvs

Indexing & Storage: Records are available from 1966 to present. It takes delivery from the county clerk before new records are available for inquiry. Records are indexed on microfiche, index cards, inhouse computer.

Searching: They only have a copy of the application form and an index to the county record. The actual certificate must be obtained from the county recorder of record. Include the following in your request-names of husband and wife, date of marriage, place or county of marriage. The following data is not released: Social Security Numbers.

Access by: mail, fax, in person, online.

Fee & Payment: The search fee is $9.00 per record. Fee payee: Bureau of Vital Statistics. Prepayment required. Credit cards accepted for fax requests only. Personal checks accepted. Credit cards accepted: MasterCard, Visa.

Mail search: Turnaround time: 6 to 10 weeks. No SASE is required.

Fax search: See expedited service.

In person search: Turnaround time while you wait.

Online search: Marriage records for 1966 to 2001 are available through a private company website at www.genlookups.com/texas_marriages/.

Expedited service: Expedited service is available for fax searches. Turnaround time: 48 to 96 hours. Add $5.00 expedited service fee, and either $8.00 for UPS ground or $13.65 for US Express mail.

Divorce Records

Texas Department of Health, Bureau of Vital Statistics, PO Box 12040, Austin, TX 78711-2040 (Courier: 1100 W 49th St, Austin, TX 78756-3191); 512-758-7366, 512-758-7711 (Fax), 8AM-5PM.

www.tdh.state.tx.us/bvs

Indexing & Storage: Records are available from 1968 to present. It takes delivery from the county district clerk before new records are available for inquiry. Records are indexed on microfiche, inhouse computer.

Searching: They only have the report of divorce form and an index that directs you to the county district court of record. A copy of the actual record must be obtained at the county level. Include the following in your request-names of husband and wife, date of divorce, year divorce case began, case number (if known).

Access by: mail, fax, in person, online.

Fee & Payment: The search fee is $9.00 per name. Fee payee: Bureau of Vital Statistics. Prepayment required. Credit cards accepted for fax requests only. Personal checks accepted. Credit cards accepted: MasterCard, Visa.

Mail search: Turnaround time: 6 to 12 weeks. No SASE is required.

Fax search: See expedited service.

In person search: Turnaround time 1-2 hours.

Online search: Divorce indexes can be downloaded and searched by year at www.tdh.state.tx.us/bvs/registra/dividx/dividx.htm . A second private company website at www.genlookups.com/texas_divorces/ offers records from 1968 to 2001.

Expedited service: Expedited service is available for fax searches at 512-458-7711. Turnaround time: 48 to 96 hours. Add $5.00 expedited service fee, and either $8.00 for UPS ground or $13.65 for US Express mail.

Workers' Compensation Records

Texas Workers' Compensation Commission, 7551 Metro Center Dr, #100, Austin, TX 78744; 512-804-4000, 512-804-4990 (Reprographics Department), 512-804-4993 (Fax), 8AM-5PM.

www.twcc.state.tx.us

Note: Claim file records are confidential; only parties to claim have access.

Indexing & Storage: Records are available from 1962. Records are indexed on inhouse computer. Records are normally destroyed after 50 years.

Searching: A signed, notarized release is required to obtain file copies. Use Form TWCC-153. Include the following in your request-claimant name, Social Security Number, date of accident. Use of TWCC 153 Form is required. The file number is required to receive copies. If you don't know the file number or date of accident, you must submit Form TWCC-155.

Access by: mail, fax, online.

Fee & Payment: The fees for TWCC-153 are $1.00 for certification, $1.00 for the first page and $.30 each additional page. The fees for TWCC-155 are $15.00 search fee and $1.00 for certification. Fee payee: Texas Workers' Compensation Commission. Prepayment required. An invoice will be sent when using TWCC 153 Form. Copies are held until payment received. Personal checks accepted. No credit cards accepted.

Mail search: Turnaround time: 4 to 6 weeks. No SASE is required.

Fax search: See expedited service.

Online search: The website gives administrative decisions for cases back to 1991 and alsoo permits searching for employers with coverage.

Expedited service: Expedited service is available for mail or fax service, using the TWCC 153 form. Fee foe expedited copy service is additional $25.00.

Driver Records

Department of Public Safety, Driver Records Section, PO Box 149246, Austin, TX 78714-9246 (Courier: 5805 N Lamar Blvd, Austin, TX 78752); 512-424-2032, 512-424-2600, 512-424-7285 (Fax), 8AM-5PM.

www.txdps.state.tx.us

Note: Tickets are only available from the court system.

Indexing & Storage: Records are available for 5 years for moving violations and suspensions, indefinite for DWIs, 11 years for SR judgments. Non-moving violations do not appear on the record. It takes 30 days before new records are available for inquiry. Records are normally destroyed after 125 years, generally.

Searching: Requesters must use Form DR-1. This form contains space for written consent if personal information is requested by a casual user. The name and driver's license number or date of birth, are needed when ordering. Note that drivers may order their own "complete" record for $6.50. While vendors or thrid parties cannot order this record by mail or walk-in, it is available online for

$7.50. The following data is not released: Social Security Numbers or medical records, class type listings

Access by: mail, in person, online.

Fee & Payment: Driving record fees of mail or walk-ins are $6.00 for a 3 year driving record, $10.00 if certified. Fee is $6.50 for online access. A license statue including latest address is $4.00 per report. There is a full charge for a "no record found." Fee payee: Texas Department of Public Safety. Prepayment required. Personal checks accepted. No credit cards accepted.

Mail search: Turnaround time: 7 to 10 days. No SASE is required.

In person search: Eligible Texas Driver License holders may request their own individual Driver Record online. The printed record is postal mailed by DPS within 5 business days. Normal turnaround time is same day.

Online search: Access is limited to only high volume users who have a permissible use and sign an agreement. Records are $6.50 for the three year record (Type 2) or $7.50 for the complete record (Type 3). Both batch and interactive modes are available. Call 512-424-2600 to receive a copy of the license agreement.

Other access: 3480 Cartridge retrieval is available for bulk purchase. Weekly updates are available. The file does not include driver history data.

Vehicle Ownership, Vehicle Identification

Department of Transportation, Vehicle Titles and Registration Division, 4000 Jackson Ave, Austin, TX 78731; 512-465-7611, 512-465-7736 (Fax), 8AM-5PM.

www.dot.state.tx.us

Note: Submit a "Request for TX Motor Vehicle Information" Form VTR-275, including a signed statement certifying that information is requested for a lawful & legitimate purpose, to be used in accordance with 18 USC, Sec2721-2725 and the TX Trans Code, Ch#730.

Indexing & Storage: Records are available as active files until there is no activity for 18 months, upon which records become inactive. After 5 years of inactivity, records are archived. Title history information is available on microfiche for 16 years to present. It takes 48 hours after entry into the system before new records are available for inquiry. Records are indexed on microfilm and microfiche; current records indexed on computer. Motor Vehicle records are indexed by VIN, title number, plate number, and expiration year. Records are normally destroyed after 16 years (title history records).

Searching: For plate checks and title histories, include a signed/completed Request for Texas Motor Vehicle Information Form VTR-275 certifying your eligibility to receive information. The state does not provide name search capability. Use Form VTR-275 for ordering a vehicle history. Personal information is not released to casual requesters without written consent of subject. The following data is not released: Social Security Numbers.

Access by: mail, phone, online.

Fee & Payment: The current fee for VIN and plate checks is $2.30 per record. The fee for a title search/history is $5.75 or $6.75 certified. Fee payee: Texas Department of Transportation.

Prepayment required. Personal checks accepted. No credit cards accepted.

Mail search: Turnaround time: 7-10 days for plates. Turnaround time for title histories is 4 weeks. Use of the state form is required.

Phone search: The department accepts phone search requests for current records The telephone current record lookups contain no personal information.

Online search: Online access is available for pre-approved accounts by contract. A $200 deposit is required, there is a $23.00 charge per month and $.12 fee per inquiry. Searching by name is not permitted. For more information, contact Production Data Control.

Other access: The department offers tape cartridge retrieval for customized searches or based on the entire database, to eligible organizations under signed contract. Weekly updates and batch inquiries are available. Database contains about 28,000,000 records.

Expedited service: The department will overnight the information requested when the customer provides their account number and service provider.

Accident Reports

Texas Department of Public Safety, Accident Records Bureau, PO Box 15999, Austin, TX 78761-5999 (Courier: 5805 N Lamar Blvd, Austin, TX 78752); 512-424-2600, 8AM-5PM.

www.txdps.state.tx.us

Indexing & Storage: Records are available for 10 years to present. It takes 30 days before new records are available for inquiry. Records are normally destroyed after ten years.

Searching: Accident reports investigated by law enforcement agencies and driver reports are open to the public. Items required to search include two or more of following: full name of any person involved, specific city/county location, and date of incident.

Access by: mail, in person.

Fee & Payment: Fee is $6.00 per uncertified report and $8.00 per certified report. There is a $6.00 charge for a no record found search. Fee payee: Texas Department of Public Safety. Prepayment required. Personal checks accepted. No credit cards accepted.

Mail search: Turnaround time: 4 to 6 weeks. No SASE is required.

In person search: Requests will be processed immediately, unless extensive lists presented.

Vessel Ownership, Vessel Registration

Parks & Wildlife Dept, 4200 Smith School Rd, Austin, TX 78744; 512-389-4828, 800-262-8755, 512-389-4900 (Fax), 8AM-5PM.

www.tpwd.state.tx.us/boat/boat.htm

Note: Record checks can be processed at any TPWD Boats Law Enforcement Field Office. All history requests must be submitted to this office.

Indexing & Storage: Records are available from 1976 to 1988 for titled boats, then from 1989 to present for all boats. Records indexed on computer. All motorized boats must be registered and titled. Sailboats 14 ft and over must be registered and titled. Lien data shows on reports. It takes less than 1 day before new records are available for inquiry. Records are normally destroyed after 10 years.

Searching: The written request must include: name & address of requestor, TX #, motor # and/or serial numbers, and the statement "The use of the information obtained will be for lawful purposes." If the history needs to be certified for court, request must show that you need a "certified history."

Access by: mail, in person.

Fee & Payment: There is a $2.00 fee for a record check and a $10.00 fee for a complete history from microfilm. Fee payee: TX Parks & Wildlife Dept. Prepayment required. Personal checks accepted. No credit cards accepted.

Mail search: Turnaround time: 2 to 3 weeks. Turnaround time is often longer in the summer. No SASE is required.

In person search: Histories are returned by mail.

Other access: Records are released in bulk format; however, requesters are screened for lawful purpose. The agency requires a copy of any item mailed or distributed as a result of purchase. Media includes tape, labels, and printed lists.

Voter Registration
Access to Records is Restricted

Secretary of State, Elections Division, PO Box 12060, Austin, TX 78711-2060; 800-252-8683, 512-475-2811 (Fax), 8AM-5PM.

www.sos.state.tx.us

Note: To do individual look-ups, one must go to the Tax Assessor-Collector at the county level. Records are open. The state will sell the entire database, for non-commercial purposes, in a variety of media and sort formats.

GED Certificates

Texas Education Agency, GED Unit CC:350, PO Box 13817, Austin, TX 78711 (Courier: 1701 N Congress Ave, Austin, TX 78701-1494); 512-463-9292, 512-305-9493 (Fax), 8AM-5PM.

www.tea.state.tx.us/ged

Indexing & Storage: Records are available from 1944 to present. It takes 2 weeks before new records are available for inquiry. Records are indexed on mainframe computer.

Searching: Include the following in your request- name, DOB, SSN. A signed release is needed for transcript, but not need for only a verification.

Access by: mail, phone, fax, in person.

Fee & Payment: There is no fee for verification, but $5.00 fee for a record of transcripts. Also, if the subject did not pay the GED fees and the record is prior to 1994, a fee may be charged to the requester. Fee payee: TEA-GED

Mail search: Turnaround time: 1 to 2 days. No SASE is required.

Phone search: If a SSN is presented, this agency will verify if a person has a GED.

Fax search: Verifications can be done by fax. To receive copy of grades fax requests require a signed release.

In person search: Over-the-counter service available.

Hunting and Fishing License Information

TX Parks & Wildlife Department, License Section, 4200 Smith School Rd, Austin, TX 78744; 512-389-4820, 512-389-4330 (Fax), 8AM-5PM.

www.tpwd.state.tx.us

Indexing & Storage: Records are available from 09/01/96 forward and are computerized.

Searching: All requests must be in writing on their official Form, unless request is for self. They will release address, status, and date of issue. Include the driver's license number and/or SSN and or DOB. Requests must be in writing and signed by requester. Include requester's address and phone.

Access by: mail, fax, in person.

Fee & Payment: There is no fee.

Mail search: Turnaround time: 10 days. Up to 5 names can be requested by mail.

Fax search: Up to 5 names can be requested by fax. Results are mailed or can be faxed.

In person search: Over-the-counter service available.

Texas State Licensing Agencies

Licenses Searchable Online

Acupuncturist #30 .... http://reg.tsbme.state.tx.us/onlineverif/phys_noticeverif.asp?

Air Conditioning/Refrigeration Contractor #14 .... www.license.state.tx.us/LicenseSearch/

Alarm Installer/Company/Sales #35 .... www.tcps.state.tx.us/individual/individual_search.aspx

Alarm/Security Instructor #35 .... www.tcps.state.tx.us/individual/individual_search.aspx

Alcoholic Beverage Dist./Mfg./Retailer #46 .... www.tabc.state.tx.us/pubinfo/rosters/default.htm

Alcoholic Beverage Permit #46 .... www.tabc.state.tx.us/pubinfo/rosters/default.htm

Architect #61 .... www.tbae.state.tx.us/active/archnamesearch.html

Architectural Barrier #14 .... www.license.state.tx.us/LicenseSearch/

Athletic Trainer #21 .... www.tdh.state.tx.us/hcqs/plc/at_rost.txt

Attorney #40 .... www.texasbar.com

Auctioneer #14 .... www.license.state.tx.us/LicenseSearch/

Audiologist #22 .... www.tdh.state.tx.us/hcqs/plc/sprost.txt

Audiology Assistant #22 .... www.tdh.state.tx.us/hcqs/plc/sprost.txt

Bank Agency, Foreign #1 .... www.banking.state.tx.us/asp/fba/lookup.asp

Bank, State Chartered #1 .... www.banking.state.tx.us/asp/bank/lookup.asp

Barber/Barber Shop/Barber Student #2 .... www.tsbbe.state.tx.us

Barber School #2 .... www.tsbbe.state.tx.us/webpages/schoolr.htm

Boiler Inspector/Installer #14 .... www.license.state.tx.us/LicenseSearch/

Boxing/Combative Sports Event #14 .... www.license.state.tx.us/LicenseSearch/

Career Counselor #14 .... www.license.state.tx.us/LicenseSearch/

Check Seller #1 .... www.banking.state.tx.us/asp/soc/lookup.asp

Child Support Enforcement Agency, Private #1 .... www.banking.state.tx.us/pcsea/licensed.htm

Counselor, Professional #41 .... www.tdh.state.tx.us/hcqs/plc/lpc/lpc_def.htm

Courier Company #35 .... www.tcps.state.tx.us/individual/individual_search.aspx

CPA Individual/Firm/Sponsor #43 .... www.tsbpa.state.tx.us/srcmain.htm

Currency Exchange #1 .... www.banking.state.tx.us/asp/cex/lookup.asp

Dentist/Dental Hygienist #23 .... www.tsbde.state.tx.us/dbsearch/

Dental Laboratory #23 .... www.tsbde.state.tx.us/dbsearch/

Dietitian #22 .... www.tdh.state.tx.us/hcqs/plc/dtrost.txt

ECA #27 .... http://160.42.108.3/ems_web/blh_html_page1.htm

Elevator/Escalator #14 .... www.license.state.tx.us/LicenseSearch/

Emergency Medical Technician #27 .... http://160.42.108.3/ems_web/blh_html_page1.htm

Engineer #5 .... www.tbpe.state.tx.us/downloads.htm

Engineering Firm #5 .... www.tbpe.state.tx.us/downloads.htm

Fire Alarm System Contractor #53 .... www.tdi.state.tx.us/fire/fmli.html

Fire Extinguisher Contractor #53 .... www.tdi.state.tx.us/fire/fmli.html

Fire Inspector/Investigator #56 .... www.tcfp.state.tx.us

Fire Protection Sprinkler Contractor #53 .... www.tdi.state.tx.us/fire/fmli.html

Fire Suppression Specialist #56 .... www.tcfp.state.tx.us

Firearm Instructor #35 .... www.tcps.state.tx.us/individual/individual_search.aspx

Firefighter #56 .... www.tcfp.state.tx.us

Fireworks Display #53 .... www.tdi.state.tx.us/fire/fmli.html

Funeral Establ./Preneed Funeral Home #15 .... www.banking.state.tx.us/asp/pfc/lookup.asp

Funeral Prepaid Permit Holder #1 .... www.banking.state.tx.us/asp/pfc/lookup.asp

Guard Dog Company #35 .... www.tcps.state.tx.us/individual/individual_search.aspx

Hearing Instrument Dispenser/Fitter #22 .... www.tdh.state.tx.us/hcqs/plc/fdhirost.txt

Independent Instructor #28 .... www.tdh.state.tx.us/hcqs/plc/mtrosts.txt

Industrialized Housing #14 .... www.license.state.tx.us/LicenseSearch/

Insurance Adjuster #48 .... www.texasonline.state.tx.us/NASApp/tdi/TdiARManager

Insurance Agency/Agent/Company #48 .... www.texasonline.state.tx.us/NASApp/tdi/TdiARManager

Interior Designer #61 .... www.tbae.state.tx.us/active/interiornamesearch.html

Irrigator #57 .... www.tnrcc.state.tx.us/enforcement/csd/ics/lilicense.html

Landscape Architect #61 .... www.tbae.state.tx.us/active/landnamesearch.html

Lead Abatement Project Designer #55 .... www.tdh.state.tx.us/beh/lead/findmd.htm#firm

Lead Firm #55 .... www.tdh.state.tx.us/beh/lead/findmd.htm#firm

Lead Risk Assessor/Inspector #55 .... www.tdh.state.tx.us/beh/lead/findmd.htm#firm

Lead Training Program Provider #55 .... www.tdh.state.tx.us/beh/lead/TRnlist.htm

Lobbyist #50 .... www.ethics.state.tx.us/php/index.html

Manicurist/Manicurist Shop #2 .... www.tsbbe.state.tx.us

Marriage & Family Therapist #31 .... www.tdh.state.tx.us/hcqs/plc/mft.htm#rosters

Massage Therapist #28	www.tdh.state.tx.us/hcqs/plc/mtrost.txt
Massage Therapist, Temporary #28	www.tdh.state.tx.us/hcqs/plc/mtrostt.txt
Massage Therapy Establishment/School #28	www.tdh.state.tx.us/hcqs/plc/mtroste.txt
Massage Therapy School #28	www.tdh.state.tx.us/hcqs/plc/mtrosts.txt
Massage Therapy School Instructor #28	www.tdh.state.tx.us/hcqs/plc/mtrosti.txt
Medical Doctor/Physician #30	http://reg.tsbme.state.tx.us/onlineverif/phys_noticeverif.asp?
Medical Specialty (Doctor) #30	http://reg.tsbme.state.tx.us/onlineverif/phys_noticeverif.asp?
Nurse, Advanced Practice #63	https://www.bne.state.tx.us/olv/apninq.htm
Nurse, Vocational #63	https://www.bne.state.tx.us/olv/vninq.htm
Nurse/RN #63	https://www.bne.state.tx.us/olv/rninq.htm
Occupational Therapist/Assistant #17	www.ecptote.state.tx.us/license/otverif.php
Occupational/Physical Therapy Facility #17	www.ecptote.state.tx.us/license/ftverif.php
Optometrist #51	www.tob.state.tx.us/tob%20verifications.htm
Orthotics & Prosthetics Facility #26	www.tdh.state.tx.us/hcqs/plc/op_rostf.pdf
Orthotist/Prosthetist #26	www.tdh.state.tx.us/hcqs/plc/op_rost.pdf
Paramedic #27	http://160.42.108.3/ems_web/blh_html_page1.htm
Perfusionist #26	www.tdh.state.tx.us/hcqs/plc/perfusn.htm
Perpetual Care Cemetery #1	www.banking.state.tx.us/asp/pcc/lookup.asp
Personal Employment Service #14	www.license.state.tx.us/LicenseSearch/
Pharmacist / Pharmacist Intern #24	www.tsbp.state.tx.us/dbsearch/Default.htm
Pharmacy / Pharmacy Technician #24	www.tsbp.state.tx.us/dbsearch/Default.htm
Physical Therapist/Assistant #17	www.ecptote.state.tx.us/license/ptverif.php
Physician Assistant #30	http://reg.tsbme.state.tx.us/onlineverif/phys_noticeverif.asp?
Physicist, Medical #26	www.tdh.state.tx.us/hcqs/plc/mprost.txt
Podiatrist #20	www.foot.state.tx.us/verifications.htm
Political Action Committee List #50	www.ethics.state.tx.us/dfs/paclists.htm
Political Contributor #50	www.ethics.state.tx.us/php/cesearch.html
Polygraph Examiner of Sex Offenders #26	www.tdh.state.tx.us/hcqs/plc/csp.htm
Private Business Letter of Auth. #35	www.tcps.state.tx.us/individual/individual_search.aspx
Private Investigator #35	www.tcps.state.tx.us/individual/individual_search.aspx
Property Tax Consultant #14	www.license.state.tx.us/LicenseSearch/
Psychological Associate #19	www.tsbep.state.tx.us/
Psychologist #19	www.tsbep.state.tx.us/
Psychologist, Provisionally Licensed #19	www.tsbep.state.tx.us/
Public Accountant-CPA, Individ'l /Firm #43	www.tsbpa.state.tx.us/srcmain.htm
Public Accountant-CPA Educator/Sponsor #43	www.tsbpa.state.tx.us/srcmain.htm
Radiology Technician #16	www.tdh.state.tx.us/hcqs/plc/mrtrost.txt
Real Estate Agent/Broker/Sales #52	www.trec.state.tx.us/publicinfo/
Real Estate Appraiser #47	www.talcb.state.tx.us/appraisers/Appraiser_Search.asp
Real Estate Inspector #52	www.trec.state.tx.us/publicinfo/
Representative Offices (Foreign Banks) #1	www.banking.state.tx.us/asp/rep/lookup.asp
Respiratory Care Practitioner #29	www.tdh.state.tx.us/hcqs/plc/rcrost.txt
Sanitarian #22	www.tdh.state.tx.us/hcqs/plc/rs_rost.txt
School Psychology Specialist #19	www.tsbep.state.tx.us/
Security Agent/Service/Sales #35	www.tcps.state.tx.us/individual/individual_search.aspx
Service Contract Provider #14	www.license.state.tx.us/LicenseSearch/
Sex Offender Treatment Provider #26	www.tdh.state.tx.us/hcqs/plc/csotrost.txt
Social Worker #26	www.tdh.state.tx.us/hcqs/plc/lsw/lsw_default.htm#roster
Speech-Language Pathologist #22	www.tdh.state.tx.us/hcqs/plc/sprost.txt
Staff Leasing #14	www.license.state.tx.us/LicenseSearch/
STAP Vendor #6	www.puc.state.tx.us/relay/stapc/vendors.cfm
Surveyor, Land #4	http://txls.state.tx.us/sect03/rosters.html
Talent Agency #14	www.license.state.tx.us/LicenseSearch/
Tax Appraisal Professional #59	www.txbtpe.state.tx.us
Teacher #42	https://secure.sbec.state.tx.us/virtcert/
Temporary Common Worker #14	www.license.state.tx.us/LicenseSearch/
Transportation Service Provider #54	www.license.state.tx.us/LicenseSearch/
Trust Company #1	www.banking.state.tx.us/asp/trustco/lookup.asp
Underground Storage Tank Installer #60	www.tnrcc.state.tx.us/enforcement/csd/ics/ustlicense.html
Vehicle Protection Provider #14	www.license.state.tx.us/LicenseSearch/
Veterinarian #18	www.tbvme.state.tx.us/verify.htm
Water Well & Pump Installer #14	www.license.state.tx.us/LicenseSearch/
Weather Modification Service #14	www.license.state.tx.us/LicenseSearch/

Texas Licensing Quick Finder

Acupuncturist #30 ... 512-305-7030
Agricultural Specialties, Perishable #11 512-463-7476
Air Conditioning/Refrig'n Contr. #14 ... 512-463-6599
Alarm Installer/Company/Sales #35 ... 512-238-5858
Alarm/Security Instructor #35 ... 512-238-5858
Alcoholic Beverage Dist./Mfg./Retailer #46 ... 512-206-3360
Alcoholic Beverage Permit #46 ... 512-206-3360
Architect #61 ... 512-305-9000
Architectural Barrier #14 ... 512-463-6599
Asbestos Abatement Contr.#12 . 512-834-6600 x2789
Asbestos Air Monitoring Tech. #12 ... 512-834-6600 x2789
Asbestos Consultant/Inspector #12 ... 512-834-6600x2789
Asbestos Mgmt Planner #12 ... 512-834-6600 x2789
Asbestos Worker #12 ... 512-834-6600 x2789
Athletic Agent #38 ... 512-475-1769
Athletic Trainer #21 ... 512-834-6615
Attorney #40 ... 512-463-1463
Auctioneer #14 ... 512-463-6599
Audiologist #22 ... 512-834-6627
Audiology Assistant #22 ... 512-834-6627
Automobile Club #38 ... 512-475-1769
Bank Agency, Foreign #1 ... 512-475-1300
Bank, State Chartered #1 ... 512-475-1300
Barber #2 ... 512-936-6333
Barber School #2 ... 512-936-6333
Barber Shop #2 ... 512-936-6333
Barber Student #2 ... 512-936-6333
Beauty Shop/Salon #8 ... 512-380-7659
Boiler Inspector/Installer #14 ... 800-722-7843
Boxing/Combative Sports Event #14 ... 512-463-5101
Business Opportunity #38 ... 512-475-1769
Career Counselor #14 ... 512-463-6599
Check Seller #1 ... 512-475-1290
Child Care Facility/Administrator #49 ... 512-438-3269
Child Support Enforcem't Agency, Private #1 ... 512-475-1300
Chiropractic Facility #25 ... 512-305-6700
Chiropractic Radiologic Tech. #25 ... 512-305-6700
Chiropractor #25 ... 512-305-6700
Contact Lens Dispenser #26 ... 512-834-4515
Cosmetologist #8 ... 512-380-7659
Counselor, Professional #41 ... 512-834-6658
Counselor, Professional Supr. #41 ... 512-834-6658
County Librarian #44 ... 512-463-5466
Courier Company #35 ... 512-238-5858
Court Reporter #9 ... 512-463-1630
Court Reporting Firm #9 ... 512-463-1630
CPA Individual/Firm/Sponsor #43 ... 512-305-7853
Credit Service Organization #38 ... 512-463-6906
Currency Exchange #1 ... 512-475-1290
Day Care Center #49 ... 512-438-3269
Day Care, Residential #49 ... 512-438-3269
Dental Assistant #23 ... 512-463-6400
Dental Hygienist #23 ... 512-463-6400
Dental Laboratory #23 ... 512-463-6400
Dentist #23 ... 512-463-6400
Dietitian #22 ... 512-834-6601
Dog Racing/Dog Racing Prof'l #36 ... 512-833-6697
ECA #27 ... 512-834-6700
Egg License #11 ... 512-463-7476
Elevator/Escalator #14 ... 512-463-6599
Emergency Medical Technician #27 ... 512-834-6700
Engineer #5 ... 512-440-7723
Engineering Firm #5 ... 512-440-7723
Family Home Day Care #49 ... 512-438-3269
Farm/Agricultural Svc Company #11 ... 512-463-7476
Fire Alarm System Contr. #53 ... 512-305-7935
Fire Extinguisher Contractor #53 ... 512-305-7934
Fire Inspector/Investigator #56 ... 512-239-4911
Fire Protection Sprinkler Contr. #53 ... 512-305-7933
Fire Suppression Specialist #56 ... 512-239-4911
Firearm Instructor #35 ... 512-238-5858
Firefighter #56 ... 512-239-4911
Fireworks Display #53 ... 512-305-7930
Fish Farmer #11 ... 512-463-7476
Fishing Guide #45 ... 512-389-4818
Funeral Director #15 ... 512-936-2474
Funeral Establ./Preneed Funeral Home #15 ... 512-936-2474
Funeral Prepaid Permit Holder #1 ... 512-475-1290
Grain Warehouser #11 ... 512-463-7476
Guard Dog Company #35 ... 512-238-5858
Health Related Registry #22 ... 512-834-6602
Health Spa #38 ... 512-463-6906
Hearing Instr't Dispenser/Fitter #22 ... 512-834-6784
Home Equity & Secondary Mortgage Lenders #7 ... 512-936-7600
Home Health Agency #26 ... 512-834-6646
Horse Racing/Horse Racing Professional #36 ... 512-833-6697
Independent Instructor #28 ... 512-834-6616
Industrialized Housing #14 ... 512-463-7353
Insurance Adjuster #48 ... 512-322-3503
Insurance Agency/Agent #48 ... 512-322-3503
Insurance Company #48 ... 512-322-3507
Interior Designer #61 ... 512-305-9000
Interpreter for the Deaf #6 ... 512-407-3250
Investment Advisor #39 ... 512-305-8332
Irrigator #57 ... 512-239-6719
Landscape Architect #61 ... 512-305-9000
Law Enforcement Officer #58 ... 512-936-7700
Lead Abatement Project Designer #55 . 512-834-6612
Lead Abatement Worker/Supv'r #55 ... 512-834-6612
Lead Firm #55 ... 512-834-6612
Lead Risk Assessor/Inspector #55 ... 512-834-6612
Lead Training Program Provider #55 ... 512-834-6612
Loan Company #7 ... 512-936-7600
Loan Officer #37 ... 512-475-1350
Lobbyist #50 ... 512-463-5800
LPG-Liquefied Petrol. Gas Tech. #11 .. 512-462-1441
Mammography System #16 ... 512-834-6688 x2037
Manicurist/Manicurist Shop #2 ... 512-936-6333
Marriage & Family Therapist #31 ... 512-834-6657
Massage Therapist #28 ... 512-834-6616
Massage Therapist, Temporary #28 ... 512-834-6616
Massage Therapy Establishm't/School #28 ... 512-834-6616
Massage Therapy School Instr. #28 ... 512-834-6616
Medical Doctor/Physician #30 ... 512-305-7030
Medical Laboratory Practitioner #22 ... 512-834-6602
Medical Specialty (Doctor) #30 ... 512-305-7030
Medication Aide #13 ... 512-231-5827
Membership Camping Resort #38 ... 512-463-6906
Mortgage Banker #37 ... 512-475-1350
Mortgage Broker #37 ... 512-475-1350
Motor Vehicle Sales Finance Co. #7 ... 512-936-7600
Notary Public #33 ... 512-463-5705
Notary Public #38 ... 512-475-5705
Nurse, Advanced Practice #63 ... 512-305-6809
Nurse, Vocational #63 ... 512-305-6809
Nurse/RN #63 ... 512-305-6809
Nursery/Floral #11 ... 512-463-7476
Nurses' Aide #13 ... 512-231-5829
Nursing Home Administ'r/Facility #13 .. 512-231-5825
Occupational Therapist/Assistant #17 .. 512-305-6900
Occupational/Physical Therapy Facility #17 ... 512-305-6900
Optician #26 ... 512-834-6661
Optometrist #51 ... 512-305-8500
Organic Grower #11 ... 512-463-7476
Orthotics & Prosthetics Facility #26 ... 512-834-4520
Orthotist/Prosthetist #26 ... 512-834-4520
Paramedic #27 ... 512-834-6700
Pawn Shop #7 ... 512-936-7600
Perfusionist #26 ... 512-834-6751
Perpetual Care Cemetery #1 ... 512-475-1290
Personal Employment Service #14 ... 512-463-6599
Pesticide Applicator/Dealer #10 ... 512-475-1639
Pharmacist #24 ... 512-305-8012
Pharmacist Intern #24 ... 512-305-8011
Pharmacy #24 ... 512-305-8022
Pharmacy Technician #24 ... 512-305-8031
Physical Therapist/Assistant #17 ... 512-305-6900
Physician Assistant #30 ... 512-305-7030
Physicist, Medical #26 ... 512-834-6655
Plumber Master/Journeyman #3 . 512-458-2145 x227
Plumbing Inspector #3 ... 512-458-2145 x227
Podiatrist #20 ... 512-305-7000
Political Action Committee List #50 ... 512-463-5800
Political Contributor #50 ... 512-463-5800
Polygraph Examiner #34 ... 512-424-2058
Polygraph Examiner of Sex Offenders #26 ... 512-834-6655
Private Business Letter of Auth. #35 ... 512-238-5858
Private Investigator #35 ... 512-238-5858
Property Rights #38 ... 512-475-1769
Property Tax Consultant #14 ... 512-463-6599
Psychological Associate #19 ... 512-305-7700
Psychologist #19 ... 512-305-7700
Psychologist, Provisional #19 ... 512-305-7700
Public Accountant-CPA #43 ... 512-305-7853
Public Accountant-CPA Educator/Sponsor #43 ... 512-305-7853
Public Accountant-CPA Firm #43 ... 512-305-7853
Public Safety Organiz'n, Promoter #38. 512-475-0775
Radiology Technician #16 ... 512-834-6617
Real Estate Agent/Broker/Sales #52 ... 512-459-6544
Real Estate Appraiser #47 ... 512-465-3950
Real Estate Inspector #52 ... 512-459-6544
Representative Ofc., Foreign Bank #1 .. 512-475-1300
Respiratory Care Practitioner #29 ... 512-834-6632
Sanitarian #22 ... 512-834-4517
Sanitation Code Enforcem't Officer #22 512-834-6635
Savings & Loan Association #37 ... 512-475-1350
Savings Bank #37 ... 512-475-1350
School Psychology Specialist #19 ... 512-305-7700
Securities Agent/Salesperson #39 ... 512-305-8332
Securities Broker/Dealer #39 ... 512-305-8332
Security Agency, Private #35 ... 512-238-5858
Security Agent/Service/Sales #35 ... 512-238-5858
Seed Dealer #11 ... 512-463-7476
Service Contract Provider #14 ... 512-463-6599
Sex Offender Treatment Provider #26 .. 512-834-4530
Shorthand Reporter #9 ... 512-463-1630
Social Worker #26 ... 512-719-3521
Speech-Language Pathologist #22 ... 512-834-6627
Staff Leasing #14 ... 512-475-2896
STAP Vendor #6 ... 512-407-3250
Surveyor, Land #4 ... 512-452-9427
Surveyor, Out-of-Texas #4 ... 512-452-9427
Surveyor, State Land #4 ... 512-452-9427
Talent Agency #14 ... 512-463-6599
Tax Appraisal Professional #59 ... 512-305-7300
Teacher #42 ... 512-238-3200
Telephone Solicitation #38 ... 512-475-0775
Temporary Common Worker #14 ... 512-463-6599
Third Part Debt Collector #38 ... 512-463-6906
Transportation Service Provider #54 ... 512-465-3500
Trust Company #1 ... 512-475-1300
Underground Storage Tank Instal. #60. 512-239-2191
Vehicle Protection Provider #14 ... 512-463-6599
Veterans Organization Solicitation #38. 512-475-0775
Veterinarian #18 ... 512-305-7555
Water Well & Pump Installer #14 ... 512-463-7880
Weather Modification Service #14 ... 512-463-6599
Weigher, Public #11 ... 512-463-7607
Weights/Measures Service #11 ... 512-463-7607
Wig Specialist #2 ... 512-936-6333
Wrestling Promoter #38 ... 512-463-6906
X-ray Machine #16 ... 512-834-6688 x2202

Texas Licensing Agency Information

1 Banking Department, 2601 N Lamar Blvd, Austin, TX 78705-4294; 512-475-1300, Fax: 512-475-1313. www.banking.state.tx.us Search Database at www.banking.state.tx.us/itds.htm

2 Board of Barber Examiners, 5717 Balcones Dr. #217, Austin, TX 78701; 512-936-6333, Fax: 512-458-4901. www.tsbbe.state.tx.us Email: glenn.parker@tsbbe.state.tx.us Search Database at www.tsbbe.state.tx.us/index.html Note: Online search of individuals requires license number. Cost of bulk record request is estimated based on amount of information requested. Also see cosmetology board for add'l manicurist licenses.

3 Board of Plumbing Examiners, PO Box 4200, Austin, TX 78765-4200; 512-458-2145, Fax: 512-450-0637. www.tsbpe.state.tx.us Email: info@tsbpe.state.tx.us

4 Board of Professional Land Surveying, 7701 N Lamar, #400, Austin, TX 78752; 512-452-9427, Fax: 512-452-7711. www.txls.state.tx.us Email: lois.coleman@mail.capnet.state.tx.us Search Database at http://txls.state.tx.us/sect03/rosters.html

5 Board of Registration for Professional Engineers, 1917 IH35 S (78760), Austin, TX 78741; 512-440-7723, Fax: 512-442-1414. www.tbpe.state.tx.us Email: peboard@tbpe.state.tx.us Search Database at www.tbpe.state.tx.us/downloads.htm Note: Licensing data available as pdf downloads; lists updated twice monthly.

6 Commission for the Deaf & Hard of Hearing, PO Box 12904, Austin, TX 78711; 512-407-3250 Voice; 512-407-3251 TTY, Fax: 512-451-9316. www.tcdhh.state.tx.us Email: angelab@tcdhh.tx.us

7 Office of Consumer Credit Commissioner, 2601 N Lamar Blvd, Austin, TX 78705-4207; 512-936-7600, Fax: 512-936-7610. www.occc.state.tx.us Email: info@occc.state.tx.us

8 Cosmetology Commission, 5717 Balcones Dr, Austin, TX 78755; 512-380-7659, Fax: 512-419-9885. www.txcc.state.tx.us Email: licensing@txcc.state.tx.us

9 Court Reporter Certification Board, PO Box 13131, Austin, TX 78711-3131; 512-463-1630, Fax: 512-463-1117. www.crcb.state.tx.us Email: info@crcb.state.tx.us Note: Interested parties may submit an open records request for a list. Refer to our website link "Making requests from CRCB".

10 Department of Agriculture, Pesticide Program, P.O. Box 12847 (1700 Congress Ave), Austin, TX 78711; 512-475-1639, Fax: 512-475-1618. www.agr.state.tx.us/pesticide/index.htm Email: contact@agr.state.tx.us

11 Department of Agriculture, Regulatory Programs, PO Box 12847 (1700 N Congress, Stephen F Austin Bldg), Austin, TX 78711; 512-463-7476, 800-835-5832, Fax: 512-463-1104. www.agr.state.tx.us Email: contact@agr.state.tx.us

12 Department of Health, Toxic Substances Control Division, Asbestos Programs Branch, 1100 W 49th St, Austin, TX 78756; 512-834-6600 x2789, Fax: 512-834-6644. www.tdh.state.tx.us/beh/asbestos/ Email: todd.wingler@tdh.state.tx.us Note: Make in person requests at 8407 Wall St, #N320, Austin, TX.

13 Department of Human Services, Long Term Care Regulatory Credentialing Dept, PO Box 149030, Mail Code Y979 (701 W. 51st St), Austin, TX 78714-9030; 512-231-5800, Fax: 512-834-6764. www.dhs.state.tx.us/programs/ltc/credentialing/index.html   Email: ltcr@dhs.state.tx.us

14 Department of Licensing & Regulation, PO Box 12157 (920 Colorado), Austin, TX 78711-2157; 512-463-6599, Fax: 512-475-2854. www.license.state.tx.us Search Database at www.license.state.tx.us/LicenseSearch

15 Funeral Service Commission, PO Box 12217 (510 S Congress Ave, #206), Austin, TX 78704-1718; 512-936-2474, Fax: 512-479-5064. www.tfsc.state.tx.us   Email: info@tfsc.state.tx.us

16 Department of Health, Bureau of Radiation Control, 1100 West 49th St, Austin, TX 78756-3189; 512-834-6688, Fax: 512-834-6690. www.tdh.state.tx.us/radiation/ir.htm

17 Executive Council on Physical Therapy & Occupational Therapy Examiners, 333 Guadalupe St, Tower 2, #510, Austin, TX 78701; 512-305-6900, Fax: 512-305-6951. www.ecptote.state.tx.us Email: ecptote@mail.capnet.state.tx.us Search Database at www.ecptote.state.tx.us/license/otverif.php Note: Will sell mailing lists for licensees.

18 Health Department, State Veterinary Board, 333 Guadalupe, Tower 2, #330, Austin, TX 78701-3998; 512-305-7555, Fax: 512-305-7556. www.texasonline.state.tx.us/tbvme Email: Vet.Board@tbvme.state.tx.us

19 Board of Examiners of Psychologists, 333 Guadalupe, #2-450, Austin, TX 78701; 512-305-7700, Fax: 512-305-7701. www.tsbep.state.tx.us Email: brenda.skiff@tsbep.state.tx.us

20 Board of Podiatric Medical Examiners, 333 Guadalupe, #2-320, Austin, TX 78701; 512-305-7000, Fax: 512-305-7003. www.foot.state.tx.us Email: hemant.makan@foot.state.tx.us Search Database at www.foot.state.tx.us/verifications.htm

21 Health Department, Advisory Board of Athletic Trainers, 1100 W 49th St, Austin, TX 78756; 512-834-6615, Fax: 512-834-6677. www.tdh.state.tx.us/hcqs/plc/at.htm Email: at@tdh.state.tx.us Search Database at www.tdh.state.tx.us/hcqs/plc/at_rost.txt

22 Department of Health, Professional Licensing & Certification - Medical, 1100 W 49th St, Austin, TX 78756-3183; 512-834-6635, Fax: 512-834-6707. www.tdh.state.tx.us/license.htm Email: registry@licc.tdh.state.tx.us

23 Health Department, Dental Board, 333 Guadalupe, Tower 3, #800, Austin, TX 78701; 512-463-6400, Fax: 512-463-7452. www.tsbde.state.tx.us Email: webmaster@tsbde.state.tx.us Search Database at www.tsbde.state.tx.us/dbsearch

24 Health Department, Board of Pharmacy, 333 Guadalupe, Box 21, Tower 3, #600, Austin, TX 78701-3942; 512-305-8000, Fax: 512-305-8082. www.tsbp.state.tx.us Email: openrec@tsbp.state.tx.us   Search Database at www.tsbp.state.tx.us/dbsearch/Default.htm

25 Texas Board of Chiropractic Examiners, 333 Guadalupe, Tower 3, #825, Austin, TX 78701; 512-505-6700, Fax: 512-305-6705. www.tbce.state.tx.us   Email: tbce@tbce.state.tx.us Search Database at www.texasonline.com

26 Department of Health, Professional Licensing & Certification Div, 1100 W 49th St, Austin, TX 78756-3180; 512-834-6658, Fax: 512-834-6789. www.tdh.state.tx.us/hcqs/plc/plcd.htm Email: lpc@licc.tdh.state.tx.us

27 Health Department, Bureau of Emergency Management, 1100 W 49th St, Austin, TX 78756; 512-834-6700, Fax: 512-834-6736. www.tdh.state.tx.us/hcqs/ems/emshome.htm Email: emscert@ems.tdh.state.tx.us Search Database at http://160.42.108.3/ems_web/blh_html_page1.htm

28 Health Department, Professional Licensure & Certification, Massage Therapy Registration Program, 1100 W 49th St, Austin, TX 78756; 512-834-6616, Fax: 512-834-6677. www.tdh.state.tx.us/hcqs/plc/massage.htm Email: massage@tdh.state.tx.us

29 Health Department, Professional Licensure & Certification, Respiratory Care Division, 1100 W 49th St, Austin, TX 78756; 512-834-6632, Fax: 512-834-4518. www.tdh.state.tx.us/hcqs/plc/resp.htm Email: resp@tdh.state.tx.us Search Database at www.tdh.state.tx.us/hcqs/plc/rcrost.txt

30 Board of Medical Examiners, MC 240, PO Box 2018, Austin, TX 78768-2018; 512-305-7010, Fax: 512-463-9416. www.tsbme.state.tx.us Email: verifcic@tsbme.state.tx.us Search Database at http://reg.tsbme.state.tx.us/onlineverif/phys_notice verif.asp? Note: Also search physician on private national website at www.docboard.org/tx/df/txsearch.htm.

31 Health Department, Professional Licensure & Certification, Marriage & Family Therapists, 1100 W 49th St, Austin, TX 78756; 512-834-6657, Fax: 512-834-6677. www.tdh.state.tx.us/hcqs/plc/mft.htm Email: mft@licc.tdh.state.tx.us Search Database at www.tdh.state.tx.us/hcqs/plc/mft.htm#rosters

33 Office of Secretary of State, Notary Public Unit, PO Box 13375 (1019 Brazos, Rm 214), Austin, TX 78711; 512-463-5705. www.sos.state.tx.us/statdoc/index.shtml Email: ckramer@sos.state.tx.us

34 Polygraph Examiner Board, PO Box 4087, Austin, TX 78773-4087; 512-424-2058, Fax: 512-424-5739. www.tpeb.state.tx.us Email: polygraph.board@mail.capnet.state.tx.us Note: There is a poloygraph examiners association that posts its member list; http://polygraph.org/states/tape/members_roster.htm. However, this association list is not generated by the official state board.

35 Commission on Private Security, PO Box 15999, Austin, TX 78761-5999; 512-238-5858, Fax: 512-238-5853. www.tcps.state.tx.us Search Database at www.tcps.state.tx.us/individual/individual_search.aspx

36 Racing Commission, 8505 Cross Park Dr, #110, Austin, TX 78754; 512-833-6699, Fax: 512-833-6907.

37 Savings & Loan Department, 2601 N Lamar Blvd, #201, Austin, TX 78705-4241; 512-475-1350, Fax: 512-475-1360. www.tsld.state.tx.us   Email: tsld@tsld.state.tx.us

38 Secretary of State, Statuatory Documents Section, PO Box 12887 (10119 Bravos), Austin, TX 78711-2887; 512-475-1769, Fax: 512-475-2815.   www.sos.state.tx.us

39 Securities Board, 208 E 10th St, 5th Fl, Austin, TX 78701; 512-305-8300, Fax: 512-305-8310. www.ssb.state.tx.us   Email: webmaster@ssb.state.tx.us

40 State Bar of Texas, 1414 Colorado, #300, Austin, TX 78701-1627; 512-463-1463 x1383, Fax: 512-462-1475.   www.texasbar.com Search Database at www.texasbar.com Note: You may also search attorneys by name at a private website at www.texaslegaldirectories.com/find.html.

41 Board of Examiners for Professional Counselors, 1100 W 49th St, Austin, TX 78756; 512-834-6658, Fax: 512-834-6789. www.tdh.state.tx.us/hcqs/plc/lpc/lpc_def.htm Email: lpc@tdh.state.tx.us Search Database at www.tdh.state.tx.us/hcqs/plc/lpc/lpc_def.htm

42 Board for Educator Certification, PO Box 12728, Austin, TX 78711-2728; 512-936-8275, Fax: 512-936-8277. www.sbec.state.tx.us   Email: sbec@sbec.state.tx.us Search Database at https://secure.sbec.state.tx.us/virtcert/

43 Board of Public Accountancy, 333 Guadalupe St, Tower III, #900, Austin, TX 78701-3900; 512-305-7800, Fax: 512-505-7875. www.tsbpa.state.tx.us   Search Database at www.tsbpa.state.tx.us/srcmain.htm

44 Library & Archives Commission, P.O. Box 12927, Austin, TX 78711-2927; 512-463-5466, Fax: 512-463-8800. www.tsl.state.tx.us   Email: ld@tsl.state.tx.su

45 State Parks & Wildlife Department, 4200 Smith School Rd, Austin, TX 78744; 512-389-4800, Fax: 512-389-4349. www.tpwd.state.tx.us

46 Alcoholic Beverage Commission, PO Box 13127 (5806 Mesa Dr), Austin, TX 78711; 512-206-3333, Fax: 512-451-0240. www.tabc.state.tx.us Note: Information regarding licenses/permits to the public in various formats such as 8 1/2" X 11" printouts, PC disks, mailing labels and 3480 tapes for a fee.

47 Appraisers Licensing & Certification Board, 1101 Camino La Costa, Austin, TX 78752; 512-465-3950, Fax: 512-465-3953. www.talcb.state.tx.us Search Database at www.talcb.state.tx.us/appraisers/Appraiser_Search.asp

48 Department of Insurance, 333 Guadalupe, Austin, TX 78701; 512-463-6169, Fax: 512-475-2025.   www.tdi.state.tx.us Email: consumer_protection@tdi.state.tx.us Search Database at www.texasonline.state.tx.us/NASApp/tdi/TdiARManager Note: Company downloads are at www.tdi.state.tx.us/general/forms/colists.html; agents downloads at www.tdi.state.tx.us/general/forms/agentlists.html.

49 Department of Protective & Regulatory Services, Child Care Licensing Division, 701 W 51st St, #E-550, Austin, TX 78751; 512-438-4800, Fax: 512-438-3848. www.tdprs.state.tx.us or www.txchildcaresearch.org

50 Ethics Commission, PO Box 12070, Austin, TX 78711-2070; 512-463-5800, Fax: 512-463-5777.   www.ethics.state.tx.us Email: disclosure@ethics.state.tx.us   Search Database at www.ethics.state.tx.us/dfs/dfs.htm

51 Optometry Board, 333 Guadalupe St, #2-420, Austin, TX 78701-3942; 512-305-8500, | Fax: 512-305-8501. www.tob.state.tx.us Email: donna.stauffer@mail.capnet.st.tx.us Search Database at www.tob.state.tx.us/tob%20verifications.htm Note: Also, you may search licensees at the national website at www.arbo.org/odfinder/LicSearch.asp.

52 Real Estate Commission, PO Box 12188, (1101 Camino La Costa), Austin, TX 78711-2188; 512-459-6544, Fax: 512-465-3913. www.trec.state.tx.us Email: glen.bridge@trec.state.tx.us Search Database at www.trec.state.tx.us/publicinfo

53 State Fire Marshal, 333 Guadalupe, Austin, TX 78701; 512-305-7900, Fax: 512-305-7922. www.tdi.state.tx.us/fire/fmli.html

54 Department of Transportation, Transportation Service Licensing Dept., 4203 Bull Creek, Austin, TX 78731; 512-465-3500, Fax: 512-465-3535. www.dot.state.tx.us

55 Department of Health, Toxic Substances Control Division, Environmental Lead Program, 1100 W 49th St, Austin, TX 78756-3199; 512-834-6612, Fax: 512-834-6644. www.tdh.state.tx.us/beh/TSCD/ Email: peter.tadin@tdh.state.tx.us

56 Commission on Fire Protection, 12015 Park 35 Circle #570, PO Box 2286, Austin, TX 78768-2286; 512-239-4911, Fax: 512-239-4917. www.tcfp.state.tx.us Email: info@tcfp.state.tx.us

57 Commission on Environmental Quality MC178, PO Box 13087, Austin, TX 78711-3087; 512-239-6719, Fax: 512-239-0533. www.tceq.state.tx.us/ Email: irrclerk@tnrcc.state.tx.us   Search Database at www.tnrcc.state.tx.us/enforcement/csd/ics/lilicense.html

58 Commission on Law Enforcement Officer, 6330 U.S. 290 East #200, Austin, TX 78723; 512-936-7700, Fax: 512-936-7714. www.tcleose.state.tx.us/ Email: kris.faldyn@mail.capnet.state.tx.us

59 Board of Tax Professional Examiners, 333 Guadalupe St, Tower II #520, Austin, TX 78701; 512-305-7300, Fax: 512-305-7304. www.txbtpe.state.tx.us Email: btpe@mail.compact.state.tx.us Search Database at www.txbtpe.state.tx.us Note: To search online, the board member number is required.

60 Natural Resource Conservation Commission, PO Box 13087, Austin, TX 78711-3087; 512-239-2191, Fax: 512-239-0533. www.tnrcc.state.tx.us Email: wkurio@tnrcc.state.tx.us Search Database at www.tnrcc.state.tx.us/enforcement/csd/ics/ustlicense.html

61 Board of Architectural Examiners, PO Box 12337, Austin, TX 78711-2337; 512-305-9000, Fax: 512-305-8900. www.tbae.state.tx.us   Search Database at www.tbae.state.tx.us/active/registrants.html

63 Board of Nurse Examiners, 333 Guadalupe #3-460, Austin, TX 78701; 512-305-7400, Fax: 512-305-7401. https://www.bne.state.tx.us/   Search Database at https://www.bne.state.tx.us/olv/rninq.htm

Texas Federal Courts

The following list indicates the district and division name for each county in the state. If the bankruptcy court location is different from the district court, then the location of the bankruptcy court appears in parentheses.

County/Court Cross Reference

County	District	Division
Anderson	Eastern	Tyler
Andrews	Western	Midland (Midland/Odessa)
Angelina	Eastern	Texarkana (Beaumont)
Aransas	Southern	Corpus Christi
Archer	Northern	Wichita Falls
Armstrong	Northern	Amarillo
Atascosa	Western	San Antonio
Austin	Southern	Houston
Bailey	Northern	Lubbock
Bandera	Western	San Antonio
Bastrop	Western	Austin
Baylor	Northern	Wichita Falls
Bee	Southern	Corpus Christi
Bell	Western	Waco
Bexar	Western	San Antonio
Blanco	Western	Austin
Borden	Northern	Lubbock
Bosque	Western	Waco
Bowie	Eastern	Texarkana
Brazoria	Southern	Galveston (Houston)
Brazos	Southern	Houston
Brewster	Western	Pecos (Midland/Odessa)
Briscoe	Northern	Amarillo
Brooks	Southern	Corpus Christi
Brown	Northern	San Angelo (Lubbock)
Burleson	Western	Austin
Burnet	Western	Austin
Caldwell	Western	Austin
Calhoun	Southern	Victoria (Corpus Christi)
Callahan	Northern	Abilene (Lubbock)
Cameron	Southern	Brownsville (Corpus Christi)
Camp	Eastern	Marshall
Carson	Northern	Amarillo
Cass	Eastern	Marshall
Castro	Northern	Amarillo
Chambers	Southern	Galveston (Houston)
Cherokee	Eastern	Tyler
Childress	Northern	Amarillo
Clay	Northern	Wichita Falls
Cochran	Northern	Lubbock
Coke	Northern	San Angelo (Lubbock)
Coleman	Northern	San Angelo (Lubbock)
Collin	Eastern	Sherman (Plano)
Collingsworth	Northern	Amarillo
Colorado	Southern	Houston
Comal	Western	San Antonio
Comanche	Northern	Fort Worth
Concho	Northern	San Angelo (Lubbock)
Cooke	Eastern	Sherman (Plano)
Coryell	Western	Waco
Cottle	Northern	Wichita Falls
Crane	Western	Midland (Midland/Odessa)
Crockett	Northern	San Angelo (Lubbock)
Crosby	Northern	Lubbock
Culberson	Western	Pecos (Midland/Odessa)
Dallam	Northern	Amarillo
Dallas	Northern	Dallas
Dawson	Northern	Lubbock
De Witt	Southern	Victoria (Houston)
Deaf Smith	Northern	Amarillo
Delta	Eastern	Sherman (Plano)
Denton	Eastern	Sherman (Plano)
Dickens	Northern	Lubbock
Dimmit	Western	San Antonio
Donley	Northern	Amarillo
Duval	Southern	Corpus Christi
Eastland	Northern	Abilene (Lubbock)
Ector	Western	Midland (Midland/Odessa)
Edwards	Western	Del Rio (San Antonio)
El Paso	Western	El Paso
Ellis	Northern	Dallas
Erath	Northern	Fort Worth
Falls	Western	Waco
Fannin	Eastern	Sherman (Plano)
Fayette	Southern	Houston
Fisher	Northern	Abilene (Lubbock)
Floyd	Northern	Lubbock
Foard	Northern	Wichita Falls
Fort Bend	Southern	Houston
Franklin	Eastern	Texarkana
Freestone	Western	Waco
Frio	Western	San Antonio
Gaines	Northern	Lubbock
Galveston	Southern	Galveston (Houston)
Garza	Northern	Lubbock
Gillespie	Western	Austin
Glasscock	Northern	San Angelo (Lubbock)
Goliad	Southern	Victoria (Corpus Christi)
Gonzales	Western	San Antonio
Gray	Northern	Amarillo
Grayson	Eastern	Sherman (Plano)
Gregg	Eastern	Tyler
Grimes	Southern	Houston
Guadalupe	Western	San Antonio
Hale	Northern	Lubbock
Hall	Northern	Amarillo
Hamilton	Western	Waco
Hansford	Northern	Amarillo
Hardeman	Northern	Wichita Falls
Hardin	Eastern	Beaumont
Harris	Southern	Houston
Harrison	Eastern	Marshall
Hartley	Northern	Amarillo
Haskell	Northern	Abilene (Lubbock)
Hays	Western	Austin
Hemphill	Northern	Amarillo
Henderson	Eastern	Tyler
Hidalgo	Southern	McAllen (Corpus Christi)
Hill	Western	Waco
Hockley	Northern	Lubbock
Hood	Northern	Fort Worth
Hopkins	Eastern	Sherman (Plano)
Houston	Eastern	Texarkana (Beaumont)
Howard	Northern	Abilene (Lubbock)
Hudspeth	Western	Pecos (Midland/Odessa)
Hunt	Northern	Dallas
Hutchinson	Northern	Amarillo
Irion	Northern	San Angelo (Lubbock)

Jack	Northern	Fort Worth
Jackson	Southern	Victoria (Corpus Christi)
Jasper	Eastern	Beaumont
Jeff Davis	Western	Pecos (Midland/Odessa)
Jefferson	Eastern	Beaumont
Jim Hogg	Southern	Laredo (Houston)
Jim Wells	Southern	Corpus Christi
Johnson	Northern	Dallas
Jones	Northern	Abilene (Lubbock)
Karnes	Western	San Antonio
Kaufman	Northern	Dallas
Kendall	Western	San Antonio
Kenedy	Southern	Corpus Christi
Kent	Northern	Lubbock
Kerr	Western	San Antonio
Kimble	Western	Austin
King	Northern	Wichita Falls
Kinney	Western	Del Rio (San Antonio)
Kleberg	Southern	Corpus Christi
Knox	Northern	Wichita Falls
La Salle	Southern	Laredo (Corpus Christi)
Lamar	Eastern	Sherman (Plano)
Lamb	Northern	Lubbock
Lampasas	Western	Austin
Lavaca	Southern	Victoria (Houston)
Lee	Western	Austin
Leon	Western	Waco
Liberty	Eastern	Beaumont
Limestone	Western	Waco
Lipscomb	Northern	Amarillo
Live Oak	Southern	Corpus Christi
Llano	Western	Austin
Loving	Western	Pecos (Midland/Odessa)
Lubbock	Northern	Lubbock
Lynn	Northern	Lubbock
Madison	Southern	Houston
Marion	Eastern	Marshall
Martin	Western	Midland (Midland/Odessa)
Mason	Western	Austin
Matagorda	Southern	Galveston (Houston)
Maverick	Western	Del Rio (San Antonio)
McCulloch	Western	Austin
McLennan	Western	Waco
McMullen	Southern	Laredo (Houston)
Medina	Western	San Antonio
Menard	Northern	San Angelo (Lubbock)
Midland	Western	Midland (Midland/Odessa)
Milam	Western	Waco
Mills	Northern	San Angelo (Lubbock)
Mitchell	Northern	Abilene (Lubbock)
Montague	Northern	Wichita Falls
Montgomery	Southern	Houston
Moore	Northern	Amarillo
Morris	Eastern	Marshall
Motley	Northern	Lubbock
Nacogdoches	Eastern	Texarkana (Beaumont)
Navarro	Northern	Dallas
Newton	Eastern	Beaumont
Nolan	Northern	Abilene (Lubbock)
Nueces	Southern	Corpus Christi
Ochiltree	Northern	Amarillo
Oldham	Northern	Amarillo
Orange	Eastern	Beaumont
Palo Pinto	Northern	Fort Worth
Panola	Eastern	Tyler
Parker	Northern	Fort Worth
Parmer	Northern	Amarillo
Pecos	Western	Pecos (Midland/Odessa)
Polk	Eastern	Texarkana (Beaumont)
Potter	Northern	Amarillo
Presidio	Western	Pecos (Midland/Odessa)
Rains	Eastern	Tyler
Randall	Northern	Amarillo
Reagan	Northern	San Angelo (Lubbock)
Real	Western	San Antonio
Red River	Eastern	Sherman (Plano)
Reeves	Western	Pecos (Midland/Odessa)
Refugio	Southern	Victoria (Corpus Christi)
Roberts	Northern	Amarillo
Robertson	Western	Waco
Rockwall	Northern	Dallas
Runnels	Northern	San Angelo (Lubbock)
Rusk	Eastern	Tyler
Sabine	Eastern	Texarkana (Beaumont)
San Augustine	Eastern	Texarkana (Beaumont)
San Jacinto	Southern	Houston
San Patricio	Southern	Corpus Christi
San Saba	Western	Austin
Schleicher	Northern	San Angelo (Lubbock)
Scurry	Northern	Lubbock
Shackelford	Northern	Abilene (Lubbock)
Shelby	Eastern	Texarkana (Beaumont)
Sherman	Northern	Amarillo
Smith	Eastern	Tyler
Somervell	Western	Waco
Starr	Southern	McAllen (Corpus Christi)
Stephens	Northern	Abilene (Lubbock)
Sterling	Northern	San Angelo (Lubbock)
Stonewall	Northern	Abilene (Lubbock)
Sutton	Northern	San Angelo (Lubbock)
Swisher	Northern	Amarillo
Tarrant	Northern	Fort Worth
Taylor	Northern	Abilene (Lubbock)
Terrell	Western	Del Rio (San Antonio)
Terry	Northern	Lubbock
Throckmorton	Northern	Abilene (Lubbock)
Titus	Eastern	Texarkana
Tom Green	Northern	San Angelo (Lubbock)
Travis	Western	Austin
Trinity	Eastern	Texarkana (Beaumont)
Tyler	Eastern	Texarkana (Beaumont)
Upshur	Eastern	Marshall
Upton	Western	Midland (Midland/Odessa)
Uvalde	Western	Del Rio (San Antonio)
Val Verde	Western	Del Rio (San Antonio)
Van Zandt	Eastern	Tyler
Victoria	Southern	Victoria (Corpus Christi)
Walker	Southern	Houston
Waller	Southern	Houston
Ward	Western	Pecos (Midland/Odessa)
Washington	Western	Austin
Webb	Southern	Laredo (Houston)
Wharton	Southern	Houston
Wheeler	Northern	Amarillo
Wichita	Northern	Wichita Falls
Wilbarger	Northern	Wichita Falls
Willacy	Southern	Brownsville (Corpus Christi)
Williamson	Western	Austin
Wilson	Western	San Antonio
Winkler	Western	Pecos (Midland/Odessa)
Wise	Northern	Fort Worth
Wood	Eastern	Tyler
Yoakum	Northern	Lubbock
Young	Northern	Wichita Falls
Zapata	Southern	Laredo (Houston)
Zavala	Western	Del Rio (San Antonio)

Standards for Federal Courts: The search fee is $20.00 per item (one party name or case number). Certification fee is $7.00 per document. Copy fee is $.50 per page. All fees standard unless noted in profile. Mail Search: always enclose a stamped self addressed envelope unless otherwise noted. Most courts accept fax requests or will suggest a copying/search vendor. Before releasing records, all courts require prepayment unless noted in profile.

Open records are located at the court unless otherwise noted. District courts index by defendant and plaintiff as well as by case number. Bankruptcy courts usually index by debtor and case number. While most courts now have their indexes on computer, many still maintain index card files as well.

The universal PACER sign-up number is 800-676-6856. Find PACER and the Party/Case Index on the Web at http://pacer.psc.uscourts.gov. PACER dial-up access is $.60 per minute. Also, courts offering internet access via RACER, PACER, Web-PACER or the new CM-ECF charge $.07 per page fee unless noted as free.

US District Court

Eastern District of Texas

Beaumont Division PO Box 3507, Beaumont, TX 77704 (courier: Room 104, 300 Willow, Beaumont, TX 77701), 409-654-7000. www.txed.uscourts.gov

Counties: Delta*, Fannin*, Hardin, Hopkins*, Jasper, Jefferson, Lamar*, Liberty, Newton, Orange, Red River. Counties marked with an asterisk are called the Paris Division, whose case records are maintained here.

Indexing & Storage: New cases available in the index immediately after filing date. Records are also indexed on microfiche. District wide searches are available for records from 3/86 from this division. This division maintains records for the Paris Division also.

Fee & Payment: Payment may be made by money order, cashier check, personal check. Payee: Clerk, U.S. District Court.

Phone Search: Only docket information available by phone.

Mail Search: A SASE not required.

In Person Search: Fee charged if court conducts your in person search for you. Public copy machine available.

PACER: PACER is available online at http://pacer.txed.uscourts.gov. Document images available on the RACER system. Records purged once per year. New records are online after 1 day.

Electronic Filing: Electronic filing information online at https://ecf.txed.uscourts.gov

Lufkin Division 104 N. Third St., Lufkin, TX 75901 (Use mail address for courier delivery) 936-632-2739. www.txed.uscourts.gov

Counties: Angelina, Houston, Nacogdoches, Polk, Sabine, San Augustine, Shelby, Trinity, Tyler.

Indexing & Storage: New cases available in the index 1 day after filing date. Records are also indexed on microfiche.

Fee & Payment: Payment may be made by money order, cashier check, personal check. Payee: U.S. District Court.

Phone Search: Only docket information available.

In Person Search: Fee charged if court conducts your in person search for you.

PACER: PACER is available online at http://pacer.txed.uscourts.gov. Document images available on the RACER system. New records are online after 1 day.

Electronic Filing: Currently in the process of implementing CM/ECF.

Marshall Division PO Box 1499, Marshall, TX 75671-1499 (courier address: 100 E Houston, Marshall, TX 75670), 903-935-2912, Fax: 903-938-2651. www.txed.uscourts.gov

Counties: Camp, Cass, Harrison, Marion, Morris, Upshur.

Indexing & Storage: New cases available in the index 1 day after filing date. Records are also indexed on microfiche.

Fee & Payment: Payment may be made by money order, cashier check, personal check. Payee: U.S. District Court.

Phone Search: Only docket information available.

In Person Search: Fee charged if court conducts your in person search for you.

PACER: PACER is available online at http://pacer.txed.uscourts.gov. Document images available on the RACER system. Records purged once per year. New records are online after 1 day.

Electronic Filing: Electronic filing information online at https://ecf.txed.uscourts.gov

Sherman Division 101 E Pecan St Rm112, Sherman, TX 75090 (courier address: Use mail address for courier delivery) 903-892-2921. www.txed.uscourts.gov

Counties: Collin, Cooke, Denton, Grayson.

Indexing & Storage: New cases available in the index 1 day after filing date. Records are also indexed on microfiche. District wide searches are available from this division.

Fee & Payment: Payment may be made by money order, cashier check, personal check. Payee: Clerk, U.S. District Court.

Phone Search: Docket information available by phone.

In Person Search: Fee charged if court conducts your in person search for you.

PACER: PACER is available online at http://pacer.txed.uscourts.gov. Document images available on the RACER system. Records purged once per year. New records are online after 1 day.

Electronic Filing: Electronic filing information online at https://ecf.txed.uscourts.gov

Texarkana Division Clerk's Office, 500 State Line Ave, Room 301, Texarkana, TX 75501 (courier address: Use mail address for courier delivery) 903-794-8561, Fax: 903-794-0600. www.txed.uscourts.gov

Counties: Bowie, Franklin, Titus.

Indexing & Storage: New cases available in the index 1-2 days after filing date. Records are also indexed on microfiche. There is no set time when cases are sent to the Fort Worth Federal Records Center.

Fee & Payment: Payment may be made by money order, cashier check, personal check. Payee: Clerk, U.S. District Court.

In Person Search: Fee charged if court conducts your in person search for you.

PACER: PACER is available online at http://pacer.txed.uscourts.gov. Document images available on the RACER system. Records purged once per year. New records are online after 1 day.

Electronic Filing: Electronic filing information online at https://ecf.txed.uscourts.gov

Tyler Division Clerk, Room 106, 211 W Ferguson, Tyler, TX 75702 (courier address: Use mail address for courier delivery) 903-590-1000. www.txed.uscourts.gov

Counties: Anderson, Cherokee, Gregg, Henderson, Panola, Rains, Rusk, Smith, Van Zandt, Wood.

Indexing & Storage: New cases available in the index 1-2 days after filing date. Records are also indexed on microfiche. There is no set time when cases are sent to the Fort Worth Federal Records Center.

Fee & Payment: Payment may be made by money order, cashier check, personal check. Payee: Clerk, U.S. District Court.

Phone Search: Only docket information available.

Mail Search: A SASE not required.

In Person Search: Fee charged if court conducts your in person search for you.

PACER: PACER is available online at http://pacer.txed.uscourts.gov. Document images available on the RACER system. Records purged once per year. New records are online after 1 day.

Electronic Filing: Electronic filing information online at https://ecf.txed.uscourts.gov

U.S. Bankruptcy Court

Eastern District of Texas

Beaumont Division Suite 100, 300 Willow, Beaumont, TX 77701 (courier address: Use mail address for courier delivery) 409-839-2617. www.txeb.uscourts.gov

Counties: Angelina, Hardin, Houston, Jasper, Jefferson, Liberty, Nacogdoches, Newton, Orange, Polk, Sabine, San Augustine, Shelby, Trinity, Tyler.

Indexing & Storage: Cases indexed by debtor as well as by case number. New cases available in the index 1 day after filing date.

Fee & Payment: Payment may be made by money order, cashier check, personal check. Debtor's checks are not accepted. Payee: Clerk, U.S. Bankruptcy Court.

Phone Search: Only docket information available by phone. Automated voice case information service (VCIS) is available. Call VCIS at 800-466-1694 or 903-590-1217.

In Person Search: Permitted. Searchers must fill out a card with their phone number, the date, and the case number.

PACER: PACER is available online at http://pacer.txeb.uscourts.gov. Document images available. Records purged every six months. New civil records are online after 1 day.

Electronic Filing: Electronic filing information online at https://ecf.txeb.uscourts.gov

Marshall Division c/o Tyler Division, 200 E Ferguson, Tyler, TX 75702 (courier address: Use mail address for courier delivery) 903-590-1212, Fax: 903-590-1226. www.txeb.uscourts.gov

Counties: Camp, Cass, Harrison, Marion, Morris, Upshur.

Indexing & Storage: Cases indexed by as well as by case number. New cases available in the index after filing date. Open records are located at the Tyler Division.

Fee & Payment: Payment may be made by money order, cashier check. Business checks are not accepted. Personal checks are not accepted.

Phone Search: Automated voice case information service (VCIS) is available. Call VCIS at 800-466-1694 or 903-590-1217.

Mail Search: A SASE not required.

In Person Search: Permitted.

PACER: PACER is available online at http://pacer.txeb.uscourts.gov. Document images available. Records purged every six months. New civil records are online after 1 day.

Electronic Filing: Electronic filing information online at https://ecf.txeb.uscourts.gov

Plano Division Suite 300B, 660 N Central Expressway, Plano, TX 75074 (courier address: Use mail address for courier delivery) 972-509-1240, Fax: 972-509-1245. www.txeb.uscourts.gov

Counties: Collin, Cooke, Delta, Denton, Fannin, Grayson, Hopkins, Lamar, Red River.

Indexing & Storage: Cases indexed by debtor and creditors as well as by case number. New cases available in the index 24 hours after filing date.

Fee & Payment: Payment may be made by money order, cashier check, personal check. Payee: Clerk, U.S. Bankruptcy Court.

Phone Search: Only docket information available by phone. Automated voice case information service (VCIS) is available. Call VCIS at 800-466-1694 or 903-590-1217.

In Person Search: Fee charged if court conducts your in person search for you.

PACER: PACER is available online at http://pacer.txeb.uscourts.gov. Document images available. Records purged every six months. New civil records are online after 1 day.

Electronic Filing: Electronic filing information online at https://ecf.txeb.uscourts.gov

Texarkana Division c/o Plano Division, Suite 300B, 660 N Central Expressway, Plano, TX 75074 (courier address: Use mail address for courier delivery) 972-509-1240, Fax: 972-509-1245. www.txeb.uscourts.gov

Counties: Bowie, Franklin, Titus.

Indexing & Storage: Cases indexed by as well as by case number. New cases available in the index after filing date. Open records are located at the Plano Division.

Fee & Payment: Payment may be made by money order, cashier check. Business checks are not accepted. Personal checks are not accepted.

Phone Search: Automated voice case information service (VCIS) is available. Call VCIS at 800-466-1694 or 903-590-1217.

Mail Search: A SASE not required.

In Person Search: Permitted.

PACER: PACER is available online at http://pacer.txeb.uscourts.gov/. Document images available. Records purged every six months. New civil records are online after 1 day.

Electronic Filing: Electronic filing information online at https://ecf.txeb.uscourts.gov

Tyler Division 200 E Ferguson, 2nd Floor, Tyler, TX 75702 (courier address: Use mail address for courier delivery) 903-590-1212, Fax: 903-590-1226. www.txeb.uscourts.gov

Counties: Anderson, Cherokee, Gregg, Henderson, Panola, Rains, Rusk, Smith, Van Zandt, Wood.

Indexing & Storage: Cases indexed by debtor as well as by case number. New cases available in the index 1 day after filing date. Records are also indexed on microfiche. Card index is only for cases prior to October 1987. District wide searches are available for information from 10/87 from this court. This court maintains automated case records and all finance records for the other divisions in this district.

Fee & Payment: Payment may be made by money order, cashier check, personal check. Payee: Clerk, U.S. Bankruptcy Court.

Phone Search: This court will answer questions pertaining to information not available from VCIS. Automated voice case information service (VCIS) is available. Call VCIS at 800-466-1694 or 903-590-1217.

Mail Search: A SASE not required.

In Person Search: Permitted.

PACER: PACER is available online at http://pacer.txeb.uscourts.gov. Document images available. Records purged every six months. New civil records are online after 1 day.

Electronic Filing: Electronic filing information online at https://ecf.txeb.uscourts.gov

U.S. District Court

Northern District of Texas

Abilene Division PO Box 1218, Abilene, TX 79604 (courier address: Room 2008, 341 Pine St, Abilene, TX 79601), 915-677-6311. www.txnd.uscourts.gov

Counties: Callahan, Eastland, Fisher, Haskell, Howard, Jones, Mitchell, Nolan, Shackelford, Stephens, Stonewall, Taylor, Throckmorton.

Indexing & Storage: New cases available in the index 2 days after filing date. A computer index is planned for early 1996. District wide searches can be conducted from this court for information from 1983.

Fee & Payment: Payment may be made by money order, cashier check, personal check. Payee: Clerk, U.S. District Court.

Phone Search: Only a name or case number will be released over the phone.

Mail Search: A SASE not required.

In Person Search: Fee charged if court conducts your in person search for you.

PACER: PACER is available online at http://pacer.txnd.uscourts.gov. Document images

available. Records purged once per year. New records are online after 1 day.

Electronic Filing: Electronic filing information online at https://ecf.txnd.uscourts.gov

Amarillo Division 205 E 5th St, Amarillo, TX 79101 (courier address: Use mail address for courier delivery) 806-324-2352. www.txnd.uscourts.gov

Counties: Armstrong, Briscoe, Carson, Castro, Childress, Collingsworth, Dallam, Deaf Smith, Donley, Gray, Hall, Hansford, Hartley, Hemphill, Hutchinson, Lipscomb, Moore, Ochiltree, Oldham, Parmer, Potter, Randall, Roberts, Sherman, Swisher, Wheeler.

Indexing & Storage: New cases available in the index immediately after filing date. Records are also indexed on microfiche.

Fee & Payment: Payment may be made by money order, cashier check, personal check. Payee: Clerk, U.S. District Court.

Phone Search: No party information is released over the phone. Only pleadings are released over the phone.

Mail Search: A SASE not required.

In Person Search: Fee charged if court conducts your in person search for you.

PACER: PACER is available online at http://pacer.txnd.uscourts.gov. Document images available. Records purged once per year. New records are online after 1 day.

Electronic Filing: Electronic filing information online at https://ecf.txnd.uscourts.gov

Dallas Division Room 1452, 1100 Commerce St, Dallas, TX 75242 (courier address: Use mail address for courier delivery) 214-753-2200. www.txnd.uscourts.gov

Counties: Dallas, Ellis, Hunt, Johnson, Kaufman, Navarro, Rockwall.

Indexing & Storage: New cases available in the index 2 days after filing date. Computer index goes back to 1990 for the entire district. Records are also indexed on microfiche since 1957. District wide searches are available for information from 1957 forward from this division.

Fee & Payment: Payment may be made by money order, cashier check, personal check, Visa, Mastercard. Payee: Clerk, U.S. District Court.

Phone Search: Only computerized docket information will be released over the phone.

In Person Search: Fee charged if court conducts your in person search for you.

PACER: PACER is available online at http://pacer.txnd.uscourts.gov. Document images available. Records purged once per year. New records are online after 1 day.

Electronic Filing: Electronic filing information online at https://ecf.txnd.uscourts.gov

Fort Worth Division Clerk's Office, 501 W Tenth St, Room 310, Fort Worth, TX 76102 (courier address: Use mail address for courier delivery) 817-978-3132. www.txnd.uscourts.gov

Counties: Comanche, Erath, Hood, Jack, Palo Pinto, Parker, Tarrant, Wise.

Indexing & Storage: New cases available in the index 1 day after filing date. Computer records go back to 1994 for civil cases and 1993 for criminal cases. Records are also indexed on microfiche.

District wide searches for information from 1957 are available from this court.

Fee & Payment: Payment may be made by money order, cashier check, personal check. Payee: Clerk, U.S. District Court.

Phone Search: The court will only release minimal information about a case when the caller already has a case number. They will not search for case numbers over the phone.

Mail Search: A SASE not required.

In Person Search: Fee charged if court conducts your in person search for you.

PACER: PACER is available online at http://pacer.txnd.uscourts.gov. Document images available. Records purged once per year. New records are online after 1 day.

Electronic Filing: Electronic filing information online at https://ecf.txnd.uscourts.gov

Lubbock Division Clerk, Room 209, 1205 Texas Ave, Lubbock, TX 79401 (courier address: Use mail address for courier delivery) 806-472-7624. www.txnd.uscourts.gov

Counties: Bailey, Borden, Cochran, Crosby, Dawson, Dickens, Floyd, Gaines, Garza, Hale, Hockley, Kent, Lamb, Lubbock, Lynn, Motley, Scurry, Terry, Yoakum.

Indexing & Storage: New cases available in the index 1 day after filing date. Records are also indexed on microfiche. No records have been sent to the Federal Records Center.

Fee & Payment: Payment may be made by money order, cashier check, personal check. Payee: Clerk, U.S. District Court.

In Person Search: Fee charged if court conducts your in person search for you. An in person request must be made in writing.

PACER: PACER is available online at http://pacer.txnd.uscourts.gov. Document images available. Records purged once per year. New records are online after 1 day.

Electronic Filing: Electronic filing information online at https://ecf.txnd.uscourts.gov

San Angelo Division Clerk's Office, Room 202, 33 E Twohig, San Angelo, TX 76903 (courier address: Use mail address for courier delivery) 325-655-4506, Fax: 325-658-6826. www.txnd.uscourts.gov

Counties: Brown, Coke, Coleman, Concho, Crockett, Glasscock, Irion, Menard, Mills, Reagan, Runnels, Schleicher, Sterling, Sutton, Tom Green.

Indexing & Storage: New cases available in the index immediately after filing date. Records are also indexed on microfiche. Civil records are retained for 3 years. Criminal records are retained for 7 to 8 years.

Fee & Payment: Payment may be made by money order, cashier check, personal check. Payee: Clerk, U.S. District Court.

Phone Search: Only docket information available.

In Person Search: Fee charged if court conducts your in person search for you.

PACER: PACER is available online at http://pacer.txnd.uscourts.gov. Document images available. Records purged once per year. New records are online after 1 day.

Electronic Filing: Electronic filing information online at https://ecf.txnd.uscourts.gov

Wichita Falls Division PO Box 1234, Wichita Falls, TX 76307 (courier address: Room 203, 1000 Lamar, Wichita Falls, TX 76301), 940-767-1902, Fax: 940-767-2526. www.txnd.uscourts.gov

Counties: Archer, Baylor, Clay, Cottle, Foard, Hardeman, King, Knox, Montague, Wichita, Wilbarger, Young.

Indexing & Storage: New cases available in the index immediately after filing date. Records are also indexed on microfiche.

Fee & Payment: Payment may be made by money order, cashier check, personal check. Payee: Clerk, U.S. District Court.

Phone Search: Only docket information available.

In Person Search: Fee charged if court conducts your in person search for you.

PACER: PACER is available online at http://pacer.txnd.uscourts.gov. Document images available. Records purged once per year. New records are online after 1 day.

Electronic Filing: Electronic filing information online at https://ecf.txnd.uscourts.gov

U.S. Bankruptcy Court

Northern District of Texas

Amarillo Division PO Box 15960, Amarillo, TX 79105 (courier address: 624 Polk St, Suite 100, Amarillo, TX 79101), 806-324-2302. www.txnb.uscourts.gov

Counties: Armstrong, Briscoe, Carson, Castro, Childress, Collingsworth, Dallam, Deaf Smith, Donley, Gray, Hall, Hansford, Hartley, Hemphill, Hutchinson, Lipscomb, Moore, Ochiltree, Oldham, Parmer, Potter, Randall, Roberts, Sherman, Swisher, Wheeler.

Indexing & Storage: Cases indexed by debtor as well as by case number. New cases available in the index immediately after filing date. Card index available prio to June 1988.

Fee & Payment: Payment may be made by money order, cashier check, business check. Personal checks are not accepted. Law firm checks are accepted. Payee: Clerk, U.S. Bankruptcy Court.

Phone Search: Only docket information available by phone. Automated voice case information service (VCIS) is available. Call VCIS at 800-886-9008 or 214-753-2128.

In Person Search: Permitted. The $20.00 search fee is required should the court have to pull the file and count pages. Court does not charge to do in person name searches.

PACER: PACER is available online at https://pacer.txnb.uscourts.gov. Document images available. Records purged every six months. New civil records are online after 1 day.

Electronic Filing: Electronic filing information online at https://ecf.txnb.uscourts.gov

Dallas Division 1100 Commerce St, Suite 12A24, Dallas, TX 75242-1496 (courier address: Use mail address for courier delivery) 214-753-2000. www.txnb.uscourts.gov

Counties: Dallas, Ellis, Hunt, Johnson, Kaufman, Navarro, Rockwall.

Indexing & Storage: Cases indexed by debtor and creditors as well as by case number. New cases available in the index 1-2 days after filing date.

District wide searches are available for records from 8/92 to the present from this division. This court maintains records for the Wichita Falls Division.

Fee & Payment: Payment may be made by money order. Business checks are not accepted. Personal checks are not accepted. There is no search fee for searching docket sheets or claim registers. Payee: Clerk, U.S. Bankruptcy Court.

Phone Search: Only docket information available by phone. Automated voice case information service (VCIS) is available. Call VCIS at 800-886-9008 or 214-753-2128.

In Person Search: Fee charged if court conducts your in person search for you. There is no search fee for searching docket sheets or claims registers. An onsite copy service is The Court System, 214-744-0585, which will provide copies.

PACER: PACER is available online at https://pacer.txnb.uscourts.gov. Document images available. Records purged every six months. New civil records are online after 1 day.

Electronic Filing: Electronic filing information online at https://ecf.txnb.uscourts.gov

Fort Worth Division 501 W 10th, Suite 147, Fort Worth, TX 76102 (courier address: Use mail address for courier delivery) 817-333-6000, Fax: 817-333-6001. www.txnb.uscourts.gov

Counties: Comanche, Erath, Hood, Jack, Palo Pinto, Parker, Tarrant, Wise.

Indexing & Storage: Cases indexed by debtor as well as by case number. New cases available in the index 1-2 days after filing date. Records up to 1986 are on index cards. Complete August 1, 1992 through the present are indexed on computer. From 1987 to August 1, 1992, records are indexed manually. Closed cases are held in house as long as there is space to store them. They are sent opnce at year end to the Fort Worth Federal Records Center.

Fee & Payment: Payment may be made by money order, cashier check, personal check. Debtor's checks are not accepted. Payee: Clerk, U.S. Bankruptcy Court.

Phone Search: Only docket information available by phone. A record can be searched over the phone by debtor's name for records from 1987 to the present. Automated voice case information service (VCIS) is available. Call VCIS at 800-886-9008 or 214-753-2128.

In Person Search: Fee charged if court conducts your in person search for you.

PACER: PACER is available online at https://pacer.txnb.uscourts.gov. Document images available. Records purged every six months. New civil records are online after 1 day.

Electronic Filing: Electronic filing information online at https://ecf.txnb.uscourts.gov

Lubbock Division 306 Federal Bldg, 1205 Texas Ave, Lubbock, TX 79401-4002 (courier address: Use mail address for courier delivery) 806-472-5000. www.txnb.uscourts.gov

Counties: Bailey, Borden, Brown, Callahan, Cochran, Cooke, Coleman, Concho, Crockett, Crosby, Dawson, Dickens, Eastland, Fisher, Floyd, Gaines, Garza, Glasscock, Hale, Haskell, Hockley, Howard, Irion, Jones, Kent, Lamb, Lubbock, Lynn, Menard, Mills, Mitchell,Motley, Nolan, Reagan, Runnels, Schleicher, Scurry, Shackelford,

Stephens, Sterling, Stonewall, Sutton, Taylor, Terry, Throckmorton, Tom Green, Yoakum.

Indexing & Storage: Cases indexed by debtor as well as by case number. New cases available in the index 1-2 days after filing date.

Fee & Payment: Payment may be made by money order, cashier check, business check. Personal checks are not accepted. Debtor's checks are not accepted. Payee: Clerk, U.S. Bankruptcy Court.

Phone Search: Only docket information available by phone. A record can be searched over the phone by debtor's name for records from 1987 to the present. Automated voice case information service (VCIS) is available. Call VCIS at 800-886-9008 or 214-753-2128.

In Person Search: Permitted.

PACER: PACER is available online at https://pacer.txnb.uscourts.gov. Document images available. Records purged every six months. New civil records are online after 1 day.

Electronic Filing: Electronic filing information online at https://ecf.txnb.uscourts.gov

Wichita Falls Division c/o Dallas Division, Suite 12A24, 1100 Commerce St, Dallas, TX 75242-1496 (Use mail address for courier delivery) 214-753-2000. www.txnb.uscourts.gov

Counties: Archer, Baylor, Clay, Cottle, Foard, Hardeman, King, Knox, Montague, Wichita, Wilbarger, Young.

Indexing & Storage: Cases indexed by as well as by case number. New cases available in the index after filing date. Open records are located at the Dallas Division.

Fee & Payment: Payment may be made by money order, cashier check. Business checks are not accepted. Personal checks are not accepted.

Phone Search: Automated voice case information service (VCIS) is available. Call VCIS at 800-886-9008 or 214-753-2128.

In Person Search: Permitted.

PACER: PACER is available online at https://pacer.txnb.uscourts.gov. Document images available. Records purged every six months. New civil records are online after 1 day.

Electronic Filing: Electronic filing information online at https://ecf.txnb.uscourts.gov

U.S. District Court

Southern District of Texas

Brownsville Division 600 E Harrison St Rm 101, Brownsville, TX 78520-7114 (courier address: Use mail address for courier delivery., 600 E Harrison St #101,), 956-548-2500, Fax: 956-548-2598. www.txsd.uscourts.gov

Counties: Cameron, Willacy.

Indexing & Storage: New cases available in the index 2 days after filing date. Records are also indexed on microfiche.

Fee & Payment: Payment may be made by money order, cashier check, personal check. Payee: Clerk, U.S. District Court.

Phone Search: Only docket information available.

In Person Search: Fee charged if court conducts your in person search for you.

PACER: PACER is available online at http://pacer.txs.uscourts.gov. Document images

available. Records purged every six months. New records are online after 1 day.

Electronic Filing: Currently in the process of implementing CM/ECF.

Corpus Christi Division Clerk's Office, 1133 N. Shoreline Blvd., #208, Corpus Christi, TX 78401 (Use mail address for courier delivery) 361-888-3142. www.txsd.uscourts.gov

Counties: Aransas, Bee, Brooks, Duval, Jim Wells, Kenedy, Kleberg, Live Oak, Nueces, San Patricio.

Indexing & Storage: New cases available in the index 3 to 5 days after filing date. Records are also indexed on microfiche.

Fee & Payment: Payment may be made by money order, cashier check, personal check. Payee: Clerk, U.S. District Court.

Phone Search: No searching by telephone.

In Person Search: Permitted. Request for copies taken and filled as personnel are available. The court will assist in searches.

PACER: PACER is available online at http://pacer.txs.uscourts.gov. Document images available. Records purged every six months. New records are online after 1 day.

Electronic Filing: Currently in the process of implementing CM/ECF.

Galveston Division Clerk's Office, PO Box 2300, Galveston, TX 77553 (courier address: 601 Rosenberg, Room 411, Galveston, TX 77550), 409-766-3530. www.txsd.uscourts.gov

Counties: Brazoria, Chambers, Galveston, Matagorda.

Indexing & Storage: New cases available in the index 1 day after filing date. Records are also indexed on microfiche.

Fee & Payment: Payment may be made by money order, cashier check, business check. Personal checks are not accepted. Payee: Clerk, U.S. District Court.

Phone Search: Only the status of the case and the trial settings will be released over the phone.

In Person Search: Fee charged if court conducts your in person search for you.

PACER: PACER is available online at http://pacer.txs.uscourts.gov. Document images available. Records purged every six months. New records are online after 1 day.

Electronic Filing: Currently in the process of implementing CM/ECF.

Houston Division PO Box 61010, Houston, TX 77208 (courier address: Room 1217, 515 Rusk, Houston, TX 77002), 713-250-5500. www.txsd.uscourts.gov

Counties: Austin, Brazos, Colorado, Fayette, Fort Bend, Grimes, Harris, Madison, Montgomery, San Jacinto, Walker, Waller, Wharton.

Indexing & Storage: New cases available in the index 2 days after filing date. Mail searches must be coordinated through the court's copy service (IKON). Call 713-236-0903. They charge $8.12 per search plus $.29 per page for copies. Records are also indexed on microfiche. District wide searches are available for information from 1979 forward from this court. Criminal docketing for the district is performed in Houston.

Fee & Payment: Payment may be made by money order, cashier check, personal check. Payee: Clerk, U.S. District Court.

Phone Search: No searching by telephone.

Mail Search: A SASE not required.

In Person Search: Fee charged if court conducts your in person search for you. Court personnel will assist in searches. Copy service is available, call 713-236-0903.

PACER: PACER is available online at http://pacer.txs.uscourts.gov. Document images available. Records purged every six months. New records are online after 1 day.

Electronic Filing: Currently in the process of implementing CM/ECF.

Laredo Division PO Box 597, Laredo, TX 78042-0597 (courier address: Room 319, 1300 Matamoros, Laredo, TX 78040), 956-723-3542, Fax: 956-726-2289. www.txsd.uscourts.gov

Counties: Jim Hogg, La Salle, McMullen, Webb, Zapata.

Indexing & Storage: New cases available in the index immediately after filing date. The style of the case is needed to search.

Fee & Payment: Payment may be made by cashier check. Business checks are not accepted. Personal checks are not accepted. Payee: Clerk, U.S. District Court.

Phone Search: No searching by telephone.

Mail Search: A SASE not required.

In Person Search: Fee charged if court conducts your in person search for you.

PACER: PACER is available online at http://pacer.txs.uscourts.gov. Document images available. Records purged every six months. New records are online after 1 day.

Electronic Filing: Currently in the process of implementing CM/ECF.

McAllen Division Suite 1011, 1701 W Business Hwy 83, McAllen, TX 78501 (courier address: Use mail address for courier delivery) 956-618-8065. www.txsd.uscourts.gov

Counties: Hidalgo, Starr.

Indexing & Storage: New cases available in the index 1 day after filing date. This court has only been in operation for about 4 years.

Fee & Payment: Payment may be made by money order, cashier check, business check. Personal checks are not accepted. Payee: Clerk, U.S. District Court.

Phone Search: Only docket information available.

In Person Search: Fee charged if court conducts your in person search for you.

PACER: PACER is available online at http://pacer.txs.uscourts.gov. Document images available. Records purged every six months. New records are online after 1 day.

Electronic Filing: Currently in the process of implementing CM/ECF.

Victoria Division Clerk U.S. District Court, PO Box 1638, Victoria, TX 77902 (courier address: Room 406, 312 S Main, Victoria, TX 77901), 361-788-5000. www.txsd.uscourts.gov

Counties: Calhoun, De Witt, Goliad, Jackson, Lavaca, Refugio, Victoria.

Indexing & Storage: New cases available in the index 2 days after filing date.

Fee & Payment: Payment may be made by money order, cashier check, personal check. Payee: Clerk, U.S. District Court.

Phone Search: Only docket information available.

In Person Search: Permitted.

PACER: PACER is available online at http://pacer.txs.uscourts.gov. Document images available. Records purged every six months. New records are online after 1 day.

Electronic Filing: Currently in the process of implementing CM/ECF.

U.S. Bankruptcy Court

Southern District of Texas

Corpus Christi Division 1133 N. Shoreline Blvd. - 3rd Fl., Corpus Christi, TX 78401 (courier address: Use mail address for courier delivery) 361-888-3484. www.txsd.uscourts.gov

Counties: Aransas, Bee, Brooks, Calhoun, Cameron, Duval, Goliad, Hidalgo, Jackson, Jim Wells, Kenedy, Kleberg, Lavaca, Live Oak, Nueces, Refugio, San Patricio, Starr, Victoria, Willacy.Files from Brownsville, Corpus Christi, and McAllen are maintained here.

Indexing & Storage: Cases indexed by debtor as well as by case number. New cases available in the index 1-2 days after filing date. Records are also indexed on microfiche. Until further notice as of 9/1/97, this office will continue to hold case records for the Victoria Division.

Fee & Payment: Payment may be made by money order, cashier check, personal check. Payee: Clerk, U.S. Bankruptcy Court.

Phone Search: Automated voice case information service (VCIS) is available. Call VCIS at 800-745-4459 or 713-250-5049.

In Person Search: Fee charged if court conducts your in person search for you. There are dollar and coin-operated copiers for public use.

PACER: PACER is available online at http://pacer.txs.uscourts.gov. Document images available. Records purged every six months. New civil records are online after 1-3 days.

Electronic Filing: Electronic filing information online at https://ecf.txsb.uscourts.gov

Houston Division Room 1217, 515 Rusk Ave, Houston, TX 77002 (courier address: Use mail address for courier delivery) 713-250-5500. www.txsd.uscourts.gov

Counties: Austin, Brazoria, Brazos, Chambers, Colorado, De Witt, Fayette, Fort Bend, Galveston, Grimes, Harris, Jim Hogg*, La Salle*, Madison, Matagorda, McMullen*, Montgomery, San Jacinto, Walker,Waller, Wharton, Webb* Zapata*. Open case records for the counties marked with an asterisk are being moved to the Laredo Division.

Indexing & Storage: Cases indexed by debtor as well as by case number. New cases available in the index 1-2 days after filing date. Records are also indexed on microfiche. Some case files are maintained here from as early as 1978. Case files for the new Laredo Division are being moved to 1300 Matamors, Laredo, TX 78040, 956-726-2236 as of 9/1/97.

Fee & Payment: Payment may be made by money order, cashier check, personal check. Payee: Clerk, U.S. Bankruptcy Court.

Phone Search: Only docket information available by phone. Automated voice case information service (VCIS) is available. Call VCIS at 800-745-4459 or 713-250-5049.

In Person Search: Fee charged if court conducts your in person search for you. There is an on-site copy service. Call 713-236-0903 for information.

PACER: PACER is available online at http://pacer.txs.uscourts.gov. Document images available. Records purged every six months. New civil records are online after 1-3 days.

Electronic Filing: Electronic filing information online at https://ecf.txsb.uscourts.gov

U.S. District Court

Western District of Texas

Austin Division Room 130, 200 W 8th St, Austin, TX 78701 (courier address: Use mail address for courier delivery) 512-916-5896. www.txwd.uscourts.gov

Counties: Bastrop, Blanco, Burleson, Burnet, Caldwell, Gillespie, Hays, Kimble, Lampasas, Lee, Llano, McCulloch, Mason, San Saba, Travis, Washington, Williamson.

Indexing & Storage: New cases available in the index 1 day after filing date. Records are also indexed on microfiche.

Fee & Payment: Payment may be made by money order, cashier check, personal check. Payee: Clerk, U.S. District Court.

Phone Search: Only docket information available by phone. The caller must have the case number.

In Person Search: Fee charged if court conducts your in person search for you.

PACER: PACER is available online at http://pacer.txwd.uscourts.gov. Records purged every six months. New records are online after 1 day.

Del Rio Division Room L100, 111 E Broadway, Del Rio, TX 78840 (courier address: Use mail address for courier delivery) 830-703-2054. www.txwd.uscourts.gov

Counties: Edwards, Kinney, Maverick, Terrell, Uvalde, Val Verde, Zavala.

Indexing & Storage: New cases available in the index 1 month after filing date.

Fee & Payment: Payment may be made by money order, cashier check, personal check. Payee: Clerk, U.S. District Court.

Phone Search: Only docket information available.

In Person Search: Fee charged if court conducts your in person search for you.

PACER: PACER is available online at http://pacer.txwd.uscourts.gov. Records purged every six months. New records are online after 1 day.

El Paso Division U.S. District Clerk's Office, Room 350, 511 E San Antonio, El Paso, TX 79901 (courier address: Use mail address for courier delivery) 915-534-6725. www.txwd.uscourts.gov

Counties: El Paso.

Indexing & Storage: New cases available in the index 1-2 days after filing date. Microfiche also available.

Fee & Payment: Payment may be made by money order, cashier check, personal check. Payee: Clerk, U.S. District Court.

Phone Search: Only docket information available.

In Person Search: Fee charged if court conducts your in person search for you.

PACER: PACER is available online at http://pacer.txwd.uscourts.gov. Records purged every six months. New records are online after 1 day.

Midland Division Clerk, U.S. District Court, 200 E Wall St, Rm 107, Midland, TX 79701 (courier address: Use mail address for courier delivery) 432-686-4001. www.txwd.uscourts.gov

Counties: Andrews, Crane, Ector, Martin, Midland, Upton.

Indexing & Storage: New cases available in the index immediately after filing date. Records are also indexed on microfiche.

Fee & Payment: Payment may be made by money order, cashier check, personal check. Payee: Clerk, U.S. District Court.

Phone Search: Most information will be released over the phone.

In Person Search: Fee charged if court conducts your in person search for you. For self-serve copies, bring your own change. They will not provide change.

PACER: PACER is available online at http://pacer.txwd.uscourts.gov. Records purged every six months. New records are online after 1 day.

Pecos Division U.S. Courthouse, 410 S Cedar St, Pecos, TX 79772 (courier address: Use mail address for courier delivery) 432-445-4228. www.txwd.uscourts.gov

Counties: Brewster, Culberson, Hudspeth, Jeff Davis, Loving, Pecos, Presidio, Reeves, Ward, Winkler.

Indexing & Storage: New cases available in the index immediately after filing date.

Fee & Payment: Payment may be made by money order, cashier check, personal check. Debtor's checks are not accepted. Payee: Clerk, U.S. District Court.

Phone Search: No searching by telephone.

In Person Search: Fee charged if court conducts your in person search for you.

PACER: PACER is available online at http://pacer.txwd.uscourts.gov. Records purged every six months. New records are online after 1 day.

San Antonio Division U.S. Clerk's Office, 655 E Durango Blvd, Suite G-65, San Antonio, TX 78206 (Use mail address for courier delivery) 210-472-6550. www.txwd.uscourts.gov

Counties: Atascosa, Bandera, Bexar, Comal, Dimmit, Frio, Gonzales, Guadalupe, Karnes, Kendall, Kerr, Medina, Real, Wilson.

Indexing & Storage: New cases available in the index 1-2 days after filing date. Records are also indexed on microfiche.

Fee & Payment: Payment may be made by money order, cashier check, personal check. Payee: Clerk, U.S. District Court.

Phone Search: Only docket information available.

In Person Search: Fee charged if court conducts your in person search for you.

PACER: PACER is available online at http://pacer.txwd.uscourts.gov. Records purged every six months. New records are online after 1 day.

Waco Division Clerk, Room 303, 800 Franklin, Waco, TX 76701 (courier address: Use mail address for courier delivery) 254-750-1501. www.txwd.uscourts.gov

Counties: Bell, Bosque, Coryell, Falls, Freestone, Hamilton, Hill, Leon, Limestone, McLennan, Milam, Robertson, Somervell.

Indexing & Storage: New cases available in the index 1-2 days after filing date.

Fee & Payment: Payment may be made by money order, cashier check, personal check. Payee: Clerk, U.S. District Court.

Phone Search: Only docket information available by phone.

In Person Search: Fee charged if court conducts your in person search for you.

PACER: PACER is available online at http://pacer.txwd.uscourts.gov. Records purged every six months. New records are online after 1 day.

U.S. Bankruptcy Court

Western District of Texas

Austin Division Homer Thornberry Judicial Bldg, 903 San Antonio, Room 322, Austin, TX 78701 (Use mail address for courier delivery) 512-916-5237. www.txwb.uscourts.gov

Counties: Bastrop, Blanco, Burleson, Burnet, Caldwell, Gillespie, Hays, Kimble, Lampasas, Lee, Llano, Mason, McCulloch, San Saba, Travis, Washington, Williamson.

Indexing & Storage: Cases indexed by debtor and creditors as well as by case number. New cases available in the index 24 hours after filing date. Records are also indexed on microfiche.

Fee & Payment: Payment may be made by money order, cashier check, personal check, Visa or Mastercard. Debtor's checks are not accepted. Payee: U.S. Bankruptcy Court.

Phone Search: Only docket information available by phone. Automated voice case information service (VCIS) is available. Call VCIS at 888-436-7477 or 210-472-4023.

In Person Search: Fee charged if court conducts your in person search for you. Xerox copies available in lobby. Fee is $.25 per page plus tax.

PACER: PACER is available online at http://pacer.txwb.uscourts.gov. Records purged every 6-8 months. New civil records are online after 1 day.

Electronic Filing: Electronic filing information online at http://ecf.txwb.uscourts.gov

El Paso Division PO Box 971040, El Paso, TX 79925 (courier: 8515 Lockheed, El Paso, TX 79997-1040), 915-779-7362, Fax: 915-779-5693. www.txwb.uscourts.gov

Counties: El Paso.

Indexing & Storage: Cases indexed by debtor as well as by case number. New cases available in the index 24 hours after filing date. The computer index goes back to 1987. Prior to that there is a card index to 1987 and microfiche up to 1980.

Fee & Payment: Payment may be made by money order, cashier check, personal check. Payee: Clerk, U.S. Bankruptcy Court.

Phone Search: Only docket information available by phone. Automated voice case information service (VCIS) is available. Call VCIS at 888-436-7477 or 210-472-4023.

In Person Search: Fee charged if court conducts your in person search for you.

PACER: PACER is available online at http://pacer.txwb.uscourts.gov. Records purged every 6-8 months. New civil records are online after 1 day.

Electronic Filing: Electronic filing information online at http://ecf.txwb.uscourts.gov

Midland/Odessa Division U.S. Post Office Annex, Room P-163, 100 E Wall St, Midland, TX 79701 (Use mail address for courier delivery) 432-683-1650. www.txwb.uscourts.gov

Counties: Andrews, Brewster, Crane, Culberson, Ector, Hudspeth, Jeff Davis, Loving, Martin, Midland, Pecos, Presidio, Reeves, Upton, Ward, Winkler.

Indexing & Storage: Cases indexed by debtor as well as by case number. New cases available in the index immediately after filing date. Records are also indexed on microfiche. Records from the Pecos Division, which has been closed, have been transferred here.

Fee & Payment: Payment may be made by money order, cashier check, personal check. Payee: Clerk, U.S. Bankruptcy Court.

Phone Search: Only docket information available by phone. Automated voice case information service (VCIS) is available. Call VCIS at 888-436-7477 or 210-472-4023.

In Person Search: Fee charged if court conducts your in person search for you. For self-serve copies, bring your own change. They will not provide change.

PACER: PACER is available online at http://pacer.txwb.uscourts.gov. Records purged

every 6-8 months. New civil records are online after 1 day.

Electronic Filing: Electronic filing information online at http://ecf.txwb.uscourts.gov

San Antonio Division PO Box 1439, San Antonio, TX 78295 (courier address: 615 E Houston St, San Antonio, TX 78205), 210-472-6720, Fax: 210-472-5916. www.txsd.uscourts.gov/

Counties: Atascosa, Bandera, Bexar, Comal, Dimmit, Edwards, Frio, Gonzales, Guadalupe, Karnes, Kendall, Kerr, Kinney, Maverick, Medina, Real, Terrell, Uvalde, Val Verde, Wilson, Zavala.

Indexing & Storage: Cases indexed by debtor as well as by case number. New cases available in the index 24 hours after filing date. District wide searches are available for records within a 10 year span from this division.

Fee & Payment: Payment may be made by cashier check. Business checks are not accepted, American Express, Visa, or Mastercard. Personal checks are not accepted.

Phone Search: Automated voice case information service (VCIS) is available. Call VCIS at 888-436-7477 or 210-472-4023.

In Person Search: Permitted. There is a copy service on site.

PACER: PACER is available online at http://pacer.txwb.uscourts.gov. Records purged every 6-8 months. New civil records are online after 1 day.

Electronic Filing: Electronic filing information online at http://ecf.txwb.uscourts.gov

Waco Division St. Charles Place, Ste. 20, 600 Austin Ave, Waco, TX 76701 (courier address: Use mail address for courier delivery) 254-754-1481, Fax: 254-754-8385. www.txwb.uscourts.gov

Counties: Bell, Bosque, Coryell, Falls, Freestone, Hamilton, Hill, Leon, Limestone, McLennan, Milam, Robertson, Somervell.

Indexing & Storage: Cases indexed by debtor as well as by case number. New cases available in the index 1 day after filing date. Records are also indexed on microfiche.

Fee & Payment: Payment may be made by money order, cashier check, personal check. Payee: Clerk, U.S. Bankruptcy Court.

Phone Search: Only docket information available by phone. Automated voice case information service (VCIS) is available. Call VCIS at 888-436-7477 or 210-472-4023.

In Person Search: Fee charged if court conducts your in person search for you.

PACER: PACER is available online at http://pacer.txwb.uscourts.gov. Records purged every 6-8 months. New civil records are online after 1 day.

Electronic Filing: Electronic filing information online at http://ecf.txwb.uscourts.gov

Texas County Courts

Court	Jurisdiction	No. of Courts	How Organized
District Courts*	General	172	420 Districts
County Constitutional Courts*	Limited	254	254 Counties
County Courts at Law Courts*	Limited	81	81 Counties
Justice of the Peace Courts	By Precinct	835	
Municipal Courts	Municipal	882	
Probate Courts*	Probate	17	10 Counties

* Profiled in this Sourcebook.

Court	CIVIL								
	Tort	Contract	Real Estate	Min. Claim	Max. Claim	Small Claims	Estate	Eviction	Domestic Relations
District Courts*	X	X	X	$200	No Max				X
County Courts*	X	X	X	$200	Varies		X		X
Justice of the Peace Courts	X	X		$0	$5000	$5000		X	
Municipal Courts									
Probate Courts*							X		

Court	CRIMINAL				
	Felony	Misdemeanor	DWI/DUI	Preliminary Hearing	Juvenile
District Courts*	X				X
County Courts*		X	X		X
Justice of the Peace Courts		X		X	
Municipal Courts		X			
Probate Courts*					

ADMINISTRATION   Office of Court Administration, PO Box 12066, Austin, TX, 78711; 512-463-1625, Fax: 512-463-1648. www.courts.state.tx.us

COURT STRUCTURE   The legal court structure for Texas is explained extensively in the "Texas Judicial Annual Report." Generally, Texas District Courts have general civil jurisdiction and exclusive felony jurisdiction, along with typical variations such as contested probate and divorce. As of 01/15/04, four additional District Courts were implemented.

The County Court structure consists of two forms of courts - "Constitutional" and "at Law. " The Constitutional upper cliam limit is $100,000 while the At Law upper limit is $5,000. For civil matters up to $5000, we recommend searchers start at the Constitutional County Court as they, generally, offer a shorter waiting time for cases in urban areas. In some counties the District Court or County Court handles evictions.

District Courts handle felonies. County Courts handle misdemeanors and general civil cases.

We have indicated when a record search is automatically combined for two courts, for example a District and County court or both county courts.

ONLINE ACCESS   Appellate court case information is searchable for free on the Internet from the web site of each appellate court, reached from the web site mentioned above. Court of Criminal Appeals opinions are found at www.cca.courts.state.tx.us. A number of local county courts offer online access to their records, but there is no statewide system of local level court records.

PROBATE COURTS   Probate is handled in Probate Court in the 10 largest counties and in District Courts or County Courts at Law elsewhere. However, the County Clerk is responsible for the records in every county.

Anderson County

District Court PO Box 1159, Palestine, TX 75802-1159; 903-723-7412. Hours: 8AM-Noon, 1-5PM (CST). *Felony, Civil.*

www.co.anderson.tx.us

Note: The court also holds family Cases.

Civil Records: Access: Phone, mail, in person. Both court and visitors may perform in person searches. Search fee: $5.00 per name. Required to search: name, years to search. Civil cases indexed by defendant, plaintiff. Civil records on computer from 1984; prior on card index back to 1946.

Criminal Records: Access: Mail, in person. Both court and visitors may perform in person searches. Search fee: $5.00 per name. Required to search: name, years to search, DOB, SSN. Criminal records on computer from 1984; prior on index.

General Information: Public Access terminal is available. No juvenile or adoption records released. Will not fax results. Copy fee: $1.00 per page. Cert fee: $1.00 per page. Payee: Anderson County District Clerk. Personal checks accepted. Prepayment required. Mial requests require SASE. Mail turnaround time 2 days.

County Court 500 N Church, Palestine, TX 75801; 903-723-7432. Hours: 8AM-5PM (CST). *Misdemeanor, Civil, Probate.*

Civil Records: Access: Mail, in person. Both court and visitors may perform in person searches. Search fee: $5.00 per name. Required to search: name, years to search. Civil cases indexed by defendant, plaintiff. Civil records on computer from 1982, land cases from 1983.

Criminal Records: Access: Mail, in person. Both court and visitors may perform in person searches. Search fee: $5.00 per name. Required to search: name, years to search, DOB. Criminal records on computer from 1969.

General Information: Copy fee: $1.00 per page. Cert fee: $5.00. Payee: County Clerk. Personal checks accepted. Prepayment required. Mial requests require SASE. Mail turnaround time 1 week.

Andrews County

District Court PO Box 328, Andrews, TX 79714; 432-524-1417. Hours: 8AM-5PM (CST). *Felony, Civil.*

Civil Records: Access: Mail, in person. Only the court performs in person searches; visitors may not. Search fee: $5.00 per name. Required to search: name, years to search. Civil cases indexed by defendant, plaintiff. Civil records computerized since 1975.

Criminal Records: Access: Mail, in person. Only the court performs in person searches; visitors may not. Search fee: $5.00 per name. Required to search: name, years to search, DOB; also helpful: SSN. Criminal records computerized since 1975; prior to 1910.

General Information: No juvenile, mental, sealed, terminations or adoption records released. Will not fax results. Copy fee: $1.00 for first page, $.25 each add'l. Cert fee: $2.00. Payee: District Clerk. Personal checks accepted. Prepayment required. Mial requests require SASE. Mail turnaround time 1 day.

County Court PO Box 727, Andrews, TX 79714; 432-524-1426. Hours: 8AM-5PM (CST). *Misdemeanor, Civil, Probate.*

Civil Records: Access: Phone, mail, in person. Both court and visitors may perform in person searches. Search fee: $10.00 per name. Required to search: name, years to search. Civil cases indexed by defendant, plaintiff. Civil records on computer since 1980; prior records in manual index.

Criminal Records: Access: Phone, mail, in person. Both court and visitors may perform in person searches. Search fee: $10.00 per name. Required to search: name, years to search, DOB or SSN; also helpful: sex. Criminal records on computer since 1985; prior records in manual index.

General Information: No juvenile, mental, sealed, or adoption records released. Copy fee: $1.00 per page. Cert fee: $5.00. Payee: F. Wm. Hoermann County Clerk. Personal checks accepted if in state. Prepayment required. Mail turnaround time 1 day.

Angelina County

District Court PO Box 908, Lufkin, TX 75902; 936-634-4312; Fax: 936-634-5915. Hours: 8AM-5PM (CST). *Felony, Civil.*

Civil Records: Access: Mail, in person. Both court and visitors may perform in person searches. Search fee: $5.00 per name. Required to search: name, years to search. Civil cases indexed by defendant, plaintiff. Civil records on computer from 1986, on index books from 1800s. Must state whether search is on plaintiff or defendant.

Criminal Records: Access: Mail, in person. Both court and visitors may perform in person searches. Search fee: $5.00 per name. Required to search: name, years to search, DOB; also helpful: SSN. Criminal records on computer from 1984, on index books from 1800s.

General Information: Public Access terminal is available. No juvenile, mental, sealed, or adoption records released. Will fax results for a $5.00 fee. Copy fee: $1.00 per page. Cert fee: $2.00. Payee: District Clerk. Personal checks not accepted. Prepayment required. Mial requests require SASE. Mail turnaround time 2-3 days.

County Court PO Box 908 (215 E Lufkin Ave), Lufkin, TX 75902; 936-634-8339; Fax: 936-634-8460. Hours: 8AM-5PM (CST). *Misdemeanor, Civil, Probate.*

www.angelinacounty.net

Civil Records: Access: Mail, in person. Both court and visitors may perform in person searches. Search fee: $5.00 per name plus 10-year period. Required to search: name, years to search. Civil cases indexed by defendant, plaintiff. Civil records go back to 1893; computerized records go back to Aug 95.

Criminal Records: Access: Mail, in person. Both court and visitors may perform in person searches. Search fee: $5.00 per name plus 10-year period. Will search back to 1984. Required to search: name, years to search; also helpful: DOB. Criminal records go back to 1893; computerized records go back to 1983.

General Information: No mental or sealed records released. These records are not filed in our office. Will not fax results. Copy fee: $1.00 per page. Cert fee: $5.00. Payee: County Clerk. Business checks accepted. Prepayment required. Mial requests require SASE. Mail turnaround time 1-2 days.

Aransas County

District Court 301 N Live Oak, Rockport, TX 78382; 361-790-0128; Fax: 361-790-5211. Hours: 8AM-5PM (CST). *Felony, Civil.*

Civil Records: Access: Mail, in person. Both court and visitors may perform in person searches. Search fee: $5.00 per name. Required to search: name, years to search. Civil cases indexed by defendant, plaintiff. Civil records in index books from 1800s, computerized since 1999.

Criminal Records: Access: Mail, in person. Both court and visitors may perform in person searches. Search fee: $5.00 per name. Required to search: name, years to search. Criminal records in index books from 1800s, computerized since 1999.

General Information: Public Access terminal is available. No juvenile, mental, sealed, or adoption records released. Copy fee: $1.00 per page. Cert fee: $1.00. Payee: District Clerk. Personal checks accepted. Prepayment required. Mial requests require SASE. Mail turnaround time 1-2 days.

County Court 301 N Live Oak, Rockport, TX 78382; 361-790-0122. Hours: 8AM-4:30PM (CST). *Misdemeanor, Civil, Probate.*

Civil Records: Access: Mail, no fax, because we require the $5.00 search fee before we do the search, (if court does the search), in person. Both court and visitors may perform in person searches. Search fee: $5.00 per name. Required to search: name, years to search. Civil cases indexed by defendant, plaintiff. Civil records in index books from 1947, computerized records go back to 1998.

Criminal Records: Access: Mail, no fax, because we require the $5.00 search fee before we do the search, (if court does the search), in person. Both court and visitors may perform in person searches. Search fee: $5.00 per name. Required to search: name, years to search, DOB. Criminal records in index books from 1947; computerized records go back to 1995.

General Information: Public Access terminal is available. No mental or sealed records released; we do not have juvenile or adoption records in our office. Will fax results to local or toll free line. Copy fee: $1.00 per page. Cert fee: $5.00. Payee: County Clerk. Personal checks accepted. Prepayment required. Mial requests require SASE. Mail turnaround time 2 days.

Archer County

District Court PO Box 815, Archer City, TX 76351; 940-574-4615. Hours: 8:30AM-5PM (CST). *Felony, Civil.*

Civil Records: Access: Mail, in person. Both court and visitors may perform in person searches. Search fee: $5.00 per name. Fee is per index searched. Required to search: name, years to search. Civil cases indexed by defendant, plaintiff. Civil records in index books from 1900s.

Criminal Records: Access: Mail, in person. Both court and visitors may perform in person searches. Search fee: $5.00 per name. Fee is per index searched. Required to search: name, years to search. Criminal records in index books from 1900s.

General Information: No juvenile, mental, sealed, or adoption records released. Will fax results after search fee is received. Copy fee: $1.00 per page. Cert fee: $1.00. Payee: District Clerk. Personal checks accepted. Prepayment required. Mial requests require SASE. Mail turnaround time 2-3 days.

County Court PO Box 427, Archer City, TX 76351; 940-574-4302. Hours: 8:30AM-5PM (CST). *Misdemeanor, Civil, Probate.*

Civil Records: Access: Phone, mail, in person. Both court and visitors may perform in person searches. Search fee: $5.00 per name. Fee is per index searched. Required to search: name, years to search. Civil cases indexed by defendant, plaintiff. Civil records in index books from 1900s.

Criminal Records: Access: Phone, mail, in person. Both court and visitors may perform in person searches. Search fee: $5.00 per name. Fee is per index searched. Required to search: name, years to search. Criminal records in index books from 1900s.

General Information: No juvenile, mental, sealed, or adoption records released. Copy fee: $1.00 per page. Cert fee: $5.00. Payee: County Clerk. Personal checks accepted. Prepayment required. Mial requests require SASE. Mail turnaround time 1 day.

Armstrong County

District & County Court PO Box 309, 100 Trice St., Claude, TX 79019; 806-226-2081; Fax: 806-226-5301. Hours: 8AM-Noon, 1-5PM (CST). *Felony, Misdemeanor, Civil, Probate.*

Civil Records: Access: Mail, in person. Both court and visitors may perform in person searches. Search fee: $5.00 per name. Required to search: name, years to search. Civil cases indexed by defendant, plaintiff. Civil records in index books from 1800s.

Criminal Records: Access: Mail, in person. Both court and visitors may perform in person searches. Search fee: $5.00 per name. Required to search: name, years to search. Criminal records in index books from 1800s; computerized back to 1992.

General Information: No juvenile, mental, sealed, or adoption records released. Copy fee: $1.00 per page. Cert fee: $5.00. Payee: County Clerk. Personal checks accepted. Prepayment required. Mial requests require SASE. Mail turnaround time 1-2 days.

Atascosa County

District Court Courthouse Circle #4-B, Jourdanton, TX 78026; 830-769-3011. Hours: 8AM-Noon, 1-5PM (CST). *Felony, Civil.*

Civil Records: Access: Mail, in person. Both court and visitors may perform in person searches. Search fee: $5.00 per name. Required to search: name, years to search; also helpful: address. Civil cases indexed by defendant, plaintiff. Civil records in index books from 1857.

Criminal Records: Access: Mail, in person. Both court and visitors may perform in person searches. Search fee: $5.00 per name. Required to search: name, years to search; also helpful: DOB, SSN. Criminal records in index books from 1857.

General Information: No juvenile, mental, sealed, or adoption records released. Fee to fax results is $2.00 per page. Copy fee: $1.00 per page. Cert fee: $1.00. Payee: District Clerk. Personal checks accepted. Prepayment required. Mial requests require SASE. Mail turnaround time 6 days.

County Court #1 Courthouse Cirlce, #102, Jourdanton, TX 78026; 830-767-2511. Hours: 8AM-5PM (CST). *Misdemeanor, Civil, Probate.*

Civil Records: Access: Mail, in person. Both court and visitors may perform in person searches. No search fee. Required to search: name, years to search. Civil cases indexed by defendant, plaintiff. Civil records in index books from 1900s; on computer back to 2000.

Criminal Records: Access: In person only. Visitors must perform in person searches for themselves. No search fee. Required to search: name, years to search. Criminal records in index books from 1900s; on computer back to 2000.

General Information: No juvenile, mental, sealed, or adoption records released. Copy fee: $1.00 per page. Cert fee: $5.00. Payee: County Clerk. Personal checks accepted. Prepayment required. Mial requests require SASE. Mail turnaround time same day.

Austin County

District Court 1 E Main, Bellville, TX 77418-1598; 979-865-5911 x121. Hours: 8AM-Noon, 1-5PM (CST). *Felony, Civil.*
www.austincounty.com/dclerk.html
Note: The 155 District web site is www.cvtv.net/~tx155district/.

Civil Records: Access: Mail, in person. Both court and visitors may perform in person searches. Search fee: $5.00 per name. Required to search: name, years to search. Civil cases indexed by defendant, plaintiff. Civil records in index books from 1843; on computer back to 1995.

Criminal Records: Access: Mail, in person. Both court and visitors may perform in person searches. Search fee: $5.00 per name. Required to search: name, years to search; also helpful: DOB, SSN. Criminal records in index books from 1843; on computer back to 1996.

General Information: Public Access terminal is available. No juvenile, mental, sealed, or adoption records released. Fee to fax results is $2.00 per document. Copy fee: $1.00 per page. Cert fee: Included in copy fee, if document complete. Payee: District Clerk. Personal checks accepted. Prepayment required. Mial requests require SASE.

County Court at Law 1 E Main, Bellville, TX 77418; 979-865-5911; Fax: 979-865-0336. Hours: 8AM-5PM (CST). *Misdemeanor, Civil, Probate.*

Civil Records: Access: Mail, in person. Both court and visitors may perform in person searches. Search fee: $5.00 per name. Required to search: name, years to search. Civil cases indexed by defendant, plaintiff. Civil records on computer from 06/95, index books from 1843.

Criminal Records: Access: Mail, in person. Both court and visitors may perform in person searches. Search fee: $5.00 per name. Required to search: name, years to search, DOB; also helpful: SSN. Criminal records on computer from 05/95, index books from 1876.

General Information: Public Access terminal is available. No juvenile, mental, sealed, or adoption records released. Will fax results for $2.00 per page. Copy fee: $1.00 per page. Cert fee: $5.00. Payee: Carrie Gregor, County Clerk. Prepayment required. Mial requests require SASE. Mail turnaround time 2 days.

Bailey County

District Court 300 S 1st St, Muleshoe, TX 79347; 806-272-3165; Fax: 806-272-3124. Hours: 8AM-5PM (CST). *Felony, Civil.*

Civil Records: Access: Phone, mail, fax, in person, online. Both court and visitors may perform in person searches. Search fee: $5.00 per name. Required to search: name, years to search. Civil cases indexed by defendant, plaintiff. Civil records in index books, archived from 1925, computerized back to 1995. Online access is through www.idocket.com; registration and password required. Records go back to 12/31/1995.

Criminal Records: Access: Phone, mail, in person, online. Both court and visitors may perform in person searches. Search fee: $5.00 per name. Required to search: name, years to search. Criminal records in index books, archived from 1925, computerized back to 1995. Online access is through www.idocket.com; registration and password required. Records go back to 12/31/1995.

General Information: No juvenile, mental, sealed, or adoption records released. Will fax results for $1.00 per page. Copy fee: $1.00 per page. Cert fee: $1.00. Payee: District Clerk. Personal checks accepted. Prepayment required. Mial requests require SASE. Mail turnaround time 1 day.

County Court 300 S 1st St, Muleshoe, TX 79347; 806-272-3044; Fax: 806-272-3538. Hours: 8:30AM-N, 1-5PM (CST). *Misdemeanor, Civil, Probate.*

Civil Records: Access: Mail, in person, online. Both court and visitors may perform in person searches. Search fee: $10.00 per name. Required to search: name, years to search. Civil cases indexed by defendant, plaintiff. Civil records in index books, archived from 1925. Online access is through www.idocket.com; registration and password required. Civil records go back to 12/31/1995 and 13/31/96 for probate.

Criminal Records: Access: Mail, in person, online. Both court and visitors may perform in person searches. Search fee: $10.00 per name. Required to search: name, years to search. Criminal records in index books, archived from 1925. Online access is through www.idocket.com; registration and password required. Records go back to 12/31/1996.

General Information: No juvenile, mental, sealed, or adoption records released. Will fax results. Copy fee: $1.00 per page. Cert fee: $5.00. Payee: County Clerk. Personal checks accepted. Prepayment required. Mial requests require SASE. Mail turnaround time 10 days.

Bandera County

District Court PO Box 2688 (500 Main St), Bandera, TX 78003; 830-796-4606; Fax: 830-796-8499. Hours: 7:30AM-4:30PM (CST). *Felony, Civil, Probate.*
www.banderacounty.org/departments/district_clerk.htm

Civil Records: Access: Phone, fax, mail, in person, online. Both court and visitors may perform in person searches. Search fee: $5.00 per name. Required to search: name, years to search; also helpful: address. Civil cases indexed by defendant, plaintiff. Civil records on computer back to 1988, index books from 1857. Civil case information is free online at www.idocket.com. Registration and password required. Free searching is limited. Records go back to 12/31/1990.

Criminal Records: Access: Fax, mail, in person, online. Both court and visitors may perform in person searches. Search fee: $5.00 per name. Required to search: name, years to search, signed release; also helpful: address, DOB, SSN. Criminal records on computer back to 1988, index books from 1857. Felony records access is through www.idocket.com; registration and password required. Records go back to 12/31/1990.

General Information: Public Access terminal is available. No juvenile, mental or sealed records released. Fee to fax results is $2.00 for 1st page, $1.00 each add'l. Copy fee: $1.00 per page certified; non-certified is $1.00 1st pg, $.25 each add'l. Cert fee: $5.00. Payee: Bandera County District Clerk. Personal checks accepted. Prepayment required. Mial requests require SASE. Mail turnaround time 2 days.

County Court PO Box 823 (500 Main St), Bandera, TX 78003; 830-796-3332; Fax: 830-796-8323. Hours: 8AM-4:30PM (CST). *Misdemeanor, Civil, Eviction, Probate.*

Civil Records: Access: Fax, mail, in person. Both court and visitors may perform in person searches. Search fee: $5.00 per name. Required to search: name, years to search; also helpful: address. Civil cases indexed by defendant, plaintiff. Civil records on computer from 1988, index books from 1857.

Criminal Records: Access: Fax, mail, in person. Both court and visitors may perform in person searches. Search fee: $5.00 per name. Required to search: name, years to search, signed release; also helpful: address, DOB, SSN. Criminal records on computer from 1988, index books from 1857.

General Information: No juvenile, mental or sealed records released. Fee to fax results is $2.00 for 1st page, $1.00 each add'l. Copy fee: $1.00 per page. Cert fee: $5.00. Payee: Bandera County Court Clerk. Personal checks accepted. Prepayment required. Mial requests require SASE. Mail turnaround time 2 days.

Bastrop County

District Court PO Box 770, Bastrop, TX 78602; 512-332-7244; Fax: 512-332-7249. Hours: 8AM-5PM (CST). *Felony, Civil.*

Civil Records: Access: Mail, in person, fax. Both court and visitors may perform in person searches.

Search fee: $5.00 per name. Required to search: name, years to search. Civil cases indexed by defendant, plaintiff. Civil records on microfilm from 1986, archived from early 1800s.

Criminal Records: Access: Mail, in person, fax. Both court and visitors may perform in person searches. Search fee: $5.00 per name. Required to search: name, years to search, signed release. Criminal records on computer since 1989; prior on microfilm from 1986, archived from early 1800s.

General Information: Public Access terminal is available. No juvenile, mental, sealed, or adoption records released. Copy fee: $.50 per page. Cert fee: $1.00. Payee: District Clerk. Personal checks accepted. Prepayment required. Mial requests require SASE. Mail turnaround time 1 day.

County Court PO Box 577, Bastrop, TX 78602; 512-332-7234. Hours: 8AM-5:PM (CST). *Misdemeanor, Probate.*

Criminal Records: Access: Phone, mail, in person. Both court and visitors may perform in person searches. Search fee: $5.00 per name. Required to search: name, years to search, DOB, SSN. Criminal records on computer since 1986, prior on index books.

General Information: No juvenile, mental, sealed, or adoption records released. Fee to fax results is $5.00. Copy fee: $1.00 per page. Cert fee: $5.00. Payee: Bastrop County Clerk. Personal checks accepted. Prepayment required. Mial requests require SASE. Mail turnaround time 1-2 days.

Baylor County

District & County Court PO Box 689, Seymour, TX 76380; 940-889-3322. Hours: 8:30AM-5PM (CST). *Felony, Misdemeanor, Civil, Probate.*

Civil Records: Access: Phone, mail, in person. Both court and visitors may perform in person searches. Search fee: $10.00 per name. Required to search: name, years to search. Civil cases indexed by defendant, plaintiff. Civil records in books from 1900s.

Criminal Records: Access: Phone, mail, in person. Both court and visitors may perform in person searches. Search fee: $10.00 per name. Required to search: name, years to search. Criminal records in books from 1900s.

General Information: Public Access terminal is available. No juvenile, mental, sealed, or adoption records released. Will not fax results. Copy fee: $1.00 per page. Cert fee: $2.00 felony, $5.00 misdemeanor for County Court certification. Payee: Baylor County Clerk. Personal checks accepted. Prepayment required. Mial requests require SASE. Mail turnaround time 1-2 days.

Bee County

District Court PO Box 666, Beeville, TX 78104-0666; 361-362-3242; Fax: 361-362-3282. Hours: 8AM-5PM (CST). *Felony, Civil.*

Civil Records: Access: Mail, in person, online. Both court and visitors may perform in person searches. Search fee: $5.00 per name. Required to search: name, years to search. Civil cases indexed by defendant, plaintiff. Civil records on index books from 1856, computerized since 2000. Online access is at www.idocket.com; registration and password required. This is a fee service, unless only one name searched a day. Records may go back to 12/31/1987.

Criminal Records: Access: Mail, in person, online. Both court and visitors may perform in person searches. Search fee: $5.00 per name. Required to search: name, years to search, signed release. Criminal records on index books from 1856, computerized since 2000. Felony record access is at www.idocket.com; registration and password

required. This is a fee service, unless only one name searched a day. Records may go back to 12/31/1987.

General Information: Public Access terminal is available. (Records go back to 2000.) No juvenile, mental, sealed, or adoption records released. Copy fee: $1.00 per page. Cert fee: $2.00. Payee: District Clerk. Personal checks accepted. Prepayment required. Mial requests require SASE. Mail turnaround time 1-3 days.

County Court 105 W Corpus Christi St, Rm 103, Beeville, TX 78102; 361-362-3245; Fax: 361-362-3247. Hours: 8AM-Noon, 1-5PM (CST). *Misdemeanor, Civil, Probate.*

Civil Records: Access: Phone, fax, mail, in person. Both court and visitors may perform in person searches. Search fee: $5.00 per name. Required to search: name, years to search. Civil cases indexed by defendant, plaintiff. Civil records on index books from 1900; computerized since 1995.

Criminal Records: Access: Phone, fax, mail, in person. Both court and visitors may perform in person searches. Search fee: $6.00 per name. Add $5.00 for certificate. Required to search: name, years to search, DOB; also helpful: SSN. Criminal records on index books from 1900; computerized since 1995.

General Information: Public Access terminal is available. No juvenile, mental, sealed, or adoption records released. Fee to fax results is $2.00 per page. Copy fee: $1.00 per page. Cert fee: $5.00. Payee: County Clerk. Personal checks accepted. Prepayment required. Mial requests require SASE. Mail turnaround time 1 day.

Bell County

District Court 104 S Main St, PO Box 909, Belton, TX 76513; 254-933-5197; Civil phone: 254-933-5195; Criminal phone: 254-933-5957; Fax: 254-933-5199. Hours: 8AM-5PM (CST). *Felony, Civil.*
www.bellcountytx.com/districtclerk/index.htm

Civil Records: Access: Mail, in person. Both court and visitors may perform in person searches. Search fee: $5.00 per name. Required to search: name, years to search. Civil cases indexed by defendant, plaintiff. Civil records on computer back to 1987, alpha index from 1982, chrono from 1800.

Criminal Records: Access: Mail, in person. Both court and visitors may perform in person searches. Search fee: $5.00 per name. Required to search: name, years to search, DOB; also helpful, SSN, signed release, cause number. Criminal records on computer back to 1987, alpha index from 1982, chrono from 1800.

General Information: Public Access terminal is available. No juvenile, mental, sealed, or adoption records released. Will fax results. Copy fee: $.50 per page. Cert fee: $1.00 per page. Payee: District Clerk, Bell County. Only cashiers checks and money orders accepted. Prepayment required. Mial requests require SASE. Mail turnaround time 1-2 days.

County Court Bell County Clerk's Office, PO Box 480, Belton, TX 76513; 254-933-5165; Civil phone: 254-933-5174; Criminal phone: 254-933-5170; Fax: 254-933-5176. Hours: 8AM-5PM (CST). *Misdemeanor, Civil, Probate.*

Civil Records: Access: Mail, in person. Both court and visitors may perform in person searches. Search fee: $5.00 per name. Required to search: name, years to search. Civil cases indexed by defendant, plaintiff. Civil records on computer since September, 1989.

Criminal Records: Access: Mail, in person. Both court and visitors may perform in person searches. Search fee: $5.00 per name. Required to search: name, years to search, DOB, SSN. Criminal records on computer since 1986. In person searching closed for lunch hour.

General Information: Public Access terminal is available. No juvenile, mental, sealed, or adoption records released. Copy fee: $1.00 per page. Cert fee: $1.00. Payee: County Clerk. Local checks only. Prepayment required. Mail turnaround time 5 days.

Bexar County

District Court - Central Records 100 Dolorosa, County Courthouse, Chief Court Clerk/Records, San Antonio, TX 78205; 210-335-2113; Civil phone: 210-335-2661; Criminal phone: 210-335-2591. Hours: 8AM-5PM (CST). *Felony, Civil.*
www.co.bexar.tx.us/dclerk

Note: There is a separate court clerk for civil and criminal, and fee for searching in each, though records are centralized.

Civil Records: Access: Mail, fax, online, in person. Both court and visitors may perform in person searches. Search fee: $5.00 per name. Required to search: name, years to search. Civil cases indexed by defendant, plaintiff. Civil records on computer from 1982-present, chrono index from 1909. Access to the remote online system requires $100 setup fee, plus a $25 monthly fee, plus inquiry fees. Call Jennifer Mann at 210-335-0212 for more information. Also, free online access to records is being implemented. Check www.co.bexar.tx.us/dclerk/e-Services/e-services.htm for updates. For fax requests, call court to request form, then submit form with payment with Discover Card.

Criminal Records: Access: Mail, fax, online, in person. Both court and visitors may perform in person searches. Search fee: $5.00 per name. Required to search: name, years to search, signed release, DOB. Criminal records on computer back to 1974, chrono index from 1909. Online access to criminal records is the same as civil. For fax requests, call court to request form, then submit form with payment with Discover Card.

General Information: Public Access terminal is available. No juvenile, mental, sealed, or adoption records released. Fee to fax results is $.50 per page. Copy fee: $.50 per page. Cert fee: $1.00 per page. Payee: District Clerk. Personal checks not accepted. Prepayment required. Mial requests require SASE. Mail turnaround time 5 to 10 days.

County Court - Civil Central Filing Department 100 Dolorosa, San Antonio, TX 78205-3083; 210-335-2231; Criminal phone: 210-335-2238; Probate phone: 210-335-2241. Hours: 8AM-5PM (CST). *Civil.*

Note: There are twelve hearing locations in this county where open cases are held. All closed cases are forwarded here.

Civil Records: Access: Mail, in person. Both court and visitors may perform in person searches. Search fee: $5.00 per name. Fee is for 10 year search. Required to search: name, years to search. Civil cases indexed by defendant, plaintiff. Civil records on computer go back 10 years, index books prior. Open and closed records maintained.

General Information: Public Access terminal is available. No mental, sealed records released. Will not fax results. Copy fee: $1.00 per page. Cert fee: $5.00. Payee: County Clerk. Personal checks accepted. Prepayment required. Mial requests require SASE. Mail turnaround time 5-7 days.

County Court - Criminal 300 Dolorosa, #4101, San Antonio, TX 78205; 210-335-2238; Civil phone: 210-335-2231; Criminal phone: 210-335-2238; Probate phone: 210-335-2241. Hours: 8AM-5PM (CST). *Misdemeanor.*
www.co.bexar.tx.us/dclerk

Criminal Records: Access: Mail, online, in person. Both court and visitors may perform in person searches. Search fee: $6.00 per name. Fee is per ten year period. $1.00 for each add'l year. Required to search: name, years to search, DOB, signed release; also helpful: SSN. Criminal records on computer since 1983, alpha index since 1983, on card index from 1909, records go back to 1899. Access to the criminal online system requires $100 setup fee, plus a $25 monthly fee, plus inquiry fees. Call Jennifer Mann at 210-335-0212 for more information.

General Information: Public Access terminal is available. No sealed records released. Copy fee: $1.00 per page. Cert fee: $5.00 per document. Payee: County Clerk. Personal checks must be in state. Prepayment required. Mail requests: SASE requested. Turnaround time 2-3 days.

Probate Court #2 100 Dolorosa St, Rm 108, San Antonio, TX 78205; 210-335-2241. Hours: 8AM-5PM (CST). *Probate.*
www.co.bexar.tx.us/pcourt/probatecourts.htm

Blanco County

County Court PO Box 65, Johnson City, TX 78636; 830-868-7357. Hours: 8AM-4:30PM (CST). *Misdemeanor, Civil, Probate.*

Civil Records: Access: Mail, in person. Both court and visitors may perform in person searches. Search fee: $5.00 per name. Required to search: name, years to search. Civil cases indexed by defendant, plaintiff. Civil records on computer from 1994, index books back to 1876.

Criminal Records: Access: Mail, in person. Both court and visitors may perform in person searches. Search fee: $5.00 per name. Required to search: name, years to search, DOB, SSN. Criminal records on computer from 1994, index books back to 1876.

General Information: Public Access terminal is available. No juvenile, mental, sealed, or adoption records released. Will fax search results. Copy fee: $1.00 per page. Cert fee: $5.00. Payee: County Clerk. Personal checks accepted. Prepayment required. Mial requests require SASE. Mail turnaround time 1 day.

District Court PO Box 382, Johnson City, TX 78636; 830-868-0973; Fax: 830-868-2084. Hours: 8AM-4:30PM (CST). *Felony, Civil, Probate.*
www.courts.state.tx.us/district/33rd/index.htm

Civil Records: Access: Mail, in person. Both court and visitors may perform in person searches. Search fee: $5.00 per name. Required to search: name, years to search. Civil cases indexed by defendant, plaintiff. Civil records on computer from 1994, index books back to 1876.

Criminal Records: Access: Mail, in person. Both court and visitors may perform in person searches. Search fee: $5.00 per name. Required to search: name, years to search, DOB, SSN. Criminal records on computer from 1994, index books back to 1876.

General Information: No juvenile, mental, sealed, or adoption records released. Copy fee: $1.00 for first per page; $.25 per page thereafter. Cert fee: $1.00. Payee: District Clerk. Personal checks accepted. Prepayment required. Mial requests require SASE. Mail turnaround time 1 day.

Borden County

District & County Court PO Box 124, Gail, TX 79738; 806-756-4312. Hours: 8AM-5PM (CST). *Felony, Misdemeanor, Civil, Probate.*
Civil Records: Access: Mail, in person. Both court and visitors may perform in person searches. Search fee: $5.00 per name. Required to search: name, years to search. Civil cases indexed by defendant, plaintiff. Civil records in index books, archived from 1900.
Criminal Records: Access: Mail, in person. Only the court performs in person searches; visitors may not.

Search fee: $5.00 per name. Required to search: name, years to search. Criminal records in index books, archived from 1900.

General Information: No juvenile, mental, sealed, or adoption records released. Fee to fax results is $1.00 per page. Copy fee: $1.00 per page. Cert fee: $1.00. Payee: District Clerk. Personal checks accepted. Prepayment required. Mial requests require SASE. Mail turnaround time 1 week.

Bosque County

District Court Main & Morgan St, PO Box 674, Meridian, TX 76665; 254-435-2334. Hours: 8AM-5PM (CST). *Felony, Civil.*

Civil Records: Access: Mail, in person. Both court and visitors may perform in person searches. Search fee: $5.00 per name. Required to search: name, years to search. Civil cases indexed by defendant, plaintiff. Civil records on computer from 1984, files/books from 1870s.

Criminal Records: Access: Mail, in person. Both court and visitors may perform in person searches. Search fee: $5.00 per name. Required to search: name, years to search, DOB or SSN. Computerized from 1984, criminal records on books/files from 1856.

General Information: No juvenile, mental, sealed, or adoption records released. Copy fee: $1.00 per page. Cert fee: $1.00. Payee: District Clerk. Personal checks accepted. Prepayment required. Mial requests require SASE. Mail turnaround time 1 day.

County Court PO Box 617, Meridian, TX 76665; 254-435-2201; Fax: 254-435-2152. Hours: 8AM-5PM (CST). *Misdemeanor, Civil, Probate.*

Civil Records: Access: Mail, in person. Both court and visitors may perform in person searches. Search fee: $5.00 per name. Required to search: name, years to search. Civil cases indexed by defendant, plaintiff. Civil records in index books from 1854; on computer back to 1997.

Criminal Records: Access: Mail, in person. Both court and visitors may perform in person searches. Search fee: $5.00 per name. Required to search: name, years to search, DOB, SSN. Criminal records in index books from 1854; on computer back to 1997.

General Information: Public Access terminal is available. (Civil only.) No juvenile, mental, sealed, or adoption records released. Copy fee: $1.00 per page. Cert fee: $5.00. Payee: County Clerk. In state personal checks accepted. Prepayment required. Mial requests require SASE. Mail turnaround time 1-2 days.

Bowie County

District & County Court at Law 710 James Bowie Dr, PO Box 248, New Boston, TX 75570; 903-628-6750; Probate phone: 903-628-6740. Hours: 8AM-5PM (CST). *Felony, Misdemeanor, Civil, Probate.*
www.co.bowie.tx.us/
Note: Probate records are at this address in the County Clerk's office.

Civil Records: Access: Mail, in person. Both court and visitors may perform in person searches. Search fee: $5.00 per name. Required to search: name, years to search. Civil cases indexed by defendant, plaintiff. Civil records on computer from 1978, on microfiche from 1900s, chrono index from 1800s.

Criminal Records: Access: Mail, in person. Both court and visitors may perform in person searches. Search fee: $5.00 per name. Required to search: name, years to search, DOB. Criminal records on computer from 1978, on microfiche from 1900s, chrono index from 1800s.

General Information: No juvenile, mental, sealed, or adoption records released. Will fax results for $5.00 per doc. Copy fee: $1.00 per page. Cert fee: $1.00. Payee: District Clerk. Personal checks accepted.

Prepayment required. Mial requests require SASE. Mail turnaround time 1 day.

Brazoria County

District Court 111 E Locus #500, Angleton, TX 77515-4678; 979-864-1316. Hours: 8AM-5PM (CST). *Felony, Civil.*
www.brazoria-county.com/dclerk

Civil Records: Access: Phone, mail, in person. Search fee: $5.00 per name. Fee is per 10 year period. Required to search: name, years to search. Civil cases indexed by defendant, plaintiff. Civil records on computer from 1986, index chrono from 1900, prior alpha.

Criminal Records: Access: Phone, mail, in person. Both court and visitors may perform in person searches. Search fee: $5.00 per name. Fee is per 10 year period. Required to search: name, years to search, DOB, signed release; also helpful: SSN. Criminal records on computer from 1986, index chrono from 1900, prior alpha.

General Information: Public Access terminal is available. No juvenile, mental, sealed, or adoption records released. Will fax results for $10.00 per document. Copy fee: $1.00 per page. Cert fee: $1.00. Payee: District Clerk. Only cashiers checks and money orders accepted. Prepayment required. Mial requests require SASE. Mail turnaround time up to 1 week.

County Court 111 E Locust #200, Angleton, TX 77515; Civil phone: 979-864-1385; Criminal phone: 979-864-1380; Fax: 979-848-1031 (civil); -1020 (Crim.). Hours: 8AM-5PM (CST). *Misdemeanor, Civil.*
www.brazoria-county.com

Civil Records: Access: Fax, mail, in person. Both court and visitors may perform in person searches. Search fee: $5.00 per name. Required to search: name, years to search. Civil cases indexed by defendant, plaintiff. Civil records on computer from 1984; prior on books or microfiche back to 1800s. Fee must be prepaid before faxing search request.

Criminal Records: Access: Fax, mail, in person. Both court and visitors may perform in person searches. Search fee: $5.00 per name. Required to search: name, years to search, DOB. Criminal records on computer from 1984; prior on books or microfiche back to 1800s.

General Information: Public Access terminal is available. No juvenile, mental, sealed records released. Copy fee: $1.00 per page. Cert fee: $5.00 per document. Payee: Joyce Hudman, County Clerk. Personal checks accepted. Prepayment required. Mial requests require SASE. Mail turnaround time 2 days.

Probate Court 111 E Locust #200, Angleton, TX 77515; 979-864-1367; Fax: 979-864-1031. Hours: 8AM-5PM (CST). *Probate.*

Brazos County

District Court 300 E 26th St #216 (PO Box 2208), Bryan, TX 77806; 979-361-4230; Fax: 979-361-0197. Hours: 8AM-5PM (CST). *Felony, Civil.*
www.co.brazos.tx.us/disclerk

Civil Records: Access: Mail, in person. Both court and visitors may perform in person searches. Search fee: $5.00 per name. Required to search: name, years to search. Civil cases indexed by defendant, plaintiff. Civil records on computer, index chrono from 1800s.

Criminal Records: Access: Mail, in person. Both court and visitors may perform in person searches. Search fee: $5.00 per name. Required to search: name, years to search; also helpful: DOB, SSN. Criminal records on computer, index chrono from 1800s.

General Information: No juvenile, mental, sealed, or adoption records released. Will fax results to toll free number. Copy fee: $.50 per page. Cert fee: $1.00 per page. Payee: District Clerk. Personal checks accepted. Prepayment required. Mial requests require SASE. Mail turnaround time 1-2 days.

County Court 300 E 26th St #120, Bryan, TX 77803; 979-361-4128. Hours: 8AM-5PM (CST). *Misdemeanor, Civil under $500, Probate.*
Note: County Clerk holds misdemeanor records prior to 1986 only. Newer cases are filed at the District Clerks Office.

Civil Records: Access: Mail, in person. Both court and visitors may perform in person searches. Search fee: $5.00 per name. Required to search: name, years to search. Civil cases indexed by defendant, plaintiff. Civil records on computer from 1986, index chrono from 1958.

Criminal Records: Access: Mail, in person. Both court and visitors may perform in person searches. Search fee: $5.00 per name. Required to search: name, years to search, DOB. Criminal records on computer from 1986, index chrono from 1958.

General Information: Public Access terminal is available. No juvenile, mental, sealed, or adoption records released. Copy fee: $1.00 per page. Cert fee: $5.00. Payee: County Clerk or District Clerk. Only cashiers checks and money orders accepted. Prepayment required. Mial requests require SASE. Mail turnaround time 2-3 days.

Brewster County

District Court PO Box 1024, Alpine, TX 79831; 432-837-6216; Fax: 432-837-6217. Hours: 9AM-12, 1-5PM (CST). *Felony, Civil.*

Civil Records: Access: Phone, fax, mail, in person. Both court and visitors may perform in person searches. Search fee: $8.00. Required to search: name; also helpful: years to search. Civil cases indexed by defendant, plaintiff. Civil records are computerized since 1994, indexed from 1899.

Criminal Records: Access: Phone, fax, mail, in person. Both court and visitors may perform in person searches. Search fee: $8.00. Required to search: name, DOB; also helpful: years to search. Criminal records are computerized since 1994, indexed from 1899.

General Information: No fee to fax results to local number. Copy fee: $1.00 per page. Cert fee: $5.00. Payee: District Clerk. Personal checks accepted. Prepayment required. Mail turnaround time 1-2 days.

County Court PO Box 119 (201 W Ave. E), Alpine, TX 79831; 432-837-3366; Fax: 432-837-6217. Hours: 9AM-5PM (CST). *Misdemeanor, Civil Probate.*

Civil Records: Access: Mail, fax, in person. Both court and visitors may perform in person searches. Search fee: $10.00 per name. Required to search: name, years to search. Civil cases indexed by defendant, plaintiff. Civil records in index books from 1950s; computerized since 1995.

Criminal Records: Access: Mail, fax, in person. Both court and visitors may perform in person searches. Search fee: $10.00 per name. Required to search: name, years to search, DOB, signed release; also helpful: SSN. Criminal records in index books from 1920s, computerized since 1994.

General Information: Public Access terminal is available. No juvenile, mental, sealed, or adoption records released. Fee to fax results is $2.00 per page. Copy fee: $1.00 per page. Cert fee: $5.00. Payee: County Clerk. Personal checks accepted. Prepayment required. Mial requests require SASE. Mail turnaround time 1 week.

Briscoe County

District & County Court PO Box 555, Silverton, TX 79257; 806-823-2134; Fax: 806-823-2359. Hours: 8AM-5PM (CST). *Felony, Misdemeanor, Civil, Probate.*

Civil Records: Access: Fax, mail, in person. Both court and visitors may perform in person searches. Search fee: $5.00 per name. Required to search: name, years to search. Civil cases indexed by defendant, plaintiff. Civil records in index books from 1892.

Criminal Records: Access: Fax, mail, in person. Both court and visitors may perform in person searches. Search fee: $5.00 per name. Required to search: name, years to search, DOB. Criminal records in index books from 1892.

General Information: No juvenile, mental, sealed, or adoption records released. Will fax results for $5.00 per name, if copy of check faxed first. Copy fee: $1.00 per page. Cert fee: $5.00. Payee: District or County Clerk. Personal checks accepted. Prepayment required. Mial requests require SASE. Mail turnaround time 1 day.

Brooks County

District Court PO Box 534, Falfurrias, TX 78355; 361-325-5604; Fax: 361-325-5679. Hours: 8AM-5PM (CST). *Felony, Civil.*
www.brooks-county.com

Civil Records: Access: Phone, fax, mail, online, in person. Both court and visitors may perform in person searches. Search fee: $5.00 per name. Required to search: name, years to search; also helpful: address. Civil cases indexed by defendant, plaintiff. Civil records on computer back to 1992, index books since 1920. Civil case information is online at www.idocket.com. Free searching is limited. Records go back to 12/31/1993.

Criminal Records: Access: Phone, fax, mail, online, in person. Both court and visitors may perform in person searches. Search fee: $5.00 per name. Required to search: name, years to search, DOB, SSN; also helpful: address. Criminal records on computer back to 1992, index books since 1920, microfiche since 1939. Criminal records access is through www.idocket.com; registration and password required. Records go back to 12/31/1993.

General Information: No juvenile, mental, sealed, or adoption records released. Fee to fax results is $1.00 per page. Copy fee: $1.00 per page. Cert fee: $2.00. Payee: District Clerk. Business checks accepted. Prepayment required. Mial requests require SASE. Mail turnaround time 1 week.

County Court PO Box 427, Falfurrias, TX 78355; 361-325-5604 X245,246,248. Hours: 8AM-5PM (CST). *Misdemeanor, Civil, Probate.*

Civil Records: Access: Phone, fax, mail, in person. Both court and visitors may perform in person searches. Search fee: $10.00 per name. Required to search: name, years to search. Civil cases indexed by plaintiff. Civil records in index books since 1911.

Criminal Records: Access: Phone, fax, mail, in person. Both court and visitors may perform in person searches. Search fee: $10.00 per name. Required to search: name, years to search, DOB. Criminal records in index books since 1911.

General Information: No juvenile, mental, sealed, or adoption records released. Will fax results $5.00 1st page, $2.00 each add'l. Copy fee: $1.00 per page. Cert fee: $5.00. Payee: County Clerk. Personal checks accepted. Prepayment required. Mial requests require SASE. Mail turnaround time 1-2 days.

Brown County

District Court 200 S Broadway, Brownwood, TX 76801; 325-646-5514. Hours: 8AM-5PM (CST). *Felony, Civil.*

Civil Records: Access: Mail, in person. Both court and visitors may perform in person searches. Search fee: $5.00 per name. Required to search: name, years to search. Civil cases indexed by defendant, plaintiff. Civil records on computer since 1995; prior records on books to 1930s.

Criminal Records: Access: Mail, in person, phone. Both court and visitors may perform in person searches. Search fee: $5.00 per name. Required to search: name, years to search. Criminal records on computer since 1995; prior records on books to 1930s.

General Information: Public Access terminal is available. No juvenile, mental, sealed, or adoption records released. Will not fax results. Copy fee: $1.00 per page. Cert fee: $1.00 per page. Payee: District Clerk. Business checks accepted. Prepayment required. Mial requests require SASE. Mail turnaround time 2-3 days.

County Court 200 S Broadway, Brownwood, TX 76801; 325-643-2594. Hours: 8:30AM-5PM (CST). *Misdemeanor, Civil, Probate.*

Civil Records: Access: Mail, in person. Both court and visitors may perform in person searches. Search fee: $5.00 per name. Required to search: name, years to search. Civil cases indexed by defendant, plaintiff. Civil records on computer from 1988 on microfiche from 1900s.

Criminal Records: Access: Mail, in person. Both court and visitors may perform in person searches. Search fee: $5.00 per name. Required to search: name, years to search; also helpful: DOB, SSN. Criminal records on computer from 1988, on microfiche from 1900s.

General Information: Public Access terminal is available. No juvenile, mental, sealed records released. Copy fee: $1.00 per page. Cert fee: $5.00. Payee: Brown County Clerk. Personal checks accepted. Prepayment required. Mial requests require SASE. Mail turnaround time 1-2 days.

Burleson County

District Court 100 W Buck #303, Caldwell, TX 77836; 979-567-2336. Hours: 8AM-12, 1-5PM (CST). *Felony, Civil.*

Civil Records: Access: Mail, in person. Both court and visitors may perform in person searches. Search fee: $5.00 per name. Required to search: name, years to search. Civil cases indexed by defendant, plaintiff. Civil records on microfilm from 1980, index books prior.

Criminal Records: Access: Mail, in person. Both court and visitors may perform in person searches. Search fee: $5.00 per name. Required to search: name, years to search. Criminal records on microfilm from 1980, index books prior.

General Information: No juvenile, mental, sealed, or adoption records released. Will fax to toll-free number. Copy fee: $1.00 per page. Cert fee: $1.00 per page. Payee: District Clerk. Personal checks accepted. Prepayment required. Mail requests: SASE or toll-free phone number required. Mail turnaround time 1-2 days.

County Court 100 W Buck, #203, Caldwell, TX 77836; 979-567-2329; Fax: 979-567-2376. Hours: 8AM-5PM (CST). *Misdemeanor, Civil, Probate.*

Civil Records: Access: Phone, mail, fax, in person. Visitors must perform in person searches for themselves. No search fee. Required to search: name, years to search. Civil cases indexed by defendant, plaintiff. Civil records indexed to 1900, records archived to 1900s.

Criminal Records: Access: Mail, fax, in person. Visitors must perform in person searches for themselves. No search fee. Required to search: name, years to search, DOB, SSN. Criminal records indexed to 1900, records archived to 1900s.

General Information: No juvenile, mental, or sealed records released. Fee to fax results is $1.00 per page. Copy fee: $1.00 per page. Cert fee: $5.00. Payee: County Clerk. Personal checks accepted. Prepayment required. Mial requests require SASE. Mail turnaround time 2-4 days.

Burnet County

District Court 1701 E Polk St #90, Burnet, TX 78611; 512-756-5450. Hours: 8AM-5PM (CST). *Felony, Civil.*
www.courts.state.tx.us/district/33rd/index.htm
Civil Records: Access: Mail, in person. Both court and visitors may perform in person searches. Search fee: $5.00 per name. Required to search: name, years to search. Civil cases indexed by defendant, plaintiff. Civil records on computer from 1991, index books from 1856.
Criminal Records: Access: Mail, in person. Both court and visitors may perform in person searches. Search fee: $5.00 per name. Required to search: name, years to search; also helpful: DOB, SSN. Criminal records on computer from 1988, index book from 1856.
General Information: Public Access terminal is available. No juvenile, mental, sealed, or adoption records released. Will fax results for $2.00 per page. Copy fee: $1.00 per page. Cert fee: $2.00. Payee: District Clerk. Personal checks accepted. Prepayment required. Mial requests require SASE. Mail turnaround time 2 days.

County Court 220 S Pierce, Burnet, TX 78611; 512-756-5403; Fax: 512-756-5410. Hours: 8AM-5PM (CST). *Misdemeanor, Civil, Probate.*
Civil Records: Access: Fax, mail, in person. Both court and visitors may perform in person searches. Search fee: $10.00 per name. Required to search: name, years to search. Civil cases indexed by defendant, plaintiff. Civil records on computer from 1989, on microfiche from 1852.
Criminal Records: Access: Fax, mail, in person. Both court and visitors may perform in person searches. Search fee: $10.00 per name. Required to search: name, years to search, offense, date of offense. Criminal records on computer from 1989, on microfiche from 1852.
General Information: Public Access terminal is available. No juvenile, mental, sealed, or adoption records released. Will fax results $1.00 per page. Copy fee: $1.00 per page. Cert fee: $5.00. Payee: County Clerk. Personal checks accepted. Prepayment required. Mial requests require SASE. Mail turnaround time 2 days.

Caldwell County

District Court 201 E San Antonio St, Lockhart, TX 78644; 512-398-1806. Hours: 8:30AM-Noon, 1-5PM (CST). *Felony, Civil.*
Civil Records: Access: Phone, fax, mail, in person. Both court and visitors may perform in person searches. Search fee: $5.00 per name. Required to search: name, years to search. Civil cases indexed by defendant, plaintiff. Civil records on computer since 1988, index books from 1846.
Criminal Records: Access: Phone, fax, mail, in person. Both court and visitors may perform in person searches. Search fee: $5.00 per name. Required to search: name, years to search; also helpful: DOB, SSN. Criminal records on computer since 1988, index books from 1846.

General Information: Public Access terminal is available. No juvenile, mental, sealed, or adoption records released. Will fax results to local or toll free line. Copy fee: $.50 per page. Cert fee: $1.00. Payee: District Clerk. Personal checks accepted. Prepayment required. Mial requests require SASE. Mail turnaround time 1-3 days.

County Court PO Box 906, Lockhart, TX 78644; 512-398-1804. Hours: 8:30AM-Noon, 1-5PM (CST). *Misdemeanor, Civil, Probate.*
Civil Records: Access: Mail, in person. Both court and visitors may perform in person searches. Search fee: $5.00 per name. Required to search: name, years to search. Civil cases indexed by defendant, plaintiff. Civil records in index books since 1967.
Criminal Records: Access: Mail, in person. Both court and visitors may perform in person searches. Search fee: $5.00 per name. Required to search: name, years to search, DOB, offense, date of offense. Criminal records in index books since 1967.
General Information: No juvenile, mental, sealed, or adoption records released. Copy fee: $1.00 per page. Cert fee: $5.00. Payee: Caldwell County Clerk. Personal checks accepted. Prepayment required. Mail turnaround time 2-4 days.

Calhoun County

District Court PO Box 658 (c/o District Clerk), Port Lavaca, TX 77979; 361-553-8698. Hours: 8AM-5PM (CST). *Felony, Civil.*
Civil Records: Access: Mail, in person. Both court and visitors may perform in person searches. Search fee: $5.00 per name. Required to search: name, years to search. Civil cases indexed by defendant, plaintiff. Civil records in index books from 1852.
Criminal Records: Access: Mail, in person. Both court and visitors may perform in person searches. Search fee: $5.00 per name. Required to search: name, years to search, signed release; also helpful: DOB. Criminal records in index books from 1852.
General Information: No juvenile, mental, sealed, or adoption records released. Copy fee: $1.00 per page. Cert fee: $1.00. Payee: District Clerk. Personal checks accepted. Prepayment required. Mial requests require SASE. Mail turnaround time 1 day.

County Court 211 S Ann, Port Lavaca, TX 77979; 361-553-4411; Fax: 361-553-4420. Hours: 8AM-5PM (CST). *Misdemeanor, Civil, Probate.*
Note: Established 11/1986.
Civil Records: Access: Phone, mail, in person. Both court and visitors may perform in person searches. Search fee: $5.00 per name. Required to search: name, years to search. Civil cases indexed by defendant, plaintiff. Civil records in index books from 11/1986; indexed on computer back to 2000.
Criminal Records: Access: Phone, mail, in person. Both court and visitors may perform in person searches. Search fee: $5.00 per name. Required to search: name, years to search. Criminal records in index books from 11/1986; indexed on computer back to 1993.
General Information: Public Access terminal is available. No juvenile, mental, sealed, or adoption records released. Copy fee: $1.00 per page. Cert fee: $5.00. Payee: County Clerk. Personal checks accepted. Prepayment required. Mial requests require SASE. Mail turnaround time 1-2 days.

Callahan County

District Court 100 W 4th St #300, Baird, TX 79504-5396; 325-854-1800. Hours: 8AM-5PM (CST). *Felony, Civil.*
Civil Records: Access: Mail. Both court and visitors may perform in person searches. Search fee: $5.00 per name. Required to search: name, years

to search. Civil cases indexed by defendant, plaintiff. Civil records in index books since 1879.
Criminal Records: Access: Mail, in person. Both court and visitors may perform in person searches. Search fee: $5.00 per name. Required to search: name, years to search. Criminal records in index books since 1879.
General Information: No juvenile, mental, sealed, or adoption records released. Copy fee: $1.00 per page. Cert fee: $1.00. Payee: District Clerk. Personal checks accepted. Prepayment required. Mial requests require SASE. Mail turnaround time 1-2 days.

County Court 100 W 4th St, #104, Baird, TX 79504-5300; 325-854-1217; Fax: 325-854-1227. Hours: 8AM-5PM (CST). *Misdemeanor, Civil, Probate.*
Civil Records: Access: Mail, in person. Both court and visitors may perform in person searches. Search fee: $6.00 per name. Required to search: name, years to search. Civil cases indexed by defendant, plaintiff. Civil records go back to 1877; computerized records go back to 1992.
Criminal Records: Access: Phone, fax, mail, in person. Both court and visitors may perform in person searches. Search fee: $6.00 per name. Required to search: name, years to search. Criminal records go back to 1877; computerized records go to 1992.
General Information: Public Access terminal is available. No juvenile, mental, sealed, or adoption records released. Fee to fax results is $1.50 per page. Copy fee: $1.00 per page. Cert fee: $5.00. Payee: Jeanie Bohannon, County Clerk. Personal checks accepted. Prepayment required. Mial requests require SASE. Mail turnaround time 1 day.

Cameron County

District Court 974 E Harrison St, Brownsville, TX 78520; 956-544-0839. Hours: 8Am-5PM (CST). *Felony, Civil.*
Civil Records: Access: Mail, online, in person. Both court and visitors may perform in person searches. Search fee: $5.00 per name. Required to search: name, years to search. Civil cases indexed by defendant, plaintiff. Civil records on computer from 1989. Online access is at www.idocket.com; registration and password required. This is a fee service, unless only one name search a day. Records may go back to 12/31/1988.
Criminal Records: Access: Mail, in person, online. Only the court performs in person searches; visitors may not. Search fee: $5.00 per name. Required to search: name, years to search, DOB, SSN, signed release, offense. Criminal records on computer since 1987. Felony records access is at www.idocket.com; registration and password required. This is a fee service, unless only one name search a day. Records may go back to 12/31/1988.
General Information: Public Access terminal is available. (Civil only.) No juvenile, mental, sealed, or adoption records released. Copy fee: $1.00 per page. No cert fee. Payee: Cameron County District Clerk. Personal checks accepted. Prepayment required. Mial requests require SASE. Mail turnaround time 1 week. On cases prior to 1990 turnaround can be more than 1 week.

County Court No. 1, 2 & 3 PO Box 2178, Brownsville, TX 78522-2178; Civil phone: 956-544-0867; Criminal phone: 956-544-0848; Probate phone: 956-544-0867; Fax: 956-544-0894. Hours: 8AM-5PM (CST). *Misdemeanor, Civil, Probate.*
www.co.cameron.tx.us
Civil Records: Access: Mail, in person. Both court and visitors may perform in person searches. Search fee: $5.00 per name. Required to search: name, years to search. Civil cases indexed by defendant, plaintiff.

Civil records on optical imaging since 1994, on computer from 1987, index books from 1912.

Criminal Records: Access: Mail, in person. Both court and visitors may perform in person searches. Search fee: $5.00 per name. Required to search: name, years to search, DOB. Criminal records on optical imaging since 1994, on computer from 1987, index books from 1912.

General Information: Public Access terminal is available. No juvenile, mental, sealed, or adoption records released. Will fax results $4.25 1st page, $2.25 each add'l. All fees must be prepaid. Copy fee: $1.00 per page. Cert fee: $5.00 per document. Payee: Joe G Rivera, County Clerk. Personal checks not accepted. Prepayment required. Mial requests require SASE. Mail turnaround time 1-2 days.

Camp County

District Court 126 Church St Rm 203, Pittsburg, TX 75686; 903-856-3221; Fax: 903-856-0560. Hours: 8AM-5PM (CST). *Felony, Civil.*

Civil Records: Access: Mail, fax, in person. Both court and visitors may perform in person searches. Search fee: $5.00 per name. Required to search: name, years to search. Civil cases indexed by defendant, plaintiff. Civil records in index books from 1874; computerized since 1995.

Criminal Records: Access: Mail, in person. Both court and visitors may perform in person searches. Search fee: $5.00 per name. Required to search: name, years to search, signed release. Criminal records in index books from 1874; computerized since 1993.

General Information: No juvenile, mental, sealed, or adoption records released. Fee to fax results is $.25 per page. Copy fee: $.50 per page. Cert fee: $2.00 for 1st page, $.25 each add'l. Payee: District Clerk. Personal checks accepted. Prepayment required. Mial requests require SASE. Mail turnaround time 1 week.

County Court 126 Church St Rm 102, Pittsburg, TX 75686; 903-856-2731; Fax: 903-856-2309. Hours: 8AM-Noon, 1-5PM (CST). *Misdemeanor, Civil, Probate.*

Civil Records: Access: Fax, mail, in person. Both court and visitors may perform in person searches. Search fee: $10.00 per name. Required to search: name, years to search. Civil cases indexed by defendant, plaintiff. Civil records in index books from 1960; computerized since 1999. Fax access is only allowed with prepayment of fees.

Criminal Records: Access: Fax, mail, in person. Both court and visitors may perform in person searches. Search fee: $10.00 per name. Required to search: name, years to search, signed release, offense. Criminal records in index books from 1960; computerized since 1999.

General Information: No juvenile, mental, sealed, or adoption records released. Copy fee: $1.00 per page. Cert fee: $5.00 plus $1.00 per page. Payee: Camp County Clerk. Personal checks accepted. Prepayment required. Mial requests require SASE. Mail turnaround time 1 day.

Carson County

District & County Court PO Box 487, Panhandle, TX 79068; 806-537-3623; Fax: 806-537-3623. Hours: 8AM-Noon, 1-5PM (CST). *Felony, Misdemeanor, Civil, Probate.*

Civil Records: Access: Mail, fax, in person. Both court and visitors may perform in person searches. Search fee: $5.00 per name. Required to search: name, years to search. Civil cases indexed by defendant, plaintiff. Civil records on computer from 1981, index books from 1800s.

Criminal Records: Access: Mail, fax, in person. Both court and visitors may perform in person

searches. Search fee: $5.00 per name. Required to search: name, years to search. Criminal records on computer from 1981, index books from 1800s.

General Information: Public Access terminal is available. No juvenile, mental, sealed, or adoption records released. Will fax results if fees have been paid. Copy fee: $1.00 per page. Cert fee: $5.00 per page. Payee: Carson County Clerk. Personal checks accepted. Prepayment required. Mial requests require SASE. Mail turnaround time 1 day.

Cass County

District Court PO Box 510, Linden, TX 75563; 903-756-7514. Hours: 8AM-5PM (CST). *Felony, Civil.*

Civil Records: Access: Mail, in person. Both court and visitors may perform in person searches. Search fee: $5.00 per name. Required to search: name, years to search. Civil cases indexed by defendant, plaintiff. Civil records on computer from 1968, index books from 1900s.

Criminal Records: Access: Mail, in person. Both court and visitors may perform in person searches. Search fee: $5.00 per name. Required to search: name, years to search. Criminal records on computer from 1968, index books from 1900s.

General Information: Public Access terminal is available. No juvenile, mental, sealed, or adoption records released. Fee to fax results is $.25 per minute; minimum $3.00. Copy fee: $1.00 per page. Cert fee: $1.00 per page. Payee: District Clerk. Personal checks accepted. Prepayment required. Mial requests require SASE. Mail turnaround time 1 day.

County Court PO Box 449, Linden, TX 75563; 903-756-5071. Hours: 8AM-5PM (CST). *Misdemeanor, Probate.*

Criminal Records: Access: Mail, in person. Both court and visitors may perform in person searches. Search fee: $10.00 per name. Required to search: name, years to search. Criminal records in index books from 1983, computerized since 1999.

General Information: No juvenile, mental, sealed, or adoption records released. Copy fee: $1.00 per page. Cert fee: $5.00 plus $1.00 per page. Payee: County Clerk. Money order or cashiers check accepted. Prepayment required. Mial requests require SASE. Mail turnaround time 1 day.

Castro County

District & County Court 100 E Bedford, Rm 101, Dimmitt, TX 79027; 806-647-3338. Hours: 8AM-5PM (CST). *Felony, Misdemeanor, Civil, Probate.*

www.242ndcourt.com

Civil Records: Access: Mail, in person. Both court and visitors may perform in person searches. No search fee. Required to search: name, years to search. Civil cases indexed by defendant, plaintiff. Civil records in index books.

Criminal Records: Access: Mail, in person. Both court and visitors may perform in person searches. Search fee: $5.00 per name. Required to search: name, years to search; also helpful: DOB, SSN. Criminal records in index books; computerized records since 2000.

General Information: No juvenile, mental, sealed, or adoption records released. Copy fee: $1.00 per page. Cert fee: $5.00 (county) per document, $1.00 (district) per page. Payee: County or District Court Clerk. Personal checks accepted. Prepayment required. Mial requests require SASE. Mail turnaround time 1 day.

Chambers County

District Clerk Drawer NN, Anahuac, TX 77514; 409-267-8276. Hours: 8AM-Noon, 1-5PM (CST). *Felony, Civil.*

Civil Records: Access: Mail, in person. Both court and visitors may perform in person searches. Search fee: $5.00 per name. Required to search: name, years to search. Civil cases indexed by defendant, plaintiff. Civil records on computer back to 1800s.

Criminal Records: Access: Mail, in person. Both court and visitors may perform in person searches. Search fee: $5.00 per name. Required to search: name, years to search, DOB, SNN. Criminal records on computer back to 1940s.

General Information: No juvenile, mental, sealed, or adoption records released. Copy fee: $1.00 per page. Cert fee: $5.00. Payee: R B Scherer Jr, District Clerk. Personal checks accepted. Prepayment required. Mial requests require SASE. Mail turnaround time 1 day.

County Court PO Box 728, Anahuac, TX 77514; 409-267-8315; Fax: 409-267-4453. Hours: 8AM-5PM (CST). *Misdemeanor, Civil, Probate.*

www.co.chambers.tx.us

Civil Records: Access: Mail, in person. Both court and visitors may perform in person searches. Search fee: $5.00 per name. Required to search: name, years to search; also helpful: address. Civil cases indexed by defendant, plaintiff. Civil records on computer from 2000, index books in office from 1905.

Criminal Records: Access: Mail, in person. Both court and visitors may perform in person searches. Search fee: $5.00 per name. Required to search: name, years to search, DOB, offense; also helpful: address. Criminal records on computer from 2000, index books in office from 1905.

General Information: No juvenile or mental records released. Will fax results for $1.00 per page plus copy charge -local; fee of $1.50 per page -long distance plus copy charge. Copy fee: $1.00 per page. Cert fee: $5.00. Payee: Chambers County Clerk. Personal checks accepted. Prepayment required. Mial requests require SASE. Mail turnaround time 2-3 days.

Cherokee County

District Court Drawer C, Rusk, TX 75785; 903-683-6908 clerk; Civil phone: 903-683-5945/5883; Criminal phone: 903-683-4533. Hours: 8AM-Noon, 1-5PM (CST). *Felony, Civil.*

Civil Records: Access: Mail, fax, in person. Both court and visitors may perform in person searches. Search fee: $5.00 per name. Required to search: name, years to search. Civil cases indexed by defendant, plaintiff. Civil records on computer from 1992, index books from 1848.

Criminal Records: Access: Mail, fax, in person. Both court and visitors may perform in person searches. Search fee: $5.00 per name. Required to search: name, years to search. Criminal records on computer from 1992, index books from 1848.

General Information: Public Access terminal is available. No juvenile, mental, sealed, or adoption records released. Will not fax results. Copy fee: $.50 per page. Cert fee: $1.00 per page. Payee: District Clerk. Personal checks accepted. Prepayment required. Mial requests require SASE. Mail turnaround time 1-2 days.

County Court Cherokee County Clerk, PO Box 420, Rusk, TX 75785; 903-683-2350; Fax: 903-683-5931. Hours: 8AM-5PM (CST). *Misdemeanor, Civil, Probate.*

Civil Records: Access: Mail, in person. Both court and visitors may perform in person searches. Search fee: $5.00 per name. Required to search: name, years to search. Civil cases indexed by defendant, plaintiff.

Civil records on computer back to 1987, index books from 1846.

Criminal Records: Access: Mail, in person. Both court and visitors may perform in person searches. Search fee: $10.00 per name. Required to search: name, years to search. Criminal records on computer back to 1987, index books from 1920s.

General Information: Public Access terminal is available. No juvenile, mental, sealed, or adoption records released. Copy fee: $1.00 per page. Cert fee: $10.00. Payee: County Clerk. Personal checks accepted. Prepayment required. Mial requests require SASE. Mail turnaround time 2-4 days.

Childress County

District & County Court Courthouse Box 4, Childress, TX 79201; 940-937-6143; Fax: 940-937-3479. Hours: 8:30AM-Noon, 1-5PM (CST). *Felony, Misdemeanor, Civil, Probate.*

Civil Records: Access: Mail, in person. Both court and visitors may perform in person searches. Search fee: $5.00 per name. Required to search: name, years to search. Civil cases indexed by defendant, plaintiff. Civil records on computer from 1995, index books from 1920.

Criminal Records: Access: Mail, in person. Both court and visitors may perform in person searches. Search fee: $5.00 per name. Required to search: name, years to search, DOB. Criminal records on computer from 1995, index books from 1920.

General Information: No juvenile, mental, sealed, or adoption records released. Copy fee: $1.00 per page. Cert fee: $1.00. County Court certification fee is $5.00. Payee: District or County Clerk. Personal checks accepted. Prepayment required. Mail turnaround time 1 day.

Clay County

District Clerk PO Box 568, Henrietta, TX 76365; 940-538-4561; Fax: 940-538-4431. Hours: 8AM-Noon, 1-5PM (CST). *Felony, Civil.*

Civil Records: Access: Mail, in person. Both court and visitors may perform in person searches. Search fee: $5.00 per name. Required to search: name, years to search. Civil cases indexed by defendant, plaintiff. Civil records in index books from 1873.

Criminal Records: Access: Mail, in person. Both court and visitors may perform in person searches. Search fee: $5.00 per name. Required to search: name, years to search. Criminal records in index books from 1873.

General Information: No juvenile, mental, sealed, or adoption records released. Copy fee: $.50 per page. Cert fee: $1.00 per page. Payee: District Clerk. Personal checks accepted. Prepayment required. Mial requests require SASE. Mail turnaround time 1-2 days.

County Court PO Box 548, Henrietta, TX 76365; 940-538-4631. Hours: 8AM-5PM (CST). *Misdemeanor, Civil, Probate.*

Civil Records: Access: Mail, in person, fax. Both court and visitors may perform in person searches. Search fee: $5.00 per name. Required to search: name, years to search. Civil cases indexed by defendant, plaintiff. Civil records in index books from 1873, reecords go back to 1910; no computerized records.

Criminal Records: Access: Mail, in person. Both court and visitors may perform in person searches. Search fee: $5.00 per name. Required to search: name, years to search. Criminal records in index books from 1873, records go back to 1910; no computerized records.

General Information: No juvenile, mental, sealed, or adoption records released. Copy fee: $1.00 per page. Cert fee: $5.00. Payee: County Clerk. Personal checks

accepted. Prepayment required. Mial requests require SASE. Mail turnaround time 2-4 days.

Cochran County

District & County Court County Courthouse Rm 102, Morton, TX 79346; 806-266-5450; Fax: 806-266-9027. Hours: 8AM-5PM (CST). *Felony, Misdemeanor, Civil, Probate.*

Civil Records: Access: Phone, fax, mail, in person. Both court and visitors may perform in person searches. Search fee: $5.00 per name. Required to search: name, years to search. Civil cases indexed by defendant, plaintiff. Civil records in index books go back to 1925. Email address for search requests is cclerk@door.net.

Criminal Records: Access: Fax, mail, in person. Both court and visitors may perform in person searches. Search fee: $5.00 per name. Required to search: name, years to search, DOB; also helpful: sex. Criminal records in index books go back to 1925. Email address for search requests is cclerk@door.net.

General Information: No juvenile, mental, sealed, or adoption records released. Will fax results to 800 # only. Copy fee: $1.00 per page. Cert fee: $5.00. Payee: District or County Clerk. Personal checks accepted. Prepayment required. Mial requests require SASE. Mail turnaround time 1 day.

Coke County

District & County Court PO Box 150, Robert Lee, TX 76945; 325-453-2631; Fax: 325-453-2650. Hours: 8AM-5PM (CST). *Felony, Misdemeanor, Civil, Probate.*

Civil Records: Access: Mail, in person. Both court and visitors may perform in person searches. Search fee: $5.00 per name. Required to search: name, years to search. Civil cases indexed by defendant, plaintiff. Civil records in index books since 1889, computerized since 1993.

Criminal Records: Access: Mail, in person. Both court and visitors may perform in person searches. Search fee: $5.00 per name. Required to search: name, years to search. Criminal records in index books since 1889.

General Information: No juvenile, mental, sealed, or adoption records released. Will fax results $2.00 per page. Copy fee: $1.00 per page. Cert fee: $5.00. Payee: Coke County Clerk. Personal checks accepted. Prepayment required. Mail turnaround time 2 days.

Coleman County

District Court PO Box 512, Coleman, TX 76834; 325-625-2568. Hours: 8AM-4:30PM (CST). *Felony, Civil.*

Civil Records: Access: Mail, in person. Both court and visitors may perform in person searches. Search fee: $5.00 per name. Required to search: name, years to search. Civil cases indexed by defendant, plaintiff. Civil records in index books since 1934; earlier records not indexed.

Criminal Records: Access: Mail, in person. Both court and visitors may perform in person searches. Search fee: $5.00 per name. Required to search: name, years to search; also helpful are DOB, SSN. Criminal records in index books since 1931; earlier records not indexed.

General Information: No juvenile, mental, sealed, or adoption records released. Will not fax results. Copy fee: $1.00 per page. Cert fee: $1.00. Payee: District Clerk. Personal checks accepted. Prepayment required. Mial requests require SASE. Mail turnaround time up to 5 days.

County Court PO Box 591, Coleman, TX 76834; 325-625-2889. Hours: 8AM-5PM (CST). *Misdemeanor, Civil, Probate.*

Civil Records: Access: Mail, in person. Both court

and visitors may perform in person searches. Search fee: $5.00 per name. Required to search: name, years to search. Civil cases indexed by defendant, plaintiff. Civil records in index books from 1971.

Criminal Records: Access: Mail, in person. Both court and visitors may perform in person searches. Search fee: $5.00 per name. Required to search: name, years to search. Criminal records in index books from 1977, archived ffrom 1900s.

General Information: No juvenile, mental, sealed, or adoption records released. Copy fee: $1.00 per page. Cert fee: $5.00. Payee: County Clerk. Personal checks accepted. Prepayment required. Mial requests require SASE. Mail turnaround time 1-2 days.

Collin County

District Clerk PO Box 578, McKinney, TX 75070; Civil phone: 972-548-4320; Criminal phone: 972-548-4430. Hours: 8AM-4:30PM (CST). *Felony, Civil.*

www.co.collin.tx.us/district_courts/index.jsp

Civil Records: Access: Mail, fax, online, in person. Both court and visitors may perform in person searches. Search fee: $5.00 per name. Required to search: name, years to search. Civil cases indexed by defendant, plaintiff. Civil records on computer and microfiche from 1986 (some records are on computer through the 1970s), index books from 1846. name and case look up is at www.co.collin.tx.us/ShowCaseLookupServlet. Search case schedules for free at www.co.collin.tx.us/ShowScheduleSearchServlet. There is also a commercial system (see county courts). Fax service only to ongoing subscriber. Call Patty Ostrom at 972-548-4503 for subscription information.

Criminal Records: Access: Mail, fax, online, in person. Both court and visitors may perform in person searches. Search fee: $5.00 per name. Required to search: name, years to search, DOB. Criminal records on computer and microfiche from 1986 (some records are on computer through the 1970s), index books from 1846. Online access to criminal records is the same as civil. Fax service only to ongoing subscriber.

General Information: Public Access terminal is available. No juvenile, mental, sealed, or adoption records released. Will return by fax, if subscriber. Copy fee: $1.00 per page. No cert fee. Payee: District Clerk. Personal checks accepted. Prepayment required. Mial requests require SASE. Mail turnaround time 2-3 days.

County Court AT Law 1800 N Graves #110, McKinney, TX 75069; 972-548-6420; Probate phone: 972-548-6465; Fax: 972-548-6433. Hours: 8AM-4:30PM (CST). *Misdemeanor, Civil, Probate.*

www.co.collin.tx.us/county_court_law/index.jsp

Note: Probate is in #115.

Civil Records: Access: Mail, online, in person. Both court and visitors may perform in person searches. Search fee: $5.00 per name. Required to search: name, years to search. Civil cases indexed by defendant, plaintiff. Civil records on computer and microfiche from 1975. Online access is free at www.co.collin.tx.us/ShowCaseLookupServlet?district_or_county_court=county.

Criminal Records: Access: Mail, online, in person. Both court and visitors may perform in person searches. Search fee: $5.00 per name. Required to search: name, DOB. Criminal records computerized since early 1970s. Online access to misdemeanor records is the same as civil.

General Information: Public Access terminal is available. No juvenile, mental, sealed, or adoption records released. Will not fax results. Copy fee: $1.00 per page. Cert fee: $5.00. Payee: County Clerk.

Personal checks accepted. Prepayment required. Mail turnaround time 2-4 days.

Collingsworth County

District & County Court County Courthouse, Rm 3, 800 W Ave, Box 10, Wellington, TX 79095; 806-447-2408; Fax: 806-447-5418. Hours: 9AM-5PM (CST). *Felony, Misdemeanor, Civil, Probate.*
Civil Records: Access: Phone, fax, mail, in person. Both court and visitors may perform in person searches. Search fee: $10.00 per name. Required to search: name, years to search. Civil cases indexed by defendant, plaintiff. Civil records on index books from 1800s.
Criminal Records: Access: Mail, in person. Both court and visitors may perform in person searches. Search fee: $10.00 per name. Required to search: name, years to search, DOB. Criminal records on index books from 1800s.
General Information: No juvenile, mental health, sealed, or adoption records released. Will fax results for $1.50 per page. Copy fee: $1.00 per page. Cert fee: $5.00. Payee: Collingsworth County Clerk. Personal checks accepted. Prepayment required. Mial requests require SASE. Mail turnaround time 2 days.

Colorado County

District Court County Courthouse, RM 210E, 400 Spring St, Columbus, TX 78934; 979-732-2536. Hours: 8AM-Noon, 1-5PM (CST). *Felony, Civil.*
Civil Records: Access: Mail, in person. Both court and visitors may perform in person searches. Search fee: $5.00 per name. Required to search: name, years to search. Civil cases indexed by defendant, plaintiff. Civil records in index books from 1837.
Criminal Records: Access: Mail, in person. Both court and visitors may perform in person searches. Search fee: $5.00 per name. Required to search: name, years to search. Criminal records in index books from 1837.
General Information: No juvenile, mental, sealed, or adoption records released. Copy fee: $1.00 per page. Cert fee: $2.00. Payee: District Clerk. Personal checks accepted. Prepayment required. Mial requests require SASE. Mail turnaround time 1 day.

County Court PO Box 68, County Courthouse, Columbus, TX 78934; 979-732-2155; Fax: 979-732-8852. Hours: 8AM-5PM (CST). *Misdemeanor, Civil, Probate.*
Civil Records: Access: Mail, in person. Both court and visitors may perform in person searches. Search fee: $10.00 per name. Required to search: name, years to search. Civil cases indexed by defendant, plaintiff. Civil records in index books from 1850, computerized since 1996.
Criminal Records: Access: Mail, in person. Both court and visitors may perform in person searches. Search fee: $10.00 per name. Required to search: name, years to search. Criminal records in index books from 1850, computerized since 1996.
General Information: No juvenile, mental, sealed, or adoption records released. Copy fee: $1.00 per page. Cert fee: $5.00. Payee: County Clerk. Personal checks accepted. Prepayment required. Mial requests require SASE. Mail turnaround time 1-2 days.

Comal County

District Court 150 N Seguin #304, New Braunfels, TX 78130-5161; 830-620-5574; Fax: 830-608-2006. Hours: 8AM-4:30PM (CST). *Felony, Civil.*
www.co.comal.tx.us
Civil Records: Access: Fax, mail, in person, online. Both court and visitors may perform in person searches. Search fee: $5.00 per name. Required to search: name, years to search. Civil cases indexed by

defendant, plaintiff. Civil records on computer from 1984, index books from 1846. Online access to county judicial records is free at www.co.comal.tx.us/Search/judsrch.htm. Search by either party name.
Criminal Records: Access: Fax, mail, in person, online. Both court and visitors may perform in person searches. Search fee: $5.00 per name. Required to search: name, years to search, DOB; also helpful: SSN, sex. Criminal records on computer from 1984, index books from 1846. Online access to county criminal judicial records is at www.co.comal.tx.us/Search/judsrch.htm. Search by defendant name.
General Information: Public Access terminal is available. No juvenile, sealed, or adoption records released. Will fax results $5.00 per page. Fee is for incoming and outgoing faxes. Copy fee: $1.00 for first page, $.25 each add'l. Cert fee: $1.00 per page. Payee: District Clerk. Personal checks accepted. Prepayment required. Mial requests require SASE. Mail turnaround time 3 days.

County Court at Law 100 Main Plaza, #303, New Braunfels, TX 78130; Civil phone: 830-620-5586; Criminal phone: 830-620-5582; Probate phone: 830-620-5539; Fax: 830-608-2021. Hours: 8AM-4:30PM (CST). *Misdemeanor, Civil, Probate.*
www.comalcounty.net
Civil Records: Access: Phone, fax, mail, in person, online. Both court and visitors may perform in person searches. Search fee: $5.00 per name. Required to search: name, years to search. Civil cases indexed by defendant, plaintiff. Civil records on computer since 1977. Online access to county judicial records is free at www.comalcounty.net/JudicialSearch/JudSrch.htm. Search by either party name.
Criminal Records: Access: Phone, fax, mail, in person. Both court and visitors may perform in person searches. Search fee: $5.00 per name. Required to search: name, years to search; also helpful: address, DOB. Criminal records on computer since 1977. Online access to county criminal judicial records is free at www.comalcounty.net/JudicialSearch/JudSrch.htm. Search by defendant name.
General Information: Public Access terminal is available. No juvenile, mental, sealed or adoption records released. Will fax results $1.00 per page. Copy fee: $1.00 per page. Cert fee: $5.00. Payee: County Court at Law. Only cashiers checks and money orders accepted. Credit cards accepted. Prepayment required. Mail turnaround time 1 week.

Comanche County

District Court County Courthouse, Box 206, Comanche, TX 76442; 325-356-2342; Fax: 325-356-2150. Hours: 8:30AM-Noon, 1-5PM (CST). *Felony, Civil.*
Civil Records: Access: Mail, in person. Only the court performs in person searches; visitors may not. Search fee: $5.00 per name. Required to search: name, years to search. Civil cases indexed by defendant, plaintiff. Civil records on computer back 1 year, index books from 1876.
Criminal Records: Access: Mail, in person. Only the court performs in person searches; visitors may not. Search fee: $5.00 per name. Required to search: name, years to search. Criminal records on computer from 1990, index books from 1876.
General Information: No juvenile, mental, sealed, or adoption records released. Copy fee: $1.00 per page. Cert fee: $2.00. Payee: District Clerk. Personal checks accepted. Prepayment required. Mial requests require SASE. Mail turnaround time 1 day.

County Court County Courthouse, Comanche, TX 76442; 325-356-2655. Hours: 8:30AM-5PM (CST). *Misdemeanor, Civil, Probate.*
Civil Records: Access: Mail, in person. Both court and visitors may perform in person searches. Search fee: $5.00 per name. Required to search: name, years to search. Civil cases indexed by defendant, plaintiff. Civil records in index books from 1856.
Criminal Records: Access: Mail, in person. Both court and visitors may perform in person searches. Search fee: $5.00 per name. Required to search: name, years to search. Criminal records in index books from 1856.
General Information: No juvenile, mental, sealed, or adoption records released. Wll fax back results for $1.50 per fax. Copy fee: $1.00 per page. Cert fee: $5.00. Payee: County Clerk. Personal checks accepted. Prepayment required. Mial requests require SASE. Mail turnaround time 1 day.

Concho County

District & County Court PO Box 98, Paint Rock, TX 76866; 325-732-4322; Fax: 325-732-2040. Hours: 8:30AM-5PM (CST). *Felony, Misdemeanor, Civil, Probate.*
Civil Records: Access: Phone, mail, in person. Both court and visitors may perform in person searches. Search fee: $5.00 per name. Required to search: name, years to search. Civil cases indexed by defendant, plaintiff. Civil records in index books from 1879; computerized back to 1994.
Criminal Records: Access: Mail, in person. Only the court performs in person searches; visitors may not. Search fee: $5.00 per name. Required to search: name, years to search, DOB; also helpful: SSN. Criminal records in index books from 1879; computerized back to 1994.
General Information: No juvenile, mental, sealed, or adoption records released. Will fax results for $1.00 per page, plus a $5.00 fax fee. Copy fee: $1.00 per page. Cert fee: $5.00. Payee: District or County Clerk. Personal checks accepted. Prepayment required. Mial requests require SASE. Mail turnaround time 1 day.

Cooke County

District Court County Courthouse, 100 S Dixon, Gainesville, TX 76240; 940-668-5450; Fax: 940-668-5476. Hours: 8AM-5PM (CST). *Felony, Civil.*
Civil Records: Access: Mail, in person. Both court and visitors may perform in person searches. Search fee: $5.00 per name. Required to search: name, years to search. Civil cases indexed by defendant, plaintiff. Civil records on microfiche from late 1900s, index books from 1800s. Must request specifically if you wish to go back more than 10 years.
Criminal Records: Access: Mail, in person. Both court and visitors may perform in person searches. Search fee: $5.00 per name. Required to search: name, years to search. Criminal records on microfiche from late 1900,s, index books from 1800s.
General Information: No juvenile, mental, sealed, or adoption records released. Copy fee: $.50 per page. Cert fee: $1.00. Payee: District Clerk. Only cashiers checks and money orders accepted. Prepayment required. Mial requests require SASE. Mail turnaround time 2 days.

County Court County Courthouse, Gainesville, TX 76240; 940-668-5422. Hours: 8AM-5PM (CST). *Misdemeanor, Civil, Probate.*
Civil Records: Access: Mail, in person. Both court and visitors may perform in person searches. Search fee: $5.00 per name. Required to search: name, years to search. Civil cases indexed by defendant, plaintiff. Civil records in index books and original papers from late 1850s.

Criminal Records: Access: Mail, in person. Both court and visitors may perform in person searches. Search fee: $5.00 per name. Required to search: name, years to search, DOB. Criminal records go back to 1969.

General Information: No juvenile, mental, sealed, or adoption records released. Will fax results of search to toll free lines or when pre-paid. Copy fee: $1.00 per page. Cert fee: $5.00. Payee: Cooke County Clerk. Personal checks accepted. Prepayment required. Mail turnaround time 1 day.

Coryell County

District Court PO Box 4, Gatesville, TX 76528; 254-865-5911; Fax: 254-865-5064. Hours: 8AM-5PM (CST). *Felony, Civil.*

Civil Records: Access: Fax, mail, in person. Both court and visitors may perform in person searches. Search fee: $5.00 per name. Required to search: name, years to search. Civil cases indexed by defendant, plaintiff. Civil records in index books from 1854; computerized back to 2000.

Criminal Records: Access: Fax, mail, in person. Both court and visitors may perform in person searches. Search fee: $5.00 per name. Required to search: name, years to search, DOB, SSN. Criminal records in index books from 1854; computerized back to 2000.

General Information: Public Access terminal is available. No juvenile, sealed, or adoption records released. Fee to fax results is $1.00 per page. Copy fee: $1.00 per page. No cert fee. Payee: District Clerk. Personal checks accepted from Coryell County residents only. Money order, cashiers check or credit card accepted for others. Prepayment required. Mial requests require SASE. Mail turnaround time 1 day.

County Court PO Box 237, Gatesville, TX 76528; 254-865-5016; Fax: 254-865-8631. Hours: 8AM-Noon, 1-5PM (CST). *Misdemeanor, Civil, Probate.*

Civil Records: Access: Mail, in person. Visitors must perform in person searches for themselves. Search fee: $10.00 per name per 10 years, when court does mail search. Required to search: name, years to search. Civil cases indexed by defendant, plaintiff. Civil records on computer back to 1993, index books from 1846.

Criminal Records: Access: Mail, in person. Visitors must perform in person searches for themselves. Search fee: $10.00 per name per 10 years, when court does mail search. Required to search: name, years to search, DOB, SSN. Criminal records on computer back to 1993; index books from 1846.

General Information: Public Access terminal is available. No juvenile, mental, sealed, or adoption records released. Will fax results $1.00 per page. Fax fee for out of county request is $5.00 plus $1.00 per page. Copy fee: $1.00 per page. Cert fee: $5.00 plus $1.00 per page. Payee: County Clerk. Business checks accepted. Personal checks must be in county. Prepayment required. Mial requests require SASE. Mail turnaround time 1-5 days.

Cottle County

District & County Court PO Box 717, Paducah, TX 79248; 806-492-3823. Hours: 9AM-Noon, 1-5PM (CST). *Felony, Misdemeanor, Civil, Probate.*

Civil Records: Access: Mail, in person. Both court and visitors may perform in person searches. Search fee: $5.00 per name. Required to search: name, years to search. Civil cases indexed by defendant, plaintiff. Civil records in index books from 1892.

Criminal Records: Access: Mail, in person. Both court and visitors may perform in person searches. Search fee: $5.00 per name. Required to search:

name, years to search. Criminal records in index books from 1892.

General Information: No juvenile, mental, sealed, or adoption records released. Copy fee: $1.00 per page. Cert fee: $1.00 for District documents; $5.00 for county documents. Payee: Cottle County Clerk. Personal checks accepted. Prepayment required. Mial requests require SASE. Mail turnaround time 2-3 days.

Crane County

District & County Court PO Box 578, Crane, TX 79731; 432-558-3581. Hours: 9AM-12 1-5PM (CST). *Felony, Misdemeanor, Civil, Probate.*

Civil Records: Access: Mail, in person. Visitors must perform in person searches for themselves. Search fee: $5.00 per name per 10 years searched. Required to search: name, years to search. Civil cases indexed by defendant, plaintiff. Limited civil records on computer from 1990; index books from 1927.

Criminal Records: Access: Mail, in person. Both court and visitors may perform in person searches. Search fee: $5.00 per name per ten year searched. Required to search: name, years to search, offense. Limited criminal records on computer from 1990; index books from 1927.

General Information: Public Access terminal is available. No juvenile, mental, sealed or adoption records released. Copy fee: $1.00 per page. Cert fee: County = $5.00. District = $1.00. Payee: District or County Clerk. Only cashiers checks and money orders accepted. Prepayment required. Mial requests require SASE. Mail turnaround time 2-5 days.

Crockett County

District & County Court PO Drawer C, Ozona, TX 76943; 325-392-2022. Hours: 8AM-5PM (CST). *Felony, Misdemeanor, Civil, Probate.*

Civil Records: Access: Mail, in person. Both court and visitors may perform in person searches. Search fee: $10.00 per name. Required to search: name, years to search. Civil cases indexed by defendant, plaintiff. Civil records on computer from 1982, index books from 1800s.

Criminal Records: Access: Mail, in person. Both court and visitors may perform in person searches. Search fee: $10.00 per name. Required to search: name, years to search, DOB, SSN, signed release. Criminal records on computer from 1982, index books from 1800s.

General Information: No juvenile, mental, sealed, or adoption records released. Fee to fax results is $1.00 per page. Copy fee: $1.00 per page. Cert fee: $5.00. Payee: District or County Clerk. Personal checks accepted. Prepayment required. Mail turnaround time 1 week.

Crosby County

District Court 201 W Aspen St #207, Crosbyton, TX 79322-2500; 806-675-2071; Fax: 806-675-2433. Hours: 8AM-Noon, 1-5PM (CST). *Felony, Civil.*

Civil Records: Access: Phone, fax, mail, in person. Both court and visitors may perform in person searches. Search fee: $5.00 per name. Required to search: name, years to search. Civil cases indexed by defendant, plaintiff. Civil records in index books from 1896.

Criminal Records: Access: Phone, fax, mail, in person. Both court and visitors may perform in person searches. Search fee: $5.00 per name. Required to search: name, years to search. Criminal records in index books from 1896.

General Information: No juvenile, mental, sealed, or adoption records released. No fee to fax results. Only for local or toll free calls. Copy fee: $1.00 per page. Cert fee: $1.00. Payee: District Clerk. Personal checks

accepted. Prepayment required. Mial requests require SASE. Mail turnaround time 1 day.

County Court 201 W Aspen St #102, Crosbyton, TX 79322-2500; 806-675-2334. Hours: 8AM-noon, 1:00PM-5PM (CST). *Misdemeanor, Civil, Probate.*

Civil Records: Access: Mail, in person. Both court and visitors may perform in person searches. No search fee. Required to search: name, years to search. Civil cases indexed by defendant, plaintiff. Civil records on microfiche from 1990, index books from 1886.

Criminal Records: Access: Mail, in person. Both court and visitors may perform in person searches. Search fee: $5.00 per name. Required to search: name, years to search. Criminal records on microfiche from 1990, index books from 1886.

General Information: No juvenile, mental, sealed, or adoption records released. Will fax results for $1.00 per page. Copy fee: $1.00 per page. Cert fee: $5.00. Payee: County Clerk. Personal checks accepted. Prepayment required. Mail turnaround time 1 day.

Culberson County

District & County Court PO Box 158, Van Horn, TX 79855; 432-283-2058. Hours: 8AM-noon; 1PM-5PM (CST). *Felony, Misdemeanor, Civil, Probate.*

Civil Records: Access: Phone, mail, fax, in person. Both court and visitors may perform in person searches. Search fee: $5.00 per name. Required to search: name, years to search. Civil cases indexed by defendant, plaintiff. Civil records in index books since 1911.

Criminal Records: Access: Phone, mail, fax, in person. Both court and visitors may perform in person searches. Search fee: $5.00 per name. Required to search: name, years to search, signed release. Criminal records in index books since 1911.

General Information: No juvenile, mental, sealed, or adoption records released. Fee to fax results is $1.00 per page. Copy fee: $1.00 per page. Cert fee: $5.00. Payee: District or County Clerk. Personal checks accepted. Prepayment required. Mial requests require SASE. Mail turnaround time 2 days.

Dallam County

District & County Court PO Box 1352, Dalhart, TX 79022; 806-244-4751; Fax: 806-249-2252. Hours: 9AM-5PM (CST). *Felony, Misdemeanor, Civil, Probate.*

Civil Records: Access: Fax, mail, in person. Both court and visitors may perform in person searches. Search fee: $5.00 per name. Required to search: name, years to search. Civil cases indexed by defendant, plaintiff. Civil records in index books from 1800s; computerized since 1991.

Criminal Records: Access: Fax, mail, in person. Both court and visitors may perform in person searches. Search fee: $5.00 per name. Required to search: name, years to search. Criminal records in index books from 1800s; computerized since 1991.

General Information: No juvenile, mental, sealed, or adoption records released. Fee to fax results $5.00 1st page, $1.00 each add'l. Copy fee: $1.00 per page. Cert fee: $5.00. Payee: Dallam County Clerk. Personal checks accepted. Prepayment required. Mial requests require SASE. Mail turnaround time 1 day.

Dallas County

District Court - Civil 600 Commerce St, Dallas, TX 75202-4606; 214-653-7421. Hours: 8AM-6:00PM (CST). *Civil.*
www.dallascounty.org

Civil Records: Access: Mail, online, in person. Both court and visitors may perform in person searches. Search fee: $5.00 per name. Required to search:

name, years to search, DOB. Civil cases indexed by defendant, plaintiff. Civil records on computer since 1967; on dockets back to 1940; records prior to 1940 are maintained by Texas Historical Div. of the Dallas Public Library. Two electronic sources are available. Public Access System allows remote access at $1.00 per minute to these and other court/public records. Dial-in access number is 900-263-INFO. ProComm Plus is recommended. Searching is by name or case number. Call the Public Access Administrator at 214-653-7717 for more info and order $2.00 set-up CD-rom. Also, name search for free at www.dallascounty.org/applications/english/record-search/intro.html; index includes DOB. Fee for documents. Save by becoming a subscriber for $75 per year. Includes civil, criminal, probate, marriages, UCC, and soon, real estate. Call 972-866-3911 for info.

General Information: Public Access terminal is available. No sealed records released. Fee to fax results is $1.00 per page. Copy fee: $1.00 per page. Payee: District Clerk. Only cashiers checks and money orders accepted. Prepayment required.

District Court - Criminal 133 N Industrial Blvd, LB12, Attn: District Clerk, Dallas, TX 75207-4313; 214-653-5950; Fax: 214-653-5986. Hours: 8AM-4:30PM (CST). *Felony.*

www.dallascounty.org

Criminal Records: Access: Mail, online, in person. Both court and visitors may perform in person searches. Search fee: $5.00 per name. Required to search: name, years to search, DOB. Criminal records on computer from 1972, on microfiche from 1979. Two electronic sources are available. Public Access System allows remote access at $1.00 per minute to these and other court/public records. Dial-in access number is 900-263-INFO. ProComm Plus is recommended. Searching is by name or case number. Call the Public Access Administrator at 214-653-7717 for more info and order $2.00 set-up CD-rom. Also, name search for free at www.dallascounty.org/applications/english/record-search/intro.html; index includes DOB. Fee for documents. Save by becoming a subscriber for $75 per year. Includes civil, criminal, probate, marriages, UCC, and soon, real estate. Call 972-866-3911 for info.

General Information: Public Access terminal is available. No juvenile, mental, sealed, or adoption records released. Copy fee: $1.00 per page. Cert fee: $1.00 per page. Payee: District Clerk. Only cashiers checks and money orders accepted. Prepayment required. Mial requests require SASE. Mail turnaround time 1-2 days.

County Court - Misdemeanor 133 N Industrial Blvd LB43, Dallas, TX 75207-4313; 214-653-5740. Hours: 8AM-4PM (CST). *Misdemeanor.*

www.dallascounty.org

Criminal Records: Access: Mail, online, in person. Both court and visitors may perform in person searches. Search fee: $5.00 per name. Required to search: name, years to search, DOB. Criminal records on computer from 1972. For older searches call 214-653-5763. Two electronic sources are available. Public Access System allows remote access at $1.00 per minute to these and other court/public records. Dial-in access number is 900-263-INFO. ProComm Plus is recommended. Searching is by name or case number. Call the Public Access Administrator at 214-653-7717 for more info and order $2.00 set-up CD-rom. Also, name search for free at www.dallascounty.org/applications/english/record-search/intro.html; index includes DOB. Fee for documents. Save by becoming a subscriber for $75 per year. Includes civil, criminal, probate, marriages,

UCC, and soon, real estate. Call 972-866-3911 for info.

General Information: Public Access terminal is available. No juvenile, mental, sealed, or adoption records released. Copy fee: $1.00 per page. Cert fee: $5.00. Payee: County Clerk. Only cashiers checks and money orders accepted or cash if in person. Prepayment required. Mial requests require SASE. Mail turnaround time 2-3 weeks.

County Court - Civil 509 W Main, 3rd Fl, Dallas, TX 75202; 214-653-7131; Civil phone: 214-653-7441; Criminal phone: 214-653-5740; Probate phone: 214-653-7442. Hours: 8AM-4:30PM (CST). *Civil.*

www.dallascounty.org

Note: No civil claims limit as of 05/23/97 in Dallas County

Civil Records: Access: Phone, mail, online, in person. Both court and visitors may perform in person searches. Search fee: $5.00 per name per 10 years. Required to search: name, years to search. Civil cases indexed by defendant, plaintiff. Civil records on computer from 1964, index books from 1800s. Two electronic sources are available. Public Access System allows remote access at $1.00 per minute to these and other court/public records. Dial-in access number is 900-263-INFO. ProComm Plus is recommended. Searching is by name or case number. Call the Public Access Administrator at 214-653-7717 for more info and order $2.00 set-up CD-rom. Also, name search for free at www.dallascounty.org/applications/english/record-search/intro.html; index includes DOB. Fee for documents. Save by becoming a subscriber for $75 per year. Includes civil, criminal, probate, marriages, UCC, and soon, real estate. Call 972-866-3911 for info.

General Information: Public Access terminal is available. No juvenile, mental, sealed, or adoption records released. Will not fax results. Copy fee: $1.00 per page. Cert fee: $5.00. Payee: County Clerk. Personal checks accepted. Prepayment required. Mial requests require SASE. Mail turnaround time 1 day.

Probate Court #3 509 Main St, Records Bldg, 2nd Fl, Dallas, TX 75202; 214-653-7243. Hours: 8AM-4:30PM (CST). *Probate.*

Note: The remote access system for civil and criminal records in this county also includes probate records. You may also name search for free at www.dallascounty.org/applications/english/record-search/intro.html; there is a fee for documents.

Dawson County

District Court Drawer 1268, Lamesa, TX 79331; 806-872-7373; Fax: 806-872-9513. Hours: 8:30AM-5PM (CST). *Felony, Civil.*

Civil Records: Access: Mail, in person. Both court and visitors may perform in person searches. Search fee: $5.00 per name. Required to search: name, years to search. Civil cases indexed by defendant, plaintiff. Civil records in index books/files from 1900; computerized records since 1995.

Criminal Records: Access: Mail, in person. Both court and visitors may perform in person searches. Search fee: $5.00 per name. Required to search: name, years to search, signed release. Criminal records in index books/files from 1900s; computerized records since 1995.

General Information: No juvenile, mental, sealed, or adoption records released. Will fax results $1.00 per page. Copy fee: $1.00 per page. Cert fee: $1.00 per page. Payee: Dawson County District Clerk. Personal checks accepted. Prepayment required. Mail turnaround time 1 day.

County Court Drawer 1268, Lamesa, TX 79331; 806-872-3778; Fax: 806-872-2473. Hours: 8:30AM-1200-15PM (CST). *Misdemeanor, Civil, Probate.*

Civil Records: Access: Fax, mail, in person. Both court and visitors may perform in person searches. Search fee: $5.00 per name. Required to search: name, years to search. Civil cases indexed by defendant, plaintiff. Civil records in index files since 1906, on computer back to 1992. Fees must be prepaid before fax access is allowed.

Criminal Records: Access: Mail, in person. Both court and visitors may perform in person searches. Search fee: $5.00 per name. Required to search: name, years to search, DOB; also helpful-signed release, offense, date of offense. Criminal records in index files since 1906; on computer back to 1986. Fees must be prepaid before fax access is allowed.

General Information: No juvenile, mental or sealed records released. Fee to fax results is $5.00 per document and $1.00 per page. Copy fee: $1.00 per page. Cert fee: $5.00 + $1.00 per page. Payee: County Clerk. Personal checks accepted. Prepayment required. Mail turnaround time 1 day.

De Witt County

County Court 307 N Gonzales, Cuero, TX 77954; 361-275-3724; Fax: 361-275-8994. Hours: 8AM-5PM (CST). *Misdemeanor, Probate.*

Civil Records: Access: Phone, fax, mail, in person. Search fee: $5.00 per name. Required to search: name, years to search. Civil cases indexed by defendant, plaintiff. Civil records go back to 1960s; on computer back to 1998.

Criminal Records: Access: Mail, in person. Both court and visitors may perform in person searches. Search fee: $5.00 per name. Required to search: name, years to search; also helpful: DOB, SSN. Criminal records go back to 1960s; on computer back to 1998.

General Information: No juvenile, mental, sealed, or adoption records released. Fee to fax results is $1.00 per page. Copy fee: $1.00 per page. Cert fee: $5.00. Payee: DeWitt County Clerk. Personal checks accepted. Prepayment required. Mial requests require SASE.

District Court PO Box 845, Cuero, TX 77954; 361-275-2221. Hours: 8AM-5PM (CST). *Felony, Civil.*

Civil Records: Access: Mail, in person. Both court and visitors may perform in person searches. Search fee: $5.00 per name. Required to search: name, years to search. Civil cases indexed by defendant, plaintiff.

Criminal Records: Access: Mail, in person. Both court and visitors may perform in person searches. Search fee: $5.00 per name. Required to search: name, years to search, DOB, SSN, signed release. Criminal records maintained on books.

General Information: No juvenile, mental, sealed, or adoption records released. Copy fee: $1.00 per page. Cert fee: $1.00. Payee: District Clerk. Personal checks accepted. Prepayment required. Mial requests require SASE. Mail turnaround time 1 week.

Deaf Smith County

District Court 235 E 3rd St, Rm 304, Hereford, TX 79045; 806-364-3901; Fax: 806-363-7007. Hours: 8AM-5PM (CST). *Felony, Civil.*

Civil Records: Access: Fax, mail, in person. Both court and visitors may perform in person searches. Search fee: $5.00 per name. Required to search: name, years to search. Civil cases indexed by defendant, plaintiff. Civil records on computer from 2/1993; prior on microfiche from 5/15/1981.

Criminal Records: Access: Fax, mail, in person. Both court and visitors may perform in person searches. Search fee: $5.00 per name. Required to search: name, years to search; also helpful: DOB, SSN, case number. Criminal records on computer from 2/1993; prior on microfiche from 5/15/1981.

General Information: Public Access terminal is available. No juvenile, mental, sealed, or adoption records released. Fee to fax results is $2.00 per page. Copy fee: $1.00 per page. Cert fee: $1.00. Payee: District Clerk. Personal checks accepted. Prepayment required. Mial requests require SASE. Mail turnaround time 1 day.

County Court Deaf Smith Courthouse, 235 E Third, Rm 203, Hereford, TX 79045; 806-363-7077. Hours: 8AM-5PM (CST). *Misdemeanor, Civil, Probate.*

Civil Records: Access: Mail, in person. Both court and visitors may perform in person searches. Search fee: $5.00 per name. Required to search: name, years to search. Civil cases indexed by defendant, plaintiff. Civil records on computer from 1989, microfiche from 1981, index books from early 1900s.

Criminal Records: Access: Mail, in person. Both court and visitors may perform in person searches. Search fee: $5.00 per name. Required to search: name, years to search. Criminal records on computer from 1989, microfiche from 1981, index books from early 1900s.

General Information: Public Access terminal is available. No juvenile, mental, sealed, or adoption records released. Will fax results for the $1.00 copy fee for each page faxed. Copy fee: $1.00 per page. Cert fee: $5.00. Payee: County Clerk. Personal checks accepted. Prepayment required. Mail turnaround time 1 day.

Delta County

District & County Court PO Box 455, Cooper, TX 75432; 903-395-4400 x223; Fax: 903-395-2178. Hours: 8AM-5PM (CST). *Felony, Misdemeanor, Civil, Probate.*

Civil Records: Access: Phone, mail, in person. Both court and visitors may perform in person searches. Search fee: $5.00 per name. Required to search: name, years to search. Civil cases indexed by defendant, plaintiff. Civil records in index books from late 1800s. Phone searches must be pre-paid.

Criminal Records: Access: Phone, mail, in person. Both court and visitors may perform in person searches. Search fee: $5.00 per name. Required to search: name, years to search, DOB. Criminal records in index books from late 1800s. Phone searches must be prepaid.

General Information: Public access terminal available for civil in person searches. No juvenile, mental, sealed, or adoption records released. Fee to fax results is $2.50 per page plus $1.00 per document. Copy fee: $1.00 per page. Cert fee: $5.00. Payee: County or District Clerk. Personal checks accepted. Prepayment required. Mial requests require SASE. Mail turnaround time 1 day.

Denton County

District Court PO Box 2146, Denton, TX 76202; 940-349-2200; Civil phone: 940-349-2205; Criminal phone: 940-349-2210; Fax: 940-349-2201. Hours: 8AM-4:30PM (CST). *Felony, Civil.*
http://dentoncounty.com/dept/main.asp?Dept=26

Civil Records: Access: Phone, mail, fax, online, in person. Both court and visitors may perform in person searches. Search fee: $5.00 per name. Required to search: name, years to search. Civil cases indexed by defendant, plaintiff. Civil records on computer from 1990, archived from 1936. Civil searches at http://justice.dentoncounty.com at no charge. Search by name or cause number.

Criminal Records: Access: Mail, fax, online, in person. Both court and visitors may perform in person

searches. Search fee: $5.00 per name. Required to search: name, years to search, DOB. Criminal records on computer from 1990, archived from 1936. Criminal searches are at http://justice.dentoncounty.com at no charge. Records go back to 1994 forward. Access also includes sheriff bond and jail records.

General Information: Public Access terminal is available. No juvenile, mental, sealed, expunctions or adoption records released. Fee to fax results is $1.00 per page. Copy fee: $1.00 per page. Cert fee: $1.00. Payee: District Clerk. Personal checks accepted. Visa, MC accepted. Use of credit card requires a 5% surcharge. Prepayment required. Mial requests require SASE. Mail turnaround time 1-2 weeks.

County Court Attn: County Clerk, PO Box 2187, Denton, TX 76202-2187; 940-349-2012; Civil phone: 940-349-2016; Criminal phone: 940-349-2013; Probate phone: 940-349-2036. Hours: 8AM-5PM (CST). *Misdemeanor, Civil, Probate.*
http://dentoncounty.com/dept/main.asp?Dept=17

Civil Records: Access: Mail, in person, online. Both court and visitors may perform in person searches. Search fee: $5.00 per name. Add $1.00 per year prior to 1989. Required to search: name, years to search. Civil cases indexed by defendant, plaintiff. Civil records on computer from 1989, microfiche from 1968. Online access to civil court records is free at http://justice.dentoncounty.com/CivilSearch/civfrmd.htm.

Criminal Records: Access: Mail, in person, online. Both court and visitors may perform in person searches. Search fee: $5.00 per name. Add $1.00 per year over first 5. Required to search: name, years to search, DOB. Criminal records on computer from 1989, microfiche from 1968. Online access to county criminal records is free at http://justice.dentoncounty.com/CrimSearch/crimfrmd.htm. Jail, bond, and parole data are also available at http://justice.dentoncounty.com. Search for registered sex offenders by ZIP Code at http://sheriff.dentoncounty.com/sex_offenders/default.htm.

General Information: Public Access terminal is available. No juvenile, mental, sealed, or adoption records released. Will not fax results. Copy fee: $1.00 per page. Cert fee: $5.00. Payee: Denton County Clerk. Only cashiers checks and money orders accepted. Prepayment required. Mial requests require SASE. Mail turnaround time 1-2 weeks.

Dickens County

District & County Court PO Box 120, Dickens, TX 79229; 806-623-5531; Fax: 806-623-5319. Hours: 8AM-5PM (CST). *Felony, Misdemeanor, Civil, Probate.*

Civil Records: Access: Mail, fax, phone, in person. Both court and visitors may perform in person searches. Search fee: $5.00 per name. Required to search: name, years to search, DOB, SSN and signed release. Civil cases indexed by defendant, plaintiff. Civil records in index books since late 1891.

Criminal Records: Access: Mail, fax, phone, in person. Both court and visitors may perform in person searches. Search fee: $5.00 per name. Required to search: name, years to search; also helpful: DOB, SSN and signed release. Criminal records in index books since late 1891.

General Information: No juvenile, mental, sealed or adoption records released. Will fax results for $1.00 per page. Copy fee: $1.00 per page. Cert fee: $5.00. Payee: District Court. Personal checks accepted. Prepayment required. Mial requests require SASE. Mail turnaround time 1-2 days.

Dimmit County

District Court 303 S 5th, Carrizo Springs, TX 78834; 830-876-2323 #244; Fax: 830-876-5036. Hours: 8AM-Noon; 1PM-5PM (CST). *Felony, Civil.*

Civil Records: Access: Mail, in person. Both court and visitors may perform in person searches. Search fee: $5.00 per name. Required to search: name, years to search; also helpful: address. Civil cases indexed by defendant, plaintiff. Civil records in index books, archived from 1936.

Criminal Records: Access: Mail, in person. Both court and visitors may perform in person searches. Search fee: $5.00 per name. Required to search: name, years to search; also helpful: DOB, SSN. Criminal records in index books, archived from 1936.

General Information: No juvenile, mental, sealed, or adoption records released. Copy fee: $1.00 per page. Cert fee: $1.00 per page. Payee: District Clerk. Personal checks accepted. Prepayment required. Mial requests require SASE. Mail turnaround time 2-3 days.

County Court 103 N 5th, Carrizo Springs, TX 78834; 830-876-2323 x232; Fax: 830-876-4205. Hours: 8AM-5PM (CST). *Misdemeanor, Civil, Probate.*

Civil Records: Access: Phone, fax, mail, in person. Both court and visitors may perform in person searches. Search fee: $5.00 per name. Required to search: name, years to search. Civil cases indexed by defendant, plaintiff. Civil records on microfiche from 1992, index books prior.

Criminal Records: Access: Phone, fax, mail, in person. Both court and visitors may perform in person searches. Search fee: $5.00 per name. Required to search: name, years to search, signed release, DOB; also helpful: sex, SSN. Criminal records on microfiche from 1992, computerized since 1996.

General Information: No juvenile, mental, sealed, or adoption records released. Fee to fax results is $2.00 1st page; $1.00 each add'l. Copy fee: $1.00 per page. Cert fee: $5.00. Payee: County Clerk. Personal checks accepted. Prepayment required. Mial requests require SASE. Mail turnaround time 1 day.

Donley County

District & County Court PO Drawer U, Clarendon, TX 79226; 806-874-3436; Fax: 806-874-5146. Hours: 8AM-Noon, 1-5PM (CST). *Felony, Misdemeanor, Civil, Probate.*

Civil Records: Access: Mail, in person. Both court and visitors may perform in person searches. Search fee: $5.00 per name. Required to search: name, years to search. Civil cases indexed by defendant, plaintiff. Civil records on computer from 1991, index books from 1890s.

Criminal Records: Access: Mail, in person. Both court and visitors may perform in person searches. Search fee: $5.00 per name. Required to search: name, years to search, DOB, signed release, aliases; also helpful: SSN. Criminal records on computer from 1991, index books from 1890s.

General Information: Public Access terminal is available. No juvenile, mental, sealed, or adoption records released. Copy fee: $1.00 per page. Cert fee: $1.00. Payee: County Clerk. Personal checks accepted. Prepayment required. Mial requests require SASE. Mail turnaround time 1 day.

Duval County

District Court PO Drawer 428, San Diego, TX 78384; 361-279-3322 X239. Hours: 8AM-5PM (CST). *Felony, Civil.*

Civil Records: Access: Mail, in person. Both court and visitors may perform in person searches. Search fee: $15.00 per name. Fee is for large cases. Required to search: name, years to search. Civil cases indexed by defendant, plaintiff. Civil records on index books from 1900s.

Criminal Records: Access: Phone, mail, in person. Both court and visitors may perform in person searches. Search fee: $15.00 per name. Fee is for large cases. Required to search: name, years to search. Criminal records not computerized, indexed in books since 1900s.

General Information: No sealed, or adoption records released. Copy fee: $1.00 per page. Cert fee: $5.00. Payee: District Clerk. Personal checks accepted. Prepayment required. Mial requests require SASE. Mail turnaround time 1-2 days.

County Court PO Box 248, San Diego, TX 78384; 361-279-3322. Hours: 8AM-Noon, 1-5PM (CST). *Misdemeanor, Civil, Probate.*

Civil Records: Access: Mail, in person. Both court and visitors may perform in person searches. Search fee: $10.00 per name. Required to search: name, years to search. Civil cases indexed by defendant, plaintiff. Civil records in index books from 1800s, records go back to the early 1900s.

Criminal Records: Access: Mail, in person. Both court and visitors may perform in person searches. Search fee: $10.00 per name. Required to search: name, years to search, offense, date of offense. Criminal records in index books from 1800s.

General Information: No juvenile, mental, sealed, or adoption records released. Copy fee: $1.00 per page. Cert fee: $5.00. Payee: County Clerk. Personal checks accepted. Prepayment required. Mial requests require SASE. Mail turnaround time 2 days.

Eastland County

District Court 100 W Main St, #206, Eastland, TX 76448; 254-629-2664; Fax: 254-629-6070. Hours: 8AM-5PM (CST). *Felony, Civil.*

Civil Records: Access: Phone, fax, mail, in person. Both court and visitors may perform in person searches. Search fee: $5.00. Required to search: name, years to search. Civil cases indexed by defendant, plaintiff. Civil records on computer from 1930.

Criminal Records: Access: Phone, fax, mail, in person. Both court and visitors may perform in person searches. Search fee: $5.00. Required to search: name, years to search. Criminal records on computer from 1976, archived from 1875.

General Information: No juvenile, mental, sealed, or adoption records released. Will fax results to toll free line. Copy fee: $1.00 per page. Cert fee: $5.00. Payee: District Clerk. Personal checks accepted. Prepayment required. Mial requests require SASE. Mail turnaround time 1 day.

County Court PO Box 110, Eastland, TX 76448; 254-629-1583. Hours: 8AM-5PM (CST). *Misdemeanor, Probate.*

Note: No civil records after 1977; criminal and probate records only thereafter.

Criminal Records: Access: Mail, in person. Both court and visitors may perform in person searches. Search fee: $5.00 per name. Required to search: name, years to search, DOB; also helpful: SSN. Signed release required if subject is a minor. Criminal records in index books from 1873. Name searches only.

General Information: No juvenile, mental, sealed, or adoption records released. Copy fee: $1.00 per page. Cert fee: $5.00. Payee: Eastland County Clerk. Personal checks accepted. Checks must have phone number & DL number on check. Prepayment required. Mail turnaround time 1-2 days.

Ector County

District Court County Courthouse, 300 N Grant, Rm 301, Odessa, TX 79761; 432-498-4290; Fax: 432-498-4292. Hours: 8AM-5PM (CST). *Felony, Civil.*

Civil Records: Access: Phone, fax, mail, in person. Both court and visitors may perform in person searches. Search fee: $5.00 per name. Required to search: name, years to search. Civil cases indexed by defendant, plaintiff. Civil records on computer from 1989, index books from 1880.

Criminal Records: Access: Phone, mail, in person. Both court and visitors may perform in person searches. Search fee: $5.00 per name. Required to search: name, years to search. Criminal records on computer from 1989, index books from 1880.

General Information: Public Access terminal is available. No juvenile, mental, sealed, or adoption records released. Will fax results $2.00 per page. Copy fee: $.25 per page. Cert fee: $1.00 per page. Payee: Ector County District Clerk. Business checks accepted. Prepayment required. Mial requests require SASE. Mail turnaround time 2 weeks.

County Court PO Box 707, Odessa, TX 79760; 432-498-4130. Hours: 8AM-4:30PM (CST). *Misdemeanor, Civil, Probate.*

Civil Records: Access: Mail, in person. Both court and visitors may perform in person searches. Search fee: $5.00 per name per ten years. Required to search: name, years to search. Civil cases indexed by defendant, plaintiff. Civil records on computer from 1992, index books from 1900s.

Criminal Records: Access: Mail, in person. Both court and visitors may perform in person searches. Search fee: $5.00 per name per ten years. Required to search: name, years to search; also helpful: DOB, SSN. Criminal records on computer from 1989, index books from 1900s.

General Information: Public Access terminal is available. No juvenile, mental, sealed, or adoption records released. Fee to fax results is $2.00 per document. Copy fee: $1.00 per page. Cert fee: $5.00. Payee: County Clerk. Personal checks accepted. Prepayment required. Mial requests require SASE. Mail turnaround time 2 days.

Edwards County

District & County Court PO Box 184, Rocksprings, TX 78880; 830-683-2235; Fax: 830-683-5376. Hours: 8AM-Noon, 1-5PM (CST). *Felony, Misdemeanor, Civil, Probate.*

Civil Records: Access: Phone, fax, mail, in person. Both court and visitors may perform in person searches. Search fee: $10.00 per name. Required to search: name, years to search. Civil cases indexed by defendant, plaintiff. Civil records on computer from 1991, Real Property on computer from 1960, index books from 1885.

Criminal Records: Access: Phone, fax, mail, in person. Both court and visitors may perform in person searches. Search fee: $10.00 per name. Required to search: name, years to search. Criminal records on computer from 1991, index books from 1960.

General Information: No juvenile, mental, sealed, or adoption records released. Fee to fax results is $2.50 1st page, $.50 per page thereafter. Copy fee: $1.00 per page. Cert fee: $5.00. Payee: Edwards County Clerk. Personal checks accepted. Prepayment required. Mial requests require SASE. Mail turnaround time 1 day.

El Paso County

District Court 500 E San Antonio Rm 103, El Paso, TX 79901; 915-546-2021; Civil phone: 915-834-8256; Criminal phone: 915-834-8255. Hours: 8AM-4:45PM (MST). *Felony, Civil.*

www.co.el-paso.tx.us/districtclerk

Civil Records: Access: Mail, in person, online. Both court and visitors may perform in person searches. Search fee: $5.00 per name. Fee is per 10 year period. Required to search: name, years to search. Civil cases indexed by defendant, plaintiff. Civil records on computer from 1976, microfiche from 1971, index books from 1800s. Online access to civil court records is free at www.epcounty.com/search.htm. Also, access is through www.idocket.com; registration and password required. Civil records go back to 12/31/2000.

Criminal Records: Access: Mail, in person, online. Both court and visitors may perform in person searches. Search fee: $5.00 per name. Fee is per 10 year period. Required to search: name, years to search, DOB, signed release; also helpful: sex. Criminal records on computer from 1986, microfiche from 1971, index books from 1800s. Online access to criminal court records is free at www.epcounty.com/search.htm. Also, online access is through www.idocket.com; registration and password required; records go back to 6/1/2001.

General Information: Public Access terminal is available. No juvenile, mental, sealed, or adoption records released. Copy fee: $.25 per page. Cert fee: $1.00. Payee: District Clerk. Business checks accepted. Visa/MC accepted, but only by mail or phone. Prepayment required. Mial requests require SASE. Mail turnaround time 1-3 days.

County Court 500 E San Antonio St Rm 105, El Paso, TX 79901; 915-546-2072. Hours: 8AM-4:45PM (MST). *Misdemeanor, Civil.*

www.co.el-paso.tx.us

Civil Records: Access: Mail, fax, in person, online. Both court and visitors may perform in person searches. Search fee: $5.00 per name. Required to search: name, years to search. Civil cases indexed by defendant, plaintiff. Civil records on computer from 1989, on microfiche and archived from 1952. Online access to civil court records is free at www.co.el-paso.tx.us/search.htm. Also, search vital records and recordings. Also, access is through www.idocket.com; registration and password required. Civil and probate records go back to 12/31/1986.

Criminal Records: Access: Phone, mail, fax, in person, online. Both court and visitors may perform in person searches. Search fee: $5.00 per name. Required to search: name, years to search, DOB, SSN. Criminal records computerized since 1989. Online access to misdemeanor criminal records is the same as civil.

General Information: Public Access terminal is available. No juvenile, mental, sealed, or adoption records released. Copy fee: $1.00 per page. Cert fee: $5.00. Payee: County Clerk. Personal checks or credit cards accepted. Prepayment required. Mial requests require SASE. Mail turnaround time up to 1 week.

Probate Court 500 E San Antonio, Rm 703, El Paso, TX 79901; 915-546-2161; Fax: 915-533-4448. Hours: 8AM-12:00,1-5PM (MST). *Probate.*

Note: Access probate records at through www.idocket.com; registration and password required.Records go back to 12/31/1986.

Ellis County

District Court 305 E Franklin, Waxahachie, TX 75165; 972-825-5091. Hours: 8AM-5PM (CST). *Felony, Civil.*

Civil Records: Access: Mail, in person. Both court and visitors may perform in person searches. Search fee: $5.00 per name. Required to search: name, years to search. Civil cases indexed by defendant, plaintiff. Civil records on computer from 1992, index books from 1800s.

Criminal Records: Access: Mail, in person. Both court and visitors may perform in person searches. Search fee: $5.00 per name. Required to search: name, years to search, DOB, offense. Criminal records on computer from 1992, index books from 1800s.

General Information: Public Access terminal is available. No juvenile, mental, sealed, or adoption records released. Copy fee: $.50 per page. Cert fee: $1.00 per page. Payee: District Clerk's Office. Only cashiers checks and money orders accepted. Prepayment required. Mial requests require SASE. Mail turnaround time 1 week.

County Court PO Box 250, Waxahachie, TX 75168; 972-923-5070. Hours: 8AM-4:30PM (CST). *Misdemeanor, Civil, Probate.*
www.co.ellis.tx.us

Civil Records: Access: Mail, in person. Both court and visitors may perform in person searches. Search fee: $5.00 per name. Fee is per 5 year period. Required to search: name, years to search. Civil cases indexed by defendant, plaintiff. Civil records on computer go back to 1995. Prior to computer records go back to 1969.

Criminal Records: Access: Mail, in person. Both court and visitors may perform in person searches. Search fee: $10.00 per name. Fee is per 10 year period. Required to search: name, years to search, DOB, SSN. Criminal records on computer since 1992, index books from 1959.

General Information: Public Access terminal is available. No juvenile, mental, sealed, or adoption records released. Copy fee: $1.00 per page. Cert fee: $5.00. Payee: Ellis County Clerk. Personal checks accepted. Prepayment required. Mial requests require SASE. Mail turnaround time 1-5 days.

Erath County

District Court 112 W College, Courthouse Annex, Stephenville, TX 76401; 254-965-1486; Fax: 254-965-7156. Hours: 8AM-5PM (CST). *Felony, Civil.*
Note: District Court Phone # is 254-965-1485; Fax is 254--965-4287

Civil Records: Access: Mail, fax, in person. Both court and visitors may perform in person searches. Search fee: $5.00 per name. Fee is per name per search. Required to search: name, years to search. Civil cases indexed by defendant, plaintiff. Limited civil records on computer last 10 years, in person must be done using docket books.

Criminal Records: Access: Mail, fax, in person. Both court and visitors may perform in person searches. Search fee: $5.00 per name. Required to search: name, years to search, DOB; also helpful: SSN. Limited criminal records on computer last 10 years, in person must be done using docket books.

General Information: No juvenile, mental, sealed, or adoption records released. Fee to fax results is $1.00 per page. Copy fee: $1.00 per page. Cert fee: $5.00. Payee: District Clerk. Personal checks accepted. Prepayment required. Mial requests require SASE. Mail turnaround time 1-2 days.

County Court Erath County Courthouse, Stephenville, TX 76401; 254-965-1482. Hours: 8AM-4PM (CST). *Misdemeanor, Civil, Probate.*

Civil Records: Access: Mail, in person. Both court and visitors may perform in person searches. Search fee: $10.00 per name. Required to search: name, years to search. Civil cases indexed by defendant, plaintiff. Civil records on computer back to 1993, index books since 1970.

Criminal Records: Access: Mail, in person. Both court and visitors may perform in person searches. Search fee: $10.00 per name. Required to search: name, years to search, DOB. Criminal records on computer back to 1993, index books from 1960.

General Information: Public Access terminal is available. No juvenile, mental, sealed, or adoption records released. Copy fee: $1.00 per page. Cert fee: $5.00 plus $1.00 per page. Payee: County Clerk. Personal checks accepted. Prepayment required. Mial requests require SASE. Mail turnaround time 1 week.

Falls County

District Court 3rd Fl, NW Corner, 125 Bridge St. Rm 301, Marlin, TX 76661; 254-883-1419. Hours: 8AM-Noon, 1-4:30PM (CST). *Felony, Civil.*
Note: Mail requests to PO Box 229. In care of the District Clerk.

Civil Records: Access: Mail, in person. Both court and visitors may perform in person searches. Search fee: $5.00 per name. Required to search: name, years to search. Civil cases indexed by defendant, plaintiff. Overall records go back to 1850s. Computerized records go back to 1998.

Criminal Records: Access: Mail, in person. Both court and visitors may perform in person searches. Search fee: $5.00 per name. Required to search: name, years to search; also helpful: DOB. Criminal records in index books.

General Information: Public Access terminal is available. No juvenile, mental, sealed, child support or adoption records released. Copy fee: $1.00 per page. No cert fee. Payee: District Clerk. Personal checks accepted. Prepayment required. Mial requests require SASE. Mail turnaround time 1-5 days.

County Court PO Box 458, Marlin, TX 76661; 254-883-1408. Hours: 8AM-5PM (CST). *Misdemeanor, Civil, Probate.*

Civil Records: Access: Phone, mail, in person. Both court and visitors may perform in person searches. Search fee: $5.00 per name. Required to search: name, years to search. Civil cases indexed by defendant, plaintiff. Civil records in index books from 1985. Phone search only if fee prepaid.

Criminal Records: Access: Phone, mail, in person. Both court and visitors may perform in person searches. Search fee: $5.00 per name. Required to search: name, years to search, DOB, SSN. Criminal records in index books from 1985. Phone search only if fee is prepaid.

General Information: No juvenile, mental, sealed, or adoption records released. Copy fee: $1.00 per page. Cert fee: $5.00. Payee: County Clerk. Local personal and business checks accepted. Prepayment required. Mial requests require SASE. Mail turnaround time 1 day.

Fannin County

District Court Fannin County Courthouse #201, Bonham, TX 75418; 903-583-7459; Fax: 903-640-1826. Hours: 8AM-Noon, 1-5PM (CST). *Felony, Civil.*

Civil Records: Access: Fax, mail, in person. Both court and visitors may perform in person searches. Search fee: $5.00 per name. Required to search: name, years to search. Civil cases indexed by

defendant, plaintiff. Civil records in index books, archived from 1865.

Criminal Records: Access: Fax, mail, in person. Both court and visitors may perform in person searches. Search fee: $5.00 per name. Fee is for felonies only. Required to search: name, years to search, address, DOB, SSN. Criminal records on computer from 1985, books from 1975, archived from 1865.

General Information: No juvenile, mental, sealed, or adoption records released. No fee to fax results. Fax available to 800 numbers only. Copy fee: $1.00 per page. Cert fee: $2.00. Payee: District Clerk, Fannin County. Personal checks accepted. Prepayment required. Mial requests require SASE. Mail turnaround time 2 days.

County Court County Courthouse, 101 E Sam Rayburn #102, Bonham, TX 75418; 903-583-7486; Civil phone: 903-640-2008; Criminal phone: 903-583-7488; Probate phone: 903-640-2008; Fax: 903-583-7811. Hours: 8AM-5PM (CST). *Misdemeanor, Civil, Probate.*

Civil Records: Access: Phone, mail, in person. Both court and visitors may perform in person searches. Search fee: $5.00 per name. Required to search: name, years to search. Civil cases indexed by defendant, plaintiff. Civil records in index books.

Criminal Records: Access: Phone, mail, in person. Both court and visitors may perform in person searches. Search fee: $5.00 per name. Required to search: name, years to search, DOB; also helpful-SSN. Criminal records on computer back to 1979; prior on index books.

General Information: No juvenile, mental, sealed, or adoption records released. Copy fee: $1.00 per page. Cert fee: $5.00. Payee: County Clerk. Personal checks accepted. Prepayment required. Mial requests require SASE. Mail turnaround time 1 day.

Fayette County

District Court Fayette County Courthouse, 151 N Washington, La Grange, TX 78945; 979-968-3548; Fax: 979-968-2618. Hours: 8AM-5PM (CST). *Felony, Civil.*
www.cvtv.net/~tx155district

Civil Records: Access: Mail, in person. Both court and visitors may perform in person searches. Search fee: $5.00 per name. Required to search: name, years to search. Civil cases indexed by defendant, plaintiff. Civil records in index books, on computer since 1992.

Criminal Records: Access: Mail, in person. Both court and visitors may perform in person searches. Search fee: $5.00 per name. Required to search: name, years to search. Criminal records in index books, on computer since 1990.

General Information: Public Access terminal is available. No juvenile, mental, sealed, or adoption records released. Copy fee: $1.00 per page. Cert fee: $2.00. Payee: Fayette County District Clerk. Personal checks accepted. Prepayment required. Mial requests require SASE. Mail turnaround time 2-3 days.

County Court PO Box 59, La Grange, TX 78945; 979-968-3251. Hours: 8AM-5PM (CST). *Misdemeanor, Civil, Probate.*

Civil Records: Access: Phone, mail, in person. Both court and visitors may perform in person searches. Search fee: $5.00 per name. Required to search: name, years to search. Civil cases indexed by defendant, plaintiff. Civil records in index books, archived from 1970.

Criminal Records: Access: Phone, mail, in person. Both court and visitors may perform in person searches. Search fee: $5.00 per name. Required to search: name, years to search. Criminal records on computer from 1980, index books prior.

General Information: No juvenile, mental, sealed, or adoption records released. Copy fee: $1.00 per page. Cert fee: $5.00 plus $1.00 per page. Payee: County Clerk. Personal checks accepted. Prepayment required. Mial requests require SASE. Mail turnaround time 1 day.

Fisher County

32nd District Court PO Box 88, Roby, TX 79543; 325-776-2279; Fax: 325-776-3253. Hours: 8AM-5PM (CST). *Felony, Civil.*

Civil Records: Access: Mail, fax, in person. Both court and visitors may perform in person searches. Search fee: $5.00 per name. Required to search: name, years to search; also helpful: address. Civil cases indexed by defendant, plaintiff. Civil records in index books from 1886.

Criminal Records: Access: Mail, fax, in person. Both court and visitors may perform in person searches. Search fee: $5.00 per name. Required to search: name, years to search, signed release; also helpful: address, DOB. Criminal records in index books from 1886.

General Information: No juvenile, mental, sealed, or adoption records released. Fee to fax results is $1.00 per page. Copy fee: $.50 per page. Cert fee: $1.00 per page. Payee: District Clerk. Business checks accepted. Prepayment required. Mial requests require SASE. Mail turnaround time 1-2 days.

County Court Box 368, Roby, TX 79543-0368; 325-776-2401. Hours: 8AM-Noon, 1-5PM (CST). *Misdemeanor, Civil, Probate.*

Civil Records: Access: Mail, in person. Both court and visitors may perform in person searches. Search fee: $5.00 per name. Required to search: name, years to search. Civil cases indexed by defendant, plaintiff. Civil records on computer from 1994 index books from 1880.

Criminal Records: Access: Mail, in person. Both court and visitors may perform in person searches. Search fee: $5.00 per name. Required to search: name, years to search, signed release, offense. Criminal records on computer from 1994, index books from 1886.

General Information: No juvenile, mental, sealed, or adoption records released. Copy fee: $1.00 per page. Cert fee: $5.00. Payee: Fisher County Clerk. Personal checks accepted. Prepayment required. Mial requests require SASE. Mail turnaround time 1 day.

Floyd County

District Court PO Box 67, Floydada, TX 79235; 806-983-4923. Hours: 8:30AM-Noon, 1-4:45PM (CST). *Felony, Civil.*

Civil Records: Access: Phone, mail, in person. Both court and visitors may perform in person searches. Search fee: $5.00 per name. Required to search: name, years to search. Civil cases indexed by defendant, plaintiff. Civil records in index books from early 1891.

Criminal Records: Access: Mail, in person. Both court and visitors may perform in person searches. Search fee: $5.00 per name. Required to search: name, years to search. Criminal records in index books from early 1891.

General Information: No juvenile, mental, sealed, or adoption records released. Copy fee: $1.00 1st page, $.25 each add'l. Cert fee: $1.00. Payee: District Clerk. Personal checks accepted. Prepayment required. Mial requests require SASE. Mail turnaround time 1 day.

County Court Courthouse, Rm 101, Main St, Floydada, TX 79235; 806-983-4900. Hours: 8:30AM-Noon, 1-5PM (CST). *Misdemeanor, Civil, Probate.*

Civil Records: Access: Phone, mail, in person. Both court and visitors may perform in person searches. Search fee: $10.00 per name. Required to search:

name, years to search. Civil cases indexed by defendant, plaintiff. Civil records in index books from 1890.

Criminal Records: Access: Phone, mail, in person. Both court and visitors may perform in person searches. Search fee: $10.00 per name. Required to search: name, years to search, DOB. Criminal records in index books from 1890.

General Information: No juvenile, mental, sealed, or adoption records released. Will fax results for $1.00 per page. Copy fee: $1.00 per page. Cert fee: $5.00. Payee: County Clerk. Personal checks accepted. Prepayment required. Mail turnaround time 1-5 days.

Foard County

District & County Court PO Box 539, Crowell, TX 79227; 940-684-1365. Hours: 9AM-4:30PM (CST). *Felony, Misdemeanor, Civil, Probate.*

Civil Records: Access: Mail, in person. Both court and visitors may perform in person searches. Search fee: $10.00 per name. Required to search: name, years to search. Civil cases indexed by defendant, plaintiff. Civil records go back to 1908, civil records in index books from 1910; on computer from 1989.

Criminal Records: Access: Mail, in person. Both court and visitors may perform in person searches. Search fee: $10.00 per name. Required to search: name, years to search, DOB. Criminal records go back to 1908, criminal records in index books from 1910; on computer from 1989.

General Information: No juvenile, mental, sealed, or adoption records released. Fee to fax results is $2.50 1st page, $.25 per page each add'l. Copy fee: $1.00 per page. Cert fee: $5.00. Payee: District or County Clerk. Personal checks accepted. Prepayment required. Mial requests require SASE. Mail turnaround time varies.

Fort Bend County

District Court 301 Jackson, Richmond, TX 77469; 281-341-4515; Civil phone: 281-341-4562; Criminal phone: 281-341-4542; Fax: 281-341-4519. Hours: 8AM-5PM (CST). *Felony, Civil.*
Note: Physical court location is 401 Jackson.

Civil Records: Access: Phone, mail, online, in person. Both court and visitors may perform in person searches. Search fee: $5.00 per name. Required to search: name, years to search. Civil cases indexed by defendant, plaintiff. Civil records on computer from 1991, index books from early 1900s. There are 2 online modes. The commercial system is via a 900 number service; fee is $.55 per minute plus a deposit. DOBs are included on this system. Call 281-341-4522 for information. Search for free at http://courtcn.co.fort-bend.tx.us/. Records go back to 9/2000; no DOBs.

Criminal Records: Access: Mail, online, in person. Both court and visitors may perform in person searches. Search fee: $5.00 per name. Required to search: name, years to search, DOB, SSN. Criminal records on computer from 1981, index books from early 1900s. Criminal records from 1987 are on the same commercial pay online system as civil records. Criminal records are not on the website.

General Information: Public Access terminal is available. (Located at 401 Jackson, Rm 100, Richmond, TX 77469.) No juvenile, mental, sealed, termination or adoption records released. Copy fee: $.50 per page. Include $1.00 for postage. Fee for microfilm copies $.50 per page. Cert fee: $.50 per page. Payee: District Clerk. No out of state personal checks accepted. For legal ease account info call 281-341-4508. Prepayment required. Mial requests require SASE. Mail turnaround time 2-3 weeks.

County Court Attn: Clerk, 301 Jackson St, #101, Richmond, TX 77469; 281-341-8685; Fax: 281-341-4520. Hours: 8AM-4PM (CST). *Misdemeanor, Civil, Probate, Juvenile.*
www.co.fort-bend.tx.us

Civil Records: Access: Mail, online, in person. Both court and visitors may perform in person searches. Search fee: $10.00 per name. Search fee is for each type record to be searched. Required to search: name, years to search. Civil cases indexed by defendant, plaintiff. Civil records on computer from 1984, also 1984-present optical imaged. Online access to the civil records index free at www.co.fort-bend.tx.us/Admin_of_Justice/County_Clerk/index_info_research.htm. Includes Probate records index online.

Criminal Records: Access: Mail, online, in person. Both court and visitors may perform in person searches. Search fee: $10.00 per name. A search fee for each type record to be searched required. Required to search: name, years to search, DOB. Criminal records on computer from 1983, also 1983 to present optical imaged. Online access to the criminal index is the same as civil.

General Information: Public Access terminal is available. No juvenile, mental, sealed, or adoption records released. Fee to fax results is $1.00 per page. Copy fee: $1.00 per page. Cert fee: $5.00. Payee: Ft Bend County Clerk. Personal checks accepted. Visa, MC accepted. Prepayment required. Mail turnaround time 1-2 days.

Franklin County

District Court PO Box 750, Mount Vernon, TX 75457; 903-537-4786. Hours: 8AM-5PM (CST). *Felony, Civil.*

Civil Records: Access: Mail, in person. Both court and visitors may perform in person searches. Search fee: $5.00 per name. Required to search: name, years to search. Civil cases indexed by defendant, plaintiff. Civil records on computer from 1987, on microfiche from 1986, index books from 1800s.

Criminal Records: Access: Mail, in person. Both court and visitors may perform in person searches. Search fee: $5.00 per name. Required to search: name, years to search; also helpful: DOB, SSN. Criminal records on computer from 1987, on microfiche from 1986, index books from 1800s.

General Information: No juvenile, mental, sealed, or adoption records released. Will fax results for $1.00 per page. Copy fee: $1.00 per page. Cert fee: $5.00. Payee: District Clerk. Personal checks accepted. Prepayment required. Mial requests require SASE. Mail turnaround time 1 day.

County Court PO Box 68, Mount Vernon, TX 75457; 903-537-4252 ext 6; Fax: 903-537-4252. Hours: 8AM-5PM (CST). *Misdemeanor, Civil, Probate.*

Civil Records: Access: Mail, fax, in person. Both court and visitors may perform in person searches. Search fee: $5.00 per name. Required to search: name, years to search. Civil cases indexed by defendant, plaintiff. Civil records on computer from 1993, index books from 1847.

Criminal Records: Access: Mail, fax, in person. Both court and visitors may perform in person searches. Search fee: $5.00 per name. Required to search: name, years to search, DOB and SSN. Criminal records on computer from 1993, index books from 1847.

General Information: Public Access terminal is available. No juvenile, mental, sealed, or adoption records released. Fee to fax results is $1.00 per page. Copy fee: $1.00 per page. Cert fee: $5.00. Payee: County Clerk. Personal checks accepted. Prepayment required. Mial requests require SASE. Mail turnaround time 1 week.

Freestone County

District Court PO Box 722, Fairfield, TX 75840; 903-389-2534. Hours: 8AM-5PM (CST). *Felony, Civil.*

Civil Records: Access: Phone, mail, in person. Both court and visitors may perform in person searches. Search fee: $5.00 per name. Required to search: name, years to search. Civil cases indexed by defendant, plaintiff. Civil records in index books from 1830s.

Criminal Records: Access: Phone, mail, in person. Both court and visitors may perform in person searches. Search fee: $5.00 per name. Required to search: name, years to search. Criminal records in index books from 1830s.

General Information: No juvenile, mental, sealed, or adoption records released. Copy fee: $1.00 per page. Cert fee: $1.00. Payee: District Clerk. Personal checks accepted. Prepayment required. Mial requests require SASE. Mail turnaround time 1 day.

County Court PO Box 1010, Fairfield, TX 75840; 903-389-2635. Hours: 8AM-5PM (CST). *Misdemeanor, Civil, Probate.*

Civil Records: Access: Mail, in person. Both court and visitors may perform in person searches. Search fee: $5.00 per name. Required to search: name, years to search. Civil cases indexed by defendant, plaintiff. Civil records in index books from 1967.

Criminal Records: Access: Mail, in person. Both court and visitors may perform in person searches. Search fee: $5.00 per name. Required to search: name, years to search. Criminal records in index books from 1967.

General Information: No juvenile, mental, sealed, or adoption records released. Copy fee: $1.00 per page. Cert fee: $5.00. Payee: Freestone County Clerk. Personal checks accepted. Prepayment required. Mial requests require SASE. Mail turnaround time 2 days.

Frio County

District Court 500 E San Antonio Box 8, Pearsall, TX 78061; 830-334-8073; Fax: 830-334-0047. Hours: 8AM-5PM (CST). *Felony, Civil.*

Civil Records: Access: Mail, in person. Both court and visitors may perform in person searches. Search fee: $5.00 per name. Required to search: name, years to search; also helpful: address. Civil cases indexed by defendant, plaintiff. Civil records in index books from 1948.

Criminal Records: Access: Mail, in person. Both court and visitors may perform in person searches. Search fee: $5.00 per name. Required to search: name, years to search, DOB; also helpful: address. Criminal records in index books from 1950.

General Information: No juvenile, mental, sealed, or adoption records released. Fee to fax results is $2.00 per page. Copy fee: $1.00 per page. Cert fee: $1.00. Payee: District Clerk. Business checks accepted. Prepayment required. Mial requests require SASE. Mail turnaround time 2-3 days.

County Court 500 E San Antonio St #6, Pearsall, TX 78061; 830-334-2214; Fax: 830-334-0021. Hours: 8AM-5PM (CST). *Misdemeanor, Civil, Probate.*

Civil Records: Access: Fax, mail, in person. Both court and visitors may perform in person searches. Search fee: $10.00 per name. Required to search: name, years to search. Civil cases indexed by defendant, plaintiff. Civil records go back to 1800s, civil records in index books from 1876, no computerized records.

Criminal Records: Access: Fax, mail, in person. Both court and visitors may perform in person searches. Search fee: $10.00 per name. Required to

search: name, years to search. Criminal records go back to 1800s, criminal records in index books from 1876; no computerized records.

General Information: No juvenile, mental, sealed, or adoption records released. Will fax results $2.00 per page. Copy fee: $1.00 per page. Cert fee: $5.00. Payee: County Clerk. Personal checks accepted. Prepayment required. Mial requests require SASE. Mail turnaround time 2-4 days.

Gaines County

District Court 101 S Main Rm 213, Seminole, TX 79360; 432-758-4013; Fax: 432-758-4036. Hours: 8AM-Noon, 1-5PM (CST). *Felony, Civil.*

Civil Records: Access: Phone, mail, in person. Only the court performs in person searches; visitors may not. Search fee: $5.00 per name. Required to search: name, years to search. Civil cases indexed by defendant, plaintiff. Civil records on computer from 1980, index books from 1900s.

Criminal Records: Access: Phone, mail, in person. Only the court performs in person searches; visitors may not. Search fee: $5.00 per name. Required to search: name, years to search. Criminal records on computer from 1980, index books from 1900s.

General Information: No juvenile, mental, sealed, or adoption records released. Will fax results to local or toll free line. Copy fee: $1.00 per page. Cert fee: $5.00. Payee: District Clerk. Personal checks accepted. Prepayment required. Mial requests require SASE. Mail turnaround time 1 day.

County Court 101 S Main Rm 107, Seminole, TX 79360; 432-758-4003. Hours: 8AM-5PM (CST). *Misdemeanor, Civil, Probate.*

Civil Records: Access: Mail, in person. Both court and visitors may perform in person searches. No search fee. Required to search: name, years to search. Civil cases indexed by defendant, plaintiff. Civil records available from 1800s, computerized since 1991.

Criminal Records: Access: Mail, in person. Both court and visitors may perform in person searches. No search fee. Required to search: name, years to search. Criminal records available from 1800s, computerized since 1991. Probate records may be accessed with same criteria as civil records.

General Information: Public Access terminal is available. No juvenile, mental, sealed, or adoption records released. Will fax results for $1.00 per page pluss $2.00 call. Copy fee: $1.00 per page. Cert fee: $5.00. Payee: County Clerk. Personal checks accepted. Prepayment required. Mial requests require SASE. Mail turnaround time 1 day.

Galveston County

District Court 722 Moody St Rm 404, Galveston, TX 77550; 409-766-2424; Fax: 409-766-2292. Hours: 8AM-5PM (CST). *Felony, Civil.*

www.co.galveston.tx.us/District_Courts/default.htm

Civil Records: Access: Fax, mail, in person. Search fee: $5.00 per name. Required to search: name, years to search. Civil cases indexed by defendant, plaintiff. Civil records on computer from 1984, on microfiche from 1982, archived from 1849. Online access to Judge's daily calendars is free at the website. Fax access is only allowed with prepaid accounts.

Criminal Records: Access: Fax, mail, in person. Both court and visitors may perform in person searches. Search fee: $5.00 per name. Required to search: name, years to search, DOB. Criminal records on computer from 1984, on microfiche from 1982, archived from 1849. Online access to Judge's daily calendars is free at the website.

General Information: Public Access terminal is available. No juvenile, mental, sealed, or adoption records released. Copy fee: $1.00 per page. Cert fee:

$2.00 for an affidavit. Payee: District Clerk. Personal checks accepted. Prepayment required. Mial requests require SASE. Mail turnaround time 2-5 days.

County Court PO Box 2450, Galveston, TX 77553-2450; 409-766-2200; Civil phone: 409-766-2203; Criminal phone: 409-770-5112; Probate phone: 409-766-2202. Hours: 8AM-5PM (CST). *Misdemeanor, Civil, Probate.*

www.co.galveston.tx.us/County_Courts

Civil Records: Access: Mail, in person. Both court and visitors may perform in person searches. Search fee: $5.00 per name. Required to search: name, years to search. Civil cases indexed by defendant, plaintiff. Civil records on computer from 1984, index books from 1947. Access to the GCNET remote online service has been suspended. Requires $200 escrow account plus a $.25 per minute fee. For more information, call 409-770-5115.

Criminal Records: Access: Mail, in person. Both court and visitors may perform in person searches. Search fee: $5.00 per name. Required to search: name, years to search, DOB; also helpful: SSN. Criminal records on computer from 1984, index books from 1947.

General Information: Public Access terminal is available. No juvenile, mental, sealed, or adoption records released. Copy fee: $1.00 per page. Cert fee: $5.00 per document. Payee: County Clerk. Prepayment required. Mial requests require SASE. Mail turnaround time 1-2 days.

Garza County

District & County Court PO Box 366, Post, TX 79356; 806-495-4430; Fax: 806-495-4431. Hours: 8AM-Noon,1-5PM (CST). *Felony, Misdemeanor, Civil, Probate.*

Civil Records: Access: Mail, in person. Both court and visitors may perform in person searches. Search fee: $5.00 per name. Required to search: name, years to search. Civil cases indexed by defendant, plaintiff. Civil records on index books.

Criminal Records: Access: Mail, in person. Both court and visitors may perform in person searches. Search fee: $5.00 per name. Required to search: name, years to search, DOB or SSN. Criminal records on index books.

General Information: Fee to fax results is $4.00 per document. Copy fee: $1.00 per page. Cert fee: $5.00. Payee: District or County Clerk. Personal checks accepted. Prepayment required. Mail turnaround time 2-3 days.

Gillespie County

District Court 101 W Main Rm 204, Fredericksburg, TX 78624; 830-997-6517. Hours: Public hours 8AM-5PM (CST). *Felony, Civil.*

Civil Records: Access: Mail, in person. Both court and visitors may perform in person searches. Search fee: $5.00 per name. Required to search: name, years to search. Civil cases indexed by defendant, plaintiff. Civil records in index books from 1800s. Index #1 from 1800s-1927, Index #2 from 1927-1988, Index #3 from 1989-present.

Criminal Records: Access: Mail, in person. Both court and visitors may perform in person searches. Search fee: $5.00 per name. Required to search: name, years to search; also helpful: DOB, SSN. Criminal records in index books from 1800s. Index #1 from 1800s-1927, Index #2 from 1927-1988, Index #3 from 1989-present.

General Information: No juvenile, mental, sealed, or adoption records released. Copy fee: $1.00 for first page, $.25 each add'l. Cert fee: $1.00 per page. Payee: Gillespie County District Clerk. Personal checks accepted. Prepayment required. Mial requests require SASE. Mail turnaround time 1-2 days.

County Court 101 W Main Unit #13, Fredericksburg, TX 78624; 830-997-6515; Fax: 830-997-9958. Hours: 8AM-4PM (CST). *Misdemeanor, Civil, Probate.*

Civil Records: Access: Mail, in person. Both court and visitors may perform in person searches. Search fee: $5.00 per name. Required to search: name, years to search; also helpful: address. Civil cases indexed by defendant, plaintiff. Civil records on computer from 1988, on microfiche from 1990, index books from 1900s.

Criminal Records: Access: Mail, in person. Both court and visitors may perform in person searches. Search fee: $5.00 per name. Required to search: name, years to search, aliases; also helpful: DOB, SSN. Criminal records on computer from 1987, on microfiche from 1990, index books from 1900s.

General Information: Public Access terminal is available. No juvenile, mental, sealed, or adoption record released. Copy fee: $1.00 per page. Cert fee: $10.00. Payee: Mary Lynn Rusche County Clerk. No out-of-town personal checks accepted. Prepayment required. Mial requests require SASE. Mail turnaround time 1-2 days.

Glasscock County

District & County Court PO Box 190, 117 E Currie, Garden City, TX 79739; 432-354-2371. Hours: 8AM-4PM (CST). *Felony, Misdemeanor, Civil, Probate.*

Civil Records: Access: Mail, in person. Both court and visitors may perform in person searches. Search fee: $10.00 per name. Required to search: name, years to search. Civil cases indexed by defendant, plaintiff. Civil records in index books from 1893.

Criminal Records: Access: Mail, in person. Both court and visitors may perform in person searches. Search fee: $10.00 per name. Required to search: name, years to search, DOB. Criminal records in index books from 1893.

General Information: No juvenile, mental, or adoption records released. Will fax results for $2.00 per page. Copy fee: $1.00 per page. Cert fee: $5.00. Payee: District or County Clerk. Personal checks accepted. Prepayment required. Mial requests require SASE. Mail turnaround time 2 days.

Goliad County

District & County Court PO Box 50 (127 N Courthouse Sq.), Goliad, TX 77963; 361-645-3294; Fax: 361-645-3858. Hours: 8AM-5PM, closed 1 hour at noon (CST). *Felony, Misdemeanor, Civil, Probate.* Note: May be at 218 S Commercial St through 2003, after will be at 127 N Courthouse Sq.

Civil Records: Access: Mail, in person. Both court and visitors may perform in person searches. Search fee: $10.00 per name. Fee is per court. Required to search: name, years to search; also helpful: address. Civil cases indexed by defendant, plaintiff. Civil records on computer since 1983 (real property only), on microfiche and index books from 1870.

Criminal Records: Access: Mail, in person. Both court and visitors may perform in person searches. Search fee: $10.00 per name. Fee is per court. Required to search: name, years to search; also helpful: address, DOB, SSN, offense. Criminal records on microfiche and index books from 1870.

General Information: Public Access terminal is available. No juvenile, mental, sealed, or adoption records released. Fee to fax results is $1.00 per page. Copy fee: $1.00 per page. Cert fee: Fee is $5.00 for County Court; $1.00 for District Court plus $1.00 per page. Payee: Goliad County/District Clerk. Personal checks accepted. Prepayment required. Mail turnaround time 1-2 days.

Gonzales County

District Court PO Box 34, Gonzales, TX 78629-0034; 830-672-2326; Fax: 830-672-9313. Hours: 8AM-Noon 1-5PM (CST). *Felony, Civil.*

Civil Records: Access: Phone, fax, mail, in person. Both court and visitors may perform in person searches. Search fee: $5.00 per name. Required to search: name, years to search; also helpful: address. Civil cases indexed by defendant, plaintiff. Civil records on computer from 1991, index books from 1800s.

Criminal Records: Access: Phone, fax, mail, in person. Both court and visitors may perform in person searches. Search fee: $5.00 per name. Required to search: name, years to search; also helpful: address, DOB, SSN. Criminal records on computer from 1991, index books from 1800s.

General Information: No juvenile, mental, sealed, or adoption records released. Fee to fax results is $1.00 per page. Copy fee: $1.00 per page. No cert fee. Payee: District Clerk. Personal checks accepted. Prepayment required. Mial requests require SASE. Mail turnaround time 1-2 days.

County Court PO Box 77, Gonzales, TX 78629; 830-672-2801; Fax: 830-672-2636. Hours: 8AM-5PM (CST). *Misdemeanor, Civil, Probate.*

Civil Records: Access: Fax, mail, in person. Both court and visitors may perform in person searches. Search fee: $5.00 per name. Required to search: name, years to search. Civil cases indexed by defendant, plaintiff. Civil records on computer since 1993, original jackets since 1975, index books from 1900s.

Criminal Records: Access: Mail, in person. Both court and visitors may perform in person searches. Search fee: $5.00 per name. Required to search: name, years to search, offense, date of offense. Criminal records on computer since 1993, original jackets, index books from 1900s.

General Information: Public Access terminal is available. No mental or drug dependant commitment records released. Fee to fax results is $5.00. Copy fee: $1.00 per page. Cert fee: $5.00. Payee: County Clerk. Personal checks accepted. Prepayment required. Mial requests require SASE. Mail turnaround time 1-2 days.

Gray County

District Court PO Box 1139, Pampa, TX 79066-1139; 806-669-8010; Fax: 806-669-8053. Hours: 8:30AM-5PM (CST). *Felony, Civil.*

Civil Records: Access: Fax, mail, in person. Both court and visitors may perform in person searches. Search fee: $5.00 per name. Required to search: name, years to search, DOB. Civil cases indexed by defendant, plaintiff. Civil records on computer from 1940, index books from 1910. All requests must be in writing.

Criminal Records: Access: Fax, mail, in person. Both court and visitors may perform in person searches. Search fee: $5.00 per name. Required to search: name, years to search; also helpful: DOB. Criminal records go back to 1930; criminal records on computer from 1965. All requests must be in writing.

General Information: No juvenile, mental, sealed, or adoption records released. Will fax results $1.00 per page. Copy fee: $.50 per page. Cert fee: $1.00 per page. Payee: District Clerk. Personal checks accepted. Prepayment required. Mial requests require SASE. Mail turnaround time 1-2 days.

County & Probate Court PO Box 1902, Pampa, TX 79066-1902; 806-669-8004; Fax: 806-669-8054. Hours: 8:30AM-5PM (CST). *Misdemeanor, Civil, Probate.*

Civil Records: Access: Phone, fax, mail, in person. Both court and visitors may perform in person searches. Search fee: $10.00 per name. Fee is per index. Required to search: name, years to search. Civil cases indexed by defendant, plaintiff. Civil records on type written indices from 1900s.

Criminal Records: Access: Phone, fax, mail, in person. Both court and visitors may perform in person searches. Search fee: $10.00 per name. Fee is per index. Required to search: name, years to search, DOB. Criminal records on type written indices from 1900s.

General Information: No juvenile, mental, sealed, or adoption records released. They will not release any records with the SSN on it. Will fax results $2.50 1st page, $1.00 each add'l. Copy fee: $1.00 per page. Cert fee: $5.00. Payee: Susan Winborne, County Clerk. Personal checks accepted. Prepayment required. Mial requests require SASE. Mail turnaround time 1-2 days.

Grayson County

District Court 200 S Crockett Rm 120-A, Sherman, TX 75090; 903-813-4352. Hours: 8AM-5PM (CST). *Felony, Civil, Family.*
www.co.grayson.tx.us

Civil Records: Access: Mail, in person. Both court and visitors may perform in person searches. Search fee: $5.00 per name. Required to search: name, years to search. Civil cases indexed by defendant, plaintiff. Civil records on computer from 1988, microfilm since 1939, index books since 1900s.

Criminal Records: Access: Mail, in person. Both court and visitors may perform in person searches. Search fee: $5.00 per name. Required to search: name, years to search, DOB; also helpful: SSN. Criminal records on computer since 1988, microfilm since 1939, index books since 1900s.

General Information: Public Access terminal is available. No juvenile, mental, sealed, expunction or adoption records released. Will not fax results. Copy fee: $1.00 per page. Cert fee: $1.00. Payee: District Clerk. Personal checks accepted. Prepayment required. Mial requests require SASE. Mail turnaround time 1-2 days.

County Court 200 S Crockett, Sherman, TX 75090; 903-813-4336; Civil phone: 903-813-4335; Probate phone: 903-813-4241; Fax: 903-892-8300. Hours: 8AM-5PM (CST). *Misdemeanor, Civil, Probate.*
www.co.grayson.tx.us

Civil Records: Access: Mail, in person, online. Both court and visitors may perform in person searches. Search fee: $5.00 per name. Required to search: name, years to search. Civil cases indexed by defendant, plaintiff. Civil records on computer since 1992, index books since 1952. Online access to civil records free at www.co.grayson.tx.us:3004/judsrch.asp. Also includes sheriffs' bail, and sheriff's jail searching.

Criminal Records: Access: Mail, in person, online. Both court and visitors may perform in person searches. Search fee: $5.00 per name. Required to search: name, years to search, also helpful: DOB, SSN. Criminal records on computer from 1982. Online access to criminal records is the same as civil.

General Information: Public Access terminal is available. No juvenile, mental, sealed, or adoption records released. Will fax results if prepaid. Copy fee: $1.00 per page. Cert fee: $5.00. Payee: County Clerk. Personal checks accepted. Prepayment required. Mial requests require SASE. Mail turnaround time 1-2 days.

Gregg County

District Court PO Box 711, Longview, TX 75606; 903-237-2663. Hours: 8AM-5PM (CST). *Felony, Civil.*
www.co.gregg.tx.us/government/courts.asp
Civil Records: Access: Phone, fax, mail, in person, online. Both court and visitors may perform in person searches. Search fee: $5.00 per name. Required to search: name, years to search. Civil cases indexed by defendant, plaintiff. Civil records on computer back to 1981, index books from 1873. Online access to county judicial records is free at www.co.gregg.tx.us/judsrch.htm. Search by name, cause number, status.
Criminal Records: Access: Phone, fax, mail, in person, online. Both court and visitors may perform in person searches. Search fee: $5.00 per name. Required to search: name, years to search. Criminal records on computer back to 1977, index books from 1873. Online access to criminal records is the same as civil. Also includes jail and bond search.
General Information: Public Access terminal is available. No juvenile, mental, sealed, or adoption records released. Will fax results $1.00 per page. Copy fee: $1.00 per page. Cert fee: $1.00 per page. Payee: District Clerk. Only cashiers checks and money orders accepted. Prepayment required. Mial requests require SASE. Mail turnaround time 1-2 days.

County Court 101 E methvin, #200, Longview, TX 75606; 903-236-8430. Hours: 8AM-5PM (CST). *Misdemeanor, Civil, Probate.*
www.co.gregg.tx.us/government/commissionersCourt/county_judge.asp
Civil Records: Access: Mail, in person, online. Both court and visitors may perform in person searches. Search fee: $5.00 per name. Required to search: name, years to search. Civil cases indexed by defendant, plaintiff. Civil records on computer from 1983, index books after 1962. Online access to county judicial records is free at www.co.gregg.tx.us/judsrch.htm. Search by name, cause number, or status.
Criminal Records: Access: Mail, in person, online. Both court and visitors may perform in person searches. Search fee: $5.00 per name. Required to search: name, years to search, DOB or SSN. Criminal records on computer from 1983, index books after 1932. Online access to criminal records is the same as civil. Jail and bond search also available.
General Information: Public Access terminal is available. No juvenile, mental, sealed, or adoption records released. Fee to fax results is $1.00 per page. Copy fee: $1.00 per page. Cert fee: $5.00. Payee: Gregg County Clerk. Only in state personal checks accepted. Prepayment required. Mial requests require SASE. Mail turnaround time 1 week.

Grimes County

District Court PO Box 234, Anderson, TX 77830; 936-873-2111/2606; Fax: 936-873-2415. Hours: 8AM-4:45PM (CST). *Felony, Civil.*
Civil Records: Access: Phone, fax, mail, in person. Both court and visitors may perform in person searches. Search fee: $5.00 per name. Required to search: name, years to search. Civil cases indexed by defendant, plaintiff. Civil records on computer from 1990, index books from 1800s.
Criminal Records: Access: Phone, fax, mail, in person. Both court and visitors may perform in person searches. Search fee: $5.00 per name. Required to search: name, years to search, DOB, SSN. Criminal

records on computer from 1990, index books from 1800s.
General Information: No juvenile, mental, sealed, or adoption records released. Will fax results for $1.00 per page. Copy fee: $1.00 per page. Cert fee: $1.00. Payee: District Clerk. Personal checks accepted. Prepayment required. Mail turnaround time 1-2 days.

County Court PO Box 209, Anderson, TX 77830; 936-873-2606 X251. Hours: 8AM-4:45PM (CST). *Misdemeanor, Civil, Probate.*
Civil Records: Access: Mail, in person. Only the court performs in person searches; visitors may not. Search fee: $5.00 per name. Required to search: name, years to search. Civil cases indexed by defendant, plaintiff. Civil records in index books from 1850.
Criminal Records: Access: Mail, in person. Only the court performs in person searches; visitors may not. Search fee: $5.00 per name. Required to search: name, years to search, offense, date of offense. Criminal records in index books from 1850.
General Information: No juvenile, mental, sealed, or adoption records released. Will not fax results. Copy fee: $1.00 per page. Cert fee: $5.00. Payee: County Clerk. Personal checks accepted. Prepayment required. Mial requests require SASE. Mail turnaround time 1-2 days.

Guadalupe County

District Court 101 E Court St, Seguin, TX 78155; 830-303-4188; Fax: 830-379-1943. Hours: 8AM-5PM (CST). *Felony, Civil.*
www.co.guadalupe.tx.us/
Note: Will not do name searches, but will loook up case information if case number is known.
Civil Records: Access: In person, online. Visitors must perform in person searches for themselves. No search fee. Required to search: name, years to search. Civil cases indexed by defendant, plaintiff. Civil records on computer from 1990, index books from 1846. Online access is at www.idocket.com; one free search per day; subscription required for more. Online records go back to 12/31/1991.
Criminal Records: Access: In person, online. Visitors must perform in person searches for themselves. No search fee. Required to search: name, years to search, DOB; also helpful: SSN. Criminal records on computer from 1985, index books from 1846. Felony records access is through www.idocket.com; registration and password required. Records go back to 12/31/1991.
General Information: Public Access terminal is available. No juvenile, mental, sealed, or adoption records released. Copy fee: $.25 per page. Cert fee: $1.00 per page. Payee: District Clerk. Personal checks accepted. Visa, MC, AmEx accepted. Prepayment required.

County Court 101 E Court St, Seguin, TX 78155; 830-303-4188 X266,234,232; Fax: 830-372-1206. Hours: 8AM-4:30PM (CST). *Misdemeanor, Civil, Probate.*
Civil Records: Access: Mail, in person. Both court and visitors may perform in person searches. Search fee: $10.00 per name. Required to search: name, years to search. Civil cases indexed by defendant, plaintiff. Civil records on computer from 1988, index books from 1968.
Criminal Records: Access: Mail, in person. Both court and visitors may perform in person searches. Search fee: $10.00 per name. Required to search: name, years to search, DOB; also helpful: SSN. Criminal records on computer from 1988, index books from 1968.
General Information: Public Access terminal is available. No juvenile, mental, sealed, or adoption

records released. Copy fee: $1.00 per page. Cert fee: $5.00. Payee: County Clerk. Personal checks accepted. Checks accepted for civil fees. Prepayment required. Mail requests require SASE. Mail turnaround time 5 days.

Hale County

District Court 500 Broadway #200, Plainview, TX 79072-8050; 806-291-5226; Fax: 806-291-5206. Hours: 8AM-Noon; 1-5PM (CST). *Felony, Civil.*
www.242ndcourt.com
Civil Records: Access: Phone, fax, mail, in person. Both court and visitors may perform in person searches. Search fee: $5.00 per name. Required to search: name, years to search. Civil cases indexed by defendant, plaintiff. Civil records on computer back to 1989; index cards from 1975; prior back to 1897.
Criminal Records: Access: Phone, fax, mail, in person. Both court and visitors may perform in person searches. Search fee: $5.00 per name. Required to search: name, years to search, SSN; also helpful: DOB. Criminal records on computer back to 1988, index cards from 1975; prior back to 1897.
General Information: Public Access terminal is available. No juvenile, mental, sealed, or adoption records released. Will fax results for $2.00 per document. Copy fee: $1.00 per page. Cert fee: $1.00 each. Payee: District Clerk. Personal checks and credit cards accepted. Prepayment required. Mial requests require SASE. Mail turnaround time 1-2 days.

County Court 500 Broadway #140, Plainview, TX 79072-8030; 806-291-5261; Fax: 806-291-9810. Hours: 8AM-Noon, 1-5PM (CST). *Misdemeanor, Civil, Probate.*
Civil Records: Access: Mail, fax, in person. Both court and visitors may perform in person searches. Search fee: $5.00 per name. Required to search: name, years to search, address. Civil cases indexed by defendant, plaintiff. Civil records in index books from 1928; on computer back to 1995.
Criminal Records: Access: Mail, fax, in person. Both court and visitors may perform in person searches. Search fee: $5.00 per name. Required to search: name, years to search, DOB. Criminal records in index books from 1928; on computer back to 1995, limited records back to 1990.
General Information: Public Access terminal is available. No juvenile, mental, sealed, or adoption records released. Copy fee: $1.00 per page. Cert fee: $5.00 plus $1.00 per page. Payee: County Clerk. Personal checks accepted. Prepayment required. Mial requests require SASE. Mail turnaround time 1-2 days.

Hall County

District & County Court County Courthouse, 512 Main St #8, Memphis, TX 79245; 806-259-2627; Fax: 806-259-5078. Hours: 8:30AM-Noon; 1-5PM (CST). *Felony, Misdemeanor, Civil, Probate.*
Civil Records: Access: Phone, mail, in person. Both court and visitors may perform in person searches. Search fee: $5.00 per name. Required to search: name, years to search. Civil cases indexed by defendant, plaintiff. Civil records on computer from 1992, index books from 1890.
Criminal Records: Access: Phone, mail, in person. Both court and visitors may perform in person searches. Search fee: $5.00 per name. Required to search: name, years to search, offense. Criminal records on computer from 1992, index books from 1890.
General Information: No juvenile, mental, sealed, or adoption records released. Will fax results to local or toll free line. Copy fee: $1.00 per page. Cert fee: $5.00. Payee: Hall County Clerk. Personal checks

accepted. Prepayment required. Mial requests require SASE. Mail turnaround time 1-2 days.

Hamilton County

District Court County Courthouse, Hamilton, TX 76531; 254-386-3417; Fax: 254-386-8610. Hours: 8AM-5PM M-Th; 8AM-4:30PM F (CST). *Felony, Civil.*

Civil Records: Access: Fax, mail, in person. Both court and visitors may perform in person searches. Search fee: $5.00 per name. Required to search: name, years to search. Civil cases indexed by defendant, plaintiff. Civil records since 1985 in index books, computerized since 1999.

Criminal Records: Access: Fax, mail, in person. Both court and visitors may perform in person searches. Search fee: $5.00 per name. Required to search: name, years to search. Criminal records in index books since 1985, computerized since 1999.

General Information: No juvenile, mental, sealed, or adoption records released. No fee to fax results. Copy fee: $1.00 per page. Cert fee: $2.00. Payee: District Clerk. Personal checks accepted. Prepayment required. Mial requests require SASE. Mail turnaround time 2-4 days.

County Court County Courthouse, Hamilton, TX 76531; 254-386-3518; Fax: 254-386-8727. Hours: 8AM-5PM (CST). *Misdemeanor, Civil, Probate.*

Civil Records: Access: Mail, fax, in person. Both court and visitors may perform in person searches. Search fee: $5.00 per name. Required to search: name, years to search. Civil cases indexed by defendant, plaintiff. Civil records in index books; on computer since.

Criminal Records: Access: Mail, fax, in person. Both court and visitors may perform in person searches. Search fee: $5.00 per name. Required to search: name, years to search, DOB or SSN. Criminal records in index books; on computer since.

General Information: No juvenile, mental, sealed, or adoption records released. Will fax results for fee. Copy fee: $1.00 per page. Cert fee: $1.00. Payee: County Clerk. Personal checks accepted. Prepayment required. Mial requests require SASE. Mail turnaround time 1-2 days.

Hansford County

District & County Court PO Box 397, Spearman, TX 79081; 806-659-4110; Fax: 806-659-4168. Hours: 8:00AM-5PM (CST). *Felony, Misdemeanor, Civil, Probate.*

Civil Records: Access: Phone, fax, mail, in person. Both court and visitors may perform in person searches. Search fee: $5.00 per name. Required to search: name, years to search. Civil cases indexed by defendant, plaintiff. Civil records on computer from 01/92, index books from 1900s.

Criminal Records: Access: Phone, fax, mail, in person. Both court and visitors may perform in person searches. Search fee: $5.00 per name. Required to search: name, years to search; also helpful: DOB, SSN. Criminal records on computer since 06/92, archived form 1900s.

General Information: Public Access terminal is available. No juvenile, mental, sealed, or adoption records released. Will fax results for $5.00 1st page, $1.00 each add'l. Copy fee: $1.00 per page. Cert fee: $2.00 for District Court records; $5.00 for County Court records. Payee: District/County Clerk. Personal checks accepted. Prepayment required. Mial requests require SASE. Mail turnaround time 1-2 days.

Hardeman County

District & County Court PO Box 30, Quanah, TX 79252; 940-663-2901. Hours: 8:30AM-5PM (CST). *Felony, Misdemeanor, Civil, Probate.*

Civil Records: Access: Mail, in person. Both court and visitors may perform in person searches. Search fee: $10.00 per name. Required to search: name, years to search. Civil cases indexed by defendant, plaintiff. Civil records in index books from 1900s.

Criminal Records: Access: Mail, in person. Both court and visitors may perform in person searches. Search fee: $10.00 per name. Required to search: name, years to search. Criminal records in index books from 1920.

General Information: No juvenile, mental, sealed, or adoption records released. Copy fee: $1.00 per page. Cert fee: $5.00. Payee: District Clerk. Personal checks accepted. Prepayment required. Mial requests require SASE. Mail turnaround time 1-2 days.

Hardin County

District Court PO Box 2997, 300 Monroe, Kountze, TX 77625; 409-246-5150. Hours: 8AM-4PM (CST). *Felony, Civil.*

Civil Records: Access: Mail, in person. Both court and visitors may perform in person searches. Search fee: $5.00 per name. Required to search: name, years to search. Civil cases indexed by defendant, plaintiff. Civil records in index books since 1920, computerized since 1997.

Criminal Records: Access: Mail, in person. Both court and visitors may perform in person searches. Search fee: $5.00 per name. Required to search: name, years to search, DOB; also helpful: SSN, sex. Criminal records in index books since 1920, computerized since 1997.

General Information: No juvenile, mental, sealed, or adoption records released. Fee to fax results is $1.00 per page. Copy fee: $1.00 per page. Cert fee: $2.00. Payee: District Clerk. Business checks accepted. Prepayment required. Mial requests require SASE. Mail turnaround time 1-2 days.

County Court PO Box 38, Kountze, TX 77625; 409-246-5185. Hours: 8AM-5PM (CST). *Misdemeanor, Civil, Probate.*

Civil Records: Access: Mail, in person, phone. Both court and visitors may perform in person searches. Search fee: $5.00 per name. Required to search: name, years to search. Civil cases indexed by defendant, plaintiff. Civil records in index books since 1850; on computer back to 1999.

Criminal Records: Access: Mail, in person, phone. Both court and visitors may perform in person searches. Search fee: $5.00 per name. Required to search: name, years to search. Criminal records on computer since 1992, index books from 1850.

General Information: No juvenile, mental, sealed, or adoption records released. Copy fee: $1.00 per page. Cert fee: $6.00. Payee: Hardin County Clerk. Personal checks accepted. Prepayment required. Mail turnaround time 1-2 days.

Harris County

District Court District Clerk, PO Box 4651, Houston, TX 77210-4651; 713-755-5734; Civil phone: 713-755-5711 x2; Criminal phone: 713-755-7801; Fax: 713-755-5480 (civil). Hours: 8AM-6PM (CST). *Felony, Misdemeanor, Civil Over $100,000.*
www.hcdistrictclerk.com
Note: Phone and mail requests are managed by a private company at 888-545-5577; fee is $5.00 per name ($1.65 after the 1st 3). Visa/MC/AmEx, personal checks accepted.

Civil Records: Access: Online, in person (phone, mail - see note above). Both court and visitors may

perform in person searches. Search fee: $5.00 per name. Required to search: name, years to search. Civil cases indexed by defendant, plaintiff. Civil records on computer from 1969. First, an online case lookup service is free at www.hcdistrictclerk.com/CFTS/CaseLocationSearch. asp. Online records go back to 10/1989. Second, register for the free-to-view e-docs service at https://e-docs.hcdistrictclerk.com/eDocs.Web/Login.aspx and pay $1 per page (credit cards accepted) for documents. You choose the delivery method. Also, access to records is to qualified JIMs subscribers at www.jims.hctx.net.

Criminal Records: Access: Online, in person (phone, mail - see note above). Both court and visitors may perform in person searches. Search fee: $5.00 per name. Required to search: name, years to search, DOB. Criminal records on computer since 1976. Online access to criminal records is same as civil.

General Information: Public Access terminal is available. No juvenile or sealed records released. Fax-service requires credit card pre-payment. Copy fee: $1.00 per page. Cert fee: $6.00. Payee: District Clerk. Court: business check accepted from attorney with TX Bar Card number, corporate or company check with Harris Co. address. Prepayment required. Mail requests: SASE not required at private company.

County Court PO Box 1525, Civil Courts Bldg, 301 Fannin, Rm 101, Houston, TX 77251-1525; 713-755-6421. Hours: 8AM-4:30PM (CST). *Civil Under $100,000.*
www.cclerk.hctx.net
Note: The Information Department (for record information) telephone is 713-755-6405, located at County Admin Bldg, 1001 Preston, 4th Fl. Small claims and evictions are handled by county Justice of Peace Courts; usually there are two per precinct.

Civil Records: Access: Phone, mail, online, in person. Both court and visitors may perform in person searches. Search fee: $5.00 for mail requests. Required to search: name, years to search. Civil cases indexed by defendant, plaintiff. Civil records on computer and microfiche from 1963. Online access is free at www.cclerk.hctx.net. System includes civil data search and county civil settings inquiry and other county clerk functions. For further information, visit the website or call 713-755-6421. Also, online access is at www.idocket.com; registration and password required. This is a fee service, unless only one name search a day. Records go back to 12/31/1997.

General Information: Public Access terminal is available. (Public terminal for Civil and Probate records only.) Copy fee: $1.00 per page. Cert fee: $5.00. Payee: Harris County Clerk. Business checks accepted. Visa, MC, Discover, AmEx accepted. Prepayment required. Mial requests require SASE. Mail turnaround time 24-48 hours.

Probate Court 1115 Congress, 6th Fl, Houston, TX 77002; 713-755-6425; Fax: 713-755-5468. Hours: 8AM-4:30PM (CST). *Probate.*
Note: Probate dockets are available through the Harris County online system. Call 713-755-7815 for information. Dockets are available free at www.cclerk.hctx.net/coolice/default.asp?Category=Pr obateCourt&Service=pc_inquiry. Records go back to 1837.

Harrison County

71st District Court PO Box 1119, Marshall, TX 75671-1119; 903-935-8409. Hours: 8AM-5PM (CST). *Felony, Civil.*
www.co.harrison.tx.us
Civil Records: Access: Mail, in person. Both court and visitors may perform in person searches. Search fee: $5.00 per name. Required to search: name, years

to search; also helpful: address. Civil cases indexed by defendant, plaintiff. Civil records on computer from 1988, index books from 1845.

Criminal Records: Access: Mail, in person. Both court and visitors may perform in person searches. Search fee: $5.00 per name. Required to search: name, years to search, DOB; also helpful: address, SSN. Criminal records on computer from 1988, index books from 1845.

General Information: Public Access terminal is available. No juvenile, mental, sealed, or adoption records released. Copy fee: $1.00 per page. No cert fee. Payee: Harrison County District Clerk. Personal checks accepted. Prepayment required. Mial requests require SASE. Mail turnaround time 1-2 days.

County Court PO Box 1365, Marshall, TX 75671; 903-935-8403. Hours: 8AM-5PM (CST). *Misdemeanor, Civil, Probate.*

Civil Records: Access: Mail, in person. Both court and visitors may perform in person searches. Search fee: $5.00 per name. Required to search: name, years to search. Civil cases indexed by defendant, plaintiff. Civil records in docket books from 1800; on computer back to 2001.

Criminal Records: Access: Mail, in person. Both court and visitors may perform in person searches. Search fee: $5.00 per name. Required to search: name, years to search, DOB. Criminal records in docket books from 1800; on computer back to 2001.

General Information: No juvenile, mental, sealed, birth, death or adoption records released. Fee to fax results is $1.00 per page. Copy fee: $1.00 per page. Cert fee: $5.00 plus $1.00 per page. Payee: County Clerk. In state personal checks accepted. Prepayment required. Mail turnaround time 10 days.

Hartley County

District & County Court PO Box Q, Channing, TX 79018; 806-235-3582; Fax: 806-235-2316. Hours: 8:30AM-Noon, 1-5PM (CST). *Felony, Misdemeanor, Civil, Probate.*

Civil Records: Access: Mail, in person. Both court and visitors may perform in person searches. Search fee: $5.00 per name. Charge is for each book searched. Required to search: name, years to search. Civil cases indexed by defendant, plaintiff. Civil records on computer from 1994, index books from 1890.

Criminal Records: Access: Mail, in person. Both court and visitors may perform in person searches. Search fee: $5.00 per name, per book searched (misdemeanor or felony). Required to search: name, years to search, DOB. Criminal records on computer from 1994, index books from 1890.

General Information: No juvenile, mental, sealed, or adoption records released. Will fax results if prepaid. Copy fee: $1.00 per page. Cert fee: $5.00. Payee: Hartley County Clerk. Personal checks accepted. Prepayment required. Mial requests require SASE. Mail turnaround time 1-2 days.

Haskell County

District Court PO Box 27, Haskell, TX 79521; 940-864-2030. Hours: 8:30AM-Noon, 1-5PM M-Th; 8:30AM-4:30PM F (CST). *Felony, Civil.*

Civil Records: Access: Mail, in person. Both court and visitors may perform in person searches. Search fee: $5.00 per name. Required to search: name, years to search. Civil cases indexed by defendant, plaintiff. Civil records on computer from 1992, index books from 1896.

Criminal Records: Access: Mail, in person. Both court and visitors may perform in person searches. Search fee: $5.00 per name. Required to search: name, years to search, signed release. Criminal

records on computer from 1992, index books from 1896.

General Information: No juvenile, mental, sealed, or adoption records released. Copy fee: $1.00 per page. Cert fee: $1.00. Payee: District Clerk. Business checks accepted. In-state checks accepted. Prepayment required. Mial requests require SASE. Mail turnaround time 1-2 days.

County Court PO Box 725, Haskell, TX 79521; 940-864-2451. Hours: 8AM-Noon, 1-5PM (CST). *Misdemeanor, Civil, Probate.*

Civil Records: Access: Phone, fax, mail, in person. Both court and visitors may perform in person searches. Search fee: $5.00 per name. Required to search: name, years to search. Civil cases indexed by defendant, plaintiff. Civil records in index books from 1903; computerized records since 1994.

Criminal Records: Access: Fax, mail, in person. Both court and visitors may perform in person searches. Search fee: $5.00 per name. Required to search: name, years to search. Criminal records in index books from 19; computerized records since 1994.

General Information: No juvenile, mental, sealed, or adoption records released. Will fax results $2.00 per page. Copy fee: $1.00 per page. Cert fee: $5.00. Payee: County Clerk. Personal checks accepted. Prepayment required. Mail requests: SASE helpful. Turnaround time 1-2 days.

Hays County

District Court 110 E Martin Luther King, #123, San Marcos, TX 78666; 512-393-7660; Fax: 512-393-7674. Hours: 8AM-5PM (CST). *Felony, Civil.* www.co.hays.tx.us

Civil Records: Access: Phone, mail, in person, online. Both court and visitors may perform in person searches. Search fee: $5.00 per name. Required to search: name, years to search. Civil cases indexed by defendant, plaintiff. Civil records on computer from 1987, index books from 1890s. Online access is through www.idocket.com; registration and password required. Records go back to 12/31/1986.

Criminal Records: Access: Phone, mail, in person, online. Both court and visitors may perform in person searches. Search fee: $5.00 per name. Required to search: name, years to search; also helpful: DOB, SSN. Criminal records on computer from 1987, index books from 1890s. Online access is through www.idocket.com; registration and password required. Records go back to 12/31/1986.

General Information: Public Access terminal is available. No sealed or adoption records released. Copy fee: $.50 per page. Cert fee: $1.00 plus $1.00 per page. Payee: District Clerk. Personal checks accepted. Prepayment required. Mial requests require SASE. Mail turnaround time 1-5 days.

County Court Justice Center, 110 E Martin L King Dr, San Marcos, TX 78666; 512-393-7738; Civil phone: 512-393-7739; Criminal phone: 512-393-7738; Probate phone: 512-393-7734; Fax: 512-393-7735. Hours: 8AM-5PM (CST). *Misdemeanor, Civil, Probate.* www.co.hays.tx.us

Civil Records: Access: Mail, in person, online. Both court and visitors may perform in person searches. Search fee: $5.00 per name. Required to search: name, years to search. Civil cases indexed by defendant, plaintiff. Civil records on computer from 1988, index books from 1848. Online access is through www.idocket.com; registration and password required. Includes probate, Records from 01/88.

Criminal Records: Access: Mail, in person, online. Both court and visitors may perform in person searches. Search fee: $5.00 per name. Required to search: name, years to search, DOB. Criminal records

on computer from 1988, index books from 1848. Misdemeanor records access is through www.idocket.com; registration and password required. Records go back to 12/31/1987.

General Information: Public Access terminal is available. No juvenile, mental, sealed, or adoption records released. Copy fee: $1.00 per page. Cert fee: $5.00. Payee: Hays County Clerk. Personal checks accepted. Prepayment required. Mail turnaround time 1-2 weeks.

Hemphill County

District & County Court PO Box 867, Canadian, TX 79014; 806-323-6212. Hours: 8AM-5PM (CST). *Felony, Misdemeanor, Civil, Probate.*

Civil Records: Access: Phone, mail, in person. Both court and visitors may perform in person searches. Search fee: $5.00 per name. Required to search: name, years to search. Civil cases indexed by defendant, plaintiff. Civil rrecords indexed from 1890s, in storage.

Criminal Records: Access: Phone, mail, in person. Both court and visitors may perform in person searches. Search fee: $5.00 per name. Required to search: name, years to search, DOB. Criminal records indexed from 1890s, in storage.

General Information: Public Access terminal is available. No juvenile, mental, sealed, or adoption records released. Copy fee: $1.00 per page. Cert fee: $5.00 per page. Payee: Hemphill County Clerk. Personal checks accepted. Prepayment required. Mial requests require SASE. Mail turnaround time 1-2 weeks.

Henderson County

District Court District Clerk Henderson County, 100 E Tyler, Rm 203, Athens, TX 75751; 903-675-6115. Hours: 8AM-5PM (CST). *Felony, Civil.*

Civil Records: Access: Mail, in person, phone, fax. Both court and visitors may perform in person searches. Search fee: $5.00 per name. Required to search: name, years to search. Civil cases indexed by defendant, plaintiff. Civil records on computer from 1987, index books from 1849.

Criminal Records: Access: Mail, in person. Both court and visitors may perform in person searches. Search fee: $5.00 per name. Required to search: name, years to search, DOB; also helpful: SSN. Criminal records on computer from 1987, index books from 1849.

General Information: Public Access terminal is available. No juvenile, mental, sealed, or adoption records released. Copy fee: $1.00 per page. No cert fee. Payee: District Clerk. Personal checks accepted. Prepayment required. Mial requests require SASE. Mail turnaround time 1-2 days.

County Court PO Box 632, Athens, TX 75751; 903-675-6140; Civil phone: 903-675-6144; Criminal phone: 903-677-7205; Probate phone: 903-677-7206; Fax: 903-675-6105. Hours: 8AM-5PM (CST). *Misdemeanor, Civil, Probate.*

Civil Records: Access: Phone, mail, fax, in person. Both court and visitors may perform in person searches. Search fee: $5.00 per name. Required to search: name, years to search. Civil cases indexed by defendant, plaintiff. Civil records on computer back to 1984, index books from 1960s.

Criminal Records: Access: Mail, fax, in person. Both court and visitors may perform in person searches. Search fee: $5.00 per name. Required to search: name, years to search, DOB, SSN. Criminal records on computer back to 1984, index books from 1960s.

General Information: Public Access terminal is available. No juvenile, mental, sealed, or adoption records released. Fee to fax results is $2.00 per page.

Copy fee: $1.00 per page. Cert fee: $1.00 per document. Payee: County Clerk. Personal checks accepted. Prepayment required. Mial requests require SASE. Mail turnaround time 1-2 weeks.

Hidalgo County

District Court 100 N Closner, Box 87, Edinburg, TX 78540; 956-318-2200. Hours: 8AM-5PM (CST). *Felony, Civil.*

Civil Records: Access: Mail, in person, online. Only the court performs in person searches; visitors may not. Search fee: $5.00 per name. Required to search: name, years to search. Civil cases indexed by defendant, plaintiff. Civil records on computer from 1987. Online access is through www.idocket.com; registration and password required. Records go back to 12/31/1986.

Criminal Records: Access: Mail, in person, online. Only the court performs in person searches; visitors may not. Search fee: $5.00 per name. Required to search: name, years to search, DOB. Criminal records on computer from 1987. Online access is through www.idocket.com; registration and password required. Records go back to 12/31/1986.

General Information: No juvenile, mental, sealed, or adoption records released. Will not fax results. Copy fee: $.25 per page. Cert fee: $1.00. Payee: District Clerk. Business checks accepted. Prepayment required. Mial requests require SASE. Mail turnaround time 1-2 days.

County Court PO Box 58, Edinburg, TX 78540; 956-318-2100. Hours: 7:30AM-5:00PM (CST). *Misdemeanor, Civil, Probate.*

Civil Records: Access: Mail, in person, online. Both court and visitors may perform in person searches. Search fee: $5.00 per name. Required to search: name, years to search. Civil cases indexed by defendant, plaintiff. Civil records on computer from 1985, index books before 1985. Online access is through www.idocket.com; registration and password required. Civil and probate records go back to 12/31/1986.

Criminal Records: Access: Mail, in person, online. Both court and visitors may perform in person searches. Search fee: $5.00 per name. Required to search: name, years to search. Criminal records on computer from 1985, index books before 1985. Misdemeanor records access is through www.idocket.com; registration and password required. Records go back to 12/31/1991.

General Information: Public Access terminal is available. No juvenile, mental, sealed, or adoption records released. Copy fee: $1.00 per page. Cert fee: $5.00. Payee: County Clerk. Business checks accepted. Prepayment required. Mial requests require SASE. Mail turnaround time 1-2 days.

Hill County

District Court PO Box 634, Hillsboro, TX 76645; 254-582-4023. Hours: 8AM-5PM (CST). *Felony, Misdmeanor, Civil.*

Civil Records: Access: Mail, in person, online. Both court and visitors may perform in person searches. Search fee: $5.00 per name. Required to search: name, years to search. Civil cases indexed by defendant, plaintiff. Civil records on optical imaging from September, 1993, on computer from 1991, microfilm from 1930s to 1950s, index books from 1900s. Online access to court records is through www.idocket.com. One search a day is free; subcription required for more. Records go back to 12/31/1990.

Criminal Records: Access: Mail, in person. Both court and visitors may perform in person searches. Search fee: $5.00 per name. Required to search: name, years to search; also helpful: DOB, SSN.

Criminal records on optical imaging from September, 1993, on computer from 1989, microfilm from 1930s to 1950s, index books from 1900s. Criminal records access is through www.idocket.com; registration and password required. Records go back to 12/31/1990.

General Information: Public Access terminal is available. (Allows civil searches only.) No juvenile, mental, sealed, or adoption records released. Will fax results for $1.50 per page. Copy fee: $1.00 per page. Cert fee: $1.00. Payee: District Clerk. Personal checks accepted in person. Prepayment required. Mial requests require SASE. Mail turnaround time 1-2 days.

County Court PO Box 398, Hillsboro, TX 76645; 254-582-4012; Probate phone: 254-582-4030; Fax: 254-582-4003. Hours: 8AM-5PM (CST). *Probate.*

Hockley County

District Court 802 Houston St, #316, Levelland, TX 79336; 806-894-8527; Fax: 806-894-3891. Hours: 9AM-5PM (CST). *Felony, Civil.*

Civil Records: Access: Phone, mail, in person. Both court and visitors may perform in person searches. Search fee: $5.00 per name. Required to search: name, years to search. Civil cases indexed by defendant, plaintiff. Civil records on computer from 1990, archived from 1922.

Criminal Records: Access: Phone, mail, in person. Both court and visitors may perform in person searches. Search fee: $5.00 per name. Required to search: name, years to search. Criminal records on computer from 1990, archived from 1922.

General Information: Public Access terminal is available. No juvenile, mental, sealed, or adoption records released. Copy fee: $1.00 per page. Cert fee: $2.00. Payee: District Clerk. Only cashiers checks and money orders accepted. Prepayment required. Mial requests require SASE. Mail turnaround time 1-2 days.

County Court County Courthouse, 802 Houston St, #213, Levelland, TX 79336; 806-894-3185. Hours: 9AM-5PM (CST). *Misdemeanor, Civil, Probate.*

Civil Records: Access: Mail, in person. Both court and visitors may perform in person searches. No search fee. Required to search: name, years to search. Civil cases indexed by defendant, plaintiff. Civil records on computer from 1990, index books from 1960.

Criminal Records: Access: Mail, in person. Both court and visitors may perform in person searches. Search fee: $5.00 per name. Required to search: name, years to search; also helpful: DOB. Criminal records on computer from 1990, index books from 1960.

General Information: Public Access terminal is available. No juvenile, mental, sealed, or adoption records released. Copy fee: $1.00 per page. Cert fee: $5.00. Payee: Hockley County Clerk. Only cashiers checks and money orders accepted. Prepayment required. Mial requests require SASE. Mail turnaround time 1-2 days.

Hood County

District Court County Courthouse, 100 E Pearl, #21, Granbury, TX 76048; 817-579-3236; Fax: 817-579-3239. Hours: 8AM-5PM (CST). *Felony, Civil.*

Civil Records: Access: Mail, in person. Both court and visitors may perform in person searches. Search fee: $5.00 per name. Required to search: name, years to search. Civil cases indexed by defendant, plaintiff. Civil records on computer and microfiche from 1983, index books before 1983.

Criminal Records: Access: Mail, in person. Both court and visitors may perform in person searches. Search fee: $5.00 per name. Required to search:

name, years to search, DOB, SSN, signed release. Criminal records on computer and microfiche from 1983, index books before 1983.

General Information: No juvenile, mental, sealed, or adoption records released. Copy fee: $1.00 1st. Page $.25 add'l. Cert fee: $1.00 per page. Payee: District Clerk. Personal checks accepted. Prepayment required. Mial requests require SASE. Mail turnaround time 1-2 days.

County Court PO Box 339, Granbury, TX 76048; 817-579-3222; Fax: 817-579-3227. Hours: 8AM-5PM (CST). *Misdemeanor, Civil, Probate.*

Civil Records: Access: Mail, in person. Both court and visitors may perform in person searches. Search fee: $5.00 per name. Required to search: name, years to search. Civil cases indexed by defendant, plaintiff. Civil records in index books.

Criminal Records: Access: Mail, in person. Both court and visitors may perform in person searches. Search fee: $5.00 per name. Required to search: name, years to search; also helpful: DOB. Criminal records on computer and microfiche from 1982, index books before 1982.

General Information: No juvenile, mental, sealed, or adoption records released. Will fax results if prepaid. Copy fee: $1.00 per page. Cert fee: $5.00. Payee: Hood County Clerk. Personal checks accepted. Prepayment required. Mial requests require SASE. Mail turnaround time 1 day.

Hopkins County

District Court 118 Church St, Sulphur Springs, TX 75483; 903-438-4081; Civil phone: 903-438-4084; Criminal phone: 903-438-4083; Probate phone: 903-438-4078. Hours: 8AM-5PM (CST). *Felony, Civil.*

Note: Probate Court located at 411 College St.

Civil Records: Access: Mail, in person. Both court and visitors may perform in person searches. Search fee: $5.00 per name. Required to search: name, years to search. Civil cases indexed by defendant, plaintiff. Civil records on computer from 1987, index books from 1840.

Criminal Records: Access: Mail, in person. Both court and visitors may perform in person searches. Search fee: $5.00 per name. Required to search: name, years to search. Criminal records on computer from 1987, index books from 1840, archived from 1890.

General Information: Public Access terminal is available. No juvenile, mental, sealed, or adoption records released. Will fax results. Copy fee: $1.00 per page. Cert fee: $2.00. Payee: District Clerk. Personal checks accepted. Prepayment required. Mial requests require SASE. Mail turnaround time 2 days.

County Court PO Box 288, Sulphur Springs, TX 75483; 903-438-4074; Fax: 903-438-4110. Hours: 8AM-5PM (CST). *Misdemeanor, Civil, Probate.* www.hopkinscountytx.org/departments.htm

Civil Records: Access: Mail, in person. Both court and visitors may perform in person searches. Search fee: $5.00 per name. Required to search: name, years to search. Civil cases indexed by defendant, plaintiff. Civil records on computer since 1992, index books from 1846.

Criminal Records: Access: Mail, in person. Both court and visitors may perform in person searches. Search fee: $5.00 per name. Required to search: name, years to search; also helpful-DOB, SSN, signed release. Criminal records on computer from 1985, index books from 1846.

General Information: Public Access terminal is available. No juvenile, mental, or sealed records released. Copy fee: $1.00 per page. Cert fee: $5.00. Payee: County Clerk. Personal checks accepted.

Prepayment required. Mial requests require SASE. Mail turnaround time 1-2 days.

Houston County

District Court County Courthouse, 401 E Houston, PO Box 1186, Crockett, TX 75835; 936-544-3255 x222; Fax: 936-544-9523. Hours: 8AM-4:30PM (CST). *Felony, Civil.*

Civil Records: Access: Fax, mail, in person. Both court and visitors may perform in person searches. Search fee: $5.00 per name. Required to search: name, years to search. Civil cases indexed by plaintiff. Civil records on computer from 10/99, index books since 1800s.

Criminal Records: Access: Fax, mail, in person. Both court and visitors may perform in person searches. Search fee: $5.00 per name. Required to search: name, years to search, signed release; also helpful: DOB, SSN. Criminal records on computer since 10/99, index books since 1800s.

General Information: Public Access terminal is available. No juvenile, mental, sealed, or adoption records released. Will fax results $3.50 1st page, $.50 each add'l. Copy fee: $1.00 per page. No cert fee. Payee: District Clerk. Personal checks accepted. Prepayment required. Mial requests require SASE. Mail turnaround time 1-2 days.

County Court PO Box 370, Crockett, TX 75835; 936-544-3255; Fax: 936-544-1954. Hours: 8AM-4:30 (CST). *Misdemeanor, Civil, Probate.*

Civil Records: Access: Mail, in person. Both court and visitors may perform in person searches. Search fee: $5.00 per name. Required to search: name, years to search. Civil cases indexed by defendant, plaintiff. Civil records on computer since 2000, microfiche since 1983, index books since 1881 (probate).

Criminal Records: Access: Mail, in person. Both court and visitors may perform in person searches. Search fee: $5.00 per name. Required to search: name, years to search. Criminal records on computer since 2000, index books since 1881.

General Information: Public Access terminal is available. No juvenile, mental, sealed, or adoption records released. Will fax results to local or toll-free number for $1.00 per page. Copy fee: $1.00 per page. Cert fee: $5.00. Payee: County Clerk. Personal checks accepted. Prepayment required. Mail turnaround time 1-2 days.

Howard County

District Court PO Box 2138, Big Spring, TX 79721; 432-264-2223; Fax: 432-264-2256. Hours: 8AM-5PM (CST). *Felony, Civil.*

Civil Records: Access: Mail, in person. Both court and visitors may perform in person searches. Search fee: $5.00 per name. Required to search: name, years to search. Civil cases indexed by defendant, plaintiff. Civil records on computer from 1990, index books from 1881.

Criminal Records: Access: Mail, in person. Both court and visitors may perform in person searches. Search fee: $5.00 per name. Required to search: name, years to search. Criminal records on computer from 1990, index books from 1881.

General Information: No juvenile, mental, sealed or adoption records released. Fee to fax results is $1.00 per page. Copy fee: $1.00 per page. Cert fee: $1.00 per page. Payee: District Clerk. Personal checks accepted. Prepayment required. Mial requests require SASE. Mail turnaround time 1-2 days.

County Court PO Box 1468, Big Spring, TX 79721; 432-264-2213; Fax: 432-264-2215. Hours: 8AM-5PM (CST). *Misdemeanor, Civil, Probate.*

Civil Records: Access: Phone, mail, in person. Both court and visitors may perform in person searches. Search fee: $5.00 per name. Required to search:

name, years to search. Civil cases indexed by defendant, plaintiff. Civil records in index books since 1881.

Criminal Records: Access: Phone, mail, in person. Both court and visitors may perform in person searches. Search fee: $5.00 per name. Required to search: name, years to search. Criminal records in index books since 1881.

General Information: Public Access terminal is available. No juvenile, mental, sealed, or adoption records released. Will fax results $5.00 per doc. Copy fee: $1.00 per page. Cert fee: $5.00. Payee: County Clerk. Business checks accepted. Prepayment required. Mail turnaround time 1-2 days.

Hudspeth County

District & County Court PO Drawer 58, Sierra Blanca, TX 79851; 915-369-2301; Fax: 915-369-3005. Hours: 8AM-5PM (MST). *Felony, Misdemeanor, Civil, Probate.*

Civil Records: Access: Phone, fax, mail, in person. Both court and visitors may perform in person searches. Search fee: $5.00 per name. Required to search: name, years to search. Civil cases indexed by defendant, plaintiff. Civil records in index books from 1900s; on computer since 1988.

Criminal Records: Access: Phone, fax, mail, in person. Both court and visitors may perform in person searches. Search fee: $5.00 per name. Required to search: name, years to search, DOB. Criminal records in index books from 1900s; on computer since 1998.

General Information: Public Access terminal is available. No juvenile, mental, sealed, or adoption records released. Will fax results $1.00 per page. Copy fee: $1.00 per page. Cert fee: $5.00. Payee: District/County Clerk. Personal checks accepted. Prepayment required. Mial requests require SASE. Mail turnaround time 1-2 days.

Hunt County

District Court Court Clerk, PO Box 1437, Greenville, TX 75403; 903-408-4172. Hours: 8AM-5PM (CST). *Felony, Civil.*

Civil Records: Access: Mail, in person. Both court and visitors may perform in person searches. Search fee: $5.00 per name. Required to search: name, years to search. Civil cases indexed by defendant, plaintiff. Civil records on computer from 1992, microfiche from 1973, index books from 1900s.

Criminal Records: Access: Mail, in person. Both court and visitors may perform in person searches. Search fee: $5.00 per name. Required to search: name, years to search, DOB. Criminal records on computer from 1992, microfilm from 1973, index books from 1900s.

General Information: No juvenile, sealed, or adoption records released. Copy fee: $1.00 per page. Cert fee: $1.00. Payee: District Clerk. Personal checks accepted. Prepayment required. Mial requests require SASE. Mail turnaround time 1-2 days.

County Court PO Box 1316, Greenville, TX 75403-1316; 903-408-4130. Hours: 8AM-5PM (CST). *Misdemeanor, Civil, Probate.*

Civil Records: Access: Mail, in person. Both court and visitors may perform in person searches. Search fee: $5.00 per name. Required to search: name, years to search. Civil cases indexed by defendant, plaintiff. Civil records on computer since 1986, index books from 1940; on microfilm prior to 1986.

Criminal Records: Access: Mail, in person. Both court and visitors may perform in person searches. Search fee: $5.00 per name. Required to search: name, years to search, DOB. Criminal records on computer since 1986, index books from 1940; on microfilm prior to 1986.

General Information: Public Access terminal is available. No juvenile, mental, sealed, or adoption records released. No fax results available. Copy fee: $1.00 per page. Cert fee: $5.00. Payee: County Clerk. Personal checks accepted. Prepayment required. Mial requests require SASE. Mail turnaround time 1-2 days.

Hutchinson County

District Court PO Box 580, Stinnett, TX 79083; 806-878-4017; Fax: 806-878-4042. Hours: 9AM-5PM (CST). *Felony, Civil.*

Civil Records: Access: Mail, in person. Both court and visitors may perform in person searches. Search fee: $5.00 per name. Required to search: name, years to search. Civil cases indexed by defendant, plaintiff. Civil records on computer from 1989, docket books from 1920.

Criminal Records: Access: Mail, in person. Both court and visitors may perform in person searches. Search fee: $5.00 per name. Required to search: name, years to search, signed release; also helpful: DOB, SSN. Criminal records on computer from 1989, docket books from 1920.

General Information: Public Access terminal is available. No juvenile, mental, sealed, or adoption records released. Fee to fax results is $1.00 per page. Copy fee: $.25 per page. $1.00 minimum. Cert fee: $1.00 per page. Payee: District Clerk. Personal checks accepted. Prepayment required. Mial requests require SASE. Mail turnaround time 2 days.

County Court PO Box 1186, Hutchinson County Clerk, Stinnett, TX 79083; 806-878-4002. Hours: 9AM-5PM (CST). *Misdemeanor, Civil, Probate.*

Civil Records: Access: Mail, in person. Both court and visitors may perform in person searches. Search fee: $5.00 per name. Required to search: name, years to search. Civil cases indexed by defendant, plaintiff. Civil records in index books from 1900s.

Criminal Records: Access: Mail, in person. Both court and visitors may perform in person searches. Search fee: $5.00 per name. Required to search: name, years to search, signed release, DOB or SSN. Criminal records on computer since 1990, index books from 1900s.

General Information: Public Access terminal is available. No juvenile, mental, sealed, or adoption records released. Copy fee: $1.00 per page. Cert fee: $5.00. Payee: Hutchinson County Clerk. Business checks accepted. Prepayment required. Mail turnaround time 2 days.

Irion County

District & County Court PO Box 736, Mertzon, TX 76941-0736; 325-835-2421; Fax: 325-835-2008. Hours: 8AM-5PM (CST). *Felony, Misdemeanor, Civil, Probate.*

Civil Records: Access: Mail, fax, in person. Both court and visitors may perform in person searches. Search fee: $5.00 per name. Fee is per court. Required to search: name, years to search. Civil cases indexed by defendant, plaintiff. Civil records in index books from 1886.

Criminal Records: Access: Mail, fax, in person. Both court and visitors may perform in person searches. Search fee: $5.00 per name. Fee is per court. Required to search: name, years to search; also helpful: DOB, SSN. Criminal records on index books from 1886.

General Information: No juvenile, mental, or sealed records released. Will fax results $1.00 per page. Copy fee: $1.00 per page. Cert fee: $1.00. County Court certification fee $5.00. Payee: District/County Clerk. Personal checks accepted. Prepayment required. Mial requests require SASE. Mail turnaround time 5-20 days.

Jack County

District Court 100 Main, County Courthouse, Jacksboro, TX 76458; 940-567-2141; Fax: 940-567-2696. Hours: 8AM-5PM (CST). *Felony, Civil.*
Civil Records: Access: Mail, in person. Both court and visitors may perform in person searches. Search fee: $10.00 per name. Required to search: name, years to search. Civil cases indexed by defendant, plaintiff. Civil records in index books from 1857.
Criminal Records: Access: Mail, in person. Both court and visitors may perform in person searches. Search fee: $10.00 per name. Required to search: name, years to search. Criminal records in index books from 1857.
General Information: No juvenile, mental, sealed, or adoption records released. Copy fee: $.50 per page. Cert fee: $10.00. Payee: Jack County District Clerk. Personal checks accepted. Prepayment required. Mial requests require SASE. Mail turnaround time 2 days.

County Court 100 Main, Jacksboro, TX 76458; 940-567-2111. Hours: 8AM-5PM (CST). *Misdemeanor, Civil, Probate.*
Civil Records: Access: Mail, in person. Both court and visitors may perform in person searches. Search fee: $5.00 per name. Required to search: name, years to search. Civil cases indexed by defendant, plaintiff. Civil records in index books from 1856, computerized sicne 1999.
Criminal Records: Access: Phone, mail, in person. Both court and visitors may perform in person searches. Search fee: $5.00 per name. Required to search: name, years to search. Criminal records in index books from 1856, computerized since 1999.
General Information: No juvenile, mental, sealed, or adoption records released. Copy fee: $1.00 per page. Cert fee: $5.00. Payee: Jack County Clerk. Personal checks accepted. Prepayment required. Mial requests require SASE. Mail turnaround time 1-2 days.

Jackson County

District Court 115 W Main, Rm 203, Edna, TX 77957; 361-782-3812. Hours: 8AM-5PM (CST). *Felony, Civil.*
Civil Records: Access: Phone, mail, in person. Both court and visitors may perform in person searches. Search fee: $5.00 per name. Required to search: name, years to search. Civil cases indexed by defendant, plaintiff. Civil records in index books from 1850.
Criminal Records: Access: Mail, in person. Both court and visitors may perform in person searches. Search fee: $5.00 per name. Required to search: name, years to search. Criminal records on microfiche from 1981, index books from 1850.
General Information: No sealed, or adoption records released. Copy fee: $1.00 per page. Cert fee: $1.00. Payee: District Clerk. Personal checks accepted. Prepayment required. Mial requests require SASE. Mail turnaround time 1-2 days.

County Court 115 W Main, Rm 101, Edna, TX 77957; 361-782-3563. Hours: 8AM-5PM (CST). *Misdemeanor, Civil, Probate.*
Civil Records: Access: Mail, in person. Both court and visitors may perform in person searches. Search fee: $5.00 per name. Required to search: name, years to search. Civil cases indexed by defendant, plaintiff. Civil records in index books from 1900s; computerized back to 1993.
Criminal Records: Access: In person only. Both court and visitors may perform in person searches. Search fee: $5.00 per name. Required to search: name, years to search, DOB, offense, date of offense. Criminal records in index books from 1900s; deed records computerized back to 1993.

General Information: No juvenile, mental, sealed, or adoption records released. Fee to fax results is $4.25 for the 1st page and $2.25 per page thereafter. Copy fee: $1.00 per page. Cert fee: $5.00. Payee: County Clerk. Personal checks accepted. Prepayment required. Mail turnaround time 1-2 days.

Jasper County

District Court County Courthouse, #202, PO Box 2088, Jasper, TX 75951; 409-384-2721. Hours: 8AM-4:30PM (CST). *Felony, Civil.*
Civil Records: Access: Mail, in person. Only the court performs in person searches; visitors may not. Search fee: $5.00 per name. Required to search: name, years to search. Civil cases indexed by defendant, plaintiff. Civil records on computer since 1991, index books and microfilm since 1850s.
Criminal Records: Access: Mail, in person. Only the court performs in person searches; visitors may not. Search fee: $5.00 per name. Required to search: name, years to search. Criminal records on computer since 12/96; index books and microfilm since 1850s.
General Information: Public Access terminal is available. No juvenile, mental, sealed, or adoption records released. Copy fee: $1.00 per page. No cert fee. Payee: District Clerk/Court. Personal checks accepted. Prepayment required. Mial requests require SASE. Mail turnaround time 1-2 days.

County Court Rm 103, Courthouse, Main at Lamar, PO Box 2070, Jasper, TX 75951; 409-384-2632; Fax: 409-384-7198. Hours: 8AM-4:30PM (CST). *Misdemeanor, Civil, Probate.*
Civil Records: Access: Phone, mail, fax, in person. Both court and visitors may perform in person searches. Search fee: $10.00 per name. There is no fee if you do the search yourself. Required to search: name, years to search. Civil cases indexed by defendant, plaintiff. Civil records in index books; on computer back to 1987.
Criminal Records: Access: Phone, mail, fax, in person. Both court and visitors may perform in person searches. Search fee: $10.00 per name. There is no fee if you do the search yourself. Required to search: name, years to search, DOB; also helpful: SSN. Criminal records in index books; on computer back to 1987.
General Information: Public Access terminal is available. No juvenile, mental, sealed, or adoption records released. Fee to fax results is $3.00 1st page; $1.00 each add'l. Copy fee: $1.00 per page. Cert fee: $5.00. Payee: Debbie Newman County Clerk. Personal checks require drivers license. Prepayment required. Mail turnaround time 1 day.

Jeff Davis County

District & County Court PO Box 398, Fort Davis, TX 79734; 432-426-3251; Fax: 432-426-3760. Hours: 9AM-Noon, 1-5PM (CST). *Felony, Misdemeanor, Civil, Probate.*
Civil Records: Access: Mail, in person. Both court and visitors may perform in person searches. Search fee: $5.00 per name. Required to search: name, years to search. Civil cases indexed by defendant, plaintiff. Civil records in index books.
Criminal Records: Access: Mail, in person, fax. Both court and visitors may perform in person searches. Search fee: $5.00 per name. Required to search: name, years to search. Criminal records in index books.
General Information: No juvenile, mental, sealed, or adoption records released. Will fax results to local or toll free line. Copy fee: $1.00 per page. Cert fee: $5.00. Payee: County Clerk. Personal checks accepted. Prepayment required. Mail requests: SASE helpful. Turnaround time 2 days.

Jefferson County

District Court PO Box 3707 (Pearl St Courthouse), Beaumont, TX 77704; 409-835-8580; Fax: 409-835-8527. Hours: 8AM-5PM (CST). *Felony, Civil.*
www.co.jefferson.tx.us
Civil Records: Access: Mail, online, in person. Both court and visitors may perform in person searches. Search fee: 10.00 per name. Required to search: name, years to search. Civil cases indexed by defendant, plaintiff. Civil records on computer and index books since 1940s. Online access to the civil records index at www.co.jefferson.tx.us/dclerk/civil_index/main.htm. Search by defendant or plaintiff by year 1985 to present. Also, you may search at http://jeffersontxclerk.hartic.com/search.asp?cabinet=civil. Index goes back to 1995; images back to 12/1998. Search results are not certified unless done by the court itself.
Criminal Records: Access: Mail, online, in person. Both court and visitors may perform in person searches. Search fee: $10.00 per name. Required to search: name, years to search; also helpful: DOB, SSN. Criminal records on computer and index books since 1940s. Online access to the criminal records index is at www.co.jefferson.tx.us/dclerk/criminal_index/main.htm. Search by name by year 1981 to present. Also, felony records may soon be free at http://jeffersontxclerk.hartic.com/search.asp?cabinet=criminal. Add'l criminal records are being added.
General Information: Public Access terminal is available. (Civil, Family, and E-file on selected cases.) No juvenile, mental, sealed, or adoption records released. Copy fee: $1.00 per page. Cert fee: $5.00. Payee: District Clerk. Only cashiers checks and money orders accepted. Prepayment required. Mial requests require SASE. Mail turnaround time 2-4 days.

County Court PO Box 1151, Beaumont, TX 77704; 409-835-8479; Probate phone: 409-835-8483; Fax: 409-839-2394. Hours: 8AM-5PM (CST). *Misdemeanor, Civil, Probate.*
http://jeffersontxclerk.hartintercivic.com/
Note: Search probate records back to 1988 free at http://jeffersontxclerk.hartic.com/search.asp?cabinet=probate. Images go back to 1998.
Civil Records: Access: Mail, in person and online. Both court and visitors may perform in person searches. Search fee: $10.00 per name. Required to search: name, years to search. Civil cases indexed by defendant, plaintiff. Civil records on computer since 11/1/95, index books to 1836. Search the county clerk's civil database free at http://jeffersontxclerk.hartintercivic.com/search.asp?cabinet=civil. Index goes back to 1995; images back to 12/1998.
Criminal Records: Access: Mail, in person, online. Both court and visitors may perform in person searches. Search fee: $10.00 per name. Required to search: name, years to search, DOB. Criminal records on computer since 1-1-82, index books to 1836. Access to Class A&B and C Misdemeanor that are appealed records back to 1982 are free at http://jeffersontxclerk.hartintercivic.com/search.asp?cabinet=criminal. Add'l criminal records are being added.
General Information: Public Access terminal is available. No juvenile, mental, sealed, or adoption records released. Will fax results for $2.50 1st page, $.25 each add'l. Copy fee: $1.00 per page. Cert fee: $5.00. Payee: County Clerk. Personal checks accepted. Credit cards accepted. Prepayment required. Mail turnaround time 1 day.

Jim Hogg County

District & County Court PO Box 878, Hebbronville, TX 78361; 361-527-4031; Fax: 361-527-5843. Hours: 9AM-5PM (CST). *Felony, Misdemeanor, Civil, Probate.*

Civil Records: Access: Mail, fax, in person. Both court and visitors may perform in person searches. Search fee: $15.00 per name. Required to search: name, years to search. Civil cases indexed by defendant, plaintiff. Civil records in index books.

Criminal Records: Access: In person only. Only the court performs in person searches; visitors may not. Search fee: $15.00. Required to search: name, years to search. Criminal records in index books.

General Information: No juvenile, mental, sealed, or adoption records released. Fee to fax results is $3.00 per page. Copy fee: $1.00 per page. Cert fee: $5.00. Payee: District Clerk. Personal checks accepted. Prepayment required. Mial requests require SASE. Mail turnaround time 2-4 days.

Jim Wells County

79th District Court PO Drawer 2219, Alice, TX 78333; 361-668-5717. Hours: 8AM-Noon, 1-5PM (CST). *Felony, Civil.*

Civil Records: Access: Mail, in person. Both court and visitors may perform in person searches. Search fee: $5.00 per name. Required to search: name, years to search. Civil cases indexed by defendant, plaintiff. Civil records on computer since 1992, index books since 1912.

Criminal Records: Access: Mail, in person. Both court and visitors may perform in person searches. Search fee: $5.00 per name. Required to search: name, years to search; also helpful: SSN. Criminal records on computer since 1992, index books since 1912.

General Information: No juvenile, mental, sealed, or adoption records released. Copy fee: $1.00 per page. Cert fee: $2.00. Payee: District Clerk. Personal checks accepted. Prepayment required. Mial requests require SASE. Mail turnaround time 2 days.

County Court PO Box 1459, 200 N Almond, Alice, TX 78333; 361-668-5702. Hours: 8:00AM-Noon, 1-5PM (CST). *Misdemeanor, Civil, Probate.*

Civil Records: Access: Mail, in person. Both court and visitors may perform in person searches. Search fee: $10.00 per name. Required to search: name, years to search. Civil cases indexed by defendant, plaintiff. Civil records in index books from 1911.

Criminal Records: Access: Phone, mail, in person. Both court and visitors may perform in person searches. Search fee: $10.00 per name. Required to search: name, years to search, address, DOB. Criminal records on computer since 1992, index books from 1911.

General Information: No juvenile, mental, sealed, or adoption records released. Copy fee: $1.00 per page. Cert fee: $5.00. Payee: County Clerk. Personal checks accepted. Prepayment required. Mail turnaround time 1 day.

Johnson County

District Court PO Box 495, Cleburne, TX 76033-0495; 817-556-6839; Fax: 817-556-6120. Hours: 8AM-5PM (CST). *Felony, Civil.*

Civil Records: Access: Fax, mail, in person. Both court and visitors may perform in person searches. Search fee: $5.00 per name. Required to search: name; also helpful: years to search. Civil cases indexed by defendant, plaintiff. Civil records on computer from 1980, index books back to 1800s.

Criminal Records: Access: Fax, mail, in person. Both court and visitors may perform in person searches. Search fee: $5.00 per name. Required to

search: name; also helpful: years to search, aliases. Criminal records on computer from 1980, index books back to 1800s.

General Information: Public Access terminal is available. No juvenile, mental, sealed, or adoption records released. Fee to fax results is $1.00 per page. Copy fee: $.50 per page. Cert fee: $1.00. Payee: District Clerk. Business checks accepted. Prepayment required. Mial requests require SASE. Mail turnaround time 2-4 days.

County Court Rm 104, PO Box 662, Cleburne, TX 76033-0662; 817-556-6300; Civil phone: 817-556-6870; Criminal phone: 817-556-6319; Probate phone: 817-556-6322. Hours: 8AM-Noon, 1-4:30PM (CST). *Misdemeanor, Civil, Probate.*
www.johnsoncountytx.org

Civil Records: Access: Mail, in person. Both court and visitors may perform in person searches. Search fee: $5.00 per name. Required to search: name, years to search. Civil cases indexed by defendant, plaintiff. Civil records on computer since 1988, index books from 1985.

Criminal Records: Access: Mail, in person. Both court and visitors may perform in person searches. Search fee: $5.00 per name. Required to search: name, years to search, and DOB or SSN. Criminal records on computer since 1988, index books from 1985.

General Information: Public Access terminal is available. No juvenile, mental, sealed, or adoption records released. Copy fee: $1.00 per page. Cert fee: $5.00. Payee: County Clerk. Business checks accepted. Prepayment required. Mial requests require SASE. Mail turnaround time 1-2 days.

Jones County

District Court PO Box 308, Anson, TX 79501; 325-823-3731; Fax: 325-823-4200. Hours: 8AM-5PM (CST). *Felony, Misdemeanor, Civil.*

Civil Records: Access: Mail, in person. Both court and visitors may perform in person searches. Search fee: $5.00 per name. Required to search: name, years to search. Civil cases indexed by defendant, plaintiff. Civil records on computer since 1990, index books since 1881.

Criminal Records: Access: Mail, in person. Both court and visitors may perform in person searches. Search fee: $5.00 per name. Required to search: name, years to search, DOB. Criminal records on computer since 1986, index books since 1881.

General Information: No juvenile, mental, sealed, or adoption records released. Will fax results to local or toll free line. Copy fee: $1.00 per page. Cert fee: $2.00. Payee: Nona Carter, District Clerk. Personal checks accepted. Can set up deposit account. Prepayment required. Mial requests require SASE. Mail turnaround time same day.

Karnes County

District Court County Courthouse, 101 N Panna Maria Ave, Karnes City, TX 78118-2930; 830-780-2562; Fax: 830-780-3227. Hours: 8AM-Noon, 1-5PM (CST). *Felony, Civil.*

Civil Records: Access: Mail, in person, fax. Both court and visitors may perform in person searches. Search fee: $5.00 per name. Required to search: name, years to search. Civil cases indexed by defendant, plaintiff. Civil records in index books form 1858.

Criminal Records: Access: Mail, in person. Both court and visitors may perform in person searches. Search fee: $5.00 per name. Required to search: name, years to search. Criminal records in index books form 1906.

General Information: No juvenile, mental, sealed, or adoption records released. Copy fee: $1.00 per page.

Cert fee: $2.00. Payee: District Clerk. Personal checks accepted. Prepayment required. Mial requests require SASE. Mail turnaround time 1-2 days.

County Court 101 N Panna Maria Ave, #9 Courthouse, Karnes City, TX 78118-2929; 830-780-3938; Fax: 830-780-4576. Hours: 8AM-5PM (CST). *Misdemeanor, Civil, Probate.*

Civil Records: Access: Mail, in person. Both court and visitors may perform in person searches. Search fee: $10.00 per name. Required to search: name, years to search. Civil cases indexed by defendant, plaintiff. Civil records in index books from 1920, no computerization.

Criminal Records: Access: Mail, in person. Both court and visitors may perform in person searches. Search fee: $10.00 per name. Required to search: name, years to search. Criminal records in index books from 1900, computerized since 1991.

General Information: No juvenile, mental, sealed, or adoption records released. Fee to fax results is $2.00 per page. Copy fee: $1.00 per page. Cert fee: $5.00. Payee: Alva Jonas, County Clerk. Personal checks accepted. Prepayment required. Mial requests require SASE. Mail turnaround time 2 days.

Kaufman County

District Court County Courthouse, 100 W Mulberry St, Kaufman, TX 75142; 972-932-4331 X214. Hours: 8AM-5PM (CST). *Felony, Civil.*

Civil Records: Access: Mail, in person. Both court and visitors may perform in person searches. Search fee: $5.00 per name. Required to search: name, years to search. Civil cases indexed by defendant, plaintiff. Civil records on computer or books from 1849.

Criminal Records: Access: Mail, in person. Both court and visitors may perform in person searches. Search fee: $5.00 per name. Required to search: name, years to search. Criminal records on computer or books from 1849.

General Information: Public Access terminal is available. No sealed, or adoption records released. Copy fee: $1.00 per page. Cert fee: $1.00. Payee: Kaufman Distric Clerk. Personal checks accepted. Prepayment required. Mial requests require SASE. Mail turnaround time up to 1 week.

County Court County Courthouse, Kaufman, TX 75142; 972-932-4331 x220. Hours: 8AM-4:30PM (CST). *Misdemeanor, Civil, Probate.*
http:www.kaufmancounty.net

Civil Records: Access: Mail, in person. Both the court and visitors may perform in person searches. Search fee: $5.00 per name; probate is $10.00 per name. Required to search: name, years to search. Civil cases indexed by defendant, plaintiff. Civil records on computer from 1985, index books to 1959.

Criminal Records: Access: Mail, in person. Both the court and visitors may perform in person searches. Search fee: $5.00 per name. Required to search: name, years to search. Criminal records on computer from 1985, index books to 1870.

General Information: Public Access terminal is available. No juvenile, mental, sealed, or adoption records released. Will fax results for $3.00 per document. Copy fee: $1.00 per page. Cert fee: $5.00. Payee: County Clerk. Personal checks accepted. Prepayment required. Mial requests require SASE. Mail turnaround time 10 days.

Kendall County

District Court 201 E San Antonio, #201, Boerne, TX 78006; 830-249-9343. Hours: 8AM-Noon, 1-5PM (CST). *Felony, Civil.*

Civil Records: Access: Mail, in person. Both court and visitors may perform in person searches. Search fee: $5.00 per name. Required to search: name, years

to search. Civil cases indexed by defendant, plaintiff. Civil records in index books back to early 1900s.

Criminal Records: Access: Mail, in person. Both court and visitors may perform in person searches. Search fee: $5.00 per name. Required to search: name, DOB, years to search, signed release; also helpful: SSN. Criminal records in index books back to early 1900s.

General Information: No juvenile, mental, sealed, or adoption records released. Copy fee: $.50 per page. Cert fee: $1.00 per page. Payee: District Clerk. Personal checks accepted. Prepayment required. Mial requests require SASE. Mail turnaround time 2-4 days.

County Court 201 E San Antonio, #127, Boerne, TX 78006; 830-249-9343; Fax: 830-249-3472. Hours: 8AM-5PM (CST). *Misdemeanor, Probate.*

Civil Records: Access: Mail, in person. Both court and visitors may perform in person searches. Search fee: $10.00 per name. Required to search: name, years to search. Civil cases indexed by defendant, plaintiff. Civil records in index books from 1860s.

Criminal Records: Access: Mail, in person. Both court and visitors may perform in person searches. Search fee: $10.00 per name. Required to search: name, years to search. Criminal records in index books from 1860s.

General Information: No juvenile, mental, sealed, or adoption records released. No fee to fax results. Copy fee: $1.00 per page. Cert fee: $5.00. Payee: County Clerk. Personal checks accepted. Prepayment required. Mial requests require SASE. Mail turnaround time 2-4 days.

Kenedy County

District & County Court PO Box 227, Sarita, TX 78385; 361-294-5220; Fax: 361-294-5218. Hours: 8:30AM-Noon, 1PM-4:30PM (CST). *Felony, Misdemeanor, Civil, Probate.*

Civil Records: Access: Phone, mail, in person. Both court and visitors may perform in person searches. Search fee: $5.00 per name. Required to search: name, years to search. Civil cases indexed by defendant, plaintiff. Civil records on microfilm since 1991, minute books since 1921.

Criminal Records: Access: Phone, mail, in person. Both court and visitors may perform in person searches. Search fee: $5.00 per name. Required to search: name, years to search. Criminal records on microfilm since 1991, minute books since 1921.

General Information: No juvenile, mental, sealed, or adoption records released. Copy fee: $1.00 per page. Cert fee: $5.00. Payee: District/County Clerk. Personal checks accepted. Prepayment required. Mail turnaround time 5 days.

Kent County

District & County Court PO Box 9, Jayton, TX 79528; 806-237-3881; Fax: 806-237-2632. Hours: 8:30AM-Noon, 1-5PM (CST). *Felony, Misdemeanor, Civil, Probate.*

Civil Records: Access: Mail, in person. Both court and visitors may perform in person searches. Search fee: $5.00 per name. Required to search: name, years to search. Civil cases indexed by defendant, plaintiff. Civil records in index books.

Criminal Records: Access: Mail, in person. Both court and visitors may perform in person searches. Search fee: $5.00 per name. Required to search: name, years to search. Criminal records in index books.

General Information: No juvenile, mental, sealed, or adoption records released. Copy fee: $1.00 per page. Cert fee: $5.00 plus $1.00 per page. Payee: County Clerk. Only cashiers checks and money orders

accepted. Prepayment required. Mial requests require SASE. Mail turnaround time ASAP.

Kerr County

District Court 700 Main, County Courthouse, Kerrville, TX 78028; 830-792-2281. Hours: 8AM-5PM (CST). *Felony, Civil.*

Civil Records: Access: Mail, in person. Both court and visitors may perform in person searches. Search fee: $5.00 per name. Required to search: name, years to search. Civil cases indexed by defendant, plaintiff. Civil records on computer from late 1991, index books prior to 1991.

Criminal Records: Access: Mail, in person. Both court and visitors may perform in person searches. Search fee: $5.00 per name. Required to search: name, years to search, DOB, SSN. Criminal records on computer from late 1990, index books prior.

General Information: Public Access terminal is available. No juvenile, mental, sealed, or adoption records released. Fee to fax results is $1.00 per page. Copy fee: $1.00 1st page; $.25 each add'l. Cert fee: $1.00 per page. Payee: District Clerk. Personal checks accepted. 1989. Prepayment required. Mial requests require SASE. Mail turnaround time 2-4 days.

County Court & County Court at Law 700 Main St, #122, Kerrville, TX 78028-5389; 830-792-2262; Probate phone: 830-792-2298; Fax: 830-792-2274. Hours: 8AM-5PM (CST). *Misdemeanor, Civil, Probate.*

www.kerrcounty.org

Civil Records: Access: Phone, mail, fax, in person. Both court and visitors may perform in person searches. Search fee: $5.00 per name. Required to search: name, years to search. Civil cases indexed by defendant, plaintiff. Civil records on computer since 1988, microfiche since 1985, index books prior to 1985.

Criminal Records: Access: Phone, mail, fax, in person. Both court and visitors may perform in person searches. Search fee: $5.00 per name. Required to search: name, years to search, DOB; also helpful: SSN. Criminal records on computer since 1985, index books prior to 1918.

General Information: Public Access terminal is available. No juvenile, mental, sealed, or adoption records released. Fee to fax results is $1.00 per page. Copy fee: $1.00 per page. Cert fee: $5.00. Payee: Kerr County Clerk. Only cashiers checks and money orders accepted. Prepayment required. Mail turnaround time 3 days.

Kimble County

District & County Court 501 Main St, Junction, TX 76849; 325-446-3353; Fax: 325-446-2986. Hours: 8AM-Noon, 1-5PM (CST). *Felony, Misdemeanor, Civil, Probate.*

Civil Records: Access: In person only. Visitors must perform in person searches for themselves. No search fee. Required to search: name, years to search. Civil cases indexed by defendant, plaintiff. Civil records in index books (records are micro-filmed for security only).

Criminal Records: Access: Mail, in person. Both court and visitors may perform in person searches. Search fee: $5.00 per name. Required to search: name, years to search, DOB. Criminal records in index books (records are micro-filmed for security only). The clerk will search back 7 years. Request for criminal search must be in writing and can be faxed if you have prearranged for payment.

General Information: No juvenile, mental, sealed, or adoption records released. Will fax results to local or toll free line. Copy fee: $1.00 per page. Cert fee: $5.00. Payee: Kimble County/District Clerk. Personal

checks accepted. Prepayment required. Mial requests require SASE. Mail turnaround time 3-4 days.

King County

District & County Court PO Box 135, Guthrie, TX 79236; 806-596-4412; Civil phone: 806-596-4412; Criminal phone: 806-596-4412; Probate phone: 806-596-4412; Fax: 806-596-4664. Hours: 9AM-Noon, 1-5PM (CST). *Felony, Misdemeanor, Civil, Probate.*

Civil Records: Access: Mail, in person. Both court and visitors may perform in person searches. Search fee: $5.00 per name. Required to search: name, years to search. Civil cases indexed by defendant, plaintiff. Civil records in index books.

Criminal Records: Access: Mail, in person. Both court and visitors may perform in person searches. Search fee: $5.00 per name. Required to search: name, years to search, DOB. Criminal records in index books.

General Information: No juvenile, mental, sealed, or adoption records released. Will fax results for $1.00 per page. Copy fee: $1.00 per page. Cert fee: $5.00. Payee: District Clerk. Personal checks accepted. Prepayment required. Mial requests require SASE. Mail turnaround time 2-4 days.

Kinney County

District & County Court PO Drawer 9, Brackettville, TX 78832; 830-563-2521; Fax: 830-563-2644. Hours: 8AM-5PM (CST). *Felony, Misdemeanor, Civil, Probate.*

Civil Records: Access: Phone, fax, mail, in person. Both court and visitors may perform in person searches. Search fee: $10.00 per name. Required to search: name, years to search. Civil cases indexed by defendant, plaintiff. Civil records in index books from late 1800s; computerized back to 1996.

Criminal Records: Access: Phone, fax, mail, in person. Both court and visitors may perform in person searches. Search fee: $10.00 per name. Required to search: name, years to search, DOB. Criminal records in index books from late 1800s; computerized records back to 1996.

General Information: No juvenile, mental, sealed, or adoption records released. Will fax results for $3.00 for 1st page; $2.00 each add'l. Copy fee: $1.00 per page. Cert fee: $5.00 County; $1.00 District. Payee: County & District Clerk. Personal checks accepted. Prepayment required. Mial requests require SASE. Mail turnaround time 1 week.

Kleberg County

District & County Court at Law PO Box 312, Kingsville, TX 78364-0312; 361-595-8561; Fax: 361-595-8525. Hours: 8AM-Noon, 1-5 PM (CST). *Felony, Civil.*

Civil Records: Access: Phone, fax, mail, in person, online. Both court and visitors may perform in person searches. Search fee: $5.00 per name. Required to search: name, years to search. Civil cases indexed by defendant, plaintiff. Civil records in index books since 1916. Computerized records go back to 1992. Online access is at www.idocket.com; registration and password required. This is a $$ fee service, unless only one name search is done a day. Records go back to 12/31/1991.

Criminal Records: Access: Phone, fax, mail, in person, online. Both court and visitors may perform in person searches. Search fee: $5.00 per name. Required to search: name, years to search; also helpful: DOB, SSN. Criminal records in index books since 1916. Computerized records go to 1992. Online access is at www.idocket.com; registration and password required. There is a fee service, unless only one name search is done a day. Records go back to 12/31/1995.

General Information: Public Access terminal is available. No sealed or adoption records released. Will fax results $5.00 per doc; incoming fax fee $1.00. Copy fee: $1.00 1st page, $.25 ea add'l. Cert fee: $1.00. Payee: District Clerk. Local personal checks accepted. Prepayment required. Mial requests require SASE. Mail turnaround time 2-3 days.

County Court - Criminal PO Box 1327, Kingsville, TX 78364; 361-595-8548. Hours: 8AM-noon; 1-5PM (CST). *Misdemeanor, Probate.*
Note: Court also handles civil cases dealing with occupational licenses and bond forfeitures.

Criminal Records: Access: Phone, mail, in person. Both court and visitors may perform in person searches. Search fee: $10.00 per name per 10 years. Required to search: name, years to search, DOB. Criminal records on computer since 1989, index books since 1913.

General Information: No juvenile or mental records released. Copy fee: $1.00 per page. Cert fee: $5.00. Payee: Kleberg County Clerk. Business checks accepted. Prepayment required. Mial requests require SASE. Mail turnaround time same day.

Knox County

District & County Court PO Box 196, Benjamin, TX 79505; 940-459-2441. Hours: 8AM-Noon, 1-5PM (CST). *Felony, Misdemeanor, Civil, Probate.*

Civil Records: Access: Mail, in person. Both court and visitors may perform in person searches. Search fee: $5.00 per name. Required to search: name, years to search. Civil cases indexed by defendant, plaintiff. Civil records in index books.

Criminal Records: Access: Mail, in person. Both court and visitors may perform in person searches. Search fee: $5.00 for a misdemeanor search; $5.00 for a felony search. Required to search: name, years to search, DOB, SSN, signed release. Criminal records in index books back to 1885.

General Information: No juvenile, mental, sealed, or adoption records released. Fee to fax results is $1.00 per page. Copy fee: $1.00 per page. Cert fee: $5.00. Payee: District/County Clerk. Personal checks accepted. Prepayment required. Mial requests require SASE. Mail turnaround time 1 day.

La Salle County

District Court PO Box 340, Cotulla, TX 78014; 830-879-4434. Hours: 8AM-5PM (CST). *Felony, Civil.*

Civil Records: Access: Phone, mail, in person. Both court and visitors may perform in person searches. Search fee: $5.00 per name. Required to search: name, years to search. Civil cases indexed by defendant, plaintiff. Civil records on computer back to 1990, prior in index books.

Criminal Records: Access: Mail, in person. Both court and visitors may perform in person searches. Search fee: $5.00 per name. Required to search: name, years to search. Criminal records on computer back to 1990, prior in index books.

General Information: No juvenile, mental, sealed, or adoption records released. Copy fee: $1.00 per page. Cert fee: $5.00. Payee: District Clerk. Personal checks accepted. Prepayment required. Mial requests require SASE. Mail turnaround time 1-2 days.

District & County Courts PO Box 340, Cotulla, TX 78014; 830-879-4432; Fax: 830-879-2933. Hours: 8AM-5PM (CST). *Misdemeanor, Civil, Probate.*

Civil Records: Access: Mail, in person. Both court and visitors may perform in person searches. Search fee: $5.00 per name. Required to search: name, years to search. Civil cases indexed by defendant, plaintiff.

Civil records on computer since 1994, prior on index books.

Criminal Records: Access: Mail, in person. Both court and visitors may perform in person searches. Search fee: $5.00 per name. Required to search: name, years to search. Criminal records on computer since 1994, prior on index books to 1988.

General Information: No juvenile, mental, sealed, or adoption records released. Copy fee: $1.00 per page. Cert fee: $5.00. Payee: County Clerk. Personal checks accepted. Prepayment required. Mial requests require SASE. Mail turnaround time 1-2 days.

Lamar County

District Court 119 N Main, Rm 306, Paris, TX 75460; 903-737-2427. Hours: 8AM-5PM (CST). *Felony, Civil.*
www.co.lamar.tx.us
Civil Records: Access: Mail, in person, online. Both court and visitors may perform in person searches. Search fee: $5.00 per name. Required to search: name, years to search. Civil cases indexed by defendant, plaintiff. Civil records on computer since January, 1994, index books prior to 1994. Access to county judicial records is free at http://209.223.255.254/. Search by either party name.
Criminal Records: Access: Mail, in person, online. Both court and visitors may perform in person searches. Search fee: $5.00 per name. Required to search: name, years to search. Criminal records on computer since January, 1994, index books prior to 1994. Access to county judicial records is free online at http://209.223.255.254/. Search by defendant name.
General Information: Public Access terminal is available. No juvenile, mental, sealed, or adoption records released. Copy fee: $1.00 per page. No cert fee. Payee: District Clerk. Personal checks accepted. Prepayment required. Mial requests require SASE. Mail turnaround time 1-2 days.

County Court 119 N Main, Paris, TX 75460; 903-737-2420. Hours: 8AM-5PM (CST). *Misdemeanor, Civil, Probate.*
www.co.lamar.tx.us
Civil Records: Access: Phone, fax, mail, in person, online. Both court and visitors may perform in person searches. Search fee: $5.00 per name. Required to search: name, years to search. Civil cases indexed by defendant, plaintiff. Civil records in index books since 1913; on computer back to 1998. Access to county judicial records is free online at http://209.223.255.254/. Search by either party name.
Criminal Records: Access: Phone, fax, mail, in person, online. Both court and visitors may perform in person searches. Search fee: $5.00 per name. Required to search: name, years to search, DOB; SSN or drivers license number also required. Criminal records on computer back to 1988, index books since 1913. Access to county judicial records is free online at http://209.223.255.254/. Search by defendant name.
General Information: No juvenile, mental, sealed, or adoption records released. Will not fax results. Copy fee: $1.00 per page. Cert fee: $5.00 (for land records only). Payee: County Clerk. Business checks accepted. Personal checks must be local. Prepayment required. Mail turnaround time 2-3 days.

Lamb County

District Court 100 6th, Rm 212, Courthouse, Littlefield, TX 79339; 806-385-4222. Hours: 8AM-Noon, 1-5PM (CST). *Felony, Civil.*
Civil Records: Access: Mail, in person. Both court and visitors may perform in person searches. Search fee: $5.00 per name. Required to search: name, years to search. Civil cases indexed by defendant, plaintiff. Civil records on computer since 1987; on index books back to 1940.

Criminal Records: Access: Mail, in person. Both court and visitors may perform in person searches. Search fee: $5.00 per name. Required to search: name, years to search; also helpful: DOB, SSN. Criminal records in index books to 1940s; on computer since 1987.

General Information: No juvenile, mental, sealed, or adoption records released. Will fax results to local or toll free line. Copy fee: $1.00 per page. Cert fee: $1.00 per page. Payee: District Court. Personal checks accepted. Prepayment required. Mial requests require SASE. Mail turnaround time 2-3 days.

County Court County Courthouse, Rm 103, Box 3, Littlefield, TX 79339-3366; 806-385-4222 X214; Fax: 806-385-6485. Hours: 8:30AM-12:00-1-5PM (CST). *Misdemeanor, Civil, Probate.*
Civil Records: Access: Mail, in person. Both court and visitors may perform in person searches. Search fee: $5.00 per name. Required to search: name, years to search. Civil cases indexed by defendant, plaintiff. Civil records in index books.
Criminal Records: Access: Mail, in person. Both court and visitors may perform in person searches. Search fee: $5.00 per name. Required to search: name, years to search; also helpful: DOB, SSN. Criminal records in index books.
General Information: No juvenile, mental, sealed, or adoption records released. Copy fee: $1.00 per page. Cert fee: $5.00. Payee: Lamb County Clerk. Personal checks accepted. Prepayment required. Mial requests require SASE. Mail turnaround time 1-2 days.

Lampasas County

District Court PO Box 327, Lampasas, TX 76550; 512-556-8271 X240; Fax: 512-556-9463. Hours: 8AM-5PM (CST). *Felony, Civil.*
Civil Records: Access: Mail, in person. Both court and visitors may perform in person searches. Search fee: $5.00 per name. Required to search: name, years to search. Civil cases indexed by defendant, plaintiff. Civil records in index books, computerized since 1997.
Criminal Records: Access: Mail, in person. Both court and visitors may perform in person searches. Search fee: $5.00 per name. Required to search: name, years to search. Criminal records in index books; on computer for 5 years.
General Information: No juvenile, mental, sealed, or adoption records released. Fee to fax results is $1.00 per page. Copy fee: $1.00 per page. Cert fee: $2.00. Payee: District Clerk. Business checks accepted. Prepayment required. Mial requests require SASE. Mail turnaround time 2-4 days.

County Court PO Box 347, Lampasas, TX 76550; 512-556-8271 X37. Hours: 8AM-5PM (CST). *Misdemeanor, Civil, Probate.*
Civil Records: Access: Mail, in person. Both court and visitors may perform in person searches. Search fee: $5.00 per name. Required to search: name, years to search. Civil cases indexed by defendant, plaintiff. Civil records in index books.
Criminal Records: Access: Mail, in person. Both court and visitors may perform in person searches. Search fee: $5.00 per name. Required to search: name, years to search; also helpful: DOB, SSN. Criminal records in index books.
General Information: No juvenile, mental, sealed, or adoption records released. Copy fee: $1.00 per page. Cert fee: $5.00. Payee: County Clerk. Personal checks must be in state. Prepayment required. Mail requests: SASE requested. Turnaround time 1-2 days.

Lavaca County

District Court PO Box 306, Hallettsville, TX 77964; 361-798-2351. Hours: 8AM-Noon, 1-5PM (CST). *Felony, Civil.*

Civil Records: Access: Phone, mail, in person. Both court and visitors may perform in person searches. Search fee: $5.00 per name. Required to search: name, years to search. Civil cases indexed by defendant, plaintiff. Civil records in index books from 1847. Information released to attorneys only.

Criminal Records: Access: Mail, in person. Both court and visitors may perform in person searches. Search fee: $5.00 per name. Required to search: name, years to search. Criminal records in index books from 1847. Information released to law enforcement only.

General Information: No juvenile, Department of Human Services, adoptions and expunction records released. Will fax results to local or toll free line. Copy fee: $1.00 per page. Cert fee: $2.00. Payee: Lavaca County District Clerk. Personal checks accepted. Prepayment required. Mial requests require SASE. Mail turnaround time same day.

County Court PO Box 326, Hallettsville, TX 77964; 361-798-3612. Hours: 8AM-5PM (CST). *Misdemeanor, Civil, Probate.*

Civil Records: Access: Mail, in person. Both court and visitors may perform in person searches. Search fee: $5.00 per name per 5 years. Required to search: name, years to search, DOB; also helpful: address, SSN, DL#. Civil cases indexed by defendant, plaintiff. Civil records on computer go back to late 1993; earlier in index books.

Criminal Records: Access: Mail, in person. Both court and visitors may perform in person searches. Search fee: $5.00 per name per 5 years. Required to search: name, years to search; also helpful: address, DOB, DL#, SSN. Records on computer go back to late 1993; earlier in index books.

General Information: No mental health or sealed records released. Copy fee: $1.00 per page. Cert fee: $5.00 plus 1.00 per page. Payee: County Clerk. Personal checks accepted. Prepayment required. Mail turnaround time same day as received.

Lee County

District Court PO Box 176, Giddings, TX 78942; 979-542-2947; Fax: 979-542-2444. Hours: 8AM-Noon, 1-5PM (CST). *Felony, Civil.*

Civil Records: Access: Mail, in person. Both court and visitors may perform in person searches. Search fee: $5.00 per name. Required to search: name, years to search. Civil cases indexed by defendant, plaintiff. Civil records on index books from 1800s.

Criminal Records: Access: Mail, in person. Both court and visitors may perform in person searches. Search fee: $5.00 per name. Required to search: name, years to search; also helpful: DOB, SSN. Criminal records on computer since 1989.

General Information: No juvenile or adoption records released. Will fax results to local or toll free line. Copy fee: $1.00 per page. Cert fee: $2.00. Payee: District Clerk, Lee County. Personal checks accepted. Prepayment required. Mail turnaround time 1-2 days.

County Court PO Box 419, Giddings, TX 78942; 979-542-3684; Fax: 979-542-2623. Hours: 8AM-5PM (CST). *Misdemeanor, Civil, Probate.*

Civil Records: Access: Mail, in person. Both court and visitors may perform in person searches. Search fee: $5.00 per name. Required to search: name, years to search. Civil cases indexed by defendant, plaintiff. Civil records in index books since 1874 (beginning 1995 on computer).

Criminal Records: Access: Mail, in person. Both court and visitors may perform in person searches.

Search fee: $5.00 per name. Required to search: name, years to search. Criminal records on computer since 1992, index books since 1874.

General Information: No juvenile, mental, sealed or adoption records released. Will fax results to local or toll free line. Copy fee: $1.00 per page. Cert fee: $5.00. Payee: County Clerk. Personal checks accepted. Prepayment required. Mial requests require SASE. Mail turnaround time 1-3 days.

Leon County

District Court PO Box 39, Centerville, TX 75833; 903-536-2227. Hours: 8AM-5PM (CST). *Felony, Civil.*

Note: Physical add; 139 E Main St.,Centerville,Tx.75833

Civil Records: Access: Mail, in person. Both court and visitors may perform in person searches. Search fee: $5.00 per name. Required to search: name, years to search. Civil cases indexed by defendant, plaintiff. Civil records in index books.

Criminal Records: Access: Mail, in person. Only the court performs in person searches; visitors may not. Search fee: $5.00 per name. Required to search: name, years to search. Criminal records in index books.

General Information: No juvenile, mental, sealed, or adoption records released. Copy fee: $1.00 per page. Cert fee: $2.00. Payee: Leon County District Clerk. Personal checks accepted. Prepayment required. Mial requests require SASE. Mail turnaround time 2-4 days.

County Court PO Box 98, Centerville, TX 75833; 903-536-2352. Hours: 8AM-5PM (CST). *Misdemeanor, Civil, Probate.*

Civil Records: Access: Mail, in person. Both court and visitors may perform in person searches. Search fee: $5.00 per name. Required to search: name, years to search. Civil cases indexed by defendant, plaintiff. Civil records in index books.

Criminal Records: Access: Mail, in person. Both court and visitors may perform in person searches. Search fee: $5.00 per name. Required to search: name, years to search, signed release. Criminal records in index books.

General Information: No juvenile, mental, sealed, or adoption records released. Copy fee: $1.00 per page. Cert fee: $5.00. Payee: Leon County Clerk. Business checks accepted. Personal checks accepted in person only. Prepayment required. Mial requests require SASE. Mail turnaround time 1-3 days.

Liberty County

District Court 1923 Sam Houston, Rm 303, Liberty, TX 77575; 936-336-4600. Hours: 8AM-Noon, 1-5PM (CST). *Felony, Civil.*

Civil Records: Access: Mail, in person. Both court and visitors may perform in person searches. Search fee: $5.00 per name. Required to search: name, years to search. Civil cases indexed by defendant, plaintiff. Civil records on computer since 1993, index books prior.

Criminal Records: Access: Mail, in person. Both court and visitors may perform in person searches. Search fee: $5.00 per name. Required to search: name, years to search. Criminal records on computer since 1993, index books prior.

General Information: Public Access terminal is available. No juvenile, mental, sealed, or adoption records released. Copy fee: $1.00 per page. Payee: District Clerk. Personal checks accepted. Prepayment required. Mial requests require SASE. Mail turnaround time 2-4 days.

County Court

County Court PO Box 369, Liberty, TX 77575; 936-336-4670. Hours: 8AM-5PM (CST). *Misdemeanor, Civil, Probate.*

Civil Records: Access: Mail, in person. Both court and visitors may perform in person searches. Search fee: $5.00 per name. Required to search: name, years to search. Civil cases indexed by defendant, plaintiff. Civil records in index books; later on computer.

Criminal Records: Access: Mail, in person. Both court and visitors may perform in person searches. Search fee: $5.00 per name. Required to search: name, years to search, DOB, SSN, signed release. Criminal records in index books; later on computer.

General Information: Public Access terminal is available. No juvenile, mental, sealed, or adoption records released. Will not fax results. Copy fee: $1.00 per page. Cert fee: $5.00. Payee: County Clerk. Business checks accepted. Personal checks accepted in person only. Prepayment required. Mial requests require SASE. Mail turnaround time 2-4 days.

Limestone County

District Court PO Box 230, Groesbeck, TX 76642; 254-729-3206; Fax: 254-729-2960. Hours: 8AM-5PM (CST). *Felony, Civil.*

Civil Records: Access: Phone, fax, mail, in person. Both court and visitors may perform in person searches. Search fee: $5.00 per name. Required to search: name, years to search. Civil cases indexed by defendant, plaintiff. Civil records on computer since September 1990, index books since 1883.

Criminal Records: Access: Phone, fax, mail, in person. Both court and visitors may perform in person searches. Search fee: $5.00 per name. Required to search: name, years to search, DOB; also helpful: SSN. Criminal records on computer since September 1990, index books since 1911.

General Information: Public Access terminal is available. No juvenile, mental, sealed, or adoption records released. Will fax results for $1.00 1st page, $.25 each add'l. Copy fee: $1.00 per document or $.50 per single page. Cert fee: $2.00. Payee: District Clerk. Personal checks accepted. Prepayment required. Mail turnaround time 1 week.

County Court PO Box 350, Groesbeck, TX 76642; 254-729-5504; Fax: 254-729-2951. Hours: 8AM-5PM (CST). *Misdemeanor, Civil, Probate.*

Civil Records: Access: Mail, in person. Both court and visitors may perform in person searches. Search fee: $5.00 per name. Required to search: name, years to search. Civil cases indexed by defendant, plaintiff. Civil records in index books to early 1900s, computerized since 1985.

Criminal Records: Access: Mail, in person. Both court and visitors may perform in person searches. Search fee: $5.00 per name. Required to search: name, years to search; also helpful: DOB, SSN, signed release. Criminal records in index books to 1900s, comupterized since 1985.

General Information: Public Access terminal is available. No juvenile, mental, sealed, or adoption records released. Fee to fax results is $2.00 per page. Copy fee: $1.00 per page. Cert fee: $5.00. Payee: Limestone County Clerk. Personal checks accepted. Prepayment required. Mail turnaround time 2 days.

Lipscomb County

District & County Court PO Box 70, Lipscomb, TX 79056; 806-862-3091; Fax: 806-862-3004. Hours: 8:30AM-Noon, 1-5PM (CST). *Felony, Misdemeanor, Civil, Probate.*

Civil Records: Access: Fax, mail, in person. Both court and visitors may perform in person searches. Search fee: $10.00 per name. Required to search: name. Civil cases indexed by defendant, plaintiff.

Civil records in index books since 1887; on computer back to 1999.

Criminal Records: Access: Fax, mail, in person. Both court and visitors may perform in person searches. Search fee: $5.00 per name. Required to search: name; also helpful: DOB. Criminal records in index books since 1887; on computer back to 1999.

General Information: No juvenile, mental, sealed, or adoption records released. Will fax results $1.00 1st page, $.50 each add'l. Copy fee: $1.00 per page. Cert fee: $5.00 per County Court or $1.00 per District Court. Payee: County Clerk. Personal checks accepted. Prepayment required. Mail turnaround time 2 days.

Live Oak County

District Court PO Drawer 440, George West, TX 78022; 361-449-2733 X105. Hours: 8AM-5PM (CST). *Felony, Civil.*

Civil Records: Access: Phone, fax, mail, in person. Both court and visitors may perform in person searches. Search fee: $10.00 per name. Required to search: name, years to search. Civil cases indexed by defendant, plaintiff. Civil records in index books and microfiche since 1850s.

Criminal Records: Access: Phone, fax, mail, in person. Both court and visitors may perform in person searches. Search fee: $10.00 per name. Required to search: name, years to search, DOB; also helpful: SSN. Criminal records in index books and microfiche since 1850s.

General Information: No juvenile, mental, sealed, or adoption records released. Copy fee: $1.00 per page. Cert fee: $1.00. Payee: District Clerk. Personal checks accepted. Prepayment required. Mial requests require SASE. Mail turnaround time 1-2 days.

County Court PO Box 280, George West, TX 78022; 361-449-2733 X3; Civil phone: X103; Criminal phone: X129; Probate phone: X103. Hours: 8AM-5PM (CST). *Misdemeanor, Civil, Probate.*

Civil Records: Access: Mail, in person. Both court and visitors may perform in person searches. Search fee: $10.00 per name. Required to search: name, years to search. Civil cases indexed by defendant, plaintiff. Civil records in index books.

Criminal Records: Access: Mail, in person. Both court and visitors may perform in person searches. Search fee: $10.00 per name. Required to search: name, years to search. Criminal records in index books.

General Information: No juvenile, mental, sealed, or adoption records released. No fax machine. Copy fee: $1.00 per page. Cert fee: $5.00. Payee: County Clerk. Personal checks accepted. Prepayment required. Mial requests require SASE. Mail turnaround time 1-2 days.

Llano County

District Clerk PO Box 877, Llano, TX 78643-0877; 325-247-5036; Fax: 325-248-0492. Hours: 8AM-4:30PM (CST). *Felony, Civil.*
www.courts.state.tx.us/district/33rd/index.htm

Civil Records: Access: Mail, in person. Both court and visitors may perform in person searches. Search fee: $5.00 per name. Fee is per 5 year period. Required to search: name, years to search. Civil cases indexed by defendant, plaintiff. Civil records in index books back to 1900, computerized back to 1995.

Criminal Records: Access: Mail, in person. Both court and visitors may perform in person searches. Search fee: $5.00 per name. Fee is per 5 year period. Required to search: name, years to search. Criminal records in index books back to 1900, computerized back to 1995.

General Information: Public Access terminal is available. No juvenile, mental, sealed, or adoption

records released. Will fax results to local or toll free line. Copy fee: $1.00 per page. Cert fee: $1.00 per page. Payee: Llano County District Clerk. Personal checks accepted. Visa, MC accepted. 5% handling fee charged. Prepayment required. Mial requests require SASE. Mail turnaround time 1-3 days.

County Court PO Box 40, Llano, TX 78643-0040; 325-247-4455. Hours: 8AM-4:30PM (CST). *Misdemeanor, Civil, Probate.*

Civil Records: Access: Phone, mail, in person. Both court and visitors may perform in person searches. Search fee: $5.00 per name. Required to search: name, years to search. Civil cases indexed by defendant, plaintiff. Civil records on computer since 1985, index books prior.

Criminal Records: Access: Phone, mail, in person. Both court and visitors may perform in person searches. Search fee: $5.00 per name. Required to search: name, years to search; also helpful: DOB. Criminal records on computer since 1985, index books prior.

General Information: Public Access terminal is available. No juvenile, mental, sealed, or adoption records released. Will fax results to local or toll free line. Copy fee: $1.00 per page. Cert fee: $5.00. Payee: County Clerk. Personal checks accepted. Prepayment required. Mail turnaround time 2-4 days.

Loving County

District & County Court PO Box 194, Mentone, TX 79754; 432-377-2441; Fax: 432-377-2701. Hours: 9AM-Noon, 1-5PM (CST). *Felony, Misdemeanor, Civil, Probate.*

Civil Records: Access: Phone, fax, mail, in person. Both court and visitors may perform in person searches. Search fee: $5.00 per name. Required to search: name, years to search. Civil cases indexed by defendant, plaintiff. Civil records in index books from 1935; computerized back to 1987.

Criminal Records: Access: Phone, fax, mail, in person. Both court and visitors may perform in person searches. Search fee: $5.00 per name. Required to search: name, years to search. Criminal records in index books from 1935; computerized back to 1987.

General Information: No juvenile, mental, sealed, or adoption records released. Fee to fax results is $1.50 per page. Copy fee: $1.00 per page. Cert fee: $5.00. Payee: Loving County Clerk. Personal checks accepted. Prepayment required. Mial requests require SASE. Mail turnaround time 2 days.

Lubbock County

District Court PO Box 10536 (904 Broadway #105), Lubbock, TX 79408-3536; 806-775-1623; Probate phone: 806-775-1051; Fax: 806-775-1382. Hours: 8AM-5PM (CST). *Felony, Civil.*
www.co.lubbock.tx.us/DClerk/d_clerk.htm
Note: Probate is a separate office at the same address.

Civil Records: Access: Fax, mail, in person. Both court and visitors may perform in person searches. Search fee: $5.00 per name. Required to search: name, years to search. Civil cases indexed by defendant, plaintiff. Civil records on computer back to 1983, in index books to 1908.

Criminal Records: Access: Fax, mail, in person. Both court and visitors may perform in person searches. Search fee: $5.00 per name. Required to search: name, years to search, DOB; also helpful: SSN, signed release. Criminal records on computer back to 1983, in index books to 1908.

General Information: Public Access terminal is available. No juvenile, mental, sealed, or adoption records released. Will fax results for $5.00 per document plus $1.00 per page. Copy fee: $1.00 per page. Cert fee: $1.00. Payee: District Clerk. Visa/MC accepted, also money order and cashier's check.

Prepayment required. Mial requests require SASE. Mail turnaround time 2 buisness days.

County Courts Courthouse, Rm 207, PO Box 10536, Lubbock, TX 79408; Civil phone: 806-775-1051; Criminal phone: 806-775-1044; Probate: 806-775-1048. Hours: 8:30AM-5PM (CST). *Misdemeanor, Civil, Probate.*
www.co.lubbock.tx.us/CCourt/c_courts.htm

Civil Records: Access: Mail, in person. Both court and visitors may perform in person searches. Search fee: $10.00 per name. Fee is for each 10 year period. Required to search: name, years to search. Civil cases indexed by defendant, plaintiff. Civil records on computer back to 1986, index books prior.

Criminal Records: Access: Mail, in person. Both court and visitors may perform in person searches. Search fee: $10.00 per name. Required to search: name, years to search. Criminal records on computer back to 1986, index books prior.

General Information: Public Access terminal is available. No juvenile, mental, sealed, or adoption records released. Copy fee: $1.00 per page. Cert fee: $5.00. Payee: County Clerk. Personal checks accepted. Prepayment required. Mial requests require SASE. Mail turnaround time 3-5 days.

Lynn County

District Court PO Box 939, Tahoka, TX 79373; 806-561-4274; Fax: 806-561-4151. Hours: 8:30AM-5PM (CST). *Felony, Civil.*

Civil Records: Access: Fax, mail, in person. Both court and visitors may perform in person searches. Search fee: $5.00 per name. Required to search: name, years to search. Civil cases indexed by defendant, plaintiff. Civil records on computer from 1997, index books from 1916.

Criminal Records: Access: Fax, mail, in person. Both court and visitors may perform in person searches. Search fee: $5.00 per name. Required to search: name, years to search. Criminal records on computer from 1997, index books from 1916.

General Information: No juvenile, mental, sealed, or adoption records released. Will fax results $2.00 per page. Copy fee: $1.00 per page. Cert fee: $1.00 per page. Payee: District Clerk. Personal checks accepted. Prepayment required. Mial requests require SASE. Mail turnaround time 2 days.

County Court PO Box 937, Tahoka, TX 79373; 806-561-4750; Fax: 806-561-4988. Hours: 8:30AM-5PM (CST). *Misdemeanor, Civil, Probate.*

Civil Records: Access: Mail, in person. Both court and visitors may perform in person searches. Search fee: $5.00. Required to search: name, years to search. Civil cases indexed by defendant, plaintiff. Civil records in index books from 1903; on computer back to 1997.

Criminal Records: Access: Mail, in person. Both court and visitors may perform in person searches. Search fee: $5.00. Required to search: name, years to search. Criminal records in index books from 1903; on computer back to 1997.

General Information: Public Access terminal is available. No juvenile, mental, sealed, or adoption records released. Fee to fax results is $2.00 per page. Copy fee: $1.00 per page. Cert fee: $5.00. Payee: Lynn County Clerk. Personal checks accepted. Prepayment required. Mial requests require SASE. Mail turnaround time 2-4 days.

Madison County

District Court 101 W Main,Rm 226, Madisonville, TX 77864; 936-348-9203. Hours: 8AM-Noon, 1-5PM (CST). *Felony, Civil.*

Civil Records: Access: Mail, in person. Both court and visitors may perform in person searches. Search fee: $5.00 per name. Required to search: name, years

to search. Civil cases indexed by defendant, plaintiff. Civil records in index books to 1935.

Criminal Records: Access: Mail, in person. Both court and visitors may perform in person searches. Search fee: $5.00 per name. Required to search: name, years to search. Criminal records in index books to 1835.

General Information: No juvenile, mental, sealed, or adoption records released. Copy fee: $1.00 per page. No cert fee. Payee: District Clerk. Personal checks accepted. Prepayment required. Mial requests require SASE. Mail turnaround time 1 day.

County Court 101 W Main,Rm 102,
Madisonville, TX 77864; 936-348-2638; Fax: 936-348-5858. Hours: 8AM-4:30PM (CST). *Misdemeanor, Civil, Probate.*
www.co.madison.tx.us/coclerk.html
Civil Records: Access: Mail, in person, fax. Both court and visitors may perform in person searches. Search fee: $10.00 per name. Required to search: name, years to search. Civil cases indexed by defendant. Civil records on computer from 1/00; index books back to 1970.

Criminal Records: Access: Mail, in person. Only the court performs in person searches; visitors may not. Search fee: $10.00 per name. Required to search: name, years to search, DOB. Criminal records on computer from 1982; records go back to early 1900s (not indexed).

General Information: No juvenile, mental, sealed, or adoption records released. Fee to fax results is $1.00 per page. Copy fee: $1.00 per page. Cert fee: $5.00. Payee: Madison County Clerk. Personal checks accepted. Prepayment required. Mial requests require SASE. Mail turnaround time as soon as fees are paid.

Marion County

District Court PO Box 628, Jefferson, TX 75657; 903-665-2441/2013. Hours: 8AM-5PM (CST). *Felony, Civil.*
Civil Records: Access: Mail, in person. Both court and visitors may perform in person searches. Search fee: $5.00 per name. Required to search: name, years to search. Civil cases indexed by defendant, plaintiff. Civil records on computer from 1997, index books up to 1986.

Criminal Records: Access: Mail, in person. Both court and visitors may perform in person searches. Search fee: $5.00 per name. Required to search: name, years to search. Criminal records on computer from 1997, index books up to 1986.

General Information: No juvenile, mental, sealed, or adoption records released. Copy fee: $1.00 per page. Cert fee: $1.00. Payee: District Clerk. Personal checks accepted. Prepayment required. Mial requests require SASE. Mail turnaround time 1 week.

County Court PO Box 763, Jefferson, TX 75657;
903-665-3971. Hours: 8AM-Noon, 1-5PM (CST). *Misdemeanor, Probate.*
Criminal Records: Access: Phone, mail, in person. Both court and visitors may perform in person searches. No search fee. Required to search: name, years to search. Criminal records in index books from 1966; computerized back to 1997.

General Information: No juvenile, mental, sealed, or adoption records released. Copy fee: $1.00 per page. Cert fee: $5.00. Payee: County Clerk. Personal checks accepted. Prepayment required. Mial requests require SASE. Mail turnaround time 2-4 days.

Martin County

District & County Court PO Box 906, Stanton, TX 79782; 432-756-3412; Fax: 432-607-2212. Hours: 8AM-Noon, 1-5PM (CST). *Felony, Misdemeanor, Civil, Probate.*
Civil Records: Access: Mail, in person. Both court and visitors may perform in person searches. Search fee: $5.00 per name. Required to search: name, years to search. Civil cases indexed by defendant, plaintiff. Civil records in index books to 1900.

Criminal Records: Access: Mail, in person. Both court and visitors may perform in person searches. Search fee: $5.00 per name. Required to search: name, years to search. Criminal records in index books to 1900, computerized since 1980.

General Information: No juvenile, mental, sealed, or adoption records released. Fee to fax results is $1.00 per page. Copy fee: $1.00 per page. Cert fee: $5.00. Payee: County/District Clerk. Personal checks accepted. Prepayment required. Mial requests require SASE. Mail turnaround time 2-4 days.

Mason County

District & County Court PO Box 702, Mason, TX 76856; 325-347-5253; Fax: 325-347-6868. Hours: 8AM-Noon, 1-4PM (CST). *Felony, Misdemeanor, Civil, Probate.*
Civil Records: Access: Mail, in person. Both court and visitors may perform in person searches. Search fee: $10.00 per name. Required to search: name, years to search. Civil cases indexed by defendant, plaintiff. Civil records in index books to 1858; on computer back to 1993.

Criminal Records: Access: Mail, in person. Both court and visitors may perform in person searches. Search fee: $10.00 per name. Required to search: name, years to search; also helpful: DOB, SSN. Criminal records igo back to 1877; on computer back to 1993.

General Information: Public Access terminal is available. No juvenile, mental, sealed, or adoption records released. Copy fee: $1.00 per page. Cert fee: $5.00. Payee: County/District Clerk. Personal checks accepted. Prepayment required. Mial requests require SASE. Mail turnaround time 2 days.

Matagorda County

District Court 1700 7th St,Rm 307, Bay City, TX 77414-5092; 979-244-7621. Hours: 8AM-Noon, 1-5PM (CST). *Felony, Civil.*
www.co.matagorda.tx.us
Civil Records: Access: Mail, in person. Both court and visitors may perform in person searches. Search fee: $5.00 per name. Required to search: name, years to search. Civil cases indexed by defendant, plaintiff. Civil records in index books and card files back to 1910; computerized back to 1994.

Criminal Records: Access: Mail, in person. Both court and visitors may perform in person searches. Search fee: $5.00 per name. Required to search: name, years to search, DOB. Criminal records in index books back to 1910; computerized back to 1994.

General Information: No juvenile, sealed, or adoption records released. Will not fax results. Copy fee: $1.00 per page. Cert fee: $2.00. Payee: District Clerk. Personal checks accepted. Prepayment required. Mial requests require SASE. Mail turnaround time 1-2 days.

County Court 1700 7th St,Rm 202, Bay City, TX
77414-5094; 979-244-7680; Fax: 979-244-7688. Hours: 8AM-5PM (CST). *Misdemeanor, Civil, Probate.*
Civil Records: Access: Mail, in person. Both court and visitors may perform in person searches. Search

fee: $5.00 per name. Required to search: name, years to search. Civil cases indexed by defendant, plaintiff. Civil records on computer from 1994, index books prior.

Criminal Records: Access: Mail, in person. Both court and visitors may perform in person searches. Search fee: $5.00 per name. Required to search: name, years to search, DOB, SSN. Criminal records on computer from 1994, index books prior.

General Information: Public Access terminal is available. No juvenile, mental, sealed, or adoption records released. Fee to fax results is $2.00 per document. Copy fee: $1.00 per page. Cert fee: $5.00. Payee: County Clerk. Personal checks accepted. Visa, MC accepted. Prepayment required. Mial requests require SASE. Mail turnaround time 1-2 days.

Maverick County

District Court 500 Quarry St, #5, Eagle Pass, TX 78853; 830-773-2629. Hours: 8AM-5PM (CST). *Felony, Civil.*
Civil Records: Access: Mail, in person. Both court and visitors may perform in person searches. Search fee: $5.00 per name. Required to search: name, years to search. Civil cases indexed by defendant, plaintiff. Civil records in index books; recent records computerized.

Criminal Records: Access: Mail, in person. Both court and visitors may perform in person searches. Search fee: $5.00 per name. Required to search: name, years to search. Criminal records in index books; recent records computerized.

General Information: No juvenile, mental, sealed, or adoption records released. Fee to fax results is $1.00 per page. Copy fee: $1.00 per page. Cert fee: $5.00. Payee: District Clerk. Personal checks not accepted. Prepayment required. Mial requests require SASE. Mail turnaround time 2-4 days.

County Court 500 Quarry St, 2, Eagle Pass, TX
78853; 830-773-2829; Civil phone: X228; Criminal phone: X228; Probate phone: X228. Hours: 8AM-5PM (CST). *Misdemeanor, Civil, Probate.*
Civil Records: Access: Mail, in person. Both court and visitors may perform in person searches. Search fee: $10.00 per name. Required to search: name, years to search. Civil cases indexed by defendant, plaintiff. Civil records on index books.

Criminal Records: Access: Mail, in person. Both court and visitors may perform in person searches. Search fee: $5.00 per name. Required to search: name, years to search, DOB, SSN. Criminal records on index books.

General Information: No juvenile, mental, sealed, or adoption records released. Fee to fax results is 1.00 per page. Copy fee: $1.00 per page. Cert fee: $5.00. Payee: County Clerk. Personal checks accepted. Prepayment required. Mial requests require SASE. Mail turnaround time 1-2 days.

McCulloch County

District Court County Courthouse,Rm 205, Brady, TX 76825; 325-597-0733; Fax: 325-597-0606. Hours: 8:30AM-5PM (CST). *Felony, Civil.*
Civil Records: Access: Mail, fax, in person, online. Both court and visitors may perform in person searches. Search fee: $5.00 per name. Required to search: name, years to search. Civil cases indexed by defendant, plaintiff. Civil records in index books. Civil case information is free at www.idocket.com. Free searching is limited. Records go back to 12/31/1995.

Criminal Records: Access: Mail, fax, in person, online. Both court and visitors may perform in person searches. Search fee: $5.00 per name. Required to search: name, years to search; also helpful: DOB, SSN. Criminal records in index books back to 1990;

on computer back to 1995. Criminal records access is through www.idocket.com; registration and password required. Records go back to 12/31/1995.

General Information: Public Access terminal is available. No juvenile, mental, sealed, or adoption records released. Will fax results for $5.00 per page. Copy fee: $1.00 per page. Cert fee: $2.00. Payee: District Clerk. Personal checks accepted. Prepayment required. Mial requests require SASE. Mail turnaround time 2-4 days.

County Court County Courthouse, Brady, TX 76825; 325-597-0733. Hours: 8AM-12:00-1-5PM (CST). *Misdemeanor, Civil, Probate.*

Civil Records: Access: Mail, in person, online. Both court and visitors may perform in person searches. Search fee: $5.00 per name. Required to search: name, years to search. Civil cases indexed by defendant, plaintiff. Civil records in index books since early 1900s, computerized since 10/95. Online access is through www.idocket.com; registration and password required. Records go back to 12/31/1996; includes probate records.

Criminal Records: Access: Mail, in person, online. Both court and visitors may perform in person searches. Search fee: $5.00 per name. Required to search: name, years to search. Criminal records in index books since 1900s, computerized since 10/95. Criminal records access is through www.idocket.com; registration and password required. Records go back to 12/31/1996.

General Information: No juvenile, mental, sealed, or adoption records released. Copy fee: $1.00 per page. Cert fee: $1.00. Payee: County Clerk. Personal checks accepted. Prepayment required. Mial requests require SASE. Mail turnaround time 7 days.

McLennan County

District Court PO Box 2451, Waco, TX 76703; Civil phone: 254-757-5057; Criminal phone: 254-757-5054; Fax: 254-757-5060. Hours: 8AM-5PM (CST). *Felony, Civil.*
www.co.mclennan.tx.us

Civil Records: Access: Fax, mail, in person. Both court and visitors may perform in person searches. Search fee: $5.00 per name. Required to search: name, years to search. Civil cases indexed by defendant, plaintiff. Civil records on computer since 1986, index books from 1850.

Criminal Records: Access: Mail, in person. Both court and visitors may perform in person searches. Search fee: $5.00 per name. Required to search: name, years to search. Criminal records on computer since 1959, index books from 1850.

General Information: Public Access terminal is available. No juvenile, mental, sealed, or adoption records released. Copy fee: $1.00 per page. No cert fee. Payee: Joe Johnson, District Clerk. Personal checks accepted. Prepayment required. Mial requests require SASE. Mail turnaround time 2 days.

County Clerk's Office PO Box 1727, Waco, TX 76703; 254-757-5185; Civil phone: 254-757-5189; Criminal phone: 254-757-5140; Probate phone: 254-757-5186; Fax: 254-757-5146. Hours: 8AM-5PM (CST). *Misdemeanor, Civil, Probate.*

Civil Records: Access: Mail, in person. Both court and visitors may perform in person searches. Search fee: $5.00 per name. Required to search: name, years to search. Civil cases indexed by defendant, plaintiff. Civil records in index books back to 1876 computerized since 2000. Probate to 1850, computerized since 1967.

Criminal Records: Access: Mail, in person. Both court and visitors may perform in person searches. Search fee: $5.00 per name. Required to search: name, years to search; also helpful: DOB, SSN.

Criminal records on computer since 1993; in index books to 1935.

General Information: Public Access terminal is available. No mental or sealed records released. Copy fee: $1.00 per page. Cert fee: $5.00. Payee: County Clerk. Business checks accepted. Prepayment required. Mial requests require SASE. Mail turnaround time 2-4 days.

McMullen County

District & County Court PO Box 235, Tilden, TX 78072; 361-274-3215; Fax: 361-274-3858. Hours: 8AM-4PM (CST). *Felony, Misdemeanor, Civil, Probate.*

Civil Records: Access: Mail, in person. Both court and visitors may perform in person searches. Search fee: $5.00 per name. Required to search: name, years to search. Civil cases indexed by defendant, plaintiff. Civil records in index books from 1918.

Criminal Records: Access: Mail, in person. Both court and visitors may perform in person searches. Search fee: $5.00 per name. Required to search: name, years to search. Criminal records in index books form 1918.

General Information: No juvenile, mental, sealed, or adoption records released. Will fax results for a fee of $ 3.00 1st page $1.00 add'l. Copy fee: $1.00 per page. Cert fee: $5.00 plus $1.00 per page. Payee: County Clerk. Personal checks accepted. Prepayment required. Mial requests require SASE. Mail turnaround time 2-4 days.

Medina County

District Court County Courthouse,Rm 209, Hondo, TX 78861; 830-741-6070. Hours: 8AM-5PM (CST). *Felony, Civil.*

Civil Records: Access: Phone, mail, in person. Both court and visitors may perform in person searches. Search fee: $5.00 per name. Required to search: name, years to search. Civil cases indexed by defendant, plaintiff. Civil records on computer since 1990, index books since 1849.

Criminal Records: Access: Mail, in person. Both court and visitors may perform in person searches. Search fee: $5.00 per name. Required to search: name, years to search, DOB, SSN. Criminal records on computer since 1990, index books since 1849.

General Information: Public Access terminal is available. No juvenile, mental, sealed, or adoption records released. Copy fee: $1.00 first page; $.50 each page thereaafter. Cert fee: $1.00 per page. Payee: Medina County District Clerk. Out-of-state checks not accepted. Prepayment required. Mial requests require SASE. Mail turnaround time 2 days.

County Court at Law 1100 16th St, Rm 203, Hondo, TX 78861; 830-741-6040. Hours: 8AM-Noon, 1-5PM (CST). *Misdemeanor, Civil, Probate.*

Civil Records: Access: Phone, mail, in person. Both court and visitors may perform in person searches. Search fee: $5.00 per name. Required to search: name, years to search. Civil cases indexed by defendant, plaintiff. Civil records on computer since late 1993, index books prior to 1881.

Criminal Records: Access: Phone, mail, in person. Both court and visitors may perform in person searches. Search fee: $5.00 per name. Required to search: name, years to search; also helpful: address, DOB, SSN. Criminal records on computer since late 1993, index books prior to 1953.

General Information: Public Access terminal is available. No juvenile, mental, or sealed records released. Will fax results for $3.00 1st page +$1.00 Add'l. Copy fee: $1.00 per page. Cert fee: $5.00. Payee: County Clerk. Personal checks accepted. Prepayment required. Mial requests require SASE. Mail turnaround time 1-2 days.

Menard County

District & County Court PO Box 1038, Menard, TX 76859; 325-396-4682; Fax: 325-396-2047. Hours: 8AM-Noon, 1-5PM (CST). *Felony, Misdemeanor, Civil, Probate.*

Civil Records: Access: Fax, mail, in person. Both court and visitors may perform in person searches. Search fee: $10.00 per name. Required to search: name, years to search. Civil cases indexed by defendant, plaintiff. Civil records in index books.

Criminal Records: Access: Mail, in person. Both court and visitors may perform in person searches. Search fee: $10.00 per name. Required to search: name, years to search. Criminal records in index books.

General Information: No juvenile, mental, sealed, or adoption records released. Will fax results for $1.00 per page. Copy fee: $1.00 per page. Cert fee: $5.00. Payee: District/County Clerk. Personal checks accepted. Prepayment required. Mial requests require SASE. Mail turnaround time 2-4 days.

Midland County

District Court 200 W Wall, 301, Midland, TX 79701; 432-688-4500. Hours: 8AM-5PM (CST). *Felony, Civil.*
www.co.midland.tx.us/DC/default.asp

Civil Records: Access: Mail, in person, online. Both court and visitors may perform in person searches. Search fee: $5.00 per name. Required to search: name, years to search. Civil cases indexed by defendant, plaintiff. Civil records on computer back to 1965, index books prior. Online access to the district Clerk database is at www.co.midland.tx.us/DC/Database/search.asp. Registration and password is required; contact the clerk for access restrictions.

Criminal Records: Access: Mail, in person, online. Both court and visitors may perform in person searches. Search fee: $5.00 per name. Required to search: name, years to search. Criminal records on computer back to 1940, index books prior. Online access to criminal records is the same as civil.

General Information: Public Access terminal is available. No juvenile, mental, sealed, or adoption records released. Fee to fax results is $1.00 per page. Copy fee: $1.00 per page. No cert fee. Payee: District Clerk. Business checks accepted. Prepayment required. Mial requests require SASE. Mail turnaround time 2 days.

County Court PO Box 211, Midland, TX 79702; 432-688-4402; Fax: 432-688-8973. Hours: 8AM-5PM (CST). *Misdemeanor, Civil, Probate.*
www.co.midland.tx.us/CC/default.asp

Civil Records: Access: Mail, in person, online. Both court and visitors may perform in person searches. Search fee: $5.00 per name. Required to search: name; also helpful: years to search, address. Civil cases indexed by defendant, plaintiff. Civil records on computer since 1987, index books since 1885. Probate records on computer since 1887. Online access to the County Clerk database is free at www.co.midland.tx.us/CC/Database/default.asp.

Criminal Records: Access: Mail, in person, online. Both court and visitors may perform in person searches. Search fee: $5.00 per name. Required to search: name; also helpful: years to search, address, DOB, SSN. Criminal records on computer since 1978, index books since 1885. Online access to criminal records is the same as civil.

General Information: Public Access terminal is available. No juvenile, mental, sealed, or adoption records released. Copy fee: $1.00 per page. Cert fee: $5.00. Payee: County Clerk. Only cashiers checks and money orders accepted. Prepayment required. Mail turnaround time 1-2 days.

Milam County

District Court PO Box 999, Cameron, TX 76520; 254-697-7052. Hours: 8AM-5PM (CST). *Felony, Civil.*

Civil Records: Access: Mail, in person. Both court and visitors may perform in person searches. Search fee: $5.00 per name. Required to search: name, years to search. Civil cases indexed by defendant, plaintiff. Civil records on microfilm and index books.

Criminal Records: Access: Mail, in person. Both court and visitors may perform in person searches. Search fee: $5.00 per name. Required to search: name, years to search. Criminal records on microfilm and index books.

General Information: No juvenile, mental, sealed, or adoption records released. Copy fee: $1.00 per page. Cert fee: $1.00. Payee: District Clerk. Only cashiers checks and money orders accepted. Prepayment required. Mial requests require SASE. Mail turnaround time same day.

County Court 107 W Main St, Cameron, TX 76520; 254-697-7049; Fax: 254-697-7055. Hours: 8AM-5PM (CST). *Misdemeanor, Civil, Probate.*

Civil Records: Access: Mail, in person. Both court and visitors may perform in person searches. Search fee: $5.00 per name. Required to search: name, years to search. Civil cases indexed by defendant, plaintiff. Civil records in books go back to 1874, computerized since 1992.

Criminal Records: Access: Mail, in person. Both court and visitors may perform in person searches. Search fee: $5.00 per name. Required to search: name, years to search, signed release, SSN. Criminal records in books go back to 1874, computerized since 1992.

General Information: Public Access terminal is available. No juvenile, mental, sealed, or adoption records released. Fee to fax results is $2.00 plus $1.00 per page. Copy fee: $1.00 per page. Cert fee: $5.00. Payee: Milam County Clerk. Personal checks accepted. Prepayment required. Mial requests require SASE. Mail turnaround time 1-2 days.

Mills County

District & County Court PO Box 646, Goldthwaite, TX 76844; 325-648-2711; Fax: 325-648-3251. Hours: 8AM-Noon, 1-5PM (CST). *Felony, Misdemeanor, Civil, Probate.*

Civil Records: Access: Fax, mail, in person. Both court and visitors may perform in person searches. Search fee: $5.00 per name. Required to search: name, years to search; also helpful: cause number. Civil cases indexed by defendant, plaintiff. Civil records in index books since 1887; no computerized records.

Criminal Records: Access: Mail, fax, in person. Both court and visitors may perform in person searches. Search fee: $5.00 per name. Required to search: name, years to search, DOB, signed release; also helpful: cause number. Criminal records in index books since 1887; no computerized records.

General Information: No juvenile, mental, sealed, or adoption records released. Copy fee: $1.00 per page. Cert fee: $5.00. Payee: County-District Clerk. Personal checks accepted. Prepayment required. Mail requests: SASE requested. Turnaround time 1-2 days.

Mitchell County

District Court County Courthouse, Colorado City, TX 79512; 325-728-5918. Hours: 9AM-4PM (CST). *Felony, Civil.*

Civil Records: Access: Mail, in person. Both court and visitors may perform in person searches. Search

fee: $5.00 per name. Required to search: name, years to search. Civil cases indexed by defendant, plaintiff. Civil records in index books.

Criminal Records: Access: Mail, in person. Only the court performs in person searches; visitors may not. Search fee: $5.00 per name. Required to search: name, years to search. Criminal records in index books.

General Information: No juvenile, mental, sealed, or adoption records released. Copy fee: $.35 per page. Cert fee: $1.00 per page. Payee: District Clerk. Personal checks accepted. Prepayment required. Mial requests require SASE. Mail turnaround time 1 day.

County Court 349 Oak St, Rm 103, Colorado City, TX 79512; 325-728-3481; Fax: 325-728-5322. Hours: 8AM-Noon, 1-5PM (CST). *Misdemeanor, Civil, Probate.*

Civil Records: Access: Fax, mail, in person. Both court and visitors may perform in person searches. Search fee: $5.00 per name. Required to search: name, years to search. Civil cases indexed by defendant, plaintiff. Civil records in index books back to 1882, on computer from 9-1-1998 to present.

Criminal Records: Access: Mail, in person. Both court and visitors may perform in person searches. Search fee: $5.00 per name. Required to search: name, years to search; also helpful: DOB. Criminal records in index books back to 1948, on computer from 9-1-1998 to present.

General Information: Public Access terminal is available. No juvenile, mental, sealed, or adoption, commitment records released. Will fax results for $3.00 for 1st page, $1.00 per page thereafter, long distance.
Will fax results for fee of $2.00 for the 1st page and $1.00 per page thereafter, local. Copy fee: $1.00 per page. Cert fee: $5.00. Payee: Mitchell County Clerk. No out of state personal checks. Money order accepted. Credit Cards accepted (4% flat fee). Prepayment required. Mail turnaround time 2-4 days.

Montague County

District Clerk PO Box 155, Montague, TX 76251; 940-894-2571. Hours: 8AM-5PM (CST). *Felony, Civil.*

Civil Records: Access: Mail, in person. Both court and visitors may perform in person searches. Search fee: $5.00 per name. Required to search: name, years to search. Civil cases indexed by defendant, plaintiff. Civil records on computer and index books.

Criminal Records: Access: Mail, in person. Both court and visitors may perform in person searches. Search fee: $5.00 per name. Required to search: name, years to search. Criminal records on computer and index books.

General Information: No juvenile, mental, sealed, or adoption records released. Copy fee: $1.00 per page. No cert fee. Payee: District Clerk. Personal checks not accepted. Prepayment required. Mial requests require SASE. Mail turnaround time 2-4 days.

County Court PO Box 77, Montague, TX 76251; 940-894-2461. Hours: 8AM-5PM (CST). *Misdemeanor, Civil, Probate.*

Civil Records: Access: Mail, in person. Both court and visitors may perform in person searches. Search fee: $10.00 per 10 years per name. Required to search: name, years to search. Civil cases indexed by defendant, plaintiff. Civil records on computer since 1993, index books prior.

Criminal Records: Access: Mail, in person. Both court and visitors may perform in person searches. Search fee: $5.00 per 10 years per name. Required to search: name, years to search, DOB. Criminal records on computer since 1993, index books prior.

General Information: No juvenile, mental, sealed, or adoption records released. Will fax results for $2.75

1st page, $.75 each add'l page. Copy fee: $1.00 per page. Cert fee: $5.00. Payee: County Clerk. Personal checks accepted; also credit cards. Prepayment required. Mial requests require SASE. Mail turnaround time 1-2 days.

Montgomery County

District Court PO Box 2985, Conroe, TX 77305; 936-539-7855. Hours: 8AM-4PM M-T,Th-F; 8AM-4:30PM W (CST). *Felony, Civil.*
www.co.montgomery.tx.us/dcourts/index.shtml
Civil Records: Access: Mail, in person. Both court and visitors may perform in person searches. Search fee: $5.00 per name. Required to search: name, years to search. Civil cases indexed by defendant, plaintiff. Civil records in index books since 1900, on computer since 1990.

Criminal Records: Access: Mail, in person. Both court and visitors may perform in person searches. Search fee: $5.00 per name. Required to search: name, years to search. Criminal records in index books since 1900, on computer since 1990.

General Information: Public Access terminal is available. No juvenile, mental, sealed, or adoption records released. Copy fee: $1.00 per page. No cert fee. Payee: Barbara Adamick, District Clerk. Personal checks not accepted. Prepayment required. Mail requests: SASE is required. Mail turnaround time 3-6 days.

County Court PO Box 959, Conroe, TX 77305; 936-539-7885; Fax: 936-760-6990. Hours: 8AM-5PM (CST). *Misdemeanor, Civil, Probate.*
www.co.montgomery.tx.us
Civil Records: Access: Mail, in person. Both court and visitors may perform in person searches. Search fee: $5.00 per name. Required to search: name, years to search, DOB or SSN. Civil cases indexed by defendant, plaintiff. Civil records on computer since 1971, and index books.

Criminal Records: Access: Mail, in person. Both court and visitors may perform in person searches. Search fee: $5.00 per name. Required to search: name, years to search, DOB or SSN. Criminal records on computer since 1985, and index books.

General Information: Public Access terminal is available. No mental or sealed records released. Fee to fax results is $2.00 per page. Copy fee: $1.00 per page. Cert fee: $5.00. Payee: County Clerk. Personal checks accepted. Prepayment required. Mial requests require SASE. Mail turnaround time 2-5 days.

Moore County

District Court 715 Dumas Ave, #109, Dumas, TX 79029; 806-935-4218; Fax: 806-935-6325. Hours: 8:30AM-5PM (CST). *Felony, Civil.*

Civil Records: Access: Mail, in person. Both court and visitors may perform in person searches. Search fee: $5.00 per name. Required to search: name, years to search. Civil cases indexed by defendant, plaintiff. Civil records on computer back to 1990; docket books and original files prior.

Criminal Records: Access: Mail, in person. Both court and visitors may perform in person searches. Search fee: $5.00 per name. Required to search: name, years to search, DOB; also helpful: SSN. Criminal records on computer back to 1990; docket books and original files prior.

General Information: Public Access terminal is available. No juvenile, mental, sealed, or adoption records released. Will fax results to a toll free number. Copy fee: $1.00 per page. Cert fee: $1.00. Payee: District Clerk. Personal checks accepted. Prepayment required. Mial requests require SASE. Mail turnaround time 1 day.

County Court 715 Dumas Ave, Rm 105, Dumas, TX 79029; 806-935-6164/2009; Fax: 806-935-9004. Hours: 8:30AM-5PM (CST). *Misdemeanor, Civil, Probate.*
Civil Records: Access: Mail, in person. Both court and visitors may perform in person searches. Search fee: $5.00 per name. Required to search: name, years to search. Civil cases indexed by defendant, plaintiff. Civil records on computer back to 1996, in index books prior.
Criminal Records: Access: Mail, fax, in person. Both court and visitors may perform in person searches. Search fee: $5.00 per name. Required to search: name, years to search, signed release, DOB or SSN. Criminal records on computer back to 1987, in index books prior.
General Information: Public Access terminal is available. No juvenile, mental, sealed, or adoption records released. Fee to fax results is $5.00 plus $1.00 per page. Copy fee: $1.00 per page. Cert fee: $5.00. Payee: Moore County Clerk. Business checks accepted. Prepayment required. Mial requests require SASE. Mail turnaround time 24 hours.

Morris County

District Court 500 Broadnax, Daingerfield, TX 75638; 903-645-2321. Hours: 8AM-5PM (CST). *Felony, Civil.*
Civil Records: Access: Mail, in person. Both court and visitors may perform in person searches. Search fee: $5.00 per name. Required to search: name, years to search. Civil cases indexed by defendant, plaintiff. Civil records in index books and file folders from 1930s, computerized since 2000.
Criminal Records: Access: Mail, in person. Both court and visitors may perform in person searches. Search fee: $5.00 per name. Required to search: name, years to search, DOB. Criminal records in index books and file folders from 1930s, computerized since 2000.
General Information: No juvenile, mental, sealed, or adoption records released. Copy fee: $1.00 per page. No cert fee. Payee: Morris County District Clerk. Personal checks accepted. Prepayment required. Mial requests require SASE. Mail turnaround time 1 day.

County Court 500 Broadnax, Daingerfield, TX 75638; 903-645-3911. Hours: 8AM-5PM (CST). *Misdemeanor, Probate.*
Criminal Records: Access: Mail, in person. Both court and visitors may perform in person searches. Search fee: $5.00 per name. Required to search: name, DOB, years to search. Criminal record on index books, computerized since 1999.
General Information: No juvenile, mental, sealed, or adoption records released. Copy fee: $1.00 per page. Cert fee: $5.00. Payee: County Clerk. Personal checks accepted. Prepayment required. Mail requests: SASE requested. Turnaround time 1 day.

Motley County

District & County Court PO Box 660, Matador, TX 79244; 806-347-2621; Fax: 806-347-2220. Hours: 9AM-Noon, 1-5PM (CST). *Felony, Misdemeanor, Civil, Probate.*
Civil Records: Access: Mail, fax, in person. Both court and visitors may perform in person searches. Search fee: $10.00 per name. Required to search: name, years to search, address. Civil cases indexed by defendant, plaintiff. Civil records in docket books, archived from 1891.
Criminal Records: Access: Mail, fax, in person. Only the court performs in person searches; visitors may not. Search fee: $10.00 per name. Required to search: name, years to search, DOB. Criminal records in docket books, archived from 1891.

General Information: No juvenile, mental, sealed or adoption records released. Will fax results to local or toll free number. Copy fee: $1.00 per page. Cert fee: $5.00. Payee: Motley County Clerk. Personal checks accepted. Prepayment required. Mial requests require SASE. Mail turnaround time 1-2 days.

Nacogdoches County

District Court 101 W Main, #215, Nacogdoches, TX 75961; 936-560-7730; Fax: 936-560-7839. Hours: 8AM-5PM (CST). *Felony, Civil.*
Civil Records: Access: Mail, in person. Both court and visitors may perform in person searches. Search fee: $5.00 per name. Required to search: name, years to search. Civil cases indexed by defendant, plaintiff. Civil records on computer from 1987, index books prior.
Criminal Records: Access: Mail, in person. Both court and visitors may perform in person searches. Search fee: $5.00 per name. Required to search: name, years to search, signed release. Criminal records on computer from 1987, index books prior.
General Information: Public Access terminal is available. No juvenile, mental, sealed, or adoption records released. Will fax results to local or toll free line. Copy fee: $1.00 per page. No cert fee. Payee: Nacogdoches County. Business checks accepted. Prepayment required. Mial requests require SASE. Mail turnaround time 5-6 days.

County Court County Clerk, 101 W Main, Rm 205, Nacogdoches, TX 75961; 936-560-7733. Hours: 8AM-5PM (CST). *Misdemeanor, Civil, Probate.* www.co.nacogdoches.tx.us/
Note: The County Clerk is the Clerk for County Court at Law, except for Juvenile, Family Law, including Divorce & Adoption. For these cases the District Clerk is the clerk for the County Court at Law.
Civil Records: Access: Mail, in person. Both court and visitors may perform in person searches. Search fee: $5.00 per name. Required to search: name, years to search. Civil cases indexed by defendant, plaintiff. Civil records on computer since June of 1986, index books prior.
Criminal Records: Access: Mail, in person. Both court and visitors may perform in person searches. Search fee: $5.00 per name. Required to search: name, years to search. Criminal records on computer since 1986, index books prior.
General Information: Public Access terminal is available. No sealed released. Will fax results to local or toll free line. Copy fee: $1.00 per page. Cert fee: $5.00. Payee: County Clerk. Personal checks accepted. Prepayment required. Mial requests require SASE. Mail turnaround time 2-4 days.

Navarro County

District Court PO Box 1439, Corsicana, TX 75151; 903-654-3040; Fax: 903-654-3088. Hours: 8AM-5PM (CST). *Felony, Civil.* www.navarrocounty.org
Civil Records: Access: Phone, fax, mail, online, in person. Both court and visitors may perform in person searches. Search fee: $5.00 per name. Required to search: name, years to search. Civil cases indexed by defendant, plaintiff. Civil records on computer since 1990, index books and microfiche since 1900s. Civil case information is online at www.idocket.com. Free searching is limited. Records go back to 12/31/1990.
Criminal Records: Access: Phone, fax, mail, in person, online. Both court and visitors may perform in person searches. Search fee: $5.00 per name. Required to search: name, years to search. Criminal records on computer since 1990, index books and microfiche since 1900s. Criminal records access is through www.idocket.com; registration and password required. Records go back to 12/31/1990.

General Information: Public Access terminal is available. No juvenile, sealed, or adoption records released. Will fax results $5.00 1st page, $1.00 each add'l. Copy fee: $1.00 for first page, $.25 each add'l. Cert fee: $1.00 per page. Payee: District Clerk. Personal checks accepted. Prepayment required. Mial requests require SASE. Mail turnaround time 1-2 days.

County Court PO Box 423, Corsicana, TX 75151; 903-654-3035. Hours: 8AM-4:45PM (CST). *Misdemeanor, Civil, Probate.*
Civil Records: Access: Mail, in person. Both court and visitors may perform in person searches. Search fee: $5.00 per name. Fee is for 10 year period. Required to search: name, years to search. Civil cases indexed by defendant, plaintiff. Civil records in index books to 1960s; on computer back to 1999.
Criminal Records: Access: Mail, in person. Both court and visitors may perform in person searches. Search fee: $5.00 per name. Fee is for 10 year period. Required to search: name, years to search, DOB or SSN. Criminal records in index books to 1930s; on computer back to 1999.
General Information: Public Access terminal is available. No juvenile, mental, sealed, or adoption records released. Copy fee: $1.00 per page. Cert fee: $5.00. Payee: County Clerk. Personal checks accepted. Prepayment required. Mial requests require SASE. Mail turnaround time 2-4 days.

Newton County

District Court PO Box 535, Newton, TX 75966; 409-379-3951. Hours: 8AM-4:30PM (CST). *Felony, Civil.*
Civil Records: Access: Mail, in person. Both court and visitors may perform in person searches. Search fee: $5.00 per name. Required to search: name, years to search. Civil cases indexed by defendant, plaintiff. Civil records in index books.
Criminal Records: Access: Mail, in person. Both court and visitors may perform in person searches. Search fee: $5.00 per name. Required to search: name, years to search. Criminal records in index books.
General Information: No juvenile, mental, sealed, or adoption records released. Will fax results for $2.00 per page. Copy fee: $1.00 per page. Cert fee: $2.00. Payee: District Clerk. Personal checks accepted. Prepayment required. Mial requests require SASE. Mail turnaround time same day.

County Court PO Box 484, Newton, TX 75966; 409-379-5341; Fax: 409-379-9049. Hours: 8AM-4:30PM (CST). *Misdemeanor, Civil, Probate.*
Civil Records: Access: Mail, in person. Both court and visitors may perform in person searches. Search fee: $5.00 per name. Required to search: name, years to search. Civil cases indexed by defendant, plaintiff. Civil records on index books from 1953.
Criminal Records: Access: Mail, in person. Both court and visitors may perform in person searches. Search fee: $5.00 per name. Required to search: name, years to search. Criminal records on index books from 1953.
General Information: No juvenile, mental, sealed, or adoption records released. Fee to fax results is $.50 per page. Copy fee: $1.00 per page. Cert fee: $5.00. Payee: County Clerk. Personal checks accepted. Prepayment required. Mail turnaround time 1-2 days.

Nolan County

District Court 100 E 3rd, #200A, Sweetwater, TX 79556; 325-235-2111. Hours: 8:30AM-Noon, 1-5PM (CST). *Felony, Civil.*
Civil Records: Access: Mail, in person. Both court and visitors may perform in person searches. Search fee: $5.00 per name. Required to search: name, years

to search. Civil cases indexed by defendant, plaintiff. Civil records in index books, records are not computerized.

Criminal Records: Access: Mail, in person. Only the court performs in person searches; visitors may not. Search fee: $5.00 per name. Required to search: name, years to search. Criminal records in index books, records are not computerized. Include which years to search.

General Information: No juvenile, mental, sealed, or adoption records released. Copy fee: $1.00 for first page, $.50 each add'l. Cert fee: $1.00 per page. Payee: District Clerk. Personal checks accepted. Prepayment required. Mial requests require SASE. Mail turnaround time same day.

County Court 100 E 3rd St, #108, Sweetwater, TX 79556-4546; 325-235-2462. Hours: 8:30AM-Noon, 1-5PM (CST). *Misdemeanor, Civil, Probate.*

Civil Records: Access: Mail, in person. Both court and visitors may perform in person searches. Search fee: $5.00 per name. Required to search: name, years to search. Civil cases indexed by defendant, plaintiff. Civil records in index books, computerized since 1999.

Criminal Records: Access: Mail, in person. Both court and visitors may perform in person searches. Search fee: $5.00 per name. Required to search: name, years to search. Criminal records in index books, computerized since 1999.

General Information: Public Access terminal is available. No juvenile, mental, sealed, or adoption records released. Copy fee: $1.00 per page. Cert fee: $5.00. Payee: County Clerk. Personal checks accepted. Prepayment required. Mial requests require SASE. Mail turnaround time 2-4 days.

Nueces County

District & County Court PO Box 2987, Corpus Christi, TX 78403-2987; 361-888-0450; Criminal phone: 361-888-0495; Fax: 361-888-0571. Hours: 8AM-5PM (CST). *Felony, Civil.*
www.co.nueces.tx.us/districtclerk/
Note: The records from the District Courts and County Courts in this county are combined at this location.

Civil Records: Access: Mail, in person, online. Both court and visitors may perform in person searches. Search fee: $5.00 per name. Required to search: name, years to search. Civil cases indexed by defendant, plaintiff. Civil records on computer since 1980, index books prior. Online access to civil District & County Court records are free at www.co.nueces.tx.us/districtclerk/. Click on Civil/Criminal Case Search, register, then search by name, company, or cause number.

Criminal Records: Access: Mail, in person, online. Both court and visitors may perform in person searches. Search fee: $5.00 per name. Required to search: name, years to search. Criminal records on computer since 1980, index books prior. Online access to criminal District & County Court records are free at www.co.nueces.tx.us/districtclerk/. Click on Civil/Criminal Case Search, register, then search by name, SID number, or cause number.

General Information: Public Access terminal is available. (Civil only.) No juvenile, mental, sealed, or adoption records released. Copy fee: $1.00 per page for civil, $1.00 per page for criminal. Cert fee: $1.00. Payee: District Clerk. Personal checks accepted. Prepayment required. Mial requests require SASE. Mail turnaround time 2-4 days.

Ochiltree County

District Court 511 S Main, Perryton, TX 79070; 806-435-8054; Fax: 806-435-8058. Hours: 8:30AM-5PM (CST). *Felony, Civil.*

Civil Records: Access: Fax, mail, in person. Both court and visitors may perform in person searches. Search fee: $5.00* per name. Required to search: name, years to search. Civil cases indexed by defendant, plaintiff. Civil records in index books; on computer back to 1995.

Criminal Records: Access: Fax, mail, in person. Only the court performs in person searches; visitors may not. Search fee: $5.00 per name. Required to search: name, years to search. Criminal records in index books; on computer back to 1995.

General Information: No juvenile, mental, sealed, or adoption records released. No fee to fax results. Copy fee: $1.00 per page. Cert fee: $1.00. Payee: District Clerk. Personal checks accepted. Prepayment required. Mial requests require SASE. Mail turnaround time 7 days.

County Court 511 S Main St, Perryton, TX 79070; 806-435-8039; Fax: 806-435-2081. Hours: 8:30AM-Noon, 1-5PM (CST). *Misdemeanor, Civil, Probate.*

Civil Records: Access: Fax, mail, in person. Both court and visitors may perform in person searches. Search fee: $5.00 per name. Required to search: name, years to search. Civil cases indexed by defendant, plaintiff. Civil records in index books.

Criminal Records: Access: Fax, mail, in person. Both court and visitors may perform in person searches. Search fee: $5.00 per name. Required to search: name, years to search. Criminal records in index books.

General Information: No juvenile, mental, sealed, or adoption records released. Will fax results for $2.00 1st page, $1.00 each add'l. Copy fee: $1.00 per page. Cert fee: $5.00. Payee: Ochiltree County Clerk. Personal checks accepted. Prepayment required. Fax fees may be billed. Mail turnaround time usually mailed out same day of receipt.

Oldham County

District & County Court PO Box 360, Vega, TX 79092; 806-267-2667. Hours: 8:30AM-Noon, 1-5PM (CST). *Felony, Misdemeanor, Civil, Probate.*

Civil Records: Access: Mail, in person. Both court and visitors may perform in person searches. Search fee: $5.00 per name. Required to search: name, years to search. Civil cases indexed by defendant, plaintiff. Civil records in index books.

Criminal Records: Access: Mail, in person. Both court and visitors may perform in person searches. Search fee: $5.00 per name. Required to search: name, years to search. Criminal records in index books.

General Information: No juvenile, mental, sealed, or adoption records released. Copy fee: $1.00 per page. Cert fee: $5.00 for county, $1.00 for district. Payee: Oldham County/District Clerk. Personal checks accepted. Prepayment required. Mial requests require SASE. Mail turnaround time 2-4 days.

Orange County

District Court PO Box 427, Orange, TX 77630; 409-883-7740. Hours: 8AM-5PM (CST). *Felony, Civil.*

Civil Records: Access: Mail, in person. Both court and visitors may perform in person searches. Search fee: $5.00 per name. Required to search: name, years to search. Civil cases indexed by defendant, plaintiff. Civil records on computer since 1985, index books prior.

Criminal Records: Access: Mail, in person, fax. Both court and visitors may perform in person searches. Search fee: $5.00 per name. Required to search: name, years to search. Criminal records computerized since 1989.

General Information: Public Access terminal is available. No juvenile, mental, sealed, or adoption records released. Copy fee: $1.00 per page $.50 self serve. Cert fee: $1.00. Payee: District Clerk. Only cashiers checks and money orders accepted. Prepayment required. Mial requests require SASE. Mail turnaround time 2-4 days.

County Court 123 S 6th St, Orange, TX 77630; 409-882-7055; Fax: 409-882-7812. Hours: 8AM-5PM (CST). *Misdemeanor, Civil, Probate.*
www.co.orange.tx.us

Civil Records: Access: Phone, fax, mail, in person. Both court and visitors may perform in person searches. No search fee. Required to search: name, years to search. Civil cases indexed by defendant, plaintiff. Civil records back to 1852; on computer back to 1982.

Criminal Records: Access: Phone, fax, mail, in person. Both court and visitors may perform in person searches. No search fee. Required to search: name, years to search. Criminal records back to 1897, on computer back to 1897.

General Information: Public Access terminal is available. No juvenile, mental, sealed. Fee to fax results is $1.00 per page. Copy fee: $1.00 per page. Cert fee: $5.00. Payee: Karen Jo Vance, County Clerk. Personal checks accepted. Prepayment required. Mail turnaround time 7-10 days.

Palo Pinto County

District Court PO Box 189, Palo Pinto, TX 76484-0189; 940-659-1279. Hours: 8AM-4:30PM (CST). *Felony, Civil.*

Civil Records: Access: Mail, in person. Both court and visitors may perform in person searches. Search fee: $5.00 per name. Required to search: name, years to search. Civil cases indexed by defendant, plaintiff. Civil records on computer since 1993, index books prior.

Criminal Records: Access: Mail, in person. Both court and visitors may perform in person searches. Search fee: $5.00 per name. Required to search: name, years to search. Criminal records on computer since 1993, index books prior.

General Information: No juvenile, mental, sealed, or adoption records released. Copy fee: $1.00 per page. Cert fee: $1.00. Payee: District Clerk. Personal checks accepted. Prepayment required. Mial requests require SASE. Mail turnaround time 1-2 days.

County Court PO Box 219, Palo Pinto, TX 76484; 940-659-1277; Fax: 940-659-2590. Hours: 8:30AM-4:30PM (CST). *Misdemeanor, Civil, Probate.*

Civil Records: Access: Mail, in person, phone. Both court and visitors may perform in person searches. Search fee: $5.00 per name. Required to search: name, years to search. Civil cases indexed by defendant, plaintiff. Civil records on computer back to 1998 index books from 1857.

Criminal Records: Access: Mail, in person. Both court and visitors may perform in person searches. Search fee: $5.00 per name. Required to search: name, years to search, DOB; also helpful: SSN. Criminal records on computer back to 1986; index books from 1857.

General Information: No juvenile, mental, sealed, or adoption records released. Copy fee: $1.00 per page. Cert fee: $5.00. Payee: County Clerk. Personal checks accepted in person, not by mail. Prepayment required. Mail turnaround time next day.

Panola County

District Court County Courthouse, Rm 227, Carthage, TX 75633; 903-693-0306; Fax: 903-693-6914. Hours: 8AM-5PM (CST). *Felony, Civil.*
Civil Records: Access: Mail, in person. Both court and visitors may perform in person searches. Search fee: $5.00 per name. Required to search: name, years to search. Civil cases indexed by defendant, plaintiff. Civil records in index books from 1865; computerized back to 1994.
Criminal Records: Access: Mail, in person. Both court and visitors may perform in person searches. Search fee: $5.00 per name. Required to search: name, years to search, DOB. Criminal records in index books from 1900s; computerized back to 1994.
General Information: No juvenile, mental, sealed, or adoption records released. Fee to fax results is $1.00 per page. Copy fee: $1.00 per page. Cert fee: $1.00 per page. Payee: District Clerk. Personal checks accepted. Prepayment required. Mial requests require SASE. Mail turnaround time 3 days.

County Court County Courthouse, Rm 201, Carthage, TX 75633; 903-693-0302. Hours: 8AM-5PM (CST). *Misdemeanor, Civil, Probate.*
Civil Records: Access: Mail, in person. Both court and visitors may perform in person searches. Search fee: $5.00 per name. Required to search: name, years to search. Civil cases indexed by defendant, plaintiff. Civil records in index books; computerized since 1996.
Criminal Records: Access: Mail, in person, fax. Both court and visitors may perform in person searches. Search fee: $5.00 per name. Required to search: name, years to search, DOB. Criminal records in index books; computerized since 1996.
General Information: No juvenile, mental, sealed, or adoption records released. Copy fee: $1.00 per page. Cert fee: $5.00. Payee: County Clerk. Personal checks require ID. Prepayment required. Mail turnaround time 2-4 days.

Parker County

District Court 117 Ft Worth Ave (PO Box 2050), Weatherford, TX 76086; 817-599-6591; Civil phone: 817-598-6114; Criminal phone: 817-598-6194 or x6200/x6214; Fax: 817-598-6131. Hours: 8AM-5PM (CST). *Felony, Civil.*
www.parkercountytx.com
Note: 9/03 County Court at Law cases filed with District Clerk. All civil cases in county to be filed with District Court.
Civil Records: Access: Mail, in person, online. Both court and visitors may perform in person searches. Search fee: $5.00 per name. Required to search: name, years to search, and/or cause number. Civil cases indexed by defendant, plaintiff. Civil records in index books. Access to court records back to 1/03 is free at www.parkercountytx.com.
Criminal Records: Access: Mail, in person, online. Both court and visitors may perform in person searches. Search fee: $5.00 per name. Required to search: name, years to search, DOB, and/or cause number; also helpful: SSN. Criminal records in index books; on comptuer back to 7/1988. Access to criminal records and sheriff inmates and bonds searching is free at www.parkercountytx.com. Online court records go back to 1/03 and modified cases.
General Information: No juvenile, mental, sealed, or adoption records released. Will not fax results. Copy fee: $1.00 per page. Cert fee: $1.00 per page. Payee: District Clerk. Personal checks accepted. Prepayment required. Mial requests require SASE. Mail turnaround time same day.

County Court Parker County Clerk - Court Division, PO Box 819, Weatherford, TX 76086-0819; 817-594-1632. Hours: 8AM-Noon, 1-4PM (CST). *Misdemeanor.*
Note: As of 9/1/03 county court cases are filed with District Clerk. 11/04 new County Court At Law #2 (a second county court location) will begin taking cases. All civil cases will be filed with District Clerk.
Civil Records: Access: Phone, mail, in person. Both court and visitors may perform in person searches. Search fee: $5.00 per name. Required to search: name, years to search. Civil cases indexed by defendant, plaintiff. Civil records in index books; on computer since 8/1985.
Criminal Records: Access: Phone, mail, in person. Both court and visitors may perform in person searches. Search fee: $5.00 per name. Required to search: name, years to search, DOB; signed release. Criminal records on computer since 8/1985, index books and archived since 1900s.
General Information: Public Access terminal is available. No juvenile, mental, sealed, or adoption records released. Copy fee: $1.00 per page. Cert fee: $5.00. Payee: County Clerk. Personal checks accepted. Prepayment required. Mial requests require SASE. Mail turnaround time 1-2 days.

Probate Court 1112 Santa Fe Dr, PO Box 819, Weatherford, TX 76086; 817-594-7461. Hours: 8AM-5PM (CST). *Probate.*

Parmer County

District Court PO Box 195, Farwell, TX 79325-0195; 806-481-3419; Fax: 806-481-9416. Hours: 8:30AM-Noon, 1-5PM (CST). *Felony, Civil.*
Civil Records: Access: Fax, mail, in person, online. Both court and visitors may perform in person searches. Search fee: $5.00 per name. Required to search: name, years to search. Civil cases indexed by defendant, plaintiff. Civil records in index books since 1917. Online access is through www.idocket.com; registration and password required. Records go back to 12/31/1995.
Criminal Records: Access: Fax, mail, in person, online. Both court and visitors may perform in person searches. Search fee: $5.00 per name. Required to search: name, years to search. Criminal records in index books since 1917. Online access is through www.idocket.com; registration and password required. Records go back to 12/31/1995.
General Information: No juvenile, mental, sealed, or adoption records released. Will fax results $1.00 per page. Copy fee: $1.00 per page. No cert fee. Payee: District Clerk. Personal checks accepted. Prepayment required. Mial requests require SASE. Mail turnaround time 1 day.

County Court PO Box 356, Farwell, TX 79325; 806-481-3691. Hours: 8:30AM-Noon; 1-5PM (CST). *Misdemeanor, Civil, Probate.*
Civil Records: Access: Mail, in person. Both court and visitors may perform in person searches. Search fee: $5.00 per name. Required to search: name, years to search. Civil cases indexed by defendant, plaintiff. Civil records in index books to 1924, computerized since 1996.
Criminal Records: Access: Mail, in person. Both court and visitors may perform in person searches. Search fee: $5.00 per name. Required to search: name, years to search. Criminal records in index books to 1920, computerized since 1996.
General Information: Public Access terminal is available. No juvenile, mental, sealed, or adoption records released. Will fax results for $1.50 per page. Copy fee: $1.00 per page. Cert fee: $5.00. Payee: County Clerk. Personal checks accepted. Prepayment

required. Mial requests require SASE. Mail turnaround time 2-4 days.

Pecos County

District Court 400 S Nelson, Fort Stockton, TX 79735; 432-336-3503; Fax: 432-336-6437. Hours: 8AM-5PM (CST). *Felony, Civil.*
Civil Records: Access: Fax, mail, in person. Both court and visitors may perform in person searches. Search fee: $5.00 per name. There is a $10.00 fee per year, when going back further than 7 years. Required to search: name, years to search, SSN. Civil cases indexed by defendant, plaintiff. Civil records on computer since 1996, index books prior to the 1920s. A seven year search is performed.
Criminal Records: Access: Fax, mail, in person. Both court and visitors may perform in person searches. Search fee: $5.00 per name. There is a $10.00 fee per year, when going back further than 7 years. Required to search: name, years to search, DOB, signed release; also helpful-address, SSN. Criminal records on computer since 1996, index books prior to 1924.
General Information: No juvenile, mental, sealed, or adoption records released. Fee to fax results is $1.00 per page. Copy fee: $1.00 per page. No cert fee. Payee: District Clerk. Personal checks accepted. Prepayment required. Mial requests require SASE. Mail turnaround time 2-4 days.

County Court 103 W Callaghan, Fort Stockton, TX 79735; 432-336-7555; Fax: 432-336-7557. Hours: 8AM-5PM (CST). *Misdemeanor, Civil, Probate.*
Civil Records: Access: Mail, in person. Both court and visitors may perform in person searches. Search fee: $8.00 per name. Required to search: name, years to search. Civil cases indexed by defendant, plaintiff. Civil records on computer and index books to 1955.
Criminal Records: Access: Mail, in person. Both court and visitors may perform in person searches. Search fee: $8.00 per name. Required to search: name, years to search. Criminal records on computer and index books to 1955.
General Information: No juvenile, mental, sealed, or adoption records released. Fee to fax results is $1.00 per page. Copy fee: $1.00 per page. Cert fee: $5.00. Payee: County Clerk. Personal checks accepted. Prepayment required. Mial requests require SASE. Mail turnaround time same day.

Polk County

District Court 101 W Church, #205, Livingston, TX 77351; 936-327-6814. Hours: 8AM-5PM (CST). *Felony, Civil.*
Civil Records: Access: Mail, in person. Both court and visitors may perform in person searches. Search fee: $5.00 per name. Fee is per 10 year period. Required to search: name, years to search. Civil cases indexed by defendant, plaintiff. Civil records in index books, computerized since 1996.
Criminal Records: Access: Mail, in person. Both court and visitors may perform in person searches. Search fee: $5.00 per name. Fee is per 10 year period. Required to search: name, years to search; also helpful: DOB. Criminal records in index books, computerized since 1996.
General Information: Public Access terminal is available. No juvenile, mental, sealed, or adoption records released. Copy fee: $1.00 per page. Cert fee: $2.00. Payee: District Clerk. Personal checks accepted. Prepayment required. Mial requests require SASE. Mail turnaround time 2-4 days.

County Court PO Drawer 2119, Livingston, TX 77351; 936-327-6804; Criminal phone: 936-327-6805; Fax: 936-327-6874. Hours: 8AM-5PM (CST). *Misdemeanor, Civil, Probate.*

Civil Records: Access: Mail, in person. Both court and visitors may perform in person searches. Search fee: $5.00 per name. Required to search: name, years to search. Civil cases indexed by defendant, plaintiff. Civil records in index books, on computer since 1988, available since 1846.

Criminal Records: Access: Mail, in person. Only the court performs in person searches; visitors may not. Search fee: $5.00 per name. Required to search: name, years to search; also helpful: DOB, SSN. Criminal records in index books; on computer back to 1982.

General Information: Public Access terminal is available. No mental records released. Fee to fax results is $2.00 per document and $1.00 per page. Copy fee: $1.00 per page. Cert fee: $5.00. Payee: County Clerk. Personal checks accepted for civil only. Prepayment required. Mial requests require SASE. Mail turnaround time 2-4 days.

Potter County

District Court PO Box 9570, Amarillo, TX 79105-9570; 806-379-2300. Hours: 7:30AM-5:30PM (CST). *Felony, Civil.*
www.co.potter.tx.us/districtclerk

Civil Records: Access: Phone, fax, mail, online, in person. Both court and visitors may perform in person searches. Search fee: $5.00 per name. Required to search: name, years to search. Civil cases indexed by defendant, plaintiff. Civil records on computer since 9/87, index books prior. Civil case information from 1988 forward is online at www.idocket.com. Free case searching is limited.

Criminal Records: Access: Fax, mail, online, in person. Both court and visitors may perform in person searches. Search fee: $5.00 per name. Required to search: name, years to search. Criminal records on computer since 9/87, index books prior. Online access to criminal records is the same as civil.

General Information: Public Access terminal is available. No juvenile, mental, sealed, or adoption records released. Will fax results $1.00 per page plus 5% of transaction total for credit card fee. Copy fee: $.50 per page. Cert fee: $1.00 per page. Payee: District Clerk. Business checks accepted. Visa, MC accepted. Prepayment required. Mial requests require SASE. Mail turnaround time 2-4 days.

County Court & County Courts at Law 1 & 2 PO Box 9638, Amarillo, TX 79105; 806-379-2285; Fax: 806-379-2296. Hours: 8AM-5PM (CST). *Misdemeanor, Civil, Probate.*
www.co.potter.tx.us/countyclerk/index.html
Note: Limited civil records filed here, most are with the District Clerk.

Civil Records: Access: Mail, in person. Both court and visitors may perform in person searches. Search fee: None, but must pay the certification fee. Required to search: exact name, years to search. Civil cases indexed by defendant, plaintiff. Civil records on computer since 1990, index books and microfiche since 1889. Probate records available since 1800s.

Criminal Records: Access: Mail, in person. Both court and visitors may perform in person searches. Search fee: None, but must pay the certification fee. Required to search: exact name, years to search, DOB. Criminal records on computer since 1990, index books and microfiche since 1889.

General Information: Public Access terminal is available. No juvenile, mental or sealed records released. Will fax results for fee. Copy fee: $1.00 per page. Cert fee: $5.00 for Certification of Fact. Payee: Potter County Clerk. Personal checks accepted. Visa,

MC accepted. Prepayment required. Mial requests require SASE. Mail turnaround time 1-2 days.

Presidio County

District & County Court PO Box 789, Marfa, TX 79843; 432-729-4812; Fax: 432-729-4313. Hours: 8AM-Noon, 1-4PM (CST). *Felony, Misdemeanor, Civil, Probate.*

Civil Records: Access: Mail, in person. Both court and visitors may perform in person searches. Search fee: $6.00 per name. Required to search: name, years to search. Civil cases indexed by defendant, plaintiff. Civil records in index books. Requests must be in writing.

Criminal Records: Access: Mail, in person. Both court and visitors may perform in person searches. Search fee: $6.00 per name. Required to search: name, years to search. Criminal records in index books. Requests must be in writing.

General Information: No juvenile, mental, sealed, or adoption records released. Copy fee: $1.00 per page. Cert fee: $5.00. Payee: District Clerk. Personal checks accepted. Prepayment required. Mial requests require SASE. Mail turnaround time 2-4 days.

Rains County

District & County Court PO Box 187, Emory, TX 75440; 903-474-9999; Fax: 903-474-9390. Hours: 8AM-5PM (CST). *Felony, Misdemeanor, Civil, Probate.*
Note: Fax for District Court criminal is 903-473-0163

Civil Records: Access: Mail, fax, in person. Both court and visitors may perform in person searches. Search fee: $5.00 per name. Required to search: name. Civil cases indexed by defendant, plaintiff. Civil records on computer back to 1989, index books prior to 1903.

Criminal Records: Access: Mail, fax, in person. Both court and visitors may perform in person searches. Search fee: $5.00 per name. Required to search: name; also helpful: DOB. Criminal records on computer back to 1989, index books prior to 1880.

General Information: No juvenile, mental, sealed, or adoption records released. Copy fee: $1.00 per page. Cert fee: $5.00. Payee: Linda Wallace County Clerk or Deborah Traylor, District Clerk. Personal checks accepted. Prepayment required. Mial requests require SASE. Mail turnaround time same day.

Randall County

District Courts PO Box 1096, Canyon, TX 79015; 806-468-5600; Fax: 806-468-5604. Hours: 8AM-5PM (CST). *Felony, Civil.*
www.randallcounty.org

Civil Records: Access: Fax, mail, online, in person. Both court and visitors may perform in person searches. Search fee: $5.00 per name. Required to search: name, years to search. Civil cases indexed by defendant, plaintiff. Civil records on computer since 1984. Civil case information is free online at www.idocket.com. Free searching is limited. Records from 12/31/84.

Criminal Records: Access: Fax, mail, online, in person. Both court and visitors may perform in person searches. Search fee: $5.00 per name. Required to search: name, years to search. Criminal records on computer since 1985; prior in docket books. Online access to criminal records is the same as civil.

General Information: Public Access terminal is available. No juvenile, mental, sealed, or adoption records released. Fee to fax results is $5.00 1st pg; $1.00 each add'l. Copy fee: $.50 per page. Cert fee: $1.00 per page. Payee: District Clerk. Personal checks accepted. Visa, MC accepted. Prepayment required. Mail turnaround time 1-2 days.

County Court PO Box 660, Canyon, TX 79015; 806-468-5505. Hours: 8AM-5PM (CST). *Misdemeanor, Civil, Probate.*
www.randallcounty.org/cclerk/default.htm

Civil Records: Access: Phone, mail, fax, in person, email. Both court and visitors may perform in person searches. Search fee: $10.00 per name. Required to search: name, years to search, SASE. Civil cases indexed by defendant, plaintiff. Civil records in index books 1900 to present. Civil case information is online from idocket at http://idocket.com/counties.htm. Free searching is limited. Records go back to 12/31/1999; probate back to 12/31/1969.

Criminal Records: Access: Phone, mail, fax, in person, online, email. Both court and visitors may perform in person searches. Search fee: $10.00 per name. Required to search: name, years to search; also helpful: DOB. Criminal records on computer since 1984; prior records in index books. Criminal case information is online from idocket at http://idocket.com/counties.htm. Online records go back to 12/31/1991.

General Information: Public Access terminal is available. No juvenile, mental, sealed, or adoption records released. Fee to fax results is $1.00 per page, $5.00 fee add'l if call is long distance. Copy fee: $1.00 per page. Cert fee: $5.00. Payee: Randall County Clerk. Personal checks accepted. Prepayment required. Mial requests require SASE. Mail turnaround time 2-4 days.

Reagan County

District & County Court PO Box 100, Big Lake, TX 76932; 325-884-2442; Fax: 325-884-1503. Hours: 8:30AM-5PM (CST). *Felony, Misdemeanor, Civil, Probate.*

Civil Records: Access: Mail, in person. Both court and visitors may perform in person searches. Search fee: $5.00 per name. Required to search: name, years to search. Civil cases indexed by defendant, plaintiff. Civil records in index books to 1903.

Criminal Records: Access: Mail, in person. Both court and visitors may perform in person searches. Search fee: $5.00 per name. Required to search: name, years to search. Criminal records in index books to 1903.

General Information: No juvenile, mental, sealed, or adoption records released. Will fax results $5.00 per doc; no fee to toll-free number. Copy fee: $1.00 per page. Cert fee: $5.00. Payee: County/District Clerk. Personal checks not accepted if out-of-state. Prepayment required. Mial requests require SASE. Mail turnaround time same day.

Real County

District & County Court PO Box 750, Leakey, TX 78873; 830-232-5202; Fax: 830-232-6888. Hours: 8AM-5PM (CST). *Felony, Misdemeanor, Civil, Probate.*

Civil Records: Access: In person only. Visitors must perform in person searches for themselves. No search fee. Required to search: name, years to search. Civil cases indexed by defendant, plaintiff. Civil records in index books.

Criminal Records: Access: In person only. Visitors must perform in person searches for themselves. No search fee. Required to search: name, years to search, DOB. Criminal records in index books.

General Information: No juvenile, mental, sealed, or adoption records released. Copy fee: $1.00 per page. Cert fee: $5.00. Payee: District/County Court. Personal checks accepted. Prepayment required.

Red River County

District Court 400 N Walnut, Clarksville, TX 75426; 903-427-3761; Fax: 903-427-1201. Hours: 8:30AM-Noon, 1-5PM (CST). *Felony, Civil.*

Civil Records: Access: Mail, in person. Both court and visitors may perform in person searches. Search fee: $5.00 per name. Required to search: name, years to search. Civil cases indexed by defendant, plaintiff. Civil records in index books and on microfilm to 1800s.

Criminal Records: Access: Mail, in person. Both court and visitors may perform in person searches. Search fee: $5.00 per name. Required to search: name, years to search. Criminal records in index books and on microfilm to 1800s.

General Information: Public Access terminal is available. No juvenile, mental, sealed, or adoption records released. Will fax results to local or toll free line. Copy fee: $1.00 per page. Cert fee: $1.00. Payee: District Clerk. Personal checks accepted. Prepayment required. Mial requests require SASE. Mail turnaround time same day.

County Court 200 N Walnut, Clarksville, TX 75426; 903-427-2401. Hours: 8:30AM-5PM (CST). *Misdemeanor, Probate.*

Criminal Records: Access: Mail, in person. Both court and visitors may perform in person searches. Search fee: $5.00 per name. Required to search: name, years to search, SSN. Criminal records on computer (name only) since 1980, in index books since 1960s.

General Information: Public Access terminal is available. No mental, sealed, or adoption records released. Copy fee: $1.00 per page. Cert fee: $5.00. Payee: County Clerk. Personal checks accepted. Prepayment required. Mial requests require SASE. Mail turnaround time 1-2 days.

Reeves County

District Court PO Box 848, Pecos, TX 79772; 432-445-2714; Probate phone: 432-445-5467; Fax: 432-445-7455. Hours: 8AM-Noon, 1-5PM (CST). *Felony, Civil.*

Note: Probate records handled by County Clerk.

Civil Records: Access: Phone, mail, in person. Both court and visitors may perform in person searches. Search fee: $5.00 per name. Required to search: name, years to search. Civil cases indexed by defendant, plaintiff. Civil records on computer since 01/91, index books prior.

Criminal Records: Access: Mail, in person. Both court and visitors may perform in person searches. Search fee: $5.00 per name. Required to search: name, years to search. Criminal records on computer back to 01/90, index books prior.

General Information: No juvenile, mental, sealed, or adoption records released. Copy fee: $.25 per page. Cert fee: $1.00 per page. Payee: District Clerk Reeves County. Personal checks accepted. Prepayment required. Mial requests require SASE. Mail turnaround time 2-4 days.

County Court PO Box 867, Pecos, TX 79772; 432-445-5467. Hours: 8AM-5PM (CST). *Misdemeanor, Civil, Probate.*

Civil Records: Access: Mail, in person. Both court and visitors may perform in person searches. Search fee: $10.00 per name. Required to search: name, years to search; also helpful: address. Civil cases indexed by defendant, plaintiff. Civil records on computer go back 10 years, index books prior.

Criminal Records: Access: Mail, in person. Both court and visitors may perform in person searches. Search fee: $10.00 per name. Required to search: name, years to search, DOB; also helpful: address.

Criminal records on computer go back 10 years; index books prior.

General Information: No juvenile, mental, sealed, or adoption records released. Will fax results $.50 per page. Copy fee: $1.00 per page. Cert fee: $5.00. Payee: Reeves County Clerk. Personal checks accepted. Prepayment required. Mial requests require SASE. Mail turnaround time 5 days.

Refugio County

District Court PO Box 736, Refugio, TX 78377; 361-526-2721. Hours: 8AM-Noon, 1-5PM (CST). *Felony, Civil.*

Civil Records: Access: Mail, in person. Both court and visitors may perform in person searches. Search fee: $5.00 per name. Required to search: name, years to search. Civil cases indexed by defendant, plaintiff. Civil records on computer back to 1992, index books back to 1879.

Criminal Records: Access: Mail, in person. Both court and visitors may perform in person searches. Search fee: $5.00 per name. Required to search: name, years to search, date of birth; also helpful-SSN, signed release. Criminal records on computer back to 1992, index books back to 1879.

General Information: No juvenile, mental, sealed, or adoption records released. Copy fee: $1.00 per page. Cert fee: $1.00. Payee: District Clerk. Personal checks accepted. Prepayment required. Mial requests require SASE. Mail turnaround time 2-4 days.

County Court PO Box 704, Refugio, TX 78377; 361-526-2233. Hours: 8AM-5PM (CST). *Misdemeanor, Civil, Probate.*

Civil Records: Access: Mail, in person. Both court and visitors may perform in person searches. Search fee: $5.00 per name. Required to search: name, years to search. Civil cases indexed by defendant, plaintiff. Civil records in index books, began computerization in 2003.

Criminal Records: Access: Mail, in person. Both court and visitors may perform in person searches. Search fee: $5.00 per name. Required to search: name, years to search. Criminal records on computer since 1992, index books prior.

General Information: No juvenile, mental, sealed, or adoption records released. Will fax results to local or toll free line. Copy fee: $1.00 per page. Cert fee: $5.00. Payee: Ruby Garcia, County Clerk. Personal checks accepted. Prepayment required. Mail turnaround time 5-10 days.

Roberts County

District & County Court PO Box 477, Miami, TX 79059; 806-868-2341. Hours: 8AM-Noon, 1-5PM (CST). *Felony, Misdemeanor, Civil, Probate.*

Civil Records: Access: Mail, in person. Both court and visitors may perform in person searches. Search fee: $5.00 per name. Required to search: name, years to search. Civil cases indexed by defendant, plaintiff. Civil records in index books.

Criminal Records: Access: Mail, in person. Both court and visitors may perform in person searches. Search fee: $5.00 per name. Required to search: name, years to search, DOB, SSN. Criminal records in index books.

General Information: No juvenile, mental, sealed, or adoption records released. Will fax results $3.00 first pg; $1.00 each add'l. Copy fee: $1.00 per page. Include postage with copy fee. Cert fee: County Court certification fee is $5.00, District is $1.00. Payee: Roberts County. Personal checks accepted. Prepayment required. Mial requests require SASE. Mail turnaround time 2-4 days.

Robertson County

District Court PO Box 250, Franklin, TX 77856; 979-828-3636. Hours: 8AM-5PM (CST). *Felony, Civil.*

www.robertsoncountycourthouse.com

Civil Records: Access: Mail, in person. Both court and visitors may perform in person searches. Search fee: $5.00 per name. Required to search: name, years to search, SSN. Civil cases indexed by defendant, plaintiff. Civil records on computer since 1987 and index books.

Criminal Records: Access: Mail, in person. Both court and visitors may perform in person searches. Search fee: $5.00 per name. Required to search: name, years to search, DOB; also helpful: SSN. Criminal records on computer since 1987 and index books.

General Information: No juvenile, sealed, or adoption records released. Copy fee: $1.00 per page. Cert fee: $1.00 per page. Payee: Robertson County District Clerk. Personal checks accepted. Prepayment required. Mial requests require SASE. Mail turnaround time 1-2 days.

County Court PO Box 1029, Franklin, TX 77856; 979-828-4130. Hours: 8AM-5PM (CST). *Misdemeanor, Civil, Probate.*

Civil Records: Access: Mail, fax, in person. Both court and visitors may perform in person searches. Search fee: $5.00 per name. Required to search: name, years to search. Civil cases indexed by defendant, plaintiff. Civil records on computer back from 1990 to present, index books from 1985 to present.

Criminal Records: Access: Mail, fax, in person. Both court and visitors may perform in person searches. Search fee: $5.00 per name. Required to search: name, years to search, DOB. Criminal records on computer back to 1986 to present, index books from 1918.

General Information: No juvenile, mental, sealed, or adoption records released. Copy fee: $1.00 per page. Cert fee: $5.00. Payee: Robertson County Clerk. Personal checks accepted. Prepayment required. Mail turnaround time same day.

Rockwall County

District Court 1101 Ridge Rd, #209, Rockwall, TX 75087; 972-882-0260; Fax: 972-882-0268. Hours: 8AM-5PM (CST). *Felony, Civil.*

www.rockwallcountytexas.com

Civil Records: Access: Mail, in person. Both court and visitors may perform in person searches. Search fee: $5.00 per name. Fee is per 5 year period. Required to search: name, years to search. Civil cases indexed by defendant, plaintiff. Civil records on computer back to 1994, index books prior.

Criminal Records: Access: Mail, in person. Both court and visitors may perform in person searches. Search fee: $5.00 per name. Required to search: name, years to search, DOB. Criminal records on computer back to 1980, index books prior.

General Information: Public Access terminal is available. No juvenile, mental, sealed, or adoption records released. Will not fax results. Copy fee: $1.00 per page. Cert fee: $1.00. Payee: District Clerk. Personal checks accepted. Prepayment required. Mial requests require SASE. Mail turnaround time 2-4 days.

County Court 1101 Ridge Rd, #101, Rockwall, TX 75087; 972-882-0220; Fax: 972-882-0229. Hours: 8AM-5PM (CST). *Misdemeanor, Civil, Probate.*

www.rockwallcountytexas.com

Civil Records: Access: Phone, mail, in person, online. Both court and visitors may perform in person searches. Search fee: $5.00 per name. Required to search: name, years to search. Civil cases indexed by defendant, plaintiff. Civil records on computer back to 1985 and in index books from 1800s. Look case index information at the website.

Criminal Records: Access: Phone, mail, in person, online. Both court and visitors may perform in person searches. Search fee: $5.00 per name. Required to search: name, years to search. Criminal records on computer back to 1987 and in index books from 1800s. Look case index information at the website.

General Information: Public Access terminal is available. No juvenile, mental, sealed, or adoption records released. Fee to fax results is $5.00 per document. Copy fee: $1.00 per page. Cert fee: $5.00. Payee: County Clerk. Personal checks accepted. Prepayment required. Mial requests require SASE. Mail turnaround time 2-4 days.

Runnels County

District Court PO Box 166, Ballinger, TX 76821; 325-365-2638; Fax: 325-365-9229. Hours: 8:30AM-5PM (CST). *Felony, Civil.*

Civil Records: Access: Phone, fax, mail, in person. Both court and visitors may perform in person searches. Search fee: $5.00 per name. Required to search: name; also helpful: years to search. Civil cases indexed by defendant, plaintiff. Civil records in index books since 1882.

Criminal Records: Access: Phone, fax, mail, in person. Both court and visitors may perform in person searches. Search fee: $5.00 per name. Required to search: name; also helpful: years to search, DOB, SSN. Criminal records in index books since 1882.

General Information: No juvenile, mental, sealed or adoption records released. Will fax results $1.00 per page. Copy fee: $1.00 per page. Cert fee: $1.00. Payee: District Clerk. Personal checks accepted. Prepayment required. Mial requests require SASE. Mail turnaround time 1-2 days.

County Court PO Box 189, Ballinger, TX 76821; 325-365-2720; Fax: 325-365-3408. Hours: 8:30AM-Noon, 1-5PM (CST). *Misdemeanor, Civil, Probate.*

Civil Records: Access: Phone, mail, in person. Both court and visitors may perform in person searches. Search fee: $5.00. Required to search: name, years to search. Civil cases indexed by defendant, plaintiff. Civil records in docket books with alphabetical index and file jacket by number; computerized since 1992.

Criminal Records: Access: Phone, mail, in person. Both court and visitors may perform in person searches. Search fee: $5.00. Required to search: name, years to search; also helpful: DOB. Criminal records in docket books with alphabetical index and file jacket by number; computerized since 1992.

General Information: No juvenile or mental records released. Will fax results to toll-free number. Copy fee: $1.00 per page. Cert fee: $5.00. Payee: County Clerk, Runnels County. Personal checks accepted. Prepayment required. Mail turnaround time 1-2 days.

Rusk County

District Court PO Box 1687, Henderson, TX 75653; 903-657-0353; Fax: 903-657-1914. Hours: 8AM-5PM (CST). *Felony, Civil.*

Civil Records: Access: Mail, in person. Both court and visitors may perform in person searches. Search fee: $5.00 per name. Required to search: name, years to search. Civil cases indexed by defendant, plaintiff. Civil records in index books; on computer back to 1973.

Criminal Records: Access: Mail, in person. Both court and visitors may perform in person searches. Search fee: $5.00 per name. Required to search: name, years to search, DOB, SSN, signed release. Criminal records in index books; on computer back to 1973.

General Information: No juvenile, mental, sealed, or adoption records released. Copy fee: $1.00 per page. Cert fee: $1.00. Payee: District Clerk. Only cashiers checks and money orders accepted. Prepayment required. Mial requests require SASE. Mail turnaround time 2-4 days.

County Court at Law PO Box 758, Henderson, TX 75653-; 903-657-0330; Fax: 903-657-0300. Hours: 8AM-5PM (CST). *Misdemeanor, Civil, Probate.*

Note: Misdemeanor & Probate records are at County Clerk, PO Box 758, phone 903-657-0330.

Civil Records: Access: Mail, in person. Both court and visitors may perform in person searches. Search fee: $5.00 per name. Required to search: name, years to search. Civil cases indexed by defendant, plaintiff. Civil records in index books.

Criminal Records: Access: Mail, in person. Both court and visitors may perform in person searches. Search fee: $5.00 per name. Required to search: name, years to search, DOB, SSN. Criminal records are not computerized, are indexed in books.

General Information: No juvenile, mental, sealed, or adoption records released. Copy fee: $1.00 per page. No cert fee. Payee: District Clerk. Business checks accepted. Prepayment required. Mial requests require SASE. Mail turnaround time 2-4 days.

Sabine County

District Court PO Box 850, Hemphill, TX 75948; 409-787-2912. Hours: 8AM-4:00PM (CST). *Felony, Civil.*

Civil Records: Access: Mail, in person. Both court and visitors may perform in person searches. Search fee: $10.00 per name. Required to search: name, years to search. Civil cases indexed by defendant, plaintiff. Civil records on computer since 1992. Overall records go back to 1900.

Criminal Records: Access: Mail, in person. Both court and visitors may perform in person searches. Search fee: $10.00 per name. Required to search: name, years to search. Criminal records on computer since 1992. Overall records go back to 1900.

General Information: No juvenile, mental, sealed, or adoption records released. Will not fax results. Copy fee: $1.00 per page. No cert fee. Payee: District Clerk. Personal checks accepted. Prepayment required. Mial requests require SASE. Mail turnaround time 1-2 days.

County Court PO Drawer 580, Hemphill, TX 75948-0580; 409-787-2889. Hours: 8AM-4PM (CST). *Misdemeanor, Probate.*

Criminal Records: Access: Mail, in person. Both court and visitors may perform in person searches. Search fee: $10.00 per name. Required to search: name, years to search. Criminal records on computer since 1992, index books prior.

General Information: No juvenile, mental, sealed, or adoption records released. Will not fax results. Copy fee: $1.00 per page. Cert fee: $5.00. Payee: Sabine County Clerk. Business checks accepted. Prepayment required. Mial requests require SASE. Mail turnaround time 2 days.

San Augustine County

District Court County Courthouse, Rm 202, San Augustine, TX 75972; 936-275-2231; Fax: 936-275-2389. Hours: 8AM-4:15PM (CST). *Felony, Civil.*

Civil Records: Access: Phone, mail, in person. Both court and visitors may perform in person searches. Search fee: $5.00 per name. Required to search: name, years to search. Civil cases indexed by plaintiff. Civil records in index books.

Criminal Records: Access: Phone, mail, in person. Only the court performs in person searches; visitors

may not. Search fee: $5.00 per name. Required to search: name, years to search. Criminal records in index books.

General Information: No juvenile, mental, sealed, or adoption records released. Will fax results to local or toll free line. Copy fee: $1.00 per page. Cert fee: $1.00. Payee: District Clerk. Personal checks accepted. Prepayment required. Mial requests require SASE. Mail turnaround time 2-4 days.

County Court 100 W Columbia, Rm #106, San Augustine, TX 75972; 936-275-2452; Fax: 936-275-9579. Hours: 8AM-4:30PM (CST). *Misdemeanor, Probate.*

Criminal Records: Access: Phone, mail, in person. Both court and visitors may perform in person searches. Search fee: $10.00 per name. Required to search: name, years to search; also helpful: address, DOB, SSN. Criminal records go back to 1984; on computer since 1990. Criminal information may be obtained over the phone, but copies must be paid for in advance. Will fax back if $5.00 paid in advance.

General Information: No juvenile, mental, sealed, or adoption records released. Copy fee: $1.00 per page. Cert fee: $5.00. Payee: County Clerk. Personal checks accepted. Prepayment required. Mial requests require SASE. Mail turnaround time 2-3 days.

San Jacinto County

District Court 1 State Hwy 150, Rm #4, Coldspring, TX 77331; 936-653-2909. Hours: 8AM-Noon, 1-5PM (CST). *Felony, Civil.*

Civil Records: Access: Mail, in person. Both court and visitors may perform in person searches. Search fee: $5.00 per name. Required to search: name, years to search. Civil cases indexed by defendant, plaintiff. Civil records in index books.

Criminal Records: Access: Mail, in person. Both court and visitors may perform in person searches. Search fee: $5.00 per name. Required to search: name, years to search. Criminal records on computer since 1986.

General Information: Public Access terminal is available. No juvenile, mental, sealed, or adoption records released. Copy fee: $1.00 per page. Cert fee: $5.00. Payee: District Clerk. Personal checks accepted. Prepayment required. Mial requests require SASE. Mail turnaround time 2-4 days.

County Court 1 State Hwy 150, Rm #2, Coldspring, TX 77331; 936-653-2324. Hours: 8AM-4:30PM (CST). *Misdemeanor, Civil, Probate.*
www.co.san-jacinto.tx.us

Civil Records: Access: Mail, in person. Both court and visitors may perform in person searches. Search fee: $9.00 per name. Required to search: name, years to search. Civil cases indexed by defendant, plaintiff. Civil records in index books.

Criminal Records: Access: Mail, in person. Both court and visitors may perform in person searches. Search fee: $9.00 per name. Required to search: name, years to search; also helpful: address, DOB, SSN. Criminal records in index books.

General Information: Public Access terminal is available. No juvenile, mental, sealed, or adoption records released. Will fax results to toll free or local number. Copy fee: $1.00 per page. Cert fee: $5.00. Payee: County Clerk. Personal checks accepted. Only cashiers checks and money orders accepted for criminal searches. Prepayment required. Mial requests require SASE. Mail turnaround time 2 weeks.

San Patricio County

District Court PO Box 1084, Sinton, TX 78387; 361-364-6225. Hours: 8AM-5PM (CST). *Felony, Civil.*

Civil Records: Access: Mail, in person. Both court and visitors may perform in person searches. Search

fee: $5.00 per name. Fee is per division. Required to search: name, years to search. Civil cases indexed by defendant, plaintiff. Civil records in index books from 1800s; computerized back to 1993.

Criminal Records: Access: Mail, in person. Both court and visitors may perform in person searches. Search fee: $5.00 per name. Fee is per division. Required to search: name, years to search. Criminal records in index books from 1800s; computerized back to 1993.

General Information: Public Access terminal is available. No juvenile, mental, sealed, or adoption records released. Will fax results. Copy fee: $1.00 per page. Cert fee: $1.00. Payee: District Clerk. Business checks accepted. Prepayment required. Mial requests require SASE. Mail turnaround time 2-4 days.

County Court PO Box 578, Sinton, TX 78387; 361-364-6290; Fax: 361-364-6112. Hours: 8AM-5PM (CST). *Misdemeanor, Civil, Probate.*

Civil Records: Access: Phone, mail, in person. Both court and visitors may perform in person searches. Search fee: $5.00 per name. Required to search: name, years to search; also helpful: address. Civil cases indexed by defendant, plaintiff. Civil records in index books and microfilm, some as far back as 1824; computerized back to 2002.

Criminal Records: Access: Phone, mail, in person. Both court and visitors may perform in person searches. Search fee: $5.00 per name. Required to search: name, years to search; also helpful: address, DOB, SSN, anything. Criminal records in index books and microfilm; computerized back to 2002.

General Information: No juvenile, mental, or sealed records released. Copy fee: $1.00 per page. Cert fee: $5.00. Payee: County Clerk. Personal checks accepted. Prepayment required. Mial requests require SASE. Mail turnaround time 2-3 days.

San Saba County

District & County Court County Courthouse, 500 E Wallace, #202, San Saba, TX 76877; 325-372-3375. Hours: 8AM-Noon, 1-4:30PM (CST). *Felony, Misdemeanor, Civil, Probate.*
www.courts.state.tx.us/district/33rd/index.htm

Civil Records: Access: Phone, mail, in person. Both court and visitors may perform in person searches. Search fee: $10.00 per name. Required to search: name, years to search. Civil cases indexed by defendant, plaintiff. Civil records in index books.

Criminal Records: Access: Mail, in person. Both court and visitors may perform in person searches. Search fee: $10.00 per name. Required to search: name, years to search; also helpful: DOB. Criminal records in index books.

General Information: No juvenile, mental, sealed, or adoption records released. Copy fee: $1.00 per page. Cert fee: $5.00. Payee: District/County Clerk. Personal checks accepted. Prepayment required. Mial requests require SASE. Mail turnaround time 2-3 days.

Schleicher County

District & County Court PO Drawer 580, Eldorado, TX 76936; 325-853-2833; Fax: 325-853-2768. Hours: 9AM-Noon, 1-5PM (CST). *Felony, Misdemeanor, Civil, Probate.*

Civil Records: Access: Mail, in person. Both court and visitors may perform in person searches. Search fee: $10.00 per name. Required to search: name, years to search. Civil cases indexed by defendant, plaintiff. Civil records in index books.

Criminal Records: Access: Mail, in person. Both court and visitors may perform in person searches. Search fee: $10.00 per name. Required to search: name, years to search. Criminal records in index books.

General Information: No juvenile, mental, sealed, or adoption records released. Will fax results for $2.00 per page, must be paid before search. Copy fee: $1.00 per page. Cert fee: $5.00. Payee: District/County Clerk. Personal checks accepted. Prepayment required. Mial requests require SASE. Mail turnaround time 2-3 days.

Scurry County

132nd District Court 1806 25th St, #402, Snyder, TX 79549; 325-573-5641. Hours: 8AM-5PM (CST). *Felony, Civil.*

Civil Records: Access: Mail, in person. Both court and visitors may perform in person searches. Search fee: $5.00 per name. Required to search: name, years to search. Civil cases indexed by defendant, plaintiff. Civil records go back to 1890; computerized records since 1994. All requests must be in writing.

Criminal Records: Access: Mail, in person. Both court and visitors may perform in person searches. Search fee: $5.00 per name. Required to search: name, years to search, address, DOB, SSN, sex. Criminal records go back to 1890; computerized records since 1994. All requests must be in writing.

General Information: No juvenile, mental, sealed, or adoption records released. Fee to fax results is $1.00 per page. Copy fee: $1.00 for first page, $.25 each add'l. Cert fee: $1.00 per page. Payee: District Clerk. Personal checks accepted. Prepayment required. Mial requests require SASE. Mail turnaround time 2-3 days.

County Court County Courthouse, 1806 25th St, #300, Snyder, TX 79549; 325-573-5332. Hours: 8:30AM-5PM (CST). *Misdemeanor, Civil, Probate.*

Civil Records: Access: Mail, in person. Both court and visitors may perform in person searches. Search fee: $10.00 per name. Required to search: name, years to search. Civil cases indexed by defendant, plaintiff. Civil records in index books since 1900s; on computer back to 1996.

Criminal Records: Access: Mail, in person. Both court and visitors may perform in person searches. Search fee: $5.00 per name. Fee includes copies. Required to search: name, years to search; also helpful: address, DOB, SSN. Criminal records in index books since 1900s; on computer back to 1996. Written request always required.

General Information: Public Access terminal is available. No mental or sealed records released. Fee to fax results is $1.00 per page. Copy fee: $1.00 per page. Cert fee: $5.00. Payee: County Clerk Scurry County. Personal checks accepted. Prepayment required. Mial requests require SASE. Mail turnaround time 1-2 days.

Shackelford County

District & County Court PO Box 247, Albany, TX 76430; 325-762-2232. Hours: 8:30AM-5PM (CST). *Felony, Misdemeanor, Civil, Probate.*

Civil Records: Access: Mail, in person. Both court and visitors may perform in person searches. Search fee: $5.00 per name. Fee is per court. Required to search: name, years to search. Civil cases indexed by defendant, plaintiff. Civil records on computer since 1987, index books since 1867.

Criminal Records: Access: Mail, in person. Both court and visitors may perform in person searches. Search fee: $5.00 per name. Fee is per court. Required to search: name, years to search. Criminal records on computer since 1987, index books since 1867.

General Information: No juvenile, mental, sealed, or adoption records released. Copy fee: $1.00 per page. Cert fee: $5.00. Payee: Clerk, Shackelford County. Personal checks accepted. Prepayment required. Mial requests require SASE. Mail turnaround time 3 days after receipt.

Shelby County

District Court PO Drawer 1953, Center, TX 75935; 936-598-4164. Hours: 8AM-4:30PM (CST). *Felony, Civil.*

Civil Records: Access: Mail, in person. Both court and visitors may perform in person searches. Search fee: $5.00 per name. Required to search: name, years to search. Civil cases indexed by defendant, plaintiff. Civil records in index books; on computer back to 2000.

Criminal Records: Access: Mail, in person. Both court and visitors may perform in person searches. Search fee: $5.00 per name. Required to search: name, years to search, signed release. Criminal records in index books; on computer back to 2000.

General Information: No juvenile, mental, sealed, or adoption records released. Copy fee: $1.00 per page. Cert fee: $1.00. Payee: District Clerk. Will accept attorney checks. Prepayment required. Mial requests require SASE. Mail turnaround time 2-3 days.

County Court PO Box 1987, Center, TX 75935; 936-598-6361; Fax: 936-598-3701. Hours: 8AM-4:30PM (CST). *Misdemeanor, Civil, Probate.*

Civil Records: Access: Mail, in person. Both court and visitors may perform in person searches. Search fee: $10.00 per name. Required to search: name, years to search. Civil cases indexed by defendant, plaintiff. Civil & probate records in index books back to 1882; on computer back to 1990.

Criminal Records: Access: Mail, in person. Both court and visitors may perform in person searches. Search fee: $10.00 per name. Required to search: name, years to search, SSN, DOB; also helpful: signed release. Criminal records in index books back to 1920; on comptuer back to 1990. All requests must be in writing.

General Information: No juvenile, mental, sealed, or adoption records released. Copy fee: $1.00 per page. Cert fee: $5.00. Payee: Shelby County Clerk. Personal checks accepted. Prepayment required. Mial requests require SASE. Mail turnaround time 1-2 days.

Sherman County

District & County Court PO Box 270, Stratford, TX 79084; 806-366-2371; Fax: 806-366-5670. Hours: 8AM-Noon, 1-5PM (CST). *Felony, Misdemeanor, Civil, Probate.*

Civil Records: Access: Mail, in person. Both court and visitors may perform in person searches. Search fee: $15.00 per name. Required to search: name, years to search. Civil cases indexed by plaintiff. Civil records to 1930.

Criminal Records: Access: Mail, in person. Both court and visitors may perform in person searches. Search fee: $15.00 per name. Required to search: name, years to search. Criminal records to 1947.

General Information: No juvenile, mental, sealed, or adoption records released. Will fax results for $5.00 1st page, plus $1.00 each add'l pg. Copy fee: $1.00 per page. Cert fee: $5.00. Payee: Sherman County Clerk. Personal checks accepted. Prepayment required. Mial requests require SASE. Mail turnaround time 2-3 days.

Smith County

District Court PO Box 1077, Tyler, TX 75710; 903-535-0666; Fax: 903-535-0683. Hours: 8AM-5PM (CST). *Felony, Civil.*
www.smith-county.com/dc_desc.htm

Civil Records: Access: Mail, in person. Both court and visitors may perform in person searches. Search fee: $5.00 per name. Required to search: name, years to search. Civil cases indexed by defendant, plaintiff. Civil records in index books.

Criminal Records: Access: Mail, in person. Both court and visitors may perform in person searches. Search fee: $5.00 per name. Required to search: name, years to search. Criminal records in index books to 1846, computerized since 1/99.

General Information: No juvenile, mental, sealed, or adoption records released. Will not fax results. Copy fee: $1.00 per page. Cert fee: $1.00. Payee: District Clerk. Cashiers checks and money orders accepted. Prepayment required. Mial requests require SASE. Mail turnaround time 2-3 days.

County Court at Law PO Box 1018, 200 E. Ferguson, #300, Tyler, TX 75710; 903-535-0630; Civil phone: 903-535-0636/37/38; Criminal phone: 903-535-0645/46/47; Probate phone: 903-535-0634; Fax: 903-535-0684. Hours: 8AM-5PM (CST). *Misdemeanor, Civil, Probate.*

Note: There are three Courts at Law at this location.

Civil Records: Access: Mail, in person. Both court and visitors may perform in person searches. Search fee: $5.00 per name. Required to search: name, years to search. Civil cases indexed by defendant, plaintiff. Civil records in index books.

Criminal Records: Access: Mail, in person. Both court and visitors may perform in person searches. Search fee: $5.00 per name. Required to search: name, years to search; also helpful: DOB, SSN. Criminal records in index books.

General Information: No juvenile, mental, sealed, or adoption records released. Will fax results for $1.00 per page. Copy fee: $1.00 per page. $5.00 certified copies. Cert fee: $5.00. Payee: Smith County Clerk. Personal checks accepted. Prepayment required. Mial requests require SASE. Mail turnaround time 2-4 days.

Somervell County

District & County Court PO Box 1098, Glen Rose, TX 76043; 254-897-4427; Fax: 254-897-3233. Hours: 8AM-5PM (CST). *Felony, Misdemeanor, Civil, Probate.*

Note: Evictions are handled by Justice of the Peace, POB 237, Glen Rose, TX 76043, 254-897-2120.

Civil Records: Access: Mail, in person. Both court and visitors may perform in person searches. Search fee: $5.00 per name. Required to search: name, years to search; also helpful: address. Civil cases indexed by defendant, plaintiff. Civil records on computer since 1991, microfilm since 1980, index books since 1875.

Criminal Records: Access: Mail, in person. Both court and visitors may perform in person searches. Search fee: $5.00 per name. Required to search: name, years to search, DOB, SSN, signed release; also helpful: address. Criminal records on computer since 1991, microfilm since 1980, index books since 1875.

General Information: No juvenile, mental, sealed, or adoption records released. Fee to fax results is $1.00 per page. Copy fee: $1.00 per page. Cert fee: $5.00. Payee: County/District Clerk. Personal checks accepted. Prepayment required. Mail requests: SASE preferred. Turnaround time same day.

Starr County

District & County Court Starr County Courthouse, Rm 304, Rio Grande City, TX 78582; 956-487-8482 (Dist) 487-8485 (County); Fax: 956-487-8493. Hours: 8AM-5PM (CST). *Felony, Misdemeanor, Civil, Probate.*

Note: Handles civil county court cases.

Civil Records: Access: Phone, fax, mail, in person. Both court and visitors may perform in person searches. Search fee: $7.00 per name. Required to search: name, years to search. Civil cases indexed by defendant, plaintiff. Civil records on index books from 1920s, computerized since 1992.

Criminal Records: Access: Phone, fax, mail, in person. Only the court performs in person searches; visitors may not. Search fee: $7.00 per name. Required to search: name, years to search, SSN; also helpful: DOB. Criminal records on computer since 1992; in docket books to 1800s.

General Information: No adoption records released. Will fax results $5.00 1st oage; $1.00 each add'l. Copy fee: $1.00 per page. Cert fee: $5.00. Payee: District Clerk. Personal checks accepted. Prepayment required. Mial requests require SASE. Mail turnaround time 2 days.

County Court Starr County Courthouse, Rm 201, Rio Grande City, TX 78582; 956-487-8032; Fax: 956-487-8674. Hours: 8AM-5PM (CST). *Misdemeanor, Probate.*

Note: See District & County Court for civil county court cases.

Criminal Records: Access: Mail, in person, online. Both court and visitors may perform in person searches. Search fee: $10.00 per name. Required to search: name, years to search; also helpful: SSN, DOB. Criminal records on computer since 1997, in index books since 1984, archived prior. Online access is at www.idocket.com; registration and password required. This is a $$ fee service, unless only one name search is done a day. Records go back to 12/31/1996.

General Information: No juvenile, mental, sealed, or adoption records released. Fee to fax results is $1.00 per page. Copy fee: $1.00 per page. Cert fee: $5.00. Payee: County Clerk. Personal checks accepted. Prepayment required. Mail requests: SASE requested. Turnaround time 2-4 days.

Stephens County

District Court 200 W Walker, Breckenridge, TX 76424; 254-559-3151; Fax: 254-559-8127. Hours: 8:30AM-5PM (CST). *Felony, Civil, Misdemeanor.*

Civil Records: Access: Fax, mail, in person. Both court and visitors may perform in person searches. Search fee: $5.00 per name. Required to search: name, years to search. Civil cases indexed by defendant, plaintiff. Civil records in index books, archived from 1900; on comptuer back to 1995.

Criminal Records: Access: Fax, mail, in person. Both court and visitors may perform in person searches. Search fee: $5.00 per name. Required to search: name, years to search, DOB. Criminal records in index books, archived from 1900; on comptuer back to 1995.

General Information: No juvenile, mental, sealed, or adoption records released. Will fax results $1.00 per page; available to local and 800 numbers only. Copy fee: $1.00 per page. Cert fee: $1.00. Payee: District Clerk. Personal checks accepted. Prepayment required. Mial requests require SASE. Mail turnaround time same day.

County Clerk 200 W Walker, Breckenridge, TX 76424; 254-559-3700. Hours: 8:30AM-5PM (CST). *Probate.*

Sterling County

District & County Court PO Box 55, Sterling City, TX 76951; 325-378-5191. Hours: 8:30AM-4PM M-Th; -1:30PM F (CST). *Felony, Misdemeanor, Civil, Probate.*

Civil Records: Access: Mail, in person. Both court and visitors may perform in person searches. No search fee. Required to search: name, years to search; also helpful: address. Civil cases indexed by defendant, plaintiff. Civil records in index books from 1900s.

Criminal Records: Access: Mail, in person. Both court and visitors may perform in person searches. No

search fee. Required to search: name, years to search; also helpful: DOB, SSN. Criminal records in index books from 1900s.

General Information: No juvenile, mental, sealed, or adoption records released. Fee to fax results is $1.00 per page. Copy fee: $1.00 per page. Cert fee: $5.00. Payee: Sterling County/District Clerk. Personal checks accepted. Prepayment required. Mial requests require SASE. Mail turnaround time 1-2 days.

Stonewall County

District & County Court PO Drawer P, Aspermont, TX 79502; 940-989-2272. Hours: 8AM-Noon, 1-4:30PM (CST). *Felony, Misdemeanor, Civil, Probate.*

Civil Records: Access: Phone, mail, in person. Both court and visitors may perform in person searches. No search fee. Required to search: name, years to search. Civil cases indexed by defendant, plaintiff. Civil records in index books to 1900s.

Criminal Records: Access: Phone, mail, in person. Both court and visitors may perform in person searches. No search fee. Required to search: name, years to search. Criminal records in index books to 1900s.

General Information: No juvenile, mental, sealed, or adoption records released. Will fax results for $2.00 per page. Copy fee: $1.00 per page. Cert fee: $5.00. Payee: County Clerk. Personal checks accepted. Prepayment required. Mial requests require SASE. Mail turnaround time 2 days.

Sutton County

District & County Court 300 E Oak, #3, Sonora, TX 76950; 325-387-3815. Hours: 8:30AM-4:30PM (CST). *Felony, Misdemeanor, Civil, Probate.*

Civil Records: Access: Phone, mail, in person. Both court and visitors may perform in person searches. Search fee: $10.00 per name. Required to search: name, years to search. Civil cases indexed by defendant, plaintiff. Civil records on computer back to 1992, index books prior.

Criminal Records: Access: Mail, in person. Both court and visitors may perform in person searches. Search fee: $10.00 per name. Required to search: name, years to search. Criminal records on computer back to 1995, index books prior to 1890.

General Information: No juvenile, mental, sealed, or adoption records released. Will fax results to local or toll free line. Copy fee: $1.00 per page. Cert fee: $5.00. Payee: County Clerk. Personal checks accepted. Prepayment required. Mial requests require SASE. Mail turnaround time 2-4 days.

Swisher County

District & County Court County Courthouse, 119 S Maxwell, Tulia, TX 79088; 806-995-4396; Fax: 806-995-4121. Hours: 8AM-5PM (CST). *Felony, Misdemeanor, Civil, Probate.*
www.242ndcourt.com

Civil Records: Access: Mail, fax, in person, email. Both court and visitors may perform in person searches. Search fee: $5.00 per name. Required to search: name, years to search. Civil cases indexed by defendant, plaintiff. Civil records on computer since 1992, index books prior.

Criminal Records: Access: Mail, fax, in person, email. Both court and visitors may perform in person searches. Search fee: $5.00 per name. Required to search: name, years to search, DOB and SSN. Criminal records on computer since 1992, index books prior to early 1900s.

General Information: No juvenile, mental, sealed, or adoption records released. Fee to fax results is $3.00 per page $1.00 each add'l page. Copy fee: $1.00 per page. Cert fee: $1.00. Payee: County/District Clerk.

Personal checks and credit cards accepted. Prepayment required. Mail requests: SASE requested. Turnaround time 1-2 days.

Tarrant County

District Court 401 W Belknap, Tarrant County District Clerk's Office, Fort Worth, TX 76196-0402; 817-884-1574 (884-1265 Family Division); Civil phone: 817-884-1240; Criminal phone: 817-884-1342. Hours: 8AM-5PM (CST). *Felony, Civil.*
www.tarrantcounty.com
Civil Records: Access: Mail, online, in person. Both court and visitors may perform in person searches. Search fee: $5.00 per name if the office does the search. Required to search: full name and DOB. Civil cases indexed by defendant, plaintiff. Civil records on computer since 1989, file jackets prior to 1989; records go back to 1800s. Access to the web-based online system requires $50 deposit and monthly fee of $35 per month. Call Ms. Witthaus at 817-884-1345 for more information.
Criminal Records: Access: Mail, online, in person. Both court and visitors may perform in person searches. Search fee: $5.00 per name if the office does the search. Required to search: full name, years to search, DOB; also helpful: SSN. Criminal records on computer back to 1975, microfilm since 1970, index books and case files since 1800s. Online access same as civil.
General Information: Public Access terminal is available. No juvenile, mental, sealed, or adoption records released. Copy fee: $.35 per page. Cert fee: $1.00 per page. Payee: Thomas A Wilder, District Clerk. Business checks accepted. Prepayment required. Mail turnaround time 1-3 days.

County Court - Criminal 401 W Belknap, Tarrant County District Clerk's Office, Fort Worth, TX 76196-0402; 817-884-1195; Fax: 817-884-3295. Hours: 7:30AM-4:30PM (CST). *Misdemeanor.*
www.tarrantcounty.com
Note: Small Claims, Evictions, and low-level civil cases are handled by JP/Municipal Courts.
Criminal Records: Access: Mail, online, in person. Both court and visitors may perform in person searches. Search fee: $5.00 per name. Required to search: name, years to search, DOB. Criminal records on computer back to 1980s. Access to the remote online system requires $50 setup that includes software. The per minute fee is $.05 plus $25 per month. Call Mr. Hinojosa at 817-884-1419 for more information.
General Information: Public Access terminal is available. No juvenile, mental, sealed, or adoption records released. Copy fee: $.30 per page. Cert fee: $5.00. Business checks accepted. Prepayment required. Mial requests require SASE. Mail turnaround time 1-3 days.

Probate Court County Courthouse, 100 W Weatherford St, Probate Court #1, Rm 260A, Fort Worth, TX 76196; 817-884-1200; Probate phone: 817-884-1254; Fax: 817-884-3178. Hours: 8AM-4:30PM (CST). *Probate.*
http://cc.co.tarrant.tx.us
Note: Search probate records at http://cc.co.tarrant.tx.us/CCPublicAccess/ASP/Probate/ProbatePublicBrowse.asp?tc_countyclerkNav=|

Taylor County

District Court 300 Oak St, Abilene, TX 79602; 325-674-1316. Hours: 8AM-Noon, 1-5PM (CST). *Felony, Civil.*
Civil Records: Access: Mail, in person. Both court and visitors may perform in person searches. Search fee: $5.00 per name. Required to search: name, years to search. Civil cases indexed by defendant, plaintiff.

Civil records on computer since 1996; prior records in index books to 1885.
Criminal Records: Access: Mail, in person. Both court and visitors may perform in person searches. Search fee: $5.00 per name. Required to search: name, years to search, DOB; also helpful: SSN. Criminal records on computer since 1996; prior records in index books to 1885.
General Information: Public Access terminal is available. No juvenile, mental, sealed, or adoption records released. Copy fee: $1.00 per page. Cert fee: $1.00. Payee: Taylor County District Clerk. Business checks accepted. Prepayment required. Mial requests require SASE. Mail turnaround time 5 days.

County Court PO Box 5497, Abilene, TX 79608; 325-674-1202; Fax: 325-674-1279. Hours: 8AM-5PM (CST). *Misdemeanor, Civil, Probate.*
www.taylorcountytexas.org
Civil Records: Access: Mail, in person. Both court and visitors may perform in person searches. Search fee: $5.00 per name. Fee is per 10 years. Required to search: name, years to search. Civil cases indexed by defendant, plaintiff. Civil records on computer less than ten years, index books prior.
Criminal Records: Access: Mail, in person. Both court and visitors may perform in person searches. Search fee: $5.00 per name. Fee is per 10 years. Required to search: name, years to search, DOB; also helpful: address, SSN. Criminal records on computer back to 1980; overall records go back to 1949.
General Information: Public Access terminal is available. No juvenile, mental, sealed, or adoption records released. Fee to fax results is $1.00 per page, $2.00 per doc. Copy fee: $1.00 per page. Cert fee: $5.00. Payee: County Clerk. Personal checks accepted. Prepayment required. Mial requests require SASE. Mail turnaround time 2-4 days.

Terrell County

District & County Court PO Drawer 410, Sanderson, TX 79848; 432-345-2391; Fax: 432-345-2653. Hours: 9AM-Noon, 1-5PM (CST). *Felony, Misdemeanor, Civil, Probate.*
Civil Records: Access: Mail, in person. Both court and visitors may perform in person searches. No search fee. Required to search: name, years to search. Civil cases indexed by defendant, plaintiff. Civil records in index books. All requests must be in writing.
Criminal Records: Access: Mail, in person. Both court and visitors may perform in person searches. Search fee: $5.00 per name. Required to search: name, years to search. Criminal records in index books. All requests must be in writing.
General Information: No juvenile, mental, sealed, or adoption records released. Copy fee: $1.00 per page. No cert fee. Payee: County Clerk. Personal checks accepted. Prepayment required. Mail turnaround time 2-4 days.

Terry County

District Court 500 W Main, Rm 209E, Brownfield, TX 79316; 806-637-4202. Hours: 8:30AM-5PM (CST). *Felony, Civil.*
Civil Records: Access: Mail, in person. Both court and visitors may perform in person searches. Search fee: $5.00 per name. Required to search: name, years to search. Civil cases indexed by defendant, plaintiff. Civil records in index books and on computer.
Criminal Records: Access: Mail, in person. Only the court performs in person searches; visitors may not. Search fee: $5.00 per name. Required to search: name, years to search, DOB; also helpful: SSN. Criminal records in index books and on computer.
General Information: No juvenile, mental, sealed, or adoption records released. Will fax results to local or

toll free line. Copy fee: $1.00 per page. Cert fee: $1.00. Payee: District Clerk. Personal checks accepted. Prepayment required. Mial requests require SASE. Mail turnaround time same day.

County Court 500 W Main, Rm 105, Brownfield, TX 79316-4398; 806-637-8551; Fax: 806-637-4874. Hours: 8:30AM-5PM (CST). *Misdemeanor, Civil, Probate.*
Civil Records: Access: Mail, in person. Both court and visitors may perform in person searches. Search fee: $10.00 per name. Required to search: name, years to search. Civil cases indexed by defendant, plaintiff. Civil records in index books to 1904, computerized since 1981.
Criminal Records: Access: Mail, in person. Both court and visitors may perform in person searches. Search fee: $10.00 per name. Required to search: name, years to search; also helpful: address, DOB, SSN. Criminal records in index books back to 1904, computerized since 1981.
General Information: No juvenile, mental, sealed, or adoption records released. Fee to fax results is $1.00 per page. Copy fee: $1.00 per page. Cert fee: $5.00. Payee: County Clerk. Personal checks accepted. Prepayment required. Mial requests require SASE. Mail turnaround time 1-2 days.

Throckmorton County

District & County Court PO Box 309, Throckmorton, TX 76483; 940-849-2501. Hours: 8AM-Noon, 1-4:30PM M-Th; 8AM-Noon Friday (CST). *Felony, Misdemeanor, Civil, Probate.*
Civil Records: Access: Phone, mail, in person. Both court and visitors may perform in person searches. Search fee: $10.00 per name. Required to search: name, years to search; also helpful: address. Civil cases indexed by defendant, plaintiff. Civil records in index books; computerized records go back to 1990.
Criminal Records: Access: Mail, in person. Both court and visitors may perform in person searches. Search fee: $10.00 per name. Required to search: name, years to search. Criminal records in index books; computerized records go back to 1990.
General Information: No juvenile, mental, sealed, or adoption records released. Copy fee: $1.00 per page. No cert fee. Payee: County/District Clerk. Personal checks accepted. Prepayment required. Mial requests require SASE. Mail turnaround time 2-4 days.

Titus County

District Court 105 W 1st St, PO Box 492, Mount Pleasant, TX 75455; 903-577-6721; Fax: 903-577-6719. Hours: 8AM-5PM (CST). *Felony, Civil.*
Civil Records: Access: Phone, mail, in person. Both court and visitors may perform in person searches. Search fee: $5.00 per name. Required to search: name, years to search. Civil cases indexed by defendant, plaintiff. Civil records in index books from 1895; computerized back to 1992.
Criminal Records: Access: Phone, mail, in person. Both court and visitors may perform in person searches. Search fee: $5.00 per name. Required to search: name, years to search. Criminal records in index books from 1895; computerized back to 1992.
General Information: Public Access terminal is available. No juvenile, mental, sealed, or adoption records released. Copy fee: $1.00 per page. Cert fee: $5.00. Payee: District Clerk. Personal checks accepted. Prepayment required. Mial requests require SASE. Mail turnaround time 2-3 days.

County Court 100 W 1st St, #204, Mount Pleasant, TX 75455; 903-577-6796; Fax: 903-577-6793. Hours: 8AM-5PM (CST). *Misdemeanor, Civil, Probate.*
Civil Records: Access: Mail, in person. Both court and visitors may perform in person searches. Search

fee: $10.00 per name. Required to search: name, years to search; also helpful: address. Civil cases indexed by defendant, plaintiff. Civil records on computer since January 1994, index books since 1895.

Criminal Records: Access: Mail, in person. Both court and visitors may perform in person searches. Search fee: $10.00 per name. Required to search: name, years to search; also helpful: address, DOB, SSN. Criminal records on computer since January 1994, index books since 1930.

General Information: No juvenile, mental, sealed, or adoption records released. Copy fee: $1.00 per page. Cert fee: $5.00. Payee: County Clerk. Business checks accepted. Prepayment required. Mial requests require SASE. Mail turnaround time 1 week to 10 days.

Tom Green County

District Court County Courthouse, 112 W Beauregard, San Angelo, TX 76903; 325-659-6579; Fax: 325-659-3241. Hours: 8AM-5PM (CST). *Felony, Civil.*

www.co.tom-green.tx.us/distclrk

Civil Records: Access: Mail, in person, online. Both court and visitors may perform in person searches. Search fee: $5.00 per name per 5 years searched. Required to search: name, years to search; also helpful. Civil cases indexed by defendant, plaintiff. Civil records in index books from 1900s; on computer back to 1993. Online access to civil case records back to 1994 is online at http://justice.co.tom-green.tx.us. Search by name, case number.

Criminal Records: Access: Mail, in person, online. Both court and visitors may perform in person searches. Search fee: $5.00 per name per 5 years searched. Required to search: name, years to search, DOB. Criminal records in index books from 1900s; on computer back to 1993. Online access to criminal records is the same as civil.

General Information: Public Access terminal is available. No juvenile, mental, sealed, or adoption records released. Fee to fax results is $1.00 per page. Copy fee: $1.00 per page, $.25 if self-service. No cert fee. Payee: District Clerk. Personal checks accepted. Prepayment required. Mial requests require SASE. Mail turnaround time 1 week.

County Court 124 W Beauregard, San Angelo, TX 76903; 325-659-6555. Hours: 8AM-4:30PM (CST). *Misdemeanor, Civil, Probate.*

http://justice.co.tom-green.tx.us

Civil Records: Access: Mail, in person, online. Both court and visitors may perform in person searches. Search fee: $5.00 per name. Required to search: name, years to search; also helpful: address. Civil cases indexed by defendant, plaintiff. Civil records on computer since 1994, index books prior. Online access to civil records back to 1994 is free at the website.

Criminal Records: Access: Mail, in person, online. Both court and visitors may perform in person searches. Search fee: $5.00 per name. Required to search: name, years to search, DOB; also helpful: address, SSN. Criminal records on computer since 1994, index books prior. Online access to criminal records is the same as civil. website also includes Sheriff jail and bond records.

General Information: Public Access terminal is available. No juvenile, mental, sealed, or adoption records released. Will fax results to local or toll free line. Copy fee: $1.00 per page. Cert fee: $5.00. Payee: County Clerk. Prepayment required. Mial requests require SASE. Mail turnaround time same day.

Travis County

District Court PO Box 1748, Austin, TX 78767; Civil phone: 512-854-9457; Criminal phone: 512-854-9420; Fax: 512-854-9549 Civil; 512-854-4566 Crim. Hours: 8AM-5PM (CST). *Felony, Civil.*

www.co.travis.tx.us

Civil Records: Access: Phone, mail, in person. Both court and visitors may perform in person searches. Search fee: $5.00 per name. Add $2.00 per year prior to 1988. Required to search: name, years to search. Civil cases indexed by defendant, plaintiff. Civil records on computer since 1986, microfiche and index books.

Criminal Records: Access: Phone, mail, in person. Both court and visitors may perform in person searches. Search fee: $5.00 per name. Add $2.00 per year prior to 1988. Required to search: name, years to search, DOB. Criminal records on computer since 1988, index books prior to 1988.

General Information: Public Access terminal is available. No juvenile, mental, sealed, or adoption records released (all felony cases are public record). Copy fee: $.50 per page. No cert fee. Payee: District Clerk. Personal checks accepted. Visa, MC, Discover accepted. Prepayment required. Mial requests require SASE. Mail turnaround time 2-3 days, normally.

County Court PO Box 1748, Austin, TX 78767-1748; Civil phone: 512-854-9090; Criminal phone: 512-854-9440; Probate phone: 512-854-9595; Fax: 512-854-4220. Hours: 8AM-5PM (CST). *Misdemeanor, Civil, Probate.*

www.co.travis.tx.us

Note: Records include appeals from the Travis County JP Courts.

Civil Records: Access: Phone, mail, in person, online. Both court and visitors may perform in person searches. Search fee: $5.00 per name. Fee applies to cases opened prior to June 1986. Required to search: name, years to search. Civil cases indexed by defendant, plaintiff. Civil records on computer since 06/86, microfilm prior to 1845, probate from 1992 forward. Also, access to probate court records only is free at http://deed.co.travis.tx.us/search.aspx?cabinet=probate.

Criminal Records: Access: Phone, mail, in person. Both court and visitors may perform in person searches. Search fee: $5.00 per name. $10.00 per name for microfilm. Required to search: name, years to search; also helpful: address, DOB, SSN. Criminal misdemeanor records on computer since 1981; prior records on microfilm to 1845.

General Information: Public Access terminal is available. No juvenile, mental, sealed, or adoption records released. Copy fee: $1.00 per page. Cert fee: $5.00 per document. Payee: Travis County Clerk. Personal checks accepted. Prepayment required. Mail turnaround time 2-5 days.

Trinity County

District Court PO Box 548, Groveton, TX 75845; 936-642-1118. Hours: 8AM-5PM (CST). *Felony, Civil.*

Civil Records: Access: Mail, in person. Both court and visitors may perform in person searches. Search fee: $5.00 per name. Required to search: name, years to search. Civil cases indexed by defendant, plaintiff. Civil records on computer since 1980, index books prior.

Criminal Records: Access: Mail, in person. Both court and visitors may perform in person searches. Search fee: $5.00 per name. Required to search: name, years to search. Criminal records on computer since 1980, index books prior.

General Information: No juvenile, mental, sealed, or adoption records released. Will not fax results. Copy fee: $1.00 per page. Cert fee: $1.00 per page. Payee: District Clerk. Personal checks accepted. Prepayment required. Mail turnaround time is 1 day.

County Court PO Box 456, Groveton, TX 75845; 936-642-1208; Fax: 936-642-3004. Hours: 8AM-5PM (CST). *Misdemeanor, Civil, Probate.*

Civil Records: Access: Mail, in person. Both court and visitors may perform in person searches. Search fee: $10.00 per name. Required to search: name, years to search; also helpful: address. Civil cases indexed by defendant, plaintiff. Civil records in index books back to 1982. Date of birth helpful for searching.

Criminal Records: Access: Mail, in person. Both court and visitors may perform in person searches. Search fee: $10.00 per name. Required to search: name, years to search, SSN; also helpful: address, DOB, sex. Criminal records in index books back to 1982. Date of birth required for searching.

General Information: No juvenile, mental, sealed, or adoption records released. Fee to fax results is $1.00 per page. Copy fee: $1.00 per page. Cert fee: $5.00. Payee: County Clerk. Personal checks accepted. Prepayment required. Mial requests require SASE. Mail turnaround time 1-2 days.

Tyler County

District Court 203 Courthouse, 100 W Bluff, Woodville, TX 75979; 409-283-2162. Hours: 8AM-Noon, 1-4:30PM (CST). *Felony, Civil.*

Civil Records: Access: Mail, in person. Both court and visitors may perform in person searches. Search fee: $5.00 per name. Required to search: name, years to search. Civil cases indexed by defendant, plaintiff. Civil records in index books.

Criminal Records: Access: Mail, in person. Both court and visitors may perform in person searches. Search fee: $5.00. Required to search: name, years to search. Criminal records in index books.

General Information: No juvenile, mental, sealed, or adoption records released. Copy fee: $1.00 per page. Payee: District Clerk. Business checks accepted. Prepayment required. Mial requests require SASE. Mail turnaround time same day.

County Court County Courthouse, Rm 110, 100 W Bluff, Woodville, TX 75979; 409-283-2281; Fax: 409-283-6305. Hours: 8AM-4:30PM (CST). *Misdemeanor, Civil, Probate.*

Civil Records: Access: Phone, mail, in person. Both court and visitors may perform in person searches. Search fee: $5.00 per name. Required to search: name, years to search. Civil cases indexed by defendant, plaintiff. Civil records on computer back to 1989, microfilm since 1973, index books from 1800s.

Criminal Records: Access: Mail, in person. Both court and visitors may perform in person searches. Search fee: $5.00 per name. Required to search: name, years to search; also helpful: address, DOB, SSN. Criminal records on computer back to 1989, microfilm since 1973, index books from 1800s.

General Information: Public Access terminal is available. No juvenile, mental, sealed or adoption records released. Will fax results for $3.00 per page. Copy fee: $1.00 per page. Cert fee: $5.00. Payee: County Clerk. Personal checks accepted. Prepayment required. Mail turnaround time 1-2 days.

Upshur County

District Court PO Box 950, Gilmer, TX 75644; 903-680-8283; Fax: 903-843-3540. Hours: 8AM-5PM (CST). *Felony, Misdemeanor, Civil, Probate.*

www.countyofupshur.com

Civil Records: Access: Mail, in person. Both court and visitors may perform in person searches. Search fee: $5.00 per name. Required to search: name, years

to search. Civil cases indexed by defendant, plaintiff. Civil records in index books to 1800s.

Criminal Records: Access: Mail, in person. Both court and visitors may perform in person searches, but in county court, only the court may search. Search fee: $5.00 per name. Required to search: name, years to search. Criminal records in index books to 1800s.

General Information: No juvenile, mental, sealed or adoption records released. Copy fee: $1.00 per page. Cert fee: $1.00 per document. Payee: County Clerk. No personal checks accepted. Prepayment required. Mial requests require SASE. Mail turnaround time same day.

County Court PO Box 730, Gilmer, TX 75644; 903-680-8126; Fax: 903-843-5492. Hours: 8AM-5PM (CST). *Misdemeanor, Civil, Probate.*

Civil Records: Access: Mail, in person. Both court and visitors may perform in person searches. Search fee: $5.00 per name. Fee is per 10 year period. Required to search: name, years to search. Civil cases indexed by defendant, plaintiff. Civil records in index books to 1936; on computer back to 1979.

Criminal Records: Access: Mail, in person. Both court and visitors may perform in person searches, but in county court, only the court may search. Search fee: $5.00 per name. Fee is per 10 year period. Required to search: name, years to search, DOB, offense, signed release. Criminal records in index books to 1936; on computer back to 1979.

General Information: Public Access terminal is available. No juvenile, mental, sealed or adoption records released. Will fax results for $1.00 per page,prepaid. Copy fee: $1.00 per page. Cert fee: $5.00. Payee: County Clerk. Personal checks accepted. Prepayment required. Mial requests require SASE. Mail turnaround time same day.

Upton County

District & County Court PO Box 465, Rankin, TX 79778; 432-693-2861; Fax: 432-693-2129. Hours: 8AM-5PM (CST). *Felony, Misdemeanor, Civil, Probate.*
www.co.upton.tx.us
Civil Records: Access: Fax, mail, in person. Both court and visitors may perform in person searches. Search fee: $5.00 per name. Required to search: name, years to search. Civil cases indexed by defendant, plaintiff. Civil records on computer back to 1987; in index books to 1910.

Criminal Records: Access: Fax, mail, in person. Both court and visitors may perform in person searches. Search fee: $5.00 per name. Required to search: name, years to search, signed release; also helpful: address, DOB. Criminal records on computer back to 1987; in index books to 1910.

General Information: No juvenile, mental, sealed, or adoption records released. Fee to fax results is $2.00 per page. Copy fee: $1.00 per page. Cert fee: $5.00. Payee: District/County Clerk. Personal checks accepted. Prepayment required. Mial requests require SASE. Mail turnaround time 1-2 days.

Uvalde County

District Court County Courthouse, #15, Uvalde, TX 78801; 830-278-3918. Hours: 8AM-5PM (CST). *Felony, Civil.*
Civil Records: Access: Phone, mail, in person. Both court and visitors may perform in person searches. Search fee: $5.00 per name. Required to search: name, years to search. Civil cases indexed by defendant, plaintiff. Civil records in index books.

Criminal Records: Access: Phone, mail, in person. Both court and visitors may perform in person searches. Search fee: $5.00 per name. Required to search: name, years to search, DOB, SSN. Criminal records in index books.

General Information: No juvenile, mental, sealed, or adoption records released. Copy fee: $.75 per page. Cert fee: $1.00 per page. Payee: District Clerk. Personal checks accepted. Prepayment required. Mial requests require SASE. Mail turnaround time 2-3 days.

County Clerk PO Box 284, Uvalde, TX 78802; 830-278-6614. Hours: 8AM-5PM (CST). *Misdemeanor, Civil, Probate.*
Civil Records: Access: Mail, in person. Both court and visitors may perform in person searches. Search fee: $10.00 per name. The fee covers a 10 year search. Required to search: name, years to search. Civil cases indexed by defendant, plaintiff. Civil records in index books from 1856, computerized records from 1997.

Criminal Records: Access: Mail, in person. Both court and visitors may perform in person searches. Search fee: $10.00 per name. The fee covers a 10 year search. Required to search: name, years to search, DOB, SSN. Criminal records in index books from 1856, computerized records from 1997.

General Information: Public Access terminal is available. No juvenile, mental, sealed, or adoption records released. Copy fee: $1.00 per page. Cert fee: $5.00. Payee: Lucille C Hutcherson, Uvalde County Clerk. Personal checks accepted. Prepayment required. Mail turnaround time 1-2 days.

Val Verde County

District Court PO Box 1544, Del Rio, TX 78841; 830-774-7538; Civil phone: 830-774-7538; Criminal phone: 830-774-7539. Hours: 8AM-4:30PM (CST). *Felony, Civil.*
Civil Records: Access: Mail, in person. Both court and visitors may perform in person searches. Search fee: $5.00 per name. Required to search: name, years to search. Civil cases indexed by defendant, plaintiff. Civil records on computer since 1990, index books prior.

Criminal Records: Access: Mail, in person. Both court and visitors may perform in person searches. Search fee: $5.00 per name. Required to search: name, years to search. Criminal records on computer since 1990, index books prior.

General Information: Public Access terminal is available. No juvenile, mental, sealed, or adoption records released. Will not fax results. Copy fee: $.50 per page. Cert fee: $1.00 per page. Payee: District Clerk. Business and local checks accepted. Prepayment required. Mial requests require SASE. Mail turnaround time 2-5 days.

County Court PO Box 1267, Del Rio, TX 78841-1267; 830-774-7564. Hours: 8AM-4:30PM (CST). *Misdemeanor, Civil, Probate.*
Criminal Records: Access: Mail, in person. Both court and visitors may perform in person searches. Search fee: $5.00 per name. Required to search: name, years to search; also helpful: address, DOB, SSN. Criminal records in index books, computerized since 1999.

General Information: No juvenile, mental, sealed, or adoption records released. Copy fee: $1.00 per page. Cert fee: $5.00. Payee: County Clerk. Personal checks accepted. Prepayment required. Mial requests require SASE. Mail turnaround time 1-2 days.

Van Zandt County

District Court 121 E Dallas St, Rm 302, Canton, TX 75103; 903-567-6576; Fax: 903-567-1283. Hours: 8AM-5PM (CST). *Felony, Civil.*
Civil Records: Access: Phone, fax, mail, in person. Both court and visitors may perform in person searches. Search fee: $5.00 per name. Required to search: name, years to search. Civil cases indexed by defendant, plaintiff. Civil records in index books back to 1800s; on computer back to 1980.

Criminal Records: Access: Mail, fax, in person. Both court and visitors may perform in person searches. Search fee: $5.00 per name. Required to search: name, years to search, DOB. Criminal records in index books back to 1800s; on computer back to 1980.

General Information: Public Access terminal is available. No juvenile, mental, sealed, or adoption records released. Will fax results for $1.00 per page. Copy fee: $1.00 per page. Cert fee: $1.00. Payee: District Clerk. Personal checks accepted. Prepayment required. Mial requests require SASE. Mail turnaround time 2-4 days.

County Court 121 E Dallas St, #202, Canton, TX 75103; 903-567-6503; Fax: 903-567-6722. Hours: 8AM-5PM (CST). *Misdemeanor, Civil, Probate.*
Civil Records: Access: Mail, in person. Both court and visitors may perform in person searches. Search fee: $5.00 per name. Required to search: name, years to search. Civil cases indexed by defendant, plaintiff. Civil records in index books to 1820s; on computer back to 1987.

Criminal Records: Access: Mail, in person. Both court and visitors may perform in person searches. Search fee: $5.00 per name. Required to search: name, years to search; also helpful: address, DOB, SSN. Criminal records in index books back to 1850s; on computer back to 1987.

General Information: Public Access terminal is available. No juvenile, mental, sealed, or adoption records released. Fee to fax results is $3.00 per doc, plus $1 per page. Copy fee: $1.00 per page. Cert fee: $10.00 first page; $1.00 each add'l page. Payee: County Clerk. Personal checks accepted. Prepayment required. Mial requests require SASE. Mail turnaround time 2-4 days.

Victoria County

District Court PO Box 2238, Victoria, TX 77902; 361-575-0581; Fax: 361-572-5682. Hours: 8AM-5PM (CST). *Felony, Civil.*
Civil Records: Access: Mail, in person, online. Both court and visitors may perform in person searches. Search fee: $5.00 per name. Required to search: name, years to search. Civil cases indexed by defendant, plaintiff. Civil records on computer since 1989, index books since 1838. Online access is through www.idocket.com; registration and password required. Records go back to 12/31/1993.

Criminal Records: Access: Mail, in person, online. Both court and visitors may perform in person searches. Search fee: $5.00 per name. Required to search: name, years to search, DOB. Criminal records on computer since 1989, index books since 1838s. Online access is through www.idocket.com; registration and password required. Records go back to 12/31/1993.

General Information: Public Access terminal is available. No juvenile, mental, sealed, or adoption records released. No fee for local fax; Long distance fax fee $5.00 plus $1.00 per pg. Copy fee: $1.00 per page. Cert fee: $1.00. Payee: District Clerk. Personal checks accepted. Prepayment required. Mial requests require SASE. Mail turnaround time 1-2 days.

County Court 115 N Bridge, Rm 103, Victoria, TX 77901; 361-575-1478; Fax: 361-575-6276. Hours: 8AM-5PM (CST). *Misdemeanor, Civil, Probate.*
Civil Records: Access: Phone, mail, in person, online. Both court and visitors may perform in person searches. Search fee: $10.00 per name. Required to search: name, years to search. Civil cases indexed by defendant, plaintiff. Civil records on Cox index back to 1836; on comptuer back to 1991. Online access is through www.idocket.com; registration and password required. Records go back to 12/31/1991.

Criminal Records: Access: Phone, fax, mail, in person, online. Both court and visitors may perform in person searches. Search fee: $10.00 per name. Required to search: name, years to search; also helpful: address, DOB, SSN. Criminal records on Cox index back to 1836; on computer back to 1989. Online access is through www.idocket.com; registration and password required. Records go back to 12/31/1989.

General Information: Public Access terminal is available. No juvenile, mental, sealed, birth, death or adoption records released. Will fax results $3.50 per doc, or $3.50 plus $1.50 per page to non toll-free number. Copy fee: $1.00 per page, Cert fee: $5.00. Payee: Victoria County Clerk. Personal checks accepted. Prepayment required. Mial requests require SASE. Mail turnaround time 1 day.

Walker County

District Court 1100 University Ave, Rm 301, Huntsville, TX 77340; 936-436-4972. Hours: 8AM-Noon, 1-5PM (CST). *Felony, Civil.*

Civil Records: Access: Mail, in person. Both court and visitors may perform in person searches. Search fee: $5.00 per name. Required to search: name, years to search. Civil cases indexed by defendant, plaintiff. Civil records on index books.

Criminal Records: Access: Mail, in person. Both court and visitors may perform in person searches. Search fee: $5.00 per name. Required to search: name, years to search. Criminal records on index books.

General Information: No juvenile, mental, sealed, abortion or adoption records released. Will fax results to local or toll free line. Copy fee: $1.00 per page. No cert fee. Payee: District Clerk. Business checks accepted. Prepayment required. Mial requests require SASE. Mail turnaround time 1-2 days.

County Court PO Box 210, Huntsville, TX 77342-0210; 936-436-4922; Fax: 936-436-4928. Hours: 8AM-4:45PM (CST). *Misdemeanor, Civil, Probate.*

Note: Criminal fax # 936-436-4962.

Civil Records: Access: Mail, in person. Both court and visitors may perform in person searches. Search fee: $5.00 per name. Required to search: name, years to search. Civil cases indexed by defendant, plaintiff. Civil records in index books.

Criminal Records: Access: Mail, in person. Both court and visitors may perform in person searches. Search fee: $5.00 per name. Required to search: name, years to search; also helpful: address, DOB, SSN. Criminal records in index books to 1977, computerized since 1998.

General Information: Public Access terminal is available. (Criminal only.) No juvenile, mental, sealed, or adoption records released. Copy fee: $1.00 per page. Cert fee: $5.00. Payee: County Clerk. Personal checks accepted. Prepayment required. Mial requests require SASE. Mail turnaround time 2-3 days.

Waller County

District Court 836 Austin St, Rm 318, Hempstead, TX 77445; 979-826-7735. Hours: 8AM-Noon, 1-5PM (CST). *Felony, Civil.*

www.cvtv.net/~tx155district

Civil Records: Access: Mail, in person. Both court and visitors may perform in person searches. Search fee: $5.00 per name. Required to search: name, years to search, DOB, SSN. Civil cases indexed by defendant, plaintiff. Civil records on index books to 1866, computerized in 2002.

Criminal Records: Access: Mail, in person. Both court and visitors may perform in person searches. Search fee: $5.00 per name. Required to search:

name, years to search, DOB, SSN. Criminal records on computer since 9/99, archived to early 1900s.

General Information: Public Access terminal is available. (Terminal is for civil only.) No juvenile, mental, sealed, or adoption records released. Copy fee: $1.00 per page. Cert fee: $1.00. Payee: District Clerk. Personal checks accepted. Prepayment required. Mial requests require SASE. Mail turnaround time 2 days.

County Court 836 Austin St, Rm 217, Hempstead, TX 77445; 979-826-7711. Hours: 8AM-Noon, 1-5PM (CST). *Misdemeanor, Civil, Probate.*

Civil Records: Access: Mail, in person. Both court and visitors may perform in person searches. Search fee: $5.00 per name. Required to search: name, years to search. Civil cases indexed by defendant, plaintiff. Civil records in index books; on computer back to 1994.

Criminal Records: Access: Mail, in person. Both court and visitors may perform in person searches. Search fee: $5.00 per name. Required to search: name, years to search, signed release; also helpful: DOB, SSN. Criminal records in index books; on computer back to 1994.

General Information: Public Access terminal is available. No juvenile, mental, sealed, or adoption records released. Copy fee: $1.00 per page. Cert fee: $5.00. Payee: Waller County Clerk. No personal checks accepted for copies. Prepayment required. Mial requests require SASE. Mail turnaround time 2-3 days.

Ward County

District Court PO Box 440, Monahans, TX 79756; 432-943-2751; Fax: 432-943-3810. Hours: 8AM-Noon-1-5PM (CST). *Felony, Civil.*

Civil Records: Access: Mail, in person. Both court and visitors may perform in person searches. Search fee: $5.00 per name. Required to search: name, years to search. Civil cases indexed by defendant, plaintiff. Civil records on computer since 1980, index books prior.

Criminal Records: Access: Mail, in person. Both court and visitors may perform in person searches. Search fee: $5.00 per name. Required to search: name, years to search, signed release, also DOB or SSN. Criminal records on books, computerized since 1980.

General Information: No juvenile, mental, sealed, or adoption records released. Will fax results for $1.00 per page. Only if prepaid. Copy fee: $.50 per page. Cert fee: $1.00 per page. Payee: District Clerk. Business checks accepted. Prepayment required. Mial requests require SASE. Mail turnaround time 1-2 days.

County Court County Courthouse, Monahans, TX 79756; 432-943-3294; Fax: 432-943-6054. Hours: 8AM-5PM (CST). *Misdemeanor, Civil, Probate.*

Civil Records: Access: Mail, in person. Both court and visitors may perform in person searches. Search fee: $5.00 per name. Required to search: name, years to search. Civil cases indexed by defendant, plaintiff. Civil records in index books; computerized records go back 10 years. In person requests must be accompanied by written request.

Criminal Records: Access: Mail, in person. Both court and visitors may perform in person searches. Search fee: $5.00 per name. Required to search: name, years to search, DOB, signed release; also helpful: address, SSN. Criminal records in index books; computerized records go back 10 years. In person requests must be accompanied by a written request.

General Information: No juvenile, mental, sealed, or adoption records released. Fee to fax results is $3.00 per page. Copy fee: $1.00 per page. Cert fee: $5.00

plus $1.00 per page. Payee: County Clerk. Personal checks accepted. Prepayment required. Mial requests require SASE. Mail turnaround time 1-2 days.

Washington County

District Court 100 E Main, #304, Brenham, TX 77833-3753; 979-277-6200. Hours: 8AM-5PM (CST). *Felony, Civil.*

Civil Records: Access: Mail, in person. Both court and visitors may perform in person searches. Search fee: $5.00 per name. Required to search: name, years to search. Civil cases indexed by defendant, plaintiff. Civil records in index books since 1800s; on computer back to 1988.

Criminal Records: Access: Mail, in person. Both court and visitors may perform in person searches. Search fee: $5.00 per name. Required to search: name, years to search; also helpful: DOB. Criminal records in index books since 1800s; on computer back to 1988.

General Information: Public Access terminal is available. No juvenile, mental, sealed, or adoption records released. Will fax results to local or toll free line. Copy fee: $.50 per page. Cert fee: $1.00 per page. Payee: District Clerk. Personal checks accepted. Prepayment required. Mail turnaround time 1-2 days.

County Court 100 E Main, #102, Brenham, TX 77833; 979-277-6200; Fax: 979-277-6278. Hours: 8AM-5PM (CST). *Misdemeanor, Civil, Probate.*

Civil Records: Access: Mail, in person. Both court and visitors may perform in person searches. Search fee: $5.00 per name. Required to search: name, years to search. Civil cases indexed by defendant, plaintiff. Civil records in index books from 1868; computerized back to 1985. In person request must be accompanied by a written request.

Criminal Records: Access: Mail, in person. Both court and visitors may perform in person searches. Search fee: $5.00 per name. Required to search: name, years to search; also helpful: address, DOB, SSN. Criminal records in index books from 1870; computerized back to 1992. In person requests must be accompanied by a written request.

General Information: Public Access terminal is available. No juvenile, mental, sealed, or adoption records released. Fee to fax results is $1.00 per page and must be pre-paid. Copy fee: $1.00 per page. Cert fee: $5.00 per instrument. Payee: Washington County Clerk. Personal checks accepted. Prepayment required. Mial requests require SASE. Mail turnaround time 1-2 days.

Webb County

District Court PO Box 667, Laredo, TX 78042-0667; 956-523-4268; Fax: 956-523-5063. Hours: 8AM-5PM (CST). *Felony, Civil.*

www.webbcounty.com

Civil Records: Access: Phone, mail, fax, in person, online. Both court and visitors may perform in person searches. Search fee: $5.00 per name. Required to search: name, years to search, address; also helpful: DOB, SSN. Civil cases indexed by defendant, plaintiff. Civil records on computer back to 11/1988, index books prior. Online access is through www.idocket.com; registration and password required. Records go back to 12/31/1988.

Criminal Records: Access: Mail, fax, in person, online. Both court and visitors may perform in person searches. Search fee: $5.00 per name. Required to search: name, years to search, DOB or SSN, signed release. Criminal records on computer back to 11/1988, index books prior. Online access is through www.idocket.com; registration and password required. Records go back to 12/31/1988.

General Information: Public Access terminal is available. No juvenile, mental, sealed, or adoption records released. Will fax results for $5.00 plus add'l $1.00 per page. Copy fee: $1.00 per page. Cert fee: $1.00 per page. Payee: District Clerk. Personal checks accepted. Prepayment required. Mial requests require SASE. Mail turnaround time 1 week.

County Court 1110 Victoria, #201, Laredo, TX 78040; 956-523-4266; Civil phone: 956-523-4262; Criminal phone: 956-523-4261; Probate phone: 956-523-4257; Fax: 956-523-5035. Hours: 8AM-5PM (CST). *Misdemeanor, Civil Under $5,000, Probate.*
Civil Records: Access: Mail, in person, online. Both court and visitors may perform in person searches. Search fee: $5.00 per name. Required to search: name, years to search. Civil cases indexed by defendant, plaintiff. Civil records on computer since 1988, index books prior. Online access is through www.idocket.com; registration and password required. Includes probate.
Criminal Records: Access: Mail, in person, online. Both court and visitors may perform in person searches. Search fee: $5.00 per name. Required to search: name, years to search, DOB; also helpful: address, SSN. Criminal records on computer since 1988, index books prior to 10/75. Criminal records access is through www.idocket.com; registration and password required. Records go back to 12/31/1989.
General Information: Public Access terminal is available. No juvenile, mental, sealed, or adoption records released. Will fax results $4.00 for 1st page; $.50 each add'l page; half that fee per page for incoming faxes. Copy fee: $1.00 per page. Cert fee: $5.00. Payee: County Clerk. Personal checks accepted. Prepayment required. Mial requests require SASE. Mail turnaround time 2-3 days.

Wharton County

District Court PO Drawer 391, Wharton, TX 77488; 979-532-5542; Fax: 979-532-1299. Hours: 8AM-5PM (CST). *Felony, Civil.*
Civil Records: Access: Mail, fax, in person. Both court and visitors may perform in person searches. Search fee: $5.00 per name. Required to search: name, years to search. Civil cases indexed by defendant, plaintiff. Civil records on computer since 1989, index books prior to 1848.
Criminal Records: Access: Mail, fax, in person. Both court and visitors may perform in person searches. Search fee: $5.00 per name. Required to search: name, years to search. Criminal records on computer since 1989, index books prior to 1932.
General Information: No juvenile, mental, sealed, or adoption records released. Will fax results for $5.00 plus add'l $1.00 per page. Copy fee: $1.00 per page. Cert fee: $2.00. Payee: District Clerk of Wharton. Personal checks accepted. Prepayment required. Mial requests require SASE. Mail turnaround time same day.

County Court PO Box 69, Wharton, TX 77488; 979-532-2381. Hours: 8AM-5PM (CST). *Misdemeanor, Civil, Probate.*
Civil Records: Access: Mail, in person. Both court and visitors may perform in person searches. Search fee: $5.00 per name per 10 years searched. Required to search: name, years to search. Civil cases indexed by defendant, plaintiff. Civil records on computer since 1991, index books since 1978, prior indexes in storage to 1893.
Criminal Records: Access: Mail, in person. Both court and visitors may perform in person searches. Search fee: $5.00 per name per 10 years searched. Required to search: name, years to search, DOB, signed release; also helpful: address, SSN, copy of ID. Criminal records on computer since 1991, index books since 1978, prior indexes in storage to 1893.
General Information: Public Access terminal is available. No juvenile, mental, sealed, or adoption

records released. Fee to fax results is $2.00 plus $1.00 per page. Copy fee: $1.00 per page. Cert fee: $5.00. Payee: County Clerk. Business checks accepted. Prepayment required. Mial requests require SASE. Mail turnaround time 1-2 days.

Wheeler County

District Court PO Box 528, Wheeler, TX 79096; 806-826-5931; Fax: 806-826-5503. Hours: 8AM-5PM (CST). *Felony, Civil.*
Civil Records: Access: Phone, mail, in person. Both court and visitors may perform in person searches. Search fee: $5.00 per name. Required to search: name, years to search. Civil cases indexed by defendant, plaintiff. Civil records in index books.
Criminal Records: Access: Phone, mail, in person. Both court and visitors may perform in person searches. Search fee: $5.00 per name. Required to search: name, years to search. Criminal records in index books.
General Information: No juvenile, mental, sealed, or adoption records released. Copy fee: $1.00 per page. Cert fee: $1.00. Payee: District Clerk. Personal checks accepted. Prepayment required. Mail turnaround time 2-3 days.

County Court PO Box 465, Wheeler, TX 79096; 806-826-5544; Fax: 806-826-3282. Hours: 8AM-5PM (CST). *Misdemeanor, Civil, Probate.*
Civil Records: Access: Mail, in person. Both court and visitors may perform in person searches. Search fee: $10.00 per name. Required to search: name, years to search. Civil cases indexed by defendant, plaintiff. Civil records in index books back to 1800s.
Criminal Records: Access: Mail, in person. Both court and visitors may perform in person searches. Search fee: $10.00 per name. Required to search: name, years to search; also helpful: DOB, SSN. Criminal records in index books.
General Information: No juvenile, mental, sealed, or adoption records released. Will fax results for $1.00 per page. Copy fee: $1.00 per page. Cert fee: $5.00. Payee: County Clerk. Business checks accepted. Prepayment required. Mial requests require SASE. Mail turnaround time 1 day.

Wichita County

District Court PO Box 718, Wichita Falls, TX 76307; 940-766-8190. Hours: 8AM-5PM (CST). *Felony, Civil.*
Civil Records: Access: Phone, mail, in person. Both court and visitors may perform in person searches. Search fee: $5.00 per name. Required to search: name, years to search. Civil cases indexed by defendant, plaintiff. Civil records on computer since 1984, index books prior. Phone searches must be prepaid.
Criminal Records: Access: Phone, mail, in person. Both court and visitors may perform in person searches. Search fee: $5.00 per name. Required to search: name, years to search. Criminal records on computer since 1984, index books before. Phone searches must be prepaid.
General Information: Public Access terminal is available. No juvenile, mental, sealed, or adoption records released. Will not fax results. Copy fee: $1.00 per page. Cert fee: $1.00. Payee: District Clerk. Personal checks accepted. Prepayment required. Mial requests require SASE. Mail turnaround time 2-3 days.

County Court PO Box 1679, Wichita Falls, TX 76307; 940-766-8160; Criminal phone: 940-766-8173; Probate phone: 940-766-8172; Fax: 940-716-8554. Hours: 8AM-5PM (CST). *Misdemeanor, Probate.*
Criminal Records: Access: Phone, mail, in person. Both court and visitors may perform in person

searches. Search fee: $10.00 per name searched. Required to search: name, years to search; also helpful: DOB, SSN. Criminal records on computer or printed index from 1980 to present.
General Information: Public Access terminal is available. No juvenile, mental, sealed, or adoption records released. Mental can be released with an order from the judge. Will fax to toll-free numbers only. Copy fee: $1.00 per page. Cert fee: $5.00 per document. Payee: Wichita County Clerk. No personal checks accepted. Prepayment required. Mial requests require SASE. Mail turnaround time 1 week or less.

Wilbarger County

District Court 1700 Wilbarger, Rm 33, Vernon, TX 76384; 940-553-3411; Fax: 940-553-2316. Hours: 8AM-5PM (CST). *Felony, Civil.*
Civil Records: Access: Mail, in person. Both court and visitors may perform in person searches. Search fee: $5.00 per name. Required to search: name, years to search. Civil cases indexed by defendant, plaintiff. Civil records go back to 1800s; computerized records go back 4 years.
Criminal Records: Access: Mail, in person. Both court and visitors may perform in person searches. Search fee: $5.00 per name. Required to search: name, years to search, DOB. Criminal records go back to 1800s; computerized records go back 4 years.
General Information: No juvenile, mental, sealed, or adoption records released. Will return results by fax or phone if an 800 number is provided. Will fax results to toll-free number. Copy fee: $1.00 per page. Cert fee: $5.00. Payee: District Clerk. Business checks accepted. Prepayment required. Mial requests require SASE. Mail turnaround time 2-3 days.

County Court 1700 Wilbarger, Rm 15, Vernon, TX 76384; 940-552-5486. Hours: 8AM-5PM (CST). *Misdemeanor, Civil, Probate.*
Civil Records: Access: Mail, in person. Both court and visitors may perform in person searches. Search fee: $10.00 per name. Required to search: name, years to search. Civil cases indexed by defendant. Civil records go back to 1887; no computerized records.
Criminal Records: Access: Mail, in person. Both court and visitors may perform in person searches. Search fee: $10.00 per name. Required to search: name, years to search; also helpful: address, DOB, SSN. Criminal records go back to 1887; computerized records go back to 1999.
General Information: No juvenile, mental, sealed, or adoption records released. Fee to fax results is $1.00 per page. Copy fee: $1.00 per page. Cert fee: $5.00 plus $1.00 per page. Payee: County Clerk. Personal checks accepted. Prepayment required. Mial requests require SASE. Mail turnaround time same day.

Willacy County

District Court County Courthouse, Raymondville, TX 78580; 956-689-2532; Fax: 956-689-5713. Hours: 8AM-5PM (CST). *Felony, Civil.*
Civil Records: Access: Mail, in person, phone. Both court and visitors may perform in person searches. Search fee: $8.00 per name. Required to search: name, years to search. Civil cases indexed by defendant, plaintiff. Civil records in index books.
Criminal Records: Access: Mail, in person. Both court and visitors may perform in person searches. Search fee: $8.00 per name. Required to search: name, years to search. Criminal records in index books.
General Information: No juvenile, mental, sealed, or adoption records released. Will fax results for $2.00 per page. Copy fee: $1.00 per page. Payee: District Clerk. Personal checks accepted. Prepayment required. Mial requests require SASE. Mail turnaround time 2-3 days.

County Court 540 W Hidalgo, Raymondville, TX 78580; 956-689-2710. Hours: 8AM-Noon, 1-5PM (CST). *Misdemeanor, Civil, Probate.*

Civil Records: Access: Mail, fax, in person. Both court and visitors may perform in person searches. Search fee: $5.00 per name. Required to search: name, years to search; also helpful: address. Civil cases indexed by defendant, plaintiff. Civil records go back to 1920s.

Criminal Records: Access: Mail, in person. Both court and visitors may perform in person searches. Search fee: $5.00 per name. Required to search: name, years to search; also helpful: address, DOB, SSN. Criminal records go back to 1921, computerized since 1990.

General Information: No juvenile, mental, sealed, or adoption records released. Fee to fax results is $2.00 per page. Copy fee: $1.00 per page. Cert fee: $5.00. Payee: County Clerk. Personal checks accepted. Prepayment required. Mial requests require SASE. Mail turnaround time 2-3 days.

Williamson County

District Court PO Box 24, Georgetown, TX 78627; 512-943-1212; Fax: 512-943-1222. Hours: 8AM-5PM (CST). *Felony, Civil.*
www.williamson-county.org

Civil Records: Access: Mail, in person. Both court and visitors may perform in person searches. Search fee: $5.00 per name. Required to search: name, years to search. Civil cases indexed by defendant, plaintiff. Civil records on computer since 1989, index books prior.

Criminal Records: Access: Mail, in person. Both court and visitors may perform in person searches. Search fee: $5.00 per name. Required to search: name, years to search, DOB, signed release; also helpful: SSN. Criminal records on computer since 1989, index books prior. Sheriff bond and inmate data is at http://judicialsearch.wilco.org.

General Information: Public Access terminal is available. No juvenile, mental, sealed, or adoption records released. Will not fax results. Copy fee: $1.00 1st pg; $.25 each add'l. Cert fee: $1.00. Payee: District Clerk. Personal checks accepted. Prepayment required. Mial requests require SASE. Mail turnaround time 2-3 days.

County Court 405 MLK St, Box 14, Georgetown, TX 78626; Civil phone: 512-943-1140; Criminal phone: 512-943-1150; Probate phone: 512-943-1140; Fax: 512-943-1154 (civil). Hours: 8AM-5PM (CST). *Misdemeanor, Civil, Probate.*

Civil Records: Access: Mail, in person, online. Both court and visitors may perform in person searches. Search fee: $10.00 per name. Required to search: name, years to search. Civil records indexed by defendant, plaintiff. Civil records on computer since 1985, index books since 1848.GA. Access to limited civil case records is free at http://judicialsearch.wilco.org.

Criminal Records: Access: Mail, in person, online. Both court and visitors may perform in person searches. Search fee: $10.00 per name. Required to search: name, years to search; also helpful: DOB, SSN. Criminal records on computer since 1983. Overall records go back to 1800. Access to a limited number of criminal case records is free at http://judicialsearch.wilco.org. Sheriff bond and inmate data is also available.

General Information: Public Access terminal is available. No juvenile, mental, sealed, or adoption records released. Fee to fax results is $1.00 per page. Copy fee: $1.00 per page. Cert fee: $5.00. Payee: County Clerk. Personal checks accepted. Prepayment required. Mial requests require SASE. Mail turnaround time 2 days.

Wilson County

District Court PO Box 812, Floresville, TX 78114; 830-393-7322; Fax: 830-393-7319. Hours: 8AM-Noon, 1-4:30PM (CST). *Felony, Civil.*
Note: Request must be in writing if court personnel are to do search.

Civil Records: Access: Fax, mail, in person. Both court and visitors may perform in person searches. Search fee: $5.00 per name. Required to search: name, years to search. Civil cases indexed by defendant, plaintiff. Civil recordsgo back to 1960.

Criminal Records: Access: Fax, mail, in person. Both court and visitors may perform in person searches. Search fee: $5.00 per name. Required to search: name, years to search; also helpful: DOB. Criminal records go back to 1975.

General Information: No juvenile, mental, sealed, or adoption records released. Will fax results to local or toll free line. Copy fee: $1.00 per page. Cert fee: $1.00. Payee: District Clerk. Personal checks accepted. Prepayment required. Mial requests require SASE. Mail turnaround time 2 days.

County Court PO Box 27, Floresville, TX 78114; 830-393-7308. Hours: 8AM-5PM (CST). *Misdemeanor, Civil, Probate.*

Civil Records: Access: Phone, mail, fax, in person. Both court and visitors may perform in person searches. No search fee. Required to search: name, years to search. Civil cases indexed by defendant, plaintiff. Civil records available from 1862.

Criminal Records: Access: Phone, mail, fax, in person. Both court and visitors may perform in person searches. No search fee. Required to search: name, years to search, DOB. Criminal records stored since 1917, computerized since 11/2002.

General Information: No juvenile, mental, sealed, or adoption records released. Will not fax results. Copy fee: $1.00 per page. Cert fee: $5.00. Payee: Eva S Martinez, County Clerk. Personal checks accepted. Prepayment required. Mial requests require SASE. Mail turnaround time same day.

Winkler County

District Court PO Box 1065, Kermit, TX 79745; 432-586-3359. Hours: 8AM-5PM (CST). *Felony, Civil.*

Civil Records: Access: Phone, mail, in person. Both court and visitors may perform in person searches. Search fee: $5.00 per name. Required to search: name, years to search. Civil cases indexed by defendant, plaintiff. Civil records on computer since 1991 (child-support only), index books prior.

Criminal Records: Access: Mail, in person. Both court and visitors may perform in person searches. Search fee: $5.00 per name. Required to search: name, years to search, DOB, SSN. Criminal records on computer since 1991, index books prior.

General Information: No juvenile, mental, sealed, or adoption records released. Copy fee: $1.00 per page. Payee: District Clerk. Personal checks accepted. Prepayment required. Mial requests require SASE. Mail turnaround time 3-4 days.

County Court PO Box 1007, Kermit, TX 79745; 432-586-3401. Hours: 8AM-5PM (CST). *Misdemeanor, Civil, Probate.*

Civil Records: Access: Mail, in person. Visitors must perform in person searches for themselves. Search fee: $5.00 per name. Required to search: name, years to search. Civil cases indexed by defendant, plaintiff. All civil records in index books.

Criminal Records: Access: Mail, in person. Visitors must perform in person searches for themselves. Search fee: $5.00 per name. Required to search: name, years to search; also helpful: address, DOB,

SSN. Criminal records on computer back to 1991; prior in index books.

General Information: No juvenile, mental, sealed, or adoption records released. Copy fee: $1.00 per page. Cert fee: $5.00. Payee: County Clerk. Business checks accepted. Prepayment required. Mial requests require SASE. Mail turnaround time 2-3 days.

Wise County

District Court PO Box 308, Decatur, TX 76234; 940-627-5535; Fax: 940-627-0705. Hours: 8AM-5PM (CST). *Felony, Civil.*

Civil Records: Access: Mail, in person. Both court and visitors may perform in person searches. Search fee: $5.00 per name. Required to search: name, years to search. Civil cases indexed by defendant, plaintiff. Civil records in index books since 1895, computerized since 1999.

Criminal Records: Access: Mail, in person. Both court and visitors may perform in person searches. Search fee: $5.00 per name. Required to search: name, years to search; also helpful-DOB, SSN. Criminal records in docket books to 1896, computerized since 1999.

General Information: Public Access terminal is available. No juvenile, mental, sealed, or adoption records released. Will fax results. Copy fee: $1.00 per page. Cert fee: $2.00. Payee: Wise County District Clerk. Personal checks accepted. Prepayment required. Mial requests require SASE. Mail turnaround time same day.

County Court at Law PO Box 359, Decatur, TX 76234; 940-627-3351; Fax: 940-627-2138. Hours: 8AM-5PM (CST). *Misdemeanor, Civil, Probate.*

Civil Records: Access: Mail, in person. Both court and visitors may perform in person searches. Search fee: $10.00 per name. Required to search: name, years to search. Civil cases indexed by defendant, plaintiff. Civil records in index books since sovereignty; on computer back to 1998.

Criminal Records: Access: Mail, in person. Both court and visitors may perform in person searches. Search fee: $10.00 per name. Required to search: name, years to search; also helpful: DOB, SSN. Criminal records in index books since sovereignty; on computer back to 1997.

General Information: Public Access terminal is available. No mental health or sealed records released. Will fax results for fee. Copy fee: $1.00 per page. Cert fee: $5.00. Payee: Wise County Clerk. Personal checks accepted. Prepayment required. Mial requests require SASE. Mail turnaround time 1 day.

Wood County

District Court PO Box 1707, Quitman, TX 75783; 903-763-2361; Fax: 903-763-1511. Hours: 8AM-5PM (CST). *Felony, Civil.*
www.co.wood.tx.us/dclerk.html

Civil Records: Access: Mail, fax, in person. Both court and visitors may perform in person searches. Search fee: $5.00 per name. Required to search: name, years to search. Civil cases indexed by defendant, plaintiff. Civil records on computer since 1990, microfilm since 1981, index books since 1890.

Criminal Records: Access: Mail, fax, in person. Both court and visitors may perform in person searches. Search fee: $5.00 per name. Required to search: name, years to search; also helpful: DOB, SSN. Criminal records on computer since 1990, microfilm since 1981, index books since 1890.

General Information: Public Access terminal is available. No juvenile, mental, sealed, or adoption records released. Copy fee: $1.00 per page. Cert fee: $1.00. Payee: District Clerk. Personal checks accepted. Prepayment required. Mial requests require SASE. Mail turnaround time 2-3 days.

County Court PO Box 1796, Quitman, TX 75783; 903-763-2711; Fax: 903-763-5641. Hours: 8AM-5PM (CST). *Misdemeanor, Civil, Probate.*
Civil Records: Access: Mail, in person. Both court and visitors may perform in person searches. Search fee: $5.00 per name. Required to search: name, years to search. Civil cases indexed by defendant, plaintiff. Civil records on computer since 1980; index books since early 1900s.
Criminal Records: Access: Mail, in person. Both court and visitors may perform in person searches. Search fee: $5.00 per name. Required to search: name, years to search; also helpful DOB, SSN, signed release, DL#. Criminal records on computer back to 1986; index books from 1965, archived to 1900.
General Information: Public Access terminal is available. No mental or sealed records released. Will fax results for $2.00 per page. Copy fee: $1.00 per page. Cert fee: $5.00. Payee: Wood County Clerk. Personal checks accepted. Mial requests require SASE. Mail turnaround time same day.

Yoakum County

District Court PO Box 899, Plains, TX 79355; 806-456-7453; Fax: 806-456-8767. Hours: 8AM-5PM (CST). *Felony, Civil.*
Civil Records: Access: Fax, mail, in person. Both court and visitors may perform in person searches. Search fee: $5.00 per name. Required to search: name, years to search. Civil cases indexed by defendant, plaintiff. Civil records on computer since 1980, index books since 1907.
Criminal Records: Access: Fax, mail, in person. Both court and visitors may perform in person searches. Search fee: $5.00 per name. Required to search: name, years to search, DOB; also helpful: SSN. Criminal records on computer since 1980, index books since 1930.
General Information: Public Access terminal is available. No juvenile, mental, sealed, or adoption records released. Copy fee: $1.00 1st page, $.25 ea add'l. Cert fee: $1.00 per page. Payee: District Clerk. Personal checks accepted. Mial requests require SASE. Mail turnaround time same day.

County Court PO Box 309, Plains, TX 79355; 806-456-2721; Fax: 806-456-6175 (County Judge Office). Hours: 8AM-5PM (CST). *Misdemeanor, Civil, Probate.*
Civil Records: Access: Phone, mail, in person. Both court and visitors may perform in person searches. Search fee: $5.00 per name. Required to search: name, years to search; also helpful: address. Civil cases indexed by defendant, plaintiff. Civil records in minutes books and microfilm since 9/1986; on computer back to 1/1986.
Criminal Records: Access: Mail, in person. Both court and visitors may perform in person searches. Search fee: $5.00 per name. Required to search: name, years to search, DOB; also helpful: address, SSN. Criminal minutes books and microfilm since 9/1986; on computer back to 1/1986.
General Information: Public Access terminal is available. No juvenile or mental records released. Will fax results for $2.00 per fax plus $1.00 per page. Copy fee: $1.00 per page. Cert fee: $5.00. Payee: County Clerk, Yoakum County. Personal checks accepted.

Prepayment required. Mail turnaround time same day.

Young County

District Court 516 4th St, Rm 201, Courthouse, Graham, TX 76450; 940-549-0029; Fax: 940-549-4874. Hours: 8:30AM-Noon, 1-5PM (CST). *Felony, Civil.*
Civil Records: Access: Phone, fax, mail, in person. Both court and visitors may perform in person searches. Search fee: $5.00 per name. Required to search: name, years to search. Civil cases indexed by defendant, plaintiff. Civil records on computer since 1988, index books prior.
Criminal Records: Access: Phone, fax, mail, in person. Both court and visitors may perform in person searches. Search fee: $5.00 per name. Required to search: name, years to search; also helpful: DOB, SSN. Criminal records on computer since 1988, index books prior.
General Information: No juvenile, mental, sealed, or adoption records released. No fee to fax results. Copy fee: $1.00 for first page, $.25 each add'l. Cert fee: $1.00 per page. Payee: District Clerk. Personal checks accepted. Prepayment required. Mial requests require SASE. Mail turnaround time 1-2 days.

County Court 516 4th St, Rm 104, Graham, TX 76450; 940-549-8432; Fax: 940-521-0305. Hours: 8:30AM-Noon, 1-5PM (CST). *Misdemeanor, Civil, Probate.*
Civil Records: Access: Mail, in person. Both court and visitors may perform in person searches. Search fee: $5.00 per name. Required to search: name, years to search. Civil cases indexed by defendant, plaintiff. Civil records on computer since 1991, index books prior to 1800s.
Criminal Records: Access: Mail, in person. Both court and visitors may perform in person searches. Search fee: $5.00 per name. Required to search: name, years to search. Criminal records on computer since 1991, index books prior to 1800s.
General Information: Public Access terminal is available. No juvenile, mental, sealed, or adoption records released. Fee to fax results is $1.00 per page. Copy fee: $1.00 per page. Cert fee: $5.00. Payee: County Clerk. Personal checks accepted. Prepayment required. Mail turnaround time same day.

Zapata County

District Court PO Box 788, Clerk's Office, Zapata, TX 78076; 956-765-9930; Fax: 956-765-9931. Hours: 8AM-Noon, 1-5PM (CST). *Felony, Civil.*
Civil Records: Access: Fax, mail, in person. Both court and visitors may perform in person searches. Search fee: $5.00 per name. Required to search: name, years to search. Civil cases indexed by plaintiff. Civil records in index books.
Criminal Records: Access: Fax, mail, in person. Both court and visitors may perform in person searches. Search fee: $5.00 per name. Required to search: name, years to search. Criminal records in index books.
General Information: No juvenile, mental, sealed, or adoption records released. Will fax results $4.00 for 1st page, $1.00 each add'l. Copy fee: $1.00 per page. Cert fee: $5.00. Payee: District Clerk/County Clerk.

Personal checks accepted. Prepayment required. Mial requests require SASE. Mail turnaround time 1-3 days.

County Court PO Box 789, Zapata, TX 78076; 956-765-9915; Fax: 956-765-9933. Hours: 8AM-Noon, 1-5PM (CST). *Misdemeanor, Civil, Probate.*
Civil Records: Access: Mail, in person. Both court and visitors may perform in person searches. Search fee: $5.00 per name. Required to search: name, years to search. Civil cases indexed by plaintiff only. Civil records in index books since 1800s, computerized records back to 1990.
Criminal Records: Access: Mail, in person. Both court and visitors may perform in person searches. Search fee: $5.00 per name. Required to search: name, years to search, DOB, SSN. Criminal records in index books since 1800s, computerized records back to 1930.
General Information: No juvenile, mental, sealed, or adoption records released. Will fax results $4.00 for 1st page, $1.00 each add'l. Copy fee: $1.00 per page. Cert fee: $5.00. Payee: Consuelo R Villarreal, County Clerk. Personal checks accepted. Prepayment required. Mail turnaround time 1-2 days.

Zavala County

District Court PO Box 704, Crystal City, TX 78839; 830-374-3456. Hours: 8AM-Noon, 1-5PM (CST). *Felony, Civil.*
Civil Records: Access: Phone, mail, in person. Both court and visitors may perform in person searches. Search fee: $5.00 per name. Required to search: name, years to search. Civil cases indexed by defendant, plaintiff, in index books from 1900s.
Criminal Records: Access: Phone, mail, in person. Both court and visitors may perform in person searches. Search fee: $5.00 per name. Required to search: name, years to search. Criminal records in index books from 1900s.
General Information: No juvenile, mental, sealed, or adoption records released. Copy fee: $1.00 per page. No cert fee. Payee: Zavala County District Clerk. Personal checks accepted. Mial requests require SASE. Mail turnaround time 1-2 days.

County Court Zavala County Courthouse, 200 E Uvalde, Crystal City, TX 78839; 830-374-2331; Fax: 830-374-5955. Hours: 8AM-5PM (CST). *Misdemeanor, Civil, Probate.*
Civil Records: Access: Mail, in person. Both court and visitors may perform in person searches. Search fee: $10.00 per name. Required to search: name, years to search. Civil cases indexed by defendant, plaintiff. Civil records in index books from 1880s.
Criminal Records: Access: Mail, in person. Both court and visitors may perform in person searches. Search fee: $10.00 per name. Required to search: name, years to search, DOB. Criminal records in index books from 1880s.
General Information: No juvenile, mental, sealed, or adoption records released. Copy fee: $1.00 per page. Cert fee: $1.00. Payee: Zavala County Clerk. Personal checks accepted. Prepayment required. Mial requests require SASE. Mail turnaround time 1-2 days.

Texas Recording Offices

ORGANIZATION: 254 counties, 254 recording offices. The recording officer is County Clerk. 252 counties are in the Central Time Zone (CST) and 2 are in the Mountain Time Zone (MST).

REAL ESTATE RECORDS: Some counties will perform real estate searches. Copy fees are usually $1.00 per page. Certification usually costs $5.00 per document. Each county has an "Appraisal District" which is responsible for collecting taxes.

UCC RECORDS: Financing statements are filed at the state level, except for real estate related collateral, which are filed with the County Clerk. Most Texas recording offices will perform UCC searches. Searches fees are usually $10.00 per debtor name using the approved UCC-11 request form, but may be $15.00 for using a non-Texas form. Copy fees are usually $1.00-2.00 per page.

TAX LIEN RECORDS: Federal tax liens on personal property of businesses are filed with the Secretary of State. Other federal and all state tax liens are filed with the County Clerk. All counties will perform tax lien searches. Search fees and copy fees can vary, but records are usually provided as part of the UCC search.

OTHER LIENS: Mechanics, judgment, hospital, labor, lis pendens.

ONLINE ACCESS: Numerous counties offer online access to assessor and recorded document data. There are two private companies that offer access via the web to multiple counties' tax assessor data. Visit www.txcountydata.com or www.taxnetusa.com. Some counties can be accessed from either site.

www.txcountydata.com - Assessor and property information records for over fifty Texas counties on the TXCOUNTYDATA site are available for no fee. At this site click on "County Search" then use the pull down menu in the county field to select the county to search. The County Info page for each county lists the Appraiser, mailing address, phone, fax, web site, e-mail. Generally, you can search any county account, owner name, address, or property ID number. Search allows you to access owner address, property address, legal description, taxing entities, exemptions, deed, account number, abstract/subdivision, neighborhood, valuation info, and more.

www.taxnetusa.com - TaxNetUSA offers free appraisal district and property information records for over fify-five Texas counties as well as a few counties in other states. The site also offers advanced and subscriptions services for many of the counties.

At the TaxNetUSA site, user chooses "advanced search subscribers login" (fee service) or "Appraisal Districts Online Basic Search" (no fee). For a basic search, use the pull down menu in the county field to select the county to search. Select county and click go. At the county Assessor/Tax site, follow the directions for that county. Generally, but in varying degrees from county to county, the basic search allows you to access general property information: name, address, valuation, etc., and you may search by parcel number, owner name, or address. Depending on the county, more "detailed" information may be available.

TaxNetUSA's Advanced Search Information (fee) allows most counties to be searched by any combination of criteria. Fees vary and can range from a simple $25 search to multiple county subscriptions as high as $1,500.

Anderson County

County Clerk, 500 N. Church St, Palestine, TX 75801. **Phone**-903-723-7432, R/E Recording-903-723-7484, UCC Recording-903-723-7484; fax-903-723-7801; hours 8AM-5PM
Will search UCC records prior to 7/2001 & current fixture files. Search per debtor- $10.00. Will search tax liens. Will search real estate records for the years of 1985 to present. Record copy- $1.00 per page. Cert fee: $5.00 per doc. Payee: Anderson County Clerk. **Online Access to Appraiser, Property Tax, Land, Judgment, Lien, Grantor/Grantee records:** The grantor/grantee index is at www.titlex.com. Select Anderson from the county list. Records range is 6/1972 to 12/2003. Also, property tax inquiries can be made at http://198.143.202.7/tax.html. Use the existing ID/password,click on login and then select "Tax Inquiry." For more infoformation, phone 800-305-9434 or 281-397-9525. Also, see note at beginning of section. **Other phones:** Assessor-903-723-7438; Treasurer-903-723-7408; Appraiser-903-723-2949; Elections-903-723-7438; Vital Records-903-723-7437.

Andrews County

County Clerk, PO Box 727, Andrews, TX 79714. **Phone**-County Clerk, R/E & UCC Recording- 432-524-1426; fax-432-524-1473; hours 8AM-5PM
Will not search UCC or real estate records. Tax lien search- $10.00 per debtor. UCC copy- $1.50 per page. Min. $5.00. Cert fee: $5.00 per doc. Payee: Andrews County Clerk. **Other phones:** Assessor-432-524-1409; Appraiser-432-523-9111; Elections-432-524-1426; Vital Records-432-524-1426.

Angelina County

County Clerk, PO Box 908, Lufkin, TX 75902-0908. **Phone**-936-634-8339; fax-936-634-8460; hours 8AM-4:30PM
Will search UCC records prior to 7/2001 & current fixture files. Search per debtor- $5.00. Tax liens not included in UCC search. Tax lien search- $5.00 per debtor. Will search real estate records. Record copy- $1.00 per page. Cert fee: $5.00 per cert. Payee: Angelina County Clerk. **Online Access to Appraiser, Property Tax records:** See note at beginning of section. **Other phones:** Assessor-936-634-8376; Appraiser-936-634-8456.

Aransas County

County Clerk, 301 N. Live Oak, Rockport, TX 78382. **Phone**-361-790-0122; fax-361-790-0119; hours 8AM-4:30PM
Will not search UCC or real estate records. Will do a tax lien search. RE record copy- $1.00 per page; $5.00 for certificate. UCC copy- $2.00 per page. Cert fee: $5.00 per cert. Payee: Aransas County Clerk. **Online Access to Real Estate, Deed, Lien, Judgment, Birth, Death, Appraiser, Property Tax records:** Access to recordings, land records, births, deaths is free at http://apolloplus.com then click on member counties to access Aransas Co. Also, appraiser and property tax information is at www.aransascad.org. Also see note at beginning of section. **Other phones:** Assessor-361-790-0160; Treasurer-361-790-0132; Appraiser-361-729-9733; Elections-361-729-7431; Vital Records-361-790-0122.

Archer County

County Clerk, PO Box 427, Archer City, TX 76351. **Phone**-County Clerk, R/E & UCC Recording- 940-574-4302; fax-940-574-4625; hours 8:30AM-5PM
Will search UCC records prior to 7/2001 & current fixture files. Search per debtor- $10.00. Search request using non-standard form (per name)- $25.00. Tax liens not included in UCC search. Separate federal/state combined tax lien search- $10.00 per debtor. Will not search real estate records. Record copy- $1.00 per page. Cert fee: $5.00 per cert. Payee: Archer County Clerk. **Online Access to Property Tax records:** See note at beginning of section. **Other phones:** Assessor-940-574-4531; Treasurer-940-574-4822; Appraiser-940-574-2172; Elections-940-574-4302; Vital Records-940-574-4302.

Armstrong County

County Clerk, PO Box 309, Claude, TX 79019-0309. **Phone**-County Clerk, R/E & UCC Recording- 806-226-2081; fax-806-226-5301; 8AM-Noon, 1-5PM

Will not search UCC or real estate records. Separate federal/state combined tax lien search- $5.00 per debtor. Record copy- $1.00 per page. Cert fee: $5.00 per cert. Payee: Armstrong County Clerk. **Other phones:** Assessor-806-226-4481; Treasurer-806-226-3651; Appraiser-806-226-4481; Elections-806-226-2081; Vital Records-806-226-2081.

Atascosa County

County Clerk, #1 Courthouse Circle #102, Jourdanton, TX 78026. **Phone-**County Clerk, R/E & UCC Recording- 830-767-2511; fax-830-769-1021; hours 8AM-5PM
Will search UCC records prior to 7/2001 & current fixture files. Search per debtor- $10.00. Federal/state combined tax lien search- $5.00 per search. Will not search real estate records. UCC copy- $1.00 per page. Cert fee: $5.00 per cert. Payee: Atascosa County Clerk. **Online Access to Appraiser, Property Tax records:** See note at beginning of section. **Other phones:** Assessor-830-769-3142; Treasurer-830-769-3024; Appraiser-830-742-3591; Elections-830-769-1472; Vital Records-830-767-2511.

Austin County

County Clerk, 1 E. Main, Bellville, TX 77418-1551. **Phone-**County Clerk, R/E & UCC Recording- 979-865-5911; fax-979-865-0336; hours 8AM-5PM
Will search UCC records prior to 7/2001 & current fixture files. Search per debtor- $10.00. Tax lien search- $10.00 per debtor. Will not search real estate records. Record copy- $1.00 per page. Cert fee: $5.00 per cert. Payee: Austin County Clerk. **Online Access to Appraiser, Property Tax, Land, Judgment, Lien, Grantor/Grantee records:** The grantor/grantee index is at www.titlex.com. Select Austin from the county list. Records range is 8/1997 to 8/2001. Also, search property tax records for free at www.austincad.org. Deed records not online. Also, see note at beginning of section. **Other phones:** Assessor-979-865-8633; Treasurer-979-865-5911; Appraiser-409-865-9124; Elections-979-865-5911; Vital Records-979-865-5911.

Bailey County

County Clerk, 300 S. 1st, #200, Muleshoe, TX 79347. **Phone-**County Clerk, R/E & UCC Recording- 806-272-3044; fax-806-272-3538; 8:30AM-Noon 1-5PM
Will search UCC records prior to 7/2001 & current fixture files. Search per debtor- $10.00. Search request using non-standard form (per name)- $25.00. Will not search real estate or tax lien records. Copy fee- $1.00 per page. Cert fee: $5.00 per cert and $1.00 per page. Payee: Bailey County Clerk. **Online Access to Property, Appraiser records:** Access to Bailey CAD property database is free at http://65.107.178.35/clientdb/main.asp. **Other phones:** Assessor-806-272-3022; Treasurer-806-272-3239; Appraiser-806-272-5501; Elections-806-272-3044; Vital Records-806-272-3044.

Bandera County

County Clerk, PO Box 823, Bandera, TX 78003. **Phone-**830-796-3332; fax-830-796-8323; hours 8:30AM-4:30PM
Will search UCC records prior to 7/2001 & current fixture files. Search per debtor- $10.00. Search request using non-standard form (per name)- $25.00. UCC search includes tax liens if requested. Separate federal/state combined tax lien search- $20.00 per debtor. RE owner, mortgage, property transfer searches available. RE record copy- $1.00 per page. UCC copy- $2.00 per page. Cert fee: $5.00 per cert. Payee: Bandera County Clerk. **Online Access to Property, Personal Property, Appraiser records:** Access to Bandera County Appraisal Roll Search is free at

http://hp3.quickaccess.com/bandera/. Also, See note at beginning of section. **Other phones:** Assessor-830-796-3731; Appraiser-830-796-3030; Vital Records-512-458-7111.

Bastrop County

County Clerk, PO Box 577, Bastrop, TX 78602. **Phone-**County Clerk, R/E & UCC Recording- 512-332-7234; fax-512-332-7241; hours 8AM-5PM
Will not search UCC or tax liens records. RE owner, mortgage, property transfer searches available. RE record copy- $1.00 per page. UCC copy- $2.00 per page. Cert fee: $5.00 per cert. Payee: Bastrop County Clerk. **Online Access to Appraiser, Property Tax, Land, Judgment, Lien, Grantor/Grantee records:** The grantor/grantee index is at www.titlex.com. Select Bastrop from the county list. Record range is 3/2001 to 8/31/2001. Also, access to tax office records is free at www.bastroptac.com. Also, see note at beginning of section. **Other phones:** Assessor-512-581-7160; Treasurer-512-332-7204; Appraiser-512-303-3536; Elections-512-332-7234; Vital Records-512-332-7234; Voter Registrar-512-332-7261.

Baylor County

County Clerk, PO Box 689, Seymour, TX 76380-0689. **Phone-**County Clerk, R/E & UCC Recording- 940-889-3322; fax-940-889-4300; hours 8:30AM-5PM
Will search UCC records prior to 7/2001 & current fixture files. Search per debtor- $15.00. UCC search includes tax liens if requested. Separate federal/state combined tax lien search- $15.00 per debtor. RE owner, mortgage, property transfer searches available. RE record copy- $1.00 per page. UCC copy- $1.50 per page with min. of $5.00. Cert fee: $6.00 per cert (County records). Payee: Baylor County Clerk. **Other phones:** Assessor-940-889-3169; Treasurer-940-889-1846; Appraiser-940-888-5636; Elections-940-889-3322; Vital Records-940-889-3322.

Bee County

County Clerk, 105 W. Corpus Christi St, Rm 103, Beeville, TX 78102. **Phone-**County Clerk, R/E & UCC Recording- 361-362-3245; fax-361-362-3247; hours 8AM-Noon, 1-5PM
Will search UCC records prior to 7/2001 & current fixture files. Search per debtor- $16.00. Search request using non-standard form (per name)- $31.00. UCC search includes tax liens if requested. Separate federal/state combined tax lien search- $5.00 per debtor. Will not search real estate records; written request required. RE record copy- $1.00 per page. UCC copy- $2.00 per page. Cert fee: $5.00 per cert. Payee: Bee County Clerk. **Online Access to Property Tax records:** See note at beginning of section. **Other phones:** Assessor-361-362-3250; Appraiser-361-358-0193; Elections-361-362-3245; Vital Records-361-362-3245.

Bell County

County Clerk, PO Box 480, Belton, TX 76513-0480. **Phone-**254-933-5174, R/E Recording-254-933-5171; fax-254-933-5176; hours-8AM-5PM
www.bellcountytx.com/countyclerk/index.htm
Will search UCC records prior to 7/2001 & current fixture files. Search per debtor- $10.00. Tax liens not included in UCC search. Tax lien search- $10.00 per debtor. Will not search real estate records. RE record copy- $1.00 per page. UCC copy- $2.00 per page. Cert fee: $5.00 per cert. Payee: Bell County Clerk. **Other phones:** Assessor-817-771-1108; Treasurer-817-933-5255; Appraiser-254-939-5841.

Bexar County

County Clerk, 100 Dolorosa, Rm 108, Bexar County Courthouse, San Antonio, TX 78205-3083. **Phone-**210-335-2581, 335-2273, 335-3041, R/E Recording-210-335-2581, UCC Recording-210-335-2581; hours 8AM-5PM www.countyclerk.bexar.landata.com
Will search UCC records prior to 7/2001 & current fixture files. Search per debtor- $1.00 per year. Tax liens not included in UCC search. Separate federal/state combined tax lien search- $1.00 per debtor per year RE owner, mortgage, property transfer searches available. Record copy- $1.00 per page. Cert fee: $5.00 per cert. Payee: Bexar County Clerk. **Online Access to Grantor/Grantee, Marriage, UCC, Assumed Name, Recording, Property Tax, Appraiser, Probate records:** Access to the County Clerk database is free at www.countyclerk.bexar.landata.com. Includes land records, deeds, UCCs, assumed names and foreclosure notices. Probate is recently added. Images are to be added on a new subscription service. Also, online access to the county Central Appraisal District database is free at www.bcad.org/property.htm. **Other phones:** Assessor-210-335-2251; Appraiser-210-224-8511; Elections-210-335-8683; Vital Records-210-335-2585.

Blanco County

County Clerk, PO Box 65, Johnson City, TX 78636. **Phone-**830-868-7357; fax-830-868-4158; hours 8AM-4:30PM. Will not search UCC or real estate records. Tax lien search- $5.00 per debtor. Record copy- $1.00 per page. Cert fee: $5.00 per cert. Payee: Blanco County Clerk. **Online Access to Appraiser, Property Tax records:** See note at beginning of section. **Other phones:** Assessor-830-868-7178; Treasurer-830-868-4566; Appraiser-830-868-4624.

Borden County

County Clerk, PO Box 124, Gail, TX 79738-0124. **Phone-**County Clerk, R/E & UCC Recording- 806-756-4312; fax-806-756-4405; 8AM-Noon, 1-5PM
Will search UCC records prior to 7/2001 & current fixture files. Search per debtor- $10.00. Search request using non-standard form (per name)- $25.00. Tax liens not included in UCC search. Separate federal/state combined tax lien search- $10.00 per debtor. Will not search real estate records. RE record copy- $1.00 per page. UCC copy- $2.00 per page. Cert fee: $5.00 per cert. Payee: Borden County Clerk. **Other phones:** Assessor-806-756-4391; Treasurer-806-756-4386; Appraiser-806-756-4484; Elections-806-756-4312; Vital Records-806-756-4312.

Bosque County

County Clerk, PO Box 617, Meridian, TX 76665. **Phone-**254-435-2201; fax-254-435-2152; 8AM-5PM
Will search UCC records prior to 7/2001 & current fixture files. Search per debtor- $5.00. UCC search includes tax liens if requested. Separate federal & state combined tax lien search- $5.00 per debtor. RE owner, mortgage, property transfer searches available. Record copy- $1.00 per page. Cert fee: $5.00 per cert. Payee: Bosque County Clerk. **Other phones:** Assessor-254-435-2301; Treasurer-254-435-2201 x20; Appraiser-254-435-2301; Elections-254-435-2201; Vital Records-254-435-2201.

Bowie County

County Clerk, PO Box 248, New Boston, TX 75570. **Phone-**903-628-6740; fax-903-628-6729; 8AM-5PM
Will search UCC records prior to 7/2001 & current fixture files. Search per debtor- $10.00. Tax lien search- $10.00 per debtor. Will not search real estate records. Copy fee- $1.00 per page. Cert fee: $2.00. Payee: County Clerk. **Online Access to Property Tax, Appraiser records:** Assess to Appraisal

District's Roll data is free at www.bowiecad.or
g/Search.htm. **Other phones:** Assessor-903-628-6733;
Treasurer-903-628-6722; Appraiser-903-628-6724;
Elections-903-628-6810; Vital Records-903-628-6744;
Courthouse Operator-903-628-6700.

Brazoria County

County Clerk, 111 E. Locust, #200, Angleton, TX
77515-4654. **Phone**-979-849-5711, R/E Recording-
979-864-1355 x5, UCC Recording-979-864-1355 x9;
fax-979-864-1358; hours-8AM-4:30PM
www.brazoria.tx.us.landata.com
Will search UCC records prior to 7/2001 & current
fixture files. Search per debtor- $10.00. Will search
tax liens including federal tax liens. Will not search
real estate records. Copy fee- $1.50 per page. Cert
fee: $1.50 per page; mimimum $5.00. Payee:
County Clerk. **Online Access to Appraiser, Property
Tax, Land, Grantor/Grantee records:** Access to the
county Central Appraisal District database is free at
www.brazoriacad.org. Click on "appraisal roll." Also,
the grantor/grantee index is at www.titlex.com. Select
Brazoria from the county list. Records range from
3/2001 to 1/2004. Also, see note at beginning of section.
Other phones: Assessor-979-849-1320; Treasurer-
979-849-5711; Appraiser-979-849-7792; Elections-
979-864-1355 x8; Vital Records-979-864-1355 x6.

Brazos County

County Clerk, 300 E. 26th St, #120, Bryan, TX 77803.
Phone-979-361-4132; fax-979-361-4125; 8AM-5PM
Will search UCC records prior to 7/2001 & current
fixture files. Search per debtor- $10.00. Search
request using non-standard form (per name)-
$25.00. Tax liens not included in UCC search. Tax
lien search- $10.00 per debtor. Mortgage and
property searches available. RE record copy- $1.00
per page. UCC copy- $2.00 per page. Cert fee:
$5.00 per cert. Payee: Brazos County Clerk. **Online
Access to Appraiser, Property Tax records:** Access
to County Appraisal District data is free at
www.brazoscad.org. Also, see notes at beginning of
section. **Other phones:** Assessor-979-361-7400;
Treasurer-979-361-4340; Appraiser-979-774-4100;
Elections-979-361-4124; Vital Records-979-361-4528.

Brewster County

County Clerk, PO Box 119, Alpine, TX 79831. **Phone**-
County Clerk, R/E & UCC Recording- 432-837-3366;
fax-432-837-6217; hours 8:30AM-5PM
Will search UCC records prior to 7/2001 & current
fixture files. Search per debtor- $10.00. Tax liens
not included in UCC search. Tax lien search-
$10.00 per debtor. Will search real estate records.
Copy fee- $1.00 per page. Cert fee: $5.00. **Online
Access to Property, Appraiser records:** Access to
property data is available for download from a private
company; fees apply; visit
www.ptax.org/tax_office_data.htm or phone 201-571-
0425. **Other phones:** Assessor-432-837-2214;
Treasurer-432-837-6200; Appraiser-432-837-2558;
Elections-432-837-6230; Vital Records-432-837-3366.

Briscoe County

County Clerk, PO Box 555, Silverton, TX 79257.
Phone-County Clerk, R/E & UCC Recording- 806-
823-2134; fax-806-823-2359; hours 8AM-5PM
Will search UCC records prior to 7/2001 & current
fixture files. Search per debtor- $11.00. Tax liens
not included in UCC search. Federal/state
combined tax lien search- $5.00 per debtor. Will
search real estate records. Record copy fee- $1.00 per
page. Cert fee: $5.00. Payee: County Clerk. **Other
phones:** Assessor-806-823-2136; Treasurer-806-823-
2133; Appraiser-806-823-2161; Elections-806-823-
2134; Vital Records-806-823-2134.

Brooks County

County Clerk, PO Box 427, Falfurrias, TX 78355.
Phone-361-325-5604, R/E Recording-361-325-5604
x1; fax-361-325-4944.
Will search UCC records. Search per debtor- $10.00.
Federal/state combined tax lien search- $10.00 per
search. Will not search real estate records. Copy fee-
$1.00 per page. Cert fee: $5.00 per doc + $1.00 per
page. Payee: Brooks County Clerk. **Other phones:**
Assessor-361-325-5604 x226; Treasurer-361-325-5604
x229; Appraiser-361-325-5681.

Brown County

County Clerk, 200 S. Broadway, Courthouse,
Brownwood, TX 76801. **Phone**-325-643-2594; hours
8:30AM-5PM
Will search UCC records. Search per debtor- $10.00.
Search request using non-standard form (per
name)- $25.00. Tax liens not included in UCC
search. Separate federal/state combined tax lien
search- $10.00 per debtor. Will not search real estate
records. RE record copy- $1.00 per page. UCC
copy- $1.50 per page. Cert fee: $5.00 per cert.
Payee: Brown County Clerk. **Online Access to
Appraiser, Property Tax records:** Access to
Appraisal District records is free at
http://65.107.178.35/clientdb/main.asp?id=30. Also, see
note at beginning of section. **Other phones:** Assessor-
325-643-1646; Treasurer-325-646-6033; Appraiser-
325-643-5676; Elections-325-643-2594; Vital Records-
325-643-2594.

Burleson County

County Clerk, 100 W Buck St #203, Caldwell, TX
77836. **Phone**-979-567-2329; fax-979-567-2376; hours
8AM-5PM. Will not search records. Record copy-
$1.00 per page. Cert fee: $5.00 per cert. Payee:
Burleson County Clerk. **Online Access to
Appraiser, Property Tax records:** See note at
beginning of section; www.txcountydata.com. **Other
phones:** Assessor-979-567-2336; Appraiser-979-567-
2318; Elections-979 567 2306.

Burnet County

County Clerk, 220 S. Pierce St, Burnet, TX 78611.
Phone-County Clerk, R/E & UCC Recording- 512-
756-5406; fax-512-756-5410; hours 8AM-5PM
Will search UCC records prior to 7/2001 & current
fixture files. Search per debtor- $10.00. Tax liens
not included in UCC search. Federal/state
combined tax lien search- $10.00 per debtor. Will
not search real estate records. RE record copy- $1.00
per page. UCC copy- $1.50 per page. Cert fee:
$5.00 per cert. Payee: Burnet County Clerk. **Online
Access to Appraiser, Property Tax, Land,
Grantor/Grantee records:** The grantor/grantee index
is at www.titlex.com. Select Burnet from the county list.
Records range from 1/1998 to 11/2001. Also, see note
at beginning of section. **Other phones:** Assessor-512-
756-5420; Treasurer-512-756-5498; Appraiser-512-
756-8291; Elections-512-756-5406; Vital Records-512-
756-5406.

Caldwell County

County Clerk, PO Box 906, Lockhart, TX 78644-0906.
Phone-512-398-1804; hours 8:30AM-Noon, 1-5PM
Will search UCC records prior to 7/2001 & current
fixture files. Search per debtor- $10.00. Tax liens
not included in UCC search. Tax lien search-
$5.00 per debtor. RE owner, mortgage, property
transfer searches available. Record copy- $1.00 per
page. Cert fee: $5.00 per cert. Payee: Caldwell
County Clerk. **Online Access to Appraiser, Property
Tax, Personal Property records:** Access the county
Appraisal District database now free at
www.txcountydata.com. The old website is not longer
working. Also, see notes at beginning of section. **Other

phones:** Assessor-512-398-1830; Treasurer-512-398-
1800; Appraiser-512-398-0550; Elections-512-398-
1830; Vital Records-512-398-1804.

Calhoun County

County Clerk, 211 S. Ann, Port Lavaca, TX 77979.
Phone-County Clerk, R/E & UCC Recording- 361-
553-4411; fax-361-553-4420; hours 8AM-5PM
Will search UCC records. Search per debtor- $10.00.
Tax liens not included in UCC search. Separate
federal tax lien search- $10.00; state lien- $5.00
per debtor. Will not search real estate records. Copy
fee- $1.00 per page. Min. of $5.00. Cert fee: $5.00
per cert + $1.00 per page. Payee: County Clerk.
**Online Access to Land, Grantor/Grantee,
Judgment, Lien, Grantor/Grantee records:** The
grantor/grantee index is at www.titlex.com. Select
Calhoun from the county list. Records range up to
9/2003. Also, see note at beginning of section. **Other
phones:** Assessor-361-552-8808; Treasurer-361-553-
4620; Appraiser-361-552-8808; Elections-361-553-
4440; Vital Records-361-553-4411.

Callahan County

County Clerk, 100 W. 4th, #104, Courthouse, Baird,
TX 79504. **Phone**-County Clerk, R/E & UCC
Recording- 325-854-1217; fax-325-854-1227; hours
8AM-5PM
Will search UCC records. Search per debtor- $11.00.
Search request using non-standard form (per
name)- $26.00. Tax liens not included in UCC
search. Separate federal/state combined tax lien
search- $20.00 per debtor. Will not search real estate
records. Record copy- $1.00 per page. Cert fee:
$5.00 per cert. Payee: Callahan County Clerk.
Other phones: Assessor-915-854-1020; Treasurer-
325-854-1399; Appraiser-325-854-1165; Elections-
325-854-1217; Vital Records-325-854-1217.

Cameron County

County Clerk, PO Box 2178, Brownsville, TX 78520.
Phone-County Clerk, R/E & UCC Recording- 956-
544-0815, UCC Recording-956-550-1329; fax-956-
544-0813; hours 8AM-5PM
Will search UCC records prior to 7/2001 & current
fixture files. Search per debtor- $10.00. Search
request using non-standard form (per name)-
$25.00. Federal/state combined tax lien search-
$5.00 per debtor. Will search real estate records.
Copy fee- $1.00 per page. Cert fee: $5.00 per doc.
Payee: Cameron County Clerk. **Online Access to
Appraiser, Property Tax records:** See note at
beginning of section. **Other phones:** Assessor-956-
544-0800; Treasurer-956-544-0819; Appraiser-956-
399-9322 or 541-3365; Elections-956-544-0809; Vital
Records-956-544-0817.

Camp County

County Clerk, 126 Church St, Rm 102, Pittsburg, TX
75686. **Phone**-County Clerk, R/E & UCC Recording-
903-856-2731; fax-903-856-2309; hours 8AM-5PM
Will search UCC records prior to 7/2001 & current
fixture files. Search per debtor- $10.00. Tax liens
not included in UCC search. Tax lien search-
$10.00 per debtor. Will not search real estate records.
Copy fee- $1.00 per page. Cert fee: $5.00. Payee:
Camp County Clerk. **Other phones:** Assessor-903-
856-3391; Treasurer-903-856-7862; Appraiser-903-
856-6538; Elections-903-856-2731; Vital Records-903-
856-2731.

Carson County

County Clerk, PO Box 487, Panhandle, TX 79068.
Phone-County Clerk, R/E & UCC Recording- 806-
537-3873; fax-806-537-3623; 8AM-Noon, 1-5PM
Will search UCC records prior to 7/2001 & current
fixture files. Search per debtor- $10.00. UCC search
includes tax liens if requested. Will not search real

estate records. Record copy- $1.00 per page. Cert fee: $5.00 per cert. Payee: Carson County Clerk. **Other phones:** Assessor-806-537-3412; Treasurer-806-537-3753; Appraiser-806-537-3569; Elections-806-537-3873; Vital Records-806-537-3873.

Cass County

County Clerk, PO Box 449, Linden, TX 75563. **Phone-**County Clerk, R/E & UCC Recording- 903-756-5071; fax-903-756-5732; hours 8AM-5PM. Will search UCC records prior to 7/2001 & current fixture files. Search per debtor- $10.00. Search request using non-standard form (per name)- $25.00. UCC search includes tax liens if lien filed in Deed records. Tax lien search- $10.00 per debtor. Will not search real estate records. Copy fee- $1.00 per page. Cert fee: $5.00. Payee: Cass County Clerk. **Other phones:** Assessor-903-756-5313; Treasurer-903-756-7626; Appraiser-903-756-7545; Elections-903-756-5071; Vital Records-903-756-5071.

Castro County

County Clerk, 100 E. Bedford, Rm 101, Dimmitt, TX 79027-2643. **Phone-**County Clerk, R/E & UCC Recording- 806-647-3338; hours 8AM-5PM
Will search UCC records prior to 7/2001 & current fixture files. Search per debtor- $16.00. Tax liens not included in UCC search. Federal/state combined tax lien search- $16.00 per debtor. Will not search real estate records. Record copy- $1.00 per page. Cert fee: $5.00 per cert. Payee: Castro County Clerk. **Other phones:** Assessor-806-647-5336; Treasurer-806-647-5534; Appraiser-806-647-5131; Elections-806-647-3338; Vital Records-806-647-3338.

Chambers County

County Clerk, PO Box 728, Anahuac, TX 77514. **Phone-**409-267-8309; fax-409-267-8315; 8AM-5PM
Will not search UCC or real estate records. UCC copy- $1.00 per page. Cert fee: $5.00 per cert. Payee: Chambers County Clerk. **Online Access to Property Tax, Appraiser records:** Search the appraiser property tax database for free at www.chamberscad.org. Also, see note at beginning of section. **Other phones:** Assessor-409-267-8301; Treasurer-409-267-8286; Appraiser-409-267-3795.

Cherokee County

County Clerk, PO Box 420, Rusk, TX 75785. **Phone-**County Clerk, R/E & UCC Recording- 903-683-2350; fax-903-683-5931.
Will search UCC records prior to 7/2001 & current fixture files. Search per debtor- $10.00. Search request using non-standard form (per name)- $25.00. Will not search real estate or tax lien records. **Online Access to Land, Grantor/Grantee, Judgment, Lien, Property Tax, Appraiser records:** The grantor/grantee index is at www.titlex.com. Select Cherokee from the county list. Records range from 5/1973 to 2/2004. Also, see note at beginning of section. Also, search the Cherokee CAD database for free at http://65.107.178.35/clientdb/main.asp?id=2. **Other phones:** Assessor-903-683-5478; Treasurer-903-683-4935; Appraiser-903-683-2296; Elections-903-683-2350; Vital Records-903-683-2350.

Childress County

County Clerk, Courthouse Box 4, Childress, TX 79201. **Phone-**County Clerk, R/E & UCC Recording- 940-937-6143; fax-940-937-3479; hours 8:30AM-5PM
Will search UCC records. Search per debtor- $10.00. Will not search real estate or tax lien records. Copy fee- $1.00 per page. Cert fee: $5.00 per instrument. Payee: County Clerk, Zona Prince. **Other phones:** Assessor-940-937-2232; Treasurer-940-937-6271; Appraiser-940-937-6062; Elections-940-937-6143; Vital Records-940-937-6143.

Clay County

County Clerk, PO Box 548, Henrietta, TX 76365. **Phone-**940-538-4631; hours 8AM-5PM
Will search UCC records. UCC search per debtor- $10.00. Will do tax lien search. Will not search real estate records. RE record copy- $1.00 per page. UCC copy- $2.00 per page. Cert fee: $5.00 per cert. Payee: Clay County Clerk. **Online Access to Property Tax records:** See note at beginning of section. **Other phones:** Assessor-940-538-4356; Appraiser-940-538-4311.

Cochran County

County Clerk, 100 N. Main, Courthouse, Morton, TX 79346-2598. **Phone-**County Clerk, R/E & UCC Recording- 806-266-5450; fax-806-266-9027; hours 8AM-5PM. Will search UCC records prior to 7/2001 & current fixture files. Search per debtor- $10.00. Search request using non-standard form (per name)- $25.00. Tax liens not included in UCC search. Separate federal tax lien-$10.00; state tax lien- $5.00 per debtor. RE owner, mortgage, property transfer searches available. Record copy- $1.00 per page. Cert fee: $5.00 per cert. Payee: Cochran County Clerk. **Other phones:** Assessor-806-266-5171; Treasurer-806-266-5161; Appraiser-806-266-5584; Elections-806-266-5450; Vital Records-806-266-5450.

Coke County

County Clerk, PO Box 150, Robert Lee, TX 76945. **Phone-**County Clerk, R/E & UCC Recording- 325-453-2631; fax-325-453-2650; hours 8AM-5PM
Will search UCC records prior to 7/2001 & current fixture files. Search per debtor- $10.00. Search request using non-standard form (per name)- $25.00. Tax liens not included in UCC search. Federal/state combined tax lien search- $18.00 per debtor. Will not search real estate records. RE record copy- $1.00 per page. UCC copy- $2.00 per page. Cert fee: $5.00 per cert. Payee: Coke County Clerk. **Other phones:** Assessor-325-453-2614; Treasurer-325-453-2713; Appraiser-325-453-4528; Elections-325-453-2631; Vital Records-325-453-2631.

Coleman County

County Clerk, PO Box 591, Coleman, TX 76834. **Phone-**325-625-2889; hours 8AM-5PM
Will search UCC records. Search per debtor- $10.00. Will not search real estate or tax lien records. Record copy- $1.00 per page. Cert fee: $5.00 per cert. Payee: Coleman County Clerk. **Other phones:** Assessor-325-625-2153; Treasurer-325-625-4221; Appraiser-325-625-4155.

Collin County

County Clerk, 200 S. McDonald, Annex "A", #120, McKinney, TX 75069. **Phone-**County Clerk, R/E & UCC Recording- 972-548-4134, UCC Recording-972-548-4151; hours 8AM-5PM (8AM-4PM Land Recording) www.co.collin.tx.us
Will search UCC records prior to 7/2001 & current fixture files. Search per debtor- $10.00. Search request using non-standard form (per name)- $30.00. UCC search includes tax liens if requested. Separate federal/state combined tax lien search- $20.00 per debtor. Will not search real estate records. Record copy- $1.00 per page. Cert fee: $5.00 per cert. Payee: Collin County Clerk. **Online Access to Appraiser, Property Tax, Business Personal Property, Deed, Lien, Judgment, Vital Statistic, Mortgage records:** Access to the county clerk Deeds database is free at www.collincountytexas.gov/DeedSearch. Also, search the Appraiser's property tax and business property database for free at www.collincad.org/search.php. Also, search the tax assessor and collector look up free

at www.co.collin.tx.us/tax_assessor/taxstmt_search.jsp. Also, see note at beginning of section. **Other phones:** Assessor-972-547-5020; Treasurer-972-548-4202; Appraiser-972-578-5200; Elections-972-547-1900; Vital Records-972-548-4134.

Collingsworth County

County Clerk, 800 West Ave, Box 10, Wellington, TX 79095. **Phone-**County Clerk, R/E & UCC Recording-806-447-2408; fax-806-447-5418; hours 9AM-5PM
Will search UCC records prior to 7/2001 & current fixture files. Search per debtor- $16.00. Search request using non-standard form (per name)- $31.00. Tax liens not included in UCC search. Separate federal/state combined tax lien search- $10.00 per debtor. Real estate record owner searches available. Record copy- $1.00 per page. Cert fee: $5.00 per cert. Payee: Collingsworth County Clerk. **Other phones:** Assessor-806-447-5606; Treasurer-806-447-2616; Appraiser-806-447-5172; Elections-806-447-2408; Vital Records-806-447-2408.

Colorado County

County Clerk, PO Box 68, Columbus, TX 78934. **Phone-**979-732-2155, R/E Recording-979-732-6561 or 2155, UCC Recording-979-732-6561 or 2155; fax-979-732-8852; hours 8AM-5PM
Will not search UCC or tax liens records. Will search real estate records. Record copy- $1.00 per page. Cert fee: $5.00 per cert. Payee: Colorado County Clerk. **Online Access to Land, Grantor/Grantee, Judgment, Lien, Grantor/Grantee, Cemetery records:** The grantor/grantee index is at www.titlex.com. Select Colorado from the county list. Records range is 5/1997 to 9/2001. Also, vital statistics are free from an unofficial at www.rootsweb.com/~txcolora/vitalrecords.htm. Divorces go back to 1968; deaths back to 1964; marriages back to 1966. Also, see note at beginning of section. **Other phones:** Assessor-979-732-2710; Treasurer-979-732-2865; Appraiser-979-732-8222; Vital Records-979-732-6561 or 2155.

Comal County

County Clerk, 150 N Seguin, #101, #104, New Braunfels, TX 78130. **Phone-**830-620-5513; fax-830-620-3410; hours 8AM-4:30PM www.co.comal.tx.us
Will search UCC records prior to 7/2001 & current fixture files. Search per debtor- $10.00. Search request using non-standard form (per name)- $25.00. **Other phones:** Assessor-830-620-5521; Treasurer-830-620-5506; Appraiser-830-625-8597; Elections-830-620-5538; Vital Records-830-620-5515.

Comanche County

County Clerk, Courthouse, Comanche, TX 76442. **Phone-**County Clerk, R/E & UCC Recording- 325-356-2655; fax-325-356-5764; hours 8:30-5PM
Will search UCC records prior to 7/2001 & current fixture files. Search per debtor- $10.00. Search request using non-standard form (per name)- $25.00. UCC search includes tax liens if requested. Will not search real estate records. Record copy- $1.00 per page. Cert fee: $5.00 per cert. Payee: Comanche County Clerk. **Online Access to Appraiser, Property Tax records:** See note at beginning of section. **Other phones:** Assessor-325-356-3101; Treasurer-325-356-2838; Appraiser-325-356-5253; Elections-325-356-2655; Vital Records-325-356-2655.

Concho County

County Clerk, PO Box 98, Paint Rock, TX 76866-0098. **Phone-**County Clerk, R/E & UCC Recording-325-732-4322; fax-325-732-2040; 8:30AM-5PM
Will search UCC records prior to 7/2001 & current fixture files. Search per debtor- $10.00. Search request using non-standard form (per name)-

$25.00. UCC search includes tax liens if requested. Separate federal/state combined tax lien search-$5.00 per debtor. Real estate record owner and mortgage searches available. Record copy- $1.00 per page. Cert fee: $5.00 per cert. Payee: Concho County Clerk. **Other phones:** Assessor-325-732-4460; Treasurer-325-732-4279; Appraiser-325-732-4389; Elections-325-732-4322; Vital Records-325-732-4322.

Cooke County

County Clerk, Courthouse, Gainesville, TX 76240. **Phone**-County Clerk, R/E & UCC Recording- 940-668-5420, UCC Recording-940-668-5474; fax-940-668-5440; hours 8AM-5PM

Will search UCC records prior to 7/2001 & current fixture files. Search per debtor- $10.00. Search request using non-standard form (per name)- $25.00. Tax lien search- $10.00 per debtor. Will not search real estate records. Copy fee- $1.00 per page. Cert fee: $5.00 per cert. Payee: County Clerk. **Online Access to Property, Appraiser records:** Access to the Cooke CAD Live database is free at http://65.107.178.35/clientdb/main.asp?id=10. **Other phones:** Assessor-940-668-5425; Treasurer-940-668-5423; Appraiser-940-665-7651; Elections-940-668-5420; Vital Records-940-668-5421.

Coryell County

County Clerk, PO Box 237, Gatesville, TX 76528. **Phone**-254-865-5911, R/E Recording-254-865-5911 x235; fax-254-865-8631.

Will search UCC records prior to 7/2001 & current fixture files. Search per debtor- $10.00. Will not search real estate or tax lien records. UCC copy- $1.00 per page. Cert fee: $5.00 per doc. **Online Access to Property, Appraiser, Recording, Real Estate records:** Access to the Appraisal Distrct proeprty records is avaialble free at www.coryellcad.org/searchrecords.htm. Also, real estate recording records may be at http://apolloplus.com in 2004. **Other phones:** Assessor-254-865-6593; Appraiser-254-865-6593.

Cottle County

County Clerk, PO Box 717, Paducah, TX 79248. **Phone**-806-492-3823; hours 9AM-12-1-5PM

Will search UCC records. Search per debtor- $10.00. Search request using non-standard form (per name)- $25.00. UCC search includes tax liens if requested. RE owner, mortgage, property transfer searches available. UCC copy- $1.50 per page. Cert fee: $5.00 per cert. Payee: Cottle County Clerk. **Other phones:** Assessor-806-492-3345; Treasurer-806-492-3738; Appraiser-806-492-3345.

Crane County

County Clerk, PO Box 578, Crane, TX 79731. **Phone**-432-558-3581; hours 9AM-Noon, 1-5PM

Will not search records. RE record copy- $1.00 per page. UCC copy- $2.00 per page. Cert fee: $5.00 per cert. Payee: Crane County Clerk. **Other phones:** Assessor-432-558-2622; Treasurer-432-558-3372; Appraiser-432-558-1021; Elections-432-558-3581; Vital Records-432-558-3581.

Crockett County

County Clerk, PO Drawer C, Ozona, TX 76943. **Phone**-County Clerk, R/E & UCC Recording- 325-392-2022; fax-325-392-3742.

Will search UCC records prior to 7/2001 & current fixture files. Search per debtor- $10.00. Search request using non-standard form (per name)- $25.00. Separate federal & state combined tax lien search- $10.00 per debtor. Will not search real estate records. Copy fee- $1.00 per page. Cert fee: $5.00 per cert. Payee: Crockett County Clerk. **Other phones:** Assessor-325-392-2674; Treasurer-325-392-

3376; Appraiser-325-392-2674; Elections-325-392-2022; Vital Records-325-392-2022.

Crosby County

County Clerk, 201 W Aspen St, Rm 102, Crosbyton, TX 79322. **Phone**-806-675-2334; 8AM-N, 1-5PM

Will not search UCC or real estate records. Separate federal/state combined tax lien search- $10.00 per debtor. RE record copy- $1.00 per page. UCC copy- $2.00 per page. Cert fee: $5.00 per cert. Payee: Crosby County Clerk. **Other phones:** Assessor-806-675-2311; Appraiser-806-675-2356.

Culberson County

County Clerk, PO Box 158, Van Horn, TX 79855. **Phone**-432-283-2058; fax-432-283-9234; hours 8AM-12, 1PM-5PM

Will search UCC records prior to 7/2001 & current fixture files. Search per debtor- $10.00. Search request using non-standard form (per name)- $25.00. Federal/state combined tax lien search- $10.00 per debtor. Will search real estate records. Copy fee-$1.00 per page. Copy fee is $1.00 per page. Cert fee: $5.00 per cert. Payee: County Clerk. **Other phones:** Assessor-432-283-2130; Treasurer-432-283-2115; Appraiser-432-283-2977; Elections-432-283-2058; Vital Records-432-283-2058.

Dallam County

County Clerk, PO Box 1352, Dalhart, TX 79022. **Phone**-806-249-4751, R/E Recording-806-244-4751, UCC Recording-806-244-4751; fax-806-249-2252.

Will not search UCC or real estate records. Federal/state combined tax lien search- $10.00 per debtor. RE record copy- $1.00 per page. Cert fee: $5.00 per doc. Payee: Dallam County District Clerk. **Other phones:** Assessor-806-244-2801; Appraiser-806-249-6767; Elections-806-244-4751; Vital Records-806-244-4751.

Dallas County

County Clerk, 509 Main St., Records Bldg, 2nd Fl, Dallas, TX 75202-3502. **Phone**-214-653-7275, R/E Recording-214-653-7131, UCC Recording-214-653-7135; fax-214-653-7082; hours 8AM-4:30PM www.dallascounty.org/html/citizen-serv/county-clerk/ Will search UCC records prior to 7/2001 & current fixture files. Search per debtor- $10.00; use UCC-11 form. Search request using non-standard form (per name)- $25.00. Tax liens not included in UCC search. Separate federal/state combined tax lien search- $5.00 per debtor. Will not search real estate records. RE record copy- $1.00; min. $5.00. UCC copy- $1.00 per page. Cert fee: $5.00 per cert. Payee: Dallas County Clerk. **Online Access to Property Tax, Personal Property, Voter Registration, Marriage, UCC, Assumed Name, Probate records:** Name search indices of marriages, assumed names, UCCs, probate, court records (and soon, real estate) back to 1977 on the new online records search system at www.dallascounty.org/applications/english/record-search/intro.html. Indices include DOB. Fee to view and print docs; credit cards accepted. Purchase per item or subscribe for $75 annual fee to save costs. Also, online access to the Central Appraisal District database is free at www.dallascad.org/SearchOwner.aspx. Also, access to the County Voter Registration Records is free online at www.openrecords.org/records/voting/dallas_voting. Search by name or partial name. **Other phones:** Assessor-214-653-0520; Treasurer-214-653-7321; Appraiser-214-631-0520; Elections-214-819-6300; Vital Records-314-653-7978.

Dawson County

County Clerk, PO Drawer 1268, Lamesa, TX 79331. **Phone**-806-872-3778, R/E Recording-806-872-

3778/7685, UCC Recording-806-872-3778/7685; fax-806-872-2473; hours 8:30AM-5PM

Will search UCC records prior to 7/2001 & current fixture files. Search per debtor- $10.00. Tax liens not included in UCC search. Tax lien search-$10.00 per debtor. Will not search real estate records. Record copy- $1.00 per page. Cert fee: $5.00 per cert. Payee: Dawson County Clerk. **Other phones:** Assessor-806-872-7181; Treasurer-806-872-7474; Appraiser-806-872-7060; Elections-806-872-3778; Vital Records-806-872-3778.

De Witt County

County Clerk, 307 N. Gonzales, Courthouse, Cuero, TX 77954. **Phone**-361-275-3724; fax-361-275-8994; hours 8AM-Noon, 1-5PM

Will search UCC records prior to 7/2001 & current fixture files. Search per debtor- $10.00. Search request using non-standard form (per name)- $25.00. Tax liens not included in UCC search, must search each location. Will not search real estate records. Record copy- $1.00 per page. Cert fee: $5.00 per cert. Payee: De Witt County Clerk. **Other phones:** Assessor-361-275-3410; Appraiser-361-275-5753.

Deaf Smith County

County Clerk, 235 E. 3rd, Rm 203, Hereford, TX 79045-5542. **Phone**-County Clerk, R/E & UCC Recording- 806-363-7077; fax-806-363-7023; hours 8AM-5PM

Will search UCC records prior to 7/2001 & current fixture files. Search per debtor- $10.00. Search request using non-standard form (per name)- $25.00. Tax liens not included in UCC search. Federal/state combined tax lien search- $5.00 per debtor. Will not search real estate records. Record copy- $1.00 per page. Cert fee: $5.00 per cert. Payee: Deaf Smith County Clerk. **Other phones:** Treasurer-806-363-7088; Appraiser-806-364-0625; Elections-806-363-7077; Vital Records-806-363-7077.

Delta County

County Clerk, 200 W. Dallas Ave, Cooper, TX 75432. **Phone**-903-395-4400, R/E Recording-903-395-4400 x222, UCC Recording-903-395-4400 x222; fax-903-395-2178; hours 8AM-5PM

Will search UCC records. Search per debtor- $10.00. UCC search includes tax liens if requested. Separate state/federal Tax lien search- $5.00 per debtor. RE owner, mortgage, property transfer searches available. RE record copy- $1.00 per page. UCC copy- $2.00 per page. Cert fee: $5.00 per cert. Payee: Delta County Clerk. **Other phones:** Assessor-903-395-4400 x228; Treasurer-903-395-4400 x225; Appraiser-903-395-4118; Elections-903-395-4400 x222; Vital Records-903-395-4400 x222.

Denton County

County Clerk, PO Box 2187, Denton, TX 76202-2187. **Phone**-County Clerk, R/E & UCC Recording- 940-349-2010; fax-940-349-2013/Non-filings; 8AM-5PM; 8AM-4:30, W www.dentoncounty.com/dept/ccl.htm Will search UCC records prior to 7/2001 & current fixture files. Search per debtor- $10.00. Search request using non-standard form (per name)- $25.00. Tax liens not included in UCC search. Tax lien search- $10.00 per debtor. Real estate record owner searches available. Record copy- $1.00 per page. Cert fee: $5.00 per cert, $1.00 per page. Payee: Denton County Clerk, Cynthia Mitchell. **Online Access to Real Estate, Property, Recording, Voter Registration, Most Wanted, Parollee, Sex Offender, Bond, Jail, Conviction records:** Access to the county property database indices is free for name/instrument searches. There is no fee for access, but to print is $1.00 per page. Visit https://www.texaslandrecords.com/txlr/TxlrApp/index.j

sp. And, with a full subscription, you can search full indices and download images. Also, search the voter registration rolls for free at http://elections.dentoncounty.com/VRSearch/default.as p. Search the "justice" database for free at http://justice.dentoncounty.com. Includes Parolees, sex offenders, most wanted lists, bond, jail, convictions and court records databases. **Other phones:** Assessor-940-349-3500; Treasurer-940-349-3150; Appraiser-940-349-3800; Elections-940-349-3200; Vital Records-940-349-2018; Admin-940-349-2012.

Dickens County

County Clerk, PO Box 120, Dickens, TX 79229. **Phone**-806-623-5531; fax-806-623-5319; hours 8AM-Noon, 1-5PM
Will search UCC records prior to 7/2001 & current fixture files. Search per debtor- $5.00. UCC search includes tax liens if requested. Separate state/federal Tax lien search- $10.00. Will search real estate records. Copy fee-$1.00 per page. UCC copy- $1.00 per page. Cert fee: $5.00 per cert. Payee: Dickens County Clerk. **Other phones:** Assessor-806-623-5216; Appraiser-806-623-5216; Elections-806-623-5531.

Dimmit County

County Clerk, 103 N. 5th St, Carrizo Springs, TX 78834. **Phone**-County Clerk, R/E & UCC Recording-830-876-2323 x233; fax-830-876-4205; hours 8AM-5PM
Will search UCC records prior to 7/2001 & current fixture files. Search per debtor- $10.00. Tax lien search- $10.00 per 10 years. Will search real estate records. Copy fee- $1.00 per page. **Other phones:** Assessor-830-876-4246 x1; Treasurer-830-876-4246 x3; Appraiser-830-876-3420; Elections-830-876-2323 #234; Vital Records-830-876-2323 x233.

Donley County

County Clerk, PO Drawer U, Clarendon, TX 79226. **Phone**-County Clerk, R/E & UCC Recording- 806-874-3436; fax-806-874-5146; hours 8AM-N, 1-5PM
Will search UCC records prior to 7/2001 & current fixture files. Search per debtor- $10.00. Search request using non-standard form (per name)- $25.00. Will search tax liens including federal tax liens. Tax lien search- $5.00 per debtor. Will search real estate records. UCC copy- $1.00 per page. Payee: Donley County District Clerk. **Online Access to Property, Appraiser records:** Access to property data is available for download from a private company; fees apply; visit www.ptax.org/tax_office_data.htm or phone 201-571-0425. **Other phones:** Assessor-806-874-2193; Treasurer-806-874-2328; Appraiser-806-874-2744; Elections-806-874-3436; Vital Records-806-874-3436.

Duval County

County Clerk, PO Box 248, San Diego, TX 78384. **Phone**-361-279-3322 x271/2, R/E Recording-361-279-3322 x272, UCC Recording-361-279-3322 x272; fax-361-279-3159; hours 8AM-Noon, 1-5PM
Will search UCC records prior to 7/2001 & current fixture files. Search per debtor- $10.00. Tax liens not included in UCC search. Tax lien search- $10.00 per debtor. Will search real estate records. Record copy- $1.00 per page. Cert fee: $5.00 per cert. Payee: Duval County Clerk. **Other phones:** Assessor-361-279-3322; Treasurer-361-279-6128; Appraiser-361-279-3305; Elections-361-279-3322 x272; Vital Records-361-279-3322 x272.

Eastland County

County Clerk, PO Box 110, Eastland, TX 76448-0110. **Phone**-County Clerk, R/E & UCC Recording- 254-629-1583; fax-254-629-8125; hours 8AM-5PM

Will search UCC records. Search per debtor- $10.00. Search request using non-standard form (per name)- $25.00. Tax liens not included in UCC search. Tax lien search- $5.00 per search. Will not search real estate records. Copy fee- $1.00 per page. Cert fee: $5.00 per cert. Payee: Eastland County Clerk. **Online Access to Vital Statistic records:** Access to vital statistics from an unofficial source free at http://ftp.rootsweb.com/pub/usgenweb/tx/eastland/vitals /. Births go back to 1926; deaths to 1964, Divorce to 1968, Marriages to 1966. **Other phones:** Assessor-254-629-1564; Treasurer-254-629-2672; Appraiser-254-629-8597; Elections-254-629-1583; Vital Records-254-629-1583.

Ector County

County Clerk, PO Box 707, Odessa, TX 79760. **Phone**-432-498-4130; fax-432-498-4177; 8AM-4:30PM
Will search UCC records. Search per debtor- $10.00. Search request using non-standard form (per name)- $25.00. Federal/state combined tax lien search- $10.00 per debtor. Will search real estate records if volume and page number is provided. Copy fee- $1.00 per page. Cert fee: $5.00 per cert. Payee: Linda Haney, County Clerk. **Online Access to Real Estate, Appraiser, Personal Property records:** Search the county appraisal district database for free at www.ectorcad.org/real_name.html. **Other phones:** Assessor-432-498-4050; Treasurer-432-498-4060; Appraiser-432-332-6834; Elections-432-498-4030.

Edwards County

County Clerk, PO Box 184, Rocksprings, TX 78880-0184. **Phone**-830-683-2235; fax-830-683-5376; hours 8AM-5PM. Will search UCC records. Search per debtor- $10.00. Search request using non-standard form (per name)- $25.00. Separate federal/state combined tax lien search- $10.00 per debtor. Will search real estate records. Record copy- $1.00 per page. Cert fee: $5.00 per cert. Payee: Edwards County Clerk. **Other phones:** Assessor-830-683-2337; Treasurer-830-683-5116; Appraiser-830-683-4189.

El Paso County

County Clerk, 500 E. San Antonio, Rm 105, El Paso, TX 79901-2496. **Phone**-915-546-2074; hours 8AM-4:45PM
Will search UCC records prior to 7/2001 & current fixture files. Search per debtor- $5.00. Tax liens not included in UCC search. Separate federal tax lien search- $10.00 per debtor. RE owner, mortgage, property transfer searches available. RE record copy- $1.00 per page. UCC copy- $2.00 per page. Cert fee: $5.00 per cert. Payee: El Paso County Clerk. **Online Access to Assumed Name, Property Tax, Real Estate, Vital Statistic records:** Search vital statistics (birth, death, marriage), assumed names, and property (land) records free at www.co.el-paso.tx.us/search.htm. Also, search property tax data at www.elpasocad.org. Also, see note at beginning of section. **Other phones:** Assessor-915-541-4054; Appraiser-915-780-2000; Elections-915-546-2154.

Ellis County

County Clerk, PO Box 250, Waxahachie, TX 75168. **Phone**-County Clerk, R/E & UCC Recording- 972-923-5070; fax-972-923-5075; hours 8AM-4:30PM
Will search UCC records prior to 7/2001 & current fixture files. Search per debtor- per 5 years. UCC search includes tax liens if requested. Separate state/federal Tax lien search- $10.00. RE owner, mortgage, property transfer searches available. Copy fee-$1 per page. UCC copy- $1.00 per page. Cert fee: $5.00 per cert. Payee: Ellis County Clerk. **Online Access to Appraiser, Property Tax records:** Search the property appraiser database for free at

www.elliscad.org. Also, see note at beginning of section. **Other phones:** Assessor-972-923-5150; Treasurer-972-923-5125; Appraiser-972-937-3552; Elections-972-923-5195; Vital Records-972-923-5070.

Erath County

County Clerk, 100 W. Washington St., Courthouse, Stephenville, TX 76401. **Phone**-County Clerk, R/E & UCC Recording- 254-965-1482; fax-254-965-5732; hours 8AM-4PM. Will search UCC records prior to 7/2001 & current fixture files. Search per debtor- $10.00. Search request using non-standard form (per name)- $25.00. Tax liens not included in UCC search. Separate federal/state combined tax lien search- $10.00 per debtor. Will not search real estate records. RE record copy- $1.00 per page. UCC copy- $1.50 per page. Cert fee: $5.00 per cert. Payee: Erath County Clerk. **Online Access to Property Tax, Appraiser records:** Access to the county appraisal role is free at www.erathcad.org. Also, see note at beginning of section. **Other phones:** Assessor-254-965-8990; Treasurer-254-965-1483; Appraiser-254-965-7301. Elections-254-965-1482; Vital Records-254-965-1410.

Falls County

County Clerk, PO Box 458, Marlin, TX 76661. **Phone**-County Clerk, R/E & UCC Recording- 254-883-1408; fax-254-883-1406; hours 8AM-Noon, 1-5PM
Will search UCC records prior to 7/2001 & current fixture files. Search per debtor- $10.00. Tax liens not included in UCC search. Federal/state combined tax lien search- $5.00 per lien. Will not search real estate records. Record copy- $1.00 per page. Cert fee: $5.00 per cert. Payee: Falls County Clerk. **Other phones:** Assessor-254-883-1436; Treasurer-254-883-1433; Appraiser-254-883-2543; Elections-254-883-1408; Vital Records-254-883-1408.

Fannin County

County Clerk, 101 E. Sam Rayburn Dr., Courthouse, #102, Bonham, TX 75418-4346. **Phone**-903-583-7488, R/E Recording-903-583-7486; fax-903-583-9598; hours 8AM-5PM. Will search UCC records prior to 7/2001 & current fixture files. Search per debtor- $5.00. UCC search includes tax liens if requested. Separate state/federal Tax lien search- $10.00. Will not search real estate records. Record copy- $1.00 per page. Cert fee: $5.00 per cert. Payee: Fannin County Clerk. **Online Access to Appraiser, Property Tax records:** See notes at beginning of section. **Other phones:** Assessor-903-583-9546; Appraiser-903-583-8701.

Fayette County

County Clerk, PO Box 59, La Grange, TX 78945. **Phone**-979-968-3251, R/E Recording-409-968-3251; fax-979-968-8531; hours 8AM-Noon, 1-5PM www.co.fayette.tx.us
Will not search records. RE record copy- $1.00 per page. UCC copy- $2.00 per page. Cert fee: $5.00 per cert. Payee: Fayette County Clerk. **Other phones:** Assessor-979-968-3164; Treasurer-979-968-3055; Appraiser-979-968-8383; Elections-979-968-3251; Vital Records-979-968-3251.

Fisher County

County Clerk, PO Box 368, Roby, TX 79543-0368. **Phone**-325-776-2401; fax-325-776-3274; 8AM-5PM
Will search UCC records. Search per debtor- $10.00. Tax liens not included in UCC search. Tax lien search- $5.00 per debtor. Will search real estate records. Copy fee- $1.00 per page. **Other phones:** Assessor-325-776-2181; Treasurer-325-776-3257; Appraiser-325-776-2181; Elections-325-776-2401; Vital Records-325-776-2401.

Floyd County

County Clerk, 105 Main St, Courthouse, Rm 101, Floydada, TX 79235. **Phone-**County Clerk, R/E & UCC Recording- 806-983-4900; fax-806-983-4909; hours 8:30AM-12, 1-5PM

Will search UCC records prior to 7/2001 but no current fixture (land) files. Search per debtor- $10.00. Search request using non-standard form (per name)- $25.00. UCC search includes tax liens if requested. Separate state/federal Tax lien search- $10.00. Will not search real estate records. UCC copy- $1.00 per page. Cert fee: $1.00 per cert. Payee: Floyd County Clerk. **Other phones:** Assessor-806-983-4908; Treasurer-806-983-4910; Appraiser-806-983-5256; Elections-806-983-4900; Vital Records-806-983-4900.

Foard County

County Clerk, PO Box 539, Crowell, TX 79227. **Phone-**County Clerk, R/E & UCC Recording- 940-684-1365; fax-940-684-1918; hours 9AM-4:30PM

Will search UCC records prior to 7/2001 & current fixture files. Search per debtor- $10.00. Search request using non-standard form (per name)- $25.00. Tax liens not included in UCC search. Tax lien search- $10.00 per debtor. Will search real estate records. Record copy fee- $1.00 per page. Cert fee: $5.00. Payee: Foard County Clerk. **Other phones:** Assessor-940-684-1501; Treasurer-940-684-1818; Appraiser-940-684-1225; Elections-940-684-1365; Vital Records-940-684-1365.

Fort Bend County

County Clerk, 301 Jackson, #101, Richmond, TX 77469. **Phone-**County Clerk, R/E & UCC Recording- 281-341-8685; fax-281-341-8669; hours 8AM-4PM
www.co.fort-bend.tx.us

Will search UCC records prior to 7/2001 & current fixture files. Search per debtor- $10.00. Search request using non-standard form (per name)- $25.00. Will search federal tax liens. RE record copy- $1.00 per page. Records also available on CD-ROM. UCC copy- $1.50 per page, but not less that $5.00 per debtor per request. Cert fee: $5.00 per cert. Payee: Fort Bend County Clerk. Credit cards accepted (M/C or Visa). **Online Access to Real Estate, Lien, Grantor/Grantee, Appraiser, UCC, Marriage, Death, Birth, Probate records:** Access to the county clerk database is free at www.co.fort-bend.tx.us/admin_of_justice/County_Clerk/index_info_research.htm. Search the property index by name, or the plat index. And, search county probate and court records. For information, contact Diane Shepard at 281-341-8664. UCCs records can be searched for free at http://ccweb.co.fort-bend.tx.us/ucc/uccDefault.asp.
Also, the grantor/grantee index is at www.titlex.com. Select Ft Bend from the county list. Record range is 1/1974 to 11/2001. Also, see note at beginning of section for add'l fee service for tax records and recordings. **Other phones:** Assessor-281-341-3735; Treasurer-281-341-3750; Appraiser-281-344-8623; Elections-281-341-8670; Vital Records-281-341-8685.

Franklin County

County Clerk, PO Box 68, Mount Vernon, TX 75457-0068. **Phone-**County Clerk, R/E & UCC Recording- 903-537-4252 x6, fax-903-537-2982; hours-8AM-5PM www.co.franklin.tx.us/
Will search UCC records prior to 7/2001 & current fixture files. Search per debtor- $5.00. Tax liens not included in UCC search. Tax lien search- $5.00 per debtor. RE owner, mortgage, property transfer searches available. Record copy- $1.00 per page. Cert fee: $5.00 per cert. Payee: Franklin County Clerk. **Online Access to Property Tax records:** See note at beginning of section. **Other phones:** Assessor-

903-537-2358; Treasurer-903-537-2206 x8; Appraiser-903-537-2286; Elections-903-537-4252 x3; Vital Records-903-537-4252 ext 6.

Freestone County

County Clerk, PO Box 1010, Fairfield, TX 75840. **Phone-**903-389-2635; hours 8AM-5PM M-Th; 8AM-4:30PM F
Will not search UCC or real estate records. Federal/state combined tax lien search- $10.00 per debtor. UCC copy- $1.00 per page. Cert fee: $5.00 per cert. Payee: Freestone County Clerk. **Online Access to Appraiser records:** Search the Appraiser's property tax database for free at www.freestonecad.org/. **Other phones:** Assessor-903-389-2336; Treasurer-903-389-2180; Appraiser-903-389-5510; Elections-903-389-2635; Vital Records-903-389-2635.

Frio County

County Clerk, 500 E. San Antonio St, # 6, Pearsall, TX 78061. **Phone-**County Clerk, R/E & UCC Recording-830-334-2214; fax-830-334-0021; hours 8AM-Noon; 1-5PM. Will search UCC records prior to 7/2001 & current fixture files. Search per debtor- $10.00. Search request using non-standard form (per name)- $25.00. Tax lien search- $10.00 per debtor. Will search real estate records. Copy fee- $1.00 per page. Cert fee: $5.00 per cert. Payee: Frio County Clerk. **Other phones:** Assessor-830-334-2152; Treasurer-830-334-0040; Appraiser-830-334-4163; Elections-830-334-2214; Vital Records-830-334-2214.

Gaines County

County Clerk, 101 S. Main, Rm 107, Seminole, TX 79360. **Phone-**County Clerk, R/E & UCC Recording-432-758-4003, UCC Recording-432-758-4033; fax-432-758-1442; hours 8AM-5PM
Will search UCC records. Search per debtor- $10.00. Search request using non-standard form (per name)- $20.00. Tax liens not included in UCC search. Separate federal/state combined tax lien search-20.00 per debtor. Will not search real estate records. Record copy- $1.00 per page. Cert fee: $5.00 per cert. Payee: Gaines County Clerk. **Other phones:** Assessor-432-758-4008; Treasurer-432-758-4009; Appraiser-432-758-3263; Elections-432-758-4033 or 758-4003; Vital Records-432-758-4033.

Galveston County

County Clerk, PO Box 2450, Galveston, TX 77553-2450. **Phone-**409-766-2200, R/E-409-766-2208; hours 8AM-5PM www.co.galveston.tx.us/County_Clerk/
Will search UCC records prior to 7/2001 & current fixture files. Search per debtor- $10.00. Search request using non-standard form (per name)- $25.00. UCC search includes tax liens if requested. Separate state/federal Tax lien search- $10.00 per debtor. Will not search real estate records. RE record copy- $1.00 per page. UCC copy- $1.50 per page; $5.00 min. Cert fee: $5.00 per cert. Payee: Galveston County Clerk. **Online Access to Real Estate, Lien, Appraiser, Grantor/Grantee, Property Tax, Personal Property, Sheriff Sale, Most Wanted records:** Several sources exist. Access to County online records requires $200 escrow deposit, $25 monthly fee, + $.25 per minute. Index records date back to 1965; image docs to 1/95. Lending agency information and fax back services are available. For info, contact Mr. Dickinson at 409-766-5115. Also, Central Appraisal Dist. database is free at www.galvestoncad.org/search.htm. Also, search county most wanted list at www.co.galveston.tx.us/Sheriff/most_wanted.htm.
Also, online access to sheriff sales is free at www.co.galveston.tx.us/sheriff/sheriff.htm. A Grantor/Grantee index is at www.titlex.com; select Galveston County. Records go back to 1/1965. Also, see note at beginning of section. **Other phones:** Assessor-409-

766-2280; Treasurer-409-762-8621 x345; Appraiser-409-935-1980.

Garza County

County Clerk, PO Box 366, Post, TX 79356-0366. **Phone-**County Clerk, R/E & UCC Recording- 806-495-4430; fax-806-495-4431; 8AM-Noon, 1-5PM
Will search UCC records prior to 7/2001 & current fixture files. Search per debtor- $10.00. Search request using non-standard form (per name)- $25.00. Tax liens not included in UCC search. Federal/state combined tax lien search- $20.00 per search. Will not search real estate records. RE record copy- $1.00 per page. UCC copy- $2.00 per page. Cert fee: $5.00 per cert. Payee: Garza County Clerk. **Other phones:** Assessor-806-495-4448; Treasurer-806-495-4423; Appraiser-806-495-3518; Elections-806-495-4430; Vital Records-806-495-4430.

Gillespie County

County Clerk, 101 W. Main, Rm 109, Unit #13, Fredericksburg, TX 78624. **Phone-**830-997-6515; fax-830-997-9958; hours 8AM-4PM
Will search UCC records prior to 7/2001 & current fixture files. Search per debtor- $11.00. Search request using non-standard form (per name)- $26.00. UCC search includes tax liens if requested. Separate state/federal Tax lien search- $5.00 per debtor. Will not search real estate records. RE record copy- $1.00 per page. UCC copy- $2.00 per page. Cert fee: $10.00 per cert. Payee: Gillespie County Clerk. **Online Access to Appraiser, Property Tax records:** See note at beginning of section. **Other phones:** Assessor-830-997-6519; Treasurer-830-997-6521; Appraiser-830-997-9807; Elections-830-997-6515; Vital Records-830-997-6515.

Glasscock County

County Clerk, PO Box 190, Garden City, TX 79739. **Phone-**County Clerk, R/E & UCC Recording- 432-354-2371; fax-432-354-2348; hours 8AM-4PM
Will search UCC records prior to 7/2001 & current fixture files. Search per debtor- $10.00. Search request using non-standard form (per name)- $25.00. UCC search includes tax liens if requested. Separate state/federal Tax lien search- $10.00 per debtor. RE owner, mortgage, property transfer searches available. Record copy- $1.00 per page. Cert fee: $5.00 per cert. Payee: Glasscock County Clerk. **Other phones:** Assessor-432-354-2361; Treasurer-432-354-2415; Appraiser-432-354-2580; Elections-432-354-2371; Vital Records-432-354-2371.

Goliad County

County Clerk, PO Box 50, Goliad, TX 77963. **Phone-**County Clerk, R/E & UCC Recording- 361-645-3294; fax-361-645-3858; hours 8AM-Noon, 1PM-5PM
Will search UCC records prior to 7/2001 & current fixture files. Search per debtor- $10.00. UCC search includes tax liens. Separate federal/state combined tax lien search- $10.00 per debtor. Will not name search real estate records. Copy fee- $1.00 per page. Cert fee: $5.00 per cert + $1.00 per page. Payee: County Clerk. **Online Access to Real estate, Grantor/Grantee, Judgment, Lien, Property records:** The grantor/grantee index is at www.titlex.com. Select Goliad from the county list. Records range is 1/1950 to 12/2003. Also, see note at beginning of section. **Other phones:** Assessor-361-645-3354 or 2541; Treasurer-361-645-3551; Appraiser-361-645-2492; Elections-361-645-3294; Vital Records-361-645-3294.

Gonzales County

County Clerk, PO Box 77, Gonzales, TX 78629. **Phone-**County Clerk, R/E & UCC Recording- 830-672-2801; fax-830-672-2636.

Will search UCC records. UCC search per debtor-$5.00 per name. Will search tax liens including federal tax liens. Tax lien search- $5.00 per debtor. Will not search real estate records. RE record copy-$1.00 per page. UCC copy- $1.50 per page. Cert fee: $5.00 per instrument. Payee: County Clerk. **Other phones:** Assessor-830-627-2841; Treasurer-830-627-2621; Appraiser-830-672-2879; Vital Records-830-672-2801.

Gray County

County Clerk, PO Box 1902, Pampa, TX 79066-1902. **Phone-**County Clerk, R/E & UCC Recording- 806-669-8004; fax-806-669-8054; hours 8:30AM-Noon, 1-5PM
Will search UCC records. Search per debtor- $10.00 per name. Will not search real estate or tax lien records. Record copy- $1.00 per page. Cert fee: $5.00 per cert. Payee: Gray County Clerk. **Other phones:** Assessor-806-669-8018; Treasurer-806-669-8009; Appraiser-806-665-0791; Elections-806-669-8004; Vital Records-806-669-8004.

Grayson County

County Clerk, 100 W. Houston #17, Sherman, TX 75090. **Phone-**903-813-4243, R/E Recording-903-813-4238, UCC Recording-903-813-4239; fax-903-870-0829; 8AM-5PM www.co.grayson.tx.us/main.htm
Will search UCC records prior to 7/2001 & current fixture files. Search per debtor- $16.00. Will search federal tax liens. Will search real estate records. RE record copy- $1.00 per page. UCC copy- $2.00 per page. Cert fee: $5.00 per cert. Payee: Grayson County Clerk. **Online Access to Property Tax, Bad Check, Sheriff Sale, Sheriff Bond, Jail, Appraiser records:** Search the Grayson CAD system for property, mortgage, and property data at http://65.107.178.35/clientdb/main.asp. Also search Appraiser property data for free at www.graysoncad.org. Also, sheriff sales data is at www.co.grayson.tx.us/Tax%20Office/ssale.pdf. Also, search the county attorney's hot check list at www.co.grayson.tx.us/Attorney/HC%20List.PDF. Search the sheriff bond records and jail data at http://co.grayson.tx.us:3004/judsrch.asp. Also, see note at beginning of section regarding other sources of Appraiser information. **Other phones:** Assessor-903-893-8683; Treasurer-903-813-4251; Appraiser-903-893-9673; Elections-903-813-4260; Vital Records-903-813-4243.

Gregg County

County Clerk, PO Box 3049, Longview, TX 75606. **Phone-**903-236-8430, R/E Recording-903-236-8430 x746, UCC Recording-903-236-8430 X746 or 846; fax-903-237-2574; hours 8AM-5PM www.co.gregg.tx.us
Will search UCC records prior to 7/2001 & current fixture files. Search per debtor- $10.00. Search request using non-standard form (per name)- $25.00. UCC search does not include tax liens Separate federal/state combined tax lien search- $10.00 per debtor. Will not search real estate records. Record copy- $1.00 per page. Cert fee: $5.00 per cert. Payee: Gregg County Clerk. **Online Access to Property Tax, Real Estate, Grantor/Grantee, Deed, Mortgage, Vital Statistic, UCC records:** Access to the County Clerk's recording database is free to view at www.co.gregg.tx.us/hartIAM/. Fee to copy documents. Also, search property tax records for free at www.co.gregg.tx.us/tax/viking.asp. Also, the grantor/grantee index is at www.titlex.com. Select Gregg from the county list. Records range is 4/1977 to 2/2004. Also, see note at beginning of section. **Other phones:** Assessor-903-759-0015; Treasurer-903-236-8430 X853; Appraiser-903-238-8823; Elections-903-237-2652; Vital Records-903-236-8430 X637.

Grimes County

County Clerk, PO Box 209, Anderson, TX 77830. **Phone-**County Clerk, R/E & UCC Recording- 936-873-2111, UCC Recording-936-873-2606 x252; fax-936-873-3308; hours 8AM-Noon, 1-4:45PM
Will search UCC records prior to 7/2001 & current fixture files. Search per debtor- $15.00. Search request using non-standard form (per name)- $25.00. Will not search real estate or tax lien records. RE record copy- $1.00 per page. UCC copy- $2.00 per page. Cert fee: $5.00 per cert. Payee: Grimes County Clerk. **Other phones:** Assessor-936-873-2606 x231; Treasurer-936-873-2606 x233; Appraiser-936-873-2163; Elections-936-873-2606 x246; Vital Records-936-873-2606 x250.

Guadalupe County

County Clerk, PO Box 990, Seguin, TX 78156-0990. **Phone-**County Clerk, R/E & UCC Recording- 830-303-4188 x236; fax-830-401-0300; 8AM-4:30PM
Will search UCC records prior to 7/2001 & current fixture files. Search per debtor- $10.00. Search request using non-standard form (per name)- $25.00. UCC search includes tax liens if requested. Separate federal/state combined tax lien search- $20.00 per debtor. Will not search real estate records. Record copy- $1.00 per page. Cert fee: $5.00 per cert. Payee: Guadalupe County Clerk. **Online Access to Property Tax, Appraiser records:** Access to the county Appraisal District database is free at http://65.107.178.35/clientdb/main.asp?id=27. Name search here, but other methods are allowed at this website. Also, see note at beginning of section. **Other phones:** Assessor-830-303-3421 x354; Treasurer-830-303-4188 x338; Appraiser-830-372-2871 or 830-303-3313; Elections-830-303-6363; Vital Records-830-303-4188 x233.

Hale County

County Clerk, 500 Broadway #140, Plainview, TX 79072-8030. **Phone-**806-291-5261; fax-806-291-9810; hours 8AM-Noon,1-5PM. Will search UCC records prior to 7/2001 & current fixture files. Search per debtor- $10.00. Search request using non-standard form (per name)- $25.00. Tax liens not included in UCC search. Federal/state combined tax lien search- $15.00 per debtor. Will search real estate records. Written requests only. Record copy- $1.00 per page. Cert fee: $5.00 per cert. Payee: Hale County Clerk. **Online Access to Property, Appraiser records:** Access to property data is free at http://65.107.178.35/clientdb/main.asp?id=8. **Other phones:** Assessor-806-291-5276; Treasurer-806-291-5213; Appraiser-806-293-2547; Elections-806-291-5261; Vital Records-806-291-5219.

Hall County

County Clerk, Courthouse, Box 8, Memphis, TX 79245. **Phone-**806-259-2627; fax-806-259-5078; hours 8:30AM-5PM. Will search UCC records prior to 7/2001 & current fixture files. Search per debtor-$10.00. Search request using non-standard form (per name)- $25.00. Tax liens not included in UCC search. Tax lien search- $10.00 per debtor. RE owner, mortgage, property transfer searches available. UCC copy- $1.00 per page. Cert fee: $5.00 per cert. Payee: Hall County Clerk. **Other phones:** Assessor-806-259-2125; Treasurer-806-259-2421; Appraiser-806-259-2393.

Hamilton County

County Clerk, Main St, Courthouse, Hamilton, TX 76531. **Phone-**County Clerk, R/E & UCC Recording-254-386-3518; fax-254-386-8727; hours 8AM-5PM
Will search UCC records prior to 7/2001 & current fixture files. Search per debtor- $15.00. Search request using non-standard form (per name)-

$30.00. Tax lien search- $5.00 per debtor. Will not search real estate records. RE record copy- $1.00 per page. Cert fee: $1.00 per doc. Payee: Hamilton County Clerk. **Other phones:** Assessor-254-386-5114; Treasurer-254-386-5315; Appraiser-254-386-8945; Elections-254-386-3518; Vital Records-254-386-3518.

Hansford County

County Clerk, 15 N.W. Court, Spearman, TX 79081. **Phone-**County Clerk, R/E & UCC Recording- 806-659-4110; fax-806-659-4168; hours 8AM-5PM
Will search UCC records prior to 7/2001 & current fixture files. Search per debtor- $5.00. Tax lien search- $5.00 per search. Will not search real estate records. UCC copy- $1.00 per page. **Online Access to Property, Appraiser, Personal Property records:** Access to property data is free at www.ptax.org/offices/hansford/hansfordcad.htm. **Other phones:** Assessor-806-659-4120; Treasurer-806-659-4125; Appraiser-806-659-5575; Elections-806-659-4110; Vital Records-806-659-4110.

Hardeman County

County Clerk, PO Box 30, Quanah, TX 79252-0030. **Phone-**County Clerk, R/E & UCC Recording- 940-663-2901; fax-940-663-5161; hours 8:30AM-5PM
Will search UCC records prior to 7/2001 & current fixture files. Search per debtor- $10.00. Tax liens not included in UCC search. Separate federal/state combined tax lien search- $10.00 per debtor. Will not search real estate records. Record copy- $1.00 per page. Cert fee: $5.00 per cert. Payee: Hardeman County Clerk. **Other phones:** Assessor-940-663-5221; Treasurer-940-663-5401; Appraiser-940-663-2532; Elections-940-663-2901; Vital Records-940-663-2901.

Hardin County

County Clerk, PO Box 38, Kountze, TX 77625. **Phone-**County Clerk, R/E & UCC Recording- 409-246-5185; hours 8AM-5PM
Will not search UCC or real estate records. Separate federal/state combined tax lien search- $5.00 per search. Record copy- $1.00 per page. Cert fee: $6.00 per cert. Payee: Hardin County Clerk. **Other phones:** Assessor-409-246-5180; Treasurer-409-246-5121; Appraiser-409-246-2507; Elections-409-246-5185; Vital Records-409-246-5185.

Harris County

County Clerk, PO Box 1525, Houston, TX 77251-1525. **Phone-**County Clerk, R/E & UCC Recording-713-755-6405, UCC Recording-713-755-6439; fax-713-755-4977; hours-8AM-4:30PM www.co.harris.tx.us/cclerk
Personal checks are not accepted for mail requests. Will search UCC records prior to 7/2001 & current fixture files. Search per debtor- $10.00. Search request using non-standard form (per name)- $25.00. Tax liens not included in UCC search. Separate Tax lien search- $10.0 per debtor. Will not search real estate records. RE record copy- $1.00 per page. UCC copy- $5.00 for 1-3 pages; $1.50 each add'l. Cert fee: $5.00 per doc. Payee: Harris County Clerk. **Online Access to Real Estate, Lien, Appraiser, Voter, UCC, Assumed Name, Grantor/Grantee, Vital Statistic, Personal Property, Delinquent Tax records:** Access to Assumed Name records, UCC filings, vital statistic, Real Property are at www.cclerk.hctx.net/coolice/default.asp?Category=RealProperty&Service=mastermenu. Appraiser records are at www.hcad.org/Records. County Court Civil, marriage and informal marriage records are also available. Also, the grantor/grantee index is at www.titlex.com. Select Harris from the county list. Records range is 6/2000 to 11/2001. **Other phones:**

Assessor-713-368-2200; Appraiser-713-957-5291; Elections-713-755-5792; Vital Records-713-755-6438.

Harrison County

County Clerk, PO Box 1365, Marshall, TX 75671. **Phone**-County Clerk, R/E & UCC Recording- 903-935-4858; fax-903-935-4877; hours 8AM-5PM
Will search UCC records prior to 7/2001 & current fixture files. Search per debtor- $5.00. UCC search includes tax liens if requested. Separate federal/state combined tax lien search- $15.00 per debtor. Will not search real estate records. Record copy- $1.00 per page. Cert fee: $5.00 per cert. Payee: Harrison County Clerk. **Online Access to Property Tax records:** Search the appraiser database for free at www.harrisoncad.org. Also, see note at beginning of section. **Other phones:** Assessor-903-935-1991; Treasurer-903-935-4820; Appraiser-903-935-1991; Elections-903-935-4822; Vital Records-903-935-4858.

Hartley County

County Clerk, PO Box Q, Channing, TX 79018. **Phone**-County Clerk, R/E & UCC Recording- 806-235-3582; fax-806-235-2316; 8:30AM-N, 1-5PM
Will not search UCC or real estate records. Separate federal/state combined tax lien search- $10.00 per debtor. RE record copy- $1.00 per page. Cert fee: $5.00 per doc + $1.00 per page copy fee. Payee: Hartley County Clerk. **Online Access to Property, Appraiser, Personal Property records:** Access to property data is free at www.ptax.org/of fices/hartley/hartley01.html. **Other phones:** Assessor-806-365-4515; Treasurer-806-235-3572; Appraiser-806-365-4515; Elections-806-235-3582; Vital Records-806-235-3582; Judge-806-235-3142.

Haskell County

County Clerk, PO Box 725, Haskell, TX 79521-0725. **Phone**-County Clerk, R/E & UCC Recording- 940-864-2451; fax-940-864-6164; hours 8AM-5PM
Will search UCC records prior to 7/2001 & current fixture files. Search per debtor- $10.00. Federal/state combined tax lien search- $10.00 per page. Will search real estate records. Copy fee-$1.00 per page. Copy fee is $1.00 per page. Cert fee: $5.00 per doc. Payee: Haskell County Clerk. **Other phones:** Assessor-940-864-2181; Treasurer-940-864-3448; Appraiser-940-864-3805; Elections-940-864-2451; Vital Records-940-864-2451.

Hays County

County Clerk, 137 N. Guadalupe, Hays County Records Bldg., San Marcos, TX 78666. **Phone**-512-393-7329; fax-512-393-7337; hours 8AM-5PM www.co.hays.tx.us
Will search UCC records prior to 7/2001 & current fixture files. Search per debtor- $10.00. Tax liens not included in UCC search. Federal/state combined tax lien search- $10.00 per 10 year search. Will search real estate records. Copy fee-$1.00 per page. Cert fee: $5.00. Payee: Hays County Clerk. **Online Access to Appraiser, Property Tax records:** See notes at beginning of section. **Other phones:** Assessor-512-393-5545; Treasurer-512-393-2236; Appraiser-512-268-2522; Elections-512-393-7310.

Hemphill County

County Clerk, PO Box 867, Canadian, TX 79014. **Phone**-County Clerk, R/E & UCC Recording- 806-323-6212; hours 8AM-5PM
Will search UCC records. Search per debtor- $10.00. Tax liens not included in UCC search. Tax lien search- $10.00 per debtor. Will search real estate records. Record copy- $1.00 per page. Cert fee: $5.00 per cert. Payee: Hemphill County Clerk. **Other phones:** Assessor-806-323-6661; Treasurer-

806-323-6671; Appraiser-806-323-8022; Elections-806-323-6212; Vital Records-806-323-6212.

Henderson County

County Clerk, PO Box 632, Athens, TX 75751-0632. **Phone**-County Clerk, R/E & UCC Recording- 903-675-6140; fax-903-675-6105; hours 8AM-5PM
Will search UCC records prior to 7/2001 & current fixture files. Search per debtor- $10.00. Tax liens not included in UCC search. Federal/state combined tax lien search- $5.00 per debtor. Will not search real estate records. Record copy- $1.00 per page. Cert fee: $5.00 per cert. Payee: Henderson County Clerk. **Online Access to Property, Appraiser records:** Access to property data is free at www.hendersoncad.org. Also, see note at beginning of section. **Other phones:** Assessor-903-675-6149; Treasurer-903-675-6119; Appraiser-903-675-9296; Elections-903-675-6140; Vital Records-903-675-6140.

Hidalgo County

County Clerk, PO Box 58, Edinburg, TX 78540. **Phone**-956-318-2100; fax-956-318-2105; hours 7:30AM-5:30PM www.hidalgo.tx.us.landata.com/
Will search UCC records prior to 7/2001 & current fixture files. Search per debtor- $11.00. Search request using non-standard form (per name)- $26.00. Will not search real estate or tax lien records. RE record copy- $1.00 per page. UCC copy- $2.00 per page. Cert fee: $5.00 per cert. Payee: Hidalgo County Clerk. **Online Access to Appraiser, Property Tax records:** See note at beginning of section. **Other phones:** Assessor-956-318-2180; Appraiser-956-782-2255; Elections-956-318-2570.

Hill County

County Clerk, PO Box 398, Hillsboro, TX 76645. **Phone**-254-582-4030, R/E Recording-254-582-2161; hours 8AM-5PM
Will search UCC records prior to 7/2001 & current fixture files. Search per debtor- $10.00. Tax liens not included in UCC search. Tax lien search- $10.00 per debtor. RE owner, mortgage, property transfer searches available. UCC copy- $1.00 per page. Cert fee: $5.00 per cert. Payee: Hill County Clerk. **Online Access to Property, Appraiser, Personal Property records:** Saccess to Appraisal district property records is free at www.hillcad.org/in/reportshome.php. Also, see note at beginning of section. **Other phones:** Assessor-254-582-4000; Treasurer-254-582-2632; Appraiser-254-582-2508.

Hockley County

County Clerk, 800 Houston St, #213, Levelland, TX 79336. **Phone**-County Clerk, R/E & UCC Recording-806-894-3185; hours 9AM-5PM
Will search UCC records prior to 7/2001 only. Search per debtor- $10.00. UCC search includes tax liens if requested. Separate federal/state combined tax lien search- $14.00 per debtor Will not search real estate records. Record copy- $1.00 per page. Cert fee: $5.00 per cert. Payee: Hockley County Clerk. **Other phones:** Assessor-806-894-4938; Treasurer-806-894-3718; Appraiser-806-894-9654; Elections-806-894-3185; Vital Records-806-894-3185.

Hood County

County Clerk, PO Box 339, Granbury, TX 76048-0339. **Phone**-817-579-3222; fax-817-579-3227; 8AM-5PM
Will search UCC records prior to 7/2001 & current fixture files. Search per debtor- $5.00 per search. Will not search tax liens. RE owner, mortgage, property transfer searches available. Record copy- $1.00 per page. Cert fee: $5.00 per cert. Payee: Hood County Clerk. **Online Access to Appraiser, Property Tax records:** Search the county appraisal

roll for free at www.hoodcad.org. Also, see note at beginning of section. **Other phones:** Assessor-817-579-3295; Treasurer-817-579-3208; Appraiser-817-573-2471; Elections-817-408-3455; Vital Records-817-408-3455.

Hopkins County

County Clerk, PO Box 288, Sulphur Springs, TX 75483. **Phone**-903-438-4074, R/E Recording-903-885-4074; fax-903-438-4110; hours 8AM-5PM www.hopkinscountytx.org
Will search UCC records prior to 7/2001 & current fixture files. Search per debtor- $16.00. Search request using non-standard form (per name)- $31.00. Tax liens not included in UCC search. Separate federal/state combined tax lien search- $15.00 per debtor. Will not search real estate records. RE record copy- $1.00 per page. UCC copy- $2.00 per page. Cert fee: $5.00 per cert. Payee: Hopkins County Clerk. **Other phones:** Assessor-903-438-4063; Treasurer-903-438-4003; Appraiser-903-885-2173; Elections-903-438-4074; Vital Records-903-438-4074; Voter Registrar-903-438-4063.

Houston County

County Clerk, PO Box 370, Crockett, TX 75835-0370. **Phone**-936-544-3255, R/E Recording-936-544-3255 x241, UCC Recording-936-544-3255 x241; fax-936-544-1954; hours 8AM-4:30PM
Will search UCC records prior to 7/2001 & current fixture files. Search per debtor- $10.00. Search request using non-standard form (per name)- $25.00. UCC search includes tax liens if requested. Separate federal/state combined tax lien search- $20.00 per debtor. Will search real estate records. Record copy- $1.00 per page. Cert fee: $5.00 per cert. Payee: Houston County Clerk. **Other phones:** Assessor-936-544-2761; Treasurer-936-544-3255 x236; Appraiser-936-544-9655; Elections-936-544-3255 x241; Vital Records-936-544-3255 x241.

Howard County

County Clerk, PO Box 1468, Big Spring, TX 79721-1468. **Phone**-County Clerk, R/E & UCC Recording-432-264-2213, UCC Recording-432-264-2214; fax-432-264-2215; hours 8AM-5PM www.howard-county.net
Will search UCC records prior to 7/2001. Search per debtor- $15.00. Tax liens not included in UCC search. Tax lien search- $2.00 per debtor. Will not search real estate records. Record copy- $1.00 per page; $5.00 min. Cert fee: $5.00 per cert. Payee: Howard County Clerk. **Other phones:** Assessor-432-264-2232; Treasurer-432-264-2218; Appraiser-432-263-8301; Elections-432-264-2214; Vital Records-432-264-2214.

Hudspeth County

County Clerk, PO Drawer A, Sierra Blanca, TX 79851. **Phone**-County Clerk, R/E & UCC Recording- 915-369-2301; fax-915-369-2361.
Will search UCC records prior to 7/2001 & current fixture files. Search per debtor- $10.00. Tax lien search- $5.00 per debtor. Will search real estate records. Copy fee- $1.00 per page. Cert fee: $5.00 per doc. Payee: County Clerk. **Other phones:** Assessor-915-369-2331; Treasurer-915-369-3511; Appraiser-915-369-4118; Elections-915-369-2301; Vital Records-915-369-2301.

Hunt County

County Clerk, PO Box 1316, Greenville, TX 75403-1316. **Phone**-County Clerk, R/E & UCC Recording-903-408-4130; hours 8AM-5PM
Will search UCC records prior to 7/2001 & current fixture files. Search per debtor- $10.00. Tax liens not included in UCC search. Federal/state combined tax lien search- $10.00 per debtor +

$5.00 each add'l lien search. Will not search real estate records. RE record copy- $1.00 per page. UCC copy- $1.50 per page. Cert fee: $5.00 per cert. Payee: Hunt County Clerk. **Online Access to Appraiser, Property Tax records:** See notes at beginning of section. Taxes only found at www.huntcounty.net. **Other phones:** Assessor-903-408-4000; Treasurer-903-408-4171; Appraiser-903-408-3510; Elections-903-454-5467; Vital Records-903-408-4130.

Hutchinson County

County Clerk, PO Box 1186, Stinnett, TX 79083. **Phone**-County Clerk, R/E & UCC Recording- 806-878-4002; hours 9AM-5PM
Will not search UCC or real estate records. Record copy- $1.00 per page. Cert fee: $5.00 per cert. Payee: Hutchinson County Clerk. **Other phones:** Assessor-806-878-4005; Treasurer-806-878-4010; Appraiser-806-274-2294; Elections-806-878-4002; Vital Records-806-878-4002.

Irion County

County Clerk, PO Box 736, Mertzon, TX 76941-0736. **Phone**-County Clerk, R/E & UCC Recording- 325-835-2421; fax-325-835-2008; 8AM-N; 1PM-5PM
Will search UCC records prior to 7/2001 & current fixture files. Search per debtor- $10.00. Search request using non-standard form (per name)- $25.00. Will search state tax liens. Federal/state combined tax lien search-$10.00 per debtor. Will search real estate records. Request must be in writing. Record copy- $1.00 per page. Cert fee: $5.00 per doc. Payee: Irion County Clerk. **Other phones:** Assessor-325-835-7771; Treasurer-325-835-4111; Appraiser-325-835-3551; Elections-325-835-2421; Vital Records-325-835-2421.

Jack County

County Clerk, 100 Main St, Jacksboro, TX 76458. **Phone**-County Clerk, R/E & UCC Recording- 940-567-2111; hours 8AM-5PM
Will search UCC records. Search per debtor- $5.00. Tax liens not included in UCC search. Tax lien search- $5.00 per debtor. Will not search real estate records. RE record copy- $1.00 per page. UCC copy- $2.00 per page. Cert fee: $5.00 per cert. Payee: Jack County Clerk. **Other phones:** Assessor-940-567-2352; Treasurer-940-567-2251; Appraiser-940-567-6301; Elections-940-567-2111; Vital Records-940-567-2111.

Jackson County

County Clerk, 115 W. Main, Rm 101, Edna, TX 77957. **Phone**-361-782-3563; fax-361-782-3132; 8AM-5PM
Will search UCC records prior to 7/2001. Search per debtor- $10.00. Search request using non-standard form (per name)- $25.00. UCC search includes tax liens if requested. Separate federal/state combined tax lien search- $5.00 per debtor. Will not search real estate records. Record copy- $1.00 per page. Cert fee: $5.00 per cert. Payee: Jackson County Clerk. **Online Access to Real Estate, Grantor/Grantee, Judgment, Lien records:** The grantor/grantee index is at www.titlex.com or county records.com. Select Jackson from the county list. Records range is 1/1993 to 9/2003. Also, see note at beginning of section. **Other phones:** Assessor-361-782-3473; Treasurer-361-782-3402; Appraiser-361-782-7115; Elections-361-782-3563; Vital Records-361-782-3563.

Jasper County

Deputy Clerk, PO Box 2070, Jasper, TX 75951. **Phone**-Deputy Clerk, R/E & UCC Recording- 409-384-2632; fax-409-384-7198; hours 8AM-4:30PM
Will search UCC records prior to 7/2001 & current fixture files. Search per debtor- $10.00. Search

request using non-standard form (per name)-$25.00. Tax liens not included in UCC search. Tax lien search- $10.00 per debtor. Will not search real estate records. Copy fee- $1.00 per page. Cert fee: $5.00. Payee: County Clerk. **Other phones:** Assessor-409-384-6896; Treasurer-409-384-2461; Appraiser-409-384-2544; Elections-409-384-3399; Vital Records-409-384-2632.

Jeff Davis County

County Clerk, PO Box 398, Fort Davis, TX 79734. **Phone**-432-426-3251; fax-432-426-3760.
Will search UCC records prior to 7/2001 & current fixture files. Search per debtor- $10.00. Tax liens not included in UCC search. Federal/state combined tax lien search- $10.00 per debtor. Will not search real estate records. RE record copy- $1.00 per page. UCC copy- $100 per page. Cert fee: $5.00 per doc. Payee: County Clerk. **Other phones:** Assessor-432-426-3213; Treasurer-432-426-3242; Appraiser-432-857-3333 or 426-3210.

Jefferson County

County Clerk, PO Box 1151, Beaumont, TX 77704-1151. **Phone**-County Clerk, R/E & UCC Recording-409-835-8475; fax-409-839-2394; hours 8AM-5PM www.co.jefferson.tx.us
Will search UCC records prior to 7/2001 and current fixture files only on personal property. Search per debtor- $10.00. Search request using non-standard form (per name)- $25.00. State tax liens not included in UCC search. Will search only federal tax liens. Separate federal tax lien search-$10.00 per debtor. Will not search real estate records. RE record copy- $1.00 per page. UCC copy- $1.50 per page; $5.00 min. Cert fee: $5.00 per cert. Payee: Jefferson County Clerk. **Online Access to Recording, Deed, Lien, Judgment, Property Tax, Marriage, UCC, Assumed Name records:** Access to the recorder database is free at http://jeffersontxclerk.hartic.com. Recording index goes back to 1983; images to 1989. Marriages go back to 1995; UCCs to 7/2001. Also, search the appraiser database for free at www.jcad.org/search2.asp. Also, see note at beginning of section. **Other phones:** Assessor-409-835-8516; Treasurer-409-835-8509; Appraiser-409-835-4611; Elections-409-835-8760; Vital Records-409-835-8475.

Jim Hogg County

County Clerk, PO Box 878, Hebbronville, TX 78361. **Phone**-County Clerk, R/E & UCC Recording- 361-527-4031; fax-361-527-5843; hours 9AM-5PM
Will search UCC records prior to 7/2001 & current fixture files. Search per debtor- $15.00. Tax lien search- $10.00 per debtor. Will search real estate records. Copy fee- $1.00 per page. Cert fee: $5.00 per doc. Payee: Jim Hogg- County Clerk. **Other phones:** Assessor-361-527-3237; Treasurer-361-527-3164; Appraiser-361-527-4033; Elections-361-527-4031; Vital Records-361-527-4031.

Jim Wells County

County Clerk, PO Box 1459, Alice, TX 78333. **Phone**-361-668-5702; hours 8AM-Noon, 1-5PM
Will search UCC records prior to 7/2001 & current fixture files. Search per debtor- $10.00. Tax lien search- $10.00 per debtor per lien. Will not search real estate records. UCC copy- $1.00 per page. Cert fee: $5.00 per cert. Payee: Jim Wells County Clerk. **Other phones:** Assessor-361-668-5711; Treasurer-361-668-5713; Appraiser-361-668-9656.

Johnson County

County Clerk, PO Box 662, Cleburne, TX 76033-0662. **Phone**-County Clerk, R/E & UCC Recording- 817-556-6314, UCC Recording-817-556-6310; fax-817-

556-6326; hours 8AM-Noon, 1-4:30PM www.johnsoncountytx.org
Will search UCC records prior to 7/2001 & current fixture files. Search per debtor- $10.00. UCC search includes tax liens if requested. Copy fee- $1.00 per page. Cert fee: $5.00 per doc. **Online Access to Appraiser, Property Tax records:** Records from the County Appraiser are free at www.johnsoncad.com/search.htm. Also, see note at beginning of section. **Other phones:** Assessor-817-556-6100; Treasurer-817-566-6340; Appraiser-817-558-8100; Elections-817-556-6197; Vital Records-817-556-6311.

Jones County

County Clerk, PO Box 552, Anson, TX 79501-0552. **Phone**-County Clerk, R/E & UCC Recording- 325-823-3762; fax-325-823-4223; hours 8AM-5PM
Will search UCC records prior to 7/2001 & current fixture files. Search per debtor- $5.00. Search request using non-standard form (per name)-$10.00. UCC search includes tax liens if requested. Separate federal/state combined tax lien search-$5.00 Will not search real estate records. UCC copy-$1.00 per page. Cert fee: $5.00. Payee: Jones County Clerk. **Other phones:** Assessor-325-823-2437; Treasurer-325-823-3742; Appraiser-325-823-2422; Elections-Vital Records-325-823-3762.

Karnes County

County Clerk, 101 N. Panna Maria Ave., Courthouse - #9, Karnes City, TX 78118-2929. **Phone**-County Clerk, R/E & UCC Recording- 830-780-3938; fax-830-780-4576; hours 8AM-5PM
Will search UCC records prior to 7/2001 & current fixture files. Search per debtor- $10.00. Search request using non-standard form (per name)-$25.00. Tax liens not included in UCC search. Tax lien searches are available. Federal/state combined tax lien search- $10.00 per ten year period. Will not search real estate records. RE record copy- $1.00 per page. UCC copy- $1.50 per page. Cert fee: $1.00 per page. Payee: Karnes County Clerk. **Online Access to Property, Appraiser records:** Access to property data is available for download from a private company; fees apply; visit www.ptax.org/tax_office_data.htm or phone 201-571-0425. **Other phones:** Assessor-830-780-2431; Treasurer-830-780-2312; Appraiser-830-780-2433; Elections-830-780-3938; Vital Records-830-780-3938.

Kaufman County

County Clerk, Courthouse, Kaufman, TX 75142. **Phone**-County Clerk, R/E & UCC Recording- 972-932-4331; fax-972-932-7628; hours 8AM-5PM www.kaufmancounty.net
Will not search UCC records. Tax lien search- $10.00 per debtor. Will search real estate records. Record copy- $1.00 per page. Cert fee: $6.00 1st page, $2.00 each add'l. Payee: Kaufman County Clerk. **Online Access to Appraiser, Property Tax, Real Estate, Grantor/Grantee, Deed, Lien records:** The grantor/grantee index is at www.titlex.com. Click on Jackson on the county list. Records range is 5/1969 to 7/2003. Also, see note at beginning of section. Also, search appraisal roll data for free at www.kaufmancad.org. www.texaslandrecords.com. **Other phones:** Assessor-972-932-4331; Treasurer-972-932-4331; Appraiser-972-932-6081; Elections-972-932-4331; Vital Records-972-932-4331.

Kendall County

County Clerk, 201 E. San Antonio, #127, Boerne, TX 78006. **Phone**-County Clerk, R/E & UCC Recording-830-249-9343; fax-830-249-3472; hours 8AM-5PM
Will search UCC records. Search per debtor- $10.00. Tax liens not included in UCC search. Tax lien search- $10.00 per debtor. RE owner, mortgage,

property transfer searches available. Record copy-$1.00 per page. Cert fee: $5.00 per cert. Payee: Kendall County Clerk. **Online Access to Appraiser, Property Tax records:** See note at beginning of section. **Other phones:** Assessor-830-249-9343; Treasurer-830-249-9343; Appraiser-830-249-8012; Elections-830-249-9343; Vital Records-830-249-9343.

Kenedy County

County Clerk, PO Box 227, Sarita, TX 78385-0227. **Phone-**County Clerk, R/E & UCC Recording- 361-294-5220; fax-361-294-5218; hours 8:30AM-Noon, 1-4:30PM. Will search UCC records prior to 7/2001 & current fixture files. Search per debtor- $5.00. UCC search includes tax liens if requested. RE owner, mortgage, property transfer searches available. Record copy- $1.00 per page. Cert fee: $5.00 per cert. Payee: Kenedy County Clerk. **Other phones:** Assessor-361-294-5202; Treasurer-361-294-5304; Appraiser-361-321-1695; Elections-361-294-5220; Vital Records-361-294-5220.

Kent County

County Clerk, PO Box 9, Jayton, TX 79528-0009. **Phone-**County Clerk, R/E & UCC Recording- 806-237-3881; fax-806-237-2632; 8:30AM-N, 1-5PM Will not search UCC records. Separate federal/state combined tax lien search- $5.00 per debtor per instrument. Mortgage searches available. Record copy- $1.00 per page. Cert fee: $5.00 per cert. Payee: Kent County Clerk. **Other phones:** Assessor-806-237-3801; Treasurer-806-237-3075; Appraiser-806-237-3036; Elections-Vital Records-806-237-3881.

Kerr County

County Clerk, 700 Main, Courthouse, Rm 122, Kerrville, TX 78028-5389. **Phone-**County Clerk, R/E & UCC Recording- 830-792-2255; fax-830-792-2274; hours 8AM-5PM www.ktc.com Will search UCC records prior to 7/2001 & current fixture files. Search per debtor- $10.00. Search request using non-standard form (per name)- $25.00. Will not search real estate or tax lien records. UCC copy- $1.00 per page. **Online Access to Appraiser, Property Tax records:** See note at beginning of section. **Other phones:** Assessor-830-792-2242; Treasurer-830-792-2275; Appraiser-830-895-5223; Elections-Vital Records-830-792-2255.

Kimble County

County Clerk, 501 Main St, Junction, TX 76849. **Phone-**County Clerk, R/E & UCC Recording- 325-446-3353; fax-325-446-2986; 8AM-Noon, 1-5PM Will not search records. Record copy- $1.00 per page. Cert fee: $5.00 per cert. Payee: Kimble County Clerk. **Other phones:** Assessor-325-446-3717; Treasurer-325-446-2847; Appraiser-325-446-3717; Elections-Vital Records-325-446-3353.

King County

County Clerk, PO Box 135, Guthrie, TX 79236. **Phone-**County Clerk, R/E & UCC Recording- 806-596-4412; fax-806-596-4664; 9AM-Noon, 1-5PM Will search UCC records prior to 7/2001 & current fixture files. Search per debtor- $5.00. Tax liens not included in UCC search. Tax lien search- $5.00 per debtor. Will not search real estate records. Record copy- $1.00 per page. Cert fee: $5.00 per cert. Payee: King County Clerk. **Other phones:** Assessor-806-596-4318; Treasurer-806-596-4319; Appraiser-806-596-4588; Elections-806-596-4412; Vital Records-806-596-4412.

Kinney County

County Clerk, PO Drawer 9, Brackettville, TX 78832. **Phone-**County Clerk, R/E & UCC Recording- 830-563-2521; fax-830-563-2644; hours 8AM-Noon; 1-5PM

Will search UCC records. Search per debtor- $5.00. Search request using non-standard form (per name)- $25.00. Tax lien search- $5.00 per debtor. Will not search real estate records. Copy fee- $1.00 per page. Cert fee: $5.00 per page. Payee: County Clerk. **Other phones:** Assessor-830-563-2688; Treasurer-830-563-2777; Appraiser-830-563-2323; Elections-830-563-2521; Vital Records-830-563-2521.

Kleberg County

County Clerk, PO Box 1327, Kingsville, TX 78364-1327. **Phone-**County Clerk, R/E & UCC Recording-361-595-8548; fax-361-593-1355; 8AM-N, 1-5PM Will search UCC records prior to 7/2001 & current fixture files. Search per debtor-(5 years) $10.00. Search request using non-standard form (per name)- $25.00. Tax liens not included in UCC search. Tax lien search- $10.00 per debtor. Will not search real estate records. Record copy- $1.00 per page. Cert fee: $5.00 per cert. Payee: Kleberg County Clerk. **Online Access to Property Tax records:** See note at beginning of section. **Other phones:** Assessor-361-595-8542; Treasurer-361-595-8535; Appraiser-361-595-5775; Elections-361-595-8548; Vital Records-361-595-8548.

Knox County

County Clerk, PO Box 196, Benjamin, TX 79505. **Phone-**940-454-2441, R/E Recording-940-459-2441, UCC Recording-940-459-2441; fax-940-454-2005; hours 8AM-12, 1-5PM Will not search UCC or real estate records. Separate federal/state combined tax lien search- $5.00 per debtor. Record copy- $1.00 per page. Cert fee: $5.00 per cert. Payee: Knox County Clerk. **Other phones:** Assessor-940-459-2411; Treasurer-817-459-2251; Appraiser-940-459-3891.

La Salle County

County Clerk, 101 Courthouse Squ #107, Cotulla, TX 78014. **Phone-**830-879-4432; fax-830-879-2933; hours 8AM-12; 1PM-5PM Will search UCC records prior to 7/2001 & current fixture files. Search per debtor- $5.00. Tax lien search- $5.00 per debtor. Will not search real estate records. Copy fee is $1.00 per page. Cert fee: $5.00 per cert. Payee: LaSalle Co Clerk. **Online Access to Property, Appraiser records:** Access to property data is available for download from a private company; fees apply; visit www.ptax.org/tax_office_data.htm or phone 201-571-0425. **Other phones:** Assessor-830-879-4437; Treasurer-830-879-4440; Appraiser-830-879-2547; Elections-830-879-4432; Vital Records-830-879-4432.

Lamar County

County Clerk, 119 N. Main #109, Courthouse, Paris, TX 75460. **Phone-**County Clerk, R/E & UCC Recording- 903-737-2420; fax-903-782-1100; hours 8AM-5PM. Will search UCC records prior to 7/2001 & current fixture files. Search per debtor- $10.00. Search request using non-standard form (per name)- $25.00. Tax liens not included in UCC search. Federal/state combined tax lien search- $10.00 per search. Will not search real estate records. Copy fee- $1.00 per page. Cert fee: $5.00 per cert. Payee: Lamar County Clerk. **Online Access to Inmate, Sheriff Bond, Sex Offender, Death records:** Access to the sheriff's inmates and bond lists is free at http://209.223.255.254/. Access to the sheriff's sex offender registry is free at www.lcsom.com/disclaimer.html Cemetery records in Lamar County are at http://userdb.rootsweb.com/cemeteries/TX/Lamar.

Other phones: Assessor-903-785-7822; Treasurer-903-737-2418; Appraiser-903-785-7822; Elections-903-737-2420; Vital Records-903-737-2420.

Lamb County

County Clerk, 100 6th Dr., Rm 103 Box 3, Littlefield, TX 79339-3366. **Phone-**806-385-4222 x210, R/E Recording-806-385-4222; fax-806-385-6485; hours 8:30AM-5PM Will search UCC records prior to 7/2001 & current fixture files. Search per debtor- $11.00. Search request using non-standard form (per name)-$26.00. Tax liens not included in UCC search. Federal tax lien search- $10.00; state lien-$5.00 per debtor. Will not search real estate records. RE record copy- $1.00 per page. UCC copy- $2.00 per page. Cert fee: $5.00 per cert. Payee: Lamb County Clerk. **Online Access to Appraiser, Property Tax records:** See note at beginning of section. **Other phones:** Assessor-806-385-4222; Treasurer-806-385-3770; Appraiser-806-385-6474.

Lampasas County

County Clerk, PO Box 347, Lampasas, TX 76550. **Phone-**512-556-8271; hours 8AM-5PM Will search UCC records prior to 7/2001 & current fixture files. Search per debtor- $21.00. Search request using non-standard form (per name)- $25.00. Tax liens not included in UCC search. Federal tax lien search- $15.00; state lien- $5.00 per debtor. Property transfer searches available. UCC copy- $1.00 per page. Cert fee: $5.00 per cert. Payee: Lampasas County Clerk. **Other phones:** Assessor-512-556-8271; Treasurer-512-556-8058; Appraiser-512-556-8058.

Lavaca County

County Clerk, PO Box 326, Hallettsville, TX 77964-0326. **Phone-**County Clerk, R/E & UCC Recording-361-798-3612; hours 8AM-5PM Will search UCC records. Search per debtor- $10.00. Search request using non-standard form (per name)- $25.00. Will not search real estate or tax lien records. RE record copy- $1.00 per page. UCC copy- $2.00 per page. Cert fee: $5.00 per cert. Payee: County Clerk. **Other phones:** Assessor-361-798-3601; Treasurer-361-798-2181; Appraiser-361-798-4396; Elections-Vital Records-361-798-3612.

Lee County

County Clerk, PO Box 419, Giddings, TX 78942. **Phone-**County Clerk, R/E & UCC Recording- 979-542-3684; fax-979-542-2623; hours 8AM-5PM Will not search records. RE record copy- $1.00 per page. UCC copy- $1.50 per page. Cert fee: $5.00 per cert. Payee: Lee County Clerk. **Other phones:** Assessor-979-542-2640; Treasurer-979-542-2161; Appraiser-979-542-9618; Elections-Vital records-979-542-3684.

Leon County

County Clerk, PO Box 98, Centerville, TX 75833. **Phone-**County Clerk, R/E & UCC Recording- 903-536-2352; hours 8AM-5PM Will not search records. UCC copy- $1.00 per page. Cert fee: $5.00. Payee: Leon County Clerk. **Online Access to Property, Appraiser records:** Downloadable property data is available from a private company; fees apply; visit www.ptax.org/tax_office_data.htm or phone 201-571-0425. **Other phones:** Assessor-903-536-2543; Treasurer-903-536-2915; Appraiser-903-536-2252; Elections-903-536-2352; Vital Records-903-536-2352.

Liberty County

County Clerk, PO Box 369, Liberty, TX 77575. **Phone-**936-336-4673, R/E Recording-409-336-4673; hours 8AM-5PM Will search UCC records prior to 7/2001 & current fixture files. Search per debtor- $10.00. UCC search includes tax liens if requested. Separate federal/state combined tax lien search- $10.00 per debtor. Will not search real estate records. Record copy- $1.00 per page. Cert fee: $5.00 per cert. Payee: Liberty County Clerk. **Online Access to Appraiser, Property Tax records:** See note at beginning of section. **Other phones:** Assessor-936-336-4629; Appraiser-409-336-5722.

Limestone County

County Clerk, PO Box 350, Groesbeck, TX 76642. **Phone-**254-729-5504, R/E Recording-254-729-3009; fax-254-729-2951; hours 8AM-5PM
Will search UCC records prior to 7/2001 & current fixture files. Search per debtor- $10.00. Tax liens not included in UCC search. Tax lien search-$10.00 per debtor. Real estate record owner searches available. UCC copy- $1.00 per page. Cert fee: $5.00 per cert. Payee: Limestone County Clerk. **Online Access to Appraiser, Property Tax records:** See notes at beginning of section. **Other phones:** Assessor-254-729-3405;   Treasurer-254-729-3314; Appraiser-254-729-5504.

Lipscomb County

County Clerk, PO Box 70, Lipscomb, TX 79056. **Phone-**806-862-3091; fax-806-862-3004; hours 8AM-12 1PM-5PM
Will not search UCC records. Tax lien search- $10.00 per debtor. Will search real estate records. RE record copy- $1.00 per page. Cert fee: $5.00. **Online Access to Property, Appraiser records:** Access to property data is by subscription from a private company; visit www.ptax.org/tax_office_data.htm or phone 201-571-0425. **Other phones:** Assessor-806-862-2911;   Treasurer-806-862-3821;   Appraiser-806-624-2881.

Live Oak County

County Clerk, PO Box 280, George West, TX 78022. **Phone-**361-449-2733 x3, R/E Recording-361-449-2733, UCC Recording-361-449-2733 x103 or 129; hours 8AM-Noon, 1-5PM
May or may not search UCC records. Search per debtor- $10.00. Search request using non-standard form (per name)- $25.00. Will do tax lien search. Will not search real estate records. UCC copy- $1.00 per page. Cert fee: $5.00 per cert. Payee: Live Oak County Clerk. **Other phones:** Assessor-361-449-2733; Treasurer-361-449-2641 x109; Appraiser-361-449-2641; Elections-361-449-2733 x129 or 103; Vital Records-361-449-2733 x129 or 103.

Llano County

County Clerk, PO Box 40, Llano, TX 78643-0040. **Phone-**325-247-4455; fax-325-247-2406; 8AM-5PM
Will search UCC records prior to 7/2001 & current fixture files. Search per debtor- $15.00. Search request using non-standard form (per name)- $25.00. UCC search includes tax liens if requested. Separate federal/state combined tax lien search-$5.00 per debtor. Will not search real estate records. Record copy- $1.00 per page. Cert fee: $5.00 per cert. Payee: Llano County Clerk. **Online Access to Appraiser, Property Tax records:** See note at beginning of section. **Other phones:** Assessor-325-247-4165; Treasurer-325-247-7743; Appraiser-325-247-3065.

Loving County

County Clerk, PO Box 194, Mentone, TX 79754. **Phone-**County Clerk, R/E & UCC Recording- 432-377-2441; fax-432-377-2701; hours 9AM-N, 1-5PM
Will search UCC records. Search per debtor- $15.00. Will not search tax liens. Will not search real estate records. UCC copy- $1.00 per page. Cert fee: $5.00. Payee: County Clerk. **Other phones:** Assessor-432-377-2411;   Treasurer-432-377-2311;

Appraiser-432-377-2201;   Elections-432-377-2441; Vital Records-432-377-2441.

Lubbock County

County Clerk, PO Box 10536, Lubbock, TX 79408-0536. **Phone-**806-775-1060; fax-806-775-1660; hours 8:30AM-5PM www.co.lubbock.tx.us
Will search UCC records prior to 7/2001. Search per debtor- $15.00. Search request using non-standard form (per name)- $25.00. Will not search real estate records. RE record copy- $1.00 per page. UCC copy- $1.50 per page. Cert fee: $5.00 per doc. Payee: Lubbock County Clerk. **Online Access to Election, Appraiser, Property Tax records:** Access to the county clerks records is limited to election results at   www.co.lubbock.tx.us/CClerk/county_clerk.htm. Also, search the property appraiser database for free at www.lubbockcad.org/Appraisal/PublicAccess/. **Other phones:** Treasurer-806-775-1018; Appraiser-806-762-5000; Elections-806-775-1339; Vital Records-806-775-2926 (birth/death), 806-775-1054(marriage); Tax Assessor-806-775-1344; State Compt.-806-762-5000.

Lynn County

County Clerk, PO Box 937, Tahoka, TX 79373. **Phone-**County Clerk, R/E & UCC Recording- 806-561-4750; fax-806-561-4988; hours 8:30AM-5PM
Will search UCC records prior to 7/2001 & current fixture files. Search per debtor- $10.00. Tax liens not included in UCC search. Tax lien search-$5.00 per book. Separate federal/state combined tax lien search-$10.00 per debtor. Will not search real estate records. Record copy- $1.00 per page. Cert fee: $5.00 per cert. Payee: Lynn County Clerk. **Other phones:** Assessor-806-561-4112; Treasurer-806-561-4055;   Appraiser-806-561-5477; Elections-806-561-4750; Vital Records-806-561-4750.

Madison County

County Clerk, 101 W. Main, Rm 102, Madisonville, TX 77864. **Phone-**County Clerk, R/E & UCC Recording- 936-348-2638; fax-936-348-5858; hours 8AM-4:30PM
Will search UCC records. Search per debtor- $10.00. Search request using non-standard form (per name)- $25.00. UCC search includes tax liens if requested. Will not search real estate records. Record copy- $1.00 per page. Cert fee: $5.00 per cert. Payee: Madison County Clerk. **Other phones:** Assessor-936-348-2654;   Treasurer-936-348-5141; Appraiser-936-348-2783;   Elections-936-348-2638; Vital Records-936-348-2638.

Marion County

County Clerk, PO Box 763, Jefferson, TX 75657. **Phone-**County Clerk, R/E & UCC Recording- 903-665-3971; fax-903-665-8732; 8AM-Noon, 1-5PM
Will search UCC records prior to 7/2001 & current fixture files. Search per debtor- $16.00. Tax liens not included in UCC search. Federal/state combined tax lien search- $5.00 per book. RE owner, mortgage, property transfer searches available. RE record copy- $1.00 per page. UCC copy- $2.00 per page. Cert fee: $5.00 per cert. Payee: Marion County Clerk. **Other phones:** Assessor-903-665-3281;   Treasurer-903-665-2472; Appraiser-903-665-2519; Elections-Vital Records-903-665-3971.

Martin County

County Clerk, PO Box 906, Stanton, TX 79782. **Phone-**County Clerk, R/E & UCC Recording- 432-756-3412; fax-432-607-2212; hours 8AM-5PM
Will search UCC records prior to 7/2001. Search per debtor- $10.00. UCC search includes tax liens if requested. Separate federal/state combined tax lien search- $15.00 per debtor. Will not search real estate records. Record copy- $1.00 per page. Cert fee: $5.00 per cert. Payee: Martin County Clerk. **Other

phones:** Assessor-432-756-3397; Treasurer-432-756-3631;   Appraiser-432-756-2823;   Elections-432-756-3412; Vital Records-432-756-3412.

Mason County

County Clerk, PO Box 702, Mason, TX 76856-0702. **Phone-**County Clerk, R/E & UCC Recording- 325-347-5253; fax-325-347-6868; hours 8AM-Noon, 1-4PM
Will search UCC records prior to 7/2001 & current fixture files. Search per debtor- $10.00. Search request using non-standard form (per name)- $25.00. UCC search includes tax liens if requested. Separate federal/state combined tax lien search-$10.00 per debtor. Will not search real estate records. RE record copy- $1.00 per page. UCC copy- $2.00 per page. Cert fee: $5.00 per cert. Payee: Mason County Clerk. **Other phones:** Assessor-325-347-6937;   Treasurer-325-347-5251;   Appraiser-325-347-5989; Elections-Vital Records-325-347-5253.

Matagorda County

County Clerk, 1700 7th St, Rm 202, Bay City, TX 77414. **Phone-**County Clerk, R/E & UCC Recording-979-244-7680; fax-979-244-7688; M-F 8AM-5PM
Will search UCC records prior to 7/2001 & current fixture files. Search per debtor- $10.00. Search request using non-standard form (per name)- $25.00. Tax lien search- $5.00 per person. Will not search real estate records. Copy fee- $1.00 per page. Cert fee: $5.00 per doc. Payee: County Clerk. **Online Access to Property, Appraiser records:** Access to the County CAD data is free at http://65.107.178.35/clientdb/main.asp?id=25. **Other phones:** Assessor-979-244-7670; Treasurer-979-244-7609;   Appraiser-979-244-2031;   Elections-Vital Records-979-244-7680.

Maverick County

County Clerk, 500 Quarry St, #2, Eagle Pass, TX 78852. **Phone-**County Clerk, R/E & UCC Recording-830-773-2829; fax-830-752-4479; 8AM-12, 1-5PM
Will search UCC records prior to 7/2001 & current fixture files. Search per debtor- $10.00. UCC search includes tax liens if requested. Will not search real estate records. RE record copy- $1.00 per page. UCC copy- $2.00 per page. Cert fee: $5.00 per cert. Payee: Maverick County Clerk. **Online Access to Appraiser, Property Tax records:** Access to county CAD property data is free at http://65.107.178.35/clientdb/main.asp?id=19. Also, see note at beginning of section. **Other phones:** Assessor-830-773-9273;   Treasurer-830-773-2413; Appraiser-830-773-0255; Elections-Vital Records-830-773-2829.

McCulloch County

County Clerk, Courthouse, Brady, TX 76825. **Phone-**County Clerk, R/E & UCC Recording- 325-597-0733; fax-325-597-1731; hours 8AM-12; 1PM-5PM
Will search UCC records prior to 7/2001 & current fixture files. Search per debtor- $5.00. Tax lien search- $5.00 per debtor. Will search real estate records. Copy fee-$1.00 per page. Copy fee is $1.00 per page. Cert fee: $5.00 per instrument or $1.00 per page. Payee: McCulloch County Clerk. **Online Access to Criminal Record, Misdemeanor Record,   Felony   Record   records:** http://idocket.com/homepage2.htm. **Other phones:** Assessor-325-597-7607;   Treasurer-325-597-0733 x116;   Appraiser-325-597-1627;   Elections-325-597-7607; Vital Records-325-597-0733.

McLennan County

County Clerk, PO Box 1727, Waco, TX 76703-1727. **Phone-**254-757-5078; fax-254-757-5146; 8AM-5PM
Will search UCC records prior to 7/2001 & current fixture files. Search per debtor- $10.00. Search request using non-standard form (per name)-

$25.00. Tax liens not included in UCC search. Separate federal/state combined tax lien search- $10.00 per debtor. Will not search real estate records. RE record copy- $1.00 per page. UCC copy- $1.50 per page. Cert fee: $5.00 per cert. Payee: McLennan County Clerk. **Online Access to Appraiser, Property Tax, Real Estate, Grantor/Grantee, Real Estate Recording records:** The grantor/grantee index is at www.titlex.com. Select McLennan from the county list. Records range from 1/1996 to 12/2002. Also, see note at beginning of section. Also, real estate appraisal records are at www.mclennancad.org. Also, land records are at https://www.etitlesearch.com/services.asp. You can do a name search; choose from $50.00 monthly subscription or per-click account. Also, see note at beginning of section. **Other phones:** Appraiser-254-752-9864; Elections-254-757-5043.

McMullen County

County Clerk, PO Box 235, Tilden, TX 78072-0235. **Phone-**361-274-3215; fax-361-274-3618; 8AM-4PM
Will search UCC records prior to 7/2001 & current fixture files. Search per debtor- $10.00. Search request using non-standard form (per name)- $25.00. Tax liens not included in UCC search. Separate federal/state combined tax lien search- $5.00 per debtor. Property transfer searches available. RE record copy- $1.00 per page. UCC copy- $2.00 per page. Cert fee: $5.00 per cert. Payee: McMullen County Clerk. **Other phones:** Assessor-361-274-3233; Treasurer-361-274-3685; Appraiser-361-274-3233.

Medina County

County Clerk, 16th St Courthouse, Rm 109, Hondo, TX 78861. **Phone-**County Clerk, R/E & UCC Recording-830-741-6041; fax-830-741-6015.
Will search UCC records prior to 7/2001 & current fixture files. Search per debtor- $10.00. Search request using non-standard form (per name)- $25.00. **Other phones:** Assessor-830-741-6100; Treasurer-830-741-6110; Appraiser-830-741-3035; Elections-830-741-6040; Vital Records-830-741-6041.

Menard County

County Clerk, PO Box 1038, Menard, TX 76859. **Phone-**County Clerk, R/E & UCC Recording- 325-396-4682; fax-325-396-2047; 8AM-noon; 1-5PM
Will search UCC records prior to 7/2001 & current fixture files. Search per debtor- $10.00. Tax lien search- $10.00 per debtor. Will search real estate records. Real estate copy fee- $1.00 per page. UCC copy- $1.00 per page. Cert fee: $5.00. Payee: Menard County Clerk. **Other phones:** Assessor-325-396-4523; Treasurer-325-396-2748; Appraiser-325-396-4784; Elections-325-396-4682; Vital Records-325-396-4682.

Midland County

County Clerk, PO Box 211, Midland, TX 79702. **Phone-**County Clerk, R/E & UCC Recording- 432-688-4401; fax-432-688-8914; hours 8AM-5PM www.co.midland.tx.us
Will search UCC records prior to 7/2001. Search per debtor- $10.00. Search request using non-standard form (per name)- $25.00. Tax liens not included in UCC search. Federal/state combined tax lien search- $5.00 per debtor/search. Will not search real estate records. RE record copy- $1.00 per page. UCC copy- $1.50 per page. Cert fee: $5.00 per cert and $1.00 per page. Payee: Midland County Clerk. **Online Access to Property Appraiser, Voter Registration records:** Access to the property tax database is free at www.co.midland.tx.us/Tax/Property/Database/search.asp. Also, search property data on the mapping page at www.midcad.org/Search/index.htm. Online access to

the voter registration database is free at www.co.midland.tx.us/Elections/VoterDatabase/input.asp. **Other phones:** Assessor-432-688-4810; Treasurer-432-688-4880; Appraiser-432-699-4991; Elections-432-688-4890; Vital Records-432-688-4401.

Milam County

County Clerk, 100 S. Fannin, Cameron, TX 76520-3939. **Phone-**254-697-6596, R/E Recording-254-697-7049, UCC Recording-254-697-7049; fax-254-697-7055; hours 8AM-5PM
Will search UCC records prior to 7/2001 & current fixture files. Search per debtor- $10.00. Search request using non-standard form (per name)- $25.00. UCC search includes tax liens if requested. Separate federal/state combined tax lien search- $10.00 per debtor searched. Will not search real estate records. UCC copy- $1.00 per page. Cert fee: $5.00 per cert. Payee: Milam County Clerk. **Online Access to Appraiser, Property Tax, Land, Grantor/Grantee, Judgment, Lien records:** The grantor/grantee index is at www.titlex.com. Select Milam from the county list. Records range is 5/2000 to 8/2001. Also, see note at beginning of section. **Other phones:** Assessor-254-697-7017; Treasurer-254-697-7032; Appraiser-254-697-6638; Elections-254-697-7049; Vital Records-254-697-7049.

Mills County

County Clerk, PO Box 646, Goldthwaite, TX 76844-0646. **Phone-**County Clerk, R/E & UCC Recording-325-648-2711; fax-325-648-3251; 8AM-N, 1-5PM
Will not search UCC or real estate records. Will do tax lien search. Federal/state combined tax lien search- $5.00 per debtor. UCC copy- $1.00 per page. Cert fee: $5.00 per cert. Payee: Mills County Clerk. **Other phones:** Assessor-325-648-3879; Treasurer-325-648-2636; Appraiser-325-648-2253; Elections-325-648-2711; Vital Records-325-648-2711.

Mitchell County

County Clerk, 349 Oak St. #103, Colorado City, TX 79512-6213. **Phone-**County Clerk, R/E & UCC Recording- 325-728-3481; fax-325-728-5322; hours 8AM-Noon 1-5PM
Will search UCC records prior to 7/2001. Search per debtor- $21.00. Tax liens not included in UCC search. Tax lien search- $5.00 per debtor. Will not search real estate records. Record copy- $1.00 per page, min. $5.00. Cert fee: $5.00 per cert. Payee: Mitchell County Clerk. **Other phones:** Assessor-325-728-2606; Treasurer-325-728-8356; Appraiser-325-728-5028; Elections-325-728-2606; Vital Records-325-728-3481.

Montague County

County Clerk, PO Box 77, Montague, TX 76251-0077. **Phone-**940-894-2461; fax-940-894-3110; 8AM-5PM
Will search UCC records prior to 7/2001 & current fixture files. Search per debtor- $10.00. Search request using non-standard form (per name)- $25.00. Tax liens not included in UCC search. Tax lien search- $10.00 per 10 years. Will not search real estate records. Copy fee- $1.00 per page. Cert fee: $5.00 per doc. **Other phones:** Assessor-940-894-3881; Treasurer-940-894-2161; Appraiser-940-894-2081.

Montgomery County

County Clerk, PO Box 959, Conroe, TX 77305. **Phone-**936-539-7893, R/E Recording-936-539-7885, UCC Recording-936-539-7885; fax-936-760-6990; hours 8:30AM-4:30PM www.co.montgomery.tx.us
Will search UCC records prior to 7/2001 & current fixture files. Search per debtor- $10.00. Search request using non-standard form (per name)- $25.00. Tax liens not included in UCC search. Separate federal tax lien search- $10.00 per debtor.

Will not search real estate records. RE record copy- $1.00 per page. UCC copy- $1.50 per page. Cert fee: $5.00 per cert. Payee: Montgomery County Clerk. **Online Access to Grantor/Grantee, Judgment, Lien, Recording records:** The grantor/grantee index is at www.titlex.com. Select Montgomery from the county list. Records go back to 1/1966. **Other phones:** Assessor-936-539-7897; Treasurer-936-759-7844; Appraiser-936-756-3354; Elections-936-539-7843; Vital Records-936-538-8114.

Moore County

County Clerk, 715 Dumas Ave, Rm 105, Dumas, TX 79029. **Phone-**806-935-2009; fax-806-935-9004; hours 8:30AM-5PM
Will search UCC records prior to 7/2001 & current fixture files. Search per debtor- $15.00. Tax liens not included in UCC search. Federal/state combined tax lien search- $15.00 per debtor. Will not search real estate records. RE record copy- $1.00 per page. UCC copy- $2.00 per page. Cert fee: $5.00 per cert. Payee: Moore County Clerk. **Other phones:** Assessor-806-935-2008; Treasurer-806-935-2019; Appraiser-806-935-4193; Elections-806-935-2009; Vital Records-806-935-2009.

Morris County

County Clerk, 500 Broadnax St, Daingerfield, TX 75638. **Phone-**County Clerk, R/E & UCC Recording-903-645-3911; fax-903-645-4026; hours 8AM-5PM
Will search UCC records prior to 7/2001 & current fixture files. Search per debtor- $10.00. Search request using non-standard form (per name)- $25.00. UCC search includes tax liens if requested. Separate federal/state combined tax lien search- $20.00 per debtor. Will not search real estate records. Record copy- $1.00 per page. Cert fee: $5.00 per cert. Payee: Morris County Clerk. **Other phones:** Assessor-903-645-2446; Treasurer-903-645-2916; Appraiser-903-645-5061; Elections-903-645-3911; Vital Records-903-645-3911.

Motley County

County Clerk, PO Box 660, Matador, TX 79244. **Phone-**County Clerk, R/E & UCC Recording- 806-347-2621; fax-806-347-2220; hours 8:30AM-5PM
Will search UCC records. Search per debtor- $10.00. Federal/state combined tax lien search- $10.00 per debtor. Will search real estate records. Copy fee- $1.00 per page. Cert fee: $5.00 per cert. Payee: Motley County Clerk. **Other phones:** Assessor-806-347-2252; Treasurer-806-347-2800; Appraiser-806-347-2273; Elections-806-347-2621; Vital Records-806-347-2621.

Nacogdoches County

County Clerk, 101 W. Main, Rm 205, Nacogdoches, TX 75961. **Phone-**County Clerk, R/E & UCC Recording- 936-560-7733; fax-936-559-5926; hours 8AM-5PM www.co.nacogdoches.tx.us
Will search UCC records prior to 7/2001 & current fixture files. Search per debtor- $10.00. Search request using non-standard form (per name)- $25.00. Tax liens not included in UCC search. Tax lien search- $10.00 per debtor. Will not search real estate records. Record copy- $1.00 per page. Cert fee: $5.00 per cert. Payee: Nacogdoches County Clerk. **Online Access to Real Estate, Lien, Judgment, Deed, Vital Statistic, Property Tax records:** Access to view and search the county Real Property (recorder) index is free at https://www.texaslandrecords.com/txlr/TxlrApp/index.jsp. Monthly subscription is recommended but there is a pay as you go plan for $1 per document. Access to the county Central Appraisal District Appraisal Roll from TaxNetUSA MAY be at www.taxnetusa.com/nacogdoches/. Access to civil, criminal or misdemeanor records at www.idocket.com.

Fees involved. **Other phones:** Assessor-936-560-3447; Treasurer-936-560-7703; Appraiser-409-560-3447; Elections-936-560-7825; Vital Records-936-560-7733.

Navarro County

County Clerk, PO Box 423, Corsicana, TX 75151. **Phone**-903-654-3035; hours 8AM-5PM

Will search UCC records & current fixture files. Search per debtor- $10.00 per 10 years. Will not search tax liens. Will search real estate records. Record copy- $1.00 per page. Cert fee: $5.00 per cert. Payee: Navarro County Clerk. **Online Access to Appraiser, Property Tax records:** See note at beginning of section for "Advanced" fee service. **Other phones:** Assessor-903-654-3080; Treasurer-903-654-3090; Appraiser-903-872-2476.

Newton County

County Clerk, PO Box 484, Newton, TX 75966-0484. **Phone**-County Clerk, R/E & UCC Recording- 409-379-5341; fax-409-379-9049; hours 8AM-4:30PM

Will search UCC records prior to 7/2001 & current fixture files. Search per debtor- $10.00. Search request using non-standard form (per name)- $25.00. UCC search includes tax liens if requested. Will not search real estate records. Record copy- $1.00 per page. Cert fee: $5.00 per cert. Payee: Newton County Clerk. **Online Access to Appraiser, Property Tax, Death records:** For Appraiser/property tax: see note at beginning of section. Death records in this county may be accessed over the Internet at www.jas.net/jas.htm (site may be temporarily down). **Other phones:** Assessor-409-379-4241; Treasurer-409-379-8127; Appraiser-409-379-3710; Vital Records-409-379-5341.

Nolan County

County Clerk, 100 E 3rd St #108, Sweetwater, TX 79556-0098. **Phone**-325-235-2462, R/E Recording-915-235-2462, UCC Recording-915-235-2462; fax-325-236-9416; hours 8:30AM-Noon, 1-5PM

Will search UCC records prior to 7/2001 & current fixture files. Search per debtor- $16.00. Search request using non-standard form (per name)- $31.00. Tax liens not included in UCC search. Federal/state combined tax lien search- $5.00 per debtor. Will not search real estate records. RE record copy- $1.00 per page. UCC copy- $1.50 per page. Cert fee: $5.00 per cert. Payee: Nolan County Clerk. **Other phones:** Assessor-325-235-3331; Treasurer-915-236-6932; Appraiser-915-235-8421; Elections-915-235-2462; Vital Records-915-235-2462.

Nueces County

County Clerk, PO Box 2627, Corpus Christi, TX 78403. **Phone**-361-888-0111, R/E Recording-361-888-0611, UCC Recording-361-888-0580; fax-361-888-0329; hours 8AM-5PM www.co.nueces.tx.us

Will search UCC records prior to 7/2001 & current fixture files. Search per debtor- $14.00. Search request using non-standard form (per name)- $29.00. Tax liens not included in UCC search. Tax lien search- $5.00 per debtor. Will not search real estate records. RE record copy- $1.00 per page. UCC copy- $1.50 per page. Cert fee: $5.00 per cert. Payee: Nueces County Clerk. **Online Access to Real Estate, Recordings, Deed, Judgment, Lien, Appraiser, Property Tax records:** Access to county clerk recording records is free at www.co.nueces.tx.us/countyclerk/records/ Also, records from the County Appraiser are free at www.nuecescad.net. Also, see notes at beginning of section. **Other phones:** Assessor-361-888-0475; Treasurer-361-888-0515; Appraiser-361-881-8022; Elections-361-888-0483; Vital Records-361-888-0580.

Ochiltree County

County Clerk, 511 S. Main, Perryton, TX 79070. **Phone**-County Clerk, R/E & UCC Recording- 806-435-8039; fax-806-435-2081; 8:30AM-Noon, 1-5PM

Will search UCC records prior to 7/2001 & current fixture files. Search per debtor- $10.00. Search request using non-standard form (per name)- $25.00. Tax liens not included in UCC search. Separate federal/state combined tax lien search- $10.00 per debtor. Will not search real estate records. RE record copy- $1.00 per page. UCC copy- $1.50 per page. Cert fee: $5.00 per cert. Payee: Ochiltree County Clerk. **Online Access to Property, Appraiser records:** Access to property data is available for download from a private company; fees apply; visit www.ptax.org/tax_office_data.htm or phone 201-571-0425. **Other phones:** Assessor-806-435-8025; Treasurer-806-435-8046; Appraiser-806-435-9623; Elections-806-435-8039; Vital Records-806-435-8039.

Oldham County

County Clerk, PO Box 360, Vega, TX 79092. **Phone**-806-267-2667; hours 8:30AM-5PM. Will search UCC records prior to 7/2001 & current fixture files. Search per debtor- $10.00. Search request using non-standard form (per name)- $25.00. UCC search includes tax liens if requested. Separate federal/state combined tax lien search- $10.00 per debtor. Will not search real estate records. RE record copy- $1.00 per page. UCC copy- $2.00 per page. Cert fee: $5.00 per cert. Payee: Oldham County Clerk. **Other phones:** Assessor-806-267-2280; Treasurer-806-267-2329; Appraiser-806-267-2442; Elections-806-267-2667; Vital Records-806-267-2667.

Orange County

County Clerk, PO Box 1536, Orange, TX 77631-1536. **Phone**-County Clerk, R/E & UCC Recording- 409-882-7055; fax-409-882-7012; hours 8AM-5PM www.co.orange.tx.us

Will search UCC records. Search per debtor- $10.00. Search request using non-standard form (per name)- $25.00. UCC search includes tax liens. Separate federal tax lien search- $10.00 per debtor. Will search real estate records. Copy fee- $1.00 per page. Cert fee: $5.00 per doc. Payee: County Clerk. **Online Access to Property, Appraiser records:** Access to the county appriasal district records is free at www.orangecad.org. **Other phones:** Assessor-409-882-7971; Treasurer-409-882-7991; Appraiser-409-745-4777; Elections-409-882-7055; Vital Records-409-882-7055.

Palo Pinto County

County Clerk, PO Box 219, Palo Pinto, TX 76484. **Phone**-County Clerk, R/E & UCC Recording- 940-659-1277; fax-940-659-3628; hours 8:30AM-4:30PM

Will search UCC records. Search per debtor- $10.00. Search request using non-standard form (per name)- $25.00. Tax liens not included in UCC search. Tax lien search- federal $10.00 per debtor; state- $5.00. Will not search real estate records. RE record copy- $1.00 per page. UCC copy- $2.00 per page. Cert fee: $5.00 per cert. Payee: Palo Pinto County Clerk. **Other phones:** Assessor-940-659-1271; Treasurer-940-659-1260; Appraiser-940-659-1281; Elections-940-659-1277; Vital Records-940-659-1277.

Panola County

County Clerk, Sabine & Sycamore, Courthouse Bldg, Rm 201, Carthage, TX 75633. **Phone**-County Clerk, R/E & UCC Recording- 903-693-0302; fax-903-693-2726; hours 8AM-5PM

Will search UCC records prior to 7/2001 & current fixture files. Search per debtor- $5.00. UCC search includes tax liens if requested. Separate

federal/state combined tax lien search- $10.00 per debtor. Will not search real estate records. UCC copy- $1.00 per page. Cert fee: $5.00 per cert. Payee: Panola County Clerk. **Other phones:** Assessor-903-693-0340; Treasurer-903-693-0325; Appraiser-903-693-2891; Elections-903-693-0370; Vital Records-903-693-0302.

Parker County

County Clerk, PO Box 819, Weatherford, TX 76086. **Phone**-817-599-6185, R/E Recording-817-599-6591; fax-817-598-6183; hours 8AM-4PM

Will search UCC records prior to 7/2001 & current fixture files. Search per debtor- $16.00. UCC search includes tax liens if requested. Separate federal/state combined tax lien search- $1.00 per year. Will not search real estate records. UCC copy- $1.00 per page. Cert fee: $5.00 per cert. Payee: Parker County Clerk. **Online Access to Appraiser, Property Tax records:** See note at beginning of section for "Advanced" fee service. **Other phones:** Assessor-817-599-7671; Treasurer-817-596-0078; Appraiser-817-596-0077.

Parmer County

County Clerk, PO Box 356, Farwell, TX 79325. **Phone**-County Clerk, R/E & UCC Recording- 806-481-3691; fax-806-481-9154; hours 8:30AM-5PM

Will search UCC records prior to 7/2001 & current fixture files. Search per debtor- $10.00. Search request using non-standard form (per name)- $25.00. UCC search includes tax liens if requested. Will not search real estate records. Record copy- $1.00 per page. Cert fee: $5.00 per cert. Payee: Parmer County Clerk. **Other phones:** Assessor-806-481-3845; Treasurer-806-481-9152; Appraiser-806-481-1405; Elections-806-481-3691; Vital Records-806-481-3691.

Pecos County

County Clerk, 103 W. Callaghan St, Fort Stockton, TX 79735. **Phone**-432-336-7555; fax-432-336-7557; hours 8AM-5PM. Will search UCC records prior to 7/2001 & current fixture files. Search per debtor- $10.00. Search request using non-standard form (per name)- $25.00. Separate federal & state combined tax lien search- $10.00 per debtor. Will not search real estate records. Copy fee- $1.00 per page. **Other phones:** Assessor-432-336-3386; Treasurer-432-336-3461; Appraiser-432-336-7587; Elections-432-336-7555; Vital Records-432-336-7555.

Polk County

County Clerk, PO Drawer 2119, Livingston, TX 77351. **Phone**-County Clerk, R/E & UCC Recording- 936-327-6804; fax-936-327-6874; hours 8AM-5PM

Will search UCC records prior to 7/2001 & current fixture files. Search per debtor- $5.00. Tax liens not included in UCC search. Federal/state combined tax lien search- $5.00 per debtor. Will search real estate records. Record copy- $1.00 per page. Cert fee: $5.00 per cert. Payee: Polk County Clerk. **Other phones:** Assessor-936-327-6880; Treasurer-936-327-6816; Appraiser-936-327-2174; Elections-936-327-6852; Vital Records-936-327-6804; Court Clerk-936-327-6805.

Potter County

County Clerk, PO Box 9638, Amarillo, TX 79105. **Phone**-806-379-2275; fax-806-379-2296; hours 8AM-5PM www.prad.org

Will search UCC records back to 7/2001. Search per debtor- $15.00. Tax liens not included in UCC search. Separate federal tax lien search- $10.00. Will not search real estate records. RE record copy- $1.00 per page. (Does not include certificate). UCC copy- $.10 per page. Cert fee: $5.00 per cert + $1.00 per page. Payee: Potter County Clerk.

Online Access to Appraiser, Property Tax records: Records on the Potter-Randall Appraisal District database are free at www.prad.org/search.html. Records periodically updated; for current tax information call Potter (806-342-2600) or Randall (806-665-6287). Also, see note at beginning of section for "Advanced" fee service. **Other phones:** Assessor-806-342-2600; Treasurer-806-349-4832; Appraiser-806-358-1601; Elections-806-379-2299; Vital Records-806-379-2290.

Presidio County

County Clerk, PO Box 789, Marfa, TX 79843. **Phone-**County Clerk, R/E & UCC Recording- 432-729-4812; fax-432-729-4313; hours 8AM-Noon; 1-4PM
Will search UCC records prior to 7/2001 & current fixture files. Search per debtor- $10.00. Search request using non-standard form (per name)- $25.00. Tax lien search- $6.00 per debtor. Will search real estate records. Copy fee- $1.00 per page. Cert fee: $5.00 per cert. Payee: Presidio County Clerk. **Other phones:** Assessor-432-729-4081; Treasurer-432-729-4076; Appraiser-432-729-3431; Elections-432-729-4812; Vital Records-432-729-4812.

Rains County

County Clerk, PO Box 187, Emory, TX 75440. **Phone-**County Clerk, R/E & UCC Recording- 903-474-9999; fax-903-474-9390; hours 8AM-5PM. Will search UCC records prior to 7/2001 & current fixture files. Search per debtor- $5.00. UCC search does not include tax liens. Separate federal/state combined tax lien search- $10.00 per debtor. Will not search real estate records. Record copy- $1.00 per page. Cert fee: $5.00 per cert. Payee: Rains County Clerk. **Other phones:** Assessor-903-474-9999; Treasurer-903-474-9999; Appraiser-903-473-2391; Elections-903-474-9999; Vital Records-903-474-9999.

Randall County

County Clerk, PO Box 660, Canyon, TX 79015. **Phone-**County Clerk, R/E & UCC Recording- 806-468-5505; fax-806-656-6430; hours 8AM-5PM
www.randallcounty.org
Will search UCC records prior to 7/2001 & current fixture files. Search per debtor- $15.00. Search request using non-standard form (per name)- $30.00. Tax liens not included in UCC search. Separate federal/state combined tax lien search- $10.00 per debtor. Copies of liens are $1.50 if federal, $1.00 each if state. Will not search real estate records. RE record copy- $1.00 per page. UCC copy- $1.50 per page. Cert fee: $5.00 per cert. Payee: Randall County Clerk. **Online Access to Appraiser, Property Tax, Business Personal Property, Sheriff Sale records:** Randall County records are combined online with Potter County; see Potter County for access information or www.prad.org. Also, see notes at beginning of section. Criminal, Probate and Civil records found at www.idocket.com. **Other phones:** Assessor-806-468-5540; Treasurer-806-468-5535; Appraiser-806-358-1601; Elections-806-468-5510; Vital Records-806-468-5505.

Reagan County

County Clerk, PO Box 100, Big Lake, TX 76932. **Phone-**County Clerk, R/E & UCC Recording- 325-884-2442; fax-325-884-1503; hours 8:30AM-5PM
Will search UCC records prior to 7/2001 & current fixture files. Search per debtor- $10.00. UCC search includes tax liens if requested. Separate federal/state combined tax lien search- $10.00 per debtor. Will not search real estate records. RE record copy- $1.00 per page. UCC copy- $2.00 per page. Cert fee: $5.00 per cert. Payee: Reagan County Clerk. **Other phones:** Assessor-325-884-2131; Treasurer-325-884-2090; Appraiser-325-884-3275; Elections-325-884-2442; Vital Records-325-884-2442.

Real County

County Clerk, PO Box 750, Leakey, TX 78873-0750. **Phone-**County Clerk, R/E & UCC Recording- 830-232-5202; fax-830-232-6888; hours 8AM-5PM
www.realcountytexas.com
Will search UCC records prior to 7/2001 & current fixture files. Search per debtor- $5.00. Will not search real estate or tax lien records. Copy fee- $1.00 per page. Cert fee: $5.00 per doc. Payee: Bella A. Rubio, County Clerk. **Other phones:** Assessor-830-232-6210; Treasurer-830-232-6627; Appraiser-830-232-6248; Elections-830-232-5202; Vital Records-830-232-5202.

Red River County

County Clerk, 200 N. Walnut, Courthouse Annex, Clarksville, TX 75426-3075. **Phone-**County Clerk, R/E & UCC Recording- 903-427-2401; fax-903-427-3589; hours 8:30AM-5PM. Will search UCC records prior to 7/2001 & current fixture files. Search per debtor- $10.00. Tax liens not included in UCC search. Tax lien search- $5.00 per debtor. Real estate record owner searches available. Record copy- $1.00 per page. Cert fee: $5.00 per cert. Payee: Red River County Clerk. **Online Access to Property, Appraiser records:** Access to county appraisal district records is free at www.redrivercad.org. **Other phones:** Assessor-903-427-3009; Treasurer-903-427-3748; Appraiser-903-427-4181; Elections-903-427-2401; Vital Records-903-427-2401.

Reeves County

County Clerk, PO Box 867, Pecos, TX 79772. **Phone-**County Clerk, R/E & UCC Recording- 432-445-5467; fax-432-445-3997; hours 8AM-5PM
Will search UCC records prior to 7/2001 & current fixture files. Search per debtor- $10.00. Tax lien search- $10.00 per debtor. Will not search real estate records. Copy fee- $1.00 per page. Cert fee: $5.00 per cert. Payee: Reeves County Clerk. **Other phones:** Assessor-432-445-5473; Treasurer-432-445-2631; Appraiser-432-445-5122; Elections-432-445-5467; Vital Records-432-445-5467.

Refugio County

County Clerk, PO Box 704, Refugio, TX 78377. **Phone-**361-526-2233; fax-361-526-1325; 8AM-5PM
Will search UCC records prior to 7/2001 & current fixture files. Search per debtor- $10.00. Search request using non-standard form (per name)- $25.00. UCC search includes tax liens if requested. Separate federal/state combined tax lien search- $10.00 per debtor. Real estate record owner and property searches available. Record copy- $1.00 per page. Cert fee: $5.00 per cert. Payee: Refugio County Clerk. **Online Access to Marriage, Birth, Death, Divorce records:** Access to 19th & 20th century marriage, birth (1951 forward) and death records is free at www.rootsweb.com/~txrefugi/Marriageshome.htm. Also, you can search individual years for births (1926-1995), deaths (1964-1999), marriages (1966-2001), divorces (1968-2001) for free at www.rootsweb.com/~usgenweb/tx/refugio/refugtoc.htm. **Other phones:** Assessor-361-526-2023; Treasurer-361-526-4223; Appraiser-361-526-5994; Vital Records-361-526-2233.

Roberts County

County Clerk, PO Box 477, Miami, TX 79059-0477. **Phone-**806-868-2341; fax-806-868-3381; hours 8AM-Noon; 1-5PM
Will not search records. RE record copy- $1.00 per page. UCC copy- $1.50 per page. Cert fee: $5.00 per doc. Payee: Pay fees to Robert Co Clerk. **Other phones:** Assessor-806-868-3611; Treasurer-806-868-3201; Appraiser-806-868-5281; Vital Records-806-868-2341.

Robertson County

County Clerk, PO Box 1029, Franklin, TX 77856. **Phone-**County Clerk, R/E & UCC Recording- 979-828-4130; fax-979-828-1260; hours 8AM-5PM
Will search UCC records prior to 7/2001 & current fixture files. Search per debtor- $11.00. Search request using non-standard form (per name)- $25.00. UCC search includes tax liens if requested. Separate federal/state combined tax lien search- $11.00 per debtor. Will not search real estate records. Record copy- $1.00 per page. Cert fee: $5.00 per cert. Payee: Robertson County Clerk. **Other phones:** Assessor-979-828-3337; Treasurer-979-828-3201; Appraiser-979-828-5800; Elections-979-828-4130; Vital Records-979-828-4130.

Rockwall County

County Clerk, 1101 Ridge Rd, S-101, Rockwall, TX 75087. **Phone-**County Clerk, R/E & UCC Recording- 972-882-0220, UCC Recording-972-882-0225; fax-972-882-0229; hours 8AM-5PM
Will search UCC records prior to 7/2001 & current fixture files. Search per debtor- $10.00. Search request using non-standard form (per name)- $25.00. UCC search includes tax liens if requested. Separate federal/state combined tax lien search- $10.00 per debtor. Will not search real estate records. Record copy- $1.00 per page. Cert fee: $5.00 per cert. Payee: Rockwall County Clerk. **Online Access to Appraiser, Property Tax, Deed records:** For Deed records go to www.texaslandrecords.com. **Other phones:** Assessor-972-882-0350; Treasurer-972-882-0290; Appraiser-972-771-2034; Elections-972-882-0220; Vital Records-972-882-0220.

Runnels County

County Clerk, PO Box 189, Ballinger, TX 76821-0189. **Phone-**County Clerk, R/E & UCC Recording- 325-365-2720; fax-325-365-3408; 8:30AM-Noon, 1-5PM
Will search UCC records prior to 7/2001 & current fixture files. Search per debtor- $10.00. Search request using non-standard form (per name)- $25.00. Tax liens not included in UCC search. Tax lien search- $10.00 per debtor. Will not search real estate records. Record copy- $1.00 per page. Cert fee: $5.00 per cert. Payee: County Clerk, Runnels County. **Other phones:** Assessor-325-365-2339; Treasurer-325-365-2428; Appraiser-325-365-3583; Elections-325-365-2720; Vital Records-325-365-2720.

Rusk County

County Clerk, PO Box 758, Henderson, TX 75653-0758. **Phone-**County Clerk, R/E & UCC Recording- 903-657-0330; hours 8AM-5PM
Will search UCC records prior to 7/2001 & current fixture files. Search per debtor- $10.00. Search request using non-standard form (per name)- $25.00. UCC search includes tax liens if requested. Separate federal/state combined tax lien search- $10.00 per debtor. Will not search real estate records. Record copy- $1.00 per page. Cert fee: $5.00 per cert. Payee: Rusk County Clerk. **Online Access to Property Tax, Real Estate, Grantor/Grantee, Judgment, Lien records:** The grantor/grantee index is at www.titlex.com. Select Rush from the county list. Record range is 1/1979 to 11/2003. Also, see note at beginning of section. **Other phones:** Assessor-903-657-0321; Treasurer-903-657-0352; Appraiser-903-657-3578; Elections-903-657-0301; Vital Records-903-657-0301; 903-657-0327.

Sabine County

County Clerk, PO Drawer 580, Hemphill, TX 75948-0580. **Phone-**County Clerk, R/E & UCC Recording- 409-787-3786; fax-409-787-2044; 8AM-4:30PM
Will search UCC records. Search per debtor- $10.00. Search request using non-standard form (per

name)- $25.00. Tax liens not included in UCC search. Will not search real estate records. UCC copy- $1.00 per page. Cert fee: $5.00. **Other phones:** Assessor-409-787-2257; Treasurer-409-787-2210; Appraiser-409-787-2777; Elections-409-787-3786; Vital Records-409-787-3786.

San Augustine County

County Clerk, 100 W. Columbia, #106 Courthouse, San Augustine, TX 75972-1335. **Phone**-County Clerk, R/E & UCC Recording- 936-275-2452; fax-936-275-9579; hours 8AM-4:30PM

Will search UCC records. UCC search per debtor- $10.00 per name. Tax lien search- $10.00 per debtor. Will not search real estate records. RE record copy- $1.00 per page. UCC copy- $1.50 but not less than $5.00 per debtor. Cert fee: $5.00 per cert. Payee: San Augustine County Clerk. **Other phones:** Assessor-936-275-2300; Treasurer-936-275-9472; Appraiser-936-275-3496; Elections-936-275-2452; Vital Records-936-275-2452.

San Jacinto County

County Clerk, PO Box 669, Coldspring, TX 77331. **Phone**-County Clerk, R/E & UCC Recording- 936-653-2324; fax-936-653-2324; hours 8AM-4:30PM

Will search UCC records prior to 7/2001 & current fixture files. Search per debtor- $10.00. Will not search real estate or tax lien records. RE record copy- $1.00 per page. UCC copy- $2.00 per page. Cert fee: $5.00 per cert. Payee: San Jacinto County Clerk. **Online Access to Appraiser, Property Tax records:** See note at beginning of section. **Other phones:** Assessor-936-653-2311; Treasurer-936-653-2353; Appraiser-936-653-4481; Elections-936-653-2324; Vital Records-936-653-2324.

San Patricio County

County Clerk, PO Box 578, Sinton, TX 78387. **Phone**-361-364-6290, R/E Recording-361-364-6290 x241 or 242, UCC Recording-361-364-6290 x241 or 242; fax-361-364-6112; hours 8AM-5PM

Will search UCC records prior to 7/2001 & current fixture files. Search per debtor- $10.00. Search request using non-standard form (per name)- $25.00. Tax liens not included in UCC search. Tax lien search- $10.00 per debtor. Will not search real estate. Copy fee- $1.00 per page. Cert fee: $5.00 per cert. Payee: San Patricio County Clerk. **Online Access to Appraiser, Property Tax, Personal Property records:** Search the Appraiser database for free at www.sanpatriciocad.org/sanpatsearch.html. Also see note at beginning of section. **Other phones:** Assessor-361-364-6161; Treasurer-361-364-6228; Appraiser-361-364-5402; Elections-361-364-6290 x236; Vital Records-361-364-6290 x238.

San Saba County

County Clerk, 500 E. Wallace, San Saba, TX 76877. **Phone**-325-372-3614; fax-325-372-5746; hours 8AM-4:30PM www.sansabacounty.org

Will search UCC records prior to 7/2001 & current fixture files. Search per debtor- $10.00. Tax lien search- $10.00 per debtor. Will not search real estate records. Copy fee- $1.00 per page. Cert fee: $5.00 per cert. Payee: Clerk. **Other phones:** Assessor-325-372-5325; Treasurer-325-372-3337; Appraiser-325-372-5031; Elections-325-372-3614; Vital Records-325-372-3614.

Schleicher County

County Clerk, PO Drawer 580, Eldorado, TX 76936. **Phone**-325-853-2833 ext 72, R/E Recording-325-853-2833; fax-325-853-2768; hours 9AM-12:00-1-5PM

Will search UCC records prior to 7/2001 & current fixture files. Search per debtor- $10.00. Search request using non-standard form (per name)- $25.00. Will not search real estate records. UCC copy- $1.00 per page. Cert fee: $6.00. Payee: Schleicher County Clerk. **Other phones:** Assessor-325-853-3066; Appraiser-325-853-2671.

Scurry County

County Clerk, 1806 25th St, #300, Snyder, TX 79549-2530. **Phone**-325-573-5332; fax-325-573-7396; hours 8:30AM-5PM

Will search UCC records prior to 7/2001 & current fixture files. Search per debtor is $10.00. Federal/state combined tax lien search- $10.00 per debtor. Will not search real estate records. Copy fee- $1.00 per page. Cert fee: $5.00 per doc. **Other phones:** Assessor-325-573-9316; Treasurer-325-573-5382; Appraiser-325-573-8549.

Shackelford County

County Clerk, PO Box 247, Albany, TX 76430. **Phone**-County Clerk, R/E & UCC Recording- 325-762-2232; hours 8:30AM-Noon, 1-5PM. Will search UCC records. Search per debtor- $10.00. Search request using non-standard form (per name)- $25.00. Tax liens not included in UCC search. Tax lien search- $5.00 per debtor. Will search real estate records. Record copy fee- $1.00 per page. Cert fee: $5.00 per cert. Payee: Shackelford County Clerk. **Other phones:** Assessor-325-762-2232; Treasurer-325-762-2232; Appraiser-325-762-2207; Elections-325-762-2232; Vital Records-325-762-2232.

Shelby County

County Clerk, PO Box 1987, Center, TX 75935. **Phone**-936-598-6361; fax-936-598-3701; hours 8AM-4:30PM

Will search UCC records prior to 7/2001 & current fixture files. Search per debtor- $10.00. Search request using non-standard form (per name)- $25.00. UCC search includes tax liens if requested. Will not search real estate records. RE record copy- $1.00 per page. UCC copy- $1.50 per page. Cert fee: $5.00 per cert. Payee: Shelby County Clerk. **Other phones:** Assessor-936-598-4441; Treasurer-936-598-3581; Appraiser-936-598-6171; Elections-936-598-6361; Vital Records-936-598-6361.

Sherman County

County Clerk, PO Box 270, Stratford, TX 79084. **Phone**-806-366-2371; fax-806-366-5670; hours 8AM-12:00-1-5PM

Will search UCC records prior to 7/2001 & current fixture files. Search per debtor- $10.00. Search request using non-standard form (per name)- $25.00. Will not search real estate records. UCC copy- $1.00 per page. Cert fee: $5.00. Payee: Sherman County Clerk. **Other phones:** Assessor-806-396-2150; Treasurer-806-396-5842; Appraiser-806-396-5566.

Smith County

County Clerk, PO Box 1018, Tyler, TX 75710. **Phone**-903-535-0630, R/E Recording-903-535-0652; fax-903-535-0684; hours 8AM-5PM

Will search UCC records prior to 7/2001. Search per debtor- $10.00. Search request using non-standard form (per name)- $25.00. Tax lien search- $5.00 per debtor. Cert fee: $5.00 per cert. Payee: Smith County Clerk. **Online Access to Property, Appraiser records:** Access to county appraisal district records is free at www.smithcad.org. Also, see note at beginning of section. **Other phones:** Assessor-903-535-0835; Treasurer-903-535-0555; Appraiser-903-510-8600; Elections-903-535-0657; Vital Records-903-535-0650.

Somervell County

County/District Clerk, PO Box 1098, Glen Rose, TX 76043. **Phone**-County/District Clerk, R/E & UCC Recording- 254-897-4427; fax-254-897-3233; hours 8AM-5PM

Will search UCC records prior to 7/2001 & current fixture files. Search per debtor- $10.00. Search request using non-standard form (per name)- $25.00. Will not search real estate or tax lien records. Record copy- $1.00 per page. Cert fee: $5.00 per cert. Payee: Somervell County Clerk. **Online Access to Appraiser, Property Tax records:** See note at beginning of section. **Other phones:** Assessor-254-897-2419; Treasurer-254-897-4814; Appraiser-254-897-4094; Elections-254-897-4427; Vital Records-254-897-4427.

Starr County

County Clerk, Courthouse, Rio Grande City, TX 78582. **Phone**-956-487-8032; fax-956-487-8624; hours 8AM-5PM. Will search UCC records. Search per debtor- $10.00. Tax liens not included in UCC search. Separate federal/state combined tax lien search- $10.00 per debtor. RE owner, mortgage, property transfer searches available. Record copy- $1.00 per page. Cert fee: $5.00 per cert. Payee: Starr County Clerk. **Other phones:** Assessor-956-487-8136; Treasurer-956-487-8106; Appraiser-956-487-5613; Vital Records-956-487-8032.

Stephens County

County Clerk, Courthouse, Breckenridge, TX 76424. **Phone**-County Clerk, R/E & UCC Recording- 254-559-3700; hours 8AM-5PM

Will search UCC records prior to 7/2001 & current fixture files. Search per debtor- $10.00. Search request using non-standard form (per name)- $25.00. UCC search includes tax liens if requested. Separate federal/state combined tax lien search- $5.00 per doc. Will not search real estate records. RE record copy- $1.00 per page. UCC copy- $2.00 per page. Cert fee: $5.00 per cert. Payee: Stephens County Clerk. **Other phones:** Assessor-254-559-2732; Treasurer-254-559-3181; Appraiser-254-559-8233; Elections-254-559-3700; Vital Records-254-559-3700.

Sterling County

County Clerk, PO Box 55, Sterling City, TX 76951-0055. **Phone**-County Clerk, R/E & UCC Recording-325-378-5191; fax-325-378-2266; hours 8AM-4PM M-Th; 8AM-1:30PM Fri.

Will search UCC records prior to 7/2001 & current fixture files. Search per debtor- $10.00. Search request using non-standard form (per name)- $25.00. Tax liens not included in UCC search. Federal/state combined tax lien search- $5.00 each. Will not search real estate records. Record copy- $1.00 per page. Cert fee: $5.00 per cert. Payee: Sterling County Clerk. **Other phones:** Assessor-325-378-7711; Treasurer-325-378-8511; Appraiser-325-378-7711; Elections-325-378-5191; Vital Records-325-378-5191.

Stonewall County

County Clerk, PO Drawer P, Aspermont, TX 79502. **Phone**-County Clerk, R/E & UCC Recording- 940-989-2272; hours 8AM-4:30PM

Will search UCC records prior to 7/2001 & current fixture files. Search per debtor- $10.00. Tax liens not included in UCC search. Tax lien search- $5.00 per search. RE owner, mortgage, property transfer searches available. Record copy- $1.00 per page. Cert fee: $5.00 per cert. Payee: Stonewall County Clerk. **Other phones:** Assessor-940-989-2633; Treasurer-940-989-3520; Appraiser-940-989-3363; Elections-940-989-2272; Vital Records-940-989-2272.

Sutton County

County Clerk, 300 E. Oak, #3, Sutton County Annex, Sonora, TX 76950. **Phone**-325-387-3815; hours 8:30AM-4:30PM. Will search UCC records prior to

7/2001 & current fixture files. Search per debtor-$10.00. Tax liens not included in UCC search. Separate federal Tax lien search- $10.00 per debtor. RE owner, mortgage, property transfer searches available. Record copy- $1.00 per page. Cert fee: $5.00 per cert. Payee: Sutton County Clerk. **Other phones:** Assessor-325-387-2342; Treasurer-325-387-2886; Appraiser-325-387-2809.

Swisher County

County Clerk, 119 S. Maxwell, Courthouse, Tulia, TX 79088. **Phone-**County Clerk, R/E & UCC Recording-806-995-3294; fax-806-995-4121; hours 8AM-5PM
Will not search UCC or real estate records. Separate federal/state combined tax lien search- $5.00 per debtor, $5.00 each add'l name. UCC copy- $1.00 per page. Cert fee: $5.00 per cert. Payee: Swisher County Clerk. **Online Access to Appraiser, Property Tax records:** Search the appraisal tax rolls for free at www.txcountydata.com/county.asp?County=219. Also see notes at beginning of section. Will search Spouses names with no additional charge. **Other phones:** Assessor-806-995-3513; Treasurer-806-995-2204; Appraiser-806-995-4118; Elections-806-995-3294; Vital Records-806-995-3294.

Tarrant County

County Clerk, 100 W. Weatherford, Courthouse, Rm 130, Ft. Worth, TX 76196. **Phone-**817-884-1060; hours 8AM-4:30PM
www.tarrantcounty.com/tc_countyclerk/site/default.asp
Will search UCC records prior to 7/2001 & current fixture files. Search per debtor- $16.00. Search request using non-standard form (per name)-$31.00. Will not search real estate or tax lien records. UCC copy- $1.00 per page. Cert fee: $5.00 per cert. Payee: Tarrant County Clerk. **Online Access to Property Tax, Appraiser, Real Estate, Grantor/Grantee, Lien records:** Access to the county Appraisal District Property data is free at www.tad.org/Datasearch/datasearch.htm. Also, online access to the county clerk's real estate and grantor/grantee index is free at www.tarrantcounty.com/tc_countyclerk/lib/tc_countyclerk/search.asp, also at www.titlex.com where records range from 4/1997 to 11/2001 only. Also, online access to property tax data is free at www.tad.org/Datasearch/datasearch.htm. Also, see note at beginning of section. **Other phones:** Assessor-817-284-0024; Appraiser-817-284-0024; Elections-817-884-1115.

Taylor County

County Clerk, PO Box 5497, Abilene, TX 79608. **Phone-**325-674-1202; fax-325-674-1279; hours 8AM-5PM www.taylorcad.org
Will search UCC records prior to 7/2001 until 6/30/2006. Search per debtor- $10.00. Tax liens not included in UCC search. Federal tax lien search-$10.00; state lien-$5.00 per debtor. Will not search real estate records. Record copy- $1.00 per page. Cert fee: $5.00 per cert. Payee: Taylor County Clerk. **Online Access to Appraiser, Property Tax, Personal Property, Unclaimed Property records:** Access to the county Central Appraisal District database is free at www.taylorcad.org/tayname.html. Search is by name; other methods are at the website listed above. Search business personal property at www.taylorcad.org/tayppname.html. Also, search the treasurer's database of unclaimed property free at www.taylorcountytexas.org/unclaime.html. Real Property records at www.taylorcountytexas.org. Also, see note at beginning of section. **Other phones:** Assessor-325-672-4870; Treasurer-325-674-1231; Appraiser-325-676-9381; Elections-325-674-1216; Vital Records-325-674-1202.

Terrell County

County Clerk, PO Drawer 410, Sanderson, TX 79848. **Phone-**County Clerk, R/E & UCC Recording- 432-345-2391; fax-432-345-2740; hours 9AM-5PM
Will search UCC records prior to 7/2001 & current fixture files. Search per debtor- $10.00. UCC copy-$1.00 per page. Cert fee: $5.00. Payee: Terrell County Clerk. **Online Access to Property, Appraiser records:** Access to the county appriasal records is free at http://65.107.178.35/clientdb/main.asp?id=16. **Other phones:** Assessor-432-345-2525; Appraiser-432-345-2251.

Terry County

County Clerk, 501 W. Main, Rm 105, Brownfield, TX 79316-4398. **Phone-**County Clerk, R/E & UCC Recording- 806-637-8551; fax-806-637-4874; hours 8:30AM-5PM
Will search UCC records prior to 7/2001 & current fixture files. Search per debtor standard form-$10.00. Search per debtor non-standard form-$25.00. Tax lien search- $15.00 per debtor. Will not search real estate records. RE record copy- $1.50 per page. UCC copy- $1.00 per page. Cert fee: $5.00 per doc. Payee: Terry County Clerk. **Other phones:** Assessor-806-637-6966; Treasurer-806-637-3616; Appraiser-806-637-6966; Elections-806-637-8551; Vital Records-806-637-8551.

Throckmorton County

County Clerk, PO Box 309, Throckmorton, TX 76483. **Phone-**County Clerk, R/E & UCC Recording- 940-849-2501; fax-940-849-3220; hours 8AM-Noon; 1:00-5:00PM
Will search UCC records prior to 7/2001 & current fixture files. Search per debtor- $10.00. Tax lien search- $10.00 per debtor. RE record copy- $1.00 per page. Cert fee: $1.00 per page. Payee: County/Disrtict Clerk. **Other phones:** Assessor-940-849-9421; Treasurer-940-849-2921; Appraiser-940-849-5691; Elections-Vital Records-940-849-2501.

Titus County

County Clerk, 100 W. 1 St., 2nd Fl, #204, Mount Pleasant, TX 75455. **Phone-**903-577-6796; fax-903-572-5078; hours 8AM-5PM
Will not search UCC or real estate records. Separate federal/state combined tax lien search- $10.00 per debtor. UCC copy- $1.00 per page. Cert fee: $5.00 per cert. Payee: Titus County Clerk. **Online Access to Property, Appraiser records:** Access to property data is available for download from a private company; fees apply; visit www.ptax.org/tax_office_data.htm or phone 201-571-0425. **Other phones:** Assessor-903-572-6712; Treasurer-903-572-8723; Appraiser-903-577-7939.

Tom Green County

County Clerk, 124 W. Beauregard, San Angelo, TX 76903-5835. **Phone-**County Clerk, R/E & UCC Recording- 325-659-6552, UCC Recording-325-659-3262; fax-325-659-3251; hours 8AM-4:30PM
Will not search UCC records. Federal/state combined tax lien search- $15.00 per debtor. Will search real estate records. RE record copy- $1.00 per page. UCC copy- $1.50 per page. Cert fee: $5.00 per cert. Payee: Tom Green County Clerk. **Other phones:** Appraiser-325-658-5575; Elections-325-659-6541; Vital Records-325-659-6556.

Travis County

County Clerk, PO Box 149325, Austin, TX 78714-9325. **Phone-**512-854-9188, R/E Recording-512-854-4526; fax-512-854-4526; hours 8AM-5PM www.traviscad.org
For Recording, Elections, Accounting and Admin Div, courier address is: 5501 Airport Blvd, Austin, TX

78751. Will search UCC records prior to 7/2001 & current fixture files. Search per debtor- $10.00. Search request using non-standard form (per name)- $25.00. Tax liens not included in UCC search. Tax lien search- $10.00 per debtor. RE owner, mortgage, property transfer searches available. Record copy- $1.00 per page. Cert fee: $5.00 per cert. Payee: Travis County Clerk. **Online Access to Appraiser, Property Tax, Business Property, Voter Registration, Grantor/Grantee, Recording, UCC, Marriage, Probate records:** Access to recorders official records is free at http://deed.co.travis.tx.us/search.aspx?cabinet=opr. Access to the Central Appraisal District database is free at www.traviscad.org/search.htm. Also search business personal property. Also, search voter registration rolls free at www.texasonline.com/travisco/voter/home.htm. Also, search on the county tax payment system at www.texasonline.state.tx.us/NASApp/rap/BaseRap. Also, See note at beginning of section. **Other phones:** Assessor-512-854-9473; Treasurer-512-854-9000; Appraiser-512-854-9317; Elections-512-854-9075; Vital Records-512-458-7111.

Trinity County

County Clerk, PO Box 456, Groveton, TX 75845. **Phone-**County Clerk, R/E & UCC Recording- 936-642-1208; fax-936-642-3004; hours 8AM-5PM
Will search UCC records. Search per debtor- $10.00. Tax liens not included in UCC search. Tax lien search- $10.00 per debtor. Will search real estate records. Record copy- $1.00 per page. Cert fee: $5.00 per cert. Payee: Trinity County Clerk. **Other phones:** Assessor-936-642-1637; Treasurer-936-642-1443; Appraiser-936-642-1502; Elections-936-642-1208; Vital Records-936-642-1208.

Tyler County

County Clerk, 110 W. Bluff, Rm 110, Woodville, TX 75979. **Phone-**409-283-2281, R/E Recording-409-283-2281 x10, UCC Recording-409-283-2281 x13; hours 8AM-4:30PM
Searches are not guaranteed, they are only a computerized index print out. Will search UCC records prior to 7/2001 & current fixture files. Search per debtor- $10.00. Search request using non-standard form (per name)- $25.00. Tax liens not included in UCC search. Tax lien search- $10.00 per debtor. RE owner, mortgage, property transfer searches available. RE record copy- $1.00 per page. UCC copy- $2.00 per page. Cert fee: $5.00 per cert. Payee: Tyler County Clerk. **Online Access to Property, Appraiser records:** Access to the county appraisal district records is free at www.tylercad.org. **Other phones:** Assessor-409-283-2734; Treasurer-409-283-3054; Appraiser-409-283-3736; Elections-409-283-2281 x10; Vital Records-409-283-2281 x15.

Upshur County

County Clerk, PO Box 730, Gilmer, TX 75644. **Phone-**903-843-4014, R/E Recording-903-680-8123, 8124, 8125, UCC Recording-903-843-4015; fax-903-843-5492; hours 8AM-5PM
Will search UCC records prior to 7/2001 & current fixture files. Search per debtor- $10.00. Tax liens not included in UCC search. Federal/state combined tax lien search- $5.00 per debtor. RE owner, mortgage, property transfer searches available. Record copy- $1.00 per page. Cert fee: $5.00 per cert. Payee: Upshur County Clerk. **Online Access to Appraiser, Property Tax, Real Estate, Grantor/Grantee, Lien, Judgment records:** The grantor/grantee index is at www.titlex.com. Select Upshur from the county list. Records go back to 4/1978. Also, see note at beginning of section. **Other phones:** Assessor-903-843-3085; Treasurer-903-680-8135, 8136, 8138; Appraiser-903-843-3041; Elections-903-

680-8126; Vital Records-903-680-8123; Civil, Criminal & Probate-903-680-8126, 8127.

Upton County

County Clerk, PO Box 465, Rankin, TX 79778. **Phone-**County Clerk, R/E & UCC Recording- 432-693-2861; fax-432-693-2129; hours-8AM-5PM www.co.upton.tx.us
Will search UCC records. Search per debtor- $10.00. Search request using non-standard form (per name)- $25.00. Federal/state combined tax lien search- $5.00 per search. Will search real estate records. Copy fee- $1.00 per page. Cert fee: $5.00. Payee: Upton County Clerk. **Other phones:** Assessor-432-693-2572; Treasurer-432-693-2401; Appraiser-432-652-3221; Elections-432-693-2861; Vital Records-432-693-2861.

Uvalde County

County Clerk, PO Box 284, Uvalde, TX 78802-0284. **Phone-**County Clerk, R/E & UCC Recording- 830-278-6614; hours 8AM-5PM
Will search UCC records prior to 7/2001 & current fixture files. Search per debtor- $10.00 per 10 year. Search request using non-standard form (per name)- $25.00. UCC search includes tax liens if requested. RE owner, mortgage, property transfer searches available. UCC copy- $1.00 per page. Cert fee: $5.00 per cert. Payee: Uvalde County Clerk. **Online Access to Property, Appraiser records:** Access to the county appriasal district tax information is free at www.eztaxonline.com/uvalde/main.jsp. **Other phones:** Assessor-830-278-3225; Treasurer-830-278-5821; Appraiser-830-278-1106; Elections-830-278-6614; Vital Records-830-278-6614.

Val Verde County

County Clerk, PO Box 1267, Del Rio, TX 78841-1267. **Phone-**830-774-7564; hours 8AM-4:30PM
Will not search UCC or tax liens records. Will search real estate records only with volume and page number. RE record copy- $1.00 per page. UCC copy- $2.00 per page. Cert fee: $5.00 per cert. Payee: Val Verde County Clerk. **Other phones:** Assessor-830-774-7535; Treasurer-210-774-4602; Appraiser-830-774-4602.

Van Zandt County

County Clerk, 121 E. Dallas St, Courthouse - Rm 202, Canton, TX 75103. **Phone-**County Clerk, R/E & UCC Recording- 903-567-6503; fax-903-567-6722; hours 8AM-5PM
Will search UCC records. Search per debtor- $10.00. Federal/state combined tax lien search- $10.00 per debtor. Will not search real estate records. RE record copy- $2.00 per page. UCC copy- $1.00 per page. Cert fee: $6.00 1st page, $2.00 each add'l. Payee: Van Zandt County Clerk. **Online Access to Property Appraisal, Land, Grantor/Grantee, Judgment, Lien records:** Search the county appraisal rolls for free at www.vanzandtcad.org. Also includes plat maps online. The grantor/grantee index is at www.titlex.com. Select Van Zandt from the county list. Record range is 1/1971 to 9/2003. Also, see note at beginning of section. **Other phones:** Assessor-903-567-6171; Treasurer-903-567-2551; Appraiser-903-567-6171; Elections-903-567-6503; Vital Records-903-567-6503.

Victoria County

County Clerk, PO Box 1968, Victoria, TX 77902. **Phone-**County Clerk, R/E & UCC Recording- 361-575-1478; fax-361-575-6276; hours 8AM-5PM
Will search UCC records prior to 7/2001 & current fixture files. Search per debtor- $10.00. Search request using non-standard form (per name)- $25.00. Tax liens not included in UCC search. Tax lien search- $10.00 per debtor. Will not search real

estate records. RE record copy- $1.00 per page. UCC copy- $1.50 per page. Cert fee: $5.00 per cert. Payee: Victoria County Clerk. **Online Access to Appraiser, Property Tax, Land, Grantor/Grantee, Judgment, Lien records:** The grantor/grantee index is at www.titlex.com. Select Victoria from the county list. Records go back to 1/1964. Also, access to appriasal district records is free at www.victoriacad.org. Also, see note at beginning of section. **Other phones:** Assessor-361-576-3671; Treasurer-361-575-8588; Appraiser-361-576-3621; Elections-361-576-0124; Vital Records-361-575-1478 (county); Vital Records (city)-361-485-3040.

Walker County

County Clerk, PO Box 210, Huntsville, TX 77342-0210. **Phone-**County Clerk, R/E & UCC Recording-936-436-4922; fax-936-436-4928; 8AM-4:45PM
Will search UCC records prior to 7/2001 & current fixture files. Search per debtor- $10.00. UCC search includes tax liens if requested. RE owner, mortgage, property transfer searches available. RE record copy- $1.00 per page. UCC copy- $1.50 per page. $5.00 Min. Cert fee: $5.00 per cert. Payee: James D. Patton, County Clerk. **Online Access to Property, Appraiser records:** Access to appraisal district records is free at http://65.107.178.35/client db/main.asp?id=4. **Other phones:** Assessor-936-436-4959; Treasurer-936-436-4933; Appraiser-936-295-0402; Elections-936-436-4950; Vital Records-936-436-4922.

Waller County

County Clerk, 836 Austin St, Rm 217, Hempstead, TX 77445. **Phone-**County Clerk, R/E & UCC Recording-979-826-7711; hours 8AM-Noon, 1-5PM
Will search UCC records prior to 7/2001 & current fixture files. Search per debtor- $10.00. Search request using non-standard form (per name)- $25.00. Will not search real estate or tax lien records. Record copy- $1.00 per page. Cert fee: $5.00 per cert. Payee: Waller County Clerk. **Online Access to Appraiser, Property Tax records:** See note at beginning of section. **Other phones:** Assessor-979-826-7620; Treasurer-979-826-7707; Appraiser-409-396-6100; Elections-979-826-7643; Vital Records-979-826-7711.

Ward County

County Clerk, Corner of 4 & Allen, Monahans, TX 79756. **Phone-**432-943-3294; hours 8AM-5PM
Will not search UCC or real estate records. Federal/state combined tax lien search- $10.00 per debtor. Record copy- $1.00 per page. Cert fee: $5.00 + $1.00 per page. Payee: Ward County Clerk. **Other phones:** Assessor-432-943-2546; Treasurer-432-943-2841; Appraiser-432-943-3224; Elections-432-943-3294; Vital Records-432-943-3294.

Washington County

County Clerk, 100 E. Main, #102, Brenham, TX 77833. **Phone-**979-277-6200; fax-979-277-6278; hours 8AM-5PM www.co.washington.tx.us/cclerk/index.html
Will search UCC records prior to 7/2001 & current fixture files. Search per debtor- $5.00. Tax lien search- $5.00 per debtor. Will search real estate records. Copy fee-$1.00 per page. Copy fee is $1.00 per page. Cert fee: $5.00 per doc. Payee: Washington County Clerk. **Online Access to Recording, Land, Marriage, Death, Birth, Military Discharge, Grantor/Grantee, Judgment, Lien records:** Access to county clerk's recordings is free at www.apolloplus.com/edocket/washington/washingtonc c.htm. Also, the grantor/grantee index is at www.titlex.com. Select Washington from the county list. Record range-1/1965 to 12/2003. Also, appraisal district records may be at www.washingtoncad.org or www.co.washington.tx.us/taxac.html. Also, see note at

beginning of section. **Other phones:** Assessor-979-277-6200; Treasurer-979-277-6200; Appraiser-979-277-6528; Elections-979-277-6200; Vital Records-979-277-6200.

Webb County

County Clerk, PO Box 29, Laredo, TX 78042. **Phone-**956-523-4622, R/E Recording-956-523-4266, UCC Recording-956-523-4266; fax-956-523-5035; hours 8AM-5PM www.webbcounty.com
Will search UCC records prior to 7/2001 & current fixture files. Search per debtor- $10.00. Search request using non-standard form (per name)- $25.00. UCC search includes tax liens if requested. Separate federal/state combined tax lien search- %5.00 per 10 years. RE owner, mortgage, property transfer searches available. Record copy- $1.00 per page. Cert fee: $5.00 per cert. Payee: Webb County Clerk. **Online Access to Appraiser, Property Tax records:** Search the county Central Appraisal District database at www.webbcad.org/search1.htm. Also, See note at beginning of section. **Other phones:** Assessor-956-523-4200; Treasurer-956-523-4150; Appraiser-956-718-4091; Elections-956-523-4050; Vital Records-956-523-4266 (outside city limits); Vital Records (inside city limits)-956-795-4929.

Wharton County

County Clerk, PO Box 69, Wharton, TX 77488. **Phone-**County Clerk, R/E & UCC Recording- 979-532-2381; fax-979-532-8426; hours 8AM-5PM
Will not search UCC or real estate records. Tax lien search- $10.00 per debtor. RE record copy- $1.00 per page. UCC copy- $2.00 per page. Cert fee: $5.00 per cert. Payee: Wharton County Clerk. **Online Access to Appraiser, Property Tax, Real Estate, Grantor/Grantee, Judgment, Lien records:** The grantor/grantee index is at www.titlex.com. Select Wharton from the county list. Records go up to 11/2003. Also, see note at beginning of section. **Other phones:** Assessor-979-532-3312; Treasurer-979-532-2971; Appraiser-979-532-8931; Elections-979-532-2381; Vital Records-979-532-2381.

Wheeler County

County Clerk, PO Box 465, Wheeler, TX 79096. **Phone-**806-826-5544; fax-806-826-3282; hours 8AM-5PM
Will search UCC records prior to 7/2001. Search per debtor- $10.00. Search request using non-standard form (per name)- $25.00. Will search tax liens including federal tax liens. Separate federal/state tax lien search- $10.00 per debtor. Will not search real estate records. Record copy- $1.00 per page. Cert fee: $5.00 per cert. Payee: Wheeler County Clerk. **Other phones:** Assessor-806-826-3131; Treasurer-806-826-3122; Appraiser-806-826-5900.

Wichita County

County Clerk, PO Box 1679, Wichita Falls, TX 76307-1679. **Phone-**940-766-8144, R/E Recording-940-766-8160, UCC Recording-940-766-8160; fax-940-716-8554; hours 8AM-5PM
Will search UCC records prior to 7/2001 & current fixture files. Search per debtor- $10.00. Search request using non-standard form (per name)- $25.00. Tax liens not included in UCC search. Federal/state combined tax lien search- $10.00 per debtor. Will not search real estate records. Record copy- $1.00 per page. Cert fee: $5.00 per cert. Payee: Wichita County Clerk. **Online Access to Property, Appraisal records:** Access to county appraisal district records is free at www.wadtx.com/search.php. Also, see note at beginning of section. **Other phones:** Assessor-940-322-2435; Treasurer-940-766-8245; Appraiser-940-322-2435; Elections-940-766-8174; Vital Records-940-766-8144.

Wilbarger County

County Clerk, 1700 Main St. #15, Courthouse, Vernon, TX 76384. **Phone-**County Clerk, R/E & UCC Recording- 940-552-5486; fax-940-553-2320; hours 8AM-5PM

Will search UCC records prior to 7/2001 & current fixture files. Search per debtor- $13.00. Tax liens not included in UCC search. Separate federal Tax lien search- $5.00 per debtor. Will not search real estate records. UCC copy- $1.00 per page. Cert fee: $5.00 per cert. Payee: Wilbarger County Clerk. **Online Access to Property Tax, Personal Property records:** Search the appraisal rolls for free at www.taxnetusa.com/cfmsite/Wilbarger/default.html. Also see note at beginning of section. **Other phones:** Assessor-940-552-9341; Treasurer-940-553-2302; Appraiser-940-553-1857; Elections-940-552-5486; Vital Records-940-552-5486.

Willacy County

County Clerk, 540 W. Hidalgo Ave, Courthouse Bldg, 1st Fl, Raymondville, TX 78580. **Phone-**County Clerk, R/E & UCC Recording- 956-689-2710; fax-956-689-0937; hours 8AM-Noon, 1-5PM

Will search UCC records prior to 7/2001 & current fixture files. Search per debtor- $10.00. Search request using non-standard form (per name)- $25.00. UCC search includes tax liens. Will not search real estate records. UCC copy- $1.00 per page. Cert fee: $5.00 per cert. Payee: Willacy County Clerk. **Online Access to Proeprty, Appraiser, Real Estate, Grantor/Grantee, Judgment, Lien records:** The grantor/grantee index is at www.titlex.com. Select Willacy from the county list. Record range is 8/1998 to 1/2004. Also, see note at beginning of section. **Other phones:** Assessor-956-689-3621; Treasurer-956-689-2772; Appraiser-956-689-5979; Elections-956-689-2710; Vital Records-956-689-2710.

Williamson County

County Clerk, PO Box 18, Georgetown, TX 78627-0018. **Phone-**County Clerk, R/E & UCC Recording-512-943-1515, UCC Recording-512-943-1514; fax-512-943-1616; hours 8AM-5PM www.wilco.org

Will search UCC records prior to 7/2001. Search per debtor- $10.00. Tax liens not included in UCC search. Federal/state combined tax lien search-$10.00 per lien. Will not search real estate records. RE record copy- $1.00 per page. UCC copy- $1.50 if less than 5 copies requested. Cert fee: $5.00 per cert. Payee: Williamson County Clerk. **Online Access to Appraiser, Property Tax, Tax Sale, Land, Grantor/Grantee, Judgment, Lien, Jail, Sheriff Bond records:** The grantor/grantee index is at www.titlex.com. Select Williamson from the county list. Records go back to 5/1999. Also, online access to the appraiser database is free at www.wcad.org/. Also, see note at beginning of section. Search the county jail inmate list at http://judicialsearch.wilco.org/SherSearch/jailfrmd.htm. Also, online access to the monthly delinquent tax sale list is free at www.williamson-county.org/Assessor/Tax.html. Also, search the sheriff's bond database at http://judicialsearch.wilco.org/S

herSearch/bondfrmd.htm. **Other phones:** Assessor-512-943-1603; Treasurer-512-943-1587; Appraiser-512-930-3787; Elections-512-943-1630; Vital Records-512-943-1512.

Wilson County

County Clerk, PO Box 27, Floresville, TX 78114. **Phone-**County Clerk, R/E & UCC Recording- 830-393-7308; fax-830-393-7334; hours 8AM-5PM

Will search UCC records prior to 7/2001 & current fixture files. Search per debtor- $10.00. UCC search includes tax liens if requested. Separate federal/state combined tax lien search- $10.00 per debtor. Real estate record owner searches available. Record copy- $1.00 per page. Cert fee: $5.00 per cert. Payee: Wilson County Clerk. **Online Access to Property Tax, Appraiser records:** Access to the county CAD records is free at http://65.107.178.35/clientdb/main.asp?id=22. Also, see note at beginning of section. **Other phones:** Assessor-830-393-7380; Treasurer-830-393-7310; Appraiser-830-393-3065; Elections-830-393-7368; Vital Records-830-393-7308.

Winkler County

County Clerk, PO Box 1007, Kermit, TX 79745. **Phone-**432-586-3401; hours 8AM-5PM

Will not search UCC or real estate records. Tax lien search- $5.00 per debtor. RE record copy- $1.00 per page. UCC copy- $1.50 per page. Cert fee: $5.00 per cert. Payee: Winkler County Clerk. **Other phones:** Assessor-432-586-3465; Treasurer-432-586-6604; Appraiser-432-586-2832.

Wise County

County Clerk, PO Box 359, Decatur, TX 76234. **Phone-**940-627-3351; fax-940-627-2138; 8AM-5PM

Will search UCC records prior to 7/2001 & current fixture files. Search per debtor- $10.00. Will search real estate records. UCC copy- $1.00 per page. Cert fee: $5.00 per cert. Payee: Wise County Clerk. **Online Access to Property, Appraiser records:** Access to appriasal district records is free at www.wisecad.org. **Other phones:** Assessor-940-627-3523; Treasurer-940-627-3540; Appraiser-940-627-3081; Elections-940-627-3523; Vital Records-940-627-3351.

Wood County

County Clerk, PO Box 1796, Quitman, TX 75783. **Phone-**County Clerk, R/E & UCC Recording- 903-763-2711; fax-903-763-5641; hours 8AM-5PM www.co.wood.tx.us

Will not search records. RE record copy- $1.00 per page. UCC copy- $2.00 per page. Cert fee: $5.00 per cert. Payee: Wood County Clerk. **Other phones:** Assessor-903-763-2261; Treasurer-903-763-4186; Appraiser-903-763-4946; Elections-903-763-2711; Vital Records-903-763-2711.

Yoakum County

County Clerk, PO Box 309, Plains, TX 79335. **Phone-**806-456-2721; fax-806-456-2258; hours 8AM-5PM

Until 2008, they will search UCC records prior to 7/2001 & current fixture files. Search per debtor- $5.00. UCC search includes tax liens if requested. Real estate record owner and property transfer searches available. Record copy- $1.00 per page. Cert fee: $5.00 per cert. Payee: Yoakum County Clerk. **Other phones:** Assessor-806-456-2825; Treasurer-806-456-8794; Appraiser-806-456-7101; Elections-806-456-2721; Vital Records-806-456-2721.

Young County

County Clerk, 516 Fourth St #104, Graham, TX 76450-3063. **Phone-**940-549-8432, R/E Recording-940-539-8432, UCC Recording-940-539-8432; fax-940-521-0305; hours 8:30AM-5PM

Will not search UCC or real estate records. Tax lien search- $10.00 per debtor. RE record copy- $1.00 per page. UCC copy- $2.00 per page. Cert fee: $5.00 per cert. Payee: Young County Clerk. **Online Access to Property, Appraiser records:** Access to property data is available for download from a private company; fees apply; visit www.ptax.org/tax_office_data.htm or phone 201-571-0425. **Other phones:** Assessor-940-549-1393; Treasurer-940-549-2633; Appraiser-940-549-2392; Elections-940-549-5132; Vital Records-940-539-8432; 940-539-8433.

Zapata County

County Clerk, PO Box 789, Zapata, TX 78076. **Phone-**956-765-9915; fax-956-765-9933; hours 8AM-5PM

Will search UCC records prior to 7/2001 & current fixture files. Search per debtor- $10.00. UCC search includes tax liens if requested. Tax lien search- $5.00 per debtor. RE owner, mortgage, property transfer searches available. RE record copy- $1.00 per page. UCC copy- $1.50 per page but not less than 5. Cert fee: $5.00 per cert. Payee: Zapata County Clerk. **Online Access to Property, Appraiser records:** Access to appraisal district records is free at www.zapatacad.org. **Other phones:** Assessor-956-765-9971; Treasurer-956-765-9925; Appraiser-956-765-9971.

Zavala County

County Clerk, Zavala Courthouse, Crystal City, TX 78839. **Phone-**County Clerk, R/E & UCC Recording-830-374-2331; fax-830-374-5955; hours 8AM-5PM

Will search UCC records prior to 7/2001 & current fixture files. Search per debtor- $10.00. UCC search includes tax liens if requested. Tax lien search- $10.00 per debtor. RE owner, mortgage, property transfer searches available. Record copy- $1.00 per page. Cert fee: $1.00 per cert. Payee: Zavala County Clerk. **Other phones:** Assessor-830-347-2351; Treasurer-830-374-2442; Appraiser-830-374-3476..

Texas County Locator

You will usually be able to find the city name in the City/County Cross Reference below. In that case, it is a simple matter to determine the county from the cross reference. However, only the official US Postal Service city names are included in this index. We have also included a ZIP/City Cross Reference immediately following the City/County Cross Reference. If you know the ZIP Code but the city name does not appear in the City/County Cross Reference index, look up the ZIP Code in the ZIP/City Cross Reference, find the city name, then look up the city name in the City/County Cross Reference.

Texas City/County Cross Reference

ABBOTT (76621) Hill(94), McLennan(5)
ABERNATHY (79311) Hale(68), Lubbock(31)
ABILENE (79601) Taylor(77), Jones(16), Callahan(3), Shackelford(2)
ABILENE (79602) Taylor(94), Callahan(5)
ABILENE Taylor
ACE Polk
ACKERLY (79713) Martin(38), Dawson(29), Howard(25), Borden(7)
ADDISON Dallas
ADKINS (78101) Bexar(82), Wilson(17)
ADRIAN (79001) Oldham(70), Deaf Smith(30)
AFTON Dickens
AGUA DULCE Nueces
AIKEN Floyd
ALAMO Hidalgo
ALANREED Gray
ALBA (75410) Wood(72), Rains(27)
ALBANY Shackelford
ALEDO (76008) Parker(84), Tarrant(15)
ALICE (78332) Jim Wells(98), Duval(1)
ALICE Jim Wells
ALIEF Harris
ALLEN Collin
ALLEYTON Colorado
ALLISON Wheeler
ALPINE Brewster
ALTAIR Colorado
ALTO Cherokee
ALVARADO Johnson
ALVIN (77511) Brazoria(93), Galveston(6)
ALVIN Brazoria
ALVORD Wise
AMARILLO (79124) Potter(93), Randall(6)
AMARILLO (79121) Randall(76), Potter(23)
AMARILLO Potter
AMARILLO Randall
AMHERST Lamb
ANAHUAC Chambers
ANDERSON Grimes
ANDREWS Andrews
ANGLETON Brazoria
ANNA Collin
ANNONA Red River
ANSON Jones
ANTHONY El Paso
ANTON (79313) Hockley(74), Lamb(17), Lubbock(5), Hale(1)
APPLE SPRINGS Trinity
AQUILLA (76622) Hill(92), McLennan(7)
ARANSAS PASS (78336) San Patricio(88), Aransas(11)
ARANSAS PASS San Patricio
ARCHER CITY Archer
ARGYLE Denton
ARLINGTON Tarrant
ARMSTRONG Kenedy
ARP Smith
ART Mason
ARTESIA WELLS La Salle
ARTHUR CITY Lamar
ASHERTON Dimmit
ASPERMONT Stonewall
ATASCOSA Bexar
ATHENS (75751) Henderson(98), Anderson(1)

ATHENS (75752) Henderson(93), Van Zandt(6)
ATLANTA Cass
AUBREY Denton
AUSTIN (78737) Hays(57), Travis(42)
AUSTIN (78728) Travis(94), Williamson(5)
AUSTIN (78736) Travis(97), Hays(2)
AUSTIN (78750) Travis(51), Williamson(48)
AUSTIN (78729) Williamson(92), Travis(7)
AUSTIN Travis
AUSTIN Williamson
AUSTWELL Refugio
AVALON Ellis
AVERY (75554) Red River(95), Bowie(4)
AVINGER (75630) Marion(55), Cass(44)
AXTELL (76624) McLennan(95), Limestone(4)
AZLE (76020) Tarrant(51), Parker(45), Wise(3)
AZLE Parker
BACLIFF Galveston
BAGWELL Red River
BAILEY Fannin
BAIRD Callahan
BALLINGER Runnels
BALMORHEA Reeves
BANDERA Bandera
BANGS (76823) Brown(88), Coleman(11)
BANQUETE Nueces
BARDWELL Ellis
BARKER Harris
BARKSDALE (78828) Edwards(68), Real(31)
BARNHART (76930) Irion(58), Crockett(41)
BARRY Navarro
BARSTOW Ward
BARTLETT (76511) Bell(53), Williamson(28), Milam(18)
BASTROP Bastrop
BATESVILLE Zavala
BATSON Hardin
BAY CITY Matagorda
BAYSIDE Refugio
BAYTOWN (77521) Harris(96), Chambers(3)
BAYTOWN Harris
BEASLEY Fort Bend
BEAUMONT Jefferson
BEBE Gonzales
BECKVILLE Panola
BEDFORD Tarrant
BEDIAS Grimes
BEEVILLE Bee
BELLAIRE Harris
BELLEVUE (76228) Clay(88), Montague(11)
BELLS Grayson
BELLVILLE Austin
BELMONT Gonzales
BELTON Bell
BEN ARNOLD Milam
BEN BOLT Jim Wells
BEN FRANKLIN Delta
BEN WHEELER Van Zandt
BENAVIDES Duval
BEND San Saba
BENJAMIN Knox
BERCLAIR Goliad
BERGHEIM Kendall

BERTRAM Burnet
BIG BEND NATIONAL PARK Brewster
BIG LAKE Reagan
BIG SANDY (75755) Upshur(52), Wood(47)
BIG SANDY Upshur
BIG SPRING (79720) Howard(98), Glasscock(1)
BIG SPRING Howard
BIG WELLS Dimmit
BIGFOOT Frio
BIROME Hill
BISHOP Nueces
BIVINS Cass
BLACKWELL (79506) Nolan(55), Coke(44)
BLANCO (78606) Blanco(90), Comal(7), Kendall(1)
BLANKET (76432) Brown(94), Comanche(5)
BLEDSOE Cochran
BLEIBLERVILLE Austin
BLESSING Matagorda
BLOOMBURG Cass
BLOOMING GROVE Navarro
BLOOMINGTON Victoria
BLOSSOM Lamar
BLUE RIDGE (75424) Collin(92), Fannin(7)
BLUEGROVE Clay
BLUFF DALE (76433) Erath(72), Hood(17), Somervell(9)
BLUFFTON Llano
BLUM Hill
BOERNE (78015) Bexar(64), Kendall(32), Comal(3)
BOERNE (78006) Kendall(82), Bexar(16), Comal(1)
BOGATA Red River
BOLING (77420) Wharton(92), Matagorda(6), Fort Bend(1)
BON WIER Newton
BONHAM Fannin
BOOKER (79005) Lipscomb(63), Ochiltree(36)
BORGER Hutchinson
BOVINA Parmer
BOWIE (76230) Montague(87), Jack(8), Clay(4)
BOYD (76023) Wise(96), Parker(3)
BOYS RANCH (79010) Oldham(83), Potter(16)
BRACKETTVILLE Kinney
BRADY (76825) McCulloch(98), Mason(1)
BRANDON Hill
BRASHEAR (75420) Hopkins(96), Rains(3)
BRAZORIA Brazoria
BRECKENRIDGE Stephens
BREMOND (76629) Robertson(95), Falls(4)
BRENHAM Washington
BRIDGE CITY Orange
BRIDGEPORT (76426) Wise(95), Jack(4)
BRIGGS Burnet
BRISCOE (79011) Hemphill(59), Wheeler(40)
BROADDUS San Augustine
BRONSON (75930) Sabine(72), San Augustine(27)
BRONTE (76933) Coke(61), Runnels(38)
BROOKELAND (75931) Sabine(82), Jasper(16)

BROOKESMITH (76827) Brown(98), Coleman(1)
BROOKSHIRE (77423) Waller(94), Fort Bend(5)
BROOKSTON Lamar
BROWNFIELD Terry
BROWNSBORO (75756) Henderson(94), Van Zandt(5)
BROWNSVILLE Cameron
BROWNWOOD Brown
BRUCEVILLE (76630) McLennan(97), Falls(2)
BRUNI (78344) Webb(91), Duval(8)
BRYAN (77808) Brazos(91), Robertson(8)
BRYAN Brazos
BRYSON Jack
BUCHANAN DAM Llano
BUCKHOLTS Milam
BUDA (78610) Hays(75), Travis(22), Caldwell(2)
BUFFALO (75831) Leon(96), Freestone(3)
BUFFALO GAP Taylor
BULA (79320) Bailey(81), Lamb(18)
BULLARD (75757) Smith(70), Cherokee(29)
BULVERDE Comal
BUNA Jasper
BURKBURNETT Wichita
BURKETT Coleman
BURKEVILLE Newton
BURLESON (76028) Johnson(77), Tarrant(22)
BURLESON Johnson
BURLINGTON (76519) Milam(50), Bell(37), Falls(11)
BURNET (78611) Burnet(96), Llano(3)
BURTON Washington
BUSHLAND Potter
BYERS Clay
BYNUM Hill
CACTUS Moore
CADDO Stephens
CADDO MILLS Hunt
CALDWELL Burleson
CALL (75933) Newton(71), Jasper(28)
CALLIHAM McMullen
CALVERT Robertson
CAMDEN Polk
CAMERON Milam
CAMP WOOD (78833) Real(84), Edwards(15)
CAMPBELL Hunt
CAMPBELLTON (78008) Atascosa(97), Live Oak(2)
CANADIAN (79014) Hemphill(93), Lipscomb(6)
CANTON Van Zandt
CANUTILLO El Paso
CANYON Randall
CANYON LAKE Comal
CARBON Eastland
CAREY Childress
CARLSBAD Tom Green
CARLTON (76436) Hamilton(61), Comanche(35), Erath(2)
CARMINE (78932) Fayette(95), Washington(4)
CARRIZO SPRINGS Dimmit

CARROLLTON (75007) Denton(90), Dallas(9)
CARROLLTON Dallas
CARROLLTON Denton
CARTHAGE Panola
CASON Morris
CASTELL (76831) Llano(65), Mason(35)
CASTROVILLE Medina
CAT SPRING (78933) Colorado(64), Austin(35)
CATARINA Dimmit
CAYUGA Anderson
CEDAR CREEK (78612) Bastrop(93), Travis(6)
CEDAR HILL Dallas
CEDAR LANE Matagorda
CEDAR PARK (78613) Williamson(85), Travis(14)
CEDAR PARK Williamson
CEE VEE Cottle
CELESTE (75423) Hunt(95), Fannin(4)
CELINA (75009) Collin(95), Denton(4)
CENTER (75935) Shelby(98), San Augustine(1)
CENTER POINT Kerr
CENTERVILLE Leon
CENTRALIA Trinity
CHALK Cottle
CHANDLER (75758) Henderson(88), Van Zandt(11)
CHANNELVIEW Harris
CHANNING (79018) Hartley(58), Moore(41)
CHAPMAN RANCH Nueces
CHAPPELL HILL (77426) Washington(90), Austin(9)
CHARLOTTE Atascosa
CHATFIELD Navarro
CHEROKEE San Saba
CHESTER (75936) Tyler(72), Polk(27)
CHICO (76431) Wise(96), Jack(3)
CHICOTA Lamar
CHILDRESS (79201) Childress(95), Cottle(2), Hall(2)
CHILLICOTHE (79225) Hardeman(93), Wilbarger(6)
CHILTON Falls
CHINA Jefferson
CHINA SPRING (76633) McLennan(91), Bosque(8)
CHIRENO Nacogdoches
CHRIESMAN Burleson
CHRISTINE Atascosa
CHRISTOVAL (76935) Tom Green(78), Schleicher(21)
CIBOLO (78108) Guadalupe(80), Bexar(17), Comal(1)
CISCO (76437) Eastland(92), Callahan(4), Stephens(3)
CLARENDON (79226) Donley(88), Armstrong(7), Hall(1), Briscoe(1)
CLARKSVILLE Red River
CLAUDE (79019) Armstrong(93), Randall(6)
CLAY Burleson
CLAYTON Panola
CLEBURNE (76033) Johnson(97), Somervell(1)
CLEBURNE Johnson
CLEVELAND (77328) Montgomery(40), San Jacinto(38), Liberty(20)
CLEVELAND Liberty
CLIFTON Bosque
CLINT El Paso
CLUTE Brazoria
CLYDE Callahan
COAHOMA (79511) Howard(76), Borden(23)
COLDSPRING San Jacinto
COLEMAN Coleman
COLLEGE STATION Brazos
COLLEGEPORT Matagorda
COLLEYVILLE Tarrant

COLLINSVILLE (76233) Grayson(75), Cooke(24)
COLMESNEIL Tyler
COLORADO CITY Mitchell
COLUMBUS Colorado
COMANCHE Comanche
COMBES Cameron
COMFORT (78013) Kendall(87), Kerr(12)
COMMERCE Hunt
COMO (75431) Hopkins(78), Wood(21)
COMSTOCK Val Verde
CONCAN Uvalde
CONCEPCION Duval
CONCORD Leon
CONE Crosby
CONROE Montgomery
CONVERSE Bexar
COOKVILLE Titus
COOLIDGE Limestone
COOPER Delta
COPEVILLE Collin
COPPELL Dallas
COPPERAS COVE (76522) Coryell(94), Lampasas(5)
CORPUS CHRISTI Nueces
CORRIGAN Polk
CORSICANA Navarro
COST Gonzales
COTTON CENTER Hale
COTULLA La Salle
COUPLAND (78615) Williamson(68), Travis(31)
COVINGTON Hill
COYANOSA Pecos
CRANDALL Kaufman
CRANE Crane
CRANFILLS GAP (76637) Bosque(98), Hamilton(1)
CRAWFORD McLennan
CRESSON (76035) Hood(56), Parker(33), Johnson(9)
CROCKETT Houston
CROSBY Harris
CROSBYTON Crosby
CROSS PLAINS (76443) Callahan(90), Brown(7), Coleman(2)
CROWELL (79227) Knox(59), Foard(40)
CROWLEY (76036) Tarrant(81), Johnson(18)
CRYSTAL CITY (78839) Zavala(98), Dimmit(1)
CUERO De Witt
CUMBY (75433) Hopkins(96), Hunt(3)
CUNEY Cherokee
CUNNINGHAM Lamar
CUSHING (75760) Nacogdoches(87), Rusk(12)
CYPRESS Harris
D HANIS Medina
DAINGERFIELD Morris
DAISETTA Liberty
DALE (78616) Caldwell(90), Bastrop(9)
DALHART (79022) Dallam(68), Hartley(30)
DALLARDSVILLE Polk
DALLAS (75252) Collin(97), Dallas(2)
DALLAS (75287) Collin(49), Denton(48), Dallas(2)
DALLAS Dallas
DAMON (77430) Fort Bend(53), Brazoria(46)
DANBURY Brazoria
DANCIGER Brazoria
DANEVANG Wharton
DARROUZETT Lipscomb
DAVILLA Milam
DAWN Deaf Smith
DAWSON Navarro
DAYTON (77535) Liberty(94), Chambers(5)
DE BERRY Panola
DE KALB Bowie
DE LEON Comanche
DEANVILLE Burleson
DECATUR (76234) Wise(98), Denton(1)

DEER PARK Harris
DEL RIO Edwards
DEL RIO Val Verde
DEL VALLE (78617) Travis(86), Bastrop(13)
DELL CITY Hudspeth
DELMITA (78536) Starr(86), Hidalgo(13)
DENISON Grayson
DENNIS Parker
DENTON Denton
DENVER CITY (79323) Yoakum(94), Gaines(5)
DEPORT (75435) Lamar(86), Red River(13)
DESDEMONA (76445) Eastland(82), Comanche(15), Erath(1)
DESOTO Dallas
DETROIT (75436) Red River(89), Lamar(10)
DEVERS Liberty
DEVINE Medina
DEWEYVILLE Newton
DIANA (75640) Upshur(67), Harrison(31), Marion(1)
DIBOLL Angelina
DICKENS Dickens
DICKINSON Galveston
DIKE Hopkins
DILLEY Frio
DIME BOX Lee
DIMMITT (79027) Castro(97), Lamb(1)
DINERO Live Oak
DOBBIN Montgomery
DODD CITY Fannin
DODGE Walker
DODSON (79230) Collingsworth(83), Childress(16)
DONIE (75838) Freestone(79), Limestone(20)
DONNA Hidalgo
DOOLE McCulloch
DOSS Gillespie
DOUCETTE Tyler
DOUGHERTY Floyd
DOUGLASS Nacogdoches
DOUGLASSVILLE Cass
DRIFTWOOD Hays
DRIPPING SPRINGS (78620) Hays(90), Travis(9)
DRISCOLL Nueces
DRYDEN Terrell
DUBLIN (76446) Erath(85), Comanche(14)
DUMAS Moore
DUMONT King
DUNCANVILLE Dallas
DUNN Scurry
DYESS AFB Taylor
EAGLE LAKE (77434) Colorado(98), Wharton(1)
EAGLE PASS Maverick
EARLY Brown
EARTH (79031) Lamb(77), Castro(18), Bailey(3)
EAST BERNARD (77435) Wharton(78), Fort Bend(20), Colorado(1)
EASTLAND Eastland
EASTON Gregg
ECLETO Karnes
ECTOR Fannin
EDCOUCH Hidalgo
EDDY (76524) McLennan(77), Falls(22)
EDEN Concho
EDGEWOOD Van Zandt
EDINBURG Hidalgo
EDMONSON Hale
EDNA Jackson
EDROY San Patricio
EGYPT Wharton
EL CAMPO Wharton
EL INDIO Maverick
EL PASO (79938) El Paso(97), Hudspeth(2)
EL PASO El Paso

ELBERT Throckmorton
ELDORADO Schleicher
ELECTRA (76360) Wichita(88), Wilbarger(11)
ELGIN (78621) Bastrop(77), Travis(13), Lee(5), Williamson(3)
ELIASVILLE Young
ELKHART Anderson
ELLINGER Fayette
ELM MOTT McLennan
ELMATON Matagorda
ELMENDORF (78112) Bexar(98), Wilson(1)
ELMO Kaufman
ELSA Hidalgo
ELYSIAN FIELDS Harrison
EMORY Rains
ENCINAL La Salle
ENCINO Brooks
ENERGY Comanche
ENLOE Delta
ENNIS (75119) Ellis(98), Navarro(1)
ENNIS Ellis
ENOCHS (79324) Bailey(93), Lamb(6)
EOLA (76937) Tom Green(69), Concho(30)
ERA Cooke
ESTELLINE Hall
ETOILE Nacogdoches
EULESS Tarrant
EUSTACE (75124) Henderson(77), Van Zandt(22)
EVADALE Jasper
EVANT (76525) Coryell(65), Hamilton(25), Lampasas(8)
FABENS El Paso
FAIRFIELD Freestone
FALCON HEIGHTS Starr
FALFURRIAS (78355) Brooks(95), Jim Wells(4)
FALLS CITY (78113) Wilson(41), Karnes(36), Atascosa(21)
FANNIN Goliad
FARMERSVILLE (75442) Collin(87), Hunt(12)
FARNSWORTH Ochiltree
FARWELL (79325) Parmer(92), Bailey(7)
FATE Rockwall
FAYETTEVILLE (78940) Fayette(86), Austin(12)
FENTRESS Caldwell
FERRIS (75125) Ellis(83), Dallas(16)
FIELDTON Lamb
FISCHER Comal
FLAT Coryell
FLATONIA (78941) Fayette(87), Bastrop(6), Gonzales(5)
FLINT Smith
FLOMOT (79234) Motley(85), Floyd(14)
FLORENCE (76527) Williamson(97), Bell(1), Burnet(1)
FLORESVILLE Wilson
FLOWER MOUND Denton
FLOYDADA (79235) Floyd(96), Crosby(3)
FLUVANNA (79517) Scurry(71), Borden(28)
FLYNN Leon
FOLLETT Lipscomb
FORESTBURG (76239) Montague(73), Cooke(26)
FORNEY (75126) Kaufman(97), Rockwall(2)
FORRESTON Ellis
FORSAN Howard
FORT DAVIS Jeff Davis
FORT HANCOCK Hudspeth
FORT MC KAVETT (76841) Menard(87), Kimble(8), Schleicher(3)
FORT STOCKTON Pecos
FORT WORTH (76126) Tarrant(87), Parker(12)
FORT WORTH (76178) Tarrant(96), Denton(3)
FORT WORTH Tarrant

FOWLERTON (78021) La Salle(80), Atascosa(10), McMullen(10)
FRANCITAS Jackson
FRANKLIN Robertson
FRANKSTON (75763) Anderson(52), Henderson(47)
FRED Tyler
FREDERICKSBURG (78624) Gillespie(86), Kendall(13)
FREDONIA (76842) Mason(54), San Saba(40), McCulloch(5)
FREEPORT Brazoria
FREER Duval
FRESNO Fort Bend
FRIENDSWOOD (77546) Galveston(68), Harris(31)
FRIENDSWOOD Galveston
FRIONA (79035) Parmer(94), Deaf Smith(4), Castro(1)
FRISCO (75034) Collin(55), Denton(44)
FRISCO Collin
FRITCH (79036) Hutchinson(94), Carson(5)
FROST Navarro
FRUITVALE Van Zandt
FULSHEAR Fort Bend
FULTON Aransas
GAIL Borden
GAINESVILLE Cooke
GALENA PARK Harris
GALLATIN Cherokee
GALVESTON Galveston
GANADO Jackson
GARCIASVILLE Starr
GARDEN CITY (79739) Glasscock(84), Reagan(15)
GARDENDALE Ector
GARLAND (75048) Dallas(80), Collin(19)
GARLAND Dallas
GARRISON (75946) Nacogdoches(53), Rusk(46)
GARWOOD Colorado
GARY (75643) Panola(94), Shelby(5)
GATESVILLE (76528) Coryell(97), Bell(2)
GATESVILLE Coryell
GAUSE Milam
GENEVA Sabine
GEORGE WEST Live Oak
GEORGETOWN Williamson
GERONIMO Guadalupe
GIDDINGS Lee
GILCHRIST Galveston
GILLETT Karnes
GILMER (75645) Upshur(98), Gregg(1)
GILMER Upshur
GIRARD Kent
GIRVIN Pecos
GLADEWATER (75647) Gregg(52), Upshur(37), Smith(9)
GLEN FLORA Wharton
GLEN ROSE Somervell
GLIDDEN Colorado
GOBER Fannin
GODLEY Johnson
GOLDEN Wood
GOLDSBORO (79519) Taylor(38), Coleman(33), Runnels(27)
GOLDSMITH Ector
GOLDTHWAITE Mills
GOLIAD Goliad
GONZALES Gonzales
GOODFELLOW AFB Tom Green
GOODRICH Polk
GORDON (76453) Palo Pinto(86), Erath(13)
GORDONVILLE Grayson
GOREE (76363) Knox(96), Haskell(2), Throckmorton(1)
GORMAN (76454) Eastland(73), Comanche(26)
GOULDBUSK Coleman
GRAFORD Palo Pinto

GRAHAM (76450) Young(93), Stephens(3), Palo Pinto(3)
GRANBURY (76048) Hood(98), Somervell(1)
GRANBURY (76049) Hood(96), Parker(2)
GRAND PRAIRIE (75052) Dallas(62), Tarrant(36)
GRAND PRAIRIE (75054) Tarrant(71), Dallas(28)
GRAND PRAIRIE Dallas
GRAND SALINE (75140) Van Zandt(98), Smith(1)
GRANDFALLS Ward
GRANDVIEW (76050) Johnson(90), Ellis(5), Hill(4)
GRANGER Williamson
GRAPELAND (75844) Houston(73), Anderson(26)
GRAPEVINE (76051) Tarrant(98), Dallas(1)
GRAPEVINE Tarrant
GREENVILLE Hunt
GREENWOOD Wise
GREGORY San Patricio
GROESBECK Limestone
GROOM (79039) Carson(64), Gray(33), Donley(1)
GROVES Jefferson
GROVETON Trinity
GRULLA Starr
GRUVER (79040) Hansford(60), Sherman(39)
GUERRA (78360) Jim Hogg(80), Starr(20)
GUNTER Grayson
GUSTINE Comanche
GUTHRIE King
GUY (77444) Fort Bend(75), Brazoria(24)
HALE CENTER (79041) Hale(97), Lamb(2)
HALLETTSVILLE Lavaca
HALLSVILLE Harrison
HALTOM CITY Tarrant
HAMILTON Hamilton
HAMLIN (79520) Jones(95), Fisher(4)
HAMSHIRE (77622) Jefferson(91), Chambers(8)
HANKAMER Chambers
HAPPY (79042) Randall(60), Swisher(19), Castro(12), Armstrong(7)
HARDIN Liberty
HARGILL Hidalgo
HARKER HEIGHTS Bell
HARLETON (75651) Harrison(95), Marion(4)
HARLINGEN Cameron
HARPER (78631) Gillespie(64), Kimble(26), Kerr(10)
HARROLD Wilbarger
HART (79043) Castro(76), Lamb(20), Hale(3)
HARTLEY Hartley
HARWOOD (78632) Gonzales(52), Caldwell(47)
HASKELL Haskell
HASLET (76052) Tarrant(88), Wise(6), Denton(5)
HASSE Comanche
HAWKINS Wood
HAWLEY Jones
HEARNE Robertson
HEBBRONVILLE Jim Hogg
HEDLEY Donley
HEIDENHEIMER Bell
HELOTES (78023) Bexar(91), Medina(8)
HEMPHILL Sabine
HEMPSTEAD Waller
HENDERSON Rusk
HENRIETTA (76365) Clay(98), Jack(1)
HEREFORD (79045) Deaf Smith(91), Castro(8)
HERMLEIGH (79526) Scurry(95), Fisher(3)
HEWITT McLennan
HEXT (76848) Menard(94), Mason(5)
HICO (76457) Hamilton(63), Erath(30), Bosque(5)

HIDALGO Hidalgo
HIGGINS (79046) Lipscomb(87), Hemphill(12)
HIGH ISLAND Galveston
HIGHLANDS Harris
HILLISTER Tyler
HILLSBORO Hill
HITCHCOCK Galveston
HOBSON Karnes
HOCHHEIM De Witt
HOCKLEY (77447) Harris(47), Waller(36), Montgomery(15)
HOLLAND Bell
HOLLIDAY Archer
HONDO Medina
HONEY GROVE (75446) Fannin(91), Lamar(8)
HOOKS Bowie
HOUSTON (77053) Fort Bend(56), Harris(43)
HOUSTON (77099) Harris(96), Fort Bend(3)
HOUSTON Harris
HOWE Grayson
HUBBARD (76648) Hill(91), Navarro(5), Limestone(2)
HUFFMAN Harris
HUFSMITH Harris
HUGHES SPRINGS (75656) Cass(89), Morris(10)
HULL Liberty
HUMBLE (77339) Harris(81), Montgomery(18)
HUMBLE Harris
HUNGERFORD Wharton
HUNT (78024) Kerr(96), Real(3)
HUNTINGTON Angelina
HUNTSVILLE (77320) Walker(91), San Jacinto(8)
HUNTSVILLE Walker
HURST Tarrant
HUTCHINS Dallas
HUTTO (78634) Williamson(98), Travis(1)
HYE Blanco
IDALOU Lubbock
IMPERIAL Pecos
INDUSTRY Austin
INEZ Victoria
INGLESIDE San Patricio
INGRAM Kerr
IOLA Grimes
IOWA PARK Wichita
IRA (79527) Scurry(81), Borden(18)
IRAAN Pecos
IREDELL (76649) Bosque(86), Erath(13)
IRENE Hill
IRVING Dallas
ITALY Ellis
ITASCA Hill
IVANHOE Fannin
JACKSBORO (76458) Jack(98), Wise(1)
JACKSONVILLE Cherokee
JARRELL Williamson
JASPER Jasper
JAYTON (79528) Kent(83), Stonewall(16)
JEFFERSON (75657) Marion(87), Cass(9), Harrison(2)
JERMYN (76459) Jack(95), Young(5)
JEWETT (75846) Leon(90), Limestone(9)
JOAQUIN (75954) Shelby(91), Panola(8)
JOHNSON CITY Blanco
JOINERVILLE Rusk
JONESBORO (76538) Hamilton(52), Coryell(47)
JONESVILLE (75659) Harrison(80), Rusk(20)
JOSEPHINE Collin
JOSHUA Johnson
JOURDANTON Atascosa
JUDSON Gregg
JUNCTION Kimble
JUSTICEBURG Garza
JUSTIN (76247) Denton(98), Wise(1)

KAMAY Wichita
KARNACK Harrison
KARNES CITY Karnes
KATY (77494) Fort Bend(90), Harris(8), Waller(1)
KATY (77450) Harris(69), Fort Bend(30)
KATY (77493) Harris(82), Waller(15), Fort Bend(1)
KATY Harris
KAUFMAN Kaufman
KEENE Johnson
KELLER Tarrant
KEMAH Galveston
KEMP (75143) Henderson(63), Kaufman(36)
KEMPNER (76539) Lampasas(82), Bell(8), Coryell(4), Burnet(3)
KENDALIA Kendall
KENDLETON Fort Bend
KENEDY Karnes
KENNARD (75847) Trinity(52), Houston(47)
KENNEDALE Tarrant
KENNEY Austin
KERENS Navarro
KERMIT Winkler
KERRICK Dallam
KERRVILLE (78028) Kerr(95), Gillespie(4)
KERRVILLE Kerr
KILDARE Cass
KILGORE (75662) Gregg(74), Rusk(24), Smith(1)
KILGORE Gregg
KILLEEN (76544) Bell(65), Coryell(34)
KILLEEN (76549) Bell(98), Burnet(1)
KILLEEN Bell
KINGSBURY Guadalupe
KINGSLAND (78639) Llano(87), Burnet(12)
KINGSVILLE Kleberg
KIRBYVILLE (75956) Jasper(98), Newton(1)
KIRKLAND Childress
KIRVIN Freestone
KLONDIKE Delta
KNICKERBOCKER Tom Green
KNIPPA Uvalde
KNOTT (79748) Howard(75), Martin(25)
KNOX CITY (79529) Knox(96), Haskell(3)
KOPPERL Bosque
KOSSE (76653) Limestone(87), Falls(10), Robertson(1)
KOUNTZE Hardin
KRESS (79052) Swisher(91), Hale(7), Castro(1)
KRUM Denton
KURTEN Brazos
KYLE (78640) Hays(98), Caldwell(1)
LA BLANCA Hidalgo
LA COSTE (78039) Medina(78), Bexar(21)
LA FERIA Cameron
LA JOYA Hidalgo
LA MARQUE Galveston
LA PORTE Harris
LA PRYOR Zavala
LA SALLE Jackson
LA VERNIA (78121) Wilson(76), Guadalupe(23)
LA VILLA Hidalgo
LA WARD Jackson
LADONIA (75449) Fannin(91), Hunt(8)
LAIRD HILL Rusk
LAKE CREEK Delta
LAKE DALLAS Denton
LAKE JACKSON Brazoria
LAKEVIEW Hall
LAMESA (79331) Dawson(97), Martin(1)
LAMPASAS Lampasas
LANCASTER Dallas
LANE CITY Wharton
LANEVILLE Rusk
LANGTRY Val Verde
LAREDO Webb
LARUE Henderson

LASARA Willacy
LATEXO Houston
LAUGHLIN A F B Val Verde
LAVON Collin
LAWN (79530) Taylor(93), Runnels(6)
LAZBUDDIE Parmer
LEAGUE CITY Galveston
LEAKEY Real
LEANDER (78641) Williamson(59), Travis(40)
LEANDER Travis
LEANDER Williamson
LEDBETTER (78946) Fayette(78), Washington(14), Lee(6)
LEESBURG (75451) Camp(89), Wood(6), Upshur(4)
LEESVILLE Gonzales
LEFORS Gray
LEGGETT Polk
LELIA LAKE Donley
LEMING Atascosa
LENORAH Martin
LEON JUNCTION Coryell
LEONA Leon
LEONARD (75452) Fannin(86), Hunt(7), Collin(6)
LEROY McLennan
LEVELLAND Hockley
LEWISVILLE Denton
LEXINGTON (78947) Lee(98), Milam(1)
LIBERTY Liberty
LIBERTY HILL (78642) Williamson(98), Burnet(1)
LILLIAN Johnson
LINCOLN Lee
LINDALE Smith
LINDEN Cass
LINDSAY Cooke
LINGLEVILLE Erath
LINN (78563) Hidalgo(94), Starr(5)
LIPAN (76462) Hood(45), Palo Pinto(20), Parker(16), Erath(12)
LIPSCOMB Lipscomb
LISSIE Wharton
LITTLE ELM Denton
LITTLE RIVER Bell
LITTLE RIVER ACADEMY Bell
LITTLEFIELD (79339) Lamb(92), Hockley(7)
LIVERPOOL Brazoria
LIVINGSTON Polk
LLANO Llano
LOCKHART Caldwell
LOCKNEY (79241) Floyd(97), Swisher(1)
LODI Marion
LOHN (76852) McCulloch(98), Concho(1)
LOLITA Jackson
LOMETA (76853) Lampasas(95), Mills(3)
LONDON (76854) Kimble(77), Menard(21)
LONE OAK (75453) Hunt(73), Rains(19), Hopkins(7)
LONE STAR (75668) Morris(86), Marion(11), Henderson(1)
LONG BRANCH (75669) Panola(98), Rusk(1)
LONG MOTT Calhoun
LONGVIEW (75602) Gregg(65), Harrison(34)
LONGVIEW (75603) Gregg(81), Rusk(18)
LONGVIEW (75604) Gregg(97), Upshur(2)
LONGVIEW (75605) Gregg(81), Harrison(17), Upshur(1)
LONGVIEW Gregg
LOOP Gaines
LOPENO Zapata
LORAINE (79532) Mitchell(94), Scurry(3), Nolan(2)
LORENA McLennan
LORENZO (79343) Crosby(71), Lubbock(28)
LOS EBANOS Hidalgo
LOS FRESNOS Cameron
LOS INDIOS Cameron

LOTT Falls
LOUISE (77455) Wharton(91), Jackson(8)
LOVELADY (75851) Houston(67), Trinity(32)
LOVING Young
LOWAKE Concho
LOZANO Cameron
LUBBOCK (79407) Lubbock(91), Hockley(8)
LUBBOCK Lubbock
LUEDERS (79533) Jones(58), Shackelford(37), Haskell(4)
LUFKIN Angelina
LULING (78648) Caldwell(91), Guadalupe(7), Gonzales(1)
LUMBERTON Hardin
LYFORD Willacy
LYONS Burleson
LYTLE (78052) Atascosa(79), Medina(13), Bexar(7)
MABANK (75156) Henderson(95), Kaufman(2), Van Zandt(1)
MABANK (75147) Kaufman(47), Van Zandt(46), Henderson(5)
MACDONA Bexar
MADISONVILLE Madison
MAGNOLIA (77355) Montgomery(98), Waller(1)
MAGNOLIA Montgomery
MAGNOLIA SPRINGS Bowie
MAGNOLIA SPRINGS Jasper
MALAKOFF Henderson
MALONE Hill
MANCHACA (78652) Travis(74), Hays(25)
MANOR Travis
MANSFIELD (76063) Tarrant(92), Johnson(7)
MANVEL Brazoria
MAPLE Bailey
MARATHON Brewster
MARBLE FALLS (78654) Burnet(95), Travis(4)
MARBLE FALLS (78657) Burnet(50), Llano(47), Blanco(1)
MARFA Presidio
MARIETTA Cass
MARION (78124) Guadalupe(93), Bexar(6)
MARKHAM Matagorda
MARLIN Falls
MARQUEZ Leon
MARSHALL Harrison
MART (76664) McLennan(83), Limestone(13), Falls(2)
MARTINDALE (78655) Caldwell(78), Guadalupe(21)
MARTINSVILLE Nacogdoches
MARYNEAL Nolan
MASON (76856) Mason(98), Menard(1)
MASTERSON (79058) Moore(58), Potter(41)
MATADOR Motley
MATAGORDA Matagorda
MATHIS (78368) San Patricio(94), Live Oak(5)
MAUD Bowie
MAURICEVILLE Orange
MAXWELL (78656) Caldwell(95), Hays(4)
MAY Brown
MAYDELLE Cherokee
MAYPEARL Ellis
MAYSFIELD Milam
MC CAMEY Upton
MC CAULLEY Fisher
MC COY Atascosa
MC DADE Bastrop
MC GREGOR (76657) McLennan(98), Coryell(1)
MC KINNEY Collin
MC LEOD Cass
MC NEIL Travis
MC QUEENEY Guadalupe
MCADOO (79243) Crosby(52), Dickens(47)
MCALLEN Hidalgo

MCFADDIN Victoria
MCLEAN (79057) Gray(70), Wheeler(20), Donley(9)
MEADOW (79345) Terry(86), Lynn(11), Taylor(1)
MEDINA Bandera
MEGARGEL Archer
MELISSA Collin
MELVIN (76858) McCulloch(60), Concho(39)
MEMPHIS (79245) Hall(97), Collingsworth(2)
MENARD (76859) Menard(78), Kimble(21)
MENTONE Loving
MERCEDES Hidalgo
MERETA Tom Green
MERIDIAN Bosque
MERIT Hunt
MERKEL (79536) Taylor(75), Jones(24)
MERTENS (76666) Hill(96), Navarro(3)
MERTZON Irion
MESQUITE Dallas
MEXIA (76667) Limestone(95), Freestone(4)
MEYERSVILLE (77974) De Witt(51), Victoria(48)
MIAMI (79059) Roberts(78), Gray(21)
MICO Medina
MIDFIELD Matagorda
MIDKIFF (79755) Upton(82), Midland(14), Reagan(2)
MIDLOTHIAN Ellis
MIDWAY (75852) Madison(97), Walker(1)
MILAM Sabine
MILANO (76556) Milam(98), Burleson(2)
MILES (76861) Tom Green(61), Runnels(36), Concho(1)
MILFORD (76670) Ellis(91), Navarro(7), Hill(1)
MILLERSVIEW Concho
MILLICAN Brazos
MILLSAP (76066) Parker(94), Palo Pinto(5)
MINDEN Rusk
MINEOLA (75773) Wood(91), Smith(7)
MINERAL Bee
MINERAL WELLS (76067) Palo Pinto(96), Parker(3)
MINERAL WELLS Palo Pinto
MINGUS (76463) Erath(75), Palo Pinto(23)
MIRANDO CITY Webb
MISSION Hidalgo
MISSOURI CITY (77489) Fort Bend(95), Harris(4)
MISSOURI CITY Fort Bend
MOBEETIE (79061) Wheeler(89), Gray(7), Hemphill(2)
MONAHANS Ward
MONT BELVIEU Chambers
MONTAGUE Montague
MONTALBA (75853) Anderson(98), Henderson(1)
MONTGOMERY (77356) Montgomery(98), Grimes(1)
MOODY (76557) McLennan(55), Bell(33), Coryell(10)
MOORE (78057) Medina(92), Frio(7)
MORAN (76464) Shackelford(81), Stephens(11), Callahan(6)
MORGAN Bosque
MORGAN MILL Erath
MORSE (79062) Hutchinson(87), Hansford(12)
MORTON (79346) Cochran(95), Bailey(4)
MOSCOW (75960) Polk(91), Tyler(8)
MOULTON Lavaca
MOUND Coryell
MOUNT CALM (76673) Hill(87), Limestone(9), McLennan(3)
MOUNT ENTERPRISE Rusk
MOUNT PLEASANT (75455) Titus(98), Franklin(1)
MOUNT PLEASANT Titus
MOUNT VERNON Franklin

MOUNTAIN HOME Kerr
MUENSTER Cooke
MULDOON Fayette
MULESHOE (79347) Bailey(83), Parmer(10), Lamb(4), Castro(1)
MULLIN Mills
MUMFORD Robertson
MUNDAY Knox
MURCHISON (75778) Henderson(65), Van Zandt(34)
MYRA Cooke
NACOGDOCHES Nacogdoches
NADA Colorado
NAPLES (75568) Morris(90), Cass(9)
NASH Bowie
NATALIA Medina
NAVAL AIR STATION/ JRB Tarrant
NAVASOTA Brazos
NAVASOTA Grimes
NAZARETH Castro
NECHES Anderson
NEDERLAND Jefferson
NEEDVILLE Fort Bend
NEMO (76070) Somervell(86), Johnson(13)
NEVADA Collin
NEW BADEN Robertson
NEW BOSTON Bowie
NEW BRAUNFELS (78130) Comal(83), Guadalupe(16)
NEW BRAUNFELS Comal
NEW CANEY Montgomery
NEW DEAL Lubbock
NEW HOME Lynn
NEW LONDON Rusk
NEW SUMMERFIELD Cherokee
NEW ULM (78950) Austin(64), Colorado(34)
NEW WAVERLY (77358) Walker(48), San Jacinto(39), Montgomery(12)
NEWARK (76071) Wise(96), Tarrant(3)
NEWCASTLE (76372) Young(78), Throckmorton(21)
NEWGULF Wharton
NEWPORT Clay
NEWTON (75966) Newton(95), Jasper(4)
NIXON (78140) Gonzales(88), Wilson(8), Guadalupe(3)
NOCONA Montague
NOLAN Nolan
NOLANVILLE Bell
NOME Jefferson
NORDHEIM (78141) De Witt(93), Karnes(6)
NORMANGEE (77871) Leon(59), Madison(40)
NORMANNA Bee
NORTH HOUSTON Harris
NORTH RICHLAND HILLS Tarrant
NORTH ZULCH Madison
NORTON Runnels
NOTREES Ector
NOVICE (79538) Coleman(51), Runnels(48)
NURSERY Victoria
O BRIEN Haskell
OAKHURST San Jacinto
OAKLAND Colorado
OAKVILLE Live Oak
OAKWOOD (75855) Leon(77), Freestone(22)
ODELL Hardeman
ODEM San Patricio
ODESSA (79766) Ector(89), Crane(6), Midland(3)
ODESSA (79765) Midland(52), Ector(47)
ODESSA Ector
ODONNELL (79351) Borden(40), Lynn(39), Dawson(19)
OGLESBY (76561) Coryell(90), McLennan(9)
OILTON Webb
OKLAUNION Wilbarger

OLD GLORY (79540) Stonewall(98), Haskell(1)
OLD OCEAN Brazoria
OLDEN Eastland
OLMITO Cameron
OLNEY (76374) Young(97), Archer(1), Throckmorton(1)
OLTON (79064) Lamb(79), Hale(20)
OMAHA Morris
ONALASKA Polk
ORANGE GROVE Jim Wells
ORANGEFIELD Orange
ORCHARD Fort Bend
ORE CITY (75683) Upshur(73), Marion(26)
ORLA Reeves
OTTINE Gonzales
OTTO Falls
OVALO (79541) Taylor(90), Callahan(9)
OVERTON (75684) Rusk(87), Smith(12)
OZONA (76943) Crockett(87), Val Verde(12)
PADUCAH (79248) Cottle(90), King(5), Foard(4)
PAIGE (78659) Bastrop(78), Lee(21)
PAINT ROCK Concho
PALACIOS (77465) Matagorda(73), Jackson(25)
PALESTINE (75803) Anderson(98), Henderson(1)
PALESTINE Anderson
PALMER Ellis
PALO PINTO Palo Pinto
PALUXY Hood
PAMPA (79065) Gray(97), Roberts(2)
PAMPA Gray
PANDORA Wilson
PANHANDLE (79068) Carson(97), Potter(1)
PANNA MARIA Karnes
PANOLA Panola
PARADISE Wise
PARIS Lamar
PASADENA Harris
PATTISON Waller
PATTONVILLE Lamar
PAWNEE Bee
PEACOCK Stonewall
PEAR VALLEY McCulloch
PEARLAND (77581) Brazoria(96), Harris(3)
PEARLAND Brazoria
PEARSALL Frio
PEASTER Parker
PECAN GAP (75469) Delta(91), Hunt(8)
PECOS Reeves
PEGGY Atascosa
PENDLETON Bell
PENELOPE Hill
PENITAS Hidalgo
PENNINGTON (75856) Trinity(68), Houston(31)
PENWELL Ector
PEP (79353) Hockley(96), Cochran(3)
PERRIN (76486) Jack(47), Palo Pinto(26), Parker(26)
PERRY Falls
PERRYTON Ochiltree
PETERSBURG (79250) Hale(48), Lubbock(22), Floyd(17), Crosby(11)
PETROLIA Clay
PETTUS Bee
PETTY Lamar
PFLUGERVILLE Travis
PHARR Hidalgo
PICKTON (75471) Hopkins(61), Wood(38)
PIERCE Wharton
PILOT POINT (76258) Denton(90), Grayson(9)
PINEHURST Montgomery
PINELAND Sabine
PIPE CREEK Bandera
PITTSBURG (75686) Camp(85), Upshur(7), Titus(5), Morris(1)
PLACEDO Victoria

PLAINS Yoakum
PLAINVIEW Hale
PLANO (75093) Collin(95), Denton(4)
PLANO Collin
PLANTERSVILLE (77363) Grimes(98), Waller(1)
PLEASANTON Atascosa
PLEDGER Matagorda
PLUM Fayette
POINT (75472) Rains(98), Hopkins(1)
POINT COMFORT Calhoun
POINTBLANK San Jacinto
POLLOK Angelina
PONDER Denton
PONTOTOC (76869) Llano(58), Mason(31), San Saba(9)
POOLVILLE (76487) Parker(68), Wise(22), Jack(8)
PORT ARANSAS Nueces
PORT ARTHUR Jefferson
PORT BOLIVAR Galveston
PORT ISABEL Cameron
PORT LAVACA Calhoun
PORT MANSFIELD Willacy
PORT NECHES Jefferson
PORT O CONNOR Calhoun
PORTER (77365) Montgomery(98), Harris(1)
PORTLAND San Patricio
POST (79356) Garza(91), Lynn(5), Crosby(2)
POTEET Atascosa
POTH Wilson
POTTSBORO Grayson
POTTSVILLE Hamilton
POWDERLY Lamar
POWELL Navarro
POYNOR Henderson
PRAIRIE HILL Limestone
PRAIRIE LEA Caldwell
PRAIRIE VIEW Waller
PREMONT Jim Wells
PRESIDIO Presidio
PRICE Rusk
PRIDDY Mills
PRINCETON Collin
PROCTOR Comanche
PROGRESO Hidalgo
PROSPER (75078) Collin(94), Denton(5)
PURDON Navarro
PURMELA (76566) Coryell(76), Hamilton(24)
PUTNAM Callahan
PYOTE Ward
QUAIL Collingsworth
QUANAH Hardeman
QUEEN CITY Cass
QUEMADO (78877) Maverick(98), Kinney(1)
QUINLAN (75474) Hunt(96), Kaufman(3)
QUITAQUE (79255) Briscoe(64), Motley(21), Floyd(13), Hall(1)
QUITMAN Wood
RAINBOW Somervell
RALLS Crosby
RANDOLPH Fannin
RANGER (76470) Eastland(85), Stephens(14)
RANKIN Upton
RANSOM CANYON Lubbock
RATCLIFF Houston
RAVENNA Fannin
RAYMONDVILLE Willacy
RAYWOOD Liberty
REAGAN Falls
REALITOS Duval
RED OAK (75154) Ellis(78), Dallas(21)
RED ROCK (78662) Bastrop(96), Caldwell(3)
REDFORD Presidio
REDWATER Bowie
REESE AIR FORCE BASE Lubbock
REFUGIO Refugio

REKLAW (75784) Cherokee(88), Rusk(11)
RHOME (76078) Wise(95), Denton(4)
RICE (75155) Navarro(94), Ellis(5)
RICHARDS (77873) Montgomery(54), Grimes(35), Walker(10)
RICHARDSON (75082) Collin(74), Dallas(25)
RICHARDSON (75080) Dallas(84), Collin(15)
RICHARDSON Dallas
RICHLAND Navarro
RICHLAND SPRINGS (76871) San Saba(95), Lampasas(3)
RICHMOND Fort Bend
RIESEL (76682) McLennan(96), Falls(3)
RINGGOLD (76261) Montague(92), Clay(8)
RIO FRIO Real
RIO GRANDE CITY Starr
RIO HONDO Cameron
RIO MEDINA Medina
RIO VISTA (76093) Johnson(92), Hill(7)
RISING STAR (76471) Eastland(79), Brown(16), Comanche(4)
RIVERSIDE Walker
RIVIERA Kleberg
ROANOKE (76262) Denton(63), Tarrant(36)
ROANOKE Denton
ROANS PRAIRIE Grimes
ROARING SPRINGS (79256) Motley(52), Dickens(47)
ROBERT LEE (76945) Coke(94), Tom Green(5)
ROBSTOWN Nueces
ROBY Fisher
ROCHELLE (76872) McCulloch(80), San Saba(19)
ROCHESTER Haskell
ROCK ISLAND Colorado
ROCKDALE (76567) Milam(94), Burleson(5)
ROCKLAND Tyler
ROCKPORT Aransas
ROCKSPRINGS Edwards
ROCKWALL (75087) Rockwall(97), Collin(2)
ROCKWALL Rockwall
ROCKWOOD Coleman
ROGERS (76569) Bell(86), Milam(13)
ROMA Starr
ROMAYOR Liberty
ROOSEVELT (76874) Sutton(66), Kimble(33)
ROPESVILLE (79358) Hockley(78), Lubbock(19), Terry(1)
ROSANKY (78953) Bastrop(53), Caldwell(46)
ROSCOE (79545) Nolan(93), Scurry(3), Fisher(3)
ROSEBUD (76570) Falls(85), Milam(13)
ROSENBERG Fort Bend
ROSHARON (77583) Brazoria(78), Fort Bend(21)
ROSS McLennan
ROSSER Kaufman
ROSSTON Cooke
ROTAN (79546) Fisher(95), Stonewall(3)
ROUND MOUNTAIN (78663) Blanco(88), Travis(8), Hays(3)
ROUND ROCK (78664) Williamson(95), Travis(4)
ROUND ROCK Williamson
ROUND TOP (78954) Fayette(97), Austin(2)
ROUND TOP Fayette
ROWENA (76875) Runnels(85), Concho(14)
ROWLETT (75089) Dallas(94), Rockwall(5)
ROWLETT Dallas
ROXTON Lamar
ROYALTY Ward
ROYSE CITY (75189) Rockwall(56), Hunt(26), Collin(16)

RULE (79547) Haskell(97), Stonewall(2)
RULE Haskell
RUNGE (78151) Karnes(94), De Witt(3), Goliad(1)
RUSK Cherokee
RYE Liberty
SABINAL Uvalde
SABINE PASS Jefferson
SACUL Nacogdoches
SADLER Grayson
SAINT HEDWIG Bexar
SAINT JO (76265) Montague(81), Cooke(18)
SALADO Bell
SALINENO Starr
SALT FLAT (79847) Hudspeth(74), Culberson(25)
SALTILLO (75478) Hopkins(87), Franklin(12)
SAMNORWOOD Collingsworth
SAN ANGELO Tom Green
SAN ANTONIO (78223) Bexar(98), Wilson(1)
SAN ANTONIO (78253) Bexar(89), Medina(10)
SAN ANTONIO (78264) Bexar(93), Atascosa(6)
SAN ANTONIO (78266) Comal(95), Bexar(4)
SAN ANTONIO Bexar
SAN AUGUSTINE San Augustine
SAN BENITO Cameron
SAN DIEGO (78384) Duval(94), Jim Wells(5)
SAN ELIZARIO El Paso
SAN FELIPE Austin
SAN ISIDRO Starr
SAN JUAN Hidalgo
SAN MARCOS (78666) Hays(92), Guadalupe(6), Caldwell(1)
SAN MARCOS Hays
SAN PERLITA Willacy
SAN SABA San Saba
SAN YGNACIO Zapata
SANDERSON Terrell
SANDIA (78383) Jim Wells(60), Nueces(35), Live Oak(4)
SANDY Blanco
SANFORD Hutchinson
SANGER Denton
SANTA ANNA Coleman
SANTA ELENA Starr
SANTA FE Galveston
SANTA MARIA Cameron
SANTA ROSA Cameron
SANTO Palo Pinto
SARAGOSA Reeves
SARATOGA Hardin
SARITA Kenedy
SATIN Falls
SAVOY Fannin
SCHERTZ (78154) Guadalupe(73), Bexar(23), Comal(2)
SCHULENBURG (78956) Fayette(89), Lavaca(10)
SCHWERTNER Williamson
SCOTLAND Archer
SCOTTSVILLE Harrison
SCROGGINS (75480) Franklin(95), Wood(4)
SCURRY Kaufman
SEABROOK Harris
SEADRIFT Calhoun
SEAGOVILLE (75159) Dallas(86), Kaufman(13)
SEAGRAVES (79359) Gaines(74), Terry(13), Yoakum(12)
SEALY Austin
SEBASTIAN Willacy
SEGUIN Guadalupe
SELMAN CITY Rusk
SEMINOLE Gaines
SEYMOUR (76380) Baylor(96), Knox(3)

SHAFTER Presidio
SHALLOWATER (79363) Lubbock(97), Hockley(1)
SHAMROCK (79079) Wheeler(90), Collingsworth(9)
SHAMROCK Wheeler
SHEFFIELD Pecos
SHEPHERD San Jacinto
SHEPPARD AFB Wichita
SHERIDAN Colorado
SHERMAN Grayson
SHINER (77984) Lavaca(91), Gonzales(8)
SHIRO Grimes
SIDNEY (76474) Comanche(98), Brown(1)
SIERRA BLANCA Hudspeth
SILSBEE Hardin
SILVER Coke
SILVERTON Briscoe
SIMMS Bowie
SIMONTON Fort Bend
SINTON (78387) San Patricio(92), Bee(7)
SKELLYTOWN (79080) Hutchinson(80), Carson(20)
SKIDMORE Bee
SLATON (79364) Lubbock(96), Lynn(3)
SLIDELL Wise
SMILEY Gonzales
SMITHVILLE (78957) Bastrop(98), Fayette(1)
SMYER Hockley
SNOOK Burleson
SNYDER Scurry
SOMERSET (78069) Atascosa(64), Bexar(35)
SOMERVILLE Burleson
SONORA Sutton
SOUR LAKE Hardin
SOUTH BEND Young
SOUTH HOUSTON Harris
SOUTH PADRE ISLAND Cameron
SOUTH PLAINS Floyd
SOUTHLAKE Tarrant
SOUTHLAND Garza
SOUTHMAYD Grayson
SPADE Lamb
SPEAKS Lavaca
SPEARMAN (79081) Hansford(92), Hutchinson(4), Ochiltree(3)
SPICEWOOD (78669) Travis(71), Burnet(26), Blanco(2)
SPLENDORA (77372) Montgomery(88), Liberty(11)
SPRING Harris
SPRING Montgomery
SPRING BRANCH Comal
SPRINGLAKE (79082) Lamb(84), Castro(15)
SPRINGTOWN (76082) Parker(78), Wise(21)
SPUR (79370) Dickens(89), Crosby(6), Kent(3)
SPURGER Tyler
STAFFORD (77477) Fort Bend(91), Harris(8)
STAFFORD Fort Bend
STAMFORD (79553) Jones(91), Haskell(8)
STANTON (79782) Martin(70), Glasscock(25), Midland(3)
STAPLES Guadalupe
STAR Mills
STEPHENVILLE Erath
STERLING CITY (76951) Sterling(98), Glasscock(1)
STINNETT (79083) Hutchinson(66), Moore(30), Hansford(2)
STOCKDALE Wilson
STONEWALL (78671) Gillespie(97), Blanco(2)
STOWELL Chambers
STRATFORD (79084) Sherman(95), Dallam(4)
STRAWN (76475) Eastland(76), Palo Pinto(23)

STREETMAN (75859) Freestone(65), Navarro(34)
SUBLIME Lavaca
SUDAN (79371) Lamb(62), Bailey(37)
SUGAR LAND Fort Bend
SULLIVAN CITY Hidalgo
SULPHUR BLUFF Hopkins
SULPHUR SPRINGS Hopkins
SUMMERFIELD (79085) Castro(85), Parmer(14)
SUMNER Lamar
SUNDOWN Hockley
SUNNYVALE Dallas
SUNRAY (79086) Moore(50), Sherman(48), Hansford(1)
SUNSET (76270) Montague(57), Wise(42)
SUTHERLAND SPRINGS Wilson
SWEENY (77480) Brazoria(95), Matagorda(4)
SWEET HOME Lavaca
SWEETWATER (79556) Nolan(95), Fisher(4)
SYLVESTER (79560) Fisher(89), Jones(10)
TAFT San Patricio
TAHOKA Lynn
TALCO (75487) Franklin(74), Titus(25)
TALPA (76882) Coleman(63), Runnels(36)
TARPLEY Bandera
TARZAN Martin
TATUM Rusk
TAYLOR Williamson
TEAGUE Freestone
TEHUACANA Limestone
TELEGRAPH (76883) Edwards(69), Kimble(30)
TELEPHONE Fannin
TELFERNER (77988) Lavaca(77), Victoria(22)
TELL (79259) Childress(56), Hall(43)
TEMPLE Bell
TENAHA (75974) Shelby(63), Panola(36)
TENNESSEE COLONY Anderson
TENNYSON Coke
TERLINGUA Brewster
TERRELL (75160) Kaufman(91), Hunt(8)
TERRELL Kaufman
TEXARKANA Bowie
TEXAS CITY Galveston
TEXLINE Dallam
THE COLONY Denton
THICKET Hardin
THOMASTON De Witt
THOMPSONS Fort Bend
THORNDALE (76577) Milam(95), Williamson(4)
THORNTON (76687) Limestone(73), Robertson(25)
THRALL (76578) Williamson(94), Milam(4), Lee(1)
THREE RIVERS Live Oak
THROCKMORTON Throckmorton
TILDEN McMullen
TIMPSON (75975) Shelby(97), Panola(1), Rusk(1)
TIOGA (76271) Grayson(88), Cooke(11)
TIVOLI (77990) Refugio(67), Calhoun(32)
TOKIO (79376) Yoakum(72), Terry(27)
TOLAR Hood
TOM BEAN Grayson
TOMBALL Harris
TORNILLO El Paso
TOW Llano
TOYAH Reeves
TOYAHVALE Reeves
TRENT (79561) Taylor(43), Nolan(36), Fisher(11), Jones(8)
TRENTON (75490) Fannin(97), Grayson(2)
TRINIDAD Henderson
TRINITY (75862) Trinity(95), Walker(4)
TROUP (75789) Smith(82), Cherokee(16), Rusk(1)
TROY (76579) Bell(95), Falls(4)

TRUSCOTT Knox
TULETA Bee
TULIA (79088) Swisher(96), Castro(1), Briscoe(1)
TURKEY (79261) Hall(92), Briscoe(7)
TUSCOLA Taylor
TYE Taylor
TYLER Smith
TYNAN Bee
UMBARGER Randall
UNIVERSAL CITY Bexar
UTOPIA Uvalde
UVALDE Uvalde
VALENTINE (79854) Presidio(57), Jeff Davis(42)
VALERA Coleman
VALLEY MILLS (76689) Bosque(59), McLennan(27), Coryell(13)
VALLEY SPRING Llano
VALLEY VIEW (76272) Cooke(98), Denton(1)
VAN (75790) Van Zandt(97), Smith(2)
VAN ALSTYNE (75495) Grayson(55), Collin(44)
VAN HORN Culberson
VAN VLECK Matagorda
VANCOURT (76955) Tom Green(51), Concho(48)
VANDERBILT Jackson
VANDERPOOL Bandera
VEGA (79092) Oldham(56), Deaf Smith(43)
VENUS (76084) Johnson(72), Ellis(27)
VERA (76383) Knox(91), Baylor(8)
VERIBEST Tom Green
VERNON Wilbarger
VICTORIA (77905) Victoria(91), Goliad(8)
VICTORIA Victoria
VIDOR Orange
VILLAGE MILLS Hardin
VOCA McCulloch
VON ORMY (78073) Bexar(89), Atascosa(10)
VOSS Coleman
VOTAW Hardin
VOTH Jefferson
WACO McLennan
WADSWORTH Matagorda
WAELDER (78959) Gonzales(70), Fayette(19), Bastrop(7), Caldwell(3)
WAKA Ochiltree
WALBURG Williamson
WALL Tom Green
WALLER (77484) Waller(73), Harris(21), Grimes(5)
WALLIS (77485) Austin(66), Fort Bend(32)
WALLISVILLE Chambers
WALNUT SPRINGS (76690) Bosque(75), Somervell(23), Erath(1)
WARDA Fayette
WARING Kendall
WARREN Tyler
WASKOM Harrison
WATER VALLEY Tom Green
WAXAHACHIE Ellis
WAYSIDE (79094) Armstrong(92), Swisher(7)
WEATHERFORD (76087) Parker(96), Hood(3)
WEATHERFORD Parker
WEBSTER Harris
WEESATCHE Goliad
WEIMAR (78962) Colorado(98), Fayette(1)
WEINERT Haskell
WEIR Williamson
WELCH (79377) Dawson(63), Terry(27), Gaines(9)
WELLBORN Brazos
WELLINGTON (79095) Collingsworth(94), Childress(5)
WELLMAN Terry
WELLS Cherokee
WESLACO Hidalgo
WEST McLennan

WEST COLUMBIA Brazoria
WEST POINT Fayette
WESTBROOK Mitchell
WESTHOFF De Witt
WESTMINSTER Collin
WESTON Collin
WHARTON Wharton
WHEELER Wheeler
WHEELOCK Robertson
WHITE DEER (79097) Carson(96), Gray(3)
WHITE OAK Gregg
WHITEFACE Cochran
WHITEHOUSE Smith
WHITESBORO (76273) Grayson(71), Cooke(28)
WHITEWRIGHT (75491) Grayson(73), Fannin(26)
WHITHARRAL Hockley
WHITNEY Hill
WHITSETT Live Oak
WHITT (76490) Parker(58), Palo Pinto(41)
WHON Coleman
WICHITA FALLS (76305) Wichita(62), Clay(37)
WICHITA FALLS (76310) Wichita(64), Archer(18), Clay(16)
WICHITA FALLS Wichita
WICKETT Ward
WIERGATE Newton
WILDORADO (79098) Deaf Smith(44), Randall(23), Oldham(22), Potter(9)
WILLIS (77378) Montgomery(81), San Jacinto(18)
WILLIS Montgomery
WILLOW CITY Gillespie
WILLS POINT (75169) Van Zandt(83), Hunt(9), Kaufman(6)
WILMER Dallas
WILSON Lynn
WIMBERLEY Hays
WINCHESTER Fayette
WINDOM Fannin
WINDTHORST (76389) Archer(61), Clay(29), Jack(8)
WINFIELD Titus
WINGATE (79566) Taylor(58), Runnels(34), Nolan(6)
WINK Winkler
WINNIE (77665) Chambers(98), Jefferson(1)
WINNSBORO (75494) Wood(72), Franklin(20), Hopkins(6)
WINONA Smith
WINTERS (79567) Runnels(97), Taylor(2)
WODEN Nacogdoches
WOLFE CITY (75496) Hunt(79), Fannin(20)
WOLFFORTH Lubbock
WOODLAKE Trinity
WOODLAWN Harrison
WOODSBORO Refugio
WOODSON (76491) Throckmorton(96), Stephens(3)
WOODVILLE Tyler
WOODWAY McLennan
WORTHAM (76693) Freestone(88), Navarro(7), Limestone(3)
WRIGHTSBORO Gonzales
WYLIE (75098) Collin(88), Dallas(9), Rockwall(1)
YANCEY Medina
YANTIS (75497) Wood(87), Hopkins(10), Rains(1)
YOAKUM (77995) Lavaca(51), De Witt(32), Victoria(16)
YORKTOWN De Witt
ZAPATA Zapata
ZAVALLA Angelina
ZEPHYR (76890) Brown(95), Mills(2), Comanche(1)

Texas ZIP/City Cross Reference

ZIP Range	City	ZIP Range	City	ZIP Range	City	ZIP Range	City
73301-73344	AUSTIN	75154-75154	RED OAK	75479-75479	SAVOY	75688-75688	SCOTTSVILLE
75001-75001	ADDISON	75155-75155	RICE	75480-75480	SCROGGINS	75689-75689	SELMAN CITY
75002-75002	ALLEN	75156-75156	MABANK	75481-75481	SULPHUR BLUFF	75691-75691	TATUM
75006-75008	CARROLLTON	75157-75157	ROSSER	75482-75483	SULPHUR SPRINGS	75692-75692	WASKOM
75009-75009	CELINA	75158-75158	SCURRY	75485-75485	WESTMINSTER	75693-75693	WHITE OAK
75010-75011	CARROLLTON	75159-75159	SEAGOVILLE	75486-75486	SUMNER	75694-75694	WOODLAWN
75013-75013	ALLEN	75160-75161	TERRELL	75487-75487	TALCO	75701-75713	TYLER
75014-75017	IRVING	75163-75163	TRINIDAD	75488-75488	TELEPHONE	75750-75750	ARP
75019-75019	COPPELL	75164-75164	JOSEPHINE	75489-75489	TOM BEAN	75751-75752	ATHENS
75020-75021	DENISON	75165-75165	WAXAHACHIE	75490-75490	TRENTON	75754-75754	BEN WHEELER
75022-75022	FLOWER MOUND	75166-75166	LAVON	75491-75491	WHITEWRIGHT	75755-75755	BIG SANDY
75023-75026	PLANO	75167-75168	WAXAHACHIE	75492-75492	WINDOM	75756-75756	BROWNSBORO
75027-75028	FLOWER MOUND	75169-75169	WILLS POINT	75493-75493	WINFIELD	75757-75757	BULLARD
75029-75029	LEWISVILLE	75172-75172	WILMER	75494-75494	WINNSBORO	75758-75758	CHANDLER
75030-75030	ROWLETT	75173-75173	NEVADA	75495-75495	VAN ALSTYNE	75759-75759	CUNEY
75032-75032	ROCKWALL	75180-75181	MESQUITE	75496-75496	WOLFE CITY	75760-75760	CUSHING
75034-75035	FRISCO	75182-75182	SUNNYVALE	75497-75497	YANTIS	75762-75762	FLINT
75037-75039	IRVING	75185-75187	MESQUITE	75501-75507	TEXARKANA	75763-75763	FRANKSTON
75040-75049	GARLAND	75189-75189	ROYSE CITY	75550-75550	ANNONA	75764-75764	GALLATIN
75050-75054	GRAND PRAIRIE	75200-75398	DALLAS	75551-75551	ATLANTA	75765-75765	HAWKINS
75056-75056	THE COLONY	75401-75404	GREENVILLE	75554-75554	AVERY	75766-75766	JACKSONVILLE
75057-75057	LEWISVILLE	75407-75407	PRINCETON	75555-75555	BIVINS	75770-75770	LARUE
75058-75058	GUNTER	75409-75409	ANNA	75556-75556	BLOOMBURG	75771-75771	LINDALE
75060-75063	IRVING	75410-75410	ALBA	75557-75557	MAGNOLIA SPRINGS	75772-75772	MAYDELLE
75065-75065	LAKE DALLAS	75411-75411	ARTHUR CITY	75558-75558	COOKVILLE	75773-75773	MINEOLA
75067-75067	LEWISVILLE	75412-75412	BAGWELL	75559-75559	DE KALB	75778-75778	MURCHISON
75068-75068	LITTLE ELM	75413-75413	BAILEY	75560-75560	DOUGLASSVILLE	75779-75779	NECHES
75069-75071	MC KINNEY	75414-75414	BELLS	75561-75561	HOOKS	75780-75780	NEW SUMMERFIELD
75074-75075	PLANO	75415-75415	BEN FRANKLIN	75562-75562	KILDARE	75782-75782	POYNOR
75076-75076	POTTSBORO	75416-75416	BLOSSOM	75563-75563	LINDEN	75783-75783	QUITMAN
75077-75077	LEWISVILLE	75417-75417	BOGATA	75564-75564	LODI	75784-75784	REKLAW
75078-75078	PROSPER	75418-75418	BONHAM	75565-75565	MC LEOD	75785-75785	RUSK
75080-75083	RICHARDSON	75420-75420	BRASHEAR	75566-75566	MARIETTA	75788-75788	SACUL
75084-75084	IRVING	75421-75421	BROOKSTON	75567-75567	MAUD	75789-75789	TROUP
75085-75085	RICHARDSON	75422-75422	CAMPBELL	75568-75568	NAPLES	75790-75790	VAN
75086-75086	PLANO	75423-75423	CELESTE	75569-75569	NASH	75791-75791	WHITEHOUSE
75087-75087	ROCKWALL	75424-75424	BLUE RIDGE	75570-75570	NEW BOSTON	75792-75792	WINONA
75088-75089	ROWLETT	75425-75425	CHICOTA	75571-75571	OMAHA	75797-75797	BIG SANDY
75090-75092	SHERMAN	75426-75426	CLARKSVILLE	75572-75572	QUEEN CITY	75798-75799	TYLER
75093-75094	PLANO	75428-75429	COMMERCE	75573-75573	REDWATER	75801-75803	PALESTINE
75097-75097	WESTON	75431-75431	COMO	75574-75574	SIMMS	75831-75831	BUFFALO
75098-75098	WYLIE	75432-75432	COOPER	75599-75599	TEXARKANA	75832-75832	CAYUGA
75099-75099	COPPELL	75433-75433	CUMBY	75601-75615	LONGVIEW	75833-75833	CENTERVILLE
75101-75101	BARDWELL	75434-75434	CUNNINGHAM	75630-75630	AVINGER	75834-75834	CENTRALIA
75102-75102	BARRY	75435-75435	DEPORT	75631-75631	BECKVILLE	75835-75835	CROCKETT
75103-75103	CANTON	75436-75436	DETROIT	75633-75633	CARTHAGE	75838-75838	DONIE
75104-75104	CEDAR HILL	75437-75437	DIKE	75636-75636	CASON	75839-75839	ELKHART
75105-75105	CHATFIELD	75438-75438	DODD CITY	75637-75637	CLAYTON	75840-75840	FAIRFIELD
75106-75106	CEDAR HILL	75439-75439	ECTOR	75638-75638	DAINGERFIELD	75844-75844	GRAPELAND
75109-75110	CORSICANA	75440-75440	EMORY	75639-75639	DE BERRY	75845-75845	GROVETON
75114-75114	CRANDALL	75441-75441	ENLOE	75640-75640	DIANA	75846-75846	JEWETT
75115-75115	DE SOTO	75442-75442	FARMERSVILLE	75641-75641	EASTON	75847-75847	KENNARD
75116-75116	DUNCANVILLE	75443-75443	GOBER	75642-75642	ELYSIAN FIELDS	75848-75848	KIRVIN
75117-75117	EDGEWOOD	75444-75444	GOLDEN	75643-75643	GARY	75849-75849	LATEXO
75118-75118	ELMO	75446-75446	HONEY GROVE	75644-75645	GILMER	75850-75850	LEONA
75119-75120	ENNIS	75447-75447	IVANHOE	75647-75647	GLADEWATER	75851-75851	LOVELADY
75121-75121	COPEVILLE	75448-75448	KLONDIKE	75650-75650	HALLSVILLE	75852-75852	MIDWAY
75123-75123	DE SOTO	75449-75449	LADONIA	75651-75651	HARLETON	75853-75853	MONTALBA
75123-75123	DESOTO	75450-75450	LAKE CREEK	75652-75654	HENDERSON	75855-75855	OAKWOOD
75124-75124	EUSTACE	75451-75451	LEESBURG	75656-75656	HUGHES SPRINGS	75856-75856	PENNINGTON
75125-75125	FERRIS	75452-75452	LEONARD	75657-75657	JEFFERSON	75858-75858	RATCLIFF
75126-75126	FORNEY	75453-75453	LONE OAK	75658-75658	JOINERVILLE	75859-75859	STREETMAN
75127-75127	FRUITVALE	75454-75454	MELISSA	75659-75659	JONESVILLE	75860-75860	TEAGUE
75132-75132	FATE	75455-75456	MOUNT PLEASANT	75660-75660	JUDSON	75861-75861	TENNESSEE COLONY
75134-75134	LANCASTER	75457-75457	MOUNT VERNON	75661-75661	KARNACK	75862-75862	TRINITY
75135-75135	CADDO MILLS	75458-75458	MERIT	75662-75663	KILGORE	75865-75865	WOODLAKE
75137-75138	DUNCANVILLE	75459-75459	HOWE	75666-75666	LAIRD HILL	75880-75880	TENNESSEE COLONY
75140-75140	GRAND SALINE	75460-75462	PARIS	75667-75667	LANEVILLE	75882-75882	PALESTINE
75141-75141	HUTCHINS	75468-75468	PATTONVILLE	75668-75668	LONE STAR	75884-75886	TENNESSEE COLONY
75142-75142	KAUFMAN	75469-75469	PECAN GAP	75669-75669	LONG BRANCH	75901-75915	LUFKIN
75143-75143	KEMP	75470-75470	PETTY	75670-75672	MARSHALL	75925-75925	ALTO
75144-75144	KERENS	75471-75471	PICKTON	75680-75680	MINDEN	75926-75926	APPLE SPRINGS
75146-75146	LANCASTER	75472-75472	POINT	75681-75681	MOUNT ENTERPRISE	75928-75928	BON WIER
75147-75147	MABANK	75473-75473	POWDERLY	75682-75682	NEW LONDON	75929-75929	BROADDUS
75148-75148	MALAKOFF	75474-75474	QUINLAN	75683-75683	ORE CITY	75930-75930	BRONSON
75149-75150	MESQUITE	75475-75475	RANDOLPH	75684-75684	OVERTON	75931-75931	BROOKELAND
75151-75151	CORSICANA	75476-75476	RAVENNA	75685-75685	PANOLA	75932-75932	BURKEVILLE
75152-75152	PALMER	75477-75477	ROXTON	75686-75686	PITTSBURG	75933-75933	CALL
75153-75153	POWELL	75478-75478	SALTILLO	75687-75687	PRICE	75934-75934	CAMDEN

75935-75935 CENTER	76117-76117 HALTOM CITY	76437-76437 CISCO	76571-76571 SALADO
75936-75936 CHESTER	76118-76126 FORT WORTH	76438-76438 ELIASVILLE	76573-76573 SCHWERTNER
75937-75937 CHIRENO	76127-76127 NAVAL AIR STATION/ JRB	76439-76439 DENNIS	76574-76574 TAYLOR
75938-75938 COLMESNEIL	76129-76179 FORT WORTH	76442-76442 COMANCHE	76576-76576 GATESVILLE
75939-75939 CORRIGAN	76180-76180 NORTH RICHLAND HILLS	76443-76443 CROSS PLAINS	76577-76577 THORNDALE
75941-75941 DIBOLL	76181-76181 FORT WORTH	76444-76444 DE LEON	76578-76578 THRALL
75942-75942 DOUCETTE	76182-76182 NORTH RICHLAND HILLS	76445-76445 DESDEMONA	76579-76579 TROY
75943-75943 DOUGLASS	76185-76199 FORT WORTH	76446-76446 DUBLIN	76596-76599 GATESVILLE
75944-75944 ETOILE	76201-76210 DENTON	76448-76448 EASTLAND	76621-76621 ABBOTT
75946-75946 GARRISON	76225-76225 ALVORD	76449-76449 GRAFORD	76622-76622 AQUILLA
75947-75947 GENEVA	76226-76226 ARGYLE	76450-76450 GRAHAM	76623-76623 AVALON
75948-75948 HEMPHILL	76227-76227 AUBREY	76452-76452 ENERGY	76624-76624 AXTELL
75949-75949 HUNTINGTON	76228-76228 BELLEVUE	76453-76453 GORDON	76625-76625 BIROME
75951-75951 JASPER	76230-76230 BOWIE	76454-76454 GORMAN	76626-76626 BLOOMING GROVE
75954-75954 JOAQUIN	76233-76233 COLLINSVILLE	76455-76455 GUSTINE	76627-76627 BLUM
75956-75956 KIRBYVILLE	76234-76234 DECATUR	76456-76456 HASSE	76628-76628 BRANDON
75957-75957 MAGNOLIA SPRINGS	76238-76238 ERA	76457-76457 HICO	76629-76629 BREMOND
75958-75958 MARTINSVILLE	76239-76239 FORESTBURG	76458-76458 JACKSBORO	76630-76630 BRUCEVILLE
75959-75959 MILAM	76240-76241 GAINESVILLE	76459-76459 JERMYN	76631-76631 BYNUM
75960-75960 MOSCOW	76244-76244 KELLER	76460-76460 LOVING	76632-76632 CHILTON
75961-75965 NACOGDOCHES	76245-76245 GORDONVILLE	76461-76461 LINGLEVILLE	76633-76633 CHINA SPRING
75966-75966 NEWTON	76246-76246 GREENWOOD	76462-76462 LIPAN	76634-76634 CLIFTON
75968-75968 PINELAND	76247-76247 JUSTIN	76463-76463 MINGUS	76635-76635 COOLIDGE
75969-75969 POLLOK	76248-76248 KELLER	76464-76464 MORAN	76636-76636 COVINGTON
75970-75970 ROCKLAND	76249-76249 KRUM	76465-76465 MORGAN MILL	76637-76637 CRANFILLS GAP
75972-75972 SAN AUGUSTINE	76250-76250 LINDSAY	76466-76466 OLDEN	76638-76638 CRAWFORD
75973-75973 SHELBYVILLE	76251-76251 MONTAGUE	76467-76467 PALUXY	76639-76639 DAWSON
75974-75974 TENAHA	76252-76252 MUENSTER	76468-76468 PROCTOR	76640-76640 ELM MOTT
75975-75975 TIMPSON	76253-76253 MYRA	76469-76469 PUTNAM	76641-76641 FROST
75976-75976 WELLS	76254-76254 NEWPORT	76470-76470 RANGER	76642-76642 GROESBECK
75977-75977 WIERGATE	76255-76255 NOCONA	76471-76471 RISING STAR	76643-76643 HEWITT
75978-75978 WODEN	76258-76258 PILOT POINT	76472-76472 SANTO	76644-76644 CLIFTON
75979-75979 WOODVILLE	76259-76259 PONDER	76474-76474 SIDNEY	76645-76645 HILLSBORO
75980-75980 ZAVALLA	76261-76261 RINGGOLD	76475-76475 STRAWN	76648-76648 HUBBARD
75990-75990 WOODVILLE	76262-76262 ROANOKE	76476-76476 TOLAR	76649-76649 IREDELL
76000-76007 ARLINGTON	76263-76263 ROSSTON	76481-76481 SOUTH BEND	76650-76650 IRENE
76008-76008 ALEDO	76264-76264 SADLER	76483-76483 THROCKMORTON	76651-76651 ITALY
76009-76009 ALVARADO	76265-76265 SAINT JO	76484-76484 PALO PINTO	76652-76652 KOPPERL
76010-76019 ARLINGTON	76266-76266 SANGER	76485-76485 PEASTER	76653-76653 KOSSE
76020-76020 AZLE	76267-76267 SLIDELL	76486-76486 PERRIN	76654-76654 LEROY
76021-76022 BEDFORD	76268-76268 SOUTHMAYD	76487-76487 POOLVILLE	76655-76655 LORENA
76023-76023 BOYD	76270-76270 SUNSET	76490-76490 WHITT	76656-76656 LOTT
76028-76028 BURLESON	76271-76271 TIOGA	76491-76491 WOODSON	76657-76657 MC GREGOR
76031-76033 CLEBURNE	76272-76272 VALLEY VIEW	76501-76508 TEMPLE	76660-76660 MALONE
76034-76034 COLLEYVILLE	76273-76273 WHITESBORO	76511-76511 BARTLETT	76661-76661 MARLIN
76035-76035 CRESSON	76299-76299 ROANOKE	76513-76513 BELTON	76664-76664 MART
76036-76036 CROWLEY	76301-76310 WICHITA FALLS	76517-76517 BEN ARNOLD	76665-76665 MERIDIAN
76039-76040 EULESS	76311-76311 SHEPPARD AFB	76518-76518 BUCKHOLTS	76666-76666 MERTENS
76041-76041 FORRESTON	76351-76351 ARCHER CITY	76519-76519 BURLINGTON	76667-76667 MEXIA
76043-76043 GLEN ROSE	76352-76352 BLUEGROVE	76520-76520 CAMERON	76670-76670 MILFORD
76044-76044 GODLEY	76354-76354 BURKBURNETT	76522-76522 COPPERAS COVE	76671-76671 MORGAN
76048-76049 GRANBURY	76357-76357 BYERS	76523-76523 DAVILLA	76673-76673 MOUNT CALM
76050-76050 GRANDVIEW	76359-76359 ELBERT	76524-76524 EDDY	76675-76675 OTTO
76051-76051 GRAPEVINE	76360-76360 ELECTRA	76525-76525 EVANT	76676-76676 PENELOPE
76052-76052 HASLET	76363-76363 GOREE	76526-76526 FLAT	76677-76677 PERRY
76053-76054 HURST	76364-76364 HARROLD	76527-76527 FLORENCE	76678-76678 PRAIRIE HILL
76055-76055 ITASCA	76365-76365 HENRIETTA	76528-76528 GATESVILLE	76679-76679 PURDON
76058-76058 JOSHUA	76366-76366 HOLLIDAY	76530-76530 GRANGER	76680-76680 REAGAN
76059-76059 KEENE	76367-76367 IOWA PARK	76531-76531 HAMILTON	76681-76681 RICHLAND
76060-76060 KENNEDALE	76369-76369 KAMAY	76533-76533 HEIDENHEIMER	76682-76682 RIESEL
76061-76061 LILLIAN	76370-76370 MEGARGEL	76534-76534 HOLLAND	76684-76684 ROSS
76063-76063 MANSFIELD	76371-76371 MUNDAY	76537-76537 JARRELL	76685-76685 SATIN
76064-76064 MAYPEARL	76372-76372 NEWCASTLE	76538-76538 JONESBORO	76686-76686 TEHUACANA
76065-76065 MIDLOTHIAN	76373-76373 OKLAUNION	76539-76539 KEMPNER	76687-76687 THORNTON
76066-76066 MILLSAP	76374-76374 OLNEY	76540-76547 KILLEEN	76689-76689 VALLEY MILLS
76067-76068 MINERAL WELLS	76377-76377 PETROLIA	76548-76548 HARKER HEIGHTS	76690-76690 WALNUT SPRINGS
76070-76070 NEMO	76379-76379 SCOTLAND	76549-76549 KILLEEN	76691-76691 WEST
76071-76071 NEWARK	76380-76380 SEYMOUR	76550-76550 LAMPASAS	76692-76692 WHITNEY
76073-76073 PARADISE	76383-76383 VERA	76552-76552 LEON JUNCTION	76693-76693 WORTHAM
76077-76077 RAINBOW	76384-76385 VERNON	76554-76554 LITTLE RIVER	76700-76711 WACO
76078-76078 RHOME	76388-76388 WEINERT	76554-76554 LITTLE RIVER ACADEMY	76712-76712 WOODWAY
76082-76082 SPRINGTOWN	76389-76389 WINDTHORST	76555-76555 MAYSFIELD	76714-76799 WACO
76084-76084 VENUS	76401-76402 STEPHENVILLE	76556-76556 MILANO	76801-76801 BROWNWOOD
76085-76088 WEATHERFORD	76424-76424 BRECKENRIDGE	76557-76557 MOODY	76802-76802 EARLY
76092-76092 SOUTHLAKE	76426-76426 BRIDGEPORT	76558-76558 MOUND	76803-76804 BROWNWOOD
76093-76093 RIO VISTA	76427-76427 BRYSON	76559-76559 NOLANVILLE	76820-76820 ART
76094-76094 ARLINGTON	76429-76429 CADDO	76561-76561 OGLESBY	76821-76821 BALLINGER
76095-76095 BEDFORD	76430-76430 ALBANY	76564-76564 PENDLETON	76823-76823 BANGS
76096-76096 ARLINGTON	76431-76431 CHICO	76565-76565 POTTSVILLE	76824-76824 BEND
76097-76097 BURLESON	76432-76432 BLANKET	76566-76566 PURMELA	76825-76825 BRADY
76098-76098 AZLE	76433-76433 BLUFF DALE	76567-76567 ROCKDALE	76827-76827 BROOKESMITH
76099-76099 GRAPEVINE	76435-76435 CARBON	76569-76569 ROGERS	76828-76828 BURKETT
76100-76116 FORT WORTH	76436-76436 CARLTON	76570-76570 ROSEBUD	76831-76831 CASTELL

Zip Range	Place	Zip Range	Place	Zip Range	Place	Zip Range	Place
76832-76832	CHEROKEE	77345-77347	HUMBLE	77468-77468	PLEDGER	77625-77625	KOUNTZE
76834-76834	COLEMAN	77348-77349	HUNTSVILLE	77469-77469	RICHMOND	77626-77626	MAURICEVILLE
76836-76836	DOOLE	77350-77350	LEGGETT	77470-77470	ROCK ISLAND	77627-77627	NEDERLAND
76837-76837	EDEN	77351-77351	LIVINGSTON	77471-77471	ROSENBERG	77629-77629	NOME
76841-76841	FORT MC KAVETT	77353-77355	MAGNOLIA	77473-77473	SAN FELIPE	77630-77632	ORANGE
76842-76842	FREDONIA	77356-77356	MONTGOMERY	77474-77474	SEALY	77639-77639	ORANGEFIELD
76844-76844	GOLDTHWAITE	77357-77357	NEW CANEY	77475-77475	SHERIDAN	77640-77643	PORT ARTHUR
76845-76845	GOULDBUSK	77358-77358	NEW WAVERLY	77476-77476	SIMONTON	77650-77650	PORT BOLIVAR
76848-76848	HEXT	77359-77359	OAKHURST	77477-77477	STAFFORD	77651-77651	PORT NECHES
76849-76849	JUNCTION	77360-77360	ONALASKA	77478-77479	SUGAR LAND	77655-77655	SABINE PASS
76852-76852	LOHN	77362-77362	PINEHURST	77480-77480	SWEENY	77656-77656	SILSBEE
76853-76853	LOMETA	77363-77363	PLANTERSVILLE	77481-77481	THOMPSONS	77657-77657	LUMBERTON
76854-76854	LONDON	77364-77364	POINTBLANK	77482-77482	VAN VLECK	77659-77659	SOUR LAKE
76855-76855	LOWAKE	77365-77365	PORTER	77483-77483	WADSWORTH	77660-77660	SPURGER
76856-76856	MASON	77367-77367	RIVERSIDE	77484-77484	WALLER	77661-77661	STOWELL
76857-76857	MAY	77368-77368	ROMAYOR	77485-77485	WALLIS	77662-77662	VIDOR
76858-76858	MELVIN	77369-77369	RYE	77486-77486	WEST COLUMBIA	77663-77663	VILLAGE MILLS
76859-76859	MENARD	77371-77371	SHEPHERD	77487-77487	SUGAR LAND	77664-77664	WARREN
76861-76861	MILES	77372-77372	SPLENDORA	77488-77488	WHARTON	77665-77665	WINNIE
76862-76862	MILLERSVIEW	77373-77373	SPRING	77489-77489	MISSOURI CITY	77670-77670	VIDOR
76864-76864	MULLIN	77374-77374	THICKET	77491-77494	KATY	77700-77708	BEAUMONT
76865-76865	NORTON	77375-77375	TOMBALL	77496-77496	SUGAR LAND	77709-77709	VOTH
76866-76866	PAINT ROCK	77376-77376	VOTAW	77497-77497	STAFFORD	77710-77710	BEAUMONT
76867-76867	PEAR VALLEY	77377-77377	TOMBALL	77501-77508	PASADENA	77711-77711	LUMBERTON
76869-76869	PONTOTOC	77378-77378	WILLIS	77510-77510	SANTA FE	77713-77726	BEAUMONT
76870-76870	PRIDDY	77379-77383	SPRING	77511-77512	ALVIN	77801-77808	BRYAN
76871-76871	RICHLAND SPRINGS	77384-77385	CONROE	77514-77514	ANAHUAC	77830-77830	ANDERSON
76872-76872	ROCHELLE	77386-77393	SPRING	77515-77516	ANGLETON	77831-77831	BEDIAS
76873-76873	ROCKWOOD	77396-77396	HUMBLE	77517-77517	SANTA FE	77833-77834	BRENHAM
76874-76874	ROOSEVELT	77399-77399	LIVINGSTON	77518-77518	BACLIFF	77835-77835	BURTON
76875-76875	ROWENA	77401-77402	BELLAIRE	77519-77519	BATSON	77836-77836	CALDWELL
76877-76877	SAN SABA	77404-77404	BAY CITY	77520-77522	BAYTOWN	77837-77837	CALVERT
76878-76878	SANTA ANNA	77406-77406	RICHMOND	77530-77530	CHANNELVIEW	77838-77838	CHRIESMAN
76880-76880	STAR	77410-77410	CYPRESS	77531-77531	CLUTE	77839-77839	CLAY
76882-76882	TALPA	77411-77411	ALIEF	77532-77532	CROSBY	77840-77845	COLLEGE STATION
76883-76883	TELEGRAPH	77412-77412	ALTAIR	77533-77533	DAISETTA	77850-77850	CONCORD
76884-76884	VALERA	77413-77413	BARKER	77534-77534	DANBURY	77852-77852	DEANVILLE
76885-76885	VALLEY SPRING	77414-77414	BAY CITY	77535-77535	DAYTON	77853-77853	DIME BOX
76886-76886	VERIBEST	77415-77415	CEDAR LANE	77536-77536	DEER PARK	77855-77855	FLYNN
76887-76887	VOCA	77417-77417	BEASLEY	77538-77538	DEVERS	77856-77856	FRANKLIN
76888-76888	VOSS	77418-77418	BELLVILLE	77539-77539	DICKINSON	77857-77857	GAUSE
76889-76889	WHON	77419-77419	BLESSING	77541-77542	FREEPORT	77859-77859	HEARNE
76890-76890	ZEPHYR	77420-77420	BOLING	77545-77545	FRESNO	77861-77861	IOLA
76901-76906	SAN ANGELO	77422-77422	BRAZORIA	77546-77546	FRIENDSWOOD	77862-77862	KURTEN
76908-76908	GOODFELLOW AFB	77423-77423	BROOKSHIRE	77547-77547	GALENA PARK	77863-77863	LYONS
76909-76909	SAN ANGELO	77426-77426	CHAPPELL HILL	77549-77549	FRIENDSWOOD	77864-77864	MADISONVILLE
76930-76930	BARNHART	77428-77428	COLLEGEPORT	77550-77555	GALVESTON	77865-77865	MARQUEZ
76932-76932	BIG LAKE	77429-77429	CYPRESS	77560-77560	HANKAMER	77866-77866	MILLICAN
76933-76933	BRONTE	77430-77430	DAMON	77561-77561	HARDIN	77867-77867	MUMFORD
76934-76934	CARLSBAD	77431-77431	DANCIGER	77562-77562	HIGHLANDS	77868-77869	NAVASOTA
76935-76935	CHRISTOVAL	77432-77432	DANEVANG	77563-77563	HITCHCOCK	77870-77870	NEW BADEN
76936-76936	ELDORADO	77433-77433	CYPRESS	77564-77564	HULL	77871-77871	NORMANGEE
76937-76937	EOLA	77434-77434	EAGLE LAKE	77565-77565	KEMAH	77872-77872	NORTH ZULCH
76939-76939	KNICKERBOCKER	77435-77435	EAST BERNARD	77566-77566	LAKE JACKSON	77873-77873	RICHARDS
76940-76940	MERETA	77436-77436	EGYPT	77568-77568	LA MARQUE	77875-77875	ROANS PRAIRIE
76941-76941	MERTZON	77437-77437	EL CAMPO	77571-77572	LA PORTE	77876-77876	SHIRO
76943-76943	OZONA	77440-77440	ELMATON	77573-77575	LEAGUE CITY	77878-77878	SNOOK
76945-76945	ROBERT LEE	77441-77441	FULSHEAR	77575-77575	LIBERTY	77879-77879	SOMERVILLE
76949-76949	SILVER	77442-77442	GARWOOD	77577-77577	LIVERPOOL	77880-77880	WASHINGTON
76950-76950	SONORA	77443-77443	GLEN FLORA	77578-77578	MANVEL	77881-77881	WELLBORN
76951-76951	STERLING CITY	77444-77444	GUY	77580-77580	MONT BELVIEU	77882-77882	WHEELOCK
76953-76953	TENNYSON	77445-77445	HEMPSTEAD	77581-77581	PEARLAND	77901-77905	VICTORIA
76955-76955	VANCOURT	77446-77446	PRAIRIE VIEW	77582-77582	RAYWOOD	77950-77950	AUSTWELL
76957-76957	WALL	77447-77447	HOCKLEY	77583-77583	ROSHARON	77951-77951	BLOOMINGTON
76958-76958	WATER VALLEY	77448-77448	HUNGERFORD	77584-77584	PEARLAND	77954-77954	CUERO
77000-77299	HOUSTON	77449-77450	KATY	77585-77585	SARATOGA	77957-77957	EDNA
77301-77306	CONROE	77451-77451	KENDLETON	77586-77586	SEABROOK	77960-77960	FANNIN
77315-77315	NORTH HOUSTON	77452-77452	KENNEY	77587-77587	SOUTH HOUSTON	77961-77961	FRANCITAS
77316-77316	MONTGOMERY	77453-77453	LANE CITY	77588-77588	PEARLAND	77962-77962	GANADO
77318-77318	WILLIS	77454-77454	LISSIE	77590-77592	TEXAS CITY	77963-77963	GOLIAD
77320-77320	HUNTSVILLE	77455-77455	LOUISE	77597-77597	WALLISVILLE	77964-77964	HALLETTSVILLE
77325-77325	HUMBLE	77456-77456	MARKHAM	77598-77598	WEBSTER	77967-77967	HOCHHEIM
77326-77326	ACE	77457-77457	MATAGORDA	77611-77611	BRIDGE CITY	77968-77968	INEZ
77327-77328	CLEVELAND	77458-77458	MIDFIELD	77612-77612	BUNA	77969-77969	LA SALLE
77331-77331	COLDSPRING	77459-77459	MISSOURI CITY	77613-77613	CHINA	77970-77970	LA WARD
77332-77332	DALLARDSVILLE	77460-77460	NADA	77614-77614	DEWEYVILLE	77971-77971	LOLITA
77333-77333	DOBBIN	77461-77461	NEEDVILLE	77615-77615	EVADALE	77972-77972	LONG MOTT
77334-77334	DODGE	77462-77462	NEWGULF	77616-77616	FRED	77973-77973	MCFADDIN
77335-77335	GOODRICH	77463-77463	OLD OCEAN	77617-77617	GILCHRIST	77974-77974	MEYERSVILLE
77336-77336	HUFFMAN	77464-77464	ORCHARD	77619-77619	GROVES	77975-77975	MOULTON
77337-77337	HUFSMITH	77465-77465	PALACIOS	77622-77622	HAMSHIRE	77976-77976	NURSERY
77338-77339	HUMBLE	77466-77466	PATTISON	77623-77623	HIGH ISLAND	77977-77977	PLACEDO
77340-77344	HUNTSVILLE	77467-77467	PIERCE	77624-77624	HILLISTER	77978-77978	POINT COMFORT

77979-77979 PORT LAVACA	78118-78118 KARNES CITY	78535-78535 COMBES	78636-78636 JOHNSON CITY
77982-77982 PORT O CONNOR	78119-78119 KENEDY	78536-78536 DELMITA	78638-78638 KINGSBURY
77983-77983 SEADRIFT	78121-78121 LA VERNIA	78537-78537 DONNA	78639-78639 KINGSLAND
77984-77984 SHINER	78122-78122 LEESVILLE	78538-78538 EDCOUCH	78640-78640 KYLE
77985-77985 SPEAKS	78123-78123 MC QUEENEY	78539-78541 EDINBURG	78641-78641 LEANDER
77986-77986 SUBLIME	78124-78124 MARION	78543-78543 ELSA	78642-78642 LIBERTY HILL
77987-77987 SWEET HOME	78125-78125 MINERAL	78545-78545 FALCON HEIGHTS	78643-78643 LLANO
77988-77988 TELFERNER	78130-78132 NEW BRAUNFELS	78547-78547 GARCIASVILLE	78644-78644 LOCKHART
77989-77989 THOMASTON	78133-78133 CANYON LAKE	78548-78548 GRULLA	78645-78646 LEANDER
77990-77990 TIVOLI	78135-78135 NEW BRAUNFELS	78549-78549 HARGILL	78648-78648 LULING
77991-77991 VANDERBILT	78140-78140 NIXON	78550-78553 HARLINGEN	78650-78650 MC DADE
77993-77993 WEESATCHE	78141-78141 NORDHEIM	78557-78557 HIDALGO	78651-78651 MC NEIL
77994-77994 WESTHOFF	78142-78142 NORMANNA	78558-78558 LA BLANCA	78652-78652 MANCHACA
77995-77995 YOAKUM	78143-78143 PANDORA	78559-78559 LA FERIA	78653-78653 MANOR
78001-78001 ARTESIA WELLS	78144-78144 PANNA MARIA	78560-78560 LA JOYA	78654-78654 MARBLE FALLS
78002-78002 ATASCOSA	78145-78145 PAWNEE	78561-78561 LASARA	78655-78655 MARTINDALE
78003-78003 BANDERA	78146-78146 PETTUS	78562-78562 LA VILLA	78656-78656 MAXWELL
78004-78004 BERGHEIM	78147-78147 POTH	78563-78563 LINN	78657-78657 MARBLE FALLS
78005-78005 BIGFOOT	78148-78150 UNIVERSAL CITY	78564-78564 LOPENO	78658-78658 OTTINE
78006-78006 BOERNE	78151-78151 RUNGE	78565-78565 LOS EBANOS	78659-78659 PAIGE
78007-78007 CALLIHAM	78152-78152 SAINT HEDWIG	78566-78566 LOS FRESNOS	78660-78660 PFLUGERVILLE
78008-78008 CAMPBELLTON	78154-78154 SCHERTZ	78567-78567 LOS INDIOS	78661-78661 PRAIRIE LEA
78009-78009 CASTROVILLE	78155-78156 SEGUIN	78568-78568 LOZANO	78662-78662 RED ROCK
78010-78010 CENTER POINT	78159-78159 SMILEY	78569-78569 LYFORD	78663-78663 ROUND MOUNTAIN
78011-78011 CHARLOTTE	78160-78160 STOCKDALE	78570-78570 MERCEDES	78664-78664 ROUND ROCK
78012-78012 CHRISTINE	78161-78161 SUTHERLAND SPRINGS	78572-78574 MISSION	78665-78665 SANDY
78013-78013 COMFORT	78162-78162 TULETA	78575-78575 OLMITO	78666-78667 SAN MARCOS
78014-78014 COTULLA	78163-78163 BULVERDE	78576-78576 PENITAS	78669-78669 SPICEWOOD
78015-78015 BOERNE	78164-78164 YORKTOWN	78577-78577 PHARR	78670-78670 STAPLES
78016-78016 DEVINE	78200-78299 SAN ANTONIO	78578-78578 PORT ISABEL	78671-78671 STONEWALL
78017-78017 DILLEY	78330-78330 AGUA DULCE	78579-78579 PROGRESO	78672-78672 TOW
78019-78019 ENCINAL	78332-78333 ALICE	78580-78580 RAYMONDVILLE	78673-78673 WALBURG
78021-78021 FOWLERTON	78335-78336 ARANSAS PASS	78582-78582 RIO GRANDE CITY	78674-78674 WEIR
78022-78022 GEORGE WEST	78338-78338 ARMSTRONG	78583-78583 RIO HONDO	78675-78675 WILLOW CITY
78023-78023 HELOTES	78339-78339 BANQUETE	78584-78584 ROMA	78676-78676 WIMBERLEY
78024-78024 HUNT	78340-78340 BAYSIDE	78585-78585 SALINENO	78677-78677 WRIGHTSBORO
78025-78025 INGRAM	78341-78341 BENAVIDES	78586-78586 SAN BENITO	78680-78683 ROUND ROCK
78026-78026 JOURDANTON	78342-78342 BEN BOLT	78588-78588 SAN ISIDRO	78691-78691 PFLUGERVILLE
78027-78027 KENDALIA	78343-78343 BISHOP	78589-78589 SAN JUAN	78700-78799 AUSTIN
78028-78029 KERRVILLE	78344-78344 BRUNI	78590-78590 SAN PERLITA	78801-78802 UVALDE
78039-78039 LA COSTE	78347-78347 CHAPMAN RANCH	78591-78591 SANTA ELENA	78827-78827 ASHERTON
78040-78049 LAREDO	78349-78349 CONCEPCION	78592-78592 SANTA MARIA	78828-78828 BARKSDALE
78050-78050 LEMING	78350-78350 DINERO	78593-78593 SANTA ROSA	78829-78829 BATESVILLE
78052-78052 LYTLE	78351-78351 DRISCOLL	78594-78594 SEBASTIAN	78830-78830 BIG WELLS
78053-78053 MC COY	78352-78352 EDROY	78595-78595 SULLIVAN CITY	78832-78832 BRACKETTVILLE
78054-78054 MACDONA	78353-78353 ENCINO	78596-78596 WESLACO	78833-78833 CAMP WOOD
78055-78055 MEDINA	78355-78355 FALFURRIAS	78597-78597 SOUTH PADRE ISLAND	78834-78834 CARRIZO SPRINGS
78056-78056 MICO	78357-78357 FREER	78598-78598 PORT MANSFIELD	78835-78835 DEL RIO
78057-78057 MOORE	78358-78358 FULTON	78599-78599 WESLACO	78836-78836 CATARINA
78058-78058 MOUNTAIN HOME	78359-78359 GREGORY	78602-78602 BASTROP	78837-78837 COMSTOCK
78059-78059 NATALIA	78360-78360 GUERRA	78603-78603 BEBE	78838-78838 CONCAN
78060-78060 OAKVILLE	78361-78361 HEBBRONVILLE	78604-78604 BELMONT	78839-78839 CRYSTAL CITY
78061-78061 PEARSALL	78362-78362 INGLESIDE	78605-78605 BERTRAM	78840-78842 DEL RIO
78062-78062 PEGGY	78363-78364 KINGSVILLE	78606-78606 BLANCO	78843-78843 LAUGHLIN A F B
78063-78063 PIPE CREEK	78368-78368 MATHIS	78607-78607 BLUFFTON	78847-78847 DEL RIO
78064-78064 PLEASANTON	78369-78369 MIRANDO CITY	78608-78608 BRIGGS	78850-78850 D HANIS
78065-78065 POTEET	78370-78370 ODEM	78609-78609 BUCHANAN DAM	78851-78851 DRYDEN
78066-78066 RIO MEDINA	78371-78371 OILTON	78610-78610 BUDA	78852-78853 EAGLE PASS
78067-78067 SAN YGNACIO	78372-78372 ORANGE GROVE	78611-78611 BURNET	78860-78860 EL INDIO
78069-78069 SOMERSET	78373-78373 PORT ARANSAS	78612-78612 CEDAR CREEK	78861-78861 HONDO
78070-78070 SPRING BRANCH	78374-78374 PORTLAND	78613-78613 CEDAR PARK	78870-78870 KNIPPA
78071-78071 THREE RIVERS	78375-78375 PREMONT	78614-78614 COST	78871-78871 LANGTRY
78072-78072 TILDEN	78376-78376 REALITOS	78615-78615 COUPLAND	78872-78872 LA PRYOR
78073-78073 VON ORMY	78377-78377 REFUGIO	78616-78616 DALE	78873-78873 LEAKEY
78074-78074 WARING	78379-78379 RIVIERA	78617-78617 DEL VALLE	78877-78877 QUEMADO
78075-78075 WHITSETT	78380-78380 ROBSTOWN	78618-78618 DOSS	78879-78879 RIO FRIO
78076-78076 ZAPATA	78381-78382 ROCKPORT	78619-78619 DRIFTWOOD	78880-78880 ROCKSPRINGS
78101-78101 ADKINS	78383-78383 SANDIA	78620-78620 DRIPPING SPRINGS	78881-78881 SABINAL
78102-78104 BEEVILLE	78384-78384 SAN DIEGO	78621-78621 ELGIN	78883-78883 TARPLEY
78107-78107 BERCLAIR	78385-78385 SARITA	78622-78622 FENTRESS	78884-78884 UTOPIA
78108-78108 CIBOLO	78387-78387 SINTON	78623-78623 FISCHER	78885-78885 VANDERPOOL
78109-78109 CONVERSE	78389-78389 SKIDMORE	78624-78624 FREDERICKSBURG	78886-78886 YANCEY
78111-78111 ECLETO	78390-78390 TAFT	78626-78628 GEORGETOWN	78931-78931 BLEIBLERVILLE
78112-78112 ELMENDORF	78391-78391 TYNAN	78629-78629 GONZALES	78932-78932 CARMINE
78113-78113 FALLS CITY	78393-78393 WOODSBORO	78630-78630 CEDAR PARK	78933-78933 CAT SPRING
78114-78114 FLORESVILLE	78400-78480 CORPUS CHRISTI	78631-78631 HARPER	78934-78934 COLUMBUS
78115-78115 GERONIMO	78501-78505 MCALLEN	78632-78632 HARWOOD	78935-78935 ALLEYTON
78116-78116 GILLETT	78516-78516 ALAMO	78634-78634 HUTTO	78938-78938 ELLINGER
78117-78117 HOBSON	78520-78526 BROWNSVILLE	78635-78635 HYE	78940-78940 FAYETTEVILLE
78941-78941 FLATONIA	78945-78945 LA GRANGE	78949-78949 MULDOON	78953-78953 ROSANKY
78942-78942 GIDDINGS	78946-78946 LEDBETTER	78950-78950 NEW ULM	78954-78954 ROUND TOP
78943-78943 GLIDDEN	78947-78947 LEXINGTON	78951-78951 OAKLAND	78956-78956 SCHULENBURG
78944-78944 INDUSTRY	78948-78948 LINCOLN	78952-78952 PLUM	78957-78957 SMITHVILLE

Zip Range	Name	Zip Range	Name	Zip Range	Name	Zip Range	Name
78959-78959	WAELDER	79093-79093	WAKA	79356-79356	POST	79565-79565	WESTBROOK
78960-78960	WARDA	79094-79094	WAYSIDE	79357-79357	RALLS	79566-79566	WINGATE
78961-78961	ROUND TOP	79095-79095	WELLINGTON	79358-79358	ROPESVILLE	79567-79567	WINTERS
78962-78962	WEIMAR	79096-79096	WHEELER	79359-79359	SEAGRAVES	79600-79606	ABILENE
78963-78963	WEST POINT	79097-79097	WHITE DEER	79360-79360	SEMINOLE	79607-79607	DYESS AFB
78964-78964	WINCHESTER	79098-79098	WILDORADO	79363-79363	SHALLOWATER	79608-79699	ABILENE
79001-79001	ADRIAN	79100-79189	AMARILLO	79364-79364	SLATON	79701-79712	MIDLAND
79002-79002	ALANREED	79201-79201	CHILDRESS	79366-79366	RANSOM CANYON	79713-79713	ACKERLY
79003-79003	ALLISON	79220-79220	AFTON	79367-79367	SMYER	79714-79714	ANDREWS
79005-79005	BOOKER	79221-79221	AIKEN	79368-79368	SOUTHLAND	79718-79718	BALMORHEA
79007-79008	BORGER	79222-79222	CAREY	79369-79369	SPADE	79719-79719	BARSTOW
79009-79009	BOVINA	79223-79223	CEE VEE	79370-79370	SPUR	79720-79721	BIG SPRING
79010-79010	BOYS RANCH	79224-79224	CHALK	79371-79371	SUDAN	79730-79730	COYANOSA
79011-79011	BRISCOE	79225-79225	CHILLICOTHE	79372-79372	SUNDOWN	79731-79731	CRANE
79012-79012	BUSHLAND	79226-79226	CLARENDON	79373-79373	TAHOKA	79733-79733	FORSAN
79013-79013	CACTUS	79227-79227	CROWELL	79376-79376	TOKIO	79734-79734	FORT DAVIS
79014-79014	CANADIAN	79229-79229	DICKENS	79377-79377	WELCH	79735-79735	FORT STOCKTON
79015-79016	CANYON	79230-79230	DODSON	79378-79378	WELLMAN	79738-79738	GAIL
79018-79018	CHANNING	79231-79231	DOUGHERTY	79379-79379	WHITEFACE	79739-79739	GARDEN CITY
79019-79019	CLAUDE	79232-79232	DUMONT	79380-79380	WHITHARRAL	79740-79740	GIRVIN
79021-79021	COTTON CENTER	79233-79233	ESTELLINE	79381-79381	WILSON	79741-79741	GOLDSMITH
79022-79022	DALHART	79234-79234	FLOMOT	79382-79382	WOLFFORTH	79742-79742	GRANDFALLS
79024-79024	DARROUZETT	79235-79235	FLOYDADA	79383-79383	NEW HOME	79743-79743	IMPERIAL
79025-79025	DAWN	79236-79236	GUTHRIE	79400-79464	LUBBOCK	79744-79744	IRAAN
79027-79027	DIMMITT	79237-79237	HEDLEY	79489-79489	REESE AIR FORCE BASE	79745-79745	KERMIT
79029-79029	DUMAS	79238-79238	KIRKLAND	79490-79499	LUBBOCK	79748-79748	KNOTT
79031-79031	EARTH	79239-79239	LAKEVIEW	79501-79501	ANSON	79749-79749	LENORAH
79032-79032	EDMONSON	79240-79240	LELIA LAKE	79502-79502	ASPERMONT	79752-79752	MC CAMEY
79033-79033	FARNSWORTH	79241-79241	LOCKNEY	79503-79503	STAMFORD	79754-79754	MENTONE
79034-79034	FOLLETT	79243-79243	MCADOO	79504-79504	BAIRD	79755-79755	MIDKIFF
79035-79035	FRIONA	79244-79244	MATADOR	79505-79505	BENJAMIN	79756-79756	MONAHANS
79036-79036	FRITCH	79245-79245	MEMPHIS	79506-79506	BLACKWELL	79758-79758	GARDENDALE
79039-79039	GROOM	79247-79247	ODELL	79508-79508	BUFFALO GAP	79759-79759	NOTREES
79040-79040	GRUVER	79248-79248	PADUCAH	79510-79510	CLYDE	79760-79769	ODESSA
79041-79041	HALE CENTER	79250-79250	PETERSBURG	79511-79511	COAHOMA	79770-79770	ORLA
79042-79042	HAPPY	79251-79251	QUAIL	79512-79512	COLORADO CITY	79772-79772	PECOS
79043-79043	HART	79252-79252	QUANAH	79516-79516	DUNN	79776-79776	PENWELL
79044-79044	HARTLEY	79255-79255	QUITAQUE	79517-79517	FLUVANNA	79777-79777	PYOTE
79045-79045	HEREFORD	79256-79256	ROARING SPRINGS	79518-79518	GIRARD	79778-79778	RANKIN
79046-79046	HIGGINS	79257-79257	SILVERTON	79519-79519	GOLDSBORO	79779-79779	ROYALTY
79051-79051	KERRICK	79258-79258	SOUTH PLAINS	79520-79520	HAMLIN	79780-79780	SARAGOSA
79052-79052	KRESS	79259-79259	TELL	79521-79521	HASKELL	79781-79781	SHEFFIELD
79053-79053	LAZBUDDIE	79260-79260	TRUSCOTT	79525-79525	HAWLEY	79782-79782	STANTON
79054-79054	LEFORS	79261-79261	TURKEY	79526-79526	HERMLEIGH	79783-79783	TARZAN
79056-79056	LIPSCOMB	79311-79311	ABERNATHY	79527-79527	IRA	79785-79785	TOYAH
79057-79057	MCLEAN	79312-79312	AMHERST	79528-79528	JAYTON	79786-79786	TOYAHVALE
79058-79058	MASTERSON	79313-79313	ANTON	79529-79529	KNOX CITY	79788-79788	WICKETT
79059-79059	MIAMI	79314-79314	BLEDSOE	79530-79530	LAWN	79789-79789	WINK
79061-79061	MOBEETIE	79316-79316	BROWNFIELD	79532-79532	LORAINE	79821-79821	ANTHONY
79062-79062	MORSE	79320-79320	BULA	79533-79533	LUEDERS	79830-79832	ALPINE
79063-79063	NAZARETH	79321-79321	CONE	79534-79534	MC CAULLEY	79834-79834	BIG BEND NATIONAL PARK
79064-79064	OLTON	79322-79322	CROSBYTON	79535-79535	MARYNEAL	79835-79835	CANUTILLO
79065-79066	PAMPA	79323-79323	DENVER CITY	79536-79536	MERKEL	79836-79836	CLINT
79068-79068	PANHANDLE	79324-79324	ENOCHS	79537-79537	NOLAN	79837-79837	DELL CITY
79070-79070	PERRYTON	79325-79325	FARWELL	79538-79538	NOVICE	79838-79838	FABENS
79072-79073	PLAINVIEW	79326-79326	FIELDTON	79539-79539	O BRIEN	79839-79839	FORT HANCOCK
79077-79077	SAMNORWOOD	79329-79329	IDALOU	79540-79540	OLD GLORY	79842-79842	MARATHON
79078-79078	SANFORD	79330-79330	JUSTICEBURG	79541-79541	OVALO	79843-79843	MARFA
79079-79079	SHAMROCK	79331-79331	LAMESA	79542-79542	PEACOCK	79845-79845	PRESIDIO
79080-79080	SKELLYTOWN	79336-79338	LEVELLAND	79543-79543	ROBY	79846-79846	REDFORD
79081-79081	SPEARMAN	79339-79339	LITTLEFIELD	79544-79544	ROCHESTER	79847-79847	SALT FLAT
79082-79082	SPRINGLAKE	79342-79342	LOOP	79545-79545	ROSCOE	79848-79848	SANDERSON
79083-79083	STINNETT	79343-79343	LORENZO	79546-79546	ROTAN	79849-79849	SAN ELIZARIO
79084-79084	STRATFORD	79344-79344	MAPLE	79547-79548	RULE	79850-79850	SHAFTER
79085-79085	SUMMERFIELD	79345-79345	MEADOW	79549-79550	SNYDER	79851-79851	SIERRA BLANCA
79086-79086	SUNRAY	79346-79346	MORTON	79553-79553	STAMFORD	79852-79852	TERLINGUA
79087-79087	TEXLINE	79347-79347	MULESHOE	79556-79556	SWEETWATER	79853-79853	TORNILLO
79088-79088	TULIA	79350-79350	NEW DEAL	79560-79560	SYLVESTER	79854-79854	VALENTINE
79090-79090	SHAMROCK	79351-79351	ODONNELL	79561-79561	TRENT	79855-79855	VAN HORN
79091-79091	UMBARGER	79353-79353	PEP	79562-79562	TUSCOLA	79900-79999	EL PASO
79092-79092	VEGA	79355-79355	PLAINS	79563-79563	TYE	88510-88595	EL PASO

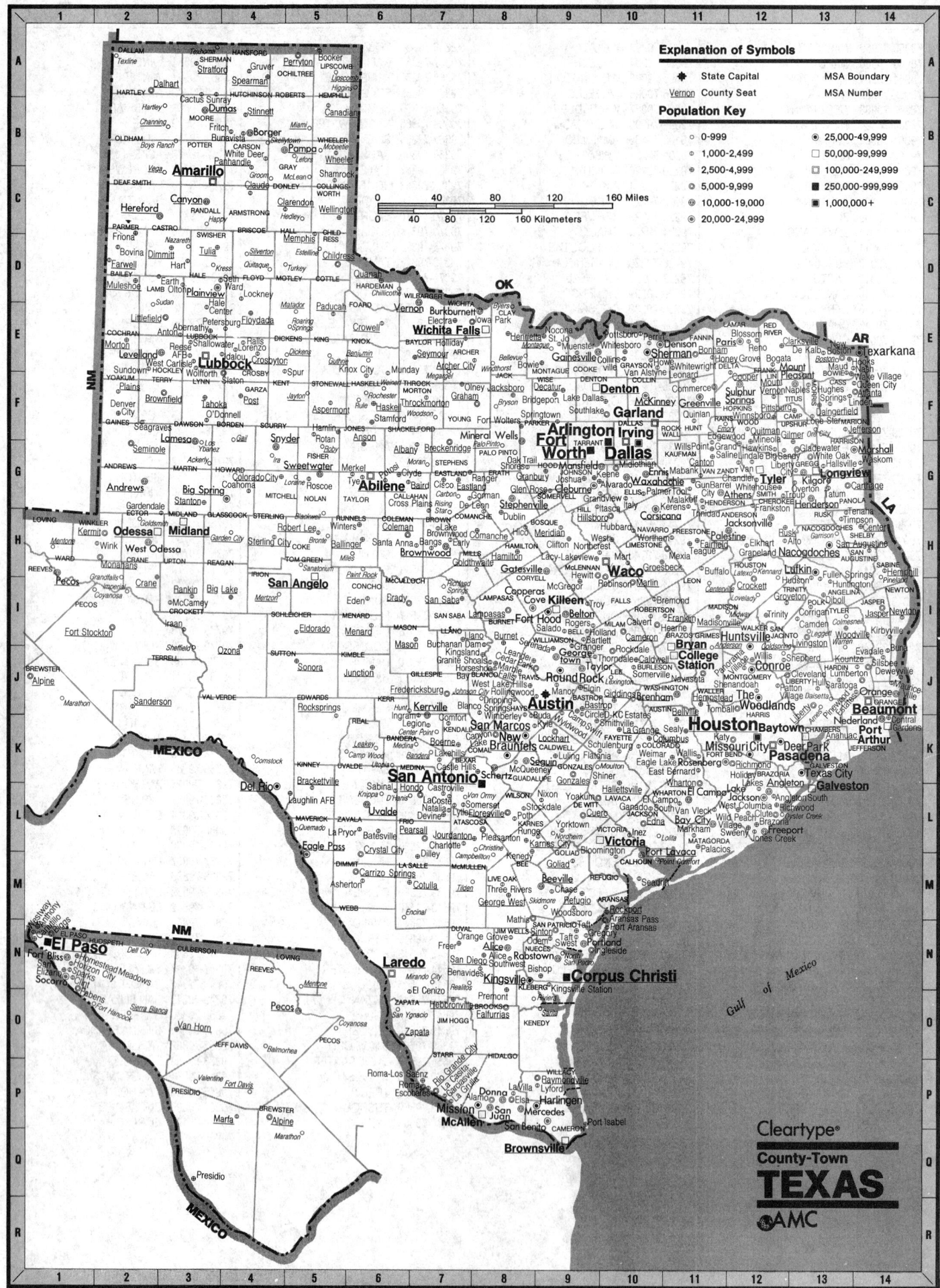

Explanation of Symbols

State Capital
County Seat
MSA Boundary
MSA Number

Population Key

○ 0-999
⊙ 1,000-2,499
⊕ 2,500-4,999
◉ 5,000-9,999
⊚ 10,000-19,000
◎ 20,000-24,999
◉ 25,000-49,999
□ 50,000-99,999
□ 100,000-249,999
■ 250,000-999,999
■ 1,000,000+

Cleartype®
County-Town
TEXAS
AMC

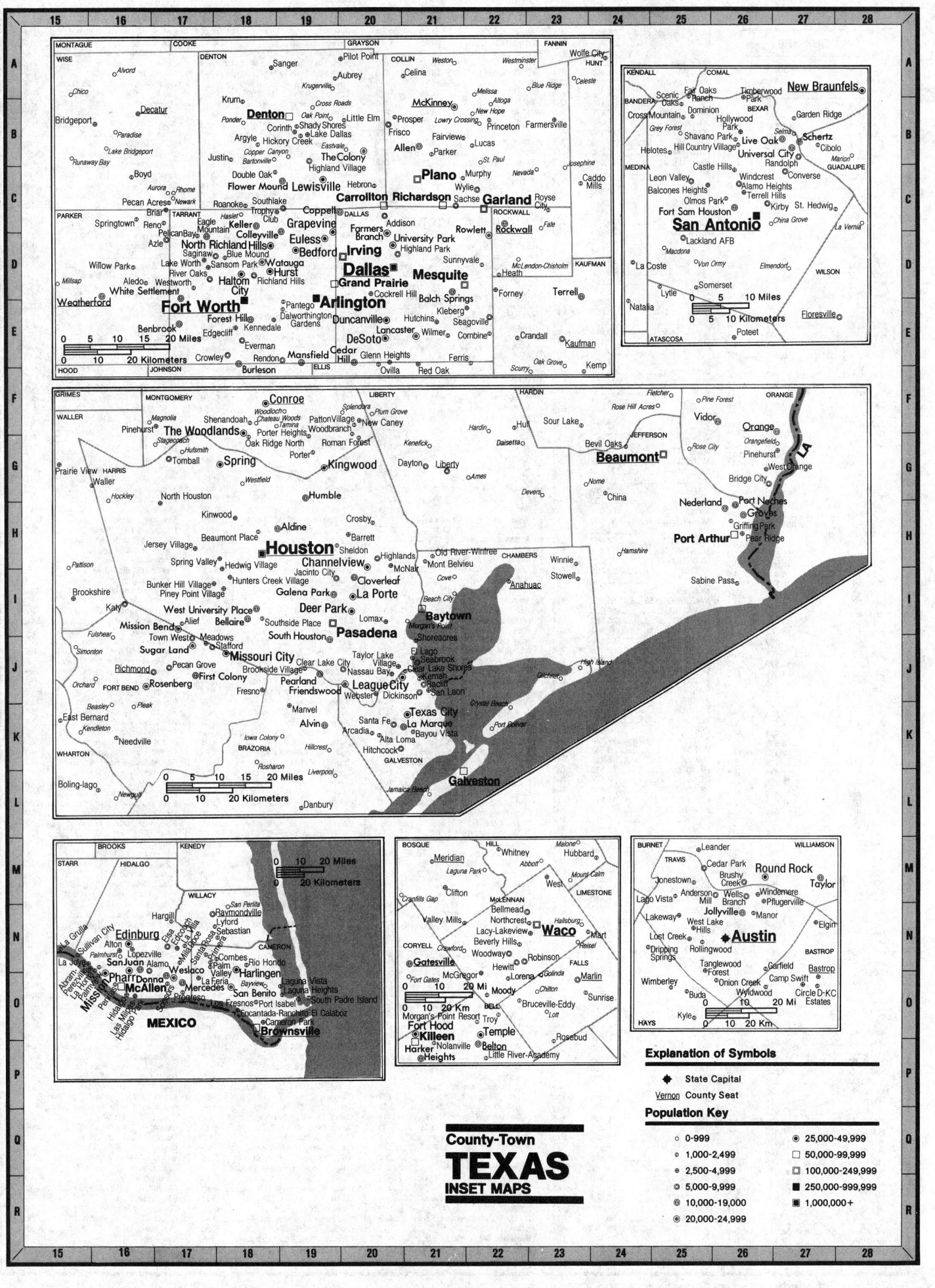

County-Town
TEXAS
INSET MAPS

Explanation of Symbols

◆ State Capital
Vernon County Seat

Population Key

○ 0-999
◉ 1,000-2,499
◉ 2,500-4,999
◉ 5,000-9,999
◉ 10,000-19,000
◉ 20,000-24,999

◉ 25,000-49,999
□ 50,000-99,999
□ 100,000-249,999
■ 250,000-999,999
■ 1,000,000+

COUNTIES

(254 Counties)

Name of County	Population	Location on Map
ANDERSON	48,024	H-11
ANDREWS	14,338	G-2
ANGELINA	69,884	I-13
ARANSAS	17,892	M-9
ARCHER	7,973	E-7
ARMSTRONG	2,021	C-4
ATASCOSA	30,533	L-7
AUSTIN	19,832	J-10
BAILEY	7,064	D-2
BANDERA	10,562	K-6
BASTROP	38,263	J-9
BAYLOR	4,385	E-6
BEE	25,135	M-8
BELL	191,088	I-9
BEXAR	1,185,394	K-7
BLANCO	5,972	J-8
BORDEN	799	F-3
BOSQUE	15,125	H-8
BOWIE	81,665	F-13
BRAZORIA	191,707	K-12
BRAZOS	121,862	I-11
BREWSTER	8,681	J-1
BRISCOE	1,971	C-4
BROOKS	8,204	O-8
BROWN	34,371	H-7
BURLESON	13,625	J-10
BURNET	22,677	I-8
CALDWELL	26,392	K-9
CALHOUN	19,053	M-10
CALLAHAN	11,859	G-6
CAMERON	260,120	Q-9
CAMP	9,904	F-12
CARSON	6,576	B-4
CASS	29,982	F-13
CASTRO	9,070	C-2
CHAMBERS	20,088	K-13
CHEROKEE	41,049	G-12
CHILDRESS	5,953	C-5
CLAY	10,024	E-8
COCHRAN	4,377	E-2
COKE	3,424	H-5
COLEMAN	9,710	H-6
COLLIN	264,036	F-10
COLLINGSWORTH	3,573	C-5
COLORADO	18,383	K-10
COMAL	51,832	K-8
COMANCHE	13,381	H-7
CONCHO	3,044	I-6
COOKE	30,777	F-9
CORYELL	64,213	I-8
COTTLE	2,247	D-5
CRANE	4,652	H-2
CROCKETT	4,078	I-3
CROSBY	7,304	F-4
CULBERSON	3,407	N-3
DALLAM	5,461	A-2
DALLAS	1,852,810	F-10
DAWSON	14,349	F-3
DEWITT	18,840	L-9
DEAF SMITH	19,153	C-2
DELTA	4,857	E-12
DENTON	273,525	F-9
DICKENS	2,571	E-4
DIMMIT	10,433	M-5
DONLEY	3,696	C-4
DUVAL	12,918	N-7
EASTLAND	18,488	G-7
ECTOR	118,934	H-2
EDWARDS	2,266	J-5
EL PASO	591,610	N-1
ELLIS	85,167	G-10
ERATH	27,991	G-8
FALLS	17,712	I-10
FANNIN	24,804	E-11
FAYETTE	20,095	J-10
FISHER	4,842	G-5
FLOYD	8,497	D-4
FOARD	1,794	E-6
FORT BEND	225,421	K-11
FRANKLIN	7,802	E-12
FREESTONE	15,818	H-11
FRIO	13,472	L-6
GAINES	14,123	F-2
GALVESTON	217,399	K-13
GARZA	5,143	F-4
GILLESPIE	17,204	J-7
GLASSCOCK	1,447	H-3
GOLIAD	5,980	L-9
GONZALES	17,205	K-9
GRAY	23,967	C-4
GRAYSON	95,021	E-10
GREGG	104,948	G-13
GRIMES	18,828	I-11
GUADALUPE	64,873	K-8
HALE	34,671	D-3
HALL	3,905	C-4
HAMILTON	7,733	H-8
HANSFORD	5,848	A-4
HARDEMAN	5,283	D-6
HARDIN	41,320	J-13
HARRIS	2,818,199	K-12
HARRISON	57,483	G-13
HARTLEY	3,634	A-2
HASKELL	6,820	F-6
HAYS	65,614	J-8
HEMPHILL	3,720	A-5
HENDERSON	58,543	G-11
HIDALGO	383,545	O-8
HILL	27,146	H-9
HOCKLEY	24,199	E-2
HOOD	28,981	G-8
HOPKINS	28,833	F-11
HOUSTON	21,375	H-12
HOWARD	32,343	G-3
HUDSPETH	2,915	N-1
HUNT	64,343	F-11
HUTCHINSON	25,689	A-4
IRION	1,629	H-4
JACK	6,981	F-8
JACKSON	13,039	L-10
JASPER	31,102	I-14
JEFF DAVIS	1,946	O-3
JEFFERSON	239,397	K-13
JIM HOGG	5,109	O-7
JIM WELLS	37,679	N-8
JOHNSON	97,165	G-9
JONES	16,490	F-6
KARNES	12,455	L-8
KAUFMAN	52,220	G-11
KENDALL	14,589	K-7
KENEDY	460	O-8
KENT	1,010	F-4
KERR	36,304	J-6
KIMBLE	4,122	J-5
KING	354	E-5
KINNEY	3,119	K-5
KLEBERG	30,274	N-8
KNOX	4,837	E-6
LA SALLE	5,254	M-6
LAMAR	43,949	E-11
LAMB	15,072	D-2
LAMPASAS	13,521	I-8
LAVACA	18,690	L-10
LEE	12,854	J-9
LEON	12,665	I-11
LIBERTY	52,726	J-13
LIMESTONE	20,946	H-10
LIPSCOMB	3,143	A-5
LIVE OAK	9,556	M-8
LLANO	11,631	I-7
LOVING	107	H-1
LUBBOCK	222,636	E-3
LYNN	6,758	F-3
MADISON	10,931	I-11
MARION	9,984	F-13
MARTIN	4,956	G-3
MASON	3,423	I-6
MATAGORDA	36,928	L-11
MAVERICK	36,378	L-5
MCCULLOCH	8,778	I-6
MCLENNAN	189,123	H-9
MCMULLEN	817	M-7
MEDINA	27,312	K-6
MENARD	2,252	I-5
MIDLAND	106,611	H-3
MILAM	22,946	I-10
MILLS	4,531	H-7
MITCHELL	8,016	G-4
MONTAGUE	17,274	E-8
MONTGOMERY	182,201	J-11
MOORE	17,865	B-3
MORRIS	13,200	F-13
MOTLEY	1,532	D-4
NACOGDOCHES	54,753	H-13
NAVARRO	39,926	H-10
NEWTON	13,569	I-14
NOLAN	16,594	G-5
NUECES	291,145	N-8
OCHILTREE	9,128	A-4
OLDHAM	2,278	B-2
ORANGE	80,509	J-14
PALO PINTO	25,055	G-8
PANOLA	22,035	G-13
PARKER	64,785	F-8
PARMER	9,863	C-2
PECOS	14,675	I-1
POLK	30,687	I-13
POTTER	97,874	B-3
PRESIDIO	6,637	P-3
RAINS	6,715	F-11
RANDALL	89,673	C-3
REAGAN	4,514	H-3
REAL	2,412	K-6
RED RIVER	14,317	E-12
REEVES	15,852	H-1
REFUGIO	7,967	M-9
ROBERTS	1,025	A-4
ROBERTSON	15,511	I-10
ROCKWALL	25,604	F-11
RUNNELS	11,294	H-5
RUSK	43,735	H-13
SABINE	9,586	H-14
SAN AUGUSTINE	7,999	H-13
SAN JACINTO	16,372	I-12
SAN PATRICIO	58,749	N-8
SAN SABA	5,401	I-7
SCHLEICHER	2,990	I-4
SCURRY	18,634	F-4
SHACKELFORD	3,316	F-6
SHELBY	22,034	H-13
SHERMAN	2,858	A-3
SMITH	151,309	G-12
SOMERVELL	5,360	G-9
STARR	40,518	O-7
STEPHENS	9,010	G-7
STERLING	1,438	H-4
STONEWALL	2,013	F-5
SUTTON	4,135	J-4
SWISHER	8,133	D-3
TARRANT	1,170,103	F-9
TAYLOR	119,655	G-6
TERRELL	1,410	J-2
TERRY	13,218	F-2
THROCKMORTON	1,880	F-6
TITUS	24,009	F-12
TOM GREEN	98,458	H-5
TRAVIS	576,407	J-8
TRINITY	11,445	I-12
TYLER	16,646	I-13
UPSHUR	31,370	F-12
UPTON	4,447	H-3
UVALDE	23,340	K-5
VAL VERDE	38,721	J-3
VAN ZANDT	37,944	G-11
VICTORIA	74,361	L-10
WALKER	50,917	I-11
WALLER	23,390	J-11
WARD	13,115	H-1
WASHINGTON	26,154	J-10
WEBB	133,239	M-5
WHARTON	39,955	L-10
WHEELER	5,879	B-5
WICHITA	122,378	E-7
WILBARGER	15,121	D-6
WILLACY	17,705	P-9
WILLIAMSON	139,551	I-9
WILSON	22,650	L-8
WINKLER	8,626	H-1
WISE	34,679	F-9
WOOD	29,380	F-12
YOAKUM	8,786	F-2
YOUNG	18,126	F-7
ZAPATA	9,279	O-6
ZAVALA	12,162	L-5
TOTAL	16,986,510	

CITIES AND TOWNS

Note: The first name is that of the city or town, second, that of the county in which it is located, then the population and location on the map.

Abernathy, Hale/Lubbock, 2,720	E-3
Abilene, Jones/Taylor, 106,654	G-6
•Abram-Perezville, Hidalgo, 3,999	O-16
Addison, Dallas, 8,783	C-20
Alamo, Hidalgo, 8,210	P-8
Alamo Heights, Bexar, 6,502	C-26
Albany, Shackelford, 1,962	G-7
•Aldine, Harris, 11,133	H-19
Aledo, Parker, 1,169	D-16
Alice, Jim Wells, 19,788	N-8
Alice Southwest, Jim Wells	N-8
Alief, Harris	I-17
Allen, Collin, 18,309	B-21
Alpine, Brewster, 5,637	J-1
Alta Loma, Galveston	K-20
Alto, Cherokee, 1,027	H-12
Alton, Hidalgo, 3,069	N-16
Alvarado, Johnson, 2,918	G-9
Alvin, Brazoria, 19,220	K-19
Amarillo, Potter/Randall, 157,615	C-3
Anahuac, Chambers, 1,993	K-13
Anderson, Grimes	J-11
•Anderson Mill, Travis/Williamson, 9,468	M-25
Andrews, Andrews, 10,678	G-2
Angleton, Brazoria, 17,140	L-12
Angleton South, Brazoria	L-12
Anson, Jones, 2,644	G-6
Anthony, El Paso, 3,328	N-1
Anton, Hockley, 1,212	E-3
Aransas Pass, Aransas/Nueces/San Patricio, 7,180	N-10
Arcadia, Galveston	K-20
Archer City, Archer, 1,748	E-8
Argyle, Denton, 1,575	B-18
Arlington, Tarrant, 261,721	G-10
Asherton, Dimmit, 1,608	M-6
Aspermont, Stonewall, 1,214	F-5
Athens, Henderson, 10,967	G-11
Atlanta, Cass, 6,118	F-14
Aubrey, Denton, 1,138	B-19
Austin, Travis/Williamson, 465,622	J-9
Azle, Parker/Tarrant, 8,868	D-17
•Bacliff, Galveston, 5,549	J-21
Baird, Callahan, 1,658	G-6
Balch Springs, Dallas, 17,406	D-21
Balcones Heights, Bexar, 3,022	C-25
Ballinger, Runnels, 3,975	H-6
Bandera, Bandera, 877	K-7
Bangs, Brown, 1,555	H-7
•Barrett, Harris, 3,052	H-20
Bartlett, Bell/Williamson, 1,439	I-9
Bastrop, Bastrop, 4,044	J-9
•Batesville, Zavala, 1,313	L-6
Bay City, Matagorda, 18,170	L-11
Bayou Vista, Galveston, 1,320	K-21
Baytown, Chambers/Harris, 63,850	I-21
Beaumont, Jefferson, 114,323	K-14
Beaumont Place, Harris	H-18
Bedford, Tarrant, 43,762	D-19
Beeville, Bee, 13,547	M-9
Bellaire, Harris, 13,842	I-18
Bellmead, McLennan, 8,336	N-23
Bellville, Austin, 3,378	K-11
Belton, Bell, 12,476	I-9
Benavides, Duval, 1,788	N-8
Benbrook, Tarrant, 19,564	E-17
Benjamin, Knox, 225	E-6
Beverly Hills, McLennan, 2,048	N-22
Bevil Oaks, Jefferson, 1,350	G-24
Big Lake, Reagan, 3,672	I-4
Big Sandy, Upshur, 1,185	G-12
Big Spring, Howard, 23,093	G-4
Biggs, El Paso	N-1
Bishop, Nueces, 3,337	N-9
Blanco, Blanco, 1,238	J-8
•Bloomington, Victoria, 1,888	M-10
Blossom, Lamar, 1,440	E-12
Blue Mound, Tarrant, 2,133	D-18
Boerne, Kendall, 4,274	K-7
Bogata, Red River, 1,421	E-12
•Boling-Iago, Wharton, 1,119	L-16
Bonham, Fannin, 6,686	E-11
Booker, Lipscomb/Ochiltree, 1,236	A-5
Borger, Hutchinson, 15,675	B-4
Bovina, Parmer, 1,549	D-2
Bowie, Montague, 4,990	E-9
Boyd, Wise, 1,041	C-17
Brackettville, Kinney, 1,740	L-5
Brady, McCulloch, 5,946	I-6
Brazoria, Brazoria, 2,717	L-12
Breckenridge, Stephens, 5,665	G-7
Bremond, Robertson, 1,110	I-10
Brenham, Washington, 11,952	J-11
•Briar, Parker/Tarrant/Wise, 3,899	C-17
Bridge City, Orange, 8,034	G-26
Bridgeport, Wise, 3,581	B-16
Brookshire, Waller, 2,922	I-15
Brookside Village, Brazoria, 1,470	J-19
Brownfield, Terry, 9,560	F-3
Brownsville, Cameron, 98,962	Q-9
Brownwood, Brown, 18,387	H-7
Bruceville-Eddy, Falls/McLennan, 1,075	O-22
•Brushy Creek, Williamson, 5,833	J-9
Bryan, Brazos, 55,002	J-11
•Buchanan Dam, Llano, 1,099	I-8
Buda, Hays, 1,795	O-11
Buffalo, Leon, 1,555	H-11
•Buna, Jasper, 2,127	J-14
Bunavista, Hutchinson	B-4
Bunker Hill Village, Harris, 3,391	I-17
Burkburnett, Wichita, 10,145	E-8
Burleson, Johnson/Tarrant, 16,113	E-18
Burnet, Burnet, 3,423	I-8
Cactus, Moore, 1,529	B-3
Caddo Mills, Hunt, 1,068	C-23
Caldwell, Burleson, 3,181	J-10
Calvert, Robertson, 1,536	I-10
Camden, Polk	I-13
Cameron, Milam, 5,580	I-10
•Cameron Park, Cameron, 3,802	O-19
•Camp Swift, Bastrop, 2,681	O-27
Canadian, Hemphill, 2,417	B-5
Canton, Van Zandt, 2,949	G-11
•Canutillo, El Paso, 4,442	N-1
Canyon, Randall, 11,365	C-3
•Canyon Lake, Comal, 9,975	K-8
Carrizo Springs, Dimmit, 5,745	M-6
Carrollton, Collin/Dallas/Denton, 82,169	C-20
Carthage, Panola, 6,496	G-13
Castle Hills, Bexar, 4,198	K-8
Castroville, Medina, 2,159	L-7
Cedar Hill, Dallas/Ellis, 19,976	E-20
Cedar Park, Travis/Williamson, 5,161	J-9
Celina, Collin, 1,737	A-21
Center, Shelby, 4,950	H-14
Centerville, Leon, 812	I-11
•Central Gardens, Jefferson, 4,026	K-14
Chandler, Henderson, 1,630	G-12
•Channelview, Harris, 25,564	H-20
Channing, Hartley, 277	B-3
Charlotte, Atascosa, 1,475	L-7
Chase, Bee	M-9
Childress, Childress, 5,055	D-5
China, Jefferson, 1,144	G-24
Cibolo, Bexar/Guadalupe, 1,757	B-27
•Circle D-KC Estates, Bastrop, 1,247	O-27
Cisco, Eastland, 3,813	G-7
Clarendon, Donley, 2,067	C-5
Clarksville, Red River, 4,311	E-12
Claude, Armstrong, 1,199	C-4
Clear Lake City, Harris	J-20
Clear Lake Shores, Galveston, 1,096	J-21
Cleburne, Johnson, 22,205	G-9
Cleveland, Liberty, 7,124	J-12
Clifton, Bosque, 3,195	H-9
Clint, El Paso, 1,035	N-1
•Cloverleaf, Harris, 18,230	I-20
Clute, Brazoria, 8,910	L-12
Clyde, Callahan, 3,002	G-6
Coahoma, Howard, 1,133	G-4
Cockrell Hill, Dallas, 3,746	D-20
Coldspring, San Jacinto, 538	J-12
Coleman, Coleman, 5,410	H-6
College Station, Brazos, 52,456	J-11
Colleyville, Tarrant, 12,724	C-19
Collinsville, Grayson, 1,033	E-10
Colorado City, Mitchell, 4,749	G-4
Columbus, Colorado, 3,367	K-10
Comanche, Comanche, 4,087	H-8
Combes, Cameron, 2,042	N-18
Combine, Dallas/Kaufman, 1,329	E-22
•Comfort, Kendall, 1,477	K-7
Commerce, Hunt, 6,825	F-11
Conroe, Montgomery, 27,610	J-12
Converse, Bexar, 8,887	C-27
Cooper, Delta, 2,153	F-12
Coppell, Dallas/Denton, 16,881	C-20
Copperas Cove, Coryell/Lampasas, 24,079	I-8
Corinth, Denton, 3,944	B-19
Corpus Christi, Kleberg/Nueces/San Patricio, 257,453	N-9
Corrigan, Polk, 1,764	I-13
Corsicana, Navarro, 22,911	H-10
Cotulla, La Salle, 3,694	M-7
Crandall, Kaufman, 1,652	E-22
Crane, Crane, 3,533	H-3
Crockett, Houston, 7,024	I-12
•Crosby, Harris, 1,811	H-20
Crosbyton, Crosby, 2,026	E-4
•Cross Mountain, Bexar, 1,112	B-25
Cross Plains, Callahan, 1,063	H-7
Crowell, Foard, 1,230	E-6
Crowley, Johnson/Tarrant, 6,974	E-18
Crystal City, Zavala, 8,263	M-6
Cuero, DeWitt, 6,700	L-9
Daingerfield, Morris, 2,572	F-13
Dalhart, Dallam/Hartley, 6,246	A-2
Dallas, Collin/Dallas/Denton/Kaufman/Rockwall, 1,006,877	G-10
Dalworthington Gardens, Tarrant, 1,758	E-19
Danbury, Brazoria, 1,447	L-19
Dayton, Liberty, 5,151	G-21
De Kalb, Bowie, 1,976	E-13
De Leon, Comanche, 2,190	H-8
De Soto, Dallas, 30,544	E-20
Decatur, Wise, 4,252	F-9
Deer Park, Harris, 27,652	K-12
Del Rio, Val Verde, 30,705	L-4
Denison, Grayson, 21,505	E-10
Denton, Denton, 66,270	F-9
Denver City, Yoakum, 5,145	F-2
Devine, Medina, 3,928	L-7
•Deweyville, Newton, 1,218	J-14
Diboll, Angelina, 4,341	I-13
Dickens, Dickens, 322	E-5
Dickinson, Galveston, 9,497	J-21
Dilley, Frio, 2,632	M-7
Dimmitt, Castro, 4,408	D-3
•Dominion, Bexar, 1,196	B-26
Donna, Hidalgo, 12,652	O-17
Double Oak, Denton, 1,664	C-19
Dripping Springs, Hays, 1,033	N-10
Dublin, Erath, 3,190	H-8
Dumas, Moore, 12,871	B-3
Duncanville, Dallas, 35,748	E-20
Eagle Lake, Colorado, 3,551	K-11
•Eagle Mountain, Tarrant, 5,847	D-17
Eagle Pass, Maverick, 20,651	M-5
Early, Brown, 2,380	H-7
Earth, Lamb, 1,228	D-3
•East Bernard, Wharton, 1,544	K-11
Eastland, Eastland, 3,690	G-7
Edcouch, Hidalgo, 2,878	N-17
Eden, Concho, 1,567	I-6
Edgecliff, Tarrant, 2,715	E-18
Edgewood, Van Zandt, 1,284	G-11
Edinburg, Hidalgo, 29,885	N-16
Edna, Jackson, 5,343	L-10
El Campo, Wharton, 10,511	L-11
El Campo South, Wharton	L-11
El Cenizo, Webb, 1,399	N-7
El Lago, Harris, 3,269	J-21
El Paso, El Paso, 515,342	N-1
Eldorado, Schleicher, 2,019	I-5
Electra, Wichita, 3,113	E-7
Elgin, Bastrop, 4,846	J-9
Elkhart, Anderson, 1,076	H-12
Elsa, Hidalgo, 5,242	P-8
Emory, Rains, 963	F-11
•Encantada-Ranchito El Calaboz, Cameron, 1,143	O-18
Ennis, Ellis, 13,883	G-10
•Escobares, Starr, 1,705	P-7
Euless, Tarrant, 38,149	D-19
•Evadale, Jasper, 1,422	J-14
Everman, Tarrant, 5,672	E-18
•Fabens, El Paso, 5,599	N-1
Fair Oaks Ranch, Bexar/Comal/Kendall, 1,860	B-25
Fairfield, Freestone, 3,234	H-11
Fairview, Collin, 1,554	B-22
Falfurrias, Brooks, 5,788	O-8
Farmers Branch, Dallas, 24,250	D-20
Farmersville, Collin, 2,640	B-23
Farwell, Parmer, 1,373	D-2
Ferris, Ellis, 2,212	E-22
•First Colony, Fort Bend, 18,327	J-17
Flatonia, Fayette, 1,295	K-9
Floresville, Wilson, 5,247	L-8
Flower Mound, Denton/Tarrant, 15,527	C-19
Floydada, Floyd, 3,896	E-4
Forest Hill, Tarrant, 11,482	E-18
Forney, Kaufman, 4,070	D-22
•Fort Bliss, El Paso, 13,915	N-1
Fort Davis, Jeff Davis	P-4
•Fort Hood, Bell/Coryell, 35,580	I-9
Fort Sam Houston, Bexar	C-26
Fort Stockton, Pecos, 8,524	I-2
Fort Wolters, Palo Pinto/Parker	F-8
Fort Worth, Denton/Tarrant, 447,619	G-9
Franklin, Robertson, 1,336	I-11
Frankston, Anderson, 1,127	G-12
Fredericksburg, Gillespie, 6,934	J-7
Freeport, Brazoria, 11,389	L-12
Freer, Duval, 3,271	N-7
•Fresno, Fort Bend, 3,182	J-18
Friendswood, Galveston/Harris, 22,814	J-20
Friona, Parmer, 3,688	D-2
Frisco, Collin/Denton, 6,141	B-20
Fritch, Hutchinson/Moore, 2,335	B-4
Fuller Springs, Angelina	I-13
Gail, Borden	G-4
Gainesville, Cooke, 14,256	E-9
Galena Park, Harris, 10,033	I-19
Galveston, Galveston, 59,070	L-13
Ganado, Jackson, 1,701	L-10
Garden City, Glasscock	H-4
Garden Ridge, Comal, 1,450	B-27
•Gardendale, Ector, 1,103	H-3
•Garfield, Bastrop/Travis, 1,336	N-26
Garland, Collin/Dallas/Rockwall, 180,650	C-22
Gatesville, Coryell, 11,492	H-9
George West, Live Oak, 2,586	M-8
Georgetown, Williamson, 14,842	J-9
Giddings, Lee, 4,093	J-10
Gilmer, Upshur, 4,822	G-13
Gladewater, Gregg/Upshur, 6,027	G-13
Glen Rose, Somervell, 1,949	G-9
Glenn Heights, Dallas/Ellis, 4,564	E-20
Goldthwaite, Mills, 1,658	H-8
Goliad, Goliad, 1,946	M-9
Gonzales, Gonzales, 6,527	K-9
Gorman, Eastland, 1,290	G-7
Graham, Young, 8,986	F-8
Granbury, Hood, 4,045	G-9
Grand Prairie, Dallas/Ellis/Tarrant, 99,616	D-19
Grand Saline, Van Zandt, 2,630	G-12
Grandview, Johnson, 1,245	G-9
Granger, Williamson, 1,190	J-9
Granite Shoals, Burnet, 1,378	J-8
Grapeland, Houston, 1,450	H-12
Grapevine, Dallas/Denton/Tarrant, 29,202	C-19

Explanation of symbols: • – Census Designated Place (CDP)

Greenville, Hunt, 23,071 ... F-11
Gregory, San Patricio, 2,458 ... N-9
Griffing Park, Jefferson ... H-26
Groesbeck, Limestone, 3,185 ... H-10
Groves, Jefferson, 16,513 ... H-26
Groveton, Trinity, 1,071 ... I-12
Gruver, Hansford, 1,172 ... A-4
Gun Barrel City, Henderson, 3,526 ... G-11
Guthrie, King ... E-5
Hale Center, Hale, 2,067 ... E-3
Hallettsville, Lavaca, 2,718 ... L-10
Hallsville, Harrison, 2,288 ... G-13
Haltom City, Tarrant, 32,856 ... D-18
Hamilton, Hamilton, 2,937 ... H-8
Hamlin, Fisher/Jones, 2,791 ... F-5
Harker Heights, Bell, 12,841 ... P-21
Harlingen, Cameron, 48,735 ... N-18
Hart, Castro, 1,221 ... D-3
Haskell, Haskell, 3,362 ... F-6
Hawkins, Wood, 1,309 ... G-12
Hearne, Robertson, 5,132 ... I-10
Heath, Rockwall, 2,108 ... D-22
©Hebbronville, Jim Hogg, 4,465 ... O-7
Hebron, Denton, 1,128 ... C-20
Hedwig Village, Harris, 2,616 ... H-18
Helotes, Bexar, 1,535 ... B-25
Hemphill, Sabine, 1,182 ... H-14
Hempstead, Waller, 3,551 ... J-11
Henderson, Rusk, 11,139 ... G-13
Henrietta, Clay, 2,896 ... E-8
Hereford, Deaf Smith, 14,745 ... C-3
Hewitt, McLennan, 8,983 ... H-9
Hickory Creek, Denton, 1,893 ... B-19
Hico, Hamilton, 1,342 ... H-8
Hidalgo, Hidalgo, 3,292 ... O-16
Highland Park, Dallas, 8,739 ... D-20
Highland Village, Denton, 7,027 ... B-19
©Highlands, Harris, 6,632 ... H-20
Hill Country Village, Bexar, 1,038 ... B-26
Hillsboro, Hill, 7,072 ... H-10
Hitchcock, Galveston, 5,868 ... K-21
Holiday Lakes, Brazoria, 1,039 ... L-12
Holland, Bell, 1,118 ... I-9
Holliday, Archer, 1,475 ... E-7
Hollywood Park, Bexar, 2,841 ... B-26
©Homestead Meadows, El Paso, 4,978 ... N-1
Hondo, Medina, 6,018 ... L-7
Honey Grove, Fannin, 1,681 ... E-11
Hooks, Bowie, 2,684 ... E-13
Horizon City, El Paso, 2,308 ... N-1
©Horseshoe Bay, Burnet/Llano, 1,546 ... J-8
Houston, Fort Bend/Harris/Montgomery, 1,630,553 ... K-12
Howe, Grayson, 2,173 ... E-10
Hubbard, Hill, 1,589 ... H-10
Hudson, Angelina, 2,374 ... I-13
Hughes Springs, Cass/Morris, 1,938 ... F-13
Hull, Liberty ... J-13
Humble, Harris, 12,060 ... G-19
Hunters Creek Village, Harris, 3,954 ... I-18
Huntington, Angelina, 1,794 ... I-13
Huntsville, Walker, 27,925 ... I-12
Hurst, Tarrant, 33,574 ... D-18
Hutchins, Dallas, 2,719 ... E-21
Idalou, Lubbock, 2,074 ... E-4
©Inez, Victoria, 1,371 ... L-10
Ingleside, San Patricio, 5,696 ... N-9
Ingram, Kerr, 1,408 ... K-7
Iowa Park, Wichita, 6,072 ... E-7
Iraan, Pecos, 1,322 ... I-3
Irving, Dallas, 155,037 ... G-10
Italy, Ellis, 1,699 ... G-10
Itasca, Hill, 1,523 ... G-9
Jacinto City, Harris, 9,343 ... I-19
Jacksboro, Jack, 3,350 ... F-8
Jacksonville, Cherokee, 12,765 ... H-12
Jasper, Jasper, 6,959 ... I-14
Jayton, Kent, 608 ... F-5
Jefferson, Marion, 2,199 ... F-13
Jersey Village, Harris, 4,826 ... H-17
Johnson City, Blanco, 932 ... J-8
©Jollyville, Travis/Williamson, 15,206 ... N-26
Jonestown, Travis, 1,250 ... M-25
Jones Creek, Brazoria, 2,160 ... L-12
Joshua, Johnson, 3,828 ... G-9
Jourdanton, Atascosa, 3,220 ... L-8
Junction, Kimble, 2,654 ... J-6
Justin, Denton, 1,234 ... C-18
Karnes City, Karnes, 2,916 ... L-8
Katy, Fort Bend/Harris/Waller, 8,005 ... I-16
Kaufman, Kaufman, 5,238 ... E-23
Keene, Johnson, 3,944 ... G-9
Keller, Tarrant, 13,683 ... C-18
Kemah, Galveston, 1,094 ... J-21
Kemp, Kaufman, 1,184 ... F-23
Kenedy, Karnes, 3,763 ... L-8
Kennedale, Tarrant, 4,096 ... E-18
Kerens, Navarro, 1,702 ... G-11
Kermit, Winkler, 6,875 ... H-2
Kerrville, Kerr, 17,384 ... J-7
Kilgore, Gregg/Rusk, 11,066 ... G-13
Killeen, Bell, 63,535 ... P-21
©Kingsland, Llano, 2,725 ... J-8
Kingsville, Kleberg, 25,276 ... N-8
Kingsville Station, Kleberg ... N-9
©Kingwood, Harris/Montgomery, 37,397 ... G-19
Kinwood, Harris ... H-18
Kirby, Bexar, 8,326 ... C-26
Kirbyville, Jasper, 1,871 ... I-14
Kleberg, Dallas ... E-22
Knox City, Knox, 1,440 ... F-6
Kountze, Hardin, 2,056 ... J-14
Krum, Denton, 1,542 ... B-18
Kyle, Hays, 2,225 ... K-8
©La Casita-Garciasville, Starr, 1,186 ... P-7
La Coste, Medina, 1,021 ... L-7
La Feria, Cameron, 4,360 ... O-17
La Grange, Fayette, 3,951 ... K-10
La Grulla, Starr, 1,335 ... P-7
©La Homa, Hidalgo, 1,403 ... O-16
La Joya, Hidalgo, 2,604 ... N-15
La Marque, Galveston, 14,120 ... K-21
La Porte, Harris, 27,910 ... I-20
©La Pryor, Zavala, 1,343 ... L-6
La Villa, Hidalgo, 1,388 ... P-8
©Lackland AFB, Bexar, 9,352 ... D-25
Lacy-Lakeview, McLennan, 3,617 ... H-9
Lago Vista, Travis, 2,199 ... M-25
©Laguna Heights, Cameron, 1,671 ... O-19
Laguna Vista, Cameron, 1,166 ... O-19
©Lake Brownwood, Brown, 1,221 ... H-7
Lake Dallas, Denton, 3,656 ... F-10
Lake Jackson, Brazoria, 22,776 ... L-12
Lake Worth, Tarrant, 4,591 ... D-17
©Lakehills, Bandera, 2,147 ... K-7
Lakeway, Travis, 4,044 ... N-25
Lamesa, Dawson, 10,809 ... G-3
Lampasas, Lampasas, 6,382 ... I-8
Lancaster, Dallas, 22,117 ... E-21
Laredo, Webb, 122,899 ... N-6
©Laughlin AFB, Val Verde, 2,556 ... L-5
League City, Galveston/Harris, 30,159 ... J-20
Leakey, Real, 399 ... K-6
Leander, Travis/Williamson, 3,398 ... J-8
Legion, Kerr ... K-7
Leon Valley, Bexar, 9,581 ... C-25
Leonard, Fannin, 1,744 ... F-11
Levelland, Hockley, 13,986 ... E-3
Lewisville, Dallas/Denton, 46,521 ... C-19
Liberty, Liberty, 7,733 ... J-13
©Liberty City, Gregg, 1,607 ... G-13
Lindale, Smith, 2,428 ... G-12
Linden, Cass, 2,375 ... F-13
Lipscomb, Lipscomb ... A-5
Little Elm, Denton, 1,255 ... B-20
Little River-Academy, Bell, 1,390 ... P-22
Littlefield, Lamb, 6,489 ... E-3
Live Oak, Bexar, 10,023 ... B-27
Livingston, Polk, 5,019 ... I-13
Llano, Llano, 2,962 ... I-7
Lockhart, Caldwell, 9,205 ... K-9
Lockney, Floyd, 2,207 ... D-4
Lomax, Harris ... I-20
Lone Star, Morris, 1,615 ... F-13
Longview, Gregg/Harrison, 70,311 ... G-13
©Lopezville, Hidalgo, 2,827 ... N-16
Lorena, McLennan, 1,158 ... O-22
Lorenzo, Crosby, 1,208 ... E-4
Los Fresnos, Cameron, 2,473 ... O-18
©Lost Creek, Travis, 4,095 ... N-25
Lubbock, Lubbock, 186,206 ... E-3
Lucas, Collin, 2,205 ... B-22
Lufkin, Angelina, 30,206 ... H-13
Luling, Caldwell, 4,661 ... K-9
Lumberton, Hardin, 6,640 ... J-14
Lyford, Willacy, 1,674 ... P-9
Lytle, Atascosa/Bexar/Medina, 2,255 ... L-7
Mabank, Henderson/Kaufman, 1,739 ... G-11
Madisonville, Madison, 3,569 ... I-11
Malakoff, Henderson, 2,038 ... G-11
Manor, Travis, 1,041 ... J-9
Mansfield, Ellis/Johnson/Tarrant, 15,607 ... G-9
Manvel, Brazoria, 3,733 ... K-19
Marble Falls, Burnet, 4,007 ... J-8
Marfa, Presidio, 2,424 ... P-4
©Markham, Matagorda, 1,206 ... L-11
Marlin, Falls, 6,386 ... I-10
Marshall, Harrison, 23,682 ... G-13
Mart, McLennan, 2,004 ... H-10
Mason, Mason, 2,041 ... I-7
Matador, Motley, 790 ... E-5
Mathis, San Patricio, 5,423 ... M-8
Maud, Bowie, 1,049 ... F-13
©Mauriceville, Orange, 2,046 ... J-14
McAllen, Hidalgo, 84,021 ... P-8
McCamey, Upton, 2,493 ... I-3
McGregor, McLennan, 4,683 ... I-9
McKinney, Collin, 21,283 ... F-10
McNair, Harris ... H-20
©McQueeney, Guadalupe, 2,063 ... K-8
Meadows, Fort Bend, 4,606 ... J-17
Memphis, Hall, 2,465 ... C-5
Menard, Menard, 1,606 ... I-6
Mentone, Loving ... H-1
Mercedes, Hidalgo, 12,694 ... P-8
Meridian, Bosque, 1,390 ... H-9
Merkel, Taylor, 2,469 ... G-6
Mertzon, Irion, 778 ... I-4
Mesquite, Dallas, 101,484 ... D-22
Mexia, Limestone, 6,933 ... H-11
Miami, Roberts, 675 ... B-5
Midland, Bay/Midland, 89,443 ... H-3
Midlothian, Ellis, 5,141 ... G-10
©Mila Doce, Hidalgo, 2,089 ... M-17
Mineola, Wood, 4,321 ... G-12
Mineral Wells, Palo Pinto/Parker, 14,870 ... G-8
Mission, Hidalgo, 28,653 ... P-8
©Mission Bend, Fort Bend/Harris, 24,945 ... I-17
Missouri City, Fort Bend/Harris, 36,176 ... J-18
Monahans, Ward/Winkler, 8,101 ... H-2
Mont Belvieu, Chambers/Liberty, 1,323 ... H-21
Montague, Montague ... E-9
Moody, McLennan, 1,329 ... O-22
Morgan's Point Resort, Bell, 1,766 ... O-22
Morton, Cochran, 2,597 ... E-2
Mount Pleasant, Titus, 12,291 ... F-13
Mount Vernon, Franklin, 2,219 ... F-12
Muenster, Cooke, 1,387 ... E-9
Muleshoe, Bailey, 4,571 ... D-2
Munday, Knox, 1,600 ... F-6
Murphy, Collin, 1,547 ... C-22
Nacogdoches, Nacogdoches, 30,872 ... H-13
Naples, Morris, 1,508 ... F-13
Nash, Bowie, 2,162 ... E-13
Nassau Bay, Harris, 4,320 ... J-20
Natalia, Medina, 1,216 ... L-7
Navasota, Grimes, 6,296 ... J-11
Nederland, Jefferson, 16,192 ... K-14
Needville, Fort Bend, 2,199 ... K-16
New Boston, Bowie, 5,057 ... E-13
New Braunfels, Comal/Guadalupe, 27,334 ... K-8
New Caney, Montgomery ... F-20
Newton, Newton, 1,885 ... I-14
Nixon, Gonzales/Wilson, 1,995 ... L-9
Nocona, Montague, 2,870 ... E-9
Nolanville, Bell, 1,834 ... P-21
North Houston, Harris ... H-17
North Richland Hills, Tarrant, 45,895 ... D-18
Northcrest, McLennan, 1,725 ... H-9
Oak Ridge North, Montgomery, 2,454 ... G-18
©Oak Trail Shores, Hood, 1,750 ... G-8
Odem, San Patricio, 2,366 ... N-9
Odessa, Ector/Midland, 89,699 ... H-3
O'Donnell, Dawson/Lynn, 1,102 ... F-3
Old River-Winfree, Chambers, 1,233 ... H-21
Olmos Park, Bexar, 2,161 ... C-26
Olney, Young, 3,519 ... F-7
Olton, Lamb, 2,116 ... D-3
©Onion Creek, Travis, 1,544 ... O-26
Orange, Orange, 19,381 ... J-14
Orange Grove, Jim Wells, 1,175 ... N-8
Overton, Rusk/Smith, 2,105 ... G-13
Ovilla, Dallas/Ellis, 2,027 ... E-20
©Ozona, Crockett, 3,181 ... J-4
Paducah, Cottle, 1,788 ... E-5
Paint Rock, Concho, 227 ... H-6
Palacios, Matagorda, 4,418 ... L-11
Palestine, Anderson, 18,042 ... H-12
Palm Valley, Cameron, 1,199 ... O-18
Palmer, Ellis, 1,659 ... G-10
Palmview, Hidalgo, 1,818 ... O-16
Palo Pinto, Palo Pinto ... G-8
Pampa, Gray, 19,959 ... B-5
Panhandle, Carson, 2,353 ... C-4
Panorama Village, Montgomery, 1,556 ... J-12
Pantego, Tarrant, 2,371 ... E-19
Paris, Lamar, 24,699 ... E-12
Parker, Collin, 1,235 ... B-21
Pasadena, Harris, 119,363 ... K-12
Patton Village, Montgomery, 1,155 ... J-12
Pear Ridge, Jefferson ... H-26
Pearland, Brazoria/Harris, 18,697 ... J-19
Pearsall, Frio, 6,924 ... L-7
©Pecan Acres, Tarrant/Wise, 1,587 ... C-17
©Pecan Grove, Fort Bend, 9,502 ... J-17
Pecos, Reeves, 12,069 ... H-1
Pelican Bay, Tarrant, 1,271 ... D-17
©Penitas, Hidalgo, 1,077 ... O-16
Perrin, Grayson ... E-10
Perryton, Ochiltree, 7,607 ... A-5
Petersburg, Hale, 1,292 ... E-4
Pflugerville, Travis, 4,444 ... N-26
Pharr, Hidalgo, 32,921 ... N-16
Pilot Point, Denton, 2,538 ... A-20
©Pinehurst, Montgomery, 3,284 ... F-16
Pinehurst, Orange, 2,682 ... G-27
©Pinewood Estates, Hardin, 1,174 ... J-13
Piney Point Village, Harris, 3,197 ... I-18
Pittsburg, Camp, 4,007 ... F-13
Plains, Yoakum, 1,422 ... F-2
Plainview, Hale, 21,700 ... D-3
Plano, Collin/Denton, 128,713 ... C-21
Pleasanton, Atascosa, 7,678 ... L-8
Port Aransas, Nueces, 2,233 ... N-10
Port Arthur, Jefferson, 58,724 ... K-14
Port Isabel, Cameron, 4,467 ... O-19
Port Lavaca, Calhoun, 10,886 ... M-10
Port Neches, Jefferson, 12,974 ... H-26
Porter, Montgomery ... G-19
©Porter Heights, Montgomery, 1,448 ... G-19
Portland, Nueces/San Patricia, 12,224 ... N-9
Post, Garza, 3,768 ... F-4
Poteet, Atascosa, 3,206 ... E-26
Poth, Wilson, 1,642 ... L-8
©Potosi, Taylor, 1,441 ... G-6
Pottsboro, Grayson, 1,177 ... E-10
Prairie View, Waller, 4,004 ... G-15
Premont, Jim Wells, 2,914 ... O-8
Presidio, Presidio, 3,072 ... Q-3
Primera, Cameron, 2,030 ... N-17
Princeton, Collin, 2,321 ... B-22
©Progreso, Hidalgo, 1,951 ... O-17
Prosper, Collin, 1,018 ... B-21
Quanah, Hardeman, 3,413 ... D-6
Queen City, Cass, 1,748 ... F-13
Quinlan, Hunt, 1,360 ... F-11
Quitman, Wood, 1,684 ... F-12
Ralls, Crosby, 2,172 ... E-4
Randolph, Bexar ... B-27
Ranger, Eastland, 2,803 ... G-7
Rankin, Upton, 1,011 ... I-3
Raymondville, Willacy, 8,880 ... P-9
Red Oak, Ellis, 3,124 ... E-21
©Reese AFB, Lubbock, 1,263 ... E-3
Refugio, Refugio, 3,158 ... M-9
©Rendon, Tarrant, 7,658 ... E-18
Reno, Lamar, 1,784 ... E-12
Reno, Parker, 2,322 ... C-17
Richardson, Collin/Dallas, 74,840 ... C-21
Richland Hills, Tarrant, 7,978 ... D-18
Richmond, Fort Bend, 9,801 ... K-12
Richwood, Brazoria, 2,732 ... L-12
©Rio Grande City, Starr, 9,891 ... P-7
Rio Hondo, Cameron, 1,793 ... N-18
River Oaks, Tarrant, 6,580 ... D-17
Roanoke, Denton, 1,616 ... C-18
Robert Lee, Coke, 1,276 ... H-5
Robinson, McLennan, 7,111 ... H-10
Robstown, Nueces, 12,849 ... N-9
Roby, Fisher, 616 ... G-5
Rockdale, Milam, 5,235 ... J-10
Rockport, Aransas, 4,753 ... M-10
Rocksprings, Edwards, 1,339 ... K-5
Rockwall, Rockwall, 10,486 ... C-22
Rogers, Bell, 1,131 ... I-9
Rollingwood, Travis, 1,388 ... J-8
Roma, Starr, 8,059 ... P-7
Roman Forest, Montgomery, 1,033 ... F-20
Roscoe, Nolan, 1,446 ... G-5
Rosebud, Falls, 1,638 ... P-23
Rosenberg, Fort Bend, 20,183 ... K-11
Rotan, Fisher, 1,913 ... F-5
Round Rock, Travis/Williamson, 30,923 ... M-26
Rowlett, Dallas/Rockwall, 23,260 ... D-22
Royse City, Collin/Rockwall, 2,206 ... C-23
Runge, Karnes, 1,139 ... L-9
Rusk, Cherokee, 4,366 ... J-12
Sabinal, Uvalde, 1,584 ... L-6
Sabine Pass, Jefferson ... I-26
Sachse, Collin/Dallas, 5,346 ... C-21
Saginaw, Tarrant, 8,551 ... D-18
Saint Hedwig, Bexar, 1,443 ... C-28
Saint Jo, Montague, 1,048 ... E-9
©Salado, Bell, 1,216 ... I-9
San Angelo, Tom Green, 84,474 ... H-5
San Antonio, Bexar, 935,933 ... K-8
San Augustine, San Augustine, 2,337 ... H-14
San Benito, Cameron, 20,125 ... O-18
San Diego, Duval/Jim Wells, 4,983 ... N-8
©San Elizario, El Paso, 4,385 ... N-1
San Juan, Hidalgo, 10,815 ... P-8
©San Leon, Galveston, 3,328 ... J-21
San Marcos, Caldwell/Hays, 28,743 ... K-8
San Saba, San Saba, 2,626 ... I-7
©Sanderson, Terrell, 1,128 ... J-2
Sanger, Denton, 3,508 ... A-18
Sansom Park, Tarrant, 3,928 ... D-17
Santa Anna, Coleman, 1,249 ... H-7
Santa Fe, Galveston, 8,429 ... K-20
Santa Rosa, Cameron, 2,223 ... N-17
Saratoga, Hardin ... J-13
Sarita, Kenedy ... O-9
©Scenic Oaks, Bexar, 2,352 ... B-25
Schertz, Bexar/Comal/Guadalupe, 10,555 ... K-8
Schulenburg, Fayette, 2,455 ... K-10
©Scissors, Hidalgo, 1,513 ... O-17
Seabrook, Chambers/Galveston/Harris, 6,685 ... J-21
Seadrift, Calhoun, 1,277 ... M-10
Seagoville, Dallas/Kaufman, 8,969 ... E-22
Seagraves, Gaines, 2,398 ... F-2
Sealy, Austin, 4,541 ... K-11
©Sebastian, Willacy, 1,598 ... N-17
Seguin, Guadalupe, 18,853 ... K-8
Seminole, Gaines, 6,342 ... G-2
©Serenada, Williamson, 3,242 ... J-9
©Seth Ward, Hale, 1,402 ... D-4
Seymour, Baylor, 3,185 ... E-7
Shady Shores, Denton, 1,045 ... B-19
Shallowater, Lubbock, 1,708 ... E-3
Shamrock, Wheeler, 2,286 ... C-5
Shavano Park, Bexar, 1,708 ... B-26
©Sheldon, Harris, 1,653 ... H-19
Shenandoah, Montgomery, 1,718 ... J-12
Shepherd, San Jacinto, 1,812 ... J-12
Sherman, Grayson, 31,601 ... E-10
Shiner, Lavaca, 2,074 ... K-9
Shoreacres, Chambers/Harris, 1,316 ... J-21
Sierra Blanca, Hudspeth ... O-2
Silsbee, Hardin, 6,368 ... J-14
Silverton, Briscoe, 779 ... D-4
Sinton, San Patricio, 5,549 ... N-9
Slaton, Lubbock, 6,078 ... F-4
Smithville, Bastrop, 3,196 ... K-9
Snyder, Scurry, 12,195 ... G-4
Socorro, El Paso, 22,995 ... N-1
Somerset, Bexar, 1,144 ... L-7
Somerville, Burleson, 1,542 ... J-11
Sonora, Sutton, 2,751 ... J-5
Sour Lake, Hardin, 1,547 ... F-23
South Houston, Harris, 14,207 ... J-19
South Padre Island, Cameron, 1,677 ... O-19
Southlake, Denton/Tarrant, 7,065 ... F-10
Southside Place, Harris, 1,392 ... I-18
©Sparks, El Paso, 1,276 ... N-1
Spearman, Hansford, 3,197 ... A-4
©Spring, Harris, 33,111 ... G-18
Spring Valley, Harris, 3,392 ... H-18
Springtown, Parker, 1,740 ... F-9
Spur, Dickens, 1,300 ... F-5
Stafford, Fort Bend/Harris, 8,397 ... J-17
Stamford, Haskell/Jones, 3,817 ... F-6
Stanton, Martin, 2,576 ... G-3
Stephenville, Erath, 13,502 ... G-8
Sterling City, Sterling, 1,096 ... H-4
Stinnett, Hutchinson, 2,166 ... B-4
Stockdale, Wilson, 1,268 ... L-8
©Stowell, Chambers, 1,419 ... I-23
Stratford, Sherman, 1,781 ... A-3
Sugar Land, Fort Bend, 24,529 ... J-17
©Sullivan City, Hidalgo, 2,371 ... N-15
Sulphur Springs, Hopkins, 14,062 ... F-12
Sundown, Hockley, 1,759 ... E-2
Sunnyvale, Dallas, 2,228 ... D-22
Sunray, Moore, 1,729 ... A-3
Sunrise, Falls ... O-23
Sweeny, Brazoria, 3,297 ... L-12
Sweetwater, Nolan, 11,967 ... G-5
Taft, San Patricio, 3,222 ... N-9
©Taft Southwest, San Patricio, 2,012 ... N-9
Tahoka, Lynn, 2,868 ... F-3
©Tanglewood Forest, Travis, 2,941 ... O-25
Tatum, Panola/Rusk, 1,289 ... G-13
Taylor, Williamson, 11,472 ... J-9
Taylor Lake Village, Harris, 3,394 ... J-20
Teague, Freestone, 3,268 ... H-11
Temple, Bell, 46,109 ... O-22
Tenaha, Shelby, 1,072 ... H-13
Terrell, Kaufman, 12,490 ... D-23
Terrell Hills, Bexar, 4,592 ... C-26
Texarkana, Bowie, 31,656 ... E-14
Texas City, Galveston, 40,822 ... K-21
The Colony, Denton, 22,113 ... B-20
©The Woodlands, Montgomery, 29,205 ... J-12
Thorndale, Milam/Williamson, 1,092 ... J-9
Three Rivers, Live Oak, 1,889 ... M-8
Throckmorton, Throckmorton, 1,036 ... F-7
Tilden, McMullen ... M-7
©Timberwood Park, Bexar, 2,578 ... B-26
Timpson, Shelby, 1,029 ... H-13
Tomball, Harris/Montgomery, 6,370 ... G-17
Tool, Henderson, 1,712 ... G-11
©Town West, Fort Bend, 6,166 ... J-17
Trinidad, Henderson, 1,056 ... H-11
Trinity, Trinity, 2,648 ... I-12
Trophy Club, Denton/Tarrant, 3,922 ... C-18
Troup, Cherokee/Smith, 1,659 ... G-12
Troy, Bell, 1,395 ... I-9
Tulia, Swisher, 4,699 ... D-3
Tye, Taylor, 1,088 ... G-6
Tyler, Smith, 75,450 ... G-12
Universal City, Bexar, 13,057 ... B-27
University Park, Dallas, 22,259 ... D-20
Uvalde, Uvalde, 14,729 ... L-6
Valley Mills, Bosque/McLennan, 1,085 ... N-21
Van, Van Zandt, 1,854 ... G-12
Van Alstyne, Grayson, 2,090 ... E-10
Van Horn, Culberson, 2,930 ... O-3
©Van Vleck, Matagorda, 1,534 ... L-11
Vega, Oldham, 840 ... C-3
Vernon, Wilbarger, 12,001 ... E-7
Victoria, Victoria, 55,076 ... L-9
Vidor, Orange, 10,935 ... F-26
Waco, McLennan, 103,590 ... H-10
Wake Village, Bowie, 4,757 ... F-13
Waller, Harris/Waller, 1,493 ... G-16
Wallis, Austin, 1,001 ... K-11
Waskom, Harrison, 1,812 ... G-14
Watauga, Tarrant, 20,009 ... D-18
Waxahachie, Ellis, 18,168 ... G-10
Weatherford, Parker, 14,804 ... D-16
Webster, Harris, 4,678 ... J-20
Weimar, Colorado, 2,052 ... K-10
Wellington, Collingsworth, 2,456 ... C-5
©Wells Branch, Travis, 7,094 ... M-26
Weslaco, Hidalgo, 21,877 ... O-17
West, McLennan, 2,515 ... H-10
West Carlisle, Lubbock ... E-3
West Columbia, Brazoria, 4,372 ... L-12
West Lake Hills, Travis, 2,542 ... J-8
©West Odessa, Ector, 16,568 ... H-2
West Orange, Orange, 4,187 ... G-26
West University Place, Harris, 12,920 ... I-18
©Westway, El Paso, 2,381 ... N-1
Westworth, Tarrant, 2,350 ... D-17
Wharton, Wharton, 9,011 ... L-11
Wheeler, Wheeler, 1,393 ... B-5
White Deer, Carson, 1,125 ... B-4
White Oak, Gregg, 5,136 ... G-13
White Settlement, Tarrant, 15,472 ... D-17
Whitehouse, Smith, 4,032 ... G-12
Whitesboro, Grayson, 3,209 ... E-10
Whitewright, Fannin/Grayson, 1,713 ... E-11
Whitney, Hill, 1,626 ... M-22
Wichita Falls, Archer/Wichita, 96,259 ... E-8
©Wild Peach Village, Brazoria, 2,440 ... L-12
Willis, Montgomery, 2,764 ... J-12
Willow Park, Parker, 2,328 ... D-16
Wills Point, Van Zandt, 2,986 ... G-11
Wilmer, Dallas, 2,479 ... E-21
©Wimberley, Hays, 2,403 ... J-8
Windcrest, Bexar, 5,331 ... C-26
©Windemere, Travis, 3,207 ... M-26
Wink, Winkler, 1,189 ... H-2
©Winnie, Chambers, 2,238 ... H-23
Winnsboro, Franklin/Wood, 2,904 ... F-12
Winters, Runnels, 2,905 ... H-6
Wolfe City, Hunt, 1,505 ... A-24
Wolfforth, Lubbock, 1,941 ... E-3
Woodbranch, Montgomery, 1,312 ... F-20
Woodsboro, Refugio, 1,731 ... M-9
Woodville, Tyler, 2,636 ... I-13
Woodway, McLennan, 8,695 ... N-22
Wortham, Freestone, 1,020 ... H-11
©Wyldwood, Bastrop, 1,764 ... O-26
Wylie, Collin/Dallas/Rockwall, 8,716 ... C-22
Yoakum, DeWitt/Lavaca, 5,611 ... L-9
Yorktown, DeWitt, 2,207 ... L-9
©Zapata, Zapata, 7,119 ... O-6

Explanation of symbols: © - Census Designated Place (CDP)

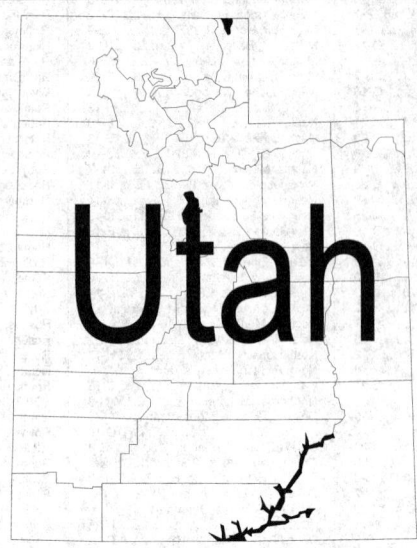

General Help Numbers:

Governor's Office
210 State Capitol
Salt Lake City, UT 84114
www.governor.utah.gov

801-538-1000
Fax 801-538-1528
8AM-5PM

Attorney General's Office
236 State Capitol
Salt Lake City, UT 84114
http://attorneygeneral.utah.gov

801-538-9600
Fax 801-538-1121
8AM-5:30PM

State Court Administrator
Office of Legislative Research and General Counsel
436 State Capitol
Salt Lake City, UT 84114
http://le.utah.gov

801-538-1588
Fax 801-538-1712
8AM-5PM

State Archives
PO Box 141021
Salt Lake City, UT 84114-1021
www.archives.state.ut.us

801-538-3012
Fax 801-538-3354
8AM-5PM M-F

State Specifics:

Capital:　　　　　　　　　　Salt Lake City
　　　　　　　　　　　　　　Salt Lake County

Time Zone:　　　　　　　　　　　　MST

Number of Counties:　　　　　　　　29

Population:　　　　　　　　　2,351,467

Web Site:　　　www.utah.gov/main/index

State Agencies

Criminal Records
Access to Records is Restricted

Bureau of Criminal Identification, Records Supervisor, Box 148280, Salt Lake City, UT 84114-8280 (Courier: 3888 West 5400 South, Salt Lake City, UT 84119); 801-965-4445, 801-965-4749 (Fax), 8AM-5PM.

http://bci.utah.gov

Note: Employers not identified by statute cannot request records, even with notarized release from prospective employee. This agency recommneds

the subject state in request for the report to be sent directly to the employer or third party.

The information below reflects procedures for those entitled.

Indexing & Storage: Records are available back to 1950's. It takes 3 to 7 days before new records are available for inquiry. Records are indexed on inhouse computer. Records are normally destroyed after (records maintained indefinitely unless expunged).

Searching: Records are not open to the public nor to employers not identified by statute signature. Those agencies authorized by law do not need to

submit fingerprints, but still must have subject's notarized signature. Include the following in your request-name, DOB, SSN, driver's license number, notarized signature of subject, fingerprints. Records are 100% fingerprint-supported.

Access by: mail, fax.

Fee & Payment: The fee is $10.00 per name (authorization required); $15.00 for fingerprint searches. Statutorily-required searches may include an FBI fingerprint search, additional $24.00 fee. Fee payee: Utah Bureau of Criminal Identification Prepayment required. Personal checks accepted. Accepts Visa and M/C credit cards.

Mail search: Turnaround time: 7-10 days. A SASE is required. Records are available by mail with submission of proper form.

Fax search: Records are available by fax if fingerprints are not required.

Statewide Court Records

Court Administrator, PO Box 140241, Salt Lake City, UT 84114-0241 (Courier: 450 S State, Salt Lake City, UT 84114); 801-578-3800, 801-238-7832 (Search Request Info), 801-578-3859 (Fax), 8AM-5PM.

www.utcourts.gov

Note: Information on a particular case or the case history of individuals can be acquired from the Utah Administrative Office of the Courts.

Indexing & Storage: Records are available for many district court locations since late 1980's, smaller courts from mid 1990's. Complete, consistent data is available for all district court locations since 1998. It takes 1 minute before new records are available for inquiry. Records are normally destroyed after imaged electronically, per UCJA Appendix F.

Searching: Include the following in your request-full name, DOB, specific counties or geographic area to search. The SSN is optional. The following data is not released: juvenile records, and records from Justice Courts.

Access by: mail, fax, online.

Fee & Payment: Fees for faxed or mailed search requests is $21.00 per hour with no charge for the first 15 minutes. The copy fee is $.25 per page.

Mail search: Address requests to Orvella Charging at address above.

Fax search: Fax requests to the attention of Orvella Charging.

Online search: Case information from all Utah District Court locations is available through XChange. Fees include $25.00 registration and $30.00 per month which includes 200 searches. Each additional minute is billed at $.20. Information about XChange and the subscription agreement can be found at www.utcourts.gov/records, or call 801-238-7877. One can search for supreme or appellate opinions at the website.

Sexual Offender Registry

Sex Offenders Registration Program, Records, 14717 S Minuteman Dr, Draper, UT 84020; 801-545-5908, 801-545-5911 (Fax), 8AM-5PM.

www.corrections.utah.gov/

Note: Utah Code § 77-27-21.5, requires the Utah Dept. of Corrections to operate, and maintain a registry of persons who have either been convicted of or entered a plea in abeyance to certain sex offenses. The offenses are listed in subsection (1)(e)(i).

Indexing & Storage: Records are available from 1987.

Searching: Include the following in your request-name, DOB or SSN, requester name address and phone number.

Access by: mail, phone, in person, online.

Mail search: Turnaround time: 10 days. Records are searchable by name and phone number, ZIP

Code, or by name and an identifer (such as DOB, SSN, etc.)

Phone search: Searches may be requested by phone, but results are mailed.

In person search: They will respond by mail only.

Online search: The Registry may be searched from the web page. Records are searchable by name, ZIP Code, or name and ZIP Code. The information released includes photos, descriptions, addresses, vehicles, offenses, and targets. Also, requests nay be emailed to registry@utah.gov

Incarceration Records

Utah Department of Corrections, DIQ Records, PO Box 250, Draper, UT 84020 (Courier: 14717 S Minuteman Dr, Draper, UT 84020); 801-576-7791, 801-572-7794 (Fax), 8AM-4PM.

www.cr.ex.state.ut.us

Indexing & Storage: Records are available on current and former inmates. It takes 1 to 20 days before new records are available for inquiry.

Searching: Include the following in your request-full name and DOB. The SSN and inmate number are helpful. Location, conviction and sentencing information, and release dates are provided. The following data is not released: SSN, DOB and specific prison housing location.

Access by: mail, phone, fax.

Fee & Payment: There is a $.25 fee per copy. Fee payee: Utah State Prison

Mail search: Turnaround time: 7 to 10 days. A SASE is requested.

Phone search: This service provides custody status and release dates and offers notification if an inmate is released or moved.

Fax search: Searching by fax is permitted.

Corporation, Limited Liability Company, Fictitious Name, Limited Partnership Records, Assumed Name, Trademarks/Servicemarks

Commerce Department, Corporate Division, PO Box 146705, Salt Lake City, UT 84114-6705 (Courier: 160 E 300 S, 2nd fl, Salt Lake City, UT 84111); 801-530-4849 (Call Center), 801-530-6111 (Fax), 8AM-5PM.

www.commerce.utah.gov

Indexing & Storage: Records are available for active entities only. It takes 5-10 days before new records are available for inquiry. Records are indexed on inhouse computer and via the Internet.

Searching: Include the following in your request-full name of business. In addition to the articles of incorporation, corporation records include the following information: Annual Reports, Officers, Directors, DBAs, Prior (merged) names and Reserved names.

Access by: mail, phone, fax, in person, online.

Fee & Payment: Search fee is $12.00. Certification is $12.00. Copies are $.30 per page, no charge if under 10 copies. Fax transmittals are $5.00 for the first page and $1.00 each page after. Fee payee: State of Utah. Prepayment required. Personal checks accepted. Credit cards accepted: MasterCard, Visa.

Mail search: Turnaround time: 5-10 days. A SASE is requested.

Phone search: Copies cost $.30 per page. They will answer questions on name availability, status, agent and officer information.

Fax search: Turnaround time is 5-10 days. There ia an additional fee of $5.00 for the first page and $1.00 for each add'l.

In person search: However, usually turnaround time is 5-10 days unless expedited fee paid.

Online search: A business entity/principle search service is available at www.utah.gov/services/business.html. Basic information (name, address, agent) is free. Detailed data is available for minimal fees, but registration is required. The website also offers an Unclaimed Property search page.

Other access: State allows e-mail access for orders of Certification of Existence at orders@br.state.ut.us.

Expedited service: Expedited service is available. Turnaround time: 24-48 hours. Add $75.00 per business name.

Uniform Commercial Code

Department of Commerce, UCC Division, Box 146705, Salt Lake City, UT 84114-6705 (Courier: 160 E 300 South, Heber M Wells Bldg, 2nd Floor, Salt Lake City, UT 84111); 801-530-4849, 877-526-3994 (In State), 801-530-6438 (Fax), 8AM-5PM.

www.commerce.utah.gov/cor/uccpage.htm

Note: The phone number above is the "only way in" and caller can experience 30-60 minute waits. Suggest faxing or email questions to corpucc@utah.gov

Indexing & Storage: Records are available from 1965. Records are computerized since 1995. It takes 24 hours or less before new records are available for inquiry.

Searching: Use search request form UCC-11. All tax liens are filed at the county level. Include the following in your request-file number(s) and/or debtor name(s), name and address of requesting party, and daytime phone number.

Access by: mail, fax, in person, online.

Fee & Payment: For a certified search, the fee is $12.00 per file number certified plus copies are $.30 per page. For uncertified searches, the fee is only $.30 per page. There is no fee if under 10 specifed copies. Fee payee: State of Utah. They will bill for copy charges. Personal checks accepted. Credit cards accepted: MasterCard, Visa.

Mail search: Turnaround time: 10 working days. A SASE is requested.

Fax search: Same fees and turnaround time as mail search apply. They will invoice.

In person search: Counter service is available.

Online search: UCC uncertified records are available free online at https://secure.e-utah.org/uccsearch/. Search by debtor individual name or organization, or by filing number. Certified searches may also be ordered for $12.00 per search. To receive certifed searches, you must be a registered user. The website gives details. Note there is a $50 annual registration fee which includes 10 user logins. Email requests are accepted at orders@br.state.ut.us.

Other access: Records are available on CD-ROM. Suggest writing or faxing, as the phone number above can give 30-60 minute waits.

Expedited service: Expedited service is available for mail and phone searches. Add $75.00 per name. Turnaround time is 24 hours.

Federal Tax Liens, State Tax Liens

Records not maintained by a state level agency.

Note: Records are found at the local level.

Sales Tax Registrations

Taxpayer Services, Technical Research, 210 N 1950 W, Salt Lake City, UT 84134; 801-297-2200, 801-297-7697 (Fax), 8AM-5PM.

http://tax.utah.gov/sales/index.html

Note: General forms and tax law information can be downloaded from the website.

Indexing & Storage: Records are available for 15 years for business records, for 10 years for individual records.

Searching: Requester must have written consent. This agency will only confirm that a business is registered and active if a tax permit number is provided. They will provide no other information. Records are not accessible by the public; access is limited to the owner(s) of the account(s). You can show power of attorney to access, also. Requests must be in writing.

Access by: mail, in person.

Fee & Payment: Copies are $6.50 per record. Fee payee: Utah Tax Commission. Prepayment required. Personal checks accepted. No credit cards accepted.

Mail search: Turnaround time: 1 to 2 weeks. No SASE is required.

In person search: Turnaround time is 24 hours.

Birth Certificates

Department of Health, Office of Vital Records & Statistics, Box 141012, Salt Lake City, UT 84114-1012 (Courier: 288 N 1460 W, Salt Lake City, UT 84114); 801-538-6105 (This Agency), 801-538-6380 (Vitalchek), 801-538-9467 (Fax), 9AM-5PM (walk-in counter closes at 4:30 PM).

http://health.utah.gov/vitalrecords/

Note: Must have a signed release from person of record or immediate family member.

Indexing & Storage: Records are available from 1905 on. Index computer files go back to 1978. Indexes are not available to the public. New records are available for inquiry immediately.

Searching: At the website you can download an application or order online from the state. The Expedited Service described below is for faster service via a vendor; www.vitalchek.com. Include the following in your request-full name, names of parents, mother's maiden name, date of birth, place of birth, relationship to person of record, reason for information request. Be sure to sign the request and include a daytime phone number. You may phone, fax or email to request an application form. The following data is not released: medical records.

Access by: mail, phone, fax, in person, online.

Fee & Payment: Search fee is $15.00. Fee is $50.00 if the entire index must be searched. Add $8.00 per name for second copies. Fee payee: Vital Records. Prepayment required. Personal checks accepted. Credit cards accepted: MasterCard, Visa, AmEx, Discover.

Mail search: Turnaround time: 2 to 3 weeks. No SASE is required.

Phone search: See expedited service.

Fax search: See expedited service.

In person search: Turnaround time 15 to 30 minutes.

Online search: Orders may be placed via www.vitalchek.com. See expedited service.

Expedited service: Expedited service is available for mail, phone and fax searches. Turnaround time: overnight delivery. Expedite fee is $10.00, add $5.50 if going thru Vitalchek.com. You must use a credit card. Add fees for express mail for overnight service.

Death Records

Department of Health, Office of Vital Records & Statistics, Box 141012, Salt Lake City, UT 84114-1012 (Courier: 288 N 1460 W, Salt Lake City, UT 84114); 801-538-6105 (This Agency), 801-538-6380 (Vitalchek), 801-538-9467 (Fax), 9AM-5PM (walk-in counter closes at 4:30 PM).

http://health.utah.gov/vitalrecords/

Note: Certificates can be obtained by an immediate family member or with written permission from the immediate family.

Indexing & Storage: Records are available from 1905 on. Index computer files go back since 1978. Indexes are not available to the public. New records are available for inquiry immediately.

Searching: At the website you can download an application or order online form the state. The Expedited Service described below is for faster service via a vendor; www.vitalchek.com. Include the following in your request-full name, date of death, place of death, relationship to person of record, reason for information request. If you do not know the date of death, include last known date alive. You may phone, fax or email to request an application form.

Access by: mail, phone, fax, in person, online.

Fee & Payment: Search fee is $13.00, add $8.00 per name for second copies. Fee payee: Vital Records. Prepayment required. Personal checks accepted. Credit cards accepted: MasterCard, Visa, AmEx, Discover.

Mail search: Turnaround time: 2 weeks. No SASE is required.

Phone search: See expedited service.

Fax search: See expedited service.

In person search: Turnaround time 15 to 30 minutes.

Online search: Orders can be placed via a state designated vendor. Go to www.vitalcheck.com. Extra fees are involved.

Expedited service: Expedited service is available for mail, phone and fax searches. Turnaround time: overnight delivery. Expedite fee is $10.00, add $5.50 if going thru Vitalchek.com. You must use a credit card. Add fees for express mail for overnight service.

Marriage Certificates

Department of Health, Office of Vital Records & Statictics, Box 141012, Salt Lake City, UT 84114-1012 (Courier: 288 N 1460 W, Salt Lake City, UT 84114); 801-535-6105 (This Agency), 801-538-6380 (Vitalchek), 801-538-9467 (Fax), 9AM-5PM (walk-in counter closes at 4:30 PM).

http://health.utah.gov/vitalrecords/

Note: Certification of marriage occurring in Utah from 1978 through 2001 are issued in this office. Requests for certified copies of marriage prior to 1978 are issued by the county where the marriage occurred.

Searching: Records are certification summaries and not copies of the original records. Download an application at the Forms link on the website navigation bar. Mail or bring the application to the Service Window in-person, or you may write a letter. Include the following in your request-date & place of occurrence, groom's name, bride's maiden name. You may phone, fax or email to request an application form.

Access by: mail, phone, in person, online.

Fee & Payment: $9.00 is for the abstract certificate. Fee payee: Vital Records. Prepayment required Personal checks accepted Credit cards accepted: MasterCard, Visa, AmEx, Discover.

Mail search: Turnaround time: 2-3 weeks.

Phone search: See expedited service.

In person search: Turn in your order form for a certificate before 4:30 p.m., and wait while it is processed. Requests received at the counter after 4:30 p.m. are processed the following day.

Online search: Orders can be placed via a state designated vendor. Go to www.vitalcheck.com. Extra fees are involved.

Expedited service: Expedited service is available for mail, phone and fax searches. Turnaround time: same day service. Expedite fee is $10.00, add $5.50 if going thru Vitalchek.com. You must use a credit card. Add fees for express mail for overnight service.

Divorce Records

Department of Health, Office of Vital Records & Statistics, Box 141012, Salt Lake City, UT 84114-1012 (Courier: 288 N 1460 W, Salt Lake City, UT 84114); 801-538-6101 (This Agency), 801-538-6380 (Vitalchek), 801-538-9467 (Fax), 9AM-5PM (walk-in counter closes at 4:30 PM).

http://health.utah.gov/vitalrecords/

Note: The offices releases certificates of abstract. Actual copies can only be obtained from the state by an immediate family member or with written permission from the immediate family.

Indexing & Storage: Records are available from 1978 to present. Requests for certified copies of divorce prior to 1978 are issued by the county where the divorce occurred.

Searching: Records are certification summaries and not copies of the original records. Download an application at the Forms link on the website navigation bar. Mail or bring the application to the Service Window in-person, or you may write a letter. Include the following in your request-date and place of occurrence, date and place of marriage, husband's name, wife's name. You may phone or fax to request an application form.

Access by: mail, phone, in person, online.

Fee & Payment: $8.00 for an abstract only. Fee payee: Vital Records. Prepayment required Personal checks accepted Credit cards accepted: Visa, MasterCard, Discover, AmEx.

Mail search: Turnaround time: 2-3 weeks.

Phone search: See expedited service.

In person search: Turn in your order form for a certificate before 4:30 p.m., and wait while it is processed the same day.

Online search: Orders can be placed via a state designated vendor. Go to www.vitalcheck.com. Extra fees are involved.

Expedited service: For phone credit card phone orders only. Turnaround time: 1-2 days. Expedite fee is $10.00, add $5.50 if going thru Vitalchek.com. You must use a credit card. Add fees for express mail for overnight service.

Workers' Compensation Records

Labor Commission, Division of Industrial Accidents, PO Box 146610, Salt Lake City, UT 84114-6610 (Courier: 160 E 300 S, 3rd Floor, Salt Lake City, UT 84114); 801-530-6800, 801-530-6804 (Fax), 8AM-5PM.

www.laborcommission.utah.gov

Indexing & Storage: Records are available from 1970 to 1988 on microfiche, from 1989 to present on computer. It takes one week before new records are available for inquiry. Records are normally destroyed after 75 years.

Searching: Must have a notarized release from claimant (not over 90 days old). If a conditional job has been offered, then include a statement of such with employer's name and signature. Include the following in your request-Social Security Number, date of birth, as well as release form. Phone or fax to request form.

Access by: mail, fax, in person.

Fee & Payment: The search fee is $15.00 per name, copies are $.50 per page. Fee payee: Division of Industrial Accidents. Prepayment required. Personal checks accepted. No credit cards accepted.

Mail search: Turnaround time: 2 to 3 days. Include requester's telephone number so they can call with the total charge, which must be paid before records are released. No SASE is required.

Fax search: Prepayment is required.

In person search: Same criteria as mail requests.

Driver Records

Department of Public Safety, Driver License Division, Customer Service Section, PO Box 30560, Salt Lake City, UT 84130-0560 (Courier: 4501 South 2700 West, 3rd Floor South, Salt Lake City, UT 84119); 801-965-4437, 801-965-4496 (Fax), 8AM-5PM.

http://driverlicense.utah.gov

Note: Copies of tickets can be purchased for $5.00 per record.

Indexing & Storage: Records are available for 3 years for moving violations, 10 years for DWIs and 3 years for suspensions (alcohol related suspensions are 10 years). Records on commercial drivers are kept for 10 years. It takes 2 weeks to 6 months before new records are available for

inquiry. Records are normally destroyed after 10 years.

Searching: Interstate speeding convictions less than 10 mph over are not shown. Accidents are reported only if driver had citation. Addresses removed from report to comply with DPPA. Requests must comply with DPPA permissible uses. The driver's full name and DOB and/or license number are needed when ordering. Also helpful: SSN. The following data is not released: medical records or addresses.

Access by: mail, fax, in person, online.

Fee & Payment: The fee is $4.25 per record, $7.25 if online. Fee payee: Department of Public Safety. Prepayment required. Personal checks accepted.

Mail search: Turnaround time: approx. 1 week. Will FedEx if requester has account or submits pre-paid envelope. A SASE is requested.

Fax search: Requests may be faxed, but results are returned by mail.

In person search: Up to 10 requests can be processed immediately; any additional requests are available the next day. Driving records can be obtained at any one of 17 branch offices throughout the state.

Online search: Driving records are available to eligible organizations through the eUtah. The system is available 24 hours daily. The fee per driving record is $7.25, there is an annual $50.00 subscription fee, also. For more information, visit the website at www.utah.gov/government/onlineservices.html. The main web page for the agency gives Utah drivers the ability to order their own record.

Vehicle and Vessel Ownership and Registration

State Tax Commission, Motor Vehicle Records Section, 210 North 1950 West, Salt Lake City, UT 84134; 801-297-3507, 801-297-3578 (Fax), 8AM-5PM.

http://dmv.utah.gov/

Indexing & Storage: Records are available for 15 years. All boats 1985 or newer must be titled. All motors over 25 HP must be titled. All boats, except canoes, must be registered. It takes 2 weeks before new records are available for inquiry.

Searching: Access is not open to casual requesters without consent of subject. Requesters should use Form TC-890. The name or the vehicle ID or registration number or hull ID is needed to search. The agency will not do a name check. The following data is not released: medical records or Social Security Numbers.

Access by: mail, phone, in person, online.

Fee & Payment: The current fee is $3.00 per record and $6.50 for each microfilm record requested. State has established accounts for dealerships and financial institutions requesting lien-holder information. Fee payee: State Tax Commission. Prepayment required. Personal checks accepted. No credit cards accepted.

Mail search: Turnaround time: 5 - 7 days. Boat records can take as long as 1 week to process.

Phone search: Searching is available for pre-approved, established accounts.

In person search: Turnaround time while you wait for small amounts.

Online search: Motor Vehicle Dept. titles, liens, and registration searches are available at www.utah.gov/government/onlineservices.html; registration is required.

Accident Reports

Driver's License Division, Accident Reports Section, PO Box 30560, Salt Lake City, UT 84130-0560 (Courier: 4501 South 2700 West, 3rd Floor South, Salt Lake City, UT 84119); 801-965-4428, 801-964-4536 (Fax), 8AM-5PM.

Indexing & Storage: Records are available from 1994 to 2002 on microfilm and 2002 to present on optical imaging system. It takes 2 weeks or more before new records are available for inquiry. Records are indexed on 10 years. Records are normally destroyed after placed on microfilm.

Searching: Include the following in your request-full name, date of accident, location of accident.

Access by: mail, fax, in person.

Fee & Payment: The fee is $5.00 per record. Fee payee: Department of Public Safety. Prepayment required. The state will allow ongoing requesters to pre-pay with an account. Personal checks accepted. Credit cards accepted if in person.

Mail search: Turnaround time: 2 weeks or more.

Fax search: Money must be received up front before records can be returned by fax.

In person search: Records will be mailed, or can be picked up if pre-paid.

Voter Registration

Access to Records is Restricted

Elections Office, Utah Capitol Complex, East Office Bldg - #E325, Salt Lake City, UT 84114-2325; 801-538-1041, 801-538-1133 (Fax), 8AM-5PM.

http://elections.utah.gov

Note: Individual record requests are referred to the county clerk offices. Records that have not been secured by the registrant are open to the public; however, the counties will not release the SSN or DL. The entire state voter registration database (current records only) can be purchased from this office for approximately $1,050. The website indicates some financial disclosures regarding political parties, action groups, lobbyists, and corporations.

GED Certificates

Utah State Office of Education, GED Testing Records, PO Box 144200, Salt Lake City, UT 84114-4200; 801-538-7921, 801-538-7868 (Fax), 8AM-4PM.

www.usoe.k12.ut.us/adulted/ged/index.html

Note: Records prior to 1990 may be at the testing sites in hard copy. Storage depends on the site. Testing sites may have fees to verify or release records.

Indexing & Storage: Records are available from 1970 to present.

Searching: Include the following in your request-Social Security Number, signed release), name at time of testing, current name if different, anme and phone number of the requester. The following information is not required to search, but is very helpful: date/year of test, date of birth, and city of test.

Access by: mail, fax, in person.

Fee & Payment: There is no fee for verification.

Mail search: Turnaround time: 2 to 3 days. No SASE is required.

Fax search: Same criteria as phone searching.

In person search: Searchers should call first.

Hunting and Fishing License Information

Utah Division of Wildlife Resources, PO Box 146301, Salt Lake City, UT 84114-6301 (Courier: 1594 West North Temple, #2110, Salt Lake City, UT 84116); 801-538-4700, 877-592-5169, 801-538-4709 (Fax), 8AM-5PM.

www.wildlife.utah.gov/

Indexing & Storage: Records are available ffor the currentt year plus the 3 previous years are kept on computer. Records are indexed on inhouse computer. Records are normally destroyed after 4 years.

Searching: Must use the official request form supplied by this agency. You must show a reasonable purpose in order to obtain information. Include the following in your request-name. DOB and SSN are helpful. The following data is not released: telephone numbers and other perosnal information.

Access by: mail, fax.

Fee & Payment: Fees are based upon actual cost of computer time, personnel time plus copy fee of $.25 per page. Fee payee: Utah Division of Wildlife Resources. Prepayment required. Personal checks accepted. No credit cards accepted.

Mail search: Turnaround time: 10 days. No SASE is required.

Fax search: Requests accpeted by fax.

Other access: Draw lists are provided for a fee at the time of big game drawing.

Utah State Licensing Agencies

Licenses Searchable Online

Accounting Firm #5	https://secure.utah.gov/llv/llv
Acupuncturist #5	https://secure.utah.gov/llv/llv
Alarm Company #5	https://secure.utah.gov/llv/llv
Alarm Company Agent/Response Runner #5	https://secure.utah.gov/llv/llv
Animal Euthanasia Agency #5	https://secure.utah.gov/llv/llv
Arbitrator, Alternate Dispute Resolution #5	https://secure.utah.gov/llv/llv
Architect #5	https://secure.utah.gov/llv/llv
Athletic Event Promoter #5	https://secure.utah.gov/llv/llv
Athletic Judge/Athletic Manager #5	https://secure.utah.gov/llv/llv
Attorney #9	www.utahbar.org/html/find_a_lawyer.html
Banks #10	www.dfi.utah.gov/Banks.htm
Barber / Barber School/Instructor #5	https://secure.utah.gov/llv/llv
Bedding/Upholstery Mfg/Whlse/Dealer #3	http://ag.utah.gov/licenses/Cur_Lic.html
Beekeeper #3	http://ag.utah.gov/licenses/Cur_Lic.html
Boxer #5	https://secure.utah.gov/llv/llv
Brand Inspector #3	http://ag.utah.gov/licenses/Cur_Lic.html
Building Inspector/Trainee #5	https://secure.utah.gov/llv/llv
Building Trades, General #5	https://secure.utah.gov/llv/llv
Burglar Alarm Agent #5	https://secure.utah.gov/llv/llv
Check Cashier/Payday Lender #10	www.dfi.utah.gov/ckcash.htm
Chiropractor #5	https://secure.utah.gov/llv/llv
Consumer Lenders #10	www.dfi.utah.gov/consumer.htm
Contractor #5	https://secure.utah.gov/llv/llv
Controlled Substance Precursor Dist. #5	https://secure.utah.gov/llv/llv
Cosmetologist #5	https://secure.utah.gov/llv/llv
Cosmetology School/Instructor #5	https://secure.utah.gov/llv/llv
Counselor Trainee, Professional #5	https://secure.utah.gov/llv/llv
Counselor, Professional #5	https://secure.utah.gov/llv/llv
Credit Unions #10	www.dfi.utah.gov/CreditUn.htm
Deception Detection Examiner/Intern #5	https://secure.utah.gov/llv/llv
Dental Hygienist #5	https://secure.utah.gov/llv/llv
Dentist #5	https://secure.utah.gov/llv/llv
Dietitian #5	https://secure.utah.gov/llv/llv
Egg & Poultry Inspector #3	http://ag.utah.gov/licenses/Cur_Lic.html
Electrician, Apprentice/Journeyman/Master #5	https://secure.utah.gov/llv/llv
Electrologist #5	https://secure.utah.gov/llv/llv
Employee Leasing Company #5	https://secure.utah.gov/llv/llv
Employment Provider, Professional #5	https://secure.utah.gov/llv/llv
Endowment Care/Cemetery #5	https://secure.utah.gov/llv/llv
Engineer #5	https://secure.utah.gov/llv/llv
Engineer, Structural Professional #5	https://secure.utah.gov/llv/llv
Environmental Health Specialist #5	https://secure.utah.gov/llv/llv
Escrow Agents #10	www.dfi.utah.gov/escrow.htm
Feed #3	http://ag.utah.gov/licenses/Cur_Lic.html
Food & Dairy Inspector #3	http://ag.utah.gov/licenses/Cur_Lic.html
Funeral Service Director/Apprentice/Establishment #5	https://secure.utah.gov/llv/llv
Genetic Counselor #5	https://secure.utah.gov/llv/llv
Geologist #7	https://secure.utah.gov/llv/llv
Grain & Seed #3	http://ag.utah.gov/licenses/Cur_Lic.html
Health Care Assistant #5	https://secure.utah.gov/llv/llv
Health Facility Administrator #5	https://secure.utah.gov/llv/llv
Hearing Aid Specialist #5	https://secure.utah.gov/llv/llv
Hearing Instrument Prof./Intern #5	https://secure.utah.gov/llv/llv
Holding Company #10	www.dfi.utah.gov/hlslist.htm
Industrial Banks #10	www.dfi.utah.gov/industbk.htm
Insurance Agent #8	www.insurance.state.ut.us/companies.html
Insurance Establishment #8	www.insurance.state.ut.us/companies.html
Laboratory, Analytical #5	https://secure.utah.gov/llv/llv
Landscape Architect #5	https://secure.utah.gov/llv/llv

Lien Recovery Fund Member #5	https://secure.utah.gov/llv/llv
Manufactured Housing Dealer/Salesman #5	https://secure.utah.gov/llv/llv
Marriage & Family Therapist/Trainee #5	https://secure.utah.gov/llv/llv
Massage Technician/Apprentice #5	https://secure.utah.gov/llv/llv
Meat Inspector #3	http://ag.utah.gov/licenses/Cur_Lic.html
Mediator, Alternate Dispute Resolution #5	https://secure.utah.gov/llv/llv
Medical Doctor/Surgeon #5	https://secure.utah.gov/llv/llv
Midwife Nurse #5	https://secure.utah.gov/llv/llv
Mortgage Broker, Residential #2	www.commerce.state.ut.us/dre/database.html
Mortgage Loan Services #10	www.dfi.utah.gov/mortgage.htm
Naturopath #5	https://secure.utah.gov/llv/llv
Naturopathic Physician #5	https://secure.utah.gov/llv/llv
Negotiator, Alternate Dispute Resolution #5	https://secure.utah.gov/llv/llv
Nuclear Pharmacy #5	https://secure.utah.gov/llv/llv
Nurse / Nurse-LPN #5	https://secure.utah.gov/llv/llv
Occupational Therapist/Assistant #5	https://secure.utah.gov/llv/llv
Optometrist #5	https://secure.utah.gov/llv/llv
Osteopathic Physician #5	https://secure.utah.gov/llv/llv
Pesticide Dealer/Applicator #3	http://ag.utah.gov/licenses/Cur_Lic.html
Pharmaceutical Admin. Facility #5	https://secure.utah.gov/llv/llv
Pharmaceutical Dog Trainer #5	https://secure.utah.gov/llv/llv
Pharmaceutical Researcher #5	https://secure.utah.gov/llv/llv
Pharmaceutical Teaching Org. #5	https://secure.utah.gov/llv/llv
Pharmaceutical Whse./Dist./Mfg. #5	https://secure.utah.gov/llv/llv
Pharmacist/Pharmacist Intern #5	https://secure.utah.gov/llv/llv
Pharmacy/Pharmacy Technician #5	https://secure.utah.gov/llv/llv
Pharmacy, Institutional/Hospital #5	https://secure.utah.gov/llv/llv
Physical Therapist #5	https://secure.utah.gov/llv/llv
Physician Assistant #5	https://secure.utah.gov/llv/llv
Plumber Apprentice/Journeyman #5	https://secure.utah.gov/llv/llv
Podiatrist #5	https://secure.utah.gov/llv/llv
Polygraph Examiner #5	https://secure.utah.gov/llv/llv
Preneed Provider/Sales Agent #5	https://secure.utah.gov/llv/llv
Probation Provider, Private #5	https://secure.utah.gov/llv/llv
Psychological Assistant #5	https://secure.utah.gov/llv/llv
Psychologist #5	https://secure.utah.gov/llv/llv
Public Accountant-CPA #5	https://secure.utah.gov/llv/llv
Radiology Practical Technician #5	https://secure.utah.gov/llv/llv
Radiology Technologist #5	https://secure.utah.gov/llv/llv
Real Estate Agent/Broker #2	www.commerce.state.ut.us/dre/database.html
Real Estate Appraiser #2	www.commerce.state.ut.us/dre/database.html
Real Estate Establishment #5	https://secure.utah.gov/llv/llv
Recreational Therapist #5	https://secure.utah.gov/llv/llv
Recreational Vehicle Dealer #5	https://secure.utah.gov/llv/llv
Referee #5	https://secure.utah.gov/llv/llv
Respiratory Care Practitioner #5	https://secure.utah.gov/llv/llv
Sanitarian #5	https://secure.utah.gov/llv/llv
Savings & Loans #10	www.dfi.utah.gov/sls.htm
Securities Broker/Dealer #5	https://secure.utah.gov/llv/llv
Security Officer/Company, Armed/Unarmed Private #5	https://secure.utah.gov/llv/llv
Shorthand Reporter #5	https://secure.utah.gov/llv/llv
Social Service Aide/Worker/Trainee #5	https://secure.utah.gov/llv/llv
Social Worker #5	https://secure.utah.gov/llv/llv
Speech Pathologist/Audiologist #5	https://secure.utah.gov/llv/llv
Substance Abuse Counselor #5	https://secure.utah.gov/llv/llv
Surveyor, Land #5	https://secure.utah.gov/llv/llv
Third Party Payment Issuers #10	www.dfi.utah.gov/montrans.htm
Title Lender #10	www.dfi.utah.gov/titlelen.htm
Trade Instructor #5	https://secure.utah.gov/llv/llv
Trust Company #10	www.dfi.utah.gov/trslist.htm
Veterinarian/Veterinary Intern #5	https://secure.utah.gov/llv/llv
Veterinary Pharmaceutical Outlet #5	https://secure.utah.gov/llv/llv
Weights & Measures #3	http://ag.utah.gov/licenses/Cur_Lic.html
Wine Store #1	www.alcbev.state.ut.us/Stores/wine_stores.html

Utah Licensing Quick Finder

Accounting Firm #5	801-530-6628	
Acupuncturist #5	801-530-6628	
Alarm Company #5	801-530-6628	
Alarm Company Agent/Response Runner #5	801-530-6628	
Animal Euthanasia Agency #5	801-530-6628	
Arbitrator, Alternate Dispute Resolution #5	801-530-6628	
Architect #5	801-530-6628	
Athletic Event Promoter #5	801-530-6628	
Athletic Judge/Athletic Manager #5	801-530-6628	
Attorney #9	801-531-9077	
Bank #10	801-538-8835	
Barber #5	801-530-6628	
Barber School/Instructor #5	801-530-6628	
Bedding/Upholstery Mfg/Whlse/Dealer #3	801-538-7151	
Beekeeper #3	801-538-7184	
Boxer #5	801-530-6628	
Brand Inspector #3	801-538-7137	
Building Inspector/Trainee #5	801-530-6628	
Building Trades, General #5	801-530-6628	
Burglar Alarm Agent #5	801-530-6964	
Check Cashier/Payday Lender #10	801-538-8842	
Chiropractor #5	801-530-6628	
Consumer Lenders #10	801-538-8830	
Contractor #5	801-530-6628	
Controlled Substance Precur'r Dist. #5	801-530-6964	
Cosmetologist #5	801-530-6628	
Cosmetology School/Instructor #5	801-530-6628	
Counselor Trainee, Professional #5	801-530-6628	
Counselor, Professional #5	801-530-6628	
Credit Union #10	801-538-8840	
Deception Detection Examin'r/Intern #5	801-530-6628	
Dental Hygienist #5	801-530-6628	
Dental Hygienist/Local Anesthesia #5	801-530-6628	
Dentist #5	801-530-6628	
Dietitian #5	801-530-6628	
Egg & Poultry Inspector #3	801-538-7124	
Electrician, Apprentice/Journeyman/Master #5	801-530-6628	
Electrologist #5	801-530-6628	
Employee Leasing Company #5	801-530-6628	
Employment Provider, Professional #5	801-530-6628	
Endowment Care/Cemetery #5	801-530-6628	
Engineer #5	801-530-6628	
Engineer, Structural Professional #5	801-530-6628	
Environmental Health Specialist #5	801-530-6628	
Escrow Agents #10	801-538-8842	
Feed #3	801-538-7183	
Food & Dairy Inspector #3	801-538-7145	
Funeral Svc Director/Apprentice #5	801-530-6628	
Funeral Service Establishment #5	801-530-6628	
Genetic Counselor #5	801-530-6628	
Geologist #7	801-537-6628	
Grain & Seed #3	801-538-7183	
Health Care Assistant #5	801-530-6628	
Health Facility Administrator #5	801-530-6628	
Hearing Aid Specialist #5	801-530-6964	
Hearing Instrument Prof./Intern #5	801-530-6628	
Holding Company #10	801-538-8842	
Industrial Banks #10	801-538-8841	
Insurance Agent / Establishment #8	801-538-3805	
Interpreter for the Deaf #12	801-263-4860	
Laboratory, Analytical #5	801-530-6628	
Landscape Architect #5	801-530-6628	
Lien Recovery Fund Member #5	801-530-6628	
Liquor License #1	801-977-6800	
Liquor Store (Retail Liquor License) #1	801-977-6800	
Manufactured Housing Dealer/Salesman #5	801-530-6628	
Marriage & Family Therapist/Trainee #5	801-530-6628	
Massage Technician/Apprentice #5	801-530-6964	
Meat Inspector #3	801-538-7161	
Mediator, Alternate Dispute Resolution #5	801-530-6628	
Medical Doctor/Surgeon #5	801-530-6628	
Midwife Nurse #5	801-530-6628	
Mortgage Broker, Residential #2	801-530-6747	
Mortgage Loan Services #10	801-538-8830	
Naturopath/Naturopathic Physician #5	801-530-6628	
Negotiator, Alternate Dispute Resolution #5	801-530-6628	
Notary Public #4	801-530-6078	
Nuclear Pharmacy #5	801-530-6628	
Nurse #5	801-530-6628	
Nurse-LPN #5	801-530-6628	
Occupational Therapist/Assistant #5	801-530-6628	
Optometrist #5	801-530-6628	
Osteopathic Physician #5	801-530-6628	
Pesticide Dealer/Applicator #3	801-538-7188	
Pharmaceutical Admin. Facility #5	801-530-6628	
Pharmaceutical Dog Trainer #5	801-530-6628	
Pharmaceutical Researcher #5	801-530-6628	
Pharmaceutical Teaching Org. #5	801-530-6628	
Pharmaceutical Whse./Dist./Mfg. #5	801-530-6628	
Pharmacist/Pharmacist Intern #5	801-530-6628	
Pharmacy Out-of-State Mail Svc. #5	801-530-6628	
Pharmacy Retail/Branch #5	801-530-6628	
Pharmacy Technician #5	801-530-6628	
Pharmacy, Institutional/Hospital #5	801-530-6628	
Physical Therapist #5	801-530-6628	
Physician Assistant #5	801-530-6628	
Plumber Apprentice/Journeyman #5	801-530-6628	
Podiatrist #5	801-530-6628	
Polygraph Examiner #5	801-530-6964	
Preneed Provider/Sales Agent #5	801-530-6628	
Probation Provider, Private #5	801-530-6628	
Psychological Assistant #5	801-530-6628	
Psychologist #5	801-530-6628	
Public Accountant-CPA #5	801-530-6628	
Radiology Practical Technician #5	801-530-6628	
Radiology Technologist #5	801-530-6628	
Real Estate Agent/Broker #2	801-530-6747	
Real Estate Appraiser #2	801-530-6747	
Real Estate Establishment #5	801-530-6628	
Recreational Therapist #5	801-530-6628	
Recreational Vehicle Dealer #5	801-530-6628	
Referee #5	801-530-6628	
Respiratory Care Practitioner #5	801-530-6628	
Sanitarian #5	801-530-6628	
Savings & Loan #10	801-538-8842	
School Administrator #6	801-538-7740	
School Librarian #6	801-538-7740	
Securities Broker/Dealer #5	801-530-6628	
Security Company #5	801-530-6628	
Security Officer, Armed/Unarmed Private #5	801-530-6964	
Shorthand Reporter #5	801-530-6964	
Social Svc Aide/Worker/Trainee #5	801-530-6628	
Social Worker #5	801-530-6628	
Social Worker, Clinical #5	801-530-6628	
Speech Pathologist/Audiologist #5	801-530-6628	
Substance Abuse Counselor #5	801-530-6628	
Surveyor, Land #5	801-530-6628	
Teacher #6	801-538-7740	
Third Party Payment Issuers #10	801-538-8842	
Title Lender #10	801-538-8842	
Trade Instructor #5	801-530-6628	
Trust Company #10	801-538-8842	
Veterinarian/Veterinary Intern #5	801-530-6628	
Veterinary Pharmaceutical Outlet #5	801-530-6628	
Weights & Measures #3	801-538-7158	
Wine Store #1	801-977-6800	

Utah Licensing Agency Information

1 Alcoholic Beverage Control Department, 1625 S 900 W, Salt Lake City, UT 84130; 801-977-6800, Fax: 801-977-6888. www.alcbev.state.ut.us Email: abcmain.hotline@state.ut.us

2 Commerce Department, Real Estate Division, PO Box 146711 (160 E 300 S, 2nd Fl, 84145), Salt Lake City, UT 84114-6711; 801-530-6747, Fax: 801-530-6749. www.commerce.utah.gov/dre Email: realest@br.state.ut.us Search Database at www.commerce.state.ut.us/dre/database.html

3 Department of Agriculture and Food, Regulatory Services, PO Box 146500, Salt Lake City, UT 84114-6500; 801-538-7100, Fax: 801-538-7126. http://ag.utah.gov/about.html Search Database at http://ag.utah.gov/licenses/Cur_Lic.html

4 Division of Cooperations & Commercial Code, State Office Building, Rm 1160, Salt Lake City, UT 84114-6705; 801-530-1040. www.commer ce.state.ut.us/corporat/notarypublic.htm Email: kbachman@br.stateut.us

5 Department of Commerce, Division of Occupational & Professional Licensing, PO Box 146741 (160 E 300 S, Heber M Wells Bldg, 84111), Salt Lake City, UT 84114-6741; 801-530-6628, Fax: 801-530-6511. www.dopl.utah.gov Email: doplweb@utah.gov Search Database at https://secure.utah.gov/llv/llv

6 Educator Licensing, Office of Education, PO Box 144200 (250 E 500 S), Salt Lake City, UT 84114-4200; 801-538-7740, Fax: 801-538-7973. www.usoe.k12.ut.us Note: The CACTUS teacher information system at www.uen.org/training/free/cactus.cgi?c_id=11341 &a_id requires user name and password.

7 Division of Occupational and Professional Licensing, Geologist Licensing Board, PO Box 146741, Salt Lake City, UT 84114-6741; 801-530-6628, Fax: 801-530-6511. www.dopl.utah.gov Search Database at https://secure.utah.gov/llv/llv

8 Insurance Department, 3110 State Office Bldg, Salt Lake City, UT 84114-6901; 801-538-3805, Fax: 801-538-3829. www.insurance.state.ut.us Search Database at www.insurance.state.ut.us/companies.html

9 State Bar Association, 645 S 200 E, Salt Lake City, UT 84111; 801-531-9077, Fax: 801-531-0660. www.utahbar.org Email: john.baldwin@utahbar.org Search Database at www.utahbar.org/html/find_a_lawyer.html

10 Department of Financial Institutions, 324 S State #201, PO Box 146800, Salt Lake City, UT 84114-6800; 801-538-8830, Fax: 801-538-8894. www.dfi.utah.gov Search Database at www.dfi.utah.gov

12 Division of Services for the Deaf & Hard of Hearing, Interpreter Program, 5709 S 1500 W, Salt Lake City, UT 84123; 801-263-4860, Fax: 801-263-4865. www.aslterps.utah.gov Email: mfjensen@utah.gov

Utah Federal Courts

County/Court Cross Reference

All counties report to Salt Lake City.

Standards for Federal Courts: The search fee is $20.00 per item (one party name or case number). Certification fee is $7.00 per document. Copy fee is $.50 per page. All fees standard unless noted in profile. Mail Search: always enclose a stamped self addressed envelope unless otherwise noted. Most courts accept fax requests or will suggest a copying/search vendor. Before releasing records, all courts require prepayment unless noted in profile.

Open records are located at the court unless otherwise noted. District courts index by defendant and plaintiff as well as by case number. Bankruptcy courts usually index by debtor and case number. While most courts now have their indexes on computer, many still maintain index card files as well.

The universal PACER sign-up number is 800-676-6856. Find PACER and the Party/Case Index on the Web at http://pacer.psc.uscourts.gov. PACER dial-up access is $.60 per minute. Also, courts offering internet access via RACER, PACER, Web-PACER or the new CM-ECF charge $.07 per page fee unless noted as free.

US District Court

District of Utah

Clerk's Office, Room 150, 350 S Main St, Salt Lake City, UT 84101-2180 (courier address: Use mail address for courier delivery) 801-524-6100, Fax: 801-526-1175. www.utd.uscourts.gov

Counties: All counties in Utah. Although all cases are heard here, the district is divided into Northern and Central Divisions. The Northern Division includes the counties of Box Elder, Cache, Rich, Davis, Morgan and Weber, and the Central Division includes all other counties.

Indexing & Storage: New cases available in the index 1 day after filing date. Older records are on microfiche.

Fee & Payment: Payment may be made by money order, cashier check, personal check, Visa, Mastercard. Payee: Clerk, U.S. District Court.

Phone Search: Only limited information will be released over the telephone.

Mail Search: A SASE not required.

In Person Search: Fee charged if court conducts your in person search for you. Public access terminals available.

PACER: PACER is available online at http://pacer.utd.uscourts.gov. Document images available. Case records go back to July 1, 1989. Records never purged. New records are online after 1 day.

Electronic Filing: Currently in the process of implementing CM/ECF.

U.S. Bankruptcy Court

District of Utah

Clerk of Court, Frank E Moss Courthouse, 350 S Main St, Room 301, Salt Lake City, UT 84101 (courier address: Use mail address for courier delivery) 801-524-6687, Fax: 801-524-4409. www.utb.uscourts.gov

Counties: All counties in Utah. Although all cases are handled here, the court divides itself into two divisions. The Northern Division includes the counties of Box Elder, Cache, Rich, Davis, Morgan and Weber, and the Central Division includes the remaining counties. Court is held once per week in Ogden for Northern cases.

Indexing & Storage: Cases indexed by debtor and creditors as well as by case number. New cases available in the index as soon as the work load permits after filing date.

Fee & Payment: Payment may be made by money order, cashier check, personal check. Debtor's checks are not accepted. Payee: Clerk, U.S. Bankruptcy Court. A contract copy service will fax back docket listings for a fee.

Phone Search: Only docket information available by phone. Automated voice case information service (VCIS) is available. Call VCIS at 800-733-6740 or 801-524-3107. A contract copy service will fax back docket listings for a fee.

In Person Search: Fee charged if court conducts your in person search for you. Imaged copies available.

PACER: PACER is available online at http://pacer.utb.uscourts.gov. Document images available. Records purged after 12 months. New civil records are online after 2 days or more.

Electronic Filing: Recent case filings reports are free. Electronic filing information online at https://ecf.utb.uscourts.gov

Opinions Online: Court opinions are online at www.utb.uscourts.gov/OPINIONS/opin.htm

Utah County Courts

Court	Jurisdiction	No. of Courts	How Organized
District Courts*	General	41	8 Districts
Justice Courts	Limited	147	128 Cities/ Counties
Juvenile Courts	Special		8 Juvenile Districts

* Profiled in this Sourcebook.

CIVIL									
Court	Tort	Contract	Real Estate	Min. Claim	Max. Claim	Small Claims	Estate	Eviction	Domestic Relations
District Courts*	X	X	X	$20,000	No Max	$5000	X	X	X
Justice Courts	X	X		$0	$1000	$7500			
Juvenile Courts									

CRIMINAL					
Court	Felony	Misdemeanor	DWI/DUI	Preliminary Hearing	Juvenile
District Courts*	X	X	X	X	
Justice Courts		X	X		
Juvenile Courts					X

ADMINISTRATION

Court Administrator, 450 S State Street, Salt Lake City, UT, 84114; 801-578-3800, Fax: 801-578-3843. http://www.utcourts.gov/

COURT STRUCTURE

41 District Courts are arranged in eight judicial districts. Branch courts in larger counties, such as Salt Lake, which were formerly Circuit Courts and elevated to District Courts have full jurisdiction over felony as well as misdemeanor cases. Justice Courts are established by counties and municipalities and have the authority to deal with class B and C misdemeanors, violations of ordinances, small claims, and infractions committed within their territorial jurisdiction. The Justice Court shares jurisdiction with the Juvenile Court over minors 16 or 17 years old, who are charged with certain traffic offenses. Automobile homicide, alcohol or drug related traffic offenses, reckless driving, fleeing an officer, and driving on a suspended license are excepted. Those charges are handled through Juvenile Court.

ONLINE ACCESS

Case information from all Utah District Court locations is available through XChange. Fees include $25.00 registration and $30.00 per month which includes 200 searches. Each additional minute is billed at $.20. Records go back to at least 1998 for all District Courts. Information about XChange and the subscription agreement can be found at www.utcourts.gov/records/xchange or call 801-238-7877.

One may search for supreme or appellate opinions at the web site.

ADDITIONAL INFORMATION

Information on a particular case or the case history of individuals can be acquired from the You may submit record requests by mail to at the address listed above or fax 801-578-3859. Fee for faxed or mailed search requests is $21.00 per hour with no charge for the first 15 minutes. The copy fee is $.25 per page.

UT Code Rule 4-202.08 sets fees for county record searches at the same rate mentioned above. But, at the county level, there is a wide variance of per hour charges statewide. The standard hourly search fee depends on which office person does the search; the basic clerk is $15.00. Yet, many courts still report their search fee as $10.00 per hour, many without the first 15 minutes free.

Salt Lake, Ogden, Provo and Orem District Courts have automated information phone lines that provide court appearance look-up, outstanding fine balance look-up, and judgment/divorce decree lookup. Use these numbers:

- Salt Lake District Court - 801-238-7830
- Ogden & Roy District Court - 801-395-1111
- Provo & Orem District Court - 801-429-1000

Beaver County

5th Judicial District Court PO Box 1683, Beaver, UT 84713; 435-438-5309; Fax: 435-438-5395. Hours: 8AM-5PM (MST). *Felony, Misdemeanor, Civil, Eviction, Probate.*

Civil Records: Access: Fax, mail, in person, online. Both court and visitors may perform in person searches. Search fee: $15.00 per hour. Required to search: name, years to search. Civil cases indexed by defendant, plaintiff. Civil records archived from 1800s, are on computer back to 1997. Online access through Xchange, see www.utcourts.gov/records/. Also, see state introduction.

Criminal Records: Access: Fax, mail, in person, online. Both court and visitors may perform in person searches. Search fee: $15.00 per hour. Required to search: name, years to search, DOB. Criminal records archived from 1896, are on computer back to 1997. Online access through Xchange, see www.utcourts.gov/records/. Also, see state introduction.

General Information: No adoption, juvenile, sealed records released. Fee to fax results is $.25 per page. Copy fee: $.25 per page. Cert fee: $4.00 plus $.50 per page. Payee: 5th District Court. Personal checks accepted. Prepayment required. Mail requests: SASE required. Mail turnaround time 2-7 days.

Box Elder County

1st District Court 43 N Main, PO Box 873, Brigham City, UT 84302; 435-734-4600; Fax: 435-734-4610. Hours: 8AM-5PM (MST). *Felony, Misdemeanor, Civil, Eviction, Small Claims, Probate.*

Civil Records: Access: Phone, fax, mail, online, in person. Both court and visitors may perform in person searches. Search fee: $15.00 per name. Required to search: name, years to search. Civil cases indexed by defendant, plaintiff. Civil records on computer from 3/87, books, microfiche, archived from 1856. Online access through Xchange, see www.utcourts.gov/records/. Also, see state introduction.

Criminal Records: Access: Fax, mail, online, in person. Both court and visitors may perform in person searches. Search fee: $15.00 per name. Required to search: name, years to search; also helpful: DOB, SSN. Criminal records on computer from 3/87, books, microfiche, archived from 1856. Online access through Xchange, see www.utcourts.gov/records/. Also, see state introduction.

General Information: Public Access terminal is available. No adoptions, sealed records released. Fee to fax results is $5.00 for up to 10 pages, then $1.00 ea add'l page. Copy fee: $.25 per page. Cert fee: $4.00 plus $.50 per page. Payee: 1st District Court. Personal checks accepted. Visa, MC accepted. Prepayment required. Mail requests: SASE required. Mail turnaround time 1 week.

Cache County

1st District Court 135 N 100 W, Logan, UT 84321; 435-750-1300; Fax: 435-750-1355. Hours: 8AM-5PM (MST). *Felony, Misdemeanor, Civil, Eviction, Small Claims, Probate.*

Civil Records: Access: Phone, mail, online, in person. Both court and visitors may perform in person searches. Search fee: $15.00 per hour. Required to search: name, years to search. Civil cases indexed by defendant, plaintiff. Civil records on computer from 11-87, archived from 1983, microfiche in Salt Lake City. Online access through Xchange, see www.utcourts.gov/records/. Also, see state introduction.

Criminal Records: Access: Phone, mail, online, in person. Both court and visitors may perform in person

searches. Search fee: $15.00 per hour. Required to search: name, years to search; also helpful: DOB, SSN. Criminal records on computer from 11-87, archived from 1983, microfiche in Salt Lake City. Online access through Xchange, see www.utcourts.gov/records/. Also see state introduction.

General Information: Public Access terminal is available. No sealed records released. Fee to fax results is $5.00 per page up to 10 pages. Copy fee: $.25 per page. Cert fee: $4.00 plus $.50 per page. Payee: 1st Judicial District. Personal checks accepted. Visa, MC accepted. Prepayment required. Mail requests: SASE required. Mail turnaround time 2 weeks.

Carbon County

7th District Court 149 E 100 S, Price, UT 84501; 435-636-3400; Fax: 435-637-7349. Hours: 8AM-5PM (MST). *Felony, Misdemeanor, Civil, Eviction, Small Claims, Probate.*

Civil Records: Access: Phone, mail, online, in person. Both court and visitors may perform in person searches. Search fee: $10.00 per hour. First 20 minutes no charge. Required to search: name, years to search. Civil cases indexed by defendant, plaintiff. Civil records on computer from 1988, on microfiche from 1985, archived prior to 1988. Online access through Xchange, see www.utcourts.gov/records/. Also see state introduction.

Criminal Records: Access: Phone, mail, online, in person. Both court and visitors may perform in person searches. Search fee: $10.00 per hour. First 20 minutes no charge. Required to search: name, years to search, DOB; also helpful: SSN. Criminal records on computer from 1988, on microfiche from 1985, archived prior to 1988. Online access through Xchange, see www.utcourts.gov/records/. Also see state introduction.

General Information: Public Access terminal is available. No sealed records released. Fee to fax results is $5.00 1st page, $1.00 each add'l. Copy fee: $.25 per page. Cert fee: $4.00 plus $.50 per page. Payee: 7th District Court. Personal checks accepted. Credit cards accepted: Visa. Prepayment required. Will bill fax fees. Mail requests: SASE required. Mail turnaround time 48 hrs after receipt.

Daggett County

8th District Court PO Box 219, Manila, UT 84046; 435-784-3154; Fax: 435-784-3335. Hours: 8AM-Noon, 1-5PM (MST). *Felony, Misdemeanor, Civil, Eviction, Probate.*

Civil Records: Access: Phone, fax, mail, in person, online. Both court and visitors may perform in person searches. Search fee: $15.00 per hour, 1st 15 minutes no charge. Required to search: name, years to search. Civil cases indexed by defendant, plaintiff. Civil records archived from 1918. Online access through Xchange, see www.utcourts.gov/records/. Also see state introduction. Fax access requires prior approval.

Criminal Records: Access: Fax, mail, in person, online. Both court and visitors may perform in person searches. Search fee: $15.00 per hour, 1st 15 minutes no charge. Required to search: name, years to search, DOB; signature and record request form required. Criminal records archived from 1918. Online access through Xchange, see www.utcourts.gov/records/. Also see state introduction.

General Information: No sealed records released. Fee to fax results is $5.00 per document up to 10 pages plus $.50 per page additional. Copy fee: $.25 per page. Cert fee: $4.00 plus $.50 per page. Payee: Daggett County. Personal checks accepted. Prepayment required. Mail requests: SASE required. Mail turnaround time 10 days.

Davis County

2nd District Court PO Box 769, Farmington, UT 84025; 801-447-3800; Fax: 801-447-3881. Hours: 8AM-5PM (MST). *Felony, Civil, Probate.*

Civil Records: Access: Phone, mail, online, in person. Both court and visitors may perform in person searches. Search fee: $15.00 per hour. First 15 minutes no charge. Required to search: name, years to search. Civil cases indexed by defendant, plaintiff. Civil records on computer back to 1982, prior on microfiche and archived to 1896. Online access through Xchange, see www.utcourts.gov/records/. Also see state introduction.

Criminal Records: Access: Phone, mail, online, in person. Both court and visitors may perform in person searches. Search fee: $15.00 per hour. First 15 minutes no charge. Required to search: name, years to search, DOB; also helpful: SSN. Criminal records on computer back to 1989, prior on microfiche and archived to 1896. Online access through Xchange, see www.utcourts.gov/records/. Also see state introduction.

General Information: Public Access terminal is available. No adoption, criminal pre-sentence investigation records released. Will fax results; no fee indicated. Copy fee: $.25 per page. Certified copies $.50 per page. Cert fee: $4.00 plus $.50 per page. Payee: 2nd District Court. Personal checks accepted. Prepayment required. Mail requests: SASE required. Mail turnaround time 2-3 days.

2nd District Court - Bountiful Department 805 S Main, Bountiful, UT 84010; Civil phone: 801-397-7004; Criminal phone: 801-397-7008; Fax: 801-397-7010. Hours: 8AM-5PM (MST). *Felony, Misdemeanor, Civil, Eviction, Small Claims, Probate.*

Note: Small Claims at 397-7002 and Traffic at 397-7000.

Civil Records: Access: Phone, mail, online, in person. Both court and visitors may perform in person searches. No search fee. Required to search: name, years to search; also helpful: address. Civil cases indexed by defendant, plaintiff. Civil records on computer since 10/86. Online access through Xchange, see www.utcourts.gov/records/. Also see state introduction. For in person searching, call ahead.

Criminal Records: Access: Phone, mail, online, in person. Both court and visitors may perform in person searches. No search fee. Required to search: name, years to search, DOB, signed release. Criminal records on computer since 10/86. Online access through Xchange, see www.utcourts.gov/records/. Also see state introduction. For in person searching, call ahead.

General Information: Public Access terminal is available. Will fax results to toll-free line for $5.00 for 1st 10 pages, then $.25 per page. Copy fee: $.25 per page. Cert fee: $4.00 plus $.50 per page. Payee: District Court. Personal checks accepted. Prepayment required. Mail requests: SASE required. Mail turnaround time 5 days.

2nd District Court - Layton Department 425 Wasatch Dr, Layton, UT 84041; 801-444-4300. Hours: 8AM-5PM (MST). *Felony, Misdemeanor, Civil, Eviction, Small Claims, Probate.*

Civil Records: Access: Online, in person. Visitors must perform in person searches for themselves. No search fee. Required to search: name, years to search. Civil cases indexed by defendant, plaintiff. Civil records on computer from 1988, archived from start of court. Computer index alpha and case number, archives by alpha from 1982, prior to 1982 not indexed. Online access through Xchange, see www.utcourts.gov/records/. Also see state introduction.

Criminal Records: Access: Mail, online, in person. Both court and visitors may perform in person searches. No search fee. Required to search: name, years to search; also helpful: DOB, SSN. Criminal records on computer from 1988, archived from start of court. Computer index alpha and case number, archives by alpha from 1982, prior to 1982 not indexed. Online access through Xchange, see www.utcourts.gov/records/. Also see state introduction.

General Information: Public Access terminal is available. No confidential records, probation reports, sealed records released. Will fax results for $5.00 per page. Copy fee: $.25 per page. Cert fee: $4.00 plus $.50 per add'l page. Payee: 2nd District Court. Personal checks accepted. Prepayment required. Mail requests: SASE requested. Turnaround time 1 day.

Duchesne County

8th District Court PO Box 990, Duchesne, UT 84021; 435-738-2753; Fax: 435-738-2754. Hours: 8AM-5PM (MST). *Felony, Misdemeanor, Civil, Eviction, Small Claims, Probate.*

Civil Records: Access: Phone, mail, fax, online, in person. Both court and visitors may perform in person searches. Search fee: $15.00 per hour. First 15 minutes no charge. Required to search: name, years to search. Civil cases indexed by defendant, plaintiff. Civil records on computer back to 6/1993, civil on microfiche back to 1912. Online access through Xchange, see www.utcourts.gov/records/.

Criminal Records: Access: Phone, mail, fax, online, in person. Both court and visitors may perform in person searches. Search fee: $15.00 per hour. First 15 minutes no charge. Required to search: name, years to search. Criminal records on computer back to 1993; index books back to 1912. Criminal records access through Xchange. For information contact Jolene Cox 578-3831. Also, see state introduction.

General Information: Public Access terminal is available. No confidential records released. Fee to fax results is $1.00 per page. Copy fee: $.25 per page; $.50 if certified. Cert fee: $4.00 plus $.50 per page. Payee: 8th District Court. Personal checks accepted. Accepts Visa/MC, money order. Prepayment required. Mail requests: SASE required. Mail turnaround time 1-5 days.

8th District Court - Roosevelt Department

PO Box 1286, Roosevelt, UT 84066; 435-722-0235; Fax: 435-722-0236. Hours: 8AM-5PM (MST). *Felony, Misdemeanor, Civil, Eviction, Probate.*

Civil Records: Access: Mail, online, in person. Both court and visitors may perform in person searches. Search fee: $15.00 per hour. First 15 minutes no charge. Required to search: name, years to search. Civil cases indexed by defendant, plaintiff. Civil records on computer since 1993. Online access through Xchange, see www.utcourts.gov/records/. Also see state introduction.

Criminal Records: Access: Mail, online, in person. Both court and visitors may perform in person searches. Search fee: $15.00 per hour. First 15 minutes no charge. Required to search: name, years to search; also helpful: DOB. Criminal records on computer since 1994. Online access through Xchange, see www.utcourts.gov/records/. Also see state introduction.

General Information: Public Access terminal is available. No confidential, sealed, expunged or juvenile records released. Will fax results for $5.00 per document. Copy fee: $.25 per page. Cert fee: $4.00 plus $.50 per page. Personal checks accepted. Prepayment required. Mail turnaround time 2-5 days.

Emery County

7th District Court PO Box 635, Castle Dale, UT 84513; 435-381-2619; Fax: 435-381-5625. Hours: 8AM-5PM (MST). *Felony, Misdemeanor, Civil, Eviction, Probate.*

Note: Phone for hearing impaired is 800-992-0172.

Civil Records: Access: Phone, fax, mail, in person, online. Both court and visitors may perform in person searches. Search fee: $10.00 per hour. First 20 minutes no charge. Required to search: name, years to search. Civil cases indexed by defendant, plaintiff. Civil records on computer from 1997, microfilm and archived from start of district court. Online access through Xchange, see www.utcourts.gov/records/. Also see state introduction.

Criminal Records: Access: Phone, fax, mail, in person, online. Both court and visitors may perform in person searches. Search fee: $10.00 per hour. First 20 minutes no charge. Required to search: name, years to search, DOB. Criminal records on computer from 1997, microfilm and archived from start of district court. Online access through Xchange, see www.utcourts.gov/records/. Also see state introduction.

General Information: Public Access terminal is available. No adoption, sealed records released. Will fax results $2.00 1st page, $1.00 each add'l. Copy fee: $.25 per page. Cert fee: $4.00 plus $.50 per page. Payee: 7th District Court. Personal checks accepted. Prepayment required. Mail requests: SASE required. Mail turnaround time 1 week unless large request.

Garfield County

6th District Court PO Box 77, Panguitch, UT 84759; 435-676-8826 X104; Fax: 435-676-8239. Hours: 9AM-5PM (MST). *Felony, Misdemeanor, Civil, Eviction, Small Claims, Probate.*

Civil Records: Access: Phone, fax, mail, in person, online. Only the court performs in person searches; visitors may not. Search fee: $15.00 per hour. Required to search: name, years to search. Civil cases indexed by defendant, plaintiff. Civil records archived for 100 years; on computer back to 2000. Online access through Xchange, see www.utcourts.gov/records/. Also see state introduction.

Criminal Records: Access: Fax, mail, in person, online. Only the court performs in person searches; visitors may not. Search fee: $15.00 per hour. Required to search: name, years to search. Criminal records archived for 100 years; on computer back to 2000. Online access through Xchange, see www.utcourts.gov/records/. Also see state introduction.

General Information: No adoption records released. Fee to fax results is $1.00 for 1st page, $.50 each add'l. Copy fee: $.25 per page. Cert fee: $4.00 plus $.50 per page. Payee: 6th District Court. Personal checks accepted. Prepayment required. Mail requests: SASE not required. Mail turnaround time 1 day.

Grand County

7th District Court 125 E Center, Moab, UT 84532; 435-259-1349; Fax: 435-259-4081. Hours: 8AM-5PM (MST). *Felony, Misdemeanor, Civil, Eviction, Probate.*

Civil Records: Access: Phone, mail, online, in person. Both court and visitors may perform in person searches. Search fee: None for 1st 20 minutes; $15.00 per hour thereafter. Required to search: name, years to search. Civil cases indexed by defendant, plaintiff. District records on computer from Spring 1990, Circuit from spring 1989, archived since court started. Online access through Xchange, see www.utcourts.gov/records/. Also see state introduction.

Criminal Records: Access: Phone, mail, online, in person. Both court and visitors may perform in person searches. Search fee: None for 1st 20 minutes; $15.00 per hour thereafter. Required to search: name, years to search; also helpful: DOB, SSN. District records on computer from spring 1990, Circuit from spring 1989, archived since court started. Online access through Xchange, see www.utcourts.gov/records/. Also see state introduction.

General Information: Public Access terminal is available. No adoption, expunged records released. Will fax results $2.00 1st page, $1.00 each add'l. Copy fee: $.25 per page. Cert fee: $4.00 plus $.50 per page. Payee: 7th District Court. Personal checks accepted. Visa, MC accepted. Prepayment required. Mail requests: SASE required. Mail turnaround time same day.

Iron County

5th District Court 40 N 100 E, Cedar City, UT 84720; 435-867-3250; Fax: 435-867-3212. Hours: 8AM-5PM (MST). *Felony, Misdemeanor, Civil, Eviction, Small Claims, Probate.*

Note: Hearing location also in Parawon, but records held here.

Civil Records: Access: Mail, phone, online, in person. Both court and visitors may perform in person searches. Search fee: Varies. Required to search: name. Civil cases indexed by defendant, plaintiff. District records on computer from 4/89, former Circuit Court records on computer from 1987, archived from 1900. Online access through Xchange, see www.utcourts.gov/records/. Also see state introduction.

Criminal Records: Access: Mail, phone, online, in person. Both court and visitors may perform in person searches. Search fee: Varies. Required to search: name, years to search, DOB, SSN. District records on computer from 4/89, former Circuit Court records on computer from 1987, archived from 1900. Online access through Xchange, see www.utcourts.gov/records/. Also see state introduction.

General Information: Public Access terminal is available. No sealed records released. Copy fee: $.25 per page. Cert fee: $4.00 plus $.50 per page. Payee: 5th District Court. Personal checks accepted. Prepayment required. Mail requests: SASE required. Mail turnaround time 2-3 days.

Juab County

4th District Court 160 N Main, PO Box 249, Nephi, UT 84648; 435-623-0901; Fax: 435-623-0922. Hours: 8AM-5PM (MST). *Felony, Misdemeanor, Civil, Eviction, Probate.*

Civil Records: Access: Phone, mail, online, in person. Both court and visitors may perform in person searches. Search fee: $15.00 per hour. First 15 minutes are no charge. Required to search: name, years to search. Civil cases indexed by defendant, plaintiff. Civil records on computer from 11/94, archived since court started. Online access through Xchange, see www.utcourts.gov/records/. Also see state introduction.

Criminal Records: Access: Phone, mail, online, in person. Both court and visitors may perform in person searches. Search fee: $15.00 per hour. First 15 minutes are no charge. Required to search: name, years to search. Criminal records on computer from 11/94, archived since court started. Online access through Xchange, see www.utcourts.gov/records/. Also see state introduction.

General Information: Public Access terminal is available. All records must be viewed in this office. Copy fee: $.25 per page. Cert fee: $4.00 plus $.50 per page. Payee: 4th District Court. Personal checks

accepted. Prepayment required. Mail requests: SASE required. Mail turnaround time 1 week.

Kane County

6th District Court 76 N Main, Kanab, UT 84741; 435-644-2458; Fax: 435-644-2052. Hours: 8AM-5PM (MST). *Felony, Misdemeanor, Civil, Eviction, Small Claims, Probate.*

Civil Records: Access: Phone, fax, mail, in person, online. Only the court performs in person searches; visitors may not. Search fee: First 15 minutes of search is free, thereafter $25.00 per hour. Required to search: name, years to search. Civil cases indexed by defendant, plaintiff. Civil records on computer from 1985, archived since court started. Online access through Xchange, see www.utcourts.gov/records/. Also see state introduction.

Criminal Records: Access: Phone, fax, mail, in person, online. Only the court performs in person searches; visitors may not. Search fee: First 15 minutes of search is free, thereafter $25.00 per hour. Required to search: name, years to search. Criminal records on computer from 1985, archived since court started. Online access through Xchange, see www.utcourts.gov/records/. Also see state introduction.

General Information: No sealed, expunged records released. Fee to fax results is $.50 per page. Copy fee: $.25 per page. Cert fee: $4.00 plus $.50 per page. Payee: Kane County. Personal checks accepted. Prepayment required. Mail requests: SASE requested. Turnaround time 2-3 days.

Millard County

4th District Court 765 S Hwy 99, #6, Fillmore, UT 84631; 435-743-6223; Fax: 435-743-6923. Hours: 8AM-5PM (MST). *Felony, Misdemeanor, Civil, Eviction, Small Claims, Probate.*

Civil Records: Access: Phone, mail, online, in person. Both court and visitors may perform in person searches. Search fee: $10.00 per hour. Required to search: name, years to search. Civil cases indexed by defendant, plaintiff. Civil records on computer from 1988, archived from 1896. Online access through Xchange, see www.utcourts.gov/records/. Also see state introduction.

Criminal Records: Access: Phone, mail, online, in person. Both court and visitors may perform in person searches. Search fee: $10.00 per hour. Required to search: name, years to search. Criminal records on computer from 1988, archived from 1896. Online access through Xchange, see www.utcourts.gov/records/. Also see state introduction.

General Information: Public Access terminal is available. No pre-sentence, expunged or sealed records released. Copy fee: $.25 per page. Cert fee: $4.00 plus $.50 per page. Payee: 4th District Court. Business checks accepted. Prepayment required. Mail requests: SASE required. Mail turnaround time 1 day.

Morgan County

2nd District Court PO Box 886, Morgan, UT 84050; 801-845-4020; Fax: 801-829-6176. Hours: 8AM-5PM (MST). *Felony, Misdemeanor, Civil, Eviction, Small Claims, Probate.*

Civil Records: Access: Phone, fax, mail, online, in person. Both court and visitors may perform in person searches. Search fee: $25.00 per name, if extensive. Required to search: name, years to search. Civil cases indexed by defendant, plaintiff. Civil records on computer since 1990; on microfiche, books, archived from 1862. Online access through Xchange, see www.utcourts.gov/records/. Also see state introduction. Extensive (special) search requests must be in writing.

Criminal Records: Access: Phone, fax, mail, online, in person. Both court and visitors may perform in person searches. Search fee: $25.00 per name, if extensive. Required to search: name, years to search, DOB; also helpful: SSN. Criminal records on computer since 1990, prior in books. Online access through Xchange, see www.utcourts.gov/records/. Also see state introduction. Extensive (special) search requests must be in writing.

General Information: Public Access terminal is available. No sealed records released. No fee to fax results. Copy fee: $.25 per page. Cert fee: $4.00 plus $.50 per page. Payee: Morgan District. Personal checks accepted. Prepayment required. Mail requests: SASE requested. Turnaround time same day.

Piute County

6th District Court PO Box 99, Junction, UT 84740; 435-577-2840; Fax: 435-577-2433. Hours: 9AM-Noon, 1-5PM (MST). *Felony, Misdemeanor, Civil, Eviction, Small Claims, Probate.*

Civil Records: Access: Mail, in person, online. Both court and visitors may perform in person searches. Search fee: $15.00 per hour. Required to search: name, years to search. Civil cases indexed by defendant, plaintiff. Civil records archived from 1889. Online access through Xchange, see www.utcourts.gov/records/. Also see state introduction.

Criminal Records: Access: Mail, in person, online. Both court and visitors may perform in person searches. Search fee: $15.00 per hour. Required to search: name, years to search. Criminal records archived from 1889. Online access through Xchange, see www.utcourts.gov/records/. Also see state introduction.

General Information: No sealed records released. Copy fee: $.50 per page. Cert fee: $4.00 plus $.50 per page. Payee: Piute County District Court. Personal checks accepted. Search fees may be billed if prior arrangement made. Mail requests: SASE required. Mail turnaround time 2-3 days.

Rich County

1st District Court PO Box 218, Randolph, UT 84064; 435-793-2415; Fax: 435-793-2410. Hours: 9AM-5PM (MST). *Felony, Misdemeanor, Civil, Eviction, Probate.*

Civil Records: Access: Phone, fax, mail, in person, online. Both court and visitors may perform in person searches. Search fee: $10.00 per hour. Required to search: name, years to search; also helpful: address. Civil cases indexed by defendant, plaintiff. Civil records ago back to 1896; computerized records since 1999. Online access through Xchange, see www.utcourts.gov/records/. Also see state introduction.

Criminal Records: Access: Phone, fax, mail, in person, online. Both court and visitors may perform in person searches. Search fee: $10.00 per hour. Required to search: name, years to search; also helpful: address, DOB, SSN. Criminal records go back to 1896; computerized records since 1999. Online access through Xchange, see www.utcourts.gov/records/. Also see state introduction.

General Information: No sealed records released. Will fax results to local or toll free line. Copy fee: $.25 per page. Cert fee: $4.00 plus $.50 per page. Payee: Rich County. Personal checks accepted. Prepayment required. Mail requests: SASE required. Mail turnaround time 2-3 days.

Salt Lake County

3rd District Court - Salt Lake Dept. 450 S State St, Salt Lake City, UT 84111; 801-238-7300; Fax: 801-238-7396. Hours: 8AM-5PM (MST). *Felony, Misdemeanor, Civil, Eviction, Small Claims, Probate.*

Civil Records: Access: Mail, online, in person. Both court and visitors may perform in person searches. Search fee: First 20 minutes no charge. Required to search: name, years to search. Civil cases indexed by defendant, plaintiff. Civil records on computer from 1985, archived after 1969. Online access through Xchange, see www.utcourts.gov/records/. Also see state introduction. An automated court information line allows phone access to court dates, fine balances, and judgment/divorce decrees (case or citation number required) at 801-238-7830.

Criminal Records: Access: Mail, online, in person. Both court and visitors may perform in person searches. Search fee: First 20 minutes no charge. Required to search: name, years to search, DOB; also helpful: SSN. Criminal records on computer from 1986, archived after satisfaction or dismissal, destroyed prior to 1985. Online access through Xchange, see www.utcourts.gov/records/. Also see state introduction.

General Information: Public Access terminal is available. No confidential records released. Will fax results $5.00 up to 10 pages; $.50 per each add'l page. Copy fee: $.25 per page. Cert fee: $4.00 and $.50 a page. Payee: 3rd District Court. Business checks accepted. Visa, MC accepted. Prepayment required. Mail turnaround time 2-3 days.

3rd District Court - Sandy Department 210 W 10,000 S, Sandy, UT 84070-3282; 801-565-5714; Fax: 801-565-5703. Hours: 8AM-5PM (MST). *Felony, Misdemeanor, Civil, Eviction, Small Claims.*

Civil Records: Access: Phone, mail, online, in person. Both court and visitors may perform in person searches. Search fee: $15.00 per hour. Required to search: name, years to search. Civil cases indexed by defendant, plaintiff. Civil records on computer from 1986, civil archived from 1985. Online access through Xchange, see www.utcourts.gov/records/. Also see state introduction.

Criminal Records: Access: Phone, mail, online, in person. Both court and visitors may perform in person searches. Search fee: $15.00 per hour. Required to search: name, years to search. Criminal records on computer from 1986, civil archived from 1985. Online access through Xchange, see www.utcourts.gov/records/. Also see state introduction.

General Information: No police reports, pre-sentence records released. Public access terminal is available by appointment. Copy fee: $.50 per page. Cert fee: $4.50 plus $.50 per page. Payee: 3rd District Court-Sandy Dept. No two-party checks accepted. Visa, MC accepted. Prepayment required. Mail requests: SASE required. Mail turnaround time 1-2 weeks.

3rd District Court - West Valley Department 3636 S Constitution Blvd, West Valley, UT 84119; 801-982-2400; Fax: 801-967-9857. Hours: 8AM-5PM (MST). *Felony, Misdemeanor, Civil, Eviction.*

Civil Records: Access: Mail, online, in person. Both court and visitors may perform in person searches. Search fee: First 15 minutes free; $15.00 per hour thereafter is assisted by staff clerk. Mail requests may send blank check. Required to search: name, years to search. Civil cases indexed by defendant, plaintiff. Civil records on computer since 1986, archived from 1983. Online access through Xchange, see www.utcourts.gov/records/. Also see state introduction.

Criminal Records: Access: Mail, online, in person. Both court and visitors may perform in person searches. Search fee: First 15 minutes free; $15.00 per hour thereafter is assisted by staff clerk. Mail requests may send blank check. Required to search: name, years to search. Criminal records on computer since 1986, archived from 1983. Online access through Xchange, see www.utcourts.gov/records/. Also see state introduction.

General Information: Public Access terminal is available. No sealed records released. Copy fee: $.25 per page. Cert fee: $4.00 plus $.50 per page. Payee: 3rd District Court. Personal checks accepted. Prepayment required. Mail requests: SASE required. Mail turnaround time 1 week.

San Juan County

7th District Court PO Box 68, Monticello, UT 84535; 435-587-2122; Fax: 435-587-2372. Hours: 8AM-5PM (MST). *Felony, Misdemeanor, Civil, Eviction, Probate.*

Civil Records: Access: Phone, mail, fax, online, in person. Both court and visitors may perform in person searches. Search fee: $15.00 per hour. Required to search: name, years to search. Civil cases indexed by defendant, plaintiff. Civil records on computer since 1991; on index books from 1919 to 1991. Online access through Xchange, see www.utcourts.gov/records/. Also see state introduction.

Criminal Records: Access: Mail, fax, online, in person. Both court and visitors may perform in person searches. Search fee: $15.00 per hour. Required to search: name, years to search. Criminal records on computer since 1991; on index books from 1919 to 1991. Online access through Xchange, see www.utcourts.gov/records/. Also see state introduction.

General Information: Public Access terminal is available. No juvenile records released. Fee to fax results is $5.00 up to 10 pages; $.50 per each add'l page. Copy fee: $.25 per page. Cert fee: $4.00 plus $.50 per page. Payee: 7th District Court. Personal checks accepted. Visa, MC accepted. Visa, MC accepted in person and by phone. Prepayment required. Mail requests: SASE required. Mail turnaround time 1 week.

Sanpete County

6th District Court 160 N Main, Manti, UT 84642; 435-835-2121; Fax: 435-835-2135. Hours: 8AM-5PM (MST). *Felony, Misdemeanor, Civil, Eviction, Small Claims, Probate.*

Civil Records: Access: Phone, fax, mail, in person, online. Both court and visitors may perform in person searches. Search fee: $15.00 per hour after first 15 minutes free. Required to search: name, years to search. Civil cases indexed by defendant, plaintiff. Civil records on computer from 1998. Online access through Xchange, see www.utcourts.gov/records/. Also see state introduction.

Criminal Records: Access: Phone, fax, mail, in person, online. Both court and visitors may perform in person searches. Search fee: $15.00 per hour. Required to search: name, years to search; also helpful: DOB. Criminal records on computer from 1998. Online access through Xchange, see www.utcourts.gov/records/. Also see state introduction.

General Information: Public Access terminal is available. No criminal, expunged, or sealed records released. Will fax results $.50 1st page. Copy fee: $.25 per page. Cert fee: $4.00 plus $.50 per page. Payee: 6th District Court. Personal checks accepted.

Prepayment required. Mail requests: SASE requested. Turnaround time 10 days.

Sevier County

6th District Court 895 E 300 N, Richfield, UT 84701-2345; 435-896-2700; Fax: 435-896-8047. Hours: 8AM-5PM (MST). *Felony, Misdemeanor, Civil, Eviction, Probate.*

Civil Records: Access: Fax, mail, online, in person. Both court and visitors may perform in person searches. Search fee: $15.00 per hour. For search requiring 15 minutes or less, no charge. Required to search: name, years to search. Civil cases indexed by defendant, plaintiff. Circuit records on computer from 1989, District on computer from 1991. Online access through Xchange, see www.utcourts.gov/records/. Also see state introduction.

Criminal Records: Access: Fax, mail, online, in person. Both court and visitors may perform in person searches. Search fee: $15.00 per hour. For search requing 15 minutes or less, no charge. Required to search: name, years to search, DOB, SSN. Circuit records on computer from 1989, District on computer from 1991. Online access through Xchange, see www.utcourts.gov/records/. Also see state introduction.

General Information: Public Access terminal is available. No sealed records released. Will fax results $2.50 1st page, $.50 each add'l. Copy fee: $.25 per page. Cert fee: $4.00 plus $.50 per page. Payee: 6th District Court. Personal checks accepted. Prepayment required. Mail turnaround time 2-3 days.

Summit County

3rd District Court PO Box 128, 60 N Main, Coalville, UT 84017; 435-336-3205; Probate phone: 435-336-3205; Fax: 435-336-3061. Hours: 8AM-5PM (MST). *Probate.*

Note: The courts is open 2 to 3 days a week.

3rd District Court 6300 N Silver Creek, Park City, UT 84098; 435-615-4300. *Felony, Misdemeanor, Civil, Small Claims, Evictions, Probate.*

Civil Records: Access: Mail, online, in person. Both court and visitors may perform in person searches. Search fee: $10.00 per hour, first 20 minutes free. Required to search: name, years to search; also helpful: DOB. By plaintiff and defendant. All indexes on computer back to 1993, records archived back to 1900s. Online access through Xchange, see www.utcourts.gov/records/. Also see state introduction.

Criminal Records: Access: Mail, online, in person. Both court and visitors may perform in person searches. Search fee: $10.00 per hour. First 20 minutes no charge. Required to search: name, years to search; also helpful: DOB. Criminal records on computer since 1993. Online access through Xchange, see www.utcourts.gov/records/. Also see state introduction.

General Information: Public Access terminal is available. Copy fee: $.25 per page. Cert fee: $4.00 plus $.50 per page.

Tooele County

3rd District Court 47 S Main, Tooele, UT 84074; 435-843-3210; Fax: 435-882-8524. Hours: 8AM-5PM (MST). *Felony, Misdemeanor, Civil, Eviction, Small Claims, Probate.*

Civil Records: Access: Fax, mail, online, in person. Both court and visitors may perform in person searches. Search fee: $15.00 per hour. First 20 minutes no charge. Required to search: name, years to search. Civil cases indexed by defendant, plaintiff. Civil records on computer from 1982, archived since court started. Online access through Xchange, see

www.utcourts.gov/records/. Also see state introduction.

Criminal Records: Access: Fax, mail, online, in person. Both court and visitors may perform in person searches. Search fee: $15.00 per hour. First 20 minutes no charge. Required to search: name, years to search; also helpful: SSN. Criminal records on computer back to 1989, archived since court started. Online access through Xchange, see www.utcourts.gov/records/. Also see state introduction.

General Information: Public Access terminal is available. No adoption records released. Will fax results $5.00 for 10 pages; $.50 each add'l. Copy fee: $.25 per page. Cert fee: $4.00 plus $.50 per page. Payee: 3rd District Court. Personal checks accepted. Prepayment required. Mail requests: SASE required. Mail turnaround time 2-3 days.

Uintah County

8th District Court 920 E Hwy 40, Vernal, UT 84078; 435-781-9300; Fax: 435-789-0564. Hours: 8AM-5PM (MST). *Felony, Misdemeanor, Civil, Eviction, Probate.*

Civil Records: Access: Mail, online, in person. Both court and visitors may perform in person searches. Search fee: $15.00 per hour. First 20 minutes no charge. Required to search: name, years to search. Civil cases indexed by defendant, plaintiff. Circuit records on computer from 1987, everything else from 1989, archived since court started. Online access through Xchange, see www.utcourts.gov/records/. Also see state introduction.

Criminal Records: Access: Mail, online, in person. Both court and visitors may perform in person searches. Search fee: $15.00 per hour. First 20 minutes no charge. Required to search: name, years to search. Circuit records on computer from 1987, everything else from 1989, archived since court started. Online access through Xchange, see www.utcourts.gov/records/. Also see state introduction.

General Information: Public Access terminal is available. No sealed records released. Will fax results to local or toll free line. Copy fee: $.25 per page. Cert fee: $4.00 plus $.50 per page. Payee: 8th District Court. Personal checks accepted. Prepayment required. Mail requests: SASE required. Mail turnaround time 2-3 days.

Utah County

4th District Court 125 N 100 W, Provo, UT 84601; 801-429-1000; Civil phone: 1-801-429-1172; Criminal phone: 1-801-429-1171; Probate phone: 1-801-429-1172; Fax: 801-429-1033. Hours: 8AM-5PM (MST). *Felony, Misdemeanor, Civil, Eviction, Small Claims, Probate.*

www.utcourts.gov

Civil Records: Access: Phone, mail, fax, in person. Both court and visitors may perform in person searches. Search fee: $15.00 per hour. Required to search: name, years to search. Civil cases indexed by defendant, plaintiff. Civil and probate on computer from 1986, judgments, tax liens, and divorce decrees on microfiche from 1900 to 1975, archived from 1900s. Online access through Xchange, see www.utcourts.gov/records/. Also see state introduction.

Criminal Records: Access: Phone, mail, fax, in person. Both court and visitors may perform in person searches. Search fee: $15.00 per hour. Required to search: name, years to search, DOB. Felony on computer from 1989; archived from 1900s. Online access through Xchange, see www.utcourts.gov/records/. Also see state introduction.

General Information: Public Access terminal is available. No sealed records released. Copy fee: $.25 per page. Cert fee: $4.00 for 1st page and $.50 per page thereafter. Payee: 4th District Court. Personal checks accepted. Visa, MC accepted. Accepted in person only. Prepayment required. Mail requests: SASE required. Mail turnaround time 7-10 days.

4th District Court - Orem Department 97
E Center, Orem, UT 84057; 801-764-5865/5864; Fax: 801-226-5244. Hours: 8AM-5PM (MST). *Misdemeanor, Civil, Eviction, Small Claims.*

Civil Records: Access: Mail, online, in person. Both the court and visitors may perform in person searches. Search fee: $15.00 per hour. First 20 minutes no charge. Required to search: name, years to search. Civil cases indexed by defendant, plaintiff. Civil records on computer since 1988. Online access through Xchange, see www.utcourts.gov/records/. Also see state introduction.

Criminal Records: Access: Mail, online, in person. Both the court and visitors may perform in person searches. Search fee: $15.00 per hour. First 20 minutes no charge. Required to search: name, years to search; also helpful: DOB. Criminal records on computer since 1988. Online access through Xchange, see www.utcourts.gov/records/. Also see state introduction.

General Information: Public Access terminal is available. No sealed, expunged or confidential records released. Copy fee: $.25 per page. Cert fee: $4.00 plus $.50 per page. Payee: 4th District Court. Personal checks accepted. Visa, MC accepted. Prepayment required. Mail turnaround time 5-7 days.

4th District Court - Spanish Forks Department
40 S Main St, Spanish Forks, UT 84660; 801-798-8674; Fax: 801-798-1377. Hours: 8AM-5PM (MST). *Felony, Misdemeanor, Civil, Eviction, Small Claims.*

Civil Records: Access: Phone, fax, mail, online, in person. Both court and visitors may perform in person searches. Search fee: $15.00 per hour. First 15 minutes no charge. Required to search: name, years to search. Civil cases indexed by defendant, plaintiff. Civil records stored from 1978, on computer since 1987. Online access through Xchange, see www.utcourts.gov/records/. Also see state introduction.

Criminal Records: Access: Phone, fax, mail, online, in person. Both court and visitors may perform in person searches. Search fee: $15.00 per hour. First 15 minutes no charge. Required to search: name, years to search; also helpful: DOB. Criminal records stored from 1978, on computer since 1987. Online access through Xchange, see www.utcourts.gov/records/. Also see state introduction.

General Information: Public Access terminal is available. No sealed, expunged or confidential records released. No fee to fax results. Fax requires prior arrangement. Copy fee: $.25 per page. Cert fee: $4.00 plus $.50 per page. Payee: 4th District Court. Personal checks accepted. Visa, MC accepted. Prepayment required. Mail turnaround time 5-7 days.

4th District Court - American Fork Department
75 E 80 N, #202, PO Box 986, American Fork, UT 84003-0986; 801-756-9654; Fax: 801-763-0153. Hours: 8AM-5PM (MST). *Misdemeanor, Civil, Eviction, Small Claims.*

Civil Records: Access: Mail, online, in person. Both court and visitors may perform in person searches. Search fee: $10.00 per hour. First 20 minutes no charge. Required to search: name, years to search. Civil cases indexed by defendant, plaintiff. Civil records on computer since 1988. Online access

through Xchange, see www.utcourts.gov/records/. Also see state introduction.

Criminal Records: Access: Mail, online, in person. Both court and visitors may perform in person searches. Search fee: $10.00 per hour. First 20 minutes no charge. Required to search: name, years to search; also helpful: DOB. Criminal records stored since 1988. Online access through Xchange, see www.utcourts.gov/records/. Also see state introduction.

General Information: Public Access terminal is available. No sealed, expunged or confidential records released. Will fax results for $5.00 per fax. Copy fee: $.25 per page. Cert fee: $4.00 plus $.50 per page. Payee: 4th District Court. Personal checks accepted. Visa, MC accepted. Prepayment required. Mail requests: SASE required. Mail turnaround time 5-7 days.

Wasatch County

4th District Court 1361 S Hwy 40, PO Box 730, Heber City, UT 84032; 435-654-4676; Fax: 435-654-5281. Hours: 8AM-5PM (MST). *Felony, Misdemeanor, Civil, Eviction, Probate.*

Note: Small claims are handled at one of two Justice Courts in the county. Heber City Justice Courts can be reached at 435-654-1662, Wasatch County Justice Court at 435-654-2679.

Civil Records: Access: Phone, fax, mail, online, in person. Both court and visitors may perform in person searches. No search fee. Required to search: name, years to search. Civil cases indexed by defendant, plaintiff. Civil records on computer since 01/95; records archived since court started. Online access through Xchange, see www.utcourts.gov/records/. Also see state introduction.

Criminal Records: Access: Phone, fax, mail, online, in person. Both court and visitors may perform in person searches. No search fee. Required to search: name, years to search; also helpful: DOB, signed release. Criminal records on computer since 01/95; records archived since court started. Online access through Xchange, see www.utcourts.gov/records/. Also see state introduction.

General Information: Public Access terminal is available. No adoption records released. Fee to fax results is $1.00 plus $.25 per page. Copy fee: $.25 per page. Cert fee: $4.00 plus $.50 per page. Payee: 4th District Court. Personal checks accepted. Prepayment required. Mail requests: SASE required. Mail turnaround time 1-2 days.

Washington County

5th District Court 220 N 200 E, St. George, UT 84770; Civil phone: 435-986-5701; Criminal phone: 435-986-5700; Fax: 435-986-5723. Hours: 8AM-5PM (MST). *Felony, Misdemeanor, Civil, Eviction, Small Claims, Probate.*

Civil Records: Access: Mail, online, in person, fax. Both court and visitors may perform in person searches. No search fee. Required to search: name. Civil cases indexed by defendant, plaintiff. District Court records on computer from April, 1990; Circuit Court on computer from 1987. Online access through Xchange, see www.utcourts.gov/records/. Also see state introduction.

Criminal Records: Access: Mail, online, in person, fax. Both court and visitors may perform in person searches. No search fee. Required to search: name, years to search. District Court records on computer from April, 1990; Circuit Court on computer from 1987. Online access through Xchange, see www.utcourts.gov/records/. Also see state introduction.

General Information: Public Access terminal is available. No mental health, adoption records released. Fee to fax results is extra $.25 per page.(min $5.00 charge). Copy fee: $.25 per page. Cert fee: $4.00 plus $.50 per page. Payee: 5th District Court. Personal checks accepted. Visa, MC accepted. Prepayment required. Mail requests: SASE required. Mail turnaround time 2-3 days.

Wayne County

6th District Court PO Box 189, Loa, UT 84747; 435-836-2731; Fax: 435-836-2479. Hours: 9AM-5PM (MST). *Felony, Misdemeanor, Civil, Eviction, Small Claims, Probate.*

Civil Records: Access: Phone, mail, fax, in person, online. Both court and visitors may perform in person searches. Search fee: $15.00 per hour. Required to search: name, years to search. Civil cases indexed by defendant, plaintiff. Civil records archived since court started; computerized from Oct. 2000. Online access through Xchange, see www.utcourts.gov/records/. Also see state introduction.

Criminal Records: Access: Phone, mail, fax, in person, online. Both court and visitors may perform in person searches. Search fee: $15.00 per hour. Required to search: name, years to search; also helpful: SSN. Criminal records archived since court started; computerized from Oct 2000. Online access through Xchange, see www.utcourts.gov/records/. Also see state introduction.

General Information: No sealed records released. Fee to fax results is $1.00 per page. Copy fee: $.25 per page. Cert fee: $4.00 plus $.50 per page. Payee: 6th District Court. Personal checks accepted. Prepayment required. Mail requests: SASE required. Mail turnaround time 2-3 days.

Weber County

2nd District Court 2525 Grant Ave, Ogden, UT 84401; 801-395-1060; Civil phone: 801-395-1091; Criminal phone: 801-395-1102; Probate phone: 801-395-1173. Hours: 8AM-5PM (MST). *Felony, Misdemeanor, Civil, Eviction, Small Claims, Probate.*

Note: Until 12/02, there was a Disctrict Court also in Roy. However, this court is now a Justice Court.

Civil Records: Access: Phone, mail, online, in person. Both court and visitors may perform in person searches. Search fee: $15.00 per hour. First 15 minutes no charge. Required to search: name, years to search. Civil cases indexed by defendant, plaintiff. Civil records on computer the past 10 years, books prior to that. Online access through Xchange, see www.utcourts.gov/records/. Also see state introduction. An automated court information line allows phone access to court dates, fine balances, and judgment/divorce decrees (case or citation number required) at 801-395-1111.

Criminal Records: Access: Phone, mail, online, in person. Both court and visitors may perform in person searches. Search fee: $15.00 per hour. First 15 minutes no charge. Required to search: name, years to search, DOB, SSN. Criminal records on computer the past 10 years, books prior to that. Online access through Xchange, see www.utcourts.gov/records/. Also see state introduction.

General Information: Public Access terminal is available. No adoption, voluntary commitments, expunged criminal records released. Will fax results $5.00 per page. Copy fee: $.25 per page. Cert fee: $4.00 plus $.50 per page. Payee: Ogden District Court. Personal checks accepted. Visa, MC accepted. Prepayment required. Mail requests: SASE required. Mail turnaround time 2-9 days.

Utah Recording Offices

ORGANIZATION: 29 counties 29 recording offices. The recording officers are County Recorder and Clerk of District Court (state tax liens). The entire state is in the Mountain Time Zone (MST).

REAL ESTATE RECORDS: County Recorders will not perform real estate searches. Copy fees vary, and certification fees are usually $2.00 per document.

UCC RECORDS: Financing statements are filed at the state level, except for real estate related collateral, which are filed with the Register of Deeds (and at the state level in certain cases). Many filing offices will not perform UCC searches. Copy fees vary, but is usually $1.00. Certification usually costs $5.00 per document.

TAX LIEN RECORDS: All federal tax liens are filed with the County Recorder. They do not perform searches. All state tax liens are filed with Clerk of District Court, many of which have on-line access. Refer to the County Court section for information about Utah District Courts.

ONLINE ACCESS: A number of counties offer online access, some are fee-based.

Beaver County

County Recorder, PO Box 431, Beaver, UT 84713. **Phone**-435-438-6480; fax-435-438-6481; hours 9AM-5PM
Will search UCC records. UCC search per debtor-fee determined by length of search. UCC search includes federal tax liens. Will not search real estate records. UCC copy- $1.00 per page. Cert fee: $5.00 per cert. Payee: Beaver County Recorder. **Other phones:** Assessor-435-438-6400; Treasurer-435-438-6410; Appraiser/ Auditor-435-438-6460.

Box Elder County

County Recorder, 1 S. Main, Courthouse, Brigham City, UT 84302-2599. **Phone**-435-734-2031, R/E Recording-435-734-3391; fax-435-734-2038; hours 8AM-5PM www.boxeldercounty.org
Will not search records. RE record copy- $1.00 per doc. UCC copy- $1.00 per doc. Cert fee: $5.00 per doc. **Other phones:** Assessor-435-734-3333; Treasurer-435-734-3333; Appraiser/ Auditor-435-734-3317; Elections-435-734-3391.

Cache County

County Recorder, 179 N. Main St #101, Logan, UT 84321. **Phone**-County Recorder, R/E & UCC Recording- 435-716-7180; fax-435-716-7187; hours 8AM-5PM
Will not search records. Copy fee- $1.00 per page. Cert fee: $5.00 per doc. Payee: Cache County Recorder. **Online Access to Recording, Grantor/Grantee, Lien, Property records:** Access to recording records is via subscription at www.landlight.com. Choose from 3 subscription plans; short free trial is offered. Grantor/Grantee Index goes back to 10/1980; Abstracts to 7/1984; images to 12/1992. Call 435-787-9003 for more information regarding online access. **Other phones:** Assessor-435-716-7100; Treasurer-435-716-8394; Appraiser/ Auditor-435-716-7123.

Carbon County

County Recorder, 120 E Main, Courthouse Bldg., Price, UT 84501. **Phone**-County Recorder, R/E & UCC Recording- 435-636-3244; fax-435-637-6757; hours 8AM-5PM
Will not search records. UCC copy- $.25 per page. Cert fee: $5.00. Payee: Carbon County Recorder. **Other phones:** Assessor-435-636-3249; Treasurer-435-636-3258; Appraiser/ Auditor-435-636-3227; Elections-435-636-3220.

Daggett County

County Recorder, PO Box 219, Manila, UT 84046-0219. **Phone**-435-784-3210; fax-435-784-3335; hours 9AM-Noon; 1-5PM
Will not search records. RE record copy- $.25 per page. Cert fee: $5.00 per page. Payee: Dagget Co. Recorder. **Other phones:** Assessor-435-784-3222; Treasurer-435-784-3154; Appraiser/ Auditor-435-784-3210; Elections-435-784-5154.

Davis County

County Recorder, PO Box 618, Farmington, UT 84025. **Phone**-801-451-3225, R/E Recording-385-451-3225; fax-801-451-3141;   hours-8:30AM-5PM www.co.davis.ut.us
Will not search records. Copy fee- $1.00 per page. Cert fee: $5.00 per doc. Payee: Davis County Recorder. **Online Access to Real Estate, Lien records:** Access to the county land records database requires written registration and $15.00 per month fee + $.10 per transaction. Records go back to 1981. For information and sign-up, contact Janet at 801-451-3347. **Other phones:** Assessor-385-451-3252; Treasurer-385-451-3243; Appraiser/ Auditor-385-451-3214; Elections-385-451-3213; Vital Records-801-451-3337.

Duchesne County

County Recorder, PO Box 916, Duchesne, UT 84021. **Phone**-County Recorder, R/E & UCC Recording- 435-738-1160; fax-435-738-5522; hours 8:30AM-5PM
Will not search records. Copy fee- $1.00 per copy. Cert fee: $3.00. Payee: County Recorder. **Other phones:** Assessor-435-738-1115; Treasurer-435-738-1193; Appraiser/ Auditor-435-738-1123; Elections-435-738-1101.

Emery County

County Recorder, PO Box 698, Castle Dale, UT 84513-0698. **Phone**-435-381-2414; fax-435-381-2614; hours 8:30AM-5:00PM www.emerycounty.com
Will not search records. Copy fee- $.25 per page. Cert fee: $5.00 per cert plsu $.50 per page. Payee: Emery County Recorder. **Online Access to Plat. records:**. **Other phones:** Assessor-435-381-2474; Treasurer-435-381-2510; Appraiser/ Auditor-435-381-2474; Elections-435-381-5106.

Garfield County

County Recorder, PO Box 77, Panguitch, UT 84759. **Phone**-435-676-1112 x112; fax-435-676-8239; hours 9-12:00-1-5PM
Will not search records. Copy fee- $.50 per page. Cert fee: $5.00. Payee: Garfield County Recorder.

Other phones: Assessor-435-676-1107; Treasurer-435-676-1109; Appraiser/ Auditor-435-676-8826 x100.

Grand County

County Recorder & Deputies, 125 E. Center St., Moab, UT 84532. **Phone**-County Recorder & Deputies, R/E & UCC Recording- 435-259-1331; fax-435-259-1320.
Will not search records. RE record copy- $1.00 per page. Cert fee: $5.00 1st page; $1.00 each add'l. Payee: Grand County Recorder. **Other phones:** Assessor-435-295-1329; Treasurer-435-295-1337,8,9; Appraiser/ Auditor-435-259-1322.

Iron County

County Recorder, PO Box 506, Parowan, UT 84761. **Phone**-435-477-8350; hours 8:30AM-5PM
Will not search records. Record copy- $1.00 per page. Cert fee: $5.00 per cert. Payee: Iron County Recorder. **Other phones:** Assessor-435-477-8311; Treasurer-435-477-8360; Appraiser/ Auditor-435-477-8331.

Juab County

County Recorder, 160 N. Main, Nephi, UT 84648. **Phone**-435-623-3430; hours 8:30AM-5PM
Will search UCC records. UCC search per debtor-$10.00. Will not do federal tax lien search. Will not search real estate records. UCC copy- $1.00 per page. Cert fee: $5.00 per cert. Payee: Juab County Recorder. **Other phones:** Assessor-435-623-3425; Treasurer-435-623-0096; Appraiser/ Auditor-435-623-3410.

Kane County

County Recorder, 76 N. Main St, #14, Kanab, UT 84741-3209. **Phone**-435-644-2360; 8AM-N, 1-5PM
Will not search records. RE record copy- $.50 per page. UCC copy- $1.00 per page. Cert fee: $5.00 per cert. Payee: Kane County Recorder. **Other phones:** Assessor-435-644-2649; Treasurer-435-644-5659; Elections-435-644-2458.

Millard County

County Recorder, 50 S. Main, Fillmore, UT 84631. **Phone**-County Recorder, R/E & UCC Recording- 435-743-6210; fax-435-743-4221; hours 8AM-5PM
Will not search UCC records unless specific doc number given. Will not search real estate or tax lien records. RE record copy- $1.00 per page. Cert fee: $5.00 1st page, $.50 each add'l. Payee: Millard County Recorder. **Other phones:** Assessor-435-743-5719; Treasurer-435-743-5322; Appraiser/ Auditor-435-743-5227.

Morgan County

County Recorder, PO Box 886, Morgan, UT 84050. **Phone**-County Recorder, R/E & UCC Recording- 801-829-3277, UCC Recording-801-845-4036; fax-801-845-4066; hours 8AM-5PM www.morgan-county.net Will not search records. Copy fee- $1.50 per page. Cert fee: $5.00 per doc + $1.50 per page. Payee: Morgan Co. Recorder. **Other phones:** Assessor-801-845-4000; Treasurer-801-845-4030; Appraiser/ Auditor-801-845-4011.

Piute County

County Recorder, PO Box 116, Junction, UT 84740. **Phone**-435-577-2505; fax-435-577-2433; 9AM-5PM Will search records. Search per debtor- $10.00. Will not search tax liens as a practice; if so, fee is $10.00 per search. Will not search real estate records as a practice. UCC copy- $1.00 per page. Cert fee: $4.50. Payee: Piute County Recorder. **Other phones:** Assessor-435-577-2988; Treasurer-435-577-2505; Appraiser/ Auditor-435-577-2840.

Rich County

County Recorder, PO Box 322, Randolph, UT 84064. **Phone**-435-793-2005; hours 9AM-Noon,1-5PM Will not search records. Cert fee: $5.00 per cert. Payee: Rich County Recorder. **Other phones:** Assessor-435-793-5215; Treasurer-435-793-5155; Appraiser/ Auditor-435-793-2415.

Salt Lake County

County Recorder, 2001 S. State St, Rm N-1600, Salt Lake City, UT 84190-1150. **Phone**-801-468-3391; hours 8AM-5PM www.co.slc.ut.us Will search UCC records. Will not do federal tax lien search. Will not search real estate records. UCC copy- $2.00 per page. Cert fee: $5.00 per cert. Payee: Salt Lake County Recorder. **Online Access to Assessor, Property Tax, Land records:** Two sources are available. Records on the county Truth-In-Tax Information website are free at www.slpropertyinfo.org. Also, access assessor, real estate, appraisal, abstracts, and GIS mapping for $150.00 fee on the online system at http://rec.co.slc.ut.us/polaris/default.cfm. Search by GIS, name, or property information. Register online or call 801-468-3013. **Other phones:** Assessor-801-468-2165; Treasurer-801-468-3140; Appraiser/ Auditor-801-468-3389.

San Juan County

County Recorder, PO Box 789, Monticello, UT 84535. **Phone**-County Recorder, R/E & UCC Recording- 435-587-3228; fax-435-587-2425; hours 8AM-5PM Will not search records. RE record copy- $.75 per page. UCC copy- $1.00 per page. Cert fee: $5.00 per doc. Payee: San Juan County Recorder. **Other phones:** Assessor-435-587-3221; Treasurer-435-547-3237; Appraiser/ Auditor-435-587-3223; Elections-435-587-3223; Vital Records-435-587-2021.

Sanpete County

County Recorder, 160 N. Main, Manti, UT 84642. **Phone**-435-835-2181; fax-435-835-2182; hours 8:30AM-5PM Will not search records. Record copy- $1.00 per page. Cert fee: $5.00 per cert. Payee: Sanpete County Recorder. **Other phones:** Assessor-435-835-

2111; Treasurer-435-835-2101; Appraiser/ Auditor-435-835-2142; Elections-435-835-2131.

Sevier County

County Recorder, 250 N. Main, Richfield, UT 84701. **Phone**-County Recorder, R/E & UCC Recording- 435-896-9262 x210; fax-435-896-8888; hours 8AM-5PM Will not search records. Copy fee- $.25 per page. Cert fee: $5.00 per doc. Payee: Sevier County Recorder. **Other phones:** Assessor-435-896-9262 x230; Treasurer-435-896-9262 x240; Appraiser/ Auditor-435-896-9262 x203; Elections-435-896-9262 x201.

Summit County

County Recorder, PO Box 128, Coalville, UT 84017. **Phone**-County Recorder, R/E & UCC Recording- 435-336-3238; fax-435-336-3055; hours 8AM-5PM M-F Will not search records. Copy fee- $.25 per page. Cert fee: $5.00 per certification. Payee: Summit County Recorder. **Other phones:** Assessor-435-336-3248; Treasurer-435-336-3266; Appraiser/ Auditor-435-336-3254.

Tooele County

County Recorder, 47 S. Main St, Rm 213, Tooele, UT 84074-2194. **Phone**-County Recorder, R/E & UCC Recording- 435-843-3180; fax-435-882-7317; hours 8:30AM-5PM www.co.tooele.ut.us Will search UCC records. Will not search real estate records. Copy fee- $1.00 per page. Cert fee: $7.00 1st page, $2.00 each add'l. **Online Access to Property Tax records:** Access to the property information database may be operational at www.co.tooele.ut.us/taxinfo.html. **Other phones:** Assessor-435-843-3101; Treasurer-435-843-3191; Appraiser/ Auditor-435-843-3130; Elections-435-843-3140; Vital Records-435-843-2300.

Uintah County

County Recorder, 147 E. Main St., County Bldg., Vernal, UT 84078. **Phone**-435-781-5461, R/E Recording-435-781-5398; fax-435-781-5319; hours 8AM-5PM www.co.uintah.ut.us Will not search records. Copy fee- $.50 per page. Cert fee: $2.00 per cert. Payee: Uintah County Recorder. **Other phones:** Assessor-435-781-5349; Treasurer-435-781-5362; Appraiser/ Auditor-435-781-5360.

Utah County

County Recorder, PO Box 122, Provo, UT 84603. **Phone**-County Recorder, R/E & UCC Recording- 801-370-8179; fax-801-370-8181; hours 8:30AM-5PM www.utahcountyonline.org Will not search records. Record copy- $1.00 per page. Cert fee: $5.00 per cert. Payee: Utah County Recorder. **Online Access to Recorder, Deed, Real Estate, Lien, Assessor, Delinquent Tax, Property Tax records:** Access to the land records database and also map searching is free at www.utahcountyonline.com/dept/record/landrecordsandmaps/index.asp. Indexes go back to 1978; parcel indexes back to 1981. Document images go back to 1994. Building and GIS information is also online. **Other phones:** Assessor-801-370-8275; Treasurer-801-370-8259; Appraiser/ Auditor-801-370-8291; Elections-801-370-8123; Vital Records-801-370-4526.

Wasatch County

County Recorder, 25 N. Main, Heber, UT 84032. **Phone**-435-657-3210; hours 8AM-5PM www.co.wasatch.ut.us/d/recorder.html Will not search records. Copy fee- $.50 per page. Cert fee: $5.00 per cert. Payee: Wasatch County Recorder. **Online Access to Real Property, Grantor/Grantee, Marriage records:** Access to a limited grantor/grantee index also maps and subdivisions are at www.co.wasatch.ut.us/web_access.htm. Only docs from 10/15/1998 to present are accessible. Grantor/Grantee can only be searched for data since 5/20/2002. Use "Advanced Search." Includes marriages. Also, the county GIS Dept. plans to have "metadata" property information free at its GIS mapping site at www.co.wasatch.ut.us/d/dpgis.html. **Other phones:** Assessor-435-657-3221; Treasurer-435-657-3217; Appraiser/ Auditor-435-657-3221; Vital Records-435-654-2700.

Washington County

County Recorder, 87 N 200 E, #101, St. George, UT 84770. **Phone**-County Recorder, R/E & UCC Recording- 435-634-5709; fax-435-652-5895; hours 8AM-5PM www.washco.state.ut.us Will not search records. Copy fee- $1.00 per page. Cert fee: $5.00 per cert + $1.00 per page. Payee: Washington County Recorder. **Online Access to Property, Tax Roll records:** Access to the tax roll database is free at www.washco.state.ut.us/index.php?page=taxes&sub=taxsearch. **Other phones:** Assessor-435-634-5703; Treasurer-435-652-5711; Appraiser/ Auditor-435-634-5703; Elections-435-634-5712.

Wayne County

County Recorder, PO Box 187, Loa, UT 84747-0187. **Phone**-435-836-1303; fax-435-836-2479; hours 9AM-5PM www.waynecnty.com Will search UCC records. Will not search real estate records. UCC copy- $.25 per page. Cert fee: $5.00. Payee: Wayne County Recorder. **Other phones:** Assessor-435-836-2709; Treasurer-435-836-2765; Clerk/Auditor-435-836-2731.

Weber County

County Recorder, 2380 Washington Blvd, #370, Ogden, UT 84401. **Phone**-County Recorder, R/E & UCC Recording- 801-399-8441; hours 8AM-5PM http://www1.co.weber.ut.us Will search UCC records. Fees vary depending on difficulty of search. Will not search real estate or tax lien records. UCC copy- $1.00 per page. Cert fee: $5.00 per cert. Payee: Weber County Recorder. **Online Access to Real Estate records:** Property records on the County Parcel Search site are free at www.co.weber.ut.us/gis/2002/psearch/. Also, Abstract Title Registration is found at http://www1.co.weber.ut.us/recorder/register.php. **Other phones:** Assessor-801-399-8572; Treasurer-801-399-8454; Appraiser/ Auditor-801-399-8400; Elections-801-399-8400.

Utah County Locator

You will usually be able to find the city name in the City/County Cross Reference below. In that case, it is a simple matter to determine the county from the cross reference. However, only the official US Postal Service city names are included in this index. There are an additional 40,000 place names that people use in their addresses. Therefore, we have also included a ZIP/City Cross Reference immediately following the City/County Cross Reference.

If you know the ZIP Code but the city name does not appear in the City/County Cross Reference index, look up the ZIP Code in the ZIP/City Cross Reference, find the city name, then look up the city name in the City/County Cross Reference. For example, you want to know the county for an address of Menands, NY 12204. There is no "Menands" in the City/County Cross Reference. The ZIP/City Cross Reference shows that ZIP Codes 12201-12288 are for the city of Albany. Looking back in the City/County Cross Reference, Albany is in Albany County.

Utah City/County Cross Reference

ALPINE Utah
ALTAMONT Duchesne
ALTON Kane
ALTONAH Duchesne
AMERICAN FORK Utah
ANETH San Juan
ANNABELLA Sevier
ANTIMONY Garfield
AURORA Sevier
AXTELL Sanpete
BEAR RIVER CITY Box Elder
BERYL Iron
BICKNELL Wayne
BINGHAM CANYON Salt Lake
BLANDING San Juan
BLUEBELL Duchesne
BLUFF San Juan
BONANZA Uintah
BOULDER Garfield
BOUNTIFUL Davis
BRIAN HEAD Iron
BRIDGELAND Duchesne
BRIGHAM CITY Box Elder
BRYCE Garfield
BRYCE CANYON Garfield
CACHE JUNCTION Cache
CANNONVILLE Garfield
CASTLE DALE Emery
CEDAR CITY Iron
CEDAR VALLEY Utah
CENTERFIELD Sanpete
CENTERVILLE Davis
CENTRAL Washington
CHESTER Sanpete
CIRCLEVILLE Piute
CISCO Grand
CLARKSTON Cache
CLAWSON Emery
CLEARFIELD Davis
CLEVELAND Emery
COALVILLE Summit
COLLINSTON Box Elder
CORINNE Box Elder
CORNISH Cache
CROYDON Morgan
DAMMERON VALLEY Washington
DELTA Millard
DEWEYVILLE Box Elder
DRAPER Salt Lake
DUCHESNE Duchesne
DUCK CREEK VILLAGE Kane
DUGWAY Tooele
DUTCH JOHN Daggett
EAST CARBON Carbon
ECHO Summit
EDEN Weber
ELBERTA Utah
ELMO Emery
ELSINORE Sevier
EMERY Emery
ENTERPRISE Washington
EPHRAIM Sanpete
ESCALANTE Garfield

EUREKA Juab
FAIRVIEW Sanpete
FARMINGTON Davis
FAYETTE Sanpete
FERRON Emery
FIELDING Box Elder
FILLMORE Millard
FORT DUCHESNE Uintah
FOUNTAIN GREEN Sanpete
FRUITLAND Duchesne
GARDEN CITY Rich
GARLAND Box Elder
GARRISON Millard
GLENDALE Kane
GLENWOOD Sevier
GOSHEN Utah
GRANTSVILLE Tooele
GREEN RIVER Emery
GREENVILLE Beaver
GREENWICH Piute
GROUSE CREEK Box Elder
GUNLOCK Washington
GUNNISON Sanpete
GUSHER Uintah
HANKSVILLE Wayne
HANNA Duchesne
HATCH Garfield
HEBER CITY Wasatch
HELPER Carbon
HENEFER Summit
HENRIEVILLE Garfield
HIAWATHA Carbon
HILDALE Washington
HILL AFB Davis
HINCKLEY Millard
HOLDEN Millard
HONEYVILLE Box Elder
HOOPER (84315) Weber(92), Davis(7)
HOWELL Box Elder
HUNTINGTON Emery
HUNTSVILLE Weber
HURRICANE Washington
HYDE PARK Cache
HYRUM Cache
IBAPAH Tooele
IVINS Washington
JENSEN Uintah
JOSEPH Sevier
JUNCTION Piute
KAMAS (84036) Summit(86), Wasatch(13)
KANAB Kane
KANARRAVILLE Iron
KANOSH Millard
KAYSVILLE Davis
KENILWORTH Carbon
KINGSTON Piute
KOOSHAREM Sevier
LA SAL San Juan
LA VERKIN Washington
LAKE POWELL San Juan
LAKETOWN Rich
LAPOINT Uintah
LAYTON Davis

LEAMINGTON Millard
LEEDS Washington
LEHI Utah
LEVAN Juab
LEWISTON Cache
LINDON Utah
LOA Wayne
LOGAN Cache
LYMAN Wayne
LYNNDYL Millard
MAGNA Salt Lake
MANILA Daggett
MANTI Sanpete
MANTUA Box Elder
MAPLETON Utah
MARYSVALE Piute
MAYFIELD Sanpete
MEADOW Millard
MENDON Cache
MEXICAN HAT San Juan
MIDVALE Salt Lake
MIDWAY Wasatch
MILFORD Beaver
MILLVILLE Cache
MINERSVILLE Beaver
MOAB Grand
MODENA Iron
MONA Juab
MONROE Sevier
MONTEZUMA CREEK San Juan
MONTICELLO San Juan
MONUMENT VALLEY San Juan
MORGAN Morgan
MORONI Sanpete
MOUNT CARMEL Kane
MOUNT PLEASANT Sanpete
MOUNTAIN HOME Duchesne
MYTON (84052) Duchesne(75), Uintah(24)
NEOLA Duchesne
NEPHI Juab
NEW HARMONY Washington
NEWCASTLE Iron
NEWTON Cache
NORTH SALT LAKE Davis
OAK CITY Millard
OAKLEY Summit
OASIS Millard
OGDEN (84405) Weber(87), Davis(12)
OGDEN Weber
ORANGEVILLE Emery
ORDERVILLE Kane
OREM Utah
PANGUITCH Garfield
PARADISE Cache
PARAGONAH Iron
PARK CITY (84060) Summit(96), Wasatch(3)
PARK CITY Summit
PARK VALLEY Box Elder
PAROWAN Iron
PAYSON Utah
PEOA Summit
PINE VALLEY Washington

PLEASANT GROVE Utah
PLYMOUTH Box Elder
PORTAGE Box Elder
PRICE Carbon
PROVIDENCE Cache
PROVO Utah
RANDLETT Uintah
RANDOLPH Rich
REDMOND Sevier
RICHFIELD Sevier
RICHMOND Cache
RIVERSIDE Box Elder
RIVERTON Salt Lake
ROOSEVELT (84066) Duchesne(94), Uintah(5)
ROY Weber
RUSH VALLEY Tooele
SAINT GEORGE Washington
SALEM Utah
SALINA Sevier
SALT LAKE CITY Salt Lake
SANDY Salt Lake
SANTA CLARA Washington
SANTAQUIN Utah
SCIPIO Millard
SEVIER Sevier
SIGURD Sevier
SMITHFIELD Cache
SNOWVILLE Box Elder
SOUTH JORDAN Salt Lake
SPANISH FORK Utah
SPRING CITY Sanpete
SPRINGVILLE Utah
STERLING Sanpete
STOCKTON Tooele
SUMMIT Iron
SUNNYSIDE Carbon
SYRACUSE Davis
TABIONA Duchesne
TALMAGE Duchesne
TEASDALE Wayne
THOMPSON Grand
TOOELE Tooele
TOQUERVILLE Washington
TORREY Wayne
TREMONTON Box Elder
TRENTON Cache
TRIDELL Uintah
TROPIC Garfield
VERNAL Uintah
VERNON Tooele
VEYO Washington
VIRGIN Washington
WALES Sanpete
WALLSBURG Wasatch
WELLINGTON Carbon
WELLSVILLE Cache
WENDOVER Tooele
WEST JORDAN Salt Lake
WHITEROCKS Uintah
WILLARD Box Elder
WOODRUFF Rich
WOODS CROSS Davis

Utah ZIP/City Cross Reference

ZIP Range	City	ZIP Range	City	ZIP Range	City	ZIP Range	City
84001-84001	ALTAMONT	84078-84079	VERNAL	84523-84523	FERRON	84715-84715	BICKNELL
84002-84002	ALTONAH	84080-84080	VERNON	84525-84525	GREEN RIVER	84716-84716	BOULDER
84003-84003	AMERICAN FORK	84082-84082	WALLSBURG	84526-84526	HELPER	84717-84717	BRYCE CANYON
84004-84004	ALPINE	84083-84083	WENDOVER	84527-84527	HIAWATHA	84718-84718	CANNONVILLE
84006-84006	BINGHAM CANYON	84084-84084	WEST JORDAN	84528-84528	HUNTINGTON	84719-84719	BRIAN HEAD
84007-84007	BLUEBELL	84085-84085	WHITEROCKS	84529-84529	KENILWORTH	84720-84721	CEDAR CITY
84008-84008	BONANZA	84086-84086	WOODRUFF	84530-84530	LA SAL	84722-84722	CENTRAL
84010-84011	BOUNTIFUL	84087-84087	WOODS CROSS	84531-84531	MEXICAN HAT	84723-84723	CIRCLEVILLE
84012-84012	BRIDGELAND	84088-84088	WEST JORDAN	84532-84532	MOAB	84724-84724	ELSINORE
84013-84013	CEDAR VALLEY	84089-84089	CLEARFIELD	84533-84533	LAKE POWELL	84725-84725	ENTERPRISE
84014-84014	CENTERVILLE	84090-84094	SANDY	84534-84534	MONTEZUMA CREEK	84726-84726	ESCALANTE
84015-84016	CLEARFIELD	84095-84095	SOUTH JORDAN	84535-84535	MONTICELLO	84728-84728	GARRISON
84017-84017	COALVILLE	84097-84097	OREM	84536-84536	MONUMENT VALLEY	84729-84729	GLENDALE
84018-84018	CROYDON	84098-84098	PARK CITY	84537-84537	ORANGEVILLE	84730-84730	GLENWOOD
84020-84020	DRAPER	84100-84199	SALT LAKE CITY	84539-84539	SUNNYSIDE	84731-84731	GREENVILLE
84021-84021	DUCHESNE	84201-84244	OGDEN	84540-84540	THOMPSON	84732-84732	GREENWICH
84022-84022	DUGWAY	84301-84301	BEAR RIVER CITY	84542-84542	WELLINGTON	84733-84733	GUNLOCK
84023-84023	DUTCH JOHN	84302-84302	BRIGHAM CITY	84601-84606	PROVO	84734-84734	HANKSVILLE
84024-84024	ECHO	84304-84304	CACHE JUNCTION	84620-84620	AURORA	84735-84735	HATCH
84025-84025	FARMINGTON	84305-84305	CLARKSTON	84621-84621	AXTELL	84736-84736	HENRIEVILLE
84026-84026	FORT DUCHESNE	84306-84306	COLLINSTON	84622-84622	CENTERFIELD	84737-84737	HURRICANE
84027-84027	FRUITLAND	84307-84307	CORINNE	84623-84623	CHESTER	84738-84738	IVINS
84028-84028	GARDEN CITY	84308-84308	CORNISH	84624-84624	DELTA	84739-84739	JOSEPH
84029-84029	GRANTSVILLE	84309-84309	DEWEYVILLE	84626-84626	ELBERTA	84740-84740	JUNCTION
84030-84030	GUSHER	84310-84310	EDEN	84627-84627	EPHRAIM	84741-84741	KANAB
84031-84031	HANNA	84311-84311	FIELDING	84628-84628	EUREKA	84742-84742	KANARRAVILLE
84032-84032	HEBER CITY	84312-84312	GARLAND	84629-84629	FAIRVIEW	84743-84743	KINGSTON
84033-84033	HENEFER	84313-84313	GROUSE CREEK	84630-84630	FAYETTE	84744-84744	KOOSHAREM
84034-84034	IBAPAH	84314-84314	HONEYVILLE	84631-84631	FILLMORE	84745-84745	LA VERKIN
84035-84035	JENSEN	84315-84315	HOOPER	84632-84632	FOUNTAIN GREEN	84746-84746	LEEDS
84036-84036	KAMAS	84316-84316	HOWELL	84633-84633	GOSHEN	84747-84747	LOA
84037-84037	KAYSVILLE	84317-84317	HUNTSVILLE	84634-84634	GUNNISON	84749-84749	LYMAN
84038-84038	LAKETOWN	84318-84318	HYDE PARK	84635-84635	HINCKLEY	84750-84750	MARYSVALE
84039-84039	LAPOINT	84319-84319	HYRUM	84636-84636	HOLDEN	84751-84751	MILFORD
84040-84041	LAYTON	84320-84320	LEWISTON	84637-84637	KANOSH	84752-84752	MINERSVILLE
84042-84042	LINDON	84321-84323	LOGAN	84638-84638	LEAMINGTON	84753-84753	MODENA
84043-84043	LEHI	84324-84324	MANTUA	84639-84639	LEVAN	84754-84754	MONROE
84044-84044	MAGNA	84325-84325	MENDON	84640-84640	LYNNDYL	84755-84755	MOUNT CARMEL
84046-84046	MANILA	84326-84326	MILLVILLE	84642-84642	MANTI	84756-84756	NEWCASTLE
84047-84047	MIDVALE	84327-84327	NEWTON	84643-84643	MAYFIELD	84757-84757	NEW HARMONY
84049-84049	MIDWAY	84328-84328	PARADISE	84644-84644	MEADOW	84758-84758	ORDERVILLE
84050-84050	MORGAN	84329-84329	PARK VALLEY	84645-84645	MONA	84759-84759	PANGUITCH
84051-84051	MOUNTAIN HOME	84330-84330	PLYMOUTH	84646-84646	MORONI	84760-84760	PARAGONAH
84052-84052	MYTON	84331-84331	PORTAGE	84647-84647	MOUNT PLEASANT	84761-84761	PAROWAN
84053-84053	NEOLA	84332-84332	PROVIDENCE	84648-84648	NEPHI	84762-84762	DUCK CREEK VILLAGE
84054-84054	NORTH SALT LAKE	84333-84333	RICHMOND	84649-84649	OAK CITY	84763-84763	ROCKVILLE
84055-84055	OAKLEY	84334-84334	RIVERSIDE	84650-84650	OASIS	84764-84764	BRYCE
84056-84056	HILL AFB	84335-84335	SMITHFIELD	84651-84651	PAYSON	84765-84765	SANTA CLARA
84057-84059	OREM	84336-84336	SNOWVILLE	84652-84652	REDMOND	84766-84766	SEVIER
84060-84060	PARK CITY	84337-84337	TREMONTON	84653-84653	SALEM	84767-84767	SPRINGDALE
84061-84061	PEOA	84338-84338	TRENTON	84654-84654	SALINA	84770-84771	SAINT GEORGE
84062-84062	PLEASANT GROVE	84339-84339	WELLSVILLE	84655-84655	SANTAQUIN	84772-84772	SUMMIT
84063-84063	RANDLETT	84340-84340	WILLARD	84656-84656	SCIPIO	84773-84773	TEASDALE
84064-84064	RANDOLPH	84341-84341	LOGAN	84657-84657	SIGURD	84774-84774	TOQUERVILLE
84065-84065	RIVERTON	84400-84415	OGDEN	84660-84660	SPANISH FORK	84775-84775	TORREY
84066-84066	ROOSEVELT	84501-84501	PRICE	84662-84662	SPRING CITY	84776-84776	TROPIC
84067-84067	ROY	84510-84510	ANETH	84663-84663	SPRINGVILLE	84779-84779	VIRGIN
84068-84068	PARK CITY	84511-84511	BLANDING	84664-84664	MAPLETON	84780-84780	WASHINGTON
84069-84069	RUSH VALLEY	84512-84512	BLUFF	84665-84665	STERLING	84781-84781	PINE VALLEY
84070-84070	SANDY	84513-84513	CASTLE DALE	84667-84667	WALES	84782-84782	VEYO
84071-84071	STOCKTON	84515-84515	CISCO	84701-84701	RICHFIELD	84783-84783	DAMMERON VALLEY
84072-84072	TABIONA	84516-84516	CLAWSON	84710-84710	ALTON	84784-84784	HILDALE
84073-84073	TALMAGE	84518-84518	CLEVELAND	84711-84711	ANNABELLA	84790-84791	SAINT GEORGE
84074-84074	TOOELE	84520-84520	EAST CARBON	84712-84712	ANTIMONY		
84075-84075	SYRACUSE	84521-84521	ELMO	84713-84713	BEAVER		
84076-84076	TRIDELL	84522-84522	EMERY	84714-84714	BERYL		

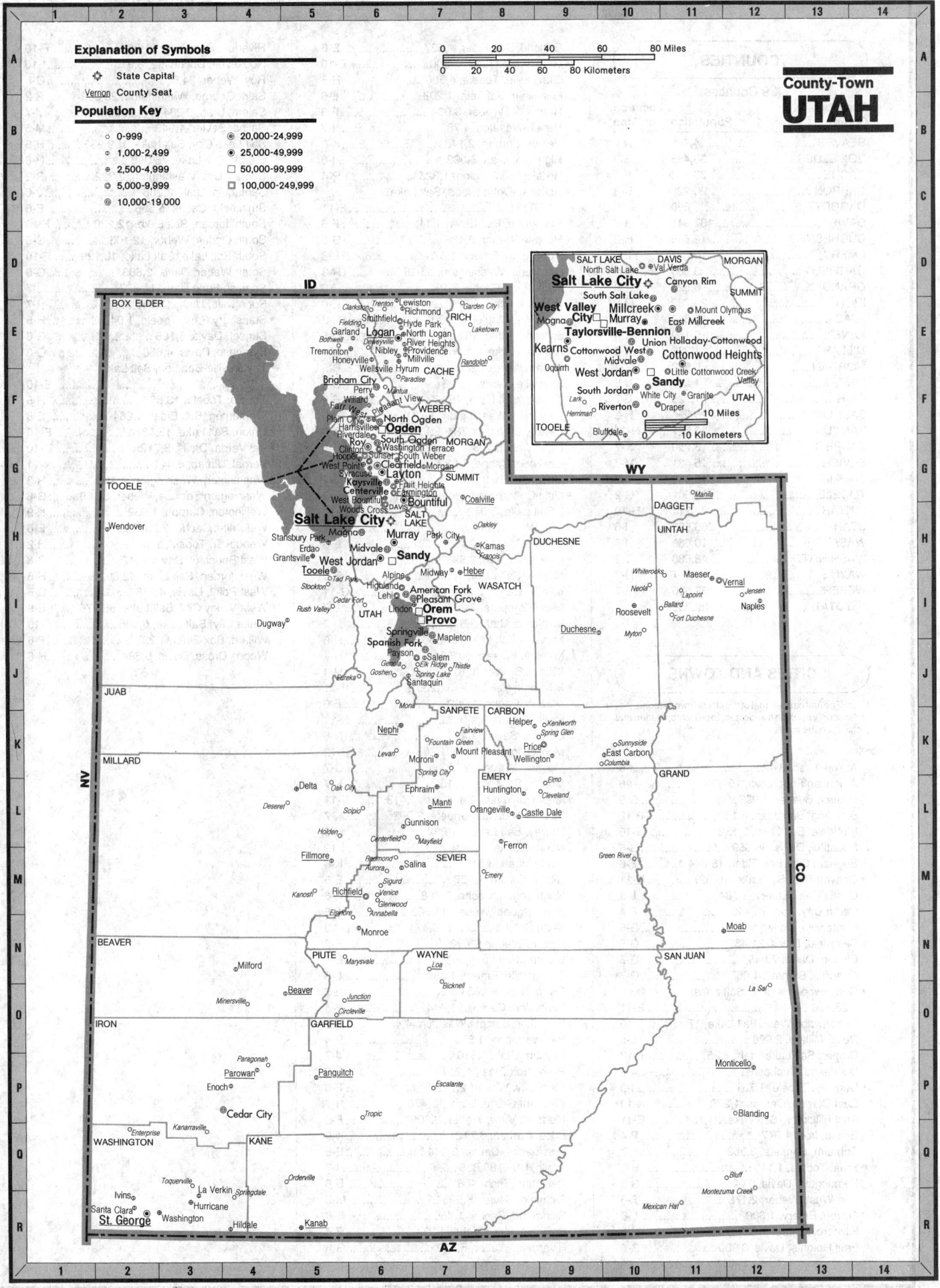

Explanation of Symbols

◇ State Capital
Vernon County Seat

Population Key

- ○ 0-999
- ⊙ 1,000-2,499
- ⊕ 2,500-4,999
- ◎ 5,000-9,999
- ◉ 10,000-19,000
- ⊛ 20,000-24,999
- ● 25,000-49,999
- □ 50,000-99,999
- ▢ 100,000-249,999

County-Town
UTAH

0 20 40 60 80 Miles
0 20 40 60 80 Kilometers

COUNTIES

(29 Counties)

Name of County	Population	Location on Map
BEAVER	4,765	N-2
BOX ELDER	36,485	E-2
CACHE	70,183	F-7
CARBON	20,228	K-8
DAGGETT	690	G-10
DAVIS	187,941	H-6
DUCHESNE	12,645	H-8
EMERY	10,332	L-8
GARFIELD	3,980	O-5
GRAND	6,620	K-10
IRON	20,789	O-2
JUAB	5,817	J-2
KANE	5,169	Q-4
MILLARD	11,333	K-2
MORGAN	5,528	G-7
PIUTE	1,277	N-5
RICH	1,725	E-7
SALT LAKE	725,956	H-6
SAN JUAN	12,621	N-11
SANPETE	16,259	K-7
SEVIER	15,431	M-7
SUMMIT	15,518	G-7
TOOELE	26,601	G-2
UINTAH	22,211	H-10
UTAH	263,590	I-6
WASATCH	10,089	I-8
WASHINGTON	48,560	Q-2
WAYNE	2,177	N-7
WEBER	158,330	F-7
TOTAL	**1,722,850**	

CITIES AND TOWNS

Note: The first name is that of the city or town, second, that of the county in which it is located, then the population and location on the map.

Alpine, Utah, 3,492 .... I-6
American Fork, Utah, 15,696 .... I-6
Beaver, Beaver, 1,998 .... O-5
Blanding, San Juan, 3,162 .... P-12
Bluffdale, Salt Lake, 2,152 .... G-10
Bountiful, Davis, 36,659 .... G-6
Brigham City, Box Elder, 15,644 .... F-6
• Canyon Rim, Salt Lake, 10,527 .... D-11
Castle Dale, Emery, 1,704 .... L-8
Cedar City, Iron, 13,443 .... P-4
Centerville, Davis, 11,500 .... G-6
Clearfield, Davis, 21,435 .... G-6
Clinton, Davis, 7,945 .... G-6
Coalville, Summit, 1,065 .... G-7
• Cottonwood Heights, Salt Lake,
   28,766 .... E-11
• Cottonwood West, Salt Lake, 17,476 .... E-10
Delta, Millard, 2,998 .... L-5
Draper, Salt Lake/Utah, 7,257 .... F-10
Duchesne, Duchesne, 1,308 .... I-9
• Dugway, Tooele, 1,761 .... I-5
East Carbon, Carbon, 1,270 .... K-10
• East Millcreek, Salt Lake, 21,184 .... E-11
Enoch, Iron, 1,947 .... P-4
Ephraim, Sanpete, 3,363 .... L-7
• Erda, Tooele, 1,113 .... H-5
Farmington, Davis, 9,028 .... G-6
Farr West, Weber, 2,178 .... F-6
Ferron, Emery, 1,606 .... L-8
Fillmore, Millard, 1,956 .... M-5
Fruit Heights, Davis, 3,900 .... G-6

Garland, Box Elder, 1,637 .... E-6
• Granite, Salt Lake, 3,300 .... E-10
Grantsville, Tooele, 4,500 .... H-5
Gunnison, Sanpete, 1,298 .... L-6
Harrisville, Weber, 3,004 .... F-6
Heber, Wasatch, 4,782 .... I-7
Helper, Carbon, 2,148 .... K-8
Highland, Utah, 5,002 .... I-6
Hildale, Washington, 1,325 .... R-4
• Holladay-Cottonwood, Salt Lake,
   14,095 .... E-11
Honeyville, Box Elder, 1,112 .... F-6
• Hooper, Weber, 3,468 .... G-6
Huntington, Emery, 1,875 .... L-8
Hurricane, Washington, 3,915 .... R-3
Hyde Park, Cache, 2,190 .... E-6
Hyrum, Cache, 4,829 .... E-6
Ivins, Washington, 1,630 .... R-2
Junction, Piute, 132 .... O-5
Kamas, Summit, 1,061 .... H-8
Kanab, Kane, 3,289 .... R-5
Kaysville, Davis, 13,961 .... G-6
• Kearns, Salt Lake, 28,374 .... E-9
La Verkin, Washington, 1,771 .... R-3
Layton, Davis, 41,784 .... G-6
Lehi, Utah, 8,475 .... I-6
Lewiston, Cache, 1,532 .... E-6
Lindon, Utah, 3,818 .... I-7
• Little Cottonwood Creek Valley,
   Salt Lake, 5,042 .... E-10
Loa, Wayne, 444 .... N-7
Logan, Cache, 32,762 .... E-6
• Maeser, Uintah, 2,598 .... I-11
• Magna, Salt Lake, 17,829 .... E-9
Manila, Daggett, 207 .... G-11
Manti, Sanpete, 2,268 .... L-7
Mapleton, Utah, 3,572 .... I-7
Midvale, Salt Lake, 11,886 .... H-6
Midway, Wasatch, 1,554 .... H-7
Milford, Beaver, 1,107 .... N-4
• Millcreek, Salt Lake, 32,230 .... E-11
Millville, Cache, 1,202 .... F-6
Moab, Grand, 3,971 .... N-11
Monroe, Sevier, 1,472 .... N-6
Monticello, San Juan, 1,806 .... P-12
Morgan, Morgan, 2,023 .... G-7
Moroni, Sanpete, 1,115 .... K-7
• Mount Olympus, Salt Lake, 7,413 .... E-11
Mount Pleasant, Sanpete, 2,092 .... K-7
Murray, Salt Lake, 31,282 .... H-6
Naples, Uintah, 1,334 .... I-12
Nephi, Juab, 3,515 .... K-6
Nibley, Cache, 1,167 .... E-6
North Logan, Cache, 3,768 .... E-6
North Ogden, Weber, 11,668 .... F-6
North Salt Lake, Davis, 6,474 .... D-10
Ogden, Weber, 63,909 .... F-6
• Oquirrh, Salt Lake, 7,593 .... E-9
Orangeville, Emery, 1,459 .... L-8
Orem, Utah, 67,561 .... I-7
Panguitch, Garfield, 1,444 .... P-5
Park City, Summit/Wasatch, 4,468 .... H-7
Parowan, Iron, 1,873 .... P-4
Payson, Utah, 9,510 .... J-7
Perry, Box Elder, 1,211 .... F-6
Plain City, Weber, 2,722 .... F-6
Pleasant Grove, Utah, 13,476 .... I-7
Pleasant View, Weber, 3,603 .... F-6
Price, Carbon, 8,712 .... K-9
Providence, Cache, 3,344 .... E-6
Provo, Utah, 86,835 .... I-7
Randolph, Rich, 488 .... E-8
Richfield, Sevier, 5,593 .... M-6
Richmond, Cache, 1,955 .... E-6
River Heights, Cache, 1,274 .... E-6
Riverdale, Weber, 6,419 .... G-6

Riverton, Salt Lake, 11,261 .... F-10
Roosevelt, Duchesne, 3,915 .... I-10
Roy, Weber, 24,603 .... G-6
Saint George, Washington, 28,502 .... R-2
Salem, Utah, 2,284 .... J-7
Salina, Sevier, 1,943 .... M-6
Salt Lake City, Salt Lake, 159,936 .... H-6
Sandy, Salt Lake, 75,058 .... H-6
Santa Clara, Washington, 2,322 .... R-2
Santaquin, Utah, 2,386 .... J-6
Smithfield, Cache, 5,566 .... E-6
South Jordan, Salt Lake, 12,220 .... F-10
South Ogden, Weber, 12,105 .... G-6
South Salt Lake, Salt Lake, 10,129 .... E-10
South Weber, Davis, 2,863 .... G-6
Spanish Fork, Utah, 11,272 .... J-7
Springville, Utah, 13,950 .... I-7
• Stansbury Park, Tooele, 1,049 .... H-5
Sunset, Davis, 5,128 .... G-6
Syracuse, Davis, 4,658 .... G-6
• Taylorsville-Bennion, Salt Lake,
   52,351 .... E-10
Tooele, Tooele, 13,887 .... H-5
Tremonton, Box Elder, 4,264 .... E-6
• Union, Salt Lake, 13,684 .... E-10
• Val Verda, Davis, 3,712 .... D-10
Vernal, Uintah, 6,644 .... I-11
Washington, Washington, 4,198 .... R-3
Washington Terrace, Weber, 8,189 .... G-6
Wellington, Carbon, 1,632 .... K-9
Wellsville, Cache, 2,206 .... E-6
Wendover, Tooele, 1,127 .... H-2
West Bountiful, Davis, 4,477 .... G-6
West Jordan, Salt Lake, 42,892 .... H-6
West Point, Davis, 4,258 .... G-6
West Valley City, Salt Lake, 86,976 ...... E-9
• White City, Salt Lake, 6,506 .... F-10
Willard, Box Elder, 1,298 .... F-6
Woods Cross, Davis, 5,384 . ... H-6

Explanation of symbols: • – Census Designated Place (CDP)

Vermont

General Help Numbers:

Governor's Office
Pavillion Office Bldg
109 State St
Montpelier, VT 05609-0101
www.vermont.gov/governor/

802-828-3333
Fax 802-828-3339
7:45AM-4:30PM

Attorney General's Office
109 State St
Montpelier, VT 05609-1001
www.atg.state.vt.us/

802-828-3171
Fax 802-828-2154
7:45AM-4:30PM

Legislative Records
State House-Legislative Council
115 State Street, Drawer 33
Montpelier, VT 05633
www.leg.state.vt.us

802-828-2231
Fax 802-828-2424
8AM-4:30PM

State Archives
State Archives Division
26 Terrace-Redstone Bldg
Montpelier, VT 05609-1103
http://vermont-archives.org

802-828-2308
Fax 802-828-1135
7:45AM-4:30PM

State Specifics:

Capital:	Montpelier Washington County
Time Zone:	EST
Number of Counties:	14
Population:	619,107
Web Site:	http://vermont.gov/

State Agencies

Criminal Records

Access to Records is Restricted

State Repository, Vermont Criminal Information Center, 103 S. Main St., Waterbury, VT 05671-2101; 802-244-8727, 802-241-5552 (Fax), 8AM-4:30PM.

www.dps.state.vt.us

Note: Records are not publicly available and can only be accessed by those authorized by law and by subject for personal review. Those authorized include employers with employees working with children, elderly or disabled. Otherwise, search at the county level. 35% of records are fingerprint supported. 96% of records have dispositions. A sex offender registry is not available online to the public.

Statewide Court Records

Court Administrator, Administrative Office of Courts, 109 State St, Montpelier, VT 05609-0701; 802-828-3278, 802-828-3457 (Fax), 7:45AM-4:30PM.

www.vermontjudiciary.org/

Note: Except for certain online research capabilities, all court record access must be done at the local level.

Access by: online.

Online search: Court calendars for all Superior, District, and Family courts are shown at the website above. Supreme Court opinions are available also from the website. In addition, Supreme Court opinions are maintained by the Vermont Department of Libraries at http://dol.state.vt.us.

Sexual Offender Registry

Access to Records is Restricted

State Repository, Vermont Criminal Information Center, 103 S. Main St., Waterbury, VT 05671-2101; 802-244-8727, 802-241-5552 (Fax), 8AM-4:30PM.

www.dps.state.vt.us/cjs/s_registry.htm

Note: In 1996, with the passage of Vermont Annotated Statutes, 13 VSA, Chapter 167, Subchapter 3, the Vermont Sex Offender Registry was established. Records are not publicly available and can only be access by those authorized by law or the subject. Those authorized include employers with employees working with children, elderly, or disabled. Otherwise, requesters must search at local level.

Incarceration Records

Vermont Department of Corrections, Inmate Information Request, 103 S. Main Street, Waterbury, VT 05671-1001; 802-241-2276, 802-241-2565 (Fax), 8AM-4:30PM.

www.doc.state.vt.us

Indexing & Storage: Records are available on current and former inmates. It takes about 3 days before new records are available for inquiry. Records are normally destroyed after six years, depending on the DN.

Searching: Computerized records go back to 1988. Include the following in your request-first and last name. DOB and SSN are helpful. Location, conviction and sentencing information, and release dates are provided.

Access by: mail, phone, fax, online.

Fee & Payment: Requester may be asked to pay reproduction and research fees.

Mail search: Turnaround time: 5 to 7 days. Requests in writing must be specific about information requested. No SASE is required.

Phone search: Searching by telephone permitted if request also in writing.

Fax search: Searching by fax permitted.

Online search: The website provides an Incarcerated Offender Locator to ascertain where an inmate is located. Click on the link at bottom of main page, or go directly to www.doc.state.vt.us:81/cgi-bin/public.cgi. This is not designed to provide complete inmate records nor is it a database of all inmates past and present in the system.

Corporation, Limited Liability Company, Limited Liability Partnerships, Limited Partnerships, Trademarks/Servicemarks

Secretary of State, Corporation Division, 81 River St, Drawer 9, Montpelier, VT 05609-1104; 802-828-2386, 802-828-2853 (Fax), 7:45AM-4:30PM.

www.sec.state.vt.us/

Indexing & Storage: Records are available from beginning of record keeping. Records are on computer if active. Inactive records are indexed by a card file.

Searching: Include the following in your request-full name of business.

Access by: mail, phone, fax, in person, online.

Fee & Payment: There is no search fee. The fee for certification is $20.00 plus $1.00 per page for copies. Fee payee: Secretary of State. Personal checks accepted. No credit cards accepted.

Mail search: Turnaround time: 3 to 5 days. SASE requested.

Phone search: They will only confirm if business is active.

Fax search: Same criteria as mail searching. They will return a page or two by fax if local number, otherwise results are mailed.

In person search: Simple requests may be processed while you wait.

Online search: Information on Corporate and trademark records can be accessed from the Internet for no fee. For the Corporation Name Finder, go to www.sec.state.vt.us/seek/database.htm#2. Many records, included corporation, UCC, trademark, tradename, and name look-ups are available. The Trade Name Finder is at www.sec.state.vt.us/seek/TRADSEEK.HTM.

Other access: There is an option on the Internet to download the entire corporation (and tradename) database.

Uniform Commercial Code

UCC Division, Secretary of State, 81 River St, Drawer 4, Montpelier, VT 05609-1101; 802-828-2386, 802-828-2853 (Fax), 7:45AM-4:30PM.

www.sec.state.vt.us/corps/corpindex.htm

Indexing & Storage: Records are available from 1967. All active records are computerized. It takes 3 to 5 days before new records are available for inquiry.

Searching: Use search request form UCC-11. All tax liens are filed at the town/city level. Include the following in your request-debtor name, business name.

Access by: mail, fax, in person, online.

Fee & Payment: Certified searches are $20.00 per name. Fee payee: Secretary of State. Personal checks accepted. No credit cards accepted.

Mail search: Turnaround time: 4 days. A SASE is requested.

Fax search: Same criteria as mail searching.

In person search: Turnaround time depends on workload, may not be immediate.

Online search: Searches are available from the Internet site. You can search by debtor or business name, there is no fee.

Federal Tax Liens, State Tax Liens

Records not maintained by a state level agency.

Note: Records are found at the local town level.

Sales Tax Registrations

Administrative Agency/Tax Department, Taxpayers Services Division, 109 State St, Montpelier, VT 05609-1401; 802-828-2551, 802-828-5787 (Fax), 7:45AM-4:30PM.

www.state.vt.us/tax/

Indexing & Storage: Records are available for 4 years on computer database, then records are archived.

Searching: This agency will only confirm that a business is registered. Taxpayer records are considered confidential, as provded by law. Include the following in your request-business name or tax permit number or owner name or federal tax ID.

Access by: mail, phone, fax.

Fee & Payment: There is no fee to confirm whether a business is registered to collect sales tax.

Mail search: Turnaround time: 7 to 10 days. A SASE is requested.

Phone search: No fee for telephone request.

Fax search: Requests may be faxed.

Birth Certificates

Reference & Research, Vital Records Section, US Rte 2, Drawer 33, Montpelier, VT 05633-7601; 802-828-3286, 802-828-3710 (Fax), 8AM-4PM.

www.bgs.state.vt.us/gsc/pubrec/referen

Note: For records for the past 5 years only, contact the Department of Health at 802-863-7300.

Indexing & Storage: Records are available from 1760 to 1998. New records are available for inquiry immediately. Records are indexed on index cards, inhouse computer.

Searching: The records are open to the public. Include the following in your request-full name, names of parents, mother's maiden name, date of birth, place of birth.

Access by: mail, phone, fax, in person.

Fee & Payment: The search fee is $9.50 per name. Fee payee: BGS State of VT Prepayment required. Personal checks accepted. Credit cards accepted: MasterCard, Visa, AmEx, Discover.

Mail search: Turnaround time: 2 to 3 days. A SASE is requested.

Phone search: See expedited service.

Fax search: See expedited service.

In person search: You may view the records for no charge.

Expedited service: Expedited service is available for fax searches. Turnaround time: 1 to 2 days. Add $6.00 for use of credit card and $17.50 for overnight shipping.

Death Records

Reference & Research, Vital Records, US Rte 2, Drawer 33, Montpelier, VT 05633-7601; 802-828-3286, 802-828-3710 (Fax), 8AM-4PM.

www.bgs.state.vt.us/gsc/pubrec/referen

Note: For records up to 5 years old, contact the Department of Health at 802-863-7300.

Indexing & Storage: Records are available from 1760 to 1998. New records are available for inquiry immediately. Records are indexed on index cards, inhouse computer.

Searching: Records are open to the public. Include the following in your request-full name, date of death, place of death, names of parents.

Access by: mail, phone, fax, in person.

Fee & Payment: The search fee is $9.50 per name. Fee payee: BGS State of VT Prepayment required. Credit cards accepted. Personal checks accepted.

Mail search: Turnaround time: 2 to 3 days. A SASE is requested.

Phone search: See expedited service.

Fax search: See expedited service.

In person search: You may view records at no charge.

Expedited service: Add $6.00 for use of credit card and $17.50 for overnight delivery. Turnaround time: 1 to 2 days.

Marriage Certificates

Reference & Research, Vital Records Section, US Rte 2, Drawer 33, Montpelier, VT 05633-7601; 802-828-3286, 802-828-3710 (Fax), 8AM-4PM.

www.bgs.state.vt.us/gsc/pubrec/referen

Note: For records up to 5 years old, contact the VT Department of Health at 802-863-7300.

Indexing & Storage: Records are available from 1760 to 1998. New records are available for inquiry immediately. Records are indexed on index cards, inhouse computer.

Searching: Records are open. Include the following in your request-names of husband and wife, date of marriage, place or county of marriage, names of parents.

Access by: mail, phone, fax, in person.

Fee & Payment: The search fee is $9.50 per name. Fee payee: BGS State of VT Prepayment required. Personal checks accepted. Credit cards accepted.

Mail search: Turnaround time: 2 to 3 days. A SASE is requested.

Phone search: See expedited service.

Fax search: See expedited service.

In person search: Records may be viewed in person at no charge.

Expedited service: Available for phone and fax requests. Turnaround time: 1-2 days. Add $6.00 for use of credit card and $17.50 for overnight delivery.

Divorce Records

Research & Reference, Vital Records Section, US Rte 2, Drawer 33, Montpelier, VT 05633-7601; 802-828-3286, 802-828-3710 (Fax), 8AM-4PM.

www.bgs.state.vt.us/gsc/pubrec/referen

Note: For records less than 5 years old, contact the VT Department of Health at 802-863-7300.

Indexing & Storage: Records are available from 1760 to 1998. New records are available for inquiry immediately. Records are indexed on index cards, inhouse computer.

Searching: Records are open. Include the following in your request-names of husband and wife, date of divorce, place of divorce.

Access by: mail, phone, fax, in person.

Fee & Payment: The search fee is $9.50 per name. Fee payee: BGS/Satte of VT Prepayment required. Personal checks and credit cards accepted.

Mail search: Turnaround time: 2 to 3 days. A SASE is requested.

Phone search: See expedited service.

Fax search: See expedited service.

In person search: There is no fee to view records.

Expedited service: Available for phone and fax requests. Turnaround time: 1-2 days. Add $6.00 for use of credit card and $17.50 for overnight delivery.

Workers' Compensation Records

Labor and Industry, Workers Compensation Division, Drawer 20, Montpelier, VT 05620-3401 (Courier: National Life Bldg, Montpelier, VT 05620); 802-828-2286, 802-828-2195 (Fax), 7:45AM-4:30PM.

www.state.vt.us/labind/wcindex.htm

Indexing & Storage: Records are available from 1997 on. Records prior to 1997 are in the State Archives. New records are available for inquiry

immediately. Records are indexed on inhouse computer. Records are normally destroyed after last activity after 13 years.

Searching: Must be a party to or have a signed release from the claimant. You also will get only the employer's first report of injury. Include the following in your request-claimant name, Social Security Number, place of employment at time of accident. Will release for employment purposes only if an offer of employment has been made. The following data is not released: medical records.

Access by: mail, fax, in person.

Fee & Payment: No search fee, copy fee is $.04 per page. Fee payee: State of Vermont. Personal checks accepted. No credit cards accepted.

Mail search: Turnaround time: 2 weeks. A SASE is requested.

Fax search: Turnaround time is 2 weeks.

In person search: Turnaround time is while you wait if staff is available.

Driver Records, Driver License Information

Department of Motor Vehicles, DI - Records Unit, 120 State St, Montpelier, VT 05603-0001; 802-828-2050, 802-828-2098 (Fax), 7:45AM-4:30PM.

www.aot.state.vt.us/dmv/dmvhp.htm

Note: This office is closed on Wed. mornings. Ticket information is available from the Vermont Judicial Bureau, PO Box 607, White River Junction, VT 05001, 802-295-8869. There is no charge, but no information is given over the phone.

Indexing & Storage: Records are available for convictions and accidents. Records are sold as 3 year records or as complete (8+ years) records. It takes 5-7 days normally before new records are available for inquiry.

Searching: Ongoing permissible users must use Form TA-VG-118. Otherwise, use TA-VG-116 for written authorization from the subject to release personal information to the requester. Include the following in your request-name, DOB, signed release, if necessary. Mail or walk-in requesters need the driver's full name and DOB; the license number is optional. Online requesters need only the license number, but the last name and DOB are helpful. The following data is not released: addresses, Social Security Numbers, medical information or personal information (height, weight, sex, eye color, etc.).

Access by: mail, in person, online.

Fee & Payment: The charge is $8.00 for 3 year record and $16.00 for the "complete" record. There is a full charge for a "no record found." Fee payee: Vermont Department of Motor Vehicles. Prepayment required. Personal checks accepted. No credit cards accepted.

Mail search: Turnaround time: 5 to 7 days. A SASE is requested.

In person search: Normal turnaround time is while you wait.

Online search: Online access costs $8.00 per 3 year record. The system is called "GovNet." Two methods are offered-single inquiry and batch mode. The system is open 24 hours a day, 7 days a week (except for file maintenance periods). Only the license number is needed when ordering, but it is suggested to submit the name and DOB also.

For more information, call Driver Improvement at 802-828-2053.

Other access: This agency will sell its license file to approved requesters, but customization is not available.

Vehicle Ownership, Vehicle Identification, Vessel Ownership, Vessel Registration

Department of Motor Vehicles, Registration & License Information/Records, 120 State St, Montpelier, VT 05603; 802-828-2000, 802-828-2872 (Fax), 7:45AM-4:30PM (on Wed only 1PM-4:30PM).

www.dmv.state.vt.us

Indexing & Storage: Records are available from 09/71 to present. Vessel records go back to the late 1980s and are removed after 14 years of inactivity. All motorized boats must be registered. It takes 1 to 3 weeks before new records are available for inquiry. Records are normally destroyed after 2 years 1 month after expiration.

Searching: Ongoing permissible users must be authorized first. Occasional requesters must use form TA-VG 116. If record use is not "permissible" per DPPA, written authorization is needed from subject. Otherwise, records with no personal data are released. You must have name and DOB or plate # or VIN. To receive personal information, you must include signed release by individual, unless ongoing account. Use of Vermont DMV Record Request Form is advised. The following data is not released: Social Security Numbers, residence addresses, bulk information or lists for commercial purposes or medical information.

Access by: mail, in person.

Fee & Payment: $6.00 for each group (1-4) of registration records and $20.00 for an ownership (lien) search. Vessel fees are different: registration check is $6.00, title search with lien is $20.00. Statistical research is $35.00 per hour. Fee payee: Vermont Department of Motor Vehicles. Prepayment required. Personal checks accepted. No credit cards accepted.

Mail search: Turnaround time: 7 to 10 days. A SASE is requested.

In person search: The turnaround time is generally 30 minutes for vehicle records. Vessel records are returned by mail.

Other access: High volume requesters can obtain records via magnetic tape. Bulk release of the database is not available except for statistical purposes. Apply to the Commissioner's Office.

Accident Reports

Department of Motor Vehicles, Accident Report Section, 120 State St, Montpelier, VT 05603; 802-828-2050, 7:45AM-4PM.

Note: The office is closed Wednesday mornings.

Indexing & Storage: Records are available for 5 years to present. Only records involving damage in excess of $1,000 or if injuries involved are reportable. It takes 45 days after the incident before new records are available for inquiry.

Searching: Include the following in your request-full name, date of accident, location of accident. If accident involves a criminal action it may take up to 3 months after accident date to get the report. The following data is not released: Social Security Numbers.

Access by: mail, in person.

Fee & Payment: The fee for certified copies are $1500 for the police report, $10.00 for a copy of the individual's report, and $6.00 for insurance information of the accident. Fee payee: Vermont Department of Motor Vehicles. Prepayment required. Personal checks accepted. No credit cards accepted.

Mail search: Turnaround time: 15 days. A SASE is requested.

In person search: Simple requests may be processed while you wait.

Voter Registration

Records not maintained by a state level agency.

Note: There is no statewide database. All records are kept at the municipal level.

GED Certificates

Department of Education, GED Testing, 120 State Street, Montpelier, VT 05620; 802-828-5161, 802-828-3146 (Fax), 8AM-4:30PM.

www.vermontcareers.org

Indexing & Storage: Records are available from 1941 Records are indexed on computer since 1997. Older records must be looked up on paper file.

Searching: Include the following in your request- name, date of birth, Social Security Number, signed release.

Access by: mail, phone, fax, in person.

Fee & Payment: The fee is $3.00 for a transcript copy. There is no fee for a simple verification. Fee payee: Treasurer, State of Vermont. Prepayment required. Personal checks accepted. No credit cards accepted.

Mail search: Turnaround time: 1 week.

Phone search: The agency will give a verification over the phone.

Fax search: You may use the fax to verify a GED, but not for a transcript purchase unless money previously sent.

In person search: If staff available, requests will be processed while you wait.

Hunting and Fishing License Information

Records not maintained by a state level agency.

Note: Although they maintain a central database on computer, the records are not open to the public. Vendors forward records on a yearly basis (July).

Vermont State Licensing Agencies

Licenses Searchable Online

Accounting Firm #15...www.vtprofessionals.org
Acupuncturist #15..www.vtprofessionals.org
Anesthesiologist Assistant #14...........................www.healthyvermonters.info/bmp/bmp.shtml#data
Architect #15..www.vtprofessionals.org
Armed Courier #15...www.vtprofessionals.org
Athletic Trainer #15...www.vtprofessionals.org
Auctioneer #15...www.vtprofessionals.org
Bank #5..www.bishca.state.vt.us/BankingDiv/banking_index.htm
Barber #15..www.vtprofessionals.org
Body Piercer #15..www.vtprofessionals.org
Boxing Manager/Promoter/Professional #15...................www.vtprofessionals.org
Chemical Suppression TQP Cert #8.....................www.state.vt.us/labind/weblic/cstqpcert.htm
Chimney Sweep #8..www.state.vt.us/labind/weblic/cswtqpcert.htm
Chiropractor #15...www.vtprofessionals.org
Cosmetologist #15...www.vtprofessionals.org
Credit Union #5..www.bishca.state.vt.us/BankingDiv/banking_index.htm
Crematory #15..www.vtprofessionals.org
Dentist/Dental Assistant #15................................www.vtprofessionals.org
Dental Hygienist #15...www.vtprofessionals.org
Dietitian #15...www.vtprofessionals.org
Electrician #8...www.state.vt.us/labind/weblic/elicenses.htm
Electrologist #15..www.vtprofessionals.org
Elevator Mechanic/Inspector #8..........................www.state.vt.us/labind/elevator/forms.htm
Embalmer #15..www.vtprofessionals.org
Engineer #15..www.vtprofessionals.org
Esthetician #15..www.vtprofessionals.org
Fire Alarm System Installer/Dealer #8................www.state.vt.us/labind/weblic/fatqpcert.htm
Fire Sprinkler System Designer #8......................www.state.vt.us/labind/weblic/slicenses.htm
Fire Sprinkler System Installer #8.......................www.state.vt.us/labind/weblic/sstqpcert.htm
Funeral Director #15..www.vtprofessionals.org
Hearing Aid Dispenser #15...................................www.vtprofessionals.org
LPG/Propane Installer #8.....................................www.state.vt.us/labind/weblic/gpicert.htm
Manicurist #15..www.vtprofessionals.org
Marriage & Family Therapist #15..........................www.vtprofessionals.org
Medical Doctor/Surgeon #14................................www.healthyvermonters.info/bmp/bmp.shtml#data
Mental Health Counselor, Clinical #15................www.vtprofessionals.org
Midwife, Licensed #15..www.vtprofessionals.org
Natural Gas System Installer #8..........................www.state.vt.us/labind/weblic/gnicert.htm
Naturopathic Physician #15..................................www.vtprofessionals.org
Notary Public #15..www.vtprofessionals.org
Nurse/Nurse Practitioner/LNA #15.......................www.vtprofessionals.org
Nursing Home Administrator #15..........................www.vtprofessionals.org
Occupational Therapist #15..................................www.vtprofessionals.org
Oil Burning Equipment Installer #8......................www.state.vt.us/labind/weblic/oicert.htm
Optician #15...www.vtprofessionals.org
Optometrist #15...www.vtprofessionals.org
Osteopathic Physician #15...................................www.vtprofessionals.org
Pharmacist #15..www.vtprofessionals.org
Pharmacy #15..www.vtprofessionals.org
Photographer, Itinerant #15.................................www.vtprofessionals.org
Physical Therapist/Assistant #15........................www.vtprofessionals.org
Physician Assistant #14..www.healthyvermonters.info/bmp/bmp.shtml#data
Plumber #8...www.state.vt.us/labind/weblic/plicenses.htm
Podiatrist #14...www.healthyvermonters.info/bmp/bmp.shtml#data
Private Investigator #15..www.vtprofessionals.org
Psychoanalyst #15..www.vtprofessionals.org
Psychologist/Psychotherapist #15.......................www.vtprofessionals.org
Public Accountant-CPA #15..................................www.vtprofessionals.org
Race Driver/Track Personnel #15.........................www.vtprofessionals.org

Racing Promoter #15...www.vtprofessionals.org
Radiologic Technologist #15.....................................www.vtprofessionals.org
Real Estate Agent/Broker/Sales #12.......................www.vtprofessionals.org/
Real Estate Appraiser #12..www.vtprofessionals.org/
Security Guard #15...www.vtprofessionals.org
Social Worker, Clinical #15.......................................www.vtprofessionals.org
Surveyor, Land #15...www.vtprofessionals.org
Tattoo Artist #15...www.vtprofessionals.org
Vendor, Itinerant #15..www.vtprofessionals.org
Veterinarian #15..www.vtprofessionals.org
Waste Water Treatment Plant Operator #1 ....www.anr.state.vt.us/dec/ww/opcert.htm

Vermont Licensing Quick Finder

Accounting Firm #15.............................802-828-2363
Acupuncturist #15..................................802-828-2363
Alcohol & Drug Abuse Counselor #18..802-878-7776
Anesthesiologist Assistant #14..............802-657-4223
Architect #15..802-828-2363
Armed Courier #15.................................802-828-2363
Asbestos Abatement Contractor/Worker #19
....802-863-7231
Athletic Trainer #15................................802-828-2363
Attorney #2..802-828-3281
Auctioneer #15.......................................802-828-2363
Bank #5..802-828-3307
Barber #15..802-828-2363
Body Piercer #15....................................802-828-2363
Boiler & Pressure Vessel Inspector #9..802-879-2107
Boxing Manager/Promoter #15...............802-828-2363
Boxing Professional #15.........................802-828-2363
Chemical Suppression TQP Cert #8....802-828-2107
Chimney Sweep #8................................802-828-2107
Chiropractor #15.....................................802-828-2363
Cosmetologist #15..................................802-828-2363
Credit Union #5......................................802-828-3307
Crematory #15..802-828-2363
Dealer/Repairer Weighing & Measuring Devices #4
....802-244-2436
Dental Assistant #15...............................802-828-2363
Dental Hygienist #15..............................802-828-2363
Dentist #15...802-828-2363
Dietitian #15...802-828-2363
Driver Training Instructor #11.................802-828-2114
Driving Instructor/School, Commercial #11
....802-828-2114
Electrician #8...802-828-2107
Electrologist #15.....................................802-828-2363
Elevator Mechanic/Inspector #8............802-828-0743
Embalmer #15..802-828-2363
Emergency Care Attendant #7..............802-863-7310
Emergency Medical Technician #7......802-863-7310

Engineer #15..802-828-2363
Esthetician #15.......................................802-828-2363
Fire Alarm System Installer/Dealer #8.802-828-2107
Fire Sprinkler System Designer #8......802-828-2107
Fire Sprinkler System Installer #8........802-828-2107
Funeral Director #15...............................802-828-2363
Hearing Aid Dispenser #15..................802-828-2363
Horse Racing Trainers/Owners/Professional #17
....802-786-5050
Insurance Adjuster #5...........................802-828-3303
Insurance Agent/Consultant #5............802-828-3303
Insurance Appraiser #5.........................802-828-3303
Insurance Broker #5..............................802-828-3303
Investment Advisor #5...........................802-828-3420
Issuer Agent #5.....................................802-828-3420
Lead Abatement Contr'r/Worker #19....802-863-7231
Lightning Rod Installer/Dealer #8........802-828-2107
Liquor, Retail/Wholesale #10...............802-828-2339
Livestock Dealer #4..............................802-828-2421
Lottery Retailer #16...............................802-479-5686
LPG/Propane Installer #8.....................802-828-2107
Manicurist #15..802-828-2363
Marriage & Family Therapist #15..........802-828-2363
Meat Inspection Laboratory #4.............802-244-4510
Medical Doctor/Surgeon #14................802-657-4223
Mental Health Counselor, Clinical #15..802-828-2363
Midwife, Licensed #15...........................802-828-2363
Milk & Cream Tester #4........................802-244-4510
Natural Gas System Installer #8..........802-828-2107
Naturopathic Physician #15..................802-828-2363
Notary Public #15..................................802-828-2363
Nurse/Nurse Practitioner/LNA #15.......802-828-2363
Nursing Home Administrator #15..........802-828-2363
Occupational Therapist #15..................802-828-2363
Oil Burning Equipment Installer #8.......802-828-2107
Optician #15...802-828-2363
Optometrist #15......................................802-828-2363
Osteopathic Physician #15....................802-828-2363

Pari-Mutuel Seller #17.........................802-786-5050
Pesticide Applicator #4.........................802-244-2431
Pharmacist #15......................................802-828-2363
Pharmacy #15..802-828-2363
Photographer, Itinerant #15.................802-828-2363
Physical Therapist/Assistant #15.........802-828-2363
Physician Assistant #14.......................802-657-4223
Plumber #8..802-828-2107
Podiatrist #14..802-657-4223
Polygraph Examiner #3.........................802-244-8781
Private Investigator #15........................802-828-2363
Psychoanalyst #15................................802-828-2363
Psychologist/Psychotherapist #15.......802-828-2363
Public Accountant-CPA #15..................802-828-2363
Public Adjuster #5.................................802-828-3303
Race Driver/Track Personnel #15........802-828-2363
Racing Promoter #15.............................802-828-2363
Radiologic Technologist #15..................802-828-2363
Real Estate Agent/Broker/Sales #12...802-828-3228
Real Estate Appraiser #12....................802-828-3228
School Guidance Counselor #6............802-828-2445
School Librarian/Media Specialist #6..802-828-2445
School Principal/Superintendent #6.....802-828-2445
Securities Broker/Dealer #5.................802-828-3420
Securities Sales Rep. #5......................802-828-3420
Security Guard #15................................802-828-2363
Social Worker, Clinical #15..................802-828-2363
Surveyor, Land #15...............................802-828-2363
Tattoo Artist #15....................................802-828-2363
Teacher #6..802-828-2445
Vehicle Dealer #11...............................802-828-2038
Vendor, Itinerant #15............................802-828-2363
Veterinarian #15....................................802-828-2363
Vocational Education Teacher #6........802-828-2445
Waste Water Treatment Plant Operator #1
....802-241-3822

Vermont Licensing Agency Information

1 Agency of Natural Resources, Department of Environmental Conservation, 103 S Main St, The Sewing Bldg, Waterbury, VT 05671-0405; 802-241-3822, Fax: 802-241-2596.
www.anr.state.vt.us
Email: carole.fowler@anr.state.vt.us

2 Board of Bar Examiners, 109 State St, Montpelier, VT 05609-0702; 802-828-3281, Fax: 802-828-3457.
www.vermontjudiciary.org
Email: licensing@mail.crt.state.vt.us
Note: They do not sell mailing lists.

3 Commission of Public Safety, 103 S Main St, Waterbury State Complex, Waterbury, VT 05671-2101; 802-244-8781, Fax: 802-241-5551.
www.dps.state.vt.us

4 Department of Agriculture, Consumer Assurance, 103 S Main St, Waterbury, VT 05671; 802-244-4510, Fax: 802-241-3008.
www.state.vt.us/agric/pidconsumer.htm

5 Department of Banking, Securities, Insurance & Health Care Admin., 89 Main St, City Ctr, Drawer 20, Montpelier, VT 05620-3101; 802-828-3301, Fax: 802-828-3306.
www.bishca.state.vt.us

6 Department of Education, Licening Professional Standards, 120 State St, Montpelier, VT 05620-2501; 802-828-2445, Fax: 802-828-5107.
www.state.vt.us/educ/new/html/maincert.html
Email: licensing@doe.state.vt.us

7 Department of Health, Emergency Medical Services Division, 108 Cherry St, (PO Box 70, 05402-0070), Burlington, VT 05402; 802-863-7310, Fax: 802-863-7577.
www.healthyvermonters.info/hp/ems/emshome.shtml

8 Department of Labor & Industry, Fire Prevention Division, Drawer 20, National Life Bldg, Montpelier, VT 05620-3401; 802-828-2106, Fax: 802-828-2195.
www.state.vt.us/labind/fpindex.htm
Email: fireinfo@labind.state.vt.us

9 Department of Labor & Industry, Fire Prevention Division - Boiler Inspector, 372 Hurricane Ln #102, Williston, VT 05495-2080; 802-879-2304, Fax: 802-879-2312.
www.state.vt.us/labind/Fire/Boiler.htm
Email: malcolm.wheel@labind.state.vt.us

10 Department of Liquor Control, PO Drawer 20, (13 Green Mountain Dr), Montpelier, VT 05620-4501; 802-828-2345, Fax: 802-828-2803.
www.state.vt.us/dlc/

11 Department of Motor Vehicles, 120 State St, Montpelier, VT 05603; 802-828-2114, Fax: 802-828-2092.
www.dmv.state.vt.us

12 Real Estate Commission, 81 Riverside St., Heritage Bldg, Montpelier, VT 05609-1106; 802-828-3228, Fax: 802-828-2368.
www.sec.state.vt.us
Email: real_estate@sec.state.vt.us
Search Database at www.vtprofessionals.org

14 Board of Medical Practice, Department of Health, PO Box 70 (108 Cherry St), Burlington, VT 05402-0070; 802-657-4220 (800-745-7371 within Vermont), Fax: 802-657-4227.
www.healthyvermonters.info/bmp/bmp.shtml
Email: medicalboard@vdh.state.vt.us
Search Database at
www.healthyvermonters.info/bmp/bmp.shtml
Note: Written verifications are available for $20

each; it is suggested to search files (dbf, delimited or excel) at the website, although seraching is also available from a private company at www.docboard.org/vt/df/vtsearch.htm.

15 Secretary of State, Office of Professional Regulation, 26 Terrace St, Drawer 09, Montpelier, VT 05609-1106; 802-828-2363, Fax: 802-828-2496.
www.sec.state.vt.us
Email: docketclerk@sec.state.vt.us
Search Database at www.vtprofessionals.org

16 Lottery Commission, PO Box 420, Rt. 14, South Barre, VT 05670-0429; 802-479-5686 or 1-800-322-8800; Fax: 802-479-4294.
www.vtlottery.com

17 Racing Commission, 88 Merchants Row #500, Rutland, VT 05701-3449; 802-786-5050, Fax: 802-786-5051.

18 Alcohol & Drug Abuse Certification Board, PO Box 135, St. Albans, VT 05478-0135; 802-878-7776, Fax: 802-879-6211.
Email: vadacb@together.net

19 Department of Health, Environmental Health, PO Box 70, (108 Cherry St), Burlington, VT 05402; 802-863-7200, Fax: 802-863-7754.
www.state.vt.us/health

Vermont Federal Courts

The following list indicates the district and division name for each county in the state. If the bankruptcy court location is different from the district court, then the location of the bankruptcy court appears in parentheses.

County/Court Cross Reference

Addison	Rutland	Lamoille	Burlington (Rutland)
Bennington	Rutland	Orange	Rutland
Caledonia	Burlington (Rutland)	Orleans	Burlington (Rutland)
Chittenden	Burlington (Rutland)	Rutland	Rutland
Essex	Burlington (Rutland)	Washington	Burlington (Rutland)
Franklin	Burlington (Rutland)	Windham	Rutland
Grand Isle	Burlington (Rutland)	Windsor	Rutland

Standards for Federal Courts: The search fee is $20.00 per item (one party name or case number). Certification fee is $7.00 per document. Copy fee is $.50 per page. All fees standard unless noted in profile. Mail Search: always enclose a stamped self addressed envelope unless otherwise noted. Most courts accept fax requests or will suggest a copying/search vendor. Before releasing records, all courts require prepayment unless noted in profile.

Open records are located at the court unless otherwise noted. District courts index by defendant and plaintiff as well as by case number. Bankruptcy courts usually index by debtor and case number. While most courts now have their indexes on computer, many still maintain index card files as well.

The universal PACER sign-up number is 800-676-6856. Find PACER and the Party/Case Index on the Web at http://pacer.psc.uscourts.gov. PACER dial-up access is $.60 per minute. Also, courts offering internet access via RACER, PACER, Web-PACER or the new CM-ECF charge $.07 per page fee unless noted as free.

US District Court

District of Vermont

Burlington Division Clerk's Office, PO Box 945, Burlington, VT 05402-0945 (courier address: Room 506, 11 Elmwood Ave, Burlington, VT 05401), 802-951-6301. www.vtd.uscourts.gov

Counties: Caledonia, Chittenden, Essex, Franklin, Grand Isle, Lamoille, Orleans, Washington. However, cases from all counties in the state are assigned randomly to either Burlington or Brattleboro. Brattleboro is a hearing location only, not listed here.

Indexing & Storage: New cases available in the index 1 working day after filing date. New cases filed January 1, 1991 to present are on the automated in house system. Pre-1991 cases are indexed on microfiche or microfilm.

Fee & Payment: Payment may be made by money order, cashier check, personal check. Payee: Clerk, U.S. District Court.

Phone Search: Only general information which can be accessed by computer will be released over the phone.

In Person Search: Fee charged if court conducts your in person search for you.

PACER: Access/Login to PACER at https://pacer.login.uscourts.gov/cgi-bin/login.pl?court_id=r_vtdc. Case records go back to January 1991. Records never purged. New records are online after 1 day.

Opinions Online: Court opinions are online at http://nysd.uscourts.gov/cwrulings.fwx?mode=rptform&cascode=D02VTXC

Other Online Access: Search monthly court calendar at www.vtd.uscourts.gov/Calendars.htm. RACER has been replaces by PACER.

Rutland Division PO Box 607, Rutland, VT 05702-0607 (courier: 151 West St, Rutland, VT 05701), 802-773-0245. www.vtd.uscourts.gov

Counties: Addison, Bennington, Orange, Rutland, Windsor, Windham. However, cases from all counties in the state are randomly assigned to either Burlington or Brattleboro. Rutland is a hearing location only, not listed here.

Indexing & Storage: New cases available in the index 1 day after filing date. New cases filed January 1, 1991 to present are on the automated in house system. Pre-1991 cases are indexed on microfiche or microfilm. There is no judge sitting in Rutland itself, but one is in Brattleboro.

Fee & Payment: Payment may be made by money order, cashier check, personal check. Payee: Clerk, U.S. District Court.

Phone Search: Only docket information available.

In Person Search: Fee charged if court conducts your in person search for you.

PACER: Access/Login to PACER at https://pacer.login.uscourts.gov/cgi-bin/login.pl?court_id=r_vtdc. Case records go back to January 1991. Records never purged. New records are online after 1 day.

Opinions Online: Court opinions are online at http://nysd.uscourts.gov/cwrulings.fwx?mode=rptform&cascode=D02VTXC

Other Online Access: Search monthly court calendar at www.vtd.uscourts.gov/Calendars.htm. RACER has been replaces by PACER.

U.S. Bankruptcy Court

District of Vermont

Rutland Division PO Box 6648, Rutland, VT 05702-6648 (courier address: 67 Merchants Row, Rutland, VT 05701), 802-776-2000, Fax: 802-776-2020. www.vtb.uscourts.gov

Counties: All counties in Vermont.

Indexing & Storage: Cases indexed by debtor and creditors as well as by case number. New cases available in the index immediately after filing date.

Fee & Payment: Payment may be made by money order, cashier check, personal check, Visa or Mastercard. Payee: U.S. Bankruptcy Court. Copy fees apply to faxed dockets.

Phone Search: Docket information is available by phone. Automated voice case information service (VCIS) available.; 800-260-9956 or 802-776-2007.

Mail Search: A SASE not required.

In Person Search: Fee charged if court conducts your in person search for you.

PACER: PACER is available online at http://pacer.vtb.uscourts.gov. Document images available. Case records go back to 1994 (limited information prior). Records never purged. New civil records are online after 1 day.

Electronic Filing: Electronic filing information online at https://ecf.vtb.uscourts.gov

Vermont County Courts

Court	Jurisdiction	No. of Courts	How Organized
Superior Courts*	General	11	14 Counties
District Courts*	Limited	11	3 Circuits
Combined Courts*		3	
Probate Courts*	Probate	18	
Family Courts	Special	14	14 Counties
Environmental Court	Special	1	

* Profiled in this Sourcebook.

Court	CIVIL								
	Tort	Contract	Real Estate	Min. Claim	Max. Claim	Small Claims	Estate	Eviction	Domestic Relations
Superior Courts*	X	X	X	$0	No Max	$3500		X	
District Courts*									
Probate Courts*							X		
Family Courts									X

Court	CRIMINAL				
	Felony	Misdemeanor	DWI/DUI	Preliminary Hearing	Juvenile
Superior Courts*					
District Courts*	X	X	X	X	
Family Courts					X

ADMINISTRATION

Administrative Office of Courts, Court Administrator, 109 State St, Montpelier, VT, 05609-0701; 802-828-3278, Fax: 802-828-3457. www.vermontjudiciary.org

COURT STRUCTURE

As of September, 1996, all small claims came under the jurisdiction of Superior Court, the court of general jurisdiction. All counties have a diversion program in which first offenders go through a process that includes a letter of apology, community service, etc. and, after 2 years, the record is expunged. These records are never released.

The Vermont Judicial Bureau has jurisdiction over Traffic, Municipal Ordinance, and Fish and Game, Minors in Possession, and hazing.

ONLINE ACCESS

Court calendars for all Superior, District, and Family courts are shown at the web site above. Supreme Court opinions are available also from the web site. In addition, Supreme Court opinions are maintained by the Vermont Department of Libraries at http://dol.state.vt.us. There is no statewide system of local court records.

ADDITIONAL INFORMATION

There are statewide search, certification and copy fees, as follows: Search fee - $10.00 per name; Certification Fee - $5.00 per document plus copy fee; Copy Fee - $.25 per page with a $1.00 minimum.

Addison County

Superior Court 7 Mahady Ct, Middlebury, VT 05753; 802-388-7741. Hours: 8:30AM-4:30PM (EST). *Civil, Eviction, Small Claims.*
Civil Records: Access: Mail, in person. Only the court performs in person searches; visitors may not. No search fee. Required to search: name, years to search. Civil cases indexed by defendant, plaintiff. Civil records on index cards and recording books, computerized since 1995.
General Information: No sealed or unserved records released. Copy fee: $.25 per page. Cert fee: $5.00. Payee: Addison Superior Court. Personal checks

accepted. Prepayment required. Mail turnaround time 2-3 days.

District Court 7 Mahady Ct, Middlebury, VT 05753; 802-388-4237. Hours: 8AM-4:30PM (EST). *Felony, Misdemeanor.*
Criminal Records: Access: Mail, in person. Only the court performs in person searches; visitors may not. Search fee: $10.00 per name. Required to search: name, years to search, DOB. Criminal records on computer since mid 1991; prior on dockets and index cards.
General Information: No adoptions, juvenile, sealed, or expunged records released. Copy fee: $.25 per page, $1.00 minimum. Cert fee: $5.00 per

document. Payee: Addison District Court. Personal checks accepted. Prepayment required. Mail turnaround time up to 1 week.

Probate Court 7 Mahady Court, Middlebury, VT 05753; 802-388-2612. Hours: 8AM-4:30PM (EST). *Probate.*

Bennington County

Superior Court 207 South St, PO Box 4157, Bennington, VT 05201; 802-447-2700; Criminal phone: 802-447-2727; Probate phone: 802-447-2705; Fax: 802-447-2703. Hours: 8AM-4:30PM (EST). *Civil, Eviction, Small Claims.*
Civil Records: Access: Phone, mail, in person. Both

court and visitors may perform in person searches. No search fee. Required to search: name, years to search. Civil cases indexed by defendant, plaintiff. Civil records on computer from 1989, index from 1968.

General Information: No deposition, adoption, juvenile, sealed or expunged records released. Copy fee: $.25 per page. Cert fee: $5.00. Payee: Bennington County. Personal checks accepted. Prepayment required. Mail turnaround time 2-3 days.

District Court 200 Veterans Memorial Dr #13, Bennington, VT 05201; 802-447-2727; Fax: 802-447-2750. Hours: 7:45AM-4:30PM (EST). *Felony, Misdemeanor.*

Criminal Records: Access: Mail, in person. Both court and visitors may perform in person searches. Search fee: $10.00 per name. Required to search: name, years to search, DOB. Criminal records on index cards, docket books, and computer.

General Information: No sealed, diversion case records released. Will fax results to toll free line. Copy fee: $.25 per page. $1.00 minimum. Cert fee: $5.00. Payee: Vermont District Court. Personal checks accepted. Prepayment required. Mail requests: SASE requested. Turnaround time varies.

Probate Court - Bennington District 207 South St, PO Box 65, Bennington, VT 05201; 802-447-2705; Fax: 802-447-2703 (Attn: Probate Court). Hours: 8:30 am-Noon, 1:00-4:30pm (EST). *Probate.*

Probate Court - Manchester District PO Box 446, Manchester, VT 05254; 802-362-1410. Hours: 8AM-Noon, 1-4:20PM (EST). *Probate.*

Caledonia County

Superior Court 1126 Main St #1, St Johnsbury, VT 05819; 802-748-6600; Fax: 802-748-6603. Hours: 8AM-4:30PM (EST). *Civil, Eviction, Small Claims.*

Civil Records: Access: Phone, mail, in person. Only the court performs in person searches; visitors may not. No search fee. Required to search: name, years to search. Civil cases indexed by defendant, plaintiff. Civil records on computer from 1992, in archives before 1985, index from 1985, all other records on index cards.

General Information: No adoption, juvenile, sealed or expunged records released. Will fax results $2.00 per page. Copy fee: Superior Court $1.00 minimum; Family Court $.25 per page, $1.00 minimum. Cert fee: $5.00 plus $.25 per page. Payee: Caledonia Superior Court. Personal checks accepted. Prepayment required. Mail requests: SASE requested. Turnaround time 1 week.

District Court 1126 Main St #1, St Johnsbury, VT 05819; 802-748-6600; Fax: 802-748-6603. Hours: 8AM-4:30PM (EST). *Felony, Misdemeanor.*

Criminal Records: Access: Fax, mail, in person. Both court and visitors may perform in person searches. Search fee: $10.00 per name. Required to search: name, years to search; also helpful: DOB. Criminal records on computer since 1991, prior on index cards to 1950.

General Information: Public Access terminal is available. No adoptions, juvenile, sealed or expunged records released. Will fax results $2.00 per page. Copy fee: $.25 per page. $1.00 minimum. Cert fee: $5.00. Payee: Caledonia District Court. Personal checks accepted. Prepayment required. Mail requests: SASE not required. Mail turnaround time less than 1 week.

Probate Court 1126 Main St, PO Box 406, St Johnsbury, VT 05819; 802-748-6605; Fax: 802-748-6603. Hours: 8AM-4:30PM (EST). *Probate.*

Chittenden County

Superior Court 175 Main St (PO Box 187), Burlington, VT 05402; 802-863-3467. Hours: 8AM-4:30PM (EST). *Civil, Eviction, Small Claims.* www.chittendensuperiorcourt.com

Civil Records: Access: Phone, mail, in person, online. Only the court performs in person searches; visitors may not. No search fee. Required to search: name, years to search. Civil cases indexed by defendant, plaintiff. Civil records on computer back to 1983, small claims since 1996, prior records on books from 1800s. The web page offers online access to court case information on cases filed in the last five years.

General Information: No adoption, juvenile, sealed or expunged records released. Copy fee: $.25 per page. $1.00 minimum. Cert fee: $5.00. Payee: Chittenden County Superior Court. Personal checks accepted. Prepayment required. Mail turnaround time 1 week.

District Court 32 Cherry St #300, Burlington, VT 05401; 802-651-1800. Hours: 8AM-4:30PM (EST). *Felony, Misdemeanor.*

Criminal Records: Access: Mail, in person. Both court and visitors may perform in person searches. Search fee: $10.00 per name. Required to search: name, years to search; also helpful: DOB. Criminal records on new computer from 6/90, on old computer from 6/85 to 06/90, books by alpha name from 12/69 to 1980, on index cards from 1970.

General Information: Public Access terminal is available. No adoption, juvenile, sealed or expunged records released. Copy fee: $.25 per page. Cert fee: $5.00. Payee: Vermont District Court. Personal checks accepted. Prepayment required. Mail turnaround time 1-2 days.

Probate Court PO Box 511, Burlington, VT 05402; 802-651-1518. Hours: 8AM-4:30PM (EST). *Probate.*

Essex County

District & Superior Court Box 75, Guildhall, VT 05905; 802-676-3910; Fax: 802-676-3463. Hours: 8AM-4:30PM (EST). *Felony, Misdemeanor, Civil, Eviction, Small Claims.* www.state.vt.us/courts

Civil Records: Access: Phone, fax, mail, in person. Only the court performs in person searches; visitors may not. No search fee. Required to search: name, years to search. Civil cases indexed by defendant, plaintiff. Civil records indexed from 1974; on computer from 5/94. Calendar information on website. Will not accept phone requests for more than 2 names.

Criminal Records: Access: Mail, in person. Only the court performs in person searches; visitors may not. Search fee: $10.00 per name. Required to search: name, years to search, DOB. Criminal records indexed from 1974; on computer from 5/94. Calendar information on website. Will not accept phone requests for more than 2 names.

General Information: No adoptions, juvenile, sealed or expunged records released. Will fax results $1.00 per page. Copy fee: $.25 per page. $1.00 minimum. Cert fee: $5.00 plus $.25 per page. Payee: Depends on court (Superior or District). Only cashiers checks and money orders accepted. Prepayment required. Mail requests: SASE required. Mail turnaround time 1 week.

Probate Court PO Box 426, Island Pond, VT 05846; 802-723-4770; Fax: 802-723-4770. Hours: 8:30AM-Noon, 1-3:30PM (EST). *Probate.*

Franklin County

Superior Court PO Box 808, Church St, St Albans, VT 05478; 802-524-3863; Fax: 802-524-7996. Hours: 8AM-4:30PM (EST). *Civil, Eviction, Small Claims.*

Civil Records: Access: Mail, in person. Only the court performs in person searches; visitors may not. No search fee. Required to search: name, years to search. Civil cases indexed by defendant, plaintiff. Civil records on computer since 1996; prior on index cards from 1840.

General Information: No adoption, juvenile, sealed or expunged records released. Copy fee: $.25 per page. $1.00 minimum. Cert fee: $5.00. Payee: Franklin Superior Court. Personal checks accepted. Prepayment required. Mail requests: SASE required. Mail turnaround time 1 week.

District Court 36 Lake St, St Albans, VT 05478; 802-524-7997; Fax: 802-524-7946. Hours: 8AM-4:30PM (EST). *Felony, Misdemeanor.*

Criminal Records: Access: Mail, in person. Both court (time permitting) and visitors may perform in person searches. Search fee: $10.00 per name. Required to search: name, years to search; also helpful: DOB, SSN. Criminal records on computer since 1987.

General Information: Public Access terminal is available. No adoption, juvenile, sealed or expunged records released. Fee to fax results is $1.00 per document and $.25 per page. Copy fee: $.25 per page. Cert fee: $5.00. Payee: Vermont District Court. Personal checks accepted. Prepayment required. Mail requests: SASE required. Mail turnaround time 7-10 days.

Franklin Probate Court 17 Church St, St Albans, VT 05478; 802-524-4112. Hours: 8AM-Noon, 1-4:30PM (EST). *Probate.*

Grand Isle County

District & Superior Court PO Box 7, North Hero, VT 05474; 802-372-8350; Fax: 802-372-3221. Hours: 8AM-4:30PM (EST). *Felony, Misdemeanor, Civil, Eviction, Small Claims.*

Civil Records: Access: Phone, fax, mail, in person. Both court and visitors may perform in person searches. No search fee. Required to search: name, years to search. Civil cases indexed by defendant, plaintiff. Civil records on computer from 1990, on index 1940, in-house from 1970.

Criminal Records: Access: Phone, fax, mail, in person. Both court and visitors may perform in person searches. Search fee: $10.00 per name. Required to search: name, years to search; also helpful: DOB, SSN. Criminal records on computer from 1990, on index from 1940, in-house from 1979.

General Information: No adoption, juvenile, sealed or expunged records released. Will not fax results. Copy fee: $.25 per page. $1.00 minimum. Cert fee: $5.25. Payee: Grand Isle Superior or District Court. Personal checks accepted. Prepayment required. Mail turnaround time 1-2 days.

Probate Court PO Box 7, North Hero, VT 05474; 802-372-8350; Fax: 802-372-3221. Hours: 8AM-4:30PM (EST). *Probate.*

Lamoille County

Superior Court Box 490, Hyde Park, VT 05655; 802-888-2207. Hours: 8AM-12:00-12:30-4:30PM (EST). *Civil, Eviction, Small Claims.*

Civil Records: Access: Mail, in person. Only the court performs in person searches; visitors may not. No search fee. Required to search: name, years to search. Civil cases indexed by defendant, plaintiff.

Civil records on computer from 1989, index from 1970s.

General Information: No adoption, juvenile, sealed or expunged records released. Will not fax results. Copy fee: $.25 per page. Cert fee: $5.50. Payee: Lamoille Superior Court. Personal checks accepted. Prepayment required. Mail requests: SASE required. Mail turnaround time 1 week.

District Court PO Box 489, Hyde Park, VT 05655-0489; 802-888-3887; Civil phone: 802-888-2207; Probate phone: 802-888-3306; Fax: 802-888-2591. Hours: 8AM-4:30PM (EST). *Felony, Misdemeanor.*

Criminal Records: Access: Mail, in person. Only the court performs in person searches; visitors may not. Search fee: $10.00 per name. Required to search: name, DOB; also helpful: years to search. Criminal records on computer since 06/88; prior on index cards.

General Information: No adoption, juvenile, sealed or expunged records released. Will fax results to toll free or local lines only. Copy fee: $.25 per page. $1.00 minimum. Cert fee: $5.00. Payee: Vermont District Court. Personal checks accepted. Prepayment required. Mail requests: SASE required. Mail turnaround time 3 days if record on-site, 1 week if off-site.

Probate Court PO Box 102, Hyde Park, VT 05655-0102; 802-888-3306; Fax: 802-888-0669. Hours: 8AM-noon, 12:30-4:30PM (EST). *Probate.*

Orange County

District & Superior Court 5 Court St, Chelsea, VT 05038-9746; 802-685-4610; Fax: 802-685-3246. Hours: 8AM-4:30PM (EST). *Felony, Misdemeanor, Civil, Eviction, Small Claims.*

Civil Records: Access: Fax, mail, in person. Only the court performs in person searches; visitors may not. No search fee. Required to search: name, years to search; also helpful: address. Civil cases indexed by defendant, plaintiff. Civil records on computer from 7/94, on index from 1967.

Criminal Records: Access: Phone, fax, mail, in person. Only the court performs in person searches; visitors may not. Search fee: $10.00 per name. Required to search: name, years to search, DOB; also helpful: address. Criminal records on computer from 1990, on index from 1967.

General Information: No adoption, juvenile, sealed or expunged records released. Fee to fax results is $1.00 per page. Copy fee: $.25 per page. $1.00 minimum. Cert fee: $5.00. Payee: District Court. Personal checks accepted. Prepayment required. Mail turnaround time 1 week.

Probate Court 5 Court St, Chelsea, VT 05038-9746; 802-685-4610; Fax: 802-685-3246. Hours: 8AM-Noon, 1-4:30PM (EST). *Probate.*

Note: The Bradford and Randolph Districts were consolidated into this one probate court as of June 1, 1994.

Orleans County

Superior Court 247 Main St #1, Newport, VT 05855-1203; 802-334-3344; Fax: 802-334-3385. Hours: 8AM-4:30PM (EST). *Civil, Eviction, Small Claims.*

Civil Records: Access: Phone, fax, mail, in person. Only the court performs in person searches; visitors may not. No search fee. Required to search: name; also helpful: years to search. Civil cases indexed by defendant, plaintiff. Civil records on computer since 1994; prior records on index from 1800s.

General Information: No juvenile records released. Copy fee: $.25 per page. $1.00 minimum. Cert fee: $5.00. Payee: Orleans Superior Court. Personal

checks accepted. Prepayment required. Mail requests: SASE required. Mail turnaround time 1 week.

District Court 217 Main St, #4, Newport, VT 05855; 802-334-3325. Hours: 8AM-4:30PM (EST). *Felony, Misdemeanor.*

Criminal Records: Access: Mail. Only the court performs in person searches; visitors may not. Search fee: $10.00 per name. Required to search: name, years to search, DOB. Criminal records on computer since 01/91; prior on index cards back to 1971. History checks of three or more names must be in writing.

General Information: No adoption, juvenile, sealed or expunged records released. Will fax results to an "800" number. Above fees apply. Copy fee: $.25 per page. $1.00 minimum; Add $4.00 if copies retrieved from public records. Cert fee: $5.00. Payee: District Court of Vermont. Personal checks accepted. Prepayment required. Mail requests: SASE required. Mail turnaround time 1 week.

Probate Court 247 Main St, Newport, VT 05855; 802-334-3366; Fax: 802-334-3385. Hours: 8AM-Noon, 1-4:30PM (EST). *Probate.*

Rutland County

Superior Court 83 Center St, Rutland, VT 05701; 802-775-4394. Hours: 8AM-4:30PM (EST). *Civil, Eviction, Small Claims.*

Civil Records: Access: Mail, in person. Only the court performs in person searches; visitors may not. No search fee. Required to search: name, years to search. Civil cases indexed by defendant, plaintiff. Civil records on computer from 1987, on index from late 1700s.

General Information: No adoption, juvenile, sealed or expunged records released. Will fax results to local or toll free line. Copy fee: $.25 per page. $1.00 minimum. Cert fee: $5.00. Payee: Rutland Superior Court. Personal checks accepted. Prepayment required. Mail requests: SASE required. Mail turnaround time 1 week.

District Court 92 State St, Rutland, VT 05701-2886; 802-786-5880. Hours: 8AM-4:30PM (EST). *Felony, Misdemeanor.*

Criminal Records: Access: Phone, mail, in person. Both court and visitors may perform in person searches. Search fee: $10.00 per name. Required to search: name, years to search, DOB; also helpful: SSN. Criminal records on computer the past 10 years.

General Information: Public Access terminal is available. No sealed, expunged records released. Copy fee: $.25 per page. $1.00 minimum. Cert fee: $5.00. Payee: District Court of Vermont. Personal checks accepted. Prepayment required. Mail requests: SASE required. Mail turnaround time 1 week.

Probate Court - Fair Haven District 3 North Park Place, Fair Haven, VT 05743; 802-265-3380; Fax: 802-265-3380. Hours: 8AM-4PM (EST). *Probate.*

Probate Court - Rutland District 83 Center St, Rutland, VT 05701; 802-775-0114; Fax: 802-775-1671. Hours: 8AM-4:30PM (EST). *Probate.*

Washington County

Superior Court 65 State St, Montpelier, VT 05602-3594; 802-828-2091. Hours: 8AM-4:30PM (EST). *Civil, Eviction, Small Claims #828-5551.*

Civil Records: Access: Phone, mail, in person. Only the court performs in person searches; visitors may not. No search fee. Required to search: name, years to search; also helpful: address. Civil cases indexed by defendant, plaintiff. Civil records on computer from 1987, archives from 1900s.

General Information: No adoption, juvenile or expunged records released. Will fax results for $1.00

per page. Copy fee: $.25 per page. $1.00 minimum. Cert fee: $5.00. Payee: Washington County Superior Court. Personal checks accepted. Prepayment required. Mail requests: SASE requested. Turnaround time 1-2 days.

District Court 255 N Main, Barre, VT 05641; 802-479-4252. Hours: 8AM-4:30PM (EST). *Felony, Misdemeanor.*

Criminal Records: Access: Mail, in person. Only court may perform in person searches. Search fee: $10.00 per name. Required to search: name, years to search; also helpful: DOB. Criminal records on computer since 1989; prior records in index form 1970s.

General Information: No adoption, juvenile, sealed or expunged records released. Copy fee: $.25 per page. $1.00 minimum. Cert fee: $5.00. Payee: Washington District Court. Personal checks accepted. Prepayment required. Mail requests: SASE requested. Turnaround time 3-5 days.

Probate Court 10 Elm St #2, Montpelier, VT 05602; 802-828-3405. Hours: 8AM-Noon, 1-4:30PM M-Th; 8AM-Noon, 1-4PM F (EST). *Probate.*

Windham County

Superior Court Box 207, Newfane, VT 05345; 802-365-7979; Fax: 802-365-4360. Hours: 9AM-4PM (EST). *Civil, Eviction, Small Claims.*

Civil Records: Access: Phone, fax, mail, in person. Both court and visitors may perform in person searches. No search fee. Required to search: name, years to search. Civil cases indexed by defendant, plaintiff. Civil records on computer from 1994, on index from 1919. Fax available only in emergency.

General Information: No adoption, juvenile, sealed or expunged records released. No fee to fax results. Copy fee: $.25 per page. $1.00 minimum. Cert fee: $5.00. Payee: Windham Superior Court. Personal checks accepted. Prepayment required. Mail requests: SASE required. Mail turnaround time 1-2 days.

District Court 30 Putney Rd #2, Brattleboro, VT 05301; 802-257-2800; Fax: 802-257-2853. Hours: 8AM-4:30PM (EST). *Felony, Misdemeanor, Civil Suspension.*

www.vermontjudiciary.org/courts/district/index.htm#Windham

Criminal Records: Access: Mail, in person. Both court and visitors may perform in person searches. Search fee: $10.00 per name. Required to search: name, years to search; also helpful: address, DOB, SSN. Criminal record go back to 1969s; computer since 1990; prior on index cards and docket books.

General Information: Public Access terminal is available. No adoption, juvenile, sealed or expunged records released. Fee to fax results is $.25 per page. Copy fee: $.25 per page($1.00 Min). Cert fee: $5.00. Payee: Vermont District Court. Personal checks accepted. Prepayment required. Mail requests: SASE requested. Turnaround time 5-7 days.

Probate Court - Marlboro District PO Box 523, Brattleboro, VT 05302; 802-257-2898. Hours: 8AM-Noon, 1-4:30PM (EST). *Probate.*

Probate Court - Westminster District PO Box 47, 39 Square, Bellows Falls, VT 05101-0047; 802-463-3019; Fax: 802-463-0144. Hours: 8AM-Noon,1-4:30PM (EST). *Probate.*

Windsor County

Superior Court Box 458, Woodstock, VT 05091; 802-457-2121; Fax: 802-457-3446. Hours: 8AM-4:30PM (EST). *Civil, Eviction, Small Claims.*

Civil Records: Access: Phone, mail, in person. Only the court performs in person searches; visitors may not. Search fee: Up to $10.00, depending on extent fo search. Required to search: name, years to search. Civil cases indexed by defendant, plaintiff. Civil records available since on computer 1990.

General Information: No sealed or expunged records released. Copy fee: $.25 per page. $1.00 minimum. Cert fee: $5.00. Payee: Windsor County Clerk or Windsor Superior Court. Personal checks accepted. Prepayment required. Mail requests: SASE required. Mail turnaround time 1-2 weeks.

District Court Windsor Circuit Unit 1, 82 Railroad Row, White River Junction, VT 05001-1962; 802-295-8865; Fax: 802-295-8897. Hours: 8AM-4:30PM (EST). *Felony, Misdemeanor.*

Criminal Records: Access: Mail, in person. Only the court performs in person searches; visitors may not. Search fee: $10.00 per name. Required to search: name, years to search; also helpful: DOB, SSN. Criminal records on computer from 1989, index from 1968. They have request forms available.

General Information: No adoption, juvenile, sealed or expunged records released. Copy fee: $.25 per page. $1.00 minimum. Cert fee: $5.00. Payee: Vermont District Court. Personal checks accepted. Prepayment required. Mail requests: SASE requested. Turnaround time 7 days.

Probate Court - Hartford District PO Box 275, Woodstock, VT 05091; 802-457-1503; Fax: 802-457-3446. Hours: 8AM-Noon, 1-4:30PM (EST). *Probate.*

Probate Court - Windsor District PO Box 402, Rt 106, Cota Fuel Bldg, North Springfield, VT 05150; 802-886-2284. Hours: 8AM-Noon, 1-4:30PM (EST). Probate.

Vermont Recording Offices

ORGANIZATION: 14 counties and 246 towns/cities, 246 recording offices. The recording officer is Town/City Clerk. There is no county administration in Vermont. Many towns are so small that their mailing addresses are in different towns. Four towns/cities have the same name as counties - Barre, Newport, Rutland, and St. Albans. The entire state is in the Eastern Time Zone (EST).

Many towns are now charging a $2.00 per hour vault time fee for in-person searchers.

REAL ESTATE RECORDS: Most towns/cities will not perform real estate searches. Copy fees and certification fees vary. Certified copies are generally $5.00 per page total. Deed copies usually cost $2.00 flat.

UCC RECORDS: This was a dual filing state until 12/31/94. From 01/01/95, only consumer goods and real estate related collateral were filed with Town/City Clerks. Starting 07/01/2001, only real estate collateral is filed at the local level. Most recording offices will perform UCC searches. Use search request form UCC-11. Search fees are usually $10.00 per name, more if non-standard form used, and copy fees vary.

TAX LIEN RECORDS: All federal and state tax liens on personal property and on real property are filed with the Town/City Clerk in the lien/attachment book and indexed in real estate records. Most towns/cities will not perform tax lien searches.

OTHER LIENS: Mechanics, local tax, judgment, foreclosure.

ONLINE ACCESS: While there is virtually no online access to county recorded documents, state recorded UCC data is available online from the Vermont Secretary of State.

Addison Town

Town Clerk, 7099 VT Rte 22A, Addison, VT 05491. **Phone**-802-759-2020; fax-802-759-2233; hours 8:30AM-Noon, 1PM-4:30PM
Will not search records. Copy fee is $1.00 per page. Payee: Addison Town Clerk.

Albany Town

Town Clerk, PO Box 284, Albany, VT 05820-0284. **Phone**-802-755-6100; hours 9AM-4PM T,Th; 9AM-7PM W. UCC record search per debtor- $10.00. UCC request on non-standard form- $15.00. Will not search real estate or tax lien records. Copy fee- $1.00 per page. Payee: Albany Town Clerk.

Alburg Town

Town Clerk, PO Box 346, Alburg, VT 05440-0346. **Phone**-802-796-3468; fax-802-796-3939; hours 9:00AM-Noon; 1:00-5:00PM
UCC record search per debtor- $10.00. UCC request on non-standard form- $15.00. Will not search real estate or tax lien records. RE record copy- $1.00 per deed. Cert fee: $2.00 per doc. Payee: Town of Alburg. **Other phones:** Assessor-802-796-4061; Treasurer-802-796-3468; Elections-802-796-3468.

Andover Town

Town Clerk, 953 Weston-Andover Rd., Andover, VT 05143. **Phone**-802-875-2765; fax-802-875-6647; hours 9AM-1PM except Wed (11AM-3PM W)
Will not search UCC or real estate records. Federal/state combined tax lien search- $2.00 per hour. Cert fee: $7.00 per doc. Payee: Town of Andover. **Other phones:** Assessor-802-875-2765.

Arlington Town

Town Clerk, PO Box 304, Arlington, VT 05250. **Phone**-802-375-2332; hours 9AM-2PM
Will not search records. Cert fee: $7.00. Payee: Arlington Town Clerk. **Other phones:** Assessor-802-375-9022; Treasurer-802-375-1260.

Athens Town

Town Clerk, 56 Brookline Rd., Athens, VT 05143. **Phone**-802-869-3370; fax-802-869-3370; hours 9AM-1PM or by appointment
UCC record search per debtor- $10.00. UCC request on non-standard form- $15.00. UCC search includes tax liens. Separate federal/state combined tax lien search- $5.00 per debtor. Will search real estate records. RE record copy- $2.00 per page. Cert fee: $5.00 per page. Payee: Athens Town Clerk. **Other phones:** Assessor-802-869-3995.

Bakersfield Town

Town Clerk, Box 203, Bakersfield, VT 05441. **Phone**-802-827-4495; fax-802-527-3106.
UCC record search per debtor- $10.00. UCC request on non-standard form- $15.00. Will not search real estate or tax lien records. Copy fee- $1.00 per page. Cert fee: $7.00 per page. Payee: Joyce-Town Clerk. **Other phones:** Assessor-802-827-4495; Treasurer-802-827-4495; Appraiser-802-827-4495; Elections-802-827-4495; Vital Records-802-827-4495.

Baltimore Town

Town Clerk, 1902 Baltimore Rd., Baltimore, VT 05143. **Phone**-802-263-5419; fax-802-263-9423; hours 10AM-Noon Sat. UCC record search per debtor- $2.00 per hour. Will not search tax liens. Will search real estate records. Copy fee- $1.00 per page. Cert fee: $10.00 per doc. Payee: Town of Baltimore.

Barnard Town

Town Clerk, PO Box 274, Barnard, VT 05031-0274. **Phone**-802-234-9211, R/E Recording-802-243-9211, UCC Recording-802-243-9211; 8AM-3:30PM M-W
Will not search records. Copy fee- $1.00 per page. Cert fee: $7.00 per page. Payee: Town of Barnard. **Other phones:** Assessor-802-243-9576; Treasurer-802-243-9050; Appraiser-802-243-9576; Elections-802-243-9211; Vital Records-802-243-9211.

Barnet Town

Town Clerk, Box 15, Barnet, VT 05821-0015. **Phone**-802-633-2256; fax-802-633-4315; hours 9AM-N, 1-4:30PM
UCC record search per debtor- $10.00. UCC request on non-standard form- $15.00. Will search tax liens including federal tax liens. Will not search real estate records. RE record copy- $1.00 per doc, uncertified. UCC copy- $1.00 per doc. Cert fee: $7.00 per page. Payee: Town of Barnet.

Barre City

Town Clerk, Box 418, Barre, VT 05641. **Phone**-Town Clerk, R/E & UCC Recording- 802-476-0242; fax-802-476-0264; hours 8AM-4PM
Will not search records. Copy fee- $1.00 per page. Cert fee: $7.00 per page. Payee: Barre City. **Other phones:** Assessor-802-476-0244; Treasurer-802-476-0242; Appraiser-802-476-0244; Elections-802-476-0242; Vital Records-802-476-0242.

Barre Town

Town Clerk, PO Box 124, Websterville, VT 05678-0124. **Phone**-Town Clerk, R/E & UCC Recording-802-479-9391; fax-802-479-9332; hours 8AM-4:30 M-F www.barretown.org
UCC record search per debtor- $10.00. Will not search real estate or tax lien records. Record copy fee- $1.00 per page. Cert fee: $7.00 per page. Payee: Town of Barre. **Other phones:** Assessor-802-479-2595; Treasurer-802-479-9391; Appraiser-802-479-2595; Elections-802-479-9391; Vital Records-802-479-9391; Town Manager-802-479-9331.

Barton Town

Town Clerk, PO Box 657, Barton, VT 05822-1386. **Phone**-Town Clerk, R/E & UCC Recording- 802-525-6222; fax-802-525-8856; hours 7:30AM-4PM
Will not search records. Copy fee is $2.00 per UCC. Cert fee: $7.00. Payee: Barton Town Clerk. **Other phones:** Assessor-802-525-6222; Treasurer-802-525-6222; Appraiser-802-525-6222; Elections-802-525-6222; Vital Records-802-525-6222.

Belvidere Town

Town Clerk, 3996 Vermont Rt 109, Belvidere Center, VT 05492. **Phone**-802-644-6621; hours 8:30AM-3:30PM T W Th

Will not search records. RE record copy- $6.00 per page if certified, $.40 if not certified plus postage. UCC copy- $6.00 per page. Cert fee: $6.00 per page total. Payee: Belvidere Town Clerk.

Bennington Town

Town Clerk, 205 South St, Bennington, VT 05201. **Phone**-802-442-1043; fax-802-442-1068; hours 8AM-5PM www.bennington.com/local.html
UCC record search per debtor- $10.00. UCC request on non-standard form- $15.00. Will not search real estate records. **Online Access to Property, Assessor records:** the Grand List search program is free at www.bennington.com/government/grandlist/index.html . No name searching at this time; site is under construction and data is incomplete. **Other phones:** Assessor-802-442-1042; Treasurer-802-442-1041; Appraiser-802-442-1042.

Benson Town

Town Clerk, PO Box 163, Benson, VT 05731-0163. **Phone**-802-537-2611; fax-802-537-2612; hours 9AM-12:00-1-5PM
UCC record search per debtor- $10.00. UCC request on non-standard form- $15.00. Will not search real estate or tax lien records. UCC copy- $1.00 per page. Cert fee: $7.00. Payee: Benson Town Clerk.

Berkshire Town

Town Clerk, RFD 1 Box 2560, Enosburg Falls, VT 05450. **Phone**-802-933-2335; fax-802-933-5913; hours 9AM-Noon, 1-4PM M,T,Th,F; 9AM-Noon W
Will not search records. Copy fee-$1.00 per page. UCC copy- $1.00 per name. Cert fee: $6.00 per page. Payee: Berkshire Town Clerk.

Berlin Town

Town Clerk, 108 Shed Rd., Berlin, VT 05602. **Phone**-Town Clerk, R/E & UCC Recording- 802-229-9298; fax-802-229-9530; hours 8:30AM-Noon,1-4:30PM (July-August 8:30AM-Noon, 1-3
Will search UCC records prior to 7/2001. Search per debtor- $10.00. Will not search real estate or tax lien records. UCC copy- $.25 per page. Payee: Berlin Town Clerk. **Other phones:** Assessor-802-229-4880; Treasurer-802-229-9380; Elections-802-229-9298; Vital Records-802-229-9298; Zoning Admin.-802-229-2529.

Bethel Town

Town Clerk, PO Box 404, Bethel, VT 05032. **Phone**-Town Clerk, R/E & UCC Recording- 802-234-9722; fax-802-234-6840; hours 8AM-4PM, M, TH; 8AM-Noon, T, F
UCC record search per debtor- $10.00. UCC request on non-standard form- $15.00. Will not search real estate or tax lien records. RE record copy- $1.00 per page. **Other phones:** Assessor-802-234-9722; Treasurer-802-234-9722; Elections-802-234-9722; Vital Records-802-234-9722.

Bloomfield Town

Town Clerk, PO Box 336, No. Stratford, NH, VT 03590. **Phone**-802-962-5191; fax-802-962-5191; hours 9AM-3PM Tues & Thurs
Will not search records. Copy fee- $1.00 per page. Cert fee: $7.00 per page. Payee: Town Clerk.

Bolton Town

Town Clerk, RD 1 Box 445, Waterbury, VT 05676. **Phone**-Town Clerk, R/E & UCC Recording- 802-434-3064; fax-802-434-6404; hours 7AM-4PM M-TH

UCC record search per debtor-$5.00 per hour. Will not search real estate or tax lien records. Copy fee-$1.00 per page. Cert fee: $10.00 per page. Payee: Town of Bolton. **Other phones:** Assessor-802-434-3064; Treasurer-802-434-5075; Appraiser-802-434-3064; Elections-Vital Records-802-434-5075.

Bradford Town

Town Clerk, PO Box 339, Bradford, VT 05033-0339. **Phone**-802-222-4727; fax-802-222-3520.
Will not search records. RE record copy- $1.00 per page. UCC copy- $1.00 per UCC. Cert fee: $7.00 per page. Payee: Town of Bradford. **Other phones:** Assessor-802-222-4727; Treasurer-802-222-4727; Appraiser-802-222-4727; Elections-802-222-4727; Vital Records-802-222-4727.

Braintree Town

Town Clerk, 932 VT Route 12A, Braintree, VT 05060. **Phone**-802-728-9787; fax-802-728-9787; hours 8AM-noon 1-5PM Tu & Th; 1-5PM Wed.
UCC record search per debtor- $10.00. UCC request on non-standard form- $15.00. Will not search real estate or tax lien records. RE record copy- $1.00 per page. UCC copy- $2.00 per page. Cert fee: $7.00 per page total. Payee: Braintree Town Clerk. **Other phones:** Assessor-802-728-9787.

Brandon Town

Town Clerk, 49 Center St, Brandon, VT 05733. **Phone**-Town Clerk, R/E & UCC Recording- 802-247-5721; fax-802-247-5481; hours-8AM-4PM www.town.brandon.vt.us
Will not search records. RE record copy- $1.00 per page. UCC copy- $20.00 per doc. Cert fee: $7.00 per page. Payee: Town of Brandon. **Other phones:** Assessor-802-247-0226; Treasurer-802-247-5721; Appraiser-802-247-0226; Elections-802-247-5721; Vital Records-802-247-5721.

Brattleboro Town

Town Clerk, 230 Main St #108, Brattleboro, VT 05301-2885. **Phone**-802-254-4541, R/E Recording-802-254-4541 x126, UCC Recording-802-254-4541 x126; fax-802-257-2312; hours 8:30AM-5PM www.brattleboro.org
UCC record search per debtor- $10.00. Will not search real estate or tax lien records. Copy fee-$1.00 per page. ($2.00 mimimun). Cert fee: $7.00 per page. Payee: Brattleboro Town Clerk. **Other phones:** Assessor-802-254-4541 x119; Treasurer-802-254-4541 x123; Appraiser-802-254-4541 x119; Elections-802-254-4541 x129; Vital Records-802-254-4541 x126.

Bridgewater Town

Town Clerk, PO Box 14, Bridgewater, VT 05034. **Phone**-Town Clerk, R/E & UCC Recording- 802-672-3334; fax-802-672-5395; hours 8AM-4PM M-Th; 8AM-Noon F
Will not search records. Copy fee- $1.00 per page. Cert fee: $7.00 per page. Payee: Town of Bridgewater. **Other phones:** Assessor-802-672-3334; Treasurer-802-672-3334; Appraiser-802-672-3334; Elections-802-672-3334; Vital Records-802-672-3334.

Bridport Town

Town Clerk, Box 27, Bridport, VT 05734-0027. **Phone**-Town Clerk, R/E & UCC Recording- 802-758-2483; hours 9AM-4PM M T F; 9AM-Noon 1-4PM W
Town clerk will perform searches as a private contractor. Will not search records. UCC copy- $.10 per page. Cert fee: $7.00 per page total. Payee: Bridport Town Clerk. **Other phones:** Assessor-802-758-2483; Treasurer-802-758-2483.

Brighton Town

Town Clerk, PO Box 377, Island Pond, VT 05846. **Phone**-Town Clerk, R/E & UCC Recording- 802-723-4405; fax-802-723-4405; hours 8:00-3:30PM M-F
Will not search records. RE copy fee- $1.00 per page. UCC copy- $.25 per page. Cert fee: $10.00 per doc. Payee: Brighton Town Clerk. **Other phones:** Assessor-802-723-4405; Treasurer-802-723-4405; Appraiser-802-723-6672; Elections-802-732-4405; Vital Records-802-732-4405.

Bristol Town

Town Clerk, Box 249, Bristol, VT 05443. **Phone**-802-453-2486; fax-802-453-5188; hours 8AM-4:30PM
Will not search UCC or real estate records. **Other phones:** Assessor-802-453-2486.

Brookfield Town

Town Clerk, PO Box 463, Brookfield, VT 05036-0463. **Phone**-802-276-3352; fax-802-276-3926; hours 8:30AM-4:30PM M,T,F. Will not search records. Copy fee- $1.00 each. Cert fee: $7.00 per page total. Payee: Town of Brookfield.

Brookline Town

Town Clerk, PO Box 403, Brookline, VT 05345. **Phone**-802-365-4648; fax-802-365-4648; hours 9AM-2PM Wed. UCC record search per debtor- $10.00. UCC request on non-standard form- $15.00. Will not search real estate or tax lien records. RE record copy- $.50 per page. Cert fee: $6.00 per page total. Payee: Brookline Town Clerk.

Brownington Town

Town Clerk, 509 Dutton Brook Ln, Orleans, VT 05860. **Phone**-802-754-8401; fax-802-754-8401; hours 8:30-11AM M; 9AM-3:30PM W; 9AM-Noon Th
UCC record search per debtor- $10.00. UCC request on non-standard form- $15.00. UCC search includes tax liens if requested. Tax lien search-federal and/or state $2.00 per hour. Real estate owner, mortgage, and property transfer searches available. Copy fee- $1.00 per page. Cert fee: $6.00 per page total. Payee: Brownington Town Clerk. **Other phones:** Treasurer-802-754-6559; Appraiser-802-754-8401.

Brunswick Town

Town Clerk, RFD 1, Box 470, 4495 Vermont Rte. 102, Brunswick, VT 05905. **Phone**-Town Clerk, R/E & UCC Recording- 802-962-5283; hours M-Sat by appointment. UCC record search per debtor- $10.00. UCC request on non-standard form- $15.00. UCC search includes tax liens. Separate federal/state combined tax lien search-no charge. Real estate owner, mortgage, and property transfer searches available. RE record copy- $1.00 per page. Cert fee: $2.00 per page. Payee: Brunswick Town Clerk. **Other phones:** Assessor-802-962-3450; Treasurer-802-962-5283; Elections-802-962-5283; Vital Records-802-962-5283.

Burke Town

Town Clerk, 212 School St, West Burke, VT 05871. **Phone**-Town Clerk, R/E & UCC Recording- 802-467-3717; fax-802-467-8623; hours 8AM-4PM
Will not search records. **Other phones:** Assessor-802-467-3717; Treasurer-802-467-3717.

Burlington City

Town Clerk, 149 Church St, City Hall, Rm 20, Burlington, VT 05401. **Phone**-802-865-7135; R/E Recording-802-865-7133; fax-802-865-7014; hours 8AM-4:30PM
UCC record search per debtor- $20.00. UCC request on non-standard form- $25.00. UCC search includes tax liens if requested. Separate

federal/state combined tax lien search- $20.00 Will not search real estate records. UCC copy- $2.00 per page. Cert fee: $20.00. Payee: Burlington City Clerk. **Other phones:** Assessor-802-865-7111; Treasurer-802-865-7000; Appraiser-802-865-7111; Elections-802-865-7136; Vital Records-802-865-7000.

Cabot Town

Town Clerk, PO Box 36, Cabot, VT 05647-0036. **Phone**-Town Clerk, R/E & UCC Recording- 802-563-2279; fax-802-563-2423; hours 9AM-5PM M-Th; 9AM-1PM F
Will not search records. RE record copy- $2.00 per page. **Other phones:** Assessor-802-563-2279; Treasurer-802-563-2279; Appraiser-802-563-2279; Elections-802-563-2279; Vital Records-802-563-2279.

Calais Town

Town Clerk, 668 W. County Rd., Calais, VT 05648. **Phone**-Town Clerk, R/E & UCC Recording- 802-223-5952, UCC Recording-802-223-5952; hours 8AM-5PM M,T,Th; 8AM-Noon Sat
UCC record search per debtor- $10.00. UCC request on non-standard form- $15.00. Will not search real estate records. Copy fee- $1.00 per page. Cert fee: $6.00 per page total. Payee: Calais Town Clerk. **Other phones:** Assessor-802-223-5952; Treasurer-802-223-5952; Appraiser-802-223-5952; Elections-802-223-5952; Vital Records-802-223-5952.

Cambridge Town

Town Clerk, PO Box 127, Jeffersonville, VT 05464. **Phone**-Town Clerk, R/E & UCC Recording- 802-644-2251; fax-802-644-8348; hours 8AM-4PM
UCC record search per debtor- $10.00. UCC request on non-standard form- $15.00. Will not search real estate or tax lien records. **Other phones:** Appraiser-802-644-2200; Vital Records-802-644-2251.

Canaan Town

Town Clerk, PO Box 159, Canaan, VT 05903-0159. **Phone**-Town Clerk, R/E & UCC Recording- 802-266-3370; fax-802-266-7085; hours 9AM-3PM
UCC record search per debtor- $10.00. UCC request on non-standard form- $15.00. UCC search includes tax liens if requested. Separate federal/state combined tax lien search- $.50 per page. Real estate owner, mortgage, and property transfer searches available. Copy fee- $.25 per page. Cert fee: $7.00 per page. Payee: Town of Canaan. **Other phones:** Assessor-802-266-3370; Treasurer-802-266-3370; Appraiser-802-266-3370; Elections-802-266-3370; Vital Records-802-266-3370.

Castleton Town

Town Clerk, PO Box 727, Castleton, VT 05735. **Phone**-802-468-2212, R/E Recording-802-468-2212 x214, UCC Recording-802-468-2212 x 214; fax-802-468-5482; hours 8AM-N, 1-4PM
Will not search records. Cert fee: $7.00 per page. Payee: Town of Castleton. **Other phones:** Treasurer-802-468-5319; Appraiser-802-468-2751; Elections-802-468-2212 x214; Vital Records-802-468-2212 x214.

Cavendish Town

Town Clerk, PO Box 126, Cavendish, VT 05142-0126. **Phone**-Town Clerk, R/E & UCC Recording- 802-226-7292; fax-802-226-7790; 9AM-Noon, 1PM-4:30PM
Will not search records. RE record copy- $1.00 per page. Cert fee: $5.00 per page. Payee: Cavendish Town Clerk. **Other phones:** Assessor-802-226-7292; Treasurer-802-226-7292; Appraiser-802-226-7292; Elections-802-226-7292; Vital Records-802-226-7292.

Charleston Town

Town Clerk, 5063 Vermont Rt 105, West Charleston, VT 05872-7902. **Phone**-802-895-2814; fax-802-895-2814; hours 9AM-3PM (Closed Wed)
Will not search records. Copy fee- $1.00 per page. Cert fee: $7.00 per page. Payee: Town of Charleston.

Charlotte Town

Town Clerk, PO Box 119, Charlotte, VT 05445-0119. **Phone**-Town Clerk, R/E & UCC Recording- 802-425-3071; fax-802-425-4241; hours 8AM-4PM www.vermont-towns.org/charlotte
UCC record search per debtor- $10.00. Will search real estate records. RE record copy- $1.00 per page. Cert fee: $7.00 per page. Payee: Town of Charlotte. **Other phones:** Assessor-802-425-3855; Treasurer-802-425-3071; Appraiser-802-425-3855; Elections-802-425-3071; Vital Records-802-425-3071; Planning & Zoning-802-425-3533.

Chelsea Town

Town Clerk, PO Box 266, Chelsea, VT 05038. **Phone**-802-685-4460; fax-802-685-4460; 8AM-N, 1-4PM
UCC record search per debtor- $10.00. UCC search includes tax liens if requested. Real estate owner, mortgage, and property transfer searches available. Copy fee- $1.00 per page. Payee: Chelsea Town Clerk. **Other phones:** Assessor-802-685-4460.

Chester Town

Town Clerk, PO Box 370, Chester, VT 05143. **Phone**-802-875-2173; fax-802-875-2237; hours 8AM-5PM
UCC record search per debtor- $10.00. UCC request on non-standard form- $15.00. Will not search real estate or tax lien records. UCC copy- no charge. Payee: Town of Chester.

Chittenden Town

Town Clerk, PO Box 89, Chittenden, VT 05737. **Phone**-802-483-6647; hours 1:30-5PM
Chittenden is in Rutland County, not Chittenden County. Uninformed secured parties continue to attempt filings at the county level here even though there is no county filing in Vermont. Will not search records. Cert fee: $7.00 per page total. Payee: Chittenden Town Clerk. **Other phones:** Treasurer-802-483-647.

Clarendon Town

Town Clerk, PO Box 30, North Clarendon, VT 05759-0030. **Phone**-Town Clerk, R/E & UCC Recording- 802-775-4274; fax-802-775-4274.
Will not search records. RE record copy- $1.00 per page. UCC copy- $2.00 per UCC. Cert fee: $7.00 per page. Payee: Town of Clarendon. **Other phones:** Assessor-802-775-1536; Treasurer-802-775-1536; Appraiser-802-775-1536; Elections-802-775-4274; Vital Records-802-775-4274.

Colchester Town

Town Clerk, PO Box 55, Colchester, VT 05446. **Phone**-802-655-0812, R/E Recording-802-654-0727, UCC Recording-802-654-0700; fax-802-654-0757; hours 8AM-4PM www.colchestervt.org
Will search UCC records by mail. Search per debtor- $10.00. UCC request on non-standard form- $15.00. Will not search real estate or tax lien records. RE record copy- $1.00 per page. UCC copy- $2.00 per UCC. Cert fee: $7.00 per page. Payee: Town od Colchester. **Other phones:** Assessor-802-655-0863; Treasurer-802-655-0812; Appraiser-802-655-0863; Elections-203-654-0727; Vital Records-203-654-0727.

Concord Town

Town Clerk, PO Box 317, Concord, VT 05824-0317. **Phone**-802-695-2220; fax-802-695-2220; hours 7:30AM-3:30PM
UCC record search per debtor- $10.00. UCC request on non-standard form- $15.00. Will not search real estate records. **Other phones:** Assessor-802-695-2220; Treasurer-802-695-2220; Appraiser-802-695-2220; Elections-802-695-2220; Vital Records-802-695-2220.

Corinth Town

Town Clerk, PO Box 461, Corinth, VT 05039. **Phone**-Town Clerk, R/E & UCC Recording- 802-439-5850; fax-802-439-5850; hours M 8:30AM-3:30PM;Tu 11AM-3PM;Th 10AM-3PM;F 8:30-3PM
Will not search UCC or real estate records. Cert fee: $7.00 per page. Payee: Town of Corinth. **Other phones:** Assessor-802-439-5098; Treasurer-802-439-5850; Elections-802-439-5850; Vital Records-802-439-5850.

Cornwall Town

Town Clerk, 2629 Route 30, Cornwall, VT 05753-9299. **Phone**-802-462-2775; fax-802-462-2606.
UCC record search per debtor- $10.00. UCC request on non-standard form- $15.00. **Other phones:** Assessor-802-462-2855.

Coventry Town

Town Clerk, PO Box 104, Coventry, VT 05825. **Phone**-802-754-2288; fax-802-754-6274; hours 8AM-Noon M,T,Th, F; 7AM-4PM, W
UCC record search per debtor- $10.00. UCC search includes tax liens if requested. Separate federal & state combined tax lien search- $1.00 Will not search real estate records. UCC copy- $1.00 per page. Cert fee: $7.00. Payee: Coventry Town Clerk.

Craftsbury Town

Town Clerk, Box 55, Craftsbury, VT 05826. **Phone**-802-586-2823; fax-802-586-2823.
UCC record search per debtor- $10.00. UCC request on non-standard form- $15.00. Will search tax liens. Will search real estate records. Copy fee- $1.00 per page. **Other phones:** Assessor-802-586-2835.

Danby Town

Town Clerk, Box 231, Danby, VT 05739-0231. **Phone**-Town Clerk, R/E & UCC Recording- 802-293-5136; fax-802-293-5311; hours 9AM-N, 1-4PM M-Th
Will not search records. **Other phones:** Assessor-802-293-5136; Treasurer-802-293-5136; Appraiser-802-293-5136; Elections-802-293-5136; Vital Records-802-293-5136.

Danville Town

Town Clerk, PO Box 183, Danville, VT 05828. **Phone**-802-684-3352; fax-802-684-9606.
Will not search records. Copy fee- $1.00 per page. Cert fee: $7.00 per page. Payee: Town of Danville.

Derby Town

Town Clerk, PO Box 25, Derby, VT 05829. **Phone**-802-766-4906; fax-802-766-2027; hours 8AM-4PM
Will not search UCC or tax liens records. Will search real estate records. Copy fee- $1.00 per page. Cert fee: $7.00. Payee: Derby Town Clerk. **Other phones:** Assessor-802-766-4906; Treasurer-802-766-4906; Appraiser-802-766-2012; Elections-802-766-4906; Vital Records-802-766-4906.

Dorset Town

Town Clerk, 112 Mad Tom Rd, Town Hall, East Dorset, VT 05253. **Phone**-802-362-1178; fax-802-362-5156.
UCC record search per debtor- $10.00. Will not search real estate or tax lien records. UCC copy-

$1.00 per page. Cert fee: $7.00. Payee: Dorset Town Clerk. **Other phones:** Assessor-802-362-0162.

Dover Town

Town Clerk, PO Box 527, Dover, VT 05356-0527. **Phone-**Town Clerk, R/E & UCC Recording- 802-464-5100; fax-802-464-8721; hours 9AM-5PM
Will not search records. UCC copy- $2.00 per page. Cert fee: $7.00. Payee: Dover Town Clerk. **Other phones:** Assessor-802-464-8720; Treasurer-802-464-5100; Appraiser-802-464-8720; Elections-802-464-5100; Vital Records-802-464-5100.

Dummerston Town

Town Clerk, 1523 Middle Rd., E. Dummerston, VT 05346. **Phone-**802-257-1496; fax-802-257-4671.
UCC record search per debtor- $10.00. UCC request on non-standard form- $15.00. Will not search real estate records.

Duxbury Town

Town Clerk, 3316 Crossett Hill Rd, Waterbury, VT 05676. **Phone-**802-244-6660; fax-802-244-5442; hours 8AM-4PM M-Th
Will not search records. Cert fee: $7.00 per page total. Payee: Town of Duxbury.

East Haven Town

Town Clerk, PO Box 10, East Haven, VT 05837-0010. **Phone-**Town Clerk, R/E & UCC Recording- 802-467-3772; hours 1-6PM T; 8AM-1PM Th; and by appt.
Will not search records. RE record copy- $1.00 per page. Cert fee: $7.00 per page total. Payee: East Haven Town Clerk. **Other phones:** Assessor-802-467-3772; Treasurer-802-467-3772; Appraiser-802-467-3772; Elections-802-467-3772; Vital Records-802-467-3772.

East Montpelier Town

Town Clerk, PO Box 157, East Montpelier, VT 05651-0157. **Phone-**Town Clerk, R/E & UCC Recording-802-223-3313; fax-802-223-3314; hours 9AM-5PM M-Th; 9AM-Noon F
UCC record search per debtor- $10.00. UCC request on non-standard form- $15.00. Will not search real estate or tax lien records. RE record copy- $1.00 per page. UCC copy- $2.00 per page. Cert fee: $7.00 per page total. Payee: East Montpelier Town Clerk. **Other phones:** Assessor-802-223-3313; Treasurer-802-223-3313; Appraiser-802-223-3313; Elections-802-223-3313; Vital Records-802-223-3313.

Eden Town

Town Clerk, 71 Old Schoolhouse Rd., Eden Mills, VT 05653. **Phone-**802-635-2528; fax-802-635-1724; hours 8AM-12:30-1-4:30PM,M-Th
Will not search records. UCC copy- $1.00 per page. Cert fee: $7.00. Payee: Eden Town Clerk. **Other phones:** Assessor-802-635-2528; Vital Records-802-635-2528.

Elmore Town

Town Clerk, PO Box 123, Lake Elmore, VT 05657. **Phone-**802-888-2637; fax-802-888-2637; hours 9AM-3PM T,W,Th. Will search UCC records. Will not search real estate or tax lien records. UCC copy-$1.00 per page. Payee: Elmore Town Clerk. **Other phones:** Assessor-802-888-2637.

Enosburgh Town

Town Clerk, PO Box 465, Enosburg Falls, VT 05450. **Phone-**Town Clerk, R/E & UCC Recording- 802-933-4421; fax-802-933-4832; hours 8AM4PM (closed on Wednesdays)
UCC record search per debtor- $20.00. Will not search real estate or tax lien records. Cert fee: $7.00 per doc. **Other phones:** Assessor-802-933-4421; Treasurer-802-933-4421; Appraiser-802-933-

4421; Elections-802-933-4421; Vital Records-802-933-4421.

Essex Town

Town Clerk, 81 Main St, Essex Junction, VT 05452. **Phone-**Town Clerk, R/E & UCC Recording- 802-879-0413; fax-802-878-1353; hours 7:30AM-4:30PM www.essex.org
UCC record search per debtor- $20.00. UCC request on non-standard form- $20.00. Will not search real estate or tax lien records. UCC copy- $1.00 per copy. Cert fee: $7.00 per page. Payee: Town of Essex. **Other phones:** Assessor-802-878-1345; Treasurer-802-879-0413; Appraiser-802-878-1345; Elections-802-879-0413; Vital Records-802-879-0413.

Fair Haven Town

Town Clerk, 3 N. Park Pl, Fair Haven, VT 05743. **Phone-**Town Clerk, R/E & UCC Recording- 802-265-3610; fax-802-265-2158; hours M-F 8-4PM
UCC record search per debtor- $10.00. UCC request on non-standard form- $15.00. Will not search real estate or tax lien records. Copy fee- $1.00 per page. Cert fee: $7.00. Payee: Town of Fair Haven. **Other phones:** Assessor-802-265-3610; Treasurer-802-265-3010; Appraiser-802-265-3610; Elections-802-265-3610; Vital Records-802-265-3610.

Fairfax Town

Town Clerk, PO Box 27, Fairfax, VT 05454. **Phone-**Town Clerk, R/E & UCC Recording- 802-849-6111; hours 9AM-4PM, M-F
Will not search records. Copy fee- $1.00 per page. Cert fee: $7.00 per page. Payee: Fairfax Town Office. **Other phones:** Assessor-802-849-6111; Treasurer-802-849-6111; Vital Records-802-849-6111.

Fairfield Town

Town Clerk, PO Box 5, Fairfield, VT 05455. **Phone-**802-827-3261; hours 10AM-2PM
Will not search records.

Fairlee Town

Town Clerk, PO Box 95, Fairlee, VT 05045-0095. **Phone-**Town Clerk, R/E & UCC Recording- 802-333-4363; fax-802-333-9214; hours 8:30AM-4:30PM M-T, 10AM-6PM W, or by app't.
Will not search records. RE record copy- $1.00 per page. UCC copy- $1.00 per page, $2.00 min. Cert fee: $6.00 per page. Payee: Fairlee Town Clerk. **Other phones:** Assessor-802-333-9829; Treasurer-802-333-4363; Appraiser-802-333-9829; Elections-802-333-4363; Vital Records-802-333-4363; Zoning Admin-802-333-4158.

Fayston Town

Town Clerk, 866 N. Fayston Rd., No. Fayston, VT 05660. **Phone-**802-496-2454; fax-802-496-9850; hours 9AM-Noon, 12:30-3:30PM
Will not search records. Copy fee- $1.00 per page. Cert fee: $7.00 per page total. Payee: Town of Fayston. **Other phones:** Assessor-802-496-2454 x24.

Ferrisburgh Town

Town Clerk, PO Box 6, Ferrisburgh, VT 05456-0006. **Phone-**802-877-3429; fax-802-877-6757; hours 8AM-4PM
UCC record search per debtor- $10.00. UCC request on non-standard form- $15.00. Will not search real estate records. RE record copy- $7.00 per page. Cert fee: $7.00 per doc. Payee: Town of Ferrisburg.

Fletcher Town

Town Clerk, 215 Cambridge Rd, Cambridge, VT 05444. **Phone-**Town Clerk, R/E & UCC Recording-802-849-6616; fax-802-849-2500; hours 9AM-3:30PM

Will not search records. Copy fee- $1.00 per page. Cert fee: $7.00 per page. Payee: Town of Fletcher. **Other phones:** Assessor-802-849-6616; Treasurer-802-849-6616; Appraiser-802-849-6616; Elections-802-849-6616; Vital Records-802-849-6616.

Franklin Town

Town Clerk, PO Box 82, Franklin, VT 05457-0082. **Phone-**Town Clerk, R/E & UCC Recording- 802-285-2101; hours 9AM-4PM M,T,F; 9AM-7PM Th; 9AM-Noon W
UCC record search per debtor- $10.00. UCC request on non-standard form- $15.00. Will not search real estate or tax lien records. RE record copy- $2.00 per doc. UCC copy- $1.00 per page/ $2.00 min. Cert fee: $2.00 per cert. Payee: Town of Franklin. **Other phones:** Assessor-802-285-2101; Treasurer-802-285-2101; Appraiser-802-285-2101; Elections-802-285-2101; Vital Records-802-285-2101.

Georgia Town

Town Clerk, 47 Town Common Rd North, St. Albans, VT 05478. **Phone-**Town Clerk, R/E & UCC Recording- 802-524-3524; fax-802-524-3543; hours 8:00AM-5PM M-Th; 8:00AM-4:00PM Fri.
Will charge in person searches for vault time-$2.00 per hour. Will not search records. Record copy fee- $1.00 per page. Cert fee: $7.00 per page. Payee: Town of Georgia. **Other phones:** Assessor-802-524-3543; Treasurer-802-524-3524; Appraiser-802-524-3543; Elections-802-524-3524; Vital Records-802-524-3524; Town Administrator-802-524-9794.

Glover Town

Town Clerk, 51 Bean Hill, Glover, VT 05839. **Phone-**Town Clerk, R/E & UCC Recording- 802-525-6227; fax-802-525-4115; hours 8AM-4PM, M-F
Will not search records. Copy fee- $1.00 per page. Cert fee: $7.00 per page. Payee: Town of Glover. **Other phones:** Assessor-802-525-6227; Treasurer-802-525-6227; Appraiser-802-525-6227; Elections-802-525-6227; Vital Records-802-525-6227.

Goshen Town

Town Clerk, 50 Carlisle Hill Rd., Goshen, VT 05733. **Phone-**802-247-6455; fax-none; hours 9-1PM Tues.
UCC record search per debtor- $10.00. Will do tax lien search. Will not search real estate records. UCC copy- $1.00 per page. Cert fee: $6.00 per page total. Payee: Madine J. Reed, Town Clerk. **Other phones:** Assessor-802-247-6455.

Grafton Town

Town Clerk, PO Box 180, Grafton, VT 05146. **Phone-**802-843-2419; hours 9AM-Noon, 1-4PM M,T,Th,F
Will not search records. Copy fee- $1.00 per page. Cert fee: $6.00 per page. Payee: Grafton Town Clerk.

Granby Town

Town Clerk, PO Box 56, Granby, VT 05840. **Phone-**802-328-3611; fax-802-328-3611; hours By appointment only.
UCC record search per debtor- $10.00. UCC request on non-standard form- $15.00. Tax lien search-$2.00 per debtor. UCC copy- $1.00 per page. Cert fee: $2.00 per page. Payee: Town of Grandby. **Other phones:** Assessor-802-328-2191.

Grand Isle Town Clerk

Town Clerk, PO Box 49, Grand Isle, VT 05458. **Phone-**Town Clerk, R/E & UCC Recording- 802-372-8830; fax-802-372-8815; hours 8:30AM-3:30PM
Will not search records. Copy fee- $7.00 per page (is certified). Payee: Town of Grand Isle. **Other phones:** Assessor-802-372-8830; Treasurer-802-372-8830; Appraiser-802-372-8830; Elections-802-372-8830; Vital Records-802-372-8830.

Granville Town

Town Clerk, PO Box 66, Granville, VT 05747-0066. **Phone**-802-767-4403; fax-802-767-3968; hours 9AM-3PM M-Th (Closed F)
UCC record search per debtor- $10.00. UCC request on non-standard form- $15.00. Will not search real estate or tax lien records. Copy fee- $1.00 per page. Cert fee: $7.00 per page total. Payee: Granville Town Clerk. **Other phones:** Assessor-802-767-4403.

Greensboro Town

Town Clerk, Box 119, Greensboro, VT 05841. **Phone**-802-533-2911; hours 8:30AM-Noon, 1-4PM
UCC record search per debtor- $10.00. UCC request on non-standard form- $15.00. Will not search real estate or tax lien records. Cert fee: $6.00 per page total. Payee: Greensboro Town Clerk.

Groton Town

Town Clerk, 314 Scott Highway, Groton, VT 05046. **Phone**-Town Clerk, R/E & UCC Recording- 802-584-3276; fax-802-584-3276; hours 7AM-N, 12:30-3:30PM M-Th
UCC record search per debtor- $10.00. UCC request on non-standard form- $15.00. Will not search real estate or tax lien records. Record copy fee- $1.00 per page. Cert fee: $7.00 per doc. Payee: Town of Groton. **Other phones:** Assessor-802-584-3276/ 584-3131; Treasurer-802-584-3276; Appraiser-802-584-3131; Elections-802-584-3276; Vital Records-802-584-3276.

Guildhall Town

Town Clerk, PO Box 10, Guildhall, VT 05905. **Phone**-802-676-3797; fax-802-676-3518; hours 9AM-12:00PM, T, TH, or by Appt.
UCC record search per debtor- $10.00. UCC request on non-standard form- $15.00. Will not search real estate records. UCC copy- per page.

Guilford Town

Town Clerk, 236 School Rd., Guilford, VT 05301-8319. **Phone**-Town Clerk, R/E & UCC Recording-802-254-6857; fax-802-257-5764; hours 9AM-4PM M T TH F; 09AM-Noon & 6:30-8:00 PM W
UCC record search per debtor- $10.00. UCC request on non-standard form- $15.00. Will not search real estate or tax lien records. Copy fee- $1.00 per page. Cert fee: $7.00 per page. Payee: Town of Guilford. **Other phones:** Assessor-802-254-6857; Treasurer-802-254-6857; Appraiser-802-254-6857; Elections-802-254-6857; Vital Records-802-254-6857.

Halifax Town

Town Clerk, PO Box 45, West Halifax, VT 05358. **Phone**-Town Clerk, R/E & UCC Recording- 802-368-7390; fax-802-368-7390; hours 9AM-4PM M,T,F; 9AM-Noon Sat
Will not search records. RE record copy- $1.00 per page. UCC copy- $.25 per copy. Cert fee: $7.00 per page total. Payee: Halifax Town Clerk. **Other phones:** Assessor-802-368-7390; Treasurer-802-368-7698; Appraiser-802-368-7390; Elections-802-368-7390; Vital Records-802-368-7390.

Hancock Town

Town Clerk, PO Box 100, Hancock, VT 05748. **Phone**-802-767-3660; fax-802-767-3660; hours 8AM-3PM T-TH; Monday by appt. only; Sat 8-10AM
Will not search records. RE record copy- $1.00 per page for land records or $.10 for others. UCC copy- $1.00 per page, $2.00 min. Cert fee: $7.00 per page total. Payee: Town of Hancock. **Other phones:** Assessor-802-767-3301; Treasurer-802-767-3660; Appraiser-802-767-3660; Elections-802-767-3660; Vital Records-802-767-3660.

Hardwick Town

Town Clerk, Box 523, Hardwick, VT 05843. **Phone**-Town Clerk, R/E & UCC Recording- 802-472-5971; fax-802-472-3793; hours 9AM-4PM
UCC record search per debtor- $10.00. UCC request on non-standard form- $15.00. Will not search tax liens or real estate records. RE record copy- $1.00 per page. UCC copy- $2.00 per page. Cert fee: $7.00 per page. Payee: Town of Hardwick. **Other phones:** Assessor-802-472-5971; Treasurer-802-472-5971; Appraiser-802-472-5971; Elections-802-472-5971; Vital Records-802-472-5971.

Hartford Town

Town Clerk, 171 Bridge St, White River Junction, VT 05001-1920. **Phone**-Town Clerk, R/E & UCC Recording- 802-295-2785; hours 8AM-Noon, 1-5PM
www.hartford-vt.org
UCC record search per debtor- $10.00. UCC request on non-standard form- $15.00. Will not search real estate or tax lien records. RE record copy- $1.00 per page. UCC copy- $2.00 per copy. Cert fee: $7.00 per page total. Payee: Town of Hartford. **Other phones:** Assessor-802-295-3077; Treasurer-802-295-3002; Appraiser-802-295-3077; Elections-802-295-2785; Vital Records-802-295-2785.

Hartland Town

Town Clerk, PO Box 349, Hartland, VT 05048-0349. **Phone**-Town Clerk, R/E & UCC Recording- 802-436-2444; fax-802-436-2444; hours 8AM-4PM
UCC record search per debtor- $10.00. UCC request on non-standard form- $15.00. Will not search real estate records. Copy fee- $1.00 per page. Cert fee: $7.00 per page. Payee: Town of Hartland. **Other phones:** Assessor-802-436-2464; Treasurer-802-436-2464; Elections-802-436-2444; Vital Records-802-436-2444.

Highgate Town

Town Clerk, PO Box 67, Highgate Center, VT 05459. **Phone**-802-868-4697; 8:30AM-12, 1PM-4:30PM
Will not search records. Payee: Town of Highgate. **Other phones:** Assessor-802-868-2741.

Hinesburg Town

Town Clerk, PO Box 133, Hinesburg, VT 05461. **Phone**-802-482-2281; fax-802-482-5404.
Will not search records. RE record copy- $1.00 per page. Cert fee: $7.00 per page. Payee: Town of Hinesburg. **Other phones:** Assessor-802-482-3619.

Holland Town

Town Clerk, 120 School Rd., Holland/Derby Line, VT 05830. **Phone**-Town Clerk, R/E & UCC Recording-802-895-4440; fax-802-895-4440; hours 9AM-2PM except Wed (closed)
Will not search records. RE record copy- $1.00 per page. Cert fee: $7.00 per doc. Payee: Town of Holland. **Other phones:** Assessor-802-895-4440; Treasurer-802-895-4440; Elections-802-895-4440; Vital Records-802-895-4440.

Hubbardton Town

Town Clerk, 1831 Monument Hill Rd, Castleton, VT 05735. **Phone**-802-273-2951; fax-802-273-3729; hours 9AM-2PM M,W,F
UCC record search per debtor- $5.00 min. UCC search includes tax liens if requested. Real estate owner, mortgage, and property transfer searches available. Cert fee: $6.00 per page total. Payee: Hubbardton Town Clerk.

Huntington Town

Town Clerk, 4930 Main Rd., Huntington, VT 05462. **Phone**-Town Clerk, R/E & UCC Recording- 802-434-2032; fax-802-434-4731; hours 8AM-4PM M,W; 7AM-2PM Tu,F; 8AM-6PM Th
Will not search records. Record copy fee- $1.00 per page. Cert fee: $6.00 per page total. Payee: Town of Huntington. **Other phones:** Assessor-802-434-5783; Treasurer-802-434-2032; Appraiser-802-434-5783; Elections-802-434-2032; Vital Records-802-434-2032; Administrator-802-434-4779.

Hyde Park Town

Town Clerk, PO Box 98, Hyde Park, VT 05655-0098. **Phone**-Town Clerk, R/E & UCC Recording- 802-888-2300; fax-802-888-6878; hours 8AM-4PM
Will not search UCC or real estate records. Will do tax lien search, no charge for short list. Federal/state combined tax lien search is $2.00 per hour. Record copy- $1.00 per page. Cert fee: $7.00 per record. Payee: Town Clerk. **Other phones:** Assessor-802-888-7786; Treasurer-802-888-2300; Appraiser-802-888-7786; Elections-802-888-2300; Vital Records-802-888-2300; Zoning/Health Officer-802-888-7784.

Ira Town

Town Clerk, 808 Route 133, West Rutland, VT 05777. **Phone**-Town Clerk, R/E & UCC Recording- 802-235-2745; hours 9AM-2:30PM M; 2-7PM T
Will not search records. UCC copy- $1.00 per page. Cert fee: $7.00 per page total. Payee: Ira Town Clerk. **Other phones:** Assessor-802-235-2745; Treasurer-802-235-2745; Appraiser-802-235-2745; Elections-802-235-2745; Vital Records-802-235-2745.

Irasburg Town

Town Clerk, Box 51, Irasburg, VT 05845. **Phone**-Town Clerk, R/E & UCC Recording- 802-754-2242; hours 9AM-3PM M,W,Th
UCC record search per debtor- $10.00. UCC request on non-standard form- $15.00. Will search tax liens. Will search real estate records. Copy fee- $1.00 per page. Cert fee: $2.00 per page. Payee: Irasburg Town Clerk. **Other phones:** Assessor-802-754-2242; Treasurer-802-754-2242; Appraiser-802-754-2242; Elections-802-754-2242; Vital Records-802-754-2242.

Isle La Motte Town

Town Clerk, PO Box 250, Isle La Motte, VT 05463. **Phone**-Town Clerk, R/E & UCC Recording- 802-928-3434; fax-802-928-3002; hours 8AM-3PM Tu,Th; 8AM-Noon Sat.
UCC record search per debtor- $10.00. UCC request on non-standard form- $15.00. Will not search real estate records. Copy fee- $1.00 per page. Cert fee: $7.00 per doc. Payee: Isle LaMotte Town Clerk. **Other phones:** Assessor-802-928-3434; Treasurer-802-928-3434; Appraiser-802-928-3434; Elections-802-928-3434; Vital Records-802-928-3434.

Jamaica Town

Town Clerk, PO Box 173, Jamaica, VT 05343. **Phone**-802-874-4681; hours 9AM-Noon, 1-4PM T,W,Th,F
UCC record search per debtor- $10.00. UCC request on non-standard form- $15.00. Will not search real estate or tax lien records. UCC copy- $1.00 per page. Cert fee: $7.00 per page total. Payee: Town of Jamaica. **Other phones:** Assessor-802-874-4908.

Jay Town

Town Clerk, 1036 Vermont Rte. 242, Jay, VT 05859-9820. **Phone**-Town Clerk, R/E & UCC Recording-802-988-2996; fax-802-988-2996; hours 7AM-4PM (Closed M)
Will not search UCC records except to find records and make copies for qualified researchers. Will not search real estate or tax lien records. Copy fee- $1.00 per page, $2.00 min. Cert fee: $7.00 per page. Payee: Town of Jay.

Jericho Town

Town Clerk, PO Box 67, Jericho, VT 05465. **Phone-**Town Clerk, R/E & UCC Recording- 802-899-4936; fax-802-899-5549; hours 8-5 M-TH, 8-3 F www.jerichovt.gov
Will not search records. Copy fee- $1.00 per page. Cert fee: $7.00 per page. Payee: Town of Jericho. **Other phones:** Assessor-802-899-2640; Treasurer-802-899-4936; Appraiser-802-899-2640; Elections-802-899-4936; Vital Records-802-899-4936.

Johnson Town

Town Clerk, PO Box 383, Johnson, VT 05656. **Phone-**Town Clerk, R/E & UCC Recording- 802-635-2611; fax-802-635-9523; hours 7:30AM-4PM
Will not search records. Record copy fee- $1.00 per page. **Other phones:** Assessor-802-635-2611; Treasurer-802-635-2611; Appraiser-802-635-2611; Elections-802-635-2611; Vital Records-802-635-2611.

Killington Town

Town Clerk, PO Box 429, Killington, VT 05751-0429. **Phone-**Town Clerk, R/E & UCC Recording- 802-422-3243; fax-802-422-3030; hours 9AM-3PM www.killingtontown.com/staff.htm
Formerly known as the Town of Sherburne. Will not search records. Copy fee- $1.00 per page. Cert fee: $7.00 per page. Payee: Killington Town Clerk. **Other phones:** Treasurer-802-422-3241; Elections-802-422-3243; Vital Records-802-422-3243.

Kirby Town

Town Clerk, 346 Town Hall Rd., Town of Kirby, Lyndonville, VT 05851-9802. **Phone-**Town Clerk, R/E & UCC Recording- 802-626-9386; fax-802-626-9386; hours 8AM-3PM; T,TH
UCC record search per debtor- $10.00. UCC request on non-standard form- $15.00. **Other phones:** Assessor-802-626-9386; Treasurer-802-626-9386; Appraiser-802-626-9386; Elections-802-626-9386; Vital Records-802-626-9386.

Landgrove Town

Town Clerk, Box 508, Londonderry, VT 05148. **Phone-**Town Clerk, R/E & UCC Recording- 802-824-3716; fax-802-824-3716; hours 9AM-1PM
UCC record search per debtor- $10.00. UCC request on non-standard form- $15.00. Tax liens not included in UCC search. Federal/state combined tax lien search- $10.00 per page. Will not search real estate records. Record copy- $7.00 per page (is certified). Payee: Landgrove Town Clerk. **Other phones:** Assessor-802-824-3716; Treasurer-802-824-3716; Appraiser-802-824-3716; Elections-802-824-3716; Vital Records-802-824-3716.

Leicester Town

Town Clerk, 44 Schoolhouse Rd., Leicester, VT 05733. **Phone-**Town Clerk, R/E & UCC Recording- 802-247-5961; hours 1-4PM M-W
Will not search records. RE record copy- $1.00 per page. UCC copy- $20.00 per UCC. Cert fee: $7.00 per page total. Payee: Leicester Town Clerk. **Other phones:** Assessor-802-247-5961; Treasurer-802-247-5961; Appraiser-802-247-5961; Elections-802-247-5961; Vital Records-802-247-5961.

Lemington Town

Town Clerk, 2549 RIver Rd, VT 102, Lemington, VT 05903. **Phone-**802-277-4814; hours 11AM-2PM W
Will not search UCC or tax liens records. Real estate owner, mortgage, and property transfer searches available. Cert fee: $6.00 per page total. Payee: Town of Lemington.

Lincoln Town

Town Clerk, 62 Quaker St., Lincoln, VT 05443. **Phone-**802-453-2980; fax-802-453-2975; hours 9AM-Noon, 1PM-4PM T-F; 9AM-Noon Sat, Closed Monday
Will not search records. Copy fee- $1.00 per page.

Londonderry Town

Town Clerk, PO Box 118, South Londonderry, VT 05155-0118. **Phone-**802-824-3356; hours 9AM-3PM T-F; 9AM-12 Sat
UCC record search per debtor- $10.00. UCC request on non-standard form- $15.00. UCC search includes tax liens if requested. Real estate owner, mortgage, and property transfer searches available. RE record copy- $1.00 per page. Cert fee: $7.00 per page total. Payee: Londonderry Town Clerk.

Lowell Town

Town Clerk, 2170 VT Rt. 100, Lowell, VT 05847-0007. **Phone-**802-744-6559; fax-802-744-2357; hours 9AM-2:30PM Mon & Th
Will not search records. Copy fee- $1.00 per record. Cert fee: $7.00 per record. Payee: Lowell Town.

Ludlow Town

Town Clerk, PO Box 307, Ludlow, VT 05149. **Phone-**Town Clerk, R/E & UCC Recording- 802-228-3232; fax-802-228-8399; hours 8:30AM-4:30PM
Will not search records. Copy fee- $1.00 per page. Cert fee: $7.00 per page. Payee: Town of Ludlow. **Other phones:** Assessor-802-228-7206; Treasurer-802-228-3232; Appraiser-802-228-7206; Elections-802-228-3232; Vital Records-802-228-3232.

Lunenburg Town

Town Clerk, PO Box 54, Lunenburg, VT 05906. **Phone-**Town Clerk, R/E & UCC Recording- 802-892-5959; fax-802-892-5100; hours 8:30AM-Noon, 1-4PM
UCC record search per debtor- $10.00. UCC request on non-standard form- $15.00. Will search tax liens. Will not search real estate records. RE record copy- $.50 per page. UCC copy- $15.00 per UCC. Cert fee: $15.00. Payee: Lunenburg Town Clerk. **Other phones:** Assessor-802-892-1162; Treasurer-802-892-5959; Appraiser-802-892-1162; Elections-802-892-5959; Vital Records-802-892-5959.

Lyndon Town

Town Clerk, PO Box 167, Lyndonville, VT 05851. **Phone-**Town Clerk, R/E & UCC Recording- 802-626-5785; fax-802-626-1265; hours 7:30AM-4:30PM
UCC record search per debtor- $10.00. UCC request on non-standard form- $15.00. Will only do searches for property taxes if you know the book/page or the 2 parties names and date. Will not search real estate records. Copy fee is $1.00 per page. Cert fee: $6.00 per page. Payee: Lyndon Town Clerk. **Other phones:** Assessor-802-626-1270; Treasurer-802-626-5785; Appraiser-802-626-1270; Elections-802-626-5785; Vital Records-802-626-5785.

Maidstone Town

Town Clerk, PO Box 118, Maidstone, VT 05905-0118. **Phone-**Town Clerk, R/E & UCC Recording- 802-676-3210; fax-802-676-3210; hours 9AM-11AM M-TH
UCC record search per debtor- $10.00. UCC request on non-standard form- $15.00. Tax liens not included in UCC search. Separate federal & state combined tax lien search- $5.00 per hour. Will search real estate records. Copy fee- $1.00 per page. ($2.00 min.). Cert fee: $7.00 per page. Payee: Maidstone Town Clerk. **Other phones:** Elections-802-676-3210; Vital Records-802-676-3210.

Manchester Town

Town Clerk, PO Box 830, Manchester Center, VT 05255. **Phone-**Town Clerk, R/E & UCC Recording- 802-362-1315; fax-802-362-1315; hours 8:30AM-1PM, 2-4:30PM M-T-Th-F; 10:00AM-6PM W www.manchester.vt.us
UCC record search per debtor- $10.00. UCC request on non-standard form- $15.00. Tax liens not included in UCC search. Tax lien search- $5.00 per debtor. Will search real estate records. RE record copy- $1.00 per page. UCC copy- $2.00 per copy. Payee: Manchester Town Clerk. **Other phones:** Assessor-802-362-1373; Treasurer-802-362-1197; Appraiser-802-362-1373; Elections-802-362-1315; Vital Records-802-362-1315; Town Manager-802-362-1313; Planning/Zoning-802-362-4824.

Marlboro Town

Town Clerk, PO Box E, Marlboro, VT 05344-0305. **Phone-**Town Clerk, R/E & UCC Recording- 802-254-2181; fax-802-257-2447; hours 9AM-4PM M,W,Th
UCC record search per debtor- $10.00. Will not search tax liens. Will do minor checking on specifically-named real estate records at clerk's discretion. Copy fee- $1.00. Cert fee: $7.00 per page total. Payee: Town of Marlboro. **Other phones:** Assessor-802-254-2181; Treasurer-802-254-2181; Appraiser-802-254-2181; Elections-802-254-2181; Vital Records-802-254-2181.

Marshfield Town

Town Clerk, 122 School St, Rm 1, Marshfield, VT 05658. **Phone-**Town Clerk, R/E & UCC Recording- 802-426-3305; fax-802-426-3045.
UCC record search per debtor- $10.00. UCC request on non-standard form- $15.00. Will not search tax liens. Copies- $1.00 per page, $2.00 min. Cert fee: $7.00 per page. Payee: Town of Marshfield. **Other phones:** Assessor-802-426-3305; Treasurer-802-426-3305; Appraiser-802-426-3305; Elections-802-426-3305; Vital Records-802-426-3305.

Mendon Town

Town Clerk, 34 US Route 4, Mendon, VT 05701. **Phone-**Town Clerk, R/E & UCC Recording- 802-775-1662; fax-802-773-9682; hours 8AM-3PM,M-W; 8AM-1PM,TH; CLOSED F
Will not search UCC or real estate records. UCC copy- $1.00 per page. Cert fee: $7.00. Payee: Mendon Town Clerk. **Other phones:** Assessor-802-496-9689; Treasurer-802-775-1662; Elections-802-775-1662; Vital Records-802-775-1662.

Middlebury Town

Town Clerk, 94 Main St, Middlebury, VT 05753-1334. **Phone-**802-388-4041, R/E Recording-802-388-4048 x222, UCC Recording-802-388-4048 x222; fax-802-388-4364; hours 8:30AM-4:30PM
Will not search records. Copy fee- $1.00 per copy. Cert fee: $7.00 per page total. Payee: Middlebury Town Clerk. **Other phones:** Assessor-802-388-8108; Treasurer-802-388-8102; Appraiser-802-388-4352; Elections-802-388-8102; Vital Records-802-388-4048 x222.

Middlesex Town

Town Clerk, 5 Church St., Middlesex, VT 05602. **Phone-**Town Clerk, R/E & UCC Recording- 802-223-5915; fax-802-223-0569; hours M-Th 8:30-Noon 1:00-4:30PM www.middlesex-vt.org/
Will not search UCC or real estate records. Copy fee- $1.00 per page. Cert fee: $7.00 per cert. Payee: Town Clerk. **Other phones:** Assessor-802-223-5915; Treasurer-802-223-5915; Appraiser-802-223-5915; Elections-802-223-5915; Vital Records-802-223-5915.

Middletown Springs Town

Town Clerk, PO Box 1232, Middletown Springs, VT 05757-1197. **Phone**-802-235-2220; fax-802-235-2066; hours 9AM-noon, 1-4PM M, Tu; 1-4PM F,9AM-12:00PM
UCC record search per debtor- $10.00. UCC request on non-standard form- $15.00. Will not search real estate or tax lien records. UCC copy- $1.00 per page. Cert fee: $7.00 per page. Payee: Middletown Springs Town Clerk.

Milton Town

Town Clerk, PO Box 18, Milton, VT 05468. **Phone**-Town Clerk, R/E & UCC Recording- 802-893-4111; fax-802-893-1005; hours 8AM-5PM
UCC record search per debtor- $10.00. UCC request on non-standard form- $7.00. Will not search real estate or tax lien records. UCC copy- $1.00 per page. Cert fee: $7.00 per page. Payee: Town of Milton. **Other phones:** Assessor-802-893-4325; Treasurer-802-893-4111; Appraiser-802-893-4325; Elections-802-893-4111; Vital Records-802-893-4111.

Monkton Town

Town Clerk, 280 Yorkton Ridge, North Ferrisburg, VT 05473-9509. **Phone**-Town Clerk, R/E & UCC Recording- 802-453-3800; hours 8AM-1PM M,T,Th,F; 8:30AM-Noon Sat
Will not search records. Copy fee- $1.00 per page. Cert fee: $1.00 per page. Payee: Monkton Town Clerk. **Other phones:** Assessor-802-453-4515; Treasurer-802-453-3800; Appraiser-802-453-3800; Elections-802-453-3800; Vital Records-802-453-3800.

Montgomery Town

Town Clerk, PO Box 356, Montgomery Center, VT 05471-0356. **Phone**-Town Clerk, R/E & UCC Recording- 802-326-4719; fax-802-326-4939; hours 9AM-Noon 1PM-4PM M T TH F; 9AM-Noon W www.vermont-towns.org/montgomery'
Will not search records. **Other phones:** Assessor-802-326-4719; Treasurer-802-326-4719; Appraiser-802-326-4719; Elections-802-326-4719; Vital Records-802-326-4719.

Montpelier City

City Clerk, 39 Main St, City Hall, Montpelier, VT 05602. **Phone**-802-223-9500; fax-802-223-9523.
UCC record search per debtor- $10.00. UCC request on non-standard form- $15.00. Will not search real estate or tax lien records. RE record copy- $.50 per page. UCC copy- $2.00 per page. Cert fee: $7.00 per page. **Other phones:** Assessor-802-223-9504.

Moretown Town

Town Clerk, PO Box 666, Moretown, VT 05660. **Phone**-802-496-3645; hours 9AM-noon, 1-4:30PM M-Th; 9AM-3:30PM F
UCC record search per debtor- $10.00. UCC request on non-standard form- $15.00. Will not search real estate or tax lien records. Copy fee- $1.00 per page. Cert fee: $6.00 per page total. Payee: Moretown Town Clerk.

Morgan Town

Town Clerk, PO Box 45, Morgan, VT 05853-0045. **Phone**-802-895-2927; fax-802-895-4204; hours 9AM-3PM M,T,Th; 8AM-5PM Wed; 9AM-N Fri.
Will not search records. RE record copy- $1.00 per page, $2.00 min. Cert fee: $7.00 per page total. Payee: Morgan Town Clerk, Town of Morgan. **Other phones:** Assessor-802-895-2858; Treasurer-802-895-2927; Appraiser-802-875-2858; Elections-802-895-2927; Vital Records-802-895-2927.

Morristown Town

Town Clerk, PO Box 748, Morrisville, VT 05661-0748. **Phone**-802-888-6370; fax-802-888-6375; hours 8:30AM-4:30PM, M,T,TH, F; 8:30AM-12:30PM, W www.morristownvt.org
UCC record search per debtor- $5.00 per hour. UCC request on non-standard form- $15.00. Federal and/or state combined tax lien search- $5.00 per hour. Will not search real estate records. RE record copy- $1.00 per page. UCC copy- $2.00 per page. Cert fee: $7.00 per page. Payee: Town of Morristown. **Other phones:** Assessor-802-888-6371.

Mount Holly Town

Town Clerk, PO Box 248, Mount Holly, VT 05758. **Phone**-Town Clerk, R/E & UCC Recording- 802-259-2391; fax-802-259-2391; hours 8:30AM-4PM M-TH
Will not search records. RE record copy- $1.00 per page. Cert fee: $7.00 per page. Payee: Town Clerk. **Other phones:** Assessor-802-259-2391; Treasurer-802-259-2391; Appraiser-802-259-2391; Elections-802-259-2391; Vital Records-802-259-2391.

Mount Tabor Town

Town Clerk, PO Box 245, Mt. Tabor, VT 05739. **Phone**-Town Clerk, R/E & UCC Recording- 802-293-5282; fax-802-293-5287; hours Tues & Wed 9AM-12PM
UCC record search per debtor- $10.00. UCC request on non-standard form- $15.00. Tax lien search-$10.00 per search. Cert fee: $7.00 per copy. Payee: Mt. Tabor Town Clerk. **Other phones:** Assessor-802-293-5282; Treasurer-802-293-5741; Appraiser-802-293-5282; Elections-802-293-5282; Vital Records-802-293-5282.

New Haven Town

Town Clerk, 78 North St., New Haven, VT 05472. **Phone**-802-453-3516; fax-802-453-3516; hours 9AM-3PM www.newhavenvt.com
Will not search records. RE record copy- $1.00 per page. UCC copy- $2.00 per page. Cert fee: $7.00 per page total. Payee: New Haven Town Clerk.

Newark Town

Town Clerk, 1336 Newark St, Newark, VT 05871. **Phone**-802-467-3336; hours 9AM-4PM M,W,Th
Will not search records. UCC copy- $1.00 per page. Cert fee: $7.00 per page total. Payee: Newark Town Clerk.

Newbury Town

Town Clerk, PO Box 126, Newbury, VT 05051. **Phone**-Town Clerk, R/E & UCC Recording- 802-866-5521; fax-802-866-5301; hours 8:30AM-2:30PM, M-F; 2:30-6PM T www.cohase.org
UCC record search per debtor- $10.00. UCC request on non-standard form- $15.00. Will not search real estate or tax lien records. RE record copy- $1.00 per page. Cert fee: $7.00 per page. Payee: Newbury Town Clerk. **Other phones:** Assessor-802-866-5521; Treasurer-802-866-5521; Appraiser-802-866-5521; Elections-802-866-5521; Vital Records-802-866-5521.

Newfane Town

Town Clerk, PO Box 36, Newfane, VT 05345-0036. **Phone**-802-365-7772; fax-802-365-7692; hours 9AM-3PM
UCC record search per debtor- $10.00. UCC request on non-standard form- $15.00. Will not search real estate records.

Newport City

Town Clerk, 222 Main St, Newport, VT 05855. **Phone**-Town Clerk, R/E & UCC Recording- 802-334-2112; fax-802-334-5632; hours 8:30AM-4:30PM

UCC record search per debtor- $10.00. Will not search real estate records. UCC copy- $1.00 per page. Cert fee: $7.00 per page. Payee: City of Newport. **Online Access to Assessor, Property records:** Access to Newport City assessor data is free at http://data.visionappraisal.com/newportvt/. **Other phones:** Assessor-802-334-6992; Treasurer-802-334-2112; Appraiser-802-334-6992; Elections-802-334-2112; Vital Records-802-334-2112.

Newport Town

Town Clerk, PO Box 85, Newport Center, VT 05857. **Phone**-802-334-6442; fax-802-334-6442; hours 7AM-4:30PM,M-Th, Closed F
Will not search records. UCC copy- $1.00 per page. Cert fee: $7.00. Payee: Newport Town Clerk.

North Hero Town

Town Clerk, PO Box 38, North Hero, VT 05474-0038. **Phone**-Town Clerk, R/E & UCC Recording- 802-372-6926; fax-802-372-3806; hours 9AM-4PM
Will not search records. Copy fee- $1.00 per page. Cert fee: $7.00 per page. Payee: Town of North Hero+. **Other phones:** Assessor-802-372-6926; Treasurer-802-372-6926; Appraiser-802-372-6926; Elections-802-372-6926; Vital Records-802-372-6926.

Northfield Town

Town Clerk, 51 S. Main St, Northfield, VT 05663. **Phone**-Town Clerk, R/E & UCC Recording- 802-485-5421; fax-802-485-8426.
UCC record search per debtor- $10.00. UCC request on non-standard form- $15.00. Will not search real estate or tax lien records. Copy fee- $1.00 per page. Cert fee: $7.00 per page. Payee: Town of Northfield. **Other phones:** Assessor-802-485-6004; Treasurer-802-485-5421; Appraiser-802-485-6004; Elections-802-485-5421; Vital Records-802-485-5421.

Norton Town

Town Clerk, VT Route 1145, Norton, VT 05907. **Phone**-Town Clerk, R/E & UCC Recording- 802-822-9935; fax-802-822-9935; hours Appointment Only
Will not search records. Copy fee- $2.00 per page. Cert fee: $6.00 per page total. Payee: Norton Town Clerk. **Other phones:** Treasurer-802-822-9935; Elections-802-822-9935; Vital Records-802-822-9935.

Norwich Town

Town Clerk, PO Box 376, Norwich, VT 05055. **Phone**-802-649-1419; fax-802-649-0123; hours 8:30-4:30
8:30-4:30,M,T,W,F, 8:30-7PM Th
Will not search records. UCC copy- $1.00 per page. Cert fee: $7.00. Payee: Norwich Town Clerk. **Other phones:** Assessor-802-649-1116.

Orange Town

Town Clerk, PO Box 233, East Barre, VT 05649. **Phone**-802-479-2673; fax-802-479-2673; hours 8AM-Noon, 1-4PM
Will not search records. Copy fee- $1.00 per page. Cert fee: $7.00. Payee: Town Clerk.

Orwell Town

Town Clerk, PO Box 32, Orwell, VT 05760-0032. **Phone**-802-948-2032; hours 9:30AM-Noon, 1-3:30PM M, T, Th, F
Will not search records. UCC copy- $2.00 per page; $5.00 if oversize. Cert fee: $7.00 per page. Payee: Town of Orwell. **Other phones:** Assessor-802-948-2032.

Panton Town

Town Clerk, PO Box 174, Vergennes, VT 05491-0174. **Phone**-802-475-2333; fax-802-475-2785; hours 9AM-5PM M,Th; 9AM-2PM Tu, F; 4-7PM W
UCC record search per debtor- $10.00. UCC request on non-standard form- $15.00. Will not search real

estate or tax lien records. UCC copy- $7.00 per page. Cert fee: $7.00 per page total. Payee: Panton Town Clerk. **Other phones:** Assessor-802-496-9689.

Pawlet Town

Town Clerk, PO Box 128, Pawlet, VT 05761-0128. **Phone-**Town Clerk, R/E & UCC Recording- 802-325-3309, UCC Recording-802-335-3309; fax-802-325-6109; 9:00AM-3:00PM T-TH; 9:00AM-Noon F
UCC record search per debtor- $2.00 per hour. UCC request on non-standard form- $15.00. Tax lien search- $2.00 per hour per debtor. Will not search real estate records. Copy fee- $1.00 per page. Cert fee: $6.00 per page. Payee: Town of Pawlet. **Other phones:** Assessor-802-325-3309; Treasurer-802-335-3309; Elections-802-335-3309; Vital Records-802-335-3309.

Peacham Town

Town Clerk, Box 244, Peacham, VT 05862. **Phone-**802-592-3218; fax-802-592-3011; hours 8:30AM-Noon T,W,Th,F; 4:30PM-7:30PM W. www.peacham.net
UCC record search per debtor- $10.00. UCC request on non-standard form- $15.00. Will not search real estate or tax lien records. UCC copy- $1.00 per page. Cert fee: $1.00 per page. Payee: Town of Peacham. **Other phones:** Assessor-802-592-3011; Appraiser-802-592-3011.

Peru Town

Town Clerk, Box 127, Peru, VT 05152. **Phone-**802-824-3065; fax-802-824-3065; 8:30AM-4PM T, Th
Will not search records. RE record copy- $1.00 per page. Cert fee: $7.00 per page. Payee: Town of Peru.

Pittsfield Town

Town Clerk, PO Box 556, Pittsfield, VT 05762-0556. **Phone-**802-746-8170; hours Noon-6PM T; 9AM-3PM W,Th
Will not search UCC records. Real estate owner, mortgage, and property transfer searches available. UCC copy- $1.00 per page. Cert fee: $7.00 per page. Payee: Town of Pittsfield. **Other phones:** Assessor-802-746-8113; Treasurer-802-746-8050.

Pittsford Town

Town Clerk, PO Box 10, Pittsford, VT 5763. **Phone-**802-483-2931, R/E Recording-802-483-6500 x12, UCC Recording-802-483-6500 x12; fax-802-483-6612; hours 8AM-4:30PM
UCC record search per debtor- $10.00. UCC request on non-standard form- $15.00. Tax lien search- $10.00 per debtor. Will not search real estate records. RE record copy- $1.00 per page. UCC copy- $1.00 per UCC. Cert fee: $7.00 per page. Payee: Town of Pittsford. **Other phones:** Assessor-802-483-6500 x15; Treasurer-802-483-6500 x12; Appraiser-802-483-6500 x12; Elections-802-483-6500 x12; Vital Records-802-483-6500 x12.

Plainfield Town

Town Clerk, PO Box 217, Plainfield, VT 5667. **Phone-**Town Clerk, R/E & UCC Recording- 802-454-8461; fax-802-454-8461; hours 7:30AM-4PM M,W,F
Will not search records. Records available for in person searching M/W/F 7:30AM-4PM. Record copy- $1.00 per deed. **Other phones:** Assessor-802-454-8461; Treasurer-802-454-8461; Appraiser-802-454-8461; Elections-802-454-8461.

Plymouth Town

Town Clerk, 68 Town Office Rd., Plymouth, VT 05056. **Phone-**802-672-3655; fax-802-672-5466; hours 8:30-11:30AM, 12:30-3:30PM

Will not search records. UCC copy- $1.00 per page. Cert fee: $7.00. Payee: Plymouth Town Clerk. **Other phones:** Assessor-802-672-3655.

Pomfret Town

Town Clerk, PO Box 64, South Pomfret, VT 05067. **Phone-**802-457-3861; fax-none; hours 8:30AM-2:30PM M,W,F
Will not search records. Payee: Pomfret Town Clerk. **Other phones:** Assessor-802-457-3861; Elections-802-457-3861.

Poultney Town

Town Clerk, 9 Main St, #2, Poultney, VT 05764. **Phone-**802-287-5761; hours 8:30AM-12:30, 1:30-4PM
Husband and wife considered as one debtor for searching fee computation. Partnership name plus two partner names considered one name on filing for fee computation. See Filing Facts for further clarification. UCC record search per debtor- $10.00. UCC request on non-standard form- $15.00. Will not search real estate or tax lien records. RE record copy- $1.00 per page. UCC copy- $2.00 per page. Cert fee: $7.00 per cert. Payee: Poultney Town Clerk. **Other phones:** Assessor-802-287-5761.

Pownal Town

Town Clerk, PO Box 411, Pownal, VT 05261. **Phone-**Town Clerk, R/E & UCC Recording- 802-823-7757; fax-802-823-0116; hours 9-2
UCC record search per debtor- $10.00. UCC request on non-standard form- $15.00. UCC search includes tax liens if requested. Separate federal/state combined tax lien search- $5.00 hr Will not search real estate records. UCC copy- $3.00 per page. Cert fee: $7.00. Payee: Pownal Town Clerk. **Other phones:** Assessor-802-823-5644.

Proctor Town

Town Clerk, 45 Main St, Proctor, VT 05765. **Phone-**802-459-3333; fax-802-459-2356; hours 8AM-4PM
Will not search records.

Putney Town

Town Clerk, PO Box 233, Putney, VT 05346. **Phone-**802-387-5862; hours 9AM-2PM M, Th, F; 9AM-2PM, 7-9PM W; 9AM-Noon Sat
UCC record search per debtor- $10.00. Search request using standard form (per name)- $15.00. Will not search real estate or tax lien records. UCC copy- $1.00 per page. Cert fee: $5.00 per cert. Payee: Putney Town Clerk.

Randolph Town

Town Clerk, Drawer B, Randolph, VT 05060. **Phone-**Town Clerk, R/E & UCC Recording- 802-728-5682; fax-802-728-5818; hours 8AM-Noon, 1-4:30PM www.randolphvt.com
UCC record search per debtor- $20.00. Will not search real estate or tax lien records. RE record copy- $1.00 per page. UCC copy- $2.00 per page. Cert fee: $7.00 per page. Payee: Town of Randolph. **Other phones:** Assessor-802-728-5682; Treasurer-728-5682; Elections-802-728-5682; Vital Records-802-728-5682.

Reading Town

Town Clerk, PO Box 72, Reading, VT 05062. **Phone-**Town Clerk, R/E & UCC Recording- 802-484-7250; fax-802-454-7250. www.readingvt.govoffice.com/
Will not search records. Copy fee- $1.00 per page. Cert fee: $7.00 per page. Payee: Town of Reading. **Other phones:** Assessor-802-484-7258; Treasurer-802-484-7250; Appraiser-802-484-7258; Elections-802-484-7250; Vital Records-802-484-7250.

Readsboro Town

Town Clerk, PO Box 187, Readsboro, VT 05350. **Phone-**Town Clerk, R/E & UCC Recording- 802-423-5405; fax-802-423-5423; hours 8AM-2PM M,T; 6-8PM M Eve; 8AM-1PM W,Th; Closed F
Will search UCC records. Will not search tax liens. Will search real estate records. Copy fee- $1.00 per page. Cert fee: $7.00 per page. Payee: Town of Readsboro. **Other phones:** Assessor-802-423-5405; Vital Records-802-423-5405.

Richford Town

Town Clerk, PO Box 236, Richford, VT 05476-0236. **Phone-**Town Clerk, R/E & UCC Recording- 802-848-7751; fax-802-848-7752; hours 8:30AM-4PM www.richfordvt.com
Will not search records. Copy fee- $1.00 per page, $2.00 min. Cert fee: $7.00 per page. Payee: Town of Richford. **Other phones:** Assessor-802-848-7751; Treasurer-802-848-7751; Appraiser-802-848-7751; Elections-802-848-7751; Vital Records-802-848-7751.

Richmond Town

Town Clerk, PO Box 285, Richmond, VT 05477. **Phone-**802-434-2221; hours 8AM-6PM M; 8AM-4PM T-Th, 8AM-1PM F
Will not search records. Record copy fee- $1.00 per page. Cert fee: $7.00 per doc. Payee: Town of Richmond.

Ripton Town

Town Clerk, Box 10, Ripton, VT 05766-0010. **Phone-**802-388-2266; 2-6PM M; 9AM-1PM T,W,Th,F
Will not search records. Cert fee: $5.00 per page. Payee: Town of Ripton. **Other phones:** Assessor-802-388-2266.

Rochester Town

Town Clerk, PO Box 238, Rochester, VT 05767-0238. **Phone-**Town Clerk, R/E & UCC Recording- 802-767-3631; fax-802-767-6028; hours 8AM-4PM T-F, 8AM-N Sat.
UCC record search per debtor- $10.00. UCC request on non-standard form- $15.00. Will do tax lien search. Federal/state combined tax lien search- $7.00 per page. Will not search real estate records. RE record copy- $7.00 per page. UCC copy- $2.00 per page. Cert fee: $7.00 per page. Payee: Town of Rochester. **Other phones:** Assessor-802-767-9872; Treasurer-802-767-3631; Elections-802-767-3631; Vital Records-802-767-3631.

Rockingham Town

Town Clerk, PO Box 339, Bellows Falls, VT 05101-0339. **Phone-**Town Clerk, R/E & UCC Recording- 802-463-4336; fax-802-463-1228; 8:30AM-4:30PM
UCC record search per debtor-$10.00 per search. Will not search real estate or tax lien records. Record copy- $1.00 per page. $2.00 min. Cert fee: $7.00 per page total. Payee: Town of Rockingham. **Other phones:** Assessor-802-463-1229; Treasurer-802-463-3964; Elections-802-463-4336; Vital Records-802-463-4336; Health & Zoning-802-463-3964.

Roxbury Town

Town Clerk, Box 53, Roxbury, VT 05669. **Phone-**Town Clerk, R/E & UCC Recording- 802-485-7840; fax-802-485-7860; hours 9AM-Noon; 1PM-4PM T-F
UCC record search per debtor- $10.00. UCC request on non-standard form- $15.00. Will not search real estate or tax lien records. Copy fee- $1.00 per page. **Other phones:** Assessor-802-485-7840 or 485-7860; Treasurer-802-485-7860; Appraiser-802-485-7840 or 485-7860; Elections-802-485-7840; Vital Records-802-485-7840.

Royalton Town

Town Clerk, PO Box 680, South Royalton, VT 05068-0680. **Phone-**Town Clerk, R/E & UCC Recording-802-763-7207; fax-802-763-7307. www.royaltonvt.com

UCC record search per debtor- $10.00. UCC request on non-standard form- $15.00. Will not search real estate or tax lien records. Copy fee- $1.00 per page. Cert fee: $2.00 per page. Payee: Town of Royalton. **Other phones:** Assessor-802-763-2202; Treasurer-802-763-7207; Elections-802-763-7207; Vital Records-802-763-7207; Second phone-802-763-7967.

Rupert Town

Town Clerk, Box 140, West Rupert, VT 05776. **Phone-**Town Clerk, R/E & UCC Recording- 802-394-7728; fax-802-394-2524; hours 2-7PM M; 12-5PM W; 10AM-3PM Th

UCC record search per debtor- $10.00. UCC request on non-standard form- $15.00. Will not search real estate or tax lien records. RE record copy- $1.00 per page. UCC copy- $7.00 per page. Cert fee: $7.00 per page total. Payee: Rupert Town Clerk. **Other phones:** Assessor-802-394-7728; Treasurer-802-394-7728; Elections-802-394-7728; Vital Records-802-394-7728.

Rutland City

City Clerk, PO Box 969, Rutland, VT 05702. **Phone-**City Clerk, R/E & UCC Recording- 802-773-1801; hours 9AM-4:45PM www.rutlandcity.com

Will not search records. Copy fee- $1.00 per page. Cert fee: $7.00 per page total. Payee: Rutland City Clerk. **Other phones:** Assessor-802-773-1800; Treasurer-802-773-1800; Appraiser-802-773-1800; Elections-802-773-1801; Vital Records-802-773-1801.

Rutland Town

Town Clerk, PO Box 225, Center Rutland, VT 05736. **Phone-**Town Clerk, R/E & UCC Recording- 802-773-2528; fax-802-773-7295; hours 8AM-4:30PM

Will not search records. UCC copy- $1.00 per page. Cert fee: $7.00. Payee: Rutland Town Clerk. **Other phones:** Assessor-802-773-2528; Treasurer-802-773-2528.

Ryegate Town

Town Clerk, PO Box 332, Ryegate, VT 05042. **Phone-**Town Clerk, R/E & UCC Recording- 802-584-3880; fax-802-584-3880; hours 1-5PM M,T,W; 9AM-1PM F.

Will not search records. RE record copy- $1.00 per page if given book/page number. UCC copy- $1.00 per page. Cert fee: $10.00 per doc. Payee: Town of Ryegate. **Other phones:** Assessor-802-584-4247; Treasurer-802-584-3880; Appraiser-802-584-3880; Elections-802-584-3880; Vital Records-802-584-3880.

Salisbury Town

Town Clerk, PO Box 66, Salisbury, VT 05769-0066. **Phone-**802-352-4228; fax-802-352-9832; hours 9AM-3PM T-F; 1st/3rd Sat 9AM-Noon

UCC record search per debtor- $10.00. Tax liens not included in UCC search. Tax lien search- $7.00 per page. Will not search real estate records. UCC copy- $1.00 per page.

Sandgate Town

Town Clerk, 3266 Sandgate Rd., Sandgate, VT 05250. **Phone-**802-375-9075; fax-802-375-8350; hours 10AM-4PM T; 9AM-3PM W

Will not search records. Record copy fee- $1.00 per page. Cert fee: $7.00 per cert. Payee: Sandgate Town Clerk. **Other phones:** Assessor-802-375-9075;

Treasurer-802-375-9075; Appraiser-802-375-9075; Elections-802-375-9075; Vital Records-802-375-9075.

Searsburg Town

Town Clerk, PO Box 157, Wilmington, VT 05363. **Phone-**Town Clerk, R/E & UCC Recording- 802-464-8081; hours 8AM-Noon M,T,F

Will search UCC records. Search per hour- $2.00. Tax liens not included in UCC search. Tax lien search- $2.00 per hour. Will not search real estate records. Copy fee- $1.00 per page. Cert fee: $5.00 per page. Payee: Searsburg Town Clerk. **Other phones:** Assessor-802-464-8081; Treasurer-802-464-8081; Elections-802-464-8081; Vital Records-802-464-8081.

Shaftsbury Town

Town Clerk, PO Box 409, Shaftsbury, VT 05262. **Phone-**802-442-4038; fax-802-442-0955; hours 9AM-5PM, M ;9AM-3:00PM T-F

Will not search records. UCC copy- $1.00 per page. Cert fee: $7.00. Payee: Shaftsbury Town Clerk. **Other phones:** Assessor-802-442-5740; Treasurer-802-442-6242.

Sharon Town

Town Clerk, PO Box 250, Sharon, VT 05065. **Phone-**802-763-8268; fax-802-763-7392; hours 7AM-12PM,1-6PM M,T,Th; 6:30AM-1PM W

Will not search records. Real estate owner and property transfer searches available. Cert fee: $7.00 per cert. Payee: Sharon Town Clerk.

Sheffield Town

Town Clerk, PO Box 165, Sheffield, VT 05866-0165. **Phone-**802-626-8862; hours 8AM-2PM,MWF, Closed T,Th

UCC record search per debtor- $10.00. UCC request on non-standard form- $15.00. Will not search real estate or tax lien records. UCC copy- $1.00 per page. Cert fee: $5.00 per page. Payee: Sheffield Town Clerk. **Other phones:** Assessor-802-626-9273.

Shelburne Town

Town Clerk, PO Box 88, Shelburne, VT 05482. **Phone-**Town Clerk, R/E & UCC Recording- 802-985-5116; fax-802-985-9550; hours 8:30AM-4:30PM www.shelburneVT.org

Will not search records. Copy fee- $1.00 per page. Cert fee: $7.00 per doc. **Other phones:** Assessor-802-985-5115; Treasurer-802-985-5116; Appraiser-802-985-5115; Elections-802-985-5116; Vital Records-802-985-5116; 802-985-5117.

Sheldon Town

Town Clerk, PO Box 66, Sheldon, VT 05483. **Phone-**802-933-2524; fax-802-933-4951; hours 8AM-3PM

UCC record search per debtor- $10.00. UCC request on non-standard form- $15.00. Will not search tax liens. Real estate record owner searches available. Cert fee: $5.00 per cert. Payee: Sheldon Town Clerk.

Shoreham Town

Town Clerk, 297 Main St., Shoreham, VT 05770-9759. **Phone-**Town Clerk, R/E & UCC Recording- 802-897-5841; fax-802-897-2545; 9AM-4P; closed Thurs.

UCC record search per debtor- $10.00. UCC request on non-standard form- $15.00. Will not search real estate or tax lien records. RE record copy- $1.00 per page. Copy fee is $2.00 per doc. Cert fee: $7.00 per page. Payee: Town of Shoreham. **Other phones:** Assessor-802-897-5841; Treasurer-802-897-5841; Elections-802-897-5841; Vital Records-802-897-5841.

Shrewsbury Town

Town Clerk, 9823 Cold River Rd., Shrewsbury, VT 05738. **Phone-**802-492-3511; fax-802-492-3511; hours 10AM-3PM M-TH

UCC record search per debtor- $10.00. UCC request on non-standard form- $15.00. Tax liens not included in UCC search. Tax lien search- $5.00 per hour. Will not search real estate records. RE record copy- $1.00 per page uncertified. Cert fee: $7.00 per page. Payee: Anne Haley, Town Clerk. **Other phones:** Treasurer-802-492-3558.

South Burlington City

Town Clerk, 575 Dorset St, South Burlington, VT 05403. **Phone-**Town Clerk, R/E & UCC Recording- 802-846-4105; hours 8AM-4:30PM, M T TH F; 8am-6:30PM, W

Will not search records. **Other phones:** Assessor-802-846-4103; Treasurer-802-846-4119; Appraiser-802-846-4103; Elections-802-846-4105; Vital Records-802-846-4105; Taxes-802-846-4109.

South Hero Town

Town Clerk, PO Box 175, South Hero, VT 05486. **Phone-**Town Clerk, R/E & UCC Recording- 802-372-5552; hours 8:30AM-Noon, 1-4:30PM M-W; 8:30AM-Noon,1-5PM Th

Will not search records. RE record copy- $1.00 per page. Cert fee: $7.00 per page. Payee: Town of South Hero. **Other phones:** Assessor-802-372-5552; Treasurer-802-372-5552; Appraiser-802-372-5552; Elections-802-372-5552; Vital Records-802-372-5552.

Springfield Town

Town Clerk, 96 Main St, Springfield, VT 05156. **Phone-**Town Clerk, R/E & UCC Recording- 802-885-2104; fax-802-885-1617; hours 8AM-4:30PM

UCC record search per debtor- $10.00. UCC request on non-standard form- $15.00. Tax lien search- $10.00 per hour. Will search real estate records. RE record copy- $1.00 per page. ($2.00 min.). UCC copy- $2.00 per page. Cert fee: $7.00 per page. Payee: Town of Springfield. **Other phones:** Assessor-802-885-2104; Treasurer-802-885-2104; Appraiser-802-885-2104; Elections-802-885-2104; Vital Records-802-885-2104.

St. Albans City

City Clerk, PO Box 867, St. Albans, VT 05478-0867. **Phone-**City Clerk, R/E & UCC Recording- 802-524-1501; hours 7:30AM-4PM

UCC record search per debtor- $10.00. UCC request on non-standard form- $15.00. Will not search real estate or tax lien records. UCC copy- $2.00 per page. Payee: St. Albans City. **Other phones:** Assessor-802-524-1502; Treasurer-802-524-1501; Appraiser-802-524-1502; Elections-802-524-1501; Vital Records-802-524-1501; Water/Sewer-802-524-1504; Accounting-802-524-1506.

St. Albans Town

Town Clerk, PO Box 37, St. Albans Bay, VT 05481. **Phone-**Town Clerk, R/E & UCC Recording- 802-524-2415; fax-802-524-9609; hours 8AM-4PM; closed to public on Wednesdays

UCC record search per debtor- $20.00. UCC request on non-standard form- $25.00. Will not search real estate or tax lien records. Copy fee- $1.00 per page. Cert fee: $6.00 per page + $1.00 per copy. Payee: Town of St. Albans. **Other phones:** Assessor-802-524-7589; Treasurer-802-524-2415; Appraiser-802-524-2415.

St. George Town

Town Clerk, 1 Barber Rd., St. George, VT 05495. **Phone-**802-482-5272; fax-802-482-5548; hours M-F 8-12PM

Will not search UCC or real estate records. Copy fee-$1.00 per copy. **Other phones:** Assessor-802-496-9689.

St. Johnsbury Town

Town Clerk, 1187 Main St, #2, St. Johnsbury, VT 05819-2288. **Phone-**Town Clerk, R/E & UCC Recording- 802-748-4331; fax-802-748-1268; hours 8AM-5PM/ Summer Hrs. 7AM-4PM www.town.st-johnsbury.vt.us
UCC record search per debtor- $10.00. UCC request on non-standard form- $15.00. Will not search real estate or tax lien records. RE record copy- $1.00 per page. UCC copy- $2.00 per page. Cert fee: $7.00 per page. Payee: Town of Johnsbury. **Other phones:** Assessor-802-748-4272; Treasurer-802-748-1260; Appraiser-802-748-4272; Vital Records-802-748-4331.

Stamford Town

Town Clerk, 986 Main Rd., Stamford, VT 05352-9601. **Phone-**Town Clerk, R/E & UCC Recording- 802-694-1361; hours 11AM-4PM T & W; Noon-4PM, 7-9PM Th; Noon-4PM F
UCC record search per debtor- $10.00. UCC request on non-standard form- $15.00. Will not search real estate or tax lien records. RE record copy- $1.00 per page. UCC copy- $2.00 per page. Cert fee: $7.00 per page. Payee: Town of Stamford. **Other phones:** Assessor-802-694-1361; Treasurer-802-694-1361; Appraiser-802-694-1361; Elections-802-694-1361; Vital Records-802-694-1361.

Stannard Town

Town Clerk, PO Box 94, Greensboro Bend, VT 05842-0094. **Phone-**802-533-2577; hours 8AM-Noon W
UCC record search per debtor- $10.00. UCC request on non-standard form- $15.00. Will not search real estate or tax lien records. RE record copy- $2.00 per page. UCC copy- $1.00 per page. Cert fee: $7.00 per page. Payee: Stannard Town Clerk.

Starksboro Town

Town Clerk, PO Box 91, Starksboro, VT 05487-0091. **Phone-**Town Clerk, R/E & UCC Recording- 802-453-2639; fax-802-453-7293; hours 8:30AM-4:30PM M-Th
Will not search records. Copy fee-$1.00 per page. UCC copy- $1.00 per page. Cert fee: $1.00 per page. Payee: Town of Starksboro. **Other phones:** Assessor-802-453-6364; Treasurer-802-453-2639; Elections-802-453-2639; Vital Records-802-453-2639.

Stockbridge Town

Town Clerk, PO Box 39, Stockbridge, VT 05772-0039. **Phone-**802-746-8400; fax-802-746-8400; hours 8AM-4:30PM T W TH; 8AM-Noon F
UCC record search per debtor- $10.00. UCC request on non-standard form- $15.00. Will not search real estate or tax lien records. Copy fee is $1.00 per page. Cert fee: $7.00 per page. Payee: Town of Stockbridge.

Stowe Town

Town Clerk, PO Box 248, Stowe, VT 05672. **Phone-**Town Clerk, R/E & UCC Recording- 802-253-6133; fax-802-253-6143; hours 7:30AM-4:30PM
UCC record search per debtor- $20.00. UCC request on non-standard form- $25.00. Will not search real estate or tax lien records. UCC copy- $.50 per page. Cert fee: $7.00. Payee: Stowe Town Clerk. **Other phones:** Assessor-802-253-6144; Treasurer-802-253-6133; Appraiser-802-253-6144; Elections-802-253-6133; Vital Records-802-253-6133.

Strafford Town

Town Clerk, PO Box 27, Strafford, VT 05072. **Phone-**802-765-4411; fax-802-765-9621; hours 8AM-5PM T,W; 8AM-7PM Th; 8AM-Noon F
Will not search records. UCC copy- $1.00 per page. Cert fee: $7.00 per page. Payee: Town of Strafford. **Other phones:** Assessor-802-765-4411.

Stratton Town

Town Clerk, PO Box 166, West Wardsboro, VT 05360. **Phone-**Town Clerk, R/E & UCC Recording- 802-896-6184; fax-802-896-6630; hours 9:00AM-3:00PM M-TH
Will not search records. Copy fee- $1.00 per page. Cert fee: $7.00 per page. Payee: Town of Stratton. **Other phones:** Assessor-802-896-6184; Treasurer-802-896-6184; Appraiser-802-896-6184; Elections-802-896-6184; Vital Records-802-896-6184.

Sudbury Town

Town Clerk, 36 Blacksmith Ln., Sudbury, VT 05733. **Phone-**Town Clerk, R/E & UCC Recording- 802-623-7296; fax-802-623-7296; hours 9AM-4PM M; 7PM-9PM W,9AM-3PM F.
UCC record search per debtor- $10.00 per page; $15.00 after two pages. Will search tax liens. Search fee- $5.00 per hour. Will not search real estate records. Copy fee is $1.00 per page. Cert fee: $7.00 per page. Payee: Sudbury Town Clerk. **Other phones:** Assessor-802-623-7296; Treasurer-802-623-7296; Appraiser-802-623-7296; Elections-802-623-7296; Vital Records-802-623-7296.

Sunderland Town

Town Clerk, PO Box 295, East Arlington, VT 05252. **Phone-**802-375-6106; hours 8AM-2PM M,T,Th; 8AM-Noon, 6-8PM W
Will not search records. UCC copy- $1.00 per page. Cert fee: $7.00 per page total. Payee: Sunderland Town Clerk. **Other phones:** Assessor-802-362-2284.

Sutton Town

Town Clerk, Box 106, Sutton, VT 05867. **Phone-**802-467-3377; fax-802-467-1052; hours 9AM-5PM,M,T,Th, F; 9am-12:00PM, W
Will not search records. UCC copy- $1.00 per page. Cert fee: $7.00. Payee: Sutton Town Clerk.

Swanton Town

Town Clerk, PO Box 711, Swanton, VT 05488. **Phone-**Town Clerk, R/E & UCC Recording- 802-868-4421; fax-802-868-4957; hours 8AM-4PM
UCC record search per debtor- $10.00. UCC request on non-standard form- $15.00. Will not search tax liens or real estate records. Record copy- $1.00 per page. Cert fee: $6.00 per cert. Payee: Town of Swanton. **Other phones:** Assessor-802-868-4421; Treasurer-802-868-4421; Appraiser-802-868-4421; Elections-802-868-4421; Vital Records-802-868-4421.

Thetford Town

Town Clerk, PO Box 126, Thetford Center, VT 05075-0126. **Phone-**Town Clerk, R/E & UCC Recording- 802-785-2922; fax-802-785-2031; 8:30AM-3PM
UCC record search per debtor- $10.00. UCC request on non-standard form- $15.00. Will not search real estate or tax lien records. Copy fee- $1.00 per page. Cert fee: $7.00 per page. Payee: Town of Thetford. **Other phones:** Assessor-802-785-2922 x15; Treasurer-802-785-2922 x19; Appraiser-802-785-2922 x15; Elections-802-785-2922; Vital Records-802-785-2922.

Tinmouth Town

Town Clerk, 515 North End Rd., Tinmouth, VT 05773. **Phone-**Town Clerk, R/E & UCC Recording- 802-446-

2498; fax-802-446-2498; hours 8AM-12, 1-5PM M & Th & 8AM-Noon Sat Jan-May only.
UCC record search per debtor- $10.00. Will not search real estate or tax lien records. RE record copy- $1.00 per page. UCC copy- no fee, usually. **Other phones:** Assessor-802-446-2498; Treasurer-802-446-2498; Appraiser-802-446-2498; Elections-802-446-2498; Vital Records-802-446-2498.

Topsham Town

Town Clerk, PO Box 69, Topsham, VT 05076. **Phone-**Town Clerk, R/E & UCC Recording- 802-439-5505; fax-802-439-5505; 1-6PM Mon.; 9AM-4PM T-F
Will not search records. Copy fee- $1.00 per page. Cert fee: $7.00 per page. Payee: Topsham Town. **Other phones:** Assessor-802-439-5505; Treasurer-802-439-5505; Appraiser-802-439-5505; Elections-802-439-5505; Vital Records-802-439-5505; Tax Collector-802-439-5550.

Townshend Town

Town Clerk, PO Box 223, Townshend, VT 05353-0223. **Phone-**802-365-7300; fax-none; hours 9AM-4PM M-W & F
Will not search records. RE record copy- $1.00 per page. UCC copy- $.10 per page. Cert fee: $7.00 per page. Payee: Town of Townshend. **Other phones:** Assessor-802-365-7300.

Troy Town

Town Clerk, PO Box 80, North Troy, VT 05859. **Phone-**802-988-2663; fax-802-988-4692; hours 8AM-Noon, 1-4PM
UCC record search per debtor- $5.00. UCC search includes tax liens if requested. Separate federal/state combined tax lien search-no charge. Will not search real estate records. UCC copy- $1.00 per page; $2.00 min. Cert fee: $5.00 per cert. Payee: Troy Town Clerk.

Tunbridge Town

Town Clerk, PO Box 6, Tunbridge, VT 05077. **Phone-**Town Clerk, R/E & UCC Recording- 802-889-5521; fax-802-889-3744; hours 8AM-Noon 1-4PM
Will not search records. Cert fee: $7.00 per page. **Other phones:** Assessor-802-889-5521; Treasurer-802-889-5521; Appraiser-802-889-3571; Elections-802-889-5521; Vital Records-802-889-5521.

Underhill Town

Town Clerk, PO Box 32, Underhill, VT 05490. **Phone-**Town Clerk, R/E & UCC Recording- 802-899-4434; fax-802-899-2137; hours 8AM-4PM M T TH F; 8AM-6PM W
Will not search records. **Other phones:** Assessor-802-899-4434; Treasurer-802-899-4434; Appraiser-802-899-4434; Elections-802-899-4434; Vital Records-802-899-4434.

Vergennes City

Town Clerk, PO Box 35, Vergennes, VT 05491-0035. **Phone-**Town Clerk, R/E & UCC Recording- 802-877-2841; fax-802-877-1160; hours 8AM-4:30PM
Will not search records. Copy fee- $1.00 per page. Cert fee: $7.00 per page. Payee: City Clerk. **Other phones:** Assessor-802-877-2841; Treasurer-802-877-2841; Appraiser-802-877-2841; Elections-802-877-2841; Vital Records-802-877-2841.

Vernon Town

Town Clerk, 567 Governor Hunt Rd., Vernon, VT 05354. **Phone-**Town Clerk, R/E & UCC Recording- 802-257-0292; fax-802-254-3561; hours 8AM-4PM
Will not search records. Copy fee- $1.00 per page. Cert fee: $7.00 per page. Payee: Town Clerk. **Other phones:** Assessor-802-257-0292; Treasurer-802-257-0292; Appraiser-802-257-0292; Elections-802-257-0292; Vital Records-802-257-0292.

Vershire Town

Town Clerk, 6894 Vermont Rte. 113, Vershire, VT 05079. **Phone**-Town Clerk, R/E & UCC Recording-802-685-2227; hours 8:30AM-3PM T-Th
UCC record search per debtor- $10.00. UCC request on non-standard form- $15.00. Will not search real estate or tax lien records. RE record copy- $1.00 per page. Cert fee: $7.00 per page total. Payee: Vershire Town Clerk. **Other phones:** Assessor-802-685-2227; Treasurer-802-685-2227.

Victory Town

Town Clerk, PO Box 609, North Concord, VT 05858. **Phone**-802-328-2400; fax-802-328-2400; hours 10AM-4PM T-F
Will not search UCC or real estate records. Copy fee-$2.00 per page. Copy fee is $6.00 per page. Cert fee: $6.00 per page total. Payee: Victory Town Clerk. **Other phones:** Treasurer-802-328-2400.

Waitsfield Town

Town Clerk, 9 Bridge St, Waitsfield, VT 05673-0390. **Phone**-Town Clerk, R/E & UCC Recording- 802-496-2218; fax-802-496-9284; hours 9AM-4PM
UCC record search per debtor- $10.00. UCC request on non-standard form- $15.00. Will not search real estate or tax lien records. Cert fee: $7.00 per page. Payee: Town of Waitsfield. **Other phones:** Assessor-802-496-9689; Treasurer-802-496-2218; Elections-802-496-2218; Vital Records-802-496-2218.

Walden Town

Town Clerk, 12 Vt. Rte. 215, West Danville, VT 05873. **Phone**-802-563-2220; fax-802-563-3008; hours 9AM-3PM
UCC record search per debtor- $10.00. UCC request on non-standard form- $15.00. Will search tax liens. Will not search real estate records. Record copy-$1.00 per page. Cert fee: $7.00 per page total. Payee: Walden Town Clerk.

Wallingford Town

Town Clerk, PO Box 327, Wallingford, VT 05773. **Phone**-802-446-2336; fax-802-446-3174; hours 8AM-4:30PM M-Th; 8AM-Noon Friday. www.wallingfordvt.com
Will not search records. Copy fee- $2.00 per page. Cert fee: $7.00 per page. Payee: Wallingford Town Clerk. **Other phones:** Assessor-802-446-2336.

Waltham Town

Town Clerk, PO Box 175, Vergennes, VT 05491. **Phone**-802-877-3641; fax-802-877-3641; hours 9AM-3PM T; 9AM-3PM F
UCC record search per debtor- $10.00. UCC request on non-standard form- $15.00. UCC search includes tax liens if requested. Separate federal/state combined tax lien search- $5.00 per debtor. Will not search real estate records. UCC copy-$1.00 per page. Cert fee: $1.00 per page. Payee: Waltham Town Clerk.

Wardsboro Town

Town Clerk, PO Box 48, Wardsboro, VT 05355-0048. **Phone**-802-896-6055; fax-802-896-1000; hours 9AM-Noon, 1-4:30PM M-Th
Will search UCC records. UCC search includes tax liens if requested. Will search real estate records. UCC copy- $1.00 per page. Cert fee: $7.00. Payee: Wardsboro Town Clerk. **Other phones:** Assessor-802-896-6055.

Warren Town

Town Clerk, PO Box 337, Warren, VT 05674. **Phone**-802-496-2709, R/E Recording-802-496-2709 x21, UCC Recording-802-496-2709 x21; fax-802-496-2418; hours 9AM-4:30PM

Will not search records. Record copy- $1.00 per page. Cert fee: $7.00 per page. Payee: Warren Town Clerk. **Other phones:** Assessor-802-496-2709 x26; Treasurer-802-496-2709 x25; Appraiser-802-496-2709 x26; Elections-802-496-2709 x21; Vital Records-802-496-2709 x21.

Washington Town

Town Clerk, Rte. 110, Clerk's Office, Washington, VT 05675. **Phone**-Town Clerk, R/E & UCC Recording-802-883-2218; hours 8:30AM-2PM M,T
UCC record search per debtor- $10.00. UCC request on non-standard form- $15.00. UCC search includes tax liens if requested. Separate federal & state combined tax lien search- $5.00 per search. Real estate record owner searches available. Copy fee-$1.00 per page. Cert fee: $1.00 per page. Payee: Washington Town Clerk. **Other phones:** Assessor-802-883-2218; Treasurer-802-883-2218; Elections-802-883-2218; Vital Records-802-883-2218.

Waterbury Town

Town Clerk, 51 S. Main St, Waterbury, VT 05676. **Phone**-Town Clerk, R/E & UCC Recording- 802-244-8447; fax-802-244-1014; hours 8AM-4:30PM www.waterburyvt.com
Will not search records. Copy fee- $1.00 per page. Cert fee: $7.00 per page. Payee: Town Clerk. **Other phones:** Assessor-802-244-8447; Treasurer-802-244-8447; Appraiser-802-244-8447; Elections-802-244-8447; Vital Records-802-244-8447.

Waterford Town

Town Clerk, PO Box 56, Lower Waterford, VT 05848. **Phone**-Town Clerk, R/E & UCC Recording- 802-748-2122; fax-802-748-8196; hours 8:30AM-3:30PM, M, TH, F; Noon-6PM, T. Will not search UCC or real estate records. Copy fee- $1.00 per page. Cert fee: $7.00 per page. Payee: Town of Waterford. **Other phones:** Assessor-802-748-2122; Treasurer-802-748-2122; Appraiser-802-748-2122; Elections-802-748-2122; Vital Records-802-748-2122.

Waterville Town

Town Clerk, PO Box 31, Waterville, VT 05492. **Phone**-Town Clerk, R/E & UCC Recording- 802-644-8865; fax-802-644-8865; hours 9AM-1:30PM M,T,Th; closed W & F
UCC record search per debtor- $10.00. UCC request on non-standard form- $15.00. Federal/state combined tax lien search- $5.00 per hour. Will not search real estate records. Copy fee- $1.00 per page. Cert fee: $1.00 per page. **Other phones:** Assessor-802-644-8865; Treasurer-802-644-8865; Appraiser-802-644-8865; Elections-802-644-8865; Vital Records-802-644-8865.

Weathersfield Town

Town Clerk, PO Box 550, Weathersfield, VT 05030-0304. **Phone**-802-674-2626; hours 9AM-4PM M-T-W; 9AM-5PM Th
Will not search records. UCC copy- $1.00 per page. Cert fee: $7.00 per page total. Payee: Weathersfield Town Clerk. **Other phones:** Assessor-802-674-2626.

Wells Town

Town Clerk, PO Box 585, Wells, VT 05774. **Phone**-802-645-0486; fax-802-645-0464; 8:30AM-4PM
Will not search UCC records. Will search real estate records. UCC copy- $1.00 per page. Cert fee: $7.00 per page total. Payee: Wells Town Clerk. **Other phones:** Treasurer-802-645-0188.

West Fairlee Town

Town Clerk, Box 615, West Fairlee, VT 05083. **Phone**-802-333-9696; fax-802-333-9611; hours 10AM-4PM M,W,F

UCC record search per debtor-$1.00 per page. Federal/state combined tax lien search- $1.00 per page. Will not search real estate records. $1.00 per page. UCC copy- $1.00 per page. Payee: Town of West Fairlee. **Other phones:** Assessor-802-333-9696; Elections-802-333-9696.

West Haven Town

Town Clerk, 2919 Main Rd., West Haven, VT 05743-9610. **Phone**-802-265-4880; fax-802-265-4880; hours 1PM-3:30PM
Will search UCC records. Search per hour- $2.00. UCC search includes tax liens. Separate federal/state combined tax lien search- $5.00 per hour. Will not search real estate records. RE record copy- $1.00 per page. UCC copy- $2.00 per hour. Cert fee: $5.00 per doc. Payee: Town of West Haven. **Other phones:** Assessor-802-265-7996; Treasurer-802-265-3675; Appraiser-802-265-7996; Elections-802-265-4880; Vital Records-802-265-4880.

West Rutland Town

Town Clerk, 35 Marble St., West Rutland, VT 05777. **Phone**-Town Clerk, R/E & UCC Recording- 802-438-2204; fax-802-438-5133; hours 9AM-4PM M-Th.; Fri. by appointment. www.wrutland.net
UCC record search per debtor- $10.00. UCC request on non-standard form- $15.00. Will not search real estate or tax lien records. RE record copy- $1.00 per page. UCC copy- $2.00 per page, $5.00 per page if over 5" by 8". Cert fee: $7.00 per page. Payee: Town of West Rutland. **Other phones:** Assessor-802-438-2263; Treasurer-802-438-2263; Appraiser-802-438-2263; Elections-802-438-2204; Vital Records-802-438-2204.

West Windsor Town

Town Clerk, Box 6, Brownsville, VT 05037. **Phone**-Town Clerk, R/E & UCC Recording- 802-484-7212; fax-802-484-3518.
UCC record search per debtor- $10.00. UCC request on non-standard form- $15.00. Will not search real estate records. **Other phones:** Assessor-802-484-7212; Treasurer-802-484-7212; Appraiser-802-484-7212.

Westfield Town

Town Clerk, 1257 Vermont Rte. 100, Westfield, VT 05874. **Phone**-Town Clerk, R/E & UCC Recording-802-744-2484; fax-802-744-2484; hours 8AM-5PM M & W; 10AM-5PM Tu.
Will not search records. Copy fee- $1.00 per copy. Cert fee: $6.00 per page total. Payee: Westfield Town Clerk. **Other phones:** Assessor-802-744-2484; Treasurer-802-744-2484; Vital Records-802-744-2484.

Westford Town

Town Clerk, 1713 Vermont Route 128, Westford, VT 05494. **Phone**-Town Clerk, R/E & UCC Recording-802-878-4587; fax-802-879-6503; hours 8:30AM-4:30PM
Will not search records. Copy fee- $1.00 per page. Cert fee: $7.00 per page. Payee: Town of Westford. **Other phones:** Assessor-802-878-4587; Treasurer-802-878-4587; Appraiser-802-878-4587; Elections-802-878-4587; Vital Records-802-878-4587.

Westminster Town

Town Clerk, PO Box 147, Westminster, VT 05158-0147. **Phone**-Town Clerk, R/E & UCC Recording-802-722-9101; fax-802-722-9816; hours 8:30AM-4PM http://westminster.govoffice.com
UCC record search per debtor- $10.00. UCC request on non-standard form- $15.00. Will not search real estate records. Copy fee- $1.00 per page. Cert fee: $7.00 per page. Payee: Town of Westminster. **Other phones:** Assessor-802-722-9516; Treasurer-802-722-4091; Appraiser-802-722-9516; Elections-802-722-4091; Vital Records-802-722-4091.

Westmore Town

Town Clerk, 54 Hinton Hill Rd., Orleans, VT 05860. **Phone**-802-525-3007; fax-802-525-3007; hours M 9AM-Noon;1-7PM, T&Th 9AM-Noon; 1-4PM, F 9AM-12PM. Will not search records. UCC copy-$1.00 per page. Cert fee: $7.00 per page. Payee: Town of Westmore.

Weston Town

Town Clerk, PO Box 98, Weston, VT 05161. **Phone**-802-824-6645; fax-802-824-4121; hours 9AM-1PM Will not search records. Copy fee- $1.00 per page. Cert fee: $7.00 per page. Payee: Town Clerk.

Weybridge Town

Town Clerk, 1727 Quaker Village Rd., Weybridge, VT 05753. **Phone**-Town Clerk, R/E & UCC Recording-802-545-2450; fax-802-545-2624; hours 9AM-2PM M,T,TH,F

UCC record search per debtor- $10.00. UCC request on non-standard form- $15.00. Will search tax liens including federal tax liens. Tax lien search-$10.00 per debtor. Will not search real estate records. Copy fee- $1.00 per page. Cert fee: $1.00 per page. Payee: Weybridge Town. **Other phones:** Assessor-802-545-2450; Treasurer-802-545-2450; Appraiser-802-545-2450; Elections-802-545-2450; Vital Records-802-545-2450.

Wheelock Town

Town Clerk, PO Box 1328, Lyndonville, VT 05851-1328. **Phone**-Town Clerk, R/E & UCC Recording-802-626-9094; fax-802-626-9094; hours 8AM-4PM M-W, 10AM-6PM Th

Will not search UCC records. Will search tax liens. Real estate record owner searches available. Record copy- $1.00 per page. Cert fee: $7.00 per page total. Payee: Wheelock Town Clerk. **Other phones:** Assessor-802-626-9094; Treasurer-802-626-9094; Elections-802-626-9094; Vital Records-802-626-9094.

Whiting Town

Town Clerk, 29 S. Main St., Whiting, VT 05778. **Phone**-Town Clerk, R/E & UCC Recording- 802-623-7813; hours 9AM-Noon M,W,F and by App't

UCC record search per debtor- $10.00. UCC request on non-standard form- $15.00. UCC search includes tax liens if requested. Real estate owner, mortgage, and property transfer searches available. RE record copy- $1.00 per page. UCC copy- $.25 per page. Cert fee: $7.00 per page total. Payee: Whiting Town Clerk. **Other phones:** Assessor-802-623-7813; Treasurer-802-623-7813.

Whitingham Town

Town Clerk, PO Box 529, Jacksonville, VT 05342. **Phone**-Town Clerk, R/E & UCC Recording- 802-368-7887; fax-802-368-7519; hours 9AM-2PM (5:30-7:30PM W); 1st Sat of month 9AM-2PM

UCC record search per debtor- $2.00 per hour. UCC search includes tax liens if requested. Real estate owner, mortgage, and property transfer searches available. Copy fee is $1.00 per page. Cert fee: $7.00 per cert. Payee: Whitingham Town Clerk. **Other phones:** Assessor-802-368-2838; Treasurer-802-368-7543; Appraiser-802-368-2838; Elections-802-368-7887; Vital Records-802-368-7887.

Williamstown Town

Town Clerk, PO Box 646, Williamstown, VT 05679. **Phone**-802-433-5455; fax-802-433-2160; hours 8AM-Noon,12:30-4:30PM M; 8AM-Noon T-F www.williamstownvt.org

Will search UCC records as time permits. No search fee. UCC search includes tax liens if requested. Tax lien search-N/C. Will not search real estate records. Copy fee- $1.00 per page. Cert fee: $5.00 per cert. Payee: Williamstown Town Clerk. **Other phones:** Assessor-802-433-5455; Treasurer-802-433-5455; Appraiser-802-433-5455; Elections-802-433-5455; Vital Records-802-433-5455.

Williston Town

Town Clerk, 7900 Williston Rd., Williston, VT 05495. **Phone**-Town Clerk, R/E & UCC Recording- 802-878-5121; fax-802-764-1140; hours 8AM-4:30PM

St. George is a separate town with a Williston mailing address. UCC record search per debtor- $10.00. UCC request on non-standard form- $15.00. Will not search real estate or tax lien records. Record copy-$1.00 per page. Cert fee: $7.00 per page. Payee: Town of Williston. **Other phones:** Assessor-802-878-1091; Treasurer-802-878-5121; Appraiser-802-878-1091; Elections-802-878-5121; Vital Records-802-878-5121.

Wilmington Town

Town Clerk, PO Box 217, Wilmington, VT 05363-0217. **Phone**-Town Clerk, R/E & UCC Recording-802-464-5836; fax-802-464-1238; hours 8:30-N, 1-4PM M-W; 8:30AM-4PM Th; 8:30AM-6:30PM F www.wilmingtonvermont.us

Will not search records. Copy fee- $1.00 per page. Cert fee: $7.00 per page. Payee: Town of Wilmington. **Other phones:** Assessor-802-464-8591; Treasurer-802-464-8591; Appraiser-802-464-8591; Elections-802-464-5836; Vital Records-802-464-5836.

Windham Town

Town Clerk, 5976 Windham Hill Rd, Windham, VT 05039. **Phone**-802-874-4211; fax-802-874-4144; hours 10AM-3PM T,Th,F. This office's jurisdiction includes ONLY Windham Town; do not confuse Windham Town with Windham County. UCC record search per debtor- $10.00. UCC request on non-standard form- $15.00. Will not search real estate or tax lien records. Cert fee: $7.00 per page total. Payee: Windham Town Clerk.

Windsor Town

Town Clerk, PO Box 47, Windsor, VT 05089. **Phone**-Town Clerk, R/E & UCC Recording- 802-674-5610; fax-802-674-1017; hours 8AM-4:30PM M,W,Th; 8AM-6PM Tues; 8AM-2PM F

Will not search records. Copy fee- $1.00 per page. Cert fee: $7.00 per page. Payee: Town Clerk. **Other phones:** Assessor-802-674-5414; Treasurer-802-674-6788; Appraiser-802-674-5414; Elections-802-674-5610; Vital Records-802-674-5610.

Winhall Town

Town Clerk, Box 389, Bondville, VT 05340. **Phone**-Town Clerk, R/E & UCC Recording- 802-297-2122; hours 9AM-Noon (Closed Th)

Will not search records. Cert fee: $7.00 per page total. Payee: Winhall Town Clerk. **Other phones:** Assessor-802-297-2119; Treasurer-802-297-1994;

Appraiser-802-297-2151; Elections-802-297-2122; Vital Records-802-297-2122.

Winooski City

Town Clerk, 27 W. Allen St, Winooski, VT 05404. **Phone**-802-655-6419; fax-802-655-6414; hours 8-4PM

UCC record search per debtor- $10.00. UCC request on non-standard form- $15.00. Tax liens not included in UCC search. Will not search real estate records. UCC copy- $1.00 per page. Cert fee: $7.00. Payee: Winooski City. **Other phones:** Assessor-802-655-6410.

Wolcott Town

Town Clerk, PO Box 100, Wolcott, VT 05680-0100. **Phone**-Town Clerk, R/E & UCC Recording- 802-888-2746; fax-802-888-2746; hours 8AM-4PM T-F; Tues Evening 6-8PM

UCC record search per debtor- $5.00 per hour. Will not search tax liens. Will search real estate records. Copy fee- $1.00 per page. Cert fee: $7.00 per page. Payee: Town of Wolcott. **Other phones:** Assessor-802-888-2746; Treasurer-802-888-2746; Appraiser-802-888-6858; Elections-802-888-2746; Vital Records-802-888-2746.

Woodbury Town

Town Clerk, PO Box 123, Woodbury, VT 05681. **Phone**-802-456-7051; hours 8:30AM-1PM T-W-Th; 6-8PM Th evening

UCC record search per debtor- $10.00. UCC request on non-standard form- $15.00. Will not search real estate or tax lien records. RE record copy- $1.00 per page, $2.00 min. Cert fee: $6.00 per page total. Payee: Woodbury Town Clerk. **Other phones:** Assessor-802-456-8836.

Woodford Town

Town Clerk, 1391 Vermont Rte. 9, Bennington, VT 05201. **Phone**-Town Clerk, R/E & UCC Recording-802-442-4895; fax-802-442-4816; hours 8:30AM-N Will not search records. UCC copy- $1.00 per page. Cert fee: $7.00 per page. Payee: Town Clerk. **Other phones:** Assessor-802-442-4895; Treasurer-802-442-4895; Appraiser-802-442-4895; Elections-802-442-4895; Vital Records-802-442-4895.

Woodstock Town

Town Clerk, 31 The Green, Woodstock, VT 05091. **Phone**-802-457-3611; fax-802-457-2329; hours 8:00AM-Noon, 1:00-4:30PM www.townofwoodstock.org

Will not search records. Copy fee- $1.00 per page. Cert fee: $7.00 per page. Payee: Town of Woodstock. **Other phones:** Assessor-802-457-2607; Treasurer-802-457-3456.

Worcester Town

Town Clerk, Drawer 161, Worcester, VT 05682-0161. **Phone**-802-223-6942; fax-802-229-5216; hours 8AM-4PM M,T,Th; 8AM-1PM F

UCC record search per debtor- $10.00. UCC request on non-standard form- $15.00. Will not search real estate or tax lien records. Copy fee- $1.00 per page. Cert fee: $7.00 per page. Payee: Town of Worcester.

Vermont County Locator

You will usually be able to find the city name in the City/County Cross Reference below. In that case, it is a simple matter to determine the county from the cross reference. However, only the official US Postal Service city names are included in this index. We have also included a ZIP/City Cross Reference immediately following the City/County Cross Reference. If you know the ZIP Code but the city name does not appear in the City/County Cross Reference index, look up the ZIP Code in the ZIP/City Cross Reference, find the city name, then look up the city name in the City/County Cross Reference.

Vermont City/County Cross Reference

ADAMANT Washington
ALBANY Orleans
ALBURG Grand Isle
ARLINGTON Bennington
ASCUTNEY Windsor
AVERILL Essex
BAKERSFIELD Franklin
BARNARD Windsor
BARNET Caledonia
BARRE Washington
BARTON Orleans
BEEBE PLAIN Orleans
BEECHER FALLS Essex
BELLOWS FALLS Windham
BELMONT Rutland
BELVIDERE CENTER Lamoille
BENNINGTON Bennington
BENSON Rutland
BETHEL Windsor
BOMOSEEN Rutland
BONDVILLE Bennington
BRADFORD Orange
BRANDON (05733) Rutland(94),
    Addison(5)
BRATTLEBORO Windham
BRIDGEWATER Windsor
BRIDGEWATER CORNERS Windsor
BRIDPORT Addison
BRISTOL Addison
BROOKFIELD Orange
BROWNSVILLE Windsor
BURLINGTON Chittenden
CABOT (05647) Washington(98),
    Caledonia(1)
CAMBRIDGE (05444) Chittenden(94),
    Franklin(3), Lamoille(2)
CAMBRIDGEPORT Windham
CANAAN Essex
CASTLETON Rutland
CAVENDISH Windsor
CENTER RUTLAND Rutland
CHARLOTTE Chittenden
CHELSEA Orange
CHESTER Windsor
CHESTER DEPOT Windsor
CHITTENDEN Rutland
COLCHESTER Chittenden
CONCORD Essex
CORINTH Orange
COVENTRY Orleans
CRAFTSBURY Orleans
CRAFTSBURY COMMON Orleans
CUTTINGSVILLE Rutland
DANBY Rutland
DANVILLE Caledonia
DERBY Orleans
DERBY LINE Orleans
DORSET Bennington
EAST ARLINGTON Bennington
EAST BARRE (05649) Washington(93),
    Orange(6)
EAST BERKSHIRE Franklin
EAST BURKE Caledonia
EAST CALAIS Washington
EAST CHARLESTON Orleans
EAST CORINTH Orange
EAST DORSET (05253) Bennington(98),
    Rutland(1)
EAST DOVER Windham
EAST FAIRFIELD Franklin

EAST HARDWICK Caledonia
EAST HAVEN Essex
EAST MIDDLEBURY Addison
EAST MONTPELIER Washington
EAST POULTNEY Rutland
EAST RANDOLPH Orange
EAST RYEGATE Caledonia
EAST SAINT JOHNSBURY Caledonia
EAST THETFORD Orange
EAST WALLINGFORD Rutland
EDEN Lamoille
EDEN MILLS Lamoille
ELY Orange
ENOSBURG FALLS Franklin
ESSEX Chittenden
ESSEX JUNCTION Chittenden
FAIR HAVEN Rutland
FAIRFAX (05454) Chittenden(93),
    Franklin(6)
FAIRFIELD Franklin
FAIRLEE Orange
FERRISBURG Addison
FLORENCE Rutland
FOREST DALE Rutland
GAYSVILLE Windsor
GILMAN Essex
GLOVER Orleans
GRAFTON Windham
GRANBY Essex
GRAND ISLE Grand Isle
GRANITEVILLE (05654) Washington(88),
    Orange(11)
GRANVILLE Addison
GREENSBORO Orleans
GREENSBORO BEND Orleans
GROTON Caledonia
GUILDHALL Essex
HANCOCK Addison
HARDWICK Caledonia
HARTFORD Windsor
HARTLAND Windsor
HARTLAND FOUR CORNERS Windsor
HIGHGATE CENTER Franklin
HIGHGATE SPRINGS Franklin
HINESBURG Chittenden
HUNTINGTON Chittenden
HYDE PARK Lamoille
HYDEVILLE Rutland
IRASBURG Orleans
ISLAND POND Essex
ISLE LA MOTTE Grand Isle
JACKSONVILLE Windham
JAMAICA Windham
JEFFERSONVILLE Lamoille
JERICHO Chittenden
JOHNSON Lamoille
JONESVILLE Chittenden
KILLINGTON Rutland
LAKE ELMORE Lamoille
LONDONDERRY Windham
LOWELL Orleans
LOWER WATERFORD Caledonia
LUDLOW Windsor
LUNENBURG Essex
LYNDON Caledonia
LYNDON CENTER Caledonia
LYNDONVILLE Caledonia
MANCHESTER Bennington
MANCHESTER CENTER Bennington
MARLBORO Windham

MARSHFIELD Washington
MC INDOE FALLS Caledonia
MIDDLEBURY Addison
MIDDLETOWN SPRINGS Rutland
MILTON (05468) Chittenden(96),
    Franklin(3)
MONKTON Addison
MONTGOMERY Franklin
MONTGOMERY CENTER (05471)
    Franklin(97), Orleans(2)
MONTPELIER Washington
MORETOWN Washington
MORGAN Orleans
MORRISVILLE Lamoille
MOSCOW Lamoille
MOUNT HOLLY Rutland
NEW HAVEN Addison
NEWBURY Orange
NEWFANE Windham
NEWPORT Orleans
NEWPORT CENTER Orleans
NORTH BENNINGTON Bennington
NORTH CLARENDON Rutland
NORTH CONCORD Essex
NORTH FERRISBURG Addison
NORTH HARTLAND Windsor
NORTH HERO Grand Isle
NORTH HYDE PARK Lamoille
NORTH MONTPELIER Washington
NORTH POMFRET Windsor
NORTH POWNAL Bennington
NORTH SPRINGFIELD Windsor
NORTH THETFORD Orange
NORTH TROY Orleans
NORTHFIELD Washington
NORTHFIELD FALLS Washington
NORTON Essex
NORWICH Windsor
ORLEANS Orleans
ORWELL (05760) Addison(97), Rutland(2)
PASSUMPSIC Caledonia
PAWLET (05761) Rutland(98),
    Bennington(1)
PEACHAM Caledonia
PERKINSVILLE Windsor
PERU Bennington
PITTSFIELD (05762) Rutland(96),
    Windsor(3)
PITTSFORD Rutland
PLAINFIELD Washington
PLYMOUTH Windsor
POST MILLS Orange
POULTNEY Rutland
POWNAL Bennington
PROCTOR Rutland
PROCTORSVILLE Windsor
PUTNEY Windham
QUECHEE Windsor
RANDOLPH Orange
RANDOLPH CENTER Orange
READING Windsor
READSBORO Bennington
RICHFORD Franklin
RICHMOND Chittenden
RIPTON Addison
ROCHESTER (05767) Windsor(97),
    Addison(1)
ROXBURY (05669) Addison(91),
    Washington(7), Orange(1)
RUPERT Bennington

RUTLAND Rutland
SAINT ALBANS BAY Franklin
SAINT JOHNSBURY Caledonia
SAINT JOHNSBURY CENTER Caledonia
SALISBURY Addison
SAXTONS RIVER Windham
SHAFTSBURY Bennington
SHARON Windsor
SHEFFIELD Caledonia
SHELBURNE Chittenden
SHELDON Franklin
SHELDON SPRINGS Franklin
SHOREHAM Addison
SOUTH BARRE Washington
SOUTH BURLINGTON Chittenden
SOUTH HERO Grand Isle
SOUTH LONDONDERRY Windham
SOUTH NEWFANE Windham
SOUTH POMFRET Windsor
SOUTH ROYALTON Windsor
SOUTH RYEGATE Caledonia
SOUTH STRAFFORD Orange
SOUTH WOODSTOCK Windsor
SPRINGFIELD Windsor
STARKSBORO Addison
STOCKBRIDGE Windsor
STOWE Lamoille
STRAFFORD Orange
SUTTON Caledonia
SWANTON Franklin
TAFTSVILLE Windsor
THETFORD Orange
THETFORD CENTER Orange
TOWNSHEND Windham
TROY Orleans
TUNBRIDGE Orange
UNDERHILL Chittenden
UNDERHILL CENTER Chittenden
VERGENNES Addison
VERNON Windham
VERSHIRE Orange
WAITSFIELD Washington
WALLINGFORD Rutland
WARDSBORO Windham
WARREN Washington
WASHINGTON Orange
WATERBURY (05676) Washington(86),
    Chittenden(13)
WATERBURY Washington
WATERBURY CENTER Washington
WATERVILLE Lamoille
WEBSTERVILLE Washington
WELLS Rutland
WELLS RIVER Orange
WEST BURKE Caledonia
WEST CHARLESTON Orleans
WEST DANVILLE Caledonia
WEST DOVER Windham
WEST DUMMERSTON Windham
WEST FAIRLEE Orange
WEST GLOVER Orleans
WEST HALIFAX Windham
WEST HARTFORD Windsor
WEST NEWBURY Orange
WEST PAWLET (05775) Rutland(98),
    Bennington(2)
WEST RUPERT Bennington
WEST RUTLAND Rutland
WEST TOPSHAM Orange
WEST TOWNSHEND Windham

WEST WARDSBORO Windham
WESTFIELD Orleans
WESTFORD Chittenden
WESTMINSTER Windham
WESTMINSTER STATION Windham

WESTON Windsor
WHITE RIVER JUNCTION Windsor
WHITING (05778) Addison(96), Rutland(3)
WHITINGHAM Windham
WILDER Windsor

WILLIAMSTOWN Orange
WILLIAMSVILLE Windham
WILLISTON Chittenden
WILMINGTON Windham
WINDSOR Windsor

WINOOSKI Chittenden
WOLCOTT Lamoille
WOODBURY Washington
WOODSTOCK Windsor
WORCESTER Washington

Vermont ZIP/City Cross Reference

05001-05009	WHITE RIVER JUNCTION
05030-05030	ASCUTNEY
05031-05031	BARNARD
05032-05032	BETHEL
05033-05033	BRADFORD
05034-05034	BRIDGEWATER
05035-05035	BRIDGEWATER CORNERS
05036-05036	BROOKFIELD
05037-05037	BROWNSVILLE
05038-05038	CHELSEA
05039-05039	CORINTH
05040-05040	EAST CORINTH
05041-05041	EAST RANDOLPH
05042-05042	EAST RYEGATE
05043-05043	EAST THETFORD
05044-05044	ELY
05045-05045	FAIRLEE
05046-05046	GROTON
05047-05047	HARTFORD
05048-05048	HARTLAND
05049-05049	HARTLAND 4 CORNERS
05050-05050	MC INDOE FALLS
05051-05051	NEWBURY
05052-05052	NORTH HARTLAND
05053-05053	NORTH POMFRET
05054-05054	NORTH THETFORD
05055-05055	NORWICH
05056-05056	PLYMOUTH
05058-05058	POST MILLS
05059-05059	QUECHEE
05060-05060	RANDOLPH
05061-05061	RANDOLPH CENTER
05062-05062	READING
05065-05065	SHARON
05067-05067	SOUTH POMFRET
05068-05068	SOUTH ROYALTON
05069-05069	SOUTH RYEGATE
05070-05070	SOUTH STRAFFORD
05071-05071	SOUTH WOODSTOCK
05072-05072	STRAFFORD
05073-05073	TAFTSVILLE
05074-05074	THETFORD
05075-05075	THETFORD CENTER
05076-05076	EAST CORINTH
05077-05077	TUNBRIDGE
05079-05079	VERSHIRE
05081-05081	WELLS RIVER
05083-05083	WEST FAIRLEE
05084-05084	WEST HARTFORD
05085-05085	WEST NEWBURY
05086-05086	WEST TOPSHAM
05088-05088	WILDER
05089-05089	WINDSOR
05091-05091	WOODSTOCK
05101-05101	BELLOWS FALLS
05141-05141	CAMBRIDGEPORT
05142-05142	CAVENDISH
05143-05143	CHESTER
05144-05144	CHESTER DEPOT
05146-05146	GRAFTON
05148-05148	LONDONDERRY
05149-05149	LUDLOW
05150-05150	NORTH SPRINGFIELD
05151-05151	PERKINSVILLE
05152-05152	PERU
05153-05153	PROCTORSVILLE
05154-05154	SAXTONS RIVER
05155-05155	SOUTH LONDONDERRY
05156-05156	SPRINGFIELD
05158-05158	WESTMINSTER
05159-05159	WESTMINSTER STATION
05161-05161	WESTON
05201-05201	BENNINGTON
05250-05250	ARLINGTON

05251-05251	DORSET
05252-05252	EAST ARLINGTON
05253-05253	EAST DORSET
05254-05254	MANCHESTER
05255-05255	MANCHESTER CENTER
05257-05257	NORTH BENNINGTON
05260-05260	NORTH POWNAL
05261-05261	POWNAL
05262-05262	SHAFTSBURY
05301-05304	BRATTLEBORO
05340-05340	BONDVILLE
05341-05341	EAST DOVER
05342-05342	JACKSONVILLE
05343-05343	JAMAICA
05344-05344	MARLBORO
05345-05345	NEWFANE
05346-05346	PUTNEY
05350-05350	READSBORO
05351-05351	SOUTH NEWFANE
05352-05352	READSBORO
05353-05353	TOWNSHEND
05354-05354	VERNON
05355-05355	WARDSBORO
05356-05356	WEST DOVER
05357-05357	WEST DUMMERSTON
05358-05358	WEST HALIFAX
05359-05359	WEST TOWNSHEND
05360-05360	WEST WARDSBORO
05361-05361	WHITINGHAM
05362-05362	WILLIAMSVILLE
05363-05363	WILMINGTON
05401-05402	BURLINGTON
05403-05403	SOUTH BURLINGTON
05404-05404	WINOOSKI
05405-05406	BURLINGTON
05407-05407	SOUTH BURLINGTON
05439-05439	COLCHESTER
05440-05440	ALBURG
05441-05441	BAKERSFIELD
05442-05442	BELVIDERE CENTER
05443-05443	BRISTOL
05444-05444	CAMBRIDGE
05445-05445	CHARLOTTE
05446-05446	COLCHESTER
05447-05447	EAST BERKSHIRE
05448-05448	EAST FAIRFIELD
05449-05449	COLCHESTER
05450-05450	ENOSBURG FALLS
05451-05451	ESSEX
05452-05453	ESSEX JUNCTION
05454-05454	FAIRFAX
05455-05455	FAIRFIELD
05456-05456	FERRISBURG
05457-05457	FRANKLIN
05458-05458	GRAND ISLE
05459-05459	HIGHGATE CENTER
05460-05460	HIGHGATE SPRINGS
05461-05461	HINESBURG
05462-05462	HUNTINGTON
05463-05463	ISLE LA MOTTE
05464-05464	JEFFERSONVILLE
05465-05465	JERICHO
05466-05466	JONESVILLE
05468-05468	MILTON
05469-05469	MONKTON
05470-05470	MONTGOMERY
05471-05471	MONTGOMERY CENTER
05472-05472	NEW HAVEN
05473-05473	NORTH FERRISBURG
05474-05474	NORTH HERO
05476-05476	RICHFORD
05477-05477	RICHMOND
05478-05479	SAINT ALBANS
05481-05481	SAINT ALBANS BAY

05482-05482	SHELBURNE
05483-05483	SHELDON
05485-05485	SHELDON SPRINGS
05486-05486	SOUTH HERO
05487-05487	STARKSBORO
05488-05488	SWANTON
05489-05489	UNDERHILL
05490-05490	UNDERHILL CENTER
05491-05491	VERGENNES
05492-05492	WATERVILLE
05494-05494	WESTFORD
05495-05495	WILLISTON
05601-05633	MONTPELIER
05640-05640	ADAMANT
05641-05641	BARRE
05647-05647	CABOT
05648-05648	CALAIS
05649-05649	EAST BARRE
05650-05650	EAST CALAIS
05651-05651	EAST MONTPELIER
05652-05652	EDEN
05653-05653	EDEN MILLS
05654-05654	GRANITEVILLE
05655-05655	HYDE PARK
05656-05656	JOHNSON
05657-05657	LAKE ELMORE
05658-05658	MARSHFIELD
05660-05660	MORETOWN
05661-05661	MORRISVILLE
05662-05662	MOSCOW
05663-05663	NORTHFIELD
05664-05664	NORTHFIELD FALLS
05665-05665	NORTH HYDE PARK
05666-05666	NORTH MONTPELIER
05667-05667	PLAINFIELD
05669-05669	ROXBURY
05670-05670	SOUTH BARRE
05671-05671	WATERBURY
05672-05672	STOWE
05673-05673	WAITSFIELD
05674-05674	WARREN
05675-05675	WASHINGTON
05676-05676	WATERBURY
05677-05677	WATERBURY CENTER
05678-05678	WEBSTERVILLE
05679-05679	WILLIAMSTOWN
05680-05680	WOLCOTT
05681-05681	WOODBURY
05682-05682	WORCESTER
05701-05702	RUTLAND
05730-05730	BELMONT
05731-05731	BENSON
05732-05732	BOMOSEEN
05733-05733	BRANDON
05734-05734	BRIDPORT
05735-05735	CASTLETON
05736-05736	CENTER RUTLAND
05737-05737	CHITTENDEN
05738-05738	CUTTINGSVILLE
05739-05739	DANBY
05740-05740	EAST MIDDLEBURY
05741-05741	EAST POULTNEY
05742-05742	EAST WALLINGFORD
05743-05743	FAIR HAVEN
05744-05744	FLORENCE
05745-05745	FOREST DALE
05746-05746	GAYSVILLE
05747-05747	GRANVILLE
05748-05748	HANCOCK
05750-05750	HYDEVILLE
05751-05751	KILLINGTON
05753-05753	MIDDLEBURY
05757-05757	MIDDLETOWN SPRINGS
05758-05758	MOUNT HOLLY

05759-05759	NORTH CLARENDON
05760-05760	ORWELL
05761-05761	PAWLET
05762-05762	PITTSFIELD
05763-05763	PITTSFORD
05764-05764	POULTNEY
05765-05765	PROCTOR
05766-05766	MIDDLEBURY
05766-05766	RIPTON
05767-05767	ROCHESTER
05768-05768	RUPERT
05769-05769	SALISBURY
05770-05770	SHOREHAM
05772-05772	STOCKBRIDGE
05773-05773	WALLINGFORD
05774-05774	WELLS
05775-05775	WEST PAWLET
05776-05776	WEST RUPERT
05777-05777	WEST RUTLAND
05778-05778	WHITING
05819-05819	SAINT JOHNSBURY
05820-05820	ALBANY
05821-05821	BARNET
05822-05822	BARTON
05823-05823	BEEBE PLAIN
05824-05824	CONCORD
05825-05825	COVENTRY
05826-05826	CRAFTSBURY
05827-05827	CRAFTSBURY COMMON
05828-05828	DANVILLE
05829-05829	DERBY
05830-05830	DERBY LINE
05832-05832	EAST BURKE
05833-05833	EAST CHARLESTON
05836-05836	EAST HARDWICK
05837-05837	EAST HAVEN
05838-05838	EAST SAINT JOHNSBURY
05839-05839	GLOVER
05840-05840	GRANBY
05841-05841	GREENSBORO
05842-05842	GREENSBORO BEND
05843-05843	HARDWICK
05845-05845	IRASBURG
05846-05846	ISLAND POND
05847-05847	LOWELL
05848-05848	LOWER WATERFORD
05849-05849	LYNDON
05850-05850	LYNDON CENTER
05851-05851	LYNDONVILLE
05853-05853	MORGAN
05855-05855	NEWPORT
05857-05857	NEWPORT CENTER
05858-05858	NORTH CONCORD
05859-05859	NORTH TROY
05860-05860	ORLEANS
05861-05861	PASSUMPSIC
05862-05862	PEACHAM
05863-05863	SAINT JOHNSBURY CENTER
05866-05866	SHEFFIELD
05867-05867	SUTTON
05868-05868	TROY
05871-05871	WEST BURKE
05872-05872	WEST CHARLESTON
05873-05873	WEST DANVILLE
05874-05874	WESTFIELD
05875-05875	WEST GLOVER
05901-05901	AVERILL
05902-05902	BEECHER FALLS
05903-05903	CANAAN
05904-05904	GILMAN
05905-05905	GUILDHALL
05906-05906	LUNENBURG
05907-05907	NORTON

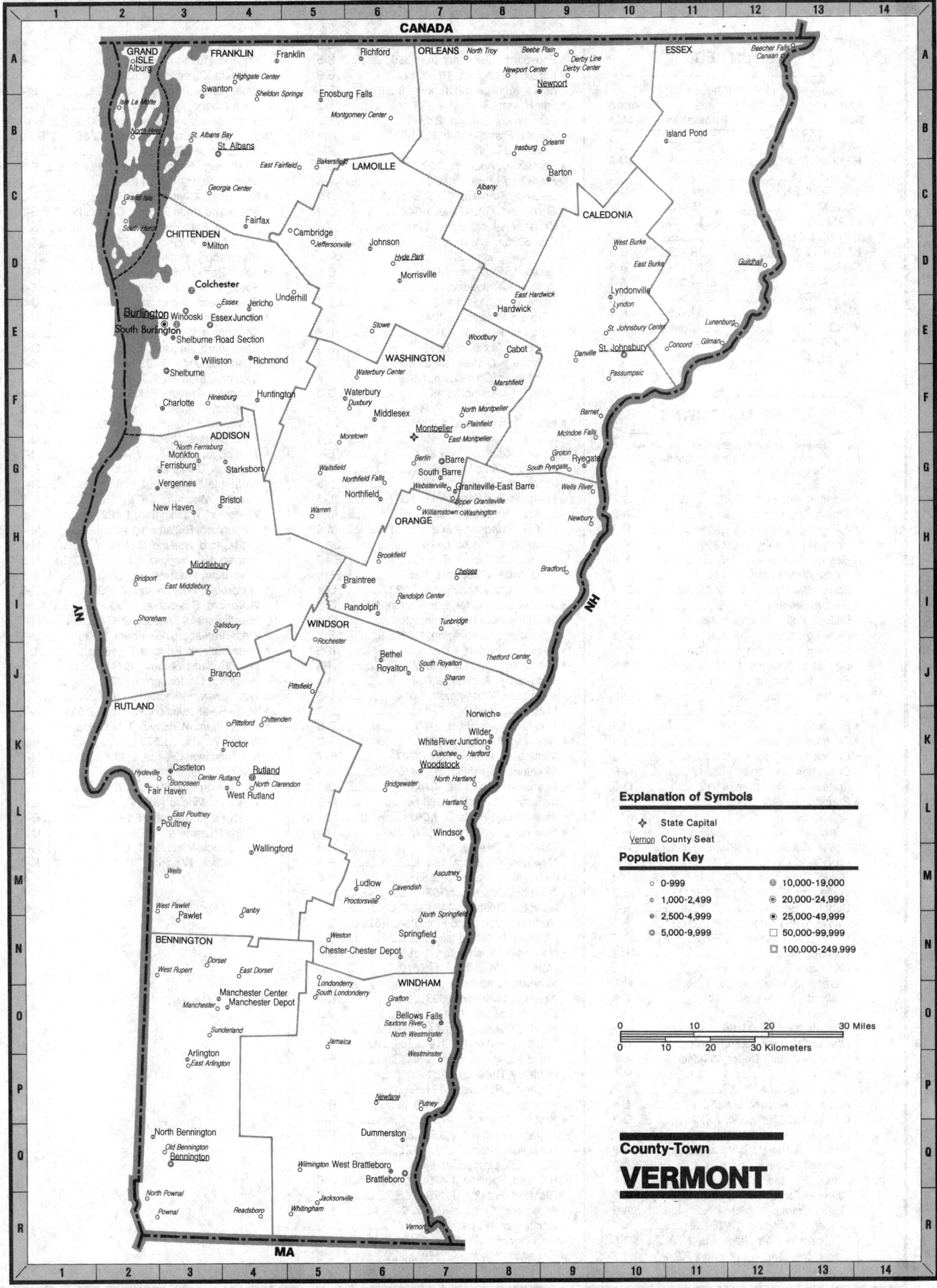

CANADA

| | 1 | 2 | 3 | 4 | 5 | 6 | 7 | 8 | 9 | 10 | 11 | 12 | 13 | 14 |

GRAND ISLE
Alburg
Isle La Motte
North Hero
Grand Isle
South Hero

FRANKLIN Franklin
Highgate Center
Swanton
Sheldon Springs
Enosburg Falls
Montgomery Center
St. Albans Bay
St. Albans
East Fairfield
Bakersfield
Georgia Center
Fairfax

Richford
ORLEANS North Troy
Newport Center
Newport
Irasburg Orleans

Beebe Plain
Derby Line
Derby Center
ESSEX
Island Pond
Beecher Falls
Canaan

LAMOILLE
Albany
Barton
CALEDONIA
West Burke
Guildhall
East Burke
Lyndonville
Lyndon
Lunenburg
St. Johnsbury Center
Gilman
Danville St. Johnsbury Concord
Passumpsic

Cambridge
Jeffersonville
Johnson
Hyde Park
Morrisville
East Hardwick
Hardwick
Woodbury
Cabot
Stowe
Marshfield

CHITTENDEN
Milton
Colchester
Essex Jericho
Burlington Winooski
Essex Junction
South Burlington
Shelburne Road Section
Williston Richmond
Shelburne
Charlotte Hinesburg Huntington
Waterbury Center
WASHINGTON
Waterbury
Duxbury
Middlesex
North Montpelier
Plainfield
Montpelier
East Montpelier
Moretown
Barnet
McIndoe Falls

ADDISON
North Ferrisburg
Monkton
Ferrisburg
Starksboro
Vergennes
Bristol
New Haven
Waitsfield
Northfield Falls
Berlin Barre
South Barre
Websterville Graniteville-East Barre
Upper Graniteville Wells River
Williamstown Washington
Groton Ryegate
South Ryegate
Northfield
Warren
ORANGE
Newbury

Bridport
Middlebury
East Middlebury
Brookfield
Chelsea
Bradford
Shoreham Salisbury
Braintree
Randolph Center
Randolph
Rochester
WINDSOR
Tunbridge
Bethel
Royalton South Royalton
Thetford Center
Sharon

Brandon
Pittsfield
RUTLAND
Pittsford Chittenden
Proctor
Norwich
Wilder
White River Junction
Quechee Hartford
Woodstock
Bridgewater North Hartland
Hartland
Castleton
Hydeville Center Rutland
Bomoseen Rutland North Clarendon
Fair Haven West Rutland
East Poultney
Poultney
Wallingford
Windsor
Ascutney
Wells
West Pawlet
Pawlet
Danby
Ludlow Cavendish
Proctorsville
North Springfield
Weston Springfield
BENNINGTON
Chester-Chester Depot
Dorset East Dorset
West Rupert
Londonderry
South Londonderry
WINDHAM
Manchester Center
Manchester Depot Grafton
Manchester
Sunderland Bellows Falls
Saxtons River
Jamaica North Westminster
Arlington
East Arlington Westminster

North Pownal
Newfane
Putney
North Bennington
Old Bennington
Bennington
Dummerston
Wilmington West Brattleboro
Brattleboro
North Pownal
Pownal Readsboro
Jacksonville
Whitingham
Vernon

NY

NH

MA

Copyright American Map Corporation

Explanation of Symbols

✦ State Capital
Vernon County Seat

Population Key

○ 0-999	⊕ 10,000-19,000
◌ 1,000-2,499	◉ 20,000-24,999
⊙ 2,500-4,999	⬤ 25,000-49,999
◉ 5,000-9,999	☐ 50,000-99,999
	▣ 100,000-249,999

0   10   20   30 Miles
0   10   20   30 Kilometers

County-Town

VERMONT

COUNTIES

(14 Counties)

Name of County	Population	Location on Map
ADDISON	32,953	G-3
BENNINGTON	35,845	N-3
CALEDONIA	27,846	C-9
CHITTENDEN	131,761	D-3
ESSEX	6,405	A-11
FRANKLIN	39,980	A-3
GRAND ISLE	5,318	A-2
LAMOILLE	19,735	C-6
ORANGE	26,149	H-6
ORLEANS	24,053	A-7
RUTLAND	62,142	J-2
WASHINGTON	54,928	E-6
WINDHAM	41,588	O-6
WINDSOR	54,055	I-5
TOTAL	562,758	

CITIES AND TOWNS

Note: The first name is that of the city or town, second, that of the county in which it is located, then the population and location on the map.

Addison, Addison, 1,023 ....G-3
Alburg, Grand Isle, 1,362 ....A-2
Arlington, Bennington, 1,311 ....P-3
Arlington, Bennington, 2,299 ....P-3
Barnet, Caledonia, 1,415 ....F-9
Barre, Washington, 7,411 ....G-7
Barre, Washington, 9,482 ....G-7
Barton, Orleans, 2,967 ....C-9
Bellows Falls, Windham, 3,313 ....O-7
Bennington, Bennington, 16,451 ....Q-3
● Bennington, Bennington, 9,532 ....Q-3
Berkshire, Franklin, 1,190 ....A-5
Berlin, Washington, 2,561 ....G-6
▲ Bethel, Windsor, 1,866 ....J-6
Bradford, Orange, 2,522 ....I-9
▲ Braintree, Orange, 1,174 ....I-5
● Brandon, Rutland, 1,902 ....J-3
Brandon, Rutland, 4,223 ....J-3
Brattleboro, Windham, 12,241 ....Q-6
● Brattleboro, Windham, 8,612 ....Q-6
▲ Bridport, Addison, 1,137 ....I-2
Brighton, Essex, 1,562 ....B-11
Bristol, Addison, 1,801 ....H-4
Bristol, Addison, 3,762 ....H-4
▲ Brookfield, Orange, 1,089 ....H-6
Burke, Caledonia, 1,406 ....D-10
Burlington, Chittenden, 39,127 ....E-3
Cabot, Washington, 1,043 ....E-8
Calais, Washington, 1,521 ....F-7
Cambridge, Lamoille, 2,667 ....D-5
Canaan, Essex, 1,121 ....A-12
▲ Castleton, Rutland, 4,278 ....K-3
Cavendish, Windsor, 1,323 ....M-6
Charlotte, Chittenden, 3,148 ....F-3
Chelsea, Orange I-7
Chelsea, Orange, 1,166 ....I-7
Chester, Windsor, 2,832 ....N-6
● Chester-Chester Depot, Windsor,
  1,057 ....N-6
Chittenden, Rutland, 1,102 ....K-4
Clarendon, Rutland, 2,835 ....L-4
▲ Colchester, Chittenden, 14,731 ....D-3
Concord, Essex, 1,093 ....E-11
Corinth, Orange, 1,244 ....H-8
Cornwall, Addison, 1,101 ....I-3
Danby, Rutland, 1,193 ....M-4
Danville, Caledonia, 1,917 ....E-9
Derby, Orleans, 4,479 ....A-9
Dorset, Bennington, 1,918 ....N-3
▲ Dummerston, Windham, 1,863 ....Q-6
East Montpelier, Washington, 2,239 ....G-7

Enosburg, Franklin, 2,535 ....B-5
Enosburg Falls, Franklin, 1,350 ....B-5
Essex, Chittenden, 16,498 ....E-3
Essex Junction, Chittenden, 8,396 ....E-3
● Fair Haven, Rutland, 2,432 ....L-2
Fair Haven, Rutland, 2,887 ....L-2
▲ Fairfax, Franklin, 2,486 ....C-4
Fairfield, Franklin, 1,680 ....B-4
▲ Ferrisburg, Addison, 2,317 ....G-3
Franklin, Franklin, 1,068 ....A-4
Georgia, Franklin, 3,753 ....C-3
Grand Isle, Grand Isle, 1,642 ....C-2
● Graniteville-East Barre, Washington,
  2,189 ....G-7
▲ Guildhall, Essex, 270 ....D-12
Guilford, Windham, 1,941 ....R-6
Hardwick, Caledonia E-8
Hardwick, Caledonia, 2,964 ....E-8
Hartford, Windsor, 9,404 ....K-8
Hartland, Windsor, 2,988 ....L-7
Highgate, Franklin, 3,020 ....A-4
Hinesburg, Chittenden, 3,780 ....F-3
▲ Huntington, Chittenden, 1,609 ....F-4
Hyde Park, Lamoille, 457 ....D-6
Hyde Park, Lamoille, 2,344 ....D-6
● Island Pond, Essex, 1,222 ....B-11
Jericho, Chittenden, 1,405 ....E-4
Jericho, Chittenden, 4,302 ....E-4
Johnson, Lamoille, 1,470 ....D-6
Johnson, Lamoille, 3,156 ....D-6
Londonderry, Windham, 1,506 ....L-5
Ludlow, Windsor, 1,123 ....M-6
Ludlow, Windsor, 2,302 ....M-6
Lunenburg, Essex, 1,176 ....E-12
Lyndon, Caledonia, 5,371 ....E-10
Lyndonville, Caledonia, 1,255 ....E-10
Manchester, Bennington, 3,622 ....O-4
● Manchester Center, Bennington, 1,574 .. O-3
Manchester Depot, Bennington O-4
Marshfield, Washington, 1,331 ....F-8
Mendon, Rutland, 1,049 ....K-5
● Middlebury, Addison, 6,007 ....I-3
Middlebury, Addison, 8,034 ....I-3
Middlesex, Washington, 1,514 ....F-6
Milton, Chittenden, 1,578 ....D-3
Milton, Chittenden, 8,404 ....D-3
▲ Monkton, Addison, 1,482 ....G-3
Montpelier, Washington, 8,247 ....G-7
Moretown, Washington, 1,415 ....F-6
Morristown, Lamoille, 4,733 ....D-6
Morrisville, Lamoille, 1,984 ....D-6
Mount Holly, Rutland, 1,093 ....M-5
▲ New Haven, Addison, 1,375 ....H-4
Newbury, Orange, 1,985 ....H-9
Newfane, Windham, 164 ....P-6
Newfane, Windham, 1,555 ....P-6
Newport, Orleans, 1,367 ....A-9
Newport, Orleans, 4,434 ....A-9
North Bennington, Bennington, 1,520 .....Q-2
North Hero, Grand Isle B-2
Northfield, Washington, 1,889 ....G-6
Northfield, Washington, 5,610 ....G-6
Norwich, Windsor K-8
Norwich, Windsor, 3,093 ....K-8
Orwell, Addison, 1,114 ....J-2
▲ Pawlet, Rutland, 1,314 ....N-3
Pittsford, Rutland, 2,919 ....K-4
Plainfield, Washington, 1,302 ....F-7
Poultney, Rutland, 1,731 ....L-3
Poultney, Rutland, 3,498 ....L-3
Pownal, Bennington, 3,485 ....R-2
▲ Proctor, Rutland, 1,979 ....K-4
Putney, Windham, 2,352 ....P-7
Randolph, Orange I-6
Randolph, Orange, 4,764 ....I-6
Richford, Franklin, 1,425 ....A-6
Richford, Franklin, 2,178 ....A-6
▲ Richmond, Chittenden, 3,729 ....F-4
Rochester, Windsor, 1,181 ....I-5
Rockingham, Windham, 5,484 ....O-7
▲ Royalton, Windsor, 2,389 ....J-6

Rutland, Rutland, 3,781 ....L-4
Rutland, Rutland, 18,230 ....L-4
▲ Ryegate, Caledonia, 1,058 ....G-9
Saint Albans, Franklin, 4,606 ....B-4
Saint Albans, Franklin, 7,339 ....B-4
● Saint Johnsbury, Caledonia, 6,424 ....E-10
Saint Johnsbury, Caledonia, 7,608 ....E-10
▲ Salisbury, Addison, 1,024 ....I-4
Shaftsbury, Bennington, 3,368 ....P-3
Sharon, Windsor, 1,211 ....J-7
▲ Shelburne, Chittenden, 5,871 ....F-3
Shelburne Road Section, Chittenden E-3
Sheldon, Franklin, 1,748 ....B-4
Shoreham, Addison, 1,115 ....I-3
Shrewsbury, Rutland, 1,107 ....L-4
● South Barre, Washington, 1,314 ....G-7
South Burlington, Chittenden, 12,809 ......E-3
South Hero, Grand Isle, 1,404 ....C-2
Springfield, Windsor, 4,207 ....N-7
Springfield, Windsor, 9,579 ....N-7
▲ Starksboro, Addison, 1,511 ....G-4
Stowe, Lamoille, 3,433 ....E-6
Swanton, Franklin, 2,360 ....B-3
Swanton, Franklin, 5,636 ....B-3
Thetford, Orange, 2,438 ....J-8
Townshend, Windham, 1,019 ....P-6
Troy, Orleans, 1,609 ....B-7
▲ Tunbridge, Orange, 1,154 ....I-7
Underhill, Chittenden, 2,799 ....D-5
Vergennes, Addison, 2,578 ....G-3
Vernon, Windham, 1,850 ....R-7
Waitsfield, Washington, 1,422 ....G-5
● Wallingford, Rutland, 1,148 ....M-4
Wallingford, Rutland, 2,184 ....M-4
Warren, Washington, 1,172 ....H-5
Waterbury, Washington, 1,702 ....F-5
Waterbury, Washington, 4,589 ....F-5
Waterford, Caledonia, 1,190 ....F-10
Weathersfield, Windsor, 2,674 ....M-7
● West Brattleboro, Windham, 3,135 ....Q-6
● West Rutland, Rutland, 2,246 ....L-4
West Rutland, Rutland, 2,448 ....L-4
Westford, Chittenden, 1,740 ....D-4
Westminster, Windham, 3,026 ....P-7
White River Junction, Windsor, 2,521 .....K-8
Whitingham, Windham, 1,177 ....R-5
● Wilder, Windsor, 1,576 ....K-8
Williamstown, Orange, 2,839 ....H-7
▲ Williston, Chittenden, 4,887 ....E-3
Wilmington, Windham, 1,968 ....Q-5
▲ Windsor, Windsor, 3,714 ....L-7
Winooski, Chittenden, 6,649 ....E-3
Wolcott, Lamoille, 1,229 ....D-7
Woodstock, Windsor, 1,037 ....K-7
Woodstock, Windsor, 3,212 ....K-7

Explanation of symbols: ● – Census Designated Place (CDP)   ● *italics* – Township shown which is also a CDP   *italics* – Townships (not shown on the map)
▲ *italics* – Townships (shown on the map)

General Help Numbers:

Governor's Office
Capitol Bldg, 3rd Floor
Richmond, VA 23219
www.governor.state.va.us

804-786-2211
Fax 804-371-6351
8:30AM-5:30PM

Attorney General's Office
900 E Main St
Richmond, VA 23219
www.oag.state.va.us

804-786-2071
Fax 804-786-1991
8:30AM-5PM

Legislative Records
Information & Public Relations
PO Box 406
Richmond, VA 23218
http://legis.state.va.us

804-698-1500
Fax 804-786-3215
8AM-5PM

State Archives
800 E. Broad St
Richmond, VA 23219-8000
www.lva.lib.va.us

804-692-3500
Fax 804-692-3556
9AM-5PM TU-SA

State Specifics:

Capital:	Richmond Richmond City County
Time Zone:	EST
Number of Counties:	95
Population:	7,386,330
Web Site:	www.myvirginia.org

State Agencies

Criminal Records

Virginia State Police, CCRE, PO Box C-85076, Richmond, VA 23261-5076 (Courier: 7700 Midlothian Turnpike, Richmond, VA 23235); 804-323-2277, 804-323-0861 (Fax), 8AM-5PM.

www.vsp.state.va.us

Indexing & Storage: Records are available from 1966. It takes 1 to 3 days before new records are available for inquiry. Records are indexed on inhouse computer.

Searching: Section 19.2-389 Code of Virginia outlines that non-criminal entities can receive conviction only records. Certain agencies may receive complete records. The website gives complete details. Include the following in your request-full name, date of birth, Social Security Number, sex, race. Turnaround time is 4-6 weeks. The general public and employers not covered by statute must have a signed release form from person of record, including notarized signatures

for both subject and requester. These requesters must use form "SP-167" which is downloadable from website. The following data is not released: dismissals, nolled pressed, whenever the disposition is missing

Access by: mail, online.

Fee & Payment: The fee is $15.00 per name; $20 if sex offender registry search included. When required, statutorily-required fingerprint check is $13.00; $37.00 if an FBI fingerpirnt check is also required. Fee payee: Virginia State Police. Prepayment required. Pay by certified check or money order. MasterCard and Visa are accepted.

Mail search: Turnaround time: 8 to 10 business days. General users must use the state form SP-167 which can be downloaded from the web at www.vsp.state.va.us/forms.htm. There is also a form SP-24 or SP-230 which you can use depending on your exempt status. A SASE is requested.

Online search: Certain entities, including screening companies, are can apply for online access via the NCJI System. The system is ONLY available to IN-STATE accounts and allows you to submit requests faster. Fees are same as manual submission-$15.00 per record. Username and password required. There is a minimum usage requirement of 25 requests per month. Turnaround time is 24-72 hours.

Statewide Court Records

Executive Secretary, Administrative Office of Courts, 100 N 9th St, 3rd Floor, Richmond, VA 23219; 804-786-6455, 804-786-4542 (Fax), 8AM-5PM.

www.courts.state.va.us

Access by: online. No searching by mail.

Online search: There are 3 available systems. None are statewide; each county must be searched separately. Cases from 132 General District Courts may be searched free at http://208.210.219.132/courtinfo/vadistrict/select.jsp?court=. You can search records from over 90 Circuit courts at http://208.210.219.132/courtinfo/vacircuit/select.jsp?court=. While these systems do not include DOBs, SSNs and Addresses, but another access system known as LOPAS does. There are no fees to use LOPAS, but access is granted on a request-by-request basis. Call 804-786-6455 for details. The main webpage above offers access to Supreme Court and Appellate opinions.

Sexual Offender Registry

Virginia State Police, Sex Offender and Crimes Against Minors Registry, PO Box 85076, Richmond, VA 23261-5076 (Courier: 7700 Midlothian Turnpike, Richmond, VA 23235); 804-323-2153, 804-323-0862 (Fax), 8AM-5PM.

http://sex-offender.vsp.state.va.us/cool-ICE/

Indexing & Storage: Records are available from 1994 when the Registry was implemented. It takes 1 to 3 days before new records are available for inquiry. Records are normally destroyed after death of offender.

Searching: There are two searches. One is distinguished as a search for Crimes Against Minors (use form SP-266). The other is a Sex Offender Registry Name Request (use form SP-230 or SP-167). Include the following in your request-name, race, sex, DOB; also helpful-SSN, residence address. The following data is not released: DOB, SSN

Access by: mail, online.

Fee & Payment: $15.00 for mail searches, either type of search. No fee for the Internet search. No personal checks accepted. Visa/MC accepted.

Mail search: Turnaround time: 1 to 2 weeks. It is suggested to use one of the two forms described above.

Online search: Search by name, city, county or ZIP Code from the website.

Incarceration Records

Virginia Department of Corrections, Central Criminal Records Section, PO Box 26963, Richmond, VA 23261-6963 (Courier: 6900 Atmore Drive, Richmond, VA 23225); 804-323-2153, 804-323-0462 (Fax), 8AM-5PM.

www.vadoc.state.va.us

Note: Requesters can email requests to clasrec@vadoc.state.va.us. Contact Virginia State Police to perform criminal background checks.

Indexing & Storage: Records are available on current and former inmates (only current if request is online). It takes up to 10 days before new records are available for inquiry.

Searching: Computer records go back to 1986. Include the following in your request-full name; DOB and SSN helpful. Location, conviction and sentencing information, and release dates are provided.

Access by: mail, phone, online.

Fee & Payment: There is no fee.

Mail search: Turnaround time: 1 to 2 days. No SASE is required.

Phone search: For phone search, dial 804-674-3131, press 0 for the operator. Provides inmate location, address, and approximate release date.

Online search: At www.vipnet.org/cgi-bin/vadoc/doc.cgi is an Incarcerated Offender Locator to ascertain where an inmate is located. This is not designed to provide complete inmate records nor is it a database of all inmates past and present in the system. Also, a private company at www.vinelink.com/index.jsp offers free web access at DOC records. Also, there is a DOC wanted/fugitives list at www.vadoc.state.va.us/offenders/wanted/fugitives.htm.

Corporation, Limited Liability Company, Fictitious Name, Limited Partnership, Business Trust Records

State Corporation Commission, Clerks Office, PO Box 1197, Richmond, VA 23218-1197 (Courier: Tyler Bldg, 1st Floor, 1300 E Main St, Richmond, VA 23219); 804-371-9733, 804-371-9133 (Fax), 8:15AM-5PM.

www.state.va.us/scc/division/clk/index.htm

Indexing & Storage: Records are available for all active entities on computer. Older inactive records must be researched from the State Library.

Searching: Records are public and are open for inspection. Original documents are microfilmed/imaged. Images are maintained permanently at the VA State Library. Include the following in your request-full name of business. In addition to the articles of incorporation, corporation records, the following information is available: Annual Reports, Officers, Directors, DBAs, Prior (merged) names, Inactive (back to 1976 on computer) and Reserved names, and Registered Agents.

Access by: mail, phone, fax, in person, online.

Fee & Payment: Plain copies cost $1.00 per page for the first two pages and $.50 for each additional page thereafter. Certification is $3.00. Fee payee: Treasurer of Virginia. Prepayment required. Requesters with billing accounts are encouraged to fax orders. Personal checks accepted. No credit cards accepted.

Mail search: Turnaround time: 3 to 5 business days. Be sure to include your phone number and contact person with all written requests. No SASE is required.

Phone search: No fee for telephone request. Agency will provide only limited information (screen data only) and name availability over the phone.

Fax search: Turnaround time is 3-5 business days.

In person search: Information is available via public access terminals and microfilm Certificates of Fact and Good Standing are generally available in 3 to 5 business days.

Online search: Their system is called Clerk's Information System and is available at www.state.va.us/scc/division/clk/diracc.htm. There are no fees. A wealth of information is available on this system.

Other access: Magnetic tape purchase is offered to those who wish the entire database.

Trademarks, Service Marks

State Corporation Commission, Virginia Securities Division, PO Box 1197 (1300 Main St, 9th Fl),

Richmond, VA 23218 (Courier: 1300 Main St, 9th Fl, Richmond, VA 23219); 804-371-9187, 804-371-9911 (Fax), 8:15AM-5PM.

www.state.va.us/scc/index.html

Indexing & Storage: Records are available from as early as the 1920s. Records are computerized since the 1970s. It takes less than 1 day before new records are available for inquiry. Records are normally destroyed after they have been inactive for 1 year.

Searching: Include the following in your request-name of mark or owner.

Access by: mail, phone, fax, in person, online.

Fee & Payment: There is no search fee. The copy fee is $2.00 for the first 2 pages and $.50 each additional page. Fee payee: Treasurer of Virginia. Prepayment required. Personal checks accepted. No credit cards accepted.

Mail search: Turnaround time: 1 to 2 days.

Phone search: Limited to 1 or 2 searches per call.

Fax search: Fax searching available.

In person search: You may make copies at $.50 per page.

Online search: Searching Trademarks and Service Marks are available at http://securities.scc.state.va.us/pls/SERFIS/wbq_tmsm$.startup.

Uniform Commercial Code, Federal Tax Liens

UCC Division, State Corporation Commission, PO Box 1197, Richmond, VA 23218-1197 (Courier: 1300 E Main St, 1st Floor, Richmond, VA 23219); 804-371-9733, 804-371-9744 (Fax), 8:15AM-5PM.

www.state.va.us/scc/division/clk/index.htm

Indexing & Storage: Records are available from the 1960s on microfiche and from mid 1992 on computer.

Searching: Use search request form UCC-11. The search includes federal tax liens on businesses if specifically requested. Federal tax liens on individuals and all state tax liens are filed at the local level, which may be a county or independent city. Include the following in your request-debtor name. Turnaround time for copies of UCC searches is generally 5 days.

Access by: mail, phone, fax, in person, online.

Fee & Payment: Search request - $7.00; copies - $1.00 for each of the first 2 pages and $.50 for each additional page; certification - $1.00. Fee payee: State Corporation Commission. Prepayment required. Personal checks accepted. No credit cards accepted.

Mail search: Turnaround time: 5 days. A SASE is requested.

Phone search: No fee for telephone request. They will do limited verification on a yes or no basis.

Fax search: Only available to those with billing accounts. Limit of 10 pages on return.

In person search: Counter service provides free access to microfilm records.

Online search: Their system is called Clerk's Information System and is available at www.state.va.us/scc/division/clk/diracc.htm. There are no fees. A wealth of information is available on this system.

State Tax Liens

Records not maintained by a state level agency.

Note: All information is found at the local city or county level.

Sales Tax Registrations

Taxation Department, Sales Tax Licenses, PO Box 1115, Richmond, VA 23218-1115 (Courier: 2220 W Broad St, Richmond, VA 23220); 804-367-8037, 804-786-2670 (Fax), 8:30AM-4:30PM.

www.tax.state.va.us/

Note: Registration information of businesses is available from the Corporation Commission.

Indexing & Storage: Records are available for three years on computer, then put on microfilm for ten years, then purged.

Searching: This agency will provide no information without a written, signed, notarized authorization from the business itself; they will then provide the business name, address, phone, and tax permit number. Include the following in your request-business name, tax permit number.

Access by: mail.

Mail search: Turnaround time: 1 week to 10 days. No SASE is required. No fee for mail request.

Birth Certificates

State Health Department, Office of Vital Records, PO Box 1000, Richmond, VA 23218-1000 (Courier: 1601 Willow Lawn Drive, #275, Richmond, VA 23220); 804-662-6200, 8AM-4:45PM, Closed on major holidays.

www.vdh.state.va.us/vitalrec/

Note: An application for certification may be downloaded from the website.

Indexing & Storage: Records are available from 1912 on. Records from 1853 to 1896 are located at the State Archives. New records are available for inquiry immediately. Records are indexed on microfiche, inhouse computer.

Searching: Vital records are available to immediate family members only. Birth records are public information 100 years after the date of the event. Include the following in your request-name at birth, date of birth, place of birth, mother's maiden name, father's name, relationship to the person on the certificate, photocopy ID of requester. Include your area code and daytime phone number, your return address, and be sure to sign your request and provide copy of ID.

Access by: mail, phone, fax, in person.

Fee & Payment: The fee is $12.00 per certificate. If certificate needs to be authorized, fee is additional an $12.00 per authentication. Fee payee: The State Health Department. Prepayment required. Personal checks accepted. Credit cards accepted: MasterCard, Visa, AmEx, Discover.

Mail search: Turnaround time is 4-6 weeks, unless birth occurred between 1940-1978, then time is 2-5 days. No SASE is required.

Phone search: You must use a credit card. See Expedited Service.

Fax search: You must use a credit card. See Expedited Service.

In person search: Turnaround time 15 minutes.

Expedited service: Expedited service is available from VitalChek Express Service. Phone 877-572-6333, select option #2. Website: www.vitalchek.com; e-mail: vitals.reply@vitalchek.com. Turnaround time: 2 - 5 days. Fee is $46.00.

Death Records

State Health Department, Office of Vital Records, PO Box 1000, Richmond, VA 23218-1000 (Courier: 1601 Willow Lawn Drive, #275, Richmond, VA 23220); 804-662-6200, 8AM-4:45PM, Closed on major holidays.

www.vdh.state.va.us/vitalrec/

Note: An application for certification may be downloaded from website.

Indexing & Storage: Records are available from 1912 on. Records from 1853 to 1896 are located at the State Archives. New records are available for inquiry immediately. Records are indexed on microfiche, inhouse computer.

Searching: Vital records are available to immediate family members only. Death records are public information 50 years after the date of the event. Include the following in your request-name of deceased, date of death, place of death, relationship to the deceased, reason for the certificate. Include your area code and daytime phone number, your return address, and be sure to sign your request and provide copy of ID.

Access by: mail, phone, fax, in person.

Fee & Payment: The fee is $12.00 per certificate. If certificate needs to be authorized, fee is additional an $12.00 per authentication. Fee payee: The State Health Department. Prepayment required. Personal checks accepted. Credit cards accepted: MasterCard, Visa, AmEx, Discover.

Mail search: Turnaround time: 4 to 6 weeks. No SASE is required.

Phone search: You must use a credit card. See Expedited Service.

Fax search: You must use a credit card. See Expedited Service.

In person search: Turnaround time 15 minutes.

Expedited service: Expedited service is available from VitalChek Express Service. Phone 877-572-6333, select option #2. Check their website at www.vitalchek.com; e-mail to vitals.reply@vitalchek.com. Turnaround time: 2 - 5 days. Fee is $46.00.

Marriage Certificates

State Health Department, Office of Vital Records, PO Box 1000, Richmond, VA 23218-1000 (Courier: 1601 Willow Lawn Drive, #275, Richmond, VA 23220); 804-662-6200, 8AM-4:45PM, Closed on major holidays.

www.vdh.state.va.us/vitalrec/

Note: An application for certification may be downloaded from website.

Indexing & Storage: Records are available from 1853 to present. New records are available for inquiry immediately. Records are indexed on microfiche, inhouse computer.

Searching: Vital records are available to immediate family members only. Marriage records are public information 50 years after the date of the event. Include the following in your request-name, date of marriage, place of marriage,

relationship to the person on the certificate, reason for the certificate. Include your area code and daytime phone number, your return address, and be sure to sign your request.

Access by: mail, phone, fax, in person.

Fee & Payment: The fee is $12.00 per certificate. If certificate needs to be authorized, fee is additional an $12.00 per authentication. Fee payee: The State Health Department. Prepayment required. Personal checks accepted. Credit cards accepted: MasterCard, Visa, AmEx, Discover.

Mail search: Turnaround time: 4 to 6 weeks. No SASE is required.

Phone search: You must use a credit card. See Expedited Service.

Fax search: You must use a credit card. See Expedited Service.

In person search: Turnaround time 15 minutes.

Expedited service: Expedited service is available from VitalChek Express Service. Phone 877-572-6333, select option #2. See their website at www.vitalchek.com or e-mail to vitals.reply@vitalchek.com for fee information. Turnaround time: 2 - 5 days. Fee is $46.00.

Divorce Records

State Health Department, Office of Vital Records, PO Box 1000, Richmond, VA 23218-1000 (Courier: 1601 Willow Lawn Drive, #275, Richmond, VA 23220); 804-662-6200, 8AM-4:45PM, Closed on major holidays.

www.vdh.state.va.us/vitalrec/

Note: An application for certification may be downloaded from website.

Indexing & Storage: Records are available 1918 to present. New records are available for inquiry immediately. Records are indexed on microfiche, inhouse computer.

Searching: Vital records are available to immediate family members only. Divorce records are public information 50 years after the date of the event. Include the following in your request-name, date of divorce, place of divorce, relationship to the person on the certificate, reason for the certificate. Include your area code and daytime phone number, your return address, and be sure to sign your request and provide copy of ID.

Access by: mail, phone, fax, in person.

Fee & Payment: The fee is $12.00 per certificate. If certificate needs to be authorized, fee is additional an $12.00 per authentication. Fee payee: The State Health Department. Prepayment required. Personal checks accepted. Credit cards accepted: MasterCard, Visa, AmEx, Discover.

Mail search: Turnaround time: 4 to 6 weeks. No SASE is required.

Phone search: You must use a credit card. See Expedited Service.

Fax search: You must use a credit card. See Expedited Service.

In person search: Turnaround time 15 minutes.

Expedited service: Expedited service is available from VitalChek Express Service. Phone 877-572-6333, select option #2. See their website at www.vitalchek.com or e-mail to vitals.reply@vitalchek.com for fee information. Turnaround time: 2 - 5 days. Fee is $46.00.

Workers' Compensation Records

Workers' Compensation Commission, 1000 DMV Dr, Richmond, VA 23220; 804-367-8633, 877-664-2566, 804-367-9740 (Fax), 8:15AM-5PM.

www.vwc.state.va.us/

Indexing & Storage: Records are available from 1977 on. New records are available for inquiry immediately. Records are indexed on microfilm, inhouse computer.

Searching: To receive file copies, you must have a notarized release from the claimant. They will release a "yes or no" answer when presented with a list. Awards issued are public information. Include the following in your request-claimant name, Social Security Number, claim number. All requests must be in writing. The following data is not released: sealed records.

Access by: mail, in person.

Fee & Payment: The search fee is $10.00. No copy fee for first 10 pages, then $.50 per page. Fee payee: Treasurer - State of Virginia. Prepayment required. Personal checks accepted. No credit cards accepted.

Mail search: Turnaround time: 1 to 4 days.

In person search: Request must be in writing.

Driver Records

Motorist Records Services, Attn: Records Request Work Center, PO Box 27412, Richmond, VA 23269; 804-367-0538, 8:30AM-5:30PM M-F; 8:30AM-12:30PM S.

www.dmv.state.va.us

Note: Copies of tickets from non-computerized courts are available at this address for $8.00 per record only to driver or driver's authorized representative. Ticket information from computerized courts must be obtained from each court.

Indexing & Storage: Records are available for 3 years for moving violations & misc convictions, 5 years for speeding & unauthorized use of a motor vehicle, 11 years for 3 reckless driving offenses and DWI, and 24 months from the complied date for suspensions. It takes 12 days from receipt before new records are available for inquiry. Records are indexed on inhouse computer.

Searching: Access to records follows DPPA guidelines. Casual requesters can only obtain records with consent using from CRD93 (formerly form DL93). Include the following in your request-full name, date of birth, sex. Insurance records display 5 years, employment records the last 7 years. Surrendered licenses are purged after 5 years.

Access by: mail, in person, online.

Fee & Payment: The current fee is $8.00 for mail or walk-in requests and $7.00 for online requests. Add $5.00 for certification. Fee payee: Department of Motor Vehicles. Prepayment required. Personal checks accepted. No credit cards accepted.

Mail search: Turnaround time: 5 days. The driver's name, DOB, and sex must "match" to get a record. Request must be on a DMV form or on letterhead. A SASE is requested.

In person search: Normal turnaround time is while you wait. There are 72 field offices where records can be requested.

Online search: Online service is provided by the Virginia Information Providers Network (VIPNet). Online reports are provided via the Internet on an interactive basis 24 hours daily. There is a $75 annual administrative fee and records are $7.00 each. Go to www.vipnet.org for more information (search "premium services") or call 804-786-4718.

Other access: Magnetic tape ordering for batch requests is available from VIPnet. No records are sold for marketing purposes.

Vehicle Ownership, Vehicle Identification

Department of Motor Vehicles, Vehicle Records Work Center, PO Box 27412, Richmond, VA 23269; 804-367-0538, 8:30AM-5:30PM M-F; 8:30AM-12:30PM S.

www.dmv.state.va.us

Note: Lien information is only released to lending institutions, collection agencies, and businesses.

Indexing & Storage: It takes 12 days from receipt before new records are available for inquiry.

Searching: Casual requesters cannot obtain records without consent. High volume requesters must sign an agreement or contract and will be assigned a user number. Records cannot be purchased and resold for marketing purposes. Include the following in your request-Form CRD93. Private investigators who are registered as compliance agents by the Department of Justice Services may obtain address information by submitting a license plate number.

Access by: mail, in person, online.

Fee & Payment: The fee is $8.00 for vehicle ownership and registration information or $8.00 per vehicle on a name search. There is a full charge for a "no record found." Add $5.00 for verification. Fee payee: Department of Motor Vehicles. Prepayment required. Personal checks accepted. No credit cards accepted.

Mail search: Turnaround time: 5 days. A SASE is requested.

In person search: Turnaround time: while you wait, usually limited to five at one time.

Online search: The online system, managed by the Virginia Information Providers Network (VIPNet), is an interactive system open 24 hours daily. There is an annual $75.00 administration fee and records are $7.00 each. All accounts must be approved by both the DMV and VIPNet. Call 804-786-4718 to request an information use agreement application. The URL is www.vipnet.org.

Other access: Bulk release of vehicle or ownership information is not available except for statistical and vehicle recall purposes.

Accident Reports

Department of Motor Vehicles, Driver Records Work Center, Rm 516, PO Box 27412, Richmond, VA 23269; 804-367-0538, 866-368-5463, 804-367-0390 (Fax), 8:30AM-5:30PM M-F; 8:30AM-12:30PM S.

www.dmv.state.va.us

Indexing & Storage: Records are available for 40 months to present. Records are indexed on computer. It takes 25-30 days before new records are available for inquiry.

Searching: All requests must be in writing. Records are only released to those involved or

with a tangible interest. Include the following in your request-full name of driver, date of accident, location of accident.

Access by: mail, fax, in person.

Fee & Payment: The fee is $8.00 per report. Prepayment is required, except for attorneys and insurance companies. Fee payee: Department of Motor Vehicles. Prepayment required. Personal checks accepted. Credit cards accepted: MasterCard, Visa.

Mail search: Turnaround time: 5 days.

Fax search: Must pay with a credit card.

In person search: Turnaround time is while you wait, if personnel available.

Vessel Ownership, Vessel Registration

Game & Inland Fisheries Dept, 4010 W Broad St, Richmond, VA 23230; 804-367-6135, 877-898-2628, 804-367-1064 (Fax), 8:15AM-5PM.

www.dgif.virginia.gov

Indexing & Storage: Records are available from 1960 to the present. Records are indexed on computer from 1984 to the present. All motorized boats must be registered. All motorboats, or sailboats if over 18 ft are titled. Lien information will show on record. It takes 24 hours before new records are available for inquiry.

Searching: All requests must be in writing. One of the following is required for a search: name, SSN, title #, hull #.

Access by: mail, in person, online.

Fee & Payment: If history or extensive research is required, there is a fee of $50.00 per boat. Fee payee: Game & Inland Fisheries Dept. Prepayment required. Personal checks and credit cards accepted.

Mail search: Turnaround time: 3 to 4 working days. No SASE is required.

In person search: Turnaround time is usually immediate.

Online search: The VA boat registration database may be searched on the web at www.vipnet.org. There is both a free service and a more advanced pay service, but both require a subscription which is $75.00 a year. Other motor vehicle records are available.

Voter Registration

Access to Records is Restricted

State Board of Elections, 200 N 9th Street, #101, Richmond, VA 23219; 804-786-6551, 804-371-0194 (Fax), 8:30AM-5PM.

www.sbe.state.va.us

Note: Individual searches must be done at the county or city level with the General Registrars. The state will sell all or portions of its statewide database (95 counties, 40 cities) to organizations promoting voter registration and participation.

GED Certificates

Virginia Dept of Education, GED Services, PO Box 2120, Richmond, VA 23218-2120; 804-786-4642, 804-225-3352 (Fax), 8:15AM-5PM.

www.pen.k12.va.us

Indexing & Storage: Records are available from 1942. Records for non-passers for tests are not maintained. It takes 6 weeks before new records are available for inquiry.

Searching: To search, all of the following is required: a signed release, name, DOB, SSN, and year of test.

Access by: mail, in person.

Fee & Payment: There is a $5.00 fee for a verification or for a transcript. Add $5.00 for certification. Fee payee: VA Department of Education - GED Srvs. Prepayment required. Personal checks are accepted. No credit cards accepted.

Mail search: Turnaround time: 5 to 10 days. A SASE is requested.

In person search: Turnaround time is typically immediate.

Hunting and Fishing License Information

Records not maintained by a state level agency.

Note: They do not have a central database because there are hundreds of vendors throughout the state that sell licenses.

Virginia State Licensing Agencies

Licenses Searchable Online

Acupuncturist #6	www.vipnet.org/dhp/cgi-bin/search_publicdb.cgi
Alcoholic Beverage Distributor #1	www.abc.state.va.us/proj/enft/enforcement/jsp/firstpage.jsp
Architect #10	www.dpor.state.va.us/regulantlookup/
Asbestos-Related Occupation #10	www.dpor.state.va.us/regulantlookup/
Athletic Trainer #6	www.vipnet.org/dhp/cgi-bin/search_publicdb.cgi
Attorney/Attorney Associate #14	www.vsb.org/attorney/attSearch.asp?S=D
Auctioneer/Auction Company #10	www.dpor.state.va.us/regulantlookup/
Audiologist #6	www.vipnet.org/dhp/cgi-bin/search_publicdb.cgi
Barber/Barber School/Business #10	www.dpor.state.va.us/regulantlookup/
Boxer #10	www.dpor.state.va.us/regulantlookup/
Carpenter #10	www.dpor.state.va.us/regulantlookup/
Cemetery Company/Seller #10	www.dpor.state.va.us/regulantlookup/
Check Casher #16	www.state.va.us/scc/division/banking/chk_cash.htm
Chiropractor #6	www.vipnet.org/dhp/cgi-bin/search_publicdb.cgi
Clinical Nurse Specialist #6	www.vipnet.org/dhp/cgi-bin/search_publicdb.cgi
Contractor #10	www.dpor.state.va.us/regulantlookup/
Cosmetic Procedure Certification #6	www.vipnet.org/dhp/cgi-bin/search_publicdb.cgi
Cosmetologist/Cosmetology School/Business #10	www.dpor.state.va.us/regulantlookup/
Counselor, Professional #6	www.vipnet.org/dhp/cgi-bin/search_publicdb.cgi
Crematory #6	www.vipnet.org/dhp/cgi-bin/search_publicdb.cgi
Dentist / Dental Hygienist #6	www.vipnet.org/dhp/cgi-bin/search_publicdb.cgi
Embalmer #6	www.vipnet.org/dhp/cgi-bin/search_publicdb.cgi
Engineer #10	www.dpor.state.va.us/regulantlookup/
Funeral Director/Establ./Trainee/Service Provider #6	www.vipnet.org/dhp/cgi-bin/search_publicdb.cgi
Gas Fitter #10	www.dpor.state.va.us/regulantlookup/
Geologist #10	www.dpor.state.va.us/regulantlookup/
Hair Braider #10	www.dpor.state.va.us/regulantlookup/
Hearing Aid Specialist #10	www.dpor.state.va.us/regulantlookup/
Home Inspector #10	www.dpor.state.va.us/regulantlookup/
Humane Society #6	www.vipnet.org/dhp/cgi-bin/search_publicdb.cgi
Interior Designer #10	www.dpor.state.va.us/regulantlookup/
Investment Advisor/Advisor Agency #12	http://securities.scc.state.va.us/pls/SERFIS/wbq_ai$.startup
Landscape Architect #10	www.dpor.state.va.us/regulantlookup/
Lead-Related Occupation #10	www.dpor.state.va.us/regulantlookup/
Lobbyist #11	www.commonwealth.virginia.gov/Lobbyist/database.cfm
Marriage & Family Therapist #6	www.vipnet.org/dhp/cgi-bin/search_publicdb.cgi
Massage Therapist #6	www.vipnet.org/dhp/cgi-bin/search_publicdb.cgi
Medical Doctor #6	www.vipnet.org/dhp/cgi-bin/search_publicdb.cgi
Medical Equipment Supplier #6	www.vipnet.org/dhp/cgi-bin/search_publicdb.cgi
Medical Wholesaler/Mfg #6	www.vipnet.org/dhp/cgi-bin/search_publicdb.cgi
Money Transmitter #16	www.state.va.us/scc/division/banking/moneytrans.htm
Mortgage Lender/Broker #16	www.state.va.us/scc/division/banking/vamortgagelist.htm
Nail Technician #10	www.dpor.state.va.us/regulantlookup/
Nurse/Nurse's Aide #6	www.vipnet.org/dhp/cgi-bin/search_publicdb.cgi
Nurse-LPN / RN #6	www.vipnet.org/dhp/cgi-bin/search_publicdb.cgi
Nursing Home Administrator/Preceptor #6	www.vipnet.org/dhp/cgi-bin/search_publicdb.cgi
Occupational Therapist #6	www.vipnet.org/dhp/cgi-bin/search_publicdb.cgi
Optician #10	www.dpor.state.va.us/regulantlookup/
Optometrist #6	www.arbo.org/odfinder/LicSearch.asp
Oral/Maxillofacial Surgeon #6	www.vipnet.org/dhp/cgi-bin/search_publicdb.cgi
Osteopathic Physician #6	www.vipnet.org/dhp/cgi-bin/search_publicdb.cgi
Payday Lender #16	www.state.va.us/scc/division/banking/paydaylend.htm
Pharmacist/Pharmacy #6	www.vipnet.org/dhp/cgi-bin/search_publicdb.cgi
Physical Therapist #6	www.vipnet.org/dhp/cgi-bin/search_publicdb.cgi
Physician #6	www.vipnet.org/dhp/cgi-bin/search_publicdb.cgi
Physician Assistant #6	www.vipnet.org/dhp/cgi-bin/search_publicdb.cgi
Pilot, Branch #10	www.dpor.state.va.us/regulantlookup/
Podiatrist #6	www.vipnet.org/dhp/cgi-bin/search_publicdb.cgi
Polygraph Examiner #10	www.dpor.state.va.us/regulantlookup/
Prescriptive Authorization #6	www.vipnet.org/dhp/cgi-bin/search_publicdb.cgi

Property Association #10 .... www.dpor.state.va.us/regulantlookup/
Psychologist / Psychology School #6 .... www.vipnet.org/dhp/cgi-bin/search_publicdb.cgi
Radiologic Technologist-limited #6 .... www.vipnet.org/dhp/cgi-bin/search_publicdb.cgi
Real Estate Agent/Business/School #10 .... www.dpor.state.va.us/regulantlookup/
Real Estate Appraiser/Appraiser Business #10 .... www.dpor.state.va.us/regulantlookup/
Rehabilitation Provider #6 .... www.vipnet.org/dhp/cgi-bin/search_publicdb.cgi
Respiratory Care Practitioner #6 .... www.vipnet.org/dhp/cgi-bin/search_publicdb.cgi
Securities Broker/Dealer/Dealer Agent #12 .... http://securities.scc.state.va.us/pls/SERFIS/wbq_ai$.startup
Social Worker, Clinical/Registered #6 .... www.vipnet.org/dhp/cgi-bin/search_publicdb.cgi
Soil Scientist #10 .... www.dpor.state.va.us/regulantlookup/
Speech Pathologist/Audiologist #6 .... www.vipnet.org/dhp/cgi-bin/search_publicdb.cgi
Substance Abuse Counselor #6 .... www.vipnet.org/dhp/cgi-bin/search_publicdb.cgi
Substance Abuse Treatment Practitioner #6 .... www.vipnet.org/dhp/cgi-bin/search_publicdb.cgi
Surveyor, Land #10 .... www.dpor.state.va.us/regulantlookup/
Tradesman #10 .... www.dpor.state.va.us/regulantlookup/
University Limited Medical License #6 .... www.vipnet.org/dhp/cgi-bin/search_publicdb.cgi
Veterinarian/Veterinary Technician #6 .... www.vipnet.org/dhp/cgi-bin/search_publicdb.cgi
Warehouser, Medical #6 .... www.vipnet.org/dhp/cgi-bin/search_publicdb.cgi
Waste Management Facility Operator #10 .... www.dpor.state.va.us/regulantlookup/
Waste Water Treatment Plant Operator #10 .... www.dpor.state.va.us/regulantlookup/
Wax Technician #10 .... www.dpor.state.va.us/regulantlookup/
Wrestler #10 .... www.dpor.state.va.us/regulantlookup/

Virginia Licensing Quick Finder

Acupuncturist #6 804-662-9908
Alcoholic Beverage Distributor #1 804-213-4400
Architect #10 804-367-8506
Asbestos-Related Occupation #10 804-367-8595
Atheletic Trainer #6 804-662-9900
Attorney/Attorney Associate #14 804-775-0500
Auctioneer/Auction Company #10 804-367-8506
Audiologist #6 804-662-9900
Bank #16 804-371-9704
Barber/Barber School/Business #10 804-367-8509
Boxer #10 804-367-0186
Cardiac Technical Professional #15 804-371-3500
Carpenter #10 804-367-8511
Cemetery Company/Seller #10 804-367-2039
Check Casher #16 .... 804/371-9701
Chiropractor #6 804-662-9908
Clinical Nurse Specialist #6 804-662-9909
Contractor #10 804-367-8511
Cosmetic Procedure Certification #6 804-662-9900
Cosmetologist/Cosmetology School/Business #10
.... 804-367-8509
Counselor, Professional #6 804-662-9912
Credit Union #16 804-371-9267
Crematory #6 804-662-9900
Dental Hygienist #6 804-662-9906
Dentist #6 804-662-9906
Embalmer #6 804-662-9907
Emergency Medical Technician #15 804-371-3500
Engineer #10 804-367-8506
Funeral Director/Establ./Trainee #6 804-662-9907
Funeral Service Provider #6 804-662-9900
Gas Fitter #10 804-367-8511
Geologist #10 804-367-0524
Hair Braider #10 804-367-8509
Hearing Aid Specialist #10 804-367-8509
Home Inspector #10 804-367-8595
Horse Racing Professional #13 804-966-7400
Humane Society #6 804-662-9900
Insurance Agent/Agency #2 804-371-9631
Interior Designer #10 804-367-8506

Investment Advisor/Advisor Agency #12
.... 804-371-9686
Landscape Architect #10 804-367-8506
Lead-Related Occupation #10 804-367-8595
Lobbyist #11 804-786-2441
Marriage & Family Therapist #6 804-662-9912
Massage Therapist #6 804-662-9900
Medical Doctor #6 804-662-9908
Medical Equipment Supplier #6 804-662-9921
Medical Wholesaler/Mfg #6 804-662-9900
Money Transmitter #16 .... 804/371-9701
Mortgage Lender/Broker #16 .... 804/371-9701
Nail Technician #10 804-367-8509
Notary Public #9 804-786-2441
Nurse/Nurse's Aide #6 804-662-9909
Nurse-LPN #6 804-662-9909
Nurse-RN #6 804-662-9900
Nursing Home Administrator/Preceptor #6
.... 804-662-7423
Occupational Therapist #6 804-662-9908
Optician #10 804-367-8509
Optometrist #6 804-662-9910
Oral/Maxillofacial Surgeon #6 804-662-9900
Osteopathic Physician #6 804-662-9908
Paramedic #15 804-371-3500
Payday Lender #16 .... 804/371-9701
Personal Protection Specialist #5 804-786-0460
Pesticide Applicator (Private) #4 804-786-3798
Pesticide Applicator/Company (Commercial) #4
.... 804-786-3798
Pharmacist/Pharmacy #6 804-662-9921
Physical Therapist #6 804-662-9908
Physician #6 804-662-9968
Physician Assistant #6 804-662-9900
Pilot, Branch #10 804-367-8514
Podiatrist #6 804-662-9908
Polygraph Examiner #10 804-367-6166
Prescriptive Authorization #6 804-662-9900
Private Investigator #5 804-786-0460
Property Association #10 804-367-8500

Psychologist at School #6 804-662-9900
Psychologist, Clinical/Applied #6 804-662-9913
Psychology School #6 804-662-9913
Radiologic Technologist-limited #6 804-662-9900
Real Estate Agent/Business/School #10
.... 804-367-8526
Real Estate Appraiser/Appraiser Business #10
.... 804-367-2039
Rehabilitation Provider #6 804-662-9912
Respiratory Care Practitioner #6 804-662-9908
Savings Institution #16 804-371-9704
School Guidance Counselor #8 804-371-2522
School Library Media Specialist #8 804-371-2522
School Principal/Superintendent #8 804-371-2522
Securities Broker/Dealer/Dealer Agent #12
.... 804-371-9686
Securities Brokerage #12 804-371-9187
Security Officer, Unarmed/Armed #5 ... 804-786-0460
Security Tech., Electronic Security #5 .. 804-786-0460
Shock/Trauma Professional #15 804-371-3500
Shorthand Reporter #3 703-768-8122
Social Worker, Clinical/Registered #6.. 804-662-9914
Soil Scientist #10 804-367-2785
Speech Pathologist at School #6 804-662-9900
Speech Pathologist/Audiologist #6 804-662-9111
Substance Abuse Counselor #6 804-662-9912
Substance Abuse Treatment Practitioner #6
.... 804-662-9912
Surveyor, Land #10 804-367-8506
Teacher #8 804-371-2522
Tradesman #10 804-367-8511
University Limited Medical License #6 . 804-662-9900
Veterinarian/Veterinary Tech. #6 804-662-9915
Veterinary Facility #6 804-662-9915
Warehouser, Medical #6 804-662-9900
Waste Mgmt. Facility Operator #10 804-367-8595
Waste Water Treatment Plant Operator #10
.... 804-367-2176
Wax Technician #10 804-367-8509
Wrestler #10 804-367-0186

Virginia Licensing Agency Information

1 Alcoholic Beverage Control Board, 2901 Hermitage Rd, Richmond, VA 23220; | 804-213-4577, Fax: 804-213-4586. www.abc.state.va.us Search Database at www.abc.state.va.us/proj/enft/enforcement/jsp/firs tpage.jsp

2 Bureau of Insurance, Financial Regulation-State Corporation Commission, PO Box 1157, (Tyler Building, 1300 E. Main St., Richmond, VA 23219), Richmond, VA 23218; 804-371-9631, Fax: 804-371-9349. www.state.va.us/scc/division/boi/index.htm

3 CSR Contact Person, 2404 Belle Haven Meadows, Alexandria, VA 22306; 703-768-8122, Fax: 703-768-8921.

4 Department of Agriculture & Consumer Services, Office of Pesticide Services, PO Box 1163, Richmond, VA 23218; 804-786-3798, 371-6558, Fax: 804-371-8598 Admin ofc.; 786-9149 lic. app. www.vdacs.state.va.us/pesticides/ Email: rgilliam@vdacs.state.va.us

5 Department of Criminal Justice, Private Security, 805 E Broad St, 10th Fl, Richmond, VA 23219; 804-786-4000, Fax: 804-786-6344. www.dcjs.state.va.us

6 Department of Health Professions, 6603 W Broad St, 5th Fl, Richmond, VA 23230-1712; 804-662-9900 (DHP), Fax: 804-662-9943/9200. www.medbd@dhp.virginia.gov Email: webmaster@dhp.virginia.gov

Search Database at www.vipnet.org/dhp/cgi-bin/search_publicdb.cgi Note: A license and case decision alert service allows you to track licensing status and disciplinary actions for health care professionals. Visit www.vipnet.org/dhp/de mo/dhpserviceinfo.html to join. Licensee lists are also available. Credit cards accepted.

8 Department of Education, Division of Teacher Education & Licensure, PO Box 2120 (101 N 14th St, James Monroe Bldg.), Richmond, VA 23218-2120; 804-371-2522, Fax: 804-786-6759. www.pen.k12.va.us Email: ppitts@mail.vak12ed.edu

9 Secretary of the Commonwealth, Notary Public Division, PO Box 1795, Richmond, VA 23218; 804-786-2441, Fax: 804-371-0017. www.soc.state.va.us Email: mford@gov.state.va.us

10 Department of Professional & Occupation Regulation, 3600 W Broad St, Richmond, VA 23230-4917; 804-367-8583, Fax: 804-367-2475. www.state.va.us/dpor Email: lexie.borkey@dpor.virginia.gov Search Database at www.dpor.state.va.us/regulantlookup/ Note: Board of Accountancy is Suite #696.

11 Secretary of the Commonwealth, 830 E Main Street, 14th Fl, Richmond, VA 23219; 804-781-2441, Fax: 804-371-0017. www.soc.state.va.us Email: lobbyist@gov.state.va.us Search Database at www.commonwealth.virginia.gov/Lobbyist/databa se.cfm

12 Corporation Commission, Securities Division, PO Box 1197 (1300 E Main, 9th Fl), Richmond, VA 23218; 804-371-9187, Fax: 804-371-9911. www.state.va.us/scc/division/srf Search Database at http://securities.scc.s tate.va.us/pls/SERFIS/wbq_ai$.startup

13 Virginia Racing Commission, 10700 Horsemans Road, PO Box 208, New Kent, VA 23124; 804-966-7400, Fax: 804-966-7418. www.vrc.state.va.us Email: shorland@vrc.state.va.us

14 State Bar Association, 707 E Main St, #1500, Richmond, VA 23219-2800; 804-775-0500, Fax: 804-775-0501. www.vsb.org Search Database at www.vsb.org/attorney/attSearch.asp?S=D

15 Department of Health, Emergency Medical Services, 109 Governor St, Richmond, VA 23219; 804-371-3500, Fax: 804-371-3543. www.vdh.state.va.us/oems

16 Corporation Commission, Bureau of Financial Institutions, PO Box 640 (1300 E. Main St #800), Richmond, VA 23218-0640; 804-371-9701, Fax: 804-371-9416. www.state.va.us/scc/division/banking/index.htm Email: bfiquestions@scc.state.va.us Search Database at www.state.va.us/scc/division/banking/licreg.htm

Virginia Federal Courts

The following list indicates the district and division name for each county in the state. If the bankruptcy court location is different from the district court, then the location of the bankruptcy court appears in parentheses.

County/Court Cross Reference

County	District	Division
Accomack	Eastern	Norfolk
Albemarle	Western	Charlottesville (Lynchburg)
Alexandria City	Eastern	Alexandria
Alleghany	Western	Roanoke (Harrisonburg)
Amelia	Eastern	Richmond
Amherst	Western	Lynchburg
Appomattox	Western	Lynchburg
Arlington	Eastern	Alexandria
Augusta	Western	Harrisonburg
Bath	Western	Harrisonburg
Bedford	Western	Lynchburg
Bedford City	Western	Lynchburg
Bland	Western	Roanoke
Botetourt	Western	Roanoke
Bristol City	Western	Abingdon (Roanoke)
Brunswick	Eastern	Richmond
Buchanan	Western	Abingdon (Roanoke)
Buckingham	Western	Lynchburg
Buena Vista City	Western	Lynchburg (Harrisonburg)
Campbell	Western	Lynchburg
Caroline	Eastern	Richmond
Carroll	Western	Roanoke
Charles City	Eastern	Richmond
Charlotte	Western	Danville (Lynchburg)
Charlottesville City	Western	Charlottesville (Lynchburg)
Chesapeake City	Eastern	Norfolk
Chesterfield	Eastern	Richmond
Clarke	Western	Harrisonburg
Clifton Forge City	Western	Roanoke (Harrisonburg)
Colonial Heights City	Eastern	Richmond
Covington City	Western	Roanoke (Harrisonburg)
Craig	Western	Roanoke
Culpeper	Western	Charlottesville (Lynchburg)
Cumberland	Western	Lynchburg
Danville City	Western	Danville (Lynchburg)
Dickenson	Western	Big Stone Gap (Roanoke)
Dinwiddie	Eastern	Richmond
Emporia City	Eastern	Richmond
Essex	Eastern	Richmond
Fairfax	Eastern	Alexandria
Fairfax City	Eastern	Alexandria
Falls Church City	Eastern	Alexandria
Fauquier	Eastern	Alexandria
Floyd	Western	Roanoke
Fluvanna	Western	Charlottesville (Lynchburg)
Franklin	Western	Roanoke
Franklin City	Eastern	Norfolk
Frederick	Western	Harrisonburg
Fredericksburg City	Eastern	Richmond
Galax City	Western	Roanoke
Giles	Western	Roanoke
Gloucester	Eastern	Newport News
Goochland	Eastern	Richmond
Grayson	Western	Roanoke
Greene	Western	Charlottesville (Lynchburg)
Greensville	Eastern	Richmond
Halifax	Western	Danville (Lynchburg)
Hampton City	Eastern	Newport News
Hanover	Eastern	Richmond
Harrisonburg City	Western	Harrisonburg
Henrico	Eastern	Richmond
Henry	Western	Danville (Lynchburg)
Highland	Western	Harrisonburg
Hopewell City	Eastern	Richmond
Isle of Wight	Eastern	Norfolk
James City	Eastern	Newport News
King George	Eastern	Richmond
King William	Eastern	Richmond
King and Queen	Eastern	Richmond
Lancaster	Eastern	Richmond
Lee	Western	Big Stone Gap (Roanoke)
Lexington City	Western	Lynchburg (Harrisonburg)
Loudoun	Eastern	Alexandria
Louisa	Western	Charlottesville (Lynchburg)
Lunenburg	Eastern	Richmond
Lynchburg City	Western	Lynchburg
Madison	Western	Charlottesville (Lynchburg)
Manassas City	Eastern	Alexandria
Manassas Park City	Eastern	Alexandria
Martinsville City	Western	Lynchburg
Mathews	Eastern	Newport News
Mecklenburg	Eastern	Richmond
Middlesex	Eastern	Richmond
Montgomery	Western	Roanoke
Nelson	Western	Charlottesville (Lynchburg)
New Kent	Eastern	Richmond
Newport News City	Eastern	Newport News
Norfolk City	Eastern	Norfolk
Northampton	Eastern	Norfolk
Northumberland	Eastern	Richmond
Norton City	Western	Big Stone Gap (Roanoke)
Nottoway	Eastern	Richmond
Orange	Western	Charlottesville (Lynchburg)
Page	Western	Harrisonburg
Patrick	Western	Danville (Lynchburg)
Petersburg City	Eastern	Richmond
Pittsylvania	Western	Danville (Lynchburg)
Poquoson City	Eastern	Newport News
Portsmouth City	Eastern	Norfolk
Powhatan	Eastern	Richmond
Prince Edward	Eastern	Richmond
Prince George	Eastern	Richmond
Prince William	Eastern	Alexandria
Pulaski	Western	Roanoke
Radford City	Western	Roanoke
Rappahannock	Western	Charlottesville (Harrisonburg)
Richmond	Eastern	Richmond
Richmond City	Eastern	Richmond
Roanoke	Western	Roanoke
Roanoke City	Western	Roanoke
Rockbridge	Western	Lynchburg (Harrisonburg)
Rockingham	Western	Harrisonburg
Russell	Western	Abingdon (Roanoke)
Salem City	Western	Roanoke
Scott	Western	Big Stone Gap (Roanoke)
Shenandoah	Western	Harrisonburg
Smyth	Western	Abingdon (Roanoke)
South Boston City	Western	Danville (Lynchburg)
Southampton	Eastern	Norfolk
Spotsylvania	Eastern	Richmond
Stafford	Eastern	Alexandria
Staunton City	Western	Harrisonburg
Suffolk City	Eastern	Norfolk
Surry	Eastern	Richmond
Sussex	Eastern	Richmond
Tazewell	Western	Abingdon (Roanoke)
Virginia Beach City	Eastern	Norfolk
Warren	Western	Harrisonburg
Washington	Western	Abingdon (Roanoke)
Waynesboro City	Western	Harrisonburg
Westmoreland	Eastern	Richmond
Williamsburg City	Eastern	Newport News
Winchester City	Western	Harrisonburg
Wise	Western	Big Stone Gap (Roanoke)
Wythe	Western	Roanoke
York	Eastern	Newport News

Standards for Federal Courts: The search fee is $20.00 per item (one party name or case number). Certification fee is $7.00 per document. Copy fee is $.50 per page. All fees standard unless noted in profile. Mail Search: always enclose a stamped self addressed envelope unless otherwise noted. Most courts accept fax requests or will suggest a copying/search vendor. Before releasing records, all courts require prepayment unless noted in profile.

Open records are located at the court unless otherwise noted. District courts index by defendant and plaintiff as well as by case number. Bankruptcy courts usually index by debtor and case number. While most courts now have their indexes on computer, many still maintain index card files as well.

The universal PACER sign-up number is 800-676-6856. Find PACER and the Party/Case Index on the Web at http://pacer.psc.uscourts.gov. PACER dial-up access is $.60 per minute. Also, courts offering internet access via RACER, PACER, Web-PACER or the new CM-ECF charge $.07 per page fee unless noted as free.

US District Court

Eastern District of Virginia

Alexandria Division 401 Courthouse Square, Alexandria, VA 22314 (courier address: Use mail address for courier delivery) 703-299-2100. www.vaed.uscourts.gov

Counties: Arlington, Fairfax, Fauquier, Loudoun, Prince William, Stafford, City of Alexandria, City of Fairfax, City of Falls Church, City of Manassas, City of Manassas Park.

Indexing & Storage: New cases available in the index 1 day after filing date. Records are indexed and stored in numerical order.

Fee & Payment: Payment may be made by money order, cashier check, personal check. Payee: Clerk, U.S. District Court.

Phone Search: Only docket information available by phone.

In Person Search: Fee charged if court conducts your in person search for you. A copy service is available.

PACER: PACER is available online at http://pacer.vaed.uscourts.gov. New records are online after 1 day.

Newport News Division Clerk's Office, PO Box 494, Newport News, VA 23607 (courier address: U.S. Post Office Bldg, Room 201, 101 25th St, Newport News, VA 23607), 757-247-0784. www.vaed.uscourts.gov

Counties: Gloucester, James City, Mathews, York, City of Hampton, City of Newport News, City of Poquoson, City of Williamsburg.

Indexing & Storage: New cases available in the index 1 day after filing date.

Fee & Payment: Payment may be made by money order, cashier check, personal check. Payee: Clerk, U.S. District Court.

Phone Search: Only docket information available by phone. The court will not honor requests for lists of names over the phone.

In Person Search: Fee charged if court conducts your in person search for you. No charge to use public access computer. If extensive copies are requested, a search fee will be charged.

PACER: PACER is available online at http://pacer.vaed.uscourts.gov. New records are online after 1 day.

Norfolk Division U.S. Courthouse, Room 193, 600 Granby St, Norfolk, VA 23510 (courier address: Use mail address for courier delivery) 757-222-7204. www.vaed.uscourts.gov

Counties: Accomack, City of Chesapeake, City of Franklin, Isle of Wight, City of Norfolk, Northampton, City of Portsmouth, City of Suffolk, Southampton, City of Virginia Beach.

Indexing & Storage: New cases available in the index 1 day after filing date. Records are also indexed by microfiche from January 1981 to June 1991. Records prior to 1981 are in the card index.

Fee & Payment: Payment may be made by money order, cashier check, business check. Personal checks are not accepted. Payee: Clerk, U.S. District Court.

Phone Search: No searching by telephone. Only limited docket information is available by phone.

In Person Search: Permitted. This court will only do searches if the public terminal is down.

PACER: PACER is available online at http://pacer.vaed.uscourts.gov. New records are online after 1 day.

Richmond Division Lewis F Powell, Jr Courthouse Bldg, 1000 E Main St, Room 305, Richmond, VA 23219-3525 (courier address: Use mail address for courier delivery) 804-916-2200. www.vaed.uscourts.gov

Counties: Amelia, Brunswick, Caroline, Charles City, Chesterfield, Dinwiddie, Essex, Goochland, Greensville, Hanover, Henrico, King and Queen, King George, King William, Lancaster, Lunenburg, Mecklenburg, Middlesex, New Kent, Northumberland, Nottoway, City of Petersburg, Powhatan, Prince Edward, Prince George, Richmond, City of Richmond, Spotsylvania, Surry, Sussex, Westmoreland, City of Colonial Heights, City of Emporia, City of Fredericksburg, City of Hopewell.

Indexing & Storage: New cases available in the index 1 day after filing date. Records are indexed by case number and stored at the court.

Fee & Payment: Payment may be made by money order, cashier check, personal check. Payee: Clerk's Office, U.S. District Court.

Phone Search: Only docket information available by phone. The court will not honor requests for lists of names over the phone.

Mail Search: A SASE not required.

In Person Search: Fee charged if court conducts your in person search for you. A copy service is available.

PACER: PACER is available online at http://pacer.vaed.uscourts.gov. New records are online after 1 day.

U.S. Bankruptcy Court

Eastern District of Virginia

Alexandria Division PO Box 19247, Alexandria, VA 22320-0247 (courier address: Suite 100, 200 S Washington St, Alexandria, VA 22314), 703-258-1200. www.vaeb.uscourts.gov

Counties: City of Alexandria, Arlington, Fairfax, City of Fairfax, City of Falls Church, Fauquier, Loudoun, City of Manassas, City of Manassas Park, Prince William, Stafford.

Indexing & Storage: Cases indexed by debtor as well as by case number. New cases available in the index 2 days after filing date. A creditor register is also kept for each case. Index card are for cases prior to December 1989.

Fee & Payment: Payment may be made by money order, cashier check, personal check. Debtor's checks are not accepted. Payee: Clerk, U.S. Bankruptcy Court.

Phone Search: Docket information is available by phone. Automated voice case information service (VCIS) is available. Call VCIS at 800-326-5879 or 804-771-2736.

In Person Search: Permitted. Copies can also be made by an on-ite copy service, IKON Mgmt. Svcs, 703-706-0494.

PACER: PACER access is available online through CM/ECF at the web site. This replaces the free NIBS system. Case records go back to mid 1989. Records never purged. New civil records are online after 1 day.

Electronic Filing: Electronic filing information online at http://ecf.vaeb.uscourts.gov

Other Online Access: Court now participates in the U.S. party case index.

Newport News Division Norfolk Bankruptcy Court, PO Box 1938, Norfolk, VA 23501-1938 (courier address: Walter E Hoffman U.S. Courthouse, Room 400, 600 Granby St, Norfolk, VA 23510), 757-222-7500. www.vaeb.uscourts.gov

Counties: Newport News City. Records are at the Norfolk Bankruptcy Court.

Indexing & Storage: Cases indexed by debtor as well as by case number. New cases available in the index 2 days after filing date.

Fee & Payment: Payment may be made by money order, cashier check, personal check. The search fee checks should be made to the clerk. Debtor checks are not accepted. Payee: Clerk, U.S. Bankruptcy Court.

Phone Search: Call for name, case number, chapter, filing date, judge, attorney for debtor, trustee, Social Security number and date discharged. Automated voice case information service (VCIS) is available. Call VCIS at 800-326-5879 or 804-771-2736.

In Person Search: Fee charged if court conducts your in person search for you. Copying available from copy service.

PACER: PACER access is available online through CM/ECF at the web site. This replaces the free NIBS system. New civil records are online after 7 days.

Electronic Filing: Electronic filing information online at http://ecf.vaeb.uscourts.gov

Other Online Access: Court now participates in the U.S. party case index.

Norfolk Division PO Box 1938, Norfolk, VA 23501-1938 (courier: Walter E Hoffman U.S. Courthouse, Rm 400, 600 Granby St, Norfolk, VA 23510), 757-222-7500. www.vaeb.uscourts.gov

Counties: Accomack, City of Cape Charles, City of Chesapeake, City of Franklin, Gloucester, City of Hampton, Isle of Wight, James City, Matthews, City of Norfolk, Northampton, City of Poquoson, City of Portsmouth, Southampton, City of Suffolk, City of Virginia Beach, City of Williamsburg, York.

Indexing & Storage: Cases indexed by debtor as well as by case number. New cases available in the index 2 days after filing date.

Fee & Payment: Payment may be made by money order, cashier check, personal check. The search fee checks should be made to the clerk. The searcher must use Ikon Manag

Mgmt Svcs for copies. The copy fee checks should be made to Ikon Mgmt Svcs. Debtor checks are not accepted. Payee: Clerk, U.S. Bankruptcy Court.

Phone Search: Call for name, case number, chapter, filing date, judge, attorney for debtor, trustee, Social Security number and date discharged. Automated voice case information service (VCIS) is available. Call VCIS at 800-326-5879 or 804-771-2736.

In Person Search: Fee charged if court conducts your in person search for you. Copying available from copy service.

PACER: PACER access is available online through CM/ECF at the web site. This replaces the free NIBS system. New civil records are online after 7 days.

Electronic Filing: Electronic filing information online at http://ecf.vaeb.uscourts.gov

Other Online Access: Court now participates in the U.S. party case index.

Richmond Division Office of the clerk, 1100 E Main St, Room 310, Richmond, VA 23219-3515 (courier address: 1100 E Main St, Room 301, Richmond, VA 23219), 804-916-2400. www.vaeb.uscourts.gov

Counties: Amelia, Brunswick, Caroline, Charles City, Chesterfield, City of Colonial Heights, Dinwiddie, City of Emporia, Essex, City of Fredericksburg, Goochland, Greensville, Hanover, Henrico, City of Hopewell, King and Queen, King George, King William, Lancaster, Lunenburg, Mecklenburg, Middlesex, New Kent, Northumberland, Nottoway, City of Petersburg, Powhatan, Prince Edward, Prince George, Richmond, City of Richmond, Spotsylvania, Surry, Sussex, Westmoreland.

Indexing & Storage: Cases indexed by debtor as well as by case number. New cases available in the index 1 day after filing date.

Fee & Payment: Payment may be made by money order, cashier check, personal check. The court will not send statements. Debtor checks are not accepted. Dave Jones & Assoc Copy Svc handles search requests. You must fax your request to them at 804-780-0652. They will call you back with the fees. Payee: Clerk, U.S. Bankruptcy Court.

Phone Search: Only docket information available by phone. Automated voice case information

service (VCIS) is available. Call VCIS at 800-326-5879 or 804-771-2736.

In Person Search: Fee charged if court conducts your in person search for you. Copying available from copy service.

PACER: PACER access is available online through CM/ECF at the web site. This replaces the free NIBS system.

Electronic Filing: Electronic filing information online at http://ecf.vaeb.uscourts.gov

Other Online Access: Court now participates in the U.S. party case index.

U.S. District Court
Western District of Virginia

Abingdon Division Clerk's Office, PO Box 398, Abingdon, VA 24212 (courier address: 180 W Main St, Abingdon, VA 24210), 276-628-5116, Fax: 276-628-1028. www.vawd.uscourts.gov

Counties: Buchanan, City of Bristol, Russell, Smyth, Tazewell, Washington.

Indexing & Storage: New cases available in the index immediately after filing date.

Fee & Payment: Payment may be made by money order, cashier check, personal check. Court will bill for searches and copies. Payee: Clerk, U.S. District Court.

Phone Search: Docket information available by phone.

Mail Search: A SASE not required.

In Person Search: Fee charged if court conducts your in person search for you.

PACER: PACER is available online at http://pacer.vawd.uscourts.gov. Case records go back to Mid 1990. Records never purged. New records are online after 1 day.

Electronic Filing: Electronic filing information online at https://ecf.vawd.uscourts.gov

Big Stone Gap Division PO Box 490, Big Stone Gap, VA 24219 (courier address: 322 Wood Ave E, Room 204, Big Stone Gap, VA 24219), 276-523-3557, Fax: 276-523-6214. www.vawd.uscourts.gov

Counties: Dickenson, Lee, Scott, Wise, City of Norton.

Indexing & Storage: New cases available in the index immediately after filing date. The style of the case is needed to conduct a search. A civil action number is very helpful. A microfilm index is also maintained for older cases.

Fee & Payment: Payment may be made by money order, cashier check, personal check. Payee: Clerk, U.S. District Court. Will fax docket listings.

Phone Search: Only docket information available by phone. Will fax docket listings.

In Person Search: Fee charged if court conducts your in person search for you.

PACER: PACER is available online at http://pacer.vawd.uscourts.gov. Case records go back to Mid 1990. Records never purged. New records are online after 1 day.

Electronic Filing: Electronic filing information online at https://ecf.vawd.uscourts.gov

Charlottesville Division Clerk, Room 304, 255 W Main St, Charlottesville, VA 22902 (courier address: Use mail address for courier delivery) 434-296-9284. www.vawd.uscourts.gov

Counties: Albemarle, Culpeper, Fluvanna, Greene, Louisa, Madison, Nelson, Orange, Rappahannock, City of Charlottesville.

Indexing & Storage: New cases available in the index immediately after filing date. Records are indexed on microfiche from 1981 to 1991, and on card prior to that. District wide searches are available from this court for any information within the district.

Fee & Payment: Payment may be made by money order, cashier check, personal check. Payee: Clerk, U.S. District Court.

Phone Search: No searching by telephone.

In Person Search: Fee charged if court conducts your in person search for you. Court only searches computer index. You may search microfiche index.

PACER: PACER is available online at http://pacer.vawd.uscourts.gov. Case records go back to Mid 1990. Records never purged. New records are online after 1 day.

Electronic Filing: Electronic filing information online at https://ecf.vawd.uscourts.gov

Danville Division PO Box 1400, Danville, VA 24543-0053 (courier address: Dan Daniel Post Office Bldg, Room 202, 700 Main St, Danville, VA 24541), 434-793-7147, Fax: 434-793-0284. www.vawd.uscourts.gov

Counties: Charlotte, Halifax, Henry, Patrick, Pittsylvania, City of Danville, City of Martinsville, City of South Boston.

Indexing & Storage: New cases available in the index immediately after filing date.

Fee & Payment: Payment may be made by money order, cashier check, personal check. Payee: Clerk, U.S. District Court.

Phone Search: If there is an expedited request and the $15.00 search fee is prepaid, the court will call to give the information, and follow with a written response.

Mail Search: A SASE not required.

In Person Search: Fee charged if court conducts your in person search for you.

PACER: PACER is available online at http://pacer.vawd.uscourts.gov. Case records go back to Mid 1990. Records never purged. New records are online after 1 day.

Electronic Filing: Electronic filing information online at https://ecf.vawd.uscourts.gov

Harrisonburg Division Clerk, PO Box 1207, Harrisonburg, VA 22803 (courier address: Post Office Bldg, 116 N Main St, Room 314, Harrisonburg, VA 22802), 540-434-3181. www.vawd.uscourts.gov

Counties: Augusta, Bath, Clarke, Frederick, Highland, Page, Rockingham, Shenandoah, Warren, City of Harrisonburg, City of Staunton, City of Waynesboro, City of Winchester.

Indexing & Storage: New cases available in the index 1-2 days after filing date. Records are indexed on computer for civil cases from 1991 and criminal cases from 1993. District wide searches are available from this court 1-2 days after it is filed, but the court prefers that searches be conducted where the case is filed.

Fee & Payment: Payment may be made by money order, cashier check, personal check. Payee: Clerk, U.S. District Court.

Phone Search: Limited information available by phone.

Mail Search: A SASE not required.

In Person Search: Fee charged if court conducts your in person search for you.

PACER: PACER is available online at http://pacer.vawd.uscourts.gov. Case records go back to Mid 1990. Records never purged. New records are online after 1 day.

Electronic Filing: Electronic filing information online at https://ecf.vawd.uscourts.gov

Lynchburg Division Clerk, PO Box 744, Lynchburg, VA 24505 (courier address: Room 212, 1100 Main St, Lynchburg, VA 24504), 434-847-5722. www.vawd.uscourts.gov

Counties: Amherst, Appomattox, Bedford, Buckingham, Campbell, Cumberland, Rockbridge, City of Bedford, City of Buena Vista, City of Lexington, City of Lynchburg.

Indexing & Storage: New cases available in the index immediately after filing date. The computer index goes back to 1989.

Fee & Payment: Payment may be made by money order, cashier check, personal check. Payee: Clerk, U.S. District Court.

Phone Search: Only docket information available by phone.

Mail Search: A SASE not required.

In Person Search: Fee charged if court conducts your in person search for you.

PACER: PACER is available online at http://pacer.vawd.uscourts.gov. Case records go back to Mid 1990. Records never purged. New records are online after 1 day.

Electronic Filing: Electronic filing information online at https://ecf.vawd.uscourts.gov

Roanoke Division Clerk, PO Box 1234, Roanoke, VA 24006 (courier: 210 Franklin Rd SW, Roanoke, VA 24011), 540-857-5100, Fax: 540-857-5110. www.vawd.uscourts.gov

Counties: Alleghany, Bland, Botetourt, Carroll, Craig, Floyd, Franklin, Giles, Grayson, Montgomery, Pulaski, Roanoke, Wythe, City of Covington, City of Clifton Forge, City of Galax, City of Radford, City of Roanoke, City of Salem.

Indexing & Storage: New cases available in the index immediately after filing date. Records are also indexed on microfiche. The automated in house system is available for records from 1994. District wide searches are available for all records from this court.

Fee & Payment: Payment may be made by money order, cashier check, personal check. Payee: Clerk, U.S. District Court.

Phone Search: If there is an expedited request and the $15.00 search fee is prepaid, the court will call to give the information. However, a written response will follow.

Mail Search: A SASE not required.

In Person Search: Fee charged if court conducts your in person search for you.

PACER: PACER is available online at http://pacer.vawd.uscourts.gov. Case records go back to Mid 1990. Records never purged. New records are online after 1 day.

Electronic Filing: Electronic filing information online at https://ecf.vawd.uscourts.gov

U.S. Bankruptcy Court

Western District of Virginia

Harrisonburg Division PO Box 1407, Harrisonburg, VA 22803 (courier address: 116 N Main St, Harrisonburg, VA 22801), 540-434-8327, Fax: 540-434-9715. www.vawb.uscourts.gov

Counties: Alleghany, Augusta, Bath, City of Buena Vista, Clarke, City of Clifton Forge, City of Covington, Frederick, City of Harrisonburg, Highland, City of Lexington, Page, Rappahannock, Rockbridge, Rockingham, Shenandoah, City of Staunton, Warren, City ofWaynesboro, City of Winchester.

Indexing & Storage: Cases indexed by debtor as well as by case number. New cases available in the index immediately after filing date. The computer index goes back to 1986. Older cases are on a card index.

Fee & Payment: Payment may be made by money order, cashier check, business check. Personal checks are not accepted. Payee: Clerk, U.S. Bankruptcy Court.

Phone Search: Only docket information available by phone, and only if it is available from the computer.

In Person Search: Fee charged if court conducts your in person search for you.

PACER: PACER is available online at https://pacer.vawb.uscourts.gov. Case records go back to March 1986. Records never purged. New civil records are online after 1 day.

Electronic Filing: Currently in the process of implementing CM/ECF.

Lynchburg Division PO Box 6400, Lynchburg, VA 24505 (courier address: 1100 Main St, Room 226, Lynchburg, VA 24504), 434-845-0317. www.vawb.uscourts.gov

Counties: Albemarle, Amherst, Appomattox, Bedford, City of Bedford, Buckingham, Campbell, Charlotte, City of Charlottesville, Culpeper, Cumberland, City of Danville, Fluvanna, Greene, Halifax, Henry, Louisa, City of Lynchburg,

Madison, City of Martinsville, Nelson, Orange, Patrick, Pittsylvania, City of South Boston.

Indexing & Storage: Cases indexed by debtor as well as by case number. New cases available in the index 24 hours after filing date. The computer index goes back to 1986.

Fee & Payment: Payment may be made by money order, cashier check, business check. Personal checks are not accepted. Payee: Clerk, U.S. Bankruptcy Court.

Phone Search: Only the name, date filed and chapter will be released over the phone.

In Person Search: Fee charged if court conducts your in person search for you.

PACER: PACER is available online at https://pacer.vawb.uscourts.gov/. New civil records are online after 1 day.

Electronic Filing: Currently in the process of implementing CM/ECF.

Roanoke Division PO Box 2390, Roanoke, VA 24010 (courier: Commonwealth Bldg, 210 Church Ave, Roanoke, VA 24011), 540-857-2391, Fax: 540-857-2873. www.vawb.uscourts.gov

Counties: Bland, Botetourt, City of Bristol, Buchanan, Carroll, Craig, Dickenson, Floyd, Franklin, City of Galax, Giles, Grayson, Lee, Montgomery, City of Norton, Pulaski, City of Radford, Roanoke, City of Roanoke, Russell, City of Salem, Scott, Smyth, Tazewell, Washington, Wise, Wythe.

Indexing & Storage: Cases indexed by debtor and creditors as well as by case number. New cases available in the index same day if possible after filing date. Records are indexed numerically (for example: 7-92-00123 = office number, year and 5 digit case number).

Fee & Payment: Payment may be made by money order, cashier check. Business checks are not accepted. Personal checks are not accepted. Only firm checks will be accepted. Payee: Clerk, U.S. Bankruptcy Court.

Phone Search: No searching by telephone. Only the number of pages of the requested items will be given over the phone.

In Person Search: Fee charged if court conducts your in person search for you.

PACER: PACER is available online at https://pacer.vawb.uscourts.gov/. Case records go back to 1988. Records never purged. New civil records are online after 1 day.

Electronic Filing: Currently in the process of implementing CM/ECF.

Virginia County Courts

Court	Jurisdiction	No. of Courts	How Organized
Circuit Courts*	General	117	31 Circuits
District Courts*	Limited	132	
Combined Courts*		11	

* Profiled in this Sourcebook.

Court	CIVIL								
	Tort	Contract	Real Estate	Min. Claim	Max. Claim	Small Claims	Estate	Eviction	Domestic Relations
Circuit Courts*	X	X	X	$3,000	No Max		X		X
District Courts*	X	X	X	$0	$15,000	$2,000		X	X

Court	CRIMINAL				
	Felony	Misdemeanor	DWI/DUI	Preliminary Hearing	Juvenile
Circuit Courts*	X				
District Courts*		X	X	X	X

ADMINISTRATION   Executive Secretary, Administrative Office of Courts, 100 N 9th Street, 3rd Fl, Supreme Court Building, Richmond, Virginia, 23219; 804-786-6455, Fax: 804-786-4542. www.courts.state.va.us

COURT STRUCTURE   The Circuit Courts in 31 districts are the courts of general jurisdiction. There are 132 District Courts of limited jurisdiction. Please note that a district can comprise a county or a city. Records of civil action from $3000 to $15,000 can be at either the Circuit or District Court as either can have jurisdiction. It is necessary to check both record locations as there is no concurrent database nor index.

ONLINE ACCESS   There are 3 available systems. None are statewide; each county must be searched separately.

132 General District Courts (many are combined courts) may be searched free at http://208.210.219.132/courtinfo/vadistrict/select.jsp?court=. Here you can search both active and inactive cases.

Also, Virginia has the growing "Circuit Court Case Information Pilot Project" with free access to Circuit Court records. You may search records from over 90 courts at http://208.210.219.132/courtinfo/vacircuit/select.jsp?court=

While these systems do not include DOBs, SSNs and Addresses, another access system known as LOPAS does. There are no fees to use LOPAS, but access is granted on a request-by-request basis. All courts except Fairfax County and Alexandria City Circuit Courts are on LOPAS. Anyone wishing to establish an account or receive information on LOPAS must contact the Supreme Court of Virginia, 100 N 9th St, Richmond VA 23219 or by phone at 804-786-6455 or fax at 804-786-4542. This is a difficult sign to "get on" as it is an old dial-up system with 20 phone lines serving requesters.

The www.courts.state.va.us site offers access to Supreme Court and Appellate opinions.

ADDITIONAL INFORMATION   In many jurisdictions, the certification fee is $2.00 per document plus copy fee. The copy fee is $.50 per page.

Accomack County

2nd Circuit Court PO Box 126, Accomac, VA 23301; 757-787-5776; Fax: 757-787-1849. Hours: 9AM-5PM (EST). *Felony, Civil Actions Over $15,000, Probate.*
Civil Records: Access: Fax, mail, online, in person. Both court and visitors may perform in person searches. No search fee. Required to search: name, years to search. Civil cases indexed by defendant, plaintiff. Civil records on microfiche and archived from 1663; on computer back to 1984. Remote online

access to court case indexes is via LOPAS; call 804-786-5511 to apply.
Criminal Records: Access: Fax, mail, online, in person. Both court and visitors may perform in person searches. No search fee. Required to search: name, years to search, DOB; also helpful: SSN. Criminal records on microfiche and archived from 1663; on computer back to 1984. Remote online access to court case indexes is via LOPAS; call 804-786-5511 to apply.
General Information: Public Access terminal is available. No juvenile, sealed, probate, tax return or adoption records released. Fee to fax results is $2.00

1st page, $.50 each add'l. Copy fee: $.50 per page. Cert fee: $2.00. Payee: Samuel H Cooper Jr, Clerk of Court. Personal checks accepted. Prepayment required. Mail requests: SASE not required. Mail turnaround time 1-2 days.

2A General District Court PO Box 276, Accomac, VA 23301; 757-787-0923. Hours: 8:30AM-4:30PM (EST). *Misdemeanor, Civil Actions Under $15,000, Eviction, Small Claims.*
Civil Records: Access: Phone, mail, online, in person. Both court and visitors may perform in person searches. No search fee. Required to search: name,

years to search. Civil cases indexed by defendant. Civil records retained ten years. Search at http://208.210.219.132/courtinfo/vadistrict/select.jsp?court=. Also, online access case indexes is via LOPAS; call 804-786-5511 to apply.

Criminal Records: Access: Phone, mail, online, in person. Both court and visitors may perform in person searches. No search fee. Required to search: name, years to search, DOB; also helpful: SSN. Criminal records retained ten years. Online access to criminal records is the same as civil.

General Information: Public Access terminal is available. No juvenile, sealed, adoption records released. Copy fee: $1.00 for first 2 pages. Add $.50 per page thereafter. No cert fee. Payee: Accomack District Court. Personal checks accepted. Visa, MC accepted. Prepayment required. Mail requests: SASE required. Mail turnaround time 1-3 days.

Albemarle County

16th Circuit & District Court 501 E Jefferson St, Charlottesville, VA 22902; 434-972-4085; Fax: 434-972-4071. Hours: 8:30AM-4:30PM (EST). *Felony, Misdemeanor, Civil, Eviction, Probate.*

Civil Records: Access: Mail, online, in person. Both court and visitors may perform in person searches. Search fee: $5.00 per name. Required to search: name, years to search. Civil records on microfiche from 1980 to present and archived from 1700s to 1990. Select and search Circuit Courts online at http://208.210.219.132/courtinfo/vacircuit/select.jsp?court= and District Courts at http://208.210.219.132/courtinfo/vadistrict/select.jsp?court=. Also search via LOPAS; call 804-786-5511.

Criminal Records: Access: Mail, online, in person. Both court and visitors may perform in person searches. Search fee: $5.00 per name. Required to search: name, years to search. Criminal records on microfiche from 1980 to present and archived from 1700s to 1990. Remote online access to court case indexes is via LOPAS; call 804-786-5511 to apply.

General Information: No juvenile, sealed records released. Copy fee: $.50 per page. Cert fee: $2.00. Payee: Albemarle Clerk of Court. Personal checks accepted. Prepayment required. Mail turnaround time 7-10 days.

Alexandria City

18th Circuit Court 520 King St, #307, Alexandria, VA 22314; Civil phone: 703-838-4044; Criminal phone: 703-838-4047; Probate phone: 703-838-4055. Hours: 9AM-5PM (EST). *Felony, Civil Actions Over $15,000, Probate.*
http://ci.alexandria.va.us/courts/courts_index.html
Civil Records: Access: In person only. Visitors must perform in person searches for themselves. No search fee. Required to search: name, years to search. Civil cases indexed by defendant, plaintiff. Civil records on computer from 1983 to present, microfiche from 1970s to present.

Criminal Records: Access: In person only. Visitors must perform in person searches for themselves. No search fee. Required to search: name, years to search; also helpful: DOB. Criminal records on computer since 7/87.

General Information: Public Access terminal is available. No juvenile, sealed, adoption or expunged records released. Copy fee: $.50 per page. Cert fee: $2.00. Payee: Clerk of Court. Only cashiers checks and money orders accepted. Prepayment required.

18th District Court 520 King St, #201, Alexandria, VA 22314; 703-838-4041 (traffic); Civil phone: 703-838-4021; Criminal phone: 703-838-4030. Hours: 8AM-4PM (EST). *Misdemeanor, Civil Actions Under $15,000, Eviction, Small Claims.*
Note: Mail can go to PO Box 20206, Zip is 22320.

Civil Records: Access: Online, in person. Both court and visitors may perform in person searches. No search fee. Required to search: name, years to search. Civil cases indexed by defendant. Civil records on computer from 1993 to present, index cards prior to 1986. Search free at http://208.210.219.132/courtinfo/vadistrict/select.jsp?court=. Also search via LOPAS; call 804-786-5511.

Criminal Records: Access: Online, in person. Visitors must perform in person searches for themselves. No search fee. Required to search: name. Criminal records on computer from 1993 to present. Online access to criminal records is the same as civil.

General Information: Public Access terminal is available. Copy fee: $1.00 first 2 pages, $.50 each addl. No cert fee.

Alleghany County

25th Circuit Court PO Box 670, Covington, VA 24426; 540-965-1730; Fax: 540-965-1732. Hours: 8:30AM-5PM M-F; 9AM-Noon Sat (EST). *Felony, Civil Actions Over $15,000, Probate.*
www.alleghanycountyclerk.com
Civil Records: Access: Online, in person. Visitors must perform in person searches for themselves. No search fee. Required to search: name. Civil cases indexed by plaintiff. Civil records available from 1822, all on microfilm. Search free online at http://208.210.219.132/courtinfo/vacircuit/select.jsp?court=. Also search via LOPAS; call 804-786-5511.

Criminal Records: Access: Online, in person. Visitors must perform in person searches for themselves. No search fee. Required to search: name. Criminal records available from 1822, all on microfilm. Online access to criminal records is the same as civil.

General Information: Public Access terminal is available. No juvenile, adoption or sealed records released. Copy fee: $.50 per page. Cert fee: $2.00. Payee: Michael D Wolfe, Clerk of Court. Personal checks accepted. Prepayment required.

25th General District Court PO Box 139, Covington, VA 24426; 540-965-1720; Fax: 540-965-1722. Hours: 9AM-5PM (EST). *Misdemeanor, Civil Actions Under $15,000, Eviction, Small Claims.*

Civil Records: Access: Online, in person. Visitors must perform in person searches. No search fee. Required to search: name, years to search. Civil cases indexed by defendant, plaintiff, on computer from 1/90, prior on index cards. Search free at http://208.210.219.132/courtinfo/vadistrict/select.jsp?court=. Also search via LOPAS; call 804-786-5511.

Criminal Records: Access: Online, in person. Visitors must perform in person searches. No search fee. Required to search: name, years to search; also helpful: DOB, SSN. Criminal records on computer from 1/90, prior on index cards. Online access to criminal records is the same as civil.

General Information: Public Access terminal is available. No juvenile, sealed records released. Copy fee: $1.00 each for first 2 pages; $.50 each add'l. No cert fee. Personal checks accepted. Visa, MC accepted. Acepted for fines and cost only. Prepayment required.

Amelia County

11th Circuit Court PO Box 237 (1 E Main St, B-5), Amelia, VA 23068; 804-561-2128. Hours: 8:30AM-4:30PM (EST). *Felony, Civil Actions Over $15,000, Probate.*
www.governdata.com/amelia.htm
Note: Will search on telephone request if not busy.

Civil Records: Access: Mail, online, in person. Both court and visitors may perform in person searches. No search fee. Required to search: name, years to search. Civil cases indexed by defendant, plaintiff. Civil

records on microfiche 1735 to present, indexed on books. Search free online at http://208.210.219.132/courtinfo/vacircuit/select.jsp?court=. Also search via LOPAS; call 804-786-5511.

Criminal Records: Access: Mail, online, in person. Both court and visitors may perform in person searches. No search fee. Required to search: name, years to search, DOB; also helpful: SSN. Criminal records on microfiche 1735 to present, indexed on books. Online access to criminal records is the same as civil.

General Information: Public Access terminal is available. No juvenile, sealed records released. Copy fee: $.50 per page. Cert fee: $2.00. Payee: Amelia County Circuit Court. Personal checks accepted. Prepayment required. Mail requests: SASE required. Mail turnaround time 3-5 days.

11th General District Court PO Box 24, Amelia, VA 23002; 804-561-2456; Fax: 804-561-6956. Hours: 8:30AM-4:30PM (EST). *Misdemeanor, Civil Actions Under $15,000, Eviction, Small Claims.*

Civil Records: Access: Online, in person. Visitors must perform in person searches for themselves. No search fee. Required to search: name, years to search. Civil cases indexed by defendant, plaintiff. Civil records on computer since 12/20/92, prior records on index cards. Search free at http://208.210.219.132/courtinfo/vadistrict/select.jsp?court=. Also search via LOPAS; call 804-786-5511.

Criminal Records: Access: Online, in person. Visitors must perform in person searches themselves. No search fee. Required to search: name, years to search, DOB; also helpful: SSN. Criminal records on computer since 12/20/92, prior records on index cards. Online access to criminal records is the same as civil.

General Information: Public Access terminal is available. No juvenile, sealed records released. Copy fee: $1.00 for 1st two pages, $.50 each add'l page. No cert fee. Payee: Amelia District Court. Personal checks accepted. Prepayment required.

Amherst County

24th Circuit Court PO Box 462, Amherst, VA 24521; 434-946-9321; Fax: 434-946-9323. Hours: 8AM-5PM (EST). *Felony, Civil Actions Over $15,000, Probate.*

Civil Records: Access: Online, in person. Visitors must perform in person searches for themselves. No search fee. Required to search: name, years to search. Civil cases indexed by defendant, plaintiff. Civil records on index books from 1761; on computer back to 1997. Remote online access to court case indexes is via LOPAS; call 804-786-5511 to apply.

Criminal Records: Access: Online, in person. Visitors must perform in person searches for themselves. No search fee. Required to search: name, years to search, date of offense. Criminal records on index books back to 1761; on comptuer back to 1997. Remote online access to court case indexes is via LOPAS; call 804-786-5511 to apply.

General Information: Public Access terminal is available. No juvenile, sealed or adoption records released. Copy fee: $.50 per page. Cert fee: $2.00. Payee: Clerk of Circuit Court. Personal checks accepted. Prepayment required.

24th General District Court PO Box 513, Amherst, VA 24521; 434-946-9351; Fax: 434-946-9359. Hours: 8AM-4PM (EST). *Misdemeanor, Civil Actions Under $15,000, Eviction, Small Claims.*
Note: Has handled misdemeanor cases since 1985.

Civil Records: Access: Mail, fax, online, in person. Both court and visitors may perform in person searches. Search fee: $10.00. Required to search: name, years to search. Civil cases indexed by defendant, plaintiff. Civil records on computer 10 years prior. Search free at http://208.210.219.132/courtinfo/vadistrict/select.jsp? court=. Also search via LOPAS; call 804-786-5511.

Criminal Records: Access: Mail, online, in person. Both court and visitors may perform in person searches. Search fee: $10.00. Required to search: name, years to search, DOB, SSN. Criminal records on computer 10 years prior. Online access to criminal records is the same as civil.

General Information: Public Access terminal is available. No sealed records released. Will fax results. Copy fee: $1.00 per page. No cert fee. Payee: Clerk of Court. Personal checks accepted. Visa, MC accepted. Prepayment required. Mail turnaround time is 48 hours.

Appomattox County

10th Circuit Court PO Box 672, 125 Court St., Appomattox, VA 24522; 434-352-5275; Fax: 434-352-2781. Hours: 8:30AM-4:30PM (EST). *Felony, Civil Actions Over $15,000, Probate.*

Civil Records: Access: Online, in person. Visitors must perform in person searches for themselves. No search fee. Required to search: name, years to search. Civil cases indexed by defendant, plaintiff. Civil records on books from 1892 to present; on computer since 1997. Search free online at http://208.210.219.132/courtinfo/vacircuit/select.jsp?c ourt=. Also search via LOPAS; call 804-786-5511.

Criminal Records: Access: Online, in person. Visitors must perform in person searches for themselves. No search fee. Required to search: name, years to search. Criminal records on books from 1892 to present; on computer since 1997. Online access to criminal records is the same as civil.

General Information: Public Access terminal is available. (Records start as of 01/01/01.) No juvenile, sealed records released. Copy fee: $.50 per page. No cert fee. Payee: Clerk of Circuit Court. Personal checks accepted. Prepayment required.

10th General District Court PO Box 187, 121 Court St., Appomattox, VA 24522; 434-352-5540; Fax: 434-352-0717. Hours: 8:30AM-4:30PM (EST). *Misdemeanor, Civil Actions Under $15,000, Eviction, Small Claims.*

Civil Records: Access: Fax, mail, online, in person. Both court and visitors may perform in person searches. No search fee. Required to search: name, years to search. Civil cases indexed by defendant, plaintiff. Civil records on card file from 1992 to present, prior in Circuit Court. Search free at http://208.210.219.132/courtinfo/vadistrict/select.jsp? court=. Also search via LOPAS; call 804-786-5511.

Criminal Records: Access: Fax, mail, online, in person. Both court and visitors may perform in person searches. No search fee. Required to search: name, years to search; also helpful: SSN. Criminal records on card file from 1992 to present, prior in Circuit Court. Online access to criminal records is the same as civil.

General Information: Public Access terminal is available. No juvenile, sealed records released. No fee to fax results. Copy fee: $1.00 1st page; $.50 each add'l. No cert fee. Payee: General District Court. Personal checks accepted. Visa, MC accepted. Turnaround time 1-5 days.

Arlington County

17th Circuit Court 1425 N Courthouse Rd, Arlington, VA 22201; 703-228-7010. Hours: 8AM-4PM (EST). *Felony, Civil Actions Over $15,000, Probate.*

http://158.59.15.115/arlington

Civil Records: Access: Online, in person. Visitors must perform in person searches for themselves. No search fee. Required to search: name, years to search. Civil cases indexed by defendant, plaintiff. Civil records on computer from 1987; prior on books from mid-1930 to present. Online access free at http://208.210.219.132/courtinfo/vacircuit/select.jsp?c ourt=. For information about the statewide online systems, see the state introduction.

Criminal Records: Access: Online, in person. Visitors must perform in person searches for themselves. No search fee. Required to search: name, years to search. Criminal records on computer from 1987; prior on books from mid-1930 to present. Online access to criminal records is the same as civil.

General Information: Public Access terminal is available. (Criminal only.) No juvenile, adoption or sealed records released. Copy fee: $.50 per page. Cert fee: $2.00. Payee: Clerk of Court. Personal checks accepted. Prepayment required.

17th General District Court 1425 N Courthouse Rd, Rm 2500, Arlington, VA 22201; 703-228-7900; Civil phone: 703-228-4485. Hours: 8AM-4PM (EST). *Misdemeanor, Civil Actions Under $15,000, Eviction, Small Claims.*

Note: Phone access limited to 4 requests.

Civil Records: Access: Phone, mail, online, in person. Both court and visitors may perform in person searches. No search fee. Required to search: name, years to search, case number. Civil cases indexed by defendant. Civil records on computer back to 1990, books from early 1970s. Search free at http://208.210.219.132/courtinfo/vadistrict/select.jsp? court=. Also search via LOPAS; call 804-786-5511.

Criminal Records: Access: Phone, mail, online, in person. Both court and visitors may perform in person searches. No search fee. Required to search: name, years to search, DOB; also helpful-SSN. Criminal records on computer back to 1990. Online access to criminal records is the same as civil.

General Information: Public Access terminal is available. No juvenile, sealed records released. Copy fee: $1.00 first 2 pages, $.25 each add'l. Cert fee: $2.00. Payee: Clerk of Court. Personal checks accepted. Prepayment required. Mail turnaround time 5 days.

Augusta County

25th Circuit Court PO Box 689, Staunton, VA 24402-0689; 540-245-5321; Fax: 540-245-5318. Hours: 8AM-5PM (EST). *Felony, Civil Actions Over $15,000, Probate.*

Note: Court prefers that searches be done in person. Mail access is limited; they will only search back to 1987. Phone available for very short search only.

Civil Records: Access: Mail, in person. Both court and visitors may perform in person searches. No search fee. Required to search: name, years to search. Civil cases indexed by defendant, plaintiff. Civil records on computer from 1987 to present, books from 1745 to 1986. Online access free at http://208.210.219.132/courtinfo/vacircuit/select.jsp?c ourt=. For information about the statewide online systems, see the state introduction.

Criminal Records: Access: Mail, in person. Both court and visitors may perform in person searches. No search fee. Required to search: name, years to search; also helpful: DOB, SSN. Criminal records go back to 1987 felonies only. Online access to criminal records is the same as civil.

General Information: Public Access terminal is available. No juvenile, adoption or sealed records released. Copy fee: $.50 per page. Cert fee: $2.00. Payee: Clerk, Augusta County Circuit Court. Personal checks accepted. Prepayment required. Mail requests: SASE required. Mail turnaround time 1-2 days.

25th General District Court 6 E Johnson St, 2nd Fl, Staunton, VA 24401; 540-245-5300; Fax: 540-245-5365. Hours: 8:30AM-4:30PM (EST). *Misdemeanor, Civil Actions Under $15,000, Eviction, Small Claims.*

Note: This court also handles traffic infractions.

Civil Records: Access: Mail, online, in person. Both court and visitors may perform in person searches. No search fee. Required to search: name, years to search. Civil cases indexed by defendant, plaintiff. Civil records kept for 10 years on computer, then archived or destroyed. Search free at http://208.210.219.132/courtinfo/vadistrict/select.jsp? court=. Also search via LOPAS; call 804-786-5511.

Criminal Records: Access: Mail, online, in person. Both court and visitors may perform in person searches. No search fee. Required to search: name, years to search. Criminal records kept for 10 years on computer, then archived or destroyed. Online access to criminal records is the same as civil.

General Information: Public Access terminal is available. Will not fax results. Copy fee: $.50 per page. No cert fee. Payee: Augusta General District Court. Personal checks accepted. Visa, MC accepted. Prepayment required. Mail requests: SASE requested. Turnaround time 2-3 days.

Bath County

25th Circuit Court PO Box 180, Warm Springs, VA 24484; 540-839-7226; Fax: 540-839-7248. Hours: 8:30AM-4:30PM (EST). *Felony, Civil Actions Over $15,000, Probate.*

Civil Records: Access: Mail, online, in person. Both court and visitors may perform in person searches. No search fee. Required to search: name, years to search. Civil cases indexed by defendant, plaintiff. Civil records on books from 1791 to present. Remote online access to court case indexes is via LOPAS; call 804-786-5511 to apply.

Criminal Records: Access: Online, in person. Visitors must perform in person searches for themselves. No search fee. Required to search: name, years to search; also helpful: DOB, SSN. Criminal records on books from 1791 to present. Online access to criminal records is the same as civil.

General Information: Public Access terminal is available. No juvenile, sealed or adoption records released. Copy fee: $.50 per page. Cert fee: $2.00. Payee: Bath County Circuit Court. Personal checks accepted. Prepayment required. Mail turnaround time 1-2 days.

25th General District Court PO Box 96, Warm Springs, VA 24484; 540-839-7242; Fax: 540-839-7248. Hours: 8:30AM-4:30PM (EST). *Misdemeanor, Civil Actions Under $15,000, Eviction, Small Claims.*

Civil Records: Access: Phone, fax, mail, online, in person. Both court and visitors may perform in person searches. No search fee. Required to search: name, years to search. Civil cases indexed by defendant, plaintiff. Civil records on files from 1985 to present, Prior records in Circuit Court. Search free at http://208.210.219.132/courtinfo/vadistrict/select.jsp? court=. Also search via LOPAS; call 804-786-5511.

Criminal Records: Access: Phone, fax, mail, online, in person. Both court and visitors may perform in person searches. No search fee. Required to search: name, years to search, DOB; also helpful: SSN. Criminal records on files back 10 years, Prior records in Circuit Court. Online access to criminal records is the same as civil.

General Information: Public Access terminal is available. No juvenile, sealed records released. Copy fee: $.50 per page. No cert fee. Payee: Bath County Combined Court. Personal checks accepted. Visa, MC accepted. Prepayment required. Mail requests: SASE requested. Turnaround time 2 days; will give immediate response on phone if not an extensive search.

Bedford County

County Circuit Court 123 E Main St, #201, Bedford, VA 24523; 540-586-7632; Fax: 540-586-6197. Hours: 8:30AM-5PM (EST). *Felony, Civil Actions Over $15,000, Probate.*

Civil Records: Access: Online, in person. Visitors must perform in person searches for themselves. No search fee. Required to search: name, years to search. Civil cases indexed by defendant, plaintiff. Civil records on computer from 1988, index books. Online access free at http://208.210.219.132/courtinfo/vacircuit/select.jsp?court=. For information about the statewide online systems, see the state introduction.

Criminal Records: Access: Online, in person. Visitors must perform in person searches for themselves. No search fee. Required to search: name, years to search, DOB. Criminal records on computer from 1988, index books. Remote online access to court case indexes is via LOPAS; call 804-786-5511 to apply.

General Information: Public Access terminal is available. No juvenile, sealed records released. Copy fee: $.50 per page. Cert fee: $.50 per page. Payee: Bedford Clerk of Court. Personal checks accepted. Prepayment required.

24th General District Court 123 E Main St, #202, Bedford, VA 24523; 540-586-7637; Fax: 540-586-7684. Hours: 8AM-4PM (EST). *Misdemeanor, Civil Actions Under $15,000, Eviction, Small Claims, Traffic.*

Note: The court will not perform name searches.

Civil Records: Access: Online, in person. Visitors must perform in person searches for themselves. No search fee. Required to search: name. Civil cases indexed by defendant. Civil records on computer for ten years. Search free at http://208.210.219.132/courtinfo/vadistrict/select.jsp?court=. Also search via LOPAS; call 804-786-5511.

Criminal Records: Access: Online, in person. Visitors must perform in person searches for themselves. No search fee. Required to search: name. Criminal records on computer for ten years. Online access to criminal records is the same as civil.

General Information: Public Access terminal is available. No sealed records released. Copy fee: $1.00 1st 2 pages, $.50 each additional page. No cert fee. Payee: Bedford General District Court. Personal checks accepted. Visa, MC accepted. Prepayment required.

Bedford City

Circuit & District Courts Note: See Bedford County

Bland County

27th Circuit Court PO Box 295, Bland, VA 24315; 276-688-4562; Fax: 276-688-4562. Hours: 8AM-6PM (EST). *Felony, Civil Actions Over $15,000, Probate.*

Civil Records: Access: Phone, fax, mail, online, in person. Both court and visitors may perform in person searches. Search fee: $10.00 per name. Required to search: name, years to search. Civil cases indexed by defendant, plaintiff. Civil records on books from 1861 to present. Search free online at http://208.210.219.132/courtinfo/vacircuit/select.jsp?court=. Also search via LOPAS; call 804-786-5511.

Criminal Records: Access: Phone, fax, mail, online, in person. Both court and visitors may perform in person searches. Search fee: $10.00 per name. Required to search: name, years to search, signed

release; also helpful: SSN. Criminal records on books from 1861 to present. Online access to criminal records is the same as civil.

General Information: No juvenile, sealed or adoption records released. Will fax results $1.00 per page. Copy fee: $.50 per page. Cert fee: $2.00. Payee: Clerk of Court. Personal checks accepted. Prepayment required. Mail turnaround time 2 days.

27th General District Court PO Box 157, Bland, VA 24315; 276-688-4433; Fax: 276-688-4789. Hours: 8AM-5PM (EST). *Misdemeanor, Civil Actions Under $15,000, Eviction, Small Claims.*

Civil Records: Access: Phone, fax, mail, online, in person. Both court and visitors may perform in person searches. No search fee. Required to search: name, years to search. Civil cases indexed by defendant. Civil records on computer from 4/23/92, card index back to 1985. Search free at http://208.210.219.132/courtinfo/vadistrict/select.jsp?court=. Also search via LOPAS; call 804-786-5511.

Criminal Records: Access: Phone, fax, mail, online, in person. Both court and visitors may perform in person searches. No search fee. Required to search: name, years to search; also helpful: DOB, SSN. Criminal records on computer from 4/23/92, card index back to 1985. Online access to criminal records is the same as civil. Phone access limited to specific cases only.

General Information: Public Access terminal is available. No juvenile, sealed or adoption records released. Copy fee: $1.00 1st 2 pages, $.50 each additional page. No cert fee. Payee: General District Court. Personal checks accepted. Visa, MC accepted. Mail requests: SASE requested. Turnaround time 1-2 days.

Botetourt County

25th Circuit Court PO Box 219, Fincastle, VA 24090; 540-473-8274; Fax: 540-473-8209. Hours: 8:30AM-4:30PM (EST). *Felony, Civil Actions Over $15,000, Probate.*

Civil Records: Access: Mail, online, in person. Both court and visitors may perform in person searches. No search fee. Required to search: name, years to search. Civil cases indexed by defendant, plaintiff. Civil records on computer 7/1/91 to present, books back to 1770. Search free online at http://208.210.219.132/courtinfo/vacircuit/select.jsp?court=. Also search via LOPAS; call 804-786-5511.

Criminal Records: Access: Mail, online, in person. Both court and visitors may perform in person searches. No search fee. Required to search: name, years to search, DOB, SSN. Criminal records on computer 7/1/91 to present, books back to 1770. Online access to criminal records is the same as civil.

General Information: No juvenile, sealed or adoption records released. Copy fee: $.50 per page. Cert fee: $2.00. Payee: Clerk of Court. Personal checks accepted. Prepayment required. Mail requests: SASE required. Mail turnaround time same day.

25th General District Court PO Box 858, Fincastle, VA 24090-0858; 540-473-8244; Fax: 540-473-8344. Hours: 8AM-4PM (EST). *Misdemeanor, Civil Actions Under $15,000, Eviction, Small Claims.*

Civil Records: Access: Mail, online, in person. Both court and visitors may perform in person searches. No search fee. Required to search: name, years to search. Civil cases indexed by defendant, plaintiff. Civil records on computer from 1992 to present. Civil records on files back to 1994. Search free at http://208.210.219.132/courtinfo/vadistrict/select.jsp?court=. Also search via LOPAS; call 804-786-5511.

Criminal Records: Access: Mail, online, in person. Both court and visitors may perform in person searches. No search fee. Required to search: name,

years to search. Criminal records on computer from 1994 to present. Online access to criminal records is the same as civil.

General Information: Public Access terminal is available. No juvenile, sealed records released. Copy fee: $.50 per page. No cert fee. Personal checks accepted. Checks that require verification calls not accepted. Visa, MC accepted. Mail requests: SASE requested. Turnaround time 3-4 days.

Bristol City

28th Circuit Court 497 Cumberland St, Bristol, VA 24201; 276-645-7321; Fax: 276-821-6097. Hours: 9AM-5PM (EST). *Felony, Civil Actions Over $15,000, Probate.*

Civil Records: Access: Online, in person. Visitors must perform in person searches for themselves. No search fee. Required to search: name, years to search. Civil cases indexed by defendant, plaintiff. Civil records indexed from 1890 to present. Search free online at http://208.210.219.132/courtinfo/vacircuit/select.jsp?court=. Also search via LOPAS; call 804-786-5511.

Criminal Records: Access: Online, in person. Visitors must perform in person searches for themselves. No search fee. Required to search: name, years to search. Criminal records indexed from 1890 to present. Online access to criminal records is the same as civil.

General Information: Public Access terminal is available. No juvenile, sealed or adoption records released. Copy fee: $.50 per page. Cert fee: $1.00. Payee: Clerk of Circuit Court. Personal checks accepted. Prepayment required.

28th General District Court 497 Cumberland St, Bristol, VA 24201; 276-645-7341; Fax: 276-645-7342. Hours: 8:30AM-4PM (EST). *Misdemeanor, Civil Actions Under $15,000, Eviction, Small Claims.*

Civil Records: Access: Mail, fax, online, in person. Both court and visitors may perform in person searches. No search fee. Required to search: name, years to search. Civil cases indexed by defendant, plaintiff. Civil records on computer from 1989, card file 1983 to 1988. Search free at http://208.210.219.132/courtinfo/vadistrict/select.jsp?court=. Also search via LOPAS; call 804-786-5511.

Criminal Records: Access: Mail, fax, online, in person. Visitors must perform in person searches for themselves. No search fee. Required to search: name, years to search, DOB, SSN. Criminal records on computer from 1989, card file 1983 to 1988. Online access to criminal records is the same as civil.

General Information: No juvenile, sealed records released. Copy fee: $.50 per page. Cert fee: $2.00. Payee: General District Court. Personal checks accepted. Visa, MC accepted. Prepayment required. Mail requests: SASE requested. Turnaround time 15 days.

Brunswick County

6th Circuit Court 216 N Main St, Lawrenceville, VA 23868; 434-848-2215; Fax: 434-848-4307. Hours: 8:30AM-5PM (EST). *Felony, Civil, Probate.*

Civil Records: Access: In person, online. Visitors must perform in person searches for themselves. Search fee: none. Required to search: name, years to search. Civil cases indexed by defendant, plaintiff. Civil records in books back to 1732; on computer since 1992 (office use only). Search free online at http://208.210.219.132/courtinfo/vacircuit/select.jsp?court=. Also search via LOPAS; call 804-786-5511.

Criminal Records: Access: In person, online. Visitors must perform in person searches for themselves. Search fee: none. Required to search: name, years to search. Criminal records in books back

to 1732; on computer back to 1992 (office use only). Online access to criminal records is the same as civil.
General Information: Public Access terminal is available. (Land records and wills; no case information.) No juvenile, sealed or adoption records released. Copy fee: $.50 per page. Cert fee: $2.00. Payee: Clerk of Court. Personal checks accepted. Prepayment required.

6th General District Court 202 Main St, Lawrenceville, VA 23868-0066; 434-848-2315; Fax: 434-848-2550. Hours: 8:30AM-4:30PM (EST). *Misdemeanor, Civil Actions Under $15,000, Eviction, Small Claims.*
Civil Records: Access: Mail. Both the court (time permitting) and visitors may perform in person searches. No search fee. Required to search: name, years to search. Civil cases indexed by defendant, plaintiff. Civil records computerized since 1988, records go back to 1988. Search free at http://208.210.219.132/courtinfo/vadistrict/select.jsp?court=. Also search via LOPAS; call 804-786-5511.
Criminal Records: Access: Mail, in person, online. Both the court (time permitting) and visitors may perform in person searches. No search fee. Required to search: name, years to search, DOB; also helpful: SSN, signed release. Criminal records computerized since 1991; records go back ten years. Online access to misdemeanor records is the same as civil.
General Information: Public Access terminal is available. No juvenile, sealed records released. No copy fee. No cert fee. Mail requests: SASE required. Mail turnaround time 1-2 days.

Buchanan County

29th Circuit Court PO Box 929, Grundy, VA 24614; 276-935-6567. Hours: 8:30AM-5PM (EST). *Felony, Misdemeanor, Civil Actions Over $15,000, Probate.*
Civil Records: Access: Phone, mail, online, in person. Both court and visitors may perform in person searches. No search fee. Required to search: name, years to search; also helpful: address. Civil cases indexed by defendant, plaintiff. Civil records on computer back to 1991, in books back to 1923. Remote online access to court case indexes is via LOPAS; call 804-786-5511 to apply.
Criminal Records: Access: Online, in person. Visitors must perform in person searches for themselves. No search fee. Required to search: name, years to search, DOB; also helpful: address, SSN. Criminal records on computer back to 1991; in books back to 1928. Remote online access to court case indexes is via LOPAS; call 804-786-5511 to apply.
General Information: Public Access terminal is available. No juvenile, sealed records released. Fee to fax results is $3.00 per document. Copy fee: $.50 per page. Cert fee: $.50. Payee: Clerk of Circuit Court. Personal checks accepted if in state. Turnaround time 1-2 days.

29th Judicial District Court PO Box 654, Grundy, VA 24614; 276-935-6526; Fax: 276-935-5479. Hours: 8AM-4PM (EST). *Civil Actions Under $15,000, Eviction, Small Claims.*
Civil Records: Access: Fax, mail, in person, phone, online. Both court and visitors may perform in person searches. No search fee. Required to search: name; also helpful: years to search. Civil cases indexed by defendant, plaintiff. Civil Records are indexed for 10 years, computerized back to 1993. Search free at http://208.210.219.132/courtinfo/vadistrict/select.jsp?court=. Also search via LOPAS; call 804-786-5511.
General Information: Public Access terminal is available. Will fax to toll-free or local numbers only. No copy fee. No cert fee. Prepayment required. Mail turnaround time is 1 week.

Buckingham County

10th Circuit Court Rte 60, PO Box 107, Buckingham, VA 23921; 434-969-4734; Fax: 434-969-2043. Hours: 8:30AM-4:30PM (EST). *Felony, Civil Actions Over $15,000, Probate.*
Civil Records: Access: Mail, online, in person. Both court and visitors may perform in person searches. No search fee. Required to search: name, years to search. Civil cases indexed by defendant, plaintiff. Civil records on books from 1869 to present, computerized since 2001. Remote online access to court case indexes is via LOPAS; call 804-786-5511 to apply.
Criminal Records: Access: In person, online. Only the court performs in person searches; visitors may not. No search fee. Required to search: name, years to search; also helpful: DOB. Criminal records on books from 1869 to present. Remote online access to court case indexes is via LOPAS; call 804-786-5511 to apply.
General Information: Public Access terminal is available. (Civil records only.) No juvenile, sealed or adoption records released. Copy fee: $.50 per page. Cert fee: $2.00. Payee: Clerk of Court. Personal checks accepted.

Buckingham General District Court PO Box 127, Buckingham, VA 23921; 434-969-4755; Fax: 434-969-1762. Hours: 8:30AM-4:30PM (EST). *Misdemeanor, Civil Actions Under $15,000, Eviction, Small Claims.*
Civil Records: Access: Mail, online, in person, fax. Only the court performs in person searches; visitors may not. No search fee. Required to search: name, years to search. Civil cases indexed by defendant. Civil records on computer or hard copy from 1993, prior records on index cards. Search free at http://208.210.219.132/courtinfo/vadistrict/select.jsp?court=. Also search via LOPAS; call 804-786-5511.
Criminal Records: Access: Mail, online, in person, fax. Only the court performs in person searches; visitors may not. No search fee. Required to search: name, years to search, DOB, SSN, signed release. Criminal records on computer or hard copy from 1993, prior records on index cards. Online access to criminal records is the same as civil.
General Information: No juvenile, sealed records released. No copy fee. No cert fee. Payee: Buckingham. Personal checks accepted. Visa, MC accepted. Prepayment required. Mail turnaround time 2 weeks.

Buena Vista City

25th Circuit & District Court 2039 Sycamore Ave, Buena Vista, VA 24416; 540-261-8627 X626/627; Fax: 540-261-8625. Hours: 8:30AM-5PM (EST). *Felony, Misdemeanor, Civil, Eviction, Probate.*
Civil Records: Access: Mail, online, in person. Both court and visitors may perform in person searches. No search fee. Required to search: name, years to search. Civil cases indexed by defendant, plaintiff. Civil records on manual records 1892 to present, computerized since 1996. Select and search Circuit Courts online at http://208.210.219.132/courtinfo/vacircuit/select.jsp?court= and District Courts at http://208.210.219.132/courtinfo/vadistrict/select.jsp?court=. Also search via LOPAS; call 804-786-5511.
Criminal Records: Access: Mail, online, in person. Both court and visitors may perform in person searches. No search fee. Required to search: name, years to search. Criminal records on manual records 1892 to present, computerized since 1996. Online access to criminal records is the same as civil.
General Information: Public Access terminal is available. No juvenile, sealed records released. Will

fax results $1.00 per page. Copy fee: $.50 per page. Cert fee: $2.00. Payee: Buena Vista Circuit Court. Personal checks accepted. Prepayment required. Mail requests: SASE required. Mail turnaround time 1 day.

Campbell County

24th Circuit Court 732 Village Hwy, PO Box 7, Rustburg, VA 24588; 434-592-9517. Hours: 8:30AM-4:30PM (EST). *Felony, Civil Actions Over $15,000, Probate.*
Civil Records: Access: Mail, online, in person. Both court and visitors may perform in person searches. No search fee. Required to search: name, years to search. Civil cases indexed by defendant, plaintiff. Civil records on index books. Remote online access to court case indexes is via LOPAS; call 804-786-5511 to apply.
Criminal Records: Access: Mail, online, in person. Both court and visitors may perform in person searches. No search fee. Required to search: name, years to search; also helpful: DOB. Criminal records on index books. Remote online access to court case indexes is via LOPAS; call 804-786-5511 to apply.
General Information: Public Access terminal is available. No juvenile, sealed or adoption records released. Copy fee: $.50 per page. Cert fee: $2.00. Payee: Clerk of Court. Personal checks accepted. Prepayment required. Mail requests: SASE required. Mail turnaround time 5 days.

24th General District Court 1st Fl, New Courthouse Bldg, PO Box 97, Rustburg, VA 24588; 434-332-9546; Fax: 434-332-9694. Hours: 8AM-4PM (EST). *Misdemeanor, Civil Actions Under $15,000, Eviction, Small Claims.*
Civil Records: Access: Online, in person. Visitors must perform in person searches for themselves. No search fee. Required to search: name, years to search. Civil cases indexed by defendant, plaintiff. Civil records on computer for 10 years. Search free at http://208.210.219.132/courtinfo/vadistrict/select.jsp?court=. Also search via LOPAS; call 804-786-5511.
Criminal Records: Access: Online, in person, Mail. Visitors must perform in person searches for themselves. No search fee. Required to search: name, years to search. Criminal records on computer for 10 years. Online access to criminal records is the same as civil.
General Information: Copy fee: $1.00 for 1st 2 copies $.50 per add'l page. No cert fee. Payee: Clerk of Court. Prepayment required. Mail requests: SASE required. Mail turnaround time is 5 days.

Caroline County

15th Circuit Court Main St & Courthouse Ln, PO Box 309, Bowling Green, VA 22427-0309; 804-633-5800. Hours: 8:30AM-4PM (EST). *Felony, Civil Actions Over $15,000, Probate.*
Civil Records: Access: Online, in person. Visitors must perform in person searches for themselves. No search fee. Required to search: name, years to search. Civil cases indexed by defendant, plaintiff. Civil records on books from early 1800s to present. Remote online access to court case indexes is via LOPAS; call 804-786-5511 to apply.
Criminal Records: Access: Online, in person. Visitors must perform in person searches for themselves. No search fee. Required to search: name, years to search; also helpful: DOB. Criminal records on books from early 1800s to present, computerized since 1992. Remote online access to court case indexes is via LOPAS; call 804-786-5511 to apply.
General Information: Public Access terminal is available. No juvenile, sealed, adoption records released. Copy fee: $.50 per page. Cert fee: $2.50. Payee: Clerk of Court. Personal checks accepted.

Accepted for payment of fines & costs only. Not accepted over the phone. Prepayment required.

15th General District Court
PO Box 511, Bowling Green, VA 22427; 804-633-5720; Fax: 804-633-3033. Hours: 8AM-4PM (EST). *Misdemeanor, Civil Actions Under $15,000, Eviction, Small Claims.*
Civil Records: Access: Mail, online, fax, in person. Both court and visitors may perform in person searches. No search fee. Required to search: name, years to search. Civil cases indexed by defendant, plaintiff. Civil records on computer from 1/92. Search free at http://208.210.219.132/courtinfo/vadistrict/select.jsp?court=. Also search via LOPAS; call 804-786-5511.
Criminal Records: Access: Mail, online, in person. Both court and visitors may perform in person searches. No search fee. Required to search: name, years to search, SSN. Criminal records on computer from 1/92. Online access to criminal records is the same as civil.
General Information: Public Access terminal is available. No cert fee. Turnaround time 5 days.

Carroll County

27th Circuit Court
PO Box 218, Hillsville, VA 24343; 276-728-3117. Hours: 8AM-5PM (EST). *Felony, Civil Actions Over $15,000, Probate.*
Civil Records: Access: Online, mail, in person. Both court and visitors may perform in person searches. Search fee: $5.00 for five years searched. Required to search: name, years to search, also helpful: SSN. Civil cases indexed by defendant, plaintiff. Civil records on books from 1842 to present, on computer back to 1985. Search free online at http://208.210.219.132/courtinfo/vacircuit/select.jsp?court=. Also search via LOPAS; call 804-786-5511.
Criminal Records: Access: Online, in person. Both court and visitors may perform in person searches. Search fee: $5.00 for five years serached. Required to search: name, years to search; also helpful: SSN. Criminal records on books from 1842 to present; on computer back to 1985. Online access to criminal records is the same as civil.
General Information: Public Access terminal is available. No juvenile, sealed, adoption records released. Copy fee: $.50 per page. Cert fee: $2.00. Payee: Clerk of Court. Personal checks accepted. Prepayment required. Mail turnaround time is 1-3 days.

Carroll Combined District Court
PO Box 698, Hillsville, VA 24343; 276-728-7751; Fax: 276-728-2582. Hours: 8AM-4:30PM (EST). *Misdemeanor, Civil Actions Under $15,000, Eviction, Small Claims.*
Civil Records: Access: In person only. Visitors must perform in person searches for themselves. No search fee. Required to search: name, years to search. Civil cases indexed by defendant, plaintiff. Civil records on books from 1800s, on computer from 1988; no plaintiff index prior to computerization. Search free at http://208.210.219.132/courtinfo/vadistrict/select.jsp?court=. Also search via LOPAS; call 804-786-5511.
Criminal Records: Access: In person, online. Visitors must perform in person searches for themselves. No search fee. Criminal records on books from 1800s, on computer 10 years. Online access to misdemeanor records is the same as civil.
General Information: Public Access terminal is available. No juvenile, sealed records released. No copy fee. No cert fee. Payee: General District Court. Personal checks accepted. Visa, MC accepted. Prepayment required.

Charles City

9th Circuit Court
10700 Courthouse Rd, PO Box 86, Charles City, VA 23030-0086; 804-829-9212; Fax: 804-829-5647. Hours: 8:30AM-4:30PM (EST). *Felony, Civil Actions Over $15,000, Probate.*
Civil Records: Access: Mail, online, in person. Both court and visitors may perform in person searches. No search fee. Required to search: name, years to search. Civil cases indexed by defendant, plaintiff. Civil records on computer from 2000, on books from 1789-2000. Search free online at http://208.210.219.132/courtinfo/vacircuit/select.jsp?court=. Also search via LOPAS; call 804-786-5511.
Criminal Records: Access: Mail, online, in person. Both court and visitors may perform in person searches. No search fee. Required to search: name, years to search, DOB, SSN, signed release. Criminal records on computer from 2000, on books from 1789-2000. Online access to criminal records is the same as civil.
General Information: No juvenile, sealed records released. Fee to fax results is $.50 per page. Copy fee: $.50 per page. Cert fee: $2.00. Payee: Clerk of Circuit Court. Personal checks accepted. Prepayment required. Mail turnaround time 2-5 days.

9th General District Court
Charles City Courthouse, PO Box 57, Charles City, VA 23030; 804-829-9224; Fax: 804-829-5109. Hours: 8:30AM-4PM (EST). *Misdemeanor, Civil Actions Under $15,000, Eviction, Small Claims.*
Civil Records: Access: Mail, online, in person. Both court and visitors may perform in person searches. No search fee. Required to search: name, years to search. Civil cases indexed by defendant, plaintiff. Civil records on computer back to 1989; on books from 1700s. Search free at http://208.210.219.132/courtinfo/vadistrict/select.jsp?court=. Also search via LOPAS; call 804-786-5511.
Criminal Records: Access: Mail, online, in person. Both court and visitors may perform in person searches. No search fee. Required to search: name, years to search, DOB, SSN. Criminal records on computer back to 1989; on books from 1700s. Online access to criminal records is the same as civil.
General Information: Public Access terminal is available. No juvenile, sealed records released. No copy fee. Cert fee: $2.00. Payee: Circuit Court. Personal checks accepted. Prepayment required. Mail requests: SASE required. Mail turnaround time 3 days.

Charlotte County

10th Circuit Court
PO Box 38, Charlotte Courthouse, VA 23923; 434-542-5147. Hours: 8:30AM-4:30PM (EST). *Felony, Civil Actions Over $15,000, Probate.*
Civil Records: Access: In person only. Visitors must perform in person searches for themselves. No search fee. Required to search: name, years to search. Civil cases indexed by defendant, plaintiff. Civil records on books from 1765, in folders by case number. Remote online access to court case indexes is via LOPAS; call 804-786-5511 to apply.
Criminal Records: Access: In person only. Visitors must perform in person searches for themselves. No search fee. Required to search: name, years to search, DOB. Criminal records on books from 1765, in folders by case number.
General Information: No juvenile, sealed records released. Copy fee: $.50 per page. Cert fee: $3.00. Payee: Clerk of Circuit Court. Personal checks accepted. Prepayment required.

Charlotte General District Court
PO Box 127, Charlotte Courthouse, VA 23923; 434-542-5600; Fax: 434-542-5902. Hours: 8:30AM-4:30PM (EST). *Misdemeanor, Civil Actions Under $15,000, Eviction, Small Claims.*
Civil Records: Access: Online, in person. Visitors must perform in person searches for themselves. No search fee. Required to search: name, years to search. Civil cases indexed by defendant, plaintiff. Civil records on computer back to 5/95, on books from 1988. Search free online at http://208.210.219.132/courtinfo/vadistrict/select.jsp?court=. Also search via LOPAS; call 804-786-5511.
Criminal Records: Access: Online, in person. Visitors must perform in person searches for themselves. No search fee. Required to search: name, years to search, DOB; also helpful-SSN, signed release. Criminal records on computer back to 5/95, on books from 1988. Online access to criminal records is the same as civil.
General Information: Public Access terminal is available. No juvenile, sealed records released. Copy fee: $.50 per page. No cert fee. Payee: Clerk of General District Court. Personal checks accepted. Visa, MC accepted. Prepayment required.

Charlottesville City

16th Circuit Court
315 E High St, Charlottesville, VA 22902; 434-295-3182. Hours: 8:30AM-4:30PM (EST). *Felony, Civil Actions Over $15,000, Probate.*
Civil Records: Access: Online, in person. Visitors must perform in person searches for themselves. No search fee. Required to search: name, years to search. Civil cases indexed by defendant, plaintiff. Civil records on books from 1888 to present. Remote online access to court case indexes is via LOPAS; call 804-786-5511 to apply.
Criminal Records: Access: Online, in person. Visitors must perform in person searches for themselves. No search fee. Required to search: name, years to search; also helpful: DOB. Criminal records on books from 1888 to present. Remote online access to court case indexes is via LOPAS; call 804-786-5511 to apply.
General Information: No juvenile, sealed or adoption records released. Copy fee: $.50 per page. Cert fee: $2.00. Payee: Charlottesville Circuit Court Clerk's Office. No out of state checks accepted. Prepayment required.

Charlottesville General District Court
606 E Market St, PO Box 2677, Charlottesville, VA 22902; 434-970-3385; Civil phone: 434-970-3392; Criminal phone: 434-970-3388; Fax: 434-970-3387. Hours: 8:30AM-4:30PM (EST). *Misdemeanor, Civil Actions Under $15,000, Eviction, Small Claims.*
Civil Records: Access: Mail, online, in person. Both court and visitors may perform in person searches. No search fee. Required to search: name, years to search. Civil cases indexed by defendant, plaintiff. Civil records kept for 10 years. Search free at http://208.210.219.132/courtinfo/vadistrict/select.jsp?court=. Also search via LOPAS; call 804-786-5511.
Criminal Records: Access: Mail, online, in person. Both court and visitors may perform in person searches. No search fee. Required to search: name, years to search; also helpful: DOB, SSN. Criminal records kept for 10 years. Online access to criminal records is the same as civil.
General Information: Public Access terminal is available. No juvenile, sealed, confidential records released. Copy fee: $1.00 for first page, $.50 each add'l. No cert fee. Payee: General District Court. Personal checks accepted. Prepayment required. Mail requests: SASE required, turnaround time 3 days.

Chesapeake City

1st Circuit Court 307 Albemarle Dr, #300A, Chesapeake, VA 23322-5579; 757-382-3000; Fax: 757-382-3035. Hours: 8:30AM-4PM (EST). *Felony, Civil Actions Over $15,000, Probate.*
Civil Records: Access: Mail, fax, online, in person. Visitors must perform in person searches for themselves. No search fee. Required to search: name, years to search. Civil cases indexed by defendant, plaintiff. Civil records on books from 1637, on computer from 1989. Online access free at http://208.210.219.132/courtinfo/vacircuit/select.jsp?court=. For information about the statewide online systems, see the state introduction.
Criminal Records: Access: Mail, fax, online, in person. Visitors must perform in person searches for themselves. Search fee: none. Required to search: name, years to search, DOB; also helpful: SSN, sex, signed release. Criminal records on books from 1800s; on computer from 1989. Online access to criminal records is the same as civil.
General Information: Public Access terminal is available. No juvenile, sealed records released. Fee to fax results is $.50 per page. Copy fee: $.50 per page. Cert fee: $2.00. Payee: Clerk of Circuit Court. Personal checks accepted. Prepayment required. Mail requests: SASE required. Mail turnaround time 1 week.

1st General District Court 307 Albemarle Dr, #100, Chesapeake, VA 23322; Civil phone: 757-382-3143; Criminal phone: 757-382-3134; Fax: 757-382-3171. Hours: 8AM-4PM (EST). *Misdemeanor, Civil Actions Under $15,000, Eviction, Small Claims.*
Note: Indicate division (civil, criminal or traffic) in address.
Civil Records: Access: Mail, online, in person. Both court and visitors may perform in person searches. Search fee: $15.00 per name. Required to search: name, years to search. Civil cases indexed by defendant, plaintiff. Civil records on computer back to 1990; prior on books. Select and search District Courts at www.courts.state.va.us. For information about the statewide online systems, see the state introduction.
Criminal Records: Access: Mail, online, in person. Both court and visitors may perform in person searches. Search fee: $15.00 per name. Required to search: name, years to search, DOB; also helpful: SSN. Criminal records on computer back to 1990; prior on books. Online access to criminal records is the same as civil.
General Information: Public Access terminal is available. No juvenile, sealed records released. Copy fee: $1.00 per page. Cert fee: $2.00. Payee: General District Court. Personal checks accepted. Visa, MC accepted. Prepayment required. Mail turnaround time 2-14 days.

Chesterfield County

12th Circuit Court 9500 Courthouse Rd, PO Box 125, Chesterfield, VA 23832; 804-748-1241; Fax: 804-796-5625. Hours: 8:30AM-5PM (EST). *Felony, Civil Actions Over $15,000, Probate.*
www.co.chesterfield.va.us/JusticeAdministration/CircuitCourtClerk/clerhome.asp
Note: The probate clerk will not search probate court records for you.
Civil Records: Access: Mail, in person. Both court and visitors may perform in person searches. Search fee: none. Required to search: name, years to search. Civil cases indexed by defendant, plaintiff. Civil records on computer go back to 1989; prior on index books. Remote online access to court case indexes is via LOPAS; call 804-786-5511 to apply.

Criminal Records: Access: Mail, in person. Only the court performs in person searches; visitors may not. No search fee. Required to search: name, years to search; also helpful: DOB, SSN, charge. Criminal records on computer go back to 1989, prior on index books.
General Information: Public Access terminal is available. (Civil only.) No juvenile, adoption, sealed records released. Copy fee: $.50 per page. Cert fee: $2.00. Payee: Chesterfield Circuit Court. Personal checks accepted. Prepayment required. Mail requests: SASE required. Mail turnaround time 1-2 days.

12th General District Court PO Box 144, Chesterfield, VA 23832; 804-748-1231; Fax: 804-748-1757. Hours: 8AM-4PM (EST). *Misdemeanor, Civil Actions Under $15,000, Eviction, Small Claims.*
www.courts.state.va.us/courts/gd/Chesterfield/home.html
Civil Records: Access: Mail, online, in person. Both court and visitors may perform in person searches. No search fee. Required to search: name, years to search. Civil cases indexed by defendant, plaintiff. Civil records on computer from 1986 to present, index books from 1975 to 1986. Search free at http://208.210.219.132/courtinfo/vadistrict/select.jsp?court=. Also search via LOPAS; call 804-786-5511.
Criminal Records: Access: Mail, online, in person. Both court and visitors may perform in person searches. No search fee. Required to search: name, years to search, DOB, SSN. Criminal records on computer from 1986 to present, index books from 1975 to 1986. Online access to criminal records is the same as civil.
General Information: Public Access terminal is available. No sealed records released. Copy fee: $.50 per page. Cert fee: $2.00. Personal checks accepted. Visa, MC accepted. Turnaround time 2 days.

Clarke County

26th Circuit Court PO Box 189, Berryville, VA 22611; 540-955-5116; Fax: 540-955-0284. Hours: 9AM-5PM (EST). *Felony, Civil Actions Over $15,000, Probate.*
Civil Records: Access: Phone, mail, fax, online, in person. Visitors must perform in person searches for themselves. No search fee. Required to search: name, years to search. Civil cases indexed by defendant, plaintiff. Civil records on books from 1920s. Remote online access to court case indexes is via LOPAS; call 804-786-5511 to apply.
Criminal Records: Access: Online, in person. Visitors must perform in person searches for themselves. No search fee. Required to search: name, years to search, signed release. Criminal records on books from 1920s. Remote online access to court case indexes is via LOPAS; call 804-786-5511 to apply.
General Information: No juvenile, sealed or adoption records released. No criminal records by mail. Fee to fax results is $.50 per page. Copy fee: $.50 per page. No cert fee. Payee: Clerk of Court. Personal checks accepted. Prepayment required. Mail requests: SASE requested. Turnaround time 1-2 days.

General District Court 104 N Church St (PO Box 612), Berryville, VA 22611; 540-955-5128; Fax: 540-955-1195. Hours: 8:30AM-4:30PM (EST). *Misdemeanor, Civil Actions Under $15,000, Eviction, Small Claims.*
www.co.clarke.va.us
Civil Records: Access: Online, in person. Visitors must perform in person searches for themselves. No search fee. Required to search: name, years to search. Civil cases indexed by defendant, plaintiff. Civil records on computer from 1994, on index cards for 1991. Search free at http://208.210.219.132/courtinfo/vadistrict/select.jsp?court=. Also search via LOPAS; call 804-786-5511.

Criminal Records: Access: Online, in person. Visitors must perform in person searches for themselves. No search fee. Required to search: name, years to search, DOB, SSN, date of conviction, charge; also helpful: docket number, defendant's name. Criminal records on computer from 1994. Online access to criminal records is the same as civil.
General Information: Public Access terminal is available. Copy fee: $.50 per page. Payee: Clarke County General District Court. Personal checks require name and address.

Clifton Forge City

25th Circuit Court, VA. *Felony, Civil Actions Over $15,000, Probate.*
Note: This court closed 7/1/01 and was combined with the Alleghany County Circuit Court.

25th General District Court PO Box 139, Covington, VA 24426; 540-965-1720; Fax: 540-965-1722. Hours: 9AM-5PM (EST). *Misdemeanor, Civil Actions Under $15,000, Eviction, Small Claims.*
Note: As of 7/1/2001, the Clifton Forge Court is combined with the Alleghany County District Court to form the 25th Combined District Court.

Colonial Heights City

12th Circuit Court 401 Temple Ave, PO Box 3401, Colonial Heights, VA 23834; 804-520-9364. Hours: 8:30AM-5PM (EST). *Felony, Civil Actions Over $15,000, Probate.*
Civil Records: Access: Mail, online, in person. Both court and visitors may perform in person searches. Search fee: $5.00 per name. Required to search: name, years to search. Civil cases indexed by defendant, plaintiff. Civil records on books from 1961, on computer from 1990. Remote online access to court case indexes is via LOPAS; call 804-786-5511 to apply.
Criminal Records: Access: Mail, online, in person. Both court and visitors may perform in person searches. Search fee: $5.00 per name. Required to search: name, years to search; also helpful: DOB, SSN. Criminal records on books from 1961, on computer from 1990. Remote online access to court case indexes is via LOPAS; call 804-786-5511 to apply.
General Information: No juvenile, sealed or adoption records released. Copy fee: $.50 per page. Cert fee: $2.00. Payee: Clerk of Circuit Court. Personal checks accepted. Prepayment required. Mail requests: SASE required. Mail turnaround time 2 days.

12th General District Court 401 Temple Ave, PO Box 279, Colonial Heights, VA 23834; 804-520-9346 (Dial 0); Fax: 804-520-9370. Hours: 8AM-4PM (EST). *Misdemeanor, Civil Actions Under $15,000, Eviction, Small Claims.*
Civil Records: Access: Mail, fax, online, in person. Both court and visitors may perform in person searches. No search fee. Required to search: name, years to search. Civil cases indexed by defendant, plaintiff. Civil records on computer from 1989 to present, index cards from 1985. Search free at http://208.210.219.132/courtinfo/vadistrict/select.jsp?court=. Also search via LOPAS; call 804-786-5511.
Criminal Records: Access: Mail, fax, online, in person. Both court and visitors may perform in person searches. No search fee. Required to search: name, years to search, DOB, SSN. Criminal records on computer from 1989 to present, index cards from 1985. Online access to criminal records is the same as civil.
General Information: Public Access terminal is available. No juvenile, sealed records released. Copy fee: $.50 per page. Cert fee: $.50. Payee: Colonial

Heights Combined Court. Personal checks accepted. Visa, MC accepted. Prepayment required. Mail requests: SASE requested. Turnaround time 1 week.

Covington City

Circuit & District Courts Note: See Alleghany County

Craig County

25th Circuit Court PO Box 185, New Castle, VA 24127-0185; 540-864-6141. Hours: 9AM-5PM (EST). *Felony, Civil Actions Over $15,000, Probate.*
Civil Records: Access: Online, in person. Visitors must perform in person searches for themselves. No search fee. Required to search: name, years to search. Civil cases indexed by defendant. Civil records on books from mid 1800s. Remote online access to court case indexes is via LOPAS; call 804-786-5511 to apply.
Criminal Records: Access: Online, in person. Visitors must perform in person searches for themselves. No search fee. Required to search: name, years to search; also helpful: SSN. Criminal records on books from mid 1800s. Online access to criminal records is the same as civil.
General Information: No juvenile, sealed or adoption records released. Copy fee: $.50 per page. Cert fee: $2.00. Payee: Clerk of Court. Personal checks accepted. Prepayment required.

25th General District Court Craig County General District Court, PO Box 232, New Castle, VA 24127; 540-864-5989. Hours: 8:15AM-4:45PM (EST). *Misdemeanor, Civil Actions Under $15,000, Eviction, Small Claims.*
Civil Records: Access: Mail, online, in person. Visitors must perform in person searches for themselves. No search fee. Required to search: name, years to search. Civil cases indexed by defendant, plaintiff. Civil records in files 10 years back. Search free at http://208.210.219.132/courtinfo/vadistrict/select.jsp?court=. Also search via LOPAS; call 804-786-5511.
Criminal Records: Access: Mail, online, in person. Visitors must perform in person searches for themselves. No search fee. Required to search: name, years to search; also helpful: SSN. Criminal records in files 10 years back. Online access to criminal records is the same as civil. Lengthy searches must be performed in person.
General Information: Public Access terminal is available. No juvenile, sealed records released. Copy fee: $1.00 per page. No cert fee. Payee: Craig County District Court. Personal checks accepted. Visa, MC accepted. Mail requests: SASE required.

Culpeper County

16th Circuit Court 135 W Cameron St, Culpeper, VA 22701-3097; 540-727-3438. Hours: 8:30AM-4:30PM (EST). *Felony, Civil Actions Over $15,000, Probate.*
Civil Records: Access: In person. Visitors must perform in person searches for themselves. No search fee. Required to search: name, years to search. Civil cases indexed by defendant, plaintiff. Civil records on computer from 1991, docket books from 1800s; records go back to 1950. Remote online access to court case indexes is via LOPAS; call 804-786-5511 to apply.
Criminal Records: Access: In person. Visitors must perform in person searches for themselves. No search fee. Required to search: name, years to search, signed release. Criminal records on computer from 1991, docket books from 1800s, roecords go back to 1950. Online access to criminal records is the same as civil.
General Information: Public Access terminal is available. No juvenile, sealed records released. Copy

fee: $.50 per page. Cert fee: $2.00. Payee: Clerk of Court. Personal checks accepted. Prepayment required.

16th General District Court 135 W Cameron St, Culpeper, VA 22701; 540-727-3417; Fax: 540-727-3474. Hours: 8:30AM-4:30PM (EST). *Misdemeanor, Civil Actions Under $15,000, Eviction, Small Claims.*
Civil Records: Access: Mail, online, in person. Both court and visitors may perform in person searches. No search fee. Required to search: name, years to search. Civil cases indexed by defendant, plaintiff. Civil records on computer from 1987 to present, prior on index cards. Search free at http://208.210.219.132/courtinfo/vadistrict/select.jsp?court=. Also search via LOPAS; call 804-786-5511.
Criminal Records: Access: Mail, online, in person. Both court and visitors may perform in person searches. No search fee. Required to search: name, years to search. Criminal records on computer from 1987 to present, prior on index cards. Online access to criminal records is the same as civil.
General Information: Public Access terminal is available. No juvenile, sealed records released. Copy fee: $1.00 for 1st two copies, $.50 each add'l page. Cert fee: $1.00. Payee: General District Court. Personal checks accepted. Prepayment required. Mail requests: SASE required. Mail turnaround time 1-5 days.

Cumberland County

10th Circuit Court PO Box 8, Cumberland, VA 23040; 804-492-4442. Hours: 8:30AM-4:30PM (EST). *Felony, Civil Actions Over $15,000, Probate.*
Civil Records: Access: Online, in person. Visitors must perform in person searches for themselves. No search fee. Required to search: name, years to search. Civil cases indexed by defendant, plaintiff. Civil records in files. Search free online at http://208.210.219.132/courtinfo/vacircuit/select.jsp?court=. Also search via LOPAS; call 804-786-5511. Phone access only for simple requests.
Criminal Records: Access: Online, in person. Visitors must perform in person searches for themselves. No search fee. Required to search: name, years to search. Criminal records in files. Online access to criminal records is the same as civil.
General Information: No juvenile, sealed records released. Copy fee: $.50 per page. Cert fee: $.50 per page. Payee: Clerk of Circuit Court. Personal checks accepted. Prepayment required.

10th General District Court PO Box 24, Cumberland, VA 23040; 804-492-4848; Fax: 804-492-9455. Hours: 8:30AM-4:30PM (EST). *Misdemeanor, Civil Actions Under $15,000, Eviction, Small Claims.*
Civil Records: Access: Phone, fax, mail, online, in person. Only the court performs in person searches; visitors may not. No search fee. Required to search: name, years to search. Civil cases indexed by defendant, plaintiff. Civil records on computer from 1993. Select and search District Courts at http://208.210.219.132/vadistrict/select.jsp. For information about the statewide online systems, see the state introduction.
Criminal Records: Access: Phone, fax, mail, online, in person. Only the court performs in person searches; visitors may not. No search fee. Required to search: name, years to search; also helpful: DOB, SSN, sex. Criminal records on computer from 1993. Online access to criminal records is the same as civil.
General Information: No juvenile, sealed records released. Will not fax results. Copy fee: $1.00 per page. No cert fee. Payee: Clerk of District Court. Personal checks accepted. Visa, MC accepted.

Prepayment required. Mail requests: SASE required. Mail turnaround time 2 days.

Danville City

22nd Circuit Court PO Box 3300 (401 Patton St), Danville, VA 24543; 434-799-5168; Fax: 434-799-6502. Hours: 9AM-4:30PM (EST). *Felony, Civil Actions Over $15,000, Probate.*
www.danville-va.gov/home.asp
Civil Records: Access: Online, in person. Visitors must perform in person searches for themselves. No search fee. Required to search: name, years to search. Civil cases indexed by defendant, plaintiff. Civil records in index books from 1841, judgments on computer since 1990. Online access free at http://208.210.219.132/courtinfo/vacircuit/select.jsp?court=. For information about the statewide online systems, see the state introduction. Also, search daily docket from the web page.
Criminal Records: Access: Online, in person. Visitors must perform in person searches for themselves. No search fee. Required to search: name, years to search. Criminal records in index books from 1841. Criminal records on computer from 1988. Online access to criminal records is the same as civil.
General Information: Public Access terminal is available. No juvenile, sealed or adoption records released. Will not fax results. Copy fee: $.50 per page. Cert fee: $2.00. Payee: Gerald A Gibson, Clerk. Personal checks accepted. Prepayment required.

22nd General District Court PO Box 3300, Danville, VA 24543; 434-799-5179; Fax: 434-797-8814. Hours: 8:30AM-4:30PM (EST). *Misdemeanor, Civil Actions Under $15,000, Eviction, Small Claims.*
Civil Records: Access: Mail, online, in person. Both court and visitors may perform in person searches. No search fee. Required to search: name, years to search. Civil cases indexed by defendant, plaintiff. Civil records go back 10 years; on computer back to 1994. Select and search District Courts at http://208.210.219.132/courtinfo/vadistrict/select.jsp?court=. For information about the statewide online systems, see the state introduction.
Criminal Records: Access: Mail, online, in person. Both court and visitors may perform in person searches. No search fee. Required to search: name, years to search. Criminal records go back 10 years; on computer back to 1994. Select and search District Courts at http://208.210.219.132/courtinfo/vadistrict/select.jsp?court=.
General Information: Public Access terminal is available. No juvenile, sealed records released. Copy fee: $1.00 1st 2 pages, $.50 each additional page. No cert fee. Payee: General District Court. Personal checks accepted. Visa, MC accepted. Prepayment required. Mail requests: SASE requested. Turnaround time 2 days.

Dickenson County

29th Circuit Court PO Box 190, Clintwood, VA 24228; 276-926-1616; Fax: 276-926-6465. Hours: 8:30AM-4:30PM (EST). *Felony, Civil Actions Over $15,000, Probate.*
Civil Records: Access: Mail, online, in person. Both court and visitors may perform in person searches. No search fee. Required to search: name, years to search. Civil cases indexed by defendant, plaintiff. Civil records on computer from 1989, index book from 1880. Online access free at http://208.210.219.132/courtinfo/vacircuit/select.jsp?court=. For information about the statewide online systems, see the state introduction.
Criminal Records: Access: Mail, online, in person. Both court and visitors may perform in person

searches. No search fee. Required to search: name, years to search, DOB; also helpful: SSN. Criminal records on computer from 1989, index book from 1880. Online access to criminal records is the same as civil.

General Information: Public Access terminal is available. No juvenile, sealed, adoption, confidential records released. Will not fax results. Copy fee: $.50 per page. Cert fee: $2.00. Payee: Joe Tate, Clerk of Circuit Court. Personal checks not accepted. Prepayment required. Mail requests: SASE requested. Turnaround time 1 week.

29th General District Court PO Box 128, Clintwood, VA 24228; 276-926-1630; Fax: 276-926-4815. Hours: 8:30AM-4:30PM (EST). *Misdemeanor, Civil Actions Under $15,000, Eviction, Small Claims.*

Civil Records: Access: Phone, mail, in person. Both court and visitors may perform in person searches. No search fee. Required to search: name, years to search. Civil cases indexed by defendant. Civil records on index cards 10 yrs back, on computer from 5/93. Search free at http://208.210.219.132/courtinfo/vadistrict/select.jsp?court=. Also search via LOPAS; call 804-786-5511.

Criminal Records: Access: Phone, mail, in person. Both court and visitors may perform in person searches. No search fee. Required to search: name, years to search. Criminal records on index cards 10 yrs back, on computer from 5/93. Online access to criminal records is the same as civil.

General Information: Public Access terminal is available. No juvenile, sealed records released. Copy fee: $.10 per page. No cert fee. Payee: Dickenson Combined Court or General District Court. Personal checks accepted. Visa, MC accepted. Prepayment required. Mail requests: SASE requested. Turnaround time 1 week.

Dinwiddie County

11th Circuit Court PO Box 63, Dinwiddie, VA 23841; 804-469-4540. Hours: 8:30AM-4:30PM (EST). *Felony, Civil Actions Over $15,000, Probate.*
Civil Records: Access: Mail, online, in person. Both court and visitors may perform in person searches. No search fee. Required to search: name, years to search; also helpful: address. Civil cases indexed by defendant, plaintiff. Civil records on index cards from 1833; deeds on computer since 1989. Select and search Circuit Courts online at http://208.210.219.132/courtinfo/vadistrict/select.jsp?court=. For information about the statewide online systems, see the state introduction.
Criminal Records: Access: Mail, online, in person. Both court and visitors may perform in person searches. No search fee. Required to search: name, years to search; also helpful: DOB, SSN. Criminal records on index cards from 1833; deeds on computer since 1989. Online access to criminal records is the same as civil.
General Information: No juvenile, sealed or expunged records released. Copy fee: $.50 per page. Cert fee: $2.00 plus $.50 per page. Payee: Clerk of Court. Personal checks accepted. Prepayment required. Mail requests: SASE requested. Turnaround time 3 days.

11th General District Court PO Box 280, Dinwiddie, VA 23841; 804-469-4533; Fax: 804-469-5383. Hours: 8:30AM-4:30PM (EST). *Misdemeanor, Civil Actions Under $15,000, Eviction, Small Claims, Traffic.*
Civil Records: Access: Mail, online, in person. Only the court performs in person searches; visitors may not. No search fee. Required to search: name, years to search. Civil cases indexed by defendant, plaintiff. Civil records on index cards from 1800s, on computer

from 1989. Search free at http://208.210.219.132/courtinfo/vadistrict/select.jsp?court=. Also search via LOPAS; call 804-786-5511.
Criminal Records: Access: Mail, online, in person. Only the court performs in person searches; visitors may not. No search fee. Required to search: name, years to search. Criminal records on index cards from 1800s, on computer from 1989. Online access to criminal records is the same as civil.
General Information: No juvenile, sealed records released. Copy fee: $1.00 per page. Cert fee: $2.00. Payee: District Court. Personal checks accepted. Visa, MC accepted. Prepayment required. Mail requests: SASE required. Mail turnaround time 3 days.

Emporia City

Circuit Court Note: See Greensville County

6th General District Court 315 S Main, Emporia, VA 23847; 434-634-5400. Hours: 8:30AM-4:30PM (EST). *Misdemeanor, Civil Actions Under $15,000, Eviction, Small Claims.*
Civil Records: Access: Online, in person. Visitors must perform in person searches for themselves. No search fee. Required to search: name, years to search. Civil cases indexed by defendant, plaintiff. Civil records on computer back to 1991. Search free at http://208.210.219.132/courtinfo/vadistrict/select.jsp?court=. Also search via LOPAS; call 804-786-5511.
Criminal Records: Access: Online, in person. Visitors must perform in person searches for themselves. No search fee. Required to search: name, years to search. Criminal records on computer back to 1991. Online access to criminal records is the same as civil.
General Information: Public Access terminal is available. No juvenile records released. Copy fee: $1.00 plus $.25 add'l. No cert fee.

Essex County

15th Circuit Court PO Box 445, 305 Prince St, Tappahannock, VA 22560; 804-443-3541. Hours: 8:30AM-5PM (EST). *Felony, Civil Actions Over $15,000, Probate.*
Civil Records: Access: In person only. Visitors must perform in person searches for themselves. No search fee. Required to search: name, years to search. Civil cases indexed by defendant, plaintiff. Civil records on books from 1656; deed index on computer back to 1977. Remote online access to court case indexes is via LOPAS; call 804-786-5511 to apply.
Criminal Records: Access: In person only. Visitors must perform in person searches for themselves. No search fee. Required to search: name, years to search. Criminal records on books from 1656. Online access to criminal records is the same as civil.
General Information: No juvenile, sealed records released. Copy fee: $.50 per page. Cert fee: $2.00. Payee: Clerk of Court. Personal checks accepted. Prepayment required.

15th General District Court PO Box 66, Tappahannock, VA 22560; 804-443-3744; Fax: 804-443-4122. Hours: 8AM-12:30PM, 1-4:30PM (EST). *Misdemeanor, Civil Actions Under $15,000, Eviction, Small Claims.*
Civil Records: Access: Mail, online, in person. Both court and visitors may perform in person searches. No search fee. Required to search: name, years to search. Civil cases indexed by defendant, plaintiff. Civil records on computer from 5/92, prior on index cards. Search free at http://208.210.219.132/courtinfo/vadistrict/select.jsp?court=. Also search via LOPAS; call 804-786-5511.
Criminal Records: Access: Online, in person. Visitors must perform in person searches for themselves. No search fee. Required to search: name, years to search, DOB, SSN. Criminal records on

computer from 5/92, prior on index cards. Online access to criminal records is the same as civil.
General Information: Public Access terminal is available. No juvenile, sealed records released. No copy fee. No cert fee. Prepayment required. Mail turnaround time 1-2 days.

Fairfax County

19th Circuit Court 4110 Chain Bridge Rd, Fairfax, VA 22030; Civil phone: 703-691-7320 x311; Criminal phone: 703-246-2228. Hours: 8AM-4PM (EST). *Felony, Civil Actions Over $15,000, Probate.* www.fairfaxcounty.gov/courts/circuit
Civil Records: Access: In person, online. Visitors must perform in person searches for themselves. No search fee. Required to search: name, years to search. Civil cases indexed by defendant, plaintiff. Civil records computerized from 1979, index books for prior years. Remote online access to current court case indexes is via CPAN; call 703-246-2366 to apply. Fee is $25.00 per month per user.
Criminal Records: Access: In person only. Visitors must perform in person searches for themselves. No search fee. Required to search: name, years to search, DOB; also helpful: SSN. Criminal records computerized from 1979. Online access to criminal records is not currently available.
General Information: Public Access terminal is available. No juvenile, sealed records released. Copy fee: $.50 per page. Cert fee: $2.00. Payee: Fairfax Circuit Court. Personal checks not accepted. Visa/MC accepted only for criminal division. Prepayment required.

19th General District Court 4110 Chain Bridge Rd, Fairfax, VA 22030; 703-246-2153; Civil phone: 703-246-3012; Criminal phone: 703-691-7320; Fax: 703-591-2349. Hours: 8AM-4PM (EST). *Misdemeanor, Civil Actions under $15,000, Eviction, Small Claims.*
www.fairfaxcounty.gov/living/legal/
Note: Traffic Division: 703-246-3764.

Civil Records: Access: Phone, in person, online. Visitors must perform in person searches for themselves. No search fee. Required to search: name, years to search. Civil cases indexed by defendant, plaintiff. Civil indexes for 10 years; onsite records held only 3 years before archiving; on computer back 10 years. Remote online access to current court case indexes is via CPAN; call 703-246-2366 to apply. Fee is $25.00 per month per user.
Criminal Records: Access: Phone, in person, online. Both court and visitors may perform in person searches. No search fee. Required to search: name, years to search; also helpful: DOB, SSN. Criminal & traffic records on computer for 10 years; onsite records held only 3 years before archiving. Online access to criminal & traffic records at http://208.210.219.132/courtinfo/vadistrict/select.jsp?court=. For information about the statewide online systems, see the state introduction.
General Information: Public Access terminal is available. No juvenile, sealed records released. Copy fee: $.50 per page. No cert fee. Payee: Fairfax General District Court. Personal checks accepted. Prepayment required.

Fairfax City

Circuit Court Note: See Fairfax County

19th General District Court 10455 Armstrong St, #304, Fairfax, VA 22030; 703-385-7866; Fax: 703-352-3195. Hours: 8:30AM-4:30PM (EST). *Misdemeanor, Traffic.*
www.ci.fairfax.va.us/Services/Courts/Courts.htm
Note: Find Circuit Court cases and General District civil cases for this city in the Fairfax County listing

Criminal Records: Access: Mail, in person. Only the court performs in person searches; visitors may not. No search fee. Required to search: name, years to search; also helpful: SSN. Criminal records on computer and index from 1985.

General Information: No juvenile or sealed records released. Will not fax results. Copy fee: $1.00 for first 2 pages; each add'l page $.50. No cert fee. Payee: General District Court. Personal checks accepted. Visa, MC accepted. Prepayment required. Mail requests: SASE requested. Turnaround time same day.

Falls Church City

Circuit Court Note: See Arlington County

17th District Courts Combined Falls Church District, 300 Park Ave, Falls Church, VA 22046-3305; 703-248-5096 (GDC); Civil phone: 703-248-5098; Fax: 703-241-1407. Hours: 8AM-4PM (EST). *Misdemeanor, Civil Actions Under $15,000, Eviction, Small Claims.*
www.ci.falls-church.va.us
Note: Small claims phone is 703-248-5157; juvenile and domestic relations is 703-248-5099.

Civil Records: Access: Fax, online. Only the court performs in person searches; visitors may not. No search fee. Required to search: name, years to search. Civil cases indexed by defendant, plaintiff. Civil records on computer from 1993 & 1983 thru 1985. Search free at http://208.210.219.132/courtinfo/vadistrict/select.jsp?court=. Also search via LOPAS; call 804-786-5511.

Criminal Records: Access: Fax, online, in person. Only the court performs in person searches; visitors may not. No search fee. Required to search: name, years to search; also helpful: DOB, SSN. Criminal records on computer back to 1993. Online access to criminal records is the same as civil.

General Information: No juvenile or sealed records released. No fee to fax results. Copy fee: $.50 per page. No cert fee. Payee: Falls Church District Court. Personal checks accepted. Visa, MC accepted. Prepayment required.

Fauquier County

Circuit Court 40 Culpeper St, Warrenton, VA 20186-3298; 540-347-8610; Civil phone: 540-347-8601; Criminal phone: 540-347-8605; Probate phone: 540-347-8606. Hours: 8AM-4:30PM (EST). *Felony, Civil Actions Over $15,000, Probate.*
www.fauquiercounty.gov/government/departments/circuitcourt
Note: Chancery court can be reached at 540-347-8607.

Civil Records: Access: Online, in person. Both court and visitors may perform in person searches. Search fee: $5.00. Required to search: name, years to search. Civil cases indexed by defendant, plaintiff. Civil records on computer back to 1988. Online access free at http://208.210.219.132/vacircuit/select.jsp. For information about the statewide online systems, see the state introduction.

Criminal Records: Access: Online, in person. Visitors must perform in person searches for themselves. Court recommends you contact the VA State Police. No search fee. Required to search: name, years to search. Criminal records on computer back to 1988. Online access to criminal records is the same as civil.

General Information: Public Access terminal is available. No juvenile, sealed, adoption records released. Copy fee: $.50 per page. Cert fee: $2.00. Payee: Clerk of Fauquier Circuit Court. Personal checks not accepted. Prepayment required.

20th General District Court 6 Court St, Warrenton, VA 20186; Civil phone: 540-347-8676; Criminal phone: 540-347-8624; Fax: 540-347-5756. Hours: 8:30AM-4:30PM (EST). *Misdemeanor, Civil Actions Under $15,000, Eviction, Small Claims.*

Civil Records: Access: Online, in person. Visitors must perform in person searches for themselves. No search fee. Required to search: name, years to search. Civil cases indexed by defendant, plaintiff. Civil records on computerized back 10 years. Search free at http://208.210.219.132/courtinfo/vadistrict/select.jsp?court=. Also search via LOPAS; call 804-786-5511.

Criminal Records: Access: Online, in person. Visitors must perform in person searches for themselves. No search fee. Required to search: name, years to search. Criminal records computerized back 10 years, criminal records only go back 10 years. Online access to criminal records is the same as civil.

General Information: Public Access terminal is available. No juvenile, sealed records released. Copy fee: $1.00 1st 2 pages, $.50 each additional page. No cert fee. Payee: General District Court. Personal checks accepted. Prepayment required.

Floyd County

27th Circuit Court 100 E Main St, #200, Floyd, VA 24091; 540-745-9330. Hours: 8:30AM-4:30PM M-F, 8:30AM-Noon Sat (EST). *Felony, Civil Actions Over $15,000, Probate.*
Note: Closed on Saturdays only if it is a holiday.

Civil Records: Access: Online, in person. Visitors must perform in person searches for themselves. No search fee. Required to search: name, years to search. Civil cases indexed by defendant, plaintiff. Civil records on files from 1831. Search free online at http://208.210.219.132/courtinfo/vacircuit/select.jsp?court=. Also search via LOPAS; call 804-786-5511.

Criminal Records: Access: Online, in person. Visitors must perform in person searches for themselves. No search fee. Required to search: name, years to search; also helpful: DOB, SSN. Criminal records on files from 1831. Online access to criminal records is the same as civil.

General Information: Public Access terminal is available. No juvenile, sealed records released. Will not fax results. Copy fee: $.50 per page. Cert fee: $2.00. Payee: Clerk of Circuit Court. Personal checks accepted. Prepayment required.

27th General District Court 100 E Main St, Floyd, VA 24091-2101; 540-745-9327; Fax: 540-745-9329. Hours: 8AM-4:30PM (EST). *Misdemeanor, Civil Actions Under $15,000, Eviction, Small Claims.*

Civil Records: Access: Online, in person. Visitors must perform in person searches for themselves. No search fee. Required to search: name, years to search. Civil cases indexed by defendant, plaintiff. Civil records computerized since 1993. Select and search District Courts at http://208.210.219.132/courtinfo/vadistrict/select.jsp?court=. Also, remote online access to court case indexes is via LOPAS; call 804-786-5511 to apply. Phone search results may be of limited content.

Criminal Records: Access: Online, in person. Visitors must perform in person searches for themselves. No search fee. Required to search: name, years to search, DOB. Criminal records computerized since 1993. Online access to criminal records is the same as civil. Phone search results may be of limited content.

General Information: Public Access terminal is available. No juvenile, sealed records released. Copy fee: $.50 per page. No cert fee. Payee: Clerk of District Court. Prepayment required.

Fluvanna County

16th Circuit Court PO Box 550, Palmyra, VA 22963; 434-591-1970; Fax: 434-591-1971. Hours: 8:AM-4:30PM (EST). *Felony, Civil Actions Over $15,000, Probate.*

Civil Records: Access: Mail, in person. Both court and visitors may perform in person searches. Search fee: $5.00 per name. Required to search: name, years to search. Civil cases indexed by defendant, plaintiff. Civil records on index books from 1777; computerized back to 1985. Search free online at http://208.210.219.132/courtinfo/vacircuit/select.jsp?court=. Also search via LOPAS; call 804-786-5511.

Criminal Records: Access: Mail, in person, online. Both court and visitors may perform in person searches. Search fee: $5.00 per name. Required to search: name, years to search, DOB; also helpful: SSN. Criminal records on index books from 1777; computerized back to 1985. Online access to criminal records is the same as civil.

General Information: No juvenile or sealed records released. Fee to fax results is $2.00 per document. Copy fee: $.50 per page. Cert fee: $2.00. Payee: Clerk of Circuit Court. Personal checks accepted. Prepayment required. Mail requests: SASE required. Mail turnaround time same 1-2 days.

16th General District Court Fluvanna County Courthouse, PO Box 417, Palmyra, VA 22963; 434-591-1980; Fax: 434-591-1981 press 4. Hours: 8:30AM-4:30PM (EST). *Misdemeanor, Civil Actions Under $15,000, Eviction, Small Claims.*

Civil Records: Access: Online, in person. Visitors must perform in person searches for themselves. No search fee. Required to search: name, years to search. Civil cases indexed by defendant, plaintiff. Civil records on computer since 12/91, on books since 1984. Search free at http://208.210.219.132/courtinfo/vadistrict/select.jsp?court=. Also search via LOPAS; call 804-786-5511.

Criminal Records: Access: Online, in person. Visitors must perform in person searches for themselves. No search fee. Required to search: name, years to search; also helpful: DOB, SSN. Criminal records on computer since 12/91, on books since 1984. Online access to criminal records is the same as civil.

General Information: Public Access terminal is available. No juvenile records released. Copy fee: $.50 per page. No cert fee. Payee: Fluvanna District Court. Personal checks accepted. Prepayment required.

Franklin County

22nd Judicial Circuit Court PO Box 567, 275 S Main St, #212, Rocky Mount, VA 24151; 540-483-3065; Fax: 540-483-3042. Hours: 8:30AM-5PM (EST). *Felony, Civil Actions Over $15,000, Probate.*
www.courts.state.va.us/courts/circuit/Franklin/home.html
Note: Note that Franklin City is not the same as Franklin County. Only Franklin County information is given here.

Civil Records: Access: In person, online. Visitors must perform in person searches for themselves. No search fee. Required to search: name. Civil cases indexed by defendant, plaintiff. Criminal records file on computer. Select and search Circuit Courts online at http://208.210.219.132/courtinfo/vacircuit/select.jsp?court=. For information about the statewide online systems, see the state introduction.

Criminal Records: Access: In person, online. Visitors must perform in person searches for themselves. No search fee. Required to search: name, years to search. Criminal records file on computer. Online access to criminal records is the same as civil.

General Information: Public Access terminal is available. No juvenile records released. Copy fee: $.25 per page. Prepayment required.

22nd General District Court

PO Box 569, 275 S Main St, #111, Rocky Mount, VA 24151; 540-483-3060; Fax: 540-483-3036. Hours: 8:30AM-4:30PM (EST). *Misdemeanor, Civil Actions Under $15,000, Eviction, Small Claims.*
www.courts.state.va.us/courts/combined/Franklin_City/home.html

Civil Records: Access: Online, in person. Visitors must perform in person searches for themselves. No search fee. Required to search: name, years to search. Civil cases indexed by defendant, plaintiff. Civil records file on computer from 1994. Search free at http://208.210.219.132/courtinfo/vadistrict/select.jsp?court=. Also search via LOPAS; call 804-786-5511.

Criminal Records: Access: Online, in person. Visitors must perform in person searches for themselves. No search fee. Required to search: name, years to search. Criminal records file on computer from 1994. Online access to criminal records is the same as civil.

General Information: Public Access terminal is available. Will not fax results. Copy fee: $.25 per page. No cert fee. Personal checks accepted. Visa, MC accepted. Prepayment required.

Franklin-City

5th Judicial General District Combined

1020 Pretlow St, Franklin, VA 23851; 757-562-8550; Fax: 757-562-8561. Hours: 8AM-4PM (EST). *Misdemeanor, Civil Actions Under $15,000, Eviction, Traffic.*
www.courts.state.va.us/courts/combined/Franklin_City/home.html

Note: Southampton County serves as the Circuit Court for the City of Franklin.

Civil Records: Access: Mail, online, in person. Both court and visitors may perform in person searches. Search fee: $5.00 per name. Required to search: name, years to search. Civil cases indexed by plaintiff. Civil records on computer since 1990, prior on docket books since 1700s. Select and search Circuit Courts online at http://208.210.219.132/courtinfo/vadistrict/select.jsp?court=. For information about the statewide online systems, see the state introduction.

Criminal Records: Access: Mail, online, in person. Both court and visitors may perform in person searches. Search fee: $5.00 per name. Required to search: name, years to search; also helpful: SSN. Criminal records on computer since 1990, prior on docket books since 1700s. Online access to criminal records is the same as civil.

General Information: Public Access terminal is available. No juvenile records released. Copy fee: $.50 per page. Cert fee: $2.00. Payee: Clerk of the Circuit Court. Personal checks accepted. Turnaround time 2-5 days.

Frederick County

Circuit Court

5 N Kent St, Winchester, VA 22601; 540-667-5770. Hours: 9AM-5PM (EST). *Felony, Misdemeanor, Civil, Probate.*
www.winfredclerk.com

Civil Records: Access: Mail, in person. Both court and visitors may perform in person searches. No search fee. Required to search: name, years to search. Civil cases indexed by defendant, plaintiff. Civil records on books from 1970s. Search free online at http://208.210.219.132/courtinfo/vacircuit/select.jsp?court=. Also search via LOPAS; call 804-786-5511. Mail access limited to simple requests.

Criminal Records: Access: In person, online. Visitors must perform in person searches for themselves. No search fee. Required to search: name, years to search. Criminal records on books from 1970s. Online access to criminal records is the same as civil.

General Information: Public Access terminal is available. No juvenile, sealed or adoption records released. Copy fee: $.50 per page. Cert fee: $3.00. Payee: Clerk of Circuit Court. Personal checks accepted. Prepayment required. Mail turnaround time 1-2 days.

26th District Court

5 N Kent St, Winchester, VA 22601; 540-722-7208; Fax: 540-722-1063. Hours: 8AM-4PM (EST). *Misdemeanor, Civil Actions up to $15,000.*

Civil Records: Access: In person, online. Visitors must perform in person searches for themselves. No search fee. Required to search: name, years to search. Search free at http://208.210.219.132/courtinfo/vadistrict/select.jsp?court=. Also search via LOPAS; call 804-786-5511.

Criminal Records: Access: In person, online. Visitors must perform in person searches for themselves. No search fee. Required to search: name, years to search. Online access to criminal records is the same as civil.

General Information: Public Access terminal is available. Copy fee: $.50 per page. Cert fee: $.50. Payee: Frederick District Court. Personal checks accepted. Prepayment required.

Fredericksburg City

15th Circuit Court

815 Princess Anne St, PO Box 359, Fredericksburg, VA 22404-0359; 540-372-1066. Hours: 8AM-4PM (EST). *Felony, Civil Actions Over $15,000, Probate.*

Civil Records: Access: Online, in person. Visitors must perform in person searches for themselves. No search fee. Required to search: name, years to search. Civil cases indexed by defendant, plaintiff. Civil records on index books from 1765; computerized records since 1987. Online access free at www.courts.state.va.us/. For information about the statewide online systems, see the state introduction.

Criminal Records: Access: Online, in person. Visitors must perform in person searches for themselves. No search fee. Required to search: name, years to search, DOB; also helpful: SSN. Criminal records on index books from 1765; computerized records since 1987. Online access to criminal records is the same as civil.

General Information: Public Access terminal is available. No juvenile, probate tax returns, sealed or adoption records released. Copy fee: $.50 per page. Cert fee: $2.00. Payee: Clerk of Circuit Court. Personal checks accepted. Prepayment required.

15th General District Court

PO Box 180, Fredericksburg, VA 22404; 540-372-1044; Civil phone: 540-372-1044; Criminal phone: 540-372-1043. Hours: 8AM-4PM (EST). *Misdemeanor, Civil Actions Under $15,000, Eviction, Small Claims.*

Civil Records: Access: Mail, online, in person. Both court and visitors may perform in person searches. No search fee. Required to search: name, years to search. Civil cases indexed by defendant, plaintiff. Civil records on computer the past 10 years, prior on index books. Search free at http://208.210.219.132/courtinfo/vadistrict/select.jsp?court=. Also search via LOPAS; call 804-786-5511.

Criminal Records: Access: Mail, online, in person. Both court and visitors may perform in person searches. No search fee. Required to search: name, years to search, DOB, SSN. Criminal records on computer the past 10 years, prior on index books. Online access to criminal records is the same as civil.

General Information: Public Access terminal is available. No sealed records released. Copy fee: $.50 per page. Cert fee: $2.00. Payee: Fredericksburg District Court. Personal checks accepted. Prepayment required. Mail requests: SASE required. Mail turnaround time 1-10 days.

Galax City

Circuit Court, VA.

Note: See Carroll County for Hillsville area and Grayson County for Independence area.

27th General District Court

353 N Main St, PO Box 214, Galax, VA 24333-0214; 276-236-8731; Fax: 276-236-2754. Hours: 8AM-4:30PM (EST). *Misdemeanor, Civil Actions Under $15,000, Eviction, Small Claims.*

Note: Circuit Court jurisdiction for this city can be in Carroll County or Grayson County depending on side of the city the offense occurred.

Civil Records: Access: Mail, fax, online, in person. Both court and visitors may perform in person searches. No search fee. Required to search: name, years to search. Civil cases indexed by defendant, plaintiff. Civil records on computer since 1990, prior on index books. Search free at http://208.210.219.132/courtinfo/vadistrict/select.jsp?court=. Also search via LOPAS; call 804-786-5511.

Criminal Records: Access: Mail, fax, online, in person. Both court and visitors may perform in person searches. No search fee. Required to search: name, years to search. Criminal records on computer since 1990, prior on index books. Online access to criminal records is the same as civil.

General Information: Public Access terminal is available. No juvenile, sealed records released. Copy fee: $.25 per page. No cert fee. Payee: Clerk of District Court Galax District. Personal checks accepted. Visa, MC accepted. Prepayment required. Mail turnaround time 1-5 days.

Giles County

27th Circuit Court

501 Wenonah Ave, PO Box 502, Pearisburg, VA 24134; 540-921-1722; Fax: 540-921-3825. Hours: 9AM-5PM (EST). *Felony, Civil Actions Over $15,000, Probate.*

Civil Records: Access: Mail, in person. Visitors must perform in person searches for themselves. No search fee. Required to search: name, years to search. Civil cases indexed by defendant, plaintiff. Civil records (financial) on computer since 1994. Remote online access to court case indexes is via LOPAS; call 804-786-5511 to apply.

Criminal Records: Access: In person. Visitors must perform in person searches for themselves. No search fee. Required to search: name, years to search, DOB; also helpful: SSN. Criminal records (financial) on computer since 1994. Remote online access to court case indexes is via LOPAS; call 804-786-5511 to apply.

General Information: No juvenile, sealed records released. Copy fee: $.50 per page. Cert fee: $3.00. Payee: Clerk of Circuit Court. Personal checks accepted. Prepayment required. Mail turnaround time 1-2 days.

27th General District Court

120 N Main St, #1, Pearisburg, VA 24134; 540-921-3533; Fax: 540-921-3752. Hours: 8:30AM-4:30PM (EST). *Misdemeanor, Civil Actions Under $15,000, Eviction, Small Claims.*

Civil Records: Access: Fax, mail, online, in person. Both court and visitors may perform in person searches. No search fee. Required to search: name, years to search. Civil cases indexed by defendant, plaintiff. Civil records on computer since 1990. Search free at

http://208.210.219.132/courtinfo/vadistrict/select.jsp? court=. Also search via LOPAS; call 804-786-5511.
Criminal Records: Access: Fax, mail, online, in person. Both court and visitors may perform in person searches. No search fee. Required to search: name, years to search; also helpful: SSN. Criminal records on computer since 1990. Online access to criminal records is the same as civil.
General Information: Public Access terminal is available. No juvenile, sealed records released. Fee to fax results is $1.00 per page. Copy fee: $1.00 for first page, $.50 each add'l. No cert fee. Payee: General District Court. Personal checks accepted. Visa, MC accepted. Turnaround time 3-7 days.

Gloucester County

9th Circuit Court PO Box 2118, Gloucester, VA 23061-0570; 804-693-2502; Fax: 804-693-2186. Hours: 8AM-4:30PM (EST). *Felony, Civil Actions Over $15,000, Probate.*
www.co.gloucester.va.us
Civil Records: Access: Fax, mail, online, in person. Both court and visitors may perform in person searches. No search fee. Required to search: name, years to search. Civil cases indexed by defendant, plaintiff. Civil records on index books from 1862; on computer since 1990. Online access free at http://208.210.219.132/courtinfo/vacircuit/select.jsp?c ourt=. For information about the statewide online systems, see the state introduction.
Criminal Records: Access: Online, in person. Visitors must perform in person searches for themselves. No search fee. Required to search: name, years to search, DOB. Criminal records on index books from 1862; on computer since 1990. Online access to criminal records is the same as civil.
General Information: Public Access terminal is available. No juvenile, sealed or adoption records released. Copy fee: $.50 per page. Cert fee: $2.00, and $2.50 if judge's signature required. Payee: Clerk of Circuit Court. Personal checks accepted. Prepayment required. Mail requests: SASE requested. Turnaround time 1 day.

9th General District Court PO Box 873, Gloucester, VA 23061; 804-693-4860; Fax: 804-693-6669. Hours: 8:30AM-4:30PM (EST). *Misdemeanor, Civil Actions Under $15,000, Eviction, Small Claims.*
Civil Records: Access: Fax, mail, online, in person. Both court and visitors may perform in person searches. No search fee. Required to search: name, years to search. Civil cases indexed by defendant, plaintiff. Civil records on index books from 1985; computerized back to 1992. Search free at http://208.210.219.132/courtinfo/vadistrict/select.jsp? court=. Also search via LOPAS; call 804-786-5511.
Criminal Records: Access: Fax, mail, online, in person. Both court and visitors may perform in person searches. No search fee. Required to search: name, years to search; also helpful: DOB, SSN. Criminal records on index books for 10 years; computerized back to 1992. Online access to criminal records is the same as civil.
General Information: Public Access terminal is available. No juvenile, sealed records released. No fee to fax results. Copy fee: $.50 per page. No cert fee. Payee: Clerk of General District Court/Gloucester District Court. Personal checks accepted. Visa, MC accepted. Prepayment required. Mail requests: SASE requested. Turnaround time 1 week.

Goochland County

16th Circuit Court PO Box 196, Goochland, VA 23063; 804-556-5353. Hours: 8:30AM-4:15 PM (EST). *Felony, Civil Actions Over $15,000, Probate.*
Civil Records: Access: Online, in person. Visitors must perform in person searches for themselves. No search fee. Required to search: name, years to search. Civil cases indexed by defendant, plaintiff. Civil records on index books from 1850. Remote online access to court case indexes is via LOPAS; call 804-786-5511 to apply.
Criminal Records: Access: Online, in person. Visitors must perform in person searches for themselves. No search fee. Required to search: name, years to search. Criminal records on index books from 1850. Remote online access to court case indexes is via LOPAS; call 804-786-5511 to apply.
General Information: No juvenile, sealed or adoption records released. Copy fee: $.50 per page. Cert fee: $1.00. Payee: Clerk of Circuit Court. Personal checks accepted. Prepayment required.

General District Court PO Box 47, Goochland, VA 23063; 804-556-5309. Hours: 8:30AM-4:30PM (EST). *Misdemeanor, Civil Actions Under $15,000, Eviction, Small Claims.*
Civil Records: Access: Online, in person. Visitors must perform in person searches for themselves. No search fee. Required to search: name, years to search. Civil cases indexed by defendant, plaintiff. Civil records on index books and computer back to 1989. Search free at http://208.210.219.132/courtinfo/vadistrict/select.jsp? court=. Also search via LOPAS; call 804-786-5511.
Criminal Records: Access: Online, in person. Visitors must perform in person searches for themselves. No search fee. Required to search: name, years to search, DOB. Criminal records on index books and computer back to 1989. Online access to criminal records is the same as civil.
General Information: Public Access terminal is available. No juvenile records released. No copy fee. No cert fee. Prepayment required.

Grayson County

27th Circuit Court PO Box 130, Independence, VA 24348; 276-773-2231; Fax: 276-773-3338. Hours: 8AM-5PM (EST). *Felony, Civil Actions Over $15,000, Probate.*
Civil Records: Access: Mail, online, in person. Both court and visitors may perform in person searches. No search fee. Required to search: name, years to search. Civil cases indexed by defendant, plaintiff. Civil records on index books since 1793. Select and search Circuit Courts online at http://208.210.219.132/courtinfo/vacircuitselect.jsp?c ourt=. For information about the statewide online systems, see the state introduction.
Criminal Records: Access: Mail, online, in person. Visitors must perform in person searches for themselves. No search fee. Required to search: name, years to search, DOB. Criminal records on index books since 1793. Online access to criminal records is the same as civil.
General Information: Public Access terminal is available. No juvenile, sealed or adoption records released. Copy fee: $.50 per page. Cert fee: $2.00. Payee: Clerk of Circuit Court. Personal checks accepted. Prepayment required. Mail requests: SASE requested. Turnaround time 2-3 days.

27th General District Court PO Box 280, Independence, VA 24348; 276-773-2011. Hours: 8AM-4:30PM (EST). *Misdemeanor, Civil Actions Under $15,000, Eviction, Small Claims.*
Civil Records: Access: Mail, online, in person. Both court and visitors may perform in person searches. No

search fee. Required to search: name, years to search. Civil cases indexed by defendant. Civil records on index books from 1800s, on computer from 1989. Search free at http://208.210.219.132/courtinfo/vadistrict/select.jsp? court=. Also search via LOPAS; call 804-786-5511.
Criminal Records: Access: Mail, online, in person. Both court and visitors may perform in person searches. No search fee. Required to search: name, years to search; also helpful: DOB, SSN. Criminal records on index books from 1800s, on computer from 1989. Online access to criminal records is the same as civil.
General Information: Public Access terminal is available. No juvenile, sealed records released. Will fax results to local or toll free line. No copy fee. No cert fee. Turnaround time 1 week.

Greene County

16th Circuit Court PO Box 386, Stanardsville, VA 22973; 434-985-5208; Fax: 434-985-6723. Hours: 8:15AM-4:30PM (EST). *Felony, Civil Actions Over $15,000, Probate.*
Civil Records: Access: Mail, in person. Both court and visitors may perform in person searches. No search fee. Required to search: name, years to search. Civil cases indexed by defendant, plaintiff. Civil records on index books from 1838. Remote online access to court case indexes is via LOPAS; call 804-786-5511 to apply.
Criminal Records: Access: Mail, in person. Both court and visitors may perform in person searches. Search fee: $10.00 per name. Required to search: name, years to search. Criminal records on index books from 1838.
General Information: No juvenile, sealed or adoption records released. Will not fax results. Copy fee: $.50 per page. Cert fee: $2.00 per instrument. Payee: Clerk of Circuit Court or Greene County Circuit. Personal checks accepted. Prepayment required. Mail requests: SASE required. Mail turnaround time 7-10 days.

16th General District Court Greene County Courthouse (PO Box 245), Stanardsville, VA 22973; 434-985-5224; Fax: 434-985-1448. Hours: 8:30AM-4PM (EST). *Misdemeanor, Civil Actions Under $15,000, Eviction, Small Claims.*
Civil Records: Access: Fax, mail, online, in person. Both court and visitors may perform in person searches. No search fee. Required to search: name, years to search. Civil cases indexed by defendant, plaintiff. Civil records on index books from 1838, on computer back to 10/93. Search free at http://208.210.219.132/courtinfo/vadistrict/select.jsp? court=. Also search via LOPAS; call 804-786-5511.
Criminal Records: Access: In person only. Visitors must perform in person searches for themselves. No search fee. Required to search: name, years to search, DOB; also helpful: SSN. Criminal records on computer back to 1/92, prior on cards, books. Online access to criminal records is the same as civil.
General Information: Public Access terminal is available. No juvenile, sealed records released. No fee to fax results. Copy fee: $.50 per page. No cert fee. Payee: Clerk of General District Court or Greene County Combined Court. Personal checks accepted. Visa, MC accepted. Prepayment required. Mail turnaround time 1 week.

Greensville County

6th Circuit Court PO Box 631, Emporia, VA 23847; 434-348-4215. Hours: 9AM-5PM (EST). *Felony, Civil Actions Over $15,000, Probate.*
Civil Records: Access: Online, in person. Visitors must perform in person searches for themselves. No search fee. Required to search: name, years to search.

Civil cases indexed by defendant, plaintiff. Civil records on index books from 1781; on computer since 1989. Search free online at http://208.210.219.132/courtinfo/vacircuit/select.jsp?court=. Also search via LOPAS; call 804-786-5511.

Criminal Records: Access: Online, in person. Visitors must perform in person searches for themselves. Court does not conduct criminal searches. No search fee. Required to search: name, years to search. Criminal records on index books from 1781; on computer since 1989. Online access to criminal records is the same as civil.

General Information: Public Access terminal is available. No juvenile, sealed records released. Copy fee: $.50 per page. Cert fee: $2.00. Payee: Clerk of Circuit Court. Business checks accepted. Prepayment required.

Greenville/Emporia Combined Court

315 S Main, Emporia, VA 23847; 434-634-5460; Fax: 434-634-0049. Hours: 8:30AM-4:30PM (EST). *Misdemeanor, Civil Actions Under $15,000, Eviction, Small Claims.*

Civil Records: Access: Online, in person. Visitors must perform in person searches for themselves. No search fee. Required to search: name, years to search. Civil cases indexed by defendant, plaintiff. Civil records on index books from 1800s; on computer back 10 years. Select and search District Courts at http://208.210.219.132/courtinfo/vadistrict/select.jsp?court=. For information about the statewide online systems, see the state introduction.

Criminal Records: Access: Online, in person. Visitors must perform in person searches for themselves. No search fee. Required to search: name, years to search, DOB; also helpful: SSN. Criminal records on index books from 1800s; on computer back 10 years. Online access to criminal records is the same as civil.

General Information: Public Access terminal is available. No juvenile, sealed records released. Copy fee: $.50 per page. No cert fee. Payee: Clerk of General District Court. Personal checks accepted.

Halifax County

10th Circuit Court PO Box 729, Halifax, VA 24558; 434-476-6211; Fax: 434-476-2890. Hours: 8:30AM-4:30PM (EST). *Felony, Civil Actions Over $15,000, Probate.*

Civil Records: Access: Online, in person. Visitors must perform in person searches for themselves. No search fee. Required to search: name, years to search. Civil cases indexed by defendant, plaintiff. Civil records on computer from 1988, on index books from 1752. Online access free at http://208.210.219.132/courtinfo/vacircuit/select.jsp?court=. For information about the statewide online systems, see the state introduction.

Criminal Records: Access: Mail, online, in person. Only the court performs in person searches; visitors may not. Search fee: $5.00 per name. Required to search: name, years to search. Criminal records on computer from 1988, on index books from 1752. Online access free at http://208.210.219.132/courtinfo/vacircuit/select.jsp?court=. For information about the statewide online systems, see the state introduction.

General Information: Public Access terminal is available. No juvenile, sealed records released. Will fax results for $.50 per page plus search fee per telephone call. Copy fee: $.50 per page. Cert fee: $.50 per page. Payee: Circuit Court. Personal checks accepted. Prepayment required. Mail requests: SASE required. Mail turnaround time 1-5 days.

10th General District Court Halifax County Courthouse, PO Box 458, Halifax, VA 24558; 434-476-3385; Fax: 434-476-3387. Hours: 8:30AM-4:30PM (EST). *Misdemeanor, Civil Actions Under $15,000, Eviction, Small Claims.*

Civil Records: Access: Fax, mail, online, in person. Both court and visitors may perform in person searches. No search fee. Required to search: name, years to search, address. Civil cases indexed by defendant, plaintiff. Civil records on computer from 1993. Search free at http://208.210.219.132/courtinfo/vadistrict/select.jsp?court=. Also search via LOPAS; call 804-786-5511.

Criminal Records: Access: Fax, mail, online, in person. Both court and visitors may perform in person searches. No search fee. Required to search: name. Criminal records on computer from 1993. Online access to criminal records is the same as civil.

General Information: Public Access terminal is available. (Available T,Th,F all day, also Wed. afternoons.) No juvenile, sealed records released. Fax fee only charged for large number of pages. Copy fee: $.50 per page. No cert fee. Payee: General District Court. Personal checks accepted. Prepayment required. Mail turnaround time within 7 days.

Hampton City

8th Circuit Court 101 King's Way, PO Box 40, Hampton, VA 23669-0040; 757-727-6105. Hours: 8:30AM-4PM (EST). *Felony, Civil Actions Over $15,000, Probate.*

Civil Records: Access: Phone, mail, fax, in person, online. Both court and visitors may perform in person searches. Search fee: $10.00 per name. Required to search: name, years to search. Civil cases indexed by defendant, plaintiff. Computerized records back to 1991, civil records on index books since 1834. Online access free at http://208.210.219.132/courtinfo/vacircuit/select.jsp?court=. For information about the statewide online systems, see the state introduction.

Criminal Records: Access: Mail, online, in person, online. Both court and visitors may perform in person searches. Search fee: $10.00 per name. Required to search: name, years to search. Computerized records back to 1991, criminal records on index books since 1949. Online access to criminal records is the same as civil.

General Information: Public Access terminal is available. No pre-sentence, criminal correspondence, chancery, judges notes or medical records released. Will fax results. Copy fee: $.50 per page. Cert fee: $2.00. Payee: Clerk of Court. No out of state checks accepted. Prepayment required. Mail requests: SASE required. Mail turnaround time 3 days.

8th General District Court Courthouse, PO Box 70, Hampton, VA 23669-0070; Civil phone: 757-727-6480; Criminal phone: 757-727-6260. Hours: 8AM-4PM (EST). *Misdemeanor, Civil Actions Under $15,000, Eviction, Small Claims.*

Civil Records: Access: Online, in person. Visitors must perform in person searches for themselves. No search fee. Required to search: name, years to search. Civil cases indexed by defendant, plaintiff. Civil records on index books and computer for 10 years. Search free at http://208.210.219.132/courtinfo/vadistrict/select.jsp?court=. Also search via LOPAS; call 804-786-5511. Mail access limited to specific case and two names.

Criminal Records: Access: Online, in person. Visitors must perform in person searches for themselves. No search fee. Required to search: name, years to search. Criminal records on index books and computer for 10 years. Online access to criminal records is the same as civil.

General Information: Public Access terminal is available. No sealed records released. Copy fee: $.50 each. Cert fee: $7.00. Payee: Hampton District Court. Personal checks accepted. Credit cards accepted. Accepted for fines only. Prepayment required.

Hanover County

15th Circuit Court 7507 Library Dr, PO Box 39, Hanover, VA 23069; 804-365-6151; Civil phone: 804-365-6143; Criminal phone: 804-365-6843; Probate phone: 804-365-6478; Fax: 804-365-6278. Hours: 8:30AM-4:30PM (EST). *Felony, Civil Actions Over $15,000, Probate.*

Civil Records: Access: Online, in person. Visitors must perform in person searches for themselves. No search fee. Required to search: name, years to search. Civil cases indexed by defendant, plaintiff. Civil records index in books, older records date from 1865. Remote online access to court case indexes is via LOPAS; call 804-786-5511 to apply.

Criminal Records: Access: Online, in person. Visitors must perform in person searches for themselves. No search fee. Required to search: name, years to search. Criminal records index in books, older records date from 1850. Remote online access to court case indexes is via LOPAS; call 804-786-5511 to apply.

General Information: Public Access terminal is available. No juvenile, sealed records released. Copy fee: $.50 per page. Cert fee: $2.00. Payee: Clerk of Circuit Court. Personal checks accepted. Prepayment required.

15th General District Court Hanover County Courthouse, PO Box 176, Hanover, VA 23069; 804-365-6191; Civil phone: 804-365-6457; Fax: 804-365-6290; 804-365-6436 (Civil Fax). Hours: 8AM-4PM (EST). *Misdemeanor, Civil Actions Under $15,000, Eviction, Small Claims.*

Civil Records: Access: Mail, online, in person. Both court and visitors may perform in person searches. No search fee. Required to search: name, years to search. Civil cases indexed by defendant, plaintiff. Civil records on computer back to 1994. Search free at http://208.210.219.132/courtinfo/vadistrict/select.jsp?court=. Also search via LOPAS; call 804-786-5511.

Criminal Records: Access: Mail, online, in person. Visitors must perform in person searches for themselves. No search fee. Required to search: name, years to search, DOB; also helpful: SSN. Criminal records on computer back to 1994. Online access to criminal records is the same as civil.

General Information: Public Access terminal is available. Copy fee: $1.00 for first and second page, $.50 each add'l page thereafter up to 10 pages. No cert fee. Payee: Hanover General District Court. Personal checks accepted. Visa, MC accepted. Turnaround time is 7-10 business days.

Harrisonburg City

Circuit & District Courts   Note: See Rockingham County.

Henrico County

14th Circuit Court PO Box 27032, Richmond, VA 23273-7032; 804-501-4202; Civil phone: 804-501-5422; Criminal phone: 804-501-4758; Probate phone: 804-501-4763. Hours: 8AM-4:30PM (EST). *Felony, Civil Actions Over $15,000, Probate.*
www.co.henrico.va.us/clerk

Civil Records: Access: Mail, online, in person. Visitors must perform in person searches for themselves. No search fee. Required to search: name, years to search. Civil cases indexed by defendant, plaintiff. Civil records on computer from 11/88, on index cards from 1850. Remote online access to court case indexes is via LOPAS; call 804-786-5511 to apply.

Criminal Records: Access: Mail, online, in person. Visitors must perform in person searches for themselves. No search fee. Required to search: name, years to search. Criminal records on computer from 11/88, on index cards from 1850. Remote online access to court case indexes is via LOPAS; call 804-786-5511 to apply.

General Information: Public Access terminal is available. No juvenile, judges notes, adoption sealed records released. Copy fee: $.50 per page. Cert fee: $2.00 per document. Payee: Clerk of Circuit Court. Personal checks accepted. Prepayment required. Mail requests: SASE required. Mail turnaround time 3-5 days.

14th General District Court PO Box 27032, Richmond, VA 23273; Civil phone: 804-501-4727; Criminal phone: 804-501-4723; Fax: 804-501-4141. Hours: 8AM-4PM (EST). *Misdemeanor, Civil Actions Under $15,000, Eviction, Small Claims.*

Civil Records: Access: Online, in person. Visitors must perform in person searches for themselves. No search fee. Required to search: name, years to search. Civil cases indexed by defendant. Civil records on computer from 07/85. Search free at http://208.210.219.132/courtinfo/vadistrict/select.jsp?court=. Also search via LOPAS; call 804-786-5511.

Criminal Records: Access: Online, in person,mail. Visitors must perform in person searches for themselves. No search fee. Required to search: name, years to search, DOB. Criminal records on computer from 1993. Online access to criminal records is the same as civil.

General Information: Public Access terminal is available. No juvenile, sealed records released. Copy fee: $1.00 per page. No cert fee. Payee: Clerk of General District Court. Personal checks accepted. Credit cards accepted. Not accepted over the phone. Prepayment required. Mail requests: SASE required. Mail turnaround time is 3-4 days.

Henry County

21st Circuit Court 3160 Kings Mountain Rd, #B, Martinsville, VA 24112; 276-634-4880 or 276-634-4884 (Law); Civil phone: 276-634-4886 (Chancery); Criminal phone: 276-634-4889 or 276-634-4885; Probate phone: 276-634-4883; Hours: 9AM-5PM, except Tues 9AM-2PM (EST). *Felony, Civil Actions Over $15,000, Probate.*
www.courts.state.va.us

Civil Records: Access: Online, in person. Visitors must perform in person searches for themselves. No search fee. Required to search: name, years to search. Civil cases indexed by defendant, plaintiff. Civil records on computer since 4/92, index back to 1777. Online access free at http://208.210.219.132/courtinfo/vacircuit/select.jsp?court=. For information about the statewide online systems, see the state introduction.

Criminal Records: Access: Online, in person. Visitors must perform in person searches for themselves. No search fee. Required to search: name, years to search, DOB; also helpful: SSN. Criminal records computerized since 7/92, index back to 1777. Online access to criminal records is the same as civil.

General Information: Public Access terminal is available. No juvenile, expungments, sealed or adoption records released. Copy fee: $.50 per page. Cert fee: $2.00. Payee: Clerk of Circuit Court. Personal checks accepted. Prepayment required.

21st General District Court 3160 King's Mountain Rd, #A, Martinsville, VA 24112; 276-634-4815; Fax: 276-634-4825. Hours: 9AM-5PM (EST). *Misdemeanor, Civil Actions Under $15,000, Eviction, Small Claims.*
www.courts.state.va.us

Civil Records: Access: Online, in person. Visitors must perform in person searches for themselves. No search fee. Required to search: name, years to search; also helpful: address. Civil cases indexed by defendant, plaintiff. Civil records on computer from 1992. Search free at http://208.210.219.132/courtinfo/vadistrict/select.jsp?court=. Also search via LOPAS; call 804-786-5511.

Criminal Records: Access: Online, in person. Visitors must perform in person searches for themselves. No search fee. Required to search: name, years to search, DOB; also helpful: address, SSN. Criminal records on computer from 1992. Online access to criminal records is the same as civil.

General Information: Public Access terminal is available. No sealed records released. Copy fee: $.50 per page. No cert fee. Payee: Henry County General District Court. Visa, MC cards accepted. Prepayment required.

Highland County

25th Circuit Court PO Box 190, Monterey, VA 24465; 540-468-2447; Fax: 540-468-3447. Hours: 8:45AM-4:30PM (EST). *Felony, Civil Actions Over $15,000, Probate.*

Civil Records: Access: Mail, online, in person. Both court and visitors may perform in person searches. No search fee. Required to search: name, years to search. Civil cases indexed by defendant, plaintiff. Civil records on index books from 1868. Remote online access to court case indexes is via LOPAS; call 804-786-5511 to apply.

Criminal Records: Access: Mail, online, in person. Both court and visitors may perform in person searches. No search fee. Required to search: name, years to search. Criminal records on index books from 1868. Online access to criminal records is the same as civil.

General Information: Public Access terminal is available. No juvenile, sealed records released. Will fax results for $2.00 plus $.50 per page. Copy fee: $.50 per page. Cert fee: $2.00. Payee: Clerk of Circuit Court. Personal checks accepted. Prepayment required. Mail turnaround time up to 1 week.

25th General District Court Highland County Courthouse, PO Box 88, Monterey, VA 24465; 540-468-2445; Fax: 540-468-3449. Hours: 8:30AM-5:00PM (EST). *Misdemeanor, Civil Actions Under $15,000, Eviction, Small Claims.*

Civil Records: Access: Fax, mail, online, in person. Both court and visitors may perform in person searches. No search fee. Required to search: name, years to search. Civil cases indexed by defendant, plaintiff. Civil records on index books from 1991; computerized back to 1993. Search free at http://208.210.219.132/courtinfo/vadistrict/select.jsp?court=. Also search via LOPAS; call 804-786-5511.

Criminal Records: Access: Fax, mail, online, in person. Both court and visitors may perform in person searches. No search fee. Required to search: name, years to search; also helpful: DOB, SSN, signed release. Criminal records on index books from 1991; computerized back to 1993. Online access to criminal records is the same as civil.

General Information: Public Access terminal is available. No juvenile, sealed records released. Copy fee: $1.00 copy fee for first 2 pages. Add $.50 per page thereafter. No cert fee. Payee: General District Court. Personal checks accepted. Prepayment

required. Mail requests: SASE requested. Turnaround time 2-3 days.

Hopewell City

6th Circuit Court 100 E Broadway, PO Box 310, 2nd Fl, Rm 251, Hopewell, VA 23860; 804-541-2239; Fax: 804-541-2438. Hours: 8:30AM-4PM (EST). *Felony, Civil Actions Over $15,000, Probate.*

Civil Records: Access: Mail, online, in person. Visitors must perform in person searches for themselves. No search fee. Required to search: name, years to search. Civil cases indexed by defendant, plaintiff. Civil records on index books since 1916. Search free online at http://208.210.219.132/courtinfo/vacircuit/select.jsp?court=. Also search via LOPAS; call 804-786-5511.

Criminal Records: Access: Online, in person. Visitors must perform in person searches for themselves. No search fee. Required to search: name, years to search, DOB. Criminal records on index books since 1916. Online access to criminal records is the same as civil.

General Information: Public Access terminal is available. No juvenile, sealed records released. Copy fee: $.50 per page. Cert fee: $2.00. Payee: Clerk of Circuit Court. Personal checks accepted. Prepayment required. Mail requests: SASE required. Mail turnaround time 1 week.

Hopewell District Court 100 E Broadway, Hopewell, VA 23860; 804-541-2257; Fax: 804-541-2364. Hours: 8:30AM-4:30PM (EST). *Misdemeanor, Civil Actions Under $15,000, Eviction, Small Claims.*

Civil Records: Access: Mail, online, in person. Both court and visitors may perform in person searches. No search fee. Required to search: name, years to search. Civil cases indexed by defendant, plaintiff. Civil records on computer from 1988, older case records archived. Search free at http://208.210.219.132/courtinfo/vadistrict/select.jsp?court=. Also search via LOPAS; call 804-786-5511.

Criminal Records: Access: Mail, online, in person. Both court and visitors may perform in person searches. No search fee. Required to search: name, years to search, DOB; also helpful: SSN. Criminal records on computer from 1988, older case records are archived. Online access to criminal records is the same as civil.

General Information: Public Access terminal is available. No juvenile, sealed or domestic relations records released. Copy fee: $1.00 per page first 2 pages, then $.50 each. No cert fee. Payee: Clerk of General District Court. Personal checks accepted. Visa, MC accepted. Prepayment required. Mail requests: SASE requested. Turnaround time 3-5 days.

Isle of Wight County

5th Circuit Court 17122 Monument Circle, PO Box 110, Isle of Wight, VA 23397; 757-365-6233. Hours: 9AM-5PM (EST). *Felony, Civil Actions Over $15,000, Probate.*

Civil Records: Access: Online, in person. Visitors must perform in person searches for themselves. No search fee. Required to search: name, years to search. Civil cases indexed by defendant, plaintiff. Civil records on index books from 1800s; on computer back to 1988. Online access free at http://208.210.219.132/courtinfo/vacircuit/select.jsp?court=. For information about the statewide online systems, see the state introduction.

Criminal Records: Access: Online, in person. Visitors must perform in person searches for themselves. No search fee. Required to search: name, years to search, DOB. Criminal records on index books from 1800s; on computer back to 1988. Online access to criminal records is the same as civil.

General Information: Public Access terminal is available. No juvenile, sealed records released. Copy fee: $.50 per page. Cert fee: $2.00. Payee: Clerk of Circuit Court. Personal checks accepted. Prepayment required.

5th General District Court Isle of Wight

Courthouse, PO Box 122, Isle of Wight, VA 23397; 757-365-6243; Fax: 757-365-6246. Hours: 8AM-4PM (EST). *Misdemeanor, Civil Actions Under $15,000, Eviction, Small Claims.*

Note: The Clerk can be reached at 757-365-6244.

Civil Records: Access: Online, in person. Visitors must perform in person searches for themselves. No search fee. Required to search: name, years to search. Civil cases indexed by defendant, plaintiff. Civil records on index books back to 1800s; on computer since 1994. Search free at http://208.210.219.132/courtinfo/vadistrict/select.jsp?court=. Also search via LOPAS; call 804-786-5511.

Criminal Records: Access: Online, in person. Visitors must perform in person searches for themselves. No search fee. Required to search: name, years to search. Criminal records on index books back to 1800s; on computer since 1994. Online access to criminal records is the same as civil.

General Information: Public Access terminal is available. Juvenile, sealed, adoption records not released. Copy fee: $1.00 per page. Cert fee: $1.00. Payee: Clerk of GDC. Personal checks accepted. Visa, MC accepted. Prepayment required.

James City

Williamsburg-James City Circuit Court

5201 Monticello Ave, #6, Williamsburg, VA 23188-8218; 757-564-2242; Fax: 757-564-2329. Hours: 8:30AM-4:30PM (EST). *Felony, Civil Actions Over $15,000, Probate.*

Civil Records: Access: Mail, online, in person. Both court and visitors may perform in person searches. Search fee: $10.00 per name. Required to search: name, years to search. Civil cases indexed by defendant, plaintiff. Civil records on computer since 1987, archived from 1970, prior on index books. Online access free at http://208.210.219.132/courtinfo/vacircuit/select.jsp?court=. For information about the statewide online systems, see the state introduction.

Criminal Records: Access: Mail, online, in person. Both court and visitors may perform in person searches. Search fee: $10.00 per name. Required to search: name, years to search, DOB; also helpful: SSN. Criminal records on computer since 1987, archived from 1970, prior on index books. Online access to criminal records is the same as civil.

General Information: Public Access terminal is available. No juvenile, sealed, adoption records released. Fee to fax results is $1.00 per page. Copy fee: $.50 per page. Cert fee: $2.00. Payee: Clerk of Circuit Court. Personal checks not accepted. Prepayment required. Mail requests: SASE required. Mail turnaround time 1-2 days.

9th General District Court James City County

Courthouse, 5201 Monticello Ave, #2, Williamsburg, VA 23188-8218; 757-564-2400; Fax: 757-564-2410. Hours: 7:30AM-4PM (EST). *Misdemeanor, Civil Actions Under $15,000, Eviction, Small Claims.*

Civil Records: Access: Fax, mail, in person. Both court and visitors may perform in person searches. No search fee. Required to search: name, years to search. Civil cases indexed by defendant, plaintiff. Civil records on index books from 1994, on computer from 1994. Search free at http://208.210.219.132/courtinfo/vadistrict/select.jsp?court=. Also search via LOPAS; call 804-786-5511.

Criminal Records: Access: Fax, mail, in person. Both court and visitors may perform in person searches. No search fee. Required to search: name, years to search, DOB; also helpful: SSN. Criminal records on index books from 1994, on computer from 1994. Online access to criminal records is the same as civil.

General Information: Public Access terminal is available. No juvenile, sealed records released. Copy fee: Charges will be incurred if extensive searching or copies are needed. No cert fee. Payee: General District Court. Personal checks accepted. Visa, MC accepted. Prepayment required. Mail requests: SASE requested. Turnaround time 10 days.

King and Queen County

9th Circuit Court PO Box 67, King & Queen

Court House, VA 23085; 804-785-5984; Fax: 804-785-5698. Hours: 9AM-5PM (EST). *Felony, Civil Actions Over $15,000, Probate.*

Note: 234 Allen's Circle is the physical address.

Civil Records: Access: Mail, in person, online. Visitors must perform in person searches for themselves. No search fee. Required to search: name, years to search. Civil cases indexed by plaintiff. Civil records archived from 1864, computerized since 1995. Remote online acces to court case indexes is via LOPAS, call 804-786-5511 to apply.

Criminal Records: Access: Online, in person. Visitors must perform in person searches for themselves. No search fee. Required to search: name, years to search. Criminal records archived from 1864, computerized since 1995. Remote online acces to court case indexes is via LOPAS, call 804-786-5511 to apply.

General Information: Public Access terminal is available. No juvenile, sealed or adoption records released. Will fax results for $1.00 per page. Copy fee: $.50 per page. Cert fee: $1.00. Payee: Clerk of Circuit Court. Personal checks accepted. Prepayment required. Mail turnaround time is 1 day.

King & Queen General District Court PO

Box 86, King & Queen Courthouse, VA 23085-0086; 804-785-5982; Fax: 804-785-5694. Hours: 8:30AM-4:30PM (EST). *Misdemeanor, Civil Actions Under $15,000, Eviction.*

www.kingandqueenco.net/html/Govt/gendist.html

Note: The General District Court also holds preliminary hearings in felony cases.

Civil Records: Access: Fax, mail, online, in person. Both court and visitors may perform in person searches. No search fee. Required to search: name, years to search. Civil cases indexed by defendant, plaintiff. Civil records on computer back to 1991. Search free at http://208.210.219.132/courtinfo/vadistrict/select.jsp?court=. Also search via LOPAS; call 804-786-5511.

Criminal Records: Access: Fax, mail, online, in person. Both court and visitors may perform in person searches. No search fee. Required to search: name, years to search, DOB; also helpful: SSN, signed release. Criminal records on computer back to 1991. Online access to criminal records is the same as civil.

General Information: Public Access terminal is available. No fee to fax results. Copy fee: $1.00 for first page, $.50 each add'l. No cert fee. Payee: General District Court. Personal checks accepted. Prepayment required. Mail turnaround time 1-5 days.

King George County

15th Circuit Court 9483 Kings Hwy, #3, King

George, VA 22485; 540-775-3322. Hours: 8:30AM-4:30PM (EST). *Felony, Civil Actions Over $15,000, Probate.*

Civil Records: Access: Mail, in person. Both court and visitors may perform in person searches. Search

fee: $10.00 per name. Required to search: name, years to search. Civil cases indexed by defendant, plaintiff. Civil records on index books from 1800s; computerized records since 1990.

Criminal Records: Access: Mail, in person. Both court and visitors may perform in person searches. Search fee: $10.00 per name. Required to search: name, years to search. Criminal records on index books from 1800s; computerized records since 1990.

General Information: Public Access terminal is available. No sealed records released. Copy fee: $.50 per page. Cert fee: $2.00. Payee: Clerk of Circuit court. Personal checks accepted. Prepayment required. Mail requests: SASE required. Mail turnaround time 30 days.

15th Judicial District King George Combined Court County Courthouse PO Box

279, King George, VA 22485; 540-775-3573. Hours: 8AM-4:00PM (EST). *Misdemeanor, Civil Actions Under $15,000, Eviction, Small Claims.*

Civil Records: Access: Mail, in person. Both court and visitors may perform in person searches. No search fee. Required to search: name, years to search. Civil cases indexed by defendant, plaintiff. Civil records on index books from early 1900s; computerized records since 1992.

Criminal Records: Access: Mail, in person. Both court and visitors may perform in person searches. No search fee. Required to search: name, years to search, DOB; also helpful: SSN. Criminal records on index books from early 1900s; computerized records since 1992.

General Information: Public Access terminal is available. No juvenile, sealed records released. Copy fee: $1.00 per page for the 1st two pages, $.50 each add'l page. Cert fee: $2.00. Payee: Clerk of General District Court. Personal checks accepted. Visa, MC accepted. Prepayment required. Mail requests: SASE required. Mail turnaround time 1-5 days.

King William County

9th Circuit Court 227 Courthouse Lane, PO Box

216, King William, VA 23086; 804-769-4936. Hours: 8:30AM-4:30PM (EST). *Felony, Civil Actions Over $15,000, Probate.*

Civil Records: Access: Mail, in person, online. Both court and visitors may perform in person searches. No search fee. Required to search: name, years to search. Civil cases indexed by defendant, plaintiff. Civil records on index books from 1800s. Search free online at http://208.210.219.132/courtinfo/vacircuit/select.jsp?court=. Also search via LOPAS; call 804-786-5511.

Criminal Records: Access: Mail, in person, online. Both court and visitors may perform in person searches. No search fee. Required to search: name, years to search, DOB; also helpful: SSN. Criminal records on index books from 1800s, computerized records from 1999. Online access to criminal records is the same as civil.

General Information: Public Access terminal is available. No juvenile, sealed records released. Will fax results ot local or toll free line. Copy fee: $.50 per page. Cert fee: $2.00. Payee: Clerk of Circuit Court. Personal checks accepted. Prepayment required. Mail requests: SASE required. Mail turnaround time 1 week.

King William General District Court PO

Box 5, King William, VA 23086; 804-769-4948; Fax: 804-769-4971. Hours: 8:30AM-4:30PM (EST). *Misdemeanor, Civil Actions Under $15,000, Eviction, Small Claims.*

Civil Records: Access: Fax, mail, online, in person. Both court and visitors may perform in person searches. No search fee. Required to search: name, years to search. Civil cases indexed by defendant, plaintiff. Civil records on computer since 1992. Search free at http://208.210.219.132/courtinfo/vadistrict/select.jsp?court=. Also search via LOPAS; call 804-786-5511.

Criminal Records: Access: Fax, mail, online, in person. Both court and visitors may perform in person searches. No search fee. Required to search: name, years to search, DOB; also helpful: signed release, SSN. Criminal records on computer back to 1992. Online access to criminal records is the same as civil.

General Information: Public Access terminal is available. No juvenile, sealed records released. No fee to fax results. Copy fee: $1.00 for first page, $.50 each add'l. No cert fee. Payee: General District Court. Personal checks accepted. Prepayment required. Mail requests: SASE requested. Turnaround time 1-5 days.

Lancaster County

15th Circuit Court Courthouse Bldg, PO Box 99, Lancaster, VA 22503; 804-462-5611. Hours: 8:30AM-4:30PM (EST). *Felony, Civil Actions Over $15,000, Probate.*

Civil Records: Access: Mail, online, in person. Both court and visitors may perform in person searches. No search fee. Required to search: name, years to search. Civil cases indexed by defendant, plaintiff. Civil records on index books from 1845. Search free online at http://208.210.219.132/courtinfo/vacircuit/select.jsp?court=. Also search via LOPAS; call 804-786-5511.

Criminal Records: Access: Mail, online, in person. Both court and visitors may perform in person searches. No search fee. Required to search: name, years to search. Criminal records on index books from 1845. Online access to criminal records is the same as civil.

General Information: Public Access terminal is available. No juvenile, sealed records released. Copy fee: $.50 per page. Cert fee: $2.00. Payee: Clerk of Circuit Court. Personal checks accepted. Out of state checks not accepted. Prepayment required. Mail turnaround time same day.

15th General District Court PO 129, Lancaster, VA 22503; 804-462-0012. Hours: 8:AM-12:00-1-4:30PM (EST). *Misdemeanor, Civil Actions Under $15,000, Eviction, Small Claims.*

Civil Records: Access: Mail, online, in person. Both court and visitors may perform in person searches. No search fee. Required to search: name, years to search. Civil cases indexed by defendant. Civil records on computer from 11/93. Search free at http://208.210.219.132/courtinfo/vadistrict/select.jsp?court=. Also search via LOPAS; call 804-786-5511.

Criminal Records: Access: Mail, online, in person. Both court and visitors may perform in person searches. No search fee. Required to search: name, years to search, DOB; also helpful: SSN. Criminal records on computer from 11/93. Online access to criminal records is the same as civil.

General Information: Public Access terminal is available. No sealed records released. Copy fee: $1.00 1st.per page. $.50 add'l. No cert fee. Payee: Clerk of General District Court. Personal checks accepted. Prepayment required. Mail requests: SASE helpful. Turnaround time is 1-2 days.

Lee County

30th Circuit Court PO Box 326, Jonesville, VA 24263; 276-346-7763; Fax: 276-346-3440. Hours: 8:30AM-5PM M-F; 9AM-Noon Sat (EST). *Felony, Civil Actions Over $15,000, Probate.*

Civil Records: Access: Phone, fax, mail, online, in person. Both court and visitors may perform in person searches. No search fee. Required to search: name, years to search. Civil cases indexed by defendant, plaintiff. Civil records on index books from 1800s.

Select and search Circuit Courts online at http://208.210.219.132/courtinfo/vacircuit/select.jsp?court=. For information about the statewide online systems, see the state introduction. Phone & fax access limited to short searches.

Criminal Records: Access: Phone, fax, mail, online, in person. Both court and visitors may perform in person searches. No search fee. Required to search: name, years to search, DOB; also helpful: SSN. Criminal records on index books from 1800s. Online access to criminal records is the same as civil.

General Information: Public Access terminal is available. No juvenile, sealed records released. Will fax results to local or toll free line. Copy fee: $.50 per page. Cert fee: $2.00. Payee: Clerk of Circuit Court. Personal checks accepted. Prepayment required. Mail turnaround time 1-3 days.

30th General District Court Lee County Courthouse, PO Box 306, Jonesville, VA 24263; 276-346-7729; Fax: 276-346-7701. Hours: 8AM-4:30PM (EST). *Misdemeanor, Civil Actions Under $15,000, Eviction, Small Claims.*

Civil Records: Access: Mail, online, in person. Both court and visitors may perform in person searches. No search fee. Required to search: name, years to search. Civil cases indexed by defendant, plaintiff. Civil records on index books from 1800s, on computer from 11/7/90. Search free at http://208.210.219.132/courtinfo/vadistrict/select.jsp?court=. Also search via LOPAS; call 804-786-5511.

Criminal Records: Access: Mail, online, in person, fax. Both court and visitors may perform in person searches. No search fee. Required to search: name, years to search. Criminal records on index books from 1800s, on computer from 11/7/90. Online access to criminal records is the same as civil.

General Information: Public Access terminal is available. No juvenile, sealed records released. Copy fee: $1.00 for first page, $.50 each add'l. No cert fee. Payee: Clerk of General District Court. Personal checks accepted. Prepayment required. Mail requests: SASE helpful. Turnaround time 1-2 days.

Lexington City

Circuit & District Courts Note: See Rockbridge County

Loudoun County

20th Circuit Court 18 E Market St, Leesburg, VA 20178; 703-777-0270; Probate phone: 703-777-0272; Fax: 703-777-0376. Hours: 8:30AM-4:30PM (EST). *Felony, Civil Actions Over $15,000, Probate.* www.loudoun.gov/clerk

Civil Records: Access: Phone, mail, online, in person. Both court and visitors may perform in person searches. No search fee. Required to search: name, years to search. Civil cases indexed by defendant, plaintiff. Civil records on computer since 1995; prior on index books from 1700s. Remote online access to court case indexes is via LOPAS; call 804-786-5511 to apply. Also, docket lists are free at http://inetdocs.loudoun.gov/clerk/docs/dockets_/index.htm. Phone access limited to simple requests. Mail access for deeds and wills only.

Criminal Records: Access: Online, in person. Both court and visitors may perform in person searches. No search fee. Required to search: name, years to search, DOB; also helpful: SSN. Criminal records on computer since 1995; prior on index books from 1700s. Remote online access to court case indexes is via LOPAS; call 804-786-5511 to apply. Also, docket lists are online free at http://inetdocs.loudoun.gov/clerk/docs/dockets_/index.htm.

General Information: Public Access terminal is available. No juvenile, sealed or adoption records

released. Will not fax results. Copy fee: $.50 per page. Cert fee: $2.50. Payee: Clerk of Circuit Court. Business checks accepted. Personal checks accepted if in state. Prepayment required. Mail turnaround time 1 week.

20th General District Court 18 E Market St, Leesburg, VA 20176; 703-777-0312; Fax: 703-777-0311. Hours: 8AM-4PM (EST). *Misdemeanor, Civil Actions Under $15,000, Eviction.*

Civil Records: Access: Mail, fax, online, in person. Both court and visitors may perform in person searches. No search fee. Required to search: name, years to search. Civil cases indexed by defendant, plaintiff. Civil records on computer back 10 years. Search free at http://208.210.219.132/courtinfo/vadistrict/select.jsp?court=. Also search via LOPAS; call 804-786-5511.

Criminal Records: Access: Mail, fax, online, in person. Both court and visitors may perform in person searches. No search fee. Required to search: name, years to search. Criminal records on computer back 10 years. Online access to criminal records is the same as civil.

General Information: Public Access terminal is available. Copy fee: $.50 per page. Cert fee: $.50. Payee: General District Court. Personal checks accepted. Visa, MC accepted. Prepayment required. Mail requests: SASE required. Mail turnaround time 7-10 days.

Louisa County

16th Circuit Court Box 37, Louisa, VA 23093; 540-967-5312; Fax: 540-967-2705. Hours: 8:30AM-5PM (EST). *Felony, Civil Actions Over $15,000, Probate.*

Civil Records: Access: Online, in person. Visitors must perform in person searches for themselves. No search fee. Required to search: name, years to search. Civil cases indexed by defendant, plaintiff. Civil records archived from 1742; on computer back to 1989. Search free online at http://208.210.219.132/courtinfo/vacircuit/select.jsp?court=. Also search via LOPAS; call 804-786-5511.

Criminal Records: Access: Online, in person. Both court and visitors may perform in person searches. No search fee. Required to search: name, years to search, DOB or SSN. Criminal records archived from 1742; on computer back to 1989. Online access to criminal records is the same as civil.

General Information: No juvenile, sealed records released. Copy fee: $.50 per page. Cert fee: $2.00. Payee: Clerk of Circuit Court. Personal checks accepted. Prepayment required.

16th General District Court PO Box 452, Louisa, VA 23093; 540-967-5330; Fax: 540-967-2369. Hours: 8:30AM-4:30PM (EST). *Misdemeanor, Civil Actions Under $15,000, Eviction, Small Claims.*

Civil Records: Access: Online, in person. Visitors must perform in person searches for themselves. No search fee. Required to search: name, years to search. Civil cases indexed by defendant, plaintiff. Civil records on computer from 1991. Search free at http://208.210.219.132/courtinfo/vadistrict/select.jsp?court=. Also search via LOPAS; call 804-786-5511.

Criminal Records: Access: Online, in person. Visitors must perform in person searches for themselves. No search fee. Required to search: name, years to search. Criminal records on computer from 1991. Online access to criminal records is the same as civil.

General Information: Public Access terminal is available. No juvenile, sealed records released. Copy fee: $1.00 for first page, $.50 each add'l. Payee: Louisa District Court. Personal checks accepted. Prepayment required.

Lunenburg County

10th Circuit Court 11435 Courthouse Rd, Lunenburg, VA 23952; 434-696-2230; Fax: 434-696-3931. Hours: 8:30AM-4:30PM (EST). *Felony, Civil Actions Over $15,000, Probate.*

Civil Records: Access: Online, in person. Visitors must perform in person searches for themselves. No search fee. Required to search: name, years to search. Civil cases indexed by defendant, plaintiff. Civil records on index books from 1700s; computerized records since 2002. Search free online at http://208.210.219.132/courtinfo/vacircuit/select.jsp?court=. Also search via LOPAS; call 804-786-5511.

Criminal Records: Access: Iin person, mail. Visitors must perform in person searches for themselves. Search fee: Varies by numbers of yrs searched. Required to search: name, years to search. Criminal records on index books from 1700s; computerized records since 2002. Online access to criminal records is the same as civil.

General Information: No juvenile, sealed records released. No fee to fax results. Copy fee: $.50 per page. Cert fee: $2.00 per page. Payee: Clerk of Circuit Court. Personal checks accepted. Prepayment required. Mail turnaround time 1-2 days.

10th General District Court 11413 Courthouse Road, Lunenburg, VA 23952; 434-696-5508; Fax: 434-696-3665. Hours: 8:30AM-4:30PM (EST). *Misdemeanor, Civil Actions Under $15,000, Eviction, Small Claims.*

Civil Records: Access: Mail, online, in person. Both court and visitors may perform in person searches. No search fee. Required to search: name, years to search. Civil cases indexed by defendant, plaintiff. Civil records computerized since 1995, on index books and cards from 1991, prior to 1985 at Circuit Court. Search free at http://208.210.219.132/courtinfo/vadistrict/select.jsp?court=. Also search via LOPAS; call 804-786-5511.

Criminal Records: Access: Mail, online, in person. Both court and visitors may perform in person searches. No search fee. Required to search: name, years to search, DBO, SSN. Criminal records computerized since 1995, on index books and cards from 1991, prior to 1985 at Circuit Court. Online access to criminal records is the same as civil.

General Information: Public Access terminal is available. No juvenile records released. No cert fee. Mail requests: SASE required. Mail turnaround time 3 days.

Lynchburg City

24th Circuit Court 900 Court St, PO Box 4, Lynchburg, VA 24505-0004; 434-847-1590; Fax: 434-847-1864. Hours: 8:15AM-4:45PM (EST). *Felony, Civil Actions Over $15,000, Probate.*

Civil Records: Access: Online, in person. Both court and visitors may perform in person searches. No search fee. Required to search: name, years to search. Civil cases indexed by defendant, plaintiff. Civil records on index books from 1800s, on computer since 1993. Search free online at http://208.210.219.132/courtinfo/vacircuit/select.jsp?court=. Also search via LOPAS; call 804-786-5511.

Criminal Records: Access: Online, in person. Both court and visitors may perform in person searches. No search fee. Required to search: name, years to search; also helpful: DOB, SSN. Criminal records on index books from 1800s, on computer since 1993. Online access to criminal records is the same as civil.

General Information: Public Access terminal is available. No juvenile, sealed records released. Copy fee: $.50 per page. Cert fee: $2.00. Payee: Clerk of Circuit Court. Personal checks accepted. Prepayment required.

24th General District Court - Civil Division 905 Court St, Lynchburg, VA 24504; Civil phone: 434-455-2640; Criminal phone: 434-455-2630; Fax: 434-847-1779. Hours: 8AM-4PM (EST). *Civil Actions Under $15,000, Eviction, Small Claims.*

Civil Records: Access: Mail, online, in person. Both court and visitors may perform in person searches. No search fee. Required to search: name, years to search; also helpful: address. Civil cases indexed by defendant, plaintiff. On computer since 1987. Search free at http://208.210.219.132/courtinfo/vadistrict/select.jsp?court=. Also search via LOPAS; call 804-786-5511.

General Information: Public Access terminal is available. No juvenile, sealed records released. Copy fee: $1.00 for first 2 pages, $.50 each add'l. No cert fee. Payee: Lynchburg General District Court. Personal checks accepted. Prepayment required. Mail turnaround time 1-2 weeks.

24th General District Court - Criminal Division 905 Court St, Lynchburg, VA 24504; Criminal phone: 434-455-2630; Fax: 434-847-1779. Hours: 8AM-4PM (EST). *Misdemeanor.*

Criminal Records: Access: Online, in person. Visitors must perform in person searches for themselves. No search fee. Required to search: name, years to search. Criminal records on index books and computer go back 10 years. For information about the statewide online systems, see the state introduction. Select and search General District Courts at http://208.210.219.132/courtinfo/vadistrict/select.jsp?court=. Mail access limited to specific cases only, not name searches.

General Information: Public Access terminal is available. No juvenile, sealed records released. Copy fee: $1.00 for first 2 pages, $.50 each add'l. No cert fee. Payee: Lynchburg General District Court. Personal checks accepted. Prepayment required.

Madison County

16th Circuit Court 100 Court Sq,1 Main St (PO Box 220), Madison, VA 22727; 540-948-6888; Fax: 540-948-3759. Hours: 8:30AM-4:30PM (EST). *Felony, Civil Actions Over $15,000, Probate.*

Civil Records: Access: Mail, online, in person. Visitors must perform in person searches for themselves. No search fee. Required to search: name, years to search. Civil cases indexed by defendant, plaintiff. Civil records on index books from 1792, on computer since 1989. Select and search Combined Courts online at http://208.210.219.132/courtinfo/vacircuit/select.jsp?court=. For information about the statewide online systems, see the state introduction.

Criminal Records: Access: Mail, online, in person. Visitors must perform in person searches for themselves. No search fee. Required to search: name, years to search, DOB; also helpful: SSN. Criminal records on index books from 1792, on computer since 1989. Online access to criminal records is the same as civil.

General Information: No juvenile, sealed records released. Copy fee: $.50 per page. Cert fee: $2.00. Payee: Clerk of Circuit Court. Personal checks accepted. Prepayment required. Mail requests: SASE required. Mail turnaround time 1 week.

16th General District Court Madison County Courthouse, PO Box 470, Madison, VA 22727; 540-948-4657; Fax: 540-948-5649. Hours: 8:30AM-4:30PM (EST). *Misdemeanor, Civil Actions Under $15,000, Eviction, Small Claims.*

Civil Records: Access: Phone, fax, mail, online, in person. Only the court performs in person searches; visitors may not. No search fee. Required to search: name, years to search. Civil cases indexed by defendant, plaintiff. Civil records on index books and computer back to 1992. Search free at http://208.210.219.132/courtinfo/vadistrict/select.jsp?court=. Also search via LOPAS; call 804-786-5511.

Criminal Records: Access: Phone, fax, mail, online, in person. Only the court performs in person searches; visitors may not. No search fee. Required to search: name, years to search, DOB; also helpful: address, SSN. Criminal records on index books and computer back to 1992. Online access to criminal records is the same as civil.

General Information: No juvenile, sealed or pre-trial records released. No fee to fax results. No copy fee. No cert fee. Mail requests: SASE required. Mail turnaround time 3-4 days.

Manassas City

Circuit & District Courts Note: See Prince William County

Manassas Park City

Circuit & District Courts Note: See Prince William County

Martinsville City

21st Circuit Court PO Box 1206, Martinsville, VA 24114-1206; 276-656-5106; Fax: 276-403-5232. Hours: 9AM-5PM (EST). *Felony, Civil Actions Over $15,000, Probate.*
www.ci.martinsville.va.us/circuitclerk

Civil Records: Access: Online, in person. Visitors must perform in person searches for themselves. No search fee. Required to search: name, years to search. Civil cases indexed by defendant, plaintiff. Civil records on computer since 1988, on index books from 1942. Online access free at http://208.210.219.132/courtinfo/vacircuit/select.jsp?court=. For information about the statewide online systems, see the state introduction. Also, with password, access judgments at www.ci.martinsville.va.us/crms/.

Criminal Records: Access: Online, in person, mail, fax. Visitors must perform in person searches for themselves. No search fee. Required to search: name, years to search; also helpful: DOB, SSN. Criminal records on computer since 1988, on index books from 1942. Online access to criminal records is the same as civil.

General Information: Public Access terminal is available. No juvenile, sealed records released. Copy fee: $.50 per page. Cert fee: $2.00. Payee: Clerk of Circuit Court. Personal checks accepted. Prepayment required. Mail requests: SASE requested. Turnaround time is 1-2 days.

21st General District Court PO Box 1402, Martinsville, VA 24112; 276-656-5125; Fax: 276-403-5114. Hours: 9AM-5PM (EST). *Misdemeanor, Civil Actions Under $15,000, Eviction, Small Claims.*
www.courts.state.va.us

Civil Records: Access: Online, in person. Visitors must perform in person searches for themselves. No search fee. Required to search: name, years to search. Civil cases indexed by defendant, plaintiff. Civil records on computer since 1993. Search free at http://208.210.219.132/courtinfo/vadistrict/select.jsp?court=. Also search via LOPAS; call 804-786-5511.

Criminal Records: Access: Online, in person. Visitors must perform in person searches for themselves. No search fee. Required to search: name, years to search. Criminal records on computer since 1993. Online access to criminal records is the same as civil.

General Information: Public Access terminal is available. (Terminals available in County General District Court, 3160 Kings Mountain Rd, Martinsville, VA 24112.) No sealed or expunged records released. Copy fee: $.50 per copy. No cert fee. Prepayment required.

Mathews County

9th Circuit Court PO Box 463, Mathews, VA 23109; 804-725-2550. Hours: 8AM-4PM (EST). *Felony, Civil Actions Over $15,000, Probate.* www.courts.state.va.us/courts/circuit/Mathews/home. html

Civil Records: Access: Online, in person. Visitors must perform in person searches for themselves. No search fee. Required to search: name, years to search. Civil cases indexed by defendant, plaintiff. Civil records on index books from 1800s. Remote online access to court case indexes is via LOPAS; call 804-786-5511 to apply.

Criminal Records: Access: Online, in person. Visitors must perform in person searches for themselves. No search fee. Required to search: name, years to search; also helpful: DOB, SSN. Criminal records on index books from 1800s. Remote online access to court case indexes is via LOPAS; call 804-786-5511 to apply.

General Information: No juvenile, sealed records released. Copy fee: $.50 per page. Cert fee: $2.00. Payee: Clerk of Circuit Court. Personal checks accepted. Prepayment required.

9th General District Court PO Box 169, Saluda, VA 23149; 804-758-4312. Hours: 8:30AM-4:30PM (EST). *Misdemeanor, Civil Actions Under $15,000, Eviction, Small Claims.*

Civil Records: Access: Mail, online, in person. Both court and visitors may perform in person searches. No search fee. Required to search: name, years to search. Civil cases indexed by defendant. Civil records on computer 10 years back. Search free at http://208.210.219.132/courtinfo/vadistrict/select.jsp? court=. Also search via LOPAS; call 804-786-5511.

Criminal Records: Access: Mail, online, in person. Both court and visitors may perform in person searches. No search fee. Required to search: name, years to search, DOB, date of offense; also helpful: SSN. Criminal records on computer 10 years back. Online access to criminal records is the same as civil.

General Information: Public Access terminal is available. No juvenile, sealed records released. Copy fee: $.50 per page. No cert fee. Payee: Clerk of General District Court. Personal checks accepted. Prepayment required. Mail requests: SASE required. Mail turnaround time 7-10 days.

Mecklenburg County

10th Circuit Court PO Box 530, Boydton, VA 23917; 434-738-6191; Fax: 434-738-6861. Hours: 8:30AM-4:30PM (EST). *Felony, Civil Actions Over $15,000, Probate.*

Civil Records: Access: Online, in person. Visitors must perform in person searches for themselves. No search fee. Required to search: name, years to search. Civil cases indexed by defendant, plaintiff. Civil records on index books from 1800s, on computer from 1987. Remote online access to court case indexes is via LOPAS; call 804-786-5511 to apply.

Criminal Records: Access: Online, in person. Visitors must perform in person searches for themselves. No search fee. Required to search: name, years to search. Criminal records on index books from 1800s, on computer from 1987. Remote online access to court case indexes is via LOPAS; call 804-786-5511 to apply.

General Information: Public Access terminal is available. No juvenile, sealed or direct indictments

(drug offenses) records released. Will fax specific case file data for $1.00 per page. Copy fee: $.50 per page. Cert fee: $2.00. Payee: Clerk of Circuit Court. Personal checks accepted. Prepayment required.

10th General District Court 1294 Jefferson St (PO Box 306), Boydton, VA 23917; 434-738-6191 X223; Fax: 434-738-0761. Hours: 8:30AM-4:30PM (EST). *Misdemeanor, Civil Actions Under $15,000, Eviction, Small Claims.*

Civil Records: Access: Fax, mail, online, in person. Both court and visitors may perform in person searches. Search fee: $5.00. Required to search: name, years to search. Civil cases indexed by defendant, plaintiff. Civil records on computer since 1994. Search free at http://208.210.219.132/courtinfo/vadistrict/select.jsp? court=. Also search via LOPAS; call 804-786-5511.

Criminal Records: Access: Fax, mail, online, in person. Both court and visitors may perform in person searches. Search fee: $5.00. Required to search: name, years to search; also helpful: DOB, SSN. Criminal records on computer since 1994. Online access to criminal records is the same as civil.

General Information: Public Access terminal is available. Sealed, and adoption records not released. Will fax results for $1.00 per pge. Copy fee: $.50 per page. No cert fee. Payee: Clerk of General District Court. Personal checks accepted. Visa, MC accepted. Turnaround time is 2 days.

Middlesex County

9th Circuit Court PO Box 158, Saluda, VA 23149; 804-758-5317; Fax: 804-758-0792. Hours: 8:30AM-4:30PM (EST). *Felony, Civil Actions Over $15,000, Probate.*

Civil Records: Access: In Person only. Visitors must perform in person searches for themselves. No search fee. Required to search: name, years to search. Civil cases indexed by defendant, plaintiff. Civil records on index books from 1672; on computer back to 1992. Remote online access to court case indexes is via LOPAS; call 804-786-5511 to apply.

Criminal Records: Access: In person only. Visitors must perform in person searches for themselves. No search fee. Required to search: name, years to search, DOB, SSN. Criminal records on index books from 1674; on computer back to 1992.

General Information: No juvenile, sealed records released. Copy fee: $.50 per page. Cert fee: $3.00. Payee: Clerk of Circuit Court. Personal checks accepted. Prepayment required.

9th General District Court PO Box 169, Saluda, VA 23149; 804-758-4312. Hours: 8:30AM-4:30PM (EST). *Misdemeanor, Civil Actions Under $15,000, Eviction, Small Claims.*

Civil Records: Access: Mail, online, in person. Both court and visitors may perform in person searches. No search fee. Required to search: name, years to search. Civil cases indexed by defendant. Civil records held 10 years, computerized since 1997. Search free at http://208.210.219.132/courtinfo/vadistrict/select.jsp? court=. Also search via LOPAS; call 804-786-5511.

Criminal Records: Access: Mail, online, in person. Both court and visitors may perform in person searches. No search fee. Required to search: name, years to search. Criminal records held 10 years, computerized since 1997. Online access to criminal records is the same as civil.

General Information: Public Access terminal is available. No juvenile, sealed records released. Copy fee: $.50 per page. No cert fee. Payee: Clerk of General District Court. Personal checks accepted. Prepayment required. Mail requests: SASE required. Mail turnaround time 2-3 days.

Montgomery County

27th Circuit Court PO Box 6309, Christiansburg, VA 24068; 540-382-5760; Fax: 540-382-6937. Hours: 8:30AM-4:30PM (EST). *Felony, Civil Actions Over $15,000, Probate.*

Civil Records: Access: Phone, mail, online, in person. Both court and visitors may perform in person searches. No search fee. Required to search: name, years to search. Civil cases indexed by defendant, plaintiff. Civil records on index books from 1800s, on computer from 1/94. Online access free at http://208.210.219.132/courtinfo/vacircuit/select.jsp?c ourt=. For information about the statewide online systems, see the state introduction. Phone & mail access limited to cases filed 7/93-present.

Criminal Records: Access: Online, in person. Visitors must perform in person searches for themselves. No search fee. Required to search: name, years to search; also helpful: DOB, SSN. Criminal records on computer since 9/93, prior in books. Online access to criminal records is the same as civil.

General Information: Public Access terminal is available. No juvenile, sealed records released. Copy fee: $.50 per page. Cert fee: $2.00. Payee: Clerk of Circuit Court. Personal checks accepted. Prepayment required.

27th General District Court Montgomery County Courthouse, 1 E Main St, #201, Christiansburg, VA 24073; 540-382-5735; Civil phone: 540-394-2085; Criminal phone: 540-394-2086; Fax: 540-382-6988. Hours: 8:30AM-4:30PM (EST). *Misdemeanor, Civil Actions Under $15,000, Eviction, Small Claims.*

Civil Records: Access: Online, in person. Visitors must perform in person searches for themselves. No search fee. Required to search: name, years to search. Civil cases indexed by defendant, plaintiff. Civil records on computerized records go back ten years. Search free at http://208.210.219.132/courtinfo/vadistrict/select.jsp? court=. Also search via LOPAS; call 804-786-5511.

Criminal Records: Access: In person only. Visitors must perform in person searches for themselves. No search fee. Required to search: name, years to search. Computerized records go back ten years. Online access to criminal records is the same as civil.

General Information: Public Access terminal is available. No juvenile records released. Copy fee: $.50 per page. No cert fee. Payee: Clerk General District Court. Personal checks accepted. Prepayment required.

Nelson County

24th Circuit Court PO Box 10, Lovingston, VA 22949; 434-263-7020; Fax: 434-263-7027. Hours: 8AM-5PM (EST). *Felony, Civil Actions Over $15,000, Probate.*

Civil Records: Access: Online, in person. Visitors must perform in person searches for themselves. No search fee. Required to search: name, years to search. Civil cases indexed by defendant, plaintiff. Civil records on index books from 1800s, deeds on computer from 7/93. Online access free at http://208.210.219.132/courtinfo/vacircuit/select.jsp?c ourt=. For information about the statewide online systems, see the state introduction.

Criminal Records: Access: Online, in person. Visitors must perform in person searches for themselves. No search fee. Required to search: name, years to search; also helpful- DOB, SSN. Criminal records on index books from 1800s, deeds on computer from 7/93. Online access to criminal records is the same as civil.

General Information: Public Access terminal is available. (Deeds and marriage licenses from 6/30/93 and financing statements from 06/30/94 are on terminal.) No juvenile, sealed records released. Copy fee: $.50 per page. Cert fee: $2.00. Payee: Clerk of Circuit Court. Personal checks accepted. Prepayment required.

24th General District Court
Nelson County Courthouse, 84 Courthouse Sq, PO Box 514, Lovingston, VA 22949; 434-263-7040; Fax: 434-263-7033. Hours: 8AM-4:30PM (EST). *Misdemeanor, Civil Actions Under $15,000, Eviction, Small Claims.*

Civil Records: Access: Fax, mail, online, in person. Both court and visitors may perform in person searches. No search fee. Required to search: name, years to search. Civil cases indexed by defendant, plaintiff. Civil records on computer for 10 years. Search free at http://208.210.219.132/courtinfo/vadistrict/select.jsp?court=. Also search via LOPAS; call 804-786-5511.

Criminal Records: Access: Fax, mail, online, in person. Both court and visitors may perform in person searches. No search fee. Required to search: name, years to search. Criminal records on computer for 10 years. Online access to criminal records is the same as civil.

General Information: Public Access terminal is available. No sealed records released. No fee to fax results. Copy fee: $.50 per page. No cert fee. Payee: Clerk of General District Court. Personal checks accepted. Prepayment required. Mail requests: SASE required. Mail turnaround time 3-4 days.

New Kent County

9th Circuit Court
PO Box 98, 12001 Court House Circle, New Kent, VA 23124; 804-966-9520; Fax: 804-966-9528. Hours: 8:30AM-4:30PM (EST). *Felony, Civil Actions Over $15,000, Probate.*

Civil Records: Access: Online, in person. Visitors must perform in person searches for themselves. No search fee. Required to search: name, years to search. Civil cases indexed by defendant, plaintiff. Civil records on index books from 1865, some on cards; computerized back to 1992. Online access free at http://208.210.219.132/courtinfo/vacircuit/select.jsp?court=. For information about the statewide online systems, see the state introduction.

Criminal Records: Access: Online, in person. Visitors must perform in person searches for themselves. No search fee. Required to search: name, years to search, DOB, SSN. Criminal records on index books from 1865, some on cards; computerized back to 1992. Online access to criminal records is the same as civil.

General Information: Public Access terminal is available. No juvenile, sealed, adoption records released. Copy fee: $.50 per page. Cert fee: $2.00. Payee: Circuit Court. Personal checks accepted. Prepayment required.

9th General District Court
PO Box 127, New Kent, VA 23124; 804-966-9530; Fax: 804-966-9535. Hours: 8:30AM-4:30PM (EST). *Misdemeanor, Civil Actions Under $15,000, Eviction, Small Claims.*

Civil Records: Access: Mail, online, in person. Both court and visitors may perform in person searches. No search fee. Required to search: name, years to search. Civil cases indexed by defendant, plaintiff. Civil records go back to 1992 and on computer since 1995. Search free at http://208.210.219.132/courtinfo/vadistrict/select.jsp?court=. Also search via LOPAS; call 804-786-5511.

Criminal Records: Access: Mail, online, in person. Both court and visitors may perform in person searches. No search fee. Required to search: name, years to search; also helpful: DOB and signed release. Criminal records go back to 1992 and on computer

since 1995. Online access to criminal records is the same as civil.

General Information: Public Access terminal is available. No juvenile, sealed records released. Copy fee: $1.00 per page. No cert fee. Payee: General District Court. Personal checks accepted. Visa, MC accepted. Prepayment required. Mail requests: SASE required. Mail turnaround time 5 days.

Newport News City

7th Circuit Court
2500 Washington Ave, Newport News, VA 23607; 757-926-8561; Fax: 757-926-8531. Hours: 8AM-4:45PM (EST). *Felony, Civil Actions Over $15,000, Probate.*

Civil Records: Access: Mail, online, in person. Both court and visitors may perform in person searches. No search fee. Required to search: name, years to search. Civil cases indexed by defendant, plaintiff. Civil records on computer from 1987, prior on index books. Online access free at http://208.210.219.132/courtinfo/vacircuit/select.jsp?court=. For information about the statewide online systems, see the state introduction. Mail access only available for old records.

Criminal Records: Access: Online, in person. Visitors must perform in person searches for themselves. No search fee. Required to search: name, years to search. Criminal records on computer from 1987, on index books from 1985 to 1987, prior on judgment books. Online access to criminal records is the same as civil.

General Information: Public Access terminal is available. No adoption, juvenile, sealed records released. Copy fee: $.50 per page. Cert fee: $2.00. Payee: Clerk of Circuit Court. In state personal checks accepted. Prepayment required. Mail requests: SASE requested. Turnaround time 1 day.

7th General District Court
2500 Washington Ave, Newport News, VA 23607; Civil phone: 757-926-3520; Criminal phone: 757-926-8811; Fax: 757-926-8496. Hours: 7:30AM-4PM (EST). *Misdemeanor, Civil Actions Under $15,000, Eviction, Small Claims.*

Civil Records: Access: Phone, fax, mail, in person. Visitors must perform in person searches for themselves. No search fee. Required to search: name, years to search. Civil cases go back to 10 years. Search free at http://208.210.219.132/courtinfo/vadistrict/select.jsp?court=. Also search via LOPAS; call 804-786-5511.

Criminal Records: Access: Phone, fax, mail, online, in person. Both court and visitors may perform in person searches. No search fee. Required to search: name, years to search. Criminal records on computer on index cards since 1985, prior records at Circuit Court. Online access to criminal records is the same as civil.

General Information: Public Access terminal is available. No juvenile, sealed records released. Copy fee: $1.00 for first page, $.50 each add'l. No cert fee. Payee: General District Court. Personal checks accepted. Credit cards accepted: Visa, MC (criminal only). Prepayment required. Mail turnaround time 1-2 days.

Norfolk City

4th Circuit Court
100 St Paul's Blvd, Norfolk, VA 23510; 757-664-4380; Civil phone: 757-664-4387; Criminal phone: 757-664-4384; Probate phone: 757-664-4385; Fax: 757-664-4581. Hours: 8:45AM-4:45PM (EST). *Felony, Civil Actions Over $15,000, Probate.*

Civil Records: Access: Online, in person. Both court and visitors may perform in person searches. Search fee: $10.00. Required to search: name, years to search. Civil cases indexed by defendant, plaintiff. Civil

records on computer back to 1993, docket books back to 1800s. Online access free at http://208.210.219.132/courtinfo/vacircuit/select.jsp?court=. For information about the statewide online systems, see the state introduction.

Criminal Records: Access: Online, in person. Both the court and visitors may perform in person searches. Search fee: $10.00. Required to search: name, years to search, DOB, SSN, signed release. Criminal records go back to 1972; on computer back to 1993, docket books back to 1800s. Online access to dockets is free at http://208.210.219.132/courtinfo/vacircuit/select.jsp?court=.

General Information: Public Access terminal is available. No juvenile, sealed records released. Copy fee: $.50 per page. Cert fee: $2.00. Payee: Clerk of Circuit Court. Personal checks accepted. Prepayment required.

4th General District Court
811 E City Hall Ave, Norfolk, VA 23510; 757-664-4910; Civil phone: 757-664-4913/4; Criminal phone: 757-664-4915/6. Hours: 8AM-4PM (EST). *Misdemeanor, Civil Actions Under $15,000, Eviction, Small Claims.*

Civil Records: Access: Mail, online, in person. Visitors must perform in person searches for themselves. Search fee: $10.00 per name. Required to search: name, years to search. Civil cases indexed by defendant, plaintiff. Civil records in files, on computer from 1992. Search free at http://208.210.219.132/courtinfo/vadistrict/select.jsp?court=. Also search via LOPAS; call 804-786-5511.

Criminal Records: Access: Mail, online, in person. Visitors must perform in person searches for themselves. Search fee: $10.00. Required to search: name, years to search. Criminal records in files, on computer from 1992. Online access to criminal records is the same as civil.

General Information: Public Access terminal is available. No juvenile, sealed, or adoption records released. Copy fee: $1.00 per page. Cert fee: $1.00. Payee: Norfolk General District Court. Personal checks accepted. Prepayment required. Mail turnaround time 1-2 weeks.

Northampton County

2nd Circuit Court
PO Box 36 (16404 Courthouse Rd), Eastville, VA 23347-0036; 757-678-0465; Fax: 757-678-5410. Hours: 9AM-4:30PM (EST). *Felony, Civil Actions Over $15,000, Probate.* Note: Oldest continuous records in the USA.

Civil Records: Access: Phone, fax, mail, online, in person. Both court and visitors may perform in person searches. No search fee. Required to search: name, years to search. Civil cases indexed by defendant, plaintiff. Civil records on index books from 1632; on computer back to 1993. Search free online at http://208.210.219.132/courtinfo/vacircuit/select.jsp?court=. Also search via LOPAS; call 804-786-5511.

Criminal Records: Access: Phone, fax, mail, online, in person. Both court and visitors may perform in person searches. No search fee. Required to search: name, years to search, DOB. Criminal records on index books from 1632; on computer back to 1993, some previous. Online access to criminal index records is the same as civil.

General Information: Public Access terminal is available. (Index goes back to 7/1997.) No juvenile, sealed records released. Will fax results for $.75 per page. Copy fee: $.50 per page. Cert fee: $1.00. Payee: Clerk of Circuit Court. Personal checks accepted. Prepayment required. Mail requests: SASE required. Mail turnaround time 1 week.

Northampton General District Court PO Box 1289, Eastville, VA 23347; 757-678-0466. Hours: 8:30AM-4:30PM (EST). *Misdemeanor, Civil Actions Under $15,000, Eviction, Small Claims.*
Civil Records: Access: Mail, online, in person. Only the court performs in person searches; visitors may not. No search fee. Required to search: name, years to search. Civil cases indexed by defendant, plaintiff. Civil records on computer since 1990. Search free at http://208.210.219.132/courtinfo/vadistrict/select.jsp?court=. Also search via LOPAS; call 804-786-5511.
Criminal Records: Access: Mail, online, in person. Only the court performs in person searches; visitors may not. No search fee. Required to search: name, years to search, DOB or SSN. Criminal records on computer since 1990. Online access to criminal records is the same as civil.
General Information: Copy fee: $.50 per page. No cert fee. Payee: General District Court. Personal checks accepted. Mail requests: SASE required. Mail turnaround time 1-2 days.

Northumberland County

15th Circuit Court PO Box 217, Heathsville, VA 22473; 804-580-3700; Fax: 804-580-2261. Hours: 8:30AM-4:45PM (EST). *Felony, Civil Actions Over $15,000, Probate.*
Civil Records: Access: Mail, online, in person. Both court and visitors may perform in person searches. No search fee. Required to search: name, years to search. Civil cases indexed by defendant, plaintiff. Civil records on index books from 1650. Online access free at http://208.210.219.132/courtinfo/vacircuit/select.jsp?court=. For information about the statewide online systems, see the state introduction.
Criminal Records: Access: Mail, online, in person. Both court and visitors may perform in person searches. No search fee. Required to search: name, years to search, DOB. Criminal records on index books from 1650. Online access to criminal records is the same as civil.
General Information: No juvenile, sealed records released. Copy fee: $.50 per page. No cert fee. Payee: Clerk of Circuit Court. Personal checks accepted. Turnaround time 1-2 days.

15th General District Court Northumberland Courthouse, PO Box 114, Heathsville, VA 22473; 804-580-4323; Fax: 804-580-6702. Hours: 8AM-4:30PM (EST). *Misdemeanor, Civil Actions Under $15,000, Eviction, Small Claims.*
Civil Records: Access: Online, in person. Visitors must perform in person searches for themselves. No search fee. Required to search: name, years to search. Civil cases indexed by defendant, plaintiff. Civil records on index books; on computer since 1994. Search free at http://208.210.219.132/courtinfo/vadistrict/select.jsp?court=. Also search via LOPAS; call 804-786-5511.
Criminal Records: Access: Online, in person. Visitors must perform in person searches for themselves. No search fee. Required to search: name, years to search, DOB; also helpful: SSN. Criminal records on index books back to 1991; on computer since 1995. Online access to criminal records is the same as civil.
General Information: Public Access terminal is available. No juvenile, sealed records released. Copy fee: $1.00 for first page, $.10 each add'l. No cert fee. Payee: Clerk of District Court. Personal checks accepted. Visa, MC accepted. Prepayment required.

Norton City

Circuit & District Courts, VA.
Note: See Wise County

Nottoway County

11th Circuit Court Courthouse, PO Box 25, Nottoway, VA 23955; 434-645-9043; Fax: 434-645-2201. Hours: 8:30AM-4:30PM (EST). *Felony, Civil Actions Over $15,000, Probate.*
Civil Records: Access: Mail, online, in person. Both court and visitors may perform in person searches. Search fee: $10.00 per hour. Required to search: name, years to search. Civil cases indexed by defendant, plaintiff. Civil records on index books from late 1700s; on computer back to 2000. Search free online at http://208.210.219.132/courtinfo/vacircuit/select.jsp?court=. Also search via LOPAS; call 804-786-5511.
Criminal Records: Access: Online, in person. Visitors must perform in person searches for themselves. No search fee. Required to search: name, years to search; also helpful: DOB, SSN. Criminal records on index books from late 1700s; on computer back to 2000. Online access to criminal records is the same as civil.
General Information: Public Access terminal is available. No juvenile, sealed records released. Fee to fax results is $1.00 per document. Copy fee: $.50 per page. Cert fee: $2.00. Payee: Clerk's Office. Personal checks accepted. Prepayment required. Mail requests: SASE required. Mail turnaround time 1-2 days.

11th General District Court PO Box 25, Nottoway, VA 23955; 434-645-9312; Fax: 434-645-8584. Hours: 8AM-4:15PM (EST). *Misdemeanor, Civil Actions Under $15,000, Eviction, Small Claims.*
Civil Records: Access: Mail, online, in person. Both court and visitors may perform in person searches. No search fee. Required to search: name, years to search. Civil cases indexed by defendant, plaintiff. Civil records on index cards from 1986, on computer the past 10 years. Only court can search prior to 1989. Search free at http://208.210.219.132/courtinfo/vadistrict/select.jsp?court=. Also search via LOPAS; call 804-786-5511.
Criminal Records: Access: Mail, online, in person. Both court and visitors may perform in person searches. No search fee. Required to search: name, years to search; also helpful: DOB, SSN. Criminal records on index cards from 1986, on computer the past 10 years Only court can search prior to 1989. Online access to criminal records is the same as civil.
General Information: Public Access terminal is available. No juvenile records released. Copy fee: $1.00 for first page, $.50 each add'l. No cert fee. Payee: Nottoway District Court. Personal checks accepted. Prepayment required. Mail requests: SASE required. Mail turnaround time 2-3 days.

Orange County

16th Circuit Court PO Box 230, Orange, VA 22960; 540-672-4030; Fax: 540-672-2939. Hours: 8:30AM-4:30PM (EST). *Felony, Civil Actions Over $15,000, Probate.*
Civil Records: Access: Online, in person. Both court and visitors may perform in person searches. No search fee. Required to search: name, years to search. Civil cases indexed by defendant, plaintiff. Civil records on computer since 1989, in index books from 1734 for deeds, from 1853 for births, from 1912 for marriages. Search free online at http://208.210.219.132/courtinfo/vacircuit/select.jsp?court=. Also search via LOPAS; call 804-786-5511.
Criminal Records: Access: Phone, fax, mail, online, in person. Both court and visitors may perform in person searches. No search fee. Required to search: name, years to search, DOB; also helpful: SSN. Criminal records on computer since 1989, in index

books from 1734. Online access to criminal records is the same as civil.
General Information: Public Access terminal is available. No juvenile, sealed records released. No fee to fax results. Copy fee: $.50 per page. No cert fee. Payee: Clerk of Circuit Court. Personal checks accepted. Prepayment required. Mail turnaround time 1 week-10 days.

16th General District Court Orange County Courthouse, PO Box 821, Orange, VA 22960; 540-672-3150; Fax: 540-672-9438. Hours: 8:30AM-4:30PM (EST). *Misdemeanor, Civil Actions Under $15,000, Eviction, Small Claims.*
Civil Records: Access: Mail, online, in person. Only the court performs in person searches; visitors may not. No search fee. Required to search: name, years to search. Civil cases indexed by defendant, plaintiff. Civil records on index books from 1800s, on computer from 1990. Search free at http://208.210.219.132/courtinfo/vadistrict/select.jsp?court=. Also search via LOPAS; call 804-786-5511.
Criminal Records: Access: Mail, online, in person. Only the court performs in person searches; visitors may not. No search fee. Required to search: name, years to search, DOB; also helpful: SSN. Criminal records on index books from 1800s, on computer from 1990. Online access to criminal records is the same as civil.
General Information: No juvenile, sealed records released. Copy fee: $1.00 for first page, $.50 each add'l. Cert fee: $1.00 for 1st page, $.50 each add'l. Payee: Clerk of District Court. In state checks accepted. Visa, MasterCard accepted. Prepayment required. Mail turnaround time 1-2 days.

Page County

26th Circuit Court 116 S Court St, #A, Luray, VA 22835; 540-743-4064; Fax: 540-743-2338. Hours: 9AM-5PM (EST). *Felony, Civil Actions Over $15,000, Probate.*
Civil Records: Access: Online, in person. Visitors must perform in person searches for themselves. No search fee. Required to search: name, years to search. Civil cases indexed by defendant, plaintiff. Civil records on index books from 1831. Computerized records go back to 1995. Online access free at http://208.210.219.132/courtinfo/vacircuit/select.jsp?court=. For information about the statewide online systems, see the state introduction.
Criminal Records: Access: Online, in person. Visitors must perform in person searches for themselves. No search fee. Required to search: name, years to search, DOB; also helpful: SSN. Criminal records on index books from 1831. Computerized records go back to 1995. Online access to criminal records is the same as civil.
General Information: Public Access terminal is available. No juvenile, sealed records released. Copy fee: $.50 per page. Cert fee: $2.00. Payee: Ron Wilson, Clerk. No second party checks accepted. Prepayment required.

26th General District Court 116 S Court St, Luray, VA 22835; 540-743-5705. Hours: 8AM-4:30PM (EST). *Misdemeanor, Civil Actions Under $15,000, Eviction, Small Claims.*
Civil Records: Access: Mail, online, in person. Both court and visitors may perform in person searches. No search fee. Required to search: name, years to search. Civil cases indexed by defendant, plaintiff. Civil records on computer back to 1/90. Search free at http://208.210.219.132/courtinfo/vadistrict/select.jsp?court=. Also search via LOPAS; call 804-786-5511.
Criminal Records: Access: Mail, online, in person. Both court and visitors may perform in person searches. No search fee. Required to search: name, years to search; also helpful: DOB. Criminal records

on computer back to 1/90. Online access to criminal records is the same as civil.

General Information: Public Access terminal is available. No sealed records released. Cert fee: $1.00. Payee: District Court. Personal checks accepted. Mail requests: SASE requested. Turnaround time 7-10 days.

Patrick County

21st Circuit Court PO Box 148, Stuart, VA 24171; 276-694-7213. Hours: 9AM-5PM (EST). *Felony, Civil Actions Over $15,000, Probate.*
Civil Records: Access: In person, online. Visitors must perform in person searches for themselves. No search fee. Required to search: name, years to search. Civil cases indexed by plaintiff. Civil records on index books from 1791. Search free online at http://208.210.219.132/courtinfo/vacircuit/select.jsp?court=. Also search via LOPAS; call 804-786-5511.
Criminal Records: Access: Online, in person. Visitors must perform in person searches for themselves. No search fee. Required to search: name, years to search; also helpful: DOB, SSN. Criminal records on index books from 1791. Online access to criminal records is the same as civil.
General Information: No juvenile, sealed records released. Copy fee: $.50 per page. Cert fee: $2.00. Payee: Clerk of Circuit Court. Personal checks accepted. Prepayment required.

21st General District Court PO Box 149, Stuart, VA 24171; 276-694-7258; Fax: 276-694-5614. Hours: 8:30AM-5PM (EST). *Misdemeanor, Civil Actions Under $15,000, Eviction, Small Claims.*
Civil Records: Access: Mail, fax, online, in person. Both court and visitors may perform in person searches. No search fee. Required to search: name, years to search. Civil cases indexed by defendant, plaintiff. Civil records go back to 1992; on computer from 10/94. Search free at http://208.210.219.132/courtinfo/vadistrict/select.jsp?court=. Also search via LOPAS; call 804-786-5511.
Criminal Records: Access: Mail, online, in person. Both court and visitors may perform in person searches. No search fee. Required to search: name, years to search, DOB; also helpful: SSN. Criminal records go back to 1992; on computer from 10/94. Online access to criminal records is the same as civil.
General Information: Public Access terminal is available. No juvenile, sealed records released. No cert fee. Mail requests: SASE requested. Turnaround time 1 week.

Petersburg City

11th Circuit Court 7 Courthouse Ave, Petersburg, VA 23803; 804-733-2367; Fax: 804-732-5548. Hours: 8AM-4PM (EST). *Felony, Civil Actions Over $15,000, Probate.*
Civil Records: Access: Online, in person. Visitors must perform in person searches for themselves. Search fee: none. Required to search: name, years to search. Civil cases indexed by defendant, plaintiff. Civil records on index books back to 1784; on computer back to 1988. Online access free at http://208.210.219.132/courtinfo/vacircuit/select.jsp?court=. For information about the statewide online systems, see the state introduction.
Criminal Records: Access: Online, in person. Visitors must perform in person searches for themselves. Search fee: none. Required to search: name, years to search; also helpful: DOB, SSN. Criminal records go back to 1970; on computer back to 1996. Online access to criminal records is the same as civil.
General Information: No juvenile, sealed or adoption records released. Copy fee: $.50 per page. Cert fee: $2.00. Payee: Petersburg Circuit Court

Clerk. Personal checks accepted. Out of state checks not accepted. Prepayment required.

11th Judicial District Court 35 E Tabb St, Petersburg, VA 23803; 804-733-2374; Civil phone: X4153; Criminal phone: X4152; Fax: 804-733-2375 (Attn: Civil or Crimnal). Hours: 8AM-4PM (EST). *Misdemeanor, Civil Actions Under $15,000, Eviction, Small Claims.*
Civil Records: Access: Fax, mail, online, in person. Both court and visitors may perform in person searches. No search fee. Required to search: name, years to search. Civil cases indexed by defendant, plaintiff. Civil records on index books back to 1983, computerized since 1992. Search free at http://208.210.219.132/courtinfo/vadistrict/select.jsp?court=. Also search via LOPAS; call 804-786-5511.
Criminal Records: Access: Fax, mail, online, in person. Both court and visitors may perform in person searches. No search fee. Required to search: name, years to search, DOB; also helpful: SSN. Criminal records indexed on books for 11 years; on computer back to 1992. Online access to criminal records is the same as civil.
General Information: Public Access terminal is available. (Available M,W,TH,F after 1PM.) No sealed records released. Copy fee: $1.00 for first 2 pages. Add $.50 per page thereafter. Cert fee: $1.00 plus $.50 per page after second. Payee: General District Court. In state personal checks accepted. Prepayment required. Mail turnaround time 1 week.

Pittsylvania County

22nd Circuit Court PO Drawer 31, Chatham, VA 24531; 434-432-7887; Fax: 434-432-7913. Hours: 8:30AM-5PM (EST). *Felony, Civil Actions Over $15,000, Probate.*
Civil Records: Access: Online, in person. Visitors must perform in person searches for themselves. No search fee. Required to search: name, years to search. Civil cases indexed by defendant, plaintiff. Civil records on index books back to 1767; computerized records since 1995. Online access free at http://208.210.219.132/courtinfo/vacircuit/select.jsp?court=. For information about the statewide online systems, see the state introduction.
Criminal Records: Access: Online, in person. Visitors must perform in person searches for themselves. No search fee. Required to search: name, years to search, DOB, SSN. Criminal records on index books back to 1767; computerized records since 1995. Online access free at http://208.210.219.132/courtinfo/vacircuit/select.jsp?court=. For information about the statewide online systems, see the state introduction.
General Information: Public Access terminal is available. No juvenile, sealed records released. Copy fee: $.25 per page. Cert fee: $2.00. Payee: Clerk of Circuit Court. Personal checks accepted. Prepayment required.

22nd General District Court Pittsylvania Courthouse Annex 2nd Flr, PO Box 695, Chatham, VA 24531; 434-432-7879; Fax: 434-432-7915. Hours: 8:30AM-4:30PM (EST). *Misdemeanor, Civil Actions Under $15,000, Eviction, Small Claims.*
www.courts.state.va.us/courts/gd/Pittsylvania/home.html
Civil Records: Access: Online, in person. Visitors must perform in person searches for themselves. No search fee. Required to search: name, years to search. Civil cases indexed by defendant, plaintiff. Civil records on computer since 1994. Search free at http://208.210.219.132/courtinfo/vadistrict/select.jsp?court=. Also search via LOPAS; call 804-786-5511.
Criminal Records: Access: Online, in person. Visitors must perform in person searches for themselves. No search fee. Required to search: name,

years to search. Criminal records on computer since 1994. Online access to criminal records is the same as civil.
General Information: Public Access terminal is available. No juvenile, sealed records released. Copy fee: $.25 per page. No cert fee. Payee: General District Court. Personal checks accepted.

Poquoson City

Circuit & District Courts Note: See York County

Portsmouth City

Circuit Court PO Drawer 1217, Portsmouth, VA 23705; 757-393-8671; Fax: 757-399-4826. Hours: 8:30AM-5:30PM (EST). *Felony, Civil Actions Over $15,000, Probate.*
Civil Records: Access: Mail, online, in person. Visitors must perform in person searches for themselves. Search fee: $10.00 per name. Required to search: name, years to search. Civil cases indexed by defendant, plaintiff. Civil records on computer back to 6/1987, prior on index books back to 1858. Online access free at http://208.210.219.132/courtinfo/vacircuit/select.jsp?court=. For information about the statewide online systems, see the state introduction. Phone access limited to simple requests.
Criminal Records: Access: Mail, online, in person. Both court and visitors may perform in person searches. Search fee: $10.00 per name. Required to search: name, years to search, DOB; also helpful: SSN. Criminal records on computer back to 6/1987, prior indexed on books back to 1858. Online access to criminal records is the same as civil.
General Information: Public Access terminal is available. No juvenile, sealed records released. Copy fee: $.50 per page. Cert fee: $2.00. Payee: Cynthia P Morrison, Clerk. Business checks accepted. No credit cards accepted. Prepayment required.

General District Court PO Box 129, Portsmouth, VA 23705; Civil phone: 757-393-8624; Criminal phone: 757-393-8681; Fax: 757-393-8634. Hours: 8:30AM-4:30PM (EST). *Misdemeanor, Civil Actions Under $15,000, Eviction, Small Claims.* Note: Traffic Division: 757-393-8506.
Civil Records: Access: Online, in person. Visitors must perform in person searches for themselves. No search fee. Required to search: name, years to search. Civil cases indexed by defendant, plaintiff. Civil records on computer from 4/87, from 1983 to 4/87 paper files only. Search free at http://208.210.219.132/courtinfo/vadistrict/select.jsp?court=. Also search via LOPAS; call 804-786-5511.
Criminal Records: Access: Mail, fax, online, in person. Both court and visitors may perform in person searches. Search fee: $7.00 per name. Required to search: name, years to search; also helpful: DOB, SSN. Criminal records on computer and case (paper files) maintained for 10 years. Online access to criminal records is the same as civil.
General Information: Public Access terminal is available. Juvenile, sealed records not released. No copy fee. No cert fee. Payee: Clerk of General District Court. Personal checks accepted. Visa, MC accepted. Mail requests: SASE required. Mail turnaround time within 14 days.

Powhatan County

11th Circuit Court PO Box 37, Powhatan, VA 23139-0037; 804-598-5660; Fax: 804-598-5608. Hours: 8:30AM-5PM (EST). *Felony, Civil Actions Over $15,000, Probate.*
Civil Records: Access: In person, online. Visitors must perform in person searches for themselves. No search fee. Required to search: name, years to search.

Civil cases indexed by defendant, plaintiff. Civil records on index books from 1777, on computer from 1993. Remote online access to court case indexes is via LOPAS; call 804-786-5511 to apply.

Criminal Records: Access: In person, online. Visitors must perform in person searches for themselves. No search fee. Required to search: name, years to search, signed release; also helpful: SSN. Criminal records on index books from 1777, on computer from 1993. Remote online access to court case indexes is via LOPAS; call 804-786-5511 to apply.

General Information: Public Access terminal is available. No juvenile, sealed records released. Copy fee: $.50 per page. Cert fee: $2.00. Payee: Clerk of Court. Personal checks accepted. Prepayment required. Will bill copy fees.

11th Judicial District Court
Courthouse, 3880 D Old Buckingham Rd, Powhatan, VA 23139; 804-598-5665; Fax: 804-598-5608. Hours: 8:30AM-5PM (EST). *Misdemeanor, Civil Actions Under $15,000, Eviction, Small Claims.*

Civil Records: Access: Phone, fax, mail, online, in person. Only the court performs in person searches; visitors may not. No search fee. Required to search: name, years to search. Civil cases indexed by defendant. Civil records on index cards for 10 yrs, on computer from 1992. Search free at http://208.210.219.132/courtinfo/vadistrict/select.jsp?court=. Also search via LOPAS; call 804-786-5511.

Criminal Records: Access: Phone, fax, mail, online, in person. Only the court performs in person searches; visitors may not. No search fee. Required to search: name, years to search, DOB; also helpful: SSN. Criminal records on index cards for 10 yrs, on computer from 1993. Online access to criminal records is the same as civil.

General Information: No juvenile, sealed records released. No fee to fax results. Local faxing only. Copy fee: $.50 each for 1st two; $25. Each add'l. No cert fee. Payee: Powhatan District Court. Personal checks accepted. Turnaround time 1 week.

Prince Edward County

Circuit Court PO Box 304, Court House, 111 S St, Farmville, VA 23901-0304; 434-392-5145. Hours: 8:30AM-4:30PM (EST). *Felony, Civil Actions Over $15,000, Probate.*

Civil Records: Access: Online, in person. Visitors must perform in person searches for themselves. No search fee. Required to search: name, years to search. Civil cases indexed by defendant, plaintiff. Civil records on computer from 1990, books from 1930s. Remote online access to court case indexes is via LOPAS; call 804-786-5511 to apply.

Criminal Records: Access: Online, in person. Visitors must perform in person searches for themselves. No search fee. Required to search: name, years to search, DOB; also helpful: SSN. Criminal records on computer from 1990, books from 1930s. Online access to criminal records is the same as civil.

General Information: Public Access terminal is available. No juvenile, sealed records released. Copy fee: $.50 per page; court will charge for the time to make copies. Cert fee: $2.00. Payee: Clerk of Circuit Court. Personal checks accepted. Prepayment required.

General District Court PO Box 41, Farmville, VA 23901-0041; 434-392-4024; Fax: 434-392-3800. Hours: 8:30AM-4:30PM (EST). *Misdemeanor, Civil Actions Under $15,000, Eviction, Small Claims.*

Civil Records: Access: Phone, mail, online, in person. Visitors must perform in person searches for themselves. No search fee. Required to search: name, years to search; also helpful: address. Civil cases indexed by defendant, plaintiff. Civil records on computer go back 10 years. Search free at http://208.210.219.132/courtinfo/vadistrict/select.jsp?court=. Also search via LOPAS; call 804-786-5511.

Criminal Records: Access: Mail, online, in person. Visitors must perform in person searches for themselves. No search fee. Required to search: name, years to search; also helpful: DOB, SSN. Criminal records on computer go back 10 years. Online access to criminal records is the same as civil.

General Information: Public Access terminal is available. No juvenile, sealed records released. Will fax results or specific documents for $1.00 per page. Copy fee: $1.00 per page. No cert fee. Payee: Clerk of District Court. Personal checks accepted. Prepayment required. Mail requests: SASE required. Mail turnaround time 1 week.

Prince George County

Circuit Court PO Box 98, Prince George, VA 23875; 804-733-2640; Fax: 804-861-5721. Hours: 8:30AM-5PM (EST). *Felony, Civil Actions Over $15,000, Probate.*

Civil Records: Access: Online, in person. Visitors must perform in person searches for themselves. No search fee. Required to search: name, years to search. Civil cases indexed by defendant, plaintiff. Civil records on index books since 1930s, computerized since 04/96. Search free online at http://208.210.219.132/courtinfo/vacircuit/select.jsp?court=. Also search via LOPAS; call 804-786-5511.

Criminal Records: Access: Online, in person. Visitors must perform in person searches for themselves. No search fee. Required to search: name, years to search, DOB; also helpful: SSN. Criminal records on index books since 1930s, computerized since 01/90. Online access to criminal records is the same as civil.

General Information: Public Access terminal is available. No juvenile or sealed records released. Copy fee: $.50 per page. No cert fee. Payee: Clerk of the Circuit Court. Personal checks accepted. Prepayment required.

6th General District Court
P.C. Courthouse, PO Box 187, Prince George, VA 23875; 804-733-2783. Hours: 8:30AM-4:30PM (EST). *Misdemeanor, Civil Actions Under $15,000, Eviction, Small Claims.*

Civil Records: Access: Online, in person. Both court and visitors may perform in person searches. No search fee. Required to search: name, years to search. Civil cases indexed by defendant, plaintiff. Civil records on computer since 1991, prior on books since 1985. Search free at http://208.210.219.132/courtinfo/vadistrict/select.jsp?court=. Also search via LOPAS; call 804-786-5511.

Criminal Records: Access: Online, in person. Both court and visitors may perform in person searches. No search fee. Required to search: name, years to search; also helpful: SSN. Criminal records on computer since 1991, prior on books since 1985. Online access to criminal records is the same as civil.

General Information: Public Access terminal is available. No juvenile records released. No copy fee. No cert fee. Payee: Prince George Combined Court.

Prince William County

31st Circuit Court 9311 Lee Ave, Manassas, VA 20110; 703-792-6015; Civil phone: 703-792-6021; Criminal phone: 703-792-6031; Probate phone: 703-792-6085; Fax: 703-792-4721. Hours: 8:30AM-5PM (EST). *Felony, Civil Actions Over $15,000, Probate.*

www.pwcgov.org/ccourt

Civil Records: Access: In person only. Visitors must perform in person searches for themselves. No search fee. Required to search: name, years to search. Civil

cases indexed by defendant, plaintiff. Civil records on computer since 1989; prior on microfiche or books to 1939. Remote online access to court case indexes is via LOPAS; call 804-786-5511 to apply.

Criminal Records: Access: Mail, in person. Both court and visitors may perform in person searches. Search fee: $10.00 per name. Required to search: name, years to search, DOB; also helpful: SSN. Criminal records on computer since 1989; prior on microfiche or books to 1939.

General Information: Public Access terminal is available. No juvenile records released. Copy fee: $.50 per page. Cert fee: $2.00. Payee: Clerk of Circuit Court. Personal checks accepted. Prepayment required. Mail turnaround time 1 week.

31st General District Court
9311 Lee Ave, Manassas, VA 20110; Civil phone: 703-792-6149; Criminal phone: 703-792-6141; Fax: 703-792-6121. Hours: 8AM-4PM (EST). *Misdemeanor, Civil Actions Under $15,000, Eviction, Small Claims.*

www.courts.state.va.us/courts/gd/Prince_William/home.html

Civil Records: Access: Mail, fax, online, in person. Both court and visitors may perform in person searches. No search fee. Required to search: name, years to search. Civil cases indexed by defendant, plaintiff. Civil records on computer go back 10 years. Search free at http://208.210.219.132/courtinfo/vadistrict/select.jsp?court=. Also search via LOPAS; call 804-786-5511.

Criminal Records: Access: Mail, fax, online, in person. Both court and visitors may perform in person searches. No search fee. Required to search: name, years to search. Criminal records on computer go back 10 years. Online access to criminal records is the same as civil.

General Information: Public Access terminal is available. No juvenile or sealed records released. Copy fee: $1.00 copy fee for first 2 pages. Add $.50 per page thereafter. No cert fee. Payee: Clerk G.D.C. Personal checks accepted. Prepayment required. Mail requests: SASE required. Mail turnaround time 10 days.

Pulaski County

27th Circuit Court 45 3rd St NW #101, Pulaski, VA 24301; 540-980-7825; Fax: 540-980-7835. Hours: 8:30AM-4:30PM (EST). *Felony, Civil Actions Over $15,000, Probate.*

www.pulaskicircuitcourt.com

Civil Records: Access: Online, in person. Visitors must perform in person searches for themselves. No search fee. Required to search: name, years to search. Civil cases indexed by defendant, plaintiff. Civil records on index books from 1839, online since 1998. Online access to court records free at http://records.pulaskicircuitcourt.com/splash.jsp. Registration required; search by name, document type or number. Also, access is free at http://208.210.219.132/courtinfo/vacircuit/select.jsp?court=.

Criminal Records: Access: Online, in person. Visitors must perform in person searches for themselves. No search fee. Required to search: name, years to search, DOBV; also helpful: SSN. Criminal records on index books from 1839, online since 1998. Online access to criminal records is the same as civil. This agency will perform no record checks and refer all requests to the State Police.

General Information: Public Access terminal is available. No juvenile, sealed records released. Copy fee: $.50 per page. Cert fee: $1.00. Payee: Clerk of Court. Personal checks accepted. Prepayment required.

27th General District Court 45 3rd St NW #102, Pulaski, VA 24301; 540-980-7470; Fax: 540-980-7792. Hours: 8:30AM-4:30PM (EST). *Misdemeanor, Civil Actions Under $15,000, Eviction, Small Claims.*
Civil Records: Access: Online, in person. Visitors must perform in person searches for themselves. No search fee. Required to search: name, years to search. Civil cases indexed by defendant, plaintiff. Civil records on computer since 1991. Search free at http://208.210.219.132/courtinfo/vadistrict/select.jsp?court=. Also search via LOPAS; call 804-786-5511.
Criminal Records: Access: Online, in person. Visitors must perform in person searches for themselves. No search fee. Required to search: name, years to search, DOB; also helpful: SSN. Criminal records on computer since 1991. Online access to criminal records is the same as civil.
General Information: Public Access terminal is available. No juvenile, sealed records released. Copy fee: $.50 per page. No cert fee. Payee: Clerk of General District Court. Personal checks accepted. Visa, MC accepted. Credit cards accepted for fines & costs only. Prepayment required.

Radford City

27th Circuit Court 619 2nd St, Radford, VA 24141; 540-731-3610; Fax: 540-731-3612. Hours: 8AM-5PM (no machine receipts after 4:30PM) (EST). *Felony, Civil Actions Over $15,000, Probate.*
Civil Records: Access: Fax, mail, online, in person. Both court and visitors may perform in person searches. No search fee. Required to search: name, years to search. Civil cases indexed by defendant, plaintiff. Civil records on books from 1892; on computer back to 6/2000. Search free online at http://208.210.219.132/courtinfo/vacircuit/select.jsp?court=. Also search via LOPAS; call 804-786-5511.
Criminal Records: Access: Fax, mail, online, in person. Both court and visitors may perform in person searches. No search fee. Required to search: name, years to search, DOB, signed release; also helpful: SSN. Criminal records on books from 1892; on computer back to 6/2000. Online access to criminal records is the same as civil.
General Information: Public Access terminal is available. No juvenile, sealed or adoption records released. Will fax results $.50 per page. Copy fee: $.50 per page. Cert fee: $2.00. Payee: Radford Circuit Court. Personal checks accepted. Prepayment required. Mail requests: SASE required. Mail turnaround time same day.

27th General District Court 619 2nd St, Radford, VA 24141; 540-731-3609; Fax: 540-731-3692. Hours: 8:30AM-4:30PM (EST). *Misdemeanor, Civil Actions Under $15,000, Eviction, Small Claims.*
Civil Records: Access: Mail, online, in person. Both court and visitors may perform in person searches. Search fee: A search fee may be required. Required to search: name, years to search. Civil cases indexed by defendant, plaintiff. Search free at http://208.210.219.132/courtinfo/vadistrict/select.jsp?court=. Also search via LOPAS; call 804-786-5511.
Criminal Records: Access: Fax, mail, online, in person. Both court and visitors may perform in person searches. Search fee: None, unless it is a lengthy search. Required to search: name, years to search, DOB, SSN, signed release. Criminal records on computer since 1989. Online access to criminal records is the same as civil.
General Information: Public Access terminal is available. No juvenile, sealed records released. Will fax results $.50 per page. Copy fee: $.50 per page. No cert fee. Payee: District Court. Personal checks

accepted. Prepayment required. Mail turnaround time 7 days or longer.

Rappahannock County

20th Circuit Court 238 Gay St (PO Box 517), Washington, VA 22747; 540-675-5350. Hours: 8:30AM-4:30PM (EST). *Felony, Civil Actions Over $15,000, Probate.*
Civil Records: Access: Mail, online, in person. Visitors must perform in person searches for themselves. No search fee. Required to search: name, years to search. Civil cases indexed by defendant, plaintiff. Civil records computerized since 1995, on index cards from 1833, early records archived. Search free online at http://208.210.219.132/courtinfo/vacircuit/select.jsp?court=. Also search via LOPAS; call 804-786-5511. Mail access limited to specific cases only. Court will only do searches as time permits.
Criminal Records: Access: Mail, online, in person. Visitors must perform in person searches for themselves. Search fee: Searches performed only as time permits. Required to search: name, years to search; also helpful: DOB, SSN. Criminal records computerized since 1995, on index cards from 1833, early records archived. Online access to criminal records is the same as civil. Mail access limited to specific cases only.
General Information: Public Access terminal is available. No juvenile, sealed records released. Copy fee: $.50 per page. Cert fee: $2.50 per document. Payee: Clerk of the Circuit Court. Personal checks accepted. Prepayment required. Mail requests: SASE required. Mail turnaround time 1-2 days.

20th Combined District Court PO Box 206, Washington, VA 22747; 540-675-5356. Hours: 8:30AM-4:30PM (EST). *Misdemeanor, Civil Actions Under $15,000, Eviction, Small Claims.*
Civil Records: Access: Mail, online, in person. Both court and visitors may perform in person searches. No search fee. Required to search: name, years to search. Civil cases indexed by defendant, plaintiff. Civil records on computer back to 1994, on index cards back to 1990, prior in Circuit Court. Search free at http://208.210.219.132/courtinfo/vadistrict/select.jsp?court=. Also search via LOPAS; call 804-786-5511.
Criminal Records: Access: Mail, online, in person. Both court and visitors may perform in person searches. No search fee. Required to search: name, years to search, DOB; also helpful: SSN, signed release. Criminal records on computer back to 1994, index cards back to 1985, prior in Circuit Court. Online access to criminal records is the same as civil.
General Information: No juvenile, sealed records released. Copy fee: $1.00 per page. No cert fee. Payee: Clerk of General District Court. Personal checks accepted. Visa, MC accepted. Prepayment required. Mail requests: SASE requested. Turnaround time up to 2 weeks.

Richmond County

15th Circuit Court 101 Court Circle, PO Box 1000, Warsaw, VA 22572; 804-333-3781; Fax: 804-333-5396. Hours: 9AM-5PM (EST). *Felony, Civil Actions Over $15,000, Probate.*
Civil Records: Access: Phone, mail, in person, online. Both court and visitors may perform in person searches. No search fee. Required to search: name, years to search; also helpful: address, SSN. Civil cases indexed by defendant, plaintiff. Civil records archived from 1692. Search free online at http://208.210.219.132/courtinfo/vacircuit/select.jsp?court=. Also search via LOPAS; call 804-786-5511.
Criminal Records: Access: Mail, in person, online. Both court and visitors may perform in person searches. No search fee. Required to search: name,

years to search, DOB; also helpful: address. Criminal records archived from 1692, computerized since 1994. Online access to criminal records is the same as civil.
General Information: No juvenile, sealed records released. Will fax results to local or toll free line. Copy fee: $.50 per page; $1.00 per page if genealogy records. Cert fee: $2.00. Payee: Clerk of Circuit Court. Personal checks accepted. Prepayment required. Mail requests: SASE requested. Turnaround time same day.

15th Judicial District Court Richmond County Courthouse, PO Box 1000, Warsaw, VA 22572; 804-333-4616; Fax: 804-333-3741. Hours: 8AM-4:30PM (EST). *Misdemeanor, Civil Actions Under $15,000, Eviction, Small Claims.*
Civil Records: Access: Mail, online, in person. Both court and visitors may perform in person searches. No search fee. Required to search: name, years to search. Civil cases indexed by defendant, plaintiff. Civil records archived 10 years back; on computer from 1994. Search free at http://208.210.219.132/courtinfo/vadistrict/select.jsp?court=. Also search via LOPAS; call 804-786-5511.
Criminal Records: Access: Mail, online, in person. Both court and visitors may perform in person searches. No search fee. Required to search: name, years to search; also helpful: DOB, SSN. Criminal records archived 10 years back; on computer from 1994. Online access to criminal records is the same as civil.
General Information: Public Access terminal is available. No juvenile, sealed records released. No cert fee. Mail requests: SASE requested. Turnaround time 2 days.

Richmond City

13th Circuit Court - Division I John Marshall Courts Bldg, 400 N 9th St, Richmond, VA 23219; 804-646-6505; Civil phone: 804-646-6536; Criminal phone: 804-646-6553. Hours: 8:45AM-4:45PM (EST). *Felony, Civil Actions Over $15,000, Probate.* www.courts.state.va.us/courts/circuit/Richmond/home.html
Note: Also search for felony records at the Manchester Courthouse location, 10th & Hull St.
Civil Records: Access: Mail, online, in person. Visitors must perform in person searches for themselves. Search fee: none. Required to search: name, years to search. Civil cases indexed by defendant, plaintiff. Civil records on computer from 1987. On microfilm from 1980, on card index from 1970s, on index books from 1600s. Online access free at http://208.210.219.132/courtinfo/vacircuit/select.jsp?court=. For information about the statewide online systems, see the state introduction. A second website is www.vipnet.org/vipnet/clerks/richmondjohnmarshall.html.
Criminal Records: Access: Mail, online, in person. Visitors must perform in person searches for themselves. Search fee: none. Required to search: name, years to search; also helpful: DOB, SSN. Criminal records on computer from 1987. On microfilm from 1980, on card index from 1970s, on index books from 1782. Online access to criminal records is the same as civil.
General Information: Public Access terminal is available. No juvenile, sealed records released. Will not fax results. Copy fee: $.50 per page. Cert fee: $2.00. Payee: Bevill M Dean, Clerk. Personal checks accepted. Prepayment required.

13th General District Court - Civil Division

400 N 9th St Rm 203, Richmond, VA 23219; 804-646-6461. Hours: 8AM-4PM (EST). *Civil Actions Under $15,000, Eviction, Small Claims.*

Civil Records: Access: Phone, mail, online, in person. Both court and visitors may perform in person searches. No search fee. Required to search: name, years to search. Civil cases indexed by defendant, plaintiff. Civil records computerized since 1994 in index books from 1973. Records destroyed after 20 years & 10 years after 1985. Search free at http://208.210.219.132/courtinfo/vadistrict/select.jsp?court=. Also search via LOPAS; call 804-786-5511.

General Information: Public Access terminal is available. No juvenile, sealed records released. Will fax results to toll free line, must be prepaid. Copy fee: $.50 per page. No cert fee. Payee: Clerk of General District Court, Civil Division. Business checks accepted. Prepayment required. Mail requests: SASE required. Mail turnaround time 1-2 days.

13th General District Court - Division II

905 Decatur St, Richmond, VA 23224; 804-646-8990; Fax: 804-646-0387. Hours: 8AM-4PM (EST). *Misdemeanor, Traffic.*

Criminal Records: Access: Mail, online, in person. Both court and visitors may perform in person searches. No search fee. Required to search: name, years to search, DOB; also helpful: SSN. Criminal records on computer from 1986, records prior to 1980 destroyed. For information about the statewide online systems, see the state introduction. Select and search General District Courts at http://208.210.219.132/courtinfo/vadistrict/select.jsp?court=.

General Information: Public Access terminal is available. No juvenile, sealed records released. Copy fee: $1.00 per page. Cert fee: $2.00. Payee: Clerk of General District Court. Personal checks accepted. Prepayment required. Mail turnaround time 1-5 days.

Richmond City - Manchester County

13th Circuit Court Manchester Courthouse, 10th and Hull St, Richmond, VA 23224-4070; 804-646-8470; Fax: 804-646-8122. Hours: 8:45AM-4:45PM (EST). *Felony.*
www.vipnet.org/vipnet/clerks/richmondmanchester.html
Note: Also search for felony records at the john Marshall Courthouse (Division I) location.

Civil Records: Access: Mail, online, in person. Both the court and visitors may perform in person searches. No search fee. Required to search: name, years to search. Civil cases indexed by defendant, plaintiff. Civil records on computer from 1989, on index cards from 1961 to 1988, prior archived in Richmond. Online access free at http://208.210.219.132/courtinfo/vacircuit/select.jsp?court=. For information about the statewide online systems, see the state introduction.

Criminal Records: Access: Mail, online, in person. Both the court and visitors may perform in person searches. No search fee. Required to search: name, years to search. Criminal records on computer from 1989, on index cards from 1961 to 1988, prior archived in Richmond. Online access to criminal records is the same as civil.

General Information: Public Access terminal is available. No juvenile, sealed, adoption records released. Copy fee: $.50 per page. Cert fee: $2.00. Payee: Clerk of Circuit Court. Business checks accepted. Prepayment required. Mail requests: SASE required. Mail turnaround time 1-2 days.

Roanoke County

23rd Circuit Court PO Box 1126, Salem, VA 24153-1126; 540-387-6260. Hours: 8:30AM-4:30PM (EST). *Felony, Civil Actions Over $15,000, Probate.*
www.co.roanoke.va.us

Civil Records: Access: Online, in person. Visitors must perform in person searches for themselves. No search fee. Required to search: name, years to search. Civil cases indexed by defendant, plaintiff. Civil records on computer from 1986, on index books from 1838 to 1986, prior records to Botetourt County. Online access free at http://208.210.219.132/courtinfo/vacircuit/select.jsp?court=. For information about the statewide online systems, see the state introduction.

Criminal Records: Access: Online, in person. Visitors must perform in person searches for themselves. No search fee. Required to search: name, years to search, DOB; also helpful: SSN. Criminal records on computer from 1986, on index books from 1838 to 1986, prior records to Botetourt County. Online access to criminal records is the same as civil.

General Information: Public Access terminal is available. (Terminal is located at the City of Salem Courthouse.) No juvenile, sealed records released. Copy fee: $.50 per page. Cert fee: $2.00. Payee: Clerk of Circuit Court. Personal checks accepted. Prepayment required.

23rd General District Court PO Box 997, Salem, VA 24153; 540-387-6168; Fax: 540-387-6066. Hours: 8:15AM-4:15PM (EST). *Misdemeanor, Civil Actions Under $15,000, Eviction, Small Claims.*
www.co.roanoke.va.us

Civil Records: Access: Mail, online, in person. Both court and visitors may perform in person searches. No search fee. Required to search: name, years to search. Civil cases indexed by defendant, plaintiff. Computerized records the past 10 years, on index cards from 1980. Prior at Circuit Court or Archives. Search free at http://208.210.219.132/courtinfo/vadistrict/select.jsp?court=. Also search via LOPAS; call 804-786-5511.

Criminal Records: Access: Mail, online, in person. Both court and visitors may perform in person searches. No search fee. Required to search: name, years to search, DOB; also helpful: SSN. Computerized records the past 10 years, on index cards from 1980. Prior at Circuit Court or Archives. Online access to criminal records is the same as civil.

General Information: Public Access terminal is available. No sealed records released. Will fax results to local numbers only. Copy fee: $.50 per page. No cert fee. Payee: General. Personal checks accepted. Visa, MC accepted. Not accepted for copy fees. Prepayment required. Mail requests: SASE required. Mail turnaround time 5 days.

Roanoke City

23rd Circuit Court PO Box 2610, Roanoke, VA 24010-2610; Civil phone: 540-853-6702; Criminal phone: 540-853-6723. Hours: 8:15AM-4:45PM (EST). *Felony, Civil Actions Over $15,000, Probate.*
www.co.roanoke.va.us

Civil Records: Access: Mail, online, in person. Visitors must perform in person searches for themselves. No search fee. Required to search: name, years to search. Civil cases indexed by defendant, plaintiff. Civil records on computer from 1986, civil on microfiche from 1884, criminal on index books from 1800s, prior archived. Online access free at http://208.210.219.132/courtinfo/vacircuit/select.jsp?court=. For information about the statewide online systems, see the state introduction.

Criminal Records: Access: Mail, online, in person. Visitors must perform in person searches for themselves. No search fee. Required to search: name, years to search, DOB; also helpful: SSN. Criminal records on computer from 1986, civil on microfiche from 1884, criminal on index books from 1800s, prior archived. Online access to criminal records is the same as civil.

General Information: Public Access terminal is available. No juvenile, sealed records released. Will not fax results. Copy fee: $.50 per page. Cert fee: $2.00. Payee: Clerk of Circuit Court. Personal checks accepted. Prepayment required.

General District Court 315 W Church Ave, 2nd Flr, Roanoke, VA 24016-5007; Civil phone: 540-853-2364; Criminal phone: 540-853-2361. Hours: 8AM-4PM (EST). *Misdemeanor, Civil Actions Under $15,000, Eviction, Small Claims.*
Note: Per state law, the court cannot release DOB and SSN.

Civil Records: Access: Mail, online, in person. Both court and visitors may perform in person searches. Search fee: $1.00 per name. Required to search: name, years to search. Civil cases indexed by defendant, plaintiff. Civil records on computer from 1986, prior on index cards. Select and search District Courts at www.courts.state.va.us/. For information about the statewide online systems, see the state introduction.

Criminal Records: Access: Online, in person. Visitors must perform in person searches for themselves. No search fee. Required to search: name, years to search, DOB; also helpful: SSN. Criminal records on computer from 1986, prior on index cards. Online access to criminal records is the same as civil.

General Information: Public Access terminal is available. (Records go back 10 years.) No juvenile records released. Copy fee: $1.00 per page. No cert fee. Payee: General District Court. Business checks accepted. Prepayment required. Mail requests: SASE required. Mail turnaround time 5 days or more for FOI Act searches.

Rockbridge County

25th Circuit Court Courthouse Sq, 2 S Main St, Lexington, VA 24450; 540-463-2232; Fax: 540-463-3850. Hours: 8:30AM-4:30PM (EST). *Felony, Civil Actions Over $15,000, Probate.*

Civil Records: Access: Phone, mail, online, in person. Both court and visitors may perform in person searches. No search fee. Required to search: name, years to search. Civil cases indexed by defendant, plaintiff. Civil records on computer from 1985, on index books from 1778. Criminal records are easily obtained from the late 1960s. Prior records are not easily accessible. Search free online at http://208.210.219.132/courtinfo/vacircuit/select.jsp?court=. Also search via LOPAS; call 804-786-5511.

Criminal Records: Access: Online, in person. Visitors must perform in person searches for themselves. No search fee. Required to search: name, years to search, DOB. Criminal records on computer from 1985, on index books from 1778. Criminal records are easily obtained from the late 1960s. Prior records are not easily accessible. Online access to criminal records is the same as civil.

General Information: Public Access terminal is available. No juvenile, sealed records released. Copy fee: $.50 per page. Cert fee: $2.50. Payee: Clerk of Circuit Court. Personal checks accepted. Prepayment required. Mail turnaround time 2-3 days.

District Court 150 S Main St, Lexington, VA 24450; 540-463-3631; Fax: 540-463-4213. Hours: 8:30AM-4:30PM (EST). *Misdemeanor, Civil Actions Under $15,000, Eviction, Small Claims.*
Note: Lexington-Rockbridge is a combined district court.

Civil Records: Access: Mail, online, in person. Both court and visitors may perform in person searches. No search fee. Required to search: name, years to search. Civil cases indexed by defendant, plaintiff. Civil records on computer from 1989, on index cards from 1985 to 1989, prior to 1985 at Circuit Court. Records destroyed after 10 years. Search free at http://208.210.219.132/courtinfo/vadistrict/select.jsp?court=. Also search via LOPAS; call 804-786-5511.

Criminal Records: Access: Mail, online, in person. Both court and visitors may perform in person searches. No search fee. Required to search: name, years to search, DOB; also helpful: SSN. Criminal records on computer from late 1989, on index cards from 1985 to 1989, prior to 1985 at Circuit Court. Online access to criminal records is the same as civil.

General Information: Public Access terminal is available. No juvenile, sealed records released. Copy fee: $1.00 each for 1st two; $.50 each add'l. No cert fee. Payee: District Court. Prepayment required. Mail requests: SASE required. Mail turnaround time 5-7 days.

Rockingham County

26th Circuit Court Courthouse, Court Sq, Harrisonburg, VA 22801; Civil phone: 540-564-3114; Criminal phone: 540-564-3118; Fax: 540-564-3127. Hours: 9AM-5PM (EST). *Felony, Civil Actions Over $15,000, Probate.*

Civil Records: Access: Online, in person. Visitors must perform in person searches for themselves. No search fee. Required to search: name, years to search. Civil cases indexed by defendant, plaintiff. Civil records on index cards from the beginning of the county. Online access free at http://208.210.219.132/courtinfo/vacircuit/select.jsp?court=. For information about the statewide online systems, see the state introduction.

Criminal Records: Access: Online, in person. Visitors must perform in person searches for themselves. No search fee. Required to search: name, years to search. Criminal records on index cards from the beginning of the county. Online access to criminal records is the same as civil.

General Information: Public Access terminal is available. (Deeds only.) No juvenile, sealed records released. Copy fee: $.50 per page. Cert fee: $2.00. Payee: Clerk of Circuit Court. Personal checks accepted. Prepayment required.

26th General District Court 53 Court Sq, Harrisonburg, VA 22801; Civil phone: 540-564-3135; Criminal phone: 540-564-3130; Fax: 540-564-3096. Hours: 8AM-4PM (EST). *Misdemeanor, Civil Actions Under $15,000, Eviction, Small Claims.*

Civil Records: Access: Phone, mail, online, in person. Both court and visitors may perform in person searches. Search fee: $3.50 per each 15 minutes. Required to search: name, years to search. Civil cases indexed by defendant, plaintiff. Civil records on computer the past 10 years, on index cards from 1978, prior at Circuit Court. Search free at http://208.210.219.132/courtinfo/vadistrict/select.jsp?court=. Also search via LOPAS; call 804-786-5511.

Criminal Records: Access: Phone, mail, online, in person. Both court and visitors may perform in person searches. No search fee. Required to search: name, years to search, DOB; also helpful: SSN. Criminal records on computer from the past 10 years, on index cards from 1985, prior at Circuit Court. Online access to criminal records is the same as civil.

General Information: Public Access terminal is available. No juvenile, sealed, adoption records released. Copy fee: $.50 per page. Cert fee: included in copy fee. Payee: General District Court. Personal checks accepted. Visa, MC accepted. Prepayment required. Mail requests: SASE required. Mail turnaround time up to 1 week.

Russell County

29th Circuit Court PO Box 435, Lebanon, VA 24266; 276-889-8023; Fax: 276-889-8003. Hours: 8AM-5PM (EST). *Felony, Civil Actions Over $15,000, Probate.*

Civil Records: Access: Online, in person. Both court and visitors may perform in person searches. No search fee. Required to search: name, years to search. Civil cases indexed by defendant, plaintiff. Civil records on computer from 1990, archived from 1809. Search free online at http://208.210.219.132/courtinfo/vacircuit/select.jsp?court=. Also search via LOPAS; call 804-786-5511.

Criminal Records: Access: Online, in person. Both court and visitors may perform in person searches. No search fee. Required to search: name, years to search, signed release. Criminal records on computer from 1990, archived from 1809. Online access to criminal records is the same as civil.

General Information: Public Access terminal is available. No juvenile, sealed records released. Will not fax results. Copy fee: $.50 per page. Cert fee: $3.00. Payee: Clerk of Circuit Court. Personal checks accepted. Prepayment required.

29th General District Court Russell County Courthouse, PO Box 65, Lebanon, VA 24266; 276-889-8051; Fax: 276-889-8091. Hours: 8:30AM-4:30PM (EST). *Misdemeanor, Civil Actions Under $15,000, Eviction, Small Claims.*

Civil Records: Access: Phone, fax, mail, online, in person. Both court and visitors may perform in person searches. No search fee. Required to search: name. Civil cases indexed by defendant, plaintiff. Civil records on computer back to 1993. Search free at http://208.210.219.132/courtinfo/vadistrict/select.jsp?court=. Also search via LOPAS; call 804-786-5511.

Criminal Records: Access: Phone, fax, mail, online, in person. Both court and visitors may perform in person searches. No search fee. Required to search: name, DOB; also helpful: SSN. Criminal records on computer back to 1993; other records back to 1990. Online access to criminal records is the same as civil.

General Information: Public Access terminal is available. No juvenile, sealed records released. No fee to fax results. No copy fee. No cert fee. Turnaround time 2-5 days.

Salem City

23rd Circuit Court 2 E Calhoun St, PO Box 891, Salem, VA 24153; 540-375-3067; Fax: 540-375-4039. Hours: 8:30AM-5PM (EST). *Felony, Civil Actions Over $15,000, Probate.*

Civil Records: Access: Online, in person. Both court and visitors may perform in person searches. No search fee. Required to search: name, years to search. Civil cases indexed by defendant, plaintiff. Civil records on computer from 1985, on index books from 1968, prior at Roanoke Circuit Court. Search free online at http://208.210.219.132/courtinfo/vacircuit/select.jsp?court=. Also search via LOPAS; call 804-786-5511.

Criminal Records: Access: Online, in person. Visitors must perform in person searches for themselves. No search fee. Required to search: name, years to search, DOB; also helpful: SSN. Criminal records on computer from 1985, on index books from 1968, prior at Roanoke Circuit Court. Online access to criminal records is the same as civil.

General Information: Public Access terminal is available. No juvenile, sealed or adoption records released. Copy fee: $.50 per page. Cert fee: $2.00. Payee: Clerk of Circuit Court. Personal checks accepted. Prepayment required.

23rd General District Court 2 E Calhoun St, Salem, VA 24153; 540-375-3044; Fax: 540-375-4024. Hours: 8AM-4PM (EST). *Misdemeanor, Civil Actions Under $15,000, Eviction, Small Claims.*

Civil Records: Access: Online, in person. Visitors must perform in person searches for themselves. No search fee. Required to search: name, years to search. Civil cases indexed by defendant, plaintiff. Civil records on computer for 10 years, prior records at City of Salem Circuit Court. Search free at http://208.210.219.132/courtinfo/vadistrict/select.jsp?court=. Also search via LOPAS; call 804-786-5511.

Criminal Records: Access: Online, in person. Visitors must perform in person searches for themselves. No search fee. Required to search: name, years to search, DOB, SSN. Criminal records on computer for 10 years, prior records at City of Salem Circuit Court. Online access to criminal records is the same as civil.

General Information: Public Access terminal is available. No juvenile, sealed records released. Copy fee: $1.00 per page. Cert fee: $1.00 per page. Payee: General District Court. Personal checks accepted. Prepayment required.

Scott County

Circuit Court 104 E Jackson St, #2, Gate City, VA 24251; 276-386-3801. Hours: 8:30AM-5PM (EST). *Felony, Civil Actions Over $15,000, Probate.*

Civil Records: Access: Phone, mail, online, in person. Both court and visitors may perform in person searches. No search fee. Required to search: name, years to search. Civil cases indexed by defendant, plaintiff. Civil records on index books back to 1815; on computer back to 1999. Search free online at http://208.210.219.132/courtinfo/vacircuit/select.jsp?court=. Also search via LOPAS; call 804-786-5511.

Criminal Records: Access: Mail, online, in person. Both court and visitors may perform in person searches. No search fee. Required to search: name, years to search, DOB; also helpful: SSN. Criminal records on index books back to 1815; on computer back to 1999. Online access to criminal records is the same as civil.

General Information: Public Access terminal is available. No juvenile, sealed records released. Fee to fax results is $4.00 per page. Copy fee: $.50 per page. Cert fee: $2.00. Payee: Mark A. Taylor, Clerk. Personal checks accepted. Prepayment required. Mail requests: SASE required. Mail turnaround time 3-4 days.

30th General District Court 104 E Jackson St, #9, Gate City, VA 24251; 276-386-7341. Hours: 8:15AM-4:45PM (EST). *Misdemeanor, Civil Actions Under $15,000, Eviction, Small Claims.*

Civil Records: Access: Mail, online, in person. Only the court performs in person searches; visitors may not. No search fee. Required to search: name, years to search. Civil cases indexed by plaintiff. Civil records on index books, on computer from 1990. Search free at http://208.210.219.132/courtinfo/vadistrict/select.jsp?court=. Also search via LOPAS; call 804-786-5511.

Criminal Records: Access: Mail, online, in person. Only the court performs in person searches; visitors may not. No search fee. Required to search: name, years to search, DOB; also helpful: SSN. Criminal records on index books, on computer from 1990. Online access to criminal records is the same as civil.

General Information: No juvenile, sealed records released. Copy fee: $1.00 per page. No cert fee.

Payee: General District Court. Personal checks accepted. Prepayment required. Mail requests: SASE required. Mail turnaround time up to 1-2 days.

Shenandoah County

26th Circuit Court 112 S Main St, PO Box 406, Woodstock, VA 22664; 540-459-6150; Fax: 540-459-6155. Hours: 9AM-5PM (EST). *Felony, Civil Actions Over $15,000, Probate.*
Civil Records: Access: Mail, online, in person. Only the court may perform in person searches. No search fee. Required to search: name, years to search. Civil cases indexed by defendant, plaintiff. Civil records on computer from 1996, on index cards from 1772. Search free online at http://208.210.219.132/courtinfo/vacircuit/select.jsp?court=. Also search via LOPAS; call 804-786-5511. Mail access limited to specific cases only.
Criminal Records: Access: Online, in person. Visitors must perform in person searches for themselves. No search fee. Required to search: name, years to search, DOB; also helpful: SSN. Criminal records on computer from 1996, on index cards from 1772. Online access to criminal records is the same as civil.
General Information: No juvenile, sealed records released. Copy fee: $.50 per page. Cert fee: $2.00. Payee: Clerk of Circuit Court. Personal checks accepted. Prepayment required. Mail requests: SASE required. Mail turnaround time 1-2 days.

26th General District Court 114 W Court St, Woodstock, VA 22664; 540-459-6130; Fax: 540-459-7279. Hours: 8:30AM-4:30PM (EST). *Misdemeanor, Civil Actions Under $15,000, Eviction, Small Claims.*
Civil Records: Access: Mail, online, in person. Visitors must perform in person searches for themselves. No search fee. Required to search: name, years to search. Civil cases indexed by defendant, plaintiff. Civil records on computer from 1992, on index cards from 1985, prior at Circuit Court. Search free at http://208.210.219.132/courtinfo/vadistrict/select.jsp?court=. Also search via LOPAS; call 804-786-5511.
Criminal Records: Access: Online, mail, in person. Visitors must perform in person searches for themselves. No search fee. Required to search: name, years to search, DOB; also helpful: SSN. Criminal records on computer from 1992, on index cards from 1985, prior at Circuit Court. Online access to criminal records is the same as civil. This agency will not do criminal record checks and refer all requesters to the State Police or the online system.
General Information: Public Access terminal is available. No sealed or adoption records relapsed. Copy fee: $1.00 minimum for first 2 pages, $.50 each add'l page. No cert fee. Payee: General District Court. Personal checks accepted. Visa/MC credit cards accepted. Accepted for criminal fines only. Prepayment required.

Smyth County

28th Circuit Court 109 W Main St #144, Marion, VA 24354-2510; 276-782-4044; Fax: 276-782-4045. Hours: 9AM-5PM (EST). *Felony, Civil Actions Over $15,000, Probate.*
Civil Records: Access: Mail, fax, online, in person. Both court and visitors may perform in person searches. Search fee: $10.00 per name. Required to search: name, years to search. Civil cases indexed by defendant, plaintiff. Civil records on index cards from 1832, most are computerized since 01/90. Search free online at http://208.210.219.132/courtinfo/vacircuit/select.jsp?court=. Also search via LOPAS; call 804-786-5511.

Criminal Records: Access: Mail, fax, online, in person. Both court and visitors may perform in person searches. Search fee: $10.00 per name. Required to search: name, years to search; also helpful: DOB, SSN. Criminal records on index cards from 1832, most are computerized since 01/90. Online access to criminal records is the same as civil.
General Information: No juvenile, sealed or adoption records released. Fee to fax results is $1.00 per page. Copy fee: $.50 per page. Cert fee: $2.00. Payee: Clerk of Circuit Court. Personal checks accepted. Prepayment required. Mail requests: SASE requested. Turnaround time 1 week.

28th General District Court Smythe County Courthouse, Rm 231, 109 W Main St, Marion, VA 24354; 276-782-4047; Fax: 276-782-4048. Hours: 8:30AM-4:30PM (EST). *Misdemeanor, Civil Actions Under $15,000, Eviction, Small Claims.*
Civil Records: Access: Phone, mail, online, in person. Both court and visitors may perform in person searches. No search fee. Required to search: name, years to search; also helpful: address. Civil cases indexed by defendant, plaintiff. Civil records on computer back to 7/90. Search free at http://208.210.219.132/courtinfo/vadistrict/select.jsp?court=. Also search via LOPAS; call 804-786-5511.
Criminal Records: Access: Phone, mail, online, in person. Both court and visitors may perform in person searches. No search fee. Required to search: name, years to search, DOB; also helpful: SSN. Criminal records on computer back to 7/90. Online access to criminal records is the same as civil.
General Information: Public Access terminal is available. No juvenile, sealed records released. Copy fee: $.50 per page. No cert fee. Payee: General District Court. Personal checks accepted. Visa, MC accepted. Prepayment required. Mail turnaround time 1-2 days.

South Boston City

Circuit & District Courts Note: See Halifax County

Southampton County

5th Circuit Court PO Box 190, Courtland, VA 23837; 757-653-2200. Hours: 8:30AM-5PM (EST). *Felony, Civil Actions Over $15,000, Probate.*
Civil Records: Access: Mail, online, in person. Both court and visitors may perform in person searches. Search fee: $5.00 per name. Required to search: name, years to search. Civil cases indexed by plaintiff. Civil records on index books from 1749; on computer back to 1990. Search free online at http://208.210.219.132/courtinfo/vacircuit/select.jsp?court=. Also search via LOPAS; call 804-786-5511. Will not certify searches.
Criminal Records: Access: Mail, online, in person. Both court and visitors may perform in person searches. Search fee: $5.00. Required to search: name, years to search. Criminal records on index books from 1749; on computer back to 1990. Online access to criminal records is the same as civil. Will not certify searches.
General Information: Public Access terminal is available. No juvenile, sealed, adoption records released. Copy fee: $.50 per page. Payee: Clerk of Circuit Court. Personal checks accepted. Prepayment required. Mail turnaround time 1-5 days.

5th General District Court PO Box 347, Courtland, VA 23837; 757-653-2673. Hours: 8:30AM-4:30PM (EST). *Misdemeanor, Civil Actions Under $15,000, Eviction, Small Claims.*
Civil Records: Access: Mail, online, in person. Both court and visitors may perform in person searches. No search fee. Required to search: name, years to search. Civil cases indexed by defendant. Civil records on

index cards, docket books and computer from 1985, prior records at Circuit Court. Search free at http://208.210.219.132/courtinfo/vadistrict/select.jsp?court=. Also search via LOPAS; call 804-786-5511.
Criminal Records: Access: Mail, online, in person. Both court and visitors may perform in person searches. No search fee. Required to search: name, years to search, DOB; also helpful: SSN. Criminal records on index cards, docket books and computer from 1985, prior records at Circuit Court. Online access to criminal records is the same as civil.
General Information: Public Access terminal is available. No juvenile, sealed, adoption records released. Fee to fax results is $2.00 per document. Copy fee: $1.00 1st 2 pages; $.50 each add'l page. No cert fee. Payee: Clerk of General District Court. Personal checks accepted. Credit cards accepted. Prepayment required. Mail turnaround time 1-5 days.

Spotsylvania County

15th Circuit Court PO Box 96, 9113 Courthouse Rd, Spotsylvania, VA 22553; 540-582-7090; Fax: 540-582-2169. Hours: 8AM-4:30PM (EST). *Felony, Civil Actions Over $15,000, Probate.*
Civil Records: Access: Online, in person. Visitors must perform in person searches for themselves. No search fee. Required to search: name, years to search. Civil cases indexed by defendant, plaintiff. Civil records on computer from 1996, on index books from late 1700s. Search free online at http://208.210.219.132/courtinfo/vacircuit/select.jsp?court=. Also search via LOPAS; call 804-786-5511. Mail access limited to specific case only.
Criminal Records: Access: Online, in person. Visitors must perform in person searches for themselves. No search fee. Required to search: name, years to search, DOB, SSN. Criminal records on computer from 1996, on index books from late 1700s. Select and search Circuit Courts online at http://208.210.219.132/courtinfo/vacircuit/select.jsp?court=. For information about the statewide online systems, see the state introduction.
General Information: Public Access terminal is available. No juvenile, sealed, adoption records released. Copy fee: $.50 per page. Cert fee: $2.00. Payee: Clerk of Circuit Court. Personal checks accepted. Prepayment required.

15th General District Court Judicial Center, PO Box 339, Spotsylvania, VA 22553; 540-582-7110. Hours: 8AM-4PM (EST). *Misdemeanor, Civil Actions Under $15,000, Eviction, Small Claims.*
Civil Records: Access: Mail, online, in person. Visitors must perform in person searches for themselves. No search fee. Required to search: name, years to search. Civil cases indexed by defendant, plaintiff. Civil records go back 10 years; on computer back to 1988. Search free at http://208.210.219.132/courtinfo/vadistrict/select.jsp?court=. Also search via LOPAS; call 804-786-5511.
Criminal Records: Access: Mail, online, in person. Visitors must perform in person searches for themselves. No search fee. Required to search: name, years to search. Criminal records go back 10 years; on computer back to 1988. Select and search District Courts at http://208.210.219.132/courtinfo/vadistrict/select.jsp?court=. For information about the statewide online systems, see the state introduction.
General Information: Public Access terminal is available. No juvenile, sealed records released. Copy fee: $.50 per page. Cert fee: $2.00. Payee: Clerk of General District Court. Personal checks accepted. Prepayment required. Mail turnaround time 5 days.

Stafford County

15th Circuit Court PO Box 69, Stafford, VA 22554; 540-658-8750. Hours: 8AM-4PM (EST). *Felony, Civil Actions Over $15,000, Probate.* www.co.stafford.va.us/courts

Civil Records: Access: Mail, online, in person. Both court and visitors may perform in person searches. No search fee. Required to search: name, years to search. Civil cases indexed by defendant, plaintiff. Civil records in index books from 1699, back on computer to 1992. Search free online at http://208.210.219.132/courtinfo/vacircuit/select.jsp?court=. Also search via LOPAS; call 804-786-5511.

Criminal Records: Access: Mail, online, in person. Both court and visitors may perform in person searches. No search fee. Required to search: name, years to search, DOB; also helpful: SSN. Criminal records in index books from 1699, back on computer to 1992. Online access to criminal records is the same as civil.

General Information: Public Access terminal is available. No juvenile, sealed records released. Copy fee: $.50 per page. Cert fee: $2.00. Payee: Clerk of Circuit Court. Personal checks accepted. Prepayment required. Mail turnaround time is 2-3 weeks.

15th General District Court 1300 Courthouse Rd, PO Box 940, Stafford, VA 22555; 540-658-8763; Civil phone: 540-658-4642; Criminal phone: 540-658-8935; Fax: 540-658-4834. Hours: 8:AM-4PM (EST). *Misdemeanor, Civil Actions Under $15,000, Eviction, Small Claims.*

Civil Records: Access: Fax, mail, online, in person. Both court and visitors may perform in person searches. No search fee. Required to search: name, years to search. Civil cases indexed by defendant, plaintiff. Civil records on computer since 1986, prior at Circuit Court. Search free at http://208.210.219.132/courtinfo/vadistrict/select.jsp?court=. Also search via LOPAS; call 804-786-5511.

Criminal Records: Access: Fax, mail, online, in person. Both court and visitors may perform in person searches. No search fee. Required to search: name, years to search. Criminal records on computer since 1986, prior at Circuit Court. Online access to criminal records is the same as civil.

General Information: Public Access terminal is available. No sealed records released. No fee to fax results. Copy fee: $.50 per page. No cert fee. Payee: Clerk of General District Court. Personal checks accepted. Visa, MC accepted. Prepayment required. Mail requests: SASE requested. Turnaround time 2-7 days.

Staunton City

25th Circuit Court PO Box 1286, Staunton, VA 24402-1286; 540-332-3874; Fax: 540-332-3970. Hours: 8:30AM-5PM (EST). *Felony, Civil Actions Over $15,000, Probate.*

Civil Records: Access: Mail, online, in person. Both court and visitors may perform in person searches. No search fee. Required to search: name, years to search. Civil cases indexed by defendant, plaintiff. Civil records on index books since 1802; on computer back to 1988. Search free online at http://208.210.219.132/courtinfo/vacircuit/select.jsp?court=. Also search via LOPAS; call 804-786-5511.

Criminal Records: Access: Online, in person. Both court and visitors may perform in person searches. No search fee. Required to search: name, years to search. Criminal records on index books since 1802; on computer back to 1988. Online access to criminal records is the same as civil.

General Information: Public Access terminal is available. No juvenile, sealed or adoption records released. Fee to fax results is $.50 per page. Copy fee:

$.50 per page. Cert fee: $2.00. Payee: Clerk of Circuit Court. Personal checks accepted. Prepayment required.

Staunton General District Court 113 E Beverly St, Staunton, VA 24401-4390; 540-332-3878; Fax: 540-332-3985. Hours: 8:30AM-4:30PM (EST). *Misdemeanor, Civil Actions Under $15,000, Eviction, Small Claims.*

Civil Records: Access: Mail, phone, fax, online, in person. Both court and visitors may perform in person searches. No search fee. Required to search: name, years to search; also helpful: address. Civil cases indexed by defendant, plaintiff. Civil records on computer for 10 years. Select and search District Courts at http://208.210.219.132/courtinfo/vadistrict/select.jsp?court=. For information about the statewide online systems, see the state introduction. Records are maintained for 10 years.

Criminal Records: Access: Mail, online, in person. Both court and visitors may perform in person searches. No search fee. Required to search: name, years to search, DOB. Criminal records indexed on computer since 1991. Online access to criminal records is the same as civil. Records are maintained for 10 years.

General Information: Public Access terminal is available. Copy fee: $.50 per page. No cert fee. Payee: Staunton General District Court. Personal checks accepted. Visa, MC accepted. Credit cards accepted for criminal & traffic cases only. Prepayment required. Mail turnaround time 1-5 days.

Suffolk City

Suffolk Circuit Court PO Box 1604, Suffolk, VA 23439-1604; 757-923-2251; Fax: 757-934-3490. Hours: 8:30AM-5PM (EST). *Felony, Civil Actions Over $15,000, Probate.*

Civil Records: Access: Online, in person. Visitors must perform in person searches for themselves. No search fee. Required to search: name, years to search. Civil cases indexed by defendant, plaintiff. Civil records on computer from 1989, on index books from 1866. Search free online at http://208.210.219.132/courtinfo/vacircuit/select.jsp?court=. Also search via LOPAS; call 804-786-5511.

Criminal Records: Access: Online, in person. Visitors must perform in person searches for themselves. No search fee. Required to search: name, years to search. Criminal records on computer from 1989, on index books from 1866. Online access to criminal records is the same as civil.

General Information: Public Access terminal is available. No juvenile, sealed, adoption records released. Copy fee: $.50 per page. Cert fee: $1.50. Payee: Clerk of Circuit Court. Personal checks accepted. Visa, MC accepted. Prepayment required.

5th General District Court 150 N Main St, PO Box 1648, Suffolk, VA 23434; 757-923-2281; Fax: 757-925-1790. Hours: 8AM-4PM (EST). *Misdemeanor, Civil Actions up to $15,000, Eviction, Small Claims.*

Civil Records: Access: Mail, online, in person. Both court and visitors may perform in person searches. No search fee. Required to search: name, years to search. Civil cases indexed by defendant, plaintiff. Civil records on computer from 1992 prior on index cards. Records destroyed after 10 years. Search free at http://208.210.219.132/courtinfo/vadistrict/select.jsp?court=. Also search via LOPAS; call 804-786-5511.

Criminal Records: Access: Online, mail, in person. Visitors must perform in person searches for themselves. No search fee. Required to search: name, years to search, DOB; also helpful: SSN. Criminal records on computer from 1992, prior on index cards. Online access to criminal records is the same as civil.

General Information: Public Access terminal is available. No juvenile, sealed, adoptions records released. Copy fee: $1.00 1st page, $.50 each add'l page. No cert fee. Payee: Suffolk General District Court. Personal checks accepted. Visa, MC accepted. Prepayment required. Mail requests: SASE required. Mail turnaround time 1 week.

Surry County

6th Circuit Court 28 Colonial Trail East, PO Box 203, Surry, VA 23883; 757-294-3161; Fax: 757-294-0471. Hours: 9AM-5PM (EST). *Felony, Civil Actions Over $15,000, Probate.*

Civil Records: Access: In person, online. Visitors must perform in person searches for themselves. No search fee. Required to search: name, years to search. Civil cases indexed by defendant, plaintiff. Civil records on cards. Remote online access to court case indexes is via LOPAS; call 804-786-5511 to apply.

Criminal Records: Access: In person, online. Visitors must perform in person searches for themselves. No search fee. Required to search: name, years to search, DOB; also helpful: SSN. Criminal records on cards. Online access to criminal records is the same as civil.

General Information: Juvenile, sealed records not released. Copy fee: $.50 per page. Cert fee: $2.00. Payee: Circuit Clerk. Business checks accepted.

6th General District Court Hwy 10 and School St, PO Box 332, Surry, VA 23883; 757-294-5201; Fax: 757-294-0312. Hours: 8:30AM-4:30PM (EST). *Misdemeanor, Civil Actions Under $15,000, Eviction, Small Claims.*

Civil Records: Access: Online, in person. Visitors must perform in person searches for themselves. No search fee. Required to search: name, years to search. Civil cases indexed by defendant, plaintiff. Civil records on computer since 11/93, on books from 1985, prior at Circuit Court. Search free at http://208.210.219.132/courtinfo/vadistrict/select.jsp?court=. Also search via LOPAS; call 804-786-5511.

Criminal Records: Access: Online, in person. Visitors must perform in person searches for themselves. No search fee. Required to search: name, years to search, DOB; also helpful: SSN. Criminal records on computer since 11/93, on books from 1985, prior at Circuit Court. Online access to criminal records is the same as civil.

General Information: Public Access terminal is available. No juvenile, sealed, adoption records released. No copy fee. No cert fee.

Sussex County

6th Circuit Court PO Box 1337, Sussex, VA 23884; 434-246-5511 X3276; Fax: 434-246-2203. Hours: 9AM-5PM (EST). *Felony, Civil Actions Over $15,000, Probate.*

Civil Records: Access: Mail, online, in person. Only the court performs in person searches; visitors may not. Search fee: $5.00. Required to search: name, years to search. Civil cases indexed by defendant, plaintiff. Civil records on index books from 1754; on computer back to 1991. Remote online access to court case indexes is via LOPAS; call 804-786-5511 to apply.

Criminal Records: Access: Mail, online, in person. Visitors must perform in person searches for themselves. Search fee: $5.00. Required to search: name, years to search, DOB, SSN, signed release. Criminal records on index books from 1754; on computer back to 1991. Online access to criminal records is the same as civil.

General Information: No juvenile, sealed, adoption, confidential, or probate records released. Fee to fax results is $1.00 per page. Copy fee: $.50 per page. Cert fee: $2.00. Payee: Clerk of Circuit Court.

Personal checks accepted. Prepayment required. Mail turnaround time 1-2 days.

6th Judicial District Court
Sussex County Courthouse, 15098 Courthouse Rd, Rt 735, PO Box 1315, Sussex, VA 23884; 434-246-5511; Civil phone: x3240; Criminal phone: x3273; Fax: 434-246-6604. Hours: 8:30AM-4:30PM (EST). *Misdemeanor, Civil Actions Under $15,000, Eviction, Small Claims.*

Civil Records: Access: Online, in person. Visitors must perform in person searches for themselves. No search fee. Required to search: name, years to search. Civil cases indexed by defendant, plaintiff. Civil records on computer from 9/88, on index cards from 1985, prior in Circuit Court. Search free at http://208.210.219.132/courtinfo/vadistrict/select.jsp?court=. Also search via LOPAS; call 804-786-5511.

Criminal Records: Access: Online, in person. Visitors must perform in person searches for themselves. No search fee. Required to search: name, years to search, DOB; also helpful: SSN. Criminal records on computer from 9/88, on index cards from 1985, prior in Circuit Court. Online access to criminal records is the same as civil.

General Information: Public Access terminal is available. No juvenile, sealed, adoption records released. Copy fee: $1.00 minimum for first 2 pages, thereafter $.50 per page. No cert fee. Payee: Sussex District Court. Personal checks accepted. Visa, MC accepted. Prepayment required.

Tazewell County

29th Circuit Court
PO Box 968, Tazewell, VA 24651-0968; 276-988-1222; Fax: 276-988-7501. Hours: 8AM-4:30PM (EST). *Felony, Civil Actions Over $15,000, Probate.*

Civil Records: Access: Mail, online, in person. Both court and visitors may perform in person searches. No search fee. Required to search: name, years to search. Civil cases indexed by defendant, plaintiff. Civil records on index cards from 1800s. Online access free at http://208.210.219.132/courtinfo/vacircuit/select.jsp?court=. For information about the statewide online systems, see the state introduction.

Criminal Records: Access: Mail, online, in person. Both court and visitors may perform in person searches. No search fee. Required to search: name, years to search, signed release. Criminal records on computer from 1992. Online access to criminal records is the same as civil.

General Information: Public Access terminal is available. No juvenile, sealed records released. Will fax results to local or toll free line. Copy fee: $.50 per page. Cert fee: $2.00. Payee: Clerk of Circuit Court. Personal checks accepted. Prepayment required. Mail turnaround time 1-3 days.

29th General District Court
PO Box 566, Tazewell, VA 24651; 276-988-9057; Fax: 276-988-6202. Hours: 8AM-4:30PM (EST). *Misdemeanor, Civil Actions Under $15,000, Eviction, Small Claims.*

Civil Records: Access: Mail, fax, online, in person. Both court and visitors may perform in person searches. No search fee. Required to search: name, years to search. Civil cases indexed by defendant, plaintiff. Civil records on computer back to 1991, prior records to 1985 at Circuit Court. Search free at http://208.210.219.132/courtinfo/vadistrict/select.jsp?court=. Also search via LOPAS; call 804-786-5511.

Criminal Records: Access: Mail, fax, online, in person. Both court and visitors may perform in person searches. No search fee. Required to search: name, years to search, DOB; also helpful: SSN, signed release. Criminal records on computer back to 1991, prior records to 1985 at Circuit Court. Online access to criminal records is the same as civil.

General Information: Public Access terminal is available. No juvenile, sealed records released. Fee to fax results is $1.00 per document and $1.00 per page. Copy fee: $.50 per page. No cert fee. Payee: Clerk of General District Court. Personal checks accepted. Visa, MC accepted. Prepayment required. Mail turnaround time 1-3 days.

Virginia Beach City

2nd Circuit Court
2425 Nimmo Parkway, Virginia Beach, VA 23456-9017; 757-427-4181; Fax: 757-426-5686. Hours: 8:30AM-5PM (EST). *Felony, Civil Actions Over $15,000, Probate.*
www.vbgov.com/courts

Civil Records: Access: Online, in person. Visitors must perform in person searches for themselves. No search fee. Required to search: name, years to search. Civil cases indexed by defendant, plaintiff. Civil records on computer from 1986, on files from 1960s. Online access free at http://208.210.219.132/courtinfo/vacircuit/select.jsp?court=. For information about the statewide online systems, see the state introduction.

Criminal Records: Access: Online, in person. Visitors must perform in person searches for themselves. No search fee. Required to search: name, years to search, DOB; also helpful: SSN. Criminal records on computer from 1986, on files from 1960s. Online access to criminal records is the same as civil.

General Information: Public Access terminal is available. No juvenile, sealed, presentencing probation report, judges notes or adoption records released. Copy fee: $.50 per page. Cert fee: $2.00. Payee: Clerk of Circuit Court. Personal checks accepted. Prepayment required.

2nd General District Court
2425 Nimmo Parkway, Judicial Center, Virginia Beach, VA 23456-9057; 757-427-8531 Court Info Line; Civil phone: 757-427-4277; Criminal phone: 757-427-4707; Fax: 757-426-5672. Hours: 8:30AM-4PM (EST). *Misdemeanor, Civil Actions Under $15,000, Eviction, Small Claims.*
www.vbgov.com

Civil Records: Access: Mail, online, in person. Visitors must perform in person searches. No search fee. Required to search: name, years to search. Civil cases indexed by defendant, plaintiff. Civil records on computer from 1987. Search free at http://208.210.219.132/courtinfo/vadistrict/select.jsp?court=. Also search via LOPAS; call 804-786-5511. Civil cases decided on or before 01/01/85 retained 10 years, after that date retained 20 years.

Criminal Records: Access: Mail, online, in person. Visitors must perform in person searches. No search fee. Required to search: name, years to search, DOB; also helpful: SSN. Criminal records on computer back ten years, then destroyed. Online access to criminal records is the same as civil.

General Information: Public Access terminal is available. No juvenile, sealed, adoption or mental records released. No fee to fax results. No cert fee. Payee: Clerk of General District Court. Personal checks accepted. Prepayment required. Mail turnaround time 3-4 weeks.

Warren County

Circuit Court
1 E Main St, Front Royal, VA 22630; 540-635-2435; Fax: 540-636-3274. Hours: 9AM-5PM (EST). *Felony, Civil, Probate.*
www.courts.state.va.us/courts/circuit/warren/home.html

Civil Records: Access: Phone, fax, mail, online, in person. Both court and visitors may perform in person searches. No search fee. Required to search: name, years to search. Civil cases indexed by defendant, plaintiff. Civil records on archives from 1836; on computer since 1986. Online access free at http://208.210.219.132/courtinfo/vacircuit/select.jsp?court=. For information about the statewide online systems, see the state introduction. Phone access limited to specific case only.

Criminal Records: Access: Phone, fax, mail, online, in person. Both court and visitors may perform in person searches. No search fee. Required to search: name, years to search, DOB; also helpful: SSN. Criminal records on archives from 1836; on computer since 1986. Online access to criminal records is the same as civil.

General Information: Public Access terminal is available. No juvenile, sealed, adoption records released. Will fax results to local or toll-free line. Copy fee: $.50 per page. Cert fee: $2.00. Payee: Jennifer R Sims Clerk. Personal checks accepted. Prepayment required. Mail requests: SASE required. Mail turnaround time 1-2 days.

26th General District Court
1 E Main St, Front Royal, VA 22630; 540-635-2335; Fax: 540-636-8233. Hours: 8:15AM-4:15PM (EST). *Misdemeanor, Civil Actions Under $15,000, Eviction, Small Claims.*

Civil Records: Access: Mail, fax, online, in person. Both court and visitors may perform in person searches. No search fee. Required to search: name, years to search. Civil cases indexed by defendant. Civil records in archives back to 1800s, on computer from 1989. Search free at http://208.210.219.132/courtinfo/vadistrict/select.jsp?court=. Also search via LOPAS; call 804-786-5511.

Criminal Records: Access: Mail, fax, online, in person. Both court and visitors may perform in person searches. No search fee. Required to search: name, years to search. Criminal records in archives, on computer from 1989. Online access to criminal records is the same as civil.

General Information: Public Access terminal is available. Copy fee: $.50 per page. No cert fee. Payee: General District Court. Personal checks accepted. Prepayment required. Mail requests: SASE required. Mail turnaround time 2-3 days.

Washington County

Circuit Court
PO Box 289, Abingdon, VA 24212-0289; 276-676-6224/6226; Fax: 276-676-6218. Hours: 7:30AM-5PM; Recording Hours: 8:30AM-4PM (EST). *Felony, Civil Actions Over $15,000, Probate.*

Civil Records: Access: Mail, online, in person. Both court and visitors may perform in person searches. Search fee: Search fee is determined by time involved. Required to search: name, years to search. Civil cases indexed by defendant, plaintiff. Civil records on archives from 1777, on computer from 1991. Remote online access to court case indexes is via LOPAS; call 804-786-5511 to apply.

Criminal Records: Access: Online, in person. Visitors must perform in person searches for themselves. No search fee. Required to search: name, years to search. Criminal records on archives from 1777, on computer from 1991. Remote online access to court case indexes is via LOPAS; call 804-786-5511 to apply.

General Information: Public Access terminal is available. No juvenile, sealed or adoption records released. Will fax results to local or toll free line. Copy fee: $.50 per page. Cert fee: $2.00. Payee: Clerk, Circuit Court. Personal checks accepted. Prepayment required. Will bill copy fees. Mail requests: SASE required. Mail turnaround time 1 week.

28th General District Court 191 E Main St, Abingdon, VA 24210; 276-676-6281; Fax: 276-676-3136. Hours: 8:30AM-4:30PM (EST). *Misdemeanor, Civil Actions Under $15,000, Eviction, Small Claims.*

Civil Records: Access: Mail, online, in person. Both court and visitors may perform in person searches. No search fee. Required to search: name, years to search. Civil cases indexed by defendant, plaintiff. Civil records on archives from 1777, on computer from 1994. Search free at http://208.210.219.132/courtinfo/vadistrict/select.jsp?court=. Also search via LOPAS; call 804-786-5511.

Criminal Records: Access: Mail, online, in person. Both court and visitors may perform in person searches. No search fee. Required to search: name, years to search. Criminal records on archives from 1777, on computer from 1994. Online access to criminal records is the same as civil.

General Information: Public Access terminal is available. No sealed records released. Will not fax results. Copy fee: $1.00 for first page, $.50 each add'l. Cert fee: $2.00. Payee: General District Court. Personal checks accepted. Visa, MC accepted. Prepayment required. Mail requests: SASE required. Mail turnaround time 1-2 days.

Waynesboro City

25th Circuit Court 250 S Wayne Ave, PO Box 910, Waynesboro, VA 22980; 540-942-6616; Fax: 540-942-6774. Hours: 8:30AM-5PM (EST). *Felony, Civil Actions Over $15,000, Probate.*

Civil Records: Access: Online, in person. Visitors must perform in person searches for themselves. No search fee. Required to search: name, years to search. Civil cases indexed by defendant, plaintiff. Civil records on computer from 11/88 (some), all on index books from 5/48. Online access free at http://208.210.219.132/courtinfo/vacircuit/select.jsp?court=. For information about the statewide online systems, see the state introduction.

Criminal Records: Access: Online, in person. Visitors must perform in person searches for themselves. No search fee. Required to search: name, years to search, DOB; also helpful: SSN. Criminal records on computer from 11/88 (some), all on index books from 5/48. Online access to criminal records is the same as civil.

General Information: Public Access terminal is available. No juvenile, sealed, adoptions released. Copy fee: $.50 per page. Cert fee: $2.00. Payee: Clerk of Circuit Court. Personal checks accepted. Prepayment required.

25th General District Court - Waynesboro 250 S Wayne, PO Box 1028, Waynesboro, VA 22980; 540-942-6636; Fax: 540-942-6666. Hours: 8:30AM-4:30PM (EST). *Misdemeanor, Civil Actions Under $15,000, Eviction, Small Claims.*

Civil Records: Access: Mail, fax, online, in person. Visitors must perform in person searches for themselves. No search fee. Required to search: name, years to search. Civil cases indexed by defendant, plaintiff. Civil records on computer 10 years. Search free at http://208.210.219.132/courtinfo/vadistrict/select.jsp?court=. Also search via LOPAS; call 804-786-5511.

Criminal Records: Access: Mail, fax, online, in person. Visitors must perform in person searches for themselves. No search fee. Required to search: name, years to search. Criminal records on computer for 10 years. Online access to criminal records is the same as civil.

General Information: Public Access terminal is available. No copy fee. No cert fee. Turnaround time up to 1 week.

Westmoreland County

15th Circuit Court PO Box 307, Montross, VA 22520; 804-493-0108; Fax: 804-493-0393. Hours: 9AM-5PM (EST). *Felony, Civil Actions Over $15,000, Probate.*

Civil Records: Access: In person. Visitors must perform in person searches for themselves. No search fee. Required to search: name, years to search. Civil cases indexed by defendant, plaintiff. Civil records on index books from 1653. Remote online access to court case indexes is via LOPAS; call 804-786-5511 to apply.

Criminal Records: Access: In person. Visitors must perform in person searches for themselves. No search fee. Required to search: name, years to search, DOB; also helpful: SSN. Criminal records on index books from 1653.

General Information: No juvenile, sealed, adoption records released. Copy fee: $.50 per page. Cert fee: $3.00. Payee: Clerk of Circuit Court. No personal checks accepted. Prepayment required. Will bill copy fees.

15th General District Court PO Box 688, Montross, VA 22520; 804-493-0105. Hours: 8AM-4:30PM (EST). *Misdemeanor, Civil Actions Under $15,000, Small Claims.*

Civil Records: Access: Mail, online, in person. Both court and visitors may perform in person searches. No search fee. Required to search: name, years to search. Civil cases indexed by defendant, plaintiff. Civil records on index books/cards for 10 years; on computer back to 5/93. Search free at http://208.210.219.132/courtinfo/vadistrict/select.jsp?court=. Also search via LOPAS; call 804-786-5511.

Criminal Records: Access: Mail, online, in person. Both court and visitors may perform in person searches. No search fee. Required to search: name, years to search; also helpful: DOB, SSN, date of offense. Criminal records on index books/cards for 10 years; on computer back to 5/93. Online access to criminal records is the same as civil.

General Information: Public Access terminal is available. All records public. Copy fee: $1.00 for first page, $.50 each add'l. No cert fee. Payee: General District Court. Personal checks accepted. Attorney checks accepted. Visa, MC accepted. Prepayment required. Mail requests: SASE required. Mail turnaround time 1 week.

Williamsburg City

Circuit & District Courts Note: See James City.

Winchester City

26th Circuit Court 5 N Kent St, Winchester, VA 22601; 540-667-5770; Fax: 540-667-6638. Hours: 9AM-5PM (EST). *Felony, Civil Actions Over $15,000, Probate.*

www.winfredclerk.com

Note: The Winchester Court and the Frederick County Court Clerks are housed in the same judicial center. The offices share microfilming and deed indexing systems.

Civil Records: Access: Online, in person. Visitors must perform in person searches for themselves. No search fee. Required to search: name, years to search. Civil cases indexed by defendant, plaintiff. Civil records on computer from 1985 to present, on index books from 1790. Online access free at http://208.210.219.132/courtinfo/vacircuit/select.jsp?court=. For information about the statewide online systems, see the state introduction.

Criminal Records: Access: Mail, online, in person. Both court and visitors may perform in person searches. No search fee. Required to search: name,

years to search; also helpful: DOB, SSN. Criminal records on computer from 1985 to present, on index books from 1790. Online access to criminal records is the same as civil.

General Information: Public Access terminal is available. No juvenile, sealed, adoption records released. Copy fee: $.50 per page. Cert fee: $2.00. Payee: Clerk of Circuit Court. Personal checks accepted. Prepayment required. Mail requests: SASE required. Mail turnaround time same day.

26th General District Court 5 N Kent St, PO Box 526, Winchester, VA 22604; 540-722-7208; Fax: 540-722-1063. Hours: 8AM-4PM (EST). *Misdemeanor, Civil Actions Under $15,000, Eviction, Small Claims.*

Civil Records: Access: Online, in person. Visitors must perform in person searches for themselves. No search fee. Required to search: name, years to search. Civil cases indexed by defendant, plaintiff. Civil records on computer from 1992, on index cards from 1985 to 1987, prior at Circuit Court. Search free at http://208.210.219.132/courtinfo/vadistrict/select.jsp?court=. Also search via LOPAS; call 804-786-5511.

Criminal Records: Access: Online, in person. Visitors must perform in person searches for themselves. No search fee. Required to search: name, years to search, DOB, SSN, signed release. Criminal records on computer from 1992, on index cards from 1985 to 1987, prior at Circuit Court. Online access to criminal records is the same as civil. Forms for criminal searches available from State Police.

General Information: Public Access terminal is available. No sealed records released. Copy fee: $.50 per page. Cert fee: $2.00. Payee: Clerk of General District Court. Personal checks accepted. Prepayment required.

Wise County

30th Circuit Court PO Box 1248, Wise, VA 24293-1248; 276-328-6111; Fax: 276-328-0039. Hours: 8:30AM-5PM (EST). *Felony, Civil Actions Over $15,000, Probate.*

www.wisecircuitcourt.com

Civil Records: Access: Phone, fax, mail, online, in person. Both court and visitors may perform in person searches. Search fee: $10.00 per name. Required to search: name, years to search; also helpful: address. Civil cases indexed by defendant, plaintiff. Civil records on archives from 1856. Online access free at http://208.210.219.132/courtinfo/vacircuit/select.jsp?court=. For information about the statewide online systems, see the state introduction. Also, court indexes and images are at www.courtbar.org. Registration and a fee is required. Records go back to June, 2000.

Criminal Records: Access: Phone, fax, mail, online, in person. Both court and visitors may perform in person searches. Search fee: $10.00 per name. Required to search: name, years to search, DOB; also helpful: SSN. Criminal records on archives from 1856. Online access to criminal records is the same as civil.

General Information: Public Access terminal is available. No juvenile, sealed or adoption records released. Will not fax results. Copy fee: $.50 per page. Cert fee: $2.00 plus copy fee. Payee: Clerk of Circuit Court. Personal checks accepted. Prepayment required. Mail turnaround time 2-3 days.

30th General District Court Wise County Courthouse, PO Box 829, Wise, VA 24293; 276-328-3426; Fax: 276-328-4576. Hours: 8AM-4PM (EST). *Misdemeanor, Civil Actions Under $15,000, Eviction, Small Claims.*

Civil Records: Access: Phone, mail, online, in person. Both court and visitors may perform in person searches. No search fee. Required to search: name, years to search. Civil cases indexed by defendant, plaintiff. Civil records on computer back 10 years. Search free at http://208.210.219.132/courtinfo/vadistrict/select.jsp?court=. Also search via LOPAS; call 804-786-5511.

Criminal Records: Access: Phone, mail, online, in person. Both court and visitors may perform in person searches. No search fee. Required to search: name, years to search; also helpful: DOB, SSN. Criminal records on computer back 10 years. Online access to criminal records is the same as civil.

General Information: Public Access terminal is available. No juvenile, sealed records released. Copy fee: $.50 per page. No cert fee. Payee: General District Court. Personal checks accepted. Credit cards accepted. Prepayment required. Mail turnaround time 5 days.

Wythe County

27th Circuit Court 225 S Fourth St, Rm 105, Wytheville, VA 24382; 276-223-6050; Fax: 276-223-6057. Hours: 8:30AM-5PM (EST). *Felony, Civil Actions Over $15,000, Probate.*

Civil Records: Access: In person, online. Both court and visitors may perform in person searches. No search fee. Required to search: name, years to search. Civil cases indexed by defendant, plaintiff. Civil records on computer from 1989, on index cards/books from 1950s (some back to 1790s). Remote online access to court case indexes is via LOPAS; call 804-786-5511 to apply.

Criminal Records: Access: In person, online. Both court and visitors may perform in person searches. No search fee. Required to search: name, years to search; also helpful: DOB, SSN. Criminal records on computer from 1989, on index cards/books from 1950s (some back to 1790s). Remote online access to court case indexes is via LOPAS; call 804-786-5511 to apply.

General Information: Public Access terminal is available. No juvenile, sealed, adoption records released. Copy fee: $.50 per page. No cert fee. Payee: Clerk of Circuit Court. Personal checks accepted. Prepayment required.

Wythe General District Court 245 S. Fourth St., # 205, Wytheville, VA 24382-2595; 276-223-6075; Fax: 276-223-6087. Hours: 8AM-4:30PM (EST). *Misdemeanor, Civil Actions Under $15,000, Eviction, Small Claims.*

Civil Records: Access: Mail, fax, in person, online. Visitors must perform in person searches for themselves. No search fee. Required to search: name, years to search. Civil cases indexed by defendant, plaintiff. Civil records maintained on computer for 10 years, prior at Circuit Court. Search free at http://208.210.219.132/courtinfo/vadistrict/select.jsp?court=. Also search via LOPAS; call 804-786-5511.

Criminal Records: Access: Online, in person. Visitors must perform in person searches for themselves. No search fee. Required to search: name, years to search; also helpful: DOB, SSN. Criminal records maintained on computer for 10 years. Online access to criminal records is the same as civil.

General Information: Public Access terminal is available. Copy fee: $.50 per page. Fee is only applied to requests for excessive amounts of information. No cert fee. Payee: General District Court. Personal checks accepted. Visa, MC accepted. Prepayment required.

York County

9th Circuit Court PO Box 371, Yorktown, VA 23690; 757-890-3350; Civil phone: 757-890-4105; Criminal phone: 757-890-4104; Probate phone: 757-890-4106; Fax: 757-890-3364. Hours: 9AM-5PM (EST). *Felony, Civil Actions Over $15,000, Probate.* www.yorkcounty.gov/circuitcourt/

Note: Also includes City of Poquoson.

Civil Records: Access: Online, in person. Visitors must perform in person searches for themselves. No search fee. Required to search: name, years to search. Civil cases indexed by defendant, plaintiff. Civil records on index books from 1950, computerized since 1986. Online access free at http://208.210.219.132/courtinfo/vacircuit/select.jsp?court=. For information about the statewide online systems, see the state introduction.

Criminal Records: Access: Mail, online, in person. Visitors must perform in person searches themselves. Search fee: $5.00 per name. Required to search: name, years to search, DOB; also helpful: SSN. Criminal records on index books from 1950, computerized since 1986. Online access to criminal records is the same as civil.

General Information: Public Access terminal is available. No juvenile, sealed, adoption records released. Copy fee: $.50 per page. Cert fee: $2.00. Payee: Clerk of Circuit Court. Personal checks accepted. Prepayment required. Mail requests: SASE required. Mail turnaround time 1 week.

9th Judicial District Court York County GDC, PO Box 316, Yorktown, VA 23690-0316; 757-890-3450; Fax: 757-890-3459. Hours: 8:30AM-4:30PM (EST). *Misdemeanor, Civil Actions Under $15,000, Eviction, Small Claims.* www.yorkcounty.gov/districtcourt

Civil Records: Access: Fax, mail, online, in person. Both court and visitors may perform in person searches. No search fee. Required to search: name, years to search. Civil cases indexed by defendant, plaintiff. Civil records on computer back to 1993; prior to 1985 at Circuit Court. Search free at http://208.210.219.132/courtinfo/vadistrict/select.jsp?court=. Also search via LOPAS; call 804-786-5511.

Criminal Records: Access: Fax, mail, online, in person. Both court and visitors may perform in person searches. No search fee. Required to search: name, years to search, DOB, SSN. Criminal records on computer back to 1993; prior to 1985 at Circuit Court. Online access to criminal records is the same as civil.

General Information: Public Access terminal is available. No juvenile, sealed, adoption records released. Will fax results $1.00 1st page, $.50 each add'l. Copy fee: $1.00 for first page, $.50 each add'l. No cert fee. Payee: York County General District Court. Prepayment required. Mail turnaround time 5 days.

Virginia Recording Offices

ORGANIZATION: 95 counties and 41 independent cities, 123 recording offices. The recording officer is Clerk of Circuit Court. Fifteen independent cities share the Clerk of Circuit Court with the county - Bedford, Covington (Alleghany County), Emporia (Greenville County), Fairfax, Falls Church (Arlington or Fairfax County), Franklin (Southhampton County), Galax (Carroll County), Harrisonburg (Rockingham County), Lexington (Rockbridge County), Manassas and Manassas Park (Prince William County), Norton (Wise County), Poquoson (York County), South Boston (Halifax County), and Williamsburg (James City County. Charles City and James City are counties, not cities. The City of Franklin is not in Franklin County, the City of Richmond is not in Richmond County, and the City of Roanoke is not in Roanoke County. The entire state is in the Eastern Time Zone (EST).

REAL ESTATE RECORDS: Only a few Clerks of Circuit Court will perform real estate searches. Copy fees and certification fees vary. The independent cities may have separate Assessor Offices.

UCC RECORDS: This was a dual filing state. Until 07/2001, financing statements were filed at the state level and with the Clerk of Circuit Court, except for consumer goods, farm and real estate related collateral, which were filed only with the Clerk of Circuit Court. Now, only real estate related collateral is filed at the county level. Some recording offices will perform UCC searches. Use search request form UCC-11. Searches fees and copy fees vary.

TAX LIEN RECORDS: Federal tax liens on personal property of businesses are filed with the State Corporation Commission. Other federal and all state tax liens are filed with the county Clerk of Circuit Court. They are usually filed in a "Judgment Lien Book." Most counties will not perform tax lien searches.

OTHER LIENS: Judgment, mechanics, hospital, lis pendens.

ONLINE ACCESS: A growing number of Virginia counties and cities provide free access to real estate related information via the Internet. A limited but growing private company network named VamaNet provides free residential, commercial and vacant property and tax records for nine Virginia jurisdictions at www.vamanet.com/cgi-bin/LOCS. At the web site, click on the county name at left.

Accomack County

Clerk of Circuit Court, PO Box 126, Accomac, VA 23301-0126. **Phone-**757-787-5776; fax-757-787-1849; hours 9AM-5PM. Will not search records. UCC copy- $.50 per page. Cert fee: $2.00. Payee: Accomack County Clerk of the Circuit Court. **Other phones:** Assessor-757-787-5729.

Albemarle County

Clerk of Circuit Court, 501 E. Jefferson St., Rm 225, Charlottesville, VA 22902-5176. **Phone-**434-972-4083; fax-434-293-0298.
UCC records search per debtor- $10.00. Will not search real estate records. **Other phones:** Assessor-434-296-5856; Treasurer-434-296-5851.

Alexandria City

Clerk of Circuit Court, 520 King St, Rm 307, Alexandria, VA 22314. **Phone-**703-838-4044, R/E Recording-703-838-4066, UCC Recording-703-838-4066; hours 9AM-5PM www.ci.alexandria.va.us
Will search UCC records. Search fee is $20.00 per request. Will not search real estate or tax lien records. Copy fee- $.50 per page. Cert fee: $2.00 per cert. Payee: Alexandria City Clerk of the Circuit Court. **Online Access to Assessor, Property records:** Access to city real estate assessments is free at www.ci.alexandria.va.us/city/reasearch/. No name searching. **Other phones:** Assessor-703-838-4646; Treasurer-703-838-6420; Appraiser-703-838-4646; Elections-703-838-4050; Vital Records-703-838-4400.

Alleghany County

Clerk of Circuit Court, PO Box 670, Covington, VA 24426-0670. **Phone-**Clerk of Circuit Court, R/E & UCC Recording- 540-965-1730; fax-540-965-1732; hours 8:30AM-5PM www.alleghanycountyclerk.com
Will not search records. RE record copy- $.50 per page. UCC copy- $.50 per page + $2.00 cert fee

per doc. Payee: Alleghany County Clerk of Court. **Other phones:** Assessor-540-863-6640; Treasurer-540-863-6630.

Amelia County

Clerk of Circuit Court, PO Box 237, Amelia Court House, VA 23002-0237. **Phone-**804-561-2128; hours 8:30AM-4:30PM. Will not search records. UCC copy- $1.00 per page. Cert fee: $2.00 per cert. Payee: Amelia County Clerk of the Circuit Court. **Other phones:** Assessor-804-561-2158; Treasurer-804-561-2145; Elections-804-561-3460.

Amherst County

Clerk of Circuit Court, PO Box 462, Amherst, VA 24521. **Phone-**Clerk of Circuit Court, R/E & UCC Recording- 434-946-9321; hours 8AM-5PM
Will not search records. RE record copy- $1.00 per page, $.50 each add'l after 2 pages. UCC copy- $1.00 per page. Cert fee: $2.00 per cert. Payee: County Clerk of the Circuit Court. **Other phones:** Assessor-434-946-9310; Treasurer-434-946-9318.

Appomattox County

Clerk of Circuit Court, PO Box 672, Appomattox, VA 24522. **Phone-**434-352-5275; fax-434-352-2781; hours 8:30AM-4:30PM
UCC records search per debtor- $10.00. Will not search real estate or tax lien records. UCC copy- $.50 per page. Cert fee: None. Payee: Appomattox County Clerk of Circuit Court. **Other phones:** Assessor-434-352-7450; Treasurer-434-352-5200.

Arlington County

Clerk of Circuit Court, 1425 N. Courthouse Rd, 6th Fl, Arlington, VA 22201. **Phone-**703-228-4369; hours 8AM-4PM www.co.arlington.va.us
UCC records search per debtor- $20.00. Will not search real estate or tax lien records. Copy fee- $.50 per page. Cert fee: $2.00 per doc. Payee:

Arlington County Clerk of the Circuit Court. **Online Access to Real Estate, Assessor, Trade Name records:** Property records on the County assessor database are free at www.co.arlington.va.us/REAssessments/Scripts/DreaDefault.asp. **Other phones:** Assessor-703-228-3920.

Augusta County

Clerk of Circuit Court, PO Box 689, Staunton, VA 24402-0689. **Phone-**540-245-5321; fax-540-245-5318; hours 8AM-5PM
Will search UCC records. Will not search real estate or tax lien records. UCC copy- $.50 per page. Cert fee: $2.00 per cert. Payee: Augusta County Clerk of the Circuit Court. **Online Access to Property, Appraisal, Most Wanted records:** Click on Augusta County to search property data for free at www.vamanet.com/cgi-bin/LOCS. Search the sheriff's most wanted list for free at www.augustacountyvirginia.com/sheriff/wanted.htm. **Other phones:** Assessor-540-245-5647; Treasurer-540-245-5660.

Bath County

Clerk of Circuit Court, PO Box 180, Warm Springs, VA 24484. **Phone-**540-839-7226; 8:30AM-4:30PM
Will not search records. Copy fee- $.50 per page. Cert fee: $2.00 per cert. Payee: Bath County Clerk of the Circuit Court. **Other phones:** Assessor-540-839-7231; Treasurer-540-839-7256.

Bedford County

Clerk of Circuit Court, 123 E Main St, Bedford, VA 24523. **Phone-**540-586-7632; fax-540-586-6197; hours 8:30AM-5PM. Will not search records. Copy fee- $.50 per page. Cert fee: $2.50. Payee: Bedford County Clerk of the Circuit Court. **Online Access to Property Tax records:** Real estate records on the Bedford County GIS site are free at www.co.bedford.va.us/Res/GIS/index.htm; however, no name searching at this time. Records on the City of

Bedford (www.ci.bedford.va.us) Property Tax database are free at www.ci.bedford.va.us/taxf.shtml. Search by name, address or tax map reference number. Also, City of Bedford property info the GIS site is free at http://arcims2.webgis.net/bedfordcity/default.asp. To search by name, click on the magnifying glass with the ? in it. **Other phones:** Assessor-540-586-7626; Treasurer-540-586-7670.

Bland County

Clerk of Circuit Court, PO Box 295, Bland, VA 24315-0295. **Phone**-276-688-4562; fax-276-688-2438; hours 8AM-6PM. UCC records search per debtor- $10.00. Will not search real estate or tax lien records. UCC copy- $1.00 per page. Cert fee: $1.00 per page. Payee: Bland County Clerk of the Circuit Court. **Other phones:** Assessor-276-688-4291; Treasurer-276-688-3741.

Botetourt County

Clerk of Circuit Court, PO Box 219, Fincastle, VA 24090. **Phone**-540-473-8274; hours 8:30AM-4:30PM UCC records search per debtor- $10.00. Will not search real estate or tax lien records. UCC copy- $1.00 per page. Cert fee: $2.00. Payee: Botetourt County Clerk of the Circuit Court. **Other phones:** Assessor-540-473-8254; Treasurer-540-473-8254.

Bristol City

Clerk of Circuit Court, 497 Cumberland St, Rm 210, Bristol, VA 24201. **Phone**-276-645-7321; fax-276-645-7345; hours 9AM-5PM. Will not search UCC or real estate records. **Other phones:** Assessor-276-645-7316; Treasurer-276-645-7311.

Brunswick County

Clerk of Circuit Court, 216 N. Main St., Lawrenceville, VA 23868. **Phone**-Clerk of Circuit Court, R/E & UCC Recording- 434-848-2215; fax-434-848-4307; hours 8:30AM - 5PM
Will not search records. Copy fee- $.50 per page. Cert fee: $2.00 per doc. Payee: Clerk of Circuit Court. **Other phones:** Assessor-434-848-2313; Treasurer-434-848-2512; Appraiser-434-848-2313; Elections-434-848-4414.

Buchanan County

Clerk of Circuit Court, PO Box 929, Grundy, VA 24614. **Phone**-Clerk of Circuit Court, R/E & UCC Recording- 276-935-6567; fax-276-935-6574; hours 8:30AM - 5PM
UCC records search per debtor- $3.00. Will not search tax liens. Will search real estate records. Copy fee- $.50 per page. Cert fee: $2.50 per cert. Payee: Circuit Court Clerk. **Other phones:** Assessor-276-935-6542; Treasurer-276-935-6551; Appraiser-276-935-6541; Elections-276-935-6534; Vital Records-276-935-6575.

Buckingham County

Clerk of Circuit Court, PO Box 107, Buckingham, VA 23921. **Phone**-434-969-4734; fax-434-959-2043; hours 8:30AM-4:30PM. Will not search UCC or real estate records. UCC copy- $.50 per page. **Other phones:** Assessor-434-969-4181; Treasurer-434-969-4744.

Buena Vista City

Clerk of Circuit Court, 2039 Sycamore Ave., Buena Vista, VA 24416. **Phone**-Clerk of Circuit Court, R/E & UCC Recording- 540-261-8627, UCC Recording-540-261-8626; fax-540-261-8623; hours 8:30AM-5PM
Will not search records. Copy fee- $.50 per page. Cert fee: $2.00 per doc. Payee: Clerk of Circuit Court. **Other phones:** Assessor-540-261-8611; Treasurer-540-261-8621; Elections-540-261-8627.

Campbell County

Clerk of Circuit Court, PO Box 7, Rustburg, VA 24588. **Phone**-434-592-9517; hours 8:30AM-4:30PM
Will search UCC records. UCC search per debtor- $20.00. Will not search real estate or tax lien records. UCC copy- $.50 per page. Cert fee: $2.00 per cert. Payee: Campbell County Clerk of the Circuit Court. **Other phones:** Assessor-434-322-9518; Treasurer-434-332-9590.

Caroline County

Clerk of Circuit Court, PO Box 309, Bowling Green, VA 22427-0309. **Phone**-804-633-5800; hours 8:30AM-4PM (recording hours 8:30AM-3:55PM)
Will search UCC records. UCC search per debtor- $10.00 per name. Will not search real estate or tax lien records. RE record copy- $.50 per page. UCC copy- $1.00 per page. Cert fee: $2.50 per doc. Payee: Caroline County Clerk of the Circuit Court. **Online Access to Appraiser, Property records:** Click on Caroline County to search property records for free at www.vamanet.com/cgi-bin/LOCS. **Other phones:** Assessor-804-633-9834; Treasurer-804-633-5291; Elections-804-633-9083.

Carroll County

Clerk of Circuit Court, PO Box 218, Hillsville, VA 24343-0218. **Phone**-Clerk of Circuit Court, R/E & UCC Recording- 276-728-3117; fax-276-728-0255; hours 8AM-5PM www.chillsnet.org
UCC records search per debtor- $20.00. Will not search real estate or tax lien records. Copy fee- $.50 per page. Cert fee: $2.00 per doc. Payee: Clerk. **Online Access to Real Estate, Judgment, UCC, Plat records:** Access to Carroll county property information is a $25 monthly fee. Username and password required; signup through Clerk of Circuit Court, 276-728-3117. Land index and images go back to 1985; plats to 2002. Access to Town of Hillsville property information is on the gis mapping site at http://arcims2.webgis.net/Hillsville/default.asp. Click on the magnifying glass with the ? to search by name. **Other phones:** Assessor-276-728-3281; Treasurer-276-728-9421; Appraiser-276-728-3281; Elections-276-728-2332.

Charles City County

Clerk of Circuit Court, PO Box 86, Charles City, VA 23030-0086. **Phone**-Clerk of Circuit Court, R/E & UCC Recording- 804-829-9212; fax-804-829-5647.
Will not search records. Copy fee- $.50 per page. Cert fee: $2.50 per doc. Payee: Clerk, Circuit Court. **Other phones:** Assessor-804-829-9216; Treasurer-804-829-9205; Elections-804-829-9210.

Charlotte County

Clerk of Circuit Court, PO Box 38, Charlotte Court House, VA 23923. **Phone**-434-542-5147; fax-434-542-4336; hours 8:30AM-4:30PM
Will not search records. UCC copy- $.50. Cert fee: $2.00. Payee: Clerk of Circuit Court. **Other phones:** Assessor-434-542-5546; Treasurer-434-542-5725.

Charlottesville City

Clerk of Circuit Court, 315 E. High St, Charlottesville, VA 22902. **Phone**-434-295-3182; 8:30AM-4:30PM
UCC records search per debtor- $10.00. Will not search real estate or tax lien records. Copy fee- $.50 per page. Cert fee: $2.00 per cert. Payee: Charlottesville City Clerk of the Circuit Court. **Other phones:** Assessor-434-970-3136; Treasurer-434-296-5851.

Chesapeake City

Clerk of Circuit Court, 307 Albemarle Dr, #300, Chesapeake, VA 23322. **Phone**-757-382-3031, R/E

Recording-757-382-3026, UCC Recording-757-382-3032; fax-757-382-3034; hours M-F 8:30-5PM http://cityofchesapeake.net
Will search UCC records. UCC search per index $20.00. Will not search real estate or tax lien records. UCC copy- $.50 per page. Cert fee: $2.00 per doc. Payee: Clerk of Circuit Court. **Online Access to Property Appraiser, Inspection, Most Wanted records:** Access to property appraiser data is free at http://cityofchesapeake.net/rea/welcome.html. No name searching at this time Also, search city inspections for free at http://cityofchesapeake.net/Cdbidt2/IDT100A.do. Also, search the police most wanted list at http://cityofchesapeake.net/services/depart/police/police/wanted.shtml. **Other phones:** Assessor-757-382-6235; Treasurer-757-382-6281.

Chesterfield County

Clerk of Circuit Court, PO Box 125, Chesterfield, VA 23832-0125. **Phone**-Clerk of Circuit Court, R/E & UCC Recording- 804-748-1241; fax-804-796-5625; hours 8:30AM-5PM www.chesterfield.gov
Will search UCC records. UCC search per debtor- $20.00. Will not search real estate or tax lien records. Copy fee- $.50 per page. Cert fee: $2.00. Payee: Circuit Court Clerk. **Online Access to Assessor, Property Tax, Property Sale records:** Search the real estate assessment data for free at www.co.chesterfield.va.us/ManagementServices/RealEstateAssessments/Rea_Search_Home.asp. **Other phones:** Assessor-804-748-1321; Treasurer-804-748-1201; Elections-804-748-1471.

Clarke County

Clerk of Circuit Court, PO Box 189, Berryville, VA 22611. **Phone**-540-955-5116; fax-540-955-0284; hours 9AM-5PM. Will not search records. UCC copy- $.50 per page. Cert fee: None. Payee: Clarke County Clerk of Circuit Court. **Online Access to Property, Appraiser records:** Click on Clarke County to search property data for free at www.vamanet.com/cgi-bin/LOCS. **Other phones:** Assessor-540-955-5108; Treasurer-540-955-5160.

Clifton Forge City

Clerk of Circuit Court, c/o Alleghany County, PO Box 670, Clifton Forge, VA 24426. **Phone**-Clerk of Circuit Court, R/E & UCC Recording- 540-965-1730; fax-540-965-1732; hours 9AM-5PM
As of July 1, 2001, all Clifton Forge governmental functions were transferred to Alleghany County. Will not search records. Copy fee- $.50 per page. Cert fee: $2.00 per cert. Payee: Clerk of the Circuit Court. **Other phones:** Assessor-540-965-1730; Treasurer-540-965-1730; Appraiser-540-965-1730; Elections-540-965-1730.

Colonial Heights City

Clerk of Circuit Court, PO Box 3401, Colonial Heights, VA 23834. **Phone**-Clerk of Circuit Court, R/E & UCC Recording- 804-520-9364; fax-804-524-8726; hours 8:30AM-5PM. Will not search records. Copy fee- $.50 per page. Cert fee: $2.00 per doc. Payee: Colonial Heights Clerk of the Circuit Court. **Other phones:** Assessor-804-520-9272; Treasurer-804-520-9320; Elections-804-520-9277.

Craig County

Clerk of Circuit Court, PO Box 185, New Castle, VA 24127-0185. **Phone**-Clerk of Circuit Court, R/E & UCC Recording-540-864-6141; hours 9AM-5PM
Will not search records. UCC copy- $.50 per page. Cert fee: $2.00 per cert. Payee: Craig County Clerk of the Circuit Court. **Other phones:** Assessor-540-864-6241; Treasurer-540-864-5641.

Culpeper County

Clerk of Circuit Court, 135 W. Cameron St, Rm 103, Culpeper, VA 22701. **Phone-**Clerk of Circuit Court, R/E & UCC Recording- 540-727-3438; hours 8:30AM-4:30PM
UCC records search per debtor- $20.00. Will not search real estate or tax lien records. Copy fee- $.50 per page. Cert fee: $2.00 per cert. Payee: Culpeper County Clerk of the Circuit Court. **Other phones:** Assessor-540-727-3443; Treasurer-540-727-3442; Vital Records-804-662-6200.

Cumberland County

Clerk of Circuit Court, PO Box 8, Cumberland, VA 23040. **Phone-**804-492-4442; fax-804-492-4876; hours 8:30AM-4:30PM
UCC records search per debtor- $10.00. Will not search real estate or tax lien records. UCC copy- $.50 per page. Cert fee: $2.00. Payee: Cumberland County Clerk of Circuit Court. **Other phones:** Assessor-804-492-4280; Treasurer-804-492-4297.

Danville City

Clerk of Circuit Court, PO Box 3300, Danville, VA 24543. **Phone-**434-799-5168; fax-434-799-6502; hours 9AM-4:30PM www.danville-va.gov/home.asp
Will search UCC records. Search fee is $20.00. Will not search real estate or tax lien records. RE record copy- $.50 per page. UCC copy- $.60 per page. Cert fee: $2.00 per doc. Payee: Danville City Clerk of the Circuit Court. **Online Access to Property, Tax Assessor records:** Access to Danville City assessor online records is free at www.danvilleavaassessor.org. **Other phones:** Assessor-434-799-5120; Treasurer-434-799- 5140; Elections-434-799-6560.

Dickenson County

Clerk of Circuit Court, PO Box 190, Clintwood, VA 24228. **Phone-**Clerk of Circuit Court, R/E & UCC Recording- 276-926-1616; fax-276-926-6465; hours 8:30AM-4:30PM www.dickensonctyva.com
Will not search records. RE record copy- $.50 per page. Cert fee: $2.00 per doc. Payee: Dickenson County Clerk. **Online Access to Real Estate, Porperty Tax records:** Access to the Commissioner of Revenue real estate data is free at www.dickensonctyva.com/html/commissioner.html. Also, tax payments data from the county Treasurer is free at www.dickensonctyva.com/html/treasurer1.html. **Other phones:** Assessor-276-926-1646; Treasurer-276-926-1610; Elections-276-926-1620.

Dinwiddie County

Clerk of Circuit Court, PO Box 63, Dinwiddie, VA 23841. **Phone-**804-469-4540; hours 8:30AM-4:30PM
Will not search records. UCC copy- $.50 per page. Cert fee: $2.00 per cert. Payee: Dinwiddie County Clerk of the Circuit Court. **Other phones:** Assessor-804-469-4507; Treasurer-804-469-4510.

Essex County

Clerk of Circuit Court, PO Box 445, Tappahannock, VA 22560. **Phone-**Clerk of Circuit Court, R/E & UCC Recording- 804-443-3541; fax-804-445-1216; hours 8:30AM-5PM. May or may not search UCC records. UCC search per debtor-$20.00 per name. Will not search real estate or tax lien records. Copy fee- $.50 per page. Cert fee: $2.00 per cert. Payee: Essex County Clerk of the Circuit Court. **Other phones:** Assessor-804-443-2661; Treasurer-804-443-4371; Elections-804-443-4611.

Fairfax County

Clerk of the Circuit Court, 4110 Chain Bridge Rd, 3rd Fl, Fairfax, VA 22030. **Phone-**Clerk of the Circuit Court, R/E & UCC Recording- 703-691-7320; hours 8AM-4PM   www.fairfaxcounty.gov/courts/circuit/land_records_info.htm
As of 1/1/88, Falls Church filings for zip codes 22041, 22042, 22043 and 22044 are filed in Fairfax County. Will not search records. Copy fee- $.50 per page. Cert fee: $2.00 per doc. Payee: Fairfax County Clerk of the Circuit Court. **Online Access to Real Estate, Property Tax, Tax Sale records:** Records on the Dept. of Tax Administration Real Estate Assessment database are free at www.www.fairfaxcounty.gov/living/taxes. Also, the Automated Information System operates Monday-Saturday 7AM-7PM at 703-222-6740. Hear about property descriptions, assessed values and sales prices. fax-back service is available. Also, the list of properties to be auctioned is free at www.fairfaxcounty.gov/dta/action.htm. Search the city Assessment roll free at www.fairfaxrealestate.org/fairfax208/LandRover.asp. No name searching. **Other phones:** Assessor-703-222-8234.

Fauquier County

Clerk of Circuit Court, 40 Culpeper St, 1st Fl, Warrenton, VA 20186. **Phone-**540-347-8608, R/E Recording-540-347-8697; hours 8AM-4:30PM www.fauquiercounty.gov/government/departments/circuitcourt
Will search UCC records. UCC search per debtor- $20.00 per search. Will not search real estate or tax lien records. Copy fee for recordings is $.50 per page. UCC copy- $1.00 per page. Cert fee: $3.00. Payee: Fauquier County Clerk of the Circuit Court. **Other phones:** Assessor-540-347-8614; Treasurer-540-347-8691; Land Records Room-540-347-8748.

Floyd County

Clerk of Circuit Court, 100 E. Main St, Rm 200, Floyd, VA 24091. **Phone-**540-745-9330; hours 8:30AM-4:30PM; 8:30AM-Noon Sat (Cls'd Sat if Hol.)
Will not search records. Copy fee- $.50 per page. Cert fee: $2.00 per cert. Payee: Floyd County Clerk of the Circuit Court. **Other phones:** Assessor-540-745-9345; Treasurer-540-745-9357.

Fluvanna County

Clerk of Circuit Court, PO Box 550, Palmyra, VA 22963-0299. **Phone-**Clerk of Circuit Court, R/E & UCC Recording- 434-591-1970; fax-434-591-1971; hours 8AM-4:30PM. Will not search records. UCC copy- $.50 per page. **Online Access to Appraiser, Property records:** Click on Fluvanna County to search property data for free at www.vamanet.com/cgi-bin/LOCS. **Other phones:** Assessor-434-591-1940; Treasurer-434-591-1945; Appraiser-434-591-1940; Elections-434-589-3593.

Franklin County

Clerk of Circuit Court, PO Box 567, Rocky Mount, VA 24151. **Phone-**540-483-3065; fax-540-483-3042; hours 9AM-4:30PM
Will not search records. RE record copy- $1.00 per page. UCC copy- $.50 in person; $1.00 per page if mailed. Cert fee: $2.00 per doc. **Other phones:** Assessor-757-562-8547; Treasurer-757-562-8540.

Frederick County

Clerk of Circuit Court, 5 N. Kent St, Winchester, VA 22601. **Phone-**540-667-5770; fax-540-545-8711; hours 9AM-5PM www.winfredclerk.com/standard.htm
Do not confuse this county with Fredericksburg, VA or Frederick, MD. Also, the City of Winchester has a separate filing office. Will not search UCC records by name. Will not search real estate or tax lien records by name. RE record copy- $.50 per page. Cert fee: $1.50 per cert. Payee: Frederick County Clerk of the Circuit Court. **Other phones:** Assessor-540-662-5303; Treasurer-540-662-6611.

Fredericksburg City

Clerk of Circuit Court, PO Box 359, Fredericksburg, VA 22404. **Phone-**540-372-1066; hours 8AM-4PM
Many Fredericksburg addresses are outside the city limits, in Stafford County or Spotsylvania County. Many residents are not themselves aware of this. Check debtor location carefully. Will search UCC records. UCC search per debtor- $20.00. Will not search real estate or tax lien records. Copy fee- $.50 per page. Cert fee: $2.00 per doc. Payee: Fredericksburg City Clerk of the Circuit Court. **Other phones:** Assessor-540-372-1004.

Giles County

Clerk of Circuit Court, PO Box 502, Pearisburg, VA 24134-0501. **Phone-**540-921-1722; fax-540-921-3825; hours 9AM-4PM. UCC records search per debtor- $10.00. Will not search real estate or tax lien records. UCC copy- $.50 per page. Cert fee: $3.00. Payee: Giles County Clerk of Circuit Court. **Online Access to Appraiser, Property records:** Click on Fluvanna County to search for property records for free at www.vamanet.com/cgi-bin/LOCS. Also, search property info on the county GIS site for free at http://arcims2.webgis.net/giles/default.asp. To name search click on the magnifying glass with the ? In it. **Other phones:** Assessor-540-921-3321; Treasurer-540-921-1240.

Gloucester County

Clerk of Circuit Court, PO Box 2118, Gloucester, VA 23061-0570. **Phone-**Clerk of Circuit Court, R/E & UCC Recording- 804-693-2502; fax-804-693-2186; hours 8AM-4:30PM www.courts.state.va.us
UCC records search per debtor- $20.00. Will not search real estate or tax lien records. Copy fee is $.50 per page. Cert fee: $2.00 per doc. Payee: Clerk of Court. **Online Access to Judgment records:** Access to Law and Chancery cases is free at http://208.210.219.132/courtinfo/vacircuit/select.jsp?court=. **Other phones:** Assessor-804-693-3451; Treasurer-804-693-2141.

Goochland County

Clerk of Circuit Court, PO Box 196, Goochland, VA 23063. **Phone-**804-556-5353; hours 8:30AM-5PM
UCC records search per debtor- $20.00. Will not search real estate or tax lien records. UCC copy- $.50 per page. Cert fee: $1.00 per page. Payee: Goochland County Clerk of the Circuit Court. **Other phones:** Assessor-804-556-5307.

Grayson County

Clerk of Circuit Court, PO Box 130, Independence, VA 24348-0130. **Phone-**276-773-2231; fax-276-773-3338; hours 8AM-5PM
UCC records search per debtor- $20.00 (not certified). Will not search real estate or tax lien records. RE record copy- $.50 per page. UCC copy- $1.00 per page. Cert fee: $2.00 per doc. Payee: Grayson Circuit Court. **Online Access to Real Estate records:** Access to Grayson county property information is free on the gis mapping site at http://arcims.webgis.net/webgis/carroll_grayson. No name searching at this time. **Other phones:** Assessor-276-773-2022; Treasurer-276-773-2571.

Greene County

Clerk of Circuit Court, PO Box 386, Stanardsville, VA 22973-0386. **Phone-**Clerk of Circuit Court, R/E & UCC Recording- 434-985-5208; fax-434-985-6723; hours 8:15AM-4:30PM
Will not search records. RE record copy- $.50 per page. Cert fee: $2.00 per instrument. Payee: Greene County Circuit Court. **Other phones:** Assessor-434-985-5211; Treasurer-434-985-5214;

Appraiser-434-985-5290; Elections-434-985-5213; Vital Records-434-985-5208.

Greensville County

Clerk of Circuit Court, PO Box 631, Emporia, VA 23847. **Phone-**Clerk of Circuit Court, R/E & UCC Recording- 434-348-4215; fax-434-348-4020; hours 9AM-5PM. Will not search records. Copy fee- $.50 per page. Cert fee: $2.00 per doc. Payee: Deputy Clerk. **Online Access to Appraiser, Property records:** Click on Grennsville County to search property data for free at www.vamanet.com/cgi-bin/LOCS. **Other phones:** Assessor-434-348-4229; Treasurer-434-348-4208.

Halifax County

Clerk of Circuit Court, PO Box 729, Halifax, VA 24558. **Phone-**434-476-6211; fax-434-476-2890. Will search UCC records. Will not search real estate records. Copy fee- $.50 per page. **Online Access to Property records:** Access the the county GIS mapping site is free at http://arcims2.webgis.net/halifax/default.asp. No name searching at this time. **Other phones:** Assessor-434-476-3314; Treasurer-434-476-3318; Vital Records-434-476-6211; 434-476-6688-.

Hampton City

Clerk of Circuit Court, PO Box 40, Hampton, VA 23669-0040. **Phone-**757-727-2440; fax-757-728-3505; hours 8:30AM-5PM. Will not search records. RE record copy- $.50 per page. UCC copy- $1.00 per page. Cert fee: $2.00 per doc. Payee: Hampton Circuit Court. **Other phones:** Assessor-757-727-6363; Treasurer-757-727-6374.

Hanover County

Clerk of Circuit Court, PO Box 39, Hanover, VA 23069-0039. **Phone-**804-537-6150, R/E Recording-804-537-6120, UCC Recording-804-537-6120; hours 8:30AM-4:30PM www.co.hanover.va.us Will search UCC records. UCC search per debtor-$20.00 per search. Will not search real estate or tax liens records. Copy fee- $.50 per page. Cert fee: $2.00 per doc. Payee: County Clerk of the Circuit Court. **Other phones:** Assessor-804-537-6029; Treasurer-804-537-6050; Registrar 804-537-6080-.

Henrico County

Clerk of Circuit Court, PO Box 27032, Richmond, VA 23273. **Phone-**804-501-4202, R/E Recording-804-501-4979, UCC Recording-804-501-5468; hours 8AM-4PM; (Recording Hours 8AM-3:30PM) www.co.henrico.va.us/clerk/ Will not search UCC or tax liens records. Will check book and page for name and date for real estate. Copy fee- $.50 per page. Cert fee: $2.00 per doc. Payee: Henrico Circuit Court Clerk. **Other phones:** Assessor-804-501-5580; Treasurer-804-501-7480; Appraiser-804-501-4217; Elections-804-501-4347; Vital Records-804-225-5000.

Henry County

Clerk of Circuit Court, 3160 Kings Mountain Rd. #B, Martinsville, VA 24112. **Phone-**Clerk of Circuit Court, R/E & UCC Recording- 276-634-4880; hours 9AM-5PM http://henrycounty.neocom.net Will search UCC records. UCC search per debtor-$.50 per page. Will not search real estate or tax liens records. UCC copy- $.50 per page. Cert fee: $2.00 per doc. Payee: Henry County Clerk of the Circuit Court. **Online Access to Property records:** Access to county property data is free at the GIS site at http://arcims2.webgis.net/henryco/default.asp. To name search click on magnifying glass with ? In it. **Other phones:** Assessor-276-634-4610; Treasurer-276-624-4675; Appraiser-276-634-4610; Elections-276-634-4697; Vital Records-276-634-4880.

Highland County

Clerk of Circuit Court, PO Box 190, Monterey, VA 24465-0190. **Phone-**Clerk of Circuit Court, R/E & UCC Recording- 540-468-2447; fax-540-468-3447; hours 8:30AM-4:30PM. Will search UCC records. Will not search real estate records. Copy fee- $.50 per page. Cert fee: $2.00 per instrument; $.50 per page to copy. Payee: Sue Dudley- Clerk. **Other phones:** Assessor-540-468-2142; Treasurer-540-465-2265; Elections-540-468-2013.

Hopewell City

Clerk of Circuit Court, PO Box 310, Hopewell, VA 23860. **Phone-**804-541-2239; fax-804-541-2438; hours 8:30AM-4PM. Will not search records. UCC copy- $.50 per page. Cert fee: $2.00 per seal. Payee: Hopewell City Clerk of the Circuit Court. **Online Access to Court Appeals Granted, Docket records:** Access to court records is free at www.courts.state.va.us. **Other phones:** Assessor-804-541-2234; Treasurer-804-541-2240.

Isle of Wight County

Clerk of Circuit Court, PO Box 110, Isle of Wight, VA 23397. **Phone-**757-355-6233; fax-757-357-0884; hours 9AM-5PM UCC records search per debtor- $10.00. Will not search real estate or tax lien records. UCC copy- $.50 per page. Cert fee: $2.00 per copy. Payee: Isle of Wight County Clerk of the Circuit Court. **Online Access to Judgment records:** Access to Law and Chancery case judgments is free at http://208.210.219.132/courtinfo/vacircuit/select2.jsp. **Other phones:** Assessor-757-365-6219; Treasurer-757-357-3191.

James City County

Clerk of Circuit Court, 5201 Monticello Ave #6, Williamsburg, VA 23188. **Phone-**757-564-2242, R/E Recording-757-564-2349; fax-757-564-2329; hours 8:30AM-4PM www.jccegov.com/resources/clerkofcircrt/index.html This office also handles filings for the City of WIlliamsburg. UCC records search per debtor- $20.00. Will not search real estate or tax lien records. Copy fee- $.50 per page. Cert fee: $2.00 per cert. Payee: Williamsburg-James City County Clerk of the Circuit Court. **Online Access to Real Estate records:** Records on the James City County Property Information database are free at www.regis.state.va.us/jcc/public/disclaimer.htm. Also, search City of Williamsburg property assessor data at www.ci.williamsburg.va.us/realestate/disclaimer.html. **Other phones:** Assessor-757-253-6650; Treasurer-757-229-6705.

King and Queen County

Clerk of Circuit Court, PO Box 67, King and Queen Court House, VA 23085. **Phone-**Clerk of Circuit Court, R/E & UCC Recording- 804-785-5984; fax-804-785-5698; hours 9AM-5PM Will not search records. UCC copy- $.50. Cert fee: $1.00. Payee: King and Queen County Clerk of Circuit Court. **Other phones:** Assessor-804-785-5976; Treasurer-804-785-5978; Elections-804-785-5980.

King George County

Clerk of Circuit Court, 9483 Kings Highway, #3, King George, VA 22485. **Phone-**Clerk of Circuit Court, R/E & UCC Recording- 540-775-3322; 8:30AM-4:30PM UCC records search per debtor- $10.00. Tax liens not included in UCC search. Real estate owner, mortgage, and property transfer searches available. UCC copy- $.50 per page. Cert fee: $2.00 per cert. Payee: King George County Clerk of the Circuit

Court. **Other phones:** Assessor-540-775-4664; Treasurer-540-775-2571.

King William County

Clerk of Circuit Court, PO Box 216, King William, VA 23086. **Phone-**804-769-4936, R/E Recording-804-769-4939, UCC Recording-804-769-4939; fax-804-769-4991; hours 8:30AM-4:30PM Will not search records. RE record copy- $.50 per page. UCC copy- $1.00 per page. Cert fee: $2.00. Payee: King William County Clerk of the Circuit Court. **Other phones:** Assessor-804-769-4942; Treasurer-804-769-4931.

Lancaster County

Clerk of Circuit Court, PO Box 99, Lancaster, VA 22503. **Phone-**Clerk of Circuit Court, R/E & UCC Recording- 804-462-5611; fax-804-462-9978; hours 8:30AM-4:30PM www.lancova.com Will search UCC records. UCC search fee-$5.00 per UCC. Will not search real estate or tax lien records. RE record copy- $.50 per page. UCC copy- $1.00 per page. Cert fee: $2.00 per cert. Payee: Lancaster County Clerk of the Circuit Court. **Online Access to Chancery, Law records:** Access to court records is free at www.courts.state.va.us. **Other phones:** Assessor-804-462-7920; Treasurer-804-462-5630; Elections-804-462-5277.

Lee County

Clerk of Circuit Court, PO Box 326, Jonesville, VA 24263. **Phone-**276-346-7763; fax-276-346-3440. UCC records search per debtor- $10.00. Will not search real estate records. UCC copy- $.50 per page. **Other phones:** Assessor-276-346-7722; Treasurer-276-346-7716.

Loudoun County

Clerk of Circuit Court, PO Box 550, Leesburg, VA 20178. **Phone-**Clerk of Circuit Court, R/E & UCC Recording- 703-777-0270; hours 8:30AM-4:30PM www.loudoun.gov/government/ Will search UCC records. Will not search real estate or tax lien records. UCC copy- $1.00 per page. Cert fee: $3.00 per cert. Payee: Loudoun County Clerk of the Circuit Court. **Online Access to Property, Assessor records:** Search the property assessor data for free at http://inter1.loudoun.gov/webpdbs/. No name searching; search by address, number, or ID only. **Other phones:** Assessor-703-777-0260; Treasurer-703-777-0280.

Louisa County

Clerk of Circuit Court, PO Box 37, Louisa, VA 23093. **Phone-**540-967-5312; hours 8:30AM-5PM (Stop Recording 4:15PM) Will not search records. UCC copy- $.50 per page. Cert fee: $2.50. Payee: Louisa County Clerk of the Circuit Court. **Other phones:** Assessor-540-967-3450.

Lunenburg County

Clerk of Circuit Court, 11435 Courthouse Rd., Lunenburg, VA 23952. **Phone-**434-696-2230; hours 8:30AM-4:30PM. Will not search records. UCC copy- $.50 per page. Cert fee: $2.50. Payee: Lunenburg County Clerk of the Circuit Court. **Other phones:** Assessor-434-696-2516.

Lynchburg City

Clerk of Circuit Court, PO Box 4, Lynchburg, VA 24505. **Phone-**434-455-2620; fax-434-847-1864; hours 8:15AM-4:45PM. Will search UCC records. Search fee is $20.00 per filing. Will not search real estate or tax lien records. Copy fee- $.50 per page. Cert fee: $2.00 per cert. Payee: Lynchburg City Clerk of the Circuit Court. **Other phones:** Assessor-434-455-3830; Treasurer-434-455-4242.

Madison County

Clerk of Circuit Court, PO Box 220, Madison, VA 22727-0220. **Phone**-540-948-6888; fax-540-948-3759; hours 8:30AM-4:30PM. Will not search records. UCC copy- $.50 per page. Cert fee: $2.00. Payee: Clerk of Circuit Court. **Other phones:** Assessor-540-948-4421; Treasurer-540-948-4409.

Martinsville City

Clerk of Circuit Court, PO Box 1206, Martinsville, VA 24114-1206. **Phone**-Clerk of Circuit Court, R/E & UCC Recording- 276-403-5106; fax-276-403-5232; hours-9AM-5PM
www.ci.martinsville.va.us/Circuitclerk
UCC records search per debtor- $20.00. Will not search real estate or tax lien records. Copy fee- $.50 per page. Cert fee: $2.00 per doc. Payee: Martinsville City Clerk of the Circuit Court. **Online Access to Property, Deed, Judgment, Will, Marriage, Delinquent Tax records:** Circuit clerk records is at www.ci.martinsville.va.us/Circuitclerk. Fee is $30.00 per month, or you may search at a rate of $1 per doc. For info, call office of Ashby Pritchett at 276-656-5106 or visit website. **Other phones:** Assessor-276-403-5131; Treasurer-276-403-5240; Other phone-276-403-5206.

Mathews County

Clerk of Circuit Court, PO Box 463, Mathews, VA 23109-0463. **Phone**-Clerk of Circuit Court, R/E & UCC Recording- 804-725-2550; hours 8AM-4PM
Will not search records. UCC copy- $1.00 per page. Cert fee: $2.00 per page. Payee: Mathews County Clerk of the Circuit Court. **Other phones:** Assessor-804-725-7168; Treasurer-804-725-2341.

Mecklenburg County

Clerk of Circuit Court, PO Box 530, Boydton, VA 23917-0530. **Phone**-434-738-6191; fax-434-738-6861; hours 8:30AM-5PM. Will search UCC records. UCC search fee is $20.00 per name. Will not search real estate or tax lien records. Copy fee- $.50 per page. Cert fee: $2.00 per instrument. Payee: Mecklenburg County Clerk of the Circuit Court.

Middlesex County

Clerk of Circuit Court, PO Box 158, Saluda, VA 23149. **Phone**-Clerk of Circuit Court, R/E & UCC Recording-804-758-5317; hours 8:30AM-4:30PM
UCC records search per debtor- $5.00. Will not search real estate or tax lien records. UCC copy- $1.00 per page. Cert fee: $2.50 per page. Payee: Middlesex County Clerk of the Circuit Court. **Other phones:** Assessor-804-758-5331; Treasurer-804-758-5302; Appraiser-804-758-5331; Elections-804-758-4420.

Montgomery County

Clerk of Circuit Court, PO Box 6309, Christiansburg, VA 24068. **Phone**-Clerk of Circuit Court, R/E & UCC Recording- 540-382-5760; fax-540-382-6937; hours 8:30AM-4:30PM
Will not search records. UCC copy- $.50 per page. **Online Access to Real Estate, Property Tax records:** Access to the county Tax Parcel Information System database is free online at www.webgis.net/montgomery/index.htm. To name search, select "owner name" in the Search box. Records on the Town of Blacksburg GIS site are free at http://arcims2.webgis.net/blacksburg/default.asp?. To name search, click on the magnifying glass with the ? In it. **Other phones:** Assessor-540-382-5717; Treasurer-540-382-5723; Appraiser-540-382-5715; Elections-540-382-5741; Vital Records-540-382-5760; Public Information Office-540-381-6887.

Nelson County

Clerk of Circuit Court, PO Box 10, Lovingston, VA 22949. **Phone**-434-263-5733; fax-434-263-8313; hours 9AM-5PM
Will not search records. UCC copy- $1.00 per page. Cert fee: $2.50 per cert. Payee: Nelson County Clerk of the Circuit Court. **Other phones:** Assessor-434-263-4009; Treasurer-434-263-4079.

New Kent County

Clerk of Circuit Court, PO Box 98, New Kent, VA 23124-0098. **Phone**-Clerk of Circuit Court, R/E & UCC Recording- 804-966-9520; fax-804-966-9528; hours 8:30AM-4:30PM
Will not search records. **Online Access to Assessor, Property records:** Access to county assessor records at http://data.visionappraisal.com/NewKentCountyVA/. Register free for full data. **Other phones:** Assessor-804-966-9610; Treasurer-804-966-9615.

Newport News City

Clerk of Circuit Court, 2500 Washington Ave, Courthouse, Newport News, VA 23607. **Phone**-757-926-8561, R/E Recording-757-926-8355, UCC Recording-757-926-8349; fax-757-926-8531.
www.newport-news.va.us
UCC records search per debtor- $20.00. Will not search real estate or tax lien records. Copy fee- $.50 per page. **Online Access to Assessor, Real Estate records:** Access to the City's "Real Estate on the Web" database is free at http://216.54.20.244/reisweb1. Search by address or parcel number; new "advanced search" may include name searching. **Other phones:** Assessor-757-247-8671; Treasurer-757-247-8731.

Norfolk City

Clerk of Circuit Court, 100 St. Paul's Blvd., Norfolk, VA 23510-2773. **Phone**-757-664-4380; hours 8:45AM-4:45PM http://norfolkgov.com/home.asp
Will search UCC records. UCC search includes tax liens if requested. Separate federal/state combined tax lien search- $10.00 per debtor. Real estate owner, mortgage, and property transfer searches available. RE record copy- $.50 per page. UCC copy- $1.00 per page. Cert fee: $2.00 per cert. Payee: Clerk, Circuit Court. **Online Access to Real Estate, Assessor, Sex Offender Registry records:** Records on the City of Norfolk Real Estate Property Assessment database are free at www.norfolk.gov/NRealEstate/search.asp. Also, sex offender registry search for free found at http://sex-offender.vsp.state.va.us/Static/Search.htm. **Other phones:** Assessor-757-664-4732; Treasurer-757-664-7800; Elections-757-664-4353.

Northampton County

Clerk of Circuit Court, PO Box 36, Eastville, VA 23347-0036. **Phone**-757-678-0465; fax-757-678-5410. Will not search records. UCC copy- $2.00 per page. Cert fee: $10.00. Payee: Northampton County Clerk of Circuit Court. **Other phones:** Assessor-757-678-0446; Treasurer-757-678-0450.

Northumberland County

Clerk of Circuit Court, PO Box 217, Heathsville, VA 22473. **Phone**-804-580-3700; hours 8:30AM-4:45PM Will search UCC records. Will not search tax liens. Real estate record owner searches available. UCC copy- $1.00 per page. Cert fee: No charge. Payee: Northumberland County Clerk of the Circuit Court. **Other phones:** Assessor-804-580-4600; Treasurer-804-580-5201.

Nottoway County

Clerk of Circuit Court, PO Box 25, Nottoway, VA 23955. **Phone**-Clerk of Circuit Court, R/E & UCC

Recording- 434-645-9043; fax-434-645-2201; hours 8:30AM-4:30PM
UCC records search per debtor- $10.00. Federal/state combined tax lien search- $10.00 per debtor. Will not search real estate records. Record copy- $.50 per page; Book and page numbers required. Cert fee: $2.00 per instrument. Payee: Clerk of Circuit Court. **Other phones:** Assessor-434-645-9317; Treasurer-434-645-9318; Appraiser-434-645-9317; Elections-434-645-8148; Vital Records-434-645-9043(marriage licenses only).

Orange County

Clerk of Circuit Court, PO Box 230, Orange, VA 22960. **Phone**-Clerk of Circuit Court, R/E & UCC Recording- 540-672-4030; fax-540-672-2939.
UCC records search per debtor- $20.00. Will not search real estate records. Copy fee is $.50 per page. **Other phones:** Assessor-540-672-4441; Treasurer-540-672-2656; Appraiser-540-672-4441.

Page County

Clerk of Circuit Court, 116 S. Court St, #A, Luray, VA 22835. **Phone**-Clerk of Circuit Court, R/E & UCC Recording- 540-743-4064; fax-540-743-2338; hours 9AM-5PM
Will search UCC records only if requested in writing on "Information Request" form. UCC search per debtor- $20.00. Will not search real estate or tax lien records. UCC copy- $.50 per page. Cert fee: $2.00 per doc. Payee: C. Ron Wilson-Clerk. **Other phones:** Assessor-540-743-3840; Treasurer-540-743-3975; Elections-540-743-3986.

Patrick County

Clerk of Circuit Court, PO Box 148, Stuart, VA 24171-0148. **Phone**-Clerk of Circuit Court, R/E & UCC Recording- 276-694-7213; fax-276-694-6943.
Will not search records. Copy fee- $.50 per page. Cert fee: $2.00 per doc. Payee: Patrick County. **Other phones:** Assessor-276-694-7131; Treasurer-276-694-7257; Elections-276-694-7206.

Petersburg City

Clerk of Circuit Court, 7 Courthouse Ave., Petersburg, VA 23803. **Phone**-804-733-2367, R/E Recording-804-733-2367 x4122, UCC Recording-804-733-2367 x4122; fax-804-732-5548; hours 8AM-4PM
www.courts.state.va.us
Will search UCC records. UCC search per debtor- $20.00 per search. Will not search real estate or tax lien records. Copy fee- $.50 per page. Cert fee: $2.00. Payee: Clerk of Court. **Other phones:** Assessor-804-733-2315; Treasurer-804-733-2321.

Pittsylvania County

Clerk of Circuit Court, PO Drawer 31, Chatham, VA 24531. **Phone**-434-432-7887, R/E Recording-434-432-7888; fax-434-432-7913; hours 8:30AM-5PM
Will not search records. Copy fee- $1.00 per page. Cert fee: $2.00 per cert. Payee: Pittsylvania County Clerk of the Circuit Court. **Online Access to Real Estate, Assessor records:** Access to county real estate data is free at www.pittgov.org/real%20search.htm. Most recent assessment data is for the previous year. See Danville City for Real Estate and Lien records online for Danville City. **Other phones:** Assessor-434-432-7949; Treasurer-434-432-7961; Elections-434-432-7971.

Portsmouth City

Clerk of Circuit Court, PO Drawer 1217, Portsmouth, VA 23705. **Phone**-757-393-8671, R/E Recording-757-393-8530; fax-757-399-4826; hours 8:30AM-5PM
Will search UCC records. Will not search real estate or tax lien records. RE record copy- $1.00 per page, $.50 each add'l after 2 pages. UCC copy- $.50 per page. Cert fee: $2.00 per cert + $.50 per

page. Payee: Portsmouth Clerk of the Circuit Court. **Other phones:** Assessor-757-393-8631; Treasurer-757-393-8651; Appraiser-757-393-8771; Elections-757-393-8644.

Powhatan County

Clerk of Circuit Court, PO Box 37, Powhatan, VA 23139-0037. **Phone-**Clerk of Circuit Court, R/E & UCC Recording- 804-598-5660; hours 8:30AM-5PM UCC records search per debtor- $10.00. Will not search real estate or tax lien records. RE record copy- $.50 per page. UCC copy- $1.00 per page. Cert fee: $2.00 per cert. Payee: Wm. E. Maxey, Jr., Clerk. **Online Access to Appraiser, Property records:** Click on Powhatan County to search property data for free at www.vamanet.com/cgi-bin/LOCS. **Other phones:** Assessor-804-598-5617; Treasurer-804-598-5626; Appraiser-804-598-5617; Elections-804-598-5604.

Prince Edward County

Clerk of Circuit Court, PO Box 304, Farmville, VA 23901. **Phone-**434-392-5145; hours 8:30AM-4:30PM Will not search records. Copy fee- $.50 per page. Cert fee: $2.50 per cert. Payee: Prince Edward County Clerk of the Circuit Court. **Other phones:** Assessor-434-392-3231; Treasurer-434-392-3404.

Prince George County

Clerk of Circuit Court, PO Box 98, Prince George, VA 23875-0098. **Phone-**804-733-2640; hours Recording Hours 8:30AM-4:30PM

Will not search records. Copy fee- $.50 per page. Cert fee: $2.00 per cert. Payee: Prince George County Clerk of the Circuit Court. **Other phones:** Assessor-804-733-2616; Treasurer-804-733-2620.

Prince William County

Clerk of Circuit Court, 9311 Lee Ave, Rm 300, Manassas, VA 20110-5598. **Phone-**Clerk of Circuit Court, R/E & UCC Recording- 703-792-6035; fax-703-792-6083. www.pwcgov.org/ccourt

UCC records search per debtor- $10.00. Will not search real estate or tax lien records. Copy fee- $.50 per page. Cert fee: $2.00 per doc. Payee: Clerk of Court. **Online Access to Land, Property Assessor records:** Records on the county Property Information database are free at www4.pwcgov.org/realestate/LandRover.asp. Also, City of Manassas Commissioner of the Revenue's real estate assessment data is at http://data.visionappraisal.com/ManassasVA/. Free registration is required to access full data. **Other phones:** Assessor-703-792-6780; Vital Records-703-792-6045 (marriage only).

Pulaski County

Clerk of Circuit Court, 45 3rd St. NW, #101, Pulaski, VA 24301. **Phone-**Clerk of Circuit Court, R/E & UCC Recording- 540-980-7825; fax-540-980-7835; hours 8:30AM-4:30PM. Will not search records. Record copy- $.50 per page. Cert fee: $1.00 per doc. Payee: Pulaski County Clerk of the Circuit Court. **Online Access to Property, GIS records:** Access to the county GIS mapping info is free at http://arcims2.webgis.net/pulaski/default.asp. No name searching. **Other phones:** Assessor-540-980-7753; Treasurer-540-980-7785; Appraiser-540-980-7753; Elections-540-980-1222.

Radford City

Clerk of Circuit Court, 619 Second St, Courthouse, Radford, VA 24141. **Phone-**540-731-3610; fax-540-731-3612; hours 8:30AM-5PM (No machine receipts after 4:30PM)

Will not search records. UCC copy- $.50 per page. Cert fee: $2.00. Payee: Radford City Clerk of the Circuit Court. **Online Access to Property records:**

Access to City property info on the GIS mapping site is free at http://arcims2.webgis.net/radfordcity/default.asp. To name search click on magnifying glass with ? In it. **Other phones:** Treasurer-540-731-3661; Elections-540-731-3639.

Rappahannock County

Clerk of Circuit Court, PO Box 517, Washington, VA 22747-1517. **Phone-**Clerk of Circuit Court, R/E & UCC Recording- 540-675-5350; fax-540-675-5351; hours 8:30AM-4:30PM. Will not search records. Copy fee- $.50 per page. Cert fee: $2.00 per doc. Payee: Rappahannock County Clerk of the Circuit Court. **Other phones:** Assessor-540-675-5370; Treasurer-540-675-5360; Appraiser-540-675-5370; Elections-540-675-5370; Vital Records-804-662-6200.

Richmond City

Clerk of Circuit Court, 400 N. 9th St., Richmond, VA 23219. **Phone-**804-646-6505; hours 8:45AM-4:45PM The City of Richmond is not in Richmond County. It is bordered by Henrico and Chesterfield Counties. Will search UCC records, no fee. Will not search real estate or tax lien records. UCC copy- $.50 per page. Cert fee: $2.00 per doc. Payee: Richmond City Clerk of the Circuit Court. **Online Access to Property, Assessor records:** Search the city's Property & Real Estate Assessment Information for free at www.ci.richmond.va.us/accessingGIS.asp. Read directions before going to search page; name searching is available. **Other phones:** Treasurer-804-646-6474; Appraiser-804-646-5616; Elections-804-646-5950; Records Rm-804-646-6530.

Richmond County

Clerk of Circuit Court, PO Box 1000, Warsaw, VA 22572-1000. **Phone-**Clerk of Circuit Court, R/E & UCC Recording- 804-333-3781; fax-804-333-5396; hours 9AM-5PM www.co.richmond.va.us

The City of Richmond is a separate filing office and is not located in this county. The following ZIP Codes are the only ones for this county: 22572, 22460, 22472, 22548, and part of 22435. UCC records search per debtor- $20.00. Tax liens not included with UCC search unless requested. The Federal/state combined tax lien search is $10.00 per debtor. Real estate record owner searches available. Copy fee- $.50 per page. Cert fee: $2.00 per cert. Payee: Richmond County Clerk of the Circuit Court. **Other phones:** Assessor-804-333-5062; Treasurer-804-333-3555; Appraiser-804-333-5062; Elections-804-333-4772; Vital Records-804-333-3781.

Roanoke City

Clerk of Circuit Court, Box 2610, Roanoke, VA 24010-2610. **Phone-**Clerk of Circuit Court, R/E & UCC Recording- 540-853-6702; hours 8:30AM-4:30PM www.ci.roanoke.va.us

Will search UCC records. UCC search fee is $20.00 per search. Will not search real estate or tax lien records. UCC copy- $.50 per page. Cert fee: $2.00 per cert. Payee: Roanoke City Clerk of the Circuit Court. **Online Access to Property, GIS records:** Access to property data is free on the City GIS website at http://gis.roanokegov.com/text.htm. **Other phones:** Treasurer-540-853-2561.

Roanoke County

Clerk of Circuit Court, PO Box 1126, Salem, VA 24153-1126. **Phone-**540-387-6205; fax-540-387-6145; hours 8:30AM-4:30PM. Will search UCC records. UCC search per debtor-$20.00 per name. Will not search real estate or tax lien records. UCC copy- $.50 per page. Cert fee: $2.00 per doc.

Rockbridge County

Clerk of Circuit Court, 2 S. Main St, Court House, Lexington, VA 24450-2599. **Phone-**Clerk of Circuit

Court, R/E & UCC Recording- 540-463-2232; fax-540-463-3850; hours 8:30AM-4:30PM

UCC records search per debtor- $20.00. Will not search real estate or tax lien records. Copy fee-$.50 per page. Cert fee: $2.50 per doc. Payee: Clerk's Office. **Online Access to Property, Appraiser records:** Access to the county GIS-property mapping site is free at http://arcims2.webgis.net/rockbridge/default.asp. However, no name searching at this time. Also, click on City of Lexington to search the city property data for free at www.vamanet.com/cgi-bin/LOCS. **Other phones:** Assessor-540-463-3431; Treasurer-540-463-2613; Appraiser-540-463-3431; Elections-540-463-7203.

Rockingham County

Clerk of Circuit Court, Courthouse, Harrisonburg, VA 22801. **Phone-**540-564-3110, UCC Recording-540-564-3126; fax-540-564-3127.

Will search UCC records. UCC search fee $20.00 per search, per name. Will not search real estate records. **Online Access to Real Estate, Deed, Lien records:** Access to records on the recorder database is free at http://rockingham.amcad.com/rockingham/. **Other phones:** Assessor-540-564-3086.

Russell County

Clerk of Circuit Court, PO Box 435, Lebanon, VA 24266. **Phone-**276-889-8023; fax-276-889-8003; hours 8:30AM-5PM. UCC records search per debtor-$20.00. Will not search real estate or tax lien records. UCC copy- $.50 per page. Cert fee: NONE. Payee: County Clerk. **Other phones:** Assessor-276-889-8014; Treasurer-276-889-8028.

Salem City

Clerk of Circuit Court, PO Box 891, Salem, VA 24153. **Phone-**540-375-3067, R/E Recording-540-375-3058; fax-540-375-4039; hours 8AM-5PM

Will not search records. UCC copy- $.50 per page. Cert fee: $2.00. Payee: Salem City Clerk of Circuit Court. **Other phones:** Elections-540-375-3058.

Scott County

Clerk of Circuit Court, 104 E. Jackson St, Courthouse, #2, Gate City, VA 24251-3417. **Phone-**Clerk of Circuit Court, R/E & UCC Recording- 276-386-3801; hours 8:30AM-5:00PM. UCC records search per debtor-$20.00. Will not search real estate or tax lien records. Copy fee- $.50 per page. Cert fee: $1.00 per cert. Payee: Scott County Clerk of the Circuit Court. **Other phones:** Assessor-276-386-7692; Treasurer-276-386-7742; Appraiser-276-386-7692; Elections-276-386-3843; Vital Records-804-662-6200; Registrar-276-386-3843.

Shenandoah County

Clerk of Circuit Court, PO Box 406, Woodstock, VA 22664-0406. **Phone-**Clerk of Circuit Court, R/E & UCC Recording- 540-459-6150; fax-540-459-6155; hours 9AM-5PM M-F. Will search UCC records. UCC search per debtor-$20.00. Will not search real estate or tax lien records. Copy fee- $.50 per page. Cert fee: $2.00 per doc. Payee: Shen. Co. Circuit Court. **Other phones:** Assessor-540-459-6170; Treasurer-540-459-6180.

Smyth County

Clerk of Circuit Court, 109 W Main St #144, Marion, VA 24354-2510. **Phone-**Clerk of Circuit Court, R/E & UCC Recording- 276-782-4044; fax-276-782-4045; hours 9AM-4:30. Will not search records. UCC copy-$.50 per page. Cert fee: $2.00. Payee: Smyth County Clerk of Circuit Court. **Online Access to Property records:** Access to property records for Smyth County including Marion, Saltville, and Chilhowie Towns are free at http://arcims2.webgis.net/smyth/default.asp. To name search click on magnifying glass with ? In it. **Other phones:** Assessor-276-782-4040; Treasurer-276-782-4059.

Southampton County

Clerk of Circuit Court, PO Box 190, Courtland, VA 23837. **Phone-**757-653-9245, R/E Recording-757-653-2200, UCC Recording-757-653-2200; 8:30AM-5PM Will search UCC records. UCC search per debtor- $20.00 per name. Will not search real estate or tax lien records. Copy fee- $.50 per page. Payee: Southampton County Clerk of the Circuit Court. **Other phones:** Assessor-757-653-3030; Treasurer-757-653-3025.

Spotsylvania County

Clerk of Circuit Court, PO Box 96, Spotsylvania, VA 22553-0096. **Phone-**540-582-7090, R/E Recording-540-582-7046, UCC Recording-540-582-7090 X233; fax-540-582-2169. Will search UCC records. UCC search fee is $20.00. Will not search real estate records. UCC copy- $.50 per page, SASE required. **Other phones:** Assessor-540-582-7132.

Stafford County

Clerk of Circuit Court, PO Box 69, Stafford, VA 22555. **Phone-**540-659-8752, R/E Recording-540-658-8752, UCC Recording-540-658-8758; hours 8AM-4PM Will not search records. RE record copy- $.50 per page. UCC copy- $1.00 per page. Cert fee: $2.00 per cert. Payee: County Clerk of the Circuit Court. **Other phones:** Assessor-540-658-4132; Treasurer-540-658-8700; Appraiser-540-658-4132.

Staunton City

Clerk of Circuit Court, PO Box 1286, Staunton, VA 24402-1286. **Phone-**Clerk of Circuit Court, R/E & UCC Recording- 540-332-3874; fax-540-332-3970. www.staunton.va.us/cityhall/spinhall.htm Will not search records. Copy fee- $.50 per page. Cert fee: $2.00 per doc. Payee: Circuit Court. **Other phones:** Assessor-540-332-3827; Treasurer-540-332-3833; Appraiser-540-332-3827; Elections-540-332-3840.

Suffolk City

Clerk of Circuit Court, PO Box 1604, Suffolk, VA 23439-1604. **Phone-**757-923-2251, R/E Recording-757-923-2264, UCC Recording-757-923-2347; hours 8:30AM-5PM. Will not search records. UCC copy- $.50 per page. Cert fee: $2.00. Payee: Suffolk City Clerk of the Circuit Court. **Other phones:** Assessor-757-923-2400.

Surry County

Clerk of Circuit Court, PO Box 203, Surry, VA 23883-0203. **Phone-**757-294-3161; hours 9AM-5PM Will not search records. Copy fee- $.50 per page. Cert fee: $2.00 per cert. Payee: Surry County Clerk of the Circuit Court. **Other phones:** Assessor-757-294-3000; Treasurer-757-294-5206; Elections-757-294-5213.

Sussex County

Clerk of Circuit Court, PO Box 1337, Sussex, VA 23884. **Phone-**Clerk of Circuit Court, R/E & UCC Recording- 434-246-5511 x3274; fax-434-246-2203; hours 9AM-5PM. UCC records search per debtor- $5.00. Will not search tax liens. Will not search real estate records. RE record copy- $.50 per page. UCC copy- $1.00 per page. Cert fee: $3.00 per cert. Payee: Sussex County Clerk of the Circuit Court. **Other phones:** Assessor-434-246-5511 x3222; Treasurer-434-246-5511 x3223.

Tazewell County

Clerk of Circuit Court, PO Box 968, Tazewell, VA 24651-0968. **Phone-**276-988-7541; fax-276-988-7585; hours 8-AM-4:30PM UCC records search per debtor- $20.00. Will not search real estate or tax lien records. UCC copy- $.50 per page. Cert fee: $2.00 per doc. Payee: Clerk of Circuit Court. **Online Access to Property records:** Access to Commission of Revenue data is free at www.smartmesh.net/tcva/html/real_estate.html. Information is not always updated in a timely manner. For more details, call 276-988-7541. **Other phones:** Assessor-276-988-7541 x305; Treasurer-276-988-7541 x315.

Virginia Beach City

Clerk of Circuit Court, 2425 Nimmo Prky, Judicial Ctr, Virginia Beach, VA 23456-9017. **Phone-**757-427-8818; fax-757-426-5686. www.vbgov.com Will not search records. UCC copy- $.50 per page. Cert fee: $2.50 per cert. **Online Access to Real Estate, Property Tax, Assessor, Marriage, Judgment, UCC, Will, Business Name records:** Online access Virginia Beach land records and recordings is free at http://vblandrecords.com/recclkshr/about.asp. But, there is a new fee for images, which is payable by credit card only. Also, notarized registration for images is required. For credit card account, call 866-793-6505. Direct general questions to Tina at 757-427-8819. Also, you may search the assessor database for free at www.vbgov.com/dept/realestate/. No name searching. **Other phones:** Assessor-757-427-4601; Treasurer-757-427-4445; Elections-757-427-8683; Public Info Office-757-427-4111; City Clerk-757-427-4303.

Warren County

Clerk of Circuit Court, 1 E. Main St, Front Royal, VA 22630-3382. **Phone-**Clerk of Circuit Court, R/E & UCC Recording- 540-635-2435; fax-540-636-3274; hours 9AM-5PM www.courts.state.va.us UCC records search per debtor- $20.00. Will not search real estate or tax lien records. Copy fee- $.50 per page. Cert fee: $2.00 per doc. Payee: Warren County Circuit Clerk. **Online Access to Recording, Deed, Land, Lien, Court, Will, Marriage, UCC records:** Access the Clerks data on the web; username and password required. For username and password contact Jennifer Sims at 540-635-2435 or at jsims@courts.state.va.us. Images go back to 1994. **Other phones:** Assessor-540-635-2651; Treasurer-540-635-2215; Appraiser-540-635-2651; Elections-540-635-4327; Vital Records-540-635-2435.

Washington County

Clerk of Circuit Court, PO Box 289, Abingdon, VA 24212. **Phone-**276-676-6226, R/E Recording-276-676-6224, UCC Recording-276-676-6224; fax-276-676-6218; hours 7:30AM-5PM Will not search records. Copy fee is $.50 per page. Cert fee: $2.00 per page. **Other phones:** Assessor-276-676-6270; Treasurer-276-676-6272; Elections-276-676-6227; Vital Records-276-676-6265.

Waynesboro City

Clerk of Circuit Court, PO Box 910, Waynesboro, VA 22980. **Phone-**540-942-6616; hours 8:30AM-5PM Will not search records. UCC copy- $.50 per page. Cert fee: $2.00 per cert. Payee: Waynesboro City Clerk of the Circuit Court. **Online Access to Porperty, Appraiser records:** Access to city property appraiser data is free at www.vamanet.com/cgi-bin/LOCS. **Other phones:** Assessor-540-942-6621/5513; Treasurer-540-942-6606.

Westmoreland County

Clerk of Circuit Court, PO Box 307, Montross, VA 22520. **Phone-**804-493-0108; hours 9AM-5PM Will not search records. Record copy- $.50 per page, $2.00 min. Payee: County Clerk of the Circuit Court. **Other phones:** Assessor-804-493-0113; Treasurer-804-493-0124; Elections-804-493-8898.

Winchester City

Clerk of Circuit Court, 5 N. Kent St, Winchester, VA 22601. **Phone-**Clerk of Circuit Court, R/E & UCC Recording- 540-667-5770; fax-540-667-6638; hours 9AM-5PM www.winfredclerk.com Will not search records. Copy fee- $.50 per page. Cert fee: $2.00 per cert. Payee: Winchester City Clerk of the Circuit Court. **Other phones:** Assessor-540-667-1815; Treasurer-540-667-1815; Appraiser-540-667-1815; Elections-540-667-1815.

Wise County

Clerk of Circuit Court, PO Box 1248, Wise, VA 24293. **Phone-**Clerk of Circuit Court, R/E & UCC Recording-276-328-6111; fax-276-328-0039; hours 8:30AM-5PM www.courtbar.org Will not search records. UCC copy- $.50 per page. **Online Access to Assessor, Real Estate, Lien, Probate, Marriage, Property Tax, Appraisal, Wanted, Fugitive records:** Includes City of Norton. For full access, a Premium User fee is $395 annually; see www.courtbar/org website. Free access is at http://arcims2.webgis.net/wise/default.asp; click on magnifying glass with ? In it. The fee service includes index and images, court orders, land docs from 1970 and links to RE tax assessments, 50-year RE, tax maps, plat maps, delinquent taxes, permit images, probate, marriage, judgment liens for 20 years, and more. UCC-1 indices for past 5 years. Also, property data is free at www.wisecad.org and also at https://www.efile.com/courts/wise/search.asp. Efile also offers a $440 per year subscription service. Also, Wants & Fugitives are at www.courtbar.org. **Other phones:** Assessor-276-328-3556; Treasurer-276-328-3666; Appraiser-276-328-3566.

Wythe County

Clerk of Circuit Court, 225 S. Fourth St, Rm 105, Wytheville, VA 24382. **Phone-**Clerk of Circuit Court, R/E & UCC Recording- 276-223-6050; fax-276-223-6057; hours 8:30AM-5PM. UCC records search per debtor- $10.00. Will not search real estate or tax lien records. Copy fee- $.50 per page. Cert fee: $1.00 per page. Payee: Clerk. **Other phones:** Assessor-276-223-6015; Treasurer-276-223-6070; Appraiser-276-223-6015; Elections-276-223-6038.

York County

Clerk of Circuit Court, PO Box 371, Yorktown, VA 23690. **Phone-**757-890-3350, R/E Recording-757-890-4103, UCC Recording- 757-890-4103; fax-757-890-3364; hours-9AM-5PM www.yorkcounty.gov/circuitcourt UCC records search per debtor- $20.00. Will not search real estate or tax lien records. Copy fee- $.50 per page. Cert fee: $2.00 fee. Payee: York County Circuit Court. **Online Access to Property records:** Property records from the County GIS site are free at www.regis.state.va.us/york/pub/disclaimer.htm. **Other phones:** Assessor-757-890-3270 (York Co); Treasurer-757-890-3420 (York Co); City of Poquoson Commissioner-757-868-3020; City of Poquoson Treasurer-757-868-3015.

Virginia County Locator

You will usually be able to find the city name in the City/County Cross Reference below. In that case, it is a simple matter to determine the county from the cross reference. However, only the official US Postal Service city names are included in this index. There are an additional 40,000 place names that people use in their addresses. Therefore, we have also included a ZIP/City Cross Reference immediately following the City/County Cross Reference.

If you know the ZIP Code but the city name does not appear in the City/County Cross Reference index, look up the ZIP Code in the ZIP/City Cross Reference, find the city name, then look up the city name in the City/County Cross Reference. For example, you want to know the county for an address of Menands, NY 12204. There is no "Menands" in the City/County Cross Reference. The ZIP/City Cross Reference shows that ZIP Codes 12201-12288 are for the city of Albany. Looking back in the City/County Cross Reference, Albany is in Albany County.

Virginia City/County Cross Reference

ABINGDON Washington
ACCOMAC Accomack
ACHILLES Gloucester
AFTON (22920) Nelson(65), Albemarle(30), Augusta(3)
ALBERTA Brunswick
ALDIE Loudoun
ALEXANDRIA (22311) Alexandria City(93), Fairfax(6)
ALEXANDRIA (22312) Fairfax(76), Alexandria City(23)
ALEXANDRIA Alexandria City
ALEXANDRIA Fairfax
ALFONSO Lancaster
ALTAVISTA Campbell
ALTON Halifax
AMELIA COURT HOUSE Amelia
AMHERST Amherst
AMISSVILLE (20106) Culpeper(62), Rappahannock(33), Fauquier(3)
AMISSVILLE Rappahannock
AMMON Dinwiddie
AMONATE Tazewell
ANDERSONVILLE Buckingham
ANDOVER Wise
ANNANDALE Fairfax
APPALACHIA Wise
APPOMATTOX (24522) Appomattox(98), Buckingham(1)
ARARAT (24053) Patrick(94), Carroll(5)
ARCOLA Loudoun
ARK Gloucester
ARLINGTON (22206) Arlington(97), Alexandria City(2)
ARLINGTON Arlington
ARODA Madison
ARRINGTON (22922) Nelson(96), Amherst(3)
ARVONIA Buckingham
ASHBURN Loudoun
ASHLAND Hanover
ASSAWOMAN Accomack
ATKINS Smyth
ATLANTIC Accomack
AUGUSTA SPRINGS Augusta
AUSTINVILLE (24312) Carroll(60), Wythe(39)
AXTON (24054) Henry(64), Pittsylvania(35)
AYLETT King William
BACOVA Bath
BANCO Madison
BANDY Tazewell
BANK AMERICARD Roanoke City
BARBOURSVILLE (22923) Orange(53), Greene(24), Albemarle(21)
BARHAMSVILLE New Kent
BARREN SPRINGS Wythe
BASKERVILLE Mecklenburg
BASSETT (24055) Henry(94), Franklin(5)
BASTIAN (24314) Bland(71), Tazewell(28)
BASYE Shenandoah
BATESVILLE Albemarle
BATTERY PARK Isle of Wight
BAVON Mathews

BEALETON Fauquier
BEAUMONT Goochland
BEAVERDAM (23015) Hanover(72), Caroline(13), Spotsylvania(12), Louisa(1)
BEAVERLETT Mathews
BEDFORD (24523) Bedford(78), Bedford City(21)
BEE Dickenson
BELLAMY Gloucester
BELLE HAVEN Accomack
BELSPRING Pulaski
BEN HUR Lee
BENA Gloucester
BENT MOUNTAIN (24059) Roanoke(92), Franklin(5), Floyd(2)
BENTONVILLE (22610) Warren(98), Page(1)
BERGTON Rockingham
BERRYVILLE Clarke
BIG ISLAND Bedford
BIG ROCK Buchanan
BIG STONE GAP (24219) Wise(97), Lee(2)
BIRCHLEAF Dickenson
BIRDSNEST Northampton
BISHOP Tazewell
BLACKSBURG Montgomery
BLACKSTONE (23824) Nottoway(91), Brunswick(8)
BLACKWATER (24221) Lee(62), Scott(37)
BLAIRS Pittsylvania
BLAKES Mathews
BLAND Bland
BLOXOM Accomack
BLUE GRASS Highland
BLUE RIDGE (24064) Botetourt(63), Bedford(36)
BLUEFIELD Tazewell
BLUEMONT (20135) Clarke(69), Loudoun(30)
BLUEMONT Loudoun
BOHANNON Mathews
BOISSEVAIN Tazewell
BOONES MILL (24065) Franklin(82), Roanoke(17)
BOSTON (22713) Culpeper(84), Rappahannock(15)
BOWLING GREEN Caroline
BOYCE Clarke
BOYDTON Mecklenburg
BOYKINS Southampton
BRACEY (23919) Mecklenburg(94), Brunswick(5)
BRANCHVILLE Southampton
BRANDY STATION Culpeper
BREAKS Dickenson
BREMO BLUFF Fluvanna
BRIDGEWATER (22812) Rockingham(80), Augusta(19)
BRIGHTWOOD Madison
BRISTOL (24202) Washington(91), Bristol City(5), Scott(2)
BRISTOL Bristol City
BRISTOW Prince William

BROAD RUN (20137) Fauquier(78), Prince William(21)
BROAD RUN Fauquier
BROADFORD (24316) Tazewell(97), Smyth(2)
BROADWAY (22815) Rockingham(98), Shenandoah(1)
BRODNAX (23920) Brunswick(76), Mecklenburg(21), Lunenburg(2)
BROOKE Stafford
BROOKNEAL (24528) Campbell(78), Charlotte(21)
BROWNSBURG Rockbridge
BRUCETOWN Frederick
BRUINGTON King and Queen
BUCHANAN Botetourt
BUCKINGHAM Buckingham
BUENA VISTA (24416) Buena Vista City(77), Rockbridge(22)
BUFFALO JUNCTION (24529) Mecklenburg(98), Halifax(1)
BUMPASS (23024) Louisa(83), Spotsylvania(13), Hanover(3)
BURGESS Northumberland
BURKE Fairfax
BURKES GARDEN Tazewell
BURKEVILLE (23922) Nottoway(91), Prince Edward(8)
BURR HILL Orange
CALLANDS (24530) Pittsylvania(98), Henry(1)
CALLAO (22435) Northumberland(98), Westmoreland(1)
CALLAWAY Franklin
CALVERTON Fauquier
CANA Carroll
CAPE CHARLES Northampton
CAPEVILLE Northampton
CAPRON Southampton
CARDINAL Mathews
CARET (22436) Essex(98), Caroline(1)
CARROLLTON Isle of Wight
CARRSVILLE Isle of Wight
CARSON (23830) Prince George(55), Dinwiddie(30), Sussex(13)
CARTERSVILLE Cumberland
CASANOVA Fauquier
CASCADE Pittsylvania
CASTLETON (22716) Rappahannock(95), Culpeper(4)
CASTLEWOOD Russell
CATAWBA (24070) Roanoke(71), Montgomery(26), Craig(1)
CATHARPIN Prince William
CATLETT Fauquier
CAUTHORNVILLE King and Queen
CEDAR BLUFF (24609) Tazewell(83), Russell(16)
CENTER CROSS (22437) Essex(79), King and Queen(20)
CENTREVILLE Fairfax
CERES (24318) Bland(67), Smyth(32)
CHAMPLAIN (22438) Essex(90), Caroline(9)

CHANCE Essex
CHANTILLY Fairfax
CHANTILLY Loudoun
CHARLES CITY Charles City
CHARLOTTE COURT HOUSE (23923) Charlotte(97), Prince Edward(2)
CHARLOTTESVILLE (22901) Albemarle(82), Charlottesville City(17)
CHARLOTTESVILLE (22903) Charlottesville City(68), Albemarle(31)
CHARLOTTESVILLE Albemarle
CHARLOTTESVILLE Charlottesville City
CHASE CITY (23924) Mecklenburg(93), Lunenburg(4), Charlotte(2)
CHATHAM Pittsylvania
CHECK Floyd
CHERITON Northampton
CHESAPEAKE Chesapeake City
CHESTER Chesterfield
CHESTER GAP Rappahannock
CHILHOWIE (24319) Smyth(76), Washington(23)
CHINCOTEAGUE Accomack
CHINCOTEAGUE ISLAND Accomack
CHRISTCHURCH Middlesex
CHRISTIANSBURG Montgomery
CHURCH ROAD (23833) Dinwiddie(89), Amelia(10)
CHURCH VIEW Middlesex
CHURCHVILLE Augusta
CITY OFFICES Roanoke City
CLAREMONT Surry
CLARKSVILLE Mecklenburg
CLAUDVILLE Patrick
CLEAR BROOK Frederick
CLEVELAND (24225) Russell(97), Dickenson(2)
CLIFFORD Amherst
CLIFTON Fairfax
CLIFTON FORGE (24422) Alleghany(95), Botetourt(3), Clifton Forge City(1)
CLINCHBURG Washington
CLINCHCO Dickenson
CLINTWOOD Dickenson
CLOVER Halifax
CLOVERDALE Botetourt
CLUSTER SPRINGS Halifax
COBBS CREEK Mathews
COBHAM Albemarle
COEBURN (24230) Wise(89), Dickenson(9), Scott(1)
COLEMAN FALLS Bedford
COLES POINT Westmoreland
COLLINSVILLE Henry
COLOGNE King and Queen
COLONIAL BEACH Westmoreland
COLONIAL HEIGHTS (23834) Colonial Heights City(70), Chesterfield(29)
COLUMBIA (23038) Goochland(56), Cumberland(21), Fluvanna(21)
CONCORD (24538) Campbell(77), Appomattox(22)
COPPER HILL Floyd
CORBIN Caroline

COURTLAND (23837) Southampton(96), Sussex(3)
COVESVILLE Albemarle
COVINGTON (24426) Alleghany(49), Covington City(49)
CRADDOCKVILLE Accomack
CRAIGSVILLE Augusta
CREWE Nottoway
CRIDERS Rockingham
CRIMORA Augusta
CRIPPLE CREEK Wythe
CRITZ Patrick
CROCKETT Wythe
CROSS JUNCTION Frederick
CROZET Albemarle
CROZIER Goochland
CRYSTAL HILL Halifax
CULLEN (23934) Charlotte(60), Prince Edward(39)
CULPEPER (22701) Culpeper(89), Orange(7), Madison(3)
CUMBERLAND (23040) Cumberland(91), Buckingham(8)
DABNEYS Louisa
DAHLGREN King George
DALEVILLE Botetourt
DAMASCUS Washington
DANTE (24237) Dickenson(68), Russell(31)
DANVILLE (24541) Danville City(77), Pittsylvania(22)
DANVILLE Danville City
DARLINGTN HTS Prince Edward
DARLINGTON HEIGHTS Prince Edward
DAVENPORT Buchanan
DAVIS WHARF Accomack
DAYTON Rockingham
DEERFIELD (24432) Augusta(98), Bath(1)
DELAPLANE Fauquier
DELTAVILLE Middlesex
DENDRON Surry
DEWITT Dinwiddie
DIGGS Mathews
DILLWYN (23936) Buckingham(96), Cumberland(3)
DINWIDDIE Dinwiddie
DISPUTANTA (23842) Prince George(92), Sussex(7)
DOE HILL Highland
DOGUE King George
DOLPHIN Brunswick
DORAN Tazewell
DOSWELL (23047) Hanover(75), Caroline(24)
DRAKES BRANCH (23937) Charlotte(94), Lunenburg(5)
DRAPER (24324) Pulaski(78), Wythe(21)
DREWRYVILLE Southampton
DRY FORK Pittsylvania
DRYDEN Lee
DUBLIN (24084) Pulaski(94), Bland(5)
DUFFIELD (24244) Scott(83), Lee(16)
DUGSPUR Carroll
DULLES Loudoun
DUMFRIES Prince William
DUNDAS (23938) Brunswick(60), Lunenburg(39)
DUNGANNON Scott
DUNN LORING Fairfax
DUNNSVILLE Essex
DUTTON (23050) Mathews(77), Gloucester(22)
DYKE (22935) Greene(68), Albemarle(31)
EAGLE ROCK Botetourt
EARLYSVILLE Albemarle
EAST STONE GAP Wise
EASTVILLE Northampton
EBONY Brunswick
EDINBURG Shenandoah
EDWARDSVILLE Northumberland
EGGLESTON Giles
ELBERON Surry
ELK CREEK Grayson

ELKTON (22827) Rockingham(90), Page(9)
ELKWOOD Culpeper
ELLISTON (24087) Montgomery(96), Roanoke(3)
EMORY Washington
EMPORIA (23847) Greensville(66), Emporia City(30), Southampton(2), Sussex(1)
ESMONT Albemarle
ETLAN Madison
EVERGREEN Appomattox
EVINGTON (24550) Campbell(89), Bedford(10)
EWING Lee
EXETER Wise
EXMORE Northampton
FABER (22938) Nelson(96), Albemarle(3)
FAIRFAX (22032) Fairfax(95), Fairfax City(4)
FAIRFAX Fairfax
FAIRFAX Fairfax City
FAIRFAX STATION Fairfax
FAIRFIELD Rockbridge
FALLS CHURCH (22044) Fairfax(93), Falls Church City(6)
FALLS CHURCH (22046) Falls Church City(69), Fairfax(30)
FALLS CHURCH Fairfax
FALLS CHURCH Falls Church City
FALLS MILLS Tazewell
FANCY GAP Carroll
FARMVILLE (23901) Prince Edward(79), Cumberland(18), Buckingham(1)
FARMVILLE Prince Edward
FARNHAM Richmond
FERRUM Franklin
FIELDALE Henry
FIFE Goochland
FINCASTLE Botetourt
FISHERS HILL Shenandoah
FISHERSVILLE Augusta
FLINT HILL Rappahannock
FONESWOOD Richmond
FORD (23850) Dinwiddie(85), Amelia(14)
FOREST (24551) Bedford(87), Campbell(11)
FORK UNION Fluvanna
FORT BELVOIR Fairfax
FORT BLACKMORE Scott
FORT DEFIANCE Augusta
FORT EUSTIS Newport News City
FORT LEE (23801) Prince George(98), Petersburg City(1)
FORT MITCHELL Lunenburg
FORT MONROE Hampton City
FORT VALLEY Shenandoah
FOSTER Mathews
FRANKLIN (23851) Franklin City(51), Southampton(41), Isle of Wight(7)
FRANKTOWN Northampton
FREDERICKSBURG (22401) Fredericksburg City(96), Spotsylvania(3)
FREDERICKSBURG (22408) Spotsylvania(95), Caroline(3)
FREDERICKSBURG Fredericksburg City
FREDERICKSBURG Spotsylvania
FREDERICKSBURG Stafford
FREE UNION (22940) Albemarle(77), Greene(22)
FREEMAN (23856) Brunswick(95), Greensville(4)
FRIES Grayson
FRONT ROYAL (22630) Warren(98), Clarke(1)
FRONT ROYAL Warren
FT MYER Arlington
FULKS RUN Rockingham
GAINESVILLE Prince William
GALAX (24333) Carroll(35), Grayson(35), Galax City(29)
GARRISONVILLE Stafford
GASBURG Brunswick

GATE CITY Scott
GLADE SPRING Washington
GLADEHILL Franklin
GLADSTONE (24553) Nelson(44), Amherst(32), Appomattox(12), Buckingham(11)
GLADYS Campbell
GLASGOW Rockbridge
GLEN ALLEN (23059) Henrico(78), Hanover(21)
GLEN ALLEN Henrico
GLEN LYN Giles
GLEN WILTON Botetourt
GLOUCESTER Gloucester
GLOUCESTER POINT Gloucester
GOLDBOND Giles
GOLDVEIN Fauquier
GOOCHLAND Goochland
GOODE Bedford
GOODVIEW Bedford
GORDONSVILLE (22942) Orange(62), Louisa(34), Albemarle(2)
GORE Frederick
GOSHEN (24439) Rockbridge(80), Augusta(19)
GRAVES MILL Madison
GREAT AMERICAN MAGAZINE Hampton City
GREAT FALLS (22066) Fairfax(96), Loudoun(3)
GREEN BAY (23942) Prince Edward(67), Lunenburg(32)
GREENBACKVILLE Accomack
GREENBUSH Accomack
GREENVILLE Augusta
GREENWAY Fairfax
GREENWOOD Albemarle
GRETNA Pittsylvania
GRIMSTEAD Mathews
GROTTOES (24441) Rockingham(81), Augusta(18)
GRUNDY Buchanan
GUM SPRING (23065) Goochland(71), Louisa(28)
GWYNN Mathews
HACKSNECK Accomack
HADENSVILLE Goochland
HAGUE Westmoreland
HALLIEFORD Mathews
HALLWOOD Accomack
HAMILTON Loudoun
HAMPDEN SYDNEY Prince Edward
HAMPTON (23665) Hampton City(52), York(47)
HAMPTON Hampton City
HANDSOM Southampton
HANOVER (23069) Hanover(41), Caroline(33), King William(24)
HARBORTON Accomack
HARDY (24101) Franklin(91), Bedford(8)
HARDYVILLE Middlesex
HARMAN Buchanan
HARRISONBURG (22802) Harrisonburg City(50), Rockingham(49)
HARRISONBURG Harrisonburg City
HARTFIELD Middlesex
HARTWOOD Stafford
HAYES Gloucester
HAYMARKET Prince William
HAYNESVILLE Richmond
HAYSI (24256) Dickenson(89), Buchanan(10)
HAYWOOD Madison
HEAD WATERS Highland
HEATHSVILLE (22473) Northumberland(98), Lancaster(1)
HENRY (24102) Franklin(92), Henry(7)
HERNDON Fairfax
HIGHLAND SPRINGS Henrico
HIGHTOWN Highland
HILLSVILLE Carroll
HILTONS (24258) Scott(85), Washington(14)

HINTON Rockingham
HIWASSEE (24347) Pulaski(89), Montgomery(10)
HONAKER (24260) Russell(87), Buchanan(12)
HOOD Madison
HOPEWELL (23860) Hopewell City(81), Prince George(18)
HORNTOWN Accomack
HORSEPEN Tazewell
HOT SPRINGS (24445) Bath(57), Alleghany(42)
HOWARDSVILLE (24562) Albemarle(48), Buckingham(38), Nelson(12)
HUDDLESTON Bedford
HUDGINS Mathews
HUME Fauquier
HUNTLY Rappahannock
HURLEY Buchanan
HURT Pittsylvania
HUSTLE Essex
HYACINTH Northumberland
INDEPENDENCE Grayson
INDIAN VALLEY Floyd
IRON GATE Alleghany
IRVINGTON Lancaster
ISLE OF WIGHT Isle of Wight
IVANHOE (24350) Wythe(57), Carroll(34), Grayson(8)
IVOR (23866) Southampton(59), Isle of Wight(40)
IVY Albemarle
JAMAICA Middlesex
JAMES STORE Gloucester
JAMESTOWN James City
JAMESVILLE Northampton
JARRATT (23867) Greensville(91), Sussex(8)
JARRATT Greensville
JAVA (24565) Pittsylvania(89), Halifax(10)
JEFFERSONTON Culpeper
JENKINS BRIDGE Accomack
JERSEY King George
JETERSVILLE (23083) Amelia(97), Nottoway(2)
JEWELL RIDGE (24622) Tazewell(89), Buchanan(10)
JONESVILLE Lee
JORDAN MINES Alleghany
KEELING Pittsylvania
KEEN MOUNTAIN Buchanan
KEENE Albemarle
KEEZLETOWN Rockingham
KELLER Accomack
KENBRIDGE Lunenburg
KENTS STORE (23084) Fluvanna(65), Goochland(20), Louisa(14)
KEOKEE Lee
KESWICK (22947) Albemarle(85), Fluvanna(11), Louisa(3)
KEYSVILLE (23947) Charlotte(51), Lunenburg(39), Prince Edward(9)
KILMARNOCK (22482) Northumberland(62), Lancaster(37)
KING AND QUEEN COURT HOUS King and Queen
KING GEORGE King George
KING WILLIAM King William
KINSALE Westmoreland
LA CROSSE (23950) Mecklenburg(87), Brunswick(12)
LACEY SPRING Rockingham
LACKEY York
LADYSMITH Caroline
LAHORE Orange
LAMBSBURG Carroll
LANEVIEW (22504) Essex(80), Middlesex(19)
LANEXA (23089) New Kent(76), James City(23)
LAUREL FORK Carroll
LAWRENCEVILLE Brunswick
LEBANON Russell

LEE MONT Accomack
LEESBURG Loudoun
LEON Madison
LEWISETTA Northumberland
LEXINGTON (24450) Rockbridge(71),
   Lexington City(28)
LIGHTFOOT York
LIGNUM Culpeper
LINCOLN Loudoun
LINDEN (22642) Warren(85), Fauquier(14)
LINVILLE Rockingham
LITTLE PLYMOUTH King and Queen
LIVELY Lancaster
LOCUST DALE Madison
LOCUST GROVE (22508) Orange(92),
   Spotsylvania(7)
LOCUST HILL Middlesex
LOCUSTVILLE Accomack
LONG ISLAND (24569) Pittsylvania(86),
   Campbell(7), Halifax(5)
LORETTO Essex
LORTON Fairfax
LOTTSBURG Northumberland
LOUISA (23093) Louisa(92), Goochland(6),
   Fluvanna(1)
LOVETTSVILLE Loudoun
LOVINGSTON Nelson
LOW MOOR Alleghany
LOWRY Bedford
LUNENBURG Lunenburg
LURAY Page
LYNCH STATION (24571) Campbell(75),
   Bedford(24)
LYNCHBURG (24502) Lynchburg City(54),
   Campbell(43), Bedford(2)
LYNCHBURG (24503) Lynchburg City(67),
   Bedford(32)
LYNCHBURG (24504) Lynchburg City(65),
   Campbell(33)
LYNCHBURG Lynchburg City
LYNDHURST (22952) Augusta(95),
   Nelson(2), Waynesboro City(1)
MACHIPONGO Northampton
MACON Powhatan
MADISON HEIGHTS Amherst
MADISON MILLS Madison
MAIDENS (23102) Goochland(79),
   Louisa(13), Hanover(6)
MANAKIN SABOT Goochland
MANASSAS (20110) Manassas City(84),
   Prince William(15)
MANASSAS (20109) Prince William(96),
   Manassas City(3)
MANASSAS (20111) Prince William(63),
   Manassas Park City(36)
MANASSAS Manassas City
MANASSAS Manassas Park City
MANASSAS Prince William
MANGOHICK King William
MANNBORO Amelia
MANQUIN King William
MAPPSVILLE Accomack
MARION Smyth
MARIONVILLE Northampton
MARKHAM Fauquier
MARSHALL Fauquier
MARTINSVILLE (24112) Henry(65),
   Martinsville City(34)
MARTINSVILLE Martinsville City
MARYUS Gloucester
MASCOT King and Queen
MASSIES MILL Nelson
MATHEWS Mathews
MATTAPONI King and Queen
MAURERTOWN Shenandoah
MAVISDALE Buchanan
MAX MEADOWS Wythe
MAXIE Buchanan
MC CLURE Dickenson
MC COY Montgomery
MC DOWELL Highland
MC GAHEYSVILLE Rockingham
MC KENNEY Dinwiddie

MC LEAN Fairfax
MEADOWS OF DAN (24120) Patrick(73),
   Floyd(16), Carroll(10)
MEADOWVIEW Washington
MEARS Accomack
MECHANICSVILLE Hanover
MEHERRIN (23954) Prince Edward(68),
   Lunenburg(31)
MELFA Accomack
MENDOTA Washington
MEREDITHVILLE Brunswick
MERRIFIELD Fairfax
MERRY POINT Lancaster
MIDDLEBROOK (24459) Augusta(88),
   Rockbridge(11)
MIDDLEBURG (20117) Loudoun(97),
   Fauquier(2)
MIDDLEBURG Loudoun
MIDDLETOWN (22645) Frederick(56),
   Warren(42)
MIDDLETOWN Warren
MIDLAND Fauquier
MIDLOTHIAN Chesterfield
MILES Chesterfield
MILFORD (22514) Caroline(98), King and
   Queen(1)
MILLBORO Bath
MILLERS TAVERN Essex
MILLWOOD Clarke
MINE RUN Orange
MINERAL (23117) Louisa(86),
   Spotsylvania(10), Goochland(2)
MINT SPRING Augusta
MITCHELLS Culpeper
MOBJACK Mathews
MODEST TOWN Accomack
MOLLUSK Lancaster
MONETA (24121) Bedford(59),
   Franklin(40)
MONROE Amherst
MONTEBELLO Nelson
MONTEREY Highland
MONTPELIER (23192) Hanover(92),
   Louisa(7)
MONTPELIER STATION Orange
MONTROSS Westmoreland
MONTVALE Bedford
MOON Mathews
MORATTICO Lancaster
MOSELEY (23120) Chesterfield(95),
   Powhatan(4)
MOUNT CRAWFORD (22841)
   Rockingham(98), Augusta(1)
MOUNT HOLLY Westmoreland
MOUNT JACKSON Shenandoah
MOUNT SIDNEY Augusta
MOUNT SOLON Augusta
MOUNT VERNON Fairfax
MOUTH OF WILSON Grayson
MUSTOE Highland
NARROWS (24124) Giles(97), Bland(2)
NARUNA Campbell
NASSAWADOX Northampton
NATHALIE Halifax
NATURAL BRIDGE Rockbridge
NATURAL BRIDGE STATION Rockbridge
NAXERA Gloucester
NELLYSFORD Nelson
NELSON Mecklenburg
NELSONIA Accomack
NEW CANTON (23123) Buckingham(95),
   Cumberland(4)
NEW CASTLE Craig
NEW CHURCH Accomack
NEW HOPE Augusta
NEW KENT (23124) New Kent(95),
   Hanover(4)
NEW MARKET (22844) Shenandoah(91),
   Rockingham(8)
NEW POINT Mathews
NEW RIVER Pulaski
NEWBERN Pulaski
NEWINGTON Fairfax

NEWPORT (24128) Giles(87), Craig(12)
NEWPORT NEWS (23605) Newport News
   City(81), Hampton City(18)
NEWPORT NEWS Hampton City
NEWPORT NEWS Newport News City
NEWSOMS Southampton
NEWTOWN King and Queen
NICKELSVILLE (24271) Scott(97),
   Russell(2)
NINDE King George
NOKESVILLE (20181) Prince William(94),
   Fauquier(5)
NOKESVILLE Prince William
NORA Dickenson
NORFOLK Norfolk City
NORGE James City
NORTH (23128) Mathews(53),
   Gloucester(46)
NORTH GARDEN Albemarle
NORTH TAZEWELL Tazewell
NORTON (24273) Norton City(72),
   Wise(27)
NORWOOD Nelson
NOTTOWAY Nottoway
NUTTSVILLE Lancaster
OAK HALL Accomack
OAKPARK Madison
OAKTON Fairfax
OAKWOOD Buchanan
OCCOQUAN Prince William
OILVILLE (23129) Goochland(96),
   Hanover(3)
OLDHAMS Westmoreland
ONANCOCK Accomack
ONEMO Mathews
ONLEY Accomack
OPHELIA Northumberland
ORANGE (22960) Orange(90), Madison(9)
ORDINARY Gloucester
ORISKANY Botetourt
ORKNEY SPRINGS Shenandoah
ORLEAN Fauquier
OYSTER Northampton
PAEONIAN SPRINGS Loudoun
PAINT BANK Craig
PAINTER Accomack
PALMYRA Fluvanna
PAMPLIN (23958) Prince Edward(57),
   Appomattox(29), Charlotte(12)
PARIS (20130) Clarke(73), Fauquier(18),
   Loudoun(8)
PARIS Fauquier
PARKSLEY Accomack
PARROTT Pulaski
PARTLOW Spotsylvania
PATRICK SPRINGS Patrick
PEARISBURG (24134) Giles(98), Bland(1)
PEMBROKE Giles
PENHOOK (24137) Franklin(79),
   Pittsylvania(20)
PENN LAIRD Rockingham
PENNINGTON GAP Lee
PETERSBURG (23803) Petersburg
   City(54), Dinwiddie(25), Chesterfield(20)
PETERSBURG (23805) Petersburg
   City(60), Prince George(26),
   Dinwiddie(13)
PETERSBURG Petersburg City
PHENIX Charlotte
PHILOMONT Loudoun
PILGRIMS KNOB Buchanan
PILOT (24138) Floyd(51), Montgomery(48)
PINEY RIVER Nelson
PITTSVILLE Pittsylvania
PLAIN VIEW King and Queen
PLEASANT VALLEY Rockingham
POCAHONTAS Tazewell
POQUOSON Poquoson City
PORT HAYWOOD Mathews
PORT REPUBLIC Rockingham
PORT ROYAL Caroline
PORTSMOUTH Portsmouth City
POUND Wise

POUNDING MILL Tazewell
POWHATAN (23139) Powhatan(97),
   Cumberland(2)
PRATTS Madison
PRINCE GEORGE Prince George
PROSPECT Prince Edward
PROVIDENCE FORGE (23140) New
   Kent(59), Charles City(40)
PUNGOTEAGUE Accomack
PURCELLVILLE Loudoun
QUANTICO Prince William
QUANTICO Stafford
QUICKSBURG Shenandoah
QUINBY Accomack
QUINQUE Greene
QUINTON New Kent
RADFORD (24141) Radford City(59),
   Pulaski(27), Montgomery(11), Floyd(1)
RADFORD Radford City
RADIANT Madison
RANDOLPH (23962) Charlotte(90),
   Halifax(9)
RAPHINE (24472) Rockbridge(70),
   Augusta(29)
RAPIDAN (22733) Culpeper(70),
   Orange(29)
RAPPAHANNOCK ACADEMY Caroline
RAVEN (24639) Tazewell(88),
   Buchanan(10), Russell(1)
RAWLINGS Brunswick
RECTORTOWN Fauquier
RED ASH Tazewell
RED HOUSE (23963) Charlotte(73),
   Campbell(21), Appomattox(5)
RED OAK (23964) Charlotte(88),
   Mecklenburg(11)
REDART Mathews
REDWOOD Franklin
REEDVILLE Northumberland
REGINA Lancaster
REMINGTON (22734) Fauquier(86),
   Culpeper(13)
REPUBLICAN GROVE Halifax
RESCUE Isle of Wight
RESTON Fairfax
REVA (22735) Culpeper(89), Madison(10)
RHOADESVILLE Orange
RICE (23966) Amelia(53), Prince
   Edward(46)
RICH CREEK Giles
RICHARDSVILLE Culpeper
RICHLANDS Tazewell
RICHMOND (23235) Chesterfield(72),
   Richmond City(27)
RICHMOND (23231) Henrico(82),
   Richmond City(13), Charles City(3)
RICHMOND (23238) Henrico(91),
   Goochland(8)
RICHMOND (23222) Richmond City(67),
   Henrico(32)
RICHMOND (23225) Richmond City(83),
   Chesterfield(16)
RICHMOND (23226) Richmond City(50),
   Henrico(49)
RICHMOND Chesterfield
RICHMOND Henrico
RICHMOND Richmond City
RIDGEWAY Henry
RILEYVILLE Page
RINER (24149) Montgomery(79), Floyd(20)
RINGGOLD Pittsylvania
RIPPLEMEAD Giles
RIXEYVILLE Culpeper
ROANOKE (24018) Roanoke(85), Roanoke
   City(14)
ROANOKE (24019) Roanoke(67),
   Botetourt(21), Roanoke City(11)
ROANOKE (24015) Roanoke City(98),
   Roanoke(1)
ROANOKE Botetourt
ROANOKE Montgomery
ROANOKE Roanoke
ROANOKE Roanoke City

ROCHELLE Madison
ROCKBRIDGE BATHS Rockbridge
ROCKVILLE (23146) Hanover(73),
   Goochland(26)
ROCKY GAP Bland
ROCKY MOUNT Franklin
ROLLINS FORK King George
ROSE HILL Lee
ROSEDALE Russell
ROSELAND (22967) Nelson(91),
   Amherst(8)
ROSELAND Amherst
ROUND HILL Loudoun
ROWE (24646) Buchanan(91), Russell(8)
RUBY Stafford
RUCKERSVILLE (22968) Greene(90),
   Albemarle(9)
RURAL RETREAT (24368) Wythe(55),
   Smyth(44)
RUSTBURG Campbell
RUTHER GLEN (22546) Caroline(98),
   Hanover(1)
RUTHVILLE Charles City
SAINT CHARLES Lee
SAINT PAUL (24283) Wise(95), Russell(3)
SAINT STEPHENS CHURCH (23148) King
   and Queen(86), Essex(13)
SALEM (24153) Salem City(63),
   Roanoke(36)
SALEM Salem City
SALTVILLE (24370) Smyth(80),
   Washington(19)
SALUDA (23149) Middlesex(49),
   Gloucester(36), King and Queen(13)
SANDSTON Henrico
SANDY HOOK Goochland
SANDY LEVEL Pittsylvania
SANDY POINT Westmoreland
SANFORD Accomack
SAXE Charlotte
SAXIS Accomack
SCHLEY Gloucester
SCHUYLER (22969) Nelson(59),
   Albemarle(40)
SCOTTSBURG Halifax
SCOTTSVILLE (24590) Fluvanna(47),
   Albemarle(44), Buckingham(8)
SEAFORD York
SEALSTON King George
SEAVIEW Northampton
SEDLEY (23878) Southampton(97),
   Sussex(2)
SELMA Alleghany
SEVEN MILE FORD Smyth
SEVERN Gloucester
SHACKLEFORDS King and Queen
SHADOW Mathews
SHARPS Richmond
SHAWSVILLE Montgomery
SHILOH King George
SHIPMAN Nelson
SHORTT GAP Buchanan
SINGERS GLEN Rockingham
SKIPPERS Greensville
SKIPWITH Mecklenburg
SMITHFIELD Isle of Wight
SOMERSET (22972) Orange(95),
   Madison(4)

SOMERVILLE Fauquier
SOUTH BOSTON Halifax
SOUTH HILL (23970) Mecklenburg(93),
   Lunenburg(6)
SPARTA Caroline
SPEEDWELL Wythe
SPENCER Henry
SPERRYVILLE (22740)
   Rappahannock(84), Culpeper(13),
   Madison(1)
SPOTSYLVANIA Spotsylvania
SPOTTSWOOD (24475) Augusta(96),
   Rockbridge(3)
SPOUT SPRING Appomattox
SPRING GROVE (23881) Prince
   George(50), Surry(49)
SPRINGFIELD Fairfax
STAFFORD (22556) Stafford(98),
   Fauquier(1)
STAFFORDSVILLE Giles
STANARDSVILLE (22973) Greene(98),
   Madison(1)
STANLEY Page
STANLEYTOWN Henry
STAR TANNERY (22654) Frederick(73),
   Shenandoah(26)
STATE FARM (23160) Powhatan(66),
   Goochland(33)
STAUNTON (24401) Staunton City(69),
   Augusta(30)
STAUNTON Augusta
STAUNTON Staunton City
STEELES TAVERN Augusta
STEPHENS CITY (22655) Frederick(98),
   Warren(1)
STEPHENSON Frederick
STERLING Loudoun
STERLING PARK Loudoun
STEVENSBURG Culpeper
STEVENSVILLE King and Queen
STONEGA Wise
STONY CREEK (23882) Sussex(71),
   Dinwiddie(28)
STRASBURG (22657) Shenandoah(84),
   Warren(15)
STRASBURG Shenandoah
STRATFORD Westmoreland
STUART Patrick
STUARTS DRAFT Augusta
STUDLEY Hanover
SUFFOLK Suffolk City
SUGAR GROVE Smyth
SUMERDUCK Fauquier
SUPPLY Essex
SURRY Surry
SUSAN Mathews
SUTHERLAND Dinwiddie
SUTHERLIN Pittsylvania
SWEET BRIAR Amherst
SWOOPE Augusta
SWORDS CREEK Russell
SYRIA Madison
TANGIER Accomack
TANNERSVILLE Tazewell
TAPPAHANNOCK (22560) Essex(94), King
   and Queen(5)
TASLEY Accomack
TAZEWELL Tazewell

TEMPERANCEVILLE Accomack
THAXTON Bedford
THE PLAINS Fauquier
THORNBURG Spotsylvania
TIMBERVILLE (22853) Rockingham(95),
   Shenandoah(4)
TOANO James City
TOMS BROOK Shenandoah
TOPPING Middlesex
TOWNSEND Northampton
TRAMMEL Dickenson
TREVILIANS Louisa
TRIANGLE Prince William
TROUT DALE (24378) Grayson(89),
   Smyth(10)
TROUTDALE (24378) Grayson(89),
   Smyth(10)
TROUTVILLE (24175) Botetourt(88),
   Roanoke(11)
TROY (22974) Fluvanna(77), Louisa(16),
   Albemarle(5)
TURBEVILLE Halifax
TYRO Nelson
UNION HALL Franklin
UNIVERSITY OF RICHMOND Richmond
   City
UPPERVILLE (20184) Fauquier(64),
   Loudoun(35)
UPPERVILLE Fauquier
URBANNA Middlesex
VALENTINES Brunswick
VANSANT Buchanan
VERNON HILL (24597) Halifax(80),
   Pittsylvania(19)
VERONA Augusta
VESTA Patrick
VESUVIUS (24483) Rockbridge(60),
   Amherst(20), Nelson(19)
VICTORIA Lunenburg
VIENNA Fairfax
VIEWTOWN (22746) Culpeper(74),
   Rappahannock(25)
VILLAGE Richmond
VILLAMONT Bedford
VINTON (24179) Bedford(50), Roanoke(49)
VIRGILINA (24598) Halifax(84),
   Mecklenburg(15)
VIRGINIA BEACH Virginia Beach City
VOLNEY Grayson
WACHAPREAGUE Accomack
WAKE Middlesex
WAKEFIELD (23888) Sussex(54),
   Southampton(25), Surry(19)
WALKERTON (23177) King and
   Queen(78), King William(21)
WALLOPS ISLAND Accomack
WARDTOWN Northampton
WARE NECK Gloucester
WARFIELD Brunswick
WARM SPRINGS Bath
WARNER Middlesex
WARRENTON Fauquier
WARSAW (22572) Richmond(93),
   Westmoreland(6)
WASHINGTON Rappahannock
WATER VIEW Middlesex
WATERFORD Loudoun
WATTSVILLE Accomack

WAVERLY Sussex
WAYNESBORO (22980) Waynesboro
   City(71), Augusta(28)
WEBER CITY Scott
WEEMS Lancaster
WEIRWOOD Northampton
WEST AUGUSTA Augusta
WEST MCLEAN Fairfax
WEST POINT (23181) King William(85),
   New Kent(11), King and Queen(3)
WESTMORELAND Westmoreland
WEYERS CAVE (24486) Augusta(85),
   Rockingham(14)
WHITE HALL Albemarle
WHITE MARSH Gloucester
WHITE PLAINS Brunswick
WHITE POST (22663) Clarke(60),
   Frederick(34), Warren(4)
WHITE STONE Lancaster
WHITETOP Grayson
WHITEWOOD Buchanan
WICOMICO Gloucester
WICOMICO CHURCH Northumberland
WILLIAMSBURG (23185) James City(46),
   Williamsburg City(27), York(25)
WILLIAMSBURG (23188) James City(78),
   York(19), Williamsburg City(1)
WILLIAMSBURG Williamsburg City
WILLIAMSVILLE (24487) Bath(64),
   Highland(36)
WILLIS (24380) Floyd(93), Carroll(6)
WILLIS WHARF Northampton
WILSONS (23894) Dinwiddie(86),
   Nottoway(13)
WINCHESTER (22601) Winchester
   City(93), Frederick(6)
WINCHESTER Frederick
WINCHESTER Winchester City
WINDSOR Isle of Wight
WINGINA (24599) Nelson(85),
   Buckingham(14)
WIRTZ Franklin
WISE Wise
WITHAMS Accomack
WOLFORD Buchanan
WOLFTOWN Madison
WOODBERRY FOREST Madison
WOODBRIDGE Prince William
WOODFORD (22580) Caroline(90),
   Spotsylvania(9)
WOODLAWN Carroll
WOODS CROSS ROADS Gloucester
WOODSTOCK Shenandoah
WOODVILLE Rappahannock
WOOLWINE Patrick
WYLLIESBURG Charlotte
WYTHEVILLE Wythe
YALE Sussex
YARDS Tazewell
YORKTOWN York
ZACATA Westmoreland
ZANONI Gloucester
ZUNI (23898) Isle of Wight(69),
   Southampton(30)

Virginia ZIP/City Cross Reference

ZIP Range	City	ZIP Range	City	ZIP Range	City	ZIP Range	City
20101-20104	DULLES	22090-22090	HERNDON	22509-22509	LORETTO	22714-22714	BRANDY STATION
20105-20105	ALDIE	22091-22091	RESTON	22511-22511	LOTTSBURG	22715-22715	BRIGHTWOOD
20106-20106	AMISSVILLE	22092-22092	HERNDON	22513-22513	MERRY POINT	22716-22716	CASTLETON
20107-20107	ARCOLA	22093-22093	ASHBURN	22514-22514	MILFORD	22718-22718	ELKWOOD
20108-20113	MANASSAS	22094-22095	HERNDON	22517-22517	MOLLUSK	22719-22719	ETLAN
20115-20116	MARSHALL	22096-22096	RESTON	22520-22520	MONTROSS	22720-22720	GOLDVEIN
20117-20118	MIDDLEBURG	22101-22102	MC LEAN	22523-22523	MORATTICO	22721-22721	GRAVES MILL
20119-20119	CATLETT	22103-22103	WEST MCLEAN	22524-22524	MOUNT HOLLY	22722-22722	HAYWOOD
20120-20122	CENTREVILLE	22106-22109	MC LEAN	22526-22526	NINDE	22723-22723	HOOD
20124-20124	CLIFTON	22110-22111	MANASSAS	22528-22528	NUTTSVILLE	22724-22724	JEFFERSONTON
20128-20128	ORLEAN	22115-22115	MARSHALL	22529-22529	OLDHAMS	22725-22725	LEON
20129-20129	PAEONIAN SPRINGS	22116-22116	MERRIFIELD	22530-22530	OPHELIA	22726-22726	LIGNUM
20130-20130	PARIS	22117-22117	MIDDLEBURG	22534-22534	PARTLOW	22727-22727	MADISON
20131-20131	PHILOMONT	22118-22120	MERRIFIELD	22535-22535	PORT ROYAL	22728-22728	MIDLAND
20132-20134	PURCELLVILLE	22121-22121	MOUNT VERNON	22538-22538	RAPPAHANNOCK	22729-22729	MITCHELLS
20135-20135	BLUEMONT	22122-22122	NEWINGTON		ACADEMY	22730-22730	OAKPARK
20136-20136	BRISTOW	22123-22123	NOKESVILLE	22539-22539	REEDVILLE	22731-22731	PRATTS
20137-20137	BROAD RUN	22124-22124	OAKTON	22540-22540	REGINA	22732-22732	RADIANT
20138-20138	CALVERTON	22125-22125	OCCOQUAN	22542-22542	RHOADESVILLE	22733-22733	RAPIDAN
20139-20139	CASANOVA	22128-22128	ORLEAN	22544-22544	ROLLINS FORK	22734-22734	REMINGTON
20140-20140	RECTORTOWN	22129-22129	PAEONIAN SPRINGS	22545-22545	RUBY	22735-22735	REVA
20141-20142	ROUND HILL	22130-22130	PARIS	22546-22546	RUTHER GLEN	22736-22736	RICHARDSVILLE
20143-20143	CATHARPIN	22131-22131	PHILOMONT	22547-22547	SEALSTON	22737-22737	RIXEYVILLE
20144-20144	DELAPLANE	22132-22132	PURCELLVILLE	22548-22548	SHARPS	22738-22738	ROCHELLE
20146-20149	ASHBURN	22134-22135	QUANTICO	22549-22549	SHILOH	22739-22739	SOMERVILLE
20151-20153	CHANTILLY	22140-22140	RECTORTOWN	22552-22552	SPARTA	22740-22740	SPERRYVILLE
20155-20156	GAINESVILLE	22141-22141	ROUND HILL	22553-22553	SPOTSYLVANIA	22741-22741	STEVENSBURG
20158-20159	HAMILTON	22150-22161	SPRINGFIELD	22554-22556	STAFFORD	22742-22742	SUMERDUCK
20160-20160	LINCOLN	22170-22170	STERLING PARK	22558-22558	STRATFORD	22743-22743	SYRIA
20163-20167	STERLING	22171-22171	THE PLAINS	22559-22559	SUPPLY	22746-22746	VIEWTOWN
20168-20169	HAYMARKET	22172-22172	TRIANGLE	22560-22560	TAPPAHANNOCK	22747-22747	WASHINGTON
20170-20172	HERNDON	22176-22176	UPPERVILLE	22565-22565	THORNBURG	22748-22748	WOLFTOWN
20175-20178	LEESBURG	22180-22185	VIENNA	22567-22567	UNIONVILLE	22749-22749	WOODVILLE
20180-20180	LOVETTSVILLE	22186-22186	WARRENTON	22568-22568	MINE RUN	22801-22807	HARRISONBURG
20181-20182	NOKESVILLE	22190-22190	WATERFORD	22570-22570	VILLAGE	22810-22810	BASYE
20184-20185	UPPERVILLE	22191-22195	WOODBRIDGE	22572-22572	WARSAW	22811-22811	BERGTON
20186-20188	WARRENTON	22199-22199	LORTON	22576-22576	WEEMS	22812-22812	BRIDGEWATER
20189-20189	DULLES	22200-22210	ARLINGTON	22577-22577	WESTMORELAND	22815-22815	BROADWAY
20190-20191	RESTON	22211-22211	FT MYER	22577-22577	SANDY POINT	22820-22820	CRIDERS
20192-20192	HERNDON	22212-22246	ARLINGTON	22578-22578	WHITE STONE	22821-22821	DAYTON
20193-20196	RESTON	22300-22336	ALEXANDRIA	22579-22579	WICOMICO CHURCH	22824-22824	EDINBURG
20197-20197	WATERFORD	22401-22412	FREDERICKSBURG	22580-22580	WOODFORD	22827-22827	ELKTON
20198-20198	THE PLAINS	22421-22421	ALFONSO	22581-22581	ZACATA	22830-22830	FULKS RUN
20199-20199	DULLES	22427-22428	BOWLING GREEN	22601-22604	WINCHESTER	22831-22831	HINTON
22001-22001	ALDIE	22430-22430	BROOKE	22610-22610	BENTONVILLE	22832-22832	KEEZLETOWN
22002-22002	AMISSVILLE	22432-22432	BURGESS	22611-22611	BERRYVILLE	22833-22833	LACEY SPRING
22003-22003	ANNANDALE	22433-22433	BURR HILL	22620-22620	BOYCE	22834-22834	LINVILLE
22009-22009	BURKE	22435-22435	CALLAO	22622-22622	BRUCETOWN	22835-22835	LURAY
22010-22010	ARCOLA	22436-22436	CARET	22623-22623	CHESTER GAP	22840-22840	MC GAHEYSVILLE
22011-22011	ASHBURN	22437-22437	CENTER CROSS	22624-22624	CLEAR BROOK	22841-22841	MOUNT CRAWFORD
22012-22012	BLUEMONT	22438-22438	CHAMPLAIN	22625-22625	CROSS JUNCTION	22842-22842	MOUNT JACKSON
22013-22013	BRISTOW	22439-22439	CHANCE	22626-22626	FISHERS HILL	22843-22843	MOUNT SOLON
22014-22014	BROAD RUN	22442-22442	COLES POINT	22627-22627	FLINT HILL	22844-22844	NEW MARKET
22015-22015	BURKE	22443-22443	COLONIAL BEACH	22630-22630	FRONT ROYAL	22845-22845	ORKNEY SPRINGS
22016-22016	CALVERTON	22446-22446	CORBIN	22637-22637	GORE	22846-22846	PENN LAIRD
22017-22017	CASANOVA	22448-22448	DAHLGREN	22638-22638	WINCHESTER	22847-22847	QUICKSBURG
22018-22018	CATHARPIN	22451-22451	DOGUE	22639-22639	HUME	22848-22848	PLEASANT VALLEY
22019-22019	CATLETT	22454-22454	DUNNSVILLE	22640-22640	HUNTLY	22849-22849	SHENANDOAH
22020-22020	CENTREVILLE	22456-22456	EDWARDSVILLE	22641-22641	STRASBURG	22850-22850	SINGERS GLEN
22021-22022	FAIRFAX	22460-22460	FARNHAM	22642-22642	LINDEN	22851-22851	STANLEY
22024-22024	CLIFTON	22461-22461	FONESWOOD	22643-22643	MARKHAM	22853-22853	TIMBERVILLE
22025-22025	DELAPLANE	22463-22463	GARRISONVILLE	22644-22644	MAURERTOWN	22900-22911	CHARLOTTESVILLE
22026-22026	DUMFRIES	22469-22469	HAGUE	22645-22645	MIDDLETOWN	22920-22920	AFTON
22027-22027	DUNN LORING	22471-22471	HARTWOOD	22646-22646	MILLWOOD	22922-22922	ARRINGTON
22030-22038	FAIRFAX	22472-22472	HAYNESVILLE	22649-22649	MIDDLETOWN	22923-22923	BARBOURSVILLE
22039-22039	FAIRFAX STATION	22473-22473	HEATHSVILLE	22650-22650	RILEYVILLE	22924-22924	BATESVILLE
22040-22047	FALLS CHURCH	22476-22476	HUSTLE	22651-22651	FRONT ROYAL	22929-22929	COBHAM
22060-22060	FORT BELVOIR	22477-22477	HYACINTH	22652-22652	FORT VALLEY	22931-22931	COVESVILLE
22065-22065	GAINESVILLE	22480-22480	IRVINGTON	22654-22654	STAR TANNERY	22932-22932	CROZET
22066-22066	GREAT FALLS	22481-22481	JERSEY	22655-22655	STEPHENS CITY	22935-22935	DYKE
22067-22067	GREENWAY	22482-22482	KILMARNOCK	22656-22656	STEPHENSON	22936-22936	EARLYSVILLE
22068-22068	HAMILTON	22485-22485	KING GEORGE	22657-22657	STRASBURG	22937-22937	ESMONT
22069-22069	HAYMARKET	22488-22488	KINSALE	22660-22660	TOMS BROOK	22938-22938	FABER
22070-22070	RESTON	22501-22501	LADYSMITH	22663-22663	WHITE POST	22939-22939	FISHERSVILLE
22071-22071	HERNDON	22502-22502	LAHORE	22664-22664	WOODSTOCK	22940-22940	FREE UNION
22075-22075	LEESBURG	22503-22503	LANCASTER	22701-22701	CULPEPER	22942-22942	GORDONSVILLE
22078-22078	PURCELLVILLE	22504-22504	LANEVIEW	22709-22709	ARODA	22943-22943	GREENWOOD
22079-22079	LORTON	22505-22505	LEWISETTA	22711-22711	BANCO	22945-22945	IVY
22080-22080	LOVETTSVILLE	22507-22507	LIVELY	22712-22712	BEALETON	22946-22946	KEENE
22081-22082	MERRIFIELD	22508-22508	LOCUST GROVE	22713-22713	BOSTON	22947-22947	KESWICK

22948-22948	LOCUST DALE
22949-22949	LOVINGSTON
22951-22951	ROSELAND
22952-22952	LYNDHURST
22953-22953	MADISON MILLS
22954-22954	MASSIES MILL
22957-22957	MONTPELIER STATION
22958-22958	NELLYSFORD
22959-22959	NORTH GARDEN
22960-22960	ORANGE
22963-22963	PALMYRA
22964-22964	PINEY RIVER
22965-22965	QUINQUE
22967-22967	ROSELAND
22968-22968	RUCKERSVILLE
22969-22969	SCHUYLER
22971-22971	SHIPMAN
22972-22972	SOMERSET
22973-22973	STANARDSVILLE
22974-22974	TROY
22976-22976	TYRO
22980-22980	WAYNESBORO
22987-22987	WHITE HALL
22989-22989	WOODBERRY FOREST
23001-23001	ACHILLES
23002-23002	AMELIA COURT HOUSE
23003-23003	ARK
23004-23004	ARVONIA
23005-23005	ASHLAND
23009-23009	AYLETT
23011-23011	BARHAMSVILLE
23013-23013	BAVON
23014-23014	BEAUMONT
23015-23015	BEAVERDAM
23016-23016	BEAVERLETT
23017-23017	BELLAMY
23018-23018	BENA
23020-23020	BLAKES
23021-23021	BOHANNON
23022-23022	BREMO BLUFF
23023-23023	BRUINGTON
23024-23024	BUMPASS
23025-23025	CARDINAL
23027-23027	CARTERSVILLE
23029-23029	CAUTHORNVILLE
23030-23030	CHARLES CITY
23031-23031	CHRISTCHURCH
23032-23032	CHURCH VIEW
23035-23035	COBBS CREEK
23037-23037	COLOGNE
23038-23038	COLUMBIA
23039-23039	CROZIER
23040-23040	CUMBERLAND
23042-23042	DABNEYS
23043-23043	DELTAVILLE
23045-23045	DIGGS
23047-23047	DOSWELL
23050-23050	DUTTON
23054-23054	FIFE
23055-23055	FORK UNION
23056-23056	FOSTER
23058-23060	GLEN ALLEN
23061-23061	GLOUCESTER
23062-23062	GLOUCESTER POINT
23063-23063	GOOCHLAND
23064-23064	GRIMSTEAD
23065-23065	GUM SPRING
23066-23066	GWYNN
23067-23067	HADENSVILLE
23068-23068	HALLIEFORD
23069-23069	HANOVER
23070-23070	HARDYVILLE
23071-23071	HARTFIELD
23072-23072	HAYES
23075-23075	HIGHLAND SPRINGS
23076-23076	HUDGINS
23079-23079	JAMAICA
23080-23080	JAMES STORE
23081-23081	JAMESTOWN
23083-23083	JETERSVILLE
23084-23084	KENTS STORE
23085-23085	KING AND QUEEN COURT HOUS
23086-23086	KING WILLIAM
23089-23089	LANEXA
23090-23090	LIGHTFOOT
23091-23091	LITTLE PLYMOUTH
23092-23092	LOCUST HILL
23093-23093	LOUISA
23101-23101	MACON
23102-23102	MAIDENS
23103-23103	MANAKIN SABOT
23104-23104	MANGOHICK
23105-23105	MANNBORO
23106-23106	MANQUIN
23107-23107	MARYUS
23108-23108	MASCOT
23109-23109	MATHEWS
23110-23110	MATTAPONI
23111-23111	MECHANICSVILLE
23112-23113	MIDLOTHIAN
23114-23114	MILES
23114-23114	MIDLOTHIAN
23115-23115	MILLERS TAVERN
23116-23116	MECHANICSVILLE
23117-23117	MINERAL
23118-23118	MOBJACK
23119-23119	MOON
23120-23120	MOSELEY
23122-23122	NAXERA
23123-23123	NEW CANTON
23124-23124	NEW KENT
23125-23125	NEW POINT
23126-23126	NEWTOWN
23127-23127	NORGE
23128-23128	NORTH
23129-23129	OILVILLE
23130-23130	ONEMO
23131-23131	ORDINARY
23137-23137	PLAIN VIEW
23138-23138	PORT HAYWOOD
23139-23139	POWHATAN
23140-23140	PROVIDENCE FORGE
23141-23141	QUINTON
23142-23142	REDART
23146-23146	ROCKVILLE
23147-23147	RUTHVILLE
23148-23148	SAINT STEPHENS CHURCH
23149-23149	SALUDA
23150-23150	SANDSTON
23153-23153	SANDY HOOK
23154-23154	SCHLEY
23155-23155	SEVERN
23156-23156	SHACKLEFORDS
23157-23157	SHADOW
23160-23160	STATE FARM
23161-23161	STEVENSVILLE
23162-23162	STUDLEY
23163-23163	SUSAN
23168-23168	TOANO
23169-23169	TOPPING
23170-23170	TREVILIANS
23173-23173	UNIVERSITY OF RICHMOND
23175-23175	URBANNA
23176-23176	WAKE
23177-23177	WALKERTON
23178-23178	WARE NECK
23179-23179	WARNER
23180-23180	WATER VIEW
23181-23181	WEST POINT
23183-23183	WHITE MARSH
23184-23184	WICOMICO
23185-23188	WILLIAMSBURG
23190-23190	WOODS CROSS ROADS
23191-23191	ZANONI
23192-23192	MONTPELIER
23200-23298	RICHMOND
23301-23301	ACCOMAC
23302-23302	ASSAWOMAN
23303-23303	ATLANTIC
23304-23304	BATTERY PARK
23306-23306	BELLE HAVEN
23307-23307	BIRDSNEST
23308-23308	BLOXOM
23310-23310	CAPE CHARLES
23313-23313	CAPEVILLE
23314-23314	CARROLLTON
23315-23315	CARRSVILLE
23316-23316	CHERITON
23320-23328	CHESAPEAKE
23336-23336	CHINCOTEAGUE
23336-23336	CHINCOTEAGUE ISLAND
23337-23337	CHINCOTEAGUE
23337-23337	WALLOPS ISLAND
23341-23341	CRADDOCKVILLE
23345-23345	DAVIS WHARF
23347-23347	EASTVILLE
23350-23350	EXMORE
23354-23354	FRANKTOWN
23356-23356	GREENBACKVILLE
23357-23357	GREENBUSH
23358-23358	HACKSNECK
23359-23359	HALLWOOD
23389-23389	HARBORTON
23395-23395	HORNTOWN
23396-23396	OAK HALL
23397-23397	ISLE OF WIGHT
23398-23398	JAMESVILLE
23399-23399	JENKINS BRIDGE
23401-23401	KELLER
23403-23403	LEE MONT
23404-23404	LOCUSTVILLE
23405-23405	MACHIPONGO
23407-23407	MAPPSVILLE
23408-23408	MARIONVILLE
23409-23409	MEARS
23410-23410	MELFA
23412-23412	MODEST TOWN
23413-23413	NASSAWADOX
23414-23414	NELSONIA
23415-23415	NEW CHURCH
23416-23416	OAK HALL
23417-23417	ONANCOCK
23418-23418	ONLEY
23419-23419	OYSTER
23420-23420	PAINTER
23421-23421	PARKSLEY
23422-23422	PUNGOTEAGUE
23423-23423	QUINBY
23424-23424	RESCUE
23426-23426	SANFORD
23427-23427	SAXIS
23429-23429	SEAVIEW
23430-23431	SMITHFIELD
23432-23439	SUFFOLK
23440-23440	TANGIER
23441-23441	TASLEY
23442-23442	TEMPERANCEVILLE
23443-23443	TOWNSEND
23450-23479	VIRGINIA BEACH
23480-23480	WACHAPREAGUE
23481-23481	CARRSVILLE
23482-23482	WARDTOWN
23483-23483	WATTSVILLE
23484-23484	WEIRWOOD
23486-23486	WILLIS WHARF
23487-23487	WINDSOR
23488-23488	WITHAMS
23500-23551	NORFOLK
23600-23603	NEWPORT NEWS
23604-23604	FORT EUSTIS
23605-23628	NEWPORT NEWS
23629-23629	GREAT AMERICAN MAGAZINE
23630-23630	NEWPORT NEWS
23630-23631	HAMPTON
23632-23632	GREAT AMERICAN MAGAZINE
23651-23651	FORT MONROE
23653-23661	HAMPTON
23662-23662	POQUOSON
23663-23681	HAMPTON
23690-23693	YORKTOWN
23694-23694	LACKEY
23696-23696	SEAFORD
23700-23709	PORTSMOUTH
23801-23801	FORT LEE
23803-23806	PETERSBURG
23821-23821	ALBERTA
23822-23822	AMMON
23824-23824	BLACKSTONE
23827-23827	BOYKINS
23828-23828	BRANCHVILLE
23829-23829	CAPRON
23830-23830	CARSON
23831-23831	CHESTER
23832-23832	CHESTERFIELD
23833-23833	CHURCH ROAD
23834-23834	COLONIAL HEIGHTS
23836-23836	CHESTER
23837-23837	COURTLAND
23838-23838	CHESTERFIELD
23839-23839	DENDRON
23840-23840	DEWITT
23841-23841	DINWIDDIE
23842-23842	DISPUTANTA
23843-23843	DOLPHIN
23844-23844	DREWRYVILLE
23845-23845	EBONY
23846-23846	ELBERON
23847-23847	EMPORIA
23850-23850	FORD
23851-23851	FRANKLIN
23856-23856	FREEMAN
23857-23857	GASBURG
23859-23859	HANDSOM
23860-23860	HOPEWELL
23866-23866	IVOR
23867-23867	JARRATT
23868-23868	LAWRENCEVILLE
23870-23870	JARRATT
23872-23872	MC KENNEY
23873-23873	MEREDITHVILLE
23874-23874	NEWSOMS
23875-23875	PRINCE GEORGE
23876-23876	RAWLINGS
23878-23878	SEDLEY
23879-23879	SKIPPERS
23881-23881	SPRING GROVE
23882-23882	STONY CREEK
23883-23883	SURRY
23884-23884	SUSSEX
23885-23885	SUTHERLAND
23887-23887	VALENTINES
23888-23888	WAKEFIELD
23889-23889	WARFIELD
23890-23891	WAVERLY
23893-23893	WHITE PLAINS
23894-23894	WILSONS
23897-23897	YALE
23898-23898	ZUNI
23899-23899	CLAREMONT
23901-23909	FARMVILLE
23911-23911	ANDERSONVILLE
23915-23915	BASKERVILLE
23917-23917	BOYDTON
23919-23919	BRACEY
23920-23920	BRODNAX
23921-23921	BUCKINGHAM
23922-23922	BURKEVILLE
23923-23923	CHARLOTTE COURT HOUSE
23924-23924	CHASE CITY
23927-23927	CLARKSVILLE
23930-23930	CREWE
23934-23934	CULLEN
23935-23935	DARLINGTN HTS
23935-23935	DARLINGTON HEIGHTS
23936-23936	DILLWYN
23937-23937	DRAKES BRANCH
23938-23938	DUNDAS
23939-23939	EVERGREEN
23941-23941	FORT MITCHELL
23942-23942	GREEN BAY
23943-23943	HAMPDEN SYDNEY
23944-23944	KENBRIDGE
23947-23947	KEYSVILLE
23950-23950	LA CROSSE
23952-23952	LUNENBURG
23954-23954	MEHERRIN
23955-23955	NOTTOWAY
23958-23958	PAMPLIN

23959-23959	PHENIX
23960-23960	PROSPECT
23962-23962	RANDOLPH
23963-23963	RED HOUSE
23964-23964	RED OAK
23966-23966	RICE
23967-23967	SAXE
23968-23968	SKIPWITH
23970-23970	SOUTH HILL
23974-23974	VICTORIA
23976-23976	WYLLIESBURG
24000-24040	ROANOKE
24041-24041	BANK AMERICARD
24042-24045	ROANOKE
24046-24046	CITY OFFICES
24048-24050	ROANOKE
24053-24053	ARARAT
24054-24054	AXTON
24055-24055	BASSETT
24058-24058	BELSPRING
24059-24059	BENT MOUNTAIN
24060-24063	BLACKSBURG
24064-24064	BLUE RIDGE
24065-24065	BOONES MILL
24066-24066	BUCHANAN
24067-24067	CALLAWAY
24068-24068	CHRISTIANSBURG
24069-24069	CASCADE
24070-24070	CATAWBA
24072-24072	CHECK
24073-24073	CHRISTIANSBURG
24076-24076	CLAUDVILLE
24077-24077	CLOVERDALE
24078-24078	COLLINSVILLE
24079-24079	COPPER HILL
24082-24082	CRITZ
24083-24083	DALEVILLE
24084-24084	DUBLIN
24085-24085	EAGLE ROCK
24086-24086	EGGLESTON
24087-24087	ELLISTON
24088-24088	FERRUM
24089-24089	FIELDALE
24090-24090	FINCASTLE
24091-24091	FLOYD
24092-24092	GLADEHILL
24093-24093	GLEN LYN
24094-24094	GOLDBOND
24095-24095	GOODVIEW
24101-24101	HARDY
24102-24102	HENRY
24104-24104	HUDDLESTON
24105-24105	INDIAN VALLEY
24111-24111	MC COY
24112-24115	MARTINSVILLE
24120-24120	MEADOWS OF DAN
24121-24121	MONETA
24122-24122	MONTVALE
24124-24124	NARROWS
24126-24126	NEWBERN
24127-24127	NEW CASTLE
24128-24128	NEWPORT
24129-24129	NEW RIVER
24130-24130	ORISKANY
24131-24131	PAINT BANK
24132-24132	PARROTT
24133-24133	PATRICK SPRINGS
24134-24134	PEARISBURG
24136-24136	PEMBROKE
24137-24137	PENHOOK
24138-24138	PILOT
24139-24139	PITTSVILLE
24141-24143	RADFORD
24146-24146	REDWOOD
24147-24147	RICH CREEK
24148-24148	RIDGEWAY
24149-24149	RINER
24150-24150	RIPPLEMEAD
24151-24151	ROCKY MOUNT
24153-24157	SALEM
24161-24161	SANDY LEVEL
24162-24162	SHAWSVILLE
24165-24165	SPENCER
24167-24167	STAFFORDSVILLE
24168-24168	STANLEYTOWN
24171-24171	STUART
24174-24174	THAXTON
24175-24175	TROUTVILLE
24176-24176	UNION HALL
24177-24177	VESTA
24178-24178	VILLAMONT
24179-24179	VINTON
24184-24184	WIRTZ
24185-24185	WOOLWINE
24201-24209	BRISTOL
24210-24212	ABINGDON
24215-24215	ANDOVER
24216-24216	APPALACHIA
24217-24217	BEE
24218-24218	BEN HUR
24219-24219	BIG STONE GAP
24220-24220	BIRCHLEAF
24221-24221	BLACKWATER
24224-24224	CASTLEWOOD
24225-24225	CLEVELAND
24226-24226	CLINCHCO
24228-24228	CLINTWOOD
24230-24230	COEBURN
24236-24236	DAMASCUS
24237-24237	DANTE
24239-24239	DAVENPORT
24243-24243	DRYDEN
24244-24244	DUFFIELD
24245-24245	DUNGANNON
24246-24246	EAST STONE GAP
24248-24248	EWING
24249-24249	EXETER
24250-24250	FORT BLACKMORE
24251-24251	GATE CITY
24256-24256	HAYSI
24258-24258	HILTONS
24260-24260	HONAKER
24263-24263	JONESVILLE
24265-24265	KEOKEE
24266-24266	LEBANON
24269-24269	MC CLURE
24270-24270	MENDOTA
24271-24271	NICKELSVILLE
24272-24272	NORA
24273-24273	NORTON
24277-24277	PENNINGTON GAP
24279-24279	POUND
24280-24280	ROSEDALE
24281-24281	ROSE HILL
24282-24282	SAINT CHARLES
24283-24283	SAINT PAUL
24285-24285	STONEGA
24289-24289	TRAMMEL
24290-24290	WEBER CITY
24292-24292	WHITETOP
24293-24293	WISE
24301-24301	PULASKI
24311-24311	ATKINS
24312-24312	AUSTINVILLE
24313-24313	BARREN SPRINGS
24314-24314	BASTIAN
24315-24315	BLAND
24316-24316	BROADFORD
24317-24317	CANA
24318-24318	CERES
24319-24319	CHILHOWIE
24321-24321	CLINCHBURG
24322-24322	CRIPPLE CREEK
24323-24323	CROCKETT
24324-24324	DRAPER
24325-24325	DUGSPUR
24326-24326	ELK CREEK
24327-24327	EMORY
24328-24328	FANCY GAP
24330-24330	FRIES
24333-24333	GALAX
24340-24340	GLADE SPRING
24343-24343	HILLSVILLE
24347-24347	HIWASSEE
24348-24348	INDEPENDENCE
24350-24350	IVANHOE
24351-24351	LAMBSBURG
24352-24352	LAUREL FORK
24354-24354	MARION
24360-24360	MAX MEADOWS
24361-24361	MEADOWVIEW
24363-24363	MOUTH OF WILSON
24366-24366	ROCKY GAP
24368-24368	RURAL RETREAT
24370-24370	SALTVILLE
24373-24373	SEVEN MILE FORD
24374-24374	SPEEDWELL
24375-24375	SUGAR GROVE
24377-24377	TANNERSVILLE
24378-24378	TROUT DALE
24378-24378	TROUTDALE
24379-24379	VOLNEY
24380-24380	WILLIS
24381-24381	WOODLAWN
24382-24382	WYTHEVILLE
24401-24407	STAUNTON
24411-24411	AUGUSTA SPRINGS
24412-24412	BACOVA
24413-24413	BLUE GRASS
24415-24415	BROWNSBURG
24416-24416	BUENA VISTA
24421-24421	CHURCHVILLE
24422-24422	CLIFTON FORGE
24426-24426	COVINGTON
24430-24430	CRAIGSVILLE
24431-24431	CRIMORA
24432-24432	DEERFIELD
24433-24433	DOE HILL
24435-24435	FAIRFIELD
24437-24437	FORT DEFIANCE
24438-24438	GLEN WILTON
24439-24439	GOSHEN
24440-24440	GREENVILLE
24441-24441	GROTTOES
24442-24442	HEAD WATERS
24444-24444	HIGHTOWN
24445-24445	HOT SPRINGS
24448-24448	IRON GATE
24449-24449	JORDAN MINES
24450-24450	LEXINGTON
24457-24457	LOW MOOR
24458-24458	MC DOWELL
24459-24459	MIDDLEBROOK
24460-24460	MILLBORO
24463-24463	MINT SPRING
24464-24464	MONTEBELLO
24465-24465	MONTEREY
24467-24467	MOUNT SIDNEY
24468-24468	MUSTOE
24469-24469	NEW HOPE
24471-24471	PORT REPUBLIC
24472-24472	RAPHINE
24473-24473	ROCKBRIDGE BATHS
24474-24474	SELMA
24475-24475	SPOTTSWOOD
24476-24476	STEELES TAVERN
24477-24477	STUARTS DRAFT
24479-24479	SWOOPE
24482-24482	VERONA
24483-24483	VESUVIUS
24484-24484	WARM SPRINGS
24485-24485	WEST AUGUSTA
24486-24486	WEYERS CAVE
24487-24487	WILLIAMSVILLE
24501-24515	LYNCHBURG
24517-24517	ALTAVISTA
24520-24520	ALTON
24521-24521	AMHERST
24522-24522	APPOMATTOX
24523-24523	BEDFORD
24526-24526	BIG ISLAND
24527-24527	BLAIRS
24528-24528	BROOKNEAL
24529-24529	BUFFALO JUNCTION
24530-24530	CALLANDS
24531-24531	CHATHAM
24533-24533	CLIFFORD
24534-24534	CLOVER
24535-24535	CLUSTER SPRINGS
24536-24536	COLEMAN FALLS
24538-24538	CONCORD
24539-24539	CRYSTAL HILL
24540-24544	DANVILLE
24549-24549	DRY FORK
24550-24550	EVINGTON
24551-24551	FOREST
24553-24553	GLADSTONE
24554-24554	GLADYS
24555-24555	GLASGOW
24556-24556	GOODE
24557-24557	GRETNA
24558-24558	HALIFAX
24562-24562	HOWARDSVILLE
24563-24563	HURT
24565-24565	JAVA
24566-24566	KEELING
24569-24569	LONG ISLAND
24570-24570	LOWRY
24571-24571	LYNCH STATION
24572-24572	MADISON HEIGHTS
24574-24574	MONROE
24576-24576	NARUNA
24577-24577	NATHALIE
24578-24578	NATURAL BRIDGE
24579-24579	NATURAL BRIDGE STATION
24580-24580	NELSON
24581-24581	NORWOOD
24585-24585	REPUBLICAN GROVE
24586-24586	RINGGOLD
24588-24588	RUSTBURG
24589-24589	SCOTTSBURG
24590-24590	SCOTTSVILLE
24592-24592	SOUTH BOSTON
24593-24593	SPOUT SPRING
24594-24594	SUTHERLIN
24595-24595	SWEET BRIAR
24596-24596	TURBEVILLE
24597-24597	VERNON HILL
24598-24598	VIRGILINA
24599-24599	WINGINA
24601-24601	AMONATE
24602-24602	BANDY
24603-24603	BIG ROCK
24604-24604	BISHOP
24605-24605	BLUEFIELD
24606-24606	BOISSEVAIN
24607-24607	BREAKS
24608-24608	BURKES GARDEN
24609-24609	CEDAR BLUFF
24612-24612	DORAN
24613-24613	FALLS MILLS
24614-24614	GRUNDY
24618-24618	HARMAN
24619-24619	HORSEPEN
24620-24620	HURLEY
24622-24622	JEWELL RIDGE
24624-24624	KEEN MOUNTAIN
24627-24627	MAVISDALE
24628-24628	MAXIE
24630-24630	NORTH TAZEWELL
24631-24631	OAKWOOD
24634-24634	PILGRIMS KNOB
24635-24635	POCAHONTAS
24637-24637	POUNDING MILL
24639-24639	RAVEN
24640-24640	RED ASH
24641-24641	RICHLANDS
24646-24646	ROWE
24647-24647	SHORTT GAP
24649-24649	SWORDS CREEK
24651-24651	TAZEWELL
24656-24656	VANSANT
24657-24657	WHITEWOOD
24658-24658	WOLFORD
24659-24659	YARDS

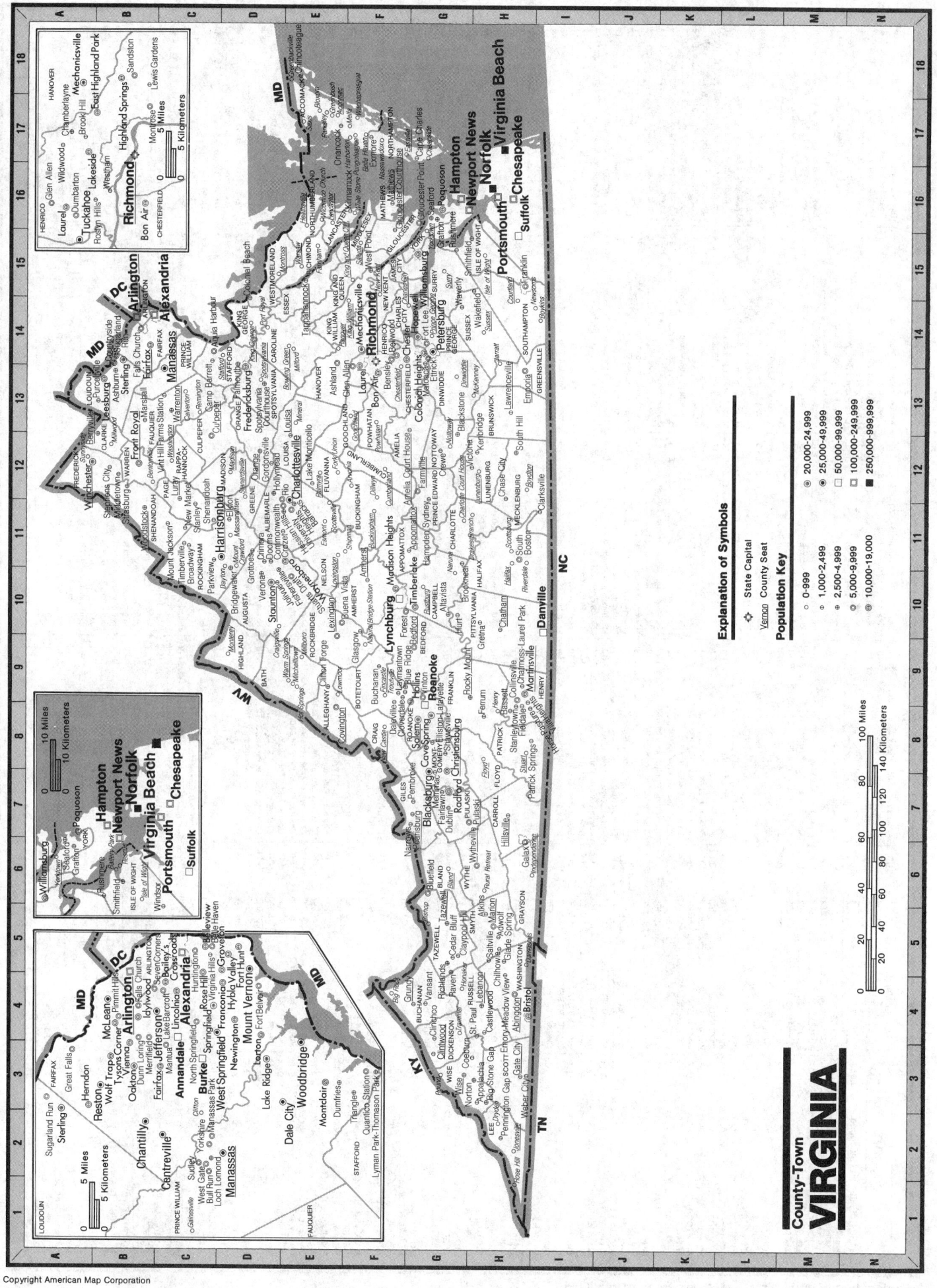

County-Town
VIRGINIA

Explanation of Symbols

State Capital
Vernon County Seat

Population Key

○ 0-999
⊙ 1,000-2,499
⊕ 2,500-4,999
◉ 5,000-9,999
◎ 10,000-19,000

◉ 20,000-24,999
◉ 25,000-49,999
□ 50,000-99,999
□ 100,000-249,999
■ 250,000-999,999

COUNTIES

(136 Counties and Independent Cities)

Name of County	Population	Location on Map
ACCOMACK	31,703	E-17
ALBEMARLE	68,040	D-11
ALLEGHANY	13,176	E-8
AMELIA	8,787	F-12
AMHERST	28,578	F-10
APPOMATTOX	12,298	F-10
ARLINGTON	170,936	B-14
AUGUSTA	54,677	D-10
BATH	4,799	D-9
BEDFORD	45,656	F-9
BLAND	6,514	G-6
BOTETOURT	24,992	F-8
BRUNSWICK	15,987	H-13
BUCHANAN	31,333	G-4
BUCKINGHAM	12,873	F-11
CAMPBELL	47,572	G-10
CAROLINE	19,217	D-14
CARROLL	26,594	H-7
CHARLES CITY	6,282	F-14
CHARLOTTE	11,688	G-11
CHESTERFIELD	209,274	F-13
CLARKE	12,101	B-12
CRAIG	4,372	F-8
CULPEPER	27,791	C-12
CUMBERLAND	7,825	F-12
DICKENSON	17,620	G-3
DINWIDDIE	20,960	G-13
ESSEX	8,689	E-14
FAIRFAX	818,584	C-14
FAUQUIER	48,741	B-12
FLOYD	12,005	H-7
FLUVANNA	12,429	E-12
FRANKLIN	39,549	G-9
FREDERICK	45,723	A-12
GILES	16,366	F-7
GLOUCESTER	30,131	F-15
GOOCHLAND	14,163	E-12
GRAYSON	16,278	H-5
GREENE	10,297	D-11
GREENESVILLE	8,853	I-13
HALIFAX	29,033	H-10
HANOVER	63,306	E-13
HENRICO	217,881	F-14
HENRY	56,942	I-8
HIGHLAND	2,635	D-9
ISLE OF WIGHT	25,053	H-15
JAMES CITY	34,859	F-15
KING AND QUEEN	6,289	E-14
KING GEORGE	13,527	D-14
KING WILLIAM	10,913	E-14
LANCASTER	10,896	E-15
LEE	24,496	H-2
LOUDOUN	86,129	A-13
LOUISA	20,325	E-12
LUNENBURG	11,419	H-12
MADISON	11,949	D-12
MATHEWS	8,348	F-16
MECKLENBURG	29,241	H-11
MIDDLESEX	8,653	F-15
MONTGOMERY	73,913	G-8
NELSON	12,778	E-10
NEW KENT	10,445	F-14
NORTHAMPTON	13,061	F-17
NORTHUMBERLAND	10,524	E-15
NOTTOWAY	14,993	G-12
ORANGE	21,421	D-13
PAGE	21,690	C-12
PATRICK	17,473	H-8
PITTSYLVANIA	55,655	H-10
POWHATAN	15,328	F-12
PRINCE EDWARD	17,320	G-11
PRINCE GEORGE	27,394	G-14
PRINCE WILLIAM	215,686	C-13
PULASKI	34,496	G-7
RAPPAHANNOCK	6,622	C-12
RICHMOND	7,273	E-15
ROANOKE	79,332	G-8
ROCKBRIDGE	18,350	E-9
ROCKINGHAM	57,482	C-10
RUSSELL	28,667	H-4
SCOTT	23,204	H-3
SHENANDOAH	31,636	B-11
SMYTH	32,370	H-5
SOUTHAMPTON	17,550	H-14
SPOTSYLVANIA	57,403	D-13
STAFFORD	61,236	D-13
SURRY	6,145	G-15
SUSSEX	10,248	G-14
TAZEWELL	45,960	G-5
WARREN	26,142	B-12
WASHINGTON	45,887	H-4
WESTMORELAND	15,480	D-14
WISE	39,573	G-3
WYTHE	25,466	G-6
YORK	42,422	G-15

Name of Independent City	Population	Location on Map
ALEXANDRIA	111,183	B-14
BEDFORD	6,073	G-9
BRISTOL	18,426	H-4
BUENA VISTA	6,406	E-10
CHARLOTTESVILLE	40,341	E-12
CHESAPEAKE	151,976	H-16
CLIFTON FORGE	4,679	E-9
COLONIAL HEIGHTS	16,064	G-14
COVINGTON	6,991	E-8
DANVILLE	53,056	I-10
EMPORIA	5,306	H-13
FAIRFAX	19,622	B-14
FALLS CHURCH	9,578	B-14
FRANKLIN	7,864	H-15
FREDERICKSBURG	19,027	D-13
GALAX	6,670	H-6
HAMPTON	133,793	G-16
HARRISONBURG	30,707	D-11
HOPEWELL	23,101	G-14
LEXINGTON	6,959	E-9
LYNCHBURG	66,049	F-10
MANASSAS	27,957	C-13
MANASSAS PARK	6,734	C-2
MARTINSVILLE	16,162	H-9
NEWPORT NEWS	170,045	G-16
NORFOLK	261,229	H-16
NORTON	4,247	H-3
PETERSBURG	38,386	G-14
POQUOSON	11,005	A-7
PORTSMOUTH	103,907	H-16
RADFORD	15,940	G-7
RICHMOND	203,056	F-14
ROANOKE	96,397	G-8
SALEM	23,756	G-8
SOUTH BOSTON	6,997	H-11
STAUNTON	24,461	D-10
SUFFOLK	52,141	H-15
VIRGINIA BEACH	393,069	H-17
WAYNESBORO	18,549	E-11
WILLIAMSBURG	11,530	G-15
WINCHESTER	21,947	A-12
TOTAL	6,187,358	

CITIES AND TOWNS

Note: The first name is that of the city or town, second, that of the county in which it is located, then the population and location on the map.

City or Town	Location on Map
Abingdon, Washington, 7,003	H-4
Accomac, Accomack, 466	E-17
•Adwolf, Smyth, 1,292	H-5
Alexandria, Independent City, 111,183	B-14
Altavista, Campbell, 3,686	G-10
Amelia Court House, Amelia	G-13
Amherst, Amherst, 1,060	F-10
•Annandale, Fairfax, 50,975	C-4
Appalachia, Wise, 1,994	H-3
Appomattox, Appomattox, 1,707	G-11
•Aquia Harbour, Stafford, 6,308	C-14
•Arlington, Arlington, 170,936	B-14
•Ashburn, Loudoun, 3,393	B-13
Ashland, Hanover, 5,864	E-14
•Atkins, Smyth, 1,130	H-5
•Bailey's Crossroads, Fairfax, 19,507	C-4
•Barracks, Albemarle, 4,710	D-12
•Bassett, Henry, 1,579	H-8
Bedford, Independent City, 6,073	G-9
Belleview, Fairfax	C-5
•Bellwood, Chesterfield, 6,178	F-14
•Bensley, Chesterfield, 5,093	F-14
Berryville, Clarke, 3,097	B-12
Big Stone Gap, Wise, 4,748	H-3
Blacksburg, Montgomery, 34,590	G-7
Blackstone, Nottoway, 3,497	G-12
Bland, Bland	G-6
•Blue Ridge, Botetourt, 2,840	F-9
Bluefield, Tazewell, 5,363	G-6
•Bon Air, Chesterfield, 16,413	F-13
Bowling Green, Caroline, 727	E-14
Boydton, Mecklenburg, 453	H-12
Bridgewater, Rockingham, 3,918	D-10
Bristol, Independent City, 18,426	H-4
Broadway, Rockingham, 1,209	C-11
Brook Hill, Henrico	A-17
Brookneal, Campbell, 1,344	G-11
Buchanan, Botetourt, 1,222	F-9
Buckingham, Buckingham	F-11
Buena Vista, Independent City, 6,406	E-10
•Bull Run, Prince William, 5,525	C-2
•Burke, Fairfax, 57,734	C-3
Camp Barrett, Stafford	C-14
Cape Charles, Northampton, 1,398	G-17
•Castlewood, Russell, 2,110	H-4
•Cave Spring, Roanoke, 24,053	G-8
Cedar Bluff, Tazewell, 1,290	G-5
•Centreville, Fairfax, 26,585	C-2
•Chamberlayne, Henrico, 4,577	A-17
•Chantilly, Fairfax, 29,337	B-2
Charles City, Charles City	F-14
Charlotte Court House, Charlotte, 531	G-11
Charlottesville, Independent City, 40,341	E-12
Chase City, Mecklenburg, 2,442	H-12
Chatham, Pittsylvania, 1,354	H-10
•Chatmoss-Laurel Park, Henry, 2,194	H-8
Chesapeake, Independent City, 151,976	H-16
•Chester, Chesterfield, 14,986	F-14
Chesterfield, Chesterfield	F-13
Chilhowie, Smyth, 1,971	H-5
Chincoteague, Accomack, 3,572	E-18
Christiansburg, Montgomery, 15,004	G-7
Clarksville, Mecklenburg, 1,243	I-11
•Claypool Hill, Tazewell, 1,468	G-5
Clifton Forge, Independent City, 4,679	E-9
Clinchco, Dickenson	G-4
Clintwood, Dickenson, 1,542	G-3
•Cloverdale, Botetourt, 1,689	F-9
Coeburn, Wise, 2,165	H-3
•Collinsville, Henry, 7,280	H-9
Colonial Beach, Westmoreland, 3,132	D-15
Colonial Heights, Independent City, 16,064	G-14
•Commonwealth, Albemarle, 5,538	D-11
•Countryside, Loudoun, 8,349	B-14
Courtland, Southampton, 819	H-14
Covington, Independent City, 6,991	E-8
Crewe, Nottoway, 2,276	G-12
•Crimora, Augusta, 1,752	D-10
•Crozet, Albemarle, 2,256	E-11
Culpeper, Culpeper, 8,581	C-12
Cumberland, Cumberland	F-12
•Dale City, Prince William, 47,170	E-3
•Daleville, Botetourt, 1,163	F-9
Danville, Independent City, 53,056	I-10
Dinwiddie, Dinwiddie	G-13
•Dooms, Augusta, 1,307	D-11
Dublin, Pulaski, 2,012	G-7
•Dumbarton, Henrico, 8,526	A-16
Dumfries, Prince William, 4,282	E-3
•Dunn Loring, Fairfax, 6,509	B-4
•East Highland Park, Henrico, 11,850	A-17
Eastville, Northampton, 185	F-17
Elkton, Rockingham, 1,935	D-11
•Elliston-Lafayette, Montgomery, 1,243	G-8
•Emory-Meadow View, Washington, 2,248	H-4
Emporia, Independent City, 5,306	H-13
•Ettrick, Chesterfield, 5,290	G-14
Exmore, Northampton, 1,115	F-17
Fairfax, Independent City, 19,622	B-14
•Fairlawn, Pulaski, 2,399	G-7
Falls Church, Independent City, 9,578	B-14
•Falmouth, Stafford, 3,541	D-14
Farmville, Cumberland/Prince Edward, 6,046	G-12
•Ferrum, Franklin, 1,514	G-8
•Fieldale, Henry, 1,018	H-8
Fincastle, Botetourt, 236	F-9
•Fishersville, Augusta, 3,230	D-11
Floyd, Floyd, 396	H-8
•Forest, Bedford, 5,624	G-10
•Fort Belvoir, Fairfax, 8,590	D-4
•Fort Hunt, Fairfax, 12,989	D-5
•Fort Lee, Prince George, 6,895	G-14
•Franconia, Fairfax, 19,882	D-4
Franklin, Independent City, 7,864	H-15
Fredericksburg, Independent City, 19,027	D-13
Front Royal, Warren, 11,880	B-12
Galax, Independent City, 6,670	H-6
Gate City, Scott, 2,214	H-3
Glade Spring, Washington, 1,435	H-5
Glasgow, Rockbridge, 1,140	F-10
•Glen Allen, Henrico, 9,010	A-16
•Gloucester Courthouse, Gloucester, 2,118	F-16
•Gloucester Point, Gloucester, 8,509	G-16
Goochland, Goochland	F-13
Gordonsville, Orange, 1,351	D-12
Grafton, York	G-16
•Great Falls, Fairfax, 6,945	A-3
Gretna, Pittsylvania, 1,339	H-10
Grottoes, Augusta/Rockingham, 1,455	D-11
•Groveton, Fairfax, 19,997	D-5
Grundy, Buchanan, 1,305	G-4
Halifax, Halifax, 688	H-11
•Hampden Sydney, Prince Edward, 1,240	G-12
Hampton, Independent City, 133,793	G-16
Hanover, Hanover	E-14
Harrisonburg, Independent City, 30,707	D-11
Heathsville, Northumberland	E-16
Herndon, Fairfax, 16,139	A-3
•Highland Springs, Henrico, 13,823	B-18
Hillsville, Carroll, 2,008	H-7
•Hollins, Botetourt/Roanoke, 13,305	G-9
•Hollymead, Albemarle, 2,628	D-12
Hopewell, Independent City, 23,101	G-14
•Horse Pasture, Henry, 2,224	H-18
•Huntington, Fairfax, 7,489	C-5
Hurt, Pittsylvania, 1,294	G-10
•Hybla Valley, Fairfax, 15,491	D-5
•Idylwood, Fairfax, 14,710	B-4
Independence, Grayson, 988	I-6
Isle of Wight, Isle of Wight	B-6
•Jefferson, Fairfax, 25,782	C-4
•Jolivue, Augusta, 1,092	D-10
Jonesville, Lee, 927	H-2
Kenbridge, Lunenburg, 1,264	H-12
Kilmarnock, Lancaster/Northumberland, 1,109	E-16
King George, King George	D-14
King William, King William	F-14
King and Queen Court House, King and Queen	F-15
•Lake Barcroft, Fairfax, 8,686	C-4
•Lake Monticello, Fluvanna, 2,331	E-12
•Lake Ridge, Prince William, 23,862	D-3
•Lakeside, Henrico, 12,081	A-17
Lancaster, Lancaster	E-16
•Laurel, Henrico, 13,011	A-16
Lawrenceville, Brunswick, 1,486	H-13
Laymantown, Botetourt, 1,942	F-9
Lebanon, Russell, 3,386	H-4
Leesburg, Loudoun, 16,202	B-13
Lewis Gardens, Henrico	B-18
Lexington, Independent City, 6,959	E-9
•Lincolnia, Fairfax, 13,041	C-4
•Loch Lomond, Prince William, 3,292	C-2
•Lorton, Fairfax, 15,385	D-4
Louisa, Louisa, 1,088	E-12
Lovingston, Nelson	E-11
Lunenburg, Lunenburg	H-12
Luray, Page, 4,587	C-12
Lyman Park-Thomason Park, Prince William	F-3
Lynchburg, Independent City, 66,049	F-10
Madison, Madison, 307	D-12
•Madison Heights, Amherst, 11,700	F-10
Manassas, Independent City, 27,957	C-13
Manassas Park, Independent City, 6,734	C-2
•Mantua, Fairfax, 6,804	C-3
Marion, Smyth, 6,630	H-5
Marshall, Fauquier	B-13
Martinsville, Independent City, 16,162	H-9
Mathews, Mathews	F-16
•McLean, Fairfax, 38,168	B-4
•Mechanicsville, Hanover, 22,027	F-14
•Merrifield, Fairfax, 8,399	B-4
•Merrimac, Montgomery, 1,713	G-7
Middletown, Frederick, 1,061	B-12
•Montclair, Prince William, 11,399	E-3
Monterey, Highland, 222	D-9
•Montrose, Henrico, 6,405	B-17
Montross, Westmoreland, 359	D-15
Mount Jackson, Shenandoah, 1,583	C-11
•Mount Vernon, Fairfax, 27,485	D-5
Narrows, Giles, 2,082	G-7
New Castle, Craig, 152	F-8
New Kent, New Kent	F-15
New Market, Shenandoah, 1,435	C-11
•Newington, Fairfax, 17,965	D-4
Newport News, Independent City, 170,045	G-16
Norfolk, Independent City, 261,229	H-16
•North Springfield, Fairfax, 8,996	C-4
Norton, Independent City, 4,247	H-3
Nottoway, Nottoway	G-12
•Oakton, Fairfax, 24,610	B-3
Onancock, Accomack, 1,434	E-17
Orange, Orange, 2,582	D-12
Palmyra, Fluvanna	E-12
Patrick Springs, Patrick	H-8
Pearisburg, Giles, 2,064	G-7
Pembroke, Giles, 1,064	G-7
Pennington Gap, Lee, 1,922	H-2
Petersburg, Independent City, 38,386	G-14
•Pimmit Hills, Fairfax, 6,019	B-4
Poquoson, Independent City, 11,005	A-7
Portsmouth, Independent City, 103,907	H-16
Powhatan, Powhatan	F-13
Prince George, Prince George	G-14
Pulaski, Pulaski, 9,985	H-7
Purcellville, Loudoun, 1,744	B-13
•Quantico Station, Prince William/Stafford, 7,425	F-3
Radford, Independent City, 15,940	G-7
•Raven, Russell/Tazewell, 2,640	G-5
•Reston, Fairfax, 48,556	B-3
Richlands, Tazewell, 4,456	G-5
Richmond, Independent City, 203,056	F-14
•Rio, Albemarle, 5,133	D-12
Roanoke, Independent City, 96,397	G-8
Rocky Mount, Franklin, 4,098	G-9
•Rose Hill, Fairfax, 12,675	C-4
Roslyn Hills, Henrico	A-16
•Rushmere, Isle of Wight, 1,064	G-15
Rustburg, Campbell	G-10
Saint Paul, Russell/Wise, 1,007	H-4
Salem, Independent City, 23,756	G-8
Saltville, Smyth/Washington, 2,300	H-5
Saluda, Middlesex	F-15
Sandston, Henrico	B-18
Seaford, York	G-16
•Seven Corners, Fairfax, 7,280	C-4
•Shawsville, Montgomery, 1,260	G-8
Shenandoah, Page, 2,213	C-11
Smithfield, Isle of Wight, 4,686	G-15
South Boston, Independent City, 6,997	H-11
South Hill, Mecklenburg, 4,217	H-12
Spotsylvania, Spotsylvania	D-13
•Spotsylvania Courthouse, Spotsylvania, 2,694	D-13
•Springfield, Fairfax, 23,706	C-4
Stafford, Stafford	D-14
Stanardsville, Greene, 257	D-12
Stanley, Page, 1,186	C-11
Stanleytown, Henry, 1,563	H-8
Staunton, Independent City, 24,461	D-10
Stephens City, Frederick, 1,186	B-12
•Sterling, Loudoun, 20,512	B-14
Strasburg, Shenandoah, 3,762	B-12
Stuart, Patrick, 965	H-8
•Stuarts Draft, Augusta, 5,087	E-10
•Sudley, Prince William, 7,321	C-2
Suffolk, Independent City, 52,141	H-15
•Sugarland Run, Loudoun, 9,357	B-14
Surry, Surry, 192	G-15
Sussex, Sussex	H-14
Tappahannock, Essex, 1,550	E-15
Tazewell, Tazewell, 4,176	G-5
•Timberlake, Campbell, 10,314	G-10
Timberville, Rockingham, 1,596	C-11
•Triangle, Prince William, 4,740	F-3
•Tuckahoe, Henrico, 42,629	A-15
•Tysons Corner, Fairfax, 13,124	B-4
•University Heights, Albemarle, 6,900	E-11
•Vansant, Buchanan, 1,187	G-4
•Verona, Augusta, 3,479	D-10
Victoria, Lunenburg, 1,830	H-12
Vienna, Fairfax, 14,852	B-3
•Villa Heights, Henry, 1,021	H-9
•Vint Hill Farms Station, Fauquier, 1,332	C-13
Vinton, Roanoke, 7,665	G-9
Virginia Beach, Independent City, 393,069	H-17
Virginia Hills, Fairfax	C-5
Wakefield, Sussex, 1,070	H-15
Warm Springs, Bath	E-9
Warrenton, Fauquier, 4,830	C-13
Warsaw, Richmond, 961	E-15
Washington, Rappahannock, 198	C-12
Waverly, Sussex, 2,223	G-14
Waynesboro, Independent City, 18,549	E-11
Weber City, Scott, 1,377	H-3
•West Gate, Prince William, 6,565	C-2
West Point, King William, 2,938	F-15
•West Springfield, Fairfax, 28,126	D-4
Westham, Henrico	B-16
Wildwood, Henrico	A-17
Williamsburg, Independent City, 11,530	G-15
Winchester, Independent City, 21,947	A-12
Windsor, Isle of Wight, 1,025	C-5
Wise, Wise, 3,193	G-3
•Wolf Trap, Fairfax, 13,133	B-3
•Woodbridge, Prince William, 26,401	E-3
Woodstock, Shenandoah, 3,182	B-11
Wytheville, Wythe, 8,038	H-6
•Yorkshire, Prince William, 5,699	C-2
Yorktown, York	G-15

Explanation of symbols: •– Census Designated Place (CDP)

Washington

General Help Numbers:

Governor's Office
PO Box 40002
Olympia, WA 98504-0002
www.governor.wa.gov

360-902-4111
Fax 360-753-4110
8AM-5PM

Attorney General's Office
PO Box 40100
Olympia, WA 98504-0100
www.atg.wa.gov/

360-753-6200
Fax 360-586-7671
8AM-5PM

Legislative Information Center
PO Box 40600
Olympia, WA 98504-0600
www1.leg.wa.gov/legislature

360-786-7573
Fax 360-786-1293
8AM-5PM

State Archives
State Archives
PO Box 40238
Olympia, WA 98504-0238
www.secstate.wa.gov/archives

360-753-5485
Fax 360-664-8814
8:30AM-4:30PM

State Specifics:

Capital:	Olympia Thurston County
Time Zone:	PST
Number of Counties:	39
Population:	6,131,445
Web Site:	http://access.wa.gov

State Agencies

Criminal Records

Washington State Patrol, Identification and Criminal History Section, PO Box 42633, Olympia, WA 98504-2633 (Courier: 3000 Pacific Ave. SE #204, Olympia, WA 98501); 360-705-5100, 360-570-5275 (Fax), 8AM-5PM.

www.wsp.wa.gov

Indexing & Storage: Records are available from 1974. Criminal history information is retained at the Identification and Criminal History Section until the offender is age seventy, or ten years from the last date of arrest, whichever is longer. It takes 30 to 45 days if manual; 2 hours if electronic before new records are available for inquiry. Records are indexed on inhouse computer. Records are normally destroyed after a court order.

Searching: Two types of records available: General Conviction - all convictions and arrests less than one year pending disposition; and Child & Adult Abuse record - only conviction of crimes against persons, certain drug crimes, and financial esploitation crimes. Include the following in your request-date of birth, Social Security Number, sex, race, name and address of subject. Fingerprints are optional. Records are 100% fingerprint-supported. Mail requests are directed to the WSP or e-mail to crimhis@wsp.gov. The following data is not released: non-conviction and arrest information over one year old without disposition.

Access by: mail, in person, online.

Fee & Payment: The fee for a name check is $10.00 per individual. For a fingerprint check, the fee is $25.00 per individual. Will not conduct FBI fingerprint checks. Fee payee: Washington State Patrol. Money orders or cashier's checks preferred.

Mail search: Turnaround time: 2 to 3 weeks.

In person search: Requests are returned by mail.

Online search: WSP offers access through a system called WATCH, which can be accessed from their website. The fee per search is $10.00. The exact DOB and exact spelling of the name, and SSN are required. Credit cards are accepted online. To set up a WATCH account, call 360-705-5100 or email watch.help@wsp.wa.gov.

Other access: See the State Court Administrator's office for information about their criminal records database (JIS-Link).

Statewide Court Records

Administrative Office of Courts, Temple of Justice, PO Box 41174, Olympia, WA 98504-1174 (Courier: 1206 Quince St SE, Olympia, WA 98504); 360-357-2121, 360-357-2127 (Fax), 8AM-5PM.

www.courts.wa.gov

Searching: Include the following in your request- name or case number.

Access by: online.

Online search: The Superior Court Management Information System (SCOMIS), the Appellate Records System (ACORDS) and the District/Municipal Court Information System (DISCIS) are on the Judicial Information System's JIS-Link. Fees include a one-time $100.00 per site, a transaction fee of $.065 per record. Case records include criminal, civil, domestic, probate, and judgments. Call 360-357-3365 or visit www.courts.wa.gov/jislink. Supreme Court and Appellate opinions can be found at www.courts.wa.gov/appellate_trial_courts.

Other access: Indexes are available electronically and via microfiche for a fee. Call the JISLink coordinator for details.

Sexual Offender Registry

Access to Records is Restricted

Washington State Patrol, SOR, PO Box 42633, Olympia, WA 98504-2633 (Courier: 3000 Pacific Ave. SE #204, Olympia, WA 98501); 360-705-5100 x3, 360-570-5275 (Fax), 8AM-5PM.

www.wsp.wa.gov

Indexing & Storage: Records are available on current and former inmates. It takes 1 to 5 days before new records are available for inquiry. Records are normally destroyed after (records not destroyed; eventually archived with Sec. of State office.).

Searching: Include the following in your request- full name, DOB; SSN is helpful. Location, CCO, parole review data, and counselor are released. For anything other than basic information, a written request is required.

Access by: online.

Online search: In cooperation with the Washington Assoc. of Sheriffs and Police Chiefs, online access to Level II and Level III sexual offenders is available at www.waspc.org. There is a link to county sex offender sites at www.waspc.org/wa_sex/index.shtml.

Incarceration Records

Washington Department of Corrections, Office of Correctional Operations, 410 W. 5th, MS-41118, Olympia, WA 98504-1118; 360-753-3317 (Basic info), 360-586-3492 (Public Disclosure), 8AM-5PM M-F.

www.doc.wa.gov

Indexing & Storage: Records are available on current and former inmates. It takes 1 to 5 days before new records are available for inquiry. Records are not destroyed; eventually archived with Sec. of State office.

Searching: Include the following in your request- full name, DOB; SSN is helpful. Location, CCO, parole review data, and counselor are released. For anything other than basic information, a written request is required.

Access by: mail, phone, online.

Fee & Payment: A copy fee is $.20 per page; a postage fee applies to all mailed documents.

Mail search: Turnaround time: 1 to 2 weeks.

Phone search: Name searching available by phone; basic information released, no personal information.

Online search: No online searching provided. Email requests can be directed to correspondence@doc1.wa.gov.

Other access: Data is available by subscription for bulk users; for information, contact the Contracts Office at 360-664-0867.

Corporation Limited Partnerships, Limited Liability Company Records Trademarks/Servicemarks

Secretary of State, Corporations Division, PO Box 40234, Olympia, WA 98504-0234 (Courier: Dolliver Bldg, 801 Capitol Way South, Olympia, WA 98501); 360-753-7115, 360-664-8781 (Fax), 8AM-5PM.

www.secstate.wa.gov/corps/

Indexing & Storage: Records are available for initial filing documents. Annual reports for the past 5 years are on microfilm, imaged since 2004. It takes less than 1 day before new records are available for inquiry. Records are normally destroyed after 20 years since lapsing, usually.

Searching: All of the information here is public record. Include the following in your request-full name of business, UBI number if available. The copies for a limited partnership are different than corporation documents. Any single document is $1.00 per page plus $.20 per copy.

Access by: mail, phone, in person, online.

Fee & Payment: Directors, Officers list is $5.00 per corporate name. Photocopies fee is $10.00 per document, $20.00 if the document needs to be certified. If file exceeds 100 pages, a surcharge of $13.00 per 50 pages is added. Trademark documents are $.50 per page. Fee payee: Secretary of State. Prepayment required. Personal checks accepted. No credit cards accepted.

Mail search: Turnaround time: variable.

Phone search: Information requests are available at this department for limited information.

In person search: Turnaround time is while you wait.

Online search: Free searching of corporation registrations is at www.secstate.wa.gov/corps/search.aspx. Information is updated daily.

Expedited service: Expedited service is available for mail and phone searches. Turnaround time: 48 hours. Add $20.00 per document.

Trade Names

Master License Service, Business & Professions Div, PO Box 9034, Olympia, WA 98507-9034 (Courier: 405 Black Lake Blvd, Olympia, WA 98507); 360-664-1400, 900-463-6000 (Trade Name Search), 360-570-7875 (Fax), 8AM-4:30PM.

www.dol.wa.gov/

Indexing & Storage: Records are available from 1984 (note that everyone re-registered trade names in 1984). It takes 3 weeks before new records are

available for inquiry. Records are normally destroyed after 10 years.

Searching: Searching may be done by business name, business address, owner's name, or UBI number. The following data is not released: Social Security Numbers, personal information (height, weight, sex, eye color, etc.), date of birth or addresses.

Access by: mail, phone, in person.

Fee & Payment: The search fee is $4.00, which includes 3 business/owner names. A name variation is considered a separate name. Certification costs an additional $2.00. Fee payee: Washington State Treasurer. Prepayment required. Personal checks accepted. No credit cards accepted.

Mail search: Turnaround time: 2 weeks. Response time is generally one week. No SASE is required.

Phone search: The 900 number fee is $4.95 for the first minute and $.50 for each additional minute. Average search is 2 minutes.

In person search: Copies cost $.25 per page. Turnaround time is while you wait.

Other access: Records can be purchased on cartridges or 9 track tapes. Information includes date of registration, owner name, state ID numbers, and cancel date if cancelled. Call same number and ask for Jody Miller.

Expedited service: Expedited service is available for fax searches. Must have deposit account.

Uniform Commercial Code, Federal Tax Liens

Department of Licensing, UCC Records, PO Box 9660, Olympia, WA 98507-9660 (Courier: 405 Black Lake Blvd, Olympia, WA 98502); 360-664-1530, 360-586-4414 (Fax), 8AM-5PM.

www.dol.wa.gov/unfc/uccfront.htm

Indexing & Storage: Records are available from 1967. Records are computerized since 1985. However, only currently active plus 1 full year are accessible. It takes 2 days before new records are available for inquiry. Records are normally destroyed after one year past lapse date.

Searching: Use search request form UCC-11. The search includes all notices of federal tax liens. State tax liens are filed at the county level. Include the following in your request-debtor name.

Access by: mail, online.

Fee & Payment: A mail or in person request for information is $18.80. A request for information with all copies is $26.57. Fee payee: Department of Licensing. Prepayment required. Credit cards are accepted for online searching only. Personal checks accepted. Major Credit cards accepted.

Mail search: Turnaround time: 2 days. No SASE is required.

Online search: For online access, go to https://fortress.wa.gov/dol/uss. There is a $15.00 search fee for a name search. Fee is $26.57 if copies included or $20.00 if partial copies included. Copies are mailed.

Other access: The database may be purchased on microfilm or CD.

State Tax Liens

Records not maintained by a state level agency.

Note: State tax liens are filed at the county level.

Sales Tax Registrations

Department of Revenue, Taxpayer Services, PO Box 47478, Olympia, WA 98504-7478; 360-486-2345, 800-647-7706, 360-486-2159 (Fax), 8AM-5PM.

www.dor.wa.gov

Indexing & Storage: Records are available from 1992 and are indexed on microfiche and optical imaging.

Searching: This agency will provide disclosable information authorized by statute such as tax registration/UBI #, owner's name, business name (DBA), address, open/closing date, account status and SIC/NAICS. For confidential information, submit a signed release. Include the following in your request-business name or owner name, UBI or tax registarion number.

Access by: mail, phone, fax, in person, online.

Fee & Payment: There is no search fee, but there is a copy fee of $.15 per page.

Mail search: Turnaround time: 5 business days.

Phone search: Only "public registration" information is available.

Fax search: Turnaround time is 5 business days.

In person search: Appointment required.

Online search: The agency provides a state business records database with free access on the Internet at http://prd.dor.wa.gov/?link/default.aspx. Lookups are by owner names, DBAs, and tax reporting numbers. Results show a myriad of data.

Birth Certificates

Department of Health, Center for Health Statistics, PO Box 9709, Olympia, WA 98507-9709 (Courier: 101 Israel Rd SE, Tumwater WA 98501); 360-236-4300 (Main Number), 360-236-4313 (Credit Card Ordering), 360-352-2586 (Fax), 9AM - 4PM.

www.doh.wa.gov

Indexing & Storage: Records are available from July 1, 1907 to present. It takes 2-3 months before new records are available for inquiry. Records are indexed on microfiche, inhouse computer.

Searching: The data on the lower portion of form is confidential. Include the following in your request-full name, names of parents, mother's maiden name, date of birth, place of birth. Please specify if father is not listed on birth certificate.

Access by: mail, phone, fax, in person, online.

Fee & Payment: The search fee is $17.00. Fee payee: Dept of Health. Prepayment required. Personal checks accepted. Major credit cards accepted.

Mail search: Turnaround time: 7 to 8 weeks. Must send your current address and daytime phone number with request. A SASE is requested.

Phone search: You must use a credit card for a $11.00 additional fee for next day processing and mail-out.

Fax search: Same criteria as phone searching. Certificate can be returned by fax for an additional $5.00 (non-certified).

In person search: Counter service is available for same day requests.

Online search: Records may requested from www.Vitalchek.com, a state-endorsed vendor.

Expedited service: Expedited service is available for phone, in person, and fax requests. Turnaround

time: next working day mail. You must use a credit card for an additional $11.00 fee and courier or Express Mail are additional costs.

Death Records

Department of Health, Vital Records, PO Box 9709, Olympia, WA 98507-9709 (Courier: 101 Israel Rd SE, Tumwater, WA 98501); 360-236-4300 (Main Number), 360-236-4313 (Credit Card Ordering), 360-352-2586 (Fax), 9AM - 4PM.

www.doh.wa.gov

Indexing & Storage: Records are available from July 1, 1907 to present. It takes 2-6 months before new records are available for inquiry. Records are indexed on microfiche, inhouse computer.

Searching: A written request is required, there is no public viewing. Include the following in your request-full name, date of death, place of death.

Access by: mail, phone, fax, in person, online.

Fee & Payment: The search fee is $17.00. Fee payee: Dept of Health. Prepayment required. Personal checks accepted. Major credit cards accepted.

Mail search: Turnaround time: 7 to 8 weeks. Must send your current address and daytime phone number with request. A SASE is requested.

Phone search: You must use a credit card for an additional $11.00 fee. Records are processed the next day.

Fax search: Same criteria as phone searching. Non-certified copies can be returned by fax for $5.00 per page.

In person search: Counter service is available for same day requests.

Online search: Records may requested from www.vitalchek.com, a state-endorsed vendor.

Expedited service: Expedited service is available for phone, fax, and in person searches. Turnaround time: next working day. You must use a credit card for an additional $11.00 fee and courier or Express Mail are additional costs.

Marriage Certificates

Department of Health, Vital Records, PO Box 9709, Olympia, WA 98507-9709 (Courier: 101 Israel Rd SE, Tumwater, WA 98501); 360-236-4300 (Main Number), 360-236-4313 (Credit Card Ordering), 360-352-2586 (Fax), 9AM - 4PM.

www.doh.wa.gov

Indexing & Storage: Records are available from 1968 to present. It takes 2-4 months before new records are available for inquiry. Records are indexed on microfiche, inhouse computer.

Searching: Written request is required, there is no public viewing. Include the following in your request-names of husband and wife, date of marriage, place or county of marriage.

Access by: mail, phone, fax, in person, online.

Fee & Payment: The search fee is $17.00. Fee payee: Dept of Health. Prepayment required. Personal checks accepted. Major credit cards accepted.

Mail search: Turnaround time: 7 to 8 weeks. Must send your current address and daytime phone number with request. A SASE is requested.

Phone search: You must use a credit card for an additional $11.00 fee. Turnaround time is next day.

Fax search: Same criteria as phone searching. Non-certified records can be returned by fax for an additional $5.00 per record.

In person search: Counter service is available for same day requests.

Online search: Records may requested from www.vitalchek.com, a state-endorsed vendor.

Expedited service: Expedited service is available for phone, fax, and in person searches. Turnaround time: overnight delivery. You must use a credit card for an additional $11.00 fee and courier or Express Mail are additional costs.

Divorce Records

Department of Health, Vital Records, PO Box 9709, Olympia, WA 98507-9709 (Courier: 101 Israel Rd SE, Tumwater, WA 98501); 360-753-4300 (Main Number), 360-753-4313 (Credit Card Ordering), 360-352-2586 (Fax), 9AM - 4PM.

www.doh.wa.gov

Indexing & Storage: Records are available from 1968 to present. It takes 2-4 months before new records are available for inquiry. Records are indexed on microfiche, inhouse computer.

Searching: Include the following in your request-names of husband and wife, date of divorce, place of divorce.

Access by: mail, phone, fax, in person, online.

Fee & Payment: The search fee is $17.00. Fee payee: Dept of Health. Prepayment required. Personal checks accepted. Major credit cards accepted.

Mail search: Turnaround time: 5 weeks. Must send your current address and daytime phone number with request. A SASE is requested.

Phone search: Phone requesters are required to use a credit card for an additional $11.00 fee. The request is processed the next day.

Fax search: Same criteria as phone searching. Non-certified documents can be returned for an additional $5.00 per record.

In person search: Counter service is available for same day requests.

Online search: Records may requested from www.vitalchek.com, a state-endorsed vendor.

Expedited service: Expedited service is available for phone, fax, and in person searches. Turnaround time: overnight delivery. You must use a credit card for an additional $11.00 fee and courier or Express Mail are additional costs.

Workers' Compensation Records

Labor and Industries, Public Disclosure Unit, PO Box 44632, Olympia, WA 98504-4632 (Courier: 7273 Linderson Way SW, Tumwater, WA 98501); 360-902-5542, 360-902-5529 (Fax), 8AM-5PM.

www.lni.wa.gov/

Indexing & Storage: Records are available for the past 3 years. Prior records are at the State Records Center, but you must go through this office for those records. It takes 1 month before new records are available for inquiry. Records are indexed on computer and microfiche. Records are normally destroyed after 75 years.

Searching: Must have signed release from the claimant. Written request only. Claims information is not released except as provided under Title 51 of the Revised Code of Washington (RCW). No out-of-state subpoenas are honored. Include the following in your request-claimant name, Social Security Number, claim number. The DOB is helpful. The following data is not released: chemically-related illness.

Access by: mail, fax, in person.

Fee & Payment: Fees depend on volume of file. First $20.00 in duplication fees are free. Fee payee: L & I Cashier. Prepayment required if over $100. Personal checks accepted. No credit cards accepted.

Mail search: Turnaround time: 3 to 5 business days. The record information that they send back is taken from microfiche only. No hard file copies released.

Fax search: Fax requests are accepted.

In person search: Must schedule by appointment.

Driver Records

Department of Licensing, Driver Record Section, PO Box 9030, Olympia, WA 98507-9030 (Courier: 1125 Washington Street SE, Olympia, WA 98504); 360-902-3921, 360-902-3900 (General Information), 360-586-9044 (Fax), 8AM-4:30PM.

www.dol.wa.gov

Note: Records available include a 3-year insurance record and the "full" employment record. The 3-year record contains employment or non-employment convictions. The full record contains both. Detailed information on access and forms are found at the web.

Indexing & Storage: It takes 2 to 3 weeks or more before new records are available for inquiry. Records are normally destroyed after 5 years.

Searching: All mail or walk-in requests require a signed authorization from the driver, exceptions are for ongoing, pre-approved accounts. Casual requesters must have written consent. Include the following in your request-licesne number, or the name and DOB. The license number is based upon a code of the name and DOB. This code can be confusing (O or 0, *'s) so it is suggested you try name and DOB first. The following data is not released: Social Security Numbers.

Access by: mail, in person, online.

Fee & Payment: The fee is $5.00 per record. Copies of tickets may be requested by the driver or driver's authorized representative. The fee is $.75 per ticket; the first 5 are free. Fee payee: Department of Licensing Prepayment required. Personal checks accepted. No credit cards accepted.

Mail search: Turnaround time: 2 weeks. There is no charge for a no record found. A SASE is requested.

In person search: Turnaround time is immediate for up to 5 requests. There is no charge for a no record found.

Online search: You may check the status of a driver license, permit or ID card online for free at https://fortress.wa.gov/dol/ddl/dsd/.

Other access: Tape retrieval is offered for high volume requesters.

Expedited service: Will expedite delivery if a prepaid envelope is provided.

Vehicle and Vessel Ownership and Registration

Department of Licensing, Vehicle Records, PO Box 2957, Olympia, WA 98507-2957 (Courier: 1125 S Washington MS-48001, Olympia, WA 98504); 360-902-3780, 360-902-3827 (Fax), 8AM-5PM.

www.dol.wa.gov

Note: It is recommended that on-going, high volume users enter into a disclosure agreement with this agency; call 360-902-3760.

Indexing & Storage: Records are available for 6 years to present. All motorized boats and sailboats must be titled. All boats must be registered unless under 16 ft with less than a 10 hp motor. It takes 2 to 3 weeks before new records are available for inquiry. Records are indexed on inhouse computer.

Searching: Washington has strict access guidelines that restrict casual requesters. Permitted requesters include attorneys, PI's, insurance companies, and business entities for use in the normal course of business. A special form is required. Include the following in your request-VIN, license plate number. Records cannot be searched by owner or driver name. Requests must be in writing.

Access by: mail, phone, in person, online.

Fee & Payment: The fee for microfilm or microfiche copies are $.75 per page. Fee for photocopy or printouts is $.15 each; no charge under $4.50. There is no charge to "view" a record. Fee payee: Department of Licensing

Mail search: Turnaround time: 2 weeks. No SASE is required.

Phone search: Phone ordering is only available for pre-approved, high volume accounts. The system processes by plate number, VIN, WN# & HIN. To set up an account, call 360-902-3760.

In person search: Simple requests may be processed while you wait.

Online search: This Internet Vehicle/Vessel Information System is a commercial subscription service and all accounts must be pre-approved. A $25.00 deposit is required and there is a fee per hit. For more information, call 360-902-3760.

Other access: Large bulk lists cannot be released for any commercial purposes. Lists are released to non-profit entities and for statistical purposes. For more information, call 360-902-3760.

Accident Reports

State Patrol, Collision Reports, PO Box 47382, Olympia, WA 98504; 360-570-2355, 360-570-2400 (Fax), 8AM-5PM.

www.wsp.wa.gov/

Indexing & Storage: Records are available for 6 years plus the present year. It takes 2 to 3 weeks before new records are available for inquiry. Records are normally destroyed after 6 years.

Searching: Include the following in your request-name, date of accident, location of accident. It is strongly suggested to use their request form - Form 300-345-008. The agency will fax a copy of the form, upon request.

Access by: mail, in person.

Fee & Payment: The fee is $5.00 per record. Fee payee: Washington State Patrol. Prepayment required. Personal checks accepted. No credit cards accepted.

Mail search: Turnaround time: 2 weeks. A SASE is requested.

In person search: Walk-in requesters may receive the report with proper credentials, if personnel are available to do the search.

Voter Registration
Access to Records is Restricted

Secretary of State, Office of Elections Division, PO Box 40220, Olympia, WA 98504-0220; 360-902-4180, 360-664-4619 (Fax), 8AM-5PM.

www.secstate.wa.gov/elections/

Note: All voter information is kept at the local level by the County Auditor (except King County where records are kept by the Dept of Records and Elections). Individual look-ups will not receive SSNs, DOBs, or telephone numbers.

GED Certificates

State Board for Community & Technical Colleges, GED Records, PO Box 42495, Olympia, WA 98504-2495 (Courier: 319 7th Ave, Olympia, WA 98504); 360-704-4410, 360-664-8808 (Fax), 8AM-5PM.

www.sbctc.ctc.edu

Searching: Include the following in your request-name, Social Security Number, date of birth, signed release. Also, the city, date of test, and any previous name the record could be under are helpful.

Access by: mail, fax, in person.

Fee & Payment: There is no fee for either verification or a transcript.

Mail search: Turnaround time: 1 week. No SASE is required.

Fax search: Same criteria as mail searching.

In person search: Verification is while you wait.

Hunting and Fishing License Information

Department of Fish & Wildlife, Attn: Public Disclosure Officer, 600 Capitol Way, N, Olympia, WA 98501-1091; 360-902-2253, 360-902-2171 (Fax), 8AM-5PM.

http://wdfw.wa.gov

Indexing & Storage: Records are available for past 5 years, in this office. It takes up to 3 months before new records are available for inquiry.

Searching: Records cannot be purchased for commercial list purposes. Include the following in your request-name and DOB. All requests must be in writing.

Access by: mail, fax, in person, online.

Fee & Payment: There is no fee unless a lengthy list is presented, then $.10 per page. Fee payee: WDFW

Mail search: Turnaround time: 1-2 weeks.

Fax search: Fax searching available.

In person search: Simple requests may be processed while you wait.

Online search: You may send an email request; check the website for the exact address.

Other access: The database can be purchased for non-commercial purposes only.

Washington State Licensing Agencies

Licenses Searchable Online

Acupuncturist #11 .... https://fortress.wa.gov/doh/hpqa1/Application/Credential_Search/profile.asp
Adult Family Home #30 .... www.aasa.dshs.wa.gov/Lookup/AFHRequestv2.asp
Animal Technician #11 .... https://fortress.wa.gov/doh/hpqa1/Application/Credential_Search/profile.asp
Announcer, Athletic Event (Ring) #27 .... https://wws2.wa.gov/dol/profquery
Applicator, Commercial #5.................................. http://agr.wa.gov/PestFert/LicensingEd/ListPrivateApplicators.htm
Architect #26.. https://wws2.wa.gov/dol/profquery/
Architect Corporation #26 .... https://wws2.wa.gov/dol/profquery/
Athlete, Professional #27................................. https://wws2.wa.gov/dol/profquery
Athletic Inspector #27 .... https://wws2.wa.gov/dol/profquery
Athletic Judge/Timekeeper/Physician #27.......... https://wws2.wa.gov/dol/profquery
Athletic Manager/Promoter/Matchmaker #27 ..... https://wws2.wa.gov/dol/profquery
Attorney #23 .... http://pro.wsba.org
Auction Company / Auctioneer #33 .... www.dol.wa.gov/main/biglist.htm
Audiologist #11 .... https://fortress.wa.gov/doh/hpqa1/Application/Credential_Search/profile.asp
Bail Bond Agent/Agency #15 .... https://wws2.wa.gov/dol/profquery
Barber #18 .... https://fortress.wa.gov/dol/dolprod/profquery/
Barber Instructor/School #18 .... https://fortress.wa.gov/dol/dolprod/profquery/
Barber Shop/Mobile/Booth #18......................... https://fortress.wa.gov/dol/dolprod/profquery/
Beauty Shop/Salon/Mobile #18 .... https://fortress.wa.gov/dol/dolprod/profquery/
Boarding Homes #30 .... www.aasa.dshs.wa.gov/Lookup/BHRequestv2.asp
Boxer #27 .... https://wws2.wa.gov/dol/profquery
Camping Resort #33... www.dol.wa.gov/main/biglist.htm
Cemetery #6 .... https://fortress.wa.gov/dol/dolprod/profquery/
Charitable Gift Annuity #25............................... www.insurance.wa.gov/cgi-bin/PubInfoApps/CharitableGA.exe
Chiropractor #11... https://fortress.wa.gov/doh/hpqa1/Application/Credential_Search/profile.asp
Collection Agency #32 .... https://fortress.wa.gov/dol/dolprod/profrequency
Contractor, General, Company #12.................... www.lni.wa.gov/contractors/contractor.asp
Cosmetologist #18.. https://fortress.wa.gov/dol/dolprod/profquery/
Cosmetology (Barber) #33................................ www.dol.wa.gov/main/biglist.htm
Cosmetology Instructor/School #18.................... https://fortress.wa.gov/dol/dolprod/profquery/
Counselor #11 .... https://fortress.wa.gov/doh/hpqa1/Application/Credential_Search/profile.asp
Court Reporter #33 .... www.dol.wa.gov/main/biglist.htm
Crematory #6 .... https://fortress.wa.gov/dol/dolprod/profquery/
Dental Hygienist #11... https://fortress.wa.gov/doh/hpqa1/Application/Credential_Search/profile.asp
Dentist #11... https://fortress.wa.gov/doh/hpqa1/Application/Credential_Search/profile.asp
Dietitian #11... https://fortress.wa.gov/doh/hpqa1/Application/Credential_Search/profile.asp
Electrical Contractor/Admin. #12 .... www.lni.wa.gov/contractors/contractor.asp
Electrician #12 .... www.lni.wa.gov/contractors/contractor.asp
Embalmer #6 .... https://fortress.wa.gov/dol/dolprod/profquery/
Emergency Medical Technician #11.................... https://fortress.wa.gov/doh/hpqa1/Application/Credential_Search/profile.asp
Employment Agency #32................................... https://wws2.wa.gov/dol/profquery
Employment Directory Service #32 .... https://wws2.wa.gov/dol/profquery
Esthetician Shop/Salon/Booth/Mobile #18 .... https://fortress.wa.gov/dol/dolprod/profquery/
Esthetician/Esthetician Instructor #18 .... https://fortress.wa.gov/dol/dolprod/profquery/
Feedlot #3.. http://agr.wa.gov/FoodAnimal/Livestock/CertifiedFeedlots.htm
Fishing, Commercial #8.................................... www.greatlodge.com/wa-fishhunt/licenses/state_fishgame_front.cgi?st=WA
Funeral Director/Establishment #6 .... https://fortress.wa.gov/dol/dolprod/profquery/
Gaming Operation #24 .... www.wsgc.wa.gov/LicSearch.asp
Gaming-related Occupation #24......................... www.wsgc.wa.gov/LicSearch.asp
Healthcare Service Company #25...................... www.insurance.wa.gov/cgi-bin/PubInfoApps/CGIAuthComp.exe
Hearing Instrument Fitter/Dispenser #11............ https://fortress.wa.gov/doh/hpqa1/Application/Credential_Search/profile.asp
HMO #25 .... www.insurance.wa.gov/cgi-bin/PubInfoApps/CGIAuthComp.exe
Home Health Care Agency #9 .... www.doh.wa.gov/Licensing.htm
Hospital #9... www.doh.wa.gov/Licensing.htm
Hypnotherapist #11... https://fortress.wa.gov/doh/hpqa1/Application/Credential_Search/profile.asp
Insurance Company #25.................................... www.insurance.wa.gov/cgi-bin/PubInfoApps/CGIAuthComp.exe
Insurance Corporation, Resident #25................. www.insurance.wa.gov/cgi-bin/PubInfoApps/CGIAuthComp.exe
Kickboxer #27 .... https://wws2.wa.gov/dol/profquery
Landscape Architect #26 .... https://wws2.wa.gov/dol/profquery/

Liquor Store #19 .... www.liq.wa.gov/services/storesearch.asp
Livestock Market #3... http://agr.wa.gov/FoodAnimal/Livestock/PublicMarkets.htm
Manicure Shop/Mobile/Booth #18 .... https://fortress.wa.gov/dol/dolprod/profquery/
Manicurist/Esthetician #33................................. www.dol.wa.gov/main/biglist.htm
Manicurist/Manicurist Instructor #18.................. https://fortress.wa.gov/dol/dolprod/profquery/
Marriage & Family Therapist #11....................... https://fortress.wa.gov/doh/hpqa1/Application/Credential_Search/profile.asp
Massage Therapist #11 .... https://fortress.wa.gov/doh/hpqa1/Application/Credential_Search/profile.asp
Medical Doctor #11 .... https://fortress.wa.gov/doh/hpqa1/Application/Credential_Search/profile.asp
Mental Health Counselor #11 .... https://fortress.wa.gov/doh/hpqa1/Application/Credential_Search/profile.asp
Midwife #11.. https://fortress.wa.gov/doh/hpqa1/Application/Credential_Search/profile.asp
Naturopathic Physician #11 .... https://fortress.wa.gov/doh/hpqa1/Application/Credential_Search/profile.asp
Notary Public #17 .... https://fortress.wa.gov/dol/dolprod/profquery/
Nurse/Nursing Assistant #11 .... https://fortress.wa.gov/doh/hpqa1/Application/Credential_Search/profile.asp
Nurse-LPN #11 .... https://fortress.wa.gov/doh/hpqa1/Application/Credential_Search/profile.asp
Nursing Home Administrator #11......................... https://fortress.wa.gov/doh/hpqa1/Application/Credential_Search/profile.asp
Nursing Homes #30 .... www.aasa.dshs.wa.gov/Professional/NFDir/directory.asp
Occupational Therapist #11................................ https://fortress.wa.gov/doh/hpqa1/Application/Credential_Search/profile.asp
Ocularist #11.. https://fortress.wa.gov/doh/hpqa1/Application/Credential_Search/profile.asp
Optician #11 .... https://fortress.wa.gov/doh/hpqa1/Application/Credential_Search/profile.asp
Optometrist #11 .... https://fortress.wa.gov/doh/hpqa1/Application/Credential_Search/profile.asp
Osteopathic Physician #11 .... https://fortress.wa.gov/doh/hpqa1/Application/Credential_Search/profile.asp
Pharmacist / Pharmacy Technician #11 .... https://fortress.wa.gov/doh/hpqa1/Application/Credential_Search/profile.asp
Physical Therapist #11 .... https://fortress.wa.gov/doh/hpqa1/Application/Credential_Search/profile.asp
Physician Assistant #11..................................... https://fortress.wa.gov/doh/hpqa1/Application/Credential_Search/profile.asp
Plumber #12 .... www.lni.wa.gov/contractors/contractor.asp
Podiatrist #11... https://fortress.wa.gov/doh/hpqa1/Application/Credential_Search/profile.asp
Private Investigative Agency/Trainer #15 .... https://wws2.wa.gov/dol/profquery
Private Investigator, Armed/Unarmed #15 .... https://wws2.wa.gov/dol/profquery
Professional Athlete #33.................................... www.dol.wa.gov/main/biglist.htm
Psychologist #11.. https://fortress.wa.gov/doh/hpqa1/Application/Credential_Search/profile.asp
Public Accountant-CPA #1 .... www.cpaboard.wa.gov/search/default.htm
Purchasing Group (Insurance) #25..................... www.insurance.wa.gov/cgi-bin/PubInfoApps/CGIRiskPG.exe
Radiologic Technologist #11............................... https://fortress.wa.gov/doh/hpqa1/Application/Credential_Search/profile.asp
Recreational Hunting #8 .... www.greatlodge.com/wa-fishhunt/licenses/state_fishgame_front.cgi?st=WA
Referee (Athletic) #27.. https://wws2.wa.gov/dol/profquery
Respiratory Therapist #11 .... https://fortress.wa.gov/doh/hpqa1/Application/Credential_Search/profile.asp
Risk Retention Group #25 .... www.insurance.wa.gov/cgi-bin/PubInfoApps/CGIRiskRG.exe
Salon #33... www.dol.wa.gov/main/biglist.htm
Security Guard, Private Armed/Unarmed #15 .... https://wws2.wa.gov/dol/profquery
Security Guard/Agency #15................................ https://wws2.wa.gov/dol/profquery
Service Contract Provider (Insurance) #25 .... www.insurance.wa.gov/cgi-bin/PubInfoApps/CGIServiceCP.exe
Sex Offender Treatment Provider #11................. https://fortress.wa.gov/doh/hpqa1/Application/Credential_Search/profile.asp
Social Worker #11 .... https://fortress.wa.gov/doh/hpqa1/Application/Credential_Search/profile.asp
Speech-Language Pathologist #11..................... https://fortress.wa.gov/doh/hpqa1/Application/Credential_Search/profile.asp
Sport Fishing #8... www.greatlodge.com/wa-fishhunt/licenses/state_fishgame_front.cgi?st=WA
Structural Pest Inspector #5 .... http://agr.wa.gov/PestFert/LicensingEd/ListStructuralPestInspectors.htm
Timeshare Seller/Company/Project #33............. www.dol.wa.gov/main/biglist.htm
Travel Agency / Travel Seller #33...................... www.dol.wa.gov/main/biglist.htm
Veterinarian #11 .... https://fortress.wa.gov/doh/hpqa1/Application/Credential_Search/profile.asp
Veterinarian, Livestock #3 .... http://agr.wa.gov/FoodAnimal/Livestock/CertifiedVeterinarians.htm
Veterinary Medical Clerk #11............................. https://fortress.wa.gov/doh/hpqa1/Application/Credential_Search/profile.asp
Viatical Settlement Provider #25........................ www.insurance.wa.gov/cgi-bin/PubInfoApps/CGIViaticalSP.exe
Whitewater River Outfitter #32........................... https://wws2.wa.gov/dol/profquery
Wrestler #27 .... https://wws2.wa.gov/dol/profquery
X-ray Technician #11.. https://fortress.wa.gov/doh/hpqa1/Application/Credential_Search/profile.asp

Washington Licensing Quick Finder

Acupuncturist #11	360-236-4700
Adult Family Home #30	360-725-2300
Animal Technician #11	360-236-4700
Announcer, Athletic Event (Ring) #27	360-664-6644
Applicator, Commercial #5	877-301-4555
Applicator, Private Commercial #5	877-301-4555
Architect #26	360-664-1388
Architect Corporation #26	360-664-1388
Athlete, Professional #27	360-664-6644
Athletic Inspector #27	360-664-6644
Athletic Judge/Timekeeper/Physician #27	360-664-6644
Athletic Mgr./Promoter/Matchmaker#27	360-664-6644
Attorney #23	206-727-8200
Auction Company / Auctioneer #33	360-664-6636
Audiologist #11	360-236-4700
Bail Bond Agent/Agency #15	360-664-6624
Bank #7	360-902-8704
Barber / Barber Instructor/School #18	360-664-6626
Barber Shop/Mobile/Booth #18	360-664-6626
Battery Collector #32	330-664-1400
Beauty Shop/Salon/Mobile #18	360-664-6626
Boarding Homes #30	360-725-2300
Boiler Inspector #13	360-902-5270
Boxer #27	360-664-6644
Brand #3	360-902-1855
Bulk Hauler #14	360-664-6466
Business Opportunity Offering #7	360-902-8760
Camping Resort #33	360-664-6646
Cemetery #6	360-664-1555
Charitable Gift Annuity #25	360-725-7000
Check Casher/Seller #7	360-902-8703
Child Care Facility #29	360-413-3209
Chiropractor #11	360-236-4700
Cigarette Retailer/Vender/Whlse #32	330-664-1400
Collection Agency #32	360-664-1389
Commodity Registration #7	360-902-8760
Concealed Weapon #15	360-664-6616
Consumer Loan Company #7	360-902-8703
Contractor, General, Company #12	360-902-5202
Contractor, General, Individual #32	330-664-1400
Cosmetologist #18	360-664-6626
Cosmetology (Barber) #33	360-664-6626
Cosmetology Instructor/School #18	360-664-6626
Counselor #11	360-236-4700
Court Reporter #33	360-664-6633
Credit Union #7	360-902-8701
Crematory #6	360-664-1555
Dental Hygienist #11	360-236-4700
Dentist #11	360-236-4700
Dietitian #11	360-236-4700
Domestic Insurance Carrier #25	360-725-7000
Egg Handler/Dealer #32	330-664-1400
Egg Inspector #4	360-902-1830
Electrical Contractor/Admin. #12	360-902-5269
Electrician #12	360-902-5269
Embalmer #6	360-664-1555
Emergency Medical Technician #11	360-236-2845
Employment Agency #32	360-664-1389
Employment Directory Service #32	330-664-1400
Engineer #35	360-664-1575
Engineering Geologist #34	360-664-1497
Engineering/Land Surveying Company #35	360-664-1575
Escrow Company/Officers #7	360-902-8703
Esthetician Shop/Salon/Booth/Mobile #18	360-664-6626
Esthetician/Esthetician Instructor #18	360-664-6626
Feedlot #3	360-902-1855
Fertilizer Distributor, Bulk #32	330-664-1400
Firearms Dealer #15	360-664-6616
Fishing, Commercial #8	360-902-2464
Foster Home #31	888-794-1794
Franchise #7	360-902-8760
Fruit/Vegetable Inspector #4	360-902-1832
Funeral Director/Establishment #6	360-664-1555
Gaming Operation #24	360-486-3440
Gaming-related Occupation #24	360-486-3440
Geologist #34	360-664-1497
Grain Inspector/Weigher/Sampler #28	360-902-1921
Healthcare Service Company #25	360-725-7000
Hearing Instrument Fitter/Dispenser #11	360-236-4700
HMO #25	360-725-7000
Home Health Care Agency #9	360-705-6611
Horse Racing-related Occupation #22	360-459-6462
Hospital #9	360-705-6611
Hydrogeologist #34	360-664-1497
Hypnotherapist #11	360-236-4700
Insurance Agent/Broker #25	360-725-7000
Insurance Broker, Resident/Non-Resident #25	360-725-7000
Insurance Company #25	360-725-7000
Insurance Corporation, Resident #25	360-725-7000
Investment Advisors #7	360-902-8760
Kickboxer #27	360-664-6644
Land Development Rep #16	306-664-6500/6488
Land Surveyor/Surveyor-in-training #35	360-664-1575
Landscape Architect #26	360-664-1388
Liquor Store #19	360-664-1600
Livestock Brand Record #3	360-902-1855
Livestock Market #3	360-902-1855
Lottery Retailer #32	330-664-1400
Manicure Shop/Mobile/Booth #18	360-664-6626
Manicurist/Esthetician #33	360-664-6626
Manicurist/Manicurist Instructor #18	360-664-6626
Manufactured Home Dealer #14	360-664-6466
Marriage & Family Therapist #11	360-236-4700
Massage Therapist #11	360-236-4700
Medical Doctor #11	360-236-4700
Mental Health Counselor #11	360-236-4700
Midwife #11	360-236-4700
Minor Worker #32	330-664-1400
Mobile Home/Travel Trailer Dealer #14	360-664-6466
Mortgage Broker #7	360-902-8703
Naturopathic Physician #11	360-236-4700
Notary Public #17	360-664-1550
Nurse/Nursing Assistant #11	360-236-4700
Nurse-LPN #11	360-236-4700
Nursery Retailer/Whlse #32	330-664-1400
Nursing Home Administrator #11	360-236-4700
Nursing Homes #30	360-725-2300
Occupational Therapist #11	360-236-4700
Ocularist #11	360-236-4700
Optician #11	360-236-4700
Optometrist #11	360-236-4700
Osteopathic Physician #11	360-236-4700
Pest Control Operator/Consultant, Public #5	877-301-4555
Pesticide Dealer/Manager #5	877-301-4555
Pesticide Operator/Applicator #5	877-301-4555
Pharmacist / Pharmacy Technician #11	360-236-4700
Physical Therapist #11	360-236-4700
Physician Assistant #11	360-236-4700
Pilot, Marine, Commercial #2	206-515-3904
Plumber #12	360-902-5207
Podiatrist #11	360-236-4700
Private Inv. Agency/Trainer #15	360-664-6611
Private Inv., Armed/Unarmed #15	360-664-6611
Professional Athlete #33	360-664-6644
Psychologist #11	360-236-4700
Public Accountant-CPA #1	360-753-2585
Purchasing Group (Insurance) #25	360-725-7000
Radiologic Technologist #11	360-236-4700
Real Estate Agent/Sales #16	360-664-6500/6488
Real Estate Appraiser, Cert./Licensed #16	306-664-6504/6488
Real Estate Broker #16	360-664-6500/6488
Real Estate LLC, LLP, Corp./Partnership #16	360-664-6500/6488
Recreational Hunting #8	360-902-2464
Referee (Athletic) #27	360-664-6644
Refrigerated Locker #32	330-664-1400
Rental Car #32	330-664-1400
Respiratory Therapist #11	360-236-4700
Risk Retention Group #25	360-725-7000
Salon #33	360-664-6626
Savings & Loan/Savings Bank #7	306-902-8704
School Counselor #20	360-725-6400
School Nurse #20	360-725-6400
School Occ./Physical Therapist #20	360-725-6400
School Principal/Superintendent #20	360-725-6400
School Program Administrator #20	360-725-6400
School Psychologist/Social Worker #20	360-725-6400
Scrap Processor #14	360-664-6466
Securities Broker/Dealer /Sales #7	306-902-8760
Security Guard, Private Armed/Unarmed #15	360-664-6611
Security Guard/Agency #15	360-664-6611
Seed Dealer #32	330-664-1400
Service Contract Provider, Insurance #25	360-725-7000
Sex Offender Treatment Provider #11	360-236-4700
Shopkeeper (non-prescript'n drug) #32	330-664-1400
Snowmobile Dealer #14	360-664-6466
Social Worker #11	360-236-4700
Speech-Language Pathologist #11	360-236-4700
Speed Pathology Audiology #20	360-725-6400
Sport Fishing #8	360-902-2464
Structural Pest Inspector #5	877-301-4555
Teacher #20	360-725-6400
Telephone Solicitor #32	330-664-1400
Timeshare Seller/Company/Project #33	360-664-6632
Tow Truck Operator #14	360-664-6466
Travel Agency / Travel Seller #33	360-664-6634
Trust Company #7	360-902-8704
Underground Storage Tank #32	330-664-1400
Vehicle Dealer/Manufacturer #14	360-664-6466
Vehicle for Hire #32	330-664-1400
Vehicle Sales/Disposal #32	330-664-1400
Vehicle Transporter #14	360-664-6466
Vessel Dealer #14	360-664-6466
Veterinarian #11	360-236-4700
Veterinarian, Livestock #3	360-902-1855
Veterinary Medical Clerk #11	360-236-4700
Viatical Settlement Provider #25	360-725-7000
Waste Tire Carrier #32	330-664-1400
Waste Tire Site Owner #32	330-664-1400
Wastewater System Designer/Inspector #35	360-664-1575
Weights & Measures #3	360-902-1857
Whitewater River Outfitter #32	330-664-1400
Wrecker #14	360-664-6466
Wrestler #27	360-664-6644
X-ray Technician #11	360-236-4700

Washington Licensing Agency Information

1 Board of Accountancy, PO Box 9131, Olympia, WA 98507-9131; 360-753-2585, Fax: 360-664-9190. www.cpaboard.wa.gov Email: webmaster@cpaboard.wa.gov   Search Database at www.cpaboard.wa.gov/search/default.htm

2 Board of Pilotage Commissioners, 2911 2nd Ave, Seattle, WA 98121-1012; 206-515-3904, Fax: 206-515-3969.   Email: larsonp@wsdot.wa.gov

3 Department of Agriculture, Livestock Division, PO Box 42560 (1111 Washington St SE), Olympia, WA 98504-2560; 360-902-1800, Fax: 360-902-2086.   http://agr.wa.gov Email: livestockid@agr.wa.gov

4 Department of Agriculture, Food Safety & Animal Health Division, PO Box 42560 (1111 Washington St SE), Olympia, WA 98504-2560; 360-902-1800, Fax: 360-902-2092. http://agr.wa.gov/default.htm

5 Department of Agriculture, Pesticides Management Division, PO Box 42589, Olympia, WA 98504-2589; 877-301-4555, Fax: 360-902-2093. http://agr.wa.gov/PestFert/default.htm Email: mtucker@agr.wa.gov   Search Database at http://agr.wa.gov/PestFert/LicensingEd/default.htm Note: Will Provide lists of business names, but not individual names.

6 Department of Licensing, Funeral & Cemetery Licensing Program, PO Box 9012, Olympia, WA 98507-9012; 360-664-1555, Fax: 360-586-4414. www.dol.wa.gov/unfc/funfront.htm Email: funerals@dol.wa.gov   Search Database at https://fortress.wa.gov/dol/dolprod/profquery/

7 Department of Financial Institutions, PO Box 41200, (150 Israel Rd SW Tumwater WA 98501), Olympia, WA 98504-1200; 360-902-8700, Fax: 360-586-5068. www.wa.gov/dfi

8 Department of Fish & Wildlife, 600 Capitol Way N, Olympia, WA 98501-1091; 360-902-2253, Fax: 360-902-2171. http://wdfw.wa.gov   Email: licensing@dfw.wa.gov

9 Department of Health, Facilities Services Licensing, PO Box 47852, Olympia, WA 98504; 360-236-2900, Fax: 360-236-2901. www.doh.wa.gov/hsqa/fsl/default.htm Email: information@doh.wa.gov   Search Database at www.doh.wa.gov/Licensing.htm

11 Department of Health, Health Professional Licensing, PO Box 47865 (310 Israel Rd, Tumwater), Olympia, WA 98504; 360-236-4700, Fax: 360-236-4818. www.doh.wa.gov/Licensing.htm Search Database at https://fortress.wa.gov/doh /hpqa1/Application/Credential_Search/profile.asp

12 Department of Labor & Industries, Construction Compliance, PO Box 44000, Olympia, WA 98504-4000; 360-902-5226, Fax: 360-902-5228. www.lni.wa.gov Email: berp235@lni.wa.gov   Search Database at www.lni.wa.gov/contractors/contractor.asp

13 Department of Labor & Industries, Boiler Section, PO Box 44410, Olympia, WA 98504-4410; 360-902-5270, Fax: 360-902-5292. www.wa.gov/lni   Email: mrod235@lni.wa.gov

14 Department of Licensing, Dealer Services, PO Box 9039, Olympia, WA 98507-9039; 360-664-6466, Fax: 360-586-0479. www.dol.wa.gov/vs/dl-lic.htm Email: dealers@dol.wa.gov

15 Licensing Dept, Public Protection Unit & Firearms Program, Private Investigator & Security Guard, PO Box 9649, Olympia, WA 98507-9649; 360-664-6611, Fax: 360-570-7888. www.wa.gov/dol   Email: Security@dol.wa.gov

16 Department of Licensing, Real Estate & Appraiser Program, PO Box 9015 (2000 4th Ave. W), Olympia, WA 98507-9015; 360-664-6500/664-6488, Fax: 360-586-0998. www.dol.wa.gov/realestate/refront.htm Email: RealEstate@dol.gov

17 Department of Licensing, Notary Section, PO Box 9027 (405 Black Lake Blvd SW), Olympia, WA 98507-9027; 360-664-1550, Fax: 360-586-4414. www.dol.wa.gov/unfc/notfront.htm Email: intnotarie@dol.wa.gov   Search Database at https://fortress.wa.gov/dol/dolprod/profquery/

18 Department of Licensing, Cosmetology Division, PO Box 9026, Olympia, WA 98507-9026; 360-664-6626, Fax: 360-664-2550. www.dol.wa.gov/plss/cosfront.htm Email: plssunit@dol.wa.gov   Search Database at https://fortress.wa.gov/dol/dolprod/profquery/

19 Liquor Control Board, 3000 Pacific Ave. SE, Olympia, WA 98504-3075; 360-664-1600, Fax: 360-753-2710. www.liq.wa.gov/default.asp Email: wslcb@liq.wa.gov   Search Database at www.liq.wa.gov/services/storesearch.asp

20 Superintendent of Public Instruction, Professional Education & Certification, PO Box 47200 (Old Capitol Bldg), Olympia, WA 98504-7200; 360-725-6400, Fax: 360-586-0145. www.k12.wa.us/cert   Email: cert@ospi.wednet.edu

22 Horse Racing Commission, 6326 Martin Way, #209, Olympia, WA 98516-5703; 360-459-6462, Fax: 360-459-6461. www.whrc.wa.gov/license.htm Email: whrc@whrc.state.wa.us

23 Bar Association, Washington State Service Center, 2101 4th Ave, 4th Fl, #400, Seattle, WA 98121-2599; 206-727-8200, Fax: 206-727-8320. www.wsba.org   Email: questions@wsba.org Search Database at http://pro.wsba.org

24 Gambling Commission, PO Box 42400, Olympia, WA 98504-2400; 360-486-3440, Fax: 360-438-7503. www.wsgc.wa.gov   Search Database at www.wsgc.wa.gov/LicSearch.asp

25 Insurance Licensing, P.O. Box 40255, Olympia, WA 98504-0255; 360-725-7003, Fax: 360-664-2782. www.insurance.wa.gov   Email: georgiac@oic.wa.gov

26 Department of Licensing, Business and Professions Division, Architects & Landscape Architects, PO Box 9045, Olympia, WA 98507-9045; 360-664-1388, Fax: 360-664-2551. www.wa.gov/dol/bpd/arcfront.htm Email: architects@dol.wa.gov   Search Database at www.wa.gov/dol/bpd/licquery.htm

27 Department of Licensing, Professional Boxing, Martial Arts & Wrestling Licensing Program, PO Box 9026, Olympia, WA 98507-9026; 360-664-6644, Fax: 360-570-4956. www.dol.wa.gov/plss/pafront.htm Email: plssunit@dol.wa.gov Search Database at https://wws2.wa.gov/dol/profquery

28 Department of Agriculture, Commodity Inspection, 3939 Cleveland Av SE, Olympia, WA 98501; 360-902-1921, Fax: 360-586-5257. http://agr.wa.gov/PestFert/default.htm Email: commodity@agr.wa.gov

29 Department of Child Care & Early Learning, PO Box 45480, Olympia, WA 98504; 360-413-3209. www.wa.gov/dol/bpd/refront.htm

30 Aging & Adult Services Administration, PO Box 45600, Olympia, WA 98504; 360-725-2300. www.aasa.dshs.wa.gov/default.htm

31 Children's Administration, Dept of Social & Health Services, P.O. Box 45715, Olympia, WA 98504-5715; 360-725-6701, Fax: 360-664-0744. http://www1.dshs.wa.gov/ca/index.asp Email: Children@dshs.wa.gov

32 Department of Licensing, Master License Service, PO Box 9034, Olympia, WA 98507-9034; 360-664-1400, Fax: 360-570-7875. www.dol.wa.gov/mls/reglic.htm Email: MLS@dol.wa.gov

33 Department of Licensing, Professional Licensing Support Services Unit, PO Box 9020 (1125 Washington St. SE), Olympia, WA 98507-9020; 360-664-1400, Fax: 360-664-2550. www.dol.wa.gov/   Email: plssunit@dol.wa.gov Search Database at www.dol.wa.gov/main/biglist.htm

34 Department of Licensing, Geologist Licensing Program, PO Box 9045, Olympia, WA 98507-9045; 360-664-1497, Fax: 360-664-2551. www.dol.wa.gov/design/geofront.htm Email: geologist@dol.wa.gov

35 Department of Licensing, Professional Engineers and Land Surveyors Section, PO Box 9025, Olympia, WA 98507-9025; 360-664-1575, Fax: 360-664-2551. www.dol.wa.gov/engineers/engfront.htm Email: engineers@dol.wa.gov

Washington Federal Courts

The following list indicates the district and division name for each county in the state. If the bankruptcy court location is different from the district court, then the location of the bankruptcy court appears in parentheses.

County/Court Cross Reference

County	District	Division
Adams	Eastern	Spokane
Asotin	Eastern	Spokane
Benton	Eastern	Spokane
Chelan	Eastern	Spokane
Clallam	Western	Tacoma (Seattle)
Clark	Western	Tacoma
Columbia	Eastern	Spokane
Cowlitz	Western	Tacoma
Douglas	Eastern	Spokane
Ferry	Eastern	Spokane
Franklin	Eastern	Spokane
Garfield	Eastern	Spokane
Grant	Eastern	Spokane
Grays Harbor	Western	Tacoma
Island	Western	Seattle
Jefferson	Western	Tacoma (Seattle)
King	Western	Seattle
Kitsap	Western	Tacoma (Seattle)
Kittitas	Eastern	Yakima (Spokane)
Klickitat	Eastern	Yakima (Spokane)
Lewis	Western	Tacoma
Lincoln	Eastern	Spokane
Mason	Western	Tacoma
Okanogan	Eastern	Spokane
Pacific	Western	Tacoma
Pend Oreille	Eastern	Spokane
Pierce	Western	Tacoma
San Juan	Western	Seattle
Skagit	Western	Seattle
Skamania	Western	Tacoma
Snohomish	Western	Seattle
Spokane	Eastern	Spokane
Stevens	Eastern	Spokane
Thurston	Western	Tacoma
Wahkiakum	Western	Tacoma
Walla Walla	Eastern	Spokane
Whatcom	Western	Seattle
Whitman	Eastern	Spokane
Yakima	Eastern	Yakima (Spokane)

Standards for Federal Courts: The search fee is $20.00 per item (one party name or case number). Certification fee is $7.00 per document. Copy fee is $.50 per page. All fees standard unless noted in profile. Mail Search: always enclose a stamped self addressed envelope unless otherwise noted. Most courts accept fax requests or will suggest a copying/search vendor. Before releasing records, all courts require prepayment unless noted in profile.

Open records are located at the court unless otherwise noted. District courts index by defendant and plaintiff as well as by case number. Bankruptcy courts usually index by debtor and case number. While most courts now have their indexes on computer, many still maintain index card files as well.

The universal PACER sign-up number is 800-676-6856. Find PACER and the Party/Case Index on the Web at http://pacer.psc.uscourts.gov. PACER dial-up access is $.60 per minute. Also, courts offering internet access via RACER, PACER, Web-PACER or the new CM-ECF charge $.07 per page fee unless noted as free.

US District Court

Eastern District of Washington

Spokane Division PO Box 1493, Spokane, WA 99210-1493 (courier: Room 840, W 920 Riverside, Spokane, WA 99201), 509-353-2150. www.waed.uscourts.gov

Counties: Adams, Asotin, Benton, Chelan, Columbia, Douglas, Ferry, Franklin, Garfield, Grant, Lincoln, Okanogan, Pend Oreille, Spokane, Stevens, Walla Walla, Whitman. Also, some cases from Kittitas, Klickitat and Yakima are heard here.

Indexing & Storage: New cases available in the index 2-3 days after filing date. Records are also indexed on microfiche. Search must be in Spokane Division for all cases before 1989. Judge McDonald's records are maintained in Yakima (Yakima County). All other cases are kept in the Spokane Division.

Fee & Payment: Payment may be made by money order, cashier check, personal check. Payee: Clerk, U.S. District Court.

Phone Search: No searching by telephone.

Mail Search: A SASE not required.

In Person Search: Fee charged if court conducts your in person search for you.

PACER: PACER is available online at http://pacer.waed.uscourts.gov. Records purged every 6 months. New records online after 2-3 days.

Yakima Division PO Box 2706, Yakima, WA 98907 (courier address: Room 215, 25 S 3rd St, Yakima, WA 98901), 509-575-5838. www.waed.uscourts.gov

Counties: Kittitas, Klickitat, Yakima. Cases assigned primarily to Judge McDonald are here. Some cases from Kittitas, Klickitat and Yakima are heard in Spokane.

Indexing & Storage: New cases available in the index 1 day after filing date. Search must be in Spokane Division for all cases before 1989. Judge McDonald's records are maintained in Yakima. All other cases are kept in the Spokane Division.

Fee & Payment: Make payments by money order, cashier check, business check. Personal checks are not accepted. Payee: Clerk, U.S. District Court.

Phone Search: Some docket information is available by phone.

In Person Search: Fee charged if court conducts your in person search for you.

PACER: PACER is available online at http://pacer.waed.uscourts.gov. Records purged every six months. New records are online after 2-3 days.

U.S. Bankruptcy Court

Eastern District of Washington

Spokane Division PO Box 2164, Spokane, WA 99210-2164 (courier address: W 904 Riverside, Suite 304, Spokane, WA 99201), 509-353-2404. www.waeb.uscourts.gov

Counties: Adams, Asotin, Benton, Chelan, Columbia, Douglas, Ferry, Franklin, Garfield, Grant, Kittitas, Klickitat, Lincoln, Okanogan, Pend Oreille, Spokane, Stevens, Walla Walla, Whitman, Yakima.

Indexing & Storage: Cases indexed by debtor and creditors as well as by case number. New cases available in the index immediately after filing date.

Fee & Payment: Payment may be made by money order, cashier check, business check. Personal checks are not accepted. Prepayment is not required for copy requests. Copies will be provided with a bill through the mail. Payee: Clerk, U.S. Bankruptcy Court.

Phone Search: Only docket information available by phone. Press extension 6. Automated voice case information service (VCIS) is available. Call VCIS at 509-353-2404.

In Person Search: Fee charged if court conducts your in person search for you. A copy service is available.

PACER: PACER is available online at http://pacer.waeb.uscourts.gov.

Electronic Filing: Electronic filing information online at https://ecf.waeb.uscourts.gov

Other Online Access: Searching records on the Internet using RACER has been replaced by PACER. Access fee is $.07 per page. Records go back to 1997.

U.S. District Court

Western District of Washington

Seattle Division Clerk of Court, 215 U.S. Courthouse, 1010 5th Ave, Seattle, WA 98104 (courier address: Use mail address for courier delivery) 206-553-5598. www.wawd.uscourts.gov

Counties: Island, King, San Juan, Skagit, Snohomish, Whatcom.

Indexing & Storage: New cases available in the index 10 days after filing date. Records are also indexed on microfiche.

Fee & Payment: Payment may be made by money order, cashier check, personal check. Payee: Clerk, U.S. District Court.

Phone Search: Docket information is available by phone for civil cases since 1994 and criminal cases since 1997.

Mail Search: A SASE not required.

In Person Search: Permitted. Outside copy service available.

PACER: PACER is available online at http://pacer.wawd.uscourts.gov. Document images available. Case records go back to 1988. Records never purged. New civil records are online after 4 days. New criminal records online after 2 days.

Electronic Filing: Electronic filing information online at https://ecf.wawd.uscourts.gov

Tacoma Division Clerk's Office, Room 3100, 1717 Pacific Ave, Tacoma, WA 98402-3200 (courier address: Use mail address for courier delivery) 253-593-6313. www.wawd.uscourts.gov

Counties: Clallam, Clark, Cowlitz, Grays Harbor, Jefferson, Kitsap, Lewis, Mason, Pacific, Pierce, Skamania, Thurston, Wahkiakum.

Indexing & Storage: New cases available in the index immediately after filing date. District wide searches are available for information from 1989. Microfiche and card indexes are available for older records.

Fee & Payment: Payment may be made by money order, cashier check, personal check. There is a $25.00 service fee if a check is returned. Payee: Clerk, U.S. District Court.

Phone Search: Only docket information available by phone.

In Person Search: Fee charged if court conducts your in person search for you.

PACER: PACER is available online at http://pacer.wawd.uscourts.gov. Document images available. Case records go back to 1988. Records never purged. New civil records are online after 4 days. New criminal records online after 2 days.

Electronic Filing: Electronic filing information online at https://ecf.wawd.uscourts.gov

U.S. Bankruptcy Court

Western District of Washington

Seattle Division Clerk of Court, 315 Park Place Bldg, 1200 6th Ave, Seattle, WA 98101 (courier address: Use mail address for courier delivery) 206-553-7545, Fax: 206-553-0131. www.wawb.uscourts.gov

Counties: Clallam, Island, Jefferson, King, Kitsap, San Juan, Skagit, Snohomish, Whatcom.

Indexing & Storage: Cases indexed by debtor and creditors as well as by case number. New cases available in the index 1 day after filing date. Open cases are stored by case number. Closed cases are stored by year closed and then by case number.

Fee & Payment: Payment may be made by money order, cashier check, personal check. Payee: Clerk, U.S. Bankruptcy Court.

Phone Search: Automated voice case information service (VCIS) is available. Call VCIS at 888-436-7477 or 206-553-8543.

In Person Search: Fee charged if court conducts your in person search for you. Outside copy service available.

PACER: PACER is available online at http://pacer.wawb.uscourts.gov. Case records go back to June 1995. Records never purged. New civil records are online after 2 days.

Electronic Filing: Electronic filing information online at https://ecf.wawb.uscourts.gov

Tacoma Division Suite 2100, 1717 Pacific Ave, Tacoma, WA 98402-3233 (courier address: Use mail address for courier delivery) 253-593-6310. www.wawb.uscourts.gov

Counties: Clark, Cowlitz, Grays Harbor, Lewis, Mason, Pacific, Pierce, Skamania, Thurston, Wahkiakum.

Indexing & Storage: Cases indexed by debtor as well as by case number. New cases available in the index 1 day after filing date. Records can be searched by debtor's name from 1987 to the present.

Fee & Payment: Payment may be made by money order, cashier check. Business checks are not accepted. Personal checks are not accepted. Attorney checks are accepted. Payee: Clerk, U.S. Bankruptcy Court.

Phone Search: Automated voice case information service (VCIS) is available. Call VCIS at 888-436-7477 or 206-553-8543.

Mail Search: A SASE not required.

In Person Search: Fee charged if court conducts your in person search for you. Outside copy service available.

PACER: PACER is available online at http://pacer.wawb.uscourts.gov. Case records go back to June 1995. Records never purged. New civil records are online after 2 days.

Electronic Filing: Electronic filing information online at https://ecf.wawb.uscourts.gov

Washington County Courts

Court	Jurisdiction	No. of Courts	How Organized
Superior Courts*	General	39	29 Districts
District Courts*	Limited	61	39 Counties
Municipal Courts	Municipal	131	131 Cities

* Profiled in this Sourcebook.

Court	CIVIL								
	Tort	Contract	Real Estate	Min. Claim	Max. Claim	Small Claims	Estate	Eviction	Domestic Relations
Superior Courts*	X	X	X	$50,000	No Max		X	X	X
District Courts*	X	X		$0	$50,000	$2500			
Municipal Courts									

Court	CRIMINAL				
	Felony	Misdemeanor	DWI/DUI	Preliminary Hearing	Juvenile
Superior Courts*	X				X
District Courts*		X	X	X	
Municipal Courts		X	X		

ADMINISTRATION   Court Administrator, Temple of Justice, PO Box 41174, Olympia, WA, 98504; 360-357-2121, Fax: 360-357-2127. www.courts.wa.gov

COURT STRUCTURE   District Courts retain civil records for 10 years from date of final disposition, then the records are destroyed. District Courts retain criminal records forever.

Washington has a mandatory arbitration requirement for civil disputes for $35,000 or less. However, either party may request a trial in Superior Court if dissatisfied with the arbitrator's decision.

The limit for civil actions in District Court has been increased from $35,000 to $50,000. The small claims maximum limit was raised to $4,000 in 2002.

ONLINE ACCESS   Appellate, Superior, and District Court records are available online. The Superior Court Management Information System (SCOMIS), the Appellate Records System (ACORDS) and the District/Municipal Court Information System (DISCIS) are on the Judicial Information System's JIS-Link. Case records available through JIS-Link from 1977 include criminal, civil, domestic, probate, and judgments. JIS-Link is generally available 24-hours daily. Minimum browser requirement is Internet Explorer 5.5 or Netscape 6.0. There is a one-time installation fee of $100.00 per site, then a $.065 charge per transaction. For information or a registration packet, contact JISLink Coordinator, Office of the Administrator for the Courts, 1206 S Quince St., PO Box 41170, Olympia WA 98504-1170, 360-357-3365 or visit www.courts.wa.gov/jislink

Supreme Court and Appellate opinions can be found at www.courts.wa.gov/appellate_trial_courts.

ADD'L INFORMATION   An SASE is required in most courts that respond to written search requests.

Adams County

Superior Court 210 W Broadway (PO Box 187), Ritzville, WA 99169-0187; 509-659-3257; Fax: 509-659-0118. Hours: 8:30AM-Noon, 1-4:30PM (PST). *Felony, Civil, Eviction, Probate.*
Civil Records: Access: Phone, fax, mail, online, in person. Only the court performs in person searches; visitors may not. Search fee: $20.00 per hour. Required to search: name, years to search; also helpful: address. Civil cases indexed by defendant, plaintiff. Civil records on computer from 1985, archived from 1900s. Index online from JIS-Link; see www.courts.wa.gov/jislink (also, see state introduction).
Criminal Records: Access: Phone, fax, mail, online, in person. Only the court performs in person searches; visitors may not. Search fee: $20.00 per hour. Required to search: name, years to search; also helpful: address, DOB, SSN. Criminal records on computer from 1985, archived from 1900s. Index remotely online from JIS-Link; see www.courts.wa.gov/jislink (also, see state introduction).

General Information: No sealed, juvenile, adoption, paternity, mental health, sex offenders (victims) records released. Will fax results $1.00 per page. Copy fee: $.50 per page. Cert fee: $2.00 plus $1.00 each add'l page. Payee: Adams County Clerk. Business checks accepted. Prepayment required. Mail requests: SASE required. Mail turnaround time 1 week.

Othello District Court 165 N 1st, Othello, WA 99344; 509-488-3935; Fax: 509-488-3480. Hours: 8:30AM-4:30PM (PST). *Misdemeanor, Civil Actions Under $50,000, Small Claims.*

Civil Records: Access: Phone, fax, mail, online, in person. Only the court performs in person searches; visitors may not. No search fee. Required to search: name, years to search; also helpful: address. Civil cases indexed by defendant, plaintiff. Civil records on computer for 10 years, prior on index cards. Index online from JIS-Link; see www.courts.wa.gov/jislink (also, see state introduction).

Criminal Records: Access: Phone, fax, mail, online, in person. Only the court performs in person searches; visitors may not. No search fee. Required to search: name, years to search, signed release; also helpful: address, DOB, SSN. Criminal records on computer for 10 years, prior on index cards. Index remotely online from JIS-Link; see www.courts.wa.gov/jislink (also, see state introduction).

General Information: No sealed, juvenile, adoption, paternity, mental health, sex offenders (victims) or (sometimes) DUI records released. No fee to fax results. Copy fee: $2.50 for first page, $1.00 each add'l. Cert fee: $6.00. Payee: Othello District Court. Personal checks accepted. Prepayment required. Mail requests: SASE required. Mail turnaround time 1-3 days.

Ritzville District Court 210 W Broadway, Ritzville, WA 99169; 509-659-1002; Fax: 509-659-0118. Hours: 8:30AM-4:30PM (PST). *Misdemeanor, Civil Actions Under $50,000, Small Claims.*

Civil Records: Access: Fax, mail, online, in person. Only the court performs in person searches; visitors may not. No search fee. Required to search: name, years to search; also helpful: address. Civil cases indexed by defendant, plaintiff. Civil records on computer from 10/90. Index online from JIS-Link; see www.courts.wa.gov/jislink (also, see state introduction).

Criminal Records: Access: Fax, mail, online, in person. Only the court performs in person searches; visitors may not. No search fee. Required to search: name, years to search, DOB; also helpful: address, SSN. Criminal records on computer from 10/90. Index remotely online from JIS-Link; see www.courts.wa.gov/jislink (also, see state introduction).

General Information: No sealed, juvenile, adoption, paternity, mental health, sex offenders (victims) or (sometimes) DUI records released. No fee to fax results. Copy fee: $1.00 per page. Cert fee: $5.00. Payee: Ritzville District Court. Personal checks accepted. Prepayment required. Mail requests: SASE required. Mail turnaround time 2 days.

Asotin County

Superior Court PO Box 159, Asotin, WA 99402-0159; 509-243-2081; Fax: 509-243-4978. Hours: 8AM-5PM (PST). *Felony, Civil, Eviction, Probate.*

Civil Records: Access: Phone, fax, mail, online, in person. Only the court performs in person searches; visitors may not. No search fee. Required to search: name, years to search; also helpful: address. Civil cases indexed by defendant, plaintiff. Civil records on computer from mid 1985, on microfiche from 1970s, archived from 1895. Index online from JIS-Link; see www.courts.wa.gov/jislink (also, see state introduction).

Criminal Records: Access: Phone, fax, mail, online, in person. Only the court performs in person searches; visitors may not. No search fee. Required to search: name, years to search, DOB; also helpful: address, SSN. Criminal records on computer from mid 1985, on microfiche from 1970s, archived from 1895. Index remotely online from JIS-Link; see

www.courts.wa.gov/jislink (also, see state introduction).

General Information: No sealed, juvenile, adoption, paternity, mental health, sex offenders (victims) or (sometimes) DUI records released. Copy fee: $2.00 for first page, $1.00 each add'l. Cert fee: included in copy fee. Payee: Asotin County Clerk. Personal checks accepted. Prepayment required. Mail requests: SASE required. Mail turnaround time 1 day.

District Court PO Box 429, Asotin, WA 99402-0429; 509-243-2027; Fax: 509-243-2091. Hours: 8AM-5PM (PST). *Misdemeanor, Civil Actions Under $50,000, Small Claims.*

Civil Records: Access: Fax, mail, online, in person. Only the court performs in person searches; visitors may not. Search fee: $6.00 per name. Required to search: name, years to search; also helpful: address. Civil cases indexed by defendant, plaintiff. Civil records on computer since 1993; prior records on log books. Index online from JIS-Link; see www.courts.wa.gov/jislink (also, see state introduction).

Criminal Records: Access: Fax, mail, online, in person. Only the court performs in person searches; visitors may not. Search fee: $6.00 per name. Required to search: name, years to search; also helpful: address, DOB, SSN. Criminal records on computer from 1993. Index remotely online from JIS-Link; see www.courts.wa.gov/jislink (also, see state introduction).

General Information: No sealed, juvenile, adoption, paternity, mental health, sex offenders (victims) or (sometimes) DUI records released. No fee to fax results. Copy fee: $.25 per page. Cert fee: $6.00. Payee: Asotin County District Court. Personal checks accepted. Prepayment required. Mail requests: SASE required. Mail turnaround time up to 2 weeks.

Benton County

Superior Court 7320 W Quinault, Kennewick, WA 99336-7690; 509-735-8388. Hours: 8AM-Noon, 1-4PM (PST). *Felony, Civil, Probate.*

Civil Records: Access: Mail, in person. Only the court performs in person searches; visitors may not. Search fee: $20.00 per hour. Required to search: name, years to search; also helpful: address. Civil cases indexed by defendant, plaintiff. Civil records on computer from 1979, pre-1979 on index books. Index online from JIS-Link; see www.courts.wa.gov/jislink (also, see state introduction).

Criminal Records: Access: Mail, in person. Only the court performs in person searches; visitors may not. Search fee: $20.00 per hour. Required to search: name, years to search; also helpful: address, DOB, SSN. Criminal records on computer from 1979, pre-1979 on index books. Index remotely online from JIS-Link; see www.courts.wa.gov/jislink (also, see state introduction).

General Information: No sealed, dependency, adoption, paternity, mental health, sex offenders (victims). Will fax results $3.00 1st page, $1.00 each add'l. Copy fee: $.25 per page. Cert fee: $2.00 plus $1.00 per page after first. Payee: Benton County Clerk. Personal checks accepted. Prepayment required. Mail requests: SASE required. Mail turnaround time 10 days.

District Court 7122 W Okanogan Place, Box E, Kennewick, WA 99336; 509-735-8476; 786-5602; Fax: 509-736-3069. Hours: 8AM-Noon, 1-4PM (PST). *Misdemeanor, Civil Actions Under $50,000, Small Claims.*

Civil Records: Access: Mail, fax, online, in person. Both court and visitors may perform in person searches. Search fee: $10.00 per name. Required to search: name, years to search; also helpful: address. Civil cases indexed by defendant, plaintiff. Civil

records on computer from 7/91. Index online from JIS-Link; see www.courts.wa.gov/jislink (also, see state introduction).

Criminal Records: Access: Mail, fax, online, in person. Both court and visitors may perform in person searches. Search fee: $10.00 per name. Required to search: name, years to search, DOB, signed release; also helpful: address, SSN. Criminal records on computer from 7/91, stored from 1988. Index remotely online from JIS-Link; see www.courts.wa.gov/jislink (also, see state introduction).

General Information: Public Access terminal is available. No sealed, juvenile, adoption, paternity, mental health, sex offenders (victims) or (sometimes) DUI records released. Copy fee: First 50 copies free, then $.15 each. Cert fee: $5.00. Payee: Benton County District Court. Personal checks accepted. Prepayment required. Mail requests: SASE requested. Turnaround time 10 days.

Chelan County

Superior Court 350 Orondo (PO Box 3025), Wenatchee, WA 98807-3025; 509-667-6380; Fax: 509-667-6611. Hours: 9AM-5PM (PST). *Felony, Civil, Eviction, Probate, Domestic.*

www.co.chelan.wa.us

Civil Records: Access: Phone, fax, mail, online, in person. Both court and visitors may perform in person searches. Search fee: $20.00 per hour. Required to search: name, years to search. Civil cases indexed by defendant, plaintiff. Civil docket records on computer back to 1984; prior on microfilm to 1900. Civil records from 1993 forward and probate from 1975 forward by online subscription at web page. Subscribers may also file online. Index online from JIS-Link; see www.courts.wa.gov/jislink (also, see state introduction). Current dockets and schedule are at www.co.chelan.wa.us/scc/scc4.htm.

Criminal Records: Access: Phone, fax, mail, online, in person. Both court and visitors may perform in person searches. Search fee: $20.00 per hour. Required to search: full name, years to search; also helpful: address, DOB, SSN. Criminal records on computer back to 1984; prior on microfilm to 1900. Records from 1992 forward by online subscription at web page. Subscribers may also file online. Index is remotely online from JIS-Link; see www.courts.wa.gov/jislink (also, see state introduction). Current dockets and schedule is at www.co.chelan.wa.us/scc/scc4.htm.

General Information: Public Access terminal is available. (Civil and criminal go back to 1996.) No sealed, juvenile, adoption, paternity, mental health, sex offenders (victims) records released. Will fax results $3.00 1st page, $1.00 each add'l. Copy fee: $2.00 for first page, $1.00 each add'l. Cert fee: The certification fee is included in the copy fee. Payee: Chelan County Clerk. Personal checks and credit cards accepted. Prepayment required. Mail requests: SASE required. Mail turnaround time 1 day.

Chelan County District Court PO Box 2182, Courthouse 4th Fl, Wenatchee, WA 98807; 509-667-6600; Fax: 509-667-6456. Hours: 8:30AM-4:30PM (PST). *Misdemeanor, Civil Actions Under $50,000, Small Claims.*

www.co.chelan.wa.us/dc/dc1.htm

Note: Physical address is 350 Orondo.

Civil Records: Access: Fax, mail, online, in person. Both court and visitors may perform in person searches. Search fee: $15.00 per name. Required to search: name; also helpful: years to search, address. Civil cases indexed by defendant, plaintiff. Civil records on computer from 1984. Records destroyed 3 years from closure. Index online from JIS-Link; see www.courts.wa.gov/jislink (also, see state introduction).

Criminal Records: Access: Fax, mail, online, in person. Both court and visitors may perform in person searches. Search fee: $15.00 per name. Required to search: name, DOB, signed release; also helpful: years to search, address, SSN, aliases. Criminal records on computer. Criminal files may be destroyed 3 years after close of case, infractions destroyed 3 years after close. Index remotely online from JIS-Link; see www.courts.wa.gov/jislink (also, see state introduction).

General Information: Public Access terminal is available. (Has records since 1986.) No sealed, domestic violence victim info, alcohol/probation evaluation records released. Copy fee: $2.00 for first page, $1.00 each add'l. Cert fee: $5.00. Payee: Chelan County District Court. Personal checks accepted. Prepayment required. Mail requests: SASE required. Mail turnaround time 1 week.

Clallam County

Superior Court 223 E Fourth St, #9, Port Angeles, WA 98362-3098; 360-417-2508. Hours: 8:30AM-4:30PM (PST). *Felony, Civil, Eviction, Probate.*
www.clallam.net/scourt
Civil Records: Access: Phone, mail, in person. Both court and visitors may perform in person searches. Search fee: $20.00 per hour. Required to search: name, years to search; also helpful: address. Civil cases indexed by defendant, plaintiff. Civil records on computer from 10/83, on microfiche from 1914, some records on index cards.
Criminal Records: Access: Phone, mail, online, in person. Both court and visitors may perform in person searches. Search fee: $20.00 per hour. Required to search: name, years to search; also helpful: address, DOB. Criminal records on computer from 10/83, on microfiche from 1914, some records on index cards. Criminal Index remotely online from JIS-Link; see www.courts.wa.gov/jislink (also, see state introduction).
General Information: Public Access terminal is available. No sealed, juvenile, adoption, paternity, mental health, sex offenders (victims) records released. Fee to fax results is $3.00 plus $1.00 per page. Copy fee: $.10 per page. Cert fee: $2.00 plus $1.00 per page after first. Payee: Clerk. Business checks accepted. Prepayment required. Mail requests: SASE required. Mail turnaround time minimum 1 week.

District Court 1 223 E 4th St, Port Angeles, WA 98362; 360-417-2560; Probate phone: 306-417-2507; Fax: 360-417-2403. Hours: 8:30AM-4:30PM (PST). *Misdemeanor, Civil Actions Under $50,000, Small Claims.*
www.clallam.net/Departments/html/dept_dc1.htm
Note: District 1 Court also has jurisdiction on Civil Anti-Harassment Petitions and Orders.
Civil Records: Access: Mail, fax, online, in person. Visitors must perform in person searches for themselves. No search fee. Required to search: name, years to search; also helpful: address. Civil cases indexed by defendant, plaintiff. Civil records on computer from 1986. Index online from JIS-Link; see www.courts.wa.gov/jislink (also, see state introduction).
Criminal Records: Access: Mail, fax, online, in person. Visitors must perform in person searches for themselves. No search fee. Required to search: name, years to search, DOB, signed release; also helpful: address, SSN, nationality. Criminal records on computer from 1986. Index remotely online from JIS-Link; see www.courts.wa.gov/jislink (also, see state introduction).

General Information: Public Access terminal is available. No sealed, juvenile, adoption, paternity, mental health, sex offenders (victims) or (sometimes) DUI records released. Copy fee: $.15 per page. Cert fee: $5.00 per document. Payee: Clallam County District Court 1. Personal checks accepted. Prepayment required. Mail turnaround time up to 1 week.

District Court II 502 E Division St, Forks, WA 98331; 360-374-6383; Fax: 360-374-2100. Hours: 8:30AM-4:30PM (PST). *Misdemeanor, Civil Actions Under $50,000, Small Claims.*
www.clallam.net/Courts/html/court_district_2.htm
Note: Clallam County District Court II serves the West End of Clallam County, including Forks, Neah Bay, Clallam Bay, Sekiu and LaPush.
Civil Records: Access: Mail, online, in person. Both court and visitors may perform in person searches. No search fee. Required to search: name, years to search; also helpful: address. Civil cases indexed by defendant, plaintiff. Civil records on computer from 1989, records go back to 1988. Index online from JIS-Link; see www.courts.wa.gov/jislink (also, see state introduction).
Criminal Records: Access: Mail, online, in person. Both court and visitors may perform in person searches. No search fee. Required to search: name, years to search DOB; also helpful: address, SSN. Criminal records on computer from 1992 (some back to 1989), on index cards from 1982-1986. Index remotely online from JIS-Link; see www.courts.wa.gov/jislink (also, see state introduction).
General Information: Public Access terminal is available. (Criminal cases only.) No sealed, juvenile, adoption, paternity, mental health, sex offenders (victims) or (sometimes) DUI records released. Fee to fax results is $1.00 per page. Copy fee: $.15 per page. Cert fee: $5.00. Payee: Clallam County District II Court. Personal checks accepted. Prepayment required. Mail turnaround time 2 weeks.

Clark County

Superior Court PO Box 5000 (1200 Franklin St), Attention-County Clerk, Vancouver, WA 98666; 360-397-2049 Court Admin.; Civil phone: 360-397-2292; Criminal phone: 360-397-2292; Fax: 360-397-6099. Hours: 8AM-4:30PM (PST). *Felony, Civil, Eviction, Probate.*
www.clark.wa.gov/courts/superior/index.html
Civil Records: Access: Phone, mail, online, in person, email. Both court and visitors may perform in person searches. Search fee: $20.00 per hour. Required to search: name, years to search. Civil cases indexed by defendant, plaintiff. Civil records on computer back to 1979 indexed, on microfiche from 1960, and index books prior to 1979. Index online from JIS-Link; see www.courts.wa.gov/jislink (also, see state introduction). Also, daily dockets are at www.clark.wa.gov/courts/superior/docket.html.
Criminal Records: Access: Phone, mail, online, in person, email. Both court and visitors may perform in person searches. Search fee: $20.00 per hour. Required to search: name, years to search, DOB; also helpful: address, signed release (if for employment). Criminal records on computer back to 1979, prior to 1988 on microfilm. Index remotely online from JIS-Link; see www.courts.wa.gov/jislink (also, see state introduction). Also, daily dockets are at www.clark.wa.gov/courts/superior/docket.html.
General Information: Public Access terminal is available. No sealed, juvenile, adoption, paternity, mental health, sex offenders (victims). Will fax results to local or toll free line. Copy fee: $2.00 for first page, $1.00 each add'l. Cert fee: $2.00. Payee: County Clerk. Only cashiers checks, money orders and

attorney checks accepted. Prepayment required. Mail turnaround time 1-3 days.

District Court PO Box 9806, 1200 Franklin St., Vancouver, WA 98666-8806; Civil phone: 360-397-2424; Criminal phone: 360-397-2424; Fax: 360-397-6044. Hours: 8AM-5PM (PST). *Misdemeanor, Civil Actions Under $50,000, Small Claims.*
www.clark.wa.gov/courts/district/index.html
Civil Records: Access: Fax, mail, online, in person. Only the court performs in person searches; visitors may not. No search fee. Required to search: name, years to search; also helpful: address. Civil cases indexed by defendant, plaintiff. Civil records on computer for approximately ten years. Index online from JIS-Link; see www.courts.wa.gov/jislink (also, see state introduction). Also, daily dockets are at www.clark.wa.gov/courts/district/docket.html.
Criminal Records: Access: Fax, mail, online, in person. Only the court performs in person searches; visitors may not. No search fee. Required to search: name, DOB, signed release; also helpful: years to search, address, SSN. Criminal records on computer for approximately five years. Index remotely online from JIS-Link; see www.courts.wa.gov/jislink (also, see state introduction). Also, daily dockets are at www.clark.wa.gov/courts/district/docket.html.
General Information: No sealed, juvenile, adoption, paternity, mental health, sex offenders (victims) or (sometimes) DUI records released. No fee to fax results. Copy fee: $.15 per page. Cert fee: $5.00. Payee: Clark County District Court. Personal checks accepted. Prepayment required. Mail turnaround time 1 week.

Columbia County

Superior Court 341 E Main St, Dayton, WA 99328; 509-382-4321; Fax: 509-382-4830. Hours: 8:30AM-Noon, 1-4:30PM (PST). *Felony, Civil, Eviction, Probate.*
Civil Records: Access: Phone, fax, mail, online, in person. Only the court performs in person searches; visitors may not. Search fee: $20.00 per hour. Required to search: name, years to search. Civil cases indexed by defendant, plaintiff. Civil records on computer from 1987, some records on index cards and books, archived from 1900s. Index online from JIS-Link; see www.courts.wa.gov/jislink (also, see state introduction).
Criminal Records: Access: Phone, fax, mail, online, in person. Only the court performs in person searches; visitors may not. Search fee: $20.00 per hour. Required to search: name, years to search. Criminal records on computer from 1987, some records on index cards and books, archived from 1900s. Index remotely online from JIS-Link; see www.courts.wa.gov/jislink (also, see state introduction).
General Information: No sealed, juvenile, adoption, paternity, mental health, sex offenders (victims). Copy fee: $1.00 per page. Cert fee: $2.00 plus $1.00 per page after first. Payee: Columbia County Clerk. Personal checks accepted. Prepayment required. Mail requests: SASE required. Mail turnaround time 1 week.

District Court 341 E Main St, Dayton, WA 99328-1361; 509-382-4812; Fax: 509-382-4830. Hours: 8:30AM-4:30PM (PST). *Misdemeanor, Civil Actions Under $50,000, Small Claims.*
Civil Records: Access: Mail, online, in person. Only the court performs in person searches; visitors may not. No search fee. Required to search: name, years to search; also helpful: address. Civil cases indexed by plaintiff. Civil records on computer since 05/96; prior on index books. Index online from JIS-Link; see www.courts.wa.gov/jislink (also, see state introduction).

Criminal Records: Access: Mail, online, in person. Only the court performs in person searches; visitors may not. Search fee: Fee may be charged if more than 1 case. Required to search: name, years to search, DOB, signed release; also helpful: address. Criminal records on computer from 1996, on books prior. Index remotely online from JIS-Link; see www.courts.wa.gov/jislink (also, see state introduction).

General Information: Will fax results for $1.00 per page. Copy fee: $1.00 per page. Cert fee: $6.00 per page. Payee: District Court. Personal checks accepted. Prepayment required. Mail requests: SASE required. Mail turnaround time 7-10 days.

Cowlitz County

Superior Court 312 SW First Ave, Attn: County Clerk, Kelso, WA 98626-1724; 360-577-3016; Criminal phone: 360-577-3017; Fax: 360-577-2323. Hours: 8:30-4:30PM (PST). *Felony, Civil, Eviction, Probate.*

www.co.cowlitz.wa.us/clerk

Civil Records: Access: Phone, fax, mail, online, in person. Both court and visitors may perform in person searches. Search fee: $10.00 per name. Required to search: name, years to search; also helpful: address. Civil cases indexed by defendant, plaintiff. Civil records on computer back to 1982; on microfilm through 1992, hard copy files from 1994. Index online from JIS-Link; see www.courts.wa.gov/jislink (also, see state introduction).

Criminal Records: Access: Phone, fax, mail, online, in person. Both court and visitors may perform in person searches. Search fee: $10.00 per name. Required to search: name, years to search; also helpful: address, DOB, SSN. Criminal records on computer back to 1982, on microfilm through 1992, hard copy files from 1993. Index remotely online from JIS-Link; see www.courts.wa.gov/jislink (also, see state introduction).

General Information: Public Access terminal is available. No sealed, juvenile, adoption, paternity, mental health records released. Will fax if prepayment received. Copy fee: $2.00 for first page, $1.00 each add'l. Cert fee: Included in copy fee. Payee: Cowlitz County Superior Court Clerk. Business checks accepted. Prepayment required. Mail requests: SASE required. Mail turnaround time 2 days.

District Court 312 SW First Ave, Kelso, WA 98626-1724; 360-577-3073. Hours: 8:30AM-5PM (PST). *Misdemeanor, Civil Actions Under $50,000, Small Claims.*

www.co.cowlitz.wa.us

Civil Records: Access: Phone, fax, mail, online, in person. Only the court performs in person searches; visitors may not. Search fee: $2 mailing fee. Required to search: name, DOB, years to search; also helpful: address. Civil cases indexed by defendant, plaintiff. Civil records on index cards back to 1992. Index online from JIS-Link; see www.courts.wa.gov/jislink (also, see state introduction).

Criminal Records: Access: Mail, fax, online, in person. Only the court performs in person searches; visitors may not. Search fee: None$2 mailing fee. Required to search: name, years to search, DOB; also helpful: address, SSN. Criminal records back to 1995. Index remotely online from JIS-Link; see www.courts.wa.gov/jislink (also, see state introduction).

General Information: Will not fax results. Copy fee: $.15 per page. Cert fee: $5.00. Payee: District Court. Personal checks accepted. Prepayment required. Mail turnaround time 2 weeks.

Douglas County

Superior Court PO Box 516, Waterville, WA 98858-0516; 509-745-9063; Fax: 509-745-8027. Hours: 8AM-5PM (PST). *Felony, Civil, Eviction, Probate.*

www.douglascountywa.net/

Note: Clerk is reached at 509-745-8529.

Civil Records: Access: Phone, fax, mail, online, in person. Both the court and visitors may performs in person searches. Search fee: $20.00 per hour. Required to search: name, years to search; also helpful: address. Civil cases indexed by defendant, plaintiff. Civil records on computer from 1985, archived and on microfiche from 1883, some records on index books. Index online from JIS-Link; see www.courts.wa.gov/jislink (also, see state introduction).

Criminal Records: Access: Phone, fax, mail, online, in person. Both the court and visitors may perform in person searches. Search fee: $20.00 per hour. Required to search: name, years to search, DOB; also helpful: address, SSN. Criminal records on computer from 1985, archived and on microfiche from 1883, some records on index books. Index remotely online from JIS-Link; see www.courts.wa.gov/jislink (also, see state introduction).

General Information: Public Access terminal is available. No sealed, juvenile, adoption, paternity, mental health, sex offenders (victims). Will fax results $2.00 1st page, $1.00 each add'l. Copy fee: $2.00 for first page, $1.00 each add'l. Cert fee: $3.00 plus $1.00 per page after first. Payee: Douglas County Clerk. Business checks accepted. Prepayment required. Mail requests: SASE required. Mail turnaround time 1 week.

District Court - Bridgeport 1206 Columbia Ave (PO Box 730), Bridgeport, WA 98813-0730; 509-686-2034; Fax: 509-686-4671. Hours: 8:30AM-4:30PM (PST). *Misdemeanor, Small Claims.*

www.douglascountywa.net/departments/district_court/

Note: This is a rural branch. If record not found in this court, request forwarded to East Wenatchee court (main court).

Civil Records: Access: Fax, mail, online, in person. Only the court performs in person searches; visitors may not. Please use the court's "Request for Information" form. Search fee: $10.00 per name. Required to search: name, years to search; also helpful: address. Civil cases indexed by defendant. Civil records on computer back to 02/95. Index online from JIS-Link; see www.courts.wa.gov/jislink (also, see state introduction).

Criminal Records: Access: Fax, mail, online, in person. Only the court performs in person searches; visitors may not. Please use the court's "Request for Information" form. Search fee: $10.00 per name. Required to search: name, years to search; also helpful: address, DOB, SSN. Criminal records on computer back to 02/95. Index remotely online from JIS-Link; see www.courts.wa.gov/jislink (also, see state introduction).

General Information: No sealed, juvenile, adoption, paternity, mental health, sex offenders (victims) or (sometimes) DUI records released. Will fax results to local or toll free line. Copy fee: $.15 per page. Cert fee: $5.00 per page. Payee: Douglas County District Court Bridgeport. Personal checks accepted. Prepayment required. Mail requests: SASE required. Mail turnaround time 10 days.

District Court - East Wenatchee 110 3rd St NE, East Wenatchee, WA 98802; 509-884-3536; Fax: 509-884-5973. Hours: 8:30AM-4:30PM (PST). *Misdemeanor, Civil Actions Under $50,000, Small Claims.*

www.douglascountywa.net/departments/district_court/index.html

Note: If record not found in this court, request forwarded to Bridgeport Branch (North) County District Court.

Civil Records: Access: Fax, mail, online, in person. Only the court performs in person searches; visitors may not. Search fee: $10.00. Required to search: name, years to search; also helpful: address. Civil cases indexed by defendant, plaintiff. Index online from JIS-Link; see www.courts.wa.gov/jislink (also, see state introduction).

Criminal Records: Access: Fax, mail, online, in person. Only the court performs in person searches; visitors may not. Search fee: $10.00. Required to search: Full name, address, DOB, SSN. Criminal records on computer back to 1992. Index remotely online from JIS-Link; see www.courts.wa.gov/jislink (also, see state introduction).

General Information: No sealed, juvenile, adoption, paternity, mental health, sex offenders (victims), Alcohol records, treatment reports released. Will fax results for $1.00 1st page, $1.00 each add'l. Local faxing only. Copy fee: $0.15 per page. Cert fee: $5.00. Payee: Douglas District Court. Personal checks accepted. Prepayment required. Mail requests: SASE required. Mail turnaround time 1 week.

Ferry County

Superior Court 350 E Delaware #4, Republic, WA 99166; 509-775-5245. Hours: 8AM-4PM (PST). *Felony, Civil, Probate.*

Civil Records: Access: Phone, mail, online, in person. Only the court may perform in person searches. Search fee: $20.00 per hour. Required to search: name, years to search; also helpful: address. Civil cases indexed by defendant, plaintiff. Civil records on computer back to 1987; other records go back to 1900. Index online from JIS-Link; see www.courts.wa.gov/jislink (also, see state introduction).

Criminal Records: Access: Phone, mail, online, in person. Only the court may perform in person searches. Search fee: $20.00 per hour. Required to search: name, years to search; also helpful: address, DOB. Criminal records on computer back to 1987; other records go back to 1900. Index remotely online from JIS-Link; see www.courts.wa.gov/jislink (also, see state introduction).

General Information: Public Access terminal is available. No sealed, adoption, paternity, mental health or sex offenders (victims). Will fax results for $2.00 for 1st page and $1.00 each add'l page. Copy fee: $2.00 for first page, $1.00 each add'l. Cert fee: $2.00 plus $1.00 each add'l page. Payee: Ferry County Clerk. Business checks accepted. Prepayment required. Mail requests: SASE required. Mail turnaround time 1-4 days.

District Court 350 E Delaware Ave #6, Republic, WA 99166-9747; 509-775-5244; Fax: 509-775-5221. Hours: 8AM-4PM (PST). *Misdemeanor, Civil Actions Under $50,000, Small Claims.*

Civil Records: Access: Fax, mail, online, in person. Only the court performs in person searches; visitors may not. No search fee. Required to search: name, years to search; also helpful: address. Civil cases indexed by case number. Civil records on computer back to 1995; others back to 1995. Index online from JIS-Link; see www.courts.wa.gov/jislink for information (also, see state introduction).

Criminal Records: Access: Mail, fax, online, in person. Only the court performs in person searches; visitors may not. No search fee. Required to search: name, years to search, DOB; also helpful: address, SSN, signed release. Criminal records on computer back to 1995; others back to 1995. Index remotely online from JIS-Link; see www.courts.wa.gov/jislink (also, see state introduction).

General Information: No sealed, juvenile, adoption, paternity, mental health, sex offenders (victims) or (sometimes) DUI records released. No fee to fax results. Copy fee: $2.00 for first page, $1.00 each add'l. Cert fee: $5.00. Payee: Ferry County District Court. Personal checks accepted. Prepayment required. Mail requests: SASE required. Mail turnaround time 1 week.

Franklin County

Superior Court 1016 N 4th Ave, Pasco, WA 99301; 509-545-3525; Fax: 509-545-2243. Hours: 8:30AM-5PM (PST). *Felony, Civil, Eviction, Probate.*

www.co.franklin.wa.us

Civil Records: Access: Mail, online, in person, email. Only the court performs in person searches; visitors may not. Search fee: $20.00 per hour. Required to search: name, years to search; also helpful: address. Civil cases indexed by defendant, plaintiff. Civil records on computer from 7/83, on index books, archived from 1900s. Index online from JIS-Link; see www.courts.wa.gov/jislink (also, see state introduction).

Criminal Records: Access: Mail, online, in person. Only the court performs in person searches; visitors may not. Search fee: $20.00 per hour. Required to search: name, years to search, DOB; also helpful: address, SSN. Criminal records on computer from 7/83, on index books, archived from 1900s. Index remotely online from JIS-Link; see www.courts.wa.gov/jislink (also, see state introduction).

General Information: No sealed, juvenile, adoption, paternity, mental health, sex offenders (victims). Fee to fax results is $3.00 1st page, $1.00 each add'l. Copy fee: $2.00 for first page, $1.00 each add'l. Cert fee: $2.00 plus $1.00 per page after first. Payee: Franklin County Superior Court Clerk. Business checks accepted, personal checks are not. Prepayment required. Mail requests: SASE required. Mail turnaround time 1 week.

District Court 1016 N 4th St, Pasco, WA 99301; 509-545-3593; Fax: 509-545-3588. Hours: 8:30AM-5PM (PST). *Misdemeanor, Civil Actions Under $50,000, Small Claims.*

Civil Records: Access: Mail, online, in person, fax. Only the court performs in person searches; visitors may not. Search fee: $10.00 per name. Required to search: name, years to search; also helpful: address. Civil cases indexed by defendant, plaintiff. Civil records on computer from 1993, prior on index cards. Index online from JIS-Link; see www.courts.wa.gov/jislink (also, see state introduction).

Criminal Records: Access: Mail, online, in person, fax. Only the court performs in person searches; visitors may not. Search fee: $10.00 per name. Required to search: name, years to search, DOB. Criminal records on computer from 1987, prior on index cards. Index remotely online from JIS-Link; see www.courts.wa.gov/jislink (also, see state introduction).

General Information: No sealed, juvenile, adoption, paternity, mental health, sex offenders (victims) or (sometimes) DUI records released. Copy fee: $.25 per page. Cert fee: $5.00. Payee: Franklin District Court. Personal checks accepted. Prepayment required. Mail

requests: SASE required. Mail turnaround time 7 days.

Garfield County

Superior Court PO Box 915, Pomeroy, WA 99347-0915; 509-843-3731; Fax: 509-843-1224. Hours: 8:30AM-Noon, 1-5PM (PST). *Felony, Civil, Eviction, Probate.*

Civil Records: Access: Phone, fax, mail, online, in person. Only the court performs in person searches; visitors may not. Search fee: $8.00 per hour. Required to search: name, years to search; also helpful: address. Civil cases indexed by defendant, plaintiff. Civil records on docket books, archived from 1882; on computer back to 1993. Index online from JIS-Link; see www.courts.wa.gov/jislink (also, see state introduction).

Criminal Records: Access: Fax, mail, online, in person, email. Only the court performs in person searches; visitors may not. Search fee: $8.00 per hour. Required to search: name, years to search, DOB; also helpful: address, SSN. Criminal records on docket books, archived from 1882; on computer back to 1993. Index remotely online from JIS-Link; see www.courts.wa.gov/jislink (also, see state introduction).

General Information: No sealed, juvenile, adoption, paternity, mental health, sex offenders (victims). Will fax results $.50 per page. Copy fee: $1.00 per page. Cert fee: $2.00 plus $1.00 per page after first. Payee: Garfield County Clerk. Personal checks accepted. Prepayment required. Mail requests: SASE requested. Turnaround time 1 week.

District Court PO Box 817, Pomeroy, WA 99347-0817; 509-843-1002; Fax: 509-843-3815. Hours: 8:30AM-5PM (PST). *Misdemeanor, Civil Actions Under $50,000, Small Claims.*

Civil Records: Access: Mail, online, in person, fax. Only the court performs in person searches; visitors may not. No search fee. Required to search: name, years to search; also helpful: address. Civil cases indexed by defendant. Civil records on index cards. Index online from JIS-Link; see www.courts.wa.gov/jislink (also, see state introduction).

Criminal Records: Access: Mail, online, in person, fax. Only the court performs in person searches; visitors may not. No search fee. Required to search: name, years to search, DOB; also helpful: address, SSN. Criminal records on index cards. Index remotely online from JIS-Link; see www.courts.wa.gov/jislink (also, see state introduction).

General Information: No sealed, juvenile, adoption, mental health, sex offenders (victims) or (sometimes) DUI records released. Copy fee: $.25 per page. Cert fee: $5.00. Payee: Garfield County District Court. Personal checks accepted. Prepayment required. Mail turnaround time 1 week.

Grant County

Superior Court PO Box 37, Ephrata, WA 98823-0037; 509-754-2011 X430; Fax: 509-754-6568. Hours: 8AM-4:30PM (PST). *Felony, Civil, Eviction, Probate.*

Civil Records: Access: Phone, mail, online, in person. Both court and visitors may perform in person searches. Search fee: $10.00 per name. Required to search: name, years to search; also helpful: address. Civil cases indexed by defendant, plaintiff. Civil records on computer from 1982, and some on index cards, archived from 1909. Index online from JIS-Link; see www.courts.wa.gov/jislink (also, see state introduction).

Criminal Records: Access: Phone, mail, online, in person. Both court and visitors may perform in person

searches. Search fee: $10.00 per name. Required to search: name, years to search; also helpful: address, DOB, SSN. Criminal records on computer from 1982, and some on index cards, archived from 1909. Index remotely online from JIS-Link; see www.courts.wa.gov/jislink (also, see state introduction).

General Information: Public Access terminal is available. No sealed, juvenile, adoption, paternity, mental health, sex offenders (victims) records released. Will not fax results. Copy fee: $2.00 for first page, $1.00 each add'l. Cert fee: $2.00 plus $1.00 per page after first. Payee: Grant County Clerk's Office. Business checks accepted. Prepayment required. Mail requests: SASE required. Mail turnaround time 2 weeks.

District Court PO Box 37, Ephrata, WA 98823-0037; 509-754-2011 X628; Fax: 509-754-6099. Hours: 8AM-5PM (PST). *Misdemeanor, Civil Actions Under $50,000, Small Claims.*

www.co.grant.wa.us

Civil Records: Access: Mail, online, in person. Only the court performs in person searches; visitors may not. Search fee: $20.00 per name. Required to search: name, years to search; also helpful: address. Civil cases indexed by defendant, plaintiff. Criminal indexed on computer per state retention schedule. Index online from JIS-Link; see www.courts.wa.gov/jislink (also, see state introduction).

Criminal Records: Access: Mail, online, in person. Only the court performs in person searches; visitors may not. Search fee: $20.00 per name. Required to search: name, years to search, DOB; also helpful: address, SSN. Criminal indexed on computer per state retention schedule. Index remotely online from JIS-Link; see www.courts.wa.gov/jislink (also, see state introduction).

General Information: No sealed, probation, juvenile, adoption, paternity, mental health, sex offenders (victims) or (sometimes) DUI records released. Will fax results per copy fee rates. Copy fee: $2.00 for first page, $1.00 each add'l. Cert fee: $5.00 per page. Payee: Grant County District Court. Personal checks accepted. Prepayment required. Mail turnaround time up to 30 days.

Grays Harbor County

Superior Court 102 W Broadway, Rm 203, Montesano, WA 98563-3606; 360-249-3842; Fax: 360-249-6381. Hours: 8AM-5PM (PST). *Felony, Civil, Eviction, Probate.*

Civil Records: Access: Phone, fax, mail, online, in person. Both court and visitors may perform in person searches. Search fee: $20.00 per name. No fee for records before 1980. Required to search: name, years to search; also helpful: address. Civil cases indexed by defendant, plaintiff. Civil records on computer from 12/80, on microfiche from 1856, on index cards. Index online from JIS-Link; see www.courts.wa.gov/jislink (also, see state introduction).

Criminal Records: Access: Phone, fax, mail, online, in person. Both court and visitors may perform in person searches. Search fee: $20.00 per name. No fee for records before 1980. Required to search: name, years to search; also helpful: address, DOB, SSN. Criminal records on computer from 12/80, on microfiche from 1856, on index cards. Index remotely online from JIS-Link; see www.courts.wa.gov/jislink (also, see state introduction).

General Information: No sealed, juvenile, adoption, paternity, mental health, sex offenders (victims). No fee to fax results. Fax available in emergency only. Copy fee: $2.00 for first page, $1.00 each add'l. Cert fee: Included in copy fee. Payee: Grays Harbor

County Clerk. Business checks accepted. Prepayment required. Mail requests: SASE required. Mail turnaround time 5 days.

District Court No 2
PO Box 142, Aberdeen, WA 98520-0035; 360-532-7061; Fax: 360-532-7704. Hours: 8AM-Noon, 1-5PM (PST). *Civil Actions Under $50,000, Small Claims.*
www.co.grays-harbor.wa.us
Note: This court no longer handles criminal cases.

Civil Records: Access: Phone, fax, mail, online, in person. Only the court performs in person searches; visitors may not. No search fee. Required to search: name, years to search; also helpful: address. Civil cases indexed by defendant, plaintiff. Civil records on computer from 4/91, on index cards. Index online from JIS-Link; see www.courts.wa.gov/jislink (also, see state introduction).

General Information: No sealed, juvenile, adoption, paternity, mental health, sex offenders (victims) or (sometimes) DUI records released. No fee to fax results. Copy fee: $.25 per page. Cert fee: $5.00. Payee: Grays Harbor District Court #2. Personal checks accepted. Prepayment required. Mail requests: SASE required. Mail turnaround time 1 week.

District Court No 1
102 W Broadway, Rm 202, Montesano, WA 98563; 360-249-3441; Fax: 360-249-6382. Hours: 8AM-Noon, 1-5PM (PST). *Misdemeanor.*
www.co.grays-harbor.wa.us/info/judicial/
Note: All civil filings and hearings are held in the District Court Dept 2 in Aberdeen.

Criminal Records: Access: Phone, fax, mail, online, in person. Only the court performs in person searches; visitors may not. No search fee. Required to search: name, years to search, DOB; also helpful: address, SSN. Criminal records on computer from 4/91, on index cards. Index remotely online from JIS-Link; see www.courts.wa.gov/jislink (also, see state introduction).

General Information: No sealed, juvenile, adoption, paternity, mental health, sex offenders (victims) records released. Will fax results for $.25 per page. Copy fee: $.25 per page. Cert fee: $5.00. Payee: Grays Harbor District Court #1. Personal checks accepted. Prepayment required. Mail requests: SASE required. Mail turnaround time 1 week.

Island County

Superior Court
PO Box 5000, Coupeville, WA 98239-5000; 360-679-7359. Hours: 8AM-4:30PM (PST). *Felony, Civil, Eviction, Probate.*
Civil Records: Access: Phone, mail, online, in person. Both court and visitors may perform in person searches. Search fee: $20.00 per hour. Required to search: name, years to search; also helpful: address. Civil cases indexed by defendant, plaintiff. Civil records on computer from 7/1984, microfiche from 1889. Archived in Bellingham, WA. Index online from JIS-Link; see www.courts.wa.gov/jislink (also, see state introduction).

Criminal Records: Access: Phone, mail, online, in person. Both court and visitors may perform in person searches. Search fee: $20.00 per hour. Required to search: name, years to search; also helpful: address, DOB. Criminal records on computer from 7/1984, microfiche from 1889. Archived in Bellingham, WA. Index remotely online from JIS-Link; see www.courts.wa.gov/jislink (also, see state introduction).

General Information: No sealed, dependency, truancy, adoption, paternity, mental health, sex offenders (victims). Copy fee: $.25 per page. Cert fee: $2.00 first page and $1.00 each add'l. Payee: Island county Clerk. Business checks accepted. Prepayment

required. Mail requests: SASE required. Mail turnaround time 1 week.

District Court
800 S 8th Ave, Oak Harbor, WA 98277; 360-675-5988; Fax: 360-675-8231. Hours: 8AM-4:30PM (PST). *Misdemeanor, Civil Actions Under $50,000, Small Claims.*
Note: Records requests are done as time permits. Bottom of priority list.

Civil Records: Access: Fax, mail, online, in person. Both court and visitors may perform in person searches. No search fee. Required to search: name, years to search; also helpful: address. Civil cases indexed by defendant. Civil records on computer from 1991, on index by alpha. Index online from JIS-Link; see www.courts.wa.gov/jislink (also, see state introduction).

Criminal Records: Access: Fax, mail, online, in person. Only the court performs in person searches; visitors may not. No search fee. Required to search: name, years to search, DOB; also helpful: address, SSN. Criminal records on computer from 1991, on index by alpha. Index remotely online from JIS-Link; see www.courts.wa.gov/jislink (also, see state introduction).

General Information: No sealed, juvenile, adoption, paternity, mental health, sex offenders (victims) or (sometimes) DUI records released. Will fax results $1.00 per page. Copy fee: $.25 per page. Cert fee: $5.00. Payee: Island District Court. Personal checks accepted. Prepayment required. Mail requests: SASE required. Mail turnaround time 1-7 days.

Jefferson County

Superior Court
PO Box 1220, Port Townsend, WA 98368-0920; 360-385-9125. Hours: 9AM-5PM (PST). *Felony, Civil, Eviction, Probate.*
Civil Records: Access: Phone, mail, online, in person. Both court and visitors may perform in person searches. Search fee: $20.00 per hour. Required to search: name, years to search. Civil cases indexed by defendant, plaintiff. Civil records on computer from 1983, on microfiche from 1890s. Archive in Bellingham, WA. Index online from JIS-Link; see www.courts.wa.gov/jislink (also, see state introduction).

Criminal Records: Access: Phone, mail, online, in person. Both court and visitors may perform in person searches. Search fee: $20.00 per hour. Required to search: name, years to search; also helpful: DOB. Criminal records on computer from 1983, on microfiche from 1890s. Archive in Bellingham, WA. Index remotely online from JIS-Link; see www.courts.wa.gov/jislink (also, see state introduction).

General Information: Public Access terminal is available. No sealed, juvenile, adoption, paternity, mental health records released. Copy fee: $.15 per page. Cert fee: $2.00 plus $1.00 per page after first. Payee: County Clerk. Personal checks accepted. Out of state checks not accepted. Prepayment required. Mail requests: SASE required. Mail turnaround time 2 days.

District Court
PO Box 1220, Port Townsend, WA 98368-0920; 360-385-9135; Fax: 360-385-9367. Hours: 8AM-5PM (PST). *Misdemeanor, Civil Actions Under $50,000, Small Claims.*
www.co.jefferson.wa.us
Civil Records: Access: Phone, fax, mail, online, in person. Only the court performs in person searches; visitors may not. No search fee. Required to search: name, years to search; also helpful: address. Civil cases indexed by defendant. Civil records on DISCIS computer from 1993, on computer from '90-'93, on log books prior to 1990. Physical files kept 10 years from disposition per retention schedule. Index online

from JIS-Link; see www.courts.wa.gov/jislink (also, see state introduction).

Criminal Records: Access: Phone, fax, mail, online, in person. Only the court performs in person searches; visitors may not. No search fee. Required to search: name, DOB; also helpful: years to search, address, SSN. Criminal records on DISCIS computer from 1993, on computer from '90-'93, on log books prior to 1990. Physical files kept 10 years from disposition per retention schedule. Index remotely online from JIS-Link; see www.courts.wa.gov/jislink (also, see state introduction).

General Information: No sealed, juvenile, adoption, paternity, mental health, sex offenders (victims) records released. Copy fee: $.15 per page. Cert fee: $6.00. Personal checks accepted. Prepayment required. Mail requests: SASE required. Mail turnaround time 1 week.

King County

Superior Court
516 Third Ave, E-609 Courthouse, Seattle, WA 98104-2386; 206-296-9300, 800-325-6165 in state. Hours: 8:30AM-4:30AM (PST). *Felony, Civil, Eviction, Probate.*
www.metrokc.gov/kcscc
Civil Records: Access: Mail, online, in person. Both court and visitors may perform in person searches. Search fee: $20.00 per hour. Fee $25.00 minimum including copies. Required to search: name, years to search. Civil cases indexed by defendant, plaintiff. Civil records on computer since 1979; prior records on microfiche back to 1935. Index online from JIS-Link; see www.courts.wa.gov/jislink (also, see state introduction).

Criminal Records: Access: Mail, online, in person. Both court and visitors may perform in person searches. Search fee: $20.00 per hour. Fee is $25.00 if number of pages unknown. Required to search: name, years to search. Criminal records on computer since 1979; prior records on microfiche back to 1938. Index remotely online from JIS-Link; see www.courts.wa.gov/jislink (also, see state introduction).

General Information: Public Access terminal is available. No sealed, juvenile, dependency, adoption, paternity (except for final judgments), mental health, sex offenders (victims) records released. Will not fax results. Copy fee: $.15 per page (self serve). Microfiche/computer image copy fee: $.25 per page. Cert fee: $2.00 plus $1.00 per page after first. Payee: King County Superior Court Clerk. Personal checks accepted if in state. Prepayment required. Mail requests: SASE required. Mail turnaround time 2 weeks.

District Court East Division - Bellevue
585 112th Ave SE, Bellevue, WA 98004; 206-296-3650; 800-325-6165 +59200; 206-205-9200; Fax: 206-296-0589. Hours: 8:30AM-4:30PM (PST). *Misdemeanor, Civil Actions Under $50,000, Small Claims.*
www.metrokc.gov/kcdc
Note: Formerly known as the Bellevue Division. Civil Filing Area: Bellevue, Eastgate, Factoria, Mercer Island, Clyde Hill, Beaux Arts, Newcastle.

Civil Records: Access: Phone, mail, online, in person. Both court and visitors may perform in person searches. No search fee. Required to search: name, years to search; also helpful: address. Civil cases indexed by defendant, plaintiff. Civil records on computer for past 10 years. Index online from JIS-Link; see www.courts.wa.gov/jislink (also, see state introduction).

Criminal Records: Access: Phone, mail, online, in person. Both court and visitors may perform in person searches. No search fee. Required to search: name, years to search, DOB; also helpful: address, SSN.

Criminal records on computer from 1987. Criminal records may be removed after 5 years from disposition. Index remotely online from JIS-Link; see www.courts.wa.gov/jislink (also, see state introduction).

General Information: No sealed, juvenile, adoption, paternity, mental health, sex offenders (victims) or (sometimes) DUI records released. Copy fee: $.15 per page. Cert fee: $5.00. Payee: KCDC, Bellevue Division. Personal checks accepted. Visa, MC accepted. Prepayment required. Mail turnaround time cannot be guaranteed for written requests.

District Court East Division - Issaquah

5415 220th Ave SW, Issaquah, WA 98029-6839; 206-205-9200; Civil phone: 206-205-1747; Fax: 206-296-0591. Hours: 8:30AM-4:30PM (PST). *Misdemeanor, Civil Actions Under $50,000, Small Claims.*
www.metrokc.gov/kcdc
Note: Formerly known as the Issaquah Division. Civil Filing Area: Issaquah, Sammamish, High Point, Preston, Fall City, Snoqualmie, North Bend, Cedar Falls, Tokul, Alpental.

Civil Records: Access: Mail, online, in person. Only the court performs in person searches; visitors may not. No search fee. Required to search: name, years to search; also helpful: address. Civil cases indexed by defendant, plaintiff. Civil records on computer back 10 years. Index online from JIS-Link; see www.courts.wa.gov/jislink (also, see state introduction).

Criminal Records: Access: Mail, online, in person. Only the court performs in person searches; visitors may not. No search fee. Required to search: name, years to search, DOB, signed release; also helpful: address. Criminal records on computer back 5 years. Index remotely online from JIS-Link; see www.courts.wa.gov/jislink (also, see state introduction).

General Information: No sealed, juvenile, sex offenders (victims) or (sometimes) DUI records released. Copy fee: $.15 per page. Cert fee: $5.00. Payee: Issaquah Division. Personal checks accepted. Prepayment required. Mail requests: SASE required. Mail turnaround time 1-5 days.

District Court East Division - Redmond

8601 160th Ave NE, Redmond, WA 98052-3548; 206-296-3667; 800-325-6165 +59200; 206-205-9200. Hours: 8:30AM-4:30PM (PST). *Misdemeanor, Civil Actions Under $50,000, Small Claims.*
www.metrokc.gov/kcdc
Note: Formerly known as the Northeast Division. Civil Filing Area: Redmond, Kirkland, Woodinville, Bothell, Duvall, Carnation, Juanita.

Civil Records: Access: Mail, online, in person. Both court and visitors may perform in person searches. No search fee. Required to search: name, years to search; also helpful: address. Civil cases indexed by defendant, plaintiff. Civil records on computer back 10 years. Index online from JIS-Link; see www.courts.wa.gov/jislink (also, see state introduction).

Criminal Records: Access: Mail, online, in person. Both court and visitors may perform in person searches. No search fee. Required to search: name, years to search, DOB; also helpful: address. Criminal records on computer back 5 years. Index remotely online from JIS-Link; see www.courts.wa.gov/jislink (also, see state introduction).

General Information: Public Access terminal is available. No sealed, juvenile, adoption, paternity, mental health, sex offenders (victims) or (sometimes) DUI records released. Copy fee: $.15 per page. Cert fee: $5.00. Payee: King County District Court. Personal checks accepted. Visa, MC accepted.

Prepayment required. Mail turnaround time 1-2 weeks.

District Court Shoreline Division 18050

Meridian Ave N, Shoreline, WA 98133-4642; 800-325-6165 +59200; 206-205-9200; Fax: 206-296-0594. Hours: 8:30AM-4:30PM (PST). *Misdemeanor, Civil Actions Under $50,000, Small Claims.*
www.metrokc.gov/kcdc
Note: Civil Filing Area: Shoreline, Kenmore, Lake Forest Park.

Civil Records: Access: Phone, fax, mail, online, in person. Both court and visitors may perform in person searches. No search fee. Required to search: name, years to search; also helpful: address. Civil cases indexed by defendant, plaintiff. Civil records on computer from 1985. Index online from JIS-Link; see www.courts.wa.gov/jislink (also, see state introduction).

Criminal Records: Access: Phone, fax, mail, online, in person. Both court and visitors may perform in person searches. No search fee. Required to search: name, years to search; also helpful: address, DOB, SSN. Criminal records on computer from 1987. Index remotely online from JIS-Link; see www.courts.wa.gov/jislink (also, see state introduction).

General Information: Public Access terminal is available. No sealed, juvenile, adoption, paternity, mental health, sex offenders (victims) or (sometimes) DUI records released. No fee to fax results. Copy fee: $.15 per page. Cert fee: $5.00. Payee: King County District Court. Personal checks accepted. Visa, MC accepted. Prepayment required. Mail requests: SASE required. Mail turnaround time 1 week.

District Court South Division - Burien

King County District Court, 601 SW 149th St, Burien, WA 98166-1935; 800-325-6165 +59200; 206-205-9200. Hours: 8:30AM-4:30PM (PST). *Misdemeanor, Civil Actions Under $50,000, Small Claims.*
www.metrokc.gov/kcdc
Note: Formerly located in Vashon. Formerly Southwest Division, name change 12/2002. All civil cases filed at South Division in Kent

Civil Records: Access: Mail, online, in person. Only the court performs in person searches; visitors may not. No search fee. Required to search: name, years to search; also helpful: address. Civil cases indexed by defendant, plaintiff. Civil records on computer back 5 years. Index online from JIS-Link; see www.courts.wa.gov/jislink (also, see state introduction).

Criminal Records: Access: Mail, online, in person. Only the court performs in person searches; visitors may not. No search fee. Required to search: name, years to search; also helpful: address, DOB, SSN. Criminal records on computer from 1987. Index remotely online from JIS-Link; see www.courts.wa.gov/jislink (also, see state introduction).

General Information: No sealed, juvenile, adoption, paternity, mental health, sex offenders (victims) or (sometimes) DUI records released. No fee to fax results. Copy fee: $.15 per page. Cert fee: $5.00. Payee: Vashon District Court. Personal checks accepted. Prepayment required. Mail turnaround time 1 day.

District Court South Division - Kent 1210

S Central, Kent, WA 98032-7426; 206-205-9200; 800-325-6165 +59200; 206-205-9200. Hours: 8:30AM-4:30PM (PST). *Misdemeanor, Civil Actions Under $50,000, Small Claims.*
www.metrokc.gov/kcdc
Note: Formerly known as Aukeen Division. Civil Filing Area: Enumclaw, Auburn, Black Diamond,

Maple Valley, Covington, Algona, Pacific, Ravensdale, Hobart, Federal Way.

Civil Records: Access: Mail, online, in person. Only the court performs in person searches; visitors may not. No search fee. Required to search: name, years to search; also helpful: address. Civil cases indexed by defendant, plaintiff. Civil records on computer 5 years back. Index online from JIS-Link; see www.courts.wa.gov/jislink (also, see state introduction).

Criminal Records: Access: Mail, online, in person. Only the court performs in person searches; visitors may not. No search fee. Required to search: name, years to search, DOB; also helpful: address, SSN. Criminal records on computer 5 years back. Index remotely online from JIS-Link; see www.courts.wa.gov/jislink (also, see state introduction).

General Information: No sealed, juvenile, adoption, paternity, mental health, sex offenders (victims) or (sometimes) DUI records released. Copy fee: $.15 per page. Cert fee: $5.00. Payee: Aukeen District Court. Personal checks accepted. Prepayment required. Mail requests: SASE required. Mail turnaround time 1 day.

District Court West Division - Seattle 516

Third Ave E-327 Courthouse, Seattle, WA 98104-3273; 800-325-6165 +59200; 206-205-9200; Civil phone: 206-296-3550; Criminal phone: 206-296-3565 (crim. traf.). Hours: 8:30AM-4:30PM (PST). *Misdemeanor, Civil Actions Under $50,000, Small Claims.*
www.metrokc.gov/kcdc
Note: Formerly known as the Seattle Division. Civil Filing Area: Seattle.

Civil Records: Access: Mail, online, in person. Visitors must perform in person searches for themselves. No search fee. Required to search: name, years to search; also helpful: address. Civil cases indexed by defendant, plaintiff. Civil records on computer from back 10 years. Index online from JIS-Link; see www.courts.wa.gov/jislink (also, see state introduction).

Criminal Records: Access: Mail, online, in person. Both court and visitors may perform in person searches. No search fee. Required to search: name, years to search, DOB, signed release; also helpful: address, SSN. Criminal records on computer from back 10 years. Index remotely online from JIS-Link; see www.courts.wa.gov/jislink (also, see state introduction).

General Information: Public Access terminal is available. (10 minute limit. 90% of info available to public, other 10% can only be searched by court staff.) No sealed, juvenile, adoption, paternity, mental health, sex offenders (victims), treatment plans or (sometimes) DUI records released. Will not fax results. Copy fee: $.15 per page. Cert fee: $5.00. Payee: King County District Court, Seattle. Personal checks accepted. Prepayment required. Mail requests: SASE required. Mail turnaround time 10 days.

Kitsap County

Superior Court 614 Division St, MS34, Port Orchard, WA 98366-4699; 360-337-7164; Fax: 360-337-4927. Hours: 8AM-4:30PM (PST). *Felony, Civil, Eviction, Probate.*
www.kitsapgov.com/sc
Civil Records: Access: Mail, online, in person. Both court and visitors may perform in person searches. Search fee: $20.00 for up to 5 names. Required to search: name, years to search. Civil cases indexed by defendant, plaintiff. Civil records on computer from 1978, on microfiche and archived from 1857. Index online from JIS-Link; see www.courts.wa.gov/jislink (also, see state introduction).

Criminal Records: Access: Mail, online, in person. Both court and visitors may perform in person searches. Search fee: $20.00 for up to 5 names. Required to search: name, years to search; also helpful: address, DOB, SSN. Criminal records on computer from 1978, on microfiche and archived from 1857. Index remotely online from JIS-Link; see www.courts.wa.gov/jislink (also, see state introduction).

General Information: Public Access terminal is available. No dependencies, adoption or mental illness records released. Will fax results for $1.00 per page. Copy fee: $2.00 for first page, $1.00 each add'l. There is an additional $5.00 handling fee if copies required. Cert fee: included in copy fee. Payee: Kitsap County Clerk. No personal checks accepted. Prepayment required. Mail requests: SASE not required. Mail turnaround time 2 weeks.

District Court 614 Division St, MS 25, Port Orchard, WA 98366-4614; 360-337-7109; Fax: 360-337-4865. Hours: 8AM-12:15PM, 1:15-4:30PM (PST). *Misdemeanor, Civil Actions Under $50,000, Small Claims.*
www.kitsapgov.com/dc
Civil Records: Access: Phone, fax, mail, online, in person. Only the court performs in person searches; visitors may not. No search fee. Required to search: name, years to search; also helpful: address. Civil cases indexed by defendant, plaintiff. Civil records on computer from 1/95, prior in archives. Index online from JIS-Link; see www.courts.wa.gov/jislink (also, see state introduction).
Criminal Records: Access: Phone, fax, mail, online, in person. Only the court performs in person searches; visitors may not. No search fee. Required to search: name, years to search; also helpful: address, DOB, SSN. Criminal records on computer from 1/95, prior in archives. Index remotely online from JIS-Link; see www.courts.wa.gov/jislink (also, see state introduction).
General Information: No fee to fax results. Local faxing only. Copy fee: $.15 per page. Cert fee: $5.00. Payee: Kitsap County District Court. Personal checks accepted. Prepayment required. Mail turnaround time 3 days.

District Court North 614 Division St, MS-25, Port Orchard, WA 98366; 360-337-7109; Fax: 360-337-4865. Hours: 8:30AM-12:15PM; 1:15-4:30PM (PST). *Misdemeanor, Civil Actions Under $50,000, Small Claims.*
Note: The court physical address is 19050 Jensen Way NE, Poulsbo, WA.
Civil Records: Access: Mail, online, in person. Only the court performs in person searches; visitors may not. No search fee. Required to search: name, years to search. Civil cases indexed by defendant, plaintiff. Civil records on computer back 8 years, on index cards for 10 years. Index online from JIS-Link; see www.courts.wa.gov/jislink (also, see state introduction). Send all mail requests to Port Orchard District court.
Criminal Records: Access: Mail, online, in person,phone(1 only). Only the court performs in person searches; visitors may not. No search fee. Required to search: name, signed release; also helpful: years to search, DOB. Criminal records on computer back 8 years, on index cards for 10 years. Index remotely online from JIS-Link; see www.courts.wa.gov/jislink (also, see state introduction). Send all mail requests to Port Orchard District Court.
General Information: Public Access terminal is available. No dependencies, adoption and mental illness records released. Copy fee: $.15 per page. Cert fee: $5.00. Payee: District Court North, Kitsap County. Only cashiers checks and money orders

accepted. Prepayment required. Mail requests: SASE required. Mail turnaround time is 2 days.

Kittitas County

Superior Court 205 W 5th Rm 210, Ellensburg, WA 98926; 509-962-7531; Fax: 509-962-7667. Hours: 9AM-Noon, 1-5PM (PST). *Felony, Misdemeanor, Civil, Eviction, Probate.*
Civil Records: Access: Phone, fax, mail, online, in person. Only the court performs in person searches; visitors may not. Search fee: $10.00 per name. Required to search: name, years to search; also helpful: address. Civil cases indexed by defendant, plaintiff. Civil records on computer from 1982, on microfiche and archived from 1890. Some records on index cards. Index online from JIS-Link; see www.courts.wa.gov/jislink (also, see state introduction).
Criminal Records: Access: Phone, fax, mail, online, in person. Only the court performs in person searches; visitors may not. Search fee: $10.00 per name. Required to search: name, years to search; also helpful: address, DOB, SSN. Criminal records on computer from 1982, on microfiche and archived from 1890. Some records on index cards. Index remotely online from JIS-Link; see www.courts.wa.gov/jislink (also, see state introduction).
General Information: No dependencies, adoption, and mental illness records released. No fee to fax results. Fax available in emergency only. Copy fee: $.15 per page. Cert fee: $2.00 first page, $1.00 each addl. Payee: Kittitas County Clerk. Personal checks accepted. Prepayment required. Mail turnaround time 2 days.

District Court Lower Kittitas 205 W 5th, Rm 180, Ellensburg, WA 98926; 509-962-7511. Hours: 9AM-5PM (PST). *Misdemeanor, Civil Actions Under $50,000, Small Claims.*
Civil Records: Access: Mail, online, in person. Only the court performs in person searches; visitors may not. No search fee. Required to search: name, years to search. Civil cases indexed by defendant, plaintiff. Civil records on computer from 8/97, archived back 10 years. Records retained for 20 years. Index online from JIS-Link; see www.courts.wa.gov/jislink (also, see state introduction).
Criminal Records: Access: Mail, online, in person. Only the court performs in person searches; visitors may not. No search fee. Required to search: name, years to search, DOB. Criminal records on computer from 8/97, archived back 10 years. Index remotely online from JIS-Link; see www.courts.wa.gov/jislink (also, see state introduction).
General Information: No dependencies, adoption, and mental illness records released. Will fax results to local or toll free line. No copy fee. Cert fee: $6.00. Payee: Lower Kittitas County District Court. Personal checks accepted. Prepayment required. Mail requests: SASE required. Mail turnaround time 7-10 days.

District Court Upper Kittitas 700 E First, Cle Elum, WA 98922; 509-674-5533; Fax: 509-674-4209. Hours: 7AM-5PM (PST). *Misdemeanor, Civil Actions Under $50,000, Small Claims.*
Civil Records: Access: Mail, online, in person. Only the court performs in person searches; visitors may not. No search fee. Required to search: name, years to search. Civil cases indexed by defendant, plaintiff. Civil records on computer since 8/91; prior records archived from 1890, some on index cards. Records retained for 10 years. Index online from JIS-Link; see www.courts.wa.gov/jislink (also, see state introduction).
Criminal Records: Access: Mail, online, in person. Only the court performs in person searches; visitors may not. No search fee. Required to search: name,

years to search, DOB, signed release; also helpful: SSN. Criminal records on computer back to 1997; prior records archived from 1890, some on index cards. Records retained for 5 years. Index remotely online from JIS-Link; see www.courts.wa.gov/jislink (also, see state introduction).
General Information: No dependencies, adoption, and mental illness records released. Fee to fax results is $1.00 per page. Copy fee: $.25 per page. Cert fee: $5.00. Payee: UKCDC. Personal checks accepted. Visa, MC accepted. Prepayment required. Mail turnaround time 1 week.

Klickitat County

Superior Court Superior Court Clerk, 205 S Columbus, MS CH-O3, Goldendale, WA 98620; 509-773-5744. Hours: 9AM-5PM (PST). *Felony, Civil, Eviction, Probate.*
Civil Records: Access: Phone, mail, online, in person. Only the court performs in person searches; visitors may not. Search fee: $8.00 per hour. Required to search: name, years to search; also helpful: address. Civil cases indexed by defendant, plaintiff. Civil records on computer from 9/87. Index online from JIS-Link; see www.courts.wa.gov/jislink (also, see state introduction).
Criminal Records: Access: Phone, mail, online, in person. Only the court performs in person searches; visitors may not. Search fee: $8.00 per hour. Required to search: name, years to search; also helpful: address, DOB, SSN. Criminal records on computer from 9/87; prior on books back to 1886. Index remotely online from JIS-Link; see www.courts.wa.gov/jislink (also, see state introduction).
General Information: No dependencies, adoption, and mental illness records released. Copy fee: $2.00 for first page, $1.00 each add'l. Cert fee: $2.00 plus $1.00 per page after first. Payee: Klickitat County Clerk. No personal checks accepted. Prepayment required. Mail requests: SASE required. Mail turnaround time 1-2 weeks or sooner.

East District Court 205 S Columbus, MS-CH11, Goldendale, WA 98620-9290; 509-773-4670; Fax: 509-773-4653. Hours: 8AM-12, 1-5pm (PST). *Misdemeanor, Civil Actions Under $50,000, Small Claims.*
Civil Records: Access: Phone, mail, fax, online, in person. Both court and visitors may perform in person searches. No search fee. Required to search: name, years to search. Civil cases indexed by defendant, plaintiff. Civil records on computer from 4/93, on index cards prior. Retained for 10 years. Index online from JIS-Link; see www.courts.wa.gov/jislink (also, see state introduction).
Criminal Records: Access: Phone, mail, fax, online, in person. Both court and visitors may perform in person searches. No search fee. Required to search: name, years to search, DOB. Criminal records on computer from 4/93, on index cards prior. Retained for 10 years. Index remotely online from JIS-Link; see www.courts.wa.gov/jislink (also, see state introduction).
General Information: No dependencies, adoption, and mental illness records released. Will fax results to local or toll free line. Copy fee: 1st 10 pages free, each additional page $.15. Cert fee: $5.00. Payee: East District Court. Personal checks accepted. Prepayment required. Mail requests: SASE required. Mail turnaround time 1 week.

West District Court PO Box 435, White Salmon, WA 98672-0435; 509-493-1190; Fax: 509-493-4469. Hours: 8AM-5PM (PST). *Misdemeanor, Civil Actions Under $50,000, Small Claims.*
Civil Records: Access: Mail, in person. Only the court performs in person searches; visitors may not. No search fee. Required to search: name, years to

search. Civil cases indexed by defendant, plaintiff. Civil records on computer from 5/93, on docket books. Index online from JIS-Link; see www.courts.wa.gov/jislink (also, see state introduction).

Criminal Records: Access: Mail, in person. Only the court performs in person searches; visitors may not. No search fee. Required to search: name, years to search, DOB; also helpful: address. Criminal records on computer from 5/93, on docket books. Index remotely online from JIS-Link; see www.courts.wa.gov/jislink (also, see state introduction).

General Information: No dependencies, adoption, sealed and mental illness records released. Copy fee: $2.00 for first page, $1.00 each add'l. Cert fee: $6.00. Payee: West District Court. Personal checks accepted. Prepayment required. Mail requests: SASE required. Mail turnaround time 3-5 days.

Lewis County

Superior Court 360 NW North St, MS:CLK 01, Chehalis, WA 98532-1900; 360-740-2704; Civil phone: 360-740-2776; Criminal phone: 360-740-1395; Probate phone: 360-740-1177; Fax: 360-748-1639. Hours: 8AM-5PM (PST). *Felony, Misdemeanor, Civil, Eviction, Probate.*
www.co.lewis.wa.us/clerk/clerk.htm

Civil Records: Access: Phone, mail, online, in person. Both the court and visitors may perform in person searches. Search fee: $8.00 per hour. Required to search: name, years to search; also helpful: address. Civil cases indexed by defendant, plaintiff. Civil records on computer from 1983, archived from 1900s. Index online from JIS-Link; see www.courts.wa.gov/jislink (also, see state introduction).

Criminal Records: Access: Phone, mail, online, in person. Both the court and visitors may perform in person searches. Search fee: $8.00 per hour. Required to search: name, years to search; also helpful: address, DOB, SSN. Criminal records on computer from 1983, archived from 1900s. Index remotely online from JIS-Link; see www.courts.wa.gov/jislink (also, see state introduction).

General Information: Public Access terminal is available. No dependencies, adoption, paternity, and mental illness records released. Fee to fax results is $.50 per page. Copy fee: $2.00 for first page, $1.00 each add'l. Copy fees include certification. Payee: Lewis County Clerk. Personal checks accepted. Prepayment required. Mail requests: SASE required. Mail turnaround time up to 7 days.

District Court PO Box 336, Chehalis, WA 98532-0336; 360-740-1203; Fax: 360-740-2779. Hours: 8AM-5PM (PST). *Misdemeanor, Civil Actions Under $50,000, Small Claims.*

Civil Records: Access: Fax, mail, online, in person. Court may perform in person searches. No search fee. Required to search: name, years to search. Civil cases indexed by defendant, plaintiff. Civil records on computer from 1983, on index cards. Records retained 10 years. Index online from JIS-Link; see www.courts.wa.gov/jislink (also, see state introduction).

Criminal Records: Access: Fax, mail, online, in person. Court may perform in person searches. No search fee. Required to search: name, years to search, DOB, sex, signed release; also helpful: address, SSN. Criminal records on computer since 1981. Records retained for 5 years. Index remotely online from JIS-Link; see www.courts.wa.gov/jislink (also, see state introduction).

General Information: No dependencies, adoption, and mental illness records released. No fee to fax results. Copy fee: $.25 per page. Cert fee: $5.00 per page.

page. Payee: Lewis County District Court. Personal checks accepted. Prepayment required. Mail requests: SASE required. Mail turnaround time 1 week.

Lincoln County

Superior Court Box 68, Davenport, WA 99122-0396; 509-725-1401; Fax: 509-725-1150. Hours: 8AM-5PM (PST). *Felony, Misdemeanor, Civil, Eviction, Probate.*

Civil Records: Access: Mail, online, in person. Both court and visitors may perform in person searches. No search fee. Required to search: name, years to search; also helpful: address. Civil cases indexed by defendant, plaintiff. Civil records on computer and microfiche from 11/82, archived from 1903. Index online from JIS-Link; see www.courts.wa.gov/jislink (also, see state introduction).

Criminal Records: Access: Mail, online, in person,phone. Both court and visitors may perform in person searches. No search fee. Required to search: name, years to search; also helpful: address, DOB, SSN. Criminal records on computer and microfiche from 11/82, archived from 1903. Index remotely online from JIS-Link; see www.courts.wa.gov/jislink (also, see state introduction).

General Information: Public Access terminal is available. No dependencies, adoption, and mental illness records released. Will not fax results. Copy fee: $1.00 per page. Cert fee: $2.00 1st page, $1.00 each add'l page. Payee: Lincoln County Clerk. Business checks accepted. Prepayment required. Mail requests: SASE required. Mail turnaround time 4 days.

District Court PO Box 329, Davenport, WA 99122-0329; 509-725-2281; Fax: 509-725-6481. Hours: 8AM-5PM (PST). *Misdemeanor, Civil Actions Under $35,000, Small Claims.*
Note: This is a small office with limited time allowable for searches.

Civil Records: Access: Mail, fax, online, in person. Both court and visitors may perform in person searches. Search fee: $25.00 per hour. Required to search: name, years to search. Civil cases indexed by defendant. Civil records on computer back to 6/93, in books from 1985. Index online from JIS-Link; see www.courts.wa.gov/jislink (also, see state introduction).

Criminal Records: Access: Mail, fax, online, in person,phone. Both the court and visitors may perform in person searches. Search fee: $25.00 per hour. Required to search: name, years to search, DOB. Criminal records on computer back to 6/93; hard copy files back to 1990. Index remotely online from JIS-Link; see www.courts.wa.gov/jislink (also, see state introduction).

General Information: Public Access terminal is available. No dependencies, adoption, and mental illness records released. Copy fee: $.50. Cert fee: $6.00 plus $1.00 per page after first. Payee: Lincoln County District Court. Business checks accepted. Prepayment required. Mail requests: SASE required. Mail turnaround time 1 week.

Mason County

Superior Court PO Box 340, Shelton, WA 98584; 360-427-9670 X346. Hours: 8:30AM-5PM (PST). *Felony, Civil, Eviction, Probate.*
www.co.mason.wa.us/Clerk

Civil Records: Access: Phone, mail, online, in person. Both court and visitors may perform in person searches. Search fee: $20.00 per hour. Required to search: name, years to search; also helpful: address. Civil cases indexed by defendant, plaintiff. Civil records on computer from 1982; on microfiche and archived from 1890; on index or docket books prior to 1982. Index online from JIS-Link; see

www.courts.wa.gov/jislink (also, see state introduction).

Criminal Records: Access: Phone, mail, online, in person. Both court and visitors may perform in person searches. Search fee: $20.00 per hour. Required to search: name, years to search; also helpful: address, DOB. Criminal records on computer from 1982; on microfiche and archived from 1890; on index or docket books prior to 1982. Index remotely online from JIS-Link; see www.courts.wa.gov/jislink (also, see state introduction).

General Information: No dependencies, adoption, and mental illness records released. Copy fee: $2.00 for 1st page, $1.00 each add'l. Cert fee: $2.00 plus $1.00 per page after first. Payee: Mason County Clerk. Attorney checks accepted. No personal checks accepted. Prepayment required. Mail requests: SASE required. Mail turnaround time 1 week.

District Court PO Box "O", Shelton, WA 98584-0090; 360-427-9670 X339; Fax: 360-427-7776. Hours: 8:30AM-5PM (PST). *Misdemeanor, Civil Actions Under $50,000, Small Claims.*

Civil Records: Access: Mail, in person. Only the court performs in person searches; visitors may not. Search fee: $20.00 per name. Fee is for extensive searching. Required to search: name, years to search; also helpful: address. Civil cases indexed by defendant, plaintiff. Civil records on computer from 12/92. Index online from JIS-Link; see www.courts.wa.gov/jislink (also, see state introduction).

Criminal Records: Access: Mail, in person. Only the court performs in person searches; visitors may not. Search fee: Will charge $20.00 for extensive search. Required to search: name, years to search, DOB, signed release; also helpful: address, SSN. Criminal records on computer from 12/92, prior on index book. Index remotely online from JIS-Link; see www.courts.wa.gov/jislink (also, see state introduction).

General Information: Copy fee: $.25 per page. Cert fee: $5.00. Payee: Mason County District Court. Personal checks accepted. Prepayment required. Mail requests: SASE required. Mail turnaround time 1 week.

Okanogan County

Superior Court PO Box 72, Okanogan, WA 98840; 509-422-7275; Fax: 509-422-7277. Hours: 8:30AM-5:00PM (PST). *Felony, Misdemeanor, Civil, Eviction, Probate.*

Civil Records: Access: Phone, fax, mail, online, in person. Both court and visitors may perform in person searches. No search fee. Required to search: name, years to search; also helpful: address. Civil cases indexed by defendant, plaintiff. Civil records on computer from 1994, on hand-written indexes from 1895. Index online from JIS-Link; see www.courts.wa.gov/jislink (also, see state introduction).

Criminal Records: Access: Phone, fax, mail, online, in person. Only the court may perform in person searches. No search fee. Required to search: name, years to search; also helpful: address, DOB, SSN. Criminal records on computer from 1994, on hand-written indexes from 1895. Index remotely online from JIS-Link; see www.courts.wa.gov/jislink (also, see state introduction).

General Information: No dependencies, adoption, and mental illness records released. Copy fee: $1.00 per page. Cert fee: $2.00 plus $1.00 per page after first. Payee: Okanogan County Clerk. Personal checks accepted. Prepayment required. Mail requests: SASE required. Mail turnaround time 1-7 days.

District Court PO Box 980, Okanogan, WA 98840-0980; 509-422-7170; Fax: 509-422-7174. Hours: 8AM-5PM (PST). *Misdemeanor, Civil Actions Under $50,000, Small Claims.*
Civil Records: Access: Phone, fax, mail, in person, online. Both court and visitors may perform in person searches. No search fee. Required to search: name, years to search. Civil cases indexed by defendant, plaintiff. Civil records on computer from 8/91, prior on index cards. Records files maintained 10 years if judgment, otherwise 3 years. Index online from JIS-Link; see www.courts.wa.gov/jislink (also, see state introduction).
Criminal Records: Access: Phone, fax, mail, in person, online. Both court and visitors may perform in person searches. No search fee. Required to search: name, years to search, DOB. Criminal records on computer from 8/91. Index remotely online from JIS-Link; see www.courts.wa.gov/jislink (also, see state introduction).
General Information: Public Access terminal is available. No alcohol related evaluations, mental illness records released. Will fax results $1.00 1st page, $.50 each add'l. Copy fee: $1.00 for first page, $.50 each add'l. Cert fee: $5.00. Payee: Okanogan County District Court. Personal checks accepted. Prepayment required. Mail requests: SASE requested. Turnaround time 7 days.

Pacific County

Superior Court PO Box 67, South Bend, WA 98586; 360-875-9320; Fax: 360-875-9321. Hours: 8:30AM-4:30PM (PST). *Felony, Civil, Eviction, Probate.*
Civil Records: Access: Phone, mail, online, in person. Both court and visitors may perform in person searches. Search fee: $20.00 per hour. Required to search: name, years to search. Civil cases indexed by defendant, plaintiff. Civil records on computer from 2/84, archived from 1887, some on docket books. Index online from JIS-Link; see www.courts.wa.gov/jislink (also, see state introduction).
Criminal Records: Access: Mail, online, in person. Both court and visitors may perform in person searches. Search fee: $20.00 per hour if searching before 1984. Required to search: name, years to search. Criminal records on computer from 2/84, archived from 1887, some on docket books. Index remotely online from JIS-Link; see www.courts.wa.gov/jislink (also, see state introduction).
General Information: No dependencies, adoption, and mental illness records released. Copy fee: $.15 per page.$1.00 by mail. Cert fee: $2.00 1st page, $1.00 each add'l page. Payee: Pacific County Clerk. Personal checks accepted. Prepayment required. Mail requests: SASE required. Mail turnaround time varies.

District Court North Box 134, South Bend, WA 98586-0134; 360-875-9354; Fax: 360-875-9351. Hours: 9AM-5PM (PST). *Misdemeanor, Civil Actions Under $50,000, Small Claims.*
Civil Records: Access: Phone, fax, mail, in person, online. Only the court may perform in person searches. No search fee. Required to search: name, years to search; also helpful: address. Civil cases indexed by defendant, plaintiff. Civil records on computer back to 3/93, prior on index cards. Depending on disposition date, civil records retained ten years. Index online from JIS-Link; see www.courts.wa.gov/jislink (also, see state introduction).
Criminal Records: Access: Phone,mail, in person. Only the court may perform in person searches. No search fee. Required to search: name, DOB; also helpful: years to search, address, SSN. Criminal

Records retained forever, on computer back to 3/93. Index remotely online from JIS-Link; see www.courts.wa.gov/jislink (also, see state introduction).
General Information: No dependencies, MVRs, defendant case histories, adoption, and mental illness records released. No fee to fax results. Copy fee: $2.00 for first page, $1.00 each add'l. Cert fee: $5.00. Payee: North District Court. Personal checks accepted. Prepayment required. Mail requests: SASE required. Mail turnaround time 1-6 weeks.

District Court South PO Box 794, Ilwaco, WA 98624; 360-642-9417; Fax: 360-642-9416. Hours: 7:30AM-4:30PM (PST). *Misdemeanor, Civil Actions Under $50,000, Small Claims.*
Civil Records: Access: Phone, fax, mail, online, in person. Only the court performs in person searches; visitors may not. No search fee. Required to search: name, years to search; also helpful: address. Civil cases indexed by defendant, plaintiff. Civil records on computer for current and open cases. Records retained for 10 years. Index online from JIS-Link; see www.courts.wa.gov/jislink (also, see state introduction).
Criminal Records: Access: Fax, mail, online, in person. Only the court performs in person searches; visitors may not. No search fee. Required to search: name; also helpful: years to search, address, DOB, SSN. Criminal records on computer for current and open cases. Records retained for 10 years. Index remotely online from JIS-Link; see www.courts.wa.gov/jislink (also, see state introduction).
General Information: No dependencies, adoption, and mental illness records released. No fee to fax results. Copy fee: $1.00 for first page, $.10 each add'l. Cert fee: $6.00. Payee: South District Court. Personal checks accepted. Prepayment required. Mail requests: SASE required. Mail turnaround time 1 week.

Pend Oreille County

Superior Court 229 S Garden Ave (PO Box 5020), Newport, WA 99156-5020; 509-447-2435; Fax: 509-447-2734. Hours: 8AM-4:30PM (PST). *Felony, Civil, Eviction, Probate.*
Civil Records: Access: Mail, in person. Both court and visitors may perform in person searches. Search fee: $20.00 per hour. Required to search: name, years to search; also helpful: address. Civil cases indexed by defendant, plaintiff. Civil records on computer and microfiche from 9/82, archived from 1911, on docket books prior to 9/82. Index online from JIS-Link; see www.courts.wa.gov/jislink (also, see state introduction).
Criminal Records: Access: Phone, mail, in person. Both court and visitors may perform in person searches. No search fee. Required to search: name, years to search; also helpful: address, DOB, SSN. Criminal records on computer and microfiche from 9/82, archived from 1911, on docket books prior to 9/82. Index remotely online from JIS-Link; see www.courts.wa.gov/jislink (also, see state introduction).
General Information: No dependencies, adoption, and mental illness records released. Fee to fax results is $3.00 for the 1st page and $1.00 per page thereafter. Copy fee: $2.00 for first page, $1.00 each add'l. Cert fee: $2.00. Payee: Pend Oreille County Clerk. Personal checks accepted. Prepayment required. Mail requests: SASE required. Mail turnaround time same day.

District Court PO Box 5030, 229 S Garden Ave, Newport, WA 99156-5030; 509-447-4110; Civil phone: 800-359-1506; Fax: 509-447-5724. Hours: 8AM-4:30PM (PST). *Misdemeanor, Civil Actions Under $50,000, Small Claims.*

Civil Records: Access: Phone, fax, mail, online, in person. Both court and visitors may perform in person searches. No search fee. Required to search: name, years to search; also helpful: address. Civil cases indexed by defendant, plaintiff. Civil records on DISCIS computer from 10/92, on computer from 1989, archived from 1972. Records retained for 10 years. Index online from JIS-Link; see www.courts.wa.gov/jislink (also, see state introduction).
Criminal Records: Access: Fax, mail, online, in person. Both court and visitors may perform in person searches. No search fee. Required to search: name, DOB; also helpful: years to search, address, SSN. Criminal records on DISCIS computer from 10/92, on computer from 1989, archived from 1972. Records retained for 10 years. Index remotely online from JIS-Link; see www.courts.wa.gov/jislink (also, see state introduction).
General Information: No dependencies, adoption, and mental illness records released. No fee to fax results. Copy fee: $.25 per page. Cert fee: $5.00. Payee: Pend Oreille County District Court. Personal checks accepted. Prepayment required. Mail requests: SASE required. Mail turnaround time 10 days.

Pierce County

Superior Court 930 Tacoma Ave South, Rm 110, Tacoma, WA 98402; 253-798-7455; Fax: 253-798-3428. Hours: 8:30AM-4:30PM (PST). *Felony, Civil, Eviction, Probate.*
www.co.pierce.wa.us/abtus/ourorg/supct/abtussup.htm
Civil Records: Access: Mail, online, in person. Both court and visitors may perform in person searches. Search fee: $10.00 per hour. Required to search: name, years to search; also helpful: address. Civil cases indexed by defendant, plaintiff. Civil records on computer from 5/81, archived from 1890. Calendars are online at the website. Also, a statewide index is remotely online (see state introduction).
Criminal Records: Access: Mail, online, in person. Both court and visitors may perform in person searches. Search fee: $10.00 per name. Required to search: name, years to search, DOB; also helpful: address, SSN. Criminal records on computer from 5/81, archived from 1890. Online access to criminal records is the same as civil.
General Information: Public Access terminal is available. No sealed, juvenile, adoption, paternity, mental health, sex offenders (victims) or (sometimes) DUI records released. Will fax results; $5.00 minimum. Copy fee: $.25 self serve $1.00 by court. Cert fee: $2.00 plus $1.00 per page after first. Payee: Pierce County Clerk. Business checks accepted. Prepayment required. Mail requests: SASE required. Mail turnaround time 2-5 days.

District Court - Civil Infractions Division 1902 96th St S, Tacoma, WA 98444; 253-798-7474; Fax: 253-798-6310. Hours: 8:30AM-4:30PM M-Th (PST). *Civil Actions Under $50,000, Small Claims, Traffic.*
www.co.pierce.wa.us/abtus/ourorg/distct/abtusd1.htm
Note: District Court #3 in Eatonville, #2 in Gig Harbor, and #4 in Buckley were closed 01/13/03, all records were transferred to this court.
Civil Records: Access: Phone, mail, online, in person. Both court and visitors may perform in person searches. No search fee. Required to search: name, years to search, DOB; also helpful: address. Civil cases indexed by defendant, plaintiff. Civil records on computer back to 1990; Records go back 5 years. Index online from JIS-Link; see www.courts.wa.gov/jislink (also, see state introduction).

General Information: No sealed, juvenile, adoption, paternity, mental health, sex offenders (victims) or some DUI records released. Will not fax results. Copy fee: $1.00 for first page, $.50 each add'l. Cert fee: $5.00. Payee: Pierce County District Court. Personal checks accepted. Visa, MC accepted. Prepayment required. Mail requests: SASE required. Mail turnaround time 1-2 weeks.

District Court - Criminal 930 Tacoma Ave S, Rm 601, Tacoma, WA 98402-2175; 253-798-7457; Fax: 253-798-6166. Hours: 8:30AM-4:30PM (PST). *Misdemeanor.*

www.co.pierce.wa.us/pc/abtus/ourorg/distct/abtusd1.htm

Note: District Court #3 in Eatonville was closed 01/13/03, all misdemeanor were transferred to this court.

Criminal Records: Access: Mail, fax, in person. Both court and visitors may perform in person searches. No search fee. Required to search: name, years to search, DOB; also helpful: address, SSN. Criminal records on computer from 8/1990. Criminal Index remotely online from JIS-Link; see www.courts.wa.gov/jislink (also, see state introduction).

General Information: No sealed, juvenile, adoption, paternity, mental health, sex offenders (victims) or some DUI records released. Will not fax results. Copy fee: $1.00 for first page, $.50 each add'l. Cert fee: $5.00. Payee: Pierce County District Court. Personal checks accepted. Visa, MC accepted. Mail requests: SASE required. Mail turnaround time 1-2 weeks.

District Court #2, WA. *Misdemeanor, Civil Actions Under $50,000, Small Claims.*

Note: This court - formerly in Gig Harbor - is closed and records are now houses at the main court in Tacoma.

District Court #3, WA. *Misdemeanor, Civil Actions Under $50,000, Small Claims.*

Note: This court was closed on 01/10/03. All records have been transferred to the Pierce County District Court in Tacoma.

District Court #4, WA. *Misdemeanor, Civil Actions Under $50,000, Small Claims.*

Note: This court was closed on 01/10/03. All records have been transferred to the Pierce County District Court in Tacoma.

San Juan County

Superior Court 350 Court St, #7, Friday Harbor, WA 98250; 360-378-2163; Fax: 360-378-3967. Hours: 8AM-5PM (PST). *Felony, Misdemeanor, Civil, Eviction, Probate.*

www.co.san-juan.wa.us

Civil Records: Access: Phone, fax, mail, online, in person. Both court and visitors may perform in person searches. Search fee: $20.00 per hour. Required to search: name, years to search; also helpful: case number. Civil cases indexed by defendant, plaintiff. Civil records on computer back to 1987, on microfilm and archived from 1890s. Index online from JIS-Link; see www.courts.wa.gov/jislink (also, see state introduction).

Criminal Records: Access: Phone, fax, mail, online, in person. Only the court may perform in person searches on computer. Search fee: $20.00 per hour. Required to search: name, years to search, DOB; also helpful: address, SSN, case number. Criminal records on computer back to 1987, on microfilm and archived from 1890s. Index remotely online from JIS-Link; see www.courts.wa.gov/jislink (also, see state introduction).

General Information: No dependencies, adoption, and mental illness records released. Will fax results

$3.00 1st page, $1.00 each add'l. Copy fee: $2.00 for first page, $1.00 each add'l. Cert fee: $2.00. Payee: San Juan County Clerk. Personal checks accepted. Credit cards accepted. Prepayment required. Mail requests: SASE required. Mail turnaround time 3 days.

District Court PO Box 127, Friday Harbor, WA 98250-0127; 360-378-4017; Fax: 360-378-4099. Hours: 8:30AM-4:30PM (PST). *Misdemeanor, Civil Actions Under $50,000, Small Claims.*

Civil Records: Access: Mail, in person. Only the court performs in person searches; visitors may not. No search fee. Required to search: name, years to search; also helpful: address. Civil cases indexed by defendant, plaintiff. Civil records on computer from 1993, on index cards prior. Records retained for 10 years. Index online from JIS-Link; see www.courts.wa.gov/jislink (also, see state introduction).

Criminal Records: Access: Mail, in person, fax. Only the court performs in person searches; visitors may not. No search fee. Required to search: name, years to search, signed release; also helpful: address, DOB, SSN. Criminal records on computer from 1993, log book prior. Retained 5 years. Index remotely online from JIS-Link; see www.courts.wa.gov/jislink (also, see state introduction).

General Information: No dependencies, adoption, confidential social files and mental illness records released. Copy fee: $2.00 for first page, $1.00 each add'l. Cert fee: $5.00. Payee: San Juan County District Court. Personal checks accepted. Credit cards are accepted through OfficialPayments.Com or 1-877-876-7619. You will need to provide them with your case # or ticket #. Prepayment required. Mail requests: SASE required. Mail turnaround time 1-3 days.

Skagit County

Superior Court 205 W Kincaid St #103, Mount Vernon, WA 98273; 360-336-9440. Hours: 8:30AM-4:30PM (PST). *Felony, Civil, Eviction, Probate.*

Civil Records: Access: Mail, online, in person. Both court and visitors may perform in person searches. Search fee: $20.00 per hour. Required to search: name, years to search. Civil cases indexed by defendant, plaintiff. Civil records on computer from 10/81, on microfilm and archived from 1878. Index online from JIS-Link; see www.courts.wa.gov/jislink (also, see state introduction).

Criminal Records: Access: Mail, online, in person. Both court and visitors may perform in person searches. Search fee: $20.00 per hour. Required to search: name, years to search. Criminal records on computer from 10/81, on microfilm and archived from 1878. Index remotely online from JIS-Link; see www.courts.wa.gov/jislink (also, see state introduction).

General Information: Public Access terminal is available. No dependencies, adoption, and mental illness, juvenile offender prior to 07/01/78 records released. Will not fax results. Copy fee: $.25 each, do-it-yourself. Self made copies cannot be certified. Cert fee: copies are $2.00 for first page, $1.00 each add'l page. Payee: Skagit County Clerk. Only cashiers checks and money orders accepted. Prepayment required. Mail requests: SASE required. Mail turnaround time 5 days.

District Court PO Box 340, Mount Vernon, WA 98273-0340; 360-336-9319; Fax: 360-336-9318. Hours: 8:30AM-4:30PM (PST). *Misdemeanor, Civil Actions Under $50,000, Small Claims.*

Civil Records: Access: Fax, mail, online, in person. Both court and visitors may perform in person searches. No search fee. Required to search: name, years to search; also helpful: address. Civil cases indexed by defendant, plaintiff. Civil records on

computer from 1986, archived for 12 years. Open records retained for 10 years. Index online from JIS-Link; see www.courts.wa.gov/jislink (also, see state introduction). Mail search requires a special form.

Criminal Records: Access: Fax, mail, online, in person. Both court and visitors may perform in person searches. No search fee. Required to search: name, years to search, DOB; also helpful: SSN. Criminal records prior to 1995 only retained for 5 years. Index remotely online from JIS-Link; see www.courts.wa.gov/jislink (also, see state introduction).

General Information: Public Access terminal is available. No dependencies, alcohol, adoption, and mental illness records released. Copy fee: $.50 per page. Cert fee: $5.00. Payee: District Court, Skagit County. Personal checks accepted. Prepayment required. Mail requests: SASE required. Mail turnaround time 3-4 days.

Skamania County

Superior Court PO Box 790, Stevenson, WA 98648; 509-427-9431; Fax: 509-427-7386. Hours: 8:30AM-5PM (PST). *Felony, Civil, Eviction, Probate.*

Civil Records: Access: Phone, mail, online, in person. Only the court performs in person searches; visitors may not. Search fee: $20.00 per hour. Required to search: name, years to search; also helpful: address. Civil cases indexed by defendant, plaintiff. Civil records on computer from 1984, on microfiche and archived from 1900. Index online from JIS-Link; see www.courts.wa.gov/jislink (also, see state introduction).

Criminal Records: Access: Phone, mail, online, in person. Only the court performs in person searches; visitors may not. Search fee: $20.00 per hour. Required to search: name, years to search; also helpful: address, DOB. Criminal records on computer from 1984, on microfiche and archived from 1900. Index remotely online from JIS-Link; see www.courts.wa.gov/jislink (also, see state introduction).

General Information: No dependencies, adoption, and mental illness records released. Will fax results to local or toll free line. Copy fee: $2.00 first page, $1.00 each add'l. Cert fee: Same as copy fee. Payee: Skamania County Clerk. Personal checks accepted. Prepayment required. Mail requests: SASE required. Mail turnaround time same day.

District Court PO Box 790, Stevenson, WA 98648; 509-427-9430; Fax: 509-427-7386. Hours: 8:30AM-5PM (PST). *Misdemeanor, Civil Actions Under $50,000, Small Claims.*

Civil Records: Access: Phone, fax, mail, online, in person. Both the court and visitors may perform in person searches. Search fee: $40.00 per hour. Required to search: name, years to search; also helpful: address. Civil cases indexed by defendant, plaintiff. Civil records on computer go back 10 years. Records retained for 10 years. Index online from JIS-Link; see www.courts.wa.gov/jislink (also, see state introduction).

Criminal Records: Access: Phone, fax, mail, online, in person. Both the court and visitors may perform in person searches. Search fee: $40.00 per hour. Required to search: name, years to search; also helpful: address, DOB, signed release. Criminal records on computer go back 10 years. Records retained for 10 years. Index remotely online from JIS-Link; see www.courts.wa.gov/jislink (also, see state introduction).

General Information: Public Access terminal is available. No dependencies, adoption, and mental illness records released. No fee to fax results. Copy fee: $3.00 for 1st page, $1.00 each add'l. Cert fee:

$6.00. Payee: Skamania County District Court. Personal checks accepted. Prepayment required. Mail requests: SASE required. Mail turnaround time 7 days.

Snohomish County

Superior Court 3000 Rockefeller, MS 605, Everett, WA 98201; 425-388-3466. Hours: 8:30AM-5PM (PST). *Felony, Civil Actions, Eviction, Probate.* www.co.snohomish.wa.us

Civil Records: Access: Phone, mail, online, in person. Both court and visitors may perform in person searches. Search fee: $20.00 per hour. Required to search: name, years to search. Civil cases indexed by defendant, plaintiff. Civil records on computer from 1978, prior on database index. Index online from JIS-Link; see www.courts.wa.gov/jislink (also, see state introduction).

Criminal Records: Access: Phone, mail, online, in person. Both court and visitors may perform in person searches. Search fee: $20.00 per hour. Required to search: name, years to search. Criminal records on computer from 1978, prior on database index. Index remotely online from JIS-Link; see www.courts.wa.gov/jislink (also, see state introduction).

General Information: Public Access terminal is available. No sealed, juvenile, adoption, paternity, mental health, sex offenders (victims). Copy fee: $.10 per page. Cert fee: $2.00 plus $1.00 per page after first. Payee: County Clerk or Snohomish County Clerk's Office. Business checks accepted; no credit cards or personal checks. Prepayment required. Mail requests: SASE requested. Turnaround time 1 week.

Cascade Division District Court 415 E

Burke St, Arlington, WA 98223; 360-435-7700; Fax: 360-435-0873. Hours: 8:30AM-5PM (PST). *Misdemeanor, Civil Actions Under $50,000, Small Claims.*

Civil Records: Access: Mail, online, in person. Both the court and visitors may perform in person searches. Search fee: $5.00 per name. Required to search: name, years to search; also helpful: address. Civil cases indexed by defendant, plaintiff. Civil records on computer from 1985. Index online from JIS-Link; see www.courts.wa.gov/jislink (also, see state introduction).

Criminal Records: Access: Mail, online, in person. Both the court and visitors may perform in person searches. Search fee: $5.00 per name. Required to search: name, years to search, DOB; also helpful: address, SSN. Criminal records on computer from 1987. Index remotely online from JIS-Link; see www.courts.wa.gov/jislink (also, see state introduction).

General Information: Public Access terminal is available. No sealed, mental health, sex offenders (victims) or some DUI records released. Copy fee: $.15 per page. Cert fee: $5.00. Payee: Cascade Division. Personal checks accepted. Visa, MC accepted. Prepayment required. Mail turnaround time 1 week.

Everett Division District Court 3000

Rockefeller Ave MS 508, Everett, WA 98201; 425-388-3331; Civil phone: 425-388-3595; Fax: 425-388-3565. Hours: 8:30AM-5PM (PST). *Misdemeanor, Civil Actions Under $50,000, Small Claims.*

Civil Records: Access: Fax, mail, online, in person. Both court and visitors may perform in person searches. No search fee. Required to search: complete name, years to search; also helpful: address. Civil cases indexed by defendant, plaintiff. Civil records on computer back to 1986. Index online from JIS-Link; see www.courts.wa.gov/jislink (also, see state introduction).

Criminal Records: Access: Fax, mail, online, in person. Both court and visitors may perform in person searches. No search fee. Required to search: complete name, years to search, DOB; also helpful: address, SSN. Criminal records on computer back to 1986. Index remotely online from JIS-Link; see www.courts.wa.gov/jislink (also, see state introduction).

General Information: Public Access terminal is available. Limited DUI records released. No fee to fax results. Copy fee: $.15 per page. Cert fee: $5.00. Payee: Everett District Court. Personal checks accepted. Visa, MC, AmEx, Discover accepted. Prepayment required. Mail requests: SASE required. Mail turnaround time 1 week.

Evergreen Division District Court 14414

179th Ave SE, PO Box 625, Monroe, WA 98272-0625; 360-805-6776; Fax: 360-805-6755. Hours: 8:30AM-5PM (PST). *Misdemeanor, Civil Actions Under $50,000, Small Claims.*

Civil Records: Access: Mail, in person. Only the court performs in person searches; visitors may not. No search fee. Required to search: name, years to search; also helpful: address. Civil cases indexed by defendant, plaintiff. Civil records on computer back 10 years; file retained until closure. Index online from JIS-Link; see www.courts.wa.gov/jislink (also, see state introduction).

Criminal Records: Access: Mail, in person. Only the court performs in person searches; visitors may not. No search fee. Required to search: name, years to search; also helpful: address, DOB. Criminal records on computer archived 3 years after closure by state. Index remotely online from JIS-Link; see www.courts.wa.gov/jislink (also, see state introduction).

General Information: No sealed, juvenile, adoption, paternity, mental health, sex offenders (victims) or some DUI records released. Copy fee: $.15 per page. Cert fee: $5.00. Payee: Evergreen District Court. Personal checks accepted. Prepayment required. Mail requests: SASE requested. Turnaround time 1 week.

South Division District Court 20520 68th

Ave W, Lynnwood, WA 98036-7406; 425-774-8803; Fax: 425-744-6820. Hours: 8:30AM-4:30PM (PST). *Misdemeanor, Civil Actions Under $50,000, Small Claims.*

Civil Records: Access: Mail, online, in person. No search fee. Required to search: name, years to search. Civil cases indexed by case number. Civil records on computer since 1987. Index online from JIS-Link; see www.courts.wa.gov/jislink (also, see state introduction).

Criminal Records: Access: Mail, online, in person. Only the court performs in person searches; visitors may not. No search fee. Required to search: name, years to search. Criminal records on computer since 1989. Index remotely online from JIS-Link; see www.courts.wa.gov/jislink (also, see state introduction).

General Information: No sealed, juvenile, adoption, paternity, mental health, sex offenders (victims) or some DUI records released. Copy fee: $.15 per page. Cert fee: $5.00. Payee: South District Court. Personal checks accepted. Prepayment required. Mail requests: SASE requested. Turnaround time 2-4 days.

Spokane County

Superior Court 1116 W Broadway, Spokane, WA 99260; 509-477-2211. Hours: 8:30AM-5PM (PST). *Felony, Civil, Eviction, Probate.* www.spokanecounty.org/clerk

Civil Records: Access: Phone, mail, online, in person. Both court and visitors may perform in person searches. Search fee: $10.00 per hour. Required to search: name, years to search. Civil cases indexed by defendant, plaintiff. Civil records on computer from 1973, archives back to 1800s, docket books prior to computer. Index online from JIS-Link; see www.courts.wa.gov/jislink (also, see state introduction).

Criminal Records: Access: Phone, mail, online, in person. Both court and visitors may perform in person searches. Search fee: $10.00 per hour. Required to search: name, years to search; also helpful: DOB. Criminal records on computer from 1973, archives back to 1800s, docket books prior to computer. Index remotely online from JIS-Link; see www.courts.wa.gov/jislink (also, see state introduction).

General Information: No sealed, juvenile, dependency, adoption, paternity, mental health records released. Copy fee: $2.00 for first page, $1.00 each add'l. Cert fee: $2.00 plus $1.00 each add'l page. Payee: Spokane County Clerk. Personal checks accepted. Prepayment required. Mail requests: SASE required. Mail turnaround time 1-3 days.

District Court 1100 Mallon W, Spokane, WA 99260; 509-477-4770. Hours: 8:30AM-5PM (PST). *Misdemeanor, Civil Actions Under $50,000, Small Claims.* www.spokanecounty.org/districtcourt

Civil Records: Access: Phone, mail, online, in person. Only the court performs in person searches; visitors may not. No search fee. Required to search: name, years to search; also helpful: address. Civil cases indexed by defendant, plaintiff. Civil records on computer go back 10 years. Index online from JIS-Link; see www.courts.wa.gov/jislink (also, see state introduction).

Criminal Records: Access: Phone, mail, online, in person. Only the court performs in person searches; visitors may not. No search fee. Required to search: name, years to search, signed release; also helpful: address, DOB. Criminal records are computer since 1984, but searches are only done for five years time. Index remotely online from JIS-Link; see www.courts.wa.gov/jislink (also, see state introduction).

General Information: Copy fee: $1.00 per page. Cert fee: $5.00. Payee: Spokane County District Court. Business checks accepted. Personal checks accepted for civil records only. Prepayment required. Mail requests: SASE required. Mail turnaround time 1 week.

Stevens County

Superior Court 215 S Oak Rm 206, Colville, WA 99114; 509-684-7575. Hours: 8AM-Noon, 1-4:30PM (PST). *Felony, Civil, Eviction, Probate.*

Civil Records: Access: Phone, mail, online, in person. Only the court performs in person searches; visitors may not. Search fee: $20.00 per hour. Required to search: name, years to search; also helpful: address. Civil cases indexed by defendant, plaintiff. Civil records on computer from 10-82, microfiche from 1889-1982, archives 1889, index cards prior to 1982. Index online from JIS-Link; see www.courts.wa.gov/jislink (also, see state introduction).

Criminal Records: Access: Mail, online, in person. Only the court performs in person searches; visitors may not. Search fee: $20.00 per hour. Required to search: name, years to search, DOB; also helpful: address, SSN. Criminal records on computer from 10-82, microfiche from 1889-1982, archives 1889, index cards prior to 1982. Index remotely online from JIS-Link; see www.courts.wa.gov/jislink (also, see state introduction).

General Information: No sealed, juvenile, adoption, paternity, mental health, sex offenders (victims). Will not fax results. Copy fee: $2.00 for 1st page, $1.00

each add'l pg. Cert fee: Included in copy fee. Payee: Stevens County Clerk. Personal checks accepted. Prepayment required. Mail requests: SASE required. Mail turnaround time same day.

District Court 215 S Oak Rm 213, Colville, WA 99114; 509-684-5249; Fax: 509-684-7571. Hours: 8AM-Noon, 1-4:30PM (PST). *Misdemeanor, Civil Actions Under $50,000, Small Claims.*
www.co.stevens.wa.us/distcourt/departments.htm
Civil Records: Access: Mail, online, in person. Only the court performs in person searches; visitors may not. Search fee: none. Required to search: name, years to search; also helpful: address. Civil cases indexed by defendant. Civil records on computer from 1/93, prior on docket books to 1988. Index online from JIS-Link; see www.courts.wa.gov/jislink (also, see state introduction).
Criminal Records: Access: Mail, online, in person. Only the court performs in person searches; visitors may not. Search fee: none. Required to search: name, years to search, DOB; also helpful: address, SSN, signed request. Criminal records on computer from 07/93, prior on docket books to 1988. Index remotely online from JIS-Link; see www.courts.wa.gov/jislink (also, see state introduction).
General Information: No sealed, juvenile, adoption, paternity, mental health, sex offenders (victims) or some DUI records released. Fee to fax results is $1.00 per page. Copy fee: $.15 per page. Cert fee: $5.00. Payee: Stevens County District Court. Business checks accepted. Prepayment required. Mail turnaround time 1 week.

Thurston County

Superior Court Thurston County Clerk, 2000 Lakeridge Dr SW, Bldg 2, Olympia, WA 98502; 360-786-5430. Hours: 8AM-5PM (PST). *Felony, Misdemeanor, Civil, Eviction, Probate.*
www.co.thurston.wa.us/clerk
Civil Records: Access: Phone, mail, in person, email. Both court and visitors may perform in person searches. Search fee: $20.00 per hour. Required to search: name, years to search; also helpful: address. Civil cases indexed by defendant, plaintiff. Civil records on computer from 07/78, archives back to 1850s. Index online from JIS-Link; see www.courts.wa.gov/jislink (also, see state introduction).
Criminal Records: Access: Phone, mail, in person, email. Both court and visitors may perform in person searches. Search fee: $20.00 per hour. Required to search: name, years to search, DOB, signed release; also helpful: address, SSN. Criminal records on computer from 07/78, archives back to 1850s. Index remotely online from JIS-Link; see www.courts.wa.gov/jislink (also, see state introduction).
General Information: Public Access terminal is available. No sealed, juvenile, adoption, paternity, mental health, sex offenders (victims). Copy fee: $2.00 for first page, $1.00 each add'l. Cert fee: $2.00 first page and $1.00 each additional. Payee: Thurston County Clerk. Business checks accepted. Prepayment required. Mail requests: SASE required. Mail turnaround time 1-7 days.

District Court 2000 Lakeridge Dr SW, Bldg 3, Olympia, WA 98502; 360-786-5450; Fax: 360-754-3359. Hours: 8:30AM-4PM (PST). *Misdemeanor, Civil Actions Under $50,000, Small Claims.*
www.co.thurston.wa.us/distcrt
Note: Daily court calendars are available at www.co.thurston.wa.us/distcrt/courtcalendars.htm.
Civil Records: Access: Phone, fax, mail, online, in person. Both court and visitors may perform in person searches. No search fee. Required to search: name,

years to search; also helpful: address. Civil cases indexed by defendant, plaintiff. Civil records on computer from 1983. Index online from JIS-Link; see www.courts.wa.gov/jislink (also, see state introduction).
Criminal Records: Access: Phone, fax, mail, online, in person. Both court and visitors may perform in person searches. No search fee. Required to search: name, years to search; also helpful: address, DOB, SSN. Criminal records on computer from 1988. Index remotely online from JIS-Link; see www.courts.wa.gov/jislink (also, see state introduction).
General Information: No sealed, juvenile, adoption, paternity, mental health, sex offenders (victims) or some DUI records released. Will fax results. Copy fee: $.25 per page. Cert fee: $5.00. Payee: Thurston County District Court. Personal checks accepted. Prepayment required. Mail requests: SASE required. Mail turnaround time 2 weeks.

Wahkiakum County

Superior Court PO Box 116, Cathlamet, WA 98612; 360-795-3558; Fax: 360-795-8813. Hours: 8AM-4PM (PST). *Felony, Misdemeanor, Civil, Eviction, Probate.*
Civil Records: Access: Mail, online, in person. Both court and visitors may perform in person searches. Search fee: $20.00 per hour. Required to search: name, years to search. Civil cases indexed by defendant, plaintiff. Civil records on computer from 1988, archives from 1850s. Index online from JIS-Link; see www.courts.wa.gov/jislink (also, see state introduction).
Criminal Records: Access: Mail, online, in person. Both court and visitors may perform in person searches. Search fee: $20.00 per hour. Required to search: name, years to search; also helpful: address, DOB. Criminal records on computer from 1988, archives from 1850s. Index remotely online from JIS-Link; see www.courts.wa.gov/jislink (also, see state introduction).
General Information: No sealed, juvenile, adoption, paternity, mental health, sex offenders (victims). Fee to fax results is $1.00 per page. Copy fee: $1.00 per page. Cert fee: $2.00. Payee: County Clerk. Personal checks accepted. Prepayment required. Mail requests: SASE required. Mail turnaround time 1 day.

District Court PO Box 144, Cathlamet, WA 98612; 360-795-3461; Fax: 360-795-6506. Hours: 8AM-4PM (PST). *Misdemeanor, Civil Actions Under $50,000, Small Claims.*
Civil Records: Access: Phone, fax, mail, online, in person. Both court and visitors may perform in person searches. No search fee. Required to search: name, years to search; also helpful: address. Civil cases indexed by defendant, plaintiff. Civil records on computer from 1997, index cards back to 1980, archived prior. Index online from JIS-Link; see www.courts.wa.gov/jislink (also, see state introduction).
Criminal Records: Access: Phone, fax, mail, online, in person. Both court and visitors may perform in person searches. No search fee. Required to search: name, years to search; also helpful: DOB. Criminal records on computer from 1997, index cards back to 1990, archived prior. Index remotely online from JIS-Link; see www.courts.wa.gov/jislink (also, see state introduction).
General Information: No sealed, juvenile, adoption, paternity, mental health, sex offenders (victims) or some DUI records released. No fee to fax results. Copy fee: $.25 per page. Cert fee: $5.00. Payee: Wahkiakum District Court. Personal checks accepted. Prepayment required. Mail requests: SASE required. Mail turnaround time 2 days.

Walla Walla County

Superior Court PO Box 836, Walla Walla, WA 99362; 509-527-3221; Fax: 509-527-3214. Hours: 9AM-4PM (PST). *Felony, Civil, Eviction, Probate.*
Civil Records: Access: Phone, mail, online, in person. Only the court performs in person searches; visitors may not. Search fee: $20.00 per hour. Required to search: name, years to search; also helpful: DOB. Civil cases indexed by defendant, plaintiff. Civil records on computer from 7/81, prior in docket books. Index online from JIS-Link; see www.courts.wa.gov/jislink (also, see state introduction).
Criminal Records: Access: Phone, mail, online, in person. Only the court performs in person searches; visitors may not. Search fee: $20.00 per hour. Required to search: name, years to search, DOB; also helpful: address, SSN. Criminal records on computer from 7/81, prior in docket books. Index remotely online from JIS-Link; see www.courts.wa.gov/jislink (also, see state introduction).
General Information: No sealed, juvenile, adoption, paternity, mental health, sex offenders (victims). Copy fee: $2.00 for first page, $1.00 each add'l. Cert fee: $2.00 plus $1.00 each add'l page. Payee: Walla Walla County Clerk. Personal checks not accepted; only cashiers checks and money orders accepted. Prepayment required. Mail turnaround time 1 day.

District Court 317 W Rose St, Walla Walla, WA 99362; 509-527-3236. Hours: 9AM-4PM (PST). *Misdemeanor, Civil Actions Under $50,000, Small Claims.*
Civil Records: Access: Mail, online, in person. Only the court performs in person searches; visitors may not. Search fee: $5.00 per name. Required to search: name, years to search. Civil cases indexed by defendant, plaintiff. Civil records on computer from 7/87, on index books. Records retained for 10 years. Index online from JIS-Link; see www.courts.wa.gov/jislink (also, see state introduction).
Criminal Records: Access: Mail, online, in person. Only the court performs in person searches; visitors may not. Search fee: $5.00 per name. Required to search: name, years to search, signed release; also helpful: address, DOB, SSN. Criminal records on computer from 7/87, on index books. Records retained for 10 years. Index remotely online from JIS-Link; see www.courts.wa.gov/jislink (also, see state introduction).
General Information: No sealed, juvenile, adoption, paternity, mental health, sex offenders (victims) or some DUI records released. Copy fee: $1.00 for first page, $.50 each add'l. Cert fee: $5.00. Payee: Walla Walla District Court. Personal checks accepted. Prepayment required. Mail requests: SASE required. Mail turnaround time 1-3 days.

Whatcom County

Superior Court PO Box 1144, Bellingham, WA 98227; 360-676-6777; Fax: 360-676-6693. Hours: 8:30-4:30PM (PST). *Felony, Civil, Eviction, Probate.*
Note: Extension 50014 for criminal; 50018 for civil.
Civil Records: Access: Phone, fax, mail, online, in person. Only the court performs in person searches; visitors may not. No search fee if record is on computer. Required to search: name, years to search; also helpful: address. Civil cases indexed by defendant, plaintiff. Civil records on computer from 1980, archives back to 1800s, index cards. Index online from JIS-Link; see www.courts.wa.gov/jislink (also, see state introduction).
Criminal Records: Access: Phone, fax, mail, online, in person. Only the court performs in person searches; visitors may not. No search fee. Required to search:

name, years to search; also helpful: address, DOB, SSN. Criminal records on computer from 1980, archives back to 1800s, index cards. Index remotely online from JIS-Link; see www.courts.wa.gov/jislink (also, see state introduction).

General Information: No sealed, juvenile, adoption, paternity, mental health, sex offenders (victims). Copy fee: $2.00 for first page, $1.00 each add'l. Cert fee: Included in copy fee. Payee: Whatcom County Clerk. Only cashiers checks and money orders accepted. Prepayment required. Mail requests: SASE required. Mail turnaround time up to 1 week.

District Court 311 Grand Ave #401, Bellingham, WA 98225; 360-676-6770; Fax: 360-738-2452. Hours: 8AM-4:30PM (PST). *Misdemeanor, Civil Actions Under $50,000, Small Claims.*
www.co.whatcom.wa.us
Civil Records: Access: Mail, online, in person. Only the court performs in person searches; visitors may not. No search fee. Required to search: name, years to search; also helpful: address. Civil cases indexed by defendant, plaintiff. Civil records on computer since 1984. Index online from JIS-Link; see www.courts.wa.gov/jislink (also, see state introduction).
Criminal Records: Access: Mail, online, in person. Only the court performs in person searches; visitors may not. No search fee. Required to search: name, years to search; also helpful: address, DOB, SSN. Criminal records on computer 10 years back, archived since 1984. Index remotely online from JIS-Link; see www.courts.wa.gov/jislink (also, see state introduction).
General Information: No sealed, juvenile, adoption, paternity, mental health, sex offenders (victims) or some DUI records released. Copy fee: $.25 per page. Cert fee: $5.00. Payee: Whatcom District Court. Personal checks accepted. Prepayment required. Mail turnaround time 2 days.

Whitman County

Superior Court Whitman County Clerk, PO Box 390, Colfax, WA 99111; 509-397-6240; Fax: 509-397-3546. Hours: 9AM-5PM (PST). *Felony, Civil, Eviction, Probate.*
Civil Records: Access: Phone, fax, mail, online, in person. Only the court performs in person searches; visitors may not. Search fee: $8.00 per hour. Required to search: name, years to search; also helpful: address. Civil cases indexed by defendant, plaintiff. Civil records on computer from 1985, archives back to 1887. Index online from JIS-Link; see www.courts.wa.gov/jislink (also, see state introduction).
Criminal Records: Access: Phone, fax, mail, online, in person. Only the court performs in person searches; visitors may not. Search fee: $8.00 per hour. Required to search: name, years to search, signed release; also helpful: address, DOB, SSN. Criminal records on computer from 1985, archives back to 1887. Index remotely online from JIS-Link; see www.courts.wa.gov/jislink (also, see state introduction).

General Information: No sealed, juvenile, adoption, paternity, mental health, sex offenders (victims). Will fax results $4.00 for 1st page, $1.00 each add'l. Copy fee: $.15 per page. Cert fee: $2.00 plus $1.00 per page after first. Payee: Whitman County Clerk. Personal checks accepted. Prepayment required. Mail requests: SASE required. Mail turnaround time 1 week.

District Court 400 N Main St, PO Box 230, Colfax, WA 99111; 509-397-6260; Fax: 509-397-5584. Hours: 8AM-5PM; Public Hours: 8:30AM-4:30PM (PST). *Misdemeanor, Civil Actions Under $50,000, Small Claims.*
Civil Records: Access: Phone, fax, mail, online, in person. Only the court performs in person searches; visitors may not. Search fee: $8.00 per hour. Required to search: name, years to search; also helpful: address. Civil cases indexed by defendant, plaintiff. Civil records on DISCIS computer system from 7/91, prior on index log. Index online from JIS-Link; see www.courts.wa.gov/jislink (also, see state introduction).
Criminal Records: Access: Phone, fax, mail, online, in person. Only the court performs in person searches; visitors may not. Search fee: $8.00 per hour. Required to search: name, years to search, DOB; also helpful: address, SSN. Criminal records on DISCIS computer system from 7/91, prior on index log. Index remotely online from JIS-Link; see www.courts.wa.gov/jislink (also, see state introduction).
General Information: Public Access terminal is available. No sealed, juvenile, adoption, paternity, mental health, sex offenders (victims) or some DUI records released. Fee to fax results is $3.00. Copy fee: $.15 per page. Cert fee: $6.00. Payee: Whitman County. Personal checks accepted. Prepayment required. Mail requests: SASE required. Mail turnaround time 2 weeks.

District Court 325 SE Paradise St, Pullman, WA 99163; 509-332-2065; Fax: 509-338-3318. Hours: 8AM-5PM (PST). *Misdemeanor, Civil Actions Under $50,000, Small Claims.*
Civil Records: Access: Fax, mail, online, in person. Only the court performs in person searches; visitors may not. Search fee: $8.00 per hour. Required to search: name, years to search; also helpful: address. Civil cases indexed by defendant, plaintiff. Civil records on DISCIS computer system from 7/91; '89-'91 on index. Index online from JIS-Link; see www.courts.wa.gov/jislink (also, see state introduction).
Criminal Records: Access: Fax, mail, online, in person. Only the court performs in person searches; visitors may not. Search fee: $8.00 per hour. Required to search: name, years to search, DOB; also helpful: address, DOB, SSN. Criminal records on DISCIS computer system from 7/91; '89-'91 on index. Index remotely online from JIS-Link; see www.courts.wa.gov/jislink (also, see state introduction).
General Information: No sealed, juvenile, adoption, paternity, mental health, sex offenders (victims) or some DUI records released. No fee to fax results. Copy fee: $.15 per page. Cert fee: $6.00. Payee: Whitman District Court. Personal checks accepted.

Prepayment required. Mail requests: SASE required. Mail turnaround time 1 week.

Yakima County

Superior Court 128 N 2nd St, Rm 314, Yakima, WA 98901; 509-574-1430. Hours: 8:30AM-4:30PM (PST). *Felony, Civil, Domestic Relations, Probate.*
www.pan.co.yakima.wa.us/clerk
Civil Records: Access: Phone, mail, in person. Only the court performs in person searches; visitors may not. Search fee: $20.00 per hour. Required to search: name, years to search. Civil cases indexed by defendant, plaintiff. Civil records on computer from 1978, archives back to 1890s. Index online from JIS-Link; see www.courts.wa.gov/jislink (also, see state introduction).
Criminal Records: Access: Phone, mail, in person. Only the court performs in person searches; visitors may not. Search fee: $20.00 per hour. Required to search: name, years to search; also helpful: DOB. Criminal records on computer from 1978, archives back to 1890s. Index remotely online from JIS-Link; see www.courts.wa.gov/jislink (also, see state introduction).
General Information: Public Access terminal is available. No sealed, juvenile, adoption, paternity, mental health, sex offenders (victims). Copy fee: $.15 per page. Microfilm copies $.25 per page. Cert fee: $2.00 plus $1.00 per page after first. Payee: Yakima County Clerk. Business checks accepted, personal checks are not. Prepayment required. Mail requests: SASE required. Mail turnaround time varies.

District Court 128 N 2nd St, Rm 217, Yakima, WA 98901-2631; 509-574-1800; Fax: 509-574-1831. Hours: 8:30AM-4:30PM (PST). *Misdemeanor, Civil Actions Under $50,000, Small Claims.*
www.co.yakima.wa.us/courts
Civil Records: Access: Phone, fax, mail, online, in person. Both court and visitors may perform in person searches. No search fee. Required to search: name, years to search; also helpful: address. Civil cases indexed by defendant, plaintiff. Civil records on computer from 1984, generally. Index online from JIS-Link; see www.courts.wa.gov/jislink (also, see state introduction). Requests must be in writing.
Criminal Records: Access: Phone, fax, mail, online, in person. Both court and visitors may perform in person searches. No search fee. Required to search: name, years to search, DOB; also helpful: address, case number, DRL, SSN. Criminal records on computer from 1984, generally. Index remotely online from JIS-Link; see www.courts.wa.gov/jislink (also, see state introduction). Requests must be in writing.
General Information: No sealed or some DUI records released. No fee to fax results. Copy fee: $.15 per page. Cert fee: $5.00. Payee: Yakima County District Court. Personal checks accepted. Credit cards accepted: Visa. Prepayment required. Mail requests: SASE requested. Turnaround time 2 days.

Washington Recording Offices

ORGANIZATION: 39 counties, 39 recording offices. The recording officer is County Auditor. County records are usually combined in a Grantor/Grantee index. The entire state is in the Pacific Time Zone (PST).

REAL ESTATE RECORDS: Many County Auditors will perform real estate searches, including record owner. Search fees and copy fees vary. Copies usually cost $1.00 per page and $2.00 for certification per document. If the Auditor does not provide searches, contact the Assessor for record owner information. Contact the Treasurer (Finance Department in King County) for information about unpaid real estate taxes.

UCC RECORDS: Financing statements are filed at the state level, except for real estate related collateral, which are filed with the County Auditor. Most recording offices will perform UCC searches. Use search request form UCC-11R. Searches fees vary, copy fee is usually $1.00.

TAX LIEN RECORDS: All federal tax liens on personal property are filed with the Department of Licensing. Other federal and all state tax liens are filed with the County Auditor. Most counties will perform tax lien searches. Search fees are usually $8.00 or $10.00 per hour.

ONLINE ACCESS: A number of counties offer access to assessor or real estate records including the larger population counties.

Adams County

County Auditor, 210 W Broadway, Ritzville, WA 99169. **Phone**-509-659-3247; fax-509-659-3254; hours 8:30AM-4:30PM www.co.adams.wa.us
UCC records search per debtor- $8.00. Tax liens not included in UCC search. Tax lien search- $8.00. Will search real estate records. Copy fee- $1.00 per page. Cert fee: $3.00 per doc. Payee: County Auditor. **Online Access to Property, Sale records:** Access to county property tax and sales records is free at www.co.adams.wa.us. No name searching. **Other phones:** Elections-509-659-3247.

Asotin County

County Auditor, PO Box 129, Asotin, WA 99402. **Phone**-509-243-2084, R/E Recording-509-246-2084; fax-509-243-2087; 9AM-5PM www.co.asotin.wa.us
UCC records search per debtor- $10.00. Separate tax lien search $10.00 per debtor. Will search real estate records. Copy fee-$1.00 per page. Copy fee is $1.00 per page. Cert fee: $3.00 per doc. Payee: Asotin County Auditor. **Other phones:** Assessor-509-243-2016; Treasurer-509-243-2014; Elections-509-243-2084; Vital Records-509-243-2084.

Benton County

County Auditor, PO Box 470, Prosser, WA 99350. **Phone**-County Auditor, R/E & UCC Recording- 509-786-5616; fax-509-786-5528; hours 8AM-5PM
The county also has a second recording office located at 5600 W. Canal, Ste B, Kennewick, WA 99336. UCC records search per debtor- $8.00 per hour. UCC search includes tax liens if requested. Separate state/federal Tax lien search- $8.00 per hour. Will search real estate records. Real estate copy fee- $1.00 per page. UCC copy- $1.00 per page. Cert fee: $2.00 per doc. Payee: Benton County Auditor. **Online Access to Assessor, Property records:** County assessor data is free at http://bentonpropertymax.governmaxa.com/propertymax/rover30.asp. Search by parcel ID#, address or map; no nmae searching. **Other phones:** Assessor-509-786-2046; Treasurer-509-786-2255; Elections-509-786-5618; Vital Records-509-786-5616.

Chelan County

County Auditor, PO Box 400, Wenatchee, WA 98807. **Phone**-County Auditor, R/E & UCC Recording- 509-667-6815; fax-509-667-6244; hours 9AM-5PM www.co.chelan.wa.us
UCC records search per debtor- $8.00 per hour; 1 hour min. Tax lien search- $8.00 per hour. Will search real estate records. Copy fee- $1.00 per page.
Cert fee: $2.00 per doc. Payee: Chelan County Auditor. **Online Access to Grantor/Grantee, Property, Marriage records:** Access to the Auditor's iCRIS database is free at www.co.chelan.wa.us/ad/ad5da.htm. Images go back to 1990; marriage images to 1990; earlier online records show indexing information only. **Other phones:** Assessor-509-667-6365; Treasurer-509-667-6405; Elections-509-667-6808; Vital Records-360-236-4300.

Clallam County

Recording Dept, 223 E. Fourth St #1, Port Angeles, WA 98362. **Phone**-Recording Dept, R/E & UCC Recording- 360-417-2220; fax-360-417-2517; hours 8:30AM-4:30PM www.clallam.net
UCC records search, information only (per debtor)- $8.00. Information and copy request (per debtor)- $10.00. Federal/state combined tax lien search- $8.00 per debtor. Will not search real estate records. Copy fee- $1.00 per page. Cert fee: $3.00 1st page, $1.00 each add'l. Payee: Clallam County Auditor. **Online Access to Property, Assessor records:** assessor property data is free at www.clallam.net/RealEstate/html/land_parcel_search.htm; search by address or property number only. Auditor property maps are also downloadable at www.clallam.net/RealEstate/html/recorded_maps.htm. Auditor records will be online at a later date. **Other phones:** Assessor-360-417-2204; Treasurer-360-417-2250; Elections-360-417-2217; Vital Records-360-417-2303.

Clark County

County Auditor, PO Box 5000, Vancouver, WA 98666-5000. **Phone**-County Auditor, R/E & UCC Recording- 360-397-2208; fax-360-397-6007; hours 8AM-5PM www.co.clark.wa.us/auditor/
Recording index, 1978 forward. UCC records search per debtor- $8.00. Tax lien search- $8.00. Will not search real estate records. Record copy- $1.00 per page. Cert fee: $2.00 per doc. Payee: Clark County Auditor. **Online Access to Real Estate, Lien, Vital Statistic, Recording, Most Wanted, Sex Offender records:** Access to County Auditor's database is at http://auditor.co.clark.wa.us/auditor_new/index.cfm.
Court documents are excluded from this index. Also, search maps online for property data at http://gis.clark.wa.gov/ccgis/mol/property.htm. No name searching. **Other phones:** Assessor-360-397-2391; Treasurer-360-397-2252; Elections-360-397-2345; Vital Records-360-397-2243; Auditor Main Line-360-397-2241.

Columbia County

County Auditor, 341 E. Main St., Dayton, WA 99328-1361. **Phone**-County Auditor, R/E & UCC Recording-509-382-4541; fax-509-382-4830; hours 8:30AM-4:30PM www.columbiaco.com
Will search UCC records. Information request- $8.00. UCC search includes tax liens if requested. Separate state/federal Tax lien search- $8.00 per hour. Will not search real estate records. Record copy- $1.00 per page. Cert fee: $2.00 per doc. Payee: Columbia County Auditor. **Other phones:** Assessor-509-382-2131; Treasurer-509-382-2641; Elections-509-382-4541.

Cowlitz County

County Auditor, 207 Fourth Ave North, Kelso, WA 98626. **Phone**-County Auditor, R/E & UCC Recording- 360-577-3006; fax-360-414-5552; hours 8:30AM-5PM www.co.cowlitz.wa.us/auditor/
UCC records search per debtor- $8.00 per hour. UCC search includes tax liens if requested. Separate state/federal Tax lien search- $8.00 per hour. Real estate record owner and mortgage searches available. Record copy- $1.00 per page. Cert fee: $2.00 per doc. Payee: Cowlitz County Auditor. **Online Access to Most Wanted, Missing Person records:** Access to sheriff's most wanted, registered sex offender and missing persons lists is free at www.co.cowlitz.wa.us/sheriff/. Also, county building permits list at http://cowlitz.solidweb.com/permits/permitsearch.asp. **Other phones:** Assessor-360-577-3010; Treasurer-360-577-3060; Elections-360-577-3002; Vital Records-360-577-5599.

Douglas County

County Auditor, PO Box 456, Waterville, WA 98858. **Phone**-509-745-8527, R/E Recording-509-745-8527 x204, UCC Recording-509-745-8527 x204; fax-509-745-8812; hours-8:30AM-4PM www.douglascountywa.net
UCC records search per debtor- $8.00 per title. Will search tax lien. Federal/state combined tax lien search- $8.00 per title. Will search real estate records. Real estate copy fee- $1.00 per page. Copy fee is $1.00 per page. Cert fee: $3.00 1st page, $1.00 each add'l. Payee: Douglas County Auditor. **Online Access to Assessor, Plat, Property records:** Access to the County Parcel Search is free at http://douglaswa.taxsifter.com/taxsifter/T-Parcelsearch.asp (may be temporarily down). **Other phones:** Assessor-509-745-8521; Treasurer-509-745-8525; Elections-509-745-8527 x203; Vital Records-509-745-8527 x204.

Ferry County

County Auditor, 350 E. Delaware #2, Republic, WA 99166. **Phone-**509-775-5200, R/E Recording-509-775-5202, UCC Recording-509-775-5202; fax-509-775-5208; hours 8AM-4PM

Will not search records. RE record copy- $1.00 per page. Cert fee: $3.00 1st page, $1.00 each add'l. Payee: Ferry County Auditor. **Other phones:** Assessor-509-775-5203; Treasurer-509-775-5238; Elections-509-775-5208; Vital Records-509-775-5200.

Franklin County

County Auditor, PO Box 1451, Pasco, WA 99301. **Phone-**County Auditor, R/E & UCC Recording- 509-545-3536; fax-509-545-3529; hours 8:30AM-5PM

Will not search records. Record copy- $1.00 per page. Cert fee: $3.00 1st page; $1 each add'l. Payee: Franklin County Auditor. **Online Access to Assessor, Property, Sex Offender records:** Search for property information by address or parcel number at www.co.franklin.wa.us/assessor. Also, search for residential sales data. Also, search level 2 sex offenders at www.co.franklin.wa.us/sheriff/?p=14&v=2. Level 3 offender at www.co.franklin.wa.us/sheriff/?p=14&v=3. **Other phones:** Assessor-509-545-3506; Treasurer-509-545-3518; Elections-509-545-3538; Vital Records-509-586-0207 X229.

Garfield County

County Auditor, PO Box 278, Pomeroy, WA 99347-0278. **Phone-**County Auditor, R/E & UCC Recording-509-843-1411; fax-509-843-3941; 8:30AM-5PM

Will look us records if customer knows recording number. Will not search records. Record copy- $1.00 per page. Cert fee: $2.00 per cert. Payee: Garfield County Auditor. **Other phones:** Assessor-509-843-3632; Treasurer-509-843-1531; Elections-509-843-1411; Vital Records-509-843-1411.

Grant County

County Auditor, PO Box 37, Ephrata, WA 98823. **Phone-**509-754-2011 x336; hours 8AM-5PM

UCC records search per debtor- $8.00. Will not search real estate or tax lien records. Record copy- $1.00 per page. Cert fee: $3.00 1st page, $1.00 each add'l. Payee: Grant County Auditor. **Other phones:** Assessor-509-754-2011 x310; Treasurer-509-754-2011 x353; Elections-509-754-2011 x377.

Grays Harbor County

County Auditor, 101 W. Broadway, #2, Montesano, WA 98563. **Phone-**360-249-4232 x331, R/E Recording-360-249-4232, UCC Recording-360-249-4232; fax-360-249-3330.

UCC records search per debtor- $8.00. Tax lien search- $8.00 per debtor, per hour. Will not search real estate records. UCC copy- $1.00 per page. Cert fee: $3.00 for 1st page, $1.00 each add'l pg. **Online Access to Assessor, Treasurer, Property Tax records:** the county Parcel Database is free at http://bentonpropertymax.governmaxa.com/propertymax/rover30.asp. Search by parcel ID#, address, legal description, but no name searching. **Other phones:** Assessor-360-249-4121; Treasurer-360-249-3751; Elections-360-249-4232.

Island County

Deputy Auditor, PO Box 5000, Coupeville, WA 98239. **Phone-**Deputy Auditor, R/E & UCC Recording- 360-679-7366; fax-360-240-5553; hours 8AM-4:30PM www.islandcounty.net/auditor/index.htm

Will not search UCC records due to incompleteness of their records. Tax lien search- $8.00 per 30 minutes. Will not search real estate records. Copy fee- $1.00 per page. Cert fee: $3.00 + $1.00 per page. Payee: Island County Auditor. **Online Access to Sex Offender records:** Search sexual offenders and kidnappers lists at www.islandcounty.net/sheriff/rsolist.htm. **Other phones:** Assessor-360-679-7303; Treasurer-360-678-5111; Elections-360-679-7366.

Jefferson County

County Auditor, PO Box 563, Port Townsend, WA 98368. **Phone-**County Auditor, R/E & UCC Recording- 360-385-9116; fax-360-385-9228; hours 8AM-5PM www.co.jefferson.wa.us/auditor/recording/Recording.asp

UCC records search per debtor- $8.00. UCC search includes tax liens. Separate federal/state combined tax lien search- $8.00 per debtor Will search single real estate records but not for a title company. RE record copy- Copy fee is $1.00 per page. Cert fee: $3.00 1st page; $1.00 each add'l. Payee: Jefferson County Auditor. **Online Access to Assessor, Real Estate, Recording, Vital Statistic, Grantor/Grantee, Lien, Deed, UCC, Permit, Voter Registration. records:** "Recorded Document Search" database at www.co.jefferson.wa.us/_hidden/disclaimer.htm. Includes records on the County Property (Tax Parcel) Database Tool as well as plats and survey images. Also, search for building permits but no name searching. Search Voter registration records at www.co.jefferson.wa.us/auditor/elections/VoterRegCard.asp. **Other phones:** Assessor-360-385-9105; Treasurer-360-385-9150; Elections-360-385-9119.

King County

Superintendent of Records, 500 4th Ave, Admin. Bldg, Rm 311, Seattle, WA 98104. **Phone-**Superintendent of Records, R/E & UCC Recording- 206-296-1570; fax-206-205-8396; 8:30AM-4:30PM www.metrokc.gov

UCC records search per debtor- $8.00 per 5-year search. Will not search tax liens. Will search real estate records. Copy fee- $1.00 per page. Cert fee: $3.00 per copy. Payee: King County Recorder's Office. **Online Access to Real Estate, Lien, Marriage, Recorder, Deed, Judgment, Vital Statistic records:** Access to the county recorder's database is free at www.metrokc.gov/recelec/records or at http://146.129.54.93:8193/localization/menu.asp. Also, property records on Dept. of Developmental and Environmental Resources database are free at www.metrokc.gov/ddes/gis/parcel. After the disclaimer page, search by parcel number, address, street, or map. **Other phones:** Assessor-206-296-7300; Treasurer-206-296-3850; Elections-206-296-1565; Vital Records-206-296-4768; Finance Dept-206-296-3850.

Kitsap County

County Auditor, 614 Division St, Rm 106 /MS 31, Port Orchard, WA 98366. **Phone-**360-337-4935, R/E Recording-360-337-7133; fax-360-337-4645; hours 8AM-4:30PM www.kitsapgov.com/aud/default.htm

UCC records search per debtor- $8.00. UCC search includes tax liens if requested. Separate federal/state combined tax lien search- $8.00 per debtor. Will not search real estate records. UCC copy- $1.00 per page. Cert fee: $3.00 1st page, $1.00 each add'l. Payee: Kitsap County Auditor. **Online Access to Auditor, Property Tax, Grantor/Grantee, Recording, Deed, Lien, Vital Statistic, Judgment records:** Access to the auditor's recording database is free at http://kcwppub4.co.kitsap.wa.us/icris/splash.jsp. Fee to print official documents. Searches can also be performed for property and tax information on the land information system site at http://kcwppub3.co.kitsap.wa.us/website/assessor/search.asp. No name searching. **Other phones:** Assessor-360-876-7160; Treasurer-360-876-7135; Elections-360-337-7128.

Kittitas County

County Auditor, 205 W. 5th, RM #105, Ellensburg, WA 98926-3129. **Phone-**County Auditor, R/E & UCC Recording- 509-962-7504; fax-509-962-7687; hours 9AM-5PM www.co.kittitas.wa.us/

UCC records search per debtor- $8.00. Tax liens not included in UCC search. Tax lien search- $8.00 per debtor. Will search real estate records. Copy fee- $1.00 per page. Cert fee: $3.00 1st page. **Other phones:** Assessor-509-962-7501; Treasurer-509-962-7535; Elections-509-962-7503; Vital Records-509-962-7504; Health Department-509-962-7515.

Klickitat County

County Auditor, 205 S. Columbus Ave, MS-CH-2, Goldendale, WA 98620. **Phone-**County Auditor, R/E & UCC Recording- 509-773-4001; fax-509-773-4244; hours 9AM-5PM www.klickitatcounty.org

UCC records search per debtor- $8.00 per hour. Tax liens not included in UCC search. Tax lien search- $8.00 per hour. Will search real estate records. Record copy- $1.00 per copy. **Other phones:** Assessor-509-773-3715; Treasurer-509-773-4664; Elections-509-773-4001; Vital Records-509-773-4001; Toll Free Auditor-800-583-8050.

Lewis County

County Auditor, PO Box 29, Chehalis, WA 98532-0029. **Phone-**County Auditor, R/E & UCC Recording-360-740-1163; fax-360-740-1421; hours 8AM-5PM

UCC records search per debtor- $8.00 per 10 years. Tax liens not included in UCC search. Tax lien search- $8.00 per debtor per 10 years. Will search real estate records; fees must be prepaid. Record copy fee- $1.00 per page. **Other phones:** Assessor-360-740-1392; Treasurer-360-740-1115.

Lincoln County

County Auditor, PO Box 28, Davenport, WA 99122. **Phone-**County Auditor, R/E & UCC Recording- 509-725-4971; fax-509-725-0820; hours 8AM-5PM

UCC records search per debtor- $11.00. Tax liens not included in UCC search. Tax lien search- $8.00 per hour. Will search real estate records. Copy fee- $1.00 per page. Cert fee: $3.00 1st page, $1.00 each add'l. Payee: Lincoln County Auditor. **Other phones:** Assessor-509-725-7011; Treasurer-509-725-5061; Elections-Vital Records-509-725-4971.

Mason County

County Auditor, PO Box 400, Shelton, WA 98584. **Phone-**360-427-9670, R/E Recording-360-427-9670 x467, UCC Recording-360-427-9670 x467; fax-360-427-8425; hours 8:30AM - 4:30PM http://auditor.co.mason.wa.us

Will search UCC records. Search fee-$8.00 per hour. Tax liens not included in UCC search. Tax lien search- $8.00 per hour. Will search real estate records. Copy fee- $1.00 per page. Cert fee: $3.00 for 1st page. Payee: Mason County Auditor. **Online Access to Assessor, Property records:** Access to the Assessor data is free at www.co.mason.wa.us/disclaimer.php. Also, auditor records from 1985 to 2004 are at www.auditor.co.mason.wa.us. **Other phones:** Assessor-360-427-9670 x491; Treasurer-360-427-9670 x484; Elections-360-427-9670 x469; Vital Records-360-427-9670 x467.

Okanogan County

County Auditor, PO Box 1010, Okanogan, WA 98840. **Phone-**509-422-7240; fax-509-422-7163; hours 8:30AM-5PM

UCC records search per debtor- $10.00. Will not search real estate or tax lien records. Record copy- $1.00 per page. Cert fee: $2.00 for 1st page. Payee: Okanogan County Auditor. **Online Access to Assessor, Property records:** Access to county assessment data is free at www.metrokc.gov/recelec/records/. As of 1/2004, only 50% of the physical real property physical addresses are available. **Other phones:** Assessor-509-422-7190; Treasurer-509-422-7180.

Pacific County

County Auditor, PO Box 97, South Bend, WA 98586-9903. **Phone**-County Auditor, R/E & UCC Recording-360-875-9318; fax-360-875-9333; hours 8:30AM-4:30PM www.co.pacific.wa.us/directory.htm
UCC records search per debtor- $8.00. Tax liens not included in UCC search. Separate federal/state combined tax lien search- $8.00 per debtor. Will not perform title searches of real estate records; will search for individual documents. Record copy- $1.00 per page. Cert fee: $3.00 per 1st page, $1.00 each add'l. Payee: Pacific County Auditor. **Other phones:** Assessor-360-875-9301; Treasurer-360-875-9421; Elections-360-875-9317; Vital Records-360-875-9318.

Pend Oreille County

County Auditor, PO Box 5015, Newport, WA 99156. **Phone**-County Auditor, R/E & UCC Recording- 509-447-3185; fax-509-447-2475; hours 8AM-4:30PM
UCC records search per debtor- $8.00 per hour. Tax liens with County Treasurer. Will search real estate records. Record copy- $1.00 per page. Cert fee: $3.00 per doc. Payee: Pend Oreille County Auditor. **Other phones:** Assessor-509-447-4312; Treasurer-509-447-3612; Elections-509-447-3185; Vital Records-360-236-4300.

Pierce County

County Auditor, 2401 S. 35th St, Rm 200, Tacoma, WA 98409. **Phone**-253-798-7440, R/E &-UCC Recording-206-591-7440; fax-253-798-2761; hours-8:30AM-4:30PM www.piercecountywa.org/auditor
UCC records search per debtor- $8.00 per hour. Tax lien search- $8.00 per hour. Will search real estate records. Cert/copy fee: $3.00 1st page, $1.00 each add'l. Payee: Pierce County Auditor. **Online Access to Assessor, Real Estate, Recording, Deed, Lien, Vital Statistic, Judgment, Assumed Name, Inmate records:** Search auditor's recording database for free at http://hartweb.piercecountywa.org/search.asp?cabinet= opr. Also, property records on County Assessor-Treasurer database are free at www.co.pierce.wa.us/C FApps/atr/TIMSNet/index.htm. After the disclaimer page, search by parcel number or site address. Also, the county sexual offender/kidnappers list is at http://pso.co.pierce.wa.us. Marriage records at http://hartweb.piercecountywa.org/search.asp?cabinet= oprmarriage. Also, search inmate info on private company website at www.vinelink.com/index.jsp. **Other phones:** Assessor-253-798-6111; Treasurer-253-798-6111; Elections-253-798-7430.

San Juan County

County Auditor, PO Box 638, Friday Harbor, WA 98250. **Phone**-360-378-2161; fax-360-378-6256; hours 8AM-4:30PM www.co.san-juan.wa.us
UCC records search per debtor- $8.00 per hour. UCC search includes tax liens if requested. Separate federal/state combined tax lien search- $8.00 per hour. Will not search real estate records. UCC copy- $1.00 per page. Cert fee: $3.00 1st page; $1.00 each add'l. Payee: San Juan County Auditor. **Online Access to Assessor, Property Tax, Auditor, Real Estate, Deed, Lien records:** Online access to assessor property records is free at www.co.san-juan.wa.us/assessor/rpsrch.asp?tp=N. No name searching. Also, access to the auditor database of real estate recording records is free at http://sjc-imaging.rockisland.com/SJCdocSearch/?. Images go back to 1997; index back to 1/1984. **Other phones:** Assessor-360-378-4729; Treasurer-360-378-2171.

Skagit County

County Auditor, PO Box 1306, Mount Vernon, WA 98273-1306. **Phone**-360-336-9420, R/E Recording-360-336-9311, UCC Recording-360-336-9311; fax-360-336-9429; hours-8:30AM-4:30PM www.skagitcounty.net
UCC records search per debtor- $8.00. UCC search includes tax liens if requested. Separate state/federal Tax lien search- $10.00 per debtor. Will search for specific real estate records only; no title searches. Copy fee- $1.00 per page. Cert fee: $2.00 per doc. Payee: Skagit County Auditor. **Online Access to Recording, Property Tax, Assessor, Treasurer, Deed, Lien, Vital Statistic records:** Assessor, Treasurer, Auditor's recorded documents as well as permits are all free at www.skagitcounty.net; click on Records Search. **Other phones:** Assessor-360-336-9370; Treasurer-360-336-9350; Elections-360-336-9305; Vital Records-360-336-9380.

Skamania County

County Auditor, PO Box 790, Stevenson, WA 98648-0790. **Phone**-County Auditor, R/E & UCC Recording-509-427-9420; fax-509-427-4165; 8:30AM-5PM www.wacounties.org/waco/county/skamania.html
UCC records search per debtor- $8.00 per hour. **Other phones:** Assessor-509-427-9400; Treasurer-509-427-9410; Elections-Vital Records-509-427-9420.

Snohomish County

County Auditor, 3000 Rockefeller Ave, Dept. R, M/S #204, Everett, WA 98201. **Phone**-425-388-3483 press 0, R/E Recording-425-388-3483 x0, UCC Recording-425-388-3483; fax-425-259-2777; hours 9AM-5PM http://www1.co.snohomish.wa.us/Departments/Auditor/
UCC records search per debtor- $8.00. Tax liens not included in UCC search. Separate federal/state combined tax lien search- $8.00 per debtor. Mortgage and property transfer searches available. UCC copy- $1.00 per page. Cert fee: $2.00 per doc. Payee: Snohomish County Auditor. **Online Access to Real Estate, Assessor, Recording, Marriage, Jail, Offender, Jail Booking records:** Access to the Auditor's office database is free at http://198.238.192.100/localization/menu.asp. Search on the recorded documents or marriage icons. Also, search the assessor property data for free at http://web5.co.snohomish.wa.us/propsys/asr-tr-propinq/ - no name searching. Search county sheriff jail register www1.co.snohomish.wa.us/Departments/Corrections/Services/default.htm. **Other phones:** Assessor-425-388-3433; Treasurer-425-388-3366; Elections-425-388-3444.

Spokane County

County Auditor, W 1116 Broadway, Spokane, WA 99260. **Phone**-County Auditor, R/E & UCC Recording- 509-477-2270; fax-509-477-6451; hours 8:30AM-5:00PM www.spokanecounty.org/auditor
UCC records search per debtor- $8.00. Tax liens not included in UCC search. Tax lien search- $8.00 per hour (1 hour min.). Will search real estate records. Record copy- $1.00 per page. Cert fee: $3.00 1st page; $1.00 each add'l. **Online Access to Property Tax, Land records:** Search the County Parcel Locator database for free at www.spokanecounty.org/pubpadal/. No name searching. **Other phones:** Assessor-509-477-5793; Treasurer-509-456-4713; Elections-509-477-2320; Vital Records-509-324-1522.

Stevens County

County Auditor, 215 S. Oak St., Colville, WA 99114. **Phone**-County Auditor, R/E & UCC Recording- 509-684-7512; fax-509-684-8310; hours 8AM-4:30PM
UCC records search per debtor- $8.00. UCC search includes tax liens. Separate federal/state combined tax lien search- $8.00 per hour. Real estate owner,

mortgage, and property transfer searches available. Record copy- $1.00 per page. Cert fee: $3.00 1st page; $1.00 each add'l. Payee: Stevens County Auditor. **Other phones:** Assessor-509-684-6161; Treasurer-509-684-2593; Elections-509-684-7514; Vital Records-509-684-7512; Auditor-509-684-7511.

Thurston County

County Auditor, 2000 Lakeridge Drive SW, Olympia, WA 98502. **Phone**-County Auditor, R/E & UCC Recording- 360-786-5405; fax-360-786-5223; hours 8AM-4:30PM www.co.thurston.wa.us/auditor
UCC records search per debtor- $8.00. Federal/state combined tax lien search- $8.00 per debtor. Will search real estate records. Record copy- $1.00 per page. Cert fee: $3 1st page; $1.00 each add'l. Payee: Thurston County Auditor. **Online Access to Assessor, Real Estate, Auditor, Recording records:** Assessor and property information on Thurston GeoData database is free at www.geodata.org/parcelsrch.asp. No name searching. Also, access the Auditor Recording I-CRIS database, no images, at www.co.thurston.wa.us/auditor. Click on online records. **Other phones:** Assessor-360-786-5410; Treasurer-360-786-5550; Elections-360-786-5408; Vital Records-360-786-5481.

Wahkiakum County

County Auditor, PO Box 543, Cathlamet, WA 98612. **Phone**-360-795-3219; fax-360-795-0824; hours 8AM-4PM www.cwcog.org/wahkiakum.html
Will not search records. Record copy- $1.00 per page. Cert fee: $3.00 1st page; $1.00 each add'l. Payee: Wahkiakum County Auditor. **Online Access to Property Sale, Sheriff Warrant records:** The assessor posts a list of property sales back about a year at www.cwcog.org/assessor.html. Click on "Current Property Sales" for the pdf list. Search sheriff's warrant list at www.sd.co.wahkiakum.wa.us. **Other phones:** Assessor-360-795-3791; Treasurer-360-795-8005; Elections-360-795-3219; Vital Records-360-795-6207.

Walla Walla County

County Auditor, PO Box 1856, Walla Walla, WA 99362-0356. **Phone**-County Auditor, R/E & UCC Recording- 509-527-3204; fax-509-526-4806; hours 9AM-4:30PM www.co.walla-walla.wa.us/Departments/auditor/auditor.htm
UCC records search per debtor- $8.00. Federal/state combined tax lien search- $8.00 per hour. Will not search real estate records. UCC copy- $1.00 per page. Cert fee: $3.00 1st page, $1.00 each add'l, per doc. Payee: Walla Walla County Auditor. **Online Access to Property Tax, Assessor, Residential Sale, Farm Sale records:** Access to the TaxSifter parcel Search is free at http://wallawallawa.taxsifter.com/taxsifter/T-Parcelsearch.asp. **Other phones:** Assessor-509-527-3216; Treasurer-509-527-3212; Appraiser/ Auditor-509-527-3216; Elections-509-527-3204.

Whatcom County

County Auditor, 311 Grand Ave #103, Bellingham, WA 98225. **Phone**-360-676-6740, R/E Recording-360-676-6740 x50013, UCC Recording-360-676-6740 x50073; fax-360-738-4556; hours 8:30AM-4:30PA www.co.whatcom.wa.us/auditor
UCC records search per debtor- $8.00. Federal/state combined tax lien search- $8.00 per search. Will search real estate records. Copy fee-$1.00 per page. UCC copy- $1.00 per page. Cert fee: $3.00 1st page, $1.00 each add'l. Payee: Whatcom County Auditor. **Online Access to Assessor, Real Estate, Voter Registration records:** Search the assessor parcel database information system free at www.co.whatcom.wa.us/cgibin/db2www/assessor/search/RPSearch.ndt/disclaimer. Also, acquire voter registration lists for political purposes only; information and request information at

www.co.whatcom.wa.us/auditor/elections/labels_lists/ordering.htm. **Other phones:** Assessor-360-676-6790; Treasurer-360-676-6774; Elections-360-676-6742; Vital Records-360-676-6740.

Whitman County

County Auditor, PO Box 350, Colfax, WA 99111-0350. **Phone-**County Auditor, R/E & UCC Recording-509-397-6270, UCC Recording-509-392-6270; fax-509-397-6351; hours 9AM-5PM (Recording Until 2:30PM) www.whitmancounty.org

UCC records search per debtor- $8.00 per hour. Tax lien search- $8.00 per debtor. Will not search real estate records. Record copy- $1.00 per page. Cert fee: $3.00 1st page, $1.00 each add'l. Payee:

Whitman County Auditor. **Other phones:** Assessor-509-397-6220; Treasurer-509-397-6230; Elections-509-397-6270; Vital Records-509-397-6270.

Yakima County

County Auditor, 128 N. 2nd St, #117, Yakima, WA 98901. **Phone-**County Auditor, R/E & UCC Recording- 509-574-1330; fax-509-574-1341; hours 9AM-4:30PM www.pan.co.yakima.wa.us

Will search UCC records. Information request- $8.00 per name per hour. Federal/state combined tax lien search- $8.00 per debtor per hour. Will search real estate records if supplied with specific document titles. Will not do chain of title or tracking of property. Copy fee- $1.00 per page. Cert fee: $3.00 1st page, $1.00

each add'l. Payee: Yakima County Auditor. **Online Access to Assessor, Real Estate, Property Tax records:** Assessor and property Assessor data are at www.co.yakima.wa.us/assessor/propinfo/asr_info.asp. No name searching. Also, access the treasurer parcel database free at www.co.yakima.wa.us/treasurer/database/taxes.asp. No name searching. Also, search the sheriff's sex offender list at www.pan.co.yakima.wa.us/Sheriff/soffenders.htm. **Other phones:** Assessor-509-574-1100; Treasurer-509-574-2800; Elections-509-574-1340; Vital Records-509-574-1330.

Washington County Locator

You will usually be able to find the city name in the City/County Cross Reference below. In that case, it is a simple matter to determine the county from the cross reference. However, only the official US Postal Service city names are included in this index. There are an additional 40,000 place names that people use in their addresses. Therefore, we have also included a ZIP/City Cross Reference immediately following the City/County Cross Reference.

If you know the ZIP Code but the city name does not appear in the City/County Cross Reference index, look up the ZIP Code in the ZIP/City Cross Reference, find the city name, then look up the city name in the City/County Cross Reference. For example, you want to know the county for an address of Menands, NY 12204. There is no "Menands" in the City/County Cross Reference. The ZIP/City Cross Reference shows that ZIP Codes 12201-12288 are for the city of Albany. Looking back in the City/County Cross Reference, Albany is in Albany County.

Washington - City/County Cross Reference

ABERDEEN Grays Harbor
ACME Whatcom
ADDY Stevens
ADNA Lewis
AIRWAY HEIGHTS Spokane
ALBION Whitman
ALLYN Mason
ALMIRA (99103) Lincoln(88), Grant(11)
AMANDA PARK Grays Harbor
AMBOY (98601) Clark(98), Cowlitz(1)
ANACORTES Skagit
ANATONE Asotin
ANDERSON ISLAND Pierce
APPLETON Klickitat
ARDENVOIR Chelan
ARIEL Cowlitz
ARLINGTON Snohomish
ASHFORD Pierce
ASOTIN Asotin
AUBURN (98092) King(92), Pierce(7)
AUBURN King
BAINBRIDGE ISLAND Kitsap
BARING King
BATTLE GROUND Clark
BAY CENTER Pacific
BEAVER Clallam
BELFAIR Mason
BELLEVUE King
BELLINGHAM (98229) Whatcom(97), Skagit(2)
BELLINGHAM Whatcom
BELMONT Whitman
BENGE Adams
BENTON CITY Benton
BEVERLY Grant
BICKLETON (99322) Klickitat(96), Yakima(3)
BINGEN (98605) Skamania(72), Klickitat(27)
BLACK DIAMOND King
BLAINE Whatcom
BLAKELY ISLAND San Juan
BOTHELL King
BOTHELL Snohomish
BOW Skagit
BOYDS Ferry
BREMERTON Kitsap
BREWSTER Okanogan
BRIDGEPORT Douglas
BRINNON Jefferson
BROWNSTOWN Yakima
BRUSH PRAIRIE Clark
BUCKLEY Pierce
BUCODA Thurston
BUENA Yakima
BURBANK Walla Walla
BURLEY Kitsap
BURLINGTON Skagit
BURTON King
CAMANO ISLAND Island
CAMAS Clark
CAMP MURRAY Pierce
CARBONADO Pierce
CARLSBORG Clallam
CARLTON Okanogan

CARNATION King
CARROLLS Cowlitz
CARSON Skamania
CASHMERE Chelan
CASTLE ROCK Cowlitz
CATHLAMET Wahkiakum
CENTERVILLE Klickitat
CENTRALIA (98531) Lewis(94), Thurston(5)
CHATTAROY Spokane
CHEHALIS Lewis
CHELAN Chelan
CHELAN FALLS Chelan
CHENEY Spokane
CHEWELAH Stevens
CHIMACUM Jefferson
CHINOOK Pacific
CINEBAR Lewis
CLALLAM BAY Clallam
CLARKSTON Asotin
CLAYTON (99110) Stevens(67), Spokane(32)
CLE ELUM Kittitas
CLEARLAKE Skagit
CLINTON Island
COLBERT Spokane
COLFAX Whitman
COLLEGE PLACE Walla Walla
COLTON Whitman
COLVILLE Stevens
CONCONULLY Okanogan
CONCRETE Skagit
CONNELL (99326) Franklin(91), Adams(8)
CONWAY Skagit
COPALIS BEACH Grays Harbor
COPALIS CROSSING Grays Harbor
COSMOPOLIS (98537) Grays Harbor(98), Pacific(1)
COUGAR Cowlitz
COULEE CITY (99115) Grant(88), Douglas(11)
COULEE DAM (99116) Okanogan(82), Douglas(15), Grant(1)
COUPEVILLE Island
COWICHE Yakima
CRESTON Lincoln
CUNNINGHAM Adams
CURLEW Ferry
CURTIS Lewis
CUSICK Pend Oreille
CUSTER Whatcom
DALLESPORT Klickitat
DANVILLE Ferry
DARRINGTON (98241) Snohomish(82), Skagit(17)
DAVENPORT (99122) Lincoln(89), Stevens(10)
DAYTON Columbia
DEER HARBOR San Juan
DEER PARK (99006) Spokane(87), Stevens(10), Pend Oreille(1)
DEMING Whatcom
DIXIE Walla Walla
DOTY Lewis
DRYDEN Chelan

DUPONT Pierce
DUVALL King
EAST OLYMPIA Thurston
EAST WENATCHEE Douglas
EASTON Kittitas
EASTSOUND San Juan
EATONVILLE Pierce
EDMONDS Snohomish
EDWALL (99008) Lincoln(80), Spokane(19)
ELBE (98330) Pierce(82), Lewis(17)
ELECTRIC CITY Grant
ELK (99009) Spokane(78), Pend Oreille(21)
ELLENSBURG Kittitas
ELMA (98541) Grays Harbor(72), Mason(27)
ELMER CITY Okanogan
ELTOPIA Franklin
ENDICOTT Whitman
ENTIAT Chelan
ENUMCLAW (98022) King(95), Pierce(4)
EPHRATA Grant
ETHEL Lewis
EVANS Stevens
EVERETT Snohomish
EVERSON Whatcom
FAIRCHILD AIR FORCE BASE Spokane
FAIRFIELD Spokane
FALL CITY King
FARMINGTON Whitman
FEDERAL WAY King
FERNDALE Whatcom
FORD (99013) Spokane(51), Stevens(46), Lincoln(1)
FORKS Clallam
FOUR LAKES Spokane
FOX ISLAND Pierce
FREELAND Island
FREEMAN Spokane
FRIDAY HARBOR San Juan
FRUITLAND Stevens
GALVIN Lewis
GARFIELD Whitman
GEORGE Grant
GIFFORD Stevens
GIG HARBOR Pierce
GLENOMA Lewis
GLENWOOD Klickitat
GOLD BAR (98251) Snohomish(96), King(3)
GOLDENDALE Klickitat
GOOSE PRAIRIE Yakima
GRAHAM Pierce
GRAND COULEE (99133) Grant(79), Lincoln(11), Douglas(8)
GRANDVIEW Yakima
GRANGER Yakima
GRANITE FALLS Snohomish
GRAPEVIEW Mason
GRAYLAND (98547) Grays Harbor(98), Pacific(1)
GRAYS RIVER Wahkiakum
GREENACRES Spokane
GREENBANK Island
HAMILTON Skagit

HANSVILLE Kitsap
HARRAH Yakima
HARRINGTON Lincoln
HARTLINE Grant
HATTON Adams
HAY Whitman
HEISSON Clark
HOBART King
HOODSPORT Mason
HOOPER Whitman
HOQUIAM Grays Harbor
HUMPTULIPS Grays Harbor
HUNTERS Stevens
HUSUM Klickitat
ILWACO Pacific
INCHELIUM Ferry
INDEX Snohomish
INDIANOLA Kitsap
IONE Pend Oreille
ISSAQUAH King
JOYCE Clallam
KAHLOTUS Franklin
KALAMA Cowlitz
KAPOWSIN Pierce
KELLER (99140) Ferry(98), Stevens(1)
KELSO Cowlitz
KENMORE King
KENNEWICK Benton
KENT King
KETTLE FALLS (99141) Stevens(88), Ferry(11)
KEYPORT Kitsap
KINGSTON Kitsap
KIRKLAND King
KITTITAS Kittitas
KLICKITAT Klickitat
LA CENTER Clark
LA CONNER Skagit
LA GRANDE Pierce
LA PUSH Clallam
LACEY Thurston
LACROSSE Whitman
LAKE STEVENS Snohomish
LAKEBAY Pierce
LAKEWOOD Pierce
LAKEWOOD Snohomish
LAMONA Lincoln
LAMONT (99017) Whitman(98), Adams(1)
LANGLEY Island
LATAH Spokane
LAURIER Ferry
LEAVENWORTH Chelan
LEBAM Pacific
LIBERTY LAKE Spokane
LILLIWAUP Mason
LIND Adams
LITTLEROCK Thurston
LONG BEACH Pacific
LONGBRANCH Pierce
LONGMIRE Pierce
LONGVIEW Cowlitz
LOOMIS Okanogan
LOON LAKE Stevens
LOPEZ ISLAND San Juan
LUMMI ISLAND Whatcom

LYLE Klickitat
LYMAN Skagit
LYNDEN Whatcom
LYNNWOOD Snohomish
MABTON Yakima
MALAGA Chelan
MALDEN Whitman
MALO Ferry
MALONE Grays Harbor
MALOTT Okanogan
MANCHESTER Kitsap
MANSFIELD Douglas
MANSON Chelan
MAPLE FALLS Whatcom
MAPLE VALLEY King
MARBLEMOUNT Skagit
MARCUS Stevens
MARLIN (98832) Grant(96), Adams(3)
MARSHALL Spokane
MARYSVILLE Snohomish
MATLOCK Mason
MATTAWA Grant
MAZAMA Okanogan
MCCLEARY Grays Harbor
MCKENNA Pierce
MEAD Spokane
MEDICAL LAKE Spokane
MEDINA King
MENLO Pacific
MERCER ISLAND King
MESA Franklin
METALINE Pend Oreille
METALINE FALLS Pend Oreille
METHOW Okanogan
MICA Spokane
MILTON (98354) Pierce(92), King(7)
MINERAL Lewis
MOCLIPS Grays Harbor
MOHLER Lincoln
MONITOR Chelan
MONROE Snohomish
MONTESANO Grays Harbor
MORTON Lewis
MOSES LAKE Grant
MOSSYROCK Lewis
MOUNT VERNON Skagit
MOUNTLAKE TERRACE Snohomish
MOXEE Yakima
MUKILTEO Snohomish
NACHES Yakima
NAHCOTTA Pacific
NAPAVINE Lewis
NASELLE Pacific
NEAH BAY Clallam
NEILTON Grays Harbor
NESPELEM Okanogan
NEWMAN LAKE Spokane
NEWPORT (99156) Pend Oreille(50),
   Spokane(49)
NINE MILE FALLS (99026) Spokane(54),
   Stevens(45)
NOOKSACK Whatcom
NORDLAND Jefferson
NORTH BEND King
NORTH BONNEVILLE Skamania
NORTH LAKEWOOD Snohomish
NORTHPORT Stevens
OAK HARBOR Island

OAKESDALE Whitman
OAKVILLE (98568) Grays Harbor(97),
   Thurston(2)
OCEAN PARK Pacific
OCEAN SHORES Grays Harbor
ODESSA (99159) Lincoln(86), Adams(13)
OKANOGAN Okanogan
OLALLA Kitsap
OLD NATIONAL BANK Spokane
OLGA San Juan
OLYMPIA Thurston
OMAK Okanogan
ONALASKA Lewis
ORCAS San Juan
ORIENT Ferry
ORONDO Douglas
OROVILLE Okanogan
ORTING Pierce
OTHELLO (99344) Adams(77), Grant(16),
   Franklin(5)
OTIS ORCHARDS Spokane
OUTLOOK Yakima
OYSTERVILLE Pacific
PACIFIC (98047) King(92), Pierce(7)
PACIFIC BEACH Grays Harbor
PACKWOOD Lewis
PALISADES Douglas
PALOUSE Whitman
PARADISE INN Pierce
PARKER Yakima
PASCO Franklin
PATEROS Okanogan
PATERSON Benton
PE ELL Lewis
PESHASTIN Chelan
PLYMOUTH Benton
POINT ROBERTS Whatcom
POMEROY (99347) Garfield(89),
   Columbia(4), Asotin(3), Whitman(1)
PORT ANGELES Clallam
PORT GAMBLE Kitsap
PORT HADLOCK Jefferson
PORT LUDLOW Jefferson
PORT ORCHARD Kitsap
PORT TOWNSEND Jefferson
POULSBO Kitsap
PRESCOTT Walla Walla
PRESTON King
PROSSER (99350) Benton(96), Klickitat(3)
PULLMAN Whitman
PUYALLUP Pierce
QUILCENE Jefferson
QUINAULT Grays Harbor
QUINCY Grant
RAINIER Thurston
RANDLE Lewis
RAVENSDALE King
RAYMOND Pacific
REARDAN (99029) Lincoln(54),
   Spokane(45)
REDMOND King
REDONDO King
RENTON King
REPUBLIC (99166) Ferry(97),
   Okanogan(2)
RETSIL Kitsap
RICE Stevens
RICHLAND Benton

RIDGEFIELD Clark
RITZVILLE Adams
RIVERSIDE Okanogan
ROCHESTER Thurston
ROCK ISLAND Douglas
ROCKFORD Spokane
ROCKPORT Skagit
ROLLINGBAY Kitsap
RONALD Kittitas
ROOSEVELT Klickitat
ROSALIA (99170) Whitman(55),
   Spokane(44)
ROSBURG Wahkiakum
ROSLYN Kittitas
ROY Pierce
ROYAL CITY Grant
RYDERWOOD Cowlitz
SAINT JOHN Whitman
SALKUM Lewis
SAMMAMISH King
SATSOP Grays Harbor
SEABECK Kitsap
SEAHURST King
SEATTLE King
SEAVIEW Pacific
SEDRO WOOLLEY (98284) Skagit(95),
   Whatcom(4)
SEKIU Clallam
SELAH Yakima
SEQUIM (98382) Clallam(98), Jefferson(1)
SEQUIM Jefferson
SHAW ISLAND San Juan
SHELTON Mason
SILVANA Snohomish
SILVER CREEK Lewis
SILVERDALE Kitsap
SILVERLAKE Cowlitz
SKAMOKAWA Wahkiakum
SKYKOMISH King
SNOHOMISH Snohomish
SNOQUALMIE King
SNOQUALMIE PASS King
SOAP LAKE Grant
SOUTH BEND Pacific
SOUTH CLE ELUM Kittitas
SOUTH COLBY Kitsap
SOUTH PRAIRIE Pierce
SOUTHWORTH Kitsap
SPANAWAY Pierce
SPANGLE Spokane
SPOKANE Spokane
SPRAGUE Lincoln
SPRINGDALE Stevens
STANWOOD Snohomish
STARBUCK Columbia
STARTUP Snohomish
STEHEKIN Chelan
STEILACOOM Pierce
STEPTOE Whitman
STEVENSON Skamania
STRATFORD Grant
SULTAN Snohomish
SUMAS Whatcom
SUMNER Pierce
SUNNYSIDE Yakima
SUQUAMISH Kitsap
TACOMA Pierce
TAHOLAH Grays Harbor

TAHUYA Mason
TEKOA (99033) Whitman(83), Spokane(16)
TENINO Thurston
THE CRESCENT STORE Spokane
THORNTON Whitman
THORP Kittitas
TIETON Yakima
TOKELAND Pacific
TOLEDO Lewis
TONASKET Okanogan
TOPPENISH Yakima
TOUCHET Walla Walla
TOUTLE Cowlitz
TRACYTON Kitsap
TROUT LAKE Klickitat
TUMTUM Stevens
TUMWATER Thurston
TWISP Okanogan
UNDERWOOD Skamania
UNION Mason
UNIONTOWN Whitman
UNIVERSITY PLACE Pierce
USK (99180) Pend Oreille(83),
   Spokane(16)
VADER Lewis
VALLEY Stevens
VALLEYFORD Spokane
VANCOUVER Clark
VANTAGE Kittitas
VASHON King
VAUGHN Pierce
VERADALE Spokane
WAHKIACUS Klickitat
WAITSBURG (99361) Walla Walla(96),
   Columbia(3)
WALDRON San Juan
WALLA WALLA Walla Walla
WALLULA Walla Walla
WAPATO Yakima
WARDEN Grant
WASHOUGAL (98671) Clark(79),
   Skamania(20)
WASHTUCNA Adams
WATERVILLE Douglas
WAUCONDA Okanogan
WAUNA Pierce
WAVERLY Spokane
WELLPINIT Stevens
WENATCHEE Chelan
WEST RICHLAND Benton
WESTPORT Grays Harbor
WHITE SALMON Klickitat
WHITE SWAN Yakima
WILBUR Lincoln
WILKESON Pierce
WILSON CREEK Grant
WINLOCK Lewis
WINTHROP Okanogan
WISHRAM Klickitat
WOODINVILLE (98077) King(92),
   Snohomish(7)
WOODLAND (98674) Cowlitz(66),
   Clark(33)
YACOLT Clark
YAKIMA Yakima
YELM Thurston
ZILLAH Yakima

Washington - City/County Cross Reference

98001-98002 AUBURN	98246-98246 BOW	98352-98352 SUMNER	98555-98555 LILLIWAUP
98003-98003 FEDERAL WAY	98247-98247 EVERSON	98353-98353 MANCHESTER	98556-98556 LITTLEROCK
98004-98009 BELLEVUE	98248-98248 FERNDALE	98354-98354 MILTON	98557-98557 MCCLEARY
98010-98010 BLACK DIAMOND	98249-98249 FREELAND	98355-98355 MINERAL	98558-98558 MCKENNA
98011-98012 BOTHELL	98250-98250 FRIDAY HARBOR	98356-98356 MORTON	98559-98559 MALONE
98013-98013 BURTON	98251-98251 GOLD BAR	98357-98357 NEAH BAY	98560-98560 MATLOCK
98014-98014 CARNATION	98252-98252 GRANITE FALLS	98358-98358 NORDLAND	98561-98561 MENLO
98015-98015 BELLEVUE	98253-98253 GREENBANK	98359-98359 OLALLA	98562-98562 MOCLIPS
98019-98019 DUVALL	98255-98255 HAMILTON	98360-98360 ORTING	98563-98563 MONTESANO
98020-98020 EDMONDS	98256-98256 INDEX	98361-98361 PACKWOOD	98564-98564 MOSSYROCK
98021-98021 BOTHELL	98257-98257 LA CONNER	98362-98363 PORT ANGELES	98565-98565 NAPAVINE
98022-98022 ENUMCLAW	98258-98258 LAKE STEVENS	98364-98364 PORT GAMBLE	98566-98566 NEILTON
98023-98023 FEDERAL WAY	98259-98259 LAKEWOOD	98365-98365 PORT LUDLOW	98568-98568 OAKVILLE
98024-98024 FALL CITY	98259-98259 NORTH LAKEWOOD	98366-98367 PORT ORCHARD	98569-98569 OCEAN SHORES
98025-98025 HOBART	98260-98260 LANGLEY	98368-98368 PORT TOWNSEND	98570-98570 ONALASKA
98026-98026 EDMONDS	98261-98261 LOPEZ ISLAND	98370-98370 POULSBO	98571-98571 PACIFIC BEACH
98027-98027 ISSAQUAH	98262-98262 LUMMI ISLAND	98371-98375 PUYALLUP	98572-98572 PE ELL
98028-98028 KENMORE	98263-98263 LYMAN	98376-98376 QUILCENE	98575-98575 QUINAULT
98029-98029 ISSAQUAH	98264-98264 LYNDEN	98377-98377 RANDLE	98576-98576 RAINIER
98030-98032 KENT	98266-98266 MAPLE FALLS	98378-98378 RETSIL	98577-98577 RAYMOND
98033-98033 KIRKLAND	98267-98267 MARBLEMOUNT	98380-98380 SEABECK	98579-98579 ROCHESTER
98035-98035 KENT	98270-98271 MARYSVILLE	98381-98381 SEKIU	98580-98580 ROY
98036-98037 LYNNWOOD	98272-98272 MONROE	98382-98382 SEQUIM	98581-98581 RYDERWOOD
98038-98038 MAPLE VALLEY	98273-98274 MOUNT VERNON	98383-98383 SILVERDALE	98582-98582 SALKUM
98039-98039 MEDINA	98275-98275 MUKILTEO	98384-98384 SOUTH COLBY	98583-98583 SATSOP
98040-98040 MERCER ISLAND	98276-98276 NOOKSACK	98385-98385 SOUTH PRAIRIE	98584-98584 SHELTON
98041-98041 BOTHELL	98277-98278 OAK HARBOR	98386-98386 SOUTHWORTH	98585-98585 SILVER CREEK
98042-98042 KENT	98279-98279 OLGA	98387-98387 SPANAWAY	98586-98586 SOUTH BEND
98043-98043 MOUNTLAKE TERRACE	98280-98280 ORCAS	98388-98388 STEILACOOM	98587-98587 TAHOLAH
98045-98045 NORTH BEND	98281-98281 POINT ROBERTS	98390-98390 SUMNER	98588-98588 TAHUYA
98046-98046 LYNNWOOD	98282-98282 CAMANO ISLAND	98392-98392 SUQUAMISH	98589-98589 TENINO
98047-98047 PACIFIC	98283-98283 ROCKPORT	98393-98393 TRACYTON	98590-98590 TOKELAND
98050-98050 PRESTON	98284-98284 SEDRO WOOLLEY	98394-98394 VAUGHN	98591-98591 TOLEDO
98051-98051 RAVENSDALE	98286-98286 SHAW ISLAND	98395-98395 WAUNA	98592-98592 UNION
98052-98053 REDMOND	98287-98287 SILVANA	98396-98396 WILKESON	98593-98593 VADER
98054-98054 REDONDO	98288-98288 SKYKOMISH	98397-98397 LONGMIRE	98595-98595 WESTPORT
98055-98059 RENTON	98290-98291 SNOHOMISH	98398-98398 PARADISE INN	98596-98596 WINLOCK
98060-98060 SEATTLE	98292-98292 STANWOOD	98401-98424 TACOMA	98597-98597 YELM
98061-98061 ROLLINGBAY	98293-98293 STARTUP	98430-98430 CAMP MURRAY	98599-98599 OLYMPIA
98062-98062 SEAHURST	98294-98294 SULTAN	98431-98439 TACOMA	98601-98601 AMBOY
98063-98063 FEDERAL WAY	98295-98295 SUMAS	98439-98439 LAKEWOOD	98602-98602 APPLETON
98064-98064 KENT	98296-98296 SNOHOMISH	98442-98466 TACOMA	98603-98603 ARIEL
98065-98065 SNOQUALMIE	98297-98297 WALDRON	98467-98467 UNIVERSITY PLACE	98604-98604 BATTLE GROUND
98068-98068 SNOQUALMIE PASS	98303-98303 ANDERSON ISLAND	98471-98492 TACOMA	98605-98605 BINGEN
98070-98070 VASHON	98304-98304 ASHFORD	98492-98492 LAKEWOOD	98606-98606 BRUSH PRAIRIE
98071-98071 AUBURN	98305-98305 BEAVER	98493-98497 TACOMA	98607-98607 CAMAS
98072-98072 WOODINVILLE	98310-98314 BREMERTON	98497-98497 LAKEWOOD	98609-98609 CARROLLS
98073-98073 REDMOND	98315-98315 SILVERDALE	98498-98499 TACOMA	98610-98610 CARSON
98074-98075 SAMMAMISH	98320-98320 BRINNON	98499-98499 LAKEWOOD	98611-98611 CASTLE ROCK
98077-98077 WOODINVILLE	98321-98321 BUCKLEY	98501-98508 OLYMPIA	98612-98612 CATHLAMET
98082-98082 BOTHELL	98322-98322 BURLEY	98509-98509 LACEY	98613-98613 CENTERVILLE
98083-98083 KIRKLAND	98323-98323 CARBONADO	98511-98511 TUMWATER	98614-98614 CHINOOK
98089-98089 KENT	98324-98324 CARLSBORG	98512-98516 OLYMPIA	98616-98616 COUGAR
98092-98092 AUBURN	98325-98325 CHIMACUM	98520-98520 ABERDEEN	98617-98617 DALLESPORT
98093-98093 FEDERAL WAY	98326-98326 CLALLAM BAY	98522-98522 ADNA	98619-98619 GLENWOOD
98100-98109 SEATTLE	98327-98327 DUPONT	98524-98524 ALLYN	98620-98620 GOLDENDALE
98110-98110 BAINBRIDGE ISLAND	98328-98328 EATONVILLE	98526-98526 AMANDA PARK	98621-98621 GRAYS RIVER
98111-98199 SEATTLE	98329-98329 GIG HARBOR	98527-98527 BAY CENTER	98622-98622 HEISSON
98200-98213 EVERETT	98330-98330 ELBE	98528-98528 BELFAIR	98623-98623 HUSUM
98220-98220 ACME	98331-98331 FORKS	98530-98530 BUCODA	98624-98624 ILWACO
98221-98221 ANACORTES	98332-98332 GIG HARBOR	98531-98531 CENTRALIA	98625-98625 KALAMA
98222-98222 BLAKELY ISLAND	98333-98333 FOX ISLAND	98532-98532 CHEHALIS	98626-98626 KELSO
98223-98223 ARLINGTON	98334-98334 SEQUIM	98533-98533 CINEBAR	98628-98628 KLICKITAT
98224-98224 BARING	98335-98335 GIG HARBOR	98535-98535 COPALIS BEACH	98629-98629 LA CENTER
98225-98229 BELLINGHAM	98336-98336 GLENOMA	98536-98536 COPALIS CROSSING	98631-98631 LONG BEACH
98230-98231 BLAINE	98337-98337 BREMERTON	98537-98537 COSMOPOLIS	98632-98632 LONGVIEW
98232-98232 BOW	98338-98338 GRAHAM	98538-98538 CURTIS	98635-98635 LYLE
98233-98233 BURLINGTON	98339-98339 PORT HADLOCK	98539-98539 DOTY	98637-98637 NAHCOTTA
98235-98235 CLEARLAKE	98340-98340 HANSVILLE	98540-98540 EAST OLYMPIA	98638-98638 NASELLE
98236-98236 CLINTON	98342-98342 INDIANOLA	98541-98541 ELMA	98639-98639 NORTH BONNEVILLE
98237-98237 CONCRETE	98343-98343 JOYCE	98542-98542 ETHEL	98640-98640 OCEAN PARK
98238-98238 CONWAY	98344-98344 KAPOWSIN	98544-98544 GALVIN	98641-98641 OYSTERVILLE
98239-98239 COUPEVILLE	98345-98345 KEYPORT	98546-98546 GRAPEVIEW	98642-98642 RIDGEFIELD
98240-98240 CUSTER	98346-98346 KINGSTON	98547-98547 GRAYLAND	98643-98643 ROSBURG
98241-98241 DARRINGTON	98348-98348 LA GRANDE	98548-98548 HOODSPORT	98644-98644 SEAVIEW
98243-98243 DEER HARBOR	98349-98349 LAKEBAY	98550-98550 HOQUIAM	98645-98645 SILVERLAKE
98244-98244 DEMING	98350-98350 LA PUSH	98552-98552 HUMPTULIPS	98647-98647 SKAMOKAWA
98245-98245 EASTSOUND	98351-98351 LONGBRANCH	98554-98554 LEBAM	98648-98648 STEVENSON

98649-98649 TOUTLE	98920-98920 BROWNSTOWN	99034-99034 TUMTUM	99161-99161 PALOUSE
98650-98650 TROUT LAKE	98921-98921 BUENA	99036-99036 VALLEYFORD	99163-99165 PULLMAN
98651-98651 UNDERWOOD	98922-98922 CLE ELUM	99037-99037 VERADALE	99166-99166 REPUBLIC
98660-98668 VANCOUVER	98923-98923 COWICHE	99039-99039 WAVERLY	99167-99167 RICE
98670-98670 WAHKIACUS	98925-98925 EASTON	99040-99040 WELLPINIT	99169-99169 RITZVILLE
98671-98671 WASHOUGAL	98926-98926 ELLENSBURG	99101-99101 ADDY	99170-99170 ROSALIA
98672-98672 WHITE SALMON	98929-98929 GOOSE PRAIRIE	99102-99102 ALBION	99171-99171 SAINT JOHN
98673-98673 WISHRAM	98930-98930 GRANDVIEW	99103-99103 ALMIRA	99173-99173 SPRINGDALE
98674-98674 WOODLAND	98932-98932 GRANGER	99104-99104 BELMONT	99174-99174 STEPTOE
98675-98675 YACOLT	98933-98933 HARRAH	99105-99105 BENGE	99176-99176 THORNTON
98682-98687 VANCOUVER	98934-98934 KITTITAS	99107-99107 BOYDS	99179-99179 UNIONTOWN
98801-98801 WENATCHEE	98935-98935 MABTON	99109-99109 CHEWELAH	99180-99180 USK
98802-98802 EAST WENATCHEE	98936-98936 MOXEE	99110-99110 CLAYTON	99181-99181 VALLEY
98807-98807 WENATCHEE	98937-98937 NACHES	99111-99111 COLFAX	99185-99185 WILBUR
98811-98811 ARDENVOIR	98938-98938 OUTLOOK	99113-99113 COLTON	99200-99256 SPOKANE
98812-98812 BREWSTER	98939-98939 PARKER	99114-99114 COLVILLE	99257-99257 THE CRESCENT STORE
98813-98813 BRIDGEPORT	98940-98940 RONALD	99115-99115 COULEE CITY	99258-99258 SPOKANE
98814-98814 CARLTON	98941-98941 ROSLYN	99116-99116 COULEE DAM	99259-99259 OLD NATIONAL BANK
98815-98815 CASHMERE	98942-98942 SELAH	99117-99117 CRESTON	99260-99299 SPOKANE
98816-98816 CHELAN	98943-98943 SOUTH CLE ELUM	99118-99118 CURLEW	99301-99302 PASCO
98817-98817 CHELAN FALLS	98944-98944 SUNNYSIDE	99119-99119 CUSICK	99320-99320 BENTON CITY
98819-98819 CONCONULLY	98946-98946 THORP	99121-99121 DANVILLE	99321-99321 BEVERLY
98821-98821 DRYDEN	98947-98947 TIETON	99122-99122 DAVENPORT	99322-99322 BICKLETON
98822-98822 ENTIAT	98948-98948 TOPPENISH	99123-99123 ELECTRIC CITY	99323-99323 BURBANK
98823-98823 EPHRATA	98950-98950 VANTAGE	99124-99124 ELMER CITY	99324-99324 COLLEGE PLACE
98824-98824 GEORGE	98951-98951 WAPATO	99125-99125 ENDICOTT	99326-99326 CONNELL
98826-98826 LEAVENWORTH	98952-98952 WHITE SWAN	99126-99126 EVANS	99327-99327 CUNNINGHAM
98827-98827 LOOMIS	98953-98953 ZILLAH	99127-99127 SAINT JOHN	99328-99328 DAYTON
98828-98828 MALAGA	99001-99001 AIRWAY HEIGHTS	99128-99128 FARMINGTON	99329-99329 DIXIE
98829-98829 MALOTT	99003-99003 CHATTAROY	99129-99129 FRUITLAND	99330-99330 ELTOPIA
98830-98830 MANSFIELD	99004-99004 CHENEY	99130-99130 GARFIELD	99332-99332 HATTON
98831-98831 MANSON	99005-99005 COLBERT	99131-99131 GIFFORD	99333-99333 HOOPER
98832-98832 MARLIN	99006-99006 DEER PARK	99133-99133 GRAND COULEE	99335-99335 KAHLOTUS
98833-98833 MAZAMA	99008-99008 EDWALL	99134-99134 HARRINGTON	99336-99338 KENNEWICK
98834-98834 METHOW	99009-99009 ELK	99135-99135 HARTLINE	99341-99341 LIND
98836-98836 MONITOR	99011-99011 FAIRCHILD AIR FORCE	99136-99136 HAY	99343-99343 MESA
98837-98837 MOSES LAKE	BASE	99137-99137 HUNTERS	99344-99344 OTHELLO
98840-98840 OKANOGAN	99012-99012 FAIRFIELD	99138-99138 INCHELIUM	99345-99345 PATERSON
98841-98841 OMAK	99013-99013 FORD	99139-99139 IONE	99346-99346 PLYMOUTH
98843-98843 ORONDO	99014-99014 FOUR LAKES	99140-99140 KELLER	99347-99347 POMEROY
98844-98844 OROVILLE	99015-99015 FREEMAN	99141-99141 KETTLE FALLS	99348-99348 PRESCOTT
98845-98845 PALISADES	99016-99016 GREENACRES	99143-99143 LACROSSE	99349-99349 MATTAWA
98846-98846 PATEROS	99017-99017 LAMONT	99144-99144 LAMONA	99350-99350 PROSSER
98847-98847 PESHASTIN	99018-99018 LATAH	99146-99146 LAURIER	99352-99352 RICHLAND
98848-98848 QUINCY	99019-99019 LIBERTY LAKE	99147-99147 LINCOLN	99353-99353 WEST RICHLAND
98849-98849 RIVERSIDE	99020-99020 MARSHALL	99148-99148 LOON LAKE	99354-99354 RICHLAND
98850-98850 ROCK ISLAND	99021-99021 MEAD	99149-99149 MALDEN	99356-99356 ROOSEVELT
98851-98851 SOAP LAKE	99022-99022 MEDICAL LAKE	99150-99150 MALO	99357-99357 ROYAL CITY
98852-98852 STEHEKIN	99023-99023 MICA	99151-99151 MARCUS	99359-99359 STARBUCK
98853-98853 STRATFORD	99025-99025 NEWMAN LAKE	99152-99152 METALINE	99360-99360 TOUCHET
98855-98855 TONASKET	99026-99026 NINE MILE FALLS	99153-99153 METALINE FALLS	99361-99361 WAITSBURG
98856-98856 TWISP	99027-99027 OTIS ORCHARDS	99154-99154 MOHLER	99362-99362 WALLA WALLA
98857-98857 WARDEN	99028-99028 SPANGLE	99155-99155 NESPELEM	99363-99363 WALLULA
98858-98858 WATERVILLE	99029-99029 REARDAN	99156-99156 NEWPORT	99371-99371 WASHTUCNA
98859-98859 WAUCONDA	99030-99030 ROCKFORD	99157-99157 NORTHPORT	99401-99401 ANATONE
98860-98860 WILSON CREEK	99031-99031 SPANGLE	99158-99158 OAKESDALE	99402-99402 ASOTIN
98862-98862 WINTHROP	99032-99032 SPRAGUE	99159-99159 ODESSA	99403-99403 CLARKSTON
98901-98909 YAKIMA	99033-99033 TEKOA	99160-99160 ORIENT	

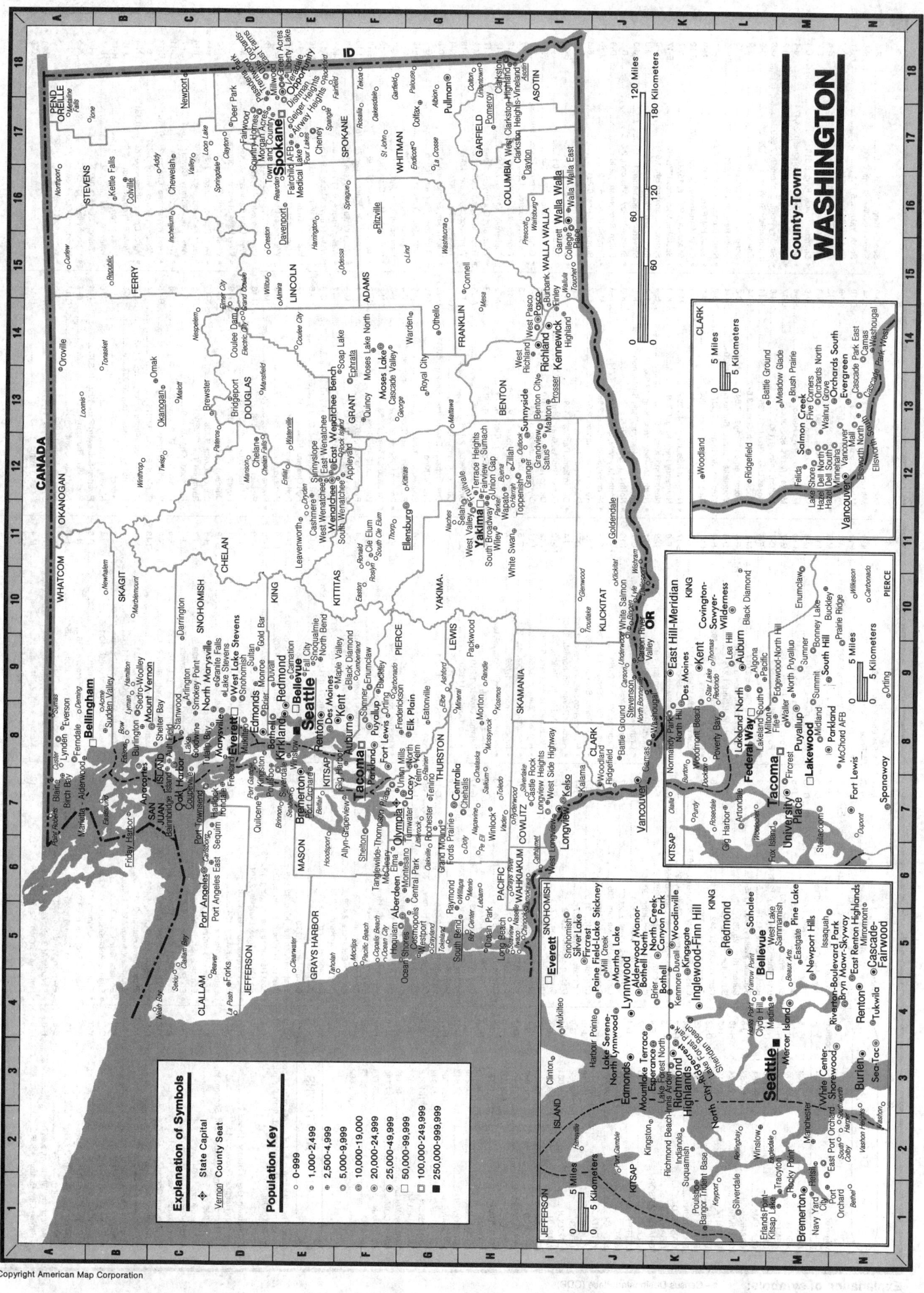

WASHINGTON

County-Town

COUNTIES

(39 Counties)

Name of County	Population	Location on Map
ADAMS	13,603	F-15
ASOTIN	17,605	I-16
BENTON	112,560	H-13
CHELAN	52,250	D-11
CLALLAM	56,464	C-4
CLARK	238,053	J-8
COLUMBIA	4,024	H-16
COWLITZ	82,119	H-7
DOUGLAS	26,205	D-13
FERRY	6,295	B-15
FRANKLIN	37,473	G-14
GARFIELD	2,248	H-17
GRANT	54,758	F-13
GRAYS HARBOR	64,175	E-4
ISLAND	60,195	C-7
JEFFERSON	20,146	D-4
KING	1,507,319	E-7
KITSAP	189,731	E-7
KITTITAS	26,725	F-10
KLICKITAT	16,616	J-10
LEWIS	59,358	G-9
LINCOLN	8,864	E-15
MASON	38,341	E-6
OKANOGAN	33,350	A-11
PACIFIC	18,882	H-6
PEND OREILLE	8,915	A-17
PIERCE	586,203	F-9
SAN JUAN	10,035	C-7
SKAGIT	79,555	B-10
SKAMANIA	8,289	H-8
SNOHOMISH	465,642	C-10
SPOKANE	361,364	E-17
STEVENS	30,948	A-16
THURSTON	161,238	G-7
WAHKIAKUM	3,327	H-6
WALLA WALLA	48,439	I-15
WHATCOM	127,780	A-10
WHITMAN	38,775	F-16
YAKIMA	188,823	G-10
TOTAL	**4,866,692**	

CITIES AND TOWNS

Note: The first name is that of the city or town, second, that of the county in which it is located, then the population and location on the map.

Aberdeen, Grays Harbor, 16,565 — G-5
Airway Heights, Spokane, 1,971 — E-17
• Alderwood Manor-Bothell North, Snohomish, 22,945 — K-4
• Algona, King, 1,694 — L-10
• Allyn-Grapeview, Mason, 1,526 — F-7
Anacortes, Skagit, 11,451 — B-8
Arlington, Snohomish, 4,037 — F-12
• Artondale, Pierce, 7,141 — L-7
Asotin, Asotin, 1,095 — H-18
Auburn, King, 33,102 — C-7
Bainbridge Island, Kitsap, 3,081 — M-3
Bangor Trident Base, Kitsap, 3,702 — K-1
Battle Ground, Clark, 3,795 — J-8
Bellevue, King, 86,874 — E-8
Bellingham, Whatcom, 52,179 — B-8
Benton City, Benton, 1,806 — H-13
• Birch Bay, Whatcom, 2,656 — A-7

Black Diamond, King, 1,422 — L-11
Blaine, Whatcom, 2,489 — A-7
Bonney Lake, Pierce, 7,494 — M-10
Bothell, King/Snohomish, 12,345 — D-8
Bremerton, Kitsap, 38,142 — E-7
Brewster, Okanogan, 1,633 — C-13
Bridgeport, Douglas, 1,498 — D-13
• Brier, Snohomish, 5,633 — D-8
• Brush Prairie, Clark, 2,650 — L-13
Bryn Mawr-Skyway, King, 12,514 — D-7
Buckley, Pierce, 3,516 — N-4
Burbank, Walla Walla, 1,745 — F-9
Burien, King, 25,089 — I-14
Burlington, Skagit, 4,349 — D-10
Camas, Clark, 6,442 — E-7
Carnation, King, 1,243 — K-8
Carson River Valley, Skamania, 1,678 — N-13
• Cascade Park East, Clark, 6,996 — N-13
• Cascade Park West, Clark, 6,656 — F-14
Cascade Valley, Grant, 1,288 — E-17
Cashmere, Chelan, 2,544 — D-4
Castle Rock, Cowlitz, 2,067 — D-10
Cathlamet, Wahkiakum, 508 — E-7
• Central Park, Grays Harbor, 2,669 — F-10
Centralia, Lewis, 12,101 — J-10
Chehalis, Lewis, 6,527 — H-7
Cheney, Spokane, 7,723 — D-12
• Chewelah, Stevens, 1,945 — E-17
Clarkston, Asotin, 6,753 — C-17
• Clarkston Heights-Vineland, Asotin, 2,832 — H-18
Cle Elum, Kittitas, 1,778 — F-11
Clinton, Island, 1,564 — I-13
Clyde Hill, King, 2,972 — I-6
Colfax, Whitman, 2,713 — G-6
College Place, Walla Walla, 6,308 — G-7
Colville, Stevens, 4,360 — H-7
Connell, Franklin, 2,005 — H-8
Cosmopolis, Grays Harbor, 1,372 — E-17
Coulee Dam, Douglas/Grant/Okanogan, 1,087 — A-16
Country Homes, Spokane, 5,126 — G-7
Coupeville, Island, 1,377 — H-6
Covington-Sawyer-Wilderness, King, 24,321 — I-15
Darrington, Snohomish, 1,042 — A-10
Davenport, Lincoln, 1,502 — F-16
Dayton, Columbia, 2,468 — H-16
Deer Park, Spokane, 2,278 — D-17
Des Moines, King, 17,283 — E-8
Dishman, Spokane, 9,671 — E-8

Duvall, King, 2,770 — M-12
• East Hill-Meridian, King, 42,696 — D-9
• East Port Orchard, Kitsap, 5,409 — L-10
• East Renton Highlands, King, 13,218 — L-10
East Wenatchee, Douglas, 2,701 — N-4
• East Wenatchee Bench, Douglas, 12,539 — E-12
• Eastgate, King, 4,434 — E-12
Eatonville, Pierce, 1,374 — M-5
Edgewood-North Hill, Pierce, 9,120 — L-9
Edmonds, Snohomish, 30,744 — G-8
Elk Plain, Pierce, 12,197 — G-11
Ellensburg, Kittitas, 12,361 — N-13
Ellsworth South, Clark, 4,423 — G-6
Elma, Grays Harbor, 3,011 — F-13
Enumclaw, King, 5,796 — M-2
Ephrata, Grant, 5,349 — K-4
• Erlands Point-Kitsap Lake, Kitsap, 2,764 — A-8
Esperance, Snohomish, 11,236 — D-8
Everett, Snohomish, 69,961 — J-4
Evergreen, Clark, 11,249 — D-8
• Everson, Whatcom, 1,490 — N-9
Fairchild AFB, Spokane, 4,854 — F-6
• Fairview-Sumach, Yakima, 2,749 — E-17
Fairwood, Spokane, 5,807 — M-4

Fall City, King, 1,582 — E-9
Federal Way, King, 67,554 — L-9
• Felida, Clark, 3,109 — M-12
Ferndale, Whatcom, 5,398 — A-8
Fife, Pierce, 3,864 — M-9
Finley, Benton, 4,897 — N-6
Fircrest, Pierce, 5,258 — D-9
• Five Corners, Clark, 6,776 — M-13
• Fords Prairie, Lewis, 2,480 — D-17
Forks, Clallam, 2,862 — H-8
Fort Lewis, Pierce, 22,224 — F-8
• Fox Island, Pierce, 2,017 — M-7
Frederickson, Pierce, 3,502 — F-8
Freeland, Island, 1,278 — D-8
Friday Harbor, San Juan, 1,492 — B-7
Fruitvale, Yakima, 4,125 — H-11
• Garrett, Walla Walla, 1,004 — E-9
Geiger Heights, Spokane — J-9
Gig Harbor, Pierce, 3,236 — N-13
Gold Bar, Snohomish, 1,078 — E-14
Goldendale, Klickitat, 3,319 — N-5
Grand Mound, Thurston, 1,394 — J-11
Granger, Yakima, 2,053 — G-7
Granite Falls, Snohomish, 1,060 — I-13
Green Acres, Spokane, 4,626 — H-12
Hadlock-Irondale, Jefferson, 2,742 — D-18
Harbour Pointe, Snohomish, 9,107 — D-7
Hazel Dell North, Clark, 6,924 — J-4
Hazel Dell South, Clark, 5,796 — M-12
Highland, Benton, 3,666 — M-12
Hoquiam, Grays Harbor, 8,972 — I-14
Indianola, Kitsap, 1,729 — H-18
Inglewood-Finn Hill, King, 29,132 — L-4
Issaquah, King, 7,786 — I-7
Kalama, Cowlitz, 1,210 — F-11
Kelso, Cowlitz, 11,820 — M-4
Kenmore, King, 8,917 — N-5
Kennewick, Benton, 42,155 — I-7
Kent, King, 37,960 — L-4
Kettle Falls, Stevens, 1,272 — I-14
Kingsgate, King, 14,259 — F-8
Kingston, Kitsap, 1,270 — B-16
Kirkland, King, 40,052 — L-5
Lacey, Thurston, 19,279 — K-2
Lake Forest North, King, 8,002 — G-7
Lake Forest Park, King, 4,031 — E-8
Lake Goodwin, Snohomish, 2,437 — G-7
Lake Serene-North Lynnwood, Snohomish, 14,290 — L-4
Lake Shore, Clark, 6,268 — E-8
Lake Stevens, Snohomish, 3,380 — K-9
• Lakeland North, King, 14,402 — N-2
• Lakeland South, King, 9,027 — L-10
Lakewood, Pierce, 58,412 — E-12
• Lea Hill, King, 6,876 — L-9
Leavenworth, Chelan, 1,692 — M-5
• Liberty Lake, Spokane, 2,015 — G-8
Long Beach, Pacific, 1,236 — D-8
Longview, Cowlitz, 31,499 — G-8
Longview Heights, Cowlitz, 3,310 — G-11
Lynden, Whatcom, 5,709 — N-13
Lynnwood, Snohomish, 28,695 — G-6
Mabton, Yakima, 1,482 — F-9
• Manchester, Kitsap, 4,031 — M-2
Maple Valley, King, 1,211 — K-4
• Marietta-Alderwood, Whatcom, 2,766 — A-8
Marysville, Snohomish, 10,155 — D-8
Martha Lake, Snohomish, 10,328 — J-4
McChord AFB, Pierce, 4,538 — D-8
McCleary, Grays Harbor, 1,235 — N-9
Meadow Glade, Clark, 1,584 — F-6
Medical Lake, Spokane, 3,664 — E-17
Medina, King, 2,981 — N-4
Mercer Island, King, 20,816 — M-4

Midland, Pierce, 5,587 — M-9
Mill Creek, Snohomish, 7,172 — J-4
Millwood, Spokane, 1,559 — D-18
Milton, King/Pierce, 4,995 — M-9
• Minnehaha, Clark, 9,661 — M-12
Mirrormont, King, 2,360 — N-6
Monroe, Snohomish, 4,278 — D-9
Montesano, Grays Harbor, 3,064 — G-6
Morgan Acres, Spokane — D-17
Morton, Lewis, 1,130 — H-8
• Moses Lake, Grant, 11,235 — F-14
Moses Lake North, Grant, 3,677 — F-14
Mount Vernon, Skagit, 17,647 — C-8
Mountlake Terrace, Snohomish, 19,320 — D-8
Mukilteo, Snohomish, 7,007 — M-7
Navy Yard City, Kitsap, 2,905 — M-2
Newport, Pend Oreille, 1,691 — C-18
Newport Hills, King, 14,736 — M-4
Normandy Park, King, 6,709 — K-9
North Bend, King, 2,578 — E-9
North City-Ridgecrest, King, 13,832 — L-4
North Creek-Canyon Park, Snohomish, 23,236 — K-5
North Hill, King, 5,706 — D-8
North Marysville, Snohomish, 18,711 — M-9
North Puyallup, Pierce, 2,886 — G-7
North Yelm, Thurston, 2,075 — C-7
Oak Harbor, Island, 17,176 — H-4
Ocean Park, Pacific, 1,409 — G-5
Ocean Shores, Grays Harbor, 2,301 — C-13
Okanogan, Okanogan, 2,370 — F-7
Olympia, Thurston, 33,840 — E-18
Omak, Okanogan, 4,117 — C-13
Opportunity, Spokane, 22,326 — M-13
Orchards North, Clark, 6,479 — A-13
Orchards South, Clark, 12,956 — F-8
Orting, Pierce, 2,106 — D-18
Oroville, Okanogan, 1,505 — M-10
Othello, Adams, 4,638 — H-9
Otis Orchards-East Farms, Spokane, 5,811 — N-2
Packwood, Lewis — L-5
Paine Field-Lake Stickney, Snohomish, 18,670 — J-4
Parkland, Pierce, 20,882 — F-8
Parkwood, Kitsap, 6,853 — D-18
Pasadena Park, Spokane — M-10
Pasco, Franklin, 20,337 — H-12
Pine Lake, King, 13,940 — M-5
Pomeroy, Garfield, 1,393 — H-17
Port Angeles East, Clallam, 2,672 — C-6
Port Orchard, Kitsap, 4,984 — E-7
Port Townsend, Jefferson, 7,001 — L-2
Poulsbo, Kitsap, 4,848 — M-9
Prairie Ridge, Pierce, 8,278 — I-13
Prosser, Benton, 4,476 — G-14
Pullman, Whitman, 23,478 — E-12
Puyallup, Pierce, 23,875 — E-12
Quincy, Grant, 3,738 — H-18
Quilcene, Jefferson — D-7
Raymond, Pacific, 2,901 — F-13
Redmond, King, 35,800 — G-5
Renton, King, 41,688 — E-8
Republic, Ferry, 940 — B-15
Richland, Benton, 32,315 — I-14
Richmond Beach-Innis Arden, King, 7,242 — I-7
Richmond Highlands, Snohomish, 26,037 — K-3
Ridgefield, Clark, 1,297 — J-7
Riverton-Boulevard Park, King, 15,337 — F-16
Rochester, Thurston, 1,250 — D-8
Royal City, Grant, 1,104 — G-13
Sahalee, King, 13,951 — L-5
Salmon Creek, Clark, 11,989 — M-12
Satus, Yakima, 1,343 — H-12
Sea-Tac, King, 22,694 — N-4

Seattle, King, 516,259 — E-8
Sedro-Woolley, Skagit, 6,031 — B-8
Selah, Yakima, 5,113 — H-11
Sequim, Clallam, 3,616 — D-7
Shelter Bay, Skagit, 1,069 — B-8
Shelton, Mason, 7,241 — F-7
Sheridan Beach, King, 6,518 — L-4
Silver Lake-Fircrest, Snohomish, 24,474 — J-4
Silverdale, Kitsap, 7,660 — M-2
Smokey Point, Snohomish, 2,620 — C-8
Snohomish, Snohomish, 6,499 — D-9
Snoqualmie, King, 1,546 — E-9
Soap Lake, Grant, 1,149 — E-13
South Bend, Pacific, 1,551 — H-5
South Broadway, Yakima, 2,735 — H-11
South Hill, Pierce, 12,963 — M-9
South Wenatchee, Chelan, 1,207 — F-12
Spanaway, Pierce, 15,001 — N-7
Spokane, Spokane, 177,196 — E-17
Stanwood, Snohomish, 1,961 — C-8
Steilacoom, Pierce, 5,728 — J-8
Stevenson, Skamania, 1,147 — J-9
Sudden Valley, Whatcom, 2,615 — B-8
Sultan, Snohomish, 2,236 — D-9
Summit, Pierce, 6,312 — M-10
Sumner, Pierce, 6,281 — F-8
Sunnyside, Yakima, 11,238 — H-12
Sunnyslope, Chelan, 1,907 — E-12
Suquamish, Kitsap, 3,105 — L-2
Tacoma, Pierce, 176,664 — F-7
Tanglewilde-Thompson Place, Thurston, 6,061 — H-12
Tenino, Thurston, 1,292 — H-12
Terrace Heights, Yakima, 4,223 — H-12
Toppenish, Yakima, 7,419 — H-12
Town and Country, Spokane, 4,921 — M-2
Tracyton, Kitsap, 2,621 — N-4
Trentwood, Spokane, 4,060 — D-8
Tukwila, King, 11,874 — G-7
Tulalip Bay, Snohomish, 1,395 — D-18
Tumwater, Thurston, 9,976 — M-10
Union Gap, Yakima, 3,120 — H-12
University Place, Pierce, 27,701 — M-7
Vancouver, Clark, 46,380 — J-4
Vancouver Mall, Clark, 6,938 — F-8
Veradale, Spokane, 7,836 — E-18
Walla Walla, Walla Walla, 26,478 — I-16
Walla Walla East, Walla Walla, 2,959 — I-16
Waller, Pierce, 6,415 — M-8
Walnut Grove, Clark, 3,906 — M-13
Wapato, Yakima, 3,795 — H-12
Warden, Grant, 1,639 — G-14
Washougal, Clark, 4,764 — K-8
Waterville, Douglas, 995 — E-12
Wenatchee, Chelan, 21,756 — E-12
West Clarkston-Highland, Asotin, 3,913 — H-18
West Lake Sammamish, King, 6,087 — M-5
West Lake Stevens, Snohomish, 12,453 — D-9
West Longview, Cowlitz, 3,163 — D-7
West Pasco, Franklin, 7,312 — F-13
West Richland, Benton, 3,962 — E-8
West Side Highway, Cowlitz, 6,594 — B-15
West Valley, Yakima, 6,594 — I-14
West Wenatchee, Chelan, 2,220 — I-7
Westport, Grays Harbor, 1,892 — G-5
White Center-Shorewood, King, 20,531 — E-12
White Salmon, Klickitat, 1,861 — J-7
White Swan, Yakima, 2,669 — F-16
Wiley, Lewis — N-4
Winlock, Lewis, 1,027 — L-3
Woodinville, King, 23,654 — J-7
Woodland, Clark/Cowlitz, 2,500 — G-13
Woodmont Beach, King, 7,493 — L-5
Yakima, Yakima, 54,827 — M-12
Yelm, Thurston, 1,337 — H-12
Zillah, Yakima, 1,911 — H-12

Explanation of symbols: • – Census Designated Place (CDP)

West Virginia

General Help Numbers:

Governor's Office

Office of the Governor   304-558-2000
1900 Kanawha Blvd, East   Fax 304-342-7025
Charleston, WV 25305-0370   8AM-6PM M-TH;
                        8AM-5PM F

www.state.wv.us/governor

Attorney General's Office

1900 Kanawha Blvd. Rm 26E   304-558-2021
Charleston, WV 25305-9924   Fax 304-558-0140
www.wvs.state.wv.us/wvag/   8:30AM-5PM

Legislative Records

West Virginia State Legislature   304-347-4830
State Capitol, Documents   Fax 304-558-1212
Charleston, WV 25305   8:30AM-4:30PM
 www.legis.state.wv.us

State Archives

Archives & History Section   304-558-0220
1900 Kanawha Blvd E   Fax 304-558-2779
Charleston, WV 25305-0300 9AM-8PM M-TH, 9-6 F-SA
www.wvculture.org/history/wvsamenu.html

State Specifics:

Capital:	Charleston Kanawha County
Time Zone:	EST
Number of Counties:	55
Population:	1,810,354
Web Site:	www.wv.gov/

State Agencies

Criminal Records

State Police, Criminal Records Section, 725 Jefferson Rd, South Charleston, WV 25309; 304-746-2277, 304-746-2402 (Fax), 8:30AM-4:30PM.

www.wvstatepolice.com

Note: The state will also sell an "incident report" of a specific criminal action for $20.00, call 304-746-2178. FBI checks only available if there is statutory authorization.

Indexing & Storage: Records are available from 1938 on computer. It takes 3 days before new records are available for inquiry. Records are indexed on in house computer (100% of names). Approximately 30% of arrest data is computerized. Records are normally destroyed after the person reaches age 80.

Searching: All searches require fingerprints, also FBI fingerprint checks. Include the following in your request-signed release of subject, SSN, DOB, race, sex, and thumbprint. You must use a WV Fingerprint Card and authorization. All records are returned by mail. Search can be initiated in person, results mailed. 100% of the records are fingerprint-supported.

Access by: mail.

Fee & Payment: The search fee is $20.00 plus $24.00 for an FBI fingerprint check. Certain statutorily-required searches are $10.00, plus the addition FBI fingercheck fee. Fee payee: West Virginia State Police. Prepayment required. Personal checks accepted. No credit cards accepted.

Mail search: Turnaround time: 5 to 10 days.

Statewide Court Records

Administrative Office, State Supreme Court of Appeals, 1900 Kanawha Blvd, Bldg 1, Rm E 100, Charleston, WV 25305-0830; 304-558-0145, 304-558-1212 (Fax), 9AM-5PM.

www.state.wv.us/wvsca

Note: Except for certain online research capabilities, all court record access must be done at the local level.

Access by: online.

Online search: Supreme Court of Appeals Opinions/Calendar is available at the web page. There are plans for a statewide system to allow access to Circuit, Family and Magistrate records, but it is not yet available. Magistrate Courts are on a private system, see www.swcg-inc.com/products/municipal_courts.html.

Sexual Offender Registry

State Police Headquarters, Sexual Offender Registry, 725 Jefferson Rd, South Charleston, WV 25309; 304-746-2133, 304-746-2403 (Fax), 8:30AM-4:30PM.

www.wvstatepolice.com/sexoff/

Note: West Virginia currently has over 1800 registered sex offenders.

Indexing & Storage: Records are available from 1994.

Access by: online. Prefer no mail requests.

Online search: Online searching is available from website, search by county or name.

Incarceration Records

West Virginia Division of Corrections, Records Room, 112 California Ave. 3rd floor, Charleston, WV 25305; 304-558-2037, 304-558-5934 (Fax), 8AM-5PM.

www.wvf.state.wv.us/wvdoc/

Indexing & Storage: Records are available on current and former inmates. It takes up to 4 days before new records are available for inquiry.

Searching: Include the following in your request-full name; DOB and SSN helpful. Location, conviction and sentencing information, and release dates are provided.

Access by: mail, phone, fax, online.

Mail search: Turnaround time: 2 to 4 weeks. SASE is required.

Phone search: Name searching permitted by phone.

Fax search: Same criteria as mail.

Online search: There is no online searching is available from this agency. However, a private company offers free web access at www.vinelink.com/index.jsp.

Corporation, Limited Liability Company, Limited Partnerships, Limited

Liability Partnerships Trademarks/Servicemarks,

Secretary of State, Corporation Division, State Capitol Bldg, Room W151, Charleston, WV 25305-0776; 304-558-8000, 304-558-5758 (Fax), 8:30AM-5PM.

www.wvsos.com

Indexing & Storage: Records are available for current active companies. It takes 24 hours before new records are available for inquiry. Records are indexed on inhouse computer.

Searching: Include the following in your request-full name of business. In addition to the initial organizing documents, business records include: Annual Reports, Officers, Directors, Prior (merged) names, Reserved names, mergers and amendments, agents of process and capital stock allocation of corporations.

Access by: mail, phone, fax, in person, online.

Fee & Payment: Copy fee is $1.00 for the first page and $.50 each additional page. Certification is $15.00 plus $5.00 for each amendment. Fee payee: Secretary of State. Prepayment required. Personal checks accepted. Credit cards accepted: MasterCard, Visa, AmEx, Discover.

Mail search: Turnaround time: 24 hours. No SASE is required.

Phone search: They will confirm if a company is active, they will only do three searches per phone call.

Fax search: Fax searching available.

In person search: Simple requests may be processed while you wait.

Online search: Corporation and business types records on the Secretary of State Business Organization Information System are available free online at www.wvsos.com/wvcorporations/. Search by organization name. Certified copies may be ordered online or via email to business@wvsos.com.

Uniform Commercial Code

UCC Division, Secretary of State, Bldg 1, West Wing, Rm 157K, Charleston, WV 25305-0440; 304-558-6000, 304-558-0900 (Fax), 8:30AM-4:30PM.

www.wvsos.com/ucc/main.htm

Note: The agency may place limited information under the website in the future.

Indexing & Storage: Records are available from July 1, 1964. It takes 1 day before new records are available for inquiry. Records are indexed on inhouse computer.

Searching: Use search request form UCC-11. All tax liens are filed at the county level. Terminated filings are researched upon request. Include the following in your request-debtor name.

Access by: mail, phone, fax, in person.

Fee & Payment: The fee is $5.00 per search and $.50 per copy. Fee payee: Secretary of State. Prepayment required. Pre-paid accounts are accepted, but do not send excess amount-search request may be returned. Personal checks accepted. Credit cards accepted: MasterCard, Visa, AmEx, Discover.

Mail search: Turnaround time: 1 day. A SASE is requested.

Phone search: They will bill for telephone searches.

Fax search: Same fees as phone or mail searches. Turnaround time in 24 hours.

In person search: Simple requests may be processed while you wait.

Federal Tax Liens, State Tax Liens

Records not maintained by a state level agency.

Note: All tax liens are filed at the county level.

Sales Tax Registrations

WV State Tax Department, Office of Business Registration, 1001 E Lee St E, Charleston, WV 25301; 304-558-8500, 304-558-8754 (Fax), 8:30AM-4:30PM.

www.state.wv.us/taxrev/

Indexing & Storage: Records are available for the current year plus four years. It takes 4 to 6 weeks before new records are available for inquiry. Records are normally destroyed after 5 years.

Searching: Will not disclose any information unless you provide a waiver form signed by the taxpayer. Without a waiver, this agency will provide only confirmation if permit is registered. The waiver form is available at www.state.wv.us/taxrev/uploads/wvari001.pdf. Include the following in your request-business name. This agency will also search by tax permit number.

Access by: mail, phone, fax, in person.

Mail search: Turnaround time: 2 weeks or less. A SASE is requested. No fee for mail request.

Phone search: No fee for telephone request.

Fax search: Fax searching available.

In person search: No fee for request. Records are still returned by mail.

Expedited service: Will expedite if requested.

Birth Certificates

Bureau of Public Health, Vital Records, 350 Capitol St, Rm 165, Charleston, WV 25305-3701; 304-558-2931, 304-558-1051 (Fax), 8:30AM-5PM.

www.wvdhhr.org/bph/oehp/hsc

Indexing & Storage: Records are available from 1917 to present. New records are available for inquiry immediately. Records are indexed on microfiche, inhouse computer.

Searching: Records released to immediate family members only. Include the following in your request-full name, names of parents, mother's maiden name, date of birth, place of birth. Online ordering is available from an approved vendor at www.vitalchek.com.

Access by: mail, phone, in person.

Fee & Payment: The fee is $5.00 per name per 3 years searched. Fee payee: Vital Registration. Prepayment required. Personal checks accepted. Credit cards accepted: MasterCard, Visa, AmEx, Discover.

Mail search: Turnaround time: 2 to 3 weeks. A SASE is requested.

Phone search: See expedited service.

In person search: Turnaround time 15 minutes.

Expedited service: Expedited service is available for fax, phone and online requests. To order by credit card and have 1 week "rush" turnaround time add $15.95. For 2 to 3 day delivery add $26.95. If overnight delivery is desired, add fee or give account number.

Death Records

Bureau of Public Health, Vital Records, 350 Capitol St, Rm 165, Charleston, WV 25305-3701; 304-558-2931, 302-343-2169 (Fax), 8AM-4PM.

www.wvdhhr.org/bph/oehp/hsc

Indexing & Storage: Records are available from 1917 on. New records are available for inquiry immediately. Records are indexed on microfiche, inhouse computer.

Searching: Record released to immediate family or anyone with a verifiable, specific interest only. Include the following in your request-full name, date of death, place of death, names of parents, Social Security Number. Online ordering is available from an approved vendor at www.vitalchek.com.

Access by: mail, phone, fax, in person.

Fee & Payment: The fee is $5.00 per name and covers a searching range of three years. Fee payee: Vital Registration. Prepayment required. Personal checks accepted. Credit cards accepted: MasterCard, Visa, AmEx, Discover.

Mail search: Turnaround time: 4 to 6 weeks. A SASE is requested.

Phone search: See expedited service.

Fax search: Access is provided by VitalChek. Use 866-870-8723 for the fax number. Use of credit card is required.

In person search: Turnaround time 15 minutes.

Expedited service: Expedited service is available for fax, phone and online requests. To order by credit card and have 1 week "rush" turnaround time add $15.95. For same day processing add $26.95. If overnight delivery is desired, add fee or give account number.

Marriage Certificates

Bureau of Public Health, Vital Records, 350 Capitol St, Rm 165, Charleston, WV 25305-3701; 304-558-2931, 304-343-2169 (Fax), 8AM-4PM.

www.wvdhhr.org/bph/oehp/hsc

Indexing & Storage: Records are available from 1921 on. Records certified from 1964 on. New records are available for inquiry immediately. Records are indexed on microfiche, inhouse computer.

Searching: You must be a family member or show cause to receive the record. Include the following in your request-names of husband and wife, date of marriage, place or county of marriage. Online ordering is available from an approved vendor at www.vitalchek.com.

Access by: mail, phone, fax, in person.

Fee & Payment: The fee is $5.00 per name and covers a searching range of three years. Fee payee: Vital Registration. Prepayment required. Personal checks accepted. Credit cards accepted: MasterCard, Visa, AmEx, Discover.

Mail search: Turnaround time: 3 to 4 weeks. A SASE is requested.

Phone search: See expedited service.

Fax search: Available from VitalChek. Use of credit card required.

In person search: Turnaround time 15 minutes.

Expedited service: Expedited service is available for fax, phone and online requests. To order by credit card and have 1 week "rush" turnaround time add $15.95. For same day processing add $26.95. If overnight delivery is desired, add fee or give account number.

Divorce Records

Records not maintained by a state level agency.

Note: Records are maintained by the Clerk of Court in the county of divorce.

Workers' Compensation Records

Workers Compensation Division, Records Management, PO Box 3151, Charleston, WV 25332; 304-558-5587, 304-926-3400, 304-558-1908 (Fax), 8AM-4:30PM.

www.state.wv.us/scripts/bep/wc/

Indexing & Storage: Records are available from 1916. New records are available for inquiry immediately. Records are indexed on microfiche.

Searching: Must have a signed release from claimant or be a representative of the employer. They suggest the use of their WC910 Form. You may call for a copy of this form, but they will release no information over the phone. Include the following in your request-claimant name, Social Security Number, date of accident, file number (if known). The following data is not released: psychiatric information.

Access by: mail, in person.

Fee & Payment: There are no fees unless extensive copies or searching is needed.

Mail search: Turnaround time: 5 to 10 days. Turnaround time is 1-2 days for microfiche copies and 5-10 days if paper copies are required. A SASE is requested.

In person search: Turnaround time is usually 1 or more days.

Driver License Information, Driver Records

Division of Motor Vehicles, 1800 Kanawha Blvd, Building 3, Rm 124, State Capitol Complex, Charleston, WV 25317; 304-558-0238, 304-558-5362, 304-558-0037 (Fax), 8:30AM-4:30PM.

www.wvdot.com/6_motorists/dmv/6G_DMV.HTM

Note: Use ZIP Code 25305 for courier deliveries.

Indexing & Storage: Records are available for 3 years for all convictions, 10 years for suspensions and revocations. A conviction not shown on the record iis speeding 10 mph or less over limit on interstate. It takes 1 week to 3 months (DUIs immediately) before new records are available for inquiry.

Searching: Casual requesters receive records without personal information, unless the subject has given written consent. The driver's license number and last name are required for a request, DOB and SSN are helpful. The following data is not released: accidents.

Access by: mail, in person, online.

Fee & Payment: The fee is $5.00 per record including no record founds. Fee payee: Division of Motor Vehicles. Prepayment required. Personal checks accepted. Credit cards accepted.

Mail search: Turnaround time: 24 hours. A SASE is requested.

In person search: Up to seven requests may be received immediately at the counter of this office. Branch offices in at least 15 cities can issue instant records for individual requests.

Online search: Online access is available 24 hours a day. Batch requesters receive return transmission about 3 AM. Users must access through AAMVAnet. A contract is required and accounts must pre-pay. Fee is $5.00 per record. For more information, call 304-558-3915.

Other access: This agency will sell its DL file to commercial vendors, but records cannot be re-sold.

Vehicle and Vessel Ownership and Registration

Division of Motor Vehicles, Information Services, 1606 Washington St East, Charleston, WV 25311; 304-558-0282, 304-558-1012 (Fax), 8:30AM-4:30PM.

www.wvdot.com/6_motorists/dmv/6g2_registration.htm

Note: This agency maintains records for unattached mobile homes.

Indexing & Storage: Records are available from 1959 for vehicles, from 1975 for boat registrations, and from 1980 for boat titles. All motorized boats and all sailboats must be registered and titled. It takes 1 to 3 days before new records are available for inquiry.

Searching: High volume requesters must be approved after stating purpose of requests. Casual requesters cannot receive personal information. If doing search by name, it is suggested to also submit address. Boat records can be searched by hull number or WV number. The following data is not released: Social Security Numbers or medical information.

Access by: mail, in person.

Fee & Payment: The fee is $1.00 for registration information, $2.00 per vehicle for lien information, $5.00 per title copy, $15.00 for a complete title history (which includes lien information), and $5.00 for message forwarding. Fee payee: Division of Motor Vehicles. Prepayment required. Do not overpay, they do not have the capacity to refund. Personal checks accepted. No credit cards accepted.

Mail search: Turnaround time: 3 to 5 business days. Return address must appear clearly on the request. A SASE is requested.

In person search: Turnaround time is while you wait if the record is on computer, or 2 days for photocopies.

Other access: The entire state's vehicle file can be purchased. Costs for customized runs depend on programming time. Further resale is prohibited. Call 304-558-0282 for more information.

Accident Reports

Department of Public Safety, Traffic Records Section, 725 Jefferson Rd, South Charleston, WV 25309-1698; 304-746-2128, 304-746-2206 (Fax), 8:30AM-5PM.

www.wvstatepolice.com

Note: It is suggested to send a letter explaining purpose of request and state if involved.

Indexing & Storage: Records are available of incidents investigated by the state police for the past 10 years. It takes 1 to 3 weeks before new records are available for inquiry. Records are normally destroyed after ten years.

Searching: If the State Police did not investigate the incident, the report must be obtained from the local investigating jurisdiction. Include the following in your request-name, date of accident, location of accident. The following data is not released: juvenile records.

Access by: mail, phone, fax, in person.

Fee & Payment: The fee is $20.00 per record. If certified, the cost is $25.00. Fee payee: Superintendent, Division of Public Safety. Prepayment required. Personal checks accepted. No credit cards accepted.

Mail search: Turnaround time: 2 to 3 weeks. A SASE is requested.

Phone search: Records are available by phone.

Fax search: For an extra $5.00 per record, the agency will send data by fax.

In person search: Turnaround time is same day, if record is readily available.

Voter Registration

Records not maintained by a state level agency.

Note: Voter information is held by the county clerks, but the state recently implemented a statewide database system. All information is public record.

GED Certificates

Dept of Education, GED Office, 1900 Kanawha Blvd E, Bldg 6, Rm 250, Charleston, WV 25305-0330; 304-558-6315, 304-558-4874 (Fax), 8AM-4PM.

www.wvabe.org/ged/

Indexing & Storage: It takes 8 weeks before new records are available for inquiry. Records are normally destroyed after 5 years.

Searching: To search, all of the following is a required: a signed release, name, year of test, date of birth, SSN, city of test, and a copy of or presentation of a photo ID and daytime phone number.

Access by: mail, fax.

Fee & Payment: There is $10.00 fee for verification. Copies of transcripts are $10.00 each. Fee payee: WV DOE Vocational Division. Prepayment required. Personal checks and money orders accepted. No credit cards accepted.

Mail search: Turnaround time: 7 to 10 days. No SASE is required.

Fax search: Only if verification is for job position.

Hunting and Fishing License Information

Natural Resources Department, Licensing Division, 1900 Kanawha Blvd E, Bldg 3, Room 624, Charleston, WV 25305; 304-558-2758, 304-558-6208 (Fax), 8:30AM-4:30PM.

www.wvweb.com/www/hunting

Indexing & Storage: Records are available for current year only. Records are indexed on inhouse computer. Records are normally destroyed after two years.

Searching: All requests must be in writing. Records are considered public records. Can request through customerservice@dnr.state.wv.us. Include the following in your request-full name, SSN.

Access by: mail, fax, in person.

Fee & Payment: The search fee is $29.00, but only if a record is found. Fee payee: Natural Resources Department. Personal checks accepted. Credit cards accepted: MasterCard, Visa.

Mail search: Turnaround time: 5 to 10 working days. No SASE is required.

Fax search: Fax requests accepted.

In person search: Request must be in writing.

West Virginia State Licensing Agencies

Licenses Searchable Online

Aesthetician #3	www.wvdhhr.org/bph/wvbc/licensees.cfm
Architect #2	http://wvbrdarch.org/roster/lic/searchdb.asp
Asbestos Clearance Air Monitor #42	www.wvdhhr.org/rtia/allair.cfm
Asbestos Contractor #42	www.wvdhhr.org/rtia/allcon.cfm
Asbestos Inspector #42	www.wvdhhr.org/rtia/allinsp.cfm
Asbestos Laboratory #42	www.wvdhhr.org/rtia/licensing.asp
Asbestos Project Designer #42	www.wvdhhr.org/rtia/alldesign.cfm
Asbestos Supervisor #42	www.wvdhhr.org/rtia/allsup.cfm
Asbestos Worker #42	www.wvdhhr.org/rtia/allwork.cfm
Attorney #14	www.wvbar.org/barinfo/mdirectory/
Barber #3	www.wvdhhr.org/bph/wvbc/licensees.cfm
Barber/Beauty Culture School #3	www.wvdhhr.org/bph/wvbc/licensees.cfm
Contractor, General #24	www.labor.state.wv.us/search/default.asp
Cosmetologist #3	www.wvdhhr.org/bph/wvbc/licensees.cfm
Electrician #40	www.wvfiremarshal.org/search.htm
Engineer #33	www.wvpebd.org
Lobbyist #39	www.wvethicscommission.org
Manicurist #3	www.wvdhhr.org/bph/wvbc/licensees.cfm
Medical Corporation #15	www.wvdhhr.org/wvbom/Directory/2003/medcorps2003.pdf
Medical Doctor #15	www.wvdhhr.org/wvbom/Directory/2003/mds2003.pdf
Medical License, Special Volunteer #15	www.wvdhhr.org/wvbom/Directory/2003/specialvolunteer2003.pdf
Medical Professional LLC/Company #15	www.wvdhhr.org/wvbom/Directory/2003/pllcs2003.pdf
Nurse-LPN #8	www.lpnboard.state.wv.us/
Occupational Therapist/Assistant #16	www.wvbot.org
Optometrist #41	www.arbo.org/odfinder/LicSearch.asp
Osteopathic Physician/Physician Assistant #17	www.state.wv.us/bdosteo
Pesticide Applicator #25	www.kellysolutions.com
Physician Assistant #15	www.wvdhhr.org/wvbom/Directory/2003/pas2003.pdf
Podiatrist #15	www.wvdhhr.org/wvbom/Directory/2003/podiatrists2003.pdf
Public Accountant-CPA #1	www.state.wv.us/scripts/wvboa/default.cfm
Radiologic Technologist #9	www.wvrtboard.org/
Real Estate Agent/Broker/Sales #35	www.arello.com/ArelloWeb/ShowPage?command=main
Real Estate Appraiser #34	www.asc.gov/content/category1/appr_by_state.asp
Respiratory Care Practitioner #43	www.wvborc.org/licensees/default.asp

West Virginia Licensing Quick Finder

Aesthetician #3	304-558-2924	
Animal Technician #22	304-558-2016	
Architect #2	304-528-5825	
Asbestos Contractor #42	304-558-6720/6768	
Asbestos Inspector /Supvr. #42	304-558-6720/6768	
Asbestos Laboratory #42	304-558-6720/6768	
Asbestos Project Designer #42	304-558-6720/6768	
Asbestos Worker #42	304-558-6720/6768	
Athlete Agent #36	304-558-6000	
Athletic Trainer #26	304-558-7010	
Attorney #14	304-558-7815	
Barber #3	304-558-2924	
Barber/Beauty Culture School #3	304-558-2924	
Boat & Canoe Expedition Provider #29	304-558-2783	
Boating Business, Whitewater #29	304-558-2783	
Charitable Organization #36	304-558-6000	
Chiropractor #4	304-746-7839	
Contractor, General #24	304-558-7890x122	
Cosmetologist #3	304-558-2924	
Counselor LPC, Professional #10	304-733-5494	
Counselor, Professional #10	304-733-5494	
Credit Service Organization #36	304-558-6000	
Dental Hygienist #6	304-252-8266	
Dentist #6	304-252-8266	
Educational Audiologist #26	304-558-7010	
Electrician #40	304-558-2191	
Embalmer #5	304-558-0302	
Emergency Medical Tech. - Paramedic #27	304-558-3956	
Engineer #33	304-558-3554	
First Responder #27	304-558-3956	
Fishing Guide #29	304-558-2783	
Forester #20	304-324-7557	
Forestry Technician #20	304-324-7557	
Fund Raiser, For-Profit Prof'l #37	800-982-8297	
Funeral Director; Funeral Home #5	304-558-0302	
Hearing Aid Specialist #12	304-558-7886	
Insurance Adjuster #30	304-558-0610	
Insurance Agency #30	304-558-0610	
Insurance Producer #30	304-558-0610	
Insurance Solicitor #30	304-558-0610	
Investment Advisor/Rep. #38	304-558-2257	
Landscape Architect #13	304-727-5501	
Lead Abatement Contractor #42	304-558-6720/6768	
Lobbyist #39	304-558-0664	
Manicurist #3	304-558-2924	
Marriage Registation #36	304-558-6000	
Medical Corporation #15	304-558-2921	
Medical Doctor #15	304-558-2921	
Medical License, Special Volunteer #15	304-558-2921	
Medical Profess'l LLC/Company #15	304-558-2921	
Midwife Nurse #8	304-558-3596	
Mine Electrician #32	304-558-1425	
Mine Surveyor/Foreman #32	304-558-1425	

Miner #32 304-558-1425	Polygraph Examiner #28 .... 304-558-7890 x122	School Social Services/Attendance Investigator #26
Notary Public #36 304-558-6000	Private Detective #36 304-558-6000	 304-558-7010
Nurse / Nurse-LPN #8 304-558-3596	Psychologist #11 304-558-0604	School Superintendent #26 304-558-7010
Nurse Anesthetist #8 304-558-3596	Public Accountant-CPA #1 304-558-3557	Securities Agent/Broker/Dealer #38 304-558-2257
Nursing Home Administrator #31 304-759-0722	Radiologic Technologist #9 304-787-4398	Security Guard #36 304-558-6000
Occupational Therapist/Assistant #16.. 304-329-0480	Radon Contractor/Trainer #42 .... 304-558-6720/6768	Shooting Reserve #29........................ 304-558-2783
Optometrist #41 304-558-5901	Rafting Outfitter, Whitewater #29 304-558-2783	Shot Firer #32................................. 304-558-1425
Osteopathic Physician/Physician Assistant #17	Real Estate Agent/Broker/Sales #35.... 304-558-3555	Social Worker #21 304-558-8816
.... 304-723-4638	Real Estate Appraiser #34 304-558-3919	Speech/Language Pathologist #26 304-558-7010
Pesticide Applicator #25 304-558-2209	Respiratory Care Practitioner #43 304-558-1382	Supervisor of Instruction #26 304-558-7010
Pharmacist #18 304-558-0558	Sanitarian, Registered/In-Training #23 . 304-558-2981	Surveyor, Land #7 304-765-0315
Physical Therapist #19 304-627-2251	School Counselor #26 304-558-7010	Teacher #26 304-558-7010
Physical Therapist Assistant #19 304-627-2251	School Nurse #26 304-558-7010	Telemarketer #37 304-558-0211
Physician Assistant #15...................... 304-558-2921	School Principal #26 304-558-7010	Veterinarian #22 304-558-2016
Podiatrist #15.......................... 304-558-2921	School Psychologist #26 304-558-7010	

West Virginia Licensing Agency Information

1 Board of Accountancy, 122 Capitol St #100, Charleston, WV 25301; 304-558-3557, Fax: 304-558-1325. www.state.wv.us/wvboa Email: wvboa@mail.wvnet.edu Search Database at www.state.wv.us/scripts/wvboa/default.cfm

2 Board of Architects, PO Box 9125, Huntington, WV 25704-0125; 304-528-5825, Fax: 304-528-5826. http://wvbrdarch.org Email: lewilex@wvnvm.wvnet.edu Search Database at http://wvbrdarch.org/roster/lic/searchdb.asp

3 Board of Barbers & Cosmetologists, 1716 Pennsylvania Ave, #7, Charleston, WV 25302; 304-558-2924, Fax: 304-558-3450. www.state.wv.us/wvbc Email: sholley@state.wv.us Search Database at www.wvdhhr.org/bph/wvbc/licensees.cfm

4 Board of Chiropractic Examiners, PO Box 8532 (415 1/2 D St, #6), South Charleston, WV 25303; 304-746-7839, Fax: 304-746-0794. www.wvboc.com/ Email: wvboc@citynet.net

5 Board of Embalmers & Funeral Directors, 179 Summers St #305, Charleston, WV 25301-2131; 304-558-0302, Fax: 304-558-0660. www.state.wv.us/funeraldirector/ Email: wvfuneralboard@msn.com Note: The Funeral Directors Assn. member list is available at www.wvfda.org/members.cfm.

6 Board of Examiners for Dentists/Dental Hygienists, 207 S. Heber St, Beckley, WV 25801; 304-252-8266, Fax: 304-252-2779. www.wvdentalboard.org Email: wvbde@charterinternet.com

7 Board of Examiners for Land Surveyors, PO Box 390 (2298 Sutton Lane), Flatwoods, WV 26621; 304-765-0315, Fax: 304-765-0316.

8 Board of Examiners for Reg. Prof. Nurses, 101 Dee Dr, Charleston, WV 25311-1620; 304-558-3596, or 1-877-743-6877, Fax: 304-558-3666. www.wvrnboard.com/ Email: rnboard@state.wv.us Note: The LPNs have a separate board at the same address; 304-558-3572; fax: 305-558-4367.

9 Board of Examiners for Radiologic Technology, PO Box 638, Cool Ridge, WV 25825; 304-787-4398, Fax: 304-787-3030. www.state.wv.us/rtboe Email: wvrtboe@charter.net Search Database at www.wvrtboard.org

10 Board of Examiners in Counseling, PO Box 129, Ona, WV 25545; 800-520-3852. www.wvbec.org/index.htm Email: counselingboard@msn.com Note: Verification requests fee is $20.00 payable to WVBEC; requests are processed in 3 working days. Will fax back results.

11 Board of Examiners of Psychologists, PO Box 3955, Charleston, WV 25339-3955; 304-558-0604, Fax: 304-558-0608. www.wvpsychbd.org Email: wvpsychbd@mail.state.wv.us

12 Board of Hearing-Aid Dealers, 619 Virginia St W, Charleston, WV 25302-2027; 304-558-7886, Fax: 304-558-7886. www.state.wv.us/bep/lmi/license/liclist.htm

13 Board of Landscape Architects, PO Box 1355, St. Albans, WV 25177; 304-727-5501, Fax: 304-727-5580.

14 Board of Law Examiners, 2006 Kanawha Blvd, Charleston, WV 25311; 304-558-2456, Fax: 304-558-2467. www.state.wv.us/wvsca Email: suerubenstein@courtswv.org Search Database at www.wvbar.org/barinfo/mdirectory/

15 Board of Medicine, 101 Dee Dr #103, Charleston, WV 25311-1620; 304-558-2921 x224, Fax: 304-558-2084. www.wvdhhr.org/wvbom

16 Board of Occupational Therapy, 119 S Price St, Kingwood, WV 26537; 304-329-0480, Fax: 304-329-0480. www.wvbot.org Email: cathywhalen@wvbot.org

17 Board of Osteopathy, 334 Penco Rd, Weirton, WV 26062-3813; 304-723-4638, Fax: 304-723-6723. www.state.wv.us/bdosteo Email: bdosteo@mail.wvnet.edu

18 Board of Pharmacy, 232 Capitol St, Charleston, WV 25301-2206; 304-558-0558, Fax: 304-558-0572. www.wvbop.com

19 WV Board of Physical Therapy, 153 W Main St, #103, Clarksburg, WV 26301; 304-627-2251, Fax: 304-627-2253. www.wvbopt.com Email: wvbopt@wvnet.edu Note: Verifications only provided based on a written request and a $25.00 fee.

20 Board of Registration for Foresters, 625 Parkway, Bluefield, WV 24701; 304-324-7557, Fax: 304-324-7512. Email: tprobert@citlink.net

21 Board of Social Work Examiners, PO Box 5459, (State Capitol Complex, Main Bldg - Rm WB9), Charleston, WV 25361; 304-558-8816, Fax: 304-558-4189. www.state.wv.us/socialworkboard Email: williju@mail.wvnet.edu

22 Board of Veterinary Medicine, 1900 Kanawha Blvd E, Charleston, WV 25305-0119; 304-558-2016, Fax: 304-558-0891. Email: goodww@mail.wvnet.edu

23 Bureau of Public Health, Sanitarian Licensing, 815 Quarrier St, Charleston, WV 25301-2616; 304-558-2981, Fax: 304-558-1071. www.wvdhhr.org

24 Contractor Licensing Board, 1900 Kanawha Blvd E, Bldg 6, Rm B-749, Charleston, WV 25305; 304-558-7890 x122, Fax: 304-558-3797. www.labor.state.wv.us Search Database at www.labor.state.wv.us/search/default.asp

25 Department of Agriculture, Pesticide Applicator Licensing, 1900 Kanawah Blvd. E., Charleston, WV 25305; 304-558-2209, Fax: 304-558-2228. www.state.wv.us/agriculture Search Database at www.kellysolutions.com/

26 Department of Education, 1900 Kanawha Blvd E, Charleston, WV 25305; 304-558-7010, Fax: 304-558-7843. http://wvde.state.wv.us Email: llkiser@access.k12.wv.us

27 Office of EMS, Bureau of Public Health, 350 Capitol St #515, Charleston, WV 25301-3716; 304-558-3956, Fax: 304-558-1437. www.wvoems.org

28 Department of Labor, State Capitol Complex, Bldg. 6, Rm 749B, Charleston, WV 25305; 304-558-7890 x122, Fax: 304-558-3797. www.state.wv.us/labor

29 Division of Natural Resources, 1900 Kanawha Blvd, East Bldg 3, Rm 837, Charleston, WV 25305; 304-558-2783, Fax: 304-558-2874. www.wvdnr.gov

30 Insurance Commissioner, 1124 Smith St, Charleston, WV 25301; 304-558-0610, Fax: 304-558-4966. www.wvinsurance.gov Email: agent.licensing@wvinsurance.gov Note: No longer licenses insurance brokers.

31 Nursing Home Administrators Licensing Board, 5303 Kensington Dr, Cross Lanes, WV 25313; 304-759-0722, Fax: 304-759-0724.

32 Office of Miners Health Safety & Training, 1615 Washington St E, Charleston, WV 25311; 304-558-1425, Fax: 304-558-1282. www.wvminesafety.org Email: MINEINFO@mines.state.wv.us

33 Board of Registration for Professional Engineers, 300 Capitol St. Ste 910, Charleston, WV 25301-2703; 304-558-3554, Fax: 304-558-6232. www.wvpebd.org Search Database at www.wvpebd.org

34 Real Estate Appraiser Licensing & Certification Board, 2110 Kanawah Blvd E, #101, Charleston, WV 25311; 304-558-3919, Fax: 304-558-3983. www.state.wv.us/appraise Email: wvappbd@wvnvm.wvnet.edu   Search Database at www.asc.gov/content/category1/appr_by_state.asp

35 Real Estate Commission, 1033 Quarrier St, #400, Charleston, WV 25301-2315; 304-558-3555, Fax: 304-558-6442. www.wvrec.org   Email: wvrec@wvrec.state.wv.us Search Database at www.arello.com/ArelloWeb/ShowPage?command=main

36 Secretary of State, 1900 Kanawha Blvd, Bldg 1, #157-K, Charleston, WV 25305-0770; 304-558-6000, Fax: 304-558-5142. www.wvsos.com   Email: wvsos@wvsos.com

37 Department of Tax & Revenue, Taypayer Services, Telemarketing Registration, PO Box 3784, Charleston, WV 25337; 304-558-3333. www.wvrevenue.gov

38 State Auditor's Office, State Capitol, Rm W110, Charleston, WV 25305; 304-558-2257, Fax: 304-558-4211. www.wvauditor.com   Email: johns@wvauditor.com

39 Ethics Commission, 1207 Quarrier St, 4th Fl, Charleston, WV 25301; 304-558-0664, Fax: 304-558-2169. www.wvethicscommission.org Email: lsuchy@wvadmin.gov Search Database at www.wvethicscommission.org

40 State Fire Marshall, 1207 Quarrier, 2nd Fl, Charleston, WV 25301; 304-558-2191, Fax: 304-558-2537. www.wvfiremarshal.org Email: info@wvfiremarshal.org   Search Database at www.wvfiremarshal.org/search.htm

41 West Virginia Board of Optometry, 723 Kanawha Boulevard #804, Charleston, WV 25301; 304-558-5901, Fax: 304-558-5908. www.wvbo.org Email: wvbdopt@westvirginia.net   Search Database at www.arbo.org/odfinder/LicSearch.asp

42 Department of Health & Human Resources, Radiation, Toxics and Indoor Air Division, 815 Quarrier St #418, Charleston, WV 25301; 304-558-2981, Fax: 304-558-1289. www.wvdhhr.org/rtia/ Search Database at www.wvdhhr.org/rtia/licensing.asp

43 Board of Respiratory Care, 106 Dee Dr, #1, Charleston, WV 25311; 304-558-1382, Fax: 304-558-1383. www.wvborc.org/topframe.html Email: info@wvborc.org Search Database at www.wvborc.org/licensees/default.asp

West Virginia Federal Courts

The following list indicates the district and division name for each county in the state. If the bankruptcy court location is different from the district court, then the location of the bankruptcy court appears in parentheses.

County/Court Cross Reference

County	District	Division	County	District	Division
Barbour	Northern	Elkins (Wheeling)	Mineral	Northern	Elkins (Wheeling)
Berkeley	Northern	Martinsburg (Wheeling)	Mingo	Southern	Huntington (Charleston)
Boone	Southern	Charleston	Monongalia	Northern	Clarksburg (Wheeling)
Braxton	Northern	Clarksburg (Wheeling)	Monroe	Southern	Bluefield (Charleston)
Brooke	Northern	Wheeling	Morgan	Northern	Martinsburg (Wheeling)
Cabell	Southern	Huntington (Charleston)	Nicholas	Southern	Beckley (Charleston)
Calhoun	Northern	Clarksburg (Wheeling)	Ohio	Northern	Wheeling
Clay	Southern	Charleston	Pendleton	Northern	Elkins (Wheeling)
Doddridge	Northern	Clarksburg (Wheeling)	Pleasants	Northern	Clarksburg (Wheeling)
Fayette	Southern	Beckley (Charleston)	Pocahontas	Northern	Elkins (Wheeling)
Gilmer	Northern	Clarksburg (Wheeling)	Preston	Northern	Elkins (Wheeling)
Grant	Northern	Elkins (Wheeling)	Putnam	Southern	Charleston
Greenbrier	Southern	Beckley (Charleston)	Raleigh	Southern	Beckley (Charleston)
Hampshire	Northern	Martinsburg (Wheeling)	Randolph	Northern	Elkins (Wheeling)
Hancock	Northern	Wheeling	Ritchie	Northern	Clarksburg (Wheeling)
Hardy	Northern	Elkins (Wheeling)	Roane	Southern	Charleston
Harrison	Northern	Clarksburg (Wheeling)	Summers	Southern	Bluefield (Charleston)
Jackson	Southern	Parkersburg (Charleston)	Taylor	Northern	Clarksburg (Wheeling)
Jefferson	Northern	Martinsburg (Wheeling)	Tucker	Northern	Elkins (Wheeling)
Kanawha	Southern	Charleston	Tyler	Northern	Clarksburg (Wheeling)
Lewis	Northern	Clarksburg (Wheeling)	Upshur	Northern	Elkins (Wheeling)
Lincoln	Southern	Huntington (Charleston)	Wayne	Southern	Huntington (Charleston)
Logan	Southern	Charleston	Webster	Northern	Elkins (Wheeling)
Marion	Northern	Clarksburg (Wheeling)	Wetzel	Northern	Wheeling
Marshall	Northern	Wheeling	Wirt	Southern	Parkersburg (Charleston)
Mason	Southern	Huntington (Charleston)	Wood	Southern	Parkersburg (Charleston)
McDowell	Southern	Bluefield (Charleston)	Wyoming	Southern	Beckley (Charleston)
Mercer	Southern	Bluefield (Charleston)			

US District Court

Northern District of West Virginia

Clarksburg Division PO Box 2857, Clarksburg, WV 26302-2857 (courier address: 500 W Pike St, Rm 301, Clarksburg, WV 26301), 304-622-8513, Fax: 304-623-4551. www.wvnd.uscourts.gov

Counties: Braxton, Calhoun, Doddridge, Gilmer, Harrison, Lewis, Marion, Monongalia, Pleasants, Ritchie, Taylor, Tyler.

Indexing & Storage: New cases available in the index 1-2 days after filing date.

Fee & Payment: Payment may be made by money order, cashier check. Business checks are not accepted. Personal checks are not accepted. Money orders are preferred unless it is a known person or business. Payee: Clerk, U.S. District Court.

Phone Search: Only docket information available.

Mail Search: A SASE not required.

In Person Search: Fee charged if court conducts your in person search for you.

PACER: PACER is available online at http://pacer.wvnd.uscourts.gov. Document images available. Records purged every 5 years. New records are online after 1 day.

Elkins Division PO Box 1518, Elkins, WV 26241 (courier: 2nd Floor, 300 3rd St, Elkins, WV 26241), 304-636-1445, Fax: 304-636-5746. www.wvnd.uscourts.gov

Counties: Barbour, Grant, Hardy, Mineral, Pendleton, Pocahontas, Preston, Randolph, Tucker, Upshur, Webster.

Indexing & Storage: New cases available in the index 1 day after filing date. Civil cases are indexed on computer from October 1994 forward, and criminal cases from October 1995 forward. District-wide searches are available from this court. Case number and cause of action is released.

Fee & Payment: Payment may be made by money order, cashier check. Business checks are not accepted. Personal checks are not accepted. Money orders are preferred unless it is a known person or business. Payee: Clerk, U.S. District Court. Will fax results $1.00 per page.

Phone Search: Only docket information available by phone. Will fax results $1.00 per page.

Mail Search: A SASE not required.

In Person Search: Fee charged if court conducts your in person search for you. If court personnel assist, search fee is charged.

PACER: PACER is available online at http://pacer.wvnd.uscourts.gov. Document images available. Records purged every 5 years. New records are online after 1 day.

Standards for Federal Courts: See Washington or Wisconsin Federal Courts Section for standards and fees for West Virginia Federal Courts.

Martinsburg Division Room 207, 217 W King St, Martinsburg, WV 25401 (Use mail address for courier delivery) 304-267-8225, Fax: 304-264-0434. www.wvnd.uscourts.gov

Counties: Berkeley, Hampshire, Jefferson, Morgan.

Indexing & Storage: New cases available in the index 2 days after filing date. The computer index is from 1994 forward.

Fee & Payment: Payment may be made by money order, cashier check. Business checks are not accepted. Personal checks are not accepted. Payee: Clerk, U.S. District Court.

Phone Search: Limited docket information is available by phone.

In Person Search: Fee charged if court conducts your in person search for you.

PACER: PACER is available online at http://pacer.wvnd.uscourts.gov. Document images available. Records purged every 5 years. New records are online after 1 day.

Wheeling Division Clerk, PO Box 471, Wheeling, WV 26003 (courier: 12th & Chapline Sts, Wheeling, WV 26003), 304-232-0011, Fax: 304-233-2185. www.wvnd.uscourts.gov

Counties: Brooke, Hancock, Marshall, Ohio, Wetzel.

Indexing & Storage: New cases available in the index immediately after filing date. Civil cases on computer since October 1994, and criminal cases since October 1995. Records have not yet been sent to the Federal Records Center from this office.

Fee & Payment: Payment may be made by money order, cashier check, personal check. Payee: Clerk, U.S. District Court.

Phone Search: All information that is not sealed is available for release over the phone.

In Person Search: Fee charged if court conducts your in person search for you.

PACER: PACER is available online at http://pacer.wvnd.uscourts.gov. Document images available. Records purged every 5 years. New records are online after 1 day.

U.S. Bankruptcy Court

Northern District of West Virginia

Wheeling Division PO Box 70, Wheeling, WV 26003 (courier address: 12th & Chapline Sts, Wheeling, WV 26003), 304-233-1655. www.wvnb.uscourts.gov

Counties: Barbour, Berkeley, Braxton, Brooke, Calhoun, Doddridge, Gilmer, Grant, Hampshire, Hancock, Hardy, Harrison, Jefferson, Lewis, Marion, Marshall, Mineral, Monongalia, Morgan, Ohio, Pendleton, Pleasants, Pocahontas, Preston, Randolph, Ritchie, Taylor, Tucker, Tyler, Upshur, Webster, Wetzel.

Indexing & Storage: Cases indexed by debtor as well as by case number. New cases available in the index 24 hours after filing date.

Fee & Payment: Payment may be made by money order, cashier check, personal check. Payee: Clerk, U.S. Bankruptcy Court.

Phone Search: Only docket information available by phone. Automated voice case information service (VCIS) is available. Call VCIS at 800-809-3028 or 304-233-7318.

In Person Search: Fee charged if court conducts your in person search for you.

PACER: PACER is available online at http://pacer.wvnb.uscourts.gov. Document images available. Case records go back to early 1990. Records never purged. New civil records are online after 1 day.

Electronic Filing: Electronic filing information online at https://ecf.wvnb.uscourts.gov

U.S. District Court

Southern District of West Virginia

Beckley Division PO Drawer 5009, Beckley, WV 25801 (courier: 110 N. Heber, Beckley, WV 25801), 304-253-7481, Fax: 304-253-3252. www.wvsd.uscourts.gov

Counties: Fayette, Greenbrier, Raleigh, Sumners, Wyoming.

Indexing & Storage: New cases available in the index immediately after filing date.

Fee & Payment: Payment may be made by money order, cashier check, personal check. Payee: Clerk, U.S. District Court.

Phone Search: Only docket information available.

In Person Search: Fee charged if court conducts your in person search for you.

PACER: PACER is available online at http://pacer.wvsd.uscourts.gov. Document images available. New records are online after 1 day.

Electronic Filing: Electronic filing information at https://ecf.wvsd.uscourts.gov/cgi-bin/login.pl

Bluefield Division Clerk's Office, PO Box 4128, Bluefield, WV 24701 (courier address: 601 Federal St, Bluefield, WV 24701), 304-327-9798. www.wvsd.uscourts.gov

Counties: McDowell, Mercer, Monroe.

Indexing & Storage: New cases available in the index immediately after filing date.

Fee & Payment: Payment may be made by money order, cashier check, personal check. Payee: Clerk, U.S. District Court.

Phone Search: One name may be searched by phone.

In Person Search: Fee charged if court conducts your in person search for you.

PACER: PACER is available online at http://pacer.wvsd.uscourts.gov. Document images available. New records are online after 1 day.

Electronic Filing: Electronic filing information at https://ecf.wvsd.uscourts.gov/cgi-bin/login.pl

Charleston Division PO Box 3924, Charleston, WV 25339 (courier address: 300 Virginia St E, #2400, Charleston, WV 25339), 304-347-3000. www.wvsd.uscourts.gov/

Counties: Boone, Clay, Jackson, Kanawha, Lincoln, Logan, Mingo, Nicholas, Putnam, Roane.

Indexing & Storage: New cases available in the index immediately after filing date. All Division records are availalble here on computer only. The fee to retrieve a record that has been sent to the Records Center is $25.00.

Fee & Payment: Payment may be made by money order, cashier check, personal check. Payee: Clerk, U.S. District Court.

Phone Search: Only docket information available.

Mail Search: A SASE not required.

In Person Search: Fee charged if court conducts your in person search for you.

PACER: PACER is available online at http://pacer.wvsd.uscourts.gov. Document images available. New records are online after 1 day.

Electronic Filing: Electronic filing information at https://ecf.wvsd.uscourts.gov/cgi-bin/login.pl

Huntington Division Clerk of Court, PO Box 1570, Huntington, WV 25716 (courier address: Room 101, 845 5th Ave, Huntington, WV 25701), 304-529-5588, Fax: 304-529-5131. www.wvsd.uscourts.gov

Counties: Cabell, Mason, Wayne.

Indexing & Storage: New cases available in the index immediately after filing date.

Fee & Payment: Payment may be made by money order, cashier check, personal check. Payee: Clerk, U.S. District Court.

Phone Search: Only docket information available.

In Person Search: Fee charged if court conducts your in person search for you.

PACER: PACER is available online at http://pacer.wvsd.uscourts.gov. Document images available. New records are online after 1 day.

Electronic Filing: Electronic filing information at https://ecf.wvsd.uscourts.gov/cgi-bin/login.pl

Parkersburg Division Clerk of Court, PO Box 1526, Parkersburg, WV 26102 (courier address: Room 5102, 425 Julianna St, Parkersburg, WV 26101), 304-420-6490, Fax: 304-420-6363. www.wvsd.uscourts.gov

Counties: Wirt, Wood.

Indexing & Storage: New cases available in the index immediately after filing date.

Fee & Payment: Payment may be made by money order, cashier check, personal check. Payee: Clerk, U.S. District Court.

Phone Search: Only docket information available.

In Person Search: Fee charged if court conducts your in person search for you.

PACER: PACER is available online at http://pacer.wvsd.uscourts.gov. Document images available. New records are online after 1 day.

Electronic Filing: Electronic filing information at https://ecf.wvsd.uscourts.gov/cgi-bin/login.pl

U.S. Bankruptcy Court

Southern District of West Virginia

Charleston Division PO Box 3924, Charleston, WV 25339 (courier: 300 Virginia St E, Room 2400, Charleston, WV), 304-347-3000. www.wvsd.uscourts.gov/bankruptcy/index.htm

Counties: Boone, Cabell, Clay, Fayette, Greenbrier, Jackson, Kanawha, Lincoln, Logan, Mason, McDowell, Mercer, Mingo, Monroe, Nicholas, Putnam, Raleigh, Roane, Summers, Wayne, Wirt, Wood, Wyoming.

Indexing & Storage: Cases indexed by debtor as well as by case number. New cases available in the index 1-2 days after filing date. Card index is maintained to December 1, 1988 after which index is on computer.

Fee & Payment: Payment may be made by money order, cashier check, personal check, Visa or Mastercard. Credit cards accepted only from law firms. Payee: Clerk, U.S. Bankruptcy Court.

Phone Search: Only docket information available by phone. Automated voice case information service (VCIS) is available. VCIS: 304-347-5337.

Mail Search: A SASE not required.

In Person Search: Fee charged if court conducts your in person search for you.

PACER: PACER is available online at http://pacer.wvsb.uscourts.gov. Document images available. Records purged every 6 months. New civil records are online after 1 day.

Electronic Filing: Electronic filing information online at https://ecf.wvsb.uscourts.gov

West Virginia County Courts

Court	Jurisdiction	No. of Courts	How Organized
Circuit Courts*	General	55	31 Circuits
Magistrate Courts*	Limited	55	55 Counties
Family Courts	Limited	55	55 Counties
Municipal Courts	Municipal	122	

* Profiled in this Sourcebook.

	CIVIL								
Court	Tort	Contract	Real Estate	Min. Claim	Max. Claim	Small Claims	Estate	Eviction	Domestic Relations
Circuit Courts*	X	X	X	$300	No Max		X		X
Magistrate Courts*	X	X		$0	$5000	$3000		X	X
Family Courts									X
Municipal Courts									

	CRIMINAL				
Court	Felony	Misdemeanor	DWI/DUI	Preliminary Hearing	Juvenile
Circuit Courts*	X				X
Magistrate Courts*		X	X	X	
Municipal Courts			X		

ADMINISTRATION Administrative Office, Supreme Court of Appeals, 1900 Kanawha Blvd, 1 E 100 State Capitol, Charleston, WV, 25305; 304-558-0145, Fax: 304-558-1212. www.state.wv.us/wvsca

COURT STRUCTURE The 55 Circuit Courts are the courts of general jurisdiction. Probate is handled by the Circuit Court. Records are held at the County Commissioner's Office.

Family Courts were created by constitutional amendment and were formed as of 01/01/02. Family courts hear cases involving such matters as divorce, annulment, separate maintenance, family support, paternity, child custody, and visitation. Family court judges also conduct final hearings in domestic violence cases.

ONLINE ACCESS The state is working towards a statewide system that will allow access to public records, but one is not yet available. Search opinions from the Supreme Court at http://www.state.wv.us/wvsca/opinions.htm.

There is a commercial system available only to law firms and government agencies that gives access to case information from six Circuit Courts and all of the Magistrate Courts. Visit http://www.swcg-inc.com/swcg/index.html for details.

ADDITIONAL INFORMATION There is a statewide requirement that search turnaround times not exceed five business days. However, most courts do far better than that limit. Release of public information is governed by WV Code Sec.29B-1-1 et seq.

Barbour County

Circuit Court 8 N Main St, Philippi, WV 26416; 304-457-3454; Fax: 304-457-2790. Hours: 8:30AM-4:30PM (EST). *Felony, Civil Actions Over $5,000, Probate.*

Note: Probate is handled by the County Clerk at this address.

Civil Records: Access: Phone, mail, in person. Both court and visitors may perform in person searches. No search fee. Required to search: name, years to search. Civil cases indexed by defendant, plaintiff. Civil records on microfiche from 1843 to 1980s on index cards back to 1862, on dockets back to 1843.

Criminal Records: Access: Phone, mail, in person. Both court and visitors may perform in person searches. No search fee. Required to search: name, years to search. Criminal records on microfiche from 1843 to 1980s on index cards back to 1862, on dockets back to 1843.

General Information: Public Access terminal is available. No sealed, juvenile, adoptions, mental health, expunged records released. No fee to fax results if one or two pages only. Copy fee: $.50 per page. Cert fee: $1.00. Payee: Barbour County Circuit Clerk. Personal checks accepted. Prepayment required. Mail requests: SASE requested. Turnaround time 1 day.

Magistrate Court PO Box 541, Philippi, WV 26416; 304-457-3676; Fax: 304-457-4999. Hours: 8:30AM-4:30PM (EST). *Misdemeanor, Civil Actions Under $5,000, Eviction, Small Claims.*

Civil Records: Access: In person, mail. Both court and visitors may perform in person searches. No search fee. Records go back 10 years, computerized since 1997. Phone access limited to one name searched from 8/93 on only.

Criminal Records: Access: In person, mail. Visitors must perform in person searches for themselves. No search fee. Required to search: name, years to search. Records go back 10 years, computerized since 1997.

General Information: Public Access terminal is available. Copy fee: $.25. Cert fee: $.50. Payee: Barbour County Magistrate Clerk. Prepayment required. Mail turnaround time varies.

Berkeley County

Circuit Court 110 W King St, Martinsburg, WV 25401-3210; 304-264-1918; Probate phone: 304-264-1940. Hours: 9AM-5PM (EST). *Felony, Civil Actions Over $5,000, Probate.*

Note: Probate is handled by Fiduciary Records Clerk, 100 W King St, Rm 2, Martinsburg, WV 25401.

Civil Records: Access: Mail, in person. Visitors must perform in person searches for themselves. No search fee. Required to search: name, years to search. Civil cases indexed by defendant, plaintiff. Civil records on computer from 1/1990, on index books from 1863. No divorce, child custody or child support information given out over phone; phote ID required or notarized copy of photo ID when requesting by mail.

Criminal Records: Access: In person only. Visitors must perform in person searches for themselves. No search fee. Required to search: name, years to search; also helpful: DOB, SSN. Criminal records on computer from 1/1990, on index books from 1800s.

General Information: Public Access terminal is available. No sealed, juvenile, adoptions, mental health, guardianship records released. Will fax results for $2.00 per page. Copy fee: $.50 per page. No cert fee. Payee: Clerk of Circuit Court. Business checks accepted. Prepayment required. Mail requests: SASE not required. Mail turnaround time 1 week.

Magistrate Court 120 W John St, Martinsburg, WV 25401; 304-264-1956; Fax: 304-263-9154. Hours: 9AM-4PM (EST). *Misdemeanor, Civil Actions Under $5,000, Eviction, Small Claims.*

Civil Records: Access: Fax, mail, in person. Both court and visitors may perform in person searches. No search fee. Records stored since 1977.

Criminal Records: Access: In person only. Both court and visitors may perform in person searches. No search fee. Required to search: name, years to search; also helpful: address, DOB, SSN. Records stored since 1977.

General Information: Public Access terminal is available. Copy fee: $.25 per page. Cert fee: $.50 per page. Payee: Berkeley County Magistrate Court. Prepayment required.

Boone County

Circuit Court 200 State St, Madison, WV 25130; 304-369-3925; Probate phone: 304-369-7337; Fax: 304-369-7326. Hours: 8AM-4PM (EST). *Felony, Civil Actions Over $5,000, Probate.*

Note: Probate is handled by County Clerk, 200 State St, Madison, WV 25130.

Civil Records: Access: Phone, fax, mail, in person. Both court and visitors may perform in person searches. No search fee. Required to search: name, years to search. Civil cases indexed by defendant, plaintiff. Civil records on computer from 1984 to present, on index books 1956 to present, on dockets back to 1900.

Criminal Records: Access: Phone, fax, mail, in person. Both court and visitors may perform in person searches. No search fee. Required to search: name, years to search, signed release. Criminal records on computer from 1984 to present, on index books 1956 to present, on dockets back to 1864.

General Information: No sealed, guardianship, juvenile, adoptions, mental health, expunged records released. Fee to fax results is $5.00 per document. Copy fee: $1.00 per page. No cert fee. Payee: Circuit Clerk. Business checks accepted. Prepayment required. Mail requests: SASE requested. Turnaround time 1 day.

Magistrate Court 200 State St., Madison, WV 25130; 304-369-7364; Fax: 304-369-1932. Hours: 8AM-4PM (EST). *Misdemeanor, Civil Actions Under $5,000, Eviction, Small Claims.*

Civil Records: Access: In person. Both court and visitors may perform in person searches. No search fee. Civil records go back to 1977; computerized since 1997.

Criminal Records: Access: In person. Visitors must perform in person searches for themselves. No search fee. Required to search: name, years to search; also helpful: DOB, SSN. Criminal records go back to 1977; computerized records since 1997.

General Information: Public Access terminal is available. Copy fee: $.25 per page. No cert fee.

Braxton County

Circuit Court 300 Main St, Sutton, WV 26601; 304-765-2837; Probate phone: 304-765-2833; Fax: 304-765-2947. Hours: 8AM-4PM (EST). *Felony, Civil Actions Over $5,000, Probate.*

Civil Records: Access: Phone, fax, mail, in person, email. Both court and visitors may perform in person searches. No search fee. Required to search: name, years to search. Civil cases indexed by defendant, plaintiff. Civil records on microfiche 1806 to 1910, on dockets back to 1810; on computer back to 1993. Probate is located across the hall in the same building.

Criminal Records: Access: Phone, fax, mail, in person. Both court and visitors may perform in person searches. No search fee. Required to search: name, years to search, signed release. Criminal records on microfiche 1806 to 1910, on dockets back to 1810.

General Information: Public Access terminal is available. No adoption, juvenile, mental hygiene records released. Will fax results $3.00 1st page, $1.00 each add'l. Copy fee: $.50 per page. No cert fee. Payee: JW Morris, Clerk. Personal checks accepted. Prepayment required. Mail requests: SASE required. Mail turnaround time 2-3 days.

Magistrate Court 307 Main St, Sutton, WV 26601; 304-765-5678; Fax: 304-765-3756. Hours: 8:30AM-4:30PM (EST). *Misdemeanor, Civil Actions Under $5,000, Eviction, Small Claims.*

Civil Records: Access: Mail, in person. Both court and visitors may perform in person searches. Search fee: $.50 per page found. Records go back to 1977; on computer back to 1998.

Criminal Records: Access: In person only. Visitors must perform in person searches for themselves. Search fee: $.50 per page found. Required to search: name, years to search, DOB; also helpful: address, SSN, signed release. Records go back to 1977; on computer back to 1998. The court will not perform criminal record searches and suggests researchers contact State Police.

General Information: Fee to fax results is $2.00 per page. Copy fee: $.50 per page. Cert fee: $.50. Payee: Braxton County Magistrate Court. Prepayment required. Mail turnaround time 1-2 weeks (civil only).

Brooke County

Circuit Court Brooke County Courthouse, PO Box 474, Wellsburg, WV 26070; 304-737-3662; Probate phone: 304-737-3661; Fax: 304-737-0352. Hours: 9AM-5PM (EST). *Felony, Civil Actions Over $5,000, Probate.*

Note: Probate is handled by County Clerk, 632 Main St, Courthouse, Wellsburg, WV 26070.

Civil Records: Access: Mail, in person. Both court and visitors may perform in person searches. Search fee: $5.00 per name. Required to search: name; also helpful: years to search. Civil cases indexed by defendant, plaintiff. Civil records on dockets and files from prior to 1960 to present, in boxes back to 1800s; computerized records since 1997.

Criminal Records: Access: Mail, in person. Both court and visitors may perform in person searches. Search fee: $5.00 per name. Required to search: name; also helpful: years to search, DOB, SSN. Criminal records on dockets and files from prior to 1960 to present, in boxes back to 1800s; computerized records since 1997.

General Information: No divorce, juvenile, mental hygiene, adoption records released. Will fax results for $5.00 per name; Fax charge is $2.00 per page. Copy fee: $.50 per page. Cert fee: $.50 per document. Payee: Brooke County Circuit Clerk. Personal checks accepted. Prepayment required. Mail turnaround time same day, longer if in archives.

Magistrate Court 632 Main St, Wellsburg, WV 26070; 304-737-1321; Fax: 304-737-1509. Hours: 9AM-4PM (EST). *Misdemeanor, Civil Actions Under $5,000, Eviction, Small Claims.*

Civil Records: Access: In person only. Both court and visitors may perform in person searches. No search fee. Civil records go back to 1977; computerized back to 1996.

Criminal Records: Access: In person only. Both court and visitors may perform in person searches. No search fee. Required to search: name; also helpful: DOB, SSN, signed release. Criminal records go back to 1977; computerized back to 1996.

General Information: Public Access terminal is available. Copy fee: $.25. Cert fee: $.50.

Cabell County

Circuit Court PO Box 0545, Huntington, WV 25710-0545; 304-526-8622; Fax: 304-526-8699. Hours: 8:30AM-4:30PM (EST). *Felony, Civil Actions Over $5,000, Probate.*

Civil Records: Access: Mail, in person. Both court and visitors may perform in person searches. No search fee. Required to search: name, years to search. Civil cases indexed by defendant, plaintiff. Civil records on computer from 1990 to present. On index books back to 1854.

Criminal Records: Access: In person, mail. Both court and visitors may perform in person searches. Search fee: $5.00. Required to search: name, years to search; also helpful: address, DOB, SSN. Criminal records on computer from 1990 to present. On index books back to 1854. Requests are directed to the state Criminal Investigation Bureau.

General Information: No sealed, juvenile, adoptions, mental health, guardianship records released. Copy fee: $.50 per page. No cert fee. Payee: Clerk of Circuit Court. Business checks accepted. Prepayment required. Mail requests: SASE required. Mail turnaround time 1 day.

Magistrate Court 750 5th Ave, Basement, Rm B 113 Courthouse, Huntington, WV 25701; 304-526-8642; Fax: 304-526-8646. Hours: 8:30AM-4:30PM (EST). *Misdemeanor, Civil Actions Under $5,000, Eviction, Small Claims.*

Civil Records: Access: In person only. Visitors must perform in person searches for themselves. No search fee. Records go back to 1977 (1987-1997 storage); on computer back to 1991.

Criminal Records: Access: In person only. Visitors must perform in person searches for themselves. No search fee. Required to search: name. Records go back to 1977 (1987-1997 storage); on computer back to 1991.

General Information: Public Access terminal is available. Will fax results for $2.00 per page. Copy fee: $.25 per page. Cert fee: $.50 per page. Payee: Magistrate Court Clerk. Prepayment required.

Calhoun County

Circuit Court PO Box 266, Grantsville, WV 26147; 304-354-6910; Fax: 304-354-6910. Hours: 8:30AM-4PM (EST). *Felony, Civil Actions Over $5,000, Probate.*

Civil Records: Access: Phone, fax, mail, in person. Both court and visitors may perform in person searches. No search fee. Required to search: name, years to search. Civil cases indexed by defendant, plaintiff. Civil records on index books from 1800s.

Criminal Records: Access: Phone, fax, mail, in person. Both court and visitors may perform in person searches. No search fee. Required to search: name, years to search; also helpful: DOB, SSN. Criminal records on dockets from 1900s.

General Information: No adoption, juvenile, divorce, domestic relations, guardianship/conservatorship records released. Will fax results $3.00 1st page, $.50 each add'l. Copy fee: $.50 per page. Cert fee: $1.00. Payee: Circuit Clerk. Personal checks accepted. Prepayment required. Mail requests: SASE helpful. Turnaround time same day received.

Magistrate Court PO Box 186, Grantsville, WV 26147; 304-354-6698; Civil phone: 304-354-6844; Fax: 304-354-6698. Hours: 8:30AM-12:00- 1-4PM (EST). *Misdemeanor, Civil Actions Under $5,000, Eviction, Small Claims.*

Civil Records: Access: In person, mail, phone. Both court and visitors may perform in person searches. No search fee. Civil records computerized since 1997.

Criminal Records: Access: In person, mail, phone. Both court and visitors may perform in person searches. No search fee. Required to search: name; also helpful: years to search, DOB, SSN. Criminal records computerized since 1997.

General Information: Public Access terminal is available. Copy fee: $.25 per page. Cert fee: $1.00 per page. Prepayment required. Mail requests: SASE required. Mail turnaround time 1 week.

Clay County

Circuit Court PO Box 129, Clay, WV 25043; 304-587-4256; Fax: 304-587-4346. Hours: 8AM-4PM (EST). *Felony, Civil Actions Over $5,000, Probate.*

Civil Records: Access: In person only. Visitors must perform in person searches for themselves. No search fee. Required to search: name, years to search, address. Civil cases indexed by defendant, plaintiff. Civil records on docket books and index books back to 1962, microfilm back to 1858; computerized back to 1998.

Criminal Records: Access: Phone, fax, mail, in person. Only the court performs in person searches; visitors may not. Court will do name only searches if time allows. No search fee. Required to search: name,

years to search, address, DOB, SSN. Criminal records on docket books and index books back to 1962, microfilm back to 1858; computerized back to 1998.

General Information: Public Access terminal is available. No juvenile, guardianship, conservatorship or mental health records released. Fee to fax results is $.50 per page. Copy fee: $.50 per page. No cert fee. Payee: Clerk of the Circuit Court. Personal checks accepted. Prepayment required. Mail requests: SASE required. Mail turnaround time 3 days.

Magistrate Court PO Box 393, Clay, WV 25043; 304-587-2131; Fax: 304-587-2727. Hours: 8:30AM-4:30PM (EST). *Misdemeanor, Civil Actions Under $5,000, Eviction, Small Claims.*

Civil Records: Access: In person, mail. Both court and visitors may perform in person searches. No search fee. Civil records go back to 1978; computerized since 2000.

Criminal Records: Access: In person, mail. Both court and visitors may perform in person searches. No search fee. Required to search: name, offense; also helpful: years to search, DOB, SSN. Criminal records go back to 1977; computerized since 2000.

General Information: Public Access terminal is available. Copy fee: $.50 per page. No cert fee. Turnaround time 5 days.

Doddridge County

Circuit Court 118 E. Court St, West Union, WV 26456; 304-873-2331. Hours: 8:30AM-4PM (EST). *Felony, Civil Actions Over $5,000, Probate.*

Civil Records: Access: Phone, mail, in person. Both court and visitors may perform in person searches. No search fee. Required to search: name, years to search. Civil cases indexed by defendant, plaintiff. Civil records on index books 1960 to present, archived from 1845 to 1960; computerized records go back to 1999.

Criminal Records: Access: Phone, mail, fax, in person. Both court and visitors may perform in person searches. No search fee. Required to search: name, years to search. Criminal records in index books and files from 1948; computerized records go back to 1999.

General Information: No juvenile, adoption, mental, domestic records released. Will fax results to local or toll free number. Copy fee: $.50 per page. No cert fee. Payee: Clerk of Circuit Court. Personal checks accepted. Prepayment required. Mail requests: SASE required. Mail turnaround time 1-5 days.

Magistrate Court PO Box 207, West Union, WV 26456; 304-873-2694; Fax: 304-873-2643. Hours: 8AM-4PM (EST). *Misdemeanor, Civil Actions Under $5,000, Eviction, Small Claims.*

Civil Records: Access: In person, mail. Both court and visitors may perform in person searches. No search fee. Civil records go back to 1977; on computer back to 1999.

Criminal Records: Access: In person, mail,fax. Both court and visitors may perform in person searches. No search fee. Required to search: name, years to search DOB, SSN, signed release; also helpful: offense. Criminal records go back to 1977; on computer back to 1999.

General Information: Public Access terminal is available. Copy fee: $.25 per page. Cert fee: $.50 per page. Payee: Magistrate Court. Checks accepted. Prepayment required. Mail requests: SASE requested. Turnaround time 5 days.

Fayette County

Circuit Court 100 Court St, Fayetteville, WV 25840; Civil phone: 304-574-4249; Criminal phone: 304-574-4303/4250; Probate phone: 304-574-4226. Hours: 8AM-4PM (EST). *Felony, Civil Actions Over $5,000, Probate.*

Note: Probate is handled by County Clerk, PO Box 569, Fayetteville, WV 25840.

Civil Records: Access: Mail, in person. Both court and visitors may perform in person searches. No search fee. Required to search: name; also helpful: years to search. Civil cases indexed by defendant, plaintiff. Civil records on computer since 1995; prior records on file 1850 to present.

Criminal Records: Access: Mail, in person. Both court and visitors may perform in person searches. No search fee. Required to search: name, years to search; also helpful: DOB, SSN. Criminal records on computer since 1995; prior records on file 1850 to present.

General Information: Public Access terminal is available. No divorce, adoption, mental, juvenile records released. Copy fee: $.50 per page. Cert fee: $2.00. Payee: Circuit Clerk of Fayette County. No personal checks accepted. Prepayment required. Mail requests: SASE not required. Mail turnaround time 1 week.

Magistrate Court 100 Church St, Fayetteville, WV 25840; 304-574-4279; Fax: 304-574-2458. Hours: 8AM-4PM (EST). *Misdemeanor, Civil Actions Under $5,000, Eviction, Small Claims.*

Civil Records: Access: In person only. Visitors must perform in person searches for themselves. No search fee. Civil records on computer back to 1997, records in-house since 1977.

Criminal Records: Access: In person only. Visitors must perform in person searches for themselves. No search fee. Required to search: name, years to search. Criminal records on computer back to 1997, records in-house since 1977.

General Information: Public Access terminal is available. Will fax search results for $2.00 per page. Copy fee: $.25. Cert fee: $.50. Payee: Magistrate Court. Prepayment required.

Gilmer County

Circuit Court Gilmer County Courthouse, 10 Howard St, Glenville, WV 26351; 304-462-7241; Fax: 304-462-7038. Hours: 8AM-4PM (EST). *Felony, Civil Actions Over $5,000, Probate.*

Civil Records: Access: Phone, mail, fax, in person. Both court and visitors may perform in person searches. No search fee. Required to search: name, years to search. Civil cases indexed by defendant, plaintiff. Civil records on dockets and files from 1845 to present; computerized back to 1999.

Criminal Records: Access: Phone, mail, fax, in person. Both court and visitors may perform in person searches. No search fee. Required to search: name, years to search. Criminal records on dockets and files from 1845 to present; computerized back to 1999.

General Information: Public Access terminal is available. No juvenile, mental, confidential records released. Fee to fax results is $1.50 per page with a $3.00 minimum. Copy fee: $.50 per page. No cert fee. Payee: Circuit Clerk. Personal checks accepted. Mail requests: SASE not required. Mail turnaround time 1 day.

Magistrate Court Courthouse Annex, Glenville, WV 26351; 304-462-7812; Fax: 304-462-8582. Hours: 8:30AM-4PM (EST). *Misdemeanor, Civil Actions Under $5,000, Eviction, Small Claims.*

Civil Records: Access: In person, mail. Both court and visitors may perform in person searches. No search fee. Civil records on computer back to 2000; other records back to 1977.

Criminal Records: Access: In person, mail. Both court and visitors may perform in person searches. No search fee. Required to search: name, years to search; also helpful: DOB, SSN. Civil records on computer back to 2000; other records back to 1977.

General Information: Public Access terminal is available. Fee to fax results is $2.00 per document. Turnaround time 1-5 days.

Grant County

Circuit Court 5 Highland Ave, Petersburg, WV 26847; 304-257-4545; Fax: 304-257-2593 (Attn: Circuit Court). Hours: 8:30AM-4:30PM (EST). *Felony, Civil Actions Over $5,000, Probate.*

Civil Records: Access: Fax, mail, in person. Both court and visitors may perform in person searches. No search fee. Required to search: name, years to search; also helpful: address. Civil cases indexed by defendant, plaintiff. Computerized records from 1999, civil records on index cards (current cases only), on index books back to 1866.

Criminal Records: Access: Fax, mail, in person. Both court and visitors may perform in person searches. No search fee. Required to search: name, years to search, DOB, SSN; also helpful: address. Computerized records from 1999, criminal records on index cards (current cases only), on index books back to 1866.

General Information: Public Access terminal is available. No juvenile, guardianship, adoptions, mental, domestic violence order records released. Fee to fax results is $1.50 1st page, $.75 each add'l page. Copy fee: $.50 per page. Cert fee: $1.50. Payee: Circuit Clerk. Business checks accepted. In state personal checks accepted. Prepayment required. Mail requests: SASE required. Mail turnaround time 1-2 days.

Magistrate Court 5 Highland Ave (PO Box 216), Petersburg, WV 26847; 304-257-4637/1289; Fax: 304-257-9501. Hours: 8:30AM-4:30PM (EST). *Misdemeanor, Civil Actions Under $5,000, Eviction, Small Claims.*

Civil Records: Access: Fax, mail, in person. Both the court and visitors may perform in person searches. Search fee: none. Required to search: Search should include DOB and SSN. Records on computer back to 1994; prior records go back to 1977.

Criminal Records: Access: Fax, mail, in person. Both the court and visitors may perform in person searches. No search fee. Required to search: name, years to search, DOB, SSN. Records on computer back to 1994; prior back to 1977.

General Information: Public Access terminal is available. Copy fee: $.50 per page. Cert fee: $.50 per page. Payee: Grant County Magistrate Court. Prepayment required. Mail turnaround time 1-2 days.

Greenbrier County

Circuit Court PO Drawer 751, Lewisburg, WV 24901; 304-647-6626; Fax: 304-647-6666. Hours: 8:30AM-4:30PM (EST). *Felony, Civil Actions Over $5,000, Probate.*

Civil Records: Access: Mail, in person. Both court and visitors may perform in person searches. No search fee. Required to search: name, years to search. Civil cases indexed by defendant, plaintiff. Civil records indexed by general and docket books from 1800s; computerized back to 1994.

Criminal Records: Access: Mail, in person. Both court and visitors may perform in person searches. No search fee. Required to search: name, years to search; also helpful: DOB, SSN, signed release. Criminal records indexed by general and docket books from 1800s; computerized back to 1995. No information

given over the telephone on criminal matters except to authorized personnel.

General Information: No juvenile, adoptions, mental health records released. Fee to fax results is $2.50 per page. Copy fee: $.50 per page. Cert fee: $1.00. Payee: Clerk of Circuit Court. Personal checks accepted. Prepayment required. Mail turnaround time 1-2 days.

Magistrate Court 200 N Court St, Lewisburg, WV 24901; 304-647-6632; Fax: 304-647-6668. Hours: 8:30AM-4:30PM (EST). *Misdemeanor, Civil Actions Under $5,000, Eviction, Small Claims.*

Civil Records: Access: Phone, mail, in person. Both court and visitors may perform in person searches. No search fee. Civil records on computer back to 1989; other records back to 1977.

Criminal Records: Access: Mail, in person. Both court and visitors may perform in person searches. No search fee. Required to search: name, years to search; also helpful: DOB, SSN. Criminal records on computer back to 1989; other records back to 1977.

General Information: Fee to fax results is $2.00 per page. Copy fee: $.25. Cert fee: $.50 plus $.25 per page. Payee: Greenbrier County Magistrate Court. Prepayment required. Mail turnaround time 1-2 days.

Hampshire County

Circuit Court PO Box 343, Romney, WV 26757; 304-822-5022; Probate phone: 304-822-5112. Hours: 9AM-4PM M-Th, 9AM-8PM Friday (EST). *Felony, Civil Actions Over $5,000, Probate.*

Note: Probate handled by County Clerk, PO Box 806, Romney, WV 26757.

Civil Records: Access: Fax, mail, in person. Both court and visitors may perform in person searches. No search fee. Required to search: name, years to search. Civil cases indexed by defendant, plaintiff. Civil records on index files from 1957 to present, on index cards in storage 1885 to 1957.

Criminal Records: Access: Fax, mail, in person. Both court and visitors may perform in person searches. Search fee: $10.00 per name. Required to search: name, years to search. Criminal records on index files from 1957 to present, on index cards in storage 1885 to 1957.

General Information: No juvenile, divorce or adoption records released. Copy fee: $.50 per page. Cert fee: $1.50. Payee: Clerk of Circuit Court. Personal checks accepted. Prepayment required. Will bill to attorneys. Mail requests: SASE required. Mail turnaround time 2 days.

Magistrate Court 239 W Birch Ln, PO Box 881, Romney, WV 26757; 304-822-4311; Fax: 304-822-3981. Hours: 8:00AM-4PM (EST). *Misdemeanor, Civil Actions Under $5,000, Eviction, Small Claims.*

Civil Records: Access: Mail, fax, in person. Both court and visitors may perform in person searches. No search fee. Civil records go back to 1977; on computer back to 1993.

Criminal Records: Access: Mail, fax, in person. Both court and visitors may perform in person searches. No search fee. Required to search: name, years to search; also helpful: DOB, SSN. Criminal records go back to 1977; on computer back to 1993.

General Information: Public Access terminal is available. Will fax to toll-free numbers no charge. Copy fee: $.25 per page. Cert fee: $.50 per page. Payee: Magistrate Court Clerk. Only cashiers checks and money orders accepted. Prepayment required. Mail turnaround time 5 days.

Hancock County

Circuit Court PO Box 428, New Cumberland, WV 26047; 304-564-3311; Fax: 304-564-5014. Hours: 8:30AM-4:30PM (EST). *Felony, Civil Actions Over $5,000, Probate.*

Note: Probate can be reached at PO Box 367.

Civil Records: Access: Fax, mail, in person, online. Both court and visitors may perform in person searches. Search fee: $5.00 per name. Required to search: name, years to search; also helpful: address. Civil cases indexed by defendant, plaintiff. Civil records on computer since 1972. Online access to court records via a pay service, see www.swcg-inc.com/courts.htm or call 800-795-8543. $125 set-up fee plus a $38.00 or $120 monthly fee plan.

Criminal Records: Access: Fax, mail, in person, online. Both court and visitors may perform in person searches. Search fee: $5.00 per name. Required to search: name, years to search, signed release; also helpful: address, DOB, SSN. Criminal records on computer since 1972. Online access to criminal records is the same as civil.

General Information: Public Access terminal is available. No adoption, juvenile, mental hygiene released. Fee to fax results is $2.00 per page. Copy fee: $.50 per page. Cert fee: $1.50. Payee: Clerk of Circuit Court. Personal checks accepted. Prepayment required. Mail requests: SASE required. Mail turnaround time same day.

Magistrate Court 106 Court St, New Cumberland, WV 26047; 304-564-3355; Fax: 304-564-3852. Hours: 8:30-4:30PM M-F (EST). *Misdemeanor, Civil Actions Under $5,000, Eviction, Small Claims.*

Civil Records: Access: In person, mail. Both court and visitors may perform in person searches. No search fee. Civil records on computer since 1996, dockets available since 1977. Phone, fax and mail access limited.

Criminal Records: Access: In person, mail. Both court and visitors may perform in person searches. No search fee. Required to search: name, years to search; also helpful: DOB, SSN. Criminal records on computer since 1996, dockets available since 1977. Phone, fax and mail access limited.

General Information: Public Access terminal is available. Copy fee: $.25 per page. Cert fee: $.50 per page. Turnaround time 1-2 days.

Hardy County

Circuit Court 204 Washington St, RM 237, Moorefield, WV 26836; 304-538-7869; Fax: 304-538-6197. Hours: 9AM-4PM (EST). *Felony, Civil Actions Over $5,000, Probate.*

Civil Records: Access: In person only. Both court and visitors may perform in person searches. No search fee. Required to search: name, years to search. Civil cases indexed by defendant, plaintiff. Civil records on docket books back to 1960 (chrono index in front of book). Computerized records go back to 1995.

Criminal Records: Access: In person only. Both court and visitors may perform in person searches. No search fee. Required to search: name, years to search, DOB; also helpful: SSN. Criminal records on docket books back to 1960 (chrono index in front of book). Computerized records go back to 1995.

General Information: No juvenile, mental, domestic records released. Will not fax results. Copy fee: $.50 per page. Cert fee: $1.00. Payee: Clerk of Circuit Court. Personal checks accepted. Prepayment required.

Magistrate Court 204 Washington St, Moorefield, WV 26836; 304-538-6836; Fax: 304-538-2072. Hours: 9AM-4PM (EST). *Misdemeanor, Civil Actions Under $5,000, Eviction, Small Claims.*
Civil Records: Access: Fax, mail, in person. Both court and visitors may perform in person searches. No search fee. Civil records on computer back to 1990; others back to 1977.
Criminal Records: Access: Fax, mail, in person. Both court and visitors may perform in person searches. No search fee. Required to search: name, years to search; also helpful: DOB, SSN. Criminal records on computer back to 1990; others back to 1977.
General Information: Public Access terminal is available. Will fax results for $2.00 per page. Copy fee: $.25 perpage. Cert fee: $.50 per page. Payee: Hardy County Magistrate Court. Prepayment required. Mail requests: SASE required. Mail turnaround time 10 days, 5 days if records on computer.

Harrison County

Circuit Court 301 W. Main, #301, Clarksburg, WV 26301-2967; 304-624-8640; Probate phone: 304-624-8673; Fax: 304-624-8710. Hours: 8:30AM-4:30PM (EST). *Felony, Civil Actions Over $5,000, Probate.*
Note: Probate is handled by County Clerk, 301 W Main St, Courthouse, Clarksburg, WV 26301.
Civil Records: Access: In person only. Visitors must perform in person searches for themselves. No search fee. Required to search: name, years to search. Civil cases indexed by defendant, plaintiff. Civil records on computer from 1990 to present. On index books back to mid-1800s.
Criminal Records: Access: In person only. Visitors must perform in person searches for themselves. No search fee. Required to search: name, years to search; also helpful: DOB, SSN (not available for search). Criminal records on computer from 1990 to present. On index books back to mid-1800s.
General Information: Public Access terminal is available. No adoption, juvenile, guardianship, mental health records released. Copy fee: $.50 per page. No cert fee. Payee: Harrison County Circuit Clerk. Only cashiers checks and money orders accepted. Prepayment required.

Magistrate Court 306 Washington Ave Rm 222, Clarksburg, WV 26301; 304-624-8645; Fax: 304-624-8740. Hours: 8AM-4PM (EST). *Misdemeanor, Civil Actions Under $5,000, Eviction, Small Claims.*
Civil Records: Access: In person, mail. Both court and visitors may perform in person searches. No search fee. Civil records go back to 1980s; computerized since 9/97.
Criminal Records: Access: In person, mail. Both court and visitors may perform in person searches. No search fee. Required to search: name, years to search; also helpful: DOB, SSN. Criminal records go back to 1980s; computerized since 9/97.
General Information: Public Access terminal is available. Copy fee: $.25 per page. Cert fee: $.50 per page. Turnaround time 5 days.

Jackson County

Circuit Court PO Box 427, Ripley, WV 25271; 304-373-2214; Fax: 304-372-6237. Hours: 9AM-4PM M-F, 9AM-Noon Sat (EST). *Felony, Civil Actions Over $5,000, Probate.*
Civil Records: Access: Phone, mail, in person. Both court and visitors may perform in person searches. No search fee. Required to search: name, years to search. Civil cases indexed by defendant, plaintiff. Civil records on index books back to 1800s. Computerized records back to 1999.

Criminal Records: Access: Phone, mail, in person. Both court and visitors may perform in person searches. No search fee. Required to search: name, years to search; also helpful: DOB, SSN. Criminal records on index books back to 1800s. Computerized records back to 1999.
General Information: No juvenile, mental, adoption, domestic records released. Will fax results for $2.00 per page. Copy fee: $.50 per page. Cert fee: $2.00. Payee: Clerk of Circuit Court. Only cashiers checks and money orders accepted. Prepayment required. Mail requests: SASE required. Mail turnaround time 1-2 days.

Magistrate Court PO Box 368, Ripley, WV 25271; 304-373-2313; Fax: 304-372-7155. Hours: 9AM-4PM (EST). *Misdemeanor, Civil Actions Under $5,000, Eviction, Small Claims.*
Civil Records: Access: In person only. Visitors must perform in person searches for themselves. No search fee. Records computerized since 1998, on dockets since 1977.
Criminal Records: Access: In person only. Visitors must perform in person searches for themselves. No search fee. Required to search: name, years to search; also helpful: DOB, SSN. Records computerized since 1998, on dockets since 1977.
General Information: Public Access terminal is available. Copy fee: $.25. Cert fee: $.50. Payee: Jackson County Magistrate Court. Prepayment required.

Jefferson County

Circuit Court PO Box 1234, Charles Town, WV 25414; 304-728-3231; Fax: 304-728-3398. Hours: 9AM-5PM (EST). *Felony, Civil Actions Over $5,000.*
Civil Records: Access: In person only. Visitors must perform in person searches for themselves. No search fee. Required to search: name, years to search. Civil cases indexed by defendant, plaintiff. Civil records on computer back to 01/85; on index books 1960 to 1985. On dockets back 1960 back to 1800s in storage.
Criminal Records: Access: In person only. Visitors must perform in person searches for themselves. No search fee. Required to search: name, years to search. Criminal records on computer back to 01/85; on index books 1960 to 1985. On dockets back 1960 back to 1800s in storage.
General Information: Public Access terminal is available. No juvenile, guardianship, adoption, or mental health records released. Copy fee: $.50 per page. Cert fee: $.50 per page; triple seal $3.00. Payee: Circuit Clerk. No personal checks accepted. Prepayment required.

Magistrate Court PO Box 607, Charles Town, WV 25414; 304-728-3233; Fax: 304-728-3235. Hours: 7:30AM-4:30PM (EST). *Misdemeanor, Civil Actions Under $5,000, Eviction, Small Claims.*
Civil Records: Access: Mail, fax, in person. Both court and visitors may perform in person searches. No search fee. Civil records on computer back to 1996; others go back to 1977.
Criminal Records: Access: In person only. Both court and visitors may perform in person searches. No search fee. Required to search: name, years to search, DOB; also helpful: SSN, signed release. Criminal records on computer back to 1996; others go back to 1977.
General Information: Public Access terminal is available. No fee to fax results. Copy fee: $.25 per page. Cert fee: $.50 per page. Payee: Magistrate Clerk. Personal checks accepted. Prepayment required.

Kanawha County

Circuit Court PO Box 2351, Charleston, WV 25328; 304-357-0440; Probate phone: 304-357-0130; Fax: 304-357-0473. Hours: 8AM-5PM (EST). *Felony, Civil Actions Over $5,000, Probate.*
Note: Probate is handled by County Clerk, 409 Virginia St East, Charleston, WV 25301.
Civil Records: Access: In person, online. Visitors must perform in person searches for themselves. No search fee. Required to search: name, years to search; also helpful: address. Civil cases indexed by defendant, plaintiff. Civil records on computer from 7/1989 to present. On microfiche back to 1800s. Online access to court records via a pay service, see www.swcg-inc.com/courts.htm or call 800-795-8543. $125 set-up fee plus a $38.00 or $120 monthly fee plan.
Criminal Records: Access: In person, online. Visitors must perform in person searches for themselves. No search fee. Required to search: name, years to search; also helpful: address, DOB, SSN. Criminal records on computer from 7/1989 to present. On microfiche back to 1800s. Online access to criminal records is the same as civil.
General Information: Public Access terminal is available. No juvenile, neglect, adoption, domestic, guardianship, mental health or conservatorship records released. Copy fee: $.50 per page. Cert fee: $.50 per page. Payee: Kanawha Circuit Clerk. Business checks accepted. Prepayment required.

Magistrate Court 111 Court St, Charleston, WV 25333; 304-357-0400; Fax: 304-357-0205. Hours: 8:30AM-5PM (EST). *Misdemeanor, Civil Actions Under $5,000, Eviction, Small Claims.*
Civil Records: Access: In person, mail. Both court and visitors may perform in person searches. No search fee. Civil records go back to 1982; computerized records since 1996.
Criminal Records: Access: In person, mail, fax. Both court and visitors may perform in person searches. No search fee. Required to search: name, years to search; also helpful: DOB, SSN. Criminal records go back to 1982; computerized records since 1991.
General Information: Public Access terminal is available. Will fax results to local or toll free line. Copy fee: $.25 per page. Cert fee: $.50 per page. Payee: Kanawha Magistrate Court. Personal checks accepted. Mail requests: SASE required. Mail turnaround time 14 days.

Lewis County

Circuit Court PO Box 69, Weston, WV 26452; 304-269-8210; Fax: 304-269-8249. Hours: 8:30AM-4:30PM (EST). *Felony, Civil Actions Over $5,000, Probate.*
Civil Records: Access: Phone, fax, mail, in person. Only the court performs in person searches; visitors may not. No search fee. Required to search: name, years to search. Civil cases indexed by defendant, plaintiff. Civil records on index books 1977 to 1992; on computer back to 1984. No index for chancery books back to 1800s.
Criminal Records: Access: Phone, fax, mail, in person. Only the court performs in person searches; visitors may not. No search fee. Required to search: name, years to search; also helpful: SSN. Criminal records on index books 1977 to 1992; on computer back to 1984. No index for chancery books back to 1800s.
General Information: No adoption, juvenile, domestic records released. Fee to fax results is $2.00 per page. Copy fee: $.50 per page. Cert fee: $.50 per page. Payee: Clerk of Circuit Court. Business checks

accepted. Prepayment required. Mail requests: SASE not required. Mail turnaround time 2 days.

Magistrate Court 111 Court St, PO Box 260, Weston, WV 26452; 304-269-8230; Fax: 304-269-8239. Hours: 8:30AM-Noon, 1-4:30PM (EST). *Misdemeanor, Civil Actions Under $5,000, Eviction, Small Claims.*

Civil Records: Access: In person, mail, fax. Both court and visitors may perform in person searches. No search fee. Required to search: name, DOB, SSN & years to search. Civil records computerized since 1991, indexed since 1977.

Criminal Records: Access: In person, mail, fax. Both court and visitors may perform in person searches. No search fee. Required to search: name, years to search; also helpful: DOB, SSN. Criminal records computerized since 1991.

General Information: Public Access terminal is available. Will fax results for $2.00 per sheet. Copy fee: $.25 per page. Cert fee: $.50 per page. Payee: Lewis County Magistrate Court. Prepayment required. Mail requests: SASE required. Mail turnaround time 5 days.

Lincoln County

Circuit Court PO Box 338, Hamlin, WV 25523; 304-824-7887 x239; Probate phone: x233; Fax: 304-824-7909. Hours: 9AM-4:30PM (EST). *Felony, Civil Actions Over $5,000, Probate.*

Note: Probate mailing address is PO Box 497; direct records requests to the county clerk at x233.

Civil Records: Access: Phone, mail, in person. Both court and visitors may perform in person searches. No search fee. Required to search: name, years to search. Civil cases indexed by defendant, plaintiff. Civil records computerized since 1991, on index books 1971 to present, on docket books back to 1909.

Criminal Records: Access: Phone, mail, in person. Both court and visitors may perform in person searches. No search fee. Required to search: name, years to search, DOB, SSN; also helpful: address. Criminal records computerized since 1991, on index books 1971 to present, on docket books back to 1909.

General Information: No juvenile, adoption, divorce or mental hygiene records released. Will fax results. No copy fee. No cert fee. Mail requests: SASE not required. Mail turnaround time: immediate to next day.

Magistrate Court PO Box 573, Hamlin, WV 25523; 304-824-5001 x235; Fax: 304-824-5280. Hours: 9AM-4PM (EST). *Misdemeanor, Civil Actions Under $5,000, Eviction, Small Claims.*

Note: Searches performed by court only on second and fourth Thursday of each month.

Civil Records: Access: In person, mail. Both court and visitors may perform in person searches. No search fee. Required to search: nmae, DOB, SSN.

Criminal Records: Access: In person, mail. Both court and visitors may perform in person searches. No search fee. Required to search: name, years to search; also helpful: DOB, SSN.

General Information: Public Access terminal is available. Will fax results to local or toll free line. Turnaround time 1-14 days.

Logan County

Circuit Court Logan County Courthouse, Rm 311, Logan, WV 25601; 304-792-8550; Fax: 304-792-8555. Hours: 8:30AM-4:30PM (EST). *Felony, Civil Actions Over $5,000, Probate.*

Civil Records: Access: In person. Visitors must perform in person searches for themselves. No search fee. Required to search: name, years to search. Civil cases indexed by defendant, plaintiff. Civil records on index books back to 1800s, on computer from 1995.

Criminal Records: Access: Mail, fax, in person. Both court and visitors may perform in person searches. No search fee. Required to search: name, years to search, SSN. Criminal records on index books back to 1800s, on computer from 1995.

General Information: No adoptions, juvenile, domestic records released. Fee to fax results is $1.00 per page. Copy fee: $.50 per page. Cert fee: $1.50 plus $.50 per page after first 2. Payee: Clerk of Circuit Court. Only cashiers checks and money orders accepted. Prepayment required. Will bill to attorneys. Mail requests: SASE not required. Mail turnaround time 1-2 days.

Logan Magistrate Court Logan County Courthouse, 300 Stratton St, Logan, WV 25601; 304-792-8651; Fax: 304-752-0790. Hours: 8:30AM-Noon; 1-4:30PM (EST). *Misdemeanor, Civil Actions Under $5,000, Eviction, Small Claims.*

Civil Records: Access: In person, mail, fax. Both court and visitors may perform in person searches. No search fee. Records are computerized since 1992.

Criminal Records: Access: In person, mail. Both court and visitors may perform in person searches. Search fee: $.50 per name. Required to search: name, years to search; also helpful: address, DOB, SSN.

General Information: Fee to fax results is $2.00 1st page and $1.50 each addl. Copy fee: $.25 per page. Cert fee: $.50 per page. Payee: Logan Magistrate Court. Prepayment required. Prepayment required for copies. Mail requests: SASE requested. Turnaround time 5 days.

Marion County

Circuit Court PO Box 1269, Fairmont, WV 26554; 304-367-5360; Fax: 304-367-5374. Hours: 8:30AM-4:30PM (EST). *Felony, Civil Actions Over $3,000.*

Civil Records: Access: Phone, fax, mail, in person. Both court and visitors may perform in person searches. No search fee. Required to search: name, years to search. Civil cases indexed by defendant, plaintiff. Civil records on computer from Jan. 1988 to present. On docket books from 1849 to 1988.

Criminal Records: Access: In person, mail, fax, phone. Visitors must perform in person searches for themselves. No search fee. Required to search: name, years to search; also helpful: DOB, SSN. Criminal records on computer from Jan. 1988 to present. On docket books from 1849 to 1988. The court refers all written requests to the Dept of Public Safety.

General Information: Public Access terminal is available. No adoptions, juvenile, mental or guardianship records released. Will fax results $5.00 1st page, $2.00 each add'l. After 10 pages fee is $1.00 per page. Copy fee: $.50 per page. Cert fee: $.50 per page. Payee: Clerk of Circuit Court. Business checks accepted. Prepayment required. Mail requests: SASE requested. Turnaround time 2-3 days.

Magistrate Court 200 Jackson St, Fairmont, WV 26554; 304-367-5330; Fax: 304-367-5336. Hours: 8:30AM-4:30PM M-T-W-F; 8:30AM-7PM Th (EST). *Misdemeanor, Civil Actions Under $5,000, Eviction, Small Claims.*

Note: No record checks performed between 11:30AM and 1:30PM.

Civil Records: Access: In person, mail. Both court and visitors may perform in person searches. No search fee. Civil records go back to 1977; computerized since 1996.

Criminal Records: Access: In person, mail. Both court and visitors may perform in person searches. No search fee. Required to search: name, years to search; also helpful: DOB, SSN. Criminal records go back to 1977; computerized since 1996.

General Information: Public Access terminal is available. Will not fax results. Copy fee: $.25 per copy. Cert fee: $.50 per page. Payee: Marion County Magistrate Clerk. Personal checks accepted. Prepayment required. Mail requests: SASE required. Mail turnaround time 5-15 days, ASAP for phone requests, time permitting.

Marshall County

Circuit Court Marshall County Courthouse, 7th St, Moundsville, WV 26041; 304-845-2130; Fax: 304-845-3948. Hours: 8:30AM-4:30PM M-Th; 8:30AM-5:30PM F (EST). *Felony, Civil Actions Over $5,000.*

Civil Records: Access: Fax, mail, in person. Both court and visitors may perform in person searches. No search fee. Required to search: name, years to search. Civil cases indexed by defendant, plaintiff. Civil records on computer since 01/98; prior records on index books and in files from 1836 to present.

Criminal Records: Access: Fax, mail, in person. Both court and visitors may perform in person searches. No search fee. Required to search: name, years to search; also helpful: DOB, SSN. Criminal records on computer since 01/98; prior records on index books and in files from 1836 to present.

General Information: No juvenile, mental, adoption, sealed, conservatorship, guardianship or divorce records released. Fee to fax results is $.50 per page. Copy fee: $.25 per page. Cert fee: $1.00. Payee: Clerk of Circuit Court. Personal checks accepted. Prepayment required. Will bill to attorneys. Mail requests: SASE not required. Mail turnaround time 1-2 days.

Mason County

Circuit Court Mason County Courthouse, Point Pleasant, WV 25550; 304-675-4400; Fax: 304-675-7419. Hours: 8:30AM-4:30PM (EST). *Felony, Civil Actions Over $5,000, Probate.*

Civil Records: Access: In person only. Visitors must perform in person searches for themselves. No search fee. Required to search: name, years to search. Civil cases indexed by defendant, plaintiff. Civil records on computer from 1994. No time limit on open cases. Index books with data back to 1800s.

Criminal Records: Access: In person only. Visitors must perform in person searches for themselves. No search fee. Required to search: name, years to search. Criminal records on computer from 1994. No time limit on open cases. Index books with data back to 1800s.

General Information: Public Access terminal is available. No divorce or juvenile records released. Copy fee: $.50 per page. No cert fee. Payee: Circuit Court Clerk. Personal checks accepted. Prepayment required. Will bill mail requests for specific document file.

Magistrate Court 200 6th St, Point Pleasant, WV 25550; 304-675-6840; Fax: 304-675-5949. Hours: 8:30AM-4:30PM (EST). *Misdemeanor, Civil Actions Under $5,000, Eviction, Small Claims.*

Note: Judges offices can be reached at 304-675-6400 and 304-675-6636.

Civil Records: Access: In person, mail. Both court and visitors may perform in person searches. No search fee. Civil records go back to 1977; computerized since 1998.

Criminal Records: Access: In person, mail. Both court and visitors may perform in person searches. No search fee. Required to search: name, years to search. Criminal records go back to 1977; computerized since 1998.

General Information: Public Access terminal is available. Copy fee: $.25 per page. Cert fee: $.50 per page. Turnaround time 3-4 days.

McDowell County

Circuit Court PO Box 400, Welch, WV 24801; 304-436-8535; Probate phone: 304-436-8544. Hours: 9AM-5PM (EST). *Felony, Civil Actions Over $5,000, Probate.*

Note: Probate is handled by County Clerk, 90 Wyoming St, #109, Welch, WV 24801.

Civil Records: Access: Mail, in person. Both court and visitors may perform in person searches. No search fee. Required to search: name, years to search. Civil cases indexed by defendant, plaintiff. Civil records on index books back to 1800s; on computer back to 1999.

Criminal Records: Access: Mail, in person. Both court and visitors may perform in person searches. No search fee. Required to search: name, years to search; also helpful: DOB, SSN. Criminal records on index books back to 1800s; on computer back to 1999.

General Information: Public Access terminal is available. No sealed, juvenile, adoption, mental health, guardianship records released. Will fax results to local or toll free line. Copy fee: $.50 per page. Cert fee: $.50 per page. Payee: Clerk of Circuit Court. Business checks accepted. Prepayment required. Mail requests: SASE required. Mail turnaround time 1 week.

Magistrate Court PO Box 447, Welch, WV 24801; 304-436-8588; Fax: 304-436-8575. Hours: 9AM-5PM (EST). *Misdemeanor, Civil Actions Under $5,000, Eviction, Small Claims.*

Civil Records: Access: Mail, fax, in person. Visitors must perform in person searches for themselves. Search fee: None; will search as time permits. Records on computer go back to 1999, accessible since 1977.

Criminal Records: Access: Mail, fax, in person. Both court and visitors may perform in person searches. Search fee: None; will search as time permits. Required to search: name, years to search, DOB, SSN. Records on computer go back to 1998, accessible since 1977. Records on criminal now go back to 1997.

General Information: Public Access terminal is available. Fee to fax results is $2.00 per page. Copy fee: $.25 per page. Cert fee: $.50 per page. Payee: Magistrate Court. Turnaround time 5 days.

Mercer County

Circuit Court 1501 W. Main St, Princeton, WV 24740; 304-487-8323; Criminal phone: 304-487-8410 / 304-487-8372; Probate phone: 304-487-8336; Fax: 304-425-8351. Hours: 8:30AM-4:30PM (EST). *Felony, Civil Actions Over $5,000.*

Note: Probate Court records are at the same address but separate office.

Civil Records: Access: Phone, fax, mail, in person. Both court and visitors may perform in person searches. No search fee. Required to search: name, years to search. Civil cases indexed by defendant, plaintiff. Civil records on computer from Oct. 1989 to present. On index books from 1930 to 1989 (Cott System). On index cards back to 1890s.

Criminal Records: Access: Phone, fax, mail, in person. Both court and visitors may perform in person searches. No search fee. Required to search: name, years to search; also helpful: DOB, SSN. Criminal records on computer from Oct. 1989 to present. On index books from 1930 to 1989 (Cott System). On index cards back to 1890s.

General Information: Public Access terminal is available. No juvenile, adoption, mental health, guardianship or conservatorship records released. Will fax results $2.00 per page. Copy fee: $.50 per page. Cert fee: $.50 per page. Payee: Circuit Court Clerk.

Business checks accepted. Prepayment required. Mail turnaround time 1-2 days.

Magistrate Court 1519 N Walker St, Princeton, WV 24740; 304-431-7115. Hours: 8:30AM-4:30PM (EST). *Misdemeanor, Civil Actions Under $5,000, Eviction, Small Claims.*

Civil Records: Access: In person only. Visitors must perform in person searches for themselves. No search fee. Civil records from 1977; computerized back to 1994.

Criminal Records: Access: In person, mail, fax. Visitors must perform in person searches for themselves. No search fee. Required to search: name, years to search; also helpful: address, DOB, SSN. Criminal records from 1977; computerized back to 1994.

General Information: Public Access terminal is available. Will fax results to local or toll free line. Copy fee: $.25 per page. Cert fee: $.50. Payee: Mercer County Magistrate Court. Cashiers checks, money orders, Visa/MC accepted. Prepayment required. Mail requests: SASE required. Mail turnaround time is 10 days.

Mineral County

Circuit Court 150 Armstrong St, Keyser, WV 26726; 304-788-1562; Fax: 304-788-4109. Hours: 8:30AM-5PM (EST). *Felony, Civil Actions Over $5,000, Probate.*

Note: Probate court is a separate office at the same address, 2nd Fl, 304-788-3924.

Civil Records: Access: Fax, mail, in person, online. Both court and visitors may perform in person searches. Search fee: $5.00 per name. Required to search: name, years to search. Civil cases indexed by defendant, plaintiff. Civil records on computer 1/1991 to present, on dockets from 1920s. Online access to court records via a pay service, see www.swcg-inc.com/courts.htm or call 800-795-8543. $125 set-up fee plus a $38.00 or $120 monthly fee plan. Fax access not guaranteed.

Criminal Records: Access: Fax, mail, in person, online. Both court and visitors may perform in person searches. Search fee: $5.00 per name. Required to search: name, years to search; also helpful: DOB, SSN. Criminal records on computer 1/1991 to present, on dockets from 1920s. Online access to criminal records is the same as civil. Fax access not guaranteed.

General Information: No juvenile, adoption, divorce, mental hygiene, conservatorship or guardianship records released. Copy fee: $.50 per page. No cert fee. Payee: Clerk of Circuit Court. Personal checks accepted. Prepayment required. Mail requests: SASE requested. Turnaround time 2-4 days.

Magistrate Court 105 West St, Keyser, WV 26726; 304-788-2625; Fax: 304-788-9835. Hours: 8:30AM-4:30PM (EST). *Misdemeanor, Civil Actions Under $5,000, Eviction, Small Claims.*

Civil Records: Access: Mail, in person. Both court and visitors may perform in person searches. Search fee: none. Required to search: name, years to search. Civil records on computer back to 1991.

Criminal Records: Access: Mail, in person. Both court and visitors may perform in person searches. No search fee. Required to search: name, years to search; also helpful: DOB, SSN. Records on computer back to 1991; prior back to 1977.

General Information: Public Access terminal is available. Copy fee: $.25 per page. Cert fee: $.50 per page. Payee: Magistrate Court. Prepayment required. Mail requests: SASE requested. Turnaround time: time permitting.

Mingo County

Circuit Court PO Box 435, Williamson, WV 25661; 304-235-0320; Probate phone: 304-235-0330; Fax: 304-235-0320. Hours: 8:30AM-4:30PM (EST). *Felony, Civil Actions Over $5,000, Probate.*

Note: Probate is handled by County Clerk, 75 E 2nd Ave, Williamson, WV 25661.

Civil Records: Access: Mail, in person. Only the court performs in person searches; visitors may not. Search fee: $10.00 per name. Required to search: name, years to search. Civil cases indexed by defendant, plaintiff. Civil records on computer from 1/91 to present, civil on index books back to 1960, chancery books back to 1800s (written or in person only).

Criminal Records: Access: Mail, in person. Both court and visitors may perform in person searches. Search fee: $10.00 per name. Required to search: name, years to search; also helpful: DOB. Criminal records on computer since 1/91, Index books back to 1955.

General Information: Public Access terminal is available. No adoption, mental hygiene, juvenile records released. Copy fee: $.50 per page. No cert fee. Payee: Mingo County Circuit Clerk. Personal checks accepted. Prepayment required. Mail requests: SASE required. Mail turnaround time 1-2 weeks.

Magistrate Court PO Box 986, Williamson, WV 25661; 304-235-2445; Fax: 304-235-3179. Hours: 8:30AM-4:30PM (EST). *Misdemeanor, Civil Actions Under $5,000, Eviction, Small Claims.*

Civil Records: Access: Phone, mail, fax, in person. Both court and visitors may perform in person searches. No search fee. Required to search: name, years to search; also helpful: DOB. Civil records go back to 1977; on computer back to 1998.

Criminal Records: Access: Phone, mail, fax, in person. Both court and visitors may perform in person searches. No search fee. Required to search: name, years to search; also helpful: DOB, SSN. Criminal records go back to 1977; on computer back to 1998.

General Information: Public Access terminal is available. Fee to fax results is $2.00 per page or free to toll-free number. Copy fee: $.25 per page. Cert fee: $.50 per page. Payee: Magistrate Court. Prepayment required. Mail turnaround time 1 week, sooner for phone requests.

Monongalia County

Circuit Court County Courthouse, 243 High St Rm 110, Morgantown, WV 26505; 304-291-7240; Probate phone: 304-291-7236; Fax: 304-291-7273. Hours: 9AM-7PM M; 9AM-5PM T-F (EST). *Felony, Civil Actions Over $5,000, Probate.*

Note: A disclaimer for the Clerk must be included by mail requesters. Estates/Probate is handled by County Clerk, 243 High St, Rm 123, Morgantown, WV 26505.

Civil Records: Access: Mail, in person. Both court and visitors may perform in person searches. Search fee: $5.00 per name. Required to search: name, years to search. Civil cases indexed by defendant, plaintiff. Civil records on computer from 1/90 to present, on index book separated by plaintiff and defendant back to 1865.

Criminal Records: Access: Mail, in person. Both court and visitors may perform in person searches. Search fee: $5.00 per name. Required to search: name, years to search; also helpful: DOB, SSN. Criminal records on computer from 1/90 to present, on index book separated by plaintiff and defendant back to 1865.

General Information: No juvenile, divorce, mental hygiene, divorce, adoption, guardianship, conservatorship or domestic records released. Fee to fax results is $1.00 per page. Copy fee: $.50 per page. No cert fee. Payee: Circuit Clerk. Business checks accepted. Prepayment required. Mail requests: SASE required. Mail turnaround time 1 day.

Magistrate Court 265 Spruce St, Morgantown, WV 26505; 304-291-7296; Fax: 304-284-7313. Hours: 8AM-7PM (EST). *Misdemeanor, Civil Actions Under $5,000, Eviction, Small Claims.*
Civil Records: Access: Mail, fax, in person. Both court and visitors may perform in person searches. Search fee: none. Required to search: name, years to search. Records on computer back to 1999; prior in books back to 1977.
Criminal Records: Access: Mail, fax, in person. Both court and visitors may perform in person searches. No search fee. Required to search: name, years to search; also helpful: DOB, SSN, signed release. Records on computer go back to 1999; prior in books back to 1977.
General Information: Public Access terminal is available. Copy fee: $.25 per page. Cert fee: $.50 per page. Payee: Magistrate Court. Prepayment required. Mail turnaround time 10-14 days.

Monroe County

Circuit Court PO Box 350, Union, WV 24983-0350; 304-772-3017; Probate phone: 304-772-3096; Fax: 304-772-4497. Hours: 8AM-4PM (EST). *Felony, Civil Actions Over $5,000, Probate.*
Civil Records: Access: Phone, mail, in person. Both court and visitors may perform in person searches. No search fee. Required to search: name, years to search. Civil cases indexed by defendant, plaintiff. Civil records on index books 1799 to present; on computer back to 2000.
Criminal Records: Access: Phone, mail, in person. Both court and visitors may perform in person searches. No search fee. Required to search: name, years to search; also helpful: DOB, SSN. Criminal records on index books 1799 to present; on computer back to 2000.
General Information: Public Access terminal is available. No juvenile, adoption, divorce records released. Will fax results to local or toll free line. Copy fee: $.50 per page. Include postage with copy fee. Cert fee: $1.00. Payee: Clerk of Circuit Court. Personal checks accepted. Prepayment required. Mail requests: SASE requested. Turnaround time 1 week.

Magistrate Court PO Box 4, Union, WV 24983; 304-772-3321/3176; Fax: 304-772-4357. Hours: 8:30AM-4:30PM (EST). *Misdemeanor, Civil Actions Under $5,000, Eviction, Small Claims.*
Civil Records: Access: Mail, In person. Both court and visitors may perform in person searches. No search fee. Required to search: name, DOB, SSN. Criminal records go back to 1977; computerized records since 2000.
Criminal Records: Access: Mail, in person, fax. Both court and visitors may perform in person searches. No search fee. Required to search: name, years to search; also helpful: DOB, SSN. Criminal records go back to 1977; computerized records since 2000.
General Information: Will fax results $2.00. Copy fee: $.25 per page. Cert fee: $.50 per page. Payee: Monroe County Magistrate Court. Personal checks accepted. Mail requests: SASE requested. Turnaround time 1-2 days.

Morgan County

Circuit Court 77 Fairfax St, #2F, Berkeley Springs, WV 25411-1501; 304-258-8554; Fax: 304-258-7319. Hours: 9AM-5PM Monday - Friday (EST). *Felony, Civil Actions Over $5,000, Probate.*
Note: Probate is located at the same address in #1A, separate office; telephone is 304-258-8547

Civil Records: Access: In person only. Visitors must perform in person searches for themselves. Search fee: none. Required to search: name, years to search. Civil cases indexed by defendant, plaintiff. Civil records on computer back to 1/93, index cards back to 1960; in person searching only on index books back to 1800s.
Criminal Records: Access: In person only. Visitors must perform in person searches for themselves. No search fee. Required to search: name, years to search; also helpful-DOB, SSN, signed release. Criminal records on computer back to 1/93, index cards back to 1960.
General Information: No juvenile, adoption, mental health, divorce records released. Copy fee: $.50 per page. No cert fee. Payee: Kimberly J Jackson, Circuit Clerk. Only cashiers checks and money orders accepted. Prepayment required. Will bill to attorneys.

Magistrate Court 111 Fairfax St, Berkeley Springs, WV 25411; 304-258-8631; Fax: 304-258-8639. Hours: 9AM-4:30PM (EST). *Misdemeanor, Civil Actions Under $5,000, Eviction, Small Claims.*
Civil Records: Access: In person only. Visitors must perform in person searches for themselves. No search fee. Civil records go back to 1977; computerized records since 1998.
Criminal Records: Access: In person only. Visitors must perform in person searches for themselves. No search fee. Required to search: name, years to search; also helpful: DOB, SSN. Criminal records go back to 1977; computerized records since 1998. Phone, fax and mail access limited.
General Information: Public Access terminal is available. Copy fee: $.25 per page. Cert fee: $.50 per page. Only cashiers checks and money orders accepted.

Nicholas County

Circuit Court 700 Main St, Summersville, WV 26651; 304-872-7810; Probate phone: 304-872-7820. Hours: 8:30AM-4:30PM (EST). *Felony, Civil Actions Over $5,000, Probate.*
Note: Probate is handled by County Clerk, 700 Main St, #2, Summersville, WV 26651.
Civil Records: Access: Mail, in person. Both court and visitors may perform in person searches. No search fee. Required to search: name, years to search. Civil cases indexed by defendant, plaintiff. Civil records on computer since 1994; prior records on index cards from 1976 to 1994 on dockets back to 1818.
Criminal Records: Access: Mail, in person. Both court and visitors may perform in person searches. No search fee. Required to search: name, years to search; also helpful: DOB, SSN. Criminal records on computer since 1994; prior records on index cards from 1976 to 1994 on dockets back to 1818.
General Information: Public Access terminal is available. No divorce, juvenile, adoption, mental, guardianship records released. Copy fee: $.50 per page. No cert fee. Payee: Circuit Clerk. Personal checks accepted. Mail requests: SASE required. Mail turnaround time 1 week.

Magistrate Court 511 Church St, #206 2nd Fl, Summersville, WV 26651; 304-872-7829; Fax: 304-872-7888. Hours: 8:30AM-4:30PM (EST). *Misdemeanor, Civil Actions Under $5,000, Eviction, Small Claims.*
Civil Records: Access: Mail, in person. Visitors must perform in person searches for themselves. No search fee. Civil records on computer back to 1990, cases available since 1977. Request must be in writing.
Criminal Records: Access: Mail, in person. Visitors must perform in person searches for themselves. No search fee. Required to search: name, years to search;

also helpful: DOB, SSN. Criminal records on computer back to 1990, cases available since 1977. Request must be in writing.
General Information: Public Access terminal is available. Copy fee: $.25. Cert fee: $.50 per page. Payee: Magistrate Court. Prepayment required.

Ohio County

Circuit Court 1500 Chapline St, City & County Bldg Rm 403, Wheeling, WV 26003; 304-234-3613; Fax: 304-232-0550. Hours: 8:30AM-5PM (EST). *Felony, Civil Actions Over $5,000, Probate.*
Civil Records: Access: Fax, mail, in person, online. Both court and visitors may perform in person searches. Search fee: $5.00 per name. Required to search: name, years to search. Civil cases indexed by defendant, plaintiff. Civil records on computer from Oct 1986 to present, on index books back to 1800s. Online access to court records via a pay service, see www.swcg-inc.com/courts.htm or call 800-795-8543. $125 set-up fee plus a $38.00 or $120 monthly fee plan.
Criminal Records: Access: Fax, mail, in person, online. Both court and visitors may perform in person searches. Search fee: $5.00 per name. Required to search: name, years to search; also helpful: DOB, SSN. Criminal records on computer from Oct 1986 to present, on index books back to 1800s. Online access to criminal records is the same as civil.
General Information: Public Access terminal is available. No domestic, juvenile, mental, adoption records released. Fee to fax results is $2.00 per page. Copy fee: $.50 per page. Cert fee: $1.50. Payee: Ohio County Circuit Court. Business checks accepted. Prepayment required. Mail requests: SASE required. Mail turnaround time 1 week for accounts only.

Magistrate Court Courthouse Annex, 26 15th St, Wheeling, WV 26003; 304-234-3709; Fax: 304-234-3898. Hours: 8:30AM-4:30PM (EST). *Misdemeanor, Civil Actions Under $5,000, Eviction, Small Claims.*
Civil Records: Access: In person, fax, mail. Both court and visitors may perform in person searches. No search fee. Required to search: name, years to search. Records go back to 1977.
Criminal Records: Access: In person, fax, mail. Both court and visitors may perform in person searches. No search fee. Required to search: name, years to search; also helpful: DOB, SSN. Records go back to 1977.
General Information: Copy fee: $.25 per page. Cert fee: $.50 per page. Mail requests: SASE requested. Turnaround time 1 week.

Pendleton County

Circuit Court PO Box 846, Franklin, WV 26807; 304-358-7067; Fax: 304-358-2152. Hours: 8:30AM-4PM (EST). *Felony, Civil Actions Over $5,000, Probate.*
Civil Records: Access: Phone, fax, mail, in person. Both court and visitors may perform in person searches. No search fee. Required to search: name, years to search. Civil cases indexed by defendant, plaintiff. Civil records on index books back to 1800s.
Criminal Records: Access: Phone, fax, mail, in person. Both court and visitors may perform in person searches. No search fee. Required to search: name, years to search; also helpful: DOB, SSN. Criminal records on index books back to 1800s.
General Information: No juvenile, divorce records released. Will fax results for $2.00 per page. Copy fee: $.50 per page. No cert fee. Payee: Pendleton County Circuit Clerk. Local checks accepted. Prepayment required. Mail requests: SASE required. Mail turnaround time 2-3 days.

Magistrate Court PO Box 637, Franklin, WV 26807; 304-358-2343; Fax: 304-358-3870. Hours: 8:30AM-4PM (EST). *Misdemeanor, Civil Actions Under $5,000, Eviction, Small Claims.*

Civil Records: Access: In person, mail. Both court and visitors may perform in person searches. No search fee. Required to search: name, years to search. Civil records computerized since 1993.

Criminal Records: Access: In person, mail. Both court and visitors may perform in person searches. No search fee. Required to search: name, years to search. Records computerized since 1993.

General Information: Public Access terminal is available. Will fax results to local or toll free line. Copy fee: $.25. Cert fee: $.50. Payee: Magistrate Court. Prepayment required. Turnaround time 5-10 days.

Pleasants County

Circuit Court 301 Court Lane, Rm 201, St. Mary's, WV 26170; 304-684-3513; Probate phone: 304-684-3542; Fax: 304-684-3514. Hours: 8:30AM-4:30PM (EST). *Felony, Civil Actions Over $5,000, Probate.*

Note: Probate is handled by County Clerk, 301 Court Lane, Rm 101, St Mary's, WV 26170.

Civil Records: Access: In person only. Visitors must perform in person searches for themselves. No search fee. Required to search: name, years to search. Civil cases indexed by defendant, plaintiff. Civil records on computer from Jan 1960 to present, on index cards from 1960 to present, on index books back to 1800s.

Criminal Records: Access: In person only. Visitors must perform in person searches for themselves. No search fee. Required to search: name, years to search. Criminal records on computer from Jan 1960 to present, on index cards from 1960 to present, on index books back to 1800s.

General Information: No domestic, marriage, adoption, juvenile or mental health records released. Copy fee: $.50 per page. Cert fee: $.50 per page. Payee: Gail E Mote, Circuit Clerk. Personal checks accepted. Prepayment required but will bill to attorneys.

Magistrate Court 301 Court Lane, Rm B-6, St Mary's, WV 26170; 304-684-7197; Fax: 304-684-3882. Hours: 8:30AM-4:30PM (EST). *Misdemeanor, Civil Actions Under $5,000, Eviction, Small Claims.*
Civil Records: Access: Phone, mail, fax, in person. Both the court and visitors may perform in person searches. Search fee: None, but there is a copy fee. Required to search: name, years to search; also helpful: DOB or SSN. Records go back to 1977, on computer since mid-2000. Will do some searches over the phone while caller holds.

Criminal Records: Access: Phone, mail, fax, in person. Both the court and visitors may perform in person searches. Search fee: None, but there is a copy fee. Required to search: name, years to search; also helpful: DOB, SSN. Records go back to 1977, on computer since mid-2000. Will do some searches over the phone while caller holds.

General Information: Public Access terminal is available. Fee to fax results is $2.00 per page. Copy fee: $.25 per page. Cert fee: $.50 per page. Payee: Pleasants County Magistrate Court. Prepayment required. Mail turnaround time 1-2 days.

Pocahontas County

Circuit Court 900-D 10th Ave, Marlinton, WV 24954; 304-799-4604; Fax: 304-799-6809. Hours: 9AM-4:30PM (EST). *Felony, Civil Actions Over $5,000, Probate.*

Civil Records: Access: Phone, mail, in person. Only the court performs in person searches; visitors may not. No search fee. Required to search: name, years to

search; also helpful: address. Civil cases indexed by defendant, plaintiff. Civil records on index books from 1948 to present, order books back to 1800s. Computerized records to 1995.

Criminal Records: Access: Phone, mail, in person. Visitors must perform in person searches for themselves. No search fee. Required to search: name, years to search; also helpful: DOB, SSN. Criminal records on index books from 1948 to present, order books back to 1800s. Computerized records to 1995.

General Information: No juvenile, domestic cases involving finances, adoption, guardianship records released. Will fax results for $1.00 per doc. Copy fee: $.50 per page. No cert fee. Payee: Clerk of Circuit Court. Personal checks accepted. Prepayment required. Mail requests: SASE required. Mail turnaround time same day.

Magistrate Court 900 10th Ave, Marlinton, WV 24954; 304-799-6603; Fax: 304-799-6331. Hours: 9AM-4:30PM (EST). *Misdemeanor, Civil Actions Under $5,000, Eviction, Small Claims.*

Civil Records: Access: In person only. Visitors must perform in person searches for themselves. No search fee. Records stored since 1977, computerized since 10-14-99.

Criminal Records: Access: In person only. Visitors must perform in person searches for themselves. No search fee. Required to search: name, years to search; also helpful: DOB, SSN. Records stored since 1977, computerized since 10-14-99.

General Information: Copy fee: $.25. Cert fee: $.25 per page. Prepayment required.

Preston County

Circuit Court 101 W. Main St, Rm 301, Kingwood, WV 26537; 304-329-0047; Probate phone: 304-329-0070; Fax: 304-329-1417. Hours: 9AM-5PM M-Th, 9AM-7PM Fri (EST). *Felony, Misdemeanor, Civil Actions Over $5,000, Probate.*

Note: Probate is handled by County Clerk, 101 W Main St, Rm 201, Kingwood, WV 26537.

Civil Records: Access: Phone, fax, mail, in person. Only the court performs in person searches; visitors may not. No search fee. Required to search: name, years to search. Civil cases indexed by defendant, plaintiff. Civil records on computer from 1/80 to present, on index books 1965 to 1980, chancery file from 1869 to 1965.

Criminal Records: Access: Phone, fax, mail, in person. Only the court performs in person searches; visitors may not. No search fee. Required to search: name, years to search, DOB, SSN. Criminal records on docket books from 1869 to 1979, records on computer since 1979.

General Information: No juvenile, adoption, domestic, mental hygiene records released. Fee to fax results is $2.00 per page. Copy fee: $.50 per page. No cert fee. Payee: Betsy Castle, Circuit Clerk. Personal checks accepted. Prepayment required. Mail requests: SASE required. Mail turnaround time 1 week.

Magistrate Court 328 Tunnelton St, Kingwood, WV 26537; 304-329-2764; Fax: 304-329-0855. Hours: 8:30AM-4:30PM (EST). *Misdemeanor, Civil Actions Under $5,000, Eviction, Small Claims.*

Civil Records: Access: In person, mail. Both court and visitors may perform in person searches. No search fee. Civil records go back to 1977; computerized records since 1987.

Criminal Records: Access: In person, mail. Both court and visitors may perform in person searches. No search fee. Required to search: name, years to search; also helpful: DOB, SSN. Criminal records go back to 1977; computerized records since 1987.

General Information: Public Access terminal is available. Copy fee: $.25 per page. Cert fee: $.50 per page. Turnaround time 1 week.

Putnam County

Circuit Court Putnam County Judicial Bldg, 3389 Winfield Rd, Winfield, WV 25213; 304-586-0203; Fax: 304-586-0221. Hours: 8:30AM-4:30PM M-F (EST). *Felony, Civil Actions Over $5,000, Probate.*

Civil Records: Access: In person, online. Both court and visitors may perform in person searches. No search fee. Required to search: name, years to search. Civil cases indexed by defendant, plaintiff. Civil records on computer from 1989 to present, on index books back to 1800s. Online access to court records via a pay service, see www.swcg-inc.com/courts.htm or call 800-795-8543. $125.00 set-up fee plus a $38.00 or $120.00 monthly fee plan.

Criminal Records: Access: In person, online. Visitors must perform in person searches for themselves. No search fee. Required to search: name, years to search; also helpful: DOB, SSN. Criminal records on computer from 1982 to present. Online access to criminal records is the same as civil.

General Information: Public Access terminal is available. No divorce records released. Copy fee: $.50 per page. No cert fee. Payee: Circuit Clerk. Business checks accepted. Prepayment required.

Magistrate Court 3389 Winfield Rd, Winfield, WV 25213; 304-586-0234; Fax: 304-586-0234. Hours: 8:30AM-4:30PM (EST). *Misdemeanor, Civil Actions Under $5,000, Eviction, Small Claims.*

Civil Records: Access: In person, mail. Both court and visitors may perform in person searches. No search fee. Records are computerized since 1996, overall records kept since 1977.

Criminal Records: Access: In person, mail. Both court and visitors may perform in person searches. No search fee. Required to search: name, years to search; also helpful: DOB, SSN. Records stored since 1977.

General Information: Copy fee: $.25 per page. Cert fee: $.50. Payee: Magistrate Court. Prepayment required. Mail turnaround time 1 week.

Raleigh County

Circuit Court 215 Main St, Beckley, WV 25801; 304-255-9135; Probate phone: 304-255-9123; Fax: 304-255-9353. Hours: 8:30AM-4:30PM (EST). *Felony, Civil Actions Over $5,000, Probate.*

Note: Probate is handled by County Clerk, 215 Main St, Courthouse, Beckley, WV 25801.

Civil Records: Access: In person only. Visitors must perform in person searches for themselves. No search fee. Required to search: name, years to search. Civil cases indexed by defendant, plaintiff. Civil records on master index books from 1977; on computer back to 1997; on dockets back to 1800s.

Criminal Records: Access: Phone, mail, in person. Both court and visitors may perform in person searches. No search fee. Required to search: name, years to search; also helpful: DOB, SSN. Criminal records on master index books from 1977; on computer back to 1997; on dockets back to 1800s.

General Information: Public Access terminal is available. No divorce, juvenile, adoption records released. Fee to fax results is $2.00 per page. Copy fee: $.50 per page. No cert fee. Payee: Clerk of Circuit Court. Business checks accepted. Prepayment required. Will bill to attorneys. Mail requests: SASE required.

Magistrate Court 115 W Prince St, #A, Beckley, WV 25801; 304-255-9197; Fax: 304-255-9354. Hours: 8AM-4PM (EST). *Misdemeanor, Civil Actions Under $5,000, Eviction, Small Claims.*

Civil Records: Access: In person only. Visitors must

perform in person searches for themselves. No search fee. Civil records go back to 1977, computerized since 1991.

Criminal Records: Access: In person only. Visitors must perform in person searches for themselves. No search fee. Required to search: name, years to search, offense, date of offense; also helpful: DOB, SSN. Criminal records go back to 1977, on computer back to 1992.

General Information: Public Access terminal is available. (Has records since 1996.) Will fax results for $2.00 per page. Copy fee: $.25 per page. Cert fee: $.50 per page. Prepayment required.

Randolph County

Circuit Court Courthouse, 2 Randolph Ave, Elkins, WV 26241; 304-636-2765; Fax: 304-637-3700. Hours: 8AM-4:30PM (EST). *Felony, Civil Actions Over $5,000, Probate.*

Civil Records: Access: In person only. Visitors must perform in person searches for themselves. No search fee. Required to search: name, years to search. Civil cases indexed by defendant, plaintiff. Civil records on computer from 1/91 to present. On index books back to late 1800s.

Criminal Records: Access: In person only. Visitors must perform in person searches for themselves. No search fee. Required to search: name, years to search. Criminal records on computer from 1/91 to present. On index books back to late 1800s.

General Information: Public Access terminal is available. No juvenile, adoption, mental health, or guardianship records released. Copy fee: $.50 per page. No cert fee. Payee: Circuit Clerk. Personal checks accepted. Prepayment required.

Magistrate Court #11 Randolph Ave, Elkins, WV 26241; 304-636-5885; Fax: 304-636-2510. Hours: 8AM-4:30PM (EST). *Misdemeanor, Civil Actions Under $5,000, Eviction, Small Claims.*

Civil Records: Access: In person, mail. Both court and visitors may perform in person searches. No search fee. Civil records go back to 1977; computerized records since 10/90.

Criminal Records: Access: In person, mail. Both court and visitors may perform in person searches. No search fee. Required to search: name, years to search; also helpful: DOB, SSN. Criminal records go back to 1977; computerized records since 10/90.

General Information: Public Access terminal is available. Will fax results for $2.00 per page prepaid. Copy fee: $.25 per page. Cert fee: $.50 per page. Prepayment required. Mail turnaround time 3 days.

Ritchie County

Circuit Court 115 E. Main St, Harrisville, WV 26362; 304-643-2164 x229; Probate phone: 304-643-2164 x229. Hours: 8AM-4PM (EST). *Felony, Civil Actions Over $5,000, Probate.*

Note: Probate office is located at the same address, but in county clerks office.

Civil Records: Access: Phone, mail, in person. Both court and visitors may perform in person searches. No search fee. Required to search: name, years to search. Civil cases indexed by defendant, plaintiff. Civil records on index cards from 1960 to present. On index books back to mid-1800s; on computer back to 2000.

Criminal Records: Access: Phone, mail, in person. Both court and visitors may perform in person searches. No search fee. Required to search: name, years to search; also helpful: DOB, SSN. Criminal records on index cards from 1960 to present. On index books back to mid-1800s; on computer back to 2000.

General Information: Public Access terminal is available. No juvenile, mental health, adoption records released. Copy fee: $.50 per page. No cert fee. Payee: Circuit Clerk. Personal checks accepted.

Prepayment required. Mail requests: SASE requested. Turnaround time 1-2 days.

Magistrate Court 319 E. Main St, Harrisville, WV 26362; 304-643-4409; Fax: 304-643-2098. Hours: 8AM-4PM (EST). *Misdemeanor, Civil Actions Under $5,000, Eviction, Small Claims.*

Civil Records: Access: In person, mail. Both court and visitors may perform in person searches. No search fee. Civil records go back to 1977; computerized from 1990. Phone, fax and mail access limited.

Criminal Records: Access: In person, mail. Both court and visitors may perform in person searches. No search fee. Required to search: name, years to search; also helpful: DOB, SSN. Criminal records go back to 1977; computerized from 1990. Phone, fax and mail access limited.

General Information: Public Access terminal is available. Will fax results for $2.00 per fax. Copy fee: $.25. Cert fee: $.50. Payee: Magistrate Court. Prepayment required. Mail turnaround time 1-2 days, 1-2 hours for phone requests.

Roane County

Circuit Court PO Box 122, Spencer, WV 25276; 304-927-2750; Fax: 304-927-2164. Hours: 8:30AM-Noon, 1-4PM M-F; 9AM-Noon Sat (EST). *Felony, Civil Actions Over $5,000, Probate.*

Civil Records: Access: Phone, fax, mail, in person. Both court and visitors may perform in person searches. No search fee. Required to search: name, years to search. Civil cases indexed by defendant, plaintiff. Civil records on index books back to early 1900s; computerized records go back to 1998.

Criminal Records: Access: Phone, fax, mail, in person. Both court and visitors may perform in person searches. No search fee. Required to search: name, years to search; also helpful: DOB, SSN. Criminal records on index books back to early 1900s; computerized records go back to 1998.

General Information: Public Access terminal is available. No sealed, juvenile, adoption records released. Will fax results $1.50 1st page; $1.00 each add'l. Copy fee: $.50 per page. Cert fee: $.50 per page. Payee: Beverly Greathouse. Local checks accepted. Prepayment required. Mail requests: SASE not required. Mail turnaround time 1-2 days, less for phone requests.

Magistrate Court 201 Main St, Spencer, WV 25276; 304-927-4750; Fax: 304-927-2754. Hours: 9AM-4PM (EST). *Misdemeanor, Civil Actions Under $5,000, Eviction, Small Claims.*

Note: Record requests can be directed to 304-746-2180.

Civil Records: Access: In person only. Visitors must perform in person searches for themselves. No search fee. Required to search: name, years to search. Records on computer back to 1997; prior records go back to 1976.

Criminal Records: Access: In person only. Visitors must perform in person searches for themselves. No search fee. Required to search: name, DOB; also helpful: years to search, SSN. Records on computer back to 1997; prior records go back to 1976.

General Information: Public Access terminal is available. Copy fee: $.25 per page. Cert fee: $.50 per page. Payee: Roane County Magistrate Court. Prepayment required. Will bill to attorneys.

Summers County

Circuit Court PO Box 1058, Hinton, WV 25951; 304-466-7103; Fax: 304-466-7124 (Attn:Circuit Court). Hours: 8:30AM-4:30PM (EST). *Felony, Civil Actions Over $5,000, Probate.*

Civil Records: Access: Phone, fax, mail, in person.

Both court and visitors may perform in person searches. No search fee. Required to search: name, years to search. Civil cases indexed by defendant, plaintiff. Civil records on index books back to late 1800s; computerized records since 1998.

Criminal Records: Access: Phone, fax, mail, in person. Both court and visitors may perform in person searches. No search fee. Required to search: name, years to search; also helpful: DOB, SSN. Criminal records on index books back to 1878, computerized since 1998.

General Information: No juvenile, adoption, child abuse records released. Will fax results $2.00 per page. Copy fee: $.50 per page. Cert fee: $1.00. Payee: Clerk of Circuit Court. Personal checks accepted. Prepayment required. Mail requests: SASE required. Mail turnaround time 1-2 days.

Magistrate Court PO Box 1059, Hinton, WV 25951; 304-466-7108; Fax: 304-466-4912. Hours: 9:00AM-4:00PM (EST). *Misdemeanor, Civil Actions Under $5,000, Eviction, Small Claims.*

Civil Records: Access: Phone, fax, mail, in person. Both court and visitors may perform in person searches. No search fee. Civil records on docket books to 1977 and computer back to 1998.

Criminal Records: Access: Phone, fax, mail, in person. Both court and visitors may perform in person searches. No search fee. Required to search: name, years to search; also helpful: DOB, SSN. Criminal records on docket books to 1977, and computer back to 1998.

General Information: Public Access terminal is available. Will fax results for $2.00 per fax. Copy fee: $.25. Cert fee: $.50 per page. Payee: Magistrate Court. Prepayment required. Mail turnaround time 1-2 days.

Taylor County

Circuit Court 214 W. Main St, Rm 104, Grafton, WV 26354; 304-265-2480. Hours: 8:30AM-Noon, 1-4:30PM (EST). *Felony, Civil Actions Over $5,000, Probate.*

Civil Records: Access: Phone, mail, in person. Both court and visitors may perform in person searches. No search fee. Required to search: name, years to search. Civil cases indexed by defendant, plaintiff. Civil records on index books back to 1844, computerized since 1996.

Criminal Records: Access: Phone, mail, in person. Both court and visitors may perform in person searches. No search fee. Required to search: name, years to search; also helpful: DOB, SSN. Criminal records on index books back to 1929, computerized since 1996.

General Information: No juvenile, adoptions, mental health records released. Fee to fax results is $2.00 per page. Copy fee: $.50 per page. No cert fee. Payee: Circuit Clerk. Prepayment required. Mail requests: SASE required; any additional fee for postage is 3 times the amount. Turnaround time 2 days.

Magistrate Court 214 W. Main St, Grafton, WV 26354; 304-265-1322; Fax: 304-265-5708. Hours: 8:30AM-4:30PM (EST). *Misdemeanor, Civil Actions Under $5,000, Eviction, Small Claims.*

Civil Records: Access: In person, mail. Both court and visitors may perform in person searches. No search fee. Overall records go back to 1976. Computerized records go back to 1992.

Criminal Records: Access: In person, mail. Both court and visitors may perform in person searches. No search fee. Required to search: name, years to search; also helpful: DOB, SSN, signed release. Overall records go back to 1976. Computerized records go back to 1992.

General Information: Public Access terminal is available. Copy fee: $.25. Cert fee: $.50. Payee: Magistrate Court. Turnaround time 1-2 days.

Tucker County

Circuit Court 215 1st St #2, Parsons, WV 26287; 304-478-2606; Fax: 304-478-4464. Hours: 8AM-4PM (EST). *Felony, Civil Actions Over $5,000.*

Civil Records: Access: Mail, fax, in person. Both court and visitors may perform in person searches. No search fee. Required to search: name, years to search. Civil cases indexed by defendant, plaintiff. Civil records on index books to 1856, 1997 to present on computer.

Criminal Records: Access: Mail, in person. Both court and visitors may perform in person searches. No search fee. Required to search: name, years to search, SSN; also helpful: DOB, case number. Criminal records on index books from 1856 to 1996; 1997 to present on rolodex.

General Information: No juvenile, domestic, guardianship,adoption or mental hygiene records released. Fee to fax results is $2.00 per page, no charge to toll free line. Copy fee: $2.00 per page. No cert fee. Payee: Circuit Court Clerk. Personal checks accepted; no out of state checks. Prepayment required. Mail requests: SASE required. Mail turnaround time 2 days.

Magistrate Court 201 Walnut St, Parsons, WV 26287; 304-478-2665; Fax: 304-478-4836. Hours: 8:30AM-4:00PM (EST). *Misdemeanor, Civil Actions Under $5,000, Eviction, Small Claims.*

Civil Records: Access: In person only. Only the court performs in person searches; visitors may not. No search fee. Civil records go back to 1977; computerized since 8/1999.

Criminal Records: Access: In person only. Only the court performs in person searches; visitors may not. No search fee. Required to search: name, years to search; also helpful: DOB, SSN. Criminal records go back to 1977; computerized since 8/1999.

General Information: Public Access terminal is available. Will not fax results. Copy fee: $.25 per page. Cert fee: $.50 per page. Prepayment required.

Tyler County

Circuit Court PO Box 8, Middlebourne, WV 26149; 304-758-4811; Fax: 304-758-4008. Hours: 8AM-4PM (EST). *Felony, Civil Actions Over $5,000.*

Civil Records: Access: Phone, mail, fax, in person. Both court and visitors may perform in person searches. No search fee. Required to search: name, years to search. Civil cases indexed by defendant, plaintiff. Civil records on index books back to 1800s; computerized back to 1997.

Criminal Records: Access: Phone, mail, fax, in person. Both court and visitors may perform in person searches. No search fee. Required to search: name, years to search; also helpful: DOB, SSN. Criminal records on index books back to 1864; computerized back to 1997.

General Information: Public Access terminal is available. No adoption, juvenile, or domestic records released. Fee to fax results is $5.00 per doc. Copy fee: $.50 per page. No cert fee. Payee: Tyler County Circuit Court Clerk. Personal checks accepted. Prepayment required. Mail requests: SASE required. Mail turnaround time 1-2 days.

Magistrate Court PO Box 127, Middlebourne, WV 26149; 304-758-2137. Hours: 9AM-4PM (EST). *Misdemeanor, Civil Actions Under $5,000, Eviction, Small Claims.*

Civil Records: Access: In person, mail. Only the court performs in person searches; visitors may not.

Search fee: none. Records go back to 1/1/77; on computer back to 1/1/2000.

Criminal Records: Access: In person, mail. Only the court performs in person searches; visitors may not. No search fee. Required to search: name, years to search; also helpful: DOB, SSN. Records go back to 1/1/77; on computer back to 1/1/2000.

General Information: Public Access terminal is available. Will fax results for $2.00 per page, in advance. Copy fee: $.25 per page. Cert fee: $.50 per page. Prepayment required. Mail turnaround time 1 week.

Upshur County

Circuit Court 38 W. Main St, Rm 304, Buckhannon, WV 26201; 304-472-2370; Probate phone: 304-472-1068; Fax: 304-472-2168. Hours: 8AM-4:30PM (EST). *Felony, Civil Actions Over $5,000, Probate.*

Note: Probate is handled by County Clerk, 40 W Main, Courthouse, Rm 101, Buckhannon, WV 26201.

Civil Records: Access: Fax, mail, in person. Visitors must perform in person searches for themselves. No search fee. Required to search: name, years to search. Civil cases indexed by defendant, plaintiff. Civil records on index books from 1900 to present, on computer from 1/90.

Criminal Records: Access: Fax, mail, in person. Both court and visitors may perform in person searches. Search fee: $5.00 per name. Required to search: name, years to search; also helpful: DOB, SSN. Criminal records on computer from 1/90 to present, on index books from 1947 to 1/90, on dockets back to 1800s.

General Information: Public Access terminal is available. No mental health, juvenile, adoption records released. Will fax results $2.00 per page. Copy fee: $.50 per page. Cert fee: $.50 per page. Payee: Circuit Clerk. Business checks accepted. Prepayment required. Mail requests: SASE requested. Turnaround time 1-2 days.

Magistrate Court 38 W Main, Rm 204 Courthouse Annex, Buckhannon, WV 26201; 304-472-2053. Hours: 8AM-4PM (EST). *Misdemeanor, Civil Actions Under $5,000, Eviction, Small Claims.*

Civil Records: Access: Mail, in person. Both court and visitors may perform in person searches. No search fee. Civil records from 1977; computerized back to 1996.

Criminal Records: Access: Mail, in person. Both court and visitors may perform in person searches. No search fee. Required to search: name; also helpful: DOB, SSN. Criminal records from 1977; computerized back to 1992.

General Information: Public Access terminal is available. Will fax results for $2.00. Copy fee: $.25 + $.50 court costs. Payee: Magistrate Court. Prepayment required. Mail turnaround time 1-2 days.

Wayne County

Circuit Court PO Box 38, Wayne, WV 25570; 304-272-6360; Probate phone: 304-272-4372. Hours: 8AM-4PM M,T,W,F; 8AM-8PM Th (EST). *Felony, Civil Actions Over $5,000, Probate.*

Note: Probate is handled by County Clerk, PO Box 248, Wayne, WV 25570.

Civil Records: Access: Phone, mail, in person. Both court and visitors may perform in person searches. No search fee. Required to search: name, years to search. Civil cases indexed by defendant, plaintiff. Civil records on computer back to 1993; prior on index books from 1960 to present. Contact Circuit Clerk for books prior to 1800s. The staff will not conduct genealogical searches.

Criminal Records: Access: In person only. Visitors must perform in person searches for themselves. No

search fee. Required to search: name, years to search, SSN; also helpful: DOB. Criminal records on computer back to 1993; prior on index books from 1960 to present. Contact Circuit Clerk for books prior to 1800s.

General Information: Public Access terminal is available. No juvenile, adoption, mental records released. Copy fee: $.50 per page. No cert fee. Payee: Clerk of Circuit Court. Business checks accepted. Prepayment required. Mail requests: SASE required. Mail turnaround time 1-2 days.

Magistrate Court PO Box 667, Wayne, WV 25570; 304-272-5648/6388. Hours: 8AM-4PM (EST). *Felony, Misdemeanor, Civil Actions Under $5,000, Eviction, Small Claims.*

Civil Records: Access: phone, fax, mail, in person. Both court and visitors may perform in person searches. No search fee. Required to search: name; also helpful: years to search, DOB, SSN. Civil records go back to 1977; on computer back to 1996.

Criminal Records: Access: phone, fax, mail, in person. Both court and visitors may perform in person searches. No search fee. Required to search: name; also helpful: years to search, DOB, SSN. Criminal records go back to 1977; on computer back to 1996.

General Information: Public Access terminal is available. Will fax results $2.00 per page. Copy fee: $.25 per page. Cert fee: $.25 per page. Payee: Wayne County Magistrate Court. Prepayment required. Mail requests: SASE required. Mail turnaround time 1-2 days, usually same day for phone requests.

Webster County

Circuit Court 2 Court Sq, Rm G-4, Webster Springs, WV 26288; 304-847-2421; Fax: 304-847-2062. Hours: 8:30AM-4PM (EST). *Felony, Civil Actions Over $5,000, Probate.*

Civil Records: Access: Phone, fax, mail, in person. Both court and visitors may perform in person searches. No search fee. Required to search: name, years to search. Civil cases indexed by defendant, plaintiff. Civil records on index cards from 1977 to present, also on computer since 08/99.

Criminal Records: Access: Phone, fax, mail, in person. Both court and visitors may perform in person searches. No search fee. Required to search: name, years to search; also helpful: DOB, SSN. Felony dockets back to 1800s. Criminal records also on computer from 08/99.

General Information: No mental health, juvenile, guardianship, adoption, paternity records released. Will fax results $1.00 per page. Copy fee: $.50 per page. No cert fee. Payee: Clerk of Circuit Court. Personal checks accepted. Prepayment required. Mail requests: SASE requested. Turnaround time 1-2 days.

Magistrate Court 2 Court Sq, Rm B-1, Webster Springs, WV 26288; 304-847-2613; Fax: 304-847-7747. Hours: 8:30AM-4PM (EST). *Misdemeanor, Civil Actions Under $5,000, Eviction, Small Claims.*

Note: They recommend that criminal searches be directed to the Court Repository in Charleston, 304-746-2180.

Civil Records: Access: Mail, in person. Visitors must perform in person searches for themselves. No search fee. Civil records go back to 1977; on computer since 2001.

Criminal Records: Access: Mail, in person. Visitors must perform in person searches for themselves. No search fee. Required to search: name, years to search; also helpful: DOB, SSN. Criminal records go back to 1977; on computer since 2001.

General Information: Public Access terminal is available. Will fax results to local or toll free line. Cert fee: $.50 per page. Payee: Magistrate Court Clerk.

Prepayment required. Mail turnaround time is 7-10 days.

Wetzel County

Circuit Court PO Box 263, New Martinsville, WV 26155; 304-455-8219; Fax: 304-455-1069. Hours: 9AM-4:30PM (EST). *Felony, Civil Actions Over $5,000.*

Civil Records: Access: Phone, mail, in person. Both court and visitors may perform in person searches. No search fee. Required to search: name, years to search. Civil cases indexed by defendant, plaintiff. Civil records on index books back to mid 1863; computerized back to 1996.

Criminal Records: Access: In person only. Visitors must perform in person searches for themselves. No search fee. Required to search: name. Criminal records on index books back to mid 1863; computerized back to 1996.

General Information: No juvenile, domestic, adoption records released. Will fax results. Copy fee: $.50 per page. No cert fee. Payee: Circuit Clerk. Personal checks accepted. Prepayment required. Mail requests: SASE required. Mail turnaround time same day.

Magistrate Court PO Box 147, New Martinsville, WV 26155; 304-455-5040\5171\2450; Fax: 304-455-2859. Hours: 8:30AM-4:30PM (EST). *Misdemeanor, Civil Actions Under $5,000, Eviction, Small Claims.*

Civil Records: Access: mail, fax, in person. Both court and visitors may perform in person searches. No search fee. Required to search: name, DOB, SSN, years to search. Civil records go back to 1995.

Criminal Records: Access: mail, fax, in person. Both court and visitors may perform in person searches. No search fee. Required to search: name, years to search; also helpful: DOB, SSN. Criminal records go back to 1980.

General Information: Public Access terminal is available. Will fax results. Turnaround time 1-2 days.

Wirt County

Circuit Court PO Box 465, Elizabeth, WV 26143; 304-275-6597; Probate phone: 304-275-4271; Fax: 304-275-3230. Hours: 8:30AM-4PM (EST). *Felony, Civil Actions Over $5,000, Probate.*

Note: Probate records located at the county clerk's office.

Civil Records: Access: Phone, fax, mail, in person. Both court and visitors may perform in person searches. No search fee. Required to search: name, years to search. Civil cases indexed by defendant, plaintiff. Civil records on index cards from 1848 to present; computerized back to 9/2000.

Criminal Records: Access: Phone, fax, mail, in person. Both court and visitors may perform in person searches. No search fee. Required to search: name, years to search; also helpful: DOB, SSN. Criminal records on index cards from 1848 to present; computerized back to 9/2000.

General Information: No divorce, juvenile or adoption records released. No fee to fax results. Copy fee: $.50 per page. Cert fee: $.50 per document. Payee: Wirt County Circuit Clerk. Personal checks accepted. Prepayment required. Mail requests: SASE required. Mail turnaround time same day if possible.

Magistrate Court PO Box 249, Elizabeth, WV 26143; 304-275-3641; Fax: 304-275-4882. Hours: 8:30AM-4PM (EST). *Misdemeanor, Civil Actions Under $5,000, Eviction, Small Claims.*

Civil Records: Access: Phone, in person. Both court and visitors may perform in person searches. No search fee. Civil records go back 10 years; computerized back to 9/2000.

Criminal Records: Access: Phone, in person. Both court and visitors may perform in person searches. No search fee. Required to search: name, years to search; also helpful: address, DOB, SSN. Criminal records go back 10 years; computerized back to 9/2000.

General Information: Public Access terminal is available. Copy fee: $.25 per page. Cert fee: $.50 per page.

Wood County

Circuit Court Wood County Judicial, #2 Government Sq, Parkersburg, WV 26101-5353; 304-424-1700; Probate phone: 304-424-1850; Fax: 304-424-1804. Hours: 8:30AM-4:30PM (EST). *Felony, Civil Actions Over $5,000, Probate.*

Note: Probate is handled by County Clerk, PO Box 1474, Parkersburg, WV 26102.

Civil Records: Access: Phone, mail, in person. Both court and visitors may perform in person searches. No search fee. Required to search: name, years to search. Civil cases indexed by defendant, plaintiff. Civil records on computer from 1978 to present, on index books back to 1885.

Criminal Records: Access: Mail, in person. Both court and visitors may perform in person searches. No search fee. Required to search: name, years to search, DOB, SSN. Criminal records on computer since 1979; prior records on index back to 1885.

General Information: Public Access terminal is available. No juvenile, adoption, mental hygiene, guardianship records released. Copy fee: $.50 per page. No cert fee. Payee: Carole Jones, Clerk. No personal checks accepted. Prepayment required. Mail turnaround time 2-3 days.

Magistrate Court 208 Avery St, Parkersburg, WV 26101; 304-422-3444. Hours: 8:30AM-4:30PM (EST). *Misdemeanor, Civil Actions Under $5,000, Eviction, Small Claims.*

Civil Records: Access: In person, mail. Both court and visitors may perform in person searches. No search fee. Required to search: name, DOB, SSN, years to search. Civil records go back to 1977;

computerized records since 1996. Fax and mail access limited.

Criminal Records: Access: In person, mail. Both court and visitors may perform in person searches. No search fee. Required to search: name, years to search, address; also helpful: DOB, SSN. Criminal records go back to 1997; computerized since 1996. Fax and mail access limited.

General Information: Public Access terminal is available. Will fax results for a fee of $2.00 pe rpage. Do not fax record search requests, however. Copy fee: $.25 per page. Cert fee: $.50 per page. Prepayment required. Mail requests: SASE required. Mail turnaround time 10 days.

Wyoming County

Circuit Court PO Box 190, Pineville, WV 24874; 304-732-8000 X238; Fax: 304-732-7262. Hours: 9AM-4PM (EST). *Felony, Civil Actions Over $5,000.*

Civil Records: Access: Phone, mail, in person. Both court and visitors may perform in person searches. No search fee. Required to search: name, years to search. Civil cases indexed by defendant, plaintiff. Civil records on index books back to 1800s.

Criminal Records: Access: Phone, mail, in person. Both court and visitors may perform in person searches. No search fee. Required to search: name, years to search; also helpful: DOB, SSN. Criminal records on index books back to 1800s.

General Information: Public Access terminal is available. No juvenile, mental hygiene, adoption, or sealed records released. Copy fee: $.50 per page. Cert fee: $.50 per page. Payee: Jack Lambert, Circuit Clerk. Business checks accepted. Prepayment required. Mail requests: SASE preferred. Turnaround time 1-2 days, less for phone requests.

Magistrate Court PO Box 598, Pineville, WV 24874; 304-732-8000 X218; Fax: 304-732-7247. Hours: 9AM-4PM M-Th, 9AM-6PM Fri (EST). *Misdemeanor, Civil Actions Under $5,000, Eviction, Small Claims.*

Civil Records: Access: Mail, in person. Both court and visitors may perform in person searches. No search fee. Civil records from 1977; computerized back to 1995.

Criminal Records: Access: Mail, in person. Both court and visitors may perform in person searches. No search fee. Required to search: name, years to search; also helpful: DOB, SSN. Criminal records from 1977; computerized back to 1995.

General Information: Public Access terminal is available. Fee to fax results is $2.00 per page. Copy fee: $.25 per copy. Cert fee: $.75. Payee: Wyoming County Magistrate Court. Prepayment required. Mail turnaround time 1-2 days.

West Virginia Recording Offices

ORGANIZATION: 55 counties, 55 recording offices. The recording officer is County Clerk. The entire state is in the Eastern Time Zone (EST).

REAL ESTATE RECORDS: Most County Clerks will not perform real estate searches. Copy fees are usually $1.50 up to two pages and $1.00 for each additional page. Certification usually costs $1.00 per document.

UCC RECORDS: Financing statements are filed at the state level, except for real estate related collateral, which are filed only with the Register of Deeds. Previous to 07/2001, collateral on consumer goods were are filed in both places, now they are only filed at the state level. Many recording offices will perform UCC searches. Use search request form UCC-11. Searches fees and copy fees vary.

TAX LIEN RECORDS: All federal and state tax liens are filed with the County Clerk. Most counties will not perform tax lien searches.

OTHER LIENS: Judgment, mechanics, lis pendens

ONLINE ACCESS: There is no state-operated system open to public, though a private company offers subscription access to land book assessment information statewide at http://digitalcourthouse.com.

Only one county – Monongalia – offers online access to assessor records.

Barbour County

County Clerk, 8 N. Main St, Courthouse, Philippi, WV 26416. **Phone**-304-457-2232; hours 8:30AM-4:30PM Will search UCC records. Search per debtor- $1.00. UCC search includes tax liens if requested. Property transfer searches available. UCC copy- $1.50 per page. Cert fee: $1.00. Payee: Barbour County Clerk. **Other phones:** Assessor-304-457-2336; Treasurer-304-457-2881.

Berkeley County

County Clerk, 100 W. King St, Rm 1, Martinsburg, WV 25401. **Phone**-304-264-1927; fax-304-267-1794. Will not search records. **Other phones:** Assessor-304-264-1901; Treasurer-304-264-1980; Sheriff-304-264-1980.

Boone County

County Clerk, 200 State St, Madison, WV 25130. **Phone**-304-369-7337; fax-304-369-7329; 8AM-4PM Will not search records. UCC copy- $1.50 per page.plus 1.00 add'l. Cert fee: $1.00. Payee: Boone County Clerk. **Other phones:** Assessor-304-369-7308; Treasurer-304-369-7391.

Braxton County

County Clerk, PO Box 486, Sutton, WV 26601-0728. **Phone**-County Clerk, R/E & UCC Recording- 304-765-2833; fax-304-765-2093; hours 8AM-4PM Will search UCC records. Search per debtor- $5.00 per doc. Will not search real estate or tax lien records. Record copy- $1.00 per page. Cert fee: $1.00 per doc. Payee: John D. Jordan-Clerk. **Other phones:** Assessor-304-765-2805; Treasurer-304-765-2830; Appraiser/ Auditor-304-765-2830; Elections-304-765-2833; Vital Records-304-765-2833.

Brooke County

County Clerk, 632 Main St, Courthouse, Wellsburg, WV 26070. **Phone**-304-737-3661; fax-304-737-4023; hours 9AM-5PM, M-F; 9AM-12, SAT Will not search records. Record copy- $1.50 for 1st pg., $1.00 each add'l pg. **Other phones:** Assessor-304-737-3667; Treasurer-304-737-3663; Elections-304-737-3668; Vital Records-304-737-3661.

Cabell County

County Clerk, 750 Fifth Ave, Rm 108, Cabell County Courthouse, Huntington, WV 25701-2083. **Phone**-County Clerk, R/E & UCC Recording- 304-526-8625, UCC Recording-304-526-8631; fax-304-526-8632; hours 8:30AM-4:30PM

Will not search records. RE record copy- $1.50 1st 2 pgs., $1.00 each add'l pg. UCC copy- $1.50 per page. Cert fee: $1.00 per doc. **Other phones:** Assessor-304-526-8601; Treasurer-304-526-8672; Elections-304-526-8633; Vital Records-304-526-8631.

Calhoun County

County Clerk, PO Box 230, Grantsville, WV 26147-0230. **Phone**-County Clerk, R/E & UCC Recording-304-354-6725; fax-304-354-6725; 8:30AM-4:00PM Will not search records. **Other phones:** Assessor-304-354-6958; Treasurer-304-354-6333; Elections-304-354-6725; Vital Records-304-354-6725.

Clay County

County Clerk, PO Box 190, Clay, WV 25043. **Phone**-304-587-4259; fax-304-587-7329; hours 8AM-4PM Will not search records. UCC copy- $1.50 per page. Cert fee: $1.00 plus copy fee. Payee: Clay Count Clerk. **Other phones:** Assessor-304-587-4258; Treasurer-304-587-4260.

Doddridge County

County Clerk, 118 E. Court St, Rm 102, West Union, WV 26456-1297. **Phone**-County Clerk, R/E & UCC Recording-304-873-2631; hours 8:30AM-4PM Will search UCC records. Search per debtor- $10.00. Will not search real estate or tax lien records. UCC copy- $1.50 per page. Cert fee: $1.00. Payee: Doddridge County Clerk. **Other phones:** Assessor-304-873-1261; Treasurer-304-873-1000; Elections-304-873-2631.

Fayette County

County Clerk, PO Box 569, Fayetteville, WV 25840. **Phone**-304-574-4226; fax-304-574-4335; 8AM-4PM Will search UCC records. UCC search per debtor- $1.00 per page. Will not search real estate or tax lien records. Record copy- $1.00 per page. Cert fee: $.50 per cert. Payee: Fayette County Clerk. **Other phones:** Assessor-304-574-4244; Treasurer-304-574-4216.

Gilmer County

County Clerk, 10 Howard St, Courthouse, Glenville, WV 26351. **Phone**-County Clerk, R/E & UCC Recording- 304-462-7641; fax-304-462-5134; hours 8AM-4PM Will not search records. Record copy- $1.50 1st 2 pages, $1.00 each add'l. Cert fee: $1.00 per doc. Payee: Gilman Count Clerk. **Other phones:** Assessor-304-462-7731; Treasurer-304-462-7441; Appraiser/ Auditor-304-462-7039; Elections-304-462-7641; Vital Records-304-462-7641.

Grant County

County Clerk, 5 Highland Ave, Petersburg, WV 26847. **Phone**-County Clerk, R/E & UCC Recording- 304-257-4550; fax-304-257-4207; hours 8:30AM-4:30PM Will search UCC records. Search per debtor- $2.00. Will not search real estate records. **Other phones:** Assessor-304-257-1050; Treasurer-304-257-1818; Appraiser/ Auditor-304-257-4550; Elections-304-257-4550; Vital Records-304-257-4550; Sheriff-304-257-1818.

Greenbrier County

County Clerk, PO Box 506, Lewisburg, WV 24901. **Phone**-County Clerk, R/E & UCC Recording- 304-647-6602; fax-304-647-6694; hours 8:30AM-4:30PM Will not search records. RE record copy- $1.00 1st page, $.75 each add'l. UCC copy- $1.50 per page. Cert fee: $3.00 per cert. Payee: Greenbrier County Clerk. **Other phones:** Assessor-304-647-6615; Treasurer-304-647-6609; Elections-304-647-6606; Vital Records-304-647-6602.

Hampshire County

County Clerk, PO Box 806, Romney, WV 26757-0806. **Phone**-County Clerk, R/E & UCC Recording- 304-822-5112; fax-304-822-4039; hours 9AM-4PM (F open until 8PM) Will not search records. UCC copy- $1.50 1st 2 pages, $1.00 each add'ls. Cert fee: $2.50. Payee: Hampshire County Clerk. **Other phones:** Assessor-304-822-3326; Treasurer-304-822-4720; Appraiser/ Auditor-304-822-3326; Elections-304-822-5112; Vital Records-304-822-5112.

Hancock County

County Clerk, PO Box 367, New Cumberland, WV 26047. **Phone**-304-564-3311 x279, R/E Recording-304-564-3311 x267, UCC Recording-304-564-3311 x281; fax-304-564-5941; hours 8:30AM-4:30PM Will not search records. RE record copy- $1.50 1st 2 pages, $1.00 each add'l. Cert fee: $3.00 + copy costs. **Other phones:** Assessor-304-564-3311 x256; Treasurer-304-564-3311 x262; Appraiser/ Auditor-304-564-3311 x256; Elections-304-564-3311 x288; Vital Records-304-564-3311 x280.

Hardy County

County Clerk, 204 Washington St, Courthouse - Rm 111, Moorefield, WV 26836. **Phone**-304-538-2929; fax-304-538-6832; hours 9am-4PM Will not search records. UCC copy- $1.50,1st 2 pages per page. Cert fee: $1.00. Payee: Hardy County Clerk. **Online Access to Deed, Mortgage,**

Grantor/Grantee records: Access to Records is free at http://66.101.143.145/. Username Id and Password is hardywv (all small letters).Index goes back to 1/1993. **Other phones:** Assessor-304-538-6139; Treasurer-304-538-2593.

Harrison County

County Clerk, 301 W. Main St, Courthouse, Clarksburg, WV 26301. **Phone-**304-624-8612; fax-304-624-8575; hours 8:30AM-4:30PM
Will not search records. UCC copy- $1.50 per page. Cert fee: $5.00. Payee: Harrison County Clerk. **Other phones:** Assessor-304-624-8510; Treasurer-304-624-8550.

Jackson County

County Clerk, PO Box 800, Ripley, WV 25271. **Phone-**304-372-2011, R/E Recording-304-373-2259, UCC Recording-304-373-2258; fax-304-372-5259; hours 9AM-4PM M-F; 9AM-Noon Sat.
Will search UCC records. Search per debtor- $5.00. Will not search real estate or tax lien records. Record copy- $1.50 for 2 pages. Cert fee: $1.00 per doc. Payee: Pay fees to Jackson-Co Clerk. **Other phones:** Assessor-304-372-2241; Treasurer-304-372-2011 x305; Elections-304-373-2249; Vital Records-304-373-2256.

Jefferson County

County Clerk, PO Box 208, Charles Town, WV 25414. **Phone-**County Clerk, R/E & UCC Recording- 304-728-3215; fax-304-728-1957; hours 9AM-5PM (F open until 7PM). Will search UCC records. Search per debtor- $4.00. Will not search real estate or tax lien records. RE record copy- $1.50 1st 2 pages; $1.00 each add'l. UCC copy- $1.50 1st 2 pages, $1.00 each add'l. Cert fee: $1.00 per cert. Payee: John Ott, County Clerk. **Other phones:** Assessor-304-728-3224; Treasurer-304-728-3220; Elections-304-728-3246; Vital Records-304-728-3215.

Kanawha County

County Clerk, PO Box 3226, Charleston, WV 25332. **Phone-**304-357-0130, R/E Recording-304-357-0244, UCC Recording-304-357-0244; fax-304-357-0585.
Will search UCC records. Search per debtor- $2.00. Will not search real estate records. RE record copy-$1.50 1st two; $1.00 each add'l. UCC copy- $1.50 1st 2 pages; $1.00 each add'l. Cert fee: $1.00 per cert. **Other phones:** Assessor-304-357-0250; Treasurer-304-357-0210; Elections-304-357-0110; Vital Records-304-357-0710.

Lewis County

County Clerk, PO Box 87, Weston, WV 26452. **Phone-**County Clerk, R/E & UCC Recording- 304-269-8215; fax-304-269-8202; hours 8:30AM-4:30PM
Will not search records. RE record copy-. UCC copy- $1.50 1st 2 pages; $1.00 each add'l. Cert fee: $2.00 per doc. Payee: Lewis County Clerk. **Other phones:** Assessor-304-269-8205; Treasurer-304-269-8222; Elections-304-269-8215; Vital Records-304-269-8215; Second Phone Line-304-269-8216.

Lincoln County

County Clerk, PO Box 497, Hamlin, WV 25523. **Phone-**304-824-3336; fax-304-824-7972.
Will not search records. UCC copy- $1.50 each 2st 2 pages; $1.00 each add'l. Cert fee: $1.00 per page. **Other phones:** Assessor-304-824-7878; Treasurer-304-824-3336.

Logan County

County Clerk, Stratton & Main St, Courthouse, Rm 101, Logan, WV 25601. **Phone-**304-792-8600, R/E Recording-304-792-8697/8603, UCC Recording-304-792-8606; fax-304-792-8621; hours 8:30AM-4:30PM

Will not search records. RE record copy- $1.50 per page. UCC copy- $2.00 per page. Cert fee: $5.00 per doc. Payee: Glen D. Adkins-County Clerk. **Other phones:** Assessor-304-792-8525; Elections-304-792-8616; Vital Records-304-792-8615.

Marion County

County Clerk, PO Box 1267, Fairmont, WV 26555-1267. **Phone-**304-367-5441, R/E Recording-304-367-5440, UCC Recording-304-367-5440; fax-304-367-5448; hours 8:30AM-4:30PM
Will search UCC records. Search per debtor- $11.00. Will not search real estate or tax lien records. RE record copy- $1.50 per page. UCC copy- $1.00 per page. Cert fee: $2.00 per page. Payee: Marion County Clerk. **Other phones:** Assessor-304-367-5410; Treasurer-304-367-5303; Appraiser/ Auditor-304-367-5310; Elections-304-367-5447; Vital Records-304-367-5453.

Marshall County

County Clerk, PO Box 459, Moundsville, WV 26041. **Phone-**County Clerk, R/E & UCC Recording- 304-845-1220; fax-304-845-5891; hours 8:30AM-4:30PM
Will search UCC records. Will not search real estate records. Copy fee- $.25 per page. Cert fee: $5.00 per copy. **Other phones:** Assessor-304-845-1490; Treasurer-304-845-1400; Elections-304-845-1220; Vital Records-304-845-1220.

Mason County

County Clerk, 200 6th St, Point Pleasant, WV 25550. **Phone-**County Clerk, R/E & UCC Recording- 304-675-1997; fax-304-675-2521; hours 8:30AM-4:30PM
Will not search records. RE record copy- $1.50 for 2 pages, $1.00 each addt'l. UCC copy- $1.50 per UCC. Cert fee: $1.00 per Cert. Payee: Mason County Clerk. **Other phones:** Assessor-304-675-2840; Treasurer-304-675-1047; Appraiser/ Auditor-304-675-2918; Elections-304-675-1997; Vital Records-304-675-1997.

McDowell County

County Clerk, 90 Wyoming St, #109, Welch, WV 24801-2487. **Phone-**304-436-8544, R/E Recording-304-436-8549, UCC Recording-304-436-8542; fax-304-436-8576; hours 9Am-5PM
Will not search records. UCC copy- $1.50 per page.$1.00 add'l. Cert fee: $1.50. Payee: McDowell County Clerk. **Other phones:** Assessor-304-436-8564; Treasurer-304-436-8527; Appraiser/ Auditor-304-436-8528; Elections-304-436-8543; Vital Records-304-436-8542.

Mercer County

County Clerk, 1501 Main St., Princeton, WV 24740. **Phone-**County Clerk, R/E & UCC Recording- 304-487-8312; fax-304-487-8351; hours 8:30AM-4PM
Will not search records. RE record copy- $1.50 for 1st 2 pages. UCC copy- $1.50 for 1st 2 pages. Cert fee: $6.00 per 5 pages. Payee: Mercer County Clerk. **Other phones:** Assessor-304-487-8329; Treasurer-304-425-8366; Elections-304-487-8339; Vital Records-304-487-8313; Probate Records-304-487-8321.

Mineral County

County Clerk, 150 Armstrong St, Keyser, WV 26726. **Phone-**County Clerk, R/E & UCC Recording- 304-788-3924; fax-304-788-4109; hours 8:30AM-5PM
Will not search records but says charge to look up a record is $2.00 per year. Record copy- $1.50 1st 2 pages, $1.00 each add'l. Cert fee: $1.50 per 2 pages. Payee: Mineral County Clerk. **Other phones:** Assessor-304-788-3753; Treasurer-304-788-0341; Appraiser/ Auditor-304-788-3753; Elections-304-788-3924; Vital Records-304-788-3924.

Mingo County

County Clerk, PO Box 1197, Williamson, WV 25661. **Phone-**304-235-0330; fax-304-235-0565; hours 8:30AM-4:30PM. Will not search records. Copy fee- $1.00 per page. Cert fee: $5.00. **Other phones:** Assessor-304-235-1850.

Monongalia County

County Clerk, 243 High St, Courthouse - Rm 123, Morgantown, WV 26505-5491. **Phone-**304-291-7230, R/E Recording-304-291-7235, UCC Recording-304-291-7235; fax-304-291-7233.
Will search UCC records. Search per debtor- $1.00. Specify type of tax lien along with name of person and year. Will search real estate records. RE record copy- $1.50 for 1st 2pages, $1.00 each add'l pg. UCC copy- $1.50 1st 2 pgs., $1.00 each add'l pg. Cert fee: $1.00 per doc. Payee: Monongalia County Clerk. **Online Access to Assessor, Real Estate records:** Records on the County Parcel Search database are free at www.assessor.org/parcelweb. Search by a wide variety of criteria including owner name and address. **Other phones:** Assessor-304-291-7222; Treasurer-304-291-7244; Elections-304-291-7238; Vital Records-304-291-7236.

Monroe County

County Clerk, PO Box 350, Union, WV 24983. **Phone-**304-772-3096; hours 8:30AM-4:30PM
Will not search records. UCC copy- $1.50 per page.$1.00 add'. Cert fee: $1.00 per doc. Payee: Monroe County Clerk. **Other phones:** Assessor-304-772-3083; Treasurer-304-772-3018.

Morgan County

County Clerk, 77 Fairfax St, #1A, #100, Berkeley Springs, WV 25411. **Phone-**County Clerk, R/E & UCC Recording- 304-258-8547; fax-304-258-8545; hours 9AM-5PM M,T,Th; 9AM-1PM W; 9AM-7PM F
Will not search records. RE record copy- $1.50 per page. UCC copy- $1.00 per page. Cert fee: $1.00 per cert. Payee: Morgan County Clerk. **Other phones:** Assessor-304-258-8570; Treasurer-304-258-8562; Appraiser/ Auditor-304-258-8570; Elections-304-258-8547; Vital Records-304-258-8547.

Nicholas County

County Clerk, 700 Main St, #2, Summersville, WV 26651. **Phone-**County Clerk, R/E & UCC Recording-304-872-7820; fax-304-872-9600; hours 8:30AM-4:30PM
Will not search UCC or real estate records. UCC copy- $1.50 1st 2 pages; $1.00 each add'l. Cert fee: $1.00. **Other phones:** Assessor-304-872-7800; Treasurer-304-872-3630 x42; Elections-304-872-7820; Vital Records-304-872-7820.

Ohio County Clerks Office

County Clerk, 1500 Chapline St Rm 205, Wheeling, WV 26003. **Phone-**304-234-3656; fax-304-234-3829; hours 8:30AM-5PM
Will not search records. Copy fee- $.50 per page. Cert fee: $1.00 per page. Payee: Ohio County Clerk. **Other phones:** Assessor-304-234-3626; Treasurer-304-234-3688.

Pendleton County

County Clerk, PO Box 1167, Franklin, WV 26807-0089. **Phone-**304-358-2505; fax-304-358-2473; hours 8:30AM-4PM
Will search UCC records. Search per debtor- $2.00. Will not search real estate or tax lien records. UCC copy- $1.50 per 2 pages. Cert fee: $1.00 per doc. **Other phones:** Assessor-304-358-2563; Treasurer-304-358-2214.

Pleasants County

County Clerk, 301 Court Lane, Rm 101, Courthouse, St. Marys, WV 26170. **Phone-**County Clerk, R/E & UCC Recording- 304-684-3542; fax-304-684-7569; hours 8:30AM-4:30PM

Will search UCC records. Search per debtor- $11.00. Will not search real estate or tax lien records. RE record copy- $1.50 1st 2 pages; $1.00 each add'l. UCC copy- $1.50 1st 2 pages; $1.00 each add'l. Cert fee: $1.00 per doc. Payee: County Clerk. **Other phones:** Assessor-304-684-3132; Treasurer-304-684-2285; Appraiser/ Auditor-304-684-3542; Elections-304-684-3542; Vital Records-304-684-3542; Sheriff-304-684-2285.

Pocahontas County

County Clerk, 900C 10th Ave, Marlinton, WV 24954. **Phone-**304-799-4549; hours 8:30AM-4:30PM

Will search UCC records. Search per debtor- $1.00. Will not search real estate or tax lien records. RE record copy- $1.50 1st 2 pages, $1.00 each add'l. UCC copy- $1.50 per page.$1.00 add'l. Cert fee: $1.00 per cert. Payee: Pocahontas County Clerk. **Other phones:** Assessor-304-799-4750; Treasurer-304-799-4710.

Preston County

County Clerk, 101 W. Main St, Rm 201, Kingwood, WV 26537. **Phone-**County Clerk, R/E & UCC Recording- 304-329-0070; fax-304-329-0198; hours 9AM-5PM (F open until 7PM)

Will search UCC records. Search per debtor- $5.00. Will not search real estate or tax lien records. UCC copy- $.50 per page. Payee: Preston County Clerk. **Other phones:** Assessor-304-329-1220; Treasurer-304-329-0105; Appraiser/ Auditor-304-329-0070; Elections-304-329-0070.

Putnam County

County Clerk, 3389 Winfield Rd., Winfield, WV 25213-9705. **Phone-**304-586-0202; fax-304-586-0280; hours 8AM-4PM

Will not search records. RE record copy- $1.50 1st 2 pages, $1.00 each add'l. Cert fee: $1.00 per cert. Payee: Putnam County Clerk. **Other phones:** Assessor-304-586-0206; Treasurer-304-586-0204.

Raleigh County

County Clerk, 215 Main St, Courthouse, Beckley, WV 25801. **Phone-**304-255-9123, R/E Recording-304-255-9125; fax-304-255-9352; hours 8:30AM-4PM

Will not search records. Copy fee-$1.50 1st 2 pages; $1.00 each add'l. **Other phones:** Assessor-304-255-9179; Treasurer-304-255-9300; Appraiser/ Auditor-304-255-9177; Elections-304-255-9127; Vital Records-304-255-9123.

Randolph County

County Clerk, PO Box 368, Elkins, WV 26241. **Phone-**304-636-0543; hours 8AM-4:30PM

Will not search records. RE record copy- $1.50 1st 2 pages, $1.00 each add'l. UCC copy- $1.50 per page.$1.00 add'l. Cert fee: $1.00 per cert. Payee: Randolph County Clerk. **Other phones:** Assessor-304-636-2114; Treasurer-304-636-2100; Sheriff-304-636-2100.

Ritchie County

County Clerk, 115 E. Main St, Courthouse - Rm 201, Harrisville, WV 26362. **Phone-**304-643-2164, R/E Recording-304-643-2164 x227, UCC Recording-304-643-2164 x227; fax-304-643-2906; hours 8AM-4PM

Will search UCC records. Search per debtor- $10.00. Will not search real estate or tax lien records. RE record copy- $1.50 1st 2 pages; $1.00 each add'l. UCC copy- $1.00 per page. Cert fee: $1.00 per

cert. Payee: Ritchie County Clerk. **Other phones:** Assessor-304-643-2164 x242; Treasurer-304-643-2164 x237; Appraiser/ Auditor-304-643-2164 x242; Elections-304-643-2164 x228; Vital Records-304-643-2164 x227; Sheriff-304-643-2164 x237.

Roane County

County Clerk, PO Box 69, Spencer, WV 25276. **Phone-**County Clerk, R/E & UCC Recording- 304-927-2860; fax-304-927-2489; hours 8:30AM-4PM M-F; 9AM-Noon Sat.

Will not search records. RE record copy- $1.50 1st 2 pages, $1.00 each add'l. UCC copy- $.50 per page. Payee: Roane County Clerk. **Other phones:** Assessor-304-927-3020; Treasurer-304-927-2540; Appraiser/ Auditor-304-927-3020; Elections-304-927-2860; Vital Records-304-927-2860; Sheriff-304-927-2540; County Commission-304-927-0078.

Summers County

County Clerk, PO Box 97, Hinton, WV 25951-0097. **Phone-**County Clerk, R/E & UCC Recording- 304-466-7104; fax-304-466-7146; hours 8:30AM-4:30PM

Will not search records. RE record copy- $1.50 per 2 pages, $1.00 each add'l. UCC copy- $1.50 per 2 pages, $1.00 each add'l. Cert fee: No charge. Payee: Summers County Clerk. **Other phones:** Assessor-304-466-7126; Treasurer-304-466-7112; Elections-304-466-7104; Vital Records-304-466-7104; Sheriff-304-466-7112.

Taylor County

County Clerk, 214 W. Main St, Rm 101, Courthouse, Grafton, WV 26354. **Phone-**County Clerk, R/E & UCC Recording- 304-265-1401; fax-304-265-3016; hours 8:30-Noon; 1-4:30PM. Will not search records. RE record copy- $1.50 1st 2 pages; $1.00 each add'l. UCC copy- $1.50 1st 2 pages; $1.00 each add'l. Payee: Taylor County Clerk. **Other phones:** Assessor-304-265-2420; Treasurer-304-265-5766; Elections-304-265-1401; Vital Records-304-265-1401.

Tucker County

County Clerk, 215 1st St. #3, Parsons, WV 26287. **Phone-**County Clerk, R/E & UCC Recording- 304-478-2414; fax-304-478-4464; hours 8AM-4PM

Will search UCC records. Search per debtor- $5.00. Will not search real estate or tax lien records. Real estate copy fee- $1.50 1st 2 pages; $1.00 each add'l. UCC copy- $1.50 1st 2 pages; $1.00 each add'l. Cert fee: $1.00 per cert. Payee: Tucker County Clerk. **Other phones:** Assessor-304-478-3727; Treasurer-304-478-2321; Elections-304-478-2414; Vital Records-304-478-2414.

Tyler County

County Clerk, PO Box 66, Middlebourne, WV 26149. **Phone-**County Clerk, R/E & UCC Recording- 304-758-2102; fax-304-758-2126; hours 8AM-4PM

Will not search records. RE record copy- $1.50 1st 2 pages; $1.00 each add'l. **Other phones:** Assessor-304-758-4781; Treasurer-304-758-4551; Elections-304-758-2102; Vital Records-304-758-2102.

Upshur County

County Clerk, 40 W. Main St, Courthouse - Rm 101, Buckhannon, WV 26201. **Phone-**County Clerk, R/E & UCC Recording- 304-472-1068; fax-304-472-1029; hours 8AM-4PM (til 6:30 on Th)

Will not search records. RE record copy- 1.50 per page. UCC copy- $1.50 per page. Cert fee: $1.00 per doc. Payee: Upshur County Clerk. **Other phones:** Assessor-304-472-4650; Treasurer-304-472-1180; Appraiser/ Auditor-304-472-4650; Elections-304-472-1068; Vital Records-304-472-1068.

Wayne County

Clerk of County Commission, PO Box 248, Wayne, WV 25570. **Phone-**Clerk of County Commission, R/E & UCC Recording- 304-272-5974; fax-304-272-5318; hours 8AM-4PM MTWF; 8AM-8PM TH

Will search UCC records. Search per debtor- $2.00. Will not search real estate or tax lien records. RE record copy- $1.50 1st 2 pages. Cert fee: $1.00 per Cert. Payee: Wayne County Clerk. **Other phones:** Assessor-304-272-6357; Treasurer-304-272-6721; Elections-304-272-6370; Vital Records-304-272-6371.

Webster County

County Clerk, 2 Court Sq, Courthouse - Rm G-1, Webster Springs, WV 26288-1054. **Phone-**County Clerk, R/E & UCC Recording- 304-847-2508; fax-304-847-5780; hours 8:30AM-4PM

Will not search records. RE record copy- $1.00 per 1st 2 pages. UCC copy- $1.50 per page; $1.00 per page after 2nd. Cert fee: $1.00 per page. Payee: Terry J. Payne, Clerk. **Other phones:** Assessor-304-847-2110; Treasurer-304-847-2006; Elections-304-847-2508; Vital Records-304-847-2508.

Wetzel County

County Clerk, PO Box 156, New Martinsville, WV 26155-0156. **Phone-**County Clerk, R/E & UCC Recording- 304-455-8224; fax-304-455-5256; hours 9AM-4:40 M,T,W,F; 9AM-4PM Th; 9-N Sat.

Will search UCC records. Search per debtor- $2.00. Will not search real estate or tax lien records. RE record copy- $1.50 1st 2 pages; $1.00 each add'l. UCC copy- $1.50 per UCC. **Other phones:** Assessor-304-455-8214; Treasurer-304-455-8218; Elections-304-455-8235; Vital Records-304-455-8224.

Wirt County

County Clerk, PO Box 53, Elizabeth, WV 26143. **Phone-**County Clerk, R/E & UCC Recording- 304-275-4271; fax-304-275-3418; hours 8:30AM-4PM

Will search UCC records. Will do tax lien search. Will not search real estate records. UCC copy- $1.50 per page. Cert fee: $1.00 per cert. Payee: Wirt County Clerk. **Other phones:** Assessor-304-275-3192; Treasurer-304-275-4222; Elections-304-275-4271; Vital Records-304-275-4271.

Wood County

County Clerk, PO Box 1474, Parkersburg, WV 26102-1474. **Phone-**304-424-1850, R/E / UCC Recording-304-424-1899; fax-304-424-1864; hours-8:30AM-4:30PM www.woodcountywv.com

Will search UCC records. Search per debtor- $11.00. Will not search real estate or tax lien records. RE record copy- $1.50 1st 2 pages; $1.00 each add'l. UCC copy- $1.50 1st 2 pages; $1.00 each add'l. Cert fee: $1.00 per cert. Payee: Wood County Clerk. **Online Access to Recording, Deed, Will, Death, Birth records:** Access is by dial-up modem; visit www.woodcountywv.com/modem.htm for instructions for free connection. Records go back to early 1990s. **Other phones:** Assessor-304-424-1875; Treasurer-304-424-1910; Appraiser/ Auditor-304-424-1875; Elections-304-424-1860; Vital Records-304-424-1844.

Wyoming County

County Clerk, PO Box 309, Pineville, WV 24874. **Phone-**304-732-8000; fax-304-732-9659.

Will search UCC records. Search per debtor- $5.00. Will not search real estate or tax lien records. UCC copy- $1.50 for 1st 2 pages, $1.00 each add'l pg. Cert fee: $2.50 per doc. Payee: Wyoming City Clerk. **Other phones:** Assessor-304-732-8000; Treasurer-304-732-8000; Sheriff-304-732-8000

West Virginia County Locator

You will usually be able to find the city name in the City/County Cross Reference below. In that case, it is a simple matter to determine the county from the cross reference. However, only the official US Postal Service city names are included in this index. There are an additional 40,000 place names that people use in their addresses. Therefore, we have also included a ZIP/City Cross Reference immediately following the City/County Cross Reference.

If you know the ZIP Code but the city name does not appear in the City/County Cross Reference index, look up the ZIP Code in the ZIP/City Cross Reference, find the city name, then look up the city name in the City/County Cross Reference. For example, you want to know the county for an address of Menands, NY 12204. There is no "Menands" in the City/County Cross Reference. The ZIP/City Cross Reference shows that ZIP Codes 12201-12288 are for the city of Albany. Looking back in the City/County Cross Reference, Albany is in Albany County.

West Virginia City/County Cross Reference

ACCOVILLE Logan
ADRIAN Upshur
ADVENT Jackson
ALBRIGHT Preston
ALDERSON (24910) Greenbrier(73),
  Summers(20), Monroe(6)
ALKOL Lincoln
ALLEN JUNCTION Wyoming
ALLOY Fayette
ALMA Tyler
ALPOCA Wyoming
ALUM BRIDGE (26321) Lewis(97),
  Doddridge(1)
ALUM CREEK (25003) Kanawha(54),
  Lincoln(45)
ALVY Tyler
AMEAGLE Raleigh
AMHERSTDALE Logan
AMIGO Wyoming
AMMA Roane
ANAWALT McDowell
ANMOORE Harrison
ANSTED Fayette
APPLE GROVE Mason
ARBOVALE Pocahontas
ARNETT Raleigh
ARNOLDSBURG Calhoun
ARTHUR Grant
ARTHURDALE Preston
ARTIE Raleigh
ASBURY Greenbrier
ASHFORD Boone
ASHLAND McDowell
ASHTON Mason
ATHENS Mercer
AUBURN Ritchie
AUGUSTA Hampshire
AURORA Preston
AUTO Greenbrier
AVONDALE McDowell
BAISDEN Mingo
BAKER Hardy
BAKERTON Jefferson
BALD KNOB Boone
BALLARD Monroe
BALLENGEE (24919) Summers(54),
  Monroe(45)
BANCROFT Putnam
BARBOURSVILLE Cabell
BARRACKVILLE Marion
BARRETT Boone
BARTLEY McDowell
BARTOW Pocahontas
BAXTER Marion
BEARDS FORK Fayette
BEAVER Raleigh
BECKLEY Raleigh
BECKWITH Fayette
BEECH BOTTOM Brooke
BEESON Mercer
BELINGTON Barbour
BELLE Kanawha
BELLEVILLE (26133) Wood(98),
  Jackson(1)
BELMONT Pleasants

BELVA (26656) Nicholas(82), Fayette(14),
  Clay(2)
BENS RUN Tyler
BENTREE Clay
BENWOOD Marshall
BEREA Ritchie
BERGOO Webster
BERKELEY SPRINGS Morgan
BERWIND McDowell
BETHANY (26032) Brooke(97), Ohio(2)
BEVERLY Randolph
BICKMORE Clay
BIG BEND Calhoun
BIG CREEK Logan
BIG RUN Wetzel
BIG SANDY McDowell
BIG SPRINGS Calhoun
BIM Boone
BIRCH RIVER (26610) Nicholas(96),
  Webster(3)
BLACKSVILLE Monongalia
BLAIR Logan
BLANDVILLE Doddridge
BLOOMERY Hampshire
BLOOMINGROSE Boone
BLOUNT Kanawha
BLUE CREEK Kanawha
BLUE JAY Raleigh
BLUEFIELD Mercer
BOB WHITE Boone
BOLT Raleigh
BOMONT Clay
BOOMER Fayette
BOOTH Monongalia
BORDERLAND Mingo
BOWDEN (26254) Randolph(96), Tucker(3)
BOZOO Monroe
BRADLEY Raleigh
BRADSHAW McDowell
BRAMWELL Mercer
BRANCHLAND (25506) Lincoln(97),
  Cabell(2)
BRANDONVILLE Preston
BRANDYWINE Pendleton
BREEDEN Mingo
BRENTON Wyoming
BRETZ Preston
BRIDGEPORT (26330) Harrison(91),
  Taylor(7), Barbour(1)
BRISTOL (26332) Harrison(97),
  Doddridge(2)
BROHARD (26138) Wirt(77), Calhoun(22)
BROOKS Summers
BROWNTON Barbour
BRUCETON MILLS Preston
BRUNO Logan
BUCKEYE Pocahontas
BUCKHANNON (26201) Upshur(95),
  Lewis(3)
BUD Wyoming
BUFFALO Putnam
BUNKER HILL Berkeley
BURLINGTON (26710) Mineral(85),
  Hampshire(14)

BURNSVILLE (26335) Braxton(55),
  Gilmer(44)
BURNWELL (25034) Kanawha(50),
  Putnam(50)
BURTON (26562) Monongalia(56),
  Wetzel(43)
CABIN CREEK Kanawha
CABINS Grant
CAIRO Ritchie
CALDWELL (24925) Greenbrier(82),
  Monroe(17)
CALVIN Nicholas
CAMDEN Lewis
CAMDEN ON GAULEY Webster
CAMERON Marshall
CAMP CREEK Mercer
CANABRAKE McDowell
CANEBRAKE McDowell
CANNELTON Fayette
CANVAS Nicholas
CAPELS McDowell
CAPON BRIDGE Hampshire
CAPON SPRINGS Hampshire
CARETTA McDowell
CAROLINA Marion
CASS Pocahontas
CASSVILLE Monongalia
CEDAR GROVE Kanawha
CEDARVILLE (26611) Braxton(56),
  Gilmer(43)
CENTER POINT Doddridge
CENTRALIA Braxton
CENTURY Barbour
CEREDO Wayne
CHAPMANVILLE (25508) Logan(89),
  Boone(10)
CHARLES TOWN Jefferson
CHARLESTON Kanawha
CHARLTON HEIGHTS Fayette
CHARMCO Greenbrier
CHATTAROY Mingo
CHAUNCEY Logan
CHESTER Hancock
CHLOE (25235) Calhoun(85), Clay(14)
CIRCLEVILLE Pendleton
CLARKSBURG Harrison
CLAY (25043) Clay(98), Nicholas(1)
CLEAR CREEK Raleigh
CLEAR FORK Wyoming
CLENDENIN (25045) Roane(40),
  Kanawha(38), Clay(20)
CLEVELAND (26215) Upshur(97),
  Webster(2)
CLIFTON Mason
CLINTONVILLE Greenbrier
CLIO Roane
CLOTHIER (25047) Boone(58), Logan(41)
COAL CITY Raleigh
COAL MOUNTAIN Wyoming
COALTON Randolph
COALWOOD McDowell
COLCORD Raleigh
COLFAX Marion
COLLIERS Brooke
COMFORT Boone
COOL RIDGE Raleigh

COPEN Braxton
CORA Logan
CORE Monongalia
CORINNE Wyoming
CORINTH Preston
COSTA Boone
COTTAGEVILLE (25239) Jackson(83),
  Mason(16)
COTTLE Nicholas
COVEL Wyoming
COWEN Webster
COXS MILLS (26342) Gilmer(98),
  Ritchie(1)
CRAB ORCHARD Raleigh
CRAIGSVILLE Nicholas
CRANBERRY Raleigh
CRAWFORD (26343) Lewis(80),
  Upshur(19)
CRAWLEY Greenbrier
CRESTON (26141) Wirt(72), Calhoun(27)
CRICHTON Greenbrier
CROWN HILL Kanawha
CRUM Wayne
CRUMPLER McDowell
CUCUMBER McDowell
CULLODEN (25510) Cabell(67),
  Putnam(21), Lincoln(10)
CUZZART Preston
CYCLONE Wyoming
DAILEY Randolph
DALLAS Marshall
DANESE Fayette
DANIELS Raleigh
DANVILLE Boone
DAVIN (25617) Logan(83), Wyoming(16)
DAVIS Tucker
DAVISVILLE Wood
DAVY (24828) McDowell(98), Wyoming(1)
DAWES Kanawha
DAWMONT Harrison
DEEP WATER Fayette
DELBARTON Mingo
DELLSLOW Monongalia
DELRAY Hampshire
DIANA Webster
DILLE (26617) Clay(98), Nicholas(1)
DINGESS Mingo
DIXIE (25059) Nicholas(85), Fayette(14)
DOROTHY Raleigh
DOTHAN Fayette
DRENNEN Nicholas
DRY CREEK Raleigh
DRYBRANCH Kanawha
DRYFORK (26263) Tucker(66),
  Randolph(33)
DUCK (25063) Clay(92), Braxton(7)
DUNBAR Kanawha
DUNLOW Wayne
DUNMORE Pocahontas
DURBIN Pocahontas
EAST BANK Kanawha
EAST LYNN Wayne
ECCLES Raleigh
ECKMAN McDowell
EDGARTON Mingo
EDMOND Fayette

EGLON Preston
ELBERT McDowell
ELEANOR Putnam
ELIZABETH (26143) Wirt(85), Ritchie(10),
   Wood(2), Jackson(1)
ELK GARDEN (26717) Mineral(79),
   Grant(20)
ELKHORN McDowell
ELKINS Randolph
ELKVIEW (25071) Kanawha(94), Roane(5)
ELLAMORE Randolph
ELLENBORO (26346) Ritchie(50),
   Pleasants(43), Tyler(6)
ELMIRA Braxton
ELTON Summers
EMMETT Logan
ENGLISH McDowell
ENTERPRISE Harrison
ERBACON Webster
ESKDALE Kanawha
ETHEL Logan
EUREKA Pleasants
EVANS (25241) Jackson(87), Mason(12)
EVERETTVILLE Monongalia
EXCHANGE Braxton
FAIRDALE Raleigh
FAIRLEA Greenbrier
FAIRMONT (26554) Marion(96),
   Monongalia(3)
FAIRMONT Marion
FAIRVIEW Marion
FALLING ROCK Kanawha
FALLING WATERS Berkeley
FALLS MILL Braxton
FANROCK Wyoming
FARMINGTON Marion
FENWICK Nicholas
FISHER Hardy
FIVE FORKS Calhoun
FLAT TOP Mercer
FLATWOODS Braxton
FLEMINGTON (26347) Taylor(67),
   Barbour(32)
FOLA Clay
FOLLANSBEE Brooke
FOLSOM Wetzel
FOREST HILL Summers
FORT ASHBY Mineral
FORT GAY Wayne
FORT SEYBERT Pendleton
FORT SPRING Greenbrier
FOSTER Boone
FOUR STATES Marion
FRAMETOWN (26623) Braxton(97),
   Gilmer(2)
FRANKFORD Greenbrier
FRANKLIN Pendleton
FRAZIERS BOTTOM (25082) Putnam(57),
   Mason(41)
FREEMAN Mercer
FRENCH CREEK Upshur
FRENCHTON Upshur
FRIARS HILL Greenbrier
FRIENDLY (26146) Tyler(54),
   Pleasants(45)
GALLAGHER (25083) Kanawha(93),
   Fayette(6)
GALLIPOLIS FERRY Mason
GALLOWAY Barbour
GANDEEVILLE Roane
GAP MILLS Monroe
GARY McDowell
GASSAWAY Braxton
GAULEY BRIDGE (25085) Fayette(61),
   Kanawha(38)
GAY (25244) Roane(55), Jackson(44)
GENOA Wayne
GERRARDSTOWN Berkeley
GHENT Raleigh
GILBERT Mingo
GILBOA Nicholas
GILMER Gilmer
GIVEN (25245) Jackson(88), Putnam(11)

GLACE Monroe
GLADY Randolph
GLASGOW Kanawha
GLEN Clay
GLEN DALE Marshall
GLEN DANIEL Raleigh
GLEN EASTON Marshall
GLEN FERRIS Fayette
GLEN FORK Wyoming
GLEN JEAN Fayette
GLEN MORGAN Raleigh
GLEN ROGERS Wyoming
GLEN WHITE Raleigh
GLENDON Braxton
GLENGARY Berkeley
GLENHAYES Wayne
GLENVILLE Gilmer
GLENWOOD (25520) Mason(54),
   Cabell(45)
GORDON Boone
GORMANIA Grant
GRAFTON Taylor
GRANT TOWN Marion
GRANTSVILLE Calhoun
GRANVILLE Monongalia
GRASSY MEADOWS Greenbrier
GREAT CACAPON Morgan
GREEN BANK Pocahontas
GREEN SPRING Hampshire
GREEN SULPHUR SPRINGS Summers
GREENVILLE Monroe
GREENWOOD (26360) Doddridge(58),
   Ritchie(31), Tyler(10)
GRIFFITHSVILLE Lincoln
GRIMMS LANDING Mason
GYPSY Harrison
HACKER VALLEY Webster
HALLTOWN Jefferson
HAMBLETON Tucker
HAMLIN (25523) Lincoln(90), Putnam(9)
HAMPDEN Mingo
HANDLEY Kanawha
HANOVER Wyoming
HANSFORD Kanawha
HARMAN (26270) Randolph(97),
   Pendleton(2)
HARMONY (25246) Roane(94), Jackson(5)
HARPER Raleigh
HARPERS FERRY Jefferson
HARRISON Clay
HARRISVILLE Ritchie
HARTFORD Mason
HARTS (25524) Lincoln(82), Logan(14),
   Wayne(2)
HAVACO McDowell
HAYWOOD Harrison
HAZELGREEN Ritchie
HAZELTON Preston
HEATERS Braxton
HEDGESVILLE (25427) Berkeley(82),
   Morgan(17)
HELEN Raleigh
HELVETIA (26224) Randolph(86),
   Upshur(13)
HEMPHILL McDowell
HENDERSON Mason
HENDRICKS Tucker
HENLAWSON Logan
HENSLEY McDowell
HEPZIBAH Harrison
HERNDON Wyoming
HERNSHAW Kanawha
HEWETT (25108) Boone(89), Logan(10)
HIAWATHA Mercer
HICO Fayette
HIGH VIEW Hampshire
HILLSBORO Pocahontas
HILLTOP Fayette
HINES Greenbrier
HINTON Summers
HOLDEN Logan
HOMETOWN Putnam
HORNER Lewis

HUGHESTON Kanawha
HUNDRED (26575) Wetzel(88),
   Monongalia(11)
HUNTINGTON (25701) Cabell(97),
   Wayne(2)
HUNTINGTON (25704) Wayne(58),
   Cabell(41)
HUNTINGTON Cabell
HUNTINGTON Wayne
HURRICANE Putnam
HUTTONSVILLE Randolph
IAEGER (24844) McDowell(87),
   Wyoming(12)
IDAMAY Marion
IKES FORK Wyoming
IMPERIAL JUNCTION (25034)
   Kanawha(50), Putnam(50)
INDEPENDENCE (26374) Preston(67),
   Monongalia(16), Taylor(15)
INDORE Clay
INDUSTRIAL Harrison
INSTITUTE Kanawha
INWOOD Berkeley
IRELAND (26376) Lewis(87), Braxton(12)
ISABAN McDowell
ITMANN Wyoming
IVYDALE Clay
JACKSONBURG (26377) Wetzel(62),
   Tyler(37)
JANE LEW (26378) Lewis(89),
   Harrison(10)
JEFFREY Boone
JENKINJONES McDowell
JESSE Wyoming
JODIE Fayette
JOLO McDowell
JONBEN Raleigh
JOSEPHINE Raleigh
JULIAN Boone
JUMPING BRANCH (25969) Summers(87),
   Raleigh(12)
JUNCTION Hampshire
JUNIOR Barbour
JUSTICE Mingo
KANAWHA FALLS Fayette
KANAWHA HEAD Upshur
KEARNEYSVILLE (25430) Jefferson(83),
   Berkeley(16)
KEARNEYSVILLE Jefferson
KEGLEY Mercer
KELLYSVILLE Mercer
KENNA Jackson
KENOVA Wayne
KENTUCK Jackson
KERENS (26276) Randolph(75),
   Tucker(24)
KERMIT (25674) Mingo(67), Wayne(32)
KESLERS CROSS LANES Nicholas
KEYSER Mineral
KEYSTONE McDowell
KIAHSVILLE Wayne
KIEFFER Greenbrier
KILSYTH Fayette
KIMBALL McDowell
KIMBERLY Fayette
KINCAID Fayette
KINGMONT Marion
KINGSTON Fayette
KINGWOOD Preston
KIRBY (26729) Hampshire(82), Hardy(17)
KISTLER Logan
KOPPERSTON Wyoming
KYLE McDowell
LAHMANSVILLE Grant
LAKE Logan
LAKIN Mason
LANARK Raleigh
LANSING Fayette
LASHMEET Mercer
LAVALETTE Wayne
LAYLAND (25864) Raleigh(78), Fayette(21)
LE ROY (25252) Roane(48), Jackson(44),
   Wirt(6)

LECKIE McDowell
LEEWOOD Kanawha
LEFT HAND Roane
LEIVASY Nicholas
LEON (25123) Mason(66), Putnam(33)
LERONA Mercer
LESAGE Cabell
LESLIE Greenbrier
LESTER Raleigh
LETART Mason
LETTER GAP Gilmer
LEVELS Hampshire
LEWISBURG Greenbrier
LIBERTY (25124) Putnam(93), Jackson(4),
   Kanawha(2)
LIMA Tyler
LINDEN Roane
LINDSIDE Monroe
LINN (26384) Gilmer(67), Lewis(31),
   Braxton(1)
LITTLE BIRCH Braxton
LITTLETON Wetzel
LIZEMORES Clay
LOCHGELLY Fayette
LOCKBRIDGE Summers
LOCKNEY Gilmer
LOGAN Logan
LONDON Kanawha
LONG BRANCH Fayette
LOOKOUT Fayette
LOONEYVILLE Roane
LORADO Logan
LORENTZ Upshur
LOST CITY Hardy
LOST CREEK Harrison
LOST RIVER Hardy
LUMBERPORT Harrison
LUNDALE Logan
LYBURN Logan
LYNCO Wyoming
MABEN Wyoming
MABIE Randolph
MABSCOTT Raleigh
MAC ARTHUR Raleigh
MACFARLAN Ritchie
MADISON Boone
MAHAN Fayette
MAIDSVILLE Monongalia
MALLORY Logan
MAMMOTH Kanawha
MAN Logan
MANNINGTON (26582) Marion(88),
   Monongalia(10), Harrison(1)
MAPLEWOOD Fayette
MARIANNA Wyoming
MARLINTON Pocahontas
MARTINSBURG Berkeley
MASON Mason
MASONTOWN (26542) Preston(88),
   Monongalia(11)
MATEWAN Mingo
MATHENY Wyoming
MATHIAS Hardy
MATOAKA (24736) Mercer(85),
   Wyoming(14)
MAXWELTON Greenbrier
MAYBEURY McDowell
MAYSEL Clay
MAYSVILLE Grant
MC COMAS Mercer
MC GRAWS Wyoming
MC MECHEN Marshall
MC WHORTER Harrison
MCMECHEN Marshall
MEADOR Mingo
MEADOW BLUFF Greenbrier
MEADOW BRIDGE (25976) Fayette(55),
   Summers(40), Greenbrier(4)
MEADOW CREEK Summers
MEADOWBROOK Harrison
MEDLEY Grant
METZ (26585) Marion(75), Wetzel(25)

MIAMI Kanawha
MIDDLEBOURNE Tyler
MIDKIFF Lincoln
MIDWAY Raleigh
MILAM (26838) Hardy(94), Pendleton(5)
MILL CREEK Randolph
MILLSTONE Calhoun
MILLVILLE Jefferson
MILLWOOD Jackson
MILTON Cabell
MINDEN Fayette
MINERAL WELLS Wood
MINGO Randolph
MOATSVILLE (26405) Barbour(84), Preston(15)
MOHAWK McDowell
MONAVILLE Logan
MONTANA MINES Marion
MONTCALM Mercer
MONTCOAL Raleigh
MONTERVILLE Randolph
MONTGOMERY (25136) Fayette(61), Kanawha(38)
MONTROSE (26283) Randolph(80), Barbour(12), Tucker(6)
MOOREFIELD Hardy
MORGANTOWN Monongalia
MOUNDSVILLE Marshall
MOUNT ALTO (25264) Jackson(65), Mason(34)
MOUNT CARBON Fayette
MOUNT CLARE Harrison
MOUNT GAY Logan
MOUNT HOPE (25880) Raleigh(59), Fayette(40)
MOUNT LOOKOUT Nicholas
MOUNT NEBO Nicholas
MOUNT OLIVE Fayette
MOUNT STORM Grant
MOUNT ZION Calhoun
MOUNTAIN Ritchie
MOYERS Pendleton
MULLENS Wyoming
MUNDAY (26152) Calhoun(92), Wirt(7)
MURRAYSVILLE (26153) Jackson(88), Wood(11)
MYRA Lincoln
MYRTLE Mingo
NALLEN (26680) Fayette(45), Nicholas(43), Greenbrier(10)
NAOMA Raleigh
NAPIER Braxton
NAUGATUCK Mingo
NEBO (25141) Clay(94), Calhoun(5)
NELLIS Boone
NEMOURS Mercer
NEOLA Greenbrier
NETTIE Nicholas
NEW CREEK (26743) Mineral(71), Grant(28)
NEW CUMBERLAND Hancock
NEW HAVEN Mason
NEW MANCHESTER Hancock
NEW MARTINSVILLE Wetzel
NEW MILTON (26411) Doddridge(90), Gilmer(9)
NEW RICHMOND Wyoming
NEWBERNE (26409) Gilmer(55), Ritchie(44)
NEWBURG Preston
NEWELL Hancock
NEWHALL McDowell
NEWTON Roane
NEWTOWN Mingo
NICUT (26633) Calhoun(62), Braxton(34), Gilmer(3)
NIMITZ Summers
NITRO (25143) Kanawha(73), Putnam(26)
NOLAN Mingo
NORMANTOWN (25267) Gilmer(91), Calhoun(4), Braxton(3)
NORTH MATEWAN Mingo
NORTH SPRING Wyoming

NORTHFORK McDowell
NORTON Randolph
OAK HILL Fayette
OAKVALE Mercer
OCEANA Wyoming
ODD (25902) Raleigh(82), Mercer(17)
OHLEY Kanawha
OLD FIELDS (26845) Hardy(97), Hampshire(2)
OMAR Logan
ONA Cabell
ONEGO Pendleton
ORGAS Boone
ORLANDO (26412) Lewis(94), Gilmer(4), Braxton(1)
ORMA Calhoun
OSAGE Monongalia
OTTAWA Boone
OVAPA (25150) Roane(63), Clay(36)
PADEN CITY (26159) Wetzel(64), Tyler(35)
PAGE Fayette
PAGETON McDowell
PALERMO Lincoln
PALESTINE Wirt
PANTHER McDowell
PARKERSBURG Wood
PARSONS (26287) Tucker(98), Preston(1)
PAW PAW (25434) Hampshire(53), Morgan(46)
PAX Fayette
PAYNESVILLE McDowell
PEACH CREEK Logan
PECKS MILL Logan
PEMBERTON Raleigh
PENCE SPRINGS Summers
PENNSBORO (26415) Ritchie(97), Tyler(2)
PENTRESS Monongalia
PERKINS Gilmer
PETERSBURG (26847) Grant(96), Hardy(3)
PETERSTOWN Monroe
PETROLEUM (26161) Ritchie(91), Wood(5), Wirt(3)
PEYTONA Boone
PHILIPPI Barbour
PICKENS (26230) Randolph(92), Webster(7)
PIEDMONT Mineral
PINCH Kanawha
PINE GROVE Wetzel
PINEVILLE Wyoming
PINEY VIEW Raleigh
PIPESTEM (25979) Summers(78), Mercer(21)
PLINY Putnam
POCA Putnam
POE Nicholas
POINT PLEASANT Mason
POINTS Hampshire
POND GAP Kanawha
POOL Nicholas
PORTERS FALLS Wetzel
POWELLTON Fayette
POWHATAN McDowell
PRATT Kanawha
PREMIER McDowell
PRENTER Boone
PRICHARD Wayne
PRINCE Fayette
PRINCEWICK Raleigh
PROCIOUS (25164) Clay(79), Roane(20)
PROCTOR (26055) Marshall(83), Wetzel(16)
PROSPERITY Raleigh
PULLMAN Ritchie
PURGITSVILLE (26852) Hardy(66), Hampshire(27), Mineral(4)
PURSGLOVE Monongalia
QUINNIMONT Fayette
QUINWOOD (25981) Greenbrier(64), Nicholas(35)
RACHEL Marion
RACINE Boone

RAGLAND Mingo
RAINELLE (25962) Fayette(94), Greenbrier(5)
RALEIGH Raleigh
RAMAGE Boone
RAMSEY Fayette
RANGER (25557) Lincoln(97), Wayne(2)
RANSON Jefferson
RAVENCLIFF Wyoming
RAVENSWOOD (26164) Jackson(88), Wood(11)
RAWL Mingo
RAYSAL McDowell
READER Wetzel
RED CREEK Tucker
RED HOUSE (25168) Putnam(68), Kanawha(31)
RED JACKET Mingo
REDSTAR Fayette
REEDSVILLE Preston
REEDY Roane
RENICK Greenbrier
REYNOLDSVILLE Harrison
RHODELL Raleigh
RICHWOOD (26261) Nicholas(98), Greenbrier(1)
RIDGELEY Mineral
RIDGEVIEW Boone
RIDGEWAY Berkeley
RIO (26755) Hampshire(64), Hardy(35)
RIPLEY Jackson
RIPPON Jefferson
RIVERTON Pendleton
RIVESVILLE (26588) Marion(87), Monongalia(12)
ROANOKE Lewis
ROBERTSBURG Putnam
ROBSON Fayette
ROCK Mercer
ROCK CASTLE Jackson
ROCK CAVE (26234) Upshur(95), Webster(4)
ROCK CREEK Raleigh
ROCK VIEW Wyoming
ROCKPORT Wood
RODERFIELD McDowell
ROMNEY Hampshire
RONCEVERTE (24970) Greenbrier(98), Monroe(1)
ROSEDALE (26636) Gilmer(46), Braxton(31), Calhoun(22)
ROSEMONT Taylor
ROSSMORE Logan
ROWLESBURG (26425) Preston(98), Tucker(1)
RUPERT Greenbrier
SABINE Wyoming
SAINT ALBANS Kanawha
SAINT GEORGE (26290) Tucker(95), Preston(4)
SAINT MARYS (26170) Pleasants(93), Ritchie(5)
SALEM (26426) Harrison(92), Doddridge(7)
SALT ROCK Cabell
SAND FORK Gilmer
SAND RIDGE Calhoun
SANDSTONE Summers
SANDYVILLE Jackson
SARAH ANN Logan
SARTON Monroe
SAULSVILLE Wyoming
SAXON Raleigh
SCARBRO Fayette
SCOTT DEPOT Putnam
SECONDCREEK Monroe
SELBYVILLE (26236) Upshur(57), Randolph(42)
SENECA ROCKS Pendleton
SETH Boone
SHADY SPRING Raleigh
SHANKS Hampshire
SHARON Kanawha
SHARPLES Logan

SHENANDOAH JUNCTION Jefferson
SHEPHERDSTOWN (25443) Jefferson(90), Berkeley(9)
SHERMAN Jackson
SHINNSTON (26431) Harrison(96), Taylor(3)
SHIRLEY Tyler
SHOALS Wayne
SHOCK (26638) Gilmer(95), Calhoun(5)
SHORT CREEK Brooke
SIAS Lincoln
SIMON Wyoming
SIMPSON Taylor
SINKS GROVE Monroe
SISTERSVILLE Tyler
SKELTON Raleigh
SKYGUSTY McDowell
SLAB FORK (25920) Raleigh(90), Wyoming(9)
SLANESVILLE Hampshire
SLATYFORK Pocahontas
SMITHBURG Doddridge
SMITHERS Fayette
SMITHFIELD (26437) Wetzel(92), Marion(7)
SMITHVILLE Ritchie
SMOOT Greenbrier
SNOWSHOE Pocahontas
SOD Lincoln
SOPHIA Raleigh
SOUTHSIDE Mason
SPANISHBURG Mercer
SPELTER Harrison
SPENCER Roane
SPRAGUE Raleigh
SPRIGG Mingo
SPRING DALE Fayette
SPRINGFIELD Hampshire
SPURLOCKVILLE (25565) Lincoln(74), Boone(25)
SQUIRE McDowell
STANAFORD Raleigh
STATTS MILLS Jackson
STEPHENSON Wyoming
STIRRAT Logan
STOLLINGS Logan
STOUTS MILLS Gilmer
STRANGE CREEK (26639) Braxton(71), Nicholas(25), Clay(3)
STUMPTOWN (25280) Gilmer(55), Calhoun(44)
SUGAR GROVE Pendleton
SUMERCO Lincoln
SUMMERLEE Fayette
SUMMERSVILLE Nicholas
SUMMIT POINT Jefferson
SUNDIAL Raleigh
SUPERIOR McDowell
SURVEYOR Raleigh
SUTTON Braxton
SWEET SPRINGS Monroe
SWEETLAND Lincoln
SWISS Nicholas
SWITCHBACK McDowell
SWITZER Logan
SYLVESTER Boone
TAD Kanawha
TALCOTT (24981) Summers(86), Monroe(14)
TALLMANSVILLE Upshur
TANNER Gilmer
TAPLIN Logan
TARIFF Roane
TEAYS Putnam
TERRA ALTA Preston
TERRY Raleigh
THACKER Mingo
THOMAS Tucker
THORNTON (26440) Taylor(67), Preston(24), Barbour(7)
THORPE McDowell
THREE CHURCHES Hampshire
THURMOND Fayette

TIOGA (26691) Nicholas(96), Webster(3)
TORNADO (25202) Lincoln(50), Kanawha(49)
TRIADELPHIA Ohio
TROY (26443) Gilmer(85), Doddridge(14)
TRUE Summers
TUNNELTON Preston
TURTLE CREEK Boone
TWILIGHT Boone
TWIN BRANCH McDowell
UNEEDA Boone
UNION Monroe
UPPER TRACT Pendleton
UPPERGLADE Webster
VALLEY BEND Randolph
VALLEY CHAPEL Lewis
VALLEY FORK Clay
VALLEY GROVE (26060) Ohio(98), Brooke(1)
VALLEY HEAD (26294) Randolph(81), Pocahontas(18)
VAN Boone
VARNEY Mingo
VERDUNVILLE Logan
VERNER (25650) Mingo(71), Logan(28)
VICTOR Fayette

VIENNA Wood
VIVIAN McDowell
VOLGA (26238) Barbour(70), Upshur(27), Harrison(1)
VULCAN Mingo
WADESTOWN Monongalia
WAITEVILLE Monroe
WALKER (26180) Wood(92), Wirt(7)
WALKERSVILLE (26447) Lewis(97), Braxton(2)
WALLACE (26448) Harrison(86), Marion(7), Doddridge(5)
WALLBACK (25285) Clay(98), Roane(1)
WALTON Roane
WANA Monongalia
WAR McDowell
WARDENSVILLE Hardy
WARRIORMINE McDowell
WASHINGTON Wood
WAVERLY (26184) Wood(62), Pleasants(37)
WAYSIDE (24985) Monroe(63), Summers(36)
WEBSTER SPRINGS Webster
WEIRTON (26062) Hancock(85), Brooke(14)

WELCH McDowell
WELLSBURG Brooke
WEST COLUMBIA Mason
WEST HAMLIN Lincoln
WEST LIBERTY Ohio
WEST MILFORD Harrison
WEST UNION (26456) Doddridge(94), Tyler(3), Ritchie(1)
WESTON Lewis
WHARNCLIFFE Mingo
WHARTON Boone
WHEELING Ohio
WHITE OAK (25989) Raleigh(98), Summers(1)
WHITE SULPHUR SPRINGS Greenbrier
WHITESVILLE (25209) Raleigh(84), Boone(15)
WHITMAN Logan
WHITMER Randolph
WICK Tyler
WIDEN Clay
WILCOE McDowell
WILEY FORD Mineral
WILEYVILLE Wetzel
WILKINSON Logan
WILLIAMSBURG Greenbrier

WILLIAMSON Mingo
WILLIAMSTOWN Wood
WILSIE Braxton
WILSONBURG Harrison
WILSONDALE (25699) Wayne(74), Mingo(20), Lincoln(5)
WINDSOR HEIGHTS Brooke
WINFIELD Putnam
WINIFREDE Kanawha
WINONA Fayette
WOLF PEN Wyoming
WOLF SUMMIT Harrison
WOLFCREEK Monroe
WOLFE Mercer
WOODVILLE Lincoln
WORTH McDowell
WORTHINGTON (26591) Marion(96), Harrison(3)
WYATT Harrison
WYCO Wyoming
WYOMING Wyoming
YAWKEY Lincoln
YELLOW SPRING Hampshire
YOLYN Logan
YUKON McDowell

West Virginia ZIP/City Cross Reference

24701-24701	BLUEFIELD
24710-24710	ALPOCA
24712-24712	ATHENS
24714-24714	BEESON
24715-24715	BRAMWELL
24716-24716	BUD
24719-24719	COVEL
24724-24724	FREEMAN
24726-24726	HERNDON
24729-24729	HIAWATHA
24731-24731	KEGLEY
24732-24732	KELLYSVILLE
24733-24733	LASHMEET
24735-24735	MC COMAS
24736-24736	MATOAKA
24737-24737	MONTCALM
24738-24738	NEMOURS
24739-24739	OAKVALE
24740-24740	PRINCETON
24747-24747	ROCK
24751-24751	WOLFE
24801-24801	WELCH
24808-24808	ANAWALT
24810-24810	ASHLAND
24811-24811	AVONDALE
24813-24813	BARTLEY
24815-24815	BERWIND
24816-24816	BIG SANDY
24817-24817	BRADSHAW
24818-24818	BRENTON
24819-24819	CANEBRAKE
24819-24819	CANABRAKE
24820-24820	CAPELS
24821-24821	CARETTA
24822-24822	CLEAR FORK
24823-24823	COAL MOUNTAIN
24824-24824	COALWOOD
24825-24825	CRUMPLER
24826-24826	CUCUMBER
24827-24827	CYCLONE
24828-24828	DAVY
24829-24829	ECKMAN
24830-24830	ELBERT
24831-24831	ELKHORN
24832-24832	ENGLISH
24834-24834	FANROCK
24836-24836	GARY
24839-24839	HANOVER
24841-24841	HAVACO
24842-24842	HEMPHILL
24843-24843	HENSLEY
24844-24844	IAEGER
24845-24845	IKES FORK
24846-24846	ISABAN
24847-24847	ITMANN
24848-24848	JENKINJONES
24849-24849	JESSE
24850-24850	JOLO
24851-24851	JUSTICE
24852-24852	KEYSTONE
24853-24853	KIMBALL
24854-24854	KOPPERSTON
24855-24855	KYLE
24856-24856	LECKIE
24857-24857	LYNCO
24859-24859	MARIANNA
24860-24860	MATHENY
24861-24861	MAYBEURY
24862-24862	MOHAWK
24866-24866	NEWHALL
24867-24867	NEW RICHMOND
24868-24868	NORTHFORK
24869-24869	NORTH SPRING
24870-24870	OCEANA
24871-24871	PAGETON
24872-24872	PANTHER
24873-24873	PAYNESVILLE
24874-24874	PINEVILLE
24877-24877	POWHATAN
24878-24878	PREMIER
24879-24879	RAYSAL
24880-24880	ROCK VIEW
24881-24881	RODERFIELD
24882-24882	SIMON
24883-24883	SKYGUSTY
24884-24884	SQUIRE
24886-24886	SUPERIOR
24887-24887	SWITCHBACK
24888-24888	THORPE
24889-24889	TWIN BRANCH
24891-24891	VIVIAN
24892-24892	WAR
24894-24894	WARRIORMINE
24895-24895	WILCOE
24896-24896	WOLF PEN
24897-24897	WORTH
24898-24898	WYOMING
24899-24899	YUKON
24901-24901	LEWISBURG
24902-24902	FAIRLEA
24910-24910	ALDERSON
24915-24915	ARBOVALE
24916-24916	ASBURY
24917-24917	AUTO
24918-24918	BALLARD
24919-24919	BALLENGEE
24920-24920	BARTOW
24923-24923	BOZOO
24924-24924	BUCKEYE
24925-24925	CALDWELL
24927-24927	CASS
24928-24928	CLINTONVILLE
24931-24931	CRAWLEY
24934-24934	DUNMORE
24935-24935	FOREST HILL
24936-24936	FORT SPRING
24938-24938	FRANKFORD
24939-24939	FRIARS HILL
24941-24941	GAP MILLS
24942-24942	GLACE
24943-24943	GRASSY MEADOWS
24944-24944	GREEN BANK
24945-24945	GREENVILLE
24946-24946	HILLSBORO
24950-24950	KIEFFER
24951-24951	LINDSIDE
24954-24954	MARLINTON
24957-24957	MAXWELTON
24958-24958	MEADOW BLUFF
24961-24961	NEOLA
24962-24962	PENCE SPRINGS
24963-24963	PETERSTOWN
24966-24966	RENICK
24970-24970	RONCEVERTE
24973-24973	SARTON
24974-24974	SECONDCREEK
24976-24976	SINKS GROVE
24977-24977	SMOOT
24980-24980	SWEET SPRINGS
24981-24981	TALCOTT
24983-24983	UNION
24984-24984	WAITEVILLE
24985-24985	WAYSIDE
24986-24986	WHITE SULPHUR SPRINGS
24991-24991	WILLIAMSBURG
24993-24993	WOLFCREEK
25002-25002	ALLOY
25003-25003	ALUM CREEK
25004-25004	AMEAGLE
25005-25005	AMMA
25007-25007	ARNETT
25008-25008	ARTIE
25009-25009	ASHFORD
25010-25010	BALD KNOB
25011-25011	BANCROFT
25013-25013	BARRETT
25014-25014	BEARDS FORK
25015-25015	BELLE
25018-25018	BENTREE
25019-25019	BICKMORE
25021-25021	BIM
25022-25022	BLAIR
25024-25024	BLOOMINGROSE
25025-25025	BLOUNT
25026-25026	BLUE CREEK
25028-25028	BOB WHITE
25030-25030	BOMONT
25031-25031	BOOMER
25033-25033	BUFFALO
25034-25034	BURNWELL
25034-25034	IMPERIAL JUNCTION
25034-25034	BURNWELL
25035-25035	CABIN CREEK
25036-25036	CANNELTON
25039-25039	CEDAR GROVE
25040-25040	CHARLTON HEIGHTS
25043-25043	CLAY
25044-25044	CLEAR CREEK
25045-25045	CLENDENIN
25046-25046	CLIO
25047-25047	CLOTHIER
25048-25048	COLCORD
25049-25049	COMFORT
25051-25051	COSTA
25052-25052	CROWN HILL
25053-25053	DANVILLE
25054-25054	DAWES
25057-25057	DEEP WATER
25059-25059	DIXIE
25060-25060	DOROTHY
25061-25061	DRYBRANCH
25062-25062	DRY CREEK
25063-25063	DUCK
25064-25064	DUNBAR
25067-25067	EAST BANK
25070-25070	ELEANOR
25071-25071	ELKVIEW
25075-25075	ESKDALE
25076-25076	ETHEL
25079-25079	FALLING ROCK
25080-25080	FOLA
25081-25081	FOSTER
25082-25082	FRAZIERS BOTTOM
25083-25083	GALLAGHER
25085-25085	GAULEY BRIDGE
25086-25086	GLASGOW
25088-25088	GLEN
25090-25090	GLEN FERRIS
25093-25093	GORDON
25095-25095	GRIMMS LANDING
25102-25102	HANDLEY
25103-25103	HANSFORD
25105-25105	HARRISON
25106-25106	HENDERSON
25107-25107	HERNSHAW
25108-25108	HEWETT
25109-25109	HOMETOWN
25110-25110	HUGHESTON
25111-25111	INDORE
25112-25112	INSTITUTE
25113-25113	IVYDALE
25114-25114	JEFFREY
25115-25115	KANAWHA FALLS
25118-25118	KIMBERLY
25119-25119	KINCAID
25120-25120	KINGSTON
25121-25121	LAKE
25122-25122	LEEWOOD

25123-25123	LEON
25124-25124	LIBERTY
25125-25125	LIZEMORES
25126-25126	LONDON
25130-25130	MADISON
25131-25131	MAHAN
25132-25132	MAMMOTH
25133-25133	MAYSEL
25134-25134	MIAMI
25135-25135	MONTCOAL
25136-25136	MONTGOMERY
25139-25139	MOUNT CARBON
25140-25140	NAOMA
25141-25141	NEBO
25142-25142	NELLIS
25143-25143	NITRO
25147-25147	OHLEY
25148-25148	ORGAS
25149-25149	OTTAWA
25150-25150	OVAPA
25152-25152	PAGE
25154-25154	PEYTONA
25156-25156	PINCH
25158-25158	PLINY
25159-25159	POCA
25160-25160	POND GAP
25161-25161	POWELLTON
25162-25162	PRATT
25163-25163	PRENTER
25164-25164	PROCIOUS
25165-25165	RACINE
25166-25166	RAMAGE
25168-25168	RED HOUSE
25169-25169	RIDGEVIEW
25172-25172	ROBERTSBURG
25173-25173	ROBSON
25174-25174	ROCK CREEK
25177-25177	SAINT ALBANS
25180-25180	SAXON
25181-25181	SETH
25182-25182	SHARON
25183-25183	SHARPLES
25185-25185	MOUNT OLIVE
25186-25186	SMITHERS
25187-25187	SOUTHSIDE
25189-25189	SUNDIAL
25193-25193	SYLVESTER
25201-25201	TAD
25202-25202	TORNADO
25203-25203	TURTLE CREEK
25204-25204	TWILIGHT
25205-25205	UNEEDA
25206-25206	VAN
25208-25208	WHARTON
25209-25209	WHITESVILLE
25211-25211	WIDEN
25213-25213	WINFIELD
25214-25214	WINIFREDE
25231-25231	ADVENT
25234-25234	ARNOLDSBURG
25235-25235	CHLOE
25237-25237	CLIFTON
25239-25239	COTTAGEVILLE
25241-25241	EVANS
25243-25243	GANDEEVILLE
25244-25244	GAY
25245-25245	GIVEN
25246-25246	HARMONY
25247-25247	HARTFORD
25248-25248	KENNA
25249-25249	KENTUCK
25250-25250	LAKIN
25251-25251	LEFT HAND
25252-25252	LE ROY
25253-25253	LETART
25255-25255	LETTER GAP
25256-25256	LINDEN
25258-25258	LOCKNEY
25259-25259	LOONEYVILLE
25260-25260	MASON
25261-25261	MILLSTONE
25262-25262	MILLWOOD
25264-25264	MOUNT ALTO
25265-25265	NEW HAVEN
25266-25266	NEWTON
25267-25267	NORMANTOWN
25268-25268	ORMA
25270-25270	REEDY
25271-25271	RIPLEY
25272-25272	ROCK CASTLE
25274-25274	SAND RIDGE
25275-25275	SANDYVILLE
25276-25276	SPENCER
25279-25279	STATTS MILLS
25280-25280	STUMPTOWN
25281-25281	TARIFF
25283-25283	VALLEY FORK
25285-25285	WALLBACK
25286-25286	WALTON
25287-25287	WEST COLUMBIA
25300-25396	CHARLESTON
25401-25402	MARTINSBURG
25410-25410	BAKERTON
25411-25411	BERKELEY SPRINGS
25413-25413	BUNKER HILL
25414-25414	CHARLES TOWN
25419-25419	FALLING WATERS
25420-25420	GERRARDSTOWN
25421-25421	GLENGARY
25422-25422	GREAT CACAPON
25423-25423	HALLTOWN
25425-25425	HARPERS FERRY
25427-25427	HEDGESVILLE
25428-25428	INWOOD
25429-25430	KEARNEYSVILLE
25431-25431	LEVELS
25432-25432	MILLVILLE
25434-25434	PAW PAW
25437-25437	POINTS
25438-25438	RANSON
25440-25440	RIDGEWAY
25441-25441	RIPPON
25442-25442	SHENANDOAH JUNCTION
25443-25443	SHEPHERDSTOWN
25444-25444	SLANESVILLE
25446-25446	SUMMIT POINT
25501-25501	ALKOL
25502-25502	APPLE GROVE
25503-25503	ASHTON
25504-25504	BARBOURSVILLE
25505-25505	BIG CREEK
25506-25506	BRANCHLAND
25507-25507	CEREDO
25508-25508	CHAPMANVILLE
25510-25510	CULLODEN
25511-25511	DUNLOW
25512-25512	EAST LYNN
25514-25514	FORT GAY
25515-25515	GALLIPOLIS FERRY
25517-25517	GENOA
25519-25519	GLENHAYES
25520-25520	GLENWOOD
25521-25521	GRIFFITHSVILLE
25523-25523	HAMLIN
25524-25524	HARTS
25526-25526	HURRICANE
25529-25529	JULIAN
25530-25530	KENOVA
25534-25534	KIAHSVILLE
25535-25535	LAVALETTE
25537-25537	LESAGE
25540-25540	MIDKIFF
25541-25541	MILTON
25544-25544	MYRA
25545-25545	ONA
25546-25546	PALERMO
25547-25547	PECKS MILL
25550-25550	POINT PLEASANT
25555-25555	PRICHARD
25557-25557	RANGER
25559-25559	SALT ROCK
25560-25560	SCOTT DEPOT
25562-25562	SHOALS
25563-25563	SIAS
25564-25564	SOD
25565-25565	SPURLOCKVILLE
25567-25567	SUMERCO
25568-25568	SWEETLAND
25569-25569	TEAYS
25570-25570	WAYNE
25571-25571	WEST HAMLIN
25572-25572	WOODVILLE
25573-25573	YAWKEY
25601-25601	LOGAN
25606-25606	ACCOVILLE
25607-25607	AMHERSTDALE
25608-25608	BAISDEN
25611-25611	BRUNO
25612-25612	CHAUNCEY
25614-25614	CORA
25617-25617	DAVIN
25620-25620	EMMETT
25621-25621	GILBERT
25623-25623	HAMPDEN
25624-25624	HENLAWSON
25625-25625	HOLDEN
25628-25628	KISTLER
25630-25630	LORADO
25631-25631	LUNDALE
25632-25632	LYBURN
25634-25634	MALLORY
25635-25635	MAN
25636-25636	MONAVILLE
25637-25637	MOUNT GAY
25638-25638	OMAR
25639-25639	PEACH CREEK
25643-25643	ROSSMORE
25644-25644	SARAH ANN
25645-25645	STIRRAT
25646-25646	STOLLINGS
25647-25647	SWITZER
25648-25648	TAPLIN
25649-25649	VERDUNVILLE
25650-25650	VERNER
25651-25651	WHARNCLIFFE
25652-25652	WHITMAN
25653-25653	WILKINSON
25654-25654	YOLYN
25661-25661	WILLIAMSON
25665-25665	BORDERLAND
25666-25666	BREEDEN
25667-25667	CHATTAROY
25669-25669	CRUM
25670-25670	DELBARTON
25671-25671	DINGESS
25672-25672	EDGARTON
25674-25674	KERMIT
25676-25676	LENORE
25678-25678	MATEWAN
25682-25682	MEADOR
25684-25684	MYRTLE
25685-25685	NAUGATUCK
25686-25686	NEWTOWN
25687-25687	NOLAN
25688-25688	NORTH MATEWAN
25690-25690	RAGLAND
25691-25691	RAWL
25692-25692	RED JACKET
25693-25693	SPRIGG
25694-25694	THACKER
25696-25696	VARNEY
25697-25697	VULCAN
25699-25699	WILSONDALE
25700-25779	HUNTINGTON
25801-25802	BECKLEY
25810-25810	ALLEN JUNCTION
25811-25811	AMIGO
25812-25812	ANSTED
25813-25813	BEAVER
25814-25814	BECKWITH
25816-25816	BLUE JAY
25817-25817	BOLT
25818-25818	BRADLEY
25820-25820	CAMP CREEK
25823-25823	COAL CITY
25825-25825	COOL RIDGE
25826-25826	CORINNE
25827-25827	CRAB ORCHARD
25828-25828	CRANBERRY
25831-25831	DANESE
25832-25832	DANIELS
25833-25833	DOTHAN
25836-25836	ECCLES
25837-25837	EDMOND
25839-25839	FAIRDALE
25840-25840	FAYETTEVILLE
25841-25841	FLAT TOP
25843-25843	GHENT
25844-25844	GLEN DANIEL
25845-25845	GLEN FORK
25846-25846	GLEN JEAN
25847-25847	GLEN MORGAN
25848-25848	GLEN ROGERS
25849-25849	GLEN WHITE
25851-25851	HARPER
25853-25853	HELEN
25854-25854	HICO
25855-25855	HILLTOP
25856-25856	JONBEN
25857-25857	JOSEPHINE
25859-25859	KILSYTH
25860-25860	LANARK
25862-25862	LANSING
25864-25864	LAYLAND
25865-25865	LESTER
25866-25866	LOCHGELLY
25867-25867	LONG BRANCH
25868-25868	LOOKOUT
25870-25870	MABEN
25871-25871	MABSCOTT
25873-25873	MAC ARTHUR
25874-25874	MAPLEWOOD
25875-25875	MC GRAWS
25876-25876	SAULSVILLE
25878-25878	MIDWAY
25879-25879	MINDEN
25880-25880	MOUNT HOPE
25882-25882	MULLENS
25901-25901	OAK HILL
25902-25902	ODD
25904-25904	PAX
25905-25905	PEMBERTON
25906-25906	PINEY VIEW
25907-25907	PRINCE
25908-25908	PRINCEWICK
25909-25909	PROSPERITY
25910-25910	QUINNIMONT
25911-25911	RALEIGH
25912-25912	RAMSEY
25913-25913	RAVENCLIFF
25914-25914	REDSTAR
25915-25915	RHODELL
25916-25916	SABINE
25917-25917	SCARBRO
25918-25918	SHADY SPRING
25919-25919	SKELTON
25920-25920	SLAB FORK
25921-25921	SOPHIA
25922-25922	SPANISHBURG
25926-25926	SPRAGUE
25927-25927	STANAFORD
25928-25928	STEPHENSON
25931-25931	SUMMERLEE
25932-25932	SURVEYOR
25934-25934	TERRY
25936-25936	THURMOND
25938-25938	VICTOR
25942-25942	WINONA
25943-25943	WYCO
25951-25951	HINTON
25957-25957	BROOKS
25958-25958	CHARMCO
25961-25961	CRICHTON
25962-25962	RAINELLE
25965-25965	ELTON
25966-25966	GREEN SULPHUR SPRINGS
25967-25967	HINES
25969-25969	JUMPING BRANCH
25971-25971	LERONA
25972-25972	LESLIE
25973-25973	LOCKBRIDGE
25976-25976	MEADOW BRIDGE
25977-25977	MEADOW CREEK
25978-25978	NIMITZ
25979-25979	PIPESTEM
25981-25981	QUINWOOD
25984-25984	RUPERT
25985-25985	SANDSTONE
25986-25986	SPRING DALE
25988-25988	TRUE
25989-25989	WHITE OAK
26003-26003	WHEELING
26030-26030	BEECH BOTTOM
26031-26031	BENWOOD
26032-26032	BETHANY
26033-26033	CAMERON
26034-26034	CHESTER
26035-26035	COLLIERS
26036-26036	DALLAS
26037-26037	FOLLANSBEE
26038-26038	GLEN DALE
26039-26039	GLEN EASTON
26040-26040	MC MECHEN
26040-26040	MCMECHEN
26041-26041	MOUNDSVILLE
26047-26047	NEW CUMBERLAND

26050-26050	NEWELL
26055-26055	PROCTOR
26056-26056	NEW MANCHESTER
26058-26058	SHORT CREEK
26059-26059	TRIADELPHIA
26060-26060	VALLEY GROVE
26062-26062	WEIRTON
26070-26070	WELLSBURG
26074-26074	WEST LIBERTY
26075-26075	WINDSOR HEIGHTS
26101-26104	PARKERSBURG
26105-26105	VIENNA
26106-26106	PARKERSBURG
26120-26121	MINERAL WELLS
26133-26133	BELLEVILLE
26134-26134	BELMONT
26135-26135	BENS RUN
26136-26136	BIG BEND
26137-26137	BIG SPRINGS
26138-26138	BROHARD
26141-26141	CRESTON
26142-26142	DAVISVILLE
26143-26143	ELIZABETH
26144-26144	EUREKA
26145-26145	FIVE FORKS
26146-26146	FRIENDLY
26147-26147	GRANTSVILLE
26148-26148	MACFARLAN
26149-26149	MIDDLEBOURNE
26150-26150	MINERAL WELLS
26151-26151	MOUNT ZION
26152-26152	MUNDAY
26153-26153	MURRAYSVILLE
26155-26155	NEW MARTINSVILLE
26159-26159	PADEN CITY
26160-26160	PALESTINE
26161-26161	PETROLEUM
26162-26162	PORTERS FALLS
26164-26164	RAVENSWOOD
26167-26167	READER
26169-26169	ROCKPORT
26170-26170	SAINT MARYS
26173-26173	SHERMAN
26175-26175	SISTERSVILLE
26178-26178	SMITHVILLE
26179-26179	TANNER
26180-26180	WALKER
26181-26181	WASHINGTON
26184-26184	WAVERLY
26185-26185	WICK
26186-26186	WILEYVILLE
26187-26187	WILLIAMSTOWN
26201-26201	BUCKHANNON
26202-26202	FENWICK
26203-26203	ERBACON
26205-26205	CRAIGSVILLE
26206-26206	COWEN
26207-26207	COTTLE
26208-26208	CAMDEN ON GAULEY
26209-26209	SNOWSHOE
26210-26210	ADRIAN
26214-26214	CENTURY
26215-26215	CLEVELAND
26217-26217	DIANA
26218-26218	FRENCH CREEK
26219-26219	FRENCHTON
26222-26222	HACKER VALLEY
26224-26224	HELVETIA
26228-26228	KANAWHA HEAD
26229-26229	LORENTZ
26230-26230	PICKENS
26234-26234	ROCK CAVE
26236-26236	SELBYVILLE
26237-26237	TALLMANSVILLE
26238-26238	VOLGA
26241-26241	ELKINS
26250-26250	BELINGTON
26253-26253	BEVERLY
26254-26254	BOWDEN
26257-26257	COALTON
26259-26259	DAILEY
26260-26260	DAVIS
26261-26261	RICHWOOD
26263-26263	DRYFORK
26264-26264	DURBIN
26266-26266	UPPERGLADE
26267-26267	ELLAMORE
26268-26268	GLADY
26269-26269	HAMBLETON
26270-26270	HARMAN
26271-26271	HENDRICKS
26273-26273	HUTTONSVILLE
26275-26275	JUNIOR
26276-26276	KERENS
26278-26278	MABIE
26280-26280	MILL CREEK
26281-26281	MINGO
26282-26282	MONTERVILLE
26283-26283	MONTROSE
26285-26285	NORTON
26287-26287	PARSONS
26288-26288	WEBSTER SPRINGS
26289-26289	RED CREEK
26290-26290	SAINT GEORGE
26291-26291	SLATYFORK
26292-26292	THOMAS
26293-26293	VALLEY BEND
26294-26294	VALLEY HEAD
26296-26296	WHITMER
26298-26298	BERGOO
26299-26299	BOGGS
26301-26306	CLARKSBURG
26320-26320	ALMA
26321-26321	ALUM BRIDGE
26322-26322	ALVY
26323-26323	ANMOORE
26325-26325	AUBURN
26327-26327	BEREA
26328-26328	BLANDVILLE
26330-26330	BRIDGEPORT
26332-26332	BRISTOL
26334-26334	BROWNTON
26335-26335	BURNSVILLE
26337-26337	CAIRO
26338-26338	CAMDEN
26339-26339	CENTER POINT
26342-26342	COXS MILLS
26343-26343	CRAWFORD
26344-26344	DAWMONT
26346-26346	ELLENBORO
26347-26347	FLEMINGTON
26348-26348	FOLSOM
26349-26349	GALLOWAY
26350-26350	GILMER
26351-26351	GLENVILLE
26354-26354	GRAFTON
26360-26360	GREENWOOD
26361-26361	GYPSY
26362-26362	HARRISVILLE
26366-26366	HAYWOOD
26367-26367	HAZELGREEN
26369-26369	HEPZIBAH
26372-26372	HORNER
26374-26374	INDEPENDENCE
26375-26375	INDUSTRIAL
26376-26376	IRELAND
26377-26377	JACKSONBURG
26378-26378	JANE LEW
26383-26383	LIMA
26384-26384	LINN
26385-26385	LOST CREEK
26386-26386	LUMBERPORT
26401-26401	MC WHORTER
26404-26404	MEADOWBROOK
26405-26405	MOATSVILLE
26407-26407	MOUNTAIN
26408-26408	MOUNT CLARE
26409-26409	NEWBERNE
26410-26410	NEWBURG
26411-26411	NEW MILTON
26412-26412	ORLANDO
26415-26415	PENNSBORO
26416-26416	PHILIPPI
26419-26419	PINE GROVE
26421-26421	PULLMAN
26422-26422	REYNOLDSVILLE
26423-26423	ROANOKE
26424-26424	ROSEMONT
26425-26425	ROWLESBURG
26426-26426	SALEM
26430-26430	SAND FORK
26431-26431	SHINNSTON
26434-26434	SHIRLEY
26435-26435	SIMPSON
26436-26436	SMITHBURG
26437-26437	SMITHFIELD
26438-26438	SPELTER
26439-26439	STOUTS MILLS
26440-26440	THORNTON
26443-26443	TROY
26444-26444	TUNNELTON
26446-26446	VALLEY CHAPEL
26447-26447	WALKERSVILLE
26448-26448	WALLACE
26451-26451	WEST MILFORD
26452-26452	WESTON
26456-26456	WEST UNION
26461-26461	WILSONBURG
26462-26462	WOLF SUMMIT
26463-26463	WYATT
26501-26508	MORGANTOWN
26519-26519	ALBRIGHT
26520-26520	ARTHURDALE
26521-26521	BLACKSVILLE
26522-26522	BOOTH
26523-26523	BRANDONVILLE
26524-26524	BRETZ
26525-26525	BRUCETON MILLS
26527-26527	CASSVILLE
26529-26529	CORE
26530-26530	CUZZART
26531-26531	DELLSLOW
26533-26533	EVERETTVILLE
26534-26534	GRANVILLE
26535-26535	HAZELTON
26537-26537	KINGWOOD
26541-26541	MAIDSVILLE
26542-26542	MASONTOWN
26543-26543	OSAGE
26544-26544	PENTRESS
26546-26546	PURSGLOVE
26547-26547	REEDSVILLE
26554-26554	FAIRMONT
26559-26559	BARRACKVILLE
26560-26560	BAXTER
26561-26561	BIG RUN
26562-26562	BURTON
26563-26563	CAROLINA
26566-26566	COLFAX
26568-26568	ENTERPRISE
26570-26570	FAIRVIEW
26571-26571	FARMINGTON
26572-26572	FOUR STATES
26574-26574	GRANT TOWN
26575-26575	HUNDRED
26576-26576	IDAMAY
26578-26578	KINGMONT
26581-26581	LITTLETON
26582-26582	MANNINGTON
26585-26585	METZ
26586-26586	MONTANA MINES
26587-26587	RACHEL
26588-26588	RIVESVILLE
26589-26589	WADESTOWN
26590-26590	WANA
26591-26591	WORTHINGTON
26601-26601	SUTTON
26610-26610	BIRCH RIVER
26611-26611	CEDARVILLE
26612-26612	CENTRALIA
26615-26615	COPEN
26617-26617	DILLE
26618-26618	ELMIRA
26619-26619	EXCHANGE
26620-26620	FALLS MILL
26621-26621	FLATWOODS
26623-26623	FRAMETOWN
26624-26624	GASSAWAY
26626-26626	GLENDON
26627-26627	HEATERS
26629-26629	LITTLE BIRCH
26631-26631	NAPIER
26633-26633	NICUT
26634-26634	PERKINS
26636-26636	ROSEDALE
26638-26638	SHOCK
26639-26639	STRANGE CREEK
26641-26641	WILSIE
26651-26651	SUMMERSVILLE
26656-26656	BELVA
26660-26660	CALVIN
26662-26662	CANVAS
26667-26667	DRENNEN
26671-26671	GILBOA
26674-26674	JODIE
26675-26675	KESLERS CROSS LANES
26676-26676	LEIVASY
26678-26678	MOUNT LOOKOUT
26679-26679	MOUNT NEBO
26680-26680	NALLEN
26681-26681	NETTIE
26683-26683	POE
26684-26684	POOL
26690-26690	SWISS
26691-26691	TIOGA
26704-26704	AUGUSTA
26705-26705	AURORA
26707-26707	BAYARD
26710-26710	BURLINGTON
26711-26711	CAPON BRIDGE
26713-26713	CORINTH
26714-26714	DELRAY
26716-26716	EGLON
26717-26717	ELK GARDEN
26719-26719	FORT ASHBY
26720-26720	GORMANIA
26722-26722	GREEN SPRING
26726-26726	KEYSER
26729-26729	KIRBY
26731-26731	LAHMANSVILLE
26734-26734	MEDLEY
26739-26739	MOUNT STORM
26743-26743	NEW CREEK
26750-26750	PIEDMONT
26753-26753	RIDGELEY
26755-26755	RIO
26757-26757	ROMNEY
26761-26761	SHANKS
26763-26763	SPRINGFIELD
26764-26764	TERRA ALTA
26765-26765	THREE CHURCHES
26767-26767	WILEY FORD
26769-26769	EGLON
26801-26801	BAKER
26802-26802	BRANDYWINE
26804-26804	CIRCLEVILLE
26806-26806	FORT SEYBERT
26807-26807	FRANKLIN
26808-26808	HIGH VIEW
26810-26810	LOST CITY
26811-26811	LOST RIVER
26812-26812	MATHIAS
26813-26813	MOYERS
26814-26814	RIVERTON
26815-26815	SUGAR GROVE
26816-26816	ARTHUR
26817-26817	BLOOMERY
26818-26818	FISHER
26823-26823	CAPON SPRINGS
26824-26824	JUNCTION
26833-26833	MAYSVILLE
26836-26836	MOOREFIELD
26838-26838	MILAM
26845-26845	OLD FIELDS
26847-26847	PETERSBURG
26851-26851	WARDENSVILLE
26852-26852	PURGITSVILLE
26855-26855	CABINS
26865-26865	YELLOW SPRING
26866-26866	UPPER TRACT
26884-26884	SENECA ROCKS
26886-26886	ONEGO

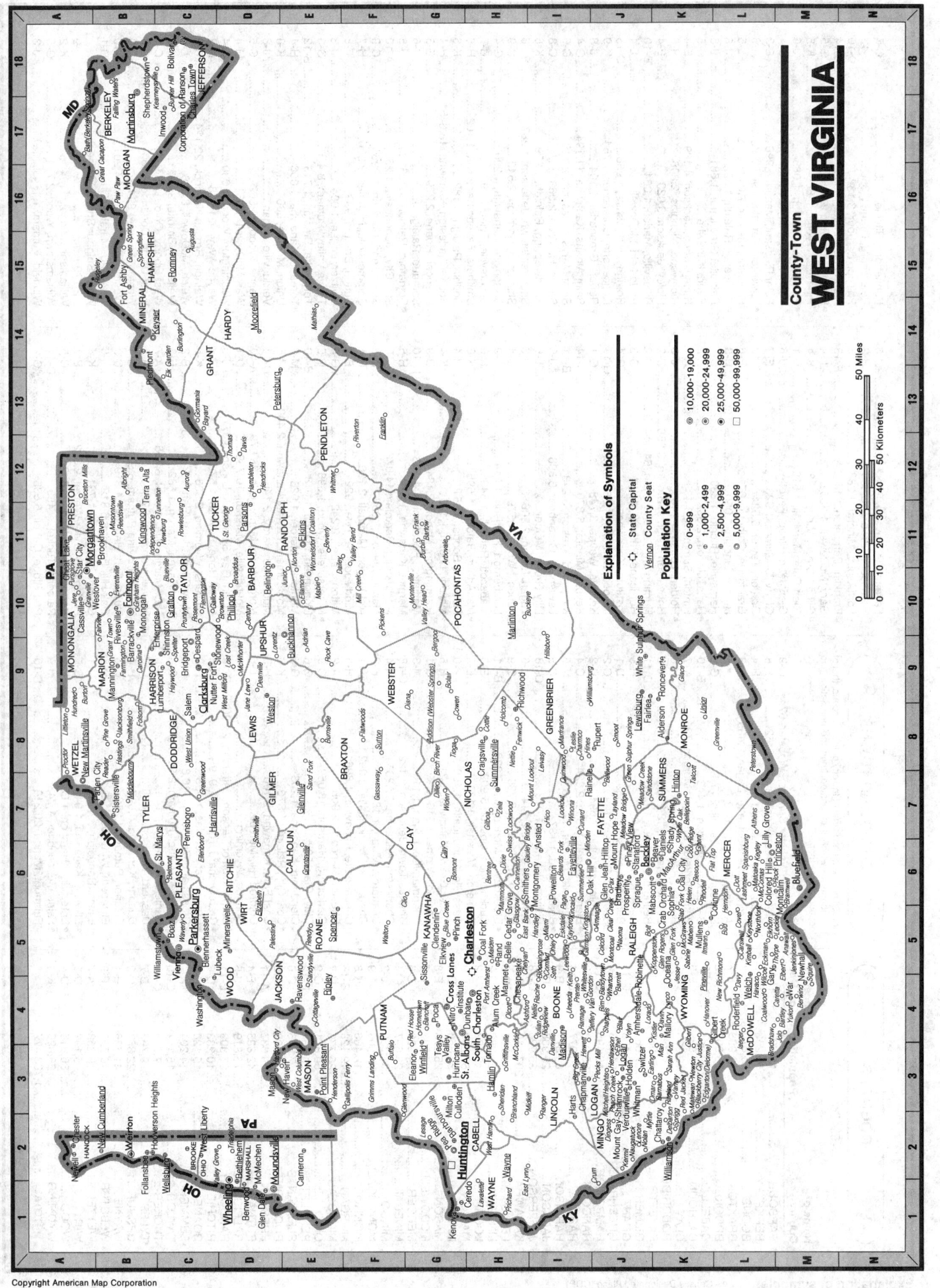

WEST VIRGINIA

County-Town

Explanation of Symbols

✧ State Capital

⊙ County Seat

Population Key

⊙	0-999
⊚	1,000-2,499
⊕	2,500-4,999
⊙	5,000-9,999
◉	10,000-19,000
⊛	20,000-24,999
◉	25,000-49,999
□	50,000-99,999

0   10   20   30   40   50 Miles

0   10   20   30   40   50 Kilometers

CITIES AND TOWNS

Note: The first name is that of the city or town, second, that of the county in which it is located, then the population and location on the map.

Explanation of symbols: ●– Census Designated Place (CDP)

Wisconsin

General Help Numbers:

Governor's Office
PO Box 7863   608-266-1212
Madison, WI 53707-7863   Fax 608-267-8983
www.wisgov.state.wi.us   8AM-5PM

Attorney General's Office
Justice Department   608-266-1221
PO Box 7857   Fax 608-267-2779
Madison, WI 53707-7857   8AM-5PM
www.doj.state.wi.us

Legislative Records
Legislative Reference Bureau   608-266-0341
PO Box 2037   Fax 608-266-5648
Madison, WI 53701-2037   7:45AM-5PM
www.legis.state.wi.us

State Archives
Archives Division   608-264-6460
816 State St   Fax 608-264-6486
Madison, WI 53706   8AM-5PM M-F, 9-4 SA
www.wisconsinhistory.org/libraryarchives/

State Specifics:

Capital: Madison
                           Dane County

Time Zone: CST

Number of Counties: 72

Population: 5,472,299

Web Site: www.wisconsin.gov

State Agencies

Criminal Records

Wisconsin Department of Justice, Crime Information Bureau, Record Check Unit, PO Box 2688, Madison, WI 53701-2688 (Courier: 17 W Main St, Madison, WI 53703); 608-266-5764, 608-266-7780 (Online Questions), 608-267-4558 (Fax), 8AM-4:30PM.

www.doj.state.wi.us

Indexing & Storage: Records are available from July 1971 (when the agencies were required to save records) and are computerized. It takes 4 days before new records are available for inquiry.

Records are indexed on inhouse computer. Records are maintained indefinitely.

Searching: Criminal record information is open to the public per statute 3-21-91. Certain statutorily-required searches require fingerprints. Include the following in your request-sex, race, full name, date of birth. Fingerprints are optional. All requests must be in writing. The following data is not released: juvenile records.

Access by: mail, fax, in person, online.

Fee & Payment: The fee is $18.00 per individual for a name search, and only $15.00 if a fingerprint search. Non-profits made submit name searches

for $7.00 per record. If a statutorily-required search also requires an FBI fingerprint check, add $24.00. Fee payee: Wisconsin Department of Justice. Prepayment required. Personal checks accepted. Credit cards accepted at web site only.

Mail search: Turnaround time: 7 to 10 days. A SASE is requested.

Fax search: Incoming fax permitted only for customers with accounts. There must be a supply of return envelopes on hand.

In person search: Records are returned by mail.

Online search: The agency offers Internet access at http://wi-recordcheck.org. An account is required. Records must be "picked up" at the website within 10 days. They are not returned by mail. Only daycare centers and other caregivers can receive immediate online response.

Other access: There is a free Internet service for access to the state's Circuit Courts' records, except for and Portage county. Visit http://wcca.wicourts.gov/index.xsl.

Statewide Court Records

Director of State Courts, Supreme Court, PO Box 1688, Madison, WI 53701-1688; 608-266-6828, 608-267-0980 (Fax), 8AM-5PM.

http://wicourts.gov

Indexing & Storage: It takes up to 4 hours before new records are available for inquiry.

Access by: online. No searching by mail.

Online search: Wisconsin Circuit Court Access (WCCA) allows users to view circuit court case information at http://wcca.wicourts.gov. Data is available from all counties. Portage County offers only probate records online. WCCA provides detailed information about circuit cases and for civil cases on either a statewide or county basis. The system displays judgment and judgment party information and offers the ability to generate reports. Appellate and Supreme Courts opinions are available from http://old.wicourts.gov/wscca/.

Other access: Bulk access to data may be arranged on contract, fees are involved. Contact the Office of Court Operations at 608-266-3121 for details.

Sexual Offender Registry

Department of Corrections, Sex Offender Registry Program, PO Box 7925, Madison, WI 53707-7925 (Courier: 3099 E Washington Avenue, Madison, WI 53704); 608-240-5830, 608-240-3355 (Fax), 7:45AM-4:30PM.

http://offender.doc.state.wi.us/public/

Note: Information stored in the database is accessible on a limited basis to victims, neighborhood watch programs, and the general public. One may also search at the local law enforcement level.

Indexing & Storage: Records are available from 1998 to present. Records are normally destroyed after the registration discharge date.

Searching: The following data is not released: victim profile and data, juvenile adjudication, exact residence address.

Access by: mail, online.

Mail search: Turnaround time: 1-2 weeks.

Online search: Search for offenders by name or location at the website. Second website address is http://widocoffenders.org.

Incarceration Records

Wisconsin Department of Corrections, Bureau of Technology Management, PO Box 8980, Madison, WI 53708-8980 (Courier: 3099 E Washington Ave, Madison, WI 53708); 608-240-5741, 608-240-3385 (Fax), 7:30AM-4PM.

www.wi-doc.com

Indexing & Storage: Records are available on current and former inmates. It takes 10 days before new records are available for inquiry. Records are indexed on inhouse computer. Records are

normally destroyed after 5 years beyond termination.

Searching: Computerized records go back to 1961. Include the following in your request-first and last name and the DOB. Location, conviction and sentencing information, and release dates are provided.

Access by: mail, phone, fax, online.

Fee & Payment: Copies are $.15 per page, there is no search fee.

Mail search: Turnaround time: 5 to 10 working days.

Phone search: For phone search, call number above.

Fax search: Requests are accepted by fax.

Online search: No online searching is available for the public from this agency, however a private company provides free web access at www.vinelink.com/index.jsp.

Corporation, Limited Partnership, Limited Liability Company, Limited Liability Partnerships

Division of Corporate & Consumer Services, Corporation Record Requests, PO Box 7846, Madison, WI 53707-7846 (Courier: 345 W Washington Ave, 3rd Floor, Madison, WI 53703); 608-261-7577, 608-267-6813 (Fax), 7:45AM-4:30PM.

www.wdfi.org

Indexing & Storage: Records are available from 1873. Any records that are not at this office are kept at the State Records Center or the State Archives, but you must go through this office for access. New records are available for inquiry immediately. Records are indexed on inhouse computer, microfilm.

Searching: Include the following in your request-full name of business. In addition to the articles of incorporation, corporation records include the following information: Annual Reports of Officers/Directors, merger information and Name Changes.

Access by: mail, phone, fax, in person, online.

Fee & Payment: ID reports are $10.00, simple copywork is $5.00 per document. Short form certificates of status are $10.00. Certified copies are $10.00 plus. In-person copies are $.25 do it yourself. Fee payee: Department of Financial Institutions. Prepayment required. Personal checks accepted. Credit cards accepted; Visa or MasterCard

Mail search: Turnaround time: 7 to 10 days. A SASE is requested.

Phone search: No fee for telephone request. They will only give a verbal response from the on-screen information.

Fax search: Requires use of a credit card.

In person search: Turnaround time is while you wait.

Online search: Selected elements of the database ("CRIS" Corporate Registration System) are available online on the department's website at www.wdfi.org/corporations/crispix.

Other access: Some data is released in database format and is available electronically via email or on CD.

Expedited service: Expedited service is available for mail searches. Turnaround time: 2 days. Add $25.00 per item.

Trademarks/Servicemarks, Trade Names

Secretary of State, Tradenames/Trademarks Division, PO Box 7848, Madison, WI 53707-7848 (Courier: 30 W Mifflin St, 10th Floor, Madison, WI 53702); 608-266-5653, 608-266-3159 (Fax), 7:45AM-4:30PM.

http://badger.state.wi.us/agencies/sos

Indexing & Storage: Records are available for the past 20 years. It takes 7-14 working days before new records are available for inquiry. Records are indexed on index cards. Records are normally destroyed after 2 years after expiration.

Searching: All information is considered public record and they will release any information they have. Note that the data is not computerized. Include the following in your request-trademark/servicemark name, name of owner, date of application.

Access by: mail, phone, fax, in person.

Fee & Payment: There is no fee to see if a mark is listed. Plain copies of one record costs $2.00. For certified copies, the cost is $6.00 minimum, depending on the number of pages in the file. Fee payee: Secretary of State. Prepayment required. Personal checks accepted. No credit cards accepted.

Mail search: Turnaround time: 7 to 10 days.

Phone search: They will pull the file and give all available information over the phone.

Fax search: Same fees apply, $2.00 per copy if returned by fax. Turnaround time in 7 to 10 days.

In person search: There is no public access to copier. Staff will pull cards and forms for free inspection; staff will make copies for fees listed.

Uniform Commercial Code, Federal and State Tax Liens

Department of Financial Institutions, CCS/UCC, PO Box 7847, Madison, WI 53707-7847 (Courier: 345 W Washington Ave 3rd Fl, Madison, WI 53703); 608-261-9548, 608-264-7965 (Fax), 7:45AM-4:30PM.

www.wdfi.org

Indexing & Storage: Records are available from 1965, if still in effect. It takes 48 hours before new records are available for inquiry. Records are indexed on inhouse computer. Records are normally destroyed after 10 years past effectiveness.

Searching: Use search request form UCC-11. Generally, the search includes federal tax liens filed on businesses. Federal tax liens filed on people, and all state tax liens are filed at the county level. Include the following in your request-debtor name.

Access by: mail, phone, fax, in person, online.

Fee & Payment: There is no search fee, copies are $4.00 per page. There is no charge for certification which must be specifically requested. Fee payee: Department of Financial Institutions. Prepayment required. Personal checks accepted. No credit cards accepted.

Mail search: Turnaround time: up to 5 days.

Phone search: Call for uncertified information, some data is given over the phone.

Fax search: Turnaround time is 2-7 days.

In person search: Simple requests may be processed while you wait.

Online search: There is free Internet access for most records. Some records may require a $1.00 fee. You may do a free debtor name search at www.wdfi.org/ucc/search/. Instant filings are available immediately.

Other access: Bulk Index data is available on CD. The initial subscription is $3,000, monthly updates are $250.00. Images are available on CD for $200 per month.

Sales Tax Registrations

Revenue Department, Income, Sales, & Excise Tax Division, PO Box 8902, Madison, WI 53708-8902 (Courier: 3125 Rimrock Rd, Madison, WI 53713); 608-266-2776, 608-267-1030 (Fax), 7:45AM-4:30PM.

www.dor.state.wi.us

Note: The information contained on the seller's permit is not tax confidential, so it may be provided to a person that inquires whether a particular seller has a seller's permit.

Indexing & Storage: Records are available from 1963. Records are indexed on inhouse computer.

Searching: The department can disclose the real name, business name, address, and seller's permit number. Include the following in your request-business name, tax permit number. The more information provided, the easier the search can be conducted. Specific account numbers (i.e., FEIN, SP, etc.) can be more easily used than can names (i.e., real or business).

Access by: mail, phone, fax, in person.

Fee & Payment: There is no search fee, no copy fee.

Mail search: Turnaround time: 2 to 3 weeks. A SASE is requested.

Phone search: Records are available by phone.

Fax search: Records may be requested via fax.

In person search: available.

Birth Certificates

Bureau of Health Information, Vital Records, PO Box 309, Madison, WI 53701-0309 (Courier: One W Wilson St, Room 158, Madison, WI 53702); 608-266-1373, 608-266-1371 (Recording), 608-267-7820 (Genealogy), 608-255-2035 (Fax), 8AM-4:15PM.

www.dhfs.state.wi.us/VitalRecords

Indexing & Storage: Records are available from 1907 on. This office has the original records. The county of issue has a copy. New records are available for inquiry immediately.

Searching: Must have a signed release from person of record or immediate family member and include the reason for the inquiry for certified copies. Uncertified copy requests do not require a release or a reason, but cannot be expedited. Include the following in your request-full name, names of parents, mother's maiden name, date of birth, place of birth, relationship to person of record, reason for information request.

Access by: mail, fax, in person, online.

Fee & Payment: The fee is $12.00 per name. Add $3.00 per name per copy for additional copies. Uncertified copies are the same price. Fee payee: State of WI Vital Records. Prepayment required. Credit cards are for fax and online service only. Personal checks accepted. Credit cards accepted: MasterCard, Visa, AmEx, Discover.

Mail search: Turnaround time: 4 weeks. A SASE is requested.

Fax search: See expedited service through Vitalchek.

In person search: Turnaround time 2 to 4 hours.

Online search: Records may be ordered online via www.vitalchek.com, a state approved vendor.

Expedited service: Expedited service is available in person from this agency for an additional $10.00. If www.vitalchek.com used (fax, online), add $6.00 for use of credit card and shipping costs.

Death Records

Bureau of Health Information, Vital Records, PO Box 309, Madison, WI 53701-0309 (Courier: One W Wilson St, Room 158, Madison, WI 53702); 608-266-1373, 608-266-1371 (Recording), 608-267-7820 (Genealogy), 608-255-2035 (Fax), 8AM-4:15PM.

www.dhfs.state.wi.us/VitalRecords

Indexing & Storage: Records are available from 1907 on. This office has the original records. The county of issue has a copy. New records are available for inquiry immediately.

Searching: Must have a signed release from immediate family member for certified copies. Uncertified copy requests do not require a release. Include the following in your request-full name, date of death, place of death, relationship to person of record, reason for information request.

Access by: mail, fax, in person, online.

Fee & Payment: The fee is $7.00 per name search. Add $3.00 per name per copy for additional copies. Uncertified copies are the same fee, but cannot be expedited. Fee payee: State of WI Vital Records. Prepayment required. Credit cards fax and online service only. Personal checks accepted. Credit cards accepted: MasterCard, Visa, AmEx, Discover.

Mail search: Turnaround time: 4 weeks. A SASE is requested.

Fax search: See expedited service through Vitalchek.

In person search: Turnaround time 2 to 4 hours.

Online search: Records may be ordered online via www.vitalchek.com, a state approved vendor.

Expedited service: Expedited service is available in person from this agency for an additional $10.00. If www.vitalchek.com used (fax, online), add $6.00 for use of credit card and shipping costs.

Marriage Certificates

Bureau of Health Information, Vital Records, PO Box 309, Madison, WI 53701-0309 (Courier: One W Wilson St, Room 158, Madison, WI 53702); 608-266-1373, 608-266-1371 (Recording), 608-267-7820 (Genealogy), 608-255-2035 (Fax), 8AM-4:15PM.

www.dhfs.state.wi.us/VitalRecords

Indexing & Storage: Records are available from 1907 on. This office has the original records. The county of issue has a copy. New records are available for inquiry immediately.

Searching: Must have a signed release from the named parties for certified copies. Requests for uncertified copies do not require a release. Include the following in your request-names of husband and wife, date of marriage, place or county of marriage, reason for information request.

Access by: mail, fax, in person, online.

Fee & Payment: The fee is $7.00 per name search. Add $3.00 per name per copy for additional copies. The fee is the same for uncertified copies, but cannot be expedited. Fee payee: State of WI Vital Records. Prepayment required. Credit cards accepted for fax and online service only. Personal checks accepted. Credit cards accepted: MasterCard, Visa, AmEx, Discover.

Mail search: Turnaround time: 4 weeks. A SASE is requested.

Fax search: See expedited service through Vitalchek.

In person search: Turnaround time 2 to 4 hours.

Online search: Records may be ordered online via www.vitalchek.com, a state approved vendor.

Expedited service: Expedited service is available in person from this agency for an additional $10.00. If www.vitalchek.com used (fax, online), add $6.00 for use of credit card and shipping costs.

Divorce Records

Bureau of Health Information, Vital Records, PO Box 309, Madison, WI 53701-0309 (Courier: One W Wilson St, Room 158, Madison, WI 53702); 608-266-1373, 608-266-1371 (Recording), 608-267-7820 (Genealogy), 608-255-2035 (Fax), 8AM-4:15PM.

www.dhfs.state.wi.us/VitalRecords

Indexing & Storage: Records are available from 1907. New records are available for inquiry immediately.

Searching: Must have a signed release from the persons of record for a certified copy. Requests for uncertified copies do not require a release. Include the following in your request-names of husband and wife, date of divorce, place of divorce, case number (if known), reason for information request.

Access by: mail, fax, in person, online.

Fee & Payment: The fee is $7.00 per name search. Add $3.00 per name per copy for additional copies. Uncertified copies are the same fee, but cannot be expedited. Fee payee: State of WI Vital Records. Prepayment required. Credit cards accepted for fax service and online only. Personal checks accepted. Credit cards accepted: MasterCard, Visa, AmEx, Discover.

Mail search: Turnaround time: 4 weeks. Uncertified requests can take up to 4 months to process. A SASE is requested.

Fax search: See expedited service through Vitalchek.

In person search: Turnaround time 2 to 4 hours if expedite fee paid.

Online search: Records may be ordered online via www.vitalchek.com, a state approved vendor.

Expedited service: Expedited service is available in person from this agency for an additional $10.00. If www.vitalchek.com used (fax, online), add $6.00 for use of credit card and shipping costs.

Workers' Compensation Records

Dept of Workforce Development, Worker's Compensation Division, PO Box 7901, Madison, WI 53707-7901 (Courier: 201 E Washington Ave, Madison, WI 53707); 608-266-1340, 608-267-0394 (Fax), 7:45AM-4:30PM.

www.dwd.state.wi.us/wc

Indexing & Storage: Records are available for 12 years from last benefit payment. New records are available for inquiry immediately. Records are indexed on microfilm, inhouse computer. Records are normally destroyed after 12 years if they are inactive. May be on microfilm if there was activity in the last couple of years.

Searching: Must have release from claimant or be a party to the claim. Must also specify what records you request. Include the following in your request-claimant name, date of accident, employer. Also, submit either the claim number or the SSN. It is suggested to call first so that they can locate records.

Access by: mail, in person.

Fee & Payment: There is a $3.00 service fee plus $.20 per copy fee, $2.00 if certified. Fee payee: Workforce Department. Prepayment required. Personal checks accepted. No credit cards accepted.

Mail search: Turnaround time: 1 to 2 weeks. A SASE is requested.

In person search: Requester must show how connected to party. If you make the copies, the fee is $.10 per page, exact change required.

Driver Records

Division of Motor Vehicles, Records & Licensing Info. Section, PO Box 7995, Madison, WI 53707-7995 (Courier: 4802 Sheboygan Ave, Room 350, Madison, WI 53707); 608-266-2353, 608-267-3636 (Fax), 7:30AM-5:15PM.

www.dot.wisconsin.gov

Note: Copies of tickets may be obtained from this address for $5.50 per citation.

Indexing & Storage: Records are available for 5 years from date of conviction for moving violations and suspensions/revocations, 55 years from date of convictions for alcohol-related violations, and 20 years withdrawal based on damage judgment. It takes no more than 15 days before new records are available for inquiry.

Searching: Driver record information can be obtained per DPPA guidelines. Casual requesters must submit Form MV2896 which requires signature of the subject. This form may be downloaded from the web. The driver license number, or full name, DOB and sex are required when ordering a record. The driver's address is included as part of the search for approved requesters. There is no public counter for walk-in requests. The following data is not released: ID card information, SSN, juvenile record entries, arrests and medical information.

Access by: mail, phone, online.

Fee & Payment: The fee is $5.00 per driving record. Fee payee: Registration Fee Trust. Prepayment required. Personal checks accepted. No credit cards accepted.

Mail search: Turnaround time: 5 business days. The Employer Notification program provides a an employee's MVR when an accident, suspension,

revocation or out of service order occurs. Cost is $20.00 to sign up and $2.00 per employee. Call 608-266-2353 to set up the program.

Phone search: Pre-approved accounts may order driving records by phone or fax. The fee is $6.00 if a human operator reads back the record or $5.00 for a digitized computer readback of record.

Online search: Commercial online access is available for high volume users only, fee is $5.00 per record. Call 608-266-2353 for more information. Also, the Department offers a Notification Program to employers of commercial drivers. Employers are notified if there is activity on an employee's record. Call 608-266-2353 for details.

Other access: The agency offers a magnetic tape retrieval system for high volume users. The agency will, also, sell its license file without histories to qualified entities. For more information, call 608-266-2353.

Vehicle Ownership, Vehicle Identification

Department of Transportation, Vehicle Records Section, PO Box 7911, Madison, WI 53707-7911 (Courier: 4802 Sheboygan Ave, Room 102, Madison, WI 53707); 608-266-3666, 608-266-1466 (Registration Laws), 608-267-6966 (Fax), 7:30AM-4:30PM.

www.dot.wisconsin.gov

Indexing & Storage: Records are available for 7 years to present. It takes 2-3 days before new records are available for inquiry. Records are normally destroyed after 7 years after expiration.

Searching: All DPPA restrictions apply. All casual or occasional requestors must submit a request form MV2896. If the request is not for a permissible use, the subject's signature is necessary. The state no longer offers in-person access to records. Depending on what record is required, records can be looked up by VIN, plate or by name & city or county.

Access by: mail, phone.

Fee & Payment: The fee is $5.00 per record, including lien searches. An additional $5.00 is charged for certification. The photocopy fee is $.25 per page. Fee payee: Registration Fee Trust. Prepayment required. Personal checks accepted. No credit cards accepted.

Mail search: Turnaround time: 5 business days. A SASE is requested.

Phone search: Approved requesters may order records by phone.

Other access: This agency offers a variety of methods of obtaining bulk registration lists on cartridge and microfiche. FTP output by a specific request list is available only to law enforcement. Call 608-266-0898 for more information. All DPPA restrictions apply.

Accident Reports

Division of Motor Vehicles, Traffic Accident Section, PO Box 7919, Madison, WI 53707-7919 (Courier: 4802 Sheboygan Ave, Room 804, Madison, WI 53707); 608-266-8753, 608-267-0606 (Fax), 7:30AM-4:30PM.

www.dot.wisconsin.gov/

Indexing & Storage: Records are available for 4 years to present. It takes 30 days, on average, from

receipt of report before new records are available for inquiry. Records are normally destroyed after 4 years.

Searching: The information is public record. Records can be accessed by driver license number, by plate number, or by accident report number. If none of these items are available, the full name, DOB, and date of accident will be used. The following data is not released: juvenile records.

Access by: mail, phone.

Fee & Payment: The fees are $6.00 for operator reports and $6.00 for police reports. Fee payee: Registration Fee Trust. Prepayment is required if charges are above $6.00. Personal checks accepted. No credit cards accepted.

Mail search: Turnaround time: 72 hours. No SASE is required.

Phone search: 24 hour automated messaging system available to request copies.

Vessel Ownership, Vessel Registration

Department of Natural Resources, Boat Registration, PO Box 7921, Madison, WI 53707 (Courier: 101 S Webster, Madison, WI 53703); 608-266-2621, 608-264-6130 (Fax), 7:45AM-4:30PM.

www.dnr.wi.gov

Indexing & Storage: Records are available from 1978 to present. Records are indexed on computer. All motorized boats and all sailboats must be registered. All motorized boats and all sailboats, if 16 ft or over, must be titled. Lien information shows on title records. Records are normally destroyed after 10 years.

Searching: To search one of the following is required: name, hull ID #, or boat registration #.

Access by: mail, phone, fax, in person.

Fee & Payment: There is no search fee unless the search is really involved, in which case the fee is $5.00 per name. Fee payee: DNR. Prepayment required. Personal checks accepted. No credit cards accepted.

Mail search: Turnaround time: 1 to 2 days. No SASE is required.

Phone search: Records are available by phone.

Fax search: Same criteria as mail searching.

In person search: Unless the search is a simple record check, records are returned by mail the next day.

Other access: Bulk lists may be purchased. Call the number above or visit the web page.

Voter Registration

Records not maintained by a state level agency.

Note: All records are maintained at the municipal level. This agency is in the process of creating a statewide voter registration list. Although records are open to the public, be advised that not all municipalities maintain voter lists. Not all voters are registered.

GED Certificates

Department of Public Instruction, GED Program, PO Box 7841, Madison, WI 53707-7841 (Courier: 125 S Webster, Madison, WI 53707); 608-267-9245, 800-441-4563, 608-264-9552 (Fax), 8AM-4:30PM.

www.dpi.state.wi.us

Indexing & Storage: It takes minutes before new records are available for inquiry. Records are normally destroyed after 7 years.

Searching: Include the following in your request- name, SSN, DOB, and year test was taken. For a transcript, include a signed release.

Access by: mail, phone, fax, in person.

Fee & Payment: there is no fee for a verification, the fee is $15.00 for a copy of a transcript. Fee payee: WI Department of Public Instruction Credit cards are accepted for transcripts.

Mail search: Turnaround time: 1 week. No SASE is required.

Phone search: A requester must leave a message, with all required data. The agency will then call back with verification.

Fax search: Same criteria as mail searching.

In person search: Simple requests may be processed while you wait.

Expedited service: Expedited service is available for mail requests. Fee is $25.00. Turnaround time: 48 hours.

Hunting and Fishing License Information

Access to Records is Restricted

Fish & Game Licensing Division, Records Manager - CS/G3, PO Box 7924, Madison, WI 53707 (Courier: 101 S Webster St, Madison, WI 53703); 608-266-2621, 608-261-0770 (List Sales), 608-261-4380 (Fax), 8AM-4:30PM.

www.dnr.state.wi.us

Note: They do not provide name searching, but will sell lists by license type. There is an opt out provision in place, and 50% of the licensees have opted out.

Wisconsin State Licensing Agencies

Licenses Searchable Online

Accounting Firm #2	http://drl.wi.gov/lookupjump.htm
Acupuncturist #4	http://165.189.238.43/plsql/plsql/Search_Ind_Health
Adjustment Service Company #6	www.wdfi.org/fi/lfs/licensee_lists
Aesthetics Establ./Instructor/Specialty School #2	http://drl.wi.gov/lookupjump.htm
Ambulance Service Provider #7	www.dhfs.state.wi.us/reg_licens/dohprog/ems/provider/wicounties.htm
Appraiser, General/Residential #1	http://drl.wi.gov/lookupjump.htm
Architect #1	http://drl.wi.gov/lookupjump.htm
Architectural Corporation #2	http://drl.wi.gov/lookupjump.htm
Art Therapist #4	http://165.189.238.43/plsql/plsql/Search_Ind_Health
Attorney #16	www.wisbar.org/lawyersearch/mainform.asp
Auction Company #2	http://drl.wi.gov/lookupjump.htm
Auctioneer #1	http://drl.wi.gov/lookupjump.htm
Audiologist #4	http://165.189.238.43/plsql/plsql/Search_Ind_Health
Bank #5	www.wdfi.org/fi/savings_institutions/licensee_lists/
Barber #1	http://drl.wi.gov/lookupjump.htm
Barber School #2	http://drl.wi.gov/lookupjump.htm
Barber/Apprentice/Instrct./Mgr. #1	http://drl.wi.gov/lookupjump.htm
Boiler Repairer #19	http://apps.commerce.state.wi.us/SB_Credential/SB_CredentialApp
Boxer #1	http://drl.wi.gov/lookupjump.htm
Boxing Club, Amateur or Prof. #2	http://drl.wi.gov/lookupjump.htm
Boxing Show Permit #2	http://drl.wi.gov/lookupjump.htm
Building Inspector #19	http://apps.commerce.state.wi.us/SB_Credential/SB_CredentialApp
Cemetery Authority/Warehouse #2	http://drl.wi.gov/lookupjump.htm
Cemetery Preneed Seller #1	http://drl.wi.gov/lookupjump.htm
Cemetery Salesperson #1	http://drl.wi.gov/lookupjump.htm
Charitable Organization #2	http://drl.wi.gov/lookupjump.htm
Check Seller #6	www.wdfi.org/fi/lfs/licensee_lists
Chiropractor #4	http://165.189.238.43/plsql/plsql/Search_Ind_Health
Collection Agency #6	www.wdfi.org/fi/lfs/licensee_lists
Cosmetologist #1	http://drl.wi.gov/lookupjump.htm
Cosmetology Instructor/Mgr./Apprentice #1	http://drl.wi.gov/lookupjump.htm
Cosmetology School #2	http://drl.wi.gov/lookupjump.htm
Counselor, Professional #4	http://165.189.238.43/plsql/plsql/Search_Ind_Health
Credit Service Organization #5	www.wdfi.org/fi/cu/chartered_lists/default.asp
Credit Union #5	www.wdfi.org/fi/cu/chartered_lists/default.asp
Currency Exchange #6	www.wdfi.org/fi/lfs/licensee_lists
Dance Therapist #4	http://165.189.238.43/plsql/plsql/Search_Ind_Health
Debt Collector #6	www.wdfi.org/fi/lfs/licensee_lists
Dental Hygienist #4	http://165.189.238.43/plsql/plsql/Search_Ind_Health
Dentist #4	http://165.189.238.43/plsql/plsql/Search_Ind_Health
Designer of Engineering Systems #1	http://drl.wi.gov/lookupjump.htm
Dietitian #4	http://165.189.238.43/plsql/plsql/Search_Ind_Health
Drug Distributor/Mfg #2	http://drl.wi.gov/lookupjump.htm
Electrical Inspector #19	http://apps.commerce.state.wi.us/SB_Credential/SB_CredentialApp
Electrician #19	http://apps.commerce.state.wi.us/SB_Credential/SB_CredentialApp
Electrologist/Electrology Instructor #1	http://drl.wi.gov/lookupjump.htm
Electrology Establ./School #2	http://drl.wi.gov/lookupjump.htm
Engineer/Engineer in Training #1	http://drl.wi.gov/lookupjump.htm
Engineering Corporation #2	http://drl.wi.gov/lookupjump.htm
Firearms Permit #2	http://drl.wi.gov/lookupjump.htm
Fireworks Manufacturer #19	http://apps.commerce.state.wi.us/SB_Credential/SB_CredentialApp
Fund Raiser, Professional #1	http://drl.wi.gov/lookupjump.htm
Fund Raising Counsel #2	http://drl.wi.gov/lookupjump.htm
Funeral Director/Director Apprentice #1	http://drl.wi.gov/lookupjump.htm
Funeral Establishment #2	http://drl.wi.gov/lookupjump.htm
Funeral Preneed Seller #1	http://drl.wi.gov/lookupjump.htm
Geologist #1	http://drl.wi.gov/lookupjump.htm

Geology Firm #2	http://drl.wi.gov/lookupjump.htm
Hearing Instrument Specialist #4	http://165.189.238.43/plsql/plsql/Search_Ind_Health
Home Inspector #1	http://drl.wi.gov/lookupjump.htm
HVAC Contractor #19	http://apps.commerce.state.wi.us/SB_Credential/SB_CredentialApp
Hydrologist #1	http://drl.wi.gov/lookupjump.htm
Hydrology Firm #2	http://drl.wi.gov/lookupjump.htm
Insurance Company #6	http://badger.state.wi.us/agencies/oci/dir_ins.htm
Insurance Premium Finance Company #6	www.wdfi.org/fi/lfs/licensee_lists
Interior Designer #1	http://drl.wi.gov/lookupjump.htm
Investment Advisor/Advisor Rep #10	www.wdfi.org/fi/securities/licensing/licensee_lists/default.asp
Land Surveyor #1	http://drl.wi.gov/lookupjump.htm
Landscape Architect #1	http://drl.wi.gov/lookupjump.htm
Loan Company #6	www.wdfi.org/fi/lfs/licensee_lists
Loan Solicitor/Originator #5	www.wdfi.org/fi/mortbank/licensee_lists/default.asp
Lobbying Organization, Principal #11	http://ethics.state.wi.us/Scripts/2003Session/OELMenu.asp
Lobbyist #11	http://ethics.state.wi.us/Scripts/2003Session/LobbyistsMenu.asp
Manicurist Establ./Specialty School #2	http://drl.wi.gov/lookupjump.htm
Manicurist/Manicurist Instructor #1	http://drl.wi.gov/lookupjump.htm
Marriage & Family Therapist #4	http://165.189.238.43/plsql/plsql/Search_Ind_Health
Massage Therapist/Bodyworker #4	http://165.189.238.43/plsql/plsql/Search_Ind_Health
Medical Doctor/Surgeon #4	http://165.189.238.43/plsql/plsql/Search_Ind_Health
Midwife Nurse #4	http://165.189.238.43/plsql/plsql/Search_Ind_Health
Mobile Home & RV Dealer #6	www.wdfi.org/fi/lfs/licensee_lists
Mortgage Banker/Broker #5	www.wdfi.org/fi/mortbank/licensee_lists/default.asp
Motorcycle Dealer #6	www.wdfi.org/fi/lfs/licensee_lists
Music Therapist #4	http://165.189.238.43/plsql/plsql/Search_Ind_Health
Nurse-RN/LPN #4	http://165.189.238.43/plsql/plsql/Search_Ind_Health
Nursing Home Administrator #1	http://drl.wi.gov/lookupjump.htm
Occupational Therapist/Assistant #4	http://165.189.238.43/plsql/plsql/Search_Ind_Health
Optometrist #4	http://165.189.238.43/plsql/plsql/Search_Ind_Health
Payday Lender #6	www.wdfi.org/fi/lfs/licensee_lists
Pesticide Applicator/Dealer/Business #9	http://datcp.state.wi.us/arm/agriculture/pest-fert/pesticides/data/
Pharmacist / Pharmacy #4	http://165.189.238.43/plsql/plsql/Search_Ind_Health
Physical Therapist #4	http://165.189.238.43/plsql/plsql/Search_Ind_Health
Physician Assistant #4	http://165.189.238.43/plsql/plsql/Search_Ind_Health
Plumber #19	http://apps.commerce.state.wi.us/SB_Credential/SB_CredentialApp
Podiatrist #4	http://165.189.238.43/plsql/plsql/Search_Ind_Health
Private Detective #1	http://drl.wi.gov/lookupjump.htm
Private Detective Agency #2	http://drl.wi.gov/lookupjump.htm
Psychologist #4	http://165.189.238.43/plsql/plsql/Search_Ind_Health
Public Accountant #1	http://drl.wi.gov/lookupjump.htm
Real Estate Agent/Broker/Sales #1	http://drl.wi.gov/lookupjump.htm
Real Estate Appraiser #1	http://drl.wi.gov/lookupjump.htm
Real Estate Business Entity #2	http://drl.wi.gov/lookupjump.htm
Respiratory Care Practitioner #4	http://165.189.238.43/plsql/plsql/Search_Ind_Health
Sales Finance/Loan Company #6	www.wdfi.org/fi/lfs/licensee_lists
Savings & Loan Sales Finance Company #6	www.wdfi.org/fi/lfs/licensee_lists
Savings Institution #5	www.wdfi.org/fi/savings_institutions/licensee_lists/
School Librarian/Media Specialist #15	www.dpi.state.wi.us/dpi/dlsis/tel/lisearch.html
School Psychology Private Practice #4	http://165.189.238.43/plsql/plsql/Search_Ind_Health
Securities Broker/Dealer/Agent #10	www.wdfi.org/fi/securities/licensing/licensee_lists/default.asp
Security Guard #1	http://drl.wi.gov/lookupjump.htm
Social Worker #4	http://165.189.238.43/plsql/plsql/Search_Ind_Health
Soil Science Firm #2	http://drl.wi.gov/lookupjump.htm
Soil Scientist #1	http://drl.wi.gov/lookupjump.htm
Soil Tester #19	http://apps.commerce.state.wi.us/SB_Credential/SB_CredentialApp
Speech Pathologist/Audiologist #4	http://165.189.238.43/plsql/plsql/Search_Ind_Health
Teacher #15	www.dpi.state.wi.us/dpi/dlsis/tel/lisearch.html
Timeshare Salesperson #1	http://drl.wi.gov/lookupjump.htm
Veterinarian/Veterinary Technician #4	http://165.189.238.43/plsql/plsql/Search_Ind_Health
Welder #19	http://apps.commerce.state.wi.us/SB_Credential/SB_CredentialApp

Wisconsin Licensing Quick Finder

Accounting Firm #2 608-261-7096
Acupuncturist #4 608-266-8794
Adjustment Counselor #6 608-261-7578
Adjustment Service Company #6 608-261-7578
Aesthetics Establ./Specialty School #2 . 608-261-2390
Aesthetics Instructor #1 608-266-2112
Ambulance Service Provider #7 608-266-1568
Appraiser, General/Residential #1 608-266-2112
Architect #1 608-266-5511
Architectural Corporation #2 608-261-7096
Art Therapist #4 608-266-8794
Asbestos Worker #17 608-261-6876
Attorney #16 608-250-6125
Auction Company #2 608-261-7096
Auctioneer #1 608-266-5511
Audiologist #4 608-266-8794
Bank #5 608-261-7578
Barber #1 608-266-2112
Barber School #2 608-261-2390
Barber/Apprentice/Instrct./Mgr. #1 608-266-2112
Beer Wholesaler #8 608-266-2776
Boiler Repairer #19 608-261-8500
Boxer #1 608-266-5511
Boxing Club, Amateur or Prof. #2 608-261-7096
Boxing Show Permit #2 608-261-2390
Building Inspector #19 608-261-8500
Business Tax Registration #8 608-266-2776
Cemetery Authority/Warehouse #2 608-261-2390
Cemetery Preneed Seller #1 608-266-5511
Cemetery Salesperson #1 608-266-5511
Charitable Gaming #14 608-270-2555
Charitable Organization #2 608-261-7096
Check Seller #6 608-261-7578
Chiropractor #4 608-266-8794
Cigarette & Tobacco Distributor/Vendor/
   Multiple Retailer #8 608-266-2776
Cigarette & Tobacco Warehouser/
   Wholesaler/Jobber #8 608-266-2776
Collection Agency #6 608-261-7578
Cosmetologist #1 608-266-2112
Cosmetology Instr./Mgr./Apprentice #1 . 608-266-2112
Cosmetology School #2 608-261-7096
Counselor, Professional #4 608-266-8794
Credit Service Organization #5 608-266-9543
Credit Union #5 608-266-9543
Currency Exchange #6 608-261-7578
Dance Therapist #4 608-266-8794
Debt Collector #6 608-261-7578
Dental Hygienist #4 608-266-8794
Dentist #4 608-266-8794
Designer of Engineering Systems #1 ... 608-266-5511
Dietitian #4 608-266-8794
Director of Instruction #15 608-266-1027

Dog Racing Professional #14 608-270-2555
Drug Distributor/Mfg #2 608-261-7096
Electrician/Electrical Inspector #19 608-261-8500
Electrologist/Electrology Instructor #1 .. 608-266-2112
Electrology Establ./School #2 608-261-7096
Employee Benefits Plan Administrator #12
   608-267-1238
EMT/Paramedic #7 608-266-1568
Engineer/Engineer in Training #1 608-266-5511
Engineering Corporation #2 608-261-7096
Excise Tax Permit #8 608-266-2776
Fertilizer #9 608-224-4541
Firearms Permit #2 608-261-7096
Fireworks Manufacturer #19 608-261-8500
Fuel Tax Permit #8 608-266-2776
Fund Raiser, Professional #1 608-266-5511
Fund Raising Counsel #2 608-261-7096
Funeral Director/Director Apprentice #1 608-266-2112
Funeral Establishment #2 608-261-2390
Funeral Preneed Seller #1 608-266-5511
Geologist #1 608-266-2112
Geology Firm #2 608-261-2390
Hearing Instrument Specialist #4 608-266-8794
Home Inspector #1 608-266-5511
HVAC Contractor #19 608-261-8500
Hydrologist #1 608-266-2112
Hydrology Firm #2 608-261-2390
Indian Gaming Vendor #14 608-270-2555
Insurance Company #6 608-261-7578
Insurance Intermediary #12 608-266-8699
Insurance Premium Fin. Company #6 .. 608-261-7578
Interior Designer #1 608-266-5511
Investment Advisor/Advisor Rep #10 ... 608-266-3693
Land Surveyor #1 608-266-5511
Landscape Architect #1 608-266-5511
Liquor, Wholesale #8 608-266-2776
Loan Company #6 608-261-7578
Loan Solicitor/Originator #5 608-261-7578
Lobbying Organization, Principal #11 .. 608-266-8123
Lobbyist #11 608-266-8123
Manicurist Establ./Specialty School #2 . 608-261-2390
Manicurist/Manicurist Instructor #1 608-266-2112
Marriage & Family Therapist #4 608-266-8794
Massage Therapist/Bodyworker #4 608-266-8794
Medical Doctor/Surgeon #4 608-266-8794
Midwife Nurse #4 608-266-8794
Mobile Home & RV Dealer #6 608-261-7578
Mortgage Banker/Broker #5 608-261-7578
Motorcycle Dealer #6 608-261-7578
Music Therapist #4 608-266-8794
Notary Public #13 608-266-5594
Nurse-RN/LPN #4 608-266-8794
Nursing Home Administrator #1 608-266-2112

Occupational Therapist/Assistant #4 ... 608-266-8794
Optometrist #4 608-266-8794
Osteopathic Physician #4 608-266-8794
Payday Lender #6 608-261-7578
Pesticide Applicator/Application Business #9
   608-224-4548
Pesticide Dealer #9 608-224-4548
Pesticide Vet Clinic #9 608-224-4548
Pharmacist #4 608-266-8794
Pharmacy #4 608-266-8794
Physical Therapist #4 608-266-8794
Physician Assistant #4 608-266-8794
Plumber #19 608-261-8500
Podiatrist #4 608-266-8794
Private Detective #1 608-266-5511
Private Detective Agency #2 608-261-7096
Psychologist #4 608-266-8794
Public Accountant #1 608-266-5511
Racing/Racing Vendor #14 608-270-2555
Real Estate Agent/Broker/Sales #1 608-266-5511
Real Estate Appraiser #1 608-266-2112
Real Estate Business Entity #2 608-261-2390
Respiratory Care Practitioner #4 608-266-8794
Sales Finance/Loan Company #6 608-261-7578
Sales Withholding Tax Registration #8 . 608-266-2776
Sanitarian #17 608-267-4784
Savings & Loan Sales Finance Company #6
   608-261-7578
Savings Institution #5 608-261-4335
School Counselor #15 608-266-1027
School Librarian/Media Specialist #15 . 608-266-1027
School Nurse #15 608-266-1027
School Principal/Superintendent/Bus. Mgr #15
   608-266-1027
School Psychologist/Social Worker #15 608-266-1027
School Psychology Private Practice #4 608-266-8794
Securities Broker/Dealer/Agent #10 608-266-3693
Security Guard #1 608-266-5511
Social Worker #4 608-266-8794
Soil Science Firm #2 608-261-7096
Soil Scientist #1 608-266-2112
Soil Tester #19 608-261-8500
Speech Pathologist/Audiologist #4 608-266-8794
Teacher #15 608-266-1027
Timeshare Salesperson #1 608-266-5511
Veterinarian/Veterinary Technician #4 .. 608-266-8794
Viatical Settlement Broker #12 608-266-8699
Vocational Education Coordinator, Local #15
   608-266-1027
Welder #19 608-261-8500
Wine Distributor, Public #8 608-266-2776

Wisconsin Licensing Agency Information

1 Department of Regulation and Licensing, Division of Business Professional Licensure & Reg - Individuals, PO Box 8935 (1400 E Washington), Madison, WI 53708-8935; 608-266-5511, Fax: 608-267-3816. www.state.wi.us/agencies/drl/ Email: dorl@drl.state.wi.us   Search Database at http://drl.wi.gov/lookupjump.htm Note: Lists may be obtained.

2 Dept of Regulation & Licensing, Division of Business Licensure & Regulation - Entities, PO Box 8935 (1400 E Washington), Madison, WI 53708-8935; 608-266-5511, Fax: 608-267-3816. http://badger.state.wi.us/agencies/drl/ Email: dorl@drl.state.wi.us   Search Database at http://drl.wi.gov/lookupjump.htm Note: Lists may be obtained.

4 Bureau of Health Services Professions, PO Box 8935 (1400 E Washington Ave), Madison, WI 53708-8935; 608-266-2112, Fax: 608-261-7083. www.state.wi.us/agencies/drl/ Email: dorl@drl.state.wi.us   Search Database at http://165.189.238.43/plsql/plsql/Search_Ind_Heal th Note: This department recommends an internet search; if not, inquire by mail. Phone verifications may not be accepted.

5 Department of Financial Institutions, Division of Banking, PO Box 7876 (345 W Washington Av, 4th Fl), Madison, WI 53707-7876; 608-261-7578, Fax: 608-261-6889. www.wdfi.org   Email: info@dfi.state.wi.us Search Database at www.wdfi.org/fi/savi ngs_institutions/licensee_lists/ Note: Division of Financial Inst. - dfi - offers both an online list system and telephone system for verifications.

6 Department of Financial Institutions, Licensed Financial Services, 345 W Washington Ave, Madison, WI 53707-7876; 608-261-7578, Fax: 608-261-7200. www.wdfi.org/fi/lfs/   Search Database at www.wdfi.org/fi/lfs/licensee_lists/ Note: Also offers an online list system for verifications.

7 Division of Public Health, Bureau of EMS and IP, 1 W Wilson St, Rm 118, Madison, WI 53703; 608-267-9777, 266-1568, Fax: 608-261-6392. www.dhfs.state.wi.us/DPH_EMSIP/ Email: webmaildph@dhfs.state.wi.us

8 Department of Revenue, 2135 Rimrock Rd, Madison, WI 53713; 608-266-2772, Fax: 608-267-1030.   www.dor.state.wi.us Email: sales10@dor.state.wi.us

9 Department of Agriculture, Trade & Consumer Protection, Applicator Certification & Licensing, 2811 Agriculture Dr, Madison, WI 53718; 608-224-4548, Fax: 608-224-4656. http://datcp.state.wi.us/core/agriculture/pest-fert/index.html Email: bonnie.bruns@datcp.state.wi.us   Search at http://datcp.state.wi.us/arm/agriculture/pest-fert/pesticides/data/

10 Department of Financial Institutions, Division of Securities, PO Box 1768, Madison, WI 53701; 608-266-3693, 608-266-1064, Fax: 608-264-7979. www.wdfi.org/fi/securities/ Email: info@dfi.state.wi.us   Search Database at www.wdfi.org/fi/securities/licensing/licensee_lists /default.asp Note: These lists only contain firm info. No agents or investment adviser reps are searchable from the DFI website.

11 Ethics Board, 44 E Mifflin St, #601, Madison, WI 53703-2800; 608-266-8123, Fax: 608-264-9319. http://ethics.state.wi.us Email: ethics@ethics.state.wi.gov   Search Database at http://ethics.state.wi.us/LobbyingRegistrationRepo rts/LobbyingOverview.htm

12 Office of the Commissioner of Insurance, 125 S Webster St, Madison, WI 53702; 608-266-3585, Fax: 608-266-9935. http://badger.state.wi.us/agencies/oci/oci_home.htm Email: agentlicensing@oci.state.wi.us Note: For list of licence types go to www.oci.wi.gov.

13 Office of Secretary of State, PO Box 7848, Madison, WI 53707-7848; 608-266-5594, Fax: 608-266-3159. www.state.wi.us/agencies/sos

14 Department of Administration, Division of Gaming/Racing, 2005 W Beltline Hwy, #201 (PO Box 8979), Madison, WI 53713; 608-270-2555, Fax: 608-270-2564. www.doa.state.wi.us/gaming/index.asp Email: racingweb@doa.state.wi.us

15 Teacher Education, Department of Public Instruction, PO Box 7841, Madison, WI 53707-7841; 608-266-1027, Fax: 608-264-9558. www.dpi.state.wi.us/dpi/dlsis/tel/ Email: tcert@dpi.state.wi.us Search Database at www.dpi.state.wi.us/dp i/dlsis/tel/lisearch.html Note: At the search page, enter the User Name "view" and the Password, "1234567" then click "ok".

16 State Bar Association, PO Box 7158 (5302 Eastpark Blvd.), Madison, WI 53707; 608-257-3838, Fax: 608-257-5502. www.wisbar.org   Email: service@wisbar.org Search Database at www.wisbar.org/lawyersearch/mainform.asp

17 Department of Health & Family Svcs, Occupational Health, 1 W Wilson St, Perry Manor, Madison, WI 53703; 608-267-2297, Fax: 608-266-9711.

19 Department of Commerce, Safety & Buildings, PO Box 2689, 201 W Washington Ave, Madison, WI 53707-2689; 608-261-8500, Fax: 608-267-0592. www.state.wv.us/wvboa   Search Database at http://apps.commerce.state.wi.us/SB_Credential/S B_CredentialApp

Wisconsin Federal Courts

The following list indicates the district and division name for each county in the state. If the bankruptcy court location is different from the district court, then the location of the bankruptcy court appears in parentheses.

County/Court Cross Reference

County	District	Location	County	District	Location
Adams	Western	Madison	Marathon	Western	Madison (Eau Claire)
Ashland	Western	Madison (Eau Claire)	Marinette	Eastern	Milwaukee
Barron	Western	Madison (Eau Claire)	Marquette	Eastern	Milwaukee
Bayfield	Western	Madison (Eau Claire)	Menominee	Eastern	Milwaukee
Brown	Eastern	Milwaukee	Milwaukee	Eastern	Milwaukee
Buffalo	Western	Madison (Eau Claire)	Monroe	Western	Madison (Eau Claire)
Burnett	Western	Madison (Eau Claire)	Oconto	Eastern	Milwaukee
Calumet	Eastern	Milwaukee	Oneida	Western	Madison (Eau Claire)
Chippewa	Western	Madison (Eau Claire)	Outagamie	Eastern	Milwaukee
Clark	Western	Madison (Eau Claire)	Ozaukee	Eastern	Milwaukee
Columbia	Western	Madison	Pepin	Western	Madison (Eau Claire)
Crawford	Western	Madison	Pierce	Western	Madison (Eau Claire)
Dane	Western	Madison	Polk	Western	Madison (Eau Claire)
Dodge	Eastern	Milwaukee	Portage	Western	Madison (Eau Claire)
Door	Eastern	Milwaukee	Price	Western	Madison (Eau Claire)
Douglas	Western	Madison (Eau Claire)	Racine	Eastern	Milwaukee
Dunn	Western	Madison (Eau Claire)	Richland	Western	Madison
Eau Claire	Western	Madison (Eau Claire)	Rock	Western	Madison
Florence	Eastern	Milwaukee	Rusk	Western	Madison (Eau Claire)
Fond du Lac	Eastern	Milwaukee	Sauk	Western	Madison
Forest	Eastern	Milwaukee	Sawyer	Western	Madison (Eau Claire)
Grant	Western	Madison	Shawano	Eastern	Milwaukee
Green	Western	Madison	Sheboygan	Eastern	Milwaukee
Green Lake	Eastern	Milwaukee	St. Croix	Western	Madison (Eau Claire)
Iowa	Western	Madison	Taylor	Western	Madison (Eau Claire)
Iron	Western	Madison (Eau Claire)	Trempealeau	Western	Madison (Eau Claire)
Jackson	Western	Madison (Eau Claire)	Vernon	Western	Madison (Eau Claire)
Jefferson	Western	Madison	Vilas	Western	Madison (Eau Claire)
Juneau	Western	Madison (Eau Claire)	Walworth	Eastern	Milwaukee
Kenosha	Eastern	Milwaukee	Washburn	Western	Madison (Eau Claire)
Kewaunee	Eastern	Milwaukee	Washington	Eastern	Milwaukee
La Crosse	Western	Madison (Eau Claire)	Waukesha	Eastern	Milwaukee
Lafayette	Western	Madison	Waupaca	Eastern	Milwaukee
Langlade	Eastern	Milwaukee	Waushara	Eastern	Milwaukee
Lincoln	Western	Madison (Eau Claire)	Winnebago	Eastern	Milwaukee
Manitowoc	Eastern	Milwaukee	Wood	Western	Madison (Eau Claire)

Standards for Federal Courts: The search fee is $20.00 per item (one party name or case number). Certification fee is $7.00 per document. Copy fee is $.50 per page. All fees standard unless noted in profile. Mail Search: always enclose a stamped self addressed envelope unless otherwise noted. Most courts accept fax requests or will suggest a copying/search vendor. Before releasing records, all courts require prepayment unless noted in profile.

Open records are located at the court unless otherwise noted. District courts index by defendant and plaintiff as well as by case number. Bankruptcy courts usually index by debtor and case number. While most courts now have their indexes on computer, many still maintain index card files as well.

PACER: The universal PACER sign-up number is 800-676-6856. Find PACER and the Party/Case Index on the Web at http://pacer.psc.uscourts.gov. PACER dial-up access is $.60 per minute. Also, courts offering internet access via RACER, PACER, Web-PACER or the new CM-ECF charge $.07 per page fee unless noted as free.

US District Court

Eastern District of Wisconsin

Milwaukee Division Clerk's Office, Room 362, 517 E Wisconsin Ave, Milwaukee, WI 53202 (courier address: Use mail address for courier delivery) 414-297-3372. www.wied.uscourts.gov

Counties: Brown, Calumet, Dodge, Door, Florence, Fond du Lac, Forest, Green Lake, Kenosha, Kewaunee, Langlade, Manitowoc, Marinette, Marquette, Menominee, Milwaukee, Oconto, Outagamie, Ozaukee, Racine, Shawano, Sheboygan, Walworth, Washington, Waukesha, Waupaca, Waushara, Winnebago.

Indexing & Storage: New cases available in the index immediately after filing date. The computer index for civil cases goes back to 1991 and for criminal cases back to 1993.

Fee & Payment: Payment may be made by money order, cashier check, personal check. Payee: Clerk, U.S. District Court.

Phone Search: Docket information available by phone if you have the case number or party names.

In Person Search: Fee charged if court conducts your in person search for you.

PACER: PACER is available online at http://pacer.wied.uscourts.gov. Case records go back to 1994. Records never purged. New records are online after 1 day.

Electronic Filing: Electronic filing information at https://ecf.wied.uscourts.gov/cgi-bin/login.pl

U.S. Bankruptcy Court

Eastern District of Wisconsin

Milwaukee Division Room 126, 517 E Wisconsin Ave, Milwaukee, WI 53202 (courier address: Use mail address for courier delivery) 414-297-3291. www.wieb.uscourts.gov

Counties: Brown, Calumet, Dodge, Door, Florence, Fond du Lac, Forest, Green Lake, Kenosha, Kewaunee, Langlade, Manitowoc, Marinette, Marquette, Menominee, Milwaukee, Oconto, Outagamie, Ozaukee, Racine, Shawano, Sheboygan, Walworth, Washington, Waukesha, Waupaca, Waushara, Winnebago.

Indexing & Storage: Cases indexed by debtor as well as by case number. New cases available in the index 1-2 days after filing date. The computer index goes back to 1986.

Fee & Payment: Payment may be made by money order, cashier check, personal check. Payee: Clerk, U.S. Bankruptcy Court.

Phone Search: Automated voice case information service (VCIS) is available. Call VCIS at 877-781-7277 or 414-297-3582.

In Person Search: Fee charged if court conducts your in person search for you.

PACER: PACER is available online at http://pacer.wieb.uscourts.gov. Records purged after case is closed. New civil records are online after 1-2 days.

Electronic Filing: Electronic filing information online at https://ecf.wieb.uscourts.gov

U.S. District Court

Western District of Wisconsin

Madison Division PO Box 432, Madison, WI 53701 (courier address: 120 N Henry St, Madison, WI 53703), 608-264-5156. www.wiw.uscourts.gov

Counties: Adams, Ashland, Barron, Bayfield, Buffalo, Burnett, Chippewa, Clark, Columbia, Crawford, Dane, Douglas, Dunn, Eau Claire, Grant, Green, Iowa, Iron, Jackson, Jefferson, Juneau, La Crosse, Lafayette, Lincoln, Marathon, Monroe, Oneida, Pepin, Pierce, Polk, Portage, Price, Richland, Rock, Rusk, Sauk, Sawyer, St. Croix, Taylor, Trempealeau, Vernon, Vilas, Washburn, Wood.

Indexing & Storage: New cases available in the index 24 hours after filing date. District wide searches are available from this court.

Fee & Payment: Payment may be made by money order, cashier check, personal check. Payee: Clerk, U.S. District Court.

Phone Search: Only docket information available by phone.

In Person Search: Fee charged if court conducts your in person search for you.

PACER: PACER is available online at http://pacer.wiwd.uscourts.gov. Case records go back to 1994. Records never purged. New records are online after 1 day.

U.S. Bankruptcy Court

Western District of Wisconsin

Eau Claire Division PO Box 5009, Eau Claire, WI 54702-5009 (courier address: 500 S Barstow Commons, Eau Claire, WI 54701), 715-839-2980, Fax: 715-839-2996. www.wiw.uscourts.gov/bankruptcy

Counties: Ashland, Barron, Bayfield, Buffalo, Burnett, Chippewa, Clark, Douglas, Dunn, Eau Claire, Iron, Jackson, Juneau, La Crosse, Lincoln, Marathon, Monroe, Oneida, Pepin, Pierce, Polk, Portage, Price, Rusk, Sawyer, St. Croix, Taylor, Trempealeau, Vernon, Vilas, Washburn, Wood. Division has satellite offices in LaCrosse and Wausau.

Indexing & Storage: Cases indexed by debtor as well as by case number. New cases available in the index 1 day after filing date. All division records are maintained here until they are forwarded to the Chicago Federal Records Center.

Fee & Payment: Payment may be made by money order, cashier check, business check. Personal checks are not accepted. Personal checks are accepted only from attorneys. Payee: Clerk, U.S. Bankruptcy Court.

Phone Search: Only limited docket information is available by phone. Automated voice case information service (VCIS) is available. Call VCIS at 800-743-8247 or 608-264-5035.

Mail Search: A SASE not required.

In Person Search: Fee charged if court conducts your in person search for you.

PACER: WebPACER is available at http://pacer.wiwb.uscourts.gov/js_index.html. Document images available. New civil records are online after 1 day.

Electronic Filing: Electronic filing information online at https://ecf.wiwb.uscourts.gov

Madison Division PO Box 548, Madison, WI 53701 (courier address: Room 340, 120 N Henry St, Madison, WI 53703), 608-264-5178. www.wiw.uscourts.gov/bankruptcy

Counties: Adams, Columbia, Crawford, Dane, Grant, Green, Iowa, Jefferson, Lafayette, Richland, Rock, Sauk.

Indexing & Storage: Cases indexed by debtor as well as by case number. New cases available in the index 24 hours after filing date.

Fee & Payment: Payment may be made by money order, cashier check, business check. Personal checks are not accepted. Payee: Clerk, U.S. Bankruptcy Court.

Phone Search: Only limited docket information is available by phone. Automated voice case information service (VCIS) is available. Call VCIS at 800-743-8247 or 608-264-5035.

Mail Search: A SASE not required.

In Person Search: Fee charged if court conducts your in person search for you.

PACER: WebPACER is available at http://pacer.wiwb.uscourts.gov/js_index.html. Document images available. New civil records are online after 1 day.

Electronic Filing: Electronic filing information online at https://ecf.wiwb.uscourts.gov

Wisconsin County Courts

Court	Jurisdiction	No. of Courts	How Organized
Circuit Courts*	General	74	69 Circuits
Municipal Courts	Municipal	226	
Probate Courts*	Probate	72	

* Profiled in this Sourcebook.

Court	CIVIL								
	Tort	Contract	Real Estate	Min. Claim	Max. Claim	Small Claims	Estate	Eviction	Domestic Relations
Circuit Courts*	X	X	X	$0	No Max	$5000	X	X	X
Municipal Courts									
Probate Courts*							X		

Court	CRIMINAL				
	Felony	Misdemeanor	DWI/DUI	Preliminary Hearing	Juvenile
Circuit Courts*	X	X	X	X	X
Municipal Courts			X		X
Probate Courts*					

ADMINISTRATION

Director of State Courts, Supreme Court, PO Box 1688, Madison, WI, 53701; 608-266-6828, Fax: 608-267-0980. http://wicourts.gov

COURT STRUCTURE

The Circuit Court is the court of general jurisdiction. The Register in Probate maintains guardianship and mental health records, most of which are sealed but may be opened for cause with a court order. In some counties, the Register also maintains termination and adoption records, but practices vary widely across the state.

Most Registers in Probate are putting pre-1950 records on microfilm and destroying the hard copies. This is done as "time and workloads permit," so microfilm archiving is not uniform across the state.

The small claims limit was raised to $5000 in mid-1995.

ONLINE ACCESS

Wisconsin Circuit Court Access (WCCA) allows users to view circuit court case information at http://wcca.wicourts.gov/ which is the Wisconsin court system web site. Data is available from all counties. Searches can be conducted statewide or county by county. WCCA provides detailed information about circuit cases and for civil cases, the program displays judgment and judgment party information. WCCA also offers the ability to generate reports. In addition, public access terminals are available at each court. Due to statutory requirements, WCCA users will not be able to view restricted cases. There are probate records for all counties. Appellate and Supreme Courts opinions are available from http://old.wicourts.gov/wscca/.

ADDITIONAL INFORMATION

The statutory fee schedule for the Circuit Courts is as follows: Search Fee - $5.00 per name; Copy Fee - $1.25 per page; Certification Fee - $5.00. In about half the Circuit Courts, no search fee is charged if the case number is provided.

The fee schedule for probate is as follows: Search Fee - $4.00 per name; Certification Fee - $3.00 per document plus copy fee; Copy Fee - $1.00 per page.

PROBATE COURTS

Probate filing is a function of the Circuit Court; however, each county has a Register in Probate who maintains and manages the probate records. Probate records are available online at the web page.

Adams County

Circuit Court PO Box 220, Friendship, WI 53934; 608-339-4208; Fax: 608-339-4503. Hours: 8AM-4:30PM (CST). *Felony, Misdemeanor, Civil, Eviction, Small Claims.*

Civil Records: Access: Phone, mail, online, in person. Both court and visitors may perform in person searches. Search fee: $5.00 per name. Required to search: name, years to search. Civil records on computer from 1993, on index cards and books from 1950. Historical societies have previous records and indexes. Organized 1848. Civil court records free online at http://wcca.wicourts.gov/index.xsl.

Criminal Records: Access: Phone, mail, online, in person. Both court and visitors may perform in person searches. Search fee: $5.00 per name. Required to search: name, years to search, DOB. Criminal records on computer from 1993, on index cards and books from 1950. Historical societies have previous records and indexes. Organized 1848. Criminal court records are free online at http://wcca.wicourts.gov/index.xsl.

General Information: Public Access terminal is available. No juvenile, paternity, financial, PSI reports released. Fee to fax results is $1.25 per page. Copy fee: $1.25 per page. Cert fee: $5.00. Payee: Clerk of Court. Personal checks accepted. Prepayment required. Mail requests require SASE. Mail turnaround time 1-2 days.

Register in Probate PO Box 200, Friendship, WI 53934; 608-339-4213; Fax: 608-339-4503. Hours: 8AM-4:30PM (CST). *Probate.*

Note: Probate records available free online at http://ccap.courts.state.wi.us/internetcourtaccess/.

Ashland County

Circuit Court Courthouse, 201 W Main St Rm 307, Ashland, WI 54806; 715-682-7016; Fax: 715-682-7919. Hours: 8AM-Noon, 1-4PM (CST). *Felony, Misdemeanor, Civil, Eviction, Small Claims.*

Civil Records: Access: Phone, fax, mail, online, in person. Both court and visitors may perform in person searches. Search fee: $5.00 per name. Required to search: name, years to search. Civil cases indexed by defendant, plaintiff. Civil records on index cards and index books concurrently from 1960. Organized 1860. Civil court records free online at http://wcca.wicourts.gov/index.xsl.

Criminal Records: Access: Fax, mail, online, in person. Both court and visitors may perform in person searches. Search fee: $5.00 per name. Required to search: name, years to search, DOB. Criminal records on computer back to 1994. Criminal court records are free online at http://wcca.wicourts.gov/index.xsl.

General Information: Public Access terminal is available. No juvenile or paternity records released. Will fax results for $1.25 per page. Copy fee: $1.25 per page. Cert fee: $5.00. Payee: Clerk of Court. Local or pre-approved checks accepted. Prepayment required. Mail requests require SASE. Mail turnaround time 1-2 days.

Register in Probate Courthouse Rm 203, 201 W Main, Ashland, WI 54806; 715-682-7009; Fax: 715-682-7919. Hours: 8AM-Noon, 1-4PM (CST). *Probate.*

Note: Probate records are available free online; see Circuit Court.

Barron County

Circuit Court Barron County Courthouse, 330 E LaSalle Ave Rm 208, Barron, WI 54812; 715-537-6265; Civil phone: 715-537-6271; Criminal phone: 715-537-6268; Probate phone: 715-537-6261; Fax: 715-537-6269. Hours: 8AM-4:30PM (CST). *Felony, Misdemeanor, Civil, Eviction, Small Claims.*

Civil Records: Access: Online, in person. Visitors must perform in person searches for themselves. No search fee. Required to search: name, years to search. Civil cases indexed by defendant, plaintiff. Civil records on computer, index cards from 1983. Organized 1859. Civil court records free online at http://wcca.wicourts.gov/index.xsl.

Criminal Records: Access: Online, in person. Visitors must perform in person searches for themselves. No search fee. Required to search: name, years to search. Criminal records on computer, index cards from 1983. Organized 1859. Criminal court records are free online at http://wcca.wicourts.gov/index.xsl.

General Information: Public Access terminal is available. No expunged, paternity or sealed records released. Copy fee: $1.25 per page. Cert fee: $5.00. Payee: Clerk of Court. Personal checks accepted. Prepayment required.

Register in Probate Barron Justice Center, 1420 State Hwy 25 N, Barron, WI 54812; 715-537-6261; Fax: 715-537-6269. Hours: 8AM-4:30PM (CST). *Probate.*

Note: Probate records are available free online; see Circuit Court.

Bayfield County

Circuit Court 117 E 5th, Washburn, WI 54891; 715-373-6108; Probate phone: 715-373-6155; Fax: 715-373-6153. Hours: 8AM-4PM (CST). *Felony, Misdemeanor, Civil, Eviction, Small Claims.*

Civil Records: Access: Mail, online, in person. Both court and visitors may perform in person searches. Search fee: $5.00 per name. Required to search: name, years to search. Civil cases indexed by defendant, plaintiff. Civil records on computer for all open cases since 1982, on index cards from 1979, index books in archives from 1845 to 1979. Civil court records free online at http://wcca.wicourts.gov/index.xsl.

Criminal Records: Access: Mail, online, in person. Both court and visitors may perform in person searches. Search fee: $5.00 per name. Required to search: name, years to search, DOB. Criminal records on computer since 03/93. Criminal court records are free online at http://wcca.wicourts.gov/index.xsl.

General Information: Public Access terminal is available. No sealed records released. Fee to fax results is $2.50 per page. Copy fee: $1.25 per page. Cert fee: $5.00. Payee: Clerk of Court. Personal checks accepted. Prepayment required. Mail requests require SASE. Mail turnaround time 1-2 days.

Register in Probate 117 E 5th, PO Box 536, Washburn, WI 54891; 715-373-6155; Fax: 715-373-6153. Hours: 8AM-4PM (CST). *Probate.*

Note: Probate records are available free online; see Circuit Court.

Brown County

Circuit Court PO Box 23600, Green Bay, WI 54305-3600; 920-448-4161; Probate phone: 920-448-4275; Fax: 920-448-4156. Hours: 8AM-4:30PM (CST). *Felony, Misdemeanor, Civil, Eviction, Small Claims.*

Civil Records: Access: Mail, online, in person. Both court and visitors may perform in person searches. Search fee: $5.00 per name. Required to search: name, years to search. Civil cases indexed by defendant, plaintiff. Civil records on computer since 1990, on microfiche from 1987-1990, archives from 1962-1990. Crossed on index cards from 1972, index books from 1982. Civil court records free online at http://wcca.wicourts.gov/index.xsl.

Criminal Records: Access: Mail, online, in person. Both court and visitors may perform in person

searches. Search fee: $5.00 per name. Required to search: name, years to search, DOB. Criminal records on computer since 1990, on microfiche from 1987-1990, archives from 1962-1990. Crossed on index cards from 1972, index books from 1982. Criminal court records are free online at http://wcca.wicourts.gov/index.xsl.

General Information: Public Access terminal is available. No juvenile or preadjudicated paternity records released. Copy fee: $1.25 per page. Cert fee: $5.00. Payee: Brown County Clerk of Court. Personal checks accepted. Prepayment required. Mail requests require SASE. Mail turnaround time 10 days.

Register in Probate PO Box 23600, Green Bay, WI 54305-3600; 920-448-4275; Fax: 920-448-6208. Hours: 8AM-4:30PM (CST). *Probate.*

Note: Probate records are available free online; see Circuit Court.

Buffalo County

Circuit Court 407 S 2nd, PO Box 68, Alma, WI 54610; 608-685-6212; Fax: 608-685-6211. Hours: 8AM-4:30PM (CST). *Felony, Misdemeanor, Civil, Eviction, Small Claims.*

Civil Records: Access: Phone, fax, mail, online, in person. Both court and visitors may perform in person searches. Search fee: $5.00 per name. Required to search: name, years to search. Civil cases indexed by defendant, plaintiff. Civil records on computer from 1994, on index cards from 1979. No civil records available before 1962. Civil court records free online at http://wcca.wicourts.gov/index.xsl.

Criminal Records: Access: Phone, fax, mail, online, in person. Both court and visitors may perform in person searches. Search fee: $5.00 per name. Required to search: name, years to search. Criminal records on computer from 1994. Felonies retained 50 years; misdemeanors 20 years. No misdemeanors available before 1962. Criminal court records are free online at http://wcca.wicourts.gov/index.xsl.

General Information: Public Access terminal is available. No closed records released. Fee to fax results is $1.25 per page. Copy fee: $1.25 per page. Cert fee: $5.00. Payee: Buffalo County Clerk of Court. Personal checks accepted. Prepayment required. Mail requests require SASE. Mail turnaround time 1 week.

Register in Probate 407 S 2nd, PO Box 68, Alma, WI 54610; 608-685-6202; Fax: 608-685-6211. Hours: 8AM-4:30PM (CST). *Probate.*

Note: Probate records are available free online; see Circuit Court.

Burnett County

Circuit Court 7410 County Road K #115, Siren, WI 54872; 715-349-2147; Probate phone: 715-349-2177. Hours: 8:30AM-4:30PM (CST). *Felony, Misdemeanor, Civil, Eviction, Small Claims.*

Civil Records: Access: Mail, online, in person. Both court and visitors may perform in person searches. Search fee: $5.00 per name. Required to search: name, years to search. Civil cases indexed by defendant, plaintiff. Civil records on computer from 10/92, on index books from 1800s. Organized 1856. Civil court records free online at http://wcca.wicourts.gov/index.xsl.

Criminal Records: Access: Mail, online, in person. Both court and visitors may perform in person searches. Search fee: $5.00 per name. Required to search: name, years to search. Criminal records on computer from 10/92, on index books from 1800s. Organized 1856. Criminal court records are free online at http://wcca.wicourts.gov/index.xsl.

General Information: Public Access terminal is available. No paternity, juvenile, sealed or confidential records released. Will fax results to local or toll free line. Fees must be paid in advance. Copy fee: $1.25 per page. Cert fee: $5.00. Payee: Clerk of Courts. Personal checks accepted. Prepayment required. Mail requests require SASE. Mail turnaround time 1-2 days.

Register in Probate 7410 County Road K #110, Siren, WI 54872; 715-349-2177 x0301; Fax: 715-349-7659. Hours: 8:30AM-4:30PM (CST). *Probate.* Note: Probate records are available free online; see Circuit Court. This court also holds Juvenile, Guardianship, Mental Commitments, Adoptions, and Term. of Parental Right.

Calumet County

Circuit Court 206 Court St, Chilton, WI 53014; 920-849-1414; Fax: 920-849-1483. Hours: 8AM-4:30PM (CST). *Felony, Misdemeanor, Civil, Eviction, Small Claims.*
Civil Records: Access: Mail, online, in person. Both court and visitors may perform in person searches. Search fee: $5.00 per name. Required to search: name, years to search. Civil cases indexed by defendant, plaintiff. Civil records on computer from 1992, index cards from 1978, index books from 1800s. Civil court records free online at http://wcca.wicourts.gov/index.xsl.
Criminal Records: Access: Mail, online, in person. Both court and visitors may perform in person searches. Search fee: $5.00 per name. Required to search: name, years to search, DOB. Criminal records on computer from 1992, index cards from 1978, index books from 1800s. Criminal court records are free online at http://wcca.wicourts.gov/index.xsl.
General Information: Public Access terminal is available. No juvenile or paternity records released. Copy fee: $1.25 per page. Cert fee: $5.00. Payee: Clerk of Court. Personal checks accepted. Prepayment required. Mail requests require SASE. Mail turnaround time 2 days.

Register in Probate 206 Court St, Chilton, WI 53014-1198; 920-849-1455; Fax: 920-849-1483. Hours: 8AM-Noon, 1-4:30PM (CST). *Probate.* Note: Probate records are available free online; see Circuit Court.

Chippewa County

Circuit Court 711 N Bridge St, Chippewa Falls, WI 54729-1879; 715-726-7758; Probate phone: 715-726-7737; Fax: 715-726-7786. Hours: 8AM-4:30PM (CST). *Felony, Misdemeanor, Civil, Eviction, Small Claims.*
Civil Records: Access: Mail, fax, online, in person. Both court and visitors may perform in person searches. Search fee: $5.00 per name. Required to search: name, years to search; also helpful: address, records sought. Civil cases indexed by defendant, plaintiff. Civil records on computer from 1990, index cards from 1979, index books from 1900s. Civil court records free online at http://wcca.wicourts.gov/index.xsl.
Criminal Records: Access: Mail, fax, online, in person. Both court and visitors may perform in person searches. Search fee: $5.00 per name. Required to search: name, years to search, DOB; also helpful: SSN. Criminal records on computer from 1990, index cards from 1979, index books from 1900s. Criminal court records are free online at http://wcca.wicourts.gov/index.xsl.
General Information: Public Access terminal is available. Paternity records released only to party or attorney of record, or with written court authorization. Fee to fax results is $2.00 for 1st page and $1.00 per page thereafter. Copy fee: $1.25 per page. Cert fee: $5.00. Payee: Chippewa County Clerk of Courts.

Personal checks accepted. Prepayment required. Mail requests require SASE. Mail turnaround time 10 days or less; up to 30 days if pre-1990.

Register in Probate 711 N Bridge St, Chippewa Falls, WI 54729; 715-726-7737; Fax: 715-738-2626. Hours: 8AM-4:30PM (CST). *Probate.* Note: Probate records are available free online; see Circuit Court.

Clark County

Circuit Court 517 Court St, Neillsville, WI 54456-1971; 715-743-5181; Fax: 715-743-5120. Hours: 8AM-4:30PM (CST). *Felony, Misdemeanor, Civil, Eviction, Small Claims.*
Civil Records: Access: Mail, online, in person. Both court and visitors may perform in person searches. Search fee: $5.00 per name. Required to search: name, years to search. Civil cases indexed by defendant, plaintiff. Civil records on computer from 1994, on index cards from 1981, index books from 1900s. Civil court records free online at http://wcca.wicourts.gov/index.xsl.
Criminal Records: Access: Mail, online, in person. Both court and visitors may perform in person searches. Search fee: $5.00 per name. Required to search: name, years to search. Criminal records on computer from 1994, on index cards from 1981, index books from 1900s. Criminal court records are free online at http://wcca.wicourts.gov/index.xsl.
General Information: Public Access terminal is available. No sealed or paternity records released. Will fax results. Copy fee: $.30 per page. Cert fee: $5.00. Payee: Clerk of Court. Personal checks accepted. Prepayment required. Mail requests require SASE. Mail turnaround time 1-2 weeks.

Register in Probate 517 Court St, Rm 403, Neillsville, WI 54456; 715-743-5172; Fax: 715-743-5120. Hours: 8AM-4:30PM (CST). *Probate.* Note: There is a $4.00 search fee. Probate records are available free online; see Circuit Court.

Columbia County

Circuit Court PO Box 587, Portage, WI 53901; 608-742-9642; Civil phone: 608-742-9624; Criminal phone: 608-742-9643; Probate phone: 608-742-9636; Fax: 608-742-9601. Hours: 8AM-4:30PM (CST). *Felony, Misdemeanor, Civil, Eviction, Small Claims.*
Civil Records: Access: Mail, online, in person. Both court and visitors may perform in person searches. Search fee: $5.00 per name. Required to search: name, years to search. Civil cases indexed by defendant, plaintiff. Civil records on computer from 1994, on microfiche to 1960s, concurrent index cards/books from 1940s. Civil court records free online at http://wcca.wicourts.gov/index.xsl.
Criminal Records: Access: Mail, online, in person. Both court and visitors may perform in person searches. Search fee: $5.00 per name. Required to search: name, years to search, DOB. Criminal records on computer from 1994, on microfiche to 1960s, concurrent index cards/books from 1940s. Criminal court records are free online at http://wcca.wicourts.gov/index.xsl.
General Information: Public Access terminal is available. No juvenile or paternity records released. Fee to fax results is $1.25 per page. Copy fee: $1.25 per page. Cert fee: $5.00. Payee: Clerk of Court. Personal checks accepted. Prepayment required. Mail requests require SASE. Mail turnaround time 1 week.

Register in Probate 400 DeWitt, PO Box 587, Portage, WI 53901; 608-742-9636, 742-9637; Fax: 608-742-9601. Hours: 8AM-4:30PM (CST). *Probate.* Note: Probate records are available free online; see Circuit Court.

Crawford County

Circuit Court 220 N Beaumont Rd, Prairie Du Chien, WI 53821; 608-326-0211; Civil phone: 608-326-0208; Criminal phone: 608-326-010; Probate phone: 608-326-0206. Hours: 8AM-4:30PM (CST). *Felony, Misdemeanor, Civil, Eviction, Small Claims.*
Civil Records: Access: Mail, online, in person. Both court and visitors may perform in person searches. Search fee: $5.00 per name. Required to search: name, years to search. Civil cases indexed by defendant, plaintiff. Civil records on computer from 1993, on index cards from 1984, index books from 1900. Historical Society has archives. Civil court records free online at http://wcca.wicourts.gov/index.xsl.
Criminal Records: Access: Mail, online, in person. Both court and visitors may perform in person searches. Search fee: $5.00 per name. Required to search: name, years to search. Criminal records on computer from 1993, on index cards from 1984, index books from 1900. Historical Society has archives. Criminal court records are free online at http://wcca.wicourts.gov/index.xsl.
General Information: Public Access terminal is available. No juvenile, paternity, mental records released. Copy fee: $1.25 per page. Cert fee: $5.00. Payee: Clerk of Court. Personal checks accepted. Prepayment required. Mail requests require SASE. Mail turnaround time 10 working days.

Register in Probate 220 N Beaumont Rd, Prairie Du Chien, WI 53821; 608-326-0206; Fax: 608-326-0288. Hours: 8AM-4:30PM (CST). *Probate.* Note: Probate records are available free online; see Circuit Court. Juvenile records also maintained at this location.

Dane County

Circuit Court 210 Martin Luther King Jr Blvd, Rm GR10, Madison, WI 53703; 608-266-4311; Probate phone: 608-266-4331; Fax: 608-267-8859. Hours: 7:45AM-4:30PM (CST). *Felony, Misdemeanor, Civil, Eviction, Small Claims.*
www.co.dane.wi.us/clrkcort/clrkhome.htm
Civil Records: Access: Fax, mail, online, in person. Both court and visitors may perform in person searches. Search fee: $5.00 per name. Required to search: name, years to search. Civil cases indexed by defendant, plaintiff. Civil records on computer from 1981, on microfiche from 1976, plaintiff index books 1848. Civil court records free online at http://wcca.wicourts.gov/index.xsl.
Criminal Records: Access: Fax, mail, online, in person. Both court and visitors may perform in person searches. Search fee: $5.00 per name. Required to search: name, years to search, DOB. Criminal records on computer from 1983, index back to 1848. Criminal court records are free online at http://wcca.wicourts.gov/index.xsl.
General Information: Public Access terminal is available. No "confidential records" released. Will fax results $.50 for 1st 5 pages, $.23 for each add'l 5 pages or fraction thereof. Copy fee: $1.25 per page. Cert fee: $5.00. Payee: Dane County Clerk of Courts. Personal checks accepted. Prepayment required. Mail requests require SASE. Mail turnaround time 2-3 days.

Register in Probate 210 Martin Luther King Jr Blvd, Rm 305, Madison, WI 53703-3344; 608-266-4331. Hours: 7:45AM-4:30PM (CST). *Probate.* Note: Probate records are available free online; see Circuit Court.

Dodge County

Circuit Court 210 W Center St, Juneau, WI 53039; 920-386-3820; Fax: 920-386-3587. Hours: 8AM-4:30PM (CST). *Felony, Misdemeanor, Civil, Eviction, Small Claims.*

Civil Records: Access: Mail, online, in person. Both court and visitors may perform in person searches. Search fee: $5.00 per name. Required to search: name, years to search. Civil cases indexed by defendant, plaintiff. Civil records on computer from 1993, on index cards from 1986, microfiche from 1972, index books from 1950s. Civil court records free online at http://wcca.wicourts.gov/index.xsl.

Criminal Records: Access: Mail, online, in person. Both court and visitors may perform in person searches. Search fee: $5.00 per name. Required to search: name, years to search, DOB. Criminal records on computer from 1993, on index cards from 1986, microfiche from 1972, index books from 1950s. Criminal court records are free online at http://wcca.wicourts.gov/index.xsl.

General Information: Public Access terminal is available. No juvenile or John Doe records released. Fee to fax results is $1.50 per page. Copy fee: $1.25 per page. Cert fee: $5.00. Payee: Clerk of Courts. Personal checks accepted. Prepayment required. Mail requests require SASE. Mail turnaround time 1-2 days.

Register in Probate 210 W Center St, Juneau, WI 53039-1091; 920-386-3550; Fax: 920-386-3933. Hours: 8AM-4:30PM (CST). *Probate.*

Note: $4.00 search fee; records computerized since 1992. Probate records are available free online; see Circuit Court.

Door County

Circuit Court PO Box 670, Sturgeon Bay, WI 54235; 920-746-2205; Fax: 920-746-2520. Hours: 8AM-4:30PM (CST). *Felony, Misdemeanor, Civil, Eviction, Small Claims.*

Civil Records: Access: Mail, online, in person. Both court and visitors may perform in person searches. Search fee: $5.00 per name. Required to search: name, years to search. Civil cases indexed by defendant, plaintiff. Civil records on computer from 4/93, on index cards from 1984. Civil court records free online at http://wcca.wicourts.gov/index.xsl.

Criminal Records: Access: Mail, online, in person. Both court and visitors may perform in person searches. Search fee: $5.00 per name. Required to search: name, years to search, DOB. Criminal records on computer from 4/93, on index cards from 1984, index books from 1900s. Criminal court records are free online at http://wcca.wicourts.gov/index.xsl.

General Information: Public Access terminal is available. No financial or paternity records released. Fee to fax results is $3.00 per document. Copy fee: $1.25 per page. Cert fee: $5.00. Payee: Clerk of Court. Personal checks accepted. Prepayment required. Mail requests require SASE. Mail turnaround time 2-3 days.

Register in Probate PO Box 670, 421 Nebraska St, Rm C375, Sturgeon Bay, WI 54235-2470; 920-746-2482; Fax: 920-746-2470. Hours: 8AM-4:30PM (CST). *Probate.*

Note: Probate records are available free online; see Circuit Court.

Douglas County

Circuit Court 1313 Belknap, Superior, WI 54880; Civil phone: 715-395-1237; Criminal phone: 715-395-1240; Fax: 715-395-1421. Hours: 8AM-4:30PM (CST). *Felony, Misdemeanor, Civil, Eviction, Small Claims.*

Civil Records: Access: Mail, online, in person. Both the court and visitors may perform in person searches. Search fee: $5.00 per name. Required to search: name, years to search. Civil cases indexed by defendant, plaintiff. Civil records on computer since 1994; prior records on index cards from 1976, index books from 1900s. Civil court records free online at http://wcca.wicourts.gov/index.xsl.

Criminal Records: Access: Mail, online, in person. Both the court and visitors may perform in person searches. Search fee: $5.00 per name. Required to search: name, years to search; also helpful: DOB. Criminal records on computer since 1994; prior records on index cards from 1976, index books from 1900s. Criminal court records are free online at http://wcca.wicourts.gov/index.xsl.

General Information: Public Access terminal is available. No juvenile or paternity records released. Copy fee: $1.25 per page. Cert fee: $5.00. Payee: Clerk of Courts. Only cashiers checks and money orders accepted. Douglas County personal checks accepted. Prepayment required. Mail requests require SASE. Mail turnaround time 1-2 weeks.

Register in Probate 1313 Belknap, Superior, WI 54880; 715-395-1229; Fax: 715-395-1421. Hours: 8AM-4:30PM (CST). *Probate.*

Note: Probate records are available free online; see Circuit Court. This court also takes care of Guardianship, Mental Commitent, Adoptions

Dunn County

Circuit Court Stokke Parkway #1500, Menomonie, WI 54751; 715-232-2611. Hours: 8AM-4:30PM (CST). *Felony, Misdemeanor, Civil, Eviction, Small Claims.*

Civil Records: Access: Mail, online, in person. Both court and visitors may perform in person searches. Search fee: $5.00 per name. Required to search: name, years to search. Civil cases indexed by defendant, plaintiff. Civil records on computer from 1987, index cards from 1977, index books from 1900s, archives from 1970. Civil court records free online at http://wcca.wicourts.gov/index.xsl.

Criminal Records: Access: Mail, online, in person. Both court and visitors may perform in person searches. Search fee: $5.00 per name. Required to search: name, years to search, DOB. Criminal records on computer from 1987, index cards from 1977, index books from 1900s, archives from 1970. Criminal court records are free online at http://wcca.wicourts.gov/index.xsl.

General Information: Public Access terminal is available. No juvenile, family financial, sealed records released. Copy fee: $1.25 per page. Cert fee: $5.00. Payee: Clerk of Court. Personal checks accepted. Prepayment required. Mail requests: SASE not required. Mail turnaround time 2-3 days.

Register in Probate 615 Stokke Parkway #1300, Menomonie, WI 54751; 715-232-6782; Fax: 715-232-6787. Hours: 8AM-4:30PM (CST). *Probate.* Note: Probate records are available free online; see Circuit Court.

Eau Claire County

Circuit Court 721 Oxford Ave, Eau Claire, WI 54703; 715-839-4816; Fax: 715-839-4817. Hours: 8AM-5PM (CST). *Felony, Misdemeanor, Civil, Eviction, Small Claims.*

Civil Records: Access: Mail, online, in person. Both court and visitors may perform in person searches. Search fee: $5.00 per name. Required to search: name, years to search. Civil cases indexed by defendant, plaintiff. Civil records on computer from 7/92, on index cards from 1970, index books from 1968. Civil court records free online at http://wcca.wicourts.gov/index.xsl.

Criminal Records: Access: Mail, online, in person. Both court and visitors may perform in person searches. Search fee: $5.00 per name. Required to search: name, years to search, DOB. Criminal records on computer from 7/92, on index cards from 1970, index books from 1968. Criminal court records are free online at http://wcca.wicourts.gov/index.xsl.

General Information: Public Access terminal is available. No paternity, financial disclosure, expungment or sealed records released. Will fax results. Copy fee: $1.25 per page. Cert fee: $5.00. Payee: Clerk of Court-Eau Claire County. Personal checks accepted. Prepayment required. Mail requests require SASE. Mail turnaround time 1-10 days.

Register in Probate 721 Oxford Ave, Rm 2201, Eau Claire, WI 54703; 715-839-4823. Hours: 8AM-5PM (CST). *Probate.*

Note: Probate records are available free online; see Circuit Court.

Florence County

Circuit Court PO Box 410, Florence, WI 54121; 715-528-3205; Fax: 715-528-5470. Hours: 8:30AM-4PM (CST). *Felony, Misdemeanor, Civil, Eviction, Small Claims.*

Civil Records: Access: Mail, online, in person. Both court and visitors may perform in person searches. Search fee: $5.00 per name. Required to search: name, years to search. Civil cases indexed by defendant, plaintiff. Civil records on computer from 1991; prior records on index books from 1900s. Civil court records free online at http://wcca.wicourts.gov/index.xsl.

Criminal Records: Access: Mail, online, in person. Both court and visitors may perform in person searches. Search fee: $5.00 per name. Required to search: name, years to search. Criminal records on computer from 1991; prior records on index books from 1900s. Criminal court records are free online at http://wcca.wicourts.gov/index.xsl.

General Information: Public Access terminal is available. No juvenile, mental health, adoption or guardianship records released. Copy fee: $1.25 per page. Cert fee: $4.00. Payee: Clerk of Courts. Personal checks accepted. Prepayment required. Mail requests require SASE. Mail turnaround time 2 weeks.

Register in Probate PO Box 410, Florence, WI 54121; 715-528-3205; Fax: 715-528-5470. Hours: 8:30AM-Noon, 1-4PM (CST). *Probate.*

Note: Probate records are available free online; see Circuit Court.

Fond du Lac County

Circuit Court 160 S Macy, Fond du Lac, WI 54936-1355; 920-929-3040; Fax: 920-929-3933. Hours: 8AM-4:30PM (CST). *Felony, Misdemeanor, Civil, Eviction, Small Claims.*

Civil Records: Access: Mail, online, in person. Both court and visitors may perform in person searches. Search fee: $5.00 per name. Required to search: name, years to search. Civil cases indexed by defendant, plaintiff. Civil records on computer from 1990, index cards from 1978, microfiche 1836 to 1978, archives prior to 1900s. Old files destroyed, on microfiche or Historical Society. Civil court records free online at http://wcca.wicourts.gov/index.xsl.

Criminal Records: Access: Mail, online, in person. Both court and visitors may perform in person searches. Search fee: $5.00 per name. Required to search: name, years to search, DOB. Criminal records on computer from 1990, index cards from 1978, microfiche 1836 to 1978, archives prior to 1900s. Old files destroyed, on microfiche or in Historical Society. Criminal court records are free online at http://wcca.wicourts.gov/index.xsl.

General Information: Public Access terminal is available. No juvenile or paternity records released. Fee to fax results is $2.00 per document. Copy fee: $1.25 per page. Cert fee: $5.00. Payee: Clerk of Circuit Court. Personal checks accepted. Prepayment required. Mail requests require SASE. Mail turnaround time 1-2 days.

Register in Probate PO Box 1576, Fond du Lac, WI 54936-1576; 920-929-3084; Fax: 920-929-7058. Hours: 8AM-4:30PM (CST). *Probate.*

Note: Probate records are available free online; see Circuit Court.

Forest County

Circuit Court 200 E Madison St, Crandon, WI 54520; 715-478-3323; Fax: 715-478-3211. Hours: 8:30AM-4:30PM (CST). *Felony, Misdemeanor, Civil, Eviction, Small Claims.*

Civil Records: Access: Mail, online, in person. Both court and visitors may perform in person searches. Search fee: $5.00 per name. Required to search: name, years to search. Civil cases indexed by defendant, plaintiff. Civil records on computer from 1994, on index cards from 1979, index books from 1920s. Civil court records free online at http://wcca.wicourts.gov/index.xsl.

Criminal Records: Access: Mail, online, in person. Both court and visitors may perform in person searches. Search fee: $5.00 per name. Required to search: name, years to search, DOB. Criminal records on computer from 1994, on index cards from 1979, index books from 1920s. Criminal court records are free online at http://wcca.wicourts.gov/index.xsl.

General Information: Public Access terminal is available. No juvenile, paternity records released. Fee to fax results is $1.25 per page. Copy fee: $1.25 per page. Cert fee: $5.00. Payee: Clerk of Court. Personal checks accepted. Prepayment required. Mail requests require SASE. Mail turnaround time 1-2 days.

Register in Probate 200 E Madison St, Crandon, WI 54520; 715-478-2418; Fax: 715-478-2430. Hours: 8:30AM-12:00,1-4:30PM (CST). *Probate.*

Note: Probate records are available free online; see Circuit Court.

Grant County

Circuit Court PO Box 110, Lancaster, WI 53813; 608-723-2752; Fax: 608-723-7370. Hours: 8AM-4:30PM (CST). *Felony, Misdemeanor, Civil, Eviction, Small Claims.*

Civil Records: Access: Phone, mail, fax, online, in person. Both court and visitors may perform in person searches. No search fee. Required to search: name, years to search. Civil cases indexed by defendant, plaintiff. Civil records on computer from 10/93, on index books from 1900s. Civil court records free online at http://wcca.wicourts.gov/index.xsl.

Criminal Records: Access: Phone, mail, fax, online, in person. Both court and visitors may perform in person searches. No search fee. Required to search: name, years to search. Criminal records on computer from 10/93, on index books from 1900s. Criminal court records are free online at http://wcca.wicourts.gov/index.xsl.

General Information: Public Access terminal is available. No juvenile, paternity records released. Will fax results to local or toll free line. Copy fee: $1.25 per page. Cert fee: $5.00 plus $1.25 per page. Payee: Clerk of Court. Personal checks accepted. Prepayment required. Mail requests require SASE. Mail turnaround time 2 weeks.

Register in Probate 130 W Maple St, Rm A360, Lancaster, WI 53813; 608-723-2697; Fax: 608-723-7370. Hours: 8AM-4:30PM (CST). *Probate.*

Note: $4.00 search fee, records computerized since 1993. Probate records are available free online; see Circuit Court.

Green County

Circuit Court 1016 16th Ave, Monroe, WI 53566; 608-328-9433; Fax: 608-328-9459. Hours: 8AM-4:30PM (CST). *Felony, Misdemeanor, Civil, Eviction, Small Claims.*

www.co.green.wi.gov

Civil Records: Access: Mail, online, in person. Both court and visitors may perform in person searches. Search fee: $5.00 per name. Required to search: name, years to search; also helpful: address. Civil cases indexed by defendant, plaintiff. Civil records on index cards from 1984, index books from 1900s; computerized back to 1994. Civil court records free online at http://wcca.wicourts.gov/index.xsl.

Criminal Records: Access: Mail, online, in person. Both court and visitors may perform in person searches. Search fee: $5.00 per name. Required to search: name, years to search; also helpful: DOB. Criminal records on index cards from 1984, index books from 1900s; computerized back to 1994. Criminal court records are free online at http://wcca.wicourts.gov/index.xsl.

General Information: Public Access terminal is available. No juvenile, paternity or sealed records released. Copy fee: $1.25 per page. Cert fee: $5.00. Payee: Clerk of Court. Personal checks accepted. Prepayment required. Mail requests require SASE. Mail turnaround time 1-2 days.

Register in Probate 1016 16th Ave, Monroe, WI 53566; 608-328-9567; Fax: 608-328-9459. Hours: 8AM-12, 1PM-4:30PM (CST). *Probate.*

Note: Probate records are available free online; see Circuit Court.

Green Lake County

Circuit Court 492 Hill St, PO Box 3188, Green Lake, WI 54941; 920-294-4142; Fax: 920-294-4150. Hours: 8AM-4:30PM (CST). *Felony, Misdemeanor, Civil, Eviction, Small Claims.*

Civil Records: Access: Mail, online, in person. Both court and visitors may perform in person searches. Search fee: $5.00 per name. Required to search: name, years to search. Civil cases indexed by defendant, plaintiff. Civil records on computer from 4/93, on index cards since 1900s. Civil court records free online at http://wcca.wicourts.gov/index.xsl.

Criminal Records: Access: Mail, online, in person. Both court and visitors may perform in person searches. Search fee: $5.00 per name. Required to search: name, years to search. Criminal records on computer from 4/93, on index cards since 1900s. Criminal court records are free online at http://wcca.wicourts.gov/index.xsl.

General Information: Public Access terminal is available. No paternity or juvenile ordinance records released. Copy fee: $1.25 per page. Cert fee: $5.00. Payee: Clerk of Circuit Clerk. Personal checks accepted. Prepayment required. Mail requests require SASE. Mail turnaround time 1-3 days.

Register in Probate 492 Hill St, PO Box 3188, Green Lake, WI 54941; 920-294-4044. Hours: 8AM-4:30PM (CST). *Probate.*

www.co.green-lake.wi.us

Note: Probate records are available free online; see Circuit Court.

Iowa County

Circuit Court 222 N Iowa St, Dodgeville, WI 53533; 608-935-0395; Probate phone: 608-935-0347; Fax: 608-935-0386. Hours: 8:30AM-4:30PM (CST). *Felony, Misdemeanor, Civil, Eviction, Small Claims.*

Civil Records: Access: Mail, online, in person. Both court and visitors may perform in person searches. Search fee: $5.00 per name. Required to search: name, years to search. Civil cases indexed by defendant, plaintiff. Civil records on computer from 1992, index cards from 1987, archives from 1917, index books from 1829. Civil court records free online at http://wcca.wicourts.gov/index.xsl.

Criminal Records: Access: Mail, online, in person. Both court and visitors may perform in person searches. Search fee: $5.00 per name. Required to search: name, years to search, DOB. Criminal records on computer from 1992, index cards from 1987, archives from 1917, index books from 1829. Criminal court records are free online at http://wcca.wicourts.gov/index.xsl.

General Information: Public Access terminal is available. No adoption, paternity or mental records released. Fee to fax results is $1.25 per page Plus $5.00 fee. Copy fee: $1.25 per page. Cert fee: $5.00. Payee: Clerk of Court. Personal checks accepted. Prepayment required. Mail requests require SASE. Mail turnaround time same day.

Register in Probate 222 N Iowa St, Dodgeville, WI 53533; 608-935-0347; Fax: 608-935-0386. Hours: 8:30AM-Noon, 12:30-4:30PM (CST). *Probate.*

Note: Probate records are available free online; see Circuit Court.

Iron County

Circuit Court 300 Taconite St, #207, Hurley, WI 54534; 715-561-4084; Fax: 715-561-4054. Hours: 8AM-4PM (CST). *Felony, Misdemeanor, Civil, Eviction, Small Claims.*

Civil Records: Access: Phone, mail, online, in person. Both court and visitors may perform in person searches. Search fee: $5.00 per name. Required to search: name, years to search. Civil cases indexed by defendant, plaintiff. Civil records on index cards from 1989, index books from 1920. Civil court records free online at http://wcca.wicourts.gov/index.xsl. Phone access for title companies only.

Criminal Records: Access: Mail, online, in person. Both court and visitors may perform in person searches. Search fee: $5.00 per name. Required to search: name, years to search, DOB. Criminal records on index cards from 1989, index books from 1920. Criminal court records are free online at http://wcca.wicourts.gov/index.xsl.

General Information: Public Access terminal is available. No juvenile or paternity records released. Will fax results to local or toll free line. Copy fee: $1.25 per page. Cert fee: $5.00. Payee: Clerk of Court. Personal checks accepted. Prepayment required. Mail requests require SASE. Mail turnaround time 2-3 days.

Register in Probate 300 Taconite St, #207, Hurley, WI 54534; 715-561-3434; Fax: 715-561-4054. Hours: 8AM-4PM (CST). *Probate.*

Note: Probate records are available free online; see Circuit Court.

Jackson County

Circuit Court 307 Main St, Black River Falls, WI 54615; 715-284-0208; Probate phone: 715-284-0213; Fax: 715-284-0270. Hours: 8AM-4:30PM (CST). *Felony, Misdemeanor, Civil, Eviction, Small Claims.*

www.co.jackson.wi.us

Civil Records: Access: Mail, online, in person. Both court and visitors may perform in person searches. Search fee: $5.00 per name. Required to search: name, years to search. Civil cases indexed by defendant, plaintiff. Civil records on computer from 6/92, on index cards from 1979, index books to 1980, files and indexes prior to 1980 destroyed. Civil court records free online at http://wcca.wicourts.gov/index.xsl.

Criminal Records: Access: Mail, online, in person. Both court and visitors may perform in person searches. Search fee: $5.00 per name. Required to search: name, years to search, DOB. Criminal records on computer from 6/92. Felonies 1879 to 1927 at State Historical Society. Criminal court records are free online at http://wcca.wicourts.gov/index.xsl.

General Information: Public Access terminal is available. No juvenile or pre-judgment paternity records released. Will fax results $3.00; must be pre-paid. Copy fee: $1.25 per page. Cert fee: $5.00. Payee: Clerk of Court. Personal checks accepted. I. Prepayment required. Prepayment required if over $5.00. Mail requests require SASE. Mail turnaround time 1-4 days.

Register in Probate 307 Main St, Black River Falls, WI 54615; 715-284-0213; Fax: 715-284-0277. Hours: 8AM-4:30PM (CST). *Probate.*
Note: Probate records are available free online; see Circuit Court.

Jefferson County

Circuit Court 320 S Main St, Jefferson, WI 53549; 920-674-7150; Fax: 920-674-7425. Hours: 8AM-4:30PM (CST). *Felony, Misdemeanor, Civil, Eviction, Small Claims.*
Civil Records: Access: Mail, online, in person. Both court and visitors may perform in person searches. Search fee: $5.00 per name. Required to search: name, years to search. Civil cases indexed by defendant, plaintiff. Civil records on computer from 1992, on index cards from 1979, index books from late 1800s. Civil court records free online at http://wcca.wicourts.gov/index.xsl.
Criminal Records: Access: Mail, online, in person. Both court and visitors may perform in person searches. Search fee: $5.00 per name. Required to search: name, years to search, DOB. Criminal records on computer from 1992, on index cards from 1979, index books from late 1800s. Criminal court records are free online at http://wcca.wicourts.gov/index.xsl.
General Information: Public Access terminal is available. No juvenile or mental health records released. Copy fee: $1.25 per page. Cert fee: $5.00. Payee: Clerk of Courts. Personal checks accepted. Prepayment required. Mail requests require SASE. Mail turnaround time 2-3 days.

Register in Probate 320 S Main St, Jefferson, WI 53549; 920-674-7245; Fax: 920-675-0134. Hours: 8AM-4:30PM (CST). *Probate.*
Note: Probate records are available free online; see Circuit Court.

Juneau County

Circuit Court 200 Oak St, Juneau County Justice Center, Mauston, WI 53948; 608-847-9356; Fax: 608-847-9360. Hours: 8AM-4:30PM (CST). *Felony, Misdemeanor, Civil, Eviction, Small Claims.*
www.wcca.wicourts.gov
Civil Records: Access: Mail, online, in person. Both court and visitors may perform in person searches. Search fee: $5.00 per name. Fee is per case. Required to search: name, years to search, DOB. Civil cases indexed by defendant, plaintiff. Civil records on computer from 1988, index cards from 1977, index books from 1900, microfiche from 1856-1900. Civil

court records free online at http://wcca.wicourts.gov/index.xsl.
Criminal Records: Access: Mail, online, fax, in person. Both court and visitors may perform in person searches. Search fee: $5.00 per name. Required to search: name, years to search, DOB. Criminal records on computer from 1988, index cards from 1977, index books from 1900, microfiche from 1856-1900. Criminal court records are free online at http://wcca.wicourts.gov/index.xsl.
General Information: Public Access terminal is available. No juvenile, confidential family or paternity records released. Copy fee: $1.25 per page. Cert fee: $5.00. Payee: Juneau County Clerk of Court. Personal checks accepted. Prepayment required. Mail requests require SASE. Mail turnaround time 1 week.

Register in Probate 200 Oak St. Rm. 2300, Mauston, WI 53948; 608-847-9346; Fax: 608-847-9349. Hours: 8AM-4:30PM (CST). *Probate.*
Note: Probate records are available free online; see Circuit Court.

Kenosha County

Circuit Court 912 56th St, Kenosha, WI 53140; 262-653-2664; Fax: 262-653-2435. Hours: 8AM-5PM (CST). *Felony, Misdemeanor, Civil, Eviction, Small Claims.*
Civil Records: Access: Mail, online, in person. Both court and visitors may perform in person searches. Search fee: $5.00 per name. Required to search: name, years to search. Civil cases indexed by defendant, plaintiff. Civil records on computer from 1989, index cards from 1960, microfiche from 1850. Civil court records free online at http://wcca.wicourts.gov/index.xsl.
Criminal Records: Access: Mail, online, in person, fax. Both court and visitors may perform in person searches. Search fee: $5.00 per name. Required to search: name, years to search; also helpful: DOB, SSN. Criminal records on computer from 1989, index cards from 1960, microfiche from 1850. Criminal court records are free online at http://wcca.wicourts.gov/index.xsl.
General Information: Public Access terminal is available. No juvenile or paternity records released. Will fax results to local or toll free line. Copy fee: $1.25 per page. Cert fee: $5.00. Payee: Clerk of Court. Personal checks accepted. Prepayment required. Mail requests require SASE. Mail turnaround time 1-2 days.

Register in Probate Courthouse Rm 304, 912 56th St, Kenosha, WI 53140; 262-653-2675; Fax: 262-653-2673. Hours: 8AM-5PM (CST). *Probate.*
Note: $4.00 per search, records indexed on computer (1992) and cards. Probate records are available free online; see Circuit Court.

Kewaunee County

Circuit Court 613 Dodge St, Kewaunee, WI 54216; 920-388-7144; Fax: 920-388-3139. Hours: 8AM-4:30PM (CST). *Felony, Misdemeanor, Civil, Eviction, Small Claims.*
Civil Records: Access: Phone, mail, online, in person. Both court and visitors may perform in person searches. Search fee: $5.00 per name. Required to search: name, years to search. Civil cases indexed by defendant, plaintiff. Computerized records from 1993, civil records on index cards from 1950, index books from 1852. Civil court records free online at http://wcca.wicourts.gov/index.xsl.
Criminal Records: Access: Phone, mail, online, in person. Both court and visitors may perform in person searches. Search fee: $5.00 per name. Required to search: name, years to search, DOB. Computerized records from 1993, criminal records on index cards

from 1950, index books from 1852. Criminal court records are free online at http://wcca.wicourts.gov/index.xsl.
General Information: Public Access terminal is available. (Public terminal for civil in person searches only.) No paternity records released. Copy fee: $1.25 per page. Cert fee: $5.00. Payee: Clerk of Circuit Court. Personal checks accepted. Prepayment required. Mail requests require SASE. Mail turnaround time 1-2 days.

Register in Probate 613 Dodge St, Kewaunee, WI 54216; 920-388-7143; Fax: 920-388-3139. Hours: 8AM-4:30PM (CST). *Probate.*
Note: Probate records are available free online; see Circuit Court.

La Crosse County

Circuit Court 333 Vine St, La Crosse, WI 54601; 608-785-9590/9573; Fax: 608-789-7821. Hours: 8:30AM-5PM (CST). *Felony, Misdemeanor, Civil, Eviction, Small Claims.*
Civil Records: Access: Phone, mail, online, in person. Both court and visitors may perform in person searches. Search fee: $5.00 per name. Required to search: name, years to search. Civil cases indexed by defendant, plaintiff. Civil records on computer from 1993, on index cards from 1983, index books from 1917. Civil court records free online at http://wcca.wicourts.gov/index.xsl.
Criminal Records: Access: Phone, mail, online, in person. Both court and visitors may perform in person searches. Search fee: $5.00 per name. Required to search: name, years to search; also helpful: DOB, SSN. Criminal records on computer from 1993, on index cards from 1983, index books from 1917. Criminal court records are free online at http://wcca.wicourts.gov/index.xsl.
General Information: Public Access terminal is available. No juvenile, paternity or finances in family records released. Fee to fax results is $1.25 per page. Copy fee: $1.25 per page. Cert fee: $5.00. Payee: Clerk of Courts. Personal checks accepted. Prepayment required. Mail requests require SASE. Mail turnaround time 1-2 days.

Register in Probate 333 Vine St, Rm 1201, La Crosse, WI 54601; 608-785-9882. Hours: 8:30AM-5PM (CST). *Probate.*
Note: Probate records are available free online; see Circuit Court.

Lafayette County

Circuit Court 626 Main St, Darlington, WI 53530; 608-776-4832; Probate phone: 608-776-4811. Hours: 8AM-4:30PM (CST). *Felony, Misdemeanor, Civil, Eviction, Small Claims.*
Civil Records: Access: Mail, online, in person. Both court and visitors may perform in person searches. Search fee: $5.00 per name. Required to search: name, years to search. Civil cases indexed by defendant. Civil records on index cards from 1973, index books from 1900; computerized back to 1993. Civil court records free online at http://wcca.wicourts.gov/index.xsl.
Criminal Records: Access: Mail, online, in person. Both court and visitors may perform in person searches. Search fee: $5.00 per name. Required to search: name, years to search. Criminal records on index cards from 1973, index books from 1900; computerized back to 1993. Criminal court records are free online at http://wcca.wicourts.gov/index.xsl.
General Information: Public Access terminal is available. No juvenile records released. Copy fee: $1.25 per page. Cert fee: $5.00. Payee: Clerk of Circuit Court. Personal checks accepted. Prepayment

required. Mail requests require SASE. Mail turnaround time 2-3 days.

Register in Probate 626 Main St, Rm 302, Darlington, WI 53530; 608-776-4811. Hours: 8AM-4:30PM (CST). *Probate.*

Note: Probate records are available free online; see Circuit Court.

Langlade County

Circuit Court 800 Clermont St, Antigo, WI 54409; 715-627-6215. Hours: 8:30AM-4:30PM (CST). *Felony, Misdemeanor, Civil, Eviction, Small Claims.*

Civil Records: Access: Mail, online, in person. Both court and visitors may perform in person searches. Search fee: $5.00 per name. Required to search: name, years to search. Civil cases indexed by defendant, plaintiff. Civil records on index books from 1905, computerized since 1993. Civil court records free online at http://wcca.wicourts.gov/index.xsl.

Criminal Records: Access: Mail, online, in person. Both court and visitors may perform in person searches. Search fee: $5.00 per name. Required to search: name, years to search. Criminal records on index books from 1905, computerized since 1993. Criminal court records are free online at http://wcca.wicourts.gov/index.xsl.

General Information: Public Access terminal is available. No confidential records released. Copy fee: $1.25 per page. Cert fee: $5.00. Payee: Clerk of Court. Personal checks accepted. Prepayment required. Mail requests require SASE. Mail turnaround time 2-3 days.

Register in Probate 800 Clermont St, Antigo, WI 54409; 715-627-6213; Fax: 715-627-6329. Hours: 8:30AM-4:30PM (CST). *Probate.*

Note: There is a $4.00 search fee. Probate records are available free online; see Circuit Court.

Lincoln County

Circuit Court 1110 E Main St, Merrill, WI 54452; 715-536-0319; Fax: 715-536-0361. Hours: 8AM-4:30PM (CST). *Felony, Misdemeanor, Civil, Eviction, Small Claims.*

Civil Records: Access: Mail, online, in person. Both court and visitors may perform in person searches. Search fee: $5.00 per name. Required to search: name, years to search. Civil cases indexed by defendant. Civil records on computer from 1990, index cards from 1982, index books from 1900s. Civil court records free online at http://wcca.wicourts.gov/index.xsl.

Criminal Records: Access: Mail, online, in person. Both court and visitors may perform in person searches. Search fee: $5.00 per name. Required to search: name, years to search; also helpful: DOB, SSN. Criminal records on computer from 1990, index cards from 1982, index books from 1900s. Criminal court records are free online at http://wcca.wicourts.gov/index.xsl.

General Information: Public Access terminal is available. No paternity or sealed records released. Will fax results for $1.00 per fax. Cannot fax Certified copies. Copy fee: $1.25 per page. Cert fee: $5.00. Payee: Clerk of Court. Local personal checks accepted. Prepayment required. Mail requests require SASE. Mail turnaround time 1-2 days.

Register in Probate 1110 E Main St, Merrill, WI 54452; 715-536-0342; 536-0378; Fax: 715-539-2762. Hours: 8:15AM-Noon, 1-4:30PM (CST). *Probate.*

Note: Probate records are available free online; see Circuit Court.

Manitowoc County

Circuit Court PO Box 2000, Manitowoc, WI 54221-2000; 920-683-4030. Hours: 8:30AM-5PM M; 8:30AM-4:30PM T-F (CST). *Felony, Misdemeanor, Civil, Eviction, Small Claims.*

Civil Records: Access: Phone, mail, online, in person. Both court and visitors may perform in person searches. Search fee: $5.00 per name. Required to search: name, years to search. Civil cases indexed by defendant, plaintiff. Civil records on computer from 1993, on index cards from 1962, index books from 1906, Historical Society has prior records. Civil court records free online at http://wcca.wicourts.gov/index.xsl. Prior written agreement with court required for phone access.

Criminal Records: Access: Phone, mail, online, in person. Both court and visitors may perform in person searches. Search fee: $5.00 per name. Required to search: name, years to search, DOB. Criminal records on computer from 1993, on index cards from 1962, index books from 1906, Historical Society has prior records. Criminal court records are free online at http://wcca.wicourts.gov/index.xsl. Prior written agreement with court required for phone access.

General Information: Public Access terminal is available. No confidential records released. Will fax results for $3.00 plus $1.25 per page, either prepaid or within 48 hours. Copy fee: $1.25 per page. Cert fee: $5.00. Payee: Clerk of Circuit Court. Personal checks accepted. Prepayment required. Mail requests: SASE requested. Turnaround time 5-7 days.

Register in Probate 1010 S 8th St Rm 116, Manitowoc, WI 54220; 920-683-4016; Fax: 920-683-5182. Hours: 8:30AM-4:30PM T-F; 8:30AM-5PM M (CST). *Probate.*

Note: Probate records are available free online; see Circuit Court.

Marathon County

Circuit Court 500 Forest St, Wausau, WI 54403; 715-261-1300; Civil phone: 715-261-1300; Fax: 715-261-1319 Civ; 261-1280 Crim. Hours: 8AM-5PM (Summer hours 8AM-4:30PM Memorial-Labor Day) (CST). *Felony, Misdemeanor, Civil, Eviction, Small Claims.*

Note: Small claims phone is 261-1310; Traffic, 261-1270. Fax for criminal is 715-261-1279.

Civil Records: Access: Mail, online, in person. Both the court and visitors may perform in person searches. Search fee: $5.00 per name. Required to search: name, years to search. Civil cases indexed by defendant, plaintiff. Civil records on computer from 1992, on index cards from 1979. Civil court records free online at http://wcca.wicourts.gov/index.xsl. All requests must be in writing, using their form if possible.

Criminal Records: Access: Mail, online, in person. Both the court and visitors may perform in person searches. Search fee: $5.00 per name. Required to search: name, years to search, DOB. Criminal records on computer from 1992, on index cards from 1979, index books from 1900s. Criminal court records are free online at http://wcca.wicourts.gov/index.xsl. All requests must be in writing, using their form if possible.

General Information: Public Access terminal is available. No mental health or juvenile records released. Will fax results to local or toll free line. Copy fee: $1.25 per page. Cert fee: $5.00. Payee: Clerk of Court. Personal checks accepted. Prepayment required. Mail requests: SASE helpful. Turnaround time 1-3 days.

Register in Probate 500 Forest St, Wausau, WI 54403; 715-261-1260; Fax: 715-261-1269. Hours: 8AM-5PM (CST). *Probate.*

Note: Probate records are available free online; see Circuit Court.

Marinette County

Circuit Court 1926 Hall Ave, Marinette, WI 54143-1717; 715-732-7450; Probate phone: 715-732-7475. Hours: 8:30AM-4:30PM (CST). *Felony, Misdemeanor, Civil, Eviction, Small Claims.*

Civil Records: Access: Mail, online, in person. Both court and visitors may perform in person searches. Search fee: $5.00 per name. Required to search: name, years to search. Civil cases indexed by defendant, plaintiff. Civil records on computer from 1989, index cards from 1980, index books from 1906, prior records at Historical Society. Civil court records 1994 to present are free online at http://wcca.wicourts.gov/index.xsl.

Criminal Records: Access: Mail, online, in person. Both court and visitors may perform in person searches. Search fee: $5.00 per name. Required to search: name, years to search, DOB. Criminal records on computer from 1989, index cards from 1980, index books from 1906, prior records at Historical Society. Criminal court records are free online at http://wcca.wicourts.gov/index.xsl.

General Information: Public Access terminal is available. No paternity records released. Will fax results to local or toll free line. Copy fee: $1.25 per page. Cert fee: $5.00. Payee: Clerk of Courts. Personal checks accepted. Prepayment required. Mail requests require SASE. Mail turnaround time 2-3 days.

Register in Probate 1926 Hall Ave, Marinette, WI 54143-1717; 715-732-7475; Fax: 715-732-7561. Hours: 8:30AM-4:30PM (CST). *Probate.*

Note: Probate records are available free online; see Circuit Court.

Marquette County

Circuit Court PO Box 187, Montello, WI 53949; 608-297-9102; Fax: 608-297-9188. Hours: 8AM-Noon, 12:30-4:30PM (CST). *Felony, Misdemeanor, Civil, Eviction, Small Claims.*

Civil Records: Access: Phone, mail, online, in person. Both court and visitors may perform in person searches. Search fee: $5.00 per name. Required to search: name, years to search. Civil cases indexed by defendant, plaintiff. Civil records on index books from 1983, prior records at Historical Society; computerized back to 1996. Civil court records free online at http://wcca.wicourts.gov/index.xsl.

Criminal Records: Access: Mail, online, in person. Both court and visitors may perform in person searches. Search fee: $5.00 per name. Required to search: name, years to search, DOB, full name. Criminal records on index books from 1900s, prior records at Historical Society; computerized back to 1996. Criminal court records are free online at http://wcca.wicourts.gov/index.xsl.

General Information: Public Access terminal is available. No adoption, juvenile, paternity, guardianship, mental or termination of parental right records released. Fee to fax results is $2.00 per page. Copy fee: $1.25 per page. Cert fee: $5.00. Payee: Clerk of Circuit Court. Personal checks accepted. Prepayment required. Mail requests: SASE requested. Turnaround time 7-10 days.

Register in Probate 77 W Park St, PO Box 749, Montello, WI 53949; 608-297-9105; Fax: 608-297-9188. Hours: 8AM-4:30PM (CST). *Probate.*

Note: Probate records are available free online; see Circuit Court profile.

Menominee County

Circuit Court PO Box 279, Keshena, WI 54135; 715-799-3313; Fax: 715-799-1322. Hours: 8AM-4:30PM (CST). *Felony, Misdemeanor, Civil, Eviction, Small Claims.*
Civil Records: Access: Mail, online, in person. Both court and visitors may perform in person searches. Search fee: $5.00 per name. Required to search: name, years to search. Civil cases indexed by defendant, plaintiff. Civil records are indexed by cards, kept in files since 1979, computerized since 1992. Ollder records are at the Historical Society. Civil court records free online at http://wcca.wicourts.gov/index.xsl.
Criminal Records: Access: Mail, online, in person, fax. Both court and visitors may perform in person searches. Search fee: $5.00 per name. Required to search: name, years to search, DOB. Criminal records are indexed by cards, kept in files since 1979, computerized since 1992. Older records are at the Historical Society. Criminal court records are free online at http://wcca.wicourts.gov/index.xsl.
General Information: Public Access terminal is available. No juvenile, mental, adoption. Will fax results to local or toll free line. Copy fee: $1.25 per page. Cert fee: $5.00. Payee: Clerk of Court. Personal checks accepted. Mail requests: SASE helpful. Turnaround time 3-4 days.

Register in Probate 311 N Main St, Rm 203, Shawano, WI 54166; 715-526-8631; Fax: 715-526-8622. Hours: 8AM-4:30PM (CST). *Probate.*
Note: Tribal probate records only in Keshena (Menominee Tribal Court); Non-tribal records are in Shawano County. Probate records are available free online; see Circuit Court.

Milwaukee County

Circuit Court - Civil 901 N. 9th St, Rm G-9, Milwaukee, WI 53233; 414-278-4128; Fax: 414-223-1256. Hours: 8AM-5PM (CST). *Civil, Eviction, Small Claims.*
http://204.194.250.11
Civil Records: Access: Mail, online, in person. Both court and visitors may perform in person searches. Search fee: $5.00 per name. Required to search: name, years to search; also helpful-DOB or SSN. Civil cases indexed by defendant, plaintiff. Civil records on computer from 1985, on microfiche from 1949, prior with County Historical Society. Civil court records free online at http://wcca.wicourts.gov/index.xsl.
General Information: Public Access terminal is available. (Terminal in Rm 114 of Safety Bldg.) No paternity records released. Copy fee: $1.25 per page. Cert fee: $5.00. Payee: Milwaukee County Clerk of Circuit Court. Personal checks accepted. Prepayment required. Mail requests require SASE. Mail turnaround time 1-2 weeks.

Circuit Court - Criminal Division 821 W State St, Milwaukee, WI 53233; 414-278-4599; Fax: 414-223-1262. Hours: 8AM-5PM (CST). *Felony, Misdemeanor.*
http://204.194.250.11
Criminal Records: Access: Fax, mail, online, in person. Both court and visitors may perform in person searches. Search fee: $5.00 per name. Required to search: name, years to search, DOB. Criminal records on computer from 10/86, index books and cards prior. Criminal court records are free online at http://wcca.wicourts.gov/index.xsl. Also, criminal case records on Milwaukee Municipal Court Case Information System database are free at www.court.ci.mil.wi.us/home.asp. Search by Case Number, by Citation Number, or by Name.

General Information: Public Access terminal is available. No sealed records released. No fee to fax results, but search fees still apply. Copy fee: $1.25 per page. Cert fee: $5.00. Payee: Clerk of Circuit Court. Personal checks accepted. Prepayment required. Mail requests require SASE. Mail turnaround time 4 days.

Register in Probate 901 N 9th St Rm 207, Milwaukee, WI 53233; 414-278-4444; Fax: 414-223-1814. Hours: 8AM-4:30PM (CST). *Probate.*
Note: Civil court records available free online at http://wcca.wicourts.gov/index.xsl.

Monroe County

Circuit Court 112 S Court St #203, Sparta, WI 54656-1764; 608-269-8745. Hours: 8AM-4:30PM (CST). *Felony, Misdemeanor, Civil, Eviction, Small Claims.*
Civil Records: Access: Fax, mail, online, in person. Both court and visitors may perform in person searches. Search fee: $5.00 per name. Required to search: name, years to search. Civil cases indexed by defendant, plaintiff. Civil records on computer and cards. Civil court records free online at http://wcca.wicourts.gov/index.xsl.
Criminal Records: Access: Fax, mail, online, in person. Both court and visitors may perform in person searches. Search fee: $5.00 per name. Required to search: name, years to search. Criminal records on computer and cards. Criminal court records are free online at http://wcca.wicourts.gov/index.xsl.
General Information: Public Access terminal is available. No paternity, medical or financial records released. Will fax results $1.25 per page; no charge to toll free line. Copy fee: $1.25 per page. Cert fee: $5.00. Payee: Clerk of Court. Local checks accepted. Prepayment required. Mail requests require SASE. Mail turnaround time 1 week.

Register in Probate 112 S Court, Rm 301, Sparta, WI 54656-1765; 608-269-8701; Fax: 608-269-8950. Hours: 8AM-Noon (CST). *Probate.*
Note: Probate records are available free online; see Circuit Court.

Oconto County

Circuit Court 301 Washington St, Oconto, WI 54153; 920-834-6855; Fax: 920-834-6867. Hours: 8AM-4PM (CST). *Felony, Misdemeanor, Civil, Small Claims.*
Civil Records: Access: Mail, online, in person. Both court and visitors may perform in person searches. Search fee: $5.00 per name. Required to search: name, years to search. Civil cases indexed by defendant, plaintiff. Civil records on computer since 1994; prior records on index books from 1930s, Historical Society has earlier records. Civil court records free online at http://wcca.wicourts.gov/index.xsl.
Criminal Records: Access: Mail, online, in person. Both court and visitors may perform in person searches. Search fee: $5.00 per name. Required to search: name, years to search, DOB. Criminal records on computer since 1994; prior records on index books from 1930s; Historical Society has earlier records. Criminal court records are free online at http://wcca.wicourts.gov/index.xsl.
General Information: Public Access terminal is available. No juvenile or paternity records released. Copy fee: $1.25 per page. Cert fee: $5.00. Payee: Oconto County Clerk of Court. Personal checks accepted. Prepayment required. Mail requests require SASE. Mail turnaround time 1-2 days.

Register in Probate 301 Washington St, Oconto, WI 54153; 920-834-6839; Fax: 920-834-6867. Hours: 8AM-4PM (CST). *Probate.*
Note: Probate records are available free online; see Circuit Court.

Oneida County

Circuit Court PO Box 400, Rhinelander, WI 54501; 715-369-6120. Hours: 8AM-4:30PM (CST). *Felony, Misdemeanor, Civil, Eviction, Small Claims.*
Civil Records: Access: Mail, online, in person. Both court and visitors may perform in person searches. Search fee: $5.00 per name. Required to search: name, years to search. Civil cases indexed by defendant, plaintiff. Civil records on computer from 1992, index cards from 1980, index books from 1900s. Civil court records free online at http://wcca.wicourts.gov/index.xsl.
Criminal Records: Access: Mail, online, in person. Both court and visitors may perform in person searches. Search fee: $5.00 per name. Required to search: name, years to search, DOB. Criminal records on computer from 1992, index cards from 1980, index books from 1900s. Criminal court records are free online at http://wcca.wicourts.gov/index.xsl.
General Information: Public Access terminal is available. No paternity records released. Will fax results for $1.25 per page. Copy fee: $1.25 per page. Cert fee: $5.00. Payee: Clerk of Court. Personal checks accepted. Prepayment required. Mail requests: SASE not required. Mail turnaround time 1 week.

Register in Probate PO Box 400, Rhinelander, WI 54501; 715-369-6159. Hours: 8AM-12, 1-4:30PM (CST). *Probate.*
http://wcca.wicourts.gov
Note: Probate records are available free online; see Circuit Court.

Outagamie County

Circuit Court 320 S Walnut St, Appleton, WI 54911; 920-832-5130; Civil phone: 920-832-5136; Fax: 920-832-5115. Hours: 8:00AM-4:30PM (CST). *Felony, Misdemeanor, Civil, Eviction, Small Claims.*
Note: Small claims and eviction records at 920-832-5135.

Civil Records: Access: In person, online mail. Visitors must perform in person searches for themselves. Search fee: $5.00. Required to search: name, years to search. Civil cases indexed by defendant, plaintiff. Civil records on computer from 10/87, index cards from 1983, index books from 1901, some records on microfiche. Civil court records free online at http://wcca.wicourts.gov/index.xsl.
Criminal Records: Access: Mail, in person. Both court and visitors may perform in person searches. Search fee: $5.00 per name. Required to search: name, years to search, DOB. Criminal records on computer from 10/87, index cards from 1983, index books from 1901, some records on microfiche.
General Information: Public Access terminal is available. No adoption or juvenile records released. Will fax results for $1.25 per page. Copy fee: $1.25 per page. Cert fee: $5.00. Payee: Clerk of Court. Personal checks accepted. Prepayment required. Mail requests require SASE. Mail turnaround time 2-3 days.

Register in Probate 320 S Walnut St, Appleton, WI 54911; 920-832-5601; Fax: 920-832-5115. Hours: 8:30AM-Noon, 1-5PM (CST). *Probate.*
Note: Probate records are available free online; see Circuit Court.

Ozaukee County

Circuit Court 1201 S Spring St, Port Washington, WI 53074; 262-284-8409; Fax: 262-284-8491. Hours: 8:30AM-5PM (CST). *Felony, Misdemeanor, Civil, Eviction, Small Claims.*
www.co.ozaukee.wi.us/ClerkCourts/default.htm
Civil Records: Access: Mail, online, in person. Both court and visitors may perform in person searches. Search fee: $5.00 per name. Required to search: name, years to search. Civil cases indexed by defendant, plaintiff. Civil records on computer from 1991, index cards from late 1950s. Civil court records free online at http://wcca.wicourts.gov/index.xsl. Access is also with the use of county "Remote Access". This data is for inquiries only and includes civil, family, and traffic courts. For info, contact the Technology Resources Dept. at 262-284-8309.
Criminal Records: Access: Mail, online, in person. Both court and visitors may perform in person searches. Search fee: $5.00 per name. Required to search: name, years to search, DOB. Criminal records on computer from 1989. Criminal court records are free online at http://wcca.wicourts.gov/index.xsl.
General Information: Public Access terminal is available. No paternity records released. Copy fee: $1.25 per page. Cert fee: $5.00. Payee: Clerk of Court. Business checks accepted. In state personal checks accepted. Prepayment required. Mail requests require SASE. Mail turnaround time 1 week.

Register in Probate PO Box 994, Port Washington, WI 53074; 262-284-8370/8409; Fax: 262-284-8491. Hours: 8:30AM-5PM (CST). *Probate.*
Note: Probate records are available free online; see Circuit Court.

Pepin County

Circuit Court PO Box 39, Durand, WI 54736; 715-672-8861; Fax: 715-672-8521. Hours: 8:30AM-Noon, 12:30-4:30PM (CST). *Felony, Misdemeanor, Civil, Eviction, Small Claims.*
Civil Records: Access: Mail, online, in person. Both court and visitors may perform in person searches. Search fee: $5.00 per name. Required to search: name, years to search. Civil cases indexed by plaintiff. Civil records on computer from 1995, index books from 1900s. Civil court records free online at http://wcca.wicourts.gov/index.xsl.
Criminal Records: Access: Mail, online, in person. Both court and visitors may perform in person searches. Search fee: $5.00 per name. Required to search: name, years to search, DOB. Criminal records on computer from 1995, index books from 1900s. Criminal court records are free online at http://wcca.wicourts.gov/index.xsl.
General Information: Public Access terminal is available. No minor or financial divorce records released. Will fax results to local or toll free line. Copy fee: $1.25 per page. Cert fee: $5.00. Payee: Clerk of Court. Personal checks accepted. Prepayment required. Mail requests require SASE. Mail turnaround time 1 week.

Register in Probate PO Box 39, Durand, WI 54736; 715-672-8859/715-672-8868; Fax: 715-672-8521. Hours: 8:30AM-Noon, 1-4:30PM (CST). *Probate.*
http://wicourts.gov
Note: Probate records are available free online; see Circuit Court Profile.

Pierce County

Circuit Court PO Box 129, Ellsworth, WI 54011; 715-273-3531. Hours: 8AM-5PM (CST). *Felony, Misdemeanor, Civil, Eviction, Small Claims.*
Civil Records: Access: Mail, online, in person. Both court and visitors may perform in person searches. Search fee: $5.00 per name. Fee is by type of case. Required to search: name, years to search. Civil cases indexed by defendant, plaintiff. Civil records are retained 20 years; on computer back to 1994. Archives in River Falls. Civil court records free online at http://wcca.wicourts.gov/index.xsl.
Criminal Records: Access: Mail, online, in person. Both court and visitors may perform in person searches. Search fee: $5.00 per name. Required to search: name, years to search, DOB. Felony records are retained 50-75 years; misdemeanors for 20. Criminal records on computer back to 1994. Archives in River Falls. Criminal court records are free online at http://wcca.wicourts.gov/index.xsl.
General Information: Public Access terminal is available. No sealed records released. Will fax results for $1.25 per page. Copy fee: $1.25 per page. Cert fee: $5.00. Payee: Clerk of Court. Personal checks accepted. Prepayment required. Mail requests require SASE. Mail turnaround time 2-3 days.

Register in Probate PO Box 97, Ellsworth, WI 54011; 715-273-3531 x6460; Fax: 715-273-6794. Hours: 8AM-5PM (CST). *Probate.*
Note: Probate records are available free online; see Circuit Court.

Polk County

Circuit Court PO Box 549, (100 Polk Plaza), Balsam Lake, WI 54810; 715-485-9299; Fax: 715-485-9262. Hours: 8:30AM-4:30PM (CST). *Felony, Misdemeanor, Civil, Eviction, Small Claims.*
Civil Records: Access: Mail, online, in person. Both court and visitors may perform in person searches. Search fee: $5.00 per name per record/file. Required to search: name, years to search. Civil cases indexed by defendant, plaintiff. Civil records go back to 1970s; on computer back to 1992. Civil court records free online at http://wcca.wicourts.gov/index.xsl.
Criminal Records: Access: Mail, online, in person. Both court and visitors may perform in person searches. Search fee: $5.00 per name. Fee is per record/file. Required to search: name, years to search, DOB. Criminal records go back to 1970s; on computer back to 1992. Criminal court records are free online at http://wcca.wicourts.gov/index.xsl.
General Information: Public Access terminal is available. No juvenile, paternity or confidential records released. Will fax results to local or toll free line. Copy fee: $1.25 per page. Cert fee: $5.00. Payee: Clerk of Court. Personal checks accepted. Prepayment required. Mail requests require SASE. Mail turnaround time 2 days.

Register in Probate 1005 W Main #500, Balsam Lake, WI 54810; 715-485-9238; Fax: 715-485-9275. Hours: 8:30AM-4:30PM (CST). *Probate.*
Note: Probate records are available free online; see Circuit Court.

Portage County

Circuit Court (Branches 1, 2 & 3) 1516 Church St, Stevens Point, WI 54481; 715-346-1364; Fax: 715-346-1236. Hours: 7:30AM-4:30PM (CST). *Felony, Misdemeanor, Civil, Eviction, Small Claims.*
Civil Records: Access: Mail, in person, online. Both court and visitors may perform in person searches. Search fee: $5.00 per name. Required to search: name, years to search. Civil cases indexed by defendant, plaintiff. Civil records on computer from 6/91, index cards from 1980, index books from 1900s. Internet access is upon approval. Request in writing to Data Processing Dept, 1462 Strong Ave, Stevens Point 54481. Explain purpose of record requests.
Criminal Records: Access: Mail, in person, online. Both court and visitors may perform in person searches. Search fee: $5.00 per name. Required to search: name, years to search, address, DOB, SSN, signed release. Criminal records on computer from 6/91, index cards from 1980, index books from 1900s. Internet access is upon approval. Request in writing to Data Processing Dept, 1462 Strong Ave, Stevens Point 54481. Explain purpose of record requests.
General Information: Public Access terminal is available. No expunged records released. Will fax results to local or toll free line. Copy fee: $1.25 per page. Cert fee: $5.00. Payee: Clerk of Court. Business checks accepted. Prepayment required. Mail requests require SASE. Mail turnaround time 10 working days.

Register in Probate 1516 Church St, Stevens Point, WI 54481; 715-346-1362; Fax: 715-346-1486. Hours: 7:30AM-4:30PM (CST). *Probate.*
Note: Probate records are available free on the Internet at http://ccap.courts.state.wi.us/internetcourtaccess.

Price County

Circuit Court Courthouse, 126 Cherry St, Phillips, WI 54555; 715-339-2353; Fax: 715-339-3079. Hours: 8AM-Noon, 1-4:30PM (CST). *Felony, Misdemeanor, Civil, Eviction, Small Claims.*
Civil Records: Access: Mail, online, in person. Both court and visitors may perform in person searches. Search fee: $5.00 per name. Required to search: name, years to search. Civil cases indexed by defendant, plaintiff. Civil records on computer from 1997, prior on index books. Civil court records free online at http://wcca.wicourts.gov/index.xsl.
Criminal Records: Access: Mail, online, in person. Both court and visitors may perform in person searches. Search fee: $5.00 per name. Required to search: name, years to search, DOB; also helpful: SSN. Criminal records on computer from 1997, prior on index books. Criminal court records are free online at http://wcca.wicourts.gov/index.xsl.
General Information: Public Access terminal is available. No confidential records per statute or order released. Will fax results to local or toll free line. Copy fee: $1.25 per page. Cert fee: $5.00. Payee: Clerk of Circuit Court. Personal checks accepted. Prepayment required. Mail requests require SASE. Mail turnaround time 1-2 days.

Register in Probate Courthouse, 126 Cherry St-Rm209, Phillips, WI 54555; 715-339-3078; Fax: 715-339-3079. Hours: 8AM-4:30PM (CST). *Probate.*
Note: Probate records are available free online; see Circuit Court.

Racine County

Circuit Court 730 Wisconsin Ave, Racine, WI 53403; 262-636-3333; Fax: 262-636-3341. Hours: 8AM-5PM (CST). *Felony, Misdemeanor, Civil, Eviction, Small Claims, Probate.*
Civil Records: Access: Mail, online, in person. Both court and visitors may perform in person searches. Search fee: $5.00 per name. Required to search: name, years to search. Civil cases indexed by defendant, plaintiff. Civil records on computer from 1990, index cards from 1970, archives prior to 1970. Civil court records free online at http://wcca.wicourts.gov/index.xsl.
Criminal Records: Access: Mail, online, in person. Both court and visitors may perform in person searches. Search fee: $5.00 per name. Required to search: name, years to search, DOB. Criminal records on computer from 1990, index cards from 1970, archives prior to 1970. Criminal court records are free online at http://wcca.wicourts.gov/index.xsl.
General Information: Public Access terminal is available. No adoption, juvenile, paternity or mental commitment records released. Will fax results to local

or toll free line. Copy fee: $1.25 per page. Cert fee: $5.00. Payee: Clerk of Court. Personal checks accepted. Prepayment required. Mail requests require SASE. Mail turnaround time 1-2 weeks.

Register in Probate 730 Wisconsin Ave, Racine, WI 53403; 262-636-3137; Fax: 262-636-3870. Hours: 8AM-5PM (CST). *Probate.*
Note: Probate records are available free online; see Circuit Court.

Richland County

Circuit Court PO Box 655, Richland Center, WI 53581; 608-647-3956. Hours: 8:30AM-4:30PM (CST). *Felony, Misdemeanor, Civil, Eviction, Small Claims.*
Civil Records: Access: Mail, online, in person. Both court and visitors may perform in person searches. Search fee: $5.00 per name. Required to search: name, years to search. Civil cases indexed by defendant, plaintiff. Civil records on index cards from 1982, index books from 1972, archives prior to 1972, on computer back to 1993. Civil court records free online at http://wcca.wicourts.gov/index.xsl.
Criminal Records: Access: Mail, online, in person. Both court and visitors may perform in person searches. Search fee: $5.00 per name. Required to search: name, years to search, DOB. Criminal records on index cards from 1982, index books from 1972, archives prior to 1972, on computer back t0 1993. Criminal court records are free online at http://wcca.wicourts.gov/index.xsl.
General Information: Public Access terminal is available. No juvenile or paternity records released. Copy fee: $1.25 per page. Cert fee: $5.00. Payee: Clerk of Circuit Court. Personal out-of-state checks not accepted. Prepayment required. Mail requests require SASE. Mail turnaround time 1 week.

Register in Probate PO Box 427, Richland Center, WI 53581; 608-647-2626; Fax: 608-647-6134. Hours: 8:30AM-Noon, 1-4:30PM (CST). *Probate.*
Note: Probate records are available free online; see Circuit Court.

Rock County

Circuit Court 51 S Main, Janesville, WI 53545; 608-743-2200; Fax: 608-743-2223. Hours: 8AM-5PM (CST). *Felony, Misdemeanor, Civil, Eviction, Small Claims.*
Civil Records: Access: Mail, online, in person. Both court and visitors may perform in person searches. Search fee: $5.00 per name. Required to search: name, years to search. Civil cases indexed by defendant, plaintiff. Civil records on computer from 6/93, on index cards from 6/91, index books from 1940, archives prior to 1940. Civil court records free online at http://wcca.wicourts.gov/index.xsl.
Criminal Records: Access: Mail, online, in person. Both court and visitors may perform in person searches. Search fee: $5.00 per name. Required to search: name, years to search, DOB. Criminal records on computer from 6/93, on index cards from 6/91, index books from 1940, archives prior to 1940. Criminal court records are free online at http://wcca.wicourts.gov/index.xsl.
General Information: Public Access terminal is available. No juvenile, paternity or sealed records released. Copy fee: $1.25 per page. Cert fee: $5.00. Payee: Clerk of Court. Personal checks accepted. Prepayment required. Mail requests require SASE. Mail turnaround time 2-3 days.

Circuit Court - South Janesville Courthouse, 51 S Main St, Janesville, WI 53545; 608-743-2200; Fax: 608-743-2223. Hours: 8AM-5PM (CST). *Felony, Misdemeanor, Civil, Eviction, Small Claims.*

Civil Records: Access: Mail, online, in person. Both court and visitors may perform in person searches. Search fee: $5.00 per name. Required to search: name, years to search. Civil cases indexed by defendant, plaintiff. Civil records on computer from mid-1993, on index cards from 1970s, index books from 1900s in vault. Civil court records free online at http://wcca.wicourts.gov/index.xsl.
Criminal Records: Access: Mail, online, in person. Both court and visitors may perform in person searches. Search fee: $5.00 per name. Required to search: name, years to search, DOB. Criminal records on computer from mid-1993, on index cards from 1970s, index books from 1900s in vault. Criminal court records are free online at http://wcca.wicourts.gov/index.xsl.
General Information: Public Access terminal is available. No paternity records released. Copy fee: $1.25 per page. Cert fee: $5.00. Payee: Clerk of Court. Personal checks accepted. Prepayment required. Mail requests require SASE. Mail turnaround time 1 week.

Register in Probate 51 S Main, Janesville, WI 53545; 608-757-5635; Fax: 608-757-5769. Hours: 8AM-5PM (CST). *Probate.*
Note: Probate records are available free online; see Circuit Court.

Rusk County

Circuit Court 311 Miner Ave East, #L350, Ladysmith, WI 54848; 715-532-2108; Probate phone: 715-532-2147. Hours: 8AM-4:30PM (CST). *Felony, Misdemeanor, Civil, Small Claims.*
Civil Records: Access: Mail, online, in person, phone, fax. Both court and visitors may perform in person searches. Search fee: $5.00 per name, no charge for persons performing their own search. Required to search: name, years to search. Civil cases indexed by defendant, plaintiff. Civil records on computer from 1992, on index cards from 1978, index books from 1901. Civil court records free online at http://wcca.wicourts.gov/index.xsl. Phone requests are accepted if the case number is known.
Criminal Records: Access: Mail, online, in person, online. Both court and visitors may perform in person searches. Search fee: $5.00 per name, no charge for persons performing their own search. Required to search: name, years to search, DOB. Criminal records on computer from 1992, on index cards from 1978, index books from 1901. Criminal court records are free online at http://wcca.wicourts.gov/index.xsl. Phone requests are accepted if the case number is known.
General Information: Public Access terminal is available. No juvenile or paternity records released. Will fax results for $1.25 per page plus $5.00 search fee per name. Copy fee: $1.25 per page. Cert fee: $5.00. Payee: Clerk of Court. Personal checks accepted. Prepayment required. Mail requests require SASE. Mail turnaround time 5 days.

Register in Probate 311 E Miner Ave, Ladysmith, WI 54848; 715-532-2147; Fax: 715-532-2266. Hours: 8AM-4:30PM (CST). *Probate.*
Note: Probate records are available free online; see Circuit Court.

Sauk County

Circuit Court 515 Oak St, Baraboo, WI 53913; 608-355-3287; Fax: 608-355-3514. Hours: 8AM-4:30PM (CST). *Felony, Misdemeanor, Civil, Eviction, Small Claims.*
Civil Records: Access: Mail, online, in person. Both court and visitors may perform in person searches. Search fee: $5.00 per name. Required to search: name, years to search. Civil cases indexed by defendant, plaintiff. Civil records on computer from

1990, index cards from 1980, index books from 1967. Civil court records free online at http://wcca.wicourts.gov/index.xsl.
Criminal Records: Access: Fax, mail, online, in person. Both court and visitors may perform in person searches. Search fee: $5.00 per name. Required to search: name, years to search. Criminal records on computer from 1990, index cards from 1980, index books from 1967. Criminal court records are free online at http://wcca.wicourts.gov/index.xsl.
General Information: Public Access terminal is available. No paternity, juvenile records released. Fee to fax results is $5.00 1st page, $1.00 each add'l plus tax. Copy fee: $1.25 per page. Cert fee: $5.00. Payee: Clerk of Court. Personal checks accepted. Prepayment required. Mail requests require SASE. Mail turnaround time 2-3 days.

Register in Probate 515 Oak St, Baraboo, WI 53913; 608-355-3226; Fax: 608-355-3480. Hours: 8AM-4:30PM (CST). *Probate, Juvenile.*
Note: Probate records are available free online; see Circuit Court profile.

Sawyer County

Circuit Court PO Box 508, Hayward, WI 54843; 715-634-4887; Fax: 715-638-3297. Hours: 8AM-4PM (CST). *Felony, Misdemeanor, Civil, Eviction, Small Claims.*
Civil Records: Access: Mail, online, in person. Both court and visitors may perform in person searches. Search fee: $5.00 per name. Required to search: name, years to search. Civil cases indexed by defendant, plaintiff. Civil records on index cards from 7/85, prior on books. Civil court records free online at http://wcca.wicourts.gov/index.xsl.
Criminal Records: Access: Mail, online, in person. Both court and visitors may perform in person searches. Search fee: $5.00 per name. Required to search: name, years to search. Criminal records on index cards from 7/85, prior on books. Criminal court records are free online at http://wcca.wicourts.gov/index.xsl.
General Information: Public Access terminal is available. No juvenile, probate or paternity records released. Copy fee: $1.25 per page. Cert fee: $5.00. Payee: Clerk of Court. Personal checks accepted. Prepayment required. Mail requests require SASE. Mail turnaround time 1 day.

Register in Probate PO Box 447, Hayward, WI 54843; 715-634-7519; Fax: 715-638-3297. Hours: 8AM-4PM (CST). *Probate.*
Note: Probate records are available free online; see Circuit Court.

Shawano County

Circuit Court 311 N Main Rm 206, Shawano, WI 54166; 715-526-9347; Probate phone: 715-526-8631; Fax: 715-526-4915. Hours: 8AM-4:30PM (CST). *Felony, Misdemeanor, Civil, Eviction, Small Claims.*
www.co.shawano.wi.us
Civil Records: Access: Fax, mail, online, in person. Both court and visitors may perform in person searches. Search fee: $5.00 per name. Required to search: name, years to search. Civil cases indexed by defendant, plaintiff. Civil records on computer from 1993, on index books from 1930s, prior in archives. Civil court records free online at http://wcca.wicourts.gov/index.xsl.
Criminal Records: Access: Fax, mail, online, in person. Both court and visitors may perform in person searches. Search fee: $5.00 per name. Required to search: name, years to search, DOB. Criminal records on computer from 1993, on index books from 1930s, prior in archives. Criminal court records are free online at http://wcca.wicourts.gov/index.xsl.

General Information: Public Access terminal is available. No juvenile, closed files or mental records released. Will fax results $1.25 per page, add $2.50 for long distance. Copy fee: $1.25 per page. Cert fee: $5.00. Payee: Clerk of Court. Personal checks accepted. Prepayment required. Mail requests require SASE. Mail turnaround time 10-20 days.

Register in Probate 311 N Main, Rm 203, Shawano, WI 54166; 715-526-8631; Fax: 715-526-8622. Hours: 8AM-4:30PM (CST). *Probate.*

Note: Probate records are available free online; see Circuit Court.

Sheboygan County

Circuit Court 615 N 6th St, Sheboygan, WI 53081; 920-459-3068; Fax: 920-459-3921. Hours: 8AM-5PM (CST). *Felony, Misdemeanor, Civil, Eviction, Small Claims.*
www.co.sheboygan.wi.us/html/d_crtclrk.html
Civil Records: Access: Mail, online, in person. Both court and visitors may perform in person searches. Search fee: $5.00 per case. Required to search: name, years to search; also helpful: address. Civil cases indexed by defendant, plaintiff. Civil records on computer since 1992; prior records on index cards from 1960, index books from 1860s, archives prior to 1971. Civil court records free online at http://wcca.wicourts.gov/index.xsl.
Criminal Records: Access: Mail, online, in person. Both court and visitors may perform in person searches. Search fee: $5.00 per case. Required to search: name, years to search, DOB; also helpful: address. Criminal records on computer since 1992; prior records on index cards from 1960, index books from 1860s, archives prior to 1971. Criminal court records are free online at http://wcca.wicourts.gov/index.xsl.
General Information: Public Access terminal is available. No juvenile or paternity records released. Will fax results for pre-paid $3.00. Copy fee: $1.25 per page. Cert fee: $5.00. Payee: Clerk of Circuit Court. Personal checks accepted. Prepayment required. Mail requests require SASE. Mail turnaround time 2-3 days.

Register in Probate 615 N 6th St, Sheboygan, WI 53081; 920-459-3050, 459-3202, 459-3051; Fax: 920-459-0541. Hours: 8AM-5PM (CST). *Probate.*

Note: There is a $4.00 search fee. Probate records are available free online; see Circuit Court.

St. Croix County

Circuit Court 1101 Carmichael Rd, Hudson, WI 54016; 715-386-4630. Hours: 8AM-5PM (CST). *Felony, Misdemeanor, Civil, Eviction, Small Claims.*
Civil Records: Access: Mail, online, in person. Both court and visitors may perform in person searches. Search fee: $5.00 per name. Required to search: name, years to search. Civil cases indexed by defendant, plaintiff. Civil records on computer from 10/92, on index cards from 1982, index books from 1965. Civil court records free online at http://wcca.wicourts.gov/index.xsl.
Criminal Records: Access: Mail, online, in person. Both court and visitors may perform in person searches. Search fee: $5.00 per name. Required to search: name, years to search, DOB. Criminal records on computer from 10/92, on index cards from 1982, index books from 1900s. Criminal court records are free online at http://wcca.wicourts.gov/index.xsl.
General Information: Public Access terminal is available. No juvenile forfeitures, paternity, some case specific documents or sealed records released. Copy fee: $1.25 per page. Cert fee: $5.00. Payee: Clerk of Court. Personal checks accepted. Prepayment

required. Mail requests require SASE. Mail turnaround time 5-10 days.

Register in Probate 1101 Carmichael Rd, Rm 2242, Hudson, WI 54016; 715-386-4618; Fax: 715-381-4318. Hours: 8AM-5PM (CST). *Probate.*

Note: Probate records are available free online; see Circuit Court.

Taylor County

Circuit Court 224 S 2nd St, Medford, WI 54451-1811; 715-748-1425; Probate phone: 715-748-1435; Fax: 715-748-2465. Hours: 8:30AM-4:30PM (CST). *Felony, Misdemeanor, Civil, Eviction, Small Claims.*
Civil Records: Access: Mail, online, in person. Both court and visitors may perform in person searches. Search fee: $5.00 per name. Required to search: name, years to search. Civil cases indexed by defendant, plaintiff. Civil records on computer from 1989; prior records index books from 1917. Civil court records free online at http://wcca.wicourts.gov/index.xsl.
Criminal Records: Access: Mail, online, in person. Both court and visitors may perform in person searches. Search fee: $5.00 per name. Required to search: name, years to search, DOB. Criminal records on computer from 1989; prior records index books from 1917. Criminal court records are free online at http://wcca.wicourts.gov/index.xsl.
General Information: Public Access terminal is available. No sealed records released. Will fax results to a local or toll free line. Copy fee: $1.25 per page. Cert fee: $5.00. Payee: Clerk of Circuit Court. Personal checks accepted. Prepayment required. Mail requests require SASE. Mail turnaround time 1-2 days.

Register in Probate 224 S 2nd, Medford, WI 54451; 715-748-1435; Fax: 715-748-1524. Hours: 8:30AM-4:30PM (CST). *Probate.*

Note: Probate records are available free online; see Circuit Court.

Trempealeau County

Circuit Court 36245 Main St, Whitehall, WI 54773; 715-538-2311. Hours: 8AM-4:30PM (CST). *Felony, Misdemeanor, Civil, Eviction, Small Claims.*
Civil Records: Access: Fax, mail, online, in person. Both court and visitors may perform in person searches. Search fee: $5.00 per name. Required to search: name, years to search. Civil cases indexed by defendant, plaintiff. Civil records on computer from 1993, on index cards from 1987, index books from 1940, archives prior to 1940. Civil court records free online at http://wcca.wicourts.gov/index.xsl. All mail requests must be in writing.
Criminal Records: Access: Fax, mail, online, in person. Both court and visitors may perform in person searches. Search fee: $5.00 per name. Required to search: name, years to search, DOB. Criminal records on computer from 1993, on index cards from 1987, index books from 1940, archives prior to 1940. Criminal court records are free online at http://wcca.wicourts.gov/index.xsl. All mail requests must be in writing.
General Information: Public Access terminal is available. No juvenile, paternity or child support records released. Will fax results $2.00 per page. Copy fee: $1.25 per page. Cert fee: $5.00. Payee: Clerk of Circuit Court. Personal checks accepted. Prepayment required. Mail requests require SASE. Mail turnaround time 2-3 days.

Register in Probate 36245 Main St, PO Box 67, Whitehall, WI 54773; 715-538-2311 X238; Fax: 715-538-4123. Hours: 8AM-4:30PM (CST). *Probate.*

Note: Probate records are available free online; see Circuit Court.

Vernon County

Circuit Court PO Box 426, Viroqua, WI 54665; 608-637-5340; Fax: 608-637-5554. Hours: 8:30AM-4:30PM (CST). *Felony, Misdemeanor, Civil, Eviction, Small Claims.*
Civil Records: Access: Phone, fax, mail, online, in person. Both court and visitors may perform in person searches. Search fee: $5.00 per name. Required to search: name, years to search, DOB. Civil cases indexed by defendant, plaintiff. Civil records on computer back to 1993; on index books & cards 1950 to 1992. Civil court records free online at http://wcca.wicourts.gov/index.xsl.
Criminal Records: Access: Phone, fax, mail, online, in person. Both court and visitors may perform in person searches. Search fee: $5.00 per name. Required to search: name, years to search; also helpful: DOB. Criminal records on computer back to 1993; on index books & cards 1950 to 1992. Criminal court records are free online at http://wcca.wicourts.gov/index.xsl.
General Information: Public Access terminal is available. No paternity or juvenile records released. Copy fee: $1.25 per page. Cert fee: $5.00. Payee: Clerk of Court. Personal checks accepted. Prepayment required. Will bill to attorneys credit agencies. Mail requests require SASE. Mail turnaround time 2-3 days.

Register in Probate PO Box 448, Viroqua, WI 54665; 608-637-5347; Fax: 608-637-5554. Hours: 8:30AM-4:30PM (CST). *Probate.*

Note: Probate records are available free online; see Circuit Court.

Vilas County

Circuit Court 330 Court St, Eagle River, WI 54521; 715-479-3632; Fax: 715-479-3740. Hours: 8AM-4PM (CST). *Felony, Misdemeanor, Civil, Eviction, Small Claims.*
Civil Records: Access: Mail, online, in person. Both court and visitors may perform in person searches. Search fee: $5.00 per name. Required to search: name, years to search. Civil records on computer back to 1992, index cards from 1978, index books from 1900s. Civil court records free online at http://wcca.wicourts.gov/index.xsl.
Criminal Records: Access: Mail, online, in person. Both court and visitors may perform in person searches. Search fee: $5.00 per name. Required to search: name, years to search, DOB. Criminal records on computer back to 1992; index cards from 1978, index books from 1900s. Criminal court records are free online at http://wcca.wicourts.gov/index.xsl.
General Information: Public Access terminal is available. No paternity records released. Fee to fax results is $1.25 per page. Copy fee: $1.25 per page. Cert fee: $5.00. Payee: Clerk of Circuit Court. Personal checks accepted. Prepayment required. Mail requests require SASE. Mail turnaround time 2 weeks.

Register in Probate 330 Court St, Eagle River, WI 54521; 715-479-3642; Fax: 715-479-3740. Hours: 8AM-4PM (CST). *Probate.*

Note: Probate records are available free online; see Circuit Court.

Walworth County

Circuit Court PO Box 1001, Elkhorn, WI 53121-1001; 262-741-4224; Probate phone: 262-741-4256/262741-4182fx; Fax: 262-741-4379. Hours: 8AM-5PM (CST). *Felony, Misdemeanor, Civil, Eviction, Small Claims.*
www.co.walworth.wi.us

Civil Records: Access: Mail, in person, online. Both court and visitors may perform in person searches. Search fee: $5.00 per name. Required to search: name, years to search. Civil cases indexed by defendant, plaintiff. Civil records on computer from 1989, index cards/books from 1836. Civil court records are free online at http://wcca.wicourts.gov/index.xsl.

Criminal Records: Access: Mail, in person, online. Both court and visitors may perform in person searches. Search fee: $5.00 per name. Required to search: name, years to search, DOB. Criminal records on computer from 1989, index cards/books from 1836 (organized). Criminal court records are free online at http://wcca.wicourts.gov/index.xsl.

General Information: Public Access terminal is available. No sealed records released. Will fax results for $1.25 per page. Copy fee: $1.25 per page. Cert fee: $5.00. Payee: County Clerk of Courts. Business checks accepted. Visa, MC accepted. Credit cards accepted in person only. Prepayment required. Mail requests require SASE. Mail turnaround time 1-2 days.

Register in Probate PO Box 1001, Elkhorn, WI 53121; 262-741-4256; Fax: 262-741-4182. Hours: 8AM-5PM (CST). *Probate.*
Note: Probate records are available free online; see Circuit Court.

Washburn County

Circuit Court PO Box 339, Shell Lake, WI 54871; 715-468-4677; Fax: 715-468-4678. Hours: 8AM-4:30PM (CST). *Felony, Misdemeanor, Civil, Eviction, Small Claims.*
Civil Records: Access: Mail, online, in person. Both court and visitors may perform in person searches. Search fee: $5.00 per name. Required to search: name, years to search. Civil cases indexed by defendant, plaintiff. Civil records on computer since 1993 (civil money judgments back to 1/1/90); on index books from 1883. Civil court records free online at http://wcca.wicourts.gov/index.xsl.
Criminal Records: Access: Mail, online, in person. Both court and visitors may perform in person searches. Search fee: $5.00 per name. Required to search: name, years to search; also helpful: DOB. Criminal records on computer since 1993; on index books from 1883. Criminal court records are free online at http://wcca.wicourts.gov/index.xsl.
General Information: Public Access terminal is available. No sealed records released. Will fax results to local or toll free line. Copy fee: $1.25 per page. Cert fee: $5.00. Payee: Clerk of Court. Personal checks accepted. Prepayment required. Mail requests require SASE. Mail turnaround time 2-3 days.

Register in Probate PO Box 316, Shell Lake, WI 54871; 715-468-4688; Fax: 715-468-4678. Hours: 8AM-4:30PM (CST). *Probate.*
Note: Probate records are available free online; see Circuit Court.

Washington County

Circuit Court PO Box 1986, West Bend, WI 53095-7986; 262-335-4341; Fax: 262-335-4776. Hours: 8AM-4:30PM (CST). *Felony, Misdemeanor, Civil, Eviction, Small Claims.*
www.co.washington.wi.us
Civil Records: Access: Mail, fax, online, in person. Both court and visitors may perform in person searches. Search fee: $5.00 per name. Required to search: name, years to search; also helpful: address. Civil cases indexed by defendant, plaintiff. Civil records on computer from 1986, index cards from 1976, index books from 1836. Civil court records free online at http://wicourts.gov/.

Criminal Records: Access: Mail, fax, online, in person. Both court and visitors may perform in person searches. Search fee: $5.00 per name. Required to search: name, years to search, DOB; also helpful: address. Criminal records on computer from 1986, index cards from 1976, index books from 1836. Criminal court records are free online at http://wcca.wicourts.gov/index.xsl.
General Information: Public Access terminal is available. No paternity records released prior to adjudication. Will fax results to local or toll free line. Copy fee: $1.25 per page. Cert fee: $5.00. Payee: Clerk of Court. Personal checks accepted. Prepayment required. Mail requests require SASE. Mail turnaround time 1 week.

Register in Probate PO Box 82, West Bend, WI 53095-0082; 262-335-4334; Fax: 262-306-2224. Hours: 8AM-4:30PM (CST). *Probate.*
www.co.washington.wi.us
Note: Probate records are available free online; see Circuit Court.

Waukesha County

Circuit Court 515 W Moreland Blvd, Waukesha, WI 53188; Civil phone: 262-548-7525; Criminal phone: 262-548-7484. Hours: 8AM-4:30PM (CST). *Felony, Misdemeanor, Civil, Eviction, Small Claims.*
www.waukeshacounty.gov
Civil Records: Access: Mail, online, in person. Both court and visitors may perform in person searches. Search fee: $5.00 per name. Required to search: name, years to search. Civil cases indexed by defendant, plaintiff. Civil records on computer back to 1994. Civil court records free online at http://wcca.wicourts.gov/index.xsl.
Criminal Records: Access: Mail, online, in person. Both court and visitors may perform in person searches. Search fee: $5.00 per name. Required to search: name, years to search, DOB. Criminal records indexed on computer, record history on computer back to 1994. Criminal court records are free online at http://wcca.wicourts.gov/index.xsl.
General Information: Public Access terminal is available. No paternity, mental commitment records released. Fee to fax results is $3.00 per document plus $1.25 per page. Copy fee: $1.25 per page. Cert fee: $5.00. Payee: Clerk of Circuit Court. Personal checks accepted. Credit cards accepted. Accepted in person only. Prepayment required. Mail requests require SASE. Mail turnaround time 2-3 days.

Register in Probate 515 W Moreland, Rm 380, Waukesha, WI 53188; 262-548-7468. Hours: 8AM-4:30PM M-F (CST). *Probate.*
circuitcourts.waukeshacounty.gov
Note: Probate records are available free online; see Circuit Court.

Waupaca County

Circuit Court 811 Harding St, Waupaca, WI 54981; 715-258-6460; Fax: 715-258-6497. Hours: 8AM-4PM (CST). *Felony, Misdemeanor, Civil, Eviction, Small Claims.*
Civil Records: Access: Mail, in person. Both court and visitors may perform in person searches. Search fee: $5.00 per name. Required to search: name, years to search. Civil cases indexed by defendant, plaintiff. Civil records on computer from 1992. Civil court records free online at http://wcca.wicourts.gov/index.xsl.
Criminal Records: Access: Mail, online, in person. Both court and visitors may perform in person searches. Search fee: $5.00 per name. Required to search: name, years to search. Criminal records on computer from 1992. Criminal court records are free online at http://wcca.wicourts.gov/index.xsl.

General Information: Public Access terminal is available. No juvenile, JO, paternity excluding past judgments released. Copy fee: $1.25 per page. Computer document copy fee $.50 per page. Cert fee: $5.00. Payee: Clerk of Court. Business checks accepted. Personal in-state checks accepted. Prepayment required. Mail requests require SASE. Mail turnaround time 3-4 days.

Register in Probate 811 Harding St, Waupaca, WI 54981; 715-258-6429; Probate phone: 715-258-6431 (Dep Reg); Fax: 715-258-6440. Hours: 8AM-4PM (CST). *Probate.*
www.co.waupaca.wi.us
Note: Probate records are available free online; see Circuit Court profile.

Waushara County

Circuit Court PO Box 507, Wautoma, WI 54982; 920-787-0441; Probate phone: 920-787-0448; Fax: 920-787-0481. Hours: 8AM-4:30PM (CST). *Felony, Misdemeanor, Civil, Eviction, Small Claims.*
Civil Records: Access: Mail, fax, online, in person. Both court and visitors may perform in person searches. Search fee: $5.00 per name. fee only if court does search. Required to search: name, years to search. Civil cases indexed by defendant. Civil records on computer from 1992, index cards prior to 1978, index books from 1900s. Civil court records free online at http://wcca.wicourts.gov/index.xsl.
Criminal Records: Access: Mail, fax, online, in person. Both court and visitors may perform in person searches. Search fee: $5.00 per name. Fee applies if court does search. Required to search: name, years to search, DOB. Criminal records on computer from 1993, prior on cards and books. Criminal court records are free online at http://wcca.wicourts.gov/index.xsl.
General Information: Public Access terminal is available. Will fax results if prepaid. Copy fee: $1.25 per page. Cert fee: $5.00. Payee: Clerk of Court. Personal in-state checks accepted; money orders for out of state requests. Prepayment required. Mail requests require SASE. Mail turnaround time 1-2 weeks.

Register in Probate PO Box 508, Wautoma, WI 54982; 920-787-0448; Fax: 920-787-0481. Hours: 8AM-4:30PM (CST). *Probate.*
Note: Probate records are available free online; see Circuit Court.

Winnebago County

Circuit Court PO Box 2808, Oshkosh, WI 54903-2808; 920-236-4848; Civil phone: 920-236-4848; Criminal phone: 920-236-4855; Probate phone: 920-236-4833; Fax: 920-424-7780. Hours: 8AM-4:30PM (CST). *Felony, Misdemeanor, Civil, Eviction, Small Claims.*
Civil Records: Access: Mail, fax, online, in person. Both court and visitors may perform in person searches. Search fee: $5.00 per name. Required to search: name, years to search. Civil cases indexed by defendant, plaintiff. Civil records are on computer since 1990, prior on books and cards to 1997. Historical Society has records to 1938. Civil court records free online at http://wcca.wicourts.gov/index.xsl.
Criminal Records: Access: Mail, fax, online, in person. Both court and visitors may perform in person searches. Search fee: $5.00 per name. Required to search: full name, years to search, DOB. Criminal records are on computer since 1990, prior on books and cards. organized since 1938. Criminal court records are free online at http://wcca.wicourts.gov/index.xsl.

General Information: Public Access terminal is available. No juvenile, paternity, financial records released. Fee to fax results is $1.25 per page. Copy fee: $1.25 per page. Cert fee: $5.00. Payee: Clerk of Courts. Personal checks accepted. Prepayment required. Mail requests require SASE. Mail turnaround time 1 week.

Register in Probate PO Box 2808, Oshkosh, WI 54903-2808; 920-236-4833; Fax: 920-424-7536. Hours: 8AM-Noon, 1-4:30PM (CST). *Probate.*

Note: There is a $4.00 search fee. Probate records are available free online; see Circuit Court.

Wood County

Circuit Court 400 Market St, Po Box 8095, Wisconsin Rapids, WI 54494-958095; 715-421-8490. Hours: 8AM-4:30PM (CST). *Felony, Misdemeanor, Civil, Eviction, Small Claims.*

Civil Records: Access: Mail, online, in person. Both court and visitors may perform in person searches. Search fee: $5.00 per name. Required to search: name, years to search. Civil cases indexed by defendant, plaintiff. Civil records on computer from 1983, microfiche from 1856-1980s. Civil court records free online at http://wcca.wicourts.gov/index.xsl.

Criminal Records: Access: Mail, online, in person. Both court and visitors may perform in person searches. Search fee: $5.00 per name. Required to search: name, years to search, DOB. Criminal records on computer from 1980; manual search required for

pre-1980 records. Criminal court records are free online at http://wcca.wicourts.gov/index.xsl.

General Information: Public Access terminal is available. No paternity or sealed records released. Will fax results to local or toll free line. Copy fee: $1.25 per page. Cert fee: $5.00. Payee: Clerk of Court. Personal checks accepted. Prepayment required. Mail requests require SASE. Mail turnaround time 2-3 days.

Register in Probate Wood County Courthouse, PO Box 8095, Wisconsin Rapids, WI 54495-8095; 715-421-8520, 421-8523; Fax: 715-421-8896. Hours: 8AM-4:30PM (CST). *Probate.*

Note: Court also holds guardianships, juveniles, mental and adoption records. Probate records are available free online; see Circuit Court.

Wisconsin Recording Offices

ORGANIZATION: 72 counties, 72 recording offices. The recording officers are Register of Deeds and Clerk of Court (state tax liens). The entire state is in the Central Time Zone (CST).

REAL ESTATE RECORDS: Registers will not perform real estate searches. Copy fees and certification fees vary. Assessor telephone numbers are for local municipalities or for property listing agencies. Counties do not have assessors. Copies usually cost $2.00 for the first page and $1.00 for each additional page. Certification usually costs $.25 per document. The Treasurer maintains property tax records.

UCC RECORDS: Financing statements are filed at the state level, except for real estate related collateral, which are filed with the Register of Deeds. However, prior to 07/2001, consumer goods and farm collateral were also filed at the Register of Deeds and these older records can be searched there. Many recording offices will no longer perform UCC searches. Use search request form UCC-11 for mail-in searches. Searches fees are usually $10.00 to $15.00 per debtor name. Copy fees are usually $2.00 1st page and $1.00 each add'l page.

TAX LIEN RECORDS: Federal tax liens on personal property of businesses are filed with the Secretary of State. Only federal tax liens on real estate are filed with the county Register of Deeds. State tax liens are filed with the Clerk of Court, and at the State Treasurer at the Dept. of Revenue. Refer to the County Court Records section for information about Wisconsin courts. Most but not all Registers will perform federal tax lien searches. Search fees vary, but copy fees are $2.00 1st page and $1.00 each add'l page.

OTHER LIENS: Judgment, mechanics, breeders.

ONLINE ACCESS: A number of cities and a few counties offer online access to assessor and property records.

Adams County

Register of Deeds, PO Box 219, Friendship, WI 53934-0219. **Phone-**608-339-4206; hours 8AM-4:30PM Will not search records. Record copy fee- $2.00 1st page, $1.00 each add'l. Payee: Adams County Register of Deeds.

Ashland County

Register of Deeds, 201 W. Main St, Rm 206, Ashland, WI 54806. **Phone-**715-682-7008; fax-715-682-7035; hours 8AM-4PM. UCC records search per debtor-$15.00. Tax liens not included in UCC search. Separate federal tax lien search- $15.00 per debtor. Will not search real estate records. Record copy fee-$2.00 1st page, $1.00 each add'l. Cert fee: $1.00 per doc. Payee: Register of deeds. **Other phones:** Treasurer-715-682-7012; Elections-715-682-7000; Vital Records-715-682-7008.

Barron County

Register of Deeds, 330 E. LaSalle, Rm 201, Barron, WI 54812. **Phone-**Register of Deeds, R/E & UCC Recording- 715-537-6210; fax-715-537-6277; hours 8AM-4PM www.co.barron.wi.us Will not search UCC or real estate records. Tax lien search- $15.00 per debtor. Record copy fee- $2.00 1st page, $1.00 each add'l. Cert fee: $1.00 per doc. Payee: Barron County Register of Deeds. **Online Access to Land, Assessor records:** county land records are at www.gcssoftware.com/product/web_se arch.asp. Registration, $300.00 annual fee, username, password required; call Yvonne at the county treasurer's office, 715-537-6280. **Other phones:** Assessor-715-537-6313; Treasurer-715-537-6280; Vital Records-715-537-6210.

Bayfield County

Register of Deeds, PO Box 813, Washburn, WI 54891. **Phone-**715-373-6119; hours 8AM-4PM Will not search records. Record copy fee- $2.00 1st page, $1.00 each add'l. Cert fee: $.25 per page. Payee: Bayfield County Register of Deeds. **Other phones:** Assessor-715-373-6131; Treasurer-715-373-6131.

Brown County

Register of Deeds, PO Box 23600, Green Bay, WI 54305-3600. **Phone-**920-448-4470, R/E Recording-920-448-4439, UCC Recording-920-448-4468; fax-920-448-4449; hours-8AM-4:30PM www.co.brown.wi.us/rod Will not search UCC or real estate records. Will search tax liens. Record copy fee- $2.00 1st page, $1.00 each add'l. Cert fee: $1.00 per doc. Payee: Register of Deeds. **Online Access to Real Estate, Recording records:** Access to Register of Deeds real estate records is by subscription at www.co.brown.wi.us/rod/LaredoTapestry/main.html. Registration and usage fees are required. Images are $.50 each. A more sophisticated subscription system, named Laredo, offers full access to land records for firms operating in Wisconsin. Land records without name searching is at www.co.brown.wi.us/tr easurer/landrecordssearch/entryform.asp. Also, Brown County land records can be downloaded from an ftp site; contact the Land Information office at 920-448-6295 to register and user information. **Other phones:** Treasurer-920-448-4074; Elections-920-448-4016; Vital Records-920-448-4474.

Buffalo County

Register of Deeds, PO Box 28, Alma, WI 54610-0028. **Phone-**608-685-6230; fax-608-685-6213. Will not search records. Record copy fee- $2.00 1st page, $1.00 each add'l. **Online Access to Land records:** Access to county land records is free at www.gcssoftware.com/applications/search/index.asp?C ounty=Buffalo. **Other phones:** Treasurer-608-685-6214.

Burnett County

Register of Deeds, 7410 County Rd K #103, Siren, WI 54872. **Phone-**Register of Deeds, R/E & UCC Recording- 715-349-2183; fax-715-349-2037; hours 8:30AM-4:30PM www.burnettcounty.com UCC records search per debtor- $10.00. UCC search does not include federal tax liens. Will not search real estate records. Record copy fee- $2.00 1st page, $1.00 each add'l. Cert fee: $1.00 per page. Payee: Burnett County Register of Deeds. **Online Access to Property, Tax Assessor records:** Access to limited county property and assessment records is free at http://burnettims.homeip.net/. No name searching. For full data, an online subscription service is $100 per year. **Other phones:** Treasurer-715-349-2187; Elections-715-349-2183.

Calumet County

Register of Deeds, 206 Court St, Chilton, WI 53014. **Phone-**920-849-1441, UCC Recording-920-849-1441 x205; fax-920-849-1469; hours 8AM-4:30PM www.co.calumet.wi.us Will not search UCC or real estate records. Record copy fee- $2.00 1st page, $1.00 each add'l. Cert fee: $1.00 per doc + copy fees. Payee: Register of Deeds. **Online Access to Assessor, Property Tax records:** Access to assessor property tax data is free at http://calum400.co.calumet.wi.us/nsccalo/nsclndrec. **Other phones:** Assessor-920-849-1457.

Chippewa County

Register of Deeds, 711 N Bridge St, Chippewa Falls, WI 54729-1876. **Phone-**715-726-7994; fax-715-726-4582; hours 8AM-4:30 PM www.co.chippewa.wi.us/Departments/RegisterDeeds UCC records search per debtor- $15.00. Will not search tax liens. Will not do a title search; will search for one or two records. Record copy fee- $2.00 1st page, $1.00 each add'l. Cert fee: $1.00. Payee: Register of Deeds. **Online Access to Recording, Deed, Judgment, Real Estate records:** Search Register of Deeds data at www.landshark.co.chippewa.wi.us, index search is free, but registration and fees apply for images and copies, $2.00 1st page, $1.00 2nd page. Credit cards accepted. **Other phones:** Treasurer-715-726-7965; Elections-715-726-7980; Vital Records-715-726-7994.

Clark County

Registrar, PO Box 384, Neillsville, WI 54456-0384. **Phone-**715-743-5162, R/E Recording-715-743-5163, UCC Recording-715-743-5163; fax-715-743-5154; hours 8AM-4:30PM www.co.clark.wi.us Will not search UCC or real estate records. Federal tax lien search-$15.00 per debtor. For state tax liens see clerk of court. Record copy fee- $2.00 1st page, $1.00 each add'l. Cert fee: $1.00 per doc. Payee: Clark County Register of Deeds. **Online**

Access to Assessor, Property records: Search for assessor/property tax data on the county GIS-site at www.co.clark.wi.us/Website/ClarkIMS/viewer.htm. Search by PIN or address. **Other phones:** Treasurer-715-743-5155; Elections-715-743-5148; Vital Records-715-743-5163.

Columbia County

Register of Deeds, PO Box 133, Portage, WI 53901. **Phone**-608-742-9677; fax-608-742-9875.
Will not search UCC or real estate records. Record copy fee- $2.00 1st page, $1.00 each add'l. Cert fee: $1.00 per record. Payee: Register of Deeds. **Online Access to Property Tax, Land records:** Search the land records system for free at www.co.columbia.wi.us/landrecords. **Other phones:** Assessor-608-742-9677; Treasurer-608-742-9613.

Crawford County

Register of Deeds, 220 N. Beaumont Rd, Prairie du Chien, WI 53821. **Phone**-Register of Deeds, R/E & UCC Recording- 608-326-0219; fax-608-326-0220. http://crawfordcounty-wi-us.org
UCC records search per debtor- $10.00. UCC search includes tax liens. Separate federal/state combined tax lien search- $10.00 per person. Will search real estate records. Record copy fee- $2.00 1st page, $1.00 each add'l. Cert fee: $2.00 per cert. Payee: Register of Deeds. **Other phones:** Treasurer-608-326-0203; Vital Records-608-326-0219.

Dane County

Register of Deeds, PO Box 1438, Madison, WI 53701. **Phone**-608-266-4141, R/E Recording-608-266-4144 (2-4 PM only), UCC Recording-608-266-4144 (2-4 PM only); fax-608-267-3110; hours 7:45AM-4PM www.co.dane.wi.us/regdeeds/rdhome.htm
The Register of Deeds will only release information over the phone between the hours of 2-4PM. You can email the agency if you have questions. Will not search UCC or tax liens records. Will search limited real estate records from 2PM-4PM only. Record copy fee- $2.00 1st page, $1.00 each add'l. Cert fee: $1.00 per doc. Payee: Register of Deeds. **Online Access to Assessor, Real Estate, Property Tax records:** A fee-based system is at www.co.dane.wi.us/regdeeds/lared otapestry/accesstorealestate.htm. Real estate recorded is at www.co.dane.wi.us/regdeeds/rdreales.htm. Also, parcel information is free at http://dc-web.co.dane.wi.us/dane/html/parcelsearch.asp.
Professional companies may register to use assessor/land record services at http://dc-web.co.dane.wi.us/dane/html/community.asp. Registration & login. Also, the City of Madison tax assessor database is accessible at www.ci.madison.wi.us/assessor/property.html. Also, search property info for Towns of Cross Plains, Mazomanie, Berry, Medina at www.wendorffassess ing.com/municipalities.htm. **Other phones:** Treasurer-608-266-4151; Elections-608-266-4121; Vital Records-608-266-4142; General Number-608-266-4141.

Dodge County

Register of Deeds, 127 E. Oak St, Admin. Bldg., Juneau, WI 53039-1391. **Phone**-Register of Deeds, R/E & UCC Recording- 920-386-3720, UCC Recording-920-386-3723; fax-920-386-3902; hours 8AM-4:30PM. Will not search records. Record copy fee-$2.00 1st page, $1.00 each add'l. Cert fee: $1.00. Payee: Dodge County Register of Deeds. **Other phones:** Assessor-920-386-3770; Treasurer-414-386-3781; Vital Records-920-386-3720.

Door County

Register of Deeds, PO Box 670, Sturgeon Bay, WI 54235-0670. **Phone**-Register of Deeds, R/E & UCC Recording- 920-746-2270, UCC Recording-608-261-9548 (Madison); fax-920-746-2525; hours 8AM-

4:30PM. Will not search UCC records. Record copy fee- $2.00 1st page, $1.00 each add'l. Cert fee: $2.00 1st page, $1.00 add'l. Payee: Register of Deeds. **Other phones:** Assessor-920-746-2905; Treasurer-920-746-2286; Vital Records-920-746-2270.

Douglas County

Register of Deeds, PO Box 847, Superior, WI 54880. **Phone**-715-395-1463, R/E Recording-715-395-1350; fax-715-395-1553; hours-8AM-4:30PM www.douglascountywi.org
Will not search records. RE record copy fee- $2.00 per page. UCC copy- $2.00 1st page; $1.00 each add'l. Cert fee: $3.00 1st page. Payee: Register of Deeds. **Other phones:** Treasurer-715-395-1348; Elections-715-395-1397; Vital Records-715-395-1463.

Dunn County

Register of Deeds, 800 Wilson Ave, Menomonie, WI 54751. **Phone**-715-232-1228; fax-715-232-1229; hours 8AM-4:30PM. Will not search UCC or real estate records. Record copy fee- $2.00 1st page, $1.00 each add'l. Cert fee: $1.00. Payee: Dunn County Register of Deeds. **Other phones:** Assessor-715-232-1401; Treasurer-715-232-3789.

Eau Claire County

Register of Deeds, PO Box 718, Eau Claire, WI 54702. **Phone**-715-839-4745; hours 8AM-5PM www.co.eau-claire.wi.us/ Will not search records. Record copy fee- $2.00 1st page, $1.00 each add'l. Cert fee: $1.00 per cert. Payee: Eau Claire County Register of Deeds. **Online Access to Warrant, Most Wanted records:** Search the sheriff's most wanted list and warrants list at www.co.eau-claire.wi.us/sheriff/sheriff.asp. **Other phones:** Treasurer-715-839-4805; Vital Records-715-839-4745.

Florence County

Register of Deeds, PO Box 410, Florence, WI 54121-0410. **Phone**-715-528-4252; fax-715-528-5470; hours M-F 8:30-4PM. Will not search UCC or tax liens records. Will do limited real estate search. Record copy fee- $2.00 1st page, $1.00 each add'l. Cert fee: $1.00. Payee: Register of Deeds. **Other phones:** Treasurer-715-528-3204.

Fond du Lac County

Register of Deeds, PO Box 509, Fond du Lac, WI 54935-0509. **Phone**-920-929-3018, R/E Recording-920-929-3021, UCC Recording-920-929-3022; fax-920-929-3293; hours 7:45AM-4:30PM www.co.fond-du-lac.wi.us
Will search UCC records, effective date to 7-1-2001. Search per debtor- $10.00. Will not do federal tax lien search. Will not search real estate records. Record copy fee- $2.00 1st page, $1.00 each add'l. Cert fee: $1.00 per doc. Payee: Fond du Lac County Register of Deeds. **Online Access to Property, Assessor, GIS Mapping records:** Access to parcel information is free through the GIS-mapping site at www.co.fond-du-lac.wi.us/Website/FondduLacIMS/vi ewer.htm. Click on search to search by address or parcel number. No name searching. **Other phones:** Assessor-920-929-3010; Treasurer-920-929-3010; Elections-920-929-3000; Vital Records-920-929-3019.

Forest County

Register of Deeds, 200 E. Madison St, Crandon, WI 54520. **Phone**-Register of Deeds, R/E & UCC Recording- 715-478-3823; 8:30AM-Noon, 1-4:30PM
UCC records search per debtor- $10.00. UCC search does not include federal tax liens. Will not search real estate records. Record copy fee- $2.00 1st page, $1.00 each add'l. Cert fee: $1.00 per cert. Payee: Forest County Register of Deeds. **Other phones:** Treasurer-715-478-2412; Elections-715-478-2422; Vital Records-715-478-3823.

Grant County

Register of Deeds, PO Box 391, Lancaster, WI 53813-0391. **Phone**-Register of Deeds, R/E & UCC Recording- 608-723-2727; fax-608-723-4048; hours 8AM-4:30PM
Will not search records. Record copy fee- $2.00 1st page, $1.00 each add'l. Cert fee: $1.00 per doc. Payee: Register of Deeds. **Online Access to Land, Assessor records:** Access to county property and assessor data is at www.gcssoftware.com/produ ct/web_search.asp. Registration, $200.00 annual fee, username, and password required; call John at the Tax Lister office, 608-723-2666. **Other phones:** Assessor-608-723-2666; Treasurer-608-723-2604; Elections-608-723-2675; Vital Records-608-723-2727.

Green County

Register of Deeds, 1016 16th Ave, Courthouse, Monroe, WI 53566. **Phone**-608-328-9439; fax-608-328-2835; hours 8AM-5PM. Will not search records. Record copy fee- $2.00 1st page, $1.00 each add'l. Payee: Green County Register of Deeds.

Green Lake County

Register of Deeds, PO Box 3188, Green Lake, WI 54941-3188. **Phone**-Register of Deeds, R/E & UCC Recording- 920-294-4021; fax-920-294-4165; hours 8AM-4:30PM www.co.green-lake.wi.us
UCC records search per debtor- $10.00. Will not search real estate or tax lien records. Record copy fee- $2.00 1st page, $1.00 each add'l. Cert fee: $1.00 per doc. **Other phones:** Treasurer-920-294-4018; Vital Records-920-294-4021.

Iowa County

Register of Deeds, 222 N. Iowa St, Dodgeville, WI 53533. **Phone**-Register of Deeds, R/E & UCC Recording- 608-935-0396; fax-608-935-3024; hours 8:30AM-4:30PM. Will not search UCC or real estate records. Record copy fee- $2.00 1st page, $1.00 each add'l. Cert fee: $1.00 plus copy fee. Payee: Iowa County Register of Deeds. **Other phones:** Treasurer-608-935-0397; Elections-608-935-0399; Vital Records-608-935-0396.

Iron County

Register of Deeds, 300 Taconite St, Hurley, WI 54534. **Phone**-Register of Deeds, R/E & UCC Recording- 715-561-2945; fax-715-561-2928.
Will not search UCC or real estate records. Record copy fee- $2.00 1st page, $1.00 each add'l. Cert fee: $2.00 per page. **Other phones:** Assessor-715-561-2883; Treasurer-715-561-2883; Appraiser/ Auditor-715-561-2883; Vital Records-715-561-2945.

Jackson County

Register of Deeds, 307 Main, Black River Falls, WI 54615. **Phone**-715-284-0205; fax-715-284-0204; hours 8AM-4PM. Will not search UCC or real estate records. Will search tax liens. Record copy fee- $2.00 1st page, $1.00 each add'l. Cert fee: $1.00 per doc. Payee: Register of Deeds. **Other phones:** Assessor-715-284-0203; Treasurer-715-284-0226.

Jefferson County

Register of Deeds, PO Box 356, Jefferson, WI 53549. **Phone**-920-674-7235; hours-8AM-4:30PM www.co.jefferson.wi.us
Will not search UCC or real estate records. Tax lien search- $10.00 per debtor. Record copy fee- $2.00 1st page, $1.00 each add'l. Cert fee: $1.00 per doc. Payee: Jefferson County Register of Deeds. **Online Access to Grantor/Grantee, Treasurer, GIS-Mapping, Assessor Property Tax records:** Call 920-674-7254 for info and fee. **Other phones:** Treasurer-920-674-7250; Elections-920-674-7140; Vital Records-920-674-7235.

Juneau County

Register of Deeds, 220 E. State St. #212, Mauston, WI 53948-1379. **Phone-**Register of Deeds, R/E & UCC Recording- 608-847-9325; fax-608-847-9402; hours 8AM-N, 12:30-4:30PM. Will not search records. Record copy fee- $2.00 1st page, $1.00 each add'l. Cert fee: $3.00 1st page, $1.00 each add'ls per real estate doc. Payee: Register of Deeds. **Other phones:** Treasurer-608-847-9308; Elections-608-847-9302; Vital Records-608-847-9325.

Kenosha County

Register of Deeds, 1010 56 St., Kenosha, WI 53140. **Phone-**262-653-2444, R/E Recording-414-653-2441; fax-262-653-2564; hours 8AM-5PM
Will not search UCC or real estate records. Record copy fee- $2.00 1st page, $1.00 each add'l. Cert fee: $1.00. Payee: Kenosha County Clerk. **Online Access to Real Estate, Lien, Vital Statistic, Assessor records:** Access to recorder records requires a set-up fee is $500, + $6.00 per hour usage fee. The system operates 24 hours daily; records date back to 5/1986. Federal tax liens and lending agency information is available. For further information, contact Joellyn Storz at 262-653-2511. Also, search Kenosha City Assessor's property database for free at www.kenosha .org/departments/assessor/search.html. No name searching. **Other phones:** Assessor-414-653-2545; Treasurer-414-653-2542; Vital Records-262-653-2444.

Kewaunee County

Register of Deeds, 613 Dodge St, Kewaunee, WI 54216-1398. **Phone-**920-388-7126, R/E Recording-920-388-7126/7127/7128; fax-920-388-7195; hours 8AM-4:30PM www.kewauneeco.org
Will not search UCC or real estate records. Record copy fee- $2.00 1st page, $1.00 each add'l. Cert fee: $1.00 per doc. Payee: Register of Deeds. **Online Access to Grantor/Grantee, Deed, Tract & Image, GIS Mapping, Property Tax records:** Access to Register of Deeds data should be at www.kewauneeco.org/subpages/Departments/ROD/Re gister%20of%20Deeds.htm. Click on Documents and Images. **Other phones:** Treasurer-920-388-7152; Elections-920-388-7133; Vital Records-920-388-7126.

La Crosse County

Register of Deeds, 400 N. 4th St, Rm 1220, Admin. Ctr, La Crosse, WI 54601-3200. **Phone-**608-785-9644, R/E Recording-608-785-9652, UCC Recording-608-785-9651; fax-608-785-9643; hours 8:30AM-5PM www.co.la-crosse.wi.us/Departments/departments.htm The county participates on the www.landrecords.net site. Fees are involved. Will not search UCC or real estate records. Will search federal tax liens. Record copy fee- $2.00 1st page, $1.00 each add'l. Cert fee: $1.00 per doc + copy fees. Payee: Register of Deeds. **Online Access to Land, Deed, Property Owner records:** Access to register of deeds records is via a private company at https://www.landrecords.net/. Subscription or pay-per search service available. Index goes back to 1992; images back to 6/1992. Also, search for property owner and land information for free at www.co.la-crosse.wi.us/Departments/LIO/main_searc h_page.htm. **Other phones:** Assessor-608-785-7525; Treasurer-608-785-9711; Vital Records-608-785-9652.

Lafayette County

Register of Deeds, PO Box 170, Darlington, WI 53530. **Phone-**Register of Deeds, R/E & UCC Recording- 608-776-4838; fax-608-776-4991; hours 8AM-4:30PM
Will not search records. Record copy fee- $2.00 1st page, $1.00 each add'l. Cert fee: $1.00. Payee: Register of Deeds. **Online Access to Land, Deed records:** Access to register of deeds records is via a private company at https://www.landrecords.net/. Subscription or pay-per search service available. **Other**

phones: Treasurer-608-776-4862; Elections-608-776-4850; Vital Records-608-776-4838.

Langlade County

Register of Deeds, 800 Clermont St, Antigo, WI 54409. **Phone-**715-627-6209; fax-715-627-6303; hours 8:30AM-4:30PM. Will not search records. Record copy fee- $2.00 1st page, $1.00 each add'l. Cert fee: $1.00. Payee: Register of Deeds. **Other phones:** Treasurer-715-627-6204.

Lincoln County

Register of Deeds, 1110 E. Main, Courthouse, Merrill, WI 54452. **Phone-**Register of Deeds, R/E & UCC Recording- 715-536-0318; fax-715-536-0360. www.co.lincoln.wi.us
UCC records search per debtor- $10.00. Will not search real estate records. Record copy fee- $2.00 1st page, $1.00 each add'l. **Online Access to Land records:** Access to county land records is free at www.lrs.co.lincoln.wi.us/apps/lrs/. No name searching. **Other phones:** Assessor-715-536-0479; Treasurer-715-536-0315; Elections-715-536-0359; Vital Records-715-536-0318.

Manitowoc County

Register of Deeds, PO Box 421, Manitowoc, WI 54221-0421. **Phone-**920-683-4010, R/E Recording-920-683-4011; fax-920-683-2702; hours 8:30AM-4:30PM www.manitowoc-county.com
UCC records search per debtor- $10.00. Will not search real estate records. Record copy fee- $2.00 1st page, $1.00 each add'l. Cert fee: $1.00 per page. Payee: Register of Deeds. **Online Access to Assessor, Real Estate records:** Records on the City of Manitowoc Assessor database are free at http://assessor.manitowoc.org/default.htm. No name searching. Also, search property data for the Villages of Mishicot and Valders as well as Town of Manitowoc at www.wendorffassessing.com/municipalities.htm. **Other phones:** Assessor-920-683-4425; Treasurer-920-683-4020; Vital Records-920-683-4509.

Marathon County

Register of Deeds, 500 Forest St, Courthouse, Wausau, WI 54403-5568. **Phone-**Register of Deeds, R/E & UCC Recording- 715-261-1470; fax-715-261-1488; hours 8AM-4:30PM www.co.marathon.wi.us
Will not search UCC or real estate records. Record copy fee- $2.00 1st page, $1.00 each add'l. Cert fee: $1.00 per doc. Payee: Register of Deeds. **Online Access to Land records:** Access county property records free at www.co.marathon.wi.us/onl ine/apps/lrs/index.asp. No name searching. **Other phones:** Assessor-715-843-1300; Treasurer-715-261-1150; Elections-715-261-1500; Vital Records-715-261-1470.

Marinette County

Register of Deeds, 1926 Hall Ave, Courthouse, Marinette, WI 54143. **Phone-**715-732-7550; fax-715-732-7532; hours 8:30AM-4:30PM. Will not search UCC or real estate records. Record copy fee- $2.00 1st page, $1.00 each add'l. Cert fee: $3.00. Payee: Marinette County. **Other phones:** Treasurer-715-732-7430.

Marquette County

Register of Deeds, PO Box 236, Montello, WI 53949-0236. **Phone-**608-297-9132, R/E Recording-608-297-9136 x232, UCC Recording-608-297-9136 x232; fax-608-297-7606; hours 8AM-Noon, 12:30-4:30PM
Will not search UCC or real estate records. Record copy fee- $2.00 1st page, $1.00 each add'l. Cert fee: $1.00 per doc. Payee: Marquette County Register of Deeds. **Other phones:** Assessor-608-297-9148; Treasurer-608-297-9148; Vital Records-608-297-9136 x232.

Menominee County

Register of Deeds, PO Box 279, Keshena, WI 54135-0279. **Phone-**Register of Deeds, R/E & UCC Recording- 715-799-3312; fax-715-799-1322; hours 8AM-4:30PM
UCC records search per debtor- $10.00. Real estate records are found at D.F.I. Record copy fee- $2.00 1st page, $1.00 each add'l. **Other phones:** Assessor-715-799-3001; Treasurer-715-799-3315; Appraiser/ Auditor-715-799-3001; Elections-715-799-3311; Vital Records-715-799-3312.

Milwaukee County

Register of Deeds, 901 N. 9th St, Rm 103, Milwaukee, WI 53233. **Phone-**414-278-4011, R/E Recording-414-278-4005, UCC Recording-414-278-4006; fax-414-223-1257. www.co.milwaukee.wi.us
UCC records search per debtor- $10.00. Record copy fee- $2.00 1st page, $1.00 each add'l. **Online Access to Assessor, Real Estate, Property Sale records:** Property, assessment data and sales data on Milwaukee City (not county) Assessor database is free at www.milwaukee.gov/display/router.asp?docid=720. No name searching. Also search Greendale City at www.gcssoftware.com/product/web_search.asp. Also, search City of Cudahy assessor property data for free at http://exch02.ci.cudahy.wi.us/Scripts/GVSWeb.dll/Sear ch, and Wauwatosa property at www.wauwatosa.net/wsp/wspAssessmentMainPage.as p. No name searching. Also, search Franklin assessor at www.ci.franklin.wi.us/dynamic/pagetemplate.cfm?tem plate=assessmentSearch.cfm. Glendale assessor is at http://ts.glendale-wi.org; West Allis at www.ci.west-allis.wi.us/asp/search_form.asp. No name searching. **Other phones:** Assessor-414-286-3651; Treasurer-414-278-4033; Elections-414-278-4060; Vital Records-414-278-4003.

Monroe County

Register of Deeds, 202 S. "K" St, Rm 2, Sparta, WI 54656. **Phone-**Register of Deeds, R/E & UCC Recording- 608-269-8716; fax-608-269-8715; hours 8AM-4:30PM www.co.monroe.wi.us
Will not search UCC records. Will do tax lien search. Real estate record owner searches available. Record copy fee- $2.00 1st page, $1.00 each add'l. Cert fee: $1.00 per cert. Payee: Monroe County Register of Deeds. **Other phones:** Treasurer-608-269-8710; Vital Records-608-269-8716.

Oconto County

Register of Deeds, 301 Washington St, Rm 2035, Oconto, WI 54153-1699. **Phone-**Register of Deeds, R/E & UCC Recording- 920-834-6807; hours 8AM-4PM www.co.oconto.wi.us
Will search UCC records through to 6/30/2001 only. Search per debtor- $15.00. UCC search includes federal tax liens if requested. Will not search real estate records. Record copy fee- $2.00 1st page, $1.00 each add'l. Cert fee: $1.00 per cert. Payee: Oconto County Register of Deeds. **Online Access to Property, Assessor records:** Access to the county SOLO tax parcel search is free or by subscription at http://solo.co.oconto.wi.us/ocontoco/. Subscription fee is $300 per calendar year. Phone 920-834-6800 for information. The free service does not include name searching. **Other phones:** Treasurer-920-834-6813; Vital Records-920-834-6807; Real Property Lister-920-834-6827.

Oneida County

Register of Deeds, PO Box 400, Rhinelander, WI 54501. **Phone-**715-369-6150; fax-715-369-6222; hours 8AM-4:30PM. UCC records search per debtor- $15.00. Record copy fee- $2.00 1st page, $1.00 each add'l. Cert fee: $1.00. Payee: Oneida County

Register of Deeds. **Other phones:** Assessor-715-369-6137; Treasurer-715-369-6137.

Outagamie County

Register of Deeds, 410 S. Walnut St, CAB 205, Appleton, WI 54911-5999. **Phone-**Register of Deeds, R/E & UCC Recording- 920-832-5095, UCC Recording-920-832-5097; fax-920-832-2177; hours 8AM-4:30PM; Summer hours: 7AM-3:30PM www.co.outagamie.wi.us
Will not search records. Record copy fee- $2.00 1st page, $1.00 each add'l. **Online Access to Inmate, Offender records:** Search inmate information for free on private company website at www.vinelink.com/index.jsp. **Other phones:** Treasurer-414-832-5065; Elections-920-832-5077; Vital Records-920-832-5095; Abstracting Phone-920-832-5114; Tax Lister-920-832-5665.

Ozaukee County

Register of Deeds, PO Box 994, Port Washington, WI 53074-0994. **Phone-**Register of Deeds, R/E & UCC Recording- 262-284-8260; fax-262-284-8100; hours 8:30AM-5:00PM www.co.ozaukee.wi.us
UCC records search per debtor- $15.00. Federal/state combined tax lien search- $15.00 per debtor. Will not search real estate records. Record copy fee- $2.00 1st page, $1.00 each add'l. Cert fee: $1.00 per doc. Payee: Register of Deeds. **Online Access to Recording, Real Estate, Grantor/Grantee, Vital Statistic, Property Tax, Tracts, Civil Court records:** Access is by "Remote Access" requiring dial-up modem. This data is for inquiries only and includes civil, family, and traffic courts with Register of Deeds (back to 1960's) and Treasurer (back 11 years) property data. Software is supplied by the county. 1st month is free, then $50.00 per month subscription. For info, contact the Technology Resources Dept. at 262-284-8309. **Other phones:** Treasurer-262-284-8280; Vital Records-262-284-8260.

Pepin County

Register of Deeds, PO Box 39, Durand, WI 54736. **Phone-**715-672-8856; fax-715-672-8677; hours 8:30AM-Noon, 12:30-4:30
Will not search UCC or real estate records. Separate federal tax lien search-$15.00 per debtor. For state tax liens see clerk of court. Record copy fee- $2.00 1st page, $1.00 each add'l. Cert fee: $1.00 per doc. Payee: Register of Deeds. **Other phones:** Treasurer-715-672-8850; Vital Records-715-672-8856.

Pierce County

Register of Deeds, PO Box 267, Ellsworth, WI 54011-0267. **Phone-**Register of Deeds, R/E & UCC Recording- 715-273-3531 x418; fax-715-273-6861; hours 8AM-5PM www.co.pierce.wi.us
Will not search UCC or real estate records. Record copy fee- $2.00 1st page, $1.00 each add'l. Cert fee: $1.00 per doc. Payee: Register of Deeds. **Online Access to Real Estate, Assessor, Property Tax records:** Access to county property data is free at www.co.pierce.wi.us/Disclaimer.htm. Click on Property Data Search. Greater assess to Register of Deeds real estate data is available to professionals on the Tapestry System or the lesser Laredo System. Registration is required and fees apply, visit www.co.pierce.wi.us/reg_of_deeds/Records.access.page.htm for information. Records go back to 1998. **Other phones:** Assessor-715-273-3531; Treasurer-715-273-3531 x307-8; Vital Records-715-273-3531 x418.

Polk County

Register of Deeds, PO Box 335, Balsam Lake, WI 54810-0335. **Phone-**Register of Deeds, R/E & UCC Recording- 715-485-9240; fax-715-485-9202; hours 8:30AM-4:30PM www.co.polk.wi.us

Will not search records. Record copy fee- $2.00 1st page, $1.00 each add'l. Cert fee: $1.00 per doc. Payee: Register of Deeds. **Other phones:** Treasurer-715-485-9254; Elections-715-485-9223; Vital Records-715-485-9240.

Portage County

Register of Deeds, 1516 Church St, County-City Bldg., Stevens Point, WI 54481. **Phone-**715-346-1428; fax-715-345-5361; hours 7:30-4:30 www.co.portage.wi.us
UCC records search per debtor- $10.00. Record copy fee- $2.00 1st page, $1.00 each add'l. Cert fee: $1.00. Payee: Register of Deeds. **Online Access to Property Tax, Assessor, Recording, Land, Deed, Criminal Complaint records:** Access to county records is free at www.co.portage.wi.us. Registration required; searching is free; fee for copies of images. Property tax data does not include Steven Point City. **Other phones:** Assessor-715-346-1553; Treasurer-715-346-1428.

Price County

Register of Deeds, 126 Cherry, Phillips, WI 54555. **Phone-**715-339-2515; hours 8AM-Noon, 1-4:30PM
Will not search UCC records. Will do tax lien search. Real estate owner, mortgage, and property transfer searches available. Record copy fee- $2.00 1st page, $1.00 each add'l. Cert fee: $1.00. Payee: Price County Register of Deeds.

Racine County

Register of Deeds, 730 Wisconsin Ave, Racine, WI 53403. **Phone-**262-636-3208; fax-262-636-3851; hours 8AM-5PM www.goracine.org
Will not search UCC or real estate records. Record copy fee- $2.00 1st page, $1.00 each add'l. Cert fee: $1.00 per doc. Payee: Racine County Register of Deeds. **Other phones:** Treasurer-262-636-3238.

Richland County

Register of Deeds, PO Box 337, Richland Center, WI 53581. **Phone-**Register of Deeds, R/E & UCC Recording- 608-647-3011; hours 8:30AM-4:30PM
UCC records search per debtor- $10.00. UCC search includes federal tax liens if requested. Will search real estate records. Record copy fee- $2.00 1st page, $1.00 each add'l. Cert fee: $.25 per cert. Payee: Richland County Register of Deeds. **Other phones:** Assessor-608-647-3658; Treasurer-608-647-3658; Vital Records-608-647-3011.

Rock County

Register of Deeds, 51 S. Main St, Janesville, WI 53545. **Phone-**608-757-5657, R/E Recording-608-757-5650; fax-608-757-5563; hours 8AM-5PM www.co.rock.wi.us/departments/reg_deeds.htm
Will not search records. Record copy fee- $2.00 1st page, $1.00 each add'l. Cert fee: $1.00 per cert. Payee: Rock County Register of Deeds. **Online Access to Assessor, Real Estate records:** Records on the City of Janesville Assessor database are free at www.ci.janesville.wi.us/Government/Assessor/Property Search/query.asp. No name searching. Also, search Evanville property assessor records for free at www.wendorffassessing.com/municipalities.htm. No name searching. **Other phones:** Vital Records-608-757-5656.

Rusk County

Register of Deeds, 311 Miner Ave. Rm#N132, Ladysmith, WI 54848-0311. **Phone-**715-532-2139; fax-715-532-2194; hours 8:00AM-4:30PM
Will not search records. Record copy fee- $2.00 1st page, $1.00 each add'l. Cert fee: $1.00. Payee: Rusk County Register of Deeds. **Online Access to Land records:** Access to the county land records data is free at www.gcssoftware.com/applications/search/index.asp?County=Rusk.

Sauk County

Register of Deeds, 505 Broadway St., Baraboo, WI 53913. **Phone-**608-355-3288; fax-608-355-3292; hours 8AM-4:30PM
Will not search UCC or real estate records. Record copy fee- $2.00 1st page, $1.00 each add'l. Cert fee: $1.00 per doc. Payee: Register of Deeds. **Online Access to Property, Assessor records:** Search Village of Spring Green property data for free at www.wendorffassessing.com/Spring%20Green%20opt ions.htm. No name searching. **Other phones:** Assessor-608-355-5581; Treasurer-608-355-3276.

Sawyer County

Register of Deeds, PO Box 686, Hayward, WI 54843-0686. **Phone-**Register of Deeds, R/E & UCC Recording- 715-634-4867; fax-715-634-6839; hours 8AM-4PM http://sawyercountygov.org
Will not search records. Record copy fee- $2.00 1st page, $1.00 each add'l. Cert fee: $1.00 per page + $2.00 per page to copy. **Other phones:** Assessor-715-634-4868; Treasurer-715-634-4868; Elections-715-634-4866; Vital Records-715-634-4867.

Shawano County

Register of Deeds, 311 N. Main, Shawano, WI 54166. **Phone-**715-524-2129; fax-715-524-5157.
Will not search UCC or real estate records. RE record copy fee- $2.00 1st page, $1.00 each add'l. UCC copy- $2.00 per page. Cert fee: $1.00 per doc. **Other phones:** Assessor-715-524-9130; Treasurer-715-524-9130.

Sheboygan County

Register of Deeds, 508 New York Ave, 2nd Fl, Sheboygan, WI 53081. **Phone-**920-459-3023; hours 8AM-5PM
Will not search UCC or real estate records. Record copy fee- $2.00 1st page, $1.00 each add'l. Cert fee: $1.00 per cert. Payee: Register of Deeds. **Online Access to Land, Deed, Real Estate, Tax Lien records:** Access to register of deeds records is via a private company at https://www.landrecords.net/. Subscription or pay-per search service available. Index goes back to 1/1992; images to 5/1994. **Other phones:** Treasurer-920-459-3015.

St. Croix County

Register of Deeds, 1101 Carmichael Rd., Hudson, WI 54016. **Phone-**715-386-4652, UCC Recording-715-386-4654; fax-715-386-4687; hours 8AM-5PM www.co.saint-croix.wi.us
Will not search UCC or real estate records. Record copy fee- $2.00 1st page, $1.00 each add'l. Cert fee: $1.00 per page. Payee: Register of Deeds. **Other phones:** Assessor-715-386-4677; Treasurer-715-386-4645; Vital Records-715-386-4653.

Taylor County

Register of Deeds, 224 S 2nd St, Medford, WI 54451-1811. **Phone-**Register of Deeds, R/E & UCC Recording- 715-748-1483; fax-715-748-1446; hours 8:30AM-4:30PM www.co.taylor.wi.us/departmen ts/registerofdeeds/rodmain.htm
UCC records search per debtor- $10.00. UCC search includes federal tax liens. Real estate owner, mortgage, and property transfer searches available. Record copy fee- $2.00 1st page, $1.00 each add'l. Cert fee: $1.00 per cert. Payee: Taylor County Register of Deeds. **Online Access to Real Estate Records - 1995 forward records:** Found at https://landshark.co.taylor.wi.us/eddie/login.jsp; username and password required. Records go back to 1998. Index search is free; images are $2.00 1st page, $1.00 each add;l. **Other phones:** Assessor-715-748-1465; Treasurer-715-748-1466; Vital Records-715-748-1483.

Trempealeau County

Register of Deeds, PO Box 67, Whitehall, WI 54773. **Phone**-715-538-2311, R/E Recording-715-538-2311 x244, UCC Recording-715-538-2311 x244; hours 8AM-4:30PM www.tremplocounty.com
Will search UCC records prior to July 1, 2001. Search per debtor- $10.00. UCC search includes federal tax liens. Will not search real estate records. Record copy fee- $2.00 1st page, $1.00 each add'l. Cert fee: $1.00 per cert. Payee: Trempealeau County Register of Deeds. **Online Access to Real Estate, Assessor records:** Access to the county assessor's database is free at www.tremplocounty.com/Search. **Other phones:** Assessor-715-538-2311 x248; Treasurer-715-538-2311 x219; Vital Records-715-538-2311 x244.

Vernon County

Register of Deeds, PO Box 46, Viroqua, WI 54665. **Phone**-Register of Deeds, R/E & UCC Recording- 608-637-3571; fax-608-637-5304; hours 8:30AM-4:30PM
Will search UCC real estate records only through 6/30/2001. Search per debtor- $15.00. Will not search real estate or tax lien records. Record copy fee- $2.00 1st page, $1.00 each add'l. Cert fee: $1.00 per cert. Payee: Vernon County Register of Deeds. **Other phones:** Assessor-608-637-3222; Treasurer-608-637-3222; Elections-608-637-5304; Vital Records-608-637-3572.

Vilas County

Register of Deeds, 330 Court St., Eagle River, WI 54521. **Phone**-Register of Deeds, R/E & UCC Recording- 715-479-3660; fax-715-479-3695; hours 8AM-4PM http://co.vilas.wi.us
Will not search UCC or real estate records. Record copy fee- $2.00 1st page, $1.00 each add'l. Cert fee: $1.00 per doc. Payee: Register of Deeds. **Other phones:** Assessor-Contact Treasurer for Info.; Treasurer-715-479-3610; Vital Records-715-479-3660.

Walworth County

Register of Deeds, PO Box 995, Elkhorn, WI 53121-0995. **Phone**-262-741-4214, R/E Recording-262-741-4233, UCC Recording-262-741-4237; fax-262-741-4947; hours 8AM-5PM www.co.walworth.wi.us
Will not search records. Record copy fee- $2.00 1st page, $1.00 each add'l. Cert fee: $1.00 per doc. Payee: Refgister of Deeds. **Online Access to Property Tax, Recording, Grantor/Grantee, Deed records:** Search the Register of Deeds index for free on the county e-government web page at www.co.walworth.wi.us. Click on "Public Records." Online records go as far back as 1976. Also, search the treasurer's tax roll list under "Tax Roll Documents" on the county e-government web page. Also search the Village of Walworth property data for free at www.wendorffassessing.com/Walworth%20options.ht

m. **Other phones:** Assessor-262-741-4251; Treasurer-262-741-4251; Elections-262-741-4241; Vital Records-262-741-4235.

Washburn County

Register of Deeds, PO Box 607, Shell Lake, WI 54871. **Phone**-Register of Deeds, R/E & UCC Recording- 715-468-4616; fax-715-468-4658; hours 8AM-4:30PM
UCC records search per debtor- $10.00. Will search tax liens including federal tax liens. Tax lien search- $10.00 per debtor. Will not search real estate records. Record copy- $2.00 1st page; $1.00 each add'l. Cert fee: $1.00 per doc. Payee: Register of deeds. **Other phones:** Assessor-715-468-4696; Treasurer-715-468-4650; Elections-715-468-4605; Vital Records-715-468-4616.

Washington County

Register of Deeds, PO Box 1986, West Bend, WI 53095-7986. **Phone**-262-335-4318, R/E Recording-262-335-4320; fax-262-335-6866; 8AM-4:30PM www.co.washington.wi.us/departments/default.htm
Will not search records. RE record copy fee- $2.00 1st page, $1.00 each add'l. UCC copy- $2.00 per page. Cert fee: $3.00 1st page; $1.00 each add'l. Payee: Register of Deeds. **Other phones:** Assessor-262-335-4370; Treasurer-262-335-4325; Elections-262-335-4468; Vital Records-262-335-4321.

Waukesha County

Register of Deeds, 1320 Pewaukee Rd, Rm 110, Waukesha, WI 53188. **Phone**-262-548-7863, R/E Recording-262-548-7590, UCC Recording-262-548-7585; hours-8AM-4:30PM www.waukeshacounty.gov/departments/register
The real estate section will only answer their phone between the hours of 3pm-4:30pm. Will not search UCC or tax liens records. Real estate owner, mortgage, and property transfer searches available. Record copy fee- $2.00 1st page, $1.00 each add'l. Cert fee: $1.00 per page. Payee: Waukesha County Register of Deeds. **Online Access to Property, Assessor, Recording, Deed, Lien, Marriage, UCC records:** Access the county recorder database is free at http://dwprd.waukeshacounty.gov/applications/producti on/ROD_TRACT_DOCUMENTS/. Also, search county tax listing at http://dwprd.waukeshacounty.go v/applications/production/ROD_TAX_LISTING/. No name searching at either of these sites. Also, search City of Waukesha assessor property database or sales lists at www.ci.waukesha.wi.us/dept/assessor/index.htm. **Other phones:** Assessor-262-542-0455; Treasurer-262-548-7576.

Waupaca County

Register of Deeds, PO Box 307, Waupaca, WI 54981. **Phone**-Register of Deeds, R/E & UCC Recording- 715-258-6250; fax-715-258-6212; hours 8AM-4PM

UCC records search per debtor- $10.00. Tax lien search- $2.00 per debtor. Will not search real estate records. Record copy fee- $2.00 1st page, $1.00 each add'l. Cert fee: $3.00 1st page, $1.00 each add'l. Payee: Register of Deeds. **Online Access to Property Tax, Assessor, Register of Deed, Land records:** Access to the county tax parcel lookup is at http://public1.co.waupaca.wi.us/is/TaxHistory/thTaxHis toryEnter.asp. Access to the Register of Deeds data requires subscription, username and password. Annual fee is $125.00. For info, call 715-258-6235 or visit http://216.56.10,105/access/default.asp?access=2. **Other phones:** Assessor-715-258-6215; Treasurer-715-258-6220; Elections-715-258-6200; Vital Records-715-258-6250.

Waushara County

Register of Deeds, PO Box 338, Wautoma, WI 54982. **Phone**-Register of Deeds, R/E & UCC Recording- 920-787-0444; fax-920-787-0425; hours 8AM-4:30PM
UCC records search per debtor- $10.00. Will not search real estate records. Record copy fee- $2.00 1st page, $1.00 each add'l. Cert fee: $1.00 per doc. Payee: Register of Deeds. **Other phones:** Treasurer-920-787-0445; Elections-920-787-0442; Vital Records-920-787-0444.

Winnebago County

Register of Deeds, PO Box 2808, Oshkosh, WI 54903-2808. **Phone**-920-236-4883, R/E Recording-920-236-4881; fax-920-303-3025; hours 8AM-4:30PM
Will not search UCC or real estate records. Separate federal tax lien search-$5.00 per debtor. Record copy fee- $2.00 1st page, $1.00 each add'l. Cert fee: $1.00 per cert. Payee: Winnebago County Register of Deeds. **Online Access to Assessor, Real Estate records:** Records on the City of Menasha Tax Roll Information database are free at www.cityofmenasha-wi.gov. Property records on the City of Oshkosh assessor database are free at www.ci.oshkosh.wi.us/assessor/ProcessSearch.asp?cmd =NewSearch. Also, City of Neenah property data is at www.ci.neenah.wi.us/propinfo/index.html but no name search. **Other phones:** Assessor-920-236-4775; Treasurer-920-236-4777; Elections-920-236-4888; Vital Records-920-236-4882.

Wood County

Register of Deeds, PO Box 8095, Wisconsin Rapids, WI 54495. **Phone**-715-421-8450; hours 8AM-4:30PM www.co.wood.wi.us
Will not search UCC or real estate records. Will not do federal tax lien search. Record copy fee- $2.00 1st page, $1.00 each add'l. Cert fee: $1.00 per cert. Payee: Wood County Register of Deeds. **Other phones:** Assessor-715-421-8484; Treasurer-715-421-8484.

Wisconsin County Locator

You will usually be able to find the city name in the City/County Cross Reference below. In that case, it is a simple matter to determine the county from the cross reference. However, only the official US Postal Service city names are included in this index. There are an additional 40,000 place names that people use in their addresses. Therefore, we have also included a ZIP/City Cross Reference immediately following the City/County Cross Reference.

If you know the ZIP Code but the city name does not appear in the City/County Cross Reference index, look up the ZIP Code in the ZIP/City Cross Reference, find the city name, then look up the city name in the City/County Cross Reference. For example, you want to know the county for an address of Menands, NY 12204. There is no "Menands" in the City/County Cross Reference. The ZIP/City Cross Reference shows that ZIP Codes 12201-12288 are for the city of Albany. Looking back in the City/County Cross Reference, Albany is in Albany County.

Wisconsin City/County Cross Reference

ABBOTSFORD (54405) Clark(71), Marathon(28)
ABRAMS Oconto
ADAMS Adams
ADELL Sheboygan
AFTON Rock
ALBANY Green
ALGOMA (54201) Kewaunee(96), Door(3)
ALGOMA Kewaunee
ALLENTON (53002) Washington(97), Dodge(2)
ALMA Buffalo
ALMA CENTER Jackson
ALMENA Barron
ALMOND (54909) Portage(88), Waushara(11)
ALTOONA Eau Claire
AMBERG Marinette
AMERY Polk
AMHERST Portage
AMHERST JUNCTION Portage
ANIWA (54408) Marathon(56), Shawano(39), Langlade(4)
ANTIGO (54409) Langlade(97), Marathon(1), Shawano(1)
APPLETON (54914) Outagamie(97), Winnebago(2)
APPLETON (54915) Outagamie(53), Calumet(32), Winnebago(13)
APPLETON Outagamie
ARCADIA (54612) Trempealeau(89), Buffalo(10)
ARENA Iowa
ARGONNE Forest
ARGYLE (53504) Lafayette(75), Green(25)
ARKANSAW (54721) Pepin(88), Pierce(6), Dunn(5)
ARKDALE Adams
ARLINGTON (53911) Columbia(93), Dane(6)
ARMSTRONG CREEK (54103) Forest(82), Marinette(16), Florence(1)
ARPIN Wood
ASHIPPUN Dodge
ASHLAND (54806) Ashland(86), Bayfield(13)
ATHELSTANE (54104) Marinette(97), Oconto(1), Forest(1)
ATHENS (54411) Marathon(97), Taylor(2)
AUBURNDALE (54412) Wood(75), Marathon(24)
AUGUSTA Eau Claire
AVALON (53505) Rock(98), Walworth(1)
AVOCA Iowa
BABCOCK Wood
BAGLEY Grant
BAILEYS HARBOR Door
BALDWIN St. Croix
BALSAM LAKE Polk
BANCROFT (54921) Portage(89), Adams(8), Waushara(1)
BANGOR La Crosse
BARABOO Sauk
BARNEVELD Iowa
BARRON Barron

BARRONETT (54813) Barron(51), Burnett(31), Washburn(16)
BASSETT Kenosha
BAY CITY Pierce
BAYFIELD Bayfield
BEAR CREEK (54922) Outagamie(54), Waupaca(45)
BEAVER DAM Dodge
BEETOWN Grant
BELDENVILLE Pierce
BELGIUM (53004) Ozaukee(98), Sheboygan(1)
BELLEVILLE (53508) Dane(72), Green(27)
BELMONT Lafayette
BELOIT Rock
BENET LAKE Kenosha
BENOIT Bayfield
BENTON Lafayette
BERLIN (54923) Green Lake(71), Waushara(25), Winnebago(3)
BIG BEND Waukesha
BIG FALLS Waupaca
BIRCHWOOD (54817) Washburn(40), Sawyer(31), Barron(24), Rusk(2)
BIRNAMWOOD (54414) Shawano(77), Marathon(21)
BLACK CREEK (54106) Outagamie(98), Shawano(1)
BLACK EARTH Dane
BLACK RIVER FALLS (54615) Jackson(98), Monroe(1)
BLAIR (54616) Trempealeau(96), Jackson(3)
BLANCHARDVILLE (53516) Lafayette(57), Green(21), Iowa(18), Dane(2)
BLENKER Wood
BLOOM CITY Richland
BLOOMER Chippewa
BLOOMINGTON Grant
BLUE MOUNDS (53517) Dane(62), Iowa(37)
BLUE RIVER (53518) Richland(70), Grant(24), Crawford(5)
BONDUEL (54107) Shawano(96), Outagamie(3)
BOSCOBEL (53805) Grant(68), Crawford(31)
BOULDER JUNCTION Vilas
BOWLER Shawano
BOYCEVILLE Dunn
BOYD (54726) Chippewa(62), Eau Claire(37)
BRANCH Manitowoc
BRANDON (53919) Fond du Lac(98), Green Lake(1)
BRANTWOOD Price
BRIGGSVILLE (53920) Marquette(67), Adams(32)
BRILL Barron
BRILLION (54110) Calumet(79), Manitowoc(18), Brown(2)
BRISTOL Kenosha
BRODHEAD (53520) Green(74), Rock(25)
BROKAW Marathon
BROOKFIELD Waukesha

BROOKLYN (53521) Green(45), Dane(31), Rock(23)
BROOKS Adams
BROWNSVILLE (53006) Dodge(70), Fond du Lac(29)
BROWNTOWN (53522) Green(92), Lafayette(7)
BRUCE Rusk
BRULE (54820) Douglas(69), Bayfield(30)
BRUSSELS Door
BRYANT Langlade
BURLINGTON (53105) Racine(67), Walworth(19), Kenosha(13)
BURNETT Dodge
BUTLER Waukesha
BUTTE DES MORTS Winnebago
BUTTERNUT (54514) Ashland(53), Price(39), Iron(7)
BYRON Fond du Lac
CABLE (54821) Bayfield(98), Sawyer(1)
CADOTT (54727) Chippewa(91), Eau Claire(8)
CALEDONIA Racine
CAMBRIA (53923) Columbia(88), Green Lake(11)
CAMBRIDGE (53523) Dane(50), Jefferson(49)
CAMERON Barron
CAMP DOUGLAS (54618) Juneau(63), Monroe(36)
CAMP LAKE Kenosha
CAMPBELLSPORT (53010) Fond du Lac(94), Washington(4)
CAROLINE Shawano
CASCADE (53011) Sheboygan(91), Fond du Lac(8)
CASCO (54205) Kewaunee(97), Door(2)
CASHTON (54619) Monroe(77), Vernon(21), La Crosse(1)
CASSVILLE Grant
CATARACT Monroe
CATAWBA Price
CATO Manitowoc
CAZENOVIA (53924) Richland(96), Sauk(3)
CECIL (54111) Shawano(90), Oconto(9)
CEDAR GROVE (53013) Sheboygan(84), Ozaukee(15)
CEDARBURG (53012) Ozaukee(95), Washington(4)
CENTURIA Polk
CHASEBURG Vernon
CHELSEA Taylor
CHETEK (54728) Barron(87), Rusk(11), Dunn(1)
CHILI (54420) Clark(96), Wood(3)
CHILTON (53014) Calumet(97), Manitowoc(2)
CHIPPEWA FALLS (54729) Chippewa(97), Eau Claire(2)
CHIPPEWA FALLS Chippewa
CLAM LAKE (54517) Ashland(93), Sawyer(6)
CLAYTON (54004) Polk(59), Barron(40)

CLEAR LAKE (54005) Polk(79), St. Croix(11), Dunn(5), Barron(3)
CLEVELAND (53015) Manitowoc(86), Sheboygan(14)
CLINTON (53525) Rock(97), Walworth(2)
CLINTONVILLE (54929) Waupaca(69), Shawano(29), Outagamie(1)
CLYMAN Dodge
COBB Iowa
COCHRANE Buffalo
COLBY (54421) Clark(74), Marathon(25)
COLEMAN (54112) Marinette(76), Oconto(23)
COLFAX (54730) Dunn(77), Chippewa(22)
COLGATE (53017) Washington(72), Waukesha(27)
COLLINS Manitowoc
COLOMA (54930) Waushara(83), Adams(14), Marquette(2)
COLUMBUS (53925) Columbia(82), Dodge(13), Dane(4)
COMBINED LOCKS Outagamie
COMSTOCK (54826) Barron(62), Polk(37)
CONOVER Vilas
CONRATH Rusk
COON VALLEY (54623) Vernon(52), La Crosse(47)
CORNELL Chippewa
CORNUCOPIA Bayfield
COTTAGE GROVE Dane
COUDERAY Sawyer
CRANDON Forest
CRIVITZ (54114) Marinette(91), Oconto(8)
CROSS PLAINS Dane
CUBA CITY (53807) Grant(86), Lafayette(13)
CUDAHY Milwaukee
CUMBERLAND (54829) Barron(91), Polk(8)
CURTISS (54422) Clark(94), Taylor(5)
CUSHING Polk
CUSTER (54423) Portage(98), Marathon(1)
DALE Outagamie
DALLAS Barron
DALTON (53926) Green Lake(72), Marquette(15), Columbia(12)
DANBURY (54830) Burnett(93), Douglas(6)
DANE Dane
DARIEN (53114) Walworth(84), Rock(15)
DARLINGTON Lafayette
DE FOREST (53532) Dane(97), Columbia(2)
DE PERE (54115) Brown(92), Outagamie(7)
DE SOTO (54624) Vernon(89), Crawford(10)
DEER PARK (54007) St. Croix(67), Polk(32)
DEERBROOK Langlade
DEERFIELD Dane
DELAFIELD Waukesha
DELAVAN Walworth
DELLWOOD Adams
DENMARK (54208) Brown(53), Kewaunee(38), Manitowoc(7)

DICKEYVILLE Grant
DODGE Trempealeau
DODGEVILLE Iowa
DORCHESTER (54425) Clark(83),
    Marathon(9), Taylor(6)
DOUSMAN (53118) Waukesha(96),
    Jefferson(3)
DOWNING (54734) Dunn(94), St. Croix(5)
DOWNSVILLE Dunn
DOYLESTOWN Columbia
DRESSER Polk
DRUMMOND Bayfield
DUNBAR Marinette
DURAND (54736) Pepin(82), Buffalo(17)
EAGLE (53119) Waukesha(93),
    Walworth(4), Jefferson(2)
EAGLE RIVER (54521) Vilas(78),
    Oneida(19), Forest(1)
EAST ELLSWORTH Pierce
EAST TROY (53120) Walworth(97),
    Racine(2)
EASTMAN Crawford
EAU CLAIRE (54703) Eau Claire(89),
    Chippewa(10)
EAU CLAIRE Eau Claire
EAU GALLE (54737) Dunn(96), Pepin(3)
EDEN Fond du Lac
EDGAR Marathon
EDGERTON (53534) Rock(84), Dane(13),
    Jefferson(2)
EDGEWATER Sawyer
EDMUND Iowa
EGG HARBOR Door
ELAND (54427) Marathon(66),
    Shawano(33)
ELCHO (54428) Langlade(96), Oneida(3)
ELDERON Marathon
ELDORADO Fond du Lac
ELEVA (54738) Eau Claire(58),
    Trempealeau(40), Buffalo(1)
ELK MOUND (54739) Dunn(62),
    Chippewa(37)
ELKHART LAKE (53020) Sheboygan(93),
    Manitowoc(3), Calumet(2)
ELKHORN Walworth
ELLISON BAY Door
ELLSWORTH Pierce
ELM GROVE Waukesha
ELMWOOD (54740) Pierce(79), Dunn(20)
ELROY (53929) Juneau(82), Monroe(11),
    Vernon(5)
ELTON Langlade
EMBARRASS Waupaca
EMERALD St. Croix
EMERALDX St. Croix
ENDEAVOR Marquette
EPHRAIM Door
ETTRICK (54627) Trempealeau(91),
    Jackson(8)
EUREKA Winnebago
EVANSVILLE (53536) Rock(96), Green(3)
EXELAND (54835) Sawyer(89), Rusk(10)
FAIRCHILD (54741) Jackson(51), Eau
    Claire(48)
FAIRWATER Fond du Lac
FALL CREEK Eau Claire
FALL RIVER (53932) Columbia(95),
    Dodge(4)
FENCE (54120) Florence(78),
    Marinette(21)
FENNIMORE Grant
FERRYVILLE (54628) Crawford(93),
    Vernon(6)
FIFIELD Price
FISH CREEK Door
FOND DU LAC Fond du Lac
FONTANA Walworth
FOOTVILLE Rock
FOREST JUNCTION Calumet
FORESTVILLE (54213) Door(85),
    Kewaunee(14)
FORT ATKINSON (53538) Jefferson(97),
    Rock(2)

FOUNTAIN CITY Buffalo
FOX LAKE Dodge
FOXBORO Douglas
FRANCIS CREEK Manitowoc
FRANKLIN Milwaukee
FRANKSVILLE Racine
FREDERIC (54837) Polk(81), Burnett(18)
FREDONIA (53021) Ozaukee(88),
    Washington(11)
FREEDOM Outagamie
FREMONT (54940) Waupaca(51),
    Waushara(29), Winnebago(14),
    Outagamie(4)
FRIENDSHIP Adams
FRIESLAND Columbia
GALESVILLE Trempealeau
GALLOWAY Marathon
GAYS MILLS Crawford
GENESEE DEPOT Waukesha
GENOA Vernon
GENOA CITY (53128) Walworth(80),
    Kenosha(19)
GERMANTOWN Washington
GILE Iron
GILLETT (54124) Oconto(87),
    Menominee(9), Shawano(2)
GILLETT Oconto
GILLETT Shawano
GILMAN (54433) Taylor(80), Chippewa(19)
GILMANTON Buffalo
GLEASON (54435) Lincoln(69),
    Langlade(30)
GLEN FLORA Rusk
GLEN HAVEN Grant
GLENBEULAH Sheboygan
GLENWOOD CITY St. Croix
GLIDDEN Ashland
GOODMAN (54125) Marinette(98),
    Forest(1)
GORDON Douglas
GOTHAM Richland
GRAFTON Ozaukee
GRAND MARSH Adams
GRAND VIEW Bayfield
GRANTON Clark
GRANTSBURG (54840) Burnett(98),
    Polk(1)
GRATIOT Lafayette
GREEN BAY Brown
GREEN LAKE Green Lake
GREEN VALLEY Shawano
GREENBUSH Sheboygan
GREENDALE Milwaukee
GREENLEAF (54126) Brown(96),
    Manitowoc(3)
GREENVILLE Outagamie
GREENWOOD Clark
GRESHAM Shawano
GURNEY Iron
HAGER CITY Pierce
HALES CORNERS Milwaukee
HAMMOND St. Croix
HANCOCK (54943) Waushara(81),
    Adams(18)
HANNIBAL Taylor
HANOVER Rock
HARSHAW Oneida
HARTFORD (53027) Washington(96),
    Dodge(3)
HARTLAND Waukesha
HATLEY Marathon
HAUGEN Barron
HAWKINS (54530) Rusk(71), Price(27)
HAWTHORNE Douglas
HAYWARD (54843) Sawyer(96),
    Washburn(3)
HAZEL GREEN (53811) Grant(94),
    Lafayette(5)
HAZELHURST Oneida
HEAFFORD JUNCTION Lincoln
HELENVILLE Jefferson
HERBSTER Bayfield
HERTEL Burnett

HEWITT Wood
HIGH BRIDGE Ashland
HIGHLAND (53543) Iowa(91), Grant(8)
HILBERT Calumet
HILLPOINT (53937) Sauk(63),
    Richland(36)
HILLSBORO (54634) Vernon(79),
    Richland(19), Juneau(1)
HILLSDALE Barron
HINGHAM Sheboygan
HIXTON Jackson
HOLCOMBE (54745) Chippewa(87),
    Rusk(12)
HOLLANDALE (53544) Iowa(97), Dane(1)
HOLMEN La Crosse
HONEY CREEK Walworth
HORICON Dodge
HORTONVILLE Outagamie
HOULTON St. Croix
HUBERTUS Washington
HUDSON St. Croix
HUMBIRD (54746) Clark(77), Jackson(22)
HURLEY Iron
HUSTISFORD Dodge
HUSTLER Juneau
INDEPENDENCE (54747)
    Trempealeau(82), Buffalo(17)
IOLA (54945) Waupaca(96); Portage(3)
IOLA Waupaca
IRMA Lincoln
IRON BELT Iron
IRON RIDGE Dodge
IRON RIVER Bayfield
IXONIA (53036) Jefferson(73), Dodge(19),
    Waukesha(6)
JACKSON Washington
JANESVILLE Rock
JEFFERSON Jefferson
JIM FALLS Chippewa
JOHNSON CREEK Jefferson
JUDA Green
JUMP RIVER Taylor
JUNCTION CITY (54443) Portage(95),
    Marathon(2), Wood(2)
JUNEAU Dodge
KANSASVILLE (53139) Racine(85),
    Kenosha(14)
KAUKAUNA (54130) Outagamie(95),
    Brown(2), Calumet(1)
KELLNERSVILLE Manitowoc
KEMPSTER Langlade
KENDALL (54638) Monroe(88), Vernon(9),
    Juneau(2)
KENNAN Price
KENOSHA Kenosha
KESHENA Menominee
KEWASKUM (53040) Washington(76),
    Sheboygan(13), Fond du Lac(9)
KEWAUNEE Kewaunee
KIEL (53042) Manitowoc(95), Calumet(4)
KIELER Grant
KIMBERLY Outagamie
KING Waupaca
KINGSTON Green Lake
KNAPP (54749) Dunn(88), St. Croix(11)
KOHLER Sheboygan
KRAKOW (54137) Shawano(76),
    Oconto(23)
LA CROSSE La Crosse
LA FARGE (54639) Vernon(93),
    Richland(6)
LA POINTE Ashland
LA VALLE (53941) Sauk(97), Juneau(1)
LAC DU FLAMBEAU (54538) Vilas(90),
    Oneida(5), Price(4)
LADYSMITH Rusk
LAKE DELTON Sauk
LAKE GENEVA Walworth
LAKE MILLS Jefferson
LAKE NEBAGAMON Douglas
LAKE TOMAHAWK Oneida
LAKEWOOD Oconto
LANCASTER Grant

LAND O LAKES Vilas
LANNON Waukesha
LAONA Forest
LARSEN Winnebago
LEBANON Dodge
LENA (54139) Oconto(98), Marinette(1)
LEOPOLIS Shawano
LEWIS Polk
LILY Langlade
LIME RIDGE Sauk
LINDEN Iowa
LITTLE CHUTE Outagamie
LITTLE SUAMICO Oconto
LIVINGSTON (53554) Grant(70), Iowa(29)
LODI (53555) Columbia(92), Dane(7)
LOGANVILLE Sauk
LOMIRA (53048) Dodge(97), Fond du
    Lac(2)
LONE ROCK (53556) Richland(83),
    Sauk(16)
LONG LAKE (54542) Forest(65),
    Florence(34)
LOWELL Dodge
LOYAL Clark
LUBLIN (54447) Taylor(97), Clark(2)
LUCK (54853) Polk(94), Burnett(5)
LUXEMBURG (54217) Kewaunee(88),
    Door(5), Brown(5)
LYNDON STATION (53944) Juneau(88),
    Sauk(11)
LYNXVILLE Crawford
LYONS Walworth
MADISON Dane
MAIDEN ROCK Pierce
MALONE (53049) Fond du Lac(92),
    Calumet(7)
MANAWA Waupaca
MANCHESTER Green Lake
MANITOWISH WATERS (54545) Vilas(98),
    Iron(1)
MANITOWOC Manitowoc
MAPLE Douglas
MAPLEWOOD Door
MARATHON Marathon
MARENGO Ashland
MARIBEL (54227) Manitowoc(98),
    Brown(1)
MARINETTE Marinette
MARION (54950) Shawano(50),
    Waupaca(49)
MARKESAN (53946) Green Lake(97),
    Fond du Lac(2)
MARQUETTE Green Lake
MARSHALL (53559) Dane(98),
    Jefferson(1)
MARSHALL FIELDS Milwaukee
MARSHFIELD (54449) Wood(93),
    Marathon(6)
MARSHFIELD Wood
MASON (54856) Bayfield(97), Ashland(2)
MATHER Juneau
MATTOON Shawano
MAUSTON Juneau
MAYVILLE Dodge
MAZOMANIE (53560) Dane(96), Iowa(3)
MC FARLAND Dane
MC NAUGHTON Oneida
MEDFORD Taylor
MEDINA Outagamie
MELLEN Ashland
MELROSE Jackson
MENASHA (54952) Winnebago(89),
    Calumet(10)
MENOMONEE FALLS Waukesha
MENOMONIE Dunn
MEQUON Ozaukee
MERCER Iron
MERRILL (54452) Lincoln(88),
    Marathon(11)
MERRILLAN (54754) Jackson(85),
    Clark(14)
MERRIMAC (53561) Sauk(86),
    Columbia(13)

MERTON Waukesha
MIDDLETON Dane
MIKANA Barron
MILAN Marathon
MILLADORE (54454) Wood(87),
  Portage(12)
MILLSTON Jackson
MILLTOWN Polk
MILTON Rock
MILWAUKEE Milwaukee
MINDORO (54644) La Crosse(96),
  Jackson(3)
MINERAL POINT (53565) Iowa(87),
  Lafayette(12)
MINOCQUA (54548) Oneida(78), Vilas(21)
MINONG (54859) Washburn(88),
  Douglas(11)
MISHICOT Manitowoc
MONDOVI (54755) Buffalo(63), Eau
  Claire(12), Dunn(11), Pepin(11)
MONROE Green
MONTELLO (53949) Marquette(98), Green
  Lake(1)
MONTFORT (53569) Grant(66), Iowa(33)
MONTICELLO Green
MONTREAL Iron
MORRISONVILLE Dane
MOSINEE (54455) Marathon(97),
  Portage(2)
MOUNT CALVARY Fond du Lac
MOUNT HOPE Grant
MOUNT HOREB Dane
MOUNT STERLING Crawford
MOUNTAIN Oconto
MUKWONAGO (53149) Waukesha(90),
  Walworth(7), Racine(1)
MUSCODA (53573) Grant(52),
  Richland(40), Iowa(7)
MUSKEGO (53150) Waukesha(98),
  Racine(1)
NASHOTAH Waukesha
NECEDAH Juneau
NEENAH Winnebago
NEILLSVILLE Clark
NEKOOSA (54457) Wood(57), Adams(39),
  Juneau(3)
NELSON Buffalo
NELSONVILLE Portage
NEOPIT Menominee
NEOSHO Dodge
NESHKORO (54960) Marquette(59),
  Waushara(35), Green Lake(5)
NEW AUBURN (54757) Chippewa(66),
  Barron(17), Dunn(9), Rusk(6)
NEW BERLIN Waukesha
NEW FRANKEN Brown
NEW GLARUS (53574) Green(98),
  Dane(1)
NEW HOLSTEIN (53061) Calumet(95),
  Fond du Lac(4)
NEW HOLSTEIN Calumet
NEW LISBON Juneau
NEW LONDON (54961) Waupaca(81),
  Outagamie(18)
NEW MUNSTER Kenosha
NEW RICHMOND (54017) St. Croix(98),
  Polk(1)
NEWBURG Washington
NEWTON Manitowoc
NIAGARA (54151) Marinette(66),
  Florence(33)
NICHOLS Outagamie
NORTH FREEDOM Sauk
NORTH LAKE Waukesha
NORTH PRAIRIE Waukesha
NORWALK Monroe
OAK CREEK Milwaukee
OAKDALE Monroe
OAKFIELD (53065) Fond du Lac(91),
  Dodge(8)
OCONOMOWOC (53066) Waukesha(94),
  Jefferson(3), Dodge(1)
OCONTO Oconto

OCONTO FALLS (54154) Oconto(96),
  Shawano(3)
ODANAH Ashland
OGDENSBURG Waupaca
OGEMA Price
OJIBWA Sawyer
OKAUCHEE Waukesha
OMRO Winnebago
ONALASKA La Crosse
ONEIDA (54155) Brown(59),
  Outagamie(40)
ONTARIO (54651) Vernon(61), Monroe(38)
OOSTBURG Sheboygan
OREGON Dane
ORFORDVILLE Rock
OSHKOSH Winnebago
OSSEO (54758) Trempealeau(71), Eau
  Claire(17), Jackson(11)
OWEN (54460) Clark(96), Taylor(3)
OXFORD (53952) Marquette(51),
  Adams(48)
PACKWAUKEE Marquette
PALMYRA Jefferson
PARDEEVILLE (53954) Columbia(96),
  Marquette(3)
PARK FALLS (54552) Price(92), Iron(7)
PATCH GROVE Grant
PEARSON Langlade
PELICAN LAKE (54463) Oneida(95),
  Langlade(4)
PELL LAKE Walworth
PEMBINE Marinette
PEPIN Pepin
PESHTIGO (54157) Marinette(98),
  Oconto(1)
PEWAUKEE Waukesha
PHELPS Vilas
PHILLIPS Price
PHLOX Langlade
PICKEREL (54465) Langlade(59),
  Forest(40)
PICKETT (54964) Winnebago(80), Fond du
  Lac(19)
PIGEON FALLS Trempealeau
PINE RIVER (54965) Waushara(98),
  Waupaca(1)
PITTSVILLE (54466) Wood(79), Clark(10),
  Jackson(9)
PLAIN Sauk
PLAINFIELD (54966) Waushara(85),
  Portage(13), Adams(1)
PLATTEVILLE (53818) Grant(95),
  Lafayette(3)
PLEASANT PRAIRIE Kenosha
PLOVER Portage
PLUM CITY Pierce
PLYMOUTH Sheboygan
POPLAR Douglas
PORT EDWARDS Wood
PORT WASHINGTON Ozaukee
PORT WING Bayfield
PORTAGE Columbia
PORTERFIELD Marinette
POSKIN Barron
POTOSI Grant
POTTER Calumet
POUND (54161) Marinette(53), Oconto(46)
POWERS LAKE Kenosha
POY SIPPI Waushara
POYNETTE Columbia
PRAIRIE DU CHIEN (53821) Crawford(98),
  Grant(1)
PRAIRIE DU SAC (53578) Sauk(90),
  Columbia(9)
PRAIRIE FARM (54762) Barron(94),
  Dunn(5)
PRENTICE Price
PRESCOTT Pierce
PRESQUE ISLE Vilas
PRINCETON (54968) Green Lake(93),
  Marquette(6)
PULASKI (54162) Shawano(62),
  Brown(28), Oconto(8)

RACINE (53403) Racine(98), Kenosha(1)
RACINE Racine
RADISSON Sawyer
RANDOLPH (53956) Dodge(57),
  Columbia(39), Green Lake(3)
RANDOLPH Columbia
RANDOM LAKE (53075) Sheboygan(93),
  Ozaukee(5)
READFIELD Waupaca
READSTOWN (54652) Vernon(96),
  Crawford(3)
REDGRANITE Waushara
REEDSBURG Sauk
REEDSVILLE Manitowoc
REESEVILLE Dodge
REWEY Iowa
RHINELANDER Oneida
RIB LAKE (54470) Taylor(96), Price(2)
RICE LAKE Barron
RICHFIELD Washington
RICHLAND CENTER Richland
RIDGELAND (54763) Dunn(84), Barron(15)
RIDGEWAY Iowa
RINGLE Marathon
RIO Columbia
RIPON (54971) Fond du Lac(82), Green
  Lake(13), Winnebago(4)
RIVER FALLS (54022) Pierce(74), St.
  Croix(25)
ROBERTS St. Croix
ROCHESTER Racine
ROCK FALLS Dunn
ROCK SPRINGS Sauk
ROCKFIELD Washington
ROCKLAND (54653) La Crosse(90),
  Monroe(9)
ROSENDALE Fond du Lac
ROSHOLT (54473) Portage(79),
  Marathon(20)
ROTHSCHILD Marathon
ROYALTON Waupaca
RUBICON Dodge
RUDOLPH (54475) Wood(86), Portage(13)
SAINT CLOUD (53079) Fond du Lac(92),
  Sheboygan(7)
SAINT CROIX FALLS Polk
SAINT FRANCIS Milwaukee
SAINT GERMAIN (54558) Vilas(89),
  Oneida(10)
SAINT JOSEPH St. Croix
SAINT NAZIANZ Manitowoc
SALEM Kenosha
SAND CREEK Dunn
SARONA (54870) Washburn(96), Barron(3)
SAUK CITY (53583) Sauk(85), Dane(13)
SAUKVILLE Ozaukee
SAXEVILLE Waushara
SAXON (54559) Iron(94), Ashland(5)
SAYNER Vilas
SCANDINAVIA (54977) Waupaca(94),
  Portage(5)
SCHOFIELD Marathon
SENECA Crawford
SEXTONVILLE Richland
SEYMOUR (54165) Outagamie(95),
  Shawano(3), Brown(1)
SHARON (53585) Walworth(96), Rock(3)
SHAWANO Shawano
SHEBOYGAN Sheboygan
SHEBOYGAN FALLS Sheboygan
SHELDON (54766) Rusk(59), Taylor(39)
SHELL LAKE (54871) Washburn(65),
  Burnett(34)
SHERWOOD Calumet
SHIOCTON (54170) Outagamie(93),
  Shawano(5)
SHULLSBURG Lafayette
SILVER LAKE Kenosha
SINSINAWA Grant
SIREN (54872) Burnett(97), Polk(2)
SISTER BAY Door
SLINGER Washington
SOBIESKI Oconto

SOLDIERS GROVE (54655) Crawford(83),
  Richland(12), Vernon(3)
SOLON SPRINGS (54873) Bayfield(50),
  Douglas(49)
SOMERS Kenosha
SOMERSET St. Croix
SOUTH MILWAUKEE Milwaukee
SOUTH RANGE Douglas
SOUTH WAYNE Lafayette
SPARTA Monroe
SPENCER (54479) Marathon(56),
  Clark(42)
SPOONER (54801) Washburn(83),
  Burnett(16)
SPRING GREEN (53588) Sauk(77),
  Iowa(21)
SPRING VALLEY (54767) Pierce(95), St.
  Croix(3), Dunn(1)
SPRINGBROOK Washburn
SPRINGFIELD Walworth
STANLEY (54768) Chippewa(73),
  Clark(16), Eau Claire(6), Taylor(2)
STAR LAKE Vilas
STAR PRAIRIE (54026) Polk(61), St.
  Croix(38)
STETSONVILLE (54480) Taylor(95),
  Marathon(4)
STEUBEN Crawford
STEVENS POINT Portage
STITZER Grant
STOCKBRIDGE Calumet
STOCKHOLM (54769) Pepin(81),
  Pierce(18)
STODDARD (54658) Vernon(89), La
  Crosse(10)
STONE LAKE (54876) Sawyer(68),
  Washburn(31)
STOUGHTON (53589) Dane(98), Rock(1)
STRATFORD Marathon
STRUM (54770) Trempealeau(76), Eau
  Claire(23)
STURGEON BAY Door
STURTEVANT (53177) Racine(91),
  Kenosha(8)
SUAMICO Brown
SULLIVAN Jefferson
SUMMIT LAKE Langlade
SUN PRAIRIE Dane
SUPERIOR Douglas
SURING (54174) Oconto(91),
  Menominee(8)
SUSSEX Waukesha
TAYLOR (54659) Jackson(91),
  Trempealeau(8)
THERESA (53091) Dodge(94),
  Washington(5)
THIENSVILLE Ozaukee
THORP (54771) Clark(92), Taylor(7)
THREE LAKES (54562) Oneida(95),
  Forest(4)
TIGERTON (54486) Shawano(92),
  Waupaca(7)
TILLEDA Shawano
TISCH MILLS Manitowoc
TOMAH Monroe
TOMAHAWK (54487) Lincoln(88),
  Oneida(11)
TONY Rusk
TOWNSEND Oconto
TREGO Washburn
TREMPEALEAU Trempealeau
TREVOR Kenosha
TRIPOLI (54564) Oneida(47), Lincoln(36),
  Price(16)
TUNNEL CITY Monroe
TURTLE LAKE (54889) Barron(76),
  Polk(23)
TWIN LAKES Kenosha
TWO RIVERS Manitowoc
UNION CENTER Juneau
UNION GROVE (53182) Racine(90),
  Kenosha(9)
UNITY (54488) Clark(68), Marathon(31)

UPSON Iron
VALDERS Manitowoc
VAN DYNE (54979) Fond du Lac(87), Winnebago(12)
VERONA Dane
VESPER Wood
VIOLA (54664) Richland(66), Vernon(33)
VIROQUA (54665) Vernon(98), Crawford(1)
WABENO Forest
WALDO Sheboygan
WALES Waukesha
WALWORTH Walworth
WARRENS (54666) Monroe(82), Jackson(17)
WASCOTT Douglas
WASHBURN Bayfield
WASHINGTON ISLAND Door
WATERFORD Racine
WATERLOO (53594) Jefferson(81), Dodge(14), Dane(3)
WATERTOWN Dodge

WAUKAU Winnebago
WAUKESHA Waukesha
WAUNAKEE Dane
WAUPACA (54981) Waupaca(91), Waushara(4), Portage(3)
WAUPUN (53963) Dodge(51), Fond du Lac(48)
WAUSAU Marathon
WAUSAUKEE Marinette
WAUTOMA (54982) Waushara(97), Marquette(2)
WAUZEKA Crawford
WEBSTER Burnett
WEST BEND Washington
WEST SALEM La Crosse
WESTBORO (54490) Taylor(95), Price(4)
WESTBY (54667) Vernon(98), La Crosse(1)
WESTFIELD (53964) Marquette(96), Adams(2), Waushara(1)
WEYAUWEGA (54983) Waupaca(90), Waushara(9)

WEYERHAEUSER Rusk
WHEELER Dunn
WHITE LAKE (54491) Langlade(91), Oconto(8)
WHITEHALL Trempealeau
WHITELAW Manitowoc
WHITEWATER (53190) Walworth(76), Rock(13), Jefferson(9)
WILD ROSE Waushara
WILLARD Clark
WILLIAMS BAY Walworth
WILMOT Kenosha
WILSON St. Croix
WILTON Monroe
WINDSOR Dane
WINNECONNE (54986) Winnebago(98), Waushara(1)
WINTER Sawyer
WISCONSIN DELLS (53965) Columbia(38), Sauk(31), Adams(23), Juneau(6)

WISCONSIN RAPIDS (54494) Wood(92), Portage(6)
WISCONSIN RAPIDS Wood
WITHEE (54498) Clark(90), Taylor(9)
WITTENBERG (54499) Shawano(71), Marathon(27), Portage(1)
WONEWOC (53968) Juneau(67), Sauk(24), Vernon(6), Richland(1)
WOODFORD Lafayette
WOODLAND Dodge
WOODMAN Grant
WOODRUFF (54568) Vilas(67), Oneida(32)
WOODVILLE St. Croix
WOODWORTH Kenosha
WRIGHTSTOWN (54180) Brown(95), Outagamie(4)
WYEVILLE Monroe
WYOCENA Columbia
ZACHOW Shawano
ZENDA Walworth

Wisconsin ZIP/City Cross Reference

53001-53001 ADELL	53066-53066 OCONOMOWOC	53149-53149 MUKWONAGO	53526-53526 COBB
53002-53002 ALLENTON	53069-53069 OKAUCHEE	53150-53150 MUSKEGO	53527-53527 COTTAGE GROVE
53003-53003 ASHIPPUN	53070-53070 OOSTBURG	53151-53151 NEW BERLIN	53528-53528 CROSS PLAINS
53004-53004 BELGIUM	53072-53072 PEWAUKEE	53152-53152 NEW MUNSTER	53529-53529 DANE
53005-53005 BROOKFIELD	53073-53073 PLYMOUTH	53153-53153 NORTH PRAIRIE	53530-53530 DARLINGTON
53006-53006 BROWNSVILLE	53074-53074 PORT WASHINGTON	53154-53154 OAK CREEK	53531-53531 DEERFIELD
53007-53007 BUTLER	53075-53075 RANDOM LAKE	53156-53156 PALMYRA	53532-53532 DE FOREST
53008-53008 BROOKFIELD	53076-53076 RICHFIELD	53157-53157 PELL LAKE	53533-53533 DODGEVILLE
53009-53009 BYRON	53077-53077 ROCKFIELD	53158-53158 PLEASANT PRAIRIE	53534-53534 EDGERTON
53010-53010 CAMPBELLSPORT	53078-53078 RUBICON	53159-53159 POWERS LAKE	53535-53535 EDMUND
53011-53011 CASCADE	53079-53079 SAINT CLOUD	53167-53167 ROCHESTER	53536-53536 EVANSVILLE
53012-53012 CEDARBURG	53080-53080 SAUKVILLE	53168-53168 SALEM	53537-53537 FOOTVILLE
53013-53013 CEDAR GROVE	53081-53083 SHEBOYGAN	53170-53170 SILVER LAKE	53538-53538 FORT ATKINSON
53014-53014 CHILTON	53085-53085 SHEBOYGAN FALLS	53171-53171 SOMERS	53540-53540 GOTHAM
53015-53015 CLEVELAND	53086-53086 SLINGER	53172-53172 SOUTH MILWAUKEE	53541-53541 GRATIOT
53016-53016 CLYMAN	53088-53088 STOCKBRIDGE	53176-53176 SPRINGFIELD	53542-53542 HANOVER
53017-53017 COLGATE	53089-53089 SUSSEX	53177-53177 STURTEVANT	53543-53543 HIGHLAND
53018-53018 DELAFIELD	53090-53090 WEST BEND	53178-53178 SULLIVAN	53544-53544 HOLLANDALE
53019-53019 EDEN	53091-53091 THERESA	53179-53179 TREVOR	53545-53548 JANESVILLE
53020-53020 ELKHART LAKE	53092-53092 THIENSVILLE	53181-53181 TWIN LAKES	53549-53549 JEFFERSON
53021-53021 FREDONIA	53093-53093 WALDO	53182-53182 UNION GROVE	53550-53550 JUDA
53022-53022 GERMANTOWN	53094-53094 WATERTOWN	53183-53183 WALES	53551-53551 LAKE MILLS
53023-53023 GLENBEULAH	53095-53096 WEST BEND	53184-53184 WALWORTH	53553-53553 LINDEN
53024-53024 GRAFTON	53097-53097 MEQUON	53185-53185 WATERFORD	53554-53554 LIVINGSTON
53026-53026 GREENBUSH	53098-53098 WATERTOWN	53186-53189 WAUKESHA	53555-53555 LODI
53027-53027 HARTFORD	53099-53099 WOODLAND	53190-53190 WHITEWATER	53556-53556 LONE ROCK
53029-53029 HARTLAND	53101-53101 BASSETT	53191-53191 WILLIAMS BAY	53557-53557 LOWELL
53031-53031 HINGHAM	53102-53102 BENET LAKE	53192-53192 WILMOT	53558-53558 MC FARLAND
53032-53032 HORICON	53103-53103 BIG BEND	53194-53194 WOODWORTH	53559-53559 MARSHALL
53033-53033 HUBERTUS	53104-53104 BRISTOL	53195-53195 ZENDA	53560-53560 MAZOMANIE
53034-53034 HUSTISFORD	53105-53105 BURLINGTON	53200-53234 MILWAUKEE	53561-53561 MERRIMAC
53035-53035 IRON RIDGE	53108-53108 CALEDONIA	53235-53235 SAINT FRANCIS	53562-53562 MIDDLETON
53036-53036 IXONIA	53109-53109 CAMP LAKE	53237-53259 MILWAUKEE	53563-53563 MILTON
53037-53037 JACKSON	53110-53110 CUDAHY	53260-53262 MARSHALL FIELDS	53565-53565 MINERAL POINT
53038-53038 JOHNSON CREEK	53114-53114 DARIEN	53263-53295 MILWAUKEE	53566-53566 MONROE
53039-53039 JUNEAU	53115-53115 DELAVAN	53400-53490 RACINE	53569-53569 MONTFORT
53040-53040 KEWASKUM	53118-53118 DOUSMAN	53501-53501 AFTON	53570-53570 MONTICELLO
53042-53042 KIEL	53119-53119 EAGLE	53502-53502 ALBANY	53571-53571 MORRISONVILLE
53044-53044 KOHLER	53120-53120 EAST TROY	53503-53503 ARENA	53572-53572 MOUNT HOREB
53045-53045 BROOKFIELD	53121-53121 ELKHORN	53504-53504 ARGYLE	53573-53573 MUSCODA
53046-53046 LANNON	53122-53122 ELM GROVE	53505-53505 AVALON	53574-53574 NEW GLARUS
53047-53047 LEBANON	53125-53125 FONTANA	53506-53506 AVOCA	53575-53575 OREGON
53048-53048 LOMIRA	53126-53126 FRANKSVILLE	53507-53507 BARNEVELD	53576-53576 ORFORDVILLE
53049-53049 MALONE	53127-53127 GENESEE DEPOT	53508-53508 BELLEVILLE	53577-53577 PLAIN
53050-53050 MAYVILLE	53128-53128 GENOA CITY	53510-53510 BELMONT	53578-53578 PRAIRIE DU SAC
53051-53052 MENOMONEE FALLS	53129-53129 GREENDALE	53511-53512 BELOIT	53579-53579 REESEVILLE
53056-53056 MERTON	53130-53130 HALES CORNERS	53515-53515 BLACK EARTH	53580-53580 REWEY
53057-53057 MOUNT CALVARY	53132-53132 FRANKLIN	53516-53516 BLANCHARDVILLE	53581-53581 RICHLAND CENTER
53058-53058 NASHOTAH	53137-53137 HELENVILLE	53517-53517 BLUE MOUNDS	53582-53582 RIDGEWAY
53059-53059 NEOSHO	53138-53138 HONEY CREEK	53518-53518 BLUE RIVER	53583-53583 SAUK CITY
53060-53060 NEWBURG	53139-53139 KANSASVILLE	53520-53520 BRODHEAD	53584-53584 SEXTONVILLE
53061-53062 NEW HOLSTEIN	53140-53144 KENOSHA	53521-53521 BROOKLYN	53585-53585 SHARON
53063-53063 NEWTON	53146-53146 NEW BERLIN	53522-53522 BROWNTOWN	53586-53586 SHULLSBURG
53064-53064 NORTH LAKE	53147-53147 LAKE GENEVA	53523-53523 CAMBRIDGE	53587-53587 SOUTH WAYNE
53065-53065 OAKFIELD	53148-53148 LYONS	53525-53525 CLINTON	53588-53588 SPRING GREEN

53589-53589 STOUGHTON	54001-54001 AMERY	54177-54177 WAUSAUKEE	54452-54452 MERRILL
53590-53591 SUN PRAIRIE	54002-54002 BALDWIN	54180-54180 WRIGHTSTOWN	54453-54453 MILAN
53593-53593 VERONA	54003-54003 BELDENVILLE	54182-54182 ZACHOW	54454-54454 MILLADORE
53594-53594 WATERLOO	54004-54004 CLAYTON	54201-54201 ALGOMA	54455-54455 MOSINEE
53595-53595 DODGEVILLE	54005-54005 CLEAR LAKE	54202-54202 BAILEYS HARBOR	54456-54456 NEILLSVILLE
53596-53596 SUN PRAIRIE	54006-54006 CUSHING	54203-54203 BRANCH	54457-54457 NEKOOSA
53597-53597 WAUNAKEE	54007-54007 DEER PARK	54204-54204 BRUSSELS	54458-54458 NELSONVILLE
53598-53598 WINDSOR	54009-54009 DRESSER	54205-54205 CASCO	54459-54459 OGEMA
53599-53599 WOODFORD	54010-54010 EAST ELLSWORTH	54206-54206 CATO	54460-54460 OWEN
53700-53794 MADISON	54011-54011 ELLSWORTH	54207-54207 COLLINS	54462-54462 PEARSON
53801-53801 BAGLEY	54012-54012 EMERALD	54208-54208 DENMARK	54463-54463 PELICAN LAKE
53802-53802 BEETOWN	54012-54012 EMERALDX	54209-54209 EGG HARBOR	54464-54464 PHLOX
53803-53803 BENTON	54013-54013 GLENWOOD CITY	54210-54210 ELLISON BAY	54465-54465 PICKEREL
53804-53804 BLOOMINGTON	54014-54014 HAGER CITY	54211-54211 EPHRAIM	54466-54466 PITTSVILLE
53805-53805 BOSCOBEL	54015-54015 HAMMOND	54212-54212 FISH CREEK	54467-54467 PLOVER
53806-53806 CASSVILLE	54016-54016 HUDSON	54213-54213 FORESTVILLE	54469-54469 PORT EDWARDS
53807-53807 CUBA CITY	54017-54017 NEW RICHMOND	54214-54214 FRANCIS CREEK	54470-54470 RIB LAKE
53808-53808 DICKEYVILLE	54020-54020 OSCEOLA	54215-54215 KELLNERSVILLE	54471-54471 RINGLE
53809-53809 FENNIMORE	54021-54021 PRESCOTT	54216-54216 KEWAUNEE	54472-54472 MARSHFIELD
53810-53810 GLEN HAVEN	54022-54022 RIVER FALLS	54217-54217 LUXEMBURG	54473-54473 ROSHOLT
53811-53811 HAZEL GREEN	54023-54023 ROBERTS	54220-54221 MANITOWOC	54474-54474 ROTHSCHILD
53812-53812 KIELER	54024-54024 SAINT CROIX FALLS	54226-54226 MAPLEWOOD	54475-54475 RUDOLPH
53813-53813 LANCASTER	54025-54025 SOMERSET	54227-54227 MARIBEL	54476-54476 SCHOFIELD
53816-53816 MOUNT HOPE	54026-54026 STAR PRAIRIE	54228-54228 MISHICOT	54479-54479 SPENCER
53817-53817 PATCH GROVE	54027-54027 WILSON	54229-54229 NEW FRANKEN	54480-54480 STETSONVILLE
53818-53818 PLATTEVILLE	54028-54028 WOODVILLE	54230-54230 REEDSVILLE	54481-54482 STEVENS POINT
53820-53820 POTOSI	54082-54082 SAINT JOSEPH	54231-54231 ALGOMA	54484-54484 STRATFORD
53821-53821 PRAIRIE DU CHIEN	54082-54082 HOULTON	54232-54232 SAINT NAZIANZ	54485-54485 SUMMIT LAKE
53824-53824 SINSINAWA	54101-54101 ABRAMS	54234-54234 SISTER BAY	54486-54486 TIGERTON
53825-53825 STITZER	54102-54102 AMBERG	54235-54235 STURGEON BAY	54487-54487 TOMAHAWK
53826-53826 WAUZEKA	54103-54103 ARMSTRONG CREEK	54240-54240 TISCH MILLS	54488-54488 UNITY
53827-53827 WOODMAN	54104-54104 ATHELSTANE	54241-54241 TWO RIVERS	54489-54489 VESPER
53901-53901 PORTAGE	54106-54106 BLACK CREEK	54245-54245 VALDERS	54490-54490 WESTBORO
53910-53910 ADAMS	54107-54107 BONDUEL	54246-54246 WASHINGTON ISLAND	54491-54491 WHITE LAKE
53911-53911 ARLINGTON	54110-54110 BRILLION	54247-54247 WHITELAW	54492-54492 STEVENS POINT
53913-53913 BARABOO	54111-54111 CECIL	54300-54344 GREEN BAY	54493-54493 WILLARD
53916-53917 BEAVER DAM	54112-54112 COLEMAN	54401-54403 WAUSAU	54494-54495 WISCONSIN RAPIDS
53919-53919 BRANDON	54113-54113 COMBINED LOCKS	54404-54404 MARSHFIELD	54498-54498 WITHEE
53920-53920 BRIGGSVILLE	54114-54114 CRIVITZ	54405-54405 ABBOTSFORD	54499-54499 WITTENBERG
53921-53921 BROOKS	54115-54115 DE PERE	54406-54406 AMHERST	54501-54501 RHINELANDER
53922-53922 BURNETT	54119-54119 DUNBAR	54407-54407 AMHERST JUNCTION	54511-54511 ARGONNE
53923-53923 CAMBRIA	54120-54120 FENCE	54408-54408 ANIWA	54512-54512 BOULDER JUNCTION
53924-53924 CAZENOVIA	54121-54121 FLORENCE	54409-54409 ANTIGO	54513-54513 BRANTWOOD
53925-53925 COLUMBUS	54123-54123 FOREST JUNCTION	54410-54410 ARPIN	54514-54514 BUTTERNUT
53926-53926 DALTON	54124-54124 GILLETT	54411-54411 ATHENS	54515-54515 CATAWBA
53927-53927 DELLWOOD	54125-54125 GOODMAN	54412-54412 AUBURNDALE	54517-54517 CLAM LAKE
53928-53928 DOYLESTOWN	54126-54126 GREENLEAF	54413-54413 BABCOCK	54519-54519 CONOVER
53929-53929 ELROY	54127-54127 GREEN VALLEY	54414-54414 BIRNAMWOOD	54520-54520 CRANDON
53930-53930 ENDEAVOR	54128-54128 GRESHAM	54415-54415 BLENKER	54521-54521 EAGLE RIVER
53931-53931 FAIRWATER	54129-54129 HILBERT	54416-54416 BOWLER	54524-54524 FIFIELD
53932-53932 FALL RIVER	54130-54130 KAUKAUNA	54417-54417 BROKAW	54525-54525 GILE
53933-53933 FOX LAKE	54131-54131 FREEDOM	54418-54418 BRYANT	54526-54526 GLEN FLORA
53934-53934 FRIENDSHIP	54135-54135 KESHENA	54419-54419 CHELSEA	54527-54527 GLIDDEN
53935-53935 FRIESLAND	54136-54136 KIMBERLY	54420-54420 CHILI	54528-54528 GURNEY
53936-53936 GRAND MARSH	54137-54137 KRAKOW	54421-54421 COLBY	54529-54529 HARSHAW
53937-53937 HILLPOINT	54138-54138 LAKEWOOD	54422-54422 CURTISS	54530-54530 HAWKINS
53939-53939 KINGSTON	54139-54139 LENA	54423-54423 CUSTER	54531-54531 HAZELHURST
53940-53940 LAKE DELTON	54140-54140 LITTLE CHUTE	54424-54424 DEERBROOK	54532-54532 HEAFFORD JUNCTION
53941-53941 LA VALLE	54141-54141 LITTLE SUAMICO	54425-54425 DORCHESTER	54534-54534 HURLEY
53942-53942 LIME RIDGE	54143-54143 MARINETTE	54426-54426 EDGAR	54536-54536 IRON BELT
53943-53943 LOGANVILLE	54149-54149 MOUNTAIN	54427-54427 ELAND	54537-54537 KENNAN
53944-53944 LYNDON STATION	54150-54150 NEOPIT	54428-54428 ELCHO	54538-54538 LAC DU FLAMBEAU
53945-53945 MANCHESTER	54151-54151 NIAGARA	54429-54429 ELDERON	54539-54539 LAKE TOMAHAWK
53946-53946 MARKESAN	54152-54152 NICHOLS	54430-54430 ELTON	54540-54540 LAND O LAKES
53947-53947 MARQUETTE	54153-54153 OCONTO	54432-54432 GALLOWAY	54541-54541 LAONA
53948-53948 MAUSTON	54154-54154 OCONTO FALLS	54433-54433 GILMAN	54542-54542 LONG LAKE
53949-53949 MONTELLO	54155-54155 ONEIDA	54434-54434 JUMP RIVER	54543-54543 MC NAUGHTON
53950-53950 NEW LISBON	54156-54156 PEMBINE	54435-54435 GLEASON	54545-54545 MANITOWISH WATERS
53951-53951 NORTH FREEDOM	54157-54157 PESHTIGO	54436-54436 GRANTON	54546-54546 MELLEN
53952-53952 OXFORD	54159-54159 PORTERFIELD	54437-54437 GREENWOOD	54547-54547 MERCER
53953-53953 PACKWAUKEE	54160-54160 POTTER	54439-54439 HANNIBAL	54548-54548 MINOCQUA
53954-53954 PARDEEVILLE	54161-54161 POUND	54440-54440 HATLEY	54550-54550 MONTREAL
53955-53955 POYNETTE	54162-54162 PULASKI	54441-54441 HEWITT	54552-54552 PARK FALLS
53956-53957 RANDOLPH	54164-54164 GILLETT	54442-54442 IRMA	54554-54554 PHELPS
53958-53959 REEDSBURG	54165-54165 SEYMOUR	54443-54443 JUNCTION CITY	54555-54555 PHILLIPS
53960-53960 RIO	54166-54166 SHAWANO	54444-54444 KEMPSTER	54556-54556 PRENTICE
53961-53961 ROCK SPRINGS	54169-54169 SHERWOOD	54445-54445 LILY	54557-54557 PRESQUE ISLE
53962-53962 UNION CENTER	54170-54170 SHIOCTON	54446-54446 LOYAL	54558-54558 SAINT GERMAIN
53963-53963 WAUPUN	54171-54171 SOBIESKI	54447-54447 LUBLIN	54559-54559 SAXON
53964-53964 WESTFIELD	54173-54173 SUAMICO	54448-54448 MARATHON	54560-54560 SAYNER
53965-53965 WISCONSIN DELLS	54174-54174 SURING	54449-54449 MARSHFIELD	54561-54561 STAR LAKE
53968-53968 WONEWOC	54175-54175 TOWNSEND	54450-54450 MATTOON	54562-54562 THREE LAKES
53969-53969 WYOCENA	54176-54176 GILLETT	54451-54451 MEDFORD	54563-54563 TONY

54564-54564 TRIPOLI	54670-54670 WILTON	54813-54813 BARRONETT	54895-54895 WEYERHAEUSER
54565-54565 UPSON	54671-54671 WYEVILLE	54814-54814 BAYFIELD	54896-54896 WINTER
54566-54566 WABENO	54701-54703 EAU CLAIRE	54816-54816 BENOIT	54901-54906 OSHKOSH
54568-54568 WOODRUFF	54720-54720 ALTOONA	54817-54817 BIRCHWOOD	54909-54909 ALMOND
54601-54603 LA CROSSE	54721-54721 ARKANSAW	54818-54818 BRILL	54911-54919 APPLETON
54610-54610 ALMA	54722-54722 AUGUSTA	54819-54819 BRUCE	54921-54921 BANCROFT
54611-54611 ALMA CENTER	54723-54723 BAY CITY	54820-54820 BRULE	54922-54922 BEAR CREEK
54612-54612 ARCADIA	54724-54724 BLOOMER	54821-54821 CABLE	54923-54923 BERLIN
54613-54613 ARKDALE	54725-54725 BOYCEVILLE	54822-54822 CAMERON	54926-54926 BIG FALLS
54614-54614 BANGOR	54726-54726 BOYD	54824-54824 CENTURIA	54927-54927 BUTTE DES MORTS
54615-54615 BLACK RIVER FALLS	54727-54727 CADOTT	54826-54826 COMSTOCK	54928-54928 CAROLINE
54616-54616 BLAIR	54728-54728 CHETEK	54827-54827 CORNUCOPIA	54929-54929 CLINTONVILLE
54617-54617 BLOOM CITY	54729-54729 CHIPPEWA FALLS	54828-54828 COUDERAY	54930-54930 COLOMA
54618-54618 CAMP DOUGLAS	54730-54730 COLFAX	54829-54829 CUMBERLAND	54931-54931 DALE
54619-54619 CASHTON	54731-54731 CONRATH	54830-54830 DANBURY	54932-54932 ELDORADO
54620-54620 CATARACT	54732-54732 CORNELL	54832-54832 DRUMMOND	54933-54933 EMBARRASS
54621-54621 CHASEBURG	54733-54733 DALLAS	54834-54834 EDGEWATER	54934-54934 EUREKA
54622-54622 COCHRANE	54734-54734 DOWNING	54835-54835 EXELAND	54935-54937 FOND DU LAC
54623-54623 COON VALLEY	54735-54735 DOWNSVILLE	54836-54836 FOXBORO	54940-54940 FREMONT
54624-54624 DE SOTO	54736-54736 DURAND	54837-54837 FREDERIC	54941-54941 GREEN LAKE
54625-54625 DODGE	54737-54737 EAU GALLE	54838-54838 GORDON	54942-54942 GREENVILLE
54626-54626 EASTMAN	54738-54738 ELEVA	54839-54839 GRAND VIEW	54943-54943 HANCOCK
54627-54627 ETTRICK	54739-54739 ELK MOUND	54840-54840 GRANTSBURG	54944-54944 HORTONVILLE
54628-54628 FERRYVILLE	54740-54740 ELMWOOD	54841-54841 HAUGEN	54945-54945 IOLA
54629-54629 FOUNTAIN CITY	54741-54741 FAIRCHILD	54842-54842 HAWTHORNE	54946-54946 KING
54630-54630 GALESVILLE	54742-54742 FALL CREEK	54843-54843 HAYWARD	54947-54947 LARSEN
54631-54631 GAYS MILLS	54743-54743 GILMANTON	54844-54844 HERBSTER	54948-54948 LEOPOLIS
54632-54632 GENOA	54744-54744 HILLSDALE	54845-54845 HERTEL	54949-54949 MANAWA
54634-54634 HILLSBORO	54745-54745 HOLCOMBE	54846-54846 HIGH BRIDGE	54950-54950 MARION
54635-54635 HIXTON	54746-54746 HUMBIRD	54847-54847 IRON RIVER	54951-54951 MEDINA
54636-54636 HOLMEN	54747-54747 INDEPENDENCE	54848-54848 LADYSMITH	54952-54952 MENASHA
54637-54637 HUSTLER	54748-54748 JIM FALLS	54849-54849 LAKE NEBAGAMON	54956-54957 NEENAH
54638-54638 KENDALL	54749-54749 KNAPP	54850-54850 LA POINTE	54960-54960 NESHKORO
54639-54639 LA FARGE	54750-54750 MAIDEN ROCK	54851-54851 LEWIS	54961-54961 NEW LONDON
54640-54640 LYNXVILLE	54751-54751 MENOMONIE	54853-54853 LUCK	54962-54962 OGDENSBURG
54641-54641 MATHER	54754-54754 MERRILLAN	54854-54854 MAPLE	54963-54963 OMRO
54642-54642 MELROSE	54755-54755 MONDOVI	54855-54855 MARENGO	54964-54964 PICKETT
54643-54643 MILLSTON	54756-54756 NELSON	54856-54856 MASON	54965-54965 PINE RIVER
54644-54644 MINDORO	54757-54757 NEW AUBURN	54857-54857 MIKANA	54966-54966 PLAINFIELD
54645-54645 MOUNT STERLING	54758-54758 OSSEO	54858-54858 MILLTOWN	54967-54967 POY SIPPI
54646-54646 NECEDAH	54759-54759 PEPIN	54859-54859 MINONG	54968-54968 PRINCETON
54648-54648 NORWALK	54760-54760 PIGEON FALLS	54861-54861 ODANAH	54969-54969 READFIELD
54649-54649 OAKDALE	54761-54761 PLUM CITY	54862-54862 OJIBWA	54970-54970 REDGRANITE
54650-54650 ONALASKA	54762-54762 PRAIRIE FARM	54864-54864 POPLAR	54971-54971 RIPON
54651-54651 ONTARIO	54763-54763 RIDGELAND	54865-54865 PORT WING	54974-54974 ROSENDALE
54652-54652 READSTOWN	54764-54764 ROCK FALLS	54866-54866 POSKIN	54975-54975 ROYALTON
54653-54653 ROCKLAND	54765-54765 SAND CREEK	54867-54867 RADISSON	54976-54976 SAXEVILLE
54654-54654 SENECA	54766-54766 SHELDON	54868-54868 RICE LAKE	54977-54977 SCANDINAVIA
54655-54655 SOLDIERS GROVE	54767-54767 SPRING VALLEY	54870-54870 SARONA	54978-54978 TILLEDA
54656-54656 SPARTA	54768-54768 STANLEY	54871-54871 SHELL LAKE	54979-54979 VAN DYNE
54657-54657 STEUBEN	54769-54769 STOCKHOLM	54872-54872 SIREN	54980-54980 WAUKAU
54658-54658 STODDARD	54770-54770 STRUM	54873-54873 SOLON SPRINGS	54981-54981 WAUPACA
54659-54659 TAYLOR	54771-54771 THORP	54874-54874 SOUTH RANGE	54982-54982 WAUTOMA
54660-54660 TOMAH	54772-54772 WHEELER	54875-54875 SPRINGBROOK	54983-54983 WEYAUWEGA
54661-54661 TREMPEALEAU	54773-54773 WHITEHALL	54876-54876 STONE LAKE	54984-54984 WILD ROSE
54662-54662 TUNNEL CITY	54774-54774 CHIPPEWA FALLS	54880-54880 SUPERIOR	54985-54985 WINNEBAGO
54664-54664 VIOLA	54801-54801 SPOONER	54888-54888 TREGO	54986-54986 WINNECONNE
54665-54665 VIROQUA	54805-54805 ALMENA	54889-54889 TURTLE LAKE	54990-54990 IOLA
54666-54666 WARRENS	54806-54806 ASHLAND	54890-54890 WASCOTT	
54667-54667 WESTBY	54810-54810 BALSAM LAKE	54891-54891 WASHBURN	
54669-54669 WEST SALEM	54812-54812 BARRON	54893-54893 WEBSTER	

County-Town
WISCONSIN

Explanation of Symbols

◇ State Capital
Vernon County Seat

Population Key

∘ 0-999
⊕ 1,000-2,499
⊕ 2,500-4,999
⊙ 5,000-9,999
◉ 10,000-19,000
◉ 20,000-24,999
● 25,000-49,999
□ 50,000-99,999
◻ 100,000-249,999
■ 250,000-999,999

Copyright American Map Corporation

Explanation of symbols: ● — Census Designated Place (CDP)

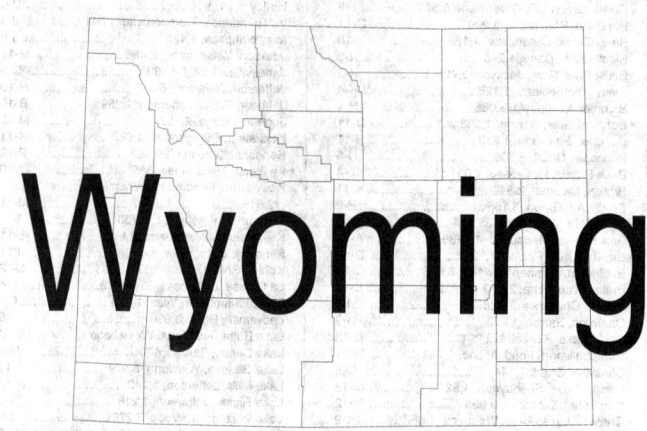

Wyoming

General Help Numbers:

Governor's Office

State Capitol Building, Rm 124   307-777-7434
Cheyenne, WY 82002-0010   Fax 307-632-3909
                        8AM-5PM
www.wyoming.gov/governor/governor_home.asp

Attorney General's Office

200 W 24thth Street   307-777-7841
Cheyenne, WY 82002   Fax 307-777-6869
http://attorneygeneral.state.wy.us   8AM-5PM

Legislative Records

Wyoming Legislature   307-777-7881
State Capitol, Room 213   8AM-5PM
Cheyenne, WY 82002
http://legisweb.state.wy.us

State Archives

Archives Division   307-777-7826
2301 Central Ave, Barrett Bldg   Fax 307-777-7044
Cheyenne, WY 82002   8AM-5PM M-F
            (Research Area 8AM-4:45PM)
http://wyoarchives.state.wy.us/index.htm

State Specifics:

Capital:	Cheyenne Laramie County
Time Zone:	MST
Number of Counties:	23
Population:	501,242
Web Site:	www.state.wy.us

State Agencies

Criminal Records

Division of Criminal Investigation, Criminal Record Unit, 316 W 22nd St, Cheyenne, WY 82002; 307-777-7523, 307-777-7252 (Fax), 8AM to 5PM.

http://attorneygeneral.state.wy.us/dci/index.html

Note: A record inquiry includes all reported felonies, high misdemeanors and other specified misdemeanors, but not municipal ordinance violations. authorized by state law, the check may include federal records held by FBI.

Indexing & Storage: Records are available from 1941 on. It takes up to 10 days before new records are available for inquiry. Records are indexed on inhouse computer.

Searching: First, obtain a Request for Criminal Record Packet ($15.00) from address above or phone. Include the following in your request-notarized waiver from subject, name, set of fingerprints, date of birth, Social Security Number, number of years to search. Use the WY standard 8" x 8" orange fingerprint card. Must also fill out waiver that is on the back of this office's

fingerprint card. The following data is not released: juvenile records.

Access by: mail, in person.

Fee & Payment: The search fee is $15.00 plus an additional $5.00 if this office must perform the fingerprinting. The fee is $10.00 if the applicant is providing volunteer services, plus the fingerprinting fee if applicable. The FBI fingerprint check is an add'l $24.00. Fee payee: Office of the Attorney General. Prepayment required. Money order, cash or certified checks only. No credit cards accepted.

Mail search: Turnaround time: 2 to 4 weeks. A SASE is requested.

In person search: Proper forms are required to be filled out.

Statewide Court Records

Court Administrator, Supreme Court Bldg, 2301 Capitol Ave, Cheyenne, WY 82002; 307-777-7583, 307-777-3447 (Fax), 8AM-5PM.

www.courts.state.wy.us

Note: Except for certain online research capabilities, all court record access must be done at the local level.

Access by: online.

Online search: Supreme Court opinions available at web, listed by date. Wyoming's statewide case management system is for internal use only. Planning is underway for a new case management system that will ultimately allow public access.

Sexual Offender Registry

Division of Criminal Investigation, ATTN: WSOR, 316 W 22nd St, Cheyenne, WY 82002-0001; 307-777-7809, 307-777-7252 (Fax), 8AM to 5PM.

http://attorneygeneral.state.wy.us/dci/index.html

Note: Wyoming law defines a sex offender subject to registration as a person convicted of a sex offense in which the victim was a minor and the offender was at least eighteen (18) years of age or an aggravated sex offense.

Searching: The County Sheriff's Office or other law enforcement agency maintains a file and forwards the information to the Wyoming Division of Criminal Investigation (DCI).

Access by: online.

Online search: The Internet is the search method offered by this agency to the public. Search is by county. The website contains offenders found to have a high risk of re-offense. Data includes name, address, date and place of birth, date and place of conviction, crime for which convicted, photograph and physical description.

Incarceration Records

Wyoming Department of Corrections, 700 W. 21st Street, Cheyenne, WY 82002; 307-777-7405, 307-777-7479 (Fax), 8AM-5PM.

http://doc.state.wy.us/corrections.asp

Indexing & Storage: Records are available on current and former inmates. It takes a minimum of 30 days before new records are available for inquiry.

Searching: Include the following in your request-full name. DOB and SSN are helpful. Location, conviction and sentencing information, and release dates are provided. Limited search requests honor via email at mbrazz@wdoc.state.wy.us. The following data is not released: probation and parole data, medical, and metal health problems

Access by: mail, phone, fax, online.

Fee & Payment: The fee is $.50 per page. Prepayment required. Personal checks accepted.

Mail search: Turnaround time: 1 to 2 weeks. A SASE is requested.

Phone search: Name searching available by phone.

Fax search: Can request via fax.

Online search: No searching online direct from this agency; a private company provides access to DOC records at www.vinelink.com/index.jsp.

Corporation, Limited Liability Company, Limited Partnership Records, Fictitious Name, Trademarks/Servicemarks

Corporations Division, Attn: Records, 200 W 24th Street, Rm 110, Cheyenne, WY 82002; 307-777-7311, 307-777-5339 (Fax), 8AM-5PM.

http://soswy.state.wy.us

Indexing & Storage: Records are available from 1800s on. The records on microfilm are inactive records before 1983. Newer records are on computer. New records are available for inquiry immediately. Records are indexed on microfilm, inhouse computer.

Searching: The Annual Report financial information (Appendix I Worksheet filed with Annual Report) is not released. Include the following in your request-full name of business. In addition to the articles of incorporation, corporation records include the following information: Annual Reports, Officers, Directors, DBAs, Prior (merged) names, Inactive and Reserved names.

Access by: mail, phone, fax, in person, online.

Fee & Payment: Copy fees are $.50 per page for the first 10 pages and $.15 for each additional page. Certification is $3.00. If you only need a couple pages and are not certifing the document (and are nice), usually there is no charge. Fee payee: Secretary of State. They will invoice for copies and certificates. Prepaid accounts are available. Personal checks accepted. No credit cards accepted.

Mail search: Turnaround time: 1 to 2 days. A SASE is requested.

Phone search: You may call for information.

Fax search: Turnaround time is 24-48 hours.

In person search: You may request information in person.

Online search: Information is available through the Internet site listed above. You can search by corporate name or even download the whole file. Also, they have 2 pages of excellent searching tips.

Uniform Commercial Code, Federal Tax Liens

Secretary of State, UCC Division - Records, 200 W 24th Street, Room 110, Cheyenne, WY 82002-0020; 307-777-5372, 307-777-5988 (Fax), 8AM-5PM.

http://soswy.state.wy.us/uniform/uniform.htm

Indexing & Storage: Records are available for five years on computer, since the "beginning" on microfiche. Records are indexed on inhouse computer and microfiche.

Searching: The search includes federal tax liens on businesses and state tax liens filed by state agencies. Include the following in your request-debtor name.

Access by: mail, fax, in person, online.

Fee & Payment: The search fee is $10.00. Copies cost $.50 each. Fee payee: Secretary of State. Personal checks accepted. No credit cards accepted.

Mail search: Turnaround time: 7 days. Please include your phone number with all requests.

Fax search: Requests may be faxed in.

In person search: Simple requests may be processed while you wait.

Online search: The online filing system permits unlimited record searching. There is a $150 annual fee, with no additional fees charged for searches. Subscribers are entitled to do filings at a 50% discount. Visit the webpage.

Other access: Lists of filings on CD or diskette are available for purchase.

State Tax Liens

Records not maintained by a state level agency.

Note: There is no state income tax. All other state tax liens are filed at the county level.

Sales Tax Registrations

Department of Revenue, Excise Tax Division, Herschler Bldg, 122 W 25th St, Cheyenne, WY 82002-0110; 307-777-5200, 307-777-3632 (Fax), 8AM-5PM.

http://revenue.state.wy.us

Indexing & Storage: Records are available for at least two years: inactive files are purged every two years. It takes 10 to 14 days before new records are available for inquiry. Records are normally destroyed after 6 to 10 years after case closure.

Searching: This agency will only confirm that the business is registered. They will provide no other information except to an owner or officer of the business. Requests may be e-mailed, visit the website for the proper e-mail address. Include the following in your request-business name, and ID of the requester. They will also search by tax permit number. Annual reports are $4.00 each.

Access by: mail, phone, in person.

Fee & Payment: For paper copies or from microfilm, copy fee is $.50 each first 10 pages, $.15 each add'l with a $10.00 minimum. For computer images, copy fee is $1.00 per page first 10 pages, then $.30 each additional with a $35.00 minimum. Fee payee: WY Dept of Revenue.

Mail search: Turnaround time: 7 to 10 days. A SASE is requested. No search fee for mail request.

Phone search: No search fee for telephone request.

In person search: No search fee for request.

Birth Certificates

Wyoming Department of Health, Vital Records Services, Hathaway Bldg, Cheyenne, WY 82002; 307-777-7591, 307-635-4103 (Fax), 8AM-5PM.

http://wdhfs.state.wy.us/vital_records

Indexing & Storage: Records are available from July 1909 to present. New records are available for inquiry immediately. Records are indexed on microfilm, inhouse computer.

Searching: Must have a signed release from person of record or parent or guardian. Include the following in your request-full name, names of parents, mother's maiden name, date of birth, place of birth, relationship to person of record. Must include signature on request and copy of photo ID.

Access by: mail, fax, in person.

Fee & Payment: Search fee is $12.00 per name per 5 years searched. Fee includes certification. Use of credit card is an additional $5.00 for expedited service. Fee payee: Vital Records Services. Prepayment required. Personal checks accepted. Credit cards accepted: MasterCard, Visa, AmEx, Discover.

Mail search: Turnaround time: 3 to 4 working days. No SASE is required.

Fax search: See expedited services.

In person search: Turnaround time is 15 minutes.

Expedited service: Expedited service is available for fax searches. Turnaround time: next day. Include $18.25 for credit card fee and for overnight delivery.

Death Records

Wyoming Department of Health, Vital Records Services, Hathaway Bldg, Cheyenne, WY 82002; 307-777-7591, 307-635-4103 (Fax), 8AM-5PM.

http://wdhfs.state.wy.us/vital_records

Indexing & Storage: Records are available from May 1945 to present. For prior records, contact the State Archives at 307-777-7826. New records are available for inquiry immediately. Records are indexed on microfilm, inhouse computer.

Searching: Must have a signed release from immediate family member. The agency will verify information to family member, such as aunts and uncles, but will not release copies. Include the following in your request-full name, date of death, place of death, relationship to person of record, reason for information request. Must include signature and copy of photo ID with request.

Access by: mail, fax, in person.

Fee & Payment: Search fee is $9.00 per name if year is known; fee is $12.00 per name per 5 years if date is unknown. All copies are certified. Use of credit card for expedited service an extra $5.00. Fee payee: Vital Records Services. Prepayment required. Personal checks accepted. Credit cards accepted: MasterCard, Visa, AmEx, Discover.

Mail search: Turnaround time: 3 to 4 working days. No SASE is required.

Fax search: See expedited services.

In person search: Turnaround time is 15 minutes.

Expedited service: Expedited service is available for fax searches. Turnaround time: next day. Include $18.25 for credit card fee and for overnight delivery.

Marriage Certificates

Wyoming Department of Health, Vital Records Services, Hathaway Bldg, Cheyenne, WY 82002; 307-777-7591, 307-635-4103 (Fax), 8AM-5PM.

http://wdhfs.state.wy.us/vital_records

Indexing & Storage: Records are available from May 1941 to present. New records are available for inquiry immediately. Records are indexed on microfilm, inhouse computer.

Searching: Must have a signed release from persons of record. Include the following in your request-names of husband and wife, date of

marriage, place or county of marriage, relationship to person of record, reason for information request, wife's maiden name. Signature and copy of photo ID must be included in request.

Access by: mail, fax, in person.

Fee & Payment: The fee is $12.00 per record and an additional $5.00 if a credit card is used for expedited service. Fee payee: Vital Records Services. Prepayment required. Personal checks accepted. Credit cards accepted: MasterCard, Visa, AmEx, Discover.

Mail search: Turnaround time: 3 to 4 working days. No SASE is required.

Fax search: See expedited services.

In person search: Turnaround time is 15 minutes.

Expedited service: Expedited service is available for fax searches. Turnaround time: next day. Include $18.25 for credit card fee and for overnight delivery.

Divorce Records

Wyoming Department of Health, Vital Records Services, Hathaway Bldg, Cheyenne, WY 82002; 307-777-7591, 307-635-4103 (Fax), 8AM-5PM.

http://wdhfs.state.wy.us/vital_records

Indexing & Storage: Records are available from May 1941 to present. New records are available for inquiry immediately. Records are indexed on microfilm, inhouse computer.

Searching: Must have a signed release from person of record. Include the following in your request-names of husband and wife, date of divorce, place of divorce, relationship to person of record. Include copy of photo ID with request.

Access by: mail, fax, in person.

Fee & Payment: Fee is $12.00 per record. Fee payee: Vital Records Services. Prepayment required. Personal checks accepted. Credit cards accepted: MasterCard, Visa, AmEx, Discover.

Mail search: Turnaround time: 3 to 4 working days.

Fax search: See expedited services.

In person search: Turnaround time is 30 minutes.

Expedited service: Expedited service is available for fax searches. Turnaround time: next day. Include $18.25 for credit card fee and for overnight delivery.

Workers' Compensation Records

Employment Department, Workers Compensation Division, 1510 E Pershing Blvd, Cheyenne, WY 82002; 307-777-7159, 307-777-5946 (Fax), 8AM-4:30PM.

http://wydoe.state.wy.us/doe.asp?ID=9

Indexing & Storage: Records are available from 1987 on computer. Records are on microfiche from 1919 to 1987. Searches on microfiche must include the date of injury, county of injury, employer and body part affected. It takes 3 days before new records are available for inquiry. Records are normally destroyed after document image saved on computer, usually several months from closure.

Searching: Only the injured party, employer or legal counsel for either party can obtain records from this agency. Include the following in your request-claimant name, Social Security Number.

The only information released is case #, date of injury, body part, employer at time of injury, or other information specifically authorized by claimant.

Access by: mail, fax.

Fee & Payment: No search fee. The copy fee is $.25 per copy. Fee payee: Wyoming Workers' Compensation

Mail search: Turnaround time: variable. Send release form with request to Gary Lord at address above. No SASE is required.

Fax search: They will fax results with appropriate request.

Driver License Information, Driver Records

Wyoming Department of Transportation, Driver Services, 5300 Bishop Blvd, Cheyenne, WY 82009-3340; 307-777-4800, 307-777-4773 (Fax), 8AM-5PM.

www.dot.state.wy.us

Note: Authorized requesters may obtain ticket information may be obtained from the address above for a fee of $5.00 per citation.

Indexing & Storage: Records are available for 3 years from offense date for moving violations, 5 years from conviction date for DWIs, and 3 to 5 years based on original charge for suspensions. Accidents are shown only if driver has no insurance. It takes 5 to 10 days before new records are available for inquiry. Records are normally destroyed after 10 years.

Searching: Companies requesting records must complete and file the DPPA form available on the website. Casual requesters cannot obtain records with personal information without signed release from subject. Include the following in your request-name and DOB and DL or SSN. The following data is not released: medical information.

Access by: mail, in person, online.

Fee & Payment: The fee is $5.00 per record, $3.00 by tape. Add $6.00 if credit card used. Fee payee: Department of Transportation. Prepayment required. Personal checks accepted. No credit cards accepted.

Mail search: Turnaround time: 2 business days.

In person search: Normal turnaround time is while you wait. Individual licensees may request a copy of their own record at any field office.

Online search: This method is available using FTP technology. Only approved vendors and permissible users are supported. Write Deb Ornelas at the above address for details.

Other access: Magnetic tape retrieval is available at $3.00 per record. The entire driver license file may be purchased for $2,500. Write or call 307-777-4842 for details.

Vehicle Ownership, Vehicle Identification

Wyoming Dept. of Transportation, Motor Vehicle Services, 5300 Bishop Blvd, Cheyenne, WY 82009-3340 (Courier: 5300 Bishop Blvd, Cheyenne, WY 82002); 307-777-4851, 307-777-4772 (Fax), 8AM-5PM.

http://wydotweb.state.wy.us/web/vehicle_services/index.html

Note: At the website, click on "Vehicle Services" for detailed WY DOT vehicle information. Also, the web site provides access to the request forms needed.

Indexing & Storage: Records are available for 40 years on titles and 80 years on registrations. It takes 3 to 15 days before new records are available for inquiry.

Searching: Requests must be for a permissible use per DPPA. A "Privacy Disclosure Agreement" will need to be signed. Casual requesters cannot obtain records unless written consent of subject is provided and reason for request is apporved by MVS. Lien records are not available from the state and must be obtained from the one of the 23 Wyoming county clerk offices.

Access by: mail, fax, in person.

Fee & Payment: The fee is $5.00 per record. Credit cards accepted for an additional $4.95 fee. Fee payee: WY Department of Transportation. Prepayment required. Personal checks accepted. No credit cards accepted.

Mail search: Turnaround time: 1 week. No SASE is required.

Fax search: Approved requetser may search by fax using a credit card.

In person search: Turnaround time is normally in a few minutes.

Other access: Bulk information is available, customized lists can be obtained, per DPPA. For more information, call the Motor Vehicle Services at 307-777-4842.

Accident Reports

Highway Safety Program, Accident Records Section, 5300 Bishop Blvd, Cheyenne, WY 82009; 307-777-4450, 307-777-4250 (Fax), 8AM-5PM.

Note: The agency refers to these reports as "Crash Reports."

Indexing & Storage: Records are available for It takes 10 to 30 days before new records are available for inquiry.

Searching: Accident reports (done by the officer) are considered open public record reports. Reports compiled by individuals involved are closed. Include the following in your request-date of accident, location of accident, full name, date of birth.

Access by: mail, phone, in person.

Fee & Payment: The fee is $3.00 per record uncertified and $5.00 certified. Fee payee: Department of Transportation. Prepayment required. Personal checks accepted. No credit cards accepted.

Mail search: Turnaround time: 1 week to 10 days. A SASE is requested.

Phone search: Searches may be done by phone, but no copies are sent until payment is received.

In person search: In-person requests are normally processed in a few of minutes.

Expedited service: Pre-paid accounts can be set up for ongoing requesters, this may speed the process.

Vessel Ownership, Vessel Registration

Wyoming Game & Fish Dept, Watercraft Section, 5400 Bishop Blvd, Cheyenne, WY 82006; 307-777-4575, 307-777-4610 (Fax), 8AM-5PM M-F.

http://gf.state.wy.us

Indexing & Storage: Records are available for the last 3 years.The state does not issue titles. All motorized boats must be registered. It takes 10 days before new records are available for inquiry. Records are indexed on computer. Records are normally destroyed after 3 years.

Searching: To search you must provide one of the following: name, Wyoming number, or hull ID number.

Access by: mail, phone, fax, in person.

Fee & Payment: There is no search fee.

Mail search: Turnaround time: 2 to 3 days. Turnaround time is 1 week if archived info is needed.

Phone search: Records are available by phone.

Fax search: Information can be faxed back.

In person search: No fee for request. Turnaround time is immediate if the file is not archived.

Other access: Printed lists are available, call for further details.

Voter Registration

Secretary of State, Election Division, Wyoming State Capitol, Cheyenne, WY 82002-0020; 307-777-7186, 307-777-7640 (Fax), 8AM-5PM.

http://soswy.state.wy.us/election/election.htm

Note: Individual look-ups can also be done at the county level. The SSN and DOB are not released. The state will sell all or part of its database, but only for political reasons. Commercial use is not permitted.

Indexing & Storage: Records are available for the last 10 years, from this office. Previous records are archived. It takes 24 hours before new records are available for inquiry. Records are normally destroyed after 10 years.

Searching: Include the following in your request-name.

Access by: mail, in person.

Fee & Payment: The fee is $.50 a page for first 10 pages and $.15 each add'l page.

Mail search: Turnaround time: 2 days. Records are available by mail.

In person search: Records are pulled within minutes, when personnel available.

GED Certificates

Deptment of WorkForce Services, GED Program, 122 W 25th Street, Cheyenne, WY 82002; 307-777-6911, 307-777-7106 (Fax), 8AM-5PM M-F.

www.wyomingworkforce.org

Indexing & Storage: Records are available from 1992 forward. New records are available for inquiry immediately.

Searching: To request a transcript or have one sent to emplyer or college, the following is required: signed release from subject, full name, SSN, and date of birth. Test date is helpful. Request form can be downloaded from webpage.

Access by: mail, fax, in person.

Fee & Payment: There is no fee for verifications or transcripts.

Mail search: Turnaround time: 24 hours. No SASE is required.

Fax search: Same criteria as mail searching.

In person search: Turnaround time is typically 10 minutes for verifications or transcripts if Chief Examiner is available. Otherwise mailed.

Hunting and Fishing License Information

Game & Fish Department, License Section, 5400 Bishop Blvd, Cheyenne, WY 82006; 307-777-4600 (Licensing Section), 307-777-4679 (Fax), 8AM-5PM.

http://gf.state.wy.us

Note: They maintain a central database for lottery (big game, moose, big horn sheep, elk, deer & antelope) permits and periodically add license permits sold by agents throughout the state.

Indexing & Storage: Records are available from 3 years present on computer, 10 years on microfiche.

Searching: Include the following in your request-full name, date of birth, Social Security Number. The following data is not released: Social Security Numbers.

Access by: mail, phone, fax, in person.

Fee & Payment: Fees are incurred if there is extensive searching or lists are involved. Call first. Fee payee: Wyoming Game and Fish. Prepayment required. Money orders and cashier's checks are preferred. No credit cards accepted.

Mail search: Turnaround time: 1 to 3 days. No SASE is required.

Phone search: Records are available by phone.

Fax search: Fax searching available.

In person search: Simple requests may be processed while you wait.

Other access: They have mailing and label lists available. Call 800-548-9453 for more information.

Wyoming State Licensing Agencies

Licenses Searchable Online

Attorney #9	www.wyomingbar.org/lawyer_directory.asp
Bank #23	http://audit.state.wy.us/banking/banking/bankingregulatedentities.htm
Check Casher #23	http://audit.state.wy.us/banking/uccc/ucclicensees.htm
Chiropractor #32	http://plboards.state.wy.us/chiropractic
Collection Agency #24	http://audit.state.wy.us/banking/cab/cablicensees.htm
Engineer #27	www.wrds.uwyo.edu/wrds/borpe/roster/roster.html
Feed/Fertilizer #1	www.kellysolutions.com/wy/
Funeral Preneed Agent #8	http://insurance.state.wy.us/search/search.asp
Geologist #18	http://wbpgweb.uwyo.edu/roster_search.asp
Guide, Outdoor #13	http://outfitte.state.wy.us/directory.html
Insurance Claims Adjuster #8	http://insurance.state.wy.us/search/search.asp
Insurance Consultant/Producer/Service Rep #8	http://insurance.state.wy.us/search/search.asp
Lender, Supervised #23	http://audit.state.wy.us/banking/uccc/ucclicensees.htm
Lobbyist #36	http://soswy.state.wy.us/election/lob-list.htm
Medical Doctor #10	http://wyomedboard.state.wy.us/roster.asp
Motor Club Agent #8	http://insurance.state.wy.us/search/search.asp
Optometrist #6	www.arbo.org/odfinder/LicSearch.asp
Outfitter #13	http://outfitte.state.wy.us/directory.html
Pawnbroker #23	http://audit.state.wy.us/banking/uccc/ucclicensees.htm
Pharmacist / Pharmacy Technician #14	http://pharmacyboard.state.wy.us/search.asp
Physician Assistant #10	http://wyomedboard.state.wy.us/PARoster.asp
Psychologist #16	http://plboards.state.wy.us/psychology
Public Accountant-CPA, Individual/Firm #29	http://cpaboard.state.wy.us/database.aspx
Real Estate Appraiser #21	www.asc.gov/content/category1/appr_by_state.asp
Rent-to-own Company #23	http://audit.state.wy.us/banking/uccc/ucclicensees.htm
Sales Finance Company #23	http://audit.state.wy.us/banking/uccc/ucclicensees.htm
Savings & Loan Association #23	http://audit.state.wy.us/banking/banking/bankingregulatedentities.htm
Surplus Line Broker, Resident #8	http://insurance.state.wy.us/search/search.asp
Surveyor, Land #27	www.wrds.uwyo.edu/wrds/borpe/roster/roster.html
Trust Company #23	http://audit.state.wy.us/banking/banking/bankingregulatedentities.htm

Wyoming Licensing Quick Finder

Architect #30	307-777-5403	
Attorney #9	307-632-9061	
Bank #23	307-777-6605	
Barber/Barber Shop #2	307-754-5237	
Bus Driver #41	307-777-4800	
Check Casher #23	307-777-6605	
Child Care Licensing #22	307-777-6595	
Child Care Subsidy #22	307-777-6848	
Chiropractor #32	307-777-3628	
Coach, Athletic #35	307-777-7291	
Collection Agency #24	307-777-3497	
Coroner/Deputy Coroner #39	307-777-7718	
Cosmetologist /Cosmetol. Instruc'r #3	307-777-3534	
Counselor, Professional #30	307-777-7387	
Dental Assistant /Hygienist #4	307-777-3628	
Dentist #4	307-777-3628	
Detention Officer #39	307-777-7718	
Dispatcher (law enforcement-related) #39	307-777-7718	
Educational Diagnostician #35	307-777-7291	
Electrical Apprentice #26	307-777-7991	
Electrician, Master/Journeyman #26	307-777-7991	
Embalmer #5	307-777-5403	
Emergency Medical Technician #40	307-777-7955	
Engineer #27	307-777-6155	
Esthetician #3	307-777-3534	
Feed/Fertilizer #1	307-777-7324	
Funeral Director #5	307-777-5403	
Funeral Preneed Agent #8	307-777-7344	
Geologist #18	307-742-1118	
Guide, Outdoor #13	307-777-5323	
Hearing Aid Specialist #7	307-777-5403	
Insurance Claims Adjuster #8	307-777-7344	
Insurance Consultant /Producer #8	307-777-7344	
Insurance Service Rep #8	307-777-7344	
Jockey/Jockey Apprentice #38	307-777-5887	
Landscape Architect #30	307-777-5403	
Law Enforcement Officer #39	307-777-7718	
Lender, Supervised #23	307-777-6605	
Lobbyist #36	307-777-7186	
Manicurist/Nail Technician #3	307-777-3534	
Marriage & Family Therapist #30	307-777-7387	
Medical Doctor #10	307-778-7053	
Mine Foreman/Inspector/Examiner #33	307-362-5222	
Motor Club Agent #8	307-777-7344	
Notary Public #36	307-777-5407	
Nurse/Nurse-LPN /Nursing Assist. #37	877-626-2681	
Nursing Home Administrator #12	307-432-0465	
Occupational Therapist #12	307-432-0488	
Occupational Therapist Assistant #12	307-432-0488	
Optometrist #6	307-777-3507	
Outfitter #13	307-777-5323	
Pari-Mutuel Employee/Official #38	307-777-5887	
Pawnbroker #23	307-777-6605	
Peace Officer #39	307-777-7718	
Pesticide Aircraft #1	307-777-7324	
Pesticide Applicator, Commercial #1	307-777-7324	
Pharmacist /Pharmacy Technician #14	307-234-0294	
Physical Therapist #15	307-777-3507	
Physician Assistant #10	307-778-7053	
Podiatrist #19	307-777-3507	
Property Tax Appraiser #25	307-777-5239	
Psychiatrist #10	307-778-7053	
Psychological Practioner #16	307-333-6529	
Psychologist #16	307-777-6529	
Public Accountant-CPA, Individual/Firm #29	307-777-7551	
Racetrack Security Employee #38	307-777-5887	
Racing Event #38	307-777-5887	
Racing Permittee/Employee/Offic'l #38	307-777-5887	
Radiation (Ionizing) Agent #17	307-777-3507	
Radiologic Technologist/Tech. #17	307-777-3507	
Radiopharmaceutical Agent #17	307-778-2068	
Real Estate Agent #21	307-777-7141	
Real Estate Appraiser #21	307-777-7141	
Rent-to-own Company #23	307-777-6605	
Sales Finance Company #23	307-777-6605	
Savings & Loan Association #23	307-777-6605	
School Counselor/Librarian #35	307-777-7291	
School Principal / Superintendent #35	307-777-7291	
School Psychologist #16	307-777-6529	
Securities Agent #34	307-777-7370	
Securities Broker/Dealer #34	307-777-7370	
Social Worker #30	307-777-7387	
Speech Pathologist/Audiologist #28	307-777-5403	
Substitute Teacher #35	307-777-7291	
Surplus Line Broker, Resident #8	307-777-7344	
Surveyor, Land #27	307-777-6155	
Teacher #35	307-777-7291	
Travel & Baggage Agent #8	307-777-7344	
Truck Driver #41	307-777-4800	
Trust Company #23	307-777-6605	
Veterinarian #20	307-777-3507	
Water Dist/Collection Operator #42	307-777-7781	
Water/Waste Water Treatment Plant Operator #42	307-777-7781	

Wyoming Licensing Agency Information

1 Technical Services Department, Board of Agriculture, 2219 Carey Ave, Cheyenne, WY 82002-0100; 307-777-7324, Fax: 307-777-6593. http://wyagric.state.wy.us/techserv/tsindex.html Email: huhden@state.wy.us Note: Will sell lists.

2 Board of Barber Examiners, 441 Sunlight Dr, Powell, WY 82435; 307-754-5237, Fax: 307-754-5580. http://soswy.state.wy.us/director/ag-bd/barber.htm

3 Board of Cosmetology, 2515 Warren Ave, #302, Cheyenne, WY 82002; 307-777-3534, Fax: 307-777-3681. http://soswy.state.wy.us/director/ag-bd/cosmet.htm Email: babern@state.wy.us

4 Board of Dental Examiners, 2020 Carey Ave #201, Cheyenne, WY 82002; 307-777-3628, Fax: 307-777-3508. http://plboards.state.wy.us/dental

5 Board of Embalming, 2020 Carey Ave, #201, Cheyenne, WY 82002; 307-777-5403, Fax: 307-777-3508.

6 Board of Examiners in Optometry, 2020 Carey Ave, #201, Cheyenne, WY 82002; 307-777-3507, Fax: 307-777-3508. http://soswy.state.wy.us/director/ag-bd/optometr.htm Email: nbrown1@missc.wy.state.us Search Database at www.arbo.org/odfinder/LicSearch.asp

7 Board of Hearing Aid Specialists, 2020 Carey Ave, #201, Cheyenne, WY 82002; 307-777-5403, Fax: 307-777-3508. http://plboards.state.wy.us/hearingaid/index.asp

8 Board of Insurance Agents Examiners, 122 W 25th St, Cheyenne, WY 82002-0040; 307-777-7344, Fax: 307-777-5895. http://insurance.state.wy.us Email: gnalde@state.wy.us Search Database at http://insurance.state.wy.us/search/search.asp

9 Board of Law Examiners, PO Box 109 (500 Randall Ave.), Cheyenne, WY 82003; 307-632-9061, Fax: 307-630-3737. www.wyomingbar.org Search Database at www.wyomingbar.org/lawyer_directory.asp

10 Board of Medicine, 211 W 19th St, 2nd Fl, Cheyenne, WY 82002; 307-778-7053, 800-438-5784, Fax: 307-778-2069. http://wyomedboard.state.wy.us Email: wyomedical@wyomedicalboard.org

12 Board of Occupational Therapy, 1114 Logan Ave, Cheyenne, WY 82002; 307-432-0488, Fax: 307-432-0492. http://plboards.state.wy.us/ Email: kspire@state.wy.us

13 Board of Outfitters & Professional Guides, 1950 Bluegrass Circle #280, Cheyenne, WY 82002; 307-777-5323, Fax: 307-777-6715. http://outfitters.state.wy.us Email: jflagg@state.wy.us Search Database at http://outfitte.state.wy.us/directory.html

14 Board of Pharmacy, 632 S David S, Casper, WY 82601-3189; 307-234-0294, Fax: 307-234-7226. http://pharmacyboard.state.wy.us Email: wybop@state.wy.us Search Database at http://pharmacyboard.state.wy.us/search.asp

15 Board of Physical Therapy, 2020 Carey Ave, #201, Cheyenne, WY 82002; 307-777-3507, Fax: 307-777-3508. http://soswy.state.wy.us/director/ag-bd/pt.htm Email: nbrown@missc.wy.state.us

16 Board of Psychology, 2020 Carey Ave, #201, Cheyenne, WY 82002; 307-777-5403, Fax: 307-777-3508. http://plboards.state.wy.us/psychology

17 Board of Radiologic Technologists, 2020 Carey Ave, #201, Cheyenne, WY 82002; 307-777-3507, Fax: 307-777-3508. http://soswy.state.wy.us/director/ag-bd/radiolog.htm Email: nbrown@missc.wy.state.us

18 Board of Registration for Professional Geologists, 1465 N. 4th Street # 109, Laramie, WY 82072-2066; 307-742-1118, Fax: 307-742-1120. http://wbpgweb.uwyo.edu Email: wbpg@state.wy.us Search Database at http://wbpgweb.uwyo.edu/roster_search.asp

19 Board of Registration in Podiatry, 2020 Carey Ave, #201, Cheyenne, WY 82002; 307-777-3507, Fax: 307-777-3508. http://soswy.state.wy.us/director/ag-bd/podiatry.htm Email: nbrown@missc.wy.state.us

20 Board of Veterinary Medicine, 2020 Carey Ave, #201, Cheyenne, WY 82002; 307-777-3507, Fax: 307-777-3508. http://soswy.state.wy.us/director/ag-bd/vet-med.htm Email: nbrown@missc.wy.state.us

21 Real Estate Appraiser Board, 2020 Carey Ave, #100, Cheyenne, WY 82002; 307-777-7141, Fax: 307-777-3796. http://realestate.state.wy.us

22 Child Care Certification Board, 2300 Capitol Ave, Hathaway Bldg., Room 337, Cheyenne, WY 82002-0490; 307-777-6350, Fax: 307-777-3659. http://dfsweb.state.wy.us

23 Department of Audit, Division of Banking, 122 W 25th St, Herschler Bldg 3 E, Cheyenne, WY 82002; 307-777-7797, Fax: 307-777-3555. http://audit.state.wy.us/banking/default.htm Email: maitchison@wyaudit.state.wy.us Search Database at http://audit.state.wy.us/banking/banking/bankingregulatedentities.htm

24 Department of Audit, Collecting Agency Board, Herschler Bldg, 3rd Fl, Cheyenne, WY 82002; 307-777-3497, Fax: 307-777-3555. http://audit.state.wy.us/banking/default.htm Email: ssmith@audit.state.wy.us Search Database at http://audit.state.wy.us/banking/cab/cablicensees.htm

25 Department of Revenue, 122 W 25th St, Herschler Bldg, 2nd Fl W, Cheyenne, WY 82002-0110; 307-777-5239. http://plboards.state.wy.us Email: jburtol@missc.state.wy.us

26 Electrical Board, Herschler Bldg, 1st Fl W, Cheyenne, WY 82002; 307-777-7288, Fax: 307-777-7119. http://soswy.state.wy.us/director/ag-bd/electric.htm Email: jnoel@state.wy.us

27 Engineers & Professional Land Surveyors, 2424 Pioneer Ave, #400, Cheyenne, WY 82001; 307-777-6155, Fax: 307-777-3403. www.wrds.uwyo.edu/wrds/borpe/borpe.html Email: wyopepls@qwest.net Search Database at www.wrds.uwyo.edu/wrds/borpe/roster/roster.html

28 Examiners for Speech Pathology & Audiology, 2020 Carey Ave, #201, Cheyenne, WY 82002; 307-777-5403, Fax: 307-777-3508. http://plboards.state.wy.us/speech/index.asp Note: Roster of Licensees available.

29 Board of Certified Public Accountants, 2020 Carey Ave, #100, Cheyenne, WY 82002; 307-777-7551, Fax: 307-777-3796. http://cpaboard.state.wy.us Email: pmorga@state.wy.us Search Database at http://cpaboard.state.wy.us/database.aspx

30 Professional Licensing Boards, 2020 Carey Ave, #201, Cheyenne, WY 82002; 307-777-5403, Fax: 307-777-3508. http://plboards.state.wy.us/architecture/index.asp

32 Board of Chiropractic Examiners, 2020 Carey Ave, #201, Cheyenne, WY 82002; 307-777-3628, Fax: 307-777-3508. http://plboards.state.wy.us/chiropractic

33 Mining Council, PO Box 1094, Rock Springs, WY 82901; 307-362-5222, Fax: 307-362-5233. http://soswy.state.wy.us/director/ag-bd/mining.htm

34 Securities Division, Office of Secretary of State, Joseph B Meyer, State Capitol Bldg, Cheyenne, WY 82002; 307-777-7370, Fax: 307-777-5339. http://soswy.state.wy.us/securiti/securiti.htm Email: securities@state.wy.us

35 Professional Teaching Standards Board, 1920 Thomes Ave. #400, Cheyenne, WY 82002; 307-777-7291, Fax: 307-777-8718. www.k12.wy.us/ptsb Email: lstowe@state.wy.us

36 Secretary of State, Elections/Notary Division, Joseph B Meyer, State Capitol Bldg, Cheyenne, WY 82002; 307-777-7378, Fax: 307-777-5466. http://soswy.state.wy.us Email: secofstate@missc.state.wy.us

37 Board of Nursing, 2020 Carey Ave, #110, Cheyenne, WY 82002; 307-777-7601; voice verification 877-626-2681, Fax: 307-777-3519. http://nursing.state.wy.us Email: rpoupp@state.wy.us Note: Call for prices.

38 Pari-Mutuel Commission, 2515 Warren Ave, #301, Cheyenne, WY 82002; 307-777-5887, Fax: 307-777-5700. http://parimutuel.state.wy.us

39 P.O.S.T. Com., 1710 Pacific Ave, Cheyenne, WY 82002; 307-777-7718, Fax: 307-638-9706.

40 Office of Emergency Medical Svcs, 2300 Capital Ave, Hathaway Bldg 4th Fl, Cheyenne, WY 82002; 307-777-7955, Fax: 307-777-5639.

41 Driver Svcs, Department of Transportation, 5300 Bishop Blvd, Cheyenne, WY 82009-3340; 307-777-4800, Fax: 307-777-4803. http://dot.state.wy.us

42 Department of Environmental Quality, Water Quality Division, 122 W 25th St, Herschler Bldg 4th Fl-W, Cheyenne, WY 82002; 307-777-7781, Fax: 307-777-5973. http://deq.state.wy.us/wqd/index.asp?pageid=5

Wyoming Federal Courts

The following list indicates the district and division name for each county in the state.

County/Court Cross Reference

Albany	Cheyenne	Natrona	Cheyenne
Big Horn	Cheyenne	Niobrara	Cheyenne
Campbell	Cheyenne	Park	Cheyenne
Carbon	Cheyenne	Platte	Cheyenne
Converse	Cheyenne	Sheridan	Cheyenne
Crook	Cheyenne	Sublette	Cheyenne
Fremont	Cheyenne	Sweetwater	Cheyenne
Goshen	Cheyenne	Teton	Cheyenne
Hot Springs	Cheyenne	Uinta	Cheyenne
Johnson	Cheyenne	Washakie	Cheyenne
Laramie	Cheyenne	Weston	Cheyenne
Lincoln	Cheyenne		

US District Court

District of Wyoming

Cheyenne Division 2120 Capitol Ave, Room 2141, Cheyenne, WY 82001 (courier: Room 2141, 2120 Capitol Ave, Cheyenne, WY 82001), 307-433-2120. www.ck10.uscourts.gov/wyoming/district/index.html

Counties: All counties in Wyoming. Some criminal records are held in Casper, but all are available electronically here.

Indexing & Storage: New cases available in the index 1-2 days after filing date. Records older than 1992 are on microfiche also.

Fee & Payment: Payment may be made by money order, cashier check, personal check. Payee: Clerk, U.S. District Court.

Phone Search: No searching by telephone.

Mail Search: A SASE not required.

In Person Search: Fee charged if court conducts your in person search for you.

PACER: PACER is available online at http://pacer.wyd.uscourts.gov. Records purged once per year. New civil records are online after 1-2 days. New criminal records online after 1 day.

Electronic Filing: Electronic filing information online at https://ecf.wyd.uscourts.gov

U.S. Bankruptcy Court

District of Wyoming

Cheyenne Division 2120 Capitol Ave, #6004, Cheyenne, WY 82001 (courier address: 6th Floor, #6004, 2120 Capitol Ave, Cheyenne, WY 82001), 307-772-2191. www.wyb.uscourts.gov

Counties: All counties in Wyoming. The Casper Bankruptcy Court records are located here.

Indexing & Storage: Cases indexed by debtor as well as by case number. New cases available in the index 24 hours after filing date.

Fee & Payment: Payment may be made by money order, cashier check, personal check. Payee: Clerk, U.S. Bankruptcy Court.

Phone Search: Automated voice case information service (VCIS) is available. Call VCIS at 888-804-5537 or 307-772-2191.

In Person Search: Fee charged if court conducts your in person search for you.

PACER: PACER is available online at http://pacer.wyb.uscourts.gov. Document images available. Records purged annually. New civil records are online after 1 day.

Electronic Filing: Electronic filing information online at https://ecf.wyb.uscourts.gov

Opinions Online: Court opinions are online at www.wyb.uscourts.gov/opinion_search.htm

Standards for Federal Courts: The search fee is $20.00 per item (one party name or case number). Certification fee is $7.00 per document. Copy fee is $.50 per page. All fees standard unless noted in profile. Mail Search: always enclose a stamped self addressed envelope unless otherwise noted. Most courts accept fax requests or will suggest a copying/search vendor. Before releasing records, all courts require prepayment unless noted in profile.

Open records are located at the court unless otherwise noted. District courts index by defendant and plaintiff as well as by case number. Bankruptcy courts usually index by debtor and case number. While most courts now have their indexes on computer, many still maintain index card files as well.

The universal PACER sign-up number is 800-676-6856. Find PACER and the Party/Case Index on the Web at http://pacer.psc.uscourts.gov. PACER dial-up access is $.60 per minute. Also, courts offering internet access via RACER, PACER, Web-PACER or the new CM-ECF charge $.07 per page fee unless noted as free.

Wyoming County Courts

Court	Jurisdiction	No. of Courts	How Organized
District Courts*	General	23	9 Districts
Circuit Courts*	Limited	27	23 Counties
Municipal Courts	Municipal	80	

* Profiled in this Sourcebook.

CIVIL									
Court	Tort	Contract	Real Estate	Min. Claim	Max. Claim	Small Claims	Estate	Eviction	Domestic Relations
District Courts*	X	X	X	$3000/ $7000	No Max		X		X
Circuit Courts*	X	X	X	$0	$7000	$3000		X	X
Municipal Courts									

CRIMINAL					
Court	Felony	Misdemeanor	DWI/DUI	Preliminary Hearing	Juvenile
District Courts*	X				X
Circuit Courts*		X	X	X	
Municipal Courts		X	X		

ADMINISTRATION
Court Administrator, 2301 Capitol Av, Supreme Court Bldg, Cheyenne, WY, 82002; 307-777-7583, Fax: 307-777-3447. www.courts.state.wy.us

COURT STRUCTURE
Each county has a District Court ("higher" jurisdiction) and a Circuit. Prior to 2003, for their "lower" jurisdiction court some counties had Circuit Courts and others had Justice Courts. Effective January 1, 2003 all Justice Courts became Circuit Courts and follow Circuit Court rules.

Circuit Courts handle civil claims up to $7,000 while Justice Courts handle civil claims up to $3,000. The District Courts take cases over the applicable limit in each county. Three counties have two Circuit Courts each: Fremont, Park, and Sweetwater. Cases may be filed in either of the two court offices in those counties, and records requests are referred between the two courts. Municipal courts operate in all incorporated cities and towns. Their jurisdiction covers all ordinance violations, and it has no civil jurisdiction. The municipal court judge may assess penalties of up to $750 and/or six months in jail.

Probate is handled by the District Court.

ONLINE ACCESS
Wyoming's statewide case management system is for internal use only. Planning is underway for a new case management system that will ultimately allow public access. Appellate and Supreme Court opinions available at web, listed by date.

Albany County

2nd Judicial District Court County Courthouse, 525 Grand, Rm 305, Laramie, WY 82070; 307-721-2508. Hours: 9AM-5PM (MST). *Felony, Civil Actions Over $7,000, Probate.*
Civil Records: Access: Phone, mail, in person. Only the court performs in person searches; visitors may not. Search fee: $10.00 per name. Required to search: name; also helpful: years to search. Civil cases indexed by defendant, plaintiff. Civil records on computer go back to 1988, prior records on card index to 1890. Limit calls to three names.
Criminal Records: Access: Mail, in person. Only the court performs in person searches; visitors may not. Search fee: $10.00 per name. Search results can be phoned back to a toll-free number only. Required to search: name, years to search, DOB. Criminal records on computer go back to 1988, prior records on card index to 1890.
General Information: No sex offenses records released, signed release required for child support cases. Will fax results to toll-free number only. Copy fee: $1.00 for first page; $.50 each add'l. No cert fee. Payee: Clerk of District Court. Personal checks accepted. Prepayment required. Mail requests: SASE required. Mail turnaround time same day.

Albany Circuit Court County Courthouse, 525 Grand, Rm 105, Laramie, WY 82070; 307-742-5747; Fax: 307-742-5610. Hours: 8AM-5PM (MST). *Misdemeanor, Civil Actions Under $7,000, Eviction, Small Claims.*

Civil Records: Access: Mail, in person. Both court and visitors may perform in person searches. Search fee: $10.00 per name. Required to search: name, years to search. Civil cases indexed by defendant, plaintiff. Civil records on computer from 1993, prior on docket books to 1984.
Criminal Records: Access: Mail, in person, fax. Both court and visitors may perform in person searches. Search fee: $10.00 per name. Required to search: name, years to search, DOB. Criminal records on computer from 1989, prior on docket books to 1984.
General Information: No SSN or family violence records released. Fee to fax results is $2.00 per document. Copy fee: $1.00 for 1st page, $.50 each add'l. Cert fee: $5.00 per document. Payee: Albany

Circuit Court. In state personal checks accepted. Prepayment required. Mail requests: SASE required. Mail turnaround time same day.

Big Horn County

5th Judicial District Court PO Box 670, Basin, WY 82410; 307-568-2381; Fax: 307-568-2791. Hours: 8AM-Noon, 1-5PM (MST). *Felony, Civil Actions Over $7,000, Probate.*

Civil Records: Access: Fax, mail, in person. Both court and visitors may perform in person searches. Search fee: $10.00 per name. Required to search: name, years to search. Civil cases indexed by defendant, plaintiff. Civil records on computer 1988, on microfiche 1982, 1970 to present on cards.

Criminal Records: Access: Fax, mail, in person. Both court and visitors may perform in person searches. Search fee: $10.00 per name. Required to search: name, years to search. Criminal records on computer 1989, on microfiche 1982, 1970 to present on cards.

General Information: Some confidential records not released. Will fax results to local or toll free line. Copy fee: $1.00 for first page, $.50 each add'l. Cert fee: $.50. Payee: Clerk of Court. Business checks accepted. Prepayment required. Mail requests: SASE required. Mail turnaround time 24 hours.

Basin Circuit Court PO Box 749, Basin, WY 82410; 307-568-2367; Fax: 307-568-2554. Hours: 8AM-5PM (MST). *Misdemeanor, Civil Actions Under $7,000, Small Claims.*

Note: Note that misdemanor records from this Basin Court and the Lovell Court are not combined.

Civil Records: Access: Fax, mail, in person. Only the court performs in person searches; visitors may not. Search fee: $10.00 per name. Required to search: name, years to search; also helpful: address. Civil cases indexed by defendant. Civil records on microfiche 1985.

Criminal Records: Access: Fax, mail, in person. Only the court performs in person searches; visitors may not. Search fee: $10.00 per name. Required to search: name, DOB; also helpful: SSN. Criminal records on computer since 1990, microfiche 1985.

General Information: No sex or juvenile offenses released. Fee to fax results is $2 per document. Copy fee: $1.00 for 1st page, $.50 each add'l. Cert fee: $5.00 per document. Payee: Basin Circuit Court. Personal checks accepted. Prepayment required. Mail turnaround time 1 day.

Lovell Circuit Court PO Box 595, Lovell, WY 82431; 307-548-7601; Fax: 307-548-9691. Hours: 8AM-5PM (MST). *Misdemeanor, Civil Actions Under $7,000, Small Claims.*

Note: Note that misdemanor records from the Basin Circuit Court and this Lovell Court are not combined.

Civil Records: Access: Fax, mail, in person. Only the court performs in person searches; visitors may not. Search fee: $10.00 per name. Required to search: name, years to search; also helpful: address. Civil cases indexed by defendant. Civil records on microfiche 1985.

Criminal Records: Access: Fax, mail, in person. Only the court performs in person searches; visitors may not. Search fee: $10.00 per name. Required to search: name, DOB; also helpful: SSN. Criminal records on computer since 1990, microfiche 1985.

General Information: No sex or juvenile offenses released. Fee to fax results is $2.00 per document. Copy fee: $1.00 for 1st page, $.50 each add'l. Cert fee: $5.00 per document. Payee: Lovell Circuit Court. Personal checks accepted. Prepayment required. Mail turnaround time 1 day.

Campbell County

6th Judicial District Court PO Box 817, 500 S Gillette, Gillette, WY 82717; 307-682-3424; Fax: 307-687-6209. Hours: 8AM-5PM (MST). *Felony, Civil Actions Over $7,000, Probate.*

Civil Records: Access: Fax, mail, in person. Visitors must perform in person searches for themselves. Search fee: $10.00 per name. Required to search: name, years to search. Civil cases indexed by defendant. Civil records archived from 1913; on computer back to 1983.

Criminal Records: Access: Fax, mail, in person. Visitors must perform in person searches for themselves. Search fee: $10.00 per name. Required to search: name, years to search. Criminal records archived from 1913; on computer back to 1983.

General Information: Public Access terminal is available. Names of victims in sex cases, confidential records not released. Will fax results $1.00 per page. Copy fee: $1.00 for first page, $.50 each add'l. No cert fee. Payee: Clerk of District Court. Personal checks accepted. Out of state checks not accepted. Prepayment required. Mail requests: SASE not required. Mail turnaround time 1-2 days.

Campbell Circuit Court 500 S Gillette Ave #301, Gillette, WY 82716; 307-682-2190; Fax: 307-687-6214. Hours: 8AM-5PM (MST). *Misdemeanor, Civil Actions Under $7,000, Eviction, Small Claims.*

Civil Records: Access: Mail, in person. Only the court performs in person searches; visitors may not. Search fee: $10.00 per name. Required to search: name, years to search; also helpful: address. Civil cases indexed by defendant, plaintiff. Civil records on computer since 1983, archives from 1979.

Criminal Records: Access: Mail, in person. Only the court performs in person searches. Search fee: $10.00 per name. Required to search: name, years to search, DOB; also helpful: address. Criminal records on computer since 1983, archives from 1979.

General Information: No sex related cases released. Fee to fax results is $2 per document. Copy fee: $1.00 for 1st page, $.50 each add'l. Cert fee: $5.00 per document. Payee: Campbell County Court. Personal checks accepted. Prepayment required. Mail requests: SASE requested. Turnaround time 1-2 days; longer for cases prior to 2001.

Carbon County

Carbon County District Court Clerk of District Court, PO Box 67, Rawlins, WY 82301; 307-328-2628; Fax: 307-328-2629. Hours: 8AM-5PM (MST). *Felony, Civil Actions Over $7,000, Probate.*

Civil Records: Access: Phone, fax, mail, in person. Both court and visitors may perform in person searches. Search fee: $10.00 per name. Required to search: name, years to search; also helpful: address. Civil cases indexed by defendant, plaintiff. Civil records on file from late 1800s, index cards, docket books, then computer 1997. Public can search on the manual index.

Criminal Records: Access: Phone, fax, mail, in person. Both court and visitors may perform in person searches. Search fee: $10.00 per name. Required to search: name, years to search; also helpful: address, DOB, SSN. Criminal records on index cards and docket books; on computer since 1997. Public can search on the manual index.

General Information: No juvenile or adoption records released. Fee to fax results depends on number of pages. Copy fee: $1.00 for first page, $.50 each add'l. No cert fee. Payee: Clerk of District Court, Carbon County. Personal checks accepted. Prepayment required. Mail requests: SASE required. Mail turnaround time 4-5 days.

Carbon Circuit Court Attn: Chief Clerk, Courthouse Bldg, 415 W Pine St, Rawlins, WY 82301; 307-324-6655; Fax: 307-324-9465. Hours: 8AM-5PM (MST). *Misdemeanor, Civil Actions Under $7,000, Eviction, Small Claims.*

Civil Records: Access: Mail, fax, in person. Only the court performs in person searches; visitors may not. Search fee: $10.00 per name. Required to search: name, years to search; also helpful: address. Civil cases indexed by defendant, plaintiff. Civil records on computer back to 3/95.

Criminal Records: Access: Mail, fax, in person. Only the court performs in person searches; visitors may not. Search fee: $10.00 per name. Required to search: name, years to search, DOB. Criminal records on computer back to 08/87.

General Information: Sex related cases not released. Will fax results to a toll-free line. Copy fee: $1.00 for 1st page, $.50 each add'l. Cert fee: $5.00 per document. Payee: Circuit Court of Carbon County. Personal checks accepted. Prepayment required. Mail requests: SASE required. Mail turnaround time 1 week.

Converse County

8th Judicial District Court Box 189, Douglas, WY 82633; 307-358-3165; Fax: 307-358-9783. Hours: 8AM-5PM (MST). *Felony, Civil Actions Over $7,000, Probate.*

Civil Records: Access: Phone, fax, mail, in person. Both court and visitors may perform in person searches. Search fee: $10.00 per name or case. Required to search: name, years to search; also helpful: address. Civil cases indexed by defendant, plaintiff. Civil records on card file from 1888.

Criminal Records: Access: Phone, fax, mail, in person. Both court and visitors may perform in person searches. Search fee: $10.00 per name or case. Required to search: name, years to search; also helpful: address, DOB, SSN. Criminal records on card file from 1800.

General Information: No juvenile, adoptions or mental cases released. Will fax results $2.00 per page. Copy fee: $.25 per page. Cert fee: $1.00 plus $.50 each add'l page. Payee: Clerk of District Court. Only cashiers checks and money orders accepted. Prepayment required. Mail turnaround time usually same day.

Converse Circuit Court 107 N 5th St #231, PO Box 45, Douglas, WY 82633; 307-358-2196; Fax: 307-358-2501. Hours: 8AM-5PM (MST). *Misdemeanor, Civil Actions Under $7,000, Eviction, Small Claims.*

Civil Records: Access: Mail, in person. Both court and visitors may perform in person searches. Search fee: $10.00 per name. Required to search: name, years to search. Civil cases indexed by defendant, plaintiff. Civil records on computer from 1994, card file prior.

Criminal Records: Access: Mail, in person. Both court and visitors may perform in person searches. Search fee: $10.00 per name. Required to search: name, years to search, DOB also helpful: address, SSN. Criminal records on computer from 1990, card file prior.

General Information: No sealed records released. Fee to fax results is $2.00 per document. Copy fee: $1.00 for 1st page, $.50 each add'l. Cert fee: $5.00 per document. Payee: Circuit Court of Converse County. Only cashiers checks and money orders accepted. Prepayment required. Mail turnaround time 1-2 days.

Crook County

6th Judicial District Court Box 904, Sundance, WY 82729; 307-283-2523; Fax: 307-283-2996. Hours: 8AM-5PM (MST). *Felony, Civil Actions Over $7,000, Probate, High Misdemeanor pre-7/1/02.*

Note: High misdemanor cases are no longer heard by this court effective 7/1/02; High misdemeanor records prior to that date can be found here.

Civil Records: Access: Mail, in person. Both court and visitors may perform in person searches. Search fee: $10.00 per name. Required to search: name, years to search; also helpful: address. Civil cases indexed by defendant, plaintiff. Civil records on card file from late 1800s; on computer back to 1999. The civil limit was raised from $3000 to $7000 effective 7/1/02. Cases prior to that date will remain with this court.

Criminal Records: Access: Mail, in person. Both court and visitors may perform in person searches. Search fee: $10.00 per name. Required to search: name, years to search; also helpful: address, DOB, SSN. Criminal records on card file from late 1800s; on computer back to 1999. As of 7/1/02, high misdemeanor cases are no longer heard by this court, however, cases prior to that date will remain here.

General Information: No sealed records released. Will fax results $3.00 for 1-10 pgs; $6.00 for 11-25 pgs; $9.00 if 25 pgs or more. Free to toll-free numbers. Copy fee: $.50 per page. Cert fee: $1.00. Payee: Clerk of District Court. Business checks accepted. Prepayment required. Mail requests: SASE required. Mail turnaround time 2 days.

Circuit Court PO Box 650, Sundance, WY 82729; 307-283-2929; Fax: 307-283-2931. Hours: 8AM-5PM (MST). *Misdemeanor, Civil Actions Under $7,000, Small Claims.*

Note: This former Justice Court became a Circuit Court on 7/1/2002.

Civil Records: Access: Mail, fax, in person. Only the court performs in person searches; visitors may not. Search fee: $10.00 per name. Required to search: name, years to search; also helpful: address. Civil cases indexed by defendant, plaintiff. Civil records on cards, archives back to 1977; on computer back to 1998.

Criminal Records: Access: Mail, fax, in person. Only the court performs in person searches; visitors may not. Search fee: $10.00 per name. Required to search: name, years to search, DOB, SSN. Criminal records go back to 1983; on computer back to 1992.

General Information: No sex related cases released. Fee to fax results is $2.00 per document; no charge if $20.00 search fee is paid. Copy fee: $1.00 for 1st page, $.50 each add'l. Cert fee: $5.00 per document. Payee: Crook County Circuit Court. Personal checks accepted. Prepayment required. Mail requests: SASE required. Mail turnaround time 3-5 days.

Fremont County

9th Judicial District Court PO Box 370, Lander, WY 82520; 307-332-1134; Fax: 307-332-1143. Hours: 8AM-Noon, 1-5PM (MST). *Felony, Civil Actions Over $7,000, Probate.*

Civil Records: Access: Phone, fax, mail, in person. Both court and visitors may perform in person searches. Search fee: $10.00 per name. Required to search: name, years to search; also helpful: address. Civil cases indexed by defendant, plaintiff. Civil records on computer since 1992, in books since 1991, on microfiche since 1939 and on card file from 1898.

Criminal Records: Access: Phone, fax, mail, in person. Both court and visitors may perform in person searches. Search fee: $10.00 per name. Required to search: name, years to search; also helpful: address, DOB, SSN. Criminal records on computer since 1992, in books since 1991, on microfiche since 1939 and on card file from 1898.

General Information: Public Access terminal is available. No juvenile, involuntary hospitalization or adoption records released. No fee to fax results. Copy fee: $.50 per page. No cert fee. Payee: Clerk of District Court. Personal checks accepted. Mail requests: SASE required. Mail turnaround time same day.

Dubois Circuit Court Box 952, Dubois, WY 82513; 307-455-2920; Fax: 307-455-2132. Hours: 8AM-2:00PM (MST). *Misdemeanor, Civil Actions Under $7,000, Eviction, Small Claims.*

Note: This is a satellite of the Lander Court.

Civil Records: Access: Mail, in person. Both court and visitors may perform in person searches. Search fee: $10.00 per name. Required to search: name, years to search. Civil cases indexed by defendant, plaintiff. Civil records on index.

Criminal Records: Access: Mail, in person. Both court and visitors may perform in person searches. Search fee: $10.00 per name. Required to search: name, years to search; also helpful: DOB. Criminal records on computer since 12/98; prior records on indexes.

General Information: No juvenile, sexual data released. Fee to fax results is $2.00 per document. Copy fee: $1.00 for 1st page, $.50 each add'l. Cert fee: $5.00 per document. Payee: Fremont County Court. Personal checks accepted. Prepayment required. Mail requests: SASE required. Mail turnaround time 2 days.

Lander Circuit Court 450 N. 2nd, Rm 230, Lander, WY 82520; 307-332-3239; Fax: 307-332-1152. Hours: 8AM-5PM (MST). *Misdemeanor, Civil Actions Under $7,000, Eviction, Small Claims.*

Note: This is the main Circuit Court for Fremont County.

Civil Records: Access: Phone, fax, mail, in person. Both court and visitors may perform in person searches. Search fee: $10.00 per name. Required to search: name, years to search; also helpful: address. Civil cases indexed by defendant, plaintiff. Civil records on computer from 1988, archive back to 1979.

Criminal Records: Access: Phone, fax, mail, in person. Both court and visitors may perform in person searches. Search fee: $10.00 per name. Required to search: name, years to search; also helpful: address, DOB, SSN. Criminal records on computer from 1988, archive back to 1979.

General Information: No juvenile or sexual data released. Fee to fax results is $2.00 per document. Copy fee: $1.00 for 1st page, $.50 each add'l. Cert fee: $5.00 per document. Payee: Circuit Court. In state personal checks accepted. Prepayment required. Mail requests: SASE required. Mail turnaround time 2 days.

Riverton Circuit Court 818 S Federal Blvd, Riverton, WY 82501; 307-856-7259; Fax: 307-857-3635. Hours: 8AM-5PM (MST). *Misdemeanor, Civil Actions Under $7,000, Eviction, Small Claims.*
www.courts.state.wy.us/Brochure_files/ccriv.htm

Civil Records: Access: Mail, in person. Only the court performs in person searches; visitors may not. Search fee: $10.00 per name. Required to search: name, years to search. Civil cases indexed by defendant, plaintiff. Civil records are computerized since 1997; prior in books to 1981.

Criminal Records: Access: Mail, in person. Only the court performs in person searches; visitors may not. Search fee: $10.00 per name. Required to search: name, years to search, DOB; also helpful: SSN. Criminal records on computer since 1989; prior in books to 1981.

General Information: No sex released cases released. Fee to fax results is $2.00 per document. Copy fee: $1.00 for 1st page, $.50 each add'l. Cert fee: $5.00 per document. Payee: Fremont County Circuit Court. In state personal checks accepted. Prepayment required. Mail requests: SASE required. Mail turnaround time 2 days.

Goshen County

8th Judicial District Court Clerk of District Court, PO Box 818, Torrington, WY 82240; 307-532-2155; Fax: 307-532-8608. Hours: 7:30AM-4PM (MST). *Felony, Civil Actions Over $7,000, Probate.*

Civil Records: Access: Mail, in person. Both court and visitors may perform in person searches. Search fee: $10.00 per name. Required to search: name, years to search; also helpful: address. Civil cases indexed by defendant, plaintiff. Civil records on index file only since 1913.

Criminal Records: Access: Mail, in person. Both court and visitors may perform in person searches. Search fee: $10.00 per name. Required to search: name, years to search; also helpful: address, DOB, SSN. Criminal records on index file only since 1913.

General Information: No juvenile records released. Will fax results, prefer toll free line. Copy fee: $1.00 for first page, $.50 each add'l. Cert fee: $.50. Payee: Clerk of District Court. In state personal checks accepted. Prepayment required. Mail requests: SASE required. Mail turnaround time 3-4 days.

Goshen Circuit Court Drawer BB, Torrington, WY 82240; 307-532-2938; Civil phone: X251; Criminal phone: X250; Fax: 307-532-5101. Hours: 7AM-4PM (MST). *Misdemeanor, Civil Actions Under $7,000, Eviction, Small Claims.*

Civil Records: Access: Mail, in person. Only the court performs in person searches; visitors may not. Search fee: $10.00 per name. Required to search: name, years to search; also helpful: address. Civil cases indexed by defendant. Civil records go back to 1988; on computer back to 3/97, prior archived.

Criminal Records: Access: Mail, in person. Only the court performs in person searches; visitors may not. Search fee: $10.00 per name. Required to search: name, years to search, DOB; also helpful: address, SSN. Criminal records go back to 10/92; on computer back to 4/1989 for disposition data, prior archived.

General Information: No juvenile records released. Fee to fax results is $2 per document. Copy fee: $1.00 for 1st page, $.50 each add'l. Cert fee: $5.00 per document. Payee: Circuit Court 8th Judicial District. Personal checks accepted. Prepayment required. Mail requests: SASE required. Mail turnaround time 3-4 days.

Hot Springs County

5th Judicial District Court 415 Arapahoe St, Thermopolis, WY 82443; 307-864-3323; Fax: 307-864-3210. Hours: 8AM-5PM (MST). *Felony, Civil Actions Over $7,000, Probate.*

Civil Records: Access: Mail, in person. Both court and visitors may perform in person searches. Search fee: $10.00 per name. Required to search: name, years to search; also helpful: address. Civil cases indexed by defendant, plaintiff. Civil records on card index back to 1900s.

Criminal Records: Access: Mail, in person. Both court and visitors may perform in person searches. Search fee: $10.00 per name. Required to search: name, years to search, DOB, SSN; also helpful: address. Criminal records on card index back to 1900s.

General Information: No juvenile, adoption or sexual data released. Will fax results to a local or toll free line. Copy fee: $.25 per page. Cert fee: $.50. Payee: Clerk of District Court. Personal checks accepted. Prepayment required. Mail requests: SASE required. Mail turnaround time 1 day.

Hot Springs Circuit Court
Hot Springs Circuit Court 417 Arapahoe St, Thermopolis, WY 82443; 307-864-5161; Fax: 307-864-2067. Hours: 8AM-5PM (MST). *Misdemeanor, Civil Actions Under $7,000, Small Claims.*
Civil Records: Access: Mail, in person. Only the court performs in person searches; visitors may not. Search fee: $10.00 per name. Required to search: name, years to search. Civil cases indexed by defendant, plaintiff. Civil records on computer from 1990, prior in card file.
Criminal Records: Access: Mail, in person. Only the court performs in person searches; visitors may not. Search fee: $10.00 per name. Required to search: name, years to search. Criminal records on computer from 1990, prior in card file to 1980.
General Information: No closed case records released. Fee to fax results is $2.00 per document. Copy fee: $1.00 for 1st page, $.50 each add'l. Cert fee: $5.00 per document. Payee: Circuit Court. Business checks accepted. Prepayment required. Mail requests: SASE required. Mail turnaround time 2-3 days.

Johnson County

4th Judicial District Court 76 N Main, Buffalo, WY 82834; 307-684-7271; Fax: 307-684-5146. Hours: 8AM-5PM (MST). *Felony, Civil Actions Over $7,000, Probate.*
Civil Records: Access: Fax, mail, in person. Both court and visitors may perform in person searches. Search fee: $10.00 per name. Required to search: name, years to search; also helpful: address. Civil cases indexed by defendant, plaintiff. Civil records on computer from 1989, card index since 1892.
Criminal Records: Access: Fax, mail, in person. Both court and visitors may perform in person searches. Search fee: $10.00 per name. Required to search: name, years to search; also helpful: address, DOB, SSN. Criminal records on computer from 1989, card index since 1892.
General Information: No adoption or juvenile records released. Will fax results for $1.00 per page. Copy fee: $.50 per page. Cert fee: $.50. Payee: Clerk of District Court. In state personal checks accepted. Prepayment required. Mail requests: SASE required. Mail turnaround time 1 week.

Circuit Court 76 N Main St, Buffalo, WY 82834-1847; 307-684-5720; Fax: 307-684-5146. Hours: 8AM-5PM (MST). *Misdemeanor, Civil Actions Under $7,000, Small Claims.*
Note: This was formally a Justice Court, it became a Circuit Courts on 1/03.
Civil Records: Access: Mail, fax, in person. Only the court performs in person searches; visitors may not. Search fee: $10.00. Required to search: name, years to search; also helpful: address. Civil cases indexed by defendant, plaintiff. Civil records on computer since 1995; prior records on index cards.
Criminal Records: Access: Mail, fax, in person. Only the court performs in person searches; visitors may not. Search fee: $10.00 per name. Required to search: name, years to search, DOB; also helpful: SSN. Criminal records on computer since 05/90, card index back to 1979.
General Information: No sex cases released. Will fax results for $2.00. Copy fee: $1.00 for 1st page; $.50 each add'l. Cert fee: $5.00 per document. Payee: Circuit Court. Personal checks accepted. Prepayment required. Mail requests: SASE required. Mail turnaround time 2 days.

Laramie County

1st Judicial District Court 309 W 20th St, #3205, PO Box 787, Cheyenne, WY 82003; 307-633-4270; Fax: 307-633-4277. Hours: 8AM-5PM (MST). *Felony, Misdemeanor, Civil Actions Over $7,000, Probate.*
http://webgate.co.laramie.wy.us/dc/dc.html
Civil Records: Access: Fax, mail, in person. Both court and visitors may perform in person searches. Search fee: $10.00 per name. Required to search: name. Civil cases indexed by defendant, plaintiff. Civil records on card index to 1890; on computer back to 1992.
Criminal Records: Access: Fax, mail, in person. Both court and visitors may perform in person searches. Search fee: $10.00 per name. Required to search: name, years to search, DOB, SSN. Criminal records on card index to 1890; on computer back to 1992.
General Information: Public Access terminal is available. No juvenile or paternity records released. No fee to fax results. Will fax to 800 numbers only. Copy fee: $1.00 for first page, $.50 each add'l. Cert fee: $.50. Payee: Laramie County Clerk of District Court. Business checks accepted. Prepayment required. Mail requests: SASE required. Mail turnaround time 2 days.

Laramie County Circuit Court 309 W 20th St Rm 2300, Cheyenne, WY 82001; 307-633-4298; Fax: 307-633-4392. Hours: 8AM-5PM (MST). *Misdemeanor, Civil Actions Under $7,000, Eviction, Small Claims.*
Civil Records: Access: Fax, mail, in person. Both court and visitors may perform in person searches. Search fee: $10.00 per name. Required to search: name, years to search; also helpful: address. Civil cases indexed by defendant, plaintiff. Civil records on computer from 1992, card index from late 1977.
Criminal Records: Access: Fax, mail, in person. Both court and visitors may perform in person searches. Search fee: $10.00 per name. Required to search: name, years to search; also helpful: address. Criminal records on computer from 1988, card index from late 1977.
General Information: Public Access terminal is available. Fee to fax results is $2.00 per document. Copy fee: $1.00 for 1st page, $.50 each add'l. Cert fee: $5.00 per document. Payee: Laramie County Circuit Court. Business checks accepted. In state checks only. Prepayment required. Mail requests: SASE required. Mail turnaround time 48 hours.

Lincoln County

3rd Judicial District Court PO Drawer 510, Kemmerer, WY 83101; 307-877-9056; Fax: 307-877-6263. Hours: 8AM-5PM (MST). *Felony, Civil Actions Over $7,000, Probate.*
Civil Records: Access: Fax, mail, in person. Both court and visitors may perform in person searches. Search fee: $10.00 per name. Required to search: name; also helpful: years to search, address. Civil cases indexed by defendant. Civil records on card index and computer back to 1916.
Criminal Records: Access: Fax, mail, in person. Both court and visitors may perform in person searches. Search fee: $10.00 per name. Required to search: name; also helpful: years to search, address, DOB, SSN. Criminal records on card index and computer back to 1916.
General Information: No juvenile, sexual or PD records released. Will fax results $5.00 per doc. Copy fee: $1.00 for first page, $.50 each add'l. Cert fee: $2.50. Payee: 3rd Judicial District Court. Personal checks accepted. Prepayment required. Mail requests: SASE required. Mail turnaround time same day.

Lincoln Circuit Court PO Box 949, Kemmerer, WY 83101; 307-877-4431; Fax: 307-877-4936. Hours: 8AM-5PM (MST). *Misdemeanor, Civil Actions Under $7,000, Eviction, Small Claims.*
Civil Records: Access: Mail, in person. Only the court performs in person searches; visitors may not. Search fee: $10.00 per name. Required to search: name, years to search. Civil cases indexed by defendant, plaintiff. Civil records on computer from 1/90, on card index from 1984, prior data in archives. All search requests must be in writing.
Criminal Records: Access: Mail, in person. Only the court performs in person searches; visitors may not. Search fee: $10.00 per name. Required to search: name, years to search, DOB; also helpful: SSN. Criminal records on computer from 10/90, card index from 1984, prior in archives. All search requests must be in writing.
General Information: No sexual or PD records released. Will fax results to local or toll free line. Copy fee: $1.00 for 1st page, $.50 each add'l. Cert fee: $5.00 per document. Payee: Lincoln Circuit Court. Business checks accepted. Out of state checks not accepted. Prepayment required. Mail requests: SASE requested. Turnaround time same day.

Natrona County

7th Judicial District Court Clerk of District Court, PO Box 2510, Casper, WY 82602; 307-235-9243; Fax: 307-235-9493. Hours: 8AM-5PM (MST). *Felony, Civil Actions Over $7,000, Probate.*
Civil Records: Access: Phone, fax, mail, in person. Both court and visitors may perform in person searches. Search fee: $10.00 per name. Required to search: name, years to search; also helpful: address. Civil cases indexed by defendant, plaintiff. Civil records on computer, microfiche from 1891.
Criminal Records: Access: Phone, fax, mail, in person. Both court and visitors may perform in person searches. Search fee: $10.00 per name. Required to search: name, years to search; also helpful: address, DOB, SSN. Criminal records on computer, microfiche from 1891.
General Information: No adoption, juvenile, paternity, mental health records released. Will fax results $.30 per page. Copy fee: $1.00 for first page, $.50 each add'l. Cert fee: $.50. Payee: Clerk of District Court. Business checks accepted. Prepayment required. Mail requests: SASE required. Mail turnaround time 5 days.

Natrona Circuit Court PO Box 1339, Casper, WY 82602; 307-235-9266; Fax: 307-235-9331. Hours: 8AM-5PM (MST). *Misdemeanor, Civil Actions Under $7,000, Eviction, Small Claims.*
Civil Records: Access: Fax, mail, in person. Only the court performs in person searches; visitors may not. Search fee: Circuit Court. Required to search: name, years to search; also helpful: address. Civil cases indexed by defendant, plaintiff. Civil records on computer from 1994, on microfiche from 1891. All search requests must be in writing.
Criminal Records: Access: Fax, mail, in person. Only the court performs in person searches; visitors may not. Search fee: $10.00 per name. Required to search: name, years to search; also helpful: address, DOB, SSN. Criminal records on computer from 1989, microfiche from 1891. All search requests must be in writing.
General Information: No sexual, abuse records released. Fee to fax results is $2.00 per document; fax available for 800 numbers only. Copy fee: $1.00 for 1st page, $.50 each add'l. Cert fee: $5.00 per document. Payee: Natrona Circuit Court. Personal checks accepted. Prepayment required. Mail requests: SASE required. Mail turnaround time 2-5 days.

Niobrara County

8th Judicial District Court Clerk of District Court, PO Box 1318, Lusk, WY 82225; 307-334-2736; Fax: 307-334-2703. Hours: 8AM-Noon, 1-4PM (MST). *Felony, Civil Actions Over $7,000, Probate.*
Civil Records: Access: Mail, in person. Visitors must perform in person searches for themselves. Search fee: $10.00 per name. Required to search: name, years to search. Civil cases indexed by defendant, plaintiff. Civil records on card index from early 1900s.
Criminal Records: Access: Mail, in person. Both court and visitors may perform in person searches. Search fee: $10.00 per name. Required to search: name, years to search, DOB, SSN. Criminal records on card index from 1913.
General Information: No juvenile or adoption related released, no PD released. Fee to fax results is $1.00 per page. Copy fee: $1.00 for first page, $.50 each add'l. Cert fee: $.50 per document. Payee: Niobrara Clerk of District Court. No personal checks accepted. Prepayment required. Mail requests: SASE required. Mail turnaround time 2 days.

Circuit Court PO Box 209, Lusk, WY 82225; 307-334-3845; Fax: 307-334-3846. Hours: 9AM-Noon, 1-5PM (MST). *Misdemeanor, Civil Actions Under $7,000, Small Claims.*
Note: This was a Justice Court until 01/03.
Civil Records: Access: Mail, in person. Both court and visitors may perform in person searches. Search fee: $10.00 per name. Required to search: name, years to search; also helpful: address. Civil cases indexed by plaintiff. Civil records on cards index.
Criminal Records: Access: Fax, mail, in person. Both court and visitors may perform in person searches. Search fee: $10.00 per name. Required to search: name, years to search, DOB, SSN, signed release; also helpful: address. Criminal records on computer from 1988, prior archived.
General Information: No juvenile data released. Fee to fax results is $2.00 per document. Copy fee: $1.00 for 1st page; $.50 each add'l. Cert fee: $5.00 per document. Payee: Niobrara Circuit Court. Personal checks accepted. Prepayment required. Mail requests: SASE requested. Turnaround time 2 days.

Park County

5th Judicial District Court Clerk of District Court, PO Box 1960, Cody, WY 82414; 307-527-8690; Fax: 307-527-8687. Hours: 8AM-5PM (MST). *Felony, Civil Actions Over $7,000, Probate.*
www.wtp.net/parkco/districtcourt.htm
Civil Records: Access: Phone, fax, mail, in person. Both court and visitors may perform in person searches. Search fee: $10.00 per name. Required to search: name, years to search; also helpful: address. Civil cases indexed by defendant, plaintiff. Civil records on computer from 1989, card index back to 1911.
Criminal Records: Access: Phone, fax, mail, in person. Both court and visitors may perform in person searches. Search fee: $10.00 per name. Required to search: name, years to search; also helpful: address, DOB, SSN. Criminal records on computer from 1989, card index back to 1911.
General Information: Public Access terminal is available. No juvenile, adoptions or PD released. Fee to fax results is $1.00 per page. Copy fee: $1.00 for first page, $.50 each add'l. Payee: Clerk of District Court. Personal checks not accepted. Prepayment required. Mail requests: SASE preferred. Turnaround time same day.

Cody Circuit Court 1002 Sheridan Ave., Cody, WY 82414; 307-527-8590; Fax: 307-527-8596. Hours: 8AM-5PM (MST). *Misdemeanor, Civil Actions Under $7,000, Eviction, Small Claims.*
Note: On January 2, 1995 this court changed status from a Justice Court to a Circuit Court. They also have records for the Powell Circuit Court Branch.
Civil Records: Access: Mail, in person. Only the court performs in person searches; visitors may not. Search fee: $10.00 per name. Required to search: name, years to search; also helpful: address. Civil cases indexed by defendant, plaintiff. Civil records on computer since 8/95; limited records available prior to 8/95.
Criminal Records: Access: Mail, in person. Only the court performs in person searches; visitors may not. Search fee: $10.00 per name. Required to search: name, years to search, DOB, SSN (one or other is required) also helpful: address. Criminal records on computer since 1990; limited records available prior to 1990.
General Information: No sexual or confidential data released. Will fax results to local or toll free line. Copy fee: $1.00 for 1st page, $.50 each add'l. Cert fee: $5.00 per document. Payee: Park County Circuit Court. Business checks accepted. Prepayment required. Mail requests: SASE required. Mail turnaround time 5 days.

Powell Circuit Court 109 W. 14th, Powell, WY 82435; 307-754-8890; Fax: 307-754-8896. Hours: 8AM-Noon, 1-5PM (MST). *Misdemeanor, Civil Actions Under $7,000, Eviction, Small Claims.*
Note: Powell court misdemeanor records are also available at the main Circuit Court in Cody.
Civil Records: Access: Mail, in person. Only the court performs in person searches; visitors may not. Search fee: $10.00 per name. Required to search: name, years to search. Civil cases indexed by defendant, plaintiff. Civil records on computer from 1995; prior records very poor.
Criminal Records: Access: Mail, in person. Only the court performs in person searches; visitors may not. Search fee: $10.00 per name. Required to search: name, years to search, DOB. Criminal records on computer from 1991; prior records very poor.
General Information: No sexual, confidential records released. Fee to fax results is $2 per document. Copy fee: $1.00 for 1st page, $.50 each add'l. No cert fee. Payee: Park County Circuit Court. Personal checks accepted. Prepayment required. Mail requests: SASE required. Mail turnaround time 1 week.

Platte County

8th Judicial District Court PO Box 158, Wheatland, WY 82201; 307-322-3857; Fax: 307-322-5402. Hours: 8AM-5PM (MST). *Felony, Civil Actions Over $7,000, Probate.*
Civil Records: Access: Mail, fax, in person. Both court and visitors may perform in person searches. Search fee: $10.00 per name. Required to search: name, years to search; also helpful: address. Civil cases indexed by defendant. Civil records on card file index last 15 yrs, then to archives.
Criminal Records: Access: Mail, fax, in person. Both court and visitors may perform in person searches. Search fee: $10.00 per name. Required to search: name, years to search; also helpful: address, DOB, SSN. Criminal records on card file index last 15 yrs, then to archives.
General Information: No juvenile data released. Will fax results to local or toll free line. Copy fee: $1.00 for first page, $.50 each add'l. Cert fee: $.50. Payee: Clerk of the Court. Personal checks accepted. Prepayment required. Mail requests: SASE required. Mail turnaround time same day.

Circuit Court PO Box 306, Wheatland, WY 82201; 307-322-3441; Fax: 307-322-1371. Hours: 8AM-5PM (MST). *Misdemeanor, Civil Actions Under $3,000, Small Claims.*
Note: This former Justice Court became a Circuit Court as of 01/03.
Civil Records: Access: Phone, mail, fax, in person. Only the court performs in person searches; visitors may not. Search fee: $10.00 per name. Required to search: name, years to search; also helpful: address. Civil cases indexed by defendant. Civil records on computer since 11/95; on card index since 1976.
Criminal Records: Access: Phone, mail, fax, in person. Only the court performs in person searches; visitors may not. Search fee: $10.00 per name. Required to search: name, years to search, signed release, DOB; also helpful: address, SSN. Criminal records on computer from 11/92, card index from 1976.
General Information: No juvenile data released. Fee to fax results is $2.00 per document. Copy fee: $1.00 for 1st page, $.50 each add'l. Cert fee: $5.00 per document. Payee: Platte County Circuit Court. Business checks accepted. Prepayment required. Mail requests: SASE required. Mail turnaround time 2 days.

Sheridan County

4th Judicial District Court 224 S. Main, #B-11, Sheridan, WY 82801; 307-674-2960; Fax: 307-674-2589. Hours: 8AM-5PM (MST). *Felony, Civil Actions Over $7,000, Probate.*
Civil Records: Access: Phone, mail, fax, in person. Both court and visitors may perform in person searches. Search fee: Circuit Court. Required to search: name, years to search. Civil cases indexed by defendant, plaintiff. Civil records archived from 1800s.
Criminal Records: Access: Phone, mail, fax, in person. Both court and visitors may perform in person searches. Search fee: $10.00 per name. Required to search: name, years to search, DOB, SSN. Criminal records archived from late 1800s.
General Information: No sex related, juvenile or adoption cases released except by judges permission. Fee to fax results is $5.00 per document. Copy fee: $1.00 for first page, $.50 each add'l. Cert fee: $.50. Payee: Clerk of District Court. Personal checks accepted. Prepayment required. Mail requests: SASE required. Mail turnaround time 1 week.

Circuit Court 224 S. Main, #B-7, Sheridan, WY 82801; 307-674-2940; Fax: 307-674-2944. Hours: 8AM-5PM (MST). *Misdemeanor, Civil Actions Under $7,000, Eviction, Small Claims.*
Civil Records: Access: Mail, in person. Only the court performs in person searches; visitors may not. Search fee: $10.00 per name. Required to search: name, years to search; also helpful: address. Civil cases indexed by defendant, plaintiff. Civil records on cards from 1983; computerized records go back to 1983.
Criminal Records: Access: Mail, in person. Only the court performs in person searches; visitors may not. Search fee: $10.00 per name. Required to search: name, years to search; also helpful: address, DOB, SSN. Criminal records on computer from 1983, on cards from 1983.
General Information: Identity of victims not released in sexual assault cases. Fee to fax results is $2.00 per document. Copy fee: $1.00 for 1st page, $.50 each add'l. Cert fee: $5.00 per document. Payee: Sheridan Circuit Court. Personal checks accepted. Prepayment required. Mail requests: SASE required. Mail turnaround time 2-3 days.

Sublette County

9th Judicial District Court PO Box 764, Pinedale, WY 82941-0764; 307-367-4376; Fax: 307-367-6474. Hours: 8AM-5PM (MST). *Felony, Civil Actions Over $7,000, Probate.*

Civil Records: Access: Mail, in person. Both court and visitors may perform in person searches. Search fee: $10.00 per name. Required to search: name; also helpful: years to search, address. Civil cases indexed by defendant, plaintiff. Civil records on card file from 1923.

Criminal Records: Access: Mail, in person. Both court and visitors may perform in person searches. Search fee: $10.00 per name. Required to search: name, years to search; also helpful: address, DOB, SSN. Criminal records go back to 1923.

General Information: No PD or juvenile records released. Will fax results for $3.00 1st page, $1.00 each add'l. Copy fee: $1.00 for first page, $.50 each add'l. No cert fee. Payee: Clerk of District Court. Personal checks accepted. Prepayment required. Mail requests: SASE required. Mail turnaround time same day.

Sublette Circuit Court PO Box 1796, Pinedale, WY 82941; 307-367-2556; Fax: 307-367-2658. Hours: 8AM-5PM (MST). *Misdemeanor, Civil Actions Under $7,000, Eviction, Small Claims.*

Civil Records: Access: Mail, in person. Only the court performs in person searches; visitors may not. Search fee: $10.00 per name. Required to search: name, years to search; also helpful: address. Civil cases indexed by defendant & plaintiff. Civil records go back 21 years, computerized from 1998.

Criminal Records: Access: Mail, in person. Only the court performs in person searches; visitors may not. Search fee: $10.00 per name. Required to search: name, years to search, DOB; also helpful: address, SSN. Criminal records go back 10 years, and are computerized.

General Information: Fee to fax results is $2.00 per document. Copy fee: $1.00 for 1st page, $.50 each add'l. Cert fee: $5.00 per document. Payee: Circuit Court of Sublette County. Will accept in state checks only. Prepayment required. Mail requests: SASE not required. Mail turnaround time 2 business days.

Sweetwater County

3rd Judicial District Court PO Box 430, Green River, WY 82935; 307-872-6440; Fax: 307-872-6439. Hours: 9AM-5PM (MST). *Felony, Civil Actions Over $7,000, Probate.*

Civil Records: Access: Phone, fax, mail, in person. Both court and visitors may perform in person searches. Search fee: $10.00 per name. Required to search: name, years to search. Civil cases indexed by defendant, plaintiff. Civil records on computer from 1985, on microfiche from 1960, archived from late 1800.

Criminal Records: Access: Phone, fax, mail, in person. Both court and visitors may perform in person searches. Search fee: $10.00 per name. Required to search: name, years to search. Criminal records on computer from 1985, on microfiche from 1960, archived from late 1800.

General Information: Public Access terminal is available. No PD, juvenile, or adoption records released. Will fax results $1.00 1st page, $.50 each add'l. Copy fee: $1.00 for first page, $.50 each add'l. Cert fee: First free, add'l documents are $.50. Payee: Clerk of District Court. Business checks accepted. Prepayment required. Mail requests: SASE required. Mail turnaround time same day.

Green River Circuit Court PO Drawer 1720, Green River, WY 82935; 307-872-6460; Fax: 307-872-6375. Hours: 8AM-5PM (MST). *Misdemeanor, Civil Actions Under $7,000, Eviction, Small Claims.*

Civil Records: Access: Mail, in person. Only the court performs in person searches; visitors may not. Search fee: Circuit Court. Required to search: name, years to search. Civil cases indexed by defendant, plaintiff. Civil records on computer from 1994, in card file from 1978-1994, archived prior to 1978. Requests must be in writing.

Criminal Records: Access: Mail, in person. Only the court performs in person searches; visitors may not. Search fee: $10.00 per name. Required to search: name, years to search, DOB; also helpful: SSN. Criminal Records computerized since 1990, on card file from 1978 to 1990. Requests must be in writing.

General Information: No sealed, sexual assault records released. Fee to fax results is $2.00 per fax. Copy fee: $1.00 for 1st page, $.50 each add'l. Cert fee: $5.00 per document. Payee: Sweetwater County Circuit Court. Business checks accepted. In-state checks only. Prepayment required. Mail turnaround time same day.

Sweetwater Circuit Court PO Box 2028, Rock Springs, WY 82902; 307-352-6817; Fax: 307-352-6758. Hours: 8AM-5PM (MST). *Misdemeanor, Civil Actions Under $7,000, Eviction, Small Claims.*

Civil Records: Access: Fax, mail, in person. Only the court performs in person searches; visitors may not. Search fee: $10.00 per name. Required to search: name, years to search; also helpful: address. Civil cases indexed by defendant, plaintiff. Civil records on computer from 1995, archived to 1981.

Criminal Records: Access: Fax, mail, in person. Only the court performs in person searches; visitors may not. Search fee: $10.00 per name. Required to search: name, years to search; also helpful: address, DOB, SSN. Criminal records on computer from 1989, archived to 1981.

General Information: No sexual assault, sealed records released. Fee to fax results is $2.00 per document. Copy fee: $1.00 for 1st page, $.50 each add'l. Cert fee: $5.00 per document. Payee: Sweetwater Circuit Court. Personal checks accepted. Prepayment required. Mail requests: SASE required. Mail turnaround time 2 days.

Teton County

9th Judicial District Court PO Box 4460, Jackson, WY 83001; 307-733-2533; Fax: 307-734-1562. Hours: 8AM-5PM (MST). *Felony, Civil Actions Over $7,000, Probate.*

Civil Records: Access: Phone, fax, mail, in person. Both court and visitors may perform in person searches. Search fee: $10.00 per name. Required to search: name, years to search; also helpful: address. Civil cases indexed by defendant, plaintiff. Civil records on computer since 1990, card index back to 1920s.

Criminal Records: Access: Phone, fax, mail, in person. Both court and visitors may perform in person searches. Search fee: $10.00 per name. Required to search: name, years to search; also helpful: address, DOB, SSN. Criminal records on computer since 1990, card index back to 1920s.

General Information: Public Access terminal is available. No juvenile or adoption records released. Will fax results to local or toll free line. Copy fee: $1.00 for first page, $.50 each add'l. Cert fee: $.50. Payee: Clerk of District Court. Personal checks accepted. Prepayment required. Mail requests: SASE required. Mail turnaround time 2 days.

Circuit Court PO Box 2906 (180 S King St), Jackson, WY 83001; 307-733-7713; Fax: 307-733-8694. Hours: 8AM-5PM (MST). *Misdemeanor, Civil Actions Under $7,000, Small Claims under $3,000.*

Note: This was a Justice Court until 01/03.

Civil Records: Access: Mail, in person. Only the court performs in person searches; visitors may not. Search fee: $10.00 per name. Required to search: name, years to search; also helpful-DOB, SSN. Civil cases indexed by defendant, plaintiff. Civil records on docket books back to 1979. Actual files 5 years.

Criminal Records: Access: Mail, in person. Only the court performs in person searches; visitors may not. Search fee: $10.00 per name. Required to search: name, years to search, DOB, SSN. Criminal records citations on computer from 1991. No citation record older than 5 years. On docket books and files back to 1979.

General Information: No juvenile, sexual or PD released. Fee to fax results is $2.00 per document. Copy fee: $1.00 for 1st page, $.50 each add'l. Cert fee: $5.00 per document. Payee: Teton County Circuit Court. Personal checks accepted. Prepayment required. Mail requests: SASE requested. Turnaround time 3-4 days; may be longer for pre-1992 criminal records.

Uinta County

3rd Judicial District Court PO Drawer 1906, Attn: Clerk of District Court, Evanston, WY 82931; 307-783-0456; Fax: 307-783-0400. Hours: 8AM-5PM (MST). *Felony, Civil Actions Over $7,000, Probate.*

www.uintacounty.com

Civil Records: Access: Mail, in person. Visitors must perform in person searches for themselves. Search fee: $10.00 per name. Required to search: name, years to search; also helpful: address. Civil cases indexed by defendant, plaintiff. Civil records on microfiche from the late 1800s.

Criminal Records: Access: Phone, fax, mail, in person. Visitors must perform in person searches for themselves. Search fee: $10.00 per name. Required to search: name, years to search, DOB, SSN; also helpful: address. Criminal records on microfiche since 1938.

General Information: Signed notarized release necessary on confidential cases. Fee to fax results is $1.00 per page, if not related to an already paid search. Copy fee: $1.00 first page; $.50 each add'l page. Cert fee: $.50 per seal. Payee: Clerk of District Court. Personal checks accepted. Prepayment required. Mail requests: SASE required. Mail turnaround time 1 day.

Uinta Circuit Court 225 9th St, 2nd Fl, Evanston, WY 82931; 307-789-2471; Fax: 307-789-5062. Hours: 8AM-5PM (MST). *Misdemeanor, Civil Actions Under $7,000, Eviction, Small Claims.*

Civil Records: Access: Mail, in person. Only the court performs in person searches; visitors may not. Search fee: $10.00 per name. Required to search: name, years to search; also helpful: address. Civil cases indexed by defendant. Civil records on computer from 1994, prior on card index. All requests must be in writing.

Criminal Records: Access: Mail, in person. Only the court performs in person searches; visitors may not. Search fee: $10.00 per name. Required to search: name, years to search; also helpful: address, DOB, SSN. Criminal records on computer since 1989, prior on index cards. All requests must be in writing.

General Information: No juvenile records released. Fee to fax results is $2.00 per document. Copy fee: $1.00 for 1st page, $.50 each add'l. Cert fee: $5.00 per document. Payee: Uinta County Court. Out of state checks not accepted. Prepayment required. Mail requests: SASE requested. Turnaround time 1 week.

Washakie County

5th Judicial District Court PO Box 862, Worland, WY 82401; 307-347-4821; Fax: 307-347-4325. Hours: 8AM-5PM (MST). *Felony, Civil Actions Over $7,000, Probate.*

Civil Records: Access: Fax, mail, in person. Both court and visitors may perform in person searches. Search fee: $10.00 per name. Required to search: name; also helpful: years to search, address. Civil cases indexed by defendant. Civil records on computer back to 1985, prior on file index.

Criminal Records: Access: Phone, fax, mail, in person. Both court and visitors may perform in person searches. Search fee: $10.00 per name. Required to search: name, years to search; also helpful: address, DOB, SSN. Criminal records on computer back to 1985, prior on file index.

General Information: No juvenile, sexual or PD released. Will fax results $1.00 per page. Copy fee: $1.00 for first page, $.50 each add'l. Cert fee: $.50. Payee: Clerk of Court. Personal checks accepted. Prepayment required. Mail requests: SASE required. Mail turnaround time same day when possible.

Justice Court PO Box 927, Worland, WY 82401; 307-347-2702; Fax: 307-347-8459. Hours: 8AM-5PM (MST). *Misdemeanor, Civil Actions Under $7,000, Small Claims.*
courts.state.wy.us.
Note: This was a Justice Court until 01/03.

Civil Records: Access: Mail, fax. Only the court performs in person searches; visitors may not Search fee: $10.00 per name. Required to search: name, years to search. Civil cases indexed by defendant. Civil records on computer since 1998, on card index from late 1970, prior archived.

Criminal Records: Access: Mail, fax, in person. Only the court performs in person searches; visitors may not Search fee: $10.00 per name. Required to search: name, years to search, DOB; also helpful: SSN. Criminal records on computer since 1995, on card index from late 1970, prior archived.

General Information: No juvenile or PD released; criminal only. Fee to fax results is $2.00 per document. Copy fee: $1.00 for 1st page; $.50 each add'l. Cert fee: $5.00 per document. Payee: Circuit Court. Personal checks accepted. Prepayment required. Mail requests: SASE not required. Mail turnaround time same day.

Weston County

6th Judicial District Court 1 W Main, Newcastle, WY 82701; 307-746-4778; Fax: 307-746-4778. Hours: 8AM-5PM (MST). *Felony, Civil Actions Over $7,000, Probate.*

Civil Records: Access: Mail, fax, in person. Both court and visitors may perform in person searches. Search fee: $10.00 per name. Required to search: name; also helpful: years to search, address. Civil cases indexed by defendant, plaintiff. Civil records on card index from 1913; computerized back to 1999.

Criminal Records: Access: Phone, fax, mail, in person. Both court and visitors may perform in person searches. Search fee: $10.00 per name. Required to

search: name; also helpful: years to search, address, DOB, SSN. Criminal records on card index from 1913; computerized back to 1999.

General Information: No juvenile, sexual or PD released. Fee to fax results is $2.00 per page. Copy fee: $1.00 for first page, $.50 each add'l. Cert fee: $.50. Payee: Clerk of District Court. Personal checks accepted. Prepayment required. Mail requests: SASE required. Mail turnaround time same day.

CircuitCourt 6 W Warwick, Newcastle, WY 82701; 307-746-3547; Fax: 307-746-3558. Hours: 8AM-5PM (MST). *Misdemeanor, Civil Actions Under $7,000, Small Claims.*
Note: This was a Justice Court until 01/03.

Civil Records: Access: Mail, fax, in person. Only the court performs in person searches; visitors may not. Search fee: $10.00. Required to search: name, DOB, years to search; also helpful: address. Civil cases indexed by defendant. Civil records in files back to 1970s; on computer back to 1998.

Criminal Records: Access: Fax, mail, in person. Only the court performs in person searches; visitors may not. Search fee: $10.00. Required to search: name, years to search, DOB; also helpful: address, offense, date of offense, SSN. Criminal records in files back to 1970s; on computer back to 1996.

General Information: Fee to fax results is $2.00 per document. Copy fee: $1.00 first page; $.50 each add'l. Cert fee: $5.00 per document. Payee: Circuit Court. Business checks accepted. Prepayment required. Mail turnaround time is minimum 1 day.

Wyoming Recording Offices

ORGANIZATION: 23 counties, 23 recording offices. The recording officer is County Clerk. The entire state is in the Mountain Time Zone (MST).

REAL ESTATE RECORDS: County Clerks will not perform real estate searches. Copy fees are usually $1.00 per page, and certification fees are usually $2.00 per document. The Assessor maintains property tax records.

UCC RECORDS: Since 07/1/2001, all filings have been centralized at the state. Prior, financing statements were usually filed with the County Clerk and accounts receivable and farm products require dula filing at the state level as well. All recording offices will perform UCC searches. Use search request form UCC-11. Searches fees are usually $10.00 per debtor name. Copy fees vary.

TAX LIEN RECORDS: Federal tax liens on personal property of businesses are filed with the Secretary of State. Other federal and all state tax liens are filed with the County Clerk. Most counties will perform tax lien searches. Search fees are usually $10.00 per name.

ONLINE ACCESS: Teton county offers online access to the County Clerk's database of recorded documents.

Albany County

County Clerk, 525 Grand Ave. Rm202, Laramie, WY 82070. **Phone**-County Clerk, R/E & UCC Recording-307-721-2547, UCC Recording-307-721-2541; fax-307-721-2544; hours 9AM-5PM
Will search UCC records. Search per debtor- $10.00. Tax lien search- $10.00 per debtor. Will not search real estate records. Copy fee- $.25 per page. Cert fee: $3.00 per copy. Payee: Albany County Clerk. **Other phones:** Assessor-307-721-2511; Treasurer-307-721-2502; Appraiser/ Auditor-307-721-2511; Elections-307-721-2546; Vital Records-307-777-7591.

Big Horn County

County Clerk, PO Box 31, Basin, WY 82410. **Phone**-County Clerk, R/E & UCC Recording- 307-568-2357; fax-307-568-9375; hours 8AM-5PM www.state.wy.us
Will search UCC records. Search per debtor- $10.00. UCC search includes tax liens. Will not search real estate records. UCC copy- $1.00 per page. Cert fee: $2.00 per doc. Payee: Big Horn County Clerk. **Other phones:** Assessor-307-568-2547; Treasurer-307-568-2578; Elections-307-568-2357; Vital Records-307-568-2357.

Campbell County

County Clerk, PO Box 3010, Gillette, WY 82717-3010. **Phone**-307-682-7285; fax-307-687-6455; 8AM-5PM
Will search UCC records. Search per debtor- $10.00. UCC search includes tax liens. Separate federal & state combined tax lien search- $10.00 per debtor. Will not search real estate records. UCC copy- $.50 each; then $.15 each after 1st 10 pages. Cert fee: $5.00 per doc. Payee: Campbell County Clerk. **Other phones:** Assessor-307-682-7266.

Carbon County

County Clerk, 415 W. Pine, PO Box 6, Courthouse, Rawlins, WY 82301. **Phone**-307-328-2679, R/E Recording-307-328-2677, UCC Recording-307-328-2667; fax-307-328-2690; hours 8AM-5PM
Will search UCC records. Search per debtor- $10.00. Federal/state combined tax lien search- $10.00 per debtor. Will not search real estate records. UCC copy- $.25 per page. Cert fee: $3.00 per cert. Payee: Carbon County Clerk. **Other phones:** Assessor-307-328-2637; Treasurer-307-328-2662; Elections-307-328-2650; Vital Records-307-328-2670.

Converse County

County Clerk, 107 North 5th St, #114, Douglas, WY 82633-0990. **Phone**-307-358-2244; fax-307-358-5998; hours 8AM-5PM
Will search UCC records. Search per debtor- $10.00. UCC search includes tax liens. Separate federal & state combined tax lien search- $10.00 per debtor. Will not search real estate records. Copy fee- $.50 per page. Cert fee: $2.00 per doc plus copy fee. **Other phones:** Assessor-307-358-2741; Treasurer-307-358-3120; Elections-307-358-2244.

Crook County

County Clerk, PO Box 37, Sundance, WY 82729. **Phone**-307-283-1323; fax-307-283-3038; 8AM-5PM
Will search UCC records. Search per debtor- $10.00. Tax liens not included in UCC search. Separate federal tax lien search- $10.00 per debtor. Will not search real estate records. UCC copy- $.50 per page. Cert fee: $3.00 per doc. Payee: Crook County Clerk. **Other phones:** Assessor-307-283-2054; Treasurer-307-283-1244.

Fremont County

County Clerk, 450 N. 2nd St, Rm 220, Lander, WY 82520. **Phone**-307-332-2405, R/E Recording-307-332-1127, UCC Recording-307-332-1125; fax-307-332-1132; hours 8AM-5PM www.fremontcounty.org
Will search UCC records. Search per debtor- $10.00. Tax lien search- $10.00 per debtor. Will search real estate records. Copy fee- $.75 per page. Cert fee: $4.00. Payee: Fremont County Clerk. **Other phones:** Assessor-307-332-1188; Treasurer-307-322-1105; Elections-307-332-1089; Vital Records-307-332-1127.

Goshen County

County Clerk, PO Box 160, Torrington, WY 82240. **Phone**-County Clerk, R/E & UCC Recording- 307-532-4051; fax-307-532-7375; hours 7:30AM-4PM www.state.wy.us
Will search UCC records. Search per debtor- $10.00. UCC search includes tax liens if requested. Will not search real estate records. UCC copy- $1.00 per page. Cert fee: $5.00. Payee: Goshen County Clerk. **Other phones:** Assessor-307-532-2349; Treasurer-307-532-5151; Elections-307-532-4051.

Hot Springs County

County Clerk, 415 Arapahoe St, Courthouse, Thermopolis, WY 82443-2783. **Phone**-307-864-3515; fax-307-864-3333; hours 8AM-5PM
Will search UCC records. Search per debtor- $10.00. Will not search real estate records. UCC copy- $.25 per page. Cert fee: $3.00 per doc. Payee: Hot Springs County Clerk. **Other phones:** Assessor-307-864-3414; Treasurer-307-864-3616.

Johnson County

County Clerk, 76 N. Main St, Buffalo, WY 82834. **Phone**-307-684-7272; fax-307-684-2708; hours 8AM-5PM
Will search UCC records. Search per debtor- $10.00. Tax liens not included in UCC search. Separate state tax lien search- $10.00 per debtor Will not search real estate records. UCC copy- $.50 per page. Cert fee: $3.00 per doc. Payee: Johnson County Clerk. **Other phones:** Assessor-307-684-7392; Treasurer-307-684-7302.

Laramie County

County Clerk, PO Box 608, Cheyenne, WY 82003. **Phone**-307-633-4351, R/E Recording-307-633-4350; fax-307-633-4240; hours 8AM-5PM www.laramiecountyclerk.com
Will search UCC records. Search per debtor- $10.00. UCC search includes tax liens if requested. Will not search real estate records. UCC copy- $.25 per page. Cert fee: $3.00 per cert. **Other phones:** Assessor-307-633-4307; Treasurer-307-633-4225; Elections-307-633-4242; Vital Records-307-777-7591.

Lincoln County

County Clerk, PO Box 670, Kemmerer, WY 83101-0670. **Phone**-307-877-9056, R/E Recording-307-877-9056 x305, UCC Recording-307-877-9056 x304; fax-307-877-3101.
Will search UCC records. Search per debtor- $10.00. Tax liens are a separate search. Tax lien search- $10.00 per debtor. Will not search real estate records. UCC copy- $.50 per page. Cert fee: $3.00 per doc. Payee: Lincoln County Clerk. **Other phones:** Assessor-307-877-9056 x330; Treasurer-307-877-9056 x345; Elections-307-877-9056 x303.

Natrona County

County Clerk, PO Box 863, Casper, WY 82602. **Phone**-307-235-9270, R/E Recording-307-235-9206, UCC Recording-307-235-9207; fax-307-235-9367; hours 8AM-5PM www.natronacounty-wy.gov
Will search UCC records. Search per debtor- $10.00. Tax lien search- $10.00 per debtor. Will not search real estate records. Copy fee is $.25 per page. Cert fee: $3.00 per doc. Payee: Natrona County Clerk. **Other phones:** Assessor-307-235-9444; Treasurer-307-235-9370; Elections-307-235-9217; Vital Records-307-777-7591.

Niobrara County

County Clerk, PO Box 420, Lusk, WY 82225. **Phone**-County Clerk, R/E & UCC Recording- 307-334-2211; fax-307-334-3013; hours 8AM-4PM
Will search UCC records. Search per debtor- $10.00. Tax lien search- $10.00 per debtor. Will not search real estate records. UCC copy- $.25 per page. Cert fee: $3.00. **Other phones:** Assessor-307-334-3201; Treasurer-307-334-2432; Elections-307-334-2211; Vital Records-307-334-2211.

Park County

County Clerk, 1002 Sheridan Ave., Courthouse, Cody, WY 82414. **Phone**-County Clerk, R/E & UCC Recording- 307-527-8600; fax-307-527-8626.
Will search UCC records. Search per debtor- $10.00. Federal/state combined tax lien search- $10.00 per debtor. Will not search real estate records. UCC copy- $.50 per page. Cert fee: $3.00 per cert. Payee: park County Clerk. **Other phones:** Assessor-307-527-8650; Treasurer-307-527-8630; Elections-307-527-8620.

Platte County

County Clerk, PO Drawer 728, Wheatland, WY 82201. **Phone**-307-322-2315, R/E Recording-307-322-1306; fax-307-322-2245; hours 7AM-4PM. Will search UCC records. Search per debtor- $10.00. Federal/state combined tax lien search- $10.00 per debtor. Will not search real estate records. UCC copy- $.50 per page. Cert fee: $3.00. Payee: Platte County Clerk. **Other phones:** Assessor-307-322-2858; Treasurer-307-322-2092; Elections-307-322-1307.

Sheridan County

County Clerk, 224 S. Main St, #B-2, Sheridan, WY 82801-9998. **Phone**-307-674-2500; fax-307-674-2529; hours 8AM-5PM
Will search UCC records. Search per debtor- $10.00. Will not search real estate or tax lien records. UCC copy- $1.00 per page. Cert fee: $5.00 per doc. Payee: Sheridan County Clerk. **Other phones:** Assessor-307-674-2535; Treasurer-307-674-6522; Elections-307-674-2515.

Sublette County

County Clerk, PO Box 250, Pinedale, WY 82941-0250. **Phone**-County Clerk, R/E & UCC Recording- 307-367-4372; fax-307-367-6396; hours 8AM-5PM
Will search UCC records. Search per debtor- $10.00. Separate federal & state combined tax lien search- $10.00 per debtor. Will not search real estate records. Copy fee- $.25 per page. Cert fee: $3.00. Payee: County Clerk. **Other phones:** Assessor-307-367-4374; Treasurer-307-367-4373; Elections-307-367-4372.

Sweetwater County

County Clerk, PO Box 730, Green River, WY 82935. **Phone**-307-872-6400, R/E Recording-307-872-6409, UCC Recording-307-872-6406 or 6407; fax-307-872-6337; hours 9AM-5PM www.co.sweet.wy.us/clerk
Will search UCC records. Search per debtor- $10.00. UCC search includes tax liens if requested. Will not search real estate records. Copy fee- $.25 per copy. Cert fee: $3.00 per doc. Payee: Sweetwater County Clerk. **Other phones:** Assessor-307-872-6416; Treasurer-307-872-6389; Appraiser/ Auditor-307-872-6400; Elections-307-872-6400; Vital Records-307-872-6407 (marriage only).

Teton County

County Clerk, PO Box 1727, Jackson, WY 83001. **Phone**-307-733-4433, R/E Recording-307-733-4430; fax-307-739-8681; hours-8AM-5PM www.tetonwyo.org/clerk/
Will search UCC records. Search per debtor- $10.00. Will search tax liens including federal tax liens. Federal/state combined tax lien search- $.25 per page. Will not search real estate records. UCC copy- $.25 per page. Cert fee: $10.00. **Online Access to**

Real Estate, Lien, Recording records: Access to the Clerk's database of scanned images is free at www.tetonwyo.org/clerk/query. Search for complete documents back to 7/1996; partial docs back to 4/1991. **Other phones:** Assessor-307-733-4960; Treasurer-307-733-4770; Elections-307-733-7733; Vital Records-307-777-7591.

Uinta County

County Clerk, PO Box 810, Evanston, WY 82931-0810. **Phone**-307-783-0308, R/E Recording-307-783-0304; fax-307-783-0511; hours 8AM-5PM www.uintacounty.com
Will search UCC records. Search per debtor- $10.00. UCC search includes tax liens. Separate federal/state combined tax lien search- $10.00 per debtor. Will not search real estate records. UCC copy- $.25 per page. Cert fee: $3.00 per doc. Payee: Uinta County Clerk.

Washakie County

County Clerk, Box 260, Worland, WY 82401-0260. **Phone**-County Clerk, R/E & UCC Recording- 307-347-3131; fax-307-347-9366; hours 8AM-5PM www.washakiecounty.net
Will search UCC records. Search per debtor- $10.00. UCC search includes tax liens if requested. Will not search real estate records. RE record copy- $1.00 per page. UCC copy- $.25 per page. Cert fee: $2.00 per doc. Payee: Washakie County Clerk. **Other phones:** Assessor-307-347-2831; Treasurer-307-347-2031; Elections-307-347-3131; Vital Records-307-347-3131.

Weston County

County Clerk, 1 W. Main, Newcastle, WY 82701. **Phone**-County Clerk, R/E & UCC Recording- 307-746-4744; fax-307-746-9505; hours 8AM-5PM
Will search UCC records. Search per debtor- $10.00. UCC search includes tax liens. Will not search real estate records. UCC copy- $.50 per page. Cert fee: $3.00. Payee: Weston County Clerk. **Other phones:** Assessor-307-746-4633; Treasurer-307-746-2852.

Wyoming County Locator

You will usually be able to find the city name in the City/County Cross Reference below. In that case, it is a simple matter to determine the county from the cross reference. However, only the official US Postal Service city names are included in this index. There are an additional 40,000 place names that people use in their addresses. Therefore, we have also included a ZIP/City Cross Reference immediately following the City/County Cross Reference.

If you know the ZIP Code but the city name does not appear in the City/County Cross Reference index, look up the ZIP Code in the ZIP/City Cross Reference, find the city name, then look up the city name in the City/County Cross Reference. For example, you want to know the county for an address of Menands, NY 12204. There is no "Menands" in the City/County Cross Reference. The ZIP/City Cross Reference shows that ZIP Codes 12201-12288 are for the city of Albany. Looking back in the City/County Cross Reference, Albany is in Albany County.

Wyoming City/County Cross Reference

AFTON Lincoln
ALADDIN Crook
ALBIN Laramie
ALCOVA Natrona
ALPINE Lincoln
ALTA Teton
ALVA Crook
ARAPAHOE Fremont
ARMINTO Natrona
ARVADA (82831) Campbell(37), Sheridan(32), Johnson(29)
AUBURN Lincoln
BAGGS Carbon
BAIROIL Sweetwater
BANNER (82832) Sheridan(80), Johnson(19)
BASIN Big Horn
BEDFORD Lincoln
BEULAH Crook
BIG HORN Sheridan
BIG PINEY Sublette
BILL Converse
BONDURANT Sublette
BOSLER Albany
BOULDER Sublette
BUFFALO Johnson
BUFORD (82052) Albany(68), Laramie(31)
BURLINGTON (82411) Big Horn(97), Park(2)
BURNS Laramie
BYRON Big Horn
CARLILE Crook
CARPENTER Laramie
CASPER Carbon
CASPER Natrona
CENTENNIAL Albany
CHEYENNE Laramie
CHUGWATER (82210) Platte(80), Goshen(20)
CLEARMONT Sheridan
CODY Park
COKEVILLE Lincoln
CORA Sublette
COWLEY Big Horn
CROWHEART Fremont
DANIEL Sublette
DAYTON Sheridan
DEAVER (82421) Big Horn(85), Park(14)
DEVILS TOWER Crook

DIAMONDVILLE Lincoln
DIXON Carbon
DOUGLAS Converse
DUBOIS Fremont
EDGERTON Natrona
ELK MOUNTAIN Carbon
EMBLEM Big Horn
ENCAMPMENT Carbon
ETNA Lincoln
EVANSTON Uinta
EVANSVILLE (82636) Natrona(97), Converse(2)
FARSON Sweetwater
FE WARREN AFB Laramie
FORT BRIDGER Uinta
FORT LARAMIE Goshen
FORT WASHAKIE Fremont
FOUR CORNERS Weston
FRANNIE Park
FREEDOM Lincoln
FRONTIER Lincoln
GARRETT Albany
GILLETTE Campbell
GLENDO (82213) Platte(98), Converse(1)
GLENROCK Converse
GRANGER Sweetwater
GRANITE CANON Laramie
GREEN RIVER Sweetwater
GREYBULL Big Horn
GROVER Lincoln
GUERNSEY Platte
HAMILTON DOME Hot Springs
HANNA Carbon
HARTVILLE Platte
HAWK SPRINGS Goshen
HILAND (82638) Natrona(87), Fremont(12)
HILLSDALE Laramie
HORSE CREEK Laramie
HUDSON Fremont
HULETT Crook
HUNTLEY Goshen
HYATTVILLE Big Horn
IRON MOUNTAIN Laramie
JACKSON Teton
JAY EM Goshen
JEFFREY CITY Fremont
JELM Albany
KAYCEE (82639) Johnson(92), Natrona(7)
KEELINE Niobrara

KELLY Teton
KEMMERER Lincoln
KINNEAR Fremont
KIRBY Hot Springs
LA BARGE Lincoln
LAGRANGE (82221) Goshen(97), Laramie(2)
LANCE CREEK Niobrara
LANDER Fremont
LARAMIE Albany
LEITER Sheridan
LINCH Johnson
LINGLE Goshen
LITTLE AMERICA Sweetwater
LONETREE Uinta
LONTETREE Uinta
LOST SPRINGS (82224) Converse(85), Niobrara(14)
LOVELL Big Horn
LUSK Niobrara
LYMAN Uinta
LYSITE Fremont
MANDERSON (82432) Park(75), Big Horn(24)
MANVILLE Niobrara
MC FADDEN Carbon
MC KINNON Sweetwater
MEDICINE BOW (82329) Carbon(77), Albany(22)
MEETEETSE Park
MERIDEN Laramie
MIDWEST Natrona
MILLS Natrona
MOORCROFT (82721) Crook(60), Campbell(39)
MOOSE Teton
MORAN Teton
MOUNTAIN VIEW Uinta
NATRONA Natrona
NEWCASTLE Weston
NODE Niobrara
OPAL Lincoln
OSAGE Weston
OSHOTO (82724) Crook(77), Campbell(22)
OTTO Big Horn
PARKMAN Sheridan
PAVILLION Fremont
PINE BLUFFS Laramie
PINEDALE Sublette

POINT OF ROCKS Sweetwater
POWDER RIVER Natrona
POWELL Park
RALSTON Park
RANCHESTER Sheridan
RAWLINS Carbon
RECLUSE Campbell
RELIANCE Sweetwater
ROBERTSON Uinta
ROCK RIVER (82083) Carbon(55), Albany(44)
ROCK SPRINGS Sweetwater
ROZET Campbell
SADDLESTRING Johnson
SAINT STEPHENS Fremont
SARATOGA Carbon
SAVERY Carbon
SHAWNEE Converse
SHELL Big Horn
SHERIDAN Sheridan
SHOSHONI Fremont
SINCLAIR Carbon
SMOOT Lincoln
STORY (82842) Sheridan(91), Johnson(8)
SUNDANCE (82729) Crook(95), Weston(4)
SUPERIOR Sweetwater
TEN SLEEP Washakie
TETON VILLAGE Teton
THAYNE Lincoln
THERMOPOLIS Hot Springs
TIE SIDING Albany
TORRINGTON Goshen
UPTON (82730) Weston(85), Crook(14)
VAN TASSELL (82242) Niobrara(59), Goshen(40)
VETERAN Goshen
WALCOTT Carbon
WAMSUTTER Sweetwater
WAPITI Park
WESTON (82731) Campbell(96), Crook(4)
WHEATLAND (82201) Platte(98), Albany(1)
WILSON Teton
WOLF Sheridan
WORLAND Washakie
WRIGHT Campbell
WYARNO Sheridan
YELLOWSTONE NATIONAL PARK Park
YODER Goshen

Wyoming ZIP/City Cross Reference

82001-82003 CHEYENNE	82321-82321 BAGGS	82631-82631 BILL	82923-82923 BOULDER
82005-82005 FE WARREN AFB	82322-82322 BAIROIL	82633-82633 DOUGLAS	82925-82925 CORA
82006-82010 CHEYENNE	82323-82323 DIXON	82635-82635 EDGERTON	82926-82926 ROCK SPRINGS
82050-82050 ALBIN	82324-82324 ELK MOUNTAIN	82636-82636 EVANSVILLE	82929-82929 LITTLE AMERICA
82051-82051 BOSLER	82325-82325 ENCAMPMENT	82637-82637 GLENROCK	82930-82931 EVANSTON
82052-82052 BUFORD	82327-82327 HANNA	82638-82638 HILAND	82932-82932 FARSON
82053-82053 BURNS	82329-82329 MEDICINE BOW	82639-82639 KAYCEE	82933-82933 FORT BRIDGER
82054-82054 CARPENTER	82331-82331 SARATOGA	82640-82640 LINCH	82934-82934 GRANGER
82055-82055 CENTENNIAL	82332-82332 SAVERY	82642-82642 LYSITE	82935-82935 GREEN RIVER
82057-82057 LARAMIE	82334-82334 SINCLAIR	82643-82643 MIDWEST	82936-82936 LONETREE
82058-82058 GARRETT	82335-82335 WALCOTT	82644-82644 MILLS	82936-82936 LONTETREE
82059-82059 GRANITE CANON	82336-82336 WAMSUTTER	82646-82646 NATRONA	82937-82937 LYMAN
82060-82060 HILLSDALE	82401-82401 WORLAND	82648-82648 POWDER RIVER	82938-82938 MC KINNON
82061-82061 HORSE CREEK	82410-82410 BASIN	82649-82649 SHOSHONI	82939-82939 MOUNTAIN VIEW
82062-82062 IRON MOUNTAIN	82411-82411 BURLINGTON	82701-82701 NEWCASTLE	82941-82941 PINEDALE
82063-82063 JELM	82412-82412 BYRON	82710-82710 ALADDIN	82942-82942 POINT OF ROCKS
82070-82073 LARAMIE	82414-82414 CODY	82711-82711 ALVA	82943-82943 RELIANCE
82080-82080 MC FADDEN	82420-82420 COWLEY	82712-82712 BEULAH	82944-82944 ROBERTSON
82081-82081 MERIDEN	82421-82421 DEAVER	82713-82713 CARLILE	82945-82945 SUPERIOR
82082-82082 PINE BLUFFS	82422-82422 EMBLEM	82714-82714 DEVILS TOWER	83001-83002 JACKSON
82083-82083 ROCK RIVER	82423-82423 FRANNIE	82715-82715 FOUR CORNERS	83011-83011 KELLY
82084-82084 TIE SIDING	82426-82426 GREYBULL	82716-82718 GILLETTE	83012-83012 MOOSE
82190-82190 YELLOWSTONE	82427-82427 HAMILTON DOME	82720-82720 HULETT	83013-83013 MORAN
NATIONAL PARK	82428-82428 HYATTVILLE	82721-82721 MOORCROFT	83014-83014 WILSON
82201-82201 WHEATLAND	82430-82430 KIRBY	82723-82723 OSAGE	83025-83025 TETON VILLAGE
82210-82210 CHUGWATER	82431-82431 LOVELL	82724-82724 OSHOTO	83101-83101 KEMMERER
82212-82212 FORT LARAMIE	82432-82432 MANDERSON	82725-82725 RECLUSE	83110-83110 AFTON
82213-82213 GLENDO	82433-82433 MEETEETSE	82727-82727 ROZET	83111-83111 AUBURN
82214-82214 GUERNSEY	82434-82434 OTTO	82729-82729 SUNDANCE	83112-83112 BEDFORD
82215-82215 HARTVILLE	82435-82435 POWELL	82730-82730 UPTON	83113-83113 BIG PINEY
82217-82217 HAWK SPRINGS	82440-82440 RALSTON	82731-82731 WESTON	83114-83114 COKEVILLE
82218-82218 HUNTLEY	82441-82441 SHELL	82732-82732 WRIGHT	83115-83115 DANIEL
82219-82219 JAY EM	82442-82442 TEN SLEEP	82801-82801 SHERIDAN	83116-83116 DIAMONDVILLE
82220-82220 KEELINE	82443-82443 THERMOPOLIS	82831-82831 ARVADA	83118-83118 ETNA
82221-82221 LAGRANGE	82450-82450 WAPITI	82832-82832 BANNER	83119-83119 FAIRVIEW
82222-82222 LANCE CREEK	82501-82501 RIVERTON	82833-82833 BIG HORN	83120-83120 FREEDOM
82223-82223 LINGLE	82510-82510 ARAPAHOE	82834-82834 BUFFALO	83121-83121 FRONTIER
82224-82224 LOST SPRINGS	82512-82512 CROWHEART	82835-82835 CLEARMONT	83122-83122 GROVER
82225-82225 LUSK	82513-82513 DUBOIS	82836-82836 DAYTON	83123-83123 LA BARGE
82227-82227 MANVILLE	82514-82514 FORT WASHAKIE	82837-82837 LEITER	83124-83124 OPAL
82228-82228 NODE	82515-82515 HUDSON	82838-82838 PARKMAN	83126-83126 SMOOT
82229-82229 SHAWNEE	82516-82516 KINNEAR	82839-82839 RANCHESTER	83127-83127 THAYNE
82240-82240 TORRINGTON	82520-82520 LANDER	82840-82840 SADDLESTRING	83128-83128 ALPINE
82242-82242 VAN TASSELL	82523-82523 PAVILLION	82842-82842 STORY	83414-83414 ALTA
82243-82243 VETERAN	82524-82524 SAINT STEPHENS	82844-82844 WOLF	
82244-82244 YODER	82601-82615 CASPER	82845-82845 WYARNO	
82301-82301 RAWLINS	82620-82620 ALCOVA	82901-82902 ROCK SPRINGS	
82310-82310 JEFFREY CITY	82630-82630 ARMINTO	82922-82922 BONDURANT	

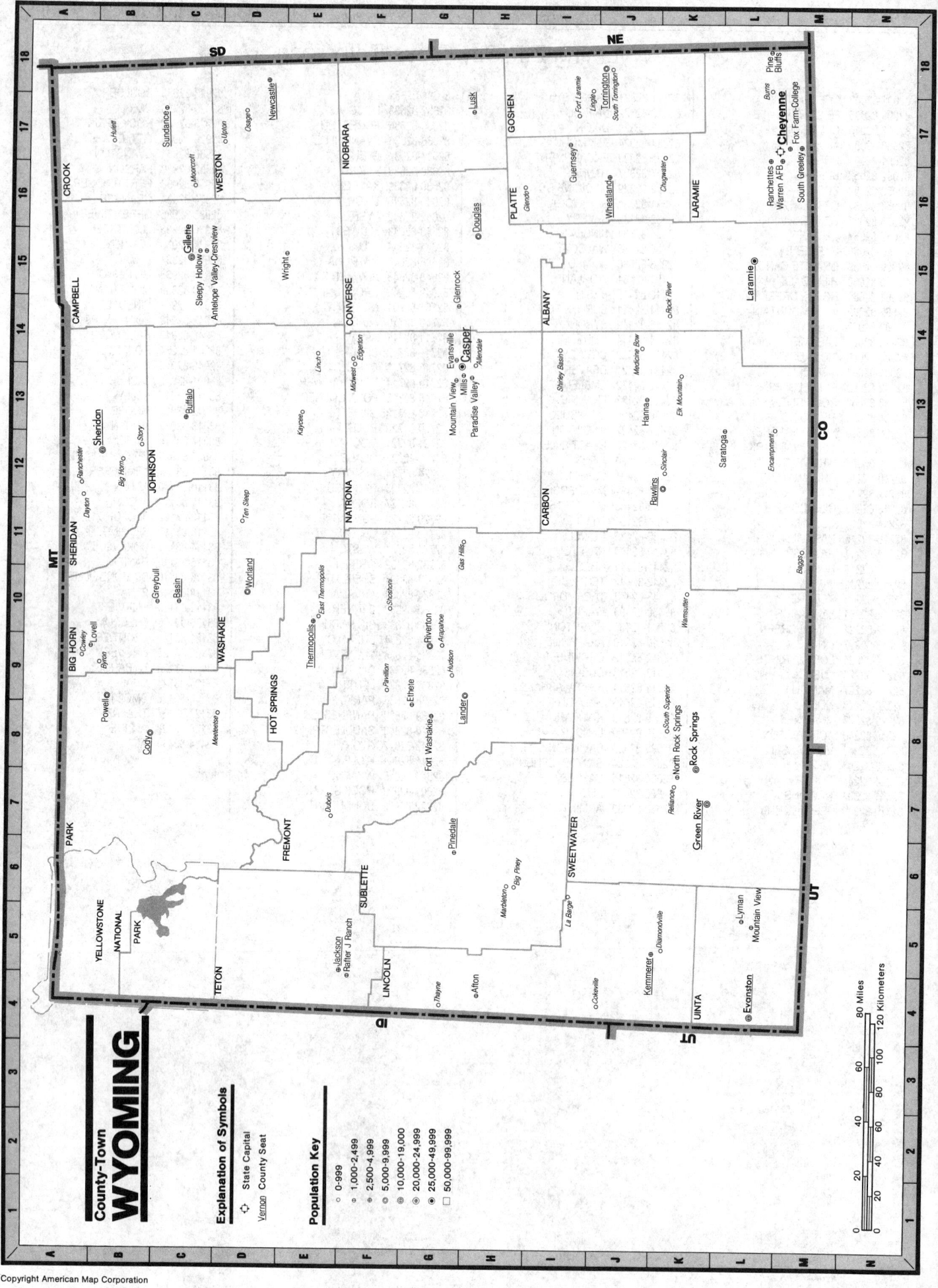

WYOMING
County-Town

Explanation of Symbols

◇ State Capital

Vernon County Seat

Population Key

- ○ 0-999
- ⊕ 1,000-2,499
- ⊙ 2,500-4,999
- ◉ 5,000-9,999
- ◎ 10,000-19,000
- ◉ 20,000-24,999
- ◉ 25,000-49,999
- □ 50,000-99,999

SD · NE · MT · CO · ID · UT

CROOK · WESTON · NIOBRARA · GOSHEN · PLATTE · LARAMIE · CAMPBELL · CONVERSE · ALBANY · SHERIDAN · JOHNSON · NATRONA · CARBON · BIG HORN · WASHAKIE · HOT SPRINGS · FREMONT · SWEETWATER · PARK · TETON · SUBLETTE · LINCOLN · UINTA

Hulett · Sundance · Moorcroft · Upton · Osage · Newcastle · Lusk · Fort Laramie · Lingle · Torrington · South Torrington · Pine Bluffs · Burns · Cheyenne · Warren AFB · Ranchettes · Fox Farm-College · South Greeley · Guernsey · Wheatland · Chugwater · Douglas · Glendo · Glenrock · Rock River · Laramie · Sleepy Hollow · Gillette · Antelope Valley-Crestview · Wright · Linch · Sheridan · Ranchester · Story · Big Horn · Dayton · Buffalo · Kaycee · Ten Sleep · Midwest · Edgerton · Mountain View · Evansville · Casper · Mills · Paradise Valley · Allendale · Shirley Basin · Medicine Bow · Hanna · Elk Mountain · Sinclair · Saratoga · Encampment · Rawlins · Baggs · Wamsutter · Greybull · Basin · Worland · Shoshoni · Gas Hills · Lovell · Cowley · Byron · Powell · Meeteetse · Cody · Thermopolis · East Thermopolis · Pavillion · Ethete · Riverton · Hudson · Arapahoe · Lander · Dubois · Fort Washakie · Pinedale · Marbleton · Big Piney · La Barge · South Superior · Reliance · North Rock Springs · Rock Springs · Green River · Lyman · Mountain View · Kemmerer · Diamondville · Cokeville · Evanston · Jackson · Rafter J Ranch · Thayne · Afton

80 Miles · 120 Kilometers

YELLOWSTONE NATIONAL PARK

COUNTIES

(23 Counties)

Name of County	Population	Location on Map
ALBANY	30,797	I-14
BIG HORN	10,525	A-9
CAMPBELL	29,370	A-14
CARBON	16,659	I-11
CONVERSE	11,128	E-14
CROOK	5,294	A-16
FREMONT	33,662	D-6
GOSHEN	12,373	H-17
HOT SPRINGS	4,809	D-8
JOHNSON	6,145	B-12
LARAMIE	73,142	K-16
LINCOLN	12,625	F-4
NATRONA	61,226	E-11
NIOBRARA	2,499	E-16
PARK	23,178	A-6
PLATTE	8,145	H-16
SHERIDAN	23,562	A-11
SUBLETTE	4,843	F-6
SWEETWATER	38,823	I-6
TETON	11,172	C-4
UINTA	18,705	K-4
WASHAKIE	8,388	C-9
WESTON	6,518	C-16
TOTAL	**453,588**	

CITIES AND TOWNS

Note: The first name is that of the city or town, second, that of the county in which it is located, then the population and location on the map.

Afton, Lincoln, 1,394 .... G-4
●Antelope Valley-Crestview, Campbell, 1,099 .... C-15
Basin, Big Horn, 1,180 .... C-10
Buffalo, Johnson, 3,302 .... C-13
Casper, Natrona, 46,742 .... G-13
Cheyenne, Laramie, 50,008 .... L-17
Cody, Park, 7,897 .... B-8
Douglas, Converse, 5,076 .... G-15
●Ethete, Fremont, 1,059 .... F-8
Evanston, Uinta, 10,903 .... L-4
Evansville, Natrona, 1,403 .... G-14
●Fort Washakie, Fremont, 1,334 .... G-8
Fox Farm-College, Laramie, 2,965 .... L-17
Gillette, Campbell, 17,635 .... C-15
Glenrock, Converse, 2,153 .... G-14
Green River, Sweetwater, 12,711 .... K-7

Greybull, Big Horn, 1,789 .... B-10
Guernsey, Platte, 1,155 .... I-17
Hanna, Carbon, 1,076 .... J-13
Jackson, Teton, 4,472 .... E-5
Kemmerer, Lincoln, 3,020 .... J-5
Lander, Fremont, 7,023 .... G-9
Laramie, Albany, 26,687 .... L-15
Lovell, Big Horn, 2,131 .... A-9
Lusk, Niobrara, 1,504 .... G-17
Lyman, Uinta, 1,896 .... L-5
Mills, Natrona, 1,574 .... G-13
●Mountain View, Natrona, 1,345 .... G-13
Mountain View, Uinta, 1,189 .... L-5
Newcastle, Weston, 3,003 .... D-18
●North Rock Springs, Sweetwater, 2,471 .... K-7
Paradise Valley, Natrona G-13
Pine Bluffs, Laramie, 1,054 .... L-18
Pinedale, Sublette, 1,181 .... G-6
Powell, Park, 5,292 .... A-9
●Rafter J Ranch, Teton, 1,092 .... F-4
●Ranchettes, Laramie, 4,038 .... L-16
Rawlins, Carbon, 9,380 .... J-12
Riverton, Fremont, 9,202 .... G-9
Rock Springs, Sweetwater, 19,050 .... K-8
Saratoga, Carbon, 1,969 .... K-13
Sheridan, Sheridan, 13,900 .... A-12
●Sleepy Hollow, Campbell, 1,194 .... C-15
●South Greeley, Laramie, 3,723 .... M-17
Sundance, Crook, 1,139 .... B-17
Thermopolis, Hot Springs, 3,247 .... E-10
Torrington, Goshen, 5,651 .... I-18
●Warren AFB, Laramie, 3,832 .... L-17
Wheatland, Platte, 3,271 .... I-16
Worland, Washakie, 5,742 .... D-10
Wright, Campbell, 1,236 .... D-15

Explanation of symbols: ●– Census Designated Place (CDP)

U.S. Territories

Guam - Puerto Rico - Virgin Islands

Guam Records

Guam Driving Records

Superior Court
Traffic Violations Bureau
120 W. O'Brien
Hagatna, Guam 96931

(671) 475-3274
(671) 472-2856 fax

Records are public. To request by mail, submit name, DOB and SSN. Include a self-addressed, stamped envelope. In person requests are permitted. The fee is $1.50 for clearance and then $1.00 per citation on the record. Make checks payable to Superior Court of Guam. They will not fax back requests.

Guam Vehicle Records

Department of Revenue & Taxation
Vehicle Records
PO Box 23607, GMF
Barrigada, Guam 96921

(671) 475-1816

Vehicle records are not considered public records.
You must have a court order and then submit request on their form

Guam Recording Office

Guam Department of Revenue & Taxation
Clerk, PO Box 23605
GMF, GU 96921

671-475-5000 x815; Fax 671-472-2643.

Will search UCC records. This agency will not do a tax lien search. Will not search real estate records.

Guam Federal Courts

Office of the Clerk of Court
520 W Soledad Ave, 4th Fl
US Courthouse, RM 460
Hagatna, Guam 96910

671-473-9100, Fax: 671-473-9152
www.gud.uscourts.gov

Counties: Guam. Address Bankruptcy requests to the Guam Bankruptcy Division.

Indexing/Storage: New cases are available in the index 24 hours after filing date. Index is manual index cards. All records including archives are located at this court. All closed case records are maintained here.

Fee & Payment: Payment may be made by. Personal checks accepted ($35 returned check fee) Credit cards not accepted. Payee: Clerk, Guam District Court.

Phone Search: Searching is not available by phone.

Mail Search: Expect a longer return time of mail.Always enclose a stamped self addressed envelope.

In Person Search: In peson searching available.
PACER: PACER is available online at https://pacer.login.uscourts.gov/cgi-bin/login.pl?court_id=gudc. Case records are available back to 2002. Records are never purged.

Other Online Access: Does not participate in the US Party case index.

Guam City/County Cross Reference

AGANA HEIGHTS Guam	DEDEDO Guam	MONGMONG Guam	TAMUNING Guam
AGAT Guam	HAGATNA Guam	PITI Guam	UMATAC Guam
ASAN Guam	INARAJAN Guam	SANTA RITA Guam	YIGO Guam
BARRIGADA Guam	MANGILAO Guam	SINAJANA Guam	YONA Guam
CHALAN PAGO Guam	MERIZO Guam	TALOFOFO Guam	

Guam ZIP/City Cross Reference

96910-96910	AGANA	96915-96915	SANTA RITA	96922-96922	ASAN	96928-96928	AGAT
96910-96910	HAGATNA	96916-96916	MERIZO	96923-96923	MANGILAO	96929-96929	YIGO
96911-96911	TAMUNING	96917-96917	INARAJAN	96924-96924	CHALAN PAGO	96930-96930	TALOFOFO
96912-96912	DEDEDO	96918-96918	UMATAC	96925-96925	PITI	96931-96931	TAMUNING
96913-96913	BARRIGADA	96919-96919	AGANA HEIGHTS	96926-96926	SINAJANA	96932-96932	AGANA
96914-96914	YONA	96921-96921	BARRIGADA	96927-96927	MONGMONG	96932-96932	HAGATNA

Puerto Rico Records

Puerto Rico Driving Records

Department of Transportation
Services Division
PO Box 41243 - Minillas Station
San Juan, PR 00940-1243

(787) 767-4425

The request must include full name and SSN, signed release from subject is suggested. The fee is $1.50 per record made payable to the Secretary of the Treasury.

Puerto Rico Federal Courts

US District Court

District of Puerto Rico

Clemente-Ruiz-Nazario U.S. Courthouse, 150 Carlos Chardon St, Hato Rey, Puerto Rico 00918 (Courier Address:), 787-772-3000, Fax: 787-766-5693. www.prd.uscourts.gov

Counties: All counties.

Indexing/Storage: Cases are indexed by as well as by case number. New cases are available in the index after filing date.

Fee & Payment: Payment may be made by. Payee: Clerk, U.S. District Court.

Phone Search: Searching is not available by phone.

Mail Search: To obtain copies by mail write to U.S. Bankruptcy Court c/o mail requests. A stamped self addressed envelope is required.

In Person Search: In peson searching available.

PACER: PACER is available online at http://pacer.prd.uscourts.gov/. Toll-free dial-up access: 800-517-2441. Local dial-up access: 787-766-5774. Records are never purged.

Other Online Access: Participates in the US Party Case Index.

US Bankruptcy Court

District of Puerto Rico

US Post Office & Courthouse Building, 300 Recinto Sur #109, San Juan, Puerto Rico 00901 (Courier Address:), 787-977-6000, Fax: 787-977-6008. www.prb.uscourts.gov/

Counties: All counties.

Indexing/Storage: Cases are indexed by as well as by case number. New cases are available in the index after filing date. Closed cases are shipped to the Missouri Federal Records Center 3 months after close of case.

Fee & Payment: Payment may be made by. Personal checks not accepted. Payee: Clerk, U.S. Bankruptcy Court.

Phone Search: Searching is not available by phone.

In Person Search: In peson searching available.

PACER: https://pacer.login.uscourts.gov/cgi-bin/login.pl?court_id=prbk. Also, document images are available on the WebPacer online system. Toll-free dial-up access: 800-792-8338. Local dial-up access: 787-977-6140.

Puerto Rico County Locator

Puerto Rico ZIP/City Cross Reference

ADJUNTAS Adjuntas
AGUADA Aguada
AGUADILLA Aguadilla
AGUAS BUENAS Aguas Buenas
AGUIRRE Guayama
AIBONITO Aibonito
ANASCO Anasco
ANGELES Utuado
ARECIBO Arecibo
ARROYO Arroyo
BAJADERO Arecibo
BARCELONETA Barceloneta
BARRANQUITAS Barranquitas
BAYAMON Bayamon
BOQUERON Cabo Rojo
CABO ROJO Cabo Rojo
CAGUAS Caguas
CAMUY Camuy
CANOVANAS Canovanas
CAROLINA (00979) San Juan(59), Carolina(40)
CAROLINA Carolina
CAROLINA San Juan
CASTANER Lares
CATANO Catano
CAYEY Cayey
CEIBA Ceiba
CIALES Ciales
CIDRA Cidra

COAMO Coamo
COMERIO Comerio
COROZAL Corozal
COTO LAUREL Ponce
CULEBRA Culebra
DORADO Dorado
ENSENADA Guanica
FAJARDO Fajardo
FLORIDA Florida
FORT BUCHANAN Bayamon
GARROCHALES Arecibo
GUANICA Guanica
GUAYAMA Guayama
GUAYAMA Guayanilla
GUAYANILLA Guayanilla
GUAYNABO Catano
GUAYNABO Guaynabo
GUAYNABO San Juan
GURABO Gurabo
HATILLO Hatillo
HORMIGUEROS Hormigueros
HUMACAO Humacao
ISABELA Isabela
JAYUYA Jayuya
JUANA DIAZ Juana Diaz
JUNCOS Juncos
LA PLATA Aibonito
LAJAS Lajas
LARES Lares

LAS MARIAS (00670) Camuy(55), Anasco(44)
LAS PIEDRAS Las Piedras
LOIZA Loiza
LUQUILLO Luquillo
MANATI Manati
MARICAO Maricao
MAUNABO Maunabo
MAYAGUEZ Mayaguez
MERCEDITA Ponce
MOCA Moca
MOROVIS Morovis
NAGUABO Naguabo
NARANJITO Naranjito
OROCOVIS Orocovis
PALMER Rio Grande
PATILLAS Patillas
PENUELAS Penuelas
PONCE Ponce
PUERTO REAL Fajardo
PUNTA SANTIAGO Humacao
QUEBRADILLAS Quebradillas
RINCON Rincon
RIO BLANCO Naguabo
RIO GRANDE (00745) Humacao(84), Rio Grande(12), Canovanas(3)
ROOSEVELT ROADS Ceiba
ROSARIO San German
SABANA GRANDE Sabana Grande

SABANA HOYOS Arecibo
SABANA SECA Toa Baja
SAINT JUST Trujillo Alto
SAINT JUST CONTRACT Trujillo Alto
SALINAS Salinas
SAN ANTONIO Aguadilla
SAN GERMAN San German
SAN JUAN San Juan
SAN LORENZO San Lorenzo
SAN SEBASTIAN San Sebastian
SANTA ISABEL Santa Isabel
ST JUST Trujillo Alto
TOA ALTA Toa Alta
TOA BAJA Toa Baja
TRUJILLO ALTO (00976) Trujillo Alto(98), San Juan(1)
TRUJILLO ALTO Trujillo Alto
UTUADO Utuado
VEGA ALTA Vega Alta
VEGA BAJA (00694) Vega Alta(59), Vega Baja(40)
VEGA BAJA Vega Baja
VIEQUES Vieques
VILLALBA Villalba
YABUCOA Yabucoa
YAUCO Yauco

Puerto Rico ZIP/City Cross Reference

00601-00601	ADJUNTAS	00664-00664	JAYUYA	00721-00721	PALMER	00778-00778	GURABO
00602-00602	AGUADA	00667-00667	LAJAS	00723-00723	PATILLAS	00780-00780	COTO LAUREL
00603-00605	AGUADILLA	00669-00669	LARES	00725-00727	CAGUAS	00782-00782	COMERIO
00606-00606	MARICAO	00670-00670	LAS MARIAS	00728-00728	PONCE	00783-00783	COROZAL
00610-00610	ANASCO	00674-00674	MANATI	00729-00729	CANOVANAS	00784-00785	GUAYAMA
00611-00611	ANGELES	00676-00676	MOCA	00730-00734	PONCE	00786-00786	LA PLATA
00612-00614	ARECIBO	00677-00677	RINCON	00735-00735	CEIBA	00791-00792	HUMACAO
00616-00616	BAJADERO	00678-00678	QUEBRADILLAS	00736-00737	CAYEY	00794-00794	BARRANQUITAS
00617-00617	BARCELONETA	00680-00682	MAYAGUEZ	00738-00738	FAJARDO	00795-00795	JUANA DIAZ
00622-00622	BOQUERON	00683-00683	SAN GERMAN	00739-00739	CIDRA	00901-00933	SAN JUAN
00623-00623	CABO ROJO	00685-00685	SAN SEBASTIAN	00740-00740	PUERTO REAL	00934-00934	FORT BUCHANAN
00624-00624	PENUELAS	00687-00687	MOROVIS	00741-00741	PUNTA SANTIAGO	00935-00940	SAN JUAN
00627-00627	CAMUY	00688-00688	SABANA HOYOS	00742-00742	ROOSEVELT ROADS	00949-00951	TOA BAJA
00631-00631	CASTANER	00690-00690	SAN ANTONIO	00744-00744	RIO BLANCO	00952-00952	SABANA SECA
00636-00636	ROSARIO	00692-00692	VEGA ALTA	00745-00745	RIO GRANDE	00953-00954	TOA ALTA
00637-00637	SABANA GRANDE	00693-00694	VEGA BAJA	00751-00751	SALINAS	00955-00955	SAN JUAN
00638-00638	CIALES	00698-00698	YAUCO	00754-00754	SAN LORENZO	00956-00961	BAYAMON
00641-00641	UTUADO	00703-00703	AGUAS BUENAS	00757-00757	SANTA ISABEL	00962-00963	CATANO
00646-00646	DORADO	00704-00704	AGUIRRE	00765-00765	VIEQUES	00964-00964	SAN JUAN
00647-00647	ENSENADA	00705-00705	AIBONITO	00766-00766	VILLALBA	00965-00971	GUAYNABO
00650-00650	FLORIDA	00707-00707	MAUNABO	00767-00767	YABUCOA	00975-00975	SAN JUAN
00652-00652	GARROCHALES	00714-00714	ARROYO	00769-00769	COAMO	00976-00977	TRUJILLO ALTO
00653-00653	GUANICA	00715-00715	MERCEDITA	00771-00771	LAS PIEDRAS	00978-00978	SAINT JUST
00656-00656	GUAYANILLA	00716-00717	PONCE	00772-00772	LOIZA	00978-00978	ST JUST
00659-00659	HATILLO	00718-00718	NAGUABO	00773-00773	LUQUILLO	00978-00978	SAINT JUST CONTRACT
00660-00660	HORMIGUEROS	00719-00719	NARANJITO	00775-00775	CULEBRA	00979-00999	CAROLINA
00662-00662	ISABELA	00720-00720	OROCOVIS	00777-00777	JUNCOS		

Virgin Islands Records

Virgin Islands Driving Records

Criminal Justice Complex
Records Bureau
St. Thomas, Virgin Islands 00802

340-774-2211 x5523

The request must include a signed release form the subject. Submit photocopy of the driver's license, a self-addressed, stamped envelope, The fee is $5.00 in certified funds, made payable to the Government of the Virgin Islands. Turnaround time is 1-2 days.

Virgin Islands Vehicle Records

Virgin Island Police Department
C/O Motor Vehicle Bureau
Sub Base
St. Thomas, Virgin Islands 00801

(340) 774-5765

They will verify information over the phone, including lien information. To do a record request, submit a license plate number of VIN, $20.00 in certified funds, and a self-addresses, stamped envelope. Make check payable to Government of the Virgin Islands.

Virgin Islands Recording Offices

St. Croix
Recorder of Deeds
1131 King St, Suite 101
Christiansted, VI 00820-4970

R/E & UCC Recording-340-773-6449; Fax-340-773-0330.

Will search UCC records. Will not search tax lien or real estate records.**Other Phones:** Assessor-340-773-6459; Treasurer-340-773-1105; Appraiser/Auditor-340-773-6459; Elections-340-773-1021; Vital Records-340-773-1311 or 773-9376.

St. Thomas
Recorder of Deeds
Division of Corporations & Trademarks
Kongens Gabe #18,
St. Thomas, VI 00802.

340-776-8515; Fax-340-776-4612. Hours: 8AM-5PM

www.ltg.gov.vi
Will search UCC records. Will not search tax lien or real estate records.

Virgin Islands County Locator

V. I. City/County Cross Reference

CHRISTIANSTED St. Croix
CHRISTIANSTED (00820) St. Croix(78), St. Thomas(21)
FREDERIKSTED St. Croix
KINGSHILL St. Croix
SAINT JOHN St. John
SAINT THOMAS St. Thomas

V. I. ZIP/City Cross Reference

00801-00805	SAINT THOMAS
00820-00824	CHRISTIANSTED
00830-00831	SAINT JOHN
00840-00841	FREDERIKSTED
00850-00851	KINGSHILL

Canada

Canadian Criminal Records
Canadian Parole/Pardon Information
Canadian Driving Records

Canadian Criminal Records

Information and Identification Services
Directorate of the Royal Canadian Mounted Police (RCMP)

Searches requests may be directed to the Royal Canadian Mounted Police's Information and Identification Services:

Mailing address:

> RCMP
> Civil Fingerprint Screening Services
> PO Box 8885
> Ottawa, Ontario K1G 3M8   Canada

Courier address:

> RCMP
> National Police Services Building, Loading Dock #1
> Information and Identification Services,
> Civil Fingerprint Screening Services,
> 1200 Vanier Parkway
> Ottawa, Ontario K1A 0R2   Canada

Telephone Information:

613-998-6362

You may follow the prompts, but in most call scenarios, you are prompted to leave a message. Please allow up to three business days for a response.

General Web Site:

> www.rcmp.gc.ca/crimrec/crimrec_e.htm

Criminal Record Checks Information Web Site:

> www.rcmp.gc.ca/crimrec/finger2_e.htm#Obtain

Email Information requests:

> civilnps@rcmp-grc.gc.ca

...continued

Searches may be performed by main and in person. A messenger and courier service may be used. Also, to speed return, include a postal paid overnight or expedited envelope; in fact, a postage paid envelope of some form is required for all mail requests.

Certified criminal records will be provided to subjects seeking employment, adoptions, Canadian citizenship, foreign travel, border crossing permits, landed immigrant status or immigration to Canada, refugee status, visa/waiver applications, work permits or volunteer positions. Criminal records are kept on file until the subject is eighty years old if no criminal activity has been reported within the last 10 years. In the case of a subject serving term of life imprisonment, of a "dangerous offender", or a subject of the age of 80 who is still incarcerated, the criminal record is retained until the sentence is completed and no additional crimes have been committed for 10 years., the subject reaches the age of 100, or the subject dies and the death is supported by fingerprints.

Search requirements: full name, DOB, sex, and SASE. A release and a fingerprint form is required. The Canadian fingerprint release form C-216C should be used when possible. If the form is not available, an official fingerprint from the police department may be substituted. The form used should be completed and signed by the officer taking the fingerprints. The form should include the reason the application (i.e. employment, etc.) Requests of records for purposes of employment or volunteer work must indicate the job title or position sought on the fingerprint form.

Records will only be released to the subject, unless a release is included with the request. The release must authorize the RCMP to provide criminal record information to a specific individual or agency. The release must also include a statement that the subject is aware that refusal to give consent to release will not negatively affect the request The consent must be an original document. A photocopied or faxed release will not be accepted.

The search fee is $25.00 (Canadian), or $18.00 (U.S.), payable to the Receiver General of Canada by certified check or money order. The fee is waived on searches done for Canadian citizenship, employment with the Canadian federal government or police forces, immigration to Canada, refugee status or volunteer work (requires written confirmation from a registered non-profit organization).

Turnaround time is 4-6 weeks. Inquiry calls regarding record requests should be directed to 613-998-6362. To receive results by courier, include prepaid return packaging. Additional funds will not be accepted for express delivery of results.

Canadian Pardons & Paroles

National Parole Board of Canada

Web Site:

www.npb-cnlc.gc.ca

The web site provides a wealth of information on parole rules and parolee records.

Canadian Pardons

For questions relating to the status of pardon applications, call this toll-free number:

1-800-874-2652

Mailing address for the Pardons Sections is:

Pardon Section
Clemency and Investigations Division
National Parole Board
410 Laurier Avenue West
Ottawa, Ontario K1A 0R1

Note: Requests must be made by the subject. Notice must include full name, date of birth, personal reference number, if available and signature.

Canadian Driving Records

Note: All record search fees are quoted in Canadian Dollars.

Alberta

Motor Vehicle Division
Alberta Service Bureau
Scctia Place, Main Floor, M23
10060 Jasper Ave
Edmonton, Alberta T5J 3R8
(780) 944-1204
(780) 423-0285 fax

www3.gov.ab.ca/gs/services/mv/

Driving Records Records are privatized and require the signed release of the subject. The cost of a record search is $27.05. Processing time is same day. The name, DOB, license number, reason for request, and a signed release from subject are required for a search. Records may be searched by mail or in person. Records may be requested by fax with a Visa or MasterCard. A fax must include cardholder's signature. Information is not available online at this time.

Vehicle Records With the exception of lien information ($17.05 fee) records are generally not released to the public. If permitted, records can be searched by owner's name, VIN number and/or by plate number.

British Columbia

Driver Services
ICBI Licensing Department
910 Government Street
PO Box 3750
Victoria, British Columbia V8W 3Y5
(250) 978-8300 or (800) 950-1498
(250) 978-8001 fax
www.icbc.com

Driving Records The cost of a record search is $5.00 (no fee if your own record). Processing time is 2 to 3 days. The name, DOB, license number and a signed release from subject are required for a search. Records may be searched by mail or in person. Will fax back. Will accept MasterCard and Visa. Information is not available online at this time.

Vehicle Records Records are not available. However, by calling (800) 464-5050, one can get a verbal verification if a vehicle was involved in an accident.

Manitoba

Division of Driver & Vehicle License
Suspension & Records
1075 Portage Ave
Winnipeg, Manitoba R3G 0S1
(204) 945-6945 (Driver)
(204) 945-0653 (Driver-fax)
(204) 945-7366 (Vehicle)

www.gov.mb.ca/tgs/ddvl/index.html

Driving Records The cost of a record search is $10.00, there is also a search on CDL drivers which is $10.00. Accident reports at $10.70. Prepayment is required, checks or money orders to be made out to Minister of Finance. The processing time is 1 to 2 days. The name, DOB, license number and a signed release from subject are required for a search. Records may be searched by mail, fax or in person and they will return by fax. MasterCard and Visa accepted.

Vehicle Records Information is not available to the general public, but they will confirm the number of vehicle owners and accident history information. To permissible users, vehicle records can be searched by owner's name, VIN number and/or by plate number. For Lien information call (204) 945-3123.

New Brunswick

Department of Public Safety
Licensing & Records Branch
Driver (or Vehicle) Records
PO Box 6000
Fredericton, New Brunswick E3B 5H1
(506) 453-2410
(506) 453-7455

www.gnb.ca/0276/index-e.asp

Driving Records The cost of a driving record search is $10.00 and **Accident Reports** are $8.00. The processing time is same day. The name, DOB and License number are required for a search. Records may be searched by mail, in person or online. Records can be returned by fax.

An online, interactive system is available from a designated vendor. Fee is $15.00 per record. For more information about setting up an account call (888) 624-2265 or fax 902-422-1675.

Vehicle Records Vehicle records searches are done through Data Entry at (506) 453-2084, fee is $8.00 per record. Vehicle records can be searched by owner's name, VIN number and/or by plate number. Credit cards are not accepted. Lien information is released only to person involved, upon request from the Registry Office at (506) 453-2817.

Newfoundland

Motor Vehicle Registration
Driver Records Division
PO Box 8710
St Johns, Newfoundland A1B 4J5
(709) 729-2519
(709) 729-2515 (Driver fax)
(709) 729-3399 (Vehicle fax)

www.gov.nf.ca/gsl/gs/mr

Driving Records The cost of a driving record search is $10.00. The processing time is in less than a week. The name and either DOB or license number, and the signature of the requester are required for a search. Records may be searched by mail or in person. Visa, MasterCard and Debit Cards are accepted. Records returned by fax incur an additional $5.00 fee.

Vehicle Records With the exception of lien information records are generally not released to the public. If permitted, records can be searched by owner's name, VIN number and/or by plate number.

Lien Records Lien searches have been privatized. Search companies are listed on the web under personal Property Registry at:

www.gov.nl.ca/gs/cca/cr/prop-about.stm

Northwest Territories

Department of Transportation
Motor Vehicle Division
Yellow Knife Registries
Box 1320
Yellow Knife, Northwest Territories
X1A 2L9
(867) 669-9964
(867) 669-9094 fax
www.gov.nt.ca

Driving Records The cost of a driving record is $12.14. Visa, MasterCard and Debit Cards are accepted. The name, DOB, license number, and a signed release from subject are required for a search. Records may be searched by mail or in person, or by fax. Processing time is 1 to 2 days. Information is not available online at this time.

Vehicle Records Vehicle records are closed and unavailable. Lien information is available from a different office, call (876) 873-7493 for more information.

Nova Scotia

Department of Transportation
PO Box 1652
Halifax, Nova Scotia B3J 2Z3
(902) 424-5851
(902) 424 0720 fax

www.gov.ns.ca/snsmr/rmv

Driving Records The cost of a record search is $10.00. Make checks payable to Registry of Motor Vehicles. Visa, MasterCard and Debit Cards are accepted. The processing time is 1 to 2 weeks by mail, immediate in person, and same day for fax. The name, DOB and a signed release from subject are required for a search. The license number is helpful. Records may be searched by mail or fax (credit card required).

An online, interactive system is available from a designated vendor. Fee is $15.00 per record. For more information about setting up an account call (888) 624-2265 or fax 902-422-1675.

Vehicle Records Vehicle record information is not available to the general public.

Lien Records Lien information is held at the Registry of Deeds at (902) 424-8571. However, you can only search in person. They recommend a vendor, Info Fax Research, at (888) 356-4636.

Ontario

Ministry of Transportation
2680 Keele
Downsview, Ontario M3M 3E6
(416) 235-2999
(416) 235-4009 fax

www.mto.gov.on.ca

Driving Records Both driving and vehicle records may be obtained from kiosks and mall kiosks. Driver's address is not released. The cost of a driving record or accident report is $12.00, add $6.00 for certification. Reports on commercial driving only is $5.00. Credit cards and debit cards are accepted with fax service. They would prefer fax requests instead of mail requests. The name, DOB and license number required for a search. Records may be ordered online, also a license check can be ordered online for $2.00. Records are turned by mail.

Vehicle Records Permitted requesters may search vehicle records by owner's name, VIN number and/or by plate number for $12.00. Addresses are not released. Lien information is shown only when a Used Vehicle Information Package is purchased for $20.00.

Prince Edward Island

Highway Safety Division
Records Division
33 Riverside Dr
PO Box 2000
Charlottetown, Prince Edward Island
C1A 7N8
(902) 368-5210
(902) 368-5236 (Driver fax)
www.gov.pe.ca/infopei/transportation/land

Driving Records   The cost of a record search is $15.00. Records may be searched by mail or in person. Processing time is 1 to 2 days for mail requests. The name, DOB, license number and a signed release from subject are required for a search. Credit cards are accepted for payment. Information is not available online at this time.

Vehicle Records   Records are closed to private individuals and the insurance industry. Lien information is released only upon request at courthouses.

Quebec

Driving Records Division
SAAQ
333 Jean LeSage
PO Box 19600
Quebec, Quebec G1K 8J6
(418) 643-7620
www.saaq.gouv.qc.ca

Driving Records   Records may be ordered by mail or at Service Centers throughout the province. The cost of a record search is $8.00. Processing time is 2 to 3 days. The full name, DOB, license number, requester's phone number, and a signed release from subject are required for a search. Records may be searched by mail or in person.

Vehicle Records   The agency will confirm, but will not do searches.

Saskatchewan

Driver Abstracts
Saskatchewan Government Insurance
2260 11th Ave
Regina, Saskatchewan S4P 2N7
(306) 775-6198
(306) 775-6681 fax

www.sgi.sk.ca

Driving Records   The cost of a record search is $10.00. MasterCard and Visa are accepted. Processing time is 1 week by mail and 1 hour if credit card signature available. The name, DOB, license number and a signed release from subject are required for a search. Records may be searched by mail or fax. Information is not available online at this time.

Vehicle Records   Vehicle records are not released to the general public. Permissible requesters can be search by owner's name, VIN number and/or by plate number. Lien information is shown.

Yukon

Motor Vehicle Department
Yukon Territory
Government of Yukon
PO Box 2703
Whitehorse, Yukon Y1A 2C6
(867) 667-5315
(867) 393-6220 fax
www.gov.yk.ca

Driving Records   The cost of a driving record is $10.00, Mastercard and Visa are accepted. Processing time is same day. The name, DOB, license number and a signed release from subject are required for a search. Records may be searched by mail or fax. Information is not available online at this time.

Vehicle Records   Vehicle records can be searched by owner's name, VIN number and/or by plate number. Records are not available unless a signed, notarized release is presented. The fee is $10.00 per record. Lien information is available from Corporate Affairs at (867) 667-5442.

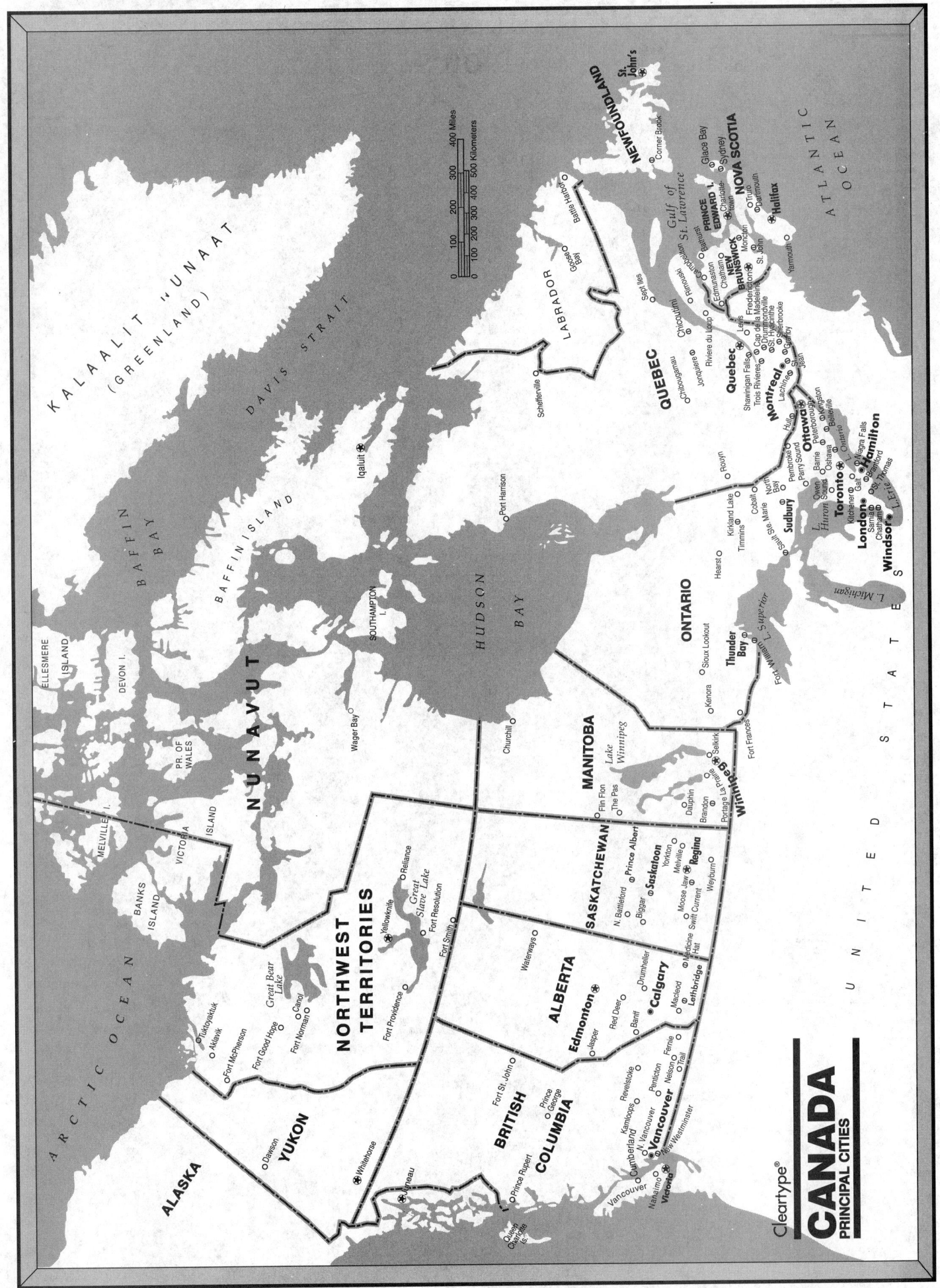

Cleartype®

CANADA
PRINCIPAL CITIES

Notes

Notes

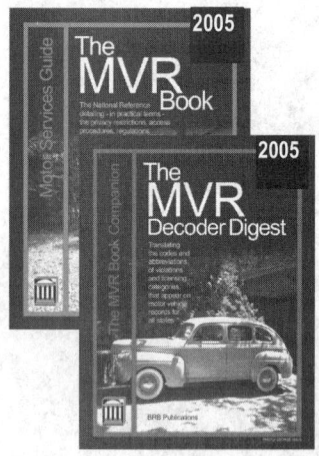

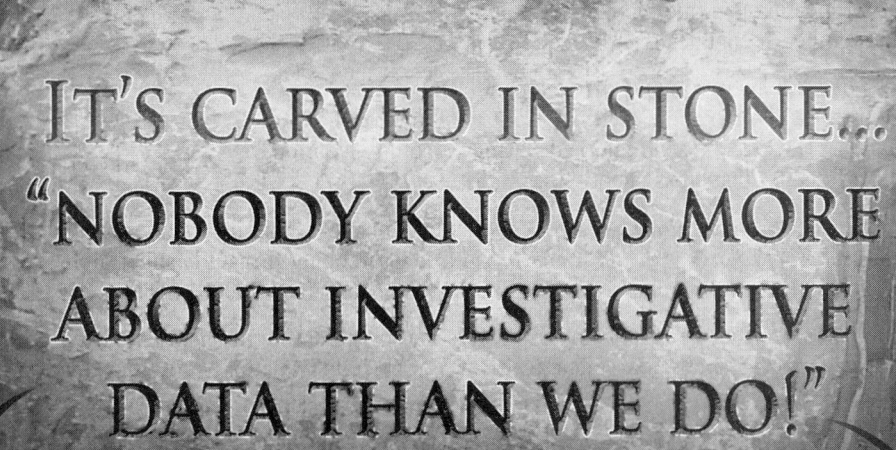